Do you understand Newton's laws of motion?

Review these basic laws of physics that all students must learn.

Pages 168–169

Have you forgotten how to calculate the area of a rectangle?

Use this table to review the most commonly needed formulas in arithmetic.

Pages 194–195

Are you having trouble with advanced math?

Work sample problems from algebra, geometry, trigonometry, and calculus. Check their solutions to make sure you are right.

Pages 196–247

Are you afraid to write research papers?

Learn how to attack the assignment step by step, from research through outline to final draft.

Pages 254–269

A checklist for outlines

1. Have you included an introduction?
2. Is your theme statement clearly presented?
3. Do your main idea headings fully cover the subject?
4. Are you sure your main idea headings do not overlap?
5. Have you arranged your main ideas in a logical order?
6. Do you have subtopic headings under each main idea?

Are you bored with the books you are reading now?

Make exciting selections from a list of some of the greatest works ever written.

Pages 320–331

Are you having trouble deciding which college to attend?

Here are some things to keep in mind while you make your choice.

Pages 334–343

Are you undecided about your future?

Find out about careers that are open to you. Make your dream future come true.

Pages 344–372

Gallery of OFFICIAL PORTRAITS *of the* PRESIDENTS *of the* UNITED STATES

George Washington
1789–1797

John Adams
1797–1801

Thomas Jefferson
1801–1809

James Madison
1809–1817

James Monroe
1817–1825

John Quincy Adams
1825–1829

Andrew Jackson
1829–1837

Martin Van Buren
1837–1841

William Henry Harrison
1841

John Tyler
1841–1845

James K. Polk
1845–1849

Zachary Taylor
1849–1850

Millard Fillmore
1850–1853

Franklin Pierce
1853–1857

James Buchanan
1857–1861

Abraham Lincoln
1861–1865

Andrew Johnson
1865–1869

Ulysses S. Grant
1869–1877

Rutherford B. Hayes
1877–1881

James A. Garfield
1881

Chester A. Arthur
1881–1885

Grover Cleveland
1885–1889, 1893–1897

Benjamin Harrison
1889–1893

William McKinley
1897–1901

Theodore Roosevelt
1901–1909

William H. Taft
1909–1913

Woodrow Wilson
1913–1921

Warren G. Harding
1921–1923

Calvin Coolidge
1923–1929

Herbert C. Hoover
1929–1933

Franklin D. Roosevelt
1933–1945

Harry S. Truman
1945–1953

Dwight D. Eisenhower
1953–1961

John F. Kennedy
1961–1963

Lyndon B. Johnson
1963–1969

Richard M. Nixon
1969–1974

Gerald R. Ford
1974–1977

Charles M. Rafshoon

JAMES E. CARTER
1977–1981

RONALD W. REAGAN
1981–1989

A. Tannenbaum/Sygma

GEORGE H. BUSH
1989–

Student Handbook

Including

Webster's New World Dictionary

Volume **2**

Student Handbook

Including

Webster's New World Dictionary

Volume 2

THE SOUTHWESTERN COMPANY
Nashville, Tennessee

WEBSTER'S NEW WORLD DICTIONARY, Second Concise Edition

Published by New World Dictionaries/Simon and Schuster
A Simon & Schuster Division of Gulf & Western Corporation

Printed in the United States of America

Table of Contents

Social Studies 2–109

Science and Mathematics 110–251

Biology 112

Chemistry 146

English and Literature 252–331

ILLUSTRATION CREDITS: *Page 3* Viking Ship Museum, Oslo; *4 (top)* National Bank of Detroit, *(bottom)* Betty Whelan; 5 *(left)* Museum of Fine Arts, Boston, *(right)* Egyptian State Tourism Administration; *7 (center)* Culver Pictures; *8* Museum of Fine Arts, Boston; *9* Gantner/Monkmeyer; *10* UPI; *11 (bottom)* EPA; *12* China News Service; *13 (bottom)* Culver Pictures; *14 (top)* Art Reference Bureau, *(bottom)* Betty Whelan; *16* EPA; *17 (top)* Pan American, *(bottom)* New York Public Library; *18* Viking Ship Museum, Oslo; *20* Culver Pictures; *21* New York Public Library, *22* Culver Pictures; *23 (top)* Metropolitan Museum of Art, *(center)* Culver Pictures, *(bottom)* Art Reference Bureau; *24 (left)* New York Public Library, *(right)* Betty Whelan; *25* Culver Pictures; *27 (both), 28* Culver Pictures; *30* New York Public Library; *31 (top)* French Embassy Press & Information Division, *(bottom)* New York Public Library; *32* Culver Pictures; *33 (top)* New York Public Library, *(bottom)* German Information Center; *34* Betty Whelan; *35* Culver Pictures; *36 (left)* Culver Pictures, *(right)* Betty Whelan; *37* Culver Pictures; *39 (top)* Walker Evans; *40 (left)* Culver Pictures, *(right)* Imperial War Museum; *41 (both)* Betty Whelan; *43 (bottom)* UPI; *44 (top)* Culver Pictures, *(bottom)* UPI; *45* UPI/Bettmann; *46, 48* Wide World Photos; *49, 50* Reuters/Bettmann; *51* AP/Wide World; *52* Culver Pictures; *53* Culver Pictures; *54 (bottom)* Culver Pictures; *55 (center left)* Morin/ Monkmeyer, *(center right)* New York Public Library, *(bottom)* Culver Pictures; *60* Washington Convention & Visitors Bureau; *64, 65* Phillip Jones/Mulvey Associates; *66 (left)* UPI, *(right)* Wide World Photos; *86 (center and right)* Library of Congress; *87 (left)* Library of Congress, *(right)* Wide World Photos; *88 (left)* New York Public Library, *(right)* Library of Congress; *89 (left)* Library of Congress, *(center)* Texas Highway Dept., *(right)* Bettmann Archive; *92 (left)* National Archives, *(right)* Library of Congress; *93 (left)* Bettmann Archive, *(center)* UPI, *(right)* Culver Pictures; *96 (left)* Lewis W. Hine, *(center)* UPI, *(right)* Library of Congress; *97 (left)* Museum of the City of New York, *(right)* Look; *98 (left and center)* UPI, *(right)* Wide World Photos; *99 (left)* Wide World Photos, *100 (left)* Wide World Photos, *(right)* Barbara Pfeffer/Peter Arnold; *101 (left)* UPI, *(center)* Rhodes/ Taurus Photos, *(right)* UPI/Bettmann; *102* New York Public Library; *105 (top left)* Squires/ Monkmeyer, *(top right)* Wide World Photos, *(bottom left)* Campell's Soup Co., *(bottom right)* Ken Karp; *107 The Wall Street Journal; 109 (center top)* New York Public Library, *(center bottom)* Dept. of the Treasury, Bureau of the Mint, *(bottom)* Wide World Photos; *111* Wexler/Monkmeyer; *112* Martin Rother/Taurus Photos; *113, 115, 116,* Peter Loewer; *117 (top left)* Nikon, Inc., *(top right)* Monkmeyer, *(center right)* Pfizer Inc., *118 (top)* Taurus photos, *(bottom)* Peter Loewer; *119–123* Peter Loewer; *124 (top left)* Carolina Biological Supply Co., *(top right)* Rhodes/Taurus Photos, *(center, both)* Goro/Monkmeyer, *(bottom left)* Hodge/Peter Arnold, *(bottom right)* Landwehr/Monkmeyer; *125–130* Peter Loewer; *127* Martin M. Rotker/Taurus Photos; *132 (left)* Eli Lilly & Co., *(right, both)* Center for Disease Control, Atlanta, Ga.; *133 (left, both)* Eli Lilly & Co., *(right, both)* Kage/Peter Arnold; *134 (left top)* Pfizer Inc., *(left center)* Grimes & Hernault/Taurus Photos, *(right)* Kage/Peter Arnold, *(art)* Peter Loewer; *135 (inset)* Carolina Biological Supply Co., *(bottom)* Bob Evans/Peter Arnold; *136 (top left)* Pfizer Inc., *(bottom left)* Bettmann Archive, *(right)* Helen Buttfiel; *137 (top)* Jane Latta, *(bottom)* Spencer/ Monkmeyer; *138 (top left)* MacGregor/Peter Arnold, *(bottom left)* Hodge/Peter Arnold, *(right)* Jane Latta, *(art)* Peter Loewer; *139 (left)* U.S. Forest Service, *(top center)* Harrison/Taurus Photos, *(top right)* Wilson/Monkmeyer, *(center right)* Hodge/Peter Arnold, *(bottom)* Peter Loewer; *140 (top left)* Carolina Biological Supply Co., *(top center)* Rother/Taurus Photos, *(bottom left)* U.S. Dept. of the Interior, Fish & Wildlife Service, *(right)* Evans/Peter Arnold; *141 (top left)* Pfletschinger/Peter Arnold, *(bottom left)* Wexler/Monkmeyer, *(top right)* Evans/Peter Arnold, *(bottom right)* Pfletschinger/Peter Arnold; *142* Phillip Jones/Mulvey Associates; *143 (top left)* Habicht/Taurus Photos, *(bottom left)* Harrison/ Monkmeyer, *(right)* New York Zoological Society; *144 (top and center top)* Martin Rother/Taurus Photos, *(center bottom)* Owczarzak/Taurus Photos, *(bottom)* Peter Arnold; *146* Migdale/Science Source/Photo Researchers; *147–152, 160, 162* Peter Loewer; *164* Mark Lyons/Image Bank; *167* UPI; *169* John Killgrew/Mulvey Associates; *171–173* Peter Loewer; *174* U.S. Dept. of Commerce, Weather Bureau; *175* John Killgrew/Mulvey Associates; *177, 178* Peter Loewer; *180* Southern Illinois University at Carbondale; *194, 195, 209, 211, 218–251* Peter Loewer; *253* EPA; *254* David Schaefer/ Monkmeyer; *257* Jesse Forde; *259 Reader's Guide to Periodical Literature; 260, 263 (top)* Ken Karp, *(bottom) The New York Times; 284* EPA; *285 (left)* Wide World Photos, *(right)* ABC, Inc.; *286 (left)* EPA, *(right)* American Shakespeare Theatre, Stratford, Conn.; *287* Wide World Photos; *290 (top)* New York Public Library, *(center bottom, bottom)* Culver Pictures; *300* EPA *301* New York Public Library, Astor, Lenox & Tilden Foundations; *303 (top)* EPA, *(center top)* Doubleday & Company, *(center bottom)* UPI, *(bottom)* Look; *306 (top and center)* New York Public Library, *(bottom left)* American Shakespeare Theatre, Stratford, Conn., *(bottom right)* Folger Shakespeare Library; *307 (both)* Martha Swope; *309 (left)* Sotheby Parke-Bernet/EPA, *(right)* Lukas/EPA; *310* New York Public Library; *314 (center top)* New York Public Library, *(center bottom)* A.F. Bradney, NY, *(bottom)* National Library of Ireland/Courtesy Embassy of Ireland; *321 (left)* Culver Pictures, *(right)* Random House, Inc.; *323 (left)* New York Public Library, *(right)* EPA; *325 (left)* New York Public Library, *(right)* John Winkler/Becky Thatcher Book Shop; *327 (left)* New York Public Library, *(right)* Culver Pictures; *333* Bell Labs; *334* Jerome Weisman; *335* Phillip Jones/Mulvey Associates; *344 (top)* Garg/Photo Researchers, *(bottom left)* Lockheed-California Co., *(bottom right)* Pratt & Whitney, United Technologies; *345* Peter Loewer; *346* Yoram Kahana/Peter Arnold; *350* Peter Loewer; *351* Yates/EPA; *352* Emery Worldwide; *355* Spencer Grant/Monkmeyer; *356 (left)* Feingersh/The Stock Market, *(right)* Seitz/Woodfin Camp; *358* Peter Loewer; *359* Jane Latta; *361 (left)* EPA, *(right)* Druskis/EPA; *365 (left)* Gschneidle/Peter Arnold *(right)* The Coca-Cola Co.; *366* Bayer/Monkmeyer; *367* Forsyth/Monkmeyer; *368* Merrim/Monkmeyer; *369 (left)* Sacks/EPA, *(right)* Leinwand/Monkmeyer; *370* Ullmann/ Taurus Photos.

Editorial development of the Student Handbook was directed by
The Hudson Group, Inc., Pleasantville, New York 10570

Administrative editors:	Gorton Carruth and Eugene Ehrlich
Editors-in-chief:	Lawrence T. Lorimer and Bryan Bunch
Editorial controllers:	Mary Egner and Hayden Carruth
Copy-editing:	Felice Levy/AEIOU, Inc.
Contributors:	Frances Barth, Marcia Golub, John Harrington, Mary Hicks, Seymour Levine, Howard Liss, Don Lorimer, Janet McHugh, Sam Plummer, Bertram Siegel, Bruce Wetterau, Richard Worth
Design and production:	Pam Forde Graphics
Design and art direction:	Pam Forde
Production:	Steven Becker, Julie Fesler, Kathleen Marks, Lynne Shenkin, Margaret Worth
Illustrations and maps:	H. Peter Loewer, Jean Loewer/Graphos Studio, Ric Del Rossi, Phillip Jones, John Killgrew, Michael O'Reilly/Mulvey Associates Betty Whelan, Nick Forde
Photo researcher:	Pat Vestal

Student Handbook

Including

Webster's New World Dictionary

Volume **2**

Social Studies

A Viking ship c 1000 A.D. *(see p. 18).*

World History

History is an account of the important events of the past, especially of those events that somehow influence the way we live and think today. This section provides a brief *chronology,* or time line, of world history, beginning with the earliest surviving records. The history has been divided into five segments. Ancient history begins with early cultures, around 3000 B.C., and ends with the fall of the Roman Empire in 476 A.D. Medieval history includes just over a thousand years, from 476 to 1478. The section on the Renaissance and the Enlightenment takes in the next 300 years, ending on the eve of the American Revolution in 1775. The modern period runs to 1945, the end of World War II. The final section on the postwar world brings events to the present day. Following the chronology is a different kind of time line showing the birth and death dates of important leaders, discoverers, and artists.

Ancient world

The modern world owes much to the early civilizations that grew up around the Mediterranean Sea in the centuries before the birth of Christ. The Hebrews developed a religion recognizing a single God; modern Judaism and Christianity have grown from this religion. The Greeks, drawing on earlier cultures, created the poetry and art that remain a standard of perfection even today. The Romans developed methods of public administration and public works that resemble our own. The great works and wisdom of these civilizations have been rediscovered many times; their history is part of our own.

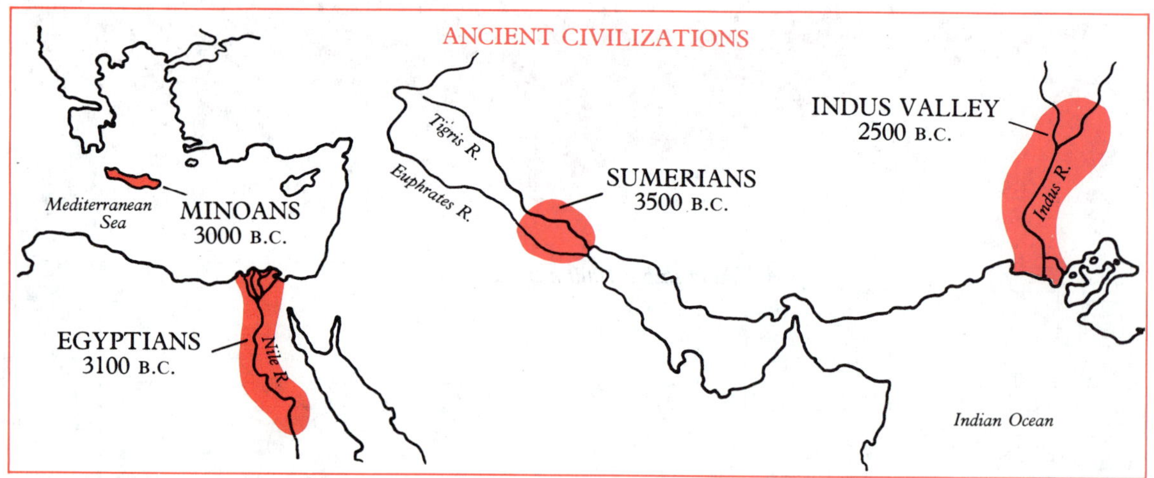

Date *Event*

c 3000 BC

Ancient civilizations. By the year 3000 BC, fairly advanced cultures had developed in Sumer, Crete, and Egypt. Sumer, located in Mesopotamia (modern Iraq), had an extensive village culture from about 4000 BC; at about this time Sumerians began to develop what became known as cuneiform writing. By 3000 BC, Sumerian civilization was centered on such flourishing cities as Erech, Lagash, and Ur. These cities rivaled one another for control of neighboring lands but were not unified until about 2300, when the Akkadians conquered them (see below).

Crete, lying off the coast of Greece, was the center of another early civilization, that of the Minoans. From about 3000, they had a flourishing Bronze Age culture. The Minoans became a maritime power in the Mediterranean (about 2000 BC), and their culture greatly influenced later civilizations on the Greek mainland.

In Egypt an advanced culture and a unified state developed early. In 3100 King Menes united Upper and Lower Egypt, two independent kingdoms that had arisen along the banks of the Nile River, and founded what was to become the great empire of Egypt. In the years after Menes, called the Early Dynastic Period (c 3100–c 2700), Egyptian culture developed rapidly and hieroglyphic writing became widespread. Government, administrative, technical, and artistic skills were also developed, providing the foundations for the Old Kingdom of Egypt (see below).

An Egyptian Pharaoh and his wife (below). *At right, the great pyramids at Giza.*

c 2700–c 2200 BC

Old Kingdom of Egypt. Period in Egyptian history following Menes's unification of Upper and Lower Egypt. During a time of prosperity and cultural flowering, the Old Kingdom was known for sun worship, pyramid building, and trading expeditions as far north as the Black Sea. The capital was located at Memphis. The rise of strong provincial rulers finally broke the Pharaoh's power and ended the Old Kingdom.

c 2600–c 2500 BC

Pyramids of Giza. Three great Egyptian pyramids built on the banks of the Nile River. They are one of the Seven Wonders of the World. The largest was built by the Pharaoh Khufu (or Cheops) about 2600 BC. It is 481 feet tall and its sides average 776 feet at the base.

c 2300–2180 BC

Akkadian Empire. Great ancient empire in Mesopotamia, in what is now Iraq. The great Akkadian ruler Sargon ruled from 2340 to 2305 and conquered lands surrounding his capital, Akkad. Eventually he controlled an empire that included all of Mesopotamia, territories extending west to the Mediterranean, and lands as far north as the Black Sea. Destruction of the empire (c 2180) by barbarian tribes plunged Mesopotamia into a period of chaos.

Date	*Event*
c 2000–c 1786 BC	**Middle Kingdom of Egypt.** Period beginning when Amenemhet I seized power at the city of Thebes (c 2000). It was marked by the conquest of lower Nubia, the standardization of writing, a literary flowering, and great commercial prosperity. The Pharaohs ruled as feudal kings, not absolute monarchs, and when their power declined the Middle Kingdom came to an end.
c 1763–c 1600 BC	**First Babylonian Empire.** Empire in Mesopotamia created by Hammurabi (fl. 1792–1750), ruler of the city-state of Babylon. He began his conquests during the last 14 years of his reign and, by them, unified Mesopotamia under his rule. Hammurabi is best known for his Law Code, one of the earliest known written legal codes. The code was inscribed on a stone tablet in cuneiform writing; it was rediscovered in 1901. The code contained provisions for criminal, civil, commercial, and family law, and is generally thought to be based on long-established Sumerian practices. Hammurabi's empire was continued by his successors, though it was considerably reduced after his death. The empire finally fell to the Kassites in about 1600 BC.
c 1720–c 1570 BC	**Hyksos rule in Egypt.** After the fall of the Middle Kingdom, a Semitic people called the Hyksos made themselves masters of Egypt (c 1720). They created a powerful and prosperous empire, moved the capital from Thebes to Avaris-Tanis in the Nile delta, and introduced the horse and chariot to Egypt. Their reign was challenged by the Theban princes, however, and the Hyksos were finally defeated (c 1570) by Amasis I at the Battle of Tanis.
c 1570–c 1085 BC	**New Kingdom in Egypt.** Last period of greatness in ancient Egypt. The New Kingdom was marked by the centralization of power in the hands of the Pharaoh (at the expense of local rulers), the expansion of the empire into Asia, the brief religious revolution of Amenhotep IV (see below), and the building of magnificent temples. The last great ruler of this period was Ramses III (ruled 1198–c 1167); after him the priests became the real rulers of Egypt. In the centuries that followed the New Kingdom, Egypt came under the control of various peoples, including the Libyans, Nubians, Persians, Macedonian Greeks, and finally the Romans (30 BC).
c 1400 BC	**Final destruction of the palace at Knossos.** By the second millennium BC, the Minoans had established a flourishing Bronze Age culture on the island of Crete. It was centered on a great palace at Knossos. The final destruction (1400) of the palace by unknown causes marked the end of the Minoan culture. Thereafter the center of Aegean culture shifted to the southern part of mainland Greece, where the Mycenaean civilization flourished (c 1400–c 1200).
c 1372–c 1354 BC	**Amenhotep's religious revolution.** The Pharaoh Amenhotep IV (Ikhnaton) in Egypt (ruled c 1372–c 1354) attempted to convert his kingdom to the worship of one god, Aton, the sun god. Amenhotep overcame the resistance of the priesthood and attempted to eliminate all references to other gods. This monotheistic worship of Aton did not survive him, however, and a successor, Tutankhamen, was forced to restore the old gods.
c 1288 BC	**Battle of Kadesh.** Great battle fought by Egyptian Pharaoh Ramses II (ruled 1292–1225) against the Hittites in Syria. Ramses took up arms against the Hittites to block their advance into Egyptian domains in Syria. Though he claimed victory, the battle is thought to have been inconclusive. War between the Egyptians and Hittites continued for ten more years before a settlement was made.
c 1260? BC	**Exodus from Egypt.** Though dating is uncertain, the Hebrews' escape from Egypt is thought to have occurred during the reign of Ramses II (c 1292–c 1225). The Bible recounts the story of the Exodus, including Moses' efforts to win the release of the Hebrews, the escape and crossing of the Red Sea, the arduous journey to Mt. Sinai, and the giving of the Ten Commandments.

c 1200 BC

Phoenician letters:

△ *D* ⊟ *H*

ᴲ *E* ○ *O*

The Phoenicians. A Canaanite people who occupied the coastal region of what is now Lebanon as early as 3000 BC. By about 1200 they were well known as traders and navigators. Between about 1000 and 800, they established a thriving commercial empire around the Mediterranean. They established trading colonies as far west as Carthage (in North Africa) and Cadiz (in modern Spain), and may well have circumnavigated Africa. After about 600 BC, the Phoenicians submitted to the Chaldeans and then the Persians. In 332 BC Alexander the Great captured and sacked the great Phoenician city of Tyre. In ensuing centuries Phoenician civilization disappeared as a distinct entity.

In addition to being renowned traders, the Phoenicians were also skilled craftsmen. Their greatest contribution, however, was the Phoenician alphabet. The Greek alphabet is thought to have been based on the Phoenician system.

c 1200 BC

Fall of Troy. The war against the city of Troy formed the basis of two great epics of ancient Greece, the *Iliad* and the *Odyssey,* by the poet Homer. These works had an immense influence on the culture of ancient Greece, though both the city and the Trojan War were long thought to be nothing more than legend. In the late 1800's, however, an archaeologist named Heinrich Schliemann (1822–1890) used details given in Homer's epics to locate the ruins of Troy in northwest Asia Minor. There, archaeological evidence indicated the city was destroyed in about 1200 BC, apparently by the conquering Greek warriors.

The Trojan horse by which the Greeks fooled the Trojans and defeated them.

c 1012–c 972 BC

King David's reign in Israel. After their exodus from Egypt, the Hebrew tribes eventually reached Palestine. There they began their wars for control of the region, but conquest was not completed until David became their leader. David created a strong kingdom with Jerusalem as the capital, and thus gave the confederated tribes a settled national state.

c 972–c 932 BC

King Solomon's reign in Israel. Under Solomon, successor to his father, King David, the ancient kingdom of Israel reached the height of its power and prosperity. Solomon brought great wealth to the kingdom by encouraging trade, built new cities throughout his domain, and constructed magnificent palaces and the first Temple at Jerusalem. He gained a legendary reputation for both his wisdom and his wealth. But the taxation required to support the luxury of his court led to unrest and, soon after Solomon's death, the kingdom split in two. The northern part became the Kingdom of Israel and the southern part became the Kingdom of Judah.

884–612 BC

Assyrian Empire. The Assyrians were a warlike, Semitic people who inhabited northern Mesopotamia from about 3000 BC. Though they expanded their domain for brief periods in previous centuries, formation of their great empire did not begin until the reign of Ashurnasirpal II (ruled 884–c 860). He was followed by other conquerors, among them Tiglath-pileser III (ruled 745–728), Sargon II (ruled 722–705), and Esarhaddon (ruled 681–668). By their conquests, these rulers created a vast empire in the Near East that extended from Egypt (conquered c 670) to the Persian Gulf. The last great Assyrian ruler was Ashurbanipal (ruled 669–633), who organized a famous library of cuneiform tablets at his capital, Nineveh. The Assyrian Empire crumbled soon after his reign, when the Babylonians and their allies captured Nineveh in 612.

c 800–c 300 BC

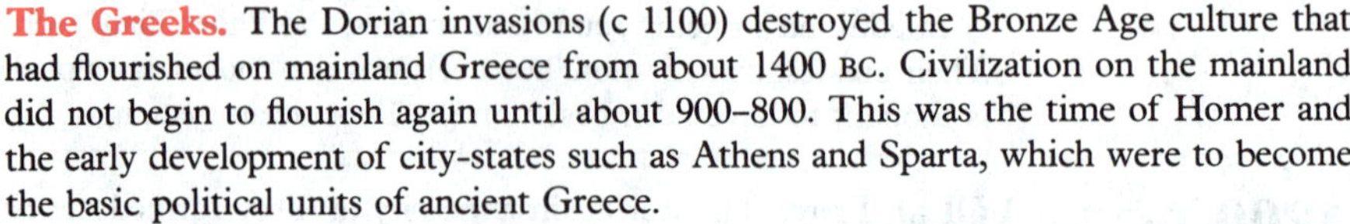

The Greeks. The Dorian invasions (c 1100) destroyed the Bronze Age culture that had flourished on mainland Greece from about 1400 BC. Civilization on the mainland did not begin to flourish again until about 900–800. This was the time of Homer and the early development of city-states such as Athens and Sparta, which were to become the basic political units of ancient Greece.

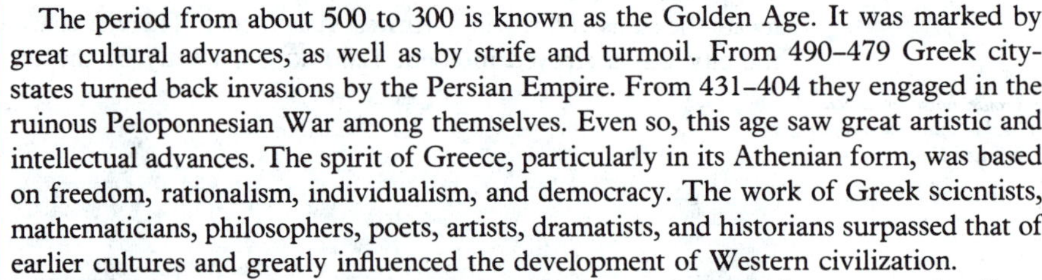

An era of colonization in faraway lands followed from about 750 to 500 BC. It received its impetus from population growth, the relatively poor soil in Greece, and the desire for land; bands of colonizers began to form independent city-states around the Mediterranean and the Black Sea.

The period from about 500 to 300 is known as the Golden Age. It was marked by great cultural advances, as well as by strife and turmoil. From 490–479 Greek city-states turned back invasions by the Persian Empire. From 431–404 they engaged in the ruinous Peloponnesian War among themselves. Even so, this age saw great artistic and intellectual advances. The spirit of Greece, particularly in its Athenian form, was based on freedom, rationalism, individualism, and democracy. The work of Greek scicntists, mathematicians, philosophers, poets, artists, dramatists, and historians surpassed that of earlier cultures and greatly influenced the development of Western civilization.

The conquests of Alexander the Great and the breakup of his great empire (from 321) marked the beginning of the decline of Greek culture on mainland Greece. But Alexander's successors helped spread Greek culture throughout the ancient world and thus brought about the Hellenistic age (see below).

A Greek vase, c 520 B.C.

776 BC

First Olympic Games. The first athletic games of what became a great tradition in ancient Greece were held at Olympia, in southern Greece, and consisted only of running events. Discontinued in the fourth century AD, the Olympic Games were revived in 1896.

753 BC

City of Rome founded. The founding of Rome is surrounded by legend, though this date is traditionally accepted. According to one legend, the brothers Romulus and Remus built the original city in 753. Soon after, the two brothers fought over the defensive wall built around it. Remus made fun of the wall by easily jumping over it. Romulus, in a rage, killed his brother and uttered the prophetic words, "Thus perish any other who leaps over my walls."

c 625–538 BC

Second Babylonian Empire in Mesopotamia. After more than a century of Assyrian domination, Babylon reestablished its independence (c 625) under Nabopolassar (ruled c 625–c 605). Some years later Nabopolassar formed an alliance with the Medes and Persians and together they brought down the Assyrian Empire by capturing its capital, Nineveh (612). With the destruction of Assyria and the great Babylonian victory over the Egyptians at Carchemish (605), the Babylonians formed a vast Mesopotamian empire. This empire reached its zenith under Nabopolassar's son, Nebuchadnezzar (ruled c 605–562), who was both a formidable warrior and a great builder. He made Babylon into the greatest city in the ancient world and built the famous Hanging Gardens of Babylon. Following two revolts by the Jews against Babylonian rule, Nebuchadnezzar destroyed their capital of Jerusalem (586) and carried off its citizens. This began the Babylonian Captivity, which lasted until the Persians conquered the Babylonian Empire in 538.

Date	*Event*
c 621 BC	**Draco institutes his legal code in Athens.** Draco's code, which according to Aristotle was the first in Athenian history, was notoriously harsh; it prescribed the death penalty for even minor offenses. The code did establish the principle that murderers were to be punished by the state, instead of the victim's family. But the severity of the laws proved so unpopular that the entire code was reformed by Solon in 594. The word *Draconian,* used to refer to repressive laws, is derived from Draco's code.
c 616–c 509 BC	**Tarquin kings rule in Rome.** Though there is much uncertainty regarding the reign of Tarquins, they were apparently Etruscans, a powerful people of Etruria in north-central Italy. The first of the Tarquins seized power in Rome c 616; they remained in power until the Romans drove them out c 509. By this time, however, Etruscan culture had greatly influenced the development of Roman civilization. The overthrow of the Tarquin kings marked the beginning of the Roman republic.
594 BC	**Solon's reforms in Athens.** Solon (c 639–c 559), one of the great Athenian statesmen, became chief magistrate in Athens amid a grave social crisis. Under the existing system, the peasants were steadily losing their land and their freedom to the nobles. Solon canceled all debts secured with personal liberty (serfdom was the penalty for failing to pay), reformed the Athenian constitution to allow all freemen to participate in the assembly, replaced the harsh Draconian code with a new law code, and made other reforms. Solon's reforms did not go unopposed, but they did lay the foundations for Athenian democracy.
c 549–330 BC	**The Persian Empire.** Beginning about 549, the Persians, under the leadership of Cyrus the Great (c 559–529), advanced from the land east of Mesopotamia (in present-day Iran) westward toward the Mediterranean, conquering Lydia and Babylonia. Within 20 years, Cyrus established the largest empire in existence before the conquests of Alexander the Great. The Greeks and Egyptians, however, held out against him. Darius the Great (521–486) was determined to conquer the Greek city-states and launched the Persian wars (see below). Following the Persian defeat in these wars, the empire sank into stagnation and collapsed before the armies of Alexander the Great. Persian intellectual and artistic achievements were derived largely from the earlier civilizations of Mesopotamia and Egypt. The Persians did, however, spread their religion, Zoroastrianism, throughout western Asia. Zoroastrians believed that Shura Mazda, god of light, created the world and mankind to be locked in endless combat with Ahriman, the god of darkness and evil. Out of these beliefs emerged Mithraism, Manicheism, and Gnosticism, all of which had a profound influence on the Roman world and on Christianity.

Sculpture from the Persian capital of Persepolis

c 538 BC

End of Babylonian Captivity. Following the conquest of the Babylonian Empire by the Persians (538), the Persian ruler Cyrus the Great permitted the Hebrews of Jerusalem to return to their city. Many, but not all, left Babylon, where they had been held captive by the Babylonians since 586 as punishment for a rebellion. Their return marked the reestablishment of Jerusalem as a center of Jewish religion and the Jewish national state.

c 528 BC

Buddha

Buddhism founded in India. Buddhism was founded by Siddhartha Gautama (c 563–c 483), who gave up a life of luxury to seek spiritual enlightenment. He found enlightenment (c 528) while meditating under a banyan tree at Buddha Gaya, in northeast India, and he devoted the rest of his life to spreading his teachings. Buddhism eventually arose as an organized religion in India, in opposition to the dominant Hindu religion. Although Buddhism later declined and nearly disappeared in India, it had spread by that time through central and eastern Asia and influenced the cultures of China, Korea, and Japan, among other countries.

508 BC

Constitution of Cleisthenes in Athens. Cleisthenes rose to power amid a political crisis in Athens and used the situation to institute reforms (508) that created the Athenian democracy. His new political system was based on political districts (demes) established by region, rather than by membership in one of the four old tribes. This broke the power of the landed aristocracy, which had previously controlled Athenian government.

c 500 BC

Confucius and the Chinese classics. By the time of Confucius (c 551–c 479), the Chinese empire had already been in existence for a thousand years or more. In his lifetime, China was torn by wars and the tyranny of feudal nobles. Confucius sought to reform government and about 531 began teaching his principles to others. His disciples later collected these teachings into the *Analects*, which is counted among the Chinese classics, along with the writings of Lao-tze (c 604–531) and Mencius (c 371–c 288). These classics continued to influence Chinese culture for some 2000 years.

500–400 BC

Golden Age of Greek drama. Greek drama evolved at Athens from ceremonies honoring the god Dionysus (Bacchus); it was raised to an art form by the four acknowledged masters of this Golden Age. Three of them, Aeschylus (525–456), Sophocles (c 496–406), and Euripides (c 480–406), developed the Greek tragedy. The fourth, Aristophanes (c 448–c 388), is known for his comedies.

490–479 BC

Persian invasions of Greece. During this period the Greek city-states united briefly to face the common enemy, Persia. The Persians invaded Greece in 490 and 480. The first invasion was ended by the great Athenian victory at Marathon (490) and the second was turned back after the Persian fleet was destroyed at Salamis (480).

c 461–429 BC

Age of Pericles in Athens. Pericles was a great statesman who strengthened the Athenian democracy and who attempted to make Athens the focus of the Greek world. By his statecraft, he brought about a period of peace and prosperity for Athens. He became a great patron of the arts, glorified Athens with many splendid buildings, and built the Acropolis of Athens. Among the buildings on the Acropolis is the world-famous Parthenon, a masterpiece of Greek architecture.

c 450–c 300 BC

Great philosophers of ancient Greece. Among the many great Greek philosophers, three have had particularly great impact on the development of Western thought. They are Socrates (469–399), his student Plato (427?–347), and Aristotle (384–322).

431–404 BC

Peloponnesian War. This great war between the rival city-states of Athens and Sparta ended in the ruin of Athens and marked the beginning of the decline of ancient Greece. The first phase of the war ended in stalemate in 421. In the second phase, Spartan naval victories culminated in destruction of the Athenian navy at the Battle of Aegospotami (405). Athens, forced to surrender in 404, never again regained its former greatness.

Date	Event

Ruins of the Parthenon at Athens, completed in 437 B.C.

c 400 BC — **Hippocrates flourishes.** Hippocrates (c 460–c 370), a renowned Greek physician, is considered the father of medicine. The Hippocratic Oath, still taken by doctors in modern times, is said to reflect his high ethical standards.

334–323 BC — **Conquests of Alexander the Great.** One of the great conquerors of the ancient world, Alexander became ruler of Macedonia, a kingdom in northern Greece, in 336. After consolidating Macedonian control over the Greek mainland, he began a series of spectacular conquests and through them became master of a vast empire that stretched from Greece to northern India. In less than ten years he conquered Persia, Phoenicia, Egypt (where he founded the great city of Alexandria), parts of central Asia, and, finally, northern India. Alexander died in 323, soon after completing these conquests, and his empire crumbled. Nevertheless, this short-lived empire helped spread Greek culture throughout the ancient world.

300 BC–476 AD — **Rome.** The Roman republic was established (509) after the overthrow of the Tarquin (Etruscan) kings. By 300 BC, the Romans had taken control of the Italian peninsula. Once they had made themselves masters of Italy, the Romans entered into conflict with Carthage in the Punic Wars (see below). The three wars (between 264 and 146 BC) ultimately resulted in Roman control over Carthage and its extensive colonial domain. Meanwhile, the Romans also conquered Macedonia, Greece, and Asia Minor. By 100 BC, Roman power extended throughout the Mediterranean.

From 133 to 31 BC, the Roman republic was torn by civil war and political unrest, which eventually led to the extinction of republican government and the establishment (27 BC) of the Roman Empire under Augustus, the first emperor. For the next 200 years, the diverse peoples of the empire enjoyed peace and prosperity. During the next three centuries, however, the western half of the empire gradually declined and was finally destroyed (476) by invading Germanic tribes.

Greco-Roman civilization continued vigorously for a thousand years in the Byzantine Empire. It profoundly influenced the Roman Catholic Church and taught Germanic invaders a civilized way of life; it also provided much of the cultural inspiration for succeeding generations.

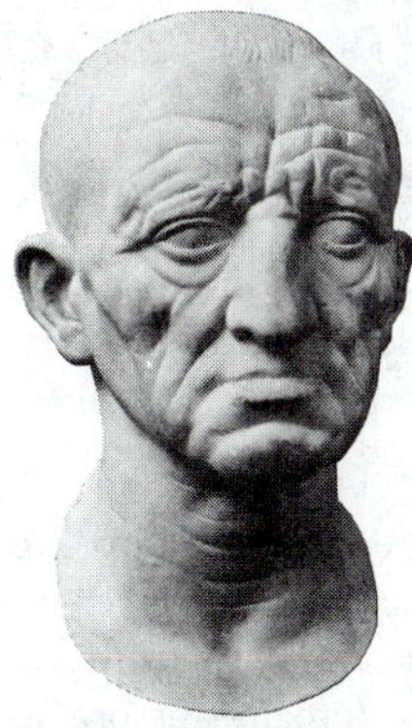

Sculpture of an old Roman, c 80 B.C.

Date	*Event*
c 300 BC	**Euclid flourishes.** Euclid, a Greek mathematician who taught at Alexandria, Egypt, is remembered for his texts on geometry and other branches of mathematics. His system of plane geometry remained largely unchallenged until the 1800's.
264–241 BC	**First Punic War.** The first of three wars in which Rome opposed and then conquered the great empire of Carthage, centered in northern Africa. The first war was fought over control of Sicily. After some serious reverses, the Romans finally destroyed the Carthaginian fleet in 241 and forced Carthage to give up Sicily.
218–201 BC	**Second Punic War.** One of the great wars of ancient times, it was sparked by Carthaginian conquests in Spain. Rome declared war and the Carthaginian general, Hannibal, responded by marching from Spain overland toward Rome. After his famous crossing of the Alps, Hannibal invaded the Italian peninsula and won a succession of decisive victories over Roman armies. He lacked sufficient supplies to attack Rome itself, however, and though he took control of most of southern Italy, the tide of the war turned against him after 212. In 203 he was recalled to Carthage to fight a Roman invasion force under Scipio Africanus Major (234–183), and was decisively defeated at the Battle of Zama (202). Carthage surrendered in 201 and never again regained its former greatness.
214 BC	**Great Wall of China.** One of the greatest manmade structures ever built, this defensive wall was originally constructed by the Chinese Emperor Shih Hwang-ti to check barbarian invasions from the north. Later rulers added to it, creating a 1500-mile-long, 25-foot-high barrier. The wall ultimately failed to check barbarian advances, however.

The Great Wall, more than 2000 years after completion

167 BC	**Revolt of the Maccabees in Palestine.** Persecution by the Seleucids (then in control of Palestine) caused the Jews to pursue a guerrilla war against Seleucid armies. Judas Maccabeus captured Jerusalem and rededicated the temple (164). By 142, the Maccabees had reestablished an independent kingdom of Judaea.
149–146 BC	**Third Punic War.** Final war by the Romans against Carthage. The Romans provoked the war and quickly laid siege to Carthage. The city refused surrender and was taken by the Romans only after hard fighting in the streets of the city itself. The city was destroyed, its surviving inhabitants were sold into slavery, and the Carthaginian domain was organized into the Roman province of Africa.

Date | *Event*

60 BC

Triumvirate in Rome. From about 133 BC there was gradual breakdown of order in Rome. Rebellions and civil war plagued Rome as various factions struggled to control the empire's vast riches. The first triumvirate, an alliance between Julius Caesar (102–44), Pompey (106–48), and Crassus (115?–53), brought a brief lull in this turmoil. Though their arrangement was not a legal form of government, the three triumvirs overcame all opposition and made themselves masters of Rome. They remained in power until Crassus's death in 53 BC.

58–51 BC

Caesar's conquest of Gaul. In 58, Caesar, one of the ruling triumvirate, was given command in Gaul. By his vigorous campaigns there, Caesar conquered all of Gaul and gained great power and prestige. More important, his victories left him at the head of a strong and loyal army.

49–31 BC

Julius Caesar

Cleopatra, queen of Egypt

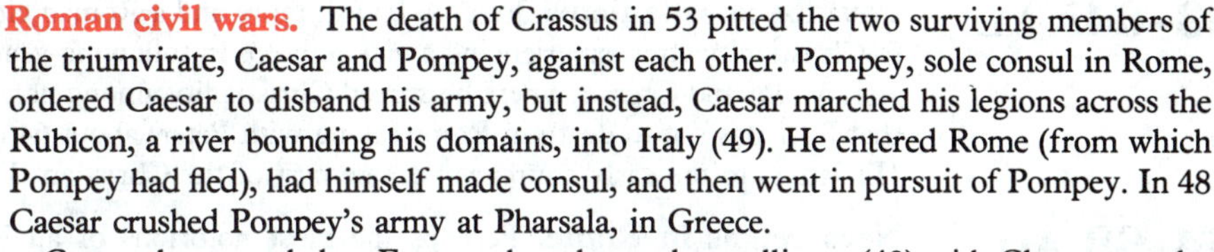

Roman civil wars. The death of Crassus in 53 pitted the two surviving members of the triumvirate, Caesar and Pompey, against each other. Pompey, sole consul in Rome, ordered Caesar to disband his army, but instead, Caesar marched his legions across the Rubicon, a river bounding his domains, into Italy (49). He entered Rome (from which Pompey had fled), had himself made consul, and then went in pursuit of Pompey. In 48 Caesar crushed Pompey's army at Pharsala, in Greece.

Caesar then traveled to Egypt, where he made an alliance (48) with Cleopatra, who had recently been deposed as queen of Egypt. Seeing in him an opportunity to regain her throne, she used her fabled charms to become his lover and keep him there. By 47 Caesar and his armies had restored her as queen of Egypt. In 45 she followed him to Rome.

By 44 Caesar had crushed the last remnants of Pompey's army, restored order in the provinces, and been made dictator for life. Resentment at his power had grown to dangerous proportions in Rome, however, and on March 15, Brutus, Cassius, Casca, and others stabbed him to death as a traitor to republican government. Caesar's death plunged Rome into a new and more deadly disorder.

In the turmoil following Caesar's assassination, Caesar's heir, Octavian (63 BC–14 AD), joined with Marc Antony (83–30 BC) and Lepidus (d. 13 BC) to form a second triumvirate to rule Rome. When they secured their position in Rome, Octavian and Antony pursued and defeated the armies of Brutus and Cassius (42). The triumvirate was renewed in 37, but in 36 Lepidus was ousted.

Meanwhile, Antony was given control of the eastern part of the Roman provinces. There he met Cleopatra; their love affair is among the most famous in history. From 42 to 40, they remained in Egypt. When Antony returned to Rome, he was forced to marry Octavian's sister, Octavia, in order to keep his power. But he soon returned to Cleopatra. The lovers went into opposition to Rome and prepared for war. Octavian's Roman forces finally defeated them in the great naval battle at Actium, off the western coast of Greece, in 31. Antony and Cleopatra fled to Egypt. Pursued by Octavian, they committed suicide. The story of Antony and Cleopatra is the nucleus of the famous play of that title by William Shakespeare.

27 BC–14 AD

Reign of Augustus in Rome. After defeating Antony, Octavian purged the Senate and began instituting reforms in Rome and the provinces. Octavian ruled as "first citizen" until 27 BC. Then he accepted the title of Augustus and became the first Roman emperor. This event also marked the end of the Roman republic and the beginning of the empire. Augustus's reign (27 BC–14 AD) was a Golden Age for Roman arts and literature. Among the great works completed were Vergil's epic poem on the founding of Rome, the *Aeneid*, and Ovid's great work, the *Metamorphoses*. For nearly 200 years after Augustus, the empire was relatively peaceful and a succession of emperors controlled a vast empire surrounding the Mediterranean.

Date	Event
AD **c 3 BC–30 AD**	**Jesus Christ.** According to the four Gospels of the Bible, Jesus was born miraculously to Mary at Bethlehem in Judea, near Jerusalem. Raised in his father's trade of carpentry, Jesus became aware of his divine calling after being baptized by John the Baptist. Following a period of solitude and meditation, Jesus chose twelve disciples and together with them he traveled through Judea. He preached that the kingdom of God had come, and his Jewish followers proclaimed him as the Messiah, a savior or new king for whom the Jews had been waiting. The Gospels tell of many miracles that Jesus accomplished, particularly in healing the sick. Jesus won a wide following but came to be regarded as a threat by Roman and Jewish authorities. He was arrested in Jerusalem (c 30 AD), turned over to Roman authorities, and crucified. But he miraculously rose from the dead. His followers soon spread his teachings through the Roman Empire, establishing churches in many cities, including Rome itself.
33–64? AD	**Paul the apostle flourishes.** A Jewish rabbi and a Roman citizen, Paul was converted to Christianity after experiencing a vision in 33. In following years he went on missions to Asia Minor and Greece, where he spread Christianity among non-Jews. Tradition suggests that Paul was put to death in Rome (along with Peter) about 64 during the reign of Nero. His letters to the early churches became part of the Christian Bible.
54–68 AD	**Nero reigns in Rome.** Perhaps the most notorious of all Roman emperors, Nero's cruelties included the murder of both his mother and his wife. Nero has also been blamed for setting the great fire that burned half of Rome in 64 AD, though this accusation has generally been discounted. Nero did blame the fire on the Christians, however, and began the first Roman persecution of Christians in 64.

Jesus and Mary, his mother

At its height, the Roman Empire circled the Mediterranean; but in 476, Rome itself was conquered.

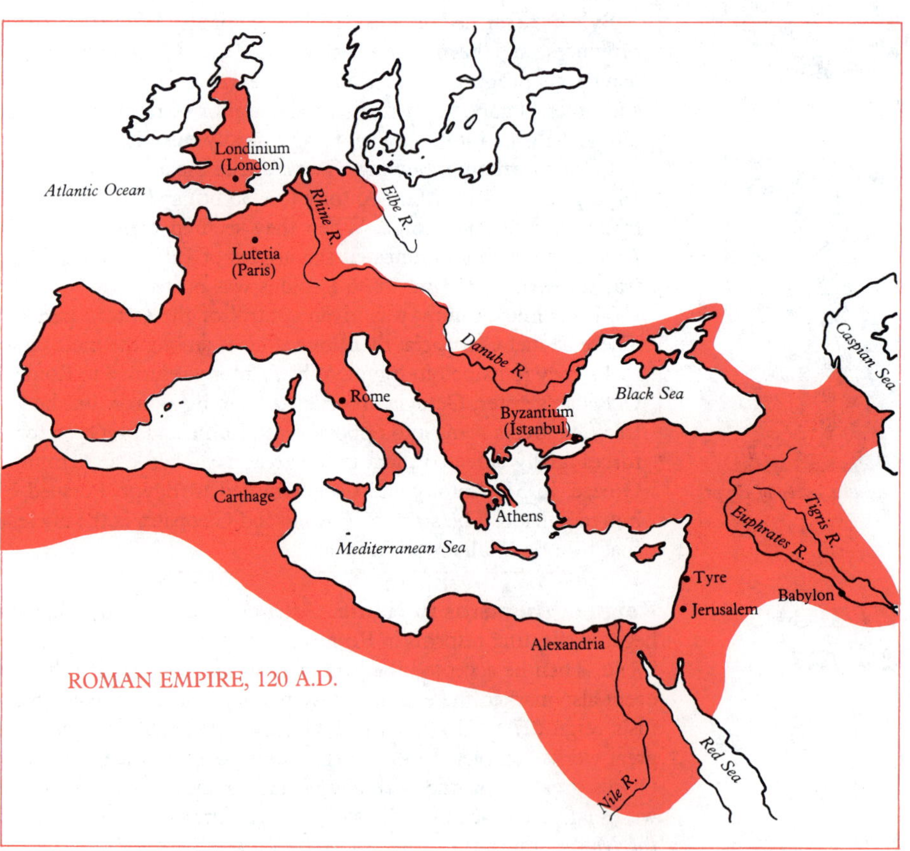

Date	*Event*
c 100 AD	**Chinese develop use of paper.** Paper was believed to have been first made by an official at the imperial court. Knowledge of papermaking spread westward, was known in Baghdad by 793, and from there was transmitted to Europe.
132–135 AD	**Revolt of the Jews.** Led by Bar Kokba (d. 135), the Jews revolted against the rule of Palestine by the Romans. The Romans crushed the revolt, founded a Roman colony on the site of Jerusalem, and refused to allow any Jew to live within the new city.
180–192 AD	**Commodius reigns in Rome.** Ill-suited for rule, Commodius brought an end to a long period of stability in Rome. Commodius's rule was harsh, and he was finally assassinated. For nearly a hundred years afterward, Roman emperors followed in quick succession, each holding on to power for only a few years before being removed.
238 AD	**First invasions by the Goths.** The Goths were a Germanic people that seriously threatened the Roman Empire. Thought to have come originally from Sweden, they migrated southward and came into conflict with the Romans by 238. They raided Greece and gradually forced Roman legions out of Dacia (now Rumania).
284–305 AD	**Diocletian reigns in Rome.** Diocletian was a strong, effective ruler who ended nearly 100 years of instability and thus checked for a time the decline of the empire.
313 AD	**Edict of Milan.** Just before becoming emperor of the Western Roman Empire in 312, Constantine accepted Christianity. The following year, Constantine convinced Licinus, emperor of the Eastern Roman Empire, to join him in proclaiming the toleration of Christianity. The resulting Edict of Milan provided religious freedom for Christians throughout the empire and ordered the restoration of property confiscated from them.
324–337 AD	**Constantine reigns as sole Roman emperor.** Constantine united the eastern and western halves of the empire, which had been administered separately. A period of peace ensued, in which Constantine attempted to strengthen the Christian church and to restore the power of the Roman Empire. He founded the great city of Constantinople (now Istanbul, Turkey), which was the center of the Byzantine Empire for nearly 1000 years. On Constantine's death in 337, however, the empire was again divided.
325 AD	**Council of Nicaea.** The rise of Arianism, a controversial doctrine on the nature of Jesus Christ, threatened to divide the Christian church during the reign of Constantine. In attempting to resolve the dispute over Arianism, Constantine convened (325) a general council of the Christian church, at Nicaea. The council condemned Arianism and formulated the Nicene Creed, which remains the orthodox doctrine on the nature of Jesus.
434–453 AD	**Attila, leader of the Huns.** The Huns were perhaps the most savage of all the barbarian invaders and their notorious leader, Attila, was sometimes called the "Scourge of God." From 434, when he became leader of the Huns, Attila menaced the Eastern Roman Empire. In 451, he marshaled an army of about half a million Huns and barbarian peoples and swept westward into Gaul. He was defeated in a bloody battle at Chalons (in modern France), but ravaged Italy the next year. He died in 453, and his empire disintegrated.
455 AD	**Vandals sack Rome.** The Vandals, a Germanic people, had been forced westward by the Huns and finally crossed from Spain into North Africa. There they captured Carthage (439) from the Romans. Their raids on Sicily and southern Italy from this base culminated in their sack of Rome in 455, soon after the Huns had swept through Italy.
476 AD	**Fall of Rome.** Disintegration of the Western Roman Empire was nearly complete when Odoacer (c 435–493), a German chieftain in Roman service, deposed the last Roman emperor, Romulus Augustulus (ruled 475–476). This marked the end of the Roman Empire in the west and the beginning of the Middle Ages in Europe. Thereafter the Roman Empire in the east became known as the Byzantine Empire.

Medieval world

In Europe, the collapse of the Roman Empire marked the beginning of the Middle Ages, a period of more than 1000 years (476–1500). This period witnessed the rise of the Roman Catholic Church, the formation of the first European nation-states, and (near its end) the rediscovery of Greek and Roman culture during the Renaissance. But in 476, the Western Roman Empire was in the hands of the European tribes the Romans called barbarians. Italy was controlled by the Ostrogoths, Gaul was undergoing a new invasion by the Franks, Spain was ruled by the Visigoths, and Africa was held by the Vandals. Only in the eastern empire, now called the Byzantine Empire, did Roman rule continue.

Date	*Event*
476–1453	**The Byzantine Empire.** Roman rule in the east continued under the Byzantine emperors, who proved able to withstand the barbarian attacks. Under Justinian (527–565), the empire recovered some lands from barbarians in the Latin West, but the Byzantine state was rarely free from the threat of invasion. Despite this, the empire successfully maintained the most prosperous economy in the medieval Christian world and achieved a dynamic and civilized society. Attacks by the Seljuk Turks after 1000 seriously weakened the empire and, for a time, it was ruled (1204–1261) by the Crusaders, European warriors who had come to help the Byzantine Christians against the Muslim Turks. After Byzantine emperors regained control in 1261, the empire continued to decline until it was finally conquered by the Turks in 1453. Throughout its long history, Byzantine culture was permeated by Christianity. But the Eastern Church, which was subject to control by the Byzantine emperors, gradually split with the Western Church over doctrinal disputes, and in 1054 the division between Eastern and Western Christianity became permanent. Byzantine art and culture greatly influenced the Slavs of Eastern Europe and helped to pass on Greek and Roman culture to Western Europe.
 *Emperor Justinian, c 560*	
c 500	**Clovis founds the Merovingian Empire in Gaul.** Clovis I (ruled 481–511) was king of the Salian Franks, a Germanic people that invaded Gaul (modern France) as Rome collapsed. By his conquests, he made himself master of Gaul and established his capital at Paris. The empire he founded was divided on his death and later was torn by internal wars, but it nevertheless provided the foundation for Charlemagne's great empire three centuries later.
527–565	**Justinian reigns in the Byzantine Empire.** Justinian retook Africa and Italy from the barbarians and ordered construction of the Hagia Sophia, the great masterpiece of Byzantine architecture. Justinian is also famous for his Justinian Code, a compilation of Roman law.
c 529	**St. Benedict's monastery founded.** Located at Monte Cassino in what is now Italy, the monastery became the symbolic center of Western monasticism. Monasteries patterned on the Benedictine model spread throughout Europe, helped Christianize the Continent, and helped preserve Latin culture during a period of great instability. The Benedictine order of monks flourished until about 1200.
590–604	**Saint Gregory I is pope.** Gregory promoted papal supremacy in spiritual matters and established papal authority in temporal matters as well. He also did much to promote monasticism and to reform church administration and liturgy.
618–907	**T'ang dynasty in China.** T'ang rulers greatly expanded the Chinese empire and by about 650 controlled regions that included China proper and parts of Korea, Manchuria, Mongolia, Tibet, and Turkistan. The T'ang period also witnessed a great flowering of the arts, especially sculpture, painting, and poetry. The rise of provincial warlords after 750 weakened and finally brought down the dynasty.

Date	*Event*
622–1258  *A Muslim mosque*	**Islam.** Muhammad (570?–632), an Arab holy man, began his prophetic mission at age 40 when God appointed him as a messenger. He named his religion Islam and called on his fellow citizens at Mecca (in modern Saudi Arabia) to forsake belief in more than one God and to seek righteousness. In 622 Muhammad and his followers were forced to leave Mecca for Medina. This exodus, called the Hegira, marks the beginning of the Muslim calendar. In 630, after consolidating his hold over Medina, Muhammad took control of Mecca. By the time he died (632), much of Arabia had submitted to him. Muhammad's successors, called caliphs, completed the conquest of Arabia and successfully attacked the Byzantines and Persians. Under the Umayyad dynasty (660–750), the empire of the caliphs reached its height and extended westward from Arabia to Spain and eastward to central Asia. In 750 the Abbasid dynasty came to power. Under Abbasid rule (750–1258), centered at Baghdad, the major cities of the Muslim empire experienced a golden age. The empire began to decline after about 900 and fell to the invading Mongols in 1258. Islam itself, however, had been established as the dominant religion from the Indian subcontinent to North Africa.
732–768	**Rise of the Frankish kingdom.** Frankish hero Charles Martel defeated the Muslim invaders at the battle of Tours in 732. Thus he ended the threat to Frankish domains and became ruler of the Franks. In 751, Pepin the Short became king, establishing the Carolingian line. Pepin donated his lands in central Italy to the pope in 756. These became the nucleus of the Papal States, which were controlled by the papacy until 1870.
768	**Charlemagne (742?–814) succeeds Pepin as ruler of the Franks.** Charlemagne embarked on series of conquests through which he created the great Carolingian Empire, defeating the Lombards in Italy, the Avars in the Danube region, and other tribes in Bavaria, Saxony, and the Spanish March (northeastern Spain). Charlemagne was crowned emperor of a reconstituted Western Roman Empire in 800. He also sought to restore education, theological studies, and art, creating a brief renaissance of learning and art.
c 800–1400  *A medieval knight*	**Age of feudalism.** Feudalism is generally believed to have been introduced in Europe during the reign of Charlemagne (768–814). It was spread across continental Europe by Frankish conquests and was introduced in England by the Normans, following their conquest in 1066. The feudal system was based on the granting of rights to lands (fiefs) in return for certain considerations. Thus, a feudal lord granted lands to his vassal (a lesser noble) in return for an oath of loyalty and the commitment to supply a number of warriors for the lord's armies. The process of subdivision (called subinfeudination) was continued by the vassals, who, in turn, divided their lands into fiefs. The vassals then became the feudal lords of the nobles who received these lands. At the bottom of the feudal hierarchy were the serfs, tenants of the feudal manor. Serfs were peasant laborers who were bound to the manor and who by farming the lands provided the economic base of the feudal system. Feudalism reached its height in the 1200's, declining thereafter until it had largely disappeared in Western Europe by about 1400. The feudal system created petty kingdoms, encouraged wars between them, and inflicted severe hardships on the peasant serfs. But feudal society, with its brave knights and strict code of chivalry, also inspired a flourishing romantic literature in late medieval times. These romances portrayed an idealized vision of courtly life and of battle, a vision that continues to hold a special fascination even today. A great body of these romances, called the Arthurian cycle, recounted and embellished tales of King Arthur, legendary English conqueror and hero; splendid Camelot, where he held court; and the Round Table, where Arthur met with his knights.

Date	Event

An early Viking ship

c 800–c 900	**Norse raiders flourish.** Norsemen were Scandinavian Vikings who, seeking plunder and new lands, ranged far from their homelands. Danes (Norsemen from Denmark) invaded England in 865 and many settled there permanently. In France, Norsemen conquered and settled what became Normandy by 912. The Norsemen who invaded Russia were called Varangians.
843	**Treaty of Verdun.** Charlemagne's successor, Louis I the Pious (ruled 814–840), held the Carolingian Empire together until he died in 840. Open warfare then broke out among his heirs. The Treaty of Verdun divided the empire into three parts: the western part became modern France and the eastern part eventually became Germany. The narrow middle section was largely absorbed into the eastern and western kingdoms.
871–899	**Alfred the Great rules in England.** From about 600, the Angles and Saxons, Germanic peoples who invaded England, had established a number of independent kingdoms. After 800, however, Norse invaders from Denmark (called Danes) threatened to overrun all of Anglo-Saxon England. Alfred, Anglo-Saxon king of Wessex, became a hero of early England by turning back the advancing Danes and preserving Anglo-Saxon rule in south and west England.
c 950	**First use of gunpowder.** Though it is not clear when gunpowder was invented, there is evidence that the Chinese were using it for fireworks by about this time. Knowledge of gunpowder was apparently transmitted from China, through the Arabs, to Europe by the 1400's.
960–1279	**Sung dynasty in China.** Following a period of chaos and warfare between petty kingdoms, Sung rulers reunited the Chinese empire and thus set the stage for one of the great epochs in Chinese history. Increased trade with India, Persia, and the Arabs brought commercial prosperity. There were many technological innovations (gunpowder, movable type for printing), Confucianism was revived, administrative reforms were instituted, and the arts flourished. Sung rulers lacked an effective military force, however, and finally succumbed to the invading Mongols, led by Kublai Khan (see below).
962	**Otto the Great founds the Holy Roman Empire.** After the division of the Carolingian Empire (843), the eastern part broke up into the duchies of Franconia, Saxony, Thuringia, Swabia, and Bavaria. As German king, Otto (ruled 936–973) reasserted imperial control over the rebellious German nobles; defeated the Magyars, a Slavic people

threatening the empire from the east; and brought Lorraine, Burgundy, and Italy under German control. Otto also fostered ties with the church and in 962 the pope crowned him emperor. This event marked the beginning of the Holy Roman Empire, a German state that remained the most formidable kingdom in Western Europe until the 1200's.

987–996

Hugh Capet, first Capetian king of France. Hugh Capet was a powerful nobleman with extensive domains around Paris. He displaced the Carolingian claimant to the throne of the western (French) part of the old empire in 987 and thereupon founded the Capetian dynasty. This dynasty ruled France until 1328. The Capetian kings greatly expanded the territories of France through wars and alliances and thus laid the foundations of modern France.

c 1000

Leif Ericsson visits North America. Raised among Norse colonists in Greenland, Leif Ericsson is known to have visited Norway in 999. On the return voyage to Greenland, however, his ship was apparently blown off course and he landed at what he called "Vinland." Though most agree he landed in North America, the exact location is a matter of conjecture.

1016–1035

Canute, Danish king of England. Canute invaded England with a large force in 1015, quickly conquered the Anglo-Saxon kingdoms, and became sole ruler of England. He succeeded to the Danish throne in 1019 and added Norway to his domain in 1028, thus creating a great but short-lived northern empire.

c 1025

Modern musical notation formulated. In order to simplify the training required for ecclesiastical singers, a Benedictine monk named Guido of Arezzo (c 990–1050) invented a new means of musical notation in about 1025. His system introduced the use of the staff and clef and thereby provided the foundation for modern musical notation in the West.

Early musical notation

1054

Schism of 1054. Doctrinal and jurisdictional disputes between the Western Christian Church, centered at Rome, and the Eastern Christian Church, centered at Constantinople, had begun centuries before. In 1054, however, the separation became permanent and formally established the independence of the Roman Catholic Church in the West and the Eastern Orthodox Church in the East.

1066

Normans conquer England. The Norman invasion was launched by William the Conqueror (c 1027–1087), duke of Normandy (in modern France), to press his claim to the English throne. William won England at the Battle of Hastings (1066), though rebellions by English noblemen continued until 1072. As king of England, William replaced the English nobles with his Norman followers and distributed English lands to them according to the feudal system. Norman customs and the Norman French language became the standard in England and remained so for two centuries among nobility.

1075–1122

Investiture controversy. Lay investiture was a medieval church practice whereby a secular ruler became involved in the selection of bishops and other clerics. The system led to widespread corruption. Pope Gregory VII (fl. c 1020–1085) ended investiture in 1075. In 1076, the Holy Roman Emperor Henry IV (ruled 1056–1105) declared the pope deposed; but within a year he was forced to submit to Gregory in a humiliating ceremony at Canossa (1077). Henry finally attacked Rome (1081–1083), forcing Gregory to flee. The struggle outlived both of them and was finally ended in 1122 by a compromise called the Concordat of Worms.

Date	Event
1095–1291	**Crusades.** By 1095 the Muslim Turks had closed access to the Holy Land (Palestine) and threatened the Christian empire of the Byzantines. In that same year Pope Urban II encouraged European noblemen to travel to the Holy Land and protect it. This first crusade (1096–1099) was successful, resulting in the capture of Jerusalem and the founding of the Crusader States in the Holy Land. Muslim victories in following years sparked new crusades—eight in all—each less successful than the last. The Christians were finally driven from the Holy Land in 1291.
1138	**Guelphs and Ghibellines in the Holy Roman Empire.** The Guelphs were partisans of the papacy. The Ghibellines supported the Hohenstaufen royal house of the Holy Roman Empire. The conflict between the Guelphs and Ghibellines continued for over a hundred years and centered on attempts by the Hohenstaufens, especially Frederick I Barbarossa (1152–1190) and Frederick II (1220–1250), to strengthen imperial power through the domination of Italy. The Hohenstaufens met stubborn resistance from the popes, feudal noblemen of Germany, and the cities of northern Italy.
1170	**St. Thomas à Becket martyred in England.** From 1162, when he was elected archbishop of Canterbury, St. Thomas valiantly resisted the efforts of King Henry II (ruled 1154–1189) to curb the powers of the church in England. The conflict ended in the murder of St. Thomas by four of the king's knights.
1198–1216	**Pope Innocent reigns.** The papacy reached the height of its power during Innocent's reign. Innocent asserted papal supremacy over secular rulers, was able to enforce his will over the Holy Roman Empire and England, and acted as overlord in Spain, Hungary, and Scandinavia.
1206–1227	**Genghis Khan.** Mongol tribes were united under the rule of Genghis Khan (1167?–1227) in 1206 and in following years he and his savage bands of warriors swept across Asia. Genghis Khan first attacked China and Korea, then turned to the west. He conquered parts of Persia and Russia and raided India. His sons continued his conquests and, by 1260, they ruled a great Mongol empire that included much of Asia and eastern Europe.
1215	**Magna Charta.** One of the most famous documents in history, the Magna Charta is an early statement of the principle of subjecting even the king to a rule of law. It was drawn up by noblemen in England to halt abuses by King John (ruled 1199–1216). The nobles forced John to sign the document at Runnymede on June 19, 1215.
c 1250	**St. Thomas Aquinas flourishes.** St. Thomas (1225–1274) was the leading philosopher of the medieval church. He taught that reason and faith are compatible and systematized the doctrines of the church. St. Thomas's writings were officially adopted (1879) by the Roman Catholic Church.
1279–1290 *Kublai Khan*	**Kublai Khan in China.** The grandson of Genghis Khan, Kublai Khan (1215?–1294) brought the Eurasian Mongol empire to its height by conquering China in 1279. Other attempts at conquests failed, however, and the sinking of his invasion fleet off Japan (1281) by a typhoon both saved Japan from the Mongols and gave rise to the term "kamikaze" (divine wind). Kublai Khan made China the seat of the Mongol empire. At what is now Peking, he built a magnificent city as his capital. His reign was prosperous and the splendor of his court was described in the famous narratives of Marco Polo (1254?–1324?), a Venetian traveler who journeyed there in 1275.
c 1308	**Dante Alighieri (1265–1321) begins work on the *Divine Comedy.*** One of the great masterpieces of Western literature, the *Divine Comedy* was written in Italian (rather than Latin, the "official" language of diplomacy and the church). It recounts the poet's imaginary journey through Hell, Purgatory, and Paradise.

Date	Event
1309–1378	**Babylonian Captivity of the papacy.** Unsettled political conditions at Rome forced the removal of the papacy to Avignon (now in France), then under papal control. The popes during this period were French and were generally under the control of the French monarchy. Pope Gregory XI (ruled 1370–1378) ended the captivity by returning the papacy to Rome. This ushered in the Great Schism (see below).
1334–c 1354	**Black Death.** This terrible epidemic began in Constantinople in 1334 and quickly spread into Europe. In the next two decades an estimated 75 percent of the population of Europe and Asia was wiped out. The social and economic consequences of the plague were enormous. It contributed to the breakup of the feudal system by creating a sudden shortage of peasant labor. Because their services became more valuable, the peasants revolted in many parts of Europe and demanded more equitable treatment.
1337–1453	**Hundred Years' War.** This protracted war left France devastated by internal revolts and famine, as well as by fighting, and cost England its extensive domains on the European Continent. Both kingdoms were further ravaged by the outbreak of the Black Death during the war. The war began when English King Edward III (ruled 1327–1377) claimed the French throne and invaded France. The first phase of the war ended favorably for the English in 1360, following important victories at Crecy (1346) and Poitiers (1356). Fighting resumed after 1369. In 1407, a civil war broke out over control of the French throne, and the English took advantage, conquering most of northern France by 1429. Then the great French heroine Joan of Arc (1412?–1431) rallied the French and drove the English back at Orleans. She was captured and burned at the stake by the English in 1431, but she provided the spark needed to bring about victory for France. Charles VII was crowned at Rheims in 1429, the civil war in France ended in 1435, and by 1453 the French had conquered all English domains on the Continent.

The English use bows and arrows to defeat the French at Crecy, 1346.

Date	*Event*
1368–1644	**Ming dynasty in China.** The Ming dynasty emperors ended the period of Mongol rule begun by Kublai Khan. They expanded their empire to include Korea, Vietnam, Burma, Turkistan, and Mongolia. Traditional Chinese culture was restored, and during this period European traders and missionaries began to penetrate China. Ineffective rulers and internal dissent finally ended the reign of the Ming emperors.
c 1369–1405	**Tamerlane.** Claiming to be a descendant of Genghis Khan, Tamerlane (c 1336–1405) had firmly established control around his capital, Samarkand (near the Caspian Sea), by about 1369. In following years, he ruthlessly conquered other territories in this region and created a short-lived empire that extended from the Black Sea to northern India.
1378–1417	**Great Schism of the Roman Catholic Church.** The return of the papacy to Rome in 1378 resulted in a split between the newly elected Italian pope and the cardinals. A faction of cardinals elected their own pope, sitting in Avignon, in opposition to the pope at Rome. The schism was ended after nearly 40 years by the Council of Constance, which deposed the rival popes and elected Martin V (ruled 1417–1431) as pope.
c 1387	***The Canterbury Tales.*** A masterpiece of early English literature, this collection of tales concerning medieval English life was written by the poet Geoffrey Chaucer (c 1340–1400) in the years after 1387.
c 1438	**Gutenberg prints with movable type.** Though the use of movable type was first discovered in China sometime between 1000 and 1100, it was apparently unknown in Europe until Johann Gutenberg (c 1400–1468?) invented it there. The discovery made books far less expensive and more accessible.
1453	**Constantinople captured by Ottoman Turks.** The fall of Constantinople marked the end of the Byzantine Empire and the ascendancy of the new and powerful Ottoman Empire. Centered in northwest Asia Minor from the 1200's, the Ottoman Turks gradually extended their control into southeastern Europe and, after displacing the Byzantines there, captured Constantinople. The empire expanded rapidly thereafter and by the late 1500's it included most of the Middle East and North Africa, the Balkans in southeastern Europe, the Crimea, and parts of Hungary. After 1600, the power of the Ottomans declined, but the regime survived until 1914.
1455–1485	**Wars of the Roses in England.** This complex dynastic war was fought by the rival houses of York and Lancaster for control of the English throne. Actual fighting occurred only sporadically. The Yorkists gained the throne in 1461, but dissension among the Yorkists led to the rise of Henry Tudor, the Lancastrian claimant to the throne. He ended the wars by defeating Yorkist King Richard III (ruled 1483–1485) at the Battle of Bosworth Field (1485), and was crowned Henry VII (ruled 1485–1509).
1469  *Ferdinand and Isabella*	**Founding of the modern Spanish state.** The Muslim invasion of the Iberian Peninsula (711) left Christians in possession of only small kingdoms in the north, and it was not until after 1000 that Spanish Christians began to retake the peninsula. In the wake of the Christian advance, various independent kingdoms were created. Their unification into the Spanish state began with the marriage of King Ferdinand of Aragon (1452–1516) and Queen Isabella of Castile (1451–1504) in 1469. The Spanish monarchs sponsored the expeditions of Christopher Columbus (see below). His discoveries gave Spain an advantage in gaining an overseas empire. By Ferdinand's death in 1516, Spain was not only united but was becoming the richest kingdom in Europe.
1478	**Spanish Inquisition.** Instituted by King Ferdinand and Queen Isabella, the Spanish Inquisition is remembered chiefly as a symbol of barbaric cruelty and persecution. In Spain the Inquisition was concerned with cases of heresy and certain other crimes. The notorious Tomás de Torquemada (1420–1498), Grand Inquisitor from 1483, devised especially cruel procedures. Only after 1600 was the severity of the Inquisition reduced.

Renaissance and Enlightenment

The European world changed greatly in the 1500's. The Renaissance in art and learning, the Reformation in religion, and the excitement of worldwide exploration all helped bring men to a new understanding of themselves and their universe. The changes also brought terrible wars and persecutions, however. By 1700, a new world view called the Enlightenment had many of the seeds of our own modern perspective; men talked of democracy and of the new world order that the modern era would one day produce.

Date *Event*

1490–1650

A sketch by Michelangelo

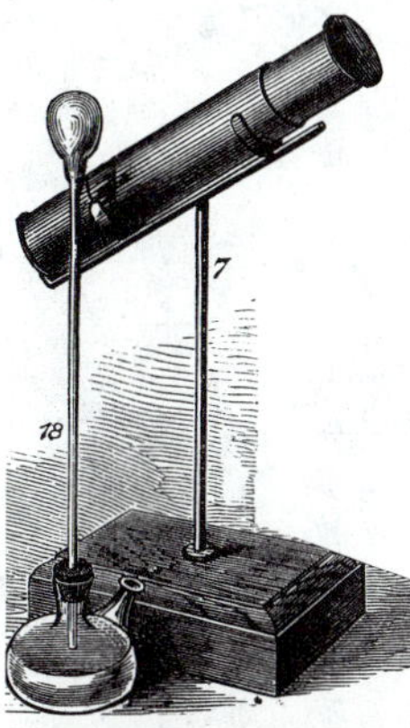

Galileo's telescope and his air thermometer

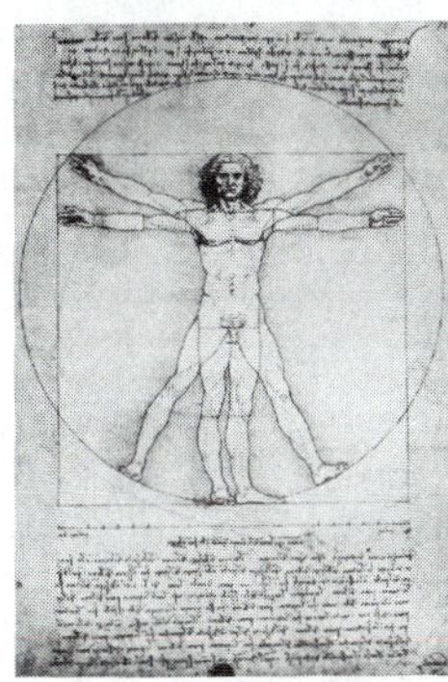

A study of proportions by Leonardo da Vinci

The Renaissance. Renaissance means literally rebirth; the term applies to the revival of classical learning and culture in Europe at the close of the Middle Ages. The reawakening began in Italy as early as 1300, and it spread gradually to other parts of Europe, mainly during the late 1400's and 1500's. The shift in viewpoint during the Renaissance was remarkable: medieval man was concerned with God, but for men in the Renaissance, man was indeed "the measure of all things."

Scholars were concerned with the secular world. Poets and philosophers were concerned with this world, not the next; with the world of nature, not that of theology; with man, not angels. Painters and sculptors sought to capture real people rather than general types, and individual personalities rather than universal human traits. Architects replaced the ornate Gothic style with a simple, classical style with straight lines and balanced proportions.

Universities concentrated heavily on secular subjects and produced large numbers of educated laymen. The "universal man"—one skilled in a variety of pursuits, from scholarship and poetry to the art of war—was the Renaissance ideal. Leonardo da Vinci (1452–1519) came closest of all to fitting this model.

The Renaissance also witnessed the consolidation of major European states under strong monarchical rule, notably in England, France, and Spain. By the early 1500's, each of these countries had achieved, approximately, its modern boundaries. Although each country developed differently, all developed a strong monarchy and centralized institutions characteristic of modern government.

Renaissance Masters

Dante, 1265–1321, *Italian poet*
Giotto, 1266–1337, *Italian painter*
Petrarch, 1304–1374, *Italian poet and humanist*
Giovanni Boccaccio, 1313–1375, *Italian writer*
Donatello, c 1386–1466, *Italian sculptor*
Leonardo da Vinci, 1452–1519, *Italian painter, sculptor, engineer, scientist*
Erasmus, 1466?–1536, *Dutch humanist scholar*
Niccolò Machiavelli, 1469–1527, *Italian writer and political philosopher*
Albrecht Dürer, 1471–1528, *German artist*
Nicolaus Copernicus, 1473–1543, *Polish astronomer*
Michelangelo, 1475–1564, *Italian painter, sculptor, architect*
Sir Thomas More, 1478–1535, *English author*
Raphael, 1483–1520, *Italian painter*
Titian, c 1490–1576, *Italian painter*
François Rabelais, 1494?–1553, *French writer*
Hans Holbein the Younger, c 1497–1543, *German artist*
Pieter Brueghel the Elder, c 1525–1569, *Flemish artist*
Michel Eyquem de Montaigne, 1533–1592, *French essayist*
Miguel de Cervantes, 1547–1616, *Spanish writer*
Francis Bacon, 1561–1626, *English philosopher*
William Shakespeare, 1564–1616, *English dramatist*
Galileo, 1564–1642, *Italian scientist*

Date *Event*

1492–1522 **Age of Discovery.** Improvements in navigation, increased knowledge about the world beyond Europe (gained during the late Middle Ages), and successful voyages along the African coast by Portuguese explorer Henry the Navigator (1394–1460), all helped set the stage for a rapid succession of voyages of discovery. That the world was round was not a new idea in Europe, but the dangers of sailing into unknown waters were legion.

Thus, in 1492, when Christopher Columbus (1451–1506) sailed westward to find a sea route to Asia, he needed both the courage of his conviction that the world was round and more than a little good fortune. News of Columbus's discovery of land (an island in the Bahamas) on October 12, 1492, aroused great interest in Europe. It touched off an era of exploration and colonization that was to profoundly affect the history of Europe and the world. While Columbus's voyages (he made four in all) opened up the New World to the Spanish, the voyage by Portuguese navigator Vasco da Gama (c 1469–1524) in 1497–1499 resulted in the discovery of a sea route to India and the establishment of Portuguese colonies in both India and east Africa. Finally, Ferdinand Magellan (c 1480–1521), a Portuguese navigator in Spanish service, set out in 1519 to find a westward route to the Spice Islands. Magellan was killed in the Philippines, but his ships continued sailing westward, and on September 6, 1522, they completed the first circumnavigation of the world.

Vasco da Gama

MAJOR VOYAGES OF EXPLORATION, 1492–1522

GREENLAND
CABOT 1497–1498
ENGLAND
NORTH AMERICA
EUROPE
ASIA
SPAIN
Atlantic Ocean
COLUMBUS 1492
Isthmus of Panama
VESPUCCI 1497–1503
AFRICA
ARABIA
INDIA
BALBOA 1513
SOUTH AMERICA
DIAS 1498
Indian Ocean
Pacific Ocean
Da GAMA 1498
MAGELLAN 1519–1522
Cape of Good Hope
Cape Horn

1509–1547 **Henry VIII reigns in England.** A strong ruler, whose actions helped shape English history, Henry is best remembered for his many wives (he had six) and for his troubles with the Roman Catholic Church. The failure of Henry's first wife to produce a male heir led him to seek papal sanction for a divorce. This was refused but Henry married a new wife, Anne Boleyn (1507?–1536), anyway. Excommunicated by the pope, he retaliated by separating the English church from Rome (1534). Henry thus created the Church of England, which is still independent of Rome today, and made himself head of the church. He then dealt ruthlessly with all opposition to the new national church. In subsequent years, Henry became increasingly despotic, treating his wives no less harshly than his subjects.

Date	*Event*

1517–1555

John Calvin

The Reformation. The Reformation began in 1517 as a revolt against corruption in the Western Church. Within 40 years, it had established several Christian churches (which came to be called Protestant) as rivals to the chuch headed by the pope (which came to be known as Roman Catholic). Widespread abuses, such as simony (sale of church offices), violation of vows of celibacy by the clergy, and the sale of indulgences (by which the pope claimed to release souls from purgatory), had sparked calls for reform in previous centuries. But it was the matter of indulgences that finally prompted action by Martin Luther (1483–1546), a professor of theology at the University of Wittenberg, in Germany. On October 31, 1517, Luther posted his famous 95 theses, attacking church corruption, on the door of the Wittenberg church. Thus began the Reformation.

Luther ultimately denied not only the doctrine of indulgences but also the infallibility of popes and church councils. Central to his emerging Protestant doctrine, however, was his assertion that salvation was achieved through faith, not sacraments and works. Luther's doctrine spread rapidly and, although he was excommunicated (1520) and put under an imperial ban by the Diet of Worms (1521), he continued to preach and teach for another 25 years. Supported by several German princes, Luther's reform movement evolved into the independent Lutheran Church.

Meanwhile, other Protestant groups appeared, including the Calvinists, led by the French theologian John Calvin (1509–1564). In 1536 Calvin organized the Reformed Church in Geneva, Switzerland, and from this beginning Calvinism grew into a second major branch of Protestantism. Calvinism differed from Lutheranism chiefly in the doctrine that salvation of individuals was predestined at the time of creation. Other more radical sects also appeared.

Attempts by Catholic princes to crush the Protestant movement in the Holy Roman Empire led to a series of rebellions and ruinous wars. The Religious Peace of Augsburg (see below) in 1555 brought a 50-year halt to the fighting, but religious antagonisms continued, playing a major role in the Thirty Years' War (1618–1648) (see below). Meanwhile, Protestantism spread quickly throughout Northern Europe and led to religious strife in France, England, Scotland, the Netherlands, Poland, and Hungary.

1519–1533

Spanish conquests in South America. After establishing themselves in the West Indies, the Spanish conquered the South American mainland. In 1519, the great Spanish conquistador Hernán Cortés (1485–1547) led a small force into what is now Mexico; by 1521 he had conquered the Mayan and Aztec empires. The Spanish extended their control into Central America in following years. In 1533 Francisco Pizarro moved against the great Inca empire, centered in Peru, and took control of it with astonishing ease. From this base, the Spanish subsequently extended their control throughout most the continent and imposed a harsh colonial regime. Native Indian cities were stripped of their fabulous wealth in gold. Indians were enslaved and forced to work in the mines to produce still more wealth for their greedy Spanish overlords.

1519–1556

Charles V (1500–1558) reigns as Holy Roman Emperor. One of the most powerful rulers of the famous Hapsburg family, Charles became king of Spain in 1516. On his succession as Holy Roman Emperor in 1519, he became the ruler of vast domains, including much of Europe and Spanish claims in the New World. His reign was marked by wars with the French and opposition to the Reformation within the Holy Roman Empire.

c 1530

Copernicus revolutionizes astronomy. Nicolaus Copernicus (1473–1543), a Polish astronomer, used his observations of heavenly bodies to disprove the traditional theory that the sun and planets rotate around Earth. Copernicus completed his book advancing a heliocentric theory (Earth and other planets rotate around the sun) in about 1530, and later came to be recognized as the founder of modern astronomy.

Date	Event
1545–1563	**Council of Trent and the Counter Reformation.** The rapid spread of Protestantism encouraged Catholic leaders to eliminate abuses and corruption in the Roman Catholic Church. The movement centered on the work of the Council of Trent, which was called by Pope Paul III (ruled 1534–1549) and which completed its work in 1563. The council instituted a reformulation of Catholic doctrine, measures to end abuses by the clergy, and liturgical reforms. The council's work was carried forward in subsequent years by reform-minded popes, as well as by reform movements within Catholic religious orders.
1547–1584	**Ivan the Terrible reigns as first Russian czar.** Following the Mongol invasions (1200's), the Duchy of Moscow rose to power as the nucleus of the Russian state. Ivan succeeded as grand duke of Moscow in 1547, but took the title of czar; he was the first Russian ruler to do so. He greatly expanded his empire eastward by defeating the Mongol Tatars and by conquering Siberia. Ivan became ruthless and erratic in the latter part of his reign and, to consolidate his power, instituted a reign of terror in which many boyars (noblemen) were killed or exiled.
1555	**Peace of Augsburg.** This agreement ended (for about 50 years) the religious strife in the Holy Roman Empire brought about by the Protestant Reformation. Warfare between rival Protestant and Catholic nobles had threatened to tear the empire apart and the nobles readily agreed to the peace, which allowed each state to adopt either Lutheranism or Catholicism. Catholics in Lutheran states were allowed to migrate to Catholic states, and vice versa. Calvinists were not included in the settlement.
1558–1603	**Queen Elizabeth reigns in England.** One of the great English monarchs, Elizabeth presided over England's rise as a major naval power, brought about a period of commercial prosperity, and oversaw the beginnings of colonization by the English. She became a champion of the Protestant cause by restoring the Church of England in 1559, after a brief renewal of Catholicism (1555–1559), and by supporting Protestant leaders in Europe. Elizabeth's reign was also marked by a great flowering of English literature, including the works of William Shakespeare (1564–1616), Christopher Marlowe (1564–1593), and Edmund Spenser (1552?–1599).
1562–1598	**Religious wars in France.** These were a series of intermittent and bloody civil wars between Catholics and French Protestants (Huguenots). The wars were sparked by persecutions of the Protestants, and were further complicated by rivalry between Protestant and Catholic nobles for control of the French monarchy. By 1584, the conflict centered around the succession of a Protestant to the French throne. The Protestant leader, King Henry IV, took the throne in 1589, but agreed to become a Catholic (1593). In 1598, he issued the Edict of Nantes, granting full liberties to Protestants.
1582	**Gregorian calendar.** Pope Gregory XIII (ruled 1572–1585) devised this calendar to improve the accuracy of the Julian calendar, which was then in use. Gregory's calendar added eleven days (at the time of its adoption) to the Julian calendar. The modern calendar uses Gregory's system.
1588	**Spanish Armada destroyed.** Spanish King Philip II assembled his famous war fleet to invade Elizabethan England and put an end to Protestantism there. But before the armada could reach English shores, it was heavily damaged (1588) and scattered by the lighter, more maneuverable English warships. Heavy storms further damaged the fleet and only half its ships returned to Spain. Spain never regained its position as a naval power, and began a long economic decline.
1592–1611	**Shakespeare flourishes.** Regarded as the world's greatest playwright, William Shakespeare (1564–1616) began his career as a playwright in London in about 1592. He wrote nearly 40 plays; among his most famous are *Romeo and Juliet, Hamlet,* and *Macbeth* (see Literature).

1600's

Building empires. During the 1500's only Spain (mainly in South America) and Portugal (mainly in Africa and the East Indies) actively sought to establish trading colonies. But in the early 1600's there began a great European movement to acquire colonial empires. The Dutch were first and they eventually dominated the East Indies. They also established footholds in India, Africa, South America, and North America (notably New Amsterdam on Manhattan Island).

By 1603 the French began the settlement of New France (Canadian coastal regions); they later expanded into the Mississippi valley region of the United States. They also founded colonies in the Caribbean islands, in Africa, and in India. The British, unable to compete with the Dutch in the East Indies, focused on India. They also established themselves in West Africa, the West Indies, coastal North America, and the Hudson Bay region of Canada. British and French colonial rivalries resulted in four colonial wars between 1689 and 1763, each a part of a larger European war. By 1763 France had lost most of her colonies and Britain emerged as the leading colonial power.

1613

Romanov dynasty comes to power in Russia. Following the collapse of the old Rurik dynasty, Russia endured a chaotic period called the Time of Troubles (1598–1613). The election of Michael Romanov (ruled 1613–1645) as czar restored order and began the long reign of the Romanov dynasty, which remained in power until the Russian Revolution in 1917.

1618–1648

Gustavus Adolphus

Thirty Years' War. This was the last of the great European wars of religion. This complex war involved the controversy between Protestants and Catholics; the power struggle between the Holy Roman Emperor and German nobles seeking to break imperial authority; and political rivalry between the Hapsburg family (which controlled the Holy Roman Empire) and England, France, Denmark, and Sweden. The war began with a revolt against Catholicism and absolutist authority in Bohemia. Order was restored by about 1623, but in 1626 Denmark invaded the empire (with some English troops) in the name of the Protestant cause. Denmark was defeated in 1629 and in 1630 the Swedes entered the war. Sweden, under the command of King Gustavus Adolphus, brought the imperial forces to near defeat, but the Peace of Prague (1635) united Protestants and Catholics in the Holy Roman Empire against the Swedes. The French then joined the Swedes and fighting spread throughout Europe. France succeeded in dragging out the war, exhausting the Hapsburgs and the Holy Roman Empire. The Peace of Westphalia ended the war in 1648 and virtually destroyed the Holy Roman Empire by making German states practically independent of imperial control. It also gave France important territories on the German frontier; forced Spain to recognize the independence of the United Provinces (the Netherlands); and granted Calvinists religious freedoms in the Holy Roman Empire.

Delegates conclude the Treaty of Westphalia, 1648.

Date	Event
1620	**Pilgrims land at Plymouth Rock.** To escape religious persecution in England, a group of Puritans obtained the backing of a London stock company and sailed to America aboard the cargo ship *Mayflower.* After a two-month voyage, the Puritans landed at Plymouth Rock (in southeastern Massachusetts) and founded the first permanent settlement in New England.
1642–1660	**Revolution and unrest in England.** During the reign of Charles I (1625–1649), members of Parliament resisted his royal prerogatives and demanded more power for themselves. The leaders of the opposition were Puritans opposed to the Church of England and often connected to the merchant class in London and other cities. The dispute broke into open warfare, and Charles was captured and finally beheaded (1649). Until 1653 Parliament governed England. Then Oliver Cromwell (1599–1658), the leader of the victorious parliamentary forces during the civil war, dissolved Parliament and set up the Protectorate (1653–1660) under his rule. By 1660, soon after Cromwell's death, the English welcomed restoration of the monarchy. The new king was Charles II (ruled 1660–1685), son of Charles I.
1643–1715  *Louis XIV*	**Louis XIV reigns in France.** One of the greatest French kings, Louis brought the absolutist powers of the monarchy to their height during his reign. He restored French finances after the Thirty Years' War, only to engage in a series of costly, expansionist wars between 1667 and 1714. In 1685 he decided to make France a Catholic state and revoked the Edict of Nantes, ending the toleration of Protestantism in France. Renewed persecution of Protestants resulted in their exodus from France by the thousands, leaving whole towns and provinces depopulated, and seriously weakening the French economy. Louis was a great spender, noted for his splendid court and his liberal patronage of the arts. His palace at Versailles is a world-famous monument to the lavish style of his reign.
1644–1912	**Ch'ing dynasty in China.** During the long reign of the Ch'ing dynasty emperors, the Chinese empire reached its greatest heights, trade with Western powers began, and Western missionaries arrived in China.
1664–1666	**Newton's laws of gravity and motion.** During this pivotal two-year period, Sir Isaac Newton (1642–1727) laid the foundations for his famous laws of motion and universal gravitation. Newton's work proved to be the crowning achievement of the scientific revolution of the 1600's.
1670–1770	**The Enlightenment.** Sometimes called the Age of Reason, the Enlightenment was an intellectual movement in Europe and America that championed rationalism, natural laws, and science. The movement grew out of the great intellectual and scientific advances of the 1600's, notably the work of René Descartes (1596–1650), John Locke (1632–1704), and Sir Isaac Newton (1642–1727). Conventional social, religious, and political doctrines were challenged by the skeptical Enlightenment thinkers. Deism, or natural religion, was a product of the Enlightenment and the ideas and spirit of this age gave impetus to both the American and French revolutions. The French *Encyclopédie,* an encyclopedia of the sciences, arts, and trades by Denis Diderot (1713–1784), was a late summary of the ideas of the Enlightenment.
1700–1721	**Great Northern War.** Sweden had become the dominant power in the Baltic region. Then, in 1700, Denmark, Russia, and Poland attacked Swedish territories in the region. Swedish King Charles XII (ruled 1697–1718) was initially victorious, but his disastrous invasion of Russia (1708) turned the tide of the war against Sweden. Charles was killed in battle in 1718 and between 1719 and 1721 peace agreements were concluded. Swedish influence was broken, and Russia, which had gained considerable Baltic territories, began its rise as a major European power.

Date	*Event*
1701–1714	**War of Spanish Succession.** When French King Louis XIV's son succeeded to the Spanish throne as King Philip V, England saw a threat in the possible unification of France and Spain. England went to war against France, joined by the Holy Roman Empire and the Netherlands. The English alliance was generally successful, and the Duke of Marlborough (John Churchill) became a great war hero for his victory at Blenheim (1704). The Peace of Utrecht (1714) ended the war. The French expansionist policies of Louis XIV were successfully checked and Philip V renounced claims to the French throne. Austria gained Spanish possessions in Europe (Spanish Netherlands, Naples, and Milan), and Britain gained French colonial possessions in Canada.
1735	**Linnaeus publishes first work on plant and animal classification.** Considered the father of modern botany, Carolus Linnaeus (1707–1778) published a number of works during his lifetime. In them he set forth what has become the modern system of classifying plants and animals by genus and species.
1740–1786	**Frederick the Great reigns in Prussia.** During Frederick's reign Prussia developed from a small German state in northern Germany to a major power. Frederick used the well-organized Prussian military to greatly enlarged Prussian territories during the War of the Austrian Succession and the Seven Years' War (see below). By the time of Frederick's death, Prussia had become the major power among the German states of the Holy Roman Empire.
1752	**Benjamin Franklin's kite.** Well known in the American colonies as the publisher of the popular *Poor Richard's Almanack,* Benjamin Franklin (1706–1790) was also interested in science. Perhaps his most famous experiment, in which he flew a kite during a thunderstorm, proved his theory that electricity and lightning are identical. This led to his invention of the lightning rod and secured his reputation as an inventor and scientist. Franklin continued his scientific explorations, but late in life he became famous as a diplomat for the newly independent American colonies. He was acknowledged there as the first "great man" the North American colonies had produced.
1756–1763	**Seven Years' War.** This war was caused by the longstanding rivalry between Austria and Prussia and by the struggle between Britain and France for the possession of colonies in America and India. Prussia started the war in 1742 by attacking Saxony, an ally of Austria. In the ensuing warfare, Britain and Portugal joined Prussia. They were opposed by Austria, France, Russia, Sweden, and Spain. In the North American colonies, fighting between British and French colonists, known as the French and Indian wars, were part of the larger European struggle. By the treaties ending the war, Prussian supremacy over Austria was assured and France was virtually stripped of its colonial empire. Britain gained French possessions in the Americas and checked French power in India. This laid the basis for the great British colonial empire.
1762–1796	**Catherine the Great reigns in Russia.** A strong and ambitious ruler, Catherine made Russia an active participant in European affairs and expanded Russian territories. She conspired to overthrow (1762) and murder her erratic husband, Emperor Peter III (ruled 1762), and took power for herself. Thereafter she proved adept at playing European politics and gained control of most of Poland. She also continued the pattern of Russian expansion into territories of the Ottoman Empire by annexing the Crimea (1762), a peninsular region of the Black Sea.
1768–1779	**Voyages of James Cook.** One of the great English navigators, James Cook (1728–1779) made three voyages of discovery in which he explored the Pacific and Antarctic regions. He charted New Zealand and the eastern coast of Australia; explored the Antarctic Ocean; and unsuccessfully searched for a sea route from the northern Pacific to the Atlantic (Northwest Passage). He was killed by natives while visiting Hawaii.

Modern world

The modern world began with a series of revolutions—political ones in America and France, and an economic one called the Industrial Revolution. Improving sanitation and health care brought perhaps the greatest revolution of all—a population explosion that has continued ever since. The modern era also saw the rise and fall of huge worldwide empires and the gradual rise of two new superstates: the United States and Russia (later called the Soviet Union). By 1945 these states had become the dominant world powers. At the same time, scores of new nations became independent.

Date	*Event*

1775–1783

American Revolution. Many historians trace the beginnings of the modern world to the revolutions of the late 1700's. The first of these was the American Revolution (1775–1781), in which 13 British colonies in North America declared their independence from the mother country and successfully resisted British military pressures for seven years.

The American patriots based their revolution on Enlightenment ideas (see above), claiming that all men have certain God-given rights. In 1788, the new United States adopted a Constitution that offered political and civil rights to a much larger part of the population than in any European country. The new republic drew both on the political traditions of Britain and on the philosophies of French thinkers (Montesquieu, Rousseau) of the mid-1700's. In turn, the American experiment inspired a new wave of revolution in Europe. (For details of the American Revolution, see U.S. History in Volume I.)

1789–1799

French Revolution. The year after the adoption of the U.S. Constitution, the French overthrew a government dominated by an absolute monarch, hereditary nobility, and higher clergy. The middle classes and landless peasants united in their opposition to the extravagance and arbitrary policies of King Louis XVI, the aristocracy, and the powerful French church.

Pressed by the need for money, Louis was forced to call the States-General (a weak parliamentary body) in 1789. The members actually began the revolution by forming the National Assembly, which they proclaimed the true representative of the French nation. The king recognized the assembly, but rumors about his intentions and serious food shortages in Paris led a mob to storm the Bastille on July 14, 1789. They freed the prisoners there (many of whom had been sentenced for political offenses). Violence soon spread to the provinces.

The National Assembly abolished feudal privileges and enacted the famous *Declaration of the Rights of Man* (August, 1789), proclaiming individual liberties for all. The king was driven from his palace at Versailles in October, and church lands were nationalized in November. The monarchy was finally abolished in 1792.

The revolution was applauded in America and by many in Europe. But other European monarchies feared the spread of revolutionary politics, and in 1792 they began a series of wars against the new French Republic. They attempted to invade France in 1792 and 1793, both times unsuccessfully.

Meanwhile, the revolution itself was entering its most radical and bloodiest phase. In January, 1793, the king and his queen, Marie Antoinette, were beheaded. Then in September, Maximilien Robespierre (1758–1794) and his radical Jacobin faction gained control of the government. They instituted the notorious Reign of Terror (1793–1794), in which some 17,000 persons were executed. Robespierre was overthrown in July, 1794, and moderate elements again took control. By 1797, Napoleon had begun his rise to power, and in 1799, he took control of the government, ending the revolutionary period.

Marie Antoinette on her way to execution, 1793

Date	*Event*

1799–1815

Napoleon

Napoleon. Napoleon carried out a revolution of his own after taking power in 1799. He reorganized France's administrative machinery to centralize control, stabilized its currency, and arranged an agreement with the Roman Catholic Church. By 1802, he had also made peace with the countries that had taken up arms against France.

Then, in December, 1804, Napoleon proclaimed the French Empire and crowned himself emperor. The countries of Europe united once more against the new empire, and Napoleon soon faced great military challenges. But he also instituted sweeping legal reforms, codifying laws that granted all citizens legal equality and property rights. The Napoleonic Code became the basis for systems of law in much of the Western world.

In 1805, Napoleon declared himself king of Italy, and was soon at war with a new alliance that included England, Russia, Austria, and other powers. Napoleon, by his military genius, conquered most of Europe in the ensuing years. At its height, his empire included most of present-day Germany, Austria, Italy, Belgium, the Netherlands, and Spain. Then, in 1812 he invaded Russia. After initial successes, his army was forced to retreat during a severe Russian winter. The army suffered disastrous losses. In 1813, at Leipzig, in eastern Germany, Napoleon confronted an alliance of European powers and was defeated at the Battle of Nations. Napoleon abdicated on April 11, 1814, and was exiled to the island of Elba in the Mediterranean. He escaped, however, and returned to France on March 1, 1815. Beginning his famous Hundred Days, Napoleon assumed power and again began the war against the allied European powers. He met final defeat in June, 1815, at the famous Battle of Waterloo in Belgium.

c 1810–c 1825

South American independence. Longstanding resentment of harsh Spanish and Portuguese colonial policies provided ample cause for rebellion in South America. While the mother countries were embroiled in the Napoleonic wars, independence fighters succeeded in throwing off colonial rule. Simón Bolívar (1783–1830) and others drove the Spanish and Portuguese off the continent by 1825.

1814–1815

Congress of Vienna. This historic conference met to decide the future of Europe following Napoleon's abdication. The purpose was to ensure a lasting peace by establishing a balance of power between rival nations. Monarchies in France, Spain, and Austria were restored and a confederation of German states was organized. New kingdoms were set up in the Netherlands and Poland. Peace in Europe was maintained for some years following the congress, largely through the skillful diplomacy of the Austrian statesman Clemens von Metternich (1773–1859). But his repressive measures met increasing opposition.

1820–1900

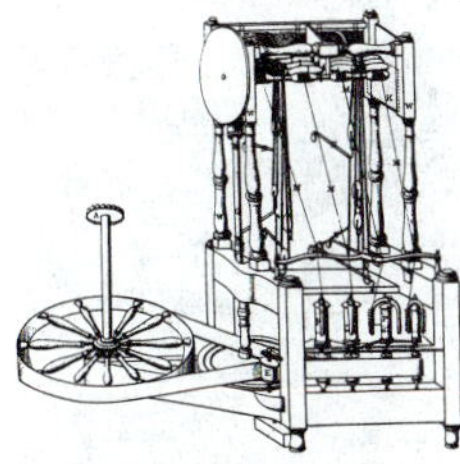

An early mill for spinning thread

Industrial Revolution. The dramatic technological and social changes of the 1800's had their roots in the development of new machines and sources of power. Machinery replaced hand tools, and water, steam, or electric power replaced the muscle of man and beast. Finally, the factory system replaced ancient home or "cottage" industries. To find employment, thousands of workers left their small farms and moved to new industrial cities. Factory owners made fabulous fortunes, but men, women, and children were forced to work long hours, often in subhuman conditions.

Gradually the workers began to fight for civil rights, labor legislation, and unionization. The pattern was repeated as the Industrial Revolution spread from Britain to France (from 1830), Germany (from 1850), and the United States (from 1860). By the late 1800's, labor was a strong political force in Europe, and it inspired growing support for legislation to ensure the social welfare of workers.

Date	*Event*
1839–1860	**Opium wars in China.** In the first war (1839–1842), the British, who had long profited from the illicit opium trade in China, defied an attempt by the Chinese to halt the trade and easily defeated the Chinese imperial armies. China was forced to cede Hong Kong to Britain and open several ports to British trade. The British, joined by the French, sparked the second war to further extend trading rights. China was again defeated. It was forced to open still other ports to European powers and to legalize the opium trade. This marked the beginning of European political influence in China, which lasted more than 100 years.
1848	**Revolutions of 1848.** Conservative European monarchs kept liberal and nationalistic movements in check from 1815 to 1830, when the new monarchy in France fell. After 1830, the conservative forces took charge again, but in 1848 widespread revolts changed the politics of Europe. The rebellions began in France, where reactionary policies of the restored monarchy led to the monarchy's overthrow and to the establishment of the short-lived French Second Republic (1848–1852). Rebellions then broke out in Austria, Hungary, and Italy. Liberal elements also gained strength in the German confederation, in Britain, and elsewhere. The 1848 uprisings prepared the way for major political changes in the second half of the 1800's.
1854–1856	**Crimean War.** The steady deterioration of the Ottoman (Turkish) Empire led to complex rivalries among European nations seeking eventual control of Ottoman lands. In 1853 Russia occupied Ottoman territories in modern Rumania, and in 1854 the Ottoman Turks, the British, and the French declared war on Russia. Fighting centered on the Crimean peninsula on the Black Sea. Hundreds of thousands were killed and wounded. It was during this war that Florence Nightingale (1820–1910) became famous for tending to the wounded. The war ended unfavorably for Russia and, by the Treaty of Paris (1856), European powers recognized the neutrality of the Black Sea and the territorial integrity of the Ottoman Empire.

An encampment during the Crimean War

Date	Event

1859

Darwin publishes *Origin of the Species*, advancing a theory of biological evolution. His explanations of evolutionary mechanisms and his voluminous observations provided the necessary scientific basis for his theory. Darwin's theory raised serious questions for both religious thinkers and philosophers of the 1800's, and it continues to be controversial today.

1861

Garibaldi

Unification of Italy. Sentiment for the unification of Italy (divided into petty states and often dominated by foreign powers since Rome's fall) had become especially strong by the mid-1800's. In 1859 Victor Emmanuel II, king of Sardinia, attempted unsuccessfully to drive the Austrians out of Italy. Other states rebelled and joined Sardinia in 1860. Then the Italian hero, Giuseppe Garibaldi (1807–1882), organized a small army and conquered (1860) the Kingdom of Two Sicilies. This brought southern Italy under King Victor Emmanuel's rule. In March, 1861, Victor Emmanuel proclaimed the Kingdom of Italy and thus founded the modern state. Venetia was added in 1866, while Rome (the last vestige of the Papal States) was seized in 1870.

1861–1865

Civil War in the United States. In March, 1861, the Southern states in the United States withdrew and set up the Confederate States of America, seeking to preserve slavery and to avoid the growing dominance of the industrial North. The Northern states, under the leadership of Abraham Lincoln, refused to grant the right of Southern states to secede, and in April, 1861, war began.

The war lasted four years, and more than 1 million men died. Parts of the Southern states were decimated. Finally, the North prevailed, largely as a result of its more advanced industrial and transportation systems. Slavery was abolished during the war, and soon afterward, former slaves received full legal citizenship. Within days of the South's surrender, President Lincoln was assassinated by a Southern patriot.

The Civil War was the first war in which telegraph communication, rapid transportation (by railroad), and automatic weapons played a large part. It served as a proving ground for equipment and tactics in later European wars.

1867

British North America Act. By this act, the British Parliament united the Canadian provinces and created the Dominion of Canada. Also written into the act was a constitutional framework for governing the new dominion.

1867–1895

***Das Kapital* published.** Publication of this voluminous work by Karl Marx (1818–1883) and Friedrich Engels (1820–1895) occurred over 28 years. With Marx's and Engels' earlier work, *The Communist Manifesto* (published 1848), *Das Kapital* developed Marxist socialism. Marx argued that revolution by workers in a capitalist society is historically inevitable. The socialist movement gradually split over this issue. Democratic socialists advocated gradual social change; Marxists, who came to be known as communists, advocated violent revolution to bring about social change.

1871

Bismarck

Unification of Germany. For decades Prussia in northeastern Germany sought to unify the loosely confederated German states. Austria, which controlled a large empire in southern Europe, consistently opposed unification. In 1862 Prussian King William I appointed a new premier, Otto von Bismarck (1815–1898), who ruthlessly brought about a united Germany. In 1866 Bismarck provoked the Austro-Prussian War and the Prussian military machine quickly crushed the Austrians. By the resulting peace treaty, a new confederation of north German states was created, without Austria and under Prussian domination. To bring the remaining south German states into the confederation, Bismarck precipitated the Franco-Prussian War of 1870–1871. The Prussian victory over France roused the German nationalist spirit and, as planned, brought about the union of northern and southern states. William I of Prussia was proclaimed emperor of Germany in January, 1871, and for the next 20 years Bismarck, nicknamed the "Iron Chancellor," dominated the new German government.

Date	*Event*

c 1875

Colonial empires. From 1820, Britain was the great colonialist country of Europe. Although it had lost the 13 colonies in North America, it gradually extended its control in India, Australia, and Canada, thus controlling large parts of three continents. In addition, Britain's smaller territories created a network of trading centers that extended around the world. By 1875, however, European powers were in a new race to acquire and control colonies. Like Britain, they were seeking new sources of raw material and new markets for manufactured goods. Germany, Belgium, France, Italy, Japan, and the United States all sought to stake out new territories. The imperialist nations carved up Africa, a large part of Asia, and the Pacific islands into colonial domains. Along with this imperialistic drive came intense rivalries among the colonial powers. These rivalries eventually led to the outbreak of World War I.

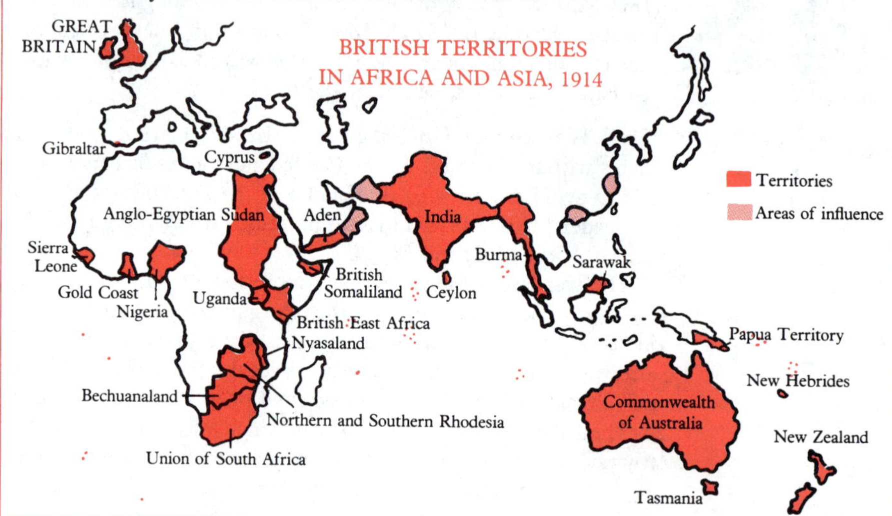

1876

Telephone invented. Alexander Graham Bell (1847–1922) was an inventor and teacher of the deaf. His experiments with telegraphic devices led to his invention of the telephone. His first working model was operational by 1876. Bell's first message over this revolutionary new device was to his assistant: "Watson, come here. I want you."

1878–1879

Practical light bulb invented. The first practical incandescent lamp, using a carbon filament inside an evacuated glass bulb, was invented in England in 1878 by Sir Joseph Swan (1828–1914). Thomas Edison (1847–1931), the famous American inventor, independently developed a similar incandescent lamp in 1879. Edison's lamp became the first widely marketed light bulb. Edison went on to create a complete electrical distribution system so that electricity could provide light and power for a whole city.

1895–1939

Freud develops psychoanalysis. Sigmund Freud (1856–1939), an Austrian doctor, began to develop his theories on the emotional life of individuals after studying patients suffering from hysteria. He asserted that much of the mind's emotional work goes on in the *unconscious*, which is not subject to the control or memory of an individual. His ideas provided the basic structure for psychoanalysis and have had a profound impact on modern society.

1898

The Curies discover radium. The French scientist Antoine H. Becquerel (1852–1891) discovered radioactivity in 1896. Soon afterward, Marie Curie (1867–1934) and Pierre Curie (1859–1906) began to investigate the mineral called pitchblende. By 1898 the Curies had isolated the previously unknown radioactive elements of radium and polonium. Their discovery was an important step toward the beginning of the atomic age.

Date	*Event*
1899–1900	**Boxer Rebellion in China.** The Boxers were a Chinese secret society that rebelled against foreign influence in China. They began by terrorizing Christian missionaries in 1899 and received unofficial support from the Chinese government. In Peking in June of 1900 many foreigners and Chinese Christians were massacred. A military expedition of French, Japanese, German, British, Russian, and American troops relieved the besieged section of the city. A peace treaty was signed in August of 1900.
1899–1902	**Boer War in South Africa.** In this colonial war, Britain sought to expand its rule throughout South Africa at the expense of the Boers (descendants of Dutch settlers). The British overwhelmed the Boers with thousands of British reinforcements. The fall of Pretoria (June, 1900) marked the end of organized fighting, but the Boers continued guerrilla warfare until 1902, when the Boer republics were made British Crown colonies.

English-speaking refugees in the Boer War

1903	**Age of the airplane begins.** Two American inventors, Orville Wright (1871–1948) and Wilbur Wright (1867–1912), flew the first successful powered airplane near Kitty Hawk, North Carolina, in December, 1903. The first flight lasted just 12 seconds.
	Ford develops mass production. Henry Ford (1863–1947) went into partnership with several backers to form the Ford Motor Company. By 1907 he was in complete control of the company and, by his development of mass production techniques, soon made it the world's largest automobile manufacturing company. He developed the moving assembly line for production of his famous Model T (1908). By the time manufacture of the car was discontinued (1927), some 15 million had been built and sold.
1904–1905	**Russo-Japanese War.** Rivalry for control of Manchuria and Korea led Japan, which had become a modern industrial state, into war against Russia. The Japanese humiliated the Russians by capturing Port Arthur, a Russian stronghold in China, and by destroying a Russian fleet. Japan ultimately won territorial concessions in Manchuria.
1905	**Einstein's theory of relativity.** Albert Einstein (1879–1955) was earning his doctorate and working in the Swiss patent office when he formulated his theory of relativity. This theory, together with his later work on relativity, revolutionized science, introducing new concepts of space, time, and gravity, and preparing the way for an understanding of nuclear physics.
1911	**Revolution in China.** The weakening of the Ch'ing dynasty, and the domination of China helped set the stage for the outbreak of revolution in October of 1911. The boy emperor, Hsüan T'ung, was forced to abdicate in 1912, ending the long rule of the Ch'ing dynasty (1644–1912). The republic was declared, and Sun Yat-sen (1866–1925), a long-time leader of revolutionary factions, served briefly as provisional president. The Nationalist Kuomintang Party became powerful under Sun Yat-sen's leadership, but it was unable to take firm control of the country. The Chinese Communist Party was formed in 1921 and in the late 1920's and 1930's the Nationalists and Communists rivaled each other for control of China.

Date	Event

1914–1918

World War I. Economic and political rivalries among European powers were rapidly increasing after 1910. War was finally precipitated by the assassination of Archduke Francis Ferdinand of Austria. The Austrian government blamed Serbia (now part of Yugoslavia) and declared war. Within weeks, Serbia's allies, including Russia, France, and Britain, had declared war, as had Austria's great ally, Germany.

In slightly over four years, the conflict was played out on several widely scattered fronts. It was the most costly war ever seen. Some 10 million men were killed and 20 million wounded, and whole regions were laid waste. The Germans and Austrians took the offensive, planning to fight on two fronts, against France in the west and Russia in the east. Resistance on the western front was stronger than had been anticipated, however, and the Balkan countries offered fierce resistance. Only in Russia were the Central Powers able to win decisively. In France and Belgium, neither side seemed able to advance. Huge armies were pinned down in trenches for weeks or months, battling over a few feet of ground. Motorized tanks, poison gas, and efficient artillery made the war a nightmare for soldiers. At sea, the Germans used submarines to destroy allied shipping. The United States remained neutral through two and a half years; in April, 1917, however, Congress declared war on Germany and its allies. The arrival of American troops helped the Allies repulse a huge German offensive at the second Battle of the Marne, in early 1918, and thus turn the tide of the war against Germany. Thereafter, military defeats and economic disorder contributed to the German decision to seek an armistice in November, 1918. The Treaty of Versailles, signed in June, 1919, formally ended the war and reorganized Europe. It resulted in the dismantling of the German colonial empire and the collapse of the Austro-Hungarian and Ottoman empires. It also marked the beginning of many present-day states, including Poland, Hungary, and Yugoslavia.

Marshal Foch of France, Allied commander

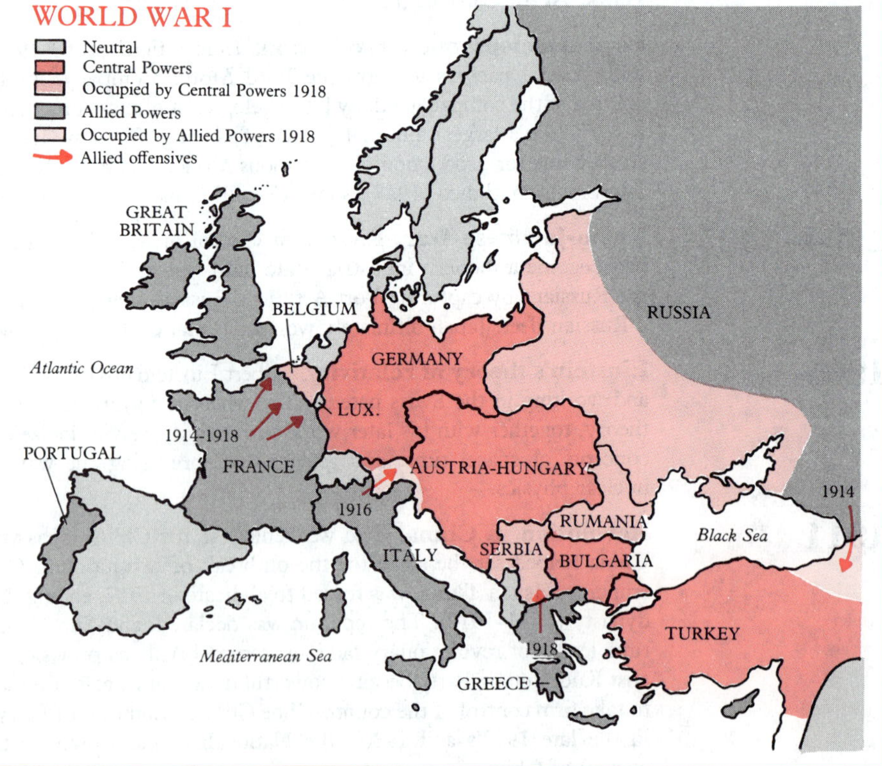

Key events in World War I

1914 Archduke Francis Ferdinand of Austria assassinated, June 28.
War declared by Austria and Germany, July 28–August 3.
Invasion of France (through Belgium and Luxembourg) begun by Germany, August 3.
Britain, soon followed by other major powers, enters the war, August 4.
Russia attacks East Prussia, opening eastern front, August 13.
Russian armies crushed at Battle of Tannenberg, August 26–29.
First Battle of the Marne (Germans halted before reaching Paris), September 5–9.
First Battle of Ypres (Germans prevented from capturing channel ports), October–November.
Trench warfare and long stalemate begins on the western front, October–November.

1915 Germans make first use of poison gas at second Battle of Ypres, April 22–May 25.
Allies' Gallipoli campaign fails to knock Ottoman Empire out of the war, April–January (1916).
Lusitania, British ocean liner, sunk by German submarine, May 7.
Italy enters war on the side of the Allies, May 23.
Allies' Salonika campaign in Greece and Balkans region begins (and is stalled soon after), October 5.

1916 Battle of Verdun in France; bloody but inconclusive German offensive, February 21–December 18.
Russian summer offensive in the east leaves both Russian and Austrian armies exhausted by tremendous losses, June 4–September 20.
Allies' Somme offensive in the west proves bloody and inconclusive, July 1–November 18.

1917 Germany begins unrestricted submarine warfare, February 1.
Russian Revolution breaks out, March; Russian army retreats in disarray.
United States enters war, April 6.
Bolsheviks seize control in Russia as Germans advance against the crumbling Russian army; Bolsheviks seek peace with Germans, November.

1918 U.S. President Wilson announces his Fourteen Points peace program, January 8.
Communist Russia concludes peace with Germany, March 3.
German Somme offensive in France is tactical success but drains German manpower, March 21–April 8.
Second Battle of Marne marks the beginning of German retreat, July 15–August 6.
Austro-Hungarian empire collapses, October.
Austria agrees to an armistice, November 4.
Germany agrees to an armistice and the war ends, November 11.

1919 Treaty of Versailles signed, formally ending the war, June 28.

1917

Russian Revolution. The czarist regime in Russia, still an unlimited monarchy, had been weak and ineffectual for years. Agitation for a constitutional form of government had brought an unsuccessful revolution in 1905. Finally, the stresses of World War I brought the old regime down. The Russian army was badly supplied and led, and it lost disastrous battles against the Germans. The government and the economy under Czar Nicholas II (ruled 1894–1917) weakened steadily.

Workers took over St. Petersburg in February, 1917. The czar was forced to abdicate, and a moderate provisional government was set up. Various Socialist parties opposed the government and undermined it and each other. Finally, the Bolshevik faction, led by Nikolai Lenin (1870–1924), staged a coup in October, set up a Communist government with Lenin at its head, and made peace with Germany. Not all Russians went along with the Bolshevik government, and soon the Reds (Bolsheviks) and the Whites (anti-Bolsheviks) were involved in a bloody civil war. The war ended with the triumph of the Reds and the exile of the Whites in 1920. Lenin ruthlessly consolidated the rule of the Communist Party in the four years before his death.

Lenin

Date	*Event*
1919	**Gandhi and nonviolent protest in India.** A national hero of India, Mohandas Gandhi (1869–1948) organized his first campaign of nonviolent civil disobedience against oppression by British colonial rulers in 1919. He eventually championed not only independence from Britain but social reforms as well. The growing success of his mass protests forced the British to grant ever greater concessions in the 1920's and 1930's and proved to be a major factor in India's fight for independence (granted in 1947).
	Treaty of Versailles. The most important of the treaties ending World War I, the treaty dealt harshly with Germany. It took away most German territories, required the payment of substantial war reparations, restricted German rearmament, and demilitarized the Rhineland along Germany's western borders. The treaty established the League of Nations (see below). The U.S. Senate refused ratification of the treaty and kept the United States out of the league.
1920	**First commercial radio station.** Wireless telegraphy, developed by the Italian physicist Guglielmo Marconi (1874–1937) at the turn of the century, was already well established when the American David Sarnoff (1891–1971) suggested establishing stations for broadcasting speech and music to the general public. Following World War I, the first commercial radio station (KDKA) was started up in Pittsburgh; it began regular programming late in 1920 and was an immediate success. Radio stations sprang up around the world, making the radio an important medium for news reporting and entertainment.
1920–1946	**League of Nations.** The league was an international organization devoted to preserving world peace and promoting international cooperation. It existed from 1920 to 1946, when it was superseded by the United Nations. Important nations (especially the United States) remained outside the league, and its peace-keeping machinery was limited. The league was unable to halt aggression by Japan, Italy, and Germany in the 1930's. Yet its work in social and economic affairs was considerable.
1922	**Mussolini and the rise of Fascism in Italy.** Benito Mussolini (1883–1945) organized the nucleus of his Fascist Party amid the strikes and unrest that overtook Italy after World War I. By appealing to nationalistic spirit and using brutal tactics against Communists and Socialists, Mussolini quickly became a formidable power in Italy. In October, 1922, King Victor Emmanuel III (ruled 1900–1946) named him premier. Mussolini immediately set about establishing himself as dictator by ruthless means.
c 1927	**Stalin takes power in the Soviet Union.** Lenin's death in 1924 touched off a complex power struggle within the Communist Party for control of the Soviet Union. Joseph Stalin (1879–1953) soon ousted his rival, Leon Trotsky (1879–1940), and established himself as sole ruler of the Soviet Union. He introduced his policy of industrialization and collectivization of agriculture in 1928 and instituted harsh measures to enforce state control over Soviet society. Stalin established his absolute dictatorship by bloody purges in the 1930's and encouraged veneration of himself as supreme leader.
	Lindbergh and *The Spirit of St. Louis.* A little-known American flier, Charles Lindbergh (1902–1974), became an American national hero overnight by making the first solo nonstop flight across the Atlantic Ocean. In May, 1927, Lindbergh piloted his plane, *The Spirit of St. Louis*, from an airfield on Long Island to Paris, France, in just over 33 hours. A folk hero during his lifetime, Lindbergh remains one of the best-known figures of the airplane age.
1928	**Penicillin discovered.** Sir Alexander Fleming (1881–1955), a Scottish biologist, first discovered penicillin and its effectiveness as an antibacterial agent. By 1941 the drug was proven to be effective in humans, and by the 1950's it was in widespread use. It was the first of a whole family of antibiotic medications.

Date *Event*

1929–1939

Soup line for the hungry

Great Depression. The economic boom of the 1920's ended late in 1929 with the catastrophic stock market crash in the United States. The crash had tragic consequences: whole fortunes were wiped out; banks failed by the thousands; and millions of workers suddenly found themselves unemployed. The economic disaster quickly spread to Europe, where the other industrial nations suffered similar consequences. In the United States, Franklin D. Roosevelt's New Deal programs marked a radical departure from previous U.S. government policy. In Europe the crisis helped pave the way for the rise of totalitarian governments. Western economies did not reach their 1929 levels until after 1945.

1931

Rise of the militarists in Japan. Militarist factions began their rise to power in the late 1920's. In 1931 the militarists provoked an incident in Manchuria, then Chinese territory, as an excuse to take control there. In 1937 they marched from Manchuria into China. By 1939 Japan had become an ally of the Axis powers (Germany and Italy). With the installation of Hideki Tojo (served 1941–1944) as prime minister in October, 1941, the militarists gained complete control of the Japanese government.

1933

Hitler's rise to power in Germany. By 1921 Adolf Hitler (1889–1945) had gained control of the fledgling Nazi Party in Germany. After 1929, Hitler's frenzied appeal to German nationalism and his use of the psychology of hate gained him a mass following. In 1933 Hitler was named chancellor of Germany and soon after, his Nazi Party gained a slim majority in the German parliament. Playing on fears of a Communist uprising, Hitler arranged to have parliament give him dictatorial powers. He thus established the Third Reich in 1933 and set about ruthlessly consolidating his power. In subsequent years, he established a totalitarian state, redirected the economy to create a powerful military machine, began the persecution (and later mass killings) of the Jews, and instituted the aggressive, nationalistic foreign policy that ultimately began World War II (see below).

1934

Fermi and the beginning of the atomic age. An Italian-born physicist, Enrico Fermi (1901–1954), first used neutrons to bombard uranium atoms during experiments from 1934 to 1937. The results of his experiments puzzled the scientific world until 1938, when three German scientists discovered that Fermi's experiments had actually split the uranium atoms by the heretofore unknown process of nuclear fission. In that year Fermi went to the United States and soon became part of the secret Manhattan Project to develop an atomic bomb. Leading a team of scientists in Chicago, Fermi produced in December, 1942, the first controlled, self-sustaining chain reaction. Fermi's experiments led to the first atom bomb and to the development of nuclear reactors for peaceful uses.

1936–1939

Spanish Civil War. This war arose from conflict between the supporters of the Spanish Republic (Loyalists) and a coalition of conservative forces (Nationalists). An election victory in 1936 by the Popular Front—republicans, liberals, Socialists, and Communists—threatened conservative interests. A right-wing rebellion broke out, led by the military, and General Francisco Franco (1892–1975) emerged as the dominant Nationalist leader. Liberal sympathizers from the United States and other nations aided Loyalists. Franco's forces, however, received large-scale aid from Nazi Germany and Fascist Italy. By 1939 Franco had defeated the Loyalists. He established dictatorial control of Spain.

The road to war. Hitler's aggressive nationalist policies first became apparent in 1936 when he remilitarized the Rhineland. He aided Franco's Fascist forces in the Spanish Civil War and in March 1938, annexed Austria. Meanwhile, the British and the French adopted a policy of appeasement toward the Axis powers. In September, 1938, they agreed to the Munich Pact, by which Germany was given a large part of Czechoslovakia. Hopes for appeasement ended in 1939, when Germany occupied all of Czechoslovakia and Italy took over Albania. Soon after Germany concluded the Pact of Steel (1939) with Italy and a nonaggression pact with the Soviet Union. With these alliances secured, Hitler ordered the invasion of Poland on September 1, 1939, and World War II began.

The swastika, the Nazis' symbol

1939–1945

World War II. World War II was a global conflict fought from 1939 to 1945 on land, sea, and in the air. The world's principal nations were divided into two groups, the Axis and the Allies. The Axis was led by Germany, Italy, and Japan. The Allies were led by Britain, France, the United States, and the Soviet Union.

The early part of the conflict was marked by sweeping German victories in Europe. Poland, Denmark, Norway, Luxembourg, the Netherlands, and Belgium quickly fell to German forces. By the end of 1940, France had collapsed and the Germans had occupied Yugoslavia and Greece. Meanwhile, British forces withstood the early assault and managed to prevent a German invasion of the British Isles.

The second stage began in June, 1941, when Germany turned on its ally, the Soviet Union, and invaded that country. At first it seemed that Germany would continue its military successes, but a Soviet counteroffensive, coinciding with the early arrival of a severe winter, caused a temporary setback for the Germans. The war was also being fought in Africa, the Mediterranean, and the Atlantic, but the fighting was inconclusive.

The third stage of the war began in the Pacific in December, 1941, when Japan attacked Pearl Harbor, in Hawaii, and brought the United States into the war. The Japanese swept through the Pacific region in a rapid series of victories, but by spring of 1942, the United States had regained several key islands.

The fourth stage began in the summer of 1942, when the Allies took the offensive on almost all fronts. The Axis powers were routed successively in North Africa, Sicily, and Italy (in 1943). In the east the Soviet Union mounted another offensive during the winter months. Finally, in June, 1944, the Allied forces invaded the coast of Normandy in France. Germany, already weakened by earlier losses, was now fighting on both eastern and western fronts. Though the Germans continued to provide stiff resistance, the Allies pushed into Germany and in May, 1945, forced the Germans to surrender. The end of the war in Europe made it possible for the Allies to concentrate on defeating Japan. Naval battles in the Pacific had broken Japanese sea power and the campaign for the Pacific islands had brought the Allies to Japan's doorstep. The final blow was an atomic-bomb attack on the cities of Hiroshima and Nagasaki in August, 1945. The Japanese surrendered on September 2, and ended World War II. The Axis powers were dealt with severely in the surrender terms set by the Allies. Germany was partitioned and occupied by the United States, the Soviet Union, Britain, and France. Japan was occupied by the United States and lost all its outlying territories. Italy, which had surrendered in 1943, lost its colonial conquests in Africa.

St. Paul's Cathedral, London, during 1940 German air raid (left). *At* right, *Soviet soldiers at Stalingrad, 1942.*

Key events in World War II

1939 Germany invades Poland and precipitates World War II, September 1.
Allied nations declare war on Germany.
The Soviets (then allies of Germany) invade Poland from then east, September 17.
Germany and the Soviet Union divide up Polish territories, September.
The Soviets attack Finland, beginning the Russo-Finnish War (1939–1940), November 30.

1940 Germany invades (and quickly conquers) Denmark and Norway, April 9.
Germany invades the Netherlands and Belgium, May 10.
Winston Churchill replaces Neville Chamberlain as British prime minister, May 10.
German victories force the famous British evacuation at Dunkirk, May 28–June 4.
France capitulates to German troops (June 21) and a puppet government under Marshal Henri Pétain is set up, June.
Germans bomb Britain, beginning the air war (the Battle of Britain), August 8.
Italy opens fighting in the North African desert by attacking British Egypt from Libya, September.

1941 German General Erwin Rommel takes over Axis forces in North Africa and begins a rapid German advance there, April.
Yugoslavia and Greece invaded by the Germans, April 6.
German battleship *Bismarck* sunk, May 27.
Germany invades the Soviet Union, ending German-Soviet alliance and bringing the Soviets into the war against Germany, June 22.
Japanese occupy French Indochina, July 21.
Germans' rapid eastward advance in the Soviet Union stalled by onset of heavy rains and freezing weather; Germans fail to capture Moscow, October–December.
Hideki Tojo becomes Japanese prime minister, October 18.
Japanese attack Pearl Harbor, beginning a rapid sweep through the Pacific region, December 7.
United States enters the war, December 8.

continued on next page

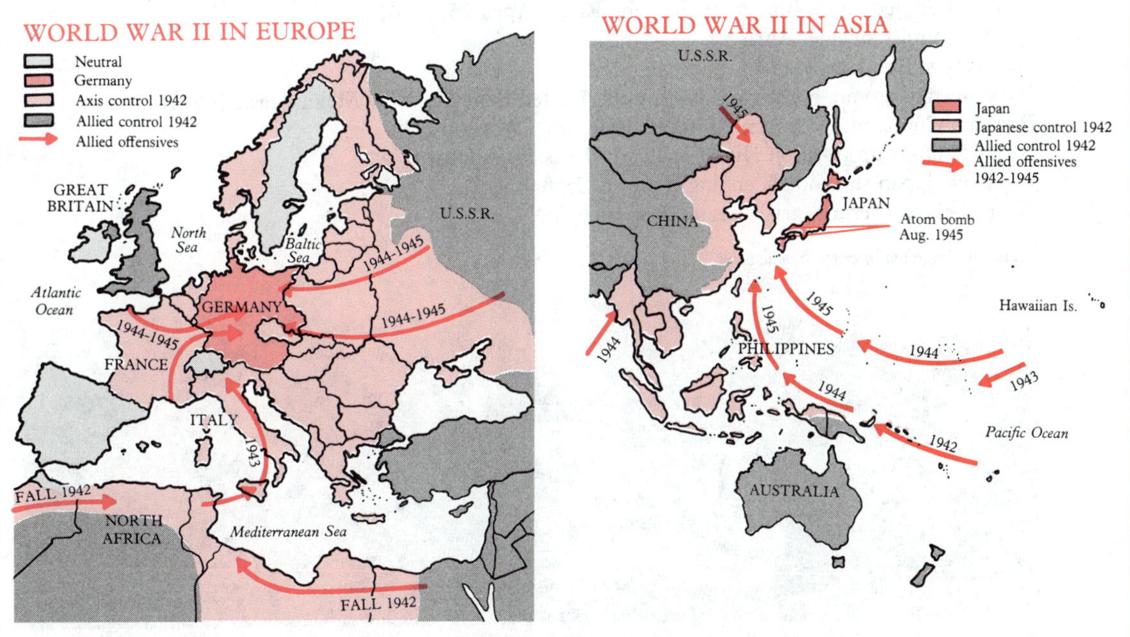

Date	Event
1942	Bataan falls, ending resistance to the Japanese in the Philippines; U.S. General Douglas MacArthur vows "I shall return," April.
	U.S. planes wreck Japanese invasion fleet at the Battle of Midway, June 3–6.
	General Dwight Eisenhower becomes head of United States operations in Europe, June 25.
	Guadalcanal landings begin U.S. counteroffensive in the Pacific, August 7.
	German eastward drive in the Soviet Union stalls at Stalingrad, August–October.
	British offensive in North Africa begins at El Alamein, Egypt, October 23.
	United States forces land in North Africa, November 8.
	Soviet counterattack at Stalingrad drives Germans into retreat, November–March (1943).
1943	Germans defeated in North Africa, May.
	Sicily invaded by Allies, June 10.
	Mussolini resigns, July 25.
	Soviets' final sustained advance against Germans begins, August.
	Italian mainland invaded; Italy surrenders (September 3) though Germans continue resistance, September.
1944	Strategic bombing of Germany begins, February 20.
	Russians enter Poland, April 2.
	Rome captured by Allies, June 4.
	D-Day. Massive amphibious invasion of Normandy begins, June 6.
	Attempt of German officers to assassinate Hitler fails, July 20.
	St.-Lô breakout in France marks the beginning of the Allied drive across Europe, July 25.
	Paris liberated, August 25.
	General MacArthur returns to the Philippines, October.
	Battle of the Bulge in Europe marks the last major German counteroffensive, December–January (1945).
1945	Allies cross the Rhine in Germany, March 7.
	U.S. forces land on Okinawa, March 26.
	U.S. President Franklin Roosevelt dies in office, April 12. Harry Truman becomes President.
	Soviets enter Berlin, April 20.
	U.S. and Soviet troops link up at the Elbe River, April 25.
	Hitler commits suicide, April 30.
	Germany surrenders, May 7.
	Experimental atomic bomb exploded by the United States in New Mexico test, July 16.
	Potsdam Conference between Allied leaders, July 17–August 2.
	Atomic bombs dropped on Hiroshima and Nagasaki, August 6, 9.
	V-J Day. Japan surrenders, ending the war, September 2.
	Nuremberg war crimes trials begin, November 20.

Ruins of Hiroshima after the atomic bomb

Postwar world

After World War II, the United States and the Soviet Union became competitors and were soon engaged in a great arms race, improving and producing weapons to be used in case of war. At the same time, other powers were emerging. China, the most populous nation on Earth, began developing its economic and military power after 1949. Scores of smaller nations sought ways to join together to make their needs and interests known. All peoples faced certain challenges together, including the threat of overpopulation, the diminishing of natural resources, and the hazards of manmade pollution.

Date *Event*

1945

United Nations established. Plans for a new international organization to replace the League of Nations were carried forward all through World War II during meetings among leaders of the Allies. Soon after Germany surrendered, delegates at the San Francisco Conference completed work on the United Nations Charter, which was ratified on October 24, 1945. The aims of the new organization were to encourage the maintenance of international peace and security, to promote cooperation in solving international, social, and economic problems, and to develop friendly relations among all nations. In subsequent years, United Nations social and economic programs achieved considerable success. But in other areas, the advent of the Cold War (see below) brought an end to the spirit of cooperation among nations that had existed during the war years. Thus, the UN's effectiveness as an international peacekeeping organization was seriously hampered soon after it was established.

United Nations insignia

1945–1949

Mao Tse-tung

Chinese civil war. Chiang Kai-shek (1887–1975), leader of the Nationalist Kuomintang Party after Sun Yat-sen's death, purged the Communists from the party in 1927 and thus began a long and bloody rivalry for control of China. The Japanese invasion in 1937 and the outbreak of World War II forced the Nationalists and Communists, now led by Mao Tse-tung (1893–1976), to work together for a number of years. But the alliance was at best an uneasy one.

At the end of World War II, both the Nationalists and Communists scrambled to take over territories once occupied by the Japanese. Civil war broke out and though the Nationalists were at first successful, the Communists turned the tide in 1947. Peking was in Communist hands by January, 1949; in July of that year, Chiang Kai-shek withdrew his forces to the island of Taiwan, where he established his Nationalist government. The victorious Communists proclaimed (October, 1949) the People's Republic of China with Mao Tse-tung as chairman.

1945–1990

Cold War. The end of World War II marked the emergence of the Soviet Union and the United States as the two great world powers. Soon the two were in conflict over ideology, and over plans for political and economic expansion. These conflicts dominated the political climate of the postwar years and remain a source of international friction even today.

Tensions first developed when the Soviet Union set up Communist governments in the East European countries it had occupied during World War II. Between 1945 and 1948, Albania, Bulgaria, Czechoslovakia, Hungary, Poland, Rumania, and Yugoslavia came under control of the Soviet Union. The United States responded with the Truman Doctrine (1947), which offered aid to countries threatened by Communism (then Greece and Turkey). In 1948, the Marshall Plan gave the countries of Western Europe large-scale U.S. aid to rebuild their war-shattered economies and to strengthen them against Communist pressures. In 1949 the North Atlantic Treaty Organization (NATO) was established to bring the European nations together for their common defense. In addition to confrontations (Berlin blockade), and warfare (Korea), the Cold War also bred the nuclear arms race and spurred space exploration.

Date *Event*

1946

Early TV star Milton Berle

The new electronic marvels: television and computers. Television, invented in the 1920's and perfected in the 1930's, became widely available soon after World War II. Regular broadcasting service was begun in the United States in 1946, when the government lifted wartime restrictions on the production of television receivers. By 1951 there were 10 million sets in use in the United States. During the next decades, the number continued to multiply in the United States and around the world.

The first fully electronic digital computer, ENIAC, was also completed in 1946. Advances during the next three decades (transistors, silicon chips, and miniaturization) transformed the computer from a bulky laboratory tool to a compact and versatile electronic "brain" that has found its way into businesses, offices, schools, and homes.

1948

Israel created; the first Arab-Israeli war. Zionist agitation for the creation of a Jewish state in Palestine finally resulted in the establishment of Israel by the United Nations in May, 1948. A Jewish state was thus established in Palestine for the first time since the days of the Romans. Arab nations vehemently opposed such a state, however, and invaded Israel the day it was officially founded. This first Arab-Israeli war lasted until January, 1949, and left Israel in possession of about 50 percent more territory than it had when war broke out. But no basis for a lasting peace was established.

1950–1953

Korean War. Following World War II, Korea was divided at the 38th parallel, with the Soviets occupying the north and the Americans occupying the south. Governments were established in both parts in 1948. In June, 1950, troops from Communist North Korea invaded the south. The United States requested the Security Council of the United Nations to authorize a police action in Korea. The Soviets boycotted the meeting and the resolution passed. In July, United Nations forces, made up primarily of United States contingents, landed in Korea under the command of General Douglas MacArthur (1880–1964). The Communist Chinese entered the fighting on the North Korean side in November, 1950. During the first year, the front shifted rapidly back and forth from North to South Korea. But in 1951 it stabilized at about the 38th parallel, where it remained for the rest of the war. In 1953, peace negotiations resulted in an armistice and the conflict ended. The 38th parallel was restored as the border between North and South Korea.

1953

Stalin's death and changes in Soviet leadership. On Joseph Stalin's death, his one-man rule of the Soviet Union was replaced for a time by collective leadership. There was a marked easing of the controls Stalin had imposed on Soviet society. In 1956 a "de-Stalinization" program introduced by Nikita Khrushchev (1894–1971) brought some further liberalization, as well as a denunciation of the worship of Stalin. De-Stalinization led to unrest within the Soviet sphere, marked by the short-lived Hungarian revolution in 1956. But Khrushchev nevertheless became the leading figure in the Soviet government and he held power until 1964.

1957

Sputnik

Sputnik and the space race. Sputnik, a 184-pound artificial satellite, was launched into orbit around Earth by the Soviets on October 4, 1957. The launch marked the beginning of the space age. On April 8, 1961, the Russian cosmonaut Yuri A. Gagarin became the first man to orbit Earth. U.S. astronaut John Glenn became the first American to orbit Earth, in February, 1962. But on July 20, 1969, the United States won a clear victory by landing the first men on the moon (Neil Armstrong and Edwin "Buzz" Aldrin, Jr.). Meanwhile, satellites and other space vehicles were perfected for a wide range of peaceful and military purposes by both sides.

1957

Common Market forms in Europe. Efforts to promote economic cooperation and the integration of Western European nations began after World War II. A major step was the creation of the Common Market (European Economic Community), which was designed to promote a complete customs union of Western European nations. In 1957 it included France, Belgium, Luxembourg, West Germany, Italy, and the Netherlands. Britain, Ireland, and Denmark became members in 1973. The success of the Common Market encouraged further cooperation among member nations, strengthening a movement toward a European community with political as well as economic ties.

1961–1963 **Kennedy administration in the United States.** John F. Kennedy (1917–1963) set the activist and idealistic tone that was to dominate U.S. government policy for much of the decade. The Kennedy years were filled with promise and with crisis. At home, Kennedy committed the federal government to civil rights for blacks during a period of mounting racial unrest, and thus began the sweeping social reform movements of the 1960's. Abroad, he actively opposed the Communists, bringing the world to the brink of nuclear war in the Cuban missile crisis (see below) and beginning the military involvement of the United States in Vietnam. The Kennedy years ended in tragedy when he was assassinated (November 22, 1963) in Dallas, Texas.

1961 **Bay of Pigs invasion of Cuba.** Fidel Castro (1927–) seized power in Cuba in 1959 and then joined the Soviet bloc in 1961. Soon afterward, Cuban exiles trained by the U.S. Central Intelligence Agency (CIA) staged what is called the Bay of Pigs invasion (April, 1961). The exiles hoped to spark a popular uprising against Castro but the attack was quickly crushed. The incident was a major embarrassment to the Kennedy administration.

Berlin wall erected. As Cold War tensions increased in 1961, the Communists moved in August to end the embarrassing flow of refugees from Communist East Germany into West Germany. The result was the Berlin wall, a 29-mile-long barrier separating East and West Berlin. In the West, the wall quickly became a symbol of Communist oppression. Although restrictions have been relaxed, the wall remains standing today.

1962 **Cuban missile crisis.** In October, 1962, the United States discovered that the Soviets were building missile sites in Cuba. President Kennedy's demand that the missile sites be dismantled and withdrawn brought the United States and the Soviet Union to the brink of nuclear war. After six days, Soviet leader Nikita Khrushchev finally backed down and agreed to withdraw the missiles. The incident was a contributing factor in Khrushchev's fall from power in 1964. However, the crisis also served to heighten public awareness of the dangerous possibility of nuclear war.

The Soviet installation of nuclear missiles in Cuba brought the United States to the brink of war.

1965–1973

Vietnam War. Fighting broke out in Vietnam soon after World War II, when followers of the Communist leader Ho Chi Minh (1890–1969) began their struggle against French rule in Indochina. The French were defeated (1954), and by the Geneva convention held that year, Vietnam was temporarily divided (at the 17th parallel) into northern and southern sectors. North Vietnam became a Communist state under Ho Chi Minh and South Vietnam became a pro-U.S. republic. South Vietnam refused to hold elections in 1956 on the reunification of Vietnam, as stipulated by the Geneva convention. In 1960 dissidents in the South were organized into the National Liberation Front (Vietcong), which had North Vietnamese backing.

The Vietcong guerrillas made significant gains against South Vietnamese government troops. The United States sent military aid to the South and brought in American military advisers in the early 1960's. By 1965 the situation had become critical. U.S. President Lyndon Baines Johnson (served 1963–1969) first ordered bombing raids on North Vietnam to halt the infiltration of North Vietnamese soldiers into the South. Soon afterward, in 1965, the first U.S. combat troops were sent to Vietnam and direct U.S. participation in the war began. Years of bloodshed followed. The United States found itself caught up in a costly and protracted war it could not win.

By 1968, over half a million U.S. troops were in Vietnam. But the Vietcong and the Soviet-backed North Vietnamese were still able to mount the demoralizing Tet offensive (February, 1968), in which cities and bases throughout the South suffered surprise attacks. The growing realization that a military victory was impossible, the pressure of world opinion, and the spread of the antiwar movement in the United States led to the opening of peace negotiations in 1968. The talks and the war dragged on until 1973, when a cease-fire agreement was reached. A complete withdrawal of U.S. forces was completed soon after, and a final offensive by the North Vietnamese brought the unconditional surrender of South Vietnam in 1975.

The Vietnam War was among the most costly and destructive ever fought. It devastated South Vietnam's economy, disrupted the social structure, decimated the population, and laid waste to the countryside. Its effect on the United States was also costly: it resulted in an unstable economy, worldwide condemnation of U.S. foreign policy, bitter internal divisions, and widespread distrust of the government's motives and credibility.

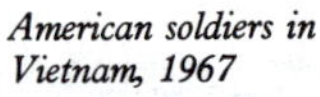

American soldiers in Vietnam, 1967

Date	*Event*
1966–1969	**Cultural revolution in China.** The cultural revolution was a ruthless campaign to purge Chinese society of ideas and people not friendly to the Communist government. Directed by Mao Tse-tung, brigades of young Maoists, called the Red Guard, spread the revolution throughout the country. Most schools were closed, and millions of city dwellers were shipped to remote collective farms for "reeducation." The movement eventually came to threaten the government itself. Beginning in about 1969, government leaders retreated from the cultural revolution and began to reestablish order in China.
1967	**Six Days' War in the Mideast.** Increasing tensions between the Arabs and the Israelis prompted the Israelis to launch a surprise attack on Egypt, Jordan, and Syria. After knocking out the Arab air force, the Israelis struck out on three fronts and quickly crushed Arab resistance. The war ended after six days of fighting with Israel in control of the Sinai Peninsula in Egypt, the West Bank in Jordan, and the Golan Heights in Syria.
1968	**Prague spring movement in Czechoslovakia.** Economic stagnation and resentment over the government's continuing hard-line policies brought the liberal Alexander Dubček to party leadership in January, 1968. Over the next few months, Dubček quickly adopted economic and political reforms, carrying Czechoslovakia closer to democratic government than any Communist bloc country before it. The Soviets became alarmed, however, and in August, 1968, the Warsaw Pact nations invaded Czechoslovakia. Dubček's liberal reforms were reversed and Dubček himself was ousted from the party leadership.
1970	**Detente.** The 1970's were the decade of detente, a new phase in relations between the United States and the Soviet Union. The two countries made a deliberate effort to ease Cold War tensions, to avoid direct confrontations, and to promote an era of negotiation and cooperation. The period saw the beginning of U.S.-Soviet trade, and important negotiations on the limitation of nuclear arms.
1971	**Communist China seated in the United Nations.** Since the Communist takeover of China in 1949, the Nationalist government on Taiwan had been recognized by the United Nations as the legitimate representative of the Chinese people. However, the Communist regime had firm political control of China's huge population. When the government moved to establish diplomatic relations with Western nations, including the United States in 1970, the last opposition to membership in the UN evaporated. The Taiwan government was unseated and the People's Republic was seated in its place.
1972	**Massacre at the Munich Olympics.** The 1970's witnessed the rise of terrorism in many parts of the world. Bombings, hijackings, and vicious murders, often of unarmed civilians, were committed for a variety of causes by small bands of fanatics. One of the most notorious of these incidents was the 1972 attack by Palestinian guerrillas at Olympic Village in Munich, Germany. Eleven Israeli athletes were massacred in the attack. One German policeman and five of the guerrillas were also killed.
1973	**Arab-Israeli war.** Mideast stability was again broken by warfare in October, 1973, when Egypt and Syria launched a surprise attack on Israel. Early advances by the two Arab states were soon nullified by Israeli victories on both the Egyptian and Syrian fronts, gained at the cost of many lives. By the end of the month, fighting had ceased, except for sporadic minor clashes that lasted into 1974. Although there was little change in territory, the Arabs had proved their fighting ability. Of greater importance, however, was the embargo on the sale of oil to Western nations imposed by Arab nations during the war. It marked the first effective use of oil as an economic and political weapon and signaled the rising power of the Arab oil-producing states.
1974	**Resignation of President Nixon.** Richard Nixon (served 1969–1974) resigned on August 9 under immediate threat of impeachment and conviction. The scandal that brought him down began with the attempted break-in at Democratic Party offices in the Watergate

apartment complex in Washington, D.C., in June, 1972. Investigations eventually revealed a wide variety of crimes and unethical acts in the Nixon administration. Many of his aides were convicted on criminal charges, but Nixon himself was given a full pardon by his successor, Gerald Ford (served 1974–1977).

1978

Camp David accords. From the time of Israel's creation in 1948, Arab states consistently refused to recognize Israel or to enter into treaties with it. The 1973 Arab-Israeli war convinced Egyptian President Anwar el-Sadat (served 1970–1981) of the importance of seeking peace with the Israelis. Negotiations culminated in a 13-day conference (September, 1978) between Sadat, Israeli Prime Minister Menachem Begin (served 1977–1983), and U.S. President Jimmy Carter (served 1977–1981). The conference was held at the Presidential retreat at Camp David, Maryland. It ended in the signing of a "framework for peace," and called for the establishment of diplomatic relations between Israel and Egypt and the gradual withdrawal of Israel from occupied Egyptian territory.

Normalized relations between the United States and China. Normalization between the two countries began when the Chinese invited an American table tennis team to China in 1971 (beginning the so-called "Ping-Pong diplomacy"). In 1973 President Richard Nixon visited China. Cultural and diplomatic exchanges increased, and China became an important new factor in international relations.

1979

Iranian revolution. The efforts of Shah Mohammed Riza Pahlevi (ruled 1941–1979) to rapidly modernize Iran led to outbreaks of violence by conservative Muslims in 1978. Soon after, the Muslim leader Ayatollah Khomeini took control of the government. The new government imposed Muslim fundamentalist culture on Iran and pursued a violently anti-American foreign policy. In November, 1979, Iranian militants, protesting the arrival of the deposed shah in the United States, seized the American Embassy in Iran and took 52 Americans hostage. In subsequent months, the Khomeini government used the incident to humiliate the United States. As negotiations for the release of the hostages bogged down, U.S. President Jimmy Carter ordered a rescue mission, but the attempt failed and cost the lives of eight servicemen. The hostages were finally released in January, 1981, after more than a year in captivity.

Soviet invasion of Afghanistan. Attempts to establish a Marxist regime in Afghanistan following a 1978 coup sparked an armed revolt by Muslim rebels. By late 1979, a Soviet-backed puppet government had been installed and the Soviets began a massive military effort to support the regime. Nearly 100,000 Soviet troops were reported in Afghanistan but guerrillas in the rugged countryside continued to mount successful resistance. The protracted conflict seriously damaged Soviet prestige and cooled Soviet relations with the United States. The last Soviet troops withdrew from Afghanistan in 1989.

1980

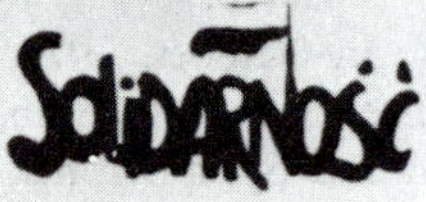

The Solidarity movement in Poland. By means of strikes and other actions, workers forced the economically hard-pressed Polish government to make major concessions. For a time it seemed that the workers were ready to topple the government. By late 1981, however, the military had taken control of the government, imprisoned Solidarity leaders, and sent the movement underground.

Iran-Iraq War. After ten months of skirmishing over the Shatt-al-Arab waterway that divides the two countries, open warfare was initiated when Iraqi bombers attacked ten Iranian oilfields. Bloody fighting ensued across both borders. In 1984 Iraq began attacks on Iranian shipping in the Persian Gulf. In 1988, after over 1 million people had been killed, a cease-fire was declared. The war was generally considered a stalemate.

1981

President Anwar el-Sadat of Egypt assassinated. The assasins were directed by Muslim extremists in the Egyptian armed forces. In the same year, U.S. President Ronald Reagan and Pope John Paul II were wounded in assassination attempts.

Date	*Event*
	Argentina invades British-held Falkland Islands. Britain recaptured the islands after a war lasting four weeks. The defeat was a major blow to Argentinan pride, and the country's military ruler resigned within days.
1982	**Israelis launch a major attack on Beirut, Lebanon.** They sought to drive out the guerrilla troops of the Palestine Liberation Army. In September, the massacre by Lebanese Christians of more than 300 Palestinians in a refugee camp prompted the sending of a peacekeeping force made up of French, Italian, and American troops to Lebanon. In October, 1983, terrorist attacks on the headquarters of the American and French forces killed over 280 people.
1983	**The United States invades Grenada.** The invasion came at the request of neighbors of the tiny Caribbean island, following a left-wing pro-Cuban coup, and in the belief that the lives of over a thousand American students on the island were in danger.
1984	**Two tragic events in India.** During a year in which religious tensions were very high, Prime Minister Indira Gandhi was assassinated by Sikh extremists. She was succeeded by her son Rajiv. Less than two months later, in the worst industrial accident in world history, over 2000 people were killed and over 150,000 injured when a cloud of toxic gas escaped from a Union Carbide chemical plant in Bhopal, India.
1986	**Dictators deposed.** In two stunning displays of popular will, Ferdinand Marcos of the Philippines and Francois "Baby Doc" Duvalier of Haiti fled into exile in the face of massive demonstrations of discontent by the people.
1987	**Missile treaty.** Ronald Reagan and Mikhail Gorbachev signed the first treaty ever to reduce the number of nuclear warheads. The treaty provides for the elimination of all medium- and short-range missiles by both countries, and establishes a mechanism for on-site inspection of the process.
1989	**Crackdown in China.** Millions of people participated in student-led demonstrations in favor of reform, provoking a political crisis. After a six-week standoff, the military brutally suppressed the movement. Hundreds of people were killed when troops opened fire on protesters in Tiananmen Square in Beijing.

Students demonstrate in Beijing's Tiananmen Square.

End of an era—Berliners anticipating the destruction of their hated wall.

1989 **The iron curtain falls.** Encouraged by reforms in the Soviet Union, the countries of the Soviet bloc in Eastern Europe moved swiftly toward democracy. Among the most dramatic events were the overwhelming Solidarity victory in Polish parliamentary elections, which forced the Communist Party to share power; the opening by East Germany of the Berlin Wall; and the violent overthrow of the Stalinist Ceausescu regime in Rumania. These changes altered radically the political and economic landscape of Europe. In 1990 East and West Germany were reunified into a single sovereign state.

1990–1991 **Changes in South Africa.** The South African government lifted a ban on the African National Congress (ANC) and freed Nelson Mandela, the leader of the ANC, from prison, where he had been detained for 28 years. Segregation in public places was outlawed and plans were made to put an end to all racial separation laws.

Nelson Mandela and South African president F. W. de Klerk

1991 **War in the Persian Gulf.** In response to the August, 1990, Iraqi invasion of Kuwait, an international coalition of forces, including the U.S. military, gathered in the Persian Gulf and in Saudi Arabia. On January 16, 1991, the coalition launched air sorties designed to destroy missile launchers and lines of supply. After 46 days of continual air attacks and five days of battle on the ground, Iraqi officials agreed to a cease-fire on March 2.

Secession and civil war in Yugoslavia. Croatia and Slovenia declared their independence, but violence broke out between Croats and ethnic Serbs in Croatia. The fighting escalated as Serbia contributed arms and supplies to the Serb rebels and the Yugoslav army engaged Croatian forces. Many cease-fires were declared, but none lasted more than a few days. The survival of Yugoslavia remained in doubt.

1985–1992

Mikhail Gorbachev.

Upheaval in the Soviet Union. In 1985 Mikhail Gorbachev was appointed general secretary of the Communist Party. In 1987 Gorbachev introduced a program of economic and social reforms, including expanded freedoms and democratization of the political process through *glasnost* (openness) and *perestroika* (restructuring), to help reshape Soviet society and government. The new era of openness coupled with an economy in its worst state since the birth of the union led to open displays of civil and ethnic unrest; workers struck and the Baltic republics demonstrated for independence.

In 1991 a coup was launched by hard-line Communist members of the Soviet military. Although the coup collapsed after only three days, it was a watershed in the demise of the Soviet Union. In the wake of the coup, Latvia, Lithuania, and Estonia asserted their independence and were recognized by the Soviet Union and the United Nations. The Russian Republic dealt the fatal blow to the union by declaring independence and creating an alliance—with Ukraine, Belarus (formerly known as Byelorussia), and eight other republics—called the Commonwealth of Independent States. On December 25, 1991, Mikhail Gorbachev resigned.

In 1992 Russia began the transition to a market economy and was faced with runaway inflation and widespread food shortages.

For Further Reference

Barnes, Julian
A History of the World
Knopf

Breasted, James H.
Conquest of Civilization
Harper & Row

Durant, Will and Ariel
Story of Civilization. 11 volumes.
Simon & Schuster

Garraty, John A.
The Columbia History of the World
Harper & Row

Grun, Bernard
The Timetables of History: A Historical Linkage of Peoples and Events
Simon & Schuster

Harrison, John B.
A Short History of Western Civilization
Knopf

Kirkler, Bernard
A Reader's Guide to Contemporary History
Quadrangle

McNeill, William H.
A World History
Oxford University Press

McNeill, William H. and Houser, Schuyler O.
Medieval Europe
Oxford University Press

Stavrianos, L.S.
Lifelines from our Past
Pantheon

Wallbank, T. Walter, et al.
Civilization Past & Present
Scott, Foresman

Wetterau, Bruce
The Macmillan Concise Dictionary of World History
Macmillan

Winks, Robin W., et al.
A History of Civilization
Prentice-Hall

Makers of world history

1000 BC to AD 2000

Peloponnesian War, 431 B.C.–404 B.C.
Hannibal crosses Alps, 218 B.C.
Caesar assassinated, 44 B.C.

1000 BC | 800 BC | 600 BC | 400 BC | 200 BC | AD 1

DAVID
c 1040–972, Hebrew king

SOLOMON
c 1000–932, Hebrew king

HOMER
fl. c 900, first Greek poet

SOLON
c 639–c 559, Greek lawmaker

NEBUCHADNEZZAR
c 630–562, Babylonian emperor

CYRUS THE GREAT
c 590–529, Persian conqueror

DARIUS THE GREAT
c 588–486, Persian king

PYTHAGORAS
581–497, Greek philosopher, scientist

BUDDHA, GAUTAMA
c 566–c 480, Indian religious leader

CONFUCIUS
c 551–479, Chinese philosopher, teacher

AESCHYLUS
c 525–456, Greek dramatist

SOPHOCLES
c 495–c 406, Greek dramatist

PERICLES
c 490–429, Athenian statesman

EURIPIDES
c 480–c 406, Greek dramatist

SOCRATES
469–399, Greek philosopher

HIPPOCRATES
c 460–c 370, "father of medicine"

THUCYDIDES
460–395, Greek historian

EUCLID
450–374, Greek geometrician

PLATO
427–347, Greek philosopher

ARISTOTLE
384–322, Greek philosopher

DEMOSTHENES
c 384–322, Athenian statesman, orator

PHILIP II
382–336, Macedonian king

PTOLEMY I
367–280, Egyptian ruler

ALEXANDER THE GREAT
356–323, Macedonian king, conqueror

CHANDAGUPTA MAURYA
ruled 322–298, king of Northern India

ASOKA
ruled c 273–232, ruler of India

PLAUTUS
c 254–c 184, Roman dramatist

HANNIBAL
247–183, Carthaginian general

CATO THE ELDER
234–149, Roman statesman

JUDAS MACCABEUS
c 200–166, led Maccabean revolt

POMPEY
106–48, Roman general, statesman

CICERO
106–43, Roman statesman, orator

JULIUS CAESAR
100–44, Roman general, statesman

LUCRETIUS
98–55, Roman poet, philosopher

MARK ANTONY
83–30, Roman soldier, politician

HEROD THE GREAT
73–4, King of Judea

VERGIL
70–19, Roman poet

CLEOPATRA
69–30, Egyptian queen

HORACE
65–8, Roman poet

AUGUSTUS CAESAR
63–AD 14, Roman emperor

Confucius

Aristotle

Alexander the Great

Statesmen, philosophers, and religious leaders

Scientists and explorers

Artists and men of letters

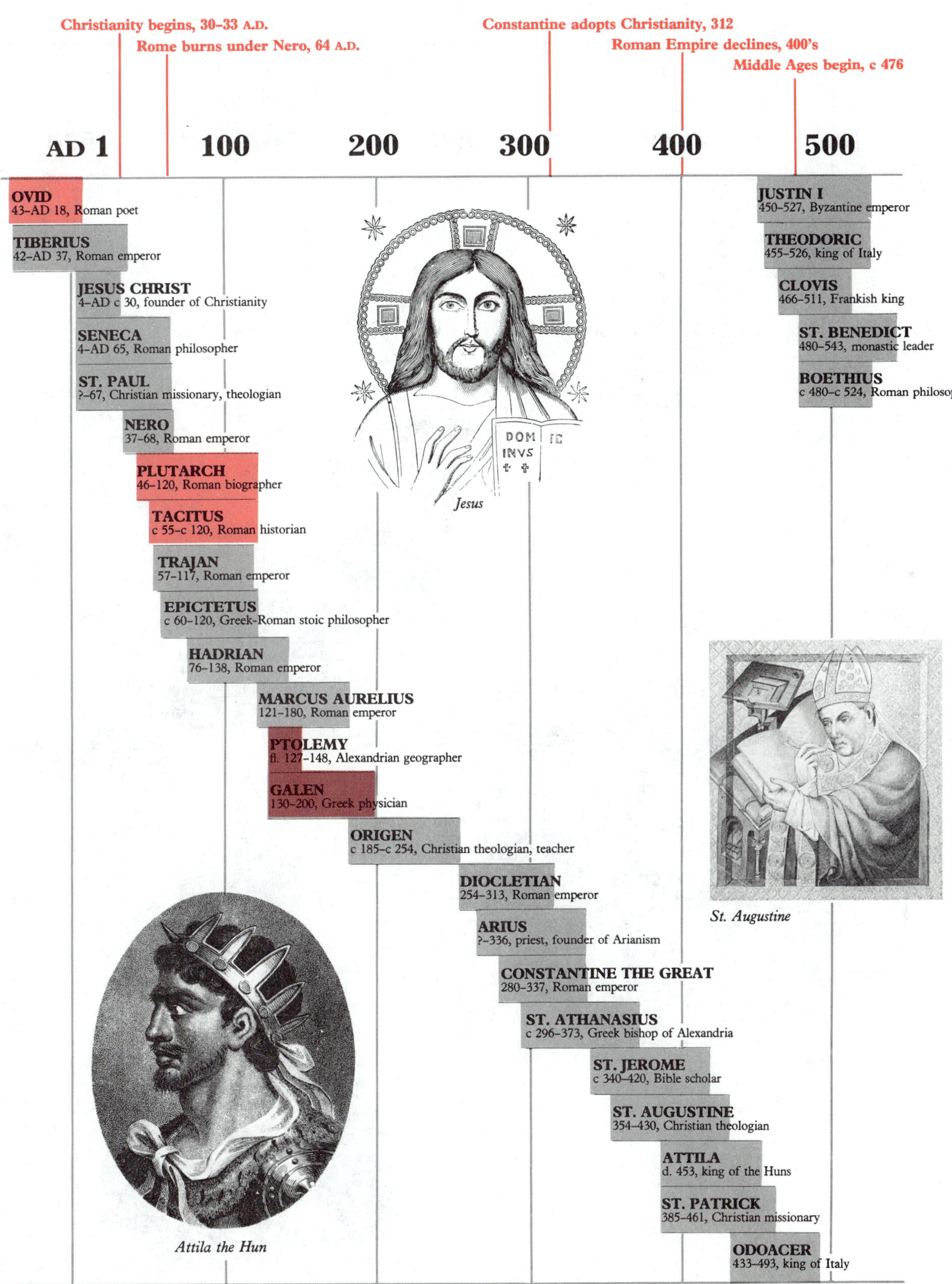

Jesus

St. Augustine

Attila the Hun

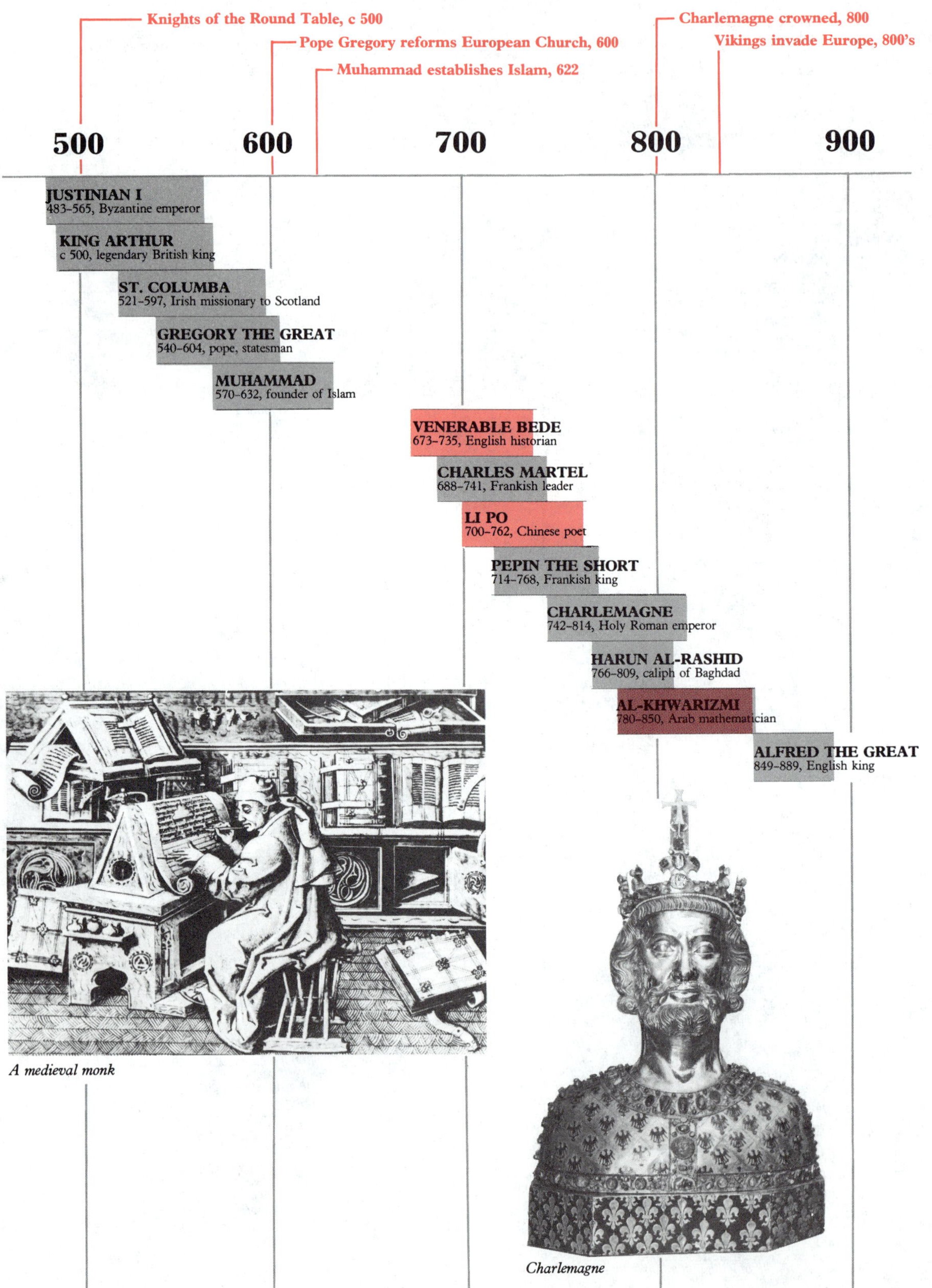

A medieval monk

Charlemagne

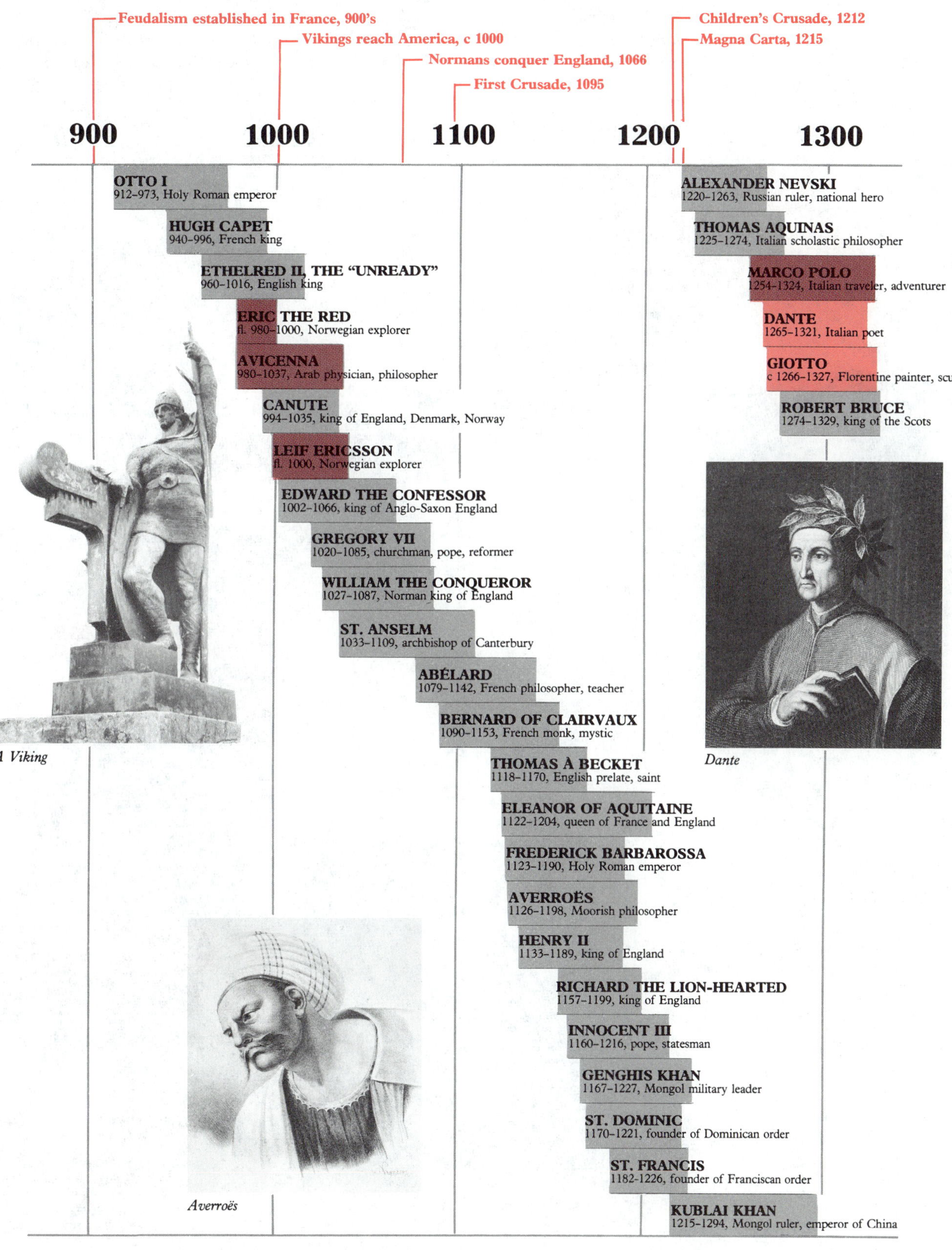

A Viking

Dante

Averroës

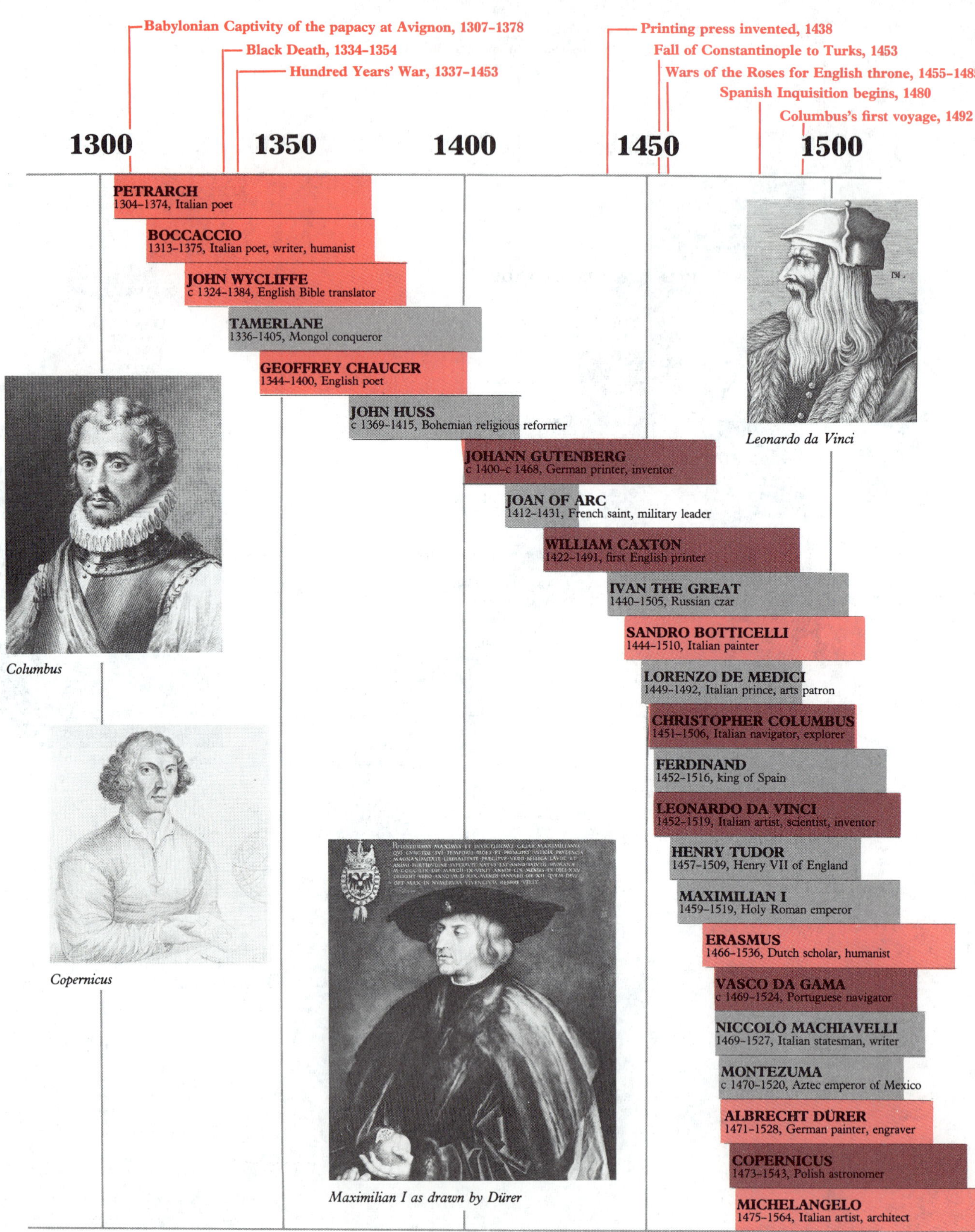

Leonardo da Vinci

Columbus

Copernicus

Maximilian I as drawn by Dürer

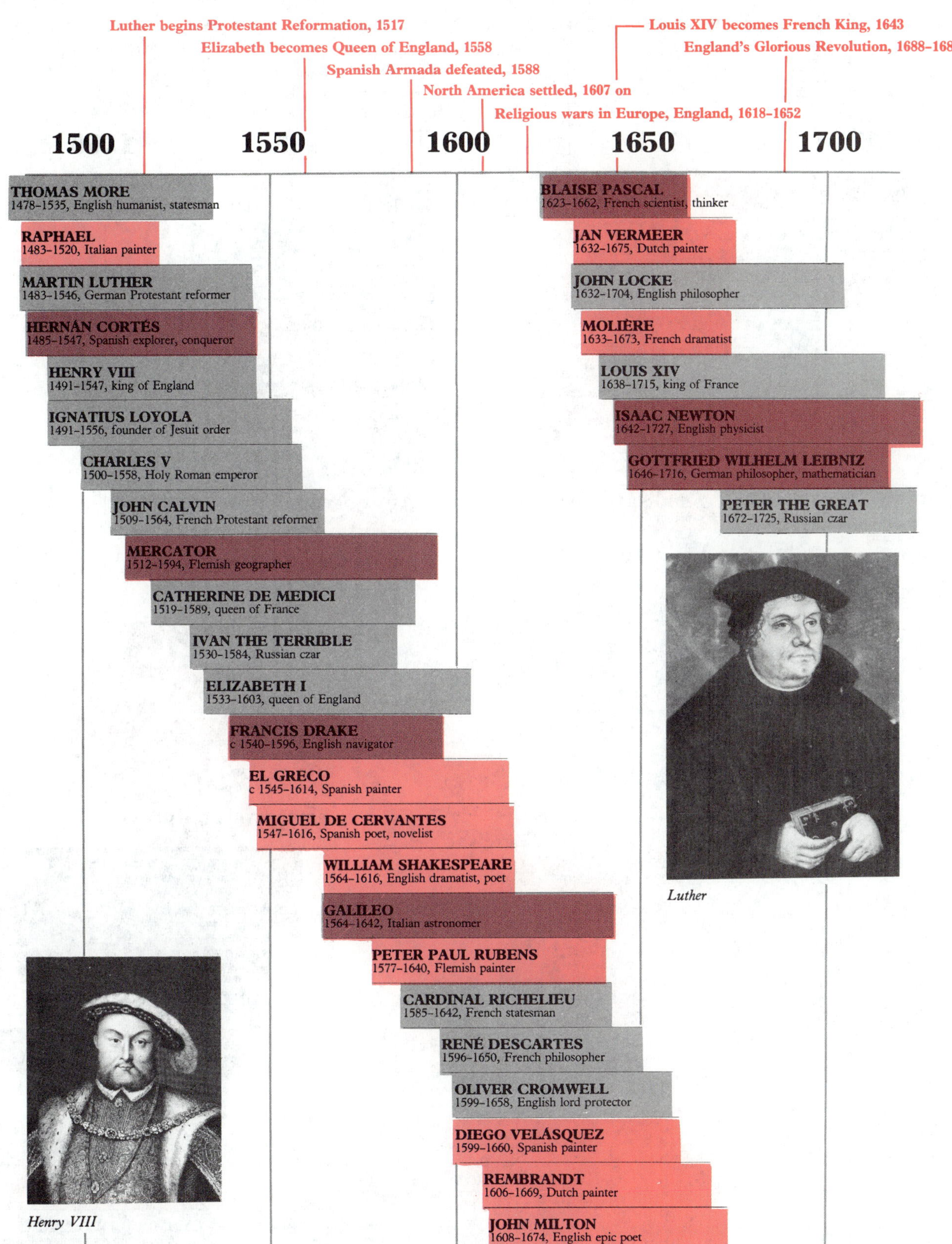

Henry VIII

Luther

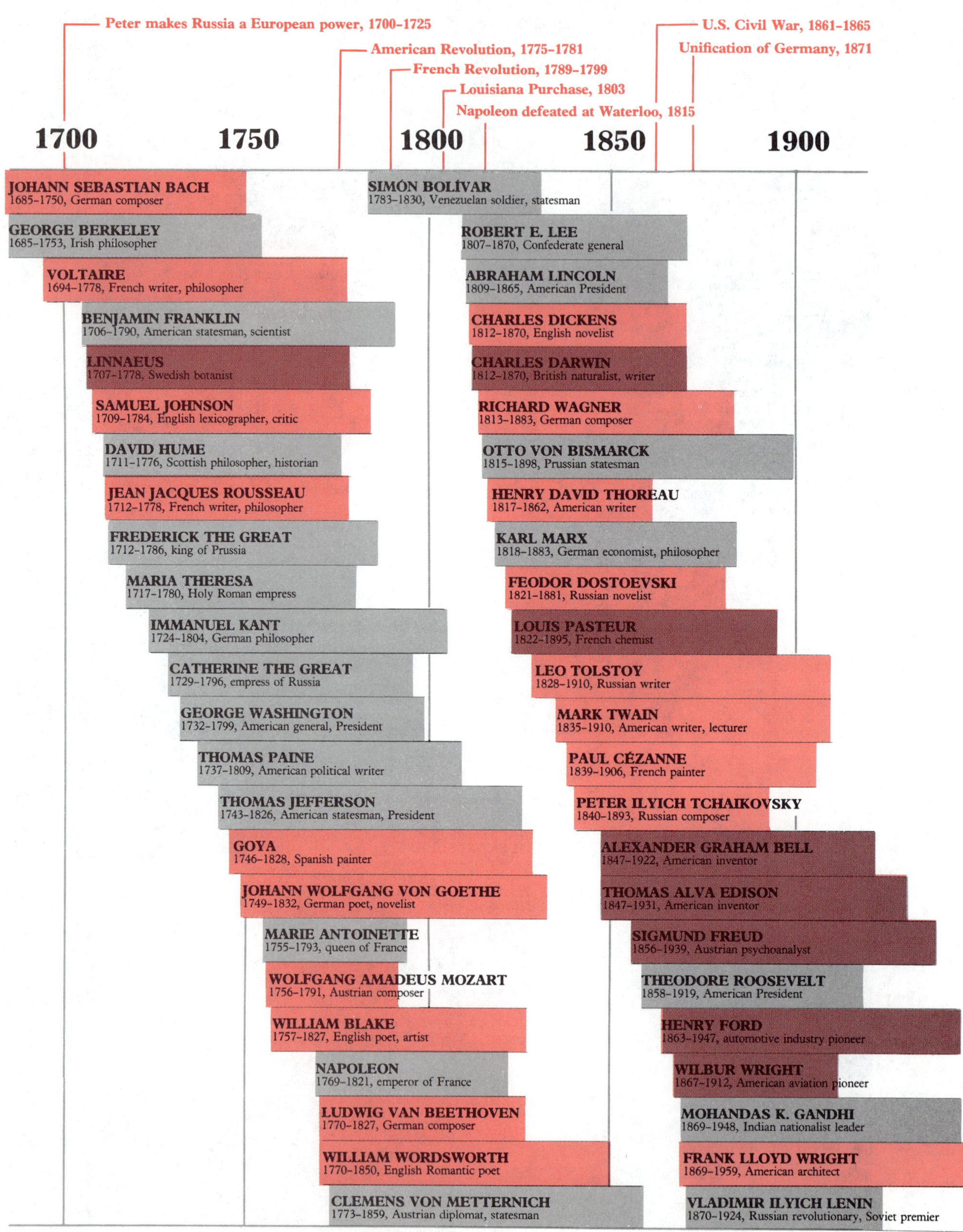

Peter makes Russia a European power, 1700–1725
American Revolution, 1775–1781
French Revolution, 1789–1799
Louisiana Purchase, 1803
Napoleon defeated at Waterloo, 1815
U.S. Civil War, 1861–1865
Unification of Germany, 1871
1700
1750
1800
1850
1900
JOHANN SEBASTIAN BACH
1685–1750, German composer
GEORGE BERKELEY
1685–1753, Irish philosopher
VOLTAIRE
1694–1778, French writer, philosopher
BENJAMIN FRANKLIN
1706–1790, American statesman, scientist
LINNAEUS
1707–1778, Swedish botanist
SAMUEL JOHNSON
1709–1784, English lexicographer, critic
DAVID HUME
1711–1776, Scottish philosopher, historian
JEAN JACQUES ROUSSEAU
1712–1778, French writer, philosopher
FREDERICK THE GREAT
1712–1786, king of Prussia
MARIA THERESA
1717–1780, Holy Roman empress
IMMANUEL KANT
1724–1804, German philosopher
CATHERINE THE GREAT
1729–1796, empress of Russia
GEORGE WASHINGTON
1732–1799, American general, President
THOMAS PAINE
1737–1809, American political writer
THOMAS JEFFERSON
1743–1826, American statesman, President
GOYA
1746–1828, Spanish painter
JOHANN WOLFGANG VON GOETHE
1749–1832, German poet, novelist
MARIE ANTOINETTE
1755–1793, queen of France
WOLFGANG AMADEUS MOZART
1756–1791, Austrian composer
WILLIAM BLAKE
1757–1827, English poet, artist
NAPOLEON
1769–1821, emperor of France
LUDWIG VAN BEETHOVEN
1770–1827, German composer
WILLIAM WORDSWORTH
1770–1850, English Romantic poet
CLEMENS VON METTERNICH
1773–1859, Austrian diplomat, statesman
SIMÓN BOLÍVAR
1783–1830, Venezuelan soldier, statesman
ROBERT E. LEE
1807–1870, Confederate general
ABRAHAM LINCOLN
1809–1865, American President
CHARLES DICKENS
1812–1870, English novelist
CHARLES DARWIN
1812–1870, British naturalist, writer
RICHARD WAGNER
1813–1883, German composer
OTTO VON BISMARCK
1815–1898, Prussian statesman
HENRY DAVID THOREAU
1817–1862, American writer
KARL MARX
1818–1883, German economist, philosopher
FEODOR DOSTOEVSKI
1821–1881, Russian novelist
LOUIS PASTEUR
1822–1895, French chemist
LEO TOLSTOY
1828–1910, Russian writer
MARK TWAIN
1835–1910, American writer, lecturer
PAUL CÉZANNE
1839–1906, French painter
PETER ILYICH TCHAIKOVSKY
1840–1893, Russian composer
ALEXANDER GRAHAM BELL
1847–1922, American inventor
THOMAS ALVA EDISON
1847–1931, American inventor
SIGMUND FREUD
1856–1939, Austrian psychoanalyst
THEODORE ROOSEVELT
1858–1919, American President
HENRY FORD
1863–1947, automotive industry pioneer
WILBUR WRIGHT
1867–1912, American aviation pioneer
MOHANDAS K. GANDHI
1869–1948, Indian nationalist leader
FRANK LLOYD WRIGHT
1869–1959, American architect
VLADIMIR ILYICH LENIN
1870–1924, Russian revolutionary, Soviet premier

World War I, 1914–1918
Russian Revolution, 1917–1920
Great Depression, 1930's
World War II, 1939–1945
Vietnam War, 1964–1973
Man walks on moon, 1969
Sadat, Egyptian leader, assassinated, 1981

1900 1950 2000

ORVILLE WRIGHT
1871–1948, American aviation pioneer

WINSTON CHURCHILL
1874–1965, English statesman

JOSEF STALIN
1879–1953, Soviet dictator

ALBERT EINSTEIN
1879–1955, German-born American physicist

POPE JOHN XXIII
1881–1963, Italian ecclesiastic, statesman

PABLO PICASSO
1881–1973, Spanish artist

FRANKLIN DELANO ROOSEVELT
1882–1945, American President

IGOR STRAVINSKY
1882–1971, Russian composer

BENITO MUSSOLINI
1883–1945, Italian dictator

DAVID BEN-GURION
1886–1973, prime minister of Israel

T. S. ELIOT
1888–1965, Anglo-American poet

ADOLF HITLER
1889–1945, German dictator

JAWAHARLAL NEHRU
1889–1964, prime minister of India

HO CHI MINH
1890–1969, Vietnamese revolutionary leader

CHARLES DE GAULLE
1890–1970, French president, general

FRANCISCO FRANCO
1892–1975, Spanish general, premier

MAO TSE-TUNG
1893–1976, Chinese Communist leader

JOMO KENYATTA
1893–1978, president of Kenya

LEONID BREZHNEV
1906–1982, Soviet leader

WERNHER VON BRAUN
1912–1977, rocket designer

JOHN F. KENNEDY
1917–1963, American President

INDIRA GANDHI
1917–1984, prime minister of India

ANWAR EL SADAT
1918–1981, president of Egypt

MARTIN LUTHER KING
1929–1968, American civil rights leader

Bach

Rousseau

Catherine the Great

Bolívar

Edison

Churchill

Gandhi

King

United States Government

The study of government is an important one for every citizen. In the United States, the will of the people is the final governmental authority through the votes cast for elected officials on the local, state, and national levels. The health of the government depends on an informed and concerned electorate. This section outlines the governmental system of the United States, considering the local, state, and federal governments in turn. In addition, there are features on the electoral system and on the importance of foreign affairs. The two concluding sections are the full text of the Constitution and its amendments, and profiles of each American President.

Federal system

At the time of the American Revolution, each of the 13 original states was a separate colony of Great Britain. When colonial representatives assembled to form an independent government, they favored a decentralized plan in which each state would maintain its sovereignty. The resulting Articles of Confederation were in force from 1780 to 1788, but experience proved that they gave too little power to the central government.

In 1787, representatives of the states met again to work out a new Constitution. The resulting document, which was ratified by all but one state by 1788, has been the basis of U.S. government ever since. It set up a *federal* system, apportioning responsibilities and authority between the new federal government and the individual states. Compared with other forms of government, the system was still decentralized, allowing considerable independence to the states.

The Constitution further divided authority in the central government among three branches—the legislative, the executive, and the judicial—providing that each of these branches serve as a check on the others. The framers were fearful of two extremes: an executive so powerful that it might claim tyrannical power, and a legislature so driven by the majority that the rights of minorities and dissenters might be overlooked.

In practice, the Constitution left the assignment of responsibility between state and central government vague enough so that power might shift between them—and among the branches of the federal government. In the 200 years since the Constitution was written, the country has grown from a small coastal enclave with fewer than 4 million people to a giant superstate covering nearly half a continent and comprising nearly 250 million people. During the 1900's, governmental power shifted to the federal government at the expense of the states. Within the federal establishment, the executive branch, headed by the President, has grown in importance at the expense of the legislative branch. Even under these changed conditions, however, the Constitution provides firm limits, and individual administrations may begin to shift power back to the states or back to the legislative branch.

Local government

Local governments include towns, counties, and a wide variety of single-function organizations such as sewer districts and consolidated school districts. These local governments all exist at the pleasure of the state government, but they operate with great independence, raising funds through local taxation and providing many essential services for local citizens. The table below summarizes some of the most important activities of local governments and their most significant powers of taxation.

Local government

Local responsibilities

Police protection	provide for safety of local citizens; local official may act as judge for minor offenses.
Fire protection	require building and fire safety standards; organize paid or volunteer fire departments; acquire equipment.
Public safety	create and enforce sanitation and other public health and safety laws.
Public works	build and maintain roads, sewer systems, public buildings, libraries, schools, parks, etc.
Education	maintain public school system through high school (small towns often cooperate in operation of higher schools; large cities may run full universities).
Social services	provide—in association with state and federal government and private organizations—assistance for the sick, the aged, the unemployed, and other needy persons.
Recreation	provide municipal parks, golf courses, and other recreation areas.
Regulation	pass and enforce zoning codes, consumer protection codes, and other laws to protect citizens.
Representation	represent local interests and needs to private and other governmental organizations through elected and appointed officials.

Local taxing powers

Property taxes	imposed as a rate or percentage of *assessed valuation* on all real property (land, buildings, homes, etc.).
User fees	paid by businesses and individuals for services received (water, registration of deeds, park fees, etc.).
Fines and penalties	for parking, overdue library books, etc.
Sales taxes	taxes on retail transactions, often excluding food and other essentials.
Income taxes	some cities and towns impose income taxes on residents and sometimes on commuters.

Local organization

Cities and towns usually have one of these two systems:

Mayor-council	mayor and council members are elected; mayor is executive, council is legislative; mayor may have many powers or few.
City manager	a nonpartisan manager is appointed as the administrative director of the city, serving at the pleasure of the mayor or council.

Larger towns and cities also have important independent organizations including the following:

School board	often separately elected, the board appoints a professional superintendent of schools and oversees educational policy.
Zoning board	usually made up of or including elected officials, the board decides on land use patterns in the town; it may control the economic development of the town.

State government

State governments are specifically recognized in the U.S. Constitution, and their existence is independent of the federal government. The Constitution specifically provides that powers not given to the federal government belong to the states. Each state has its own constitution, establishing that state's basic laws and administrative organization.

All states have provided for a governor as chief officer of the government (he or she usually serves a four-year term), and for a legislative branch with two houses resembling the Congress of the United States (only Nebraska has a one-house legislature). In addition, states have full judicial systems—trial courts, appeals courts, and supreme courts. The following table summarizes the responsibilities, taxing powers, and organization of state governments.

State government

State responsibilities

Police protection	provide state police to patrol unincorporated areas, state highways, etc.
Court system	maintain a system of courts to hear both civil cases (those between individuals, corporations, and the like) and criminal cases originating within state boundaries. State courts hear the vast majority of court cases in the United States. Parties to a case may appeal to federal courts only when federal laws or guarantees are at issue (see Federal government, Judicial branch, below).
Public safety	establish laws and regulations governing certain areas of public safety; maintain state penal institutions for those sentenced to imprisonment for serious crimes.
Public works	build and maintain state highways, buildings, universities, hospitals, parks, etc.
Education	set minimum standards for local elementary and high schools; maintain state colleges and universities.
Social services	provide assistance for needy citizens (states usually maintain public mental hospitals, set standards for other hospitals, and administer workmen's compensation, unemployment, and welfare benefits, receiving partial funding from the federal government).
Recreation	provide state parks and recreation areas.
Regulation	license corporations, drivers of motor vehicles, and practitioners of certain professions and occupations (doctors, lawyers, accountants, beauticians, etc.); regulate local tax rates and set minimum standards for certain local government services.
Representation	represent state interests to private and other governmental organizations through elected and appointed state officials.

State taxing powers

Income taxes	nearly all states levy taxes on the incomes of individual state residents, and most tax profits of corporations; tax rates vary considerably.
Sales taxes	most states levy broad sales taxes in addition to special taxes on such items as alcohol, tobacco, and gasoline.
Gambling	many states license gambling on horse races, and many have state lotteries, often to raise funds for particular activities.
User fees	these include those for drivers' and other licenses, and for the use of recreation facilities; resident students at state universities pay tuition that partly covers the cost of their education.
Fines and penalties	these include those for late payment of taxes.

Federal government

The official structure of the federal government is stated in the Constitution. The Constitution also prescribes the main responsibilities of the federal establishment. At the same time, a large body of tradition helps determine how government institutions work.

The Constitution provides that the federal government is responsible for four principal activities:

1. Regulation of affairs with other countries,
2. Defense of the country from foreign enemies and from civil disturbance,
3. Establishment of the monetary system, and
4. Regulation of relations among the states.

From these four activities have emerged an increasing number of other responsibilities. For example, only the federal government can declare war on another nation (in several instances it has fought "police actions" without declaring an official state of war). It can raise armed forces—by draft if necessary—and develop elaborate weapons systems. The largest employer in the federal government is the Department of Defense.

Similarly, the federal establishment has taken responsibility for regulating business by broad interpretation of its power to regulate commerce among the states.

The responsibilities of the government are carefully divided among the three branches: the legislative, the executive, and the judicial.

Apportionment in House of Representatives, 1982

Total: 435

	Number	*Change from 1972*		*Number*	*Change from 1972*
Alabama	7	—	Montana	2	—
Alaska	1	—	Nebraska	3	—
Arizona	5	+1	Nevada	2	+1
Arkansas	4	—	New Hampshire	2	—
California	45	+2	New Jersey	14	−1
Colorado	6	+1	New Mexico	3	+1
Connecticut	6	—	New York	34	−5
Delaware	1	—	North Carolina	11	—
Florida	19	+4	North Dakota	1	—
Georgia	10	—	Ohio	21	−2
Hawaii	2	—	Oklahoma	6	—
Idaho	2	—	Oregon	5	+1
Illinois	22	−2	Pennsylvania	23	−2
Indiana	10	−1	Rhode Island	2	—
Iowa	6	—	South Carolina	6	—
Kansas	5	—	South Dakota	1	−1
Kentucky	7	—	Tennessee	9	+1
Louisiana	8	—	Texas	27	+3
Maine	2	—	Utah	3	+1
Maryland	8	—	Vermont	1	—
Massachusetts	11	−1	Virginia	10	—
Michigan	18	−1	Washington	8	+1
Minnesota	8	—	West Virginia	4	—
Mississippi	5	—	Wisconsin	9	—
Missouri	9	−1	Wyoming	1	—

Legislative branch.

The legislative or law-making branch consists of two elected bodies collectively called the Congress. Together, the Congress is responsible for considering and passing all laws and acts necessary to the operation of the government.

The House of Representatives. The larger of the two bodies is the House of Representatives, which consists of 435 voting members apportioned to the states by population. Every ten years, in years ending in "0," a national census determines the population of each state; states are entitled to representatives in proportion to their population. Apportionment for the period 1982 to 1992 is shown in the box above. At the beginning of this period, each congressman represented about 520,000 people.

Members of the House are called either representatives or congressmen. They are elected for two-year terms, standing for election in November of even-numbered years and taking office in January.

In general, proposed laws or acts—called *bills*—may be first introduced in either House of Congress. Two kinds of bills *must* originate in the House, however; those calling for the raising or appropriating of government funds and those impeaching (bringing charges against) a President or other high government official.

The Senate. The Senate is the smaller of the two Houses of Congress. Its members are not apportioned according to population; instead, two senators are elected from each state, regardless of population. In 1980, the senators from Alaska represented a state with fewer than 500,000 people, while the senators from California represented a state with more than 24 million. Senators represent a state as a whole rather than a particular district or region.

The framers of the Constitution provided senators with terms even longer than that of the President—six years—and arranged that only a third of them would stand for election in any election year. They hoped that longer terms and a staggered election system would make the Senate more leisurely in its deliberations and less subject to sudden enthusiasms among the electorate. The framers also provided that the senators be elected by state legislatures rather than directly by voters. This provision was changed by the 17th Amendment, ratified in 1913. Since then, all senators are elected by the full electorate of their states.

The Constitution provides the Senate with a few specific duties not shared with the House. It must ratify treaties with other nations negotiated by the President or his appointees, and it must approve Presidential appointments to major Cabinet posts, diplomatic posts, and federal judgeships. If a President or other high official is impeached by the House, the Senate sits as a jury in the impeachment trial.

How a bill is passed. The Houses of Congress are organized into committees, each of which considers legislation in a particular area, such as agriculture or defense. When a bill is introduced by a congressman (or senator), it is first referred to a committee for consideration. The committee may *table* the bill, killing it for that session of Congress; *report it out* to the full body for a vote of the whole; or report it out with amendments. If the full House votes in favor of the bill, it is sent to the Senate for consideration (and vice versa). If the vote goes against the bill, it is killed and must be reintroduced.

The presiding officer of the House is the Speaker, who is elected by the majority party and has considerable power in referring bills to committees and controlling debate once a bill reaches the floor of the House. The majority leader and majority whips often work with the Speaker on bills favored by their party. The minority leader and minority whip often organize the opposition to a bill favored by the majority party.

The Senate has no officer with the power of the Speaker of the House. The Vice President of the United States normally presides, but he has no vote unless the Senate is tied. The president pro tempore of the Senate is a senior member of the majority party who presides in the absence of the Vice President, but this post is largely honorary. Majority and minority leaders and whips play roles similar to those of their counterparts in the House.

A bill passed in one House goes through the same process—introduction, committee consideration, floor debate—in the other House. If both Houses pass the bill in the same form, it has been passed by Congress and goes to the President for his signature. More often, the bills passed in the two Houses have differences. When this happens, they are referred to a *conference committee* comprised of senators and representatives who negotiate until they agree on a single form for the bill. This revised bill is then considered by both Houses for passage without further amendment. If both Houses pass the bill, it goes to the President for his signature.

The President acts as a check on the Congress. He signs routine bills and they become law. But if he opposes a bill, he may refuse to sign it. This is called a *veto.* The bill is then returned to both Houses. If they both pass the bill by two-thirds majorities, the Congress has *overridden* the President's veto and the bill becomes law without his signature. If the bill fails to pass both Houses by two-thirds, it dies and can only be resurrected by carrying it through the legislative process once again.

In practice, the President and his advisers often prepare legislation for consideration by Congress and help see it through the legislative process. But the Congress can also act as a check on the President by tabling, delaying, or voting down bills he has helped to frame. In most cases, both the President and the Congress make an effort to work together so that important legislation may be passed.

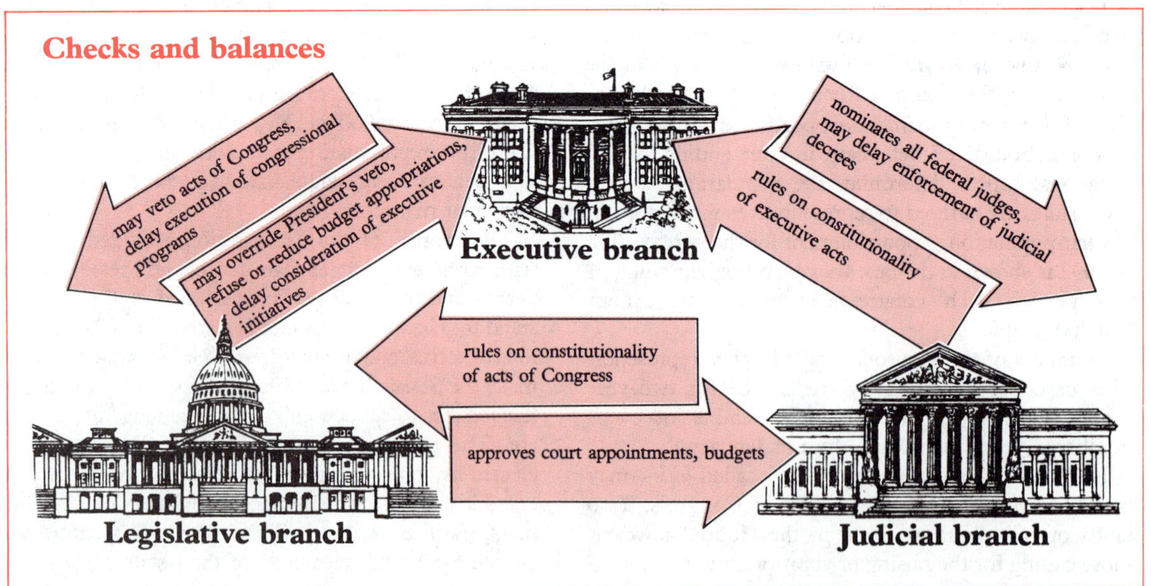

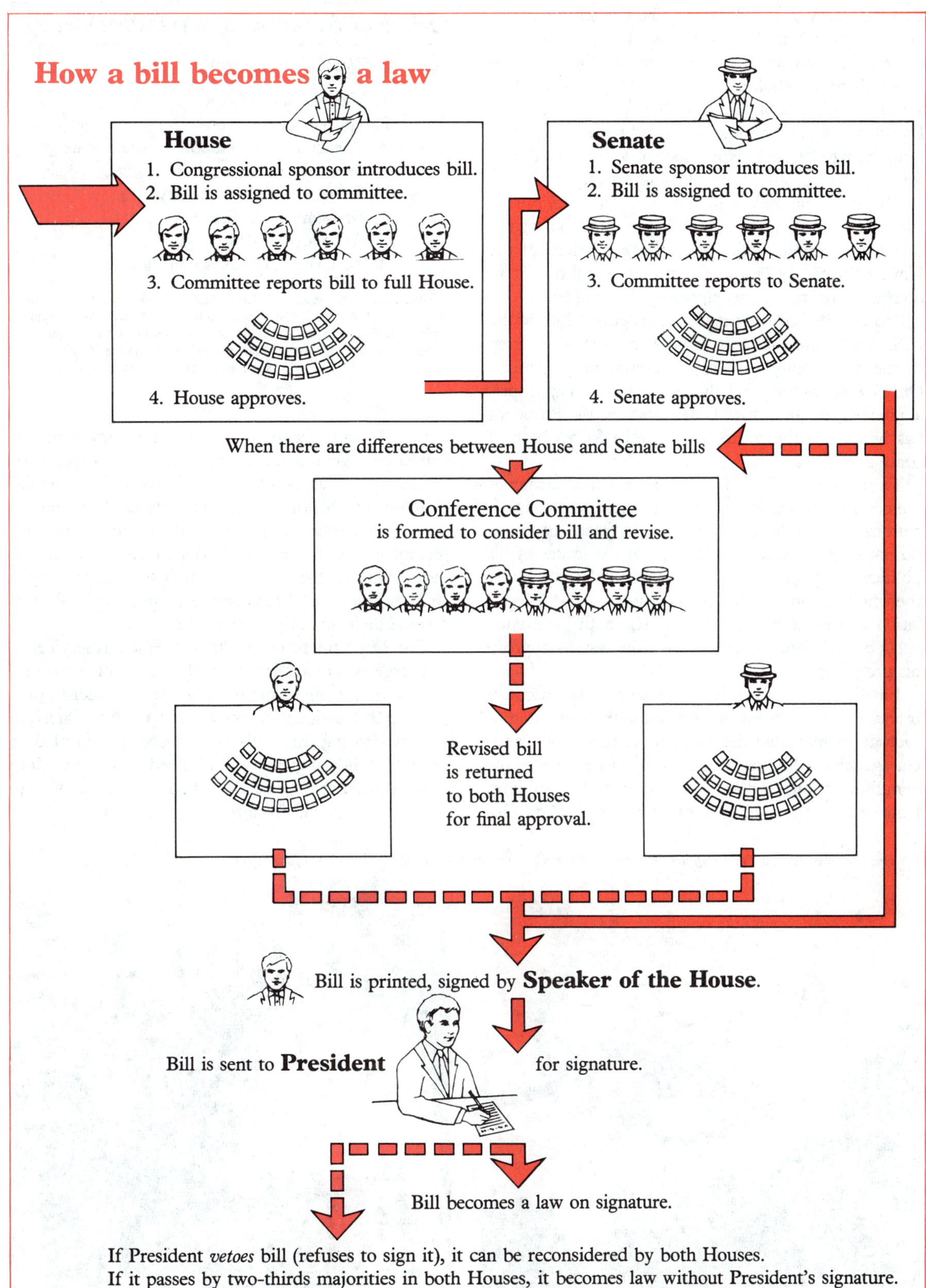
How a bill becomes a law
House
1. Congressional sponsor introduces bill.
2. Bill is assigned to committee.
3. Committee reports bill to full House.
4. House approves.
Senate
1. Senate sponsor introduces bill.
2. Bill is assigned to committee.
3. Committee reports to Senate.
4. Senate approves.
When there are differences between House and Senate bills
Conference Committee
is formed to consider bill and revise.
Revised bill
is returned
to both Houses
for final approval.
Bill is printed, signed by Speaker of the House.
Bill is sent to President for signature.
Bill becomes a law on signature.
If President vetoes bill (refuses to sign it), it can be reconsidered by both Houses.
If it passes by two-thirds majorities in both Houses, it becomes law without President's signature.

Executive branch. The Constitution provides that the President be the head of the executive branch. He and his Vice President are the only two government officeholders elected by the whole electorate of the United States. The President and the Vice President run on the same ticket and serve a four-year term, being elected in November of years divisible by four and taking office the following January.

The President serves in four important capacities. First, he is Head of State, serving as a symbol of national unity and directing the foreign relations of the United States. As Head of State, he is equivalent to other nations' monarchs, emperors, or presidents.

Second, the President is Commander in Chief of the U.S. armed forces. In this capacity, he is superior even to the most senior general or admiral in the forces. Only Congress can officially declare war and appropriate money to fight a war; but in practice, the President has broad powers to direct the armed forces both in peace and in war.

Third, the President is the chief political leader of the country. In this capacity, he is equivalent to other nations' prime ministers or presidents (many of whom do not serve as head of state). He is the leader of his political party, and as the chief officeholder elected by the whole country, he has broad powers to frame legislation and make policy. He may use both persuasion and political force to encourage Congress to approve his programs.

Finally, the President is the director of the executive branch of the government, appointing the secretaries of each department and the members of many independent agencies. The executive departments employ some 3 million civilian workers in a wide variety of jobs, from protecting wildlife to collecting taxes. The Cabinet-level departments and the more important independent agencies are listed in the box on page 67.

Among the largest of the executive departments are Defense and Health and Human Services. The Defense Department is in charge of the development and deployment of weapons both in the United States and in other parts of the world. It employs a large civilian staff engaged in defense-related work and all uniformed members of the armed forces.

The Department of Health and Human Services is in charge of administering a wide variety of social service programs, including the giant Social Security program. Most civilian workers in the United States are required to pay into this system and are entitled to benefits if they are widowed, disabled, or retired. More than 30 percent of the federal budget consists of payments made to and from this insurance fund.

Order of Succession to the Presidency*

(in case of death or disability)

1. Vice President*
2. Speaker of the House
3. President Pro Tempore of the Senate
4. Secretary of State
5. Secretary of the Treasury
6. Secretary of Defense
7. Attorney General

8–16. Other Cabinet secretaries

* The 25th Amendment to the Constitution provides a means by which a Vice President who has succeeded to the Presidency may nominate a new Vice President with the advice and consent of the Senate. The order of succession above would take effect only if the Vice President died at the same time as or soon after the President.

The President presides over foreign affairs (left) *and serves as Commander in Chief of all U.S. armed forces* (right).

Structure of the U.S. federal government.

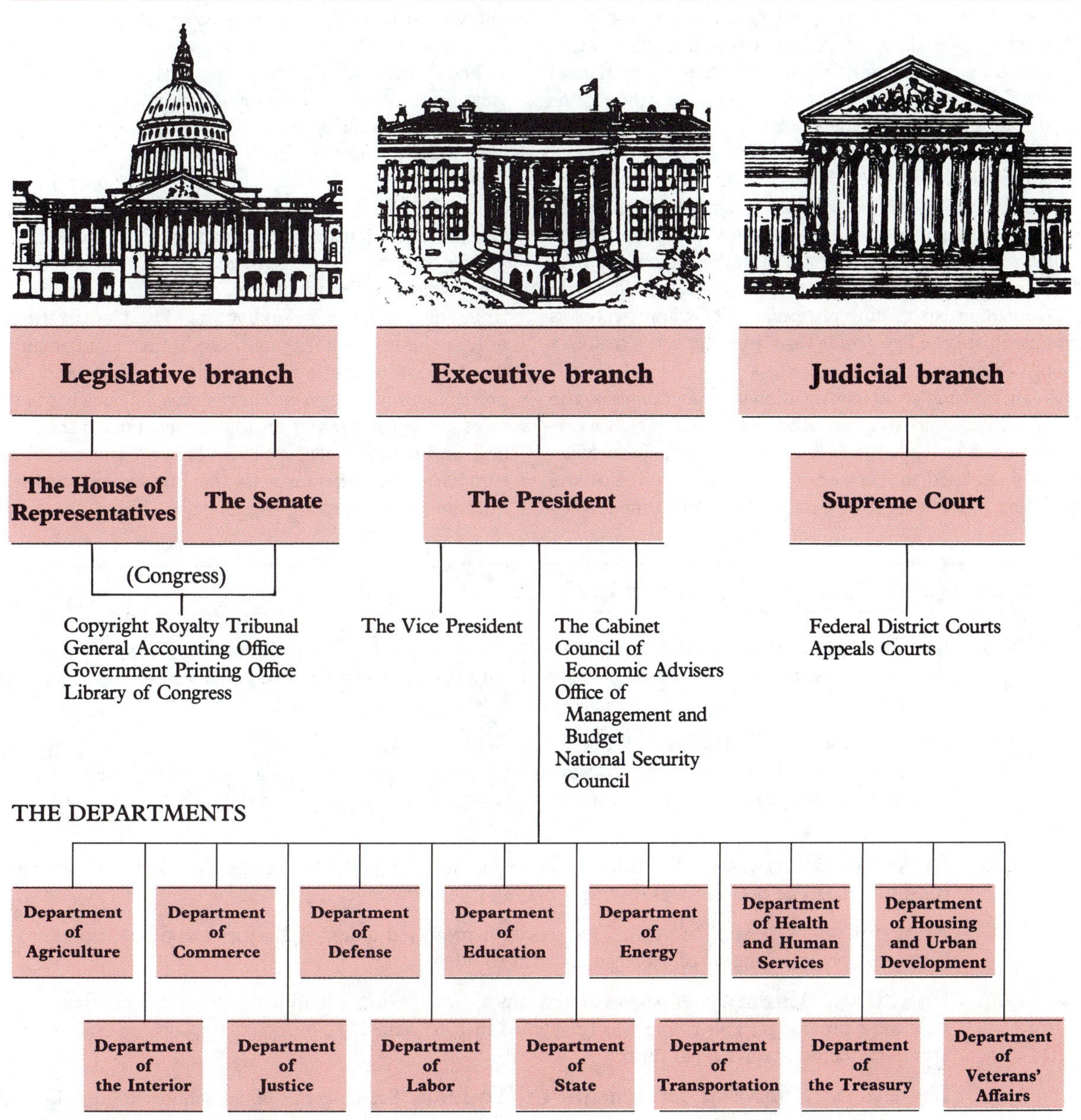

INDEPENDENT ESTABLISHMENTS

ACTION
Agency for International Development
Arms Control and Disarmament Agency
Central Intelligence Agency
Consumer Product Safety Commission
Environmental Protection Agency
Equal Employment Opportunity Commission
Federal Communications Commission
Federal Deposit Insurance Corporation
Federal Election Commission
Federal Home Loan Bank Board
Federal Mediation and Conciliation Service
Federal Reserve System
Federal Trade Commission
General Services Administration
International Communications Agency
Interstate Commerce Commission
National Aeronautics and Space Administration
National Endowment for the Arts
National Endowment for the Humanities
National Labor Relations Board
National Mediation Board
National Science Foundation
Nuclear Regulatory Commission
Postal Service, United States
Securities and Exchange Commission
Selective Services System
Small Business Administration
Smithsonian Institution
Tennessee Valley Authority
Veterans Administration

Judicial branch. The Constitution provides for a federal judiciary and gives it specific responsibility for hearing cases between states or residents of different states; cases involving other countries; and cases involving the breaking of federal laws. The only court mentioned by name in the Constitution is the Supreme Court.

Today the court system consists of federal district courts, operating in every state in the Union; nine federal circuit courts, each hearing appeals from lower courts in a region of the country; several special courts for specialized cases; and the Supreme Court, the final authority in the U.S. system of law. The Supreme Court consists of nine justices, one of whom serves as chief justice. They decide cases by vote, and a majority of justices present is required.

In addition to its constitutional responsibilities, the Supreme Court has two other important jobs. One is the function called *judicial review.* Justice John Marshall declared in *Marbury* v. *Madison* (1803) that the Court had the right to decide the constitutionality of any act of Congress. Similarly, the Court may declare the act of a President unconstitutional. This power is seldom used, but it acts as a powerful check on the Congress and the President.

The Court's second extra-constitutional job is to review cases in which individuals or groups claim that their constitutionally guaranteed rights have been violated. These *civil liberties,* as they are called, are guaranteed by the first ten amendments of the Constitution, called the *Bill of Rights.* These guarantees have been extended by later amendments to the Constitution.

The Supreme Court is asked to decide thousands of cases each year, most of which come to it *on appeal* from state or lower federal courts. The Court refuses to hear the vast majority of cases; in this circumstance, the decision of the lower court stands. When the Supreme Court does agree to hear a case, lawyers for both sides present written briefs for review. Then a time for oral arguments is set, and the lawyers present brief summaries of their cases to the justices and answer questions.

Landmark decisions of the Supreme Court

1803 **Marbury vs. Madison.** Chief Justice Marshall asserted the Court's right to judicial review—to overturn a law as unconstitutional. This decision became a central part of American governmental practice.

1857 **Dred Scott vs. Sandford.** Court ruled 6–3 that black slaves were to be considered property; that they had no rights of citizenship; and that Congress could not abolish slavery in a U.S. territory. The decision sharpened divisions that led to the Civil War in 1861. It was nullified by the 13th and 14th Amendments.

1896 **Plessy vs. Ferguson.** Court ruled that "separate but equal" facilities for blacks and whites were constitutional. The decision was reversed in 1954 (see below).

1919 **Schenck vs. United States.** Free speech is protected unless authorities can prove it presents a "clear and present danger" of violence or harm to others.

1932 **Powell vs. Alabama.** A person on trial for a capital crime is entitled to legal counsel even if the state must provide it. This ruling was broadened in 1963 and 1972 to include persons on trial for any crime that could involve a jail term.

1954 **Brown vs. Board of Education of Topeka.** Separate but equal schools for blacks and whites are unconstitutional.

1962 **Engel vs. Vitale.** Public schools cannot constitutionally require students to recite prayers.

1964 **Reynolds vs. Sims.** The U.S. House of Representatives and both houses of state legislatures must create election districts of roughly equal population. This decision forced most state legislatures to redistrict.

1973 **Doe vs. Bolton and Roe vs. Wade.** Broad state prohibitions of abortion during a woman's first six months of pregnancy are unconstitutional.

1974 **Nixon vs. United States.** The President cannot withhold information required in a criminal trial; his right to keep executive matters confidential—called "executive privilege"—is limited.

Foreign relations.

The federal government has exclusive power over the conduct of foreign relations. This responsibility is shared by the three branches. No state or individual may make a treaty or agreement with a foreign government without approval of the federal government.

Various agencies of the executive branch deal with such foreign relations concerns as immigration, customs, foreign travel by American nationals, tariffs, and trade relations. Direct relations with foreign governments are carried on by the State Department, which maintains U.S. embassies in most countries of the world and helps negotiate treaties, alliances, and other international agreements. Major foreign policy decisions are made by the President in consultation with the secretary of state and other advisers. In the case of treaties, the Senate must approve them before they take effect. Congress also has considerable influence in foreign affairs through its power to appropriate money for aid to other countries. The federal courts hear cases that involve foreign nationals and foreign governments.

The United States also participates in foreign affairs through its membership in international organizations. Some of these were established for joint defense, particularly the North Atlantic Treaty Organization (NATO). Others, such as the Organization of American States (OAS), are regional organizations seeking political and economic cooperation. Perhaps the most important among international organizations is the United Nations (the UN), whose headquarters are in New York and whose membership includes nearly every country in the world.

United Nations.

The United Nations was organized in 1945 by the victorious nations in World War II. Today it has more than 150 members and pursues a wide variety of cooperative and consultative ventures. It provides a forum for the discussion of international disputes and an administrative center for cooperation among nations in economic development, agricultural improvement, and many other matters.

The main deliberative bodies in the UN are the General Assembly, in which each member nation has a voice and a vote; and the Security Council, which is made up of five permanent members (the United States, the Soviet Union, China, Great Britain, and France), and ten rotating members who serve two-year terms. In Security Council votes on important matters, any permanent member may cast a *veto*, killing a measure even if all other members are in favor.

The United Nations has no military force of its own, but it may send peacekeeping forces from consenting member nations to supervise truces and otherwise discourage bloodshed.

The Secretariat of the UN is its executive branch, directed by the secretary-general, who is elected by member nations for a term of five years. The Secretariat coordinates the work of UN organizations in many fields (see chart). The Office of the UN High Commissioner for Refugees received the Nobel Prize for Peace in 1954 and 1981.

The United Nations is supported by assessments on member nations, apportioned by population and economic strength. The largest contributor is the United States. For a list of member nations, see *Countries of the World* in Volume I.

Organization of the United Nations

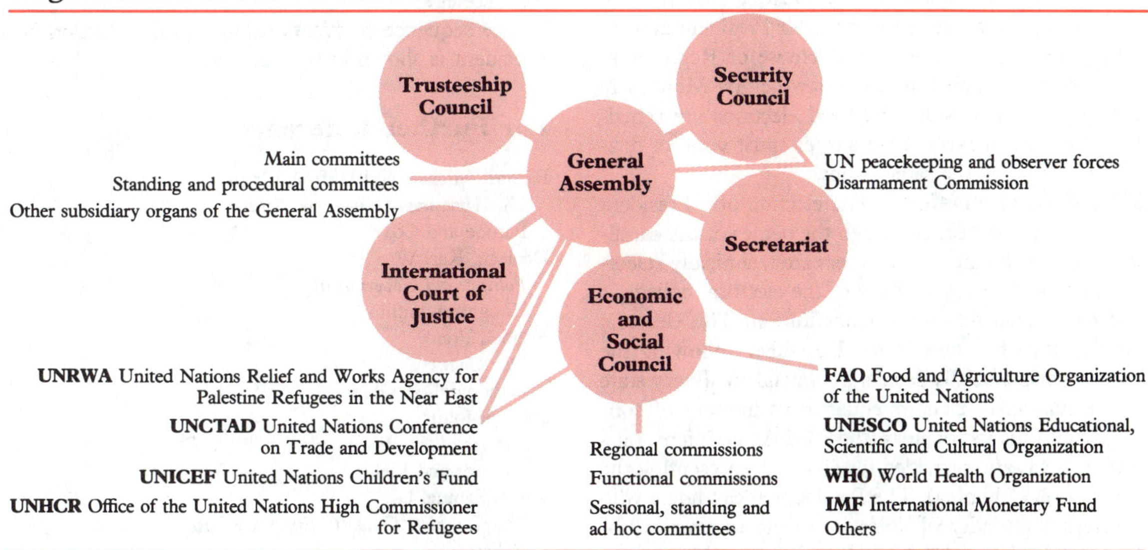

Elections

All elections for federal and state officials are held by secret ballot. The elections are preceded by a complex nomination process by which each political party chooses its nominee for office.

Nominations. Those seeking a major party nomination to state or federal office often begin campaigning a year or more before the election. In some jurisdictions, a nominee is chosen by a series of party caucuses or by the vote of delegates to a party convention on the local, state, or national level. In recent years, however, primary elections have played an increasing role in choosing nominees. In most states, voters registered in a given party choose between two or more candidates for their party's nomination two to six months before the general election. Between the primary and the general election, the nominees of the various parties campaign against each other.

Presidential candidates gain their party's nomination through a combination of state caucuses, state primary elections, and party conventions. A series of state caucuses and primaries runs from January to June of an election year. These caucuses and elections select delegates to the national convention who are committed to one candidate or another. The final vote on the nominee takes place at the convention, which is held in the summer. Often the result of this nomination vote is already determined before the convention begins.

General elections. In elections for most federal and state offices, the candidate who receives a *plurality* of the votes—one more than his nearest competitor—is elected. In some cases state laws provide that if no candidate receives a certain percentage of the vote (often 40 percent), a runoff election must be held between the two top contenders. Elections for President and for all members of the Senate and House of Representatives are held on the Tuesday after the first Monday in November. Many state and local elections are scheduled for the same day. Voters often must vote for dozens of offices on the same ballot.

Presidential elections. The election of a President is more complicated. Although the names of the candidates appear on the ballot, voters are technically selecting unnamed representatives to the electoral college, a body provided for in the Constitution. The electoral college casts its votes in the December following the election and officially selects the President. Every state has a number of electors equal to its number of congressmen plus its senators (the 23rd Amendment, ratified in 1961, also provided for electors representing the District of Columbia). The Presidential candidate who receives a plurality of votes in a state receives *all* of that state's electoral votes.

Presidential elections: a schedule

Popular election

First Tuesday in November

Candidate with plurality in each state wins that state's electoral votes.

Electoral college meetings

First Monday after second Wednesday in December

Electors meet in state capitals to cast their votes. States certify the votes and send them to Congress.

Counting the electoral vote

Results of the electoral college vote are tallied by the President of the Senate (usually the U.S. Vice President) at a joint session of Congress. If there is a tie in the electoral vote, the House of Representatives must elect the President, each state receiving *one* vote.

Inauguration

January 20

The President-elect is sworn in at noon and takes office.

To be elected President, a candidate must receive a majority of electoral votes—at least 270 of a total of 538. If no candidate receives a majority, the election is thrown into the House of Representatives. There, each state delegation receives one vote. This has happened only once, in 1824, when John Quincy Adams was elected by the House over Andrew Jackson and Henry Clay. Twice, however, a candidate who received a plurality of all popular votes cast was defeated in the electoral college.

The sequence of events leading to the election of a President is shown in the box above.

For Further Reference

Barone, Michael and Ujifusa, Grant
The Almanac of American Politics
Barone and Co.

Deutsch, Karl W.
Politics and Government
Houghton-Mifflin

Freidel, Frank
Our Country's Presidents
National Geographic

Hersey, John
Aspects of the Presidency
Ticknor and Fields

Kling, Samuel G.
The Complete Guide to Everyday Law
Follett

Constitution of the United States

Preamble

We the people of the United States, in order to form a more perfect union, establish justice, insure domestic tranquility, provide for the common defense, promote the general welfare, and secure the blessings of liberty to ourselves and our posterity, do ordain and establish this Constitution for the United States of America.

NOTE:
The titles and annotations in this column are aids to understanding. They are not part of the Constitution itself.

Article I

The Legislative Branch

Section 1. All legislative powers herein granted shall be vested in a Congress of the United States, which shall consist of a Senate and House of Representatives.

House of Representatives

Section 2. The House of Representatives shall be composed of members chosen every second year by the people of the several States, and the electors in each State shall have the qualifications requisite for electors of the most numerous branch of the State legislature.

No person shall be a Representative who shall not have attained to the age of twenty-five years, and been seven years a citizen of the United States, and who shall not, when elected, be an inhabitant of that State in which he shall be chosen.

This section set up the national census to determine how many representatives in Congress each state would have. Originally, slaves and Indians were not counted "whole persons" in the census, but the 14th Amendment gave former slaves the full rights of citizenship. The number of congressmen from each state is still determined by the number of people in the state, but the total membership of the House is limited to 435.

Representatives and direct taxes shall be apportioned among the several States which may be included within this Union, according to their respective numbers, which shall be determined by adding to the whole number of free persons, including those bound to service for a term of years, and excluding Indians not taxed, three-fifths of all other persons. The actual enumeration shall be made within three years after the first meeting of the Congress of the United States, and within every subsequent term of ten years, in such manner as they shall by law direct. The number of Representatives shall not exceed one for every thirty thousand, but each State shall have at least one Representative; and until such enumeration shall be made, the State of New Hampshire shall be entitled to choose three; Massachusetts, eight; Rhode Island and Providence Plantations, one; Connecticut, five; New York, six; New Jersey, four; Pennsylvania, eight; Delaware, one; Maryland, six; Virginia, ten; North Carolina, five; South Carolina, five; and Georgia, three.

When vacancies happen in the representation from any State, the executive authority thereof shall issue writs of election to fill such vacancies.

"Impeachment" means accusing an official of wrong conduct in office. The House of Representatives makes these charges, and the Senate acts as the court where they are tried (see Section 3).

The House of Representatives shall choose their Speaker and other officers, and shall have the sole power of impeachment.

Senate

Since the 17th Amendment was passed in 1913, senators have been chosen by direct popular vote, not by the legislatures.

Section 3. The Senate of the United States shall be composed of two Senators from each State, chosen by the legislature thereof for six years; and each Senator shall have one vote.

This clause set up a system of staggered elections to the Senate. All senators now have six-year terms, but the terms expire at different times.

Immediately after they shall be assembled in consequence of the first election, they shall be divided as equally as may be into three classes. The seats of the Senators of the first class shall be vacated at the expiration of the second year, of the second class at the expiration of the fourth year, and of the third class at the expiration of the sixth year, so that one-third may be chosen every second year; and if vacancies happen by resignation, or otherwise, during the recess of the legislature of any State, the executive thereof

In one election year, only one-third of the senators are up for election; the others still have two or four more years to serve. This gives the Senate more continuity than the House, where all members are up for election every two years. Since there is always an even number of senators, tie votes are possible, and so the Vice President was given the power to break ties.

may make temporary appointments until the next meeting of the legislature, which shall then fill such vacancies.

No person shall be a Senator who shall not have attained the age of thirty years, and been nine years a citizen of the United States, and who shall not, when elected, be an inhabitant of that State for which he shall be chosen.

The Vice-President of the United States shall be President of the Senate, but shall have no vote, unless they be equally divided.

The Senate shall choose their other officers and also a President pro tempore, in the absence of the Vice-President, or when he shall exercise the office of President of the United States.

The Senate shall have the sole power to try all impeachments. When sitting for that purpose, they shall be on oath or affirmation. When the President of the United States is tried, the Chief Justice shall preside; and no person shall be convicted without the concurrence of two-thirds of the members present.

Judgment in cases of impeachment shall not extend further than to removal from office, and disqualification to hold and enjoy any office of honor, trust, or profit under the United States; but the party convicted shall nevertheless be liable and subject to indictment, trial, judgment and punishment, according to law.

Congressional Elections

Section 4. The times, places, and manner of holding elections for Senators and Representatives shall be prescribed in each State by the legislature thereof; but the Congress may at any time by law make or alter such regulations, except as to the places of choosing Senators.

The 20th Amendment changed this meeting time to noon, January 3.

The Congress shall assemble at least once in every year, and such meeting shall be on the first Monday in December, unless they shall by law appoint a different day.

Procedures

Section 5. Each House shall be the judge of the elections, returns, and qualifications of its own members, and a majority of each shall constitute a quorum to do business; but a smaller number may adjourn from day to day, and may be authorized to compel the attendance of absent members, in such manner, and under such penalties, as each House may provide.

Each House may determine the rules of its proceedings, punish its members for disorderly behavior, and with the concurrence of two-thirds, expel a member.

In addition to the Congressional Record, which is published every day, both Houses of Congress keep a record of their proceedings.

Each House shall keep a journal of its proceedings, and from time to time publish the same, excepting such parts as may in their judgment require secrecy, and the yeas and nays of the members of either House on any question shall, at the desire of one-fifth of those present, be entered on the journal.

Neither House, during the session of Congress, shall, without the consent of the other adjourn for more than three days, nor to any other place than that in which the two Houses shall be sitting.

Payment and Privileges

These privileges are called "congressional immunity."

Section 6. The Senators and Representatives shall receive a compensation for their services, to be ascertained by law and paid out of the Treasury of the United States. They shall, in all cases except treason, felony, and breach of the peace, be privileged from arrest during their attendance at the session of their respective Houses, and in going to and returning from the same; and for any speech or debate in either House they shall not be questioned in any other place.

No Senator or Representative shall, during the time for which he was elected, be appointed to any civil office under the authority of the United

States, which shall have been created, or the emoluments whereof shall have been increased during such time; and no person holding any office under the United States shall be a member of either House during his continuance in office.

"Emoluments" are salaries. This section prevents federal officials from being members of Congress at the same time.

Section 7. All bills for raising revenue shall originate in the House of Representatives; but the Senate may propose or concur with amendments as on other bills.

Relation to Executive

Every bill which shall have passed the House of Representatives and the Senate shall, before it become a law, be presented to the President of the United States; if he approve he shall sign it, but if not he shall return it, with his objections, to that House in which it shall have originated, who shall enter the objections at large on their journal and proceed to reconsider it. If after such reconsideration two-thirds of that House shall agree to pass the bill, it shall be sent, together with the objections, to the other House, by which it shall likewise be reconsidered, and if approved by two-thirds of that House, it shall become a law. But in all such cases the vote of both Houses shall be determined by yeas and nays, and the names of the persons voting for and against the bill shall be entered on the journal of each House respectively. If any bill shall not be returned by the President within ten days (Sundays excepted) after it shall have been presented to him, the same shall be a law, in like manner as if he had signed it, unless the Congress by their adjournment prevent its return, in which case it shall not be a law.

This section describes the President's veto power. Even if a bill has been passed by both the Senate and the House, the President can veto it, or turn it down, instead of signing it and making it a law. However, a two-thirds vote by both Houses can pass the bill over his veto. Simply holding the bill when Congress is about to adjourn is a "pocket veto."

Every order, resolution or vote to which the concurrence of the Senate and House of Representatives may be necessary (except on a question of adjournment) shall be presented to the President of the United States; and before the same shall take effect shall be approved by him, or being disapproved by him, shall be repassed by two-thirds of the Senate and the House of Representatives, according to the rules and limitations prescribed in the case of a bill.

Section 8. The Congress shall have power to lay and collect taxes, duties, imposts and excises, to pay the debts and provide for the common defense and general welfare of the United States; but all duties, imposts and excises shall be uniform throughout the United States;

Specific Powers

To borrow money on the credit of the United States;

To regulate commerce with foreign nations, and among the several States, and with the Indian tribes;

To establish an uniform rule of naturalization, and uniform laws on the subject of bankruptcies throughout the United States;

To coin money, regulate the value thereof, and of foreign coin, and fix the standard of weights and measures;

To provide for the punishment of counterfeiting the securities and current coin of the United States;

To establish post offices and post roads;

To promote the progress of science and useful arts by securing for limited times to authors and inventors the exclusive right to their respective writings and discoveries;

This section allows Congress to pass laws about patents and copyrights.

To constitute tribunals inferior to the Supreme Court;

To define and punish piracies and felonies committed on the high seas, and offenses against the law of nations;

To declare war, grant letters of marque and reprisal, and make rules concerning captures on land and water;

Only Congress can declare war, but the President, as Commander in Chief, can order the armed forces to act.

To raise and support armies, but no appropriation of money to that use shall be for a longer term than two years;

To provide and maintain a navy;

To make rules for the government and regulation of the land and naval forces;

To provide for calling forth the militia to execute the laws of the Union, suppress insurrections, and repel invasions;

To provide for organizing, arming and disciplining the militia, and for governing such part of them as may be employed in the service of the United States, reserving to the States respectively the appointment of the officers, and the authority of training the militia according to the discipline prescribed by Congress;

This gave Congress the authority to establish and govern the District of Columbia.

To exercise exclusive legislation in all cases whatsoever over such district (not exceeding ten miles square) as may, by cession of particular States and the acceptance of Congress, become the seat of government of the United States, and to exercise like authority over all places purchased by the consent of the legislature of the State in which the same shall be, for the erection of forts, magazines, arsenals, dockyards, and other needful buildings;

This is sometimes called the "elastic clause" because it can be interpreted to give many powers not actually mentioned in the Constitution.

To make all laws which shall be necessary and proper for carrying into execution the foregoing powers, and all other powers vested by this Constitution in the Government of the United States, or in any department or officer thereof.

Limitations on Congress

This paragraph set up a waiting period for action on the slave trade; Congress did abolish it in 1808.

Section 9. The migration or importation of such persons as any of the States now existing shall think proper to admit shall not be prohibited by the Congress prior to the year one thousand eight hundred and eight, but a tax or duty may be imposed on such importation, not exceeding ten dollars for each person.

Habeas corpus *guards against unjust imprisonment by requiring a judge or court to decide whether a person may be held. An* ex post facto *law applies to acts committed* before *the law was passed. The 16th Amendment allowed the income tax, which is not related to the census.*

The privilege of the writ of habeas corpus shall not be suspended, unless when in cases of rebellion or invasion the public safety may require it.

No bill of attainder or ex post facto law shall be passed.

No capitation or other direct tax shall be laid, unless in proportion to the census or enumeration hereinbefore directed to be taken.

No tax or duty shall be laid on articles exported from any State.

No preference shall be given by any regulation of commerce or revenue to the ports of one State over those of another; nor shall vessels bound to or from one State be obliged to enter, clear or pay duties in another.

No money shall be drawn from the Treasury but in consequence of appropriations made by law; and a regular statement and account of the receipts and expenditures of all public money shall be published from time to time.

In fact, Presidents often exchange gifts with important foreign visitors, but the gifts are considered as gifts to the country.

No title of nobility shall be granted by the United States; and no person holding any office of profit or trust under them shall, without the consent of the Congress, accept of any present, emolument, office, or title of any kind whatever from any king, prince, or foreign state.

Limitations on States

Section 10. No State shall enter into any treaty, alliance, or confederation; grant letters of marque and reprisal; coin money; emit bills of credit; make anything but gold and silver coin a tender in payment of debts; pass any bill of attainder, ex post facto law or law impairing the obligation of contracts, or grant any title of nobility.

No State shall, without the consent of the Congress, lay any imposts or duties on imports or exports, except what may be absolutely necessary for executing its inspection laws; and the net produce of all duties and imposts, laid by any State on imports or exports, shall be for the use of the Treasury of the United States; and all such laws shall be subject to the revision and control of the Congress.

No State shall, without the consent of Congress, lay any duty of tonnage, keep troops or ships of war in time of peace, enter into any agreement or compact with another State or with a foreign power, or engage in war, unless actually invaded or in such imminent danger as will not admit of delay.

Article II

The Executive Branch
The President

Section 1. The executive power shall be vested in a President of the United States of America. He shall hold his office during the term of four years, and together with the Vice-President, chosen for the same term, be elected as follows:

Each State shall appoint, in such manner as the legislature thereof may direct, a number of Electors, equal to the whole number of Senators and Representatives to which the State may be entitled in the Congress; but no Senator or Representative, or person holding an office of trust or profit under the United States, shall be appointed an Elector.

The system for electing the President has been changed a great deal since the Constitution was written, primarily because of the rise of political parties. The so-called "electoral college" still meets, though under the 12th Amendment electors vote separately for the President and Vice President. Originally, the candidate who came in second in the Presidential race became Vice President. Since electors now are pledged to support a party's candidates, election results are actually known before the electors meet.

The Electors shall meet in their respective States and vote by ballot for two persons, of whom one at least shall not be an inhabitant of the same State with themselves. And they shall make a list of all the persons voted for, and of the number of votes for each; which list they shall sign and certify, and transmit sealed to the seat of the government of the United States, directed to the President of the Senate. The President of the Senate shall, in the presence of the Senate and House of Representatives, open all the certificates, and the votes shall then be counted. The person having the greatest number of votes shall be the President, if such number be a majority of the whole number of Electors appointed; and if there be more than one who have such majority, and have an equal number of votes, then the House of Representatives shall immediately choose by ballot one of them for President; and if no person have a majority, then from the five highest on the list the said House shall in like manner choose the President. But in choosing the President the votes shall be taken by States, the representation from each State having one vote; a quorum for this purpose shall consist of a member or members from two-thirds of the States, and a majority of all the States shall be necessary to a choice. In every case, after the choice of the President, the person having the greatest number of votes of the Electors shall be the Vice-President. But if there should remain two or more who have equal votes, the Senate shall choose from them by ballot the Vice-President.

The Congress may determine the time of choosing the Electors and the day on which they shall give their votes, which day shall be the same throughout the United States.

No person except a natural-born citizen, or citizen of the United States at the time of the adoption of this Constitution, shall be eligible to the office of President; neither shall any person be eligible to that office who shall not have attained to the age of thirty-five years, and been fourteen years a resident within the United States.

In case of the removal of the President from office, or of his death, resignation, or inability to discharge the powers and duties of the said office, the same shall devolve on the Vice-President, and the Congress may by law provide for the case of removal, death, resignation, or inability, both of the President and Vice-President, declaring what officer shall then act as President, and such officer shall act accordingly until the disability be removed or a President shall be elected.

The 25th Amendment (1967) makes further provisions for succession to the Presidency and for cases when the President is ill.

The President shall, at stated times, receive for his services a compensation, which shall neither be increased nor diminished during the period for which he shall have been elected, and he shall not receive within that period any other emolument from the United States or any of them.

Before he enter on the execution of his office he shall take the following oath or affirmation:

"I do solemnly swear (or affirm) that I will faithfully execute the office of President of the United States, and will to the best of my ability preserve, protect, and defend the Constitution of the United States."

Presidential Powers
This is the only mention of the Cabinet made in the Constitution; the first three Cabinet secretaries—state, treasury, and war—were named in 1789.
The Senate must approve Presidential appointments to important posts, such as Cabinet members, ambassadors, and Supreme Court justices.

Section 2. The President shall be Commander-in-Chief of the Army and Navy of the United States, and of the militia of the several States when called into the actual service of the United States; he may require the opinion, in writing, of the principal officer in each of the executive departments, upon any subject relating to the duties of their respective offices, and he shall have power to grant reprieves and pardons for offenses against the United States, except in cases of impeachment.

He shall have power, by and with the advice and consent of the Senate, to make treaties, provided two-thirds of the Senators present concur; and he shall nominate, and, by and with the advice and consent of the Senate, shall appoint ambassadors, other public ministers and consuls, judges of the Supreme Court, and all other officers of the United States whose appointments are not herein otherwise provided for, and which shall be established by law; but the Congress may by law vest the appointment of such inferior officers, as they think proper, in the President alone, in the courts of law, or in the heads of departments.

The President shall have power to fill up all vacancies that may happen during the recess of the Senate, by granting commissions which shall expire at the end of their next session.

Relation to Congress
The President traditionally delivers his "State of the Union" message at the start of each session of Congress. He can suggest legislation at any time.

Section 3. He shall from time to time give to the Congress information of the state of the Union, and recommend to their consideration such measures as he shall judge necessary and expedient; he may, on extraordinary occasions, convene both Houses, or either of them, and in case of disagreement between them with respect to the time of adjournment, he may adjourn them to such time as he shall think proper; he shall receive ambassadors and other public ministers; he shall take care that the laws be faithfully executed, and shall commission all the officers of the United States.

Impeachment
All federal judges are appointed for life and can be removed only by impeachment and conviction.

Section 4. The President, Vice-President and all civil officers of the United States shall be removed from office on impeachment for and conviction of treason, bribery, or other high crimes and misdemeanors.

The Judicial Branch
Courts

Article III

Section 1. The judicial power of the United States shall be vested in one Supreme Court, and in such inferior courts as the Congress may from time to time ordain and establish. The judges, both of the Supreme and inferior courts, shall hold their offices during good behavior, and shall, at stated times, receive for their services a compensation, which shall not be diminished during their continuance in office.

Jurisdiction

Section 2. The judicial power shall extend to all cases, in law and equity, arising under this Constitution, the laws of the United States, and treaties made, or which shall be made, under their authority; to all cases affecting ambassadors, other public ministers, and consuls; to all cases of admiralty and maritime jurisdiction; to controversies to which the United States shall be a party; to controversies between two or more States; between a State and citizens of another State; between citizens of different States; between citizens of the same State claiming lands under grants of different States, and between a State, or the citizens thereof, and foreign states, citizens, or subjects.

In all cases affecting ambassadors, other public ministers and consuls, and those in which a State shall be party, the Supreme Court shall have original jurisdiction. In all the other cases before mentioned the Supreme Court shall have appellate jurisdiction, both as to law and fact, with such exceptions and under such regulations as the Congress shall make.

Certain kinds of cases are taken directly to the Supreme Court. The Court can also review cases that have been tried in other federal or state courts.

The trial of all crimes, except in cases of impeachment, shall be by jury; and such trial shall be held in the State where the said crimes shall have been committed; but when not committed within any State, the trial shall be at such place or places as the Congress may by law have directed.

Treason

Section 3. Treason against the United States shall consist only in levying war against them, or in adhering to their enemies, giving them aid and comfort. No person shall be convicted of treason unless on the testimony of two witnesses to the same overt act, or on confession in open court.

The Congress shall have power to declare the punishment of treason, but no attainder of treason shall work corruption of blood or forfeiture except during the life of the person attainted.

Article IV

Relations Between the States

Full Faith and Credit

Contracts and other legal documents written in one state are valid in all other states.

Section 1. Full faith and credit shall be given in each State to the public acts, records, and judicial proceedings of every other State. And the Congress may by general laws prescribe the manner in which such acts, records, and proceedings shall be proved, and the effect thereof.

Other Obligations

Section 2. The citizens of each State shall be entitled to all privileges and immunities of citizens in the several States.

Extradition is the process by which a fugitive from justice in one state is handed over to the state in which the crime was committed.

A person charged in any State with treason, felony, or other crime, who shall flee from justice, and be found in another State, shall, on demand of the executive authority of the State from which he fled, be delivered up, to be removed to the State having jurisdiction of the crime.

This paragraph provided that runaway slaves should be returned; the 13th Amendment abolished slavery.

No person held to service or labor in one State, under the laws thereof, escaping into another, shall, in consequence of any law or regulation therein, be discharged from such service or labor, but shall be delivered up on claim to the party to whom such service or labor may be due.

New States

Section 3. New States may be admitted by the Congress into this Union; but no new State shall be formed or erected within the jurisdiction of any other State; nor any State be formed by the junction of two or more States or parts of States, without the consent of the legislatures of the States concerned as well as of the Congress.

The Congress shall have power to dispose of and make all needful rules and regulations respecting the territory or other property belonging to the United States; and nothing in this Constitution shall be so construed as to prejudice any claims of the United States or of any particular State.

Federal Guarantees

Section 4. The United States shall guarantee to every State in this Union a republican form of government, and shall protect each of them against invasion, and on application of the legislature, or of the executive (when the legislature cannot be convened) against domestic violence.

Constitutional Amendments

Article V

The Congress, whenever two-thirds of both Houses shall deem it necessary, shall propose amendments to this Constitution, or, on the application of the legislatures of two-thirds of the several States, shall call a convention for proposing amendments, which, in either case shall be valid to all intents and purposes as part of this Constitution, when ratified by the legislatures of three-fourths of the several States, or by conventions in three-fourths thereof, as the one or the other mode of ratification may be proposed by the Congress; provided that no amendment which may be made prior to the year one thousand eight hundred and eight shall in any manner affect the first and fourth clauses in the Ninth Section of the First Article; and that no State, without its consent shall be deprived of its equal suffrage in the Senate.

Federal Supremacy
John Marshall, the first chief justice, gave broad interpretations to many sections of the Constitution during his tenure from 1801 to 1835. This clause was interpreted by Marshall to mean that the Supreme Court had the power to review the constitutionality of acts of Congress, since, as stated here, the Constitution is the "supreme law of the land."

Article VI

All debts contracted and engagements entered into, before the adoption of this Constitution, shall be as valid against the United States under this Constitution as under the Confederation.

This Constitution, and the laws of the United States which shall be made in pursuance thereof, and all treaties made, or which shall be made, under the authority of the United States, shall be the supreme law of the land; and the judges in every State shall be bound thereby, anything in the constitution or laws of any State to the contrary notwithstanding.

The Senators and Representatives before mentioned and the members of the several State legislatures, and all executive and judicial officers both of the United States and of the several States, shall be bound by oath or affirmation to support this Constitution; but no religious test shall ever be required as a qualification to any office or public trust under the United States.

Ratification
The Constitution was signed by 39 delegates to the Constitutional Convention, representing 12 of the 13 colonies—all except Rhode Island.

Article VII

The ratification of the conventions of nine States shall be sufficient for the establishment of this Constitution between the States so ratifying the same.

Done in convention by the unanimous consent of the States present, the seventeenth day of September in the year of our Lord one thousand seven hundred and eighty-seven, and of the independence of the United States of America the twelfth. In witness whereof we have hereunto subscribed our names.

Amendments to the Constitution

The Bill of Rights (1791)
The first ten amendments to the Constitution were proposed—and adopted—together at the request of the states. This Bill of Rights has become an integral part of the Constitution, and its guarantees to individuals are still significant today.

The conventions of a number of the States having, at the time of their adopting the Constitution, expressed a desire, in order to prevent misconstruction or abuse of its powers, that further declaratory and restrictive clauses should be added, and as extending the ground of public confidence in the Government will best insure the beneficent ends of its institution;

Resolved, by the Senate and House of Representatives of the United States of America, in Congress assembled, two-thirds of both Houses concurring, that the following articles be proposed to the Legislatures of the several States, as amendments to the Constitution of the United States; all or any of which articles, when ratified by three-fourths of the said Legislatures, to be valid to all intents and purposes as part of the said Constitution, namely:

Amendment 1. Congress shall make no law respecting an establishment of religion, or prohibiting the free exercise thereof; or abridging the freedom of speech or of the press; or the right of the people peaceably to assemble, and to petition the government for a redress of grievances.

Freedom of Religion, Speech, Press, Assembly, and Petition

Amendment 2. A well-regulated militia, being necessary to the security of a free State, the right of the people to keep and bear arms shall not be infringed.

Right to Bear Arms
This amendment is often cited by those opposed to gun-control laws.

Amendment 3. No soldier shall, in time of peace, be quartered in any house without the consent of the owner, nor in time of war, but in a manner to be prescribed by law.

Quartering Soldiers

Amendment 4. The right of the people to be secure in their persons, houses, papers, and effects, against unreasonable searches and seizures, shall not be violated, and no warrants shall issue but upon probable cause, supported by oath or affirmation, and particularly describing the place to be searched, and the persons or things to be seized.

Searches and Seizures
Police and other officials must have specific search warrants when they make investigations of people, homes, or private property.

Amendment 5. No person shall be held to answer for a capital, or otherwise infamous crime, unless on a presentment or indictment of a grand jury, except in cases arising in the land or naval forces, or in the militia, when in actual service in time of war or public danger; nor shall any person be subject for the same offense to be twice put in jeopardy of life or limb; nor shall be compelled in any criminal case to be a witness against himself, nor be deprived of life, liberty or property, without due process of law; nor shall private property be taken for public use without just compensation.

Rights of Defendants
Several legal protections are included here—the need for a grand jury hearing; protection against "double jeopardy"; and the right not to testify against oneself in a trial or hearing.

Amendment 6. In all criminal prosecutions, the accused shall enjoy the right to a speedy and public trial, by an impartial jury of the State and district wherein the crime shall have been committed, which district shall have been previously ascertained by law, and to be informed of the nature and cause of the accusation; to be confronted with the witnesses against him; to have compulsory process for obtaining witnesses in his favor, and to have the assistance of counsel for his defense.

Jury in Criminal Cases
A 1963 Supreme Court decision ruled that the right to legal counsel in felony cases applies whether or not the accused person can afford a lawyer. If the accused cannot, the court must appoint a lawyer.

Amendment 7. In suits at common law, where the value in controversy shall exceed twenty dollars, the right of trial by jury shall be preserved, and no fact tried by a jury shall be otherwise re-examined in any court of the United States, than according to the rules of the common law.

Jury in Civil Cases

Amendment 8. Excessive bail shall not be required, nor excessive fines imposed, nor cruel and unusual punishments inflicted.

Excessive Penalties

Amendment 9. The enumeration in the Constitution of certain rights shall not be construed to deny or disparage others retained by the people.

Other Rights
These amendments protect against a too-powerful federal government.

Amendment 10. The powers not delegated to the United States by the Constitution, nor prohibited by it to the States, are reserved to the States respectively, or to the people.

Additional Amendments

Suits Against States (1798)

Amendment 11.

The judicial power of the United States shall not be construed to extend to any suit in law or equity, commenced or prosecuted against one of the United States by citizens of another State, or by citizens or subjects of any foreign state.

Presidential Elections (1804)
This amendment changed the election process so that electors voted separately for President and Vice President.

Amendment 12.

The Electors shall meet in their respective States and vote by ballot for President and Vice-President, one of whom, at least, shall not be an inhabitant of the same state with themselves; they shall name in their ballots the person voted for as President, and in distinct ballots the person voted for as Vice-President, and they shall make distinct lists of all persons voted for as President and of all persons voted for as Vice-President, and of the number of votes for each; which lists they shall sign and certify, and transmit sealed to the seat of the government of the United States, directed to the President of the Senate. The President of the Senate shall, in the presence of the Senate and House of Representatives, open all the certificates and the votes shall then be counted. The person having the greatest number of votes for President shall be the President, if such a number be a majority of the whole number of Electors appointed; and if no person have such majority, then from the persons having the highest numbers not exceeding three on the list of those voted for as President, the House of Representatives shall choose immediately, by ballot, the President. But in choosing the President the votes shall be taken by States, the representation from each State having one vote; a quorum for this purpose shall consist of a member or members from two-thirds of the States, and a majority of all the States shall be necessary to a choice. And if the House of Representatives shall not choose a President whenever the right of choice shall devolve upon them, before the fourth day of March next following, then the Vice-President shall act as President, as in the case of the death or other constitutional disability of the President.

The person having the greatest number of votes as Vice-President shall be the Vice-President, if such number be a majority of the whole number of Electors appointed; and if no person have a majority, then from the two highest numbers on the list the Senate shall choose the Vice-President; a quorum for the purpose shall consist of two-thirds of the whole number of Senators, and a majority of the whole number shall be necessary to a choice. But no person constitutionally ineligible to the office of President shall be eligible to that of Vice-President of the United States.

Abolition of Slavery (1865)
The 13th and 14th Amendments were added after the Civil War. The 13th abolished slavery in the United States. The 14th gave the rights of citizenship to former slaves.

Amendment 13

Section 1. Neither slavery nor involuntary servitude, except as a punishment for crime whereof the party shall have been duly convicted, shall exist within the United States, or any place subject to their jurisdiction.

Section 2. Congress shall have power to enforce this article by appropriate legislation.

Rights of Citizens (1868)
This section extends Bill of Rights protection to matters under state jurisdiction. It is the basis for important court decisions and legislation protecting civil rights of minorities.

Amendment 14

Section 1. All persons born or naturalized in the United States, and subject to the jurisdiction thereof, are citizens of the United States and of the State wherein they reside. No State shall make or enforce any law which shall abridge the privileges or immunities of citizens of the United States; nor shall any State deprive any person of life, liberty or property, without due process of law; nor deny to any person within its jurisdiction the equal protection of the laws.

Section 2. Representatives shall be apportioned among the several States according to their respective numbers, counting the whole number of persons in each State, excluding Indians not taxed. But when the right to vote at any election for the choice of Electors for President and Vice-President of the United States, Representatives in Congress, the executive and judicial officers of a State, or the members of the legislature thereof, is denied to any of the male inhabitants of such State, being twenty-one years of age, and citizens of the United States, or in any way abridged except for participation in rebellion or other crime, the basis of representation therein shall be reduced in the proportion which the number of such male citizens shall bear to the whole number of male citizens twenty-one years of age in such State.

This section gave the right to vote to black men; the 19th Amendment allowed women to vote; the 26th lowered the voting age to 18.

Section 3. No person shall be a Senator or Representative in Congress, or elector of President and Vice-President, or hold any office, civil or military, under the United States or under any State, who, having previously taken an oath as a member of Congress, or as an officer of the United States, or as a member of any State legislature, or as an executive or judicial officer of any State, to support the Constitution of the United States, shall have engaged in insurrection or rebellion against the same, or given aid or comfort to the enemies thereof. But Congress may, by a vote of two-thirds of each House, remove such disability.

The idea of this clause was to keep former Confederate officials out of the federal government. Special acts of Congress later allowed some to serve.

Section 4. The validity of the public debt of the United States, authorized by law, including debts incurred for payment of pensions and bounties for services in suppressing insurrection or rebellion, shall not be questioned. But neither the United States nor any State shall assume or pay any debt or obligation incurred in aid of insurrection or rebellion against the United States, or any claim for the loss or emancipation of any slave; but all such debts, obligations, and claims shall be held illegal and void.

This clause forbade both the federal government and the states to pay any debt the Confederacy owed.

Section 5. The Congress shall have power to enforce, by appropriate legislation, the provisions of this article.

Amendment 15

Black Voting Rights (1870)
This amendment was added to strengthen the 14th Amendment.

Section 1. The right of citizens of the United States to vote shall not be denied or abridged by the United States or by any State on account of race, color, or previous condition of servitude.

Section 2. The Congress shall have power to enforce this article by appropriate legislation.

Amendment 16.

Income Taxes (1913)
An amendment to allow an income tax was needed because the Constitution did not allow any direct tax.

The Congress shall have power to lay and collect taxes on incomes, from whatever source derived, without apportionment among the several States, and without regard to any census or enumeration.

Amendment 17

Senatorial Elections (1913)

Section 1. The Senate of the United States shall be composed of two Senators from each State, elected by the people thereof, for six years; and each Senator shall have one vote. The electors in each State shall have the qualifications requisite for electors of the most numerous branch of the State legislatures.

Section 2. When vacancies happen in the representation of any State in the Senate, the executive authority of such State shall issue writs of election to fill such vacancies: Provided, that the legislature of any State may empower the executive thereof to make temporary appointments until the people fill the vacancies by election as the legislature may direct.

Section 3. This amendment shall not be so construed as to affect the election or term of any Senator chosen before it becomes valid as part of the Constitution.

Prohibition (1919)
The Prohibition amendment was ineffective and so was repealed in 1933 by the 21st Amendment.

Amendment 18

Section 1. After one year from the ratification of this article the manufacture, sale or transportation of intoxicating liquors within, the importation thereof into, or the exportation thereof from the United States and all territory subject to the jurisdiction thereof, for beverage purposes, is hereby prohibited.

Section 2. The Congress and the several States shall have concurrent power to enforce this article by appropriate legislation.

Section 3. This article shall be inoperative unless it shall have been ratified as an amendment to the Constitution by the legislatures of the several States, as provided in the Constitution, within seven years from the date of the submission hereof to the States by the Congress.

Women's Suffrage (1920)

Amendment 19

Section 1. The right of citizens of the United States to vote shall not be denied or abridged by the United States or by any State on account of sex.

Section 2. Congress shall have power to enforce this article by appropriate legislation.

Terms of Office (1933)
This is known as the "lame duck" amendment because it shortened the time between congressmen's elections and the date they took office. "Lame ducks" were defeated members who, under the old system, remained in Congress long after being defeated in an election.

Amendment 20

Section 1. The terms of the President and Vice-President shall end at noon on the 20th day of January, and the terms of Senators and Representatives at noon on the 3d day of January, of the years in which such terms would have ended if this article had not been ratified; and the terms of their successors shall then begin.

Section 2. The Congress shall assemble at least once in every year, and such meetings shall begin at noon on the 3d day of January, unless they shall by law appoint a different day.

Section 3. If, at the time fixed for the beginning of the term of the President, the President-elect shall have died, the Vice-President-elect shall become President. If a President shall not have been chosen before the time fixed for the beginning of his term or if the President-elect shall have failed to qualify, then the Vice-President-elect shall act as President until a President shall have qualified; and the Congress may by law provide for the case wherein neither a President-elect nor a Vice-President-elect shall have qualified, declaring who shall then act as President, or the manner in which one who is to act shall be selected, and such person shall act accordingly until a President or Vice-President shall have qualified.

Section 4. The Congress may by law provide for the case of the death of any of the persons from whom the House of Representatives may choose a President whenever the right of choice shall have devolved upon them, and for the case of the death of any of the persons from whom the Senate may choose a Vice-President whenever the right of choice shall have devolved upon them.

Section 5. Sections 1 and 2 shall take effect on the 15th day of October following the ratification of this article.

Section 6. This article shall be inoperative unless it shall have been ratified as an amendment to the Constitution by the legislatures of three-fourths of the several States within seven years from the date of its submission.

Amendment 21

Repeal of Prohibition (1933)

Section 1. The eighteenth article of amendment to the Constitution of the United States is hereby repealed.

Section 2. The transportation or importation into any State, territory, or possession of the United States for delivery or use therein of intoxicating liquors, in violation of the laws thereof, is hereby prohibited.

Section 3. This article shall be inoperative unless it shall have been ratified as an amendment to the Constitution by conventions in the several States, as provided in the Constitution, within seven years from the date of the submission hereof to the States by the Congress.

Amendment 22

Presidential Terms (1951)
This amendment was passed after the death of Franklin D. Roosevelt, who had been elected four times. Its purpose was to prevent subsequent Presidents from serving more than two terms.

Section 1. No person shall be elected to the office of President more than twice, and no person who has held the office of President, or acted as President, for more than two years of a term to which some other person was elected President shall be elected to the office of President more than once. But this Article shall not apply to any person holding the office of President when this Article was proposed by the Congress, and shall not prevent any person who may be holding the office of President, or acting as President, during the term within which this Article becomes operative from holding the office of President or acting as President during the remainder of such term.

Section 2. This article shall be inoperative unless it shall have been ratified as an amendment to the Constitution by the legislatures of three-fourths of the several States within seven years from the date of its submission to the States by the Congress.

Amendment 23

District of Columbia Voting Rights (1961)
Before this amendment, residents of the District of Columbia could not vote.

Section 1. The District constituting the seat of Government of the United States shall appoint in such manner as the Congress may direct:

A number of electors of President and Vice-President equal to the whole number of Senators and Representatives in Congress to which the District would be entitled if it were a State, but in no event more than the least populous State; they shall be in addition to those appointed by the States, but they shall be considered, for the purposes of the election of President and Vice-President, to be electors appointed by a State; and they shall meet in the District and perform such duties as provided by the twelfth article of amendment.

Section 2. The Congress shall have power to enforce this article by appropriate legislation.

Amendment 24

Poll Tax Prohibited (1964)
Poll taxes had been used to prevent or discourage black voters from registering or voting.

Section 1. The right of citizens of the United States to vote in any primary or other election for President or Vice-President, for electors for President or Vice-President, or for Senator or Representative in Congress, shall not be denied or abridged by the United States or any State by reason of failure to pay any poll tax or other tax.

Section 2. The Congress shall have power to enforce this article by appropriate legislation.

Presidential Succession (1967)

Amendment 25

Section 1. In case of the removal of the President from office or of his death or resignation, the Vice-President shall become President.

Section 2. Whenever there is a vacancy in the office of the Vice-President, the President shall nominate a Vice-President who shall take office upon confirmation by a majority vote of both Houses of Congress.

Section 3. Whenever the President transmits to the President pro tempore of the Senate and the Speaker of the House of Representatives his written declaration that he is unable to discharge the powers and duties of his office, and until he transmits to them a written declaration to the contrary, such powers and duties shall be discharged by the Vice-President as Acting President.

Section 4. Whenever the Vice-President and a majority of either the principal officers of the executive departments or of such other body as Congress may by law provide, transmit to the President pro tempore of the Senate and the Speaker of the House of Representatives their written declaration that the President is unable to discharge the powers and duties of his office, the Vice-President shall immediately assume the powers and duties of the office as Acting President.

Thereafter, when the President transmits to the President pro tempore of the Senate and the Speaker of the House of Representatives his written declaration that no inability exists, he shall resume the powers and duties of his office unless the Vice-President and a majority of either the principal officers of the executive department or of such other body as Congress may by law provide, transmit within four days to the President pro tempore of the Senate and the Speaker of the House of Representatives their written declaration that the President is unable to discharge the powers and duties of his office. Thereupon Congress shall decide the issue, assembling within forty-eight hours for that purpose if not in session. If the Congress, within twenty-one days after receipt of the latter written declaration, or, if Congress is not in session, within twenty-one days after Congress is required to assemble, determines by two-thirds vote of both Houses that the President is unable to discharge the powers and duties of his office, the Vice-President shall continue to discharge the same as Acting President; otherwise, the President shall resume the powers and duties of his office.

Voting Age (1971)

Amendment 26

Section 1. The right of citizens of the United States, who are eighteen years of age or older, to vote shall not be denied or abridged by the United States or by any State on account of age.

Section 2. The Congress shall have power to enforce this article by appropriate legislation.

Many amendments to the Constitution have been approved by the required vote of Congress (two-thirds majorities in both houses) but have never taken effect because they were not ratified in time by the required number of states (three quarters, now 38 of the 50). The most recent amendment to fail in this way was the Equal Rights Amendment (ERA), guaranteeing no discrimination on the basis of sex, whose ratification period ended June 30, 1982. Such an amendment can be reintroduced to Congress, beginning the process again.

Presidents of the United States

The Presidents of the United States are the only officials elected by all the people of the country. From the beginning, they have had considerable prestige and power, especially in times of national crises. In recent times, as the United States has become a world power, the office has become one of the most influential—and difficult to manage—in the world.

What kind of men were those who served as President? Thirty-nine served between 1789 and 1982, for an average of about five years each. The following pages provide thumbnail sketches of each of them, from George Washington through Ronald Reagan. For each, there is information on personal life, education and occupation, political career, and years in office. On this page, there are some interesting facts about the Presidents as a group. (For portraits of the Presidents, see the color plates in the front of this volume. For more information on U.S. history, see Volume 1.)

Which Presidents served the longest and shortest times in office?

Longest: Franklin D. Roosevelt served from March, 1933, to April, 1945, a total of 12 years, 1 month. He had been elected for a fourth term and would have served 16 years had he not died in office. The 22nd Amendment (1951) limits Presidents to two terms.

Shortest: William Henry Harrison served from March 4 to April 4, 1841. He caught a cold at his inauguration and died of pneumonia just one month after taking office. One other President, James Garfield, died of an assassin's wounds in September, 1881, after serving six months.

How many Presidents died in office?

Eight. They are: William Henry Harrison, 1841, illness; Zachary Taylor, 1850, illness; Abraham Lincoln, 1865, assassination; James Garfield, 1881, assassination; William McKinley, 1901, assassination; Warren Harding, 1923, illness; Franklin D. Roosevelt, 1945, illness; and John F. Kennedy, 1963, assassination.

Which states have been the birthplace of the most Presidents?

Virginia and Ohio. Virginia, sometimes called "the cradle of Presidents," has been the birthplace of eight Presidents, including four of the first five. They are: Washington, Jefferson, Madison, Monroe, William Henry Harrison, Tyler, Taylor, and Wilson.

Ohio follows close behind with seven, all of whom served between 1869 and 1923. They are: Grant, Hayes, Garfield, Benjamin Harrison, McKinley, Taft, and Harding.

Were any Presidents related to each other?

Yes. John Adams and John Quincy Adams, the second and sixth Presidents, were father and son. William Henry Harrison and Benjamin Harrison, the ninth and 23rd Presidents, were grandfather and grandson. Theodore and Franklin Roosevelt, the 25th and 31st Presidents, were distant cousins.

Were all the Presidents married?

All except one were married at some time in their lives. The exception is James Buchanan. Several Presidents have been married more than once, usually after the death of their first wives. The only President who has received a divorce is Ronald Reagan.

Did all Presidents retire after serving as President?

Most, but not all. John Quincy Adams returned to the House of Representatives and served there for 17 years after his Presidency. William Howard Taft became a law professor and later served nine years as chief justice of the Supreme Court.

Have any Presidents been removed from office?

No. But in two cases, impeachment proceedings were begun. Andrew Johnson was impeached (accused) by the House of Representatives in 1868 and tried before the Senate. The Senate vote was one short of the two-thirds majority required for conviction. Johnson remained in office, but did not run for reelection.

Richard Nixon was the subject of committee impeachment hearings in the House in 1974. Before the full House could vote, Nixon resigned from office, on August 9, 1974. He was the first President ever to resign.

General Washington (center)

John Adams

The Capitol Building c 1800

Name/Dates in office	*Personal*	*Education/Occupation*
1st **George Washington** April 30, 1789–March 4, 1797	Born Feb. 22, 1732, Westmoreland County, Va.; died Dec. 14, 1799, Mount Vernon, Va. Raised in part by half brother Lawrence, from whom he inherited the plantation at Mount Vernon. In 1759 married Martha Dandridge Custis (1732–1802), a widow with two children.	Schooled at home, trained as a surveyor, Washington operated and expanded the farmland of Mount Vernon. Began military career in French and Indian War in 1753. Named commander in chief of Continental Army in 1775, and led troops in most major battles of American Revolution.
2nd **John Adams** March 4, 1797–March 4, 1801	Born Oct. 30, 1735, Braintree (now Quincy), Mass.; died July 4, 1826, Quincy, Mass. Member of prominent family that arrived in Massachusetts in 1636. In 1764 married Abigail Smith (1744–1818); their five children included the sixth President, John Quincy Adams.	Graduated from Harvard, 1755; studied law, and began practice in Boston. Important writer of tracts against British taxation of colonies and in support of British military action in Boston Massacre of 1770.
3rd **Thomas Jefferson** March 4, 1801–March 4, 1809	Born April 13, 1743, Goochland (now Albemarle County), Va.; died July 4, 1826, Charlottesville, Va. Son of a tobacco farmer, he was left the family estate at age 14 and later pursued literary and musical interests. In 1772 married Martha Wayles Skelton (1748–1782); they had six children, but only two daughters survived infancy.	Attended William and Mary College, 1760–1762. A lawyer, he became an important writer on a variety of topics, especially political philosophy and education. He designed buildings for the University of Virginia at Charlottesville, which he founded, as well as his own home there, Monticello.
4th **James Madison** March 4, 1809–March 4, 1817	Born March 16, 1751, Port Conway, Va.; died June 28, 1836, Montpelier, Virginia. In 1794 married Dolley Paine Todd (1768–1849), who became popular First Lady Dolley Madison and rescued important White House art works when the British burned Washington in 1814.	Graduated from College of New Jersey (now Princeton), 1771. Lawyer and public servant in Virginia prior to political career.

Shipbuilding c 1800

Lewis and Clark expedition

Jefferson's Monticello

Political career	*Highlights in office*
Member of Virginia House of Burgesses, 1758. Delegate to Continental Congresses 1774–1775. Chairman of Constitutional Convention, 1787.	Elected first President by unanimous vote of electoral college and inaugurated on balcony of Federal Hall in New York City. Established strong U.S. currency, Bank of the United States, and U.S. Military Academy at West Point. Ended the first American domestic crisis, the 1791 Whiskey Rebellion in Pennsylvania. Reelected in 1792 but declined a third term in 1796, setting a precedent followed by all Presidents until Franklin D. Roosevelt.
Organized opposition to Stamp Act in Boston. Delegate to First Continental Congress, 1774, and signer of Declaration of Independence, 1776. Commissioner to France with Benjamin Franklin, 1778; diplomat to Holland, 1780–1782; helped negotiate Treaty of Paris, ending the American Revolution, 1782–1783; first U.S. minister to England, 1785–1788. Elected Vice President, 1788, and reelected, 1792.	Elected President over Thomas Jefferson, who became Vice President. Prevented war with France in 1798 after relations were disrupted by XYZ Affair, in which French tried to bribe American officials. Permitted passage of Alien and Sedition Acts, 1798. Defeated for reelection by Jefferson, 1800.
Elected to Virginia House of Burgesses, 1769. Member of Continental Congress and author of Declaration of Independence, 1776. Governor of Virginia 1779–1781. Minister to France 1785–1789. Secretary of state to President Washington 1789–1793. Second to John Adams in 1796 Presidential election, he became Vice President.	Voted President by House of Representatives after electoral tie with Aaron Burr. Authorized and concluded Louisiana Purchase of 1803, and commissioned Lewis and Clark expedition. Negotiated Embargo Act to protect American interests while England and France were at war. Reelected by overwhelming majority in 1804 over C. C. Pinckney of South Carolina. Noted for ridding Presidency of royal trappings and Federal power-sharing with state government.
Member of Virginia Constitutional Convention, 1776, and Continental Congress, 1780. Chief recorder and influential organizer at U.S. Constitutional Convention in 1787. Author of *The Federalist* with Alexander Hamilton and John Jay. Congressman from Virginia, 1787–1797. Appointed secretary of state by President Thomas Jefferson in 1801.	Elected as opponent of free interpretation of U.S. Constitution and preserver of Jeffersonian policies, including unpopular trade embargo on English goods. Reelected in 1812 with firm support from new Western states. Trade embargo brought about War of 1812, declared by Madison on June 18 of that year and ended without victory for either side in 1815.

Early steamboat

Monroe expounds foreign policy

Name/Dates in office	*Personal*	*Education/Occupation*
5th **James Monroe** March 4, 1817–March 4, 1825	Born April 28, 1758, Westmoreland County, Va.; died July 4, 1831, New York City. Married Elizabeth Kortwright (1768–1830) of New York City in 1786; they had two daughters and a son who died in infancy.	Attended the College of William and Mary, where he studied law under Thomas Jefferson and became an adherent of his philosophy. Fought in Continental Army, being wounded at Trenton, New Jersey. Sacrificed personal wealth to political career, and died in relative poverty.
6th **John Quincy Adams** March 4, 1825–March 4, 1829	Born July 11, 1767, Braintree (now Quincy), Mass.; died Feb. 23, 1848, Washington, D.C. Son of John Adams, second President. In 1797 married Louise Catherine Johnson (1775–1852), daugher of U.S. consul in London; they had three sons and one daughter.	Attended schools in France and Holland; graduated from Harvard, 1787. Practiced law in Boston beginning in 1790 and wrote a series of pamphlets on political topics.
7th **Andrew Jackson** March 4, 1829–March 4, 1837	Born March 15, 1767, Waxhaw, S.C.; died June 8, 1845, at "The Hermitage," near Nashville, Tenn. The son of Irish immigrants, he joined the local militia at the age of 13. Married Rachel Donelson Robards (1767–1828) in 1791 and remarried her in 1793 when her divorce from a previous husband became final; they had one adopted son, Andrew Jackson, Jr., and raised several foster children.	No formal education, although he privately studied law. In Indian wars, defeated Creeks at Horseshoe Bend, Ala., 1814. Defeated British at New Orleans in 1815, not knowing War of 1812 had already ended. Defeated Seminole Indians, 1818, and became military governor of Florida, 1821.
8th **Martin Van Buren** March 4, 1837–March 4, 1841	Born Dec. 5, 1782, Kinderhook, N.Y.; died July 24, 1862, Kinderhook, N.Y. In 1807 married Hannah Hoes (1783–1819); they had four sons. As President, Van Buren was a widower, and a daughter-in-law served as White House hostess.	Privately studied law and was admitted to the bar in 1803 without attending college. Practiced law in his hometown.

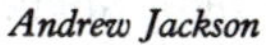

Andrew Jackson

The Alamo

Indians and soldier

Political career	*Highlights in office*
Congressman from Virginia 1783–1786; senator from Virginia 1790–1794. Minister to France 1794–1796. Governor of Virginia 1799–1802. Member of diplomatic missions, including negotiation of Louisiana Purchase in 1803. Secretary of state to James Madison 1811–1817.	Elected by overwhelming majority in 1816, and reelected with all but one electoral vote in 1820. His administration, called the "Era of Good Feeling," included the acquisition of Florida from Spain, the improvement of relations with Canada, and the Missouri Compromise on the slavery issue in 1820. The Monroe Doctrine announced that North and South American countries would unite against European interference.
Minister to Holland, 1794, and later minister to Portugal and Prussia. Senator from Massachusetts 1803–1808. Negotiated treaty to end War of 1812. Secretary of state to James Monroe 1817–1825. After Presidency returned to Congress, 1831–1848.	Elected President by House of Representatives after Andrew Jackson received more electoral and popular votes but not a majority. Expanded executive powers and passed tariff regulations that favored New England manufacturers over plantation farmers of the South. Soundly defeated by Jackson in 1828 reelection bid.
Congressman from Tennessee, 1796, and senator, 1797–1798. After military career returned to Senate, 1823–1825. Received more electoral and popular votes than John Quincy Adams in 1824 election for President, but lacked a majority and saw the House of Representatives award the office to Adams. Resigned from Senate 1825 to prepare for new Presidential campaign.	Elected by a landslide over John Quincy Adams in second attempt to gain Presidency. Instituted the "spoils system" to reward party members and oust lifelong Washington politicians. Opposed Bank of the United States and undermined its credibility by redistributing funds. Declared a policy of "let the people rule." Renominated at the first party convention and subsequently reelected,1832.
Columbia County, N.Y., surrogate 1808–1813; state senator 1812–1820; state attorney general 1815–1819. U.S. senator 1821–1828. Elected governor of New York, 1828, but resigned soon after taking office to become secretary of state to Andrew Jackson, 1829–1831. Vice President during Jackson's second administration, 1833–1837. Campaigned unsuccessfully for the Presidency twice after his single term in office.	Took office as the Panic of 1837 launched a severe economic depression. His policies to relieve the depression were ineffective, and this led to his defeat in 1840 by William Henry Harrison.

Name/Dates in office	*Personal*	*Education/Occupation*
9th **William Henry Harrison** March 4, 1841–April 4, 1841	Born Feb. 9, 1773, Berkeley, Va.; died April 4, 1841, Washington, D.C., first President to die in office. In 1795 married Anna Symmes (1775–1864); they had six sons, and grandson Benjamin Harrison became the 23rd President.	Graduated from Hampden-Sydney College in Virginia, 1790. Joined military, 1791. Defeated Indians under Tecumseh at the Tippecanoe River in Indiana, 1811, and the British at the Battle of the Thames in Indiana in 1813.
10th **John Tyler** April 6, 1841–March 4, 1845	Born March 29, 1790, Greenway, Va.; died Jan. 18, 1862, Richmond, Va. In 1813 married Letitia Christian (1790–1842); they had seven children. After her death, married Julia Gardiner (1820–1889) in an 1844 White House ceremony; they also had seven children.	Graduated from the College of William and Mary, 1807. Studied law before commencing active political career. Returned to legal practice in Richmond following Presidency.
11th **James Knox Polk** March 4, 1845–March 4, 1849	Born Nov. 2, 1795, Mecklenburg County, N.C.; died June 15, 1849, Nashville, Tenn. In 1824 married Sarah Childress (1803–1891), who served as official secretary to him in the White House.	Graduated from University of North Carolina in 1818, studied law, and moved to Nashville to begin practice there. Gained prominence as a political speaker.
12th **Zachary Taylor** March 4, 1849–July 9, 1850	Born Nov. 24, 1784, Orange County, Va.; died July 9, 1850, Washington, D.C., while in office. In 1810 married Margaret Mackall Smith (1788–1852); they had six children.	With little formal education, rose through the military ranks as a career soldier. Veteran of War of 1812 and Black Hawk and Seminole Indian wars; commander of forces in 1845 Mexican War.
13th **Millard Fillmore** July 10, 1850–March 4, 1853	Born Jan. 7, 1800, Locke (now Summerhill), N.Y.; died March 8, 1874, Buffalo, N.Y. In 1826 married Abigail Powers (1798–1853); they had two children. After her death he married Caroline McIntosh (1814–1881) in 1858.	Educated at country schools where he later taught. Privately studied law; was admitted to bar in 1823, beginning his practice in Buffalo, N.Y. Returned to Buffalo after Presidency as chancellor of University of Buffalo.
14th **Franklin Pierce** March 4, 1853–March 4, 1857	Born Nov. 23, 1804, Hillsboro, N.H.; died Oct. 8, 1869, Concord, N.H. In 1834 married Jane Means Appleton (1806–1863); their three sons all died in childhood.	Graduated from Bowdoin College in Maine, 1824, then studied law. Interrupted political career to serve in Mexican War under General Winfield Scott.
15th **James Buchanan** March 4, 1857–March 4, 1861	Born April 23, 1791, Mercersburg, Pa.; died June 1, 1868, Lancaster, Pa. Was the only President who never married.	Graduated from Dickinson College in Pennsylvania, 1809. Served as a volunteer in War of 1812, and afterward practiced law.

Political career	*Highlights in office*
Secretary of the Northwest Territory, 1798, and its delegate to Congress, 1799. First governor of the Indian Territory, 1800, and superintendent of Indian affairs, 1801–1813. Represented Ohio in Congress, 1816–1819, and in the Senate, 1825–1828. Defeated by Martin Van Buren in 1836 Presidential election.	Elected as war hero on a ticket with John Tyler for Vice President; famous for slogan "Tippecanoe and Tyler Too." Contracted pneumonia during inauguration and died one month after taking office.
Elected to Virginia House of Delegates in 1811 at the age of 21. Congressman 1816–1821; state legislator 1823–1825; governor of Virginia 1825–1827; senator from Virginia 1827–1836. Shifted from Democratic to Whig Party and elected Vice President for William Henry Harrison. After serving as President, elected to Confederate Congress, 1861.	Assumed office when William Henry Harrison died only one month into his term. Vetoed bills for a national bank, and entire Cabinet, with the exception of Daniel Webster, resigned in protest. Refused to continue spoils system of Andrew Jackson; signed bill admitting Texas to the Union; reorganized the Navy; signed trade treaty with China. Nominated for a second term, but declined.
Tennessee state legislator 1823–1825. Member of Congress 1825–1839 and Speaker of the House 1835–1839. Governor of Tennessee 1839–1841. A protégé of Andrew Jackson, he was nominated in 1844 to resolve party differences and to launch a "dark horse" candidacy based on support for the annexation of Texas.	Sent troops under Zachary Taylor to the Mexican border, precipitating war with that country that ended with U.S. annexation of California and New Mexico. Ended Oregon Territory border dispute with Canada by retreating from "54–40 or fight" demand and settling for present border at 49th parallel.
Without political experience, he was nominated for President by the Whigs on the basis of the war career that earned him the nickname "Old Rough and Ready."	Although a Southerner, he supported the Compromise of 1850 that admitted California as a free state while toughening fugitive slave laws. Did not endorse abolition of slavery, but opposed extension of it to territories and new states. Died in office of natural causes.
Member New York state legislature 1829–1832. Congressman from New York 1833–1835 and 1837–1843. Ran unsuccessfully for governor of New York, 1844. Elected Vice President for Zachary Taylor, 1848, becoming President when Taylor died in office. Unsuccessful candidate in 1856 Presidential election.	Supported Compromise of 1850 that admitted California as a free state while strengthening fugitive slave laws. His compromise policies on territorial expansion and slavery pleased few, and he was not renominated in 1852.
New Hampshire state legislator 1829–1833. Congressman 1833–1837 and senator 1837–1842. At 1852 Democratic convention, was nominated on 49th ballot as "dark horse" alternative to a three-candidate deadlock.	Elected in landslide over General Winfield Scott, formerly Pierce's commanding officer. Signed Kansas-Nebraska Act, 1854, which made slavery subject to local rather than national legislation. Approved Gadsden Purchase of southwestern lands from Mexico, 1853. Was not renominated.
Member of Pennsylvania state legislature 1814–1816. Elected to Congress in 1820, he was an important supporter of Andrew Jackson and became minister to Russia in 1831. Returned to Washington as senator from Pennsylvania, 1834–1845. Secretary of state to Polk 1845–1849. Minister to Britain 1853–1856.	Elected as Democrat against John C. Fremont of young and growing Republican Party. Supported proslavery Dred Scott Decision of 1857 and states' choice on slavery issue, but failed to act decisively against secessionist movement.

Civil War troops, 1864

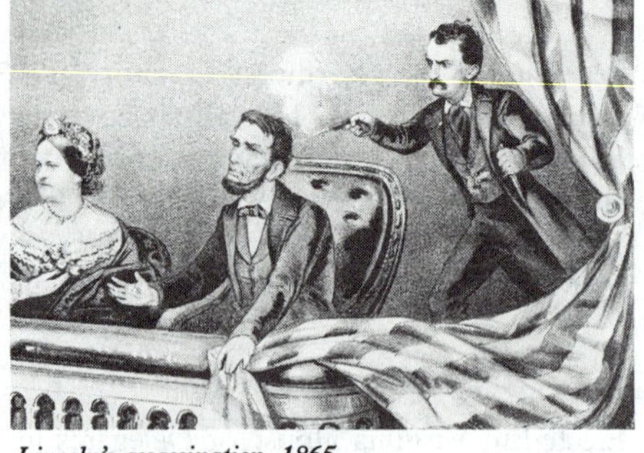

Lincoln's assassination, 1865

Name/Dates in office	*Personal*	*Education/Occupation*
16th **Abraham Lincoln** March 4, 1861–April 15, 1865	Born Feb. 12, 1809, Hardin County (now Larue), Ky.; died April 15, 1865, Washington, D.C., one day after being shot by John Wilkes Booth at Ford's Theatre. In 1842 married Mary Todd (1818–1882); they had four sons.	No formal education, but studied law privately while working as a farmer, store clerk, and riverboat pilot. Admitted to the bar in 1837; began his practice in Springfield, Ill. Became a prominent lawyer in Illinois between terms of political office, representing corporations as well as individuals.
17th **Andrew Johnson** April 15, 1865–March 4, 1869	Born Dec. 29, 1808, Raleigh, N.C.; died July 31, 1875, Carter's Station, Tenn. In 1827 married Eliza McCardle (1810–1876); they had five children.	Apprenticed as a tailor, but ran away and settled in Greenville, Tenn., where his future wife taught him to read at age 17. Supported himself with a variety of jobs while broadening his education and being drawn into politics.
18th **Ulysses Simpson Grant** March 4, 1869–March 4, 1877	Born April 27, 1822, Point Pleasant, Ohio; died July 23, 1885, Mt. McGregor, N.Y. Named at birth Hiram Ulysses Grant. In 1848 married Julia Dent (1826–1902); they had four children.	Career soldier who graduated from U.S. Military Academy at West Point in 1843. Served in Mexican War, resigned commission in 1854, and returned to Army after unsuccessful business ventures in 1861. Because of his brilliant leadership in early battles, he was made commander of Union forces late in the Civil War.
19th **Rutherford Birchard Hayes** March 4, 1877–March 4, 1881	Born Oct. 4, 1822, Delaware, Ohio; died Jan. 17, 1893, Fremont, Ohio. In 1852 married Lucy Webb (1831–1889); they had eight children.	Graduated from Kenyon College in Ohio, 1842, and from Harvard School of Law, 1845. Began practice of law in Lower Sandusky, Ohio, and became solicitor of city of Cincinnati. Served in Civil War and was wounded.

A carpetbagger

Completing the transcontinental railroad, 1869

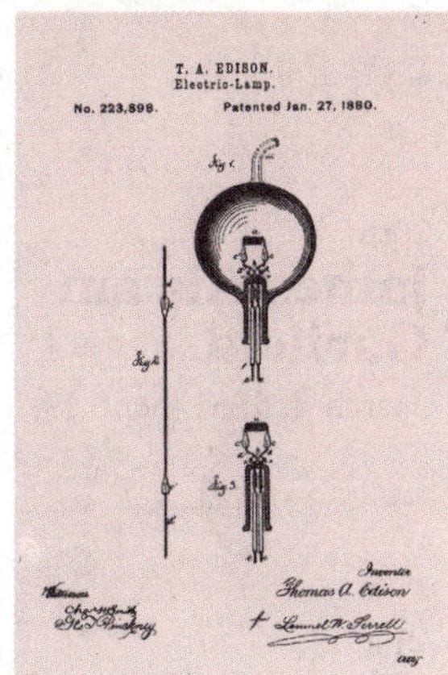

Edison's electric light, 1880

Political career	*Highlights in office*
After one unsuccessful attempt, elected to the Illinois state legislature as a Whig. Served as congressman from Illinois 1847–1849. Shifted to Republican Party established in 1854. Defeated in Senate race by Democrat Stephen A. Douglas, but his brilliance in the Lincoln-Douglas debates placed him in the front rank of antislavery Republicans and led to Republican nomination for President in 1860.	Southern states began to secede immediately following Lincoln's election to the Presidency. Lincoln began the Civil War to protect the Union, 1861. Issued Emancipation Proclamation that freed slaves in Southern states in 1863, and prepared 13th Amendment, which abolished slavery. Lincoln's many famous public addresses kept the North unified during the Civil War. Reelected in 1864, he was assassinated 43 days into his second term and five days after the Confederate surrender ended the war.
In Greenville, Tenn., elected alderman in 1828, mayor in 1830, and state representative in 1835. Served in Congress 1843–1853. Governor of Tennessee 1853–1857. Served in Senate 1857–1862. Opposed Lincoln in 1860, but was true to the Union and was named governor of occupied Tennessee in 1862. Chosen as Lincoln's running mate in 1864 to encourage return of Southern states to Union, and became President on Lincoln's assassination.	Stirred hostility by granting amnesty to Southern states and ratifying 13th Amendment abolishing slavery. Dismissed Secretary of War Edwin M. Stanton without required notification of Senate. For this the House voted to impeach him, but the Senate failed to convict by a single vote.
Appointed secretary of war by Andrew Johnson in 1867, but never confirmed by Congress. In 1868 was nominated for President by the Republicans as the hero of the Civil War, and he was elected in a close popular vote over Horatio Seymour (1810–1886), Democrat of New York.	Amnesty act for Confederate veterans and 15th Amendment to protect voting rights of all races passed during his administration. Was reelected in 1872. Grant's second administration was marred by mismanagement that permitted widespread corruption.
Congressman from Ohio 1864-1867. Governor of Ohio 1868–1872 and 1876–1877. Ran unsuccessfully for Congress, 1872.	Elected as Republican over Democrat Samuel J. Tilden in a disputed election finally decided by a special electoral commission appointed by Congress. Removed last occupation forces from the South and ended Reconstruction policies. Reformed the civil service to end evils permitted by Jackson's spoils system.

Name/Dates in office	*Personal*	*Education/Occupation*
20th **James Abram Garfield** March 4, 1881–Sept. 19, 1881	Born Nov. 19, 1831, Cuyahoga County, Ohio; died Sept. 19, 1881, Elberon, N.J.; assassinated by Charles J. Guiteau, who had been denied a government job. In 1858 married Lucretia Rudolph (1832–1918); they had seven children.	Graduated from Williams College in Massachusetts, 1856. Taught literature at Hiram College in Ohio and was its president from 1857 to 1861. Served in Civil War, distinguishing himself at Shiloh and Chickamauga.
21st **Chester Alan Arthur** Sept. 20, 1881–March 4, 1885	Born Oct. 5, 1830, Fairfield, Vt.; died Nov. 18, 1886, New York City. Son of a clergyman from Ireland. In 1859 married Ellen Herndon (1837–1880); they had three children.	Graduated from Union College in New York, 1848, and taught school at Pownall, Vermont. Studied law in New York City. Famous as an opponent of fugitive slave laws and of discrimination laws. Served in Civil War with New York militia.
22nd and 24th **Grover Cleveland** March 4, 1885–March 4, 1889 and March 4, 1893–March 4, 1897	Born March 18, 1837, Caldwell, N.J.; died June 24, 1908, Princeton, N.J. Married Frances Folsom (1864–1947) in an 1886 White House ceremony; they had five children, including two daughters born in the White House.	Never attended college. Taught at New York City Institution for the Blind and worked as a clerk in New York law offices. Admitted to the bar in 1859, and became a district attorney in Buffalo, New York, 1863.
23rd **Benjamin Harrison** March 4, 1889–March 4, 1893	Born Aug. 20, 1833, North Bend, Ohio; died March 13, 1901, Indianapolis, Ind. Grandson of ninth President, William Henry Harrison. In 1853 married Caroline Scott (1831–1892); they had two children. Married Mary Scott Dimmick (1859–1948) in 1896; they had a daughter.	Graduated from Miami University of Ohio, 1852. Was admitted to the bar in 1853 and began to practice law in Indianapolis. Served in the Civil War.
25th **William McKinley** March 4, 1897–Sept. 14, 1901	Born Jan. 29, 1843, Niles, Ohio; died Sept. 14, 1901, Buffalo, N.Y., one week after being shot by anarchist Leon Czolgosz. In 1871 married Ida Saxton (1847–1907); their two daughters both died in infancy.	Attended Allegheny College in Pennsylvania without graduating because his education was interrupted by service in the Civil War, 1861–1865. Studied law in Albany, N.Y., and in 1867 began practice in Canton, Ohio.
26th **Theodore Roosevelt** Sept. 14, 1901–March 4, 1909	Born Oct. 27, 1858, New York City; died Jan. 6, 1919, Oyster Bay, N.Y. A distant cousin of 32nd President Franklin D. Roosevelt. In 1880 married Alice Hathaway Lee (1861–1884); they had a daughter. After his wife's death, married Edith Kermit Carow (1861–1948) in 1886; they had five children.	Graduated from Harvard University, 1880; attended Columbia University Law School. Rancher and writer of travel and political books. Organized the cavalry troop known as the Rough Riders, fighting in Cuba in Spanish-American War. After leaving Presidency, pursued outdoor adventures, advocated conservation policies.

Political career	*Highlights in office*
Republican congressman from Ohio 1863–1880. Elected to the Senate in 1880, but never took his seat because he was elected to the Presidency that same year.	Began reform of postal system and efforts to establish better Latin-American relations, but was assassinated after only six months in office.
Collector of the Port of New York, 1871, but forced out by civil service reforms of President Hayes. Led a Republican faction called the "Stalwart Republicans" against Hayes. When Garfield was nominated by the Republicans in 1880, Arthur was given the Vice Presidential position to placate the Stalwarts.	Assumed Presidency upon assassination of Garfield in 1881. Continued the debate over civil service appointments, and signed into law the Civil Service Reform Act of 1883. Was not renominated for a second term by the Republicans.
Elected mayor of Buffalo, New York, in 1881, and governor of New York in 1882 as a Democrat who opposed the corruption of Tammany Hall Democrats in New York City. Elected President in 1884; defeated by Republican Benjamin Harrison in 1888; elected a second time (against Harrison) in 1892.	Labeled by the State Department the 22nd and 24th President because his terms were not consecutive. In first administration, he enlarged the civil service. In second administration, he introduced monetary reforms to counter economic depression caused by the Panic of 1893. Ended Pullman strike of 1894, a protracted railroad labor struggle. Desired a third term, but was not renominated in 1896.
Launched unsuccessful campaign for governor of Indiana in 1876. Served in Senate 1881–1887, and fought for government pension increases never granted by Grover Cleveland. Nominated by Republicans; defeated incumbent Cleveland in 1888. As an incumbent himself, was defeated by Cleveland in 1892.	Assisted in passage of Sherman Antitrust Act and expanded government pension system. Presided over era of territorial expansion that included admission to the Union of Idaho and Wyoming, homestead settlement of Oklahoma Territory, and acquisition of Samoa.
Congressman from Ohio 1877–1883 and 1885–1891. Defeated in reelection campaign for Congress in 1890, but elected governor of Ohio in 1892. Sought Presidential nomination in 1892; won it in 1896 and was elected over Democrat William Jennings Bryan (1860–1925) as a proponent of the gold standard monetary policy.	Opened the Spanish-American War after the battleship *Maine* was sunk in Havana harbor, Cuba, in 1898; the war ended in the same year when Spain ceded Puerto Rico, the Philippines, and Guam to the United States and granted independence to Cuba. Reelected in 1900, but was assassinated early in his second term.
Member of New York State Assembly 1882–1884, but left politics after death of first wife. Returned as member of U.S. Civil Service Commission, 1889–1895, and president of N.Y. Police Board, 1895–1897. Assistant secretary of Navy 1897–1898. As a war hero, elected governor of New York, 1898. Elected Vice President for McKinley's second term, 1900, he became President on McKinley's death. Reelected in 1904; deferred to fellow Republican Taft in 1908; defeated by Wilson in 1912.	Advocated "speak quietly but carry a big stick" foreign policy. Recognized Republic of Panama and planned canal there. Regulated big business and enforced antitrust laws. In 1905 negotiated peace between Russia and Japan and was awarded the Nobel Peace Prize.

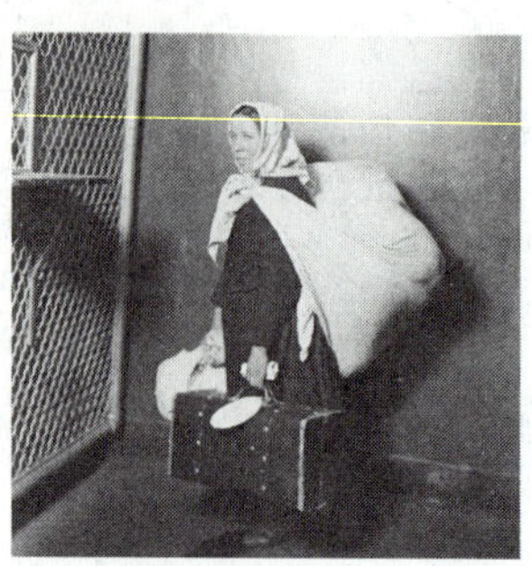

An immigrant c 1900

The sinking of the Titanic, *1912*

John D. Rockefeller

Name/Dates in office	*Personal*	*Education/Occupation*
27th **William Howard Taft** March 4, 1909–March 4, 1913	Born Sept. 15, 1857, Cincinnati, Ohio; died March 8, 1930, Washington, D.C. In 1886 married Helen Herron (1861–1943); they had two sons.	Graduated from Yale University, 1878, and Cincinnati Law School, 1880. Was a law journalist in Cincinnati, and later a district attorney. After Presidency became professor of law at Yale, 1913–1931, and chief justice of the Supreme Court, 1921–1930.
28th **Woodrow Wilson** March 4, 1913–March 4, 1921	Born Dec. 28, 1856, Staunton, Va.; died Feb. 3, 1924, Washington, D.C. In 1885 married Ellen Axson (1860–1914); they had three daughters. After her death married Edith Bolling Galt (1872–1961), a widow who assisted Wilson during illness in second term.	Graduated from Princeton University, 1879; attended University of Virginia Law School; earned Ph.D. in political science at Johns Hopkins in 1886. Taught at Princeton, 1890–1910, and served as president of the university, 1902–1910.
29th **Warren Gamaliel Harding** March 4, 1921–Aug. 2, 1923	Born Nov. 2, 1865, Corsica (now Blooming Grove), Ohio; died Aug. 2, 1923, San Francisco, Calif., of natural causes while in office. In 1391 married Florence Kling DeWolfe (1860–1924).	Attended Ohio Central College. In 1884 brought the Marion (Ohio) *Star,* an increasingly influential newspaper under his ownership and the source of his early political power.
30th **Calvin Coolidge** Aug. 2, 1923–March 4, 1929	Born July 4, 1872, Plymouth, Vt.; died Jan. 5, 1933, Northampton, Mass. In 1905 married Grace Anna Goodhue (1879–1957); they had two sons.	Graduated from Amherst College in Massachusetts in 1895. Studied law and began practice in Northampton, Massachusetts.
31st **Herbert Hoover** March 4, 1929–March 4, 1933	Born Aug. 10, 1874, West Branch, Iowa; died Oct. 20, 1964, New York City. Raised on the Indian Territory (now Oklahoma). In 1899 married Lou Henry (1874–1944); they had two sons.	Graduated from Stanford University in 1891 as an engineer and worked for U.S. Geological Survey. As a mining engineer he worked in Asia, Australia, and Europe as well as the United States.

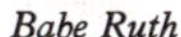
Babe Ruth

Dust storm c 1930

Political career	*Highlights in office*
U.S. solicitor general, 1890. Appointed first civil governor of the Philippines, 1901. Secretary of war to Theodore Roosevelt, 1904, and provisional governor of Cuba, 1906. Adviser and protégé of Roosevelt, who supported him for Presidency in 1908. The two later disagreed; both campaigned for President in 1912, helping Democrat Woodrow Wilson win.	Continued antitrust policies of Roosevelt, dissolving Standard Oil and other monopolies. Founded the Department of Labor. Aided ratification of 16th Amendment, which authorized income taxes.
Governor of New Jersey 1911–1913. Received Democratic nomination for President in 1912 as a reform candidate supported by William Jennings Bryan to block the party's Tammany Hall political machine. Elected in 1912 when Taft and Theodore Roosevelt, as third-party candidate, split Republican vote. Reelected in 1916 on the slogan "he kept us out of war."	In first term, created Federal Reserve System and passed Clayton Antitrust Act. In second term, oversaw American involvement in World War I. Drafted Fourteen Points for world peace, which were accepted at Treaty of Versailles conference in 1919 and earned him the Nobel Peace Prize. The points included a League of Nations. The U.S. Senate refused to enter the league despite efforts by Wilson that ultimately ruined his health.
Member of Ohio state assembly 1900–1904, and lieutenant governor of Ohio 1904–1906. After an unsuccessful campaign for the governorship in 1910, was elected to the Senate in 1915. Elected President as a Republican in 1920 with a platform that included opposition to incumbent President Wilson's plans for a League of Nations.	Convened International Conference on Limitations of Armaments in 1921, which resulted in a treaty. The end of his two-year administration was marred by the Teapot Dome scandal, in which Secretary of the Interior Albert B. Fall (1861–1944) and Attorney General Harry Daugherty (1860–1941) were charged with corruption.
Member of Massachusetts state legislature 1912–1915. Lieutenant governor of Massachusetts 1916–1919, and governor 1919–1920. Became famous for ending Boston police strike of 1919. Nominated as Vice President in 1920 by the Republicans and succeeded when Harding died of natural causes.	Presided over era of economic prosperity. Reduced national debt, provided relief for farmers, and passed legislation beneficial to industry with the slogan "the business of America is business." Reelected in a landslide in 1924 but declined a further term in 1928.
Became famous as director of relief committees supplying food to countries devastated by World War I. Secretary of commerce to Presidents Harding and Coolidge, 1921–1928. Elected President as a Republican, 1928. Following Presidency headed "Hoover commissions" on government reform and founded Hoover Institute for political study.	Election followed by stock market crash of 1929 and general collapse of American economy. During subsequent Great Depression, Hoover opposed federal aid to unemployed and other welfare measures. Was defeated in 1932 by a landslide vote for Democrat Franklin D. Roosevelt.

Franklin Roosevelt

Victory in World War II, 1945

School desegregation decision, 1954

Name/Dates in office	*Personal*	*Education/Occupation*
32nd **Franklin Delano Roosevelt** March 4, 1933–April 12, 1945	Born Jan. 30, 1882, Hyde Park, N.Y.; died April 12, 1945, Warm Springs, Ga., while in office. In 1905 married Eleanor Roosevelt (1884–1962); they had six children, one dying in infancy. Paralyzed by polio in 1921, Roosevelt could stand or walk only with assistance.	Graduated from Harvard University, 1904, and attended Columbia University Law School. Practiced law in New York City.
33rd **Harry S. Truman** April 12, 1945–Jan. 20, 1953	Born May 8, 1884, Lamar, Mo.; died Dec. 26, 1972, Independence, Mo. In 1919 married Bess Wallace (1885–1982); they had one daughter.	After high school education in Independence, Missouri, worked a series of jobs and ran family farm. Served in World War I. Opened a clothing store and studied at Kansas City Law School.
34th **Dwight David Eisenhower** Jan. 20, 1953–Jan. 20, 1961	Born Oct. 14, 1890, Denison, Texas; died March 28, 1969, Washington, D.C. Raised in Abilene, Kansas. In 1916 married Mamie Geneva Doud (1896–1979); they had two sons, one of whom died in childhood.	Graduated from West Point, 1915. Rose in rank to Supreme Allied Commander in 1943, during World War II. Launched D-Day invasion in 1944 and accepted German surrender in 1945.
35th **John Fitzgerald Kennedy** Jan. 20, 1961–Nov. 22, 1963	Born May 29, 1917, Brookline, Mass.; died Nov. 22, 1963, Dallas, Texas, assassinated while riding in a motorcade. In 1953 married Jacqueline Lee Bouvier (1929–); they had three children. One child died in infancy.	Graduated from Harvard University, 1940. Served in World War II as PT boat commander in Solomon Islands. Authored books, including *Profiles in Courage* (1953).
36th **Lyndon Baines Johnson** Nov. 22, 1963–Jan. 20, 1969	Born Aug. 27, 1908, near Stonewall, Texas; died Jan. 22, 1973, Johnson City, Texas. In 1934 married Claudia Alta (Lady Bird) Taylor (1912–); they had two daughters.	Graduated from Southwest Texas State Teachers College, 1930, and attended Georgetown University Law School in Washington, D.C., 1935. Taught public speaking in Houston, Texas, 1930–1932.

Khrushchev and Kennedy, 1963

Footprint on the moon, 1969

Political career	*Highlights in office*
New York state senator 1910–1913. Assistant secretary of Navy 1913–1920. Unsuccessful candidate for Vice President 1920. Following recovery from polio attack, governor of New York, 1929–1933. Elected President by a landslide in 1932 and reelected three times, more than any other President.	Took office during Great Depression of 1930's. Obtained emergency powers for dispensing economic relief and proclaimed New Deal for the country. Fought with the Supreme Court over executive powers. Oversaw American involvement in World War II and pledged himself to protection of Four Freedoms (of speech, worship, want, and fear). Conferred with heads of allied countries several times during war, helping shape postwar world.
Served in a series of public offices and judgeships in Missouri until election to U.S. Senate in 1934. Served in Senate until 1945. Elected Vice President for Franklin D. Roosevelt's fourth term, and became President when Roosevelt died. Elected to full term in 1948 upset victory over Thomas E. Dewey.	Ordered atomic bombs dropped on Japanese cities of Hiroshima and Nagasaki to end Pacific combat in World War II. Created NATO and the Marshall Plan to protect and assist Europe after the war. Established the Truman Doctrine to protect countries from Russian interference. With U.N. approval, sent U.S. troops to protect South Korea.
After resignation from the Army, was considered as a Presidential candidate by both parties. Accepted Republican nomination in 1952 and was elected as a war hero over Democrat Adlai E. Stevenson. Reelected in 1956, again over Stevenson. Advised three subsequent Presidents.	Ended the Korean War, but supported American involvement in Southeast Asia, including Vietnam. Sent troops to enforce desegregation of schools in Little Rock, Arkansas, in 1957. Favored strong Cold War stance against Russia, but resisted military action and warned against power of the "military-industrial complex."
As representative from Massachusetts, served in the House 1947–1953, and the Senate 1953–1961. Nominated for President by Democrats in 1960, and defeated Republican candidate Richard Nixon, later 37th President, in part because of charm and intelligence in nationally televised Presidential debates.	Unsuccessfully attempted invasion of Cuba at Bay of Pigs; successfully blockaded Cuba until Russian missile bases there were removed. Blocked proposed increases in prices by steel industry. Preserved Western European and American presence in West Berlin despite Berlin wall isolating city. Began American program of manned space flights and promised a landing on the moon by 1970, which was accomplished after his death.
Appointed to Congress to fill a vacancy in 1937 and served until 1948. Elected to Senate in 1948 and 1954, and became Democratic leader. He was elected Vice President with President John F. Kennedy. Became President when Kennedy was assassinated, and was elected to a full term in 1964.	Launched Great Society programs to increase aid for education, housing, and medical care. Signed laws to protect civil rights and to reduce taxes. Johnson's second term was marred by the unpopular war in Vietnam. Although eligible, he did not seek reelection in 1968.

March on Selma, 1965

President Lyndon Johnson signs the 1964 Civil Rights bill.

Name/Dates in office	Personal	Education/Occupation
37th **Richard Milhous Nixon** Jan. 20, 1969–Aug. 9, 1974	Born Jan. 9, 1913, Yorba Linda, Calif. In 1940 married Thelma (Patricia) Ryan (1913–); they had two daughters.	Graduated from Whittier College, California, in 1934, and Duke University Law School in 1937. Practiced law in Whittier, Calif., and served in Navy during World War II.
38th **Gerald R. Ford** Aug. 9, 1974–Jan. 20, 1977	Born July 14, 1913, Omaha, Neb., named Leslie King; raised in Grand Rapids, Mich., and renamed after his stepfather. In 1948 married Elizabeth Bloomer Warren (1918–); they had four children.	Graduated from University of Michigan in 1935 and Yale University Law School in 1941. Practiced law in Grand Rapids, Mich., before enlisting in Navy in 1942.
39th **Jimmy Carter** Jan. 20, 1977–Jan. 20, 1981	Born Oct. 1, 1924, Plains, Ga. Named James Earl Carter at birth, but was officially known as "Jimmy." In 1946 married Rosalynn Smith (1927–); they had four children.	Attended Georgia Tech and graduated from U.S. Naval Academy at Annapolis in 1946. Served in nuclear submarine program. After father's death in 1953 ran family peanut farm.
40th **Ronald Reagan** Jan. 20, 1981–Jan. 20, 1989	Born Feb. 6, 1911, Tampico, Ill. In 1940 married actress Jane Wyman (1914–); they had one child and adopted another. After a 1948 divorce, married Nancy Davis (1922–) in 1952; they also had two children.	Graduated from Eureka College in Illinois in 1932. Worked as a sports announcer and served in World War II. Became a major movie star, president of the Screen Actors Guild, and television spokesman for General Electric Co. and others.
41st **George H. Bush** Jan. 20, 1989–	Born June 12, 1924, Milton, Mass. In 1945 married Barbara Pierce (1925–); they had six children. One child died at a young age.	Served in the Navy from 1942 to 1945. Earned an economics degree at Yale University. Founded an oil company.

John Dean, Watergate testimony, 1973

Bicentennial decoration, 1976

George Bush

Political career	*Highlights in office*
U.S. congressman from California 1947–1951. Became famous as a member of House Un-American Activities Committee investigating alleged Communist links of American citizens, including Alger Hiss. Elected to Senate, 1950. Served as Vice President during both Eisenhower administrations. Republican candidate for President, 1960, defeated by John Kennedy. Elected President in 1968 and reelected in 1972.	Gradually ended American involvement in Vietnam. Visited China, recognized Communist regime there. Promoted cautious detente with Soviet Union. Second term disrupted by Watergate scandal, which revealed many unlawful and unethical actions by Nixon and his associates. After House committee voted to impeach him, Nixon resigned August 9, 1974. In September he received a legal pardon from his successor, Gerald Ford.
Elected to Congress as Republican representative from Michigan and served 25 years, becoming Republican leader in the House. Appointed Vice President in 1973 to fill vacancy created by resignation of Spiro Agnew. Became President following resignation of Richard Nixon.	Granted Richard Nixon a pardon. Visited China in 1976. Vetoed numerous spending bills in pursuit of policy of fiscal austerity. Was defeated by Democrat Jimmy Carter in campaign for a full term in 1976.
Unsuccessful candidate for governor of Georgia in 1966, but elected governor as a Democrat in 1970. Limited by law to a single term, he then launched a marathon grass roots campaign for the Presidency. Elected President in 1976 over Republican incumbent Gerald R. Ford.	Initiated human rights programs and the Camp David peace talks between Israel and Egypt. His administration was marred by the Muslim takeover of the U.S. embassy in Teheran, Iran, and the holding of American hostages. He secured their release, but was defeated for reelection by Ronald Reagan.
Originally a Democrat, he became an active Republican during Barry Goldwater's unsuccessful campaign for the Presidency in 1964. Served as governor of California 1967–1974. An unsuccessful candidate for the Republican nomination in 1976, he was nominated for the Presidency in 1980 and defeated incumbent Jimmy Carter. He was reelected in 1984.	Administration launched sweeping program of government spending reductions and tax cuts to fight economic recession. Nominated the first woman, Sandra Day O'Connor, to the Supreme Court. Initiated friendlier relations and an intermediate-range nuclear missile treaty with the Soviet Union. His second term was disrupted by the furor caused by the Iran Contra affair.
Elected to Congress as a Republican representative from Texas in 1966. Appointed U.S. delegate to the United Nations in 1970. In 1973 became Republican National chairman. Director of the Central Intelligence Agency under President Ford. Elected Vice President under Reagan. Elected President in 1988, defeating Democrat Michael S. Dukakis.	Sent troops to Panama in December, 1989, to apprehend dictator Manuel Noriega. Nominated David Souter to replace William Brennan on the Supreme Court. Deployed American troops in the Persian Gulf as part of an international coalition that drove Iraqi invaders out of Kuwait in 1991.

Economics and Business

Our word *economy* comes from the Greek term meaning "management of a household." In a broad sense, economy means the careful management of anything, such as time. The social science of economics examines the way in which society chooses to manage its money and resources and formulates plans to insure the highest possible standard of living for the members of a society. Business, the commercial exchange of goods and services, is the activity that economics studies.

This section introduces you to the study of modern economics and business. First, it describes the two great modern theories of capitalism and socialism, the ways they have been mixed in the world today, and the most recent theories about their proper interaction. It then describes the practical business world, how it is organized, and how it functions. Finally, the section discusses the so-called "public sector." The section also includes a dictionary that defines key terms related to economics and business.

Economic systems

Capitalism. The economic system of the United States is known as capitalism, or free enterprise. Capitalism is based on ownership of business by individuals rather than by the government, and on the freedom of individuals to operate businesses for personal profit. In capitalism businesses compete to supply consumers with goods and services, and this competition controls prices. Hence, capitalism is known as an "open" or a "free" economy.

The economic theory of capitalism was formulated by the Scottish professor of philosophy Adam Smith (1723–1790). In *The Wealth of Nations*, published in 1776, he argued that if businesses operated free of government intervention, the competition for consumer spending would control prices. Smith believed that a desire for profit would guide businesses to provide the goods and services demanded by society.

In capitalism, the balance between society's needs and individual self-interest is maintained by the market theory of value. Any commodity, in this theory, is worth whatever money or services it can command in the marketplace. For example, suppose a single businessman decides to manufacture pianos. Without competition, he can insist on high prices for these scarce pianos. However, if consumers demand more pianos, other capitalists will begin to manufacture them. The greater availability of pianos will lower the price they command in the marketplace, and more people will be able to afford them.

Both society and capitalists can benefit from free competition. Once too many pianos are available, capitalists will naturally turn to production of other needed goods. The same principle governs labor. If there are few piano makers, they will command high wages and others will be encouraged to learn that trade. Once there are too many piano makers, wages will fall and young workers will turn to other trades needed by their society. This is called the law of supply and demand, and it is the foundation of the system of competition central to all capitalist economies.

Marxist socialism. There are a number of modern alternatives to capitalism, but the most important is Marxist socialism. It is based on public ownership of business by large social groups, usually a nation through its government. Socialism operates on a principle of government control of industry to provide needed goods at reasonable prices. Socialism hopes to distribute wealth evenly, following the formula *from each according to his ability, to each according to his need.* Because of the government's primary role in this system, socialism is known as a "planned" or "controlled" economy.

Socialism has roots in the distant past, but modern economic socialism began in the 1800's as a reaction to unrestricted capitalism. Capitalistic abuses included unhealthy working conditions in factories, conspiracies by capitalists to keep prices high and workers' wages low, and cruel exploitation of child laborers. As a result, labor forces joined together to protect their own interests against those of wealthy capitalists.

The most important document in modern socialism is the *Communist Manifesto*, published in England in 1848 by the German intellectuals Karl Marx (1818–1883) and Friedrich Engels (1820–1895). In their view, capitalism did not serve the common good; instead, it encouraged wealthy capitalists to exploit laborers who did not have the wealth, or capital, to form their own businesses. Marx, in particular, thought that capitalism had created a growing rift between the wealthy and the poor that would result in a revolution by the workers.

The key to socialism, as formulated by Marx, is a labor theory of value that contrasts with capitalism's market theory of value. In the labor theory of value, prices are determined by the amount of labor required to produce a commodity rather than its exchange value in the marketplace. This theory includes in prices the value of indirect labor, such as the time required to construct factories and machinery. It can only operate if the government intervenes to suspend supply and demand. In a socialist economy, the government decides which commodities to supply, and it controls prices. Hence, clothing is priced according to the labor required to produce individual items rather than by consumer demand. The government maintains control over labor by deciding which jobs to create within the economy and by setting the wages for any individual job.

Mixed economic systems. Both free and controlled economies have certain flaws. In pure capitalism, capitalists may neglect factory working conditions and exploit working men and women. Socialist countries are plagued by low production standards because of a general lack of worker incentive. For this reason, neither pure capitalism nor pure socialism exists in today's world. Instead, countries organize their economies to balance between free and controlled economic principles. This is called mixed economy.

The United States has a predominantly free economy. It is based on private ownership of industries and competition among industries for consumer dollars. Consumers are allowed free choice in the goods they purchase with their wages and workers are allowed to pursue the profession of their choice. U.S. farms are privately owned; farm produce enters an open market that determines prices; and farmers gain personal profit

From ***The Communist Manifesto,***
by Marx and Engels

"The history of all hitherto existing society is the history of class struggles. . . . It has pitilessly torn asunder the motley feudal ties that bound man to his "natural superiors," and has left no other bond between man and man than naked self-interest, than callous "cash payment". . . . It has resolved personal worth into exchange value, and in place of the numberless indefeasible chartered freedoms, has set up that single, unconscionable freedom—Free Trade. In one word, for exploitation, veiled by religious and political illusions, it has substituted naked, shameless, direct, brutal exploitation."

From ***Wealth of Nations,***
by Adam Smith

"Man has almost constant occasion for the help of his brethren, and it is in vain for him to expect it from their benevolence only. He will be more likely to prevail if he can interest their self-love in his favour, and shew them that it is for their own advantage to do for him what he requires of them. . . . It is not from the benevolence of the butcher, the brewer, or the baker, that we expect our dinner, but from their regard to their own interest. We address ourselves, not to their humanity but to their self-love, and never talk to them of our own necessities but of their advantages. Nobody but a beggar chuses to depend chiefly upon the benevolence of his fellow-citizens."

from the sale of goods. Other workers are also free to sell their labor and to profit in the form of wages. Risk exists in both cases, in the form of farm losses or of unemployment.

Not all economic activity in the United States, however, is free from government control. Some industries, including farming, benefit from government financial support and are subject to government price controls. Other industries are entirely owned by government, such as the postal service, school system, and some transportation and utility companies. The government can also break up companies by enforcing antitrust laws against monopolies.

By contrast, the Soviet Union is organized into a predominantly controlled economy. Its government owns all industries, and workers have no choice but to work for the state. Both the kind and the price of consumer goods are also controlled by the state. In the Soviet Union, all farms are owned by the state or by collectives that it organizes and regulates. Farm produce is returned directly to the government for pricing and distribution.

Nevertheless, there are some aspects of free economy operating in the Soviet Union. Single craftsmen and professionals are allowed to work for themselves and to profit from their labor. Other workers can also profit from their labor by earning bonuses and productivity awards. Income, then, is not entirely equal, and those with sufficient income can privately purchase and own consumer goods such as automobiles. The Soviet Union considers its system a socialist one on its way to a pure communist one without private property or personal profit.

Most of the nations of the world fall between the free U.S. economy and the controlled Soviet economy. Great Britain, for example, is organized into a predominantly free economy; but its medical, automotive, airline, and steel industries are nationalized, or owned by the state. This makes the economy of Great Britain more controlled than that of the United States, and more free than that of the Soviet Union.

Modern economic theories. Recent history, especially the worldwide Depression of the 1930's, alerted economists to the fact that even mixed economies can fail to utilize fully a nation's resources. For this reason, economists have explored new theories of economic behavior and policy, theories that are far more complex than the pure forms of capitalism and socialism formulated by Adam Smith and Karl Marx.

The New Economics. The most important revolution in modern economics was brought about by the Englishman John Maynard Keynes (1883–1946). His *General Theory of Employment, Interest, and Money,* published in 1936, was a dramatic revision of the capitalist principles established by Adam Smith. The school of thought inspired by Keynes is called the "New Economics."

Keynes's great insight was to perceive that free competition based on supply and demand would not necessarily lead to full employment and a healthy economy. He realized this by considering the economy as a whole rather than as the single industries on which Adam Smith had based his theories. This method, now universally accepted, is known as macroeconomics. When Keynes considered total supply and total demand in a national economy, he saw that they had a more complicated relationship than had been thought. In times of little available consumer money, for example, demand could naturally decrease, causing less than full employment and undermining business. In times of available money, demand could naturally increase beyond the economy's ability to produce goods, causing inflation. While either situation might benefit single businesses, the total economy could be damaged.

Keynes's perception of this potential imbalance between supply and demand led to practical applications of the New Economics. Government could involve itself in the economy to manipulate demand, ending the old laissez-faire policy, but improving the general health of the economy. The widest application of this idea was the New Deal policy introduced in the United

Controlled and open economies

The positions of representative countries in respect to entirely free or entirely controlled economies.

Pure controlled economy		Equal mixture		Pure open economy
U.S.S.R.	India	Spain	Great Britain	U.S.
China	Laos	Peru	Denmark	Canada
Cuba	Iran	Algeria	Germany	Japan
	Zaire	Costa Rica	France	Australia

*Important economic functions include production (*top left*); distribution (grain awaiting shipment) (*top right*); marketing (*bottom left*); and services, a rapidly growing sector of the economy (*bottom right*).*

States by President Franklin D. Roosevelt. In the Depression of the 1930's, the American economy was damaged by widespread unemployment; this limited consumer ability to purchase goods and so forced businesses into bankruptcy. Using the theories of the New Economics, government entered the economy and became an employer, instituting major public works projects such as the Civilian Conservation Corps and the Tennessee Valley Authority. Government hoped to increase employment and consumer ability to purchase goods, and thus to improve the climate for private businesses. Economists disagree on how successful New Deal policies were.

Monetarism. More recent theories share the belief that government should involve itself in business, but disagree on the most effective kind of involvement. Rather than increase government spending, as in the New Deal, government could control money supply. Control of money supply is called monetarism, and it is one of the most influential economic theories today.

Monetarists believe that the manipulation of money supply (cash, savings, and credit) can quickly improve the economy without leaving the government in debt from fiscal assistance programs. Money supply can be regulated by the Federal Reserve Bank, twelve "banks for smaller banks" that hold resources and dispense credit. If there is too much money in the economy, the result is excessive spending and inflation. If there is too little money in the economy, the result is a decline in spending and unemployment. To prevent these extremes, monetarists espouse the "money supply rule": money supply should be increased in proportion to annual economic growth.

President Ronald Reagan's administration promoted a "tight money" policy to correct inflation. It also reduced income tax rates drastically with the intention of keeping more money in circulation in order to promote business investment and expand business activities. It thus addressed supply rather than demand, as was the case in the New Deal. For this reason, the Reagan administration's policy was often called "supply-side economics."

Business

Kinds of businesses.

In the American system of free enterprise, individuals are free to own and operate businesses for personal profit. There are more than 14 million businesses in the United States, ranging from small local shops to enormous companies with national networks of offices. In all cases, however, the businesses fall into one of three categories: proprietorship, partnership, or corporation.

Proprietorship. The simplest kind of business organization is the proprietorship, a company owned by a single person. This individual provides all the money needed for operation and personally absorbs all profits and losses of the business. A proprietorship can be formed without any special registration or legal documents. In comparison with the other forms of business, the proprietorship is usually a small personal enterprise. It is subject to no special taxes.

Partnership. A partnership is a business owned by more than one person; there may be two owners or several. All partners contribute money to the business, and their ownership is divided in proportion to their capital investment. This division of ownership might be sealed by contract, but a partnership can be formed without any special legal documents or registration. Profits are distributed according to ownership proportions and taxed only as personal income.

Corporation. A corporation is a business association independent of its individual owners, many of whom may not be directly involved in its operation. A corporation has its own legal status: it can own property, accumulate money, and enter into contracts. It is also liable for its own debts, and can be sued in court.

To form a corporation, individuals contribute capital and file a special certificate with their state government. The state approves the legal name of the corporation, regulates its activities, and subjects corporation profits to tax rates generally higher than those on personal income. Ownership of the corporation is divided into units called stocks. These stocks represent shares of the business proportionate to capital investment. The value of these stocks rises with the value of the business. Stockholders receive corporate profits in the form of dividends paid per share of stock; they also vote for a board of directors.

The greatest advantage of the corporation is its *limited liability.* Creditors or dissatisfied clients can sue for the assets of the corporation, but not for the personal property of the stockholders. Corporations are also able to generate new capital quickly through the sale of more stock. Corporations are less personal than proprietorships or partnerships, but they are more stable and potentially profitable.

Stocks.

In America there is only one corporation for every five unincorporated businesses. But corporations earn ten times as much money as all other businesses combined.

The stock system. One reason for this is the stock system. Corporations are able to sell stock, or shares in their business, to interested buyers. This enables them to raise capital quickly, expand their business activities, and so gain greater profits.

The stock system also permits people who are not wealthy to participate in the economy. Anyone can buy stock and so own a part, however small, in even giant corporations. Nearly 30 million Americans own stock, and most of them are "small investors," owning small shares in large corporations.

When individuals join to form a corporation, they divide the ownership into shares of stock. At that beginning point each stock is worth a fixed amount of money, called "par value." The owners might then be content to keep all shares of stock among themselves; but they might choose to issue stock as well and sell some of their shares to new investors.

The sale value of stock depends on the health of the business. In periods of profit the value of stock will rise; in periods of loss it will fall. Investors purchase stock at a certain price and hope to sell it later at a higher price. Corporations with erratic histories of profits and losses are considered risky, but if their stock is offered at a low price investors may be attracted by the chance for a sudden increase in value, a short-term gain. Corporations with histories of steady profits and slow growth are considered attractive for long-term gains. The value of their stock is not likely to rise or fall suddenly.

Many investors are drawn to the stock market because it allows them to research individual companies and invest accordingly. If a shrewd researcher can uncover information about companies and markets early enough, he can buy stock that can be expected to rise in value. As an alternative to this sort of research, many people leave decisions to professional investment advisers, who offer their services for a fee.

In addition to the chance to profit from stock sales, the stock system also rewards investors in healthy companies with *dividends.* A dividend is an amount of money paid per share of stock at regular intervals, usually quarterly. The amount of money is fixed by the board of directors of the corporation, who are usually elected by the stockholders. The dividend represents the stockholder's share of the profits of the company, and so dividends are paid only if the company itself is earning profits.

Buying and selling stock. Stock is bought and sold in the marketplace and shares are worth whatever exchange value they have in either money or other stock. Most stock is bought and sold in central places of consolidated trading, called securities exchanges. The most famous of these is the New York Stock Exchange on Wall Street. Another important one in New York City is the American Stock Exchange (Amex). Other U.S. stock exchanges are located in Chicago, Boston, Philadelphia, and San Francisco.

To have its stock bought and sold in one of these exchanges, a corporation must have distributed a certain number of shares, have a certain number of stockholders, and have a certain value in corporate assets. If a corporation does not satisfy these requirements or does not wish to be listed on an exchange, it can still sell its stock in the "over-the-counter" market.

On the stock exchanges, stock cannot be sold unless there is a buyer, and vice versa, so stock transactions are called "trading." On the New York Stock Exchange alone, tens of millions of shares are traded every day. Professional dealers, called stockbrokers, handle other people's stock, obtaining the best possible prices for their clients in return for a commission on each purchase or sale.

Here is how a typical stock transaction might take place. A person named Smith living in Kansas checks a local newspaper and sees that Consolidated Gas, Inc., was selling at $20 per share on the previous day. Thinking this a good investment, Smith calls his brokerage firm to learn the current price. The broker tells him, "20 to a quarter," which means that the stock is being bought at $20 and sold at $20.25. Smith tells the broker to buy 100 shares at the best market price (which will be between $20 and $20.25). Meanwhile, a person named Miller in Indiana has decided to sell 100 shares of Consolidated Gas and make another investment. Miller is told the same going price from another broker in New York, and he places an order to sell at the best price between $20 and $20.25. In New York, brokers from each stockholder's firm go to the place in the exchange designated for trading Consolidated Gas. Smith's broker could pay $20.25 per share, but he bargains by bidding $20\frac{1}{8}$, or $\$20.12\frac{1}{2}$. Miller's broker could sell at $20. He thinks that the bid is a good price, and so he accepts it by saying: "Sold at $20\frac{1}{8}$." Thus a trade, worth $2012.50, has been made in New York for investors in Kansas and Indiana. Both the investors and Consolidated Gas have benefited from the services offered by the public exchange.

Stock information

Here is how *The Wall Street Journal* lists the daily information about the New York Stock Exchange. Most daily newspapers provide stock tables in the same format.

1		2	3	4	5	6	7	8	9	10
61½	26⅝	GnInst	.50	1.0	15	4179	53	50½	52¼	+2¼
54¾	33	GnMills	1.84	4.0	10	799	46⅜	45⅝	45⅞	− ¼
65½	34	GMot	2.40e	3.9	21	7362	62½	61⅛	61¾	+1⅝
49¾	37	GMot	pf 5	11.	..	6	47½	47	47	− ¼
32⅞	8¾	GNC	.16	.6	27	62	28	26⅞	27¼	− ⅛
8⅛	4½	GPU		..	15	816	8	7¾	7⅞	+ ⅛
65½	33⅞	GenRe	s1.08	1.9	13	554	57¼	56⅝	57	.....
4⅞	2⅜	GnRefr		..	..	55	4⅜	4¼	4⅜	+ ⅛
47	28	GnSignl	1.68	3.7	11	247	46⅜	46	46	− ¼
11⅝	8	GTFl	pf1.25	11.	..	z100	11	11	11	.....
12	8¾	GTFl	pf1.30	11.	..	z10	11½	11½	11½	+ ¾
70	53	GTFl	pf8.16	12.	..	z200	70	70	70	+2⅛
35¼	17⅞	GTire	1.50b	4.7	22	136	32	31½	31¾	+ ½
6½	3⅝	Gensco		..	..	148	5¼	5	5⅛	+ ⅛
37½	14	GnRad	.10	.3	68	287	u38⅛	36⅛	37⅛	+1¼
20½	7⅛	Genst	g .60	..	..	245	18⅛	17¾	18⅛	+ ¼
21½	11½	Gst pf	1.68	7.8	..	1	21½	21½	21½	+ ½
47⅜	29¾	GenuPt	1.30	3.1	15	416	41⅞	41⅛	41⅝	+ ⅝
28	13¼	GaPac	.60	2.4	51	2738	24⅞	24⅜	24½	+ ⅛
32⅞	23½	GaPc	pfB2.24	7.3	..	1	30½	30½	30½	− ½
31	22	GaPc	pfC2.24	7.6	..	21	30	29½	29½	.....
28⅞	25⅜	GaPw	pf3.44	13.	..	126	27¼	26⅞	27⅛	+ ⅛
31	23½	GaPw	pf3.76	13.	..	150	30	29¼	29¼	− ⅝
21¼	16⅛	GaPw	pf2.56	13.	..	1	20¼	20¼	20¼	.....
21⅛	15½	GaPw	pf2.52	12.	..	5	21	20¾	20¾	+ ⅛
24	18½	GaPw	pf2.75	12.	..	26	23¾	23⅝	23¾	+ ⅛

1. The higest and lowest prices paid for the stock over the previous year.
2. Abbreviated name of the company.
3. Amount of last quarterly dividend; "pf" means preferred stock, no indication means common stock.
4. Yield, or the percentage of the stock price returned in its annual dividend.
5. Price-earnings ratio, the ratio between the stock's current value and the company's most recent report of earnings per share.
6. Shares traded in 100's.
7. The day's high price.
8. The day's low price.
9. The day's final price.
10. Change over the previous day; no indication means zero change.

Credit.

Corporations often have reason to borrow money in order to run their businesses efficiently. Credit is the general term for all borrowing (and lending) transactions. The amount borrowed in a credit transaction is called the *principal.* Some credit transactions require only return of the principal; however, most business credit transactions are made for a price. The price demanded for credit is called the *interest.* Interest fees are usually annual rates, or percentages, of the amount of principal borrowed. If a business borrowed $1000 for one year at an annual rate of 10 percent, it would repay the $1000 principal plus $100 interest at the end of the year.

Credit helps businesses operate, because it permits the postponement of production expenses until after the product is sold. Credit also helps businesses grow, because it can provide the capital needed to undertake more work. In the business world there are three principal "instruments of credit," or contracts for credit transactions: notes, bonds, and drafts.

Notes. A promissory note is a promise to repay a loan with interest within a short period, usually within one year. This form of short-term credit is used by individuals, corporations, and governments to meet operating expenses during certain times of the year when business activity is slow.

Bonds. A bond is a promise to repay a loan at the end of a long period, usually far more than one year, and to pay interest at regularly scheduled dates within that period. Corporations sell bonds, and promise to repay with interest rather than with shares in ownership. Governments also sell bonds, especially to undertake long-term improvements such as bridges and sewer systems. Such *municipal bonds* usually pay a lower rate of interest than corporate bonds, but income from them is partially or wholly free from taxation. The most common bonds available to individuals are federal savings bonds. They are considered especially safe investments.

Drafts. A draft is an order by one party to a second party to pay a sum of money to a third party. Personal checks are drafts: by writing a check to pay for rent you are instructing your bank to pay a sum of money to the landlord. In the business world, a draft is sometimes called a "bill of exchange," or simply a "bill." All drafts are subject to "banker's approval," or the consent of the second party involved in the transaction.

Personal credit. Credit is crucial to the business world, but it is also used by individuals in their personal finances. Home buyers obtain credit from banks and repay this loan with interest. Consumers use credit cards to buy goods and services and pay for the purchases later. Savers place their money in bank savings accounts. In effect, they are lending money to the bank to be returned with interest on demand.

The public sector.

In the United States, business is motivated by the goal of personal profit. For this reason it is called the private sector of the economy. But there is another huge part of our mixed economy that aims to provide necessary services that cannot be expected to produce profits. This public sector is funded by taxes imposed by governments for the common good. Governments run police departments, hospitals, schools, and many other essential services.

Taxes.

The United States uses three kinds of taxes to fund the public sector: on income, property, and consumption.

Income taxes, the governments' greatest source of tax revenues, are based on ability to pay. They are progressive taxes in which the tax rate rises with the amount of income. Income of $20,000 might be taxed at a rate of 20 percent, equaling $4,000, while income of $100,000 might be taxed at a rate of 40 percent, equaling $40,000.

Property taxes are paid by owners of land and buildings. The tax rate is usually fixed within a locality and remains constant whatever the amount of property. A town might levy a 2 percent property tax to pay for public sewers and other services, for example. The owner of a $50,000 home would pay $1000, and the owner of a $100,000 home would pay $2000. One would contribute more than the other to the town, but the rate would be constant for both.

Consumption taxes are levied against particular purchases or activities, and they are used to provide services related to those purchases or activities. One example is the registration fee on motor vehicles. The money is usually used to promote highway safety and adequate inspection of cars on the road. A person who does not drive would not pay this tax because he does not demand the services it provides.

Part of the public sector funded by these taxes provides programs that benefit the entire population. Federal tax dollars are used for national defense, for example, and local tax dollars provide police protection. However, the public sector has an even greater effect on the economy as a medium for *transfer payments.* Transfer payments move money from one group to another, from the employed to the unemployed, from the healthy to the sick, or from the educated to the uneducated. Agencies charged with managing these transfer payments are called nonprofit agencies, and include bureaus of unemployment insurance, hospitals, and schools. In keeping with their nonprofit role, they are exempt from business taxes.

The public sector is an essential component of the American economy. It helps to accomplish the goal of any economy: to organize resources to provide the greatest degree of well-being for the entire population.

New York City subway token

Dictionary of economics and business

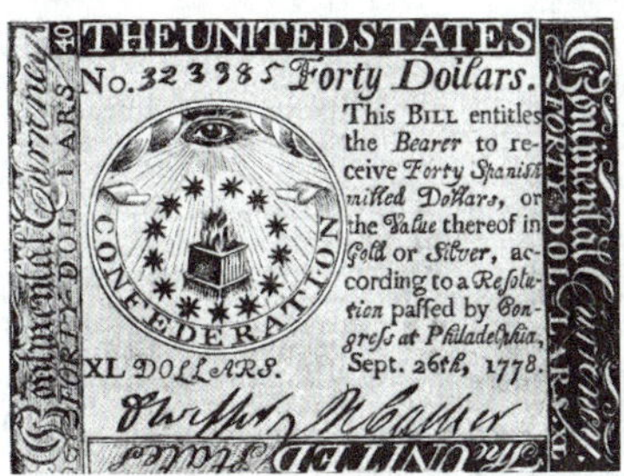

Forty dollar note, 1778

Susan B. Anthony dollar, 1979

United States savings bond

assets. Property and money resources owned by a business or owed to it. The value of assets in excess of liabilities determines the net worth of a business.

capital. Wealth used to produce goods for profit. Economics distinguishes between physical capital, such as land and machinery, and financial capital, such as money and credit. In business, capital usually refers to the money required to start production and operation.

collateral. Security pledged by a borrower as a guarantee that a loan will be repaid. In a home mortgage, the house is usually pledged as collateral, and it can be repossessed by the bank if loan payments are not made.

down payment. Partial payment made at the time a loan is secured and deducted from the principal. Often loans require a down payment computed as a percentage of the principal.

fiscal year. Business accounting period of twelve months, not necessarily beginning January 1. The U.S. government fiscal year runs from July 1 to June 30.

inflation. Rise in the prices of goods and services, and so a decline in the purchasing power of money. The reverse, a fall in prices, is called deflation.

laissez-faire. Originally a French term meaning "let (them) act," used to describe a government policy of nonintervention in private business.

liabilities. Outstanding debts owed by a business to creditors.

macroeconomics. Study of the national economy as a whole to understand the behavior of its single parts, such as industries or markets.

microeconomics. Study of parts of a national economy, such as single industries or markets, to understand the behavior of the whole economy.

mortgage. Credit agreement in which property is pledged as collateral for repayment of a loan. The most common mortgage is a loan to purchase a home, with the house being pledged as collateral.

overhead. The continuing costs of business operation, including rent, wages, credit, and supplies.

prime rate. Interest rate charged by banks for short-term loans to major corporate borrowers. The prime rate is usually lower than personal loan rates.

profit. The money remaining from a transaction after payment of necessary expenditures and settlement of liabilities.

recession. Economic decline because of falls in investment, employment, and consumption levels. When especially severe, a recession becomes a depression.

supply and demand. Balance between available goods and consumer ability and willingness to purchase them. In capitalism, the balance between supply and demand can determine the price of any item.

For Further Reference

Hurta, P. F.
ABC's of Business
Kendall-Hunt

McGann, A. F.
Introduction to Business
John Wiley & Sons

Sampson, Roy J., et al.
American Economy: Analysis, Issues, Principles
Houghton-Mifflin

Silk, Leonard
Economics in Plain English
Simon & Schuster

Sloan, Harold, and Zurcher, Arnold
Dictionary of Economics
Barnes and Noble

Science and Mathematics

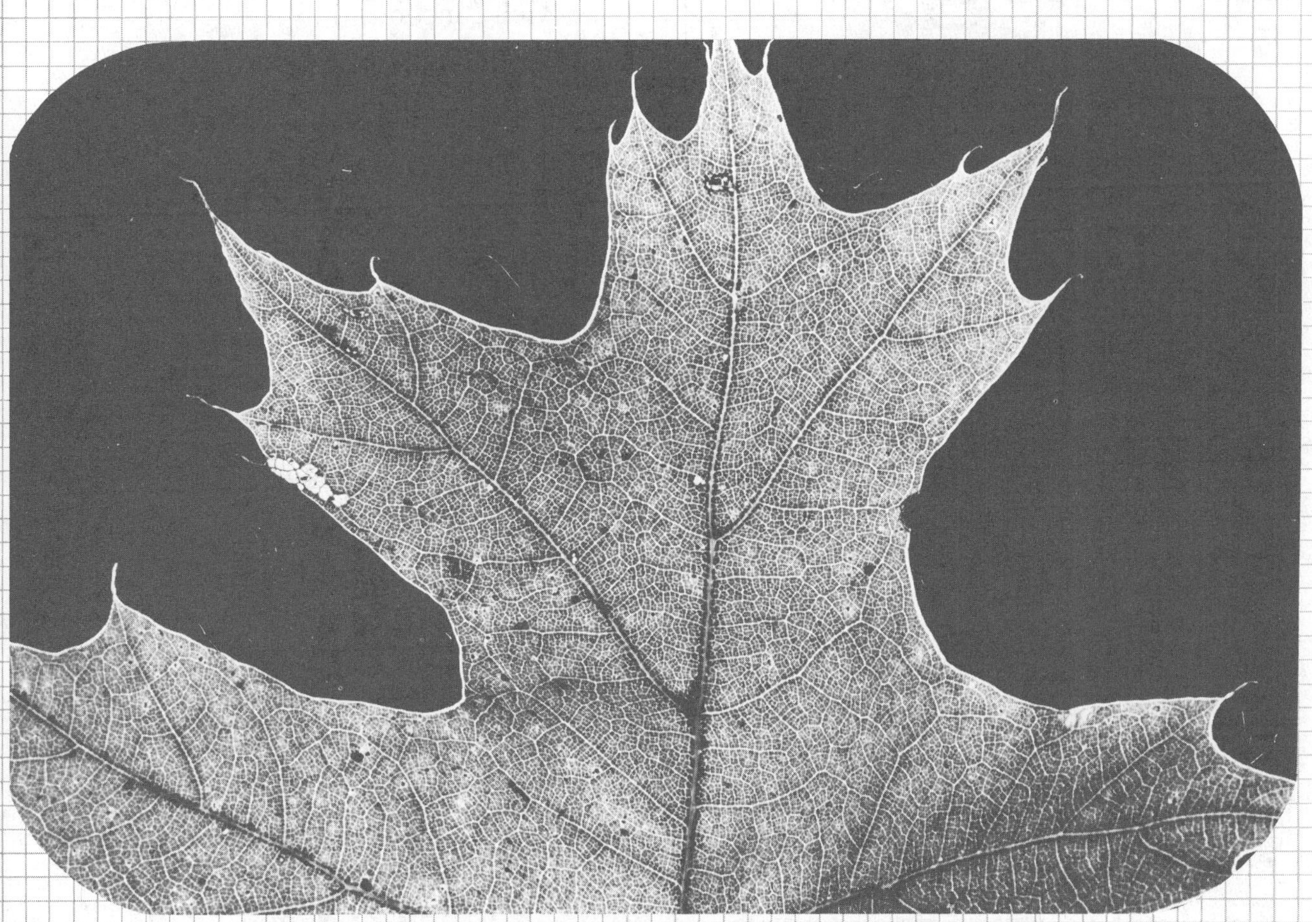

A pin oak leaf makes food from sunlight, carbon dioxide, and water (*see p. 119*).

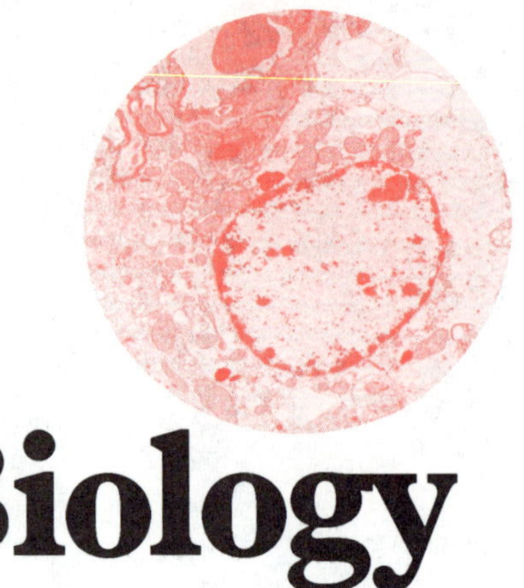

Biology

The immense variety of living things is, surprisingly, based on a few basic structures and a limited number of fundamental chemical operations. In this article, you will first encounter the most general features of life and then see how they have been combined to form the different types of living things that inhabit Earth.

Biology made a major breakthrough when scientists came to understand that all living things (except viruses, which sometimes are classed as not living) are composed of cells. Although there are many different types of cells, much of their structure and function remains the same, from microscopic bacteria to giant sequoias.

A later breakthrough has shown an even closer relationship among all living things: all life (including the viruses) is based on one of two closely related chemicals, either DNA or RNA. In fact, RNA is common to virtually all living things, although DNA is probably the more fundamental of the two giant nucleic acids.

The cell

The *cell* is a highly complex organization of matter in which the basic processes characteristic of life are performed. Monera and Protista may consist of a single cell; Plantae and Animalia, including man, may consist of billions of cells. Almost all cells are microscopic.

The cell is life's minimum unit of structure and function. Each cell must perform the processes we associate with whole organisms: taking in, storing, and releasing energy; taking in materials and metabolizing them for growth; repair; sense perception; response to stimuli; movement; and reproduction.

It is impossible to generalize about the size and shape of cells. The variety of shapes corresponds to the functions performed. Human skin cells are flat and platelike, while nerve cells are very long. A single nerve cell in a large animal may be several feet long. A bacterium may be 0.4 microns in diameter. The average diameter of a cell in man is about 10 microns (0.01 millimeters).

Organization of the cell. While there is a variety of cellular shapes and sizes, cells have certain common features. Each cell is covered by a thin *membrane* that generally allows only what the cell requires to pass through. The membrane encloses the *cytoplasm,* which itself contains many *organelles* (small organs). All cells also contain *chromosomal material* that, in many cells, is organized within a *nucleus.*

Cell membrane and cell wall. The outer boundary of a cell is a very thin, two-layered membrane. This extremely fragile and complex structure is less than 1/100,000 of a millimeter thick. This organelle controls and regulates everything that passes into and out of the cell. The membrane is made up of *protein* and *lipid* (fat) molecules. These molecules also act as adjustable pores through which molecules can selectively pass.

Multicellular organisms would collapse under their

own weight without a supporting structure of some type. Some animals have a skeletal system. Plants derive additional support from a rigid *cell wall* that lies outside the cell membrane. While there may be specialized structures that support the entire organism, each plant cell has its own wall. The function of the wall is mainly mechanical, since it is generally composed of inert cellulose. The wall does, however, play a small role in controlling the passage of material into and out of the cell.

The nucleus. The nucleus is usually the largest and most distinct organelle within the cell. Most cells contain a single nucleus, but some cells are multinucleated. The nucleus is roughly spherical and denser than the cytoplasm that surrounds it. The nucleus is held together by a double-layered nuclear membrane. This membrane has many pores that allow material to pass in and out of the nucleus.

The nucleus contains a tangled network of material called *chromatin.* Chromatin strands come together during cell division to form a number of threadlike bodies called *chromosomes.* There is a definite number of chromosomes for each species of organism, although plants often have double, triple, or even higher multiples of their species number. Chromosomes are the carriers of the cell's heredity. They direct and guide the development of the organism and maintain its order and organization. Chromatin is made up of strands of *DNA* (*deoxyribonucleic acid*) and proteins. DNA controls the hereditary characteristics of all living things and directs the production of proteins.

A spherical body called the *nucleolus* is visible within the nucleus when the cell is not dividing. The nucleolus is composed of granules rich in *RNA* (*ribonucleic acid*). RNA is essential to the formation of proteins by the cell. Cells that contain nuclei and chromosomes are called *eukaryotes.* Bacteria are simpler in organization. While they contain DNA, they have no nuclei, nuclear membranes, or chromosomes. The hereditary material of these *prokaryotes* is within the cytoplasm.

Types of cells in the human body

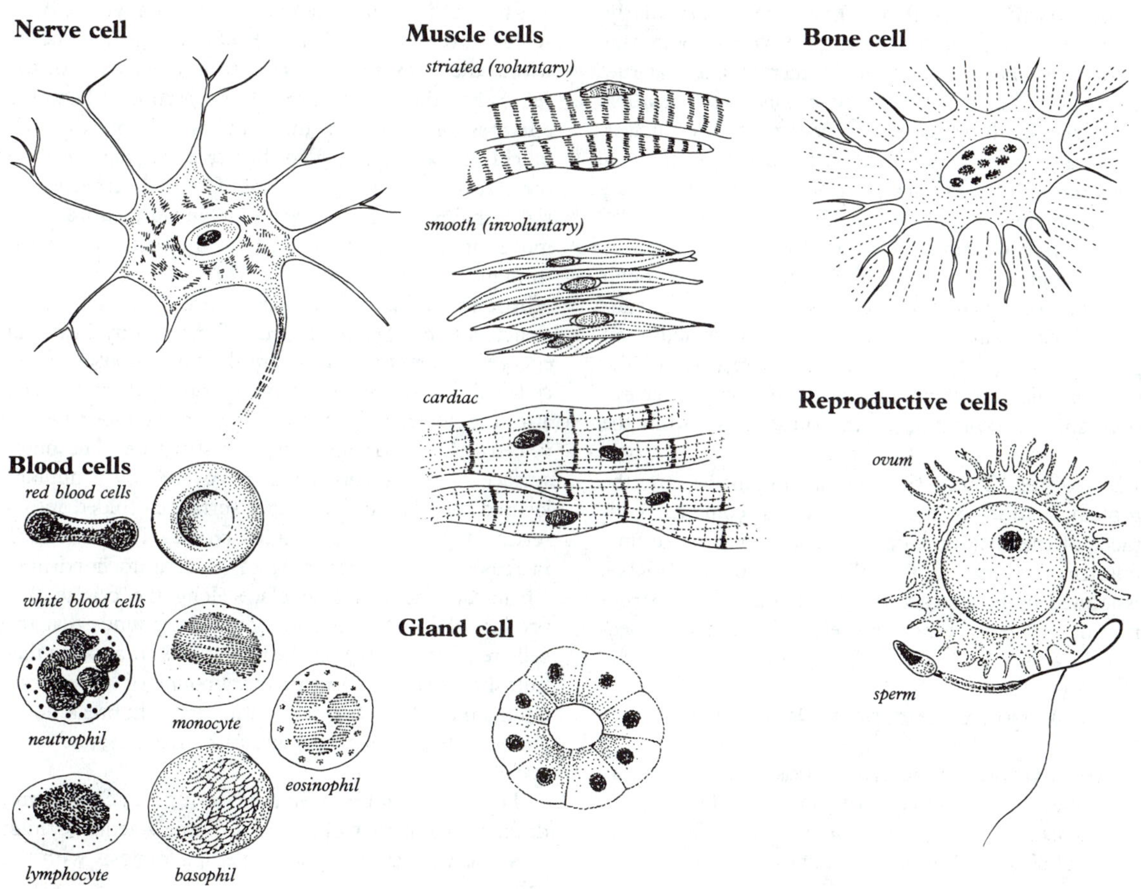

Cytoplasm. Cytoplasm is the cellular material enclosed by the cell membrane and outside the nuclear membrane. Within the cytoplasm are the several cellular organelles. The cytoplasm itself is made up mostly of water, in which are suspended carbohydrates, proteins, lipids, and other smaller molecules. Observations of living cells have shown that the viscosity of the same portion of cytoplasm varies. At one time, it will flow freely; at another, it appears to be thick and jellylike.

Cytoplasm is a *colloidal suspension*. A *colloid* is a mixture in which the motion of the particles of the solvent and the particle size of the solute (dissolved substance) are delicately balanced. The solute particles are not so large as those of a suspension, but they do not exist as individual molecules, as do the particles of a solution. The particles do not sink to the bottom of the solution unless the system itself is changed by an outside influence such as heat.

Cytoplasm is sometimes called *protoplasm*, which is the old name for all of the contents of the cell (including, of course, the cytoplasm). The word *protoplasm* reflects the incorrect idea that cell membranes were not truly living substance.

Endoplasmic reticulum. Every cell, particularly those involved in the formation of proteins, contains a network of channels bounded by membranes that run throughout the cytoplasm. This *endoplasmic reticulum* is a series of tubes that are connected to the nuclear membrane. The tubes provide a channel from the nucleus through the cytoplasm to the outside of the cell by way of the cell membrane. There are two types of endoplasmic reticulum. One is smooth; the other is rough or granular. The organelles that give the rough form its granular texture are *ribosomes*. All of the substances made within the cell must be transported to all parts of the cell for use. The main functions of the endoplasmic reticulum appear to be storage, separation, and transportation of the substances within the cell.

Ribosomes. These tiny, grainy organelles are the protein factories of the cell. Each cell contains thousands of them and in some, ribosomes may make up a quarter of the mass of the cell. Most of the cell's RNA is located in these structures. While the internal structure of ribosomes cannot be seen even under an electron microscope, two forms have been identified. One form is attached to the endoplasmic reticulum and transfers proteins to these membranes for transportation. The other form is free floating and releases proteins directly into the cytoplasm. Cells that form substances that are secreted through the cell membrane have the greatest systems of granular endoplasmic reticulum.

Golgi apparatus. Sometimes referred to as the Golgi complex, or Golgi bodies, these organelles are flat, saclike structures near the nucleus. Electron microscopy has shown that they are multilayered structures composed of smooth membranes that are probably the same as the membranes of the endoplasmic reticulum. It is thought the Golgi apparatus "packages" proteins that are secreted from the cell. While the mechanism is not known, it is thought that the molecules to be secreted are enclosed in membranous envelopes. These "packages" are sent to the surface of the cell, where they move out of the cell.

Lysosomes. These organelles seem to change their size and shape depending upon activity. They appear to be tiny drops of fluid surrounded by a membrane. The fluid consists of digestive enzymes whose function it is to break down protein, fat, and carbohydrate molecules into simpler substances. These reactions occur within the lysosome and are used in other parts of the cell. When the lysosome membrane is ruptured and the enzymes are released into the cytoplasm, the cell quickly breaks apart. The digestive enzymes also rid the cell of undigested material. The undigested material remains within the lysosome and the entire body moves to the cell surface where the waste is ejected through the membrane.

Mitochondria. *Mitochondria* are sausage-shaped structures that are the source of most body heat and energy. The mitochondria are the powerhouses of the cell and are the second largest organelles in the cell after the nucleus. Electron microscope studies have revealed their remarkably intricate structure. The outer surface of a mitochondrium is covered by a double-layered membrane. The inner surface is folded into a series of parallel ridges called *cristae*. This infolding increases the interior area of each mitochondrium. Chemical reactions take place along the cristae that produce the high energy-yielding compounds that the cells require to carry on their functions. It appears that mitochondria also control the amount of water, calcium, and other substances within the cell; break down and recycle proteins, fats, and carbohydrates; and form urea.

The mitochondria have their own genetic structure, different from that of the cell. Some scientists think they evolved separately and live in symbiosis with the cell.

Organic compounds in cells

carbohydrates	proteins	lipids	nucleic acids
sugars	enzymes	fats	DNA
starches	collagen	oils	RNA
cellulose	keratin	waxes	

Some structural components of cells and their principal functions

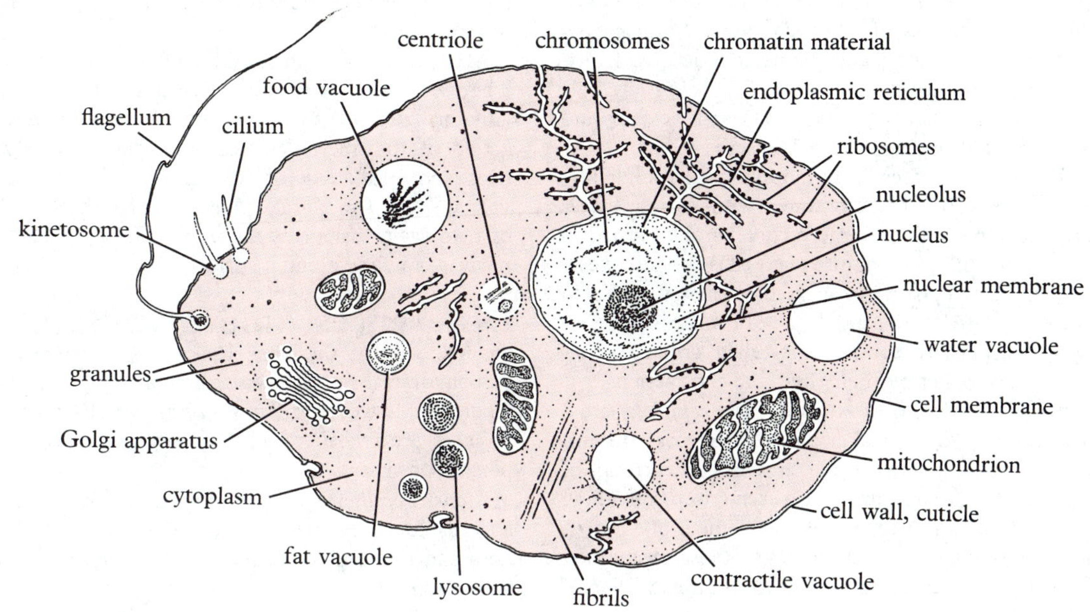

	Structure	*Function*
Nucleus	chromosomes	gene carriers, ultimate control of cell activities
	nucleolus	auxiliary to protein synthesis
	nuclear membrane	traffic control to and from cytoplasm
Cytoplasm	endoplasmic reticulum	secretion channels, connection between cell parts, attachment surfaces
	mitochondria	site of respiration
	ribosomes	site of protein synthesis
	Golgi bodies	site of specific secretion synthesis
	lysosomes	stores of hydrolytic enzymes
	chloroplasts	site of photosynthesis
	centrioles	auxiliary to cell division
	kinetosomes	anchor and control of flagella, cilia
	myofibrils	contraction
	neurofibrils	conduction
	granules, vacuoles	transport, storage, processing centers
Surface	plasma membrane	traffic control to and from cell
	cell wall	support, protection, cell shape
	cuticles, pellicles	support, protection, waterproofing
	cilia, flagella	locomotion, current creation, feeding
	pseudopodia	locomotion, feeding, phagocytosis

Plastids and vacuoles. *Plastids* are special organelles found in most plants and one-celled organisms. They are associated with the formation and storage of substances important in the metabolism of that cell. The green pigment chlorophyll occurs in *chloroplasts*, which are the sites of photosynthesis. *Chromoplasts* manufacture and store the pigments that give fruits, vegetables, and leaves their color. *Leucoplasts* are colorless and are the sites where fats and proteins are stored and glucose is converted to starch.

Vacuoles are cavities in the cytoplasm surrounded by membranes. They contain water with various other substances in solution. Large vacuoles are not found in most animal cells, but mature plant cells contain one or more in the cytoplasm. Small vacuoles may function to digest food, store food, and dispose of wastes. The *contractile vacuoles* of some single-celled organisms remove excess water by their rhythmic contractions.

Centrioles and kinetosomes. The *centrioles* are a pair of small, cylindrical bodies that lie near the nucleus. A centriole consists of a cluster of nine groups of delicate tubelike structures, with each group containing three tubules. The elements of one member of a centriole pair always lie at right angles to those of another. The centrioles play an important role in the division of the cell.

Some cells have organelles called *cilia.* At the base of each cilium is a *kinetosome*, the structure of which resembles a centriole. Some biologists think that both centrioles and kinetosomes function as units of locomotion within a cell, similar to the muscle cells of multicellular animals.

Microtubules and microfilaments. *Microtubules* are a series of long, thin cylinders that support, stiffen, and give shape to cells. They also assist in transporting substances in and out of the cell and in cellular movement. The cilia of certain cells are formed of bundles of microtubules.

Microfilaments are threadlike fibers made of protein. They seem to have the ability to contract like muscle. Cilia are attached to microfilaments. The contracting action of the microfilaments cause the cilia to wave back and forth. Microfilaments also seem to be involved in the formation of *pseudopodia*—the streaming of cytoplasm that gives the impression that the organism is crawling along a surface.

Differences among cells.

All cells are made up of the same basic substances: proteins, carbohydrates, nucleic acids, lipids, water, and salts. There are, however, differences among cells; these differences are related to whether certain organelles are present or absent.

Moneran cells are prokaryotic. The chromosome material floats throughout the cytoplasm. Monerans have no organelles that are surrounded by membranes, such as mitochondria. These prokaryotic cells cannot combine with each other to form multicellular organisms.

Protist cells are eukaryotic. They have a nucleus surrounded by a nuclear membrane. They also have many complex organelles that are separated from the cytoplasm by membranes. These organelles can be found in both plant and animal cells.

Fungus cells are all eukaryotic and can combine to

Differences among cells

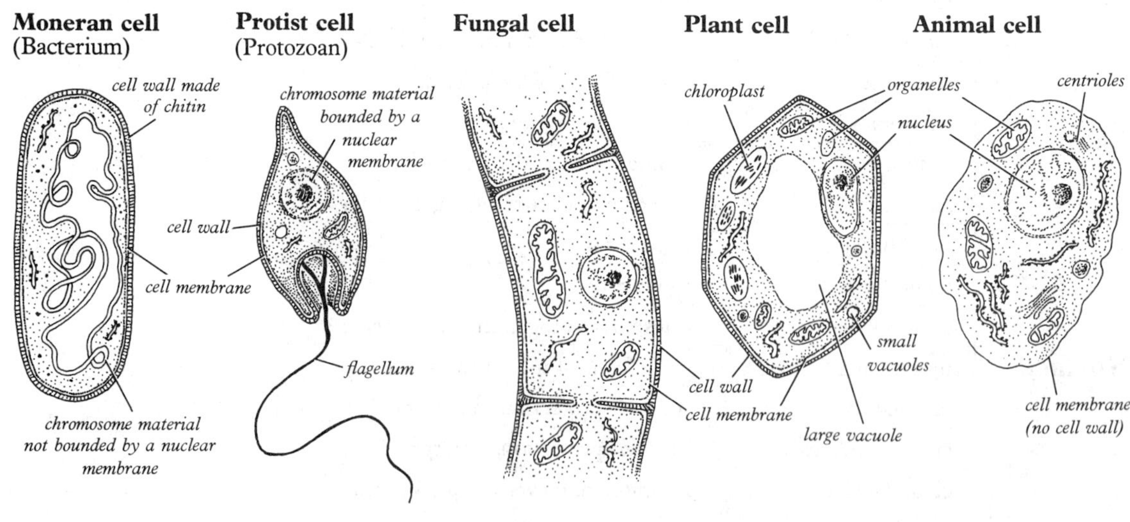

form simple, multicellular organisms. These cells are bounded by a cell wall made of chitin. Each fungus cell is usually multinucleated. The cell walls do not completely close when the cells grow and develop. Cytoplasm can circulate freely from cell to cell.

Plant cells are eukaryotic and have rigid cell walls made of cellulose. Each cell has a nucleus and many organelles. Plastids are found only in plant cells and in some protists. Each plant cell also has a large vacuole containing salt and water to help to keep the cell wall rigid and give support to the leaves and stem.

Animal cells are also eukaryotic. They have no cell walls and no plastids. Centrioles are organelles unique to animal cells.

Microscopes

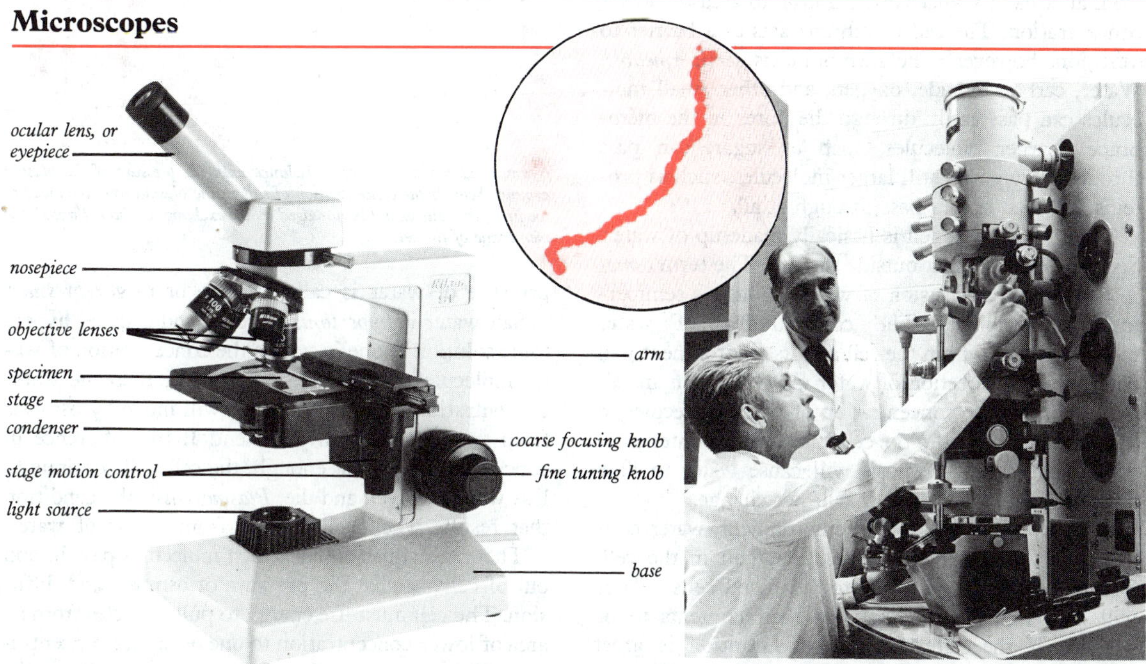

A modern optical microscope, shown at the left, provides its own illumination and a place for taking photographs. The electron microscope, shown at the right, is capable of greater resolution than the optical microscope. The inset photomicrograph of a streptococcus was made with an electron microscope.

For almost 300 years, everything that was learned about cells came from studies with the light microscope. Samples of material were cut into thin sections and stained with various dyes. The stains made certain parts of the cell show up more clearly, but they also tended to kill the cell. In the past few years, new tools and techniques have been developed that allow biologists higher magnifications, greater resolving power, and the ability to study living tissue. (The resolving power of a microscope is the limit of its useful magnification. Beyond this limit, the image is blurred.)

The Phase-Contrast Microscope is used to study living cells. This microscope is constructed in a way that causes a portion of the light passing through to slow down relative to the rest of the light. This portion of light is "out of phase." The changes in refractive power of this light show up as differences in light and shade.

Electron microscopes use electrons to form images instead of light waves. Electrons travel with a wave motion similar to that of light, but their wavelengths are over 100,000 times shorter. Therefore, their resolving power is much greater. In general, an electron microscope is an evacuated tube with an electron gun at one end. The gun accelerates a beam of electrons, which is directed onto a specimen by electromagnetic and electrostatic fields that act as lenses. The electrons interact with the atoms of the specimen, enter other lenses, and finally form an image on a viewing screen or on photographic film. The screen glows when struck by the electron beam and a camera beneath the screen records the images. Most instruments can cover a range in magnification from 50× to 800,000×. However, standard *transmission* electron microscopes, as well as standard light microscopes, can focus only a limited depth of the specimen.

The *scanning* electron microscope is used to study the surface of a specimen. A beam of electrons moves over the surface, producing an effect similar to that of a television camera. This provides a very detailed three-dimensional picture of a living subject. Magnification can range from 10× to 200,000×.

Cell functions

The materials needed by a cell to carry on its functions must come from outside the cell. Many of the substances produced by the cell, as well as the waste products of its activities, must pass out of the cell.

Diffusion is a process by which molecules will move from an area of higher concentration to areas of lower concentration. The cell membrane acts as a barrier to diffusion, however. The membrane is *semipermeable*. Water, carbon dioxide, oxygen, and other small molecules can pass easily through the pores in the membrane. Larger molecules, such as sugar, can pass through slowly, and still larger molecules, such as proteins and fats, cannot pass through at all.

The interior of a cell is basically made up of water. So is the environment outside the cell. The term *osmosis* describes the diffusion of water through a semipermeable membrane. The concentration of water molecules both within the cell and its environment will determine the direction of water movement. In an *isotonic* solution, the concentration of water molecules in the solution is equal to the concentration of water molecules in the cell. Osmosis will cause water to flow both in and out and the cell will not change.

In a *hypotonic* solution or environment, water concentration is higher in the solution than in the cell. Distilled water is hypotonic to red blood cells. Water will flow into the cells causing their contents to be diluted. If the difference in concentration is great enough, water will continue to move into the cells until they rupture. The cell walls of plant cells prevent them from rupturing. The excess water causes them to stiffen instead. The stiffness of plants that is caused by pressure of water is called *turgor*, or *turgor pressure*.

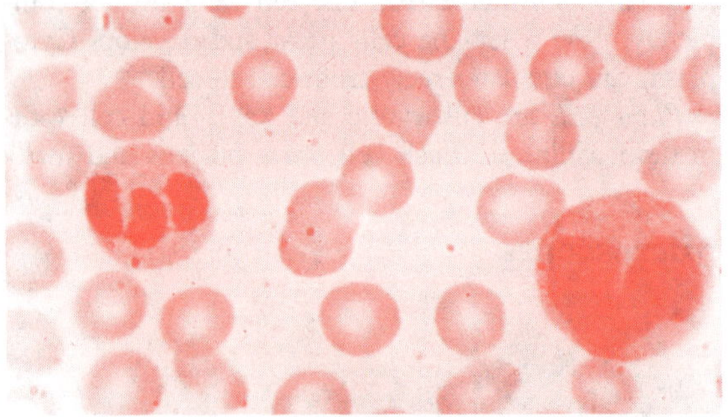

Normal red blood cells are in balance with the pressure of the plasma around them. If the concentration of salt in the plasma were too great or too little, the cells would be damaged by the exchange of fluids through the membrane of the cell.

Salt water is *hypertonic* to red blood cells. A hypertonic solution is one in which the concentration of water molecules in the solution is lower than the water concentration in the cell. Water will move by osmosis from the cell to its environment. If the difference in concentration is great enough, the cell will continue to lose water, shrivel, and die. *Plasmolysis* is the condition that results when cells shrink from a loss of water.

There are situations in which molecules pass in and out of cells against the pressure of osmosis and diffusion. The cell must use energy to pull particles from an area of lower concentration to one of higher concentration. This process, called *active transport*, allows the cell to eliminate substances that would be harmful in high concentrations and to bring in food particles in high concentrations.

Respiration

Cells perform chemical work, which includes synthesizing molecules and other chemical reactions that allow the cell to perform its activities. All cells obtain their required energy from the chemical bonds of the same molecule, ATP (adenosine triphosphate). In addition, all cells manufacture their own ATP. Energy is required to form ATP. The main source of this energy is the compound *glucose*. Certain organisms, called *autotrophs*, can transform light energy into the chemical energy of glucose, and use glucose to form the chemical bond energy of ATP. Other organisms, *heterotrophs*, cannot use light energy and must use energy in the bonds of organic molecules formed by other cells. Heterotrophic organisms digest or break down these large molecules into simpler glucose molecules.

ATP

Adenosine | **Triphosphate**

high-energy bonds

NH_2

adenine

ribose

phosphate *phosphate* *phosphate*

ATP

ADP + energy + phosphate

Photosynthesis. Autotrophic cells are found in green plants. Certain bacteria are also autotrophic. The structures within autotrophic cells that allow them to transform light energy are the *chloroplasts*. There may be as many as 50 chloroplasts in the cell of a leaf. Photosynthesis begins with the absorption of light by the *chlorophyll* in the chloroplasts.

Photosynthesis takes place in two steps or phases. The first phase requires the presence of light. During this *light reaction* phase, red wavelengths of light are absorbed by chlorophyll. This energy is used to split water molecules. The chemical energy released by this reaction is stored in two compounds called ATP and NADP. This stored energy is used in the second step of photosynthesis, which does not require light. The *dark reaction* involves synthesizing needed compounds. The energy stored in the chemical bonds of ATP and NADP is used to combine carbon dioxide with other molecules to form glucose, other carbohydrates, amino acids, fats, and proteins. Photosynthesis can be described by the following equation:

$$\text{carbon dioxide} + \text{water} \xrightarrow{\text{light + chlorophyll}} \text{glucose} + \text{oxygen} + \text{water}$$

$$6CO_2 + 12H_2O \longrightarrow C_6H_{12}O_6 + 6O_2 + 6H_2O$$

ATP and respiration. ATP is the energy-storing molecule of the cell. A molecule of ATP consists of an adenosine group with three phosphate groups bonded to it and forming a "tail." The bond between the second and third phosphate groups is the high energy bond. When this bond is broken, energy is released and the third phosphate group is freed. ADP (adenosine diphosphate) is formed. When energy is available, ADP will combine with a free phosphate, reforming ATP. Energy is thus stored for future use.

The sum total of all chemical reactions that take food molecules apart and transfer their energy to ATP is called *respiration*. Respiration is described in two steps or phases, *anaerobic* and *aerobic*. All cells are capable of performing the anaerobic phase; most cells can perform both phases.

Anaerobic respiration does not require oxygen. In this phase, glucose molecules undergo a series of chemical reactions. A glucose molecule containing six carbon atoms is split into two molecules of pyruvic acid ($C_3H_4O_3$), each containing three carbons. The energy from two molecules of ATP is used during these reactions. However, four molecules of ATP are formed by this process. For every molecule of glucose split

Photosynthesis and respiration

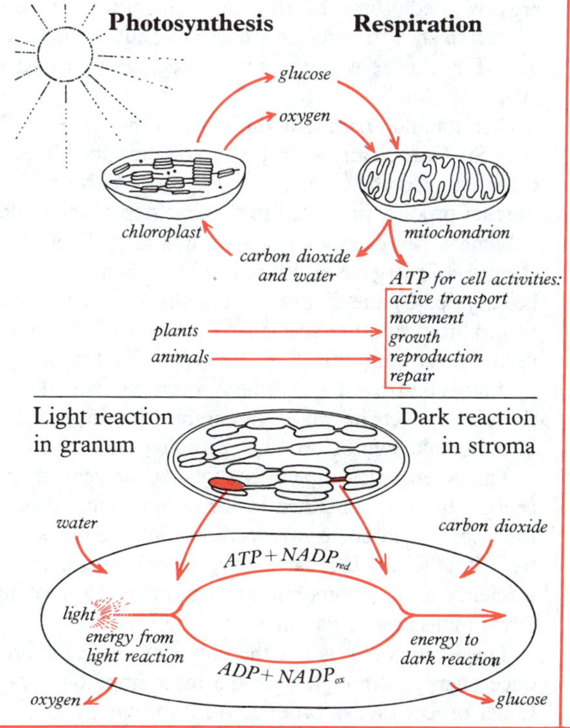

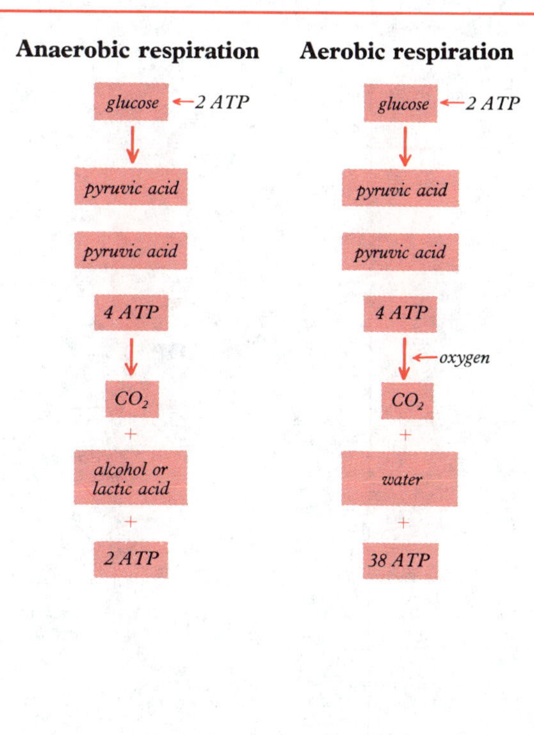

into two molecules of pyruvic acid, there is a gain of two molecules of ATP. This anaerobic phase is similar to those reactions that occur during the fermentation of yeast. The *glycolysis* reaction in muscle cells is also anaerobic. In this series of reactions, the starch glycogen is split into two glucose molecules. These are split into molecules of lactic acid.

Aerobic respiration is the second phase of cellular respiration. Oxygen is required to complete the chemical reactions involved. In this phase, the two pyruvic acid molecules formed in phase one are broken down into carbon dioxide and water. When the bonds of pyruvic acid are broken, 38 molecules of ATP have been formed from the one original glucose molecule. Sixty percent of the available energy in a glucose molecule has been made available to the cell. Carbon dioxide is given off at different stages in these reactions. Water is formed at the end, when hydrogen made available from the decomposition of the pyruvic acid combines with oxygen. Without oxygen, these reactions could not be completed and the death of cells would result, although cells live for a time using anaerobic respiration.

Enzymes and respiration. An important property of chemical reactions in the cell is that they usually occur in sequence. Most of the chemical changes take place in steps. Often 20 or more individual reactions are involved. This "production line" saves both energy and raw materials and provides the energy to produce the next reaction. A sequence of reactions enables the cell to make full use of the compounds and energy available.

Chemical compounds called *enzymes* provide the energy to start the reaction and to control the rate of the reactions within the temperature range tolerated by the substance within the cell. Enzymes are proteins and act as *catalysts*. They cause chemical reactions to occur without being changed themselves. In addition, these organic catalysts are specific. One enzyme can only catalyze one specific reaction.

In some situations, enzymes can function only when associated with smaller molecules called *coenzymes*. Certain B vitamins are coenzymes and are essential to our diets because they cannot be synthesized by cells. Enzymes are proteins and are synthesized in the cell by the series of reactions involving DNA and RNA. All energy transformations are dependent upon the ability of DNA to implement the genetic code of the cell. The molecules that react with an enzyme attach to it, and are called the *substrate*. The enzyme-molecule combination is called the *enzyme-substrate complex*.

Enzymes, coenzymes, ATP, and vitamins function in such a way that some of the basic materials needed for respiration are available at the end of the process as well as at the beginning. In other words, although energy is used, some of the same chemicals that are needed to start the process are also a result of the process. For this reason, the set of reactions is called a *cycle*.

One common name for this cycle is the *Krebs cycle*, after Sir Hans Adolf Krebs, who first described it. Another name is the *citric-acid cycle*, since citric acid is the first product produced in the first step of the cycle.

Some other chemicals needed in the cycle are destroyed as energy is produced. These chemicals must be supplied by the diet of the organism if they cannot be produced in other specialized cells because they are destroyed at each "turn" of the cycle. The key chemical that is destroyed each time is a combination of acetic acid and a coenzyme. This combination is produced in the breakdown of proteins, carbohydrates, and fats.

The Krebs cycle liberates about 60 percent of the energy that was contained in the original molecules of the acetic acid-coenzyme combination. This is extremely efficient. It is far better, for example, than the efficiency of an automobile getting energy by breaking down molecules of gasoline.

The Krebs cycle is not the only way that cells produce energy, although it is the most important way. Other processes also produce ATP for energy.

The ADP-ATP cycle

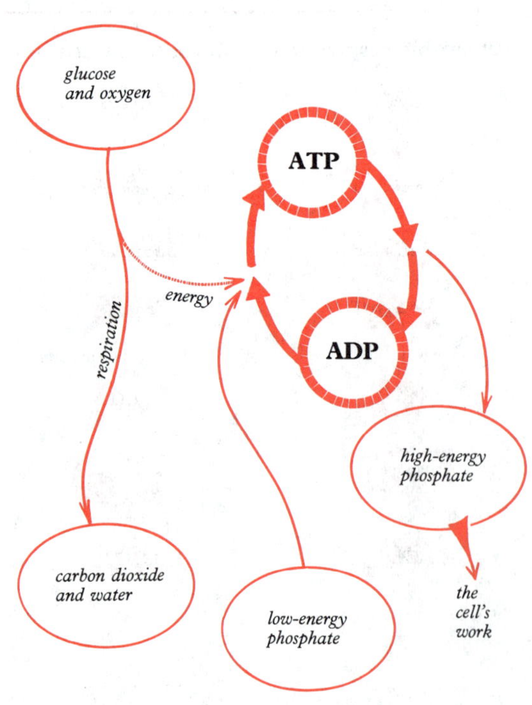

DNA

DNA, or deoxyribonucleic acid, is found only in the chromosomes of the cell. The amount of DNA is remarkably constant from cell to cell within an organism and within a single species. Only the egg cells and sperm cells contain a different amount: half the normal amount of DNA (and half the number of chromosomes) found in other body cells.

Proteins and ribonucleic acid (RNA), which are also found in the chromosomes, vary considerably in the amounts found in different tissues within a species. However, they are associated with DNA in carrying and transferring information.

The Watson-Crick model. DNA is a polymer with a high molecular weight, a giant molecule formed from a few simple molecules linked repeatedly by chemical bonds. The repeating units that form the molecule are nucleotides, each built from similar components: a phosphate group, a 5-carbon sugar, deoxyribose, and a nitrogenous base. The base may be any one of four—the purines adenine (A) or guanine (G) or the pyrimidines cytosine (C) and thymine (T). The nucleotides are connected by a bond between the phosphate group of one and the adjacent sugar (deoxyribose) of the next.

Various studies, including x-ray diffraction analyses by Maurice Wilkins, led James Watson and F.H.C. Crick to propose in 1953 the *double helix* structure of the DNA molecule. A double helix is something like a twisted ladder or zipper; the sides are made of the linked sugar-phosphate backbone, and the rungs are the bases (purines or pyrimidines). The sequence of bases in one strand determines the base sequence in the complementary strand—A matches with T, C matches with G. These bases are held together by weak hydrogen bonds, making the "ladder" firm but still able to separate during mitosis.

With this model (for which Watson, Crick, and Wilkins won the Nobel Prize in 1962), it is possible to explain how genetic information is duplicated and transmitted. When the strands of the double helix "unzip," or separate, each strand becomes a mold, or *template,* that governs the replication of its new complementary strand. The result is two DNA molecules, each identical with the original because each new strand is based on a specified pattern.

DNA replication

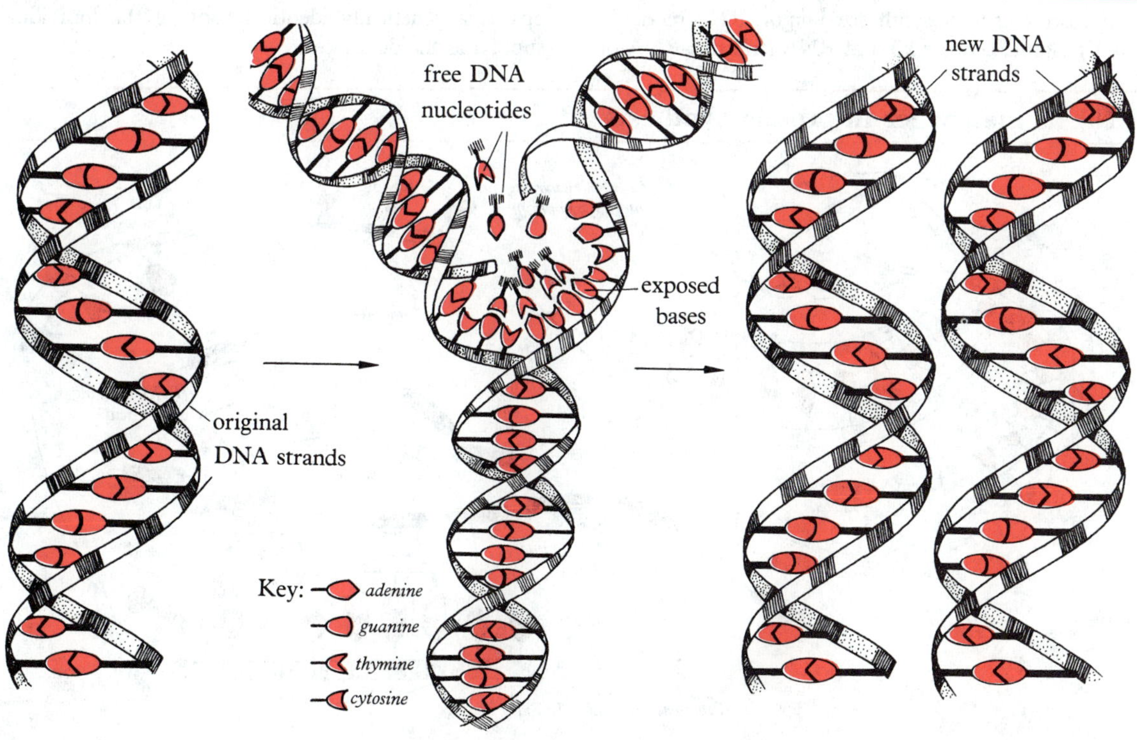

The genetic code.

DNA, according to the Watson-Crick model, carries genetic information in a kind of code, which depends on the varying sequence of the four bases in relation to each other—in effect, a four-letter alphabet. Since there are ten base pairs in each complete turn of the double helix (which is only a small part of the entire large molecule), the theoretical number of possible combinations in a turn is 4^{10} or 1,048,576. Thus, the storage potential for different items of genetic information is vast, even with only four bases to work with.

The information carried by DNA must be translated into the formation of proteins, for DNA itself is inactive in the metabolic processes of the cell. So the DNA "message" carrying the coded instructions is given to the RNA within the nucleus. Messenger RNA then transmits the information to the place in the cytoplasm where proteins are synthesized. These protein-producing areas, in the ribosomes, are another form of RNA; there a template is formed according to the coded instructions.

Proteins themselves are long chains of amino acids hooked together by peptide bonds in which the 20-odd basic amino acids are repeated several times and arranged in different orders. Even the smallest protein is a chain of 124 amino acids. The protein chains (polypeptides) form a helix that folds into a definite shape, determined by the sequence of amino acids in the chain.

For proteins to be synthesized on thc RNA model in the ribosome, another kind of RNA (transfer-RNA or t-RNA) must pick up the right amino acid and fit it to the right place in the template. When the amino acid sequence has been established, peptide bonds are formed, and the new protein "unzips" from the template to carry out its functions in the cell.

RNA structure.

Not as much is known of the structure of RNA as of DNA, though RNA plays a vital role in carrying the information from DNA and in translating the message into protein structure. Like DNA, RNA is a long-chain giant molecule (a polymer); its components are similar except that the sugar in RNA is ribose (not deoxyribose) and one of the pyrimidine bases that form the nucleotides is uracil (U) instead of thymine.

Studies of RNA have concluded that its code is read in groups of three bases (triplets or trinucleotides), with each triplet (say, GUU or AUC) coding the formation of a given amino acid. Experiments have been done to discover which triplet combinations govern the formation of which amino acids; it has been found that several different triplets may code the same amino acid.

Evidence suggests that the genetic code is universal; that is, more or less the same code governs genetic information and protein building in all living species. Interest is building in the possibility of cloning, an asexual reproduction achieved by transplanting the nucleus of a donor's cell into a fertile egg cell, whose nucleus has been removed. The cloned offspring develops as a genetically identical copy of the individual supplying the donor cell.

RNA as messenger in protein synthesis

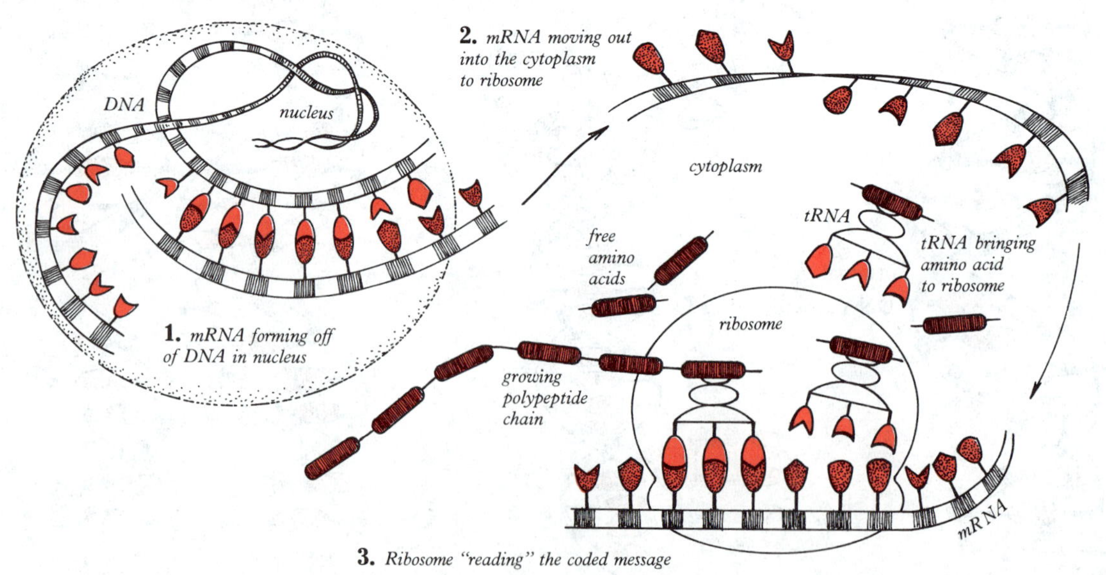

Reproduction

All cells are derived from other cells. Cells reproduce themselves by a general process called *fission*. Simple cells such as the monera seem to pinch in half to form two new cells. In eukaryotic cells, the major aspect of cell division is the duplication of the nucleus with its DNA and chromosomes in a process called *mitosis*. In addition to duplication of the nucleus, mitosis also involves duplication of the structures within the cytoplasm. Mitosis as a term refers to both nuclear and cell division. Because of mitosis, all body cells of an organism have identical molecules of DNA, and the number of chromosomes characteristic of each species remains constant.

Mitosis is a continuous process but is described in terms of five phases.

Mitosis

Interphase. This is the time between cell divisions. The amount of time a cell spends in interphase varies with the species, its age, temperature, and other factors. Most cells divide on a regular basis in order to repair or replace other cells. During interphase, each cell begins to grow to mature size, and RNA and protein synthesis occurs. DNA replication begins when the cell reaches a particular size. Each chromosome duplicates itself to form identical sister chromosomes. The DNA is duplicated, more proteins are synthesized, and the cell continues to increase in size. The cell becomes ready to divide and interphase ends.

Prophase. The chromosomes condense or coil into short, thick structures that become visible under a light microscope. The membrane around the nucleus breaks down and disappears. If centrioles are present, they begin to migrate to opposite regions of the cell, forming two poles. A football-shaped structure, the *spindle*, made of tubelike structures, forms. The spindle fibers form between the poles. The spindle forms in plant cells without centrioles. The chromosomes begin to move toward the middle of the spindle.

Metaphase. The chromosomes line up along the middle of the spindle, apparently pushed or pulled along by the spindle fibers.

Anaphase. The sister chromosomes separate from each other. Each daughter chromosome, as they are now called, migrates toward opposite poles. The chromosomes often have a V or J shape.

Telophase. The daughter chromosomes are at opposite poles of the spindle, and the spindle starts to break down. The individual chromosomes become thinner, longer, and less visible. The nuclear membrane reforms around each set of chromosomes. The centrioles replicate. A furrow or groove appears in the membrane of animal cells and a cell plate forms in plant cells. The animal cell furrow curves inward until a complete membrane separates the two daughter cells. The plant cell plate expands until a wall is formed that separates the two cells. A new interphase then begins in each daughter cell.

Mitosis

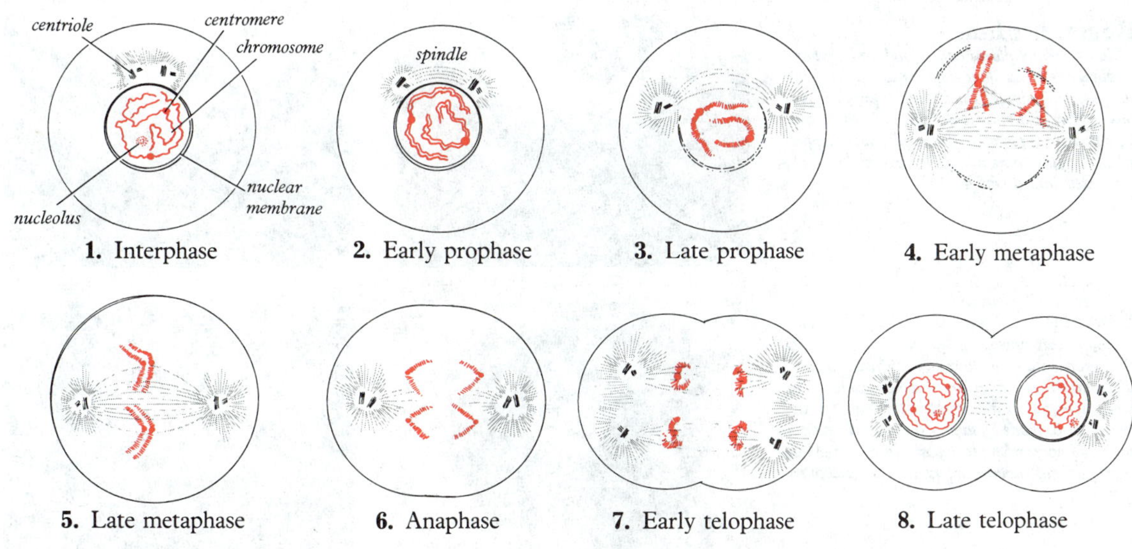

1. Interphase **2.** Early prophase **3.** Late prophase **4.** Early metaphase **5.** Late metaphase **6.** Anaphase **7.** Early telophase **8.** Late telophase

Reproduction of organisms. Cells reproduce by mitosis. Organisms reproduce either asexually or sexually. There are three types of asexual reproduction. *Vegetative* reproduction is common to many plants and some animals. In vegetative reproduction, another organism will develop from a portion of an organism that has been removed from it. Potato tubers can be cut up and planted to produce potatoes; a branch of a willow tree can grow into a new tree; the animal hydra develops buds. The buds are developing hydra that eventually separate and become independent organisms.

Regeneration means the regrowth of missing parts. If a starfish or a planarium is cut into several pieces, each may develop into an independent organism. Some organisms can only regenerate missing parts, however.

Some organisms produce specialized cells that can grow into complete organisms. These cells are called *spores*. Bread mold and mushrooms reproduce thousands of organisms by this method.

Organisms that have formed from asexual reproduction have the same exact DNA structure as their parent, and each "daughter" organism carries the exact hereditary information that is found in the parent.

bone muscle skin nerve gland blood other cells
sperm
egg
fertilized egg
immature reproductive cell
sperm or egg

A. *Fertilization produces a cell with 2n chromosomes—the diploid number.*

B. *Most of the new organism's cells maintain the 2n number by mitosis.*

C. *But the cells that divide to produce sperms or eggs halve the chromosome number by meiosis.*

Many organisms produce specialized cells that differ from spores in that they do not develop directly into a new organism. These cells, called *gametes*, will form a new individual only after they have fused or become fertilized by another gamete. Fertilization is the key event in sexual reproduction. Organisms formed by sexual reproduction are truly new and different from their parents since the organism receives DNA from each parent. To accomplish this another form of cell division, called *meiosis*, is required.

Types of asexual reproduction

Vegetative reproduction

Both plants and animals can reproduce "vegetatively." The hydra is a tiny water animal. It grows buds that break off to form "daughter" hydra. In the garden, a familiar example is the strawberry, which produces runners that root to form new plants.

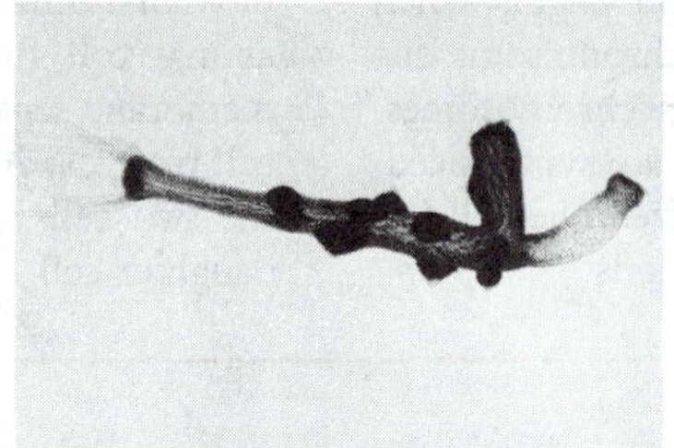

Regeneration

Although many plants can reproduce by regeneration, one of the most familiar examples is the starfish, an animal. Since starfish prey on oysters, oyster fishermen used to catch them and tear them into pieces. This practice was stopped when the fishermen realized that each piece regenerated into a new starfish.

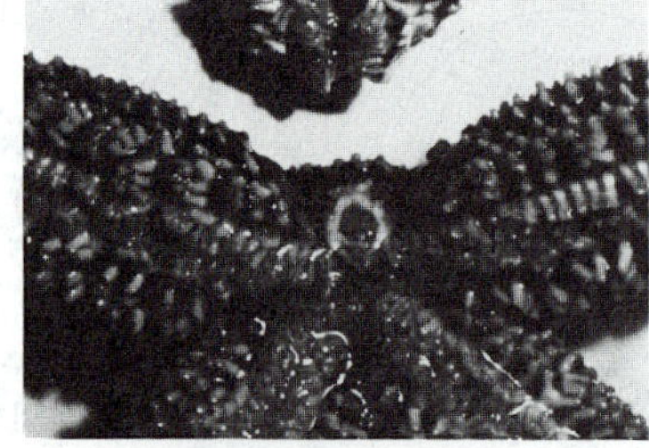

Spores

Many plants reproduce by spores, special cells that grow into new plants if they reach a suitable environment. A mushroom produces so many spores that a characteristic print (shown here) can be made by laying the mushroom on a sheet of paper, where it deposits its spores. Most spores do not survive. Ferns also reproduce by spores.

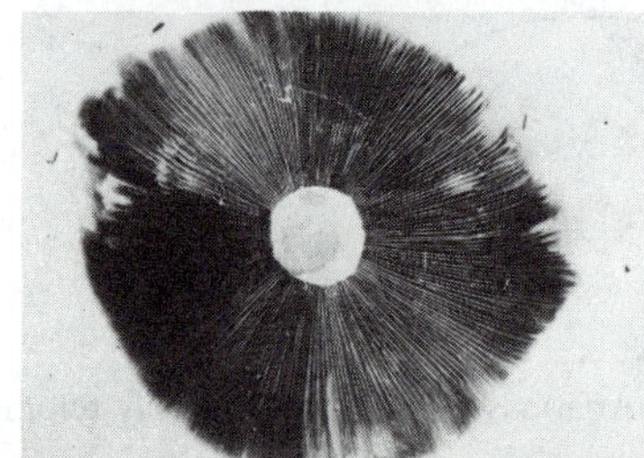

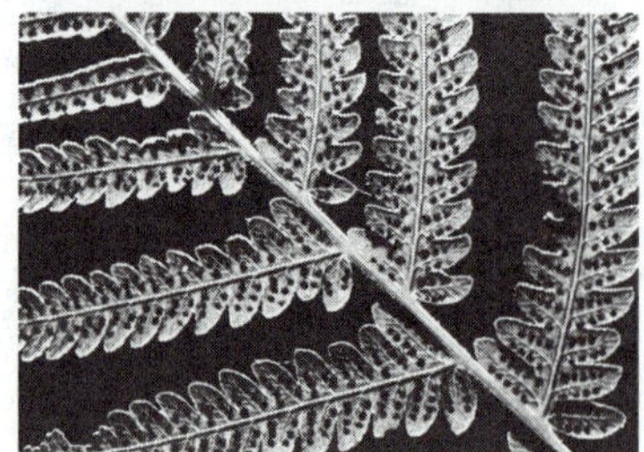

Meiosis. The chromosomes in each cell occur in pairs. In humans there are 46 chromosomes or 23 pairs. If the gametes (usually called egg and sperm) fuse, the chromosome number would double. Meiosis is a process of cell division unique to gametes where the chromosome number is halved. In this way, the proper chromosome number is ensured after fertilization occurs.

Meiosis differs from mitosis in a number of ways. In meiosis there are two cell divisions resulting in four daughter cells; the chromosomes can exchange parts; the chromosomes duplicate only once, even though there are two cell divisions; the chromosomes line up and randomly move to either pole. In this way, each gamete is unique and has one-half the chromosome number of its species. Meiosis occurs in two stages.

First meiotic division. Each chromosome has duplicated itself. Each replicated chromosome seeks out its sister. Frequently, chromosome pairs will become entangled and exchange sections of DNA. This process is called *crossing over.* The duplicated chromosomes pair up, forming a four-stranded group called a *tetrad.* As tetrads are forming, the nuclear membrane is breaking down and spindle fibers are forming. The tetrads migrate toward the center and line up randomly. Complete chromosomes gather at each pole and the cytoplasm divides either by furrowing or forming a cell plate. Each new cell now has half the chromosome number of its species (in humans, 23).

Second meiotic division. This phase is very similar to mitosis. Spindle fibers form, the paired chromosomes line up at the center of the cell, and the spindle fiber begins to draw the chromosomes apart. The chromosomes group and migrate together at each pole. The cytoplasm again divides. Four daughter cells, each with half the chromosome number, have formed. Usually in male organisms the cytoplasm divides evenly and all four cells function as sperm cells. In females, the cytoplasm divides unequally with one cell receiving the majority of the cytoplasm. This cell becomes the functioning gamete.

Meiosis produces organisms that are genetically different. Crossing over and the random assortment of chromosomes ensures that each daughter cell will be different. Additional genetic mixing will occur at fertilization when the chromosome number is restored.

Meiosis

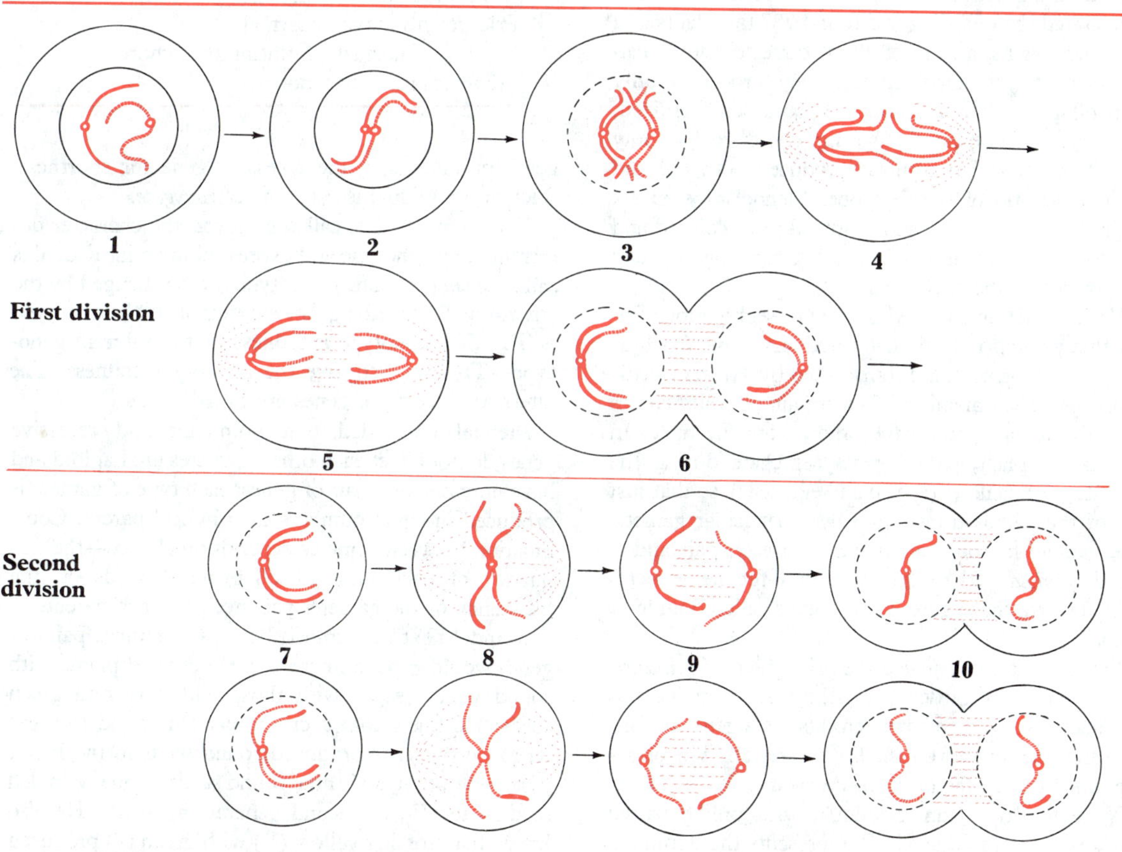

Genetics

The study of the inheritance of biological characteristics in living things—characteristics that are passed from one generation to the next—is called *genetics*. What is inherited is a code message in the genetic material (genes) of egg and sperm. The code directs embryonic development and organization of cells into tissues and organs; in addition, it directs the function of each tissue and organ. This development is also influenced by the external and internal environment. Thus, an organism is the product of interaction between genetic material and environment.

Mendelian genetics. Gregor Johann Mendel (1822–1884), an Austrian monk, analyzed the basic laws of inheritance in 1866. He proved that hereditary traits are transmitted by pairs of distinct units, later called *genes*, which reshuffle, segregate, and redistribute, rather than blend, in offspring.

Mendel used garden peas in his experiments because they hybridize easily. When a purebred tall plant was crossed with a purebred short plant, all hybrid offspring were tall, no matter which type was the mother and which the father. The hybrids self-fertilized. Mendel counted the offspring and found 787 tall plants and 277 short plants, a ratio of about three to one. When the short plants self-fertilized, they produced only short offspring, but when the tall plants self-fertilized, there were two types of offspring: one-third had only tall offspring, and two-thirds produced both tall and short in a ratio of three to one. Mendel crossed six other characters: round and wrinkled peas, colored and uncolored flowers, and yellow and green peas. He had approximately the same results.

Mendel then formulated the law of segregation. Today this principal states that hereditary traits (such as tallness or shortness) are transmitted by *zygotes* (fertilized eggs). One member of each pair of traits comes from the female parent; the other, from the male. In the mature plant, paired genes segregate during the formation of gametes (sperm and egg cells), so that just one of the pair is transmitted by a particular gamete. The gamete has only one gene from each pair and is called *haploid*. When the male and female gametes unite to form the zygote, the zygote is called double or *diploid*.

Mendel's studies showed the principle of *dominance*. For instance, in garden peas, the trait of tallness is dominant over shortness; when there is a gene for tallness and one for shortness, all peas are tall. The opposite, unexpressed factor is *recessiveness*.

To a geneticist, an individual with unlike paired genes is represented as Tt. T represents the dominant gene for tallness; t, the recessive gene for shortness. Such an individual is called a *heterozygote*.

Genetic makeup is called *genotype*; the character determined by genotype and expressed in an individual is called *phenotype*. The phenotype can be changed by the environment, but the genotype cannot. If the genotype is TT, the phenotype is tallness, but a different genotype—Tt—can also give the phenotype tallness. The alternative forms of genes are called *alleles*.

Mendel concluded that dominant and recessive genes do not affect each other; gametes are haploid and have only one of a pair of genes; each type of gamete is produced in equal numbers by a hybrid parent. Combination between gametes depends on chance—the frequency of each class of offspring depends on the frequency of the gametes produced by each parent.

Mendel next determined how two or more pairs of genes would behave in crosses. He crossed plants with round yellow seeds with those with wrinkled green seeds. He knew that a cross between round (R) and wrinkled (r) seeds produced round seeds in the F_1, or first, generation, and three round seeds to one wrinkled seed in the F_2, or second generation, plants. He also knew that crossing yellow (Y) with green (y) produced

Some traits in man that are inherited in a simple Mendelian fashion

Recessive	*Dominant*
red hair	not red hair
white forelock	normal
normal	premature grayness of hair
normal	no iris
normal	glaucoma
extreme myopia	normal
night blindness	normal
normal	congenital cataract
albinism	normal
polydactyl	normal
normal	split foot
normal	no incisor teeth
normal	rootless teeth
no A or B antigens	A and B antigens
normal	sickle cell
no Rh antigen	Rh antigen
attached ear lobe	free ear lobe
normal size	achondroplastic dwarf
St. Vitus' dance	normal
Friedreich's ataxia	normal
normal	Huntington's chorea
diabetes mellitus	normal

all yellow seeds in the F_1 and three yellow to one green in the F_2 generation. This showed the dominance of roundness and yellowness over their respective contrasting alleles. Thus, when Mendel crossed round yellow with wrinkled green, the first generation (F_1) produced all round yellow seeds.

In the second generation (F_2), a more complicated assortment of differing seed types resulted:

Type	*Proportion*
Round yellow	$\frac{9}{16}$
Round green	$\frac{3}{16}$
Wrinkled yellow	$\frac{3}{16}$
Wrinkled green	$\frac{1}{16}$

Two combinations, round green and wrinkled yellow, not present in either the parents or the first generation, have appeared. This result can be explained by Mendel's law of independent assortment, which states that members of one pair of genes segregate independently of other pairs.

Mendel also tested F_2 plants to determine whether all of a single phenotype class, such as round yellow, were alike in genotype. According to his hypothesis, there should be four different genotypes in this group: RR, YY; RR, Yy; Rr, YY; and Rr, Yy. When F_2 plants self-fertilized, he found four classes of round yellow seeded plants; the ratios fitted expectations. The breeding behavior of the F_2 round green, wrinkled yellow, and wrinkled green seeded plants also fitted the hypothesis that each pair of genes segregates independently from other pairs of genes and is transmitted independently to the next generation.

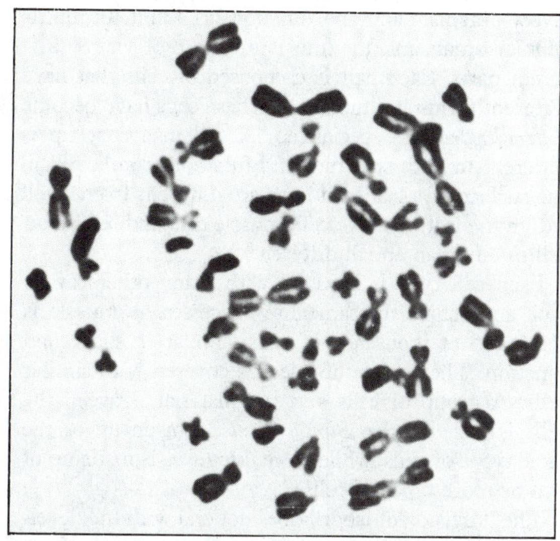

Not all traits that are thought of as hereditary are caused by the genes. Down's syndrome results from a defect in chromosomes, not from the genetic composition of the parents. Shown here are the chromosomes of a person with Down's syndrome.

Mendelian square

Phenotype parents

RRYY *round yellow* — rryy wrinkled green

Genotype 1st generation

RrYy *round yellow*

RY Ry rY ry

Gametes 2nd generation

	RY	Ry	rY	ry
ry	RrYy	Rryy	rrYy	rryy
rY	RrYY	RrYy	rrYY	rrYy
Ry	RRYy	RRyy	RrYy	Rryy
RY	RRYY	RRYy	RrYY	RrYy

Key:
R *round*
r *wrinkled*
Y *yellow*
y *green*

Sex-linked inheritance

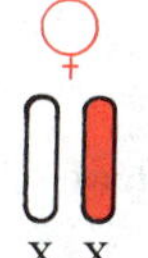

A sex-linked gene is passed on in a family through "criss-cross" transmission. A woman who has the hemophilia gene will be normal when her second X chromosome has a normal gene. But she is a carrier.

One of every two of her sons may be a bleeder. The bleeder is the son who receives an X from her that carries a hemophilia gene. His Y has no normal gene to block the effect of the X gene. All his sons (who receive only his Y chromosome) are normal.

All his daughters, though, are carriers like their grandmother. The process of transmitting the gene begins again in their families.

Multicellular organization

Every organism acts and functions as a unit. In multicellular organisms, the unit is made up of visibly different parts. Each part is composed of cells that have different forms and functions. These cells have become *differentiated* and specialized. A cell in a root tip is different in both structure and function from a cell in the surface of a leaf, and both are different from a cell within the leaf. A nerve cell, muscle cell, and red blood cell in a human are all different.

Each cell type is grouped with many others of its type and shares the same life processes. A muscle is composed of thousands of cells, similar in shape and function. The surface of a leaf is covered with similar cells. A group of cells and the material between the cells is called *tissue. Simple tissue* is made up of the same types of cells, while *composite tissue* is made up of two or more types of cells.

The "division of labor" does not end with the development of tissue. In complex organisms, groups of tissues are combined to form *organs.* An organ is a group of tissues that works together to perform a special function for the benefit of the organism. Organs can become interacting parts of an anatomical and physiological *system.* The human digestive system is a sequence of organs from the mouth through the esophagus, the stomach, and the small and large intestine to the anus. Each organ is different, but each interacts with the others to accomplish the process of digestion.

The bodies of more highly complex plants consist of four types of tissue and two organ systems.

Meristematic tissue is involved in plant growth; *protective* tissue covers and protects both organ systems; one type of *fundamental* tissue adds strength to a plant's organs while a second type is the site of photosynthesis; *conductive*, or vascular, tissue helps transport fluids and dissolved materials within the plant.

The organ systems are the *root system* and the *shoot system*, which includes the stem and leaves. Organization into systems is more common in animals than in plants. Humans and other more complex multicellular animals have ten systems.

1. The *integumentary system* encloses or covers the animal. Hair, skin, nails, scales, feathers, and hooves are parts of the integumentary system.
2. The *skeletal system* provides support, protection, and help in movement.
3. The *muscular system* provides for movement of the animal and its internal organs.
4. The *respiratory system* moves gases in and out of the organisms.
5. The *excretory system* eliminates liquid wastes from the body. A kidney is a key organ in this system.
6. The *nervous system* receives stimuli from the environment and causes organs to respond.
7. The *endocrine system*, through its *hormones*, regulates and controls the growth, development, and functions of the organism.
8. The *digestive system* changes food into a form that can be used by the individual cells.
9. The *circulatory system* moves food, hormones, and other materials throughout the body.
10. The *reproductive system* produces gametes to continue the species of organism.

Multicellular life

Tissues that function together in a leaf

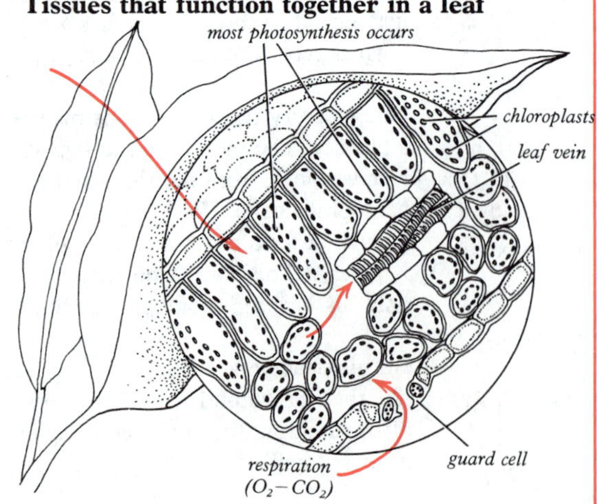

Essential functions in an animal

respiration (O_2-CO_2)
work
reproduction
metabolism
excretion
growth
sex cells
absorption
egestion
nervous and endocrine control
organic wastes
feces
digestion
ingestion
food

Tissues

Tissue			*Location*	*Function*
Epithelial	Simple squamous		Lungs	Exchange of gases
			Lining of blood/lymph vessels	Absorption by diffusion
			Surface layer of organs	Absorption by diffusion
	Stratified squamous		Skin, mouth, esophagus	Protection
	Simple columnar		Lining of stomach, intestines, and respiratory tract	Protection; secretion; absorption; moving of mucus
Muscle	Skeletal		Attached to bones and eyes	Movement
			Upper third of esophagus	First part of swallowing
	Visceral		Walls of digestive, respiratory, and genitourinary tracts	Movement of substances along respective tracts
			Walls of blood and lymph vessels	Change diameter of vessels
			In ducts of glands	Movement of substances
			Intrinsic eye muscles	Adjust vision
			Arrector muscles of hairs	Erection of hairs (gooseflesh)
	Cardiac		Wall of heart	Contraction of heart
Connective	Reticular tissue		Spleen, lymph nodes, bone marrow	Defense for harmful substances; synthesis of reticular fibers
	Loose, ordinary (areolar)		Between other tissues and organs	Connection
			Superficial fascia	Connection
	Fat		Under skin and padding at various points	Protection, insulation, support, and reserve food
	Dense fibrous		Tendons, ligaments, dermis, scars, capsule of kidney, etc.	Flexible but strong connection
	Bone		Skeleton	Support and protection
	Cartilage:	Hyaline	Nose, bones, larynx, rings in trachea and bronchi	Firm but flexible support
		Fibrous	Disks between vertebrae	
		Elastic	External ear, Eustachian tube	
	Hemopoietic:	Bone marrow	Marrow spaces of bones	Formation of red blood cells, granular leukocytes, platelets
		Lymphatic	Lymph nodes, spleen, tonsils and adenoids, thymus gland	Formation of lymphocytes and monocytes
Blood			In blood vessels	Transportation and protection
Nervous			Brain, spinal cord, nerves	Irritability; conduction

Variety of living things

Imagine trying to order items from a catalog that is completely disorganized! On a single page there might be clothing and toys as well as hardware and household appliances. In addition, none of the items is labeled, so it is almost impossible to refer to an item by its name or to distinguish it from another item. Fortunately, catalogs are not usually organized in this way. Every object is given a specific name, and similar objects are generally grouped together.

The same situation exists in the world of living things. Each living thing is given a specific name, and those living things with similar characteristics are classified together. This makes it much easier for scientists, as well as the rest of us, to study living things and to discuss them.

The variety of organisms is enormous. For instance, over 1 million animals have already been discovered and named; and there are many others yet to be investigated. By organizing this large number of creatures into groups based on similar characteristics, we can bring order to the animal kingdom and make sense of it. As more animals are discovered, they can be added to the existing classifications. If an animal is found for which no classification exists, a new one can be created.

A system of classifying living things was developed by the Swedish naturalist Linnaeus during the 18th century. (His actual name was Carl von Linné.) The largest divisions established by Linnaeus are the *kingdoms*. These include many organisms that share a few of the same characteristics. All members of the plant kingdom, for example, manufacture their own food and do not move around. Today scientists often speak of five kingdoms. These include Animalia (animal), Plantae (plant), Fungi, Protista, and Monera.

Five kingdom classification system

Kingdom Monera

Most organisms in this kingdom are made up of a simple, *prokaryotic* cell.
Some monerans make their own food; others take in food from an outside source.

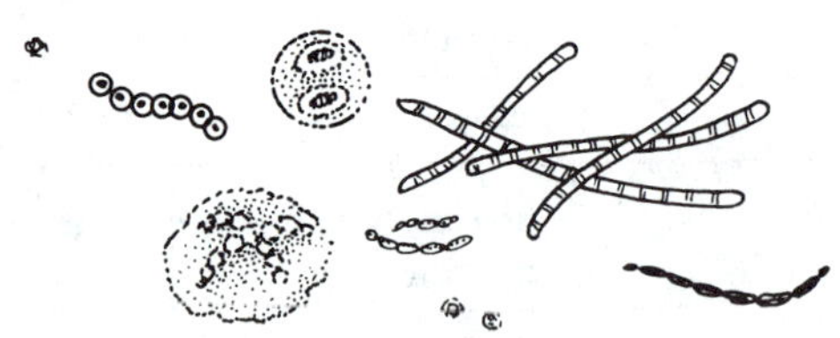

Kingdom Protista

Organisms in this kingdom are made up of a complex, *eukaryotic* cell.
Like monerans, protists either make their own food or take it in from an outside source.

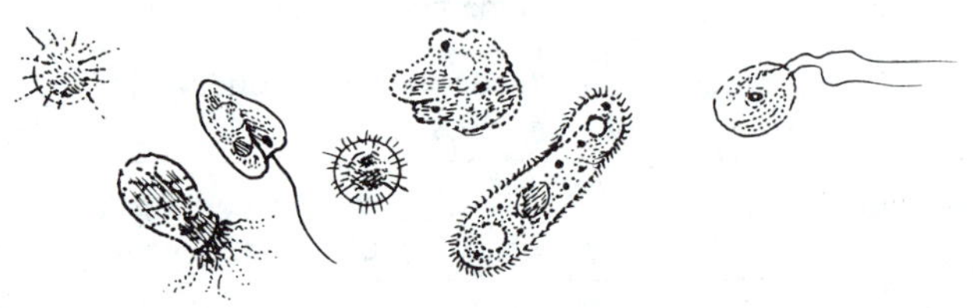

Kingdom Animalia

Members of this kingdom are multicellular, but they obtain food from *outside sources.*
Animals move from place to place to obtain food, swallow the food, and digest it inside the body.

Kingdom Fungi

These organisms are made up of many cells, but lack the ability to move about.
They obtain food by *absorbing* it from dead or living organisms.

Kingdom Plantae

Members of the plant kingdom are also multicellular, but the cells are *specialized* for different tasks—such as support or transport.
Plants use chlorophyll to *make their own food,* and so lack the ability to move about.

Every kingdom is further broken down into smaller groups. These groups have fewer organisms with more characteristics in common. Each of the various groups into which a kingdom is divided is called a *phylum*. The phyla (plural of phylum) are broken into *classes*, which are subdivided into *orders*. These, in turn, are subdivided into *families*. Finally, the families are broken down into *genera* (singular genus) and *species*. The smallest grouping is generally the species. All members of a species are very similar, and they can mate to produce fertile offspring. According to this system, the classification for humans would be:

Kingdom:	**Animalia**	Family:	HOMINIDAE
Phylum:	**CHORDATA**	Genus:	*Homo*
Class:	**Mammalia**	Species:	*sapiens*
Order:	PRIMATA		

Each living thing has its own special name, which is a combination of its genus and its species. Humans are called *Homo sapiens*. This name is unique: there is no other organism that possesses it.

Latin is the language used to label living things. When Linnaeus invented his system of classification, Latin was the language used by most scientists. Using Latin avoids confusion. Instead of calling the same species by different names in different languages, one name is used universally.

At present, all scientists do not subscribe to a single system of classification. For example, some scientists classify most of the algae as protists, while others split them between the protist and the plant kingdoms. What follows is one classification system that is accepted in the scientific community. But alternatives exist that are equally valid.

A partial classification of corn plants and men

Taxonomic rank	*Corn plant*	*Man*
phylum	**TRACHEOPHYTA** plants with vascular tissues	**CHORDATA** animals with notochords
subphylum	**PTEROPSIDA** types with large leaves	**VERTEBRATA** types with vertebral columns
superclass	**Spermatophyta** seed producers	**Tetrapoda** terrestrial; four limbs; bony skeletons
class	**Angiospermae** flowering plants; seeds inside fruits	**Mammalia** types with hair and milk glands
subclass	**Monocotyledonae** parallel-veined leaves; single seed leaf; flower parts in threes or multiples	**Eutheria** offspring develop within female parent, nourished by placenta
order	GRAMINALES grasses	PRIMATA fingers; flat nails
family	GRAMINACEAE leaves in two rows on round or flattened stem	HOMINIDAE upright posture; flat face; stereoscopic vision; large brain; hands and feet
genus	*Zea* corn plants	*Homo* double-curved spine; long life span and long youth
species	*mays* cultivated, domesticated corn plants	*sapiens* well-developed chin; high forehead; thin skull bones

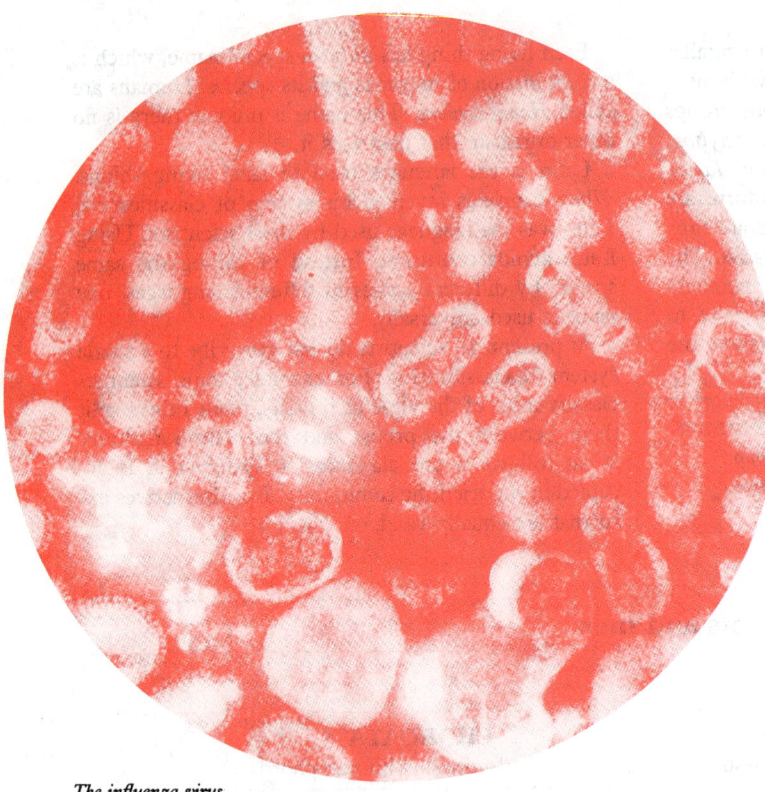

The influenza virus

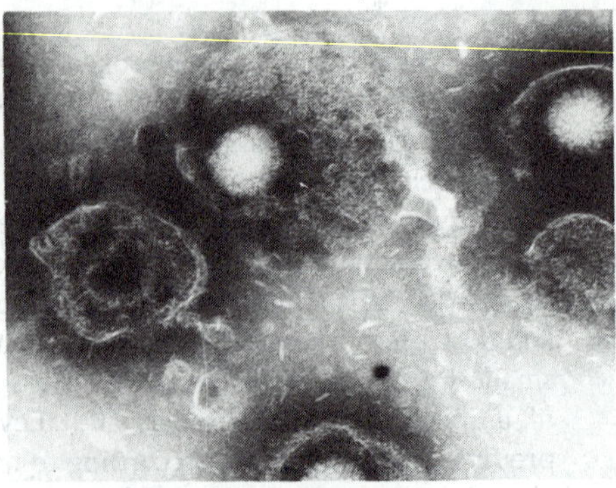

The herpes virus

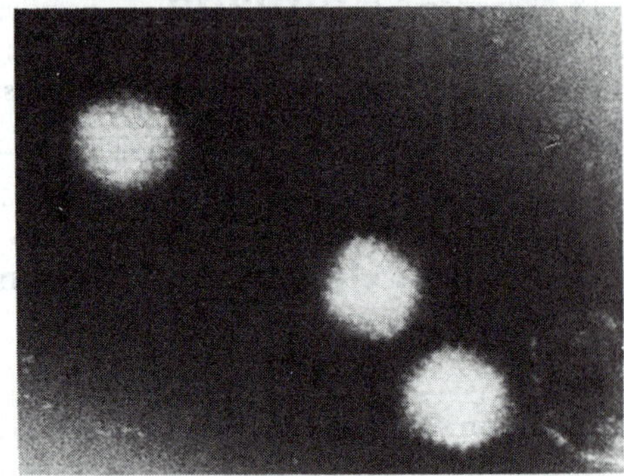

Many viruses have geometric shapes.

Virus. A virus is a piece of nucleic acid—DNA or RNA—enclosed within a protective shell of protein. A virus particle is very tiny, smaller than a bacteria cell. Under the electron microscope, some viruses have been shown to look like the bacteriaphage. Others have a rod or a helix shape.

On its own, a virus shows no signs of life; consequently, scientists cannot agree on whether it is a living thing. A virus does not move; it must be carried by air, water, or some organism. Once in contact with a cell, a virus seems to come alive. After attaching itself to the cell wall, the virus enters the cell and takes control of its reproductive mechanisms to replicate itself; in the process, it prevents the cell from operating normally.

Once a cell has been infected by a virus, it may change and become a tumor cell. While some tumors, such as warts, are benign, others are malignant, or cancerous. Viruses cause cancer in plants and animals. As the virus replicates, producing more particles, the particles may burst out of a cell, destroying it. Then the particles may be carried by the bloodstream to infect other cells. Human diseases caused by viruses include influenza, measles, mumps, polio, and the common cold.

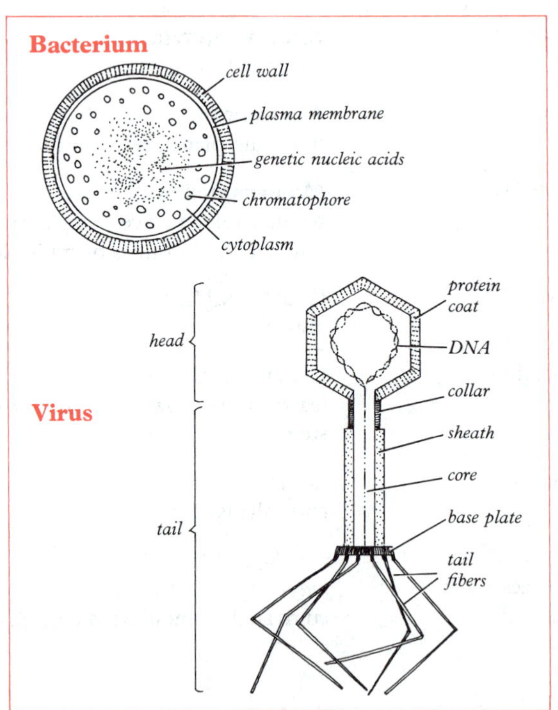

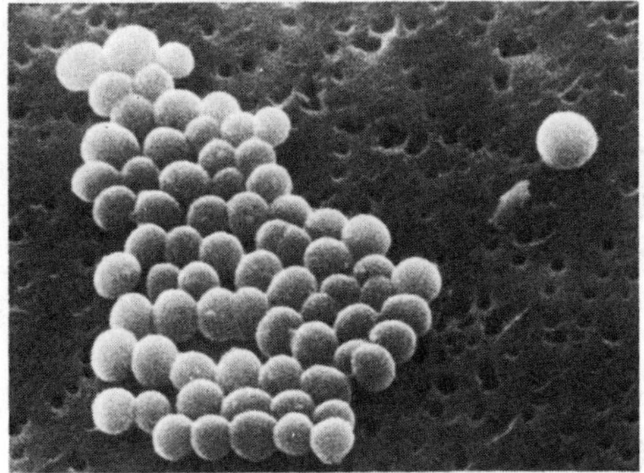

Staphylococcus

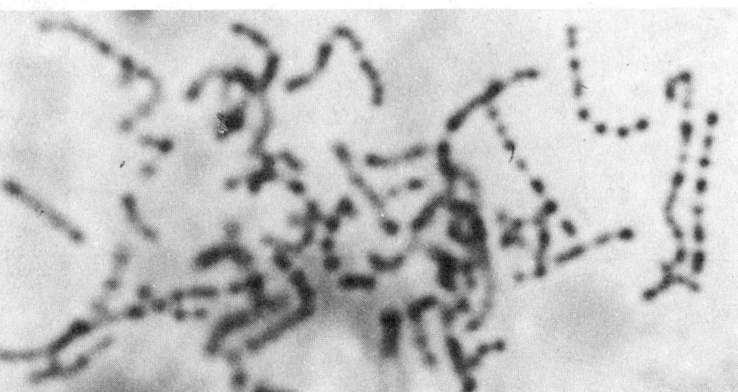

Streptococcus shows that cocci are often joined in chains.

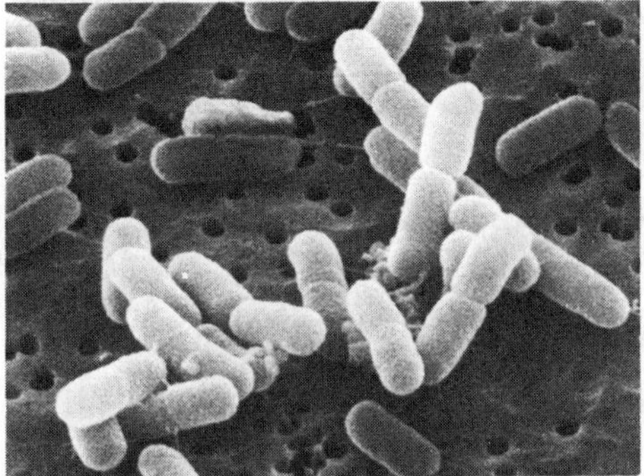

Common bacteria used in gene splicing, Escherichia coli

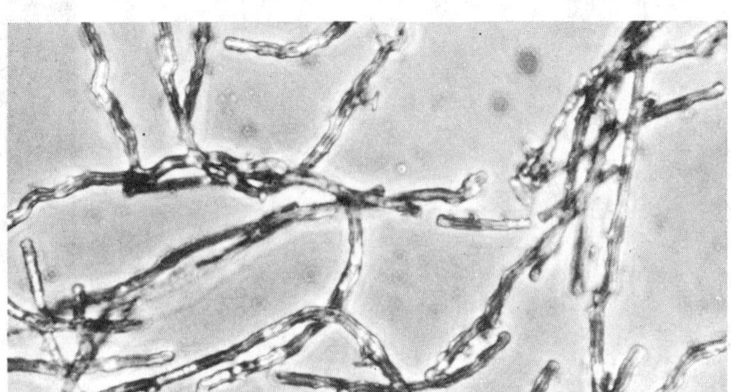

The anthrax bacterium is a typical bacillus.

Kingdom Monera. This kingdom is comprised of all bacteria. Bacteria are thought to be the most numerous type of living thing in our environment. They are grouped into two phyla: bacteria and blue-green bacteria. Formerly, the bacteria were classified as plants because bacteria have cell walls.

Bacteria are tiny organisms that generally consist of a single cell. This is called a *prokaryotic* cell. A prokaryotic cell has a definite cell wall, but, unlike the cells in other organisms, it lacks an organized nucleus. The prokaryotic cell is also missing specialized cell structures, such as mitochondria and golgi.

Bacteria generally reproduce by a process called *fission.* In fission, one cell simply divides, producing an offspring. Monerans may also reproduce sexually.

Bacteria play an essential role in the ecosystem as decomposers. After plants and animals have died, bacteria break them down, releasing vital substances such as oxygen, carbon, and sulfur, which are essential for life. Certain bacteria attached to plants "capture" nitrogen and transform it into a compound that plants can use. This process, called nitrogen fixation, is necessary for these plants to function.

Some bacteria cause serious illnesses. These illnesses include tuberculosis, cholera, typhoid fever, and tetanus. Disease-causing bacteria can be transmitted directly from one individual to another. They may also be carried by an animal, such as an insect. The bacteria that cause bubonic plague are carried by fleas from rodents to humans.

PHYLUM SCHIZOPHYTA:

BACTERIA. Bacteria exist in three different shapes. The spherical bacteria are called **cocci**. The rod-shaped bacteria are known as **bacilli**. The spiral-shaped cells are called **spirilla**. Some bacteria possess a long hairlike structure that resembles a tail. Known as a *flagellum,* it moves very rapidly and propels the bacterium.

PHYLUM CYANOPHYTA:

BLUE-GREEN BACTERIA. These are sometimes called blue-green algae. They contain chlorophyll and carry on photosynthesis, but the chlorophyll is not contained in chloroplasts as it is in other photosynthetic organisms. Blue-green bacteria may be single-celled or multicellular. They grow mainly in a freshwater environment.

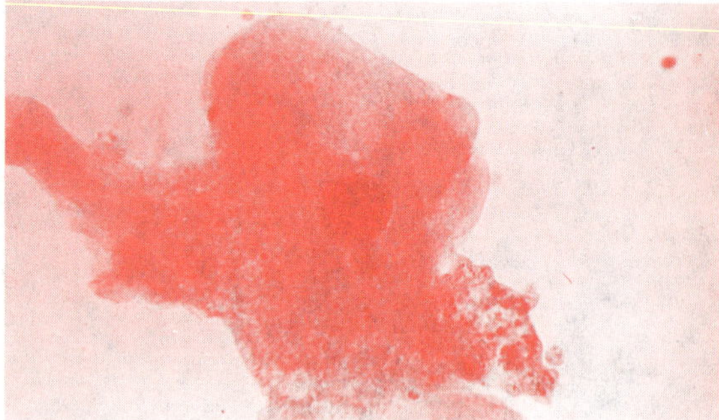

An amoeba

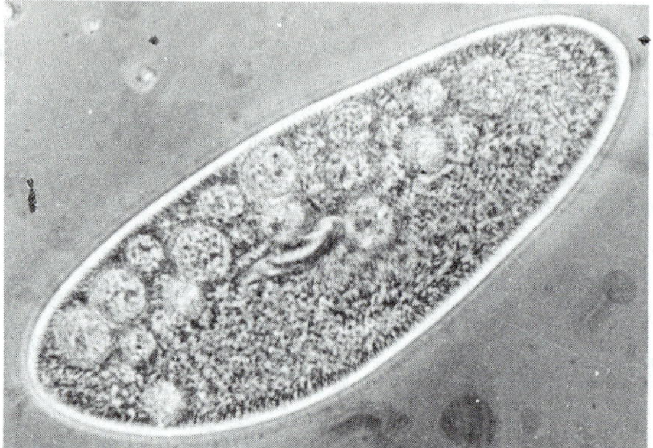

A paramecium

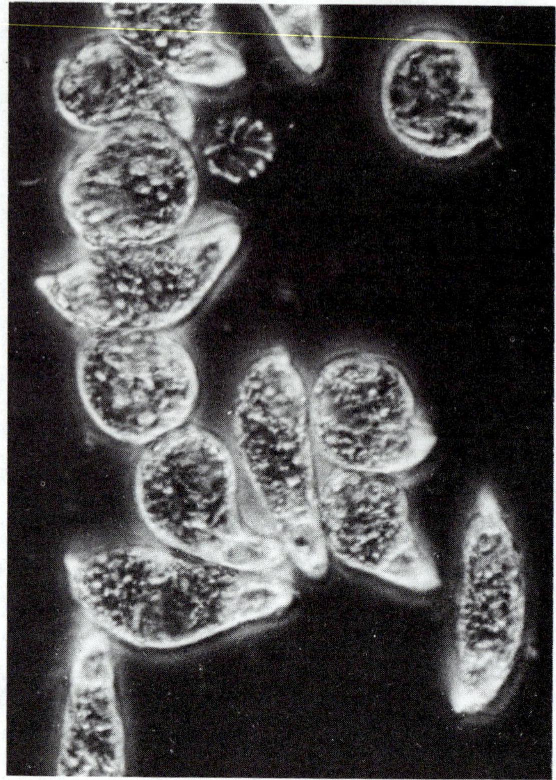

Euglena

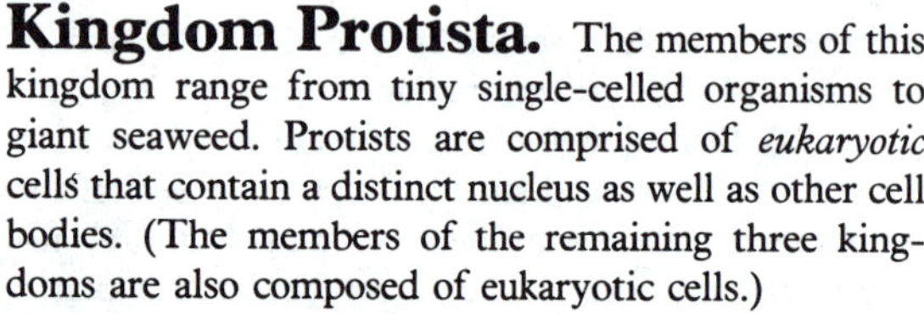

Kingdom Protista. The members of this kingdom range from tiny single-celled organisms to giant seaweed. Protists are comprised of *eukaryotic* cells that contain a distinct nucleus as well as other cell bodies. (The members of the remaining three kingdoms are also composed of eukaryotic cells.)

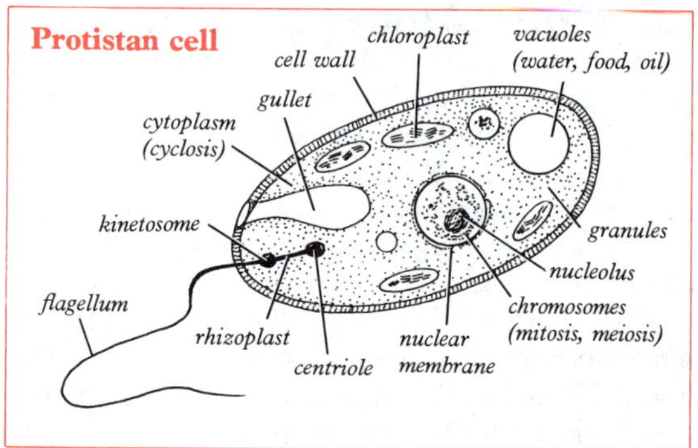

PHYLUM PROTOZOA:

Protozoa are like animals because they move and obtain their food from outside sources. They reproduce sexually and asexually. There are perhaps 30,000 species of protozoa organized into four classes.

Mastigophora. This class includes protozoa that move by means of flagella. One species causes the disease called African sleeping sickness.

Sarcodina. The best-known member of this class is the amoeba. The amoeba possesses projections, called pseudopods, used to capture food and in movement.

Ciliophora. These protozoans use hairlike projections called *cilia* to swim. The paramecium is a member of this class. Paramecia are shaped like a slipper and found in fresh water. Each cell has two nuclei. One directs reproduction and the other directs the rest of the paramecium's functions.

Sporozoa. This class includes protozoans that glide. One of them, the plasmodium, causes malaria.

The remaining phyla consist of photosynthetic organisms. There are perhaps 25,000 species of such *algae.* Most are found in water environments.

PHYLUM EUGLENOPHYTA:

EUGLENA. The euglena are protists that have characteristics of plants and animals. Euglena contain chlorophyll and can make their own food; or they can capture it. Euglena move by using flagella.

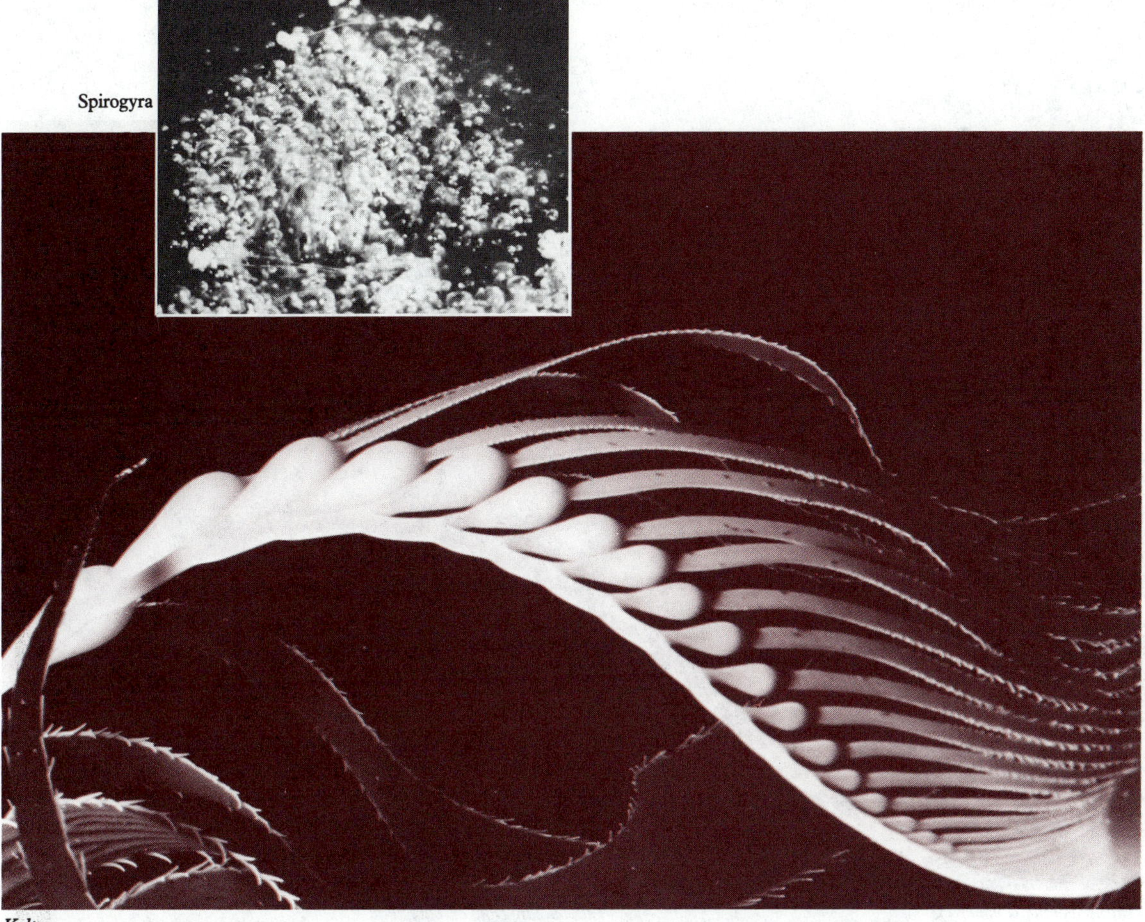
Spirogyra

Kelp

PHYLUM CHRYSOPHYTA:
GOLDEN ALGAE AND DIATOMS. In the golden algae the green chlorophyll is masked by yellow to brown pigments, giving these organisms their characteristic color. Diatoms are single-celled algae. They are among the living things that comprise *plankton*—tiny organisms that float along the water's surface. Plankton serves as food for many marine animals. Diatoms have cell walls composed of silica, which are found in a variety of shapes.

PHYLUM PYRROPHYTA:
DINOFLAGELLATES. Many of these organisms spin from the motion of their flagella. One species creates the so-called "red tide" that occurs in the Gulf of Mexico. This phenomenon is produced by a large number of dinoflagellates whose pigments create the red color. Red tides kill many types of marine life. Some species of dinoflagellates are bioluminescent; that is, they emit light.

PHYLUM CHLOROPHYTA:
GREEN ALGAE. The members of this phylum come in a variety of shapes and sizes. There are single-celled algae such as CHLAMYDOMONAS and DESMIDS. A desmid consists of two symmetrical halves connected by a bridge. The *Ulva* is a type of green algae that looks like leafy lettuce. *Spirogyra* is a long filament that makes up the scum that covers ponds. The filament consists of a series of elongated algal cells that are connected to each other. Another type of filamentous algae, *Ulothrix*, is held in place by means of a structure called a *holdfast*. It attaches to rocks and twigs. The multicellular algae have specialized cells that perform various functions.

PHYLUM PHAEOPHYTA:
BROWN ALGAE.
PHYLUM RHODOPHYTA:
RED ALGAE. These are multicelled algae known as seaweeds. The brown algae are the largest and include the giant kelp. Some of the kelps are over 40 feet in length. The kelps contain rudimentary transport systems that carry nutrients from those parts on the surface to the rest of the organism below. The giant kelps are anchored to the ocean floor by large holdfasts. Another type of brown algae, called *Fucus*, has air bladders that help its leaflike parts float on the surface.

Colony of Penicillium *mold*

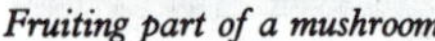

Fruiting part of a mushroom

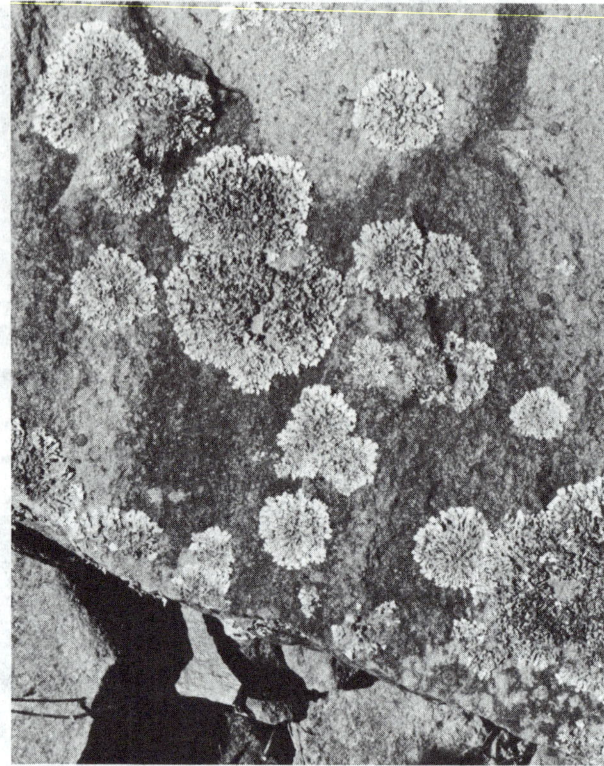

Lichens can grow on bare rock.

Kingdom Fungi. In this kingdom there are approximately 100,000 species that have been named. Fungi cannot produce their own food; they obtain it by absorbing material from other organisms. Along with bacteria and protozoa, fungi act as decomposers. They reproduce by sexual and asexual means. Some species of fungi can also cause diseases such as ringworm and athlete's foot.

Ascomycetes. These are sometimes known as "sac fungi" because of their shape. The class also includes powdery mildews and yeasts. Mildews are parasites that live on many green plants, such as lilacs and roses. Yeasts carry on a process known as *fermentation*, which is important in baking and in the production of alcoholic beverages. Truffles and morels, which are both edible fungi, are other members of this class.

Basidomycetes. This class includes mushrooms and toadstools as well as rusts and smuts. While some mushrooms are edible, others are poisonous and should be avoided. Only that part of the mushroom involved in reproduction appears above the surface; the rest remains below ground. Rusts and smuts are parasites that attack wheat, trees, and other plants. Rusts have a rusty color, while smuts are dark.

Deuteromycetes. Among these fungi are the *Penicillium* molds. Species of this mold are the source of the drug penicillin. Some species are also used in the production of cheeses such as Roquefort, blue, and Camembert. Many types of molds spoil food; for example, the *Trichothecium* grows on apples and produces rot.

Lichens. A lichen is composed of a species of algae and a species of fungi living together. The algae manufacture food, while the fungi form a framework that protects the algae. Some lichens are crustlike; others are leaflike; still others are branchy. These are hearty organisms that can survive in even the most inhospitable environments, such as the icy conditions of Antarctica, where lichens can be found living inside the outer layers of some rock formations.

PHYLUM GYMNOMYCOTA:

SLIME MOLDS. These are not true molds. In one stage, slime molds are individual cells that move around like amoeba; they are often classified in the protist kingdom. In other stages, the slime molds gather in colonies that resemble fungi. There are almost 500 species in this phylum.

Moss

Cinnamon fern

Kingdom Plantae. This kingdom consists of multicellular, photosynthetic organisms that range in size from tiny mosses to giant sequoia trees. Reproduction among the plants is both sexual and asexual.

PHYLUM BRYOPHYTA:
LIVERWORTS, HORNWORTS, MOSSES. These are nonvascular plants; that is, they do not possess a system of specialized cells for carrying water and food through the plants. As a result the bryophytes are frequently found near water, and they remain small. There are over 23,000 species.

Hepaticae. These are low, flat plants numbering about 9000 species. People in the ancient world believed these liverworts would cure diseases of the liver.

Antherocerotae. This class includes about 100 species of hornworts.

Musci. Mosses are tiny plants that grow in clumps. They have leaflike parts above ground and rootlike structures, called *rhizoids*, that absorb water and nutrients. Mosses are often called "pioneer plants" because they may be among the first species to inhabit harsh environments. Mosses growing on rocky surfaces, for example, break up the rocks and create a more fertile soil where other plants can survive. A special type of moss, called *Sphagnum*, grows in heavy mats in ponds. Sphagnum eventually forms *peat*, which is burned as a fuel and used as fertilizer in gardens. There are over 14,000 species of mosses.

PHYLUM TRACHEOPHYTA:
VASCULAR PLANTS. With vascular systems, plants can grow very tall, and even the highest branches can receive the nutrients necessary to survive. Tracheophytes have roots, stems, and leaves. Roots hold the plant in the ground. They absorb water and minerals, transport them to the rest of the plant, and act as storage areas for food. Stems also serve as transport structures. Additionally, they provide sturdiness and support for the plant's leaves and branches. Leaves manufacture food through photosynthesis.

Filicinae. Ferns are seedless plants, numbering about 11,000 species. In spring the coiled leaf buds, called *fiddleheads*, uncoil into broad fern leaves known as *fronds*. These are attached to the ferns' underground stems, or *rhyzomes*. Although ferns are generally small, some giant tree ferns grow to heights of over 40 feet.

The leaf of the gingko is easily recognized.

The mojadji cycad of South Africa

A white pine

Gymnospermae. This class comprises seed-bearing plants. Seeds consist of a tough outer shell enveloping in embryo plant and nutrients to sustain it. Seeds can survive in a very harsh environment; then, under just the right conditions, they germinate and begin to sprout. Seeds can also be carried easily by wind, water, and animals. All these advantages have helped seed-bearing plants proliferate.

Gymnosperm means "naked" or "exposed" seed. In gymnosperm plants, the seed is not enclosed by a fruit.
ORDER CYCADINAE: CYCADS. There are about 550 species of these trees, which look like palms.
ORDER GINKGOINAE: GINKGO. Only one species exists today.
ORDER CONIFERINAE: CONIFERS. There are over 500 species; they include pines, firs, spruces, hemlocks, and sequoias. The conifers, or "cone-bearers," develop their seeds in cones. They have sharp needle-like leaves that are shed at intervals throughout the year. This gives conifers the appearance of always being green; hence the term "evergreen." Vast forests of conifers stretch across Canada and the northern United States, forming a huge biome called the taiga. Conifers are important as sources of lumber.

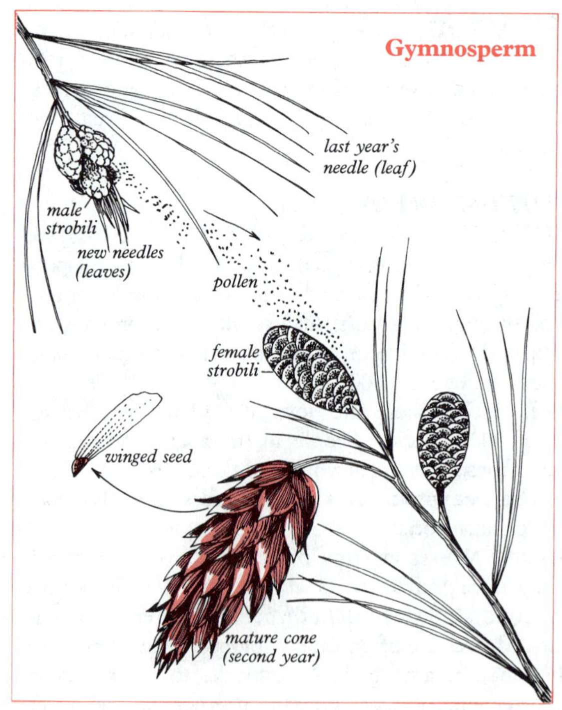

Giant saguaro cacti

The rose is a flowering plant . . .

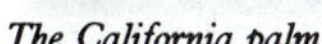

The California palm

But grasses are flowering plants, also.

Angiospermae. These flowering seed plants are the most highly developed plants. Flowers contain plants' reproductive organs. The *stamen* is the male organ. It consists of a *filament* and an *anther*. *Pollen*, which contains male reproductive cells, is produced in the anther. The *pistil*, or female reproductive organ, includes the *stigma*, the *style*, the *ovary*, and the *ovule*. An egg cell is produced inside the ovule. When the ovule is fertilized by sperm from pollen grains, it develops into a seed. The ovary enclosing the seed becomes the fruit. Pollen is frequently carried to the pistil by insects, and plants have developed a variety of methods of attracting them. These methods include colorful flowers, smells, and a sweet liquid called nectar.

The flowering plants are divided into two main groups: the *monocots*, with one seed leaf; and the *dicots*, with two seed leaves. Members of these two groups also differ in the number of their flower parts, the appearance of their leaves, and their root structure. For example, monocots have leaves with parallel veins, while the leaves of dicots have branching veins. The monocots include grasses, lilies, orchids, palms, and cattails. Dicots include oaks, maples, beeches, willows, mustards, roses, poppies, and mints.

Cross section of perfect flower

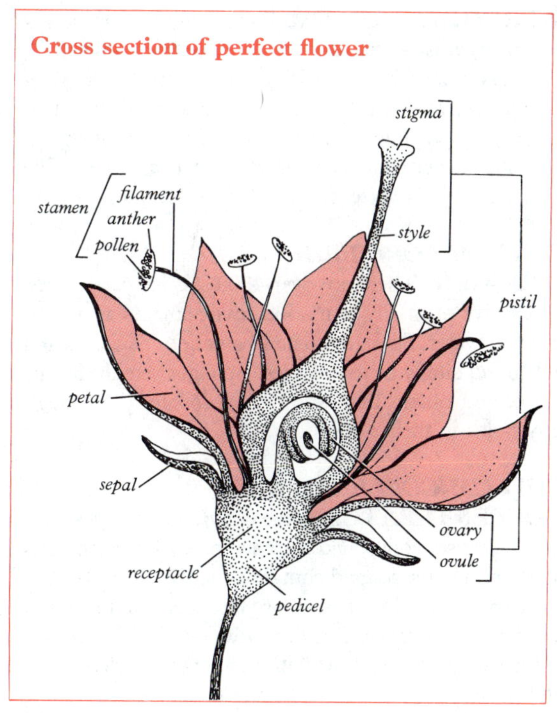

A flatworm

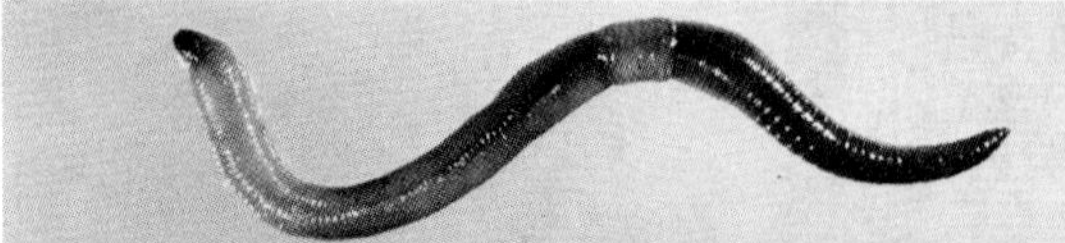
Typical segmented worm: the dew worm, or nightcrawler

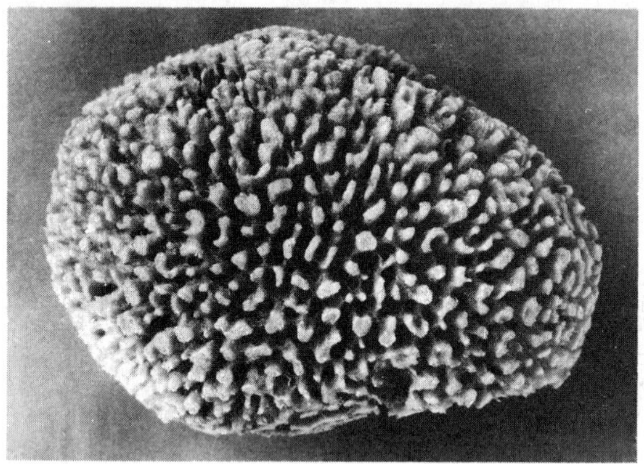
Velvet sponge

A jellyfish floating in the sea

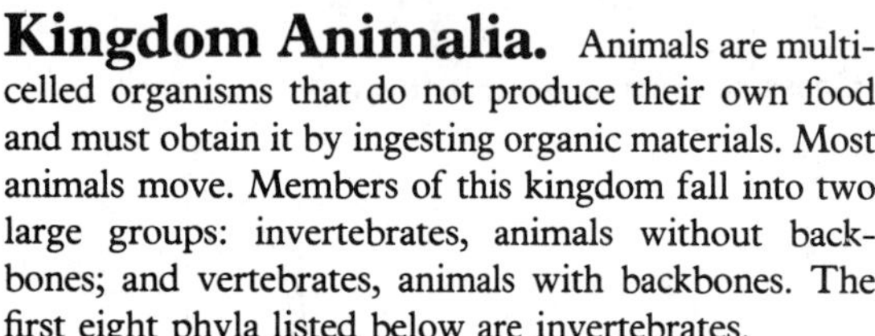

Kingdom Animalia. Animals are multicelled organisms that do not produce their own food and must obtain it by ingesting organic materials. Most animals move. Members of this kingdom fall into two large groups: invertebrates, animals without backbones; and vertebrates, animals with backbones. The first eight phyla listed below are invertebrates.

PHYLUM PORIFERA:
SPONGES. There are over 4000 species of sponges, which live primarily in marine environments as well as in fresh water. Sponges come in a variety of colors and are found singly or in colonies. Sponges remain in one place, and obtain their food by absorbing it through tiny holes in their sides.

PHYLUM COELENTERATA:
COELENTERATES. This phylum includes hydras, jellyfish, corals, and sea anemones. These animals have definite tissues and contain a saclike digestive cavity surrounded by special organs such as tentacles. Typical of this phylum is the hydra—a tiny freshwater animal shaped like a tube with stinging tentacles at one end.

PHYLUM PLATYHELMINTHES:
FLATWORMS. Flatworms have three tissue layers—ectoderm, mesoderm, and endoderm—and possess definite organs. These characteristics are shared by all the remaining phyla in the animal kingdom. This phylum includes planarians, tapeworms, and flukes. Planarians have eyespots, which are capable of detecting light but not shapes. Tapeworms and flukes are parasites that live in humans and animals.

PHYLUM NEMATODA:
ROUNDWORMS. These animals consist of an outer tube enclosing a tubular digestive system. Some are parasites, including the trichina and the hookworm. The trichina lives in pigs and other animals. If humans eat raw pork, they may ingest the trichina and develop *trichinosis.*

PHYLUM ANNELIDA:
SEGMENTED WORMS. Although the majority of these worms are found in marine habitats, the best known is the earthworm, which lives in the soil. Earthworms eat particles of soil, retain the food contained in it, and excrete the remainder in the form of *castings.*

The snail is a gastropod.

A crab is a crustacean.

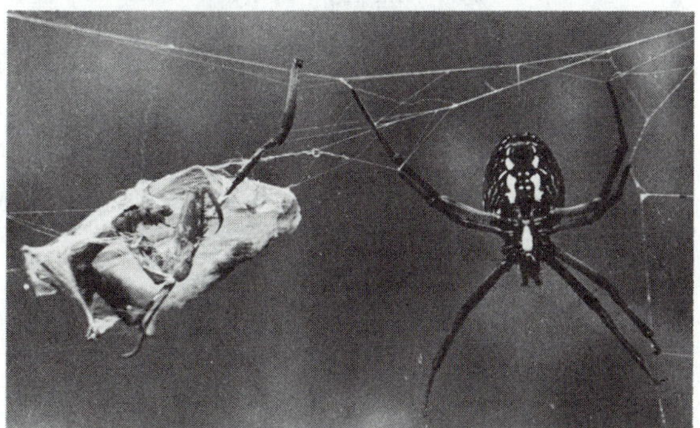

Spiders are arachnids.

Swallowtail butterfly

PHYLUM MOLLUSKA:

MOLLUSKS. These animals have a soft body and a foot protruding from it. Covering the body is a membrane, or *mantle*; some mollusks also have a shell. There are various classes, such as the PELECYPODA, or two-shelled mollusks, which include clams, mussels, and oysters. Snails and slugs are members of the class GASTROPODA, which means "stomach-footed." The snail uses his foot to move. The squid and the octopus belong to the class CEPHALODA, which means "head-footed." There are about 110,000 species.

PHYLUM ECHINODERMATA:

ECHINODERMS. Members of this phylum are starfish, sea urchins, sea cucumbers, and sand dollars. Numbering about 6000, they are animals with spiny skin found in marine environments.

PHYLUM ARTHROPODA:

ARTHROPODS. This is the largest phylum in the animal kingdom, numbering around 1 million species. Its members have paired appendages, a jointed external skeleton, and three body parts—a head, thorax, and abdomen.

Crustacea. This class includes crabs, crayfish, and lobsters. There are about 30,000 species, and most live in water.

Arachnida. Members of this class include spiders, scorpions, ticks, and mites. In spiders the head and thorax are fused, forming the *cephalothorax*. Spiders have four pairs of legs and special glands called *spinnerets*, which are used in spinning a web. When an insect prey enters the web, the spider injects it with poison to facilitate capture. There are about 35,000 species of arachnids.

Chilopoda. This class includes about 2000 species of centipedes.

Diplopoda. This class includes about 7000 species of millipedes.

Insecta. This is the largest class of arthropods, with over 700,000 insect species, including bees, mosquitoes, grasshoppers, butterflies, and fleas. These animals have three body sections, three pairs of legs, and two antennae. Many also have wings. During their lifetimes, insects generally undergo bodily changes called *metamorphoses*. The butterfly, for example, passes through four stages: egg, larva (caterpillar), pupa (cocoon), and adult.

Dissection of frog

A. Cut with scissors from tail up through skin of stomach to throat. Extend cut along all four legs.

B. Cut through bones of chest and remove them.

C. Pin back sides of body.

D. Remove muscles that overlie internal organs.

E. Locate
- Heart, arteries, veins
- Liver (large, reddish)
- Right and left lungs
- Digestive system (esophagus, stomach, intestines)
- Spleen (reddish globe attached to small intestine)
- Pancreas (in transparent membrane)
- Gallbladder (greenish globe)
- Kidneys (small, pink, under intestines)
- Backbone

Muscles

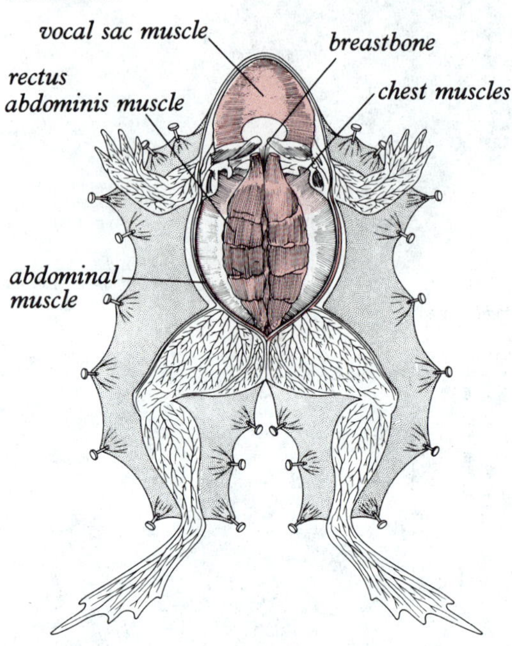

Internal organs

Digestive system

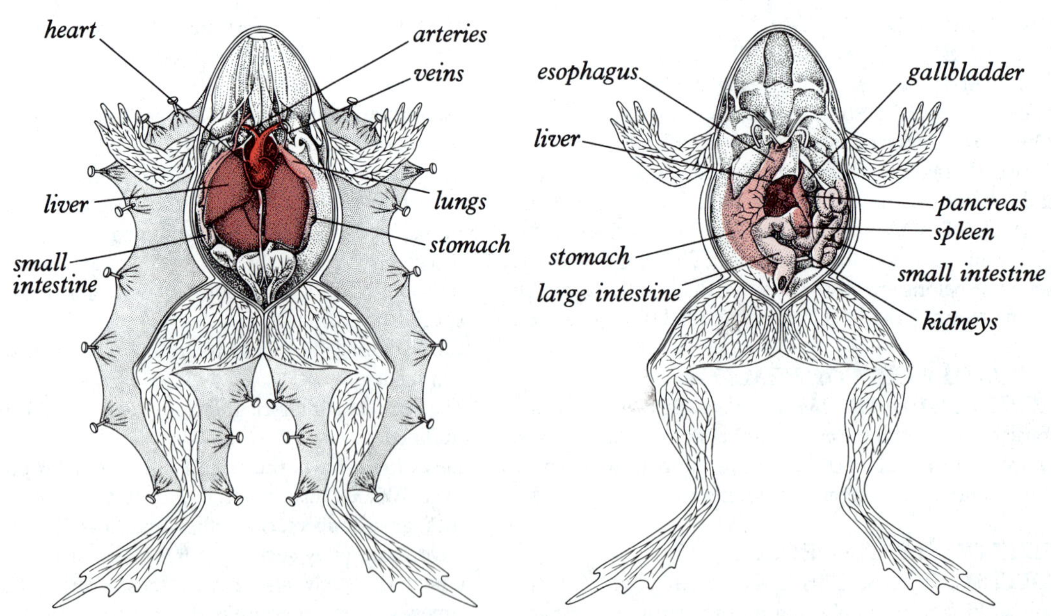

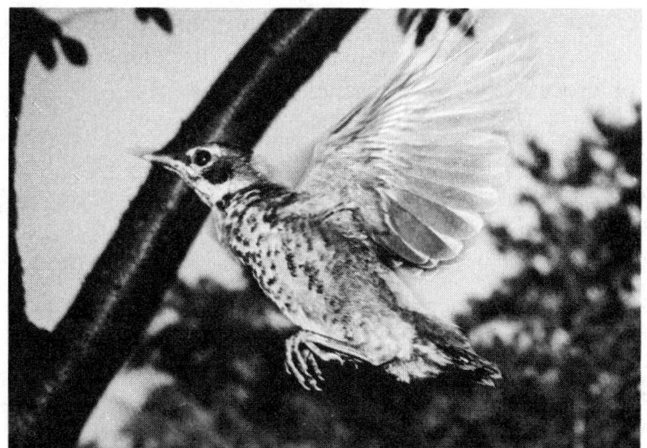

Young robin shows typical structure of birds.

The opossum is the only marsupial in North America.

Whales are placental mammals that have returned to the ocean.

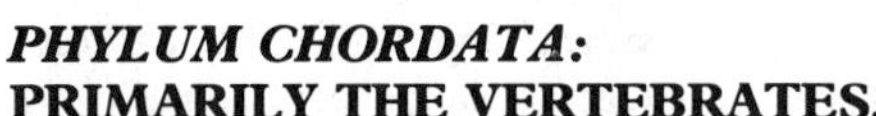

PHYLUM CHORDATA: PRIMARILY THE VERTEBRATES.

Agnatha. There are two members of this class of jawless fish: the lamprey and the hagfish. They are long, tubular fish with skeletons comprised of cartilage.

Chondrichthyes. These shark, ray, and skate fish have jaws and skeletons comprised only of cartilage.

Osteichthyes. This class consists of all the fishes we normally think of when we use the word *fish.* Their principal characteristic is the possession of true bone, either as a skeleton or a bony plate. All possess gills and live most of the time in water, but a few, such as lungfish, can breathe air or be found occasionally on land.

Amphibia. There are tailless amphibians, such as frogs; and amphibians with tails, such as salamanders. Amphibians generally lay their eggs in water and the young develop there; but the adults of many species live most of their lives on land. There are about 2000 species.

Reptilia. This class of reptiles includes snakes, turtles, and lizards. The reptile hatches from an egg that has its own water supply; this allows these animals to live and reproduce entirely on land. Like fish and amphibians, the reptiles are cold-blooded. As the temperature of the environment changes, their body temperature changes too. There are about 7000 species of reptiles.

Aves. This class is comprised of birds, all of which have feathers, and most of which fly. Birds that do not fly include penguins and ostriches. Birds and mammals are warm-blooded; that is, their body temperature remains the same regardless of the environment. There are approximately 8000 species.

Mammalia. Among the members of the mammal class are dogs, squirrels, whales, porpoises, and humans. Mammals generally have hair and nurse their young on milk from mammary glands. There are three subclasses. *Monotremes,* such as the duck-billed platypus, lay eggs. *Marsupials,* including the kangaroo and the opossum, have pouches where the young finish their development. In *placentals,* the female develops an organ called the *placenta* through which the embryo receives nourishment inside its mother's body. The young are born fully developed. Most of the animals you think about when you hear or read the word "animal" are placental, including dogs, cats, mice, cattle, and people. There are about 4500 species of mammals.

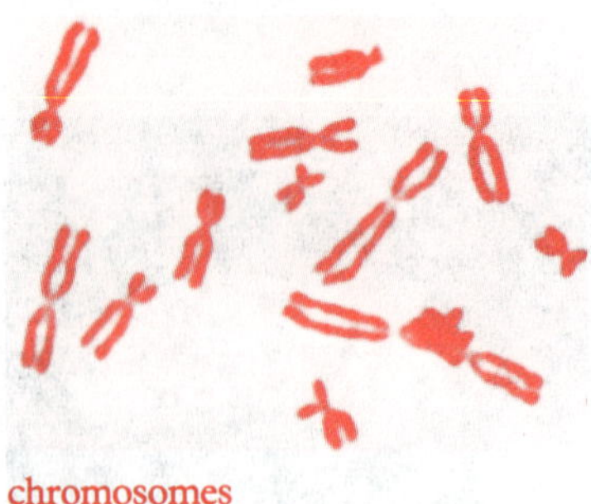
chromosomes

Dictionary of biology

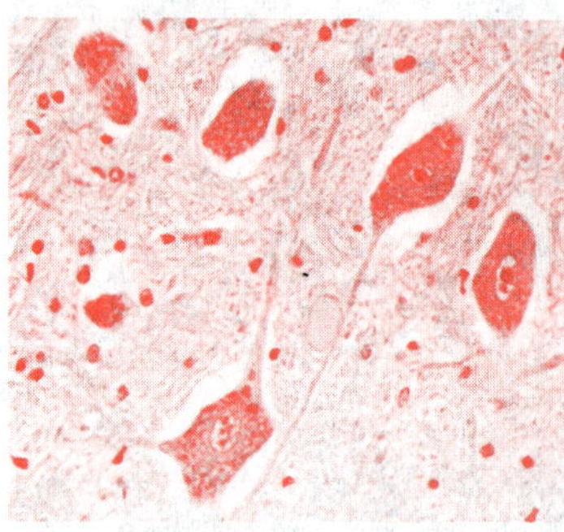
neurons

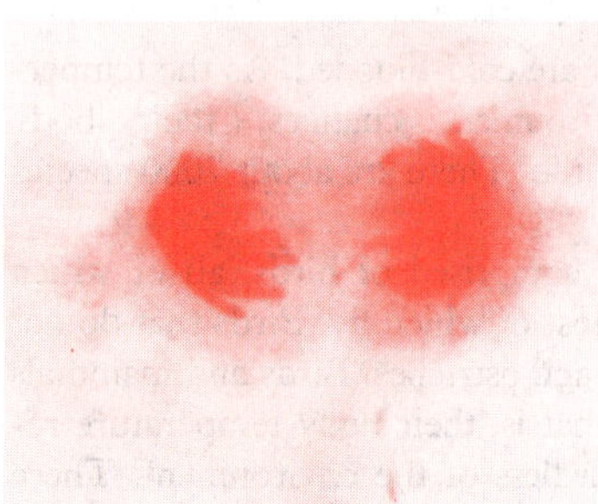
mitosis *(rough skinned newt cell)*

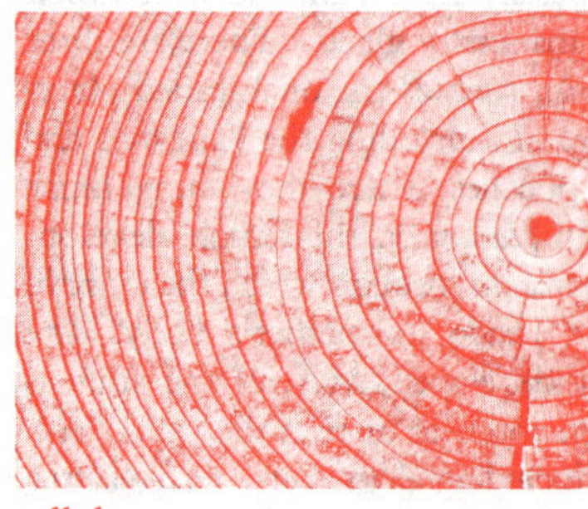
cellulose

adaptation. Means by which an organism fits itself to live and reproduce in a particular environment.

aerobic. Organisms or processes that can live or occur only in the presence of oxygen.

allele. Variant form of a gene, producing a different trait, for example, hair or eye color.

anaerobic. Indicates the absence of free oxygen.

asexual. Reproduction without male and female cells.

assimilation. Conversion of digested products into cytoplasm by an organism.

ATP (adenosine triphosphate). Compound synthesized within the cell that provides energy for cellular functions.

autotroph. Organism that can transform light energy into the chemical energy of glucose.

bacillus. Rodlike bacterium.

backbone. Column of bones (vertebrae) along the center of the back.

binary fission. Process by which an organism divides into two approximately equal parts.

cancer. Group of diseases characterized by uncontrolled cellular growth.

cell. The smallest functional unit of life.

cellulose. A complex carbohydrate. The chief component of the wall of plant cells.

chlorophyll. Green coloring matter of plants. It converts light energy into chemical energy.

chromatin. Hereditary material consisting of nucleoproteins from which chromosomes are formed during mitosis.

chromosomes. Composed of chromatin and located in the nucleus, they contain the genes.

cilia. Small hairlike bits of cytoplasm that move in unison to move cells or particles.

clone. A group of cells all descended from a single common ancestor.

cytoplasm. Cellular material between the cell membrane and the nuclear membrane; a colloidal suspension that contains the organelles of most cells.

dicot. Member of the class of flowering plants having two undeveloped leaves in the embryo of the seed.

differentiation. Specialization of cells and tissues during development for the purpose of performing particular functions.

diffusion. The movement of molecules of gases or liquids that causes them to spread out uniformly in a container.

digestion. Conversion of insoluble food substances into soluble substances that may be absorbed.

diploid. The number of chromosomes normally present in the nucleus of a cell, except the gametes.

DNA (dioxyribonucleic acid). Genetic material of all cells.

dominant. In genetics, one of any pair of opposite Mendelian characters that dominates over the other.

embryo. Organism in the earliest stages of its development.

endocrine. Any gland that produces one or more secretions that are carried by the lymph or blood to some other body part whose function they regulate.

endoplasmic reticulum. Network of thin membranes across the cytoplasm of the cell.

enzyme. Organic substance produced in cells that causes change in other substances by catalytic action.

epidermis. Outermost layer of skin in vertebrates; outermost layer of cells covering seed plants and ferns; outermost layer of the shells of many mollusks.

epithelium. Cellular membranous tissue that covers surfaces, forms glands, and lines most cavities of the body.

eukaryotes. Cells that have a nucleus surrounded by a nuclear membrane and that contain complex organelles.

fission. Form of asexual reproduction in which the parent organism divides into two or more parts, each becoming an independent individual.

flagellum. Whiplike part serving as an organ of locomotion in bacteria and certain cells.

genus. In the classification of organisms, the main subdivision of a family; includes one or more species.

haploid. Having only one set of chromosomes, as in gametes.

heredity. The transmission of characteristics from parent to offspring through genes.

heterotroph. Organism that must use the energy of the bonds of organic molecules formed by other cells.

homeostasis. Maintenance of equilibrium between an organism and its environment or between a cell and its environment.

hybrid. Offspring of two animals or plants of different species.

ingestion. Process of taking food into an organism for digestion.

meiosis. Nuclear changes in the maturation of germ cells in which the chromosome number is reduced from diploid to haploid.

metabolism. Continuous processes in cells by which food is formed into cytoplasm and by which cytoplasm is broken down into simpler substances or waste products with the release of energy.

mitochondria. Cell organelle responsible for the production of energy.

mitosis. Cell division in which the nuclear chromatin is formed into a long thread that in turn forms chromosomes that are split; two daughter cells are formed.

Monera. Kingdom of organisms having no distinct nucleus in their cells; the bacteria.

monocot. One of two groups of flowering plants with parallel veins in their leaves and flowering parts in threes or groups of threes.

mutant. Organism with inheritable characteristics different from those of the parents.

mutation. Sudden variation in some inheritable characteristic.

neuron. The structural and functional unit of the nervous system, consisting of the nerve cell body and its processes.

nucleus. Central mass of cytoplasm in most cells necessary for growth and reproduction.

organ. Group of tissues working together to perform a special function.

organelle ("small organ"). Any one of several parts of a cell that performs specific functions for that cell.

osmosis. Diffusion of water through a semipermeable membrane.

phagocyte. Any white blood cell that ingests and destroys other cells, bacteria, etc. Any cell capable of engulfing a microorganism.

phenotype. The sum of the characteristics shown by an organism.

phylum. The most broad, basic division within a kingdom.

plasmolysis. Shrinkage of cells from osmotic loss of water.

prokarocytes. Cells that do not have membrane-bound nuclei or organelles.

protist. Member of the kingdom of Protista; unicellular organism with specialized organelles.

recessive. Any one of a pair of opposite Mendelian characters that remains latent unless both characters are present.

regeneration. Growth of a new part to replace one that is injured or lost; a form of asexual reproduction in some animals.

respiration. Process by which an organism or cell takes in oxygen, utilizes it, and gives off products, especially carbon dioxide. The chemical reactions in a cell that take food molecules apart to release the food's energy, which is then stored as ATP.

RNA (ribonucleic acid). Polymer of ribonucleotides; important in protein synthesis.

species. Group of organisms that has common characteristics and is capable of interbreeding; a subdivision of a genus.

tissue. Grouping of cells and matter between the cells performing a common function.

viruses. Group of parasites composed of protein and nucleic acid; infectious agents smaller than bacteria that require host cells for replication.

zygote. Single cell formed by the union of an egg and a sperm; a fertilized ovum.

For Further Reference

Andrewes, C.H.
Natural History of Viruses
Norton Publishing

Berger, Melvin
Tools of Modern Biology
Thomas Y. Crowell

Carlquist, Sherwin
Island Life
Natural History Press

Curtiss, Helena
Invitation to Biology
Worth Publishing

Tompkins, Peter and Bird, Christopher
The Secret Life of Plants
Harper & Row

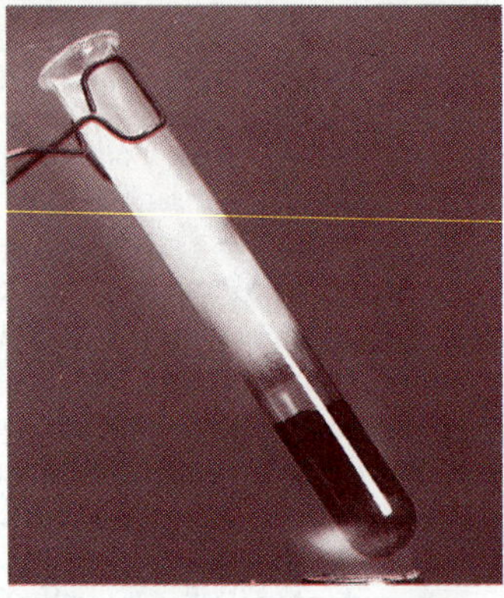

Chemistry

It is customary to break the sciences into several branches. The most familiar are biology, chemistry, and physics. Increasingly, however, our understanding of the way nature works suggests that these divisions are somewhat artificial. Scientists try to bridge the gaps between the branches by becoming biochemists, biophysicists, nuclear chemists, and so forth.

Even though the distinctions among the sciences are becoming blurred, it is still useful to be able to identify chemistry as opposed to other sciences. It is commonly said that the biologist studies the properties of life, the chemist studies the properties of matter, and the physicist studies the properties of energy. But the biologist also studies chemical interactions in living things, the chemist studies not only matter produced by living things but also the transfer of energy in some forms of matter, and the physicist intrudes into the domains of life and matter. There are, however, specific forms of matter the chemist studies.

Matter

The science of chemistry is concerned with the study of matter, its properties, its structure, its composition, and changes in its composition. *Matter* is anything that occupies space and has *mass*, which is a measure of the amount of matter in an object. Under ordinary conditions at Earth's surface, the mass of an object is the same as its weight, or nearly so. Since weight is defined as the pull of Earth's gravitation on an object, weight becomes less as matter moves away from Earth toward outer space, but its mass stays the same.

When studying samples of matter, chemists find that most are *mixtures* that can be separated by physical means into various *compounds*, which in turn can be broken down into *elements*. An element is the simplest kind of chemical substance that cannot be broken down into simpler substances by ordinary chemical means. Oxygen, hydrogen, carbon, sodium, and chlorine are examples of elements. A compound is formed by the chemical union of two or more elements. New compounds can also be formed by the chemical interaction of other compounds. Water, made up of hydrogen and oxygen, carbon dioxide, made up of carbon and oxygen, and sodium chloride, or table salt, made up of sodium and chlorine, are examples of compounds. When salt is dissolved in water, the resulting salt water is an example of a mixture. Carbon dioxide bubbled into water makes soda water, another example of a mixture.

The smallest unit of an element that can enter into chemical change is an *atom.* All atoms of a given element have the same basic structure, although they may differ slightly in mass. At present, 108 elements are known, but only 88 of these are found in nature. The rest are synthetic and are too unstable to exist in nature. The number of ways in which the elements can combine into compounds is very much greater than the number of elements. In fact, the number of compounds that are possible is so large as to be practically infinite.

Each element has been assigned a symbol consisting of one or two letters. Chemists use these symbols to write formulas for compounds. For example, the symbol for hydrogen is H, for oxygen it is O, for carbon it is C, for chlorine it is Cl; but the symbol for sodium is Na, from the Latin *natrium.*

The *formula* of a compound shows the different elements it contains and the number of each atom present, or the ratio in which the different elements are present. For most compounds, such as water and carbon dioxide, the formula represents the makeup of the *molecules* of the substance; that is, the smallest particle of the substance that can exist free and retain the properties of that substance. A molecule of water is H_2O, and a molecule of carbon dioxide is CO_2. Some compounds, such as sodium chloride, are made up of *ions*, charged particles that form when the atoms combine. In sodium chloride, there are equal numbers of positive ions of sodium (Na^+) and of negative chloride ions (Cl^-); thus, its formula is written NaCl, indicating one sodium ion to one chloride ion. Some compounds that consist of ions, such as sodium hydroxide (NaOH), contain certain combinations of elements called *polyatomic ions*. The hydroxide ion, OH^-, is a polyatomic ion in the compound sodium hydroxide. Another example is the sulfate group, SO_4^{2-}, as it occurs; for example, in aluminum sulfate, $Al_2(SO_4)_3$. This formula indicates that aluminum sulfate consists of Al^{3+} and SO_4^{2-} ions in the ratio of 2 to 3.

Phases of matter.

Matter may exist in three states or *phases*: solid, liquid, or gas. A familiar example is water, which in the solid phase is called ice or snow, in the liquid phase, water, and in the gaseous phase, steam or water vapor. The phase of any substance depends on the temperature and pressure. At atmospheric pressure, the temperature at which the solid form changes to the liquid is called the *melting point*. The temperature at which the *vapor pressure* of the liquid (that is, the pressure of the gaseous phase of the substance) in equilibrium with the liquid phase becomes equal to the atmospheric pressure, is called the *boiling point*.

Solids. A *solid* retains its shape and resists forces tending to change its shape. It is not so easy to pull apart as a liquid. The particles of some solids, such as sodium chloride, are arranged in definite patterns called crystals. Other solids, such as chalk, are not crystalline but amorphous.

Liquids. In a *liquid*, the particles are free to move about but not to separate from one another. A liquid will take the shape of the container in which it is placed, but will not expand to fill the entire space available to it.

Gases. A *gas* has no boundary surface. It will take the shape of and expand to fill any container in which it is placed. Gases respond readily to changes in pressure and temperature. The volume of the gas particles is usually only a small fraction of the total space they occupy.

Amounts of the elements (by weight)

Most of Earth's crust, including its air and water, is made from compounds. Some uncombined elements, such as oxygen in air, also occur in nature.

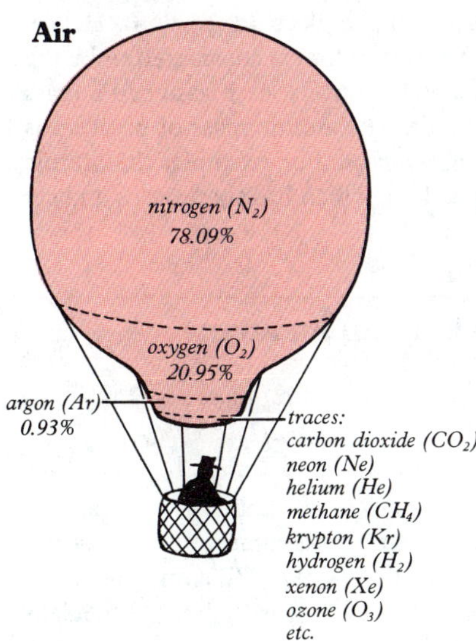

Element	*Symbol*	*Percent in earth*	*Percent in human body*
oxygen	0	47%	65%
silicon	Si	28%	trace
aluminum	Al	8%	—
iron	Fe	5%	trace
calcium	Ca	4%	2%
carbon	C	trace	18%
hydrogen	H	trace	3%
phosphorus	P	trace	1%
potassium	K	3%	trace
magnesium	Mg	2%	trace
nitrogen	N	traces	traces
sulfur	S	traces	traces
chlorine	Cl	traces	traces
fluorine	F	traces	traces
copper	Cu	traces	traces
iodine	I	traces	traces
manganese	Mn	traces	traces
zinc	Zn	traces	traces
about 70 other elements		traces	

Phases of matter

Particles of a solid vibrate. Particles of a liquid are free to move but not to separate, except at the surface. Particles of a gas are unattached.

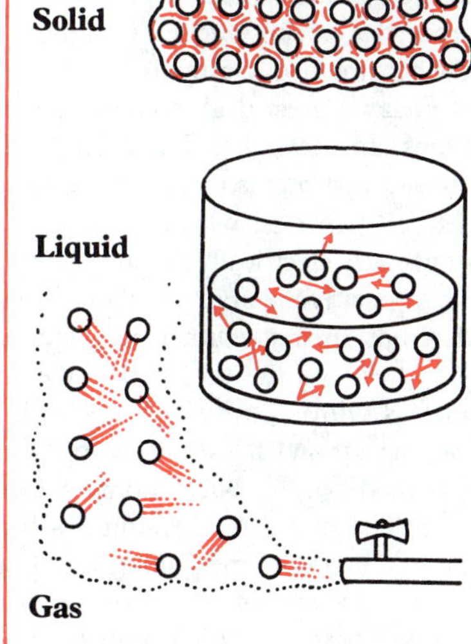

Changes in matter. The changes that matter can undergo may be classified as physical or chemical. In a *physical change*, there is no change in the composition or chemical properties of the substances involved: that is, no new combinations of elements in compounds are formed. For example, the freezing of water to form ice is a physical change, as are all changes of phase. Molecules of ice, water, or steam are all still H_2O. Physical change can also be seen in the dissolving of salt into water. Both the salt and the water retain their chemical makeup and properties, although some of their physical properties are changed.

A *chemical change* or *reaction* always results in the formation of one or more new substances. Chemical reactions take place when new combinations of atoms of elements in compounds are formed. The burning of a fuel such as gasoline is a familiar example of a chemical change. The gasoline reacts with oxygen from the air and two new substances, carbon dioxide and water, are formed.

Both physical and chemical changes involve energy changes. For example, energy is stored in water when it is changed into steam, and energy is released when gasoline burns. Energy does not change to matter, however, in physical and chemical changes.

Physical and chemical change

When water is heated and becomes steam, a physical change occurs. The molecules move apart, but their composition stays the same.

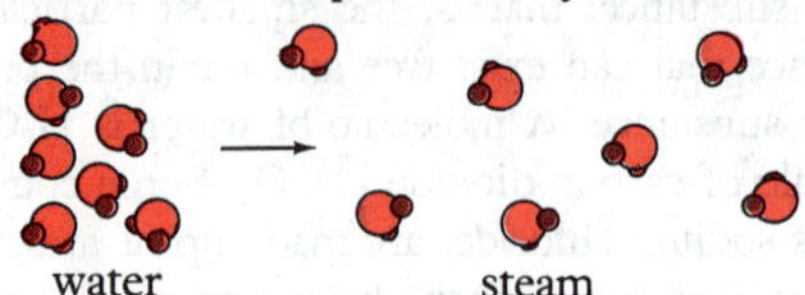

When the octane in gasoline burns, a chemical change occurs. Atoms of carbon (black spheres) and atoms of hydrogen (brown spheres) that were combined in the molecule of octane come apart and are recombined with atoms of oxygen (red spheres) to form molecules of water and carbon dioxide.

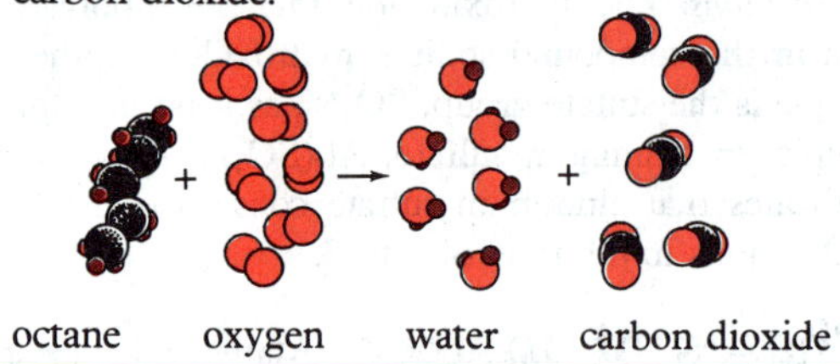

Atomic structure

The idea that matter can be divided only so far before coming to a particle, called an atom, which cannot be divided any further, was first proposed by the Greek philosophers Leucippus and Democritus about 400 B.C. More than 2000 years later, the idea became the basis for modern chemistry. In 1803, the English chemist John Dalton reformulated the atomic theory and showed that it explains a great deal about the chemical properties of substances. Since then, the atomic theory has become firmly established.

Today a great deal is known about the structure of atoms. In 1898, J.J. Thomson, an English physicist, showed that atoms can be made to give up negatively charged particles, which he called *electrons.* Since all atoms are electrically neutral, they must contain as many positive charges as they do negatively charged electrons. Ernest Rutherford, another English physicist, proposed the theory that the atom consists of a nucleus with a positive charge with enough electrons rotating around it to balance the charge. This theory was modified by Niels Bohr, a Danish physicist, in 1913. His model of the atom, as further modified by modern quantum mechanics, is still in use today.

The nucleus of the atom consists of positively charged particles called *protons*, and neutral particles called *neutrons*. Each neutron has almost exactly the same mass as a proton. Moving around the nucleus are *electrons*, equal in number to the protons in the nucleus. Electrons have a mass that is only about one two-thousandth that of a neutron or proton. When computing the mass of an atom, therefore, a chemist considers the masses of the electrons to be 0. Hence, the *atomic mass* of a given atom is considered to be the sum of its protons and neutrons, each assigned a mass of 1 atomic mass unit. The atomic mass of an atom is also called its *mass number*. For example, the atomic mass of ordinary carbon, which has six protons and six neutrons, is 12.

Particles making up an atom

Particle	*Symbol*	*Charge*	*Approximate mass (atomic mass units)*	*Location*
proton	p	1+	1 amu	nucleus
neutron	n	0	1 amu	nucleus
electron	e	1−	1/1837 amu (or 0)	outside nucleus

Bohr pictured the movement of the electrons around the nucleus as somewhat like the orbiting of the planets around the sun. Diagrams of atomic structures used to explain chemical reactions still use what is essentially the Bohr model. However, a somewhat different model, in which each electron is represented as a cloud of negative charge, is necessitated by today's more advanced theory, which describes the probabilities of electrons being found at various distances and directions from the nucleus, rather than in fixed orbits.

Three models of the atom

There are various models, or ways of representing and thinking about the atom. Here are three that are commonly used. Each is shown for boron, which has atomic number 5.

The Bohr model. Electrons are pictured as orbiting the nucleus in definite paths, somewhat in the way that planets orbit the sun. Although this is a familiar model, it is inadequate because it is now known that electrons do not follow definite paths. Nevertheless, the Bohr model is a useful way to picture the atom in some applications. It is also the easiest model to understand, so it is frequently taught in the beginning, and then followed with more sophisticated models.

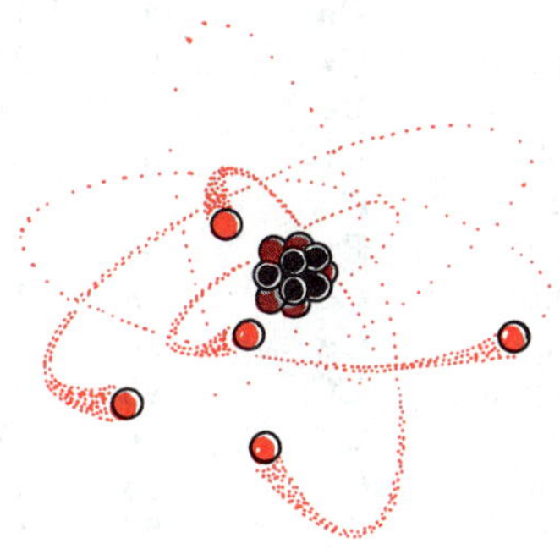

The electron-cloud model. Electrons are not shown as particles that follow precise paths in this model. Instead, the electrons are indicated by definite regions in which there is a high probability of finding electrons. These regions are often known as electron shells. In this model it is possible to picture electrons as either waves or particles. Each idea of the nature of electrons is useful in different applications.

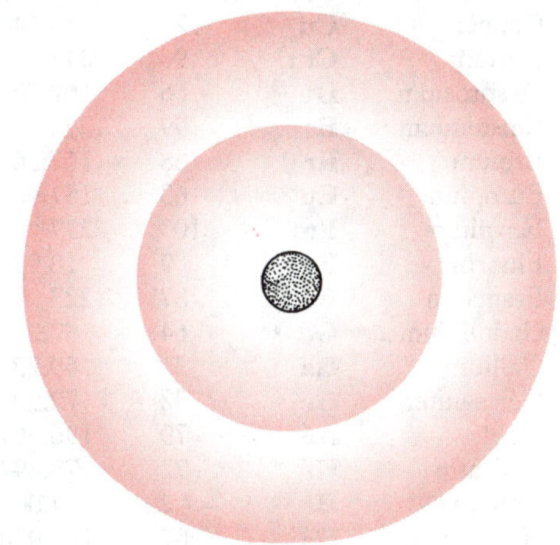

The electron-shell diagram. Chemists recognize that no model can really give an accurate picture of what an atom would look like if it were possible to see it. Therefore, it is often best to use a simplified diagram that provides information without attempting to give a physical picture of an atom. The electron-shell diagram, in which each electron is shown as a particle, and the shells are represented as concentric rings around the nucleus, provides useful information without using a physical representation that might lead to misunderstanding.

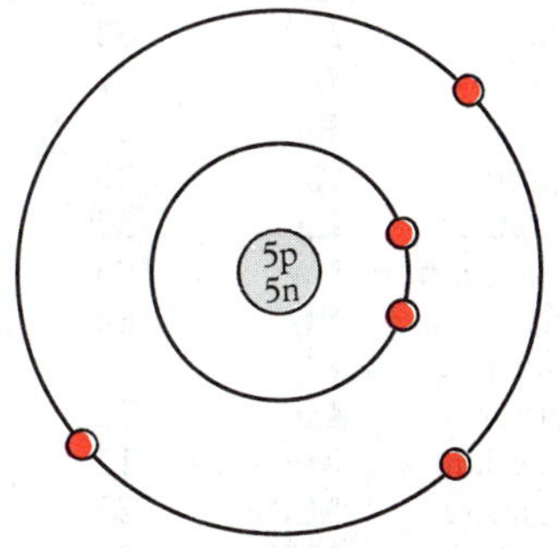

Table of atomic masses

Name	Symbol	Atomic number	Atomic mass
Actinium	**Ac**	89	227
Aluminum	**Al**	13	26.9815
Americium	**Am**	95	243
Antimony	**Sb**	51	121.75
Argon	**Ar**	18	39.948
Arsenic	**As**	33	74.9216
Astatine	**At**	85	210
Barium	**Ba**	56	137.34
Berkelium	**Bk**	97	247
Beryllium	**Be**	4	9.0122
Bismuth	**Bi**	83	208.980
Boron	**B**	5	10.811
Bromine	**Br**	35	79.904
Cadmium	**Cd**	48	112.40
Calcium	**Ca**	20	40.08
Californium	**Cf**	98	251
Carbon	**C**	6	12.01115
Cerium	**Ce**	58	140.12
Cesium	**Cs**	55	132.9055
Chlorine	**Cl**	17	35.453
Chromium	**Cr**	24	51.996
Cobalt	**Co**	27	58.9332
Copper	**Cu**	29	63.546
Curium	**Cm**	96	247
Dysprosium	**Dy**	66	162.50
Einsteinium	**Es**	99	254
Erbium	**Er**	68	167.26
Europium	**Eu**	63	151.96
Fermium	**Fm**	100	257
Fluorine	**F**	9	18.9984
Francium	**Fr**	87	223
Gadolinium	**Gd**	64	157.25
Gallium	**Ga**	31	69.72
Germanium	**Ge**	32	72.59
Gold	**Au**	79	196.967
Hafnium	**Hf**	72	178.49
Helium	**He**	2	4.0026
Holmium	**Ho**	67	164.930
Hydrogen	**H**	1	1.00797
Indium	**In**	49	114.82
Iodine	**I**	53	126.9045
Iridium	**Ir**	77	192.2
Iron	**Fe**	26	55.847
Krypton	**Kr**	36	83.80
Lanthanum	**La**	57	138.91
Lawrencium	**Lw**	103	256
Lead	**Pb**	82	207.19
Lithium	**Li**	3	6.941
Lutetium	**Lu**	71	174.97
Magnesium	**Mg**	12	24.305
Manganese	**Mn**	25	54.9380
Mendelevium	**Md**	101	258
Mercury	**Hg**	80	200.59
Molybdenum	**Mo**	42	95.94
Neodymium	**Nd**	60	144.24
Neon	**Ne**	10	20.179
Neptunium	**Np**	93	237
Nickel	**Ni**	28	58.71
Niobium	**Nb**	41	92.906
Nitrogen	**N**	7	14.0067
Nobelium	**No**	102	255
Osmium	**Os**	76	190.2
Oxygen	**O**	8	15.9994
Palladium	**Pd**	46	106.4
Phosphorus	**P**	15	30.9738
Platinum	**Pt**	78	195.09
Plutonium	**Pu**	94	244
Polonium	**Po**	84	210
Potassium	**K**	19	39.102
Praseodymium	**Pr**	59	140.9077
Promethium	**Pm**	61	147
Protactinium	**Pa**	91	231
Radium	**Ra**	88	226.0254
Radon	**Rn**	86	222
Rhenium	**Re**	75	186.2
Rhodium	**Rh**	45	102.9055
Rubidium	**Rb**	37	85.47
Ruthenium	**Ru**	44	101.07
Samarium	**Sm**	62	150.35
Scandium	**Sc**	21	44.956
Selenium	**Se**	34	78.96
Silicon	**Si**	14	28.086
Silver	**Ag**	47	107.868
Sodium	**Na**	11	22.9898
Strontium	**Sr**	38	87.62
Sulfur	**S**	16	32.064
Tantalum	**Ta**	73	180.948
Technetium	**Tc**	43	99
Tellurium	**Te**	52	127.60
Terbium	**Tb**	65	158.9254
Thallium	**Tl**	81	204.37
Thorium	**Th**	90	232.038
Thulium	**Tm**	69	168.934
Tin	**Sn**	50	118.69
Titanium	**Ti**	22	47.90
Tungsten	**W**	74	183.85
Uranium	**U**	92	238.03
Vanadium	**V**	23	50.9414
Xenon	**Xe**	54	131.30
Ytterbium	**Yb**	70	173.04
Yttrium	**Y**	39	88.9059
Zinc	**Zn**	30	65.37
Zirconium	**Zr**	40	91.22

All elements exist in more than one form, differing in atomic mass but having the same atomic number. These different forms are called *isotopes*. The element hydrogen, for example, has three isotopes. For many chemical calculations, it is important to know the atomic masses of various elements. These are relative to a standard, usually the most abundant isotope of carbon, which is assigned a value of 12, the same as its mass number. The table of atomic masses (page 150) shows that most of these values are close to whole numbers. One reason they are not whole numbers is that the atomic mass of every element is an average of the masses of the isotopes in the proportions in which they exist in nature.

For example, carbon 13 and carbon 14 are both found in small amounts in nature. Therefore the atomic mass shown for carbon in the table is 12.01115, which reflects the amount of carbon 13 and carbon 14 in a typical sample of carbon. Since the atomic mass of carbon 12 is 12, it is easy to see that most of the mass is due to carbon 12.

In the Bohr model of the atom, the electrons orbit the nucleus in definite shells. A certain maximum number of electrons can fit into each shell. The first shell, closest to the nucleus, is filled when it has two electrons. The second and third shells can each hold eight electrons. The fourth and fifth shells can each hold 18 electrons, and the sixth and seventh shells can each hold 32 electrons. It is the electrons that determine the chemical properties of atoms.

Isotopes of hydrogen

Natural elements are mixtures of different isotopes. Hydrogen has three isotopes: protium with an atomic mass of 1, deuterium, with an atomic mass of 2, and tritium, with an atomic mass of 3. Since there is a much larger percentage of protium (atomic mass = 1) than of the other isotopes, the average atomic mass of hydrogen is 1.008. Hydrogen is the only element with special names for its isotopes. It can be seen in the diagrams that all atoms of hydrogen have the same charge (number of protons) on the nucleus, and thus the same atomic number. They also all have the same number (1) of orbiting electrons. The atoms are all shown as electron-shell diagrams, which provide the essential information without trying to suggest actual "pictures" of atoms.

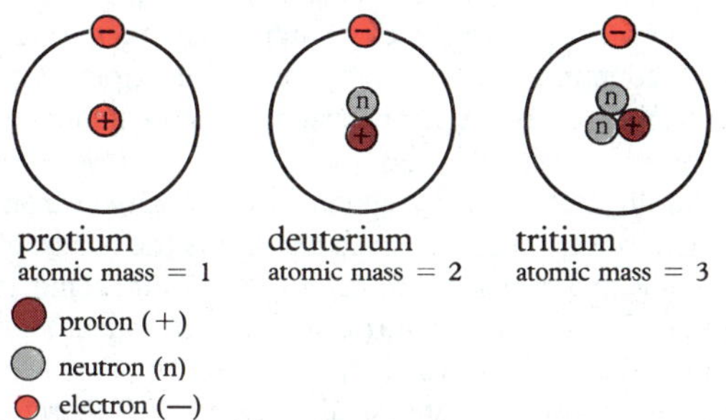

Structures of the first 18 elements

The number next to the symbol for each element is the atomic number. The diagrams reflect the pairing of electrons in the first three shells around the nucleus. The number of neutrons (n) on each nucleus is the number in the most common isotope of the element. The number of protons (p) equals the number of electrons in the atom.

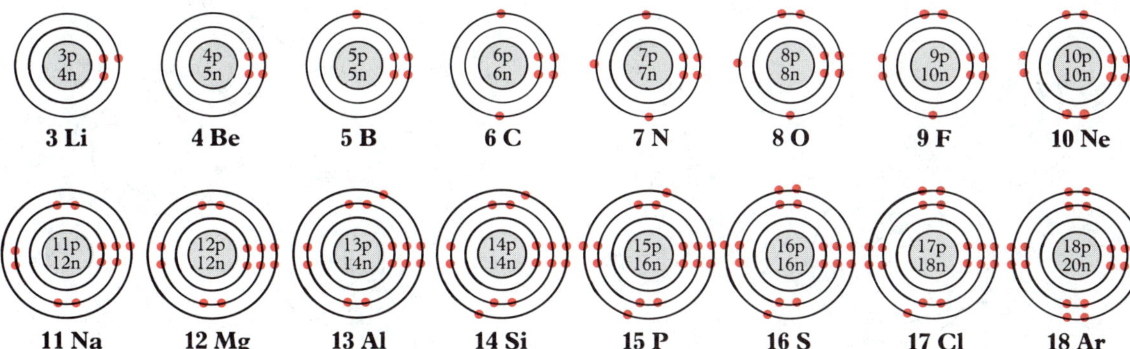

Chemical reactions

In nearly all chemical reactions, only the electrons in the outermost shell are involved. Chemical reactions consist of the transfer of electrons from some atoms to others, or the sharing of electrons between atoms. Atoms react in such a way as to reach a state of greatest stability. For elements with atomic numbers of 1 through 5 (that is, hydrogen, helium, lithium, beryllium, and boron) that state is usually two electrons in the outer shell, and for all other atoms it is usually eight electrons in the outer shell. The outer shell of an atom is called its *valence shell*, and the electrons in the valence shell are the atom's *valence electrons*. No atom can have more than eight valence electrons, even though its outer shell may be capable of holding many more; the chemical demands of the atom are satisfied by eight. There are six elements, called the inert or *noble gases*, that do not ordinarily undergo chemical reactions because in the elementary state, their valence shells contain a stable configuration of electrons. These elements are helium, neon, argon, krypton, xenon, and radon.

An illustration of a reaction in which an electron is transferred from one atom to another is the reaction of sodium and chlorine to produce sodium chloride, NaCl. The sodium atom transfers its one valence electron to the chlorine atom, which has seven. This leaves each atom with an outer shell of eight, and, therefore, with the stable electron structure of a noble gas. The loss of an electron leaves the sodium with a positive charge; the gain of an electron gives the chlorine a negative charge. That is, both become ions, which are atoms (or groups of atoms) with electric charges. The attraction between the oppositely charged ions is the bond that holds the two atoms together. This type of chemical bond is called an *ionic bond.*

Six gases that do not form compounds easily

Noble gas	*Atomic number*	*Electrons in valence shell*
helium	2	2
neon	10	8
argon	18	8
krypton	36	8
xenon	54	8
radon	86	8

Another way of completing the outer shell is for two or more atoms to share their electrons so that each has the stable configuration of a noble gas without an actual transfer. This type of chemical bond is called a *covalent bond.* Covalent bonding takes place in the formation of molecules of elements, like hydrogen (H_2), oxygen (O_2), and chlorine (Cl_2), that usually exist as diatomic molecules in the elementary state. The great majority of chemical compounds also have covalent bonds rather than ionic bonds, and exist as molecules rather than as ions. An example of covalent bonding may be seen in the sharing of electrons between a hydrogen atom and a chlorine atom in the compound hydrogen chloride, HCl. In a molecule of hydrogen chloride, the hydrogen atom has a stable structure of two electrons in its outer shell, and the chlorine atom has a stable structure of eight in its outer shell.

Electron transfer

Formation of sodium chloride (NaCl)

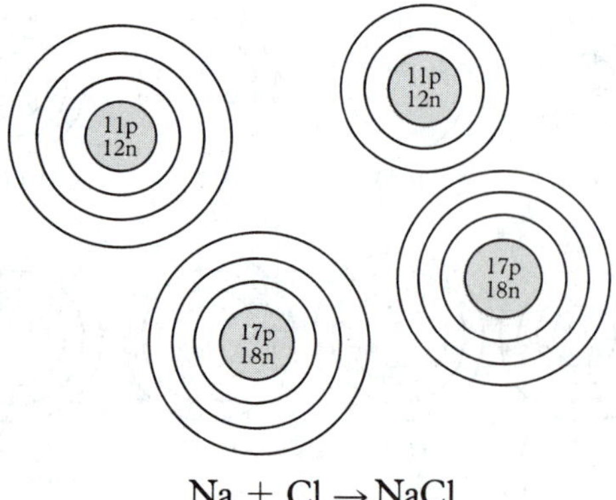

Na + Cl → NaCl

Electron sharing

Formation of hydrogen chloride (HCl)

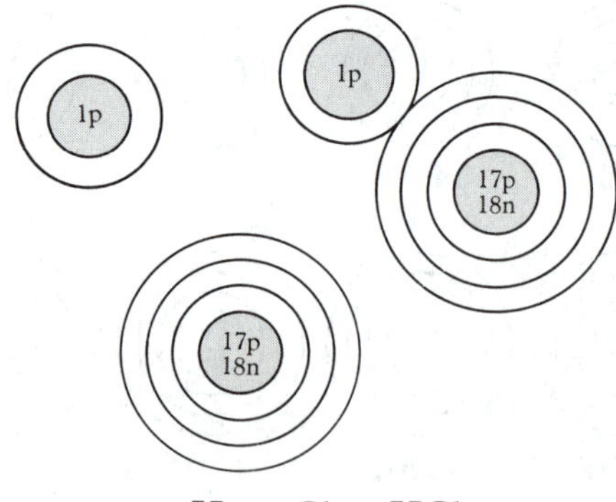

H + Cl → HCl

How to balance equations. The ratio in which atoms of elements combine to form compounds is determined by the number of electrons that the atoms lose, gain, or share when combining with other atoms. For example, when atoms of the metal calcium combine with atoms of the nonmetal fluorine, each calcium atom loses two electrons, forming Ca^{2+} ions, and each fluorine atom gains one electron, forming F^- ions. Since the compound that forms, calcium fluoride, is electrically neutral, there must be two F^- ions for each Ca^{2+} ion. Thus, the formula for the compound is written CaF_2. Formulas for many other compounds between metals and nonmetals are determined in a similar way.

When two nonmetals combine to form a compound, their atoms share electrons. Depending on various conditions, the number of electrons shared by two given elements may vary. For example, each of two atoms of oxygen may share two electrons with one atom of sulfur, which shares four electrons in the compound SO_2, sulfur dioxide. But in sulfur trioxide, SO_3, the sulfur atom shares six electrons, so three atoms of oxygen, each sharing two electrons, are required.

A chemical change or reaction can be expressed as a *chemical equation*, in which symbols and formulas for the substances involved are joined by plus signs and an arrow. The substances that appear at the left of the arrow are the *reactants*; those that appear at the right are the *products* of the reaction. For example, the equation

$$2H_2 + O_2 \rightarrow 2H_2O$$

states that two molecules of hydrogen react with one molecule of water to form two molecules of water. Since both hydrogen and oxygen exist as diatomic molecules, we write their formulas as H_2 and O_2. When an equation is *balanced*, all atoms appearing in the reactants must also appear in the products, although in different combinations. So the number 2 is written before the H_2 and the H_2O in order to balance the numbers of atoms in the equation.

Writing a laboratory report

Problem: You are presented with an unknown white crystal, which you suspect to be table salt, sodium chloride (NaCl). You perform a series of tests (which do not include tasting, since many white crystals are poisonous). Here is a format for presenting your report on the tests.

NOTE: The arrow pointing downward in a chemical equation indicates a *precipitate*, a solid that forms from a liquid and settles to the bottom of the liquid.

PROBLEM: Determine the chemical composition of an unknown white crystal.

PROCEDURE

STEP 1: Dissolved the crystal in 1/3 test tube of H_2O. (Dissolved easily.)

STEP 2: Added 2mL silver nitrate, $AgNO_3$. White precipitate appeared and settled to bottom of tube. Reaction could be

$$AgNO_3 + NaCl \rightarrow AgCl\downarrow + NaNO_3$$

STEP 3: Added 3mL dilute nitric acid, HNO_3, to solution. No effect on precipitate. (AgCl does not react with HNO_3.)

STEP 4: Poured off solution leaving precipitate in test tube. Added 5mL ammonium hydroxide. Precipitate dissolved. Reaction must be with ammonia, NH_3.

$$AgCl + 2NH_3 \rightarrow Ag(NH_3)_2Cl$$

REMARKS: After getting results outlined, concluded that the unknown crystal was salt (NaCl).

The periodic table

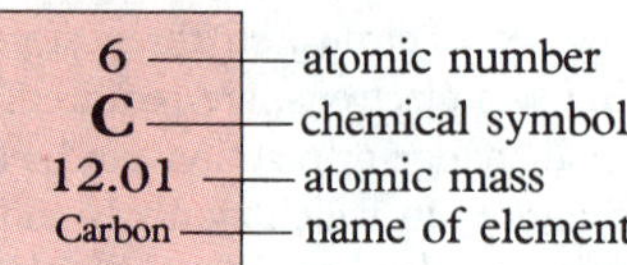

Early in the 19th century, chemists noted that the elements seemed to fall into several groups, with certain elements showing definite family resemblances. The Russian chemist Dmitri Mendeleev published the first successful periodic table of the elements in 1869. He showed that if the elements were arranged in the approximate order of increasing atomic mass, they showed a periodic change in properties from metallic to nonmetallic. The rows of the periodic table begin with the strongly metallic elements on the left; as we move across the rows, we see that the nonmetals are on the far right, with the noble gases at the extreme right. We now know that the order is actually one of increasing atomic number. The modern form of the periodic table appears on this page and the next.

In the periodic table, the number of each *period*, or horizontal row, indicates the number of electrons in the outermost, or valence, shell of each element in that period. For example, the elements in period 2 have their valence electrons in the second shell.

	alkali metals IA	**alkaline earth metals** II A	transition metals III B	IV B	V B	VI B	VII B		VIII
Period 1	1 **H** 1.01 Hydrogen								
Period 2	3 **Li** 6.94 Lithium	4 **Be** 9.01 Beryllium							
Period 3	11 **Na** 23.00 Sodium	12 **Mg** 24.31 Magnesium							
Period 4	19 **K** 39.10 Potassium	20 **Ca** 40.08 Calcium	21 **Sc** 44.96 Scandium	22 **Ti** 47.90 Titanium	23 **V** 50.94 Vanadium	24 **Cr** 52.00 Chromium	25 **Mn** 54.94 Manganese	26 **Fe** 55.85 Iron	27 **Co** 58.93 Cobalt
Period 5	37 **Rb** 85.47 Rubidium	38 **Sr** 87.62 Strontium	39 **Y** 88.91 Yttrium	40 **Zr** 91.22 Zirconium	41 **Nb** 92.91 Niobium	42 **Mo** 95.94 Molybdenum	43 **Tc** 98.91 Technetium	44 **Ru** 101.07 Ruthenium	45 **Rh** 102.91 Rhodium
Period 6	55 **Cs** 132.91 Cesium	56 **Ba** 137.34 Barium		72 **Hf** 178.49 Hafnium	73 **Ta** 180.95 Tantalum	74 **W** 183.85 Tungsten	75 **Re** 186.2 Rhenium	76 **Os** 190.2 Osmium	77 **Ir** 192.2 Iridium
Period 7	87 **Fr** (223) Francium	88 **Ra** (226) Radium		104 (261)	105 (262)	106 (263)	107 (267)		109 (266)

rare earth elements							
Lanthanide series	57 **La** 138.9 Lanthanum	58 **Ce** 140.12 Cerium	59 **Pr** 140.91 Praseodymium	60 **Nd** 144.24 Neodymium	61 **Pm** (145) Promethium	62 **Sm** 150.4 Samarium	63 **Eu** 151.96 Europium
Actinide series	89 **Ac** (227) Actinium	90 **Th** 232.03 Thorium	91 **Pa** 231.04 Protactinium	92 **U** 238.03 Uranium	93 **Np** 237.05 Neptunium	94 **Pu** (244) Plutonium	95 **Am** (243) Americium

A figure in parentheses is the isotope of longest known half-life. No stable isotope is known.

As we move from left to right in each period, the number of valence electrons increases until, at the end of the period, we reach an element whose valence shell is full. For example, at the end of period 2 is the element neon, a noble gas whose valence shell contains eight electrons.

Each element in a vertical column, or *group*, has the same number of valence electrons. For example, each element in group VIIA has seven electrons in its valence shell. Because of this similarity of structure, the elements of group VIIA have a number of similar or related physical properties and undergo many similar chemical reactions as well. For example, the elements in this group are called by a family name, the *halogens* ("salt-formers"), because of their common property of reacting with metals to form salts. A familiar example is sodium chloride, formed by the halogen chlorine when it reacts with sodium, a member of the family of *alkali metals*, in group IA of the periodic table.

nonmetals (III A – VII A)

	I B	II B	III A	IV A	V A	VI A	VII A	noble gases O
								2 **He** 4.00 Helium
			5 **B** 10.81 Boron	6 **C** 12.01 Carbon	7 **N** 14.01 Nitrogen	8 **O** 16.00 Oxygen	9 **F** 19.00 Fluorine	10 **Ne** 20.18 Neon
			13 **Al** 26.98 Aluminum	14 **Si** 28.09 Silicon	15 **P** 30.97 Phosphorus	16 **S** 32.06 Sulfur	17 **Cl** 35.45 Chlorine	18 **Ar** 39.95 Argon
28 **Ni** 58.71 Nickel	29 **Cu** 63.55 Copper	30 **Zn** 65.37 Zinc	31 **Ga** 69.72 Gallium	32 **Ge** 72.59 Germanium	33 **As** 74.92 Arsenic	34 **Se** 78.96 Selenium	35 **Br** 79.90 Bromine	36 **Kr** 83.80 Krypton
46 **Pd** 106.4 Palladium	47 **Ag** 107.87 Silver	48 **Cd** 112.40 Cadmium	49 **In** 114.82 Indium	50 **Sn** 118.69 Tin	51 **Sb** 121.75 Antimony	52 **Te** 127.60 Tellurium	53 **I** 126.90 Iodine	54 **Xe** 131.30 Xenon
78 **Pt** 195.09 Platinum	79 **Au** 196.97 Gold	80 **Hg** 200.59 Mercury	81 **Tl** 204.37 Thallium	82 **Pb** 207.2 Lead	83 **Bi** 208.98 Bismuth	84 **Po** (209) Polonium	85 **At** (210) Astatine	86 **Rn** (222) Radon

other metals

64 **Gd** 157.25 Gadolinium	65 **Tb** 158.93 Terbium	66 **Dy** 162.50 Dysprosium	67 **Ho** 164.93 Holmium	68 **Er** 167.26 Erbium	69 **Tm** 168.93 Thulium	70 **Yb** 173.04 Ytterbium	71 **Lu** 174.97 Lutetium
96 **Cm** (247) Curium	97 **Bk** (247) Berkelium	98 **Cf** (251) Californium	99 **Es** (254) Einsteinium	100 **Fm** (257) Fermium	101 **Md** (258) Mendelevium	102 **No** (255) Nobelium	103 **Lw** (256) Lawrencium

Inorganic chemistry

Inorganic chemistry deals with the reactions of all the elements with the exception, for the most part, of carbon. Many of the reactions of inorganic chemistry are known as *oxidation-reduction* reactions, in which one substance that loses electrons is *oxidized*, and another that gains electrons is *reduced*. These two processes always go on simultaneously. When one substance is oxidized, another must be reduced. All reactions of the types known as direct combination, decomposition, and single replacement are oxidation-reduction reactions. The rusting of iron, forming ferric oxide, Fe_2O_3, is a familiar example of oxidation, with the iron being oxidized and oxygen, from the air, being reduced. It is because oxygen is such a common oxidizing agent that the whole process is often called, simply, "oxidation."

Many inorganic compounds can be classified as *acids*, *bases*, and *salts*. An acid is a compound that is able to give up hydrogen ions to some other compound. The compound that receives hydrogen ions from an acid is called a base. The products of the reaction between an acid and a base are water and a salt. When the acid and base that react are of equal strength, the reaction is called *neutralization*.

For example, hydrochloric acid reacts with the base sodium hydroxide to produce the salt sodium chloride and water:

$$HCl + NaOH \longrightarrow NaCl + H_2O$$

This reaction, like all acid-base reactions, is a kind of double replacement, in which there is an exchange of ions between two compounds.

Types of inorganic reactions

Type	*Reactants*	*Products*	*Examples*
Direct combination or synthesis	element + element or compound + compound	compound	$2Na + Cl_2 \rightarrow 2NaCl$ (sodium + chlorine → sodium chloride)
			$2CO + O_2 \rightarrow 2CO_2$ (carbon monoxide + oxygen → carbon dioxide)
Decomposition or analysis	compound	two or more elements or compounds	$2HgO \rightarrow 2Hg + O_2$ (mercuric oxide → mercury + oxygen)
			$2KClO_3 \rightarrow 2KCl + 3O_2$ (potassium chlorate → potassium chloride + oxygen)
Single replacement	element + compound	element + compound	$Cl_2 + 2NaI \rightarrow I_2 + 2NaCl$ (chlorine + sodium iodide → iodine + sodium chloride)
			$Zn + H_2SO_4 \rightarrow H_2 + ZnSO_4$ (zinc + sulfuric acid → hydrogen + zinc sulfate)
Double replacement	compound + compound	compound + compound	$NaCl + AgNO_3 \rightarrow NaNO_3 + AgCl$ (sodium chloride + silver nitrate → sodium nitrate + silver chloride)
			$2\,HCl + FeS \rightarrow H_2S + FeCl_2$ (hydrochloric acid + ferrous sulfide → hydrogen sulfide + ferrous chloride)

Organic chemistry

The chemistry of most compounds of carbon is unique and is considered as a separate branch of chemistry, *organic chemistry*. It is called organic because until 1828 chemists believed that familiar carbon compounds, such as ethyl alcohol, acetic acid, and sugars, could only be produced by living things (that is, organisms). In 1828, however, the German chemist Friedrich Wöhler succeeded in making urea, a typical organic compound, from ammonium chloride and silver cyanate, typical inorganic compounds.

Carbon is unique because its atoms have the ability to link together to form chains of great size and complexity. Carbon has four electrons in its outer shell, and these are available for covalent sharing with other elements, but especially with other carbon atoms.

The number and variety of compounds that carbon forms with hydrogen, known as the *hydrocarbons*, is quite large. We can represent the simplest of these compounds, methane, CH_4, by a *structural formula* in which each dash represents a pair of shared electrons between the atoms indicated by their symbols:

$$\begin{array}{ccc} & H & \\ & | & \\ H- & C & -H \\ & | & \\ & H & \end{array}$$

Methane, the main component of natural gas, is the first in a series of hydrocarbons called the *alkanes*, characterized by *single bonds* between carbon atoms. A single bond exists when each of the atoms that share electrons contributes only one electron to the bond. The alkanes are *saturated* hydrocarbons; this means that they contain only single bonds.

A carbon atom may also share two or even three of its electrons with another carbon. The resulting compounds form other series of hydrocarbons. The *alkenes*, whose first member is ethylene (or ethene), are a series of hydrocarbons that have one *double* bond (written C=C) in their structure; and the *alkynes*, whose first member is acetylene (or alkyne), are a series that have a triple bond (written C≡C) in their structure. The *aromatics*, so-called because many members have a distinctive odor, are another important series of hydrocarbons. Each of the aromatics has a ring of six carbons that contains three double bonds. Organic compounds that contain double or triple bonds between carbon atoms are *unsaturated*, which means that they may undergo reactions in which hydrogen atoms are added at the site of the double or triple bond.

Many organic compounds that contain oxygen as well as hydrogen and carbon also form series of related compounds. Four such series are the *alcohols*, the *aldehydes*, the *ketones*, and the *organic acids*.

Structures of some hydrocarbons

Series	Hydro-carbon	Molecular formula	Structural formula
Alkane	Methane	CH_4	$\begin{array}{ccc} & H & \\ & \vert & \\ H- & C & -H \\ & \vert & \\ & H & \end{array}$
	Ethane	C_2H_6	$\begin{array}{cccc} & H & H & \\ & \vert & \vert & \\ H- & C- & C & -H \\ & \vert & \vert & \\ & H & H & \end{array}$
Alkene	Ethene	C_2H_4	$\begin{array}{ccccc} H & & & & H \\ & \diagdown & & \diagup & \\ & C & = & C & \\ & \diagup & & \diagdown & \\ H & & & & H \end{array}$
	Propene	C_3H_6	$\begin{array}{ccccc} & H & H & H & \\ & \vert & \vert & \vert & \\ H- & C= & C- & C & -H \\ & & & \vert & \\ & & & H & \end{array}$
Alkyne	Ethyne	C_2H_2	$H-C\equiv C-H$
	Propyne	C_3H_4	$\begin{array}{ccccc} & & & H & \\ & & & \vert & \\ H- & C\equiv & C- & C & -H \\ & & & \vert & \\ & & & H & \end{array}$
Aromatic	Benzene	C_6H_6	$\begin{array}{ccccc} & & H & & \\ & & \vert & & \\ & & C & & \\ & /\!/ & & \diagdown & \\ H-C & & & & C-H \\ \vert & & & & \Vert \\ H-C & & & & C-H \\ & \diagdown\!\diagdown & & / & \\ & & C & & \\ & & \vert & & \\ & & H & & \end{array}$
	Toluene	C_7H_8	$\begin{array}{ccccc} & & H & & \\ & & \vert & & \\ & & C & & \\ & /\!/ & & \diagdown & \\ H-C & & & & C-CH_3 \\ \vert & & & & \Vert \\ H-C & & & & C-H \\ & \diagdown\!\diagdown & & / & \\ & & C & & \\ & & \vert & & \\ & & H & & \end{array}$

Structures of some organic compounds of carbon, hydrogen, and oxygen

Series	*Functional group*	*Example*	*Structural formula*
Alcohols	—OH	ethyl alcohol	H H | | H—C—C—OH | | H H
Aldehydes	H | —C=	formaldehyde	H | H—C=O
Ketones	—C=O	acetone	H O H | ‖ | H—C—C—C—H | | H H
Organic acids	O // —C \\ OH	acetic acid	H O | // H—C—C | \\ H OH

The alcohols, aldehydes, ketones, and organic acids are each characterized by a *functional group*. The functional group is present in each compound and determines its properties.

Like inorganic compounds, organic compounds undergo characteristic types of reactions. These reactions include oxidation, addition, substitution, and esterfication. Examples are shown in the tables.

Some types of organic reactions

Type	*What happens*	*Example*
Oxidation of a hydrocarbon	A hydrocarbon reacts with oxygen, forming carbon dioxide and water.	H | H—C—H + $2O_2$ → CO_2 + $2H_2O$ | H methane oxygen carbon dioxide water
Addition	Atoms (or groups) are added at a double bond, resulting in the saturation of the bond.	H H H H | | | | H—C=C—H + Cl_2 → H—C—C—H | | Cl Cl ethene (or ethylene) chlorine dichloroethane
Substitution	Atoms (or groups) are replaced by atoms (or groups) of another kind.	H H H H | | | | H—C—C—H + Cl_2 → H—C—C—H + HCl | | | | H H H Cl ethane chlorine ethyl chloride (or monochloroethane) hydrogen chloride
Esterification	An organic acid reacts with an alcohol to form an ester and water.	H O H H H O H H | // | | | // | | H—C—C + H—C—C—OH → H—C—C—O—C—C—H + H_2O | \\ | | | | | H OH H H H H H acetic acid ethyl alcohol ethyl acetate (an ester) water

Nuclear chemistry

The reactions of both inorganic and organic chemistry involve changes that take place outside the nuclei of atoms. However, the nuclei of certain isotopes of many elements are unstable and break down; that is, they undergo *radioactive decay*. Isotopes whose nuclei break down in this process are called radioactive isotopes, or *radioisotopes*. When nuclei break down spontaneously, the process is called *natural radioactivity*. However, some nuclei can be made radioactive artificially, and they exhibit *induced radioactivity*.

Radioactive atoms emit three types of radiation: *alpha particles*, *beta particles*, and *gamma rays*. An alpha particle is made up of two protons and two neutrons, and is therefore identical to the nucleus of a helium atom. As such, its symbol is ${}^{4}_{2}He$, in which the 4 indicates the mass and the 2 indicates the atomic number. Symbols used for isotopes of other elements are written in the same system for the purpose of representing nuclear reactions. A beta particle is a high-speed electron coming from the nucleus, not the outer part, of the atom. Since the nucleus contains no electrons, beta particles are considered to come from the breakdown of neutrons, each of which forms a proton and an electron in the process. Gamma rays, which often accompany the emission of alpha or beta particles, are a very penetrating form of radiant energy similar to x-rays.

All the isotopes of every naturally occurring element with an atomic number above 83 are radioactive. They undergo decay, usually in a series of reactions, some with the emission of an alpha particle and some with the emission of a beta particle, ending with the formation of a stable isotope of lead. For example, uranium 238, that is, the isotope of uranium that has an atomic mass of 238, emits an alpha particle to form thorium 234, which, in turn, emits a beta particle to form protactinium 234. After a number of additional steps, the series ends with the formation of lead 206. Changes such as these, in which atoms of one element are converted into atoms of another element, are called *transmutations*.

Another example of a transmutation is the decay of carbon 14, which emits a beta particle, into nitrogen 14, which is stable. This nuclear reaction occurs naturally and is the basis for *radiocarbon dating*, a valuable technique for finding the age of objects containing carbon, such as wood, cloth, or paper. All such organic objects start out with a certain proportion of radioactive carbon 14. By determining the proportion of carbon 14 to the total carbon content, we can calculate the age of the object. In carrying out this calculation, the *half-life* of carbon 14 is used. The half-life is the period of time it takes for half of the radioactive atoms in a substance to decay. The period of time varies among different radioisotopes; for carbon 14, it is 5730 years.

Particles and symbols used in nuclear chemistry

Particle	*Symbol*	*Charge*	*Mass in atomic mass units*
Beta particle (electron)	${}^{0}_{1-}e$	negative	0 amu
Positron	${}^{0}_{1+}e$	positive	0 amu
Proton (hydrogen-1 nucleus)	${}^{1}_{1}H$	positive	1 amu
Alpha particle (helium-4 nucleus)	${}^{4}_{2}He$	positive	4 amu
Neutron	${}^{1}_{0}n$	neutral	1 amu

Particle emission and half-lives

When a radioisotope decays, it may emit an alpha particle, a beta particle, or a positron. The half-lives of radioisotopes vary from very brief to very long periods of time. Some examples are listed here.

Radioisotope	*Particle emission*	*Half-life*
carbon 14	beta	5730 years
cobalt 60	beta	5.3 years
iodine 131	beta	8.07 days
uranium 238	alpha	4.51×10^9 years
radium 226	alpha	1620 years
potassium 42	beta	12.4 hours
francium 229	alpha	27.5 seconds
bismuth 212	alpha	60.5 minutes
silver 106	positron	24.5 minutes
yttrium 88	positron	2.0 hours
plutonium 239	alpha	24,000 years
lithium 8	beta	.88 seconds
nitrogen 13	positron	9.93 minutes

The *artificial transmutation* of elements takes place as the result of the bombardment, in the laboratory, of certain atoms by particles such as alpha particles, protons, or neutrons. Ernest Rutherford, in 1919, carried out the first artificial transmutation, from stable nitrogen 14 to stable oxygen 17. Irène and Frédéric Joliot-Curie, in 1934, were the first scientists to produce, artificially, a radioactive isotope, starting with stable aluminum 27 and obtaining radioactive phosphorus 30. The phosphorus 30, having a half-life of only 3.55 minutes, was soon converted to stable silicon 30. (These reactions, and those of other nuclear changes, are shown in the table on p. 161.)

Today many radioisotopes are produced by bombardment of the same element with neutrons, without transmutation, since the atomic number, and thus the identity of the element, remains the same and only the atomic mass changes. Radioisotopes produced artificially exhibit induced radioactivity. They are used as tracers in chemical reactions, in medical diagnoses, and in industrial processes.

Nuclear energy. Two types of nuclear reactions that result in the release of enormous amounts of energy are *nuclear fission* and *nuclear fusion*. In nuclear fission, a heavy nucleus is split to produce lighter nuclei, and in nuclear fusion, light nuclei combine to produce a heavier nucleus. In both of these types of reactions, the total mass of the nuclei of the reactants is greater than the total mass of the nuclei of the products. Some mass appears to be lost, but in reality, the missing mass is converted into energy, according to Einstein's equation for the equivalence of mass and energy. In this equation, $E=mc^2$, m stands for mass and c is the velocity of light, a very large number. Thus, the amount of energy produced from the conversion of a small amount of mass is tremendous. Nuclear reactions in atomic or fission bombs, in thermonuclear or fusion bombs, and in thermonuclear fusion reactions in the sun and other stars, are remarkable for the spectacular amounts of energy released.

Both the atomic fission bomb and the nuclear reactor use a fissionable isotope, such as uranium 235, as fuel. The uranium 235 captures a neutron, splits, and releases two or three neutrons, which can enter other uranium 235 nuclei, creating a chain reaction. When materials are used to absorb some of the extra neutrons, the chain reaction is controlled, and energy is produced at a steady, slow rate. This takes place in a nuclear reactor that produces energy for conversion into electricity. But when a *critical mass* of a fissionable isotope is present, the reaction is uncontrolled, and an explosion occurs. This takes place in a fission bomb. Since the supply of naturally occurring fissionable isotopes is limited, a *breeder reactor* is used to produce fissionable materials, even new elements, such as plutonium, that do not exist in nature.

Nuclear fusion has been carried out in the laboratory but not yet developed for the production of energy in a controlled reaction. Fusion bombs have, however, been made with deuterium, or hydrogen 2, and tritium, or hydrogen 3, as the reactants. Because of the use of hydrogen isotopes in the fusion bomb, it has also been called the hydrogen bomb.

Nuclear fission and chain reaction

When a neutron traveling at the right speed strikes a uranium 235 nucleus at the right place, the nucleus splits into two smaller nuclei, krypton 92 and barium 141. Two or three neutrons and energy are also released in the reaction.

Neutrons released when an atom of uranium 235 is split can strike other uranium 235 nuclei, which split and produce additional neutrons, and so on. The chain reaction is controlled if the mass of uranium 235 is below the critical mass.

EQUATION: $^{1}_{0}n + ^{235}_{92}U \rightarrow ^{92}_{36}Kr + ^{141}_{56}Ba + 3\,^{1}_{0}n$ + energy

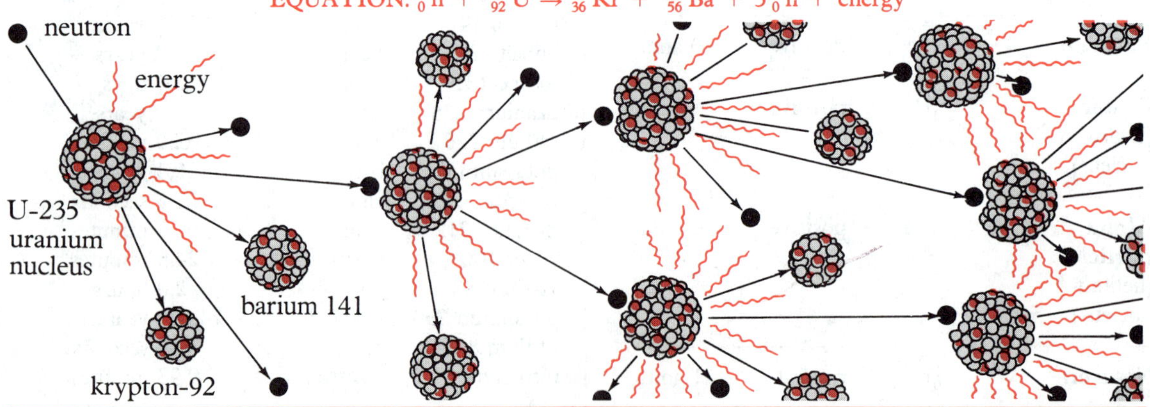

Some types of nuclear reactions

Type	*Example*	*Equation*	*Occurrence or use*
Alpha decay	emission of alpha particle by uranium 238	${}^{238}_{92}U \longrightarrow {}^{234}_{90}Th + {}^{4}_{2}He$ uranium 238 (radioactive) → thorium 234 (radioactive) + alpha particle (helium 4)	natural radioactivity
Beta decay	emission of beta particles by thorium 234	${}^{234}_{90}Th \longrightarrow {}^{234}_{91}Pa + {}^{0}_{1-}e$ thorium 234 (radioactive) → protactinium 234 (radioactive) + beta particle (electron)	natural radioactivity
Beta decay	emission of beta particle by carbon 14	${}^{14}_{6}C \longrightarrow {}^{14}_{7}N + {}^{0}_{1-}e$ carbon 14 (radioactive) → nitrogen 14 (stable) + beta particle electron)	radiocarbon dating
Artificial transmutation	bombardment of nitrogen 14 with alpha particle	${}^{14}_{7}N + {}^{4}_{2}He \longrightarrow {}^{17}_{8}O + {}^{1}_{1}H$ nitrogen 14 (stable) + alpha particle (helium 4) → oxygen 17 (stable) + proton (hydrogen 1)	Rutherford experiment
Artificial transmutation	bombardment of aluminum 27 with alpha particle	${}^{27}_{13}Al + {}^{4}_{2}He \longrightarrow {}^{30}_{15}P + {}^{1}_{0}n$ aluminum 27 (stable) + alpha particle (helium 4) → phosphorus 30 (radioactive) + neutron	Joliot-Curie experiment (step 1)
Decay of synthetic radioisotope	emission of positron by phosphorus 30	${}^{30}_{15}P \longrightarrow {}^{30}_{14}Si + {}^{0}_{1+}e$ phosphorus 30 (radioactive) → silicon 30 (stable) + positron	Joliot-Curie experiment (step 2)
Production of radioisotope of same element	bombardment of sodium 23 with neutron	${}^{23}_{11}Na + {}^{1}_{0}n \longrightarrow {}^{24}_{11}Na$ sodium 23 (stable) + neutron → sodium 24 (radioactive)	nuclear reactor
Nuclear fission	capture of neutron by uranium 235, with splitting	${}^{235}_{95}U + {}^{1}_{0}n \longrightarrow {}^{141}_{56}Ba + {}^{92}_{36}Kr + 3\,{}^{0}_{1}n + energy$ uranium 235 (radioactive) + neutron → barium 141 (radioactive) + krypton 92 + neutrons (radioactive)	nuclear reactor (controlled) or atomic fission bomb (uncontrolled)
Synthesis of new element	capture of neutron by uranium 238, with synthesis of plutonium 239	${}^{238}_{92}U + {}^{1}_{0}n \longrightarrow {}^{239}_{94}Pu + 2\,{}^{0}_{1-}e$ uranium 238 (radioactive) + neutron → plutonium 239 (radioactive) + beta particles (electrons)	breeder reactor for production of nuclear fuels
Nuclear fusion	reaction of deuterium with tritium	${}^{2}_{1}H + {}^{3}_{1}H \longrightarrow {}^{4}_{2}He + {}^{1}_{0}n + energy$ deuterium (hydrogen 2) + tritium (hydrogen 3) → proton (helium 4) + neutron	thermonuclear or hydrogen-bomb reaction

acid

Dictionary of chemistry

ester

hydrocarbon

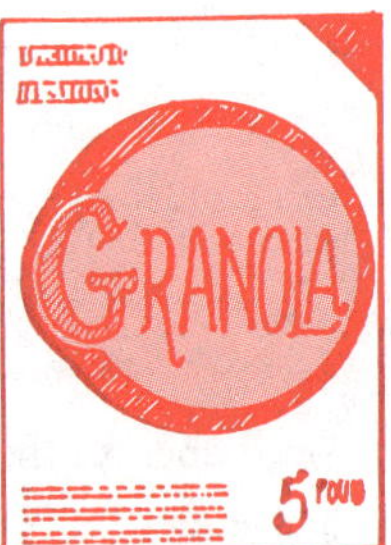

mixture

acid. Compound that produces hydrogen ions in water and that is able to donate hydrogen ions to other compounds.

addition reaction. In organic chemistry, a reaction in which one substance is added on to the structure of another, producing a single compound.

alcohol. Class of organic compounds in which the hydroxyl group (-OH) is added on to a hydrocarbon group.

alkali. Strong base formed from an alkali metal.

alkali metal. Metallic element that belongs to Group IA of the period table and that forms a strong base when combined with the hydroxide group.

alkane. Hydrocarbon in which there are only single bonds between carbon atoms.

alkene. Hydrocarbon in which there is one double bond between two carbon atoms, and the rest of the carbon-carbon bonds are single.

alkyne. Hydrocarbon in which there is one triple bond between two carbon atoms, and the rest of the carbon-carbon bonds are single.

alpha particle. Particle consisting of two protons and two neutrons; a helium nucleus.

aromatic. Hydrocarbon in which the benzene ring structure is present.

atom. Smallest unit of an element.

atomic mass. Mass of an atom compared with carbon 12, which has been assigned a mass of 12 atomic mass units.

atomic number. Number of protons in the nucleus of an atom, or the number of electrons.

base. Compound that produces hydroxide ions in water, or that is capable of receiving a hydrogen ion from an acid.

beta particle. Electron that is emitted by the nucleus of a radioactive atom.

boiling point. Temperature at which the vapor pressure of a liquid is equal to the atmospheric pressure.

breeder reactor. Nuclear reactor used to produce nuclear fuel, often in the form of synthetic elements, as well as nuclear energy.

chain reaction. Process in which the splitting of one atomic nucleus gives off neutrons that cause the splitting of other atomic nuclei.

chemical equation. A statement, consisting of symbols and formulas, that summarizes the changes that occur in a chemical reaction.

chemical reaction. Change in matter that results in a change in composition, in which new substances are formed.

chemistry. Science that deals with the composition of matter and with changes in this composition.

compound. Substance consisting of two or more elements joined by chemical bonds.

covalent bond. Chemical bond between two atoms in which electrons are shared.

crystal. Substance in the solid phase having an ordered arrangement of atoms or groups of atoms.

decomposition. A reaction, also called analysis, in which a chemical substance is broken down.

direct combination. A reaction, also called synthesis, in which two or more substances combine.

double replacement. Reaction in which there is an exchange of the positive and negative ions of two compounds.

electron. Fundamental negatively charged particle of matter.

element. Substance that cannot be broken down into simpler substances by ordinary chemical means.

esterification. Reaction between an alcohol and an acid in which the product, other than water, is an ester.

functional group. In organic chemistry, a group of atoms that characterizes a series or class of compounds.

gamma rays. High-frequency radiation, similar to x-rays, emitted by radioactive substances.

half-life. Period of time it takes for half the radioactive atoms in a given mass to decay.

hydrocarbon. Compound consisting only of hydrogen and carbon.

inorganic chemistry. Branch of chemistry that deals with the reactions of elements other than carbon.

ion. Atom or group of atoms bearing an electric charge.

ionic bond. Chemical bond formed by the transfer of electrons from one atom to another.

isotope. Form of an element differing from other forms in atomic mass but not in atomic number.

ketone. Class of organic compounds in which the carbonyl group (–CO–) is contained.

melting point. Temperature at which a solid turns into a liquid, or vice versa.

metal. Element that loses electrons easily, has a high luster, and is a good conductor of heat and electricity.

mixture. Aggregate of two or more substances that are not chemically combined.

molecule. The smallest particle of a substance that can exist free and retain the properties of that substance.

neutron. Nuclear particle having the same mass as a proton but zero electric charge.

nonmetal. Element that gains or shares electrons in chemical reactions, and whose properties contrast with those of metals.

nuclear fission. Nuclear reaction in which a large nucleus is split into smaller nuclei.

nuclear fusion. Nuclear reaction in which small atomic nuclei join to form a larger nucleus.

nuclear reactor. Device in which a nuclear reaction is controlled. to produce energy.

organic acid. Class of organic compounds in which the carboxyl group (–COOH) is contained.

organic chemistry. Chemistry of carbon compounds.

period. Horizontal row of elements in the periodic table.

phase. Physical state of matter; for example, solid, liquid, or gas.

physical change. Any change in matter that does not involve changes in the composition of substances.

polyatomic ion. Group of atoms carrying an electric charge that usually react as a unit in chemical reactions.

positron. Subatomic particle with the same mass as an electron, but with a positive electric charge.

product. Substance formed as a result of a chemical reaction, whose formula is written on the right side of the arrow in a chemical equation.

proton. Nuclear particle with the same mass as a neutron, but positive electric charge.

radioactivity. Spontaneous breakdown, or decay, of unstable atoms, during which alpha, beta, or gamma radiation is emitted.

radioisotope. Form of an element that exhibits radioactivity, or is radioactive.

reactant. Starting substance in a chemical reaction, whose formula is written on the left side of the arrow in a chemical equation.

salt. The product, other than water, of the reaction between an acid and a base.

saturated hydrocarbon. Organic compound in which carbon atoms are joined by single bonds.

single replacement. In inorganic chemistry, a reaction in which an element displaces another element in a compound, setting that element free.

substitution. In organic chemistry, a reaction in which an element or a group replaces another element or group in a molecule.

thermonuclear reaction. Atomic fusion reaction, such as the one that occurs in the fusion or hydrogen bomb.

transmutation. Nuclear change in which one element is converted into another.

unsaturated hydrocarbon. Organic compound in which some of the carbon atoms are joined by double or triple bonds.

valence electrons. Electrons in the outermost shell of an atom, which take part in the formation of chemical bonds.

vapor pressure. Pressure of the gas phase of a liquid when the two phases are in equilibrium.

For Further Reference

Asimov, Isaac
A Short History of Chemistry
Anchor Books

Asimov, Isaac
The World of Carbon
Abelard-Schuman

Day, Frank Henry
The Chemical Elements in Nature
Reinhold Co.

Patterson, E.C.
John Dalton and the Atomic Theory
Abelard-Schuman

Pottenger, Francis M.
Fundamentals of Chemistry
Scott, Foresman & Co.

Physics

Both chemistry and physics deal with matter and energy. The chemist deals mostly with the changes that matter can undergo, changes that do not affect the internal structure of atoms. The physicist, however, is more interested in energy: its various forms and how they change into one another. Physicists are also interested in the nature of matter and how matter and energy are related.

The most spectacular results of physics have been in the development of the atomic bomb and nuclear power, but physical theories are also at the heart of the transistor and the other semiconducting devices that have been changing the way people live since World War II. On a more abstract level, physics has explained the motions of the planets, the energy processes of stars, and the origin of the universe. Today's physicists continue to explore both the smallest fundamental particles of matter-energy and the largest forces and objects in the universe. The success of physics has come from the ability of physicists to describe these varied phenomena with mathematical equations. In fact, the fundamental meaning of such important physical concepts as force or energy is found in the equations that describe the concepts. For this reason, a large part of this section of the book sets forth the key relationships and equations in easy-to-use tabular form. Measurement is especially important in physics, and the tables set forth the correct units used in making each measurement.

Fundamental concepts

Measurement. Physicists make extensive and careful use of measurement. Certain units are viewed as fundamental, and all other measures are derived from them. In practice, physicists use one of two versions of the *metric system*, the centimeter-gram-second (cgs) system, or the meter-kilogram-second (mks) system. In the *customary system*, the fundamental units form the foot-pound-second (fps) system.

Mass and weight. *Mass* is the amount of matter in an object. The mass of this book would be the same anywhere in the universe. *Weight* is the pull of gravity on a given mass. This book would weigh only one-sixth of its Earth weight on the moon because the moon has one-sixth of Earth's gravitational pull. In physics, this distinction between mass and weight is carefully maintained. In ordinary life (and in engineering), however, mass and weight are treated as if they were the same. Thus, although the basic unit of *mass* in the metric system is the gram, people in ordinary life may talk about how many grams a coin *weighs*; and although the basic unit of *weight* in the U.S. customary system of measurement is the pound, people in ordinary life say that a pound is about the same as 2.2 kilograms, a measure of *mass*.

Force. Weight is one kind of *force*. A force causes motion to change in speed or direction. Force is recognized from this property. A book is acted upon by the force of gravity—that is, the book has weight. If the book is dropped, the force on the book causes it to move toward the center of Earth.

Velocity and acceleration. Motion can be categorized in various ways. A steady motion in a single direction, such as a car traveling along a straight highway at 55 kilometers per hour, is measured as *velocity*. Velocity is the rate of change of the car's position in a unit of time for such a steady motion. If the motion is changing in any way (for example, if the car is speeding up, braking, or turning), the velocity will change at every instant.

The rate of change of velocity is called *acceleration*. The unit of time occurs twice in a measure of acceleration; for example, if the driver of the car were to speed up gradually by 10 kilometers per hour every hour, the acceleration would be 10 kilometers per hour per hour. Physicists often write this as 10 km/h². While constant velocity does not produce a force, constant acceleration of a mass results in force. You can feel this force as a car picks up speed or slows down.

Velocity and acceleration

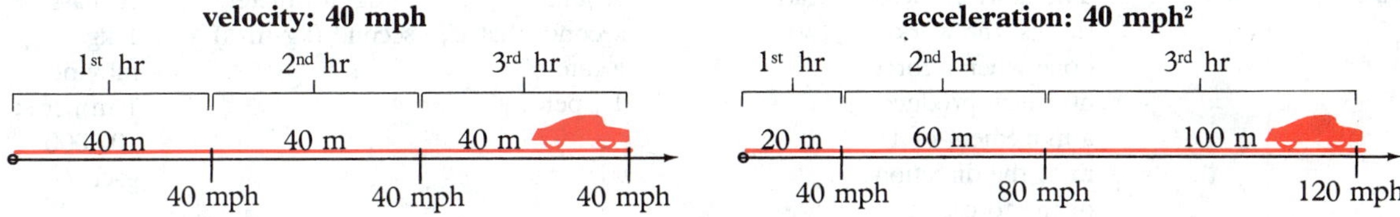

Mass and force

System	Mass Unit	Definition	Force Unit	Definition
cgs	gram (g)	Fundamental (originally the mass of 1 cubic centimeter of water under standard conditions)	dyne (dy)	The force required to accelerate a mass of 1 gram 1 cm/s²
mks	kilogram (kg)	1000 grams	newton (new)	The force required to accelerate a mass of 1 kilogram 1 m/s²; 100,000 dynes
fps	slug	The mass to which a force of 1 pound will give an acceleration of 1 ft/sec²	pound (lb)	Fundamental
Other common units	metric ton (MT or t) = 1,000,000 g = 1,000 kg milligram (mg) = 0.001 g = 0.000001 kg		(short) ton = 2000 lb (avoirdupois) ounce (oz) = 1/16 lb	

Ordinary, or engineering, usage

(short) ton = 0.907 metric tons
pound = 0.454 kilograms
ounce = 28.349 grams
slug = 32.1740 pounds

metric ton = 1.1 (short) tons
kilogram = 2.2046 pounds
gram = 0.035 ounce
milligram = 0.000035 ounce

Fundamental relationship of force, mass, and acceleration

$F = ma$		cgs	kms	fps
	where F means force in	dy	newton	lb
	m means mass in	g	kg	slugs
	a means acceleration in	cm/s²	m/s²	ft/s²

Work, energy, power, and momentum

System	Work and energy Unit	Definition	Power Unit	Definition	Momentum Unit	Definition
cgs	erg	The dyne-centimeter; that is, the work done when a force of 1 dy produces a movement of 1 cm in the direction of the force.	erg/second (erg/s)	A rate of 1 erg per s; $\frac{1}{10{,}000{,}000}$ w	gram-centimeter/second (g-cm/s)	A mass of 1 g moving 1 cm per s
mks	joule (j)	The newton-meter; that is, the work done when a force of 1 new produces a movement of 1 m in the direction of the force; 10,000,000 ergs.	watt (w)	A joule/second; that is, a rate of 1 j per s	kilogram-meter/second (kg-m/s)	A mass of 1 kg moving 1 m per s; 100,000 g-cm/s
fps	foot-pound (ft-lb)	The work done when a force of 1 lb. produces a movement of 1 ft. in the direction of the force.	foot-pound/second (ft-lb/s)	A rate of 1 ft-lb per s	slug-foot/second (slug-ft/s)	A mass of 1 slug moving 1 ft per s
Other common units	kilogram-meter (kg-m)	98,066,500 ergs	kilowatt (kw)	1000 w; 1.34 hp		
	kilocalorie (also called Calorie [kc or C])	4184.0 j	horsepower (hp)	550 ft-lb/s; 746 w		
	kilowatt-hour (kwh)	60,000 j				

Equations of work, energy, power, and momentum

$W = Fd$

where		cgs	mks	fps
W means work	in	ergs	j	ft-lb
F means force	in	dy	new	lb
d means distance	in	cm	m	ft

$PE = wh$

where PE means		cgs	mks	fps
potential energy	in	ergs	j	ft-lb
w means weight	in	dy	new	lb
h means height	in	cm	m	ft

$KE = \frac{1}{2} mv^2$

where KE means		cgs	mks	fps
kinetic energy	in	ergs	j	ft-lb
m means mass	in	g	kg	slugs
v means velocity	in	cm/s	m/s	lb/s

$E = mc^2$

where		cgs	mks	fps
E means energy	in	ergs	j	ft-lb
m means mass	in	g	kg	slugs
c means the speed of light		30 billion cm/s	300 million m/s	982.08 million ft/s

$P = \frac{W}{t}$

where		cgs	mks	fps
P means power	in	erg/s	w	lb/s
W means work	in	ergs	j	ft/lb
t means time	in	s	s	s

$P = mv$

where P means		cgs	mks	fps
momentum	in	g-cm/s	kg-m/s	slug-ft/s
m means mass	in	g	kg	slugs
v means velocity	in	cm/s	m/s	ft/s

Work.

Work is done when a force moves an object in the direction of that force. The amount or quantity of work done is the product of the force and the distance the object moved. In physics, no work is done unless motion takes place. Merely applying force to an object is not considered to be work unless motion takes place.

Energy.

This is the ability to do work. *Energy* is measured by the amount of work performed. There are many types of energy, including electrical, heat, mechanical, chemical, and nuclear. These types of energy are present in three forms.

Potential energy. This is the energy an object has stored in it. Probably the most familiar form of potential energy is energy stored in an object owing to the object's change in position. A hammer that has been raised has the potential to do work when it falls. An increase in the height to which it is raised or an increase in the weight of the hammer will increase the amount of potential energy. A spring that has been tightly coiled also contains potential energy, in much the same way. Sometimes the energy produced in chemical reactions (for example, burning a piece of coal) is thought of as potential energy.

Kinetic energy. This is the energy an object or body has because of its motion. A hammer applies the force of kinetic energy as it strikes a nail. The amount of kinetic energy of a moving body is a result of its mass and the square of its velocity. Since the velocity is squared, the kinetic energy increases rapidly when the velocity increases. Tripling the speed of an object will increase its kinetic energy nine times.

In a system, the sum of potential energy and kinetic energy is constant. For example, the potential energy that a hammer loses in falling is equal to its gain in kinetic energy.

Rest-mass energy. The third form in which energy can exist is a consequence of Albert Einstein's theory of relativity. Einstein showed that if matter could be completely annihilated, the amount of energy released would be equal to the product of the mass times the speed of light squared. It is this form of energy that is exploited in nuclear reactors and nuclear or thermonuclear bombs.

Power.

The rate at which work is done is called *power*. Power is the amount of work done per unit of time. It is generally more important to know the power of an engine than the amount of energy the engine can generate. Consequently, automobiles are rated by horsepower and electric lights by watts, both units of power.

Momentum.

Momentum is defined as the product of the mass of a moving object and its velocity. Momentum is a measure of the tendency of a body to remain in motion or the resistance of a body to being stopped.

The effect of one solid body striking another is determined largely by the momentum of the bodies. A light straw moved by a tornado to a great velocity can have enough momentum to be driven into a tree. Similarly, a very massive object, even though it is moving slowly, can crush everything in its path. In both cases, the momentum determines the result. (Of course, a massive object that is moving fast has even more momentum.)

After the pitcher accelerates a baseball to nearly 100 mph and releases it, the momentum of the ball changes only slightly as a result of gravity and friction with the air—until it is hit, when the force of the bat accelerates the ball in a new direction, or is caught by the catcher.

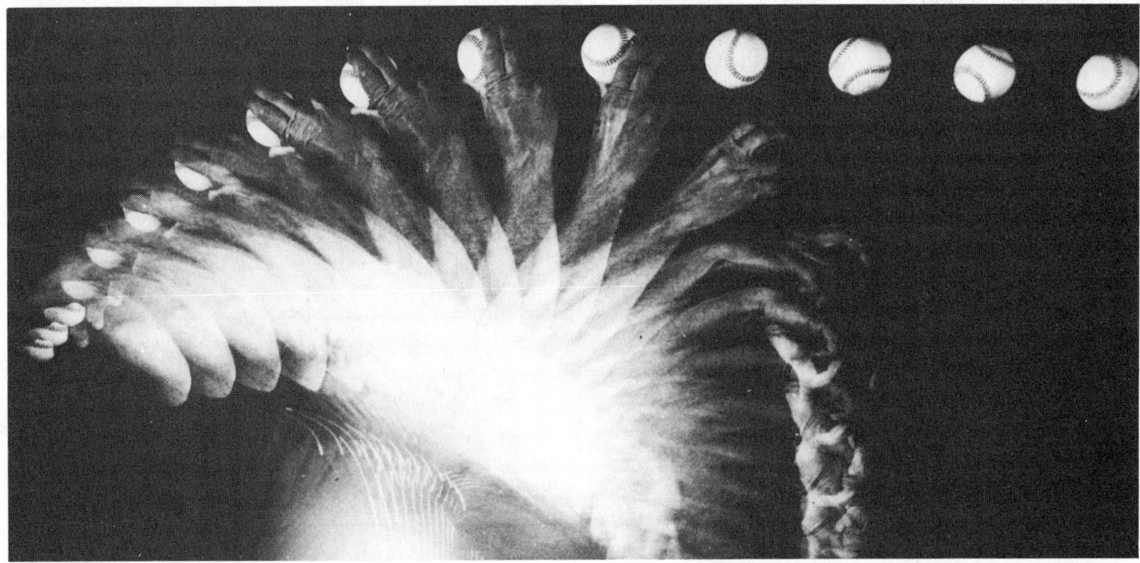

Newton's laws

Sir Isaac Newton is well known for having discovered the laws of gravity, but his fundamental laws of motion, published in 1687, are equally important. While these laws were stated earlier by Galileo, Newton was the first to express them clearly in mathematical terms. Newton's laws of motion form the basis for the branch of physics called mechanics.

The first law. A body at rest tends to remain at rest until acted upon by an outside force; a body in motion tends to remain in motion in a straight line at the same velocity unless acted upon by an outside force. The tendency of a body at rest to remain at rest and of a body in motion to remain in motion in a straight line is called *inertia*.

It is a common error to assume that a body can move in a curved path with no force acting on it. For example, students often believe that a rock that is tied to a string and swung in a circle will follow a curved path when released. In fact, inertia will cause the rock to travel in a straight line. Deviations from that straight line will be caused by forces acting on the rock. The force of gravity will cause the path of the rock to be a curve very close to a part of a parabola, but this is the same curve that the rock would follow had it been shot from a cannon.

The second law. You already know the second law of motion in the form $F = ma$ or force equals mass times acceleration. A more general statement of the law is as follows: When a body is acted upon by a constant force, its acceleration is proportional to the force and inversely proportional to the mass. In the formula $F = ma$, the units are chosen so that the constant of proportionality will be 1.

Since momentum is mv (mass times velocity), the rate of change of momentum is ma (mass times the rate of change of velocity, or mass times acceleration). Therefore, another way of stating Newton's second law is, force acting upon a body is equal to the rate of change of momentum. Newton's second law is often called the law of momentum.

Equations for laws of motion and gravity

Second law of motion

$F = ma$ where F is force
m is mass
a is acceleration

$F = \frac{mv}{t}$ where F is force
m is mass
v is velocity
t is time

Third law of motion

$m_1v_1 = m_2v_2$ where m_1 is one mass
m_2 is another mass
v_1 is the velocity of the first mass
v_2 is the velocity of the second mass

Law of gravity

$f = G\frac{m_1m_2}{r^2}$ where f is the attractive force
G is the gravitational constant (6.673×10^{-8} dyne-cm^2/g^2 in the cgs system)
m_1 is one mass
m_2 is another mass
r is the distance between masses

Motion of body falling to Earth

$v = v_0 + gt$ where v is velocity
v_0 is initial velocity
g is acceleration because of gravity (980 cm/s^2)
t is time

$s = v_0t + \frac{1}{2}gt^2$ where s is distance fallen
v_0 is initial velocity
t is time
g is acceleration because of gravity (980 cm/s^2)

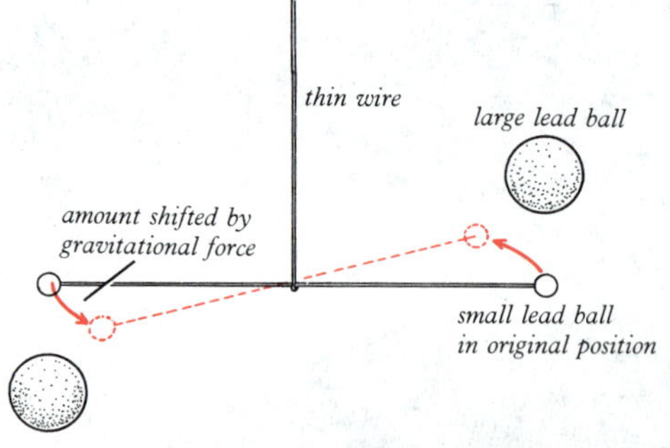

Henry Cavendish used the equipment shown to determine the gravitational constant in 1798. The gravitational force between the two lead balls moved the smaller one by an amount that could be measured.

The third law. For every action, there is an equal and opposite reaction. The third law also relates to momentum. This law can also be stated: When an object is given a certain momentum in a given direction, some other body or bodies will get an equal momentum in the opposite direction. A rocket moves forward to the rearward action of the gases from its engines. In this example, the momentum of the product of the mass of gases and their velocity is equal to the momentum of the product of the rocket's mass and its velocity.

Conservation of momentum.

Newton's laws are contained in a very general conservation law. Conservation laws describe quantities that do not change during physical interactions. The law of conservation of momentum states that in any interaction of bodies, the total momentum of the interacting bodies does not change. Application of the conservation law to different situations produces Newton's three laws:

1. If a body is at rest, it will have a momentum of 0, and will continue to have 0 momentum unless a force changes it.
2. A body in motion will continue in motion with the same momentum.
3. When two bodies interact, momentum is conserved. For example, when a stationary billiard ball is struck by a moving ball of the same mass, the momentum of the moving ball must be shared between them. If the second ball stops, the first must move off with a momentum equal to that of the second before the collision. If both billiard balls have the same mass, the velocity of the first ball will be transmitted completely to the second ball.

Law of gravity. Two bodies attract each other with a force directly proportional to the product of their masses and inversely proportional to the square of the distance between them. In 1798 Henry Cavendish established the constant of proportionality, later refined to 0.0000006673 in the cgs system.

On Earth, gravity seems to be a large force only because the mass of Earth is great. A 1-gram mass is attracted to the center of Earth with a force of about 980 dynes. Putting this into the equation $F = ma$ shows that for 980 to equal $1 \cdot a$, the acceleration owed to gravity (called g) must be 980 centimeters per second per second (in the fps system, this is about 32.2 feet per second per second).

Since gravity produces acceleration, a freely falling body will tend to travel faster and faster as it falls to Earth. At the end of 1 second, the velocity of a body that started from rest will reach 980 centimeters per second. At the end of the next second, the velocity will reach $2 \cdot 980$, or 1960 centimeters per second. Since the velocity is constantly increasing, the distance traveled in each second also increases. For the first second of fall, the *average* velocity is $\frac{0 + 980}{2} = 490$ centimeters per second, so the distance traveled is 490 centimeters. In the next second, the average velocity is $\frac{980 + 1960}{2} = 1470$ centimeters per second, and the body travels 1470 centimeters. In the third second, the body falls $\frac{1960 + 2940}{2} = 2450$ centimeters.

The total distance traveled at the end of each second varies with the *square* of the time. At the end of 1 second, the distance is $\frac{980}{2}(1^2) = 490$ centimeters; at the end of the next second, the total distance is $\frac{980}{2}(2^2) = 1960$ centimeters ($490 + 1470 = 1960$); and at the end of the third second, the total distance is $\frac{980}{2}(3^2) = 4410$ centimeters ($490 + 1470 + 2450 = 4410$).

When you push something away from you (by throwing it, for example), you impart momentum to yourself that is equal in amount and oppositely directed. Where frictional resistance to motion is small, throwing a heavy object causes motion away from the direction in which the object is thrown.

Thermodynamics

Heat. The particles that make up all matter are in a state of perpetual motion. This internal kinetic energy manifests itself as the form of energy called *heat*. The study of heat is *thermodynamics*. All matter is made up of moving particles; therefore, all matter has heat.

Heat is a form of energy and is measured in terms of the amount of work done. In the metric system, there are two units commonly used. Physicists most often use the calorie, the amount of heat needed to raise the temperature of 1 gram of water (under standard conditions) by 1° C. A kilocalorie or Calorie is the amount of heat required to raise the temperature of a kilogram of water 1°C. The Calorie with a capital C is the one used to measure the energy content of foods. In the fps system, a British thermal unit (Btu) is the amount of heat required to raise the temperature of 1 pound of water 1° F.

Temperature is not the same as heat. Temperature is a measure of the average kinetic energy of the particles of an object while heat is a measure of the total kinetic energy. The Kelvin, or absolute, scale of temperature is based on the idea that there is a temperature at which all particle motion ceases. This temperature is called absolute zero and has been calculated to be 273.16° below zero Celsius.

Conservation of mass-energy. Energy can neither be created nor destroyed but only changed in type. This law is a generalization of the first law of thermodynamics, which states that when heat is transformed into other kinds of energy, the total energy remains constant.

In nuclear reactions, however, mass is converted to energy. Since matter can be considered a third form of energy, this principle is often called the law of conservation of mass-energy.

Heat and work. To get work out of randomly moving particles, you must induce them to move predominantly in one direction or to supply energy in a single direction. Heat is transferred from any body of a higher temperature to a body of a lower temperature. The efficiency of a heat engine is proportional to this temperature difference. As heat is transferred, the difference is reduced. The fraction of the energy that flows into the cooler body becomes less available for transformation into work even though the total amount of energy is unchanged.

The statement that heat can never travel from a colder to a hotter body by any continuous, self-sustaining process is the second law of thermodynamics. That portion or quantity of energy that is lost as nonuseful heat is measured by *entropy*. Since heat in useful form is a result of particles in one place moving faster than particles somewhere else (that is, the first place is hotter than the second), entropy is also a measure of disorder. The moving particles are statistically less ordered when the temperatures at both places are the same than when the temperatures are different. As a result, another version of the second law of thermodynamics is "Entropy (disorder) tends to increase."

Thermodynamics

1 Kilocalorie (Kcal) or Calorie (Cal) = 1000 calories (cal)
= 3.968 British thermal units (Btu)

1 degree Celsius (1°C) = 1 degree Kelvin (1°K)
= 1.8 degrees Fahrenheit (1.8° F)

1 Btu = 0.252 Cal = 252 cal

1°F = 0.555°C = 0.555°K

$C = \frac{5}{9}(F - 32)$ where C means temperature in degrees Celsius
F means temperature in degrees Fahrenheit

$F = \frac{9C + 160}{5}$ where F means temperature in degrees Fahrenheit
C means temperature in degrees Celsius

$K = C + 273.16$ where K means temperature in degrees Kelvin
C means temperature in degrees Celsius

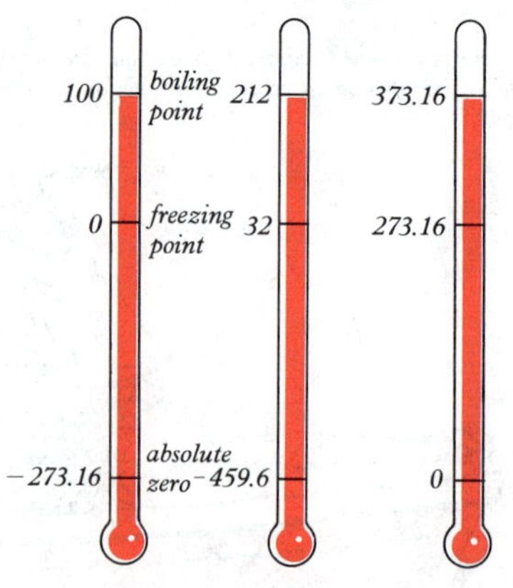

Wave motion

Energy is often transmitted in the form of *waves*, that is, back and forth or up and down vibrations. The energy of a wave travels, but the medium in which it travels only vibrates or oscillates.

There are two main types of waves. In *transverse* waves, the vibrations of the medium are perpendicular to the direction of wave motion. A common example is a boat bobbing up and down on water as waves pass. The boat moves at right angles to the direction of the waves. In *longitudinal* waves, the vibrations of the medium are parallel to the direction of the waves. Sound is a longitudinal wave.

Sound. Sound is a longitudinal vibration of a medium at frequencies the human ear can detect. The medium can be a gas, liquid, or solid. *Frequency* is the rate at which waves are produced in a unit of time. The distance from one point on a wave to a corresponding point on the next wave is the *wavelength*. Wavelength determines the *pitch* of the sound. The greater the frequency, the shorter the wavelength, and the higher the pitch of the sound produced. The *amplitude*, or loudness, of a sound is determined by the distance the particles of the medium are displaced from their original undisturbed position. A blast of a loud horn will displace particles of air much farther than a small whistle or toot.

When a tuning fork is struck it starts to vibrate at a frequency that depends upon the size of the fork and the material it is made of. This vibration sets the air particles around the tuning fork vibrating back and forth at the same frequency. When the energy reaches us, our eardrums vibrate, and we hear a tone.

Electromagnetic waves. These are transverse vibrations; that is, the oscillations are perpendicular to the direction of the wave. Light is a small portion of a large range, or *spectrum*, of transverse waves called *electromagnetic waves* because they combine both electrical and magnetic properties. Strictly speaking, however, electromagnetic waves are not what we normally think of as electricity, which is produced by moving electrons, or magnetism, which is a field that can be produced by moving electrons or in other ways. Electromagnetic waves are the wave interpretation of the motion of a particle called the *photon*.

The electromagnetic spectrum is divided into regions according to ranges in wavelength (or ranges in frequency). The units used to measure the wavelengths of the shorter waves are the micron (μ); millimicron ($m\mu$); and angstrom (Å)

$$1\mu = 10^{-6}\text{m} = 10^{-4}\text{cm}$$
$$1\text{m}\mu = 10^{-9}\text{m} = 10^{-7}\text{cm}$$
$$1\text{Å} = 10^{-10}\text{m} = 10^{-8}\text{cm}$$

In order of increasing wavelength, the electromagnetic spectrum can be divided into gamma rays, x-rays, ultraviolet rays, visible light, infrared rays, microwaves, and radio waves. Note that each type of radiation merges gradually into the next and that all electromagnetic radiations travel at the same speed in a vacuum, the speed of light.

Sound

Sound wave

Sound is a longitudinal vibration, which passes from place to place as alternate waves of compression and rarefaction of a material (most commonly for humans, the air). The same pattern can be seen in a coiled spring.

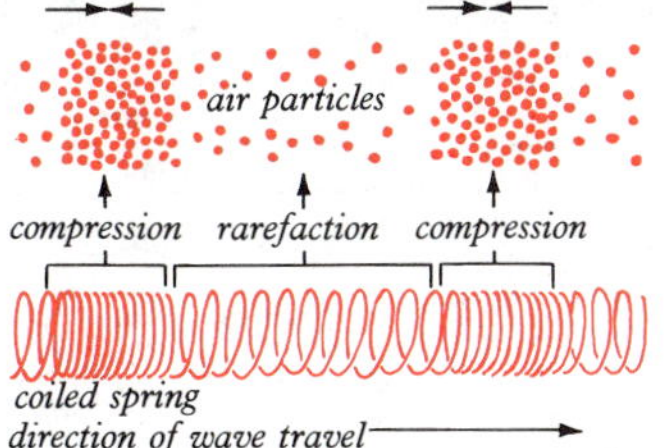

Intensity of sound

Sound	*Decibels*
threshold of hearing	0
whisper	10–20
very soft music	30
average home	40–50
automobile	40–50
conversation	60–70
heavy street traffic	70–80
loud music	90–100
threshold of pain	120
jet airplane engine	170

Speed of sound

Medium at 0° C	*ft/sec*
air	1,090
alcohol	3,890
brass	11,480
carbon dioxide	846
copper	11,670
glass	16,500
iron	16,820
steel	16,820
water	4,794
wood (pine)	10,900

The visible spectrum. The speed of light is accepted today as 2.99793 times 10^8 meters per second in a vacuum. This value is approximately 186,000 miles per second. In a more dense medium, such as glass, all electromagnetic waves, including that portion called light or the visible spectrum, will slow down. The change in direction of waves as they pass obliquely from one medium to another is called *refraction.* The *index of refraction* is an indication of how much light will bend in passing from one substance to another. The refractive index of a substance is the ratio of the speeds of light in different media.

Refraction enables us to bend and focus light with lenses, making photography, microscopes, and telescopes possible. Prisms have enabled us to separate the visible spectrum into the various wavelengths we see as colors. The wavelengths we perceive as colors travel at the same speed in a vacuum but at different speeds in matter. Red, the longest visible wavelength, is approximately 0.00007 cm in length and travels about 1 percent faster in glass than does violet, the shortest visible wavelength (0.00004 cm).

Lenses. The purpose of a lens is to change the curvature of light waves, usually to form an image. The ability of a lens to form an image is measured by its *focal length.* The distance of the principal focus from the lens is the focal length of that particular lens. Its value depends on the curvature of the two surfaces of the lens and the refractive index of its material. Convex (converging) lenses form real images. A real image can be focused on a screen and is inverted.

The law of reflection. Reflection is the return of an object or a train of waves from a surface that acts as a boundary between two media. If the surface is smooth, the incoming ray of light, the incident ray, and the ray when reflected, the reflected ray, form equal angles with the normal. The normal at the point where the rays intersect is a line perpendicular to the surface. The angle of incidence equals the angle of reflection and both angles and the normal are on the same plane. Curved mirrors called *reflectors* are used to focus light in large telescopes. Mirrors do not distort images as much as refracting lenses do.

Electromagnetic waves

Light wave

Light is a transverse wave. In the transverse waves of water the molecules travel perpendicular to the direction of the wave. Unlike water, however, light waves are not caused by the motion of a substance through which they are traveling. Light is caused by the wave properties of small particles.

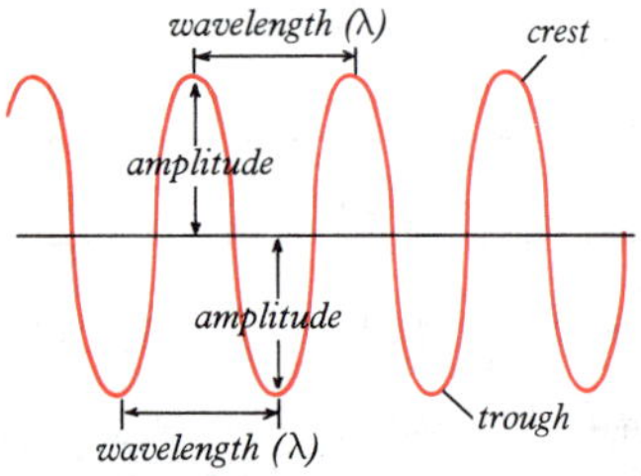

Refraction

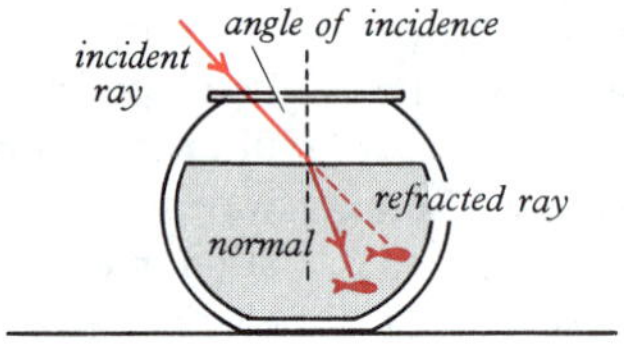

Reflection

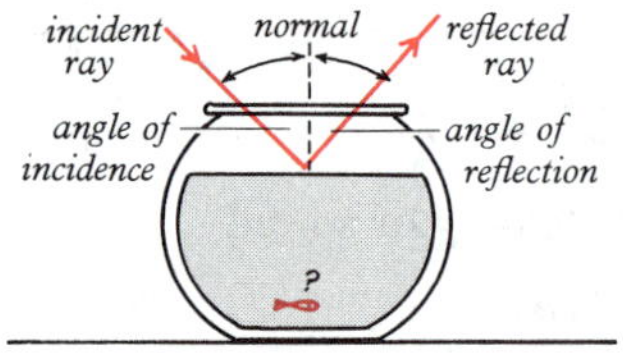

Speed of light

*Medium**	*m/sec*
vacuum	299,793,000
air (g)	299,700,000
methyl alcohol (l)	228,000,000
water (l)	226,000,000
quartz (s)	207,000,000
benzene (l)	200,000,000
ordinary glass (s)	198,000,000
sodium chloride** (s)	195,000,000
ethyl alcohol (l)	188,000,000
heat-resistant glass (s)	181,000,000
diamond (s)	124,000,000

* *s=solid; l=liquid; g=gas*
** *table salt*

Electromagnetic spectrum

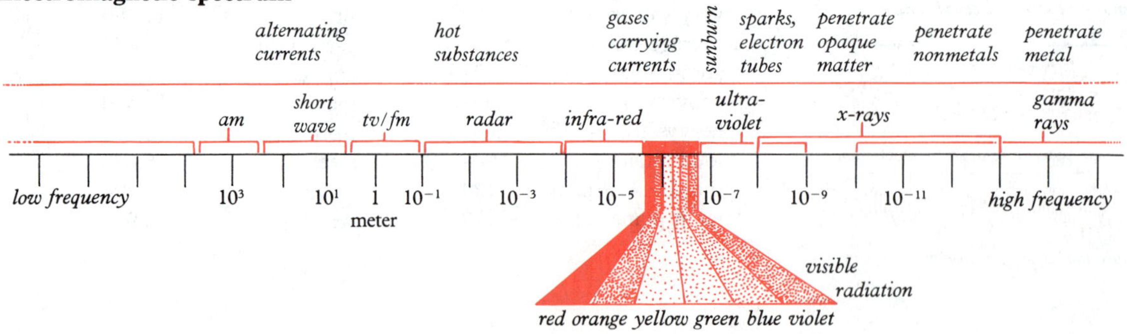

The law of inverse squares.

This law explains why we often move an object closer to a light source to see it better. It states that the *intensity* of certain effects, including the illumination of a surface, gravitational force, and sound, is inversely proportional to the square of the distance from the source. The intensity decreases as the distance increases. At 4 meters, the intensity is $\frac{1}{16}$ of what it is at 1 meter.

Applications.

The high accuracy of the speed at which electromagnetic radiation travels makes it possible to measure the distance of objects such as the moon by *radar.* Radar is an instrument that emits microwaves, bounces them off an object, and measures the time for the echo to return. Knowing the speed of the radiation, the distance to the object can be calculated with great precision.

Radar is also used by highway police to get an instantaneous reading of the speed of an automobile by taking into account the *Doppler effect.* If an object emitting a tone is receding from us, the pitch is lower than that heard when the object was at rest; that is, the wavelength appears to increase. If the object is moving toward us, the wavelength is decreased and we hear a higher pitch. The speed of a moving car can be read by the increase or decrease of the wavelength of the radar waves that are bounced off it. The Doppler effect has also been used to determine that the universe is expanding. Light of known wavelengths emitted by distant galaxies is shifted toward longer wavelengths, that is, toward the red end of the visible spectrum, indicating that these galaxies are receding from us.

The *laser* is a device that amplifies focused light waves and concentrates them in a narrow, very intense beam. The emitted light, called *coherent light,* does not spread out, so it does not lose intensity. It can deliver great energy to a small area.

Electromagnetic radiation

Wave equation

$V = v\lambda$ where V is velocity
v is frequency
λ is wavelength

Wave energy

$E = hV$ where E is energy
h is Planck's constant (6.6×10^{-27} erg sec)
V is frequency

Snell's law (index of refraction)

$n = \frac{\sin i}{\sin r}$ where n is the index
$\sin i$ is sine of incident angle
$\sin r$ is sine of refracted angle

Location of image formed by a converging lens

$\frac{1}{p} + \frac{1}{q} = \frac{1}{f}$ where p is object distance
q is image distance
f is focal length

Size of image

$\frac{h_i}{h_o} = \frac{q}{p}$ where h_i is image height
h_o is object height
q is image distance
p is object distance

Inverse square law

$E = \frac{I}{d^2}$ where E is illumination
I is intensity of the source
d is distance to the illuminated surface

Law of inverse squares

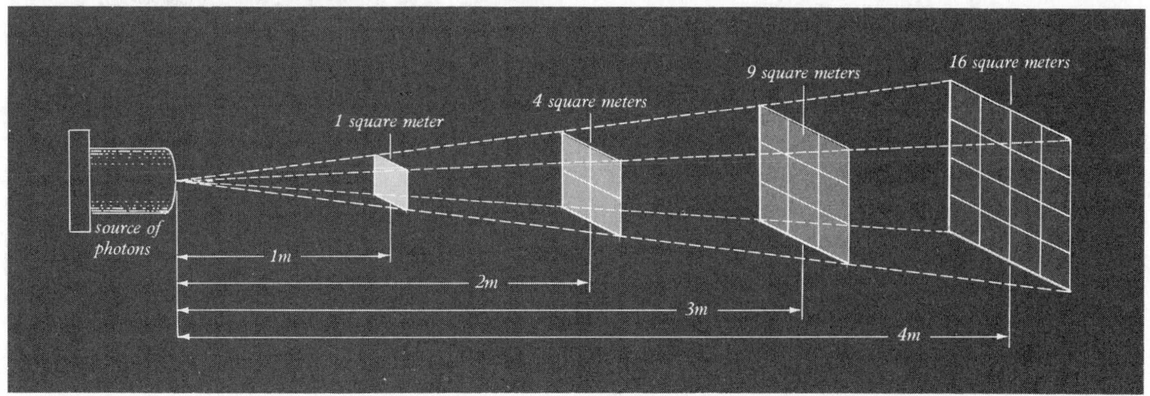

Electricity

Electricity is the term given to phenomena caused by electric charges whether they are static or in motion. There are two kinds of electric charges—positive and negative. Materials always contain both positive and negative charges, but only *electrons*, carriers of the tiny negative charge, move freely. A substance becomes positively charged when it loses electrons; a negatively charged substance has gained electrons. Electrons can be made to flow through some materials easily. Such materials are called *conductors*.

Electric current is the flow of electrons past a given point. The unit of electron flow is the *ampere*. One ampere is the flow of 1 coulomb of charge per second. A *coulomb* is a unit of quantity of electricity. It is the charge equal to 6.25 times the charge of 10^{18} electrons.

$$1 \text{ ampere} = \frac{1 \text{ coulomb}}{\text{second}}$$

The amount of work electricity can do depends on both the quantity of electrons and their potential energy. Electrical potential energy is called *voltage* and is measured in *volts*. Voltage is also referred to as electromotive force or potential difference. It can be considered as a measure of electrical pressure in a circuit and is often defined as the force required to send a current of 1 ampere through a circuit having a resistance of 1 ohm.

The *ohm* is the unit of electrical resistance. It is the resistance offered by a circuit or device to the flow of 1 ampere being driven by the force of 1 volt. The relationship between electrical pressure, current flow, and resistance is expressed in Ohm's law. *Ohm's law* states that the current through a circuit is directly proportional to the force or pressure that drives it and inversely proportional to resistance of the circuit.

Electric power. The rate at which an appliance uses electrical energy is measured in watts. One watt is the rate at which work is done when 1 ampere is moved by 1 volt. Electrical energy is sold in kilowatt hours, the power of 1000 watts for 1 hour.

Electricity

Unit	*Definition*
coulomb	Electric charge equal to 6.25×10^{18} electron charges
ampere	Flow of 1 coulomb per second past a point
volt	1 joule per coulomb
ohm	1 volt per ampere
watt	1 joule per second

Ohm's law

$I = \frac{E}{R}$ where I is current in amperes
E is potential difference in volts
R is resistance in ohms

Electric power

P = IV where P is power in watts
I is current in amperes
V is potential difference in volts

In thunderstorms, the top part of clouds and the ground become positively charged, while the midsections of clouds become strongly negative. Lightning results from the sudden resolution of these differences.

Modern physics

Relativity. Until the beginning of this century, many scientists believed that Newton's laws of motion and law of gravity offered a satisfactory basis for explaining the physical world. In 1905, Albert Einstein published his theory of special relativity, which showed that Newton's laws were really versions of more general laws. Einstein's theory is based on the following assumptions:

1. The measured value of the speed of light in a vacuum is always the same no matter how fast the observer or light source is moving.
2. The maximum velocity possible in the universe is that of light.
3. Absolute speed cannot be measured, only speed relative to some other object.

The theory states that to an observer at rest, a moving object will appear shorter and more massive than the same object at rest, and that a moving clock will appear to be going more slowly than the same one at rest.

Quantum theory. Newton believed that visible light consists of particles, while a Dutch physicist, Christiaan Huygens, and others felt that light was a wave. Today both views are believed to be correct. Radiation has the properties of both waves and particles, depending upon the experiment that is performed and the explanation that is sought. Max Planck, a German physicist, while studying radiation from so-called black bodies, concluded that his results could only be explained if energy were produced in individual bundles or packets, which he called *quanta*, rather than in waves. A *quantum* of energy emitted as visible light is called a *photon*. The amount of energy of each quantum is not the same. The amount of energy of each is proportional to the frequency of the radiation. Einstein soon showed that the *photoelectric effect*, which is the release of electrons by certain metals when irradiated by light, can only be explained in terms of the quantum theory. The quantum theory has since become the foundation of our understanding of matter.

Modern physics

Mass increases with motion

$$m = \frac{m_o}{1 - \frac{v^2}{c^2}}$$

where m is the mass of the body in motion
m_0 is the mass of the body at rest
v is the velocity of the body relative to an observer at rest
c is the speed of light

Energy of a photon is proportional to the frequency

$$E = hv = \frac{hc}{\lambda}$$

where E is energy in joules per quantum
h is Planck's constant (6.6232×10^{34} joules sec/quantum)
v is wave frequency
c is velocity of light
λ is the wavelength of radiation in meters

Einstein's photoelectric law

$$E_k = hv - w$$

where E_k is the kinetic energy of the emitted photoelectron
h is Planck's constant
v is the frequency associated with the absorbed photon
w is the work function for the surface of the photosensitive metal

According to special relativity, the boy sees the girl's watch as slower, and she sees his watch as slower. Unless the car is moving near the speed of light, however, the effect is too small to be noticed.

The principle of uncertainty.

Newton believed that if we knew the exact position and momentum (mass multiplied by velocity) of a particle at some instant, it would be possible to calculate where the particle would be at any time in the future. In 1927 Werner Heisenberg, a German physicist, showed that this is not so. He proved that it is impossible to determine both the exact position and speed of any particle at the same time, since the act of measuring disturbs the particle and introduces an error into the measurement. This *principle of uncertainty* has led to *quantum*, or *wave, mechanics*, a new way of describing atomic particles.

The uncertainty principle tells us that any statement about any individual event that occurs within the confines of this basic uncertainty has no meaning and is not admissible in physics. The discovery of this principle has given physicists deeper insight into the laws of nature, but it has not altered the general pattern of physical concepts. Most observations are carried out with materials having large numbers of particles and individual events, and are statistical in nature. The laws of probability see to it that the sum total of the events is determined, although each individual event is uncertain.

Particle physics.

At one time—around 1930—the only known particles smaller than atoms were *electrons*, *protons*, and *photons*. The electron is the carrier of negative electric charge (and some mass), the proton is the carrier of positive electric charge and mass, and the photon is the carrier of electromagnetic radiation. But there are many subatomic particles that have been found since 1930. Certain of these particles are considered basic in various theories. There are 22 of these.

More basic even than most of the 22 observed particles are *quarks*. While quarks have never been observed experimentally, 15 of the 22 particles are thought to be made from quarks. The 15 subatomic particles formed from quarks (and other very short-lived particles also formed from quarks) are called *baryons*, meaning "heavy," or *mesons*, meaning "middle." Subatomic particles that are not formed from quarks are called *leptons*, meaning "light," except for the photon, which is a class by itself. The mass of these particles is measured in millions of electron volts (MEV).

Four different forces cause the interactions between particles, including the change of an isolated particle to other particles of less mass (*decay*). These forces are gravity, the electric force, the *weak* force, and the *strong* force. (In some recent theories, the electric and the weak forces have been combined as the *electroweak* force.) Gravity is actually the weakest of the four forces.

Nearly all particles exist in at least two forms, one of which is called the *antiparticle* of the other. The antiparticle of the proton is called the *antiproton*; the antiparticle of the neutron is the *antineutron*; and so forth for most particles. However, the antiparticle of the electron, which was the first antiparticle to be discovered, is usually called the *positron*. If a particle and its antiparticle meet, say an electron and a positron, they will destroy each other completely, producing photons that carry off the masses as energy. Similarly, a photon with sufficient energy can suddenly become a pair consisting of one electron and one positron, converting part of the energy of the photon into mass. Atoms can be made from antiprotons, antineutrons, and positrons, forming *antimatter*, but they immediately interact with ordinary matter to turn into energy.

Some nuclear particles

Name	*Symbol*	*Mass (in MEV)*	*Charge*	*Average lifetime (in seconds)*
Photon	γ	0	0	Stable
LEPTONS				
Neutrino	ν	0*	0	Stable
Antineutrino	$\bar{\nu}$	0*	0	Stable
Neutrino (Muon type)	ν_μ	0*	0	Stable
Antineutrino (Muon type)	$\bar{\nu}_\mu$	0*	0	Stable
Electron	e^-	0.511	−1	Stable
Positron	e^+	0.511	+1	Stable
Muon	μ^-	105.7	−1	2.2×10^{-6}
Antimuon	μ^+	105.7	+1	2.2×10^{-6}
MESONS				
Positive Pi	π^0	139.6	+1	2.6×10^{-8}
Negative Pi	π^-	189.6	−1	2.6×10^{-8}
Neutral Pi	π^0	135	0	8×10^{-17}
Positive K	K^+	493.7	+1	1.2×10^{-8}
K-zero-short	K^0_S	497.7	0	9×10^{-11}
K-zero-long	K^0_L	497.7	0	5.2×10^{-8}
Negative K	K^-	493.7	−1	1.2×10^{-8}
BARYONS				
Proton	p	938.3	+1	Stable*
Antiproton	$\bar{p}$	938.3	−1	Stable*
Neutron	n	939.6	0	9.18×10^2
Antineutron	$\bar{n}$	939.6	0	9.18×10^2
Lambda Hyperon	Λ^0	115.6	0	3×10^{-10}
Lambda Antihyperon	$\bar{\Lambda}^0$	1115.6	0	3×10^{-10}

* Some theories challenge this.

Nuclear physics.

Nuclear physics is concerned with changes in the nuclei of atoms.

Radioactivity. Antoine Henri Becquerel, a French scientist, discovered in 1896 that uranium gives off radiation that fogs photographic film. Soon after, Marie and Pierre Curie isolated two new radioactive elements, polonium and radium. *Radioactivity* is the spontaneous disintegration of the nuclei of certain atoms. As these atoms disintegrate, energy is released. The radioactivity of a substance decreases continually with time and the rate of decrease is different for each element. The rate of radioactive decay is usually expressed as the *half-life* of that element, that is, the time for half the atoms to decompose. The half-life ranges from a fraction of a second for some isotopes to billions of years for others.

Radioactivity originates in the unstable nucleus of the atom. There are three general types of radioactive decay. The nucleus can emit a *gamma ray*, which is an electromagnetic wave of very high frequency. It can also emit an *alpha particle*, which is the equivalent of the nucleus of a helium atom containing two protons and two neutrons. Since the loss of protons means a decrease in the atomic number (the number of protons in the nucleus), and since the atomic number determines the chemistry of the atom, the result is the formation of a new element. When radium loses an alpha particle, the products are helium and radon.

The third type of radioactive decay comes from the *beta particle*, which is an electron. We can imagine a neutron losing an electron and becoming a proton. Since a proton has been gained, the atomic number changes and a new element is produced.

Nuclear fission. In 1939 Otto Hahn and Fritz Strassman, German physicists, discovered that if uranium^{235} (an isotope of uranium with the atomic weight of 235) is bombarded with neutrons, uranium^{236} is formed. This isotope is unstable and splits into several fragments in a process called *nuclear fission*. The fission process releases enormous amounts of energy because some mass is converted to energy. The theory of relativity states that when a mass is converted to energy, the energy is $E = mc^2$ where c is the speed of light. Since c^2 is a very large number, E is great even for small values of m. As an example, if the mass is 1 gram:

$$E = mc^2$$
$$E = 1\text{ g} \times (9 \times 10^8\text{ cm/sec})^2$$
$$E = 9 \times 10^{16}\text{ ergs} \quad or$$
$$E = 9 \times 10^9\text{ joules} \quad or$$
$$E = 25 \times 10^4\text{ kilowatt-hours}$$

One gram of matter is equivalent to 25 million kilowatt hours of energy!

The fission process requires a neutron to start it, but the resulting fissions produce many neutrons. If these bombard other U^{235} atoms, a *chain reaction* can occur,

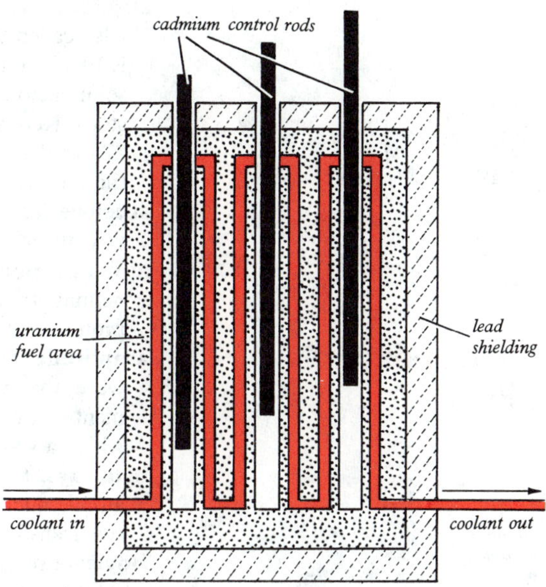

Atomic reactor

If enough uranium 235 is collected in one place, the neutrons produced will cause an explosion. In an atomic reactor, uranium 235 is mixed with the more common form, uranium 238. Enough neutrons are produced to cause continued fission, which then produces heat. Cadmium rods can be used to control the process by absorbing some of the neutrons.

producing an instantaneous explosion. This requires a certain *critical mass* of uranium, for otherwise the neutrons will escape. This is the principle behind the fission bomb.

To use the fission reaction to produce nuclear power, it is necessary to have a controlled reaction. The first controlled reaction was contained in a uranium-graphite pile into which cadmium rods were inserted. Cadmium absorbs neutrons so the reaction can be slowed down by simply pushing the rods further into the pile. This is the basic principle of today's nuclear reactors. The huge amount of heat that is produced is converted to steam which in turn drives electric generators.

Nuclear fusion. Another way to release very large amounts of energy is by fusing or combining the nuclei of certain light atoms to form heavier elements. In this process some mass is converted to energy. This fusion reaction is the source of energy of the stars, including our sun. In the sun, four hydrogen atoms fuse to make an isotope of helium. The helium nucleus formed has less mass than the sum of the four hydrogen nuclei. This mass is converted into energy. To start this reaction requires temperatures that are difficult to attain in a controlled way. We have succeeded in making hydrogen or fusion bombs by using fission bombs to attain the necessary temperatures. If we could control the fusion process, the energy problems of mankind would be over.

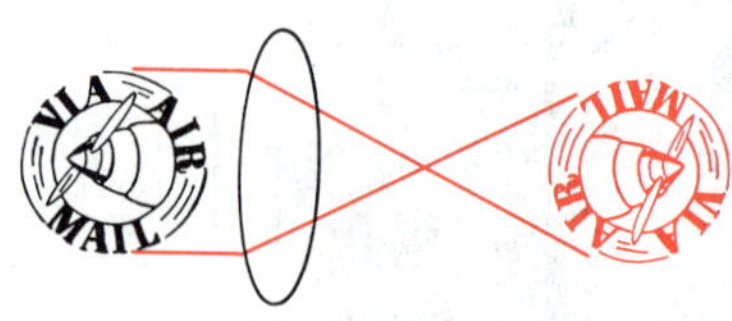

real image

Dictionary of physics

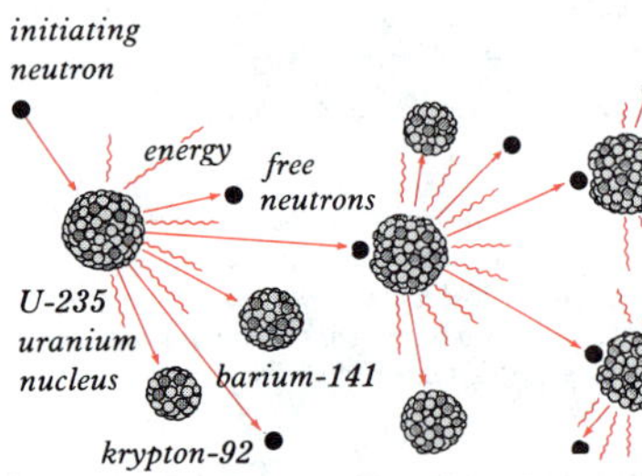

Neutrons set free by fission collide with U-235, continuing chain reaction.

fission

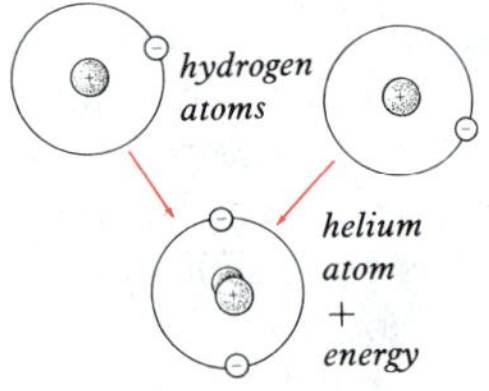

Two hydrogen atoms combine to create one atom of helium, releasing energy.

fusion

radar

absolute temperature scale. Also called the Kelvin scale, it is based on the idea that at absolute zero all molecular motion stops. Kelvin temperatures are 273.16 degrees higher than those on the Celsius scale.

acceleration. Rate of change of velocity with time.

alpha particle. Nucleus of a helium atom, consisting of two protons and two neutrons.

amplitude. Height of a crest of a wave; the maximum displacement of the medium through which a wave is traveling.

beta rays. Electrons emitted by atomic nuclei in certain radioactive transformations.

Boyle's law (for gases). At a constant temperature, the volume of a gas is inversely proportional to the pressure.

Celsius temperature scale. Based on the temperature of melted ice (assigned a value of 0°) and boiling water (assigned a value of 100°). The interval is divided into 100 degrees.

Charles's law (for gases). At a fixed pressure, the volume of a gas is directly proportional to the absolute temperature.

conservation of mass-energy, law of. In any change, the sum of the amount of matter and the amount of energy remains constant.

conservation of momentum, law of. For any system, the total momentum (mass times velocity) of all bodies involved remains unchanged.

Coulomb's law. Force is proportional to the product of charges and is inversely proportional to the square of distances between charges.

critical mass. The mass of uranium or other material in a fission nuclear bomb required for a chain reaction at a constant rate.

Doppler effect. Change in wavelength that results when the source producing the waves is moving with respect to the receiver.

electromagnetic waves. Systems of varying electrical and magnetic fields regenerating each other and traveling through space as waves.

energy. Ability to perform work.

entropy. Mathematical measure of the unavailable energy in a thermodynamic system.

Fahrenheit temperature scale. Melting ice is assigned a value of 32° and boiling water 212°. The interval is divided into 180 degrees.

force. That which causes acceleration or distortion of shape.

frequency. Number of cycles of a wave per unit time.

gamma ray. Electromagnetic radiation of very short wavelength.

gravitation, law of. The gravitational force between two bodies is directly proportional to the product of their masses and inversely proportional to the square of the distance between their centers.

half-life. Time it takes for half of the atoms of a radioactive element to become transformed as a result of radioactive decay.

image, real. Image formed when light passes from an object through a convex lens. The image is on the opposite side of the lens from the object, is always inverted, and can be projected on a screen.

inertia. Property of an object that makes it resist change in its velocity.

infrared radiation. Electromagnetic radiation of longer wavelength than visible light, with a maximum wavelength of 10^{-4}m.

inverse square law (for light). The intensity of illumination of a surface is inversely proportional to the square of the distance of the surface from the light source.

isotopes. Forms of an element with the same atomic number but different atomic weights.

Kelvin temperature scale. *See* absolute temperature scale.

longitudinal waves. Waves in which the oscillation of the moving particles is parallel to the wave direction, for example, sound.

mass. Amount of matter in a body. A measure of the inertia of an object.

microwaves. Portion of the electromagnetic spectrum between infrared and radio frequencies.

momentum. Mass of an object multiplied by its velocity.

motion, Newton's laws of:
1. A body continues in a state of rest or in a uniform straight line motion unless acted upon by an outside force.
2. The change in motion of a body is proportional to the force applied.
3. To every action, there is an equal and opposite reaction.

nuclear fission. Splitting of heavy nuclei caused by absorption of neutrons.

nuclear fusion. Creation of atomic nuclei by the fusion of light nuclei.

nuclear physics. Study of changes in atomic nuclei.

nuclear reaction. Change in an atomic nucleus caused by combination with or loss of elemental particles such as neutrons or other nuclei.

Ohm's law. Electric current is equal to the ratio of voltage and resistance.

phase. Time relation of two cyclic motions. Two motions are in phase if they reach their peaks simultaneously. In chemistry, the form in which a substance exists at room temperature, that is, solid, liquid, or gas.

photoelectric effect. Emission of electrons by an object as the result of irradiation by light.

photon. Quantum of light or other electromagnetic radiation.

pitch. Frequency of a sound wave.

Planck's constant. Ratio between the energy and frequency of a photon.

power. Rate at which work is done.

quantum. Smallest unit of quantized energy (that is, energy that can only have certain integral values). For electromagnetic energy, the quantum is called a photon.

radar. Device for detecting distant objects by reflection of microwaves.

radioactivity. Spontaneous breakdown of atomic nuclei.

real image. *See* image, real.

reflection, law of. Angle between an incident ray of light and the normal is always equal to the angle between the reflected ray and the normal.

refraction, law of. When light passes at an oblique angle from one medium into another of greater density, the velocity of light decreases and is bent toward the normal.

relativity. Principle that all frames of reference are equivalent for the description of physical events.

sound waves. Longitudinal vibrations of audible frequency.

spectrum. Continuous series of wavelengths.

temperature. Condition of a substance that determines the direction of heat flow from one object to another; a measurement of the kinetic energy of the particles of a substance.

thermodynamics. Study of the interrelationships between heat and mechanical energy.

thermodynamics, laws of:
1. When work is transformed into heat or vice versa, the amount of work is always equivalent to the amount of heat.
2. It is impossible by any continuous self-sustaining process for heat to be transferred from a colder to a hotter body.

thermonuclear. Reaction in nucleus of atoms caused by very high temperatures, which causes nuclei to fuse, forming new elements.

transmutation. Change of one element into another as the result of a nuclear event.

transverse waves. Waves in which particles move perpendicularly to the direction of the wave, for example, light.

ultraviolet. Portion of the electromagnetic spectrum lying between x-rays and visible light.

uncertainty, principle of. Theory that it is impossible to measure both the exact position and exact velocity of an atomic particle at the same time.

wave. Cyclic disturbance traveling through a medium.

wavelength. Distance between adjacent peaks of a wave.

weight. Measure of the pull of the force of gravity on a body.

work. Product of a force and the displacement of an object in the direction of the force.

x-rays. Portion of the electromagnetic spectrum between gamma rays and the ultraviolet.

For Further Reference

Asimov, Isaac
Understanding Physics (3 volumes)
Walker and Co., New York

Beiser, Arthur
Concepts of Modern Physics
McGraw-Hill, New York

Ford, Kenneth
Classical & Modern Physics (3 volumes)
John Wiley & Sons, New York

March, Robert H.
Physics for Poets
McGraw-Hill, New York

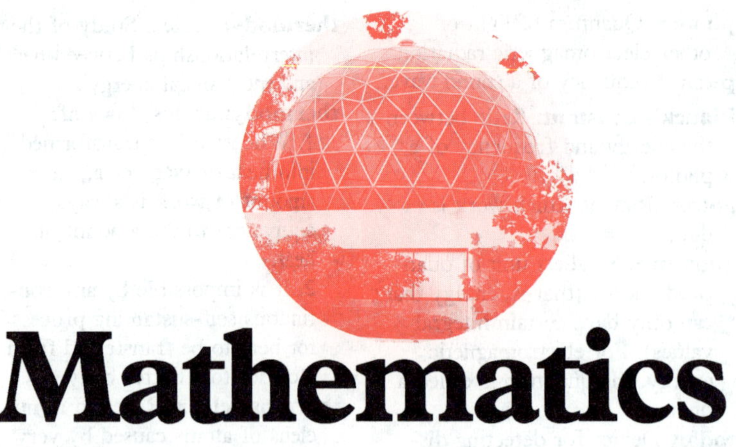

Mathematics

In this article, the entire sequence of secondary-school mathematics, from arithmetic through calculus, is presented in a simple way, with an emphasis on problem solving. Specific guidelines for difficult areas and easy-to-use summaries of essential information are presented in tabular and chart form. Special attention is paid to the use of the hand-held calculator.

Arithmetic

Whole numbers. The first numbers that one learns are sometimes called the *counting numbers,* but mathematicians call them the *natural numbers.* They are 1, 2, 3, ... Notice that 0 is not included. If 0 is included, the set of numbers is called *whole numbers.* Fractions, which are not whole numbers, present special problems; they are usually not adaptable to work on the calculator the way whole numbers are.

When you learn to factor a whole number into its *primes,* you simplify many fraction problems. A prime is a whole number that can be formed by multiplication from other whole numbers in one way only: as a product of itself with 1 (1 is not considered a prime). For example, 3 and 5 are primes, but 4 and 9 are not.

Which are prime numbers? 2, 6, 17, 51

PRIME
$2 = 2 \times 1$ or 1×2

COMPOSITE
$6 = 6 \times 1$ or 1×6
$= 2 \times 3$ or 3×2

(A *composite* number is any whole number, except 1, that is not prime.)

PRIME
$17 = 17 \times 1$ or 1×17

COMPOSITE
$51 = 51 \times 1$ or 1×51
$= 3 \times 17$ or 17×3

Factor 60 into primes.

A. Start with the least prime. Work up through the primes. The least prime is 2. Since $\frac{60}{2} = 30$, 2 is a factor of 60. (The symbol $\frac{60}{2}$ means "60 divided by 2.")

B. Now look at 30, the quotient. Since $\frac{30}{2} = 15$, 2 is a factor of 60 twice. The quotient, 15, cannot be divided evenly by 2, so look at the next higher prime, 3, as a divisor.

C. Since $\frac{15}{3} = 5$, 3 is also a prime factor of 60. The quotient, 5, is prime; therefore, the answer is
$60 = 2 \times 2 \times 3 \times 5$.

Fractions

$$\frac{3}{4} \times \frac{2}{3}$$

METHOD 1

A. Multiply the numerators (top numbers in fractions).

$$\frac{3}{4} \times \frac{2}{3} = \frac{6}{}$$

B. Multiply the denominators (bottom numbers).

$$\frac{3}{4} \times \frac{2}{3} = \frac{6}{12}$$

C. Eliminate common factors in the numerator and denominator of the product. The prime factors of 6 are shown as 2 × 3, while the prime factors of 12 are shown as 2 × 2 × 3. *Canceling* is crossing out matching prime factors in the numerator and denominator and indicating that a factor of 1 is left.

$$\frac{3}{4} \times \frac{2}{3} = \frac{\overset{1}{\cancel{2}} \times \overset{1}{\cancel{3}}}{\underset{1}{\cancel{2}} \times 2 \times \underset{1}{\cancel{3}}}$$

Multiply the 1's and any numbers not crossed out to get the "reduced" form of the product.

$$\frac{3}{4} \times \frac{2}{3} = \frac{1}{2}$$

METHOD 2

A. Cancel before you multiply.

$$\frac{3}{4} \times \frac{2}{3} = \frac{\overset{1}{\cancel{3}}}{2 \times \underset{1}{\cancel{2}}} \times \frac{\overset{1}{\cancel{2}}}{\underset{1}{\cancel{3}}}$$

Remember that factors in the numerators must be matched with factors in the denominators.

B. Multiply any factors remaining.

$$\frac{3}{4} \times \frac{2}{3} = \frac{\overset{1}{\cancel{3}}}{2 \times \underset{1}{\cancel{2}}} \times \frac{\overset{1}{\cancel{2}}}{\underset{1}{\cancel{3}}} = \frac{1}{2}$$

$$\frac{7}{8} \div \frac{5}{6}$$

A. Invert the divisor to change to multiplication.

$$\frac{7}{8} \times \frac{6}{5}$$

B. Cancel any common factors.

$$\frac{7}{8} \times \frac{6}{5} = \frac{7}{\underset{1}{\cancel{2}} \times 2 \times 2} \times \frac{\overset{1}{\cancel{2}} \times 3}{5}$$

C. Multiply the remaining numerators and denominators.

$$\frac{7}{\underset{1}{\cancel{2}} \times 2 \times 2} \times \frac{\overset{1}{\cancel{2}} \times 3}{5} = \frac{21}{20}$$

LCM's and GCD's

Least Common Multiple

Multiples are products of a number with 0, 1, 2, 3, . . . as a factor.

Examples

For 6: 0, 6, 12, 18, 24, 30, 36, 42, 48, 54, . . .

For 8: 0, 8, 16, 24, 32, 40, 48, 56, 64, 72, . . .

Common multiples of 6 and 8: 0, 24, 48, 72, . . .

The *Least Common Multiple* (LCM) of a set of numbers is the first nonzero common multiple of the numbers in the set.

The LCM of 6 and 8 is 24.

Using primes to find the LCM

24 = 2 × 2 × 2 × 3
42 = 2 × 3 × 7
The primes in 24 and 42 together are
2 (three times)
3 (once)
7 (once)
The LCM of 24 and 42 is 2 × 2 × 2 × 3 × 7 = 168.

Greatest Common Divisor

Divisor is another name for factor.

Examples

Divisors of 6: 1, 2, 3, 6

Divisors of 8: 1, 2, 4, 8

Common divisors of 6 and 8 are 1 and 2.

The *Greatest Common Divisor* (GCD) of a set of numbers is the largest common divisor of the numbers in the set.

The GCD of 6 and 8 is 2.

Using primes to find the GCD

24 = 2× 2× 2 × 3
42 = 2 × 3 × 7
The common primes in 24 and 42 are
2 (once)
3 (once)
The GCD of 24 and 42 is 2 × 3 = 6.

$2\frac{3}{4} + 1\frac{7}{8}$

METHOD 1

A. Change the mixed numbers to fractions.

$2\frac{3}{4} + 1\frac{7}{8} = \frac{11}{4} + \frac{15}{8}$

B. Use the least common multiple of the denominators as a new denominator—the *lowest common denominator,* or *LCD.*

$\frac{11}{4} + \frac{15}{8} = \frac{22}{8} + \frac{15}{8}$

C. Add the numerators and change to a mixed number.

$\frac{22}{8} + \frac{15}{8} = \frac{37}{8} = 4\frac{5}{8}$

METHOD 2

A. Write the problem in vertical form.

$$\begin{array}{r} 2\frac{3}{4} \\ +1\frac{7}{8} \\ \hline \end{array}$$

B. Rewrite the fractions with a common denominator. Add.

$$\begin{array}{rr} 2\frac{3}{4} = & 2\frac{6}{8} \\ +1\frac{7}{8} = & 1\frac{7}{8} \\ \hline & 3\frac{13}{8} \end{array}$$

C. Change the fraction to a mixed number. Since $\frac{13}{8} = 1\frac{5}{8}$, the sum is $4\frac{5}{8}$.

Mixed numbers and the calculator

Mixed numbers and improper fractions

The sum of an integer (whole number) and a fraction, when shown without a + sign, is a *mixed number.*

Examples

$3\frac{1}{2}$ means $3 + \frac{1}{2}$ | $5\frac{7}{8}$ means $5 + \frac{7}{8}$

Mixed numbers can also be shown as *improper fractions;* that is, fractions in which the numerator is greater than the denominator.

$3\frac{1}{2} = \frac{7}{2}$ | $5\frac{7}{8} = \frac{47}{8}$

Changing mixed numbers to fractions with the calculator

	Examples $3\frac{1}{2}$	$5\frac{7}{8}$
A. Whole number $\boxtimes$ denominator.	$3 \boxtimes 2 \boxed{=} 6$	$5 \boxtimes 8 \boxed{=} 40$
B. Product (step A) $\boxplus$ numerator.	$6 \boxplus 1 \boxed{=} 7$	$40 \boxplus 7 \boxed{=} 47$
C. Sum (step B) is numerator of improper fraction.	$3\frac{1}{2} = \frac{7}{\ }$	$5\frac{7}{8} = \frac{47}{\ }$
D. Original denominator is also new denominator.	$3\frac{1}{2} = \frac{7}{2}$	$5\frac{7}{8} = \frac{47}{8}$

Changing improper fractions to mixed numbers with the calculator

	Examples $\frac{11}{4}$	$\frac{28}{6}$
A. Numerator ÷ denominator.	$11 \boxed{\div} 4 \boxed{=} 2.75$	$28 \boxed{\div} 6 \boxed{=} 4.6666666$
B. Take whole part of decimal and ignore any digits after the decimal point.	2 (ignore .75)	4 (ignore .6666666)
C. Whole part (step B) × denominator.	$2 \boxtimes 4 \boxed{=} 8$	$4 \boxtimes 6 \boxed{=} 24$
D. Numerator − product (step C).	$11 \boxed{-} 8 \boxed{=} 3$	$28 \boxed{-} 24 \boxed{=} 4$
E. Whole part (step B) is the whole number.	$\frac{11}{4} = 2 -$	$\frac{28}{6} = 4 -$
F. Difference (step D) is the numerator.	$\frac{11}{4} = 2\frac{3}{\ }$	$\frac{28}{6} = 4\frac{4}{\ }$
G. Original denominator is also the new denominator.	$\frac{11}{4} = 2\frac{3}{4}$	$\frac{28}{6} = 4\frac{4}{6}$
H. Fraction may need to be put in simplest form.	Not needed	$\frac{28}{6} = 4\frac{2}{3}$

$5\frac{1}{6} - 3\frac{1}{2}$

A. Rewrite in vertical form with common denominators.

$$\begin{array}{r} 5\frac{1}{6} = 5\frac{1}{6} \\ -3\frac{1}{2} = 3\frac{3}{6} \\ \hline \end{array}$$

B. "Borrow" 1 = $\frac{6}{6}$ from 5; that is, rename $5\frac{1}{6}$ as $4\frac{7}{6}$. Subtract.

$$\begin{array}{r} 5\frac{1}{6} = 4\frac{7}{6} \\ -3\frac{1}{2} = 3\frac{3}{6} \\ \hline 1\frac{4}{6} \end{array}$$

C. Rename $\frac{4}{6}$ as $\frac{2}{3}$. The answer is $1\frac{2}{3}$.

Powers of ten

Exponents

An *exponent* is used to show how many times a number is used as a factor.

Examples

$3^2 = 3 \times 3 = 9$;
9 is the *second power* of 3.

$10^4 = 10 \times 10 \times 10 \times 10 = 10{,}000$;
10,000 is the *fourth power* of 10.

Negative and zero exponents

When a minus sign (−) is placed in front of an exponent, the power becomes the denominator of a fraction whose numerator is 1.

Examples

$3^{-2} = \frac{1}{3\times3} = \frac{1}{9}$;
$\frac{1}{9}$ is 3 *raised* to the *negative two* power.

$10^{-4} = \frac{1}{10\times10\times10\times10} = \frac{1}{10{,}000}$;
$\frac{1}{10{,}000}$ is 10 raised to the *negative four* power.

The exponent 0 always gives the value 1 to the power (except that 0^0 is not defined).

Examples

$3^0 = 1$
$10^0 = 1$

Powers of ten

The number 10 has the special property that the number of times the digit 0 is used in the power is the same as the value of the exponent. For negative exponents, this property holds true for the denominators of powers of 10 in fraction form, but it is only true for powers of 10 in decimal form if a 0 is always written in the ones place (just in front of the decimal point). Counting all the zeros then gives the negative power.

Positive exponents		Zero and negative exponents
	(0 zeros)	$10^0 = 1$, or one
$10^1 = 10$, or ten	(1 zero)	$10^{-1} = \frac{1}{10} = 0.1$, or one tenth
$10^2 = 100$, or one hundred	(2 zeros)	$10^{-2} = \frac{1}{100} = 0.01$, or one hundredth
$10^3 = 1000$, or one thousand	(3 zeros)	$10^{-3} = \frac{1}{1000} = 0.001$, or one thousandth
$10^4 = 10{,}000$, or ten thousand	(4 zeros)	$10^{-4} = \frac{1}{10{,}000} = 0.0001$, or one ten thousandth
$10^5 = 100{,}000$, or one hundred thousand	(5 zeros)	$10^{-5} = \frac{1}{100{,}000} = 0.00001$, or one hundred thousandth
$10^6 = 1{,}000{,}000$, or one million	(6 zeros)	$10^{-6} = \frac{1}{1{,}000{,}000} = 0.000001$, or one millionth
$10^7 = 10{,}000{,}000$, or ten million	(7 zeros)	$10^{-7} = \frac{1}{10{,}000{,}000} = 0.0000001$, or one ten millionth
$10^8 = 100{,}000{,}000$, or one hundred million	(8 zeros)	$10^{-8} = \frac{1}{100{,}000{,}000} = 0.00000001$, or one hundred millionth
$10^9 = 1{,}000{,}000{,}000$, or one billion	(9 zeros)	$10^{-9} = \frac{1}{1{,}000{,}000{,}000} = 0.000000001$, or one billionth

Decimals. Decimals are another way of writing fractions. The decimal point means that the denominator will be a power of 10. The particular power of 10 is indicated by the number of places to the right of the decimal point. For example, 0.3 has 1 place to the right of the decimal point, so $0.3 = \frac{3}{10^1}$, or $\frac{3}{10}$. The decimal 0.123 has 3 places to the right of the decimal point, so $0.123 = \frac{123}{10^3}$, or $\frac{123}{1000}$.

Decimals are *decimal fractions,* but they are also an extension of the numeration system used for whole numbers. The decimal point marks the ones place. A digit to the left of the point means tens, while a digit to the right means tenths.

One way to read decimals is by saying the power of 10 with a *-th* attached after reading the number. Using that system, 0.123 would be read as "one hundred twenty-three thousandths." Another way to read decimals is by reading each digit in order, saying "point" for the decimal point. Using that method, 0.123 would be read as "zero point one two three." If a decimal is greater than 1, the "point" method can still be used as before, but the *-th* method needs to be modified. You must say "and" between the whole-number part and the decimal part. Therefore, 3.14 would be read as either "three point one four" or as "three and fourteen hundredths."

3.04 + 5.6 + 0.04

A. Write in vertical form, being careful to keep the decimal points lined up.

```
  3.04
  5.6
+0.04
```

B. Add as you would for whole numbers, inserting a decimal point below the line of points. Some people prefer to write in extra zeros to make the right align.

This does not change the value of the decimals.

```
  3.04
  5.60
+0.04
------
  8.68
```

3.89 − 2.647

A. Rewrite in vertical form, keeping the decimal points lined up. Most people find filling out the zeros to be helpful.

```
  3.890
−2.647
```

B. Subtract as with whole numbers, lining up the decimal point in the difference with the ones above it.

```
  3.890
−2.647
-------
  1.243
```

Notice that it is necessary to "borrow" 1 from the 9 when you begin to subtract; that is, you must rename 9 hundredths as 8 hundredths 10 thousandths.

Many people find it easier to show this by writing a 1, the "helping number," just before the 0. They also cross out the 9 and write in a small 8 as another helping number.

```
     8 1
  3.8 9 0   (9 crossed out)
−2.6 4 7
---------
  1.2 4 3
```

Subtracting is sometimes more difficult when it is necessary to borrow across zeros.

7.006 − 4.798

A. Since you cannot borrow from the first 0, or from the second 0, proceed to the 7 to borrow 1. Then the problem, using helping numbers, looks like this:

```
 6 1
 7.006   (7 crossed out)
− 4.798
```

B. Now you can borrow from the 10. Repeat the process until you reach the 6.

```
      9 9
 6   1 1 1
 7 . 0 0 6   (7, 0, 0 crossed out)
− 4 . 7 9 8
-----------
  2 . 2 0 8
```

Multiplying by powers of 10

The key to working with decimals is understanding how powers of 10 work, since decimals are based upon powers of 10. The rules for multiplying and dividing by powers of 10 are also useful in solving many problems with whole numbers. You can memorize rules for powers of ten that are based upon counting zeros or on "moving the decimal point" to a different location to get the numeral for a different number. These rules are based on the properties of the numeration system we use.

To start with, make sure that you know the powers of 10 themselves. These are given in the table on page 183. Each positive or negative power of 10 is related in a simple way to the number of zeros shown when the number is written out in the decimal numeration system.

Whole numbers

Notice the pattern.

$3 \times 10^1 = 3 \times 10 = 30$ (1 zero)
$3 \times 10^2 = 3 \times 100 = 300$ (2 zeros)
$3 \times 10^3 = 3 \times 1000 = 3000$ (3 zeros)
$3 \times 10^4 = 3 \times 10000 = 30000$ (4 zeros)

Rule

To multiply a whole number by a non-negative power of 10, write the whole number with the same number of zeros after it as in the power of 10.
(NOTE: This will not work for negative powers.)

Examples

$7 \times 100{,}000 = 7 \times 10^5 = 700{,}000$
$40 \times 1000 = 40 \times 10^3 = 40{,}000$
(NOTE: Keep the 0 from the 40.)

Decimals

$3.455192 \times 10^0 = 3.455192 \times 1 = 3.455192$ (decimal point in same place)
$3.455192 \times 10^1 = 3.455192 \times 10 = 34.55192$ (decimal point 1 place to the right)
$3.455192 \times 10^2 = 3.455192 \times 100 = 345.5192$ (decimal point 2 places to the right)
$3.455192 \times 10^3 = 3.455192 \times 1000 = 3455.192$ (decimal point 3 places to the right)
$3.455192 \times 10^4 = 3.455192 \times 10000 = 34551.92$ (decimal point 4 places to the right)

Rule

To multiply a decimal by a non-negative power of 10, rewrite the decimal with the decimal point the same number of places to the right as the power of 10.

Examples

$27.349 \times 100 = 27.349 \times 10^2 = 2734.9$
$3.82 \times 100 = 3.82 \times 10^2 = 382. = 382$
(You need not show point.)
$3.501 \times 10{,}000 = 3.501 \times 10^4 = 35{,}010$
(You may need to write 0's.)
$57 \times 1000 = 57 \times 10^3 = 57. \times 10^3 = 57{,}000$
(The decimal rule also works for whole numbers.)

Negative exponents

$392.422 \times 10^{-1} = 392.422 \times 0.1 = 39.2422$ (decimal point 1 place to the left)
$392.422 \times 10^{-2} = 392.422 \times 0.01 = 3.92422$ (decimal point 2 places to the left)
$392.422 \times 10^{-3} = 392.422 \times 0.001 = 0.392422$ (decimal point 3 places to the left)
$392.422 \times 10^{-4} = 392.422 \times 0.0001 = 0.0392422$ (decimal point 4 places to the left)

Rule

To multiply a decimal by a negative power of 10, rewrite the decimal with the decimal point the same number of places to the left as the power of 10, ignoring the negative sign.

Examples

$495.3 \times 0.01 = 495.3 \times 10^{-2} = 4.953$
$7534.02 \times 0.0001 = 7534.02 \times 10^{-4} = 0.753402$
$37.5 \times 0.001 = 37.5 \times 10^{-3} = 0.0375$
(You may need to write more zeros to get the decimal point where you want it.)
$5028 \times 0.1 = 5028 \times 10^{-1} = 5028. \times 10^{-1} = 502.8$
(The decimal rule also works for whole numbers.)

5.9 × 2.3

A. Rewrite in vertical form and multiply as if you were dealing with whole numbers.

```
  2.3
 ×5.9
  207
 115
 1357
```

B. Count the number of decimal places in the problem as originally posed. The first factor, 2.3, has 1 decimal place. The second factor, 5.9, also has 1 digit to the right of the decimal point. Add the number of decimal places. $1 + 1 = 2$.

C. Mark off 2 decimal places in the product.

```
  2.3
 × 5.9
  207
 115
 13.57
```

You use the sum of the decimal places in the problem as the number of decimal places in the product because decimals are just fractions that have powers of 10 as their denominators. When you multiply fractions, you multiply the denominators. Using the rule for multiplying by a power of 10 (see box on page 185), the product of the denominators is the sum of the exponents of the powers of 10. 4.7 is another way of writing $\frac{47}{10^1}$ and 3.054 is another way of writing $\frac{3954}{10^3}$. The product has a numerator that is 47×3954. The product also has a denominator of $10^1 \times 10^3$, which is equal to 10^{1+3}. The answer will have 4 decimal places.

0.07 × 0.005

A. Rewrite in vertical form. Most people ignore lining up the decimal points.

```
  0.005
× 0.07
```

B. Multiply as if the problem had only the whole numbers 5 and 7 shown.

```
  0.005
× 0.07
     35
```

C. Count the number of decimal places in each of the factors: 0.005 has 3 decimal places and 0.07 has 2 decimal places. The number of decimal places in the product is $3 + 2 = 5$.

D. The number 35, however, has 2 digits only. Additional zeros must be written in front of 35.

Three additional decimal places are needed, so 3 zeros must be added.

```
  0.005
× 0.07
0.00035
```

Dividing by powers of 10

Non-negative exponents

Notice the pattern.

$872.384 \div 10^1 = 872.384 \div 10 = 87.2384$
$872.384 \div 10^2 = 872.384 \div 100 = 8.72384$
$872.384 \div 10^3 = 872.384 \div 1000 = 0.872384$

Rule

To divide a number by a non-negative power of 10, rewrite the number with the decimal point the same number of places to the left as the power of 10.

Examples

$29837.4 \div 10{,}000 = 29837.4 \div 10^4 = 2.98374$
$5.9 \div 1000 = 5.9 \div 10^3 = 0.0059$
(You may need to write more 0's.)
$293 \div 1000 = 293 \div 10^3 = 293. \div 10^3 = 0.293$

Negative exponents

$872.384 \div 10^{-1} = 872.384 \div 0.1 = 8723.84$
$872.384 \div 10^{-2} = 872.384 \div 0.01 = 87238.4$
$872.384 \div 10^{-3} = 872.384 \div 0.001 = 872{,}384$

Rule

To divide a number by a negative power of 10, rewrite the number with the decimal point the same number of places to the right as the power of 10, ignoring the negative sign.

Examples

$2957.395 \div 0.01 = 2957.395 \div 10^{-2} = 295{,}739.5$
$3.14 \div 0.0001 = 3.14 \div 10^{-4} = 31{,}400$
(You may need to write more zeros.)
$85 \div 0.1 = 85 \div 10^{-1} = 850$

Fractions, decimals, and repeating decimals

Decimals into fractions
To change a decimal to a fraction, write the decimal as a fraction that has a whole-number (omitting the decimal point) numerator over a denominator of the proper power of 10; then simplify if possible.

Examples

$0.12 = \frac{12}{100} = \frac{12 \div 4}{100 \div 4} = \frac{3}{25}$

$2.314 = \frac{2314}{1000} = 2\,\frac{314}{1000}$

NOTE: Decimals greater than 1 maybe written as mixed numbers by taking the whole-number part of the decimal as the whole-number part of the mixed number. Treat the fraction part as in the general rule.

Example

$5.02 = 5\,\frac{2}{100} = 5\,\frac{1}{50}$

Fractions into decimals
To change a fraction to a decimal, divide the numerator by the denominator.

Examples

$\frac{5}{8} = 5 \div 8$

```
    0.625
8 ) 5.000
    4 8
      20
      16
       40
       40
```

$\frac{11}{4} = 11 \div 4$

```
    2.75
4 ) 11.00
     8
     3 0
     2 8
       20
       20
```

NOTE: For mixed numbers, you may take the whole-number part of the mixed number as the whole-number part of the decimal. Treat the fraction part as in the general rule.

Example

$4\frac{1}{2} = 4 + (1 \div 2)$

```
    0.5
2 ) 1.0
    1 0
```

$4\frac{1}{2} = 4.5$

Repeating decimals
If the same remainder is encountered more than once after you begin to "bring down" zeros, the decimal will repeat the same pattern of digits over and over. This may be indicated by putting a bar over the digits that repeat.

HINT: All fractions with whole-number numerators and denominators either terminate (the remainder when you divide is zero) or repeat a set of digits. The fraction will *always* terminate if the denominator of the fraction has only the prime factors 2 and 5—so fractions with denominators of 2, 10, 4, 8, 20, 25, and so forth terminate. Otherwise the fraction will repeat with a period (the number of digits that repeat) that is less than the denominator.

Examples

The denominator of $\frac{1}{3}$ has the prime factor 3, so it repeats with a period less than 3 (its actual period is 1).

The denominator of $\frac{11}{40}$ has the factors $2^3 \times 5$, so it terminates.

The denominator of $\frac{2}{7}$ has the prime factor 7, so it repeats with a period less than 7 (its actual period is 6).

The denominator of $\frac{5}{9}$ has the prime factors 3^2, so it repeats with a period less than 9 (its actual period is 1).

Examples

$\frac{1}{3} = 1 \div 3$

$$\begin{array}{r} 0.3\overline{3} \\ 3\,)\,\overline{1.00} \\ \underline{9} \\ 10 \\ \underline{9} \\ 1 \end{array}$$

$0.3\overline{3}$ means 0.333333 . . .

$\frac{3}{11} = 3 \div 11$

$$\begin{array}{r} 0.\overline{2727} \\ 11\,)\,\overline{3.0000} \\ \underline{2.2} \\ 80 \\ \underline{77} \\ 30 \\ \underline{22} \\ 80 \\ \underline{77} \\ 3 \end{array}$$

$0.\overline{2727}$ or $0.\overline{27}$ means 0.27272727 . . .

$\frac{2}{7} = 2 \div 7$

$$\begin{array}{r} 0.\overline{285714} \\ 7\,)\,\overline{2.000000} \\ \underline{1\,4} \\ 60 \\ \underline{56} \\ 40 \\ \underline{35} \\ 50 \\ \underline{49} \\ 10 \\ \underline{7} \\ 30 \\ \underline{28} \\ 2 \end{array}$$

$0.\overline{285714}$ means 0.285714285714285714 . . .

$\frac{16.1}{2.3}$

A. Division problems are easier to do by hand if they are written in the form that corresponds to vertical form for addition, subtraction, and multiplication. This is sometimes called "example form." Rewrite the problem in example form.

$2.3\overline{)16.1}$

Table of fractions and decimals

While you can always calculate the decimal equivalent to a fraction or the fraction equivalent to a decimal, it is very handy to memorize the more common equivalents. The following table includes the equivalents that occur most often.

Fraction	*Decimal equivalent*
$\frac{1}{2}$	0.5
$\frac{1}{3}$	$0.\overline{3}$
$\frac{1}{4}$	0.25
$\frac{1}{5}$	0.2
$\frac{1}{6}$	$0.1\overline{6}$
$\frac{1}{8}$	0.125
$\frac{1}{10}$	0.1
$\frac{2}{3}$	$0.\overline{6}$
$\frac{2}{5}$	0.4
$\frac{3}{4}$	0.75
$\frac{3}{5}$	0.6
$\frac{3}{8}$	0.375
$\frac{3}{10}$	0.3
$\frac{4}{5}$	0.8
$\frac{5}{6}$	$0.8\overline{3}$
$\frac{5}{8}$	0.625
$\frac{7}{8}$	0.875
$\frac{7}{10}$	0.7
$\frac{9}{10}$	0.9

B. Division by a whole number is accomplished by dividing as if both the *divisor* (number being divided by) and the *dividend* (number being divided into) are whole numbers. The decimal point in the quotient then lines up with the decimal point in the dividend (see box on page 187 for examples). The quotient will not change if both the divisor and the dividend are multiplied by the same number. Multiply each number by the power of 10 indicated by the decimal point in the divisor. For 2.3 the power is 10^1.

$2.3.\overline{)16.1.}$

C. In this problem, both the divisor and the dividend are changed to whole numbers by multiplication, so the division is completed in the same way as for whole numbers.

```
        7
2.3.)16.1.
     16 1
```

In this case, there is no remainder. Had there been a remainder of 3, for instance, it could *not* have been written with the quotient as "R3." Instead, one would need to insert more zeros after the dividend and continue dividing.

$\frac{23.4}{0.32}$

A. Rewrite in example form.

$0.32\overline{)23.4}$

B. There are 2 decimal places in the divisor, so both the divisor and the dividend must be multiplied by 10^2. This has the effect of "moving the decimal points" each 2 places to the right. Since there is only 1 decimal place in the dividend, however, it is necessary to insert a zero to locate the "new" decimal point.

$0.32.\overline{)23.40.}$

C. Now divide as with whole numbers.

```
           73
0.32.)23.40.
       22 4
        1 00
          96
           4
```

Since there is a remainder, it is necessary to insert zeros and keep dividing until (1) you do not require any greater precision; that is, you have as many decimal places as you need; (2) the division terminates because the remainder is 0; or (3) you reach the same remainder for the second time, which indicates that you have found all of the digits that repeat.

```
           73.125
0.32.)23.40.000
       22 4
        1 00
          96
           40
           32
            80
            64
            160
            160
```

Proportion and percent

William can go 385 miles on 1 tank of gasoline. If his tank holds 11 gallons, how many gallons of gasoline will he use on a trip of 595 miles?

A. Write the problem as a *proportion.* A proportion is a statement that two *ratios* are equal. A ratio is one way to compare two amounts by division. Each ratio is a number of miles to a number of gallons. The first ratio is the number of miles per tank to the number of gallons per tank, or $\frac{385}{11}$. The second ratio is the number of miles on the trip to an unknown number of gallons. The unknown number is N. Thus, the proportion is

$$\frac{385}{11} = \frac{595}{N}.$$

B. Solve the proportion. The easiest way to solve a proportion is to use the *cross-product rule:* In a proportion, the product of the numerator of the first ratio and the denominator of the second ratio is equal to the product of the denominator of the first ratio and the numerator of the second ratio. Accordingly, you can rewrite the proportion as

$$385 \times N = 11 \times 595.$$

C. Carry out any multiplication that you can.

$$385 \times N = 6545$$

D. If $385 \times N = 6545$, then

$$N = \frac{6545}{385} = 17.$$

The answer is 17 gallons of gasoline.

Find 37% of 250.

A. A *percent* is a ratio of a whole number to 100, so 37% is the ratio $\frac{37}{100}$. Percent problems can be solved in many ways. You may use decimals, for example, to rewrite this problem as 0.37×250.

The examples here will use the proportion method for solution because it is a useful way to solve practical problems. Think not only of 37% as a ratio, but also of 250 as a ratio.

In this context, the problem "find 37% of 250" may be solved by thinking "37 is to 100 as what number (N) is to 250?"

$$\frac{37}{100} = \frac{N}{250}.$$

B. Rewrite using the cross-product rule and complete any multiplication that you can.

$$37 \times 250 = 100 \times N$$
$$9250 = 100 \times N$$

C. Divide by 100 to find N.

$$N = \frac{9250}{100} = 92.5$$

The answer is 92.5.

Notice that this method involves multiplication by whole numbers only. Also, division by 100 is simple.

What percent of 400 is 260?

A. Set up a proportion.

$$\frac{260}{400} = \frac{N}{100}$$

The ratio $\frac{N}{100}$ is the same as N%.

B. Use the cross-product rule.

$$260 \times 100 = 400 \times N$$
$$26000 = 400 \times N$$

C. Divide by 400.

$$N = \frac{26000}{400} = 65$$

The answer is 65%.

52.5 is 35% of what number?

A. Set up a proportion.

$$\frac{52.5}{N} = \frac{35}{100}$$

B. Use the cross-product rule.

$$52.5 \times 100 = N \times 35$$
$$5250 = N \times 35$$

C. Divide by 35.

$$N = \frac{5250}{35} = 150$$

The answer is 150.

Interest problems

Find the amount of interest on $1500 at a rate of 9% for 6 months.

METHOD 1

A. The interest formula is $i = prt$ where i is the interest in dollars, p is the amount of money on which interest is being paid (the *principal*), r is the rate expressed as a percent, and t is the time in years. Since t is in months, convert 6 months to years.

$$\frac{6}{12} = \frac{1}{2}$$

The time is $\frac{1}{2}$ year.

B. Substitute into the formula, using the ratio form of percent.

$$i = 1500 \times \frac{9}{100} \times \frac{1}{2}$$

C. Cancel any factors you can and multiply.

$$i = 15 \times 9 \times \frac{1}{2} = \frac{135}{2} = 67\tfrac{1}{2}$$

The answer is $67.50.

METHOD 2

A. If you are using a calculator it will be easier to work with decimals than with ratios. Use 0.09 for 9% and 0.5 for $\frac{1}{2}$.

B. Use the formula and multiply.

$$i = 1500 \times 0.09 \times 0.5 = 67.5$$

The interest is $67.50.

Find the rate of interest if the interest is $55, the principal is $1000, and the time is 11 months.

METHOD 1

A. The interest formula can be rewritten in several ways by dividing both sides of the formula by one of the factors on the right side.

$$r = \frac{i}{p \times t}$$

$$p = \frac{i}{r \times t}$$

$$t = \frac{i}{p \times r}$$

The most useful form for this problem is the first,

$$r = \frac{i}{p \times t}$$

B. Convert the time to years and substitute into the formula.

$$t = \frac{11}{12}$$

$$r = \frac{55}{1000 \times \frac{11}{12}}$$

C. Multiply and rewrite the fraction as a ratio of some number to 100.

$$r = \frac{6}{100}$$

The answer is 6%.

METHOD 2

A. If you have a calculator it is easier to work with

$$t = \frac{i}{p \times r},$$

which avoids the problem of having to convert $\frac{11}{12}$ to a decimal.

$$\frac{11}{12} = \frac{55}{1000 \times r}$$

B. Use the cross-product rule.

$$11 \times (1000 \times r) = 12 \times 55$$
$$11000 \times r = 660$$

C. Divide by 11000.

$$r = 0.06$$

The answer is 6%.

Find the amount of money that will result from investing $2500 for 9 months at 10% when the interest is computed every 3 months and left in the account.

A. When interest is is collected on the interest, it is known as *compound interest.* While you can calculate compound interest by repeatedly calculating the amount for each period, it is easier to use the *compound interest formula*:

$$A = p \times (1+i)^n$$

where A is the amount (principal plus interest), p is the original principal, i is interest rate per period of compounding, and n is the number of periods. To use the formula, convert the interest rate, which is given per year, to a per period ratio. Since the period is 3 months, the per period rate is $\frac{3}{12} \times \frac{10}{100} = \frac{25}{1000} = 2.5\%$. In 9 months, there are 3 3-month periods.

B. Substitute into the formula.

$$A = 2500 \times (1+0.025)^3$$
$$= 2500 \times 1.0768906$$
$$= 2692.2265$$

The amount is $2692.23.

Discounts and taxes

How much does a dress cost if its original price was \$80 but it is now on sale at a discount of 20%?

METHOD 1

A. Find 20% of 80.

20% of 80 = 16

B. Subtract 16 from 80.

$80-16=64$

The dress will cost \$64.

METHOD 2

A. A discount is always a *percent of decrease.* You can solve percent-of-decrease problems in one step by subtracting the percent discount from 100% and then multiplying.

$100\%-20\%=80\%$

B. Multiply.

$80\times 0.80=64$

The dress will cost \$64.

Find the total amount for a \$50 purchase if the sales tax is $5\frac{1}{2}\%$.

A. A sales tax is a *percent of increase,* so the rate of the tax may be added to 100%.

$100\%+5\frac{1}{2}\%=105\frac{1}{2}\%$

B. Convert $105\frac{1}{2}\%$ to a decimal and multiply.

$50\times 1.055=52.75$

The answer is \$52.75.

Measurement

What is the precision of a measurement of 5 centimeters when the measurement is made with a ruler that shows only centimeters and millimeters?

A. The *precision* of any measurement is the smallest unit used in making the measurement. In this case it is 1 millimeter.

B. The number of *significant digits* should be the same as the total number of units used. There are two significant digits in 50 mm. In cm, the measurement should be shown as 5.0. The result can also be expressed in scientific notation (see box on page 192) as 5.0×10^0.

What is the greatest possible error in a measurement of 28.57 meters?

A. Determine the precision of the measurement. Since the measurement is written as 28.57 meters, it was made by measuring to the nearest 0.01 meter.

B. The *greatest possible error* is one-half the precision (the measurement is closer to 0.57 than to 0.56 or 0.58). One-half of 0.01 meter is 0.005 meter, so that is the greatest possible error.

What is the relative error in a measurement of 29 centimeters?

A. Determine the greatest possible error. Since the measurement is expressed to the nearest centimeter, the greatest possible error is one-half of 1 centimeter, or 0.5 cm.

B. The *relative error* is the greatest possible error divided by the measurement. Therefore, the relative error is

$$\frac{0.5}{29}=\frac{1}{58}$$

Scientific notation and calculators

Scientists and engineers regularly use *scientific notation* to show large and small numbers. Scientific notation may also be used to show the number of significant digits in a number. In scientific notation, a number is shown as a product. One factor is a number between 1 and 10, called the *mantissa.* The other factor is a power of 10. If the number shown is exactly a power of 10, the mantissa of 1 is omitted.

Ordinary notation	*Scientific notation*
5000	5×10^3
4978	4.978×10^3
4,9780	4.978×10^4
4,978$\underline{0}$	4.9780×10^4

(NOTE: The line under the 0 in 4.9780 means that the zero is significant. The same information is provided by showing the zero in scientific notation.)

5,000,000,000	5×10^9
10,000,000,000	10^{10}
1	10^0
0.1	10^{-1}
0.20	2.0×10^{-1}
0.0000007	7×10^{-7}
0.00000073	7.3×10^{-7}

Because scientific notation is a compact way to express large numbers, a form of it is used in many hand-held calculators and in some computer languages. The displays of calculators and computers cannot indicate exponents as raised numerals, however, so the system is modified to allow for all the characters to be shown on the same line. In this form, scientific notation is often called *floating-point notation.* In the floating-point system, the exponent is shown with the letter E and the times sign may be omitted (although some calculators include the times sign). Often, the sign of the number, positive or negative, is shown.

Ordinary notation	*Scientific notation*	*Floating point*
5,000,000,000	5×10^9	+5 E+9
3,892,405,000	3.892405×10^9	+3.892405 E+9
0.0000957	9.57×10^{-5}	+9.57 E−5
−3,028	-3.028×10^3	−3.028 E+3
−0.000054	-5.4×10^{-5}	−5.4 E−5

(NOTE: A hand-held calculator will automatically round a number to the number of places that can be shown on its display. Also, many hand-held calculators will automatically show very large or small numbers in floating-point notation. Therefore, an answer of 3,892,405,000 may be shown on the calculator as 3.8924 E+9 instead of +3.892405 E+9.)

Multiplication and division in scientific notation

To multiply

Multiply the mantissas; add the exponents. You may have to adjust the mantissa of the product to get it between 1 and 10 again.

(NOTE: If significant digits are important, the mantissa of the product should be rounded to show only the number of significant digits in the factor with the least number of significant digits.)

$$(4.30\times10^{-7})\times(5.329\times10^3)=(4.30\times5.329)\times10^{-7+3}$$
$$=22.9147\times10^{-4}$$
$$=2.29147\times10^{-3},$$

which rounds to 2.29×10^{-3}.

Examples

$$(5.83\times10^7)\times(3.07\times10^5)=(5.83\times3.07)\times10^{7+5}$$
$$=17.8981\times10^{12}$$
$$=1.78981\times10^{13}$$

$$(2.04\times10^{-3})\times(3.12\times10^{-4})=(2.04\times3.12)\times10^{-3+(-4)}$$
$$=6.3648\times10^{-7}$$

$$(7.59\times10^4)\times(8.27\times10^{-3})=(7.59\times8.27)\times10^{4+(-3)}$$
$$=62.7693\times10$$
$$=6.27693\times10^2$$

To divide

Divide the mantissa; subtract the exponents. You may have to adjust the mantissa of the quotient to get it between 1 and 10 again.

Examples

$(8.214\times10^8)\div(2.24\times10^3)=(8.214\div2.24)\times10^{8-3}$
$=3.67\times10^5$ (rounded to two places)

$(5.19\times10^5)\div(4.5\times10^{-2})=(5.19\div4.5)\times10^{5-(-2)}$
$=1.2\times10^7$ (rounded to one place)

$(7.35\times10^{-3})\div(9.323\times10^{-7})=(7.35\div9.323)\times10^{-3-(-7)}$
$=0.788\times10^4$ (rounded to three places)
$=7.88\times10^3$.

Square roots and the Pythagorean theorem

The two sides of a right triangle that make up the right angle measure 9 centimeters and 40 centimeters. What is the length of the side opposite the right angle (the *hypotenuse*)?

A. This problem can be solved by using *the Pythagorean theorem,* which states that in a right triangle the square of the hypotenuse is equal to the sum of the squares of the two sides.

Therefore, if you call the length of the hypotenuse c, the following relationship is true:

$$\begin{aligned} c^2 &= 9^2 + 40^2 \\ &= 81 + 1600 \\ &= 1681 \end{aligned}$$

B. Find the square root of 1681. This is most easily accomplished on a calculator. The result is 41.

Find the square root of 30,679 to the nearest tenth without using the square root key on a calculator.

A. Estimate the square root. Since 100×100 is 10,000, the square root will be larger than 100. Use 150 as an estimate.

B. Divide the original number by your estimate.

$$\frac{30679}{150} = 204.52666$$

C. Average the quotient and your estimate. Find the average to 1 significant digit more than your original estimate. Since your estimate of 150 has 2 significant digits, find the average to 3 significant digits.

$$\frac{(150 + 204.5)}{2} = 177.25,$$

which rounds to 177.

D. Use the average as a new estimate and repeat steps A, B, and C.

$$\frac{30679}{177} = 173.32768$$

$$\frac{(177 + 173.33)}{2} = 175.165,$$

which rounds to 175.2.

E. Use that result as a new average and keep repeating steps, A, B, C, and D until the average has "settled down" in the hundredths place. Notice that the tens place, 7, has already "settled down," so the square root of 30,679 to the nearest hundred is 200.

$$\frac{30679}{175.2} = 175.10844$$

$$\frac{(175.2 + 175.108)}{2} = 175.154,$$

which rounds to 175.15.

$$\frac{30679}{175.15} = 175.15843$$

Since the hundredths place in 175.15 and in 175.15843 is the same, you have established that the square root to the nearest tenth is 175.2, which is 175.15 rounded to the nearest tenth.

Note that this method, which is called the *method of iteration* (repetition), is considerably easier to remember than the traditional square-root algorithm. Because this method gets you close to the correct answer very quickly, the closeness of the original estimate to the actual square root is not very important. Suppose that your original estimate had been 100:

$$\frac{30679}{100} = 306.79$$

$$\frac{(100+306)}{2} = 203$$

$$\frac{30679}{200} = 153.395$$

$$\frac{(200+153.4)}{2} = 176.7$$

$$\frac{30679}{177} = 173.32768$$

This is, of course, the same point as was reached in step D, so the calculations proceed exactly as in step E. It only took one more iteration starting with a poor guess than it did starting with a good one.

Formulas often used in arithmetic

	Formula	Definition	
General	$d=rt$	where d is distance r is rate t is time	
	$p=br$	where p is percent b is base r is time	
	$i=prt$	where i is interest p is percent r is rate t is time	
Length	$p=a+b+c$	where p is perimeter of a *triangle* a, b, and c are the lengths of the sides	a, b, c
	$p=2l+2w$	where p is perimeter of a *rectangle* l is length w is width	l, w, w, l
	$p=4s$	where p is perimeter of a *square* s is length of a side	s, s, s, s
	$C=\pi d$	where C is circumference of a *circle* π is pi, a number that is about 3.14 or $\frac{22}{7}$ d is the length of the diameter	d
	$C=2\pi r$	where C is the circumference of a *circle* π is pi, a number that is about 3.14 or $\frac{22}{7}$ r is the length of the radius	r
Area	$A=lw$	where A is area of a *rectangle* l is length w is width	w, l
	$A=s^2$	where A is area of a *square* s is length of a side	s
	$A=bh$	where A is area of a *parallelogram* b is length of the base h is height	h, b
	$A=\frac{1}{2}bh$	where A is area of a *triangle* b is length of the base h is height	h, b
	$A=\frac{1}{2}h(B+b)$	where A is area of a *trapezoid* h is height B is length of one parallel side b is length of the other parallel side	b, h, B
	$A=\frac{1}{2}Dd$	where A is area of a *kite* D is length of one diagonal d is length of the other diagonal	d, D
	$A=\frac{1}{2}ab$	where A is area of a *right triangle* a is length of one leg b is length of the other leg	a, b
	$A=\frac{s^2}{4}\sqrt{3}$	where A is area of an *equilateral triangle* s is length of one of the sides	s, s, s
	$A=\frac{1}{2}ap$	where A is area of a *regular polygon* a is length of an apothem p is perimeter of the polygon	a *p=perimeter*

	Formula	Definition	
	$A = \pi r^2$	where A is area of a *circle* π is pi, a number that is about 3.14 or $\frac{22}{7}$ r is length of the radius	
	$A = \sqrt{s(s-a)(s-b)(s-c)}$	where A is area of a *triangle* s is semiperimeter of the triangle; $(s = \frac{a+b+c}{2})$ a, b, and c *are the lengths of the sides*	*perimeter* $= 2s$
	$A = 2(\pi rh + \pi r^2)$ or $A = 2\pi r(h+r)$	where A is total area of a *right circular cylinder* π is pi, a number that is about 3.14 or $\frac{22}{7}$ r is length of the radius of the base h is height of the cylinder	
	$A = \pi rl + \pi r^2$ or $A = \pi r(l+r)$	where A is total area of a *right circular cone* π is pi, a number that is about 3.14 or $\frac{22}{7}$ r is length of the radius of the base l is slant height of the cone	
	$A = 4\pi r^2$	where A is area of a *sphere* π is pi, a number that is about 3.14 or $\frac{22}{7}$ r is length of the radius of the sphere	
Volume	$V = lwh$	where V is volume of a *right rectangular prism* l is length w is width h is height	
	$V = e^3$	where V is volume of a *cube* e is length of an edge of the cube	
	$V = Bh$	where V is volume of a *prism* B is area of the base h is height of the prism	B = *area of base*
	$V = \pi r^2 h$	where V is volume of a *circular cylinder* π is pi, a number that is about 3.14 or $\frac{22}{7}$ r is length of the radius of the base h is height of the cylinder	
	$V = \frac{1}{3}\pi r^2 h$	where V is volume of a *circular cone* π is pi, a number that is about 3.14 or $\frac{22}{7}$ r is length of the radius of the base h is height of the cylinder	
	$V = \frac{1}{3}Bh$	where V is volume of a *pyramid* B is area of the base of the pyramid h is height of the pyramid	B = *area of base*
	$V = \frac{4}{3}\pi r^3$	where V is volume of a *sphere* π is pi, a number that is about 3.14 or $\frac{22}{7}$ r is length of the radius of the sphere	

Algebra

The algebra that is studied in secondary schools has as its goals the ability to manipulate expressions containing variables; the ability to use equations and inequalities to solve problems; and the development of an introductory understanding of the different functions of a variable.

A *variable* is a letter or other sign used to represent any one of a set of numbers; thus, the variable x typically can represent any positive or negative number that can be expressed as a decimal, including infinite decimals such as π. (Although Greek letters are sometimes used as variables, π is a number, not a variable.)

Equations state that two expressions are equal. For example, $2x + 5 = 17$. *Inequalities* use signs such as $<$ ("is less than") or $>$ ("is greater than") to make statements. A *function* is a rule connecting the members of 2 sets. In algebra, most functions are expressed as equations in two variables, such as $y = 3x - 7$. Special notation for one of the variables is often used to indicate its functional nature, most commonly in expressions such as $f(x) = 3x - 7$, where $f(x)$, which is read f of x or f at x, means the same as y in the previous equation.

In algebra, multiplication is shown differently from the familiar $\times$ sign of arithmetic. Most commonly, the product of a number and a variable, or two variables, is shown by writing the two adjacent to each other, so $5a$ means $5 \times a$ and ab means $a \times b$. Sometimes a raised dot, $\cdot$, is used to show multiplication.

Multiplication is also indicated simply by writing two numbers adjacent to each other in parentheses, as $(2)(3) = 6$, for example.

Expressions and formulas

Rewrite $2a - 7 + 5a$ in simpler form.

A. Collect the parts with the same variable.

$$2a + 5a - 7$$

B. The distributive law permits *terms*—algebraic expressions formed by just multiplication or division—to be combined.

$$(2 + 5)a - 7$$
$$7a - 7$$

The laws of numbers

For any real numbers a, b, and c:

Closure

$a + b$ is a real number

$a \cdot b$ is a real number

Commutative law

$a + b = b + a$

$a \cdot b = b \cdot a$

Associative law

$a + (b + c) = (a + b) + c$

$a \cdot (b \cdot c) = (a \cdot b) \cdot c$

Identity elements

$a + 0 = a$

$a \cdot 1 = a$

Distributive law

$a \cdot (b + c) = a \cdot b + a \cdot c$

Laws of equality

Reflexive law	$a = a$
Symmetric law	If $a = b$, then $b = a$
Transitive law	If $a = b$ and $b = c$, then $a = c$

Laws of equations

Addition	If $a = b$, then $a + c = b + c$
Subtraction	If $a = b$, then $a - c = b - c$
Multiplication	If $a = b$, then $a \cdot c = b \cdot c$
Division	If $a = b$, then $\frac{a}{c} = \frac{b}{c}$ unless $c = 0$

Inverse elements

For each a there exists a number $-a$ such that $a + (-a) = 0$

For each a (except 0) there exists a number $\frac{1}{a}$ such that $a \cdot \frac{1}{a} = 1$

Rewrite $3x^2 + x - 2x^2 + 5y - 3x + 9xy$ in simpler form.

A. Collect like terms. *Like terms* are those with the same variables to the same powers; thus $3x^2$ is like $2x^2$ but not like $5y$, $-3x$, or $9xy$.
$3x^2 - 2x^2 + x - 3x + 5y + 9xy$

B. Combine like terms.
$(3-2)x^2 + (1-3)x + 5y + 9xy$
$x^2 - 2x + 5y + 9xy$
Notice that a factor of 1 is usually not written.

Use the formula $p = 2l + 2w$ to find the perimeter of a rectangle if l is 7 and w is 4.

A. Substitute the values of l and w into the formula.
$p = 2(7) + 2(4)$

B. Multiply.
$p = 14 + 8$

C. Add.
$p = 22$

In a trapezoid, one base is 15 centimeters, the other base is 10 centimeters, and the height is 6 centimeters. Find the area using the formula $A = \frac{1}{2}(B + b)h$.

A. Substitute.
$A = \frac{1}{2}(15 + 10) \cdot 6$

B. Follow the correct order of operations (see box) to do the arithmetic.

Start with expressions in parentheses.
$A = \frac{1}{2}(25) \cdot 6$
$= 75$

Evaluate the expression $5(3x^2 - 2x) + 4$ for $x = 3$.

A. Substitute 3 for x wherever x occurs in the expression.
$5(3 \cdot 3^2 - 2 \cdot 3) + 4$

B. Follow the correct order of operations.
$5(3 \cdot 9 - 2 \cdot 3) + 4$
$5\ (27 - 6) + 4$
$5\ (21) + 4$
$105 + 4$
109

The order of operations

Compute $(3 \cdot 4 + \frac{8}{2} - (\frac{3+7}{5} + \sqrt{10 - 1}))^2 + 2 \cdot 8$

First: Do everything in parentheses following the order of operations. If parentheses are nested (one set inside another), work from the inside set of parentheses to the outside set.
$(3 \cdot 4 + \frac{8}{2} - (\frac{10}{5} + \sqrt{9}))^2 + 2 \cdot 8$

Second: Treat the horizontal line in a fraction or in the square root symbol the same as another set of parentheses.
$(3 \cdot 4 + \frac{8}{2} - (2 + 3))^2 + 2 \cdot 8$
$(3 \cdot 4 + \frac{8}{2} - 5)^2 + 2 \cdot 8$

Third: Compute all powers as soon as possible.
$(12 + 4 - 5)^2 + 16$

Fourth: Multiply and divide from left to right.
$11^2 + 16$

Fifth: Add and subtract from left to right.
$121 + 16$
137

Signed numbers.

Algebra makes full use of the complex number system (see box), but most secondary-school algebra is confined to real numbers. Operations with real numbers are more difficult than operations with whole numbers because numbers can be both positive and negative.

A number on the number line is always less than any number to the right of it, so -3 is less than -1, for example. The *absolute value* of a real number is its distance from 0. Thus, the absolute value of -5 is 5 and the absolute value of $+7$ is 7. Absolute value is indicated by a pair of parallel lines | | that enclose the number. Therefore, $|-4|$ is the same as 4, $|+6|$ is the same as 6, and $|0|$ is the same as 0.

$$5 + (-2)$$

A. To add numbers with unlike signs, subtract the absolute value of the lesser number from the absolute value of the greater number.

$$|5| - |-2|$$
$$5 - 2$$
$$3$$

B. Affix the sign of the number with the greater absolute value. The answer is $+3$.

Sets of numbers

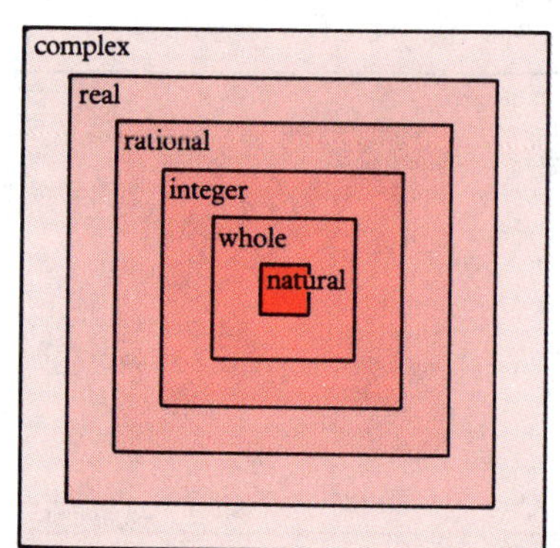

In algebra, mathematicians work with several different sets of numbers, although most often with the integers, the real numbers, or the complex numbers. Each set of numbers includes all the numbers in each of the sets above it.

Symbol	*Name and description*	*Examples*
N	**Natural numbers** (often called counting numbers): The numbers with which you count; the number of members in a nonempty set.	1, 2, 3, . . .
W	**Whole numbers** (sometimes called natural numbers): The natural numbers and 0; the number of members in any set.	0, 1, 2, . . .
I	**Integers:** Whole numbers and their opposites (or negatives).	. . ., -3, -2, -1, 0, 1, 2, 3, . . .
Q	**Rational numbers:** The quotients of any two integers (with the exception that dividing by 0 is not allowed).	0, 3, $\frac{1}{2}$, $\frac{3}{4}$, 3.2, $-\frac{7}{8}$, -57, -0.00001, $-6\frac{2}{3}$, 1,000,001
R	**Real numbers:** Any numbers that can be represented by an infinite decimal (or equivalently, by a point on a line).	0, 5, -8, $\frac{3}{7}$, π, $\sqrt{2}$, 1.01001000100001 . . ., $-\sqrt{137}$
C	**Complex numbers:** The sums found by adding a real number to the product of a real number with the square root of -1, which is shown by i.	0, i, $-i$, $4 + i$, $1 + i\sqrt{2}$, $-8 + 3i$, $8 - 9i$, $\pi - 27i$

$-4 + (-7)$

A. To add numbers with like signs, add the absolute values.
$|-4| + |-7| = 11$

B. Affix the sign of the numbers.
$-4 + (-7) = -11$

$5 - 9$

A. To subtract real numbers, replace the number to be subtracted with its *opposite* and add. The opposite of a real number is the number on the other side of 0 on the number line that has the same absolute value (the opposite of 0 is 0). Thus, the opposite of 9 is -9.
$5 - 9 = 5 + (-9)$

B. $5 + (-9) = -4$

$5(-3)$

A. To multiply two real numbers, find the product of their absolute values.
$|5| \cdot |-3| = 5 \cdot 3 = 15$

B. If the signs of the numbers are different, the product is negative.
$5(-3) = -15$

$(-8)(-4)$

A. $|-8| \cdot |-4| = 8 \cdot 4 = 32$

B. If the signs of the factors are the same, the product is positive.
$(-8)(-4) = +32$

$(-5)(0)$

The product of any real number and 0 is 0 (see box on page 196).
$(-5)(0) = 0$

$- \times - = +$

Filling a tank at $+3$ gal./min.

Five min. from now
$(+5)(+3) = +15$

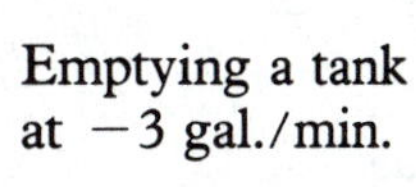

Emptying a tank at -3 gal./min.

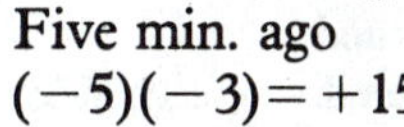

Five min. ago
$(-5)(-3) = +15$

$\frac{-10}{5}$

A. To divide one real number by another, replace the number you are dividing by with the inverse for multiplication (see box on page 196) and multiply.

The multiplicative inverse is the same as the reciprocal.
$(-10)/5 = (-10) \cdot 1/5$

$\frac{-10}{5}$ is often written as $(-10)/5$ in algebra.

B. $|-10| \cdot |1/5| = 2$

C. $(-10) \cdot 1/5 = -2$

$\frac{-35}{-7}$

A. $-35/-7 = -35 \cdot (-1/7)$

B. $|-35| \cdot |-1/7| = 5$

C. $-35 \cdot (-1/7) = +5$

"Undoing" equations

Addition method

If $x + a = b$, then add $-a$ to each side:

$$x + a + (-a) = b + (-a)$$
$$x + 0 = b - a$$
$$x = b - a$$

If $x - a = b$, then add a to each side:

$$x - a + a = b + a$$
$$x + 0 = b + a$$
$$x = b + a$$

Examples:

Solve: $x + 7 = 19$

Add -7. $x + 7 + (-7) = 19 + (-7)$

$x + 0 = 19 - 7$

$x = 12$

Solve: $x - 3 = 15$

Add 3. $x - 3 + 3 = 15 + 3$

$x + 0 = 18$

$x = 18$

Subtraction method

If $x + a = b$, then subtract a from each side:

$$x + a - a = b - a$$
$$x + 0 = b - a$$
$$x = b - a$$

Example:

Solve: $x + 3 = 11$

Subtract 3. $x + 3 - 3 = 11 - 3$

$x + 0 = 8$

$x = 8$

Multiplication method

If $ax = b$, then multiply each side by $\frac{1}{a}$ $(a \neq 0)$:

$$\frac{1}{a} \cdot ax = \frac{1}{a} \cdot b$$
$$1 \cdot x = \frac{b}{a}$$
$$x = \frac{b}{a}$$

If $\frac{x}{a} = b$, then multiply each side by a $(a \neq 0)$:

$$a \cdot \frac{x}{a} = a \cdot b$$
$$1 \cdot x = ab$$
$$x = ab$$

Examples:

Solve: $5x = 40$

Multiply by $\frac{1}{5}$. $\frac{1}{5} \cdot 5x = \frac{1}{5} \cdot 40$

$1 \cdot x = 8$

$x = 8$

Solve: $\frac{x}{3} = 13$

Multiply by 3. $3 \cdot \frac{x}{3} = 3 \cdot 13$

$1 \cdot x = 39$

$x = 39$

Division method

If $ax = b$, then divide each side by a $(a \neq 0)$:

$$\frac{ax}{a} = \frac{b}{a}$$
$$1 \cdot x = \frac{b}{a} \qquad x = \frac{b}{a}$$

Example:

Solve: $4x = 24$

Divide by 4. $\frac{4x}{4} = \frac{24}{4}$

$\frac{x}{1} = 6$

$x = 6$

Combined addition and multiplication method

If $ax + b = d$, then

First: Add $-b$ to each side:

$$ax + b + (-b) = d + (-b)$$
$$ax + 0 = d - b$$
$$ax = d - b$$

Second: Multiply each side by $\frac{1}{a}$ $(a \neq 0)$:

$$\frac{1}{a} \cdot ax = \frac{1}{a} \cdot (d - b)$$
$$1 \cdot x = \frac{d - b}{a} \qquad x = \frac{d - b}{a}$$

Examples:

Solve: $2x + 5 = 17$

Add -5. $2x + 5 + (-5) = 17 + (-5)$

$2x = 12$

Multiply by $\frac{1}{2}$. $\frac{1}{2} \cdot 2x = \frac{1}{2} \cdot 12$

$x = 6$

Solve: $\frac{x}{7} + 4 = 6$

Add -4. $\frac{x}{7} + 4 + (-4) = 6 + (-4)$

$\frac{x}{7} = 2$

Multiply by 7. $7 \cdot \frac{x}{7} = 7 \cdot 2$

$x = 14$

Equations in one variable.

See the box on page 200 for the basic rules for solving equations in one variable in which only the first power of the variable appears. The problems on this page use these rules in conjunction with ideas from the earlier pages of this section.

Solve $2x + 3 + 5x = 17$.

A. Collect like terms.
$7x + 3 = 17$

B. Add -3 to each side.
$7x = 14$

C. Divide each side by 7.
$x = 2$

Solve $3x - 5 = 4x + 11$.

A. Subtract $3x$ from each side of the equation.
$-5 = x + 11$

B. Subtract 11 from each side of the equation.
$-16 = x$

Most people prefer to write the solution as
$x = -16$

Solve $8x - 3 = 6x - 11$.

A. Subtract $6x$ from each side of the equation.
$2x - 3 = -11$

B. Add 3 to each side of the equation.
$2x = -8$

C. Divide each side by 2.
$x = -4$

Solve $2(x + 5) = 6$.

A. Eliminate parentheses.
$2x + 10 = 6$

B. Subtract 10 from each side.
$2x = -4$

C. Divide by 2.
$x = -2$

Solve $\frac{3x+4}{5} = 11$.

A. Multiply each side of the equation by 5.
$3x + 4 = 55$

B. Subtract 4.
$3x = 51$

C. Divide by 3.
$x = 17$

Solve $\frac{4x-6}{3} = 5x + 9$.

A. Multiply each side of the equation by 3.
$(4x - 6) = 3(5x + 9)$
$4x - 6 = 15x + 27$

B. Subtract $4x$.
$-6 = 11x + 27$

C. Subtract 27.
$-33 = 11x$

D. Divide by 11 and reverse.
$x = -3$

Solve $\frac{5x+4}{2} = \frac{3x-9}{4}$.

A. Multiply both sides by 2.
$(5x + 4) = \frac{2(3x - 9)}{4}$

B. Multiply both sides by 4.
$4(5x + 4) = 2(3x - 9)$

The result of these two steps is the same as the single step of following the cross-product rule for solving a proportion.

C. Complete the multiplication.
$20x + 16 = 6x - 18$

D. Subtract $6x$ and 16.
$14x = -34$

E. Divide by 14 and reduce to lowest terms.
$x = -\frac{34}{14} = -\frac{17}{7}$

Literal equations.

The rules for solving equations apply when the equation is a formula. Such an equation is called a *literal equation* because it is expressed primarily in letters instead of numbers.

Solve the formula $d = rt$ for r.

A. Divide both sides of the equation by t.

$$\frac{d}{t} = r$$

B. Rewrite the equation with r on the left side of the equals sign.

$$r = \frac{d}{t}$$

Solve $A = \frac{1}{2}bh$ for b.

A. Multiply each side by 2.

$$2A = bh$$

B. Divide by h and rewrite.

$$\frac{2A}{h} = b$$

$$b = \frac{2A}{h}$$

Solve $A = \frac{1}{2}(B + b)h$ for B.

A. Multiply each side by 2.

$$2A = (B + b)h$$

B. Divide each side by h.

$$\frac{2A}{h} = B + b$$

C. Subtract b from each side.

$$\frac{2A}{h} - b = B$$

$$B = \frac{2A}{h} - b$$

Solve $A = \frac{1}{2}(B + b)h$ for h.

A. Multiply each side by 2.

$$2A = (B + b)h$$

B. Divide each side by $B + b$.

$$\frac{2A}{B+b} = h$$

$$h = \frac{2A}{B+b}$$

Formulas often used in problem solving in algebra

Distance-rate-time problems: $d = rt$

where d is distance
r is rate
t is time

Lever problems: $l_1w_1 = l_2w_2$

where l_1 is length from fulcrum to first weight
w_1 is first weight
l_2 is length from fulcrum to second weight
w_2 is second weight

Work problems: $\frac{1}{a} + \frac{1}{b} = \frac{1}{n}$

where a is length of time it takes person A to complete a task
b is length of time it takes person B to complete the same task
n is length of time it would take A and B to complete the task together

Consecutive number problems: $n + (n + 1) = A$

where n is the first of the consecutive numbers
A is the sum of two consecutive numbers

$n(n + 2) = B$

where n is the first of a pair of even or odd consecutive numbers
B is the product of two even or odd consecutive numbers

Digit problems: $A(u + t + h) = u + 10t + 100h$

where A is multiplied by the sum of the digits
u is the ones digit of the given number
t is the tens digit of the given number
h is the hundreds digit of the given number

Coin problems: $25n + 5m = 100A$

where n is the number of quarters
m is the number of nickels
A is the total worth shown as a decimal

Solving problems

Will was 18 when he graduated from school 9 years ago. How old is he now?

A. You are probably able to solve this "in your head," but one should get in the habit of always writing down and solving an equation. Decide on a variable and its meaning. For example, let x = Will's age now.

B. Write an equation that expresses the conditions of the problem.
Will's age now: x
Will's age 9 years ago:
Either 18 or $x - 9$.
Therefore, $x - 9 = 18$.

C. Solve for x.
$x - 9 = 18$
Add 9. $x = 27$
Will is 27 years old now.

What number when multiplied by 4 can be added to 15 to produce 63?

A. Choose a variable and use it to express the conditions of the problem as an equation.
Let n = the number.
$4n + 15 = 63$

B. Solve the equation.
$4n + 15 = 63$
Subtract 15. $4n = 48$
Divide by 4. $n = 12$
The number is 12.

Sally has only quarters and nickels in her piggy bank. If the total amount is $2.65 and she has 8 nickels, how many quarters does she have?

A. Convert the problem to pennies. The total amount is 265 cents, a quarter is 25 cents, and a nickel is 5 cents. The total amount of nickels is $8 \cdot 5 = 40$ cents.

B. Let n = the number of quarters. The total amount of quarters is $25n$ cents.
$25n + 40 = 265$

C. Solve the equation.
$25n + 40 = 265$
Subtract 40. $25n = 225$
Divide by 25. $n = 9$
Sally has 9 quarters.

Find two consecutive integers such that three times the second plus the first is 47.

A. Consecutive integers are the integers that immediately follow one another. Therefore, if you let the first integer be n, then the second is $n + 1$.
$3(n + 1) + n = 47$

B. Solve the equation.
$3(n + 1) + n = 47$
Multiply. $3n + 3 + n = 47$
Combine like terms.
$4n + 3 = 47$
Subtract 3. $4n = 44$
Divide by 4. $n = 11$

C. State both parts of the answer. The consecutive integers are 11 and 12.

Find two consecutive odd integers such that 5 times the second minus 6 times the first is 21.

A. If you let the first odd integer be n, then the second is $n + 2$.
$5(n + 2) - 6n = 21$

B. Solve the equation.
$5(n + 2) - 6n = 21$
Multiply. $5n + 10 - 6n = 21$
Combine like terms.
$10 - n = 21$
Subtract 10. $-n = 11$
Multiply by -1. $n = -11$

C. State both parts of the answer. The consecutive odd integers are -11 and -9 (NOT -11 and -13!).

Candy selling for $0.29 a gram is to be mixed with candy selling for $0.39 a gram. If you want 5 grams of the mixture to sell for $0.36 a gram, how many grams of each kind of candy should be mixed?

A. Let x be the number of grams of the less expensive candy. Then $5 - x$ will be the number of grams of the candy selling for $0.39 a gram.

$$0.29x + 0.39(5 - x) = 0.36(5)$$

B. Solve the equation.

Multiply $0.29x + 1.95 - 0.39x = 1.8$

Combine like terms.

$$1.95 - 0.1x = 1.8$$

Subtract 1.95. $-0.1x = -0.15$

Multiply by -10. $x = 1.5$

C. You need to mix 1.5 grams of the $0.29 candy with 5 − 1.5, or 3.5, grams of the $0.39 candy.

A radiator system is full with 12 liters of a mixture of 30% antifreeze in water. How much should be drained and replaced by an 80% antifreeze solution to bring the antifreeze content to 60%?

A. Let x be the number of liters drained and replaced in the radiator. Then $12 - x$ is the amount of the original solution remaining in the radiator.

$$0.30(12 - x) + 0.80x = 0.60(12)$$

B. Solve the equation.

$$3.60 - 0.30x + 0.80x = 7.20$$
$$3.60 + 0.50x = 7.20$$
$$0.50x = 3.60$$
$$x = 7.2$$

C. You must drain and replace 7.2 liters.

Two trains travel toward each other from points 200 kilometers apart. If one train is traveling at 50 kilometers per hour and the other at 60 kilometers per hour, where and when will they meet if they start at the same time?

A. Let d = distance traveled by the 50 km/h train. Then $200 - d$ = distance traveled by the other train. When the two trains meet, the times they have traveled will be equal, so

$$\frac{d}{50} = \frac{200 - d}{60}$$

B. Solve the equation. Use the cross-product rule.

$$\frac{d}{50} = \frac{200 - d}{60}$$
$$60d = 50(200 - d)$$
$$60d = 10000 - 50d$$
$$110d = 10000$$
$$d = \frac{10000}{110}, \text{ or } 90.9090\ldots$$

C. Round the answer to 91. Then the trains will meet about 91 kilometers from the starting point of the 50 km/h train. The length of time is

$$t = \frac{d}{r}, \text{ or about}$$
$$t = \frac{91}{50} = 1.82,$$

which can be rounded to 1.8 hours.

Fred can complete a project in 6 days. Jack can complete the same project in 5 days, and David takes 4 days. How many days will it take if all three work together?

A. Let x = the number of days needed to do the job working together. Individually, $x/6$ of the project will be completed by Fred after x days, $x/5$ of the project by Jack, and $x/4$ by David.

B. $\frac{x}{6} + \frac{x}{5} + \frac{x}{4} = 1$

Multiply by the LCD, 60.

$$10x + 12x + 15x = 60$$

Combine like terms. $37x = 60$

Divide by 37. $x = \frac{60}{37}$

C. The project will take $\frac{60}{37}$, or slightly more than $1\frac{1}{2}$ days.

Operations with polynomials. A *monomial* is a term formed entirely by multiplication; for example $2x$, y^2, or $n/3$ (which is interpreted as the number $\frac{1}{3}$ times n). A *polynomial* is the sum of any finite number of monomials, including just 1 monomial. Certain polynomials are referred to often enough that it is useful to learn their special names:

monomial, a polynomial with one term
binomial, a polynomial with two terms
trinomial, a polynomial with three terms.

Polynomials can be added, subtracted, multiplied, and divided.

Add $3x^3 + 5x^2y - 2xy^2 + y^3$ and $2x^3 - 3y^3 + 4xy^2$.

Rearrange the two polynomials so that they are in the same order.

Write the polynomials with terms that have corresponding powers of the same variable above each other as an addition problem and add each term to the one directly below it.

$$\begin{array}{r} 3x^3 + 5x^2y - 2xy^2 + y^3 \\ +2x^3 \qquad\quad + 4xy^2 - 3y^3 \\ \hline 5x^3 + 5x^2y + 2xy^2 - 2y^3 \end{array}$$

Subtract $3abc + 2ac - 3b$ from $4bc - 3abc + 5ac$.

Arrange the two polynomials with the terms with the same variables to the same powers directly over one another.

To subtract, multiply the polynomial to be subtracted by -1 and add.

$$\begin{array}{r} 4bc - 3abc + 5ac \qquad \\ - 3abc - 2ac + 3b \\ \hline 4bc - 6abc + 3ac + 3b \end{array}$$

Multiply the monomials, $3x^2y^3$ and $4xy^2$.

Multiplication of powers of the same variable can be accomplished by following the laws of exponents (see box). The numerical parts of each monomial (called the *coefficients* of the monomials) are multiplied in the ordinary way.

$$\begin{aligned} 3x^2y^3(4xy^2) &= 12x^{2+1}y^{3+2} \\ &= 12x^3y^5 \end{aligned}$$

Laws of exponents

If a and b are not zero

$$a^na^m = a^{n+m}$$
$$(a^n)^m = a^{mn}$$
$$a^n/a^m = a^{m-n}$$
$$a^nb^n = (ab)^n$$
$$a^n/b^n = (a/b)^n$$
$$a^{-n} = 1/a^n$$

$(2x + y)(x - y)$

METHOD 1

A. Use the distributive law with $x - y$ as the factor to be distributed over $2x + y$.

$(2x + y)(x - y) = 2x(x - y) + y(x - y)$

B. Use the distributive law twice more to distribute each of the factors over $x - y$.

$(2x + y)(x - y) = 2x^2 - 2xy + xy - y^2$

C. Collect like terms.

$(2x + y)(x - y) = 2x^2 - xy - y^2$

METHOD 2

A. Use the FOIL method. FOIL is based on the fact that the product of any two binomials is always the sum of the following: The product of the

*F*irst terms;
the sum of the product of the
*O*uter terms and the
*I*nner terms;
and the product of the
*L*ast terms.

In our example, the product of the first terms is $2x^2$, the product of the outer terms is $-2xy$, the product of the inner terms is xy, and the product of the last terms is $-y^2$.

$2x^2 - 2xy + xy - y^2$

B. Collect like terms.

$(2x + y)(x - y) = 2x^2 - xy - y^2$

Divide $3x^2 + 2x - 5$ by $x + 2$.

A. Set up the problem as you would a long division problem in arithmetic.

$$x + 2\overline{)3x^2 + 2x - 5}$$

B. Divide the first term of the trinomial by the first term of the binomial to get a partial quotient. Multiply the partial quotient and the binomial. Subtract that product from the trinomial.

$$\begin{array}{r} 3x \\ x + 2\overline{)3x^2 + 2x - 5} \\ 3x^2 + 6x \\ \hline -4x - 5 \end{array}$$

C. Repeat the process from step B with the remainder of subtraction in step B.

$$\begin{array}{r} 3x - 4 \\ x + 2\overline{)3x^2 + 2x - 5} \\ 3x^2 + 6x \\ \hline -4x - 5 \\ -4x - 8 \\ \hline +3 \end{array}$$

D. The answer is $3x - 4$ with a remainder of 3, since x is not a divisor of 3.

Factoring polynomials

Factor $x^3 + 2x^2 - 6x$.

The word *factor* used as a verb means "write in factored form." You are already familiar with factoring numbers. Polynomials are factored by reversing the rules of multiplication.

In this case, x is a factor of each term of the polynomial. Use the distributive law to obtain

$$x^3 + 2x^2 - 6x = x(x^2 + 2x - 6).$$

Factor $x^3yz^4 - x^2yz^3 + 2xy^2z^2$.

A. Identify the factors that are common to each of the terms of the polynomial. They are

x, y, and z^2.

B. Use the distributive law to rewrite the polynomial in factored form.

$$x^3yz^4 - x^2yz^3 + 2xy^2z^2 = xyz^2(x^2z^2 - xz + 2y)$$

Factor $x^2 - 5x + 6$ into the product of binomials.

A. Begin by looking for possible factors for the first term. Since the first term is x^2, the only possible factors are x and x or x^2 and 1. Experience shows that, since there is no other x^2 in the trinomial, the first factors of the binomials will be x and x.

$x^2 - 5x + 6 = (x \quad\ )\ (x \quad\ )$

NOTE: It is also possible to factor x^2 as $-x$ and $-x$. However, it is customary to factor a positive first term into 2 positive factors.

B. Look for all the possible factors of the second term. These will come in pairs of 2 positive factors or 2 negative factors, since the last term is positive.

1 and 6	-1 and -6
2 and 3	-2 and -3

C. Try the possible factors in the binomials to see which pair will give a middle term that is $-5x$. The only combination that works is -2 and -3, so the correct factored form is

$$x^2 - 5x + 6 = (x - 2)\ (x - 3).$$

Factor $x^2 + 7x + 6$.

A. Once again the factors of x^2 must be x and x.

Also, the possible factors of $+6$ are the same:

1 and 6 -1 and -6
2 and 3 -2 and -3

B. Find the factors of $+6$ that, when multiplied by x and x, will add up to $+7x$. They are 1 and 6, so the factored form is $x^2 + 7x + 6 = (x + 1)(x + 6)$.

Factor $x^2 - x - 6$.

A. The pairs of factors to be examined are

-1 and 6   1 and -6
-2 and 3   2 and -3

B. The combination that will yield $-x$ is 2 and -3.
$x^2 - x - 6 = (x + 2)(x - 3)$

Factor $2x^2 - 15x + 18$.

A. The possible factors of $2x^2$ are x and $2x$, so
$2x^2 - 15x + 18 = (x \quad)(2x \quad)$.

B. The possible factors of $+18$ are

1 and 18 -1 and -18
2 and 9 -2 and -9
3 and 6 -3 and -6

C. Since the first terms of the binomial factors are different, more combinations must be checked. For example,
$1(2x) + 18(x) = +20x$
while $1(x) + 18(2x) = +37x$
The combination that produces $-15x$ for the second term of the trinomial is
$-3(x) - (-6)(2x) = -15x$.

D. The correct answer is
$2x^2 - 15x + 18 = (x - 6)(2x - 3)$.

Factor $20x^2 + 27x - 8$.

A. Possible factors of the first term are

$(x \quad)(20x \quad)$
$(2x \quad)(10x \quad)$
$(4x \quad)(5x \quad)$

B. Possible factors of the last term are

1 and -8 -1 and 8
2 and -4 -2 and 4

C. The combination that yields $+27x$ is
$-1(5x) + 8(4x) = +27x$,
so the factored form is
$20x^2 + 27x - 8 = (4x - 1)(5x + 8)$.

Often binomials can be factored into 2 polynomials. The types of binomials that can be factored in this way are either *the difference of 2 squares, the difference of 2 cubes,* or *the sum of 2 cubes.* The sum of 2 squares cannot be factored over the integers (indeed, it cannot be factored over the real numbers). The general forms for the 3 binomials that can be factored into 2 polynomials are given below. When A and B are expressions of any kind,

$A^2 - B^2 = (A - B)(A + B)$
$A^3 - B^3 = (A - B)(A^2 + AB + B^2)$
$A^3 + B^3 = (A + B)(A^2 - AB + B^2)$.

Factor $x^4 - 16$.

A. This problem should be recognized as the difference of 2 squares, since x^4 is the same as $(x^2)^2$ and 16 is 4^2. Therefore, the general form can be used with
$A = x^2$ and $B = 4$.
$x^4 - 16 = (x^2 - 4)(x^2 + 4)$

B. Notice that $x^2 - 4$ is also the difference of 2 squares, so it can be factored further. However, $x^2 + 4$ cannot be factored, so the final answer is
$x^2 - 16 = (x - 2)(x + 2)(x^2 + 4)$.

Graphing lines.

A *graph is a way of representing a set of ordered pairs. Ordered pairs* of numbers are shown in parentheses with a comma.

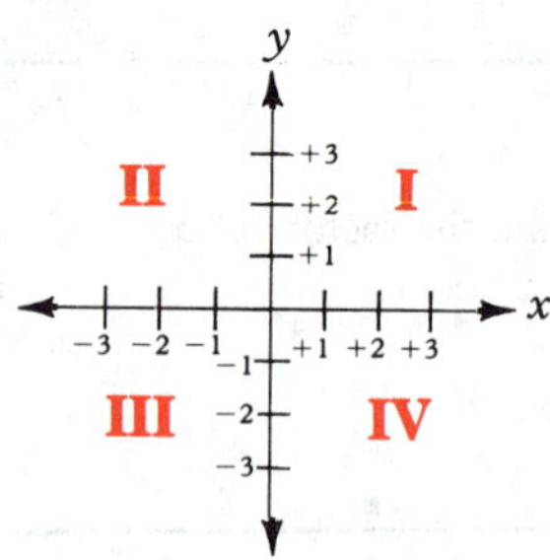

The most common way to graph ordered pairs is to use 2 number lines that are perpendicular to each other at their 0 points. The point of intersection is called the *origin* of the graph. In a graph, the first member of each pair is a directed distance from the vertical line. The distance is "directed" because a + indicates distance to the right of the origin and a − indicates distance to the left. The second member of each pair is a directed distance from the horizontal line with + indicating distance above the line and − indicating distance below it. The first members of the pair are called *abscissas* and the second members are called *ordinates.*

The axes define a plane, called the *coordinate plane,* and divide that plane into 4 regions called *quadrants.*

Locate the points (1, 1), (−1, 2), (−3, −2), and (1, −2) on the coordinate plane.

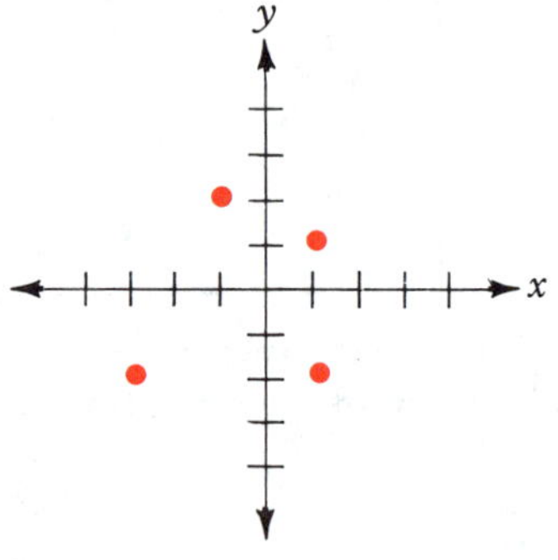

A. To find (1, 1), count 1 unit to the right from the y axis and 1 unit up from the x axis.

B. To find (−1, 2), count 1 unit to the left from the y axis and 2 units up from the x axis.

C. To find (−3, −2), count 3 units to the left from the y axis and 2 units down from the x axis.

D. To find (1, −2), count 1 unit to the right from the y axis and 2 units down from the x axis.

Graph the equation $y = 2x - 2$.

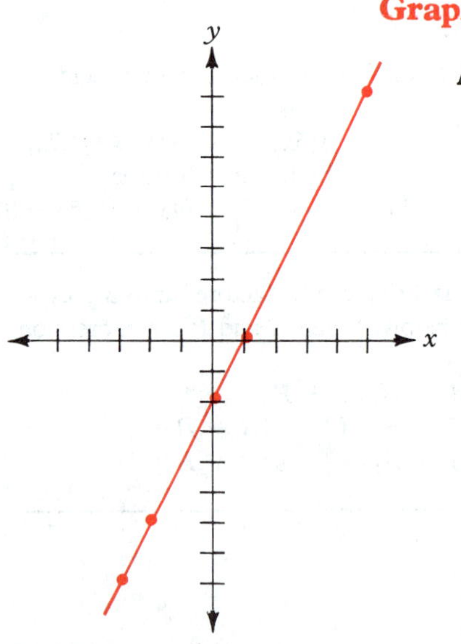

A. An equation in x and y is a way of identifying a set of ordered pairs of the form (x, y) where the relationship between x and y is given by the equation. In general, assume that x can be any real number (unless some values are prohibited by the equation, as in the case of $y = 1/x$, which cannot be graphed if x is equal to 0). Therefore, begin by assigning arbitrary values to x. For example, assign 0, 1, 5, −2, and −3.

B. Use the values assigned to x and the equation to find the values for y. For example, if x is 0, the equation becomes

$$\begin{aligned} y &= 2\,(0) - 2 \\ &= 0 - 2 \\ &= -2 \end{aligned}$$

Find the other values of y in the same way. Most people find it convenient to keep track of the values in a chart.

x	y
0	−2
1	0
5	8
−2	−6
−3	−8

C. Plot the ordered pairs indicated by the chart on the coordinate plane.

D. Since x could be any real number, there are more points in the graph than those plotted. Since all the points plotted can be connected by a straight line, the line contains *all* the points of the graph, although only a part of the line can be shown on the page.

Graph the equation $y = -x - 1$.

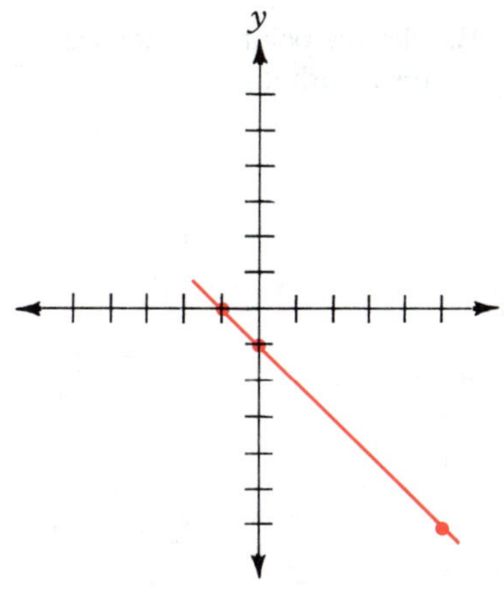

A. All equations that involve just the first power of x and the first power of y (unless the variables are enclosed in absolute-value bars, multiplied by each other, or otherwise changed by some operation other than addition, subtraction, and multiplication) have lines as graphs. Two points determine a line; therefore, only 2 points need be plotted to find the graph. Most people also plot a third point as a check.

In general, the 2 easiest plots to point are the ones where x or y is 0. The check point can use any convenient small number for x, but it is better not to use a number too close to 0, or the 3 points will be too close to each other.

x	y
0	
	0
5	

B. Fill in the other values in the chart.

$y = -(0) - 1 = -1$

$0 = -x - 1$, so $x = -1$

$y = -5 - 1 = -6$

x	y
0	-1
-1	0
5	-6

C. Plot the 3 points.

D. Draw a line between 2 of the points and use the third point as a check.

The graph of a line

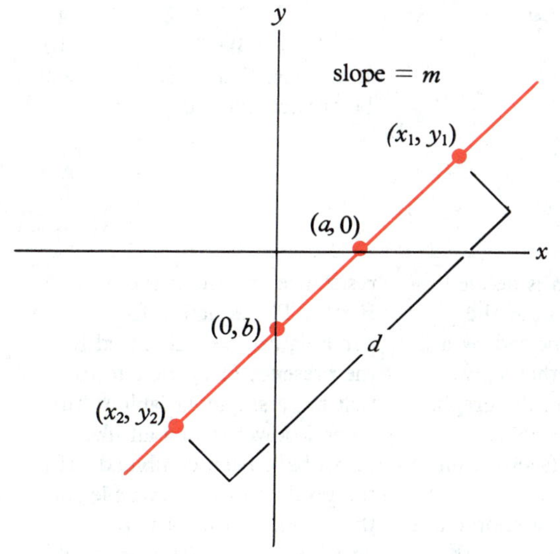

Slope:

$$m = \frac{y_2 - y_1}{x_2 - x_1}$$

Point-slope equation for the line:

$$(y - y_1) = m(x - x_1)$$

Slope-intercept equation for the line:

$$y = mx + b$$

Two-point equation for the line:

$$y - y_1 = \frac{y_2 - y_1}{x_2 - x_1}(x - x_1)$$

Intercept equation for the line:

$$\frac{x}{a} + \frac{y}{b} = 1$$

Distance from (x_1, y_1) to (x_2, y_2):

$$d = \sqrt{(x_2 - x_1)^2 + (y_2 - y_1)^2}$$

Midpoint between (x_1, y_1) and (x_2, y_2):

(x, y) is the midpoint when

$$x = \frac{x_1 + x_2}{2}, \; y = \frac{y_1 + y_2}{2}$$

Graph $3x + 2y = 30$.

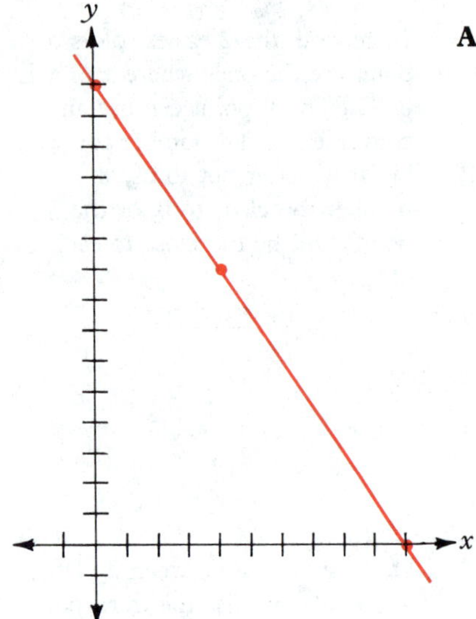

A. Since both x and y are in first degree terms, the graph will be a line. Find the points called the intercepts, where $x = 0$ and where $y = 0$, and a check point.

x	y
0	15
10	0
4	9

B. Plot the points and connect them with a line.

Graph the equation $y = x^2 - x - 2$.

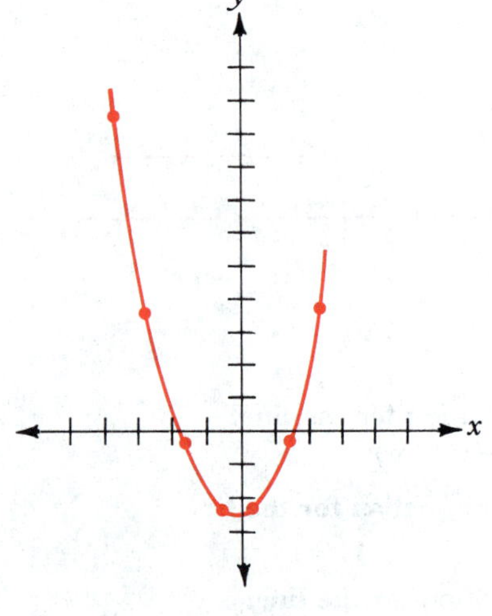

A. This equation involves a power of the variable that is different from the first power, so the graph is not a line. Therefore, choose several different points to get an idea of the shape of the graph. For example, start with

x	y
0	
1	
2	
3	
−1	
−2	
−3	

$$y = 0^2 - 0 - 2 = -2$$
$$y = 1^2 - 1 - 2 = -2$$
$$y = 2^2 - 2 - 2 = 0$$
$$y = 3^2 - 3 - 2 = 4$$

It is apparent that if x is greater than 3, then y will be greater than 4.

$$y = (-1)^2 + 1 - 2 = 0$$
$$y = (-2)^2 + 2 - 2 = 4$$
$$y = (-3)^2 + 3 - 2 = 10$$

If x is less than -3, then y will be greater than 10.

B. Use the completed table to plot the points.

x	y
0	−2
1	−2
2	0
3	4
−1	0
−2	4
−3	10

C. Since the equation is defined for all real values of x, the points can be connected by a continuous curve that shows all of the points on the graph. In this case, the curve is a form of *parabola* (see box on page 211).

A parabola is a common curve in applications, since it is the curve that a thrown or fired object makes (discounting air resistance and the curve of Earth). The equation for a parabola can be recognized by the presence of a single term that has a single variable to the second power (when all like terms have been combined). If the product of two variables or the second power of two variables is included, the graph of the equation will be another one of the conic sections.

Conic sections

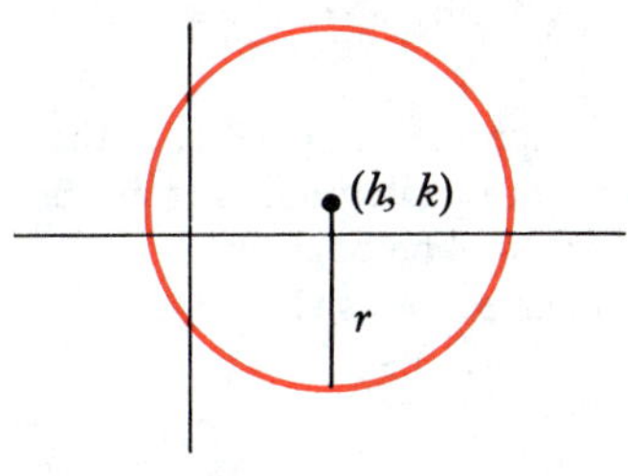

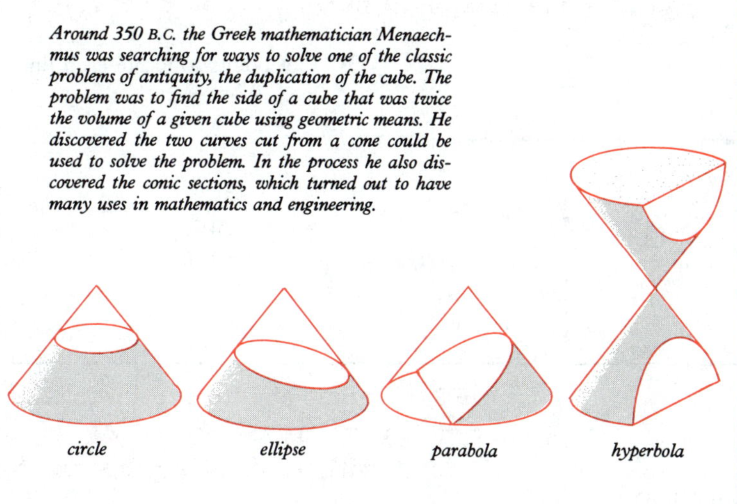

Around 350 B.C. the Greek mathematician Menaechmus was searching for ways to solve one of the classic problems of antiquity, the duplication of the cube. The problem was to find the side of a cube that was twice the volume of a given cube using geometric means. He discovered the two curves cut from a cone could be used to solve the problem. In the process he also discovered the conic sections, which turned out to have many uses in mathematics and engineering.

The circle:

Points in the same plane all at a common distance, the *radius,* from the same point, the *center.*

center: (h, k)
radius: r

$$(x - h)^2 - (y - k)^2 = r^2$$

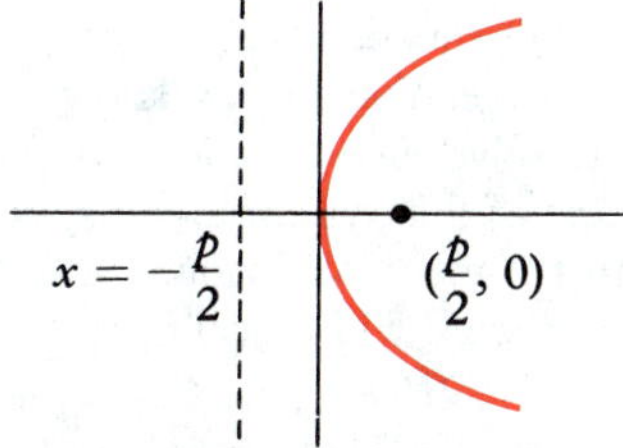

The parabola:

Points in the same plane that are the same distance from a point, the *focus,* and a line, the *directrix.*

focus: $(\frac{p}{2}, 0)$

directrix: $x = -\frac{p}{2}$

$$y^2 = 2px$$

The point on the parabola halfway between the focus and the directrix is the *vertex.*

vertex: (h, k)

$$y = a(x - h)^2 + k$$

(If a is positive, the vertex is the lowest point of the parabola. If a is negative, the vertex is the highest point.)

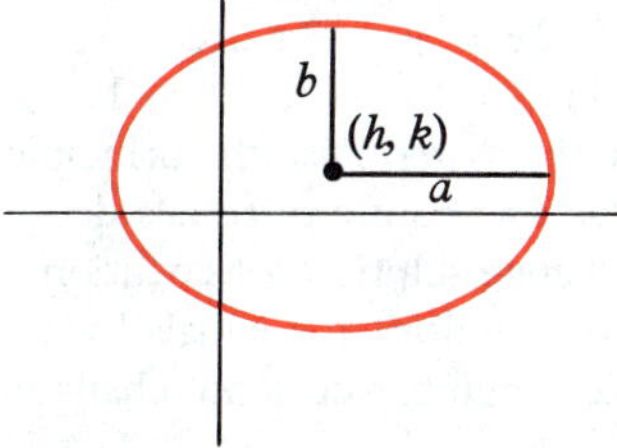

The ellipse:

Points in the same plane from which the sum of the distances from two points, the *foci,* is constant. The midpoint of the line joining the foci is the *center.* The distance from the center through one of the foci to the ellipse is the *semimajor axis;* the distance from the center to the ellipse perpendicular to the semimajor axis is the *semiminor axis.*

center: (h, k)
semimajor axis: a
semiminor axis: b

$$\frac{(x - h)^2}{a^2} + \frac{(y - k)^2}{b^2} = 1$$

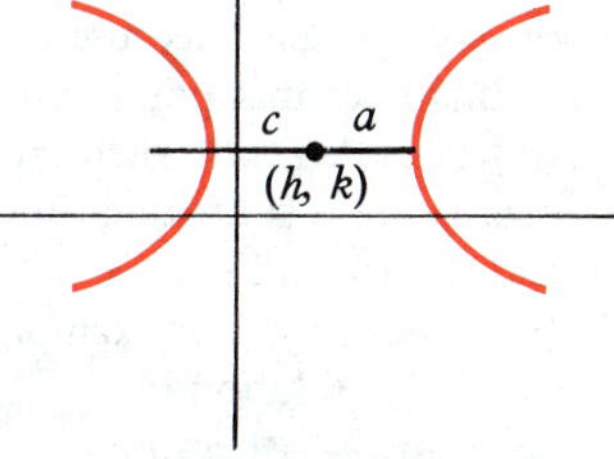

The hyperbola:

Points in the same plane from which the difference of the distances from two points, the *foci,* is constant. The midpoint of the line joining the foci is the center.

Distance from center to hyperbola: a
Distance from center to a focus: c

Let $c^2 = a^2 + b^2$,

or $b = \sqrt{c^2 - a^2}$

$$\frac{(x - h)^2}{a^2} - \frac{(y - k)^2}{b^2} = 1$$

Lines that the hyperbola gets closer to (but does not touch) are called *asymptotes.* The asymptotes are given by

$$\frac{(x - h)^2}{a^2} = \frac{(y - k)^2}{b^2}$$

or $y = \pm(\frac{b}{a})(x - h) + k.$

Systems of equations

Find the intersection of the graphs of $x + 3y = -2$ and $2x - y = 3$.

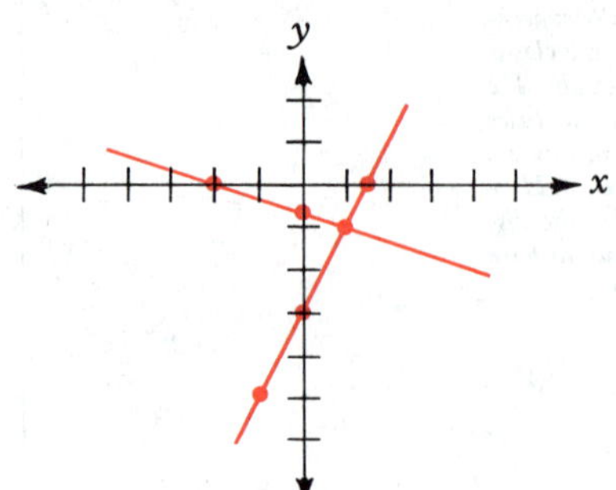

A. Plot points to locate each line.

$x + 3y = -2$		$2x - y = 3$	
x	y	x	y
0	$-\frac{2}{3}$	0	-3
-2	0	$\frac{3}{2}$	0
1	-1	-1	-5

B. Graph the lines and read the point of intersection from the graph. The point of intersection is $(1, -1)$.

Find the point of intersection of the graphs of $-2x - 6y = 4$ and $2x - y = 3$ without drawing the graphs.

METHOD 1

A. The point of intersection of two graphs is the *solution of a system of equations* because the coordinates of that point will give true statements when the x coordinate is substituted for x and the y coordinate is substituted for y. For example, $(-1, 1)$ is a solution of $-2x - 6y = 4$ because $-2(-1) - 6(1) = 4$ is true.

But $(-1, 1)$ is not a solution to the system because it does not satisfy $2x - y = 3$ since $2(-1) - (1)$ is -3, not 3. To solve the system, use the principle that adding equals to equals does not change solutions of equations and that multiplying equals by a nonzero number does not change solutions.

The strategy is to multiply and add in such a way as to obtain an *equivalent* equation that has only one variable. You already know how to solve such equations. In the case of this system it is easy to see that if the two equations are added, the x's will cancel out.

Add.
$$\begin{aligned} -2x - 6y &= 4 \\ 2x - y &= 3 \\ \hline 0 - 7y &= 7 \end{aligned}$$

B. Solve the equation $-7y = 7$ for y.

$$-7y = 7$$

Divide by -7. $\quad y = -1$

C. Use the value you have found for y in either of the original equations to find the value x must have when y is -1.

$$\begin{aligned} -2x - 6(-1) &= 4 \\ -2x + 6 &= 4 \\ -2x &= -2 \\ x &= 1 \end{aligned}$$

The point of intersection, or the solution of the system, is $(1, -1)$. Check by substituting these coordinates in the other equation.

$$\begin{aligned} 2x - y &= 3 \\ 2(1) - (-1) &= 3 \\ 2 + 1 &= 3 \\ 3 &= 3 \end{aligned}$$

METHOD 2

A. *Substitute* the value of one of the variables (determined from one of the equations) into the other equation. In this case, it is easiest to find the value of y from the second equation and substitute it into the first.

$$2x - y = 3$$

Subtract $2x$. $\quad -y = 3 - 2x$

Multiply by -1. $\quad y = 2x - 3$

B. Substitute the value obtained for y in step A into the first equation and solve.

$$\begin{aligned} -2x - 6y &= 4 \\ -2x - 6(2x - 3) &= 4 \\ -2x - 12x + 18 &= 4 \\ -14x + 18 &= 4 \\ -14x &= -14 \\ x &= 1 \end{aligned}$$

C. Use the value of x obtained in step B to find y. The easiest way to do this is to use the value for y found in step A.

$$\begin{aligned} y &= 2x - 3 \\ &= 2(1) - 3 \\ &= 2 - 3 \\ &= -1 \end{aligned}$$

Be sure to check; if you made a mistake in step A, the whole solution would be wrong.

Mary has $2.75 in her change purse. There are 14 coins and all of them are dimes or quarters. How many of each coin does she have?

A. Set up a system of equations that describes the conditions of the problem. Let d be the number of dimes and q be the number of quarters.

$$d + q = 14$$

The value of the dimes is $10d$ (in cents) and the value of quarters is $25d$. Therefore,

$$10d + 25q = 275.$$

B. Solve the system. Use substitution.

$$d = 14 - q$$

so

$$\begin{aligned} 10(14 - q) + 25q &= 275 \\ 140 - 10q + 25q &= 275 \\ 140 + 15q &= 275 \\ 15q &= 135 \\ q &= 9 \end{aligned}$$

$$\begin{aligned} d &= 14 - q \\ d &= 14 - 9 \\ d &= 5 \end{aligned}$$

The solution of the system is (5, 9).

C. Check in the other equation.

$$\begin{aligned} 10(5) + 25(9) &= 275 \\ 50 + 225 &= 275 \\ 275 &= 275 \end{aligned}$$

It checks, so Mary has 5 dimes and 9 quarters.

Larry had $7000 invested, some at 6% and some at 9%. He makes $570 a year on these investments. How much does Larry have invested at each rate?

A. Let x be the amount at 6% and y be the amount at 9%. Then,

$$\begin{aligned} 0.06x + 0.09y &= 570 \\ x + y &= 7000 \end{aligned}$$

is the system of equations that describes the conditions of the problem.

B. Solve the system. Multiply the second equation by -0.09

$$\begin{aligned} 0.06x + 0.09y &= 570 \\ -0.09x - 0.09y &= -630 \end{aligned}$$

Add.

$$\begin{aligned} -0.03x &= -60 \\ x &= 2000 \end{aligned}$$

Use the equation $x + y = 7000$ to find y.

$$y = 5000$$

C. Larry has $2000 invested at 6% and $5000 invested at 9%. Check in the other equation.

$$0.06(2000) + 0.09(5000) = 570$$

A plane trip of 3000 miles with the jet stream takes 5 hours, while the return against the jet stream takes 6 hours. How fast is the plane (in still air), and how fast is the jet stream?

A. Let x be the speed of the plane and y be the speed of the jet stream. The plane in still air would go a distance of $5x$ in 5 hours. Also, the jet stream would take it a distance of $5y$ in 5 hours, so

$$5x + 5y = 3000.$$

On the return trip, the plane travels for 6 hours at the same air speed, but the jet stream is $-6y$, so

$$6x - 6y = 3000.$$

B. The system

$$\begin{aligned} 5x + 5y &= 3000 \\ 6x - 6y &= 3000 \end{aligned}$$

is most easily solved with multiplication and addition. Multiply the first equation by 6 and the second by 5.

$$\begin{aligned} 30x + 30y &= 18000 \\ 30x - 30y &= 15000 \end{aligned}$$

Add.

$$\begin{aligned} 60x &= 33000 \\ x &= 550 \end{aligned}$$

Substitute in one of the equations to find the value of y.

$$y = 50$$

C. The solution to the system is (550, 50), so the plane's air speed is 550 mph and the wind speed is 50 mph. Check in the other equation.

Quadratic equations. A *quadratic equation* is an equation in one variable in which a second-degree term appears. For example, $x^2 = 4$ and $2x^2 - x + 6 = 0$ are both quadratic equations. A quadratic equation cannot be solved simply by adding, subtracting, multiplying, and dividing. All quadratic equations can be solved, however, if complex-number solutions are permitted (see box on page 198). In this section, all the quadratic equations will be solved for real solutions only.

There are several techniques available for solving quadratic equations, including completing the square, factoring, and using a formula, but all are fundamentally based on using one or the other of two basic rules of mathematics:

(1) *If two numbers are equal, then the square roots of those numbers are also equal.*

(2) *If the product of two numbers is equal to zero, then one or the other or both of the two numbers must be 0.*

Solve $x^2 = 64$.

METHOD 1

A. Take the square root of both sides of the equation.

$$x^2 = 64$$
$$\pm x = \pm 8$$

B. Look at all the combinations.

$$+x = +8$$
$$+x = -8$$
$$-x = +8$$
$$-x = -8$$

All combinations come down to either $x = +8$ or $x = -8$, so the solution is expressed as

$$x = \pm 8.$$

METHOD 2

A. Set the equation equal to 0.

$$x^2 - 64 = 0$$

The expression $x^2 - 64$ is the difference of 2 squares, so it can be factored as

$$(x - 8)(x + 8).$$

Therefore, another way to write the equation is

$$(x - 8)(x + 8) = 0.$$

B. By rule (2) above, if the product of two expressions is 0, then one or the other or both must also be zero. Use this to separate the equation into two first-degree equations.

$$x - 8 = 0 \textit{ or } x + 8 = 0$$

C. Solve each equation separately.

$$x = 8 \textit{ or } x = -8$$

This result can be written as

$$x = \pm 8.$$

Solve $x^2 + 2x - 8 = 0$.

METHOD 1

A. If the expression on the left were the square of a binomial, the square root of both sides could be taken. Add a number to each side to make this operation possible. This method is called *completing the square.* Since $(x + a)^2$ is

$$x^2 + 2ax + a^2,$$

the number to be added is the number that will make the term without a variable equal to the square of half the coefficient of x. The easiest way to do this is to begin by rewriting the equation with no constant term on the left.

$$x^2 + 2x = 8$$

Then add $(\frac{1}{2} \cdot 2)^2$, or 1, to each side of the equation.

$$x^2 + 2x + 1 = 9$$

B. You now have an equation that has the square of a binomial on the left and a number on the right, so you can use rule (1).

$$(x + 1)^2 = 3^2$$
$$x + 1 = \pm 3$$

C. Separate the equation into two parts,

$$x + 1 = 3 \textit{ or } x + 1 = -3$$

and solve the parts separately.

$$x = 2 \textit{ or } x = -4$$

METHOD 2

A. This equation can also be solved by *factoring.* In other words, it can be solved using rule (2). Factor the left side.

$$x^2 + 2x - 8 = 0$$
$$(x + 4)(x - 2) = 0$$

B. Separate the equation into two parts by rule (2).

$$x + 4 = 0 \textit{ or } x - 2 = 0$$

C. Solve each part separately.

$$x = -4 \textit{ or } x = 2$$

While completing the square will work for all quadratic equations, it is often awkward to use when the coefficient of x^2 is not 1; and factoring is often difficult or impossible. Another method for solving quadratic equations is often used. The general equation $ax^2 + bx + c = 0$ can be solved by completing the square. The solution is called the *quadratic formula.*

$$x = \frac{-b \pm \sqrt{b^2 - 4ac}}{2a}$$

Solve $12x^2 - 17x - 5 = 0$ using the quadratic formula.

A. Identify a, b, and c from the formula.

$$a = 12$$
$$b = -17$$
$$c = -5$$

B. Substitute the values of a, b, and c into the formula.

$$x = \frac{-(-17) \pm \sqrt{(-17)^2 - 4(12)(-5)}}{2(12)}$$
$$= \frac{17 \pm \sqrt{289 + 240}}{24}$$
$$= \frac{17 \pm \sqrt{529}}{24}$$
$$= \frac{17 \pm 23}{24}$$

C. Separate into two equations.

$$x = \frac{17 + 23}{24} \text{ or}$$
$$x = \frac{17 - 23}{24}$$
$$x = \frac{40}{24} \text{ or } x = \frac{-6}{24}$$
$$x = \frac{5}{3} \text{ or } x = -\frac{1}{4}$$

The product of two consecutive odd positive integers is 63. What is the smaller integer?

A. Let the smaller odd integer be x. Then the other integer is $x + 2$.

$$x(x + 2) = 63$$

B.

$$x^2 + 2x - 63 = 0$$
$$(x - 7)(x + 9) = 0$$
$$x - 7 = 0 \text{ or } x + 9 = 0$$
$$x = 7 \text{ or } x = -9$$

C. The problem specifies that the integers are positive. Therefore the smaller integer is 7.

There are two integers such that when 6 times an integer is subtracted from the square of that integer, the difference is 16. What are both integers with this property?

A. Call the integer with the specified property x. Then,

$$x^2 - 6x = 16.$$

B. Add $(\frac{1}{2} \cdot (-6))^2 = 9$ to each side.

$$x^2 - 6x + 9 = 25$$
$$(x - 3)^2 = 5^2$$
$$x - 3 = \pm 5$$

$$x - 3 = 5 \text{ or } x - 3 = -5$$
$$x = 8 \text{ or } x = -2$$

C. One of the integers is 8 and the other is -2. Check both in the original problem.

$$64 - 48 = 16$$
$$16 = 16$$
$$4 + 12 = 16$$
$$16 = 16$$

A rectangle is twice as long as it is wide. The number of units in its area is 4 times the number in its perimeter. How long and how wide is the rectangle?

A. If x is the width of the rectangle, then $2x$ is the length, $6x$ is the perimeter, and $2x^2$ is the area.

$$2x^2 = 24x$$

B. Divide by 2 to simplify.

$$x^2 = 12x$$
$$x^2 - 12x = 0$$
$$x^2 - 12x + 36 = 36$$
$$(x - 6)^2 = 6^2$$
$$x - 6 = \pm 6$$

$$x - 6 = 6 \text{ or } x - 6 = -6$$
$$x = 12 \text{ or } x = 0$$

C. A rectangle with a width of 0 would not be a rectangle, so only the answer $x = 12$ would be practical. Therefore, the width is 12 units and the length is 24 units.

Equations with fractions

Solve the equation $\frac{2x-1}{2} - \frac{x+2}{2x+5} = \frac{6x-5}{6}$.

A. The first step in solving any equation that contains fractions is to get rid of the fractions by multiplying both sides of the equation by the lowest common denominator of the fractions in the equation. In this case, the LCD is $6(2x + 5)$.

B. Multiplying both sides by $6(2x + 5)$ produces
$3(2x + 5)(2x - 1) - 6(x + 2) = (2x + 5)(6x - 5)$.
Multiply.
$12x^2 + 24x - 15 - 6x - 12 = 12x^2 + 20x - 25$
Collect like terms.

$$\begin{aligned} 12x^2 + 18x - 27 &= 12x^2 + 20x - 25 \\ 18x - 27 &= 20x - 25 \\ -2 &= 2x \\ x &= -1 \end{aligned}$$

Operations with fractions

Addition:

$$\frac{a}{b} + \frac{c}{b} = \frac{a+c}{b}$$

Multiplication:

$$\frac{a}{b} \cdot \frac{c}{d} = \frac{ac}{bd}$$

Exponentiation:

$$\left(\frac{a}{b}\right)^n = \frac{a^n}{b^n}$$

Subtraction:

$$\frac{a}{b} - \frac{c}{b} = \frac{a-c}{b}$$

Division:

$$\frac{a}{b} \div \frac{c}{d} = \frac{ad}{bc}$$

Square roots:

$$\sqrt{\frac{a}{b}} = \frac{\sqrt{a}}{\sqrt{b}}$$

NOTE: b, c, and d are not 0.

Solve the equation $\frac{x^2 - 4x}{6} - \frac{x-3}{3} = 1$.

A. Find the LCD. It is 6.

B. Multiply both sides by the LCD.

$$\begin{aligned} x^2 - 4x - 2(x-3) &= 6(1) \\ x^2 - 4x - 2x + 6 &= 6 \\ x^2 - 6x + 6 &= 6 \\ x^2 - 6x &= 0 \end{aligned}$$

C. This equation can be solved by the rule that if $AB = 0$, then either A or B or both is equal to 0. Factor.

$$\begin{aligned} x(x-6) &= 0 \\ x = 0 \text{ or } x - 6 &= 0 \\ x &= 6 \end{aligned}$$

There are two solutions.

$x = 0$ *or* $x = 6$

Solve the equation $2x + \frac{2x-6}{x-3} = 1$.

A. Multiply both sides by $(x - 3)$.

$$\begin{aligned} 2x(x-3) + 2x - 6 &= 1(x-3) \\ 2x^2 - 6x + 2x - 6 &= x - 3 \\ 2x^2 - 5x - 3 &= 0 \end{aligned}$$

B. Solve by factoring.

$$(2x + 1)(x - 3) = 0$$

$$2x + 1 = 0 \text{ or } x - 3 = 0$$

$$2x = -1 \text{ or } \quad x = 3$$

$$x = -\frac{1}{2}$$

C. The apparent solutions are $x = -\frac{1}{2}$ and $x = 3$; however, the apparent solution $x = 3$ is *extraneous.* When you substitute 3 in the original equation, you get

$$2(3) + \frac{2(3) - 6}{(3-3)} = 1$$

$$\frac{6+0}{0} = 1.$$

Since division by 0 is always prohibited, $x = 3$ must be eliminated. The other apparent solution, however, checks. Therefore, the only solution is $-\frac{1}{2}$. Extraneous solutions can also occur in equations that are solved by squaring both sides.

Operations with radicals. The sign $\sqrt{\ }$ is a *radical.* By itself, it means the positive square root; thus, $\sqrt{x^2} = |x|$ (NOT $\pm x$). When a number, such as n, is inserted in the radical sign, the combination means the nth root; for example, $\sqrt[3]{-27}$ is the third root of -27, or -3, since $(-3)(-3)(-3) = -27$, and $\sqrt[4]{16}$ is the fourth root of 16, or 2. Note that if n is odd, the nth root of a negative number is negative, when only real roots are considered. If n is even, there is no real nth root.

Simplify $\sqrt{72}$.

A. The product of two numbers indicated by radicals is the product of the numbers in the radicals, called the *radicands,* as long as both radicals have the same *index,* the number n that indicates the meaning of the radical. Therefore,
$\sqrt{72} = \sqrt{36 \cdot 2} = \sqrt{36} \cdot \sqrt{2}.$

B. A radical is simplified when all the real integral roots have been removed from the radicand. In this case, since 36 is a perfect square, $\sqrt{36}$ can be replaced by 6.

Therefore, the simplified form of $\sqrt{72}$ is $6\sqrt{2}$, since 2 is not a perfect square; that is, 2 does not have an integral root.

Simplify $\sqrt{20x^2y^3}$.

A. Rewrite each coefficient as a product that involves perfect squares if it is possible to do so.
$\sqrt{20x^2y^3} = \sqrt{4 \cdot 5x^2y^2y}$

B. Remove the perfect squares from the radicand.
$\sqrt{4 \cdot 5x^2y^2y} = 2|xy|\sqrt{5y}$
The answer is often given without using the absolute value sign, as $2xy\sqrt{5y}$.

In careful work, however, the absolute value sign is used unless one is certain that the values of x and y are non-negative.

Sequences and series

Arithmetic sequence:
First term: a or a_1

Constant difference: d

General term: $a_n = a + (n - 1)d$

Sequence: $a, a + d, a + 2d, a + 3d, \ldots,$
$a + (n - 1)d, \ldots$

Geometric sequence:
First term: a or a_1

Constant ratio: r

General term: $a_n = ar^{n-1}$

Sequence: $a, ar, ar^2, ar^3, \ldots, ar^{n-1}, \ldots$

Arithmetic series:
Series: $a + (a + d) + (a + 2d) + \ldots$
$+ (a + (n - 1)d) + \ldots$

Last term of finite series: l_n

Sum of finite series of n terms:

$$S_n = \frac{n}{2}(a + l_n)$$

$$= \frac{n}{2}(2a + (n - 1)d)$$

Sum of infinite series: none

Geometric series:
Series: $a + ar + ar^2 + ar^3 + \ldots + ar^{n-1} + \ldots$

Sum of finite series of n terms:

$$S_n = \frac{a - ar^n}{1 - r} \quad (r \neq 1)$$

$$= \frac{a(a - r^n)}{1 - r} \quad (r \neq 1)$$

Sum of infinite series: $S = \dfrac{a}{1 - r} \quad (|r| < 1)$

Geometry

Geometry is the study of certain properties of sets of points. These properties are arranged and developed as part of an *axiomatic system;* that is, they are proved by *deduction* from a set of first principles called *axioms.* The axioms are accepted without proof, but the remaining properties of the system must all be proved.

Certain concepts must also be accepted without definition. These *undefined terms* are *point, betweenness, congruence,* and *continuity.* Although the terms are undefined, there is a common understanding of what they mean. Thus, a point is something like a small dot, or an exact location in space. The concept of betweenness suggests that between two points, there can be another. This is different from continuity, which refers to the nature of a line.

Congruence is an essential idea in geometry. It is simply the notion that two different line segments can have the same length. (A *line segment* is the part of a line between two points, called the *endpoints,* including the points.)

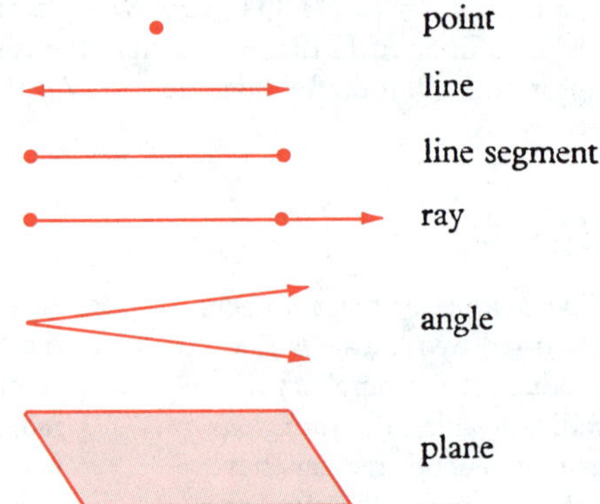

Most of the terms used in geometry, however, are defined terms based on the undefined terms. For example, a *ray* is the union of a line segment AB (A and B are the endpoints of the segment) and all points C such that B is between A and C. This figure is called ray AB, and A is the *endpoint* of the ray. An *angle* is the union of two rays that have the same endpoint.

Angles

The measure of angle A is shown as m $\angle A$.

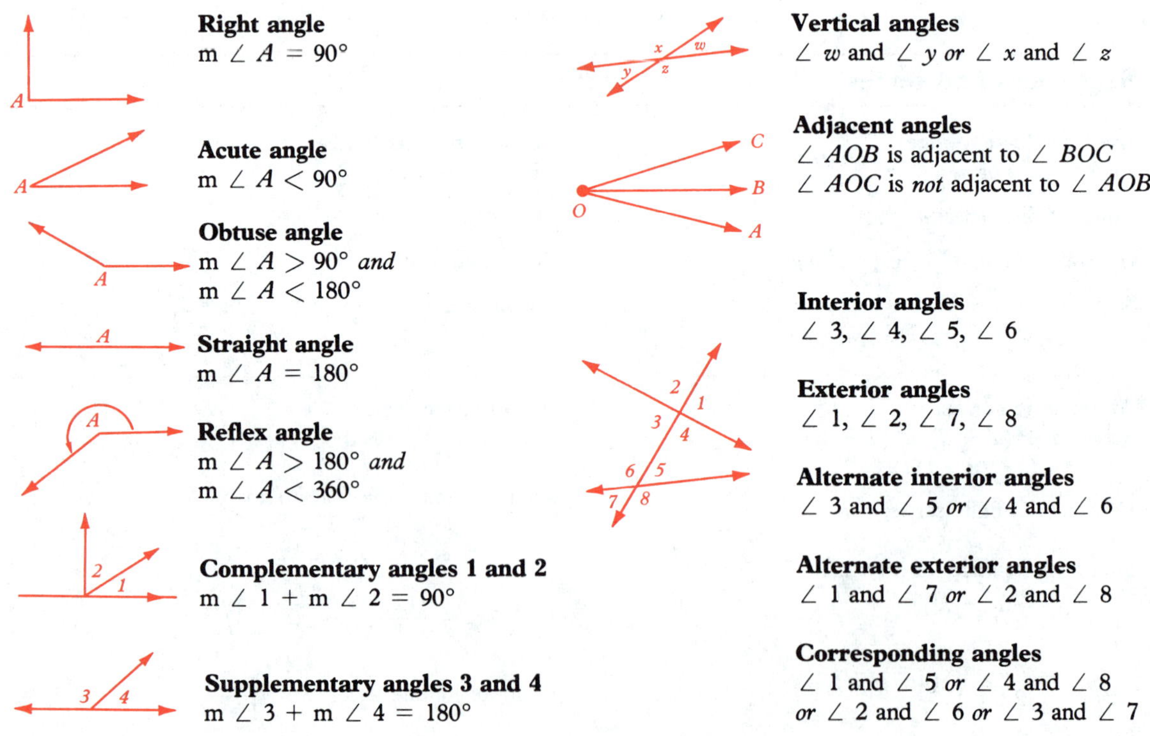

Geometric constructions. It is assumed that one can draw a line segment and extend it to become a line and that one can reproduce the distance between two points. The tools for performing these operations are called the *straightedge* and the *compass.* With a straightedge and compass, it is possible to draw theoretically exact figures, which are called *constructions.* When a construction has been given for a figure, one can take the construction as the definition, since the construction provides an essential way of reproducing the figure from points, lines, and congruent distances, all undefined concepts.

In making constructions, the compass is used to draw short circle segments called *arcs.*

Bisect a line segment *AB*.

A. Set the point of the compass at *A* and, with a radius greater than $\frac{1}{2}$ *AB,* draw a small arc above and below *AB.*

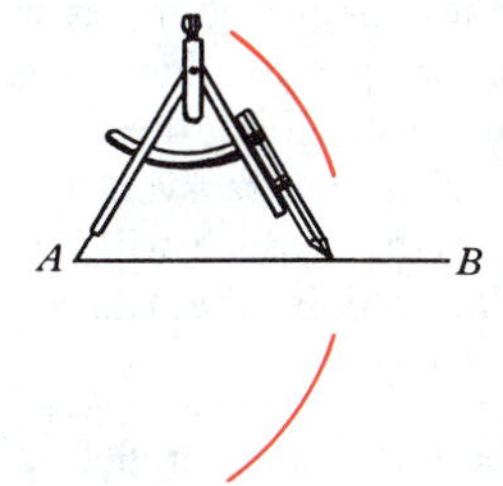

B. With the same radius, draw two arcs with the compass point at *B,* so that each of the first arcs is crossed by the second. Connect the two points of intersection of the arcs, *C* and *D,* with a line.

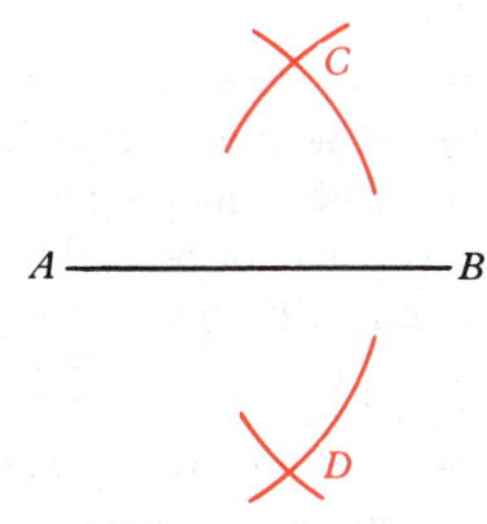

Where this line crosses *AB* at point *E,* the line *bisects AB.* In other words, *E* divides the segment into two parts that are congruent.
NOTE: *CD* is actually perpendicular to *AB.* Thus, it is the *perpendicular bisector* of *AB.*

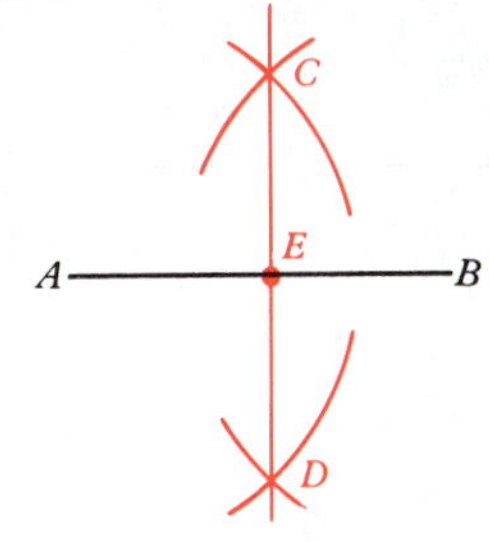

Construct a perpendicular to *AB* at *G*.

A. Set the point of the compass at *G* and draw equal arcs on *AB* that cross at *C* and *D.*

B. With a larger radius, set the compass point at *C* and draw an arc above *AB.*

C. With the same radius, draw an arc with the compass point at *D,* crossing the other arc, locating point *E.*

D. Connect *E* and *G; EG* is perpendicular to *AB* at *G.*

Construct an angle congruent to a given angle *A*.

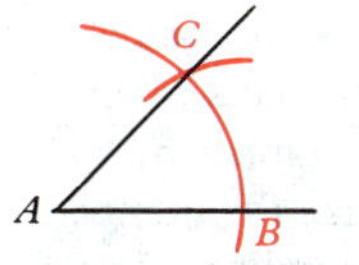

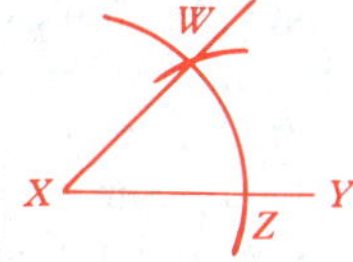

A. Draw a base line *XY.*

B. Set the compass point at *X* and draw an arc through *Z.*

C. Set the compass point at *A* to draw the same arc as in step B through the sides of angle *A* to locate points *B* and *C.*

D. Set the compass point at *B* and draw an arc through *C.*

E. Use the arc from step D with the compass point set at *Z* to locate point *W.*

F. Draw ray *XW* to complete the construction of angle *X* that is congruent to angle *A.*

Bisect angle *P*.

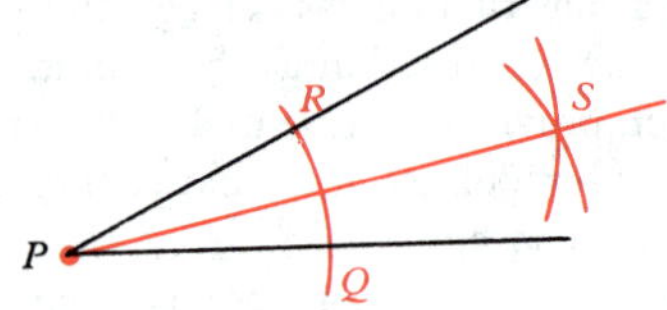

A. Draw an arc with the compass point at *P* to get points *Q* and *R*.

B. With a sufficiently large radius, set the compass point at *Q* and strike an arc.

C. Set the compass point at *R* with the same radius as in step *B*. Intersect the other arc to locate point *S*.

D. Draw ray *PS*, which is the bisector of angle *P*.

Construct a line through point *P* that is parallel to *AB*.

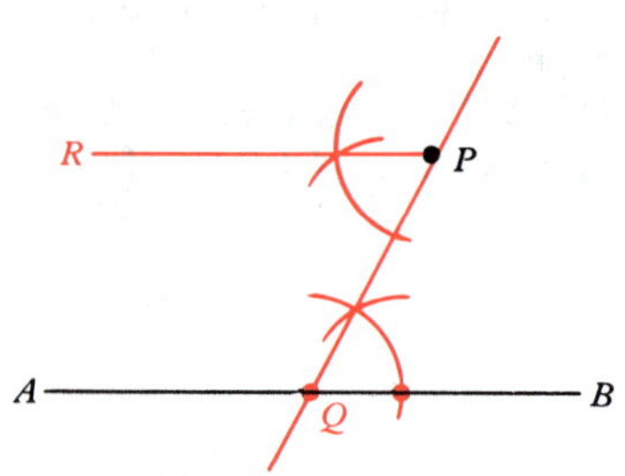

A. Two lines are *parallel* if they always maintain the same distance from each other. From this it can be inferred that parallel lines do not intersect. All lines that are not parallel do intersect in a point, a result that is not obvious. In fact, non-Euclidean geometries exist in which this property of parallels does not hold. The construction, however, does not use distance.

Instead, it relies on another property of parallel lines, which is often taken as an axiom in Euclidean geometry: A line that intersects both parallel lines—a *transversal*—makes congruent angles with the two parallel lines. Begin the construction, then, by drawing any transversal through *P*, which will intersect *AB* at a point that can be called *Q*.

B. At point *P*, construct an angle *RPQ* congruent to angle *PQB*.

The line *RP* is parallel to line *AB*.

Divide a line segment *AB* into three congruent parts.

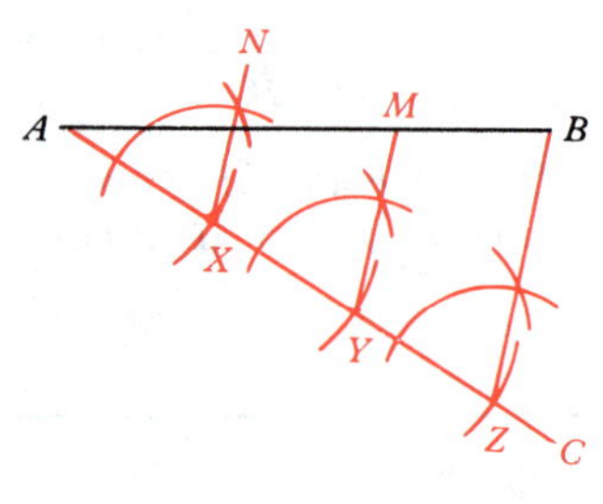

A. Draw a ray *AC* with its endpoint at *A*. This ray is an *auxiliary* ray because it is not a part of the actual division, even though it is used to make the construction.

B. With the compass point at *A*, mark point *X* any suitable distance along *AC*.

C. With the same radius as in step B, mark points *Y* with the compass point at *X*, and *Z* with the compass point at *Y*.

D. Draw line segment *ZB*, which defines angle *AZB*.

E. Construct angles at *Y* and *X* that are each congruent to angle *AZB*. The sides of these angles strike *AB* at points that you can label *N* and *M*. This completes the construction because *AN* is congruent to *NM* and to *MB*.

NOTE: You can use the same method to divide a line segment into any required number of points. Simply make the number of arcs along the auxiliary ray the same as the number of divisions of the line segment.

Triangles. Two triangles are congruent if all the corresponding sides and all the corresponding angles are congruent. Congruent triangles are used extensively in geometry. The following construction shows that equal sides imply equal angles for triangles.

Construct a triangle given three sides of length *a*, *b*, and *c*.

A. The sides of a triangle are conventionally called by the lower-case version of the name of the angle opposite the side. Therefore, the side whose length is *c* is also called *c*, since it is opposite angle *C*. Start by drawing *c*. The other name for the segment *c* is *AB*.

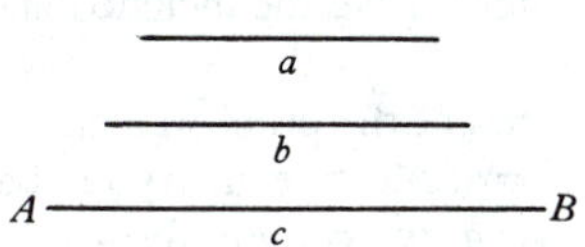

B. With the radius of the compass equal to *b*, make an arc with the compass point at *A*.

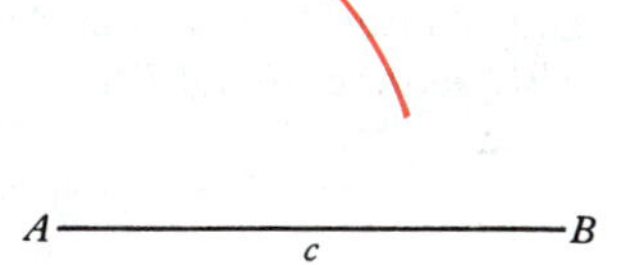

C. Set the radius of the compass to the length of *a* and make an arc with the compass point at *B* that intersects the arc drawn in step B. *C* will be where the two arcs intersect.

D. Draw *AC* and *CB*.

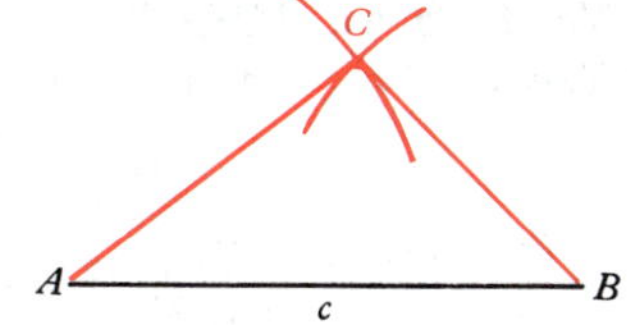

Triangles

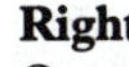

Right
One angle measures 90°.
The side opposite the right angle is called the *hypotenuse.* The other two sides are called *legs.*

Acute
All angles measure less than 90°.

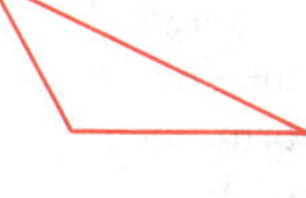

Obtuse
One angle measures more than 90°.

Equilateral
All three sides measure the same.

Isosceles
Two of the three sides measure the same.

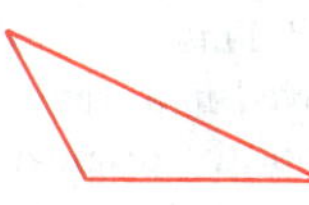

Scalene
No two sides measure the same.

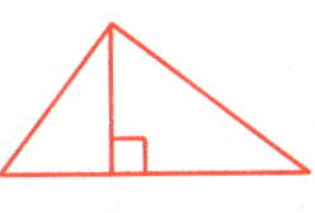

Altitude
A line segment from a vertex perpendicular to the opposite side.

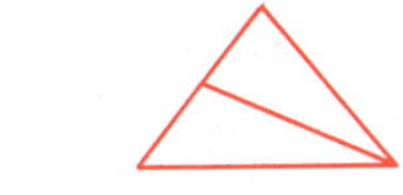

Median
A line segment from a vertex to the midpoint of the opposite side.

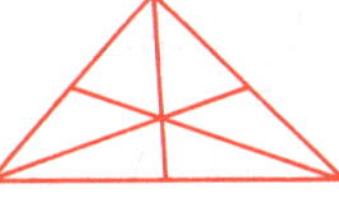

Centroid
Point where all three medians meet.

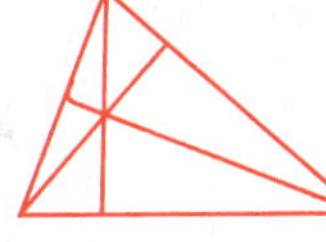

Circumcenter
Point where all three altitudes meet.

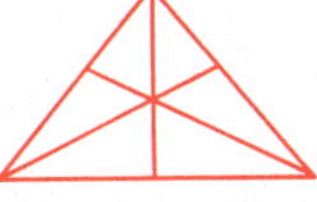

Incenter
Point where the bisectors of the angles of a triangle meet.

Proof in geometry is based on a set of axioms. In this book, the proofs that are given are examples, so it is not necessary to provide a complete set of axioms. Axioms such as the following will be used in the proofs:

- A figure is congruent to itself.
- Vertical angles are congruent.
- If two figures are each congruent to a third figure, then the two figures are also congruent to each other.
- Corresponding parts of congruent triangles are also congruent.
- If two lines are parallel, the alternate interior angles cut off by a transversal are congruent.

Prove that the angles opposite the congruent sides (the *base* angles) of an isosceles triangle are congruent.

A. First establish what is *given* in the statement of the problem. In this case, you know that the triangle is isosceles. Make a drawing of an isosceles triangle, label it, and mark the congruent sides.
You are given $AC \cong BC$.
You are also given $BC \cong AC$.

B. Next, establish what you are going to prove. In this case, you want to prove two triangles are congruent (although only one triangle is given). The second triangle is the same as the first with the sides taken in a different order. You can call the first triangle ABC and the second BAC.

If you can prove

$$\triangle ABC \cong \triangle BAC,$$

then the theorem will be true by corresponding parts of congruent triangles. Since you have two sides already given as congruent, you need either a third side or the included angle. Take the included angle.

C. Present the proof in a clear form. Most geometry textbooks use a two-column format.

Statements	*Reasons*
1. $AC \cong BC$	1. Given.
2. $BC \cong AC$	2. Given.
3. $\angle C \cong \angle C$	3. A figure is congruent to itself.
4. $\triangle ABC \cong \triangle BAC$	4. S.A.S.
5. $\angle A \cong \angle B$	5. Corresponding parts of congruent triangles are also congruent.

NOTE: The converse of a theorem is a kind of "reverse" of the theorem. If the theorem is stated in "if-then" form, then the converse can be found by interchanging the clause after "if" and the clause after "then." The if-then form of the previous theorem is, "if a triangle is isosceles, then the base angles of the triangle are congruent." Therefore, the converse of the theorem is "if the base angles of a triangle are congruent, then the triangle is isosceles." This converse can be proved in a way similar to the proof of the original theorem.

Congruence for triangles

Two triangles are congruent if any of the following conditions are true:

Property		*Abbreviation*	
Three corresponding sides are congruent (side-side-side).	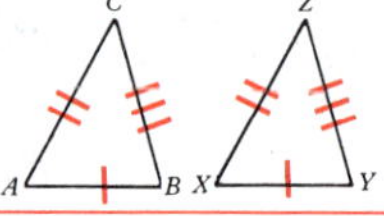	S.S.S.	$AB \cong XY$ $AC \cong XZ$ $BC \cong YZ$
Two corresponding sides and the included angle are congruent (side-angle-side).	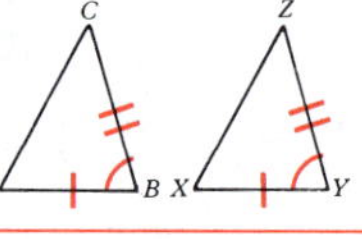	S.A.S.	$AB \cong XY$ $BC \cong YZ$ $\angle B \cong \angle Y$
Two corresponding angles and the included side are congruent (angle-side-angle).	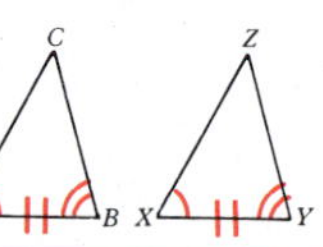	A.S.A.	$\angle A \cong \angle X$ $\angle B \cong \angle Y$ $AB \cong XY$
Two corresponding angles and the side not included are congruent (angle-angle-side).	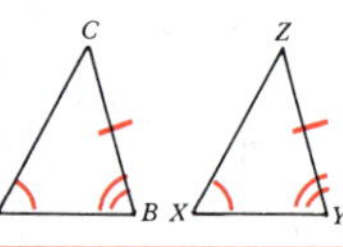	A.A.S.	$\angle A \cong \angle X$ $\angle B \cong \angle Y$ $BC \cong YZ$
In a right triangle, two corresponding hypotenuses and two corresponding legs are equal (hypotenuse-leg).	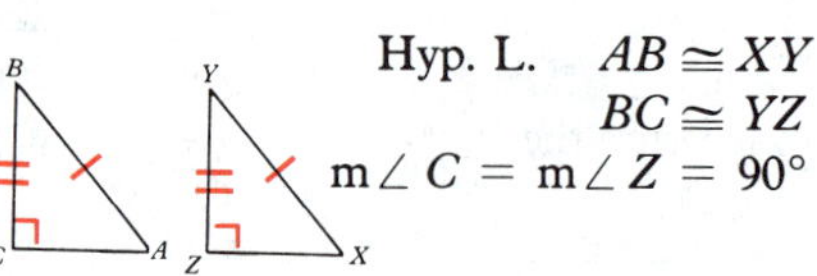	Hyp. L.	$AB \cong XY$ $BC \cong YZ$ $m\angle C = m\angle Z = 90°$

Prove that the bisector of the vertex angle of an isosceles triangle is also the bisector of the base of the triangle.

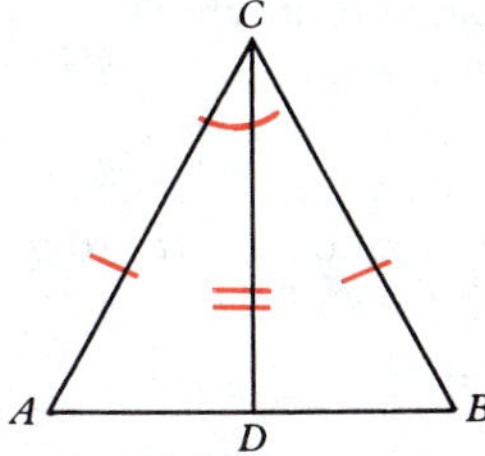

A. You are given an isosceles triangle and the angle bisector of the *vertex* angle; that is, the angle that is not one of the base angles.

B. The strategy is to use the angle bisector to divide the triangle into two triangles that can be shown to be congruent by S.A.S.

C. Express as a two-column proof.

Statements	*Reasons*
1. $AC \cong BC$	1. Definition of isosceles.
2. $\angle ACD \cong \angle BCD$	2. Definition of angle bisector.
3. $CD \cong CD$	3. Figures are congruent to themselves.
4. $\triangle ACD \cong \triangle BCD$	4. S.A.S.
5. $AD \cong DB$	5. Corresponding parts of congruent triangles are congruent.
6. D bisects AB	6. Definition of bisector.

Given two intersecting circles whose centers are O and P and whose points of intersection are A and B. Line segment AB bisects angles OAP and OBP. Prove that $BP \cong AP \cong AO \cong OB$.

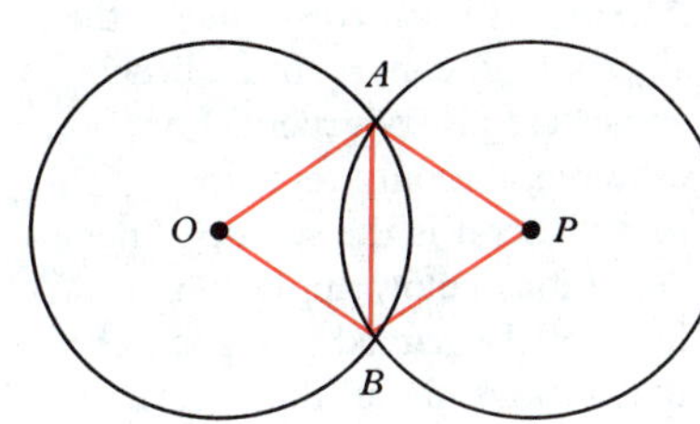

A. Establish what is given.

B. Choose a plan of attack. In this case you will want to use the definition of a circle as a set of points all at the same distance from a given point, the definition of bisect, and the theorems about isosceles triangles. The fact that there are two angles bisected in the problem suggests that A.S.A. will be useful.

C. Write a two-column proof.

Statements	*Reasons*
1. O and P are circles	1. Given.
2. $OA \cong OB$	2. Radii of the same circle are congruent by definition.
3. $\triangle OAB$ is isosceles	3. Definition of isosceles.
4. $\angle OAB \cong \angle OBA$	4. Base angles of isosceles triangles are congruent.
5. $\angle OAB \cong \angle BAP$	5. Definition of bisect.
6. $\angle OBA \cong \angle ABP$	6. Definition of bisect.
7. $AB \cong AB$	7. A figure is congruent to itself.
8. $\triangle ABO \cong \triangle ABP$	8. A.S.A.
9. $OA \cong AP$	9. Corresponding parts of congruent triangles are congruent.
10. $OB \cong BP$	10. Corresponding parts of congruent triangles are congruent.
11. $BP \cong AP \cong AO \cong OB$	11. If two figures are each congruent to a third figure, they are also congruent to each other.

Polygons

Prove that the opposite sides of a parallelogram are congruent.

A. Given $AB \parallel CD$ and $AD \parallel BC$.

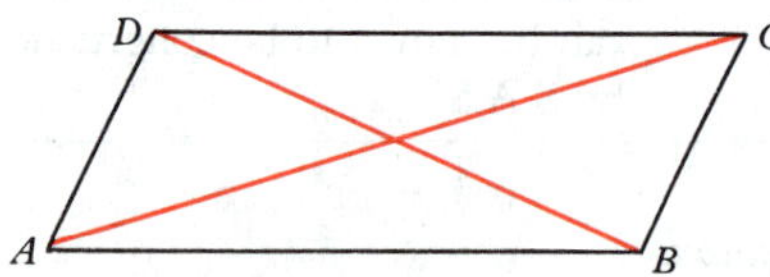

B. In more advanced work with geometry, the two-column proof is often replaced with the paragraph proof. The most important reasons and all the steps are included, but the material is presented in ordinary prose instead of in chart or list form. Since you have been exposed to theorems involving triangles, put some triangles into the figure by drawing the *diagonals* or line segments from one vertex to the opposite vertex of the parallelogram.

C. Use the result that alternate interior angles cut off by a transversal and parallel lines are congruent. This shows that $\angle BDC \cong \angle DBA$ and $\angle ADB \cong \angle DBC$. Since $DB \cong DB$, triangles ADB and BDC are congruent by A.S.A.

D. Therefore, $AD \cong BC$ and $AB \cong DC$.

NOTE: This proof applies equally to rectangles and to rhombuses. As a result, it is easy to show that all four sides of a rhombus are congruent.

Similarly, a result that you will use in the next proof is a partial converse of this theorem: if two sides of a quadrilateral are both congruent and parallel, the quadrilateral is a parallelogram.

Common polygons

Quadrilaterals: Polygons with 4 sides

Name/Defining property

Trapezoid
A quadrilateral with two parallel sides.* — $AB \parallel DC$

Isosceles Trapezoid
A trapezoid with congruent nonparallel sides. — $AB \parallel DC$, $AD \cong BC$

Kite
A quadrilateral with two pairs of adjacent congruent sides. — $AB \cong AD$, $BC \cong CD$

Parallelogram
A quadrilateral with pairs of opposite sides parallel. — $AB \parallel DC$, $AD \parallel BC$

Rhombus
A parallelogram with a pair of adjacent congruent sides. — $AB \parallel DC$, $AD \parallel BC$, $AB \cong AD$

Rectangle
A parallelogram with a right angle. — $AB \parallel DC$, $AD \parallel BC$, $m\ \angle A = 90°$

Square
A rectangle with a pair of adjacent congruent sides. — $AB \parallel DC$, $AD \parallel BC$, $m\ \angle A = 90°$, $AB \cong AD$

* *Some books use* trapezoid *only if the quadrilateral has two parallel sides and two nonparallel sides; other books permit parallelograms to be special cases of trapezoids.*

Other polygons

A polygon is called *regular* if the sides are all congruent and the angles are all congruent. For example, the only regular quadrilateral is the square. The definitions below apply to any form of the named polygon. The illustrations are all the regular forms of the polygons.

Name/Defining property

Triangle
A polygon with 3 sides.

Quadrilateral
A polygon with 4 sides.

Pentagon
A polygon with 5 sides.

Hexagon
A polygon with 6 sides.

Octagon
A polygon with 8 sides.

Decagon
A polygon with 10 sides.

It can be proved from congruent triangles that the angle formed by extending one side of a triangle (called an *exterior angle* of the triangle) is greater than the *remote interior angles* of the triangle, the angles that are not adjacent to the angle formed by extension. In the figure, angle *CBD* is an exterior angle and angles *C* and *A* are the remote interior angles.

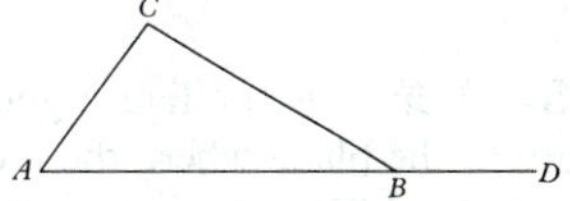

Prove that two lines are parallel if a transversal between the lines cuts off congruent alternate interior angles.

A. Make a drawing showing lines *AB* and *CD* cut by the transversal *PQ* at *A* and *D*. Then angles *BAD* and *CDA* are alternate interior angles. It is given that these two angles are congruent.

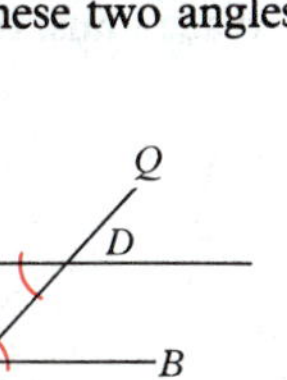

B. Assume that the opposite of what you want to prove is true; then show that such an assumption leads to a contradiction. Assume that *AB* and *CD* are not parallel. In that case, they must intersect at some point, which can be called *X*.

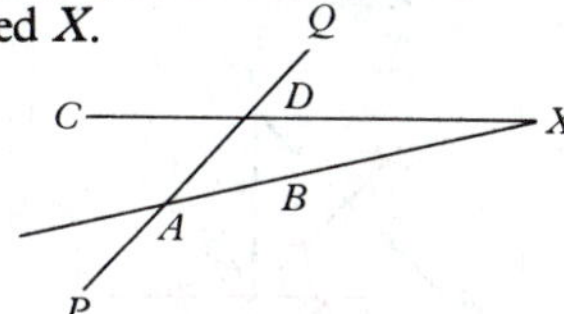

C. By the exterior angle theorem, angle *CDA* is greater than angle *BAD*. However, it is given that angles *CDA* and *BAD* are congruent. Therefore, a contradiction has been shown and the theorem is proved.

Prove that a segment joining the midpoints of two sides of a triangle is parallel to the third side and that its length is one-half the length of the third side.

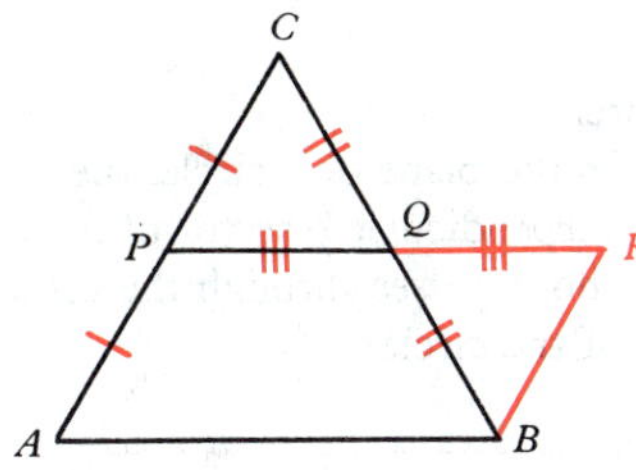

A. Draw a general triangle *ABC* and the line segment *PQ* joining the midpoints of sides *AC* and *BC*. Label *AP* and *PC* as congruent and *BQ* and *QC* as congruent.

B. The strategy will be to make *PQ* part of one side of a parallelogram, with *AB* the opposite side of the parallelogram. Construct the side containing *PQ* to be twice as long as *PQ*. Then it will be possible to prove the second part of the theorem.

C. Extend *PQ* through *Q* to point *R* so that *PR* is twice as long as *PQ*. Draw a line segment from *R* to *B*.

D. $QB \cong QC$ is given. *QR* was drawn to be congruent to *PQ*, since *PR* is twice as long as *PQ*. $\angle CQP$ and $\angle RQB$ are congruent because they are vertical angles (see box on page 218). Therefore, triangles *CPQ* and *QRB* are congruent by S.A.S.

E. Since *PC* and *RB* are corresponding parts, they are congruent. Also, *AP* is given to be congruent to *PC*. Therefore, *RB* and *AP* are congruent, since each is congruent to *PC*.

F. *CB* is a transversal between *AC* and *RB*. Angles *C* and *RBQ* are corresponding parts of congruent triangles, so they are congruent. Then, *CB* makes congruent alternate interior angles with *AC* and *RB*. Therefore, *AC* is parallel to *RB*. Since *AP* is part of *AC*, it is also parallel to *RB*. Since the conditions are both filled, *ABRP* is a parallelogram.

G. Since *ABRP* is a parallelogram, *PR* is parallel to *AB*, and, since *PQ* is part of *PR*, *PQ* is parallel to *AB*, which was the first thing to be proved. Also, *AB* is congruent to *PR*. Since *PQ* is half the length of *PR*, it is also half the length of *AB*.

Circles.

A *circle* is the figure you get when you extend an arc to the place where the arc started. More formally, a circle is the set of all points in the plane that are the same distance from a given point.

Various lines, line segments, angles, and other geometric figures connected with circles are given special names. Definitions for these figures that are related to the circle are given at the bottom of this page.

Construct a circle given three points through which the circle must pass.

A. Given the three points A, B, and C, draw line segments to connect two pairs of them, A with B and B with C.

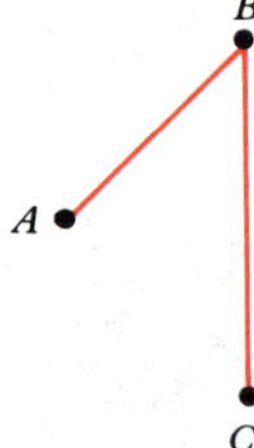

B. Construct the perpendicular bisectors of the segments AB and BC. Where the bisectors meet is the center of the circle. Note that if the three points are all in a line, the bisectors will not meet. Three *collinear* points (points on the same line) cannot be on a circle.

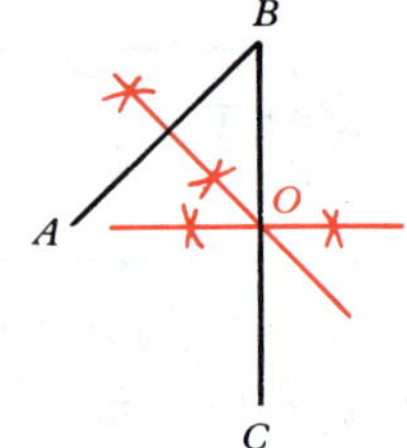

C. The distance from the intersection of the perpendiculars to one of the points is the radius of the circle. Set your compass point on the intersection and using that radius, draw the circle.

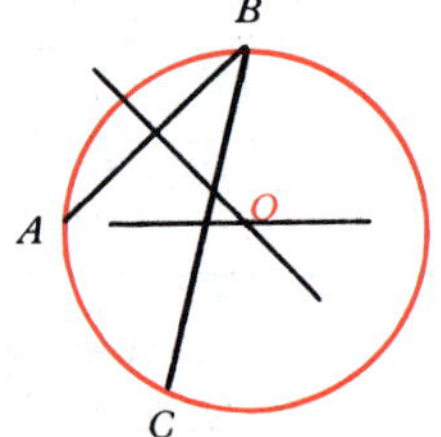

NOTE: This construction relies on this sequence of theorems about chords of circles:

1. The perpendicular from the center of a circle bisects a chord.
2. The line from the center of a circle to a chord that is not a diameter is perpendicular to the chord.
3. In the plane of a circle, the perpendicular bisector of a chord passes through the center of the circle.

Definitions

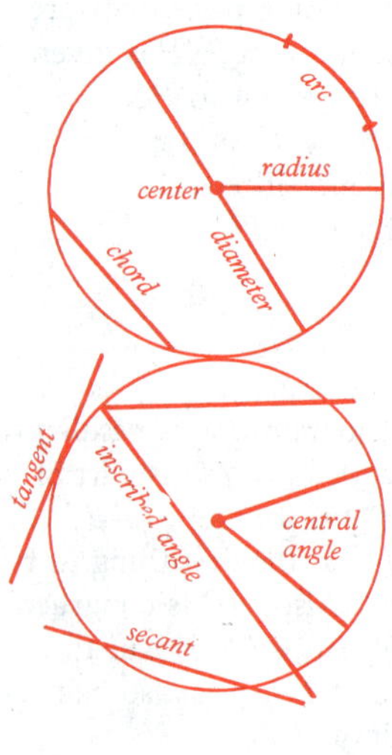

arc	Part of a circle.
center	Point from which all points of the circle are equidistant.
radius	Either the distance from the center to the circle or the line segment from the center to the circle.
diameter	Either the distance across the circle or the line segment from one side of the circle to the other that passes through the center.
chord	Line segment from one point of the circle to another point of the circle.
secant	Line passing through the circle.
tangent	Line that contains only one point of a circle.
central angle	Angle with its vertex at center of circle.
inscribed angle	Angle that intersects the circle in two points with its vertex on the circle.

Construct the two tangents to a circle from a point outside the circle.

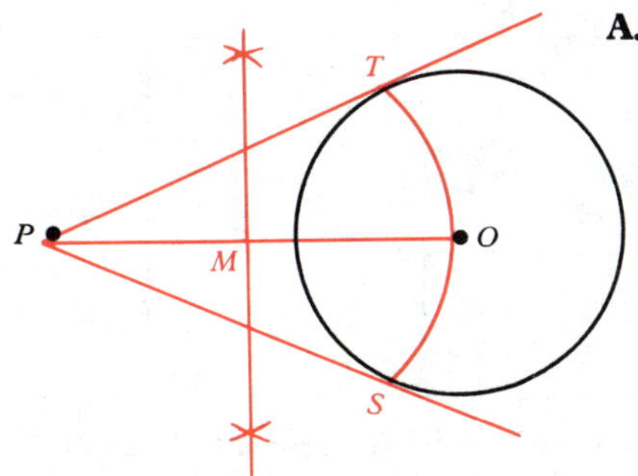

A. Call the point outside the circle *P* and the center of the circle *O*. Connect *O* to *P* and bisect *OP*. Use *M* to label the midpoint of *OP*.

B. With the compass at point *M* and a radius of *MO*, draw an arc that intersects the circle at two points, *T* and *S*. The lines *PT* and *PS* are the required tangents.

Given two circles, construct lines that are tangent to each circle and that intersect each other at a point between the two circles.

A. The tangents described are the *internal* common tangents of the two circles. Internal tangents to two circles are tangents that cross the line segment between the centers of the circles. Draw a diameter in one of the circles; construct a diameter in the other circle that is parallel to the one you drew in the first circle.

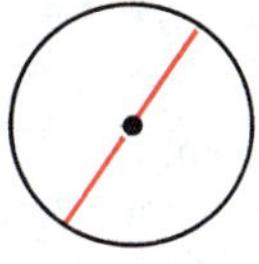

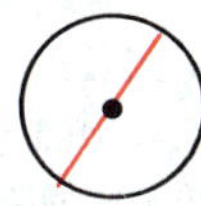

B. Connect the ends of the diameters with line segments. Where these segments cross is called the *internal center of similitude* of the two circles.

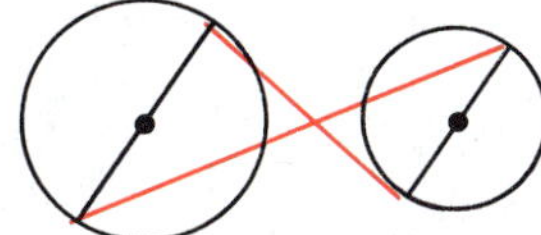

C. The common internal tangents of the circles will pass through the internal center of similitude. Therefore, to complete the construction, use this point, *S*, as the point outside the circle in the previous construction. Construct tangents to one of the circles from *S*. These will also be tangents to the other circle.

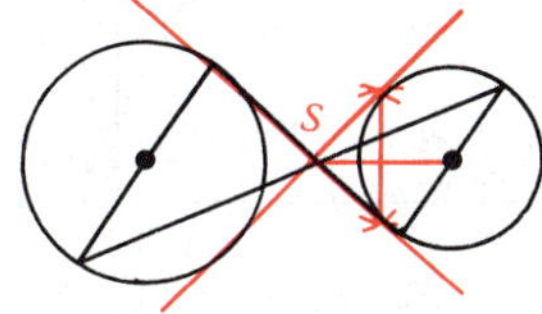

Construct the tangents to two circles from a point that is not between the two circles.

A. The tangents described are *external* common tangents; the tangents do not cross a line segment between the centers of the circles. Again, begin by drawing a diameter in one of the circles and constructing the diameter parallel to it in the other circle.

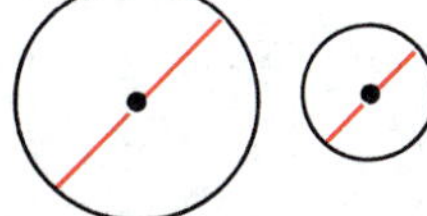

B. This time join the same ends of the diameters with lines (instead of the opposite ends with line segments). These lines will cross at a point outside the circles. Call that point *S*, since it is the *external center of similitude*.

S

C. As in the previous construction, construct tangents to one of the circles from *S*. They will also be the required tangents to both circles.

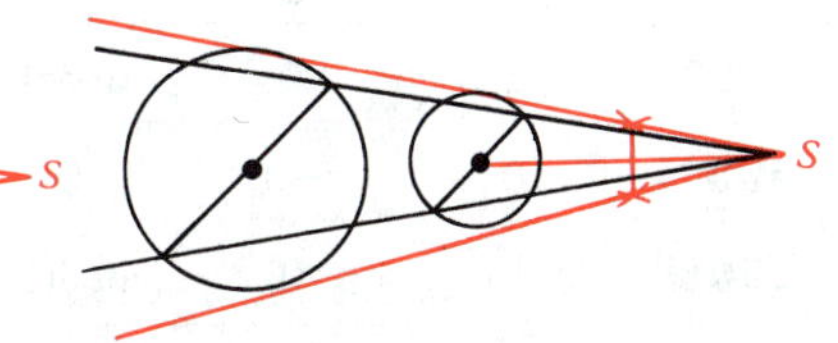

Trigonometry

Functions of angles. An angle is said to be in *standard position* in the *xy* coordinate system if its vertex is at the origin and one side, called the *initial* side, is on the positive x axis. The other side of the angle is the *terminal* side. Angles in trigonometry are measured as rotations from the initial side of the angle to the terminal side. If the terminal side is measured as a counterclockwise rotation from the initial side, the angle is *positive*. If the terminal side of an angle is viewed as having rotated in a clockwise direction, the angle is *negative*.

If θ is an angle in standard position, and p is a point on the terminal side with coordinates x and y, and if r is the distance between point p and the origin, then six *trigonometric functions* of the angle θ are defined.

$$\text{sine } \theta = \frac{y}{r} \qquad \text{tangent } \theta = \frac{y}{x} \qquad \text{secant } \theta = \frac{r}{x}$$

$$\text{cosine } \theta = \frac{x}{r} \qquad \text{cotangent } \theta = \frac{x}{y} \qquad \text{cosecant } \theta = \frac{r}{y}$$

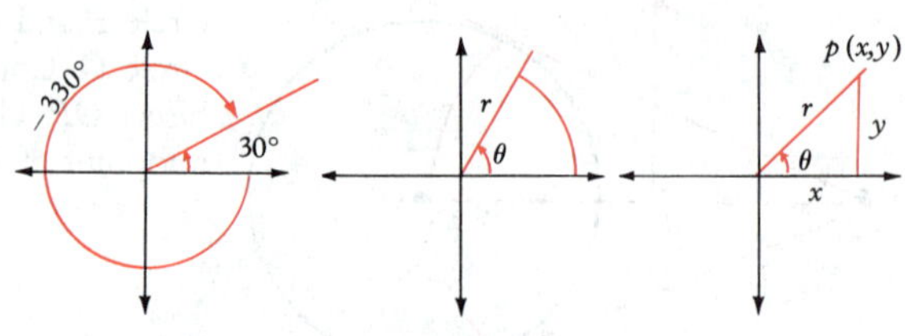

These functions are abbreviated respectively as sin θ, cos θ, tan θ, cot θ, sec θ, and csc θ.

Any angle will have six different values of the trigonometric functions (unless the denominator in the definition is 0 for a pair of values). For example, if the point is (4, 3), which is 5 units from the origin,

$$\sin \theta = \frac{3}{5} \qquad \tan \theta = \frac{3}{4} \qquad \sec \theta = \frac{5}{4}$$

$$\cos \theta = \frac{4}{5} \qquad \cot \theta = \frac{4}{3} \qquad \csc \theta = \frac{5}{3}$$

Compute the trigonometric functions when p is (8, 6).

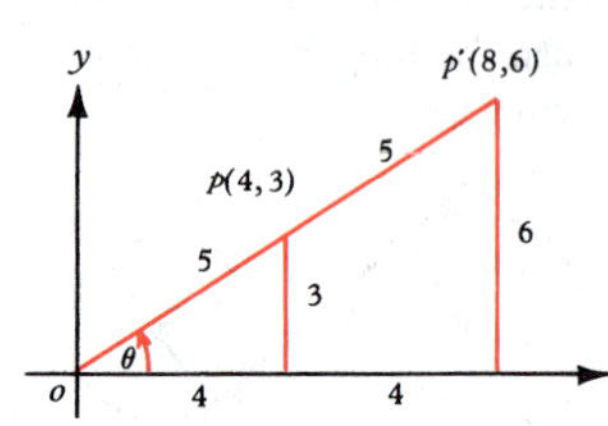

A. Find the value of r using the Pythagorean theorem. It is $\sqrt{8^2 + 6^2} = 10.$

B. Compute the ratios in lowest form.

$\sin \theta = \frac{3}{5}$ $\cot \theta = \frac{4}{3}$

$\cos \theta = \frac{4}{5}$ $\sec \theta = \frac{5}{4}$

$\tan \theta = \frac{3}{4}$ $\csc \theta = \frac{5}{3}$

Note that the point (8, 6) is on the same terminal side as (4, 3), so the values of the trigonometric functions of θ are the same. The values are determined by the angle, not the point chosen. If $x = -12$, $y = 5$, and $r = 13$, the values are

$\sin \theta = \frac{-5}{13}$ $\cot \theta = \frac{12}{5}$

$\cos \theta = \frac{-12}{13}$ $\sec \theta = \frac{13}{-12}$

$\tan \theta = \frac{5}{12}$ $\csc \theta = \frac{13}{-5}$

Notice that in this case some of the values are negative and others are positive.

Functions of special angles

Measure of θ	*Sin θ*	*Cos θ*	*Tan θ*	*Cot θ*	*Sec θ*	*Csc θ*
0°	0	1	0	undef.	1	undef.
30°	$\frac{1}{2}$	$\frac{\sqrt{3}}{2}$	$\frac{\sqrt{3}}{3}$	$\sqrt{3}$	$\frac{2\sqrt{3}}{3}$	2
45°	$\frac{\sqrt{2}}{2}$	$\frac{\sqrt{2}}{2}$	1	1	$\sqrt{2}$	$\sqrt{2}$
60°	$\frac{\sqrt{3}}{2}$	$\frac{1}{2}$	$\sqrt{3}$	$\frac{\sqrt{3}}{3}$	2	$\frac{2\sqrt{3}}{3}$
90°	1	0	undef.	0	undef.	1
180°	0	−1	0	undef.	−1	undef.
270°	−1	0	undef.	0	undef.	−1

How to read trigonometric and logarithmic tables

If you have a moderately good calculator, the values of logarithmic and trigonometric functions can be obtained by pushing the correct keys. If you do not have a calculator with such special function keys, you need to be able to read tables of values. Such tables are usually given in concise formats to enable them to contain as much information as possible. Most tables use the methods outlined below.

Trigonometric tables

Here is small section of a typical trigonometric table:

θ Deg.	Sin θ	Cos θ	Tan θ	Cot θ	Sec θ	Csc θ	
30°00′	.5000	.8660	.5774	1.7321	1.155	2.000	60°00′
10′	.5025	.8646	.5812	1.7205	1.157	1.990	50′
20′	.5050	.8631	.5851	1.7090	1.159	1.980	40′
30′	.5075	.8616	.5890	1.6977	1.161	1.970	30′
40′	.5100	.8601	.5930	1.6864	1.163	1.961	20′
50′	.5125	.8587	.5969	1.6753	1.165	1.951	10′
31°00′	.5150	.8572	.6009	1.6643	1.167	1.942	59°00′
10′	.5175	.8557	.6048	1.6534	1.169	1.932	50′
20′	.5200	.8542	.6088	1.6426	1.171	1.923	40′
30′	.5225	.8526	.6128	1.6319	1.173	1.914	30′
40′	.5250	.8511	.6168	1.6212	1.175	1.905	20′
50′	.5275	.8496	.6208	1.6107	1.177	1.896	10′
32°00′	.5299	.8480	.6249	1.6003	1.179	1.887	58°00′
10′	.5324	.8465	.6289	1.5900	1.181	1.878	50′
	Cos θ	Sin θ	Cot θ	Tan θ	Csc θ	Sec θ	θ Deg.

Notice that this table has column "headings" at both the top and the bottom. Because the sine and cosine, tangent and cotangent, and secant and cosecant are co-functions, as the values of one member of each pair increase from 0° to 90°, the other function in the pair takes on the same values in reverse order, from 90° to 0°. Therefore, one entry can serve two purposes, cutting the length of the table in half. For example, to find cos 30°, locate the column labeled Cos θ at the *top* of the page and 30° 00′ at the *left* of the page (30° 00′ is read "thirty degrees zero minutes"; one minute is $\frac{1}{60}$ of one degree). Where this column and row intersect, at .8660, is the value of cos 30°.

The same procedure works for all functions of angles of 45° or less.

For angles between 45° and 90°, start at the bottom and right instead of at the top and left. To find tan 59° 20′, first locate Tan θ at the *bottom* of the page. Then, looking from *bottom to top* first, find 59° 00′ in the *right-hand* column; keep traveling *up* that column until you get to 20′. Now look for the intersection of the row and column. If you have been careful, you should find the value of tan 59° 20′ to be 1.6864.

Logarithmic tables

N	0	1	2	3	4	5	6	7	8	9
5.5	7404	7412	7419	7427	7435	7443	7451	7459	7466	7474
5.6	7482	7490	7497	7505	7513	7520	7528	7536	7543	7551
5.7	7559	7566	7574	7582	7589	7597	7604	7612	7619	7627
5.8	7634	7642	7649	7657	7664	7672	7697	7686	7694	7701
5.9	7709	7716	7723	7731	7738	7745	7752	7760	7767	7774
6.0	7782	7789	7796	7803	7810	7818	7825	7832	7839	7846
6.1	7853	7860	7868	7875	7882	7889	7896	7903	7910	7917

Logarithmic tables are often condensed to give the logs of numbers from 1.00 to 9.99 directly. For numbers outside that range, you must make adjustments. This is the top of the second page of such a table.

To find a number such as 5.5, find 5.5 in the left column. Log 5.5 is the number in that row immediately following; that is, it is the number in the column headed 0. Although the number shown in that column is 7404, it is read as 0.7404, as all the logarithms between 1.00 and 9.99 are between 0 and 1. In fact, this is the approximate value of log 5.5, for most logarithms are irrational numbers.

To find log 5.56, look in the column headed 6 and the row labeled 5.5. The entry is 7451, or 0.7451.

For numbers less than 1.00 and greater than 9.99, treat the entry as a *mantissa* and find the *characteristic* of the logarithm. The easiest way to do this is to write the number whose logarithm you are finding in scientific notation. For example, to find the logarithm of 572, first write 572 as 5.72×10^2. The *characteristic* is the exponent of 10—in this case, 2. The *mantissa* is the logarithm of 5.72, which you know how to find in the table. The logarithm is the sum of the characteristic and the mantissa or 2.7574.

Mantissas are always kept positive. If the characteristic is negative, as it is for a number between 0 and 1.00, the method is to write the characteristic as a difference. 10 is commonly subtracted from a positive number to show the logarithm. For example, to find log 0.0584, first rewrite in scientific notation as 5.84×10^{-4}. The characteristic -4 is rewritten as $6 - 10$. The mantissa is 0.7664, so the logarithm is $6.7664 - 10$.

Interpolation.

If a function of an angle *between* what is listed in a table is desired, then *interpolation* can be employed. This is a method that assumes that the values between the values in the table increase as if they were proportional to the distance from the listed values. Interpolation gives approximate values.

Find sin 39°42′.

A. Note that 39°42′ is between 39° and 40°. In particular, it is $\frac{42}{60}$ of the way from 39° to 40°.

B. Find the corresponding values in the table.

$$\sin 39° = 0.6293$$
$$\sin 40° = 0.6428$$

C. Find the difference between the values from step B.

$$0.6428 - 0.6293 = 0.0135$$

D. Multiply the difference by the ratio from step A.

$$(\tfrac{42}{60})(0.0135) = 0.0095$$

to the nearest ten thousandth.

E. Note that the sin values increase from 0° to 90°, so you must *add* 0.0095 to sin 39°.

$$\sin 39°42' = 0.6293 + 0.0095 = 0.6388$$

Find cos 39°42′.

A. Since the cosine values decrease from 0° to 90°, the interpolation must be worked in a way opposite to that of the previous problem.

The ratio that you want is the same, however: $\frac{42}{60}$.

B.

$$\cos 39° = 0.7771$$
$$\cos 40° = 0.7660$$

C. $0.7771 - 0.7660 = 0.0111$

D. $(\frac{42}{60})(0.0111) = 0.0078$ to the nearest ten thousandth.

E. Subtract the value found in step D from the value of sin 39°.

$$\sin 39°42' = 0.7771 - 0.0078 = 0.7693$$

Solving problems.

Trigonometry can be used to solve problems; it also has many uses in higher mathematics. For most people, the first encounter with trigonometric functions is in relation to finding distances or heights that cannot be measured directly. Most problems of *indirect measurement* are solved by knowing one angle and side of a right triangle; from these it is possible to find other angles or sides.

A man stood at point *A* on one side of a river (see illustration) and noted a small tree, point *B*, across the river. He turned 90° to the right, walked 100 meters to point *C*, and then found the angle of sight to the tree to be 63°. Find *AB*, the original distance of the man from the tree.

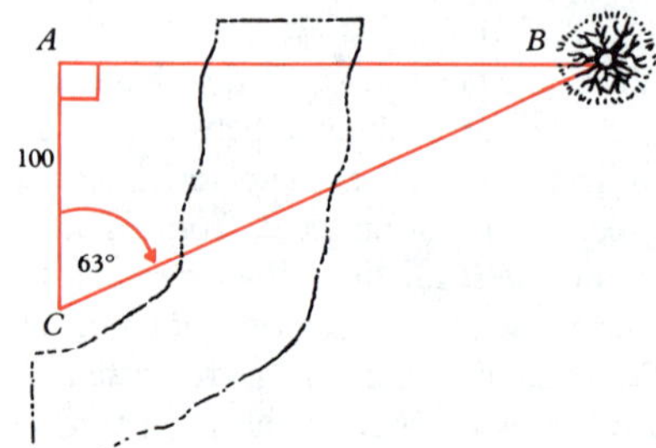

A. *ABC* is a right triangle, so the trigonometric ratios can be used as if you were using a graph. That is, *AB*/*AC* corresponds to the tangent ratio y/x on the graph for the given angle of 63°.

$$\tan 63° = \frac{AB}{AC}$$

B. From the table, or using a calculator, you find that tan 63° is about 1.9626. You know that *AC* is 100 meters, so

$$1.9626 = \frac{AB}{100}$$

C. Solve the equation.

$$AB = 196.26$$

Therefore, *AB* is 196 meters to the nearest meter.

Find the angle θ that a line makes with the x axis if the slope of the line is 0.6124.

A. The slope is the y distance over the x distance, which is also the tangent of the angle. Thus, $\tan \theta = 0.6124$.

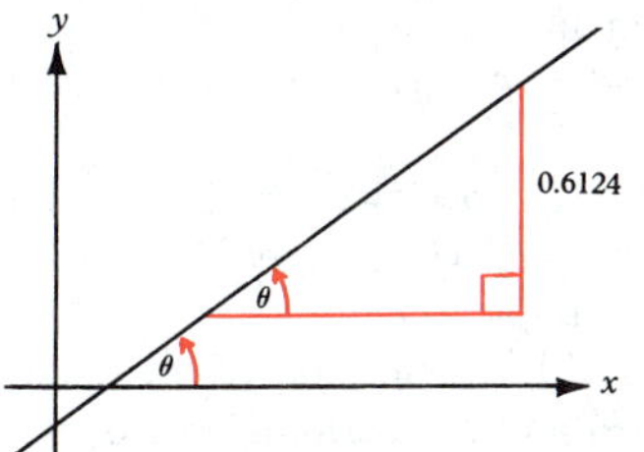

B. If you have a calculator that gives angles from the values of the trigonometric functions, get the value of θ from the calculator. Otherwise, use a table. However, the exact value 0.6124 is not in the table, so interpolate to find the angle.

$\tan 31° = 0.6009$

and $\tan 32° = 0.6249$

are the closest values to 0.6124 in the table.

C. $0.6249 - 0.6009 = 0.0240$

$0.6124 - 0.6009 = 0.0115$

Therefore, the angle desired is $\frac{0.0115}{0.024}$ of the way from 31° to 32°.

$(\frac{115}{240})(60) = 28.75$

Hence, $\theta = 31°29'$ to the nearest minute. Note that if you had used a calculator, you would have gotten the answer as 31.479°, since calculators use decimals instead of minutes and seconds.

Trigonometric graphs. So far you have measured angles in degrees, minutes, and seconds (or in degrees and decimal parts of a degree). Angles in trigonometry are often measured in *radians.* A radian is the measure of a central angle that cuts off an arc whose length is equal to the radius of the circle. Therefore, $360° = 2\pi$ radians.

From this you can calculate that

1 radian is about 57.29578 degrees

or 1 radian is about 57° 17′ 45″

and 1 degree is about 0.01745 radians.

Graphs of the trigonometric functions generally use size of angles in radians as the horizontal axis and values of a trigonometric function as the vertical axis.

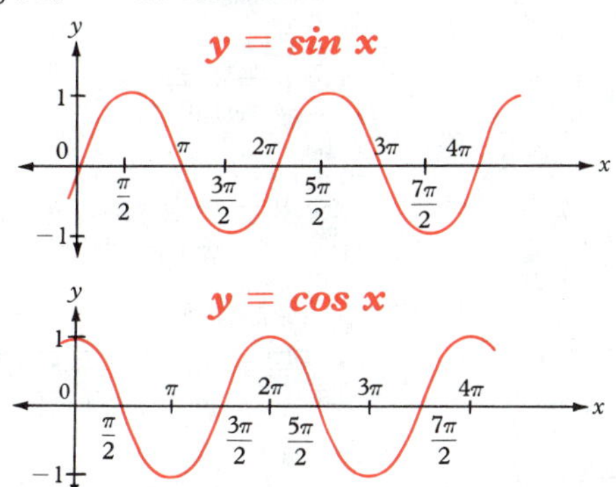

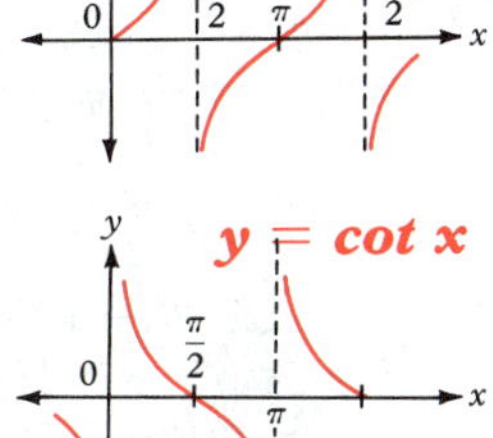

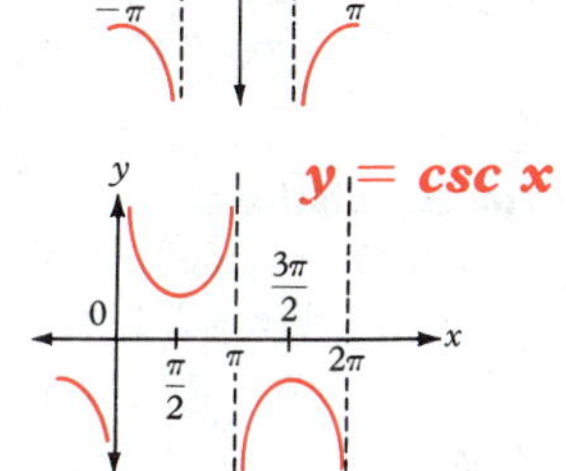

Graph $y = \sin x$.

A. If you have a calculator that gives the values of the trigonometric functions for angles measured in radians, you can use the calculator to plot the points.

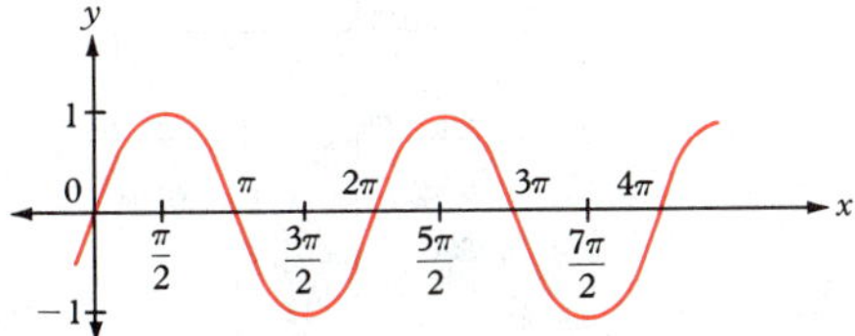

B. Otherwise, find the values in terms of fractions of radians. Notice that an angle of 90° corresponds with $\pi/4$ radians. The other values found in the box on page 228 can be found similarly. Here is a table of these values:

x	y
0	0
$\pi/6$	$\frac{1}{2} = 0.5$
$\pi/4$	$\frac{\sqrt{2}}{2}$ = about 0.7
$\pi/3$	$\frac{\sqrt{3}}{2}$ = about 0.9
$\pi/2$	1
π	0
$3\pi/2$	-1

Plot these points and a few more. Connect with a smooth curve.

Trigonometric functions. From the graphs, you can see that all trigonometric functions repeat their values at least every 360°. Also, the tangent and cotangent repeat every 180°. The distance between the repeated functional values is the *period* of the function. Thus, the period of the sine, cosine, secant, and cosecant functions is 360°, or 2π radians, as can be seen in the box on this page. The period of the tangent and cotangent functions is 180°, or π radians.

The graphs can be extended to the left of the vertical axes to obtain values of the trigonometric functions for the negative numbers. For each function, the value of the negative of an angle is either the same as the value of the angle or it is the opposite of that value. If it is the same, the function is an *even* function.

$$\cos 30° = \cos(-30°) = \sqrt{3}/2$$

illustrates that the cosine is an even function. If the value for the negative of an angle is the negative of the value for the angle, the function is *odd.* The sine is an odd function, so

$$\sin(-30°) = -\sin 30° = -\tfrac{1}{2}.$$

One other relationship that is easily established from the graphs is that both the sine and cosine functions have maximum and minimum values. The maximum value of a periodic function is its *amplitude,* so the functions $y = \sin x$ and $y = \cos x$ have amplitudes of 1.

In general, $y = a \sin bx$ and $y = a \cos bx$ have the period $2\pi/b$ and amplitude a, where a and b are both positive. Consider, for example, the graphs of $y = 3/4 \sin 2x$ and $y = 3 \sin x/2$. The amplitude of the graph of $y = 3/4 \sin 2x$ is 3/4 and the period is π. For the graph of $y = 3 \sin x/2$, the amplitude is 3 and the period is 4π.

Trigonometric identities

Reciprocal relations

$\sin\theta = \dfrac{1}{\csc\theta}$ $\quad\cos\theta = \dfrac{1}{\sec\theta}$ $\quad\tan\theta = \dfrac{1}{\cot\theta}$

$\csc\theta = \dfrac{1}{\sin\theta}$ $\quad\sec\theta = \dfrac{1}{\cos\theta}$ $\quad\cot\theta = \dfrac{1}{\tan\theta}$

Complementary cofunctions

$\sin\theta = \cos(90° - \theta)$ $\quad\tan\theta = \cot(90° - \theta)$ $\quad\sec\theta = \csc(90° - \theta)$

where $0° < \theta < 90°$

Periodic relations

$\sin(\theta + n360°) = \sin\theta$
$\cos(\theta + n360°) = \cos\theta$

$\tan(\theta + n360°) = \tan\theta$
$\tan(\theta + n180°) = \tan\theta$
$\cot(\theta + n360°) = \cot\theta$
$\cot(\theta + n180°) = \cot\theta$

$\sec(\theta + n360°) = \sec\theta$
$\csc(\theta + n360°) = \csc\theta$

Negative angles

$\sin(-\theta) = -\sin\theta$
$\csc(-\theta) = -\csc\theta$

$\cos(-\theta) = \cos\theta$
$\sec(-\theta) = \sec\theta$

$\tan(-\theta) = -\tan\theta$
$\cot(-\theta) = -\cot\theta$

Fundamental identities

$\tan\theta = \dfrac{\sin\theta}{\cos\theta}$ $\quad\cot\theta = \dfrac{\cos\theta}{\sin\theta}$

$\sin\theta = \tan\theta\cos\theta$
$\sin^2\theta + \cos^2\theta = 1$
$\sec^2\theta - \tan^2\theta = 1$
$\csc^2\theta - \cot^2\theta = 1$

$\cos\theta = \cot\theta\sin\theta$
$1 - \sin^2\theta = \cos^2\theta$
$1 + \tan^2\theta = \sec^2\theta$
$1 + \cot^2\theta = \csc^2\theta$

Trigonometric identities.

If a statement involving the relationship of trigonometric functions of the same angle is true for *all* defined values of that angle, then the statement is called an *identity.* Many common identities are shown in the box on page 232. The fundamental identities can be discovered from the definition of the functions or with the use of the Pythagorean theorem. Other identities are then proved on the basis of the reciprocal relationships or the fundamental identities.

Proving an identity is the process of verifying that a statement is true for all defined values of an angle by using algebraic factoring and simplification, and by substitution of the fundamental identities. Either transform one side of the identity into the other or reduce both sides to an expression in which it is obvious that all the defined values are true. You can operate on both sides of an equation simultaneously (for example, $\sin\theta$ to both sides) as long as the operation is reversible and yields an equation with the same solution. It is usually easier to work with the more complicated side of an identity first.

Verify the identity $\sin\theta\,(1 + \cot^2\theta) = \csc\theta$.

METHOD 1

A. Note that $\cot^2\theta$ means $(\cot\theta)^2$. One useful way to solve identities is to change both sides to sines and cosines. For example, every trigonometric function can be expressed in terms of sines.

$$\sin\theta = \sin\theta$$

$$\cos\theta = \pm\sqrt{1 - \sin^2\theta}$$

$$\tan\theta = \frac{\pm\sin\theta}{\sqrt{a - \sin^2\theta}}$$

$$\cot\theta = \frac{\pm\sqrt{1 - \sin^2\theta}}{\sin\theta}$$

$$\sec\theta = \frac{\pm 1}{\sqrt{1 - \sin^2\theta}}$$

$$\csc\theta = \frac{1}{\sin\theta}$$

The appropriate $\pm$ sign is used according to the quadrant of the angle. Try to change each side of the identity to functions of $\sin\theta$.

B. $\sin\theta\,(1 + \cot^2\theta) = \csc\theta$

$\sin\theta\,(\csc^2\theta) = \csc\theta$

$$\sin\theta\,\frac{1}{\sin^2\theta} = \frac{1}{\sin\theta}$$

$$\frac{1}{\sin\theta} = \frac{1}{\sin\theta}$$

METHOD 2

A. Multiply both sides of the identity by $\csc\theta$.
$\csc\theta\,(\sin\theta(1 + \cot^2\theta)) = \csc\theta\,(\csc\theta)$

B. Then use algebra and the fundamental identities to transform the left side of the equation to match the right.

$$\csc\theta\,(\sin\theta(1 + \cot^2\theta)) = \csc^2\theta$$
$$(\csc\theta\sin\theta)(1 + \cot^2\theta) =$$
$$1 + \cot^2\theta =$$
$$\csc^2\theta = \csc^2\theta$$

Verify the identity $\dfrac{\sin x + \tan x}{\cot x + \csc x} = \sin x \tan x$.

$$\frac{\sin x + \tan x}{\cot x + \csc x} = \sin x \tan x$$

$$\frac{\sin x + \dfrac{\sin x}{\cos x}}{\dfrac{\cos x}{\sin x} + \dfrac{1}{\sin x}} = \sin x\,\frac{\sin x}{\cos x}$$

$$\frac{\sin x\cos x + \sin x}{\cos x} \div \frac{\cos x + 1}{\sin x} = \frac{\sin^2 x}{\cos x}$$

$$\frac{\sin x\,(\cos x + 1)}{\cos x} \cdot \frac{\sin x}{\cos x + 1} = \frac{\sin^2 x}{\cos x}$$

$$\frac{\sin^2 x}{\cos x} = \frac{\sin^2 x}{\cos x}$$

Inverse functions. The *inverse trigonometric functions* can be indicated by writing "arc"; as in $y = \text{arc sin } x$, or by using a superscript of -1, as in $y = \sin^{-1} x$. Inverses are defined for *principal values* to keep them single valued.

If $x = \sin y$, then $y = \sin^{-1} x$, $-\pi/2 \leq y \leq \pi/2$.
If $x = \cos y$, then $y = \cos^{-1} x$, $0 \leq y \leq \pi$.
If $x = \tan y$, then $y = \tan^{-1} x$, $-\pi/2 \leq y \leq \pi/2$.

Find y if $y = \sin^{-1} 0.5$.

The equation $y = \sin^{-1} 0.5$ means y = the angle whose sine is 0.5.

Since $\sin 30°$ is $\frac{1}{2}$, or 0.5, $y = 30°$.

In radians, $y = \pi/6$.

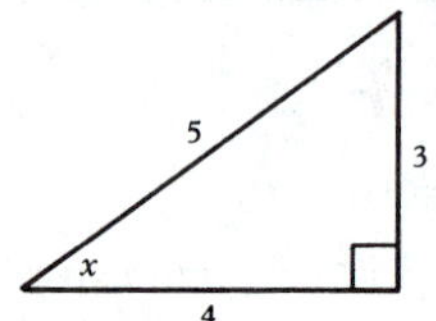

Find $\tan (\cos^{-1} \frac{4}{5})$.

A. If $\cos x = \frac{4}{5}$, then a right triangle with angle x as one of its acute angles must be the 3-4-5 triangle.

B. Since the tangent ratio in that triangle is the side opposite over the side adjacent,

$$\tan (\cos^{-1} \tfrac{4}{5}) = \tfrac{3}{4}$$

Trigonometric formulas

Sums and differences of angles

$\sin (A + B) = \sin A \cos B + \cos A \sin B$

$\cos (A + B) = \cos A \cos B - \sin A \sin B$

$$\tan (A + B) = \frac{\tan A + \tan B}{1 - \tan A \tan B}$$

$\sin (A - B) = \sin A \cos B - \cos A \sin B$

$\cos (A - B) = \cos A \cos B + \sin A \sin B$

Sums and differences of functions

$$\sin A + \sin B = 2 \sin \frac{A + B}{2} \cos \frac{A - B}{2}$$

$$\sin A - \sin B = 2 \sin \frac{A - B}{2} \cos \frac{A + B}{2}$$

$$\cos A + \cos B = 2 \cos \frac{A - B}{2} \cos \frac{A + B}{2}$$

$$\cos A - \cos B = -2 \sin \frac{A + B}{2} \sin \frac{A - B}{2}$$

Double angles

$\sin 2A = 2 \sin A \cos A$

$\cos 2A = \cos^2 A - \sin^2 A$

$$\tan 2A = \frac{2 \tan A}{1 - \tan^2 A}$$

Triple angles

$\sin 3A = 3 \sin A - 4 \sin^3 A$

$\cos 3A = 4 \cos^3 A - 3 \cos A$

Half angles

$$\sin \frac{A}{2} = \sqrt{\frac{1 - \cos A}{2}}$$

$$\cos \frac{A}{2} = \sqrt{\frac{1 + \cos A}{2}}$$

$$\tan \frac{A}{2} = \sqrt{\frac{1 - \cos A}{1 + \cos A}}$$

Products of functions

$\sin A \sin B = \frac{1}{2} (\cos (A - B) - \cos (A + B))$

$\cos A \cos B = \frac{1}{2} (\cos (A - B) + \cos (A + B))$

$\sin A \cos B = \frac{1}{2} (\sin (A + B) + \sin (A - B))$

If a triangle ABC has sides whose lengths are a, b, and c, with a opposite $\angle A$, b opposite $\angle B$, and c opposite $\angle C$, then

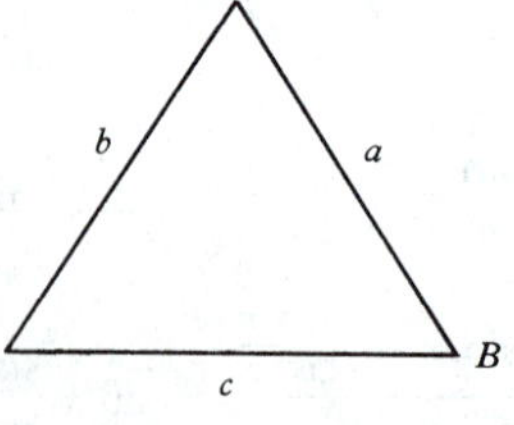

Law of sines

$$\frac{a}{\sin A} = \frac{b}{\sin B} = \frac{c}{\sin C}$$

Law of cosines

$a^2 = b^2 + c^2 - 2bc \cos A$

Area of triangle

Area $ABC = \frac{1}{2} ab \sin C$

Problem solving and applications

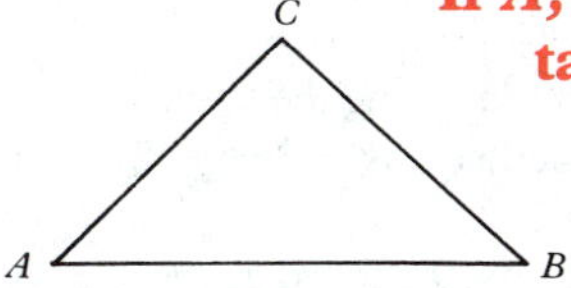

If *A, B,* and *C* are the angles of a triangle, show that $\tan A + \tan B + \tan C = \tan A \tan B \tan C$.

A. In any triangle angles A, B, and C sum to 180°, so $C = 180° - (A + B)$.

B. The tangent is periodic with a period of 180°, so $\tan x = \tan (x - 180°)$.

C. Finally, the tangent is an odd function, so
$\tan(-x) = -\tan x$.
Combine this with
$(x - 180°) = -(180° - x)$
and step B to give
$\tan(180° - x) = -\tan x$.
Thus,
$\tan C = \tan(180° - (A + B))$
$= -\tan(A + B)$

D. Proceed by the same methods you would use to verify an identity.

$$\tan A + \tan B + \tan C = \tan A + \tan B - \tan(A + B)$$
$$= \tan A + \tan B - \frac{\tan A + \tan B}{1 - \tan A \tan B}$$
$$= (\tan A + \tan B)\left(1 - \frac{1}{1 - \tan A \tan B}\right)$$
$$= (\tan A + \tan B)\frac{1 - \tan A \tan B - 1}{1 - \tan A \tan B}$$
$$= \tan A \tan B\left(-\frac{\tan A + \tan B}{1 - \tan A \tan B}\right)$$
$$= \tan A \tan B(-\tan(A + B))$$
$$= \tan A \tan B \tan C$$

Two observation posts, *A* and *B,* spot the flash of an enemy gun, *G,* at angles of 40° and 76° respectively. Posts *A* and *B* are 3 kilometers apart. Find the distance, *BG,* to the gun from post *B.*

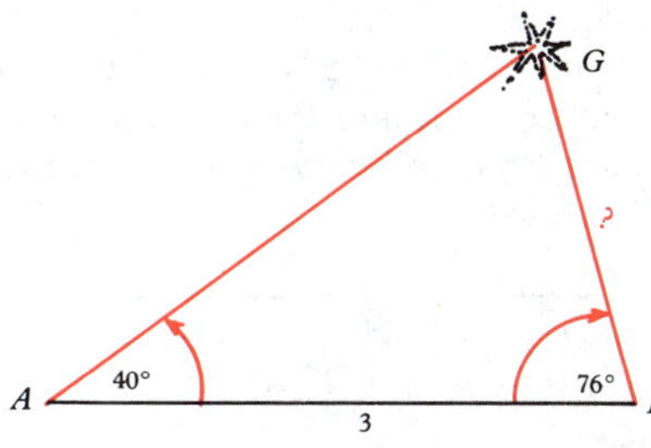

A. Note that the angle AGB must be 64°.

B. Use the law of sines to get

$$\frac{BG}{\sin 40°} = \frac{3}{\sin 64°}.$$

C.

$$BG = 3\frac{\sin 40°}{\sin 64°}$$
$$= \text{about } 3\frac{0.6428}{0.8988}$$
$$= \text{about } 2.15$$

The distance is 2.15 kilometers to the nearest hundredth of a kilometer.

A ship sails from port *P* on a bearing of N35°E at a rate of 12 kilometers per hour. In what length of time will the ship be 10 kilometers from a lighthouse that is 5 kilometers due west from the port?

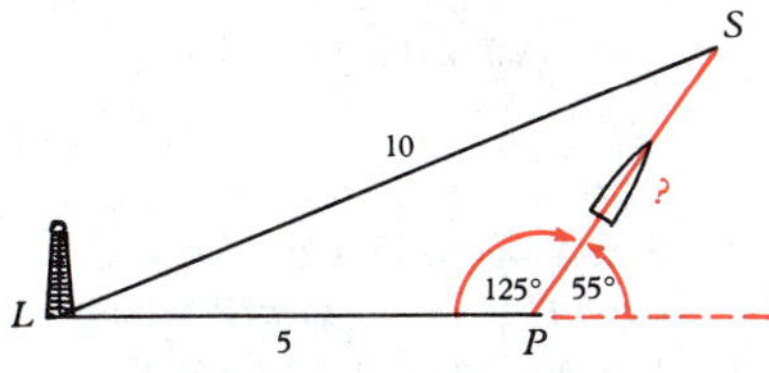

A. The heading of N35°E means that angle LPS is 125°. Use the law of cosines.

B. $\cos 125° = -\cos 55°$
From a table, $-\cos 55°$ is about -0.5736.

C. Using the law of cosines,
$LS^2 = LP^2 + PS^2 - 2(LP)(PS)\cos P$
$10^2 = 5^2 + PS^2 - 2(5)(PS)(-0.5736)$
$PS^2 + 5.736\,PS - 75 = 0$

D. The quadratic formula gives two solutions, approximately $PS = 6.2$ or $PS = -11.9$, so PS is about 6.2.

E. This means that the ship will take about (6.2)/12, or 0.52, hours to reach the designated location.

Calculus

The branch of mathematics called *calculus* (or *the calculus*) is customarily divided into two main parts, *differential* and *integral* calculus, although the techniques of calculus also involve work with infinite sequences and series. In fact, calculus is merely a part of a larger branch of mathematics that uses these same techniques. This branch of mathematics is usually called *analysis*. The major theorems of calculus, and the techniques for applying its operations to problem solving, are based on the concept of *limit*. The limit concept is basic to the development of the two main operations of the calculus that are not found in more elementary mathematics, namely *differentiation* and *integration*. In general, differentiation is used to determine instantaneous rate of change in one variable with respect to another; that is, the limit of the rate of change as the time of the change goes to zero. Similarly, integration is used to obtain an exact sum of an infinite number of parts; that is, the limit of the sum as the number of parts increases without bound.

Functions and relations. You have had some experience with the idea of a function in algebra (see page 196), but the concept of a function is much more important in calculus, so it must be described in more detail. A function such as $f(x) = x^2$ can be thought of as a rule that connects two sets of numbers. The rule is clear in the sense that, if you know a number in the set for x^2, you can determine exactly one number in the set for $f(x)$. If this is not possible (as in $y^2 = x$, where knowing the value of x as, say, 4 does not tell you whether y is $+2$ or -2), then the rule is not a function.

Rules that are not functions are called *relations*, but functions are also relations; that is, every rule connecting two sets of numbers is a relation. Frequently, this idea is expressed by using ordered pairs. All sets of ordered pairs illustrate a connection between the set of first members and the set of second members, so every set of ordered pairs shows a relation. The pairs (1, 1), (2, 4), (3, 9), and so forth, are part of the set that shows the function $f(x) = x^2$, and the pairs (1, 1), (1, -1), (4, 2), (4, -2), and so forth are part of the set that shows the relation $y^2 = x$. Notice that the pairs for the function do not repeat any first members. One way to define a function is as a relation shown by a set of ordered pairs that have no first members in common.

The variable that is connected with the first members of the ordered pairs (usually x) is called the *independent variable*. Often $f(x)$ is replaced with a variable (usually y), which is then called the *dependent variable*. The set of first members of the ordered pairs—that is, the set of values of the independent variable—is called the *domain* of the function. The set of second members of the ordered pairs—the set of values of $f(x)$ or the values of the dependent variable—is called the *range* of the function. In calculus, the domain is generally either the real or the complex numbers (see box on page 198). In this discussion, only the real numbers will be used.

If x is the independent variable, which of the following is not a function:
$x + y = 5$ or $x^2 + y^2 = 25$?

Use the *vertical-line test*.

If a vertical line can intersect the graph at more than one point, the relation is not a function.

Since the graph of $x^2 + y^2 = 25$ is a circle, it is not a function.

What is the domain and range of each of the following functions:
$f(x) = x^2$, $f(x) = \sin x$, and $f(x) = \tan x$?

A. $f(x) = x^2$ is defined for all values of x, so the domain is the set of real numbers. The range, however, is the set of non-negative real numbers, since no real numbers have squares that are negative.

B. The sine of x exists for all real numbers, so the domain of $f(x) = \sin x$ is the set of real numbers; the range, however, is the set of numbers y such that $1 \leq y \leq 1$.

C. The tangent of x does not exist for $(2n - 1)\,\pi/2$ where n is any integer, so these values are excluded from the domain of $f(x) = \tan x$. The range, however, includes all the real numbers.

The limit of a sequence. All analysis is ultimately based on the concept of the limit of a *sequence* (see box on page 217 for some basic formulas related to sequences). A sequence is the range of a function whose domain is the set of natural numbers, 1, 2, 3, . . ., arranged in the same order as the domain elements. Thus, 2, 4, 6, . . ., $2n$, . . . is the sequence of even numbers defined by the function $f(n) = 2n$. The expression that defines the function is called the *general term* of the sequence. Note that 4, 6, 2, . . ., $2n$, . . . is not the same sequence, because order is considered as part of the sequence.

What is the limit of the sequence $1, \frac{1}{2}, \frac{1}{3}, \frac{1}{4}, \ldots, 1/n, \ldots$?

A. The limit is determined as n grows larger without bound. As n grows larger, $1/n$ grows smaller. In fact, although $1/n$ is never exactly 0, it seems to be getting closer and closer to 0 as n becomes larger.

B. After n reaches a certain value, it is possible to show that all subsequent (that is, larger) values of n will leave $1/n$ closer to 0 than that value. For example, when n reaches 1,000,000, all values of $1/n$ for $n > 1{,}000{,}000$ will be closer to 0 than to 1/1,000,000. This condition shows that the limit of the sequence is 0. Another way to say the same thing is to say that the sequence *converges* to 0.

What is the limit of the sequence $\frac{1}{2}, \frac{2}{3}, \frac{3}{4}, \ldots, n/(n+1) \ldots$?

A. Rewrite the general term as

$$\frac{n}{n+1} = 1 - \frac{1}{n+1}$$

B. The limit of $\frac{1}{n+1}$ as n goes to infinity is 0 by the same arguments used in the preceding problem. This is written

$$\lim_{n\to\infty} \frac{1}{n+1} = 0.$$

Therefore, you have

$$\lim_{n\to\infty}\left(1 - \frac{1}{n+1}\right) = 1$$

What is lim a^n where a is some real number?

A. This is the same as asking for the limit of the sequence $a^1, a^2, a^3, \ldots, a^n, \ldots$ for some real number. There are several cases to consider. If $|a|$ is 1, if $|a|$ is less than 1, and if $|a|$ is greater than 1.

B. If a is 1, then the sequence is $1, 1, 1, \ldots, 1^n, \ldots$. This is a *constant sequence.* All terms of the sequence have the same value. Therefore, the terms are all very close to (in fact, equal to) the same number, in this case 1. Therefore, when $a = 1$, $\lim_{n\to\infty} a^n = 1$

C. If a is -1, then the sequence is $1, -1, 1, -1, \ldots, (-1)^n, \ldots$. This sequence never becomes arbitrarily close to any number, as each term is two units away from the preceding term. Therefore, there is no limit when a is -1.

D. If a is greater than 1, then the terms all increase. This sequence also does not have a limit, although it is sometimes stated that the sequence converges to infinity, which can be written

$$\lim_{n\to\infty} a^n = \infty \quad (a > 1)$$

E. If a is less than -1, the terms become farther and farther apart as n increases. This sequence also does not converge to a limit.

F. If $|a| < 1$, it can be shown that the limit will always exist and that it will always be 0. It is easy to see that a sequence such as the one formed when $a = \frac{1}{2}$ will converge to 0, for the terms become small quite fast, $\frac{1}{2}, \frac{1}{4}, \frac{1}{8}, \frac{1}{16}, \frac{1}{32}, \ldots$ but we will not prove that here.

The sum of an infinite series. A series is the indicated sum of a sequence. It is "indicated" because the +'s are still shown. The sequence of the first five positive even numbers is 2, 4, 6, 8, 10, so the series of the first five positive even numbers is $2 + 4 + 6 + 8 + 10$. The sum of such a *finite* series is easy to find by ordinary addition. It is just the ordinary sum, in this case 30.

For an infinite series, the sum is harder to define because there is no ordinary way to add an infinite number of addends. The *sum of an infinite series* is the limit of the sequence of partial sums, formed by adding one additional term of the series each time to form a new term of the sequence—if such a limit exists. If such a limit does not exist, an infinite series has no sum. For example, the infinite series of positive even numbers is $2 + 4 + 6 + \ldots + 2n + \ldots$. Its associated sequence of partial sums is $2, 2 + 4, 2 + 4 + 6, \ldots, 2 + 4 + 6 + \ldots + 2n, \ldots$ or $2, 6, 12, \ldots, n(n + 1), \ldots$. (You can obtain the general term from the formula for the sum of a finite arithmetic series on page 217.) It is easy to see that this infinite sequence converges to infinity; hence, the series of positive even numbers has no sum.

Based on the formula on page 217 for the sum of a finite geometric series, show that the sum of an infinite series given on that page is correct according to the definition just given.

A. The sequence of partial sums of a geometric series is

$a, a + ar, a + ar^2, \ldots,$
$(a - ar^n)/(1 - r), \ldots$

provided that r is not equal to 1.

B. The sum of an infinite geometric series, then, is the limit of the sequence in step A. To find that limit, begin by rewriting the general term as

$$\frac{a - ar^n}{1 - r} = \frac{a}{1 - r} - a \cdot \frac{r^n}{1 - r}.$$

The only part of the expression on the right that changes as n changes is

$$\frac{r^n}{1 - r}$$

If $|r|$ is less than 1, as was noted on page 237, then r^n has the limit 0 as n increases.

Thus, $a \cdot \frac{r^n}{1 - r}$ also goes to 0 at the limit. The remaining expression,

$$\frac{a}{1 - r}$$

is unchanged by changes in n, so the sum of the infinite geometric series is

$$\frac{a}{1 - r}$$

if $|r| < 1$. If $|r| > 1$, then there is no sum.

One of the many uses of infinite series is to provide definitions of some important *irrational numbers*. The irrational numbers are real numbers that are not rational (see box on page 198). You are familiar with the definition of π in terms of the circumference of a circle, for example. Since π is irrational, it can only be expressed with an infinite decimal in the Hindu-Arabic system. Expressing π as an infinite series, however, has an advantage over the infinite-decimal representation: you can use additional terms of the series to calculate π as closely as you like. For example, one series used for π is

$$\frac{\pi}{4} = 1 - \frac{1}{3} + \frac{1}{5} - \frac{1}{7} + \ldots + \frac{-1^n}{2n - 1} + \ldots.$$

Another well-known irrational number that can be calculated from an infinite series is e.

$$e = 1 + \frac{1}{1} + \frac{1}{1 \cdot 2} + \frac{1}{1 \cdot 2 \cdot 3} + \ldots.$$

Also, logarithms can be calculated in this way. For example, the logarithm of 2 to the base e has the particularly happy series representation

$$\log_e 2 = 1 - \frac{1}{2} + \frac{1}{3} - \frac{1}{4} \ldots + \frac{-1^n}{n} + \ldots.$$

Infinite series are also used regularly for representing the rational numbers, since every nonterminating decimal is an infinite series. When you see $\frac{1}{3}$ written as $0.333\ldots$, the meaning is

$$\frac{1}{3} = \frac{3}{10} + \frac{3}{10^2} + \frac{3}{10^3} + \ldots + \frac{3}{10^n} + \ldots.$$

It is easy to show that all nonterminating decimals converge and that all repeating nonterminating decimals will converge to a rational number. It is somewhat more difficult to prove that nonrepeating, nonterminating decimals converge to irrational numbers (although that result is true and is sometimes used as the definition of irrational numbers).

The limit of a function.

If $f(x)$ has a finite real-number value for all x not equal to c in an interval containing c, then the *limit of the function* $f(x)$ as x approaches c can be defined. The limit will not exist, however, unless the conditions of the definition are met. Informally, the definition is that a number L is the limit of $f(x)$ if $f(x)$ can be shown to be within any challenged closeness to L when x is chosen to be close enough to c. Formally, the definition is given in terms of two positive numbers labeled ϵ (the lower-case Greek letter epsilon) and δ (the lower-case Greek letter delta). The limit as x goes to c of $f(x)$ is L if and only if for any $\epsilon > 0$ there exists $\delta > 0$ such that, when $0 < |x - c| < \delta$, then $|f(x) - L| < \epsilon$.

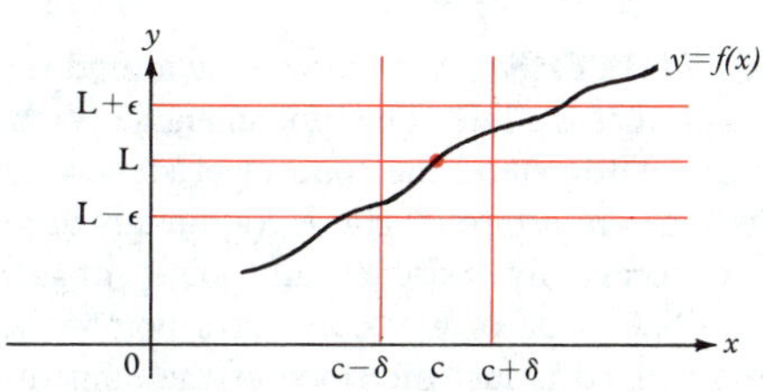

The meaning of the formal definition can be seen more clearly in the illustration, which shows how ϵ and δ are used to define a *neighborhood* around $f(c)$, the value of $f(x)$ at $x = c$. As ϵ is chosen to be smaller and smaller, δ can still be found so that $f(x)$ is still in the vicinity of L (where the vicinity is made formal by the size of ϵ).

What is the limit as x approaches $\frac{1}{2}$ of $f(x) = 2x + 1$?

A. Informally, it is easy to see that $\lim_{x \to \frac{1}{2}} 2x + 1 = 2$ since $2x$ is ever closer to 1 as x approaches $\frac{1}{2}$ from either side.

B. A more formal approach would be to note that if ϵ is some small number, then there exists another small number, δ, such that if

$$0 < |x - \frac{1}{2}| < \delta,$$

then $|2x + 1 - 2| < \epsilon$

In particular, if δ is equal to $\epsilon/2$, then when

$$|x - \frac{1}{2}| < \frac{\epsilon}{2} (= \delta)$$

it will always be true that

$$|2x + 1 - 2| < \epsilon.$$

What is the limit as x approaches $\frac{1}{2}$ of $g(x) = \dfrac{4x^2 - 1}{2x - 1}$?

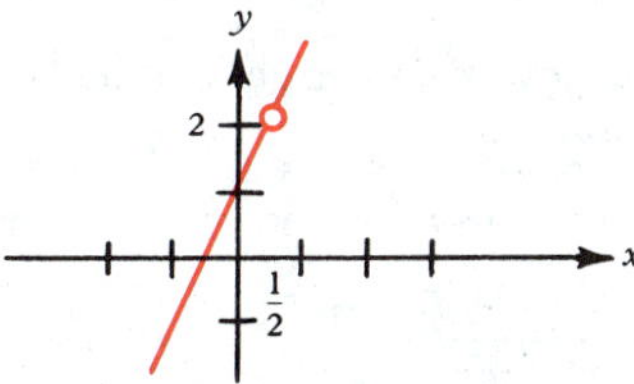

A. Note that $g(x)$ is the same as $f(x)$ in the previous problem, except that $f(x)$ is defined for $x = \frac{1}{2}$ and $g(x)$ is not defined for $x = \frac{1}{2}$. In other words, there is a "hole" at the point $(\frac{1}{2}, 2)$ on the graph of $g(x)$, not a point of the graph.

B. In the definition of a limit, however, there is no requirement that the limit L be a value of the function. Thus,

$$\lim_{n \to \frac{1}{2}} \frac{4x^2 - 1}{2x - 1} = 2$$

just as in the previous problem.

The two problems just given illustrate the difference between a *continuous* function and one that is not continuous. A function $f(x)$ is continuous at $x = c$ if $f(c)$ is defined and $\lim_{x \to c} f(x) = f(c)$.

The function $g(x)$ is not continuous at $\frac{1}{2}$ because $g(\frac{1}{2})$ is not defined. An example of a function that is defined for all real numbers but that has a discontinuity is $f(x) = -1$ for $x < 0$, $f(0) = 0$, and $f(x) = +1$ for $x > 0$. (NOTE: This is a single function $f(x)$ since it describes a set of ordered pairs in which no two of the pairs have the same first member.) Although this function is defined at $x = 0$, the limit as x approaches 0 does not exist.

In calculus, you will be most frequently concerned with functions that are continuous over all the real values of x between two given values, a set that is called an *interval.* A function is continuous over an interval from $x = a$ to $x = b$ if it is continuous at all x in $a < x < b$.

Which of the trigonometric functions are continuous?

Look at the graphs on page 231. Both the sine and cosine are continuous for all real numbers, but the other trigonometric functions have discontinuities at the places shown by dotted vertical lines.

Derivatives. You know how to find the slope of a graph that is a line. The fundamental notion of the derivative is to extend the concept of slope to include graphs that are arbitrary curves (although derivatives do not necessarily exist at all points of arbitrary curves). The slope of any curve at a point where the slope is defined is just the slope of the tangent to the curve. Except for circles, however, you do not have a definition of *tangent* to a curve. In fact, the tangent is the limit of a line through two points on the curve as the two points get closer and closer. Thus, in the figure, the tangent at point P is the limit of the line through Q as Q approaches P. The slope of the tangent is Δy over Δx (where Δ, the Greek capital delta, is a common mathematical abbreviation meaning "the change in"; thus, Δy is the change in the value of y from Q to P). As Q approaches P, both Δy and Δx approach 0, but the limit $\Delta y/\Delta x$ does not approach 0. This can be seen from the graph because the tangent to

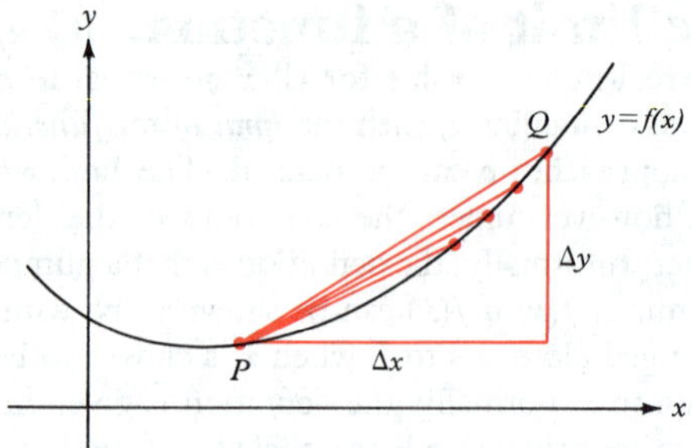

the curve (the dashed line) does not have a slope of 0.

It should be clear that the derivative does not exist if the curve has a sharp corner. For example, the graph of $|x| + |y| = 1$ is a square that has its corners at the points (0, 1), (1, 0), (0, −1), and (−1, 0). The tangent cannot exist at any of these corners, since there is no unique line that is approached as the two points get closer.

Limits and derivatives

Limit of a constant

$\lim_{x \to c} k = k$, where k is any constant

$\lim_{x \to c} k \cdot f(x) = k \cdot \lim_{x \to c} f(x)$

Derivative of a constant

If $y = k$, and k is a constant, $\frac{dy}{dx} = 0$

If $y = kx^n$, $\frac{dy}{dx} = nkx^{n-1}$

Sums, differences, products, quotients of limits

If $\lim_{x \to c} f(x) = L_1$ and $\lim_{x \to c} g(x) = L_2$,

$\lim_{x \to c} (f(x) + g(x)) = L_1 + L_2$

$\lim_{x \to c} (f(x) - g(x)) = L_1 - L_2$

$\lim_{x \to c} (f(x) \cdot g(x)) = L_1 \cdot L_2$

$\lim_{x \to c} (f(x)/g(x)) = L_1/L_2$ when $L_2 \neq 0$

Derivatives of sums, powers, products, and quotients of functions

If u and v are functions of x, and

if $y = u + v$, $\frac{dy}{dx} = \frac{du}{dx} + \frac{dv}{dx}$

if $y = u^n$, $\frac{dy}{dx} = nu^{n-1}(\frac{du}{dx})$

if $y = uv$, $\frac{dy}{dx} = u(\frac{dy}{dx}) + v(\frac{du}{dx})$

if $y = \frac{u}{v}$, $\frac{dy}{dx} = \frac{v(du/dx) - u(dv/dx)}{v^2}$

Derivatives of sine and cosine

If u is a function of x, and

if $y = \sin u$, $\frac{dy}{dx} = \cos u\,(\frac{du}{dx})$

if $y = \cos u$, $\frac{dy}{dx} = -\sin u\,(\frac{du}{dx})$

The chain rule

If x and y are functions of t, $\frac{dy}{dx} = \frac{dy/dt}{dx/dt}$

The derivative of $y = f(x)$ can be represented as either $f'(x)$ or as dy/dx. The formal definition is any one of the following:

$$f'(x) = \frac{dy}{dx} = \frac{df(x)}{dx}$$
$$= \lim_{x \to x_1} \frac{f(x_1) - f(x)}{x_1 - x}$$
$$= \lim_{h \to o} \frac{f(x + h) - f(x)}{h}$$
$$= \lim \Delta y/\Delta x.$$

The process of finding the derivative for a given function is called *differentiation.*

If the derivative of a function is taken twice (that is, if the derivative is treated as a function and then differentiated), the resulting *second derivative* is the rate of change of the rate of change. The second derivative of $y = f(x)$ is shown either as $f''(x)$ or as d^2y/dx^2.

A way to think about this in physical terms is to consider a function that gives the distance an object moves in x seconds. Then the first derivative of that function will give the velocity of the object and the second derivative will give the acceleration, which is the rate of change of the velocity.

Use the definition to find the derivative of $f(x) = x^2$.

A. In this case,
$$\frac{f(x_1) - f(x)}{x_1 - x} = \frac{x_1^2 - x^2}{x_1 - x}$$

B. If x_1 is not equal to x, the numerator equals
$$(x_1 - x)(x_1 + x)$$
and the factor $(x_1 - x)$ can be canceled, leaving $x_1 + x$.

C. Let x_1 approach x. Then the expression $x_1 + x$ will approach $x + x = 2x$. Therefore, if $f(x) = x^2$, then $f'(x) = 2x$.

Use the formulas in the box on page 240 to find the derivative of $y = (x^2 - 1)(x^2 + x)^{1/2}$.

A. The overall pattern of the function is a product, of the form $y = uv$, but u is a sum and v is a power, so it is best to think of the function first as $y = uv^{1/2}$. From the formula,
$$\frac{dy}{dx} = u \cdot \frac{1}{2} \cdot v^{-1/2} \frac{dv}{dx} + v^{1/2} \frac{du}{dx}$$

B. $u = x^2 - 1$
$$\frac{du}{dx} = \frac{d}{dx}(x^2) + \frac{d}{dx}(1)$$
$$= 2x \quad + 0$$
$$= 2x$$

C. $v = x^2 + x$
$$\frac{dv}{dx} = \frac{d}{dx}(x^2) + \frac{d}{dx}(x)$$
$$= 2x$$

D. Substituting into the expression obtained in step A gives
$$\frac{dy}{dx} = \frac{1}{2}(x^2 - 1)(x^2 + x)^{-1/2}(2x + 1) + 2x(x^2 + x)^{1/2}$$

Implicit differentiation. To obtain dy/dx in a relation that is not a function, consider that y implicitly represents one or more functions of x. It is then sometimes possible to separate these functions and differentiate each with respect to x. It is often impossible to separate a relation. Implicit differentiation uses the idea of simply differentiating each side of the equation, defining the relation with repect to x.

Differentiate the relation $x^2 + y^2 = 25$.

A. Differentiate both sides of the equation with respect to x.
$$2x + 2y\left(\frac{dy}{dx}\right) = 0$$

B. Solve the result from step A for dy/dx.
$$\frac{dy}{dx} = \frac{x}{y}$$

C. Solve the original equation for y and substitute into step B.
$$\frac{dy}{dx} = \frac{x}{\pm\sqrt{25 - x^2}}$$

Differentials. For some purposes, it is convenient to separate dy/dx into the *differentials* dy and dx. This is particularly important for the notation employed in integral calculus. Given $y = f(x)$, the differentials are defined by $dy = f'(x)dx$. (This is suggested by the notation $f'(x) = dy/dx$, which makes it easy to remember the definition. However, dy/dx is not a fraction and cannot always be treated as one.)

Applications of the derivative.

Graphing. In a continuous interval of the function $y = f(x)$, the graph is rising when $dy/dx > 0$, is falling when $dy/dx < 0$, and is at a *turning point* when $dy/dx = 0$. At a turning point the tangent to the graph is horizontal. More information can be obtained from looking at the second derivative. The slope of the graph is increasing when $d^2y/dx^2 > 0$ and is decreasing when $d^2y/dx^2 < 0$. If the second derivative and the first derivative are both 0, the graph has a *point of inflection* between upward and downward concavity. A turning point is a *relative maximum* for the interval (highest point) if the first derivative is 0 and the second is less than 0. A turning point is a *relative minimum* for the interval (lowest point) if the first derivative is 0 and the second derivative is greater than 0.

The graph of a function often can be accurately sketched by dividing the domain into intervals of rising and falling, identifying relative maximum and minimum points and points of inflection, and by calculating a few easy-to-find points, such as the intercepts.

If the domain of $y = f(x)$ is the set of all real numbers, the actual maximum or minimum value of y occurs at a turning point or is undefined (infinite). When the domain is a finite interval, the actual maximum or minimum occurs at a turning point or at an end of the interval. The process for solving maximum/minimum problems involves writing an expression for the quantity to be maximized or minimized and using the derivative to locate the relative extreme points.

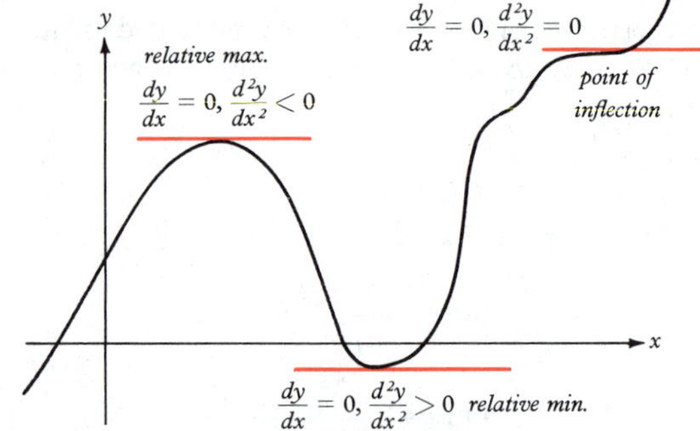

Motion and rates. If the position of an object in motion is given as a function of time, then the position, s, can be expressed as $f(t)$, $v = ds/dt$ is the velocity, and $a = dv/dt = d^2s/dt^2$ is its acceleration. The motion is in a positive direction (upward, to the right, or however defined), changing direction, or in a negative direction according to whether v is positive, zero, or negative, respectively. Similarly, the change in v is shown by the sign of a.

To find the instantaneous rate of change of a variable with respect to time, when the known conditions are in terms of other variables, write the equations relating variables and differentiate with respect to time. Then substitute in the conditions at the required instant.

Solving problems

After t seconds, the altitude of a projectile fired vertically from a platform is given in meters as $s = 10 + 200t - 4.9t^2$. Write the velocity and acceleration functions, and find the maximum altitude reached, as well as the initial velocity and altitude.

A. The velocity is ds/dt, which can be calculated from the formulas in the box on page 240.

$$v = ds/dt = 200 - 9.8t$$

This function gives results in meters per second.

B. The acceleration is dv/dt, or

$$a = dv/dt = -9.8.$$

This function is a constant expressed in meters per second per second, or m/sec^2. It should be recognizable as the acceleration due to gravity.

C. The maximum altitude is reached when the velocity is 0, as the projectile changes from rising to falling. When v is 0,

$$t = 200/9.8 = 20.4$$

to the nearest tenth of a second. Therefore, at the time 20.4 seconds,

$$s = 10 + 200(20.4) - 4.9(20.4)^2$$
$$= 10 + 4080 - 2039.184$$
$$= 2050$$

meters to the nearest 10 meters.

D. At $t = 0$, the original formula gives $s = 10$ and the first derivative gives $v = 200$.

Therefore, the initial velocity was 200 meters per second and the platform height (initial altitude) was 10 meters.

Oil is pumped into a conical tank (with the vertex of the cone down) at a constant rate of 2 cubic meters per minute. The tank is 8 meters high, and the radius of the circular top is 6 meters. At what rate is the oil level rising when the depth of the oil in the tank is 2 meters?

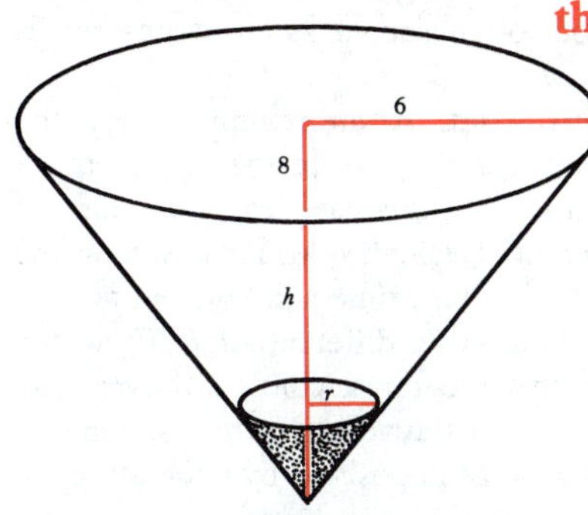

A. Call the altitude of the filled portion h and the radius of the surface of the filled portion r. By similar triangles,
$$h/r = 8/6 = 4/3.$$

B. You know that the change in volume with respect to time is 2 cubic meters per minute. Therefore, $dV/dt = 2$, where V is volume and t is time.

C. The formula for the volume of a cone (see page 195) is
$$V = \pi r^2 h/3.$$
From $h/r = 4/3$, you can obtain $r = 3h/4$.
Substitute this value into the formula for the volume to get
$$V = 3\pi h^3/16$$

D. Use implicit differentiation to obtain a second description of the rate of change of the volume (see step B).
$$dV/dt = 9\pi h^2(dh/dt)/16$$
Since the two expressions for dV/dt must be equal,
$$9\pi h^2(dh/dt)/16 \doteq 2$$

E. The derivative dh/dt is the rate that the level of the oil in the tank is rising (or falling) at any time t. From step D, this rate is $dh/dt = 32/9\pi h^2$.

F. Find the value of the rate that the oil is rising when the depth, or h, is equal to 2.

Substituting 2 for h in the formula from step E gives
$$dh/dt = 32/36\pi = 8/9\pi$$

Using 3.14 for π, the oil level is rising at a rate of about 0.28 meters per minute.

A manufacturer finds that his plant can produce up to 600 units of a certain product per week. For n units, the production cost is $c = 10n + 40$ dollars, and the expected sales income is $I = n(30 - 0.02n)$ dollars. For what production level should profit be a maximum?

A. In this case, the profit can be figured as the income minus the cost (since the cost includes overhead), so if p is the profit
$$p = I - c = 20n - 0.02n^2 - 40$$

B. The rate of change of profit with respect to the number of units produced is
$$dp/dn = 20 - 0.04n$$

C. A turning point for the profit occurs when $dp/dn = 0$. Solving $0 = 20 - 0.04n$ for n gives $n = 500$.

D. The second derivative of the profit with respect to n is
$$d^2p/dn^2 = -0.04.$$
Therefore, the turning point at $n = 500$ is a relative maximum.

E. The interval that the manufacturer can consider is from $n = 0$ to $n = 600$, since he can produce up to 600 units a week. Although 500 is a relative maximum, it should be compared with the ends of the interval to be certain that the actual maximum for that interval is also at $n = 500$.

F. Use the profit formula from step A to compute $p(n)$ for n equal to 0, 500, and 600.
$$p(0) = -40$$
$$p(500) = 4960$$
$$p(600) = 4760$$
Therefore, production of 500 units per week yields maximum profit.

Integrals. There are two seemingly unrelated approaches to integral calculus. In one of these approaches, the integral is defined directly as the area under a curve. In the other, the integral is defined in terms of the derivative. The essence of the fundamental theorem of calculus is that these two approaches produce the same result. An informal way of stating the fundamental theorem is as follows: For an interval from a to b, if you know how the slope of a curve changes in the interval, you can determine the area between the curve and the horizontal axis. We will look at the slope first.

Antiderivatives. Determining a function whose derivative is known is called *antidifferentiation.* For example, if $g'(x) = 2x$, the formula for the derivative of $g(x) = x^2$ would suggest that $g(x)$ is the antiderivative of $g'(x)$. However, it is also true that $g'(x) = 2x$ when $g(x) = x^2 + 117$ or when $g(x) = x^2 - 5$ or when $g(x)$ is any function of the form $g(x) = x^2 + C$ where C is any constant, since the derivative of a constant is 0. Therefore, the antiderivative is always defined with some arbitrary constant added to the function.

Another name for the antiderivative is the *indefinite integral.* The integral is "indefinite" because it is not a single function, but is instead a set of functions that can differ by any arbitrary constant.

The notation for the integral is based on differentials (see page 241). By definition, if $dy/dx = f(x)$, then $dy = f(x)dx$. The indefinite integral of $f(x)$ would be $y + C$, where C is the arbitrary constant. An elongated S, $\int$, is used to indicate the indefinite integral, so you can write $y = \int dy = \int f(x)dx = F(x) + C$, where $F(x)$ is defined by $F'(x) = f(x)$ and C is called *the constant of integration.* Therefore, in the case of $f(x) = g'(x) = 2x$, you can write $\int 2x\,dx = x^2 + C$. The function to be integrated (in this case, $2x$) is the expression between the integral sign and the differential. This function, often shown as an expression, is called the *integrand.*

Application to motion. As an example of how the integral works, consider the case of the motion of an object. When you look at this case from the point of view of the differential calculus, you know how the object's position varies with time and you can find its velocity and acceleration by differentiation. From the point of view of the integral calculus, however, you know the acceleration or the velocity, from which you can determine the change in position by integrating the function once or twice.

An object in motion with position s given as a function of time has the velocity $v = ds/dt$ and an acceleration $a = dv/dt$. Therefore, you can write $v = \int a\,dt$ and $s = \int v\,dt$.

For example, if a is the acceleration owed to gravity, 9.8 meters per second per second, then $a = 9.8$ so

$$v = \int 9.8\,dt = 9.8t + C.$$

Similarly, since $v = 9.8t + C$

$$\text{then } s = \int (9.8t + C)\,dt = 4.9t^2 + Ct + C'$$

where C' (read "see prime") is used to indicate that it is a different constant of integration from the one found in the first part of the problem. In an actual problem about the motion of an object, further information about the velocity, position, or the motion would be given to enable you to determine numerical values for the two constants of integration.

Find $\int x^2(x^3 - 5)^7dx$.

A. From the table on page 245, it appears that the integrand is nearly of the form $u^n du$, with $u^n = (x^3 - 5)^7$.

B. If $u = x^3 - 5$, then $du/dx = 3x^2$ and, from the definition of differential, $du = 3x^2dx$. However, when you remove u^7 from the integrand, the remaining part is just x^2dx, so you need a factor of 3. Since

$$\int k\,du = k \int du,$$

you can get the required constant factor by balancing it with a factor outside the sign of integration.

$$\int x^2 (x^3 - 5)^7 dx = 1/3 \int (x^3 - 5)(3x^2dx) = 1/3 \int u^7\,du$$

C. Now you can apply the formula to obtain

$$u^8/24 + C.$$

Substituting the value of u gives the final answer as

$$(x^3 - 5)^8/24 + C.$$

The area under a curve. Consider the problem of finding the area of a region bounded by the graph of $y = f(x)$, the vertical lines $x = a$ and $x = b$, and the x axis. Such an area is referred to as *the area under the curve* y = f(x) *in the interval between* a *and* b. An approximation to this area can be made by constructing n rectangles with equal base lengths $(b - a)/n$, which we will also call Δx (for reasons that will become clear later). The height of the rectangle can be obtained by first choosing some value c_i that is in each base, where i is a natural number $\leq n$. For example, in the illustration, the left endpoint of each subinterval is used.

The height of the ith rectangle is $f(c_i)$ and its area is $f(c_i)\,\Delta x$. All rectangles formed in this way may turn out to be too large or too small for the area under the curve, or some may be too large and others may be too small; but the sum of the areas of the rectangles is an approximation for the required area. It is obvious that if more and more rectangles were used, they would come closer to filling up the space under the curve, so the limit as n goes to infinity is the required area.

The *definite integral* is defined by this procedure.

$$\lim_{n\to\infty} \sum_{i=1}^{n} f(c_i)\,\Delta x = \int_a^b f(x)\,dx$$

Thus, the definite integral is a number, while the indefinite integral is a function. The relationship between them is the fundamental theorem of calculus, which will not be proved here.

If $$\int f(x)\,dx = F(x) + C$$
and $f(x)$ is continuous between a and b, then

$$\int_a^b f(x)\,dx = F(b) - F(a)$$

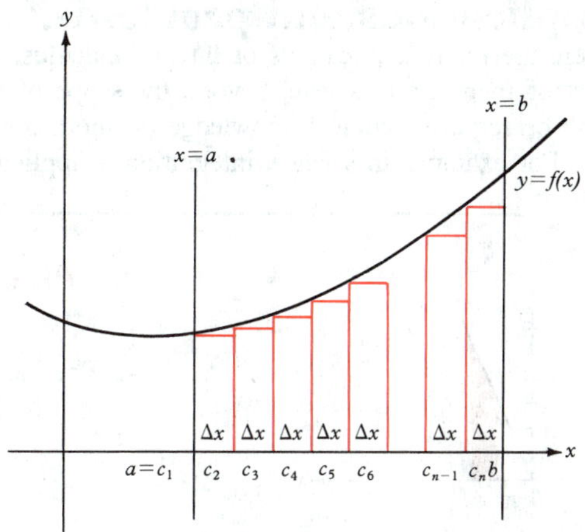

Sometimes an indefinite integral is defined by holding one of the ends of the interval constant and letting the other end vary. For example,

$$\int_a^x f(u)\,du$$

is a function of x. (The variable u is a "dummy" variable that disappears when the integration is completed.) The specific value of the function will depend on a, so an arbitrary constant must be added. In other words, if $f(u)$ and $f(x)$ are the same function with only the variables different, and $F(x)$ is a function such that $F'(x) = f(x)$, then

$$\int_a^x f(u)du = \int f(x)\,dx = F(x) + C$$

Integrals

If k is a constant, and C is an arbitrary constant,

$$\int x^k dx = \frac{x^{k+1}}{k+1} + C \quad (k \neq -1)$$

$$\int \frac{1}{x}\,dx = \log|x| + C$$

$$\int e^x dx = e^x + C$$

$$\int k^x dx = \frac{k^x}{\log k} + C \quad (k \neq 1)$$

$$\int \sin x\,dx = -\cos x + C$$

$$\int \cos x\,dx = \sin x + C$$

$$\int \csc^2 x\,dx = -\cot x + C$$

$$\int \sec^2 x\,dx = \tan x + C$$

$$\int \frac{1}{\sqrt{1-x^2}}\,dx = \sin^{-1} x + C \text{ or } -\cos^{-1} x + C \quad |x| < 1$$

$$\int \frac{1}{x+x^2}\,dx = \tan^{-1} x + C \text{ or } -\cot^{-1} x + C$$

Applications and problems.

There are many applications of integral calculus, but most of them are at a level beyond the scope of this book or require technical knowledge of another subject. For example, in science, integration is applied to problems involving center of gravity, work, voltage drop, battery power leakage, and so forth. Here are a few examples showing integration in several of its common applications, along with a few problems dealing with various aspects of integration itself.

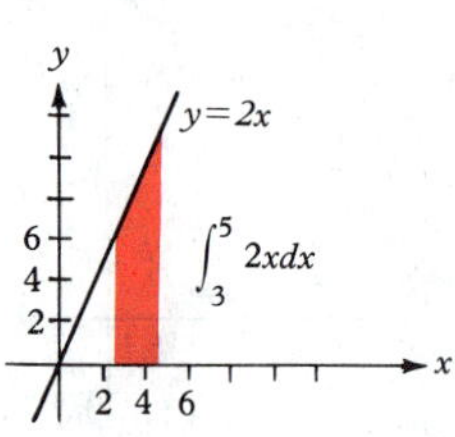

Find $\int_3^5 2x\,dx$.

A. The indefinite integral $F(x)$ is $x^2 + C$

B. The definite integral is $F(5) - F(3) = 25 - 9 = 16$

Find the area enclosed by the sine curve and the x axis in the interval from $x = 0$ to $x = 2\pi$.

A. Notice that the sine curve is partly above and partly below the x axis in the interval from 0 to 2π. If the region is below the x axis, the value of the definite integral is negative for that part of the interval. Therefore, since the area cannot be negative, break the problem down into the intervals where the graph crosses the x axis, and then take the sum of the absolute values of the areas for each interval. For the sine curve, calculate the interval from 0 to π and the interval from π to 2π separately.

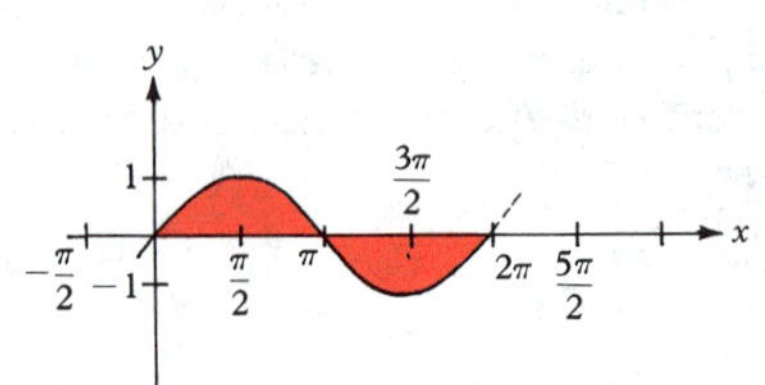

B. Find

$$\left|\int_0^{\pi} \sin x\,dx\right| + \left|\int_{\pi}^{2\pi} \sin x\,dx\right|.$$

Since the indefinite integral of $\sin x$ is $-\cos x$, the value of the definite integral is

$$|-\cos\pi - (-\cos 0)| + |-\cos 2\pi - (-\cos\pi)|$$

or $|1 - (-1)| + |-1 - 1| = 2 + 2$
$= 4$

Find $\int xe^{2x}$ where e is the base of the natural logarithms.

A. This problem requires knowledge of the formula for *integrating by parts*, which is the integral formula corresponding to the formula for differentiating a product. That is,
$dy/dx\, f(x)g(x) = f'(x)g(x) + f(x)g'(x)$
or (in integral form)
$f(x)g(x) = \int g(x)f'(x)\,dx + \int f(x)g'(x)\,dx$,
which is most useful as
$\int f(x)g'(x)\,dx = f(x)g(x) - \int g(x)f'(x)\,dx$.
This last formula may be used to solve the given problem.

B. Let $f(x) = x$ and $g'(x) = e^{2x}$.
Then, $g(x) = \int e^{2x}\,dx$
$= \frac{1}{2}\int e^{2x}(2\,dx)$
$= \frac{1}{2}e^{2x}$

C. Thus,
$\int xe^{2x}\,dx = \frac{1}{2}xe^{2x} - \int \frac{1}{2}e^{2x}\,dx$
$= \frac{1}{2}xe^{2x} - \frac{1}{4}e^{2x} + C$

The integral was defined for the area under a curve in two-dimensional space, but it could have been explained as a sum of an infinite series with no reference to the curve. This gives a flexibility to the concept of integration that permits solution of problems that involve other situations in which a region of some kind can be allowed to go to zero. In examples that conclude this discussion, volume problems are solved by letting a three-space region go to zero. More complex volume problems require advanced integration.

Suppose that a region is rotated about the x axis to form a solid. Find the volume of the solid formed by rotating the region bounded by $x = 1$, $x = 3$, and the curve $y = x^2$.

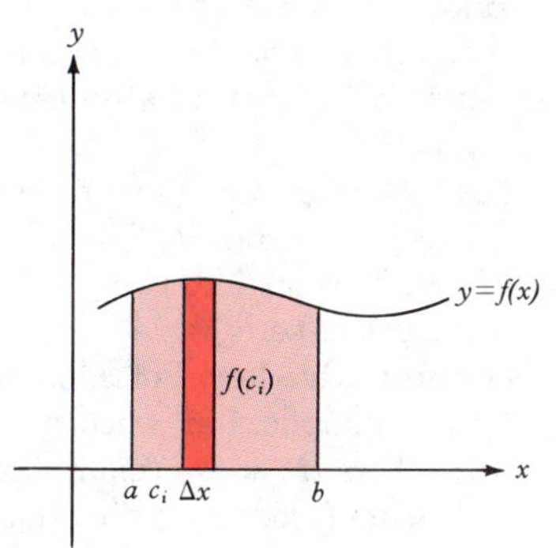

A. The volume of a solid formed by rotation around the x axis may be found by the *slice method.* Divide the interval into subintervals as was done in finding the area under a curve. In this case, however, you will be dealing with the volumes of cylinders instead of the areas of rectangles. If each cylinder has a radius of $f(c_1)$ and a thickness of x, then the volume of each will be

$$f(c_1)^2\,\Delta x$$

Taking the limit of the sum according to the definition of the definite integral gives the required volume as

$$\int_a^b \pi y^2\,dx$$

B. In this case, $a = 1$, $b = 3$, and $y = x^2$, so the volume is

$$\int_1^3 \pi x^4\,dx$$

and the indefinite integral is

$$\frac{\pi}{5}(x^5)$$

and the definite integral is

$$\frac{\pi}{5}(243 - 1) = \frac{242\pi}{5}$$

The volume is $242\pi/5$ cubic units.

Find the volume of the solid formed by rotating the region bounded by $y = 1$, $y = 3$, $x = y^2$, and the y axis about the x axis.

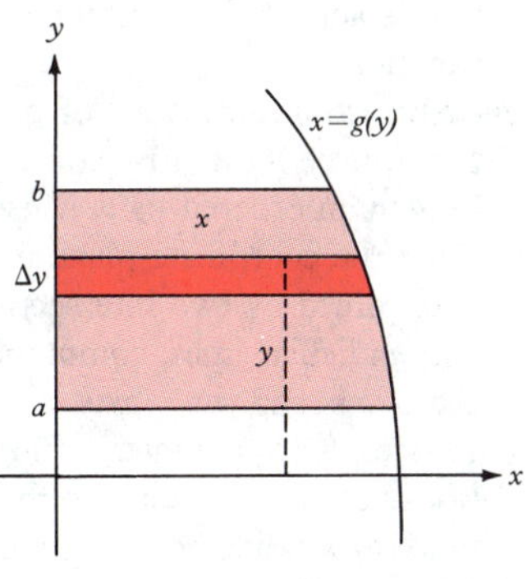

A. The slice method is not always appropriate. If the region is formed as described in the problem, it will have a hollow interior. In fact, the rotation will produce a *cylindrical shell* instead of a solid cylinder. The same general approach will work, however. Divide the region into rectangles as shown in the illustration. The volume of the cylindrical shell formed by each rectangle will be $2\pi c_i g(c_i)\,\Delta y$, and the limit as n goes to infinity will be the definite integral

$$\int_a^b 2\pi yx\,dy$$

B. For this problem, you know that $x = y^2$, so the definite integral becomes

$$\int_1^3 2\pi y^3\,dy$$

Therefore, the indefinite integral is $\frac{1}{2}\pi y^4$ and the definite integral is

$$\tfrac{1}{2}\pi(81 - 1) = 40\pi$$

Therefore, the volume of the cylindrical shell is 40π cubic units.

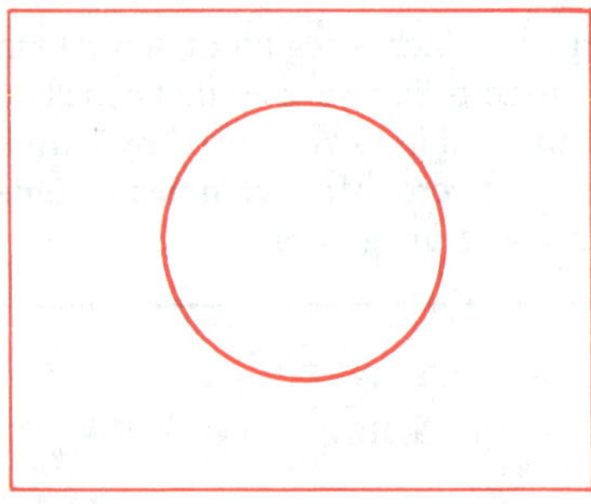
empty set

Dictionary of mathematics

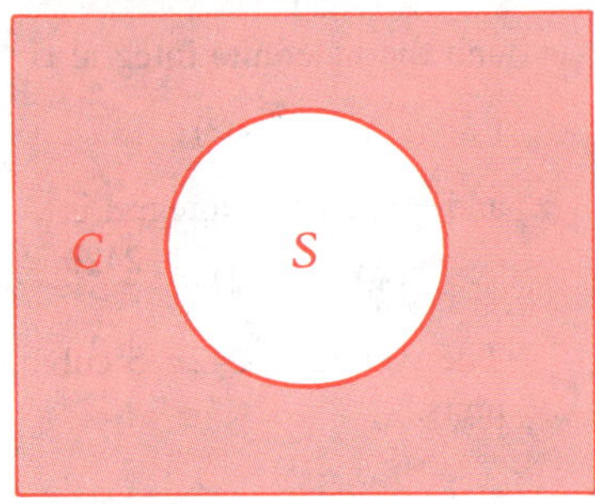

complement

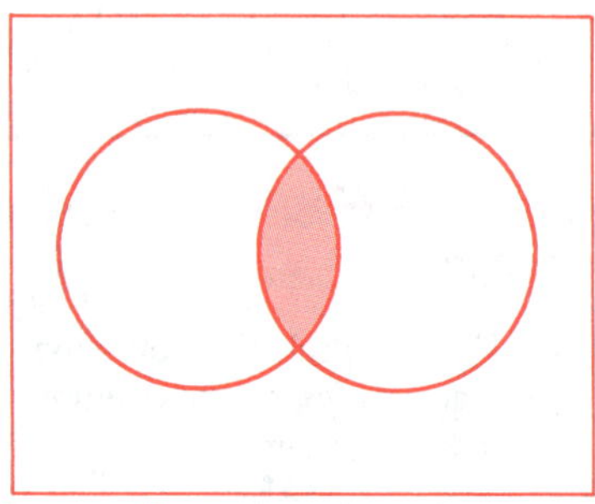
intersection

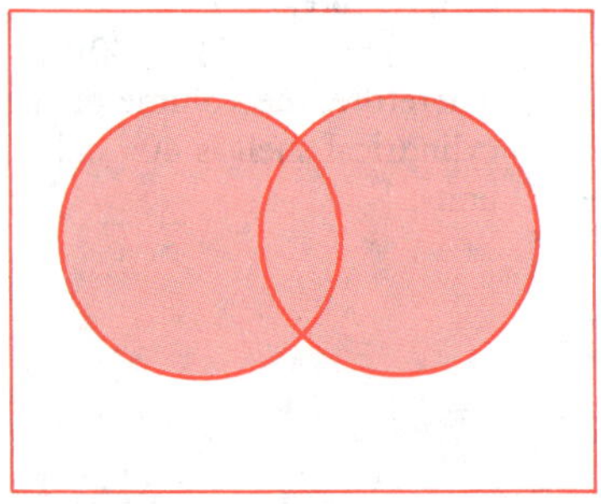
union

abscissa. Directed distance of a point from the *y* axis. In a pair of coordinates, the first member.

acute. For an angle, one with a measure of less than 90°. For a triangle, one with three acute angles.

additive identity element. A number z such that for any number in a set, z added to the number gives the original number. For the real numbers, the additive identity element is 0.

additive inverse. A number that can be added to another number to produce the additive identity element is the additive inverse of the second number. For the real numbers, the additive inverse of x is $-x$, because $x + (-x) = 0$, and 0 is the additive identity element.

amplitude. For a trigonometric function, the largest value of the function if a largest value exists.

angle. Union of two rays with a common endpoint.

arc cosine. The inverse of the cosine function; that is, the angle that has a particular value of the cosine. Abbreviated either arc cos or $\cos^{-1}$.

arc sine. The inverse of the sine function; that is, the angle that has a particular value of the sine. Abbreviated either arc sin or $\sin^{-1}$.

arc tangent. The inverse of the tangent function; that is, the angle that has a particular value of the tangent. Abbreviated either arc tan or $\tan^{-1}$.

arithmetic mean. The average; that is, the quotient formed when the numbers in a set are added and then divided by the number of numbers in the set.

arithmetic sequence. Sequence formed by adding the same amount to a given number over and over.

arithmetic series. Series formed as the indicated sum of an arithmetic sequence.

associative law. For addition and multiplication, when three numbers are added (multiplied), the sum (product) is the same when the sum (product) of the last two numbers is added to (multiplied by) the first as when the sum (product) of the first two numbers is added to (multiplied by) the last.

average. The arithmetic mean.

axiom. A statement that is accepted without proof and then used as the basis of a system of proofs.

base. Number raised to a power by an exponent.

bisect. Separate into two congruent parts.

commutative law. For addition and multiplication, when two numbers are added (multiplied), the sum (product) is the same no matter which order they are added (multiplied) in.

complement. For sets, the elements of a set with respect to another set that are not included in the first set.

complex number. A number that is the sum of a real number and an imaginary number.

constant. In algebra or calculus, a quantity that does not vary in a given situation; in calculus in particular, an unknown amount that is added to the integral of a function.

coordinate plane. A set of points that can be located by two numbers in an ordered pair. Most often the coordinate plane is determined by two intersecting perpendicular lines, commonly the x axis and the y axis.

cosecant. A trigonometric function that is defined as the distance of a point on a particular ray from the origin divided by the ordinate of the point on the ray. It is a constant for the angle that the ray makes with the positive horizontal axis.

cosine. A trigonometric function that is defined as the abscissa of a point on a particular ray from the origin divided by the distance of that point from the origin. It is a constant for the angle that the ray makes with the positive horizontal axis.

cotangent. A trigonometric function that is defined as the abscissa of a point on a particular ray divided by the ordinate of that point. It is a constant for the angle that the ray makes with the positive horizontal axis.

counting number. Natural number.

cross-product rule. In a proportion, the rule that the product of the numerator of one ratio with the denominator of the other ratio is always equal to the product of the denominator of the first ratio with the numerator of the second ratio.

cube. In geometry, a figure in three dimensions that has six congruent squares as faces.

definite integral. The area between a curve and the horizontal axis.

denominator. In a fraction, the number that tells the number of parts into which something has been divided.

dependent system of equations. System of equations in two or more variables in which each equation has the same solution.

dependent variable. In a function, the variable that represents the value of the function.

derivative. For a function, the derivative is the instantaneous rate of change of the dependent variable with respect to change in the independent variable.

differential. If the derivative of a function is $f'(x)$, then the differential dy is the product $f'(x)dx$, where dx is an independent variable.

distributive law. The product of a number and a sum is equal to the sum of the product of the number with each of the addends.

dividend. In division, the number into which you divide.

divisor. In division, the number that you divide by.

e. The base of the natural logarithms, an irrational number that is equal to about 2.71828.

element. A member of a set.

empty set. A set that is a subset of every set and that contains no members; often symbolized by $\emptyset$.

equilateral. For a triangle, having all sides congruent.

event. In probability, a set or sentence that describes the outcomes that will be considered successful.

exponent. A small numeral (superscript) written above and to the right of a number or variable. Exponents that represent natural numbers tell how many times the number or variable is used as a factor. Zero, negative, and real exponents are defined to be consistent with the meaning of natural-number exponents.

factor. In multiplication, any one of the numbers to be multiplied to form a product. When used as a verb, *factor* means to find the factors that can be used to form a given number or algebraic expression.

function. A rule that connects two sets of numbers in such a way that a member of the second set is completely specified by choosing a member of the first set.

GCF. Greatest common factor.

geometric mean. For two numbers, the positive square root of their product.

geometric sequence. Sequence formed by multiplying a given number by the same factor over and over.

geometric series. Indicated sum of a geometric sequence.

greatest common factor. Largest factor that is common to two or more numbers.

harmonic mean. For two numbers, the multiplicative inverse of the mean (average) of their multiplicative inverses.

harmonic sequence. A sequence formed by the multiplicative inverses of the terms of an arithmetic sequence.

harmonic series. Indicated sum of a harmonic sequence.

heptagon. Polygon with seven sides.

hexagon. Polygon with six sides.

***i*.** Symbol used to denote the square root of -1; when multiplied by any real number (except 0), it forms an imaginary number.

imaginary number. The product of any real number (except 0) and i, the square root of -1.

inconsistent system of equations. System of equations with no solution to the system.

indefinite integral. Function that is the antiderivative of a given function; equivalently defined as a definite integral for which one bound of the interval over which the integral is defined is allowed to vary.

independent variable. For a function, the variable over which the function is defined; that is, the variable representing the set that is the domain of the function.

inequality. Sentence containing one of the following relations: greater than, less than, not equal, greater than or equal, less than or equal.

infinite sequence. Sequence for which the domain is the entire set of natural numbers.

infinite series. Indicated sum of an infinite sequence.

infinity. In calculus, a symbol used to indicate that a variable increases without bound.

integer. Number that is either a whole number or the negative of a whole number.

integral. Either the definite or indefinite integral.

integrand. Function operated upon by a definite or indefinite integral over a given differential.

intercept. For graphs, either the point at which the graph crosses one of the axes or the distance of that point from the origin.

interpolation. Method of finding an approximate value between two values given in a table that assumes that the graph of the values in the table is a straight line.

intersection. For sets, the set that contains all the members common to two or more sets.

inverse operation. An operation that undoes the effect of a given operation; for example, addition is the inverse of subtraction and division is the inverse of multiplication.

irrational number. Real number that is not also a rational number.

isosceles. For triangles, a triangle that has two congruent sides.

kite. Polygon that has two pairs of adjacent congruent sides.

LCD. Least common denominator.

LCM. Least common multiple.

least common denominator. Least common multiple of the denominators of a set of fractions.

least common multiple. Smallest nonzero number that is a multiple of all numbers in a set of numbers.

limit. For sequences (functions), the number such that in any small neighborhood around it there will always be terms of the sequence (values of the function).

logarithm. For a particular base, the exponent by which the base must be raised to equal the number of which it is the logarithm.

mean proportional. In a proportion, a number that is both the denominator of one ratio and the numerator of the other.

member. For sets or for ordered pairs, one of the individual parts of the set or pair.

monomial. Product of number and one or more variables.

multiple. Product of a given number and a whole number.

multiplicative identity element. A number I such that for any number in a set, I times the number gives the original number. For the real numbers, the multiplicative identity element is 1.

multiplicative inverse. Number such that the product of that number and a given number is 1.

natural number. Number that is 1 or formed by starting with 1 and adding one more each time.

negative number. Number to the left of 0 on the number line.

null set. Set with no members; the empty set.

numerator. In a fraction, the number of parts represented by the fraction.

obtuse. For angles, an angle greater than 90° and less than 180°.

octagon. Polygon with eight sides.

opposite. Number that is equal in value, but opposite in sign, to a given number.

ordinate. For a point in the coordinate plane, the directed distance from the x axis; the second member of the coordinates of the point.

outcome. In probability, the result of a trial.

parallel. For lines, two lines that do not meet.

parallelogram. Quadrilateral for which both pairs of opposite sides are parallel.

pentagon. Polygon with five sides.

percent. Ratio of some number to 100.

percentage. Percent of a number.

period. For functions, a number such that when the number is added to the independent variable, the value of the function does not change.

perpendicular. For lines or line segments, two lines (segments) that meet at right angles.

pi. A Greek letter. Its lower-case form, π, is used for the ratio of the circumference of a circle to its diameter. Although pi cannot be expressed exactly as a decimal, it is 3.14159 to six decimal places.

plane. Flat surface extending infinitely far in all directions.

point of inflection. For a curve, a point at which the curve changes from being convex to being concave.

polynomial. A monomial or the sum of any finite number of monomials.

positive number. Number to the right of 0 on the number line.

power. The result when a number is used as a factor a number of times.

prime. For natural numbers, a number that has only itself and 1 as factors.

probability. Number that describes the chance that a given event will take place.

proportion. Statement that two ratios are equal.

Pythagorean theorem. For right triangles, the statement that the area of a square that has one side on the side of the triangle opposite the right angle is equal to the sum of the areas of the squares on the other two sides of the triangle.

quadrant. On the coordinate plane, one of the four regions into which the plane is separated by the axes.

quadratic equation. An equation in one variable for which the highest power of the variable is the second and all the powers of the variable are whole numbers.

quadrilateral. Polygon with four sides.

quotient. In division, the answer.

radical. Sign used to indicate that a square root of a number (or, combined with an index, another root of the number) is to be taken.

radicand. Number or expression under a radical.

ratio. Comparison of two quantities by division.

rational number. The ratio of an integer to a natural number.

real number. Any number that can be represented by an infinite decimal.

reciprocal. For a given number, the number formed by dividing the given number into 1.

rectangle. Parallelogram that contains a right angle.

relation. Any rule connecting the members of two sets.

relative maximum. Greatest value of a function in an interval.

relative minimum. Least value of a function in an interval.

rhombus. Parallelogram with adjacent sides congruent.

right angle. Angle that measures 90°.

right triangle. Triangle that contains a right angle.

root. For numbers, a number such that the product of the number repeated two (or more) times is a given number.

sample space. In probability, the set of all outcomes of a given experiment.

scalene. For triangles, one in which no two sides are equal.

secant. A trigonometric function that is defined as the distance of a point on a particular ray from the origin divided by the abscissa of the point on the ray. It is a constant for the angle that the ray makes with the horizontal axis.

secant. For circles, a line that intersects the circle in two points.

second derivative. Function formed by taking the derivative of another function twice.

sequence. Ordered values of a function over the natural numbers.

series. Indicated sum of a sequence.

set. Any collection of objects or ideas such that you can tell whether a given object or idea is a member of the collection.

signed number. Number written with a positive or negative sign.

similar figures. Geometric figures that have the same shape but not necessarily the same size.

sine. A trigonometric function that is defined as the ordinate of a point on a particular ray from the origin divided by the distance of that point from the origin. It is a constant for the angle that the ray makes with the positive horizontal axis.

slope. For a line, the quotient of rate of change of the ordinates on the line divided by the rate of change of the abscissas.

solution. In algebra, an equation that states the value of a variable that will make another given equation true.

square. A rhombus with four right angles.

straight angle. Angle whose measure is 180°.

system of equations. Set of two or more equations in two or more variables to be solved for the intersection of the solutions of the equations in the set.

tangent. Trigonometric function that is defined as the ordinate of a point on a particular ray divided by the abscissa of that point. It is a constant for the angle that the ray makes with the positive horizontal axis. For a curve, the limit of a line that intersects the curve in two points as one point approaches the other. For a circle, a line that intersects the circle at one and only one point.

tetrahedron. Four-sided solid whose faces are all triangles.

theorem. Statement that has been derived from a set of axioms according to the rules of logic.

triangle. Polygon with three sides.

trigonometric function. Function whose independent variable is an angle and whose value is defined as a quotient of one pair from the following:
abscissa
ordinate
distance from origin of a point on a ray that makes the given angle with the positive x axis.

trinomial. Polynomial that has three terms.

turning point. On a curve, point where the tangent is horizontal.

union. For two sets, the set that contains all the members of both sets.

variable. Letter or other symbol that can represent any one of a specified set of numbers.

vertical angles. Two angles formed by intersecting lines so that the angles do not have a ray in common.

For Further Reference

Bunch, Bryan H.
Mathematical Fallacies and Paradoxes
Van Nostrand Reinhold

Courant, Richard and John, Fritz
Introduction to Calculus and Analysis, Volume 1
Interscience Publisher (John Wiley & Sons)

Coxeter, H.S.M.
Introduction to Geometry
John Wiley & Sons

Pedoe, Dan
The Gentle Art of Mathematics
Dover

English and Literature

A tragic mask from an early Roman mosaic *(see "Drama," p. 300).*

Writing a Research Paper

Although most students groan when research papers are assigned, writing a term report can be stimulating, particularly if you choose a topic that interests you. A good research paper integrates the use of information gathered from various sources with your own ideas. It demonstrates your ability to think and write clearly, as well as your skill in using the library and ingenuity in finding other sources of information.

Writing a research paper is in itself a way of learning, not only about the particular topic you are investigating, but also about the process of investigation itself. You must become a kind of detective to find the facts and theories needed to come to an informed conclusion. Putting information gathered together with personal ideas is the way all investigators solve mysteries. Unlike crimes, however, research topics may have more than one possible conclusion.

In writing a good paper, you learn how to argue your point—fairly, yet persuasively. Furthermore, as you research your topic, you become an expert on it. Very few people will know more about your subject than you will after you have completed your investigation.

There are two common misconceptions about the research paper: 1) that it is a collection of strung-together quotations and paraphrases from published sources with a lot of footnotes attached so no one can accuse you of plagiarism, or 2) that it is a collection of your uninformed opinions about a topic. In reality, a research paper is a combination of the two concepts—your informed opinions and ideas based on your investigation of published, and occasionally unpublished, information.

In this section you will learn how to pick a good topic, how to find and take notes on the information you need, how to put that information and your own ideas together in logical order, and how to write the paper in an accepted manner, using the correct form for footnotes and bibliography.

Choosing a topic

The first task is choosing a suitable topic, one that interests you and on which there is enough information available. Your teacher may assign or recommend a broad subject. You are not expected to write a report on the whole subject, but to choose an aspect of it that particularly interests you. In order to do so, it is a good idea to read some general articles on the subject, such as those found in an encyclopedia. They will provide you with an overview of the subject. In the course of your reading, you will come across sections that interest you more than others. This will help you pinpoint the aspect of the subject on which you would most like to write.

Once you have a possible topic, determine whether enough research material exists on your topic. Start with the encyclopedia articles you have read. Most such articles include a *bibliography*—a list of books and authors, usually the most important works in the field. Another way to check for research material is to consult the catalog of your library (see below, page 256). If too little information is available, you will save yourself wasted effort by choosing another, more accessible topic or, if possible, by broadening the topic. You must also be careful not to choose a topic on which there is too much information. If the topic you have chosen is so well covered that you do not know where to begin, narrow it further or choose another topic.

To narrow down a topic you must move from the general to the specific. For example, if you have been studying Greek, Egyptian, and Anglo-Saxon societies, a subject such as comparing attitudes toward death could require a book, not a paper. A comparison of burial rites in those societies may be a more workable topic. If, on the other hand, you are too specific, choosing to write only about burial rites in Anglo-Saxon societies, your paper may turn out to be only three pages long.

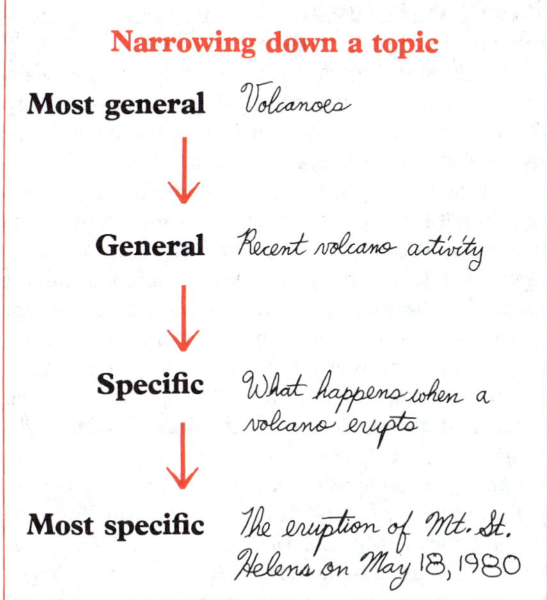

Using the library

Kinds of libraries. Most of the research you do will be conducted in a library, so it is a good idea to know how to use one. There are four basic types of libraries—circulating, reference, technical, and government depository.

Circulating libraries. These are the libraries with which you are probably most familiar. They lend books to all kinds of readers, young and old, scholars, students, and sunbathers. You are usually allowed to borrow books from circulating libraries for two to four weeks.

Reference libraries. These are places where students and scholars work. Reference libraries often have old, valuable books with essential information. Because of their fragile condition or rarity, these books usually cannot be borrowed, and one must be careful using them.

Technical libraries. These libraries are devoted to specialized fields, such as engineering, medicine, or science. Hospitals, for example, may have extensive medical libraries. You may need special permission to use such libraries.

Government depository libraries. Located in major cities throughout the United States, these libraries contain government publications and other printed material pertinent to government. You may find copies of the *Federal Register*, the daily *Congressional Record*, House and Senate *Calendars*, the *Weekly Compilation of Presidential Documents*, *Commerce Business Daily*, and many pamphlets put out by the Government Printing Office. Such pamphlets cover subjects from how to make toys out of junk to how to pump gas.

Much government material is available in general libraries. Larger libraries may have *The Index of Monthly Catalogues of U.S. Government Publications*, a complete listing of documents available. Otherwise, ask the reference librarian for help in locating government publications. *Government Publications and Their Use* by Laurence F. Schmeckebier and Roy B. Eastin is the best guide to what the government prints and how to obtain copies. Some large cities have government bookstores that sell publications printed by the government. Also, the vertical files of your circulating library may have useful pamphlets (see page 260).

All libraries are staffed by trained reference librarians who are experts in locating source material on any subject. Their purpose is to help you, as a user of the library, and you should never hesitate to ask them questions.

To obtain a price list of government pamphlets and other publications, write to

U.S. Government Printing Office
Superintendent of Documents
Washington, D.C. 20003

Book catalogs.

There are many catalogs to help you find information.

The card catalog. Most libraries use an index card filing system called the card catalog; it tells you where to locate books. Cards are usually arranged in three separate ways—by title, author, and subject. It is easiest to locate a book by its title or author, but sometimes you do not have the necessary information. For example, when you are doing preliminary research on a topic, you will initially look under different subject headings—there may be more than one that is relevant to your topic—to see how much material is available. For example, to research a paper on burial rites in Egyptian, Greek, and Anglo-Saxon societies, you might look under the following subject headings: *funerary rites, death, cremation, interment, water burial, Egypt, Greece, Anglo-Saxon society, ancient religion.*

Call numbers. A book's call number is usually found in the upper left-hand corner of the card. This is the key to its location in the library. All books are arranged numerically or alphabetically on shelves, with the call numbers on their spines matching those in the card catalog. The call number for each book is not chosen at random. The numbers or letters indicate book categories. In this way, all books pertaining to American history are grouped together, as are books on literature, science, art, etc. As long as you know the call number of the book you need, either you or the librarian will be able to find it.

Stacks and call slips. Many libraries allow you to go through their stacks, which are the open shelves of books arranged by their call numbers. Because books are arranged by categories, you may find books pertinent to your paper that you may not have known about. But not all libraries have open stacks. In reference libraries particularly, you may be required to fill out a call slip, giving the book's title, author, and call number as well as other information. The librarian will then search the closed stacks and locate the book for you.

The catalog card has more information than just the call number. In addition to the book's title and author, it may give the birth and death dates of the author, the names of editors and translators, the place and date of publication, the publisher's name, a physical description of the book (including the size and number of pages), a short description of the book's contents, information on illustrations, photographs, bibliography, explanatory notes, the subject heading, and other places in the card catalog where the book is listed.

Tracing. A "tracing," often found at the bottom of a card, indicates other subject headings under which the book is listed. When you are doing preliminary research, it is a good idea to check such tracings. They can direct you to subject headings related to your topic that may not have occurred to you.

Bound catalogs. Some large library systems, such as those in the New York City Library and the Library of Congress, use bound, printed catalogs to list their full holdings, which may be vast and distributed to many individual branches. These catalogs, alphabetically arranged by title, author, and subject, also give call numbers and publication facts. The advantage of these bound catalogs is that they are complete, listing all of that library system's holdings, and not just those in one particular branch. Furthermore, they indicate which branches of the system have the book you are looking for, since no branch exactly duplicates the holdings of another. Sometimes large libraries hold copies of each other's bound catalogs.

Typical card from subject catalog

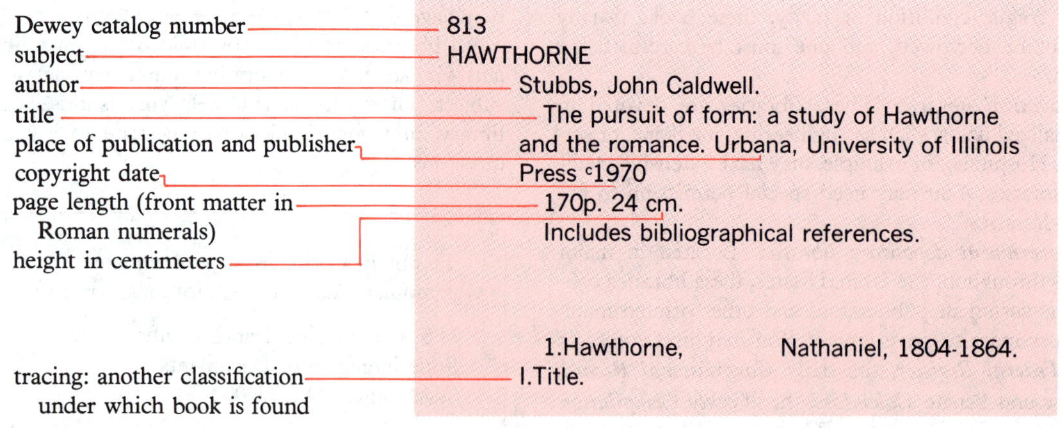

Union Catalog. This is the Library of Congress's card catalog. It usually can be found as a bound, printed catalog, although some libraries have it in index card form. Books are listed in the Union Catalog by their Library of Congress, not Dewey Decimal system, classification numbers (see below, page 258). The Library of Congress is one of the largest in the world. The Union Catalog helps researchers sift through all the books that have been printed on a subject, regardless of whether the library they are using has such books. To know which books exist is the first step in finding them, which may mean trying other libraries or taking advantage of interlibrary loan services. Many small libraries can borrow books from major libraries for the use of qualified students and researchers. Ask your neighborhood librarian if such a service is available to you and, if so, what steps are necessary to secure the needed books.

How to use the card catalog

The card catalog. This is the index of all books in a library. It is kept on cards in drawers so that it can be easily updated. Each book is listed on a separate card for author, title, and subject. The cards are arranged in alphabetical order, and the label on the front of each drawer tells you the first and the last card that it contains.

The card. The most important information on a catalog card is the call number in the upper left-hand corner. This tells you where to look for the book. The card also gives you complete information about the author, the full title of the book, its publisher and date of publication, and something about its contents. The bottom of the card indicates other listings for the same book in the catalog.

```
        Today's teen-agers

301.43  Duvall, Evelyn Ruth (Millis) 1906-
D         Today's teen-agers, by Evelyn Millis Duvall.
        New York, Association Press [c1966]
          256p.  illus.  23cm.

          Bibliography: p.225-248.


          1.Adolescence.  I.Title.

                                          10/27/66
```

The book. Books are shelved in library "stacks" of bookcases. Each book has the call number printed on its spine, and it is shelved in a place set aside for books with similar call numbers. Examination of the shelf will often lead you to books on the same or related subjects.

Classification systems. The two main systems for classifying books in the United States are the Dewey Decimal and Library of Congress systems. The first is used in most public libraries; the second, in many college libraries.

Dewey Decimal system. This system has ten major divisions, from 000 for general reference works to the 900s for history. Each major division is in turn divided into ten parts, each subdivision focusing on a particular aspect of the main class. For example, 900-909 is the subdivision under which general works of history are listed, 910-919 covers geography, 920-929 biography. The subdivisions are again divided into ten sections, and so on for increasingly specialized categories.

Library of Congress system. This system uses the letters of the alphabet to divide information into 20 categories. The letters I,O,W,X, and Y are not used. The letters E and F are both used to designate American history. As with the Dewey Decimal system, the main groups are subdivided into specialized groups, designated by arabic numerals and other letters.

Other research sources.

There are a variety of other sources worth checking.

Periodicals. In addition to books, libraries stock many periodicals, from daily newspapers to specialized magazines. Periodical indexes can be used to find relevant articles in much the same way as the card catalog is used to find books (see box).

Periodicals themselves may be found in bound volumes, or they may be available on microfilm. Since microfilm is not as easy to flip through as an actual magazine or newspaper is, it is a good idea to know the correct page before searching the microfilm. The way to find such information is by using the indexes provided.

Encyclopedias. The best multivolume general encyclopedias are the *Encyclopaedia Britannica* and the *Encyclopedia Americana.* The *World Book Encyclopedia,* which is for young adults, is also excellent.

Many specialized encyclopedias exist as well; they include the *Encyclopedia of Jazz*, the *Encyclopedia of Sports*, the *International Encyclopedia of Social Sciences*, and the *Encyclopedia of Associations* (see page 260).

Almanacs. Early almanacs contained such useful items as recipes, folk remedies, and weather predictions, but modern almanacs are a valuable source of miscellaneous information, often in tabular form. They may include a chronology of the past year's events, geographical information, statistics, lists of famous people, state mottoes, and the like. The *Old Farmer's Almanac* is a source of weather predictions and is consulted more for its quaintness than for its information. The *Information Please Almanac* and the *World Almanac* are often consulted for data on events, recent population statistics, and other general information.

Facts on File is not really an almanac but a fully

Classification systems

Dewey Decimal system

000 general works
100 philosophy
200 religion
300 sociology
400 philology
500 natural science
600 useful arts
700 fine arts
800 literature
900 history and biography

Library of Congress system

A general works
B philosophy, religion
C history
D foreign history
E, F American history
G geography, anthropology
H social sciences
J political science
K law
L education
M music
N fine arts
P language and literature
Q science
R medicine
S agriculture
T technology
U military science
V naval science
Z library science, bibliography

indexed weekly compilation of news. Current news is available in loose-leaf folders, and news from past years is bound in permanent volumes.

Bibliographies. These are comprehensive lists of books that have been written on different subjects. The librarian can help you locate specialized bibliographies. Among general bibliographies are *Books in Print*, published since 1948, indexed by title and author; *Subject Guide to Books in Print*, companion volume; and *Book Review Digest*, which excerpts reviews of books from magazines.

Atlases. Atlases are not just collections of current maps. In addition, there are maps showing historical development, climate, and many other special subjects (see box).

General atlases

Goode's World Atlas is found in many school libraries and is helpful in learning how to read maps; it is a good introduction to atlases.

The Times Atlas of the World is a comprehensive five-volume work, and includes solar system maps.

The Rand McNally New Cosmopolitan World Atlas includes ocean and solar system maps as well as historical, physical, and political maps.

Shepherd's *Historical Atlas* maps the world historically from 1450 B.C. to the present.

Periodical indexes

The Reader's Guide to Periodical Literature indexes 130 of the most popular magazines by author and subject. It has been published since 1900. It is a good idea to start with the most recent article on the subject you are investigating and work backward from there.

Poole's Index to Periodical Literature is an index of American and English periodicals published from 1802 to 1906. Articles are listed primarily by subject.

Nineteenth Century Reader's Guide can direct you to general and literary periodicals published from 1800 to 1899.

International Index to Periodicals, published since 1907, is similar to the *Reader's Guide* except that it covers scholarly journals.

The New York Times Index is the best guide to finding newspaper articles on events since the 1850's. The *Times* index can help you locate other newspaper accounts of events: once you know the date of the event, you can check other newspapers for that date.

The Public Affairs Information Service *Bulletin*, published since 1915, lists pamphlets, periodicals, government documents, and other material pertinent to economics, government, and sociology.

There are many other specialized indexes in fields such as art, medicine, literature, business, and social science.

1672 READERS' GUIDE TO PERIODICAL LITERATURE March 1980–February 1981

WILDERNESS areas—California—*Continued*

Photographs and photography

Wilderness in California: a portfolio. Liv Wildn 44:20-31 D '80

Montana

Saving the Bob [Bob Marshall Wilderness] S. M. O'Connell. il Int Wildlife 10:28D S/O '80

New York (state)

Fire Island: at last, a wilderness for New York? S. Oakes. il Sierra 65:50-3 Jl/Ag '80

Is forever wild in danger? [Adirondack Wilderness] G. Randorf. il por Conservationist 35:7-10 S/O '80

Southern States

What is this thing called wilderness? G. Morris. il South Liv 15:50-3 Ag '80

United States

See Wilderness areas

Washington (state)

After the blast [Mt St. Helens] A. Bonenko. il Nat Wildlife 18:36-9 O/N '80

Cougar Lakes: Washington's #1 wilderness battle. C. C. Raines. il Sierra 65:56-7 My/

Observing the great life chain: visiting the National Wildlife Refuges. B. Hurter. il map Peter Phot Mag 9:32-7+ O '80

Wildlife and the lens. T. A. Blake. il Sierra 65:32-4 Mr/Ap '80

Africa

See also

Elephants
Giraffes
Gorillas
Hyenas
Lions

Africa turns its guns against its animals. R. Knight. il U.S. News 89:74-5 D 8 '80

Africa, Sub-Saharan

Status of the leopard [proposal to remove from endangered status] L. J. Carter. il Science 208:269 Ap 18 '80

Alaska

On a safari in Alaska. G. Rowell. il Sierra 65:54-7 Jl/Ag '80

Alberta

Downtown deer [mule deer] V. Geist. bibl(p 101) il Natur Hist 89:56-65 Mr '80

Antarctic Regions

Dictionaries. In addition to English and other language dictionaries, libraries have specialized dictionaries in many fields, including music, biography, etymology, and art. Consult the librarian for dictionaries in your field.

The Oxford English Dictionary is the great comprehensive dictionary of the language. It provides detailed definitions and thousands of examples of use from 1150 to the present.

Biographical dictionaries include present and past editions of *Who's Who*, which provides short biographical sketches of famous living British people. *Who's Who in America* offers similar information on living Americans. There are also "who's who" publications for many different countries, as well as a *Who Was Who in America. Webster's Biographical Dictionary*, a one-volume work, briefly identifies international figures, living and dead. *Biographical Dictionaries Master Index* is a guide to over 50 "who's who" publications and other biographical dictionaries. This is a good directory to other sources of biographical sketches.

Vertical files. These files are arranged alphabetically by subject, and may include newspaper clippings, photographs, prints, pamphlets, and government publications. Ask the librarian for help.

Special collections. Many libraries have collections of films, records, and tapes. If these kinds of collections are useful to you, check the audio-visual catalog that lists the library's holdings in these areas. A number of libraries have archives of photographs, prints, and manuscripts. The librarian will help you locate these materials.

Other sources of information.

Most of your research will be done in the library. However, you may also wish to write away to various places for information.

Among the organizations or people to which you might try writing are government agencies, trade organizations, historical societies, public officials, congressmen, senators, and industries' public affairs offices. You might also wish to consult the *Encyclopedia of Associations* for ideas. This volume lists national organizations by title and subject, and gives addresses and names of key personnel. The Consumer Information Center prints a number of consumer-interest pamphlets. You may wish to write them as well for their catalog.

To obtain the Consumer Publication Catalog, write:
Consumer Information Center
Pueblo, Colorado 81009

Interviews with community leaders, experts, or concerned citizens will also provide information on your topic. Be sure you have researched your topic before an interview so you will be able to ask informed questions. Prepare your questions in advance, but be prepared to follow interesting turns if the person you are interviewing offers original insights. Use a cassette tape recorder if possible; it is the most reliable way to record statements and provide you with proof that you have quoted your source correctly. Furthermore, it frees you to concentrate on your questions and the answers rather than on taking notes.

Microforms

Because of space limitations and limited availability of some printed sources, modern libraries are now collecting microforms—material that has been photographed and reduced on film. It is intended to be read on viewers like slide projectors. The most common sorts of microforms are microfilm, or strips of film on spools, and microfiche, or flat sheets of film. Each is read on a different sort of viewer, which projects an image from the film onto a screen. Library microform materials are cataloged in the card catalog like books; they are listed by author, title, and subject.

Taking notes

A working bibliography. Once you have narrowed your subject down to a workable topic, having read at least one general encyclopedia article, it is time to set up a working bibliography. Your preliminary bibliography comes from the encyclopedia articles you have read, from your search through the library's card catalog, and, if applicable, through periodical indexes. For each possible source, enter all bibliographical information on a separate slip of paper or index card (see box).

If the article in question is from a book, you will need the book's bibliographical information, with the article's title in quotes. Make sure to have the editor's or compiler's name as well as the article's author's name. If the article is from a newspaper, you will need the exact date of the paper. If the article is from an encyclopedia, note the edition and year of publication of the encyclopedia, the volume and page numbers of the piece, and the article and encyclopedia titles.

Bibliography cards will make your task much easier when it is time to write your paper's bibliography. You may want to key your bibliography cards to your notes, using numbers or letters to signify reference sources. Some people prefer to write the author's last name on each note card.

Note cards. Before taking notes on any book or article, read the relevant pages through, making sure that you understand the material. This will make it easier to take good notes.

Write your notes on index cards, making sure to have only one note on each card, even if there are two important pieces of information on the same page of your source. This will save work later, when you are writing your outline. It is also a good idea not to write on the back on any index card. Make sure each note card has the following information:

Heading. A short key to the note, one or two words telling what the information on the card pertains to.

Source. Use either the number or letter labeling technique described above, or the author's last name, with a shortened version of the title if more than one work by an author is being used, or if two authors have the same last name. Be sure to write down the page numbers on which material was found.

Type of note. There are three basic types of notes—paraphrase, quotation, and personal comment. Make sure your note card is labeled accordingly to prevent confusion later.

Most of your notes will *paraphrase* the material you have read, or restate it in your own words.

You may wish to *quote* all or part of some sentences. This type of note must follow the author's words exactly. If you leave words out, indicate this by ellipsis points. Put the quotation in quotation marks.

Personal comment notes record your own response to something you have read. You might write, for example, that an author used faulty logic or was biased. Mark personal comments clearly so that you do not confuse them later with the author's point of view.

Bibliography cards

For a book: author
book title
(editor or translator)
city of publication
publisher's name
date of publication
call number

Sagan, Carl
The Dragons of Eden: Speculations on the Evolution of Human Intelligence
New York
Random House
1977
BF 431.S2

For an article: author (if applicable)
article title
magazine or newspaper
volume number and date
relevant page numbers

Church, George J.
"Wrestling with Social Security"
Time
vol. 120; Nov. 22, 1982
p. 71

The outline

An outline takes a broad topic and divides it into its main ideas, called subtopics, moving always from the general to the particular. Writing an outline helps to weed out irrelevant information and highlights where information is lacking; it aids in focusing an argument and determining the most logical and persuasive order for ideas.

Theme statement. After you have done some general reading on your topic and taken notes, you should have an idea of what you want to say in your paper. Try to write a statement of your theme. It should tell the purpose of your paper in one or two sentences. What is it that you are setting out to show? What aspect of a subject are you focusing on? In what direction do you want your report to move? Writing a theme statement will help you bring your research and ideas together.

Scratch outlines. With a theme statement in front of you, write a rough outline for your paper. Copy the headings from your note cards and jot down any other ideas you can think of. You may find that some of the categories you have written down are really aspects of other categories. For example, in writing a scratch outline for a paper on Nathaniel Hawthorne, you may jot down childhood and schooling as two headings only to discover that early schooling is a subtopic of childhood and that college is a separate heading. Or else you might decide to have a section on early childhood, then one on school days prior to college, and another on college. You may also discover that some categories do not fit in your paper. Put the extraneous note cards to one side. You may end up using them later, but if they do not belong it is a mistake to insert them.

This rough theme statement and scratch outline should help point out weak parts of your research and help plan further research. New subtopics—or even different ways of organizing—may occur to you as you continue reading. Don't be alarmed by this, but revise your outline accordingly.

You may also find that your theme statement needs to be modified, that new ideas and information have come your way to change your outlook. Feel free to change. Until you actually begin writing, you are not really committed to one view. Your main objective is to learn about the field you are investigating. If your research has made you change your mind about a topic, there is nothing wrong with changing your theme statement before you begin writing.

To show how a person actually goes about writing a scratch outline, let's say a student has done some reading on the life of Nathaniel Hawthorne. He has decided to focus on what made Hawthorne the type of writer that he was. The list of note headings the student has written are: Childhood, Schooling, Weird Ancestors, Puritanism. He might then jot down: College, Relationship with Family, Friends, Themes in Writing. The preliminary theme statement at this point might be, "Factors in Nathaniel Hawthorne's childhood and early adulthood made him the sort of writer that he was."

This scratch outline is inconclusive, but it lets the student know where the gaps in information are. The student must now determine the specific factors that influenced Hawthorne, the sort of writer he was, and how one thing influenced the other.

Writing a theme statement

Poor: There are many similarities and differences between life in New England today and 200 years ago.

Good: Although the past two centuries have brought many changes to New England, the region retains many of the traditional values of 200 years ago.

Revision: In the midst of many changes, life in New England remains true to the values of 200 years ago because it still revolves around the town meeting form of local government.

Sources may include people you have interviewed (above) *and newspaper stories* (below) *as well as books and magazines.*

BOMBER HITS EMPIRE STATE BUILDING, SETTING IT AFIRE AT THE 79TH FLOOR; 13 DEAD, 26 HURT; WIDE AREA ROCKED

WHERE BOMBER CRASHED INTO EMPIRE STATE BUILDING | B-25 CRASHES IN FOG

Evaluating sources

Not all sources are equally valuable. Here are some questions to ask in deciding.

1. Is the note or quotation *fact* or *opinion?*
2. If it is fact, do other sources back it up?
3. If it is opinion, who holds the opinion?
   - a participant or witness
   - a recognized expert
   - a general writer

   Each of these kinds of sources has strengths and weaknesses.
4. When was an observation or opinion made? If it is many years old, do more recent sources agree? Has new information come to light since it was made?

Evaluating notes and sources.

Once you have completed your investigation, having filled in the information gaps that the scratch outline made you aware of, it is important to read your notes carefully—to determine if any gaps remain, to eliminate notes that do not fit in, and to evaluate your sources.

Researchers divide sources into *primary* and *secondary*. Primary sources are firsthand records of events. They may include newspaper accounts written when the events occurred, autobiographies of the participants, diaries or letters of the participants, or reports of scientific experiments. If you interview people for your paper, they may be primary sources for information on events that they witnessed.

Secondary sources evaluate, analyze, criticize, relate, or otherwise deal with primary source information. Such sources include the work of historians or commentators with no firsthand knowledge of the events they write about. People you interview may be secondary sources if they are repeating what they have heard from other sources, or evaluating such information.

Both types of information sources must be evaluated for their accuracy. People who participate in events are closest to them, but may not have the objectivity necessary to relate what really happened. They often try to cast themselves or their friends in a favorable light. They also may not really know all that was going on. Secondary sources may be more objective, but they too may be biased, inaccurate, or incompetent.

One important way to judge the reliability of a source is to see if different authors support each other by presenting the same basic facts, though they may have varying slants and interpretations. Another way is to read about an author in a biographical dictionary. What professional position does the author hold? What other books has he written? What might the author's concerns be besides wanting to present his viewpoint? A paper on the scandals of the Nixon administration, for example, would treat material by those accused or convicted of illegal acts as different from material by those not involved. It is part of your job as a researcher to evaluate the accuracy of your sources and to distinguish between opinions and facts.

The finished outline. Now you are ready to put together a finished outline. It may be done in topic form or sentence form. The topic outline gives headings and subheadings in noun form, such as: Early Childhood, Learning to Write, Themes. The sentence outline gives main headings in either sentence or noun form, but the subheadings are complete sentences. Whatever style of outline you choose, be careful not to mix them up. This can lead to muddled thinking.

The first step in any outline is to write a carefully considered theme statement. Now that you have finished research on your topic, you can be more specific than you were in your rough theme statement. If you find that you are pleased with your scratch theme, you can use that or reword it. You may wish to write an entirely new theme statement, having reconsidered the focus of your paper. Keep in mind that your theme statement must still be short, no more than one or two sentences telling the reader what you will be discussing in your paper.

The preliminary theme statement we wrote for a paper on Nathaniel Hawthorne, for example, is too sketchy for a careful outline statement. Instead we might now write: *Already inclined toward introspection by nature and experience, Nathaniel Hawthorne spent twelve years after college in virtual isolation, writing and rewriting his* Twice-Told Tales *and forming the style that characterized all his literary output throughout his career.*

An outline, like the paper itself, should have an introduction, a body, and a conclusion. The introduction should state the focus or purpose of the paper. It may in fact, when you actually write the introduction, be an expanded version of the theme statement. It may also discuss in concise terms some historical background, or it may give important definitions. Its purpose is to let the reader know what the rest of the paper will cover in detail.

Most of the outline will be taken up by the body. The main ideas of your paper, and the subtopics that

Types of outlines

Topic outline

Title That Lonely Hawthorne Chamber

I. Introduction
II. Early Childhood
  A. The early years
  B. Death of father
    1. Effect on Hawthorne
    2. Self-imposed isolation of Hawthorne's mother
    3. Life with relatives
III. New England School Days
  A. Education
  B. Foot injury and subsequent two-year isolation
  C. Life in Maine
IV. Bowdoin College Days
  A. Education
  B. Companions
  C. Decision to become a writer
V. The Lonely Chamber—Learning to Write
  A. Twelve years of isolation
    1. Critics—favorable and unfavorable
    2. Writing apprenticeship
  B. Anguishing through his Puritan ancestry
  C. Emergence from the lonely chamber
VI. Themes in Hawthorne's Works Showing Early Influences
  A. Isolation of mankind
  B. Evils of Puritanism
VII. Conclusion

Sentence outline

Theme statement Burial rites among the ancient Greeks, the Egyptians, and the Anglo-Saxons differed in detail, but all three groups used cremation and interment, and the Egyptians and Anglo-Saxons both practiced burial at sea.

Title Ancient Burial Rites

I. Ancient Greeks usually burned their dead heroes.
  A. The *Iliad* recounts the cremation of Hector and Patroclus.
  B. Frequently the ashes of the dead were placed in urns.
  C. Other sections of the *Iliad* suggest interment.
    1. Erection of a barrow for Patroclus.
    2. Other evidence of the existence of barrows.
II. Egyptians interred their leaders.
  A. Pyramids are seen in the Nile valley.
  B. Archaeologists have found burial ships.
III. Anglo-Saxons practiced interment, cremation, and ship burial.
  A. There is evidence of interment in *Beowulf.*
  B. In the same poem, Beowulf is burned on a huge pyre.
  C. The Sutton Hoo find reveals the existence of ship burial.
IV. Conclusion.

A checklist for outlines

1. Have you included an introduction?
2. Is your theme statement clearly presented?
3. Do your main idea headings fully cover the subject?
4. Are you sure your main idea headings do not overlap?
5. Have you arranged your main ideas in a logical order?
6. Do you have subtopic headings under each main idea?
7. Can you provide facts to back up every main idea and subtopic heading?
8. Have you included a conclusion?

support them, should be enumerated in the body. The body may include explanations, comparisons, contrasts, examples, analogies, facts, and historical details. The level of detail should depend on the length of the paper itself. A paper of 25 pages will require a longer outline than one of ten pages.

A conclusion is also necessary. This can be a summary of points made in your paper, or it can be a restatement of the theme. It shows the reader that you have demonstrated what you set out to prove. Neither the introduction nor the conclusion have to be spelled out in the outline, since the ideas they detail are covered in the body of the outline.

Use your scratch outline to help you list the main points of your report, making sure that all relevant subject note headings, especially those added after you wrote your scratch outline, are included. Polish the language of your scratch outline headings. Most important, begin to consider how to organize your paper so that the information and ideas will be persuasive. A first step is to decide on your topic and subtopic headings. Main idea headings are more general than the supporting elements that substantiate them. Which are the main, general ideas, and which are the facts, theories, and opinions that support or substantiate those ideas?

Once you have determined your main ideas, try to think of the most logical way to present them. Do not be afraid to try different sequences. If you have taken good notes and written good headings, shuffle your note cards to try out different organizational schemes. You may find that writing the headings on a piece of paper and numbering them in different sequences is the method that works best for you.

Organization. The trickiest part of writing an outline for many people is deciding how to organize it. This becomes easier if you know the four basic types of research papers, and the main ways in which papers are organized. The four types of research papers are historical, biographical, literary, and analytical.

Historical papers are usually developed chronologically or by thoroughly analyzing the important events of an era and then discussing related side issues.

Biographical papers can be organized in either of the two ways discussed above. Your choice of organization will depend on how you have viewed the life of your subject. The emphasis placed on events will determine the order of presentation.

Literary papers may trace certain themes in the work of one or many authors. In such papers, it is common to select only the major works of the authors for analysis. If you choose to study both major and minor works, you would probably do best to analyze the major works first, then finish up with the minor ones. The works could also be treated chronologically. If you are dealing with the images in the works of a particular author, you would probably deal with the central images first, then go on to the related images. In either case, your paper would be strengthened by pertinent examples of the images.

Analytical papers dealing with problems or events might be developed by discussing the central issues first, then going on to related side issues. Thus, if you were dealing with a particularly stressful time in the history of a country, you would work through the most important aspects of the situation before covering the less important problems.

In general, the main types of orders are chronological, decreasing importance, increasing importance, compare and contrast, pro and con, geographical, cause to effect, and effect to cause. These are not the only orders possible, but they are the most common ones.

Note that in the biographical topic outline on Hawthorne, the writer chose a chronological order; the sentence outline on burial rites is organized geographically. It could have been organized by type of burial as follows:

I. Ship burial.
II. Interment.
III. Cremation.

As the writer, you have the choice of type of organization for your paper, subject to the advice and recommendations of your teacher.

You should always experiment with more than one outline organization for a research paper. Which suits your topic best? Which is closest to the recommendations of your teacher? Remember that it is always easier and faster to change the organization of the outline before you start to write than to revise a poorly planned or unfinished paper.

Writing

Oh! But he was a tight-fisted hand at the grindstone, Scrooge! a squeezing, wrenching, grasping, scraping, clutching, covetous old sinner! Hard and sharp as flint, from which no steel had ever struck out generous fire; secret, and self-contained, and solitary as an oyster. The cold within him froze his old features, nipped his pointed nose, shrivelled his cheek, stiffened his gait; made his eyes red, his thin lips blue; and spoke out shrewdly in his grating voice. A frosty rime was on his head, and on his eyebrows, and his wiry chin. He carried his own low temperature always about with him; he iced

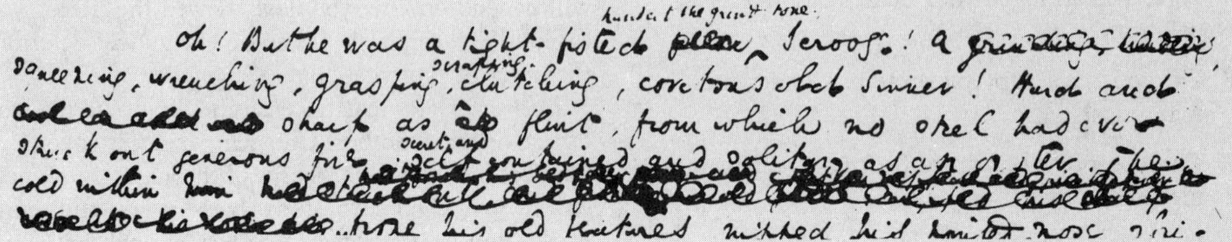

Good writers learn how to edit their own writing. Above is a passage from "A Christmas Carol" by Dickens, corrected by the author himself.

The first draft. Now that you have good notes, a theme statement, and an organized outline, it is time to begin writing a rough draft. At this point, it is a good idea not to worry too much about the way you are using language, as long as your ideas make sense and there is a logic behind the movement of your paragraphs based on your outline.

Some people find the introduction the hardest part of the paper to write, so you may wish to start writing your first draft in the middle, with one of the main ideas that particularly excites you. You can save writing the introduction for last. A good outline has the special advantage of keeping you abreast of everything you want to say. Since there is no chance you will lose your train of thought, you can concentrate on your choice of words, sentence structure, and paragraph development. Many writers prefer to write the first draft quickly, then pay attention to how they express themselves in the later draft. Just remember, this is a first draft, and no one is going to see it but you. You will have to rewrite this first draft no matter how much time you spend perfecting your sentences; you will have to change your wording around; you may even have to revise your basic outline if another order seems to work better.

Complete the first draft before you begin to rewrite. You will then have a better idea of the weak parts of your paper, where it is needlessly repetitious, and where more explanations are necessary. As you work through your first draft you may want to use certain shortcuts that experienced writers employ.

One helpful hint is to staple note cards to your first draft when the cards carry material that you want to quote word for word. Why bother to copy quotations when you are only working on a first draft? Copying takes time and it can mean making mistakes.

Another helpful hint is to set a goal for each writing session. If you set a reasonable goal for each session, you will find that you can complete that unit of writing in the time allotted. Examine your outline to see what you are going to cover in that particular writing session. The outline helps you plan your thoughts out so that the writing comes easier. It also tells you which notes you will be using for that period.

A third hint is to frequently look back at what you have already written in your first draft. Looking back helps you to pick up the thread of your discussion and helps to reacquaint you with the thoughts you are about to pursue.

Style. Good writers follow certain conventions that make their prose clear and pleasant to read. Among them are:

Avoid personal references. It is unnecessary to use "I think," "my opinion," "I've found," and other first-person phrases. When you want to make clear that you are stating an opinion, it is more acceptable to use such phrases as "many people feel," "as some critics believe," and "one opinion is."

Avoid informal language. There are many colloquial and informal uses of language that are acceptable in conversation but not in writing. Make sure you use a word correctly when you write it, both in its spelling and meaning (see Usage dictionary, page 272).

Avoid verbosity. Be as succinct as possible without sacrificing clarity. Do not write, "in the event of," instead of "if"; "in view of the fact," instead of "because"; "at the present time," instead of "now"; or "in the majority of cases," instead of "usually." Be on the lookout for other phrases of the same kind.

Use the active voice. Whenever possible, have the subject of your sentence act instead of being acted upon. "he wrote it," is more direct and forceful than "it was written by him."

Avoid exclamation marks. Except on rare occasions, exclamation marks make your prose seem hysterical.

Avoid unnecessary adjectives and adverbs. If you use the right noun or verb to begin with, you will not need many modifiers. Modifiers actually weaken prose. "The abandoned child was left behind," can be changed to "the child was abandoned." "He walked quickly" can be changed to "he hurried."

Avoid clichés. The use of clichés indicates a lazy mind. Search for ways to make your points in fresh and more effective ways.

Avoid jargon, slang, euphemism. Jargon and slang may not be understood by your reader. Even if understood, they make the tone of your paper too informal. Euphemism, the substitution of a polite, roundabout way of referring to something disturbing, can make your paper sound prissy. Don't write "passed away" for "died."

Avoid foreign expressions. Unless there is no way to say something in English, or unless the originally foreign word is common enough in English to be found in the dictionary, you should not use non-English expressions. They may not be understood and can seem pretentious. They are usually unnecessary.

Use specific, concrete language. Instead of using general nouns and abstractions, try to use specific language and solid images. "The person" is hazy, but "the middle-aged farmer" gives us a clear picture. To say "he loved nature" does not mean as much as, "he took long walks in the woods." Use analogies and anecdotes to make abstract concepts such as love, time, good, and evil come alive.

Ten useful rules for style

1. Avoid personal references.
2. Avoid informal language.
3. Avoid verbosity.
4. Use the active voice.
5. Avoid exclamation marks.
6. Avoid unnecessary adjectives and adverbs.
7. Avoid clichés.
8. Avoid jargon, slang, euphemism.
9. Avoid foreign expressions.
10. Use specific, concrete language.

The final draft.

Preparing the final draft is an important step in writing a successful research paper. This is the end product of all your work.

Editing. You may need to go over your first draft more than once, correcting spelling, punctuation, phrasing, grammar, logic, paragraphing, and the development and progression of ideas. Read your first draft for sense. Do you understand the points you are making? Check to make sure your nouns and verbs agree, being either singular or plural but not switching back and forth. Also make sure that you do not switch tenses for no reason. Are your transitions from one idea to the next smooth? If not, transitional phrases may help your paragraphs move more easily. "However," "although," "in addition," "first," "second," "third," and "moreover" are some useful transitional phrases.

In addition to editing your paper, you must make sure that you have documented your sources. All quotations, paraphrases, and ideas that you have taken from books and articles should be marked by footnotes. Well-known facts, such as the birth or death dates of famous people, do not have to be documented. Many facts and all opinions and interpretations by others should be referenced to their source. Documentation also supports the validity of your statements, providing the reader with source references to check if he doubts the accuracy of your facts.

Form. Title pages may be set up in many ways. One common way is to have the title of your paper start one-third down from the top of the page, centered, with your name on the next line. The course title should be typed one-third of the way from the bottom of the page, centered. The next line should have your teacher's name, and the line after that should have the date.

The body of the paper should be typed on unlined $8\frac{1}{2}$ inch by 11 inch white bond paper. The left margin should be $1\frac{1}{2}$ inches; the right, top, and bottom margins should be 1 inch.

Double-space the paper throughout, except for footnotes and bibliography. The page number should appear in the upper right-hand corner. Use arabic numerals.

Be sure to fix all typographical errors. Some teachers will accept small corrections made in pen or pencil in your report, but all prefer clean copy. Use a correcting fluid or correcting paper to eliminate mistakes, and type the correction in.

When typing your paper, leave one space after a comma or a semicolon and leave two spaces after a period, question mark, or colon. Indent the beginnings of paragraphs five spaces.

Footnotes. After marking footnotes numerically in the body of your report, you need to write the full citations that correspond to them. These can appear at the bottom of the page on which they are noted, but it is easier to put them at the end of your paper, on a separate piece of paper entitled "Footnotes," which should come just prior to the bibliography. Number these pages like the others in the paper.

Footnotes are single-spaced, with a line skipped between entries. The first line of each footnote is indented five spaces, with the following lines brought out to the left margin. The footnote number is typed a half line up from the note itself, just as in the body of the report. Footnotes appear in the same numerical order in which they appear in your report. The basic forms are described below and examples are shown in the box at the right.

For a book:

- Name of author in normal order, putting the first name or initials (if the author uses them instead of a first name) first. Comma after author's last name.
- Book title underlined.
- In parentheses, the city of publication, colon, publisher, comma, year of publication, end parenthesis, then a comma.
- Page numbers. Use p. for page and pp. for pages. Put a period at the end of the line.
- Note: If other information, such as the name of the editor or translator, needs to be included, put a comma after the book title and the abbreviations "ed." or "trans." followed by the name of the editor or translator. The facts of publication follow, in parentheses, with no comma between the editor's name and the starting parenthesis.
- If a volume number is needed, it comes after the comma that follows the end parenthesis. It is given in arabic numerals and is followed by a colon, then the page numbers without the abbreviations p. and pp. There must be a period at the end of the line.

For a magazine article:

- Name of author in normal order, comma.
- Article title in quotation marks, with comma before the final mark.
- Magazine title underlined, comma.
- Date of magazine, including month and year, comma. The exact date of a weekly must be given.
- Page numbers, using p. and pp. abbreviations. Period at the end of the line.
- Note: For scholarly publications, you may need to include the volume number. If so, it comes after the magazine title, with no comma between them, and is followed by the month and year of the issue in parentheses, which are followed by a colon and the page numbers of the reference without use of p. and pp. A period must be placed at the end of the line.

Sample footnotes

Book with one author (who uses initials instead of a full first name); note subtitle after colon:

[1] F. W. Bateson, *The Scholar-Critic: An Introduction to Literary Research* (London: Routledge & Kegan Paul, 1972), pp. 51-55.

Book with two (or more) authors; edition other than first:

[2] Robert Jastrow and Malcolm H. Thompson, *Astronomy: Fundamentals and Frontiers,* 3rd ed. (New York: John Wiley & Sons, 1972), p. 117.

Article in a book; note the mention of the editors:

[3] O.R. Gurney, "The Babylonians and Hittites," *Oracles and Divination,* ed. Michael Loewe and Carmen Blacker (Boulder, Colo.: Shambhala, 1981), pp. 142–168.

Article in a popular magazine; note the full date of a weekly is given:

[4] John Newhouse, "Arms and Orthodoxy," *The New Yorker,* 7 June 1982, pp. 44–103.

Article in a scholarly journal:

[5] A.K. Coomaraswamy, "Sir Gawain and the Green Knight: Indra and Namuci," *Speculum* 19 (January 1944): 104–125.

Unsigned newspaper article; if signed, the author's name would come first:

[6] "Teacher Calls Confinement in China a 'Nightmare,' " *New York Times,* 6 June 1982, sec. 1, p. 15.

Pamphlet where agency's name is used instead of author:

[7] Department of Health, Education, and Welfare, *Day Care for Your Children* (Washington, D.C.: Government Printing Office, 1974).

Article in encyclopedia; note the mention of edition and volume.

[8] "Anarcharsis," *Encyclopaedia Britannica,* 14th ed. (1965), 1:839.

Personal interview:

[9] Jules Blane, Candy-Store Owner, Brooklyn, New York, personal interview, 1 June 1981.

- The form for an article from a book combines the magazine article and book footnote forms. After the author's name, the article title comes in quotation marks, with an inner comma (the same style as for a magazine article). Instead of a magazine title, the book title is given and underlined, followed by a comma, then the editor's name, if applicable, followed by parentheses and the facts of publication. After the end parenthesis, there is a comma and the page reference, using the page abbreviations followed by a period.

Subsequent footnotes. The first time you write a footnote for a source, you must give full information. If the next footnote is from the same source, you can write "ibid.," which means "in the same place." This should be followed by a comma and the new page number, followed by a period. If the reference is on the same page as the previous one, put a period after "ibid."

If you refer later to a book already cited, you can write the author's last name, comma, and the page numbers, followed by a period.

If you have used more than one work by an author, and have previously given full reference information on the book you are now referring to, you can write the author's last name, comma, title, comma, and page numbers, period.

If you mention the author's name in the body of the text and have already given full reference information on it elsewhere, you can write "op. cit." followed by a comma, and then the page reference, period.

After the first mention of a work, use of a short title is permissible in both notes and text.

Bibliography. A bibliography is a list of all the works used in writing your paper, particularly those cited; it should also include works that helped shape your thinking on the topic, even if they were not mentioned in your report. Entries are alphabetically arranged by author's last name wherever possible. (Unsigned articles are alphabetized by the first letter of the article title; pamphlets issued by agencies are alphabetized by the first letter of the agency's name.) Bibliographies are single-spaced, with a line skipped between entries. The first line of each entry is flush with the left margin, but the rest of the entry is indented five spaces.

Entries should be typed on a separate piece of paper entitled "Bibliography." This is the last page of your report. The basic forms are as follows:

For a book:

- Author's last name, comma, first name or initials, period.
- Book title underlined, period.
- Place of publication, colon, publisher, comma, year of publication, period.

For a magazine article:

- Author's last name, comma, first name or initials, period.
- Article title in quotation marks, a period preceding the end quotation mark.
- Magazine title, underlined, comma.
- Date of issue, including month and year, comma.
- Page numbers of the article, using page abbreviations and ending the line with a period.
- Note: For an article from a book, the book title is given, underlined, after the article title in quotation marks. The period after the book title is followed by the editor or translator's name, which is followed by a period and the facts of publication, the same as for a full book reference.
- In a scholarly journal where the volume number is given, the volume number should be placed directly after the magazine title with no comma between them. The month (if possible) and year are given in parentheses, followed by a colon and the page numbers of the article. Page abbreviations are not used. There must be a period at the end of the line.
- Newspaper articles are cited by the section number, following the date, if the pages are not numbered consecutively. Unsigned newspaper articles are alphabetized by title.

Sample bibliography

"Anarcharsis." *Encyclopaedia Britannica,* 14th ed., (1965).

Bateson, F.W. *The Scholar-Critic: An Introduction to Literary Research.* London: Routledge & Kegan Paul, 1972.

Blane, Jules. Candy-Store Owner. Brooklyn, New York. Personal interview. 1 June 1981.

Coomaraswamy, A. K. "Sir Gawain and the Green Knight: Indra and Namuci." *Speculum* 19 (January 1944): 104–125.

Department of Health, Education, and Welfare. *Day Care for Your Children.* Washington, D.C.: Government Printing Office, 1974.

Gurney, O.R. "The Babylonians and Hittites." *Oracles and Divination.* Ed. Michael Loewe and Carmen Blacker. Boulder, Colo.: Shamabhala, 1981.

Jastrow, Robert, and Thompson, Malcolm H. *Astronomy: Fundamentals and Frontiers.* 3rd ed. New York: John Wiley & Sons, 1972.

Newhouse, John. "Arms and Orthodoxy." *The New Yorker,* 7 June 1982, pp. 44–103.

"Teacher Calls Confinement in China a 'Nightmare.' " *New York Times,* 6 June 1982, sec. 1, p. 15.

Punctuation review

Questions of punctuation are always a serious concern in formal writing. The following pages provide a brief review of major types of punctuation.

Good style in punctuating, especially in the use of commas, often depends on a grasp of English grammar. If you wish to review the grammar that affects punctuation, turn to pages 34–53 in Volume 1.

There are two issues in punctuating. The first is a simple question of right and wrong. A writer who ends each sentence with a colon rather than a period is simply wrong. Sentences cannot end with a colon.

The second issue is less clear-cut. For example, in some cases, the writer may choose punctuation to suit his or her taste: a semicolon to separate two closely related thoughts, or a period. Writers learn with practice which possibility to choose to make their meaning clearest.

End punctuation. There are three kinds of end punctuation: the period, the question mark, and the exclamation point. Every sentence must end with one of these marks.

The exclamation point ends an exclamatory sentence, and the question mark is at the end of a question. All other sentences end with a period.

What a good boy Paul is!
Is Paul a good boy?
Paul is a good boy.

The most common mistake in end punctuation usage is to punctuate as a sentence a group of words that is not a sentence. A sentence must, as a minimum, have a subject and a verb. In addition, it must not have been transformed into an adjective clause by the addition of a subordinate conjunction, nor into a relative clause by the use of a relative pronoun. Such clauses should not be punctuated as separate sentences, but only as parts of some other, longer sentence.

SENTENCE FRAGMENT
Although I like the design.

CORRECTIONS
(1) *I like the design.*
(2) *Although I like the design, I don't care to use it in a living room.*

Periods. Besides its use at the end of a sentence, the period is used after initials (*T. S. Eliot*) and after many other abbreviations, including those of months (*Feb.*), countries (*U.S.A.*), states (*Tenn.*), and other commonly abbreviated forms (*St., Ave., Dr., Mr.,* and so on).

Commas. The most common mistake in comma usage is to use too many. Limit comma usage to the following situations.

Compound sentences. When two simple sentences are joined together by a coordinating conjunction, put a comma before the conjunction. (This comma is often omitted when the clauses being joined are especially short.) Do not use commas when only a part of the sentence has been compounded.

She got up to close the window, but he asked her to sit down again.

Series. Use commas after all but the last item in a series.

Nonrestrictive relative clauses. A nonrestrictive relative clause is set off from the rest of the sentence by commas. So, too, are expressions that derive from nonrestrictive clauses, such as appositives and nonrestrictive participles and participial phrases.

The woman, who was smiling engagingly, told us to take our seats.
Mr. Jackson, standing on the makeshift platform, gave a rousing campaign speech.

Adverbial clauses. An adverbial clause at the beginning of a sentence is set off from the rest of the sentence by a comma. Such a clause at the end of a sentence is not set off.

When we got back from the beach, we were too tired to eat dinner.
We were too tired to eat dinner when we got back from the beach.

Parenthetical expressions. Parenthetical expressions are set off by commas. These include *yes, no,* and mild interjections (those not followed by an exclamation point), such as *well* and *oh,*

Well, it's time to leave

nouns of address,

How is your garden growing, Mary?

and such expressions as *of course* and *however.*

We will, of course, be ready; others, however, may not be.

Clarity. Sometimes—but very rarely—a comma is needed to avoid confusion and to make a sentence clearer:

To John, Matilda would always be a mystery.

Semicolons. Use a semicolon to join two sentences without using a conjunction. The semicolon is also used when two sentences are joined by such an expression as *therefore* or *however.*

Two plus two equal four; therefore, five is not an acceptable answer.

The semicolon is also used to separate the items in a series when there are already commas within individual elements of the series:

He has lived in Moline, Illinois; Boulder, Colorado; and Seattle, Washington.

Colons. The main use of a colon is to introduce a list, an example, a question, or a long quotation.

The question is this: What should we do next?

A colon used in this way should always follow a noun or a pronoun, never a verb or a preposition. It may also come after the expressions *as follows* and *the following.*

Dashes. The dash indicates a sudden break or change of emphasis in a sentence:

I have here a—now, where did I put that thing?

Dashes can also be used to set off an appositive when the appositive is to be emphasized or when it contains commas within it.

Parentheses. Parentheses set off material in a sentence that is separate or apart from the main thought.

She traveled through Davenport (a city she once lived in) and on toward Chicago.

Quotations. A direct quotation—the exact words that someone has said or written—is enclosed in quotation marks. If the quotation is included within another sentence, it is set off from the rest of the sentence by commas:

"I think," he said, "that you are on the right track."

When more than one person is being quoted, as in a conversation, begin a new paragraph for each change of speaker.

Question marks and exclamation points are placed inside the quotation marks if they are part of the quote

"Who are you?" she asked

and outside if they apply to the sentence as a whole

Who was it that said, "I shall return"?

Periods and commas are always placed inside quotation marks, while the semicolon and colon are always placed outside.

Do not use quotation marks for an indirect quotation, that is, one that does not report someone's exact words:

He said that it was raining.

Italics. Words to be set in italics are indicated in typed or handwritten material by an underline. Italics are used to single out words, phrases, or even sentences for special emphasis. Titles of books, plays, magazines, and newspapers, and the names of ships, trains, and airplanes are italicized. (Shorter works like poems and stories are put in quotation marks.)

The Adventures of Tom Sawyer
Hamlet
National Geographic
the *Titanic*
"Annabel Lee"
"The Masque of the Red Death"

Capitalization. All proper nouns (persons, places, or things) are capitalized. In addition, capitalize the first word of every sentence; the first word of a direct quotation embedded in another sentence; the names of groups, associations, and businesses; the letters of some abbreviations; and all historic events, buildings, monuments, and documents:

General Motors — *Grant's Tomb*
NASA — *Declaration of Independence*
World War II

Titles used with proper nouns are capitalized:

Dr. Brown
Senator Douglas

as are the first, last, and important words in titles of printed texts. Prepositions, articles, and conjunctions are not capitalized unless they are the first or last word of the title.

Usage dictionary

Understanding usage can be an important part of improving your writing. A careful writer is one who develops a sense for the right word at the right time and place. Careless writers, on the other hand, often confuse words that look or sound alike and are willing to settle for the approximate word.

If you have never used a usage dictionary, spend a few minutes browsing through this one to see the kind of information it offers you. The entries often comment on the difference between informal (spoken) and formal (written) English. They also provide advice on avoiding lazy writing. Once you are familiar with the contents, return to the dictionary for specific information when you are writing a paper or report.

A

a, an. These forms of the indefinite article are used to refer to one person, place, abstraction, or other "thing." They are used only with singular nouns and are unspecific, not indicating which one of many is meant. *A* is the article used before consonant sounds (*a* dog); *an* is used before any word beginning with a vowel sound (*an* ant). Since the rule is based on the opening sound of the following word, words beginning with *h* or *u* may take either article form, depending on pronunciation (*an* honor, *a* hospital, *an* underground, *a* universe).

abbreviations. Abbreviatons should not be used unless they are explained or are likely to be understood without explanation. A few abbreviations (such as Mr., A.M., B.C., and Ph.D.) are so common that avoiding them would be thought eccentric. Excessive use of abbreviations, however, is generally unpleasant, especially when the abbreviations are jargon or slang. Except for the common abbreviations discussed above, abbreviations are regarded as more informal than full forms.

about, almost. *About* in the sense of almost is informal usage in such phrases as *about done*, *about dead. See also* ALMOST.

absolutely. *See* ADVERBS.

accept, except. *Accept* is a verb meaning to receive or approve. *Except* is usually a preposition that means excluding. (I *accept* all your comments *except* the last one.)

adapt, adopt. *Adapt* means to change something to make it suitable for a new use. One may *adapt* oneself to different circumstances. A novel may be *adapted* for the stage. *Adopt* means to decide upon (a plan), to choose to treat someone as a close relative, or to vote to accept a resolution. (The committee voted to *adopt* the resolution.)

adjectives. There are many overworked and misused adjectives that should be avoided in careful writing. Something is *wonderful* if it inspires wonder; otherwise *wonderful* is an empty adjective. When you say something is *nice*, the reader politely yawns. Other adjectives to look out for are *awful*, *beautiful*, *cute*, *funny*, *incredible*, *interesting*, *lousy*, *lovely*, *marvelous*, *pretty*, *terrible*, *terrific*, and *unique* (since *unique* means one of a kind, do not write or say "the most unique"). In general, if an adjective tells a reader only that you vaguely approve or disapprove of something, a better adjective is needed.

adopt. *See* ADAPT.

adverbs. Tired adjectives can be made into exhausted adverbs, usually just by adding *-ly* to the end. In addition to *awfully*, *beautifully*, etc., watch out for overdoses of *absolutely*, *definitely*, *positively*, *quite*, *really*, and *very*.

advice, advise. *Advice* is a noun; *advise* is a verb. If you can see the *vice* in *advice*, you may find it easier to remember which is the noun. (He *advised* me against seeking *advice*.)

affect, effect. *Affect* is a verb meaning to influence or to pretend in an offensive way. (The weather *affects* my moods. She *affects* to great wealth.) *Effect* is a noun meaning result or what is accomplished. (He never considered the *effect* of his actions.) It can also be used as a verb meaning to accomplish something. (The principal *effected* changes in the school.)

aggravate. In formal speech or writing, *aggravate* is used only to mean to make worse. (The difficulty was *aggravated* by misunderstanding.) Colloquially, *aggravate* is often used to mean irritate. (His nagging *aggravated* me.) This usage is less acceptable in writing than in speech.

agree to, agree with. *Agree to* something. (I *agree to* your proposal.) *Agree with* someone. (He *agrees with* me.)

ain't. *Ain't* was originally a contraction of *am not* (compare *can't*, which in some regions is pronounced *cain't*). Over a hundred years ago, it came to be widely used also as a contraction for *are not* and even for *is not* and *have not* or *has not*. Perhaps because of the indiscriminate use, *ain't* fell into disfavor among many careful speakers. It is not used now in published writing, except in dialogue. The word is generally regarded as slang.

all of, alongside of. *See* OF.

all ready, already. *All ready* means completely ready

(I was *all ready* for the picnic) or that all of what has been referred to is ready (the boys were *all ready* to shout). *Already* is an adverbial expression meaning by or before a particular time. (The sun was *already* up when I awoke.)

all right. *See* ALRIGHT.

all the farther, as far as. In the sense of *as far as, all the farther* (that's *all the farther* he can walk) is a regional expression and should not be used in formal writing.

all together, altogether. *Altogether* means entirely. (That's an *altogether* different matter.) *All together* means in a group. (When we are *all together,* we sing.)

allude, elude. To *allude* to something is to refer to it indirectly. (The poet *alludes* subtly to King Arthur.) Note that the verb *allude* is regularly followed by the particle *to.* To *elude* something or somebody is to evade or escape. (The suspect *eluded* the police.)

allusion, illusion, delusion. An *allusion* is an indirect reference. (The poet made *allusions* to King Arthur.) An *illusion* is a false perception or idea. (What you thought you saw was an optical *illusion.*) A *delusion* is a false belief. The word connotes madness. (Hitler's fatal *delusion* was that he could never be wrong.)

almost, most. In speech, *almost* is sometimes shortened to *most*, and the shortened form is written with an initial apostrophe. (They had *'most* everything.) But *almost* is the standard form for use in writing.

a lot. *A lot* is two words.

already. *See* ALL READY.

alright, all right. Although there would be logical justification for a spelling form "alright," it is not acceptable in careful writing. *All right* is the only correct form.

although, though. These two words have the same meaning. *Although* is generally felt to be a bit more formal than *though.* The shortened forms *altho* and *tho* should be avoided in formal writing.

altogether. *See* ALL TOGETHER.

alumnus. An *alumnus* is a male graduate of a school; a female graduate is an *alumna. Alumni* are graduates, a group of all males or males and females. *Alumnae* is the plural form used to refer to a group of all female graduates.

among, between. *Among* is used when referring to more than two persons or things. (The prize money was distributed *among* three winners.) *Between* is used when referring to two persons or things. (The prize money was divided *between* the two winners.) However, many speakers and writers do not observe the distinction.

amount, number; fewer, less. *Amount* refers to quantity in bulk while *number* refers to separate units. (The *amount* of money; the *number* of dollars.) Similarly, fewer refers to numbered things while less refers to amount. (The *number* of pieces in the game was *fewer* than called for; the *amount* of sugar we needed was *less* than we thought.)

an. *See* A.

and etc. *See* ETC.

and/or. Useful as this expression is, most careful speakers and writers feel it should be confined to legal or commercial use.

anxious, eager. *Anxious* means apprehensive, worried. *Eager* means looking forward to. In writing, try to keep this distinction in mind. (I am *anxious* about the test; I am *eager* to have it over.)

anybody, anyone, each, everybody, everyone, no one, nobody, none, somebody, someone. These words are all singular and always take singular verbs. (*Everybody* is here.) When a pronoun refers back to such words, *he* and *his* are most often used. (*Everyone* knows what *he* is supposed to do.) This is formally correct but awkward when the word may refer to a man or a woman. Some writers prefer to use the plural forms *they* and *their* (someone called but *they* hung up), but this practice is not as widely accepted as the use of the masculine singular pronouns. Other writers use the phrase *he or she,* although this too can be awkward. *See also* GENDER.

anyway. This, and not *anyways,* is the correct word. It means in any case. (He went *anyway.*) *Any way* means in any of a number of ways. (She traveled *any way* the wind blew.)

anywhere, everywhere, nowhere, somewhere. None of these words takes a final *-s* in standard English. These words are considered more appropriate in writing than are the related terms *anyplace, everyplace, no place,* and *someplace.*

appraise, apprise. *Appraise* means to estimate the value of something. *Apprise* is a less common word meaning to notify or inform about.

around, 'round. *Around* in the sense of about or nearby is colloquial and should not be used in formal writing. (Let's start *around* ten o'clock. The book is *around* here somewhere.) The adverb *around* is often shortened in speech to *'round.* We are likely to say *the other way 'round,* but in formal situations we would write *the other way around.*

as. The use of *as* in the sense of because or since is often ambiguous. (We were bored *because* we knew what he would say, not, We were bored *as* we knew what he would say.) *See also* LIKE.

as far as. *See* ALL THE FARTHER.

as/like. *See* LIKE.

at. The use of *at* in such expressions as, Where is he *at*? is colloquial and should be avoided.

away. *See* 'WAY.

awful. *See* ADJECTIVES.

awhile, a while. *Awhile* means for a time. (Sleep *awhile*.) After a preposition, *a while* should be used. (Help me for *a while*.)

B

backward(s), forward(s), inward(s), outward(s), onward(s), toward(s). As adverbs, these words may or may not have a final *-s*, although the forms without *-s* are more common in this country. As adjectives, they never have a final *-s*. (The *backward* boy walked *forward*; or *forwards*.)

bad, badly. *Bad* is the adjective; *badly* is the adverb. If you say that you *feel badly*, you are not saying that you feel sick or sorry, but that your sense of touch is lacking in some way. *See also* GOOD.

barely. *See* DOUBLE NEGATIVE.

beautiful. *See* ADJECTIVES.

began, begun. These are, respectively, the standard past tense and past participial forms of the verb *begin*. (Right now, I *begin*. Yesterday, I *began*. Recently, I *have begun*.)

beside, besides. *Beside* means by the side of. (They stood *beside* each other.) *Besides* means moreover. (*Besides*, what difference does it make?)

better, best. *See* HAD BETTER.

between. *See* AMONG.

between you and me. This is the correct expression. *Between you and I* is grammatically incorrect. After a preposition such as *between*, use objective pronouns (me, him, her, them), not subjective pronouns (I, he, she, they).

borrow, lend. One *borrows from* someone and *lends* to someone. (John *borrowed* money *from* Jan. She agreed to *lend* it *to* him.)

but. *See* HELP BUT.

C

calculate, reckon. Both these words mean to compute or arrive at a conclusion after careful consideration. In regional dialects, they are used indiscriminately for such verbs as think, suppose, expect. Avoid such usages in writing.

Calvary, cavalry. *Calvary* is a proper noun, the name of the place where Jesus was crucified. *Cavalry* refers to soldiers on horseback and does not need to be capitalized unless a particular cavalry is being named (the *Ninth Cavalry*).

can, may. *Can* implies the ability to do something; *may* implies permission or chance. (He *can* drive; his father said he *may* go; *may* stay longer.)

can't. *See* AIN'T.

can't hardly. *See* DOUBLE NEGATIVE.

capital, capitol. A *capitol* is the main building of a government. (The *Capitol* in Washington is open to the public.) All other meanings of the word are spelled *capital*. A *capital* means a city that is the seat of government (Washington is the U.S. *capital*; money (How much *capital* can you invest?); or an upper-cased letter. As an adjective, *capital* describes an offense punishable by death. (Stealing was once a *capital* crime.)

case. *See* CIRCUMLOCUTION.

catalog, catalogue. Both spellings are correct.

censor, censure, censer. A *censor* is a person who undertakes to restrict the dissemination of immoral or dangerous communications (such as pornography or correspondence during war). Such a person *censors*, or cuts out objectionable material. *Censure* is blame or condemnation; to censure is to blame or to condemn. (She was *censured* by the principal for cheating.) A *censer* is a vessel in which incense is burned in religious rites.

childish, childlike. Children are both annoying and lovable. Someone who is *childish* reminds one of the annoying traits of children. (His whining and *childish* behavior lost him friends.) Someone who is *childlike* has the innocence and freshness associated with children. (He viewed the most ordinary things with a *childlike* wonder.)

circumlocution. Being concise and direct is a virtue in writing and speaking. The opposite of directness is circumlocution, or talking around a subject before getting to the point. Some words seem to invite circumlocution. One such word is *case*. *In case I can't come* is less direct than *If I can't come*. *In all except a few cases, our winters are mild* could be replaced by *Our winters are almost always mild*. Instead of using *The reason is because*, simply write *because*. Avoid sentences using *in terms of*, *as to*, *as for*, and *the fact that*. *See* WRITING A RESEARCH PAPER, page 254, for more examples.

cite, site, sight. *Cite* is a verb meaning to mention specifically as an example, illustration, or authority. (He *cited* the Constitution to support his argument.) *Site* is a noun meaning a location. (We live on the *site* of an ancient Indian village.) Sight may be a noun meaning a view, the capacity for seeing, or the aiming device on a gun; it may also be a verb meaning to identify (we *sighted* a ship in the distance) or to take aim.

citizen. *See* NATIVE.

compare to, compare with. *Compare to* means to show the similarities between two things of different classes. (He *compared* the world *to* a child's ball because both are round.) *Compare with* means to show the similarities and differences of two things in the same class. (*Compare* this house *with* the other and you'll see which is the better value.)

complement, compliment. A *complement* is that which completes; *to complement* is to complete. (That rug *complements* the room; the dessert was the *complement* to a fine meal.) A *compliment* is praise; *to compliment* is to praise. (I *complimented* him on his choice. He returned the *compliment*.)

comprehensible, comprehensive. *Comprehensible* means capable of being understood. *Comprehensive* means complete.

connote, denote. To *connote* means to suggest meanings that are incidental or dependent on associations. To *denote* means to express a specific literal meaning. Words that *denote* the same thing may have quite different *connotations*. For example, *house*, *home*, *residence*, *abode*, and *address* may denote the same structure; a careful writer will choose among these words depending on the *connotations* that seem most appropriate.

continual(ly), continuous(ly). *Continual* refers to a succession of repeated events over a long period of time (*continual* hammer blows, *continual* interruptions). *Continuous* refers to what is unbroken or uninterrupted (a *continuous* flow of traffic, the *continuous* whine of a siren).

could of. *See* OF.

could've. Though common in speech, this contraction of *could have* would normally only appear in informal writing.

council, counsel, consul. A *council* is a meeting or a group set up to govern or advise. (The *council* voted to accept the proposition.) *Counsel* means advice or, as a verb, to advise. (I offer you my *counsel*. She *counseled* him on what steps to take.) *Counsel* also means a lawyer. (The *counsel* for the defense called her first witness.) A *consul* is a government official living in a foreign country.

credible, credulous, creditable. A statement is *credible* if it is believable. A person is *credulous* if he is quick to believe whatever he is told (and hence is easily deceived). A statement or action is *creditable* when it is worthy of being praised or or being given credit.

criteria. *Criteria*, meaning standards of judgment, is plural and takes a plural verb. (Their *criteria* for giving her the promotion were sound.) The singular is *criterion*.

curriculum. The plural of the noun *curriculum*, meaning courses of study in a school, is *curricula*. (The students' *curricula* are arduous. Look at my *curriculum*.)

cute. *See* ADJECTIVES.

D

dangling modifier. A modifier is said to be dangling when the word it properly modifies does not follow immediately, leaving doubt about which word is being modified. Sentences with dangling modifiers must be rephrased to remove the ambiguity. (*At the age of three, John's father died* should be changed to, *When John was three, his father died. Coming into the room, my eyes fell on the dresser* should be changed to, *Coming into the room, I glanced at the dresser*.)

data. *Data* is the plural of *datum*; it means facts or bits of information. *Data* should take a plural verb. (These *data* suggest a good year ahead.)

deduct, deduce. To *deduce* is to reach a conclusion through reasoning. (Sherlock Holmes's method was to *deduce* the identity of the criminal from the clues he found.) To *deduct* is to subtract. (*Deduct* the amount I owe you.)

definitely. *See* ADVERBS.

delusion. *See* ALLUSION.

denote. *See* CONNOTE.

dependent. Spell *dependent* with the *-ent* ending. This is acceptable both for the noun and for the adjective.

desert, dessert. A *desert* is an arid tract of land. To *desert* means to abandon. *Dessert* is a sweet course at the end of a meal. *Deserts*, as in *just deserts*, is a noun meaning deserved reward or punishment.

device, devise. *Device* is a noun meaning an object used for a particular purpose. (The ingenious *device* was too fragile.) *Devise* is a verb meaning to think out or invent. (He *devised* a plan.)

dialog, dialogue. Either spelling is correct. *Dialogue* is more common.

did, done. The past tense of *do* is *did*. *Done* is the past participle. (He *did* it yesterday. He *has done* things like that before.)

different from, different than. *Different than* is common in speech and informal writing. In formal usage, careful writers use *different from*. (The town is *different from* what it used to be.)

differ from, differ with. To *differ from* means to be unlike. (Her methods *differ from* mine.) To *differ with* means to disagree. (He *differs with* me on the best approach to the problem.)

discreet, discrete. *Discreet* means prudent. (She was *discreet* about his secret.) *Discrete* means distinct or separate. (We must consider three *discrete* elements.)

disinterested, uninterested. Careful speakers and writers are likely to use *disinterested* only to mean impartial. *Uninterested* means indifferent.

dived, dove. Both forms are acceptable for the past tense. He *dived*—or *dove*—off the river bank. As a past participle, *dived* is standard. (He *has dived* from there many times.)

doesn't, don't. Use *doesn't* with singular subjects (except *I* and *you*) and *don't* for all others. (He *doesn't*; they *don't*.)

done. *See* DID.

double negative. Double negatives occur in sentences that use two negative words, making the meaning unclear. There are at least three types of double negatives. If one writes, *It is not unlikely that John will come*, we understand that there is some likelihood that John will come. This type of double negative is acceptable, although slightly roundabout. Such a double negative means what it says: *not unlikely* means *likely*. But *I don't have no money* is unclear. In speech, listeners would understand that this is an emphatic statement about your finances; but logically it could mean that you have some money: I don't have *no* money—I only have a little. Avoid such confusion in formal writing. A third type of double negative is that in which a negative is associated with such weak negative adverbs as *hardly, barely, scarcely*, or *but*. I don't have *but* a dollar). Avoid the use of such double negatives in formal writing or speech.

double possessive. *A friend of John's* illustrates the double possessive. This usage is acceptable.

doubt but. *See* HELP BUT.

dove. *See* DIVED.

dreamed, dreamt. Both spellings are acceptable.

drink, drank, drunk. These are the principal parts of the verb in standard English usage. (They *drink*; they *drank*; they *have drunk*.) The adjective *drunken* is acceptable when it comes before the noun it modifies (*drunken* sailor; the sailor was *drunk*.)

drowned. This is the correct form of the past tense and the past participle of the verb *drown*. Do not say or write *drownded.*

E

each. *See* ANYBODY.

eager. *See* ANXIOUS.

easy. There are some expressions in colloquial English in which *easy* is an adverb. (Take it *easy*. *Easy* come, *easy* go.) Elsewhere, the adverbial form is *easily*. (I can do that trick *easily*).

economic, economical. Both these forms are adjectives, but the first applies to general matters of finance (*economic* aid, *economic* planning) and the second to specific instances of thrift (an *economical* vacation). The adverb related to both adjectives is *economically*.

effect. *See* AFFECT.

e.g. This abbreviation, which is preceded and followed by commas, is usually used in scholarly writing to mean "for example." *See also* I.E.

egoism, egotism. *Egoism* is a term applied to self-centeredness or to the conviction that one's own personal interests must always be served. It has a philosophical connotation. *Egotism* connotes boasting and much talking about oneself.

either. *Either* goes with *or*; *neither* goes with *nor*. (*Either* you go *or* I will go. *Neither* you *nor* I can go.) *See also* NEITHER.

elicit, illicit. To *elicit* something means to bring it out. (The response they *elicited* was overwhelming.) If something is *illicit*, it is illegal or immoral. (Their *illicit* affair was kept secret.)

else's. *Anybody else's, everyone else's*, and similar forms are standard usage. *Anybody's else*, once thought to be elegant, is no longer acceptable.

elude. *See* ALLUDE.

emigrant, immigrant. These words can be easily distinguished if one recognizes that the first is formed from the Latin prefix *ex-*, meaning from or out of, while the second carries the prefix *in-*, meaning in or into. One *emigrates* from one country and *immigrates* to another. The same person is both an *emigrant* and an *immigrant*, depending on the writer's point of reference.

eminent, imminent. *Eminent* means distinguished. (The *eminent* scholar lectured at our school.) *Imminent* means about to take place. (The government's collapse is *imminent*.)

enthuse. Many people object to making a verb out of the adjective *enthusiastic*. Avoid its use in formal writing.

epic, epoch. An *epic* is a particular kind of long poem or story about a hero; as an adjective, *epic* refers to the qualities of an epic (for example, heroic, grand). An *epoch* is an historical period of time—an important one having distinct and special characteristics.

epitaph, epithet. An *epitaph* is an inscription on a gravestone. An *epithet* is a phrase that accompanies or replaces the name of a person. (The Little Tramp is an *epithet* for Charlie Chaplin.) *Epithet* may also mean a word of abuse.

epoch. *See* EPIC.

especially, specially. In some contexts, these words are interchangeable. In others, careful writers use *especially* when the meaning is particularly or most importantly, and *specially* when the meaning is uniquely. (Jack was *especially* fond of fried chicken. The car was *specially* built as a racer.)

etc. This abbreviation stands for the Latin *et cetera*, which means *and others*. Do not write "and etc." since this would mean "and and others." *Etc.* nearly always falls at the end of a sentence; in any case, it must be followed by a period since it is an abbreviation. The term is useful to suggest the rest of a long list (he took soap, shampoo, towel, etc.) but it should not be overused.

everybody, everyone. *See* ANYBODY.

every day, everyday. *Every day* describes an action that takes place day after day. (She went to work *every day.*) *Everyday* is an adjective meaning ordinary. (She wore her *everyday* clothes.)

everywhere. *See* ANYWHERE.

except. *See* ACCEPT.

expect. Expect means to look forward to or to assume something to be proper or likely. (We *expect* your arrival tomorrow at noon. He *expects* too much of me.) In formal writing, the word should not be used as a synonym for *think, suppose,* or *guess.*

F

fact, the fact that. *See* CIRCUMLOCUTION.

famous, infamous. *Famous* means widely known and it may suggest an admirable reason for the fame. *Infamous* means widely known for something considered reprehensible. (Wyatt Earp was a *famous* lawman. Billy the Kid was an *infamous* bandit.)

farther, further. Careful writers use *farther* to refer to physical distance and *further* to refer to additional ideas, thoughts, or other immaterial things. In general usage, the two words are often used interchangeably. *See also* ALL THE FARTHER.

faze. This verb, which means to disturb or to disconcert, is more common in speech than in writing. It should not be confused with *phase,* a noun that means a stage of development.

feel. *See* BAD; GOOD.

fewer. *See* AMOUNT.

figuratively. *See* LITERALLY.

fix. This word in various contexts can mean so many things that objections to what seems to be its overuse have often been voiced. More formal synonyms are available to express most of its meanings. In the sense of getting ready (she's *fixing* to go shopping), the verb usage is regional. The noun, meaning a predicament, is colloquial. (He was in a *fix.*)

flammable, inflammable. Both these words mean easy to set on fire. The negative of *flammable* is *nonflammable.*

flaunt, flout. To *flaunt* is to show off, to display boldly what others may disapprove of. To *flout* is to defy or treat with contempt. (She *flaunted* her jewels. They *flouted* the rules, showing disdain for society's laws.)

fly, flee. Birds *fly;* criminal *flee.* Figuratively, however, fugitives may be said to fly from their pursuers. *Flew* is the past tense of *fly* (the bird *flew* away), and *flown* is its past participle (the bird *has flown* away). The verb *flee* has only one past tense form—*fled.*

formally, formerly. The first is an adverb derived from *formal.* (He was *formally* offered the job in a letter from the president.) *Formerly* is the adverb derived from *former.* (He was *formerly* the owner of that car.)

former, latter. These terms apply properly to a pair of things or choices. (He had to choose between the red tie and the blue, and he chose the *latter.*) When there are more than two things or choices, *first* may be used instead of *former* and *last* instead of *latter.*

forward(s). *See* BACKWARD(S).

funny. In formal writing, this word is used to mean humorous. (She did not think the story funny at all.) The use of the word to mean odd or peculiar (there is something *funny* about him) should be avoided in formal writing. *See also* ADJECTIVES.

further. *See* FARTHER.

G

gender of singular pronouns. When a pronoun refers back to a singular subject, it is often difficult to determine what gender should be used. (One must raise *his,* or *her,* hand when *he,* or *she,* wants to be recognized.) Traditionally, the singular pronouns *he* and *his* have been used. This may be confusing when the original pronoun or noun is indefinite. In that case, one may substitute the phrases *he or she, him or her,* or *his or her.* (One must raise *his or her* hand when *he or she* wishes to be recognized.) This solution is, unfortunately, cumbersome. In most cases it is best to rewrite the sentence. *You* and *your* can often be substituted for *one* and *his.* (*You* must raise *your* hand.) Some authorities suggest using the plural pronoun even with a singular noun. (*One* must raise *their* hand.) This solution has not been widely accepted, however. In formal writing, use *he/him/his. See also* ANYBODY.

get. *Get* has acquired dozens of meanings; therefore, the use of a more specific verb is usually preferred. Such phrases as *get* smart, *get* happy, and *get* mad are acceptable in speech but not in formal writing. Some other phrases such as *get* sick and *get* home are acceptable both in speech and writing. Both *got* and *gotten* are used as the past participle.

go, went, gone. These are the principal parts of the verb *go.* In standard English, *went* is never used as the past participle. (I *go;* I *went;* I *have gone.*)

good, well. *Good* is an adjective that describes a noun (the *good* child). It also describes nouns when used with verbs of appearance, sound, taste, smell, and feel. (The dress looks *good* on her.) *Well* can be the adverb equivalent of good, and is used to describe actions. (He runs *well*). *Well* may also be an adjective meaning healthy. (I am *well.*) It is in that sense, as an adjective, that it is used in the sentence *I feel well. See also* BAD.

got to. This should be changed to *have to.* (I *have to* go; not, I *got to* go.) *See also* HAVE GOT.

H

had better, had best. These expressions are acceptable in speech and writing. (You *had better* come early.)

had of, had've. Neither of these expressions is used in standard English. Write *I wish I had worked harder* rather than *I wish I had've worked harder.*

had ought. Neither this expression nor its negative, *hadn't ought*, is acceptable in writing.

hanged, hung. The past tense of *hang* is *hung*, except when one is referring to an execution by hanging. (The coat *hung* on the hook. The man was *hanged* at dawn.)

hardly. *See* DOUBLE NEGATIVE.

have got. The use of this expression is more common in informal speech than in writing. *We have four dollars* is preferable to *We have got four dollars* in formal writing.

help but. The *but* is usually unnecessary and should be omitted. (I couldn't *help* coming here; not, I couldn't *help but* come here.) Similarly, the use of *but what* should be avoided in careful writing. (I didn't doubt that she meant it; not, I didn't doubt *but what* she meant it.)

hopefully. Careful writers and speakers avoid the use of this word to mean *I* (or *we*) *hope. I hope to be there tomorrow* is preferable to *Hopefully, I'll be there tomorrow.*

hung. *See* HANGED.

I

i.e. This abbreviation, usually found in scholarly writing, means "that is." It should be set off by commas. (Plato is concerned with the ideal, *i.e.*, the Forms in the world of Idea.)

illicit. *See* ELICIT.

illusion. *See* ALLUSION.

immigrant. *See* EMIGRANT.

imminent. *See* EMINENT.

imply, infer. To *imply* means to suggest without actually saying so. (You *implied* that I was lying.) To *infer* means to derive a conclusion from evidence, or to surmise. (We *inferred* from her tone of voice that she liked him.)

incidence, incidents. *Incidence* means frequency of occurrence. (The *incidence* of fatal car accidents is rising.) *Incidents* is the plural of *incident*, and means events. (The three *incidents* happened in one week.)

incredible, incredulous. Something that is *incredible* is hard to believe. Someone who is *incredulous* is skeptical. (I found his *incredible* story unconvincing. I was *incredulous* till he proved it was true.)

infamous. *See* FAMOUS.

infer. *See* IMPLY.

infinitive. *See* SPLIT INFINITIVE.

inflammable. *See* FLAMMABLE.

ingenious, ingenuous. *Ingenious* means clever, inventive. (The *ingenious* device could reduce fuel consumption by half.) *Ingenuous* means innocent, guileless, unsophisticated. (His *ingenuous* response disarmed the judge.)

innumerable, numerous. *Innumerable* means countless, too many to be numbered. (The *innumerable* grains of sand represent the passage of time.) *Numerous* means many. (There were *numerous* reasons why the plan failed.)

inside, inside of. *See* OF.

interesting. *See* ADJECTIVES.

intransitive verbs. *See* LIE; RAISE; SET; TRANSITIVE VERBS.

invitation, invite. In formal English, *invite* is a verb. It should not be used as a noun (I got an *invite* to the party); instead, use *invitation.*

inward(s). *See* BACKWARD(S).

irregardless. *Regardless* has a negative suffix already, so *irregardless* is not a word to be used in standard English. (He will come to the party *regardless* of her wishes.)

its, it's. *Its* is the possessive form of *it. It's* is a contraction of *it is.* (The kitten cried when *its* foot was stepped on. *It's* hard to see in the dark.)

it's I, it's me. Precise writers prefer *it's I*, which is the grammatically correct expression. But English speech insists on *it's me, it's him, it's them*, etc. Unless the occasion is very formal, use *me, him, her*, and *them.*

-ize. Be cautious of verbs formed with the *-ize* suffix. If possible use a different word that is more precise. Use *conceive* instead of *conceptualize*; *complete* instead of *finalize*; *perfect* instead of *optimize.*

J

judicial, judicious. *Judicial* is properly used to describe behavior or procedure related to or appropriate to a judge. *Judicious* is an adjective applied to carefully considered and wise conduct. (He spoke in a solemn, *judicial* manner. Although the woman was angry, she acted *judiciously.*)

K

kind of, sort of. Use of these phrases as adverbs meaning rather (I am *kind of* tired today) is informal and should be avoided in formal writing.

L

latter. *See* FORMER.

lay. *See* LIE.

learn, teach. We *learn* what teachers *teach* us. No one can *learn* us anything.

leave, let. In standard English, *leave* never means allow. *Let* is the verb with that meaning. (*Let* us go; not, *leave* us go.)

lend. *See* BORROW.

less, lesser. These are both comparative forms of *little. Lesser* is less commonly used, and it is generally confined to comparisons involving judgment of importance (as in the *lesser* of two evils). *See also* AMOUNT.

let. *See* LEAVE.

let's us. *Let's* already means let us, so *let's us* means "let us us," and is incorrect.

lie, lay. These two verbs are often confused. To *lay* an object down is to put it down; to *lie* down is to recline. *Lay* is a transitive verb, which means it must take an object. *Lie* is intransitive and does not need an object. (I *lie* down to sleep. I *lay* the pencil on the table.) The confusion arises in part because the past tense forms of *lie* are *lay* and *lain* (she *lay* back and died; he *had lain* there many days), while the past tense form of *lay* is *laid* (I *have laid* the book down; I *laid* the book down). *See also* TRANSITIVE VERBS.

like, as. Like should be used when a comparison is made between two things. (The fog lay *like* a blanket in the valley. The boys swam *like* fish.) When one part of the comparison is a quality, use *as*. (The scarf was green *as* grass. This boulder is big *as* a house.) When the comparison is between two actions, use *as* or *as if*. (Do *as* I do. She spoke her lines *as if* she were singing.)

literally, figuratively. *Literally* means really, in truth. Do not use it to be emphatic. (When he saw me he *literally* fell through the floor means that he actually did fall through the floor.) *Figuratively* means that you are using a figure of speech and are not to be taken literally.

loose, lose. Something that is *loose* is slack. (My *loose* pants are cool.) If you *lose* something, you cannot find it. (Did you *lose* an earring?)

lousy, lovely. *See* ADJECTIVES.

M

marvelous. *See* ADJECTIVES.

may. *See* CAN.

may of, must of, might of. *See* OF.

mean for. In writing, it is preferable to use *mean that*. (I didn't *mean that* you should go alone; not, *mean for* you to go alone.)

median. This word should not be confused with *medium*. It means middle and may refer to the strip that separates traffic on an expressway or to the middle number in a series. The plural of *median* is *medians*.

medium. This word has several distinct meanings. It is sometimes used to mean a means of communication. (Television is the *medium* I am most interested in.) The plural of *medium* may be either *media* or *mediums. Media* is often used to mean all means of mass communication. (The campaign manager sought to promote his candidate in all the *media*—radio, television, newspapers, and even magazines.)

mighty. The use of *mighty* as an adverb (he is *mighty* good at golf) is informal and should be avoided in formal writing.

modifer. *See* DANGLING MODIFIER.

moral, morale. *Moral* is a noun meaning the lesson taught by a story; it is also an adjective denoting ethically correct behavior. (It was the *moral* thing to do.) The plural noun *morals* refers to the general values of a person or group. (Public *morals* are not high in the matter of reporting income to the tax bureau.) *Morale* is a noun meaning the general mood of an individual or of a group of people. (After the defeat, the army's *morale* sank.)

most. *See* ALMOST.

myself. Speakers and writers sometimes use *myself* instead of *I* or *me* to sound modest. Often they sound pretentious instead. Use *myself* only where it is really required to denote a reflexive action. (They thanked my mother and *me* for our contributions. John and *I* will be the two representatives. I deceived *myself* about my talents.)

N

native, citizen. You are a *native* of the place where you were born; you are a *citizen* of the country, state, or other political unit where you have legal rights and duties.

neither, nor. *Neither* and *nor* are negatives and should not be used with other negatives. Use *either* instead. (She will *not* go to *either* place; she will go to *neither* place.) *See also* DOUBLE NEGATIVES; EITHER.

never, not. The indiscriminate use of *never* to mean *not* is colloquial. (I was late this morning because Mother did *not* wake me; not, because Mother *never* woke me.)

nice. *See* ADJECTIVES.

nobody, no one. *See* ANYBODY.

none. *See* ANYBODY.

none is, none are. Although *none* is a compound made from *no* and *one*, the word long ago ceased being only singular. The grammatical number of the verb used with it depends on the meaning of the sentence.

nor. *See* NEITHER.

not. *See* NEVER.

notable, notorious. *Notable* is an adjective meaning noted for. It has a neutral or favorable connotation. Notorious describes someone well known for traits disapproved of. (The *notable* banker died. The *notorious* bank robber died.)

nowhere. *See* ANYWHERE.
number. *See* AMOUNT.
numbers. It is customary to use figures for numbers in addresses, dates, page references, and official names such as *Public School 203,* as well as in lists of numbers, statistics, and mathematical texts. In formal writing, numbers are spelled out at the beginning of sentences. Some writers prefer to spell out all whole numbers less than one hundred and round figures in the hundreds, thousands, and millions after that. Others spell out only whole numbers up to twelve. Whichever style you choose, be consistent. Always write out a number at the beginning of a sentence.
numerous. *See* INNUMERABLE.

O

O, oh. When used as part of a vocative expression, *O* is capitalized and is not separated by punctuation from the name of what is called on. (Where is thy sting, *O* Death?) *Oh* is capitalized only at the beginning of a sentence and is often followed by a comma or exclamation mark. (*Oh*! *Oh*, Henry!) *O* is more common in poetic writing.
of. It is incorrect to use *of* when you mean *have*; could *have*, may *have*, might *have*, must *have*, ought to *have*, should *have,* would *have*, will *have* are the correct expressions, not the previous words used with *of.* (I could *have* gone; not, I could *of* gone.) *Of* is often added to expressions where it is not needed. *All, alongside, inside, off,* and *outside* often have *of* needlessly attached to them. (He took *all* my money; not, *all of* my money. (Note, however, that in a few cases the addition of *of* changes the meaning of the expression. *Inside of* can mean in less than. *Outside of* can mean excluding.)
OK, O.K., okay. This expression is America's contribution to international communication. Known and used almost everywhere in the world as an indication of approval or agreement, it is still not generally used in formal writing. When it is used in informal writing, any of the forms shown here may be used.
on, onto, on to. The prepositions *on* and *onto* sometimes mean the same thing. (She got *on*, or *onto*, the bus.) In some cases, however, *onto* indicates direction of movement and *on* does not. (He stood *on* the desk, then climbed *onto* the bookcase.) *Onto* should not be used where the adverb *on* and the preposition *to* are intended. (Go *on to* the next lesson.)
one. Use of *one* as an indefinite pronoun (*one* scarcely knew what to think) is more common in British than in American English. In most cases, American writers use a definite pronoun (*we* scarcely knew what to think) or the indefinite pronoun *you* (*you* never know).
only. Intonation in speech almost always indicates clearly what *only* should modify in a sentence. In writing, however, the word can cause ambiguity. For example, *I only gave her flowers* could mean several different things; for example, only I (and no one else) gave her flowers; I didn't give her anything else. Careful writers should be certain that the meaning of such a sentence is clear—either from its context or from the careful placement of *only* in the sentence.
onto. *See* ON.
onward(s). *See* BACKWARD(S).
or. *See* AND/OR.
ought. *See* HAD OUGHT.
outside of. *See* OF.
outward(s). *See* BACKWARD(S).

P

pass. The spelling of the past tense and past participle of *pass* is *passed.* Do not confuse it with the noun, adverb, adjective, and preposition *past.* (The *past* president *passed* the house. When he *passed* it, he thought of days gone *past.*)
per, percent. *Per* is a preposition meaning for each or by (*per* diem, *per* year, *per* student). It has a technical connotation and can usually be said more simply (*a* day, *a* year, *a* student). But the term *percent* is indispensable. This word is represented by the symbol % only when it follows a specific figure (40%).
persecute, prosecute. To *persecute* someone is to cause that person to suffer unjustly. (The dictator *persecuted* the opposition.) To *prosecute* is to take legal action against. (We *prosecuted* the company for negligence.)
personal, personnel. *Personal* means having to do with one's private life. *Personnel* refers to employees. (The personnel manager asked me too many *personal* questions.)
perspective, prospective. *Perspective* has to do with ways of seeing things or ways of understanding. (Labor and management look at assembly line work from different *perspectives.*) *Prospective* is an adjective meaning possible in the future. (His wife's pregnancy made him a *prospective* father.)
phenomenon. This word, meaning an occurrence, is singular. The preferred plural is *phenomena.* (Severe weather *phenomena* include thunderstorms, tornadoes, and blizzards.)
plenty. Use of this word as an adverb to strengthen an adjective (he was *plenty* good) is informal and should be avoided in formal writing.
politics. Like many other nouns that end in *-ics* (physics, economics, etc.), this word was originally plural but may now be used as singular. (*Politics is* a demanding profession.)

positively. *See* ADVERBS.

practicable, practical, practically. *Practicable* is an adjective meaning capable of being put into practice. *Practical* is an adjective that means sensible or likely to work to good advantage. (His plan to paint the roof from a helicopter was *practicable,* but it was not at all *practical.*) In informal usage, *practically* is sometimes made to mean almost or nearly. (He was *practically* a moron.) This usage should be avoided in formal writing.

precede, proceed. To *precede* is to go before; to *proceed* is to continue. (He was *preceded* by his wife. After the judge sits, you may *proceed.*)

precedence, precedents. *Precedence* means priority in rank or order. (The king takes *precedence* over the prince.) *Precedents,* the plural of *precedent,* are decisions or actions that have already occurred. (The *precedents* in this case favor the plaintiff's side.)

preposition at the end of a clause. In informal speech and writing, prepositions often occur at the end of clauses or sentences. Careful writers end clauses or sentences with a preposition even in formal writing, especially when alternative forms are cumbersome or awkward. (It was not the kind of party he wanted to go *to.*)

prescribe, proscribe. To *prescribe* is to require or strongly advise. To *proscribe* is to prohibit some action or to banish some person.

presently. This means in a little while. *At present* means now.

pretty. Originally an adjective, *pretty* is too often used in colloquial English as a qualifier of adjectives and adverbs (as in, the book was *pretty* good). Avoid such usage in writing.

principal, principle. As an adjective, *principal* means chief. (The *principal* reason for going was to enjoy the scenery.) *Principal* as a noun may mean a sum of money invested or borrowed; or the head person of a school or of a group of investors. A *principle* is a general rule, assumption, or moral standard. (Speaking softly was a *principle* with her. It is the first *principle* of good leadership to listen. He refused to lie on *principle* even though he knew lying might sometimes profit him.)

proceed. *See* PRECEDE.

pronouns. *See* GENDER.

prophecy, prophesy. If someone *prophesies,* that person produces a *prophecy.* (She *prophesies* doom but no one pays attention to her *prophecies.*)

proscribe. *See* PRESCRIBE.

prosecute. *See* PERSECUTE.

prospective. *See* PERSPECTIVE.

proved, proven. Both forms are used as the past participle of the verb to *prove. Proven* is less frequent, except when it modifies a noun (a *proven* evil).

Q

quantity. Uncountable things such as milk, sand, and lumber, are measured as *quantities.* Countable things should not be referred to as *quantities.* There may be a large *quantity* of sand on a beach, but *many* (not a large *quantity* of) people.

quote, quotation. *Quote* is a verb meaning to repeat what has been said or written. *Quotation* is a noun. Use of *quote* as a noun (I saw a *quote* from her in the paper) is informal and should be avoided in formal writing.

R

raise, rise. To raise means to lift or grow something. It is a transitive verb and must take an object. (I *raise* my hand. I *raise* chickens.) To *rise* means to get up or to increase in size. It is intransitive and does not need an object. (I *rise* at six. The river *rises* in the spring.) *See also* TRANSITIVE VERBS.

rarely ever, seldom ever. The *ever* is omitted from these expressions in formal writing.

rational, rationale, rationalization. *Rational* is an adjective meaning sensible. (Her behavior was *rational.*) *Rationale* is a noun meaning the reason behind an action or idea. (His *rationale* for doing so was to make money.) A *rationalization* is an excuse, usually a false one though the person rationalizing may not know it. (Excusing her theft because she was unhappy was a *rationalization.*)

real, really. *Real* is an adjective. Do not use it as an adverb. (It was *really* big; not, *real* big.) *See also* ADVERBS.

reckon. *See* CALCULATE.

regardless. *See* IRREGARDLESS.

respectfully, respectively. *Respectfully* describes courteous behavior. *Respectively* means considering several items in the order named. (The three boys, Jack, Tom, and Bob excelled in swimming, golf, and tennis, *respectively.*)

rise. *See* RAISE.

run. The past tense of this verb is *ran,* but its past participle is *run.* (The rabbit *ran* away last night. We are sorry that it *has run* away.)

S

said, same. These words, when used in legal documents, mean the person or thing identified earlier. (*Said* lessor shall have the quiet enjoyment of *same* for the term of this lease.) This is a technical usage and should be avoided in careful writing.

scarcely. *See* DOUBLE NEGATIVE.

see, saw, seen. These are the standard principal parts of the verb. (I *see* a bird. I *saw* it yesterday. I *have seen* it here often.)

seldom every. *See* RARELY EVER.

set, sit. *Sit* is usually an intransitive verb. Its past tense and past participle are *sat*. (They *sit* around the table. She *sat* beside me.) *Set* is usually a transitive verb. Its past and past participle forms are also *set*. (He *set* the dishes on the table). As an intransitive verb, *set* is used principally to describe the sun (the sun *sets* at six) and the incubation of eggs by birds (a hen *setting*).

shall, will. In declarative sentences, *shall* and *will* have come to have the same meaning. *Shall* is less often used, except when strong intention is being expressed. (I *shall* return.) In questions, however, the two words have different meanings. *Shall we go through Atlanta?* suggests that a decision to do so may be made. *Will we go through Atlanta?* suggests that the decision has been made but that the speaker is not yet aware of it.

should, would. *Should* may be used to express obligation (it's late; you *should* go to bed) or likelihood (we *should* be finished with this by noon). *Would* may express habitual action (he *would* walk in the woods each morning before we were up) or polite requests (*would* you bring something to eat?). In conditional clauses, *should* suggests uncertainty. (If she *should* come before seven, I will get to meet her.) *Would* suggests desire on the part of the speaker that the condition be fulfilled. (If only she *would* come before seven, I would be able to meet her.)

should of. *See* OF.

sight. *See* CITE.

sing. In formal English, *sang* is the past tense of *sing*, while *sung* is its past participle. (I *sing* in the morning. I *sang* yesterday. I *have sung* all my life.)

singular pronouns. *See* GENDER.

sink. Either *sank* or *sunk* may be used as the past tense of this verb (*sank* is more common). The past participle is *sunk*, except when it is used as an adjective; *sunken* may then be used. (We were searching for *sunken* treasure.)

sit. *See* SET.

site. *See* CITE.

slow(ly). Both *slow* and *slowly* are used as adverbs. *Slow* is used only in a few common expressions (go *slow*), while *slowly* is used in all other cases (he climbed the hill *slowly*).

so. In informal speech and writing, *so* is sometimes used as a qualifier meaning *very*. (He was *so* big.) This usage is not incorrect, but it can easily be overused and tiresome.

somebody, someone. *See* ANYBODY.

somewhere. *See* ANYWHERE.

sort of. *See* KIND OF.

specially. *See* ESPECIALLY.

specie, species. *Specie* is a rarely used word that means money in the form of coins; the word has no plural form. *Species*, which means a kind or class of thing, may be used either as a singular or plural noun.

split infinitive. At one time grammarians frowned on placing a word between the two parts of an infinitive verb. (He failed *to fully understand* the test.) Today, splitting the infinitive in this manner is acceptable as long as the result is not awkward.

stationary, stationery. The first of these words is an adjective meaning unchanging or fixed. The second is a noun that means writing materials.

statistics. This word is always treated as a plural noun unless it means a branch of study. (*Statistics* is a kind of applied mathematics.) The singular form *statistic* must refer to a single fact. (One *statistic* stood out from the rest: the country's growth rate.)

stayed, stood. The past tense of *stay* is *stayed*; the past tense of *stand* is *stood*. (I *stayed* up all night; not, I *stood* up all night, unless you stood on your feet all night.)

stratum. The most frequently used plural of this word, which means a layer, is *strata*.

such. Use of *such* as a mere qualifier is colloquial (as in, we had *such* a good time).

sure to. Use *sure to* and not *sure and*. (Be *sure to* bring your records; not, be *sure and* bring your records.)

swim. The past tense of *swim* is *swam*; the past participle is *swum*. (I *swam* here yesterday. I *have swum* here every summer.)

T

teach. *see* LEARN.

terrible, terrific. *See* ADJECTIVES.

than, then. *Than* means when compared with or except. (He is better equipped for it *than* you. I'd rather be anywhere *than* here.) *Then* means at that time. (*Then* I went to the store.)

that. *See* WHICH, THAT.

that there. *See* THIS (THESE) HERE.

their, theirs, there, there's, they're. *Their* and *theirs* mean belonging to them. (*Their* house is red. It's *theirs*.) *There* means at that place. (Meet me *there*.) *There* is also used to introduce a sentence. (*There* is nothing left.) *There's* is a shortened form of *there is*. (*There's* nothing left.) *They're* is a shortened form of *they are*. (*They're* going too.)

theirselves. *Themselves*, not *theirselves*, is the correct word.

then. *See* THAN.

this (these) here, that (those) there. Leave out the *here* and *there* in these expressions.

though (tho). *See* ALTHOUGH.

thru. This simplified spelling of *through* is never used in formal writing.

till, until. These words may be used interchangeably. *'Til* is not acceptable.

to, too, two. *Too* means also or more than enough. (I want some, *too.* They were *too* loud.) *Two* is the number 2. In every other case, the spelling is *to* (*to* run, give it *to* me, *to* and fro, from New York *to* California, dance *to* the music).

toward(s). *See* BACKWARD(S).

transitive verbs. A transitive verb always has to be followed by an object in order to complete its meaning. (*Lay the book* on the table. *Set it* down. *Raise the curtain.*) An intransitive verb does not require an object. (I *lie* on the bed. I *sit* in the chair. I *rise* at six.) *See also* LIE; RAISE; SET.

U

uninterested. *See* DISINTERESTED.

unique. *See* ADJECTIVES.

unless. Do not substitute *without* for *unless.* (I won't go *unless* you take me; not, *without* you taking me.)

until. *See* TILL.

used. Be careful not to drop the *d* in the past tense of *use*, especially in the expression *used to.* (I *used to* go; not, *use to* go.)

V

venal, venial. *Venal* describes corruption or corruptibility as a result of greed. *Venial* means forgivable. A *venial* sin is not a deadly sin.

very. *See* ADVERBS.

virtue, virtuosity. *Virtue* refers to merit of any sort. *Virtuosity* refers to an artist's technical skill.

W

wait for, wait on. *Wait on* means to serve. (He *waits on* tables.) In the sense of *wait for*, the use of *wait on* is colloquial. (We're *waiting for* Fred; not, we're *waiting on* Fred.)

'way, away. In informal speech, *away* is often shortened to *'way.* Avoid such usage in writing.

well. *See* BAD; GOOD.

went. *See* GO.

which, that. *Which* and *that* have the same meaning, but *which*, preceded by a comma, is usually used for nonrestrictive clauses—those that describe antecedent nouns but are not necessary to identify them. *That* is used in restrictive clauses—those that are necessary to identify the antecedent nouns. *She stroked the cat that bit her* tells you that she stroked that particular cat, the one that bit her. *She stroked the cat, which bit her* assumes that we already know which cat, and adds the information that the cat bit her after she stroked it.

which, who. Use *who* instead of *which* when you are referring to people. (The boys *who* own this car are rude.)

while. *See* AWHILE.

who, whom, whoever, whomever. Traditionally *who* and *whoever* are the subjects of sentences; *whom* and *whomever* are the objects. (*Who* is coming? *Whom* did you wish to see?) *Whom* and *whomever* are disappearing, however, and are being replaced by *who* and *whoever.* Many authorities consider it acceptable to write, *Who* did you wish to see? Using *whom* where *who* is required is a more serious error. Use *whom* only when you are sure it is the object of a sentence. Never use it to sound elegant if you are uncertain.

whose, who's. *Whose* is the possessive form of *who.* (*Whose* coat is this?) *Who's* is a contraction of *who is.* (*Who's* going to go?)

will. *See* SHALL.

-wise. This suffix should be used in formal writing to mean in the manner or direction of (*clockwise, otherwise, lengthwise*). Do not use it to mean in regard to. (I'm having *financial* trouble; not, I'm having trouble *moneywise.*)

without. *See* UNLESS.

wonderful. *See* ADJECTIVES.

would. *See* SHOULD.

Y

you. *See* ONE.

you all. This is a regional expression. *You* is the accepted singular and plural noun.

you and I. *You and I, he,* or *she* should be used as subjects. (*You and I* can do it.) As an object of a verb or preposition, use objective forms with *you.* (He called *you and me.* I must choose between *you and her.*)

your, you're. *Your* is possessive. (Take *your* hat.) *You're* is a contraction of *you are.* (*You're* going?)

For Further Reference

Ehrlich, Eugene, and Murphy, Daniel
Writing and Researching Term Papers and Reports
Bantam Books

Kurtinitis, Sandra
A Brief and Lively No-Nonsense Guide to Writing
Scott, Foresman

University of Chicago
A Manual of Style (13th ed.)
University of Chicago Press

Strunk, William, Jr., and White, E. B.
The Elements of Style (2nd ed.)
Macmillan

Turabian, Kate L.
Student's Guide for Writing College Papers (3rd ed.)
University of Chicago Press

Literature

Literature is one of our great cultural inheritances from the past; it is an essential subject for study in any complete education. This section introduces the study of literature by describing the nature of literature, the history of literature, and the great writers and literary works of the past.

There are three principal forms of literature: poetry, drama, and fiction. This section is divided into those three categories for study. Each category first defines the literary form and then explains its special value and importance. A brief history of that particular form of literature follows. Finally, each section concludes with a detailed alphabetical listing of the most important writers of the past who have worked in that literary form. The last major section is an alphabetical listing of some literary masterpieces with brief summaries of their contents.

Introduction

Literature, broadly defined, is all written matter. The medium of music is sound, the medium of visual art is form, and the medium of literature is words. Like music or art, literature may be either inspirational or utilitarian. It ranges from the sublime to the workaday, from the Shakespearean tragedy to the magazine advertisement.

Since the early 1800's, the word "literature" has come to mean primarily written expressions that are of lasting importance or value. Used in this sense, literature is the written artistic legacy of a particular time to later generations. To identify the period or society, we speak of medieval literature, 18th-century literature, or American or Russian literature.

Literature is one of the distinguishing achievements of the earliest civilized societies. Among the earliest printed symbols were Egyptian hieroglyphics and Chinese ideograms. The first literary documents were scrolls and manuscripts that were copied and recopied by hand. Written literature was available only to a select few who were important or wealthy enough to afford such documents. In modern society, literature has become available to millions, thanks to the printing press. Printing was first known in China in the ninth century, and it became a major influence on European history when the German printer Johann Gutenberg developed movable type in the 1400's.

Forms of literature. The principal forms of literary expression are poetry, drama, and fiction. Most of these forms can be traced to ancient times. They have been revived whenever their special qualities fulfilled the needs of a given age and society. Poems, plays, and fiction are considered separately in the pages that follow.

Other literary forms have also had great importance. Gutenberg's first printed book was the Bible; to this day it is the most widely printed book in most European languages.

For centuries, history was a major literary form. An

early example is *The Peloponnesian War*, written by the Greek Thucydides in about 400 B.C., an account of the struggle between the Athenians and Spartans. Most cultures produce their own accounts of the historical episodes they consider to be most important.

A history devoted to the life of a person is called a biography. The Roman writers Plutarch and Suetonius, in the first and second centuries A.D., were among the earliest known biographers. Modern biography is usually traced to the publication of James Boswell's *Life of Samuel Johnson* in England in 1791. A biographical history written by the person himself is called an autobiography. One of the earliest such works is the *Confessions* of St. Augustine, written after 400 A.D. Since that time, many famous people have recorded the story of their own lives for posterity. When not formally revised, an autobiography remains a diary. Samuel Pepys kept a remarkable and entertaining diary in the late 1600's in England. More recently, *The Diary of Anne Frank*, written by a young girl in the 1940's, has been translated into dozens of languages. It records the persecution of her family and friends by the Nazis.

Another literary form that has special historical and intellectual importance is the essay. An essay is a short composition, usually in prose, devoted to a philosophical discussion of one or more topics. The term was used by the French writer Montaigne in 1580; *essai*, in French, means "attempt." In his writings, Montaigne tries informally to define and illuminate particular topics that concern him. One of the great revivals of the essay as a literary form occurred in the 1700's in England. Joseph Addison and Richard Steele developed the occasional essay for their journal *The Spectator;* other great writers of the century, including Jonathan Swift and Samuel Johnson, also wrote probing and serious essays. Today, essays may appear as magazine articles or as feature columns in newspapers.

For the most part, however, the study of literature concentrates on the three principal literary forms—poetry, plays, and fiction. Histories, biographies, and essays are usually *denotative*: they seek to present direct and explicit meanings without obvious emotion and without ambiguity. Poems, fiction, and plays, however, communicate an emotional and intellectual impression that cannot be reduced to a single meaning. They are essentially *connotative*: they seek to present suggestive meanings that are by their very nature emotional and ambiguous. Histories and essays mean exactly what they say; poems, fiction, and plays mean far more than they say. This imaginative energy of poems, fiction, and plays provides the essential pleasures found in the study of literature.

Approaches to literature. Great works of literature can be understood in at least three ways. The first is biographical. A work of literature provides an insight into the mind and personality of the author. In this sense, literature may be approached as the study of great minds in human history. A second way is historical. Literature provides insight into other times and places. In this sense, literature may be approached as the study of the great moments in human history. A third way is interpretive. Great literary works provide insight into enduring human problems. The interpretive approach is the most difficult, but also the most rewarding. It involves close attention to the work itself free from biographical or historical distractions. The power of great literature lies in its ability to tell a reader what authors from other times and places understand about life's possibilities. As the great English essayist and poet Matthew Arnold wrote, the value of literature lies in "making us know ourselves and the world."

Literature is often meant to be read aloud as poet Dylan Thomas often did; it is also meant to tell us about our personal and collective histories, as in this TV production of Roots, *about black Americans.*

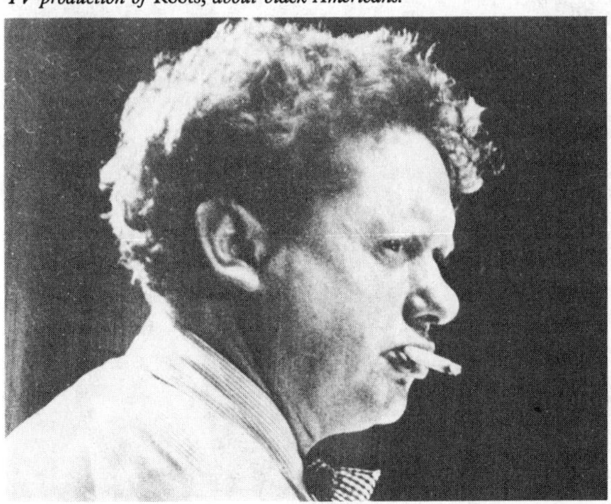

Poetry

Samuel Johnson, author of the first important dictionary of the English language, wrote that "the essence of poetry is invention, such invention as by producing something unexpected, surprises and delights." Johnson's emphasis on "invention" points up the imaginative qualities of poetry, but poetry also "surprises" in the sense that it provides knowledge. Poetry "delights" or entertains as well; from earliest times poets have seen themselves as singers.

A useful addition to Johnson's definition might be the suggestion that poetry's subject matter is the enduring emotional and philosophical problems of human existence. Ezra Pound had this timeless quality in mind when he wrote that poetry is "news that stays news."

Kinds of poetry. There are many specific kinds of poetry, but they can be reduced to three principal categories. The first is *lyric* poetry, named for the Greek lyre, a stringed musical instrument. A lyric poem is a brief musical expression of the thoughts and feelings of a single speaker. "Lyric" also refers to the words of a song, and lyric poetry includes many humorous and witty types of light verse as well as serious works.

The second category is *narrative* poetry, which is usually longer than lyric poetry and tells a story. There are many sorts of narrative poems, ranging from the ancient Greek epic the *Iliad* to such popular poems as "The Midnight Ride of Paul Revere" by Longfellow.

The third category is *dramatic* poetry, which is often written in the dialogue form of drama but is not intended for performance. Dramatic poetry is distinct for being able to present more than one speaker, although single-speaker dramatic monologues are also common.

Poetic devices. Most poetry presents certain difficulties for the reader because it attempts to present a thought that can never be paraphrased fully in prose. Its language is often compressed and "difficult," requiring closer reading than prose. A poem can change before a reader's eyes as different aspects of its language emerge.

Poetic language usually includes imagery—a visual expression of thought and feeling. A simple example is Robert Burns's line

My love is like a red red rose.

Figurative language, as in Wordsworth's simile

I wandered lonely as a cloud,

is a way to express a complex thought briefly. Poems also use symbols, things that represent a variety of associations rather than a single meaning, such as the raven in Edgar Allan Poe's poem of that name. These devices may also be found in plays and fiction.

se mai tornare degio inallegragio
Amore amore piu ke uedem
si mette im podere tuo uolontier
ro: alafine di ben tuctol contraro

A troubadour, performer of lyric poetry.

Poetic drama: Shakespeare

Poetry's unique quality is its use of rhythm and sound. From the simple repeating rhythms of folk ballads like "Barbara Allen," to the subtle use of blank (unrhymed) verse by Shakespeare, poets use the rhythm of the language to emphasize their meaning. Among poetry's sound effects are rhymes, often of words at the end of lines; and alliteration, the use of words with the same consonants. The last lines of Shakespeare's Sonnet 18 illustrate both rhyme and alliteration (words beginning with "L").

So long as men can breathe, or eyes can see,
So long lives this, and this gives life to thee.

Poets may also use visual effects. Acrostics are poems in which the first letters of each line spell out a word or name. There are even some "picture-poems" in which the lines form the shape of the object they describe, as in George Herbert's "Easter Wings."

Poetry, then, is a special reading experience in which the style of expression is as important as the content of the words. Because of its rhythm and sound, most poetry is best read aloud so that its language can be appreciated. If a reading of a poem manages to catch its invention, surprise, and delight, then the assertion of American poet Archibald MacLeish in "Ars Poetica" is fulfilled:

A poem should not mean
But be.

A modern poet: Allen Ginsberg.

Some common verse forms

ballad. Narrative poem consisting of four-line stanzas with alternating rhymes. Folk ballads were handed down from generation to generation and were originally sung. Major poets sometimes use the form, as did Keats in "La Belle Dame sans Merci."

dramatic monologue. Form of dramatic poetry in which only a single character speaks, gradually revealing his or her own dramatic situation. Robert Browning wrote many dramatic monologues. T.S. Eliot's "The Love Song of J. Alfred Prufrock" is a famous modern example.

elegy. Named from the Greek word for "lament," elegies are lyric poems on the subject of death. The death may be that of an individual, as in Auden's "In Memory of W. B. Yeats" and Milton's *Lycidas*, or in a more figurative sense that of all men, as in Donne's *Elegies* or Gray's "Elegy Written in a Country Churchyard."

epic. Long narrative poem whose subject is of major importance. The major classical epics are Homer's *Iliad* and *Odyssey* and Vergil's *Aeneid.*

hymn. Lyric poem in praise of God, or, by extension, anything of great value. The *Homeric Hymns* celebrate the Greek gods. Donne wrote "A Hymn to God the Father," and Shelley wrote a "Hymn to Intellectual Beauty."

limerick. A humorous poem of five lines. The first, second, and fifth lines rhyme, while the shorter third and fourth lines have a different rhyme. "Hickory Dickory Dock" is a limerick.

ode. Lyric poem of irregular form, often used to express deep personal feelings. Odes originated with the ancient Greek poet Pindar. English examples include Keats's "Ode to a Nightingale," and Wordsworth's "Ode: Intimations of Immortality."

romance. Long narrative poem based on legend. Among the heroes of romance are Roland in France, King Arthur and his knights in Britain, and Orlando in Italy. *Sir Gawain and the Green Knight* is the most important literary romance in English. The term also describes a type of historical novel.

sonnet. Lyric poem of 14 lines. The sonnet originated in Italy and was taken over by English poets, many of whom used a different rhyme scheme. The sonnet has been used by such English poets as Spenser, Shakespeare, Milton, and Keats.

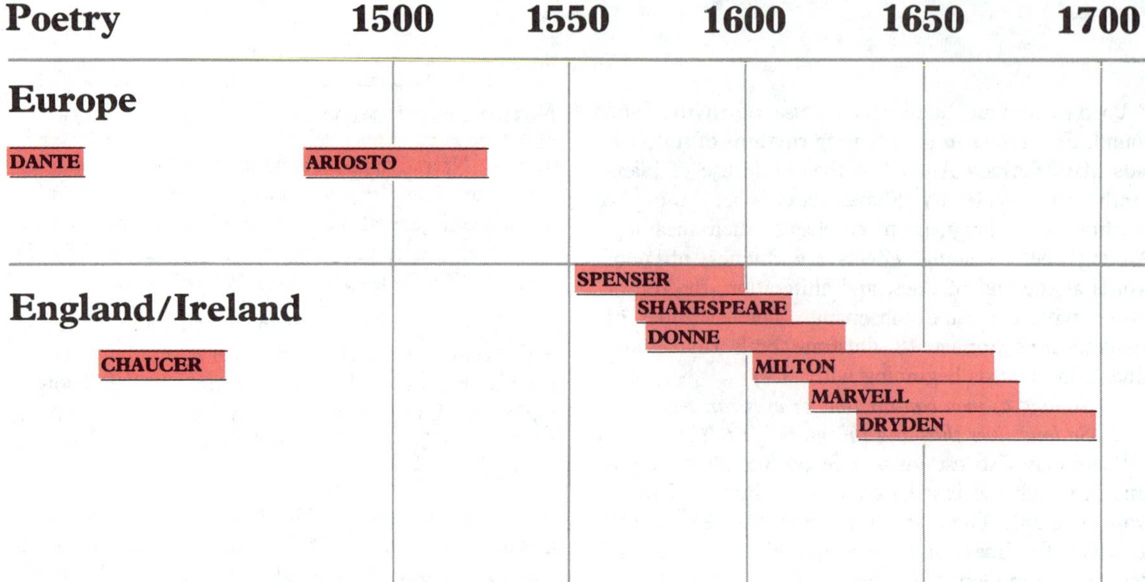

The history of poetry. Poetry is the oldest of literary forms, growing from the ancient combination of music and speech. The oldest written poems are probably written transcriptions of even older poetic legends that were originally sung or chanted by generations of traveling poet-singers or bards.

Ancient poetry. The first extant poem is the Babylonian epic *Gilgamesh*, which may date as far back as 2000 B.C. It is a collection of myths that have parallels in many later traditions. The true foundations of Western literature, however, are the Greek epics the *Iliad* and the *Odyssey.* Set down in the eighth century B.C. and attributed to the legendary poet Homer, these poems have provided a common mythology for Western literature. Their importance to Western literature is rivaled only by the Bible. The *Aeneid*, by the Latin poet Vergil, is the third great classical epic.

The Middle Ages. Poetry became moribund after the fall of Rome, when literary Latin was more and more separated from the language of everyday speech. When the new vernacular languages of Europe gained acceptance, however, poetry was reborn. Among the earliest poems were the Old English *Beowulf* in the 700's, the Gaelic-Celtic legends in the 800's, the French *Song of Roland* in the 1000's, and the Spanish *Song of the Cid* in the 1100's. These poems used new European myths, but they also portrayed their characters with a new kind of realism. Between 1050 and 1250, the troubadours of southern France completely abandoned the traditional heroic sagas to write simple love lyrics.

The Renaissance. Because of the influence of Latin, Italy was slow to accept a new vernacular language for poetry. With the appearance of Dante's *Divine Comedy* just after 1300, however, Italian culture flowered in a rebirth, or Renaissance, of its past Roman glory. Dante's vision of hell, purgatory, and heaven was filled with references to the villains and heroes of his own day, yet it owed much to the Christian church of the Middle Ages and to the Latin classics, especially to Vergil.

Chaucer's Wife of Bath, teller of one of the Canterbury Tales

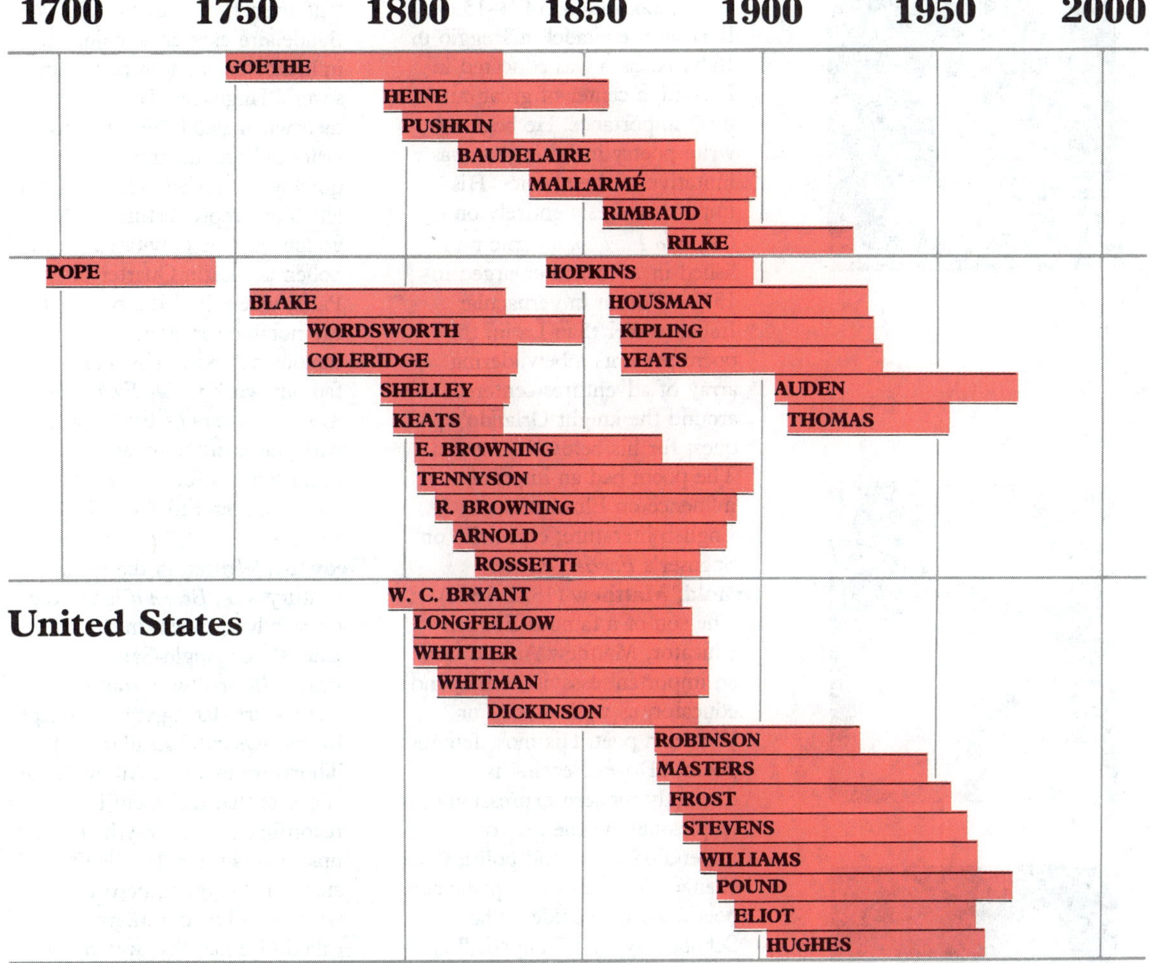

The first great English poet, Geoffrey Chaucer, visited Italy in the late 1300's and incorporated some Italian poetic innovations into his *Canterbury Tales*, but the English language waited until the late 1500's for its first great age of poetry. Then Edmund Spenser created his epic *Faerie Queene*, while Shakespeare and Donne worked most successfully in a lyric mode. In the 1600's, Milton's epic *Paradise Lost* and Andrew Marvell's lyric poems appeared. These writers still measured their works against the Greek and Latin classics. By the 1700's English poetry was being decisively challenged by prose—especially by the novel—and its golden age had passed.

Romanticism. The next great age of poetry arrived at the end of the 1700's. Romanticism was a movement that valued the natural over the artificial, the emotional over the formal, and the modern over the classical. Goethe and his contemporaries in Germany were the formulators of Romanticism, but the greatest body of Romantic poetry was written in English by Blake, Wordsworth, Coleridge, Byron, Shelley, and Keats. A movement akin to Romanticism surfaced in the mid-1800's in France in the works of Baudelaire, Mallarmé, and Rimbaud.

The American tradition in poetry was effectively begun by Longfellow, whose emphasis on historical legend was indebted to the English poets of the 1800's. In 1855, however, Walt Whitman published *Leaves of Grass*, a rowdy collection of unrhymed and unmetered free verse. It marked the beginning of modern poetry in English and became an important influence on poetry not only in America, but in many other parts of the world as well.

Modern poetry. Modern poetry has developed as a distinctly international phenomenon. Promising American poets such as T.S. Eliot and Ezra Pound emigrated to Europe. Britain's W. H. Auden and Dylan Thomas lived or traveled in the United States. The Irish poet W. B. Yeats lived much of his life in London before dying in France. The modern poets combine the conflicting impulses of classicism and Romanticism, past and present.

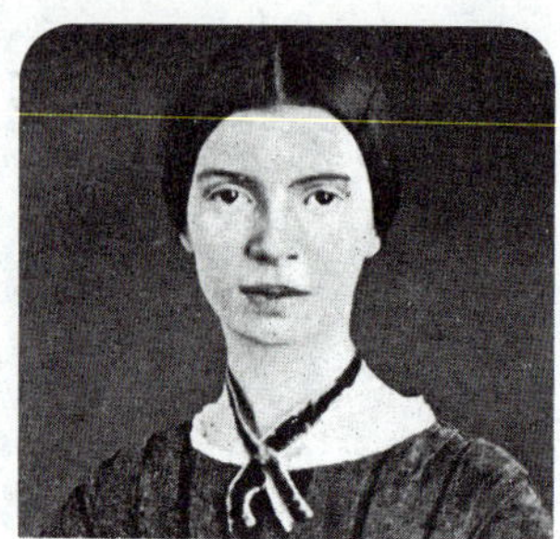
Dickinson

Poets

Whitman

Hughes

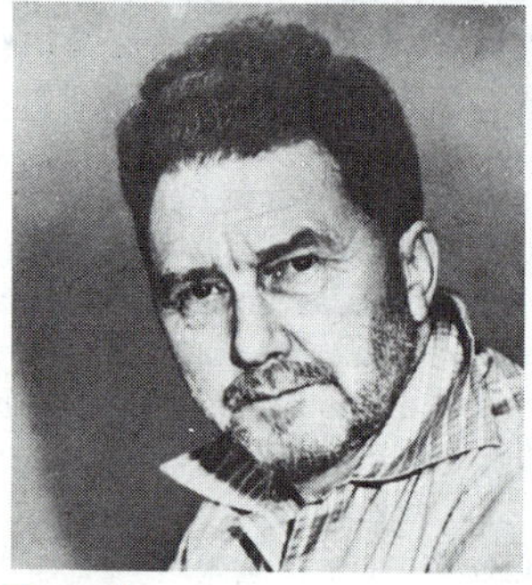
Pound

Ariosto, Lodovico (1474–1533). Born in the citadel of Reggio in Italy, Ariosto was educated in Ferrara, a center of great cultural importance. He began to write poetry in Latin that was imitative of the classics. His importance rests entirely on *Orlando Furioso*, an epic published in 1516 and enlarged in 1532. Written in vernacular Italian rather than Latin, the poem presents a bewildering array of adventures centered around the knight Orlando's quest for his beloved Angelica. The poem had an important influence on Elizabethan English literature, especially on Spenser's *Faerie Queene.*

Arnold, Matthew (1822–1888). The son of a famous English educator, Matthew Arnold was an important essayist, critic, and educator, as well as a major Victorian poet. His most famous poem, "Dover Beach," is a distinctly modern expression of helplessness in the face of impending social and political change. Arnold's other principal poetic works include "The Scholar Gypsy," "Thyrsis," and "Empedocles on Etna."

Auden, Wystan Hugh (1907–1973). The most important English poet in the first half of the 1900's, Auden fought in the Spanish Civil War in the 1930's and then left England in 1939 for residence in the United States. In England, his earliest poems brought him immediate fame because of their technical proficiency, complex forms, rhythmic patterns, and rhyme schemes. Auden also became a leading intellectual poet, one who experimented with ideas associated with Freud, with socialism, and with German rather than English or American literary history.

Baudelaire, Charles Pierre (1821–1867). The most important French poet of the 1800's, Baudelaire exerted a major influence on modern poetry in several languages. His father died when Baudelaire was six years old and his mother quickly remarried. These events left him deeply disturbed. As a young man he gravitated to the bohemian Latin Quarter of Paris, where he led a profligate life notable for affairs with famous actresses. His most famous work is *Les Fleurs du Mal* ("Flowers of Evil"), a six-part poetic autobiography of the mind famous for images and ideas that tend to shock its readers.

Beowulf. Written in the eighth century A.D., *Beowulf* is the oldest surviving poem in the Old English, or Anglo-Saxon, language. *Beowulf* was transcribed from a fire-damaged manuscript by the Icelandic scholar G. J. Thorkelin in 1787. All evidence suggests that the poem is a late recording of early myths by an unknown author. It tells the story of the young hero Beowulf, who killed a monster called Grendel that was raiding the camp of the Danish King Hrothgar. Beowulf later becomes King of the Geats and defeats a dragon in mortal combat. *Beowulf* is a great early European moral fable in which good triumphs over evil because of the direct intervention of God.

Blake, William (1757–1827). One of the most extraordinary English poets, Blake was known in his own time only as a failed painter. Self-taught, he was thoroughly absorbed by the study of the Bible and the works of Milton. Blake's major works attempt to create a modern myth that supercedes rationality about the creation and order of the world. After the short lyrics collected in *Songs of*

Blake

"The Sick Rose"

O Rose, thou art sick.
The invisible worm
That flies in the night
In the howling storm

Has found out thy bed
Of crimson joy,
And his dark secret love
Does thy life destroy.

Innocence and *Songs of Experience*, Blake began to write longer poems, such as *The Four Zoas, Milton*, and *Jerusalem*. These three poems elaborate on a visonary scheme about the hidden workings of the world; they were often illustrated with pictures in Blake's own unusual style.

Browning, Elizabeth Barrett (1806–1861). The invalid daughter of a rigidly disciplinarian father, Elizabeth Barrett married the poet Robert Browning in 1846; the couple soon left England for residence in Italy. Barrett Browning had written poetry since childhood, but her most ambitious work is the book-length poem *Aurora Leigh*, published in 1857. Termed by her a "novel-poem," *Aurora Leigh* was an attempt to write a verse epic set in contemporary Victorian surroundings rather than in the distant past. Barrett Browning was also the author of many sonnets, most of them addressed to her husband.

Browning, Robert (1812–1889). One of the preeminent poets of Victorian England, Browning was married to the poet Elizabeth Barrett Browning from 1846 until her death 15 years later. His major poems are dramatic monologues in which a character, generally a personage from European history, speaks directly to the reader and slowly reveals his or her circumstances. Browning was a prolific poet, writing many long works. In his later years he became increasingly interested in Italian history and art.

Bryant, William Cullen (1794–1878). A lawyer and editor of *The New York Evening Post*, Bryant was considered by many to be "America's Poet Laureate" because of the influence of his poems and theories about poetry in the early 1800's. His most famous work is "Thanatopsis," a meditation on death composed when he was a teenager and published after many revisions in 1817.

Byron, George Gordon (1788–1824). Lord Byron was the most popular of the English Romantic poets in his own day. This popularity was based partly on his flamboyant life, great physical beauty, and reputation as a lover. He first became known with the publication of *Childe Harold's Pilgrimage*. When fame led to a celebrated divorce, Byron left England for the Continent and continued to add to the poem. The success of a satire called *Beppo* encouraged him to begin another, and it is on the basis of the second, *Don Juan*, that Byron's reputation stands today.

Chaucer, Geoffrey (1340?–1400). The first great poet in the English language, Chaucer was a court diplomat whose travels in Europe brought him into contact with the early works and writers of the Italian Renaissance. He wrote a number of important poems, including *The Parliament of Fowls* and *Troilus and Criseyde*, but his major work was *The Canterbury Tales*. Written late in life and published after his death, the 24 tales are all told by pilgrims on the way to Canterbury Cathedral to visit the shrine of St. Thomas à Becket. Chaucer's work is written in Middle English, an early form of the language alien to modern eyes but close enough to modern English to be read without translation.

Cid, Song of the. The oldest extant poem of a longer Spanish epic cycle, *Song of the Cid* was written in 1140 A.D. and transcribed from a damaged manuscript in 1779. In almost 4000 lines, it tells the story of a

Chaucer

From The Prologue to
The Canterbury Tales

A knyght ther was, and that a worthy man,
That fro the tyme that he first bigan
To riden out, he loved chivalrie,
Trouthe and honour, fredom and curteisie.
Ful worthy was he in his lordes werre,
And therto hadde he riden, no man ferre,
As wel in Cristendom as in hetheness,
And evere honoured for his worthynesse.

The Opening of "The Wife of Bath's Tale"
from *The Canterbury Tales*

In tholde dayes of the king Arthour,
Of which that Britons speken greet honour,
All was this land fulfild of fayerye.
The elf-queen, with hir joly companye,
Daunced ful ofte in many a grene mede;
This was the olde opinion, as I rede.
I speke of manye hundred yeres ago;
But now can no man see none elves mo.

popular military leader, *El Cid*, based on the life of an actual eleventh-century leader named Rodrigo Díaz de Bivar. In the poem the hero is unjustly exiled, fights as a mercenary in the employ of both the Spaniards and their enemy the Moors, and finally returns to favor with a victory for Spain at the Battle of Valencia. In comparison with other early European epics, *Song of the Cid* is unusual for its historical accuracy and for recounting political events realistically.

Coleridge, Samuel Taylor (1772–1834). The most eccentric of the English Romantic poets, Coleridge contributed "The Rime of the Ancient Mariner," a fantastic vision, to the important collection of *Lyrical Ballads* issued in collaboration with Wordsworth in 1798. Coleridge also wrote "Kubla Khan," a dream vision about an elaborate "pleasure dome." Coleridge had immense talents and immense ambitions, but because of irregular personal habits both remained unfulfilled. He did write a number of important poems, however, including "Dejection: An Ode," "Christabel," and "The Eolian Harp," as well as a major work of literary criticism called *Biographica Literaria*.

Dante Alighieri (1265–1321). Dante was a prominent citizen of Florence, Italy, when he published his first poems in *La Vita Nuova* ("The New Life") in 1292. In 1300 he fell from political favor, however, and it was then that he set about composing his *Commedia*, which is usually referred to as the *Divine Comedy*. An epic poem, the *Divine Comedy* recounts the poet's visits to Hell (Inferno), Purgatory (Purgatorio), and Heaven (Paradiso). It is of special importance for being written in the Italian vernacular language rather than in Latin. In the poem Dante is guided through the *Inferno* and the *Purgatorio* by his poetic mentor Vergil. His guide to *Paradiso* is Beatrice, his beloved. The poem is partly concerned with political justice, and Dante places identifiable historical figures in each of the three realms of the afterlife.

Dickinson, Emily (1830–1886). Unmarried and in her later years an eccentric recluse in her father's Amherst, Massachusetts, home, Dickinson refined a very personal style and vision in more than 1800 short poems, only seven of which were published in her lifetime. Her finest poems join domestic details with larger abstractions in unlikely ways. For example, courtship is a metaphor for death in "Because I Could Not Stop for Death/He Kindly Stopped for Me." Terse and witty, her poems find wisdom in insignificant details rather than in large social or political issues.

Donne, John (1572–1631). Born into a Catholic family at a time when Catholics were persecuted in England, John Donne later became a Church of England minister and an influential preacher. He was also the most important writer of "metaphysical" poetry, in which a poetic point is made by means of surprising and often improbable analogies. In "The Flea," for example, the bite of the bug becomes a figurative representation of the love between two people. Other poems in this vein, which Donne called "far-fetched wit," include "A Fever" and "The Bait." Donne was also the author of a sequence called *Holy Sonnets* and a group of *Elegies* modeled on Ovid.

Dryden, John (1631–1700). First brought to public attention by a schoolboy elegy on the death of a young noble, Dryden was throughout his career intimately involved with the political issues of his day. He wrote *Heroic Stanzas* on the death of Cromwell, *Astraea Redux* to celebrate the return to the throne of Charles II, the satire *Absalom and Achitophel*, and major poems on his own religious odyssey. Late in his life he became a Roman Catholic. A prolific essayist, critic, dramatist, and translator, Dryden was credited by Samuel Johnson a century later with "the refinement of our language, and much of the correctness of our sentiments."

Eliot, Thomas Stearns (1888–1965). Born in St. Louis, Missouri, and educated at Harvard, Eliot went to England in 1910 and later became both a British citizen and a convert to the Church of England. His first poems, especially "The Love Song of J. Alfred Prufrock," immediately established him as one of the most important modern poets in the English language. In 1922 he published the single most important modern poem in the language, *The Waste Land*, after it had been severely edited by his fellow American expatriate Ezra Pound. Like all his major works, *The Waste Land* juxtaposes the loss of values in post-World War I society with the enduring continuities of the myths and literatures of the past. Eliot's later works include the poems in *Four Quartets*, verse dramas, and influential essays of literary criticism.

Frost, Robert (1874–1963). The great poet of New England landscapes and Yankee values, Frost lived most of his life on a small Vermont farm and wrote poems in a colloquial style that approximates the dialect of the

Dickinson

"Exultation"

Exultation is the going
Of an inland soul to sea,—
Past the houses, past the headlands,
Into deep eternity!

Bred as we, among the mountains,
Can the sailor understand
The divine intoxication
Of the first league out from land?

Hopkins

"Pied Beauty"

Glory be to God for dappled things—
For skies of couple-colour as a brinded cow;
For rose-moles all in stipple upon trout that swim;
Fresh-firecoal chestnut-falls; finches' wings;
Landscape plotted and pieced—fold, fallow, and plough;
And áll trádes, their gear and tackle and trim.
All things counter, original, spare, strange;
Whatever is fickle, freckled (who knows how?)
With swift, slow; sweet, sour; adazzle, dim;
He fathers-forth whose beauty is past change:
Praise him.

region. Important poems such as "Mending Wall," "After Apple Picking," and "The Need to Be Versed in Country Things" raise complex issues about human values and human endurance in a simple homespun style. Frost's poems are especially American in their insistence that nature is the greatest teacher, as in the famous "Stopping by Woods on a Snowy Evening."

Gilgamesh. The product of Babylonian and Assyrian society as long ago as 2000 B.C., *Gilgamesh* is the oldest surviving epic poem. The story concerns Gilgamesh's attempt to locate his dead friend Enkidu and bring him back to life. The various episodes in the poem include a great flood, such as that survived by Noah in the Bible, and feats of heroism that resemble those of Hercules and other heroes of later classical works.

Goethe, Johann Wolfgang von (1749–1832). The greatest German poet and one of the most important figures in the history of world literature, Goethe was a major novelist and playwright as well as a poet. He wrote verse from the time he was eight years old, although his education through the university level remained rather haphazard. Goethe was one of the leaders of the great German literary revolt called *Sturm und Drang* (Storm and Stress). The movement replaced conventional aesthetics with a highly dramatized sense of personal crisis, such as that affecting the suicidal title character in Goethe's novel *The Sorrows of Young Werther.* Goethe's poetic output was his greatest achievement, and it ranged from the pastoral poem *Hermann and Dorothea* to the huge two-part dramatic poem *Faust,* the story of an ambitious man's bargain with the Devil.

Heine, Heinrich (1797–1856). A German poet second in importance only to Goethe, Heinrich Heine was born in Düsseldorf to wealthy parents and was educated at a combination of local Jewish and French-speaking academies. His early reputation was based on a series of travel books and a collection of lyric poems published in 1820 and afterward set to music. He left Germany in 1831, and for a time he ceased writing poetry. In the last 15 years of his life, however, he completed a large body of poetry ranging in theme from the personal to the political.

Homer. The great bard to whom the major Greek epic poems are attributed, Homer is a legendary figure who perhaps lived in the 700's B.C. The Homeric poems are the first written transcriptions of legends that existed previous to that time. The principal Homeric poems are the *Iliad,* which tells the story of the Greek siege of Troy, and the *Odyssey,* which tells the story of the Greek Odysseus (or Ulysses) and his adventures as he returns to his homeland after the Greek victory at Troy. The events recounted in these two epics and other texts attributed to Homer are the foundation for many later literary works in English and other European languages.

Hopkins, Gerard Manley (1844–1889). Converted to Catholicism while at Oxford University, Hopkins later became a Jesuit priest. He gave up poetry for a time after entering the priesthood, although he soon resumed writing. His poems were not published until many years after his death. Hopkins' poetry is unique because of what he called "sprung rhythm," an irregular cadence indicated by accent marks over ordinarily unstressed syllables. This metrical innovation was admired by modern poets; the rhythm of such poems as "Pied Beauty" and "The Windhover" has been imitated by recent poets.

Housman, Alfred Edward (1859–1936). A. E. Housman failed his honors examination at Oxford, but he went on to become one of the great English authorities on the Latin classics. By the time he became professor of Latin at Cambridge University, he had already published his principal book of poems, *A Shropshire Lad* (1896), a gathering of poems that celebrate the beauty of nature but find it insufficient to combat a growing sense of doom and malevolent fate.

Hughes, Langston (1902–1967). The principal poet of the "Harlem Renaissance" in New York City in the 1920's, Langston Hughes described his work as an attempt to "explain and illuminate the Negro condition in America." His most famous poems, such as "The Negro Speaks of Rivers" and "Mother to Son," are written in free verse and use colloquial rhythms and idioms to communicate the special qualities of the black American experience.

Keats, John (1795–1821). The son of an English coachman and an orphan at the age of eight, Keats was a medical student who wrote a remarkable body of poetry by the time he was 24. In 1819 he completed the ballad "La Belle Dame sans Merci" and the important odes "On a Grecian Urn," "On Melancholy," and "To a Nightingale." In the autumn of the same year he wrote *The Fall of Hyperion*, a fragment of a projected longer poem, and the ode "To Autumn." Keats possessed a rapt absorption in the physical world and a passive acceptance of tragic fate and the destructive passage of time. He died of tuberculosis at the age of 26.

Kipling, Rudyard (1865–1936). Born in Bombay, India, where his father was serving in the English civil service, Kipling was sent to a brutal boarding school in England at the age of six and earned his earliest literary reputation by writing about his experiences there. He became an enormously popular poet, however, for such patriotic poems as "Danny Deever," "Tommy," and "Gunga Din," which were published while England was involved in the unpopular Boer War in Africa. Also author of *The Jungle Book* and many other novels, Kipling was awarded the Nobel Prize in 1907.

Longfellow, Henry Wadsworth (1807–1882). One of the first popular American poets, Longfellow was a precursor of the great American literary renaissance of the mid-1800's. He wrote in a traditional style, but he used new material—especially American Indian legends—that influenced many later writers. Poems such as "The Village Blacksmith" seem extremely sentimental compared with the works of younger American poets. Nevertheless, in his own day Longfellow was greatly admired, especially for such long poems as *Hyperion*, *Evangeline*, and *The Song of Hiawatha.*

Mallarmé, Stephane (1842–1898). One of the most important modern French poets, Mallarmé was also an important translator of Edgar Allan Poe into French and an essayist on ancient myths and modern music. He supported himself in Paris with these literary works while his poetry, heavily influenced by Baudelaire, slowly gained acceptance. His most important single work is *L'Apres midi d'un faune* ("Afternoon of a Faun"), for which the French composer Claude Debussy wrote a famous musical accompaniment. The body of his work is comprised of a large collection of short lyrics.

Marvell, Andrew (1621–1678). Traveling in Europe when the English Civil War erupted in 1642, Marvell returned home to support the Puritan side, which was victorious; he later became a member of Parliament. Marvell wrote many satires and political tracts, but he is principally remembered today for his lyric poetry. The most important examples are "To His Coy Mistress," "The Garden," "The Mower Against the Garden," and the longer "Upon Appleton House."

Masters, Edgar Lee (1869–1948). A Chicago lawyer, Masters was a poet without great pretensions. His *Spoon River Anthology*, published in 1915, became one of the best-selling volumes of verse in American literary history. Written in a free verse form imitative of Walt Whitman, the poems criticized the narrowness and frustrations of life in a small town.

Milton, John (1608–1674). The greatest English poet of his time, Milton was a supporter of the Puritan cause; he rose in government service during Cromwell's rule over England. During this period Milton wrote his famous poems *L'Allegro*, *Il Penseroso*, and *Lycidas*, the last an elegy on the death of his friend Edward King. With the restoration of the monarchy in 1660, Milton fell from political favor. Totally blind, he then dictated to his daughters the epic poem *Paradise Lost*, which was published in 1667. Like the epics of Homer and Vergil, Milton's poem is in twelve books; it recounts Satan's fall from God's grace and the paral-

Keats

"When I Have Fears"

When I have fears that I may cease to be
  Before my pen has gleaned my teeming brain,
Before high-pilèd books, in charact'ry,
  Hold like rich garners the full-ripened grain;
When I behold, upon the night's starred face,
  Huge cloudy symbols of a high romance,
And think that I may never live to trace
  Their shadows, with the magic hand of chance;
And when I feel, fair creature of an hour,
  That I shall never look upon thee more,
Never have relish in the faery power
  Of unreflecting love! — then on the shore
Of the wide world I stand alone, and think
Till Love and Fame to nothingness do sink.

Milton

The Opening of *Paradise Lost*

Of man's first disobedience, and the fruit
Of that forbidden tree, whose mortal taste
Brought death into the world, and all our woe,
With loss of Eden, till one greater Man
Restore us, and regain the blissful seat,
Sing, heavenly Muse, that on the secret top
Of Oreb, or of Sinai, didst inspire
That shepherd who first taught the chosen seed
In the beginning how the heavens and earth
Rose out of Chaos; or if Sion hill
Delight thee more, and Siloa's brook that flowed
Fast by the oracle of God, I thence
Invoke thy aid to my adventurous song,
That with no middle flight intends to soar
Above the Aonian mount, while it pursues
Things unattempted yet in prose or rhyme.

lel fall of man in Eden. It is the one great literary epic in English.

Ovid (43 B.C.–18 A.D.). Publius Ovidius Naso was a Latin poet born near Rome and exiled to a settlement called Tomis on the Black Sea after he ran afoul of authorities at the end of his life. He was a lawyer by profession, but he soon abandoned his practice to write poetry. His work departed from the noble vein common in Latin poetry since the *Aeneid* of Vergil. Instead, Ovid wrote verses whose irreverent and titillating qualities were suggested by his first titles: *Amores* and *The Confessions of Women*. His masterpiece is the epic *Metamorphoses*, literally "transformations," a collection of well-known legends that ponder the ambiguities of life.

Pope, Alexander (1688–1744). A recluse from refined London society because he was both a Catholic and physically deformed, Pope refined his outsider's views of political, literary, and cultural events and became the great verse satirist of English poetry. *The Rape of the Lock* is a mock epic in verse that satirizes aristocratic vanity; *The Dunciad* is a similar satire on the vanity of popular writers of the day. Pope was a scholarly classicist who insisted on high literary standards; he met these standards in his more serious works, *Essay on Criticism* and *Imitations of Horace*.

Pound, Ezra (1885–1972). The self-proclaimed "Idaho Kid," Pound left the United States after his education at the University of Pennsylvania and brought an American entrepreneurial spirit to the poetry circles in Europe. He was an important editor and influence on other poets, notably T. S. Eliot, as well as a major poet in his own right. His principal poetic works, *Personae*, a collection of short lyrics, and *Cantos*, a volume of more than 100 cantos left incomplete at his death, show an encyclopedic knowledge of literature in many Western and Eastern languages.

Pushkin, Aleksandr (1799–1837). The founder of modern Russian literature, Pushkin wrote plays, novels, and short stories that reflected the special nature of Russian life but took Western European forms. His major achievement is the long poem *Eugene Onegin*, which is the great poetic epic in the Russian tongue. The story of the unrequited love of Eugene for Tatiana over a period of several years, it was later made into an important opera by the Russian composer Tchaikovsky.

Rilke, Rainer Maria (1875–1926). One of the most important modern poets to write in the German language, Rilke was born in Prague, now the capital of Czechoslovakia. Austrian by heritage, he had an unhappy childhood and wrote early lyrics that combined elements of mysticism with a search for God outside of organized religion. Usually in poor financial circumstances, Rilke traveled considerably throughout his life in search of literary patronage. His most important work is the obscure and demanding *Duino Elegies*, which has exerted great influence on modern poets in several languages.

Rimbaud, Arthur (1854–1891). A child prodigy who wrote verse when very young, Rimbaud was a fiercely rebellious youth who ran away from home several times and served a term in a French prison while still an adolescent. He wrote what is perhaps the most important prose poem in literature, "Le Bateau Ivre" ("The Drunken Boat"), and a collection of short lyrics and prose poems, *Les Illuminations*, that is one of the key texts of modern French poetry. Subject to deep emotional stresses, he gave up writing late in life and settled in North Africa, where he may have been involved in criminal activities.

Robinson, Edwin Arlington (1869–1935). Raised in Maine and educated as a "special," or nondegree student at Harvard, Robinson wrote prosaic poems that were considered outdated even as they were published. He was acclaimed later in his career, receiving three Pulitzer Prizes, but because his poetry relied more on plot than on subtleties of language, his work had little influence on younger poets. In his later years he wrote long Arthurian narrative poems such as *Merlin* and *Tristram*, but he is best remembered today for short, storylike poems such as "Richard Cory," "Mr. Flood's Party," and "Miniver Cheevy."

Rossetti, Dante Gabriel (1828–1882). Born in London of Italian parents, Rossetti was the founder of the Pre-Raphaelite movement in England. The movement was an attempt by painters, as well as poets, including his sister Christina Rossetti, to return aesthetics to the formal purity of the time before Italian Renaissance painter Raphael. Dante Gabriel Rossetti's major poetic works include "The Blessed Damozel," "The Woodspurge," and a sonnet sequence called *The House of Life*.

Shakespeare, William (1564–1616). In addition to being the most important dramatist in Western literature, William Shakespeare was one of the major poets in English literature. He wrote two important narrative poems between 1592 and 1594, years when an epidemic closed the London theaters: *Venus and Adonis*, an adaptation of a tale from Ovid's *Metamorphoses*, and *The Rape of Lucrece*. Shakespeare's most famous poems, however, are the 154 *Sonnets*, a sequence published in 1609 and probably written over a number of years. These sonnets, full of extremely subtle wordplay, all address the subjects of love and human relationships as they are experienced by a young aristocrat; by a mysterious "dark lady"; and by a poet jealous of both.

English Romantic poets and representative works

William Blake (1757–1827)
Songs of Innocence
Songs of Experience
Jerusalem

Samuel Taylor Coleridge (1772–1834)
"The Rime of the Ancient Mariner"
"Kubla Khan"
"Dejection: An Ode"

William Wordsworth (1779–1850)
The Prelude
"Ode: Intimations of Immortality"
"Tintern Abbey"

Lord George Gordon Byron (1788–1824)
Childe Harold's Pilgrimage
Don Juan

Percy Bysshe Shelley (1792–1822)
Adonais
Prometheus Unbound
"Ode to the West Wind"

John Keats (1795–1821)
"Ode to a Nightingale"
"Ode to a Grecian Urn"
"To Autumn"

Shelley, Percy Bysshe (1792–1822). Having been expelled from Oxford and having abandoned his daughter and pregnant wife, Shelley wrote his first major poem, *Alastor*, in the misguided belief that he was about to die of tuberculosis. He did not die, but after eloping to Europe with Mary Godwin Shelley, who would write the novel *Frankenstein*, he began to write major poems in a burst of sudden genius. The most important of his works are *Adonais*, an elegy on the death of Keats, and *Prometheus Unbound*, an adaptation of the Greek tragedy *Prometheus Bound*. Shelley also wrote a number of important shorter works, including "Ode to the West Wind" and "To a Skylark."

Sir Gawain and the Green Knight. The most important verse romance in English, *Sir Gawain and the Green Knight* was written by an unknown poet at the end of the 1300's. It tells the story of Gawain, whose courage is tested when confronted by the mysterious Green Knight. The poem is most remarkable for its long digressions, including formal descriptions of King Arthur's Christmas feast, the manner in which Gawain arms himself for a journey, and elaborate hunting parties.

Song of Roland. The major epic in the French language, *Song of Roland* was composed by an unknown Norman author before 1131, when the poem was translated into Latin to reach a larger audience. The poem describes the exploits of its hero on a military expedition by

Shakespeare
Sonnet 73

That time of year thou mayst in me behold
When yellow leaves, or none, or few, do hang
Upon those boughs which shake against the cold,
Bare ruined choirs where late the sweet birds sang:
In me thou see'st the twilight of such day
As after sunset fadeth in the west,
Which by and by black night doth take away,
Death's second self that seals up all in rest:
In me thou see'st the glowing of such fire
That on the ashes of his youth doth lie
As the death-bed whereon it must expire,
Consumed with that which it was nourished by:
  This thou perceivest, which makes thy love more strong
  To love that well which thou must leave ere long.

Spenser
Sonnet 68 from *Amoretti*

Most glorious Lord of Lyfe, that on this day
Didst make thy triumph over death and sin:
And having harrowd hell, didst bring away
Captivity thence captive us to win:
This joyous day, deare Lord, with joy begin,
And grant that we for whom thou diddest dye
Being with thy deare blood clene washt from sin,
May live for ever in felicity.
And that thy love we weighing worthily,
May likewise love thee for the same againe:
And for thy sake that all lyke deare didst buy,
With love may one another entertayne.
So let us love, deare love, lyke as we ought,
Love is the lesson which the Lord us taught.

Charlemagne into Spain, a campaign that actually occurred in the year 778. Roland dies a tragic death on the return trip, when a small band of Spanish Saracens attacks the rear guard of Charlemagne's army and Roland is too proud to blow his magic horn to summon help. The poem is important in the English as well as French traditions, for when the Normans invaded England in 1066 some accounts say that Roland sung to stimulate the Norman troops before the Battle of Hastings.

Spenser, Edmund (1552–1599). One of the most important poets of early English literary history, Spenser hoped to gain preferment in the Elizabethan court with his poetry, but met with only limited success. His twelve pastoral dialogues, *The Shepheardes Calendar*, brought him some fame in 1579, but afterward he was given the mixed blessing of a government position in Ireland. His most important work is the *Faerie Queene*, a major poem that uses elements of Arthurian romance to describe allegorically the threats to Queen Elizabeth's power in the 1580's and 1590's. The *Faerie Queene* presents a panorama of characters and a series of unrelated tales rather than a single story. The first three books were published in 1590, and three more appeared in Spenser's lifetime, but fragments exist that suggest the poem was to be continued.

Stevens, Wallace (1879–1955). A lawyer employed for most of his life by an insurance company in Connecticut, Wallace Stevens quietly amassed one of the most important philosophical bodies of poetry in American literature. He often referred to his poems as "ideas of order," and many of them debate the relative merits of the order apparent in nature as opposed to the manmade order provided by art or religion. Poems such as "Sunday Morning" and "The Snow Man" test subtle intellectual distinctions between the natural and the artificial, while poems such as "The Emperor of Ice Cream" and "A High-Toned Old Christian Woman" explore the same subject in exuberant and playful ways.

Tennyson, Alfred (1809–1892). Alfred Lord Tennyson was the Poet Laureate of England from 1850 until his death. His works, many of which attempt to recover the certainties of the past in an era of great social change, are considered the major poetic expression of English sensibility in the Victorian age. In addition to many short poems such as "Mariana," "Maud," and "Audley Court," his major achievements are *In Memoriam*, an elegy on the death of his friend Arthur Hallam, and *The Idylls of the King*, an Arthurian legend published in twelve parts between 1859 and 1885.

Thomas, Dylan (1914–1953). Born in Swansea, Wales, a town he always described with bitterness, Dylan Thomas had a formal education that ended with grammar school; however, he was hailed as a major poet when he published his first book at the age of 20. From that point on, his hard-drinking, improvident life made him for many the image of the modern poet. He died from alcohol-related causes at 39. Thomas's poetry is notable for imagery from Welsh lore and the Bible, and for its intoxication with the natural world, as in "Fern Hill."

Whitman

The Opening of "Song of Myself"

I celebrate myself, and sing myself,
And what I assume you shall assume,
For every atom belonging to me as good belongs
to you.

I loafe and invite my soul,
I lean and loafe at my ease observing a spear
of summer grass.

My tongue, every atom of my blood, form'd from
this soil, this air,
Born here of parents born here from parents the
same, and their parents the same,
I, now thirty-seven years old in perfect health
begin,
Hoping to cease not till death.

Wordsworth

The Opening of *The Prelude*

O there is blessing in this gentle breeze
That blows from the green fields and from
the clouds
And from the sky: it beats against my cheek,
And seems half-conscious of the joy it gives.
O welcome messenger! O welcome friend!
A captive greets thee, coming from a house
Of bondage, from yon city's walls set free,
A prison where he hath been long immured.
Now I am free, enfranchised and at large,
May fix my habitation where I will.
What dwelling shall receive me? in what vale
Shall be my harbour? underneath what grove
Shall I take up my home? and what sweet stream
Shall with its murmurs lull me to my rest?

Vergil (70–19 B.C.). Publius Vergilius Maro was born on a farm in the north of Italy, and although he made important friends in the Roman government he continued to prefer life in the country. This interest was reflected in his early poetic works, *Eclogues* and *Georgics*. His greatest work, however, is the *Aeneid*, an epic poem in twelve books left incomplete at the time of his death. The *Aeneid* tells the story of the journey of Aeneas and a band of followers from the ruined city of Troy to the present site of Rome, and their establishment of a city there. Written just after the end of the Roman republic, the poem is the greatest legacy of that classical society.

Whitman, Walt (1819–1892). The first great American poet, Whitman was a journeyman printer from New York City who published a slim volume called *Leaves of Grass* in 1855. He then continued to enlarge and revise the book for the rest of his life. He was the great exponent of modern free verse, poetry composed of unrhymed lines of varied lengths. By means of free verse and a vocabulary of colloquialisms and slang words once considered "unpoetic," Whitman hoped to communicate in his poems the special exuberance of life in America. The most famous of the more than 400 poems finally gathered into *Leaves of Grass* include "Song of Myself," "Crossing Brooklyn Ferry," and an elegy for Abraham Lincoln, "When Lilacs Last in the Dooryard Bloom'd."

Whittier, John Greenleaf (1807–1892). Of all American poets, John Greenleaf Whittier was the most vocal supporter of the abolitionist movement to end slavery. His most famous poems on the subject were "Massachusetts to Virginia," on the fugitive slave law, and "Ichabod," an attack on Senator Daniel Webster. His story poems, such as "Snowbound," also gained wide popularity after the Civil War.

Williams, William Carlos (1883–1963). A friend of Ezra Pound, Williams decided against life in Europe and served as a practicing physician in New Jersey throughout his long literary career. He was influenced by many of the schools of modern poetry developing in Europe, but for the most part he attempted to draw attention to the minute qualities of common objects in short lyrics of unadorned American speech patterns. In his long poem *Paterson*, Williams celebrates the history and diversity of that New Jersey city in various verse forms broken by occasional passages of prose.

Wordsworth, William (1770–1850). One of the most important of all English poets, Wordsworth concentrated on rural settings and themes in all his works. He was the principal theorist behind the important collection of 1798 called *Lyrical Ballads*, which contained poems by Coleridge as well. The *Ballads* were an attempt to return poetry to a mode of common, as opposed to ornate, speech. Wordsworth also made the spiritual autobiography an accepted subject for poetry in his book-length *The Prelude* and many shorter poems. His other major poems include "Lines Composed Above Tintern Abbey" and "Ode: Intimations of Immortality."

Yeats, William Butler (1865–1939). An important essayist and playwright as well as one of the major poets of the early 1900's, Yeats was one of the founders of the Irish literary revival in the 1890's. The subjects of his major poems are derived from Celtic legends, from modern Ireland's struggle for political independence, and from mystical and symbolic elements borrowed from other European literatures. In poems such as "Byzantium" and "The Second Coming," Yeats elaborated a sweeping theory about historical cycles, but most of his important poems are tied to particular Irish places, as in "The Lake Isle of Innisfree," or to historical events, as in "Easter 1916," the date of the great Irish uprising.

Meter and rhythm in poetry

The musical qualities of poetry in English are created by the length of a single line and the arrangement of stressed syllables within it. Length determines the meter of the line. Stressed syllables give the line its rhythm.

Meter

Units of a line of poetry are syllabic groups called *feet*; the number of feet gives the meter its name.

tetrameter. One of the most common meters in English consists of four feet; it is called tetrameter:

"O West/ern wind,/ when wilt/ thou blow."

pentameter. Another very common English meter is pentameter, so named because it consists of five feet: "That time/ of year/ thou mayst/ in me/ be-hold"

hexameter. English poetry also uses the hexameter line, which has six feet. Each stanza of Spenser's *The Faerie Queene* ends with a line of hexameter:

"Fierce warres/ and faith/ full loves/
shall mor/ a-lize/ my song."

other meters. Other meters are also named according to the number of feet in the line. A line of one foot is called monometer, a line of two feet is called dimeter, and a line of three feet is called trimeter.

mixed meter. Lines of poetry can be classified as a single meter. Poems, however, usually mix meter, or alternate lines of one meter with lines of at least one other meter. This adds to the musical quality of the poem by eliminating monotonous repetition. All ballads, for example, alternate tetrameter with trimeter lines. Look at this stanza of Coleridge's ballad "The Rime of the Ancient Mariner": the first and third lines are tetrameter, the second and fourth are trimeter:

"The Wed/ ding Guest/ sat on/ a stone:
He can/ not choose/ but hear;
And thus/ spake on/ that an/ cient man,
The bright/ eyed Mar/ in-er."

Rhythm

The placement of a stressed syllable in a foot determines its rhythm and gives the foot its name. Words in poetry generally carry the same syllabic stress that they have in speech.

iambic. The most common foot in the English language is the iamb, an unstressed syllable followed by a stressed one as in the word "a-bove." Thus, the first example above would be fully described as iambic tetrameter:

"O West/ ern wind,/ when wilt / thou blow."

anapestic. If a foot consists of two unstressed syllables followed by a stressed one, it is called an anapest, as in the word "un-de-ceive." Edgar Allan Poe's poem "Annabel Lee" contains a line of anapestic trimeter:

"Of the beau / ti-ful Ann / a-bel Lee"

trochaic. The poetic foot can also begin with the stressed syllable. A stressed syllable followed by a single unstressed one is called a trochee, as in the word "hu-mor." Thus, another line from Poe, in this case from "The Raven," can be described as trochaic tetrameter:

"Once u/ pon a/ mid-night / drear-y"

dactylic. If a foot consists of a stressed syllable followed by two unstressed ones, it is called a dactyl, as in the word "mur-mur-ing." A line of three such feet would be called dactylic trimeter:

"This is the / moun-tain un/ reach-a-ble."

other rhythmic feet. Sometimes two unstressed syllables will come together in a single foot; this combination is called a pyrrhic foot. Alternately, two stressed syllables can come together in a single foot; this combination is called a spondee.

Plays	1500	1550	1600	1650	1700
Europe	LOPE DE VEGA CALDERÓN CORNEILLE MOLIÈRE RACINE				
England/Ireland	SHAKESPEARE MARLOWE JONSON				

Drama

Plays are unique among the principal literary forms in that they are meant to be performed, like music, rather than read, like poems. The word "drama" is derived from the Greek word for action. The Greek philosopher Aristotle defined all literary works as imitations of life's actions; he distinguished drama as the "imitation of action in the form of action." Hence plays are inseparable from performance; when simply read they reveal only a portion of their power and meaning.

In addition to the serious plays suggested by the word "drama," the dramatic arts include musical comedies, pantomimes, television dramas, religious pageants, and movies. In some cases plays may be "translated" into other artistic forms; the composers Rossini and Verdi based operas on Shakespeare's tragedy *Macbeth.* In other cases plays themselves may be dramatizations of other literary forms, as with the modern musical *Oliver* based on Dickens' novel *Oliver Twist.* Drama is remarkably versatile, and it has been used in a variety of ways to suit the needs of audiences and different historical eras.

Aristotle also provided the basic distinction between kinds of plays: in tragedies audiences perceive the principal characters to be more noble than people in real life; in comedies the characters are perceived to be inferior to people in real life. Tragedies tend to have sad endings, and comedies happy endings. Tragicomic plays combine elements of tragedy and comedy. History plays, dramatizations of past events, may be primarily tragic, as in Shakespeare's *Richard II,* or primarily comic, as in Shaw's *Caesar and Cleopatra.* Many distinct kinds of plays exist within these broad categories: the revenge tragedy about retribution, the domestic tragedy about everyday people, the sophisticated comedy of manners, and the low comedy of farce.

A full appreciation of plays requires three kinds of attention: first, attention to the language spoken, as in poetry; second, attention to plot, character, and setting, as in fiction; and third, attention to drama's unique qualities, including lighting, set design, interpretation of roles, and the organization of actors by the director.

The history of drama. The origin of theater as we know it is generally ascribed to an ancient Greek named Thespis, and for that reason actors are still called thespians. Thespis is said to have added a new voice to the traditional choral poetry of Athens by acting the part of a god or hero in dialogue with the chorus. Soon other characters were added and large dramatic festivals arranged. In the 400's B.C. Athens produced the oldest surviving plays: the tragedies of Aeschylus, Sophocles, and Euripides, and the comedies of Aristophanes. The earliest of these plays were formal performances combining dance and poetry. But soon attention shifted to individual characters and away from the chorus.

With the rise of Rome, the center of theater shifted to the Imperial City. Roman drama was distinguished by the tragedies of Seneca and the comedies of Plautus and Terence.

Roman drama, as shown in a carving found at Pompeii

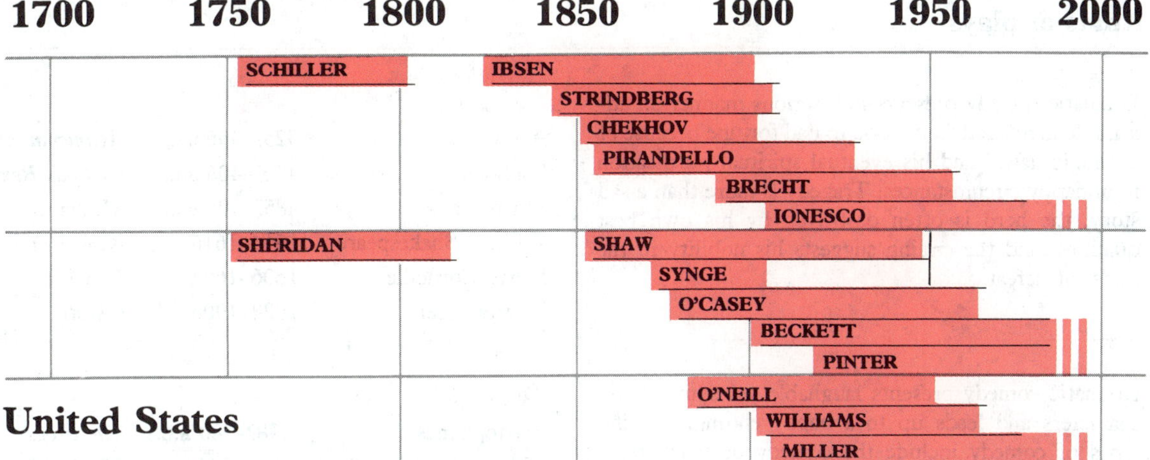

In the Middle Ages drama came to serve religious purposes. Theatrical performances included mystery plays, dramatizations of the Scriptures (also known as miracle plays), and allegorical morality plays in which actors might represent the Seven Deadly Sins or the Seven Moral Virtues.

In the 1500's, Europeans began to rediscover the classic dramas of Rome and Greece, and began once more to perform secular plays. Between 1580 and 1680, a new golden age of drama dawned in Western Europe. In England, Shakespeare transformed stage entertainments into a great literary vehicle; his plays eventually established drama as a literary form to be read as well as performed. In Spain, Shakespeare's contemporary Lope de Vega established theater as an art form so popular that he is said to have written as many as 2000 plays. In France, Corneille and Racine extended the bounds of tragedy, and Molière revived dramatic comedy as an art form.

After 1700, drama became a neglected art. In England playwrights such as Sheridan provided light comedies, and in Germany literary figures such as Schiller wrote plays as a secondary occupation, causing drama to survive only as a poor cousin to poetry and fiction.

It was in the late 1800's that drama regained its importance among the literary forms, chiefly because of the socially conscious plays of Norwegian Henrik Ibsen and Russian Anton Chekhov, and the surreal experiments of the Swedish master, Johan August Strindberg. These authors explored topics of immediate relevance to the lives of their audiences, and they favored realistic everyday speech. By the early 1900's the plays of Irish literary revival figures such as John Millington Synge and Sean O'Casey helped rouse a nation struggling for political independence.

Since then, dramatists have continued to experiment in directions first explored by Ibsen, Chekhov, and Strindberg. In America writers such as Eugene O'Neill, Tennessee Williams, and Arthur Miller have devoted themselves to contemporary dramas about common people. In Europe writers such as Luigi Pirandello, Samuel Beckett, and Eugene Ionesco have produced less realistic plays that address enduring philosophical problems.

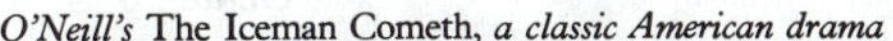

O'Neill's The Iceman Cometh, *a classic American drama*

Kinds of plays

Tragedy

Dramatic tragedy presents in a serious manner an admirable hero's fall from good to bad fortune because of a "tragic flaw," and his eventual spiritual purification in unhappy circumstances. Tragedy is more than a sad story; the hero is often destroyed by his own best qualities, and the ending suggests his nobility in the midst of defeat.

Examples

Playwright	*Lifetime*	*Work*
Aeschylus	525?–456 B.C.	*Agamemnon*
Sophocles	496?–406 B.C.	*Oedipus Rex*
Euripides	485?–406 B.C.	*Medea*
William Shakespeare	1564–1616	*King Lear*
Pierre Corneille	1606–1684	*Le Cid*
Henrik Ibsen	1828–1906	*Ghosts*

Comedy

Dramatic comedy presents laughable yet sympathetic characters and leads up to a happy ending. Specific types of comedy include the comedy of manners, a satire of sophisticated life; low comedy, a satire of cruder lifestyles; and the comedy of situation, in which the humor is provided by the plot. In all cases, the comic actions of simplified characters in an ideal world have relevance to real-life situations.

Examples

Playwright	*Lifetime*	*Work*
Aristophanes	448?–380 B.C.	*The Frogs*
William Shakespeare	1564–1616	*Much Ado About Nothing*
Ben Jonson	1572–1637	*Volpone*
Molière	1622–1673	*Tartuffe*
Richard Brinsley Sheridan	1751–1816	*The Rivals*
George Bernard Shaw	1856–1950	*Candida*

Tragicomedy

Dramatic tragicomedy, a relatively modern combination of dramatic types, presents events apparently headed for the catastrophic ending of tragedy but actually headed for a comic or ambiguous ending. Tragicomedy thus manages to combine the entertaining qualities of comedy with the serious themes of tragedy. Modern tragicomedy is a powerful vehicle for the communication of pessimistic ideas in the form of farce.

Examples

Playwright	*Lifetime*	*Work*
William Shakespeare	1564–1616	*Measure for Measure*
George Bernard Shaw	1856–1950	*St. Joan*
Anton Chekhov	1860–1904	*The Cherry Orchard*
John M. Synge	1871–1909	*The Playboy of the Western World*
Sean O'Casey	1880–1964	*Juno and the Paycock*
Samuel Beckett	b. 1906	*Waiting for Godot*

Stage terms

act. One of the major divisions of a play. Many plays of the past had five acts, and many modern plays have three acts. Short plays may have only one act.

aside. Brief comment made by an actor on the stage, but intended to be heard only by the audience.

chorus. Group on the stage that comments on but does not participate in the dramatic action. The chorus is an essential part of Greek drama, in which it consists of masked dancers who originally sang or chanted their lines.

comic relief. A humorous story or character inserted into a serious play to release tension briefly and to intensify, by contrast, tragic emotions. Shakespeare uses comic relief to this effect with the grave digger in *Hamlet* and the drunken gatekeeper in *Macbeth.*

scene. Unit within an act of a play, usually indicated by a change of setting or by a brief curtain or blackout.

soliloquy. Extended speech by a character alone on the stage, in which he often reveals truths not admitted in the presence of other characters.

Tragic masks

Dramatists

Ibsen

O'Neill

Shaw

Aeschylus (525?–456 B.C.). Author of the oldest surviving plays, Aeschylus was a Greek soldier who fought the Persians at Marathon and Salamis and later became a prominent citizen of Athens. He is thought to have written more than 80 plays, most for the Greek dramatic festival Dionysia. Seven complete plays survive in addition to many fragments. All of Aeschylus' plays are tragedies, and his most important work is the trilogy called the *Oresteia*. The three plays—*Agamemnon*, *The Libation Bearers*, and *The Eumenides*—recount the legends concerning the royal house of Atreus during the Trojan War. The other surviving plays of Aeschylus include *Seven Against Thebes* and *Prometheus Bound*.

Aristophanes (448?–380 B.C.). Younger than the great Greek tragedians, Aristophanes is the only writer of comedies of his time whose works have survived. Eleven of his 40 plays are known today. They reveal satires of Athenian political events and a bawdy humor that occasionally borders on the obscene. The satire in his plays is generally delivered by the chorus, and several plays such as *The Birds* and *The Frogs* are named for the disguises worn by the chorus on the stage. Aristophanes often ridicules specific social evils, such as excessive militarism in *Peace* and pretentious scholarship in *The Clouds*.

Beckett, Samuel (b. 1906). Born in Ireland, Beckett was educated at Trinity College, Dublin, and then traveled in Europe. He became a close friend of the Irish novelist James Joyce in Paris in the 1930's. Although he published novels, poems, and essays, Beckett remained unknown until the production of his play *Waiting for Godot* brought sudden fame in 1953. That play established him as the founder of the theater of the absurd, a school of drama devoted to the existentialist belief that inherited values and institutions are meaningless and that man must create his own identity in a malevolent world. Beckett's many plays, written in either English or French, include *Endgame* and *Krapp's Last Tape*. Also one of the most important of modern novelists, he was awarded the Nobel Prize in 1969.

Brecht, Bertolt (1898–1956). The most important modern German dramatist, Brecht was a confirmed Communist who left Germany for New York in the 1930's and settled in East Germany after World War II. It was with the Berliner Ensemble in East Berlin that he produced his major works, *Mother Courage*, *The Good Woman of Setzuan*, and *The Caucasian Chalk Circle*. These were works in what Brecht called his "epic theater," characterized by episodic scenes strung together by subtitles and short films. Brecht aimed to destroy the usual theatrical illusion of reality in search of a higher truth. He was the collaborator with composer Kurt Weill on *The Threepenny Opera*.

Calderón de la Barca (1600–1681). The successor to Lope de Vega as the leading dramatist of Spain's golden age, Calderón began his career as the author of popular mythological spectacles that used innovative scenery and lighting techniques. He became a priest in 1651, after which his work was devoted to religious themes and theological issues. His principal long work is the play *Life Is a Dream*, and he is especially famous for short *autos sacramentales*, one-act plays on religious subjects.

Chekhov, Anton (1860–1904). Chekhov was a Russian who witnessed the social transformation within his country that would lead to the Bolshevik Revolution after his death. With Henrik Ibsen of Norway, he was the leading pioneer in modern drama. Chekhov's major plays, *The Seagull*, *Uncle Vanya*, *Three Sisters*, and *The Cherry Orchard*, all explore the human drama of the decline of the Russian nobility and the rise of the middle classes. The plays are realistic and restrained, and at first audiences found them dull. Later productions of the plays by the Moscow Art Theater directed by Constantin Stanislavsky revealed the richness and subtlety of Chekhov's art, and soon his influence was international. Chekhov was also a gifted and influential writer of short stories.

Corneille, Pierre (1606–1684). The founder of France's first great age of drama, Corneille was born in Rouen and saw his first play performed there by a troup of traveling players. Brought to Paris to write plays in imitation of the classical Greek and Latin dramas, he became dissatisfied with their restrictions and as a result composed the first great tragedies in French literature. The most important of these were *Le Cid*, about the exploits of Spain's national hero, and *Andromède*, a treatment of a classical myth.

Euripides (485?–406 B.C.). Euripides was the youngest of the three great Greek tragedians. He was more individualistic and less popular in his own day than Aeschylus or Sophocles. But his emphasis on character—and on human psychology—makes his plays most like modern European classics. His plays are more often staged today than those of his predecessors. Eighteen of his tragedies survive, and all are notable for their understanding of human suffering, particularly the sufferings of women. The plays most often performed today are *Medea*, *Trojan Women*, *Electra*, and *Bacchae*.

Ibsen, Henrik (1828–1906). The most important pioneer of modern drama, Henrik Ibsen was a Norwegian who learned stagecraft as the manager of theaters in Oslo. His first works were romantic verse plays such as *Brand* and *Peer Gynt*. Gradually he moved toward more realistic plays that considered important social issues, including the status of women and the hypocrisy of the educated classes. Early performances of his plays frequently received jeers and even caused riots. The most important of his plays include *A Doll's House*, the story of a woman's search for freedom; *An Enemy of the People*; *Ghosts*; *The Wild Duck*; and *Hedda Gabler*. All of them present unflattering portraits of middle-class and small-town life.

Ionesco, Eugene (b. 1912). A leading figure in contemporary French drama, Eugene Ionesco first gained attention in the early 1950's as an exponent of the theater of the absurd, which sought to illustrate the meaninglessness of life by overturning the conventions of traditional drama. In *The Bald Soprano*, for example, relatives gather for a family reunion and exchange meaningless phrases taken from a beginning foreign language primer. Other important works include *The Lesson*, *The Chairs*, and *Jack, or The Submission*.

Jonson, Ben (1572–1637). Although he was the son of a poor London bricklayer, Ben Jonson alone among the important English dramatists of Elizabethan times was an intellectual and a classicist. Jonson differs from Shakespeare, Marlowe, and his other contemporaries in that all his major plays are satires. He ridicules lust in *Volpone*, greed in *The Alchemist*, and several common vices in *Bartholomew Fair*. After the death of Elizabeth I in 1603, Jonson wrote elaborate entertainments called *masques* for the court of James I. Masques used poetry, music, dance, and special effects to entertain court audiences.

Marlowe, Christopher (1564–1593). The son of a shoemaker from Canterbury, England, Marlowe lived a life of intrigue that ended when he was murdered in a tavern at the age of 29. The precise dating and texts of his plays are a matter of dispute, but his importance as an Elizabethan dramatist is second only to that of Shakespeare, who was born in the same year. Marlowe's great theme was heroic but excessive ambition: for political power in *Tamburlaine the Great*, for money in *The Jew of Malta*, and for knowledge in *Doctor Faustus*. Marlowe's plays are in blank verse, unrhymed but metrical lines that he could make stately and conversational at the same time.

Miller, Arthur (b. 1915). One of the most important dramatists of his generation, Miller was born in New York City. During the 1930's he developed a lasting sympathy for victims of the American ideal of success. His major work is the great domestic tragedy *Death of a Salesman*, about an aging traveling salesman named Willy Loman who has devoted himself to the codes of the business world and then finds himself a victim of that world. Miller's other important works include *The Crucible* and *After The Fall*.

Molière (1622–1673). Born Jean Baptiste Poquelin and known only by his pen name after he left home at the age of 21, Molière was an actor and stage manager as well as one of the greatest of French dramatists. He lived at the same time as Corneille and Racine, but he chose to write comedies rather than tragedies. His major works are biting satires of social pretensions and hypocrisies. Among his most important plays are *Le Bourgeois Gentilhomme* (*The Would-Be Gentleman*), *Le Misanthrope*, and *Tartuffe*. Molière was also important as a producer of plays, as a developer of the all-purpose theatrical set, and as a manager of one of the first modern repertory companies. After his death, his own company merged with others to form the Comédie Française, the national theater of France.

O'Casey, Sean (1880–1964). A working-class Irish laborer who was self-educated, O'Casey became famous as the great chronicler in drama of Ireland's struggle for political independence from England. He was discovered by the poet W. B. Yeats and other leaders of the Irish literary revival, and at Dublin's Abbey Theatre they produced his first and most important works: *Juno and the Paycock*, *The Shadow of a Gunman*, and *The Plough and the Stars*. These plays are about rather disreputable people who live on the edge of the important political events of the day. O'Casey showed the independence movement's flaws as well as its strengths, and his plays met with bitter criticism. He later left Ireland, after the Abbey Theatre rejected his play *The Silver Tassie*. While living in England, he experimented with many forms of farce, musical comedy, and expressionist drama.

O'Neill, Eugene (1888–1953). The first great American dramatist, O'Neill was born in New York City, the son of a famous actor. After some years at sea, during which he read the great plays of the past, he joined the Provincetown Players in Massachusetts and there learned stagecraft. His major works are notable for the depth of their psychological penetration and for expressionist stage techniques. Of his many plays the most important are *Mourning Becomes Electra*, which draws on Greek tragedy, *The Iceman Cometh*, *A Moon for the Misbegotten*, and *Long Day's Journey into Night*, a family drama now recognized as his masterpiece.

Pirandello, Luigi (1867–1936). The major 20th-century Italian playwright Pirandello was scarred first by poverty and then by the insanity of his wife. He remained devoted to drama, however, and formed his own theater company to produce his plays in Rome. His best known work is *Six Characters in Search of an Author*, in which actors in street clothes watch and eventually intrude on a rehearsal of another play on the same stage. His other works explore the confusion between illusion and reality. In *Henry IV*, for example, an insane man imagines himself a king.

Racine, Jean (1639–1699). The successor to Corneille as the leading tragedian of early French drama, Jean Racine wrote plays that were faithful to Aristotle's theories of drama, but innovative for their lyrical dialogue and attention to psychology. The most famous of these are love stories such as *Andromache*, *Britannicus*, and *Phèdre*, the last of which contains a leading role that has attracted French actresses from its first performance in 1677 to the present. Racine's success brought him a position in the court of Louis XIV. His disgust at cheap imitations of his greatest plays caused him to cease writing while still at the peak of his powers.

Schiller, Friedrich von (1759–1805). As co-manager of the Court Theater at Weimar with Wolfgang von Goethe, Schiller was at the center of the German literary *Sturm und Drang* (Storm and Stress) movement, which emphasized emotions of almost apocalyptic proportions. He became the movement's greatest dramatist, chiefly on the basis of *Wallenstein*, a trilogy of plays; *Mary Stuart*; and *William Tell.*

Shakespeare, William (1564–1616). The greatest of all Western dramatists, William Shakespeare is perhaps the most important literary figure of the past 500 years. He created drama as we know it by introducing a shrewd knowledge of human psychology and poetry of unparalleled beauty to a stage that had been concerned mostly with mythical and religious themes. Shakespeare's appeal is universal; his works have been translated into most modern languages and have influenced such great writers as Goethe and Tolstoy. His influence has been especially strong on English literature, since performances or readings in English reveal the full beauty and subtlety of his poetry. The plays of Shakespeare are performed more often than those of any other dramatist. They are regularly produced on Broadway with a cast of famous actors; they are also a mainstay of college and amateur theatrical companies. (See box on Shakespeare's life and works.)

M[r] WILLIAM
SHAKESPEARES
COMEDIES,
HISTORIES, and
TRAGEDIES.
Publithed according to the true Originall Copies.
The second Impression.

LONDON
Printed by [illegible], and are to be fold at the figne [illegible] Church yard. 1632.

SHAKESPEARE. 1632. SECOND FOLIO.
(*See No.* 559.)

The "First Folio" above *was the first collected edition of the plays.* Below, *the Globe theater, where many of the plays were first performed.*

Our knowledge about the life of the world's greatest playwright is limited, and fact has become entangled with legend. Baptismal records show that William Shakespeare was christened in the English market town of Stratford-on-Avon on April 26, 1564, and his birth date is thought to have been April 23 in that year. Little is known about his youth, but he was married to Anne Hathaway in Stratford in 1582 when he was 18 years old. They had three children, Susan, Hamnet, and Judith. Shakespeare seems to have moved to London in 1586. Legend says he had been accused of poaching deer in his hometown.

He found employment as an actor and manager in the city's theaters. His first plays, *The Comedy of Errors* and *Henry VI, Part I*, were written in imitation of the popular dramatic comedies and histories of the day. His first tragedy, *Titus Andronicus,* was probably written in 1594, but the great tragedies—*Othello*, *King Lear*, and *Macbeth*—were written in a burst of creativity between 1604 and 1605. In 1598, Shakespeare joined with several famous actors of the time and opened the Globe Theatre. Its success provided him with financial security, a stage for his future works, and a valuable repertory company of actors. His literary genius reached its final phase in 1610 and 1611 with *A Winter's Tale* and *The Tempest*, poetic dramas usually classified as comedies but fantastic enough in their settings and characters to be termed stage romances.

Having earned a fortune in the theater, Shakespeare retired to Stratford in 1611. He died there on April 23, 1616, at the age of 52. His plays were only gathered into the famous "First Folio" edition in 1623, and no manuscripts written in his own hand survive.

Shakespeare's plays are so important that generations of scholars have searched for more information about his life. Little of significance has been discovered, and there are even theories that the man known as Shakespeare was *not* the author of the great plays and poems. None of these theories has ever been accepted by scholars, however, so we are left only with tantalizing clues about the man—and the certainty of his great genius.

(*See also* Masterpieces of literature)

Comic characters: Pompey and Lucio in Measure for Measure (left), *and Falstaff* (right), *who appears in* Henry IV *and* Merry Wives of Windsor.

His plays

Year	Comedies	Histories	Tragedies
1590	The Comedy of Errors	King Henry VI, Part I	
1591		King Henry VI, Part II	
1592		King Henry VI, Part III	
1593	The Taming of the Shrew	Richard III	
1594	The Two Gentlemen of Verona	King John	Titus Andronicus
1595	A Midsummer Night's Dream	Richard II	
1596	Love's Labour's Lost		Romeo and Juliet
1597	The Merchant of Venice	Henry IV, Part I	
1598	As You Like It	Henry IV, Part II	
1599	Much Ado About Nothing	Henry V	Julius Caesar
1600	Twelfth Night		
	The Merry Wives of Windsor		
1601			Hamlet
			Troilus and Cressida
1603	All's Well That Ends Well		
1604	Measure for Measure		Othello
1605			King Lear
			Macbeth
1606			Timon of Athens
1607			Pericles
			Antony and Cleopatra
1608			Coriolanus
1609	Cymbeline		
1610	The Winter's Tale		
1611	The Tempest		
1613		Henry VIII	

Tragic characters: King Lear (left), *and Othello* (right). *Shakespeare's other great tragic heroes were Hamlet and Macbeth.*

Shaw, George Bernard (1856–1950). Born in Ireland, Shaw became a drama critic in London at the age of 30 and was an ardent supporter of the first productions of Ibsen's plays in English. In 1884 he joined the Fabian Society, which advocated socialism by gradual reform, and his many plays are known for their witty commentaries on social and political issues of his day. Shaw's plays are for the most part satirical, and his targets include the status of women in *Mrs. Warren's Profession*, militarism in *Arms and the Man*, and England's treatment of Ireland in *John Bull's Other Island*. His play *Pygmalion* was the basis for the musical *My Fair Lady*. He was awarded the Nobel Prize in 1925.

Sheridan, Richard Brinsley (1751–1816). Forced to turn to the theater to satisfy the luxurious lifestyle of his wife, Sheridan became the most accomplished dramatist of the late 1700's. His comedies *The Rivals* and *School for Scandal* are light, witty satires of social pretensions and hypocrisies, and are so successful on the stage that they are still regularly performed. Sheridan was also a politician and served in Parliament for more than 30 years.

Sophocles (496?–406 B.C.). About 29 years younger than Aeschylus, Sophocles was the second of the three great Greek tragedians. Sophocles is thought to have written more than 80 plays, but only seven survive. Sophocles differs from his elder, however, in that his plays dwell more on human emotions than on civic and political events. His major works are three plays about the Oedipus legend: *Oedipus Rex*, *Oedipus at Colonus*, and *Antigone*. These plays trace the fate and legacy of Oedipus, doomed to marry his mother and murder his father. Antigone, the daughter of Oedipus, is the central character of the third play. Sophocles' other surviving plays are *Ajax*, *The Women of Trachis*, *Electra*, and *Philoctetes*. The relevance to the modern world of his ideas is apparent in the fact that the psychoanalyst Sigmund Freud gave the name "Oedipus complex" to one of his most important theories about the human subconscious.

Strindberg, Johan August (1848–1912). The greatest Swedish dramatist, Strindberg was some 20 years younger than Norwegian Henrik Ibsen. His early works, such as *The Father* and *Miss Julie*, were realistic studies of romantic involvements resembling Ibsen's plays in style. Later, however, Strindberg began to explore the possibilities of "expressionist" styles, seeking a new kind of realism through portraying a character's inner state, as in *A Dream Play* and *The Ghost Sonata*. In order to stage these last works, he experimented with new setting and lighting techniques at his own theater in Stockholm.

Synge, John Millington (1871–1909). The most important dramatist of the Irish literary revival, Synge was working as a translator in Paris when the Irish poet W. B. Yeats urged him to return to Ireland. Synge then went to the Aran Islands on Ireland's western coast, learned the Gaelic language, and began to write plays about peasant life in a distinctive "Kiltartan" English dialect. The first of these plays were the one-act *In the Shadow of the Glen* and *Riders to the Sea*. Synge's most important work is the three-act play *The Playboy of the Western World*, a story about a braggart's conquest of gullible peasants. At its opening night in Dublin, audiences rioted, believing the play demeaned the Irish people. Now, however, *The Playboy* is recognized as a masterpiece about universal human pretensions. Synge had nearly completed the mythological tragedy *Deirdre of the Sorrows* when he died in Dublin at 38.

Vega, Lope de (1562–1635). A veteran of the Spanish Armada defeated by the English in 1588, Lope de Vega was his country's first great dramatist and the leading figure in the Spanish golden age. He was two years older than Shakespeare. He claimed to have written more than 2000 plays to satisfy the enormous demand by Spanish audiences for new dramas; of these, more than 300 survive. His works characteristically stress the triumph of good over evil rather than the tragic ambiguities common in the English drama of the time. De Vega's most famous play is *Fuenteovejuna* (*The Sheepfold*), in which peasant villagers revolt against a cruel nobleman and require protection from their king.

Williams, Tennessee (1911–1983). Thomas Lanier Williams was born in Mississippi and lived for a time in the state for which he is nicknamed. He was an obscure writer of poems and short stories as well as plays until *The Glass Menagerie* became a major theatrical event in New York in 1945. It was followed by a string of other Broadway successes, including *The Rose Tattoo, Sweet Bird of Youth, A Streetcar Named Desire*, and *Suddenly Last Summer*. Williams's plays are generally set in the southern United States, and feature characters whose unhappiness has roots in the past. He is considered now one of America's foremost playwrights.

Fiction

Today prose fiction is by far the most popular of the three principal literary forms. Originally the word "fiction" included any imaginative creation with a story, whether in poetry, drama, or prose. In modern times, however, fiction is usually used to refer to prose.

Poems and plays are governed by strict conventions such as meter and structure. In contrast, prose fiction is less confined and is the most natural and informal kind of literary presentation. In it a storyteller speaks and provides an account of imaginary events for the entertainment of an audience. In fact, storytelling as a folk art may be the earliest of all literary arts, but one that is lost because the stories were passed from one generation to another without being written down.

Since the 1700's, literary fiction has branched in many directions. Some writers have explored the past, as in *Ivanhoe* by Sir Walter Scott. Some have explored particular settings, as in *Moby-Dick* by Melville. Others have chosen to explore the mind and emotions of an individual, as in *Crime and Punishment* by Dostoevski. Many have concentrated on the social relationships of their own times, whether in England during Victorian times or the United States today.

There are also particular types of stories called *genres* of fiction. These include the Gothic novel, detective stories, satirical fiction, and science fiction.

In all fiction, appreciation hinges on recognition of four principal elements. The first is plot, or the order of events in a narrative. These events are not always presented in chronological order, but the cause and effect relationship between different events in a story is often crucial to a full understanding of it. The second element is character, or the specific qualities attached to each of the people in a narrative. Most stories feature both major and minor characters, distinguished by the amount of attention they receive, but the virtues and vices of all are important to the meaning of the story. The third element is setting, or the time and place in which the narrative occurs. The setting usually changes in the course of a narrative, and this often signals a change in the kind of action likely to occur and its probable outcome. Attention to the setting and its influence on the story's outcome may help illuminate the writer's ideas and purposes in writing the story. The fourth element is the teller of the story. Some stories are told by an objective third-person narrator who knows all the circumstances and thoughts of all the characters. Many others are told by a subjective first-person narrator whose knowledge and understanding of the story is limited.

Some philosophers and religious thinkers have always objected to fiction because it is "untrue," and some modern readers continue to prefer nonfiction—biographies, histories, and books on current affairs. But in a sense, a great novel or story may be more real than a biography or history, using the writer's imagination to help understand not only what happened but why it happened, and how it felt to those who were there. The great power of fiction is that it can let a reader experience events in another time and place and discover how different, yet how much the same, other people's lives can be.

A storyteller (left) *was the first maker of fiction. Early written stories, like Defoe's* Robinson Crusoe (right) *have often been illustrated.*

Fiction	1500	1550	1600	1650	1700
Europe		CERVANTES			
England/Ireland				BUNYAN	
				DEFOE	

The history of fiction.

Prose fiction is the youngest of the three principal literary forms. Its earliest ancestors date from the 1300's: the romance tales in the *Decameron* by the Italian Boccaccio, presented as indoor entertainment during a plague, and *The Canterbury Tales* by the English poet Chaucer, presented as entertainment during a pilgrimage. More immediate sources for the novel lie in the 1600's, when Cervantes' *Don Quixote* added psychological realism to the earlier episodic tales and John Bunyan's *Pilgrim's Progress* presented a religious allegory with characters and dialogue in prose.

Fiction as we know it, however, awaited the greater availability of printing presses, widespread literacy, and a middle class capable of purchasing books. Most of the important early novels were published in England in the first half of the 1700's, where these requirements had been fulfilled. Three milestones were Daniel Defoe's *Robinson Crusoe,* which drew on the travel literature of the time, Samuel Richardson's *Pamela,* which provided entertainment for a predominantly female audience, and Henry Fielding's *Tom Jones,* a novel with strong satirical and comic elements. Most early English novels were similar to one of these three strains until Jane Austen's more sophisticated work in the early 19th century made the novel a witty forum for social commentary.

In Europe, novels remained primarily a hobby of philosophers such as Rousseau until the great German literary figure Goethe described through letters a suicidal youth in *The Sorrows of Young Werther.* Later, he established the *bildungsroman,* or "formation novel," with *The Apprenticeship of Wilheim Meister.* In France in the early 1800's, the romantic fictions of Victor Hugo caused great excitement. Stendhal's panoramic saga of war, *The Red and the Black,* and Balzac's series of socially conscious novels, collectively called *The Human Comedy,* are among the great classics of modern fiction.

Perhaps the most important single phase of the novel occurred in Victorian England, where philosophical controversies surrounding Darwin's *Origin of the Species* and the effects of the Industrial Revolution created a concerned reading public and great novelists of social interaction. The decade of the 1840's alone saw the publication of *Jane Eyre* and *Wuthering Heights* by the Brontë sisters, Thackeray's *Vanity Fair,* and Dickens' *Martin Chuzzlewit* and *David Copperfield.* Most Victo-

Frontispiece of Vanity Fair, *drawn by Thackeray*

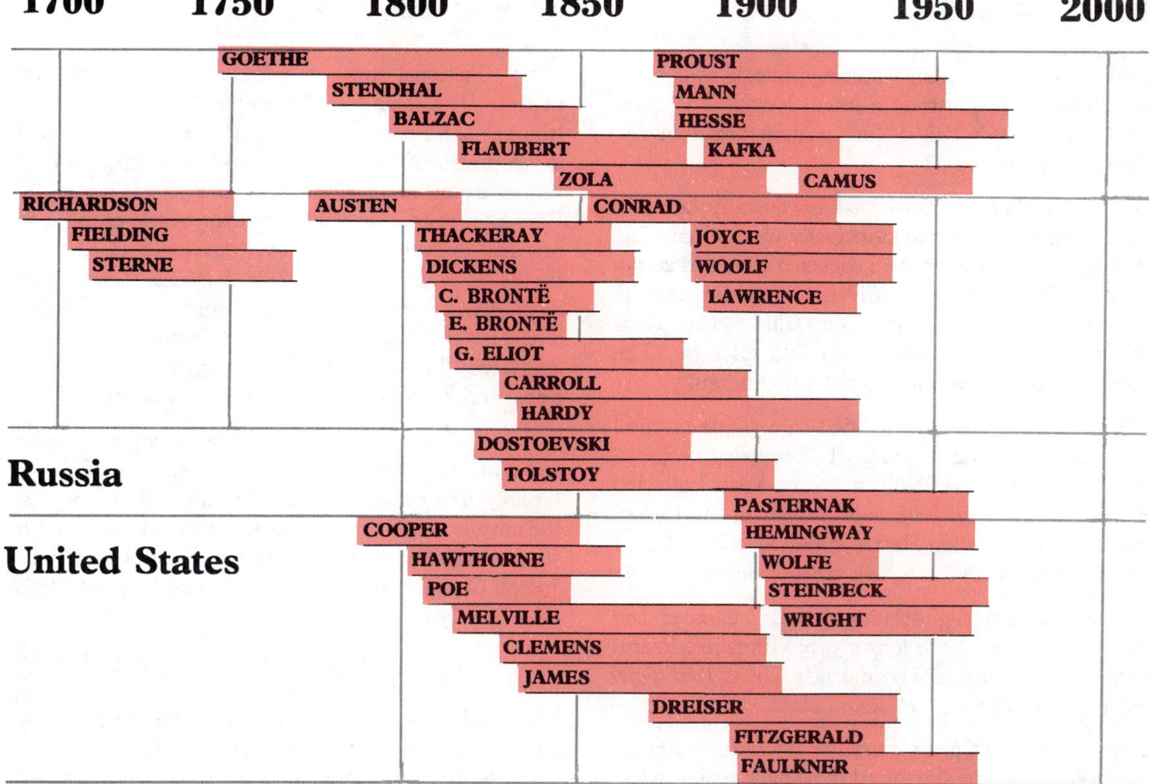

rian novels were published first in magazine installments, then as "triple decker" book trilogies to be rented at lending libraries. Most also told a story that ended with a successful marriage, a convention that survived through George Eliot's *Middlemarch* in 1872. By the time of Thomas Hardy's series of novels beginning in the 1890's, however, British novels had begun to end on a gloomier note. Readers can no longer expect a happy ending in serious fiction.

In 19th-century America, the novel tradition began with the frontier sagas of James Fenimore Cooper, the Puritanical stories and novels of Nathaniel Hawthorne, and the mysterious works of Edgar Allan Poe. The greatest American novels were not written until the second half of the century, when Melville's symbolic *Moby-Dick*, Mark Twain's colloquial *Huckleberry Finn*, and Henry James's complex novels all broke new ground. The success of these writers created a national appetite for a "great American novel," a work of sufficient breadth to capture the essence of the American experience. Most agree that no such work exists, although the possibility of one continues to tantalize critics and novelists alike.

The roots of the modern novel lie primarily in Europe. Flaubert's *Madame Bovary* of 1857 and Émile Zola's *Nana* of 1880 brought a new realism and emphasis on the misfortunes of characters of low social status. Tolstoy's wartime saga in *War and Peace* was followed in the Russian tradition by the religious symbolism and sense of alienation presented in Dostoevski's novels *Crime and Punishment* and *The Brothers Karamazov*.

The great European novels of the early 20th century added a complexity of style that firmly established the novel as an advanced art form on the order of painting or music. Proust in French, Mann and Kafka in German, and Joyce, Woolf, and Conrad in English all developed idiosyncratic styles in order to imitate the workings of the human mind. All of these writers (except Proust) were also the authors of important short stories or novellas, forms which gained a new importance as serious literature.

In America, early 20th-century writers of fiction split their interests between following European experiments and describing the dynamic new world of American values. F. Scott Fitzgerald became the most successful writer of his time with the novel *The Great Gatsby* and his immensely popular short stories, but the longer careers and greater productivity of William Faulkner, who wrote complex fictions about families in the American South, and Ernest Hemingway, who wrote in a restrained style about brave heroes doomed by large social forces, have brought them greater esteem since that time.

Kinds of short fiction

fable. Brief story, often featuring animals as characters, intended to illustrate a moral lesson. The most famous is *Aesop's Fables*, first written down in the 300's B.C. in Greece.

fairy tale. Short narrative that is generally fantastic and is today read or told principally to children. The most famous fairy tales were collected from old storytellers in Germany in the early 1800's by the brothers Jakob and Wilhelm Grimm. The Danish writer Hans Christian Andersen imitated old folk tales in "The Ugly Duckling" and other stories for children.

folk tale. Anonymous story tied to a single cultural group and handed down orally before being recorded in writing. The poet William Butler Yeats collected many such works in *Irish Folk Stories*. In the United States, Joel Chandler Harris collected folk tales of black Americans in *Tales from Uncle Remus*.

tale. Short story slightly unrealistic in character and event and related to the longer prose romance. Examples include Nathaniel Hawthorne's *Twice-Told Tales* and Herman Melville's *Piazza Tales*.

short story. Brief prose narrative describing a limited number of characters involved in a single major event. Descended from the forms described above, the modern short story has become increasingly realistic in the hands of such writers as Guy de Maupassant and Anton Chekhov.

Important short story writers

America	Washington Irving, 1783–1859 Edgar Allan Poe, 1809–1849 Bret Harte, 1836–1902 O.Henry (W.S. Porter), 1862–1910 Stephen Crane, 1871–1900 Sherwood Anderson, 1876–1941 Jack London, 1876–1916 James Thurber, 1894–1961 Flannery O'Connor, 1925–1964
Russia	Ivan Turgenev, 1818–1883 Anton Chekhov, 1860–1904 Maxim Gorky, 1868–1936 Isaac Babel, 1894–1941
France	Guy de Maupassant, 1850–1893
England	Saki (H.H. Munro), 1870–1916 W. Somerset Maugham, 1874–1965
Ireland	Frank O'Connor, 1903–1966

Kinds of long fiction

novel. Fictional story of considerable length written in prose. The name comes from the Italian for "[a] new [thing]." The novel's special purpose is to stress the development of its characters and to describe in detail the environment in which they live. *Don Quixote* by Cervantes is an important precursor of the novel. The first real examples of the novel developed in England in the 1700's. Daniel Defoe's *Robinson Crusoe* and *Moll Flanders* brought new realism to longer fiction. The first true literary novels, by Samuel Richardson and Henry Fielding, added a new interest in the emotional and psychological lives of their characters.

novella. Short novel, a distinction measured by the scope of the work as well as by the number of pages. Usually limited in number of characters and events, the novella combines some of the qualities of the short story and the novel. Important examples include Joseph Conrad's *Heart of Darkness* and Henry James's *The Turn of the Screw.*

picaresque. Novel-length story consisting of many individual episodes, usually a series of adventures encountered by a single hapless hero called a picaroon. Early picaresque narratives, such as the anonymous Spanish *Lazarillo de Tormes*, were written in the 1500's and precede the rise of the novel. Defoe's *Moll Flanders* has picaresque qualities, and later writers also used the form. Important examples are *Candide* by Voltaire and *Jonathan Wild* by Henry Fielding.

romance. Novel-length story that is exotic and slightly fabulous rather than realistic. Related to earlier verse romances, prose romances, usually set in historical times, became popular in the 1800's. Examples include Sir Walter Scott's *Ivanhoe.* James Fenimore Cooper's *Leatherstocking Tales*, about the American frontier, might also be considered a romance.

bildungsroman. A German term meaning "formation novel" used to describe novels about an adolescent's initiation into adulthood. *Bildungsromans* in English include Dickens' *David Copperfield* and Samuel Butler's *The Way of All Flesh.*

roman à clef. A novel in which actual persons are described under fictitious names. Such novels are often satirical. *Clef* is French for "key"; the *roman à clef* provides clues as keys to the real identities of its characters. In Aldous Huxley's novel *Point Counter Point,* for example, the character John Bidlake is identifiable as the novelist D. H. Lawrence.

Special types of fiction

Satirical fiction

Satirical fiction ridicules vanities and pretensions by means of exaggeration. The exaggeration may take the form of implausible events in fantastic settings, or it may sarcastically simplify realistic characters and environments. In either case, satirical fiction is comical in tone, for it attacks its targets by making them laughable to the reader. Jonathan Swift defined this form as "ridicule of the foibles of men with the hope of reforming them."

Examples

Author	*Lifetime*	*Work*
Jonathan Swift	1667–1745	*Gulliver's Travels*
Voltaire	1694–1778	*Candide*
Samuel Johnson	1709–1784	*Rasselas*
Lewis Carroll	1832–1898	*Alice's Adventures in Wonderland*
Aldous Huxley	1894–1963	*Point Counter Point*
George Orwell	1903–1950	*Animal Farm*
Evelyn Waugh	1903–1966	*Scoop*

Gothic fiction

Gothic fiction is a form of romance describing supernatural events in exotic and eerie surroundings. The creatures and ghosts common in Gothic fiction are at once thrilling entertainments and versions of psychological and spiritual conditions. In modern times these Gothic elements are often found in combination with a melodramatic love story. Because it is so unrealistic, Gothic fiction is often considered a kind of prose romance.

Examples

Author	*Lifetime*	*Work*
Horace Walpole	1717–1797	*The Castle of Otranto*
William Beckford	1760–1844	*Vathek*
Anne Radcliffe	1764–1823	*The Mysteries of Udolfo*
Matthew Lewis	1775–1818	*The Monk*
Mary Shelley	1797–1851	*Frankenstein*
Edgar Allan Poe	1809–1849	"The Fall of the House of Usher"
Henry James	1843–1916	*The Turn of the Screw*
Bram Stoker	1847–1912	*Dracula*

Detective fiction

Detective fiction opens with a crime and leads up to a final explanation about how the hero has identified the villian through the evidence of various clues. At its purest, detective fiction is an exercise in pure logic. It also frequently dwells on the psychology of both the detective and the other characters as well as the social nature of the evil they confront.

Examples

Author	*Lifetime*	*Work*
Edgar Allan Poe	1809–1849	"The Purloined Letter"
Arthur Conan Doyle	1859–1930	*Adventures of Sherlock Holmes*
Raymond Chandler	1888–1959	*The Big Sleep*
Agatha Christie	1891–1976	*Murder on the Orient Express*
Dashiell Hammett	1894–1961	*The Maltese Falcon*
Mickey Spillane	b. 1918	*I the Jury*

Science fiction

Science fiction deals with the nature and effects of scientific advancement, its values and dangers. Often set in the future and in outer space, it nevertheless provides a commentary on present society by imagining the future effects of present decisions or by creating an allegorical version of traditional conflicts. The imaginary world created in science fiction may be either a utopia, or perfect world, or a dystopia, or imperfect one. Because of its essentially allegorical purpose, science fiction is a modern form of a type of fiction as old as Sir Thomas More's *Utopia,* published in Latin in 1516.

Examples

Author	*Lifetime*	*Work*
Jules Verne	1828–1905	*Twenty Thousand Leagues Under the Sea*
H. G. Wells	1866–1946	*The Time Machine*
Aldous Huxley	1894–1963	*Brave New World*
C. S. Lewis	1898–1963	*Out of the Silent Planet*
Arthur C. Clarke	b. 1917	*The Lost Worlds of 2001*
Isaac Asimov	b. 1920	*I, Robot*
Ray Bradbury	b. 1920	*Fahrenheit 451*
Ursula K. LeGuin	b. 1929	*The Left Hand of Darkness*

Flaubert

Fiction writers

George Eliot

Clemens

Joyce

Austen, Jane (1775–1817). Although she lived a placid life as an English gentlewoman, Jane Austen wrote four very important novels: *Sense and Sensibility*, *Pride and Prejudice*, *Mansfield Park*, and *Emma*. Each is a parlor drama leading to a marriage, and each takes place in similar upper-middle-class surroundings. All make subtle observations on the manners of the time and lend themselves to larger generalizations about the conflict between social role and personal desire.

Balzac, Honoré de (1799–1850). The most prolific of French novelists, Balzac wrote a long series of novels that are together given the title *The Human Comedy*. His project was to write about a broad spectrum of contemporary French life and to create a panorama in fiction that included the very rich, the very poor, and the classes in between. Events and characters recur from novel to novel, and the effect of any event on a different group of characters is an important theme in this social history in fiction. The most famous of the individual novels are *Père Goriot*, *Cousin Bette*, and *Louis Lambert*.

Brontë, Charlotte (1816–1855). The sister of Emily Brontë, Charlotte Brontë published *Jane Eyre* under the pseudonym Currer Bell in 1847. It is the story of the title character's experiences in a brutal boarding school and of her subsequent love for the handsome but evil Mr. Rochester. *Jane Eyre* granted a greater degree of freedom and passion to the female character than did any previous English novel. Charlotte Brontë was a forerunner of modern feminist ideas.

Brontë, Emily (1818–1848). The sister of Charlotte Brontë, Emily Brontë published *Wuthering Heights* under the pseudonym Ellis Bell in 1847, the same year in which her sister's novel *Jane Eyre* appeared. *Wuthering Heights* is one of the great romantic novels in the English language. It employs devices of Gothic fiction to heighten the grandeur and mystical intensity of wealthy Catherine Linton's doomed love for Heathcliff.

Bunyan, John (1628–1688). The most important English precursor of the modern novelist, John Bunyan was a Puritan imprisoned twice for his religious beliefs. During his second imprisonment he wrote *Pilgrim's Progress* (1678). A religious allegory about the quest of a man named Christian, it became a great influence on many more realistic modern writers. It was among the most popular books in English for more than 200 years.

Camus, Albert (1913–1960). A French novelist born in Algeria, Camus earned a degree in philosophy, worked as a journalist, and fought for the French Resistance during the German occupation of Paris in World War II. He became the most famous spokesman in fiction for the French school of existentialism, which argued that each man creates his own life by his actions. His novels include *The Stranger*, *The Plague*, and *The Fall*. An essayist and playwright as well, he was awarded the Nobel Prize in 1957.

Carroll, Lewis (1832–1898). Charles Lutwidge Dodgson, a shy and retiring professor of mathematics, published books under the name Lewis Carroll. He is best known for *Alice's Adventures in Wonderland* and *Through the Looking-Glass*. Both books are of interest to readers of all ages for their play with language, their satire of adult life, and their whimsical, surreal qualities. Lewis Carroll also wrote poems, literary riddles, and miscellaneous works.

Cervantes, Miguel de (1547–1616). Born into an aristocratic family in northern Spain that had recently lost its fortune, Cervantes made a living as a soldier through most of his life. He is said to have written more than 20 plays, although only two survive. Late in life he began *Don Quixote*, the cornerstone of the novel tradition. Published in two parts in 1605 and 1615, it tells the story of the elderly and eccentric Alonzo Quixano, who dubs himself Don Quixote and sets off on a series of comic chivalrous adventures with his squire Sancho Panza. The book describes a misguided but noble attempt to relive the heraldic past, and plays on Quixote's confusion between illusion and reality.

Clemens, Samuel (Mark Twain) (1835–1910). An American novelist, Sam Clemens grew up in Missouri and served as an apprentice on a Mississippi River steamboat. Later, he traveled to Nevada and began to write humorous newspaper accounts of life in the West. *The Adventures of Tom Sawyer* was his first big success, and its sequel, *Huckleberry Finn*, is considered to be his masterpiece. Huck, the outcast son of the town drunk, travels down the Mississippi on a raft with Jim, an escaped slave. The book, told in Huck's own words, is funny and exciting, but it also raises important moral and social issues. Clemens's other novels include *Pudd'nhead Wilson* and *The Prince and the Pauper*.

Conrad, Joseph (1857–1924). Born Josef Korzeniowski in the Polish Ukraine, Conrad served in the French navy and only began to write novels in English after he retired, at the age of nearly 40. One of the most important modern novelists in English, he drew on his sea adventures in *The Nigger of the Narcissus*, *Lord Jim*, and *Heart of Darkness*. Although English was his second language, Conrad became one of the most famous prose stylists in the language.

Cooper, James Fenimore (1789–1851). The son of the wealthy family for which Cooperstown, New York, is named, Cooper was expelled from Yale University, shipped out on a European sailing ship, and later joined the U.S. Navy. He wrote several adventure stories about life at sea, but he is best known for the series of novels collectively called *Leatherstocking Tales*. The stories relate the frontier adventures of the woodsman Natty Bumppo, his combat and friendship with the Indians, and his resigned surrender of the woods to the civilized manners of the American pioneers. Important novels in the saga include *The Deerslayer*, *The Last of the Mohicans*, and *The Pathfinder*.

Defoe, Daniel (1659?–1731). Called by some the first true novelist, Defoe was born in London. He began his adult life as a businessman constantly threatened with debtor's prison. He first wrote political tracts to raise money; these were popular enought to embarrass the government and land the author in jail. Sensing the reading public's desire for information about faroff places, Defoe wrote *Robinson Crusoe*, a fictionalized version of the experiences of a man named Alexander Selkirk. The success of this landmark novel led Defoe to write a string of other adventure stories, some set at sea, such as *Captain Jack*, and some in London, such as *Moll Flanders*.

Dickens, Charles (1812–1870). Born into a poor and debt-ridden English family, Dickens first became a journalist. His early works of fiction, *Sketches by Boz* and *The Pickwick Papers*, brought him immediate fame. His major novels are indictments of the deprivation suffered by working-class people in England of the mid-1800's. Among them are *Oliver Twist*, *David Copperfield*, *Hard Times*, and *Bleak House*. Most of Dickens' novels were first published in magazine installments. Their suspenseful episodes and vivid characters helped create anticipation for the next installment.

Dostoevski, Feodor (1821–1881). Born in Moscow, Dostoevski was a political activist as a young man. Arrested by the czarist regime in Russia, he was condemned to death, a sentence that was later commuted to exile in Siberia from 1850 to 1859. Dostoevski began to write after returning to Moscow, and his works pondered questions about guilt and redemption that are more moral than political in nature. His most important novels are *Crime and Punishment*, *The Idiot*, and *The Brothers Karamazov*.

Dreiser, Theodore (1871–1945). Born in Indiana, Dreiser was for the most part self-educated. He became a Chicago newspaperman. His first novel, *Sister Carrie*, was published in 1900. It tells the story of a pure girl from the Midwest who prospers because she becomes unscrupulous. This reversal of traditional morality was so shocking that Dreiser's own publisher suppressed the novel. Among his later novels were *Jennie Gerhard*, about a kept woman, and

An American Tragedy, about a youth who becomes the victim of class prejudice in New York.

Eliot, George (1819–1880). Born Mary Ann Evans, George Eliot adopted a male pseudonym for her fiction because of the prejudice against women novelists in Victorian England. Encouraged by her lifelong companion George Henry Lewes, she began to publish under the name George Eliot the novels on which her reputation now rests: *Adam Bede*, *The Mill on the Floss*, *Silas Marner*, and *Middlemarch*. The last, her major achievement, is a long novel about Dorothea Brooke's attempt to preserve her distinctly feminine intellect and imagination despite the stern society of the time.

Faulkner, William (1897–1962). Born into a Mississippi family whose fortunes had been destroyed by the Civil War, Faulkner spent a vagrant youth and then began to write a series of novels about the American South. His principal works take place in the fictional Yoknapatawpha County in Mississippi, and they examine life there through the minds of a wide range of white and black characters. His novels in this group include *The Sound and the Fury*, *Light in August*, *Absalom, Absalom*, and a collection of interrelated short stories called *Go Down, Moses*. Faulkner was awarded the Nobel Prize in 1950.

Fielding, Henry (1707–1754). A lawyer by profession, Fielding was also a prolific playwright and journalist. In 1741 he published *Shamela*, a parody of Samuel Richardson's popular novel *Pamela*. This launched his career as one of the great comic novelists in English literature. His works include *Joseph Andrews*, subtitled "written in imitation of the manner of Cervantes"; *Jonathan Wild*, also a picaresque; and *Tom Jones*, an eventful and chaotic story about an orphan's improbable journey toward wealth and happiness.

Fitzgerald, F. Scott (1896–1940). Born in St. Paul, Minnesota, Fitzgerald came east to be educated at Princeton University. Married to the debutante beauty Zelda Sayre in 1920, he became famous as the chronicler of the adventures of young people in the "jazz age" of the roaring '20's. His short stories brought him national fame and considerable wealth, but Zelda's mental illness and Fitzgerald's alcoholism brought them both to early deaths. His greatest novel, *The Great Gatsby*, examines the self-destructive side of the American dream. In addition to many short stories, his works include the novels *Tender Is the Night* and *The Last Tycoon*, which was left unfinished at his death.

Flaubert, Gustave (1821–1880). A former student of law in Paris, Flaubert was the pioneer of a new realism in the French novel. His ideal was to pay close attention to the grim realities of life, and to relate them in a disciplined style free from older novelistic conventions. His most important realistic novels are *Madame Bovary*, the story of a deteriorating marriage, and *The Sentimental Education*. *Madame Bovary* is among the most admired of all novels and has had great influence on many later novelists.

Goethe, Johann Wolfgang von (1749–1832). The greatest of all German writers, Goethe was born in Frankfurt and studied law while writing his early lyric poems. He became famous as leader of the German *Sturm und Drang* (Storm and Stress) movement, which advocated a heightened sense of personal emotion in art and literature. Goethe's contributions to the movement include the novels *The Sorrows of Young Werther*, consisting principally of letters from a suicidal young man, and *The Apprenticeship of Wilhelm Meister*. These early novels were models for many later novelists. *See also* Goethe in Poetry Glossary.

Hardy, Thomas (1840–1928). Born in rural Dorset, England, a region he recreated as the fictional Wessex in his novels, Thomas Hardy left an apprenticeship in architecture to pursue his literary ambitions. He wrote a great number of novels, including *The Mayor of Casterbridge*, *The Return of the Native*, *Tess of the D'Urbervilles*, and *Jude the Obscure*. The last two were publicly condemned as immoral, and Hardy spent his later years writing poetry. The central theme of the novels is the way in which people trapped in the working classes are frustrated in their efforts to improve themselves morally and socially.

Hawthorne, Nathaniel (1804–1864). A resident of Salem, Massachusetts, for most of his life, Hawthorne was a friend of Herman Melville and a member of the intellectual circle that included Henry David Thoreau and Ralph Waldo Emerson. He was a solitary and conventional man, but his works include some of the first important examples of American fiction. His great novel *The Scarlet Letter* is about the adulteress Hester Prynne and her punishment by the stern and sometimes hypocritical elders of Puritan Boston. Hawthorne's other works include many short stories and the novel *The House of the Seven Gables*.

Hemingway, Ernest (1899–1961). Born in Illinois, Heming-

Openings of novels

Moby-Dick, by Herman Melville (1851):
Call me Ishmael. Some years ago—never mind how long precisely—having little or no money in my purse, and nothing particular to interest me on shore, I thought I would sail about a little and see the watery part of the world.

Pride and Prejudice, by Jane Austen (1813):
It is a truth universally acknowledged, that a single man in possession of a good fortune, must be in want of a wife.

A Tale of Two Cities, by Charles Dickens (1859):
It was the best of times, it was the worst of times, it was the age of wisdom, it was the age of foolishness, it was the epoch of belief, it was the epoch of incredulity, it was the season of light, it was the season of darkness, it was the spring of hope, it was the winter of despair, we had everything before us, we had nothing before us, we were all going direct to heaven, we were all going direct the other way—in short, the period was so far like the present period, that some of its noisiest authorities insisted on its being received for good or for evil, in the superlative degree of comparison only.

The Portrait of a Lady, by Henry James (1880):
Under certain circumstances there are few hours in life more agreeable than the hour dedicated to the ceremony known as afternoon tea.

Adam Bede, by George Eliot (1859):
With a single drop of ink for a mirror, the Egyptian sorcerer undertakes to reveal to any chance comer far-reaching visions of the past. This is what I undertake to do for you, reader.

The Adventures of Huckleberry Finn, by Samuel Clemens (Mark Twain, 1884):
You don't know about me without you have read a book by the name of *The Adventures of Tom Sawyer;* but that ain't no matter. That book was made by Mr. Mark Twain, and he told the truth, mainly. There was things which he stretched, but mainly he told the truth. That is nothing. I never seen anybody but lied one time or another, without it was Aunt Polly, or the widow, or maybe Mary. Aunt Polly—Tom's Aunt Polly, she is—and Mary and the Widow Douglas is all told about in that book, which is mostly a true book, with some stretchers, as I said before.

Anna Karenina, by Leo Tolstoy (1876):
All happy families are like one another; each unhappy family is unhappy in its own way.

way was wounded while serving as an ambulance driver for the Italian army in World War I, an experience he later described in the novel *A Farewell to Arms.* As a journalist in Paris, he began to refine the spare prose style he made famous in his major novels, including *The Sun Also Rises, To Have and Have Not*, and *For Whom the Bell Tolls.* In both his novels and his many short stories Hemingway used both war and such sports as bullfighting, hunting, and fishing as metaphors for the workings of daily life. His solitary heroes are doomed, but seek to maintain their personal honor. He was awarded the Nobel Prize for Literature in 1954.

Hesse, Hermann (1877–1962). A German novelist and visionary thinker, Hesse wrote unusual novels that brought him the Nobel Prize in 1946. He has retained a devoted following since. His works are mystical and surreal, and they attempt to incorporate the discoveries of modern psychology into older philosophies and spiritual schemes. Among his novels are *Siddhartha* and *Steppenwolf.*

James, Henry (1843–1916). Born into a famous New York intellectual family, Henry James permanently settled in England in 1876 and became a British citizen in the year before his death. In novels such as *The Ambassadors*, *The American*, and *Daisy Miller*, he subtly contrasts the imaginations of his American characters with those of their European counterparts. James experimented with relating events through a character's own point of view and with describing subtle shades of emotion in long, complex sentences. In addition to novels he wrote more than 70 short stories, plays, and critical essays.

Joyce, James (1882–1941). Born and educated in Dublin, Ireland, Joyce lived all of his adult life in Europe but wrote only about his home country. After publishing a group of lyrical poems, he wrote the collection of stories called *Dubliners*, understated accounts of the paralysis of the Irish imagination. This was followed by the autobiographical novel *Portrait of the Artist as a Young Man*, a story about coming of age in Ireland that ends with a flight to Europe like Joyce's own. His two long masterpieces are *Ulysses* and *Finnegans Wake*, which are experimental in form and language and rank as major landmarks in the history of the modern novel.

Kafka, Franz (1883–1924) Born in Prague, Czechoslovakia, Kafka worked as a civil servant throughout his adult life. His rather fantastic novels and stories use improbable metaphors to describe his deep alienation from social and familial aspects of life. His important short stories include "The Metamorphosis," in which Gregor Samsa is transformed into an insect. In novels such as *The Trial* and *The Castle,* which were published after his death, Kafka gives us a sensitive hero who is nightmarishly mistreated by public authorities.

Lawrence, David Herbert (1885–1930). The son of a humble coal miner and an ambitious mother, D. H. Lawrence described his own rise above dreary surroundings in *Sons and Lovers*. He later developed a complicated ethic about sexual relations in novels such as *Women in Love*, *The Rainbow*, and *Lady Chatterley's Lover*. These books outraged the reading public, and Lawrence, with his German-born wife Frieda, spent his later years in ill health wandering to Italy, Australia, Mexico, and the southwest United States.

Mann, Thomas (1875–1955). The most important modern German novelist, Thomas Mann first wrote a family saga called *Buddenbrooks*; he became an international spokesman on German issues because of it. His 1924 novel *The Magic Mountain* described the rise of the new German nationalism as it appeared in an isolated health sanitarium. Mann was forced to immigrate to the United States in 1933 because of his criticism of the Nazi movement. He returned to Germany after World War II, and in novels such as *Dr. Faustus*, *Joseph and His Brothers*, and *Death in Venice*, he experimented with new treatments of the complex cultural relations between art and politics.

Melville, Herman (1819-1891). A New York City native who shipped out as a young man on sailing vessels bound for Pacific islands, Melville became a popular American novelist with early adventure novels such as *Typee*, *Omoo*, and *Mardi*. With *Moby-Dick* in 1851, however, he began to pursue a more complexly metaphysical vision that cost him his popularity. *Moby-Dick* tells of Captain Ahab's obsessive search for the white whale he believes personifies evil. It includes whole chapters about the art of whaling and other apparently extraneous material. Since Melville's death his artistry has been rediscovered, and he has been recognized as one of the greatest of all American novelists.

Pasternak, Boris (1890–1960). An important Russian poet and translator as well as a novelist, Pasternak wrote his famous novel *Doctor Zhivago* in secret and had it smuggled to Paris, where it was published in 1957. It describes the experiences of a doctor and poet named Yurii Zhivago in the years of the Russian Revolution. Because it unflatteringly contrasted Bolshevik ruthlessness with Zhivago's peaceful instincts, the book was considered subversive in Russia. When Pasternak was awarded the Nobel Prize in 1958, he could not accept it for fear of persecution in his country.

Poe, Edgar Allan (1809–1849). The son of traveling actors and orphaned at an early age, Edgar Allan Poe made a marginal living as a journalist before turning to fiction. He wrote eerie short stories in the Gothic style that became classics of the type, especially "The Fall of the House of Usher," "Ligeia," "The Pit and the Pendulum," and "The Cask of Amontillado." He was also the originator of the modern detective story with "The Purloined Letter," and was an important poet. Personally, Poe was erratic and alcoholic, and he died in his 40th year.

Proust, Marcel (1871–1922). The most important French novelist in the early 1900's, Proust was a sickly man who lived in Paris all his life. He became reclusive in his later years and seldom left his darkened rooms. As early as age 19 he began to make notes for what proved to be his life's work: the seven-novel-long *Rememberance of Things Past*. This work attempts to explore the workings of the mind and memory by dwelling at length on apparently insignificant details and pursuing long digressive recollections. Although he did complete all seven novels, the final one did not appear until five years after Proust's death.

Richardson, Samuel (1689–1751). A prosperous master printer, Richardson became one of the first great English novelists. His first book, *Pamela: or Virtue Rewarded*, is often considered the first true novel. It consisted of a long series of letters from Pamela, an attractive serving girl, to other characters, and it became immensely popular. In *Clarissa*, a seven-volume work (1747–1748), Richardson refined the new novel form, and his interest in the psychology of his characters attracted a huge new reading public. His prudish morality was satirized by Henry Fielding in *Shamela* and other novels.

Steinbeck, John (1902–1968). Born in Salinas, California, Steinbeck became the great chronicler of the lives of migrant farmers and "down-and-outers" during the Great Depression of the 1930's. His major works include *Of Mice and Men* and *The Grapes of Wrath*, about the migrant Joad family's desperate search for a decent life in California. Awarded the Nobel Prize in 1962, he was also the author of *East of Eden*, *The Winter of Our Discontent*, and short stories.

Stendhal (1783–1842). Marie Henri Beyle, who wrote under the name Stendhal, was one of the first great French novelists. His fiction showed how the great political events of his day affected individuals and society. His major work was *The Red and the Black*, about Julien Sorel's futile attempt to rise in the church hierarchy ("the black"), and about his encounters with important military events ("the red"), such as the Battle of Waterloo. His novels were panoramic in their historical and social scope, but later French realists such as Flaubert and Zola criticized them as melodramatic in style.

Sterne, Laurence (1713–1768). Born in Ireland but raised and educated in England, Sterne gained lasting fame as the author of *The Life and Opinions of Tristram Shandy, Gentleman.* The narrator and title character is so digressive that he does not describe his birth until Volume IV of the nine-volume work and is not involved in most of the book's later events. The novel hilariously illustrates the limitations of erudite knowledge through the conversations and actions of Tristram's father Walter and his Uncle Toby. The book also plays with the conventions of the printed text, including several blank pages and bizarre diagrams. Sterne's whimsical humor and support of "sentiment" over cold reason influenced many later writers.

Thackeray, William Makepeace (1811–1863). The first great novelist of Victorian England, Thackeray was born in India, where his father served in the British foreign service. Sent to London for his education, Thackeray later became famous as a journalist, humorist, and illustrator of his own novels. The most important of these novels was *Vanity Fair*, first published in installments in 1847 and 1848. A satirical study of aristocratic pretensions, the book is centered on the unscrupulous social climber Becky Sharp and is set in the early 1800's, during the Napoleonic wars. A prolific novelist, Thackeray is also known for a series of historical novels that includes *Henry Esmond.*

Tolstoy, Leo (1828–1910). A major Russian novelist whose influence has been worldwide, Tolstoy was born into a noble family and became interested in writing only after his military experience in the Crimean War. His reputation largely rests on the 1869 novel *War and Peace*, a panoramic account of life in Russia during the Napoleonic wars, and on the 1876 novel *Anna Karenina*, about the conflicting personal and social allegiances of the title character. A moralist and social reformer as well as a novelist, Tolstoy also wrote short stories and novellas, including *The Death of Ivan Ilich.*

Twain, Mark. *See* Clemens, Samuel.

Wolfe, Thomas (1900–1938). A North Carolinian famous for his excesses in both his life and his work, Thomas Wolfe wrote the autobiographical novel *Look Homeward, Angel*, a sprawling and mostly affectionate look at his hometown of Asheville and at his own family. His novels began as huge boxes of manuscript, which he shortened and organized with the help of his editors. Many of his short stories were originally episodes cut out of the manuscript for one of the novels.

Woolf, Virginia (1882–1941). The most important writer in England's Bloomsbury Group of intellectuals, Virginia Woolf rejected the objective treatment of events in earlier English novels and sought to portray the inner life of her characters. In *To the Lighthouse*, *The Waves*, and *Mrs. Dalloway*, rather uneventful stories are told from the perspective of individual characters, with the emphasis falling on the lyrical movements of their thoughts and emotions.

Wright, Richard (1908–1960). Born on a Mississippi plantation, Wright began as a short story writer. It was his first novel *Native Son*, however, that established him as the most important American chronicler of the black experience. This book was followed by *Black Boy*, a violent story about the victimization of one race by another. His short stories are collected in the volumes *Uncle Tom's Children* and *Eight Men.*

Zola, Émile (1840–1902). Along with Flaubert, Zola was the pioneer of realism in the French novel. His novels portrayed the low levels of life in the France of his day, and suggested that social class and environment are the greatest influences on a person's character and fortunes. Critics charged that his novels were obscene and immoral, but Zola replied that he was scientifically recording the facts of life. His great achievement was the 20-volume Rougon and Macquart families series, including *Nana* and *Germinal.*

Masterpieces of literature

Great works of literature have been produced in a number of forms: poetry, drama, fiction, and essay. This selection concentrates on longer works, ones that are often studied in schools or colleges or that have had great influence on the history of Western literature. Most are works of fiction—whether in poetic, dramatic, or prose form.

Five early anonymous epics are briefly described under "Poets," beginning on page 290. They are *Beowulf* (old English), *Song of the Cid* (early Spanish), *Gilgamesh* (ancient Babylonian), *Sir Gawain and the Green Knight* (Middle English), and *Song of Roland* (early French). For further information on Shakespeare and his plays, see pages 306–307.

Aeneid. A Latin epic poem by the Roman poet Vergil dated 19 B.C.; it is the classic work telling of the founding of Rome by the Trojan hero Aeneas. It narrates Aeneas's wanderings before he reaches the seven hills of Rome, his love and abandonment of Dido, queen of Carthage, his descent into Hell, his war against a rival, Turnus, and his marriage to Lavinia, for continuation of his lineage. It closely follows Homer's great epic the *Iliad.*

All's Well That Ends Well. Shakespeare's comedy beginning when Count Bertram departs for the king's court and is followed by the maid Helena, who is the secret admirer of the count. Helena administers to the sick king a cure inherited from her father. Recovered, the king gives Helena a ring and grants her Bertram as a husband. Displeased, Bertram sends the low-born Helena to his mother, flees to Florence, and promises to be her true husband when she can get his ring and bear his child. Helena travels to Florence, changes place with a local maid in Bertram's bed, and switches his ring with hers. Believing Helena dead, Bertram returns home. The king sees Helena's ring on the count's hand and demands an explanation. Helena appears and confesses the plot. Claiming that she has fulfilled both parts of Bertram's requirements, Helena gains him as a true husband.

Animal Farm. Anti-Utopian novel by British author George Orwell (Eric Blair), published in 1945, and written in the form of a beast fable. A group of animals overthrow their human masters and set up a communal society. Events in the animal Utopia closely parallel events in the Soviet Union, and the majority of animals are more cruelly victimized by their new masters than they were by the old. The chief animal villain, the pig Napoleon, is easily recognized as Stalin.

Antony and Cleopatra. Shakespeare's tragedy in which Antony, torn between reason and passion for Cleopatra, realizes he is losing respect and position in Rome. He reconciles with his fellow rulers, Lepidus and Octavius, and marries Octavius's sister. Cleopatra, enraged, knows Antony will return to her one day because Octavius's sister is unattractive. The situation degenerates until Antony and Octavius do battle at Actium. Antony loses that battle and another in Egypt and returns to Rome. Cleopatra attempts to woo him back by sending word that she is dead. Grief-stricken, Antony kills himself. Cleopatra also commits suicide.

Arthurian legend. The cycle of verse and prose tales concerning the mythical King Arthur of Britain and his knights of the Round Table forms the Arthurian legend. The legend provided one of the principal themes of medieval romance throughout Europe. The Arthur of romance is of marvelous birth. He is conceived by Queen Igraine when his father Uther Pendragon magically disguises himself as Igraine's husband. Arthur is marked for kingship as a young boy when he proves to be the only one who can remove the sword Excalibur from a stone in which it is embedded. This is interpreted as a sign of the true king. (In a common variant, Arthur receives Excalibur from the mysterious Lady of the Lake, who hands it up to him through the water.) Arthur marries Guinevere and establishes his court at Camelot, where he is advised by the wizard Merlin, and where he gathers at his Round Table the flower of knighthood. The adventures and love affairs of the various knights constitute the bulk of the legend. Finally, the adulterous love of Arthur's favorite knight Lancelot and his queen Guinevere leads to the disintegration of the fellowship of the Round Table. Arthur's treacherous nephew Mordred attempts to usurp his throne. Though Arthur kills Mordred in battle, he is severely wounded. In some versions he dies and is buried in Glastonbury, England. In others, Sir Bedivere throws Excalibur into the lake. The Lady's hand reaches out to receive it. A barge appears and carries Arthur to the isle of Avalon, from which he is expected to return some day, healed of his wounds.

The legends are of Celtic origin and have a complicated history. There is some evidence that Arthur was a historical figure, a Celtic chieftain of the sixth century who repelled an invasion of Saxons into Welsh territory. The earliest stories about Arthur are Welsh and emphasize his magic helpers (or hinderers), Merlin and his sister Morgan le Fay.

Arthur was given a place in history as a conqueror of

STORM, SHIPWRECK, EARTHQUAKE, AND WHAT HAPPENED TO DR. PANGLOSS, TO CANDIDE AND THE ANABAPTIST JACQUES

CHAPTER V

HALF the enfeebled passengers, suffering from that inconceivable anguish which the rolling of a ship causes in the nerves and in all the humours of bodies shaken in contrary directions, did not retain strength enough even to trouble about the danger. The other half screamed and prayed; the sails were torn, the masts broken, the vessel leaking. Those worked who could, no one co-operated, no one commanded. The Anabaptist tried to help the crew a little; he was on the main-deck; a furious sailor struck him violently and stretched him on the deck; but the blow he delivered gave him so violent a shock that he fell head-first out of the ship. He remain[illegible] and clinging to part [illegible] mast. The good

King Arthur, hero of legends in English and other literatures. Candide, the innocent hero of Voltaire's fable, in an edition designed by Rockwell Kent.

Europe by the chronicler Geoffrey of Monmouth in his largely fictitious *History of the Kings of Britain*, written in Latin in the twelfth century. In the 15th century, the English prose *Morte d'Arthur* by Sir Thomas Malory fixed the legend in its traditional form. Modern versions include Alfred Tennyson's poems *Idylls of the King* and the novel *The Once and Future King* by T. H. White.

As You Like It. A comedy by Shakespeare in which Rosalind is expelled from court by her uncle Frederick, usurper of her father's throne. Disguised as Ganymede, a country lad, she travels with her cousin Celia to the Forest of Arden, where her secret love, Orlando, has joined the followers of her exiled father, Duke Senior. Ganymede pretends to help Orlando rid himself of his infatuation by encouraging him to make love to her as though she were Rosalind. Orlando is on his way to one of their lovers' meetings when he kills a lion and saves the life of his wicked brother Oliver, who has actually come to kill Orlando. Oliver is full of remorse and asks Ganymede's forgiveness for the delay and falls in love with Celia. The two couples are married, and Duke Senior regains his lands from the penitent Frederick.

Babbitt. A novel by American writer Sinclair Lewis published in 1922. Its hero, George Babbitt, a small-town businessman and town booster, whose horizons are limited to Zenith, the "greatest little city in the world," gave his name to an emergent social type. Although Babbitt comes to vaguely realize that the narrow aspirations of Zenith are not the whole of life, he is never able to act on this idea.

Brothers Karamazov, The. This novel has often been considered the masterpiece of the Russian novelist Feodor Dostoevski; it was published in 1879–1880. It deals with the murder of a corrupt landowner, Karamazov, and the reactions of his three sons. The eldest, Dmitri, a wild, impulsive, hard-drinking former soldier, a rival of his father for the favors of the fair Grushenka, is unjustly accused of the crime. The second son, Ivan, a proud and cold intellectual incapable of love, feels guilty of the intellectual crime of despising his father and wishing him dead. The youngest son, Alyosha, is a figure of saintlike innocence, capable of undivided love. In addition to being a suspenseful story of crime and mystery, the work explores Dostoevski's religious and social ideas. The atheism and despair of Ivan are weighed against the faith of Alyosha, but there is no easy choice between them. The novel introduces a multitude of characters, divided in heart and lacerated in feeling, whose motivations Dostoevski probes relentlessly.

Candide. A satirical novel by the French author Voltaire published in 1759; it is directed against the notion that "everything happens for the best in this best of all possible worlds." The plot, thick with farcical misadventures (most of the incidents having some precedent in history), is concerned with the sometimes divided fortunes of Candide, his beloved Cunegonde, and his tutor Dr. Pangloss, who is the embodiment of optimism. In the end, after a series of personal disasters, Candide decides the best wisdom is to "tend one's own garden." He resignedly marries Cunegonde and settles down to grow vegetables.

Canterbury Tales, The. A collection of tales, mostly in verse, by Geoffrey Chaucer. It is both his masterpiece and one of the great works in English literature. The tales were written between about 1387 and 1400, the year of Chaucer's death. They tell of the poet joining a company of pilgrims on their way to Canterbury to visit the shrine of St. Thomas à Becket. To while away the journey, their host, Harry Bailey, suggests that each pilgrim tell two stories going, and two coming back: the pilgrim judged to have told the best tale is to get a free dinner. Chaucer completed 24 of the tales, from chivalric romance to folk tale to sermon to bawdy fable. The pilgrims, who come from all walks of life, are vividly described by Chaucer, and within the framework of the pilgrimage he brilliantly develops their personalities.

Catcher in the Rye, The. Novel by American author J. D. Salinger published in 1951; it concerns youth's disenchantment with a hostile adult world. It is cast as a long monologue spoken by Holden Caulfield, who has run away from his prep school and gone to New York. In spite of his external sophistication, Holden maintains an incorruptible innocence during a weekend of disillusioning experiences.

Christmas Carol, A. A story of Christmas by Charles Dickens, published in 1843. Old Ebenezer Scrooge, a "clutching, covetous old sinner" and Tiny Tim, the crippled child of Bob Cratchit, Scrooge's downtrodden clerk, are two of the main characters. It is the story of Scrooge's regeneration: fantastic visitations by three spirits of Christmas (the ghosts of Christmas Past, Christmas Present, and Christmas Yet to Come) change him from an unfeeling money-lover to a benevolent human being who sends a turkey to the Cratchit family to make their Christmas merry.

Comedy of Errors, The. Shakespeare's first play. Two brothers, both named Antipholus, "the one so like the other as could not be distinguished," and their servants named Dromio, "male twins, both alike," are separated in infancy during a shipwreck. Bachelors Antipholus and Dromio of Syracuse, searching for their brothers, enter Ephesus, where they meet two women who claim to be their wives. Going home with them, Antipholus and Dromio enter into a comedy of errors, in which merchants, wives, and servants mistake the pair with their twins until the confusion finally clears up and all is sorted out.

Crime and Punishment. This masterly novel by the Russian writer Feodor Dostoevski, published in 1866, develops the theme of redemption through suffering. The penniless student Raskolnikov believes that his natural superiority places him above the moral law of common men. He finds good reasons for committing for gain two brutal murders, and the novel furnishes an examination of these reasons, which, one by one, prove to be insupportable. Conscience will not permit Raskolnikov to use the money obtained through his crime, and his anguish slowly leads him to confess and embrace the consequent punishment—hard labor in Siberia—that is the gateway to his redemption.

David Copperfield. A novel by Charles Dickens, published in 1849–1850. It is a sentimental story of an orphan's struggles. It deals with the sufferings of young David after his mother's death, and his cruel treatment by his stepfather, schoolmasters, and employers. The hypocritical Uriah Heep is one of the book's many memorable characters. David finds friends, too—his aunt Betsy Trotwood, the optimistic Mr. Micawber, and the kite-flying Mr. Dick. With their help, he becomes a successful writer.

Death of a Salesman. A play by American writer Arthur Miller, first performed in 1949, this is the modern tragedy of an ordinary man, Willie Loman, an aging traveling salesman. Faced with loss of his livelihood, and the failure of his sons, whom he has inculcated with his values of achieving success through being "well-liked," Willie is bewildered by his fate. Unable to understand why this familiar American dream worked for others but not for him, Willie commits suicide in a final, pathetic effort to rescue his family through his insurance money.

Divine Comedy, The. A long, allegorical poem written about 1307–1321 by the Italian poet Dante Alighieri. This work has been considered the supreme literary achievement of the Middle Ages. It expresses the poet's vision of the divine plan for justice in this world and the next. Dante originally called it *The Comedy*, because it begins in sorrow and ends happily, and also because it was written in Italian at a time when serious works were written in Latin.

The first book, *Inferno*, begins with a prologue. In the middle of his life, the poet finds himself stranded in a dark wood (the world of sin and error). Unable to escape, he is helped by the intervention of his idealized beloved Beatrice (divine grace), who has been dead for ten years and is now in Heaven. The Roman poet Vergil (the highest representative of human reason and pagan ethics) guides Dante out of the wood by a roundabout journey through the Afterlife. On Good Friday in the year 1300, they enter Hell, descending through nine circles in which the sinners become increasingly more infamous and their torments more hideous. There Dante sees well-known historical figures, princes, popes, and personal enemies, all vividly characterized. The lowest circle is reserved for traitors such as Judas Iscariot, Cassius, and Brutus.

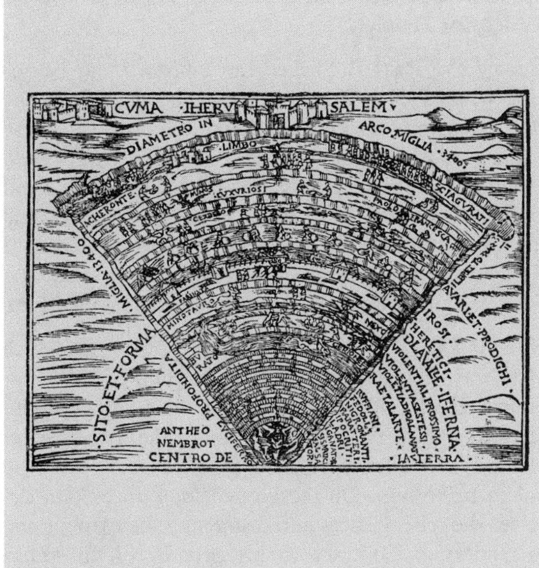

The circles of Hell in Dante's Inferno. *Lucifer, the Devil, is at the bottom, encased in ice.*

Don Quixote and his make-believe world of chivalry, as shown by Gustave Doré.

In the second book, *Purgatorio*, Vergil leads Dante through Purgatory, where he is purged of his sins, as far as the gates of Paradise. As that is as far as human reason can go, Vergil leaves and Beatrice guides Dante through the nine ascending circles of Paradise. In the tenth circle, St. Bernard becomes his guide, and Dante briefly experiences a vision of the Eternal Light, Divine Wisdom, or God.

The number three, symbolizing the Trinity, is used throughout as a structural principle. Thus, the work is divided into three books, each having 33 cantos. The cantos are written in *terza rima*, a three-line verse form invented by Dante specifically for this work.

Don Quixote de la Mancha, The Ingenious Gentleman. This picaresque novel, published in two parts in 1605 and 1615, is the masterpiece of the Spanish writer Miguel de Cervantes. It was a satire of the romances of chivalry popular in Cervantes's day.

An impoverished old gentleman, Alonzo Quixano, infatuated with knight errantry, changes his name to Don Quixote de la Mancha. With an uncouth peasant, Sancho Panza, as his squire, he embarks on a series of misadventures. His valorous deeds, such as tilting at windmills that he believes to be giants, are inspired by a peasant girl whom he believes to be the Lady Dulcinea. Ironically, he dies thinking he has been a failure, although in his pursuit of his illusory ideals he has shown far greater nobility than his sane, materialistic contemporaries.

Don Quixote has had a lasting influence on Western literature, and Sancho Panza ranks with the great comic characters of all time. It is the greatest prose work of Spanish literature, and its episodic structure was a major influence on the form of fiction for more than 200 years.

Faust. Faust, a figure in numerous legends and literary works, is based on the few facts known of the life of a 16th-century charlatan and magician. Faust is archetypical of the overreacher, one with an insatiable desire for power and knowledge.

The Tragical History of Doctor Faustus, a play by English dramatist Christopher Marlowe (published in 1604), is one of the most famous dramatizations of the legend. It is based on the *Faustbuch*, published in 1587 at Frankfurt am Main by Johann Spies. The play is in the morality tradition and anti-papist. Faustus, a good and learned man, sells his soul to Mephistopheles (the Devil), practices necromancy, and plays tricks on the pope. When payment is due, he despairs and is taken to Hell.

Faust, a dramatic poem by German writer Johann Wolfgang von Goethe (published in two parts in 1808 and 1832), is another famous version of the legend. Faust is tempted by the Devil, and although he sins seriously, he remains aware of truth and goodness and is saved.

For Whom the Bell Tolls. This novel by the American novelist Ernest Hemingway, published in 1940, is a tragic story of courage and compassion. Its hero, Robert Jordan, an American who volunteers in the Spanish Civil War, grows beyond a cold concern for his military objective and dies with the awareness that his struggle was for all men.

Great Expectations. A novel by Charles Dickens, published in 1861, this is the story of Pip, a village boy who longs for riches and social station, and suddenly receives from an unknown source wealth and the chance for an education. His "great expectations" lead him to attempt to act like a fine gentleman, but when they disappear he returns to a sense of real values.

Great Gatsby, The. This novel by F. Scott Fitzgerald, published in 1925 and generally regarded as his greatest completed work, is set in New York and is a searing exposure of the desperate boredom and spiritual bankruptcy of the Jazz Age, and of the thoughtless cruelty of great wealth. Its violent plot is concerned with the efforts of Jay Gatsby, a wealthy racketeer who poses as a businessman, to win his idealized love, the spoiled and wealthy Daisy, cousin of Nick Carraway, the story's narrator. Not only does Gatsby fail, he dies alone and deserted even by the hangers-on who had flocked to his lavish parties.

Gulliver's Travels. A satire by Jonathan Swift published in 1726 that tells of Lemuel Gulliver's voyages to imaginary lands. In Book I he goes to the island of Lilliput, where he finds himself a giant prisoner of a race of people 6 inches tall, but every bit as vain and pompous as the people of his homeland. In Book II he goes to Brobdingnag, the land of the giants, where he suffers the indignities of being swallowed and burped up by a squalling infant, and being carried away by a puppy. In Book III he goes to various countries, chief of which is the floating island of Laputa, the Cloud Cuckooland of eccentric scholars. In Book IV he arrives in the country of the Houyhnhnms, a land where horses with an intelligence superior to that of mankind carry on an ideal government, despite the fact that they share their island with an inferior race of Yahoos who cannot participate in it.

Hamlet, Prince of Denmark. Shakespearean tragedy in which Hamlet's father's ghost orders Hamlet to avenge his father's "foul and unnatural death." Claudius, murderer of the dead Danish king, marries Queen Gertrude, Hamlet's mother, and takes the throne. Feigning madness while awaiting his opportunity, Hamlet misleads Polonius, father of Ophelia, into thinking that love for Ophelia is causing Hamlet's strange behavior. Hamlet enlists the aid of an itinerant band of actors to recreate a poisoning scene and, with his friend Horatio, watches Claudius closely during the performance. Gertrude calls Hamlet to her chamber, where he rashly stabs eavesdropping Polonius. Subsequently, Ophelia, mad from grief, drowns herself. Claudius attempts to remove Hamlet to England, but fails. He plots with Polonius's son Laertes to fence with Hamlet and wound him with a poisoned foil. Hamlet is mortally wounded, Laertes and Claudius are killed, and Gertrude dies after drinking a cup of poison intended for Hamlet.

Henry IV, Part I. Shakespeare's history play beginning when Henry Percy, called Hotspur, refuses the king's demand for prisoners taken in recent wars. The ensuing battle against Henry's forces aligns Percy, Douglas, and Prince Hal against Henry. Prince Hal and his friend Falstaff have been carousing together and accosting travelers on the king's highway. Hal kills Hotspur in the battle of Shrewsbury, but Falstaff, who has come upon the body, pretends to have killed him.

Henry IV, Part II. Shakespeare's play in which Mowbray, Hastings, and the Archbishop of York war against Henry. Pressed with debts and charged with recruiting soldiers, Falstaff examines the men Justices Shallow and Silence present. He picks the ones who fail to bribe him. On the battlefield, Prince John deceives the rebel leaders into dismissing their troops and surrendering. Contrary to his promise, John orders them executed. Prince Hal visits the dying king, dreads the anxiety a crown entails, and promises his father he will mend his ways. During the coronation, Falstaff's familiar greetings incense Henry V, who orders his old friend banished.

Henry V. A sequel to Shakespeare's history plays about Henry IV. England's claim by hereditary right from Edward III to certain French dukedoms evokes an insulting reply from the Dauphin. Henry vows to invade France. A French assassination plot is uncovered, and Henry has the traitorous lords pass their own sentences of execution. Falstaff dies in London, and his comrades join the battles in France, during which Nym and Bardolph are hanged and a frightened Pistol decides to return to England. The French town of Harfleur falls to the English. Henry, after going disguised among his weary but valiant men, leads his troops to fight the larger French armies at Agincourt, a decisive English victory. Henry marries Katherine, the daughter of the defeated French king. Their son becomes Henry VI, king of France and England.

Huckleberry Finn, The Adventures of. Novel by American writer Mark Twain (Samuel Langhorne Clemens), generally considered his masterpiece. The story, told in the vernacular of Huck, a true child of nature, deals with his daring act of helping Jim, a runaway slave, to escape. Huck and Jim, floating down the Mississippi on a raft, enjoy a peace and freedom and mutual respect that is in sharp contrast to the meanness of society in the river towns where they stop. Twain uses the irony of Huck's innocent view of life to criticize the barbarity of "sivilization." Huck Finn is also a character in *The Adventures of Tom Sawyer*, published eight years earlier in 1876.

Gulliver in the land of the Lilliputians, captured by the tiny race.

Huck Finn (right) *and Tom Sawyer—a statue in Mark Twain's hometown of Hannibal, Missouri.*

Iceman Cometh, The. Tragedy by American playwright Eugene O'Neill, produced in 1946, that is often considered his greatest work. Through an intricate network of religious symbolism, O'Neill tells the story of a man's death brought about by loss of hope.

Iliad. Greek epic poem by Homer. A recitative poem in the ancient bardic tradition, it was orally composed in about the ninth century B.C. and first transcribed in the sixth century B.C.

It is an heroic account of the Greek victory in the Trojan War. Started by the elopement of Paris and Helen (the wife of Menelaus, the Greek commander and the brother of King Agamemnon), the war enlists all of the Greek and Trojan heroes, including Achilles, Odysseus, Hector, and Troilus, and most of the gods. The conflict is decided by Zeus, who gives victory to the Greeks.

Generally considered the greatest literary work of Western civilization, the *Iliad* is the starting point for virtually every epic of Greco-Roman literature—for instance, the *Odyssey* and the *Aeneid*—and the model for every later epic in the classical tradition.

Jane Eyre. Novel by British writer Charlotte Bronte published in 1847; it deals with the love of a modest and plain but intelligent governess and her ill-tempered, discourteous employer Rochester. The impediment to their love, and the cause of Rochester's moodiness, is an insane wife he has kept hidden in the house. When Jane learns of the wife's existence, she leaves. Later, when the wife is killed and Rochester is blinded in a fire, the lovers are reunited.

Julius Caesar. Shakespearean tragedy beginning when Caesar refuses the crown three times before falling into a fit. Caesar belittles his wife's fears and the warnings of a soothsayer before going to the capital on the Ides of March. Brutus, convinced he is acting for the good of Rome, joins a group of conspirators led by Cassius. They assassinate Caesar. At Caesar's funeral, Mark Antony speaks ironically of the "honorable" conspirators and teases the crowd with Caesar's "will." A civil war ensues. Cassius and Brutus both commit suicide, and Brutus is proclaimed "the noblest Roman of them all" by Antony.

King Lear. This tragedy is considered one of Shakespeare's most important plays. Lear's loving daughter Cordelia refuses to follow her sisters Goneril and Regan in false flattery of their father. The Earl of Kent is banished for defending Cordelia, and the king of France accepts disinherited Cordelia as his wife, as Lear leaves his kingdom divided between his two other daughters. Suddenly stripped of his remaining rights, Lear goes mad from knowledge of his error and wanders out in a storm accompanied by his fool. He rails against the ingratitude of children. Aided by Goneril and Regan, Edmund causes his father, the Earl of Gloucester, to be blinded for aiding Lear. Kent sends Lear to Cordelia's care in Dover, while Gloucester's true son Edgar tends his father. Victorious over the invading French, Edmund executes Cordelia and causes Lear to die of grief. With Gloucester dead, Regan killed by Goneril, who then commits suicide, and Edmund executed, England is rebuilt by Edgar and Kent.

Leatherstocking Tales. Novels of early frontier life by James Fenimore Cooper. All have the same hero, the scout Leatherstocking or Natty Bumppo, who combines knowledge of the woods with Yankee ingenuity. The series contains *The Pioneers* (1823), *The Last of the Mohicans* (1826), *The Prairie* (1827), *The Pathfinder* (1840), and *The Deerslayer* (1841). These books remained popular throughout Europe long after their reputation declined in the United States.

Long Day's Journey into Night. A domestic tragedy by Eugene O'Neill, the most personal and intimate of all his works. Written about 1941, it was not performed until 1956, after the author's death. The play embodies all the bitterness and ambivalence of the author's feelings toward his family. It is set in a country house in the year 1912. The characters—the four members of the Tyrone family—are patterned on O'Neill's family. The father is a famous actor, the mother a drug addict who lives on memories of her innocent Catholic girlhood. The elder son is an alcoholic, and the younger son (O'Neill), while struggling to break away to a new life, learns he is stricken with tuberculosis.

Look Homeward, Angel. Novel by Thomas Wolfe, published in 1929, of the type called in German a *Kunstlerroman*, a novel of an artist's development. Its autobiographical hero Eugene Gant, a physical giant and precocious genius, loves and hates his hometown of Altamont (Asheville, North Carolina), struggles against the limited horizons of his family, receives vague indications of immortality from a few sympathetic people, and finally sets out on a quest for fame and fortune as a writer.

Lord Jim. Novel by Joseph Conrad written in 1900; it deals with a young English seaman who impulsively abandons his sinking ship carrying Muslim pilgrims. Unable to understand or to reconcile this ignoble act with his own self-image, Jim cannot face returning home. He lives out his life among the South Sea Island natives, whose love and admiration for him are expressed in their nickname *Tuan* (Lord) Jim. But luck is against Jim. Unwittingly he betrays his native friends and meets death at their hands, a fate that finally resolves his guilt.

Lord of the Rings, The. Trilogy of fantasy novels with allegorical overtones written by the English scholar J. R. R. Tolkien. It consists of *The Fellowship of the Ring* (1954), *The Two Towers* (1954), and *The Return of the King* (1955). It deals with the long and often grim and terrible quest of the Hobbits to destroy the magic ring they possess in order to keep it from falling into the hands of evil powers.

The trilogy carries on a story first introduced in Tolkien's *The Hobbit* (1937), a fantasy written for children. Tolkien, a scholar of Old English and Old Norse literature, drew on old legends for the setting and atmosphere of "Middle-earth."

Macbeth. Shakespearean tragedy based on Scottish history. The victorious generals Banquo and Macbeth are met by witches, who prophesy that Macbeth is to be thane of Cawdor and king. Macbeth travels to Duncan and finds that the first prophecy has come true. Lady Macbeth presses her husband to make the second prophecy true by killing Duncan during his visit, but Macbeth is reluctant. After he does murder Duncan, Banquo, and Macduff's child and wife, Macbeth rules tyrannically while Lady Macbeth goes mad from the sins of too much blood. Another visit to the witches assures Macbeth that "none of woman born" shall harm him. He returns home satisfied that he is safe. After Lady Macbeth's suicide, Macbeth resolutely faces Macduff, who was delivered by Caesarian section. Macbeth is killed, and Duncan's son Malcolm succeeds Macbeth as king of Scotland.

Measure for Measure. Shakespeare's comedy written immediately before his greatest tragedies. Lord Angelo is ruling in the absence of the Duke of Vienna. To observe the justice of Lord Angelo's rule, the duke disguises himself as Friar Ludovick and returns to move among his people. Just at that time, Angelo revives capital punishment for immoral behavior. Unable to marry his beloved Juliet, young Claudio is unjustly seized and sentenced to immediate execution. Claudio's sister Isabella leaves her nunnery to plead for mercy from Angelo, who offers her brother's life in exchange for her honor. Indignant, Isabella refuses but, at Ludovick's direction, consents and is replaced by Mariana, who once was betrothed to Angelo. Later, Angelo orders the execution of Claudio, but the prison official disobeys. The Duke of Vienna removes his disguise and confronts Angelo. The duke then pardons Angelo, who marries Mariana while the duke marries Isabella and Claudio marries Juliet.

Merchant of Venice, The. Shakespeare's play opening when the Venetian Jewish moneylender Shylock demands a pound of flesh of Antonio if Antonio fails to repay a loan Shylock has made to Antonio's friend Bassanio. While Bassanio is at Belmont winning the hand of Portia by correctly choosing one of three chests, as stipulated in her father's will, Shylock's daughter Jessica flees Venice with her father's money and her lover Lorenzo. Antonio's message to Bassanio, warning him that the debt has fallen due, causes Bassanio to rush to court. Shylock refuses late payment of the money due him, ignores pleas of mercy, and demands his payment in the form of a pound of flesh

Natty Bumppo (right), *hero of James Fenimore Cooper's* Leatherstocking Tales.

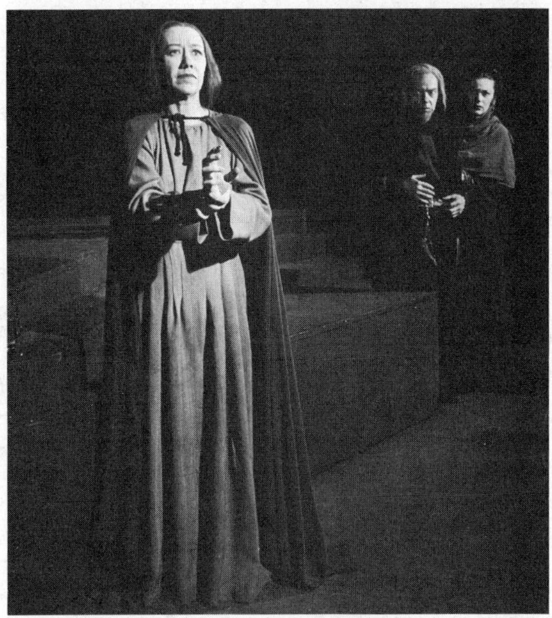

Lady Macbeth, after encouraging her husband to murder, gradually approaches madness.

taken from around the heart. Portia disguises herself as a lawyer and grants Shylock's request, but warns him that the death of Antonio that may result will leave Shylock open to charges of threatening the life of a Venetian citizen. Shylock is ordered to give up his money to Antonio and to the state. By Antonio's wish, Shylock is permitted to give the money to Jessica.

Merry Wives of Windsor, The. Shakespeare's comedy in which Sir John Falstaff writes identical letters to the wives of Windsor gentlemen Ford and Page, professing his love. The honest wives pretend to offer encouragement but plan revenge on the knight. The Pages' daughter Anne meanwhile is courted by Dr. Caius, Slender, and her favorite, Fenton. Falstaff is humiliated on his first visit to Mistress Ford when the basket of dirty clothes in which he hides from Ford is dumped into a muddy ditch. On his second visit, he disguises himself as a woman whom Ford hates. Falstaff is beaten for his trouble. The wives and their husbands humiliate Falstaff a third time when mock fairies pinch and burn him while Anne elopes with Fenton.

Midsummer Night's Dream, A. Shakespearean play in which Egeus, father of Hermia, promises her to Demetrius despite her love for Lysander. Athenian Duke Theseus supports Egeus's decision, so Hermia and Lysander plan to meet in the woods and elope. Helena, in love with Demetrius, reveals Hermia's plan to Demetrius and he sets out to search for the lovers. In the woods, various tradesmen rehearse a play of which Peter Quince is the director and vain Nick Bottom is the star. The play is to be presented in honor of the duke's marriage to the Amazon Queen Hippolyta. The woods are enchanted by fairies who have come to bless the royal wedding. Oberon, who is the fairy king, and the mischievous sprite Puck, play outrageous tricks on everybody until Theseus and Egeus arrive. The various spells are undone, and the couples are sorted out and happily married.

Moby-Dick. A novel by American author Herman Melville (1851), *Moby-Dick* is considered by many to be the finest American novel ever written. This tale of Captain Ahab's search for the great while whale that has crippled him is rich in symbolism and philosophical overtones. At the same time, the book is an exciting narrative and a precise description of the New England whaling industry of the time. The narrator, Ishmael, is the only survivor of the mad quest.

Much Ado About Nothing. A comedy by Shakespeare in which Claudio is in love with Hero, daughter of the Governor of Messina. His own wedding date set, Claudio arranges for his friend Benedick and Hero's cousin Beatrice to fall in love. Don John, seeking revenge on his brother Don Pedro, prince of Arragon, attempts to wreck the marriage of Claudio, Pedro's favorite. Claudio witnesses a clandestine meeting between Hero's maid and one of Don John's men. Thinking Hero unfaithful, Claudio disgraces her at church, provoking Benedick to challenge Claudio to a duel. Then Hero's presumed lover confesses the plot, and Claudio agrees to marry one of Hero's cousins to gain forgiveness. At last, Claudio and Hero are married, along with Benedick and Beatrice.

Nineteen Eighty-Four. This novel written in 1949 by the English satirist George Orwell (Eric Blair) offers a prophetic forecast of the future under totalitarian rule. It is a terrifying projection of life in the superstate watched over by Big Brother, where no one dares to trust another, and each lives in dread that his secret thoughts ("thought crimes") may be revealed on his face ("face crime").

Odyssey. Homer's epic of Odysseus, king of Ithaca and one of the foremost of the Greek chiefs in the Trojan War. The *Odyssey* describes the ten years of wandering and hardship Odysseus endures on his voyage home from the war. He touches upon the shores of the Lotus Eaters in Africa. He escapes death from the one-eyed Cyclops Polyphemus by his courageous trickery, blinding the giant and concealing himself beneath one of the Cyclops's sheep as they crowd out of the cave. He remains one year with Circe, the enchantress, and seven years with the ocean nymph Calypso on her island. He braves the dangers of Scylla and Charybdis and hears the Sirens sing while he is bound to the mast, thus escaping them. He is shipwrecked on the shores of Phaeacia and there cared for by Nausicaa and her father, who give him ships to continue his voyage home.

At last he reaches Ithaca disguised as a beggar, to find his wife Penelope surrounded by a host of insolent suitors, each coveting the kingdom. With the aid of his son Telemachus and his faithful herdsman Eumaeus, he slays them all and reigns another good 16 years.

Oliver Twist. Novel by British writer Charles Dickens published serially from 1837 to 1839; it is a melodramatic tale of poverty and the London underworld. Oliver, an unknown waif, escapes from a workhouse only to fall into the hands of Fagin, the master of a den of thieves. Fagin forces Oliver to break into a house. Oliver is caught by his intended victims, who recognize at once that he is no common criminal. Through their kindly interest, Oliver discovers his true parentage; Fagin and his crew are brought before the law, and Oliver is adopted by a wealthy gentleman.

One Day in the Life of Ivan Denisevich. A novel by Russian writer Alexander Solzhenitsyn, published in 1962, which describes a typical "good" day in the life of a prisoner in a Soviet concentration camp in Siberia. Ivan counts the day good because he manages to conceal a little extra food for himself, because he incurs no unusual punishment for misconduct, and because he avoids the dreaded sentence to solitary confinement in a freezing cell.

Othello, the Moor of Venice. Shakespeare's tragedy opening when Desdemona, bride of Othello, is entrusted to the care of Iago while Othello rushes to defend Cyprus from a Turkish invasion, which soon is ended by a storm. Iago, insulted by Othello's preference for Cassio as top lieutenant, plots revenge and enlists the aid of Roderigo in disgracing Cassio and making Othello jealous. Roderigo's brawl with Cassio gains the first objective, and Desdemona's handkerchief, obtained by unsuspecting Emilia and placed by her husband Iago in Cassio's possession, gains the second. Obsessed by jealousy, Othello kills his wife, takes his own life, and leaves Iago, murderer of Emilia, to be punished for his treachery.

Our Town. An elegiac play by the American writer Thornton Wilder, performed first in 1938. *Our Town* deals with the cycle of life in a New England town called Grovers Corners, but meant to be Everytown. A narrator comments on the town's activities and leading citizens. A girl and young man fall in love and marry. The young wife dies in childbirth and is buried among her fellow townsmen in the local cemetery.

Paradise Lost. Epic poem in blank verse by John Milton published in 1667; its purpose is "to justify the ways of God to man." It relates how some of the angels revolted against God and were cast out of Heaven into Hell. They decide to revenge themselves upon the Almighty by invading Earth and leading man to sin. Satan, chief of the fallen angels, corrupts Adam and Eve, the first human beings, and brings about their expulsion from Paradise. *Paradise Lost* is regarded as the greatest epic in the English language. A sequel, *Paradise Regained* (1671), deals with the theme of redemption.

Pilgrim's Progress, The. Allegory by the English preacher John Bunyan, the first part of which was issued in 1678; it describes the adventures of its hero, Christian, on his way from the City of Destruction to the Celestial City. He fights with Apollyon, looks on Vanity Fair, passes the castle of Giant Despair, and, after these and many other trials, reaches the Delectable Mountains and crosses the Black River to the Shining Gate. The plain, direct style was welcomed by the common people and was as popular in New England as in the author's own country.

Playboy of the Western World, The. Play by the Irish dramatist John Millington Synge, performed in 1907, about a young country lad, Christie Mahon, who thinks he has killed his father and, horrified, flees his home. But he is received as though he were a hero, bold and brave, and the flattering attentions bring about a complete change in his naturally timid personality. Christie's moment of glory is over when his father turns up alive. The play is greatly admired for the richness of its language, and is still remembered for the outrage with which its early performances in Ireland

Odysseus is tied to the mast of his ship so that he can resist the allure of the Sirens in the Odyssey.

and America were greeted, resulting in the "Playboy Riots" in Dublin, New York, and Philadelphia.

Pride and Prejudice. The first novel by Jane Austen, written in 1796 (when she was 21 years old) and published in 1813. The scene is laid in the English countryside, and the plot concerns the Bennett family's attempts to find suitable husbands for three daughters. The intimate drawing of the book's middle-class characters is done with humor and charm. Prejudice is represented by Elizabeth Bennett; Pride, by Mr. Darcy, her wealthy suitor. As Darcy overcomes his pride, Elizabeth overcomes her prejudice, and the two are married at last, giving this comedy of manners a happy ending.

Red Badge of Courage, The. Novel by Stephen Crane, published in 1895 when the author was about 24 years old; it is a study of a man's feelings in battle, written by one who had never seen battle. Henry Fleming, a raw country boy, enlists at the outset of the Civil War. The book describes his mental states as he waits for action, his panic under fire, and his final conquest of cowardice through identification with his comrades. It is one of the first books to treat battle realistically rather than as a theater for displays of gallantry.

Richard II. Shakespearean tragedy beginning when the Duke of York warns Richard of the dangers of his policy of confiscation of the lands of the dying John of Gaunt, and Richard departs for Ireland. Gaunt's son and heir, Henry Bolingbroke, exiled as a result of a quarrel with the Duke of Norfolk, seeks revenge by invading England. When Richard returns from Ireland, Bolingbroke seizes him, forces Richard's abdication, and imprisons Richard in Pomfret Castle. Loyal York foils Aumerle's plot against Henry IV. Sir Pierce, hoping to please his king, murders Richard and is banished by Henry, who pledges a Holy Land pilgrimage to gain forgiveness.

Richard III. In this early Shakespeare tragedy, the deformed Richard, duke of Gloucester, plots to secure the throne. By manipulating his brother, sickly King Edward IV, Richard causes the death of another brother, the Duke of Clarence. Edward dies, and Richard sends Edward's two sons to the tower, presumably to await coronation, while Richard arranges to be crowned king of England. King Richard then murders the two young princes and plans to kill his wife in order to marry his niece Elizabeth, who is sought after by the Lancastrian Earl of Richmond. Richmond's forces march on London. Richard is slain, and Richmond accepts the crown. He plans to marry Elizabeth and join forever the houses of Lancaster and York.

Riders to the Sea. A one-act play by John Millington Synge, first performed in Dublin in 1904. It is among the finest achievements of the Irish literary renaissance. A starkly tragic play, it pictures a day like any other day in an Aran Island fishing village. But it is the day when the old woman Maurya, who has lost four sons at sea, sees her youngest son Bartley brought home drowned. The characters speak a dialect that is at once plain and poetic, and the language gives the play special dignity and warmth.

Romeo and Juliet. Shakespeare's first great tragedy. The Montagues and Capulets are warring houses. Romeo Montague meets Juliet Capulet at a ball and falls in love at once. He professes his love in Juliet's garden, and they decide to marry. They go the next morning to Friar Laurence for the ceremony. Soon, new fighting occurs and Romeo's friend Mercutio is killed by Juliet's cousin Tybalt, who is then killed by Romeo, later banished for his crime. Juliet, desperate for help, plans at the friar's insistence to take a potion that will cause a deathlike trance from which Romeo will rescue her. Romeo fails to hear of the plan. Learning of Juliet's death, he visits the tomb and kills himself. Juliet awakens, sees Romeo dead, and kills herself. Filled with remorse, the families reconcile through their common grief.

Stranger, The. Novel by the Algerian-born French philosopher Albert Camus, published in 1942. It embodies the author's belief that life in the modern world is "absurd," or meaningless. It views man as a "stranger" in the world, and is about a man named Meursault, who is unable to find any reason for living or to experience any kind of emotional reaction, even to harrowing events. Faced with death, however, he discovers that the simple fact of life itself is enough to justify existence.

Streetcar Named Desire, A. Play by the American author Tennessee Williams, performed in 1947, and awarded a Pulitzer Prize. The play concerns Blanche Dubois, an aging, unstable Southern belle who comes to stay with her sister, Stella. Her refined behavior and coquettish manner provoke a conflict with her earthy brother-in-law, Stanley Kowalski. The title sums up the theme of the play, which is set in the French Quarter of New Orleans, where a streetcar named "Desire" shares its track with one named "Cemetery."

Taming of the Shrew, The. This popular Shakespeare play concerns Katharina, a beautiful but harsh-tongued and obstinate girl no one wants to marry. Petruchio agrees to marry Katharina, and her father, Baptista of Padua, allows his younger daughter Bianca to be courted by Gremio, Hortensio, and Lucentio. Lucentio wins Bianca's hand. Petruchio, on his own wedding day, arrives late at church dressed like a madman, swears throughout the service, and leaves Padua immediately with Katharina before the wedding reception. In Verona Petruchio tames Katharina by torturing her with mock kindness: her food is not good enough to eat, her bed not fit to sleep in, her clothes unfit to wear. Katharina, for the sake of peace, gives in and returns to Padua a model wife, amazing the henpecked husband of once-gentle Bianca by lecturing on the duties of a wife to her husband.

Tempest, The. One of William Shakespeare's last plays. Prospero, duke of Milan, has been ousted from his throne by Antonio, his brother. Set adrift on the sea with his daughter Miranda, Prospero finds his way to an island, the place of banishment of the witch Sycorax. Prospero releases Ariel and other spirits imprisoned by Sycorax, and they now obey Prospero's orders. The sole inhabitant of the island, the witch's son Caliban, also obeys Prospero's orders. Prospero lives on the island with Miranda for twelve years, when a ship carrying Antonio and the king of Naples and his son Ferdinand is wrecked on the island. Everyone is rescued, but Ferdinand is separated from the others and thought to be dead. In turn, Ferdinand believes all the others are dead. Ferdinand and Miranda fall in love. Acting under Prospero's orders, Ariel terrorizes Antonio and the king of Naples. The king repents his past cruelty and reconciles with Prospero and restores him to his throne in place of the frightened Antonio. Leaving Caliban behind, all the other mortals prepare to leave the island.

Tom Jones. Properly called *The History of Tom Jones, a Foundling*, this comic romance by Henry Fielding, one of the founders of the English novel, was published in 1749. It relates the adventures of high-spirited, impulsive, and generous Tom, who, despite many discreditable escapades, at last wins the confidence of his foster father, Squire Allworthy, and the love of beautiful Sophia Western. The novel is remarkable for its vitality and sweeping picture of 18th-century London and country life.

Tom Sawyer, The Adventures of. This classic of small-town American boyhood written by Mark Twain (Samuel Langhorne Clemens) in 1876 was based on his memories of growing up in Hannibal, Missouri. Tom, an imaginative boy who is fond of adventure stories, finds himself involved in a real-life adventure when he and his friend Huck Finn witness a murder committed by Injun Joe. The terrified boys run away, but return in time to prevent an innocent man from being condemned for the crime.

Two Gentlemen of Verona. Shakespearean comedy in which fickle Proteus woos Julia in Verona, while constant Valentine falls in love with Silvia, daughter of the Duke of Milan. Proteus is ordered to Milan. After pledging undying love to Julia, Proteus proceeds to the court, where he also falls in love with Silvia and reveals to the duke Valentine's plan to elope with Silvia. Valentine is banished from the court and becomes the leader of a group of outlaws in a nearby forest. Proteus, with the help of a page named Sebastian, really Julia in disguise, bids openly for Silvia's hand in marriage. Silvia flees in search of Valentine but is caught by Proteus, who tries to force his attentions upon her.

Napoleon (center) *invades Russia in 1812, in a film version of Tolstoy's* War and Peace.

Caught by Valentine, Proteus begs and receives forgiveness. The duke has a change of heart and allows Valentine and Silvia to be reunited as Julia, her true identity disclosed, is joined with Proteus.

Ulysses. Novel by the Irish writer James Joyce, first published in 1922; it has become a landmark of psychological and naturalistic fiction. The story takes place in Dublin in one day, June 16, 1904. The ordinary events of that day experienced by the leading characters—the autobiographical Stephen Dedalus; Leopold Bloom, a Jewish advertising salesman; his wife Molly Bloom, the eternal daughter of Eve—are carefully recorded. Joyce uses the method of free-association interior monologue (stream of consciousness) and sometimes interpolates a variety of other styles that are brilliant literary parodies.

War and Peace. Epic novel by Russian novelist Leo Tolstoy published in 1864–1869; it gives a view of all of Russian society at the beginning of the 19th century, focusing on the Napoleonic wars. It expresses an optimistic view of life in which evil can be successfully resisted by love and family happiness.

Winter's Tale, The. This tragicomedy was written late in Shakespeare's life. Leontes, king of Sicily, mistakenly suspects his wife Hermione of infidelity with Polixenes, king of Bohemia. He seeks to kill Polixenes and imprisons Hermione. When Hermione bears a daughter, the king orders that the baby be left to die. Hermione is reported to have died of grief. The baby, Perdita, survives and is brought up by a shepherd. She falls in love with Florizel, son of Polixenes, and goes with him to Leontes' court. Her true identity is revealed, a statue of Hermione turns out to be the living Hermione, and the young lovers are married.

Wuthering Heights. The one novel by Emily Brontë, published in 1847, *Wuthering Heights* is a somber tale of love and vengeance. Its central character is the orphaned Heathcliff, whose thwarted love for Catherine Earnshaw leads him to take revenge on her and her family.

For Further Reference

Abacarion, Richard and Klutz, Marvin
Literature: The Human Experience
St. Martin's Press

Abel, Darrel
American Literature (3 vols.)
Barron's

Beckoff, G., et al.
English Literature (5 vols.)
Random House

Cudden, J. A.
Dictionary of Literary Terms
Doubleday

Holman, C. Hugh
Handbook to Literature
Odyssey Press

Scholes, Robert
Elements of Literature: Essay, Fiction, Poetry, Drama, Film
Oxford University Press

Education and Careers

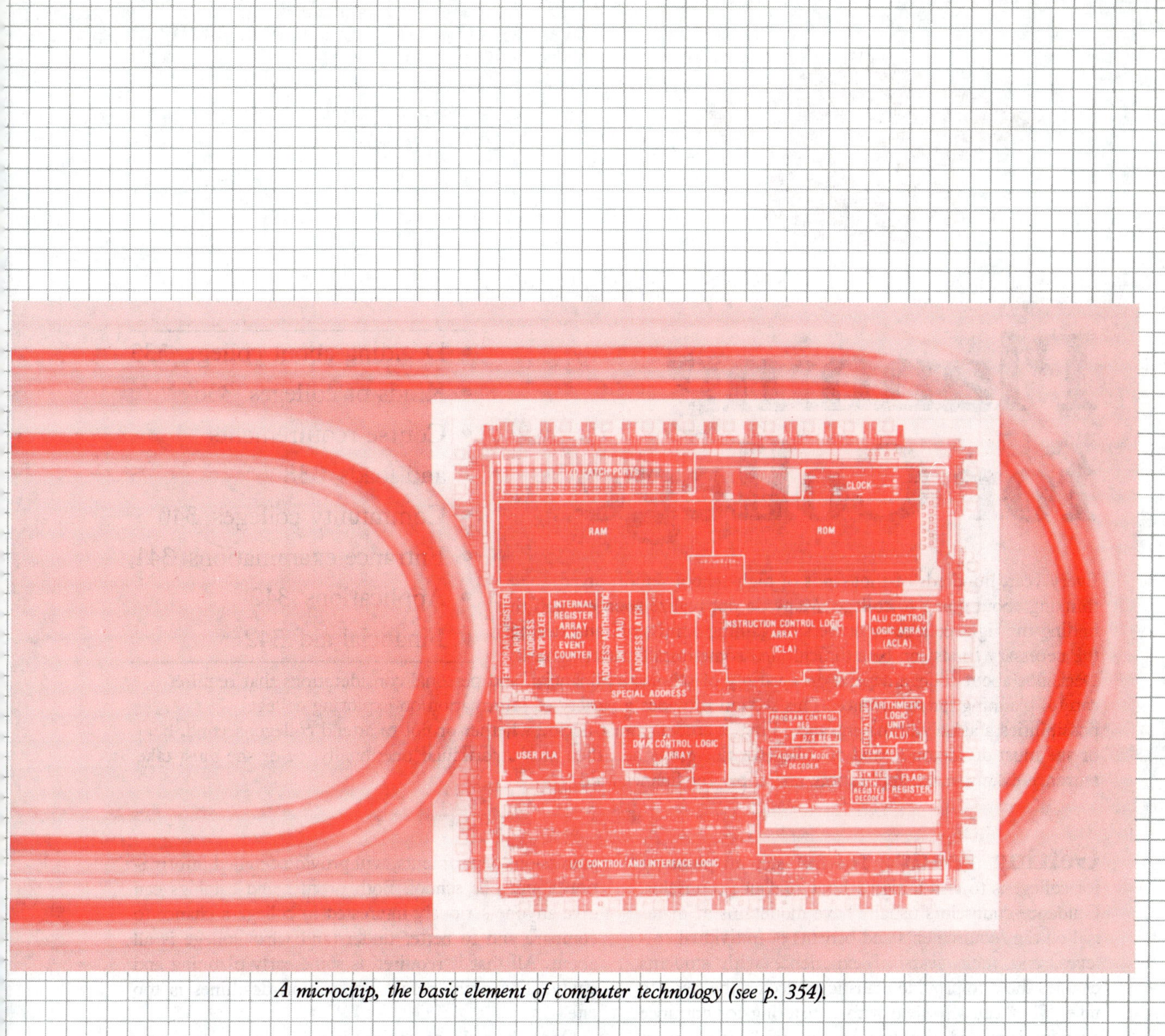

A microchip, the basic element of computer technology (see p. 354).

Planning for College

Every year, hundreds of thousands of high-school seniors start thinking about going to college. Many do not realize soon enough that finding the right college or university, gaining admission, and raising the necessary funds can be a difficult and sometimes frustrating task. Decisions about college depend on a variety of scholastic, financial, and personal considerations that require careful planning far in advance. This section provides a variety of information on exploring college possibilities and on gaining entrance. First, a student must decide whether or not to attend college; second, he or she must decide on a kind of college or university and then pick a particular one; finally, he or she must take entrance exams, make application, and apply for financial aid.

Getting ready. The first step in planning for college is to visit a high school guidance counselor. Guidance counselors usually have mountains of material on the requirements and benefits of individual colleges, and their years of experience with students enables them to provide realistic advice on the steps to take. They can also help with registering for entrance examinations and applying for financial aid to meet college expenses.

Many high schools arrange "college nights." College admissions officers come to meet personally with prospective students. Such events remind students that a wide variety of colleges and other educational institutions exist. Most colleges distribute free literature that will be useful for future reference.

The best published sources of information about college are commercial volumes of "profiles" of American colleges and the catalogs of the colleges themselves. Both are usually available in high-school and many public libraries. The profile volumes condense information about entrance requirements, tuition costs, facilities, and student life at all American colleges, making it possible to compare schools. An individual college catalog, free of charge from most college admissions departments, will provide detailed information about one school. Both profiles and catalogs can give anyone seriously interested in college a chance to compare and to better understand what college is all about. All that is required is some early planning and study. The night before application deadlines is too late.

Once the field of choices has been narrowed, prospective students should visit any colleges under serious consideration if at all possible. College admissions departments actively encourage such visits, and if asked in advance they will arrange tours and, in some cases, overnight accommodations. Visits to prospective colleges also provide a chance to talk with enrolled students, who may be far franker in their advice than admissions officers.

This sort of research can be time-consuming, but it is an essential beginning step in planning for a college education. Such research can be especially rewarding in today's world of higher education. Rising costs and falling enrollments have created a "buyer's market" for colleges; promising students may actually find themselves actively recruited by a particular college or university if applications are made early.

Deciding about college

The percentage of high-school graduates going straight to college has declined in recent years. In 1981, about one-third of high-school seniors entered college in the same year that they graduated. This suggests that many college places are going unfilled; opportunities for students seriously interested in college are growing, but the decision to attend college should be a deliberate one. College does offer access to a world of intellectual activity and necessary preparation for professional fields such as law or medicine. But, there are also many alternatives to a traditional college education—study at a community college, vocational training, or immediate entry into the business world. These may prove better suited to the needs of some high-school graduates.

A primary consideration when deciding about college is the scholastic background necessary for admission. The level of scholastic achievement required varies according to the nature and status of individual colleges. Nearly all colleges, however, require a high-school diploma and particular high-school courses, such as four years of English, three of mathematics, and one of American history. These entrance requirements are itemized in all college catalogs. Colleges also require reports of grades in the form of a transcript provided by the high school. The admissions department at a college will interpret the transcript according to its own requirements. An engineering school will place great stress on science grades, for example, while a liberal arts school will be more interested in language arts grades. Many colleges require a minimum grade-point average from applicants.

Another consideration is achievement on standardized entrance examinations, which are described below.

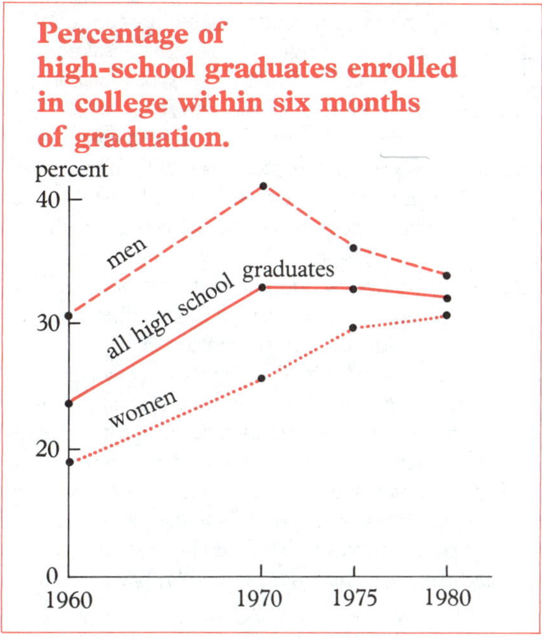

Average entrance examination scores for individual schools can be found in the aforementioned profiles of American colleges. Students whose own scores on these tests are substantially below the school's average may have trouble gaining admission.

Finally, tuition costs and residence costs must be considered by all applicants. There are many available sources of financial aid, but the cost of higher level education remains an essential consideration for any high-school graduate contemplating college.

Education career paths

Those who do not attend college may limit their potential, but they also gain work experience sooner.

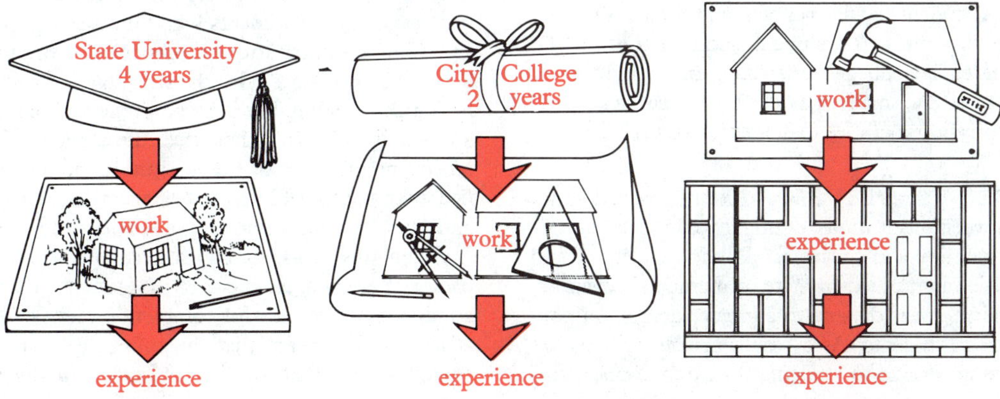

Kinds of colleges

There are approximately 3000 institutions of higher education in the United States, including community colleges. Each has its individual strengths, weaknesses, and particular character. For this reason, any college candidate is well advised at the outset of his or her search to consider a variety of kinds of colleges and universities. Some preferences may not survive the shock of a campus visit, and unexpected possibilities can become preferences in the course of the search for an acceptable institution.

Choosing the right school the first time is especially important because transferring from one college to another can be a difficult and frustrating experience. At most colleges, standards for transfer applicants are more demanding than those for first-year applicants. Many transfer students find themselves denied credit for past courses, forced to repeat required courses, or asked to meet new and unforeseen requirements. In all cases, the result is slower progress toward a degree and loss of tuition dollars. One's initial choice, then, should be thoughtful, realistic, and, preferably, permanent.

Large vs. small. The basic distinctions between large and small schools are suggested by the distinction between a university and a college. *Universities* are generally large institutions with graduate research departments and professional schools for doctors and lawyers. *Colleges* are usually smaller institutions entirely devoted to four-year programs that end in a bachelor's degree.

Universities, in keeping with their greater size and broader purpose, have extensive classroom, dormitory, laboratory, library, and athletic facilities. Many have among their faculty well-known scholars. Some students will find the size and prestige of a university stimulating, but others may find the same atmosphere impersonal and discouraging.

Colleges, in contrast, are known for their primary interest in teaching rather than research, their greater degree of student-faculty contact, and their more personal environment for student social activities. To some students, a college's relatively limited number of courses of study, smaller student body, and lack of extensive physical facilities may seem undesirable.

Public vs. private. Another basic distinction between institutions of higher education is between public and private. Public colleges and universities are funded by state or municipal revenues, while private ones depend to a greater degree on payments from students. As a result, private schools are far more expensive to students than public ones. Enrollments at public institutions have grown far faster in recent years than those at private institutions.

There are also other differences between public and private schools. Private schools, which include many church-related institutions, are often able to pursue a single educational or philosophical goal with greater freedom than public ones. Some private schools also retain a special prestige. Eastern private universities such as Harvard and Yale, for example, maintain high academic standards and attract students from all parts of the country. On the average, however, private institutions and public ones have similar academic standards and offer similar courses of study.

A third way of classifying institutions of higher learning is by whether their students live on campus or at home. Traditional private colleges and universities have a high percentage of resident students. Many city and state universities enroll most or all of their students from the local area. A student may want to consider the advantages and disadvantages of going away to school. Residence in a distant college may provide friends and business contacts valuable in later life. But if a student plans to enter a business or profession in his or her hometown, study at a good local university may be more advantageous (as well as less expensive). Friendships made with others in the same profession or business can give the hometown student an advantage over those who go away to study.

General vs. specialized. A final distinction between institutions of higher education rests on whether they offer general or specialized courses of study. The most common sorts of specialized schools are those that concentrate on teaching or engineering. A liberal arts college offers a wide spectrum of courses, but it is usually stronger in the humanities and social sciences; often it cannot offer advanced courses in the sciences. Specialized institutions offer the advantage of many courses within a single field, but they may prove unsatisfactory for students who find their interests and ambitions changed after enrollment. By the same token, general colleges offer the advantage of a multitude of courses of study but less comprehensive offerings in any single field. In either case, the student body will reflect the purposes of the institution: broadly diversified with multiple interests or specialized, consisting entirely of students pursuing a single profession.

Given this range of educational opportunities, the choice of a school is crucial to the student's chances for admission and successful completion of a degree. It is at least as important that the college be suited to the student as it is that the student qualify for the college.

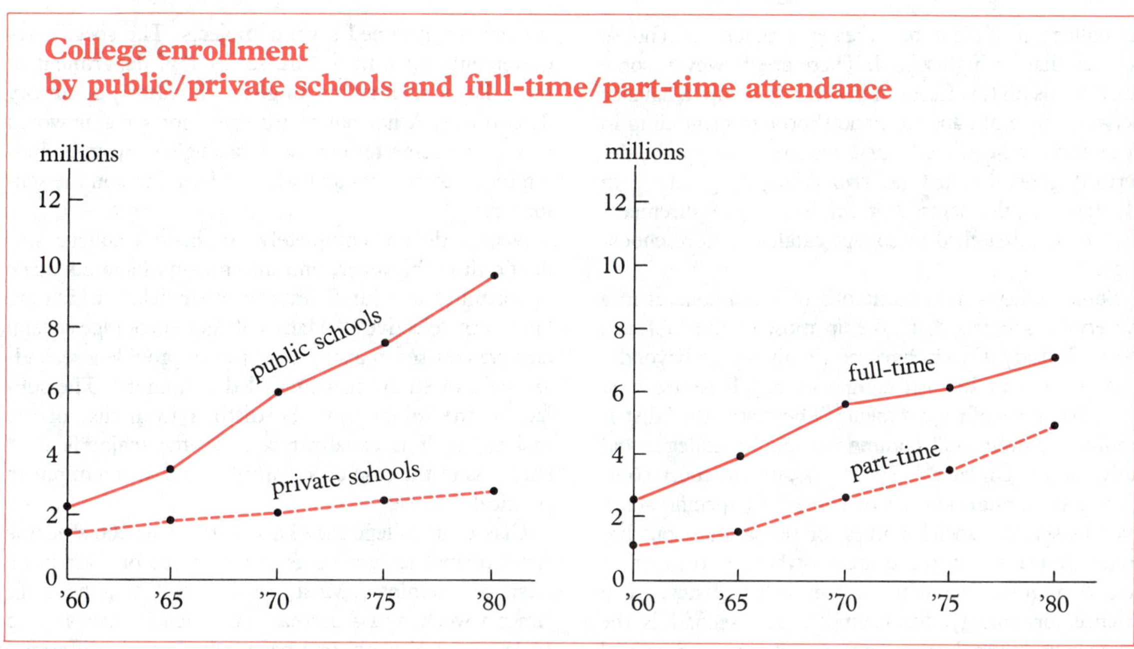

College enrollment
by public/private schools and full-time/part-time attendance

Classifying colleges

Type	*Study*	*Examples*
Large public		
State Universities	general and professional studies	University of California
City Universities (city owned)		City University of New York
Large private		
"Prestige" Universities	general and professional studies	Harvard University
Commuter Universities		New York University
Engineering and Technical Schools	specialized studies	Massachusetts Institute of Technology
Professional Schools	law, medicine, etc.	Wharton School of Business
Small public		
State Colleges	general studies	(includes many smaller state- and city-operated colleges; for those in your region, consult directories or ask a guidance counselor)
Community Colleges		
Agricultural and Technical Colleges	specialized studies	
Small private		
Liberal Arts Colleges	general undergraduate studies	(includes many church-related liberal arts and Bible colleges and independent colleges with regional following; proprietary schools are operated for profit)
Christian and Bible Colleges	specialized undergraduate studies	
Proprietary Business and Secretarial Schools	specialized nondegree programs	

Course requirements and loads

In college a student has greater freedom to choose courses than in high school. There are, however, some restrictions on this freedom in order to insure a balance between general education and thorough grounding in at least one discipline. Course requirements can be described generally, but no two colleges operate with identical requirements. For this reason, requirements should be researched in college catalogs before choosing a school.

Some colleges have numerous required courses in a variety of subjects that take up most of the first two years of study. Others have no requirements beyond a basic course in English composition. There are only two basic sorts of requirements. The first is the "distribution requirement," common in public colleges and universities. Under this system, a student must complete a minimum number of courses in specific areas, such as science, social studies, or humanities, but has some choice within those areas—whether to satisfy a science requirement with courses in chemistry, earth science, or biology, for example. The second is the "core curriculum," common in private universities and colleges. Under this system, a student must complete specific courses, usually broadly defined surveys that touch on more than one field of study. As a rule, private schools have more requirements than public ones. In many colleges, credit may also be earned through independent study projects pursued during recesses.

The college course "load" is the number of courses taken during a fall or a spring semester, with the average load being four or five courses each semester. The student's four-year course load is organized around a primary field of study called a "major," which is usually chosen formally late in the second year, after the student has sampled several subjects. The specific requirements for a major are set by that department of the college, such as the English, chemistry, or history department. A normal requirement for a major would be ten one-semester courses in a single subject, including required courses and advanced seminars in the senior year.

Majors do not completely dominate a college student's time, however, and all students have adequate opportunity to take courses in other fields, which are known as "electives." Many colleges encourage several elective courses in a single subject to provide a secondary field of study, usually called a "minor." The subject of the minor must be distinct from that of the major, but it is usually related to the major field of study, as in the case of a history major with a minor in political science.

Classes in college may have as many as 200 students for a formal lecture or as few as three or four in an advanced seminar. Most classes meet two or three times a week, and a normal course load consists of 15 to 18 hours of class time per week. The big difference from high school is that students must take much greater personal responsibility for studying and for mastering new material on their own. Attendance at classes is often not required, leaving students free to choose *not* to attend if they can master the material on their own. (Attendance is generally wise, of course, and students seldom succeed by cutting classes.)

Many first-year college students find their new freedom a great temptation. They fail to budget their time early in a school term, then find themselves studying all night as papers come due and examinations are given.

Typical course requirements and loads

A typical core curriculum requirement
Students are required to complete two semesters of work in each of the following courses:

1. History of Ideas and Civilizations
2. Survey of Literature and the Arts
3. Problems and Methods in Social Science
4. Problems in Science and Mathematics

A typical distribution requirement
Students are required to complete a minimum of two semesters of course work in each of the following areas:

Area A: Foreign languages, classics, philosophy, religion

Area B: English literature, music, art history, fine arts

Area C: Economics, history, political science, sociology, psychology, American studies

Area D: Chemistry, mathematics, physics, biology

Sample college curriculums

Humanities *(English major; history minor)*

First year	*Second year*	*Third year*	*Fourth year*
English composition	Introduction to literature	Shakespeare	Literature seminar
Foreign language	American literature	A literature course	Independent study in literature
Science or mathematics	A social science course	A literature course	A literature course
World history	American history	A history course	Elective
Elective	Elective	Elective	

Teaching *(elementary school)*

First year	*Second year*	*Third year*	*Fourth year*
English composition	General psychology	Reading techniques	Student teaching
Speech	Educational psychology	Child psychology	Seminar on teaching science in elementary school
Music or art	Health education	English in elementary school	
Mathematics	Social science in elementary school	Elementary curriculum	
Elective	Elective	Field experience	

Engineering *(electrical engineering)*

First year	*Second year*	*Third year*	*Fourth year*
English composition	Electrical engineering	Computer analysis	Electrical project
Chemistry	Chemistry	Electromagnetism	Systems laboratory
Mechanical drawing	Computer science	Circuits design	Social science course
Calculus	Calculus	Digital logic	Elective
Physics	Physics	Humanities elective	Elective

Pre-med *(biochemistry major; computer science minor)*

First year	*Second year*	*Third year*	*Fourth year*
English composition	Calculus	General biochemistry	Biochemistry
Foreign language	General physics	Organic chemistry	Biochemistry lab
Biology	Laboratory	Organic chemistry lab	Biochemistry seminar
Chemistry	Computer science	Computer science	Computer science
Laboratory skills	Elective	Elective	Elective

Social Work

First year	*Second year*	*Third year*	*Fourth year*
English composition	Sociology	Social work methods	Social work methods
Foreign language	Foreign language	Human development	History of social welfare
Psychology	Psychology	Research methods	Field practice in social work
History	Political science	Elective	Elective
Elective	Elective	Elective	

Accounting

First year	*Second year*	*Third year*	*Fourth year*
English composition	Principles of economics	Principles of business administration	Advanced accounting
Mathematics	Business statistics	Cost accounting	The law of business transactions
Introduction to computer information systems	Computer programming and data processing	Economics	Controllership
Principles of accounting	Intermediate accounting	Income tax	Business finance
Science elective	Science elective	Business law	Marketing

Community colleges

One alternative to a traditional college education is enrollment in a community college, sometimes called a junior or two-year college. There are now well over 1000 such institutions across the country. Community college enrollment doubled between 1970 and 1980 to reach a total of more than 4 million students.

Most community colleges are open to anyone who has received a high-school diploma or its equivalent. At the end of two years of full-time study or the equivalent part-time study, a successful student is awarded an Associate in Arts (AA) or Associate in Science (AS) degree. The student is then eligible, if willing and qualified by grades, to transfer to a traditional four-year college with credit for the work already completed. Community colleges are far less expensive than four-year institutions, with annual tuition fees usually falling between $500 and $1000.

Community colleges vary considerably in quality. It is clear, however, that they offer a route to higher education for high-school graduates who have postponed college or who require remedial work before they can satisfy college-level requirements. Community colleges are also known for practical and professional course offerings in fields such as automobile technology, secretarial skills, and business administration. Finally, community colleges maintain evening programs to serve part-time students and those who must support a family while pursuing higher education.

It is fairly common for community college students in academic subjects to transfer to four-year institutions after two years. It should be noted, however, that community colleges can offer no guarantee of acceptance at a four-year institution after completion of the AA or AS program. Also, many of their students may be doing remedial work, so the academic atmosphere may not be stimulating for high-school graduates already qualified for traditional colleges. Virtually all community college students commute to school, so such colleges offer little of the campus atmosphere common at four-year institutions.

The national trend toward community college education, however, indicates that these schools serve a growing need in the field of higher education. For this reason they represent an option that should be considered against the particular needs and qualifications of the high-school graduate interested in college.

Sample community college curriculums

Business administration

First semester	*Second semester*	*Third semester*	*Fourth semester*
English composition	English composition	Management	Marketing
Accounting	Accounting	Psychology	Sociology
Economics	Economics	Science lab	Science lab
Business law	Business law	Business elective	Business elective
Elective	Elective	Elective	Elective

Industrial electronics

First semester	*Second semester*	*Third semester*	*Fourth semester*
English composition	Principles of circuits	Circuits and systems	Industrial electronics
Industrial controls	Industrial controls	Electronic graphics	Automated systems
Electronic formulas	Digital elements	Physics	Electrical troubleshooting
Mathematics	Wiring skills	Machine shop	Elective
Elective	Elective	Elective	Elective

Dental assistant

First semester	*Second semester*	*Third semester*	*Fourth semester*
Anatomy and physiology	Anatomy and physiology	General psychology	Pharmacology
English composition	Speech	Oral pathology	Peridontology
Introduction to clinical hygiene	Clinical services	Peridontology	Dental internship
Dental anatomy	Dental anatomy	Dental health education	
Dental Hygiene	Dental hygiene	Clinical services	

Entrance examinations

Most college applications require scores on standardized entrance examinations. These are helpful to colleges because they provide a uniform test of intellectual ability for students of very different high-school backgrounds. Entrance examinations are conducted by independent testing agencies, notably the College Entrance Examination Board (CEEB) and the American College Testing program (ACT). Their tests are scheduled on dates in the months preceding application deadlines, so candidates for college should arrange to take entrance examinations even if they have not yet selected specific colleges. Applicants can register for the examinations by mail or by obtaining forms from guidance counselors. Fees range from $7.50 to $25, depending on the kind and number of tests taken.

Virtually all college applicants take aptitude tests, which measure ability to do college-level work; these include the Scholastic Aptitude Tests (SAT) prepared by the CEEB and the American College Tests (ACT). Many students also take achievement tests, which measure knowledge of a specific subject. The CEEB also provides the College Level Examination Program (CLEP) for older students having high-school equivalency diplomas.

The SAT and ACT aptitude tests each require about three hours to complete. The SAT consists of two sections, verbal and math, with separate scores reported on a scale of 200 to 800. ACT consists of four sections: English usage, math usage, social studies reading, and natural science reading. Scores for each section of ACT are reported as a percentage of correct answers.

Achievement tests are one-hour examinations in subjects such as English composition, mathematics, American history, and foreign languages. They are used by colleges for purposes of placement as well as admission. High test scores sometimes free accepted students from required courses.

Most bookstores contain manuals for preparing for all of these tests. The usefulness of these manuals is a matter of current debate, but students will certainly find useful information about the nature of the tests and the kinds of questions asked.

Sample test questions

Verbal and English usage questions

Antonyms: Choose the word most nearly opposite in meaning to the word in capital letters.

DISINTERESTED: (a) bored (b) selfish (c) generous (d) rapt (e) lonely

Sentence Completion: Choose the word that would best complete the meaning of the sentence.

The________________of gloom pervaded the room.
(a) aura (b) atmosphere (c) redolence (d) foreboding (e) murmur

Analogy: Select the pair of words with the same relationship as those in capital letters.

KING: CROWN:: (a) conductor: podium (b) monarch: throne (c) musician: instrument (d) judge: gavel (e) dentist: drill

SUBJECT: OBJECT:: (a) child: man (b) house: roof (c) bat: ball (d) calf: cow (e) sun: desert

answers: b, b, d, c

Math and math usage questions

Percents: If a city had a population of 650,000 in 1950 and a growth rate of 5 percent in the next decade, what was its population in 1960?

(a) 715,000 (b) 682,500 (c) 975,000 (d) 700,000 (e) none of these

Formulas: Change 90° Celsius into the Fahrenheit scale using the formula $F° = \frac{9}{5} C° + 32$. Answer:

(a) 194° (b) 144° (c) 162° (d) 210° (e) none of these

Geometry: The area of a trapezoid equals $\frac{1}{2}$ height $(b_1 + b_2)$. If the bases of a trapezoid are 20 and 30 and its area is 100, what is its height?

(a) 1 (b) 7 (c) 4 (d) 5 (e) none of these

Algebra: If $\frac{1}{x} = 6$, and $Y = 6$, what is X in terms of Y?

(a) $\frac{1}{y}$ (b) 6Y (c) 6 − Y (d) Y − 6

(e) none of these

answers: b, a, c, a

Applications

Students seriously interested in any college should immediately request by mail its application packet. College applications are generally due by the March preceding fall admission, and it is wise to request application materials well in advance. Application packets are provided by colleges without charge, but submission of the completed application usually requires a fee of about $20.00. This fee is the only restriction on the number of applications a student can make. Application to several colleges is advisable.

The college application form asks the candidate to supply information about high-school achievement, extra-curricular activities, including sports, and personal data about family, part-time jobs, and involvement in civic groups. In addition, the application may ask the candidate to list favorite books, magazines, newspapers, and movies. A key consideration in most admissions departments is the overall personality of the candidate apart from his or her scholastic achievement. This is best provided by an application that is completed honestly, thoughtfully, and in detail.

In many cases, the application packet will also provide a form for an essay by the candidate about his or her interest in that particular college. Such essays enable admissions officers to distinguish serious from half-hearted applicants. For that reason, a single essay will not do for all applications; the candidate should instead address each essay to the particular qualities and goals stressed by the college in its catalog.

Finally, application packets usually include recommendation forms to be completed by a candidate's high-school teachers. For as personal and effective a recommendation as possible, candidates should request recommendations as early as possible and discuss them with the teacher in question. Recommendations from other adults are also advantageous, and they may be submitted even if forms for this purpose are not provided by the college. All these materials are placed in a folder labeled with the candidate's name, and all will be taken into consideration by an admissions officer.

In some cases, colleges will request an interview with candidates residing within a specific area. Such interviews are the single most effective way to convey one's personal attributes to an admissions officer, and they should be arranged whenever required or encouraged by an admissions department.

Most colleges will report decisions on applicants in the April preceding fall enrollment. At that time the candidate is either accepted, not accepted, or placed on a waiting list for later decision. Some colleges, however, operate on a system of "rolling admission" in which decisions are made whenever the application is turned in; in such cases it is especially advantageous to submit one's application as early as possible.

A typical application packet

Instructions and information

Application, including personal data and space for an essay

Two recommendation forms to be completed by teachers

Envelope for submission of high-school transcript

Form for enclosure of application fee

Dormitory room application (optional)

Financial aid

Expenses are, of course, a primary consideration in all decisions about college. Tuition and residence costs have been rising rapidly at both private and public colleges. In 1980 the tuition, board, and dormitory rates for full-time resident students averaged $6000 to $7000 per year at private schools and $2500 to $3000 at public ones. Itemized lists of predicted expenses at any college can be found in the catalogs and in the commercial profiles of American colleges. Obviously, the greatest saving can be achieved by attendance at a local school while living at home. Commuting to college can reduce costs by more than half.

There are numerous opportunities for financial aid that can be used to cover the total expenses of enrollment in college. Students should be aware that individual sources of aid can be combined into a package that can substantially reduce costs even if the individual sources of aid are limited. Guidance counselors and college financial aid offices are the primary sources of information on locating and securing sources of financial aid. In recent years, private agencies have been organized to provide, for a fee, research on commonly ignored sources of financial aid for students and parents. Students and parents should also be aware that each year there are potential sources of financial aid that go unclaimed.

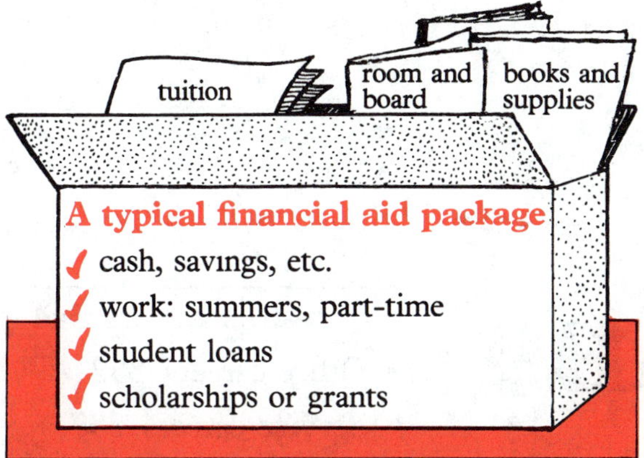

There are four basic types of financial aid. *Scholarships* are awarded on the basis of scholastic achievement. *Grants* are awarded on the basis of financial need. *Loans* require the student or the parents to be responsible for repayment. Finally, assistance of various sorts, including athletic scholarships and student employment, can by arranged by individual colleges.

The most important scholarship programs are operated by the federal government and by individual state governments. Information about these sources can be obtained from the national or state agencies of higher education. High schools usually inform students about the National Merit Scholarship Corporation located in Evanston, Illinois. It awards, on the basis of test scores and financial need, the National Merit Scholarships and the National Achievement Scholarship Program for Outstanding Negro Students. Other sources of scholarships, which must be contacted individually, include prominent corporations, civic groups such as the Rotarians, and veterans' organizations such as the American Legion.

The most accessible grants for college students are distributed by the federal Basic Educational Opportunity program. Commonly called Pell grants, after the program's founder, Senator Claiborne Pell, these grants were awarded on the basis of financial need to some 2.5 million students in 1980. The same program distributes the Supplementary Educational Opportunity Grants to minority students. Applications for either sort of grant can be obtained from guidance counselors or from the program headquarters in Iowa City, Iowa.

Loan programs worth up to $10,000 over four years are operated by the federal government in conjunction with local banks. The primary types are the Guaranteed Student Loan and the National Direct Student Loan. Both are repayable by the student over a ten-year period beginning soon after graduation or withdrawal from college. Interest rates are well below commercial lending rates. Educational loans made to parents rather than to students are usually called Tuition Deferment Plans. These plans generally include terms for repayment over six years at market interest rates. Information can be obtained from local banks.

College financial aid offices offer a variety of assistance programs, and they are especially useful for coordinating packages of financial aid. They offer a variety of scholarships and grants funded by their own resources and by alumni associations. They also offer part-time employment within the college that can be arranged around class time. Applications for financial aid are usually submitted with applications for admission. Financial aid requests are made by completing either the Family Financial Status form or the Family Aid Form. Both forms ask for confidential information on a family's income and financial assets. The forms can be obtained from colleges on request.

A great many college students finance their educations themselves through money earned in summer work. The book you are reading was sold by a college student during his or her summer vacation, and the profit made will go toward that student's college expenses. These students gain much more than money, however. They gain the satisfaction of helping to finance their own education.

Inspection of expected expenses at any college can be a shocking experience for students and their families. It should be remembered, however, that even at the most expensive universities, the majority of students receive some assistance. Most students and families qualify for some aid. This aid, however limited, can often provide a basis for a realistic budget.

For Further Reference

Barre, Mary E.
College Information and Guidance
Houghton-Mifflin

Barron's Profiles of American Colleges
Barron's

Gruber, Gary R.
Preparation for the Scholastic Aptitude Test (SAT)
Contemporary Books

Hawes, Gene R.
Hawes' Comprehensive Guide to College
New American Library

Kohl, Kenneth and Irene
Financing College Education
Harper & Row

Lovejoy's College Guide
Simon & Schuster

The Working World

In any gathering of Americans—at a movie, a picnic, or on a train—you will find dozens of jobs represented. Nearly everyone has a different way of making a living. For most people, the choice was no accident. Successful career choices reflect careful plans. The first step is to see the overall picture, to learn where your job interests fit in the whole world of work. In these pages, you will get that overall view, helping you move closer to a job decision that may last you a lifetime.

Industrial careers

The great appeal of work in industry is seeing the finished product—whether it is a home, a car, a transistor radio, or a book. Every industrial process requires a wide variety of workers—from planners and designers to assemblers and cleanup people.

Architects and *engineers* create models of buildings, airplanes, radios, or chairs of plastic or wood. Then comes the complex process of designing equipment to make the product, obtaining materials, and finally assembling it and finishing it. The largest number of jobs open to beginners is in the assembly phase. Such jobs offer training in fashioning such materials as wood, metals, and plastics. There are many other jobs in maintaining and repairing manufactured products.

Design engineers (left) *and assembly workers* (right) *are both important to aircraft manufacturing.*

Automotive and aircraft work.

Hundreds of thousands of workers in Michigan, California, and Washington state were attracted by offers of ready employment and high wages. The American automobile manufacturing industry is centered in Michigan near Detroit. On the West Coast are manufacturing facilities that turn out most of the world's commercial and military airplanes. When times are good, they are very good indeed in those industries. But when economic hard times set in, thousands are laid off and prospects for new employees dwindle.

During the 1970's, American car makers lost their dominance of worldwide markets. Japan and Germany were able to produce four-cylinder, economical small cars and to undersell the American models. Domestic car sales dropped sharply. On the West Coast, similar reversals were rocking the airframe industry.

The 1980's saw an enormous change in the career outlook for young people who wanted to make their livings in the automobile and airplane manufacturing industries. But the picture is not all gloomy. Detroit has begun to change with the times, and plans to recapture a large share of the world market with its new, small, fuel-efficient cars. Even though fewer workers are employed in manufacturing commercial airliners, military planes and rockets continue to be made in California and Washington, and workers are still employed in those factories.

Careers in the automobile and airplane industries

	Job	*Training*
Design	**Draftsmen**	two years of college; on-the-job training
	Engineers	four or more years of college
	Metallurgists	four or more years of college
	Tool and die makers	six or eight years of apprenticeship
	Molders	on-the-job training
Manufacture	**Punch press operators**	on-the-job training
	Welders	high school and special classes
	Riveters	high school and special classes
	Lift operators	on-the-job training
	Assemblers	on-the-job training
	Polishers	on-the-job training
Maintenance and repair (autos at car dealers and service stations; planes at airports)	**Mechanics**	high school; armed forces or special classes
	Electrical specialists	two years of college; company training course
	Foremen and supervisors	usually, a college degree plus a management training course; long experience as a working mechanic

Two views of an automobile engine

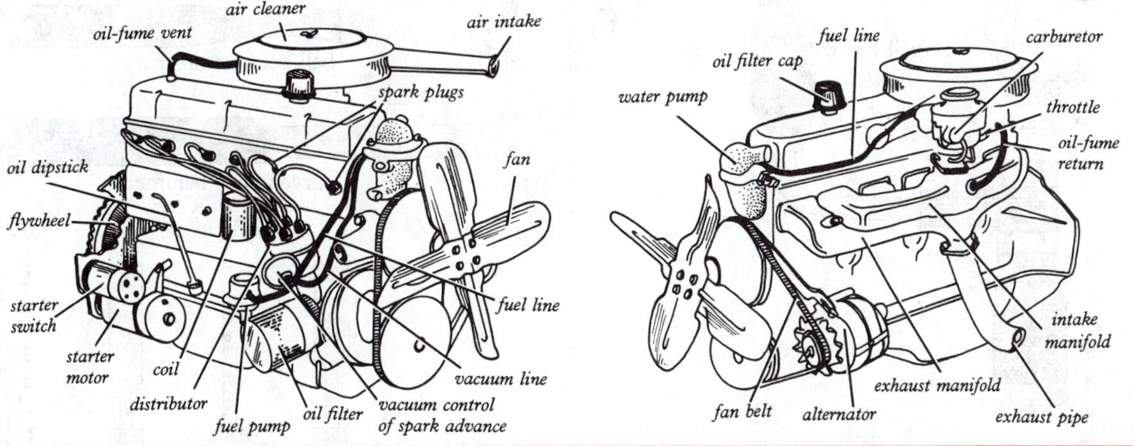

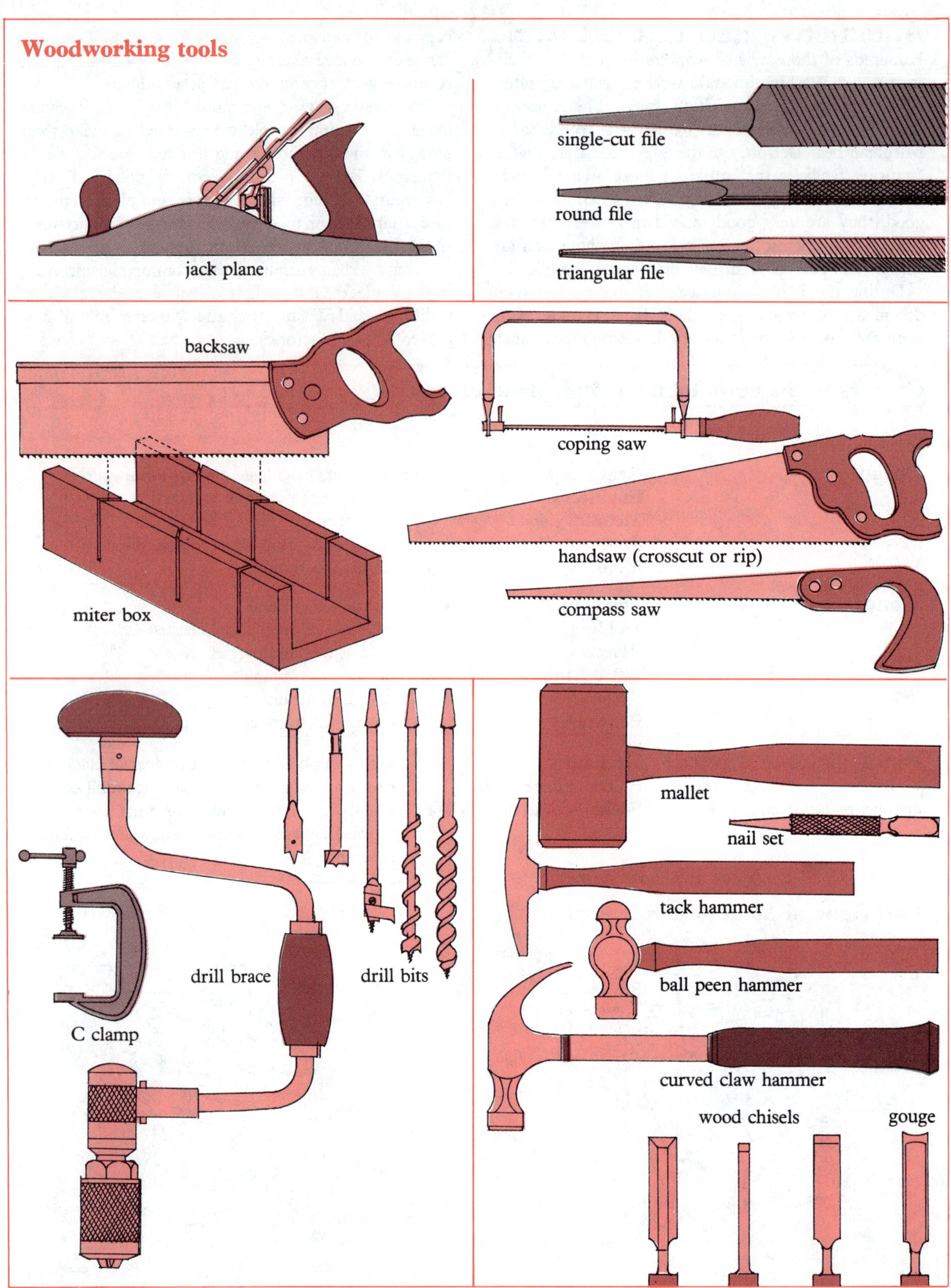
Woodworking tools
jack plane
single-cut file
round file
triangular file
backsaw
coping saw
handsaw (crosscut or rip)
compass saw
miter box
mallet
nail set
tack hammer
ball peen hammer
drill brace
drill bits
C clamp
curved claw hammer
wood chisels
gouge

Woodworking. Carpentry has always been an essential part of our economy, and carpenters will continue to be needed. Because the training period for a first-class craftsman is long and hard, master carpenters are much in demand. One of them is Jason Chadwick, who works in the New York town of Mt. Kisco. Here is what he says about his work.

"Even in the years when housing starts were way down, I've been lucky. I get more jobs than I can handle, maybe because I've been around a long time, and people know me. I was born in Maine, and my father was a ship's cabinetmaker. I grew up using his tools summers and after school, and liked it. I liked it more than college, which I quit after two years. Carpentry was what I wanted to do.

"The hardest thing for an apprentice to learn is *take your time.* I don't mean work slow. But instead, plan it carefully before you start. Know exactly what stud goes on which bottom plate, and where the screwholes are. Get the insulation in solid, before you close up the wall. Or take the time to get concrete footings exactly level, before the beams go on them. All these things that you do at the start of a job pay off, many times over, at the end.

"I like working outside in all seasons. And I like the different kinds of work I get to do. We just finished a big job I got from an architect I know. It was making over an old barn into a big, tightly insulated house. An architect did the plans. I did all the building.

"Before that I built a deck—we used to call them porches—on back of an old colonial house. And before that we lifted the roof of a ranch house, added two dormers, and gave them two new bedrooms."

Mr. Chadwick is an independent contractor, so he must also be a businessman. He must charge enough to pay for a new van every few years, pay his helpers and apprentices, insurance, and many other expenses. He must also put money aside to pay living expenses during bad weather and during slack periods when there is not enough work.

Lumber types, grades, and sizes

Type:	**Softwood** *(pine, redwood, Douglas fir, etc.)*	**Hardwood** *(oak, maple, mahogany, teak, etc.)*
Grade:	Selects Grade A Grade B Grade C Grade D Common boards (less than 2 inches nominal thickness) No. 1 No. 2 No. 3 No. 4 No. 5 Common dimensions (2 inches or more nominal thickness) No. 1 No. 2 No. 3 No. 4	Firsts Seconds Selects No. 1 common No. 2 common Sound wormy No. 3A common No. 3B common

Lumber is measured before it has been planed, so its *nominal* size is always larger than its *actual* size. A 2-by-4, for example, actually measures only $1\frac{1}{2}$ inches thick and $3\frac{1}{2}$ inches wide

Nominal size	*Actual size*	*Nominal size*	*Actual size*
Boards (up to 2 inches nominal thickness)			
1×2	$\frac{3}{4} \times 1\frac{1}{2}$	$1\frac{1}{2} \times 2$	$1\frac{1}{4} \times 1\frac{1}{2}$
1×4	$\frac{3}{4} \times 3\frac{1}{2}$	$1\frac{1}{2} \times 4$	$1\frac{1}{4} \times 3\frac{1}{2}$
1×5	$\frac{3}{4} \times 4\frac{1}{2}$	$1\frac{1}{2} \times 5$	$1\frac{1}{4} \times 4\frac{1}{2}$
1×6	$\frac{3}{4} \times 5\frac{1}{2}$	$1\frac{1}{2} \times 6$	$1\frac{1}{4} \times 5\frac{1}{2}$
1×7	$\frac{3}{4} \times 6\frac{1}{2}$	$1\frac{1}{2} \times 7$	$1\frac{1}{4} \times 6\frac{1}{2}$
1×8	$\frac{3}{4} \times 7\frac{1}{4}$	$1\frac{1}{2} \times 8$	$1\frac{1}{4} \times 7\frac{1}{4}$
1×9	$\frac{3}{4} \times 8\frac{1}{4}$	$1\frac{1}{2} \times 9$	$1\frac{1}{4} \times 8\frac{1}{4}$
1×10	$\frac{3}{4} \times 9\frac{1}{4}$	$1\frac{1}{2} \times 10$	$1\frac{1}{4} \times 9\frac{1}{4}$
1×11	$\frac{3}{4} \times 10\frac{1}{4}$	$1\frac{1}{2} \times 11$	$1\frac{1}{4} \times 10\frac{1}{4}$
1×12	$\frac{3}{4} \times 11\frac{1}{4}$	$1\frac{1}{2} \times 12$	$1\frac{1}{4} \times 11\frac{1}{4}$
Dimensions (2 inches up to 5 inches nominal thickness)			
2×2	$1\frac{1}{2} \times 1\frac{1}{2}$	3×3	
$2 \times 2\frac{1}{2}$	$1\frac{1}{2} \times 2$	3×4	$2\frac{1}{2} \times 2\frac{1}{2}$
2×3	$1\frac{1}{2} \times 2\frac{1}{2}$	3×6	$2\frac{1}{2} \times 3\frac{1}{2}$
2×4	$1\frac{1}{2} \times 3\frac{1}{2}$	3×10	$2\frac{1}{2} \times 5\frac{1}{2}$
2×6	$1\frac{1}{2} \times 5\frac{1}{2}$	3×12	$2\frac{1}{2} \times 9\frac{1}{4}$
2×10	$1\frac{1}{2} \times 9\frac{1}{4}$	4×4	$2\frac{1}{2} \times 11\frac{1}{4}$
2×12	$1\frac{1}{2} \times 11\frac{1}{4}$	4×6	$3\frac{1}{2} \times 3\frac{1}{2}$
$2\frac{1}{2} \times 3$	$2 \times 2\frac{1}{2}$	4×10	$3\frac{1}{2} \times 5\frac{1}{2}$
$2\frac{1}{2} \times 4$	$2 \times 3\frac{1}{2}$	4×12	$3\frac{1}{2} \times 9\frac{1}{4}$
$2\frac{1}{2} \times 6$	$2 \times 5\frac{1}{2}$		$3\frac{1}{2} \times 11\frac{1}{4}$
$2\frac{1}{2} \times 10$	$2 \times 9\frac{1}{4}$		
$2\frac{1}{2} \times 12$	$2 \times 11\frac{1}{4}$		

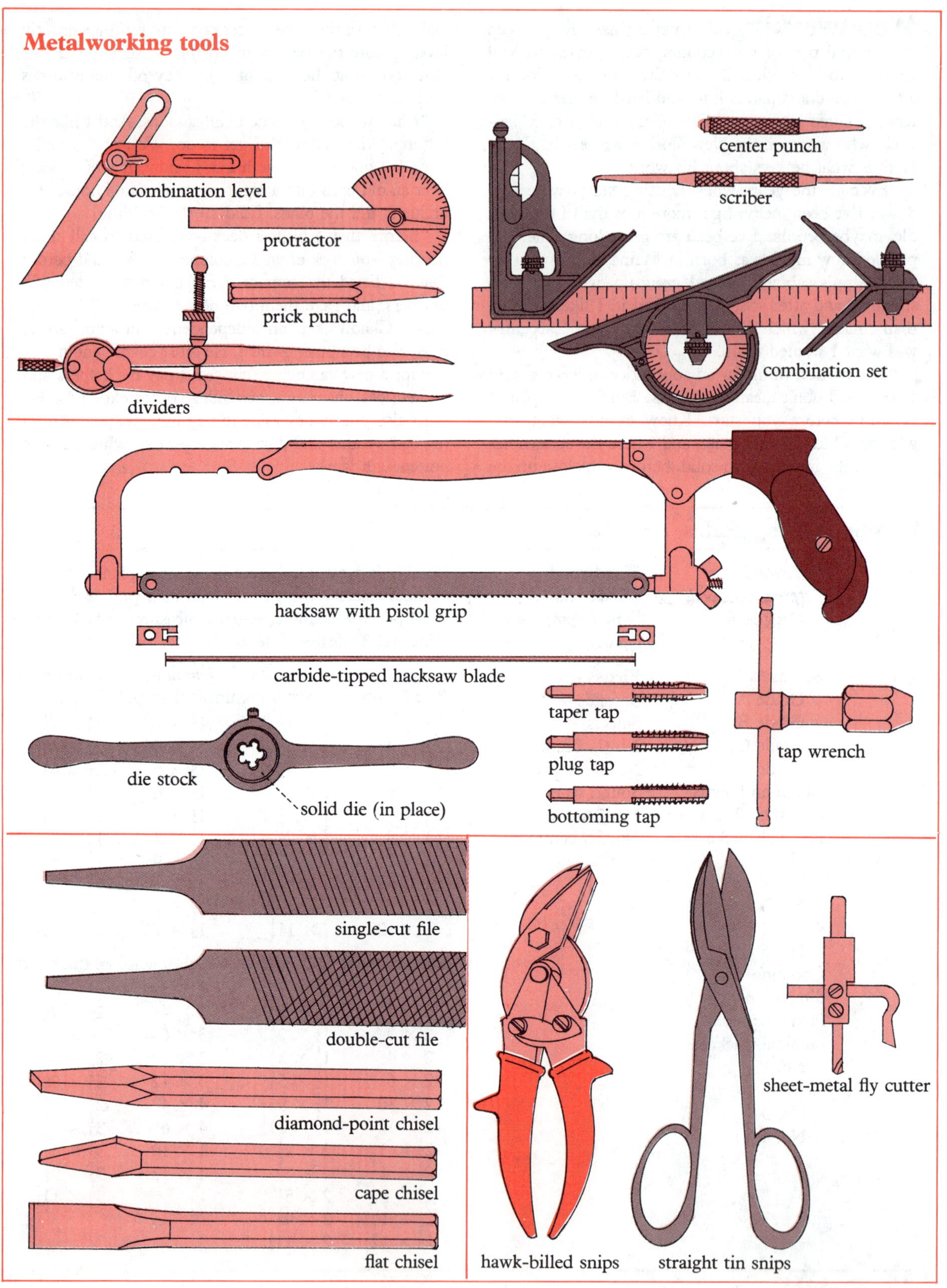
Metalworking tools
combination level
protractor
prick punch
dividers
center punch
scriber
combination set
hacksaw with pistol grip
carbide-tipped hacksaw blade
taper tap
plug tap
bottoming tap
tap wrench
die stock
solid die (in place)
single-cut file
double-cut file
diamond-point chisel
cape chisel
flat chisel
hawk-billed snips
straight tin snips
sheet-metal fly cutter

Metalworking.

Metalworking is essential to modern living. Automobiles, the structural elements of many buildings, pipes for water, ducts for air conditioning, small appliances, and many other products are made primarily from metal. Metalworkers include those employed in industry and in construction and maintenance. Among the second group are plumbers and heating and air-conditioning technicians.

Working with plastics.

Plastics may replace wood, metals, and glass. Carpenters use plastics for windows and insulation; plumbers use plastic pipes, tanks, and joints. Air-conditioning installers use plastic tubing and housings for humidifiers. The processes for plastics are similar to those for wood and metal. But plastics can be shaped by relatively low degrees of heat and joined by chemical bonding.

Working with metals and plastics

Types of metal

cast iron. Hard, strong, easily machined. Too brittle for use in tools. Iron rusts, other metals do not.

wrought iron. Tough, malleable (can be shaped); heated and then hammered into shape.

steel. Carbon is added to iron, then heated to extremely high temperatures. When nickel or chromium is added, it becomes *stainless steel.*

aluminum. Extremely light and soft, an excellent conductor of electricity.

copper. Long-wearing, malleable, perfect for pipes, roofing, and conducting electricity, but very expensive.

lead. Heavy, soft, often used for lining and sheathing wooden construction.

tin. Almost never used in a pure state, it is important in preventing rust, as in the plated coverings over steel in "tin" cans.

zinc. "Galvanized" iron has a coating of corrosion-resistant zinc.

Metal shaping and finishing processes

rolling. Bars of metal are rolled between huge steel cylinders, emerging as sheets of any desired thickness. The sheets can then be cut, stamped, or fabricated.

stamping. Thin sheets of steel or tin or copper are placed on a die; pressure is applied, and the metal is forced into the die's image.

soldering. Wires, pipes, and engine components are permanently joined together by applying heat to the two parts and fusing them together.

grinding. A grinding wheel can smooth metal parts. A cloth *buffing wheel* can give a lustrous polish to a metallic surface.

Using metal in plumbing, heating, air conditioning

cutting. Galvanized iron sheets, usually 1/16th of an inch thick, are formed into ducts (through which heated or cooled air is moved). They are cut easily with a large pair of tin snips. Pipe is cut with a hacksaw, or by using a specialized chain link pipe cutter.

riveting. Ductwork is connected by drilling holes through overlapping edges, placing a screwlike rivet in the hole, and flattening the rivet with a hammer. Self-tapping screws, easier than rivets to apply, are replacing rivets as fasteners.

Plastic shaping processes

planning and marking. Sheets of rigid plastic are sold with protective paper layers glued to both surfaces. All marking, cutting, and drilling is done with the paper still on, to prevent scratching or marring of the surface.

cutting. Thin sheets of plastic are cut with a knife and straightedge. Thicker sheets require the use of a power saw or handsaw. If saw blades are not sharp, the heat may melt or distort the plastic.

sanding. Slow-speed sanders, geared at about 1500 rpm, are used to avoid the danger of overheating the plastic.

buffing. Disks of cotton cloth, used on a portable drill or bench grinder motor, are impregnated with buffing compound. They are used to remove scratches.

drilling and carving. Portable drills can be fitted with a variety of bits and tools for making holes and interior shapes in plastic.

gluing and joining. Surfaces can be joined together by (a) drilling a hole and securing the surfaces with a bolt and nut; (b) fastening two lengths of pipe with a metal hose clamp; (c) heating the two surfaces, fusing them together; (d) gluing and clamping them together tightly.

Electrical work. Watch an electric company lineman as he rides a cherry picker toward the top of a 30-foot pole where twelve heavy wires cross the pole. He selects various tools—cutters, pliers, insulation strippers, screwdrivers—from the heavy belt he is wearing, and takes apart one of the wires.

Where did he gain the skill that gives him all that confidence? From an intensive training course that teaches high-school graduates all they need to know to become skilled technicians.

The students learn how electricity is generated, stored, and transmitted. Utility company linemen repair and maintain transmission systems—above ground wires and transformers and underground cables. At the point where wires enter residences or other buildings, the electric company's responsibility stops. Privately employed electricians and maintenance engineers take over.

The yellow pages of any large city's phone directory list dozens of *electricians* and *electrical contractors.*

The two ads reproduced here cover most of the work that electricians are called on to do. Bob Emery runs his own shop, and charges $25 an hour for calls he makes in his specially outfitted van. He learned the business by going to work for the phone company right after graduating from high school. After eight years, he knew enough and had enough money saved to start his own business.

EMERY ELECTRICIANS
COMPLETE ELECTRIC SERVICE
ELECTRIC HEATING

24 HOUR SERVICE, ANY DAY ANY HOUR

RESIDENTIAL • COMMERCIAL • INDUSTRIAL
FIRE & BURGLAR ALARM SYSTEMS
EMERGENCY GENERATORS INSTALLED

RTE. 166 **244-8686**
NORTHFIELD NITES, SUN., HOLIDAYS 244-1710

ROGERS ELECTRIC CORP.
LICENSED ELECTRICAL CONTRACTORS
244-2000

All Types of Wiring
Complete Installations & Repairs
Residential • Commercial • Industrial

WIRING FOR
AIR CONDITIONING
OUTDOOR LIGHTING
INCREASE 220 VOLT POWER
ATTIC VENTILATORS

142 WILSON AVE.
Northfield

Rogers Electric does the same kind of work, but its customers tend to be commercial establishments. Hank Rogers is an electrical engineer and has a Bachelor of Science (B.S.) degree from the state university.

Careers in electronics

More than 500,000 workers are employed in manufacturing electronic devices such as radios, television equipment, radar, lasers, and diagnostic instruments.

plant jobs. Engineers, scientists, and technicians work on research and development. B.S. or M.S. (Master of Science) degrees in electrical engineering are required, and starting salaries are fairly high.

assemblers. These semi-skilled workers are trained in the plant. No formal education beyond high school is required.

laboratory jobs. Physicists and electrical engineers staff the laboratories maintained by universities, large manufacturing corporations, and government agencies. B.S. and M.S. degrees are required in such specialties as electrochemistry, microscopy, and transistor and laser technology. Laboratory assistants almost always have at least two years of college training, although some lower-paying jobs exist. They require only a high-school diploma and a few years of on-the-job training.

A basic electric wiring system

A three-wire system for a house, with connections to an outside utility pole. The service entrance wires are connected to the meter and then to the panelboard. The diagram gives an example of one branch circuit leading from the panelboard to an outlet, a light switch, and a lighting fixture.

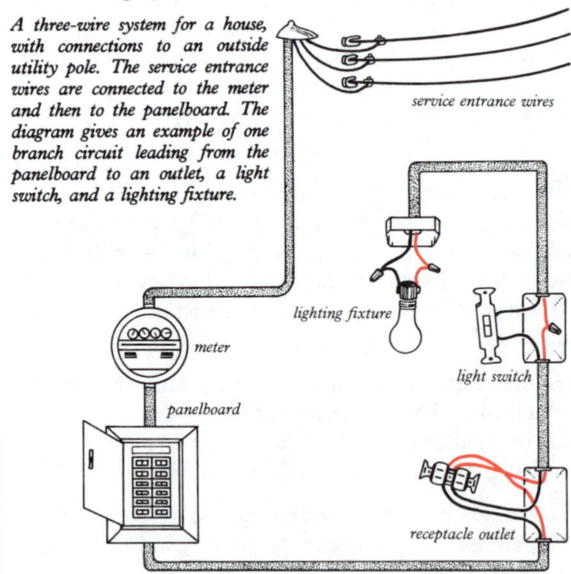

Graphic arts. A growing field that attracts increasing numbers of high-school graduates, the graphic arts industry has much to commend it. New technologies are being introduced, creating new job opportunities. The work is stimulating, with artistic and personal elements that give workers a sense of full involvement. The field attracts intelligent, interesting people, so the interaction among employees can be a source of high job satisfaction.

Newspapers, magazines, food packages, signs, and television commercials are some of the places that we see the results of graphic artists' work. Workers may be employed in advertising agencies, at newspapers, or with magazine or book publishers. Graphic artists may also go into business for themselves.

A stripper checks the film of a book before printing plates are made.

Careers in the graphic arts

Job	*Where employed*	*Salary level*	*Training*
Art director	advertising agency; publisher; television station	high	art courses; experience as pasteup person and artist
Copywriter	advertising agency; publisher	high	college journalism courses; junior writer of sales promotion copy
Agency supervisor	advertising agency	very high	college marketing courses; sales or writing experience
Agency secretary	advertising agency	low	high school; preferably, college; secretarial skills
Typesetter	compositor	medium	high school; preferably, college; heavy on-the-job training; must know how to spell and proofread
Photographer	free lance	very high	high school; special courses; many years as assistant photographer
Photographer's assistant	photo studio	low	high school; special courses
Photostat technician	stat laboratory	medium	high school; on-the-job training
Pasteup artist	advertising agency; publisher	low	high school; preferably, college; on-the-job training (traditional first job for someone breaking into art field)
Stripper	printing house	medium	high school; on-the-job training
Platemaker	printing house	medium	high school; extensive on-the-job training, starting as apprentice
Printer	printing house	high	high school; many years as apprentice pressman (unions are strong, control hiring, keep wages high)

Office careers

In every town, large and small, jobs in offices are widely available. They range from a one-employee reception desk in the waiting room of a dentist's office to a football field-sized array of desks in a governmental department or insurance company.

In general, the work experience needed to perform well at these jobs is minimal. Typing and filing are the main skills required. The starting salary levels are fairly low.

When further education or training is required, the pay scale rises. Office jobs are often stepping stones to positions with higher responsibilities and larger salaries. High-school graduates who are willing to work their way up can begin rewarding careers with minimal office skills, and gain essential experience as they progress upward. They may be able to learn administrative skills or the details of a specific business.

Desk jobs exist in nearly every type of business. Note computer terminal at right.

Office careers

	Job	*Work skills*	*Salary level*	*Training*
Bank	**Teller**	simple math; operate computer terminal	low	high school; brief training course
	Secretary	typing; word processing	low	high school
Real estate	**Phone receptionist**	typing; switchboard	low	high school
	Secretary	typing; word processeng	low	high school
Stock market	**"Back office" clerk**	electronic data processing; filing	medium	high school; on-the-job training course
Publishing	**Editorial assistant**	handle phone inquiries; help obtain facts; typing	medium	B.A. degree
	Secretary	typing; filing	low	high school
Wholesale	**Receptionist**	typing; switchboard	low	high school
	Billing clerk	electronic data processing	medium	high school; on-the-job training courses
Advertising	**Account assistant**	prepare account executive's paperwork; help obtain facts	medium	college marketing or journalism degree
	Secretary	typing; filing	low	high school
Government	**General clerk**	typing; filing	low	high school
Medical or dental office	**Assistant receptionist**	phone answering; simple math; typing	low to medium	high school

Clerical, administrative jobs.

Of the millions of office workers now employed in the United States, by far the greatest number work at clerical or general administrative jobs. Secretaries are included in this wide range of work responsibilities, as are office managers, general assistants, and file clerks.

Traditionally, these jobs serve as an entry place for young people hoping to work their way upward through a company. A general high-school education is often sufficient to get started, although some college is an advantage in some kinds of business. Starting salaries are low.

Ambitious junior clerks and secretaries should keep their eyes open, and notice which areas of the business interest them most. If it is accounting, for example, an evening course in accountancy and finance may eventually lead to a position in the accounting department. Often, the company will pay the tuition fees. Another clerical worker might be interested in the work done by the public relations director. Expertise in word processing and a good grasp of English may bring a job in that department. (*Word processing* is a fairly recent electronic advancement. The processor may be used as a typewriter, but it also stores information, which can be printed out in a variety of typefaces and can be edited to bring old information up to date.)

Among the larger employers of administrative and clerical workers are manufacturing concerns, governmental offices, the medical profession, insurance companies, and public utilities (electric and phone companies). There are also jobs (though not as many) in many specialized fields. A clerical job in the right field may give a young worker a chance to break into a glamour profession (see page 368).

Where to find office jobs

General offices	One of the nation's largest manufacturers of hardware and tools is located in central Connecticut. The office employs 18 file clerks, 24 secretaries and word processors, 12 billing clerks, 3 office boys, 2 receptionists, and 11 administrator/managers. Within five miles of that office is an insurance company that employs a total of 450 people in similar jobs—and a real estate broker's office staffed by one boss and one general assistant. This suggests the wide variety of working situations available.
Personnel offices	File clerks, general assistants, and secretaries are essential to help personnel specialists and administrators run their offices. The higher level people talk to employees, write job descriptions, and interview applicants. The clerical staff sorts out resumes, answers questions, types correspondence, and maintains orderly files.
Education	Offices in schools and universities create mountains of paperwork. Each year, as many as 35,000 applicants try for admission to a single graduate school of business administration. A file of at least ten pieces of paper is created for each of them. Each of the documents must be processed—typed, filed, or entered on a computer.
Institutions and government	Managers, correspondents, word processors, file clerks, and mail clerks are employed in every county in federal and local administrative offices. County clerks' and tax receivers' offices, jails, military installations, courthouses, and elected officials' staff offices are some of the places in which they work. The work is steady, the pay is low, and the opportunities for advancement are predictable. (See also Government services, page 363.)
Arts and specialized careers	When museums, magazines, talent agents, or modeling agencies advertise for staff assistants, they usually specify "typing skills" or "receptionist." Once inside the company, an enterprising young person can learn the ropes and make himself or herself valuable in numerous ways. Even though the applicant may be a college graduate, office skills remain the necessary ticket of admission. This was once true only for women, but today it is true for both men and women. Clerical skills—and willingness to do clerical chores—can be essential.

The computer. The computer has gradually revolutionized office life and procedures. It has also replaced thousands of semiskilled workers who were once required to keep detailed clerical records—of orders, billings, payments, and so on—by hand. On the other hand, the computer has created many new jobs that did not exist before. Among these are jobs for programmers, operators, and word processors. Many general clerical workers are now required to do much of their business at computer terminals. They work at varied functions in fields such as car rentals, airline reservations, accounting and bookkeeping, inventory control, and mail advertising.

What is a computer? A single computer may be small enough to fit comfortably on a desk top or large enough to fill a large room. The same machine may be able to accomplish many different jobs, depending on the *program* it is using at the moment. It may hold all the bookkeeping records for a company; allow financial planners to test out assumptions about future sales and expenses; turn out letters to be sent to customers who have not paid their bills; or help the custodial staff by reminding them to order new supplies.

The computer itself may be self-contained on its desk top, or it may be a large "mainframe" connected to a dozen or more terminals. National companies may have a central computer connected by telephone lines to terminals in each of their offices around the country or around the world. The computer itself and its main accessories—monitors, memory storage units, etc.—are called *hardware.*

In order for a computer to do a job, it must be *programmed.* Skilled programmers are in great demand and may earn exceptionally high salaries. They must know both about the electronic makeup of a particular computer and about the job the owner of the computer wants done. The program may be entered into the machine in various ways:

- it may be hard-wired—technicians may actually convert the programmer's plan into a new set of electrical connections;
- it may be typed into a computer terminal using a computer language the machine is equipped to understand;
- it may be put on a magnetic disc or magnetic tape and "read" into the computer—home video game equipment is programmed in this way. Such programs are called *software.*

Once the computer has been programmed, it is ready to do its assigned job. This generally requires at least one operator, and in some cases there may be hundreds of operators receiving and entering information at separate terminals. Some of the common operators' jobs are listed in the table below.

Careers as a computer operator

Industry	*Job*	*Computer application*
Airline	**Reservation clerk**	Central computer keeps track of all reservations on every flight. Clerk may check flights to assure there is space, enter new reservations, cancel reservations, etc.
Manufacturing	**Inventory control**	Computer keeps track of stock of each item. Control operator may check stock at any time, request production of new stock, keep track of warehouse space available, etc.
	Sales	Same computer as above may keep track of sales, be used to send out invoices, compute balances due, record payments, etc. Sales clerk may enter information or recall existing information for writing reports, determining credit, etc.
General business	**Personnel**	Records of all employees may be entered on computer. Personnel clerk may enter new information, such as salary increase; may also recall information in any order (for example, names in order of hiring date).
	Finance	Finance clerks may keep track of company income and expenditures on computers. The computer may be programmed to calculate tax withholdings and net pay for employees, to keep track of sales and expenses by category, to project income and expenses for the future, etc. Some computers can even print out charts or graphs, expressing information in easy-to-understand form.

Word processing. One of the more recent uses for computers has been in the area of word processing. Often a word processor (or sometimes a secretary) has a desk-top computer programmed for processing words for his or her personal use. This type of computer may be used as a "thinking typewriter." Some of its advantages are:

- *Instant correction.* If a typist has completed a long report on a conventional typewriter and discovers that a sentence was left out of an early paragraph, the report may have to be retyped completely. If, on the other hand, the report has been typed on a word processing machine, the sentence may be added at the appropriate spot. The computer automatically "retypes" the remainder of the report with the lines properly broken and with no additional errors.
- *"Boiler-plate."* Many offices send out hundreds of similar letters in a year. If the word processor has in its memory paragraphs often used in such letters, the operator can assemble particular letters by choosing from these "boiler-plate" paragraphs.
- *Formatting.* The word processor's memory can also hold particular forms (such as an application form or a monthly sales report form). The operator can call the form up on the screen, fill in the blanks, then instruct the processor to print out the finished form.
- *Spelling checks and other special features.* Some word processors are equipped with a whole dictionary in their memories and can be instructed to search a finished letter or report for misspellings. The processor will display each word that it does not have in its dictionary, allowing the operator either to correct it (if the word is really misspelled) or to override the check (if the word is simply a word or word form not in the computer dictionary). Other special features include provision for word counts and line counts, and the ability to substitue one word for another wherever it appears in a letter or report.

There are two kinds of word processors. Some are manufactured only for word processing; these are called "dedicated" machines. Other word processors are simply micro- or desk-top computers using a special word-processing program. These machines may be easily reprogrammed to handle numbers, or even to produce graphs, bar charts, and other graphics.

The diagram on this page shows the parts of a typical microcomputer set up for word processing.

Word-processing system

1. Keyboard: the operator's main means of giving commands and entering data.

2. Monitor: The operator receives information from the computer on this televisionlike screen and sees what she *enters* through the keyboard.

3. Central processing unit: the "brain" of the computer, which directs its functions.

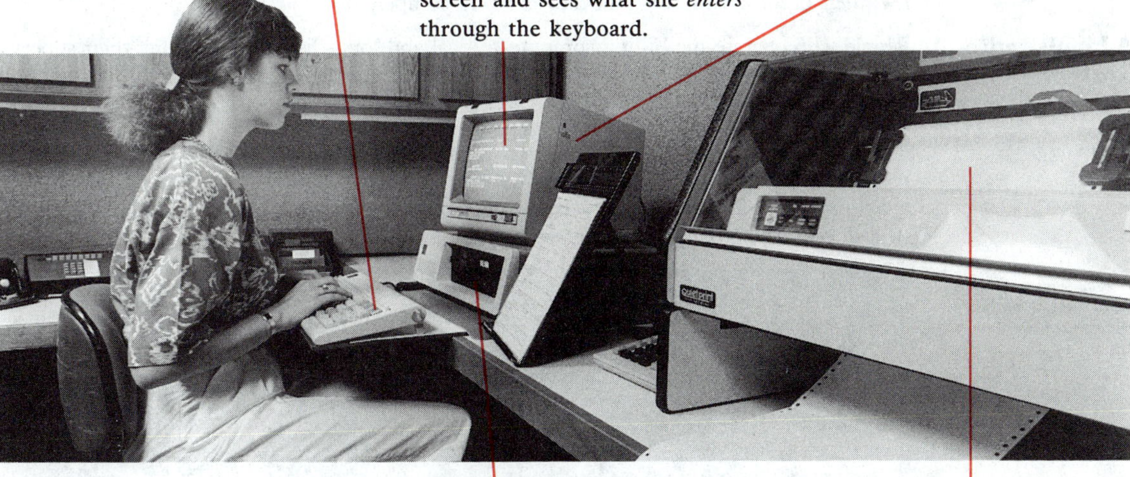

4. Disk drive: Magnetic disks can be used to *enter* a program, preparing the computer to work, or to *store* data—letters, manuscripts, tables, etc.

5. Printer: When data have been entered, checked, and corrected, they can be printed on command at speeds up to several hundred words per minute.

Telephone work. Nearly 100 million of the world's 200 million telephones are in the United States. This huge industry has created a wide variety of jobs that fall into two general categories: jobs outside the telephone companies, and those directly for telephone companies.

Careers in telephone work

Outside

Receptionists Sit near the front doors of offices and factories. When a visitor arrives, they ask who he is there to see, then phone that person and announce the visitor. While the job requires little more than patience and a pleasant personality, it frequently is the first step in a long career.

Switchboard operators Control most of the incoming calls to dozens, or hundreds, of individuals in a company. New transistorized automatic dialing equipment allows most calls to bypass the switchboard and go directly to an individual phone, but there will continue to be a need for an operator of some sort in larger offices for at least the next 20 years or so.

Direct-by-phone salespeople Use a carefully prepared script to give sales talks to customers. They work for a small salary plus a high percentage of the sales they make. If their companies employed outside salespeople and paid their travel expenses and salaries, the companies might pay as much as $50 per sales call. Obviously, it is more economical to employ a well-trained telephone seller and pay him generously for his expertise.

Inside

Equipment manufacturing workers Companies, loosely related to the phone utilities, offer dozens of factory-centered jobs for designers, molders, electricians, assemblers, office workers, drivers, supervisors, and even food handlers. There is a ready market for their products, so the work is steady and secure.

Maintenance workers Responsible for uninterrupted performance of intricate switching equipment. They are highly trained troubleshooters, most of whom have B.S. degrees in electrical engineering.

Repair crews Crews we see in trucks rushing to restore service after a damaging wind or snowstorm. They are highly paid technicians whose jobs require long, hard hours of work and lengthy training; their union guarantees that they are well compensated.

Administrative workers People who operate the billing computers, local and long-distance operators, their supervisors, and the executives who make decisions that affect the company's future. All of them enjoy good salaries, high job security, and better-than-average working conditions.

Sales agents Trained to call on the office managers of local businesses, offer them advice on their communications problems, and persuade them to use more telephone service. Among sales jobs, it is not one in the higher pay range, but sales agents do have the job security and extra benefits that all phone company employees receive.

*Telephone systems require installers (*left*) and communications technicians (*right*).*

Service careers

The fastest growing part of the U.S. economy is the service sector. A decreasing proportion of people are engaged in producing *goods*—food, clothing, all manufactured items—and an increasing proportion, ranging from barbers and beauticians to police and firemen, provide services. The service professions—doctors, lawyers, teachers—also fall within this broad category. The following pages give a sampling of occupations in the service area.

Food service and hospitality.

Changing patterns of life have brought changes to the food service and hotel/motel industries. Since both parents in a family often work full time, families are eating out more than ever before. This creates new opportunities in the prepared food industry. The gradual rise of car travel has created a giant motel industry. The following table describes some of the major job opportunities in these related fields.

Careers in food service and motels

Job	*Responsibilities*	*Training*	*Salary level*
Food processor	prepare vegetables for canning or freezing; in factories, make candy, jelly, soup, etc.	none beyond on-the-job supervision	low, but with union benefits
Baker	mix doughs, supervise baking	experience as an apprentice	medium
Butcher	assembly line work in packing plants; semiskilled work in retail stores	experience as an apprentice	medium
Chef	order raw food, cook it with no mistakes	culinary school after high school; long apprenticeship	medium to high
Assistant chef	prepare raw foods for chef's cooking	none beyond on-the-job supervision	low
Route salesperson	deliver milk, soda, bread, etc., to food stores	driving skill; salesmanship	low to medium
Supermarket manager	supervise stock, cash receipts, store's cleanliness	high-school or college graduate; company training; work as clerk and assistant manager	medium
Fast food chain manager	supervise quality of food and service, personnel, cash receipts	high-school or college graduate; company training; work as clerk or assistant manager	medium
Waitress, waiter	serve food to diners	on-the-job training	low
Dietitian	see that all meals are nutritionally balanced; devise menus for special needs	college degree plus special courses	medium
Motel desk clerk	see that guests are registered, billed properly; maintain order	high-school graduate; on-the-job training	low
Banquet manager	sell hotel's services to people who buy 25 to 300 meals at once	college degree; high level of salesmanship	medium to high
Chambermaid	clean guest rooms, make beds	unskilled	low

Beauty culture. In your grandparents' time, beauty parlors and barber shops were fortresses of strictly preserved femininity or masculinity. Women received their permanent waves or manicures from friendly, gossipy female operators, and exchanged neighborhood news with other patrons. Men had their favorite barber, who knew just how they wanted their hair trimmed, and who treated them to the latest jokes, sports news, and town gossip.

Today those sexual barriers are disappearing. Men and women are customers in the same establishments, and might be served by operators of the same or opposite sexes. There are still many neighborhood establishments that serve men or women exclusively, but even there female barbers and male hairdressers are appearing in increasing numbers.

Hairstyles change constantly. In the 1920's, flappers' shingled or permanently waved hair was the fashion. The 1930's saw movie star Jean Harlow's bleached blond hair widely imitated. In the 1960's versions of Jacqueline Kennedy's bouffant hairdo were seen in shopping centers across the nation. Hairdressers must keep up with changing styles in general and also with their customers' individual needs and tastes, which are certain to vary with age and other factors.

Training and governmental regulations. Because of the obvious hazards to customers' health and safety, and to the operators themselves, all states require cosmetologists and hairdressers to be licensed. A high-school education is required, though tenth grade will suffice in some instances. Further, the candidate must receive at least six months' training in a licensed school. The licensing examination is readily passed by students who have attended the lectures, demonstrations, and practice sessions.

Our federal government carefully regulates the manufacture of hairsprays, dyes, face creams, and all other cosmetics. Even though a product is certified "safe," cosmeticians must be alert against accidental misuse, or problems from a customer's unexpected allergic reaction.

A related consideration is the matter of sanitation and hygiene. State and local inspectors check to see that water and sewage facilities are clean, hair is swept thoroughly away from floors and counters, and combs and towels are sterilized. Yet, to be successful, the operator's attitude toward hygiene must go far beyond licensing requirements. Customers respond quickly to any hint of unsanitary conditions; they take their business to shops in which they feel no threat of disease.

Hairstyles: before and after

Hairstyles can offset irregular or less attractive features. In each pair of sketches, the one at the left is *before.* On the right, a hairstylist has played up the client's good features and minimized the less desirable ones.

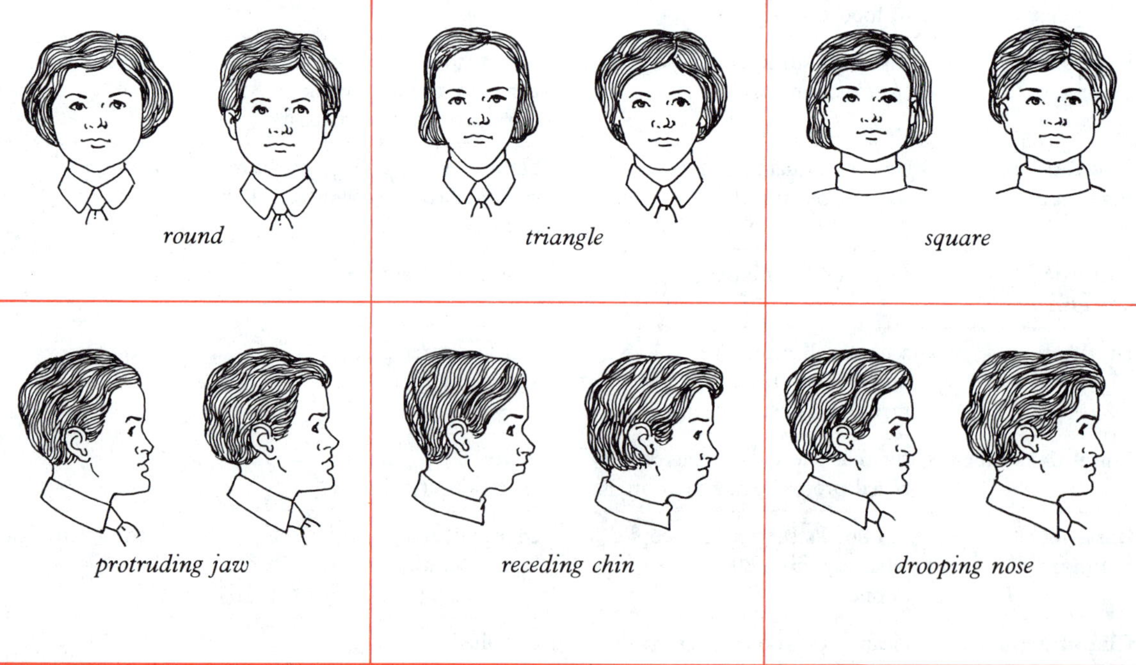

Careers in cosmetology

Education

public vocational schools	department head guidance counselor teacher (cosmetology) substitute teacher
private beauty schools	school owner director supervisor or dean teacher (cosmetology)
outside of beauty culture schools	state board member state board inspector manufacturer's sales staff guest artists

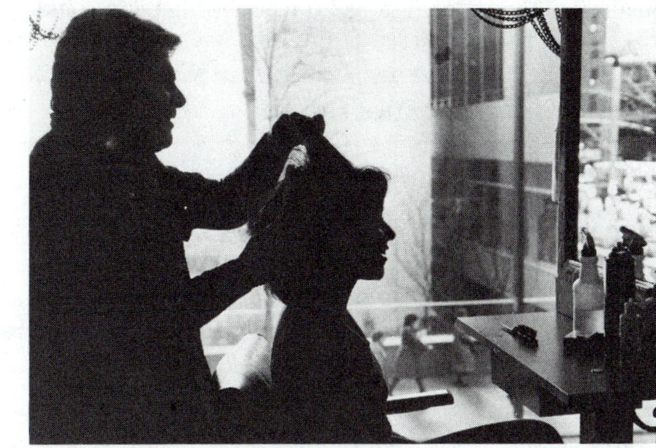

Many hairstylists operate their own businesses.

Salons

salon owner or concessionaire

salon supervisor

permanent wave technician | hairstylist-barber | wig stylist | hair straightening specialist

hair coloring technician | scalp and hair specialist

facial expert | makeup artist | manicurist | receptionist electrolysist

Cosmetics manufacturers' staffs

An increasing number of women are finding gratifying, well-paid careers working for manufacturers of hair, skin, and nail preparations. After graduating from high school, they are sent to company training schools for four to ten weeks. They learn rules of makeup, skin, and hair physiology—and sales techniques.

There are a variety of jobs for these women. *Guest instructors* at schools, clubs, and department stores demonstrate beauty techniques. *Department store salespeople* staff counters leased by major manufacturers of cosmetics. These trained operators receive low salaries but high commissions on all products sold; if the saleswoman is successful, she can earn a high weekly income. *In-home sales agents* ("Avon ladies") are a familiar part of the American scene. They are highly trained professionals who set their own schedules, go out alone, and enjoy feelings of independence. They are compensated with a high percentage of each sales dollar. The better organized salespeople make extremely good livings. Most, however, find the work too difficult, and drop out after a few months' trial.

Men's hairdressing

Once a man is licensed as a barber, he must find work as an apprentice. Barbershop owners pay new men very little—they can get all the apprentices they want—so the tips that young barbers receive from satisfied customers become very important.

After a few years, the shop owner may make a more generous offer. He will be inclined to do so if the new man is personable, well liked by customers, and has added to the shop's growth. At the same time, the young barber may be thinking of opening his own shop. He should be aware that many barbers fail as shop owners. They may not have enough steady customers to follow them to the new location, or they may not be prepared with enough capital for rent, taxes, supplies, advertising, and employees' wages.

Transportation. Moving people and products across the nation and around the world is a major business activity. Even in bad times, getting people and goods from one place to another is a constant activity.

Jobs in the transportation industry tend to be low paying. Exceptions—airline pilots, ship captains, air

Careers in transportation

Air

Management	Passenger airlines and cargo carriers employ specialists whose backgrounds include college degrees and on-the-job training to schedule their flights. Purchasing agents buy vast amounts of printed matter, food, and furniture; they, too, have college degrees, usually in business administration, and several years' on-the-job experience. Large office staffs perform the customary data processing and clerical functions. (See Office careers, page 352.)
Reservation and ticket clerks	A high-school diploma is required, and at least two years of college is preferred for these demanding jobs. Learning how to read complicated schedules and how to write tickets correctly is a difficult task. Dealing with cranky passengers requires patience and tact.
Pilots and flight engineers	Because these jobs require extraordinarily high degrees of concentration, skill, and experience, they pay extremely well. Senior pilots earn more than $75,000 yearly and receive generous job benefits. A strong union protects pilots and engineers from excessive demands and from loss of benefits. Engineering degrees are required, and most pilots have served in the Air Force, where they received thorough flight training.
Stewardesses	A difficult and far from glamorous job, being a stewardess nevertheless attracts thuosands of young women to the airlines' training programs. (Young men are employed as stewards in lesser numbers.) The hours are irregular, and hard physical work leaves stewardesses exhausted at the end of many flights. But being part of an elite, much-admired group with limitless opportunities to travel offsets the difficulties. Pay is in the medium range.
Maintenance and ground personnel	Airlines, both passenger and cargo, employ large staffs of mechanics to keep their planes in peak condition. Every airport is also staffed by tractor operators, fuel and fire engine drivers, baggage handlers, and various other workers. High-school degrees are the basic requirement, but further training is a necessity; the airlines run fully staffed schools where skills are taught to trainees. Pay scales are low for baggage handlers, medium for beginning mechanics, and fairly high for master mechanics.

Motor

Management	The office staffs of bus, auto rental, and trucking companies have duties and pay scales similar to those of airlines. The similarities also hold for reservation and ticket clerks, and for maintenance staffs.
Bus drivers	Two somewhat different job opportunities are open for experienced, mature drivers. The drivers can operate an interstate bus on the open highways or a city bus on crowded streets. Both require patience, alertness, and tact in dealing with the public. No formal education beyond high school is necessary, and the pay is in the low-to-medium range.
Car and truck rental clerks	Three large corporations and dozens of smaller ones maintain truck and car rental offices in cities all across the nation. The business is highly competitive; the efficiency of a company's clerks often makes the difference between success and failure. In spite of their importance, the rental firms' clerks do not command high salaries. Most rental clerks, unless they are promoted to supervisor, do not remain at their jobs for more than a year or two.
Salespeople for trucking lines	Large interstate trucking companies retain sales forces in each city. Salesmen call on manufacturers' traffic managers, and attempt to convince them of their trucks' on-time performance. (See Sales, page 364, for a general description of job duties.) Their compensation is on a commission basis; depending on their skill, they can earn $25,000 to $40,000 yearly.

traffic controllers—do exist, but the general range is on the low side. Workers are highly unionized, so job security and benefits partially make up for lesser wages.

Important job categories in the transportation field are listed in the following table, organized by type of transportation.

Transportation careers include many in the shipment of freight—by air, land, or sea.

Rail

Management	The office staffs of railroads are similar to those of airlines, as are the duties and pay scales of mechanics and maintenance crews.
Engineers	Those who work on interstate railroads are highly trained, experienced people whose pay is high. They have served long apprenticeships, and belong to a powerful, well-organized union. Engineers in cities' rapid transit systems—above ground and subway—have less demanding jobs, and so earn less money. Neither category of engineer requires a college degree, but the on-the-job training is detailed and thorough.
Conductors	Semiskilled workers who receive low pay. However, most like the work they do, and tend to remain at their jobs until retirement. A strong union guarantees them job security and retirement benefits.

Water

Ships' officers and crews	Trucks and planes have replaced ships as the world's principal transport for moving goods; and sophisticated machinery has replaced manpower aboard freighters and passenger liners. Consequently, inland and ocean shipping companies employ far fewer officers and crews than they did two decades ago. The federal government seeks to maintain at least a minimum level of efficient, well-trained sailors. It finances an excellent Merchant Marine Academy, and nearly all ships' officers are graduates of it. A high-school education is required before entrance examinations can be taken; the tests are hard, and admission is restricted to several hundred applicants per year. Pay for new officers is relatively low, but promotions are fairly steady, and at retirement age officers' salaries are in the higher brackets. Seamen, whose duties are hard, belong to a powerful union that has gained them good living conditions and medium-range wages.

Health services. One of the fastest growing industries in the United States is health-related services. New technology and longer life spans have combined to attract many thousands of young people into the field each year.

In addition to the specialized personnel listed here, hospitals, laboratories, and manufacturers employ people trained in various other aspects of health services. Among these careers are:

Drivers of ambulances and trucks.
Salespeople for doctors', dentists', and hospitals' equipment; for pharmaceutical companies.
Office workers and administrators in hospitals and medical and dental offices.
Electricians and mechanics in hospitals, laboratories, and factories.
Food service specialists in hospitals.
Security guards in hospitals.

Careers in health services

	Job	*Training*	*Salary level*
Dentistry	**Assistant**	high school; on-the-job training	low
	Hygienist	two years of college; special courses	medium
	Dentist	B.S.; four years of dental school; additional years for surgery, peridontia, or orthodontia	extremely high
Medicine	**Assistant** (appointments and billing)	high school; typing; on-the-job training	low
	Doctor	B.S.; four years of medical school; additional years for surgery, psychiatry, or obstetrics	extremely high
Nursing	**Licensed practical nurse**	high school; one to two years of training	medium
	Registered nurse	high school; two years of training; B.S. and M.S. degrees to qualify for higher salary	medium to high
Laboratory	**Assistant**	high school; on-the-job training	low
	Technician	B.S.; special courses	medium
	X-ray technician	B.S.; special courses	medium
Veterinary	**Assistant**	high school; on-the-job training	low
	Animal doctor	B.S.; four years of veterinary medicine	medium to high
Hospital staff	**Administrator** (managerial)	B.S.; post-graduate courses in hospital administration	high
	Orderly	on-the-job training	low
	Paramedic	high school; on-the-job training	low
	Social worker	Master's degree	medium
	Physical therapist	B.S.; special courses	medium
	Dietitian	see Food service and hospitality page 357	low

Government services. Governments are the largest service employers in the United States. Between them, municipal, state, and federal governments employ some 16 million people—one out of every six working Americans. Many government workers are office workers, staffing a variety of government offices (see Office careers, page 352). Many others provide a wide range of services—from fire and police protection to elementary school teaching.

On the average, government employees receive somewhat lower salaries than workers doing comparable jobs for private businesses. But they receive many benefits in return. The chief among these is a large degree of job security. Other benefits include generous retirement plans (after 20 years of service regardless of age for many uniformed workers); free training after employment; and good provisions for holidays, vacation, sick leave, and the like.

Careers in government

Police, fire and sanitation forces	Examinations are held annually for admission to these uniformed forces. In most years, particularly during economic downturns, many more men and women apply than are accepted. Studying for a few months at local academies or through mail courses is a decided help. Unions are strong in these fields; racial and sexual discrimination, once quite high, is disappearing in many city and town forces. Benefits are generous and generally are in proportion to the risk of the jobs.
Postal workers	The U.S. Postal Service is a "private" company, but for all practical purposes it is part of the federal government. Appointments are by examination; veterans, handicapped workers, and racial minorities receive preference where scores are equal. Nearly all workers join the powerful union.
Military	In peacetime, the Army, Navy, Air Force, Marines, and Coast Guard offer careers to a total of 2 million men and women. During wars and national emergencies, the total rises to a huge 12 or 15 million. Recruiting goes on constantly. The armed services have a never-ending need for serious young people who are willing to learn quickly and to discipline themselves. Though training is hard and the life sometimes rugged, the rewards can be high. Promotions come at regular intervals, and there are many opportunities to learn marketable skills.
Teachers and librarians	Once among the more poorly paid workers in our society, these professionals now earn decent, middle-class wages. Masters' degrees are standard requirements for starting salaries that range from $10,000 to about $20,000, and that can advance to $35,000 or more. Employment opportunities are greatest in growing communities that attract young families.
Security and correctional forces	Penitentiaries and jails are maintained by federal, state, and county governments. Each institution requires round-the-clock guards and security officers. Other governmental buildings with requirements for trained security officers include courthouses, detention centers for youthful offenders, and educational institutions. The work is sometimes unpleasant; unchanging routines can lead to boredom and physical hazards are always present. For these reasons, security jobs are not as widely sought after as other governmental positions. Those who work at them tend to keep them, however, probably because of the generous retirement benefits.
Park services	Jobs for rangers, forest wardens, and conservation officers are among those that attract the largest numbers of applicants in federal and state examinations. Qualification standards are high, and go higher every year. While some opportunities for high-school graduates remain, successful applicants tend to have college degrees in forest services or biology. As in military service, duties are well defined and continue round the clock, yet furlough time is compensatingly high. People who retire after only 20 years of service may qualify for high-paying second careers with major corporations.

Other career fields

Among careers that do not fit neatly into the preceding categories are those in a wide variety of sales fields, the often attractive field of small independent business, and the well-publicized "glamour" jobs to which so many people aspire, in journalism, the fine arts, and the performing arts.

Sales and marketing. In an industrial society such as that in the United States, millions of workers turn out the goods and services that all of us buy and use. But nothing would happen—nothing would be bought and society would come to a halt—if there weren't an in-between step. Someone has to *sell* something to someone else. The *distribution* of products and services is a necessary part of our economy, in good times and in bad. That is why marketers—salespeople—are among the highest paid members of nearly every community.

The jobs listed here are in direct sales. These are usually easiest to obtain and may lead eventually to administrative positions (sales management) or to positions in marketing. Marketing consists of formulating sales plans and may include making market surveys and evaluating past sales performance. Marketing executives are often college graduates with advanced study in business administration.

Careers in sales

Job	*Description*
Route salesman	This work is the traditional entry path for jobs in the distributive industries. Many routes are busy enough to require a helper for the driver/salesman. Companies run once-a-month training sessions, and require helpers and route salesmen to learn sales promotion, display, and merchandising techniques. Union membership is often a must after the helper has learned the ropes and before he can become a regular driver.
Pharmaceutical "detail" sales	After an intensive training period, detail salespeople are assigned "territories"—whole cities or states. They call on doctors in offices and hospitals, and explain the superiorities of their companies' new drugs. Doctors have very little spare time, so the detailers become skilled at compressing their stories into two- or three-minute presentations. The pay is high; so are the companies' performance requirements.
Direct-in-home sales	Among the attractions of this work are its part-time aspects, four or five hours a day being the norm. Working mothers, students, and partially employed people find this convenient. Companies train new salespeople thoroughly, then put them on their own. Earnings are nearly all "commissions," or a share of sales dollars. For this reason, the range of income is from very low—for inefficient salespeople—to extremely high, for men and women who take the job seriously and work long hours.
Retail sales	Nearly everyone has worked in a retail establishment at one time or another. But not everyone develops the selling skills necessary for success in this competitive field. It does not all "come naturally." Trainees must learn to listen to customers, find out what they are really looking for, answer their objections, and push to close the sale. Merchandising display abilities, knowledge of promotional techniques, and the ability to supervise others are important skills for professional retailers.
Commercial and industrial sales	These jobs range from steady, 9-to-5 positions with travel agencies and phone companies to varied, "road" sales jobs with manufacturing concerns. Salespeople who travel large distances—usually for manufacturers, calling on wholesalers and retailers—are on their own most of the time. They plan their own work week, solve their own sales problems, and are responsible for maintaining an expense account. As they become more and more important to the firms that employ them, they begin to earn impressively high incomes.

Even within one company, sales can range from routine route sales (left) *to commercial sales of major systems or equipment* (right).

Where the work is	*Training*	*Could lead to*
soda bottlers magazine and newspaper publishers bakers food manufacturers	salesmanship possession of driver's license familiarity with city streets merchandising	supervisor sales manager corporation executive
medical laboratories medical equipment manufacturers hospital supply manufacturers	salesmanship basic biology and chemistry	regional sales manager national sales manager corporation executive
cosmetic and soap manufacturers reference book and magazine publishers funeral directors clothing manufacturers insurance companies	salesmanship knowledge of Americans' family habits persistence product knowledge	regional sales manager national sales manager marketing director
banks, airlines department stores supermarkets shops of all kinds: pet, sports, book, antique, food, jewelry, clothing, art, hardware, gas stations	salesmenship product knowledge merchandising simple mathematics	store manager chain store executive shopping center executive independent wholesaler or broker
travel agencies manufacturers of office equipment, cars, planes, paper, building materials, textiles, chemicals employment agencies insurance agencies electric companies	salesmanship telephone techniques product knowledge	bank officer travel agency owner regional sales manager national sales manager marketing manager

Starting a small business. If photography is your hobby, you've probably thought about putting your camera to work. Add sales and merchandising skills to your photographic talent, and you are ready to start. Other small business fields include mail order sales, general and special contracting, retailing, and varied service establishments.

Important advice. Before you have your business cards printed, you would do well to consider the move carefully. Successful small businessmen need more than ordinary self-confidence and ingenuity. At first, income may be irregular, and you are likely to make mistakes. Unless you enjoy fending for yourself and taking chances, you would probably be better off working for someone else. Think about the following six tips. They come from the experiences of thousands of young people who started their own businesses. Some of them were successful and made money, but some had only disappointments. All agree these pointers are important.

The nursery and garden supply business requires skill with plants and training.

Advice for starting a business

1. **Test the market.** Being a lawn doctor might seem ideal if you like working outdoors and have a knack for making things grow. But maybe your neighborhood cannot support a business of that kind. There may be several reasons: too many lawn maintenance firms already operating; not enough high-income families; a deceitful operator from ten years ago is still remembered by homeowners. So ask around. See if people are willing to buy your services *before* you spend money to start a business.

2. **Do only what you know best.** If you are good with dogs, and want to board them and groom them, you will probably be successful at it. But do not be tempted to include training or breeding dogs in your services if you are not familiar with those specialties. You are more than likely to fail when you have less than complete control over your offerings.

3. **Start small, grow later.** Your biggest business asset, at first, is your own ability. Do not dilute it by offering to sell more than you can handle personally. If you are selling homemade bread and cakes, start by selling only the things you bake in your own oven. You can't afford to be responsible for someone else's errors. Later, when you are successful, you can expand by carefully training other bakers. Right now, you don't have the time.

4. **Get all the help you can.** Ask lawyers and accountants about general business practices. Ask salespeople how they do their selling. Watch your competitors; see what they are doing right, and—most important—where they are making mistakes. Write it all down and you've got a *business plan.* Follow that plan as closely as you can.

5. **Watch out for too much of a good thing.** Be suspicious of a friend who can get capital for you at far below the normal interest rate. Look twice at an offer of "below wholesale" paper bags, or a "demonstration model" pickup truck, or "surplus merchandise" you can sell at 300 percent profit. Realize that no one will lose money to help you get started. Expect to pay full value for everything you buy.

6. **All businesses require business skills.** You may intend to make a living doing auto repairs, or taking care of small children while their mothers work. In either case, you have to *sell* your services. You will also be keeping a set of account books, buying the supplies you need, and making sure you get paid on time. Those are business skills that are nearly as important as the main talent you bring to your new career.

Popular fields for small businesses

Photography

Familes pay surprisingly large amounts of money for photo albums of their weddings, anniversaries, and birthday parties. Companies want product shots and annual meetings recorded. Passport photos, real estate shots, and insurance file photos are other specialties. A well-equipped darkroom can bring in additional dollars from fellow photographers who will buy meticulous, trouble-free film processing.

Lawn and tree care

Fertilizing, mowing, and raking lawns are the most common services offered in this kind of business. Equipment is inexpensive, but a truck is needed. Tree care requires chain saws and a power sprayer. It pays to work for an established operator for a year or so to learn how to diagnose and treat various plant problems. Winter months are a good time to plan advertising and sales campaigns, necessities in this competitive business.

Mail order

Craftsmen who can produce their own jewelry, pottery, candies, or furniture can build profitable mail-order businesses. Others who have a flair for advertising might consider putting together a catalog and mailing it to 1000 names. A common problem is profit. Products must be purchased cheaply enough to afford a profit after catalog preparation and postage and mailing expenses are paid.

Moving and messenger services

A van or pickup truck can be the means for a small, spare-time business. Phone book ads and postcard mailings will bring in home moving and commercial delivery jobs. A strong-backed assistant usually can be found among local high-school or college students. In larger cities, office buildings are sources of steady customers for messenger services.

Specialty foods

Talent for cooking and baking is exceptionally well suited to profitable small businesses. Ethnic specialties—Italian, Greek, Mexican, and Japanese are a few—help a beginning business stand out from its competition, and help build a local reputation. Weddings and parties often require outside cooking services; sometimes dishes and tables and chairs must be provided, but those larger jobs should be turned aside until you are established. To begin, orders for homemade foods and cakes can be placed through delicatessens and food markets. Food can be sold from a cart or van outside factories and office buildings.

Music

Trios, combos, and groups are in demand for parties in homes, offices, churches, clubs, and schools. The leader, who makes booking arrangements, usually is asked to play a cassette recording of his group's performance when selling his services to a client. Advertising is important, yet more jobs are sold through word-of-mouth recommendations from satisfied clients. A trend in recent years toward chamber duos, trios, and quartets continues to provide part-time income for amateur violinists and flutists.

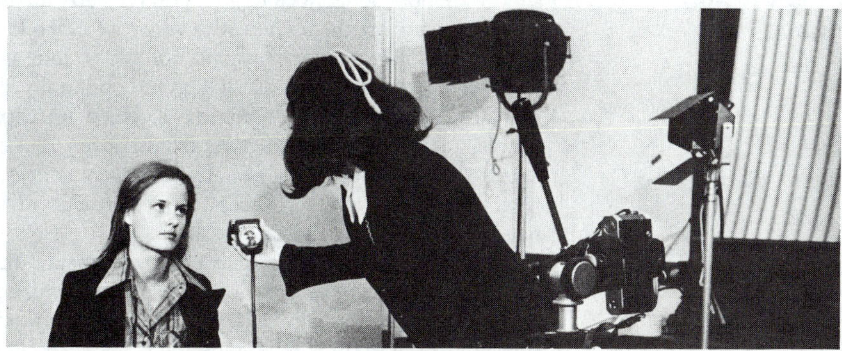

Studio or location photography can offer good business possibilities for a skilled and enterprising person.

"Glamour" jobs.

Workers in the arts and entertainment fields are somehow thought to lead lives more glamorous than the rest of us. To some extent, they do. Their work is often stimulating and well paid, and they are the focus of more than ordinary attention.

Yet it *is* work. "Glamour" jobs are among the most competitive in the market, and dozens fail at them for every one who succeeds. They require long apprenticeships, attention to detail, and absorbing dedication. The rewards can be high—but the work and the pressure can be extremely demanding.

Musical performance is an exceptionally competitive glamour field.

Careers in glamour professions

Music

People in the world of music fall into two categories—those who compose and perform the melodies, and those who bring them to us.

Composers

Writing classical music is an extremely limited field. Demand for the music is small, and the training it requires is long and costly. Writing popular songs is much easier; though many more amateurs try it than can possibly succeed, the rewards sometimes are remarkable.

Musicians

The best country and jazz musicians were playing their instruments all through their high-school years. They perfected their technique, then went to the big cities after graduation. They mingled with nightclub and recording professionals, kept learning, and eventually got opportunities to work. Belonging to the musicians' union is necessary, as is an ability to bounce back after disappointments.

Classical musicians require years of college and specialized training. Their employment opportunities are severely limited. Anyone considering the field should discuss it thoroughly with high-school or college music instructors.

Recording technicians, agents, publishers

Composers and musicians have *agents* who line up work for them. The agents' fees usually are 15 percent of the money their clients earn. Agents know "everybody" in the business, and never rest. Working for an established agent, then later striking out on your own, is the only way to break in.

Sound engineers and recording technicians

These are specialists who are familiar with electric circuitry, sound patterns, and acoustic waves. They learned their trades by taking apart radios and hi-fi equipment, and in vocational schools, night schools, or mail order courses. They usually have easy-going personalities that allow them to adapt to performers' quirks.

Movies, television, theater, and dance

The performing arts attract thousands of young, talented performers each year. However, few of them make it to the top, or even make the barest living at it. There simply are not enough jobs to go around. Nearly all aspiring actors and dancers find they must support themselves with other work while trying to break through.

The steps necessary for progress follow. 1. Join an amateur group, appear in as many productions as possible. Church, community, high-school, and college productions all add important credits. 2. Keep up contacts with a wide variety of people. Job tips most often come from friends. 3. Register with a reputable talent agent. 4. Keep a portfolio of photos and press notices, and have a clear, uncluttered résumé. Ask several older, successful performers' advice. 5. Read all the trade journals and professional magazines.

An active, exciting part of every performance takes place behind the scenes. *Lighting, costume, set design, writing* and *directing* specialists all are needed to make the production come alive. Here, too, the supply of young hopefuls exceeds the capacity of the theaters to employ them.

Broadcasting careers include both technical and on-the-air positions.

Illustrators may produce work for advertising, children's books, or for film and television.

Journalism

Newspapers, radio, and television newsrooms require writers and broadcast reporters. While the number of employers remains level, job opportunities are created when reporters move on to other positions. Reporters in the top ranks of television newscasting make huge salaries: $100,000 to $1 million yearly. But for every one of those super earners, there are dozens at the $25,000 range.

A bachelor of arts degree in journalism is practically a necessity when applying for a first job as a reporter or caption writer. But beyond that, professionals all agree that practice—on high-school, college, and local papers—is an essential ingredient for success. Filling page after page, and submitting those pages to editors, is the proven way to become a writer.

Painting and crafts

The plastic arts are probably the hardest to convert to a livelihood. Every community has its share of painters, sculptors, weavers, potters, leatherworkers, and other craftsmen. Most would like to sell their creations, but only a handful are lucky enough to make substantial amounts of money. Artists who study illustration or graphic design can find work in advertising agencies, on publications, and in television studios. These jobs pay well, and there are opportunities in nearly every city. Most artists and craftspeople come to accept that they will not be able to support themselves through their talent. Yet they continue to exhibit and sell an occasional piece. A few eventually support themselves.

Sports

High-school athletes sometimes go on to win college scholarships. When they do, they have cashed in on the training, practice, and skill they have worked so hard to develop. Athletes may hope for playing careers as professionals in tennis, golf, baseball, football, and basketball. Yet most athletes, by the time they have gone through four years of college playing, realize they lack the talent. Many find satisfying careers as teachers or continue to be involved with sports—but only a very few will be top-ranking professionals.

Modeling

Modeling is a natural profession for photogenic young men and women. Careers usually begin during high-school years, with the model posing for retail store ads that appear in local papers.

A full portfolio of professional photos, either paid for by the model herself or compiled from clippings from newspapers and magazines, is a necessity. Full-time professionals move to New York, Chicago, or Los Angeles, where the national business is centered. They make the rounds of agencies, and—if they're lucky—are called for shooting sessions. Each session may last for as little as an hour, or as much as eight hours. The pay can be $200 or more an hour.

The work is hard, and getting work is even harder. Many more models are trying to break into the business than it can ever absorb. Models seem to know this, and work at other, easier-to-find jobs while making the rounds of the agencies.

How to get a job

When you have decided what kind of career path you would like to follow, there are two important steps along the way. One is to get in touch with the people who might hire you; the second is to "package" yourself attractively for their attention.

Organize a job search. The first task is to locate a job opening. These four steps should set you on your way.

Read the ads. Look in your local paper to see if anyone is in the market for your services. If your career is in the arts or encompasses a specialized skill, go to the library. Read New York, San Francisco, Atlanta and other big-city newspaper want ads. Be sure to read the classified ads in specialized magazines, trade papers, and newsletters—they are often the best sources of leads.

Register with employment agencies. Private agencies charge a fee that is usually paid by the employer. States regulate agencies' conduct; do not pay more than the approved rate, and never pay in advance. Walk away from any agency that has a "registration fee" or "enrollment charge" of any kind.

State and federal employment offices charge no fees, but they are understaffed and overcrowded. High school and college placement centers may be of some help.

Mail out résumés. Get a list of likely employers from a directory in the library. Tell the librarian what you are looking for. She will know which book has the right data.

Address each envelope by name, not title. Enclose a résumé and a brief one- or two-sentence covering note. Do not send your letters to personnel directors. Instead, use the name of an executive in charge of the actual work you will be doing.

Circulate and get known. This is the hardest, but most important, part of a job search. Most jobs are found through word of mouth, or recommendations from insiders. Get to know some insiders, and you are ahead of your competitors.

How do you crack the inner circle? By being a little pushy, a little aggressive. Attend meetings, join associations, write to people whose names you read in trade magazines. Ask to meet with them for ten minutes. Tell them you want to break into the business, and would appreciate their help. When you do meet, use those ten minutes wisely. Don't let that important person say "What a nice kid. But so shy." People want to help someone they respect, someone who seems aggressive enough to get things done in a competitive world.

The interview is your chance to make a good personal impression. Employers look for signs of honesty, good sense, and reliability, and are as interested in how you present yourself as in what you say.

Come across as a strong person, one who is convinced of his own abilities. (Read the six bosses' opinions on page 372, and be guided by them.) Be sure to have a copy of your résumé with you to leave with the person with whom you are meeting. Also, ask if there is anyone else in your field who would talk to you. Get all the names and addresses you can from everyone you see.

Package yourself attractively.

The "package" that prospective employers see at first, days before they have a chance to see you in person, is your résumé. Your whole job-finding process can fail before it begins if the package is unappealing or lacks the necessary information.

A sample résumé. Look at Karen Howard's résumé and see if you know what is wrong with each of the lettered portions.

- **A.** No need to say "Résumé of." It is evident this is Karen's résumé.
- **B.** Address and phone number should go up at the top, under Karen's name. If the employer wants to reach her, he wants the data right near her name.
- **C.** Don't date the résumé. Six months from now, Karen may still be looking for a job. She shouldn't tip off prospective employers that she hasn't connected in all that time.
- **D.** Do not include any career goal. Karen is pinning herself down too tightly. A boss may be looking for a general assistant, or law librarian, or administrative aide. Why should Karen disqualify herself from those opportunities?

Résumé "before"

A Résumé of Karen Howard C May 15, 1983
D Career Goal: Paralegal Aide
F Education: Graduate, 1980, James Madison H.S., Oakville PA.
Certificate, Law & Justice School, Milton
Community College, Milton PA. 1982.
Work Experience:

G	June 77 – Dec 78	Cashier, First National Store, Milton PA. Worked at Checkout Counter, adding up **H** Customers' purchase's, using **E** Electronic Register.
	Jan 79 – Feb 80 **I**	Counter girl, Burger King, Milton PA. Took orders, delivered Hamburgers and Beverages to Customer's. Promoted to shift Chief. Left to work in Law Office.
J	Summers 76 81 82	Lifeguard at Town Pool, Milton PA. Passed Red Cross Junior Lifesaver Test, high marks, when only 13 year's old. Was employed by Town Clerk for Summer work.
K	Mar 80 – current	Clerk and Junior Aide, Law Offices of Delehanty, Rourke & Shapiro, Milton PA.
L	References:	Peter Crowther, Pastor, Milton First Methodist Ch. Dr. Armand Fiore MD, Family Doctor Jane Fulton, Director, Milton Recreation Dept.
M	Hobbies:	Swimming, Reading, Bicycle Touring.
B	Address:	108 Narrows Road Oakville PA 11706 Phone (123) 456-7890

Résumé "after"

Karen Howard

108 Narrows Road
Oakville PA 11706
Phone (123) 456-7890

1980 – current	Clerk and junior aide, law offices of Delehanty, Rourke & Shapiro, Milton PA. Assist legal associates and partners in research, prepare data for briefs. Work with legal secretaries in photocopying and typing.
1979 – 1980	Shift chief, Burger King, Milton PA. Supervised work of six counter girls, responsible for prompt service and correct cash register totals. Worked up from trainee. Store manager said, "Karen is one of quickest learners I ever had. Wish there were ten more like her."
Education	Certificate, Law & Justice School, Milton Community College, Milton PA. June, '82. Graduate, James Madison H.S., Oakville PA, June, '80.
References	Howard Stein, Dean, Law & Justice School, Milton Community College, (123) 666-6060. Reardon Delehanty, managing partner, Delehanty, Rourke & Shapiro, 418 Center Street, Milton PA 11777. (123) 666-5000.

E. Throughout the page, Karen uses capital letters—Goal, Aide, Checkout, Counter, Electronic—when small letters are correct. Only proper nouns should be capitalized.

F. Karen's education is less important to the employer than her work experience. The order should be reversed. Within both categories, items should be listed in reverse order: latest date comes first, then the one that occurred before that, and so forth.

G. Omit the months from work chronologies. Employers are only interested in years—the big picture. Karen should omit that whole First National entry. It doesn't mean anything; her Burger King work can be more impressive, and it sufficiently covers the retail field.

H. Karen has been infected with apostrophe-itis, an epidemic among young people. None belongs in the words *purchases*, *customers* (in the Burger King entry), *years*.

I. Karen's promotion to shift chief should be highlighted. No need to tell that she "took orders, delivered hamburgers and beverages to customers." She should begin with a shift chief's responsibilities, tell how many counter clerks she supervised.

J. No. Entirely wrong. No employer cares what Karen did during her summer vacation, or how old she was when she became a junior lifesaver.

K. This is the most important part of the résumé—and Karen has buried it down near the bottom. She should build it up, tell more about the work she does for Delehanty, Rourke. And she should kill the capital letters in junior aide.

L. References are fine on a résumé, if they are appropriate. Two-thirds of these are inappropriate. No employer wants to waste time calling an applicant's pastor or doctor; what will he learn from them? Jane Fulton is okay, but her address and phone number should be included.

M. Listing hobbies downgrades the seriousness of an applicant's purpose, and may seem to minimize her real accomplishments.

Now look at Karen's résumé as it looks after revision. It is shorter, but contains more relevant information. Job applicants just out of school would rarely have a résumé much longer than this one. Avoid the temptation to "pad" a résumé. A good résumé is brief and to the point.

Typical comments from employers

1. **A personnel manager.** "I see a lot of job applicants, and they all hand me a résumé. If I can't get the information off it in a hurry, I just don't bother. If the résumé is sloppy, or filled with unimportant details, I figure it reflects the person who wrote it. If they can't get this first step right, I don't want to trust them with any other steps."

2. **A plant manager.** "The guy who gives me straight, direct answers to my questions is the guy I hire. We have no time to fool around here in the plant. So I appreciate anyone who comes right out with a no-nonsense answer. Another thing. If he seems human, doesn't blow himself up—and maybe has a little humor in what he says—I appreciate that, too. We're looking for people we want to work with year in and year out."

3. **An art director.** "So many kids come in here with the wrong kind of portfolio. It is a showing of all the scraps they've done in their whole lifetime. Seems like it starts with the kindergarten drawing their mother taped to the refrigerator door. What I want to see is a handful of their best stuff. Layouts of imaginary ads, if they have no actual ones. But every piece should be the kind of *work* we turn out here. It should reflect business sense. I imagine that's true for anyone who's looking for a job. He only has one crack at the interviewer. He better use it to show two or three realistic pieces—not a whole mess of junk."

4. **A store manager.** "When we talk to new salespeople here, we see what kinds of questions they ask. If they don't understand the job, how can they do it right? And if they're too shy to ask, what will happen when they run into a hard-nosed customer? Maybe I'm wrong, but I think the questions an applicant asks are the most important part of an interview. The smartest kids are the ones who plan a couple of good questions before they come in here. I go for that."

5. **An office manager.** "I've seen a lot of young people come in here. And if they don't work out, I remember an interesting thing about them. Often, on their interviews, they had very little idea of what the pay scale was. Or exactly what the job involved. Of course, I told them, but their own ideas were unrealistic. So over the years I've learned to be suspicious of an applicant who hasn't bothered to learn the facts. He ought to take the time to find out just a few things before he shows up. I tend to steer clear of those muddle-headed kids nowadays."

6. **A foreman.** "At the end of the second interview, there's a point where the talk gets serious. What the pay is, and when we want you to start. If I hear a stall, or he isn't ready to start, that's it. Sure, he ought to consider his options. But when I offer him a job that starts in two weeks, I'm serious. If he can't make up his mind to take it, I'm sorry. I'll find someone else who can."

The interview. The next step is to interview for the job. There is no reason to be frightened of the interview, but there is good reason to think it through ahead of time and make some preparations:

- Dress neatly, but don't be flashy.
- Get a good night's sleep so that you'll feel fresh and alert.
- Think about the questions the interviewer will ask and about what your answers will be.
- Put down questions you may want to ask—about the job's responsibilities, hours, pay, etc.

What counts most in an interview is the impression you make on the person who is doing the hiring. If you have made him turn to an associate after the interview and say, "That's the one I've got to hire," you've connected. Listed above are six typical bosses and their views on what makes them sit up and take notice.

For Further Reference

Fredrickson, Ronald H.
Career Information
Prentice-Hall

Hawes, Gene
Careers Today: A Guide to Good Jobs Without a Degree
Taplinger
Occupational Opportunities for Everywoman
Sterling

Sinick, Daniel
Occupational Information and Guidance
Houghton-Mifflin

Wright, John W.
The American Almanac of Jobs and Salaries
Avon

Index

How to use the index. The INDEX to the *Student Handbook* is arranged alphabetically according to a letter-by-letter system. All entries, regardless of punctuation or spaces between words, are in precise alphabetical order; there are no exceptions:

Marshall Islands
Marshall, John
Marshall Plan
Mars (planet)

Names beginning with Mac or Mc are also arranged in strict alphabetical order. The abbreviation St. is indexed as if it were spelled out as Saint.

Each entry ends with a period. Following the period is the number **1** or **2** followed by a colon. These boldfaced numbers indicate the volume in which each page can be found. The page number follows the colon. A semicolon separates the volumes, when applicable:

Lincoln, Abraham. 1: 93, 95; **2:** 33, 85, 92–93

Most main entries are indexed under the main element of the name, e.g., Sinai, Mount (not Mount Sinai); Marathon, Battle of (not Battle of Marathon); Verdun, Treaty of (not Treaty of Verdun). Handy cross-references are provided when a listing may be ambiguous or confusing.

Few abbreviations are used in the index, and those that are used are so standard as to eliminate the need for an abbreviations list.

Books, plays, and other titles are not indexed, but authors, artists, composers, etc., are, and the great works will almost invariably be found on the pages listed under their creators' names. Anonymous works (e.g., *Beowulf*) have their own listings.

A

B

C

D

E

F

G

H

J

M

N

O

P

Q

R

S

T

U

V

W

X

Y

Z

SECOND CONCISE EDITION

WEBSTER'S NEW WORLD DICTIONARY

SECOND CONCISE EDITION

WEBSTER'S NEW WORLD DICTIONARY

David B. Guralnik, GENERAL EDITOR

SIMON AND SCHUSTER

WEBSTER'S NEW WORLD DICTIONARY, Second Concise Edition

This book is based upon and includes material from WEBSTER'S NEW WORLD DICTIONARY, Second College Edition, copyright © 1970, 1972, 1974, 1976, 1978, 1979, 1980, 1982 by Simon & Schuster, a Division of Gulf & Western Corporation.

Published by New World Dictionaries/Simon and Schuster
A Simon & Schuster Division of Gulf & Western Corporation
Simon & Schuster Building
Rockefeller Center
1230 Avenue of the Americas
New York, New York 10020

Manufactured in the United States of America

3 5 7 9 10 8 6 4

LIBRARY OF CONGRESS CATALOG CARD NO.: 81-85761
Webster's New World Dictionary.

New York: Simon & Schuster
882 p. Concise ed.
8201 811119

ISBN 0-671-41816-5 plain edged
ISBN 0-671-41817-3 indexed

Previous editions of this book were published by The World Publishing Company, William Collins +World Publishing Co., Inc. and William Collins Publishers, Inc.

PRINTED IN THE UNITED STATES OF AMERICA

CONTENTS

EDITORIAL STAFF

Editor in Chief	David B. Guralnik
Managing Editor	Samuel Solomon
Associate Editors	Clark C. Livensparger *(Supervising),* Thomas Layman, Andrew N. Sparks, Christopher T. Hoolihan, Paul B. Murry, Ruth Kimball Kent
Assistant Editors	Eleanor Rickey Stevens, Jonathan L. Goldman, Roslyn Block, Lois Engintunca, Thomas V. Sullivan
Office Assistants	Virginia C. Becker, Dorothy H. Benedict, Cynthia Sadonick, Joan McDaniel, Sharon Preisler, Gertrude Tullar
Chief Proofreader	Shirley M. Miller
Illustrator	Anita S. Rogoff

FOREWORD

The *Second Concise Edition* of WEBSTER'S NEW WORLD DICTIONARY is still another addition to the family of word reference books that have been serving America's dictionary needs for over two decades. It has been prepared by the same permanent lexicographical staff that brought out the highly acclaimed *Second College Edition*, using the same data base compiled for that work. The success of the earlier *Concise Edition*, first published in 1956, has made it clear that there are many professional and business people, secondary-school students, office workers, word-game addicts, learners of English as a second language, and others who want a comprehensive and up-to-date dictionary, but who have less need for the extensive etymologies, highly technical or arcane terms, rare meanings, and certain other features found in the *Second College Edition*. For such persons, the *Second Concise Edition* should prove highly serviceable.

The word stock of this edition, over 105,000 vocabulary entries, was selected on the basis of frequency of occurrence in general publications and books of general interest. It is of primary importance that a contemporary dictionary make every effort to incorporate the burgeoning vocabulary that reflects our rapidly expanding technology and the changes that are taking place in our life styles. That very term *life style* typifies the kind of coinage that the lexicographer must be constantly on the alert to identify and to incorporate in the ongoing record of language usage that we term a dictionary. In selecting for inclusion in this *Second Concise Edition* items from our vast citation file, we have been careful to cull only those terms that have acquired a stability of form and meaning and that show some promise of surviving in the language, at least for a time. We have equally sought to avoid expending space on the merely faddish or ephemeral terms that appear suddenly and then die within a year or two.

Obsolete and archaic terms and senses that are frequently found in the Bible or in standard works of literature have been included. Also, such technical terms and meanings of specialized fields as are encountered in general writings have been entered, usually prefaced by a field label. The abbreviations for these various labels will be found in the List of Abbreviations immediately preceding the first page of the vocabulary. With the aid of the United States Trademark Association, every effort has been made to establish the status of terms suspected of being trademarks and to properly label those so identified.

A great many prefixes, suffixes, and combining forms have been entered, and these will enable the user of this dictionary to determine the meanings of thousands of additional words that are themselves too specialized for entry in a work of this scope. In the interest of conserving space, many words derived from main words, such as nouns ending in *-tion*, *-er*, or *-ness*, adjectives ending in *-like* or *-less*, and adverbs ending in *-ly* have been run in at the end of the entry for the base word. Such run-ins are syllabified and, where necessary, pronounced, and irregular inflected forms, if any, are shown. The meaning of any such run-in can easily be determined from the meanings of the base word and the suffix. Any derivative that has an important meaning not readily inferred from its separate parts is entered separately and defined.

Among the words whose spelling offers difficulty to many people are the principal parts of so-called irregular verbs, plurals that are formed in some way other than by adding *-s* or *-es*, and comparisons of adjectives that may or may not double the consonant before adding *-er* and *-est*. Rather than leave these forms to guesswork or to reliance on a number of rules to which many exceptions exist, we have shown them in full or in shortened form immediately after the appropriate part-of-speech label.

As a convenience to the user of this dictionary, all vocabulary entries, including proper names as of persons and places, abbreviations, affixes, and unnaturalized foreign terms frequently met up with in English contexts, have been entered in one alphabetical listing. There is no need to rummage among a number of appendixes in order to find lexical information of any sort. The pages following the dictionary proper have been restricted to useful nonlexical aids, such as tables of weights and measures and guides to punctuation, spelling, and the like.

The continuing popular interest in language resulted in our decision to include brief etymologies within these entries. The history of the origin and development of a word, in addition to satisfying the curiosity that many people have about the language they speak, can often help one to understand more clearly the current meaning of the word and to remember that meaning when the word is reencountered. Those who seek even more detailed etymologies, including the ultimate Indo-European roots from which most of our vocabulary derives, can find that information in the *Second College Edition* of WEBSTER'S NEW WORLD DICTIONARY.

The pronunciations recorded here are those that at the present time are most frequently used by cultivated speakers of the major dialects of the American language. Common variants are also shown, as well as native pronunciations of foreign words and proper names. Transcription is in a simple, easily read key that is nevertheless phonemically precise, and a short form of that key appears on every right-hand page of the dictionary text. A more detailed explanation will be found in the introductory Guide to the Dictionary and inside the front cover of this book.

Through the use of the latest technological advances in composition, this dictionary has been set by computer in modern type that is clear, attractive, and of the largest practicable size. To help the reader find more quickly the information he is seeking, various type faces are used for the different elements within the entry. More than 500 illustrations have been included where it was felt that a picture would help to expand or sharpen the definition. The actual sizes of animals have been given in feet or inches, and tools and instruments have been shown in use to make even clearer their function and relative size.

To help the user get the full benefit of the language information included in this dictionary, we have prepared a detailed *Guide to the Use of the Dictionary*, which appears on the following pages. You are urged to read it.

David B. Guralnik

GUIDE TO THE USE OF THE DICTIONARY

I. THE MAIN ENTRY WORD

A. Arrangement of Entries

All main entries, including single words, hyphenated and unhyphenated compounds, proper names, prefixes, suffixes, and abbreviations, are listed in strict alphabetical order and are set in large, boldface type.

black (blak) *adj.* . . .
black-and-blue (-ən blo͞o′) *adj.* . . .
black·ber·ry (-ber′ē) *n.* . . .
black flag . . .
Black Forest . . .
Black·pool (blak′po͞ol′) . . .
-blast (blast) . . .
bldg. . . .
bleach (blēch) *vt., vi.* . . .

Note that in the biographical entry only the last, or family, name (that part coming before the comma) has been considered in alphabetization. When two or more persons with the same family name are entered, they are dealt with in a single entry block, arranged in alphabetical order by first names. Biographical and geographical names that are identical in spelling are kept in separate blocks.

Jack·son (jak′s'n) [after A. JACKSON] capital of Miss., in the SW part: pop. 154,000
Jack·son (jak′s'n) **1. Andrew,** 1767–1845; 7th president of the U.S. (1829–37) **2. Thomas Jonathan,** (nickname *Stonewall Jackson*) 1824–63; Confederate general in the Civil War

Strict alphabetical order is followed for "Saint" and "St." when they appear as a part of proper names that are not the names of canonized persons.

Saint Agnes's Eve
Saint Bernard (dog)
sainted
Saint-Gaudens, Augustus
stain
St. George's Channel
stick
St. John (city)

Canonized persons are entered by their given names, which appear in the regular alphabetical listing. Thus **Augustine,** the saint, will be found in the A's, but **St. Augustine,** the city in Florida, will be found in the S's.

B. Variant Spellings & Forms

When variant spellings of a word are some distance apart in alphabetical listing, the definition appears at the spelling most frequently used. Other spellings of the word are cross-referred to that spelling. Sometimes such a cross-reference indicates that the variant is British, dialectal, slang, obsolete, or the like.

ae·on . . . *n. same as* EON
kerb . . . *n. Brit. sp. of* CURB (*n.* 4)
shew . . . *n., vt., vi.* . . . *archaic sp. of* SHOW

If two variant spellings would appear close to each other in alphabetical order and are used with nearly equal frequency, they are placed together at the head of the entry. Neither spelling is considered to be "more correct," even though the one listed first may be used somewhat more often.

the·a·ter, the·a·tre . . . *n.* . . .

If a variant spelling is close in alphabetical order to the main-entry spelling and pronounced exactly like it but is used less often, such a spelling or spellings are given at the end of the entry block or pertinent definition.

Az·er·bai·jan . . . Also sp. **Azerbaidzhan, Azerbaydzhan**
co·op·er·a·te, co-op·er·ate . . . *vi.* . . . : also **co·öp′er·ate′**

When related words with the same meaning would appear in alphabetical order close to each other, the less frequently used word is placed at the end of the entry block or pertinent definition for the more common word.

laud·a·to·ry . . . *adj.* . . . : also **laud′a·tive**
in·fu·so·ri·an . . . *n.* . . . —*adj.* . . . : also **in′fu·so′ri·al**

C. Cross-references

In all entries or senses that consist simply of a cross-reference to another entry having the same meaning, the entry cross-referred to is shown in small capitals.

gay·e·ty . . . *n.* . . . *same as* GAIETY
ca·ble . . . *n.* **1.** . . . **2.** . . . **3.** *same as* CABLE LENGTH
aer·o·plane . . . *n.* . . . *Brit. var. of* AIRPLANE
chaunt . . . *n., vt., vi. archaic var. of* CHANT
lark·spur . . . *n. a common name for* DELPHINIUM
ma·jor·ette . . . *n. short for* DRUM MAJORETTE
re·pro . . . *n. shortened form of* REPRODUCTION PROOF
lib . . . *n. clipped form of* LIBERATION

D. Homographs

Main entries that are spelled exactly alike but are different in meaning and origin, as **bat** (a club), **bat** (the animal), and **bat** (to wink), are entered in separate blocks and are marked with small, raised numerals just after the boldface spellings.

bat¹ . . . *n.* . . .
bat² . . . *n.* . . .
bat³ . . . *vt.* . . .

Cross-references to such entries are identified by these small, raised numerals.

Indian corn *same as* CORN¹ (sense 2)

E. Foreign Terms

Foreign words and phrases that appear fairly often in English speech and writing but are not yet felt as a part of the English vocabulary, are marked with a double dagger (‡) at the beginning of the entry. This mark indicates that such a term is usually printed in italic type.

‡au na·tu·rel . . . [Fr.] . . .

F. Prefixes, Suffixes, & Combining Forms

Prefixes and combining forms used at the beginning of words are indicated in the dictionary by a hyphen placed after the entry form.

re- . . . *a prefix meaning:* **1.** back *[repay]* **2.** again, anew *[reappear]* . . .

Suffixes and combining forms used at the end of words are indicated in the dictionary by a hyphen placed before the entry form.

-hood . . . *a suffix meaning:* **1.** state, quality, condition *[childhood]* **2.** the whole group of (a specified class, profession, etc.) *[priesthood]*

Many such forms are entered here and make it possible for the reader to figure out the meaning of words that are made with these forms but that are not entered in the dictionary.

G. Syllabification

Center dots in the entry words indicate where the words can be divided if they need to be broken at the end of a written or printed line. In actual copy, a hyphen is used in place of the center dot. For example, **car·niv·o·rous** can be broken at the end of a line in the following ways (*car-* or *carniv-* or *carnivo-*), depending on how much space is available.

If the stress given to the syllables of a word shifts when that word is used as another part of speech, the syllabification shown may properly apply only to the use of the word as the first part of speech given. In the case of a word such as *progress,* the writer may wish to change the syllabification from **prog·ress** when the noun is meant to **pro·gress** when the verb is meant; the pronunciation shown for the verb serves as a guide for this change.

All the syllables of a word are marked (for example, **might·y, a·ban·don**) although it is not customary in written or printed matter to break a word after the first syllable or before the last if that syllable consists of only a single letter or generally, in the case of a long word, of only two letters.

II. PRONUNCIATION

A. Introduction

The pronunciations recorded in this dictionary are for the most part those found in the normal, relaxed conversation of educated speakers. For some words, pronunciations that are dialectal, British, Canadian, etc. are given along with the usual American pronunciation.

neph·ew (nef′yo͞o; *chiefly Brit.* nev′-) . . .

B. Key to Pronunciation

An abbreviated form of this key appears at the bottom of every right-hand page of the vocabulary.

Symbol	*Key Words*	*Symbol*	*Key Words*
a	ask, fat, parrot	**b**	bed, fable, dub
ā	ape, date, play	**d**	dip, beadle, had
ä	ah. car, father	**f**	fall, after, off
		g	get, haggle, dog
e	elf, ten, berry	**h**	he, ahead, hotel
ē	even, meet, money	**j**	joy, agile, badge
		k	kill, tackle, bake
i	is, hit, mirror	**l**	let, yellow, ball
ī	ice, bite, high	**m**	met, camel, trim
		n	not, flannel, ton
ō	open, tone, go	**p**	put, apple, tap
ô	all, horn, law	**r**	red, port, dear
o͞o	ooze, tool, crew	**s**	sell, castle, pass
o͝o	look, pull, moor	**t**	top, cattle, hat
yo͞o	use, cute, few	**v**	vat, hovel, have
yo͝o	united, cure, globule	**w**	will, always, swear
oi	oil, point, toy	**y**	yet, onion, yard
ou	out, crowd, plow	**z**	zebra, dazzle, haze
u	up, cut, color	**ch**	chin, catcher, arch
ʉr	urn, fur, deter	**sh**	she, cushion, dash
		th	thin, nothing, truth
ə	**a** in ago	***th***	then, father, lathe
	e in agent	**zh**	azure, leisure
	i in sanity	**ŋ**	ring, anger, drink
	o in comply	**’**	[see explanatory note below and also *Foreign sounds* below]
	u in focus		
ər	perhaps, murder		

The symbols in the key above can be easily understood from the key words in which they are shown, and a speaker of any dialect of American English will automatically read his own pronunciation into any symbol shown here. Explanatory notes on some of these symbols follow.

ä This symbol represents the vowel of *car.* Some words shown with **ä**, such as *alms* (ämz), *hot* (hät), *rod* (räd), etc., are heard in the speech of some persons with the vowel sound **ô** (ômz), (hôt), (rôd). Such variations may be assumed although they are not recorded in this dictionary.

e This symbol represents the vowel of *ten.* It is also used, followed by **r,** to represent the vowel sound of *care* (ker); for this sound, vowels ranging from **ā** (kār *or* kā′ər) to **a** (kar) are sometimes heard and may be assumed as variants although they are not recorded in this dictionary.

ē This symbol represents the vowel of *meet* and is also used for the vowel in the unstressed final syllable of such words as *lucky* (luk′ē), *pretty* (prit′ē), etc.

i This symbol represents the vowel of *hit* and is also used for the vowel in the unstressed syllables of such words as *garbage* (gär′bij), *goodness* (go͝od′nis), *preface* (pref′is), *deny* (di nī′), *curate* (kyo͝or′it), etc. In such unstressed syllables, the schwa (ə) is often heard (gär′bəj), (go͝od′nəs), etc. and may be assumed as a variant although not recorded in this dictionary. This symbol is also used, followed by **r,** to represent the vowel sound of *dear* (dir); for this sound, vowels ranging to **ē** (dēr *or* dē′ər) are sometimes heard and, although not here recorded, may be assumed as variants.

ô This symbol represents the vowel of *all.* When followed by **r**, as in *more* (môr), vowels ranging to **ō** (mōr *or* mō′ər) are often heard and, although not here recorded, may be assumed as variants. In certain words shown with **ô,** such as *cough* (kôf), *lawn* (lôn), etc., vowel sounds ranging all the way to **ä** (käf), (län), etc. are heard and may be assumed as variants although not generally recorded in this dictionary.

ʉr and **ər** These two symbols represent, in order, the stressed and the unstressed r-colored vowels heard in the two syllables of *murder* (mʉr′dər). Where these symbols are shown, some speakers, especially in the South and along the Eastern seaboard, will "drop their *r*'s" in pronouncing them.

ə This symbol, called the schwa, represents the neutral vowel heard in the unstressed syllables of *ago, agent, focus,* etc. In many words, such as *colitis,* this vowel is sometimes heard as **i** (kō līt′is).

ŋ This symbol represents the nasal sound indicated in spelling by the *ng* of *sing* and occurring also for **n** before the consonants **k** and **g**, as in *drink* (driŋk) and *finger* (fiŋ′gər).

’ The apostrophe occurring before **l, m,** and **n** indicates that the following consonant is a syllabic consonant, with little or no vowel sound accompanying it, as in *apple* (ap′’l) or *happen* (hap′’n). Some persons pronounce such words with a vowel sound close to the schwa (ə), as in *happen* (hap′ən), but such variants are not entered in this dictionary.

Foreign Sounds

Most of the symbols in the key above have been used to transcribe pronunciations in foreign languages, although it should be understood that these sounds will vary somewhat from language to language. The additional symbols below will cover those situations that cannot be adequately dealt with using the general key.

ȧ This symbol, representing the *a* in French *bal* (bȧl) can best be described as intermediate between (a) and (ä).

ë This symbol represents the sound of the vowel cluster in French *coeur* (kër) and can be approximated by rounding the lips as for (ô) and pronouncing (e).

ö This symbol variously represents the sound of *eu* in French *feu* (fö) or of *ö* (or *oe*) in German *Göthe* (or *Goethe*) (gö′tə) and can be approximated by rounding the lips as for (ō) and pronouncing (ā).

ȏ This symbol represents a range of sounds varying from (ō) to (ô) and heard with such varying quality in French *coq* (kȏk), German *doch* (dȏkh), Italian *poco* (pȏ′kȏ), Spanish *torero* (tȏ *re*′rȏ), etc.

ü This symbol variously represents the sound of *u* in French *duc* (dük) and in German *grün* (grün) and can be approximated by rounding the lips as for (o͞o) and pronouncing (ē).

kh This symbol represents the sound heard in German *doch* (dȏkh). It can be approximated by arranging the speech organs as for (k) but allowing the breath to escape in a stream, as in pronouncing (h).

H This symbol represents a sound similar to the preceding but formed by friction against the forward part of the palate, as in German *ich* (iH). It is sometimes misheard, and hence pronounced, by English speakers as (sh).

n This symbol indicates that the vowel sound immediately preceding it is nasalized; that is, the nasal passage is left open so that the breath passes through both the mouth and nose in voicing the vowel, as in French *mon* (mō*n*).

r This symbol represents any of various sounds used in languages other than English for the consonant *r*. It may represent the tongue-point trill or uvular trill of the *r* in French *reste* (*r*est) or *sur* (sü*r*), German *Reuter* (*r*oi′tər), Italian *ricotta* (*r*ē kȏt′tä), Russian *gorod* (gȏ′*r*ȏd), etc.

’ The apostrophe is used after final *l* and *r*, in certain French pronunciations, to indicate that they are voiceless after an unvoiced consonant, as in *lettre* (let′*r*’). In Russian words the "soft sign" in the Cyrillic spelling is indicated by (y’). The sound can be approximated by pronouncing an unvoiced (y) directly after the consonant involved, as in *Sevastopol* (se′väs tȏ′pəl y’).

C. General Styling of Pronunciation

Pronunciations are given inside parentheses, immediately following the boldface entry. A single space is used between syllables. A primary, or strong, stress is indicated by a heavy stroke (′) immediately following the syllable so stressed. A secondary, or weak, stress is indicated by a lighter stroke (′) following the syllable so stressed. All notes, labels, or other matter inside the parentheses are in italics.

D. Truncation

Variant pronunciations are truncated wherever possible, with only that syllable or those syllables in which change occurs shown. A hyphen after the truncated variant shows that it is the beginning of the word; one before the variant, that it is the end; and hyphens before and after the variant, that it is within the word.

ac·cept (ək sept′, ak-) . . .
rec·ti·tude (rek′tə to͞od′, -tyo͞od′) . . .
fu·tu·ri·ty (fyo͝o to͝or′ə tē, -tyo͝or′-, -cho͝or′-) . . .

Truncations of variant pronunciations involving different parts of speech in the same entry block appear as follows:

pre·cip·i·tate (pri sip′ə tāt′; *also, for adj. & n.,* -tit) . . .

Truncated pronunciations are also given for a series of words having the same first part, after the pronunciation of this first part has been established.

le·git·i·ma·tize (lə jit′ə mə tīz′) . . .
le·git·i·mist (-mist) . . .
le·git·i·mize (-mīz′) . . .

Similarly, with a series made up of compounds and derived forms:

time-hon·ored (tīm′än′ərd) . . .
time-keep·er (-kē′pər) . . .
time-lapse (-laps′) . . .
time·less (-lis) . . .
time loan . . .
time·ly (-lē) . . .

Full pronunciations are given with words in a series of the following kind when the stress in the first part is changed in some way.

bi·o·as·tro·nau·tics (bī′ō as′trə nô′tiks) . . .
bi·o·chem·is·try (-kem′is trē) . . .
bi·o·cide (bī′ə sīd′) . . .
bi·o·de·grad·a·ble (bī′ō di grā′də b'l) . . .
bi·o·en·gi·neer·ing (-en′jə nir′iŋ) . . .

E. Variants

Where two or more pronunciations for a single word are given, the order in which they are entered does not necessarily mean that the first is preferred or is more correct. In most cases, the order indicates that on the basis of available information, the form given first is the one more frequent in general cultivated use. Unless a variant is qualified, as by *now rarely* or *occasionally* or some such note, it is understood that any pronunciation here entered represents a standard use.

III. PART-OF-SPEECH LABELS

Part-of-speech labels are given for lower-case main entries that are solid or hyphenated forms, except for prefixes, suffixes, and abbreviations. The following labels for the parts of speech into which words are classified in traditional English grammar are used in this dictionary. They appear in boldface italic type following the pronunciations.

n.	noun	*prep.*	preposition
vt.	transitive verb	*conj.*	conjunction
vi.	intransitive verb	*pron.*	pronoun
adj.	adjective	*interj.*	interjection
adv.	adverb		

In addition, the following labels are sometimes used:

n.pl. plural noun
v.aux. auxiliary verb
v.impersonal impersonal verb
n.fem. feminine noun
n.masc. masculine noun

When an entry word is used as more than one part of speech, long dashes introduce each different part of speech in the entry block and each part-of-speech label appears in boldface italic type.

round[1] . . . *adj.* . . . —*n.* . . . —*vt.* . . . —*vi.* . . . —*adv.* . . . —*prep.* . . .

Two or more part-of-speech labels are given jointly for an entry when the definition or definitions, or the cross-reference, will suffice for both or all.

lip-read . . . *vt., vi.* . . . to recognize (a speaker's words) by lip reading . . .
hal·lo, hal·loa . . . *interj., n., vi., vt. same as* HALLOO

Part-of-speech labels are not used for names of persons and places, or for given names, figures in religion, mythology, literature, etc. However, usages have sometimes developed from these that can be classified as parts of speech and these are indicated.

A·don·is . . . *Gr. Myth.* a young man loved by Aphrodite —*n.* any very handsome young man . . .

It is theoretically possible to use almost any word as whatever part of speech is required. Thus any transitive verb can be used absolutely as an intransitive verb, with the object understood ("Shall I *use* this lotion?" "Yes, but *use* sparingly.") Such absolute uses are entered only when they are relatively common. In the same way nouns used as adjectives (a *cloth* cover; a *family* affair) are indicated only for the most frequent uses.

IV. INFLECTED FORMS

Inflected forms regarded as irregular or offering difficulty in spelling are entered in small boldface immediately following the part-of-speech labels. They are truncated where possible, and syllabified and pronounced where necessary.

A. Plurals of Nouns

Plurals formed regularly by adding *-s* to the singular (or *-es* after *s, x, z, ch,* and *sh*), as *bats, boxes,* are not normally indicated.

Plurals are shown when formed irregularly, as for nouns with a *-y* ending that changes to *-ies*, and for those with an *-o* ending, those inflected by some change within the word, those having variant forms, those having different forms for different meanings, compound nouns, etc.

cit·y . . . *n., pl.* **cit′ies** . . .
bo·le·ro . . . *n., pl.* **-ros** . . .
tooth . . . *n., pl.* **teeth** (tēth) . . .
a·moe·ba . . . *n., pl.* **-bas, -bae** (-bē) . . .
die[2] . . . *n., pl.*, for 1 **dice** (dīs); for 2 **dies** (dīz)
son-in-law . . . *n., pl.* **sons′-in-law′** . . .

If an irregular plural is so altered in spelling that it would appear at some distance from the singular form, it is entered additionally in its proper alphabetical place.

lice . . . *n. pl. of* LOUSE

B. Principal Parts

Verb forms regarded as regular and not normally indicated include:

a) present tenses formed by adding *-s* to the infinitive (or *-es* after *s, x, z, ch,* and *sh*), as *waits, searches;*

b) past tenses and past participles formed by simply adding *-ed* to the infinitive with no other changes in the verb form, as *waited, searched;*

c) present participles formed by simply adding *-ing* to the infinitive with no other change in the verb form, as *waiting, searching.*

Principal parts are given for irregular verbs, including those in which the final *e* is dropped in forming the present participle.

Where two inflected forms are given for a verb, the first is the form for the past tense and the past participle, and the second is the form for the present participle.

make . . . *vt.* **made, mak′ing** . . .
sip . . . *vt., vi.* **sipped, sip′ping** . . .

Where three forms are given, separated from one another by commas, the first represents the past tense, the second the past participle, and the third the present participle.

swim . . . *vi.* **swam, swum, swim′ming** . . .

Where there are alternative forms for any of the principal parts, these are indicated as follows:

trav·el . . . *vi.* **-eled** or **-elled, -el·ing** or **el·ling**
drink . . . *vt.* **drank** or archaic **drunk, drunk** or now colloq. **drank** or archaic **drunk′en, drink′ing** . . .

If a principal part of a verb is so altered in spelling that it would appear at some distance from the infinitive form, it is entered additionally in its proper alphabetical place.

said . . . *pt. & pp. of* SAY

C. Comparatives & Superlatives of Adjectives & Adverbs

Comparatives and superlatives formed by simply adding *-er* or *-est* to the base, as *taller, tallest,* are not indicated.

Those formed irregularly, as by adding *-r* and *-st* (*rare, rarer, rarest*), by changing final *-y* to *-i-* (*happy, happier, happiest*), or by some radical change in form (*good, better, best* or *well, better, best*), are indicated with the positive form.

The positive form is also noted at the comparative and superlative forms when these are entered and defined at some distance from it.

best . . . *adj. superl. of* GOOD . . . *—adv. superl. of* WELL² . . .

V. THE ETYMOLOGY

Brief etymologies, or little histories of the words in this dictionary have been included so that they may help the user to a clearer understanding of the current meanings of these words. The etymology will be found immediately before the definition, set off in heavy brackets. The symbols, as < for "derived from," and the abbreviations of language labels, etc. used in the etymologies are dealt with in full in the list of Abbreviations and Symbols immediately preceding page 1 of the vocabulary.

ex·er·cise (ek′sər sīz′) ***n.*** **[**< OFr. < L. < pp. of *exercere*, to drive out (farm animals to work) < *ex-*, out + *arcere*, to enclose**]** **1.** active use or operation . . .
es·cape (ə skāp′, e-) ***vi.*** **-caped′, -cap′ing [**< ONormFr. < L. *ex-*, out of + *cappa*, cloak (i.e., leave one's cloak)**]** **1.** to get free; get away . . .

For some words etymologies are shown by means of cross-references (in small capitals) to the elements of which they are formed and which are dealt with separately in the dictionary.

en·dog·a·my (en däg′ə mē) ***n.*** **[**ENDO- + -GAMY**]** **1.** the custom of marrying only within one's own tribe, clan, etc.; inbreeding . . .
ra·don (rā′dän) ***n.*** **[**RAD(IUM) + -ON**]** a radioactive gaseous chemical element . . .

No etymology is shown where one is not needed, as because the elements making up the word are immediately apparent to the user (**precondition**) or because the definition that follows clearly explains the derivation (see **bluebottle**).

Where no etymology is known for certain, that fact is indicated by the following: **[**< ?**]**

A special effort has been made to include as many etymologies as possible for place names in the United States.

VI. THE DEFINITIONS

A. Order of Senses

The definitions, or senses, of a longer entry have been arranged in an order which shows how the word has developed from its etymology and its earliest meanings and how the meanings of the word are related to one another. Senses that need to be labeled as colloquial, slang, archaic, obsolete, or the like are given after the general senses. Next, any technical senses are given, arranged in alphabetical order according to their special field labels. Sometimes an obsolete sense may be given first, preceded by "originally" (abbreviated "orig.") or "formerly," to serve as a link between the etymology and the current senses.

B. Numbering & Grouping of Senses

Senses are numbered consecutively within any given part of speech in boldface numerals. A new series of numerals is used for each new part of speech and for each idiomatic phrase.

tap² . . . ***n.*** **1.** . . . **2.** . . . **3.** . . . ***—vt.*** **1.** . . . **2.** . . . **3.** . . . **—on tap** **1.** . . . **2.** . . .

Where a primary sense of a word can easily be subdivided into several closely related meanings, this has been done; such meanings are indicated by italicized letters after the pertinent numbered or labeled sense. The words "especially" or "specifically" (abbreviated "esp." and "specif.") are often used after an introductory definition to introduce such a grouping of related senses.

bind·er . . . ***n.*** **1.** a person who binds; specif., a bookbinder **2.** a thing that binds; specif., *a)* a band, cord, etc. *b)* a substance, as tar, that binds things together *c)* a detachable cover for holding sheets of paper together **3.** a device attached to a reaper . . .

C. Capitalization

If a main-entry word is capitalized in all its senses, the entry word itself is printed with a capital letter.

Eur·a·sian (-zhən; *chiefly Brit.* -shən) ***adj.*** **1.** of Eurasia **2.** of mixed European and Asian descent ***—n.*** a person with one European parent and one Asian parent . . .

If a capitalized main-entry word has a sense or senses that are uncapitalized, these are marked with the corresponding lower-case letter enclosed in brackets, sometimes with a qualifying word, such as "usually," "often," "also," etc.

Pur·i·tan . . . ***n.*** . . . **1.** . . . **2.** **[p-]** . . . ***—adj.*** **1.** . . . **2.** **[p-]** . . .

If a lower-case main-entry word has a sense or senses that are capitalized, these are marked with the corresponding upper-case letter enclosed in brackets, sometimes with a qualifying word, such as "usually," "often," "also," etc.

north . . . ***n.*** . . . **1.** . . . **2.** . . . **3.** [*often* **N-**] . . . ***—adj.*** **1.** . . . **2.** . . . **3.** [**N-**] . . .

D. Plural Forms

The designation "[*pl.*]" (or "[*often pl.*]," "[*usually pl.*]," etc.) before a definition indicates that it is the plural form of the entry word (or *often* or *usually* the plural form) that has the meaning given in the definition.

lim·it . . . ***n.*** . . . **1.** . . . **2.** [*pl.*] bounds . . .
look . . . ***vi.*** . . . ***—n.*** **1.** . . . **2.** . . . **3.** [Colloq.] *a)* [*usually pl.*] appearance . . . *b)* [*pl.*] personal appearance, esp. of a pleasing nature . . .

If such a plural sense is construed as singular, the designation "*with sing. v.*" is added inside the brackets.

bone . . . ***n.*** . . . **6.** [*pl.*] *a)* flat sticks used as clappers in minstrel shows *b)* [*with sing. v.*] the end man in a minstrel show . . .

The note "*usually used in pl.*" at the end of a singular noun definition means that although the definition applies to the given singular form of the entry word, the word is usually used in the plural and with a plural meaning.

ex·trem·i·ty (ik strem′ə tē) ***n.***, *pl.* **-ties** . . . **5.** an extreme measure; strong action: *usually used in pl.* . . .

If a plural noun entry is construed as singular, the designation "[*with sing. v.*]" is placed after the ***n.pl.*** label or, in some cases, with the numbered sense to which it applies.

ger·i·at·rics . . . ***n.pl.*** [*with sing. v.*] . . . the branch of medicine that deals with the diseases and hygiene of old age . . .
a·cous·tics . . . ***n.pl.*** **1.** the qualities of a room, etc. that have to do with how clearly sounds can be heard in it **2.** [*with sing. v.*] the branch of physics dealing with sound

E. Prepositions Accompanying Verbs

Where certain verbs are, in usage, always or usually followed by a specific preposition or prepositions, this has been indicated in the following ways: the preposition has been worked into the definition, italicized and enclosed in parentheses, or a note has been added in parentheses indicating that the preposition is so used.

strike . . . ***—vi.*** . . . **9.** to come suddenly (*on* or *upon*) [*we struck* on an idea] . . . **16.** *U.S. Navy* to be in training (*for* a specified rating) . . .
hit . . . ***—vi.*** . . . **4.** to come by accident or after search (with *on* or *upon*) . . .

Note: Such uses of verbs with specific prepositions should not be confused with verb sets consisting of a verb form with an adverb, which are entered as idiomatic phrases under the key verb (**make out, make over,** and **make up** at the entry **make**).

F. Objects of Transitive Verbs

In definitions of transitive verbs the specific or generalized objects of the verb, where given, are enclosed in parentheses since such objects are not part of the definition.

ob·serve . . . ***vt.*** . . . **1.** to adhere to or keep (a law, custom, duty, etc.) **2.** to celebrate (a holiday, etc.) according to custom **3.** *a)* to notice or perceive (something) *b)* to pay special attention to . . .

In some cases the transitive verb can be defined jointly with the intransitive verb.

chis·el . . . —*vi., vt.* . . . **1.** to cut or shape with a chisel . . .

G. Additional Information & Notes

Additional information or any note or comment on the definition proper is preceded by a colon.

Cau·ca·soid . . . *adj.* . . . designating or of one of the major groups of mankind that includes the native peoples of Europe, North Africa, the Near East, India, etc.: loosely called the *white race,* although skin color varies . . .
ma·ture . . . *adj.* . . . **4.** due: said of a note, bond, etc. . . .
mil·li·gram . . . *n.* . . . : also, chiefly Brit. sp., **mil′li·gramme′**

If the note or comment applies to all the senses or parts of speech preceding it, it begins with a capital letter and no colon introduces it.

rest[2] . . . *n.* . . . **1.** what is left; remainder **2.** [*with pl. v.*] the others Used with *the* . . .

H. Illustrative Examples of Entry Words in Context

Examples of a word in use have been given where such examples help make the meaning clearer or show more exactly the differences in meaning among the different senses. Such examples of usage are enclosed in slanted brackets, and the word being defined is set in italics.

spir·it . . . *n.* . . . **5.** an individual person or personality *[*a brave *spirit]* **6.** [*usually pl.*] disposition; mood *[*high *spirits]* **7.** vivacity, courage, enthusiasm, etc. **8.** enthusiasm and loyalty *[*school *spirit]* **9.** real meaning; true intention *[*to follow the *spirit* if not the letter of the law*]* **10.** an essential quality or prevailing tendency *[*the *spirit* of the Renaissance*]* **11.** . . .

I. Cross-references

Entry words (or tables, illustrations, etc.) to which the reader is being cross-referred are given in small capitals.

cap·i·tal[1] . . . —*n.* . . . **8.** . . . : distinguished from LABOR
ca·tab·o·lism . . . *n.* . . . : opposed to ANABOLISM
civil disobedience . . . : see also NONCOOPERATION, PASSIVE RESISTANCE
clause . . . *n.* . . . **1.** . . . : cf. MAIN CLAUSE, SUBORDINATE CLAUSE **2.** . . .
ev·o·lu·tion . . . *n.* . . . **5.** . . . : see DARWINIAN THEORY
Gem·i·ni . . . : see ZODIAC, illus.
Holy Land *same as* PALESTINE (sense 1)
sol[1] . . . *n.* . . . *see* MONETARY UNITS, table (Peru)

VII. USAGE LABELS & NOTES

It is generally understood that usage varies among groups of people according to locality, level of education, social environment, occupation, etc. More specifically, usage can vary in the speech of any person depending upon the particular situation in which he is involved and the purpose his language must serve. The language that a scientist uses in preparing a report on his work may be quite different from the language he uses in writing a letter to a friend. What is good usage in a literary essay may not be the best usage in the lyrics to a popular song or in casual conversation. Certain occasions call for language that is more or less formal, and others, language that is more or less informal.

Dictionaries can reasonably be expected to assign usage labels, as, for example, to those terms that the record shows are regularly used in informal or highly informal contexts. The conventional usage labels are so well known that they can be used if their meaning is clearly understood in advance. The labels, and what they are intended to indicate, are given below. If the label, which is placed in brackets (and in some cases abbreviated), occurs directly after a part-of-speech label or after a boldface entry term, it applies to all senses given with that part of speech or that term; if it occurs after a numeral or letter, it applies only to the sense so numbered or lettered.

Colloquial: The term or sense is generally characteristic of conversation and informal writing. It is not to be regarded as substandard or illiterate.
Slang: The term or sense is not generally regarded as conventional or standard usage but is used, even by the best speakers, in highly informal contexts. Slang consists of both coined terms and of new or extended meanings attached to established terms. Slang terms tend either to pass into disuse in time or to move toward standard usage.
Obsolete: The term or sense is no longer used but occurs in earlier writings.
Archaic: The term or sense is rarely used today except in certain restricted contexts, as in church ritual, but occurs in earlier writings.
Poetic: The term or sense is used chiefly in poetry, especially in earlier poetry, or in prose where a poetic quality is desired.
Dialect: The term or sense is used regularly only in some geographical areas or in a certain designated area (*South, Southwest, West,* etc.) of the United States.
British (or Canadian, Scottish, etc.): The term or sense is characteristic of British (or Canadian, etc.) English rather than of that spoken in the United States. When preceded by *chiefly,* the label indicates an additional, though less frequent, American usage. *British dialect* indicates that the term or sense is used regularly only in certain geographical areas of Great Britain, usually in northern England.

In addition to the above usage labels, additional information is often given after the definition, indicating whether the term or sense is generally regarded as vulgar, substandard, or derogatory, or used for ironic, familiar, or exaggerated effect, etc. Where there are some objections to common usages, that fact is also indicated (for example, **who, whom**).

VIII. FIELD LABELS

Labels for specialized fields of knowledge and activity appear in italics (in abbreviated form where practical) immediately before the sense involved. In long entry blocks having many general and specialized senses, these labels, arranged in alphabetical order, help the user to quickly find the special sense or senses he is seeking.

base[1] . . . *n.* . . . **8.** *Chem.* . . . **9.** *Geom.* . . . **10.** *Linguis.* . . . **11.** *Math.* . . .

IX. IDIOMATIC PHRASES

Idiomatic phrases are run in on an entry block in alphabetical order after the definition or definitions of the main-entry word. The entry for each phrase is set in small boldface with a dash preceding it. Such phrases have been entered wherever possible under the key word.

busi·ness . . . *n.* . . . **—business is business** . . . **—do business with** . . . **—give** (or **get**) **the business** . . . **—mean business** . . .

Alternative forms are indicated inside parentheses, as above in **give** (or **get**) **the business.** In the phrase **(at) full tilt** under the entry **tilt,** both the longer phrase, **at full tilt,** and the shorter, **full tilt,** are being recorded.

X. RUN-IN DERIVED ENTRIES

It is possible in English to form an almost infinite number of derived forms simply by adding certain prefixes or suffixes to the base word. This dictionary includes as run-in entries in small boldface type only those words one might reasonably expect to meet up with in literature or ordinary usage, and then only when the meaning of such derived words can be immediately understood from the meanings of the base word and the affix. Thus, **greatness, liveliness,** and **newness** are run in at the end of the entries for **great, lively,** and **new,** the meanings of the derived forms being clearly understood from the base word and the suffix **-ness,** which is found as a separate entry in this dictionary and means "state, quality, or instance of being." Many words formed with common suffixes such as **-able, -er, -less, -like, -ly, -tion,** etc. are similarly treated as run-in entries with the base word from which they are derived. All such entries are syllabified and either accented to show stress in pronunciation or, where necessary, pronounced in full or in part. Each run-in derived form is preceded by a dash.

If two run-in derived forms have the same meaning and share a part-of-speech label, the more frequently used form appears first and the part-of-speech label is given after the second form. Note the plural form following the first run-in:

prac·ti·cal . . . *adj.* . . . **—prac′ti·cal′i·ty** (-kal′ə tē), *pl.* **-ties, prac′ti·cal·ness** *n.*

When a derived word has a meaning or meanings different from those which can be deduced from the sum of its parts, it has been entered in a block of its own, pronounced, and fully defined (for example, **producer**).

ABBREVIATIONS AND SYMBOLS USED IN THIS DICTIONARY

abbrev. abbreviated; abbreviation
abl. ablative
acc. accusative
adj. adjective
adv. adverb
Aeron. Aeronautics
Afr. African
Afrik. Afrikaans
alt. alternative
Am. American
AmFr. American French
AmInd. American Indian
AmSp. American Spanish
Anat. Anatomy
Anglo-Fr. Anglo-French
Anglo-Ind. Anglo-Indian
Anglo-Ir. Anglo-Irish
Anglo-L. Anglo-Latin
Anglo-N. Anglo-Norse
Anglo-Norm. Anglo-Norman
Ar. Arabic
Aram. Aramaic
Archaeol. Archaeology
Archit. Architecture
Arith. Arithmetic
Arm. Armenian
art. article
assoc. associated
Assyr. Assyrian
Astrol. Astrology
Astron. Astronomy
at. no. atomic number
at. wt. atomic weight
Bab. Babylonian
Beng. Bengali
Biochem. Biochemistry
Biol. Biology
Bohem. Bohemian
Bot. Botany
Braz. Brazilian
Bret. Breton
Brit. British
Bulg. Bulgarian
C Celsius; Central
c. century (in etym.); circa
Canad. Canadian
CanadFr. Canadian French
cap. capital
Celt. Celtic
cent. century; centuries
cf. compare
Ch. Chaldean; Church
Chem. Chemistry
Chin. Chinese
Chr. Chronicles
Col. Colossians
comp. compound
compar. comparative
conj. conjunction
contr. contracted; contraction
Cop. Coptic
Cor. Corinthians
Corn. Cornish
cu. cubic
Cym. Cymric
Dan. Daniel; Danish
dat. dative
deriv. derivative
Deut. Deuteronomy
Dial., dial. dialectal
dim. diminutive
Du. Dutch
E East; eastern
E. East; English (in etym.& pronun.
Early ModDu. Early modern Dutch
Early ModG. Early modern German
EC east central
Eccl. Ecclesiastes
Eccles. Ecclesiastical
Ecol. Ecology
Econ. Economics
Educ. Education
e.g. for example
Egypt. Egyptian
Elec. Electricity
Eng. English
Eph. Ephesians
equiv. equivalent
Esk. Eskimo
esp. especially
est. estimated
Esth. Esther
Eth. Ethiopic
etym. etymology
Ex. example; Exodus
exc. except
Ezek. Ezekiel
F Farenheit
fem. feminine
ff. following (entry, sense, etc.)
fig. figurative; figuratively
Finn. Finnish
Fl. Flemish
fl. flourished
Fr. French
Frank. Frankish
freq. frequentative
Fris. Frisian
ft. feet
fut. future
G. German (in etym. & pronun.)
Gael. Gaelic
Gal. Galatians
gal. gallon; gallons
Gaul. Gaulish
Gen. Genesis
gen. genitive
Geog. Geography
Geol. Geology
Geom. Geometry
Ger. German
ger. gerund
Gmc. Germanic
Goth. Gothic
Gr. Greek
Gram. Grammar
Hab. Habakkuk
Hag. Haggai
Haw. Hawaiian
Heb. Hebrew; Hebrews
Hort. Horticulture
Hos. Hosea
Hung. Hungarian
hyp. hypothetical
Ice. Icelandic
i.e. that is
imper. imperative
imperf. imperfect
in. inch; inches
incl. including
Ind. Indian
indic. indicative
inf. infinitive
infl. influenced
intens. intensive
interj. interjection
Ir. Irish
Iran. Iranian
IrGael. Irish Gaelic
irreg. irregular
Isa. Isaiah
It. Italian
Jap. Japanese
Jas. James
Jer. Jeremiah
Josh. Joshua
Judg. Judges
KJV King James Version
L Late
L. Latin
Lam. Lamentations
lb. pound

Abbreviations and Symbols

Lev. Leviticus
LGr. Late Greek
Linguis. Linguistics
lit. literally
Lith. Lithuanian
LL. Late Latin
LME. Late Middle English
LXX Septuagint
M Middle; Medieval
Mal. Malachi
Math. Mathematics
Matt. Matthew
MDu. Middle Dutch
ME. Middle English
Mech. Mechanics
Med. Medicine; Medieval
met. metropolitan
Meteorol. Meteorology
Mex. Mexican
MexSp. Mexican Spanish
MFr. Middle French
MGr. Medieval Greek
MHG. Middle High German
mi. mile; miles
Mic. Micah
Mil. Military
ML. Medieval Latin
MLowG. Middle Low German
Mod, Mod. Modern
ModE. Modern English
ModGr. Modern Greek
ModHeb. Modern Hebrew
ModL. Modern Latin
Mongol. Mongolic
Myth. Mythology
N North; northern
N. North
n. noun
Nah. Nahum
Naut., naut. nautical usage
NC north central
NE northeastern
Neh. Nehemiah
neut. neuter
n.fem. feminine form of noun
n.masc. masculine form of noun
nom. nominative
Norm, Norm. Norman
Norw. Norwegian
n.pl. plural form of noun
n.sing. singular form of noun
N.T. New Testament
Num. Numbers
NW northwestern
O Old
Ob. Obadiah
Obs, obs. obsolete
occas. occasionally
OE. Old English
OFr. Old French
OHG. Old High German
OIr. Old Irish
OIt. Old Italian
OL. Old Latin
ON. Old Norse
ONormFr. Old Norman French
orig. origin; originally
OS. Old Saxon
O.T. Old Testament
oz. ounce
P Primitive
p. page
part. participle
pass. passive
Per. Persian
perf. perfect
pers. person
Peruv. Peruvian
Pet. Peter
Phil. Philippians
Philem. Philemon
Philos. Philosophy
Phoen. Phoenician
Phonet. Phonetics
Photog. Photography
phr. phrase
Phys. Ed. Physical Education
Physiol. Physiology
PidE. Pidgin English
pl. plural
Poet. Poetic
Pol. Polish
pop. popular; population
Port. Portuguese
poss. possessive
pp. pages; past participle
Pr. Provençal
prec. preceding
prep. preposition
pres. present
prin. pts. principal parts
prob. probably
pron. pronoun
pronun. pronunciation
Prov. Proverbs; Provincial
prp. present participle
Ps. Psalms
pseud. pseudonym
Psychol. Psychology
pt. past tense
qt. quart; quarts
R.C.Ch. Roman Catholic Church
redupl. reduplication
refl. reflexive
Rev. Revelation
Rom. Roman; Romans
R.S.F.S.R. Russian Soviet Federated Socialist Republic
RSV Revised Standard Version
Russ. Russian
S South; southern
S. South
Sam. Samuel
Sans. Sanskrit
SC south central
Scand. Scandinavian
Scot, Scot. Scottish
ScotGael. Scottish Gaelic
SE southeastern
Sem. Semitic
Serb. Serbian
sing. singular
Sinh. Sinhalese
Slav. Slavic
S. of Sol. Song of Solomon
Sp. Spanish
sp. spelled; spelling
specif. specifically
sq. square
S.S.R. Soviet Socialist Republic
subj. subjunctive
superl. superlative
SW southwestern
Sw. Swedish (in etym. & pronun.)
Swed. Swedish
Syr. Syriac
Tag. Tagalog
Theol. Theology
Thess. Thessalonians
Tim. Timothy
Tit. Titus
transl. translation
Turk. Turkish
TV television
ult. ultimately
UN United Nations
U.S. United States
U.S.S.R. Union of Soviet Socialist Republics
v. verb
var. variant; variety
v.aux. auxiliary verb
Vet. Veterinary Medicine
vi. intransitive verb
VL. Vulgar Latin
voc. vocative
vt. transitive verb
Vulg. Vulgate
W West; western
W. Welsh; West
WAfr. West African
WC west central
WGmc. West Germanic
WInd. West Indian
yd. yard; yards
Yid. Yiddish
Zech. Zechariah
Zeph. Zephaniah
Zool. Zoology

‡ foreign word or phrase
* hypothetical
+ plus
< derived from
? uncertain; possibly; perhaps
& and

A

A, a (ā) ***n.**, pl.* **A's, a's** **1.** the first letter of the English alphabet **2.** a sound of *A* or *a* **3.** *a symbol for* the first in a sequence or group

A (ā) ***n.*** **1.** *Educ.* a grade indicating excellence **2.** *Music a)* the sixth tone in the ascending scale of C major *b)* the scale having A as the keynote —***adj.*** shaped like *A*

a (ə; *stressed* ā) ***adj., indefinite article*** [form of AN[1]] **1.** one; one sort of **2.** each; any one *A* connotes a thing not previously noted or recognized; *the*, a thing previously noted or recognized **3.** [orig. a prep. < OE. *an*, in, on, at] to each; in each; per *[*once *a* day*]* Before words beginning with a consonant sound or a sounded *h*, *a* is used *[a* child, *a* home, *a* uniform*]*; before words beginning with a vowel sound or a silent *h*, *an* is used *[an* eye, *an* ultimatum, *an* honor*]*

a-[1] [weakened form of OE. *an, on*, in, on, at] *a prefix meaning:* **1.** in, into, on, at, to *[abed, ashore]* **2.** in the act or state of *[asleep]*

a-[2] *a prefix of various origins and meanings:* **1.** [OE. *a-*, out of, up] up, out: now generally an intensive *[awake, arise]* **2.** [OE. *of-, af-*] off, of *[akin]* **3.** [Gr. *a-, an-*, not] not, without *[atypical]*: before vowels *an-* is used *[anastigmatic]*

A. **1.** Absolute **2.** angstrom

a. **1.** about **2.** acre(s) **3.** adjective **4.** alto **5.** ampere **6.** anode **7.** anonymous **8.** answer

AA, A.A. **1.** Alcoholics Anonymous **2.** antiaircraft

AAA, A.A.A. American Automobile Association

Aa·chen (ä′kən; *G.* ä′khən) city in W West Germany, on the Belgian border: pop. 177,000

aard·vark (ärd′värk′) ***n.*** [obs. Afrik., earth pig] a burrowing African mammal that feeds on ants and termites: it has a long snout

AARDVARK
(c. 2 ft. high at shoulder)

aard·wolf (-woolf′) ***n.**, pl.* **-wolves′** (-woolvz′) [Afrik., earth wolf] a mammal of S and E Africa resembling the hyena but feeding chiefly on termites and insect larvae

Aar·on (er′ən) [LL. < Gr. < Heb. *aharōn*, lit., the exalted one]**·** **1.** a masculine name **2.** *Bible* the older brother of Moses and first high priest of the Hebrews

Ab (äb; *Heb.* äv) ***n.*** [Heb.] the eleventh month of the Jewish year: see JEWISH CALENDAR

ab- [L.] *a prefix meaning* away, from, from off, down *[abdicate]*: shortened to *a-* before *m, p,* and *v;* often *abs-* before *c* or *t [abstract]*

A.B. [ML. *Artium Baccalaureus*] Bachelor of Arts

a·ba (ä′bə) ***n.*** [Ar.] **1.** a fabric of wool or hair fiber with a felted finish **2.** a loose, sleeveless robe worn by Arabs

a·ba·cá (ab′ə kə) ***n.*** [Tag.] **1.** *same as* MANILA HEMP (sense 1) **2.** the Philippine plant yielding Manila hemp

a·back (ə bak′) ***adv.*** **1.** [Archaic] backward; back **2.** backward against the mast, as sails in a wind from ahead —**taken aback** startled and confused

ab·a·cus (ab′ə kəs, ə bak′əs) ***n.**, pl.* **-cus·es, -ci′** (-sī′) [L. < Gr. *abax*] **1.** a frame with beads or balls sliding back and forth on wires or in slots, for doing arithmetic **2.** *Archit.* a slab forming the uppermost part of the capital of a column

ABACUS

A·ba·dán (ä′bä dän′) city in W Iran, on an island in the Shatt-al-Arab: pop. 302,000

a·baft (ə baft′) ***adv.*** [< OE. *on*, on + *bæftan* < *be*, by + *æftan*, behind] at or toward the stern of a ship; aft —***prep.*** *Naut.* behind

ab·a·lo·ne (ab′ə lō′nē) ***n.*** [AmSp. < AmInd. *aulun*] a sea mollusk with an oval, somewhat spiral shell lined with mother-of-pearl

a·ban·don (ə ban′dən) ***vt.*** [< OFr. < *mettre a bandon*, to put under (someone else's) ban] **1.** to give up (something) completely **2.** to forsake; desert **3.** to yield (oneself) completely, as to a feeling —***n.*** unrestrained freedom of action or emotion —**a·ban′don·ment** ***n.***

a·ban·doned (-dənd) ***adj.*** **1.** forsaken; deserted **2.** shamefully wicked **3.** unrestrained

a·base (ə bās′) ***vt.*** **a·based′, a·bas′ing** [< OFr. < ML. *abassare*, to lower < L. *ad-*, to + LL. *bassus*, low] to humble or humiliate —**a·base′ment** ***n.***

a·bash (ə bash′) ***vt.*** [OFr. *esbahir*, to astonish < L. *ex* + *ba*, interj. of surprise] to make ashamed and ill at ease —**a·bashed′** ***adj.***

a·bate (ə bāt′) ***vt.*** **a·bat′ed, a·bat′ing** [< OFr. *abattre*, to beat down: see AD- & BATTER[1]] **1.** to make less in amount, degree, etc. **2.** to deduct **3.** *Law* to put a stop to; end —***vi.*** to become less; subside —**a·bate′ment** ***n.***

ab·a·tis, ab·at·tis (ab′ə tis) ***n.**, pl.* **-a·tis, -at·tis** [Fr.: see prec.] a barricade of felled trees with branches facing the enemy

ab·at·toir (ab′ə twär′, ab′ə twär′) ***n.*** [Fr.: see ABATE] a slaughterhouse

ab·ba·cy (ab′ə sē) ***n.**, pl.* **-cies** an abbot's position, jurisdiction, or term of office

ab·bé (a′bā; *Fr.* à bā′) ***n.*** [Fr. < LL.: see ABBOT] a French title of respect for a priest, minister, etc.

ab·bess (ab′əs) ***n.*** [< LL.: see ABBOT] a woman who is head of an abbey of nuns

ab·bey (ab′ē) ***n.*** **1.** a monastery headed by an abbot or a convent of nuns headed by an abbess **2.** the monks or nuns in such a place, collectively **3.** a church or building belonging to an abbey

ab·bot (ab′ət) ***n.*** [< OE. < LL. < Gr. < Aram. *abbā*, father] a man who heads an abbey of monks

abbr., abbrev. **1.** abbreviated **2.** abbreviation

ab·bre·vi·ate (ə brē′vē āt′) ***vt.*** **-at′ed, -at′ing** [< LL. pp. of *abbreviare* < L. < *ad-*, to + *brevis*, short] **1.** to make shorter **2.** to shorten (a word or phrase) by leaving out or substituting letters —**ab·bre′vi·a′tor** ***n.***

ab·bre·vi·a·tion (ə brē′vē ā′shən) ***n.*** **1.** a making shorter **2.** the state or fact of being made shorter **3.** a shortened form of a word or phrase, as *N.Y.* for *New York, Mr.* for *Mister, lb.* for *pound*

A B C (ā′ bē′ sē′) ***n.**, pl.* **A B C's** **1.** [*usually pl.*] the alphabet **2.** the basic elements (*of* a subject); rudiments

ABC American Broadcasting Company

ABC soil a vertical section of soil in three distinct layers: the top layer (*A-horizon*) is mostly humus, the middle layer (*B-horizon*) is of clay and other oxidized material, and the bottom layer (*C-horizon*) consists of loose rock and other mineral materials

ab·di·cate (ab′də kāt′) ***vt., vi.*** **-cat′ed, -cat′ing** [< L. pp. of *abdicare* < *ab-*, off + *dicare*, to proclaim] **1.** to give up formally (a high office, etc.) **2.** to surrender (a right, responsibility, etc.) —**ab′di·ca′tion** ***n.*** —**ab′di·ca′tor** ***n.***

ab·do·men (ab′də mən, ab dō′-) ***n.*** [L.] **1.** the part of the body between the diaphragm and the pelvis, containing the intestines, etc.; belly **2.** in insects and crustaceans, the hind part of the body —**ab·dom·i·nal** (ab däm′ə n'l) ***adj.***

ab·duct (ab dukt′) ***vt.*** [<L. pp. of *abducere* < *ab-*, away + *ducere*, to lead] **1.** to kidnap (a person) **2.** to move (a part of the body) away from the median axis of the body —**ab·duc′tion** ***n.*** —**ab·duc′tor** ***n.***

a·beam (ə bēm′) ***adv.*** abreast (*of*) the middle of a ship's side

a·bed (ə bed′) ***adv., adj.*** in bed; on a bed

A·bel (ā′b'l) [L. < Gr. < Heb. *hebel*, lit., breath] **1.** a masculine name 2. *Bible* the second son of Adam and Eve, killed by his brother Cain: Gen. 4

Ab·é·lard (à bā lȧr′), **Pierre** (pyer) 1079–1142; Fr. philosopher & teacher: Eng. name **Peter Ab·e·lard** (ab′ə lärd′) : see also HÉLOÏSE

Ab·er·deen (ab′ər dēn′) seaport in E Scotland, on the North Sea: pop. 182,000 —**Ab′er·do′ni·an** (-dō′nē ən) ***adj., n.***

ab·er·rant (a ber′ənt) ***adj.*** [< L. prp. of *aberrare* < *ab-*, from + *errare*, to wander] deviating from what is true, normal, or typical —**ab·er′rance, ab·er′ran·cy** ***n.***

ab·er·ra·tion (ab′ər ā′shən) ***n.*** **1.** a departure from what is right, true, etc. **2.** a deviation from the normal or typical **3.** mental derangement or lapse **4.** *Optics a)* the failure of light rays from one point to converge to a single focus *b)* an error in a lens or mirror causing this

a·bet (ə bet′) ***vt.*** **a·bet′ted, a·bet′ting** [< OFr. *abeter*, to incite < *a-*, to + *beter*, to BAIT] to incite or help, esp. in wrongdoing —**a·bet′ment** ***n.*** —**a·bet′tor, a·bet′ter** ***n.***

a·bey·ance (ə bā′əns) ***n.*** [< Anglo-Fr. < OFr. *abeance*, expectation < *a-*, at + *bayer*, to gape] temporary suspension, as of an activity or function

ab·hor (əb hôr′, ab-) ***vt.*** **-horred′, -hor′ring** [< L. *abhorrere* < *ab-*, away, from + *horrere*, to shudder] to shrink from in disgust or hatred; detest —**ab·hor′rence** ***n.***

ab·hor·rent (-ənt) ***adj.*** **1.** causing disgust, hatred, etc.; detestable **2.** opposed (*to*) *[abhorrent* to his principles*]* —**ab·hor′rent·ly** ***adv.***

a·bide (ə bīd′) ***vi.*** **a·bode′** or **a·bid′ed, a·bid′ing** [OE. *abidan* < *a-* (intens.) + *bidan*, to remain] **1.** to stand fast; remain **2.** [Archaic] to stay; reside (*in* or *at*) —***vt.*** **1.** to await **2.** to submit to; put up with —**abide by** **1.** to live up to (a promise, etc.) **2.** to submit to and carry out (a rule, decision, etc.) —**a·bid′ance** ***n.***

a·bid·ing (ə bīd′iŋ) ***adj.*** enduring; lasting —**a·bid′ing·ly** ***adv.***

Ab·i·djan (äb′i jän′) seaport and capital of the Ivory Coast: pop. 282,000

Ab·i·gail (ab′ə gāl′) [Heb. *abīgayil*, lit., father is rejoicing] a feminine name: dim. *Abby, Gail*

Ab·i·lene (ab′ə lēn′) [ult. < Luke 3:1] city in C Tex.: pop. 98,000

a·bil·i·ty (ə bil′ə tē) ***n.,*** *pl.* **-ties** [see ABLE] **1.** a being able; power to do **2.** skill or talent

-a·bil·i·ty (ə bil′ə tē) *pl.* **-ties** [L. *-abilitas:* see -ABLE & -ITY] *a suffix used to form nouns from adjectives ending in* -ABLE *[durability]*

ab·i·o·gen·e·sis (ab′ē ō jen′ə sis) ***n.*** [ModL. < Gr. *a-*, without + BIOGENESIS] *same as* SPONTANEOUS GENERATION

ab·ject (ab′jekt, ab jekt′) ***adj.*** [< L. pp. of *abjicere* < *ab-*, away, from + *jacere*, to throw] **1.** of the lowest degree; miserable *[abject* poverty*]* **2.** lacking self-respect; degraded —**ab′ject·ly** ***adv.*** —**ab′ject·ness, ab·jec′tion** ***n.***

ab·jure (əb joor′, ab-) ***vt.*** **-jured′, -jur′ing** [< L. *abjurare* < *ab-*, away, from + *jurare*, to swear] **1.** to give up (rights, allegiance, etc.) on oath; renounce **2.** to give up (opinions) publicly; recant —**ab·ju·ra·tion** (ab′jə rā′shən) ***n.*** —**ab·jur′er** ***n.***

ab·late (ab lāt′) ***vt.*** **-lat′ed, -lat′ing** [back-formation < *ablation* < LL. < L. *ablatus:* see ff.] **1.** to remove, as by surgery **2.** *Astrophysics* to melt, vaporize, etc. (surface material) during high-speed movement through the atmosphere —***vi.*** to become ablated —**ab·la′tion** ***n.***

ab·la·tive (ab′lə tiv; *for adj. 2* ab lāt′iv) ***n.*** [< L. < *ablatus*, pp. of *auferre* < *ab-*, away + *ferre*, to carry] **1.** the grammatical case in Latin and some other languages expressing removal, deprivation, direction from, or source, cause, etc. **2.** a word in this case —***adj.*** **1.** of or in the ablative **2.** *Astrophysics* that ablates

ab·laut (äb′lout, ab′-; *G.* äp′lout) ***n.*** [G. < *ab-*, off, from + *laut*, sound] the change of base vowels in related words to show changes in tense, meaning, etc. (Ex.: dr*i*nk, dr*a*nk, dr*u*nk) —***adj.*** of or characterized by ablaut

a·blaze (ə blāz′) ***adj.*** **1.** flaming; gleaming **2.** greatly excited; eager

a·ble (ā′b′l) ***adj.*** **a′bler** (-blər), **a′blest** (-blist) [< OFr. < L. *habilis*, handy < *habere*, to have, hold] **1.** having enough power, skill, etc. (*to* do something) **2.** having much power of mind; skilled; talented —**a′bly** ***adv.***

-a·ble (ə b′l) [< OFr. < L. *-abilis*] *a suffix meaning:* **1.** able to *[durable]* **2.** capable of being *[drinkable]* **3.** worthy of being *[lovable]* **4.** having qualities of *[comfortable]* **5.** tending or inclined to *[peaceable]*

a·ble-bod·ied (ā′b′l bäd′ēd) ***adj.*** healthy and strong

able-bodied seaman a trained, skilled sailor

a·bloom (ə bloom′) ***adj.*** in bloom; in flower

ab·lu·tion (ab loo′shən, əb-) ***n.*** [< L. *ablutio* < *abluere* < *ab-*, off + *luere*, to LAVE] a washing of the body, esp. as a religious ceremony

-a·bly (ə blē) *a suffix used to form adverbs from adjectives ending in* -ABLE *[peaceably]*

ABM anti-ballistic missile

ab·ne·gate (ab′nə gāt′) ***vt.*** **-gat′ed, -gat′ing** [< L. pp. of *abnegare* < *ab-*, away, from + *negare*, to deny] to give up (rights, claims, etc.); renounce —**ab′ne·ga′tion** ***n.*** —**ab′ne·ga′tor** ***n.***

Ab·ner (ab′nər) [L. < Heb. *'abnēr*, lit., the father is a light] a masculine name

ab·nor·mal (ab nôr′m′l) ***adj.*** [earlier *anormal* < Fr. < LL. < Gr. *anōmalos* (see ANOMALOUS) infl. by L. *abnormis* < *ab-*, from + *norma*, NORM] not normal; not average; not typical; irregular, esp. to a considerable degree —**ab·nor′mal·ly** ***adv.***

ab·nor·mal·i·ty (ab′nôr mal′ə tē) ***n.*** **1.** the condition of being abnormal **2.** *pl.* **-ties** an abnormal thing

a·board (ə bôrd′) ***adv.*** **1.** on board; on, in, or into a ship, airplane, etc. **2.** alongside —***prep.*** on board of; on; in —**all aboard!** get on! get in!: a warning that the train, car, etc. will start soon

a·bode[1] (ə bōd′) ***n.*** [see ABIDE] a place where one lives or stays; home; residence

a·bode[2] (ə bōd′) *alt. pt. and pp. of* ABIDE

a·bol·ish (ə bäl′ish) ***vt.*** [< OFr. < L. *abolescere*, to decay < L. *abolere*, to destroy] to do away with; put an end to; annul —**a·bol′ish·ment** ***n.***

ab·o·li·tion (ab′ə lish′ən) ***n.*** **1.** an abolishing or being abolished; annulment **2.** [*occas.* **A-**] the abolishing of slavery in the U.S. —**ab′o·li′tion·ar′y** ***adj.***

ab·o·li·tion·ist (-ist) ***n.*** one in favor of abolishing some law, custom, etc.; specif., [*occas.* **A-**] one who favored the abolition of slavery in the U.S. —**ab′o·li′tion·ism** ***n.***

ab·o·ma·sum (ab′ə mā′səm) ***n.,*** *pl.* **-ma′sa** (-sə) [ModL. < L. *ab-*, from + *omasum*, paunch] the fourth, or digesting, chamber of the stomach of a cud-chewing animal, as the cow

A-bomb (ā′bäm′) ***n.*** *same as* ATOMIC BOMB —***vt.*** to attack with an atomic bomb

a·bom·i·na·ble (ə bäm′ə nə b′l) ***adj.*** [see ABOMINATE] **1.** disgusting; vile; loathsome **2.** disagreeable; very bad —**a·bom′i·na·bly** ***adv.***

Abominable Snowman a large, hairy, manlike animal reputed to live in the Himalayas

a·bom·i·nate (ə bäm′ə nāt′) ***vt.*** **-nat′ed, -nat′ing** [< L. pp. of *abominari*, to regard as an ill omen] **1.** to feel hatred and disgust for; loathe **2.** to dislike very much —**a·bom′i·na′tor** ***n.***

a·bom·i·na·tion (ə bäm′ə nā′shən) ***n.*** **1.** hatred and disgust **2.** anything hateful and disgusting

ab·o·rig·i·nal (ab′ə rij′ə n′l) ***adj.*** **1.** existing from earliest days; first; indigenous **2.** of aborigines

ab·o·rig·i·ne (ab′ə rij′ə nē′) ***n.,*** *pl.* **-nes′** [L. < *ab-*, from + *origine*, the beginning] **1.** any of the earliest known inhabitants of a region; native **2.** [*pl.*] the native animals or plants of a region

a·born·ing (ə bôr′niŋ) ***adv.*** while being born or created *[*the plan died *aborning]*

a·bort (ə bôrt′) ***vi.*** [< L. pp. of *aboriri*, to miscarry] **1.** to have a miscarriage **2.** to fail to be completed —***vt.*** **1.** to cause to have an abortion **2.** to check (a disease) before fully developed **3.** to cut short (an operation of an aircraft, missile, etc.) as because of an equipment failure

a·bor·tion (ə bôr′shən) ***n.*** **1.** expulsion of a fetus from the womb before it is viable; miscarriage **2.** an aborted fetus **3.** anything immature and incomplete —**a·bor′tion·ist** ***n.***

a·bor·tive (ə bôr′tiv) ***adj.*** **1.** coming to nothing; unsuccessful **2.** *Biol.* rudimentary **3.** *Med.* causing abortion —**a·bor′tive·ly** ***adv.***

ABO system the system of classifying human blood types in accordance with their compatibility for transfusion: there are four major types (A, B, AB, and O), determined by the antigens inherited

a·bound (ə bound′) ***vi.*** [< OFr. < L. *abundare*, to overflow < *ab-*, away + *undare*, to rise in waves < *unda*, a wave] **1.** to be plentiful **2.** to have plenty; be rich (*in*) or teem (*with*)

a·bout (ə bout′) ***adv.*** [< OE. *onbutan*, around, on the outside (of)] **1.** all around *[*look *about]* **2.** here and there *[*travel *about]* **3.** near *[*it is somewhere *about]* **4.** in the opposite direction *[*turn it *about]* **5.** in succession or rotation *[*play fair—turn and turn *about]* **6.** nearly *[about* four years old*]* **7.** [Colloq.] almost *[*just *about* ready*]* —***adj.*** [*used only in the predicate*] **1.** active *[*he is up and *about* again*]* **2.** in the vicinity *[*typhoid is *about]* —***prep.*** **1.** around; on all sides of **2.** here and there in; everywhere in **3.** near to **4.** with; on (one's person) *[*have your wits *about* you*]* **5.** attending to *[*go *about* your business*]* **6.** intending; on the point of *[*he is *about* to speak*]* **7.** having to do with; concerning **8.** in connection with —**how** (or **what**) **about** [Colloq.] what is your wish or opinion concerning? —**how about that!** [Colloq.] isn't that interesting!

a·bout-face (ə bout′fās′; *for v.* ə bout′fās′) ***n.*** **1.** a sharp turn to the opposite direction, esp. in response to a military command **2.** a sharp change, as in opinion —***vi.*** **-faced′, -fac′ing** to turn or face in the opposite direction

a·bove (ə buv′) ***adv.*** [OE. *abufan*] **1.** in, at, or to a higher place; overhead; up **2.** in or to heaven **3.** at a previous place (in a piece of writing) **4.** higher in power, status, etc. ***—prep.*** **1.** higher than; over **2.** beyond; past [the road *above* the town] **3.** at a point upstream of **4.** better than [*above* the average] **5.** more than [*above* fifty dollars] ***—adj.*** placed, found, mentioned, etc. above or earlier ***—n.*** something that is above **—above all** most of all; mainly

a·bove·board (-bôrd′) ***adv., adj.*** without dishonesty or concealment

ab·ra·ca·dab·ra (ab′rə kə dab′rə) ***n.*** [LL.] **1.** a word supposed to have magic powers, used in incantations, etc. **2.** foolish or meaningless talk

ab·rade (ə brād′) ***vt., vi.*** **-rad′ed, -rad′ing** [< L. *abradere* < *ab-*, away + *radere*, to scrape] to rub off; wear away by scraping **—ab·rad′er *n.***

A·bra·ham (ā′brə ham′) [Heb., lit., father of many] **1.** a masculine name: dim. *Abe;* var. *Abram* **2.** *Bible* the first patriarch and ancestor of the Hebrews

a·bran·chi·ate (ā braŋ′kē it, -āt′) ***adj.*** [< Gr. *a-*, not + *branchia*, gills + -ATE[1]] without gills ***—n.*** an animal without gills Also **a·bran′chi·al** (-əl)

ab·ra·sion (ə brā′zhən) ***n.*** **1.** a scraping or rubbing off, as of skin **2.** an abraded spot or area

ab·ra·sive (ə brā′siv) ***adj.*** causing abrasion ***—n.*** a substance used for grinding, polishing, etc.

a·breast (ə brest′) ***adv., adj.*** [A-[1] + BREAST] **1.** side by side [walking four *abreast*] **2.** informed (*of*) or conversant (*with*) recent developments

a·bridge (ə brij′) ***vt.*** **a·bridged′, a·bridg′ing** [< OFr. < LL. *abbreviare:* see ABBREVIATE] **1.** to reduce in scope, extent, etc. **2.** to shorten by using fewer words but keeping the main contents **3.** to lessen (rights, authority, etc.) **—a·bridg′a·ble, a·bridge′a·ble *adj.* —a·bridg′er *n.***

a·bridg·ment, a·bridge·ment (ə brij′mənt) ***n.*** **1.** an abridging or being abridged **2.** an abridged form of a book, etc.

a·broad (ə brôd′) ***adv.*** **1.** broadly; far and wide **2.** circulating [a report is *abroad* that he is ill] **3.** outdoors [to stroll *abroad*] **4.** to or in foreign countries **—from abroad** from a foreign land

ab·ro·gate (ab′rə gāt′) ***vt.*** **-gat′ed, -gat′ing** [< L. pp. of *abrogare*, to repeal < *ab-*, away + *rogare*, to propose] to cancel or repeal by authority; annul **—ab′ro·ga·ble** (-gə b′l) ***adj.*** **—ab′ro·ga′tion *n.* —ab′ro·ga′tive *adj.* — ab′ro·ga′tor *n.***

a·brupt (ə brupt′) ***adj.*** [< L. pp. of *abrumpere* < *ab-*, off + *rumpere*, to break] **1.** sudden; unexpected **2.** curt or brusque **3.** very steep **4.** jumping from topic to topic; disconnected **—a·brupt′ly *adv.* —a·brupt′ness *n.***

Ab·sa·lom (ab′sə ləm) *Bible* David's favorite son, who rebelled against his father: II Sam. 18

ab·scess (ab′ses) ***n.*** [< L. < *abscidere* < *ab(s)-*, from + *cedere*, to go] a swollen, inflamed area in body tissues, in which pus gathers ***—vi.*** to form an abscess **—ab′scessed *adj.***

ab·scis·sa (ab sis′ə) ***n., pl.*** **-sas, -sae** (-ē) [L. *abscissa* (*linea*), (a line) cut off < pp. of *abscindere* < *ab-*, from, off + *scindere*, to cut] *Math.* in a system of coordinates, the distance of a point from the vertical axis as measured along a line parallel to the horizontal axis: cf. ORDINATE

ABSCISSA
(x, the abscissa of P; y, the ordinate of P)

ab·scond (əb skänd′, ab-) ***vi.*** [< L. *abscondere* < *ab(s)-*, from, away + *condere*, to hide] to run away and hide, esp. in order to escape the law

ab·sence (ab′s′ns) ***n.*** **1.** the state of being absent, or away **2.** the time of being away **3.** the fact of being without; lack [in the *absence* of proof]

ab·sent (ab′s′nt; *for v.* ab sent′) ***adj.*** [< OFr. < L. prp. of *abesse* < *ab-*, away + *esse*, to be] **1.** not present; away **2.** not existing; lacking **3.** not attentive; absorbed in thought ***—vt.*** to keep (oneself) away [he *absents* himself from classes] **—ab′sent·ly *adv.***

ab·sen·tee (ab′s′n tē′) ***n.*** a person who is absent, as from work ***—adj.*** designating or of a landlord who lives away from the property he owns

ab·sen·tee·ism (-iz′m) ***n.*** absence from work, school, etc., esp. when deliberate or habitual

ab·sent-mind·ed (ab′s′nt mīn′did) ***adj.*** **1.** so lost in thought as not to pay attention to what is going on around one **2.** habitually forgetful **—ab′sent-mind′ed·ly *adv.* —ab′sent-mind′ed·ness *n.***

ab·sinthe, ab·sinth (ab′sinth) ***n.*** [< OFr. < L. < Gr. *apsinthion* < OPer.] **1.** wormwood **2.** a green liqueur with the flavor of wormwood and anise

ab·so·lute (ab′sə lo͞ot′, ab′sə lo͞ot′) ***adj.*** [< L. pp. of *absolvere:* see ABSOLVE] **1.** perfect; complete [*absolute* silence] **2.** not mixed; pure **3.** not limited; unrestricted [an *absolute* ruler] **4.** positive; definite **5.** actual; real [an *absolute* truth] **6.** without reference to anything else **7.** *Gram.* *a*) forming part of a sentence, but not in the usual relations of syntax [in the sentence "The weather being good, they went," *the weather being good* is an *absolute* construction] *b*) with no expressed object: said of a verb usually transitive *c*) used alone, with the noun understood: said of a pronoun or an adjective, such as *ours* and *brave* in the sentence "Ours are the brave." ***—n.*** something that is absolute **—ab′so·lute′ly *adv.* — ab′so·lute′ness *n.***

absolute pitch the ability to identify the pitch of any tone, or to sing a given tone, without having a known pitch sounded beforehand

absolute temperature temperature measured from absolute zero

absolute zero a point of temperature theoretically equal to −273.15° C or −459.67° F: the hypothetical point at which a substance would have no molecular motion and no heat

ab·so·lu·tion (ab′sə lo͞o′shən) ***n.*** [<OFr. < L. *absolutio* < *absolvere:* see ABSOLVE] **1.** a formal freeing (*from* guilt); forgiveness **2.** *a*) remission (*of* sin or its penalty); specif., in some churches, such remission formally given by a priest in the sacrament of penance *b*) the formula stating such remission

ab·so·lut·ism (ab′sə lo͞o′tiz′m) ***n.*** government in which the ruler has unlimited powers; despotism **—ab′so·lut′ist *n., adj.***

ab·solve (əb zälv′, ab-; -sälv′) ***vt.*** **-solved′, -solv′ing** [< L. *absolvere* < *ab-*, from + *solvere*, to loose] **1.** to pronounce free from guilt or blame; acquit **2.** *a*) to give religious absolution to *b*) to remit (a sin) **3.** to free (someone *from* an obligation) **—ab·solv′ent *adj., n.* —ab·solv′er *n.***

ab·sorb (əb zôrb′, ab-; -sôrb′) ***vt.*** [< L. *absorbere* < *ab-*, from + *sorbere*, to drink in] **1.** to suck up [sponges *absorb* water] **2.** to take up fully the attention of; engross **3.** to take in and incorporate; assimilate **4.** to take in (a shock, jolt, etc.) with little or no recoil or reaction **5.** to take in and not reflect (light, sound, etc.) **—ab·sorbed′ *adj.* —ab·sorb′ing *adj.* —ab·sorb′ing·ly *adv.***

ab·sorb·ent (əb zôr′b′nt, ab-; -sôr′-) ***adj.*** capable of absorbing moisture, light, etc. ***—n.*** a thing that absorbs moisture, etc. **—ab·sorb′en·cy *n.***

ab·sorp·tion (əb zôrp′shən, ab-; -sôrp′-) ***n.*** **1.** an absorbing or being absorbed **2.** great interest; engrossment **3.** *Biol.* the passing of nutrient material into the blood or lymph **—ab·sorp′tive *adj.* —ab′sorp·tiv′i·ty *n.***

ab·stain (əb stān′, ab-) ***vi.*** [< OFr. < L. *abstinere* < *ab(s)-*, from + *tenere*, to hold] to do without voluntarily; refrain (*from*) **—ab·stain′er *n.***

ab·ste·mi·ous (əb stē′mē əs, ab-) ***adj.*** [< L. < *ab(s)-*, from + root of *temetum*, strong drink] moderate, esp. in eating and drinking; temperate **—ab·ste′mi·ous·ly *adv.* —ab·ste′mi·ous·ness *n.***

ab·sten·tion (əb sten′shən, ab-) ***n.*** an abstaining; specif., a refraining from voting on some issue

ab·sti·nence (ab′stə nəns) ***n.*** **1.** an abstaining from some or all food, drink, or other pleasures **2.** an abstaining from alcoholic liquors **— ab′sti·nent *adj.* —ab′sti·nent·ly *adv.***

ab·stract (ab strakt′; *also, and for n. 1 & v. 4 always*, ab′strakt) ***adj.*** [< L. pp. of *abstrahere* < *ab(s)-*, from + *trahere*, to draw] **1.** thought of apart from any particular instances or material objects **2.** expressing a quality so thought of ["beauty" is an *abstract* word] **3.** not easy to understand; abstruse **4.** theoretical; not practical or applied **5.** designating or of art that does not depict objects realistically but in patterns or forms of lines, masses, or colors ***—n.*** **1.** a brief statement of the essential thoughts of a book, article, etc.; summary **2.** an abstract thing, condition, etc. ***—vt.*** **1.** to take away **2.** to steal **3.** to think of (a quality) apart from any particular instance or from any object that has it **4.** to summarize; make an abstract of **—in the abstract** in theory as apart from practice **—ab·stract′er *n.* —ab·stract′ly *adv.* —ab·stract′ness *n.***

ab·stract·ed (ab strak′tid) ***adj.*** **1.** removed or separated (*from* something) **2.** withdrawn in mind; preoccupied **—ab·stract′ed·ly *adv.***

abstract expressionism a style of painting popular after World War II, in which the artist's self-expression is carried out by applying paint freely in compositions that do not represent known objects

ab·strac·tion (ab strak′shən) ***n.*** **1.** an abstracting or being abstracted 2. formation of an idea, as of the qualities of a thing, by separating it mentally from any particular instances or material objects 3. an idea so formed, or a word for it ["honesty" is an *abstraction*] 4. an unrealistic notion 5. mental withdrawal; preoccupation 6. a picture, sculpture, etc. that is wholly or partly abstract —**ab·strac′tion·ism** *n.* —**ab·strac′tion·ist** *n.*

ab·struse (ab stro͞os′) *adj.* [< L. pp. of *abstrudere* < *ab(s)-*, away + *trudere*, to thrust] hard to understand; deep —**ab·struse′ly** *adv.* —**ab·struse′ness** *n.*

ab·surd (əb surd′, ab-; -zurd′) *adj.* [< Fr. < L. *absurdus*, not to be heard of < *ab-*, intens. + *surdus*, dull, deaf] so clearly untrue or unreasonable as to be laughable or ridiculous —**ab·surd′ly** *adv.* —**ab·surd′ness** *n.*

ab·surd·i·ty (əb sur′də tē, ab-; -zur′-) *n.* 1. the quality or state of being absurd; foolishness 2. *pl.* **-ties** an absurd idea or thing

a·bun·dance (ə bun′dəns) *n.* [< OFr. < L. prp. of *abundare*: see ABOUND] 1. a great supply; more than sufficient quantity 2. wealth —**a·bun′dant** *adj.* —**a·bun′dant·ly** *adv.*

a·buse (ə byo͞oz′; *for n.* ə byo͞os′) *vt.* **a·bused′, a·bus′ing** [< OFr. < L. pp. of *abuti*, to misuse < *ab-*, away, from + *uti*, to use] 1. to use wrongly; misuse 2. to mistreat 3. to use insulting language about or to; revile 4. [Obs.] to deceive —*n.* 1. wrong or excessive use 2. mistreatment; injury 3. a bad or corrupt custom or practice 4. insulting language —**a·bus′er** *n.*

a·bu·sive (ə byo͞os′iv) *adj.* 1. abusing; mistreating 2. insulting in language; scurrilous —**a·bu′sive·ly** *adv.* —**a·bu′sive·ness** *n.*

a·but (ə but′) *vi.* **a·but′ted, a·but′ting** [< OFr. < *a-*, to + *bout*, end] to end (*on*) or lean (*upon*) at one end; border (*on*) —*vt.* to border upon

a·but·ment (-mənt) *n.* 1. an abutting 2. that part of a support which carries the weight of an arch 3. the supporting structure at either end of a bridge

ABUTMENT

a·but·ter (-ər) *n.* the owner of an abutting, or adjacent, piece of land

a·buzz (ə buz′) *adj.* 1. filled with buzzing 2. full of activity, talk, etc.

a·bysm (ə biz′'m) *n.* [Poet.] *same as* ABYSS

a·bys·mal (ə biz′m'l) *adj.* 1. of or like an abyss; bottomless 2. immeasurably bad [*abysmal* poverty] —**a·bys′mal·ly** *adv.*

a·byss (ə bis′) *n.* [< L. < Gr. < *a-*, without + *byssos*, bottom] 1. a deep fissure in the earth; bottomless gulf; chasm 2. anything too deep for measurement [an *abyss* of shame] 3. the ocean depths 4. *Theol.* the primeval chaos before the Creation —**a·bys·sal** (ə bis′'l) *adj.*

Ab·ys·sin·i·a (ab′ə sin′ē ə) *same as* ETHIOPIA —**Ab′ys·sin′i·an** *adj., n.*

-ac (ak, ək) [Fr. *-aque* < L. *-acus* < Gr. *-akos* (or directly < any of these)] *a suffix meaning:* 1. characteristic of [*elegiac*] 2. of; relating to [*cardiac*] 3. affected by or having [*maniac*]

Ac *Chem.* actinium

AC, A.C., a.c. alternating current

A/C, a/c *Bookkeeping* 1. account 2. account current

a·ca·cia (ə kā′shə) *n.* [< OFr. < L. < Gr. *akakia*, thorny tree; prob. < *akē*, a point] 1. a tree or shrub of the legume family, with clusters of yellow or white flowers: some yield gum arabic or dyes 2. the flower3. *same as* LOCUST (sense 3)

ac·a·dem·ic (ak′ə dem′ik) *adj.* [see ACADEMY] 1. of colleges, universities, etc.; scholastic 2. having to do with liberal rather than technical or vocational education 3. following fixed rules; formalistic 4. merely theoretical [an *academic* question] Also **ac′a·dem′i·cal** —*n.* a teacher or student at a college or university —**ac′a·dem′i·cal·ly** *adv.*

academic freedom freedom of a teacher or student to hold and express views without fear of arbitrary interference by officials

a·cad·e·mi·cian (ə kad′ə mish′ən, ak′ə də-) *n.* a member of an academy (sense 3)

a·cad·e·my (ə kad′ə mē) *n., pl.* **-mies** [< Fr. < L. < Gr. *akadēmeia*, the grove of *Akadēmos* (legendary figure), where Plato taught] 1. a private secondary or high school 2. a school offering training in a special field 3. an association of scholars, writers, artists, etc., for advancing literature, art, or science

A·ca·di·a (ə kā′dē ə) [< Fr., prob. < native name of Nova Scotia] French colony (1604–1713) that became Nova Scotia and New Brunswick —**A·ca′di·an** *adj., n.*

a·can·thus (ə kan′thəs) *n., pl.* **-thus·es, -thi** (-thī) [L. < Gr. *akantha*, thorn < *akē*, a point] 1. a thistlelike Mediterranean plant with lobed, often spiny leaves 2. *Archit.* a conventional representation of its leaf, esp. on the capitals of Corinthian columns —**a·can′thine** (-thin) *adj.*

a cap·pel·la (ä′ kə pel′ə) [It., in chapel style < L. *ad*, to + ML. *capella*, CHAPEL] without instrumental accompaniment: said of choral singing

acc. 1. accompanied 2. account 3. accusative

ac·cede (ak sēd′) *vi.* **-ced′ed, -ced′ing** [< L. *accedere* < *ad-*, to + *cedere*, to yield] 1. to enter upon the duties (of an office); attain (*to*) 2. to give assent; give in; agree (*to*) —**ac·ced′ence** *n.* —**ac·ced′er** *n.*

ac·cel·er·an·do (ak sel′ə ran′dō; *It.* ät che′le rän′dô) *adv., adj.* [It.] *Music* with gradually quickening tempo

ac·cel·er·ate (ək sel′ə rāt′, ak-) *vt.* **-at′ed, -at′ing** [< L. pp. of *accelerare* < *ad-*, to + *celerare*, to hasten < *celer*, swift] 1. to increase the speed of 2. to cause to progress more rapidly 3. *Physics* to cause a change in the rate of velocity of (a moving body) 4. to cause to happen sooner —*vi.* to go or progress faster —**ac·cel′er·a′tive** *adj.*

ac·cel·er·a·tion (ək sel′ə rā′shən, ak-) *n.* 1. an accelerating or being accelerated 2. change in velocity, or the rate of such change

ac·cel·er·a·tor (ək sel′ə rāt′ər, ak-) *n.* 1. one that accelerates 2. a device, as the foot throttle of an automobile, for speeding up something 3. *Chem.* a substance that speeds up a reaction 4. *Nuclear Physics* a device that accelerates charged particles to high energies

ac·cent (ak′sent; *for v. also* ak sent′) *n.* [Fr. < L. < *ad-*, to + *cantus*, pp. of *canere*, to sing] 1. the emphasis given to a particular syllable or word in speaking it 2. a mark used to show this emphasis, as primary (′) and secondary (′) accents 3. a mark used to distinguish between various sounds of the same letter [in French there are acute (´), grave (`), and circumflex (^) *accents*] 4. a distinguishing regional or national way of pronouncing 5. [*pl.*] [Poet.] speech; words [in *accents* mild] 6. something that lends emphasis, as by contrast with its surroundings 7. special emphasis [to put the *accent* on safety] 8. *Music* emphasis or stress on a note or chord 9. *Prosody* rhythmic stress or beat —*vt.* 1. to pronounce with special stress 2. to mark with an accent 3. to emphasize

ac·cen·tu·al (ak sen′cho͞o wəl) *adj.* 1. of or having to do with accent 2. having rhythm based on stress, as some poetry —**ac·cen′tu·al·ly** *adv.*

ac·cen·tu·ate (ak sen′cho͞o wāt′) *vt.* **-at′ed, -at′ing** 1. to pronounce or mark with an accent or stress 2. to emphasize —**ac·cen′tu·a′tion** *n.*

ac·cept (ək sept′, ak-) *vt.* [< OFr. < L. *acceptare* < *accipere* < *ad-*, to + *capere*, to take] 1. to take (what is offered or given); receive willingly 2. to receive favorably; approve 3. to agree or give assent to 4. to believe in 5. to understand as having a certain meaning 6. to reply affirmatively to; say "yes" to [to *accept* an invitation] 7. *Business* to agree to pay —*vi.* to accept something offered —**ac·cept′er** *n.*

ac·cept·a·ble (ək sep′tə b'l, ak-) *adj.* worth accepting; satisfactory or, sometimes, merely adequate —**ac·cept′a·bil′i·ty** *n.* —**ac·cept′a·bly** *adv.*

ac·cept·ance (ək sep′təns, ak-) *n.* 1. an accepting or being accepted 2. approving reception; approval 3. belief in; assent 4. a written order to pay a certain sum at a set future time

ac·cep·ta·tion (ak′sep tā′shən) *n.* the generally accepted meaning (of a word or expression)

ac·cept·ed (ək sep′tid, ak-) *adj.* generally regarded as true, proper, etc.; conventional; approved

ac·cess (ak′ses) *n.* [< OFr. < L. pp. of *accedere*, ACCEDE] 1. a coming toward; approach 2. a means of approaching, using, etc. 3. the right to enter, approach, or use 4. increase 5. an outburst [an *access* of anger] 6. the onset (*of* a disease) —*vt.* to gain or have access to [branch officials can *access* the central data bank]

ac·ces·sa·ry (ək ses′ər ē, ak-) *adj., n., pl.* **-ries** *same as* ACCESSORY

ac·ces·si·ble (ak ses′ə b'l) *adj.* [see ACCESS] 1. that can be approached or entered 2. easy to approach or enter 3. obtainable 4. open to the influence of (with *to*) [not *accessible* to pity] —**ac·ces′si·bil′i·ty** *n.* —**ac·ces′si·bly** *adv.*

ac·ces·sion (ak sesh′ən) *n.* [see ACCESS] 1. the act of attaining (a throne, power, etc.) 2. assent 3. *a*) increase by addition *b*) an item added, as to a library —**ac·ces′sion·al** *adj.*

ac·ces·so·rize (ək ses′ə rīz′, ak-) *vt.* **-rized′, -riz′ing** to equip, decorate, supplement, etc. with accessories

ac·ces·so·ry (ək ses′ər ē, ak-) *adj.* [< ML. < L. pp. of *accedere*, ACCEDE] 1. helping in a secondary way; extra; additional 2. *Law* helping in an unlawful act —*n., pl.* **-ries** 1. something extra added to help in a secondary way; specif., *a*) an article to complete one's costume, as a purse, gloves, etc. *b*) a piece of optional equipment for convenience, comfort, etc. 2. *Law* an accomplice —**accessory before** (or **after**) **the fact** one who, though absent at the commission of a felony, aids the accused before (or after) its commission —**ac·ces·so·ri·al** (ak′sə sôr′ē əl) *adj.*

access time in computers, the time between the moment when information is requested from (or presented for) storage and the moment of its delivery (or storage)

ac·ci·dence (ak′sə dəns) ***n.*** **[**see ff.**]** the part of grammar dealing with inflection of words

ac·ci·dent (ak′sə dənt) ***n.*** **[**< OFr. < L. prp. of *accidere*, happen < *ad-*, to + *cadere*, to fall**]** **1.** a happening that is not expected, foreseen, or intended **2.** an unintended happening that results in injury, loss, etc. **3.** chance *[*to meet by *accident]* **4.** an attribute that is not essential

ac·ci·den·tal (ak′sə den′t'l) ***adj.*** **1.** happening by chance **2.** belonging but not essential; incidental **—*n.*** **1.** a nonessential quality **2.** *Music a)* a sign, as a sharp or flat, placed before a note to show a chromatic change of pitch *b)* the tone of such a note **—ac′ci·den′tal·ly *adv.***

ac·ci·dent-prone (ak′sə dənt prōn′) ***adj.*** tending to become involved in accidents

ac·claim (ə klām′) ***vt.*** **[**< L. *acclamare* < *ad-*, to + *clamare*, to cry out**]** **1.** to greet with loud applause or strong approval **2.** to announce with much applause or praise; hail *[*they *acclaimed* him president*]* **—*n.*** loud applause or strong approval

ac·cla·ma·tion (ak′lə mā′shən) ***n.*** **1.** an acclaiming or being acclaimed **2.** loud applause or strong approval **3.** an enthusiastic approving vote by voice without an actual count **—ac·clam·a·to·ry** (ə klam′ə tôr′ē) ***adj.***

ac·cli·mate (ak′lə māt′, ə klī′mət) ***vt., vi.*** **-mat′ed, -mat′ing [**< Fr.: see AD- & CLIMATE**]** to accustom or become accustomed to a different climate or environment **—ac′cli·ma′tion *n.***

ac·cli·ma·tize (ə klī′mə tīz′) ***vt., vi.*** **-tized′, -tiz′ing** *same as* ACCLIMATE **—ac·cli′ma·ti·za′tion *n.***

ac·cliv·i·ty (ə kliv′ə tē) ***n., pl.*** **-ties [**< L. < *ad-*, up + *clivus*, hill**]** an upward slope of ground **—ac·cli·vous** (ə klī′vəs) ***adj.***

ac·co·lade (ak′ə lād′) ***n.*** **[**Fr. < Pr. < It. pp. of *accollare*, to embrace < L. *ad*, to + *collum*, neck**]** **1.** formerly, an embrace (now, a touch with a sword) used in conferring knighthood **2.** anything done or given as a sign of great respect, appreciation, etc.

ac·com·mo·date (ə käm′ə dāt′) ***vt.*** **-dat′ed, -dat′ing [**< L. pp. of *accommodare* < *ad-*, to + *com-*, with + *modus*, a measure**]** **1.** to adjust; adapt **2.** to reconcile (differences) **3.** to help by supplying (*with* something) **4.** to do a favor for **5.** to have room for **—*vi.*** to become adjusted, as the lens of the eye in focusing **—ac·com′mo·da′tive *adj.* —ac·com′mo·da′tor *n.***

ac·com·mo·dat·ing (-dāt′iŋ) ***adj.*** ready to help; obliging **—ac·com′mo·dat′ing·ly *adv.***

ac·com·mo·da·tion (ə käm′ə dā′shən) ***n.*** **1.** adaptation (*to* a purpose); adjustment **2.** reconciliation of differences **3.** willingness to do favors **4.** a help or convenience **5.** [*pl.*] lodgings or space, as in a hotel, on a ship, etc. **6.** the self-adjustment of the lens of the eye in focusing

ac·com·pa·ni·ment (ə kump′ni mənt, ə kum′pə nē-mənt) ***n.*** **1.** anything that accompanies something else **2.** *Music* a part performed, as on a piano, together with the main part, as with a vocal solo

ac·com·pa·nist (ə kum′pə nist) ***n.*** a person who plays an accompaniment

ac·com·pa·ny (ə kum′pə nē, ə kump′nē) ***vt.*** **-nied, -ny·ing [**< MFr. < *ac-*, to + OFr. *compagnon:* see COMPANION[1]**]** **1.** to go or be together with **2.** to supplement *[*to *accompany* words with acts*]* **3.** to play an accompaniment for or to

ac·com·plice (ə käm′plis) ***n.*** **[**< A-[1] + OFr. *complice* < LL. *complex*, accomplice: see COMPLEX**]** a person who knowingly helps another in an unlawful act

ac·com·plish (ə käm′plish) ***vt.*** **[**< OFr. < L. *ad-*, intens. + *complere:* see COMPLETE**]** to do; succeed in doing; complete **—ac·com′plish·a·ble *adj.***

ac·com·plished (-plisht) ***adj.*** **1.** done; completed **2.** skilled; proficient **3.** trained in the social arts or skills; polished

ac·com·plish·ment (-plish mənt) ***n.*** **1.** an accomplishing or being accomplished; completion **2.** something done successfully; achievement **3.** a social art or skill: *usually used in pl.*

ac·cord (ə kôrd′) ***vt.*** **[**< OFr. < L. *ad-*, to + *cor* (gen. *cordis*), heart**]** **1.** to make agree; reconcile **2.** to grant or concede **—*vi.*** to agree or harmonize (*with*) **—*n.*** **1.** mutual agreement; harmony **2.** an informal agreement, as between nations **3.** harmony of sound, color, etc. **—of one's own accord** willingly, without being asked **—with one accord** all agreeing

ac·cord·ance (-'ns) ***n.*** agreement; conformity **—ac·cord′ant *adj.* —ac·cord′ant·ly *adv.***

ac·cord·ing (-iŋ) ***adj.*** agreeing; in harmony **—according as** to the degree that **—according to** **1.** in agreement with **2.** in the order of *[*seated *according to* age*]* **3.** as stated by

ac·cord·ing·ly (-iŋ lē) ***adv.*** **1.** in a way that is fitting and proper **2.** therefore

ac·cor·di·on (ə kôr′dē ən) ***n.*** **[**< G., prob. < It. *accordare*, be in tune**]** a musical instrument with a bellows which is pulled out and pressed together to produce tones by forcing air through metal reeds opened by fingering keys **—*adj.*** having folds, or folding, like an accordion's bellows **—ac·cor′di·on·ist *n.***

ACCORDION

ac·cost (ə kôst′, -käst′) ***vt.*** **[**< Fr. < It. < L. < *ad-*, to + *costa*, rib, side**]** to approach and speak to, esp. in a bold or forward manner

ac·couche·ment (ə ko͞osh′mənt; *Fr.* ä ko͞osh män′) ***n.*** **[**Fr. < OFr. *acoucher:* see AD- & COUCH**]** confinement for giving birth to a child; childbirth

ac·count (ə kount′) ***vt.*** **[**< OFr. < *a-*, to + *conter*, to tell < L. *computare:* see COMPUTE**]** to consider to be; deem **—*vi.*** **1.** to furnish a reckoning of money received and paid out **2.** to make satisfactory amends (*for*) *[*made to *account* for his crime*]* **3.** to give satisfactory reasons or an explanation (*for*) **4.** to be the cause or source of (with *for*) **5.** to do away with as by killing (with *for*) **—*n.*** **1.** *a)* a record of the financial transactions of a person, business, etc. *b) same as* CHARGE ACCOUNT *c)* a business that is a customer or client, esp. on a credit basis **2.** *same as* BANK ACCOUNT **3.** worth; importance *[*a thing of small *account]* **4.** an explanation **5.** a report; description **—call to account** **1.** to demand an explanation of **2.** to reprimand **—give a good account of oneself** to acquit oneself well **—on account** as partial payment **—on account of** because of **—on no account** under no circumstances **—take account of** **1.** to allow for **2.** to take notice of **—take into account** to take into consideration **—turn to account** to get use from

ac·count·a·ble (-ə b'l) ***adj.*** **1.** obliged to account for one's acts; responsible **2.** that can be accounted for; explainable **—ac·count′a·bil′i·ty *n.* —ac·count′a·bly *adv.***

ac·count·an·cy (ə kount′'n sē) ***n.*** the work of an accountant

ac·count·ant (ə kount′'nt) ***n.*** a person whose work is to inspect or keep financial accounts: see CERTIFIED PUBLIC ACCOUNTANT

ac·count·ing (ə koun′tiŋ) ***n.*** **1.** the principles or practice of setting up and auditing financial accounts **2.** a settling or balancing of accounts

ac·cou·ter (ə ko͞ot′ər) ***vt.*** **[**Fr., prob. < L. *con-*, together + *suere*, to sew**]** to equip or attire: also **ac·cou′tre -tred, -tring**

ac·cou·ter·ments, ac·cou·tre·ments (ə ko͞ot′ər mənts, -ko͞o′trə-) ***n.pl.*** **1.** clothes; dress **2.** equipment; furnishings; trappings

Ac·cra (ə krä′) capital of Ghana, on the Atlantic: pop. 533,000

ac·cred·it (ə kred′it) ***vt.*** **[**< Fr.: see CREDIT**]** **1.** to bring into credit or favor **2.** to give credentials to **3.** to take as true **4.** to certify as meeting certain standards **5.** to attribute; credit **—ac·cred′it·a′tion** (-ə tā′shən) ***n.***

ac·cre·tion (ə krē′shən) ***n.*** **[**< L. *accretio* < *accrescere* < *ad-*, to + *crescere*, to grow**]** **1.** growth in size, esp. by addition or accumulation **2.** a growing together of separate parts **3.** accumulated matter **4.** a part added separately **5.** a whole resulting from such growth **—ac·cre′tive *adj.***

ac·crue (ə kro͞o′) ***vi.*** **-crued′, -cru′ing [**< OFr. < L.: see ACCRETION**]** **1.** to come as a natural growth, advantage, or right (*to*) **2.** to be added periodically as an increase: said esp. of interest on money **—ac·cru′al *n.***

acct. account

ac·cul·tu·rate (ə kul′chə rāt′) ***vi., vt.*** **-rat′ed, -rat′ing** to undergo, or alter by, acculturation

ac·cul·tu·ra·tion (ə kul′chə rā′shən) ***n.*** **[**AC- (see AD-) + CULTUR(E) + -ATION**]** **1.** the conditioning of a child to the patterns of a culture **2.** a becoming adapted to a different culture **3.** the mutual influence of different cultures in close contact

ac·cu·mu·late (ə kyo͞om′yə lāt′) ***vt., vi.*** **-lat′ed, -lat′ing [**< L. pp. of *accumulare* < *ad-*, to + *cumulare*, to heap**]** to pile up or collect, esp. over a period of time **—ac·cu′mu·la·ble** (-lə b'l) ***adj.***

ac·cu·mu·la·tion (ə kyo͞om′yə lā′shən) ***n.*** **1.** an accumulating; collection **2.** accumulated or collected material

ac·cu·mu·la·tive (ə kyo͞om′yə lāt′iv) ***adj.*** **1.** resulting from accumulation **2.** tending to accumulate **—ac·cu′mu·la′tive·ly *adv.* —ac·cu′mu·la′tive·ness *n.***

ac·cu·mu·la·tor (-lāt′ər) ***n.*** **1.** one that accumulates

fat, āpe, cär; ten, ēven; is, bīte; gō, hôrn, to͞ol, look; oil, out; up, fur; get; joy; yet; chin; she; thin, *th*en; zh, leisure; ŋ, ring; ə for *a* in *ago*, *e* in *agent*, *i* in *sanity*, *o* in *comply*, *u* in *focus*; ' as in *able* (ā′b'l); Fr. bal; ë, Fr. coeur; ö, Fr. feu; Fr. mo*n*; ô, Fr. coq; ü, Fr. duc; *r*, Fr. cri; H, G. ich; kh, G. doch; ‡foreign; *hypothetical; < derived from. See inside front cover.

2. [Brit.] a storage battery 3. a device, as in a computer, that stores a quantity and that will add to that quantity others, storing the sum

ac·cu·ra·cy (ak′yər ə sē) ***n.*** the quality or state of being accurate; precision

ac·cu·rate (ak′yər it) ***adj.*** [< L. pp. of *accurare,* to take care < *ad-,* to + *cura,* care] **1.** careful and exact **2.** free from errors; precise **3.** adhering closely to a standard —**ac′cu·rate·ly** ***adv.*** —**ac′cu·rate·ness** ***n.***

ac·curs·ed (ə kur′sid, -kurst′) ***adj.*** **1.** under a curse; ill-fated **2.** deserving to be cursed; damnable Also **ac·curst′** (-kurst′) —**ac·curs′ed·ly** ***adv.*** —**ac·curs′ed·ness** ***n.***

ac·cu·sa·tion (ak′yə zā′shən) ***n.*** **1.** an accusing or being accused **2.** the wrong that one is accused of

ac·cu·sa·tive (ə kyōō′zə tiv) ***adj.*** [< L. < pp. of *accusare:* see ACCUSE] **1.** designating or in the grammatical case, as in Latin, used for the direct object of a verb and after certain prepositions **2.** accusatory —***n.*** **1.** the accusative case **2.** a word in this case —**ac·cu′sa·ti′val** (-tī′v'l) ***adj.*** —**ac·cu′sa·tive·ly** ***adv.***

ac·cu·sa·to·ry (-tôr′ē) ***adj.*** making or containing an accusation; accusing

ac·cuse (ə kyōōz′) ***vt.*** **-cused′, -cus′ing** [< OFr. < L. *accusare* < *ad-,* to + *causa,* a cause or lawsuit] **1.** to find at fault; blame **2.** to bring formal charges against (*of* breaking the law, etc.) —**the accused** *Law* the person formally charged with committing a crime —**ac·cus′er** ***n.*** —**ac·cus′ing·ly** ***adv.***

ac·cus·tom (ə kus′təm) ***vt.*** to make used (*to* something) as by custom or regular use; habituate

ac·cus·tomed (-təmd) ***adj.*** **1.** customary; usual; characteristic **2.** used (*to*); in the habit of

ace (ās) ***n.*** [< L. *as,* unit] **1.** a playing card, domino, etc. marked with one spot **2.** *a)* a serve, as in tennis, that one's opponent is unable to return *b)* the point thus made **3.** *Golf* a hole in one: see entry HOLE **4.** a combat pilot who has destroyed many enemy planes **5.** an expert —***adj.*** [Colloq.] first-rate; expert *[an ace salesman]* —***vt.*** **aced** (āst), **ac′ing** to score an ace against (an opponent) in tennis, or on (a hole) in golf —**within an ace of** on the verge of

-a·ce·a (ā′shə, ā′shē ə) [L., neut. pl. of *-aceus*] a plural suffix used in forming zoological names of classes or orders: see -ACEOUS

-a·ce·ae (ā′si ē′) [L., fem. pl. of *-aceus*] a plural suffix used in forming botanical names of families: see -ACEOUS

ace-high (ās′hī′) ***adj.*** [orig. a poker term] [Colloq.] highly esteemed; respected

ace in the hole **1.** *Stud Poker* an ace dealt and kept face down until the deal is over **2.** [Slang] any advantage held in reserve

-a·ceous (ā′shəs) [L. *-aceus*] *a suffix meaning* of the nature of, like, belonging to, producing, etc.: often used to form adjectives corresponding to nouns ending in -ACEA, -ACEAE

ac·er·bate (as′ər bāt′) ***vt.*** **-bat′ed, -bat′ing** [< L. pp. of *acerbare*] **1.** to make sour or bitter **2.** to irritate; vex

a·cer·bi·ty (ə sur′bə tē) ***n.,*** *pl.* **-ties** [< Fr. < L. < *acerbus,* bitter] **1.** a sour, astringent quality **2.** sharpness or harshness of temper, words, etc.

ac·e·tab·u·lum (as′ə tab′yoo ləm) ***n.,*** *pl.* **-la** (-lə), **-lums** [L., orig. vinegar cup < *acetum:* see ACETO-] *Anat.* the cup-shaped socket of the hipbone

ac·e·tal (as′ə tal′) ***n.*** [ACET(O)- + -AL] a colorless, volatile liquid, $C_6H_{14}O_2$, used as a hypnotic

ac·et·an·i·lide (as′ə tan′ə līd′, -′l id) ***n.*** [ACET(O)- + ANIL(INE) + -IDE] a white, crystalline organic substance, C_8H_9NO, used to lessen pain and fever

ac·e·tate (as′ə tāt′) ***n.*** [ACET(O)- + -ATE[2]] **1.** a salt or ester of acetic acid **2.** *same as* CELLULOSE ACETATE —**ac′e·tat′ed** ***adj.***

a·ce·tic (ə sēt′ik, -set′-) ***adj.*** [< L. *acetum:* see ACETO-] of, like, containing, or producing acetic acid or vinegar

acetic acid a sour, colorless liquid, $C_2H_4O_2$, having a sharp odor: it is found in vinegar

a·cet·i·fy (ə set′ə fī′, -sēt′-) ***vt., vi.*** **-fied′, -fy′ing** to change into vinegar or acetic acid —**a·cet′i·fi·ca′tion** ***n.***

ac·e·to- [< L. *acetum,* vinegar] *a combining form meaning* of or from acetic acid: also, before a vowel, **ac·et-**

ac·e·tone (as′ə tōn′) ***n.*** [ACET(O)- + -ONE] a colorless, flammable, volatile liquid, C_3H_6O, used as a solvent for certain oils, etc. —**ac′e·ton′ic** (-tän′ik) ***adj.***

ac·e·to·phe·net·i·din (ə sēt′ō fə net′ə din) ***n.*** [ACETO- + PHEN(O)- + ET(HYL) + -ID(E) + -IN[1]] a white, crystalline powder, $C_{10}H_{13}O_2N$, used to reduce fever and to relieve headaches and muscular pains; phenacetin

a·cet·y·lene (ə set′'l ēn′) ***n.*** [ACET(O)- + -YL + -ENE] a colorless, poisonous, highly flammable gaseous hydrocarbon, C_2H_2, used for lighting and, with oxygen, in blowtorches, etc.

ac·e·tyl·sal·i·cyl·ic acid (ə sēt′'l sal′ə sil′ik, as′ə t'l-) *same as* ASPIRIN

ace·y-deuc·y (ā′sē dōō′sē) ***n.*** [< ACE + DEUCE[1]] a variation of backgammon

A·chae·an (ə kē′ən) ***adj.*** **1.** of Achaea, an ancient province in the Peloponnesus, or its people **2.** loosely, Greek —***n.*** **1.** a native or inhabitant of Achaea **2.** loosely, a Greek

A·cha·tes (ə kāt′ēz) in Virgil's *Aeneid,* a loyal friend of Aeneas —***n.*** a loyal friend

ache (āk) ***vi.*** **ached, ach′ing** [OE. *acan*] **1.** to have or give dull, steady pain **2.** to feel pity, etc. (*for*) **3.** [Colloq.] to yearn or long: with *for* or an infinitive —***n.*** a dull, continuous pain

a·chene (ā kēn′) ***n.*** [< ModL. < Gr. *a-,* not + *chainein,* to gape] any small, dry, one-seeded fruit that ripens without bursting —**a·che′ni·al** ***adj.***

a·chieve (ə chēv′) ***vt.*** **a·chieved′, a·chiev′ing** [< OFr. < *a-,* to + *chief:* see CHIEF] **1.** to succeed in doing; accomplish **2.** to get by exertion; attain; gain —***vi.*** to bring about a desired result —**a·chiev′a·ble** ***adj.*** —**a·chiev′er** ***n.***

a·chieve·ment (-mənt) ***n.*** **1.** an achieving **2.** a thing achieved, esp. by skill, work, etc.; feat

A·chil·les (ə kil′ēz) *Gr. Myth.* Greek hero in the Trojan War, who killed Hector and was killed by Paris with an arrow that struck his vulnerable heel: he is the hero of Homer's *Iliad*

Achilles' heel (one's) vulnerable spot

Achilles' tendon the tendon connecting the back of the heel to the muscles of the calf of the leg

ach·ro·mat·ic (ak′rə mat′ik) ***adj.*** [< Gr. < *a-,* without + *chrōma,* color + -IC] **1.** colorless **2.** refracting white light without breaking it up into its component colors **3.** forming visual images whose outline is free from prismatic colors *[an achromatic lens]* **4.** *Music same as* DIATONIC —**ach′ro·mat′i·cal·ly** ***adv.***

a·chro·mic (ā krō′mik) ***adj.*** [< Gr. < *a-,* without + *chrōma,* color + -IC] without color: also **a·chro′mous** (-məs)

ach·y (ā′kē) ***adj.*** **ach′i·er, ach′i·est** having an ache, or dull, steady pain

ac·id (as′id) ***adj.*** [L. *acidus,* sour] **1.** sharp and biting to the taste; sour **2.** sharp or sarcastic in speech, etc. **3.** of or being an acid **4.** having too much acid —***n.*** **1.** a sour substance **2.** [Slang] *same as* LSD **3.** *Chem.* any compound that reacts with a base to form a salt, produces hydrogen ions in water solution, and turns blue litmus red —**ac′id·ly** ***adv.*** —**ac′id·ness** ***n.***

a·cid·ic (ə sid′ik) ***adj.*** **1.** forming acid **2.** acid

a·cid·i·fy (ə sid′ə fī′) ***vt., vi.*** **-fied′, -fy′ing** **1.** to make or become sour or acid **2.** to change into an acid —**a·cid′i·fi′a·ble** ***adj.*** —**a·cid′i·fi·ca′tion** ***n.*** —**a·cid′i·fi′er** ***n.***

a·cid·i·ty (-tē) ***n.,*** *pl.* **-ties** **1.** *a)* acid quality or condition; sourness *b)* the degree of this **2.** *same as* HYPERACIDITY

ac·i·do·sis (as′ə dō′sis) ***n.*** *Med.* a condition in which the body's alkali reserve is below normal —**ac′i·dot′ic** (-dät′ik) ***adj.***

acid test [orig., a *test* of gold by *acid*] a crucial, final test of value or quality

a·cid·u·late (ə sij′oo lāt′) ***vt.*** **-lat′ed, -lat′ing** to make somewhat acid or sour —**a·cid′u·la′tion** ***n.***

a·cid·u·lous (-ləs) ***adj.*** [< L. dim. of *acidus,* sour] **1.** somewhat acid or sour **2.** somewhat sarcastic Also **a·cid′u·lent** (-lənt)

ac·i·nus (as′i nəs) ***n.,*** *pl.* **-ni′** (-nī′) [L., a grape] *Anat.* any of the small sacs of a compound gland —**ac′i·nar** (-nər), **ac′i·nous** (-nəs) ***adj.***

-a·cious (ā′shəs) [< L. *-ax* (gen. *-acis*) + -OUS] *a suffix meaning* characterized by, inclined to, full of *[tenacious]*

-ac·i·ty (as′ə tē) *a suffix corresponding to* -ACIOUS *[tenacity]*

ack-ack (ak′ak′) ***n.*** [echoic; prob. expansion of abbrev. *A.A.,* antiaircraft artillery] [Slang] an antiaircraft gun or its fire

ac·knowl·edge (ək näl′ij, ak-) ***vt.*** **-edged, -edg·ing** [< ME. *knowleche* (see KNOWLEDGE): infl. by ME. *aknowen* < OE. *oncnawan,* to understand] **1.** to admit to be true; confess **2.** to recognize the authority or claims of **3.** to recognize and answer (a greeting or introduction) **4.** to express thanks for **5.** to state that one has received (a letter, gift, etc.) **6.** *Law* to certify in legal form *[to acknowledge a deed]* —**ac·knowl′edge·a·ble** ***adj.***

ac·knowl·edg·ment, ac·knowl·edge·ment (-mənt) ***n.*** **1.** an acknowledging; admission **2.** something done or given in acknowledging, as thanks **3.** recognition of the authority or claims of **4.** a legal avowal or certificate

ACLU, A.C.L.U. American Civil Liberties Union

ac·me (ak′mē) ***n.*** [Gr. *akmē,* a point, top] the highest point; peak

ac·ne (ak′nē) ***n.*** [ModL., ? orig. error for Gr. *akmē:* see prec.] a common skin disease characterized by chronic inflammation of the sebaceous glands, usually causing pimples on the face, etc.

ac·o·lyte (ak′ə līt′) ***n.*** [< ML. < Gr. *akolouthos,* follower] **1.** *R.C.Ch.* a member of the highest of the four minor orders, who serves at Mass **2.** *same as* ALTAR BOY **3.** an attendant

A·con·ca·gua (ä′kôn kä′gwä) mountain of the Andes in W Argentina: 22,835 ft.
ac·o·nite (ak′ə nīt′) ***n.*** [< L. < Gr. *akoniton*] **1.** any of a genus of plants of the buttercup family, with blue, purple, or yellow hoodlike flowers: most species are poisonous **2.** a drug made from the dried roots of one species, formerly used in medicine
a·corn (ā′kôrn′) ***n.*** [< OE. *æcern*, nut] the fruit of the oak tree; oak nut
acorn squash a kind of winter squash, acorn-shaped with a dark-green, ridged skin
a·cous·tic (ə ko͞os′tik) ***adj.*** [< Fr. < Gr. < *akouein*, to hear] **1.** having to do with hearing or with sound as it is heard **2.** of acoustics Also **a·cous′ti·cal** —**a·cous′ti·cal·ly *adv.***
a·cous·tics (-tiks) ***n.pl.*** **1.** the qualities of a room, etc. that have to do with how clearly sounds can be heard in it **2.** [*with sing. v.*] the branch of physics dealing with sound
ac·quaint (ə kwānt′) ***vt.*** [< OFr. < ML. < L. *ad*, to + *cognitus*, pp. of *cognoscere*, to know thoroughly] **1.** to let know; make aware **2.** to cause to know personally; make familiar (*with*)
ac·quaint·ance (-'ns) ***n.*** **1.** knowledge (of something) got from personal experience or study **2.** the state of being acquainted (*with* someone) **3.** a person whom one knows only slightly —**ac·quaint′ance·ship′ *n.***
ac·qui·esce (ak′wē es′) ***vi.*** **-esced′, -esc′ing** [< Fr. < L. *acquiescere* < *ad-*, to + *quiescere:* see QUIET] to consent quietly without protest, but without enthusiasm (often with *in*) —**ac′qui·es′cence *n.*** —**ac′qui·es′cent *adj.*** —**ac′qui·es′cent·ly *adv.***
ac·quire (ə kwīr′) ***vt.*** **-quired′, -quir′ing** [L. *acquirere* < *ad-*, to + *quaerere*, to seek] **1.** to get or gain by one's own efforts or actions **2.** to get as one's own —**ac·quir′a·ble *adj.***
acquired character *Biol.* a modification of structure or function caused by environmental factors: now generally regarded as not inheritable: also **acquired characteristic**
ac·quire·ment (ə kwīr′mənt) ***n.*** **1.** an acquiring **2.** something acquired, as a skill, etc.
ac·qui·si·tion (ak′wə zish′ən) ***n.*** **1.** an acquiring or being acquired **2.** something acquired
ac·quis·i·tive (ə kwiz′ə tiv) ***adj.*** eager to acquire; good at getting and holding wealth, ideas, etc. —**ac·quis′i·tive·ly *adv.*** —**ac·quis′i·tive·ness *n.***
ac·quit (ə kwit′) ***vt.*** **-quit′ted, -quit′ting** [< OFr. < ML. *acquitare*, to settle a claim < L. *ad*, to + *quietare*, to quiet] **1.** to release from a duty, etc. **2.** to declare not guilty of a charge; exonerate **3.** to conduct (oneself); behave —**ac·quit′tal *n.*** —**ac·quit′ter *n.***
ac·quit·tance (-'ns) ***n.*** **1.** a settlement of, or release from, debt or liability **2.** a record of this; receipt
a·cre (ā′kər) ***n.*** [OE. *æcer*, field; akin to L. *ager*] **1.** a measure of land, 43,560 sq. ft. **2.** [*pl.*] specific holdings in land; lands
a·cre·age (ā′kər ij, ā′krij) ***n.*** acres collectively
ac·rid (ak′rid) ***adj.*** [< L. *acris*, sharp; form infl. by ACID] **1.** sharp, bitter, or irritating to the taste or smell **2.** bitter or sarcastic in speech, etc. —**a·crid·i·ty** (a krid′ə tē, ə-), **ac′rid·ness *n.*** —**ac′rid·ly *adv.***
ac·ri·mo·ny (ak′rə mō′nē) ***n.*** [< L. < *acer*, sharp] bitterness or harshness of manner or speech; asperity —**ac′ri·mo′ni·ous *adj.***
ac·ro- [< Gr. *akros*, at the end or top] *a combining form meaning* highest, at the extremities [*acrogen*]
ac·ro·bat (ak′rə bat′) ***n.*** [< Fr. < Gr. *akrobatos*, walking on tiptoe < *akros* (see prec.) + *bainein*, to go] an expert performer of tricks in tumbling or on the trapeze, tightrope, etc.; skilled gymnast —**ac′ro·bat′ic *adj.*** —**ac′ro·bat′i·cal·ly *adv.***
ac·ro·bat·ics (ak′rə bat′iks) ***n.pl.*** [*also with sing. v.*] **1.** the skill or tricks of an acrobat **2.** tricks requiring great skill [mental *acrobatics*]
ac·ro·gen (ak′rə jən) ***n.*** [ACRO- + -GEN] a plant, such as a fern or moss, having a perennial stem with the growing point at the tip —**a·crog·e·nous** (ə kräj′ə nəs), **ac′ro·gen′ic** (-jen′ik) ***adj.***
ac·ro·meg·a·ly (ak′rō meg′ə lē) ***n.*** [< Fr.: see ACRO- & MEGALO-] abnormal enlargement of the bones of the head, hands, and feet, resulting from overproduction of growth hormone by the pituitary gland —**ac′ro·me·gal′ic** (-mə gal′ik) ***adj.***
ac·ro·nym (ak′rə nim) ***n.*** [< ACRO- + Gr. *onyma*, name] a word formed from the first (or first few) letters of a series of words, as *radar*, from *ra*dio *d*etecting *a*nd *r*anging —**ac′ro·nym′ic *adj.***
ac·ro·pho·bi·a (ak′rə fō′bē ə) ***n.*** [ACRO- + PHOBIA] an abnormal fear of being in high places
a·crop·o·lis (ə kräp′'l is) ***n.*** [< Gr. < *akros* (see ACRO-) + *polis*, city] the fortified upper part of an ancient Greek city, esp. [A-] that of Athens, on which the Parthenon was built

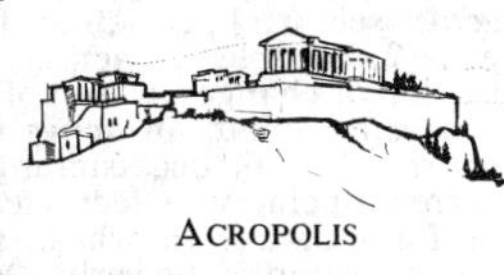
ACROPOLIS

a·cross (ə krôs′) ***adv.*** **1.** crossed; crosswise **2.** from one side to the other **3.** on or to the other side —***prep.*** **1.** from one side to the other of; so as to cross **2.** on or to the other side of; over **3.** into contact with by chance [he came *across* a friend]
a·cros·tic (ə krôs′tik) ***n.*** [< Gr. < *akros* (see ACRO-) + *stichos*, line of verse] a verse or arrangement of words in which certain letters in each line, as the first or last, when taken in order spell out a word, motto, etc. —***adj.*** of or like an acrostic —**a·cros′ti·cal·ly *adv.***
a·cryl·ic fiber (ə kril′ik) [ult. < ACR(ID) + -YL + -IC] any of a group of synthetic fibers derived from a compound of hydrogen cyanide and acetylene, and made into fabrics
acrylic resin any of a group of transparent thermoplastic resins, as Lucite
act (akt) ***n.*** [< Fr. < L. *actus*, a doing, *actum*, thing done, pp. of *agere*, to do] **1.** a thing done; deed **2.** an action; doing **3.** a decision (of a court, legislature, etc.) **4.** a document formally stating what has been done, etc. **5.** one of the main divisions of a drama or opera **6.** any of the separate performances on a variety program **7.** insincere behavior, put on just for effect —***vt.*** **1.** to play the part of **2.** to perform in (a play) **3.** to behave like [don't *act* the child] —***vi.*** **1.** to perform on the stage; play a role **2.** to behave as though playing a role **3.** to behave; comport oneself **4.** to do something **5.** to serve or function **6.** to serve as spokesman (*for*) **7.** to have an effect [acids *act* on metal] **8.** to appear to be —**act up** [Colloq.] **1.** to be playful **2.** to misbehave **3.** to become inflamed, painful, etc.
act·a·ble (ak′tə b'l) ***adj.*** that can be acted: said of a play, a role, etc. —**act′a·bil′i·ty *n.***
ACTH [<*a*(*dreno*)*c*(*ortico*)*t*(*rophic*) *h*(*ormone*)] a hormone secreted by the anterior lobe of the pituitary gland, that stimulates the growth and hormone production of the adrenal cortex
act·ing (ak′tiŋ) ***adj.*** **1.** adapted for performance [an *acting* version of a play] **2.** that acts; functioning **3.** temporarily taking over the duties of a position [the *acting* chairman] —***n.*** the art or occupation of performing in plays
ac·tin·ic (ak tin′ik) ***adj.*** having to do with actinism —**ac·tin′i·cal·ly *adv.***
actinic rays violet or ultraviolet rays that produce chemical changes, as in photography
ac·ti·nide series (ak′tə nīd′) a group of radioactive chemical elements from element 89 (actinium) through element 103 (lawrencium)
ac·tin·ism (ak′tən iz'm) ***n.*** [< Gr. *aktis* (gen. *aktinos*), ray & -ISM] that property of ultraviolet light, X-rays, etc. by which chemical changes are produced
ac·tin·i·um (ak tin′ē əm) ***n.*** [ModL. < Gr. *aktis* (gen. *aktinos*), ray] a radioactive chemical element found in pitchblende and other minerals: symbol, Ac; at. wt., 227 (?); at. no., 89
ac·ti·noid (ak′tə noid′) ***adj.*** star-shaped
ac·ti·no·my·cin (ak′ti nō mī′s'n) ***n.*** [< ModL. *Actinomyces*, a genus of bacteria] any of various antibiotic substances derived from soil bacteria
ac·ti·no·zo·an (ak′ti nō zō′ən) ***n.*** [< Gr. *aktis* (gen. *aktinos*), ray + *zōion*, animal] *same as* ANTHOZOAN
ac·tion (ak′shən) ***n.*** [< OFr. < L. *actio* < pp. of *agere:* see ACT] **1.** the doing of something; a being in motion **2.** an act or thing done **3.** [*pl.*] behavior; habitual conduct **4.** bold and energetic activity **5.** an effect [the *action* of a drug] **6.** the way of moving, working, etc., as of a machine **7.** the moving parts or mechanism, as of a gun, piano, etc. **8.** the happenings in a story or play **9.** a legal proceeding; lawsuit **10.** military combat **11.** [Slang] activity or excitement —**bring action** to start a lawsuit —**see action** to take part in military combat —**take action** **1.** to become active **2.** to start a lawsuit
ac·tion·a·ble (-ə b'l) ***adj.*** *Law* that gives cause for an action, or lawsuit
ac·ti·vate (ak′tə vāt′) ***vt.*** **-vat′ed, -vat′ing** **1.** to make active **2.** to put (an inactive military unit) on an active status **3.** to make radioactive **4.** to make capable of reacting or of accelerating a chemical reaction **5.** to treat (sewage) with air so that aerobes will purify it —**ac′ti·va′tion *n.*** —**ac′ti·va′tor *n.***
activated carbon a highly porous carbon that can adsorb gases, vapors, and colloidal particles

ac·tive (ak′tiv) ***adj.*** [< OFr. < L. *activus* < base *act-* as in *actus:* see ACT] **1.** acting, functioning, working, moving, etc. **2.** capable of acting, functioning, etc. **3.** causing motion or change **4.** full of action; lively, busy, quick, etc. [an *active* mind, an *active* boy] **5.** involving action [an *active* role] **6.** necessitating action [*active* sports] **7.** in current operation, effect, etc. **8.** *Gram.* denoting the voice or form of a verb whose subject is shown as performing the action of the verb —***n.*** *Gram.* the active voice —**ac′tive·ly** ***adv.***

ac·tiv·ism (ak′tə viz'm) ***n.*** the doctrine or policy of taking positive, direct action, esp. for political or social ends —**ac′tiv·ist** ***adj., n.***

ac·tiv·i·ty (ak tiv′ə tē) ***n., pl.*** **-ties** **1.** the state of being active; action **2.** energetic action; liveliness **3.** an active force **4.** any specific action [recreational *activities*]

ac·tiv·ize (ak′tə vīz′) ***vt.*** **-ized′, -iz′ing** *same as* ACTIVATE

act of God *Law* an occurrence, esp. a disaster, that is due to the forces of nature and could not reasonably have been prevented

Ac·ton (ak′t'n), Lord (*John Emerick Edward Dalberg-Acton*) 1834–1902; Eng. historian

ac·tor (ak′tər) ***n.*** **1.** a person who does something **2.** a person who acts in plays, movies, etc.

ac·tress (ak′tris) ***n.*** a woman or girl who acts in plays, movies, etc.

Acts (akts) a book of the New Testament, ascribed to Luke: full title, **The Acts of the Apostles**

ac·tu·al (ak′choo wəl) ***adj.*** [< LL. < L. *actus:* see ACT] **1.** existing in reality or fact; not merely possible, but real **2.** existing at present or at the time

ac·tu·al·i·ty (ak′choo wal′ə tē) ***n.*** **1.** the state of being actual; reality **2.** *pl.* **-ties** an actual thing or condition; fact

ac·tu·al·ize (ak′choo wə līz′) ***vt.*** **-ized′, -iz′ing** to make actual or real —**ac′tu·al·i·za′tion** ***n.***

ac·tu·al·ly (ak′choo wəl ē, ak′chə lē) ***adv.*** as a matter of actual fact; really

ac·tu·ar·y (ak′choo wer′ē) ***n., pl.*** **-ar′ies** [L. *actuarius,* clerk < *actus:* see ACT] a person who calculates risks, premiums, etc. for insurance —**ac′tu·ar′i·al** ***adj.*** —**ac′tu·ar′i·al·ly** ***adv.***

ac·tu·ate (ak′choo wāt′) ***vt.*** **-at′ed, -at′ing** **1.** to put into action or motion **2.** to cause to take action —**ac′tu·a′tion** ***n.*** —**ac′tu·a′tor** ***n.***

a·cu·i·ty (ə kyoo′ə tē) ***n.*** [< Fr. < L. *acus,* a needle] keenness, as of thought or vision; acuteness

a·cu·men (ə kyoo′mən, ak′yoo-) ***n.*** [L., a point < *acuere,* to sharpen] keenness and quickness of mind

a·cu·mi·nate (ə kyoo′mə nit; *for v.* -nāt′) ***adj.*** [< L. pp. of *acuminare* < *acumen:* see prec.] pointed; tapering to a point —***vt.*** **-nat′ed, -nat′ing** to make sharp or pointed —**a·cu′mi·na′tion** ***n.***

ac·u·punc·ture (ak′yoo puŋk′chər) ***n.*** [< L. *acus,* needle + PUNCTURE] the ancient practice, esp. as carried on by the Chinese, of piercing parts of the body with needles in seeking to treat disease or relieve pain

a·cute (ə kyoot′) ***adj.*** [< L. pp. of *acuere:* see ACUMEN] **1.** having a sharp point **2.** keen or quick of mind; shrewd **3.** sensitive [*acute* hearing] **4.** severe and sharp, as pain, jealousy, etc. **5.** severe but of short duration, as some diseases; not chronic **6.** very serious; critical [an *acute* shortage] **7.** of less than 90° [an *acute* angle] —**a·cute′ly** ***adv.*** —**a·cute′ness** ***n.***

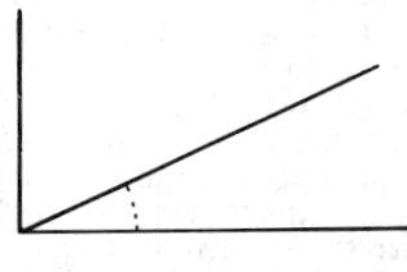

ACUTE ANGLE

acute accent a mark (´) used to show: **1.** the quality or length of a vowel, as in French *idée* **2.** primary stress, as in *týpewriter*

-a·cy (ə sē) [variously < Fr. < L. < Gr. *-ateia*] *a suffix meaning* quality, condition, position, etc. [*celibacy, curacy*]

ad[1] (ad) ***n.*** [Colloq.] an advertisement

ad[2] (ad) ***n.*** *Tennis* advantage; the first point scored after deuce

ad- [L., to, at, toward; akin to AT] *a prefix meaning variously* motion toward, addition to, nearness to [*admit, adjoin, adrenal*]: assimilated in words of Latin origin to **ac-, af-, ag-, al-, an-, ap-, ar-, as-, at-,** and **a-** before certain consonants

A.D. [L. *Anno Domini,* in the year of the Lord] of the Christian era: used with dates

A·da, A·dah (ā′də) [Heb. *'ādhā,* beauty] a feminine name

ad·age (ad′ij) ***n.*** [Fr. < L. < *ad-,* to + *aio,* I say] an old saying that has been popularly accepted as a truth

a·da·gio (ə dä′jō, -jē ō) ***adv.*** [It. *ad agio,* lit., at ease] *Music* slowly and leisurely —***adj.*** slow —***n., pl.*** **-gios** **1.** a slow movement in music **2.** a slow ballet dance, esp. by a mixed couple

Ad·am (ad′əm) [Heb. < *ādām,* a human being] **1.** a masculine name **2.** *Bible* the first man: Gen. 1–5 —**not know (a person) from Adam** not know (a person) at all

ad·a·mant (ad′ə mənt, -mant′) ***n.*** [OFr. < L. < Gr. *adamas* (gen. *adamantos*) < *a-,* not + *daman,* to subdue] a substance of unbreakable hardness —***adj.*** **1.** too hard to be broken **2.** not giving in or relenting; unyielding—**ad′a·man′tine** (-man′tēn, -tīn, -tin) ***adj.*** —**ad′a·mant·ly** ***adv.***

Ad·ams (ad′əmz) **1. Henry (Brooks),** 1838–1918; U.S. historian & writer **2. John,** 1735–1826; 2d president of the U.S. (1797–1801) **3. John Quin·cy** (kwin′sē), 1767–1848; 6th president of the U.S. (1825–29): son of *prec.* **4. Samuel,** 1722–1803; Am. statesman & Revolutionary leader

Adam's apple the projection formed in the front of the throat by the thyroid cartilage, seen chiefly in men

A·da·na (ä′dä nä′) city in S Turkey: pop. 290,000

a·dapt (ə dapt′) ***vt.*** [< Fr. < L. *adaptare* < *ad-,* to + *aptare,* to fit] **1.** to make fit or suitable by changing or adjusting **2.** to adjust (oneself) to new or changed circumstances —***vi.*** to adjust oneself —**a·dapt′a·bil′i·ty** ***n.*** —**a·dapt′a·ble** ***adj.*** —**a·dapt′er, a·dap′tor** ***n.***

ad·ap·ta·tion (ad′əp tā′shən) ***n.*** **1.** an adapting or being adapted **2.** a thing resulting from adapting [a movie *adaptation* of a novel] **3.** *Biol.* a change in structure, function, etc. of a plant or animal that produces better adjustment to the environment Also **a·dap·tion** (ə dap′shən)

a·dap·tive (ə dap′tiv) ***adj.*** **1.** showing adaptation **2.** able to adapt —**a·dap′tive·ly** ***adv.***

A·dar (ä där′) ***n.*** [Heb.] the sixth month of the Jewish year: see JEWISH CALENDAR

A.D.C., ADC aide-de-camp

add (ad) ***vt.*** [< L. *addere* < *ad-,* to + *dare,* to give] **1.** to join or unite (*to*) so as to increase the quantity, number, etc. **2.** to state further **3.** to combine (numbers) into a sum or total —***vi.*** **1.** to cause an increase (*to*) **2.** to figure a total —**add up** to seem reasonable —**add up to** **1.** to reach a total of **2.** to mean; signify

Ad·dams (ad′əmz), **Jane** 1860–1935; U.S. social worker & writer

ad·dax (ad′aks) ***n.*** [L. < native Afr. word] a large antelope of N Africa, with long, twisted horns

ad·dend (ad′end, ə dend′) ***n.*** [< ff.] a number or quantity to be added to another

ad·den·dum (ə den′dəm) ***n., pl.*** **-da** (-də) [L., gerundive of *addere:* see ADD] a thing added; esp., an appendix or supplement

ad·der (ad′ər) ***n.*** [ME. < *nadder* (by faulty separation of *a nadder*) < OE. *nædre*] **1.** a small poisonous snake of Europe; common viper **2.** any of various other snakes, as the puff adder (sense 1), the milk snake, etc.

ad·der's-tongue (ad′ərz tuŋ′) ***n.*** **1.** *same as* DOGTOOTH VIOLET **2.** a fern with a narrow spike

ad·dict (ə dikt′; *for n.* ad′ikt) ***vt.*** [< L. pp. of *addicere,* to give assent < *ad-,* to + *dicere,* to say] **1.** to give (oneself) up (*to* some strong habit): usually in the passive **2.** to make an addict of —***n.*** one addicted to a habit, esp. to the use of a narcotic drug —**ad·dic′tion** ***n.*** —**ad·dic′tive** ***adj.***

Ad·dis A·ba·ba (ä′dis ä′bə bə) capital of Ethiopia: pop. 644,000

Ad·di·son (ad′ə s'n), **Joseph** 1672–1719; Eng. essayist & poet —**Ad′di·so′ni·an** (-sō′nē ən) ***adj.***

Ad·di·son's disease (ad′ə s'nz) [after T. *Addison,* 19th-c. Eng. physician] a disease of the adrenal glands, characterized by weakness, skin discolorations, etc.

ad·di·tion (ə dish′ən) ***n.*** **1.** an adding of numbers to get a number called the sum **2.** a joining of a thing to another thing **3.** a thing or part added **4.** a room or rooms added to a building —**in addition (to)** besides; as well (as) —**ad·di′tion·al** ***adj.*** —**ad·di′tion·al·ly** ***adv.***

ad·di·tive (ad′ə tiv) ***adj.*** **1.** showing or relating to addition **2.** to be added —***n.*** a substance added to another in small quantities for a desired effect, as a preservative added to food

ad·dle (ad′'l) ***adj.*** [< OE. *adela,* mire, mud] **1.** rotten: said of an egg **2.** muddled; confused: often in compounds [*addlebrained*] —***vt., vi.*** **-dled, -dling** **1.** to make or become rotten **2.** to make or become muddled or confused

ad·dle·brained (-brānd′) ***adj.*** having an addle brain; muddled: also **ad′dle·head′ed, ad′dle·pat′ed** (-pāt′id)

ad·dress (ə dres′; *for n., esp. 2, 3, & 4, also* ad′res) ***vt.*** [< OFr. < *a-,* to + *dresser,* to direct < L. *dirigere:* see DIRECT] **1.** to direct (spoken or written words *to*) **2.** to speak to or write to **3.** to write the destination on (a letter or parcel) **4.** to use a proper form in speaking to **5.** to apply (oneself) or direct (one's energies) **6.** to take a stance, as in aiming the club at (a golf ball), facing (a target), etc. —***n.*** **1.** a speech, esp. a formal one **2.** the place to which mail can be sent to one; place where one lives or works **3.** the writing on mail showing its destination **4.** the location in a computer's storage compartment of an item of information **5.** social skill and tact **6.** conversational manner —**ad·dress′er, ad·dres′sor** ***n.***

ad·dress·ee (ad′res ē′) ***n.*** the person to whom mail, etc. is addressed

ad·duce (ə doos′, -dyoos′) ***vt.*** **-duced′, -duc′ing** [< L. *ad-*

ducere < *ad-*, to + *ducere:* see DUCT] to give as a reason or proof; cite —**ad·duc′er** *n.* —**ad·duc′i·ble, ad·duce′a·ble** *adj.*
ad·duct (a dukt′, ə-) *vt.* [< L. pp. of *adducere:* see prec.] to pull (a part of the body) toward the median axis: said of a muscle —**ad·duc′tor** *n.*
ad·duc·tion (a duk′shən, ə-) *n.* **1.** an adducing or citing **2.** an adducting
-ade (ād) [ult. < L. *-ata*] *a suffix meaning:* **1.** the act of *[blockade]* **2.** the result or product of *[pomade]* **3.** participant(s) in an action *[brigade]* **4.** [after LEMONADE] drink made from *[limeade]*
Ad·e·laide (ad′'l ād′) [< Fr. < G. < OHG. *Adalheit,* lit., nobility] **1.** a feminine name: dim. *Addie;* var. *Adeline, Adelina, Adele* **2.** city in S Australia: pop. 727,000
A·den (äd′'n, ād′-) **1.** former Brit. colony in SW Arabia: now part of YEMEN (sense 2) **2.** seaport in this region: pop. 250,000 **3. Gulf of,** arm of the Arabian Sea, between S Arabia and E Africa
ad·e·nine (ad′'n ēn′) *n.* [ADEN(O)- + -INE[4]] a white, crystalline purine base, $C_5H_5N_5$, found in nucleic acid in the spleen, pancreas, etc.
ad·e·no- [< Gr. *adēn,* gland] *a combining form meaning* of a gland or glands: also, before a vowel, **aden-**
ad·e·noi·dal (ad′'n oid′'l) *adj.* **1.** *a)* glandular *b)* of or like lymphoid tissue: also **ad′e·noid′** **2.** having adenoids **3.** having the characteristic difficult breathing or nasal tone due to enlarged adenoids
ad·e·noids (ad′'n oidz′) *n.pl.* [< ADEN(O)- & -OID] lymphoid growths in the throat behind the nose: they can swell up and obstruct breathing
ad·e·no·ma (ad′'n ō′mə) *n.* [ADEN(O)- + -OMA] a benign tumor of glandular origin or glandlike cell structure
a·den·o·sine (ə den′ə s'n, -sēn′) *n.* [arbitrary blend < ADENINE + RIBOSE] a white crystalline powder, $C_{10}H_{13}N_5O_4$, obtained from the hydrolysis of yeast nucleic acid: see also ADP, ATP
ad·ept (ə dept′; *for n.* ad′ept) *adj.* [< L. pp. of *adipisci* < *ad-,* to + *apisci,* to pursue, attain] highly skilled; expert —*n.* an expert —**ad·ept′ly** *adv.* —**ad·ept′ness** *n.*
ad·e·quate (ad′ə kwət) *adj.* [< L. pp. of *adaequare* < *ad-,* to + *aequare,* to make equal < *aequus,* level] **1.** enough or good enough; sufficient; suitable **2.** barely satisfactory —**ad′e·qua·cy** (-kwə sē), **ad′e·quate·ness** *n.* —**ad′e·quate·ly** *adv.*
ad·here (əd hir′, ad-) *vi.* **-hered′, -her′ing** [< L. *adhaerere* < *ad-,* to + *haerere,* to stick] **1.** to stick fast; stay attached **2.** to stay firm in supporting or approving —**ad·her′er** *n.*
ad·her·ence (əd hir′əns, ad-) *n.* an adhering; attachment or devotion (*to* a person, cause, etc.)
ad·her·ent (-ənt) *adj.* **1.** sticking fast; attached **2.** *Bot.* grown together —*n.* a supporter or follower (*of* a person, cause, etc.)
ad·he·sion (əd hē′zhən, ad-) *n.* [Fr. < L. *adhaesio* < *adhaerere:* see ADHERE] **1.** a sticking or being stuck together **2.** devoted attachment; adherence **3.** *Med. a)* the joining together, by fibrous tissue, of bodily parts normally separate *b)* such fibrous tissue **4.** *Physics* the force that holds together the molecules of unlike substances in surface contact: distinguished from COHESION
ad·he·sive (əd hē′siv, ad-; -ziv) *adj.* **1.** sticking and not coming loose; clinging **2.** gummed; sticky —*n.* an adhesive substance, as glue —**ad·he′sive·ly** *adv.* —**ad·he′siveness** *n.*
adhesive tape tape with a sticky substance on one side, used for holding bandages in place, etc.
ad hoc (ad′ häk′) [L., to this] for a special case or purpose only *[an ad hoc committee]*
ad·i·a·bat·ic (ad′ē ə bat′ik) *adj.* [< Gr. < *a-,* not + *dia,* through + *bainein,* to go] *Physics* involving expansion or compression without loss or gain of heat —**ad′i·a·bat′i·cal·ly** *adv.*
a·dieu (ə dyōō′, -dōō′; *Fr.* à dyö′) *interj., n., pl.* **a·dieus′;** Fr. **a·dieux′** (-dyö′) [Fr. < OFr. < L. *ad,* to + *Deus,* God] goodbye
ad in·fi·ni·tum (ad in′fə nīt′əm) [L., to infinity] endlessly; forever; without limit
ad in·ter·im (ad in′tər im) [L.] **1.** in the meantime **2.** temporary
a·di·os (a′dē ōs′, ä′-; *Sp.* ä dyôs′) *interj.* [Sp. *adiós* < L. *ad,* to + *Deus,* God] goodbye
ad·i·pose (ad′ə pōs′) *adj.* [< ModL. < L. *adeps* (gen. *adipis*), fat] of, like, or containing animal fat; fatty —*n.* animal fat in the connective tissue —**ad′i·pos′i·ty** (-päs′ə tē) *n.*
Ad·i·ron·dack Mountains (ad′ə rän′dak) mountain range of the Appalachians, in NE N.Y.: also **Ad′i·ron′dacks**
ad·it (ad′it) *n.* [< L. pp. of *adire* < *ad-,* to + *ire,* to go] an approach or entrance
adj. **1.** adjective **2.** adjourned **3.** adjutant
ad·ja·cent (ə jā′s'nt) *adj.* [< L. prp. of *adjacere* < *ad-,* to + *jacere,* to lie] near or close (*to* something); adjoining —**ad·ja′cen·cy** *n.* —**ad·ja′cent·ly** *adv.*
adjacent angles two angles having the same vertex and a side in common
ad·jec·tive (aj′ik tiv) *n.* [< L. < pp. of *adjicere,* to add to < *ad-,* to + *jacere,* to throw] **1.** any of a class of words used to limit or qualify a noun or other substantive *[good, every,* and *Aegean* are *adjectives]* **2.** any phrase or clause similarly used —*adj.* of, or having the nature or function of, an adjective —**ad′jec·ti′val** (-tī′v'l) *adj.* —**ad′jec·ti′val·ly** *adv.*
ad·join (ə join′) *vt.* [< OFr. < L. *adjungere* < *ad-,* to + *jungere:* see JOIN] to be next to; be contiguous to —*vi.* to be next to each other; be in contact —**ad·join′ing** *adj.*
ad·journ (ə jurn′) *vt.* [< OFr. < *a,* at + *jorn,* day < L. *diurnum,* daily < *dies,* day] to put off or suspend until a future day —*vi.* **1.** to close a session or meeting for a time **2.** [Colloq.] to go (*to* another place) *[let's adjourn to the patio]* —**ad·journ′ment** *n.*
ad·judge (ə juj′) *vt.* **-judged′, -judg′ing** [< OFr. < L. *adjudicare* < *ad-,* to + *judicare,* to judge < *judex,* JUDGE] **1.** to judge or decide by law **2.** to declare or order by law **3.** to award (costs, etc.) by law **4.** [Rare] to regard; deem
ad·ju·di·cate (ə jōō′də kāt′) *vt.* **-cat′ed, -cat′ing** [< L. pp. of *adjudicare:* see prec.] *Law* to hear and decide (a case); adjudge —*vi.* to serve as a judge (*in* or *on* a matter) —**ad·ju′di·ca′tion** *n.* —**ad·ju′di·ca′tive** *adj.* —**ad·ju′di·ca′tor** *n.* —**ad·ju′di·ca·to′ry** (-kə tôr′ē) *adj.*
ad·junct (aj′uŋkt) *n.* [< L. pp. of *adjungere:* see ADJOIN] **1.** a thing added to something else, but secondary **2.** a subordinate associate **3.** *Gram.* a modifier —*adj.* connected in a subordinate way —**ad·junc·tive** (ə juŋk′tiv) *adj.* —**ad·junc′tive·ly** *adv.* —**ad′junct·ly** *adv.*
ad·jure (ə joor′) *vt.* **-jured′, -jur′ing** [< L. *adjurare* < *ad-,* to + *jurare:* see JURY[1]] **1.** to charge solemnly, often under oath or penalty **2.** to entreat earnestly —**ad·ju·ra·tion** (aj′oo rā′shən) *n.* —**ad·jur′a·to′ry** (-ə tôr′ē) *adj.* —**ad·jur′er, ad·ju′ror** *n.*
ad·just (ə just′) *vt.* [< OFr. < *a-,* to + *j(o)uster* (see JOUST); infl. by OFr. *juste* < L. *justus,* JUST[1]] **1.** to change so as to fit, conform, make suitable, etc. **2.** to regulate *[to adjust a watch]* **3.** to settle or arrange rightly **4.** to resolve or bring into accord **5.** to decide how much is to be paid on (an insurance claim) —*vi.* to adapt oneself, as to one's surroundings —**ad·just′a·ble** *adj.* —**ad·just′er, ad·jus′tor** *n.*
ad·just·ment (-mənt) *n.* **1.** an adjusting or being adjusted **2.** a means by which parts are adjusted to one another **3.** the settlement of a claim
ad·ju·tant (aj′ə tənt) *n.* [< L. prp. of *adjutare* < *adjuvare* < *ad-,* to + *juvare,* to help] **1.** an assistant **2.** *Mil.* a staff officer who is an administrative assistant to the commanding officer **3.** a large stork of India and Africa
adjutant general *pl.* **adjutants general** **1.** an army officer who is the chief administrative assistant of a commanding general **2.** [A- G-] *U.S. Army* the general in charge of the department that handles records, correspondence, etc.

ADJUTANT STORK (to 60 in. high)

ad-lib (ad′lib′) *vt., vi.* **-libbed′, -lib′bing** [< ff.] [Colloq.] to improvise (words, etc. not in the script); extemporize —*n.* [Colloq.] an ad-libbed remark: also **ad lib** —*adj.* spoken or done extemporaneously —*adv.* [Colloq.] extemporizing freely: also **ad lib**
ad lib·i·tum (ad′ lib′i təm) [ML. < L. *ad,* at + *libitum* < *libet,* it pleases] at pleasure; as one pleases: used esp. as a musical direction that a section may be altered to suit the performer
Adm. **1.** Admiral **2.** Admiralty
ad·man (ad′man′) *n., pl.* **-men′** (-men′) a man whose work or business is advertising: also **ad man**
ad·meas·ure (ad mezh′ər) *vt.* **-ured, -ur·ing** [see AD- & MEASURE] to measure out shares of; apportion —**admeas′ure·ment** *n.*
ad·min·is·ter (əd min′ə stər, ad-) *vt.* [< OFr. < L. *administrare* < *ad-,* to + *ministrare,* to serve] **1.** to manage or direct **2.** to give out or dispense (punishment, etc.) **3.** to give or apply (medicine, etc.) **4.** to direct the taking of (an oath, pledge, etc.) **5.** *Law* to act as executor or administrator of (an estate) —*vi.* **1.** to act as manager or administrator **2.** to furnish help or be of service —**ad·min′is·tra·ble** (-ə strə b'l) *adj.* —**ad·min′is·trant** (-ə strənt) *n., adj.*
ad·min·is·trate (əd min′ə strāt′, ad-) *vt.* **-trat′ed, -trat′ing** *same as* ADMINISTER

ad·min·is·tra·tion (əd min′ə strā′shən, ad-) *n.* **1.** management, specif. of the affairs of a government, business, etc. **2.** *a)* [*often* A-] the executive officials of a government, business, etc., and their policies *b)* their term of office **3.** the administering (*of* medicine, an oath, etc.) **4.** *Law* the management and settling (*of* an estate) —**ad·min′is·tra′tive** *adj.* —**ad·min′is·tra′tive·ly** *adv.*

ad·min·is·tra·tor (əd min′ə strāt′ər, ad-) *n.* **1.** one who administers, or manages affairs **2.** *Law* one appointed by a court to settle an estate: cf. EXECUTOR —**ad·min′is·tra′trix** (-strā′triks) *n.fem., pl.* **-tra′tri·ces′** (-tri sēz′), **-trix·es**

ad·mi·ra·ble (ad′mər ə b'l) *adj.* inspiring or deserving admiration or praise; splendid —**ad′mi·ra·bil′i·ty** *n.* —**ad′mi·ra·bly** *adv.*

ad·mi·ral (ad′mər əl) *n.* [< OFr. < Ar. *amīr a' āli*, high leader; sp. infl. by ADMIRABLE] **1.** the commanding officer of a navy or fleet **2.** a naval officer of the highest rank **3.** [orig. ADMIRABLE] any of certain colorful butterflies

ad·mi·ral·ty (-tē) *n., pl.* **-ties** **1.** the rank, position, or authority of an admiral **2.** *a)* [*often* A-] the governmental department for naval affairs, as in England *b)* maritime law or court

ad·mi·ra·tion (ad′mə rā′shən) *n.* **1.** an admiring **2.** wonder, delight, and pleased approval at anything fine, skillful, beautiful, etc. **3.** a thing or person inspiring such feelings

ad·mire (əd mīr′, ad-) *vt.* **-mired′, -mir′ing** [< OFr. < L. *admirari* < *ad-*, at + *mirari*, to wonder] **1.** to regard with wonder, delight, and approval **2.** to have high regard for **3.** [Dial.] to like or wish (*to* do something) —**ad·mir′er** *n.* —**ad·mir′ing·ly** *adv.*

ad·mis·si·ble (əd mis′ə b'l, ad-) *adj.* [Fr. < L. pp. of *admittere*, ADMIT] **1.** that can be properly accepted or allowed **2.** that ought to be admitted —**ad·mis′si·bil′i·ty** *n.* —**ad·mis′si·bly** *adv.*

ad·mis·sion (əd mish′ən, ad-) *n.* **1.** an admitting or being admitted **2.** the right to enter **3.** an entrance fee **4.** a conceding, or granting **5.** an acknowledging or confessing **6.** a thing conceded, acknowledged, or confessed —**admis′sive** *adj.*

ad·mit (əd mit′, ad-) *vt.* **-mit′ted, -mit′ting** [< L. *admittere* < *ad-*, to + *mittere*, to send] **1.** to permit to enter or use **2.** to entitle to enter **3.** to allow, or leave room for **4.** to have room for; hold **5.** to concede; grant **6.** to acknowledge or confess **7.** to permit to practice [*admitted* to the bar] —*vi.* **1.** to give entrance (*to* a place) **2.** to allow or warrant (with *of*)

ad·mit·tance (-'ns) *n.* **1.** an admitting or being admitted **2.** permission or right to enter **3.** *Elec.* the reciprocal of impedance

ad·mit·ted·ly (əd mit′id lē) *adv.* by admission or agreement; confessedly [*admittedly* afraid]

ad·mix (ad miks′) *vt., vi.* [< ff.] to mix (a thing) in; mix with something

ad·mix·ture (-chər) *n.* [< L. pp. of *admiscere* < *ad-*, to + *miscere*, to mix + -URE] **1.** a mixture **2.** a thing or ingredient added in mixing

ad·mon·ish (əd män′ish, ad-) *vt.* [< OFr. < L. *admonere* < *ad-*, to + *monere*, to warn] **1.** to caution against specific faults; warn **2.** to reprove mildly **3.** to urge or exhort **4.** to inform or remind, by way of a warning —**ad·mon′ish·ing·ly** *adv.* —**ad·mon′ish·ment** *n.*

ad·mo·ni·tion (ad′mə nish′ən) *n.* **1.** an admonishing, or warning to correct some fault **2.** a mild rebuke; reprimand

ad·mon·i·tor (əd män′ə tər, ad-) *n.* a person who admonishes —**ad·mon′i·to′ry** (-tôr′ē) *adj.*

ad nau·se·am (ad′ nô′zē əm, -shē-, -sē-) [L., to nausea] to the point of disgust

a·do (ə do͞o′) *n.* [ME. < dial. inf. *at do*, to do] fuss; trouble; excitement

a·do·be (ə dō′bē) *n.* [Sp. < Ar. < Coptic *tōbe*, brick] **1.** unburnt, sun-dried brick **2.** the clay of which such brick is made **3.** a building made of adobe, esp. in the Southwest

ad·o·les·cence (ad′'l es′'ns) *n.* **1.** the state or quality of being adolescent **2.** the time of life between puberty and maturity

ad·o·les·cent (-'nt) *adj.* [Fr. < L. prp. of *adolescere*, to mature < *ad-*, to + *alescere*, to increase, grow up < *alere*, to feed] **1.** developing from childhood to maturity; growing up **2.** of or characteristic of adolescence; youthful, exuberant, immature, etc. —*n.* a boy or girl from puberty to adulthood; person in his teens

Ad·olph (ad′älf, ā′dôlf) [< L. < OHG. < *adal*, nobility + *wolf*, wolf] a masculine name

A·don·is (ə dän′is, -dō′nis) *Gr. Myth.* a young man loved by Aphrodite —*n.* any very handsome young man —**A·don′ic** (-ik) *adj.*

a·dopt (ə däpt′) *vt.* [< L. *adoptare* < *ad-*, to + *optare*, to choose] **1.** to choose and bring into a certain relationship; specif., to take into one's own family by legal process and raise as one's own child **2.** to take up and use (an idea, etc.) as one's own **3.** to choose and follow (a course) **4.** to vote to accept (a motion, etc.) **5.** to select as a required textbook —**a·dopt′a·ble** *adj.* —**a·dopt′er** *n.* —**a·dop′tion** *n.*

a·dop·tive (ə däp′tiv) *adj.* **1.** of adoption **2.** having become so by adopting [*adoptive* parents]

a·dor·a·ble (ə dôr′ə b'l) *adj.* **1.** [Now Rare] worthy of adoration **2.** [Colloq.] delightful; charming —**a·dor′a·bil′i·ty** *n.* —**a·dor′a·bly** *adv.*

ad·o·ra·tion (ad′ə rā′shən) *n.* **1.** a worshiping or paying homage **2.** great love or devotion

a·dore (ə dôr′) *vt.* **a·dored′, a·dor′ing** [< OFr. < L. *adorare* < *ad-*, to + *orare*, to speak] **1.** to worship as divine **2.** to love or honor greatly; idolize **3.** [Colloq.] to like very much —**a·dor′er** *n.* —**a·dor′ing·ly** *adv.*

a·dorn (ə dôrn′) *vt.* [< OFr. < L. *adornare* < *ad-*, to + *ornare*, to deck out] **1.** to be an ornament to; add beauty or distinction to **2.** to put decorations on; ornament —**a·dorn′ment** *n.*

ADP [A(DENOSINE) *d*(*i*)*p*(*hosphate*)] a vital substance, $C_{10}H_{15}N_5O_{10}P_2$, of all living cells, that is essential to the energy processes of life

ad·re·nal (ə drē′n'l) *adj.* [AD- + RENAL] **1.** near the kidneys **2.** of or from the adrenal glands —*n. same as* ADRENAL GLAND

adrenal gland either of a pair of endocrine organs lying immediately above the kidney and producing a variety of hormones

Ad·ren·al·in (ə dren′'l in) [ADRENAL + -IN[1]] *a trademark for* EPINEPHRINE —*n.* [a-] epinephrine: also **ad·ren′al·ine** (-in)

ad·re·no- *a combining form meaning:* **1.** adrenal glands **2.** epinephrine Also, before a vowel, **adren-**

A·dri·at·ic (Sea) (ā′drē at′ik) arm of the Mediterranean between Italy and Yugoslavia

a·drift (ə drift′) *adv., adj.* **1.** floating freely without being steered; drifting **2.** without any particular aim or purpose

a·droit (ə droit′) *adj.* [Fr. *à*, to + *droit*, right < L. pp. of *dirigere*, DIRECT] skillful in a physical or mental way; clever —**a·droit′ly** *adv.* —**a·droit′ness** *n.*

ad·sorb (ad sôrb′, -zôrb′) *vt.* [< AD- + L. *sorbere* (cf. ABSORB)] to collect (a gas, liquid, or dissolved substance) in condensed form on a surface —**ad·sorb′a·ble** *adj.* —**ad·sor′bent** *adj., n.*

ad·sorp·tion (ad sôrp′shən, -zôrp′-) *n.* adhesion of the molecules of a gas, liquid, or dissolved substance to a surface —**ad·sorp′tive** *adj.*

ad·u·late (aj′ə lāt′) *vt.* **-lat′ed, -lat′ing** [< L. pp. of *adulari*, to fawn upon] to praise or flatter too greatly —**ad′u·la′tion** *n.* —**ad′u·la′tor** *n.* —**ad′u·la·to′ry** (-lə tôr′ē) *adj.*

a·dult (ə dult′, ad′ult) *adj.* [< L. pp. of *adolescere*: see ADOLESCENT] **1.** grown up; fully developed in size, strength, mind, etc. **2.** of or for adult persons —*n.* **1.** a mature person **2.** a mature animal or plant **3.** a person who has reached the age at which he has full legal rights and responsibilities —**a·dult′hood** *n.* —**a·dult′ness** *n.*

a·dul·ter·ant (ə dul′tər ənt) *n.* a substance used to adulterate something —*adj.* adulterating

a·dul·ter·ate (ə dul′tə rāt′) *vt.* **-at′ed, -at′ing** [< L. pp. of *adulterare*, to falsify < *ad-*, to + *alter*, other] to make inferior, impure, etc. by adding a harmful, inferior, or unnecessary substance —**a·dul′ter·a′tion** *n.* —**a·dul′ter·a′tor** *n.*

a·dul·ter·er (ə dul′tər ər) *n.* a person (esp. a man) who commits adultery —**a·dul′ter·ess** *n.fem.*

a·dul·ter·ous (-əs) *adj.* of, or having committed, adultery —**a·dul′ter·ous·ly** *adv.*

a·dul·ter·y (ə dul′tər ē) *n., pl.* **-ter·ies** [L. *adulterium* < *adulter*: see ADULTERATE] voluntary sexual intercourse between a married person and another not the spouse

ad·um·brate (ad um′brāt, ad′əm brāt′) *vt.* **-brat·ed, -brat·ing** [< L. pp. of *adumbrari* < *ad-*, to + *umbra*, shade] **1.** to outline vaguely; sketch **2.** to foreshadow vaguely **3.** to obscure; overshadow —**ad′um·bra′tion** *n.* —**ad·um′bra·tive** *adj.*

adv. **1.** adverb **2.** adverbial **3.** advertisement **4.** advisory **5.** advocate

ad va·lo·rem (ad′ və lôr′əm) [L.] in proportion to the value: said of duties levied on imports according to their invoiced value: abbrev. **ad val.**

ad·vance (əd vans′) *vt.* **-vanced′, -vanc′ing** [< OFr. *avancer*, to forward < L. *ab-*, from + *ante*, before] **1.** to bring or move forward **2.** to raise in rank, importance, etc. **3.** to help; further **4.** to put forward; propose **5.** to cause to happen earlier **6.** to raise the rate of **7.** to pay (money) before due **8.** to lend —*vi.* **1.** to go forward **2.** to improve; progress; develop **3.** to rise in rank, importance, price, etc. —*n.* **1.** a moving forward **2.** an improvement; progress **3.** a rise in value or cost **4.** [*pl.*] approaches to gain favor, become acquainted, etc. **5.** a payment made before due, as of wages **6.** a loan —*adj.*

1. in front *[advance* guard*]* **2.** beforehand *[advance* information*]* —**in advance** **1.** in front **2.** ahead of time

ad·vanced (əd vanst′) ***adj.*** **1.** in advance; in front **2.** far on in life; old **3.** ahead or beyond in progress, complexity, etc. *[advanced* studies*]* **4.** higher than usual *[advanced* prices*]*

ad·vance·ment (əd vans′mənt) ***n.*** **1.** an advancing or being advanced **2.** promotion, as to a higher rank **3.** progress or improvement; furtherance

ad·van·tage (əd van′tij) ***n.*** [< OFr. < *avant,* before < L. *ab ante,* from before] **1.** a more favorable position; superiority or a better chance **2.** a favorable circumstance, event, etc. **3.** gain or benefit **4.** *Tennis* the first point scored after deuce —***vt.*** **-taged, -tag·ing** to give an advantage to —**take advantage of** **1.** to use for one's own benefit **2.** to impose upon —**to advantage** producing a good effect

ad·van·ta·geous (ad′vən tā′jəs) ***adj.*** favorable; profitable —**ad′van·ta′geous·ly** ***adv.***

Ad·vent (ad′vent) ***n.*** [< L. pp. of *advenire* < *ad-,* to + *venire,* to come] **1.** the period including the four Sundays just before Christmas **2.** *Theol. a)* Christ's birth *b) same as* SECOND COMING **3.** [**a-**] a coming or arrival

Ad·vent·ist (ad′vən tist) ***n.*** a member of a Christian sect based on the belief that Christ's second coming will soon occur —**Ad′vent·ism** ***n.***

ad·ven·ti·tious (ad′vən tish′əs) ***adj.*** [< L., coming from abroad: see ADVENT] **1.** added from outside; accidental **2.** *Biol.* occurring in unusual or abnormal places *[adventitious* leaves on a plant*]* —**ad′ven·ti′tious·ly** ***adv.*** —**ad′ven·ti′tious·ness** ***n.***

ad·ven·tive (ad ven′tiv) ***adj.*** *Bot.* not native to the environment

ad·ven·ture (əd ven′chər) ***n.*** [< OFr. < L. *advenire:* see ADVENT] **1.** the encountering of, or a liking for, danger **2.** an exciting and dangerous undertaking **3.** an unusual, stirring experience, often of a romantic nature **4.** a business venture or speculation —***vt.*** **-tured, -tur·ing** to risk or venture —***vi.*** **1.** to engage in adventure **2.** to take a risk

ad·ven·tur·er (-ər) ***n.*** **1.** a person who has or likes to have adventures **2.** *same as* SOLDIER OF FORTUNE **3.** a financial speculator **4.** a person who seeks to become rich, powerful, etc. by dubious schemes —**ad·ven′tur·ess** ***n.fem.***

ad·ven·ture·some (-səm) ***adj.*** willing to take risks; adventurous

ad·ven·tur·ism (-iz'm) ***n.*** actions, esp. in international relations, regarded as reckless and risky —**ad·ven′tur·ist** ***n., adj.***

ad·ven·tur·ous (-əs) ***adj.*** **1.** fond of adventure; daring **2.** full of danger; risky —**ad·ven′tur·ous·ly** ***adv.*** —**ad·ven′tur·ous·ness** ***n.***

ad·verb (ad′vurb) ***n.*** [< L. *adverbium* < *ad-,* to + *verbum,* a word] **1.** any of a class of words used to modify a verb, adjective, or another adverb, by expressing time, place, manner, degree, cause, etc. **2.** any phrase or clause similarly used —**ad·ver′bi·al** ***adj.,*** ***n.*** —**ad·ver′bi·al·ly** ***adv.***

ad·ver·sar·y (ad′vər ser′ē) ***n.,*** *pl.* **-sar′ies** [< OFr. < L. < *adversus,* ADVERSE] a person who opposes or fights against another; opponent; enemy

ad·ver·sa·tive (ad vur′sə tiv, əd-) ***adj.*** [< LL. < L. pp. of *adversari,* to be opposed to] expressing opposition or antithesis —***n.*** an adversative word, such as *but, yet, however*

ad·verse (ad vurs′, əd-; ad′vərs) ***adj.*** [< OFr. < L. *adversus,* turned opposite to, pp. of *advertere:* see ADVERT] **1.** opposite in position or direction **2.** unfavorable; harmful —**ad·verse′ly** ***adv.***

ad·ver·si·ty (ad vur′sə tē, əd-) ***n.*** **1.** a state of wretchedness; poverty and trouble **2.** *pl.* **-ties** a disaster; calamity

ad·vert (ad vurt′, əd-) ***vi.*** [< OFr. < L. *advertere* < *ad-,* to + *vertere,* to turn: see VERSE] to call attention (*to*); refer

ad·vert·ent (-'nt) ***adj.*** attentive; heedful —**ad·vert′ence, ad·vert′en·cy** ***n.*** —**ad·vert′ent·ly** ***adv.***

ad·ver·tise (ad′vər tīz′) ***vt.*** **-tised′, -tis′ing** [< OFr. *advertir,* to call attention to < L. *advertere:* see ADVERT] **1.** to tell about or praise (a product, etc.), as through newspapers, radio, or the like, so as to promote sales **2.** to make known —***vi.*** **1.** to call the public's attention to things for sale, for rent, etc., as by printed notices **2.** to ask (*for*) publicly by printed notice, etc. *[advertise* for a maid*]* —**ad′ver·tis′er** ***n.***

ad·ver·tise·ment (ad′vər tīz′mənt, əd vur′tiz mənt) ***n.*** **1.** the act of advertising **2.** a public announcement, usually paid for, as of things for sale, needs, etc.

ad·ver·tis·ing (ad′vər tī′ziŋ) ***n.*** **1.** printed or spoken matter that advertises **2.** the business or work of preparing and issuing advertisements

ad·ver·tize (ad′vər tīz′) ***vt., vi.*** **-tized′, -tiz′ing** *same as* ADVERTISE —**ad′ver·tize′ment** ***n.***

ad·vice (əd vīs′) ***n.*** [< OFr. < ML. *advisum* < pp. of *advidere* < L. < *ad-,* at + *videre,* to look] **1.** opinion given as to what to do; counsel **2.** [*usually pl.*] information or report

ad·vis·a·ble (əd vī′zə b'l) ***adj.*** proper to be advised or recommended; being good advice —**ad·vis′a·bil′i·ty** ***n.*** —**ad·vis′a·bly** ***adv.***

ad·vise (əd vīz′) ***vt.*** **-vised′, -vis′ing** [< OFr. < ML. *advisum:* see ADVICE] **1.** to give advice to; counsel **2.** to offer as advice; recommend **3.** to notify; inform —***vi.*** **1.** to discuss or consult (*with*) **2.** to give advice —**ad·vis′er, ad·vi′sor** ***n.***

ad·vised (əd vīzd′) ***adj.*** showing or resulting from thought or advice: now chiefly in WELL-ADVISED, ILL-ADVISED

ad·vis·ed·ly (əd vī′zid lē) ***adv.*** with due consideration; deliberately

ad·vise·ment (əd vīz′mənt) ***n.*** careful consideration —**take under advisement** to consider carefully

ad·vi·so·ry (əd vī′zər ē) ***adj.*** **1.** advising or empowered to advise **2.** relating to, or containing, advice —***n.,*** *pl.* **-ries** a warning, esp. one about weather conditions

ad·vo·ca·cy (ad′və kə sē) ***n.*** an advocating; a speaking or writing in support (*of* something)

ad·vo·cate (ad′və kit, -kāt′; *for v.* -kāt′) ***n.*** [< OFr. < L. *advocatus,* a counselor < *ad-,* to + *vocare,* to call] **1.** a person who pleads another's cause; specif., a lawyer **2.** a person who speaks or writes in support of something —***vt.*** **-cat′ed, -cat′ing** to speak or write in support of; be in favor of —**ad′vo·ca′tor** ***n.***

advt. *pl.* **advts.** advertisement

adz, adze (adz) ***n.*** [OE. *adesa*] an axlike tool for trimming and smoothing wood, etc., with a curved blade at right angles to the handle

ADZ

A.E.C., AEC Atomic Energy Commission

a·ë·des (ā ē′dēz) ***n.,*** *pl.* **a·ë′des** [ModL. < Gr. *aēdēs* < *a-,* not + *hēdys,* sweet] the mosquito that carries the virus of yellow fever

ae·dile (ē′dīl) ***n.*** [< L. < *aedes,* building] in ancient Rome, an official in charge of buildings, roads, public games, etc.

Ae·ge·an (Sea) (ē jē′ən) sea between Greece and Turkey: an arm of the Mediterranean

ae·gis (ē′jis) ***n.*** [L. < Gr. *aigis,* goatskin] **1.** *Gr. Myth.* a shield borne by Zeus and, later, by Athena **2.** a protection **3.** sponsorship; auspices

Ae·ne·as (i nē′əs) *Gr. & Rom. Myth.* a Trojan warrior who escaped from ruined Troy and wandered for years before coming to Latium

Ae·ne·id (i nē′əd) a Latin epic poem by Virgil, about Aeneas and his adventures

Ae·o·li·an (ē ō′lē ən) ***adj.*** **1.** of Aeolus **2.** [*often* **a-**] of the wind

aeolian harp a boxlike stringed instrument that makes musical sounds when air blows on it

Ae·o·lus (ē′ə ləs) *Gr. Myth.* the god of the winds

ae·on (ē′ən, ē′än) ***n.*** *same as* EON

ae·o·ni·an (ē ō′nē ən) ***adj.*** lasting for eons; eternal

aer·ate (er′āt′, ā′ər-) ***vt.*** **-at′ed, -at′ing** [AER(O)- + -ATE[1]] **1.** to expose to air, or cause air to circulate through **2.** to supply oxygen to (the blood) by respiration **3.** to charge (liquid) with gas, as in making soda water —**aer·a′tion** ***n.*** —**aer′a′tor** ***n.***

aer·i- *same as* AERO-

aer·i·al (er′ē əl; *occas. for adj.* ā ir′ē əl) ***adj.*** [< L. *aerius* < *aer* (see AIR) + -AL] **1.** of, in, or by the air **2.** like air; light as air **3.** not substantial; unreal; imaginary **4.** high up **5.** of, for, or by means of aircraft or flying **6.** growing in the air instead of in soil or water —***n.*** an antenna (sense 2) —**aer′i·al·ly** ***adv.***

aer·i·al·ist (er′ē əl ist) ***n.*** an acrobat who performs on a trapeze, high wire, etc.

aer·ie (er′ē, ir′ē) ***n.*** [< OFr. < ML. *aeria,* area; sp. & meaning infl. by L. *aer,* air & ME. *ei,* egg] **1.** the nest of an eagle or other bird of prey that builds in a high place **2.** a house or stronghold on a high place

aer·o (er′ō, ā′ə rō′) ***adj.*** of or for aeronautics or aircraft

aer·o- [< Gr. *aēr,* air] *a combining form meaning:* **1.** air; of the air *[aerolite]* **2.** of aircraft or flying *[aerostatics]* **3.** of gases *[aerodynamics]*

aer·obe (er′ōb) ***n.*** [< AERO- + Gr. *bios,* life] a microorganism that can live and grow only where free oxygen is present

aer·o·bic (er ō′bik) ***adj.*** **1.** of, characteristic of, or produced by aerobes **2.** designating or involving exercise, such as running, that increases the efficiency of oxygen intake by the body —***n.*** [*pl.*] aerobic exercises

aer·o·drome (er′ə drōm′) ***n.*** *Brit. var. of* AIRDROME
aer·o·dy·nam·ics (er′ō dī nam′iks) ***n.pl.*** [*with sing. v.*] the branch of aeromechanics dealing with the forces exerted by air or other gases in motion —**aer′o·dy·nam′ic** ***adj.*** —**aer′o·dy·nam′i·cal·ly** ***adv.***
aer·o·em·bo·lism (er′ō em′bə liz'm) ***n.*** **1.** *same as* DECOMPRESSION SICKNESS **2.** nitrogen bubbles formed in the blood during decompression sickness
aer·o·lite (er′ə līt′) ***n.*** [AERO- + -LITE] a stony meteorite —**aer′o·lit′ic** (-lit′ik) ***adj.***
aer·ol·o·gy (er äl′ə jē) ***n.*** [AERO- + -LOGY] the branch of meteorology concerned with the study of air, esp. in the upper atmosphere
aer·o·me·chan·ics (er′ō mə kan′iks) ***n.pl.*** [*with sing. v.*] the branch of mechanics dealing with air or other gases in motion or equilibrium: it includes aerodynamics and aerostatics —**aer′o·me·chan′ic** ***adj.***
aer·o·nau·tics (er′ə nôt′iks) ***n.pl.*** [*with sing. v.*] [AERO- + Gr. *nautēs*, sailor + -ICS] the science, art, or work of designing, making, and operating aircraft —**aer′o·nau′ti·cal, aer′o·nau′tic** ***adj.*** —**aer′o·nau′ti·cal·ly** ***adv.***
aer·o·pause (er′ō pôz′) ***n.*** a region at the upper level of the earth's atmosphere, regarded as the boundary between the atmosphere and outer space
aer·o·plane (er′ə plān′) ***n.*** *Brit. var. of* AIRPLANE
aer·o·pulse (-puls′) ***n.*** [AERO- + PULSE[1]] *same as* PULSEJET (ENGINE)
aer·o·sol (-sôl′, -säl′, -sōl′) ***n.*** [AERO- + SOL[3]] a suspension of colloidal particles in a gas —***adj.*** of or dispensed by a container in which gas under pressure is used to aerate liquid and eject it as a spray or foam
aer·o·space (er′ō spās′) ***n.*** [altered < AIR + SPACE] the earth's atmosphere and the space outside it, considered as one continuous field
aer·o·stat (-stat′) ***n.*** [< Fr.: see AERO- & -STAT] a dirigible, balloon, or other airship that is lifted by a contained gas lighter than air
aer·o·stat·ics (er′ō stat′iks) ***n.pl.*** [*with sing. v.*] the branch of aeromechanics dealing with the equilibrium of air or other gases, and with the equilibrium of solid bodies floating in air or other gases —**aer′o·stat′ic** ***adj.***
aer·y (er′ē, ir′ē) ***n.*** *same as* AERIE
Aes·chy·lus (es′kə ləs) 525?–456 B.C.; Gr. writer of tragedies —**Aes′chy·le′an** (-lē′ən) ***adj.***
Aes·cu·la·pi·us (es′kyoo lā′pē əs) *Rom. Myth.* the god of medicine and of healing: identified with the Greek god Asclepius —**Aes′cu·la′pi·an** ***adj.***
Ae·sir (ā′sir, ē′-) ***n.pl.*** [ON., pl. of *ass*, a god] the principal gods of Norse mythology
Ae·sop (ē′säp, -səp) real or legendary Gr. author of fables: supposed to have lived 6th cent. B.C. —**Ae·so·pi·an** (ē sō′pē ən) ***adj.***
aes·thete (es′thēt′) ***n.*** [Gr. *aisthētēs*, one who perceives] **1.** a person highly sensitive to art and beauty **2.** a person who artificially cultivates artistic sensitivity or makes a cult of art and beauty —**aes·thet·i·cism** (es thet′ə siz'm) ***n.***
aes·thet·ic (es thet′ik) ***adj.*** **1.** of aesthetics **2.** of beauty **3.** sensitive to art and beauty; artistic Also **aes·thet′i·cal** —***n.*** the aesthetic principle —**aes·thet′i·cal·ly** ***adv.***
aes·thet·ics (-iks) ***n.pl.*** [*with sing. v.*] the study or theory of beauty and of the psychological responses to it; specif., the branch of philosophy dealing with art and its forms, effects, etc.
aes·ti·vate (es′tə vāt′) ***vi.*** **-vat′ed, -vat′ing** *same as* ESTIVATE
aet., aetat. [L. *aetatis*] at the age of
ae·ther (ē′thər) ***n.*** *earlier var. of* ETHER
Aet·na (et′nə) *same as* ETNA
a.f., A.F. audio-frequency
a·far (ə fär′) ***adv.*** [Poet. or Archaic] at or to a distance —**from afar** from a distance
AFB Air Force Base
A.F.C., AFC automatic frequency control
a·feard, a·feared (ə fird′) ***adj.*** [< OE. < *a-* (intens.) + *faeran*, to frighten] [Dial. or Archaic] frightened; afraid
af·fa·ble (af′ə b'l) ***adj.*** [< L. *affabilis* < *ad-*, to + *fari*, to speak: see FAME] **1.** easy to approach and talk to; friendly **2.** gentle and kindly *[an affable smile]* —**af′fa·bil′i·ty** ***n.*** —**af′fa·bly** ***adv.***
af·fair (ə fer′) ***n.*** [< OFr. < *a faire*, to do < L. *ad-*, to + *facere*, to do] **1.** a thing to be done; business **2.** [*pl.*] matters of business or concern **3.** any matter, occurrence, or thing **4.** an event arousing public controversy **5.** a social gathering **6.** a sexual relationship outside of marriage
af·fect[1] (ə fekt′; *for n.* af′ekt) ***vt.*** [< L. *affectare*, to strive after < pp. of *afficere*, to influence < *ad-*, to + *facere*, to do] **1.** to have an effect on; influence **2.** to move or stir the emotions of —***n.*** *Psychol.* emotion or emotional response
af·fect[2] (ə fekt′) ***vt.*** [< OFr. < L. *affectare*, AFFECT[1]] **1.** to like to have, use, wear, etc. *[she affects plaid coats]* **2.** to pretend to have, feel, like, etc.; feign *[to affect indifference]*
af·fec·ta·tion (af′ek tā′shən) ***n.*** **1.** an affecting or pretending to like, have, etc.; show or pretense **2.** artificial behavior meant to impress others
af·fect·ed[1] (ə fek′tid) ***adj.*** **1.** attacked by disease **2.** influenced; acted upon **3.** emotionally moved
af·fect·ed[2] (ə fek′tid) ***adj.*** **1.** assumed for effect; artificial **2.** behaving in an artificial way to impress people —**af·fect′ed·ly** ***adv.*** —**af·fect′ed·ness** ***n.***
af·fect·ing (ə fek′tiŋ) ***adj.*** emotionally touching; causing one to feel pity, sympathy, etc.
af·fec·tion (ə fek′shən) ***n.*** **1.** a tendency or disposition **2.** fond or tender feeling; warm liking **3.** a disease; ailment **4.** an affecting or being affected
af·fec·tion·ate (-it) ***adj.*** full of affection; tender and loving —**af·fec′tion·ate·ly** ***adv.***
af·fec·tive (ə fek′tiv) ***adj.*** of affects, or feelings; emotional —**af·fec′tive·ly** ***adv.*** —**af·fec·tiv·i·ty** (af′ek tiv′ə tē) ***n.***
af·fer·ent (af′ər ənt) ***adj.*** [< L. prp. of *afferre* < *ad-*, to + *ferre*, to BEAR[1]] *Physiol.* bringing inward to a central part; specif., designating nerves that transmit impulses toward a nerve center: opposed to EFFERENT
af·fi·ance (ə fī′əns) ***vt.*** **-anced, -anc·ing** [< OFr. *afier* < ML. < *ad-*, to + *fidare*, to trust] to betroth
af·fi·ant (ə fī′ənt) ***n.*** [< prp. of OFr. *afier*: see prec.] a person who makes an affidavit
af·fi·da·vit (af′ə dā′vit) ***n.*** [ML., he has made oath] a written statement made on oath as before a notary public
af·fil·i·ate (ə fil′ē āt′; *for n.* -it) ***vt.*** **-at′ed, -at′ing** [< ML. pp. of *affiliare*, to adopt as a son < L. *ad-*, to + *filius*, son] **1.** to take in as a member or branch **2.** to connect or associate (oneself *with*) —***vi.*** to associate oneself; join —***n.*** an affiliated person or organization —**af·fil′i·a′tion** ***n.***
af·fin·i·ty (ə fin′ə tē) ***n.***, *pl.* **-ties** [< OFr. < L. < *affinis*, adjacent < *ad-*, to + *finis*, end] **1.** relationship by marriage **2.** close relationship; connection **3.** a similarity of structure implying common origin **4.** a natural liking; esp., a mutual attraction between a man and a woman **5.** a person of the opposite sex who especially attracts one **6.** the force that causes the atoms of certain elements to combine and stay combined —**af·fin′i·tive** ***adj.***
af·firm (ə furm′) ***vt.*** [< OFr. < L. *affirmare* < *ad-*, to + *firmare*, to make firm] **1.** to declare positively; assert to be true **2.** to confirm; ratify (a law, decision, or judgment) —***vi.*** *Law* to declare solemnly, but not under oath —**af·firm′a·ble** ***adj.*** —**af·firm′er,** *Law* **af·firm′ant** ***n.***
af·fir·ma·tion (af′ər mā′shən) ***n.*** **1.** an affirming **2.** a positive declaration; assertion **3.** *Law* a solemn declaration, but not under oath, made by one having conscientious objections to taking oaths
af·firm·a·tive (ə fur′mə tiv) ***adj.*** **1.** answering "yes" **2.** bold or positive, as in asserting —***n.*** **1.** a word or expression indicating assent or agreement **2.** an affirmative statement —**the affirmative** the side upholding the proposition being debated —**af·firm′a·tive·ly** ***adv.***
affirmative action a policy or program for correcting the effects of discrimination in the employment or education of members of certain groups, as women, blacks, etc.
af·fix (ə fiks′; *for n.* af′iks) ***vt.*** [< L. pp. of *affigere* < *ad-*, to + *figere*, FIX] **1.** to fasten; attach **2.** to add at the end —***n.*** **1.** a thing affixed **2.** a prefix, suffix, or infix —**af′fix·al** ***adj.***
af·fla·tus (ə flāt′əs) ***n.*** [L. < pp. of *afflare* < *ad-*, to + *flare*, to blow] inspiration, as of an artist
af·flict (ə flikt′) ***vt.*** [< L. *afflictare* < pp. of *affligere* < *ad-*, to + *fligere*, to strike] to cause pain or suffering to; distress very much
af·flic·tion (ə flik′shən) ***n.*** **1.** pain; suffering **2.** anything causing pain or distress; calamity
af·flic·tive (-tiv) ***adj.*** causing pain or misery —**af·flic′tive·ly** ***adv.***
af·flu·ence (af′loo wəns; *now sometimes* af lōō′-) ***n.*** [< L. < *affluere* < *ad-*, to + *fluere*, to flow] **1.** great plenty; abundance **2.** abundant riches; wealth; opulence
af·flu·ent (-wənt) ***adj.*** **1.** plentiful; abundant **2.** wealthy; rich —***n.*** a stream flowing into a river; tributary —**af′flu·ent·ly** ***adv.***
af·ford (ə fôrd′) ***vt.*** [OE. *geforthian*, to advance < *forthian*, to further] **1.** to have enough or the means for; bear the cost of without serious inconvenience: usually with *can* or *be able* **2.** to be able (*to* do something) with little risk **3.** to give; yield; furnish *[it affords much pleasure]*
af·fray (ə frā′) ***n.*** [< OFr. < *esfraer*, to frighten < L. *ex*, out of + Gmc. base *frith-*, peace] a noisy brawl or quarrel
af·fri·cate (af′rə kit) ***n.*** [< L. pp. of *affricare* < *ad-*, to + *fricare*, to rub] *Phonet.* a sound produced when a slowly released stop is followed immediately by a fricative, as the (ch) in *latch* —**af·fric·a·tive** (ə frik′ə tiv) ***n., adj.***
af·fright (ə frīt′) ***vt.*** [Archaic] to frighten; terrify —***n.*** [Archaic] great fright or terror

af·front (ə frunt′) *vt.* [< OFr. *afronter,* to encounter < ML. < *ad-,* to + *frons,* forehead] **1.** to insult openly or on purpose **2.** to confront defiantly —*n.* an open or intentional insult

Af·ghan (af′gan, -gən) *n.* **1.** a native of Afghanistan **2.** any of a breed of hunting dog with silky hair and a long, narrow head **3.** [**a-**] a soft blanket or shawl, crocheted or knitted, esp. in a geometrical design —*adj.* of Afghanistan, its people, etc.

af·ghan·i (af gan′ē) *n., pl.* **-is** *see* MONETARY UNITS, table (Afghanistan)

Af·ghan·i·stan (af gan′ə stan′) country in SW Asia, between Iran and Pakistan: 250,000 sq. mi.; pop. 16,516,000; cap. Kabul

a·fi·cio·na·do (ə fish′ə nä′dō, -fis′ē ə-; *Sp.* ä fē′syô nä′thô) *n., pl.* **-dos** (-dōz; *Sp.* *-thôs*) [Sp., pp. of *aficionar,* to be devoted to < L. *affectio,* warm liking] a devoted follower of some sport, art, etc.; fan

a·field (ə fēld′) *adv.* **1.** in, on, or to the field **2.** away (from home) **3.** off the right path; astray

a·fire (ə fīr′) *adv., adj.* **1.** on fire **2.** greatly excited

a·flame (ə flām′) *adv., adj.* **1.** in flames **2.** glowing **3.** greatly excited

AFL-CIO American Federation of Labor and Congress of Industrial Organizations

a·float (ə flōt′) *adv.* **1.** floating freely **2.** on board ship; at sea **3.** flooded *[*the deck is *afloat]* **4.** drifting about **5.** in circulation; current *[*rumors are *afloat]* **6.** free of trouble, debt, etc.

a·flut·ter (ə flut′ər) *adv., adj.* in a flutter

a·foot (ə foot′) *adv.* **1.** on foot; walking **2.** in motion or operation; in progress; astir

a·fore (ə fôr′) *adv., prep., conj.* [Archaic or Dial. except in compounds and nautical use] before

a·fore·men·tioned (ə fôr′men′shənd) *adj.* mentioned before or previously

a·fore·said (-sed′) *adj.* spoken of before; mentioned previously

a·fore·thought (-thôt′) *adj.* thought out beforehand; premeditated

a for·ti·o·ri (ā fôr′tē ôr′ē, -shē ôr′ī) [L., for a stronger (reason)] all the more: said of a conclusion following with even greater logical necessity another already accepted

a·foul (ə foul′) *adv., adj.* in a collision or a tangle —**run** (or **fall**) **afoul of** to get into trouble with

Afr. **1.** Africa **2.** African

a·fraid (ə frād′) *adj.* [< ME. pp. of *affraien,* to frighten: see AFFRAY] feeling fear; frightened (with *of, that,* or an infinitive): often used colloquially to indicate regret *[*I'm *afraid* I can't go*]*

A-frame (ā′frām′) *n.* a structural framework, as of a house, with steeply angled sides meeting at the top like the sides of the letter A

a·freet (af′rēt, ə frēt′) *n.* [Ar. *'ifrīt*] *Arabic Myth.* a strong, evil demon: also sp. **af′rit**

a·fresh (ə fresh′) *adv.* again; anew

Af·ri·ca (af′ri kə) second largest continent, in the Eastern Hemisphere, south of Europe: c. 11,500,000 sq. mi.; pop. c. 345,000,000

Af·ri·can (-kən) *adj.* of Africa, its peoples (esp. Negro peoples), their cultures, etc. —*n.* **1.** a member of an indigenous ethnic group of Africa, esp. a Negro **2.** any native or inhabitant of Africa

African violet any of several tropical African plants with hairy, dark-green leaves, often grown as house plants

Af·ri·kaans (af′ri känz′, -käns′, -kanz′) *n.* [Afrik. < *Afrika,* Africa] an official language of South Africa, a development from 17th-cent. Dutch

Af·ri·ka·ner (af′ri kän′ər) *n.* [Du.] a South African of European, esp. Dutch, ancestry; Boer

Af·ro (af′rō) *adj.* [< ff.] designating or of a full, bouffant hair style, as worn by some Negroes

Af·ro- *a combining form meaning:* **1.** Africa **2.** African Also, before a vowel, **Afr-**

Af·ro-A·mer·i·can (af′rō ə mer′ə kən) *adj.* of Negro Americans, their culture, etc. —*n.* a Negro American

aft (aft) *adv.* [< OE. < *afta,* behind] at, near, or toward the stern of a ship or rear of an aircraft

af·ter (af′tər) *adv.* [OE. *æfter* < *of,* off + *-ter,* old compar. suffix] behind in place or time; later or next —*prep.* **1.** behind in place **2.** behind in time; later than **3.** in search of **4.** as a result of *[after* what has happened, he won't go*]* **5.** in spite of *[after* all his bad luck, he is still cheerful*]* **6.** following next to in rank or importance **7.** in the manner of *[*a novel *after* Dickens' style*]* **8.** for; in honor of *[*named *after* Lincoln*]* **9.** concerning *[*she asked *after* you*]* —*conj.* following the time when —*adj.* **1.** next; later **2.** nearer the rear (esp. of a ship or aircraft)

af·ter·birth (-burth′) *n.* the placenta and fetal membranes expelled from the womb after childbirth

af·ter·burn·er (-bur′nər) *n.* **1.** a device for obtaining additional thrust in a jet engine by using the hot exhaust gases to burn extra fuel **2.** a device, as on an incinerator, for burning undesirable exhaust gases

af·ter·damp (-damp′) *n.* an asphyxiating gas left in a mine after an explosion of firedamp

af·ter·ef·fect (-ə fekt′) *n.* an effect coming later, or as a secondary result

af·ter·glow (-glō′) *n.* **1.** the glow remaining after a light has gone, as after sunset **2.** a pleasant feeling after an enjoyable experience

af·ter·im·age (-im′ij) *n.* a visual image that continues after the external stimulus is withdrawn

af·ter·math (-math′) *n.* [AFTER + dial. *math* < OE. *mæth,* cutting of grass] a result or consequence, esp. an unpleasant one

af·ter·most (-mōst′) *adj.* **1.** hindmost; last **2.** nearest to the stern

af·ter·noon (af′tər nōōn′, af′tər nōōn′) *n.* the time of day from noon to evening —*adj.* of, in, or for the afternoon

af·ter·noons (-nōōnz′) *adv.* during every afternoon or most afternoons

af·ter·taste (af′tər tāst′) *n.* **1.** a taste lingering on in the mouth, as after eating **2.** the feeling remaining after an experience

af·ter·thought (-thôt′) *n.* **1.** an idea, explanation, etc. coming or added later **2.** a thought coming too late to be apt, useful, etc.

af·ter·ward (-wərd) *adv.* at a later time; subsequently: also **af′ter·wards**

Ag [L. *argentum*] *Chem.* silver

AG Adjutant General

Ag. August

A.G. Attorney General

a·gain (ə gen′; *chiefly Brit.* -gān′) *adv.* [OE. *ongegn* < *on-,* toward + *gegn,* direct] **1.** [Rare] in return *[*answer *again]* **2.** back into a former condition **3.** once more; anew **4.** besides; further **5.** on the other hand —**again and again** often; repeatedly —**as much again** twice as much

a·gainst (ə genst′; *chiefly Brit.* -gānst′) *prep.* [see AGAIN] **1.** in opposition to *[against* my will*]* **2.** toward so as to strike *[*throw the ball *against* the wall*]* **3.** opposite to the direction of *[*drive *against* the traffic*]* **4.** in contrast with *[*green *against* the gold*]* **5.** next to; adjoining **6.** in preparation for *[*we provided *against* a poor crop*]* **7.** as a charge on *[*a bill was entered *against* his account*]* —**over against** **1.** opposite to **2.** as compared with

Ag·a·mem·non (ag′ə mem′nän, -nən) *Gr. Myth.* king of Mycenae and commander in chief of the Greek army in the Trojan War

A·ga·ña (ä gän′yə) capital of Guam: pop. 900

a·gape[1] (ə gāp′) *adv., adj.* [A-[1] + GAPE] **1.** with the mouth wide open, as in wonder **2.** wide open

ag·a·pe[2] (ä′gä pā′, ag′ə pē) *n.* [< LL. < Gr. *agapē,* love] *Christian Theol.* **1.** God's love for man **2.** spontaneous, altruistic love

a·gar-a·gar (ä′gär ä′gär, ag′ər ag′ər) *n.* [Malay] a gelatinous extract of seaweed, used for bacterial cultures, as a laxative, etc.: also **a′gar**

ag·ar·ic (ə ger′ik, ag′ər ik) *n.* [< L. < Gr. < Agaria, ancient E European town] any gill fungus, as the common edible mushroom, etc.

Ag·as·siz (ag′ə sē), **(Jean) Louis (Rodolphe)** 1807–73; U.S. zoologist & geologist, born in Switzerland

ag·ate (ag′ət) *n.* [OFr. < L. < Gr. *achatēs* < ?] **1.** a hard, semiprecious stone, a variety of chalcedony, with striped or clouded coloring **2.** a little ball made of this stone or of glass, used in playing marbles **3.** a small size of type, 5½ point

Ag·a·tha (ag′ə thə) [L. < Gr. *Agathē,* lit., good, fem. of *agathos,* good] a feminine name

a·ga·ve (ə gä′vē) *n.* [ModL. < Gr. *Agauē,* a proper name, lit., illustrious] any of several American desert plants, as the century plant, having tall flower stalks and fleshy leaves: some agaves yield a rope fiber

a·gaze (ə gāz′) *adv., adj.* gazing

age (āj) *n.* [< OFr. < L. *aetas*] **1.** the time that a person or thing has existed since birth or beginning **2.** the lifetime **3.** a stage of life *[*the awkward *age]* **4.** the condition of being old *[*bent with *age]* **5.** a generation **6.** a period in history or in prehistoric or geologic time **7.** [*often pl.*] [Colloq.] a long time —*vi.* **aged, ag′ing** or **age′ing** to grow old or become mature —*vt.* to make old or cause to become mature —**of age** having reached the age of full legal rights

-age (ij, əj) [OFr. < LL. *-aticum,* belonging to] *a noun-forming suffix meaning:* **1.** the act, condition, or result of

fat, āpe, cär, ten, ēven, is, bīte; gō, hôrn, tōōl, look; oil, out; up, fur; get; joy; yet; chin; she; thin, *th*en; zh, leisure; ŋ, ring; ə for *a* in *ago, e* in *agent, i* in *sanity, o* in *comply, u* in *focus;* ′ as in *able* (ā′b′l); Fr. bål; ë, Fr. coeur; ö, Fr. feu; Fr. mon; ô, Fr. coq; ü, Fr. duc; *r,* Fr. cri; H, G. ich; kh, G. doch; ‡foreign; *hypothetical; < derived from. See inside front cover.

[usage] **2.** amount or number of *[acreage]* **3.** cost of *[postage]* **4.** place of *[steerage]* **5.** collection of *[peerage]* **6.** home of *[hermitage]*

a·ged (ā′jid *for 1 & 2;* ājd *for 3 & 4*) ***adj.*** **1.** grown old **2.** of old age **3.** brought to a desired state of aging **4.** of the age of *[*a boy *aged* ten*]* —**the aged** (ā′jid) old people

age·ism (āj′iz′m) ***n.*** [AGE + (RAC)ISM] discrimination against people on the basis of age; specif., discrimination against, and prejudicial stereotyping of, older people —**age′ist** ***adj., n.***

age·less (āj′lis) ***adj.*** **1.** seemingly not growing older **2.** eternal —**age′less·ly** ***adv.***

age·long (-lôŋ′) ***adj.*** lasting a very long time

age-mate (-māt′) ***n.*** a person or animal of the same age, or nearly the same age, as another

a·gen·cy (ā′jən sē) ***n., pl.*** **-cies** [see AGENT] **1.** action; power **2.** means; instrumentality **3.** the business or place of business of any person, firm, etc. authorized to act for another **4.** an administrative division of government

a·gen·da (ə jen′də) ***n., pl.*** **-das** [L., pl. of *agendum* < *agere,* ACT] program of things to be done; specif., a list of things to be dealt with at a meeting: also **a·gen′dum** (-dəm), *pl.* **-da** (-də), **-dums**

a·gent (ā′jənt) ***n.*** [< L. *agens* (gen. *agentis*), prp. of *agere,* ACT] **1.** a person or thing that performs an action **2.** a force or substance that produces an effect *[*chemical *agent]* **3.** a person, firm, etc. authorized to act for another **4.** a representative of a government agency **5.** [Colloq.] a traveling salesman —**a·gen·tial** (ā jen′shəl) ***adj.***

‡**a·gent pro·vo·ca·teur** (á zhän′ prô vô kà tėr′) *pl.* **a·gents pro·vo·ca·teurs** (á zhän′ prô vô kà tėr′) [Fr.] a secret agent hired to join some group in order to incite its members to commit unlawful acts

age of consent *Law* the age of a girl, specified by law, before which sexual intercourse with her may be classified as statutory rape

age-old (āj′ōld′) ***adj.*** ages old; ancient

ag·er·a·tum (aj′ə rāt′əm) ***n.*** [ModL. < Gr. < *agēratos,* not growing old < *a-,* not + *gēras,* old age] a plant of the composite family, with small bluish flowers

ag·glom·er·ate (ə gläm′ə rāt′; *for adj. & n.* -ər it) ***vt., vi.*** **-at′ed, -at′ing** [< L. pp. of *agglomerare* < *ad-,* to + *glomerare,* to form into a ball] to gather into a mass or ball —***adj.*** gathered into a mass or ball —***n.*** a jumbled heap, mass, etc. —**ag·glom′er·a′tion** ***n.*** —**ag·glom′er·a′tive** ***adj.***

ag·glu·ti·nant (ə glo͞ot′'n ənt) ***adj.*** [see ff.] sticking together —***n.*** a sticky substance

ag·glu·ti·nate (ə glo͞ot′'n it; *for v.* -āt′) ***adj.*** [< L. pp. of *agglutinare* < *ad-,* to + *gluten,* glue] **1.** stuck together, as with glue **2.** *Linguis.* forming words by agglutination —***vt., vi.*** **-nat′ed, -nat′ing** **1.** to stick together, as with glue **2.** *Linguis.* to form (words) by agglutination **3.** *Med. & Bacteriology* to clump, as blood cells, microorganisms, etc. suspended in fluid —**ag·glu′ti·na′tive** ***adj.***

ag·glu·ti·na·tion (ə glo͞ot′'n ā′shən) ***n.*** **1.** an agglutinating or being agglutinated **2.** a mass of agglutinated parts **3.** *Linguis.* the combining of words into compounds without marked change of form or loss of meaning

ag·gran·dize (ə gran′dīz′, ag′rən-) ***vt.*** **-dized′, -diz′ing** [< Fr. < *a-,* to + *grandir,* to increase < L. *grandire* < *grandis,* great] **1.** to make (esp. oneself) greater, more powerful, richer, etc. **2.** to make seem greater —**ag·gran′dize·ment** (-diz mənt) ***n.*** —**ag·gran′diz′er** ***n.***

ag·gra·vate (ag′rə vāt′) ***vt.*** **-vat′ed, -vat′ing** [< L. pp. of *aggravare* < *ad-,* to + *gravis,* heavy] **1.** to make worse; make more burdensome, troublesome, etc. **2.** [Colloq.] to exasperate; annoy —**ag′gra·va′tion** ***n.***

ag·gre·gate (ag′rə gət; *for v.* -gāt′) ***adj.*** [< L. pp. of *aggregare* < *ad-,* to + *gregare,* to herd < *grex* (gen. *gregis*), a herd] gathered into, or considered as, a whole; total —***n.*** a group or mass of distinct things gathered into, or considered as, a whole; total —***vt.*** **-gat′ed, -gat′ing** **1.** to gather into a whole or mass **2.** to amount to; total —**in the aggregate** taken all together; on the whole —**ag′gre·ga′tion** ***n.***

ag·gress (ə gres′) ***vi.*** [< L. pp. of *aggredi,* to attack < *ad-,* to + *gradi,* to step] to start a quarrel or make an attack

ag·gres·sion (ə gresh′ən) ***n.*** **1.** an unprovoked attack or warlike act **2.** the practice or habit of being aggressive, or quarrelsome **3.** *Psychiatry* forceful or hostile behavior

ag·gres·sive (ə gres′iv) ***adj.*** **1.** aggressing or inclined to aggress **2.** ready to engage in direct action **3.** full of enterprise; bold and active —**ag·gres′sive·ly** ***adv.***

ag·gres·sor (-ər) ***n.*** a person, nation, etc. that is guilty of aggression, or makes an unprovoked attack

ag·grieve (ə grēv′) ***vt.*** **-grieved′, -griev′ing** [< OFr. < L. *aggravare,* AGGRAVATE] **1.** to cause grief or injury to; offend **2.** to injure in one's legal rights

a·ghast (ə gast′) ***adj.*** [< ME. < *a-* (intens.) + *gastan* < OE. *gæstan,* to terrify < *gast,* GHOST] feeling great horror or dismay; horrified

ag·ile (aj′'l; *chiefly Brit.* -īl) ***adj.*** [Fr. < L. < *agere,* ACT] **1.** quick and easy of movement; nimble **2.** keen and lively *[*an *agile* wit*]* —**ag′ile·ly** ***adv.*** —**a·gil·i·ty** (ə jil′ə tē) ***n.***

ag·ism (āj′iz′m) ***n.*** *same as* AGEISM —**ag′ist** ***adj., n.***

ag·i·tate (aj′ə tāt′) ***vt.*** **-tat′ed, -tat′ing** [< L. pp. of *agitare,* to put in motion < *agere,* ACT] **1.** to move violently; stir up or shake up **2.** to disturb the feelings of —***vi.*** to stir up support through speeches and writing so as to produce changes *[*to *agitate* for reform*]* —**ag′i·tat′ed·ly** ***adv.***

ag·i·ta·tion (aj′ə tā′shən) ***n.*** **1.** an agitating or being agitated; violent motion **2.** emotional disturbance **3.** discussion meant to stir up people and produce changes

‡**a·gi·ta·to** (ä′jē tä′tô) ***adj., adv.*** [It.: see AGITATE] *Music* fast and with excitement

ag·i·ta·tor (aj′ə tāt′ər) ***n.*** **1.** a person who tries to stir up people in support of a social or political cause: often used in disapproval **2.** an apparatus for shaking or stirring

ag·it·prop (aj′it präp′) ***adj.*** [< Russ. *agit(atsiya) prop(aganda),* agitation propaganda] of or for agitating and propagandizing

a·gleam (ə glēm′) ***adv., adj.*** gleaming

a·gley (ə glē′, -glī′, -glā′) ***adv.*** [Scot.] awry

a·glow (ə glō′) ***adv., adj.*** in a glow (of color or emotion)

Ag·nes (ag′nis) [< Fr. < L. < Gr. *hagnē,* fem. of *hagnos,* chaste] a feminine name: dim. *Aggie*

ag·nos·tic (ag näs′tik) ***n.*** [< Gr. < *a-,* not + base of *gignōskein,* to know] a person who believes that one cannot know whether there is a God, or anything beyond material phenomena —***adj.*** of or characteristic of an agnostic —**ag·nos′ti·cal·ly** ***adv.*** —**ag·nos′ti·cism** ***n.***

Ag·nus De·i (äg′no͞os dā′ē; ag′nəs dē′ī) [L., Lamb of God] **1.** a representation of Christ as a lamb, often holding a cross or flag **2.** *R.C.Ch.* a prayer in the Mass, beginning *Agnus Dei,* or music for it

a·go (ə gō′) ***adj.*** [< OE. *agan* < *a-,* away + *gan,* go] gone by; past *[*years *ago]* —***adv.*** in the past *[*long *ago]*

a·gog (ə gäg′) ***adv., adj.*** [OFr. < *a-,* to + *gogue,* joyfulness] with eager interest or excitement

-a·gogue, -a·gog (ə gäg′, -gôg′) [< Gr. prp. of *agein,* to lead] *a combining form meaning* leading, directing, inciting *[demagogue]*

ag·o·nize (ag′ə nīz′) ***vi.*** **-nized′, -niz′ing** **1.** to make convulsive efforts; struggle **2.** to be in agony —***vt.*** to torture —**ag′o·niz′ing·ly** ***adv.***

ag·o·ny (ag′ə nē) ***n., pl.*** **-nies** [< L. < Gr. *agōnia,* a contest < *agōn,* an assembly < *agein,* to lead] **1.** very great mental or physical pain **2.** death pangs **3.** a convulsive struggle **4.** a sudden, strong outburst (*of* emotion)

ag·o·ra¹ (ag′ə rə) ***n., pl.*** **-rae′** (-rē′), **-ras** [Gr. < *ageirein,* to assemble] in ancient Greece, an assembly or a place of assembly, esp. a marketplace

a·go·ra² (ä′gō rä′) ***n., pl.*** **-rot′** (-rōt′) [ModHeb. *'āgōrāh*] *see* MONETARY UNITS, table (Israel)

ag·o·ra·pho·bi·a (ag′ər ə fō′bē ə) ***n.*** [AGORA¹ + -PHOBIA] an abnormal fear of being in open spaces

a·gou·ti, a·gou·ty (ə go͞o′tē) ***n., pl.*** **-tis, -ties:** see PLURAL, II, D, 1 [Fr. < Sp. < Guarani] a rodent related to the guinea pig, found in tropical America

AGOUTI (17–25 in. long)

A·gra (ä′grə) city in N India: site of the Taj Mahal: pop. 509,000

a·grar·i·an (ə grer′ē ən) ***adj.*** [< L. < *ager,* a field, land] **1.** relating to land or to the ownership or division of land **2.** of agriculture —***n.*** a person who favors a more even division of land among those who work it —**a·grar′i·an·ism** ***n.***

a·gree (ə grē′) ***vi.*** **-greed′, -gree′ing** [< OFr. < *a gre,* favorably < L. *ad,* to + *gratus,* pleasing] **1.** to consent or accede (*to*) **2.** to be in harmony **3.** to be of the same opinion; concur (*with*) **4.** to arrive at a satisfactory understanding (*about* prices, etc.) **5.** to be suitable, healthful, etc. (followed by *with*) *[*the climate *agrees* with him*]* **6.** *Gram.* to be inflected so as to correspond in number, person, case, or gender —***vt.*** to grant or acknowledge *[*we *agreed* that it was true*]*

a·gree·a·ble (-ə b'l) ***adj.*** **1.** pleasing or pleasant **2.** willing or ready to consent **3.** conformable; in accord —**a·gree′a·bil′i·ty, a·gree′a·ble·ness** ***n.*** —**a·gree′a·bly** ***adv.***

a·greed (ə grēd′) ***adj.*** settled by mutual consent *[*pay the *agreed* price*]*

a·gree·ment (ə grē′mənt) ***n.*** **1.** an agreeing, or being in harmony **2.** an understanding between two or more people, countries, etc. **3.** a contract

ag·ri·busi·ness (ag′rə biz′nis) ***n.*** [AGRI(CULTURE) + BUSINESS] farming and the businesses associated with farming

ag·ri·cul·ture (ag′ri kul′chər) ***n.*** [Fr. < L. < *ager,* a field (see ACRE) + *cultura,* cultivation] the science and art of farming; work of cultivating the soil, producing crops, and raising livestock —**ag′ri·cul′tur·al** ***adj.*** —**ag′ri·cul′tur·al·ly** ***adv.***

ag·ri·cul·tur·ist (ag′ri kul′chər ist) ***n.*** **1.** an expert in agriculture **2.** a farmer Also **ag′ri·cul′tur·al·ist**

ag·ri·mo·ny (ag′rə mō′nē) ***n.,*** *pl.* **-nies** [< OE. & OFr. < L. < Gr. *argemōnē*] a plant of the rose family, having little yellow flowers on spiky stalks and bearing burlike fruits

ag·ro·bi·ol·o·gy (ag′rō bī äl′ə jē) ***n.*** the science of plant growth and nutrition as applied to improvement of crops and control of soil

a·gron·o·my (ə grän′ə mē) ***n.*** [< Fr. < Gr. < *agros,* field + *nemein,* to manage] the science and economics of crop production; management of farm land —**ag·ro·nom·ic** (ag′rə näm′ik), **ag′ro·nom′i·cal** ***adj.*** —**a·gron′o·mist** ***n.***

a·ground (ə ground′) ***adv., adj.*** on or onto the shore, a reef, etc. [the ship ran *aground*]

agt. agent

a·gue (ā′gyo͞o) ***n.*** [< OFr. < ML. (*febris*) *acuta,* violent (fever)] **1.** a fever, usually that of malaria, marked by regularly recurring chills **2.** a chill; fit of shivering

ah (ä, ô) ***interj.*** an exclamation expressing pain, delight, regret, disgust, surprise, etc.

a·ha (ä hä′) ***interj.*** an exclamation expressing satisfaction, pleasure, triumph, etc., often mixed with irony or mockery

A·hab (ā′hab) *Bible* a wicked king of Israel, husband of Jezebel: I Kings 16:29

a·head (ə hed′) ***adv., adj.*** **1.** in or to the front **2.** forward; onward **3.** in advance **4.** winning or leading **5.** having something as a profit or advantage —**get ahead** to advance socially, financially, etc. —**get ahead of** to outdo or excel

a·hem (ə hem′; *conventionalized pronun.*) ***interj.*** a cough or similar sound made to get attention, fill a pause, etc.

a·him·sa (ə him′sä) ***n.*** [< Sans. < *a-,* not + *himsā,* injury] the Buddhist and Hindu principle of not harming any living creature

Ah·med·a·bad, Ah·mad·a·bad (ä′məd ə bäd′) city in W India: pop. 1,206,000

A-ho·ri·zon (ā′hə rī′z'n) ***n.*** *see* ABC SOIL

a·hoy (ə hoi′) ***interj.*** *Naut.* a call used in hailing [ship *ahoy!*]

A·hu·ra Maz·da (ä′hoo rə maz′də) *same as* ORMAZD

a·i (ä′ē) ***n.,*** *pl.* **a′is** (-ēz) [Tupi *ai hai* < the animal's cry] a S. American sloth with three toes

aid (ād) ***vt., vi.*** [< OFr. < L. *adjutare:* see ADJUTANT] to give help (to); assist —***n.*** **1.** help; assistance **2.** a helper; assistant **3.** a helpful device **4.** *same as* AIDE-DE-CAMP

aide (ād) ***n.*** [Fr.: see AID] **1.** an assistant **2.** *same as* AIDE-DE-CAMP

aide-de-camp (ād′də kamp′) ***n.,*** *pl.* **aides-de-camp** [Fr., lit., camp assistant] an officer in the army, navy, etc. serving as assistant and confidential secretary to a superior

aid·man (ād′man′) ***n.,*** *pl.* **-men′** (-men′) an enlisted man in a medical corps in a combat area

ai·grette, ai·gret (ā′gret, ā gret′) ***n.*** [see EGRET] **1.** the long, white plumes of the egret, once worn for ornament by women **2.** any ornament like this

Ai·ken (āk′'n), **Conrad** (**Potter**) 1889–1973; U.S. poet & fiction writer

ail (āl) ***vt.*** [< OE. *eglian,* to afflict with dread, trouble < *egle,* harmful] to be the cause of pain to; trouble —***vi.*** to be in poor health; be ill

ai·lan·thus (ā lan′thəs) ***n.,*** *pl.* **-thus·es** [ModL. < native name in Malacca] a tree with pointed leaflets, fine-grained wood, and greenish flowers with an unpleasant odor

Ai·leen (ī lēn′, ā-) *var. of* EILEEN

ai·le·ron (ā′lə rän′) ***n.*** [Fr. < OFr. < *aile* < L. *ala,* wing] a movable hinged section of an airplane wing for controlling rolling movements

ail·ing (āl′iŋ) ***adj.*** in poor health; sickly

ail·ment (āl′mənt) ***n.*** an illness, esp. a mild one

aim (ām) ***vi., vt.*** [< OFr. *aesmer* < L. < *ad-,* to + *aestimare,* to estimate] **1.** to point (a weapon) or direct (a blow, remark, etc.) **2.** to direct (one's efforts) **3.** to try or intend (*to* do or be) —***n.*** **1.** the act of aiming **2.** the direction of a missile, blow, etc. **3.** intention or purpose —**take aim** to point a weapon, as by viewing along a sight

aim·less (ām′ləs) ***adj.*** having no aim or purpose —**aim′less·ly** ***adv.*** —**aim′less·ness** ***n.***

ain't (ānt) [early assimilation of *amn't,* contr. of *am not;* later confused with *a'nt* (*are not*), *i'nt* (*is not*), *ha'nt* (*has not, have not*)] [Colloq.] am not: also a dialectal or substandard contraction for *is not, are not, has not,* and *have not: ain't* was formerly standard for *am not* and is still sometimes defended as a useful contraction for *am not* in questions [I'm going too, *ain't* I?]

Ai·nu (ī′no͞o) ***n.*** [Ainu, lit., man] **1.** *pl.* **-nus, -nu** a member of a native, light-skinned people of Japan **2.** their language, unrelated to any other

air (er) ***n.*** [< OFr. < L. *aer* < Gr. *aēr,* air, mist] **1.** the elastic, invisible mixture of gases (chiefly nitrogen and oxygen, as well as hydrogen, carbon dioxide, etc.) that surrounds the earth; atmosphere **2.** space above the earth; sky **3.** a movement of air; breeze; wind **4.** *same as* COMPRESSED AIR **5.** an outward appearance [an *air* of luxury] **6.** a person's manner or bearing **7.** [*pl.*] affected, superior manners **8.** public expression [give *air* to your opinions] **9.** transportation by aircraft **10.** the medium through which radio signals are transmitted: a figurative use **11.** a song or melody —***adj.*** of aircraft, air forces, etc. —***vt.*** **1.** to let air into or through **2.** to publicize —***vi.*** to become aired, dried, etc. —**give** (or **get**) **the air** [Slang] to reject (or be rejected) —**in the air** **1.** prevalent **2.** not decided —**on** (or **off**) **the air** *Radio & TV* that is (or is not) broadcasting or being broadcast —**take the air** to go outdoors, as for fresh air —**up in the air** not settled or decided —**walk on air** to feel very happy or exalted

air bag a bag of nylon, plastic, etc. that inflates automatically within an automobile at the impact of a collision, to protect riders from being thrown forward

air base a base of operations for military aircraft

air bladder a sac with air or gas in it, found in most fishes and in some other animals and some plants

air·borne (er′bôrn′) ***adj.*** **1.** carried by or through the air **2.** aloft or flying

air brake **1.** a brake operated by the action of compressed air on a piston **2.** any flap on an airplane for reducing its speed in flight

air·brush (er′brush′) ***n.*** a kind of atomizer operated by compressed air and used for spraying on paint or other liquid: also **air brush** —**air′brush′** ***vt.***

air chamber a cavity or compartment full of air, esp. one used in hydraulics

air command *U.S. Air Force* the largest organizational unit

air conditioning a method of filtering air and regulating its humidity and temperature in buildings, cars, planes, etc. —**air′con·di′tion** ***vt.*** —**air conditioner**

air-cooled (er′ko͞old′) ***adj.*** cooled by having air passed over, into, or through it —**air′-cool′** ***vt.***

air·craft (er′kraft′) ***n.,*** *pl.* **-craft′** any machine designed for flying, whether heavier or lighter than air; airplane, balloon, helicopter, etc.

aircraft carrier a warship that carries aircraft, with a large, flat deck for taking off and landing

air curtain (or **door**) a downward draft of air at an open entrance for maintaining even temperatures within

air·drome (er′drōm′) ***n.*** [AIR + -DROME] the physical facilities of an air base

air·drop (-dräp′) ***n.*** the delivery of supplies or troops by parachute from an aircraft —***vt.*** **-dropped′, -drop′ping** to deliver by airdrop

Aire·dale (er′dāl′) ***n.*** [after *Airedale* in Yorkshire, England] a large terrier having a hard, wiry, tan coat with black markings

AIREDALE
(23 in. high at shoulder)

air·field (er′fēld′) ***n.*** a field where aircraft can take off and land

air·foil (-foil′) ***n.*** a part with a flat or curved surface, as a wing, rudder, etc., used to keep an aircraft up or control its movements

air force **1.** the aviation branch of the armed forces **2.** *U.S. Air Force* a unit lower than an air command

air gun **1.** a gun operated by compressed air **2.** a gunlike device used to spray paint, insecticide, etc. by compressed air

air hole **1.** a hole that permits passage of air **2.** an unfrozen or open place in the ice covering a body of water

air·i·ly (er′ə lē) ***adv.*** in an airy or gay, light manner; jauntily; breezily

air·i·ness (-ē nis) ***n.*** **1.** a being airy, or full of fresh air **2.** gay lightness; jauntiness

air·ing (-iŋ) ***n.*** **1.** exposure to the air, as for drying **2.** exposure to public knowledge **3.** a walk or ride outdoors

air lane a prescribed route for travel by air; airway

air·less (-lis) ***adj.*** **1.** without air or without fresh air **2.** without wind or breeze

air·lift (-lift′) ***n.*** a system of transporting troops, supplies, etc. by aircraft, as when ground routes are blocked —***vt.*** to transport by airlift

air·line (-līn′) ***n.*** **1.** a direct line; beeline: also **air line** **2.** a system or company for moving freight and passengers

by aircraft **3.** a route for travel by air *—adj.* of or on an airline
air·lin·er (-lī′nər) ***n.*** a large aircraft for carrying passengers
air lock an airtight compartment, with adjustable air pressure, between places that do not have the same air pressure
air·mail (-māl′) ***n.*** **1.** the system of transporting mail by aircraft **2.** mail so transported *—vt.* to send by airmail
air·man (-mən) ***n.,*** *pl.* **-men** **1.** an aviator **2.** an enlisted man or woman in the U.S. Air Force
air mass *Meteorol.* a large body of air having virtually uniform conditions of temperature and moisture in a horizontal cross section
air-mind·ed (er′mīn′dəd) ***adj.*** interested in or promoting aviation, aircraft, air power, etc.
air·plane (er′plān′) ***n.*** an aircraft, heavier than air, that is kept aloft by the aerodynamic forces of air upon its wings and is driven forward by a screw propeller, by jet propulsion, etc.
air pocket an atmospheric condition that causes an aircraft to make sudden, short drops
air·port (-pôrt′) ***n.*** a place where aircraft can land and take off, usually with facilities for repair, accommodations for passengers, etc.
air power total capacity of a nation for air war
air pressure the pressure of atmospheric or compressed air
air·proof (-pro͞of′) ***adj.*** not penetrable by air *—vt.* to make airproof
air pump a machine for removing or compressing air or for forcing it through something
air raid an attack by aircraft, esp. bombers
air rifle a rifle in which the force of compressed air is used to shoot BB's, etc.
air sac any of the air-filled cavities in a bird's body, having connections to the lungs
air shaft **1.** a passage through which fresh air can enter a tunnel, mine, etc. **2.** *same as* AIR WELL
air·ship (-ship′) ***n.*** any self-propelled aircraft that is lighter than air and can be steered
air·sick (-sik′) ***adj.*** sick or nauseated from traveling in an aircraft —**air′sick′ness *n.***
air·space (-spās′) ***n.*** **1.** space for maneuvering an aircraft **2.** the space extending upward above a particular land area
air·speed (-spēd′) ***n.*** the speed of an aircraft relative to the air rather than to the ground
air·strip (-strip′) ***n.*** a hard-surfaced area used as a temporary airplane runway
air taxi a small commercial airplane that carries passengers to places not regularly served by scheduled airlines
air·tight (er′tīt′) ***adj.*** **1.** too tight for air or gas to enter or escape **2.** giving no opening for attack; without weak points *[*an *airtight* alibi*]*
air·waves (-wāvz′) ***n.pl.*** the medium through which radio signals are transmitted
air·way (-wā′) ***n.*** **1.** *same as: a)* AIR SHAFT (sense 1) *b)* AIR LANE *c)* *[pl.]* AIRWAVES **2.** a passage for air, as to the lungs
air well an open shaft passing through the floors of a building, for ventilation
air·wor·thy (-wur′*th*ē) ***adj.*** fit and safe to fly: said of aircraft —**air′wor′thi·ness *n.***
air·y (er′ē) ***adj.*** **air′i·er, air′i·est** **1.** in the air; high up **2.** of air **3.** open to the air; breezy **4.** unsubstantial as air; visionary **5.** light as air; delicate; graceful **6.** lighthearted; gay **7.** flippant **8.** [Colloq.] putting on airs; affected
aisle (īl) ***n.*** [< OFr. *aile:* see AILERON: the *-s-* is through confusion with ISLE] **1.** a part of a church set off by a row of columns or piers **2.** a passageway, as between rows of seats —**aisled** (īld) ***adj.***
Aisne (ān) river in N France: 175 mi.
A·jac·cio (ä yät′chô) chief city of Corsica: birthplace of Napoleon: pop. 41,000
a·jar¹ (ə jär′) ***adv., adj.*** [ME. *on char* < OE. *cier,* a turn: see CHORE] slightly open, as a door
a·jar² (ə jär′) ***adv., adj.*** [A-¹, on + JAR, *v.*] not in harmony
A·jax (ā′jaks) *Gr. Myth.* a Greek hero in the Trojan War
AK Alaska
a·kim·bo (ə kim′bō) ***adv., adj.*** [ME. *in kenebowe,* lit., in keen bow; a folk etym. < ON. < *keng,* bent + *bogi,* a bow] with hands on hips and elbows bent outward *[*with arms *akimbo]*
a·kin (ə kin′) ***adj.*** **1.** of one kin; related **2.** having similar qualities; similar
Ak·ron (ak′rən) [< Gr. *akron,* highest point] city in N Ohio: pop. 237,000 (met. area 660,000)
-al (əl, ′l) [< Fr. < L. *-alis*] **1.** *an adj.-forming suffix meaning* of, like, or suitable for *[comical, hysterical]* **2.** a suffix of nouns originally adjectives *[perennial, annual]* **3.** *a n.-forming suffix meaning* the act or process of *[avowal]* **4.** [AL(DEHYDE)] *Chem. a n.-forming suffix denoting: a)* an aldehyde *[chloral] b)* a barbiturate *[phenobarbital]*
Al *Chem.* aluminum
a·la (ā′lə) ***n.,*** *pl.* **a′lae** (-lē) [L., a wing] **1.** *Zool.* a wing **2.** a winglike structure, as the ear lobe

à la, a la (ä′lə, -lä; al′ə) [Fr.] **1.** to, in, or at the **2.** in the manner or style of **3.** according to
Al·a·bam·a (al′ə bam′ə) [< Fr. < AmInd. tribal name] Southern State of SE U.S.: 51,609 sq. mi.; pop. 3,890,000; cap. Montgomery: abbrev. **Ala., AL** —**Al′a·bam′i·an** (-ē ən) ***adj., n.***
al·a·bas·ter (al′ə bas′tər) ***n.*** [< OFr. < L. < Gr., prob. < Egypt. name for "vessel of (the goddess) Bast"] **1.** a translucent, whitish, fine-grained variety of gypsum **2.** a streaked or mottled variety of calcite —**al′a·bas′trine** (-trin) ***adj.***
a la carte (ä′lə kärt′, al′ə-) [Fr., by the bill of fare] with a separate price for each item on the menu: opposed to TABLE D'HÔTE
a·lack (ə lak′) ***interj.*** [A(H) + LACK] [Archaic] an exclamation of regret, surprise, dismay, etc.
a·lac·ri·ty (ə lak′rə tē) ***n.*** [< OFr. < L. < *alacer,* lively] eager willingness or readiness, often shown by quick, lively action —**a·lac′ri·tous *adj.***
A·lad·din (ə lad′'n) a boy in *The Arabian Nights* who found a magic lamp and a magic ring
à la king (ä′lə kiŋ′) [lit., in kingly style] diced and served in a sauce containing mushrooms, pimentos, and green peppers
Al·a·me·da (al′ə mē′də, -mā′-) [Sp. < *álamo,* poplar tree] city on an island in San Francisco Bay, Calif.: pop. 64,000
Al·a·mo (al′ə mō′) [see prec.] Franciscan mission at San Antonio, Tex.: scene of a siege and massacre of Texans by Mexican troops (1836)
a la mode (al′ə mōd′, ä′lə) [Fr. *à la mode*] **1.** in the fashion; stylish **2.** made or served in a certain style, as (pie) with ice cream, or (beef) braised with vegetables in sauce Also **à la mode, alamode**
Al·an (al′ən) [ML. *Alanus,* of Breton origin] a masculine name
a·lar (ā′lər) ***adj.*** [< L. < *ala,* a wing] **1.** of or like a wing **2.** having wings
A·lar·cón (ä′lär kôn′), **Pe·dro An·to·nio de** (pe′*th*rô än tô′nyô de) 1833–91; Sp. writer
Alarcón y Men·do·za (ē men dô′thä), **Juan Ru·iz de** (hwän ro͞o′ēth de) 1581?–1639; Sp. dramatist
Al·a·ric (al′ə rik) 370–410 A.D.; king of the Visigoths (395?–410): captured Rome (410)
a·larm (ə lärm′) ***n.*** [< OFr. < It. *all'arme,* to arms] **1.** [Archaic] a sudden call to arms **2.** a signal, sound, etc. to warn of danger **3.** a mechanism designed to warn of danger or trespassing *[a* burglar *alarm]* **4.** the bell, buzzer, etc. of an alarm clock **5.** fear caused by the sudden realization of danger *—vt.* **1.** to warn of approaching danger **2.** to frighten
alarm clock a clock that can be set to ring, buzz, or flash a light at any particular time, as to awaken a person from sleep
a·larm·ing (-iŋ) ***adj.*** that alarms, or makes suddenly afraid; frightening —**a·larm′ing·ly *adv.***
a·larm·ist (-ist) ***n.*** **1.** one who habitually spreads alarming rumors, etc. **2.** one who usually expects the worst to happen *—adj.* of or like an alarmist
a·lar·um (ə ler′əm, -lär′-) ***n.*** *archaic var. of* ALARM (esp. sense 1)
a·las (ə las′) ***interj.*** [< OFr. < *a,* ah + *las,* wretched < L. *lassus,* weary] an exclamation of sorrow, pity, regret, etc.
A·las·ka (ə las′kə) [< Esk. *Aláskhak*] **1.** State of the U.S. in NW N. America: 586,400 sq. mi.; pop. 400,000; cap. Juneau: abbrev. **Alas., AK** **2. Gulf of,** inlet of the Pacific in the S coast of Alaska —**A·las′kan *adj., n.***
Alaska Highway highway between E British Columbia, Canada, and Fairbanks, Alas.: 1,523 mi.
Alaska Range mountain range in SC Alaska: highest peak, Mount McKinley
Alaska Standard Time *see* STANDARD TIME
a·late (ā′lāt) ***adj.*** [< L. < *ala,* a wing] having wings or winglike attachments: also **a′lat·ed**
alb (alb) ***n.*** [< OE. *albe,* ult. < L. *albus,* white] a long, white linen robe with sleeves tapering to the wrist, worn by a priest at Mass
al·ba·core (al′bə kôr′) ***n.,*** *pl.* **-cores′, -core′:** see PLURAL, II, D, 1 [Port. < Ar. *al,* the + *bakūrah,* albacore] **1.** *a)* a warm-water tuna with unusually long pectoral fins *b) same as* TUNA¹ **2.** any of several related saltwater fishes, as the bonito
Al·ba·ni·a (al bā′nē ə, -bān′yə) country in the W Balkan Peninsula, on the Adriatic: 11,099 sq. mi.; pop. 2,019,000; cap. Tirana —**Al·ba′ni·an *adj., n.***
Al·ba·ny (ôl′bə nē) [after the Duke of York and *Albany,* later JAMES II] **1.** capital of N.Y., on the Hudson: pop. 102,000 **2.** city in SW Ga.: pop. 74,000
al·ba·tross (al′bə trôs′, al′bə träs′) ***n.,*** *pl.* **-tross′es, -tross′:** see PLURAL, II, D, 1 [<

ALB

Spanish < Port. < Ar. *al qādūs,* water container < Gr. *kados,* cask; prob. < Heb. *kad,* water jug] **1.** any of several large, web-footed sea birds related to the petrel **2.** [from the bird used as a guilt symbol in a poem by S. T. COLERIDGE] a source of worry or trouble, esp. when it keeps one from doing things effectively: often in the phrase **an albatross around one's neck**

al·be·it (ôl bē′it, al-) ***conj.*** [ME. *al be it,* al(though) it be] although; even though

Al·bé·niz (äl bā′nith, -nis), **Isaac (Manuel Francisco)** 1860–1909; Sp. composer & pianist

Al·bert (al′bərt) [Fr. < OHG. *Adalbrecht,* lit., bright through nobility] **1.** a masculine name: dim. *Al, Bert;* var. *Adelbert, Elbert* **2.** Prince, (*Albert of Saxe-Coburg Gotha*) 1819–61; husband of Queen Victoria of England

Al·ber·ta (al bʉr′tə) [fem. of ALBERT] **1.** a feminine name: var. *Albertina, Albertine* **2.** [after Princess Louise *Alberta,* 4th daughter of Queen Victoria] province of SW Canada: 255,285 sq. mi.; pop. 1,838,000; cap. Edmonton: abbrev. **Alta.**

Al·ber·tus Mag·nus (al bʉr′təs mag′nəs), Saint (*Count von Bollstädt*) 1193?–1280; Ger. scholastic philosopher

Al·bi·gen·ses (al′bə jen′sēz) ***n.pl.*** a religious sect in France c.1020–1250 A.D.: it was suppressed for heresy —**Al′bi·gen′si·an** (-sē ən) ***adj., n.***

al·bi·no (al bī′nō) ***n., pl.*** **-nos** [< Port. < L. *albus,* white] **1.** a person whose skin, hair, and eyes lack normal coloring: albinos have a white skin, whitish hair, and pink eyes **2.** any animal or plant abnormally lacking in color —**al·bin′ic** (-bin′ik) ***adj.*** —**al·bi·nism** (al′bə niz′m) ***n.***

Al·bi·on (al′bē ən) *poet. name for* ENGLAND

al·bum (al′bəm) ***n.*** [L., neut. of *albus,* white] **1.** a book with blank pages for mounting pictures, clippings, stamps, etc., or for collecting autographs **2.** *a*) a booklike holder for phonograph records *b*) a set of records in such a holder *c*) a single long-playing record, not part of a set **3.** an anthology, picture book, or the like

al·bu·men (al byōō′mən) ***n.*** [L. < *albus,* white] **1.** the white of an egg **2.** the nutritive protein substance in germinating plant and animal cells **3.** *same as* ALBUMIN

al·bu·min (al byōō′mən) ***n.*** [ALBUM(EN) + -IN[1]] any of a class of water-soluble proteins found in milk, egg, muscle, blood, and in many plants

al·bu·mi·nous (-mə nəs) ***adj.*** of, like, or containing albumin or albumen

Al·bu·quer·que (al′bə kʉr′kē) [after the Duke of *Albuquerque,* Mex. Viceroy (1702–11)] city in C N.Mex.: pop. 332,000

al·bur·num (al bʉr′nəm) ***n.*** [< L. < *albus,* white] *same as* SAPWOOD

al·cai·de, al·cay·de (al kī′dē; *Sp.* äl kä′ē *the*) ***n.*** [Sp. < Ar. < *qāda,* to lead] **1.** a governor of a Spanish fortress **2.** a warden of a Spanish prison

al·cal·de (al kal′dē; *Sp.* äl käl′de) ***n.*** [Sp. < Ar. < *qada,* to judge] the mayor of a Spanish or Spanish-American town, who also acts as a judge

Al·ca·traz (al′kə traz′) [< Sp. *Isla de Alcatraces,* Island of Pelicans] small island in San Francisco Bay: site of a Federal prison (1934–63)

al·caz·ar (al′kə zär′, al kaz′ər; *Sp.* äl kä′thär) ***n.*** [Sp. < Ar. *al-qasr,* the castle] a palace or fortress of the Moors in Spain; specif., [**A-**] such a palace in Seville, later used by the Spanish kings

al·che·mist (al′kə mist) ***n.*** one who practiced alchemy —**al′che·mis′tic** (-mis′tik) ***adj.***

al·che·my (al′kə mē) ***n.*** [< OFr. < ML. < Ar. *al-kīmiyā* < ? Gr. *cheein,* to pour] **1.** an early form of chemistry studied in the Middle Ages: its chief aims were to change the baser metals into gold and to find the elixir of perpetual youth **2.** a means of transmutation; esp., the seemingly miraculous change of a thing into something better —**al·chem·ic** (al kem′ik), **al·chem′i·cal** ***adj.*** —**al·chem′i·cal·ly** ***adv.***

Alc·me·ne (alk mē′nē) *see* AMPHITRYON

al·co·hol (al′kə hôl′, -häl′) ***n.*** [ML. < Ar. *al kuhl,* powder of antimony] **1.** a colorless, volatile, pungent liquid, C_2H_5OH: it can be burned as fuel, is used in industry and medicine, and is the intoxicating element in whiskey, wine, beer, etc.: also called *ethyl alcohol* **2.** any intoxicating liquor with this liquid in it **3.** any of a series of similarly constructed organic compounds with a hydroxyl group, as methyl (or wood) alcohol

al·co·hol·ic (al′kə hôl′ik, -häl′-) ***adj.*** **1.** of, containing, or caused by alcohol **2.** suffering from alcoholism —***n.*** one who has chronic alcoholism

al·co·hol·ism (al′kə hôl′iz′m, -häl′-) ***n.*** the habitual drinking of alcoholic liquor to excess, or a diseased condition caused by this

al·co·hol·ize (al′kə hôl īz′, -häl-) ***vt.*** **-ized′, -iz′ing** **1.** to saturate or treat with alcohol **2.** to convert into alcohol

Al·cott (ôl′kət), **Louisa May** 1832–88; U.S. novelist

al·cove (al′kōv) ***n.*** [Fr. < Sp. < Ar. < *al,* the + *qubba,* an arch, vault] **1.** a recessed section of a room **2.** a secluded bower in a garden

Ald., Aldm. Alderman

Al·deb·a·ran (al deb′ər ən) a brilliant red star in the constellation Taurus

al·de·hyde (al′də hīd′) ***n.*** [< AL(COHOL) + L. *de,* without + HYD(ROGEN)] **1.** a colorless, volatile fluid, CH_3CHO, with a strong, unpleasant odor, obtained from alcohol by oxidation **2.** any of a class of organic compounds containing the CHO group —**al′de·hy′dic** (-hī′dik) ***adj.***

Al·den (ôl′d′n), **John** 1599?–1687; Pilgrim settler in Plymouth Colony

al·der (ôl′dər) ***n.*** [< OE. *alor*] any of a group of trees and shrubs of the birch family, having durable wood and growing in cool, moist regions

al·der·man (ôl′dər mən) ***n., pl.*** **-men** [< OE. < *eald,* old + *man,* man] **1.** in some U.S. cities, a member of the municipal council, usually representing a certain district or ward **2.** in England and Ireland, a senior member of a county or borough council —**al′der·man·cy** (-sē) ***n.*** —**al′der·man′ic** (-man′ik) ***adj.***

Al·der·ney (ôl′dər nē) ***n., pl.*** **-neys** any of a breed of small dairy cattle originally from Alderney, one of the Channel Islands

ale (āl) ***n.*** [< OE. *ealu*] a fermented drink made from malt and hops, like beer, but produced by rapid fermentation at a relatively high temperature

a·le·a·to·ry (ā′lē ə tôr′ē) ***adj.*** [< L. < *alea,* chance] depending on chance or luck: also **a′le·a·to′ric**

a·lee (ə lē′) ***adv., adj.*** *Naut.* on or toward the lee; leeward

ale·house (āl′hous′) ***n.*** a place where ale is sold and served; saloon; tavern

A·leich·em, Sho·lom *see* SHOLOM ALEICHEM

Alembert, Jean le Rond d' *see* D'ALEMBERT

a·lem·bic (ə lem′bik) ***n.*** [< OFr. < ML. < Ar. < *al,* the + *anbīq,* a still < Gr. *ambix,* a cup] **1.** an apparatus of glass or metal, formerly used for distilling **2.** anything that refines or purifies

a·leph (ä′lif) ***n.*** [Heb., lit., ox, leader] the first letter of the Hebrew alphabet

A·lep·po (ə lep′ō) city in NW Syria: pop. 563,000

a·lert (ə lʉrt′) ***adj.*** [< Fr. < It. *all' erta,* on the watch < L. *erigere,* to ERECT] **1.** watchful; vigilantly ready **2.** quick and active; nimble —***n.*** **1.** a warning signal, as of an expected air raid **2.** the period when such a warning is in effect —***vt.*** to warn to be ready or watchful *[the troops were alerted]* —**on the alert** watchful; vigilant —**a·lert′ly** ***adv.*** —**a·lert′ness** ***n.***

A·leut (ə lōōt′, al′ōōt) ***n.*** [< Russ. < ? native name] **1.** *pl.* **A·leuts′, A·leut′** any of a native people of the Aleutian Islands and parts of mainland Alaska **2.** either of their two languages

A·leu·tian (ə lōō′shən) ***adj.*** **1.** of the Aleutian Islands **2.** of the Aleuts, their culture, etc. —***n.*** *same as* ALEUT

Aleutian Islands chain of islands of Alaska, extending c. 1,200 miles from the SW coast

ale·wife (āl′wīf′) ***n., pl.*** **-wives′** (-wīvz′) [< ?] an edible N. American fish resembling the herring

Al·ex·an·der (al′ig zan′dər) [< L. < Gr. < *alexein,* to defend + *andros,* gen. of *anēr,* man] **1.** a masculine name: dim. *Alex* **2. Alexander II** 1818–81; czar of Russia (1855–81): son of NICHOLAS I

Alexander Nev·ski (nef′skē) 1220?–63; Russ. military hero, statesman, & saint

Alexander the Great 356–323 B.C.; king of Macedonia (336–323); military conqueror

Al·ex·an·dri·a (al′ig zan′drē ə) **1.** seaport in Egypt, on the Mediterranean: pop. 1,513,000 **2.** [< prec., but with allusion to the *Alexander* family, owners of the town site] city in NE Va., near Washington, D.C.: pop. 103,000

al·ex·an·drine (al′ig zan′drin, -drēn) ***n.*** [*occas.* **A-**] *Prosody* an iambic line having six feet; iambic hexameter —***adj.*** of an alexandrine or alexandrines

a·lex·i·a (ə lek′sē ə) ***n.*** [ModL. < Gr. *a-,* without + *lexis,* speech < *legein,* to speak] a loss of the ability to read, caused by brain injury

al·fal·fa (al fal′fə) ***n.*** [Sp. < Ar. *al-fasfaṣah,* the best fodder] a deep-rooted plant of the legume family, used extensively in the U.S. for fodder, pasture, and as a cover crop

‡al fi·ne (äl fē′ne) [It.] *Music* to the end (of a repeated section)

Al·fred (al′frid) [OE *Ælfred,* lit., wise counselor] a masculine name: dim. *Al, Alf*

Alfred the Great 849–900? A.D.; king of Wessex (871–900?)
al·fres·co (al fres′kō) ***adv.*** [It. < *al* (for *a il*), in the + *fresco,* fresh, cool] in the open air; outdoors —***adj.*** outdoor Also **al fresco**
Alg. 1. Algeria **2.** Algerian
alg. algebra
al·gae (al′jē) ***n.pl., sing.*** **al′ga** (-gə) [pl. of L. *alga,* seaweed] a group of plants, variously one-celled or colonial, containing chlorophyll and other pigments, and having no true root, stem, or leaf: algae are found in water or damp places and include seaweeds —**al′gal** (-gəl) ***adj.***
al·ge·bra (al′jə brə) ***n.*** [ML. < Ar. < *al,* the + *jabr,* reunion of broken parts] a mathematical system used to generalize certain arithmetical operations by permitting letters or other symbols to stand for numbers: it is used esp. in the solution of polynomial equations —**al′ge·bra′ic** (-brā′ik), **al′ge·bra′i·cal** ***adj.*** —**al′ge·bra′i·cal·ly** ***adv.*** —**al′ge·bra′-ist** ***n.***
Al·ger (al′jər), **Horatio** 1832–99; U.S. writer of boys' stories
Al·ge·ri·a (al jir′ē ə) country in N Africa, on the Mediterranean: c. 919,000 sq. mi.; pop. 13,547,000; cap. Algiers —**Al·ge′ri·an** ***adj., n.***
Al·ger·non (al′jər nən) [prob. < OFr. *al grenon,* with a mustache] a masculine name: dim. *Algie, Algy*
-al·gi·a (al′jə, -jē ə) [< Gr. *algos,* pain] *a n.-forming suffix meaning* pain *[neuralgia]*
al·gid (al′jid) ***adj.*** [< Fr. < L. *algidus*] cold; chilly —**al·gid·i·ty** (al jid′ə tē) ***n.***
Al·giers (al jirz′) capital of Algeria; seaport on the Mediterranean: pop. 943,000
Al·gon·qui·an (al gäŋ′kē ən, -kwē-) ***adj.*** designating or of a widespread family of languages used by a number of N. American Indian tribes, including the Arapaho, Cheyenne, Blackfoot, etc. —***n.*** **1.** this family of languages **2.** a member of any tribe using one of these languages
Al·gon·quin (al gäŋ′kwin, -kin) ***n.*** [< AmInd.] **1.** a member of a tribe of Algonquian Indians who live in the area of the Ottawa River, Canada **2.** their Algonquian language
al·go·rism (al′gər iz′m) ***n.*** [< ME. & OFr. < ML. *algorismus* < name of 9th-c. Ar. mathematician] **1.** the Arabic, or decimal, system of counting **2.** any method of computing
al·go·rithm (-*ith*′m) ***n.*** [altered (after ARITHMETIC) < prec.] *Math.* any special method of solving a certain kind of problem; specif., the repetitive calculations used in finding the greatest common divisor of two numbers
Al·ham·bra (al ham′brə) [Sp. < Ar. *al ḥamrā′,* lit., the red (house)] **1.** early palace of the Moorish kings near Granada, Spain **2.** city in SW Calif.: pop. 65,000 —**Al′-ham·bresque′** (-bresk′) ***adj.***
a·li·as (ā′lē əs, āl′yəs) ***n., pl.*** **a′li·as·es** [< L. < *alius,* other] an assumed name; another name —***adv.*** otherwise named; called by the assumed name of *[*Bell *alias* Jones*]*
A·li Ba·ba (ä′lē bä′bə, al′ē bab′ə) in *The Arabian Nights,* a poor woodcutter who finds the treasure of forty thieves in a cave
al·i·bi (al′ə bī′) ***n., pl.*** **-bis′** [L., contr. < *alius ibi,* elsewhere] **1.** *Law* the plea or fact that an accused person was elsewhere than at the scene of the crime **2.** [Colloq.] an excuse —***vi.*** **-bied′, -bi′ing** [Colloq.] to offer an excuse
Al·ice (al′is) [< OFr. < OHG. *Adalheit:* see ADELAIDE] a feminine name: dim. *Elsie;* var. *Alicia*
al·ien (āl′yən, -ē ən) ***adj.*** [< OFr. < L. *alienus* < *alius,* other] **1.** belonging to another country or people; foreign **2.** not natural; repugnant (*to*) *[*ideas *alien* to him*]* **3.** of aliens —***n.*** **1.** a foreigner **2.** a foreign-born resident in a country who is not a naturalized citizen **3.** an outsider
al·ien·a·ble (-ə b′l) ***adj.*** capable of being transferred to a new owner —**al′ien·a·bil′i·ty** ***n.***
al·ien·ate (-āt′) ***vt.*** **-at′ed, -at′ing 1.** to transfer the ownership of (property) to another **2.** to make unfriendly; estrange *[*behavior that *alienated* his friends*]* **3.** to cause to be withdrawn or detached, as from society **4.** to cause a transference of (affection) —**al′ien·a′tor** ***n.***
al·ien·a·tion (āl′yə nā′shən, -ē ə-) ***n.*** **1.** an alienating or being alienated **2.** insanity
al·ien·ee (āl′yə nē′, āl′ē ə-) ***n.*** a person to whom property is transferred or conveyed
al·ien·ist (āl′yən ist, āl′ē ən-) ***n.*** a psychiatrist, esp. one who testifies in a law court
al·ien·or (-ôr′, -ər) ***n.*** a person from whom property is transferred or conveyed
al·i·form (al′ə fôrm′, ā′lə-) ***adj.*** [< L. *ala,* a wing + -FORM] shaped like a wing
a·light[1] (ə līt′) ***vi.*** **a·light′ed** or **a·lit′, a·light′ing** [< ME. < *a-,* out, off + *lihtan,* to dismount] **1.** to get down or off; dismount **2.** to come down after flight **3.** [Rare] to come (*on* or *upon*) accidentally
a·light[2] (ə līt′) ***adj.*** lighted up; glowing
a·lign (ə līn′) ***vt.*** [< Fr. < *a,* to + *ligner* < *ligne,* LINE[1]] **1.** to bring into a straight line **2.** to bring (parts, as the wheels of a car) into proper coordination **3.** to bring into agreement, close cooperation, etc. *[*he *aligned* himself with the liberals*]* —***vi.*** to come into line; line up
a·lign·ment (-mənt) ***n.*** **1.** an aligning or being aligned; esp., *a)* arrangement in a straight line *b)* a condition of close cooperation **2.** a line or lines formed by aligning
a·like (ə līk′) ***adj.*** [< OE. *gelic, onlike:* see A-[1] & LIKE[1]] like one another; similar: usually in the predicate —***adv.*** **1.** in the same manner; similarly **2.** to the same degree; equally —**a·like′ness** ***n.***
al·i·ment (al′ə mənt; *for v.* -ment′) ***n.*** [L. *alimentum* < *alere,* to nourish] **1.** anything that nourishes; food **2.** means of support —***vt.*** to nourish —**al′i·men′tal** (-men′t′l) ***adj.***
al·i·men·ta·ry (al′ə men′tər ē) ***adj.*** [see prec.] **1.** connected with food or nutrition **2.** nourishing **3.** furnishing support or sustenance
alimentary canal (or **tract**) the passage in the body through which food passes to be digested: it extends from the mouth to the anus
al·i·men·ta·tion (al′ə men tā′shən) ***n.*** **1.** nourishment; nutrition **2.** support; sustenance —**al′i·men′ta·tive** (-men′tə tiv) ***adj.***
al·i·mo·ny (al′ə mō′nē) ***n.*** [< L. < *alere,* to nourish] an allowance paid, esp. to a woman, by the spouse or former spouse after a legal separation or divorce
a·line (ə līn′) ***vt., vi.*** **a·lined′, a·lin′ing** *same as* ALIGN —**a·line′ment** ***n.***
al·i·quant (al′ə kwənt) ***adj.*** [< L. < *alius,* other + *quantus,* how much] *Math.* that does not divide a number evenly but leaves a remainder *[*8 is an *aliquant* part of 25*]* : cf. ALIQUOT
al·i·quot (al′ə kwət) ***adj.*** [L. < *alius,* other + *quot,* how many] *Math.* that divides a number evenly and leaves no remainder *[*8 is an *aliquot* part of 24*]* : cf. ALIQUANT
Al·i·son (al′ə s′n) [< OFr.: see ALICE] a feminine name
a·lit (ə lit′) *alt. pt. & pp. of* ALIGHT[1]
a·live (ə līv′) ***adj.*** [< OE. *on,* in + *life,* life] [*usually used in the predicate*] **1.** having life; living **2.** in existence, operation, etc. *[*to keep his memory *alive]* **3.** lively; alert *Alive* is used as an interjection in such phrases as *man alive! sakes alive!* etc. —**alive to** fully aware of; perceiving —**alive with** teeming with; full of
a·liz·a·rin (ə liz′ər in) ***n.*** [G., ult. < Ar. *al aṣārah,* the juice < *aṣara,* to press] a reddish-yellow crystalline compound, $C_{14}H_8O_4$, used in dyes: also **a·liz′a·rine** (-in, -ēn′)
al·ka·li (al′kə lī′) ***n., pl.*** **-lies′, -lis′** [< Ar. *al,* the + *qili,* ashes (of saltwort)] **1.** any base or hydroxide, as soda, potash, etc., that gives a high concentration of hydroxyl ions in solution **2.** any soluble mineral salt or mixture of salts found in desert soils and capable of neutralizing acids
alkali metals the group of metallic chemical elements consisting of lithium, sodium, potassium, rubidium, cesium, and francium
al·ka·line (al′kə lin, -līn′) ***adj.*** of, like, or containing an alkali; basic —**al′ka·lin′i·ty** (-lin′ə tē) ***n.***
al·ka·line-earth metals (al′kə lin urth′, -līn′-) a group of metallic chemical elements, including calcium, strontium, barium, and sometimes beryllium, magnesium, and radium: the oxides of these metals are called **alkaline earths**
al·ka·lin·ize (al′kə lə nīz′) ***vt.*** **-ized′, -iz′ing** *same as* ALKALIZE —**al′ka·lin·i·za′tion** ***n.***
al·ka·lize (al′kə līz′) ***vt.*** **-lized′, -liz′ing** to make alkaline —**al′ka·li·za′tion** ***n.***
al·ka·loid (-loid′) ***n.*** [ALKAL(I) + -OID] any of a number of colorless, bitter, basic organic substances, as caffeine, morphine, quinine, etc., found in certain plants —**al′ka·loid′al** ***adj.***
Al·ko·ran (al′kō ran′, -rän′) ***n.*** the Koran
al·kyd (al′kid) ***n.*** [ult. < ALKALI + ACID] any of several synthetic resins used as coatings, and in paints, varnishes, etc.: also **alkyd resin**
all (ôl) ***adj.*** [OE. *eall*] **1.** the whole quantity, extent, or number of *[all* the gold, *all* day*]* **2.** every one of *[all* men must eat*]* **3.** the greatest possible *[*said in *all* sincerity*]* **4.** any; any whatever *[*true beyond *all* question*]* **5.** every *[all* manner of men*]* **6.** alone; only *[*life is not *all* pleasure*]* **7.** seeming to be nothing but *[*he was *all* arms and legs*]* —***pron.*** **1.** *[with pl. v.]* everyone *[all* are present*]* **2.** *[with pl. v.]* every one *[all* of us are going*]* **3.** everything *[all* is over between them*]* **4.** every part or bit *[all* of it is eaten*]* —***n.*** **1.** everything one has *[*give your *all]* **2.** a totality; whole —***adv.*** **1.** wholly; entirely *[all* worn out*]* **2.** apiece *[*a score of thirty *all]* —**after all** nevertheless; in spite of everything —**all but 1.** all except **2.** nearly; almost —**all in** [Colloq.] very tired —**all in all 1.** considering everything **2.** as a whole —**all over 1.** ended **2.** everywhere; in every part of; throughout **3.** [Colloq.] typically *[*that's Mary *all over]* —**all the (better, worse,** etc.**)** so much the (better, worse, etc.) —**all the (farther, closer,** etc.**)** [Colloq. or Dial.]

as (far, close, etc.) as —**all the same** 1. nevertheless 2. of no importance —**at all** 1. in the least 2. in any way 3. under any conditions —**for all** in spite of —**in all** altogether
all- *a combining form meaning:* 1. wholly; entirely *[all-American]* 2. for every *[all-purpose]* 3. of every part *[all-inclusive]*
Al·lah (al′ə, ä′lə, ä lä′) [Ar. *Allāh* < *al,* the + *ilāh,* god] *the Moslem name for* GOD
Al·la·ha·bad (al′ə hä bäd′) city in N India, on the Ganges: pop. 431,000
all-A·mer·i·can (ôl′ə mer′ə kən) *adj.* 1. made up wholly of Americans or of American elements 2. representative of the U.S. as a whole, or chosen as best in the U.S. 3. of all the Americas —*n.* 1. a hypothetical football (or other) team of college players voted the best of the year in the U.S. 2. a player chosen for such a team
Al·lan (al′ən) *var. of* ALAN
all-a·round (ôl′ə round′) *adj.* having many abilities, talents, or uses; versatile
al·lay (ə lā′) *vt.* **-layed′, -lay′ing** [< OE. < *a-,* down + *lecgan,* to lay] 1. to put (fears, etc.) to rest; calm 2. to lessen or relieve (pain, etc.)
all-clear (ôl′klir′) *n.* a siren or other signal that an air raid or practice alert is over
al·le·ga·tion (al′ə gā′shən) *n.* 1. an alleging 2. something alleged; assertion 3. an assertion made without proof 4. *Law* an assertion which its maker proposes to support with evidence
al·lege (ə lej′) *vt.* **-leged′, -leg′ing** [ME. *aleggen,* to produce as evidence < OFr., ult. < L. *ex-,* out of + *litigare:* see LITIGATE] 1. to declare or assert 2. to assert or declare without proof 3. to give as a plea, excuse, etc. —**al·lege′a·ble** *adj.* —**al·leg′er** *n.*
al·leged (ə lejd′, ə lej′id) *adj.* 1. so declared, but without proof *[the alleged assassin]* 2. so-called *[his alleged friends]* —**al·leg′ed·ly** *adv.*
Al·le·ghe·ny (al′ə gā′nē) [< AmInd. < ?] river in W Pa., joining the Monongahela to form the Ohio: 325 mi.
Allegheny Mountains mountain range of the Appalachians, in C Pa., Md., Va., and W.Va.: also **Al′le·ghe′nies**
al·le·giance (ə lē′jəns) *n.* [< OFr. *a-,* to + *ligeance* < *liege:* see LIEGE] 1. the obligation of support and loyalty to one's ruler, government, or country 2. loyalty or devotion, as to a cause, person, etc. —**al·le′giant** (-jənt) *adj., n.*
al·le·gor·i·cal (al′ə gôr′i k′l, -gär′-) *adj.* 1. of or characteristic of allegory 2. that is or contains an allegory Also **al′le·gor′ic** —**al′le·gor′i·cal·ly** *adv.*
al·le·go·rist (al′ə gôr′ist, -gər ist) *n.* one who writes allegories —**al′le·go·ris′tic** *adj.*
al·le·go·rize (al′ə gə rīz′) *vt.* **-rized′, -riz′ing** 1. to make into or treat as an allegory 2. to interpret in an allegorical sense —*vi.* to make or use allegories —**al′le·go·ri·za′tion** *n.* —**al′le·go·riz′er** *n.*
al·le·go·ry (al′ə gôr′ē) *n., pl.* **-ries** [< L. < Gr. < *allos,* other + *agoreuein,* to speak < *agora,* AGORA[1]] 1. a story in which people, things, and events have a symbolic meaning: allegories are used for teaching or explaining ideas, moral principles, etc. 2. the presenting of ideas by such stories 3. any symbol or emblem
al·le·gret·to (al′ə gret′ō) *adj., adv.* [It., dim. of ALLEGRO] *Music* moderately fast; somewhat slower than *allegro* —*n., pl.* **-tos** an allegretto movement or passage
al·le·gro (ə leg′rō, -lā′grō) *adj., adv.* [It. < L. *alacer,* brisk] *Music* fast, but not so fast as *presto* —*n., pl.* **-gros** a fast movement or passage
al·lele (ə lēl′) *n.* [G. *allel* < Gr. *allēlōn,* of one another] either of a pair of genes in the same position on both members of a pair of chromosomes and bearing characters inherited alternatively according to Mendelian law: also **al·le·lo·morph** (ə lel′ə môrf′, ə lē′lə-) —**al·le′lic** *adj.*
al·le·lu·ia (al′ə lo͞o′yə) *interj., n. same as* HALLELUJAH
Al·len (al′ən) *var. of* ALAN
Al·len·town (al′ən toun′) [after Wm. *Allen,* the founder] city in E Pa.: pop. 104,000
al·ler·gen (al′ər jən) *n.* [G. < *allergie,* ALLERGY + *-gen,* -GEN] a substance inducing an allergic state or reaction —**al′ler·gen′ic** (-jen′ik) *adj.*
al·ler·gic (ə lʉr′jik) *adj.* 1. of or caused by allergy 2. having an allergy 3. unwilling or not inclined (*to*): a humorous usage *[allergic to study]*
al·ler·gist (al′ər jist) *n.* a doctor who specializes in treating allergies
al·ler·gy (al′ər jē) *n., pl.* **-gies** [< G. < Gr. *allos,* other + *-ergeia,* as in *energeia* (see ENERGY)] 1. abnormal sensitivity to a specific substance (such as a food, pollen, dust, etc.) or condition (as heat or cold) which in like amounts is harmless to most people 2. a strong dislike
al·le·vi·ate (ə lē′vē āt′) *vt.* **-at′ed, -at′ing** [< LL. pp. of *alleviare* < L. < *ad-,* to + *levis,* light] 1. to make less hard to bear; relieve (pain, etc.) 2. to reduce or decrease *[to alleviate poverty]* —**al·le′vi·a′tion** *n.* —**al·le′vi·a′tive** *adj.* —**al·le′vi·a′tor** *n.* —**al·le′vi·a·to′ry** (-ə tôr′ē) *adj.*
al·ley (al′ē) *n., pl.* **-leys** [< OFr. *alee,* a going < *aler* (Fr. *aller*), to go < ML. < L. *ambulare,* to walk] 1. a lane in a garden or park 2. a narrow street or walk; specif., a lane behind a row of buildings 3. *Bowling a)* the long, narrow lane along which the balls are rolled: now usually LANE *b)* [*occas. pl.*] a bowling establishment —**up** (or **down**) **one's alley** [Slang] suited to one's tastes or abilities
al·ley·way (al′ē wā′) *n.* 1. an alley between buildings 2. any narrow passageway
All Fools' Day *same as* APRIL FOOLS' DAY
all hail [Archaic] all health: a greeting
All·hal·lows (ôl′hal′ōz) *n.* [< OE. *ealle halgan:* see ALL & HALLOW[1]] [Archaic] *same as* ALL SAINTS' DAY: also called **All′hal′low·mas** (-hal′ō məs)
al·li·ance (ə lī′əns) *n.* [< OFr. < *alier:* see ALLY] 1. an allying or being allied; specif., a union, as of families by marriage 2. *a)* a close association for a common goal, as of nations, parties, etc. *b*) the agreement for such an association *c*) the countries, groups, etc. in such association 3. similarity or relationship in characteristics
al·lied (ə līd′; *also, esp. for 3,* al′īd) *adj.* 1. united by kinship, treaty, etc. 2. closely related *[allied sciences]* 3. **[A-]** of the Allies
Al·lies (al′īz′, ə līz′) *n.pl.* 1. in World War I, the nations allied by treaty against Germany and the other Central Powers; orig., Great Britain, France, and Russia, later joined by the U.S., Italy, Japan, etc. 2. in World War II, the nations associated against the Axis; esp., Great Britain, the Soviet Union, and the U.S.: see UNITED NATIONS
al·li·ga·tor (al′ə gāt′ər) *n.* [< Sp. *el,* the + *lagarto* < L. *lacerta,* LIZARD] 1. a large reptile of the crocodile group, found in tropical rivers and marshes of the U.S. and in China 2. a leather made from its hide

ALLIGATOR (8–12 ft. long)

alligator pear *same as* AVOCADO
all-im·por·tant (ôl′im pôr′t′nt) *adj.* essential
al·lit·er·ate (ə lit′ə rāt′) *vi., vt.* **-at′ed, -at′ing** to show or cause to show alliteration
al·lit·er·a·tion (ə lit′ə rā′shən) *n.* [< ML. < L. *ad-,* to + *littera,* letter] repetition of a beginning sound, usually of a consonant, in two or more words of a phrase, line of poetry, etc. (Ex.: "Sing a song of sixpence")
al·lit·er·a·tive (ə lit′ə rāt′iv, -ər ə tiv) *adj.* of, showing, or using alliteration —**al·lit′er·a′tive·ly** *adv.* —**al·lit′er·a′tive·ness** *n.*
al·lo- [< Gr. *allos,* other] *a combining form signifying* variation or reversal *[allotropy]*
al·lo·cate (al′ə kāt′) *vt.* **-cat′ed, -cat′ing** [< ML. pp. of *allocare* < L. *ad-,* to + *locus,* a place] 1. to set apart for a specific purpose 2. to distribute in shares; allot 3. to locate —**al′lo·ca·ble** (-kə b′l) *adj.* —**al′lo·ca′tion** *n.*
al·lom·er·ism (ə läm′ər iz′m) *n.* [< ALLO- + Gr. *meros,* part + -ISM] variation in chemical makeup without change in crystalline form —**al·lom′er·ous** (-əs) *adj.*
al·lo·path (al′ə path′) *n.* a person who practices or advocates allopathy: also **al·lop·a·thist** (ə läp′ə thist)
al·lop·a·thy (ə läp′ə thē) *n.* [< G.: see ALLO- & -PATHY] treatment of disease by remedies that produce effects different from those produced by the disease: opposed to HOMEOPATHY —**al·lo·path·ic** (al′ə path′ik) *adj.* —**al′lo·path′i·cal·ly** *adv.*
al·lo·phone (al′ə fōn′) *n.* [ALLO- + -PHONE[1]] *Linguis.* any of the variant forms of a phoneme
al·lot (ə lät′) *vt.* **-lot′ted, -lot′ting** [OFr. *aloter* < *a-,* to + *lot,* lot] 1. to distribute by lot or in shares; apportion 2. to give or assign as one's share *[each speaker is allotted five minutes]* —**al·lot′ta·ble** *adj.* —**al·lot′ter** *n.*
al·lot·ment (-mənt) *n.* 1. an allotting or being allotted 2. a thing allotted; portion 3. *Mil.* a regular deduction from one's pay
al·lo·trope (al′ə trōp′) *n.* an allotropic form
al·lo·trop·ic (al′ə träp′ik) *adj.* of or having allotropy: also **al′lo·trop′i·cal** —**al′lo·trop′i·cal·ly** *adv.*
al·lot·ro·py (ə lät′rə pē) *n.* [< Gr. < ALLO- + *tropos,* way, manner] the property that certain chemical elements have of existing in two or more different forms: also **al·lot′ro·pism**
al·lot·tee (ə lät′ē′) *n.* a person to whom something is allotted

all-out (ôl′out′) ***adj.*** complete or wholehearted [*an all-out effort*]

al·low (ə lou′) ***vt.*** [< OFr. *alouer* < ML. < L. < *ad-*, to + *locus*, a place: associated with OFr. *alouer* < L. *ad-*, to + *laudare*, to praise] **1.** to let do, happen, etc.; permit [*allowed* to rot] **2.** to let have [*allowed* no vacation] **3.** to let enter [dogs not *allowed*] **4.** to admit (a claim or the like); acknowledge as true **5.** to provide or allot (an amount, period, etc.) for a purpose [*allow* an inch for shrinkage] **6.** [Dial.] *a*) to think; give as one's opinion *b*) to intend —**allow for** to keep in mind [*allow for* the difference in time] —**allow of** to be subject to

al·low·a·ble (-ə b'l) ***adj.*** that can be allowed; permissible —**al·low′a·bly** ***adv.***

al·low·ance (-əns) ***n.*** **1.** an allowing, permitting, etc. **2.** something allowed, as an amount of money, food, etc. given regularly, as to a child, or for a specific purpose, as to a soldier **3.** a reduction in price in consideration of a large order, a trade-in, etc. —***vt.*** **-anced, -anc·ing** **1.** to put on an allowance **2.** to apportion economically —**make allowance** (or **allowances**) to take circumstances into consideration —**make allowance** (or **allowances**) **for** **1.** to excuse because of mitigating factors **2.** to leave room, time, etc. for

al·low·ed·ly (ə lou′id lē) ***adv.*** admittedly

al·loy (al′oi; *also, and for v. usually*, ə loi′) ***n.*** [< Anglo-Fr. < OFr. < L. *alligare*: see ALLY] **1.** a substance that is a mixture of two or more metals, or of a metal and something else **2.** *a*) formerly, a less valuable metal mixed with a more valuable one, often to give hardness *b*) something that lowers the value of another thing when mixed with it —***vt.*** **1.** to make (a metal) less pure by mixing with a less valuable metal **2.** to mix (metals) to form an alloy **3.** to debase by mixing with something inferior

all-pur·pose (ôl′pur′pəs) ***adj.*** useful in many ways

all-right (-rīt′) ***adj.*** [Slang] honest, honorable, good, etc. [an *all-right* guy]

all right **1.** satisfactory; adequate **2.** unhurt; safe **3.** correct **4.** yes; very well **5.** [Colloq.] certainly [he's the one, *all right*]

all-round (ôl′round′) ***adj.*** *same as* ALL-AROUND

All Saints' Day an annual church festival (November 1) in honor of all the saints

All Souls' Day in some Christian churches, a day (usually November 2) of prayer for the dead

all-spice (ôl′spīs′) ***n.*** **1.** the berry of a West Indian tree of the myrtle family **2.** the spice made from this berry: its flavor seems to combine the tastes of several spices **3.** the tree itself

all-star (-stär′) ***adj.*** made up entirely of outstanding or star performers

all-time (-tīm′) ***adj.*** unsurpassed up to the present time [an *all-time* record]

al·lude (ə lo͞od′) ***vi.*** **-lud′ed, -lud′ing** [L. *alludere*, to jest < *ad-*, to + *ludere*, to play] to refer in a casual or indirect way (*to*)

al·lure (ə loor′) ***vt., vi.*** **-lured′, -lur′ing** [< OFr. < *a-*, to + *lurer*, to LURE] to tempt with something desirable; attract; entice —***n.*** the power of alluring; fascination —**al·lure′·ment** ***n.*** —**al·lur′er** ***n.***

al·lur·ing (ə loor′iŋ) ***adj.*** tempting strongly; highly attractive; charming —**al·lur′ing·ly** ***adv.***

al·lu·sion (ə lo͞o′zhən) ***n.*** **1.** an alluding **2.** an indirect reference; casual mention

al·lu·sive (ə lo͞os′iv) ***adj.*** **1.** containing an allusion **2.** using allusion; full of allusions —**al·lu′sive·ly** ***adv.*** —**al·lu′sive·ness** ***n.***

al·lu·vi·al (ə lo͞o′vē əl) ***adj.*** of, composed of, or found in alluvium —***n.*** *same as* ALLUVIUM

al·lu·vi·um (ə lo͞o′vē əm) ***n.*** **-vi·ums, -vi·a** (-vē ə) [< L. < *alluere* < *ad-*, to + *luere*, to LAVE] sand, clay, etc. gradually deposited by moving water, as along a river bed

al·ly (ə lī′; *also, and for n. usually*, al′ī) ***vt.*** **-lied′, -ly′ing** [< OFr. *alier* < L. *alligare* < *ad-*, to + *ligare*, to bind] **1.** to unite for a specific purpose, as families by marriage or nations by treaty **2.** to relate by similarity of structure, qualities, etc.: usually in the passive [the onion is *allied* to the lily] —***vi.*** to become allied —***n.***, *pl.* **-lies** **1.** a country or person joined with another for a common purpose: see also ALLIES **2.** a plant, animal, or thing closely related in structure, etc. to another **3.** an associate; helper

Al·ma (al′mə) [L. fem. of *almus*, nourishing] a feminine name

Al·ma-A·ta (äl′mə ä′tə) capital of the Kazakh S.S.R.: pop. 673,000

al·ma ma·ter (al′mə mät′ər, māt′ər) [L., fostering mother] **1.** the college or school that one attended **2.** its anthem, or hymn

al·ma·nac (ôl′mə nak′, al′-) ***n.*** [< ML. < LGr. *almenichiaka*, calendar] **1.** a calendar with astronomical data, weather forecasts, etc. **2.** a book published annually, containing information, usually statistical, on many subjects

al·might·y (ôl mīt′ē) ***adj.*** [< OE. < *eal*, all + *mihtig*, mighty] **1.** having unlimited power; all-powerful **2.** [Slang] great; extreme —***adv.*** [Slang] extremely —**the Almighty** God —**al·might′i·ly** ***adv.*** —**al·might′i·ness** ***n.***

al·mond (ä′mənd, am′ənd, al′mənd) ***n.*** [< OFr. < L. < Gr. *amygdalē*] **1.** the edible, nutlike kernel of a small, dry, peachlike fruit **2.** the tree bearing this fruit —**al′mond-like′** ***adj.***

al·mon·er (al′mən ər, ä′mən-) ***n.*** one who distributes alms, as for a church, etc.

al·most (ôl′mōst, ôl′mōst′) ***adv.*** [OE. *eallmæst*: see ALL & MOST] very nearly; all but

alms (ämz) ***n.***, *pl.* **alms** [< OE. < LL. < Gr. *eleēmosynē*, alms < *eleos*, pity] money, food, etc. given to poor people —**alms′giv′er** ***n.***

alms·house (-hous′) ***n.*** formerly, a home for people too poor to support themselves; poorhouse

al·oe (al′ō) ***n.***, *pl.* **-oes** [< L. < Gr. *aloē* < ? Heb.] **1.** a South African plant of the lily family, with fleshy, spiny leaves **2.** [*pl., with sing. v.*] a laxative drug made from the juice of certain aloe leaves

a·loft (ə lôft′) ***adv.*** [ME. *o, on*, on + *loft* < ON. *lopt*: see LOFT] **1.** far above the ground **2.** in the air; flying **3.** high above a ship's deck

a·lo·ha (ə lō′ə, ä lō′hä) ***n., interj.*** [Haw., lit., love] a word used as a greeting or farewell

a·lone (ə lōn′) ***adj., adv.*** [ME. < *al*, ALL + *one*, ONE] **1.** apart from anything or anyone else [the hut stood *alone* in the woods] **2.** without any other person [to walk *alone*] **3.** with nothing more; only [the box *alone* weighs two pounds] **4.** without equal or peer —**let alone** **1.** to refrain from bothering **2.** not to mention [we hadn't a dime, *let alone* a dollar] —**let well enough alone** to be content with things as they are —**a·lone′ness** ***n.***

a·long (ə lôŋ′) ***prep.*** [< OE. *andlang*, along < *and-*, over against + *-lang*, long] **1.** on or beside the length of [*along* the wall is a hedge] **2.** in conformity with [to think *along* certain lines] —***adv.*** **1.** in a line; lengthwise **2.** progressively onward [he walked *along* by himself] **3.** as a companion [come *along* with us] **4.** with one [she took her book *along*] **5.** advanced [well *along* in years] **6.** [Colloq.] approaching [*along* toward evening] —**all along** from the very beginning —**along with** **1.** together with **2.** in addition to —**be along** [Colloq.] to come or arrive [I'll *be along* soon] —**get along** **1.** to go forward **2.** to contrive **3.** to succeed **4.** to agree **5.** [Colloq.] to go away

a·long·shore (ə lôŋ′shôr′) ***adv.*** along the shore; near or beside the shore

a·long·side (-sīd′) ***adv.*** at or by the side; side by side —***prep.*** at the side of; side by side with —**alongside of** at the side of; beside

a·loof (ə lo͞of′) ***adv.*** [*a-*, on + *loof* < Du. *loef*, LUFF, to windward] at a distance but in view; apart —***adj.*** **1.** at a distance; removed **2.** distant in sympathy, interest, etc. [an *aloof* manner] —**a·loof′ly** ***adv.*** —**a·loof′ness** ***n.***

a·loud (ə loud′) ***adv.*** **1.** loudly **2.** with the normal voice [read the letter *aloud*]

Al·o·ys·i·us (al′ə wish′əs) [< ML.; prob. < OFr. *Loeis*: see LOUIS] a masculine name

alp (alp) ***n.*** [< L. *Alpes*, the Alps] a high mountain, esp. in Switzerland: see ALPS

al·pac·a (al pak′ə) ***n.***, *pl.* **-pac′as, -pac′a**: see PLURAL, II, D, 1 [Sp. < SAmInd. *allpaca*] **1.** a domesticated S. American mammal related to the llama, with long, fleecy wool **2.** this wool **3.** a cloth woven from this wool, often mixed with other fibers **4.** a glossy cloth of cotton and wool

al·pen·horn (al′pən hôrn′) ***n.*** [G., Alpine horn] a curved, wooden, powerful-sounding horn, from five to twelve feet long, used by Swiss Alpine herdsmen for signaling: also **alp′horn′**

al·pen·stock (-stäk′) ***n.*** [G., Alpine staff] an iron-pointed staff used by mountain climbers

al·pha (al′fə) ***n.*** [Gr. < Phoen. name whence Heb. *āleph*: see ALEPH] **1.** the first letter of the Greek alphabet (A, α) **2.** the beginning of anything **3.** the brightest star in a constellation

alpha and omega **1.** the first and last letters of the Greek alphabet **2.** the beginning and the end

al·pha·bet (al′fə bet′) ***n.*** [< LL. < LGr. < Gr.: see ALPHA & BETA] **1.** the letters of a language, arranged in a traditional order **2.** a system of signs or symbols to indicate letters or speech sounds **3.** the first elements, as of a subject

al·pha·bet·i·cal (al′fə bet′i k'l) ***adj.*** **1.** of or using an alphabet **2.** in the usual order of the alphabet Also **al′pha·bet′ic** —**al′pha·bet′i·cal·ly** ***adv.***

al·pha·bet·ize (al′fə bə tīz′) ***vt.*** **-ized′, -iz′ing** **1.** to arrange in alphabetical order **2.** to express by or provide with an alphabet —**al′pha·bet′i·za′tion** (-bet′i zā′shən) ***n.***

al·pha·nu·mer·ic (al′fə no͞o mer′ik, -nyo͞o-) ***adj.*** [ALPHA(BET) + NUMERIC(AL)] having or using both alphabetical and numerical symbols

alpha particle a positively charged particle given off by certain radioactive substances: it consists of two protons and two neutrons

alpha ray 1. *same as* ALPHA PARTICLE 2. a stream of alpha particles, less penetrating than a beta ray

Al·pine (al′pīn) *adj.* 1. of the Alps or their inhabitants 2. [a-] *a*) of or like high mountains *b*) growing in high altitudes

al·pin·ist (al′pə nist) *n.* [*also* A-] a mountain climber

Alps (alps) mountain system of SC Europe: highest peak, Mont BLANC

al·read·y (ôl red′ē) *adv.* 1. by or before the given or implied time 2. even now or even then

al·right (ôl rīt′) *adv. var. of* ALL RIGHT: a disputed sp., but in common use

Al·sace (al sās′, al′sas; *Fr.* ål zås′) former province of NE France —**Al·sa′tian** (-sā′shən) *adj., n.*

Al·sace-Lor·raine (-lô rān′; *Fr.* -lô ren′) region in NE France consisting of the former provinces of Alsace and Lorraine

al·so (ôl′sō) *adv.* [< OE. < *eal,* all + *swa,* so] in addition; too: sometimes used in place of *and*

al·so-ran (-ran′) *n.* [Colloq.] any loser in a race, competition, election, etc.

alt. 1. alternate 2. altitude 3. alto

Alta. Alberta (Canada)

Al·ta·ic (al tā′ik) *adj.* 1. of the Altai Mountains or the people living there 2. designating or of a family of languages including Turkic and Mongolic

Al·tai Mountains (al′tī, al tī′) mountain system in SC U.S.S.R., NW China, and W Mongolia

Al·ta·ir (al tä′ir) [Ar. *al tā'ir,* the bird] the brightest star in the constellation Aquila

al·tar (ôl′tər) *n.* [< OE. & OFr.; both ult. < L. < *altus,* high] 1. a raised platform where sacrifices are made to a god, etc. 2. a table, stand, etc. used for sacred purposes in a place of worship, as the Communion table in Christian churches —**lead to the altar** to marry

altar boy a boy or man who helps a priest, vicar, etc. at religious services, esp. at Mass

al·tar·piece (-pēs′) *n.* an ornamental carving, painting, etc. above and behind an altar

al·ter (ôl′tər) *vt.* [< ML. *alterare* < L. *alter,* other] 1. to make different in details; modify 2. to resew parts of (a garment) for a better fit 3. to castrate or spay —*vi.* to become different; change —**al′ter·a·ble** *adj.* —**al′ter·a·bly** *adv.*

al·ter·ant (-ənt) *adj.* causing alteration —*n.* a thing that causes alteration

al·ter·a·tion (ôl′tə rā′shən) *n.* 1. an altering or being altered 2. the result of this; change

al·ter·a·tive (ôl′tə rāt′iv, -tər ə tiv) *adj.* 1. causing alteration 2. *Med.* gradually restoring to health —*n.* an alterative medicine or treatment

al·ter·cate (ôl′tər kāt′) *vi.* **-cat′ed, -cat′ing** [< L. pp. of *altercari,* to dispute < *alter,* other] to argue angrily; quarrel

al·ter·ca·tion (ôl′tər kā′shən) *n.* an angry or heated argument

al·ter e·go (ôl′tər ē′gō, eg′ō) [L., lit., other I] 1. another aspect of oneself 2. a very close friend or constant companion

al·ter·nate (ôl′tər nit, al′-; *for v.* -nāt′) *adj.* [< L. pp. of *alternare,* to do by turns < *alternus,* one after the other < *alter,* other] 1. succeeding each other; first one and then the other 2. every other [*alternate* Fridays] 3. being one of two or more choices; alternative 4. *Bot.* growing along the stem singly at intervals —*n.* a person chosen to take the place of another if necessary; substitute —*vt.* **-nat′ed, -nat′ing** to do, use, or make happen by turns —*vi.* 1. to act, happen, etc. by turns 2. to take turns 3. to exchange places, etc. regularly 4. *Elec.* to reverse direction periodically: said of a current —**al′ter·nate·ly** *adv.* —**al′ter·na′tion** *n.*

alternate angles two angles at opposite ends and on opposite sides of a line crossing two others

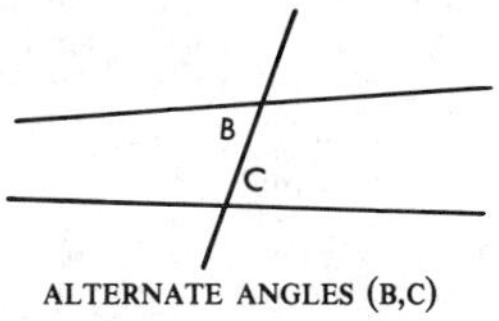

B
C

ALTERNATE ANGLES (B,C)

alternating current an electric current that reverses its direction periodically

al·ter·na·tive (ôl tur′nə tiv, al-) *adj.* providing or being a choice between two (or, less strictly, among more than two) things —*n.* 1. a choice between two or more things 2. any of the things to be chosen —**al·ter′na·tive·ly** *adv.*

al·ter·na·tor (ôl′tər nāt′ər, al′-) *n.* an electric generator or dynamo producing alternating current

al·the·a, al·thae·a (al thē′ə) *n.* [< L. < Gr. *althaia,* wild mallows] 1. any of a genus of plants in the mallow family, as the hollyhock 2. *same as* ROSE OF SHARON (sense 1)

alt·horn (alt′hôrn′) *n.* a brass-wind instrument, the alto saxhorn: also **alto horn**

al·though (ôl thō′) *conj.* [ME. < *all, al,* even (emphatic) + *though*] in spite of the fact that; though: now sometimes sp. **altho**

al·tim·e·ter (al tim′ə tər; *chiefly Brit.* al′tə mēt′ər) *n.* [< L. *altus,* high + -METER] an instrument for measuring altitude; esp., in aircraft, an aneroid barometer that tells how high the craft is flying —**al·tim′e·try** *n.*

al·ti·tude (al′tə to͞od′, -tyo͞od′) *n.* [< L. < *altus,* high] 1. height; esp., the height of a thing above the earth's surface or above sea level 2. a high place or region: *usually in pl.* 3. a high level, rank, etc. 4. *Astron.* the angular height of a planet, star, etc. above the horizon 5. *Geom.* the perpendicular distance from the base of a figure to its highest point or to the side parallel to the base —**al′ti·tu′di·nal** (-′n əl) *adj.*

al·to (al′tō) *n., pl.* **-tos** [It. < L. *altus,* high] 1. the range of the lowest female voice or, esp. formerly, the highest male voice 2. a voice or singer with such range 3. an instrument with the second highest range within a family of instruments, as the alto saxophone 4. a part for such a voice or instrument —*adj.* of, in, for, or having this range

alto clef *see* C CLEF

al·to·geth·er (ôl′tə geth′ər, ôl′tə geth′ər) *adv.* [see ALL & TOGETHER] 1. wholly; completely [*altogether* right] 2. in all [he wrote six books *altogether*] 3. on the whole [*altogether* a success] Distinguished from **all together** —**in the altogether** [Colloq.] nude

Al·too·na (al to͞o′nə) [< *Altona,* former Ger. seaport] city in C Pa.: pop. 57,000

al·tru·ism (al′tro͞o iz'm) *n.* [< Fr. < It. *altrui,* of or to others < L. *alter,* another] unselfish concern for the welfare of others —**al′tru·ist** *n.*

al·tru·is·tic (al′tro͞o is′tik) *adj.* of or motivated by altruism —**al′tru·is′ti·cal·ly** *adv.*

al·um (al′əm) *n.* [< OFr. < L. *alumen*] 1. a hydrated double sulfate of a trivalent metal and a univalent metal; esp., a double sulfate of potassium and aluminum, used in medicine and in making dyes, paper, etc. 2. aluminum sulfate: erroneous use

a·lu·mi·na (ə lo͞o′mi nə) *n.* an oxide of aluminum, Al_2O_3, present in bauxite and clay and found as different forms of corundum, including emery, sapphires, rubies, etc.

al·u·min·i·um (al′yoo min′yəm, -ē əm) *n. Brit. var. of* ALUMINUM

a·lu·mi·nize (ə lo͞o′mə nīz′) *vt.* **-nized′, -niz′ing** to cover, or treat, with aluminum

a·lu·mi·nous (-nəs) *adj.* of or containing alum, alumina, or aluminum

a·lu·mi·num (ə lo͞o′mə nəm) *n.* [ModL. < L. *alumen,* alum] a silvery, lightweight, metallic chemical element that is easily worked, resists corrosion, and is found abundantly, but only in combination: symbol, Al; at. wt., 26.9815; at. no., 13 —*adj.* of, containing, or made of aluminum

aluminum oxide *same as* ALUMINA

a·lum·na (ə lum′nə) *n., pl.* **-nae** (-nē) [L., fem. of ff.] a girl or woman alumnus

a·lum·nus (-nəs) *n., pl.* **-ni** (-nī) [L., foster son < *alere,* to nourish] a person, esp. a boy or man, who has attended or is a graduate of a particular school, college, etc.

al·ve·o·lar (al vē′ə lər) *adj.* 1. of or like an alveolus; socketlike 2. *Anat. a*) of the part of the jaws containing the sockets of the teeth *b*) designating the ridge of the gums behind the upper front teeth *c*) of the air pockets in the lungs 3. *Phonet.* formed, as English *t, d, s,* by touching or approaching the alveolar ridge with the tip of the tongue —*n. Phonet.* an alveolar sound

al·ve·o·late (-lit) *adj.* full of small cavities: also **al·ve′o·lat′ed** (-lāt′id) —**al·ve′o·la′tion** *n.*

al·ve·o·lus (al vē′ə ləs) *n., pl.* **-li′** (-lī′) [L., dim. of *alveus,* a cavity < *alvus,* the belly] 1. *Anat., Zool.* a small cavity or hollow, as an air cell of a lung, a tooth socket, etc. 2. [*usually pl.*] the alveolar ridge

Al·vin (al′v'n) [< G. < OHG. *adal,* nobility + *wini,* friend] a masculine name

al·way (ôl′wā) *adv.* [Archaic] always

al·ways (ôl′wiz, -wāz) *adv.* [see ALL & WAY] 1. in every instance; invariably [he's *always* late] 2. all the time; forever [*always* present in the atmosphere] 3. at any time [you can *always* leave]

a·lys·sum (ə lis′əm) *n.* [ModL. < Gr. < *alyssos,* curing madness < *a-,* without + *lyssa,* rage] 1. any of a genus of plants of the mustard family, with white or yellow flowers 2. *same as* SWEET ALYSSUM

am (am; *unstressed* əm) [OE. *eom:* see BE] *1st pers. sing., pres. indic., of* BE

Am *Chem.* americium

AM amplitude modulation

Am. 1. America 2. American

A.M., AM [L. *Artium Magister*] master of arts

A.M., a.m., AM [L. *ante meridiem*] before noon: used to designate the time from midnight to noon

AMA, A.M.A. American Medical Association

a·mah (ä′mə) *n.* [Anglo-Ind. < Port. *ama*] in the Orient, a woman servant, esp. one who serves as a baby's nurse

a·main (ə mān′) *adv.* [A-[1], on + MAIN[1]] [Archaic or Poet.] **1.** forcefully; vigorously **2.** at or with great speed **3.** hastily; suddenly **4.** greatly

a·mal·gam (ə mal′gəm) *n.* [< ML., prob. < Ar. < Gr. *malagma,* an emollient < *malassein,* to soften] **1.** any alloy of mercury with another metal or metals *[silver amalgam* is used as a dental filling*]* **2.** any mixture or blend

a·mal·ga·mate (-gə māt′) *vt., vi.* **-mat′ed, -mat′ing 1.** to combine in an amalgam **2.** to join together into one; unite —**a·mal′gam·a·ble** (-gəm ə b'l) *adj.* —**a·mal′ga·ma′tion** *n.* —**a·mal′ga·ma′tive** *adj.* —**a·mal′ga·ma′tor** *n.*

A·man·da (ə man′də) [L., lit., worthy to be loved < *amare,* to love] a feminine name: dim. *Mandy*

a·man·dine (ä′mən dēn′, am′ən-) *adj.* [Fr. < *amande,* almond + *-ine,* -INE[1]] prepared or garnished with thinly sliced almonds *[trout amandine]*

a·man·u·en·sis (ə man′yoo wen′sis) *n., pl.* **-ses** (-sēz) [L. < *a-* (*ab*), from + *manus,* a hand + *-ensis,* relating to] an assistant who takes dictation or copies something already written; secretary: now somewhat jocular

am·a·ranth (am′ə ranth′) *n.* [< L. < Gr. *amarantos,* unfading < *a-,* not + *marainein,* to die away] **1.** any of a genus of plants, usually with colorful leaves, including love-lies-bleeding, etc. **2.** [Poet.] an imaginary flower that never fades or dies **3.** a dark purplish red —**am′a·ran′thine** (-ran′thin) *adj.*

Am·a·ril·lo (am′ə ril′ō) [Sp., yellow] city in NW Texas: pop. 149,000

am·a·ryl·lis (am′ə ril′əs) *n.* [< L. & Gr.; conventional name for a shepherdess] **1.** a bulb plant bearing several white, purple, pink, or red lilylike flowers on a single stem **2.** any of several plants closely related to this

a·mass (ə mas′) *vt.* [< Fr. < ML. < *a-,* to + VL. *massare,* to pile up < L. *massa,* a MASS] **1.** to pile up; collect together **2.** to accumulate (esp. wealth) —**a·mass′er** *n.* —**a·mass′ment** *n.*

am·a·teur (am′ə chər, -toor, -tyoor) *n.* [Fr. < L. *amator,* a lover < *amare,* to love] **1.** a person who engages in some art, science, sport, etc. for pleasure rather than as a profession; specif., an athlete who is forbidden by rule to profit from his athletic activity **2.** a person who does something without professional skill —*adj.* **1.** of or done by or as by an amateur or amateurs **2.** being an amateur or made up of amateurs

am·a·teur·ish (am′ə choor′ish, -toor′-, -tyoor′-) *adj.* like an amateur; unskillful; not expert —**am′a·teur′ish·ly** *adv.* —**am′a·teur′ish·ness** *n.*

am·a·teur·ism (am′ə chər iz'm, -toor-, -tyoor-) *n.* **1.** an amateurish method or quality **2.** the nonprofessional status of an amateur

am·a·to·ry (am′ə tôr′ē) *adj.* [< L. pp. of *amare,* to love] of or showing love, esp. sexual love

a·maze (ə māz′) *vt.* **a·mazed′, a·maz′ing** [< OE. *amasian:* see MAZE] to fill with great surprise or sudden wonder; astonish —*n.* [Poet.] amazement —**a·maz′ed·ly** (-id lē) *adv.* —**a·maz′ing·ly** *adv.*

a·maze·ment (-mənt) *n.* an amazed condition; great wonder; astonishment

Am·a·zon (am′ə zän′, -zən) river in S. America, flowing from the Andes in Peru across N Brazil into the Atlantic: c. 3,300 mi. —*n.* [L. < Gr. < ?, but derived by folk etym. < *a-,* without + *mazos,* breast, hence the story that the Amazons cut off one breast to facilitate archery] **1.** *Gr. Myth.* any of a race of female warriors supposed to have lived in Scythia **2.** [a-] a large, strong, masculine woman —**Am′a·zo′ni·an** (-zō′nē ən) *adj.*

am·bas·sa·dor (am bas′ə dər) *n.* [< MFr. < OIt. < Pr. < hyp. *ambaissa,* task, mission] **1.** the highest-ranking diplomatic representative appointed by a government to represent it in another country: an **ambassador-at-large** is one accredited to no particular country; an **ambassador extraordinary** is one on a special diplomatic mission; an **ambassador plenipotentiary** has the power to make treaties **2.** an official messenger with a special mission —**am·bas′sa·do′ri·al** (-dôr′ē əl) *adj.* —**am·bas′sa·dor·ship′** *n.*

am·ber (am′bər) *n.* [< OFr. < Ar. *'anbar,* ambergris] **1.** a yellow or brownish-yellow translucent fossil resin used in jewelry, pipestems, etc. **2.** the color of amber —*adj.* **1.** made of or like amber **2.** having the color of amber

am·ber·gris (-grēs′, -gris′) *n.* [< OFr. < *ambre gris,* gray AMBER] a grayish, waxy substance from the intestines of sperm whales, found floating in tropical seas and used in some perfumes

am·ber·jack (-jak′) *n.* [AMBER + JACK (fish): from its color] any of several food and game fishes found in warm seas

am·bi- [L. < *ambo,* both] *a combining form meaning* both *[ambidextrous]*

am·bi·ance (am′bē əns) *n.* [Fr.: see AMBIENT] an environment or milieu: also **am′bi·ence**

am·bi·dex·trous (am′bə dek′strəs) *adj.* [< L. AMBI- + *dexter,* right hand + -OUS] **1.** able to use both hands with equal ease **2.** very skillful or versatile **3.** deceitful; double-dealing —**am′bi·dex·ter′i·ty** (-dek ster′ə tē) *n.* —**am′bi·dex′trous·ly** *adv.*

am·bi·ent (am′bē ənt) *adj.* [< L. prp. of *ambire* < *ambi-,* around + *ire,* to go] surrounding; on all sides

am·bi·gu·i·ty (am′bə gyōō′ə tē) *n.* **1.** the quality or state of being ambiguous **2.** *pl.* **-ties** an ambiguous word, statement, etc.

am·big·u·ous (am big′yoo wəs) *adj.* [< L. < *ambigere,* to wander < *ambi-,* around + *agere,* to ACT] **1.** having two or more possible meanings **2.** not clear; indefinite; vague —**am·big′u·ous·ly** *adv.* —**am·big′u·ous·ness** *n.*

am·bi·tion (am bish′ən) *n.* [< OFr. < L. *ambitio,* a going around (to solicit votes) < pp. of *ambire:* see AMBIENT] **1.** a strong desire for success, fame, power, wealth, etc. **2.** the thing so desired

am·bi·tious (-əs) *adj.* **1.** full of or showing ambition **2.** greatly desirous (*of* something) **3.** needing great effort, skill, enterprise, etc. —**am·bi′tious·ly** *adv.* —**am·bi′tious·ness** *n.*

am·biv·a·lence (am biv′ə ləns) *n.* [AMBI- + VALENCE] simultaneous conflicting feelings toward a person or thing, as love and hate —**am·biv′a·lent** *adj.* —**am·biv′a·lent·ly** *adv.*

am·ble (am′b'l) *vi.* **-bled, -bling** [< OFr. < L. *ambulare,* to walk] **1.** to move at a smooth, easy gait by raising first both legs on one side, then both on the other: said of a horse, etc. **2.** to walk in a leisurely manner —*n.* **1.** a horse's ambling gait **2.** a leisurely walking pace —**am′bler** *n.*

Am·brose (am′brōz) [< L. < Gr. < *ambrotos:* see ff.] a masculine name

am·bro·sia (am brō′zhə) *n.* [L. < Gr. < *ambrotos* < *a-,* not + *brotos,* mortal] **1.** *Gr. & Rom. Myth.* the food of the gods and immortals **2.** anything that tastes or smells delicious —**am·bro′sial** (-zhəl), **am·bro′sian** (-zhən) *adj.*

am·bu·lance (am′byə ləns) *n.* [< Fr. (*hôpital*) *ambulant* < L. prp. of *ambulare,* to walk] **1.** orig., a mobile field hospital **2.** a specially equipped vehicle for carrying the sick or wounded

am·bu·lance-chas·er (-chās′ər) *n.* [Slang] a lawyer who encourages victims of accidents to sue for damages as his clients

am·bu·lant (am′byə lənt) *adj.* moving; walking

am·bu·late (am′byə lāt′) *vi.* **-lat′ed, -lat′ing** [< L. pp. of *ambulare,* to walk] to move about; walk —**am′bu·la′tion** *n.*

am·bu·la·to·ry (-lə tôr′ē) *adj.* **1.** of or for walking **2.** able to walk and not confined to bed **3.** moving from one place to another; movable **4.** *Law* that can be changed or revoked —*n., pl.* **-ries** any sheltered place for walking, as in a cloister

am·bus·cade (am′bəs kād′; *also for n.* am′bəs kād′) *n., vt., vi.* **-cad′ed, -cad′ing** [< Fr. < OFr. *embuschier:* see ff.] *same as* AMBUSH —**am′bus·cad′er** *n.*

am·bush (am′boosh) *n.* [< OFr. *embuschier* < ML. *imboscare,* to set an ambush < *in-,* in + *boscus,* woods] **1.** an arrangement of persons in hiding to make a surprise attack **2.** *a*) the persons in hiding *b*) their place of hiding **3.** the act of so lying in wait to attack —*vt., vi.* **1.** to hide in ambush **2.** to attack from ambush —**am′bush·ment** *n.*

a·me·ba (ə mē′bə) *n., pl.* **-bas, -bae** (-bē) *same as* AMOEBA —**a·me′bic, a·me′ban** *adj.* —**a·me′boid** *adj.*

amebic dysentery a form of dysentery caused by an amoeba

a·meer (ə mir′) *n. same as* AMIR

A·me·lia (ə mēl′yə, -ē ə) [of Gmc. origin; lit., ? diligent < base of *amal,* work] a feminine name

a·mel·io·rant (ə mēl′yər ənt) *n.* a thing that ameliorates

a·mel·io·rate (ə mēl′yə rāt′) *vt., vi.* **-rat′ed, -rat′ing** [< Fr. < OFr. *ameillorer* < *a-,* to + *meillor* < L. *melior,* better] to make or become better; improve —**a·mel′io·ra·ble** (-yər ə b'l) *adj.* —**a·mel′io·ra′tion** *n.* —**a·mel′io·ra′tive** *adj.* —**a·mel′io·ra′tor** *n.*

A·men (ä′mən) *same as* AMON

a·men (ā′men′, ä′-) *interj.* [< L. < Gr. < Heb. *āmēn,* truly, certainly] may it be so! so it is!: used after a prayer or to express approval —*n.* a speaking or writing of "amen"

a·me·na·ble (ə mē′nə b'l, -men′ə-) *adj.* [Anglo-Fr. < OFr. < *a-,* to + *mener,* to lead < L. *minare,* to drive (animals)] **1.** responsible or answerable **2.** able to be controlled or influenced; responsive; submissive *[amenable* to suggestion*]* **3.** that can be tested by (with *to*) *[amenable* to the laws of physics*]* —**a·me′na·bil′i·ty** *n.* —**a·me′na·bly** *adv.*

amen corner in some rural Protestant churches, the seats to the minister's right, once occupied by those leading the responsive amens

a·mend (ə mend′) ***vt.*** [< OFr. < L. *emendare*, to correct: see EMEND] **1.** to make better; improve **2.** to remove the faults of; correct **3.** to change or revise (a legislative bill, a law, etc.) —***vi.*** to improve one's conduct —**a·mend′a·ble** ***adj.*** —**a·mend′a·to′ry** ***adj.*** —**a·mend′er** ***n.***

a·mend·ment (ə mend′mənt) ***n.*** **1.** a change for the better; improvement **2.** a correction of errors, faults, etc. **3.** a revision or addition proposed or made in a bill, law, constitution, etc.

a·mends (ə mendz′) ***n.pl.*** [< OFr., pl. of *amende*, a fine: see AMEND] [*sometimes with sing. v.*] something given or done to make up for injury, loss, etc. that one has caused [to make *amends* for rudeness by apologizing]

a·men·i·ty (ə men′ə tē, -mē′nə-) ***n.***, *pl.* **-ties** [< OFr. < L. *amoenitas* < *amoenus*, pleasant] **1.** pleasant quality; attractiveness **2.** *a*) an attractive or desirable feature, as of a place, climate, etc. *b*) anything that adds to one's comfort; convenience **3.** [*pl.*] the courtesies of polite social behavior

a·men·or·rhe·a, a·men·or·rhoe·a (ā men′ə rē′ə) ***n.*** [ModL. < Gr. *a-*, not + *mēn*, month + *rheein*, to flow] abnormal absence or suppression of menstruation

am·ent (am′ənt, ā′mənt) ***n.*** [< L. *amentum*, thong] *same as* CATKIN —**am·en·ta·ceous** (am′ən tā′shəs) ***adj.***

a·men·tia (ā men′shə) ***n.*** [L., madness < *amens* (gen. *amentis*) < *a-* (*ab*), away + *mens*, mind] severe congenital mental deficiency: cf. DEMENTIA

a·merce (ə murs′) ***vt.*** **a·merced′, a·merc′ing** [< Anglo-Fr. < OFr. *a merci*, at the mercy of] **1.** to punish by imposing an arbitrary fine **2.** to punish generally —**a·merce′ment** ***n.***

A·mer·i·ca (ə mer′ə kə) [name traditionally associated with *Amerigo* VESPUCCI, but < ? Sp. *Amerrique* (< AmInd. *Americ*), name of a Nicaraguan mountain range] **1.** North America and South America considered together **2.** either North America or South America **3.** the United States —**the Americas** America (sense 1)

A·mer·i·can (ə mer′ə kən) ***adj.*** **1.** of or in America **2.** of, in, or characteristic of the U.S., its people, etc. —***n.*** **1.** a native or inhabitant of America; specif., *a*) an American Indian *b*) a citizen of the U.S. **2.** the English language spoken in the U.S.

A·mer·i·ca·na (ə mer′ə kan′ə, -kä′nə) ***n.pl.*** [see -ANA] books, papers, objects, etc. having to do with America, its people, and its history

American cheese a kind of fairly hard, mild Cheddar cheese, popular in the U.S.

American Indian *same as* INDIAN (*n.* 2)

A·mer·i·can·ism (ə mer′ə kən is′m) ***n.*** **1.** a custom, characteristic, or belief of or originating in the U.S. **2.** a word, phrase, or usage originating in or peculiar to American English **3.** devotion or loyalty to the U.S., or to its traditions, etc.

A·mer·i·can·ize (-īz′) ***vt., vi.*** **-ized′, -iz′ing** to make or become American in character, manners, methods, ideals, etc.; assimilate to U.S. customs, speech, etc. —**A·mer′i·can·i·za′tion** ***n.***

American plan a system of hotel operation in which the charge to guests covers room, service, and meals: distinguished from EUROPEAN PLAN

American Revolution **1.** a sequence of actions (1763–83) by American colonists against British domination, culminating in the Revolutionary War **2.** the Revolutionary War (1775–83), fought by the American colonies to gain independence from England

American Samoa *see* SAMOA

American Standard Version a revision of the King James Version of the Bible, published in the U.S. in 1901

am·er·ic·i·um (am′ə rish′ē əm, -ris′-) ***n.*** [ModL. < AMERICA] a chemical element, one of the transuranic elements produced from plutonium: symbol, Am; at. wt., 243.13; at. no., 95

Am·er·ind (am′ə rind′) ***n.*** [AMER(ICAN) + IND(IAN)] an American Indian or Eskimo —**Am′er·in′di·an** ***adj., n.*** —**Am′er·in′dic** ***adj.***

am·e·thyst (am′ə thist) ***n.*** [< OFr. < L. < Gr. < *a-*, not + *methystos*, drunken (from the notion that it prevented intoxication)] **1.** a purple or violet variety of quartz, used in jewelry **2.** popularly, a purple corundum, used in jewelry: also called *Oriental amethyst* **3.** purple or violet —**am′e·thys′tine** (-this′tin, -tēn) ***adj.***

Am·har·ic (am har′ik, äm här′-) ***n.*** the Semitic language used officially in Ethiopia

‡**a·mi** (à mē′) ***n.***, *pl.* **a·mis′** (-mē′) [Fr.] a (man or boy) friend —**a·mie′** ***n. fem.***, *pl.* **a·mies′** (-mē′)

a·mi·a·ble (ā′mē ə b'l) ***adj.*** [< OFr. < LL. *amicabilis*, friendly < L. *amicus*, friend] having a pleasant, friendly disposition; good-natured —**a′mi·a·bil′i·ty** ***n.*** —**a′mi·a·bly** ***adv.***

am·i·ca·ble (am′i kə b'l) ***adj.*** [< LL. *amicabilis*: see AMIABLE] friendly in feeling; showing good will; peaceable [an *amicable* discussion] —**am′i·ca·bil′i·ty** ***n.*** —**am′i·ca·bly** ***adv.***

am·ice (am′is) ***n.*** [< OFr. < L. *amictus*, a cloak] an oblong cloth of white linen worn about the neck and shoulders by a priest at Mass

a·mi·cus cu·ri·ae (ə mī′kəs kyoor′i ē′) [L., friend of the court] *Law* a person who offers, or is called in, to advise a court on some legal matter

a·mid (ə mid′) ***prep.*** [ME. < *on*, at + *middan*, middle] in the middle of; among

am·ide (am′īd, -id) ***n.*** [AM(MONIA) + -IDE] **1.** any of a group of organic compounds containing the $CO{\cdot}NH_2$ radical or an acid radical in place of one hydrogen atom of an ammonia molecule **2.** any of the ammono bases in which one hydrogen atom of the ammonia molecule is replaced by a metal —**a·mid·ic** (ə mid′ik) ***adj.***

am·i·dol (am′ə dōl′, -dôl′) ***n.*** [< AMID(E) + (PHEN)OL] a colorless, crystalline compound used as a developer in photography

a·mid·ships (ə mid′ships) ***adv., adj.*** in or toward the middle of a ship: also **a·mid′ship**

a·midst (ə midst′) ***prep.*** *same as* AMID

a·mi·go (ə mē′gō; *Sp.* ä mē′gô) ***n.***, *pl.* **-gos** (-gōz; *Sp.* -gôs) [Sp.] a friend

a·mine (ə mēn′; am′ēn, -in) ***n.*** [AM(MONIA) + -INE[4]] *Chem.* a derivative of ammonia in which hydrogen atoms have been replaced by radicals containing hydrogen and carbon atoms

a·mi·no (ə mē′nō) ***adj.*** [< prec.] of or containing the NH_2 radical in combination with certain organic radicals

amino acids a group of organic compounds that contain the amino radical and serve as units of structure of the proteins

a·mir (ə mir′) ***n.*** [Ar.] in some Moslem countries, a ruler, prince, or commander: see also EMIR

Am·ish (ä′mish, am′ish) ***n.pl.*** [after Jacob *Ammann* (or *Amen*), the founder] Mennonites of a sect founded in the 17th cent. —***adj.*** of this sect

a·miss (ə mis′) ***adv.*** [ME.: see A-[1] & MISS[1]] in a wrong way; astray, wrongly, faultily, etc. —***adj.*** wrong, faulty, improper, etc.: used predicatively

a·mi·to·sis (ā′mī tō′sis, am′ə-) ***n.*** [A-[2] (sense 3) + MITOSIS] *Biol.* cell division by simple constriction of the nucleus into two halves: opposed to MITOSIS —**am′i·tot′ic** (-tät′ik) ***adj.***

am·i·ty (am′ə tē) ***n.***, *pl.* **-ties** [< OFr. *amistie* < L. *amicus*, friend] friendly, peaceful relations, as between nations; friendship

Am·man (äm′än) capital of Jordan: pop. 330,000

am·me·ter (am′mēt′ər) ***n.*** [AM(PERE) + -METER] an instrument for measuring the strength of an electric current in terms of amperes

am·mo (am′ō) ***n.*** [Slang] ammunition

Am·mon (am′ən) Amon, the ancient Egyptian god: identified by the Greeks (and Romans) with Zeus (and Jupiter)

am·mo·nia (ə mōn′yə) ***n.*** [< (SAL) AMMONIAC] **1.** a colorless, pungent gas, NH_3, used in fertilizers, cleaning fluids, etc. **2.** a water solution of this gas: in full, **ammonia water**

am·mo·ni·ac (ə mō′nē ak′) ***n.*** [< L. < Gr. *ammōniakon*, gum resin said to come from near the temple of Jupiter AMMON in Libya] an Asian gum resin used in perfumes, porcelain cements, etc.

am·mo·ni·ate (ə mō′n ē āt′; *for n.* -it) ***vt.*** **-at′ed, -at′ing** to mix or combine with ammonia —***n.*** any of several compounds containing ammonia —**am·mo′ni·a′tion** ***n.***

am·mo·ni·fi·ca·tion (ə mō′nə fi kā′shən, -män′ə-) ***n.*** **1.** an ammoniating **2.** the forming of ammonia by bacterial action in the decay of nitrogenous organic matter —**am·mo′ni·fy′** ***vt., vi.*** **-fied′, -fy′ing**

am·mo·nite (am′ə nīt′) ***n.*** [< L. (*cornu*) *Ammonis*, (horn) of Ammon] any of the coiled fossil shells of a Mesozoic mollusk

am·mo·ni·um (ə mō′nē əm) ***n.*** the radical NH_4, present in salts produced by the reaction of ammonia with an acid

ammonium chloride a white, crystalline compound, NH_4Cl: it is used in medicine, and also in dry cells, dyes, etc.: also called **sal ammoniac**

ammonium hydroxide an alkali, NH_4OH, formed by dissolving ammonia in water

ammonium sulfate an ammonium salt, $(NH_4)_2SO_4$, used in making fertilizers, in treating water, etc.

am·mo·no (am′ə nō′) ***adj.*** of, containing, or derived from ammonia

am·mu·ni·tion (am′yə nish′ən) ***n.*** [< Fr., by faulty separation of *la munition:* see MUNITIONS] **1.** anything hurled by a weapon or exploded as a weapon, as bullets, shells, bombs, grenades, etc. **2.** any means of attack or defense

am·ne·sia (am nē′zhə, -zhē ə) ***n.*** [ModL. < Gr. < *a-*, not + *mnasthai*, to remember] partial or total loss of memory caused by brain injury, or by shock, repression, etc. —**am·ne′si·ac′** (-zē ak′), **am·ne′sic** (-sik, -zik) ***adj., n.***

am·nes·ty (am′nəs tē) ***n.,*** *pl.* **-ties** [< Fr. < L. < Gr. *amnēstia*, a forgetting: see prec.] a general pardon, esp. for political offenses —***vt.*** **-tied, -ty·ing** to grant amnesty to; pardon

am·ni·on (am′nē ən, -än′) ***n.,*** *pl.* **-ni·ons, -ni·a** (-ə) [Gr., dim. of *amnos*, lamb] the innermost membrane of the sac enclosing the embryo of a mammal, reptile, or bird: it is filled with a watery fluid **(amniotic fluid)** —**am′ni·ot′ic** (-ät′ik) ***adj.***

a·moe·ba (ə mē′bə) ***n.,*** *pl.* **-bas, -bae** (-bē) [ModL. < Gr. *amoibē* < *ameibein*, to change] **1.** a microscopic, one-celled animal found usually in stagnant water: it moves by making continual changes in its shape and multiplies by fission **2.** a similar animal that is a parasite in higher animals and man

NUCLEUS
VACUOLE
PSEUDOPODIUM

AMOEBA

a·moe·bic (-bik) ***adj.*** **1.** of or like an amoeba or amoebas **2.** caused by amoebas Also **a·moe′ban** (-bən)

a·mok (ə muk′) ***adj., adv.*** [Malay *amoq*] in a frenzy to kill; in a violent rage —**run** (or **go**) **amok** **1.** to rush about in a frenzy to kill **2.** to lose control of oneself and attempt violence

A·mon (ä′mən) an ancient Egyptian deity, later identified with the sun god: see AMON-RE

a·mong (ə muŋ′) ***prep.*** [OE. *on gemang*, in the company (of) < *on*, in + *gemang*, a crowd < *gemengan*, to mingle] **1.** in the company of; surrounded by *[among* friends*]* **2.** from place to place in *[*pass *among* the crowd*]* **3.** in the group or class of *[*fairest *among* women*]* **4.** by or with many of *[*rebellion *among* the youth*]* **5.** as compared with *[*one *among* thousands*]* **6.** with a share for each of *[*divided *among* us*]* **7.** with one another *[*talking *among* ourselves*]* **8.** by the joint action of

a·mongst (ə muŋst′) ***prep.*** *same as* AMONG

A·mon-Re (ä′mən rā′) the ancient Egyptian sun god: also **A′mon-Ra′** (-rä′)

a·mon·til·la·do (ə män′tə lä′dō) ***n.*** [Sp. < *Montilla*, a town in Spain] a pale, rather dry sherry

a·mor·al (ā môr′əl, -mär′-) ***adj.*** **1.** not to be judged by moral values; neither moral nor immoral **2.** without moral sense or principles —**a·mor·al·i·ty** (ā′mə ral′ə tē) ***n.*** —**a·mor′al·ly** ***adv.***

am·o·rous (am′ər əs) ***adj.*** [< OFr. < LL. *amorosus* < L. *amor*, love < *amare*, to love] **1.** fond of making love **2.** in love; enamored or fond (*of*) **3.** full of or showing love or sexual desire *[amorous* words*]* **4.** of sexual love or lovemaking —**am′o·rous·ly** ***adv.*** —**am′o·rous·ness** ***n.***

a·mor·phous (ə môr′fəs) ***adj.*** [< ModL. < Gr. < *a-*, without + *morphē*, form] **1.** without definite form; shapeless **2.** indefinite, unorganized, vague, etc. **3.** *Biol.* without specialized structure **4.** *Chem., Mineralogy* not crystalline —**a·mor′phism** ***n.*** —**a·mor′phous·ly** ***adv.*** —**a·mor′phous·ness** ***n.***

am·or·tize (am′ər tīz′, ə môr′-) ***vt.*** **-tized′, -tiz′ing** [< OFr. *amortir*, to extinguish < ML. < L. *ad*, to + *mors*, death] **1.** to put money aside at intervals, as in a sinking fund, for gradual payment of (a debt, etc.) **2.** *Accounting* to write off (expenditures) by prorating over a fixed period Chiefly Brit. sp. **am′or·tise′, -tised′, -tis′ing** —**am′or·tiz′a·ble** ***adj.*** —**am′or·ti·za′tion** ***n.***

A·mos (ā′məs) [Heb. *'āmōs*, lit., borne (by God?)] **1.** a masculine name **2.** *Bible a)* a Hebrew prophet of the 8th cent. B.C. *b)* the book containing prophecies attributed to him

a·mount (ə mount′) ***vi.*** [< OFr. *amonter* < *amont*, upward < *a-* (L. *ad*), to + *mont* < L. *mons*, mountain] **1.** to add up; total *[*the bill *amounts* to $4.50*]* **2.** to be equal in meaning, value, or effect *[*her reply *amounts* to a refusal*]* —***n.*** **1.** the sum of two or more quantities; total **2.** a principal sum plus its interest **3.** a quantity

a·mour (ə moor′) ***n.*** [Fr. < Pr. < L. *amor*, love] a love affair, esp. one that is illicit or secret

‡a·mour-pro·pre (à mo͞or prô′pr′) ***n.*** [Fr.] self-love

amp. **1.** amperage **2.** ampere(s)

am·per·age (am′pər ij, am pir′-) ***n.*** the strength of an electric current, measured in amperes

am·pere (am′pir) ***n.*** [after A. M. *Ampère* (1775–1836), Fr. physicist] the standard unit for measuring the strength of an electric current; rate of flow of charge of one coulomb per second

am·per·sand (am′pər sand′) ***n.*** [< *and per se and*, lit., (the sign) & by itself (is) *and*] a sign (& or &) meaning *and*

am·phet·a·mine (am fet′ə mēn′, -min) ***n.*** [*a*lpha-*m*ethyl-beta-*ph*enyl-*et*hyl-*amine*] a compound, $C_9H_{13}N$, used as a drug to overcome depression, fatigue, etc. and to lessen the appetite

am·phi- [< Gr.] *a prefix meaning:* **1.** on both sides or ends **2.** of both kinds **3.** around; about

am·phib·i·an (am fib′ē ən) ***n.*** [see ff.] **1.** any of a class of vertebrates, including frogs, toads, salamanders, etc., that usually begin life in the water as tadpoles with gills, and later develop lungs: they are coldblooded and scaleless **2.** any amphibious animal or plant **3.** an aircraft that can take off from and come down on either land or water **4.** a vehicle that can travel on either land or water —***adj.*** **1.** of the amphibians **2.** *same as* AMPHIBIOUS

am·phib·i·ous (am fib′ē əs) ***adj.*** [< Gr. < *amphi-*, AMPHI- + *bios*, life] **1.** that can live both on land and in water **2.** that can operate on both land and water **3.** of or for a military operation involving the landing of troops from seaborne transports —**am·phib′i·ous·ly** ***adv.***

am·phi·bole (am′fə bōl′) ***n.*** [Fr. < LL. *amphibolus*, ambiguous < Gr. *amphiballein*, to be uncertain < *amphi-*, AMPHI- + *ballein*, to throw] any of a group of rock-forming minerals, as hornblende or asbestos, composed largely of silica, calcium, iron, and magnesium —**am′phi·bol′ic** (-bäl′ik) ***adj.***

am·phi·ox·us (am′fē äk′səs) ***n.*** [< AMPHI- + Gr. *oxys*, sharp] *same as* LANCELET

am·phi·pro·style (am′fə prō′stīl, am fip′rə stīl′) ***adj.*** [< L. < Gr.: see AMPHI- & PROSTYLE] *Archit.* having rows of columns only at the front and back —***n.*** an amphiprostyle building

am·phi·the·a·ter, am·phi·the·a·tre (am′fə thē′ə tər) ***n.*** [< L. < Gr.: see AMPHI- & THEATER] **1.** a round or oval building with an open space (arena) surrounded by rising rows of seats **2.** a scene of contest **3.** a level place surrounded by rising ground

Am·phi·tri·te (am′fi trīt′ē) *Gr. Myth.* goddess of the sea and wife of Poseidon

Am·phi·try·on (am fit′rē ən) *Gr. Myth.* a king of Thebes: his wife, Alcmene, became the mother of Hercules by Zeus

am·pho·ra (am′fər ə) ***n.,*** *pl.* **-rae** (-ē), **-ras** [L. < Gr. < *amphi-*, AMPHI- + *pherein*, to bear] a tall jar with a narrow neck and base and two handles, used by the ancient Greeks and Romans

am·pho·ter·ic (am′fə ter′ik) ***adj.*** [< Gr. < *amphō*, var. of AMPHI-] *Chem.* having both acid and basic properties

am·ple (am′p'l) ***adj.*** **-pler, -plest** [OFr. < L. *amplus*] **1.** large in size, extent, etc. **2.** more than enough; abundant **3.** enough; adequate —**am′ple·ness** ***n.***

am·plex·i·caul (am plek′sə kôl′) ***adj.*** [< L. pp. of *amplectari*, to twine around + *caulis*, stem] *Bot.* growing directly from the main stem and encircling it, as corn leaves

am·pli·fi·ca·tion (am′plə fi kā′shən) ***n.*** **1.** an amplifying or being amplified **2.** additional details **3.** a statement, etc. with something added

am·pli·fi·er (am′plə fī′ər) ***n.*** **1.** a person or thing that amplifies **2.** *Electronics* a device, esp. one with electron tubes or semiconductors, used to increase electrical signal strength

am·pli·fy (am′plə fī′) ***vt.*** **-fied′, -fy′ing** [< OFr. < L. *amplificare* < *amplus*, AMPLE + *facere*, to make] **1.** to make stronger; increase (power, authority, etc.) **2.** to develop more fully, as with details, examples, etc. **3.** *Electronics* to strengthen (an electrical signal) by means of an amplifier —***vi.*** to speak or write at length; expatiate

am·pli·tude (am′plə to͞od′, -tyo͞od′) ***n.*** [< L. < *amplus*, AMPLE] **1.** extent; largeness **2.** abundance; fullness **3.** scope or breadth, as of mind **4.** the extreme range of a fluctuating quantity, from the average or mean to the extreme

amplitude modulation the changing of the amplitude of the transmitting radio wave in accordance with the signal being broadcast: distinguished from FREQUENCY MODULATION

am·ply (am′plē) ***adv.*** to an ample degree

am·pul (am′pool, -pul) ***n.*** [Fr. < L. *ampulla*, AMPULLA] a small, sealed glass container for one dose of a medicine to be injected hypodermically: also **am′pule** (-pyool), **am′poule** (-po͞ol)

am·pul·la (am pul′ə, -pool′ə) ***n.,*** *pl.* **-pul′lae** (-ē) [< OE. < L. *ampulla*, dim. of AMPHORA] **1.** a nearly round bottle with two handles, used by the ancient Greeks and Romans **2.** a container used in churches for holy oil, consecrated wine, etc.

am·pu·tate (am′pyə tāt′) ***vt.*** **-tat′ed, -tat′ing** [< L. pp. of *amputare* < *am-*, for AMBI- + *putare*, to prune] to cut off (an arm, leg, etc.), esp. by surgery —**am′pu·ta′tion** ***n.*** —**am′pu·ta′tor** ***n.***

am·pu·tee (am′pyə tē′) ***n.*** [see -EE] a person who has had a limb or limbs amputated

Am·rit·sar (əm rit′sər) city in Punjab, N India: pop. 398,000

Am·ster·dam (am′stər dam′) constitutional capital of the Netherlands: pop. 868,000: see also The HAGUE

amt. amount

amu, AMU atomic mass unit

a·muck (ə muk′) ***adj., adv.*** *same as* AMOK

am·u·let (am′yə lit) ***n.*** [< Fr. < L.] something worn on the body as a charm against evil

A·mund·sen (ä′moon sən), **Ro·ald** (rō′äl) 1872–1928; Norw. polar explorer

A·mur (ä moor′) river in NE Asia, flowing along the U.S.S.R.–China border: c. 2,700 mi.

a·muse (ə myōōz′) ***vt.*** **a·mused′, a·mus′ing** [< Fr. < *ā,* at + OFr. *muser,* to stare fixedly] **1.** to keep pleasantly occupied; entertain **2.** to make laugh, smile, etc. by being humorous **—a·mus′a·ble** ***adj.*** **—a·mus′er** ***n.***

a·muse·ment (-mənt) ***n.*** **1.** the condition of being amused **2.** something that amuses or entertains

amusement park an outdoor place with devices for entertainment, as a merry-go-round, etc.

a·mus·ing (ə myōō′ziŋ) ***adj.*** **1.** entertaining; diverting **2.** causing laughter **—a·mus′ing·ly** ***adv.***

A·my (ā′mē) [< OFr. *Amee,* lit., beloved < pp. of *aimer,* to love < L. *amare*] a feminine name

a·myg·da·lin (ə mig′də lin) ***n.*** [< L. *amygdala,* almond + -IN[1]] a glucoside, $C_{20}H_{27}NO_{11}$, present in bitter almonds and used as a flavoring agent

am·yl (am′il) ***n.*** [AM(YLUM) + -YL] any of various isomeric forms of the monovalent radical C_5H_{11} **—a·myl·ic** (ə mil′ik) ***adj.***

am·y·la·ceous (am′ə lā′shəs) ***adj.*** [< AMYLUM + -ACEOUS] of or like starch

am·yl·ase (am′ə lās′) ***n.*** an enzyme that helps change starch into sugar: it is found in saliva, pancreatic juice, etc.: see also DIASTASE

am·y·loid (am′ə loid′) ***n.*** a starchy substance

am·y·lop·sin (am′ə läp′sin) ***n.*** [< ff. + TRYPSIN] the enzyme (amylase) of pancreatic juice

am·y·lum (am′ə ləm) ***n.*** [< L. < Gr.] *Chem. a technical name for* STARCH

an[1] (ən; *stressed* an) ***adj., indefinite article*** [weakened variant of ONE < OE. *an,* the numeral one] **1.** one; one sort of *[an apple pie]* **2.** each; any one *[pick an apple]* **3.** to each; in each; for each; per *[two an hour]* See also A, *adj.*

an[2], **an′** (an) ***conj.*** [< *and*] **1.** [Dial.] and **2.** [Archaic] if

an- *same as* A-[2] (not, without): used before vowels

-an (ən, ′n) [< L. *-anus*] *an adj.-forming and n.-forming suffix meaning:* **1.** (one) belonging to or having some relation to *[diocesan]* **2.** (one) born in or living in *[American]* **3.** (one) believing in or following *[Mohammedan]*

an. **1.** [L. *anno*] in the year **2.** anonymous

an·a- [L. < Gr. *ana,* up, on, again] *a prefix meaning:* **1.** up *[anadromous]* **2.** back, backward *[anagram]* **3.** again *[Anabaptist]* **4.** throughout *[analysis]* **5.** according to, similar to *[analogy]*

-a·na (an′ə, ä′nə, ā′nə) [neut. pl. of L. *-anus*] *a n.-forming suffix meaning* sayings, writings, anecdotes, or facts of *[Americana]*

An·a·bap·tist (an′ə bap′tist) ***n.*** [< LL. < Gr. < *ana-,* again + *baptizein,* to baptize] a member of a 16th-cent. Swiss sect of the Reformation, that rejected infant baptism and practiced baptism of adults **—*adj.*** of this sect **—An′a·bap′tism** ***n.***

A·nab·a·sis (ə nab′ə sis) [Gr. < *anabainein,* to go up < *ana-,* up + *bainein,* to go] **1.** the unsuccessful military expedition (401–400 B.C.) of Cyrus the Younger to overthrow Artaxerxes II **2.** a book about this by Xenophon **—*n.*** **[a-]** *pl.* **-ses′** (-sēz′) any large military expedition

an·a·bat·ic (an′ə bat′ik) ***adj.*** [Gr. *anabatikos:* see prec.] moving upward: said of air currents

an·a·bi·o·sis (an′ə bī ō′sis) ***n.*** [ModL. < Gr. < *anabioein,* to come to life again] a state of suspended animation, as in certain arthropods when desiccated **—an′a·bi·ot′ic** (-ät′ik) ***adj.***

a·nab·o·lism (ə nab′ə liz′m) ***n.*** [< Gr. *anabolē,* a rising up + -ISM] the process in a plant or animal by which food is changed into living tissue; constructive metabolism: opposed to CATABOLISM **—an·a·bol·ic** (an′ə bäl′ik) ***adj.***

a·nach·ro·nism (ə nak′rə niz′m) ***n.*** [< MGr. *anachronizein,* to refer to a wrong time < *ana-,* against + *chronos,* time] **1.** the representation of something as existing or occurring at other than its proper time **2.** anything out of its proper time in history **—a·nach′ro·nis′tic, a·nach′ro·nous** (-nəs) ***adj.*** **—a·nach′ro·nis′ti·cal·ly** ***adv.***

an·a·co·lu·thon (an′ə kə lōō′thän) ***n., pl.*** **-tha** (-thə), **-thons** [Gr. < *anakolouthos,* inconsequent < *an-,* not + *akolouthos,* following] a change from one grammatical construction to another within the same sentence, sometimes as a rhetorical device **—an′a·co·lu′thic** ***adj.***

an·a·con·da (an′ə kän′də) ***n.*** [< ? Singhalese *henakandayā,* whip snake] **1.** a long, heavy S. American snake of the boa family **2.** any similar large snake that crushes its victim in its coils

ANACONDA (to 30 ft. long)

a·nad·ro·mous (ə nad′rə məs) ***adj.*** [< Gr. < *ana-,* upward + *dramein,* to run] going up rivers to spawn: said of salmon, shad, etc.

a·nae·mi·a (ə nē′mē ə, -myə) ***n.*** *same as* ANEMIA **—a·nae′mic** ***adj.***

an·aer·obe (an er′ōb, an′ə rōb′) ***n.*** [< ff.] a microorganism that can live and grow where there is no free oxygen **—an·aer·o·bic** (an′er ō′bik, -ə rō′-) ***adj.***

an·aer·o·bi·um (an′er ō′bē əm, -ə rō′-) ***n., pl.*** **-bi·a** (-bē ə) [ModL. < Gr. *an-,* AN- + *aero-,* AERO- + *bios,* life] *same as* ANAEROBE

an·aes·the·sia (an′əs thē′zhə) ***n.*** *same as* ANESTHESIA **—an′·aes·thet′ic** (-thet′ik) ***adj., n.*** **—an·aes·the·tist** (ə nes′thə tist) ***n.*** **—an·aes′the·tize′** ***vt.*** **-tized′, -tiz′ing**

an·a·gram (an′ə gram′) ***n.*** [< ModL. < Gr. *anagrammatizein,* to transpose letters < *ana-,* back + *gramma,* letter < *graphein,* to write] **1.** a word or phrase made from another by rearranging its letters (Ex.: *now — won*) **2.** [*pl., with sing. v.*] a game in which players seek to form words by arranging letters drawn at random from a stock of them **—an′a·gram·mat′ic** (-grə mat′ik), **an′a·gram·mat′i·cal** ***adj.*** **—an′a·gram·mat′i·cal·ly** ***adv.***

an·a·gram·ma·tize (an′ə gram′ə tīz′) ***vt.*** **-tized′, -tiz′ing** to make an anagram of

An·a·heim (an′ə hīm′) [< Santa *Ana* (St. Anne, reputed mother of the Virgin Mary) + G. *heim,* home] city in SW Calif.: pop. 222,000

a·nal (ā′n′l) ***adj.*** **1.** of or near the anus **2.** *Psychoanalysis* of an early stage of psychosexual development focusing on excretory functions **—a′nal·ly** ***adv.***

an·a·lects (an′ə lekts′) ***n.pl.*** [< L. < Gr. *analegein,* to collect < *ana-,* up + *legein,* to gather] collected literary excerpts: also **an′a·lec′ta** (-lek′tə) **—the Analects** a collection of Confucius' teachings

an·a·lep·tic (an′ə lep′tik) ***adj.*** [< Gr. < *analambanein,* to recover < *ana-,* up + *lambanein,* to take] *Med.* restorative **—*n.*** an analeptic drug

an·al·ge·si·a (an′'l jē′zē ə, -sē ə) ***n.*** [ModL. < Gr. *an-,* without + *algēsia,* pain] a state of not feeling pain although fully conscious

an·al·ge·sic (-zik, -sik) ***adj.*** of or causing analgesia **—*n.*** a drug producing analgesia

analog computer an electronic computer that uses voltages to represent the numerical data of physical quantities: cf. DIGITAL COMPUTER

an·a·log·i·cal (an′ə läj′i k′l) ***adj.*** of, expressing, or based upon analogy **—an′a·log′i·cal·ly** ***adv.***

a·nal·o·gize (ə nal′ə jīz′) ***vi.*** **-gized′, -giz′ing** to use, or reason by, analogy **—*vt.*** to explain or liken by analogy **—a·nal′o·gist** (-jist) ***n.***

a·nal·o·gous (-gəs) ***adj.*** [see ANALOGY] **1.** similar or comparable in certain respects **2.** *Biol.* similar in function but not in origin and structure **—a·nal′o·gous·ly** ***adv.***

an·a·logue, an·a·log (an′ə lôg′, -läg′) ***n.*** a thing or part that is analogous **—*adj.*** of or by means of an analog computer: usually **analog**

a·nal·o·gy (ə nal′ə jē) ***n., pl.*** **-gies** [< ME. & OFr. < L. < Gr. *analogia,* proportion < *ana-,* according to + *logos,* ratio: see LOGIC] **1.** similarity in some respects; partial resemblance **2.** a comparing of something point by point with something similar **3.** *Biol.* similarity in function but not in origin and structure **4.** *Logic* the inference that certain resemblances imply probable further similarity

a·nal·y·sand (ə nal′ə sand′) ***n.*** a person who is undergoing psychoanalysis

an·a·lyse (an′ə līz′) ***vt.*** **-lysed′, -lys′ing** *chiefly Brit. sp. of* ANALYZE

a·nal·y·sis (ə nal′ə sis) ***n., pl.*** **-ses′** (-sēz′) [ML. < Gr., a dissolving < *ana-,* up, throughout + *lysis,* a loosing < *lyein,* to loose] **1.** *a)* a breaking up of any whole into its parts so as to find out their nature, function, etc. *b)* a statement of these findings **2.** *same as* PSYCHOANALYSIS **3.** *Chem.* the separation of compounds and mixtures into their constituent substances to determine the nature (*qualitative analysis*) or the proportion (*quantitative analysis*) of the constituents **4.** *Linguis.* the use of word order and function words rather than inflection to express syntactic relationships

an·a·lyst (an′ə list) ***n.*** **1.** a person who analyzes *[a news analyst]* **2.** *same as* PSYCHOANALYST

an·a·lyt·ic (an′ə lit′ik) ***adj.*** **1.** *Linguis.* characterized by analysis rather than inflection **2.** *same as* ANALYTICAL

an·a·lyt·i·cal (-i k′l) ***adj.*** **1.** of analysis or analytics **2.** skilled in or using analysis **3.** *same as* ANALYTIC (sense 1) **—an′a·lyt′i·cal·ly *adv.***

an·a·lyt·ics (-iks) ***n.pl.*** [*with sing. v.*] the part of logic having to do with analyzing

an·a·lyze (an′ə līz′) ***vt.*** **-lyzed′, -lyz′ing** [< Fr. < *analyse,* ANALYSIS] **1.** to separate into parts so as to find out their nature, function, etc. **2.** to examine in detail so as to determine the nature or tendencies of **3.** to psychoanalyze **—an′a·lyz′a·ble *adj.* —an′a·lyz′er *n.***

an·a·pest, an·a·paest (an′ə pest′) ***n.*** [< L. < Gr. < *ana-,* back + *paiein,* to strike] a metrical foot consisting of two unaccented syllables followed by an accented one, as in English verse (Ex.: "Ănd thĕ shéen/ŏf thĕir spéars/wăs lĭke stárs/ŏn thĕ séa") **—an′a·pes′tic, an′a·paes′tic *adj.***

a·naph·o·ra (ə naf′ər ə) ***n.*** [L. < Gr. < *ana-,* up, back + *pherein,* to BEAR[1]] the repetition of a word or phrase at the beginning of successive clauses or sentences as a rhetorical device

an·aph·ro·dis·i·ac (an af′rə diz′ē ak) ***adj.*** that lessens sexual desire ***—n.*** a drug, etc. that lessens sexual desire

an·ar·chic (an är′kik) ***adj.*** **1.** of, like, or promoting anarchy **2.** without controls; lawless Also **an·ar′chi·cal —an·ar′chi·cal·ly *adv.***

an·ar·chism (an′ər kiz′m) ***n.*** [ANARCH(Y) + -ISM] **1.** the theory that all forms of government interfere unjustly with individual liberty and should be replaced by a system of voluntary cooperation **2.** resistance, sometimes by terrorism, to government

an·ar·chist (-kist) ***n.*** **1.** a person who believes in anarchism **2.** a promoter of anarchy **—an′ar·chis′tic *adj.***

an·ar·chy (-kē) ***n., pl.*** **-chies** [< Gr. < *an-,* without + *archos,* leader] **1.** the complete absence of government **2.** political disorder and violence **3.** disorder in any sphere of activity

An·a·sta·sia (an′ə stā′shə, -zhə) [LL. < Gr. *Anastasios,* lit., of the resurrection] a feminine name

an·as·tig·mat·ic (an as′tig mat′ik, an′ə stig-) ***adj.*** free from, or corrected for, astigmatism

a·nas·to·mose (ə nas′tə mōz′) ***vt., vi.*** **-mosed′, -mos′ing** to join by anastomosis

a·nas·to·mo·sis (ə nas′tə mō′sis) ***n., pl.*** **-ses** (-sēz) [ModL. < Gr. *anastomōsis,* opening < *ana-,* again + *stoma,* mouth] **1.** interconnection as between blood vessels or veins of a leaf **2.** a surgical joining of one hollow or tubular organ to another

a·nas·tro·phe (ə nas′trə fē) ***n.*** [Gr. < *ana-,* back + *strephein,* to turn] reversal of the usual word order of a sentence (Ex.: "Came the dawn")

anat. **1.** anatomical **2.** anatomist **3.** anatomy

a·nath·e·ma (ə nath′ə mə) ***n., pl.*** **-mas** [LL. < Gr., thing devoted to evil < *anatithenai,* to dedicate < *ana-,* up + *tithenai,* to set] **1.** a thing or person accursed **2.** a thing or person greatly detested **3.** a formal curse, as in excommunicating a person from a church **4.** any strong curse

a·nath·e·ma·tize (ə nath′ə mə tīz′) ***vt., vi.*** **-tized′, -tiz′ing** to utter an anathema (against); curse

An·a·to·li·a (an′ə tō′lē ə) **1.** formerly, Asia Minor **2.** the part of modern Turkey that is in Asia **—An′a·to′li·an *adj., n.***

an·a·tom·i·cal (an′ə täm′i k′l) ***adj.*** **1.** of or connected with anatomy **2.** structural Also **an′a·tom′ic —an′a·tom′i·cal·ly *adv.***

a·nat·o·mist (ə nat′ə mist) ***n.*** **1.** a person skilled in anatomy **2.** a person who anatomizes

a·nat·o·mize (-mīz′) ***vt., vi.*** **-mized′, -miz′ing** [see ff.] **1.** to dissect (an animal or plant) in order to examine the structure **2.** to analyze in great detail

a·nat·o·my (ə nat′ə mē) ***n., pl.*** **-mies** [< ME. & OFr. < LL. < Gr. < *ana-,* up + *temnein,* to cut] **1.** the dissecting of an animal or plant in order to study its structure **2.** the science of the structure of animals or plants **3.** the structure of an organism or body **4.** a detailed analysis

An·ax·ag·o·ras (an′ak sag′ər əs) 500?–428? B.C.; Gr. philosopher

-ance (əns, ′ns) [< Fr. < L. *-antia, -entia,* or directly < L.] *a suffix meaning:* **1.** the act of *[utterance]* **2.** the quality or state of being *[vigilance]* **3.** a thing that *[conveyance]* **4.** a thing that is *[dissonance, inheritance]*

an·ces·tor (an′ses′tər) ***n.*** [< ME. & OFr. < L. *antecessor,* one who goes before < *ante-,* before + *cedere,* to go] **1.** any person from whom one is descended; forebear **2.** an early type of animal from which later kinds have evolved **3.** a precursor or predecessor **4.** *Law* the person from whom an estate has been inherited **—an′ces′tress** (-trəs) ***n.fem.***

an·ces·tral (an ses′trəl) ***adj.*** of or inherited from ancestors **—an·ces′tral·ly *adv.***

an·ces·try (an′ses′trē) ***n., pl.*** **-tries** **1.** family descent or lineage **2.** ancestors collectively

an·chor (aŋ′kər) ***n.*** [< OE. < L. < Gr. *ankyra,* a hook] **1.** a heavy object, usually a shaped iron weight with flukes, lowered to the bottom of water by cable or chain to keep a ship from drifting **2.** any device that holds something else secure **3.** anything regarded as giving stability or security ***—vt.*** **1.** to hold secure by or as by an anchor **2.** to act as an anchorman on ***—vi.*** **1.** to lower the anchor overboard **2.** to be or become fixed **—at anchor** anchored **—drop** (or **cast**) **anchor** **1.** to lower the anchor overboard **2.** to settle (*in* a place) **—weigh anchor** **1.** to raise the anchor **2.** to leave; go away

ANCHOR

An·chor·age (aŋ′kər ij, aŋ′krij) seaport in S Alas.: pop. 173,000

an·chor·age (aŋ′kər ij) ***n.*** **1.** money charged for the right to anchor **2.** an anchoring or being anchored **3.** a place to anchor **4.** something that can be relied on

an·cho·rite (aŋ′kə rīt′) ***n.*** [< OFr. < LL. < Gr. *anachōrētēs* < *ana-,* back + *chōrein,* to retire] a person who lives alone for religious meditation; hermit: also **an′cho·ret** (-rit) **—an′cho·ress *n.fem.* —an′cho·rit′ic** (-rit′ik) ***adj.***

an·chor·man (aŋ′kər man′) ***n.*** **1.** the final contestant, as on a relay team **2.** *Radio & TV* that member of a team of newscasters who coordinates various reports **—an′chor·wom′an *n.fem., pl.*** **-wom′en**

an·chor·per·son (-pʉr′s′n) ***n.*** *same as* ANCHORMAN: used to avoid the masculine implication of *anchorman*

an·cho·vy (an′chō′vē, -chə-; an′chō′vē) ***n., pl.*** **-vies, -vy:** see PLURAL, II, D, 1 [< Port. *anchova,* prob. ult. < Gr. *aphyē,* small fry] a very small, herringlike fish: anchovies are usually canned in oil or made into a salty paste

an·chy·lose (aŋ′kə lōs′) ***vt., vi.*** **-losed′, -los′ing** *same as* ANKYLOSE **—an′chy·lo′sis** (-lō′sis) ***n.***

‡an·cien ré·gime (än syan rā zhēm′) [Fr., old order] the former social and political system, esp. that in France before the Revolution of 1789

an·cient (ān′shənt) ***adj.*** [< OFr., ult. < L. *ante,* before] **1.** of times long past; esp., of the time before the end of the Western Roman Empire in 476 A.D. **2.** very old **3.** antiquated ***—n.*** **1.** a person who lived in ancient times **2.** an aged person **—the ancients** the people who lived in ancient times; esp., the classical writers and artists of Greco-Roman times **—an′cient·ness *n.***

an·cient·ly (-lē) ***adv.*** in ancient times

an·cil·lar·y (an′sə ler′ē) ***adj.*** [< L. < *ancilla,* maidservant] **1.** subordinate (*to*) **2.** auxiliary

an·con (aŋ′kän) ***n., pl.*** **an·co·nes** (aŋ kō′nēz) [L. < Gr. < *ankos,* a bend] a bracketlike projection supporting a cornice

-an·cy (ən sē, ′n sē) *same as* -ANCE

and (ənd, ən, ′n; *stressed* and) ***conj.*** [OE.] **1.** also; in addition; as well as: used to join elements of equal grammatical value *[apples and pears, to beg and borrow]* **2.** plus *[6 and 2 equals 8]* **3.** as a result *[he told her and she wept]* **4.** [Colloq.] to *[try and get it]* **5.** [Archaic] then *[and it came to pass]* **6.** [Obs.] if

An·da·lu·sia (an′də lōō′zhə, -shə) region of S Spain

an·dan·te (än dän′tā, an dan′tē) ***adj., adv.*** [It., prp. of *andare,* to walk] *Music* moderate in tempo ***—n.*** an andante movement or passage

an·dan·ti·no (än′dän tē′nō, an′dan-) ***adj., adv.*** [It., dim. of *andante*] *Music* slightly faster than andante ***—n., pl.*** **-nos** an andantino movement or passage

An·der·sen (an′dər s′n), **Hans Christian** 1805–75; Dan. novelist & writer of fairy tales

An·der·son (an′dər s′n) [after a Delaware Indian, Chief *Anderson*] city in EC Ind.: pop. 65,000

An·des (Mountains) (an′dēz) mountain system along the length of W S.America: highest peak, ACONCAGUA **—An·de·an** (an dē′ən, an′dē-) ***adj.***

and·i·ron (an′dī′ərn) ***n.*** [< OFr. *andier* (with ending altered after IRON)] either of a pair of metal supports with front uprights, used to hold the wood in a fireplace

and/or either *and* or *or,* according to what is meant *[personal and/or real property]*

An·dor·ra (an dôr′ə, -där′ə) republic in the E Pyrenees, between Spain and France: 180 sq. mi.; pop. 19,000 **—An·dor′ran *adj., n.***

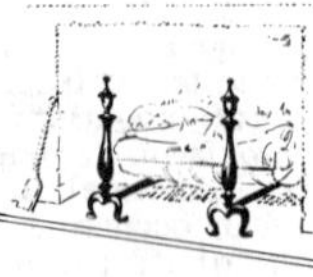
ANDIRONS

Andrea del Sarto *see* SARTO

An·drew (an′drōō) [< OFr. < L. < Gr. *Andreas,* lit., manly < *anēr* (gen. *andros*), man] **1.** a masculine name: dim. *Andy* **2.** *Bible* one of the twelve apostles

an·dro- [< Gr. *anēr* (gen. *andros*), man] *a combining form meaning:* **1.** man, male, masculine **2.** anther, stamen

An·dro·cles (an′drə klēz′) *Rom. Legend* a slave spared in the arena by a lion that recognized him as the man who had once pulled a thorn from its paw

an·droe·ci·um (an drē′shē əm, -sē-) ***n.,*** *pl.* **-ci·a** (-ə) [ModL. < ANDRO- + Gr. *oikos,* house] *Bot.* the stamens and the parts belonging to them, collectively

an·dro·gen (an′drə jən) ***n.*** [ANDRO- + -GEN] a male sex hormone that can give rise to masculine characteristics — **an′dro·gen′ic** (-jen′ik) ***adj.***

an·drog·y·nous (an dräj′ə nəs) ***adj.*** [< L. < Gr. < *anēr* (gen. *andros*), man + *gynē,* woman] **1.** hermaphroditic **2.** *Bot.* bearing both staminate and pistillate flowers in the same cluster —**an·drog′y·ny** (-ə nē) ***n.***

an·droid (an′droid) ***n.*** [ANDR(O)- + -OID] in science fiction, an automaton that looks human

An·drom·a·che (an dräm′ə kē) *Gr. Myth.* the wife of Hector

An·drom·e·da (an dräm′ə də) **1.** *Gr. Myth.* an Ethiopian princess whom Perseus rescued from a sea monster and then married **2.** *Astron.* a N constellation just south of Cassiopeia

an·dros·ter·one (an dräs′tə rōn′) ***n.*** [ANDRO- + STER(OL) + -ONE] a steroid that is a male sex hormone

-an·drous (an′drəs) [< Gr. *anēr:* see ANDRO-] *a suffix meaning* having stamens

-ane (ān) [arbitrary formation] *a suffix denoting* a hydrocarbon of the paraffin series *[methane]*

an·ec·dote (an′ik dōt′) ***n.*** [Fr. < ML. < Gr. *anekdotos,* unpublished < *an-,* not + *ek-,* out + *didonai,* to give] a short, entertaining account of some happening, usually personal or biographical —**an′ec·dot′al** (-dōt′'l) ***adj.*** —**an′ec·dot′ist** (-dōt′ist) ***n.***

an·e·cho·ic (an′e kō′ik) ***adj.*** [AN- + ECHOIC] free from echoes *[*an *anechoic* recording chamber*]*

a·ne·mi·a (ə nē′mē ə, -myə) ***n.*** [ModL. < Gr. < *a-, an-,* without + *haima,* blood] **1.** a condition in which there is a reduction of red blood corpuscles or of hemoglobin (or of both) in the bloodstream **2.** lack of vigor; lifelessness — **a·ne′mic** (-mik) ***adj.*** —**a·ne′mi·cal·ly** ***adv.***

a·nem·o·graph (ə nem′ə graf′) ***n.*** [< Gr. *anemos,* the wind + -GRAPH] an instrument for recording the velocity and direction of the wind

an·e·mom·e·ter (an′ə mäm′ə tər) ***n.*** [< Gr. *anemos,* the wind + -METER] a gauge for determining the force or speed of the wind, and sometimes its direction —**an′e·mo·met′ric** (-mō met′rik) ***adj.*** —**an′e·mom′e·try** ***n.***

a·nem·o·ne (ə nem′ə nē′) ***n.*** [L. < Gr., infl. by *anemos,* wind] **1.** any of various plants of the buttercup family, with cup-shaped flowers, usually white, purple, or red **2.** *same as* SEA ANEMONE

a·nent (ə nent′) ***prep.*** [< OE. *on efen,* lit., on even (with), level (with)] concerning; as regards

an·er·oid (an′ər oid) ***adj.*** [< Gr. *a-,* without + *nēros,* liquid + -OID] not using liquid

aneroid barometer a barometer consisting of a box in which a partial vacuum is maintained: changes in atmospheric pressure cause its elastic top to bend in or out, thus moving a pointer

an·es·the·sia (an′əs thē′zhə, -zhē ə) ***n.*** [< Gr. < *an-,* without + *aisthēsis,* feeling] **1.** a partial or total loss of the sense of pain, temperature, touch, etc. produced by disease **2.** a loss of sensation induced by an anesthetic and limited to a specific area (**local anesthesia**) or producing unconsciousness (**general anesthesia**)

an·es·the·si·ol·o·gist (an′əs thē′zē äl′ə jist) ***n.*** a doctor who specializes in anesthesiology

an·es·the·si·ol·o·gy (-jē) ***n.*** the science of anesthesia and anesthetics

an·es·thet·ic (an′əs thet′ik) ***adj.*** **1.** of or with anesthesia **2.** producing anesthesia —***n.*** a drug, gas, etc. used to produce anesthesia, as before surgery —**anesthetic to** incapable of feeling or responding to —**an′es·thet′i·cal·ly** ***adv.***

an·es·the·tist (ə nes′thə tist) ***n.*** a nurse or other person trained to administer anesthetics

an·es·the·tize (-tīz′) ***vt.*** **-tized′, -tiz′ing** to cause anesthesia in as by giving an anesthetic —**an·es′the·ti·za′tion** ***n.***

an·eu·rysm, an·eu·rism (an′yər iz'm) ***n.*** [ModL. < Gr. < *ana-,* up + *eurys,* broad] a sac formed when the wall of an artery, weakened by disease or injury, becomes enlarged — **an′eu·rys′mal, an′eu·ris′mal** (-yə riz′m'l) ***adj.***

a·new (ə nōō′, -nyōō′) ***adv.*** **1.** once more; again **2.** in a new manner or form

an·ga·ry (aŋ′gə rē) ***n.*** [L. *angaria,* enforced service < Gr. < *angaros,* a mounted courier] *International Law* the right of a belligerent to use or destroy a neutral's property if necessary, provided that indemnification is made

an·gel (ān′j'l) ***n.*** [< OFr. or OE. < L. *angelus* < Gr. *angelos,* messenger < Iran.] **1.** *Theol. a)* a messenger of God *b)* a supernatural being, either good or bad, of more than human power, intelligence, etc. **2.** a guiding spirit *[*one's good *angel]* **3.** a conventionalized image of a figure in human form with wings and a halo **4.** a person regarded as beautiful, good, etc. **5.** [Colloq.] a supporter who provides money, as for producing a play —***vt.*** [Slang] to support with money

An·ge·la (an′jə lə) [< ML. < L. *angelicus,* angelic] a feminine name: var. *Angelica, Angelina*

angel dust [*also* **A- D-**] [Slang] a phenyl-based hallucinogenic drug, sometimes sniffed in powder form

An·gel·e·no (an′jə lē′nō) ***n.,*** *pl.* **-nos** [AmSp.] a native or inhabitant of Los Angeles

an·gel·fish (ān′j'l fish′) ***n.,*** *pl.* **-fish′, -fish′es:** see FISH **1.** a shark with winglike pectoral fins **2.** any of a number of bright-colored tropical fishes with spiny fins

angel food cake a light, spongy, white cake made with egg whites and no shortening: also **angel cake**

an·gel·ic (an jel′ik) ***adj.*** **1.** of an angel or the angels **2.** like an angel in beauty, goodness, etc. Also **an·gel′i·cal** — **an·gel′i·cal·ly** ***adv.***

an·gel·i·ca (an jel′i kə) ***n.*** [ML. (*herba*) *angelica,* lit., the angelic (herb)] a plant of the parsley family, with roots and fruit used in flavoring, medicine, etc.

An·gel·i·co (an jel′ə kō′), **Fra** (frä) (*Giovanni da Fiesole*) 1387–1455; It. painter

An·ge·lus (an′jə ləs) ***n.*** [L.: see ANGEL] [*also* **a-**] *R.C.Ch.* **1.** a prayer said at morning, noon, and evening in commemoration of the Incarnation **2.** a bell rung to announce the time for this

an·ger (aŋ′gər) ***n.*** [ON. *angr,* distress, sorrow] a feeling of displeasure and hostility resulting from injury, mistreatment, opposition, etc. —***vt.*** to make angry; enrage —***vi.*** to become angry

An·ge·vin, An·ge·vine (an′jə vin) ***adj.*** [Fr.] of Anjou or the Plantagenets —***n.*** **1.** a native of Anjou **2.** any of the Plantagenets

an·gi·na (an jī′nə, an′jə-) ***n.*** [L., quinsy < Gr. < *anchein,* to squeeze] **1.** any inflammatory disease of the throat, esp. one characterized by fits of suffocation **2.** a localized spasm of pain **3.** *same as* ANGINA PECTORIS —**an·gi′nal, an·gi·nose** (an′jə nōs′), **an′gi·nous** (-nəs) ***adj.***

angina pec·to·ris (pek′tər is) [L., angina of the breast] a condition marked by recurrent pain in the chest and left arm, caused by a sudden decrease of blood to the heart

an·gi·o·ma (an′jē ō′mə) ***n.,*** *pl.* **-ma·ta** (-mə tə), **-mas** [< Gr. *angeion,* vessel + -OMA] a tumor made up mainly of blood vessels and lymph vessels

an·gi·o·sperm (an′jē ə spurm′) ***n.*** [< Gr. *angeion,* capsule + -SPERM] any flowering plant having the seeds enclosed in an ovary

Angl. **1.** Anglican **2.** Anglicized

an·gle[1] (aŋ′g'l) ***n.*** [ME. & OFr. < L. *angulus,* a corner < Gr. *ankylos,* bent] **1.** *a)* the shape made by two straight lines or plane surfaces that meet *b)* the space between such lines or surfaces *c)* the degrees of difference in direction between them **2.** a sharp corner **3.** point of view *[*consider this from all *angles]* **4.** [Colloq.] a selfish motive or tricky plan —***vt., vi.*** **-gled, -gling** **1.** to move or bend at an angle **2.** [Colloq.] to give a specific point of view to (a story, report, etc.)

an·gle[2] (aŋ′g'l) ***vi.*** **-gled, -gling** [OE. *angul,* fishhook] **1.** to fish with a hook and line **2.** to use tricks to get something *[angling* for attention*]*

angle iron an angled piece of iron or steel used for joining or reinforcing two beams, girders, etc.

angle of incidence the angle that a light ray or electromagnetic wave striking a surface makes with a line perpendicular to the surface

an·gler (aŋ′glər) ***n.*** [< ANGLE[2]] **1.** a fisherman **2.** a schemer **3.** a saltwater fish that feeds on other fish attracted by a filament on its head

ANGLE IRON

An·gles (aŋ′g'lz) ***n.pl.*** a Germanic people that settled in E England in the 5th cent. A.D. — **An′gli·an** (-glē ən) ***adj., n.***

an·gle·worm (aŋ′g'l wurm′) ***n.*** an earthworm: so called because used as fishing bait

An·gli·can (aŋ′gli kən) ***adj.*** [< ML. < *Anglicus,* of England, of the Angles] **1.** of England; English **2.** of the Church of England or any related church with the same faith and forms —***n.*** a member of an Anglican church — **An′gli·can·ism** ***n.***

An·gli·cism (aŋ′glə siz'm) ***n.*** **1.** a word or idiom peculiar to English, esp. British English; Briticism **2.** a typically English trait, custom, etc. **3.** the quality of being English
An·gli·cize (aŋ′glə sīz′) ***vt., vi.*** **-cized′, -ciz′ing** [*also* **a-**] to change to English idiom, pronunciation, customs, etc. —**An′gli·ci·za′tion** ***n.***
An·gli·fy (-fī′) ***vt.*** **-fied′, -fy′ing** *same as* ANGLICIZE
an·gling (aŋ′gliŋ) ***n.*** the act of fishing with hook and line
An·glo- [< L. *Anglus,* sing. of *Angli,* ANGLES] *a combining form meaning* English *[Anglophile]*
An·glo-A·mer·i·can (aŋ′glō ə mer′ə kən) ***adj.*** English and American —***n.*** an American of English birth or ancestry
An·glo-French (-french′) ***adj.*** English and French —***n.*** the French spoken in England from the Norman Conquest through the Middle Ages: see NORMAN FRENCH
An·glo-In·di·an (-in′dē ən) ***adj.*** **1.** of England and India **2.** of Anglo-Indians or their English speech —***n.*** **1.** a person of English and Indian ancestry **2.** words borrowed into English from the languages of India
An·glo·ma·ni·a (-mā′nē ə) ***n.*** an exaggerated liking for and imitation of English customs, manners, institutions, etc. —**An′glo·ma′ni·ac′** (-ak′) ***n.***
An·glo-Nor·man (-nôr′mən) ***adj.*** English and Norman —***n.*** **1.** a Norman settler in England after the Norman Conquest **2.** the Anglo-French dialect of such settlers
An·glo·phile (aŋ′glə fīl′) ***n.*** [*often* **a-**] a person characterized by Anglophilia
An·glo·phil·i·a (aŋ′glə fil′ē ə) ***n.*** [*often* **a-**] extreme admiration for England, its people, customs, etc.
An·glo·phobe (aŋ′glə fōb′) ***n.*** [*often* **a-**] a person characterized by Anglophobia
An·glo·pho·bi·a (aŋ′glə fō′bē ə) ***n.*** [*often* **a-**] hatred or fear of England, its people, customs, etc. —**An′glo·pho′bic** (-fō′bik) ***adj.***
An·glo-Sax·on (aŋ′glō sak′s'n) ***n.*** [< ML.: see ANGLES & SAXON] **1.** a member of the Germanic peoples (Angles, Saxons, and Jutes) living in England at the time of the Norman Conquest **2.** *same as* OLD ENGLISH **3.** plain, blunt language of Old English origin **4.** a person of English nationality or descent —***adj.*** **1.** of the Anglo-Saxons or their language **2.** of their descendants; English
An·go·la (aŋ gō′lə, an-) country on the W coast of Africa: formerly a Port. territory: 481,351 sq. mi.; pop. 6,761,000
An·go·ra (aŋ gôr′ə, an-) ***n.*** [former name of ANKARA] **1.** a kind of cat with long, silky fur **2.** *a)* a kind of goat raised for its long, silky hair *b)* a cloth made from this hair; mohair **3.** *a)* a long-eared rabbit, raised for its long, silky hair *b)* a soft yarn made from this hair Also **angora** for senses 2*b*, 3*b*
an·gos·tu·ra (bark) (an′gəs toor′ə, -tyoor′-) [after *Angostura,* former name of Ciudad Bolivar, city in Venezuela] a bitter bark used as a tonic and as a flavoring in bitters
an·gry (aŋ′grē) ***adj.*** **-gri·er, -gri·est** **1.** feeling, showing, or resulting from anger **2.** wild and stormy **3.** inflamed and sore —**an′gri·ly** (-grə lē) ***adv.*** —**an′gri·ness** ***n.***
ang·strom (aŋ′strəm) ***n.*** [after A. J. *Ångström,* 19th-c. Swed. physicist] one hundred-millionth of a centimeter, a unit used in measuring the length of light waves: also **angstrom unit**
an·guish (aŋ′gwish) ***n.*** [< OFr. < L. *angustia,* tightness < *angustus,* narrow] great suffering, as from grief or pain; agony —***vi., vt.*** to feel or make feel anguish —**an′guished** (-gwisht) ***adj.***
an·gu·lar (aŋ′gyə lər) ***adj.*** **1.** having or forming an angle or angles; having sharp corners **2.** measured by an angle *[angular* distance*]* **3.** lean; bony; gaunt **4.** without ease or grace; awkward *[*an *angular* stride*]* —**an′gu·lar·ly** ***adv.***
an·gu·lar·i·ty (aŋ′gyə lar′ə tē) ***n.,*** *pl.* **-ties** **1.** the quality of being angular **2.** [*pl.*] angular forms; angles
An·gus (aŋ′gəs) [< Gael. & Ir. < *aon,* one] a masculine name
an·hy·dride (an hī′drīd) ***n.*** [< Gr. *anhydros* (see ff.) + -IDE] **1.** an oxide that reacts with water to form an acid or a base **2.** any compound formed by the removal of water, usually from an acid
an·hy·drous (-drəs) ***adj.*** [Gr. *anhydros* < *an-,* without + *hydōr,* water] **1.** without water **2.** *Chem.* having no water of crystallization
an·il (an′il) ***n.*** [Fr. < Port. < Ar. *al,* the + *nīl,* blue] **1.** a West Indian shrub from which indigo is made **2.** *same as* INDIGO
an·i·line (an′'l in, -ēn′, -īn′) ***n.*** [prec. + -INE[4]] a colorless, poisonous, oily liquid, $C_6H_5NH_2$, a derivative of benzene, used in making dyes, synthetic resins, rocket fuel, etc.
aniline dye **1.** any dye made from aniline **2.** commonly, any synthetic dye made from coal tar
an·i·ma (an′ə mə) ***n.*** [L.] life principle; soul
an·i·mad·ver·sion (an′ə mad vʉr′zhən, -shən) ***n.*** [see ff.] **1.** a critical, esp. unfavorable, comment (*on* or *upon* something) **2.** the act of criticizing adversely
an·i·mad·vert (-vʉrt′) ***vi.*** [< L. < *animus,* mind + *advertere,* to turn: see ANIMUS & ADVERT] to comment (*on* or *upon*), esp. with disapproval; criticize adversely
an·i·mal (an′ə m'l) ***n.*** [L. < *anima, animus,* breath, life principle, soul] **1.** any living organism except a plant or bacterium: most animals can move about voluntarily and are unable to make their own food by photosynthesis, as plants do **2.** any such organism other than a human being, esp. a mammal or, sometimes, any four-footed creature **3.** a brutish person —***adj.*** **1.** of, like, or from an animal **2.** gross, bestial, sensual, etc. —**an′i·mal·ly** ***adv.***
an·i·mal·cule (an′ə mal′kyool) ***n.*** [< ModL., dim. of prec.] a very small or microscopic animal: also **an′i·mal′cu·lum** (-kyə ləm) ***n.,*** *pl.* **-la** (-lə) —**an′i·mal′cu·lar** ***adj.***
animal husbandry the raising of domesticated animals, as cattle, sheep, horses, etc.
an·i·mal·ism (an′ə m'l iz'm) ***n.*** **1.** the activity, appetites, nature, etc. of animals **2.** the doctrine that man is a mere animal with no soul —**an′i·mal·ist** ***n.*** —**an′i·mal·is′tic** ***adj.***
an·i·mal·i·ty (an′ə mal′ə tē) ***n.*** **1.** animal characteristics or nature **2.** the animal kingdom; animal life **3.** the animal instincts or nature in man
an·i·mal·ize (an′ə mə līz′) ***vt.*** **-ized′, -iz′ing** to make (a person) resemble a beast; brutalize; dehumanize —**an′i·mal·i·za′tion** ***n.***
animal magnetism **1.** *old term for* HYPNOTISM **2.** the power to attract others in a sensual way
animal spirits healthy, lively vigor
an·i·mate (an′ə māt′; *for adj.* -mit) ***vt.*** **-mat′ed, -mat′ing** [< L. pp. of *animare,* to make alive < *anima:* see ANIMAL] **1.** to give life to; bring to life **2.** to make gay or spirited; enliven **3.** to cause to act; inspire **4.** to give motion to *[*a breeze *animating* the leaves*]* **5.** to make move so as to seem lifelike *[*to *animate* puppets*]* **6.** to produce as an animated cartoon —***adj.*** **1.** living; having life, esp. animal life **2.** lively; spirited —**an′i·ma′tor, an′i·mat′er** ***n.***
an·i·mat·ed (-māt′id) ***adj.*** **1.** alive or seeming alive; living **2.** lively; spirited —**an′i·mat′ed·ly** ***adv.***
animated cartoon a motion picture made by filming a series of drawings, each slightly changed from the one before, so that the figures in them seem to move when the film is projected
an·i·ma·tion (an′ə mā′shən) ***n.*** **1.** an animating or being animated **2.** life **3.** vivacity; liveliness **4.** the making of animated cartoons **5.** *same as* ANIMATED CARTOON
‡**a·ni·ma·to** (ä′nē mä′tô) ***adj., adv.*** [It.] *Music* with animation
an·i·mism (an′ə miz'm) ***n.*** [< Fr. & G. < L. *anima:* see ANIMAL & -ISM] **1.** the doctrine that all life is produced by a spiritual force **2.** the belief that all natural objects and phenomena have souls **3.** a belief in the existence of spirits, demons, etc. —**an′i·mist** ***n.*** —**an′i·mis′tic** ***adj.***
an·i·mos·i·ty (an′ə mäs′ə tē) ***n.,*** *pl.* **-ties** [< L. *animositas,* spirit < *animus:* see ff.] ill will; hostility
an·i·mus (an′ə məs) ***n.*** [L., soul, mind, passion: see ANIMAL] **1.** an animating force; intention **2.** a feeling of ill will; animosity
an·i·on (an′ī′ən) ***n.*** [< Gr. neut. prp. of *anienai,* to go up < *ana-,* up + *ienai,* to go] a negatively charged ion: in electrolysis, anions move toward the anode —**an·i·on·ic** (an′ī än′ik) ***adj.***
an·ise (an′is) ***n.*** [< ME. & OFr. < L. < Gr. *anēson*] **1.** a plant of the parsley family, with fragrant seeds used for flavoring **2.** *same as* ANISEED
an·i·seed (an′ə sēd′) ***n.*** the seed of anise
an·i·sette (an′ə set′, -zet′) ***n.*** [Fr., dim. < *anis:* see ANISE] a sweet, anise-flavored liqueur
A·ni·ta (ə nēt′ə) [Sp. dim. of *Ana,* equiv. of ANNA] a feminine name
An·jou (an′joo; *Fr.* än zhoo′) former province of W France
An·ka·ra (aŋ′kə rə, äŋ′-) capital of Turkey: pop. 906,000
ankh (aŋk) ***n.*** [Egypt., life, soul] a cross with a loop at the top, an ancient Egyptian symbol of life
an·kle (aŋ′k'l) ***n.*** [OE. *ancleow*] **1.** the joint that connects the foot and the leg **2.** the part of the leg between the foot and calf
an·kle·bone (-bōn′) ***n.*** the bone of the ankle; talus
an·klet (aŋ′klit) ***n.*** **1.** anything worn around the ankle as an ornament or fetter **2.** a short sock
an·ky·lose (aŋ′kə lōs′) ***vt., vi.*** **-losed′, -los′ing** to stiffen or join by ankylosis
an·ky·lo·sis (aŋ′kə lō′sis) ***n.*** [Gr. < *ankyloun,* to stiffen < *ankylos,* bent] *Med.* an abnormal growing together and stiffening of a joint —**an′ky·lot′ic** (-lät′ik) ***adj.***
ann. **1.** annual **2.** annuity
An·na (an′ə) [< Fr. < L. < Gr. < Heb. *hannāh,* lit., grace] a feminine name: var. *Ann, Anne, Hannah*

an·na (an′ə, ä′nə) *n.* [Hindi *ānā*] a former coin of India, Pakistan, and Burma, equal to 1/16 of a rupee
An·na·bel, An·na·belle (an′ə bel′) [? altered < *Amabel* < L. *amabilis,* lovable < *amare,* to love] a feminine name
an·nal·ist (an′'l ist) *n.* a writer of annals —**an′nal·is′tic** *adj.*
an·nals (an′'lz) *n.pl.* [< L. < *annus,* year] **1.** a written account of events year by year in chronological order **2.** historical records; history **3.** any journal containing reports of a society, etc.
An·nam (an am′, an′am) region in EC Vietnam —**An′na·mese′** (-ə mēz′) *adj., n., pl.* **-mese′**
An·nap·o·lis (ə nap′ə lis) [< ANNA + Gr. *polis,* city] capital of Md., on Chesapeake Bay: pop. 32,000
An·na·pur·na (än′ə poor′nə, an′ə pur′-) mountain mass of the Himalayas, C Nepal: highest peak, 26,500 ft.
Ann Ar·bor (an är′bər) [prob. after *Ann* Allen, early settler] city in SE Mich.: pop. 107,000
Anne (an) **1.** a feminine name: see ANNA **2.** 1665–1714; queen of Great Britain & Ireland (1702–14)
an·neal (ə nēl′) *vt.* [OE. *anælan,* to burn < *an-,* on + *ælan,* to burn < *æl,* fire] **1.** to heat (glass, metals, etc.) and then cool slowly to prevent brittleness **2.** to temper (the mind, will, etc.) —**an·neal′er** *n.*
an·ne·lid (an′'l id) *n.* [< Fr. < L. *annellus,* dim. of *anulus,* a ring: see ANNULAR] a worm with a body made of joined segments, as the earthworm —*adj.* of such worms
An·nette (an et′, ə net′) [Fr. dim. of *Anne*] a feminine name
an·nex (ə neks′; *for n.* an′eks) *vt.* [< OFr. < L. pp. of *annectere* < *ad-,* to + *nectere,* to tie, bind] **1.** to add on or attach, esp. to something larger **2.** to add as a condition, consequence, etc. **3.** to incorporate into a state, etc. the territory of (another state, etc.) **4.** to take, esp. without asking —*n.* something added on; esp., an addition to a building —**an·nex′a·ble** *adj.* —**an·nex·a·tion** (an′ek sā′shən) *n.* —**an′nex·a′tion·ist** *n.*
An·nie Oak·ley (an′ē ōk′lē) *n.* [after woman rifle expert (1860–1926) ? because her targets resembled punched tickets] [Slang] a free ticket; pass
an·ni·hi·late (ə nī′ə lāt′) *vt.* **-lat′ed, -lat′ing** [< L. pp. of *annihilare,* to bring to nothing < *ad-,* to + *nihil,* nothing] **1.** to destroy completely; demolish **2.** to kill **3.** to conquer decisively —**an·ni′hi·la·ble** (-lə b'l) *adj.* —**an·ni′hi·la′tion** *n.* —**an·ni′hi·la′tive** *adj.* —**an·ni′hi·la′tor** *n.*
an·ni·ver·sa·ry (an′ə vur′sər ē) *n., pl.* **-ries** [< L. < *annus,* year + pp. of *vertere,* to turn] **1.** the date on which some event occurred in an earlier year **2.** the celebration of such a date —*adj.* of or connected with an anniversary
‡**an·no Do·mi·ni** (än′ō dō′mə nē, an′ō däm′ə nī) [L., lit., in the year of the Lord] in the (given) year since the beginning of the Christian Era
an·no·tate (an′ə tāt′, -ō-) *vt., vi.* **-tat′ed, -tat′ing** [< L. pp. of *annotare* < *ad-,* to + *notare,* to mark < *nota:* see NOTE] to provide critical or explanatory notes for (a literary work, etc.) —**an′no·ta′tive** *adj.* —**an′no·ta′tor** *n.*
an·no·ta·tion (an′ə tā′shən, -ō-) *n.* **1.** an annotating or being annotated **2.** a critical or explanatory note or notes
an·nounce (ə nouns′) *vt.* **-nounced′, -nounc′ing** [< OFr. < L. *annuntiare* < *ad-,* to + *nuntiare,* to report < *nuntius,* messenger] **1.** to give notice of publicly; proclaim **2.** to say or tell **3.** to make known the arrival, etc. of **4.** *Radio & TV* to be an announcer for —*vi.* **1.** to serve as an announcer **2.** to declare one's candidacy or endorsement (with *for*) —**an·nounce′ment** *n.*
an·nounc·er (-ər) *n.* a person who announces; specif., one who introduces radio or television programs, identifies the station, reads the news, etc.
an·noy (ə noi′) *vt.* [< OFr. < VL. < *in odio habere,* to have in hate: see ODIUM] **1.** to irritate, bother, or make somewhat angry **2.** to harm by repeated attacks; harass —*vi.* to be annoying —**an·noy′er** *n.* —**an·noy′ing** *adj.* —**an·noy′ing·ly** *adv.*
an·noy·ance (-əns) *n.* **1.** an annoying or being annoyed **2.** a thing or person that annoys
an·nu·al (an′yoo wəl) *adj.* [< ME. & OFr. < L. < *annus,* year] **1.** of or measured by a year **2.** happening once a year; yearly **3.** for a year's time, work, etc. *[an annual wage]* **4.** living for only one year or season —*n.* **1.** a yearly publication; specif., a yearbook of a school senior class **2.** a plant that lives only one year or season —**an′nu·al·ly** *adv.*
an·nu·i·tant (ə no͞o′ə tənt, -nyo͞o′-) *n.* a person receiving an annuity
an·nu·i·ty (ə no͞o′ə tē, -nyo͞o′-) *n., pl.* **-ties** [< ME. & OFr. < ML. < L. *annus,* year] **1.** a payment of a fixed sum of money at regular intervals, esp. yearly **2.** an investment yielding such payments
an·nul (ə nul′) *vt.* **-nulled′, -nul′ling** [< OFr. < LL. *annullare,* to bring to nothing < *ad-,* to + *nullum,* nothing: see NULL] **1.** to do away with **2.** to invalidate; cancel —**an·nul′la·ble** *adj.*
an·nu·lar (an′yoo lər) *adj.* [< L. < *anulus,* a ring] of, like, or forming a ring —**an′nu·lar′i·ty** (-lar′ə tē) *n.* —**an′nu·lar·ly** *adv.*
annular eclipse an eclipse in which a ring of sunlight can be seen around the disk of the moon
annular ligament the ligament surrounding the ankle joint or wrist joint
an·nu·late (an′yoo lit, -lāt′) *adj.* [see ANNULAR] marked with, or made up of, rings: also **an′nu·lat′ed** —**an′nu·la′tion** *n.*
an·nu·let (an′yoo lət) *n.* [< L. *anulus,* a ring + -ET] **1.** a small ring **2.** *Archit.* a ringlike molding near the top of a column
an·nul·ment (ə nul′mənt) *n.* **1.** an annulling or being annulled **2.** an invalidation, as of a marriage, by the decree of a court
an·nu·lus (an′yoo ləs) *n., pl.* **-li′** (-lī′), **-lus·es** [L. *anulus*] any ringlike part or mark
an·nun·ci·ate (ə nun′sē āt′, -shē-) *vt.* **-at′ed, -at′ing** [< L. pp. of *annuntiare*] to announce —**an·nun′ci·a′tor** *n.*
an·nun·ci·a·tion (ə nun′sē ā′shən, -shē-) *n.* **1.** an announcing or being announced **2.** [A-] *a)* the angel Gabriel's announcement to Mary that she was to give birth to Jesus: Luke 1:26–38 *b)* the church festival (March 25) commemorating this
an·ode (an′ōd) *n.* [< Gr. < *ana-,* up + *hodos,* way] **1.** a positively charged electrode, as in an electrolytic cell, electron tube, etc. **2.** the negative electrode in a battery supplying current
an·o·dize (an′ə dīz′) *vt.* **-dized′, -diz′ing** to put a protective oxide film on (a light metal) by an electrolytic process in which the metal serves as the anode
an·o·dyne (an′ə dīn′) *adj.* [< L. < Gr. < *an-,* without + *odynē,* pain] relieving or lessening pain —*n.* anything that relieves pain or soothes —**an′o·dyn′ic** (-din′ik) *adj.*
a·noint (ə noint′) *vt.* [< OFr. < L. *inungere* < *in-,* on + *ungere,* to smear] **1.** to rub oil or ointment on **2.** to put oil on in a ceremony of consecration —**a·noint′er** *n.* —**a·noint′ment** *n.*
Anointing of the Sick *R.C.Ch.* the sacrament in which a priest prays for and anoints a person dying or critically ill
a·nom·a·lis·tic (ə näm′ə lis′tik) *adj.* **1.** tending to be anomalous **2.** of an anomaly
a·nom·a·lous (ə näm′ə ləs) *adj.* [< L. < Gr. < *an-,* not + *homalos* < *homos,* the same] **1.** deviating from the general rule; abnormal **2.** being, or seeming to be, inconsistent or improper —**a·nom′a·lous·ly** *adv.* —**a·nom′a·lous·ness** *n.*
a·nom·a·ly (-lē) *n., pl.* **-lies** [< L. < Gr. *anōmalia,* inequality: see prec.] **1.** departure from the regular arrangement or usual method; abnormality **2.** anything anomalous
an·o·mie, an·o·my (an′ə mē) *n.* [< Fr. < Gr. < *a-,* without + *nomos,* law] lack of purpose, identity, or ethical values in a person or in a society; rootlessness —**a·nom·ic** (ə näm′ik) *adj.*
a·non (ə nän′) *adv.* [OE. *on an,* in one, straightway] **1.** soon; shortly; also, at another time: now nearly archaic **2.** [Archaic] at once —**ever and anon** now and then
anon. anonymous
an·o·nym (an′ə nim) *n.* [Fr. < Gr.: see ANONYMOUS] **1.** a person whose name is not known **2.** a pseudonym
an·o·nym·i·ty (an′ə nim′ə tē) *n.* the condition or fact of being anonymous
a·non·y·mous (ə nän′ə məs) *adj.* [< Gr. < *an-,* without + *onyma,* name] **1.** with no name known or acknowledged **2.** given, written, etc. by a person whose name is withheld or unknown **3.** lacking in distinctive features —**a·non′y·mous·ly** *adv.*
a·noph·e·les (ə näf′ə lēz′) *n.* [ModL. < Gr. *anōphelēs,* harmful < *an-,* without + *ophelēs,* use] the mosquito that can carry the malaria parasite and transmit the disease —**a·noph′e·line′** (-līn′, -lin) *adj.*
an·o·rex·i·a (an′ə rek′sē ə) *n.* [ModL. < Gr. < *an-,* without + *orexis,* a desire for] lack of appetite for food; specif., **anorexia ner·vo·sa** (nər vō′sə), a personality disorder, chiefly in young women, characterized by aversion to food, obsession with weight loss, etc.
an·oth·er (ə nuth′ər) *adj.* [ME. *an other*] **1.** one more; an additional **2.** a different **3.** one of the same kind as *[another Caesar]* —*pron.* **1.** one additional **2.** a different one **3.** one of the same kind
an·ox·i·a (an äk′sē ə) *n.* [AN- + OX(YGEN) + -IA] the condition of not having enough oxygen in the body tissues
ans. answer

an·ser·ine (an′sər īn′, -in) ***adj.*** [< L. < *anser,* goose] **1.** of or like a goose **2.** stupid; foolish

an·swer (an′sər) ***n.*** [< OE. < *and-,* against + *swerian,* to SWEAR] **1.** something said or written in return to a question, letter, etc. **2.** any act in response or retaliation **3.** a solution to a problem **4.** *Law* a defense —***vi.*** **1.** to reply in words, by an action, etc. **2.** to respond (*to*) [the horse *answered* to its rider's touch] **3.** to be sufficient **4.** to be responsible (*to* a person *for* an action, etc.) **5.** to correspond (*to*) [he *answers* to the description] —***vt.*** **1.** to reply to in some way **2.** to respond to the signal of (a telephone, doorbell, etc.) **3.** to comply with; serve [to *answer* a purpose] **4.** to refute (an accusation, criticism, etc.) **5.** to suit [he *answers* the description] —**answer back** [Colloq.] to reply rudely or impertinently

an·swer·a·ble (-ə b'l) ***adj.*** **1.** responsible; accountable **2.** that can be answered or shown to be wrong [an *answerable* argument]

ant (ant) ***n.*** [OE. *æmete*] any of a family of insects, generally wingless, that live in colonies with a complex division of labor

-ant (ənt, 'nt) [Fr. < L. *-antem* or *-entem,* acc. prp. ending] *a suffix meaning:* **1.** that has, shows, or does [*defiant, radiant*] **2.** a person or thing that [*occupant, accountant*]

WORKER ANT

ant. **1.** antenna **2.** antonym

ant·ac·id (ant′as′id) ***adj.*** counteracting acidity —***n.*** an antacid substance

an·tag·o·nism (an tag′ə niz'm) ***n.*** [see ANTAGONIZE] **1.** the state of being opposed or hostile to another or to each other; opposition or hostility **2.** an opposing force, principle, etc.

an·tag·o·nist (-nist) ***n.*** **1.** an adversary; opponent **2.** a muscle, drug, etc. that counteracts another

an·tag·o·nis·tic (an tag′ə nis′tik) ***adj.*** showing antagonism; acting in opposition —**an·tag′o·nis′ti·cal·ly** ***adv.***

an·tag·o·nize (an tag′ə nīz′) ***vt.*** **-nized′, -niz′ing** [< Gr. < *anti-,* against + *agōn,* a contest: see AGONY] **1.** to oppose or counteract **2.** to incur the dislike of; make an enemy of

ant·al·ka·li (ant al′kə lī′) ***n.,*** *pl.* **-lies′, -lis′** a substance that counteracts alkalinity

ant·arc·tic (ant ärk′tik, -är′-) ***adj.*** [< OFr. < L. < Gr. < *anti,* opposite + *arktikos,* ARCTIC] of or near the South Pole or the region around it —**the Antarctic** *same as* ANTARCTICA

Ant·arc·ti·ca (-ti kə) land area about the South Pole, covered by ice: c. 5,000,000 sq. mi.

Antarctic Circle [*also* **a- c-**] an imaginary circle parallel to the equator, 66°33′ south of it

Antarctic Ocean the parts of the Atlantic, Pacific, and Indian oceans surrounding Antarctica

An·tar·es (an ter′ēz) the brightest star in the constellation Scorpio

ant bear a large anteater of tropical S. America

an·te (an′tē) ***n.*** [L., before] **1.** *Poker* the stake that each player must put into the pot before receiving cards **2.** [Colloq.] the amount one must pay as his share —***vt., vi.*** **-ted** or **-teed, -te·ing** **1.** *Poker* to put in (one's stake) **2.** [Colloq.] to pay (one's share) —**ante up** to ante one's stake or share

an·te- [< L. *ante,* before] *a prefix meaning:* **1.** before, prior (to) [*antecedent, ante-*Victorian] **2.** before, in front (of) [*anteroom*]

ant·eat·er (ant′ēt′ər) ***n.*** any of several mammals that feed mainly on ants: anteaters have a long, sticky tongue and a long snout

an·te·bel·lum (an′ti bel′əm) ***adj.*** [L.] before the war; specif., before the American Civil War

an·te·cede (an′tə sēd′) ***vt., vi.*** **-ced′ed, -ced′ing** [< L. *antecedere* < *ante,* before + *cedere,* to go] to go before; precede

an·te·ced·ence (-sēd′'ns) ***n.*** [see prec.] a being prior; precedence: also **an′te·ced′en·cy** (-'n sē)

an·te·ced·ent (-sēd′'nt) ***adj.*** [see ANTECEDE] prior; previous —***n.*** **1.** any thing prior to another **2.** anything logically preceding **3.** [*pl.*] one's ancestry, past life, etc. **4.** *Gram.* the word, phrase, or clause to which a pronoun refers **5.** *Math.* the first term of a ratio —**an′te·ced′ent·ly** ***adv.***

an·te·cham·ber (an′ti chām′bər) ***n.*** [< Fr.: see ANTE- & CHAMBER] a smaller room leading into a larger or main room

an·te·date (-dāt′) ***vt.*** **-dat′ed, -dat′ing** **1.** to put a date on that is earlier than the actual date **2.** to come before **3.** to set an earlier date for —***n.*** a date fixed for an event, etc. that is earlier than the actual one

an·te·di·lu·vi·an (an′ti də lo͞o′vē ən) ***adj.*** [< ANTE- + L. *diluvium,* a flood + -AN] **1.** of the time before the Biblical Flood **2.** very old or old-fashioned —***n.*** an antediluvian person or thing

an·te·lope (an′tə lōp′) ***n.,*** *pl.* **-lopes′, -lope′**: see PLURAL, II, D, 1 [< ME. & OFr. < ML. < MGr. *antholops,* deer] **1.** *a*) any of a group of swift, cud-chewing, hollow-horned, deerlike animals related to oxen, sheep, and goats *b*) *same as* PRONGHORN **2.** leather made from an antelope's hide

ANTELOPE (to 70 in. high at shoulder)

an·te me·ri·di·em (an′tē mə rid′ē əm) [L.] before noon: abbrev. **A.M., a.m., AM**

an·ten·na (an ten′ə) ***n.*** [< L. < *antemna,* sail yard] **1.** *pl.* **-nae** (-ē), **-nas** either of a pair of movable sense organs on the head of an insect, crab, etc.; feeler **2.** *pl.* **-nas** *Radio & TV* an arrangement of wires, metal rods, etc. used in sending and receiving electromagnetic waves; aerial

an·te·pe·nult (an′ti pē′nəlt) ***n.*** [see ANTE- & PENULT] the third last syllable in a word, as *-lu-* in *an·te·di·lu·vi·an*

an·te·pe·nul·ti·mate (-pi nul′tə mit) ***adj.*** third last; third from the end —***n.*** **1.** anything third from the end **2.** an antepenult

an·te·ri·or (an tir′ē ər) ***adj.*** [L., compar. of *ante,* before] **1.** at or toward the front; forward: opposed to POSTERIOR **2.** coming before in time, order, etc.; earlier —**an·te′ri·or·ly** ***adv.***

an·te·room (an′ti ro͞om′, -ro͝om′) ***n.*** a room leading to a larger one; waiting room

an·them (an′thəm) ***n.*** [< OE. *antefn* < ML. < Gr. *antiphōnos,* sounding back < *anti-,* over against + *phōnē,* voice] **1.** a religious choral song usually based on words from the Bible **2.** a song of praise or devotion, as to a nation, college, etc.

an·ther (an′thər) ***n.*** [< Fr. < ModL. < Gr. *anthēros,* blooming < *anthos,* a flower] the part of a stamen that contains the pollen

an·ther·id·i·um (an′thə rid′ē əm) ***n.,*** *pl.* **-id′i·a** (-ə) [ModL. < prec. + Gr. dim. suffix *-idion*] in flowerless and seedless plants, the organ in which the male sex cells are developed —**an′ther·id′i·al** ***adj.***

ant·hill (ant′hil′) ***n.*** the soil carried by ants from their underground nest and heaped around its entrance

an·thol·o·gize (an thäl′ə jīz′) ***vi.*** **-gized′, -giz′ing** to make anthologies —***vt.*** to make an anthology of or include in an anthology —**an·thol′o·gist** ***n.***

an·thol·o·gy (an thäl′ə jē) ***n.,*** *pl.* **-gies** [< Gr. *anthologia,* a garland < *anthos,* flower + *legein,* to gather] a collection of poems, stories, etc. —**an·tho·log·i·cal** (an′thə läj′i k'l) ***adj.***

An·tho·ny (an′thə nē; *also, for 1 & 2,* -tə-) [< L. *Antonius,* name of a Roman gens] **1.** a masculine name: dim. *Tony;* var. *Antony* **2. Mark,** see ANTONY **3. Susan B(rownell),** 1820–1906; U.S. leader in the women's suffrage movement

an·tho·zo·an (an′thə zō′ən) ***n.*** [< ModL. < Gr. *anthos,* flower + *zōion,* animal + -AN] any of a class of sea organisms, comprising corals, sea anemones, etc. —***adj.*** of the anthozoans

an·thra·cene (an′thrə sēn′) ***n.*** [< Gr. *anthrax,* coal + -ENE] a crystalline hydrocarbon, $C_{14}H_{10}$, a product of coal-tar distillation used in making dyes and as a radiation detector

an·thra·cite (-sīt′) ***n.*** [< Gr. < *anthrax,* coal] hard coal, which gives much heat but little flame and smoke —**an′thra·cit′ic** (-sit′ik) ***adj.***

an·thrax (an′thraks) ***n.*** [L. < Gr., (burning) coal, hence carbuncle] **1.** an infectious disease of wild and domesticated animals, esp. cattle and sheep, that can be transmitted to man: it is characterized by black pustules **2.** any such pustule

an·thro·po- [< Gr. *anthrōpos,* man] *a combining form meaning* man, human [*anthropology*]: also, before a vowel, **anthrop-**

an·thro·po·cen·tric (an′thrə pə sen′trik) ***adj.*** [prec. + CENTRIC] **1.** that considers man as the central fact, or final aim, of the universe **2.** viewing everything in terms of human values

an·thro·po·gen·e·sis (-jen′ə sis) ***n.*** the study of man's origin and development: also **an′thro·pog′e·ny** (-päj′ə nē) —**an′thro·po·ge·net′ic** (-jə net′ik) ***adj.***

an·thro·poid (an′thrə poid′) ***adj.*** [ANTHROP(O)- + -OID] **1.** resembling man; manlike; esp., designating or of any of the most highly developed apes, as the chimpanzee and gorilla **2.** apelike —***n.*** any anthropoid ape —**an′thro·poi′dal** ***adj.***

an·thro·pol·o·gist (an′thrə päl′ə jist) ***n.*** a student of or specialist in anthropology

an·thro·pol·o·gy (-päl′ə jē) ***n.*** [ANTHROPO- + -LOGY] the study of man, esp. of the variety, distribution, characteristics, cultures, etc. of mankind —**an′thro·po·log′i·cal** (-pə läj′i k'l), **an′thro·po·log′ic** ***adj.*** —**an′thro·po·log′i·cal·ly** ***adv.***

an·thro·pom·e·try (-päm′ə trē) ***n.*** [ANTHROPO- + -METRY] the science dealing with measurement of the human body in comparing individual and group differences —**an′thro·po·met′ric** (-pə met′rik), **an′thro·po·met′ri·cal** ***adj.*** —**an′thro·po·met′ri·cal·ly** ***adv.***

an·thro·po·mor·phic (-pə môr′fik) ***adj.*** of, characterized by, or resulting from anthropomorphism —**an′thro·po·mor′phi·cal·ly** ***adv.***

an·thro·po·mor·phism (-pə môr′fiz'm) ***n.*** [ANTHROPOMORPH(OUS) + -ISM] the attributing of human shape or characteristics to a god, animal, or inanimate thing —**an′thro·po·mor′phist** ***n.***

an·thro·po·mor·phous (-pə môr′fəs) ***adj.*** [< Gr. < *anthrōpos,* a man + *morphē,* form, shape] having human shape and appearance

an·thro·poph·a·gi (-päf′ə jī′) ***n.pl.,*** *sing.* **-a·gus** (-ə gəs) [L. < Gr. < *anthrōpos,* man + *phagein,* to eat] cannibals

an·thro·poph·a·gy (-päf′ə jē) ***n.*** [see prec.] cannibalism —**an′thro·poph′a·gous** (-gəs), **an′thro·po·phag′ic** (-pə-faj′ik) ***adj.***

an·thu·ri·um (an thoor′ē əm) ***n.*** [ModL. < Gr. *anthos,* flower + *oura,* tail] a tropical American plant having a long spike with a flaring, heart-shaped spathe around its base

an·ti (an′tī, -tē) ***n.,*** *pl.* **-tis** [< ff.] [Colloq.] a person opposed to some policy, proposal, etc. —***prep.*** [Colloq.] opposed to; against

an·ti- (an′ti; *also variously* -tē, -tī, -tə) [< Gr. < *anti,* against] *a prefix meaning:* **1.** against; hostile to *[antilabor]* **2.** that operates against *[antiaircraft]* **3.** that prevents, cures, or neutralizes *[antitoxin]* **4.** opposite; reverse *[antimatter]* **5.** rivaling *[antipope]*

an·ti·air·craft (an′tē er′kraft, -tī-) ***adj.*** used for defense against hostile aircraft *[antiaircraft* gun*]*

an·ti·bac·te·ri·al (-bak tir′ē əl) ***adj.*** that checks the growth or effect of bacteria

an·ti·bal·lis·tic missile (-bə lis′tik) a ballistic missile intended to intercept and destroy another ballistic missile in flight

an·ti·bi·o·sis (-bī ō′sis) ***n.*** [ModL. < ANTI- + Gr. *biōsis,* way of life < *bios,* life] *Biol.* an association between organisms which is harmful to one of them

an·ti·bi·ot·ic (-bī ät′ik, -bē-) ***adj.*** **1.** of antibiosis **2.** destroying, or stopping the growth of, bacteria and other microorganisms —***n.*** an antibiotic substance produced by various microorganisms, as by bacteria or fungi

an·ti·bod·y (an′ti bäd′ē) ***n.,*** *pl.* **-bod′ies** a protein produced in the body in response to contact of the body with an antigen, serving to neutralize the antigen, thus creating immunity

an·tic (an′tik) ***adj.*** [< It. < L. *antiquus:* see ANTIQUE] **1.** [Archaic] fantastic and queer **2.** odd and funny —***n.*** **1.** a playful or silly act, trick, etc.; caper **2.** [Archaic] a clown or buffoon —***vi.*** **-ticked, -tick·ing** to perform antics; caper

an·ti·christ (an′ti krīst′, -tī-) ***n.*** an opponent of Christ —[A-] *Bible* the great antagonist of Christ: I John 2:18

an·tic·i·pant (an tis′ə pənt) ***adj.*** expecting; anticipating (with *of*) —***n.*** a person who anticipates

an·tic·i·pate (an tis′ə pāt′) ***vt.*** **-pat′ed, -pat′ing** [< L. pp. of *anticipare* < *ante-,* before + *capere,* to take] **1.** to look forward to; expect **2.** to prevent by action in advance; forestall *[to anticipate* an opponent's blows*]* **3.** to foresee and take care of in advance *[to anticipate* a request*]* **4.** to use or enjoy in advance *[to anticipate* a legacy*]* **5.** to be ahead of in doing or achieving something —**an·tic′i·pa′tor** ***n.***

an·tic·i·pa·tion (an tis′ə pā′shən) ***n.*** **1.** an anticipating or being anticipated **2.** something anticipated or expected **3.** foreknowledge; presentiment

an·tic·i·pa·tive (an tis′ə pāt′iv) ***adj.*** of or full of anticipation —**an·tic′i·pa′tive·ly** ***adv.***

an·tic·i·pa·to·ry (-pə tôr′ē) ***adj.*** of or expressing anticipation —**an·tic′i·pa·to′ri·ly** ***adv.***

an·ti·cler·i·cal (an′ti kler′ə k'l, -tī-) ***adj.*** opposed to the influence of the clergy or church in public affairs —**an′ti·cler′i·cal·ism** ***n.***

an·ti·cli·max (-klī′maks) ***n.*** **1.** a sudden drop from the dignified or important to the commonplace or trivial **2.** a final event which is in disappointing contrast to those coming before —**an′ti·cli·mac′tic** (-mak′tik) ***adj.***

an·ti·cline (an′ti klīn′) ***n.*** [< ANTI- + Gr. *klinein,* to incline] *Geol.* a fold of stratified rock in which the strata slope downward in opposite directions from the central axis: opposed to SYNCLINE —**an′ti·cli′nal** ***adj.***

an·ti·co·ag·u·lant (an′ti kō ag′yə lənt, -tī-) ***n.*** a drug or substance that delays or prevents the clotting of blood

an·ti·cy·clone (-sī′klōn) ***n.*** an extensive atmospheric condition of high barometric pressure, with the winds at the edge blowing outward —**an′ti·cy·clon′ic** (-klän′ik) ***adj.***

an·ti·de·pres·sant (-di pres′ənt) ***adj.*** designating or of any drug used to treat emotional depression —***n.*** an antidepressant drug

an·ti·dote (an′tə dōt′) ***n.*** [ME. & OFr. < L. < Gr. < *anti-,* against + *dotos,* given < *didonai,* to give] **1.** a remedy to counteract a poison **2.** anything that works against an evil or unwanted condition —**an′ti·dot′al** ***adj.***

An·tie·tam (an tēt′əm) [AmInd. < ?] creek in W Md.: site of a Civil War battle (1862)

an·ti·fed·er·al·ist (an′ti fed′ər ə list, -tī-; -fed′rə-) ***n.*** **1.** one opposed to federalism **2.** [A-] one who opposed the Federalists and the adoption of the U.S. Constitution

an·ti·freeze (an′ti frēz′, -tī-) ***n.*** a substance of low freezing point added esp. to the water in automobile radiators to prevent freezing

an·ti·gen (an′tə jən) ***n.*** [ANTI- + -GEN] an enzyme, toxin, etc. to which the body reacts by producing antibodies —**an′ti·gen′ic** (-jen′ik) ***adj.***

An·tig·o·ne (an tig′ə nē′) *Gr. Myth.* daughter of Oedipus: she defied her uncle by performing funeral rites for her brother

An·ti·gua (an tē′gə, -gwə) self-governing island under Brit. protection, in the Leeward group of the West Indies: 108 sq. mi.; pop. 57,000

an·ti·he·ro (an′ti hir′ō, -tī-) ***n.*** the main character of a novel, play, etc. who lacks the virtues of a traditional hero

an·ti·his·ta·mine (an′ti his′tə mēn′, -tī-; -mən) ***n.*** any drug used to minimize the action of histamine in such allergic conditions as hay fever and hives —**an′ti·his′ta·min′ic** (-min′ik) ***adj.***

an·ti·knock (an′ti näk′, -tī-) ***n.*** a substance added to the fuel of internal-combustion engines to do away with noise caused by too rapid combustion

an·ti·la·bor (an′ti lā′bər, -tī-) ***adj.*** opposed to labor unions or to the interests of workers

An·til·les (an til′ēz) main island group of the West Indies: see GREATER ANTILLES, LESSER ANTILLES —**An·til′le·an** (-ē ən, an′tə lē′ən) ***adj.***

an·ti·log·a·rithm (an′ti lôg′ə ri*th*'m, -tī-; -läg′-) ***n.*** the number corresponding to a given logarithm *[*the *antilogarithm* of 1 is 10*]*

an·ti·ma·cas·sar (an′ti mə kas′ər) ***n.*** [ANTI- + *macassar (oil),* a former hair oil] a small cover to protect the back or arms of a chair, etc. from soiling

an·ti·mag·net·ic (an′ti mag net′ik, -tī-) ***adj.*** made of metals that resist magnetism *[*an *antimagnetic* watch*]*

an·ti·ma·lar·i·al (-mə ler′ē əl) ***adj.*** preventing or relieving malaria —***n.*** an antimalarial drug

an·ti·mat·ter (an′ti mat′ər, -tī-) ***n.*** a form of matter in which the electrical charge or other property of each constituent particle is the reverse of that in the usual matter of our universe

an·ti·mis·sile (-mis′'l) ***adj.*** designed as a defense against ballistic missiles

an·ti·mo·ny (an′tə mō′nē) ***n.*** [< OFr. < ML. *antimonium*] a silvery-white, brittle, metallic chemical element, found only in combination: used to harden alloys, etc.: symbol, Sb; at. wt., 121.75; at. no., 51 —**an′ti·mo′nic** ***adj.*** —**an′ti·mo′nous** ***adj.***

An·ti·och (an′tē äk′) capital of ancient Syria: now, a city in S Turkey: pop. 46,000

an·ti·par·ti·cle (an′ti pär′tə k'l, an′tī-) ***n.*** any of the constituent particles of antimatter

an·ti·pas·to (an′ti pas′tō, -päs′-) ***n.*** [It. < *anti-* (L. *ante*), before + *pasto* < L. *pastus,* food] a dish of salted fish, meat, olives, etc. served as an appetizer

an·ti·pa·thet·ic (an′ti pə thet′ik) ***adj.*** **1.** having antipathy **2.** opposed or antagonistic in character, tendency, etc. Also **an′ti·pa·thet′i·cal** —**an′ti·pa·thet′i·cal·ly** ***adv.***

an·tip·a·thy (an tip′ə thē) ***n.,*** *pl.* **-thies** [< L. < Gr. < *anti-,* against + *patheia* < *pathein,* to feel] **1.** a strong dislike **2.** the object of such dislike

an·ti·per·son·nel (an′ti pur′sə nel′, -tī-) ***adj.*** directed against, or intended to destroy, people rather than material objects *[antipersonnel* mines*]*

an·ti·per·spir·ant (-pur′spər ənt) ***n.*** a substance applied to the skin to reduce perspiration

an·ti·phlo·gis·tic (-flə jis′tik) ***adj.*** counteracting inflammation —***n.*** an antiphlogistic substance

an·ti·phon (an′tə fän′) ***n.*** [< ML. < Gr.: see ANTHEM] a hymn, psalm, etc. chanted or sung in responsive, alternating parts —**an·tiph′o·nal** (-tif′ə n'l), **an′ti·phon′ic** ***adj.***

an·tiph·o·nar·y (an tif′ə ner′ē) ***n.,*** *pl.* **-nar′ies** a book of antiphons

an·ti·pode (an′tə pōd′) ***n.*** [back-formation of ff.] an exact opposite

an·tip·o·des (an tip′ə dēz′) ***n.pl.*** **[**ML. < L. < Gr., pl. of *antipous* < *anti-*, opposite + *pous*, foot**]** **1.** any two places directly opposite each other on the earth **2.** [*with pl. or sing. v.*] a place on the opposite side of the earth: in British usage, New Zealand and Australia **3.** two opposite or contrary things —**an·tip′o·dal** ***adj.*** —**an·tip′o·de′an** (-dē′ən) ***adj.*, *n.***

an·ti·pope (an′ti pōp′, -tī-) ***n.*** a pope set up against the one chosen by church laws, as in a schism

an·ti·py·ret·ic (an′ti pī ret′ik, -tī-) ***adj.*** reducing fever —***n.*** anything that reduces fever

antiq. **1.** antiquarian **2.** antiquity; antiquities

an·ti·quar·i·an (an′tə kwer′ē ən) ***adj.*** **1.** of antiques or antiquities **2.** of antiquaries **3.** of, or dealing in, rare old books —***n.*** an antiquary

an·ti·quar·y (an′tə kwer′ē) ***n.*, *pl.*** **-quar′ies** one who collects or studies relics and ancient art

an·ti·quate (-kwāt′) ***vt.*** **-quat′ed, -quat′ing** **[**< L. pp. of *antiquare* < *antiquus:* see ANTIQUE**]** to make old or obsolete; cause to become old-fashioned —**an′ti·quat′ed** ***adj.*** —**an′ti·qua′tion** ***n.***

an·tique (an tēk′) ***adj.*** **[**Fr. < L. *antiquus*, ancient < *ante*, before**]** **1.** of ancient times; ancient **2.** out-of-date; old-fashioned **3.** in the style of classical antiquity **4.** of, or in the style of, a former period **5.** dealing in antiques —***n.*** **1.** an ancient relic **2.** the ancient style, esp. of Greek or Roman sculpture, etc. **3.** a piece of furniture, silverware, etc. of a former period **4.** *Printing* a variety of boldface type —***vt.*** **-tiqued′, -tiqu′ing** to make look antique —**antique′ly** ***adv.*** —**an·tique′ness** ***n.***

an·tiq·ui·ty (an tik′wə tē) ***n.*, *pl.*** **-ties** **[**see prec.**]** **1.** the early period of history, esp. before the Middle Ages **2.** great age; oldness *[*a statue of great *antiquity]* **3.** the people of ancient times **4.** [*pl.*] *a)* relics, monuments, etc. of the distant past *b)* ancient manners, customs, etc.

an·ti·scor·bu·tic (an′ti skôr byōō′tik, -tī-) ***adj.*** that cures or prevents scurvy

an·ti-Se·mit·ic (-sə mit′ik) ***adj.*** **1.** having or showing prejudice against Jews **2.** discriminating against or persecuting Jews —**an′ti-Sem′ite** (-sem′īt) ***n.*** —**an′ti-Sem′i·tism** (-sem′ə tiz′m) ***n.***

an·ti·sep·sis (an′tə sep′sis) ***n.*** **[**ANTI- + SEPSIS**]** **1.** the technique of preventing infection, the growth of microorganisms, etc. **2.** the condition of being antiseptic **3.** the use of antiseptics

an·ti·sep·tic (-sep′tik) ***adj.*** **1.** preventing infection, decay, etc. by inhibiting the action of microorganisms **2.** using antiseptics **3.** free from infection; sterile **4.** untouched by life, its problems, etc. —***n.*** any antiseptic substance —**an′ti·sep′ti·cal·ly** ***adv.*** —**an′ti·sep′ti·cize′** ***vt.*** **-cized′, -ciz′ing**

an·ti·se·rum (an′ti sir′əm) ***n.*** a serum with antibodies in it

an·ti·slav·er·y (an′ti slā′vər ē, -tī-) ***adj.*** against slavery

an·ti·so·cial (-sō′shəl) ***adj.*** **1.** unsociable **2.** harmful to the welfare of the people generally

an·ti·spas·mod·ic (-spaz mäd′ik) ***adj.*** relieving spasms —***n.*** an antispasmodic drug

an·ti·stat·ic (-stat′ik) ***adj.*** reducing static electric charges, as on textiles, polishes, etc.

an·tis·tro·phe (an tis′trə fē) ***n.*** **[**L. < Gr. < *anti-*, opposite + *strephein*, to turn**]** **1.** *a)* the return movement, left to right, made by the chorus of an ancient Greek play in answering a strophe *b)* the part of a choric song performed during this **2.** a stanza following a strophe, often in the same form —**an·ti·stroph·ic** (an′tə sträf′ik) ***adj.***

an·ti·tank (an′ti taŋk′, -tī-) ***adj.*** for use against tanks in war

an·tith·e·sis (an tith′ə sis) ***n.*, *pl.*** **-ses′** (-sēz′) **[**L. < Gr. < *anti-*, against + *tithenai*, to place**]** **1.** a contrast of thoughts, usually in two phrases, clauses, etc. (Ex.: "Man proposes, and God disposes") **2.** a contrast or opposition **3.** the exact opposite *[*joy is the *antithesis* of sorrow*]* —**an·ti·thet·i·cal** (an′tə thet′i k′l) ***adj.*** —**an′ti·thet′i·cal·ly** ***adv.***

an·ti·tox·in (an′ti täk′sin, -tī-) ***n.*** **1.** an antibody formed by the body to act against a specific toxin **2.** a serum containing an antitoxin: taken from the blood of an immunized animal, such a serum is injected into a person to prevent a specific disease, such as diphtheria or tetanus —**an′ti·tox′ic** ***adj.***

an·ti·trades (an′ti trādz′) ***n.pl.*** winds that blow above and opposite to the trade winds

an·ti·trust (an′ti trust′, -tī-) ***adj.*** opposed to or regulating trusts, or business monopolies

an·ti·ven·in (-ven′ən) ***n.*** **[**ANTI- + VEN(OM) + -IN[1]**]** **1.** an antitoxin for venom, as of snakes, produced by gradually increased injections of the specific venom **2.** a serum containing this antitoxin

an·ti·viv·i·sec·tion (-viv′ə sek′shən) ***n.*** opposition to medical research on living animals —**an′ti·viv′i·sec′tion·ist** ***n.*, *adj.***

ant·ler (ant′lər) ***n.*** **[**< OFr. < L. < *ante-*, before + *ocularis*, of the eyes**]** **1.** the branched, deciduous horn of any animal of the deer family **2.** any branch of such a horn —**ant′lered** ***adj.***

MOOSE ANTLERS

ant lion **1.** the large-jawed larva of certain winged insects that digs a pit for trapping ants, etc. on which it feeds **2.** the adult insect

An·toi·nette (an′twə net′, -tə-) **1.** a feminine name: dim. *Nettie, Netty* **2. Marie,** *see* MARIE ANTOINETTE

An·to·ny (an′tə nē) **1.** *var. of* ANTHONY **2. Mark** or **Marc,** (L. name *Marcus Antonius*) 83?–30 B.C.; Rom. general & statesman

an·to·nym (an′tə nim′) ***n.*** **[**< Gr. < *anti-*, opposite + *onyma*, name**]** a word that is opposite in meaning to another word *[*"sad" is an *antonym* of "happy"*]* —**an·ton·y·mous** (an tän′ə məs) ***adj.***

an·trum (an′trəm) ***n.*, *pl.*** **-tra** (-trə), **-trums** **[**L. < Gr. *antron*, cave**]** *Anat.* a cavity; esp., either of a pair of sinuses in the upper jaw

Ant·werp (an′twərp) seaport in N Belgium, on the Scheldt River: pop. 240,000

A·nu·bis (ə nyōō′bis, -nōō′-) an Egyptian god, depicted with the head of a jackal, who led the dead to judgment

an·u·re·sis (an′yoo rē′sis) ***n.*** **[**ModL. < AN- + Gr. *ourēsis*, urination**]** the condition of being unable to pass one's urine

a·nus (ā′nəs) ***n.*, *pl.*** **a′nus·es, a′ni** (-nī) **[**L., a ring**]** the opening at the lower end of the alimentary canal

an·vil (an′vəl) ***n.*** **[**< OE. *anfilt* < *an-*, on + hyp. *filtan*, to beat**]** **1.** an iron or steel block on which metal objects are hammered into shape **2.** the incus, one of the three bones of the middle ear

anx·i·e·ty (aŋ zī′ə tē) ***n.*, *pl.*** **-ties** **[**see ff.**]** **1.** a state of being uneasy or worried about what may happen **2.** an eager but often uneasy desire *[anxiety* to do well*]*

anx·ious (aŋk′shəs, aŋ′-) ***adj.*** **[**L. *anxius* < *angere*, to choke**]** **1.** uneasy in mind; worried **2.** causing or full of anxiety *[*an *anxious* hour*]* **3.** eagerly wishing —**anx′ious·ly** ***adv.*** —**anx′ious·ness** ***n.***

an·y (en′ē) ***adj.*** **[**< OE. *ænig* < *an*, ONE**]** **1.** one, no matter which, of more than two *[any* pupil may answer*]* **2.** some, no matter what amount or kind *[*he hasn't *any* food*]* **3.** without limit *[*enter *any* number of times*]* **4.** every *[any* child can do it*]* —***pron. sing. & pl.*** any one or ones; any amount or number —***adv.*** to any degree or extent; at all *[*is he *any* better?*]*

an·y·bod·y (-bud′ē, -bäd′ē) ***pron.*** **1.** any person; anyone **2.** a person of fame, importance, etc.

an·y·how (-hou′) ***adv.*** **1.** no matter in what way **2.** in any case **3.** carelessly

an·y·more (-môr′) ***adv.*** now; nowadays: in standard use, only in negative constructions *[*he doesn't live here *anymore]*: also **any more**

an·y·one (-wun′) ***pron.*** any person; anybody

any one any single (person or thing)

an·y·place (en′ē plās′) ***adv.*** [Colloq.] in, at, or to any place; anywhere —**get anyplace** [Colloq.] to succeed

an·y·thing (-thiŋ′) ***pron.*** any object, event, fact, etc. —***n.*** a thing, no matter of what kind —***adv.*** in any way; at all —**anything but** not at all

an·y·way (-wā′) ***adv.*** **1.** in any manner or way **2.** in any case; anyhow **3.** haphazardly; carelessly

an·y·where (-hwer′, -wer′) ***adv.*** **1.** in, at, or to any place **2.** [Colloq.] at all; to any extent —**get anywhere** [Colloq.] to have any success

an·y·wise (-wīz′) ***adv.*** in any manner; at all

A/O, a/o account of

A-OK (ā′ō kā′) ***adj.*** **[**A(LL) OK**]** [Colloq.] excellent, fine, in working order, etc.: a generalized term of commendation: also **A′-O·kay′**

A one (ā′ wun′) [Colloq.] first-class; first-rate; superior: also **A 1, A number 1**

a·or·ta (ā ôr′tə) ***n.*, *pl.*** **-tas, -tae** (-tē) **[**ModL. < Gr. < *aeirein*, to raise**]** the main artery of the body carrying blood from the left ventricle of the heart to arteries in all organs and parts —**a·or′tic, a·or′tal** ***adj.***

a·ou·dad (ä′oo dad′) ***n.*** **[**Fr. < Moorish *audad***]** a wild North African sheep with large, curved horns and a heavy growth of hair on the chest

a·pace (ə pās′) ***adv.*** at a fast pace; swiftly

A·pach·e (ə pach′ē) ***n.*** **[**AmSp., prob. < Zuñi *ápachu*, enemy**]** **1.** *pl.* **A·pach′es, A·pach′e** any member of a group of tribes of Indians of N Mexico and the SW U.S. **2.** any of their Athapascan languages

a·pache (ə pash′, -päsh′; *Fr.* à pȧsh′) ***n.*, *pl.*** **a·pach′es** (-iz; *Fr.* à pȧsh′) **[**Fr., lit., APACHE**]** a gangster of Paris —***adj.*** designating a dance which represents an apache handling his girl brutally

a·part (ə pärt′) ***adv.*** **[**< OFr. < L. *ad*, to, at + *partem*, acc.

of *pars*, a part, side] **1.** to one side; aside **2.** away in place or time **3.** separately in function, use, etc. *[viewed apart]* **4.** in or to pieces **5.** aside; notwithstanding *[all joking apart]* ***—adj.*** *[used only in the predicate]* separated **—apart from** other than; besides **—take apart** to reduce (a whole) to its parts **—tell apart** to distinguish one from another

a·part·heid (ə pärt′hāt, -hīt) ***n.*** [Afrik., apartness] in South Africa, the policy of strict racial segregation and discrimination imposed on Negroes and other colored peoples

a·part·ment (ə pärt′mənt) ***n.*** [< Fr. < It. < *appartare*, to separate < *parte*, PART] a room or suite of rooms to live in

apartment house a building divided into a number of apartments: also **apartment building**

ap·a·thet·ic (ap′ə thet′ik) ***adj.*** [< APATHY, after PATHETIC] **1.** feeling no emotion; unmoved **2.** not interested; indifferent **—ap′a·thet′i·cal·ly *adv.***

ap·a·thy (ap′ə thē) ***n.***, *pl.* **-thies** [< Fr. < L. < Gr. < *a-*, without + *pathos*, emotion] **1.** lack of emotion **2.** lack of interest; indifference

APC tablet a tablet containing aspirin, phenacetin, and caffeine, for relieving headaches, etc.

ape (āp) ***n.*** [OE. *apa*] **1.** any of a family of large, tailless monkeys; specif., a chimpanzee, gorilla, orangutan, or gibbon **2.** any monkey **3.** a person who imitates; mimic **4.** a coarse, uncouth person ***—vt.* aped, ap′ing** to imitate or mimic **—ape′like′ *adj.***

ape-man (-man′) ***n.*** any of several extinct primates, with structural characteristics between those of man and the higher apes

Ap·en·nines (ap′ə nīnz′) mountain range in C Italy: highest peak, 9,560 ft.

a·pe·ri·ent (ə pir′ē ənt) ***adj., n.*** [< L. prp. of *aperire*: see APERTURE] *same as* LAXATIVE

a·pe·ri·od·ic (ā′pir ē äd′ik) ***adj.*** **1.** occurring irregularly **2.** *Physics* without periodic vibrations

a·pe·ri·tif (ä′pā rə tēf′) ***n.*** [< Fr. < L. *apertus*: see ff.] an alcoholic drink, esp. a wine, taken before meals to stimulate the appetite

ap·er·ture (ap′ər chər) ***n.*** [< L. < *apertus*, pp. of *aperire*, to open] **1.** an opening; hole; gap **2.** the diameter of the opening in a camera, etc., through which light passes into the lens

a·pet·a·lous (ā pet′′l əs) ***adj.*** *Bot.* without petals

a·pex (ā′peks) ***n.***, *pl.* **a′pex·es, ap′i·ces** (ap′ə sēz′, ā′pə-) [L., a point] **1.** the highest point; peak; vertex **2.** the pointed end; tip **3.** a climax

a·pha·si·a (ə fā′zhə, -zhē ə) ***n.*** [ModL. < Gr. < *a-*, not + *phanai*, to speak] a total or partial loss of the power to use or understand words **—a·pha′sic** (-zik), **a·pha′si·ac′** (-zē ak′) ***adj., n.***

a·phe·li·on (ə fē′lē ən) ***n.***, *pl.* **-li·ons, -li·a** (-ə) [ModL. < Gr. *apo*, from + *hēlios*, sun] the point farthest from the sun in the orbit around it of a planet, comet, or man-made satellite: cf. PERIHELION

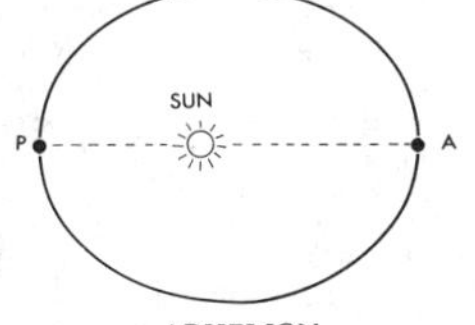

APHELION
(planet at aphelion A and at perihelion P)

a·phid (ā′fid, af′id) ***n.*** [ModL. *aphis* (pl. *aphides*) < Gr. *apheidēs*, lavish] any of a group of small insects that suck the juice from plants; plant louse: also **a·phis** (ā′fis, af′is), *pl.* **aph·i·des** (af′ə dēz′) **—a·phid·i·an** (ə fid′ē ən) ***adj., n.***

aph·o·rism (af′ə riz′m) ***n.*** [< Fr. < Gr. < *aphorizein*, to divide < *apo-*, from + *horizein*, to bound: see HORIZON] **1.** a short, concise statement of a principle **2.** a maxim or adage **—aph′o·rist *n.* —aph′o·ris′tic *adj.* —aph′o·ris′ti·cal·ly *adv.***

aph·ro·dis·i·ac (af′rə diz′ē ak′) ***adj.*** [< Gr. < ff.] arousing or increasing sexual desire ***—n.*** any aphrodisiac drug or other agent

Aph·ro·di·te (af′rə dīt′ē) *Gr. Myth.* the goddess of love and beauty: identified with the Roman Venus

a·pi·a·rist (ā′pē ə rist, -er′ist) ***n.*** a person who keeps bees **—a′pi·ar′i·an** (-er′ē ən) ***adj.***

a·pi·ar·y (ā′pē er′ē) ***n.***, *pl.* **-ar′ies** [< L. < *apis*, bee] a place where bees are kept for their honey

ap·i·cal (ap′i k′l, ā′pi-) ***adj.*** of, at, or constituting the apex

ap·i·ces (ap′ə sēz′, ā′pə-) ***n.*** *alt. pl. of* APEX

a·pi·cul·ture (ā′pə kul′chər) ***n.*** [< L. *apis*, bee + CULTURE] the raising and care of bees; beekeeping **—a′pi·cul′tur·al *adj.* —a′pi·cul′tur·ist *n.***

a·piece (ə pēs′) ***adv.*** [see A & PIECE] for each one

ap·ish (āp′ish) ***adj.*** **1.** like an ape **2.** foolishly imitative **3.** silly, affected, mischievous, etc. **—ap′ish·ly *adv.* —ap′ish·ness *n.***

a·plen·ty (ə plen′tē) ***adj., adv.*** [Colloq.] in abundance

a·plomb (ə pläm′, -plum′) ***n.*** [Fr., lit., perpendicularity < *à*, to + *plomb*, a PLUMB] self-possession; poise

ap·o- [< Gr. *apo*, off] *a prefix meaning* off, from, or away from *[apogee]*

APO Army Post Office

Apoc. 1. Apocalypse **2.** Apocrypha

a·poc·a·lypse (ə päk′ə lips′) ***n.*** [< L. < Gr. < *apokalyptein*, to disclose] any of various religious writings depicting symbolically the end of evil and the triumph of good; specif., [A-] the last book of the New Testament; book of Revelation **—a·poc′a·lyp′tic** (-lip′tik), **a·poc′a·lyp′ti·cal *adj.* —a·poc′a·lyp′ti·cal·ly *adv.***

a·po·car·pous (ap′ə kär′pəs) ***adj.*** *Bot.* having separate or partially joined carpels

a·poc·o·pe (ə päk′ə pē′) ***n.*** [< Gr. < *apo-*, from + *koptein*, to cut off] the dropping of a sound or sounds at the end of a word (Ex.: *mos'* for *most*)

a·poc·ry·pha (ə päk′rə fə) ***n.pl.*** [< LL. < Gr. *apokryphos*, hidden, obscure < *apo-*, away + *kryptein*, to hide] **1.** any writings, anecdotes, etc. of doubtful authenticity or authorship **2.** [A-] fourteen books of the Septuagint that are rejected in Judaism and regarded by Protestants as not canonical: eleven are fully accepted in the Roman Catholic canon

a·poc·ry·phal (-f′l) ***adj.*** **1.** of doubtful authorship or authenticity **2.** not genuine; false; counterfeit **3.** [A-] of or like the Apocrypha

a·pod·o·sis (ə päd′ə sis) ***n.***, *pl.* **-ses′** (-sēz′) [Gr., a giving back] the clause expressing result in a conditional sentence: opposed to PROTASIS

ap·o·gee (ap′ə jē′) ***n.*** [< Fr. < L. < Gr. < *apo-*, from + *gē*, earth] **1.** the point farthest from the earth, the moon, or another planet, in the orbit of a satellite or spacecraft around it **2.** the highest or farthest point **—ap′o·ge′an** (-jē′ən), **ap′o·ge′al *adj.***

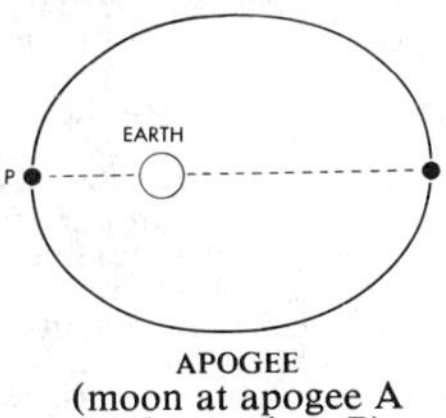

APOGEE
(moon at apogee A and at perigee P)

a·po·lit·i·cal (ā′pə lit′ə k′l) ***adj.*** not concerned with political matters **—a′po·lit′i·cal·ly *adv.***

A·pol·lo (ə päl′ō) **1.** *Gr. & Rom. Myth.* the god of music, poetry, prophecy, and medicine: later identified with HELIOS **2.** any of a series of U.S. spaceships; specif., **Apollo 11,** that first landed men on the moon (July 20, 1969) ***—n.***, *pl.* **-los** any handsome young man

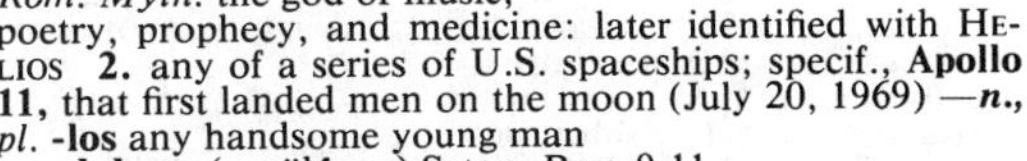

A·pol·lyon (ə päl′yən) Satan: Rev. 9:11

a·pol·o·get·ic (ə päl′ə jet′ik) ***adj.*** making apology; esp., showing realization of and regret for a fault, wrong, etc.: also **a·pol′o·get′i·cal —a·pol′o·get′i·cal·ly *adv.***

a·pol·o·get·ics (-iks) ***n.pl.*** *[with sing. v.]* [see APOLOGY] the branch of theology dealing with the defense and proofs of Christianity

ap·o·lo·gi·a (ap′ə lō′jē ə) ***n.*** an apology, esp. a formal defense of an idea, religion, etc.

a·pol·o·gist (ə päl′ə jist) ***n.*** a person who writes or speaks in defense or justification of a doctrine, faith, action, etc.

a·pol·o·gize (ə päl′ə jīz′) ***vi.*** **-gized′, -giz′ing** to make an apology; esp., to state that one is aware of and regrets a fault, wrong, etc.

ap·o·logue (ap′ə lôg′, -läg′) ***n.*** [Fr. < L. < Gr.] a short allegorical story with a moral; fable

a·pol·o·gy (ə päl′ə jē) ***n.***, *pl.* **-gies** [< LL. < Gr. *apologia*, a speaking in defense < *apo-*, from + *logos*, word] **1.** a formal spoken or written defense of some idea, doctrine, etc. **2.** an acknowledgment of some fault, wrong, etc., with an expression of regret **3.** an inferior substitute *[he is a poor apology for an actor]*

ap·o·phthegm (ap′ə them′) ***n.*** *same as* APOTHEGM

ap·o·plec·tic (ap′ə plek′tik) ***adj.*** **1.** of, like, or causing apoplexy **2.** having apoplexy **3.** seemingly about to have apoplexy *[apoplectic with rage]* Also **ap′o·plec′ti·cal *—n.*** a person having or likely to have apoplexy **—ap′o·plec′ti·cal·ly *adv.***

ap·o·plex·y (ap′ə plek′sē) ***n.*** [< ME. & OFr. < L. < Gr. < *apo-*, down + *plēssein*, to strike] sudden paralysis with some loss of consciousness and feeling, caused when a blood vessel in the brain breaks or becomes clogged; stroke

a·port (ə pôrt′) ***adv.*** *Naut.* on or to the left, or port, side

a·pos·ta·sy (ə päs′tə sē) ***n.***, *pl.* **-sies** [< LL. < Gr. < *apo-*, away + *stasis*, a standing] an abandoning of something that one once believed in, as a faith, cause, etc.

a·pos·tate (-tāt′, -tit) ***n.*** a person guilty of apostasy; renegade ***—adj.*** guilty of apostasy

a·pos·ta·tize (-tə tīz′) *vi.* **-tized′, -tiz′ing** to become an apostate

a pos·te·ri·o·ri (ā′ päs tir′ē ôr′ī, -ôr′ē) [ML., lit., from what comes later] **1.** from effect to cause, or from particular instances to a generalization; inductive or inductively **2.** based on observation or experience; empirical Opposed to A PRIORI

a·pos·tle (ə päs′'l) *n.* [< OE. & OFr. < LL. < Gr. *apostolos,* one sent forth < *apo-,* from + *stellein,* to send] **1.** a person sent out on a special mission; specif., [*usually* **A-**] any of the twelve disciples sent out by Jesus to teach the gospel **2.** the first Christian missionary in a place **3.** any of a group of early Christian missionaries **4.** an early advocate or leader, as of a reform movement **5.** any of the twelve administrative officials of the Mormon Church —**a·pos′tle·ship′** *n.*

Apostles' Creed an early statement of belief in the basic Christian doctrines, formerly thought to have been composed by the twelve Apostles

a·pos·to·late (ə päs′t'l it, -tə lāt′) *n.* the office, duties, or period of activity of an apostle

ap·os·tol·ic (ap′əs täl′ik) *adj.* **1.** of an apostle **2.** of the Apostles, their teachings, work, or times **3.** held to derive from the Apostles in a direct line of succession **4.** [*often* **A-**] of the Pope; papal Also **ap′os·tol′i·cal**

Apostolic See *R.C.Ch.* the Pope's see at Rome

a·pos·tro·phe[1] (ə päs′trə fē) *n.* [L. < Gr. *apostrophē,* a turning away to address one person < *apo-,* from + *strephein,* to turn] words addressed to a person or thing, whether absent or present —**ap·os·troph·ic** (ap′ə sträf′ik) *adj.*

a·pos·tro·phe[2] (ə päs′trə fē) *n.* [Fr. < LL. < Gr. *apostrophos (prosōdia),* averted (accent): see prec.] the mark (') used: **1.** to show the omission of a letter or letters from a word (Ex.: *it's* for *it is*) **2.** to indicate the possessive case (Ex.: *Mary's* dress, the *girls'* club) **3.** in forming some plurals, as of figures and letters (Ex.: five *6's,* dot the *i's*)

a·pos·tro·phize (-fīz′) *vt., vi.* **-phized′, -phiz′ing** to speak or write an apostrophe (to)

apothecaries' measure a system of units used in measuring liquids in pharmacy: see TABLES OF WEIGHTS AND MEASURES in the Supplements

apothecaries' weight a system of weights used in pharmacy: see TABLES OF WEIGHTS AND MEASURES in the Supplements

a·poth·e·car·y (ə päth′ə ker′ē) *n., pl.* **-car′ies** [< OFr. < ML. < L. < Gr. *apothēkē,* storehouse < *apo-,* away + *tithenai,* to put] a pharmacist, or druggist: apothecaries formerly also prescribed drugs

ap·o·thegm (ap′ə them′) *n.* [< Gr. < *apo-,* from + *phthengesthai,* to utter] a short, pithy saying (Ex.: "Brevity is the soul of wit") —**ap′o·theg·mat′ic** (-theg mat′ik), **ap′o·theg·mat′i·cal** *adj.*

a·poth·e·o·sis (ə päth′ē ō′sis, ap′ə thē′ə sis) *n., pl.* **-ses′** (-sēz′) [L. < Gr. < *apotheoun,* to deify < *apo-,* from + *theos,* a god] **1.** the act of raising a person to the status of a god; deification **2.** the glorification of a person or thing **3.** an ideal or exact type [she is the *apotheosis* of beauty]

a·poth·e·o·size (ə päth′ē ə sīz′, ap′ə thē′ə sīz′) *vt.* **-sized′, -siz′ing** [APOTHEOS(IS) + -IZE] **1.** to deify **2.** to glorify; idealize

app. **1.** appendix **2.** appointed **3.** approved **4.** approximate

ap·pal (ə pôl′) *vt.* **-palled′, -pal′ling** *same as* APPALL

Ap·pa·la·chi·a (ap′ə lā′chə, -chē ə; -lach′ə) the highland region of the E U.S., including the C and S Appalachians: characterized generally by economic depression and poverty

Ap·pa·la·chi·an Mountains (-lā′chən, -chē ən; -lach′ən) [< ? *Apalachee* Indians < ?] mountain system in E N. America, extending from S Quebec to N Ala.: highest peak, 6,684 ft.: also **Appalachians** —**Ap′pa·la′chi·an** *adj.*

ap·pall (ə pôl′) *vt.* [< OFr. *apalir* < *a-,* to + *palir,* to grow pale < L. *pallidus,* pale] to fill with horror or dismay; shock

ap·pal·ling (-iŋ) *adj.* causing horror, shock, or dismay —**ap·pal′ling·ly** *adv.*

ap·pa·loo·sa (ap′ə lo͞o′sə) *n.* [altered < *a palouse,* after the *Palouse* Indians of the NW U.S.] any of a sturdy breed of Western saddle horses with spotted markings on the rump and loins

ap·pa·nage (ap′ə nij) *n.* [< Fr. < ML. < L. *ad,* to + *panis,* bread] **1.** money, land, etc. granted by a monarch for the support of his younger children **2.** a benefit that is a perquisite or adjunct

ap·pa·ra·tus (ap′ə rat′əs, -rāt′-) *n., pl.* **-ra′tus, -ra′tus·es** [L., a making ready < *apparare* < *ad-,* to + *parare,* to prepare] **1.** the instruments, equipment, etc. for a specific use **2.** any complex device or system **3.** *Physiol.* a set of organs having a specific function [the digestive *apparatus*]

ap·par·el (ə per′əl, -par′-) *n.* [< OFr., ult. < L. *apparare:* see prec.] clothing; attire —*vt.* **-eled** or **-elled, -el·ing** or **-el·ling** **1.** to clothe; dress **2.** to adorn; bedeck

ap·par·ent (ə per′ənt, -par′-) *adj.* [< OFr. < L. prp. of *apparere,* APPEAR] **1.** readily seen; visible **2.** readily understood; obvious **3.** appearing to be real or true; seeming See also HEIR APPARENT —**ap·par′ent·ly** *adv.* —**ap·par′ent·ness** *n.*

ap·pa·ri·tion (ap′ə rish′ən) *n.* [< OFr. < ML. < L. *apparere:* see APPEAR] **1.** anything that appears unexpectedly or remarkably **2.** a ghost; phantom **3.** the act of appearing —**ap′pa·ri′tion·al** *adj.*

ap·peal (ə pēl′) *vt.* [< OFr. < L. *appellare,* to accost, appeal < *ad-,* to + *pellere:* see COMPEL] to make a request to a higher court for the rehearing of (a case) —*vi.* **1.** to appeal a law case to a higher court **2.** to make an urgent request (*to* a person *for* help, sympathy, etc.) **3.** to resort (*to*) for decision, etc. **4.** to be attractive, interesting, etc. —*n.* **1.** a call upon some authority for a decision, etc. **2.** an urgent request for help, etc. **3.** a quality that arouses interest, sympathy, etc.; attraction **4.** *Law a)* a request that a case be transferred to a higher court for rehearing or review *b)* the right to request this —**ap·peal′a·ble** *adj.* —**ap·peal′ing** *adj.* —**ap·peal′ing·ly** *adv.*

ap·pear (ə pir′) *vi.* [< OFr. < L. *apparere* < *ad-,* to + *parere,* to come forth] **1.** to come into sight **2.** to come into being **3.** to become understood [it *appears* he left] **4.** to seem; look **5.** to present oneself formally, as in court **6.** to come before the public [he *appeared* in Hamlet] **7.** to be published

ap·pear·ance (-əns) *n.* **1.** an appearing **2.** the outward aspect of anything **3.** an outward show; pretense **4.** [*pl.*] the way things seem to be —**keep up appearances** to try to give the impression of being proper, well-off, etc. —**put in an appearance** to be present for a short time, as at a party

ap·pease (ə pēz′) *vt.* **-peased′, -peas′ing** [< OFr. < *a-,* to + *pais* < L. *pax,* PEACE] **1.** to make peaceful or quiet, esp. by giving in to the demands of **2.** to satisfy or relieve [water *appeases* thirst] —**ap·peas′a·ble** *adj.* —**ap·peas′er** *n.*

ap·pease·ment (-mənt) *n.* **1.** an appeasing or being appeased **2.** the policy of giving in to demands of a hostile power in an attempt to keep peace

ap·pel·lant (ə pel′ənt) *adj. Law* relating to appeals; appealing —*n.* a person who appeals, esp. to a higher court

ap·pel·late (-it) *adj.* [< L. pp. of *appellare,* APPEAL] *Law* relating to, or having jurisdiction to review, appeals [an *appellate* court]

ap·pel·la·tion (ap′ə lā′shən) *n.* [< L. < pp. of *appellare,* APPEAL] **1.** the act of calling by a name **2.** a name or title; designation

ap·pel·la·tive (ə pel′ə tiv) *adj.* of appellation; naming —*n.* **1.** a name or title **2.** a common noun: earlier usage —**ap·pel′la·tive·ly** *adv.*

ap·pend (ə pend′) *vt.* [< OFr. < L. *appendere* < *ad-,* to + *pendere,* to suspend] to attach or affix; add as a supplement or appendix

ap·pend·age (ə pen′dij) *n.* **1.** anything appended; adjunct **2.** *Biol.* any secondary, external organ or part, as a tree branch or a dog's tail

ap·pend·ant, ap·pend·ent (-dənt) *adj.* [Fr.: see APPEND] **1.** attached or added **2.** associated with as a consequence —*n.* an appendage

ap·pen·dec·to·my (ap′ən dek′tə mē) *n., pl.* **-mies** [APPEND(IX) + -ECTOMY] the surgical removal of the vermiform appendix

ap·pen·di·ci·tis (ə pen′də sīt′əs) *n.* [< ff. + -ITIS] inflammation of the vermiform appendix

ap·pen·dix (ə pen′diks) *n., pl.* **-dix·es, -di·ces′** (-də sēz′) [L.: see APPEND] **1.** additional material at the end of a book **2.** *Anat.* an outgrowth of an organ; esp., a small sac (**vermiform appendix**) extending from the cecum of the large intestine

ap·per·ceive (ap′ər sēv′) *vt.* **-ceived′, -ceiv′ing** [< OFr. < L. *ad,* to + *percipere,* PERCEIVE] *Psychol.* to assimilate and interpret (a new perception) by the help of past experience

ap·per·cep·tion (ap′ər sep′shən) *n.* [< Fr. < *apercevoir,* APPERCEIVE] **1.** an apperceiving **2.** the state of the mind in being conscious of its own consciousness —**ap′per·cep′tive** *adj.*

ap·per·tain (ap′ər tān′) *vi.* [< OFr. < L. *appertinere* < *ad-,* to + *pertinere:* see PERTAIN] to belong properly as a function, part, etc.; pertain

ap·pe·ten·cy (ap′ə tən sē) *n., pl.* **-cies** [< L. prp. of *appetere:* see ff.] **1.** a strong desire **2.** a propensity **3.** an affinity Also **ap′pe·tence**

ap·pe·tite (ap′ə tīt′) *n.* [< ME. & OFr. < L. *appetitus,* pp. of *appetere* < *ad-,* to + *petere,* to seek] a desire or craving, esp. for food or for a specific food —**ap′pe·ti′tive** (-tīt′iv) *adj.*

ap·pe·tiz·er (-tī′zər) *n.* a small portion of a tasty food or a drink to stimulate the appetite at the beginning of a meal

ap·pe·tiz·ing (-tī′ziŋ) *adj.* **1.** stimulating the appetite **2.** savory; tasty —**ap′pe·tiz′ing·ly** *adv.*

ap·plaud (ə plôd′) *vt., vi.* [L. *applaudere* < *ad-,* to + *plaudere,* to clap hands] **1.** to show approval (of) by clap-

ping the hands, cheering, etc. 2. to praise; approve —**ap·plaud′er** *n.*
ap·plause (ə plôz′) *n.* approval or praise, esp. as shown by clapping hands, cheering, etc.
ap·ple (ap″l) *n.* [OE. *æppel*] 1. *a*) a round, firm, fleshy, edible fruit with a red, yellow, or green skin and a seed core, growing on any of a genus of trees in temperate regions *b*) any of these trees 2. any of various plants bearing applelike fruits, as the May apple
apple butter a kind of jam made from apples stewed with spices
ap·ple·jack (-jak′) *n.* brandy distilled from apple cider
apple of one's eye 1. the pupil of one's eye 2. any person or thing that one cherishes
ap·ple-pie order (ap″l pī′) [Colloq.] neat order
apple polisher [Slang] a person who curries favor by gifts, flattery, etc.
ap·ple·sauce (-sôs′) *n.* 1. apples cooked to a pulp in water 2. [Slang] nonsense; hokum
Ap·ple·seed (ap″l sēd′), **Johnny** (nickname of *John Chapman*) 1775–1845; U.S. frontiersman who planted apple trees throughout the Midwest
Ap·ple·ton (ap″l tən) [after S. *Appleton,* 19th-c. Boston philanthropist] city in E Wis.: pop. 59,000
ap·pli·ance (ə plī′əns) *n.* a device or machine for performing a specific task, esp. one worked mechanically or by electricity
ap·pli·ca·ble (ap′li kə b′l) *adj.* that can be applied; appropriate; suitable —**ap′pli·ca·bil′i·ty** *n.* —**ap′pli·ca·bly** *adv.*
ap·pli·cant (ap′li kənt) *n.* a person who applies, as for employment, help, etc.
ap·pli·ca·tion (ap′lə kā′shən) *n.* 1. the act or a way of applying or being applied 2. anything applied, esp. a remedy 3. a request, or the form filled out in making a request *[*an *application* for employment*]* 4. continued effort; diligence 5. relevance or practicality *[*this idea has no *application* to the case*]*
ap·pli·ca·tor (ap′lə kāt′ər) *n.* any device for applying medicine or paint, polish, etc.
ap·pli·ca·to·ry (-kə tôr′ē) *adj.* that can be applied or used; practical: also **ap′pli·ca′tive** (-kāt′iv)
ap·plied (ə plīd′) *adj.* used in actual practice or to work out practical problems *[applied* science*]*
ap·pli·qué (ap′lə kā′) *n.* [Fr. < L. *applicare:* see ff.] a decoration made of one material attached by sewing, etc. to another —*adj.* applied as such a decoration —*vt.* **-quéd′**, **-qué′ing** 1. to decorate with appliqué 2. to put on as appliqué
ap·ply (ə plī′) *vt.* **-plied′**, **-ply′ing** [< OFr. < L. *applicare,* to attach to < *ad-,* to + *plicare,* to fold] 1. to put on *[*to *apply* salve*]* 2. to use practically *[*to *apply* one's knowledge*]* 3. to refer to a person or thing with (an epithet, etc.) 4. to concentrate (one's faculties); employ (oneself) diligently —*vi.* 1. to make a formal request 2. to be suitable or relevant *[*this rule *applies* to everyone*]* —**ap·pli′er** *n.*

APPLIQUÉ

ap·pog·gia·tu·ra (ə päj′ə toor′ə) *n.* [It. < *appoggiare,* to lean, ult. < L. *ad-,* to + *podium,* PODIUM] *Music* an auxiliary note like a grace note but rhythmically more prominent than the melodic note that it precedes
ap·point (ə point′) *vt.* [< OFr. *apointer,* to make ready, ult. < L. *ad,* to + *punctum,* a POINT] 1. to set (a date, place, etc.); decree 2. to name for an office, etc. *[*to *appoint* a chairman*]* 3. to furnish and arrange: now usually in *well-appointed,* etc. —**ap·point·ee** (ə poin′tē′) *n.*
ap·point·ive (ə poin′tiv) *adj.* to which one is appointed, not elected *[*an *appointive* office*]*
ap·point·ment (ə point′mənt) *n.* 1. an appointing or being appointed; specif., a naming for an office, etc. 2. a person so named 3. an office held in this way 4. an arrangement to meet a person; engagement 5. [*pl.*] furnishings
Ap·po·mat·tox (Court House) (ap′ə mat′əks) [< Algonquian tribal name] former village in C Va., where Lee surrendered to Grant (April 9, 1865), ending the Civil War
ap·por·tion (ə pôr′shən) *vt.* [< OFr.: see AD- & PORTION] to divide and distribute in shares according to a plan
ap·por·tion·ment (-mənt) *n.* 1. an apportioning 2. a proportional distribution, as of U.S. Representatives among the States
ap·pose (ə pōz′) *vt.* **-posed′**, **-pos′ing** [< Fr. < L. *appositus,* pp. of *apponere* < *ad-,* near + *ponere,* to put] to put side by side, next, or near —**ap·pos′a·ble** *adj.*
ap·po·site (ap′ə zit) *adj.* [see prec.] appropriate; apt —**ap′po·site·ly** *adv.* —**ap′po·site·ness** *n.*
ap·po·si·tion (ap′ə zish′ən) *n.* 1. an apposing or being apposed 2. the position resulting from this 3. *Gram. a*) the placing of a word or expression beside another so that the second explains and has the same grammatical construction as the first *b*) the relationship between such terms *[*"my cousin" is in *apposition* with "Mary" in "Mary, my cousin, is here"*]* —**ap′po·si′tion·al** *adj.*
ap·pos·i·tive (ə päz′ə tiv) *adj.* of or in apposition —*n.* a word, phrase, or clause in apposition —**ap·pos′i·tive·ly** *adv.*
ap·prais·al (ə prā′z′l) *n.* 1. an appraising 2. an appraised value; esp., an expert valuation as for taxation or sale Also **ap·praise′ment**
ap·praise (ə prāz′) *vt.* **-praised′**, **-prais′ing** [< OFr. < LL. *appretiare* < L. *ad,* to + *pretium,* PRICE; Eng. sp. infl. by PRAISE] 1. to set a price for; decide the value of, esp. officially 2. to estimate the quantity or quality of —**ap·prais′er** *n.* —**ap·prais′ing·ly** *adv.*
ap·pre·ci·a·ble (ə prē′shə b′l, -shē ə-) *adj.* enough to be perceived; noticeable; measurable *[*an *appreciable* difference*]* —**ap·pre′ci·a·bly** *adv.*
ap·pre·ci·ate (ə prē′shē āt′) *vt.* **-at′ed**, **-at′ing** [< LL. pp. of *appretiare,* APPRAISE] 1. to think well of; enjoy; esteem 2. to recognize gratefully 3. to estimate the quality or worth of 4. to be fully or sensitively aware of 5. to raise the price of: opposed to DEPRECIATE —*vi.* to rise in value —**ap·pre′ci·a′tor** *n.* —**ap·pre′ci·a·to′ry** (-shə tôr′ē, -shē ə-) *adj.*
ap·pre·ci·a·tion (ə prē′shē ā′shən) *n.* 1. an appreciating; specif., *a*) proper estimation *b*) grateful recognition, as of a favor *c*) sensitive awareness or enjoyment, as of art *d*) an evaluation 2. a rise in value or price
ap·pre·ci·a·tive (ə prē′shə tiv, -shē ə-; -shē āt′iv) *adj.* feeling or showing appreciation —**ap·pre′ci·a·tive·ly** *adv.* —**ap·pre′ci·a·tive·ness** *n.*
ap·pre·hend (ap′rə hend′) *vt.* [< L. *apprehendere,* to take hold of < *ad-,* to + *prehendere,* to seize] 1. to take into custody; arrest 2. to perceive or understand 3. to anticipate with anxiety; dread
ap·pre·hen·si·ble (-hen′sə b′l) *adj.* that can be apprehended —**ap′pre·hen′si·bil′i·ty** *n.*
ap·pre·hen·sion (-hen′shən) *n.* 1. capture or arrest 2. perception or understanding 3. anxiety or dread
ap·pre·hen·sive (-hen′siv) *adj.* 1. perceptive 2. uneasy or fearful about the future —**ap′pre·hen′sive·ly** *adv.* —**ap′pre·hen′sive·ness** *n.*
ap·pren·tice (ə pren′tis) *n.* [< OFr. < *aprendre,* to teach < L. *apprehendere,* APPREHEND] 1. a person under legal agreement to work a specified length of time for a master craftsman in a craft or trade in return for instruction and, formerly, support 2. a person, usually a member of a labor union, learning a trade, etc. under specified conditions 3. any learner or beginner —*vt.* **-ticed**, **-tic·ing** to place or accept as an apprentice —**ap·pren′tice·ship′** *n.*
ap·prise[1], **ap·prize**[1] (ə prīz′) *vt.* **-prised′** or **-prized′**, **-pris′ing** or **-priz′ing** [< Fr. pp. of *apprendre,* to teach, inform < L. *apprehendere,* APPREHEND] to inform or notify
ap·prize[2], **ap·prise**[2] (ə prīz′) *vt.* **-prized′** or **-prised′**, **-priz′ing** or **-pris′ing** *same as* APPRAISE
ap·proach (ə prōch′) *vi.* [< OFr. < LL. *appropiare* < L. *ad,* to + *propius,* compar. of *prope,* near] to come closer or draw nearer —*vt.* 1. to come near or nearer to 2. to be similar to; approximate 3. to bring near (*to* something) 4. to make advances, a proposal, or a request to 5. to begin dealing with *[*to *approach* a task*]* —*n.* 1. a coming closer 2. an approximation 3. an advance or overture (*to* someone): *often used in pl.* 4. a way of getting to a person, place, or thing; path; road; access 5. *Golf* a shot to drive the ball from the fairway onto the putting green —**ap·proach′a·bil′i·ty** *n.* —**ap·proach′a·ble** *adj.*
ap·pro·ba·tion (ap′rə bā′shən) *n.* [< L. < *approbare,* APPROVE] official approval, permission, or praise —**ap′pro·ba′tive**, **ap·pro·ba·to·ry** (ə prō′bə tôr′ē) *adj.*
ap·pro·pri·ate (ə prō′prē āt′; *for adj.* -it) *vt.* **-at′ed**, **-at′ing** [< LL. pp. of *appropriare* < L. < *ad-,* to + *proprius,* one's own] 1. to take for one's own use 2. to take improperly, as without permission 3. to set aside for a specific use *[*to *appropriate* funds for schools*]* —*adj.* right for the purpose; suitable —**ap·pro′pri·ate·ly** (-it lē) *adv.* —**ap·pro′pri·ate·ness** *n.* —**ap·pro′pri·a′tive** (-āt′iv) *adj.* —**ap·pro′pri·a′tor** *n.*
ap·pro·pri·a·tion (ə prō′prē ā′shən) *n.* 1. an appropriating or being appropriated 2. a thing appropriated; esp., money set aside for a specific use
ap·prov·al (ə prōō′v′l) *n.* 1. an approving 2. favorable attitude or opinion 3. formal consent or permission —**on**

fat, āpe, cär, ten, ēven, is, bīte; gō, hôrn, tōōl, look; oil, out; up, fur; get; joy; yet; chin; she; thin, *th*en; zh, leisure; ŋ, ring; ə for *a* in *ago, e* in *agent, i* in *sanity, o* in *comply, u* in *focus;* ′ as in *able* (ā′b′l); Fr. bål; ë, Fr. coeur; ö, Fr. feu; Fr. mon; ô, Fr. coq; ü, Fr. duc; *r,* Fr. cri; H, G. ich; kh, G. doch; ‡foreign; *hypothetical; < derived from. See inside front cover.

approval for the customer to examine and decide whether to buy or return

ap·prove (ə pro͞ov′) *vt.* **-proved′, -prov′ing** [< OFr. < L. *approbare* < *ad-*, to + *probare*, to try, test < *probus*, good] **1.** to give one's consent to; sanction **2.** to be favorable toward; judge to be good, satisfactory, etc. —*vi.* to have a favorable opinion (*of*) —**ap·prov′er** *n.* —**ap·prov′ing·ly** *adv.*

approx. **1.** approximate **2.** approximately

ap·prox·i·mate (ə präk′sə mit; *for v.* -māt′) *adj.* [< LL. pp. of *approximare* < L. *ad*, to + *proximus*, superl. of *prope*, near] **1.** near in position **2.** much like; resembling **3.** not exact, but almost so —*vt.* **-mat′ed, -mat′ing** **1.** to come near to; be almost the same as *[a painting that approximates reality]* **2.** to bring near (*to* something) —*vi.* to come near; be almost the same —**ap·prox′i·mate·ly** *adv.*

ap·prox·i·ma·tion (ə präk′sə mā′shən) *n.* **1.** an approximating **2.** a fairly close estimate, etc.

ap·pur·te·nance (ə pʉr′t′n əns) *n.* [< Anglo-Fr. < OFr. < L. prp. of *appertinere*, APPERTAIN] **1.** something added to a more important thing; adjunct **2.** [*pl.*] accessories **3.** *Law* an additional, subordinate right or privilege —**ap·pur′te·nant** *adj., n.*

a·prax·i·a (ə prak′sē ə) *n.* [ModL. < Gr. *apraxia*, nonaction] loss of memory of how to perform complex muscular movements, resulting from brain damage —**a·prax′ic** (-prak′sik), **a·prac′tic** (-prak′tik) *adj.*

a·près (a′prā′; *Fr.* à pre′) *prep.* [Fr.] after: often in hyphenated compounds *[an après-ski party]*

a·pri·cot (ap′rə kät′, ā′prə-) *n.* [< Fr. < Port. < Ar. < MGr. < L. *praecoquus*, early matured (fruit)] **1.** a small, yellowish-orange fruit related to the peach **2.** the tree it grows on **3.** yellowish orange

A·pril (ā′prəl) *n.* [< OFr. < L. < *apero-*, second (in the ancient Rom. calendar, the year began with March)] the fourth month of the year, having 30 days: abbrev. **Apr.**

April fool a victim of jokes on April Fools' Day

April Fools' Day April 1, All Fools' Day, when practical jokes are traditionally played

a pri·o·ri (ä′prē ôr′ē, ā′prī ôr′ī) [L., from something prior] **1.** from cause to effect or from a generalization to particular instances; deductive or deductively **2.** based on theory instead of on experience or experiment **3.** before examination or analysis Opposed to A POSTERIORI

a·pron (ā′prən, -pərn) *n.* [by faulty separation < ME. *a napron* < OFr. *naperon* < *nape*, a cloth < L. *mappa*, a napkin] **1.** a garment worn over the front part of the body, usually to protect one's clothes **2.** anything like an apron; specif., *a*) a protective covering for or edging on a structure, machine, etc. *b*) the hard-surfaced area in front of a hangar *c*) a broadened part of a driveway *d*) the part of a stage in front of the curtain —*vt.* to put an apron on or provide an apron for

apron string a string for tying an apron on —**tied to one's mother's** (or **wife's,** etc.) **apron strings** dominated by one's mother (or wife, etc.)

ap·ro·pos (ap′rə pō′) *adv.* [Fr. *à propos*, to the purpose] at the right time; opportunely —*adj.* relevant; apt —**apropos of** with regard to

apse (aps) *n.* [< L. < Gr. *hapsis*, an arch, fastening < *haptein*, to fasten] a semicircular or polygonal projection of a building, esp. one at the east end of a church, with a domed or vaulted roof —**ap′si·dal** (ap′sid ′l) *adj.*

apt (apt) *adj.* [< ME. & OFr. < L. *aptus*, pp. of *apere*, to fasten] **1.** appropriate; fitting *[an apt remark]* **2.** tending or inclined; likely *[apt to rain]* **3.** quick to learn or understand *[an apt student]* —**apt′ly** *adv.* —**apt′ness** *n.*

apt. *pl.* **apts.** apartment

ap·ter·ous (ap′tər əs) *adj.* [< Gr. < *a-*, without + *pteron*, a wing] *Biol.* having no wings; wingless

ap·ter·yx (ap′tər iks) *n.* [< Gr. *a-*, without + *pteryx*, wing] *same as* KIWI

ap·ti·tude (ap′tə to͞od′, -tyo͞od′) *n.* [< ML. < L. *aptus*: see APT] **1.** the quality of being appropriate; fitness **2.** a natural tendency, inclination, or ability **3.** quickness to learn or understand

aq·ua (ak′wə, äk′-) *n., pl.* **aq′uas, aq′uae** (-wē) [L.] water; esp., *Pharm.* a solution of a substance in water —*adj.* [< AQUAMARINE] bluish-green

aq·ua·cul·ture (ak′wə kul′chər, äk′-) *n.* [prec. + CULTURE] cultivation of water plants and animals for human use —**aq′ua·cul′tur·al** *adj.*

aqua for·tis (fôr′təs) [L., strong water] *same as* NITRIC ACID

Aq·ua-lung (ak′wə luŋ′, äk′-) [AQUA + LUNG] *a trademark for* a kind of self-contained underwater breathing apparatus: see SCUBA —*n.* an apparatus of this kind: usually **a′qua·lung′**

aq·ua·ma·rine (ak′wə mə rēn′, äk′-) *n.* [L. *aqua marina*, sea water] **1.** a transparent, pale bluish-green variety of beryl, used in jewelry **2.** its color —*adj.* bluish-green

aq·ua·naut (ak′wə nôt′, äk′-) *n.* [AQUA + (ASTRO)NAUT] **1.** any of a group of persons using a watertight underwater chamber as a base for oceanographic experiments **2.** *same as* SKIN DIVER

aq·ua·plane (ak′wə plān′, äk′-) *n.* [AQUA + PLANE[4]] a board on which one rides standing up as it is pulled over water by a motorboat —*vi.* **-planed′, -plan′ing** to ride on such a board as a sport

aqua re·gi·a (rē′jē ə) [L., lit., kingly water: it dissolves the "noble metals," gold and platinum] a mixture of nitric and hydrochloric acids

a·quar·ist (ə kwer′ist) *n.* the keeper of an aquarium

a·quar·i·um (ə kwer′ē əm) *n., pl.* **-i·ums, -i·a** (-ē ə) [L., neut. of *aquarius*, of water < *aqua*, water] **1.** a tank, usually with glass sides, or a pool, bowl, etc., for keeping live water animals and water plants **2.** a building where such collections are exhibited

A·quar·i·us (ə kwer′ē əs) [L., the water carrier] **1.** a large S constellation **2.** the eleventh sign of the zodiac: see ZODIAC, illus.

a·quat·ic (ə kwät′ik, -kwat′-) *adj.* [< L. < *aqua*, water] **1.** growing or living in or upon water **2.** done in or upon the water *[aquatic sports]* —*n.* **1.** an aquatic plant or animal **2.** [*pl., often with sing. v.*] aquatic sports or performances —**a·quat′i·cal·ly** *adv.*

aq·ua·tint (ak′wə tint′, äk′-) *n.* [< Fr. < It. *acqua tinta*, dyed in water] **1.** a process by which spaces rather than lines are etched with acid to produce an etching that looks like a water color **2.** such an etching —*vt.* to etch in this way

aqua vi·tae (vīt′ē) [L., water of life] **1.** *Alchemy* alcohol **2.** brandy or other strong liquor

aq·ue·duct (ak′wə dukt′) *n.* [< L. < *aqua*, water + pp. of *ducere*, to lead] **1.** a large pipe or conduit for bringing water from a distant source **2.** a bridgelike structure for carrying a water conduit or canal across a river or valley

a·que·ous (ā′kwē əs, ak′wē-) *adj.* [see AQUA & -OUS] **1.** of, like, or containing water; watery **2.** *Geol.* formed by the action of water

aqueous humor a watery fluid in the space between the cornea and the lens of the eye

aq·ui·cul·ture (ak′wi kul′chər, äk′-) *n. same as* AQUACULTURE —**aq′ui·cul′tur·al** *adj.*

Aq·ui·la (ak′wi lə) [L., eagle] a N constellation in the Milky Way

aq·ui·line (ak′wə līn′, -lən) *adj.* [< L. < *aquila*, eagle] **1.** of or like an eagle **2.** curved or hooked like an eagle's beak *[an aquiline nose]*

A·qui·nas (ə kwī′nəs), Saint **Thomas** 1225?–74; It. theologian & philosopher

Aq·ui·taine (ak′wə tān′) region of SW France

-ar (ər) [< ME. < OFr. < L. *-aris* or *-arius;* or directly < L.] **1.** *a suffix meaning* of, relating to, like, of the nature of *[singular, polar]* **2.** *a suffix denoting* agency *[bursar, vicar]*

Ar *Chem.* argon

AR **1.** Airman Recruit **2.** Arkansas **3.** Army Regulation

Ar. **1.** Arabic **2.** Aramaic

ar. **1.** arrival **2.** arrives

A.R. Autonomous Republic

A·ra (ā′rə) [L., an altar] a S constellation

Ar·ab (ar′əb) *n.* **1.** a native or inhabitant of Arabia **2.** any of a Semitic people originating in Arabia; commonly, a Bedouin **3.** any of a breed of swift, graceful horses native to Arabia —*adj. same as* ARABIAN

ar·a·besque (ar′ə besk′) *n.* [Fr. < It. < *Arabo*, Arab < Ar. *ʿarab:* with reference to Moorish designs] **1.** an elaborate design of intertwined flowers, foliage, geometrical patterns, etc. **2.** *Ballet* a position in which one leg is extended back and the arms are extended, usually one back and one forward **3.** *Music* a light, whimsical composition —*adj.* of or done in arabesque; fantastic and elaborate

ARABESQUE

A·ra·bi·a (ə rā′bē ə) peninsula, largely a desert, in SW Asia: also **Arabian Peninsula**

A·ra·bi·an (-ən) *adj.* of Arabia or the Arabs —*n. same as* ARAB (senses 1 & 3)

Arabian Nights, The a collection of ancient tales from Arabia, India, Persia, etc.

Arabian Sea part of the Indian Ocean, between India and Arabia

Ar·a·bic (ar′ə bik) *adj.* **1.** of Arabia **2.** of the Arabs, their language, culture, etc. —*n.* the Semitic language of the Arabs, spoken in Arabia, Syria, Jordan, Iraq, northern Africa, etc.

Arabic numerals the figures 1, 2, 3, 4, 5, 6, 7, 8, 9, and the 0 (zero), orig. used in India

ar·a·ble (ar′ə b′l) *adj.* [Fr. < L. < *arare*, to plow] suita-

ble for plowing and producing crops —*n.* arable land —ar′a·bil′i·ty *n.*
Arab League a confederation of a number of Arabic-speaking nations
Ar·a·by (ar′ə bē) [Archaic or Poet.] Arabia
a·rach·nid (ə rak′nid) *n.* [ModL. < Gr. *arachnē*, spider] any of a large group of arthropods, including spiders, scorpions, and mites, with four pairs of legs and with breathing tubes or lunglike sacs —**a·rach′ni·dan** (-ni dən) *adj., n.*
Ar·a·gon (ar′ə gän′) region in NE Spain —**Ar′a·go·nese′** (-gə nēz′) *adj., n., pl.* **-nese′**
ar·ak (ar′ək) *n. same as* ARRACK
Ar·al Sea (ar′əl) inland body of salt water in SW Asiatic U.S.S.R., east of the Caspian Sea: also **Lake Aral**
Ar·am (ar′əm) [Heb.] *Biblical name for* ancient Syria —**Ar·a·mae·an, Ar·a·me·an** (ar′ə mē′ən) *adj., n.*
Aram. Aramaic
Ar·a·ma·ic (ar′ə mā′ik) *n.* a group of northwestern Semitic languages of Biblical times, including that of Palestine
A·rap·a·ho (ə rap′ə hō′) *n.* [< ? Crow, lit., enemy] **1.** *pl.* **-hos′, -ho′** any member of a tribe of Indians orig. from the area between the upper Platte and Arkansas rivers **2.** their Algonquian language
Ar·a·rat (ar′ə rat′) mountain in E Turkey: supposed landing place of Noah's Ark (Gen. 8:4)
ar·ba·lest, ar·ba·list (är′bə list) *n.* [< OFr. < L. < *arcus*, a bow + *ballista*, BALLISTA] a medieval crossbow with a steel bow
ar·bi·ter (är′bə tər) *n.* [L., orig., one who goes to a place, a witness < *ad-*, to + *baetere*, to go] **1.** a person selected to judge a dispute; umpire; arbitrator **2.** a person fully authorized to judge or decide —**ar′bi·tral** (-trəl) *adj.* —**ar′bi·tress** *n.fem.*
ar·bi·tra·ble (är′bə trə b'l) *adj.* that can be arbitrated; subject to arbitration
ar·bit·ra·ment (är bit′rə mənt) *n.* **1.** arbitration **2.** an arbitrator's verdict or award
ar·bi·trar·y (är′bə trer′ē) *adj.* [< L. < *arbiter*, ARBITER] **1.** not fixed by rules but left to one's own choice **2.** based on one's whim or notion; capricious **3.** absolute; despotic —**ar′bi·trar′i·ly** *adv.* —**ar′bi·trar′i·ness** *n.*
ar·bi·trate (är′bə trāt′) *vt.* **-trat′ed, -trat′ing** [< L. pp. of *arbitrari*, to give a decision < *arbiter*, ARBITER] **1.** to give to an arbitrator to decide **2.** to decide (a dispute) as an arbitrator —*vi.* **1.** to act as an arbitrator (*in* a dispute, *between* persons) **2.** to submit a dispute to arbitration
ar·bi·tra·tion (är′bə trā′shən) *n.* settlement of a dispute by someone chosen to hear both sides and come to a decision —**ar′bi·tra′tion·al** *adj.*
ar·bi·tra·tor (är′bə trāt′ər) *n.* a person chosen to arbitrate a dispute
ar·bor[1] (är′bər) *n.* [< OFr. < LL. *herbarium*, HERBARIUM] a place shaded by trees, shrubs, or vines: Brit. sp. **ar′bour** —**ar′bored** *adj.*
ar·bor[2] (är′bər) *n., pl.* **ar′bo·res′** (-bə rēz′) [L.] *Bot.* a tree
ar·bor[3] (är′bər) *n.* [< Fr. *arbre* < L. *arbor*, tree, beam] *Mech.* **1.** a shaft; beam **2.** a spindle; axle **3.** a bar that holds cutting tools
Arbor Day a tree-planting day observed in most States of the U.S., usually in April
ar·bo·re·al (är bôr′ē əl) *adj.* **1.** of or like a tree **2.** living in trees
ar·bo·res·cent (är′bə res′'nt) *adj.* treelike in form or growth; branching —**ar′bo·res′cence** *n.*
ar·bo·re·tum (är′bə rēt′əm) *n., pl.* **-tums, -ta** (-ə) [L.] a place where many kinds of trees and shrubs are grown for exhibition or study
ar·bor·vi·tae (är′bər vīt′ē) *n.* [L., tree of life] any of several evergreen trees related to the cypress, with flattened sprays of scalelike leaves
ar·bu·tus (är byōōt′əs) *n.* [L., wild strawberry tree] **1.** a tree or shrub of the heath family, with dark-green leaves and berries like strawberries **2.** a related trailing plant with clusters of white or pink flowers
arc (ärk) *n.* [OFr. < L. *arcus*, a bow, arch] **1.** a bowlike curved line or object **2.** *Elec.* the band of sparks or incandescent light formed when an electric discharge is conducted from one electrode or conducting surface to another **3.** *Geom. a)* any part of a curve, esp. of a circle *b)* the angular measurement of this —*vi.* **arced** or **arcked, arc′ing** or **arck′ing** **1.** to move in a curved course **2.** *Elec.* to form an arc
Arc, Jeanne d' (zhän dȧrk′) *see* JOAN OF ARC
ARC, A.R.C. American Red Cross
ar·cade (är kād′) *n.* [Fr. < Pr. < ML. < L. *arcus*, arch] **1.** a covered passageway, as through a building, often with an arched roof; esp., such a passage with shops along the sides **2.** a line of arches and their supporting columns —*vt.* **-cad′ed, -cad′ing** to make into or provide with an arcade
Ar·ca·di·a (är kā′dē ə) a pastoral district of ancient Greece —*n.* any place of rural peace and simplicity Also [Poet.] **Ar·ca·dy** (är′kə dē) —**Ar·ca·di·an** (är kā′dē ən) *adj., n.*
ar·cane (är kān′) *adj.* [see ff.] **1.** hidden or secret **2.** esoteric
ar·ca·num (-kā′nəm) *n., pl.* **-na** (-nə), **-nums** [L., hidden < *arcere*, to shut up] a secret; mystery
arch[1] (ärch) *n.* [< OFr. < ML. < L. *arcus*, a bow, arch] **1.** a curved structure, as of masonry, that supports the weight of material over an open space, as in a bridge, doorway, etc. **2.** the form of an arch **3.** anything shaped like an arch [*the arch of the foot*] —*vt.* **1.** to provide with an arch or arches **2.** to form into an arch —*vi.* **1.** to form an arch **2.** to span as an arch

ARCHES (A, semicircular; B, horseshoe; C, pointed)

arch[2] (ärch) *adj.* [< ff.] **1.** main; chief **2.** gaily mischievous; pert —**arch′ly** *adv.* —**arch′ness** *n.*
arch- [< OE. < L. < Gr. *archos*, ruler] *a prefix meaning* main, chief [*archbishop, archduke*]
-arch (ärk; *occas.* ərk) [< Gr. *archos*, ruler] *a suffix meaning* ruler [*matriarch*]
arch. **1.** archaic **2.** archaism **3.** archipelago **4.** architect **5.** architectural **6.** architecture
ar·chae·ol·o·gy (är′kē äl′ə jē) *n.* [< Gr. *archaios*, ancient < *archē*, the beginning + -LOGY] the scientific study of the life and culture of ancient peoples, as by excavation of ancient cities, artifacts, etc. —**ar′chae·o·log′i·cal** (-ə läj′i k'l) *adj.* —**ar′chae·o·log′i·cal·ly** *adv.* —**ar′chae·ol′o·gist** *n.*
ar·cha·ic (är kā′ik) *adj.* [< Gr. < *archaios*, ancient] **1.** ancient **2.** antiquated; old-fashioned **3.** that is now seldom used except in poetry, church ritual, etc., as the word *thou* —**ar·cha′i·cal·ly** *adv.*
ar·cha·ism (är′kē iz'm, -kā-) *n.* **1.** the use or imitation of archaic words, technique, etc. **2.** an archaic word, usage, etc. —**ar′cha·ist** *n.* —**ar′cha·is′tic** *adj.* —**ar′cha·is′ti·cal·ly** *adv.*
arch·an·gel (ärk′ān′j'l) *n.* a chief angel
Arch·an·gel (ärk′ān′j'l) seaport in NW R.S.F.S.R., on the White Sea: pop. 313,000
arch·bish·op (ärch′bish′əp) *n.* a chief bishop, who presides over an archbishopric or archdiocese
arch·bish·op·ric (-bish′ə prik′) *n.* the office, rank, term, or church district of an archbishop
arch·dea·con (ärch′dē′k'n) *n.* [see ARCH- & DEACON] a church official ranking just below a bishop, as in the Anglican Church —**arch′dea′con·ry** *n., pl.* **-ries**
arch·di·o·cese (-dī′ə sis, -sēs′) *n.* the diocese of an archbishop —**arch′di·oc′e·san** (-dī äs′ə sən) *adj.*
arch·du·cal (-dōōk′'l, -dyōōk′'l) *adj.* of an archduke or archduchy
arch·duch·ess (-duch′is) *n.* **1.** the wife or widow of an archduke **2.** a princess of the former Austrian royal family
arch·duch·y (-duch′ē) *n., pl.* **-ies** the territory of an archduke or of an archduchess
arch·duke (-dōōk′, -dyōōk′) *n.* a chief duke, esp. a prince of the former Austrian royal family
ar·che·go·ni·um (är′kə gō′nē əm) *n., pl.* **-ni·a** (-nē ə) [ModL. < Gr. < *archos*, first + *gonos*, offspring] the flask-shaped female reproductive organ in mosses, ferns, etc. —**ar′che·go′ni·al** *adj.*
arch·en·e·my (ärch′en′ə mē) *n., pl.* **-mies** a chief enemy —**the archenemy** Satan
ar·che·ol·o·gy (är′kē äl′ə jē) *n. same as* ARCHAEOLOGY
arch·er (är′chər) *n.* [< ME. & OFr. < VL. < L. < *arcus*, a bow] a person who shoots with bow and arrow; bowman —[A-] the constellation Sagittarius
arch·er·y (är′chər ē) *n.* **1.** the practice, art, or sport of shooting with bow and arrow **2.** an archer's equipment **3.** archers collectively
ar·che·type (är′kə tīp′) *n.* [< L. < Gr. < *archos*, first + *typos*: see TYPE, *n.*] **1.** the original pattern or model of something; prototype **2.** a perfect example of a type or group —**ar′che·typ′al** (-tīp′əl), **ar′che·typ′i·cal** (-tip′i-k'l) *adj.*
arch·fiend (ärch′fēnd′) *n.* a chief fiend —**the archfiend** Satan
Ar·chi·bald (är′chə bôld′) [of Gmc. origin, prob. nobly bold] a masculine name

ar·chi·di·ac·o·nal (är′kə dī ak′ə n'l) ***adj.*** of an archdeacon or archdeaconry —**ar′chi·di·ac′o·nate** (-nit) ***n.***
ar·chi·e·pis·co·pal (är′kē ə pis′kə p'l) ***adj.*** of an archbishop or archbishopric —**ar′chi·e·pis′co·pate** (-pət, -pāt′) ***n.***
Ar·chi·me·des (är′kə mē′dēz) 287?–212 B.C.; Gr. mathematician & inventor —**Ar′chi·me′de·an** (-mē′dē ən, -midē′ən) ***adj.***
ar·chi·pel·a·go (är′kə pel′ə gō′) ***n.,*** *pl.* **-goes′, -gos′** [< It. < MGr. < Gr. *archi-*, chief + *pelagos*, sea] **1.** a sea with many islands **2.** such a group of islands —**ar′chi·pelag′ic** (-pə laj′ik) ***adj.***
ar·chi·tect (är′kə tekt′) ***n.*** [< L. < Gr. < *archi-*, chief + *tektōn*, carpenter] **1.** a person whose profession is designing plans for buildings, bridges, etc. and generally administering construction **2.** any planner, builder, or creator
ar·chi·tec·ton·ic (är′kə tek tän′ik) ***adj.*** [see prec.] **1.** of architecture or architectural methods, etc. **2.** having structure or design like that of architecture —***n.*** *same as* ARCHITECTONICS
ar·chi·tec·ton·ics (-tän′iks) ***n.pl.*** [*with sing. v.*] **1.** the science of architecture **2.** structural design, as of a symphony
ar·chi·tec·ture (är′kə tek′chər) ***n.*** [Fr. < L. *architectura:* see ARCHITECT] **1.** the science, art, or profession of designing and constructing buildings, etc. **2.** a building, or buildings collectively **3.** a style of construction [*modern architecture*] **4.** design and construction **5.** any framework, system, etc. —**ar′chi·tec′tur·al** ***adj.*** —**ar′chi·tec′tur·al·ly** ***adv.***
ar·chi·trave (är′kə trāv′) ***n.*** [Fr. < It. < L. *archi-*, first + *trabs*, a beam] *Archit.* **1.** the lowest part of an entablature, a beam resting directly on the tops of the columns **2.** the molding around a doorway, window, etc.
ar·chives (är′kīvz) ***n.pl.*** [Fr. < L. < Gr. *archeion*, town hall < *archē*, the beginning] **1.** a place where public records, documents, etc. are kept **2.** the public records, documents, etc. kept there —**ar·chi·val** (är′kī′v'l, är kī′v'l) ***adj.***
ar·chi·vist (är′kə vist, är′kī′vist) ***n.*** a person having charge of archives
ar·chon (är′kän′) ***n.*** [< Gr. < *archein*, to be first, rule] **1.** one of the nine chief magistrates of ancient Athens **2.** a ruler
arch·priest (ärch′prēst′) ***n.*** a chief priest
arch·way (ärch′wā′) ***n.*** a passage under an arch
-ar·chy (är kē, ər kē) [< Gr. < *archein*, to rule] *a suffix meaning* a ruling, or that which is ruled [*matriarchy, monarchy*]
arc lamp a lamp in which the light is produced by an arc between electrodes: also **arc light**
arc·tic (ärk′tik, är′-) ***adj.*** [< OFr. < L. < Gr. *arktikos*, lit., of the (constellation of the) Bear (Gr. *arktos*), northern] **1.** of, characteristic of, or near the North Pole or the region around it **2.** very cold —**the Arctic** the region around the North Pole
Arctic Circle [*also* **a- c-**] an imaginary circle parallel to the equator, 66°33′ north of it
Arctic Ocean ocean surrounding the North Pole, north of the Arctic Circle
arc·tics (är′tiks, ärk′-) ***n.pl.*** [< ARCTIC] high, warm, waterproof overshoes, usually with buckles
Arc·tu·rus (ärk toor′əs, -tyoor′-) [L. < Gr. *Arktouros* < *arktos*, a bear + *ouros*, a guard] a giant red star of the first magnitude, the brightest in the constellation Boötes
arc welding the welding of metal parts using the extreme heat of an electric arc
-ard (ərd) [OFr. < MHG. *hart*, bold] *a suffix denoting* one who carries an action too far or has too much of some quality [*sluggard, drunkard*]
ar·dent (är′d'nt) ***adj.*** [< L. prp. of *ardere*, to burn] **1.** warm or intense in feeling; passionate **2.** intensely enthusiastic or devoted; zealous **3.** glowing; radiant **4.** burning; aflame —**ar′den·cy** (-d'n sē) ***n.*** —**ar′dent·ly** ***adv.***
ar·dor (är′dər) ***n.*** [< OFr. < L. < *ardere*, to burn] **1.** emotional warmth; passion **2.** enthusiasm; zeal **3.** intense heat; fire
ar·dour (är′dər) ***n.*** *Brit. sp. of* ARDOR
ar·du·ous (är′joo wəs) ***adj.*** [L. *arduus*, steep] **1.** difficult to do; laborious **2.** using much energy; strenuous **3.** steep; hard to climb —**ar′du·ous·ly** ***adv.*** —**ar′du·ous·ness** ***n.***
are[1] (är; *unstressed* ər) [OE. (Northumbrian) *aron*] *pl. & 2d pers. sing., pres. indic., of* BE
are[2] (er, är) ***n.*** [Fr. < L. *area:* see ff.] a unit of surface measure in the metric system, equal to 100 square meters (119.6 sq. yd.)
ar·e·a (er′ē ə) ***n.*** [L., vacant place, courtyard] **1.** orig., a level surface **2.** a part of the earth's surface; region **3.** the size of a surface, in square units **4.** a yard of a building **5.** a particular part of a house, city, etc. [*dining area, slum area*] **6.** a part of any surface **7.** scope or extent, as of an operation —**ar′e·al** ***adj.***
ar·e·a·way (-wā′) ***n.*** **1.** a sunken yard leading into a cellar **2.** a passage between buildings
a·re·na (ə rē′nə) ***n.*** [L., sand, sandy place, arena] **1.** the central part of an ancient Roman amphitheater, for gladiatorial contests **2.** any place like this **3.** any sphere of struggle
arena theater a theater having a central stage without a proscenium, surrounded by seats
aren't (ärnt) are not: also, occas., a substitute for a contraction of *am not* in questions: see also AIN'T
a·re·o·la (ə rē′ə lə) ***n.,*** *pl.* **-lae′** (-lē′), **-las** [L., dim. of *area:* see AREA] **1.** a small space, as between the veins of a leaf **2.** *Anat.* a small, surrounding area, as the dark ring around a nipple Also **ar·e·ole** (ar′ē ōl′) —**a·re′o·lar** (-lər) ***adj.*** —**a·re′o·late** (-lit) ***adj.*** —**ar·e·o·la·tion** (ar′ē-ə lā′shən, ə rē′ə-) ***n.***
Ar·e·op·a·gus (ar′ē äp′ə gəs) [L. < Gr. < *Areios*, of Ares + *pagos*, hill] a rocky hill northwest of the Acropolis in Athens —***n.*** the high court of justice that met there
Ar·es (er′ēz) *Gr. Myth.* the god of war: identified with the Roman god Mars
ar·ga·li (är′gə lē) ***n.,*** *pl.* **-lis, -li:** see PLURAL, II, D, 1 [Mongol.] a wild sheep of Asia, with large, curved horns

ARGALI (3–4 ft. high at shoulder)

ar·gent (är′jənt) ***n.*** [Fr. < L. *argentum*, silver] [Archaic or Poet.] silver —***adj.*** [Poet.] of silver: also **ar·gen′tal** (-jen′t'l)
ar·gen·tif·er·ous (är′jən tif′ər-əs) ***adj.*** [see prec. & -FEROUS] containing silver, as ore
Ar·gen·ti·na (är′jən tē′nə) country in S S. America: 1,084,120 sq. mi.; pop. 23,983,000; cap. Buenos Aires —**Ar′gen·tine′** (-tēn′, -tīn′), **Ar′gen·tin′e·an** (-tin′ē ən) ***adj., n.***
ar·gen·tine (är′jən tin, -tīn′, -tēn′) ***adj.*** of or like silver —***n.*** silver or a silvery substance
ar·gil·la·ceous (är′jə lā′shəs) ***adj.*** [< L. *argilla*, clay < Gr. < *argos*, white] like or containing clay
Ar·give (är′gīv, -jīv) ***adj., n.*** Greek
Ar·go (är′gō) *Gr. Myth.* the ship on which Jason sailed to find the Golden Fleece
ar·gon (är′gän) ***n.*** [Gr., inert < *a-*, without + *ergon*, work] one of the chemical elements, an inert, odorless, colorless gas forming nearly one percent of the atmosphere: it is used in radio tubes, welding, etc.: symbol, Ar; at. wt., 39.948; at. no., 18
Ar·go·naut (är′gə nôt′) ***n.*** [< L. < Gr. < ARGO + *nautēs*, sailor] *Gr. Myth.* any of the men who sailed with Jason to search for the Golden Fleece
Ar·gonne (är′gän; *Fr.* ȧr gôn′) wooded region in NE France, near the Belgian border
ar·go·sy (är′gə sē) ***n.,*** *pl.* **-sies** [earlier *ragusy* < It. (*nave*) *Ragusea*, (vessel of) Ragusa, ancient Dalmatian port; sp. infl. by ARGO] [Poet.] **1.** a large ship **2.** a fleet of such ships
ar·got (är′gō, -gət) ***n.*** [Fr., orig. (in thieves' jargon), the company of beggars < *argoter*, to beg, prob. < *ergot*, claw] the specialized vocabulary and idioms of a particular group, as the secret jargon of criminals
ar·gue (är′gyoo) ***vi.*** **-gued, -gu·ing** [< OFr. < L. *argutare*, to prattle, freq. of *arguere*, to prove] **1.** to give reasons (*for* or *against* a proposal, etc.) **2.** to have a disagreement; quarrel —***vt.*** **1.** to give reasons for and against; debate **2.** to try to prove by giving reasons; contend **3.** to give evidence of; indicate **4.** to persuade (*into* or *out of* an opinion, etc.) by giving reasons —**ar′gu·a·ble** ***adj.*** —**ar′gu·a·bly** ***adv.*** —**ar′gu·er** ***n.***
ar·gu·fy (är′gyə fī′) ***vt., vi.*** **-fied′, -fy′ing** [< ARGU(E) + -FY] [Colloq. or Dial.] to argue, esp. merely for the sake of arguing
ar·gu·ment (är′gyə mənt) ***n.*** **1.** a reason or reasons offered for or against something **2.** the offering of such reasons; reasoning **3.** discussion in which there is disagreement; dispute; debate **4.** a short statement of subject matter; summary
ar·gu·men·ta·tion (är′gyə men tā′shən) ***n.*** **1.** the process of arguing **2.** debate; discussion
ar·gu·men·ta·tive (-men′tə tiv) ***adj.*** **1.** controversial **2.** apt to argue Also **ar′gu·men′tive** —**ar′gu·men′ta·tive·ly** ***adv.*** —**ar′gu·men′ta·tive·ness** ***n.***
Ar·gus (är′gəs) [L. < Gr. < *argos*, bright] *Gr. Myth.* a giant with a hundred eyes, killed by Hermes —***n.*** an alert watchman
Ar·gus-eyed (-īd′) ***adj.*** keenly observant; vigilant
ar·gyle (är′gīl) ***adj.*** [orig. a clan tartan of *Argyll*, county of Scotland] knitted or woven in a pattern of diamond-shaped figures of different colors —***n.*** [*pl.*] argyle socks
a·ri·a (är′ē ə, er′-) ***n.*** [It. < L. *aer*, AIR] an air or melody in an opera, cantata, or oratorio, esp. for solo voice with instrumental accompaniment

-a·ri·a (er′e ə, ā′rē ə) [ModL. < L. *-arius*] *Biol. a plural suffix used in* names of taxonomic groups

Ar·i·ad·ne (ar′ē ad′nē) *Gr. Myth.* King Minos' daughter, who gave Theseus the thread by which he found his way out of the Labyrinth

Ar·i·an[1] (er′ē ən, ar′-) *n., adj. same as* ARYAN

Ar·i·an[2] (er′ē ən, ar′-) *adj.* of Arius or Arianism —*n.* a believer in Arianism

-ar·i·an (er′ē ən, ar′-) [L. *-arius* + *-anus*] *a suffix denoting:* **1.** age *[octogenarian]* **2.** sect *[Unitarian]* **3.** social belief *[utilitarian]* **4.** occupation *[antiquarian]*

Ar·i·an·ism (er′ē ə niz'm, ar′-) *n.* the doctrines of Arius, who taught that Jesus was not of the same substance as God

ar·id (ar′id, er′-) *adj.* [< L. < *arere,* to be dry] **1.** dry and barren **2.** not interesting; dull —**a·rid·i·ty** (ə rid′ə tē), **ar′id·ness** *n.* —**ar′id·ly** *adv.*

Ar·i·el (er′ē əl, ar′-) in Shakespeare's *The Tempest,* an airy spirit who is Prospero's servant

Ar·i·es (er′ēz, ar′-; -i ēz′) [L., the Ram] **1.** a N constellation **2.** the first sign of the zodiac: see ZODIAC, illus.

a·right (ə rīt′) *adv.* in a right way; correctly

ar·il (ar′il, er′-) *n.* [ModL. *arillus* < ML., dried grape] an additional covering that forms on certain seeds after fertilization —**ar′il·late′** (-ə lāt′) *adj.*

a·ri·o·so (är′ē ō′sō) *adj., adv.* [It. < *aria,* ARIA] like an aria —*n.* an arioso composition

a·rise (ə rīz′) *vi.* **a·rose′, a·ris′en** (-riz′'n), **a·ris′ing** [OE. < *a-,* out + *risan,* to rise] **1.** to get up, as from sleeping or sitting; rise **2.** to move upward; ascend **3.** to come into being; originate **4.** to result or spring (*from* something)

Ar·is·ti·des (ar′ə stī′dēz) 530?–468? B.C.; Athenian general & statesman

ar·is·toc·ra·cy (ar′ə stäk′rə sē) *n., pl.* **-cies** [< L. < Gr. < *aristos,* best + *kratein,* to rule] **1.** orig., government by the best citizens **2.** government by a privileged minority, usually of inherited wealth and social position **3.** a country with such government **4.** a privileged ruling class; nobility **5.** those considered the best in some way

a·ris·to·crat (ə ris′tə krat′, ar′is-) *n.* **1.** a member of the aristocracy; nobleman **2.** a person with the manners, beliefs, etc. of the upper class **3.** a supporter of aristocracy in government

a·ris·to·crat·ic (ə ris′tə krat′ik, ar′is-) *adj.* **1.** of or favoring aristocracy in government **2.** of an aristocracy or upper class **3.** like an aristocrat —**a·ris′to·crat′i·cal·ly** *adv.*

Ar·is·toph·a·nes (ar′ə stäf′ə nēz′) 448?–380? B.C.; Gr. writer of satirical comedies

Ar·is·to·te·li·an (ar′is tə tēl′yən, -tē′lē ən) *adj.* of Aristotle or his philosophy —*n.* **1.** a follower of Aristotle **2.** a person who is empirical or practical in his thinking —**Ar′is·to·te′li·an·ism** *n.*

Ar·is·tot·le (ar′ə stät′'l) 384–322 B.C.; Gr. philosopher, pupil of Plato

a·rith·me·tic (ə rith′mə tik; *for adj.* ar′ith met′ik) *n.* [OFr. < L. < Gr. < *arithmein,* to count < *arithmos,* number] **1.** the science of computing by positive, real numbers, specif. by adding, subtracting, multiplying, and dividing **2.** skill in this science —*adj.* of or using arithmetic: also **ar′ith·met′i·cal** —**ar′ith·met′i·cal·ly** *adv.*

a·rith·me·ti·cian (ar′ith mə tish′ən, ə rith′mə-) *n.* a person skilled in arithmetic

arithmetic mean the average obtained by dividing a sum by the number of its addends

arithmetic progression a sequence of terms each of which, after the first, is derived by adding to the preceding one a constant quantity (Ex.: 5, 9, 13)

A·ri·us (ə rī′əs, er′ē əs) 256?–336 A.D.: Christian theologian of Alexandria: see ARIANISM

Ar·i·zo·na (ar′ə zō′nə) [AmSp. < AmInd. *Arizonac,* "little springs"] State of the SW U.S., on the Mexican border: 113,909 sq. mi.; pop. 2,718,000; cap. Phoenix: abbrev. **Ariz., AZ** —**Ar′i·zo′nan, Ar′i·zo′ni·an** (-nē ən) *adj., n.*

ark (ärk) *n.* [< OE. *earc* < L. *arca* < *arcere,* to enclose] **1.** *Bible* the huge boat in which Noah, his family, and two of every kind of creature survived the Flood: Gen. 6–9 **2.** formerly, a large, flat-bottomed river boat **3.** a place of refuge **4.** *same as* ARK OF THE COVENANT

Ar·kan·sas (är′k'n sô′; *for 2, also* är kan′zəs) [< Fr. < Siouan tribal name] **1.** State of the SC U.S.: 53,104 sq. mi.; pop. 2,286,000; cap. Little Rock: abbrev. **Ark., AR** **2.** river flowing from Colorado southeast into the Mississippi: 1,450 mi. —**Ar·kan′san** (-kan′z'n) *adj., n.*

ark of the covenant *Bible* the chest containing the stone tablets inscribed with the Ten Commandments: Ex. 25:10

Ark·wright (ärk′rīt′), Sir **Richard** 1732–92; Eng. inventor of a cotton-spinning machine

Ar·ling·ton (är′liŋ tən) [orig. after a place name in England] **1.** urban county in Va., near Washington, D.C.: pop. 153,000: site of a national cemetery (**Arlington National Cemetery**) **2.** city in NE Tex.: suburb of Fort Worth: pop. 160,000

arm[1] (ärm) *n.* [OE. *earm*] **1.** an upper limb of the human body **2.** anything like this in structure or function; esp., *a)* the forelimb of a vertebrate animal *b)* any limb of an octopus, starfish, etc. *c)* a branch of a tree **3.** anything commonly in contact with the human arm; esp., *a)* a sleeve *b)* a support for the arm, as on a chair **4.** anything armlike, esp. in being connected with something larger *[*an *arm* of the sea*]* **5.** power to seize, control, etc. *[*the *arm* of the law*]* —**arm in arm** with arms interlocked —**at arm's length** at a distance; aloof —**with open arms** in a warm and friendly way —**arm′less** *adj.* —**arm′like′** *adj.*

arm[2] (ärm) *n.* [< OFr. *armes,* pl. < L. *arma,* implements, weapons] **1.** any weapon: *usually used in pl.*: see also SMALL ARMS **2.** [*pl.*] warfare; fighting **3.** [*pl.*] heraldic insignia: see COAT OF ARMS **4.** any combatant branch of the military forces —*vt.* **1.** to provide with weapons, tools, etc. **2.** to prepare for or against attack **3.** to equip with needed parts —*vi.* to equip oneself with weapons, etc., esp. for war —**bear arms** to serve in the armed forces —**take up arms** **1.** to go to war **2.** to enter a dispute —**to arms!** get ready to fight! —**under arms** equipped with weapons —**up in arms** **1.** prepared to fight **2.** indignant

ar·ma·da (är mä′də, -mā′-) *n.* [Sp. < L. *armata,* fem. pp. of *armare,* to arm < *arma:* see ARM[2]] **1.** *a)* a fleet of warships *b)* [A-] such a fleet sent against England by Spain in 1588 but destroyed: also **Spanish Armada** **2.** a fleet of military aircraft

ar·ma·dil·lo (är′mə dil′ō) *n., pl.* **-los** [Sp., dim. of *armado:* see prec.] any of a family of burrowing, chiefly nocturnal mammals of Texas and Central and South America, having an armorlike covering of bony plates

Ar·ma·ged·don (är′mə ged′'n) *Bible* the place described as the scene of the last, deciding battle between good and evil: Rev. 16:16

ar·ma·ment (är′mə mənt) *n.* [< L. < *armare:* see ARMADA] **1.** [*often pl.*] all the military forces and equipment of a nation **2.** a combat force **3.** all the military equipment of a warship, fortification, etc. **4.** an arming or being armed for war **5.** anything serving to protect or defend

ar·ma·ture (är′mə chər) *n.* [< L. *armatura,* arms, equipment < pp. of *armare:* see ARMADA] **1.** any protective covering; armor **2.** any part of an animal useful for offense or defense **3.** a soft iron bar placed across the poles of a magnet **4.** *a)* the laminated iron core wound around with wire, usually a revolving part, in a generator or motor *b)* the vibrating part in an electric relay, bell, etc. **5.** *Sculpture* a framework for supporting the clay, etc. in modeling

arm·chair (ärm′cher′) *n.* a chair with supports at the sides for one's arms or elbows

armed (ärmd) *adj.* **1.** provided with arms (weapons), armor, etc. **2.** having arms (limbs) of a specified kind *[long-armed]*

armed forces all the military, naval, and air forces of a country or group of countries

Ar·me·ni·a (är mē′nē ə, -mēn′yə) **1.** former kingdom of SW Asia, south of the Caucasus Mts. **2.** republic of the U.S.S.R., including most of this region: 11,500 sq. mi.; pop. 2,300,000; cap. Yerevan: in full, **Armenian Soviet Socialist Republic** —**Ar·me′ni·an** *adj., n.*

arm·ful (ärm′fool) *n., pl.* **-fuls** as much as the arms or one arm can hold

arm·hole (-hōl′) *n.* an opening for the arm in a garment

Ar·min·i·us (är min′ē əs), **Ja·co·bus** (jə kō′bəs) 1560–1609; Du. theologian, whose doctrines (**Ar·min′i·an·ism**) stress man's free will as against Calvinistic predestination —**Ar·min′i·an** *adj., n.*

ar·mi·stice (är′mə stis) *n.* [Fr. < L. *arma,* arms + *sistere,* to cause to stand] a temporary stopping of warfare by mutual agreement; truce

Armistice Day November 11, the anniversary of the armistice of World War I in 1918: see VETERANS DAY

arm·let (ärm′lit) *n.* **1.** a band worn for ornament around the upper arm **2.** a small inlet of the sea

arm·lock (-läk′) *n.* *Wrestling* a hold in which one contestant's arm is locked by the other's arm

ar·moire (är mwär′) *n.* [Fr. < OFr. < L. *armarium,* chest for arms] a large cupboard or clothespress

ar·mor (är′mər) *n.* [< OFr. < L. *armatura:* see ARMATURE] **1.** covering worn to protect the body against weapons **2.** any defensive or protective covering, as the shell of a turtle or the metal plating on warships **3.** armored forces, as tanks **4.** a quality, etc. serving as a defense difficult to penetrate —*vt., vi.* to put armor on

ar·mor·bear·er (-ber′ər) ***n.*** a person who carried the armor or weapons of a warrior
ar·mored (är′mərd) ***adj.*** **1.** covered with armor **2.** equipped with tanks and other armored vehicles
ar·mor·er (är′mər ər) ***n.*** **1.** formerly, one who made or repaired armor **2.** a maker of firearms **3.** *Mil.* an enlisted man in charge of small arms
ar·mo·ri·al (är môr′ē əl) ***adj.*** of coats of arms; heraldic
armor plate a protective covering of steel plates, as on a tank —**ar′mor-plat′ed** ***adj.***
ar·mor·y (är′mər ē) ***n.***, *pl.* **-mor·ies** [< OFr. < *arme:* see ARM²] **1.** an arsenal **2.** a building housing the drill hall and offices of a National Guard unit **3.** a place where firearms are made
ar·mour (är′mər) ***n., vi., vt.*** *Brit. sp. of* ARMOR
arm·pit (ärm′pit′) ***n.*** the hollow under the arm where it joins the shoulder; axilla
arm·rest (-rest′) ***n.*** a support for one's arm
ar·my (är′mē) ***n.***, *pl.* **-mies** [< OFr. < L. *armata:* see ARMADA] **1.** a large, organized body of soldiers for waging war **2.** a military unit of two or more corps **3.** [*often* **A-**] a large organization of persons for a specific cause [*the Salvation Army*] **4.** any large number of persons, animals, etc.
army ant any of certain ants that travel in large groups and devour insects and animals
army worm any of the larvae of certain moths that travel in large groups, ruining crops
Arn·hem (ärn′hem) city on the Rhine, in E Netherlands: pop. 135,000
ar·ni·ca (är′ni kə) ***n.*** [ModL.] **1.** any of a number of plants bearing bright yellow flowers **2.** a preparation made from certain of these plants, formerly used for treating sprains, bruises, etc.
Ar·nold (är′nəld) [< G. < Gmc. bases *aran*, eagle + *wald*, power] **1.** a masculine name **2. Benedict,** 1741–1801; Am. Revolutionary general who became a traitor **3. Matthew,** 1822–88; Eng. poet, essayist, & critic
a·roint (ə roint′) ***vt.*** [< ?] [Obs.] begone!: used in the imperative, usually followed by *thee*
a·ro·ma (ə rō′mə) ***n.*** [LL. < Gr. *arōma*, sweet spice] **1.** a pleasant, often spicy odor; fragrance, as of a plant, cooking, etc. **2.** a characteristic quality or atmosphere
ar·o·mat·ic (ar′ə mat′ik) ***adj.*** **1.** of or having an aroma **2.** *Chem.* containing one or more benzene rings in the molecule —***n.*** an aromatic plant, substance, or chemical —**ar′o·mat′i·cal·ly** ***adv.***
a·ro·ma·tize (ə rō′mə tīz′) ***vt.*** **-tized′, -tiz′ing** to make aromatic —**a·ro′ma·ti·za′tion** ***n.***
a·rose (ə rōz′) *pt. of* ARISE
a·round (ə round′) ***adv.*** [ME. < *a-*, on + *round*] **1.** round; esp., *a*) in a circle; along a circular course *b*) in or through a course or circuit *c*) in every direction *d*) in circumference *e*) in or to the opposite direction, belief, etc. *f*) in various places *g*) in sequence [*his turn came around*] *h*) throughout **2.** [Colloq.] nearby [*stay around*] **3.** [Colloq.] to a (specified) place [*come around to see us*] —***prep.*** **1.** round; esp., *a*) so as to encircle or envelop *b*) on the border of *c*) on all sides of *d*) in various places in or on *e*) so as to rotate about (a center) **2.** close to; about [*around 1890*] —***adj.*** [*used only in the predicate*] **1.** on the move; about [*he's up and around now*] **2.** existing [*when dinosaurs were around*] Cf. ROUND —**have been around** [Colloq.] to have had wide experience; be sophisticated See also phrases under BRING, COME, GET, etc.
a·rouse (ə rouz′) ***vt.*** **a·roused′, a·rous′ing** [A-² (sense 1) + ROUSE] **1.** to awaken, as from sleep **2.** to stir, as to action **3.** to bring forth or work up (some action or feeling); excite —***vi.*** to become aroused —**a·rous′al** ***n.***
ar·peg·gio (är pej′ō, -pej′ē ō) ***n.***, *pl.* **-gios** [It. < *arpeggiare*, to play on a harp < *arpa*, a harp] **1.** the playing of the notes of a chord in quick succession instead of simultaneously **2.** a chord so played
ar·que·bus (är′kwə bəs) ***n.*** *same as* HARQUEBUS
arr. 1. arranged **2.** arrival
ar·rack (ar′ək) ***n.*** [< Fr. < Ar. *ʿaraq*, sweat, liquor] in the Orient, strong alcoholic drink, esp. that made from rice, molasses, or coconut milk
ar·raign (ə rān′) ***vt.*** [< OFr. < ML. < L. *ad*, to + *ratio*, reason] **1.** to bring before a law court to hear and answer charges **2.** to call to account; accuse —**ar·raign′er** ***n.*** —**ar·raign′ment** ***n.***
ar·range (ə rānj′) ***vt.*** **-ranged′, -rang′ing** [< OFr. < *a-*, to + *renc*, rank: see RANGE] **1.** to put in the correct or suitable order **2.** to classify **3.** to prepare or plan **4.** to settle or adjust (matters) **5.** *Music* to adapt (a composition) to other instruments or voices than those for which it was written, or to the style of a certain band or orchestra —***vi.*** **1.** to come to an agreement (*with* a person, *about* a thing) **2.** to make plans **3.** *Music* to write arrangements —**ar·range′a·ble** ***adj.*** —**ar·rang′er** ***n.***
ar·range·ment (-mənt) ***n.*** **1.** an arranging or being arranged **2.** the way in which something is arranged **3.** something made by arranging parts in a particular way **4.** [*usually pl.*] a plan or preparation [*arrangements for the party*] **5.** a settlement or adjustment **6.** *Music* an adaptation of a composition for other instruments, voices, etc.
ar·rant (ar′ənt) ***adj.*** [var. of ERRANT] that is plainly such; out-and-out [*an arrant fool*] —**ar′rant·ly** ***adv.***
ar·ras (ar′əs) ***n.*** [after *Arras*, city in France, where it was made] **1.** an elaborate kind of tapestry **2.** a wall hanging, esp. of tapestry
ar·ray (ə rā′) ***vt.*** [< OFr. < ML. *arredare*, to put in order < *ad-*, to + Gmc. base *raid-*, order] **1.** to put in the proper order; marshal (troops, etc.) **2.** to dress in finery —***n.*** **1.** an orderly grouping, esp. of troops **2.** a military force so grouped **3.** an impressive display of persons or things **4.** fine clothes —**ar·ray′al** ***n.*** —**ar·ray′er** ***n.***
ar·rear·age (ə rir′ij) ***n.*** arrears or the state of being in arrears
ar·rears (ə rirz′) ***n.pl.*** [< OFr. *ariere*, backward < VL. < L. *ad*, to + *retro*, behind] **1.** overdue debts **2.** unfinished work, etc. —**in arrears** (or **arrear**) behind in paying a debt, in one's work, etc.
ar·rest (ə rest′) ***vt.*** [< OFr. < L. *ad-*, to + *restare*, to stop] **1.** to stop or check **2.** to seize or take into custody by authority of the law **3.** to catch and keep (one's attention, etc.) —***n.*** an arresting or being arrested —**under arrest** in legal custody, as of the police —**ar·rest′er, ar·res′tor** ***n.***
ar·rest·ing (-iŋ) ***adj.*** attracting attention; interesting; striking —**ar·rest′ing·ly** ***adv.***
Ar·rhe·ni·us (ä rā′nē oos), **Svan·te Au·gust** (svän′te ou′goost) 1859–1927; Swed. chemist
ar·rhyth·mi·a (ə rith′mē ə) ***n.*** [ModL. < Gr. < *a-*, without + *rhythmos*, measure] any irregularity in the rhythm of the heart's beating —**ar·rhyth′mic, ar·rhyth′mi·cal** ***adj.*** —**ar·rhyth′mi·cal·ly** ***adv.***
ar·ris (ar′əs) ***n.*** [< OFr. < L. *arista*, awn of grain] the edge made by two surfaces coming together at an angle, as in a molding
ar·riv·al (ə rī′v'l) ***n.*** **1.** the act of arriving **2.** a person or thing that arrives or has arrived
ar·rive (ə rīv′) ***vi.*** **-rived′, -riv′ing** [< OFr. < L. *ad-*, to + *ripa*, shore] **1.** to reach one's destination; come to a place **2.** to come [*the time has arrived*] **3.** to attain fame, etc. —**arrive at 1.** to reach by traveling **2.** to reach by thinking, etc.
‡ar·ri·ve·der·ci (ä rē′ve der′chē) ***interj.*** [It.] until we meet again; goodbye
‡ar·ri·viste (à rē vēst′) ***n.*** [Fr. < *arriver* (see ARRIVE) + *-iste*, -IST] *same as* PARVENU
ar·ro·gance (ar′ə gəns) ***n.*** [see ff.] overbearing pride or self-importance: also **ar′ro·gan·cy**
ar·ro·gant (-gənt) ***adj.*** [OFr. < L. prp. of *arrogare*, ARROGATE] full of or due to arrogance; overbearing; haughty —**ar′ro·gant·ly** ***adv.***
ar·ro·gate (-gāt′) ***vt.*** **-gat′ed, -gat′ing** [< L. pp. of *arrogare* < *ad-*, for + *rogare*, to ask] **1.** to claim or seize without right **2.** to ascribe or attribute without reason —**ar′ro·ga′tion** ***n.***
‡ar·ron·disse·ment (à rōn dēs män′) ***n.***, *pl.* **-ments′** (-män′) [Fr. < *arrondir*, to make round] in France, **1.** the largest subdivision of a department **2.** a municipal subdivision, as of Paris
ar·row (ar′ō) ***n.*** [OE. *earh, arwe*] **1.** a slender shaft, usually pointed at one end and feathered at the other, for shooting from a bow **2.** anything like an arrow in form, etc. **3.** a sign (←) used to indicate direction —**ar′row·y** ***adj.***
ar·row·head (-hed′) ***n.*** **1.** the pointed tip of an arrow **2.** anything shaped like an arrowhead, as an indicating mark **3.** a marsh plant with arrow-shaped leaves and small, white flowers
ar·row·root (-rōōt′, -root′) ***n.*** [from its use as an antidote for poisoned arrows] **1.** a tropical American plant with starchy roots **2.** the edible starch made from its roots
ar·roy·o (ə roi′ō) ***n.***, *pl.* **-os** [Sp. < L. *arrugia*, mine shaft] [Southwest] **1.** a dry gully **2.** a rivulet or stream
ar·se·nal (är′s'n əl, -snəl) ***n.*** [It. *arsenale*, a dock < Ar. *dār* (*eṣ*) *ṣināʿa*, wharf, workshop] **1.** a place for making or storing weapons and other munitions **2.** a store or collection [*an arsenal of facts used in a debate*]
ar·se·nate (är′s'n āt′, -it) ***n.*** [ARSEN(IC) + -ATE²] a salt or ester of arsenic acid
ar·se·nic (är′s'n ik, -snik; *for adj.* är sen′ik) ***n.*** [OFr. < L. < Gr. *arsenikon*, a yellow sulfide of arsenic; ult. < Per. *zar*, gold] **1.** a silvery-white, brittle, very poisonous chemical element, compounds of which are used in making insecticides, medicines, etc.: symbol, As; at. wt., 74.9216; at. no., 33 **2.** loosely, arsenic trioxide, a poisonous, tasteless, white powder, used to exterminate insects and rodents —***adj.*** of or containing arsenic, esp. with a valence of five
arsenic acid a white, poisonous, crystalline compound, H_3AsO_4, used in insecticides, etc.

ar·sen·i·cal (är sen′ə k'l) ***adj.*** of or containing arsenic —***n.*** an arsenical drug, insecticide, etc.

ar·se·ni·ous (är sē′nē əs) ***adj.*** of or containing arsenic, esp. with a valence of three: also **ar·se·nous** (är′s'n əs)

‡**ars gra·ti·a ar·tis** (ärz′ grā′shē ə är′tis; grä′tē ə) [L.] art for art's sake

ar·son (är′s'n) ***n.*** [OFr. < L. pp. of *ardere*, to burn] the crime of purposely setting fire to a building or property —**ar′son·ist** ***n.***

art[1] (ärt) ***n.*** [< OFr. < L. *ars* (gen. *artis*), art] **1.** human creativity **2.** skill **3.** any specific skill or its application **4.** any craft or profession, or its principles [*the cobbler's art*] **5.** a making or doing of things that have form and beauty; creative work: see also FINE ART **6.** any branch of creative work, esp. painting, drawing, sculpture, etc. **7.** products of creative work; paintings, statues, etc. **8.** a branch of learning; specif., [*pl.*] the liberal arts as distinguished from the sciences **9.** cunning **10.** trick; wile: *usually used in pl.* —***adj.*** of or for works of art or artists

art[2] (ärt) *archaic 2d pers. sing., pres. indic., of* BE: *used with* thou

-art (ərt) *same as* -ARD

art. **1.** article **2.** artificial

ar·te·fact (är′tə fakt′) ***n.*** *var. sp. of* ARTIFACT

Ar·te·mis (är′tə mis) *Gr. Myth.* the goddess of the moon and hunting, Apollo's twin sister: identified with the Roman goddess Diana

ar·te·ri·al (är tir′ē əl) ***adj.*** **1.** of or like an artery or arteries **2.** designating or of the bright-red, oxygenated blood in the arteries **3.** of or being a main road with many branches —**ar·te′ri·al·ly** ***adv.***

ar·te·ri·al·ize (-īz′) ***vt.*** **-ized′, -iz′ing** to change (venous blood) into arterial blood by oxygenation —**ar·te′ri·al·i·za′tion** ***n.***

ar·te·ri·ole (är tir′ē ōl′) ***n.*** a small artery

ar·te·ri·o·scle·ro·sis (är tir′ē ō sklə rō′sis) ***n.*** [see ff. & SCLEROSIS] a thickening, and loss of elasticity, of the walls of the arteries, as in old age —**ar·te′ri·o·scle·rot′ic** (-rät′ik) ***adj.***

ar·ter·y (är′tər ē) ***n.,*** *pl.* **-ter·ies** [< L. < Gr.; prob. < *aeirein*, to raise] **1.** any of the system of tubes carrying blood from the heart to all parts of the body: cf. VEIN **2.** a main road or channel

ar·te·sian well (är tē′zhən) [Fr. *artésien*, lit., of Artois, former Fr. province] a well in which ground water is forced up by hydrostatic pressure

ARTESIAN WELL

art·ful (ärt′fəl) ***adj.*** **1.** skillful or clever, esp. in achieving a purpose **2.** sly or cunning **3.** using or showing considerable art or skill **4.** artificial; imitative —**art′ful·ly** ***adv.*** —**art′ful·ness** ***n.***

ar·thral·gia (är thral′jə) ***n.*** [see ff. & -ALGIA] neuralgic pain in a joint or joints

ar·thri·tis (är thrīt′əs) ***n.*** [Gr. < *arthron*, a joint + -ITIS] inflammation of a joint or joints —**ar·thrit′ic** (-thrit′ik) ***adj.*** —**ar·thrit′i·cal·ly** ***adv.***

ar·thro·pod (är′thrə päd′) ***n.*** [< Gr. *arthron*, a joint + -POD] any member of a large group of invertebrate animals with jointed legs and a segmented body, as insects, crustaceans, arachnids, etc. —**ar·throp·o·dal** (är thräp′ə d'l), **ar·throp′o·dous** (-dəs) ***adj.***

Ar·thur (är′thər) [ML. *Arthurus*] **1.** a masculine name: dim. *Art* **2.** a legendary 6th-cent. king of Britain who led the knights of the Round Table **3. Chester Alan,** 1830–86; 21st president of the U.S. (1881–85) —**Ar·thu′ri·an** (-thoor′ē ən) ***adj.***

ar·ti·choke (är′tə chōk′) ***n.*** [< It. < Sp. < Ar. *al-ḥaršūf*] **1.** a thistlelike plant **2.** its flower head, cooked as a vegetable **3.** *short for* JERUSALEM ARTICHOKE

ar·ti·cle (är′ti k'l) ***n.*** [OFr. < L. *articulus*, dim. of *artus*, a joint] **1.** any of the sections of a written document, as of a treaty **2.** a complete piece of writing that is part of a newspaper, magazine, or book **3.** a separate item [*an article of luggage*] **4.** a commodity **5.** *Gram.* any one of the words *a*, *an*, or *the* (and their equivalents in other languages), used as adjectives —***vt.*** **-cled, -cling** to bind by the articles of an agreement or contract

ar·tic·u·lar (är tik′yə lər) ***adj.*** [< L. < *articulus:* see prec.] of a joint or joints [*an articular inflammation*]

ar·tic·u·late (är tik′yə lit; *for v.* -lāt′) ***adj.*** [< L. pp. of *articulare*, to disjoint < *articulus:* see ARTICLE] **1.** jointed: usually **ar·tic′u·lat′ed** **2.** made up of distinct syllables or words that have meaning **3.** able to speak **4.** expressing oneself easily and clearly **5.** well formulated —***vt.*** **-lat′ed, -lat′ing** **1.** to put together by joints **2.** to correlate **3.** to pronounce carefully; enunciate **4.** to express clearly —***vi.*** **1.** to speak distinctly **2.** to be jointed —**ar·tic′u·late·ly** ***adv.*** —**ar·tic′u·late·ness** ***n.*** —**ar·tic′u·la′tive** ***adj.*** —**ar·tic′u·la′tor** ***n.***

ar·tic·u·la·tion (är tik′yə lā′shən) ***n.*** **1.** a jointing or being jointed **2.** the way in which parts are joined together **3.** enunciation **4.** a spoken sound **5.** a joint between bones or similar parts **6.** *Bot.* a node, or a space between two nodes

ar·ti·fact (är′tə fakt′) ***n.*** [< L. *ars* (gen. *artis*), ART[1] + *factum*, thing made (see FACT)] any object made by human work; esp., a primitive tool, etc.

ar·ti·fice (är′tə fis) ***n.*** [Fr. < L. < *ars*, ART[1] + *facere*, to make] **1.** skill or ingenuity **2.** trickery or craft **3.** a sly or artful trick

ar·tif·i·cer (är tif′ə sər) ***n.*** [see prec. & -ER] **1.** a skilled craftsman **2.** an inventor **3.** a military mechanic

ar·ti·fi·cial (är′tə fish′əl) ***adj.*** [< OFr. < L.: see ARTIFICE] **1.** made by human work or art; not natural **2.** made in imitation of something natural; simulated [*artificial teeth*] **3.** unnatural in an affected way [*an artificial smile*] —**ar′ti·fi′ci·al′i·ty** (-fish′ē al′ə tē) ***n.,*** *pl.* **-ties** —**ar′ti·fi′cial·ly** ***adv.*** —**ar′ti·fi′cial·ness** ***n.***

artificial insemination the impregnation of a female by the introduction of semen without sexual intercourse

artificial respiration the artificial maintenance of breathing, as by forcing breath into the mouth

ar·til·ler·y (är til′ər ē) ***n.*** [< OFr. < Pr. *artilla*, fortifications; ult. < L. *ars*, ART[1]] **1.** heavy mounted guns, as cannon or missile launchers **2.** the science of guns; gunnery **3.** [Slang] small arms: a facetious usage —**the artillery** the military branch specializing in the use of artillery —**ar·til′ler·ist, ar·til′ler·y·man** (-mən) ***n.,*** *pl.* **-men**

ar·ti·san (är′tə z'n, -s'n) ***n.*** [Fr. < It.; ult. < L. *ars*, ART[1]] a skilled workman; craftsman

art·ist (är′tist) ***n.*** [ML. *artista*, craftsman < L. *ars*, ART[1]] **1.** a person who is skilled in any of the fine arts, esp. in painting, sculpture, etc. **2.** a person who does anything very well, with a feeling for form, etc. **3.** *same as* ARTISTE

ar·tiste (är tēst′) ***n.*** [Fr.] **1.** a professional in any of the performing arts **2.** a person very skilled in his work: often humorous or facetious

ar·tis·tic (är tis′tik) ***adj.*** **1.** of art or artists **2.** done skillfully and tastefully **3.** keenly sensitive to aesthetic values —**ar·tis′ti·cal·ly** ***adv.***

art·ist·ry (är′tis trē) ***n.*** artistic work or skill

art·less (ärt′lis) ***adj.*** **1.** lacking skill or art **2.** uncultured; ignorant **3.** simple; natural **4.** without guile or deceit; ingenuous —**art′less·ly** ***adv.*** —**art′less·ness** ***n.***

‡**art nou·veau** (ȧr n$\overline{oo}$ vō′) [Fr., lit., new art] an art movement of the late 19th and early 20th cent., emphasizing stylized curvilinear designs

art·sy-craft·sy (ärt′sē kraft′sē) ***adj.*** [Colloq.] of arts and crafts: usually a disparaging term connoting faddishness, amateurishness, etc.

art·y (är′tē) ***adj.*** **art′i·er, art′i·est** [Colloq.] showing artistic pretensions —**art′i·ness** ***n.***

ar·um (er′əm, ar′-) ***n.*** [L. < Gr. *aron*, the wake robin] any of a family of plants bearing small flowers on a fleshy spike enclosed by a hoodlike leaf, as the jack-in-the-pulpit

A.R.V. American (Standard) Revised Version (of the Bible), printed in 1901

-ar·y (er′ē; *chiefly Brit.* ər i) [L. *-arius, -aria, -arium*] **1.** *a suffix meaning: a)* related to; connected with [*auxiliary*] *b)* a person or thing connected with [*missionary*] *c)* a place for [*granary*] **2.** [L. *-aris*] *a suffix meaning* like; of the same kind [*military*]

Ar·y·an (er′ē ən, ar′-) ***adj.*** [< Sans. *ārya*, noble, lord (used as a tribal name)] **1.** *earlier term for* INDO-EUROPEAN **2.** *same as* INDO-IRANIAN **3.** of the Aryans —***n.*** **1.** formerly, the hypothetical language from which all Indo-European languages are supposed to be descended **2.** a person belonging to, or supposed to be a descendant of, the prehistoric peoples who spoke this language **3.** loosely, as in Nazi usage, a non-Jewish Caucasoid, a Nordic, etc.

as[1] (az; *unstressed* əz) ***adv.*** [weakened form of ALSO < OE. *ealswa*, quite so, just as: see ALSO] **1.** to the same amount or degree; equally [*he's just as happy at home*] **2.** for instance; thus [*a card game, as bridge*] **3.** when related in a specified way [*romanticism as contrasted with classicism*] —***conj.*** **1.** to the same amount or degree that [*it flew straight as an arrow*] **2.** in the same manner that [*do as he does*] **3.** at the same time that [*she wept as she spoke*] **4.** because [*as you object, we won't go*] **5.** that the consequence is [*a question so obvious as to need no reply*] **6.** though [*full as he was, he kept eating*] **7.** [Colloq.] that

[I don't know *as* I should] —*pron.* **1.** a fact that [he is tired, *as* anyone can see] **2.** that (preceded by *such* or *the same*) [the same color *as* yours (is)] —*prep.* **1.** in the role, function, capacity, or sense of [he poses *as* a friend] **2.** like [the same *as* mine] —**as . . . as** a correlative construction used to indicate the equality or sameness of two things [*as* large *as*, *as* many *as*, etc.] —**as for** with reference to; concerning —**as if** (or **though**) **1.** as it (or one) would if **2.** that [it seems *as if* she's never home] —**as is** [Colloq.] just as it is; without any changes: said of damaged goods for sale —**as it were** as if it were so; so to speak —**as of** up to, on, or from (a specified time) —**as to** **1.** concerning **2.** as if to

as² (as) *n., pl.* **as′ses** (-əz, -ēz) [L.] **1.** an ancient Roman unit of weight equal to about twelve ounces **2.** an ancient Roman coin of copper alloy

As *Chem.* arsenic

AS., A.S., A.-S. Anglo-Saxon

as·a·fet·i·da, as·a·foet·i·da (as′ə fet′ə də) *n.* [ML. *asa* < Per. *āzā*, gum + L *f(o)etida*, FETID] a bad-smelling gum resin obtained from various Asiatic plants of the parsley family, formerly used in folk medicine to repel disease

as·bes·tos, as·bes·tus (as bes′təs, az-) *n.* [< L. < Gr. *asbestos*, inextinguishable < *a-*, not + *sbennynai*, to extinguish] a grayish mineral, esp. an amphibole, that separates into long, threadlike fibers: some varieties resist heat and chemicals and are used in fireproof curtains, roofing, etc.

as·ca·rid (as′kə rid) *n.* [< Gr. *askaris*] a roundworm that is a parasite in mammals

as·cend (ə send′) *vi.* [< OFr. < L. < *ad-*, to + *scandere*, to climb] **1.** to go up; move upward; rise **2.** to slope or lead upward —*vt.* **1.** to move upward along; climb **2.** to succeed to (a throne) —**as·cend′a·ble, as·cend′i·ble** *adj.* —**as·cend′er** *n.*

as·cend·an·cy, as·cend·en·cy (-ən sē) *n.* a position of control or power; supremacy; domination: also **as·cend′ance, as·cend′ence**

as·cend·ant, as·cend·ent (-ənt) *adj.* **1.** rising; ascending **2.** in control; dominant; superior —*n.* **1.** a dominating position; ascendancy **2.** *Astrol.* the sign of the zodiac just above the eastern horizon at any given moment —**in the ascendant** at or approaching the height of power, fame, etc.

as·cen·sion (ə sen′shən) *n.* **1.** an ascending; ascent **2.** [A-] *same as* ASCENSION DAY —**the Ascension** *Bible* the bodily ascent of Jesus into heaven on the fortieth day after the Resurrection: Acts 1:9 —**as·cen′sion·al** *adj.*

Ascension Day the fortieth day after Easter, celebrating the Ascension

as·cent (ə sent′) *n.* **1.** an ascending or rising **2.** an advancement, as in rank, fame, etc. **3.** *a)* an upward slope *b)* the degree of such slope **4.** a going back in time or genealogy

as·cer·tain (as′ər tān′) *vt.* [< OFr. < *a-*, to + *certain*, CERTAIN] to find out with certainty —**as′cer·tain′a·ble** *adj.* —**as′cer·tain′ment** *n.*

as·cet·ic (ə set′ik) *adj.* [< Gr. < *askein*, to train the body] of or characteristic of ascetics or their way of life; self-denying; austere: also **as·cet′i·cal** —*n.* a person who leads a life of contemplation and rigorous self-denial, esp. for religious purposes —**as·cet′i·cal·ly** *adv.* —**as·cet′i·cism** *n.*

as·cid·i·an (ə sid′ē ən) *n.* [< Gr. *askidion:* see ff.] any of a class of sea animals that are sac-shaped and have a tough outer covering

as·cid·i·um (-əm) *n., pl.* **-i·a** (-ə) [ModL. < Gr. dim. of *askos*, a bag, bladder] *Bot.* a pitcherlike leaf or structure, as of the pitcher plant

As·cle·pi·us (as klē′pē əs) *Gr. Myth.* the god of healing and medicine: identified with the Roman god Aesculapius

as·co·my·cete (as′kə mī sēt′) *n.* [< Gr. *askos*, bladder + *mykēs*, fungus] any of a class of fungi, including the mildews, yeasts, etc., that develop spores in a saclike structure —**as′co·my·ce′tous** *adj.*

a·scor·bic acid (ə skôr′bik) [A-² (sense 3) + SCORB(UTIC) + -IC] a water-soluble vitamin, $C_6H_8O_6$, occurring in citrus fruits, tomatoes, etc.: it prevents and cures scurvy; vitamin C

as·cot (as′kət, -kät′) *n.* **1.** [A-] an annual horse-racing meet at Ascot Heath, Berkshire, England **2.** a necktie or scarf with very broad ends hanging from the knot, one upon the other

ASCOT

as·cribe (ə skrīb′) *vt.* **-cribed′, -crib′ing** [< OFr. < L. < *ad-*, to + *scribere*, to write] **1.** to put down (*to* a supposed cause); attribute **2.** to regard as belonging (*to*) or coming from someone [poems *ascribed* to Homer] —**as·crib′a·ble** *adj.*

as·crip·tion (ə skrip′shən) *n.* **1.** the act of ascribing **2.** a statement that ascribes

-ase (ās, āz) [< (DIAST)ASE] *a suffix denoting* an enzyme, esp. one of vegetable origin [*amylase*]

a·sep·sis (ā sep′sis, ə-) *n.* **1.** the condition of being aseptic **2.** aseptic treatment or technique

a·sep·tic (-tik) *adj.* not septic; free from microorganisms that cause disease —**a·sep′ti·cal·ly** *adv.*

a·sex·u·al (ā sek′shoo wəl) *adj.* **1.** having no sex or sexual organs; sexless **2.** of reproduction without the union of male and female germ cells —**a·sex′u·al′i·ty** (-wal′ə tē) *n.* —**a·sex′u·al·ly** *adv.*

As·gard (as′gärd, az′-) *Norse Myth.* the home of the gods and slain heroes: also **As′garth** (-gär*th*)

ash¹ (ash) *n.* [OE. *æsce*] **1.** the white or grayish powder left after something has been thoroughly burned **2.** fine, volcanic lava **3.** the silvery-gray color of wood ash See also ASHES

ash² (ash) *n.* [OE. *æsc*] **1.** a timber and shade tree of the olive family, having tough, elastic, straight-grained wood **2.** the wood

a·shamed (ə shāmd′) *adj.* **1.** feeling shame **2.** feeling humiliated or embarrassed **3.** reluctant because fearing shame beforehand —**a·sham·ed·ly** (ə shā′mid lē) *adv.*

A·shan·ti (ə shän′tē, -shan′-) region in C Ghana, orig. a native kingdom —*n.* **1.** *pl.* **-ti, -tis** any member of the W African people of Ashanti **2.** their language

ash·can (ash′kan′) *n.* a can for ashes and trash

ash·en¹ (ash′ən) *adj.* **1.** of ashes **2.** like ashes, esp. in color; pale; pallid

ash·en² (ash′ən) *adj.* [Archaic] of the ash tree or its wood

ash·es (ash′iz) *n.pl.* **1.** the unburned particles and grayish powder left after a thing has been burned **2.** human remains, esp. after cremation **3.** the ruins or remains of something destroyed

Ashe·ville (ash′vil) [after S. *Ashe* (1725–1813), governor of N.C.] city in W N.C.: pop. 58,000

Ash·ke·naz·im (ash′kə naz′im, äsh′kə näz′im) *n.pl., sing.* **-naz′, -naz′i** (-ē) [Heb.: cf. Jer. 51:27] the Jews who settled in C and N Europe after the Diaspora, or their descendants: cf. SEPHARDIM —**Ash′ke·naz′ic** *adj.*

ash·lar, ash·ler (ash′lər) *n.* [< OFr. < L. *assis*, board] **1.** a square, hewn stone used in building **2.** a thin, dressed, square stone used for facing masonry walls **3.** masonry made of either kind of ashlar

a·shore (ə shôr′) *adv., adj.* **1.** to or on the shore **2.** to or on land

ash·ram (ash′rəm) *n.* [< Sans. < *ā*, toward + *śrama*, fatigue, penance] a secluded place for a community of Hindus leading a life of religious meditation

Ash·to·reth (ash′tə reth′) the ancient Phoenician and Syrian goddess of love and fertility: identified with ASTARTE

ash·tray (ash′trā′) *n.* a container for smokers' tobacco ashes: also **ash tray**

A·shur (ä′shoor) *Assyr. Myth.* the chief deity, god of war and empire

Ash Wednesday the first day of Lent: from the putting of ashes on the forehead in penitence

ash·y (ash′ē) *adj.* **ash′i·er, ash′i·est** **1.** of, like, or covered with ashes **2.** of ash color; pale

A·sia (ā′zhə, -shə) largest continent, situated in the Eastern Hemisphere and separated from N Europe by the Ural Mountains: 16,900,000 sq. mi.; pop. 2,035,000,000 —**A′sian, A·si·at·ic** (ā′zhē at′ik) *adj., n.*

Asia Minor large peninsula in W Asia, between the Black Sea and the Mediterranean

Asian influenza a widespread influenza caused by a strain of virus first isolated in Singapore in 1957: also **Asian flu**

Asiatic cholera an acute, infectious disease characterized by severe diarrhea, cramps, and loss of water from the body

a·side (ə sīd′) *adv.* **1.** on or to one side **2.** away; in reserve [put this *aside* for me] **3.** out of the way; out of one's mind **4.** apart; notwithstanding [joking *aside*, I mean it] —*n.* an actor's words spoken as to the audience and supposedly not heard by the other actors —**aside from** **1.** with the exception of **2.** apart from; besides

as·i·nine (as′ə nīn′) *adj.* [< L. < *asinus*, ass] like an ass; esp., having qualities thought of as asslike; stupid, silly, obstinate, etc. —**as′i·nine′ly** *adv.* —**as′i·nin′i·ty** (-nin′ə tē) *n., pl.* **-ties**

ask (ask) *vt.* [OE. *ascian*] **1.** to use words in seeking the answer to (a question); inquire about **2.** to put a question to (a person); inquire of **3.** to request; solicit; beg **4.** to demand or expect as a price **5.** to be in need of or call for (a thing) **6.** to invite —*vi.* **1.** to make a request (*for*) **2.** to inquire (*about, after,* or *for*) **3.** to behave so as to appear to be looking (*for* trouble, etc.) —**ask′er** *n.* —**ask′ing** *n.*

a·skance (ə skans′) *adv.* [< ME. *askoin* < *a-*, on + *skwyn* < Du. *schuin*, sidewise] **1.** with a sidewise glance; obliquely **2.** with suspicion, disapproval, etc. Also [Archaic or Poet.] **a·skant′**

a·skew (ə skyoo′) *adv.* to one side; awry; crookedly —*adj.* on one side; awry

asking price the price asked by a seller, esp. when he will accept less after bargaining

a·slant (ə slant′) ***adv.*** on a slant; slantingly —***prep.*** on a slant across —***adj.*** slanting
a·sleep (ə slēp′) ***adj.*** **1.** in a condition of sleep; sleeping **2.** inactive; dull; sluggish **3.** numb except for a prickly feeling [my arm is *asleep*] **4.** dead —***adv.*** into a sleeping or inactive condition
a·slope (ə slōp′) ***adv., adj.*** at a slant
As·ma·ra (äs mä′rä) capital of Eritrea, in N Ethiopia: pop. 146,000
a·so·cial (ā sō′shəl) ***adj.*** **1.** not social; characterized by withdrawal from others **2.** selfish
asp (asp) ***n.*** [< OFr. < L. < Gr. *aspis*] any of several small, poisonous snakes of Africa and Europe, as the horned viper
as·par·a·gus (ə spar′ə gəs) ***n.*** [L. < Gr. *asparagos*, a sprout] **1.** a plant of the lily family, with small, scalelike leaves and many needlelike branches **2.** the tender shoots of this plant, eaten as a cooked vegetable
a·spar·kle (ə spär′k'l) ***adj.*** sparkling
A.S.P.C.A. American Society for the Prevention of Cruelty to Animals
as·pect (as′pekt) ***n.*** [< L. pp. of *aspicere* < *ad-*, to, at + *specere*, to look] **1.** the way a person or thing appears or looks to another; appearance **2.** the appearance of an idea, problem, etc. regarded from a specific viewpoint **3.** a facing in a given direction **4.** a side facing in a given direction [the eastern *aspect* of the house] **5.** *Astrol.* the position of stars in relation to each other or to the observer, as it supposedly influences human affairs
as·pen (as′pən) ***n.*** [OE. *æspe*] a kind of poplar tree with leaves that flutter in the least breeze —***adj.*** of or like an aspen; esp., fluttering; trembling
as·per·i·ty (as per′ə tē) ***n., pl.*** **-ties** [ME. & OFr. < L. < *asper*, rough] **1.** roughness or harshness, as of surface, sound, etc. **2.** sharpness of temper
as·perse (ə spurs′) ***vt.*** **-persed′, -pers′ing** [< L. pp. of *aspergere* < *ad-*, to + *spargere*, to sprinkle] to spread false or damaging rumors about; slander —**as·pers′er** ***n.***
as·per·sion (ə spur′zhən, -shən) ***n.*** **1.** a defaming **2.** a damaging or disparaging remark; slander
as·phalt (as′fôlt) ***n.*** [< ML. < Gr.; prob. < *a-*, not + *sphallein*, to cause to fall] **1.** a brown or black tarlike substance, a variety of bitumen, found in a natural state or obtained by evaporating petroleum **2.** a mixture of this with sand or gravel, for paving, roofing, etc. —***vt.*** to pave, roof, etc. with asphalt —**as·phal′tic** ***adj.***
as·phal·tum (as fôl′təm) ***n.*** *same as* ASPHALT
as·pho·del (as′fə del′) ***n.*** [< L. < Gr. *asphodelos*] a plant of the lily family, having fleshy roots and white or yellow flowers
as·phyx·i·a (as fik′sē ə) ***n.*** [ModL. < Gr., a stopping of the pulse < *a-*, not + *sphyzein*, to throb] loss of consciousness as a result of too little oxygen and too much carbon dioxide in the blood: suffocation causes asphyxia —**as·phyx′i·ant** ***adj., n.***
as·phyx·i·ate (-āt′) ***vt.*** **-at′ed, -at′ing** **1.** to cause asphyxia in **2.** to suffocate —***vi.*** to undergo asphyxia —**as·phyx′i·a′tion** ***n.*** —**as·phyx′i·a′tor** ***n.***
as·pic (as′pik) ***n.*** [Fr. < OFr. *aspe*, ASP] **1.** [Archaic] an asp **2.** [Fr., from its asplike colorfulness] a jelly of meat juice, tomato juice, etc., molded, often with meat, seafood, etc., and eaten as a relish
as·pi·dis·tra (as′pə dis′trə) ***n.*** [ModL. < Gr. *aspis*, a shield + *astron*, a star] a plant of the lily family, with stiff, glossy evergreen leaves
as·pir·ant (as′pər ənt, ə spīr′ənt) ***adj.*** aspiring —***n.*** a person who aspires, as after honors, etc.
as·pi·rate (as′pə rāt′; *for n. & adj.* -pər it) ***vt.*** **-rat′ed, -rat′ing** [< L. pp. of *aspirare*: see ASPIRE] **1.** to begin (a word or syllable) with the sound of English *h* **2.** to follow (a consonant) with a puff of suddenly released breath **3.** to suck in or draw in, as by inhaling **4.** *Med.* to remove (fluid or gas), as from a body cavity, by suction —***n.*** **1.** the speech sound represented by English *h* **2.** an expiratory breath puff —***adj.*** preceded or followed by an aspirate: also **as′pi·rat′ed**
as·pi·ra·tion (as′pə rā′shən) ***n.*** **1.** *a)* strong desire or ambition, as for honor, etc. *b)* the thing so desired **2.** an aspirating **3.** an aspirate
as·pi·ra·tor (as′pə rāt′ər) ***n.*** a suction apparatus for removing air, fluids, etc. as from a body cavity
as·pir·a·to·ry (ə spīr′ə tôr′ē) ***adj.*** of or suited for breathing or suction
as·pire (ə spīr′) ***vi.*** **-pired′, -pir′ing** [< L. *aspirare* < *ad-*, to + *spirare*, to breathe] **1.** to be ambitious (*to* get or do something lofty); yearn or seek (*after*) **2.** [Archaic] to rise high; tower —**as·pir′er** ***n.*** —**as·pir′ing·ly** ***adv.***
as·pi·rin (as′pər in, as′prin) ***n.*** [G. < *a(cetyl)* + *spir(säure)*, salicylic acid + -IN[1]] a white, crystalline powder, acetylsalicylic acid, $C_9H_8O_4$, used for reducing fever, relieving headaches, etc.
a·squint (ə skwint′) ***adv., adj.*** [ME. *of skwyn* (see ASKANCE): infl. by SQUINT] with a squint; out of the corner of the eye
ass (as) ***n.*** [OE. *assa* < L. *asinus*] **1.** an animal related to the horse but having longer ears and a shorter mane: donkeys and burros are domesticated asses **2.** a stupid or silly person; fool
as·sa·fet·i·da, as·sa·foet·i·da (as′ə fet′ə də) ***n.*** *same as* ASAFETIDA
‡**as·sa·i** (äs sä′ē) ***adv.*** [It.] *Music* very: used in indicating tempo [adagio *assai*]
as·sail (ə sāl′) ***vt.*** [< OFr. < L. *assilire* < *ad*, to + *salire*, to leap] **1.** to attack physically and violently **2.** to attack with arguments, etc. **3.** to begin working on (a task, etc.) with vigor **4.** to have a forceful effect on —**as·sail′a·ble** ***adj.*** —**as·sail′er** ***n.*** —**as·sail′ment** ***n.***
as·sail·ant (-ənt) ***n.*** a person who assails; attacker
As·sam (a sam′, as′am) state of NE India, between Bhutan and Bangladesh: 47,091 sq. mi.; pop. 11,873,000 —**As·sa·mese** (as′ə mēz′, -mēs′) ***adj., n., pl.*** **-mese′**
as·sas·sin (ə sas′'n) ***n.*** [Fr. < Ar. *hash-shāshīn*, hashish users < *ḥashīsh*, hemp] **1.** [A-] a member of a secret cult of Moslems who killed Crusaders, supposedly while under the influence of hashish **2.** a murderer who strikes suddenly; esp., the killer of a politically important person
as·sas·si·nate (-āt′) ***vt.*** **-nat′ed, -nat′ing** **1.** to murder (esp. a politically important person) **2.** to harm or ruin (a reputation, etc.), as by slander —**as·sas′si·na′tion** ***n.***
as·sault (ə sôlt′) ***n.*** [< OFr. < L. *ad*, to + *saltare*, to leap] **1.** a violent attack, either physical or verbal; sometimes, specif., rape **2.** *Law* an unlawful threat or unsuccessful attempt to physically harm another —***vt., vi.*** **1.** to make an assault (upon) **2.** to rape —**as·sault′ive** ***adj.***
assault and battery *Law* the carrying out of threatened physical harm or violence
as·say (as′ā, a sā′; *for v.* a sā′, ə-) ***n.*** [OFr. *essai*, trial, test < L. *exagium*, a weighing < *ex-*, out + *agere*, to ACT] **1.** an examination or testing **2.** the analysis of an ore, etc. to find out the nature and proportion of the ingredients **3.** a substance to be analyzed in this way **4.** the result or report of such analysis —***vt.*** **1.** to make an assay of; test; analyze **2.** to try; attempt —**as·say′er** ***n.***
as·sem·blage (ə sem′blij) ***n.*** **1.** an assembling or being assembled **2.** a group of persons or things gathered together; assembly **3.** a form of art in which a number of unrelated objects are arranged together to form a kind of sculptural collage
as·sem·ble (ə sem′b'l) ***vt., vi.*** **-bled, -bling** [< OFr. < L. < *ad-*, to + *simul*, together] **1.** to gather into a group; collect **2.** to fit or put together the parts of —**as·sem′bler** ***n.***
as·sem·bly (ə sem′blē) ***n., pl.*** **-blies** **1.** an assembling or being assembled **2.** a group of persons gathered together, as for a meeting **3.** [A-] in some States, the lower house of the legislature **4.** *a)* a fitting together of parts to form a complete unit *b)* such parts **5.** a call, as by bugle or drum, for soldiers to assemble in ranks
assembly line in many factories, an arrangement by which each worker does a single operation in assembling the work as it is passed along, often on a slowly moving belt or track
as·sem·bly·man (ə sem′blē mən) ***n., pl.*** **-men** (-mən, -men′) a member of a legislative assembly, esp. [A-] of a State Assembly
as·sent (ə sent′) ***vi.*** [< OFr. < L. < *assentire* < *ad-*, to + *sentire*, to feel] to express acceptance of an opinion, proposal, etc.; agree (*to*); concur —***n.*** consent or agreement —**as·sent′er** ***n.***
as·sen·ta·tion (as′en tā′shən) ***n.*** immediate and usually flattering or hypocritical assent
as·sert (ə surt′) ***vt.*** [< L. pp. of *asserere* < *ad-*, to + *serere*, to join] **1.** to state positively; declare **2.** to insist on or defend (one's rights, a claim, etc.) —**assert oneself** to insist on one's rights, or on being recognized —**as·sert′er, as·ser′tor** ***n.***
as·ser·tion (ə sur′shən) ***n.*** **1.** an asserting **2.** a positive statement; declaration
as·ser·tive (-tiv) ***adj.*** positive or confident in a persistent way —**as·ser′tive·ly** ***adv.*** —**as·ser′tive·ness** ***n.***
as·sess (ə ses′) ***vt.*** [< OFr. < ML. *assessare*, to set a rate < L. pp. of *assidere*, to sit beside, assist < *ad-*, to + *sedere*, to sit] **1.** to set an estimated value on (property, etc.) for taxation **2.** to set the amount of (damages, a fine, etc.) **3.** to impose a fine, tax, etc. on (a person or property) **4.** to impose (an amount) as a fine, tax, etc. **5.** to estimate the importance or value of
as·sess·ment (-mənt) ***n.*** **1.** an assessing **2.** an amount assessed

as·ses·sor (-ər) ***n.*** a person who assesses property, etc. for taxation —**as·ses·so·ri·al** (as′ə sôr′ē əl) ***adj.*** —**as·ses′sor·ship′** ***n.***

as·set (as′et) ***n.*** **[**< Anglo-Fr. *assetz*, enough < OFr.; ult. < L. *ad*, to + *satis*, enough**]** **1.** anything owned that has exchange value **2.** a valuable or desirable thing *[*charm is her chief *asset]* **3.** [*pl.*] *a) Accounting* the entries on a balance sheet showing all the resources of a person or business, as accounts and notes receivable, cash, property, etc. *b) Law* property, as of a bankrupt

as·sev·er·ate (ə sev′ə rāt′) ***vt.*** **-at′ed, -at′ing** **[**< L. pp. of *asseverare* < *ad-*, to + *severus*, earnest**]** to state seriously or positively; assert —**as·sev′er·a′tion** ***n.***

as·si·du·i·ty (as′ə dyo͞o′ə tē, -do͞o′-) ***n.***, *pl.* **-ties** **1.** the quality or condition of being assiduous; diligence **2.** [*pl.*] constant personal attention

as·sid·u·ous (ə sij′o͞o wəs) ***adj.*** **[**< L. < *assidere:* see ASSESS**]** working with constant and careful attention; diligent; persevering —**as·sid′u·ous·ly** ***adv.*** —**as·sid′u·ous·ness** ***n.***

as·sign (ə sīn′) ***vt.*** **[**< OFr. < L. *assignare*, to allot < *ad-*, to + *signare*, SIGN**]** **1.** to set apart or mark for a specific purpose; designate **2.** to place at some task or duty **3.** to give out as a task; allot **4.** to ascribe (a motive, reason, etc.) **5.** *Law* to transfer (a claim, property, etc.) to another —***vi.*** *Law* to transfer property, etc. to another —***n.*** [*usually pl.*] an assignee —**as·sign′a·bil′i·ty** ***n.*** —**as·sign′a·ble** ***adj.*** —**as·sign′er,** *Law* **as·sign′or** (-ər, -ôr′) ***n.***

as·sig·na·tion (as′ig nā′shən) ***n.*** **1.** an assigning **2.** anything assigned **3.** an appointment to meet, esp. one made secretly by lovers; rendezvous

as·sign·ee (ə sī′nē′) ***n.*** *Law* a person to whom a claim, property, etc. is transferred

as·sign·ment (ə sīn′mənt) ***n.*** **1.** an assigning or being assigned **2.** anything assigned, as a lesson, task, etc. **3.** *Law a)* a transfer of a claim, property, etc. *b)* a deed, etc. authorizing this

as·sim·i·late (ə sim′ə lāt′) ***vt.*** **-lat′ed, -lat′ing** **[**< L. pp. of *assimilare* < *ad-*, to + *similare*, make similar to < *similis*, like**]** **1.** to absorb (food) into the body **2.** to absorb and incorporate into one's thinking **3.** to absorb (groups of different cultures) into the main culture **4.** to make like or alike (with *to*) —***vi.*** to become assimilated —**as·sim′i·la·bil′i·ty** ***n.*** —**as·sim′i·la·ble** ***adj.*** —**as·sim′i·la′tor** ***n.***

as·sim·i·la·tion (ə sim′ə lā′shən) ***n.*** an assimilating or being assimilated; specif., *a)* the absorption of a minority group into the main culture *b) Phonet.* the process by which a sound tends to become like a neighboring sound *[*the *p* in *cupboard* has been lost by assimilation to *b] c) Physiol.* the change of digested food into the protoplasm of an animal; also, the absorption of nutritive elements by plants

as·sim·i·la·tive (ə sim′ə lāt′iv) ***adj.*** of or causing assimilation; assimilating: also **as·sim·i·la·to·ry** (ə sim′'l ə tôr′ē)

as·sist (ə sist′) ***vt.*** **[**< OFr. < L. *assistere* < *ad-*, to + *sistere*, to make stand < *stare*, to stand**]** **1.** to give help to; aid **2.** to work as an assistant to —***vi.*** to give help; aid —***n.*** **1.** an instance or act of helping **2.** *Baseball* a defensive play by a fielder enabling a teammate to make a putout **3.** *Hockey* the passing of the puck in such a way as to enable a teammate to score a goal —**assist at** to be present at; attend

as·sis·tance (ə sis′təns) ***n.*** the act of assisting or the help given; aid

as·sis·tant (-tənt) ***adj.*** assisting; helping —***n.*** **1.** a person who assists another or serves in a lower position; helper **2.** a thing that aids

as·size (ə sīz′) ***n.*** **[**< OFr. < L. *assidere:* see ASSESS**]** **1.** orig., a legislative assembly or any of its decrees **2.** [*pl.*] *a)* court sessions held periodically in each county of England to try civil and criminal cases *b)* the time or place of these

assn. association

assoc. **1.** associate **2.** associated **3.** association

as·so·ci·ate (ə sō′shē āt′, -sē-; *for n. & adj., usually* -it) ***vt.*** **-at′ed, -at′ing** **[**< L. pp. of *associare* < *ad-*, to + *sociare*, to join < *socius*, companion**]** **1.** to join together; connect; combine **2.** to bring into relationship as companion, partner, friend, etc. **3.** to connect in the mind *[*to *associate* rain with grief*]* —***vi.*** **1.** to join (*with*) as a companion, partner, friend, etc. **2.** to join together; unite —***n.*** **1.** a friend, partner, fellow worker, etc. **2.** a member of less than full status, as of a society **3.** anything joined with another thing or things **4.** a degree granted by a junior college to those completing the regular two-year course —***adj.*** **1.** joined with others, as in some work **2.** of less than full status

as·so·ci·a·tion (ə sō′sē ā′shən, -shē-) ***n.*** **1.** the act of associating **2.** companionship; fellowship; partnership **3.** an organization of persons having the same interests, purposes, etc.; society **4.** a connection in the mind between ideas, feelings, etc. —**as·so′ci·a′tion·al** ***adj.***

association football *British name for* SOCCER

as·so·ci·a·tive (ə sō′shē āt′iv, -sē-; -shə tiv) ***adj.*** **1.** of, characterized by, or causing association **2.** *Math.* of an operation, as multiplication of three numbers, in which the result is the same regardless of the way the elements are grouped

as·so·nance (as′ə nəns) ***n.*** **[**Fr. < L. prp. of *assonare* < *ad-*, to + *sonare*, to sound**]** **1.** likeness of sound, as in a series of words or syllables **2.** a partial rhyme in which the stressed vowel sounds are alike but the consonant sounds are unlike, as in *late* and *make* —**as′so·nant** ***adj., n.***

as·sort (ə sôrt′) ***vt.*** **[**< OFr. < *a-* (L. *ad*), to + *sorte*, SORT**]** **1.** to separate into classes according to sorts or kinds; classify **2.** to supply with an assortment of goods —***vi.*** **1.** to match or harmonize (*with*) **2.** to associate (*with*) —**as·sort′a·tive** ***adj.*** —**as·sort′er** ***n.***

as·sort·ed (-id) ***adj.*** **1.** of different sorts; miscellaneous **2.** sorted into groups according to kind **3.** matched *[*a poorly *assorted* pair*]*

as·sort·ment (-mənt) ***n.*** **1.** an assorting or being assorted; classification **2.** an assorted, or miscellaneous, group or collection; variety

ASSR, A.S.S.R. Autonomous Soviet Socialist Republic

asst. assistant

as·suage (ə swāj′) ***vt.*** **-suaged′, -suag′ing** **[**< OFr. < L. *ad*, to + *suavis*, sweet**]** **1.** to lessen (pain, distress, etc.); allay **2.** to calm (passion, anger, etc.); pacify **3.** to satisfy or slake (thirst, etc.) —**as·suage′ment** ***n.*** —**as·suag′er** ***n.***

as·sume (ə so͞om′, -syo͞om′) ***vt.*** **-sumed′, -sum′ing** **[**< L. *assumere*, to claim < *ad-*, to + *sumere*, to take**]** **1.** to take on or put on (the appearance, form, role, etc. *of*) **2.** to seize; usurp *[*to *assume* control*]* **3.** to take upon oneself; undertake **4.** to take for granted; suppose **5.** to pretend to have; feign —**as·sum′a·ble** ***adj.*** —**as·sum′a·bly** ***adv.*** —**as·sum′ed·ly** ***adv.*** —**as·sum′er** ***n.***

as·sum·ing (ə so͞o′miŋ, -syo͞o′-) ***adj.*** taking too much for granted; presumptuous

as·sump·tion (ə sump′shən) ***n.*** **1.** the act of assuming **2.** anything taken for granted; supposition **3.** presumption; impudence **4.** [A-] *R.C.Ch. a)* the taking up of the body and soul of the Virgin Mary into heaven after her death *b)* a church festival on August 15 celebrating this —**as·sump′tive** ***adj.***

as·sur·ance (ə shoor′əns) ***n.*** **1.** the act of assuring **2.** a being assured; sureness; confidence **3.** something that inspires confidence, as a promise, positive statement, etc.; guarantee **4.** self-confidence **5.** impudent forwardness; presumption **6.** [Chiefly Brit.] insurance

as·sure (ə shoor′) ***vt.*** **-sured′, -sur′ing** **[**< OFr. < ML. *assecurare* < L. *ad*, to + *securus*, SECURE**]** **1.** to make (a person) sure of something; convince **2.** to give confidence to *[*the news *assured* us*]* **3.** to declare to or promise confidently **4.** to make (a doubtful thing) certain; guarantee **5.** [Brit.] to insure against loss —**as·sur′er** ***n.***

as·sured (ə shoord′) ***adj.*** **1.** made sure; certain **2.** confident **3.** insured —***n.*** **1.** the person to whom an insurance policy is payable **2.** the person whose life or property is insured —**as·sur·ed·ly** (ə shoor′id lē) ***adv.*** —**as·sur′ed·ness** ***n.***

As·syr·i·a (ə sir′ē ə) ancient empire in SW Asia in the region of the upper Tigris River

As·syr·i·an (-ən) ***adj.*** of Assyria, its people, language, etc. —***n.*** **1.** a native or inhabitant of Assyria **2.** the Semitic language of the Assyrians

As·tar·te (as tär′tē) a Semitic goddess of fertility and sexual love

as·ta·tine (as′tə tēn′) ***n.*** **[**< Gr. *astatos*, unstable + -INE[4]**]** a radioactive chemical element formed from bismuth bombarded by alpha particles: symbol, At; at. wt., 210 (?); at. no., 85

as·ter (as′tər) ***n.*** **[**L. < Gr. *astēr*, star**]** a plant of the composite family, with purplish, blue, pink, or white daisylike flowers

-as·ter (as′tər) **[**L. dim. suffix**]** *a suffix meaning* inferior or worthless *[poetaster]*

as·ter·isk (as′tər isk) ***n.*** **[**< LL. < Gr. dim. of *astēr*, a star**]** a starlike sign (*) used in printing to indicate footnote references, omissions, etc. —***vt.*** to mark with this sign

as·ter·ism (as′tər iz′m) ***n.*** **[**< Gr. < *astēr*, star**]** *Astron.* a group or cluster of stars

a·stern (ə sturn′) ***adv.*** **1.** behind a ship or aircraft **2.** at or toward the back of a ship or aircraft **3.** backward; in a reverse direction

NEW ENGLAND ASTER

as·ter·oid (as′tə roid′) ***adj.*** **[**< Gr. *astēr*, star + -OID**]** like a star or starfish —***n.*** **1.** any of the many small planets with orbits between those of Mars and Jupiter; planetoid **2.** a starfish

as·the·ni·a (as thē′nē ə) ***n.*** [ML. < Gr. < *a-*, without + *sthenos*, strength] bodily weakness —**as·then′ic** (-then′ik) ***adj.***

asth·ma (az′mə) ***n.*** [Gr.] a chronic disorder characterized by wheezing, coughing, difficulty in breathing, and a suffocating feeling

asth·mat·ic (az mat′ik) ***adj.*** of or having asthma: also **asth·mat′i·cal** —***n.*** a person who has asthma —**asth·mat′ical·ly** ***adv.***

as·tig·mat·ic (as′tig mat′ik) ***adj.*** **1.** of or having astigmatism **2.** correcting astigmatism **3.** having a distorted view or judgment —**as′tig·mat′i·cal·ly** ***adv.***

a·stig·ma·tism (ə stig′mə tiz'm) ***n.*** [< Gr. *a-*, without + *stigma*, a mark + -ISM] **1.** an irregularity in the curvature of a lens, esp. of the eye, so that light rays do not meet in a single focal point and images are distorted **2.** a distorted view or judgment, as because of prejudice

a·stir (ə stur′) ***adv., adj.*** **1.** in motion; in excited activity **2.** out of bed

as·ton·ish (ə stän′ish) ***vt.*** [< OFr. < L. < *ex-*, emphatic + *tonare*, to thunder] to fill with sudden wonder or great surprise; amaze —**as·ton′ish·ing** ***adj.*** —**as·ton′ish·ing·ly** ***adv.***

as·ton·ish·ment (-mənt) ***n.*** **1.** a being astonished; great amazement **2.** anything that astonishes

As·tor (as′tər), **John Jacob** 1763–1848; U.S. fur merchant & financier, born in Germany

as·tound (ə stound′) ***vt.*** [< ME. pp. of *astonien*, ASTONISH] to astonish greatly; amaze —**as·tound′ing** ***adj.*** —**as·tound′ing·ly** ***adv.***

a·strad·dle (ə strad′'l) ***adv.*** in a straddling position

As·tra·khan (as′trə kan′; *Russ.* äs′trə khän′y') seaport in S European R.S.F.S.R.: pop. 376,000

as·tra·khan (as′trə kən) ***n.*** **1.** a loosely curled fur from the pelt of very young lambs orig. bred near Astrakhan **2.** a wool fabric made to look like this Also sp. **as′tra·chan**

as·tral (as′trəl) ***adj.*** [< L. < Gr. *astron*, star < *astēr*, star] **1.** of, from, or like the stars **2.** *Theosophy* of a substance supposedly existing at a level just beyond normal human perception

a·stray (ə strā′) ***adv.*** **1.** off the right path **2.** so as to be in error

a·stride (ə strīd′) ***adv.*** **1.** with a leg on either side; astraddle **2.** with legs far apart —***prep.*** **1.** with a leg on either side of (a horse, etc.) **2.** extending over or across

as·trin·gent (ə strin′jənt) ***adj.*** [< L. prp. of *astringere*, to contract < *ad-*, to + *stringere*, to draw] **1.** that contracts body tissues and checks secretions, capillary bleeding, etc. **2.** having a harsh, biting quality —***n.*** an astringent substance —**as·trin′gen·cy** ***n.*** —**as·trin′gent·ly** ***adv.***

as·tro- [< Gr. *astron*: see ASTRAL] *a combining form meaning* of a star or stars *[astrophysics]*

as·tro·dome (as′trə dōm′) ***n.*** a transparent dome on top of an aircraft fuselage for the navigator

astrol. **1.** astrologer **2.** astrology

as·tro·labe (as′trə lāb′) ***n.*** [< OFr. < ML. < Gr. < *astron*, a star + *lambanein*, to take] an instrument once used to find the altitude of stars, etc.

as·trol·o·gy (ə sträl′ə jē) ***n.*** [< L. & Gr. *astron*, star + *-logia*, -LOGY] **1.** orig., primitive astronomy **2.** a pseudoscience based on the notion that the positions of the moon, sun, and stars affect human affairs and that one can foretell the future by studying the stars, etc. —**as·trol′o·ger** ***n.*** —**as·tro·log·i·cal** (as′trə läj′i k'l) ***adj.*** —**as′tro·log′i·cal·ly** ***adv.***

astron. **1.** astronomer **2.** astronomy

as·tro·naut (as′trə nôt′) ***n.*** [< Fr.: see ff.] a person trained to make rocket flights in outer space

as·tro·nau·tics (as′trə nôt′iks) ***n.pl.*** [*with sing. v.*] [< Fr.: see ASTRO- & AERONAUTICS] the science that deals with spacecraft and with travel in outer space —**as′tro·nau′ti·cal** ***adj.***

as·tro·nom·i·cal (as′trə näm′i k'l) **adj.** **1.** of or having to do with astronomy **2.** extremely large, as the numbers or quantities used in astronomy Also **as′tro·nom′ic** —**as′tro·nom′i·cal·ly** ***adv.***

astronomical unit a unit of length equal to the mean radius of the earth's orbit (c. 93 million mi.) used in measuring distances in astronomy

as·tron·o·my (ə strän′ə mē) ***n.*** [< ME. & OFr. < L. < Gr. < *astron*, star + *nomos*, system of laws < *nemein*, to arrange] the science of the stars, planets, and all other heavenly bodies, dealing with their composition, motion, relative position, size, etc. —**as·tron′o·mer** ***n.***

as·tro·phys·ics (as′trō fiz′iks) ***n.pl.*** [*with sing. v.*] the science of the physical properties and phenomena of the stars, planets, etc. —**as′tro·phys′i·cal** ***adj.*** —**as′tro·phys′i·cist** (-ə sist) ***n.***

as·tute (ə stōōt′, -styōōt′) ***adj.*** [< L. < *astus*, craft, cunning] having or showing a clever or shrewd mind; keen —**as·tute′ly** ***adv.*** —**as·tute′ness** ***n.***

A·sun·ción (ä sōōn syôn′) capital of Paraguay, on the Paraguay River: pop. 305,000

a·sun·der (ə sun′dər) ***adv.*** [see SUNDER] **1.** into parts or pieces **2.** apart or separate

As·wan (äs wän′, as-; as′wän′) city on the Nile, in SE Egypt: pop. 48,000: a dam (**Aswan High Dam**) has been built just south of this city

a·sy·lum (ə sī′ləm) ***n.*** [L. < Gr. *asylon*, asylum < *a-*, without + *sylē*, right of seizure] **1.** formerly, a sanctuary, as a temple, where criminals, etc. were safe from arrest **2.** any refuge **3.** the protection given by one country to refugees from another **4.** *an old term for* a place for the care of the mentally ill, or of the aged, poor, etc.

a·sym·me·try (ā sim′ə trē) ***n.*** lack of symmetry —**a·sym·met·ri·cal** (ā′sə met′ri k'l), **a′sym·met′ric** ***adj.*** —**a′sym·met′ri·cal·ly** ***adv.***

as·ymp·tote (as′im tōt′) ***n.*** [ModL. < Gr. < *a-*, not + *syn-*, together + *piptein*, to fall] a straight line always approaching but never meeting a curve —**as′ymp·tot′ic** (-tät′ik), **as′ymp·tot′i·cal** ***adj.***

ASYMPTOTE
(A, asymptote of curve C)

at[1] (at; *unstressed* ət) ***prep.*** [OE. *æt*] **1.** on; in; near; by *[at* the office*]* **2.** to or toward *[*look *at* her*]* **3.** through *[*enter *at* the gate*]* **4.** from *[*get the facts *at* their source*]* **5.** attending *[at* the party*]* **6.** occupied in; busy with *[at* work*]* **7.** in a state of *[at* war*]* **8.** in the manner of *[at* a trot*]* **9.** because of *[*terrified *at* the sight*]* **10.** according to *[at* his discretion*]* **11.** with reference to *[*good *at* tennis*]* **12.** in the amount, degree, price, etc. of *[at* five cents each*]* **13.** from an interval of *[at* half a mile*]* **14.** on or close to the time or age of *[at* five o'clock*]* **15.** during the period of *[*to happen *at* night*]*

at[2] (ät, at) ***n.***, *pl.* **at** *see* MONETARY UNITS, table (Laos)

At *Chem.* astatine

at. **1.** airtight **2.** atmosphere **3.** atomic

At·a·brine (at′ə brin, -brēn′) [G. *atebrin*] *a trademark for* a synthetic drug used in treating malaria and other diseases —***n.*** [a-] this drug

At·a·lan·ta (at′'l an′tə) *Gr. Myth.* a beautiful, swift-footed maiden who offered to marry any man able to defeat her in a race

at·a·rac·tic (at′ə rak′tik) ***n.*** [< Gr. < *ataraxia*, calmness < *a-*, not + *tarassein*, to disturb] a tranquilizing drug —***adj.*** of tranquilizing drugs or their effects Also **at′a·rax′ic** (-rak′sik)

at·a·vism (at′ə viz'm) ***n.*** [< Fr. < L. *atavus*, ancestor < *at-*, beyond + *avus*, grandfather] **1.** the appearance in an individual of a characteristic found in an early ancestor but not in more recent ones **2.** *a)* such a characteristic *b)* an individual with such a characteristic: also **at′a·vist** —**at′a·vis′tic** ***adj.*** —**at′a·vis′ti·cal·ly** ***adv.***

a·tax·i·a (ə tak′sē ə) ***n.*** [Gr., disorder < *a-*, not + *tassein*, to arrange] inability to coordinate voluntary muscular movements —**a·tax′ic** ***adj., n.***

A·te (ā′tē) *Gr. Myth.* the goddess personifying criminal folly or reckless ambition

ate (āt; *Brit., or U.S. dial.*, et) *pt. of* EAT

-ate[1] (āt *for 1;* it, āt *for 2 & 3*) [< L. *-atus*, pp. ending] **1.** *a suffix meaning: a)* to become *[maturate]* *b)* to cause to become *[sublimate]* *c)* to produce *[salivate]* *d)* to provide or treat with *[vaccinate]* *e)* to put in the form of *[triangulate]* *f)* to arrange for *[orchestrate]* *g)* to combine or treat with *[oxygenate]* **2.** *a suffix meaning: a)* of or characteristic of *[roseate]* *b)* having or filled with *[passionate]* *c) Biol.* having or characterized by *[spatulate]* **3.** *a suffix roughly equivalent to the past participial ending -ed [animate (animated)]*

-ate[2] (āt, it) [L. *-atus*, a noun ending] *a suffix denoting:* **1.** a function, agent, or official *[directorate, potentate]* **2.** [L. *-atum*, neut. of *-atus*] *Chem.* a salt made from (an acid with a name ending in *-ic*) *[acetate, nitrate]*

at·el·ier (at′'l yā′) ***n.*** [Fr., ult. < L. *assula*, dim. of *assis*, board] a studio or workshop

a tem·po (ä tem′pō) [It.] *Music* in time: a direction to return to the original tempo

Ath·a·na·sius (ath′ə nā′shəs), Saint 296?–373 A.D.; Alexandrian bishop, who opposed Arianism —**Ath′a·na′sian** (-zhən) ***adj., n.***

Ath·a·pas·can, Ath·a·pas·kan (ath′ə pas′kən) ***adj.*** [< Cree *athap-askaw*, lit., grass here and there] designating or of the most widely scattered linguistic family of N. American Indians, including the Navajos and Apaches —***n.***

fat, āpe, cär; ten, ēven; is, bīte; gō, hôrn, tōōl, look; oil, out; up, fur; get; joy; yet; chin; she; thin, *th*en; zh, leisure; ŋ, ring; ə for *a* in *ago*, *e* in *agent*, *i* in *sanity*, *o* in *comply*, *u* in *focus*; ' as in *able* (ā′b'l); Fr. bål; ë, Fr. coeur; ö, Fr. feu; Fr. mo*n*; ô, Fr. coq; ü, Fr. duc; *r*, Fr. cri; H, G. ich; kh, G. doch; ‡foreign; *hypothetical; < derived from. See inside front cover.

an Athapascan Indian or language Also **Ath'a·bas'can, Ath'a·bas'kan** (-bas'-)

a·the·ism (ā'thē iz'm) ***n.*** [< Fr. < Gr. < *a-*, without + *theos*, god] the belief that there is no God —**a'the·ist** (-ist) ***n.*** —**a'the·is'tic, a'the·is'ti·cal** ***adj.***

A·the·na (ə thē'nə) *Gr. Myth.* the goddess of wisdom, skills, and warfare, identified with the Roman goddess Minerva: also **A·the'ne** (-nē)

Ath·e·nae·um, Ath·e·ne·um (ath'ə nē'əm) the temple of Athena at Athens, where writers and scholars met —***n.*** **[a-] 1.** a literary or scientific club **2.** a library or reading room

Ath·ens (ath''nz) capital of Greece: pop., of met. area, 2,540,000: the ancient center of Greek culture and capital of ancient Attica —**A·the·ni·an** (ə thē'nē ən) ***adj., n.***

ath·er·o·scle·ro·sis (ath'ər ō sklə rō'sis) ***n.*** [ModL. < Gr. *athērōma*, tumor filled with grainy matter + SCLEROSIS] a thickening, and loss of elasticity, of the walls of arteries, with the formation of fatty nodules —**ath'er·o·scle·rot'ic** (-rät'ik) ***adj.***

a·thirst (ə thurst') ***adj.*** **1.** thirsty **2.** eager; longing *[athirst for knowledge]*

ath·lete (ath'lēt') ***n.*** [< L. < Gr. < *athlein*, to contest for a prize < *athlon*, a prize] a person trained in exercises, games, or contests requiring physical strength, skill, speed, etc.

athlete's foot a common fungous infection of the skin of the feet; ringworm of the feet

ath·let·ic (ath let'ik) ***adj.*** **1.** of, like, or proper to athletes or athletics **2.** physically strong, skillful, muscular, etc. —**ath·let'i·cal·ly** ***adv.***

ath·let·i·cism (-ə siz'm) ***n.*** **1.** addiction to athletics **2.** an athletic quality

ath·let·ics (-iks) ***n.pl.*** [*sometimes with sing. v.*] sports, games, etc. requiring physical strength, skill, stamina, speed, etc.

at-home (ət hōm') ***n.*** an informal reception at one's home, usually in the afternoon

a·thwart (ə thwôrt') ***prep.*** **1.** from one side to the other of; across **2.** in opposition to; against **3.** *Naut.* across the course or length of —***adv.*** **1.** crosswise **2.** so as to block or thwart

-at·ic (at'ik) [< Fr. or L. < Gr. *-atikos*] *a suffix meaning* of, of the kind of *[lymphatic, chromatic]*

a·tilt (ə tilt') ***adj., adv.*** tilted

a·tin·gle (ə tiŋ'g'l) ***adj.*** tingling; excited

-a·tion (ā'shən) [< Fr. or L.] *a suffix meaning:* **1.** the act of *[alteration]* **2.** the condition of being *[gratification]* **3.** the result of *[compilation]*

-a·tive (ə tiv, āt'iv) [< Fr. or L.] *a suffix meaning* of or relating to, serving to, tending to *[demonstrative, informative, talkative]*

At·lan·ta (ət lan'tə, at-) [< Western & *Atlantic* Railroad] capital of Ga., in the NC part: pop. 425,000 (met. area 2,010,000)

at·lan·tes (ət lan'tēz) ***n.pl., sing.*** **at·las** (at'ləs) [L. < Gr. pl. of ATLAS] supporting columns in the form of standing or kneeling figures of men

At·lan·tic (ət lan'tik, at-) [< L. *Atlanticum* (*mare*), Atlantic (ocean) < *Atlanticus*, of the Atlas Mts.] ocean touching the American continents to the west and Europe and Africa to the east —***adj.*** of, in, on, or near this ocean

Atlantic City city & ocean resort in N.J., on the Atlantic: pop. 40,000

Atlantic Standard Time *see* STANDARD TIME

At·lan·tis (ət lan'tis, at-) legendary island or continent west of Gibraltar, supposed to have sunk in the Atlantic —**At·lan·te·an** (at'lan tē'ən) ***adj.***

At·las (at'ləs) [L. < Gr.; ult. < *tlan*, bearing] *Gr. Myth.* a Titan forced to hold the heavens on his shoulders —***n.*** **[a-] 1.** a book of maps **2.** a book of tables, charts, etc. on a specific subject

Atlas Mountains mountain system in NW Africa, extending across Morocco, Algeria, and Tunisia

atm. 1. atmosphere **2.** atmospheric

at·man (ät'mən) ***n.*** [Sans., breath, soul] *Hinduism* **1.** the individual soul or ego **2. [A-]** the universal soul; source of all individual souls

at·mos·phere (at'məs fir') ***n.*** [< ModL. < Gr. *atmos*, vapor + *sphaira*, sphere] **1.** all the air surrounding the earth, consisting of oxygen, nitrogen, and other gases **2.** the gaseous mass surrounding any star, etc. **3.** the air in any given place **4.** the general feeling or spirit of a place; mood **5.** [Colloq.] an interesting effect produced by decoration, etc. **6.** *Physics* a unit of pressure equal to 14.69 lb. per sq. in.

at·mos·pher·ic (at'məs fer'ik, -fir'-) ***adj.*** **1.** of or in the atmosphere **2.** caused or produced by the atmosphere **3.** creating an atmosphere, or mood Also **at'mos·pher'i·cal** —**at'mos·pher'i·cal·ly** ***adv.***

at·mos·pher·ics (-iks) ***n.pl.*** *same as* STATIC (*n.* 1)

at. no. atomic number

at·oll (a'tôl, ā'-; -täl) ***n.*** [< Maldive Is. term] a ring-shaped coral island nearly or completely surrounding a lagoon

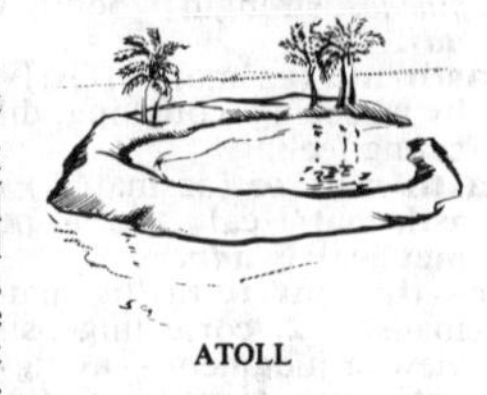

ATOLL

at·om (at'əm) ***n.*** [< OFr. < L. < Gr. *atomos*, uncut < *a-*, not + *temnein*, to cut] **1.** orig., any of the tiny particles that ancient philosophers imagined as the basic component of all matter **2.** a tiny particle; jot **3.** *Chem. & Physics* any of the smallest particles of an element that combine with similar particles of other elements to produce compounds: atoms consist of electrons revolving about a positively charged nucleus —**the atom** *same as* ATOMIC ENERGY

atom bomb *same as* ATOMIC BOMB —**at'om-bomb'** ***vt.***

a·tom·ic (ə täm'ik) ***adj.*** **1.** of an atom or atoms **2.** of or using atomic energy or atomic bombs **3.** having its atoms in an uncombined form **4.** very small; minute —**a·tom'i·cal·ly** ***adv.***

Atomic Age the period since the creation of the first self-sustaining nuclear chain reaction on December 2, 1942

atomic bomb an extremely destructive type of bomb, the power of which comes from the very great quantity of energy that is suddenly released when a chain reaction of nuclear fission is set off: first used in warfare in 1945 by the United States

atomic clock a highly accurate clock regulated by the unvarying vibrational frequency of the atoms or molecules of certain substances

atomic cocktail a dose of medicine to be swallowed, containing a radioactive element and used as in diagnosing or treating cancer

atomic energy the energy released from an atom in nuclear fission or nuclear fusion, or by radioactive decay

at·o·mic·i·ty (at'ə mis'ə tē) ***n.*** **1.** the state of being made up of atoms **2.** *Chem. a)* the number of atoms in a molecule *b) same as* VALENCE

atomic mass unit a unit of mass, exactly one twelfth of the mass of an atom of the most common isotope of carbon

atomic number *Chem.* a number representing the relative position of an element in the periodic table; number representing the number of protons in the nucleus of the atom of an element

atomic pile *early name for* NUCLEAR REACTOR

atomic theory the theory that all material objects and substances are composed of atoms

atomic weight *Chem.* a number representing the weight of one atom of an element as compared with an arbitrary number representing the weight of one atom of another element taken as the standard (now usually carbon at 12)

at·om·ize (at'ə mīz') ***vt.*** **-ized', -iz'ing 1.** to separate into atoms **2.** to reduce (a liquid) to a fine spray **3.** to destroy by atomic weapons **4.** to disintegrate; break up —**at'om·i·za'tion** ***n.***

at·om·iz·er (-mī'zər) ***n.*** a device used to shoot out a fine spray, as of medicine or perfume

atom smasher *same as* ACCELERATOR (sense 3)

a·ton·al (ā tōn''l) ***adj.*** having atonality —**a·ton'al·ism** ***n.*** —**a·ton'al·ist** ***n.*** —**a·ton'al·is'tic** ***adj.*** —**a·ton'al·ly** ***adv.***

a·to·nal·i·ty (ā'tō nal'ə tē) ***n.*** *Music* lack of tonality through intentional disregard of key; also, use of chromatic tones without relation to a central keynote

a·tone (ə tōn') ***vi.*** **a·toned', a·ton'ing** [ME. *at-onen*, become reconciled < *at one*, in accord] to make amends (*for* wrongdoing, etc.) —**a·ton'er** ***n.***

a·tone·ment (-mənt) ***n.*** **1.** an atoning **2.** satisfaction given for wrongdoing, etc.; expiation **3. [A-]** *Theol.* the reconciliation of God to man by means of Jesus' sufferings and death

a·top (ə täp') ***adv.*** on the top; at the top —***prep.*** on the top of

-a·to·ry (ə tôr'ē, ə tō'rē) [< L. *-atorius*] *a suffix meaning* of, characterized by, produced by *[accusatory]*

ATP [A(DENOSINE) *t*(*ri*)*p*(*hosphate*)] a vital substance, $C_{10}H_{16}P_3O_{13}N_5$, found in all living cells: it is the immediate source of muscular energy

at·ra·bil·ious (a'trə bil'yəs) ***adj.*** [< L. *atra bilis*, black bile: cf. MELANCHOLY] melancholy, morose, cross, etc.: also **at'ra·bil'iar** (-yər)

a·tri·um (ā'trē əm) ***n.***, *pl.* **a'tri·a** (-ə), **a'tri·ums** [L.] **1.** the main room of an ancient Roman house **2.** a hall or entrance court **3.** *Anat.* a chamber or cavity, esp. either of the upper chambers of the heart —**a'tri·al** (-əl) ***adj.***

a·tro·cious (ə trō'shəs) ***adj.*** [< L. *atrox* (gen. *atrocis*), fierce < *ater*, black + -OUS] **1.** very cruel, evil, etc. **2.** appalling or dismaying **3.** [Colloq.] very bad, offensive, inferior, etc. —**a·tro'cious·ly** ***adv.*** —**a·tro'cious·ness** ***n.***

a·troc·i·ty (ə träs'ə tē) ***n.***, *pl.* **-ties 1.** atrocious behavior; brutality, etc. **2.** an atrocious act **3.** [Colloq.] a very offensive thing

at·ro·phy (at′rə fē) ***n.*** [< Fr. < L. < Gr. < *a-*, not + *trephein*, to nourish] a wasting away, or the failure to grow, of an organ, etc., because of insufficient nutrition —***vi.*** **-phied, -phy·ing** to waste away or fail to develop —***vt.*** to cause atrophy in —**a·troph·ic** (ə träf′ik) ***adj.***

at·ro·pine (at′rə pēn′, -pin) ***n.*** [< ModL. < Gr. *Atropos* (see ff.) + -INE[4]] a poisonous, crystalline alkaloid obtained from belladonna and similar plants, used to relieve spasms or to dilate the pupil of the eye: also **at′ro·pin** (-pin)

At·ro·pos (at′rə päs′) *Gr. & Rom. Myth.* that one of the three Fates who cuts the thread of life

att. 1. attention 2. attorney

at·tach (ə tach′) ***vt.*** [< OFr. < *estachier* < *estache*, a post] **1.** to fasten by tying, etc. **2.** to join (often used reflexively) [he *attached* himself to us] **3.** to connect by ties of affection, etc. **4.** to affix (a signature, etc.) **5.** to ascribe **6.** to appoint by order **7.** *Law* to take (property or a person) into custody by writ **8.** *Mil.* to join (troops, etc.) temporarily to another unit —***vi.*** to be joined; belong —**at·tach′a·ble** ***adj.***

at·ta·ché (at′ə shā′; *chiefly Brit.* ə tash′ā; *Fr.* à tà shā′) ***n.*** [Fr., pp. of *attacher*, ATTACH] a person with special duties on the staff of an ambassador or minister

attaché case a flat, rectangular case for carrying documents, papers, etc.

at·tach·ment (ə tach′mənt) ***n.*** **1.** the act of attaching something **2.** anything that attaches; fastening **3.** devotion **4.** anything attached **5.** an accessory for an electrical appliance, etc. **6.** *Law* a taking of a person, property, etc. into custody, or a writ for this

at·tack (ə tak′) ***vt.*** [< Fr. < It. < OFr.: see ATTACH] **1.** to use force against in order to harm **2.** to speak or write against **3.** to begin working on energetically **4.** to begin acting upon harmfully —***vi.*** to make an assault —***n.*** **1.** an attacking; onslaught **2.** an onset or recurrence of a disease **3.** a beginning of a task, undertaking, etc. —**at·tack′er** ***n.***

at·tain (ə tān′) ***vt.*** [< OFr. < L. *attingere* < *ad-*, to + *tangere*, to touch] **1.** to gain through effort; achieve **2.** to reach or come to; arrive at —***vi.*** to succeed in reaching or coming (*to* a goal) —**at·tain′a·bil′i·ty, at·tain′a·ble·ness** ***n.*** —**at·tain′a·ble** ***adj.***

at·tain·der (ə tān′dər) ***n.*** [OFr. *ataindre*, to attain] the loss of a person's civil rights and property because he has been sentenced to death or outlawed: see BILL OF ATTAINDER

at·tain·ment (ə tān′mənt) ***n.*** **1.** an attaining or being attained **2.** anything attained, as a skill

at·taint (ə tānt′) ***vt.*** to punish by attainder —***n.*** an attainder

at·tar (at′ər) ***n.*** [< Per. < Ar. *'itr*, perfume] a perfume made from the petals of flowers, esp. of damask roses (**attar of roses**)

at·tempt (ə tempt′) ***vt.*** [< OFr. < L. *attemptare* < *ad-*, to + *temptare*, to try] to try to do, get, etc.; endeavor —***n.*** **1.** a try; endeavor **2.** an attack, as on a person's life —**attempt the life of** to try to kill —**at·tempt′a·ble** ***adj.***

at·tend (ə tend′) ***vt.*** [< OFr. < L. *attendere*, to give heed to < *ad-*, to + *tendere*, to stretch] **1.** [Now Rare] to take care or charge of **2.** *a*) to wait on; serve *b*) to serve as doctor to during an illness **3.** to go with **4.** to accompany as a result [success *attended* his efforts] **5.** to be present at —***vi.*** **1.** to pay attention **2.** to wait (*on* or *upon*) **3.** to devote oneself (*to*) **4.** to give the required care or attention (*to*)

at·tend·ance (ə ten′dəns) ***n.*** **1.** an attending **2.** the number of persons attending **3.** the degree of regularity in attending

at·tend·ant (-dənt) ***adj.*** **1.** attending or serving **2.** being present **3.** accompanying [*attendant* difficulties] —***n.*** **1.** one who attends or serves **2.** a person present **3.** an accompanying thing

at·ten·tion (ə ten′shən) ***n.*** **1.** *a*) the act of keeping one's mind closely on something; concentration *b*) readiness for concentration **2.** notice **3.** care or consideration **4.** *a*) thoughtful consideration for others *b*) an act of consideration, courtesy, etc.: *usually used in pl.* **5.** *Mil.* *a*) the erect, motionless posture of soldiers in readiness for a command *b*) a command to assume this posture

at·ten·tive (ə ten′tiv) ***adj.*** **1.** paying attention **2.** courteous, devoted, etc. —**at·ten′tive·ly** ***adv.*** —**at·ten′tive·ness** ***n.***

at·ten·u·ate (ə ten′yoo wāt′) ***vt.*** **-at′ed, -at′ing** [< L. pp. of *attenuare* < *ad-*, to + *tenuare* < *tenuis*, thin] **1.** to make slender or thin **2.** to dilute; rarefy **3.** to lessen or weaken —***vi.*** to become thin, weak, etc. —**at·ten′u·a·ble** ***adj.*** —**at·ten′u·a′tion** ***n.***

at·test (ə test′) ***vt.*** [< Fr. < L. *attestari* < *ad-*, to + *testari*, to bear witness < *testis*, a witness] **1.** to declare to be true or genuine **2.** to certify, as by oath **3.** to serve as proof of —***vi.*** to bear witness; testify (*to*) —**at·tes·ta·tion** (at′es tā′shən) ***n.*** —**at·test′er, at·tes′tor** ***n.***

At·tic (at′ik) ***adj.*** **1.** of Attica **2.** Athenian **3.** classical in a simple, restrained way [an *Attic* style] —***n.*** **1.** the Greek dialect of Attica, the literary language of ancient Greece **2.** an Athenian

at·tic (at′ik) ***n.*** [< Fr. < prec.] **1.** a low wall or story above the cornice of a classical façade **2.** the room or space just below the roof of a house; garret

At·ti·ca (at′i kə) province of SE Greece: in ancient times, a region dominated by Athens

At·ti·cism (at′ə siz′m) ***n.*** [*also* **a-**] an Attic idiom, style, custom, etc. —**At′ti·cize′** (-sīz′) ***vt., vi.*** **-cized′, -ciz′ing**

Attic salt, Attic wit graceful, piercing wit

At·ti·la (at′l ə, ə til′ə) 406?–453 A.D.; king of the Huns (433?–453)

at·tire (ə tīr′) ***vt.*** **-tired′, -tir′ing** [< OFr. *atirier*, put in order < *a* (L. *ad*), to + *tire*, row, order] to dress, esp. in fine garments; clothe; array —***n.*** clothes, esp. rich apparel; finery

at·ti·tude (at′ə to͞od′, -tyo͞od′) ***n.*** [Fr. < It. < LL. *aptitudo* < L. *aptus*, APT] **1.** the posture of the body in connection with an action, mood, etc. **2.** a way of acting, feeling, or thinking; one's disposition, mental set, etc. **3.** the position of an aircraft or spacecraft in relation to a given line or plane —**at′ti·tu′di·nal** ***adj.***

at·ti·tu·di·nize (at′ə to͞od′'n īz′, -tyo͞od′-) ***vi.*** **-nized′, -niz′ing** to pose for effect

at·to- [< Dan. *atten*, eighteen] *a combining form meaning* one quintillionth (10^{-18}) [*attosecond*]

at·tor·ney (ə tur′nē) ***n.***, *pl.* **-neys** [< OFr. < *a-* (L. *ad*), to + *torner:* see TURN] any person having the legal power to act for another; esp. (also **attorney at law**), a lawyer

attorney general *pl.* **attorneys general, attorney generals** **1.** the chief law officer of a national or State government **2.** [A- G-] the head of the U.S. Department of Justice

at·tract (ə trakt′) ***vt.*** [< L. pp. of *attrahere* < *ad-*, to + *trahere*, to draw] **1.** to draw to itself or oneself [a magnet *attracts* iron] **2.** to get the admiration, attention, etc. of; allure —***vi.*** to be attractive —**at·tract′a·ble** ***adj.*** —**at·tract′er, at·trac′tor** ***n.***

at·trac·tion (ə trak′shən) ***n.*** **1.** an attracting or the power of attracting; esp., charm or fascination **2.** anything that attracts **3.** *Physics* the mutual action by which bodies or particles of matter tend to draw together or cohere: opposed to REPULSION

at·trac·tive (-tiv) ***adj.*** that attracts or has the power to attract; esp., charming, pretty, etc. —**at·trac′tive·ly** ***adv.*** —**at·trac′tive·ness** ***n.***

attrib. 1. attribute 2. attributive

at·trib·ute (ə trib′yoot; *for n.* a′trə byo͞ot′) ***vt.*** **-ut·ed, -ut·ing** [< L. pp. of *attribuere* < *ad-*, to + *tribuere*, to assign < *tribus:* see TRIBE] **1.** to think of as belonging to or coming from a particular person or thing; assign or ascribe (*to*) **2.** to ascribe as a characteristic or quality —***n.*** **1.** a characteristic or quality of a person or thing **2.** an object used in the arts as a symbol for a person, office, etc. **3.** a word or phrase used as an adjective —**at·trib′ut·a·ble** ***adj.*** —**at′·tri·bu′tion** ***n.***

at·trib·u·tive (ə trib′yoo tiv) ***adj.*** **1.** attributing **2.** of or like an attribute **3.** *Gram.* joined directly to the substantive it modifies, esp., in English, coming just before it: said of an adjective —***n.*** an attributive adjective, as *black* in *black cat* —**at·trib′u·tive·ly** ***adv.***

at·tri·tion (ə trish′ən) ***n.*** [< L. < pp. of *atterere*, to wear < *ad-*, to + *terere*, to rub] **1.** a wearing away by friction **2.** any gradual wearing, or weakening **3.** loss of personnel in the normal course of events, as because of death, retirement, etc.

at·tune (ə to͞on′, -tyo͞on′) ***vt.*** **-tuned′, -tun′ing** **1.** to tune **2.** to bring into harmony or agreement

atty. attorney

at. wt. atomic weight

a·typ·i·cal (ā tip′i k'l) ***adj.*** not typical; not characteristic: also **a·typ′ic** —**a·typ′i·cal·ly** ***adv.***

Au [L. *aurum*] *Chem.* gold

au·burn (ô′bərn) ***adj., n.*** [< OFr. < L. *alburnus* < *albus*, white; meaning infl. by ME. *brun*, brown] reddish brown

Auck·land (ôk′lənd) seaport on North Island, New Zealand: pop. 152,000 (met. area 577,000)

‡au cou·rant (ō ko͞o *rän′*) [Fr., lit., with the current] fully informed; up-to-date

auc·tion (ôk′shən) ***n.*** [< L. < pp. of *augere*, to increase] **1.** a public sale at which each item is sold to the highest bidder **2.** *same as* AUCTION BRIDGE —***vt.*** to sell at auction

auction bridge a variety of the game of bridge in which the players bid for the right to say what suit shall be trump or to declare no-trump

auc·tion·eer (ôk'shə nir') *n.* one whose work is selling things at auction —*vt.* to auction

auc·to·ri·al (ôk tôr'ē əl) *adj.* [< L. *auctor,* author] of or by an author

aud. 1. audit 2. auditor

au·da·cious (ô dā'shəs) *adj.* [< L. < *audax,* bold < *audere,* to dare] 1. bold or daring; fearless 2. rudely bold; brazen; insolent —**au·da'cious·ly** *adv.* —**au·da'cious·ness** *n.*

au·dac·i·ty (ô das'ə tē) *n.* 1. bold courage; daring 2. brazen boldness; insolence 3. *pl.* **-ties** an audacious act or remark

Au·den (ôd''n), **W(ystan) H(ugh)** 1907–73; U.S. poet, born in England

au·di·ble (ô'də b'l) *adj.* [< ML. < L. *audire,* to hear] loud enough to be heard —**au'di·bil'i·ty** *n.* —**au'di·bly** *adv.*

au·di·ence (ô'dē əns) *n.* [ME. & OFr. < L. *audientia,* a hearing < prp. of *audire,* to hear] 1. a group assembled to see and hear a play, concert, etc. 2. those who are tuned in to a certain radio or TV program or who read a certain book 3. those who pay attention to what one writes or says 4. the act or state of hearing 5. an opportunity to be heard; hearing 6. a formal interview with a person in high position

au·di·o (ô'dē ō) *adj.* [< L. *audire,* hear] 1. of frequencies corresponding to sound waves that are normally audible 2. of or relating to sound reproduction, esp. to the sound phase of TV

au·di·o-fre·quen·cy (ô'dē ō frē'kwən sē) *adj.* of the band of audible sound frequencies or corresponding electric current frequencies, from about 20 to 20,000 hertz

au·di·ol·o·gy (ô'dē äl'ə jē) *n.* the science of hearing; esp., evaluation of hearing defects and rehabilitation of those who have such defects —**au'di·o·log'i·cal** (-ə läj'i k'l) *adj.* —**au'di·ol'o·gist** *n.*

au·di·om·e·ter (ô'dē äm'ə tər) *n.* an instrument for measuring hearing

au·di·o·phile (ô'dē ə fīl') *n.* a devotee of high-fidelity sound reproduction

au·di·o-vis·u·al (ô'dē ō vizh'oo wəl) *adj.* 1. involving both hearing and sight 2. designating or of such teaching aids as filmstrips, radio, etc.

au·dit (ô'dit) *n.* [< L. pp. of *audire,* to hear] 1. a formal, often periodic examination and checking of accounts or financial records 2. a settlement or adjustment of accounts 3. an account thus examined and adjusted, or a statement of this —*vt., vi.* 1. to examine and check (accounts, claims, etc.) 2. to attend (a college course) as a listener receiving no credits

au·di·tion (ô dish'ən) *n.* 1. the act or sense of hearing 2. a hearing to test the ability or fitness of an actor, musician, etc. —*vt.* to give an audition to —*vi.* to perform in an audition

au·di·tor (ô'də tər) *n.* 1. a hearer or listener 2. a person who is authorized to audit accounts 3. a person who audits a college course

au·di·to·ri·um (ô'də tôr'ē əm) *n.* 1. a room for an audience, as in a school, library, etc. 2. a building or hall for speeches, concerts, etc.

au·di·to·ry (ô'də tôr'ē) *adj.* of hearing or the sense of hearing —**au'di·to'ri·ly** *adv.*

Au·du·bon (ô'də bän'), **John James** 1785–1851; U.S. ornithologist, naturalist, & painter

‡**auf Wie·der·se·hen** (ouf vē'dər zā'ən) [G.] till we see each other again; goodbye

Aug. August

Au·ge·an (ô jē'ən) *adj.* 1. *Gr. Legend* of King Augeas or his large, filthy stable, which Hercules cleaned in one day 2. very filthy

au·ger (ô'gər) *n.* [by faulty separation of ME. *a nauger* < OE. *nafu,* nave (of a wheel) + *gar,* a spear] 1. a tool for boring holes in wood 2. a similar but larger tool, as for boring in the earth

TYPES OF AUGER

aught (ôt) *n.* [OE. *awiht* < *a,* one + *wiht,* a creature, WIGHT] 1. anything whatever [for *aught* I know] 2. [< *a naught* (see NAUGHT), wrongly divided *an aught*] a zero —*adv.* [Archaic] to any degree

aug·ment (ôg ment') *vt., vi.* [< OFr. < L. *augmentare* < *augere,* to increase] to make or become greater; increase —**aug·ment'a·ble** *adj.* —**aug·ment'er** *n.*

aug·men·ta·tion (ôg'men tā'shən) *n.* 1. an augmenting or being augmented 2. an addition; increase

aug·ment·a·tive (ôg men'tə tiv) *adj.* augmenting —*n.* an intensifying word or affix

au gra·tin (ō grät''n, ô-; -grat'-) [Fr., lit., with scrapings] made with a lightly browned crust of bread crumbs and grated cheese

Augs·burg (ôgz'bərg; *G.* ouks'boork) city in Bavaria, S West Germany: pop. 211,000

au·gur (ô'gər) *n.* [L., orig., a priest at rituals of fertility; prob. < *augere* (see AUGMENT)] 1. in ancient Rome, any of a group of officials who interpreted omens as favorable or unfavorable for an undertaking 2. a fortuneteller; soothsayer; prophet —*vt., vi.* 1. to foretell or prophesy from omens 2. to be an omen (of) —**augur ill** (or **well**) to be a bad (or good) omen

au·gu·ry (ô'gyər ē) *n., pl.* **-ries** 1. the rite conducted by an augur 2. an omen; indication

Au·gust (ô'gəst) [L. < AUGUSTUS (Caesar)] a masculine name —*n.* the eighth month of the year, having 31 days: abbrev. **Aug., Ag.**

au·gust (ô gust') *adj.* [L. *augustus,* orig., prob. "consecrated by the augurs"] 1. inspiring awe and reverence; imposing 2. worthy of respect; venerable —**au·gust'ly** *adv.* —**au·gust'ness** *n.*

Au·gus·ta (ô gus'tə) [L., fem. of AUGUSTUS] 1. a feminine name 2. city in E Ga.: pop. 60,000 3. capital of Me.: pop. 22,000

Au·gus·tan (ô gus'tən) *adj.* 1. of or characteristic of Augustus Caesar, his reign (27 B.C.–14 A.D.), or his times 2. of or like any similar age; classical; elegant —*n.* a writer living in an Augustan age

Au·gus·tine (ô'gəs tēn', ô gus't'n) [< L. dim. of AUGUSTUS] 1. a masculine name: var. *Austin, Augustin* 2. Saint *a)* 354–430 A.D.; Christian church father & bishop in North Africa *b)* ?–604? A.D.; Roman monk sent to convert the English to Christianity —**Au'gus·tin'i·an** (-tin'ē ən) *adj., n.*

Au·gus·tus (ô gus'təs) [L. < *augustus,* AUGUST] 1. a masculine name: dim. *Gus* 2. (*Gaius Julius Caesar Octavianus*) 63 B.C.–14 A.D.; 1st Roman emperor (27 B.C.–14 A.D.): grandnephew of Julius Caesar: also called *Octavian*

au jus (ō zhōō', ō jōōs'; *Fr.* ō zhü') [Fr., with the juice] served in its natural gravy: said of meat

auk (ôk) *n.* [dial. *alk* < ON. *alka*] any of a number of related diving birds of the northern seas, with webbed feet and short wings used as paddles

‡**au lait** (ō le') [Fr.] with milk

auld (ôld) *adj.* [Dial. & Scot.] old

auld lang syne (ôld' laŋ' zīn', sīn') [Scot., lit., old long since] old times; the good old days

‡**au na·tu·rel** (ō nȧ tü rel') [Fr.] 1. in the natural state 2. naked 3. prepared simply

aunt (ant, änt) *n.* [< ME. & OFr. < L. *amita,* paternal aunt] 1. a sister of one's mother or father 2. the wife of one's uncle

GREAT AUK (to 30 in. high)

aunt·ie, aunt·y (an'tē, än'-) *n.* aunt: a familiar or affectionate form

au·ra (ôr'ə) *n., pl.* **-ras, -rae** (-ē) [L. < Gr., akin to *aēr,* air] 1. an invisible emanation 2. a particular atmosphere or quality that seems to arise from and surround a person or thing

au·ral (ôr'əl) *adj.* [< L. *auris,* ear + -AL] of or received through the ear or the sense of hearing —**au'ral·ly** *adv.*

au·re·ate (ôr'ē it) *adj.* [< LL. < L. *aureus* < *aurum,* gold] 1. golden; gilded 2. splendid or brilliant, often affectedly so

Au·re·li·us (ô rē'lē əs, -rēl'yəs), **Marcus** (*Marcus Aurelius Antoninus*) 121–180 A.D.; Roman emperor (161–180) & Stoic philosopher

au·re·ole (ôr'ē ōl') *n.* [< L. *aureola* (*corona*), golden (crown) < L. *aureus:* see AUREATE] 1. a halo 2. the sun's corona Also **au·re·o·la** (ô rē'ə lə)

Au·re·o·my·cin (ôr'ē ō mīs''n) [< L. *aureus,* golden + Gr. *mykēs,* fungus + -IN[1]] *a trademark for* CHLORTETRACYCLINE

au re·voir (ō'rə vwär') [Fr. < L. < *re-,* again + *videre,* to see] until we meet again; goodbye

au·ri·cle (ôr'ə k'l) *n.* [< L. *auricula,* dim. of *auris,* ear] 1. *Anat. a)* the external part of the ear; pinna *b)* an atrium of the heart 2. *Biol.* an earlike part or organ

au·ric·u·lar (ô rik'yoo lər) *adj.* 1. of or near the ear, or having to do with the sense of hearing 2. spoken directly into the ear 3. ear-shaped 4. *Anat.* of an auricle —**au·ric'u·lar·ly** *adv.*

au·rif·er·ous (ô rif'ər əs) *adj.* [< L. < *aurum,* gold + *ferre,* to BEAR[1] + -OUS] bearing or yielding gold

au·ri·form (ôr'ə fôrm') *adj.* ear-shaped

au·rochs (ô'räks) *n., pl.* **au'rochs** [G. *auerochs* < OHG. *urohso* < *uro,* aurochs + *ohso,* ox] 1. the wild ox of Europe, now extinct 2. the nearly extinct European bison

Au·ro·ra (ô rôr'ə, ə-) [L., lit., dawn] 1. *Rom. Myth.* the goddess of dawn 2. [immediately or ult. < prec.] *a)* city in NE Ill., near Chicago: pop. 81,000 *b)* city in NC Colo., near Denver: pop. 159,000 —*n.* [a-] *pl.* **-ras, -rae** (-ē) 1.

the dawn 2. *same as* AURORA AUSTRALIS or AURORA BOREALIS —**au·ro′ral, au·ro′re·an** (-ē ən) *adj.*

aurora aus·tra·lis (ô strā′lis) [L.: see prec. & AUSTRAL] luminous bands of light like the aurora borealis, but in the Southern Hemisphere

aurora bo·re·a·lis (bôr′ē al′is) [AL.: see AURORA & BOREAS] luminous bands or streamers of light sometimes appearing in the night sky of the Northern Hemisphere; northern lights

Au·schwitz (ou′shvits) city in SW Poland: site of a Nazi concentration camp notorious as an extermination center: Pol. name, OŚWIĘCIM

aus·cul·ta·tion (ôs′kəl tā′shən) *n.* [< pp. of L. *auscultare,* to listen] **1.** a listening **2.** a listening, often with a stethoscope, to sounds in the chest, abdomen, etc., as in diagnosis —**aus′cul·tate′** *vt., vi.* **-tat′ed, -tat′ing** —**aus′cul·ta′tor** *n.*

aus·land·er (ous′lan′dər, ôs′-) *n.* [G. *ausländer* < *aus,* out + *land,* land] a foreigner; outsider

aus·pice (ôs′pis) *n., pl.* **-pi·ces′** (-pə sēz′) [Fr. < L. *auspicium,* omen] **1.** an omen, esp. a favorable one **2.** [*pl.*] guiding sponsorship; patronage

aus·pi·cious (ôs pish′əs) *adj.* **1.** of good omen; favorable **2.** favored by fortune; successful —**aus·pi′cious·ly** *adv.* —**aus·pi′cious·ness** *n.*

Aus·ten (ôs′tən), **Jane** 1775–1817; Eng. novelist

aus·tere (ô stir′) *adj.* [< OFr. < L. < Gr. *austēros* < *auos,* dry] **1.** having a stern manner; forbidding **2.** showing strict self-discipline; ascetic **3.** very plain —**aus·tere′ly** *adv.* —**aus·tere′ness** *n.*

aus·ter·i·ty (ô ster′ə tē) *n., pl.* **-ties** **1.** an austere quality, state, act, or practice **2.** tightened economy, as from shortages of goods

Aus·tin (ôs′tən) **1.** a masculine name: see AUGUSTINE **2.** [after S. F. *Austin,* Am. pioneer in Tex.] capital of Tex., on the Colorado River: pop. 345,000 (met. area 533,000)

aus·tral (ôs′trəl) *adj.* [< L. < *auster,* the south] **1.** southern; southerly **2.** [A-] Australian

Aus·tral·a·sia (ôs′trə lā′zhə, -shə) the islands of the SW Pacific; specif., *a)* Australia, New Zealand, and adjacent islands *b)* Australia, New Zealand, the Malay Archipelago, and Oceania —**Aus′tral·a′sian** *adj., n.*

Aus·tral·ia (ô strāl′yə) [< L. (*terra*) *australis,* southern (land)] **1.** island continent between the S Pacific and Indian oceans **2.** country comprising this continent and Tasmania: a member of the Commonwealth: 2,971,081 sq. mi.; pop. 12,446,000; cap. Canberra —**Aus·tral′ian** *adj., n.*

Australian ballot an official ballot listing candidates for election to public office, marked by the voter in secrecy

Aus·tra·loid (ôs′trə loid′) *adj.* [AUSTRAL(IA) + -OID] designating or of an ethnic group of mankind that includes the Australian aborigines, the Ainu, etc. —*n.* any member of this group

Aus·tri·a (ôs′trē ə) country in C Europe: 32,375 sq. mi.; pop. 7,371,000; cap. Vienna: Ger. name, ÖSTERREICH —**Aus′tri·an** *adj., n.*

Aus·tri·a-Hun·ga·ry (-huŋ′gər ē) former monarchy in C Europe (1867–1918) —**Aus·tro-Hun·gar·i·an** (ôs′trō huŋ ger′ē ən) *adj.*

Aus·tro-[1] *a combining form meaning* Austria

Aus·tro-[2] [< L. *auster,* south] *a combining form meaning* South, Southern

Aus·tro-A·si·at·ic (ôs′trō ā′zhē at′ik) *adj.* of a family of languages widely scattered throughout SE Asia, including Vietnamese

Aus·tro·ne·sia (ôs′trō nē′zhə, -shə) island area extending from Madagascar east to Hawaii and Easter Island

Aus·tro·ne·sian (-zhən, -shən) *adj.* **1.** of Austronesia, its people, etc. **2.** *same as* MALAYO-POLYNESIAN

au·tar·chy (ô′tär kē) *n., pl.* **-chies** [< Gr. < *autarchos,* absolute ruler < *autos,* self + *archos,* first, ruler] **1.** absolute rule; autocracy **2.** a country under such rule **3.** *same as* AUTARKY —**au·tar′chic, au·tar′chi·cal** *adj.*

au·tar·ky (ô′tär kē) *n.* [Gr. *autarkeia* < *autos,* self + *arkein,* to suffice] economic self-sufficiency as a national policy —**au·tar′kic, au·tar′ki·cal** *adj.*

auth. **1.** author **2.** authority **3.** authorized

au·then·tic (ô then′tik) *adj.* [< OFr. < LL. < Gr. *authentikos* < *authentēs,* one who does things himself] **1.** that can be believed; reliable [*an authentic* report] **2.** genuine; real [*an authentic* antique] **3.** legally executed, as a deed —**au·then′ti·cal·ly** *adv.* —**au·then·tic·i·ty** (ô′thən tis′ə tē) *n.*

au·then·ti·cate (-tə kāt′) *vt.* **-cat′ed, -cat′ing** to establish as authentic, or true, valid, genuine, etc. —**au·then′ti·ca′tion** *n.* —**au·then′ti·ca′tor** *n.*

au·thor (ô′thər) *n.* [< OFr. < L. *auctor* < *augere,* to increase] **1.** one who makes or originates something; creator **2.** the writer (*of* a book, article, etc.) —*vt.* to be the author of —**au′thor·ess** [Now Rare] *n.fem.* —**au·tho·ri·al** (ô thôr′ē əl) *adj.*

au·thor·i·tar·i·an (ə thôr′ə ter′ē ən, -thär′-) *adj.* believing in or characterized by unquestioning obedience to authority rather than individual freedom —*n.* a person who believes in or enforces such obedience —**au·thor′i·tar′i·an·ism** *n.*

au·thor·i·ta·tive (ə thôr′ə tāt′iv, -thär′-) *adj.* **1.** having authority; official **2.** reliable because coming from an authority or expert **3.** asserting authority; dictatorial —**au·thor′i·ta′tive·ly** *adv.* —**au·thor′i·ta′tive·ness** *n.*

au·thor·i·ty (ə thôr′ə tē, -thär′-) *n., pl.* **-ties** [< OFr. < L. *auctoritas* < *auctor:* see AUTHOR] **1.** *a)* the power or right to give commands, enforce obedience, take action, or make final decisions; jurisdiction *b)* the position of one having such power [the man in *authority*] *c)* such power as delegated; authorization **2.** power or influence resulting from knowledge, prestige, etc. **3.** a writing, decision, etc. cited in support of an opinion, action, etc. **4.** *a)* [*pl.*] persons, esp. in government, having the power to enforce orders, laws, etc. *b)* a government agency that administers a project **5.** an expert whose opinion is considered reliable **6.** self-assurance based on expertness

au·thor·ize (ô′thə rīz′) *vt.* **-ized′, -iz′ing** **1.** to give official approval to or permission for **2.** to give power or authority to; empower; commission **3.** to give justification for; warrant —**au′thor·i·za′tion** *n.* —**au′thor·iz′er** *n.*

Authorized Version the revised English translation of the Bible published in England in 1611 with the authorization of King James I: also called *King James Version*

au·thor·ship (ô′thər ship′) *n.* **1.** the profession of a writer **2.** the origin (of a book, idea, etc.) with reference to its author or originator [a story of unknown *authorship*]

au·tism (ô′tiz′m) *n.* [AUT(O)- + -ISM] *Psychol.* a state of mind characterized by self-absorption, fantasy, and a disregard of external reality —**au·tis′tic** *adj.*

au·to (ôt′ō) *n., pl.* **-tos** an automobile —*vi.* **-toed, -to·ing** to go by automobile: an earlier usage

au·to- [Gr. *autos,* self] *a combining form meaning:* **1.** of or for oneself; self [*autobiography*] **2.** by oneself or itself [*automobile*] Also, before a vowel, **aut-**

‡**Au·to·bahn** (ou′tō bän′; *E.* ôt′ə bän′) *n., pl.* **-bahn′en** (-bä′nən); E. **-bahns′** [G.] in Germany, an automobile expressway

au·to·bi·og·ra·phy (ôt′ə bī äg′rə fē, -bē-) *n., pl.* **-phies** the story of one's own life written or dictated by oneself —**au′to·bi·og′ra·pher** *n.* —**au′to·bi′o·graph′i·cal** (-bī′ə graf′i k'l), **au′to·bi′o·graph′ic** *adj.* —**au′to·bi′o·graph′i·cal·ly** *adv.*

au·to·clave (ôt′ə klāv′) *n.* [Fr. < *auto-,* AUTO- + L. *clavis,* a key] a container for sterilizing, cooking, etc. by superheated steam under pressure —*vt.* **-claved′, -clav′ing** to sterilize, etc. in this

au·toc·ra·cy (ô täk′rə sē) *n., pl.* **-cies** [< Gr. < *autokratēs:* see ff.] **1.** a government in which one person has supreme power; dictatorship **2.** unlimited power or authority over others

au·to·crat (ôt′ə krat′) *n.* [< Fr. < Gr. *autokratēs,* absolute ruler < *autos,* self + *kratos,* power] **1.** a ruler with absolute power; dictator; despot **2.** anyone having unlimited power over others **3.** any domineering, self-willed person —**au′to·crat′ic, au′to·crat′i·cal** *adj.* —**au′to·crat′i·cal·ly** *adv.*

au·to-da-fé (ôt′ō də fā′, out′-) *n., pl.* **au′tos-da-fé′** [Port., lit., act of the faith] **1.** the public ceremony in which the Inquisition judged and sentenced those tried as heretics **2.** the execution of the sentence; esp., the public burning of a heretic

au·tog·a·my (ô täg′ə mē) *n.* [AUTO- + -GAMY] self-fertilization, as in a flower receiving pollen from its own stamens —**au·tog′a·mous** *adj.*

au·to·gi·ro, au·to·gy·ro (ôt′ə jī′rō) *n., pl.* **-ros** [orig. a trademark < AUTO- + Gr. *gyros,* a circle] an earlier kind of aircraft having both a propeller and a large horizontal rotor

au·to·graph (ôt′ə graf′) *n.* [< L. < Gr. *autographos* < *autos,* self + *graphein,* to write] **1.** a person's own signature or handwriting **2.** a thing written in one's own handwriting; holograph —*vt.* **1.** to write (something) with one's own hand **2.** to write one's signature on or in —**au′to·graph′ic** *adj.* —**au′to·graph′i·cal·ly** *adv.*

au·to·hyp·no·sis (ôt′ō hip nō′sis) *n.* a hypnotizing of oneself or the state of being so hypnotized

au·to·in·tox·i·ca·tion (-in täk′sə kā′shən) *n.* poisoning by toxic substances (**autotoxins**) formed within the body —**au′to·tox′ic** *adj.*

au·to·mat (ôt′ə mat′) *n.* [see AUTOMATIC] a restaurant in which patrons get food from small compartments opened by putting coins into slots

au·to·mate (ôt′ə māt′) *vt.* **-mat′ed, -mat′ing** [back-formation < AUTOMATION] **1.** to convert (a factory, process, etc.) to automation **2.** to use the techniques of automation in

au·to·mat·ic (ôt′ə mat′ik) *adj.* [Gr. *automatos*, self-moving] **1.** done without conscious thought or volition, as if mechanically, or from force of habit **2.** involuntary or reflex, as some muscle action **3.** *a)* moving, operating, etc. by itself [*automatic* machinery] *b)* done with automatic equipment **4.** *Firearms* using the force of the explosion of a shell to eject, reload, and fire again, so that shots continue in rapid succession with one trigger pull: cf. SEMIAUTOMATIC —*n.* **1.** an automatic pistol, rifle, etc. **2.** any automatic machine —**au′to·mat′i·cal·ly** *adv.*

au·to·ma·tion (-mā′shən) *n.* [AUTOMA(TIC) + -TION] **1.** in manufacturing, a system or method in which many or all of the processes are automatically performed or controlled by machinery, electronic devices, etc. **2.** any system using equipment to replace people **3.** the state of being automated

au·tom·a·tism (ô täm′ə tiz'm) *n.* **1.** the quality or condition of being automatic **2.** automatic action **3.** *Physiol.* action independent of outside stimulus or of conscious control

au·tom·a·tize (-tīz′) *vt.* **-tized′, -tiz′ing** **1.** to make automatic **2.** *same as* AUTOMATE

au·tom·a·ton (ô täm′ə tän′, -tən) *n., pl.* **-tons′, -ta** (-tə) [Gr., neut. of *automatos:* see AUTOMATIC] **1.** anything that can move or act of itself **2.** an apparatus that works or moves by responding to preset controls or computerized instructions **3.** a person acting in a mechanical way

au·to·mo·bile (ôt′ə mə bēl′, -mō-; ôt′ə mə bēl′; ôt′ə-mō′bēl) *n.* [Fr.: see AUTO- & MOBILE] a passenger car propelled by an engine, esp. an internal-combustion engine, and used for traveling on streets or roads; motorcar

au·to·mo·tive (ôt′ə mōt′iv) *adj.* [AUTO- + -MOTIVE] **1.** moving by its own power; self-moving **2.** of or having to do with motor vehicles

au·to·nom·ic (-näm′ik) *adj.* **1.** of or controlled by the autonomic nervous system **2.** *Biol.* resulting from internal causes —**au′to·nom′i·cal·ly** *adv.*

autonomic nervous system the divisions of the nervous system that control the motor functions of the heart, lungs, intestines, smooth muscles, glands, etc.

au·ton·o·mous (ô tän′ə məs) *adj.* [< Gr. < *autos*, self + *nomos*, law] **1.** of an autonomy **2.** *a)* having self-government *b)* functioning independently **3.** *Biol.* functioning independently of other parts

au·ton·o·my (-mē) *n.* **1.** self-government **2.** *pl.* **-mies** any state that governs itself

au·top·sy (ô′täp′sē) *n., pl.* **-sies** [< ML. & Gr. *autopsia*, a seeing with one's own eyes < *autos*, self + *opsis*, a sight] an examination and dissection of a dead body to discover the cause of death, damage done by a disease, etc.; postmortem

au·to·sug·ges·tion (ôt′ō səg jes′chən) *n.* suggestion to oneself arising within oneself and having effects on one's thinking and bodily function

au·tumn (ôt′əm) *n.* [< OFr. < L. *autumnus;* prob. of Etruscan origin] **1.** the season that comes between summer and winter; fall **2.** any period of maturity or of beginning decline —*adj.* of, in, characteristic of, or like autumn —**au·tum·nal** (ô tum′n'l) *adj.* —**au·tum′nal·ly** *adv.*

aux. auxiliary

aux·il·ia·ry (ôg zil′yər ē, -zil′ər-) *adj.* [< L. < *auxilium*, aid < pp. of *augere*, AUGMENT] **1.** giving help or aid; assisting **2.** acting in a subsidiary, or subordinate, capacity **3.** additional; supplementary; reserve —*n., pl.* **-ries** **1.** an auxiliary person or thing **2.** [*pl.*] foreign troops aiding a country at war **3.** a supplementary group or organization [a women's *auxiliary*]

auxiliary verb a verb that helps form tenses, moods, or voices of other verbs, as *have, be, may, can, must, do, shall, will*

Av., av. avenue

av. **1.** average **2.** avoirdupois

A.V. Authorized Version (of the Bible)

a.v., a/v, A/V ad valorem

a·vail (ə vāl′) *vi., vt.* [< OFr. *a* (L. *ad*), to + *valoir*, to be worth < L. *valere*, to be strong] to be of use, help, worth, or advantage (to), as in accomplishing an end —*n.* effective use or help; advantage [of no *avail*] —**avail oneself of** to take advantage of (an opportunity, etc.)

a·vail·a·ble (ə vā′lə b'l) *adj.* **1.** that can be used **2.** that can be got, had, or reached; accessible **3.** qualified and willing to run for public office —**a·vail′a·bil′i·ty** *n.* —**a·vail′a·bly** *adv.*

av·a·lanche (av′ə lanch′) *n.* [Fr. (altered after *avaler*, to descend) < *lavanche* < LL. < L. < *labi*, to slip, glide down] **1.** a large mass of loosened snow, earth, rocks, etc. suddenly and swiftly sliding down a mountain **2.** anything that comes suddenly in overwhelming number [an *avalanche* of mail] —*vi., vt.* **-lanched′, -lanch′ing** to come down (on) like an avalanche

a·vant-garde (ä vänt′gärd′; *Fr.* à vän gȧrd′) *n.* [Fr., lit., advance guard] the leaders in new or unconventional movements, esp. in the arts; vanguard —*adj.* of such movements, ideas, etc. —**a·vant′-gard′ism** *n.* —**a·vant′-gard′ist** *n.*

av·a·rice (av′ər is) *n.* [< OFr. < L. < *avarus*, greedy < *avere*, to desire] too great a desire to have wealth; greed for riches; cupidity —**av·a·ri·cious** (av′ə rish′əs) *adj.* —**av′a·ri′cious·ly** *adv.* —**av′a·ri′cious·ness** *n.*

a·vast (ə vast′) *interj.* [< Du. *houd vast*, hold fast] *Naut.* stop! cease! halt!

av·a·tar (av′ə tär′) *n.* [Sans. *avatāra*, descent] **1.** *Hinduism* a god's coming down in bodily form to the earth; incarnation **2.** any embodiment

a·vaunt (ə vônt′, -vänt′) *interj.* [< OFr. < L. *ab*, from + *ante*, before] [Archaic] begone! go away!

avdp. avoirdupois

a·ve (ä′vā, ā′vē) *interj.* [L., imperative of *avere*, to be well] **1.** hail! **2.** farewell! —*n.* **1.** the salutation *ave* **2.** [A-] the prayer AVE MARIA

Ave., ave. avenue

A·ve Ma·ri·a (ä′vā mə rē′ə, -vē) [L. (Luke 1:28)] **1.** "Hail, Mary," the first words of a prayer to the Virgin Mary used in the Roman Catholic Church **2.** this prayer **3.** a musical setting of this

a·venge (ə venj′) *vt., vi.* **a·venged′, a·veng′ing** [< OFr. < *a-* (L. *ad*), to + *vengier* < L. *vindicare*, to claim: see VINDICATE] **1.** to get revenge for (an injury, wrong, etc.) **2.** to take vengeance on behalf of, as for a wrong —**a·veng′er** *n.*

av·e·nue (av′ə no͞o′, -nyo͞o′) *n.* [Fr. < L. *advenire:* see ADVENT] **1.** a road, path, or drive, often bordered with trees **2.** a way of approach to something **3.** a street, esp. a wide, principal one

a·ver (ə vʉr′) *vt.* **a·verred′, a·ver′ring** [< OFr. *averrer* < L. *ad*, to + *verus*, true] **1.** to declare to be true; affirm **2.** *Law* to state or declare formally; assert; allege —**a·ver′ment** *n.*

av·er·age (av′rij, -ər ij) *n.* [< Fr. *avarie*, damage to ship < It. < Ar. *'awār*, damaged goods; sense development from *n.* 4] **1.** the numerical result obtained by dividing the sum of two or more quantities by the number of quantities; an arithmetic mean **2.** any similar value [a grade *average* of C] **3.** the usual or normal kind, amount, quality, etc. **4.** *Marine Law a)* a loss incurred by damage to a ship or its cargo *b)* the equitable division of such a loss among the interested parties —*adj.* **1.** being a numerical average **2.** usual; normal; ordinary —*vi.* **-aged, -ag·ing** **1.** to be or amount to on the average **2.** to buy or sell more shares, goods, etc. at intervals so as to get a better average price —*vt.* **1.** to calculate the average or mean of **2.** to do, take, etc. on the average **3.** to divide proportionately among more than two —**average out** to arrive at an average eventually —**on the** (or **an**) **average** as an average quantity, rate, etc. —**av′er·age·ness** *n.*

a·verse (ə vʉrs′) *adj.* [< L. pp. of *avertere:* see AVERT] not willing; reluctant; opposed (*to*) —**a·verse′ly** *adv.* —**a·verse′ness** *n.*

a·ver·sion (ə vʉr′zhən, -shən) *n.* **1.** a strong or definite dislike; antipathy; repugnance **2.** the object arousing such dislike

a·vert (ə vʉrt′) *vt.* [< L. *avertere* < *a-* (*ab-*), from + *vertere*, to turn] **1.** to turn away [to *avert* one's eyes] **2.** to keep from happening; avoid; prevent [to *avert* a catastrophe] —**a·vert′i·ble** *adj.*

A·ves·ta (ə ves′tə) *n.* [< Per.] the sacred writings of Zoroastrianism, in an ancient Iranian language —**A·ves′tan** *adj., n.*

avg. average

a·vi·an (ā′vē ən) *adj.* [< L. *avis*, bird + -AN] of or having to do with birds

a·vi·ar·y (-er′ē) *n., pl.* **-ar′ies** [< L. *avis*, bird] a large cage or building for keeping many birds

a·vi·a·tion (ā′vē ā′shən) *n.* [Fr. < L. *avis*, bird] **1.** the art or science of flying airplanes **2.** the development and operation of heavier-than-air craft

a·vi·a·tor (ā′vē āt′ər) *n.* an airplane pilot; flier —**a′vi·a′trix** (-ā′triks) *n.fem.*

av·id (av′id) *adj.* [L. *avidus* < *avere*, to desire] **1.** having an intense desire or craving; greedy [*avid* for power] **2.** eager and enthusiastic [an *avid* reader] —**a·vid·i·ty** (ə vid′ə tē) *n.* —**av′id·ly** *adv.*

A·vi·gnon (à vē nyōn′) city in SE France: seat of the papacy (1309–77): pop. 73,000

a·vi·on·ics (ā′vē än′iks) *n.pl.* [AVI(ATION) + (ELECTR)ONICS] [*with sing. v.*] the branch of electronics dealing with the use of electronic equipment in aviation and astronautics —**a′vi·on′ic** *adj.*

av·o·ca·do (av′ə kä′dō, äv′-) *n., pl.* **-dos** [Sp. < MexSp. *aguacate* < Nahuatl *ahuacatl*] **1.** a thick-skinned, pear-shaped tropical fruit, yellowish green to purplish black, with a single large seed and yellow, buttery flesh, used in salads; alligator pear **2.** the tree that it grows on

av·o·ca·tion (av′ə kā′shən) ***n.*** [< L. pp. of *avocare* < *ab-*, away + *vocare*, to call] something one does in addition to his regular work, and usually for pleasure; hobby —**av′o·ca′tion·al** ***adj.***

av·o·cet (av′ə set′) ***n.*** [< Fr. < It.] a long-legged wading bird with webbed feet and a slender bill that curves upward

a·void (ə void′) ***vt.*** [< Anglo-Fr. < OFr. *esvuidier*, to empty < *es-* (< L. *ex*), out + *vuidier:* see VOID] **1.** to make void; annul, invalidate, or quash (a plea, etc. in law) **2.** to keep away from; shun [to *avoid* crowds] **3.** to keep from happening [to *avoid* breakage] —**a·void′a·ble** ***adj.*** —**a·void′a·bly** ***adv.*** —**a·void′ance** ***n.***

av·oir·du·pois (av′ər də poiz′, av′ər də poiz′) ***n.*** [< OFr. *aveir de peis*, goods having weight] **1.** *same as* AVOIRDUPOIS WEIGHT **2.** [Colloq.] heaviness or weight, esp. of a person

avoirdupois weight an English and American system of weights based on a pound of 16 ounces: see TABLES OF WEIGHTS AND MEASURES in Supplements

a·vouch (ə vouch′) ***vt.*** [< OFr. *avochier* < L. *advocare:* see ADVOCATE] **1.** to vouch for; guarantee **2.** to declare the truth of; affirm **3.** to acknowledge openly; avow —**a·vouch′ment** ***n.***

a·vow (ə vou′) ***vt.*** [< OFr. *avouer* < L. *advocare:* see ADVOCATE] **1.** to declare openly or admit frankly **2.** to acknowledge or claim (oneself) to be [he *avowed* himself a patriot] —**a·vowed′** ***adj.*** —**a·vow·ed·ly** (ə vou′id lē) ***adv.*** —**a·vow′er** ***n.***

a·vow·al (-əl) ***n.*** open acknowledgment or declaration; frank admission

a·vun·cu·lar (ə vuŋ′kyə lər) ***adj.*** [< L. *avunculus*, maternal uncle, dim. of *avus*, ancestor] of, like, or in the relationship of, an uncle

aw (ô, ä) ***interj.*** an exclamation of protest, dislike, disgust, sympathy, etc.

a·wait (ə wāt′) ***vt.*** [< ONormFr. < *a-* (L. *ad*), to + *waitier*, WAIT] **1.** to wait for; expect **2.** to be in store for; be ready for —***vi.*** to wait

a·wake (ə wāk′) ***vt.*** **a·woke′** or **a·waked′**, **a·waked′**, **a·wak′ing**; occas. Brit. pp. **a·woke′** or **a·wok′en** [< OE. *awacan* (*on-* + *wacan*, to arise, awake) & OE. *awacian* (*on-* + *wacian*, to be awake, watch)] **1.** to rouse from sleep; wake **2.** to rouse from inactivity; stir up **3.** to call forth (memories, etc.) —***vi.*** **1.** to come out of sleep; wake **2.** to become active **3.** to become aware (with *to*) —***adj.*** **1.** not asleep **2.** active or alert

a·wak·en (ə wāk′′n) ***vt., vi.*** to awake; wake up; rouse —**a·wak′en·er** ***n.***

a·wak·en·ing (-iŋ) ***n., adj.*** **1.** (a) waking up **2.** (an) arousing, as of impulses, interest, etc.

a·ward (ə wôrd′) ***vt.*** [< Anglo-Fr. < ONormFr. < *es-* (< L. *ex*) + Gmc. hyp. *wardon:* see GUARD] **1.** to give by the decision of a law court or arbitrator **2.** to give as the result of judging, as in a contest [*award* prizes] —***n.*** **1.** a decision, as by a judge or arbitrator **2.** something awarded; prize

a·ware (ə wer′) ***adj.*** [< OE. *gewær* < *wær*, cautious] **1.** orig., on one's guard **2.** knowing or realizing; conscious; informed —**a·ware′ness** ***n.***

a·wash (ə wôsh′, -wäsh′) ***adv., adj.*** **1.** just above the surface of the water and washed over by it **2.** floating on the water **3.** flooded with water

a·way (ə wā′) ***adv.*** [< OE. *aweg* < *on*, on + *weg*, way] **1.** from any given place; off [to run *away*] **2.** in another place, esp. the proper place [put tools *away*] **3.** in another direction [look *away*] **4.** far [*away* behind] **5.** off; aside [to clear snow *away*] **6.** from one's possession [give it *away*] **7.** out of existence [to fade *away*] **8.** at once [fire *away*] **9.** without stopping [to work *away* all night] **10.** into action [*away* we go!] —***adj.*** **1.** absent; gone [he is *away*] **2.** at a distance [a mile *away*] **3.** *Baseball* out [one *away* in this inning] —***interj.*** **1.** begone! **2.** let's go! —**away with** **1.** take away **2.** go or come away —**do away with** **1.** to get rid of **2.** to kill

awe (ô) ***n.*** [ON. *agi*] a mixed feeling of reverence, fear, and wonder, caused by something sublime, etc. —***vt.*** **awed, aw′ing** to inspire awe in; fill with awe —**stand** (or **be**) **in awe of** to respect and fear —**awe′less, aw′less** ***adj.***

a·weigh (ə wā′) ***adj.*** *Naut.* clearing the bottom; being weighed: said of an anchor

awe·some (ô′səm) ***adj.*** **1.** inspiring awe **2.** showing awe —**awe′some·ly** ***adv.*** —**awe′some·ness** ***n.***

awe-struck (ô′struk′) ***adj.*** filled with awe or wonder: also **awe′-strick′en** (-strik′ən)

aw·ful (ô′fəl) ***adj.*** [see AWE & -FUL] **1.** inspiring awe **2.** causing fear; terrifying **3.** [Colloq.] *a*) very bad, unpleasant, etc. [an *awful* joke] *b*) great [an *awful* bore] —***adv.*** [Colloq.] very; extremely [*awful* happy] —**aw′ful·ness** ***n.***

aw·ful·ly (ô′fə lē, ô′flē) ***adv.*** **1.** in a way to inspire awe **2.** [Colloq.] badly or offensively [to behave *awfully*] **3.** [Colloq.] very; extremely

a·while (ə wīl′, -hwīl′) ***adv.*** for a while; for a short time

awk·ward (ôk′wərd) ***adj.*** [< ON. *ǫfugr*, turned backward + OE. *-weard*, -WARD] **1.** not having grace or skill; clumsy; bungling **2.** hard to handle and use; unwieldy **3.** inconvenient; uncomfortable [an *awkward* position] **4.** embarrassed or embarrassing [an *awkward* remark] **5.** not easy to deal with; delicate [an *awkward* situation] —**awk′ward·ly** ***adv.*** —**awk′ward·ness** ***n.***

awl (ôl) ***n.*** [< OE. *æl, awel*] a small, pointed tool for making holes in wood, leather, etc.

awn (ôn) ***n.*** [ON. *ǫgn*, chaff] any of the bristly fibers on a head of barley, oats, etc., or, usually, such fibers collectively; beard —**awned** ***adj.*** —**awn′less** ***adj.***

awn·ing (ô′niŋ) ***n.*** [< ? MFr. *auvans*, pl. of *auvent*, window shade] a structure of canvas, metal, etc. extended before a window or door or over a patio, deck, etc. as a protection from sun or rain

a·woke (ə wōk′) *alt. pt. & occas. Brit. pp. of* AWAKE

a·wok·en (ə wōk′′n) *occas. Brit. pp. of* AWAKE

AWN

A·WOL, a·wol (ā′wôl′) ***adj.*** [*a*(*bsent*) *w*(*ith*)*o*(*ut*) *l*(*eave*)] *Mil.* absent without leave, but without intention of deserting —***n.*** one who is AWOL

a·wry (ə rī′) ***adv., adj.*** [see A-[1] (sense 1) & WRY] **1.** with a twist to a side; askew **2.** wrong; amiss [our plans went *awry*]

ax, axe (aks) ***n.***, *pl.* **ax′es** [OE. *eax, æx*] **1.** a tool with a long handle and a bladed head, for chopping trees and splitting wood **2.** any similar tool or weapon, as a battle-ax —***vt.*** **axed, ax′ing** **1.** to trim, split, etc. with an ax **2.** to get rid of —**get the ax** [Colloq.] **1.** to be beheaded **2.** to be discharged from one's job —**have an ax to grind** [Colloq.] to have an object of one's own to promote

ax·es[1] (ak′siz) ***n.*** *pl. of* AX

ax·es[2] (ak′sēz) ***n.*** *pl. of* AXIS

ax·i·al (ak′sē əl) ***adj.*** **1.** of, like, or forming an axis **2.** around or along an axis —**ax′i·al·ly** ***adv.***

ax·il (ak′sil) ***n.*** [< L. *axilla:* see ff.] the upper angle between a leaf, twig, etc. and the stem from which it grows

ax·il·la (ak sil′ə) ***n.***, *pl.* **-lae** (-ē), **-las** [L., armpit] **1.** the armpit **2.** *Bot.* an axil

ax·il·lar (ak′sə lər) ***adj.*** *same as* AXILLARY —***n.*** any of the stiff feathers on the underside of a bird's wing where it joins the body

ax·il·la·ry (ak′sə ler′ē) ***adj.*** **1.** *Anat.* of or near the axilla **2.** *Bot.* of, in, or growing from an axil —***n.***, *pl.* **-ries** *same as* AXILLAR

ax·i·om (ak′sē əm) ***n.*** [< Fr. < L. < Gr. *axiōma*, authority < *axios*, worthy] **1.** a statement widely accepted as true; truism **2.** an established principle or law of a science, art, etc. **3.** *Logic, Math.* a statement that needs no proof because its truth is obvious; self-evident proposition

ax·i·o·mat·ic (ak′sē ə mat′ik) ***adj.*** **1.** of or like an axiom; self-evident **2.** full of axioms; aphoristic —**ax′i·o·mat′i·cal·ly** ***adv.***

ax·is (ak′sis) ***n.***, *pl.* **ax′es** (-sēz) [L.] **1.** a real or imaginary straight line on which an object rotates or is regarded as rotating [the earth's *axis*] **2.** a real or imaginary straight line around which the parts of a thing, system, etc. are symmetrically or evenly arranged **3.** a straight line for reference or measurement, as in a graph [*x-axis, y-axis*] **4.** *Bot., Zool.* any of various axial or central parts, as the main stem of a plant —**the Axis** Germany and Italy (**Rome-Berlin Axis**), and later Japan, etc. (**Rome-Berlin-Tokyo Axis**), as allies in World War II

ax·le (ak′s'l) ***n.*** [< ff.] **1.** a rod on which a wheel turns, or one connected to a wheel so that they turn together **2.** a bar connecting opposite wheels, as of an automobile

ax·le·tree (-trē′) ***n.*** [< ON. < *ǫxull*, axle + *tre*, tree, beam] a bar connecting two opposite wheels of a carriage, wagon, etc.

Ax·min·ster (aks′min stər) ***n.*** [< *Axminster*, town in England] a type of carpet with a cut pile

ax·o·lotl (ak′sə lät′'l) ***n.*** [< Nahuatl, lit., water toy] a salamander of Mexico and the W U.S. that matures sexually while remaining in the larval stage

ax·on (ak′sän) ***n.*** [ModL. < Gr. *axōn*, axis] that part of a nerve cell through which impulses travel away from the cell body

ay·ah (ä′yə) ***n.*** [< Hindi < Port. *aia,* governess] a native nursemaid or lady's maid in India

ay·a·tol·lah (ī′ə tō′lə) ***n.*** [Ar., lit., sign of God] a leader of one of the sects of the Moslem religion, serving as teacher, judge, and administrator

aye[1] (ā) ***adv.*** [ON. *ei*] [Poet.] always; ever: also sp. **ay**

aye[2] (ī) ***adv.*** [< ? prec.] yes; yea —***n.*** an affirmative vote or voter Also sp. **ay**

aye-aye (ī′ī′) ***n.*** [Fr. < Malagasy: echoic of its cry] a lemur of Madagascar, with shaggy fur, large ears, fingerlike claws, and a long, bushy tail

AYE-AYE
(34–41 in. long, including tail)

AZ Arizona

a·zal·ea (ə zāl′yə) ***n.*** [ModL. < Gr. fem. of *azaleos,* dry: because it thrives in dry soil] **1.** any of several rhododendrons, having variously colored flowers and leaves that are usually shed in the fall **2.** the flower of any of these plants

Az·er·bai·jan (äz′ər bī jän′, az′-) **1.** region of NW Iran **2.** republic of the U.S.S.R., on the Caspian Sea: 33,436 sq. mi.; pop. 4,900,000; cap. Baku: in full, **Azerbaijan Soviet Socialist Republic** Also sp. **Azerbaidzhan, Azerbaydzhan**

Az·er·bai·ja·ni (-jä′nē) ***n.,*** *pl.* **-nis, -ni** **1.** a native or inhabitant of Azerbaijan **2.** the Turkic dialect spoken there

az·i·muth (az′ə məth) ***n.*** [< OFr. < Ar. *as-sumūt* < *al,* the + *sumūt,* pl. of *samt,* way, path] *Astron., Surveying,* etc. distance in angular degrees in a clockwise direction from the north point or, in the Southern Hemisphere, south point —**az′i·muth′al** (-muth′əl) ***adj.***

az·o (az′ō, ā′zō) ***adj.*** [< *azote,* obs. name for nitrogen] containing the nitrogen radical -N:N- *[azo dyes]* : used also as a prefix, **az·o-**

A·zores (ā′zôrz, ə zôrz′) group of Portuguese islands in the N Atlantic, west of Portugal

A·zov (ā′zôf; *Russ.* ä′zôf), **Sea of** northern arm of the Black Sea, in S European U.S.S.R.

Az·tec (az′tek) ***n.*** [< Nahuatl *Aztatlán,* name of their legendary place of origin] **1.** *pl.* **-tecs, -tec** a member of a people who lived in Mexico and had an advanced civilization before the conquest of Mexico by Cortés in 1519 **2.** their Uto-Aztecan language, usually called Nahuatl —***adj.*** of the Aztecs, their language, culture, etc.: also **Az′tec·an**

az·ure (azh′ər) ***adj.*** [OFr. *azur* < Ar. < Per. *lāzhuward,* lapis lazuli] of or like the color of a clear sky; sky-blue —***n.*** **1.** sky blue or any similar blue **2.** [Poet.] the blue sky

az·u·rite (azh′ə rīt′) ***n.*** [AZUR(E) + -ITE] **1.** a brilliant blue mineral, $2CuCO_3 \cdot Cu(OH)_2$, an ore of copper **2.** a semiprecious gem cut from it

az·y·gous (az′i gəs) ***adj.*** [Gr.] not one of a pair; unpaired; odd

B

B, b (bē) ***n.,*** *pl.* **B's, b's** **1.** the second letter of the English alphabet **2.** the sound of *B* or *b* **3.** *a symbol for* the second in a sequence or group

B[1] (bē) ***n.*** **1.** *Chem.* boron **2.** *Educ.* a grade indicating above-average work **3.** *Music a)* the seventh tone in the ascending scale of C major *b)* the scale having B as the keynote

B[2] *Chess* bishop

B- bomber

B. **1.** Bible **2.** British **3.** Brotherhood

B., b. **1.** bachelor **2.** bacillus **3.** *Baseball* base(man) **4.** *Music* bass **5.** bay **6.** book **7.** born **8.** brother

Ba *Chem.* barium

B.A. [*L. Baccalaureus Artium*] Bachelor of Arts

baa (bä) ***n.*** [echoic] the cry of a sheep or goat —***vi.*** to make this cry; bleat

Ba·al (bā′əl, bāl) ***n.,*** *pl.* **Ba′al·im** (-im), **Ba′als** **1.** among some ancient Semitic peoples, any of several fertility gods; later, a chief god **2.** a false god; idol —**Ba′al·ism *n.*** —**Ba′al·ist, Ba′al·ite′** (-īt′) ***n.***

bab·bitt[1] (bab′it) ***n.*** *same as* BABBITT METAL

bab·bitt[2], **Bab·bitt** (bab′it) ***n.*** [after the title character of a novel by Sinclair Lewis (1922)] a smugly conventional person interested chiefly in business and social success and indifferent to cultural values —**bab′bitt·ry, Bab′bitt·ry *n.***

Babbitt metal [after Isaac *Babbitt* (1799–1862), U.S. inventor] a soft alloy of tin, copper, and antimony, used to reduce friction in bearings, etc.

bab·ble (bab′′l) ***vi.*** **-bled, -bling** [of echoic origin] **1.** to make incoherent sounds, as a baby does; prattle **2.** to talk foolishly or too much **3.** to make a low, bubbling sound *[a babbling brook]* —***vt.*** **1.** to say indistinctly or incoherently **2.** to say foolishly; blab —***n.*** **1.** confused, incoherent vocal sounds **2.** foolish or meaningless talk **3.** a low, bubbling sound —**bab′bler *n.***

babe (bāb) ***n.*** **1.** a baby **2.** a naive, gullible, or helpless person: also **babe in the woods** **3.** [Slang] a girl or young woman

Ba·bel (bā′b'l, bab′′l) *Bible* a city where people tried to build a tower to the sky and were stopped by God, who caused them suddenly to speak in different languages: Gen. 11:1–9 —***n.*** [*also* **b-**] **1.** a confusion of voices, languages, or sounds; tumult **2.** a place of such confusion

ba·biche (bä bēsh′) ***n.*** [< CanadFr. < Algonquian] [Chiefly Canad.] thongs or lacings as of rawhide, used for tying or weaving, esp. in snowshoes

bab·i·ru·sa, bab·i·rous·sa, bab·i·rus·sa (bab′ə rōōs′ə, bä′bə-) ***n.*** [Malay *bābī,* hog + *rūsa,* deer] a wild hog of the East Indies, with large, curving tusks: the upper pair grow through the skin of the snout and curve backwards

Bab·ism (bäb′iz'm) ***n.*** a Persian religion founded c. 1844: cf. BAHAISM —**Bab′ist, Bab′ite *n., adj.***

ba·boon (ba bōōn′) ***n.*** [< OFr. *babuin,* ape, fool < *baboue,* lip (of animals) < *bab,* echoic] any of various large and fierce, short-tailed monkeys of Africa and Arabia, having a doglike snout, cheek pouches, and bare calluses on the rump —**ba·boon′er·y *n.*** —**ba·boon′ish *adj.***

BABOON
(35–58 in. long, including tail)

ba·bu, ba·boo (bäb′ōō) ***n.*** [Hindi *bābu*] **1.** a Hindu title equivalent to *Mr.* or *Sir* **2.** a native clerk in India who can write English

ba·bush·ka (bə boosh′kə) ***n.*** [Russ., grandmother] a scarf worn on the head by a woman or girl and tied under the chin

ba·by (bā′bē) ***n.,*** *pl.* **-bies** [ME. *babi*] **1.** a very young child; infant **2.** a person who behaves like an infant **3.** a very young animal **4.** the youngest or smallest in a group **5.** [Slang] *a)* a girl or young woman *b)* any person or thing —***adj.*** **1.** of or for an infant **2.** extremely young **3.** small of its kind **4.** infantile or childish —***vt.*** **-bied, -by·ing** **1.** to treat like a baby; pamper; coddle **2.** [Colloq.] to handle with great care —**ba′by·hood′ *n.*** —**ba′by·ish *adj.*** —**ba′by·ish·ly *adv.*** —**ba′by·like′ *adj.***

baby beef meat from a heifer or steer fattened for butchering when one to two years old

baby carriage a light carriage for wheeling a baby about: also **baby buggy**

baby grand a small grand piano

Bab·y·lon (bab′ə lən, -län′) ancient capital of Babylonia, famous for wealth, luxury, and wickedness

Bab·y·lo·ni·a (bab′ə lō′nē ə) ancient empire in SW Asia, in the lower valley of the Tigris & Euphrates rivers: flourished c. 2100–538 B.C. —**Bab′y·lo′ni·an *adj., n.***

ba·by's breath (bā′bēz breth′) **1.** any of several plants of the pink family, having small, delicate, white or pink flowers **2.** any of several other plants with small, sweetly scented flowers: also **ba′bies' breath**

ba·by-sit (bā′bē sit′) ***vi., vt.*** **-sat′, -sit′ting** to act as a baby sitter (to)

baby sitter a person hired to take care of a child or children, as when parents are away for an evening

bac·ca·lau·re·ate (bak′ə lôr′ē it) ***n.*** [< ML. < *baccalaris,* vassal farmer, squire (*n.* 1) < ? L. *baculum,* staff] **1.** the degree of Bachelor of Arts (or Science, etc.) **2.** a speech to a graduating class at commencement: also **baccalaureate address** (or **sermon**)

bac·ca·rat, bac·ca·ra (bak′ə rä′, bäk′-) ***n.*** [Fr. < ?] a gambling game played with cards

bac·cha·nal (bak′ə nəl, -nal′; bak′ə nal′) ***n.*** [L., place devoted to Bacchus] **1.** a worshiper of Bacchus **2.** a drunken carouser **3.** [*pl.*] the Bacchanalia **4.** a drunken party; orgy —***adj.*** **1.** of Bacchus or his worship **2.** carousing

Bac·cha·na·li·a (bak′ə nāl′yə, -nā′lē ə) ***n.pl.*** **1.** an ancient Roman festival honoring Bacchus **2.** [**b-**] a drunken party; orgy —**bac′cha·na′li·an** ***adj., n.***

bac·chant (bak′ənt, bə kant′) ***n., pl.*** **-chants, -chan′tes** (-kan′tēz) **1.** a priest or worshiper of Bacchus **2.** a drunken carouser —***adj.*** **1.** worshiping Bacchus **2.** given to carousing —**bac·chan·te** (bə kan′tē, -kant′) ***n.fem.***

Bac·chus (bak′əs) an ancient Greek and Roman god of wine and revelry: earlier called *Dionysus* by the Greeks —**Bac′chic, bac′chic** ***adj.***

bach (bach) ***vi.*** [< BACHELOR] [Slang] to live alone or keep house for oneself, as a bachelor: usually in phr. **bach it** —***n.*** [Slang] a bachelor

Bach (bäkh; *E. also* bäk) **1. Jo·hann Sebastian** (yō′hän), 1685–1750; Ger. organist & composer **2. Karl Philipp Emanuel,** 1714–88; Ger. composer: son of *prec.*

bach·e·lor (bach′′l ər, bach′lər) ***n.*** [< OFr. < ML. *baccalaris:* see BACCALAUREATE] **1.** orig., a young knight who served under another's banner **2.** a man who has not married **3.** a person who is a BACHELOR OF ARTS (or SCIENCE, etc.) —***adj.*** of or for a bachelor —**bach′e·lor·hood′** ***n.***

Bachelor of Arts (or **Science,** etc.) **1.** a degree given by a college or university to one who has completed a four-year course in the humanities (or in science, etc.) **2.** one who has this degree

bachelor's button any of several plants of the composite family, as the cornflower, with button-shaped flowers

bac·il·lar·y (bas′ə ler′ē, bə sil′ər ē) ***adj.*** [ModL. *bacillarius:* see ff.] **1.** rod-shaped: also **ba·cil·li·form** (bə sil′ə fôrm′) **2.** consisting of rodlike structures **3.** of, like, or caused by bacilli Also **ba·cil·lar** (bə sil′ər)

ba·cil·lus (bə sil′əs) ***n., pl.*** **-cil′li** (-ī) [ModL. < LL. < L. dim. of *baculus,* a stick] **1.** any of the rod-shaped bacteria **2.** [*usually pl.*] loosely, any of the bacteria, esp. those causing disease

back (bak) ***n.*** [< OE. *bæc*] **1.** the part of the body opposite to the front; in man and other animals, the part from the nape of the neck to the end of the spine **2.** the backbone **3.** the part of a chair that supports one's back **4.** the part of a garment that fits on the back **5.** the rear part of anything **6.** the part or side that is less often used, seen, etc. **7.** the part of a book where the sections are fastened together **8.** *Sports* a player or position behind the front line —***adj.*** **1.** at the rear; behind **2.** distant or remote **3.** of or for a time in the past *[back* pay*]* **4.** backward; reversed **5.** *Phonet.* with the tongue toward the back of the mouth —***adv.*** **1.** at, to, or toward the rear **2.** to or toward a former position **3.** into or toward a previous condition **4.** to or toward an earlier time **5.** in concealment *[*to hold *back* information*]* **6.** in return *[*to pay one *back]* —***vt.*** **1.** to cause to move backward (often with *up*) **2.** to stand behind **3.** to support or help **4.** to bet on **5.** to get on the back of; mount **6.** to provide with a back or backing **7.** to form the back of —***vi.*** **1.** to go backward **2.** to shift counterclockwise: said of the wind **3.** to have the back facing —**back and forth** to and fro —**back down** to withdraw from a position, etc.: also **back water** —**back out (of)** **1.** to withdraw from an enterprise **2.** to break a promise or engagement —**back up** **1.** to support **2.** to go backward: also **back away, back out,** etc. **3.** to accumulate as the result of a stoppage *[*traffic *backed up]* —**be (flat) on one's back** to be ill, bedridden, etc. —**behind one's back** without one's knowledge or consent —**get off one's back** (or **case**) [Slang] to stop nagging or harassing one —**get** (or **put**) **one's back up** to make or be obstinate —**go back on** [Colloq.] **1.** to betray **2.** to fail to keep (a promise, etc.) —**(in) back of** behind —**turn one's back on** to desert; fail —**with one's back to the wall** in a desperate position

back·ache (bak′āk′) ***n.*** an ache or pain in the back

back·bench·er (bak′ben′chər) ***n.*** a legislator who is not a leader in his party

back·bite (-bīt′) ***vt., vi.*** **-bit′, -bit′ten** or **-bit′, -bit′ing** to slander (an absent person) —**back′bit′er** ***n.***

back·board (-bôrd′) ***n.*** *Basketball* a board or flat surface just behind the basket

back·bone (-bōn′) ***n.*** **1.** the column of bones (vertebrae) along the center of the back; spine **2.** main support **3.** a main ridge of mountains **4.** willpower, courage, etc.

back·break·ing (-brāk′iŋ) ***adj.*** very tiring

back burner [from the idea of keeping a pot and its contents warm on a back burner of a stove] a state of temporary suspension, low priority, etc.: usually in phr. **on the back burner,** in or into such a state

back court **1.** *Basketball* a team's defensive half of the court **2.** *Tennis* the area from the service line to the base line on either side of the net

back·down (-doun′) ***n.*** [Colloq.] a backing down; withdrawal from a position, claim, etc.

back·drop (-dräp′) ***n.*** a curtain hung at the back of a stage, often a painted scene

backed (bakt) ***adj.*** having a (specified kind of) back *[*canvas-*backed]*

back·er (bak′ər) ***n.*** **1.** a patron; supporter **2.** a person who bets on a contestant

back·field (-fēld′) ***n.*** *Football* the players stationed behind the line of scrimmage; esp., the offensive unit

back·fill (-fil′) ***vt.*** to refill (an excavation), as with earth previously removed

back·fire (-fīr′) ***n.*** **1.** a fire started to stop a prairie fire or forest fire by creating a burned area in its path **2.** a premature explosion in a cylinder of an internal-combustion engine **3.** an explosive force toward the breech of a firearm —***vi.*** **-fired′, -fir′ing** **1.** to use or set a backfire **2.** to explode as a backfire **3.** to go awry; boomerang

back-for·ma·tion (-fôr mā′shən) ***n.*** **1.** a word formed from, but looking as if it were the base of, another word (Ex.: *burgle* from *burglar*) **2.** the forming of such a word

back·gam·mon (-gam′ən) ***n.*** [BACK + GAMMON[2]] a game played on a special board by two people, with pieces moved according to the throw of dice

back·ground (-ground′) ***n.*** **1.** the part of a scene or picture toward the back **2.** surroundings behind something, providing harmony or contrast **3.** an unimportant position **4.** the whole of one's study, training, and experience **5.** events or conditions leading up to or surrounding something, helping to explain it **6.** music (in full, **background music**) or sound effects accompanying action, as in movies

back·hand (-hand′) ***n.*** **1.** handwriting that slants up to the left **2.** a backhand catch, stroke, etc. —***adj.*** **1.** done with the back of the hand turned inward, as for a baseball catch, or forward, as for a tennis stroke, and with the arm across the body **2.** written in backhand —***adv.*** in a backhand way —***vt.*** to hit, catch, swing, etc. backhand

BACKHAND STROKE

back·hand·ed (-han′did) ***adj.*** **1.** *same as* BACKHAND **2.** not direct and open; equivocal or sarcastic *[*a *backhanded* compliment*]* —***adv.*** in a backhanded way

back·hoe (-hō′) ***n.*** an excavating machine with a hinged bucket on a long, jointed arm: it digs by drawing the bucket toward its power unit

back·ing (-iŋ) ***n.*** **1.** something forming a back for support or strength **2.** support given to a person or cause **3.** those giving such support **4.** [Slang] a musical accompaniment

back·lash (-lash′) ***n.*** **1.** a quick, sharp recoil **2.** a sudden, strong reaction, as to a political or social movement **3.** a snarl in a reeled fishing line, from an imperfect cast

back·log (-lôg′, -läg′) ***n.*** **1.** a large log at the back of a fireplace **2.** a reserve **3.** an accumulation of unfilled orders, unfinished work, etc. —***vi., vt.*** **-logged′, -log′ging** to accumulate as a backlog

back number an old issue of a periodical

back order an order not yet filled

back·pack (-pak′) ***n.*** a knapsack, often on a lightweight frame, worn by campers or hikers —***vi.*** to hike wearing a backpack —***vt.*** to carry in a backpack —**back′pack′er** ***n.***

back·ped·al (-ped′′l) ***vi.*** **-ped′aled** or **-ped′alled, -ped′al·ing** or **-ped′al·ling** **1.** to press backward on bicycle pedals in braking **2.** to move backward quickly in boxing to avoid a blow **3.** to retreat from a previously held opinion

back road a road that is away from the main road; country road, esp. an unpaved one

back seat a secondary or inconspicuous position

back-seat driver (-sēt′) an automobile passenger who offers unwanted advice about driving

back·side (bak′sīd′) ***n.*** **1.** the back or hind part **2.** the rump; buttocks

back·slide (-slīd′) ***vi.*** **-slid′, -slid′** or **-slid′den, -slid′ing** to slide backward in morals or religion —**back′slid′er** ***n.***

back·space (-spās′) ***vi.*** **-spaced′, -spac′ing** to move a typewriter carriage back a space at a time by depressing a certain key **(backspacer)**

back·spin (-spin′) ***n.*** a backward spin given to a ball, etc., making it come back as upon hitting the ground

back·stage (-stāj′) ***adv.*** in the wings or dressing rooms of a theater —***adj.*** **1.** situated backstage **2.** of the life of people in show business

back·stairs (-sterz′) ***adj.*** involving intrigue or scandal

back·stay (-stā′) ***n.*** a stay or rope extending aft from a masthead to the side or stern of the ship

back·stop (-stäp′) ***n.*** **1.** a screen, etc., as behind a baseball catcher, to stop balls from going too far **2.** anything that supports or bolsters
back·stretch (-strech′) ***n.*** the part of a race track farthest from the grandstand
back·stroke (-strōk′) ***n.*** **1.** a backhand stroke **2.** a stroke made by a swimmer lying face upward, stretching the arms alternately over the head —***vi.*** **-stroked′, -strok′ing** to perform a backstroke —***vt.*** to hit with a backstroke
back talk [Colloq.] saucy or insolent retorts
back-to-back (bak′tə bak′) ***adj.*** [Colloq.] one right after another; consecutive
back·track (-trak′) ***vi.*** **1.** to return by the same path **2.** to withdraw from a position, etc.
back·up, back-up (-up′) ***adj.*** **1.** alternate or auxiliary *[a backup pilot]* **2.** supporting *[a backup effort]* —***n.*** a backing up; specif., *a)* an accumulation because of a stoppage *b)* a support
back·ward (-wərd) ***adv.*** **1.** toward the back; behind **2.** with the back or rear foremost **3.** in reverse **4.** in a way contrary to normal **5.** into the past **6.** from a better to a worse state Also **back′wards** —***adj.*** **1.** turned or directed toward the rear or in the opposite way **2.** hesitant or shy, as in meeting people **3.** late in developing; retarded —**bend** (or **lean**) **over backward** **1.** to try earnestly (to please, pacify, etc.) **2.** to offset a tendency, bias, etc. by an effort in the opposite direction —**back′ward·ly** ***adv.*** —**back′ward·ness** ***n.***
back·wash (-wôsh′, -wäsh′) ***n.*** **1.** water moved backward, as by a ship, an oar, etc. **2.** a backward current, as of air from an airplane propeller
back·wa·ter (-wôt′ər, -wät′-) ***n.*** **1.** water moved backward or held back by a dam, etc. **2.** stagnant water in a stream **3.** a place or condition where there is no progress or growth —***adj.*** stagnant; backward
back·woods (-woodz′) ***n.pl.*** [*occas. with sing. v.*] **1.** heavily wooded areas far from centers of population **2.** any remote, thinly populated place —***adj.*** in, from, or like the backwoods: also **back′wood′** —**back′woods′man** ***n., pl.*** **-men**
ba·con (bāk′′n) ***n.*** [OFr. < OS. *baco,* side of bacon] salted and smoked meat from the back or sides of a hog —**bring home the bacon** [Colloq.] **1.** to earn a living **2.** to succeed; win
Ba·con (bāk′′n) **1. Francis,** 1561–1626; Eng. philosopher, essayist, & statesman **2. Roger,** 1214?–94; Eng. philosopher & scientist
bac·te·ri·a (bak tir′ē ə) ***n.pl., sing.*** **-ri·um** (-əm) [ModL. < Gr. dim. of *baktron,* a staff] typically one-celled microorganisms which have no chlorophyll, multiply by simple division, and occur in various forms, chiefly as cocci, bacilli, and spirilla: some bacteria cause diseases, but others are necessary for fermentation, nitrogen fixation, etc. —**bac·te′ri·al** ***adj.*** —**bac·te′ri·al·ly** ***adv.***
bac·te·ri·cide (bak tir′ə sīd′) ***n.*** [BACTERI(O)- + -CIDE] an agent that destroys bacteria —**bac·te′ri·ci′dal** ***adj.***
bac·te·ri·o- *a combining form meaning* of bacteria
bac·te·ri·ol·o·gy (bak tir′ē äl′ə jē) ***n.*** the study of bacteria, as in medicine, or for food processing, agriculture, etc. —**bac·te′ri·o·log′ic** (-ē ə läj′ik), **bac·te′ri·o·log′i·cal** ***adj.*** —**bac·te′ri·o·log′i·cal·ly** ***adv.*** —**bac·te′ri·ol′o·gist** ***n.***
bac·te·ri·o·phage (bak tir′ē ə fāj′) ***n.*** [BACTERIO- + -PHAGE] any virus that is parasitic upon certain bacteria, disintegrating them
bac·te·ri·um (-əm) ***n.*** *sing. of* BACTERIA
Bac·tri·an camel (bak′trē ən) [< *Bactria,* ancient country in W Asia] a camel with two humps, native to C Asia, shorter and hairier than the dromedary
bad[1] (bad) ***adj.*** **worse, worst** [ME.] **1.** not good; not as it should be **2.** defective in quality **3.** unfit; unskilled **4.** not pleasant; unfavorable **5.** rotten; spoiled **6.** incorrect; faulty *[bad spelling]* **7.** *a)* wicked; immoral *b)* mischievous **8.** causing injury; harmful **9.** severe *[a bad storm]* **10.** ill; in poor health **11.** sorry; distressed *[he feels bad about it]*: cf. BADLY **12.** *Law* not valid —***adv.*** [Colloq.] badly —***n.*** **1.** anything bad; bad quality or state **2.** wickedness —**in bad** [Colloq.] in trouble or disfavor —**not bad** [Colloq.] good; fairly good: also **not half bad, not so bad** —**bad′ness** ***n.***
bad[2] (bad) *archaic pt. of* BID
bad blood a feeling of (mutual) enmity
bade (bad; *occas.* bād) *alt. pt. of* BID
bad egg [Slang] a mean or dishonest person: also **bad actor, bad apple, bad hat, bad lot,** etc.
Ba·den (bäd′′n) **1.** region in SW West Germany **2.** city & health resort there: in full, **Baden-Baden**
badge (baj) ***n.*** [ME. *bage*] **1.** a token, emblem, or sign worn to show rank, membership, etc. **2.** any distinguishing mark or symbol —***vt.*** **badged, badg′ing** to provide or mark with a badge
badg·er (baj′ər) ***n., pl.*** **-ers, -er:** see PLURAL, II, D, 1 [< ? obs. n. & personal name *badger,* grain dealer] **1.** a carnivorous, burrowing mammal with thick, short legs, and long claws on the forefeet **2.** its fur —***vt.*** to nag at
bad·i·nage (bad′ə näzh′, bad′′n ij) ***n.*** [Fr. < *badiner,* to jest < Pr. < ML. *badare,* to gape] playful, teasing talk; banter —***vt.*** **-naged′, -nag′ing** to tease with playful talk
bad·lands (bad′landz′) ***n.pl.*** **1.** any section of barren land where deep erosion has cut the dry soil or soft rocks into strange shapes **2.** [B-] any section like this in the W U.S., esp. in SW S.Dak.: also **Bad Lands**
bad·ly (bad′lē) ***adv.*** **1.** in a bad manner **2.** [Colloq.] very much; greatly Also used informally as an adjective meaning "sorry" or "distressed"
bad·man (bad′man′) ***n., pl.*** **-men′** (-men′) a cattle thief, desperado, or hired gunman of the old West
bad·min·ton (bad′min t′n) ***n.*** [after *Badminton,* estate of the Duke of Beaufort] a game in which a feathered cork (*shuttlecock*) is batted back and forth with light rackets across a net
bad-tem·pered (bad′tem′pərd) ***adj.*** having a bad temper or cranky disposition; irritable
Bae·de·ker (bā′də kər) ***n.*** **1.** any of a series of guidebooks to foreign countries first published in Germany by Karl Baedeker (1801–59) **2.** loosely, any guidebook
baf·fle (baf′′l) ***vt.*** **-fled, -fling** [16th-c. Scot.; prob. respelling of obs. Scot. *bauchle*] **1.** to confuse so as to keep from understanding or solving; puzzle; confound **2.** to hinder; impede **3.** to check the interference of (sound waves) by a baffle —***n.*** **1.** a baffling or being baffled **2.** a wall or screen to deflect the flow of liquids, gases, etc.: also **baf′fle·plate′** **3.** a mounting that checks the transmission of sound waves between the front and rear of a loudspeaker —**baf′fle·ment** ***n.*** —**baf′fler** ***n.*** —**baf′fling** ***adj.***
bag (bag) ***n.*** [ON. *baggi*] **1.** a nonrigid container made of fabric, paper, leather, etc., with an opening at the top that can be closed; sack **2.** the amount a bag holds **3.** a piece of hand luggage **4.** a woman's handbag; purse **5.** *a)* a container for game *b)* the amount of game caught or killed **6.** anything shaped or bulging like a bag *[bags under the eyes]* **7.** an udder or sac **8.** [Slang] one's special sphere of interest, talent, obsession, etc. **9.** [< BAGGAGE, *3a*] [Slang] an unattractive woman **10.** *Baseball* a base —***vt.*** **bagged, bag′ging** **1.** to make bulge **2.** to enclose within a bag **3.** to capture **4.** to kill in hunting **5.** [Slang] to get —***vi.*** **1.** to swell **2.** to hang loosely —**bag and baggage** [Colloq.] **1.** with all one's possessions **2.** entirely —**be left holding the bag** [Colloq.] to be left to suffer the bad consequences or the blame —**in the bag** [Slang] having its success assured—**bag′ful′** ***n., pl.*** **-fuls′**
ba·gasse (bə gas′) ***n.*** [Fr. < Pr. *bagasso,* refuse from processing grapes, etc. < L. *baca,* berry] the part of sugar cane left after the juice has been extracted, or the residue of certain other processed plants: used for making fiberboard, etc.
bag·a·telle (bag′ə tel′) ***n.*** [Fr. < It. *bagatella,* dim. < L. *baca,* berry] **1.** something of little value; trifle **2.** a game, somewhat like billiards, played with nine balls on a table
Bag·dad (bag′dad, bäg däd′) *same as* BAGHDAD
ba·gel (bā′g′l) ***n.*** [< Yid., ult. < G. *beugen,* to bend] a hard, doughnut-shaped bread roll that is simmered in water before being baked
bag·gage (bag′ij) ***n.*** [< OFr. < *bagues,* baggage < ML. *baga,* chest] **1.** the bags and other equipment of a traveler **2.** the supplies and gear of an army **3.** *a)* [< Fr. *bagasse,* harlot, ult. < Ar. *baghīya,* adulteress: infl. by "army baggage," i.e., "camp follower"] formerly, a prostitute *b)* a saucy girl **4.** burdensome or superfluous ideas, practices, etc.
bag·gy (bag′ē) ***adj.*** **-gi·er, -gi·est** **1.** puffed in a baglike way **2.** hanging loosely *[baggy trousers]* —**bag′gi·ly** ***adv.*** —**bag′gi·ness** ***n.***
Bagh·dad (bag′dad, bäg däd′) capital of Iraq, on the Tigris River: pop. c. 1,000,000
bag·man (bag′mən) ***n., pl.*** **-men** **1.** [Brit.] a traveling salesman **2.** [Slang] a go-between, as in the numbers racket, etc.
bagn·io (ban′yō, bän′-) ***n., pl.*** **-ios** [< It. < L. < Gr. *balaneion,* bath] a house of prostitution; brothel
bag·pipe (bag′pīp′) ***n.*** [*often pl.*] a shrill-toned musical instrument with a double-reed, fingered pipe and drone pipes, all sounded by air forced from a leather bag: now chiefly Scottish —**bag′pip′er** ***n.***

BAGPIPE

ba·guette, ba·guet (ba get′) ***n.*** [< Fr. < It. < L. *baculum,* a staff] **1.** a gem, etc. cut in the shape of a narrow oblong **2.** this shape **3.** *Archit.* a small, convex molding
bah (bä, ba) ***interj.*** an exclamation expressing contempt, scorn, or disgust
Ba·hai (bə hī′, bə hä′ē) ***n., pl.*** **Ba·hais′** **1.** a believer in Bahaism **2.** *same as* BAHAISM —***adj.*** of Bahaism or a Bahai Also written **Baha'i**

Ba·ha·ism (bə hä′iz'm, -hī′-) *n.* [Ar. *ba-hā,* splendor + -ISM] a modern religion, developed orig. in Iran from Babism, that advocates universal brotherhood, social equality, etc. —**Ba·ha′ist** *n., adj.*

Ba·ha·mas (bə hä′məz, -hā′-) country consisting of a group of islands **(Bahama Islands)** in the West Indies: a member of the Commonwealth: 4,404 sq. mi.; pop. 180,000; cap. Nassau —**Ba·ha′mi·an** *adj., n.*

Bah·rain, Bah·rein (bä rān′) independent Arab sheikdom consisting of a group of islands in the Persian Gulf: a member of the Commonwealth: 231 sq. mi.; pop. 200,000

baht (bät) *n., pl.* **bahts, baht** [Thai *bāt*] *see* MONETARY UNITS, table (Thailand)

Bai·kal (bī käl′), **Lake** lake in SE Siberia: 12,000 sq. mi.

bail[1] (bāl) *n.* [OFr., power, control < *baillir,* keep in custody < L. *bajulare,* bear a burden < *bajulus,* porter] **1.** money or credit deposited with the court to get an arrested person released until his trial **2.** the release thus brought about **3.** the person giving bail —*vt.* **1.** to set (an arrested person) free on bail or have (an arrested person) set free by giving bail (often with *out*) **2.** to help out of financial or other difficulty (often with *out*) —**go bail for** to furnish bail for —**bail′a·ble** *adj.*

bail[2] (bāl) *n.* [< OFr. < VL. hyp. *bajula,* vessel < *bajulare:* see prec.] a bucket, etc. for dipping up water from a boat —*vi., vt.* **1.** to remove water from (a boat) as with a bail **2.** to dip out (water, etc.) as with a bail —**bail out** to make a parachute jump from an aircraft —**bail′er** *n.*

bail[3] (bāl) *n.* [< ON. *beygla* < *beygja,* to bend] **1.** a hoop-shaped support, as for a canopy **2.** a hoop-shaped handle for a bucket, etc. **3.** a bar on a typewriter to hold the paper against the platen

bail[4] (bāl) *n.* [< OFr., ult. < L. *bajulus,* porter] *Cricket* either of two pieces of wood laid across the three stumps to form a wicket

bai·lie (bā′lē) *n.* [Scot. < OFr. < *bailif:* see ff.] in Scotland, a municipal official corresponding to an alderman in England

bai·liff (bā′lif) *n.* [OFr. *bailif* < *baillir:* see BAIL[1]] **1.** a deputy sheriff who serves processes, etc. **2.** a court officer who guards jurors, keeps order in the courtroom, etc. **3.** in England, an administrative official of a district **4.** [Chiefly Brit.] an overseer or steward of an estate

bai·li·wick (bā′lə wik) *n.* [ME. < *bailif,* BAILIFF + *wik* < OE. *wic,* village] **1.** a bailiff's district **2.** one's particular area of activity, authority, etc.

bail·out (bāl′out′) *n.* [see BAIL[1], *vt.* 2] a helping out of one in serious financial or other difficulty; specif., a providing of government assistance, including loans, to a failing company, municipality, etc.

bails·man (bālz′mən) *n., pl.* **-men** a person who acts as surety or gives bail for another

bairn (bern) *n.* [< OE. < *beran,* to BEAR[1]] [Scot.] a child

bait (bāt) *vt.* [ON. *beita,* to make bite, caus. < *bīta,* to bite] **1.** to set attacking dogs against for sport *[to bait bears]* **2.** to torment or harass with unprovoked, repeated attacks **3.** to tease or goad **4.** to put food, etc. on (a hook or trap) so as to lure animals or fish **5.** to lure; tempt; entice —*n.* **1.** food, etc. put on a hook or trap to lure fish or animals **2.** any lure; enticement —**bait′er** *n.*

bait-and-switch (bāt′'n swich′) *adj.* of or using an unethical sales technique in which a seller lures customers by advertising an often nonexistent bargain item and then tries to switch their attention to more expensive items

baize (bāz) *n.* [< OFr. pl. of *baie* < L. *badius,* chestnut-brown] a feltlike, thick woolen cloth, often green, used to cover billiard tables, etc.

Ba·ja Ca·li·for·nia (bä′hä kä′lē fôr′nyä) peninsula in Mexico, between the Pacific & the Gulf of California: 55,634 sq. mi.

bake (bāk) *vt.* **baked, bak′ing** [OE. *bacan*] **1.** to cook (food) by dry heat, esp. in an oven **2.** to dry and harden (esp. glazed stoneware) by heat —*vi.* **1.** to bake bread, etc. **2.** to become baked —*n.* **1.** a baking **2.** a product of baking **3.** a social affair at which a baked food is served

Ba·ke·lite (bā′kə līt′) [after L. H. *Baekeland* (1863–1944), U.S. chemist] *a trademark for* a synthetic resin and plastic

bak·er (bāk′ər) *n.* **1.** one whose work or business is baking bread, etc. **2.** a small, portable oven

baker's dozen thirteen

Bak·ers·field (bāk′ərz fēld′) [after Col. *Baker,* early landowner] city in SC Calif.: pop. 106,000

bak·er·y (bāk′ər ē) *n.* **1.** *pl.* **-er·ies** a place where bread, pastries, etc. are baked or sold **2.** baked goods

bake·shop (bāk′shäp′) *n.* a bakery

baking powder a leavening agent containing baking soda and an acid substance, such as cream of tartar, which together produce carbon dioxide in the presence of water

baking soda sodium bicarbonate, $NaHCO_3$, used as a leavening agent and as an antacid

bak·sheesh, bak·shish (bak′shēsh) *n.* [via Turk. or Ar. < Per. < *bakhshidan,* to give] in Turkey, Egypt, India, etc., a tip, gratuity, or alms

Ba·ku (bä ko͞o′) capital of the Azerbaijan S.S.R., on the Caspian Sea: pop. 1,224,000

bal. balance

Ba·laam (bā′ləm) *Bible* a prophet rebuked by his donkey after he had beaten it: Num. 22–24

bal·a·lai·ka (bal′ə lī′kə) *n.* [Russ.] a Russian stringed instrument like a guitar, but with a triangular body

bal·ance (bal′əns) *n.* [OFr. < ML. < LL. *bilanx,* having two scales < L. *bis,* twice + *lanx,* a scale] **1.** an instrument for weighing, esp. one with two matched pans hanging from either end of a poised lever; scales **2.** a state of equilibrium or equipoise; equality in weight, value, importance, etc. **3.** bodily equilibrium *[he kept his balance on the tightrope]* **4.** mental or emotional stability **5.** the pleasing harmony of various elements in a work of art; harmonious proportion **6.** a weight, force, etc. that counteracts another or causes equilibrium **7.** the point along an object's length at which there is equilibrium: in full, **balance point** **8.** *a)* equality of debits and credits in an account *b)* the difference between credits and debits **9.** the amount still owed after a partial settlement **10.** a remainder **11.** a balancing **12.** *same as* BALANCE WHEEL —*vt.* **-anced, -anc·ing** **1.** to weigh in or as in a balance **2.** to compare as to relative importance, value, etc. **3.** to counterpoise or counteract; offset **4.** to put or keep in a state of equilibrium; poise **5.** to bring into proportion, harmony, etc. **6.** to make or be equal to in weight, force, etc. **7.** *a)* to find any difference between the debit and credit sides of (an account); also, to equalize the debit and credit sides of (an account) *b)* to settle (an account) —*vi.* **1.** to be in equilibrium **2.** to be equal in value, weight, etc. **3.** to have the credit and debit sides equal **4.** to waver slightly —**in the balance** in a critical, undecided state —**bal′ance·a·ble** *adj.* —**bal′anc·er** *n.*

balance beam a long, horizontal wooden beam raised about four feet above the floor, on which women gymnasts perform balancing exercises of jumps, turns, steps, etc.

balance of (international) payments a balance estimated for a given period showing an excess or deficit in total payments of all kinds between one country and another country or other countries

balance of power an even distribution of military and economic power among nations that keeps any one of them from being too strong or dangerous

balance of trade the difference in value between the imports and exports of a country

balance sheet a summarized statement showing the financial status of a business

balance wheel a wheel that swings back and forth to regulate the movement of a timepiece, etc.

bal·a·ta (bal′ə tə) *n.* [Sp. < Tupi] **1.** a tropical American tree **2.** its dried sap, a rubberlike gum used commercially

bal·bo·a (bal bō′ə) *n.* [Sp., after ff.] *see* MONETARY UNITS, table (Panama)

Bal·bo·a (bal bō′ə; *Sp.* bäl bō′ä), **Vas·co Nú·ñez de** (väs′kô no͞o′nyeth *the*) 1475?–1517?; Sp. explorer: first European to discover the Pacific Ocean

bal·brig·gan (bal brig′ən) *n.* [after *Balbriggan,* Ireland] a knitted cotton material used for hosiery, underwear, etc.

bal·co·ny (bal′kə nē) *n., pl.* **-nies** [< It., akin to OHG. *balcho,* a beam] **1.** a platform projecting from a building and enclosed by a balustrade **2.** an upper floor of seats in a theater, etc., often jutting out over the main floor

bald (bôld) *adj.* [ME. *balled* < ?] **1.** having white fur or feathers on the head, as some animals and birds **2.** having no hair on all or part of the scalp **3.** not covered by natural growth *[bald hills]* **4.** plain; unadorned **5.** frank and blunt —**bald′ly** *adv.* —**bald′ness** *n.*

bald·cy·press (bôld′sī′pris) *n.* a cone-bearing tree of SE U.S. swamps, that sheds its needles in the fall

bald eagle a large, strong eagle of N. America, with a white-feathered head and neck

Bal·der (bôl′dər) *Norse Myth.* the god of light, peace, virtue, and wisdom: also sp. **Baldr**

bal·der·dash (bôl′dər dash′) *n.* [orig., a senseless mixture of liquids] nonsensical talk or writing

bald·faced (bôld′fāst′) *adj.* brazen; shameless

bald·head (-hed′) *n.* **1.** a person who has a bald head **2.** a bald (sense 1) bird —**bald′head′ed** *adj.*

bald·ing (bôl′diŋ) *adj.* becoming bald

bald·pate (bôld′pāt′) *n.* **1.** a baldheaded person **2.** a N. American duck with a white crown

bal·dric (bôl′drik) *n.* [< OFr., ult. < L. *balteus,* a girdle] a

fat, āpe, cär, ten, ēven, is, bīte; gō, hôrn, to͞ol, look; oil, out; up, fur; get; joy; yet; chin; she; thin, *th*en; zh, leisure; ŋ, ring; ə for *a* in *ago, e* in *agent, i* in *sanity, o* in *comply, u* in *focus;* ′ as in *able* (ā′b'l); Fr. bál; ë, Fr. coeur; ö, Fr. feu; Fr. mon; ô, Fr. coq; ü, Fr. duc; *r,* Fr. cri; H, G. ich; kh, G. doch; ‡foreign; *hypothetical; < derived from. See inside front cover.

belt worn over one shoulder and across the chest to support a sword, etc.

Bald·win (bôld′win) ***n.*** [after Col. L. *Baldwin* (1740–1807), Mass. apple grower] a moderately tangy, red winter apple

bale[1] (bāl) ***n.*** [OFr. < OHG. *balla,* a ball] a large bundle, esp. a standardized quantity, as of cotton, hay, or straw, compressed and bound —***vt.*** **baled, bal′ing** to make into bales —**bal′er** ***n.***

bale[2] (bāl) ***n.*** [OE. *bealu*] [Poet.] **1.** evil; harm **2.** woe

Bal·e·ar·ic Islands (bal′ē er′ik) group of Sp. islands in the Mediterranean, east of Spain

ba·leen (bə lēn′) ***n.*** [< OFr. < L. *ballaena,* a whale] *same as* WHALEBONE

bale·ful (bāl′fəl) ***adj.*** harmful or evil; sinister —**bale′ful·ly** ***adv.*** —**bale′ful·ness** ***n.***

Ba·li (bä′lē, bal′ē) island of Indonesia, east of Java: 2,100 sq. mi. —**Ba′li·nese′** (bä′lə nēz′, bal′ə-) ***adj., n.***

balk (bôk) ***n.*** [OE. *balca,* a bank, ridge] **1.** a ridge of unplowed land between furrows **2.** a roughly hewn piece of timber **3.** a check, hindrance, disappointment, etc. **4.** *Baseball* an illegal motion by the pitcher, as an uncompleted motion to throw, entitling base runners to advance one base —***vt.*** **1.** to miss or let slip by **2.** to obstruct or foil —***vi.*** **1.** to stop and refuse to move or act **2.** to hesitate or recoil (*at*) **3.** to make a balk in baseball —**balk′er** ***n.***

Bal·kan (bôl′kən) ***adj.*** **1.** of the Balkans, their people, etc. **2.** of the Balkan Mountains

Balkan Mountains mountain range extending across C Bulgaria, from Yugoslavia to the Black Sea

Balkan Peninsula peninsula in SE Europe, between the Adriatic & the Black seas

Bal·kans (bôl′kənz) countries of the Balkan Peninsula (Yugoslavia, Bulgaria, Albania, Greece, & the European part of Turkey) & Romania: also **Balkan States**

balk·line (bôk′līn′) ***n.*** a line across one end of a billiard table, from behind which opening shots are made

balk·y (bôk′ē) ***adj.*** **balk′i·er, balk′i·est** stubbornly refusing to move or act —**balk′i·ness** ***n.***

ball[1] (bôl) ***n.*** [ME. *bal,* akin to OHG. *balla*] **1.** any round object; sphere; globe **2.** a planet or star, esp. the earth **3.** *a)* a round or egg-shaped object used in various games *b)* any of several such games, esp. baseball **4.** a throw or pitch of a ball *[a fast ball]* **5.** a solid missile for a cannon or firearm **6.** a rounded part of the body *[the ball of the foot]* **7.** *Baseball* a pitch that is wide of the plate or goes above the armpit or below the knee of the batter and is not struck at by him —***vi., vt.*** to form into a ball —**ball up** [Slang] to muddle or confuse —**be on the ball** [Slang] to be alert; be efficient —**carry the ball** [Colloq.] to assume responsibility —**get** (or **keep**) **the ball rolling** [Colloq.] to start (or maintain) some action —**have something on the ball** [Slang] to have ability —**play ball 1.** to begin or resume playing a ball game **2.** to begin or resume any activity **3.** [Colloq.] to cooperate

ball[2] (bôl) ***n.*** [Fr. *bal* < OFr. < LL. *ballare,* to dance < Gr. *ballein,* to throw] **1.** a formal social dance **2.** [Slang] an enjoyable time or experience

bal·lad (bal′əd) ***n.*** [< OFr. *ballade,* dancing song, ult. < LL. *ballare:* see prec.] **1.** a romantic or sentimental song with the same melody for each stanza **2.** a song or poem, usually of unknown authorship and handed down orally, that tells a story in short stanzas and simple words, with repetition, refrain, etc. **3.** a slow, sentimental popular song —**bal′lad·eer′** ***n.*** —**bal′lad·ry** ***n.***

bal·lade (bə läd′) ***n.*** [Fr.: see prec.] **1.** a verse form with three stanzas of eight or ten lines each and an envoy of four or five lines **2.** a romantic musical composition

ball-and-sock·et joint (bôl′′n säk′it) a joint, as that of the hip, formed by a ball in a socket, allowing limited movement in any direction

bal·last (bal′əst) ***n.*** [LowG. < ODan. *barlast* < *bar,* bare + *last,* a load] **1.** anything heavy carried in a ship, aircraft, or vehicle to give stability or in an airship to help control altitude **2.** anything giving stability and firmness to character, human relations, etc. **3.** crushed rock or gravel, as that used to make a firm bed for railroad ties —***vt.*** **1.** to furnish with ballast; stabilize **2.** to fill in (a railroad bed, etc.) with ballast

BALL-AND-SOCKET JOINT

ball bearing 1. a bearing in which the moving parts revolve on freely rolling metal balls so that friction is reduced **2.** any of these balls

bal·le·ri·na (bal′ə rē′nə) ***n.*** [It. < LL. *ballare:* see BALL[2]] a woman ballet dancer

bal·let (bal′ā, ba lā′) ***n.*** [< Fr. < It. *balletto,* dim. < *ballo,* a dance: see BALL[2]] **1.** an intricate group dance (or dancing) using pantomime and conventionalized movements to tell a story **2.** ballet dancers —**bal·let·ic** (ba let′ik) ***adj.***

bal·lis·ta (bə lis′tə) ***n., pl.*** **-tae** (-tē) [L. < Gr. *ballein,* to throw] a device used in ancient warfare to hurl heavy stones, etc.

bal·lis·tic (bə lis′tik) ***adj.*** **1.** of or connected with ballistics **2.** of the motion and force of projectiles

ballistic missile a long-range missile guided in the first part of its flight, but free-falling as it approaches its target

bal·lis·tics (bə lis′tiks) ***n.pl.*** [*with sing. v.*] **1.** the science dealing with the motion and impact of projectiles, such as bullets, rockets, bombs, etc. **2.** the study of the effects of firing on a firearm or bullet, etc.

bal·loon (bə lo͞on′) ***n.*** [< Fr. < It. *pallone* < *palla,* a ball] **1.** a large, airtight bag that rises above the earth when filled with a gas lighter than air **2.** a bag of this sort with an attached car for passengers or instruments **3.** a small, inflatable rubber bag, used as a toy **4.** the outline enclosing spoken words in a comic strip —***vt.*** to cause to swell like a balloon —***vi.*** **1.** to ride in a balloon **2.** to swell; expand —***adj.*** like a balloon —**bal·loon′ist** ***n.***

bal·lot (bal′ət) ***n.*** [It. *ballotta, pallotta,* dim. of *palla,* a ball] **1.** orig. a ball, now a ticket, paper, etc., by which a vote is registered **2.** act or method of voting, esp. secret voting by the use of ballots or voting machines **3.** the right to vote **4.** the total number of votes cast in an election **5.** a list of candidates for office; ticket —***vi.*** to decide by means of the ballot; vote —**bal′lot·er** ***n.***

ball·park (bôl′pärk′) ***n.*** a stadium for playing baseball —***adj.*** [Colloq.] reasonably accurate *[a ballpark estimate]* —**in the ballpark** [Colloq.] **1.** reasonably accurate **2.** fairly close to what is required

ball·play·er (-plā′ər) ***n.*** a baseball player

ball point pen a pen having instead of a point a small ball bearing that rolls over an ink reservoir: also **ball′-point′, ball′point′** ***n.***

ball·room (-ro͞om′) ***n.*** a large hall for dancing

ballroom dancing dancing in which two people dance as partners to a waltz, fox trot, etc.

bal·ly·hoo (bal′ē ho͞o′; *also, for v.* bal′ē ho͞o′) ***n.*** [< ?] **1.** loud talk; uproar **2.** loud or sensational advertising or propaganda —***vt., vi.*** **-hooed′, -hoo′ing** [Colloq.] to advertise or promote by sensational methods —**bal′ly·hoo′er** ***n.***

balm (bäm) ***n.*** [< OFr. < L. < Gr. *balsamon*] **1.** an aromatic gum resin obtained from certain trees and plants and used as medicine; balsam **2.** any fragrant ointment or oil **3.** anything healing or soothing, esp. to the mind or temper **4.** any of various aromatic plants of the mint family **5.** pleasant odor; fragrance

balm of Gilead 1. *a)* a small evergreen tree native to Asia and Africa *b)* an aromatic ointment formerly prepared from its resin **2.** anything healing or soothing **3.** *same as* BALSAM FIR **4.** a hybrid poplar of the northern U.S.

balm·y (bäm′ē) ***adj.*** **balm′i·er, balm′i·est 1.** having the qualities of balm; soothing, mild, pleasant, etc. **2.** [var. of BARMY] [Chiefly Brit. Slang] crazy or foolish —**balm′i·ly** ***adv.*** —**balm′i·ness** ***n.***

ba·lo·ney (bə lō′nē) ***n.*** [altered < ? *bologna,* sausage] **1.** *same as* BOLOGNA **2.** [Slang] nonsense —***interj.*** [Slang] nonsense!

bal·sa (bôl′sə) ***n.*** [Sp.] **1.** a tropical American tree that yields an extremely light and buoyant wood used for rafts, etc. **2.** the wood **3.** a raft, esp. one made up of a frame on cylindrical floats

bal·sam (bôl′səm) ***n.*** [OE. < L.: see BALM] **1.** any of various aromatic resins obtained from certain trees **2.** any of various aromatic, resinous oils or fluids **3.** anything healing or soothing; balm **4.** any of various trees that yield balsam, as the balsam fir **5.** any of various species of the impatiens —**bal·sam·ic** (bôl sam′ik) ***adj.***

balsam fir an evergreen tree of Canada and the northern U.S. with a soft wood used for pulpwood

Bal·tic (bôl′tik) ***adj.*** **1.** of the Baltic Sea **2.** of the Baltic States —***n.*** the Baltic Sea

Baltic Sea sea in N Europe, south & east of Scandinavia & west of the U.S.S.R.

Baltic States former independent countries of Latvia, Lithuania, & Estonia

Bal·ti·more (bôl′tə môr′) [after Lord *Baltimore,* George Calvert (1580?–1632), Eng. founder of Md.] seaport in N Md., on Chesapeake Bay: pop. 787,000 (met. area 2,166,000)

Baltimore oriole [from the colors of the coat of arms of Lord *Baltimore:* see prec.] a N. American oriole that has an orange body with black on the head, wings, and tail

bal·us·ter (bal′əs tər) ***n.*** [< Fr. < It. < L. < Gr. *balaustion,* flower of the wild pomegranate: from some resemblance in shape] any of the small posts supporting a railing, as on a staircase

bal·us·trade (bal′ə strād′) ***n.*** a railing held up by balusters

Bal·zac (bál zák′; *E.* bôl′zak), **Ho·no·ré de** (ô nô *rā′* də) 1799–1850; Fr. novelist

bam·bi·no (bam bē′nō) ***n., pl.*** **-nos, -ni** (-nē) [It., dim. of *bambo,* childish] **1.** a child; baby **2.** any image of the infant Jesus

bam·boo (bam bo͞o′) ***n.*** **[**Malay *bambu***]** any of a number of treelike, semitropical or tropical grasses with springy, jointed, often hollow stems, sometimes growing to heights of 120 feet: the stems are used for furniture, canes, etc., and the young shoots of some species are eaten
bamboo curtain [*often* **B- C-**] the barrier of political and ideological differences that separate China from the West
bam·boo·zle (bam bo͞o′z'l) ***vt.*** **-zled, -zling [**< ?**]** **1.** to deceive or cheat by trickery **2.** to confuse or puzzle —**bam·boo′zle·ment** ***n.*** —**bam·boo′zler** ***n.***
ban[1] (ban) ***vt.*** **banned, ban′ning [**OE. *bannan*, to summon**]** to prohibit or forbid, as by official order —***n.*** **[**< the *v.;* also < OFr. *ban*, decree < OHG. *bann***]** **1.** an excommunication or condemnation by church authorities **2.** a curse **3.** an official prohibition **4.** strong public disapproval **5.** a sentence of outlawry
ban[2] (bän) ***n.,*** *pl.* **ba·ni** (bä′nē) *see* MONETARY UNITS, table (Romania)
ba·nal (bā′n'l; bə nal′, -näl′) ***adj.*** **[**Fr. < *ban:* see BAN[1]**]** dull or stale because of overuse; trite; hackneyed —**ba·nal·i·ty** (bə nal′ə tē) ***n.,*** *pl.* **-ties** —**ba′nal·ly** ***adv.***
ba·nan·a (bə nan′ə) ***n.*** **[**Sp. & Port. < native name in W Africa**]** **1.** any of a genus of treelike, tropical plants, with long, broad leaves and large clusters of edible fruit **2.** the fruit: it is narrow and somewhat curved, and has a sweet, creamy flesh covered by a yellow or reddish skin

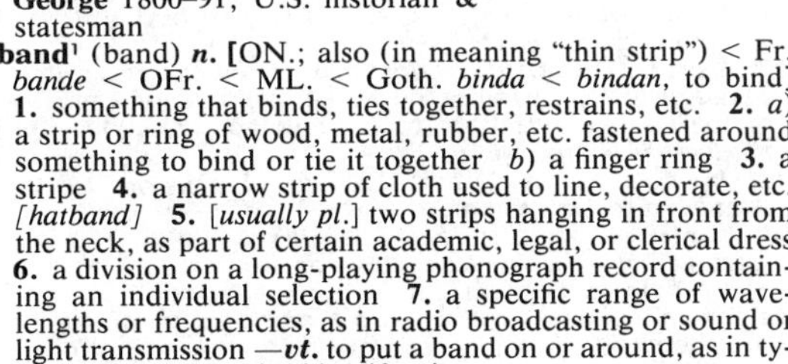
BANANA

banana oil 1. a colorless liquid acetate with a bananalike odor, used in flavorings, in making lacquers, etc. **2.** [Old Slang] insincere talk
banana republic any small Latin American country whose economy is controlled by foreign capital
Ban·croft (ban′krôft, baŋ′-), **George** 1800–91; U.S. historian & statesman
band[1] (band) ***n.*** **[**ON.; also (in meaning "thin strip") < Fr. *bande* < OFr. < ML. < Goth. *binda* < *bindan*, to bind**]** **1.** something that binds, ties together, restrains, etc. **2.** *a*) a strip or ring of wood, metal, rubber, etc. fastened around something to bind or tie it together *b*) a finger ring **3.** a stripe **4.** a narrow strip of cloth used to line, decorate, etc. *[hatband]* **5.** [*usually pl.*] two strips hanging in front from the neck, as part of certain academic, legal, or clerical dress **6.** a division on a long-playing phonograph record containing an individual selection **7.** a specific range of wavelengths or frequencies, as in radio broadcasting or sound or light transmission —***vt.*** to put a band on or around, as in tying or in marking for identification
band[2] (band) ***n.*** **[**Fr. *bande*, a troupe (orig., prob., those following the same sign) < It. *banda* < Goth. *bandwa*, a sign**]** **1.** a group of people united for a common purpose **2.** a group of musicians playing together, esp. upon wind and percussion instruments *[a dance band]* —***vi., vt.*** to unite for a common purpose (usually with *together*)
band·age (ban′dij) ***n.*** **[**Fr. < *bande*, BAND[1]**]** a strip of cloth or other dressing used to bind or cover an injured part of the body —***vt.*** **-aged, -ag·ing** to put a bandage on
Band-Aid (ban′dād′) **[**BAND(AGE) + AID**]** *a trademark for* a small prepared bandage of gauze and adhesive tape —***n.*** [**b- a-**] a bandage of this type: also **band′aid′**
ban·dan·na, ban·dan·a (ban dan′ə) ***n.*** **[**Hindi *bāndhnū*, method of dyeing**]** a large, colored handkerchief, usually with a printed pattern
band·box (band′bäks′) ***n.*** a light box of wood or pasteboard to hold hats, collars, etc.
ban·deau (ban dō′, ban′dō) ***n.,*** *pl.* **-deaux′** (-dōz′, -dōz) **[**Fr.**]** **1.** a narrow ribbon, esp. one worn around the head to hold the hair in place **2.** a narrow brassiere giving little support
ban·de·role, ban·de·rol (ban′də rōl′) ***n.*** **[**Fr. < It. dim. of *bandiera*, banner**]** a narrow flag or pennant, as one attached to a lance
ban·di·coot (ban′di ko͞ot′) ***n.*** **[**< Telugu *pandikokku*, pig rat**]** **1.** a very large rat found esp. in India and Ceylon **2.** a ratlike animal of Australia that carries its young in a pouch
ban·dit (ban′dit) ***n.,*** *pl.* **-dits, ban·dit·ti** (ban dit′ē) **[**It. *bandito* < *bandire*, to outlaw, akin to OHG. *bann* (see BAN[1], *n.*)**]** **1.** a robber, esp. one who robs travelers on the road; brigand **2.** anyone who cheats, steals, etc. —**ban′dit·ry** ***n.***
band·mas·ter (band′mas′tər) ***n.*** the leader or conductor of a military or brass band
ban·do·leer, ban·do·lier (ban′də lir′) ***n.*** **[**< Fr. < Sp. < *banda*, a scarf, ult. < Goth. *bandwa:* see BAND[2]**]** a broad shoulder belt with pockets for carrying ammunition, etc.
band saw a power saw consisting of an endless, toothed steel belt running over pulleys
band shell an outdoor platform for concerts, having a concave back serving as a sounding board
bands·man (bandz′mən) ***n.,*** *pl.* **-men** a member of a band of musicians
band·stand (band′stand′) ***n.*** **1.** an outdoor, usually roofed platform for a band or orchestra **2.** any platform for a musical band, as in a ballroom
Ban·dung (bän′do͝oŋ, ban do͝oŋ′) city in W Java, Indonesia: pop. 973,000
band·wag·on (band′wag′ən) ***n.*** a wagon for the band to ride in, as in a parade —**on the bandwagon** [Colloq.] on the popular or apparently winning side, as in an election
band·width (-width′) ***n.*** the range of frequencies within a radiation band needed to transmit a particular signal
ban·dy[1] (ban′dē) ***vt.*** **-died, -dy·ing [**Fr. *bander*, to bandy at tennis**]** **1.** to toss or hit (a ball, etc.) back and forth **2.** to pass (gossip, etc.) about carelessly **3.** to exchange (words), as in arguing
ban·dy[2] (ban′dē) ***adj.*** **[**< Fr. pp. of *bander*, to bend (as a bow)**]** bent or curved outward
ban·dy·leg·ged (-leg′id, -legd′) ***adj.*** having bandy legs; bowlegged
bane (bān) ***n.*** **[**OE. *bana*, slayer**]** **1.** [Poet.] ruin **2.** the cause of distress, death, or ruin **3.** deadly poison: now obs. except in *ratsbane*, etc.
bane·ber·ry (bān′ber′ē) ***n.,*** *pl.* **-ries 1.** any of a genus of plants of the buttercup family, with clusters of berries, some of which are poisonous **2.** the berry of any of these plants
bane·ful (-fəl) ***adj.*** causing distress, death, or ruin —**bane′ful·ly** ***adv.***
bang[1] (baŋ) ***vt.*** **[** ON. *banga*, to pound**]** **1.** to hit hard and noisily **2.** to shut (a door, etc.) noisily **3.** to handle violently —***vi.*** **1.** to make a sharp, loud noise **2.** to strike sharply (*against, into*, etc.) —***n.*** **1.** a hard blow or loud knock **2.** a sudden, loud noise **3.** *a*) [Colloq.] a display of enthusiasm or vigor *[to start with a bang]* *b*) [Slang] a thrill —***adv.*** **1.** hard and noisily **2.** suddenly or exactly —**bang up** to do physical damage to
bang[2] (baŋ) ***vt.*** **[**< ?**]** to cut (hair) short and straight across —***n.*** [*usually pl.*] banged hair worn across the forehead
Ban·ga·lore (baŋ′gə lôr′) city in S India: pop. 1,207,000
Bang·ka (bäŋ′kä) island of Indonesia, off the E coast of Sumatra: 4,610 sq. mi.
Bang·kok (baŋ′käk) capital of Thailand, a seaport in the S part: pop. 1,669,000
Ban·gla·desh (bäŋ′glə desh′) country in S Asia, at the head of the Bay of Bengal: a member of the Commonwealth: 55,134 sq. mi.; pop. 50,840,000; cap. Dacca
ban·gle (baŋ′g'l) ***n.*** **[**Hindi *bangrī*, glass bracelet**]** **1.** a decorative bracelet, armlet, or anklet **2.** a disk-shaped ornament
bang·tail (baŋ′tāl′) ***n.*** [Slang] a racehorse
bang-up (baŋ′up′) ***adj.*** [Colloq.] excellent
ban·ian[1] (ban′yən) ***n.*** *same as* BANYAN
ban·ian[2] (ban′yən) ***n.*** **[**Port., ult. < Sans. *vaṇij*, merchant**]** a Hindu merchant
ban·ish (ban′ish) ***vt.*** **[**< extended stem of OFr. *banir* < *ban:* see BAN[1]**]** **1.** to send into exile **2.** to send or put away; dismiss —**ban′ish·ment** ***n.***
ban·is·ter (ban′əs tər) ***n.*** **[**altered < BALUSTER**]** **1.** [*often pl.*] a railing and the balusters supporting it, as on a staircase **2.** the railing itself
ban·jo (ban′jō) ***n.,*** *pl.* **-jos, -joes [**of Afr. origin**]** a stringed musical instrument having a long neck and a circular body covered with taut skin —**ban′jo·ist** ***n.***

BANJO

bank[1] (baŋk) ***n.*** **[**< Fr. < It. *banca*, orig. a (moneylender's) table < OHG. *bank*, bench: see ff.**]** **1.** *a*) an establishment for receiving, lending, or, sometimes, issuing money *b*) its building **2.** *same as* PIGGY BANK **3.** the fund held, as by the dealer, in some gambling games **4.** *Med.* *a*) any place for gathering and distributing blood for transfusions or body parts for transplantation *b*) any reserve thus gathered —***vi.*** **1.** to put money in or do business with a bank **2.** to manage a bank **3.** to keep the bank, as in some gambling games —***vt.*** to deposit (money) in a bank —**bank on** [Colloq.] to depend on; rely on —**bank′a·ble** ***adj.***

bank[2] (baŋk) ***n.*** [< ON. *bakki,* akin to OHG. *bank* & OE. *benc,* BENCH] **1.** a long mound or heap; ridge **2.** a steep slope, as of a hill **3.** a stretch of rising land at the edge of a stream, etc. **4.** a shoal or shallow place, as in a sea **5.** the sloping of an airplane laterally to avoid slipping sideways on a turn **6.** the sloping of a road laterally along a curve —***vt.*** **1.** to heap dirt around for protection from cold, etc. **2.** to cover (a fire) with ashes and fuel so that it will burn longer **3.** to pile up so as to form a bank **4.** to construct (a curve in a road, etc.) so that it slopes up from the inside edge **5.** to slope (an airplane) laterally on a turn **6.** *Billiards* to stroke (a ball) so that it recoils from a cushion —***vi.*** **1.** to form a bank or banks **2.** to bank an airplane

bank[3] (baŋk) ***n.*** [< OFr. < OHG. *bank:* see prec.] **1.** a bench for rowers in a galley **2.** a row of oars **3.** a row or tier of objects **4.** a row of keys in a keyboard or console —***vt.*** to arrange in a bank

bank account money deposited in a bank and subject to withdrawal by the depositor

bank·book (baŋk′book′) ***n.*** the book in which the account of a depositor in a bank is recorded

bank·er (baŋ′kər) ***n.*** **1.** one who owns or manages a bank **2.** the keeper of the bank in some gambling games

bank·ing (-kiŋ) ***n.*** the business of a bank

bank note a promissory note issued by a bank, payable on demand: it is a form of paper money

bank·roll (baŋk′rōl′) ***n.*** a supply of money —***vt.*** [Colloq.] to finance

bank·rupt (baŋk′rupt′, -rəpt) ***n.*** [< Fr. < It. < *banca,* bench (see BANK[1]) + *rotta,* broken < L. pp. of *rumpere,* to break] a person legally declared unable to pay his debts: his property is divided among his creditors —***adj.*** **1.** that is a bankrupt **2.** lacking in some quality *[*morally *bankrupt]* **3.** that has failed completely *[*a *bankrupt* foreign policy*]* —***vt.*** to make bankrupt

bank·rupt·cy (-rupt′sē, -rəp sē) ***n., pl.*** **-cies** **1.** the state or an instance of being bankrupt **2.** complete failure; ruin; destitution

ban·ner (ban′ər) ***n.*** [< OFr. *baniere* (< WGmc. *banda,* a sign), altered after *banir,* to announce (see BANISH)] **1.** a piece of cloth bearing a design, motto, etc. **2.** a flag **3.** a headline extending across a newspaper page —***adj.*** foremost; leading

ban·nis·ter (ban′əs tər) ***n.*** *same as* BANISTER

ban·nock (ban′ək) ***n.*** [< Gael. *bannach,* a cake] [Scot.] a flat cake of oatmeal or barley meal

banns (banz) ***n.pl.*** [see BAN[1]] the proclamation, generally made in church on three successive Sundays, of an intended marriage

ban·quet (baŋ′kwit, ban′-) ***n.*** [Fr. < It. *banchetto,* dim. of *banca:* see BANK[1]] **1.** a feast **2.** a formal dinner, usually with speeches —***vt.*** to honor with a banquet —***vi.*** to dine at a banquet —**ban′quet·er** ***n.***

ban·quette (baŋ ket′) ***n.*** [Fr., dim. < Norm. *banque,* earthwork < Du. *bank,* BANK[2]] **1.** a gunners' platform along the inside of a trench or parapet **2.** [South] a sidewalk **3.** an upholstered bench along a wall

ban·shee, ban·shie (ban′shē) ***n.*** [< Ir. < *bean,* woman + *sith,* fairy] *Ir. & Scot. Folklore* a female spirit believed to wail to warn of an impending death in the family

ban·tam (ban′təm) ***n.*** [after *Bantam,* former Du. residency in Java] **1.** [*often* **B-**] any of various dwarf varieties of breeds of domestic fowl **2.** a small but aggressive person —***adj.*** like a bantam; small and aggressive

ban·tam·weight (-wāt′) ***n.*** a boxer or wrestler between a flyweight and a featherweight (in boxing, 113–118 pounds)

ban·ter (ban′tər) ***vt.*** [17th-c. slang < ? BANDY[1]] to tease in a playful way —***vi.*** to exchange banter (*with* someone) —***n.*** good-natured teasing or joking —**ban′ter·ing·ly** ***adv.***

bant·ling (bant′liŋ) ***n.*** [< G. *bänkling,* bastard < *bank,* a bench] [Archaic] a young child; brat

Ban·tu (ban′tōō) ***n.*** [Bantu *ba-ntu,* mankind] **1.** *pl.* **-tus, -tu** any member of a large group of Negroid tribes of equatorial and southern Africa **2.** any of the group of languages of these peoples —***adj.*** of the Bantus or their languages

ban·yan (ban′yən) ***n.*** [from a tree of this kind under which the *banians* (see BANIAN[2]) had built a pagoda] an East Indian fig tree whose branches take root and become new trunks

ban·zai (bän′zī′) ***interj.*** a Japanese greeting or shout, meaning "May you live ten thousand years!"

ba·o·bab (bā′ō bab′, bä′-) ***n.*** [prob. EAfr. native name] a tall tree of Africa and India, with a thick trunk and gourdlike, edible fruit

bap·tism (bap′tiz′m) ***n.*** [< OFr. < L. < Gr. < *baptizein,* to immerse] **1.** the rite or sacrament of admitting a person into a Christian church by dipping him in water or sprinkling water on him **2.** any experience that initiates, tests, or purifies —**bap·tis′mal** (-tiz′m'l) ***adj.***

bap·tist (bap′tist) ***n.*** **1.** a person who baptizes; specif., [**B-**] JOHN THE BAPTIST **2.** [**B-**] a member of a Protestant denomination holding that baptism should be given only after confession of faith and only by immersion

bap·tis·ter·y (bap′tis trē, -tis tər ē) ***n., pl.*** **-ter·ies** a place, esp. a part of a church, used for baptizing: also **bap′tis·try** (-trē), *pl.* **-tries**

bap·tize (bap′tīz, bap tīz′) ***vt.*** **-tized, -tiz·ing** **1.** to administer baptism to **2.** to purify; initiate **3.** to christen —***vi.*** to administer baptism —**bap′tiz·er** ***n.***

bar[1] (bär) ***n.*** [OFr. *barre* < ML. *barra,* barrier] **1.** any piece of wood, metal, etc. longer than it is wide or thick, often used as a barrier, lever, etc. **2.** *a)* an oblong piece *[bar* of soap*]* *b)* a small metal strip worn to show military or other rank **3.** anything that obstructs, hinders, or prevents **4.** a strip, band, or broad line **5.** the part of a law court, enclosed by a railing, where the judges or lawyers sit, or where prisoners are brought to trial **6.** *a)* a law court *b)* any place of judgment **7.** *a)* lawyers collectively *b)* the legal profession **8.** *a)* a counter at which alcoholic drinks are served *b)* a place with such a counter **9.** a handrail held onto while doing ballet exercises **10.** the mouthpiece of a horse's bit **11.** *Music a)* any of the vertical lines across a staff, dividing it into measures *b)* a measure —***vt.*** **barred, bar′ring** **1.** to fasten with or as with a bar **2.** to obstruct; shut off; close **3.** to oppose, prevent, or forbid **4.** to keep out; exclude **5.** to set aside *[barring* certain possibilities*]* —***prep.*** excluding; excepting *[*the best, *bar* none*]* —**cross the bar** to die

bar[2] (bär) ***n.*** [G. < Gr. *baros,* weight] a metric unit of pressure equal to one million dynes per square centimeter

bar. **1.** barometer **2.** barrel **3.** barrister

barb[1] (bärb) ***n.*** [< OFr. < L. *barba,* a beard] **1.** a beardlike growth near the mouth of certain animals **2.** a sharp point projecting away from the main point of a fishhook, arrow, etc. **3.** a cutting remark **4.** any of the hairlike projections from the shaft of a feather —***vt.*** to provide with a barb or barbs —**barbed** ***adj.***

barb[2] (bärb) ***n.*** [< Fr. < It. < Ar. *Barbar,* Berber] a horse of a breed native to Barbary

Bar·ba·dos (bär bā′dōz, -dōs) country on the easternmost island of the West Indies, northeast of Trinidad: a member of the Commonwealth: 166 sq. mi.; pop. 253,000 —**Bar·ba′di·an** (-dē ən) ***adj., n.***

Bar·ba·ra (bär′bər ə, -brə) [L., fem. of *barbarus,* foreign, strange] a feminine name

bar·bar·i·an (bär ber′ē ən) ***n.*** [see BARBAROUS] **1.** orig., a foreigner; esp., a non-Greek or non-Roman **2.** a member of a people with a civilization regarded as primitive, etc. **3.** a person who lacks culture **4.** a coarse or unmannerly person; boor **5.** a savage, cruel person; brute —***adj.*** of or like a barbarian; esp., uncivilized, cruel, rude, etc. —**bar·bar′i·an·ism** ***n.***

bar·bar·ic (-ik) ***adj.*** **1.** of or like barbarians; uncivilized; primitive **2.** wild; crude —**bar·bar′i·cal·ly** ***adv.***

bar·ba·rism (bär′bər iz′m) ***n.*** **1.** *a)* the use of words and expressions not standard in a language *b)* a word or expression of this sort (Ex.: "youse" for "you") **2.** the state of being primitive or uncivilized **3.** a barbarous act, custom, etc.

bar·bar·i·ty (bär ber′ə tē) ***n., pl.*** **-ties** **1.** cruel or brutal behavior **2.** a cruel or brutal act **3.** a crude or coarse taste, manner, etc.

bar·ba·rize (bär′bə rīz′) ***vt., vi.*** **-rized′, -riz′ing** to make or become barbarous —**bar′ba·ri·za′tion** ***n.***

bar·ba·rous (-bər əs) ***adj.*** [< L. < Gr. *barbaros,* foreign; prob. < echoic word describing unintelligible speech] **1.** orig., foreign or alien; esp., in the ancient world, non-Greek or non-Roman **2.** characterized by substandard usages in speaking or writing **3.** uncivilized **4.** uncultured, crude, coarse, etc. **5.** cruel; brutal —**bar′ba·rous·ly** ***adv.*** —**bar′ba·rous·ness** ***n.***

Bar·ba·ry (bär′bər ē) region in N Africa, west of Egypt, inhabited chiefly by Berbers: its coast (**Barbary Coast**) was once a center of piracy

Barbary ape a tailless, apelike monkey of North Africa and Gibraltar

bar·bate (bär′bāt) ***adj.*** [< L. < *barba,* a beard] bearded

bar·be·cue (bär′bə kyōō′) ***n.*** [< Sp. < Haitian Creole *barbacoa,* framework] **1.** orig., a framework for smoking, drying, or broiling meat **2.** a hog, steer, etc. roasted whole over an open fire **3.** any meat broiled over an open fire **4.** a party or picnic at which such meat is served **5.** a portable outdoor grill —***vt.*** **-cued′, -cu′ing** **1.** to prepare (meat) outdoors by broiling on a spit or over a grill **2.** to cook (meat) with a highly seasoned sauce (**barbecue sauce**)

barbed wire twisted wire with sharp points all along it, used for barriers

bar·bel (bär′b'l) ***n.*** [OFr., ult. < L. *barba,* a beard] **1.** a threadlike growth from the jaws of certain fishes: it is an organ of touch 2. any of several large European freshwater fishes with such growths

bar·bell (bär′bel′) ***n.*** [BAR[1] + (DUMB)BELL] a metal bar to which disks of varying weights are attached at each end, used for weight-lifting exercises: also **bar bell, bar-bell**

bar·ber (bär′bər) ***n.*** [OFr. *barbour,* ult. < L. *barba,* a beard] a person whose work is cutting hair, shaving and trimming beards, etc. —***vt.*** to cut the hair of, shave, etc. —***vi.*** to work as a barber

barber pole a pole with spiral stripes of red and white, a symbol of the barber's trade

bar·ber·ry (bär′ber′ē) ***n.,*** *pl.* **-ries** [< ML. *barberis* < Ar. *barbāris*] 1. a spiny shrub with sour, red berries 2. the berry

bar·ber·shop (bär′bər shäp′) ***n.*** a barber's place of business —***adj.*** [Colloq.] designating, characterized by, or like the close harmony of male voices *[a barbershop* quartet*]*

bar·bi·can (bär′bi kən) ***n.*** [< OFr., prob. < Per. *barbarkhānah,* house on a wall] a fortification at the gate or bridge leading into a town or castle

bar·bi·cel (bär′bə sel′) ***n.*** [< ModL. < L. *barba,* a beard] any of the tiny, hairlike extensions growing from the barbules of a feather

bar·bi·tal (bär′bi tôl′) ***n.*** [BARBIT(URIC ACID) + -AL] a drug, $C_8H_{12}O_3N_2$, in the form of a white powder, used to induce sleep

bar·bi·tu·rate (bär bich′ər it, bär′bə tyoor′it) ***n.*** any salt or ester of barbituric acid, used as a sedative or to induce sleep

bar·bi·tu·ric acid (bär′bə tyoor′ik, -toor′-) [< G. *barbitursäure* + -IC] a crystalline acid, $C_4H_4O_3N_2$, derivatives of which are used to induce sleep

bar·bule (bär′byo͞ol) ***n.*** [< L. *barba,* a beard] 1. a very small barb 2. any of the threadlike parts fringing each barb of a feather

barb·wire (bärb′wīr′) ***n.*** *same as* BARBED WIRE

bar·ca·role, bar·ca·rolle (bär′kə rōl′) ***n.*** [Fr. < It. < *barca,* boat] 1. a song sung by Venetian gondoliers 2. a piece of music imitating this

Bar·ce·lo·na (bär′sə lō′nə; *Sp.* bär′the lô′nä) seaport in NE Spain: pop. 1,697,000

bard (bärd) ***n.*** [Gael. & Ir.] 1. an ancient Celtic poet 2. any poet —**bard′ic *adj.***

Bard of Avon William Shakespeare: so called from his birthplace, Stratford-on-Avon

bare[1] (ber) ***adj.*** [OE. *bær*] 1. *a)* without the customary covering *[bare* floors*]* *b)* without clothing; naked 2. without equipment or furnishings; empty 3. simple; plain 4. without tools or weapons *[*to use one's *bare* hands*]* 5. threadbare 6. mere *[a bare* wage*]* —***vt.* bared, bar′ing** to make bare; uncover; strip —**lay bare** to uncover; expose —**bare′ness *n.***

bare[2] (ber) *archaic pt. of* BEAR[1]

bare·back (ber′bak′) ***adv., adj.*** on a horse with no saddle

bare·faced (-fāst′) ***adj.*** 1. with the face uncovered or beardless 2. unconcealed; open 3. shameless; brazen; audacious —**bare′fac′ed·ly** (-fās′id lē) ***adv.*** —**bare′fac′ed·ness *n.***

bare·foot (-foot′) ***adj., adv.*** without shoes and stockings —**bare′foot′ed *adj.***

bare·hand·ed (-han′did) ***adj., adv.*** 1. with hands uncovered 2. without weapons or other means

bare·head·ed (-hed′id) ***adj., adv.*** wearing no hat or other head covering

bare·leg·ged (-leg′id, -legd′) ***adj., adv.*** with the legs bare; without stockings on

bare·ly (ber′lē) ***adv.*** 1. openly; plainly 2. only just; scarcely 3. scantily *[barely* furnished*]*

barf (bärf) ***vi., vt.*** [echoic] [Slang] to vomit

bar·fly (bär′flī′) ***n.,*** *pl.* **-flies′** [Slang] one who spends much time drinking in barrooms

bar·gain (bär′g′n) ***n.*** [< OFr. < *bargaignier,* to haggle < Frank.] 1. a mutual agreement between parties on what should be given or done by each 2. such an agreement in terms of its worth to one of the parties *[a bad bargain]* 3. something sold at a price favorable to the buyer —***vi.*** 1. to talk over a transaction, contract, etc., trying to get the best possible terms 2. to make a bargain —***vt.*** to barter —**bargain for** 1. to try to get cheaply 2. to expect; count on: also **bargain on —into the bargain** in addition —**bar′gain·er *n.***

barge (bärj) ***n.*** [< OFr. < ML. *barga*] 1. a large, flat-bottomed boat for carrying freight on rivers, etc. 2. a large pleasure boat, used for pageants, etc. 3. a flagship's boat for use by flag officers —***vt.* barged, barg′ing** to carry by barge —***vi.*** 1. to move slowly and clumsily 2. to come or go (*in* or *into*) in a rude, abrupt way 3. to collide (*into*) —**barge′man *n.,*** *pl.* **-men**

bar graph a graph with parallel bars representing in proportional lengths the figures given in the data

Ba·ri (bä′rē) seaport in SE Italy, on the Adriatic: pop. 345,000

bar·ite (ber′īt) ***n.*** [< Gr. *barys,* weighty + -ITE] a white, crystalline mineral composed mainly of barium sulfate

bar·i·tone (bar′ə tōn′) ***n.*** [< It. < Gr. < *barys,* deep + *tonos,* tone] 1. the range of a male voice between bass and tenor 2. a voice or singer with such a range 3. any wind instrument with a similar range 4. a part for such a voice or instrument —***adj.*** of, in, for, or having this range

bar·i·um (ber′ē əm) ***n.*** [ModL. < Gr. *barys,* heavy] a silver-white, metallic chemical element: symbol, Ba; at. wt., 137.34; at. no., 56

bark[1] (bärk) ***n.*** [ON. *bǫrkr*] the outside covering of the stems and roots of trees and woody plants —***vt.*** 1. to tan (hides) with a bark infusion 2. to take the bark off (a tree) 3. [Colloq.] to scrape some skin off *[*to *bark* one's shin*]*

bark[2] (bärk) ***vi.*** [OE. *beorcan:* echoic] 1. to make the sharp, abrupt cry of a dog 2. to make a sound like this *[*the engine *barked]* 3. to speak or shout sharply; snap 4. [Colloq.] to cough 5. [Slang] to work as a barker —***vt.*** to say with a bark or a shout —***n.*** a sound made in barking —**bark up the wrong tree** to misdirect one's attack, energies, etc.

bark[3] (bärk) ***n.*** [< Fr. < It. & L. *barca* < Gr. < Coptic *bari,* small boat] 1. [Poet.] any boat, esp. a small sailing boat 2. a sailing vessel with its two forward masts square-rigged and its rear mast rigged fore-and-aft

bar·keep·er (bär′kēp′ər) ***n.*** 1. an owner or manager of a bar 2. a bartender Also **bar′keep′**

bark·en·tine (bär′kən tēn′) ***n.*** [< BARK[3] after BRIGANTINE] a sailing vessel with its foremast square-rigged and its other two masts rigged fore-and-aft

bark·er (bär′kər) ***n.*** one that barks; esp., a person in front of a sideshow, etc. who tries to attract customers by loud, lively talk about it

bar·ley (bär′lē) ***n.*** see PLURAL, II, D, 3 [< OE. *bærlic, adj.* < *bere,* barley] 1. a cereal grass 2. its grain, used in making malts, in soups, and as a feed for animals

bar·ley·corn (-kôrn′) ***n.*** barley or a grain of barley: see also JOHN BARLEYCORN

barm (bärm) ***n.*** [OE. *beorma*] the foamy yeast that appears on the surface of fermenting malt liquors

bar·maid (bär′mād′) ***n.*** a waitress who serves alcoholic drinks in a bar

bar·man (-mən) ***n.,*** *pl.* **-men** a bartender

bar mitz·vah, bar miz·vah (bär mits′və) [Heb. *bar mitswāh,* son of the commandment] [*also* **B- M-**] 1. a Jewish boy who has arrived at the age of religious responsibility, thirteen years 2. the ceremony celebrating this event

barm·y (bär′mē) ***adj.* -i·er, -i·est** 1. full of barm; foamy 2. [Brit. Slang] silly; idiotic

barn (bärn) ***n.*** [< OE. *bern, berern* < *bere,* barley + *ærn,* a building] 1. a farm building for sheltering harvested crops, livestock, etc. 2. a large building for housing streetcars, trucks, etc.

bar·na·cle (bär′nə k'l) ***n.*** [< Fr. *bernicle* & Bret. *bernik,* kind of shellfish] any of a number of saltwater shellfish that attach themselves to rocks, ship bottoms, etc. —**bar′na·cled *adj.***

barn dance a party, orig. held in a barn, at which people dance square dances

barn owl a species of brown and gray owl with a spotted white breast, commonly found in barns

barn·storm (bärn′stôrm′) ***vi., vt.*** [BARN + STORM, *vi.* 3: from occas. use of barns as auditoriums] to tour in small towns and rural districts, performing plays, giving campaign speeches, etc. —**barn′storm′er *n.*** —**barn′storm′ing *adj., n.***

barn swallow a common swallow with a long, deeply forked tail: it usually nests in barns

Bar·num (bär′nəm), **P(hineas) T(aylor)** 1810–91; U.S. showman & circus operator

barn·yard (bärn′yärd′) ***n.*** the yard or ground near a barn —***adj.*** 1. of a barnyard 2. like or fit for a barnyard; earthy, smutty, etc.

bar·o- [< Gr. *baros,* weight] *a prefix meaning* of pressure, esp. atmospheric pressure *[barograph]*

bar·o·gram (bar′ə gram′) ***n.*** the linear record traced by a barograph

bar·o·graph (-graf′) ***n.*** a barometer that records variations in atmospheric pressure automatically on a revolving cylinder —**bar′o·graph′ic *adj.***

ba·rom·e·ter (bə räm′ə tər) ***n.*** [BARO- + -METER] 1. an instrument for measuring atmospheric pressure, as by a graduated glass tube (**mercury barometer**) in which a column of mercury rises or falls as the pressure changes (see also ANEROID BAROMETER): barometers are used in forecasting the weather or finding height above sea level **2.** anything that indicates change —**bar·o·met·ric** (bar′ə-met′rik), **bar′o·met′ri·cal** *adj.* —**bar′o·met′ri·cal·ly** *adv.*

barometric pressure the pressure of the atmosphere as indicated by a barometer: in a mercury barometer it averages 29.92 inches at sea level

bar·on (bar′ən) *n.* [OFr. < Frank. hyp. *baro,* freeman, man] **1.** a member of the lowest rank of the British hereditary peerage **2.** a European or Japanese nobleman of like rank **3.** a powerful businessman or industrialist; magnate —**ba·ro·ni·al** (bə rō′nē əl) *adj.*

bar·on·age (bar′ə nij) *n.* **1.** barons as a class **2.** the peerage **3.** the rank, title, etc. of a baron

bar·on·ess (-nis) *n.* **1.** a baron's wife or widow **2.** a lady with a barony in her own right

bar·on·et (-nit, -net′) *n.* a man holding the lowest hereditary British title, below a baron but above a knight —**bar′on·et·cy** (-sē) *n., pl.* **-cies**

ba·ro·ni·al (bə rō′nē əl) *adj.* of or fit for a baron [a *baronial* mansion]

bar·on·y (bar′ə nē) *n., pl.* **-on·ies** **1.** a baron's domain **2.** the rank or title of a baron

ba·roque (bə rōk′) *adj.* [Fr. < Port. *barroco,* imperfect pearl] **1.** *a*) of or like a style of art and architecture with much ornamentation and curved rather than straight lines *b*) of or like a style of music with highly embellished melodies and fugal or contrapuntal forms **2.** of the period in which these styles flourished (c. 1550–1750) **3.** *same as* ROCOCO **4.** overdecorated, or too ornate **5.** irregular in shape: said of pearls —*n.* baroque style, baroque art, etc.

bar·o·scope (bar′ə skōp′) *n.* [BARO- + -SCOPE] an instrument indicating but not measuring changes in atmospheric pressure —**bar′o·scop′ic** (-skäp′ik) *adj.*

ba·rouche (bə ro͞osh′) *n.* [< G. < It. < LL. *birotus* < *bi-*, two + *rota,* a wheel] a four-wheeled carriage with a collapsible hood, two double seats opposite each other, and a driver's seat in front

barque (bärk) *n. same as* BARK[3]

bar·quen·tine (bär′kən tēn′) *n. same as* BARKENTINE

Bar·qui·si·me·to (bär kē′sē mā′tô) city in NW Venezuela: pop. 235,000

bar·rack (bar′ik) *n.* [< Fr. < Sp. < *barro,* clay < VL. hyp. *barrum,* clay] [*pl., often with sing. v.*] **1.** a building or group of buildings for housing soldiers **2.** a large, plain building for housing workmen, etc. —*vt., vi.* to house in barracks

barracks bag a large cloth bag to hold a soldier's equipment and personal possessions

bar·ra·cu·da (bar′ə ko͞o′də) *n., pl.* **-da, -das:** see PLURAL, II, D, 2 [Sp., prob. < native WInd. name] a fierce, pikelike fish of tropical seas

bar·rage (bə räzh′, -räj′; *for n. 3* bär′ij) *n.* [Fr. < *barrer,* to stop < *barre,* BAR[1]] **1.** a curtain of artillery fire laid down to keep enemy forces from moving, or to cover one's own forces, esp. in attack **2.** a prolonged attack of words, blows, etc. **3.** a man-made barrier in a river; dam —*vi., vt.* **-raged′, -rag′ing** to lay down a barrage (against)

bar·ran·ca (bə raŋ′kə) *n.* [Sp.] a deep ravine or a steep cliff: also **bar·ran′co** (-kō), *pl.* **-cos**

Bar·ran·qui·lla (bä′rän kē′yä) seaport in NW Colombia: pop. 498,000

bar·ra·tor, bar·ra·ter (bar′ə tər) *n.* [< OFr. *barater,* to cheat < *barate,* fraud < ON. *baratta,* quarrel] a person guilty of barratry

bar·ra·try (-trē) *n.* [see prec.] **1.** the criminal offense of habitually bringing about quarrels or lawsuits **2.** fraud or negligence on the part of a ship's officers or crew that results in a loss to the owners —**bar′ra·trous** *adj.*

barred (bärd) *adj.* **1.** having bars or stripes **2.** closed off with bars **3.** forbidden or excluded

bar·rel (bar′əl) *n.* [< OFr. *baril* < ML. *barillus* < ?] **1.** a large, wooden, cylindrical container with slightly bulging sides and flat ends, made usually of staves bound together with hoops **2.** the capacity of a standard barrel (in the U.S., usually 31½ gal.) **3.** any somewhat similar cylinder, drum, etc. [the *barrel* of a windlass] **4.** the tube of a gun, through which the projectile is fired —*vt.* **-reled** or **-relled, -rel·ing** or **-rel·ling** to put or pack in a barrel or barrels —*vi.* [Slang] to go at a high speed —**have (someone) over a barrel** [Slang] to have (someone) completely at one's mercy, esp. financially

bar·rel-chest·ed (-ches′tid) *adj.* having an especially broad, deep chest for one's height

barrel organ a mechanical musical instrument having a revolving cylinder studded with pins which open pipe valves, producing a tune

barrel roll a complete revolution made by an airplane around its longitudinal axis while in flight

bar·ren (bar′ən) *adj.* [< OFr. *baraigne,* orig. used of land] **1.** that cannot produce offspring; sterile **2.** not producing crops or fruit; having little or no vegetation **3.** unproductive; unprofitable **4.** lacking appeal, interest, or meaning; dull; boring **5.** empty; devoid [*barren* of creative spirit] —*n.* **1.** an area of unproductive land **2.** [*usually pl.*] land with shrubs, brush, etc. and sandy soil —**bar′ren·ly** *adv.* —**bar′ren·ness** *n.*

bar·rette (bə ret′, bä-) *n.* [Fr., dim. of *barre,* BAR[1]] a small bar or clasp for holding a girl's or woman's hair in place

bar·ri·cade (bar′ə kād′; *also, esp. for v.,* bar′ə kād′) *n.* [Fr. < It. pp. of *barricare,* to fortify] **1.** a barrier thrown up hastily for defense **2.** any barrier or obstruction —*vt.* **-cad′ed, -cad′ing** **1.** to shut in or keep out with a barricade **2.** to put up barricades in; obstruct

Bar·rie (bar′ē), Sir **James M(atthew)** 1860–1937; Scot. novelist & playwright

bar·ri·er (bar′ē ər) *n.* [< OFr. < *barre,* BAR[1]] **1.** an obstruction, as a fence or wall **2.** anything that holds apart or separates [racial *barriers*]

barrier reef a long ridge of coral parallel to the coastline, separated from it by a lagoon

bar·ring (bär′iŋ) *prep.* unless there should be; excepting [*barring* rain, we leave tonight]

bar·ri·o (bär′ē ō) *n., pl.* **-os** [Sp. < Ar. < *barr,* open country] in Spanish-speaking countries, a district or suburb of a city

bar·ris·ter (bar′is tər) *n.* [< BAR[1] (*n.* 6) + *-ister,* as in MINISTER] in England, a counselor-at-law who presents and pleads cases in court: distinguished from SOLICITOR

bar·room (bär′ro͞om′) *n.* a room with a bar at which alcoholic drinks are sold

bar·row[1] (bar′ō) *n.* [< OE. < *beran,* BEAR[1]] **1.** *same as:* *a*) HANDBARROW *b*) WHEELBARROW **2.** a small cart with two wheels, pushed by hand; pushcart

bar·row[2] (bar′ō) *n.* [OE. *beorg,* hill] a heap of earth or rocks marking an ancient grave

Bar·row (bar′ō), **Point** [after Sir J. *Barrow,* 19th-c. Eng. geographer] northernmost point of Alas.; cape on the Arctic Ocean

bar sinister *same as* BEND SINISTER

Bart. Baronet

bar·tend·er (bär′ten′dər) *n.* a man who mixes and serves alcoholic drinks at a bar

bar·ter (bär′tər) *vi.* [< OFr. *barater:* see BARRATOR] to trade by exchanging goods or services without using money —*vt.* to exchange (goods, etc.); trade —*n.* **1.** the act or practice of bartering **2.** anything bartered —**bar′ter·er** *n.*

Barth (bärt), **Karl** 1886–1968; Swiss theologian

Bar·thol·o·mew (bär thäl′ə myo͞o′) [< LL. < Gr. *Bartholomaios* < Aram., lit., son of Talmai] a masculine name

bar·ti·zan (bär′tə zən, bär′tə zan′) *n.* [altered < ME. *bretasce,* a parapet < OFr., prob. < OHG. *bret,* a board] a small, overhanging turret on a tower or battlement

Bart·lett pear (bärt′lət) [after E. *Bartlett* of Roxbury, Mass., the distributor] a large, juicy variety of pear

Bar·tók (bär′tôk), **Bé·la** (bā′lä) 1881–1945; Hung. composer

Bar·ton (bär′t′n), **Clara** 1821–1912; U.S. philanthropist: founder of the American Red Cross

bar·y·on (bar′ē än′) *n.* [< Gr. *barys,* heavy + (ELECTR)ON] one of a class of heavy atomic particles, including the proton and neutron

ba·ry·tes (bə rīt′ēz) *n. same as* BARITE

bar·y·tone (bar′ə tōn′) *adj., n. same as* BARITONE

bas·al (bā′s′l) *adj.* **1.** of, at, or forming the base **2.** basic; fundamental —**bas′al·ly** *adv.*

basal metabolism the quantity of energy used by any organism at rest, measured by the rate **(basal metabolic rate)** at which heat is given off by the organism

ba·salt (bə sôlt′; bās′ôlt, bas′-) *n.* [< L. *basaltes,* a dark marble] a dark, tough, fine-grained to dense, volcanic rock —**ba·sal′tic** *adj.*

bas·cule (bas′kyo͞ol) *n.* [Fr.] any device balanced like a seesaw

bascule bridge a drawbridge counterweighted so that it can be raised and lowered easily

base[1] (bās) *n., pl.* **bas′es** (-əz) [< OFr. *bas* < L. *basis,* BASIS] **1.** the thing or part on which something rests; foundation **2.** the main part, as of a plan, system, etc., on which the rest depends **3.** the principal or essential ingredient [paint with an oil *base*] **4.** a basis **5.** a goal or place of safety in certain games, as baseball **6.** the point of attachment of a part of the body **7.** a center of operations or source of supply; headquarters **8.** *Chem.* any compound that reacts with an acid to form a salt, produces hydroxyl ions in water solutions, and turns red litmus blue **9.** *Geom.* the line or plane upon which a figure is thought of as resting **10.** *Linguis.* any morpheme to which prefixes, suffixes, etc. are added; root **11.** *Math.* *a*) the number that is raised to various powers to produce the main counting units of a number system [10 is the *base* of the decimal system] *b*) the number that when raised to the logarithm of a given number produces the given number *c*) in business, etc., a figure or sum upon which certain calculations are made —*adj.* forming a base —*vt.* **based, bas′ing** **1.** to make a base for **2.** to put or rest (*on*) as a base or basis **3.** to place or station (*in* or *at* a base) —**off base 1.** *Baseball* not touching the base **2.** [Slang] taking an unsound or wrong position, attitude, etc.

base[2] (bās) ***adj.*** [< OFr. < VL. *bassus,* low] **1.** with little or no honor, courage, or decency; mean; contemptible **2.** of a menial or degrading kind **3.** inferior in quality **4.** of comparatively low worth *[*iron is a *base* metal, gold a precious one*]* **5.** debased or counterfeit **6.** [Archaic] of servile or humble birth —**base′ly** ***adv.*** —**base′ness** ***n.***

base·ball (bās′bôl′) ***n.*** **1.** a game played with a rawhide-covered ball and a bat by two opposing teams of nine players each, on a field with four bases forming a diamond **2.** the ball used in this game

base·board (-bôrd′) ***n.*** a board or molding covering the edge of a wall next to the floor

base·born (-bôrn′) ***adj.*** **1.** of humble birth or origin **2.** of illegitimate birth **3.** mean or ignoble

base·burn·er, base-burn·er (-bur′nər) ***n.*** any stove, etc. in which more coal is fed automatically from above when that at the base is consumed

base hit *Baseball* a play in which the batter hits the ball and gets on base without benefit of an opponent's error and without forcing a runner

Ba·sel (bä′z'l) city in NW Switzerland, on the Rhine: pop. 212,000

base·less (bās′lis) ***adj.*** having no basis in fact; unfounded —**base′less·ness** ***n.***

base line 1. a line serving as a base **2.** *Baseball* the lane between any two consecutive bases **3.** *Tennis* the line at the back at either end of a court

base·man (-mən) ***n.,*** *pl.* **-men** *Baseball* an infielder stationed at first, second, or third base

base·ment (bās′mənt) ***n.*** [BASE[1] + -MENT] the lowest story of a building, below the main floor and wholly or partly below the surface of the ground

ba·sen·ji (bə sen′jē) ***n.*** [Bantu < *ba-,* plural prefix + *senji* < Fr. *singe,* a monkey] any of an African breed of small dog with a reddish-brown coat

base on balls *Baseball same as* WALK

base runner *Baseball* any member of the team at bat who is on base or is trying to reach a base

bas·es[1] (bās′əz) ***n.*** *pl. of* BASE[1]

ba·ses[2] (bā′sēz) ***n.*** *pl. of* BASIS

bash (bash) ***vt.*** [echoic; akin to (< ?) ON. hyp. *basca,* to strike] [Colloq.] to strike with a violent blow; smash (*in*) —***n.*** **1.** [Colloq.] a violent blow **2.** [Slang] a gala party

bash·ful (bash′fəl) ***adj.*** [(A)BASH + -FUL] **1.** timid, shy, and easily embarrassed **2.** showing an embarrassed timidity —**bash′ful·ly** ***adv.*** —**bash′ful·ness** ***n.***

bas·ic (bā′sik) ***adj.*** **1.** of, at, or forming a base; fundamental **2.** introductory or elementary **3.** *Chem.* of, having the nature of, or containing a base; alkaline —***n.*** a basic principle, factor, etc.: *usually used in pl.* —**bas′i·cal·ly** ***adv.***

Basic English a copyrighted simplified form of English for international communication and for first steps into full English, devised by C. K. Ogden (1889–1957)

ba·sid·i·o·my·cete (bə sid′ē ō mī′sēt, -mī sēt′) ***n.*** [< ModL. < Gr. *basis,* base + ModL. dim. suffix *-idium* + -MYCETE] any of a class of fungi, including the mushrooms, rusts, etc., that reproduce through spores borne on a club-shaped structure

Bas·il (baz′'l, bā′z'l) [< L. < Gr. *Basileios,* lit., kingly < *basileus,* king] a masculine name

bas·il (baz′'l, bā′z'l) ***n.*** [< OFr. < ML. < Gr. *basilikon* (*phyton*), lit., royal (plant) < *basileus,* king] a fragrant herb of the mint family, whose leaves are used for flavoring in cooking

bas·i·lar (bas′ə lər) ***adj.*** of or at the base, esp. of the skull: also **bas′i·lar′y** (-ler′ē)

ba·sil·i·ca (bə sil′i kə) ***n.*** [L. < Gr. *basilikē* (*stoa*), royal (portico)] **1.** in ancient Rome, a rectangular building with a broad nave flanked by colonnaded aisles, used as a courtroom, etc. **2.** a Christian church in this style

bas·i·lisk (bas′ə lisk′) ***n.*** [< L. < Gr. dim. of *basileus,* king] **1.** a mythical, lizardlike monster with fatal breath and glance **2.** a tropical American lizard with a crest on its back and tail

ba·sin (bās′'n) ***n.*** [< OFr. < VL. < *bacca,* water vessel] **1.** *a*) a wide, shallow container, as for liquid *b*) its contents or capacity **2.** a washbowl or sink **3.** any shallow, esp. water-filled hollow, as a pond **4.** a bay or harbor **5.** all the land drained by a river and its branches **6.** a great hollow in the earth's surface filled by an ocean

ba·sis (bā′sis) ***n.,*** *pl.* **ba′ses** (-sēz) [L. < Gr., a base, pedestal] **1.** the base or foundation of anything **2.** a principal constituent **3.** the basic principle or theory, as of a system of knowledge

bask (bask) ***vi.*** [ME. *basken,* to wallow (in blood) < ?] **1.** to warm oneself pleasantly, as in sunlight **2.** to enjoy any pleasant or warm feeling *[*he *basked* in her favor*]*

bas·ket (bas′kit) ***n.*** [ME. < ?] **1.** a container made of interwoven cane, strips of wood, etc. **2.** the amount that a basket will hold **3.** anything used or shaped like a basket **4.** the structure hung from a balloon to carry persons, etc. **5.** *Basketball a*) the goal, a round net open at the bottom and hanging from a metal ring *b*) a score made by tossing the ball through this net

bas·ket·ball (-bôl′) ***n.*** **1.** a game played by two teams of five players each, in a zoned floor area: points are scored by tossing a ball through a basket at the opponent's end of the court **2.** the large, inflated ball used in this game

basket case [Slang] **1.** a person lacking all four limbs **2.** any helpless or emotionally distraught person **3.** anything that cannot function as it should

bas·ket·ry (bas′kə trē) ***n.*** **1.** the craft of making baskets **2.** *same as* BASKETWORK

basket weave a weave of fabrics resembling the weave used in basketwork

bas·ket·work (bas′kit wurk′) ***n.*** work that is interlaced or woven like a basket

ba·so·phile (bā′sə fīl′, -fil′) ***n.*** [< BASIC + -PHILE] a cell or tissue that is readily stained with basic dyes: also **ba′so·phil′** (-fil′) —**ba′so·phil′ic** ***adj.***

Basque (bask) ***n.*** **1.** any member of a certain people living in the W Pyrenees **2.** their unique language —***adj.*** of the Basques, their language, etc.

basque (bask) ***n.*** [Fr. < Pr. *basto* < ?] a woman's tightfitting bodice or tunic

Bas·ra (bus′rə, buz′-) port in SE Iraq: pop. 328,000

bas-re·lief (bä′rə lēf′) ***n.*** [Fr. < It. *basso-rilievo:* see BASSO & RELIEF] sculpture in which figures are carved in a flat surface so that they project only a little from the background

bass[1] (bās) ***n.*** [ME. *bas,* BASE[2]] **1.** the range of the lowest male voice **2.** a voice or singer with such a range **3.** an instrument of the lowest range; specif., *same as* DOUBLE BASS **4.** a part for such a voice or instrument —***adj.*** of, in, for, or having this range

bass[2] (bas) ***n.,*** *pl.* **bass, bass′es:** see PLURAL, II, D, 2 [< OE. *bærs*] a spiny-finned food and game fish of fresh or salt water

bass[3] (bas) ***n.*** *same as:* **1.** BAST **2.** BASSWOOD

bass clef (bās) *Music* a sign on a staff, indicating the position of F below middle C on the fourth line

bass drum (bās) the largest and lowest-toned of the double-headed drums

bas·set (bas′it) ***n.*** [OFr., orig., dim. of *bas,* BASE[2]] a kind of hunting hound with a long body, short legs, and long, drooping ears: also **basset hound**

bass horn (bās) *same as* TUBA

bas·si·net (bas′ə net′) ***n.*** [< Fr. *bercelonnette,* dim. of *berceau,* cradle] an infant's basketlike bed, often hooded and set on a stand having casters

bass·ist (bās′ist) ***n.*** a person who plays the double bass

bas·so (bas′ō; *It.* bäs′sô) ***n.,*** *pl.* **bas′sos;** It. **bas′si** (-sē) [It. < VL. *bassus,* low] a bass voice or singer

bas·soon (bə so͞on′, ba-) ***n.*** [Fr. *basson* < It. < prec.] a double-reed bass woodwind instrument having a long, curved stem attached to the mouthpiece —**bas·soon′ist** ***n.***

BASSOON

bas·so-re·lie·vo (bas′ō rə lē′vō) ***n.,*** *pl.* **-vos** *same as* BAS-RELIEF

bass viol (bās) *same as:* **1.** VIOLA DA GAMBA **2.** DOUBLE BASS

bass·wood (bas′wood′) ***n.*** **1.** any of several trees of the U.S. and Canada, with fragrant, yellowish flowers and light, soft wood **2.** the wood

bast (bast) ***n.*** [OE. *bæst*] **1.** *same as* PHLOEM **2.** fiber obtained from phloem, for making ropes, etc.

bas·tard (bas′tərd) ***n.*** [< OFr. < ?] **1.** a person born of parents not married to each other **2.** anything spurious, inferior, or varying from standard **3.** a person regarded with contempt, hatred, pity, etc. or, sometimes, with playful affection: a vulgar usage —***adj.*** **1.** of illegitimate birth or uncertain origin **2.** of a size or shape not standard **3.** not genuine or authentic; inferior; spurious —**bas′tard·ly** ***adj.*** —**bas′tard·y** ***n.,*** *pl.* **-ies**

bas·tard·ize (bas′tər dīz′) ***vt.*** **-ized′, -iz′ing** **1.** to make, declare, or show to be a bastard **2.** to make corrupt or inferior —**bas′tard·i·za′tion** *n.*

baste[1] (bāst) *vt.* **bast′ed, bast′ing** [< OFr. < OHG. *bastjan,* to sew with bast] to sew with long, loose stitches so as to keep the parts together until properly sewed —**bast′er** *n.*

baste[2] (bāst) *vt.* **bast′ed, bast′ing** [< OFr. < *bassiner,* to moisten < *bassin,* BASIN] to moisten (meat) with melted butter, drippings, etc. during roasting —**bast′er** *n.*

baste[3] (bāst) *vt.* **bast′ed, bast′ing** [ON. *beysta*] **1.** to beat soundly **2.** to attack with words; abuse

bas·tille, bas·tile (bas tēl′) *n.* [Fr. < OFr. *bastir,* to build: see BASTION] a prison —**the Bastille** a state prison in Paris until destroyed (July 14, 1789) in the French Revolution

bas·ti·na·do (bas′tə nā′dō, -nā′dō) *n., pl.* **-does** [< Sp. < *bastón,* a stick] **1.** a beating with a stick, usually on the soles of the feet, esp. as a punishment **2.** a rod or stick Also **bas′ti·nade′** (-nād′) —*vt.* **-doed, -do·ing** to inflict a bastinado on

bast·ing (bās′tiŋ) *n.* **1.** the act of sewing with loose, temporary stitches **2.** loose, temporary stitches or the thread used for them

bas·tion (bas′chən; *occas.* -tē ən) *n.* [Fr. < It. < *bastire,* to build < Gmc. *bastjan,* to make with bast, build] **1.** a projection from a fortification **2.** any strong defense or bulwark —**bas′tioned** *adj.*

bat[1] (bat) *n.* [< OE. *batt,* cudgel (prob. < W. *bat*) & < OFr. *battre,* BATTER[1]] **1.** any stout club or stick **2.** a club used to strike the ball in baseball and cricket **3.** a turn at batting, as in baseball *[to be at bat]* **4.** [Brit.] a batsman at cricket **5.** [Colloq.] a blow or hit **6.** [Old Slang] a spree —*vt.* **bat′ted, bat′ting 1.** to strike with or as with a bat **2.** to have a batting average of —*vi.* to take a turn at batting —**bat around** [Slang] to consider or discuss (an idea, plan, etc.) —**go to bat for** [Colloq.] to intervene on behalf of; defend —**(right) off the bat** [Colloq.] immediately

bat[2] (bat) *n.* [altered < ME. *bakke* < Scand.] a mouselike mammal with a furry body and membranous wings, usually seen flying at night —**blind as a bat** quite blind —**have bats in the** (or **one's**) **belfry** [Slang] to be insane; have crazy notions

bat[3] (bat) *vt.* **bat′ted, bat′ting** [ME. *baten,* to flap (wings) < OFr. *battre,* BATTER[1]] [Colloq.] to wink; blink; flutter —**not bat an eye** (or **eyelash**) [Colloq.] not show surprise

Ba·ta·vi·a (bə tā′vē ə) *former name of* JAKARTA

batch (bach) *n.* [OE. *bacan,* to bake] **1.** the amount (of bread, etc.) produced at one baking **2.** the quantity of anything needed for or made in one operation or lot **3.** a number of things or persons taken as a group

bate (bāt) *vt., vi.* **bat′ed, bat′ing** [< ABATE] to abate or lessen —**with bated breath** with the breath held in because of fear, excitement, etc.

ba·teau (ba tō′) *n., pl.* **-teaux′** (-tōz′) [Fr. < OFr. *batel* < OE. *bat,* boat] a lightweight, flat-bottomed river boat with tapering ends

bat·fish (bat′fish′) *n., pl.* **-fish′, -fish′es:** see FISH any of certain marine fishes with expanded or extended pectoral fins

Bath (bath) city in SW England: a health resort with hot springs: pop. 85,000

bath (bath) *n., pl.* **baths** (ba*th*z, baths) [OE. *bæth*] **1.** a washing or dipping of a thing, esp. the body, in water or other liquid, steam, etc. **2.** water or other liquid for bathing, or for dipping, soaking, regulating temperature, etc. **3.** a container for such liquid **4.** a bathtub **5.** a bathroom **6.** a building or set of rooms for bathing **7.** [*often pl.*] a resort where bathing is part of the medical treatment —*vt., vi.* [Brit.] *same as* BATHE

bathe (bā*th*) *vt.* **bathed, bath′ing** [OE. *bathian* < *bæth,* bath] **1.** to put into a liquid; immerse **2.** to give a bath to; wash **3.** to wet or moisten **4.** to cover as if with a liquid *[trees bathed in moonlight]* —*vi.* **1.** to take a bath **2.** to go into or be in water so as to swim, cool oneself, etc. **3.** to soak oneself in some substance or influence —*n.* [Brit.] a swim or dip —**bath′er** *n.*

bath·house (bath′hous′) *n.* **1.** a public building where people can take baths **2.** a building used by bathers for changing clothes

Bath·i·nette (bath′ə net′) [< BATH, BASSINET] *a trademark for* a portable folding bathtub for babies, made of rubberized cloth, etc. —*n.* [**b-**] a bathtub of this kind

bathing cap a tightfitting cap of rubber, etc., worn to keep the hair dry as while swimming

bathing suit a garment worn for swimming

bath·mat (bath′mat′) *n.* a mat used in or next to a bathtub, as to prevent slipping

ba·thos (bā′thäs, -thôs) *n.* [Gr., depth] **1.** an abrupt change from the lofty to the ordinary or trivial in writing or speech; anticlimax **2.** false pathos; sentimentality **3.** triteness —**ba·thet·ic** (bə thet′ik) *adj.* —**ba·thet′i·cal·ly** *adv.*

bath·robe (bath′rōb′) *n.* a long, loose coat for wear to and from the bath, in lounging, etc.

bath·room (-ro͞om′) *n.* a room with a bathtub, toilet, washstand, etc.

bath·tub (-tub′) *n.* a tub, now usually a bathroom fixture, in which to take a bath

bath·y·scaph (bath′ə skaf′) *n.* [Fr. < Gr. *bathys,* deep + *skaphē,* boat] a deep-sea diving compartment for reaching great depths without a cable

bath·y·sphere (bath′ə sfir′) *n.* [< Gr. *bathys,* deep + -SPHERE] a round, watertight observation chamber lowered by cables into sea depths

ba·tik (bə tēk′, bat′ik) *n.* [Malay] **1.** a method of dyeing designs on cloth by coating with removable wax the parts not to be dyed **2.** cloth so decorated or a design made in this way —*adj.* of or like batik

ba·tiste (ba tēst′, bə-) *n.* [Fr. < OFr. *baptiste:* after the supposed original maker, *Baptiste* of Cambrai] a fine, thin cloth of cotton, linen, rayon, etc.

bat mitz·vah, bat miz·vah (bät mits′və) [Heb. *bat mitswāh,* daughter of the commandment] [*also* **B- M-**] **1.** a Jewish girl who undergoes a ceremony analogous to that of a bar mitzvah **2.** the ceremony itself

ba·ton (bə tän′, ba-) *n.* [Fr. < OFr. < VL. hyp. *basto,* a stick] **1.** a staff serving as a symbol of office **2.** a slender stick used by a conductor in directing an orchestra, choir, etc. **3.** a hollow metal rod twirled in a showy way, as by a drum majorette **4.** the short rod passed from one runner to the next in a relay race

Bat·on Rouge (bat′'n ro͞ozh′) [Fr. transl. of Choctaw *ītu-úma,* red (boundary) pole] capital of La., on the Mississippi: pop. 219,000

ba·tra·chi·an (bə trā′kē ən) *adj.* [< ModL. < Gr. < *batrachos,* frog] of, like, or concerning amphibians without tails, as frogs and toads —*n.* an amphibian without a tail; frog or toad

bats·man (bats′mən) *n., pl.* **-men** the batter in cricket

bat·tal·ion (bə tal′yən) *n.* [< Fr. < It. < VL. *battalia,* BATTLE] **1.** a large group of soldiers arrayed for battle **2.** any large group joined together in some activity **3.** *U.S. Army* a tactical unit made up of three or more companies, batteries, or similar units

bat·ten[1] (bat′'n) *n.* [var. of BATON] **1.** a sawed strip of wood, flooring, etc. **2.** a strip of wood put over a seam between boards as a fastening or covering **3.** a strip used to fasten canvas over a ship's hatchways —*vt.* to fasten or supply with battens —**batten down the hatches** to fasten canvas over the hatches, esp. in preparing for a storm

bat·ten[2] (bat′'n) *vi.* [ON. *batna,* to improve] to grow fat; thrive —*vt.* to fatten up; overfeed

bat·ter[1] (bat′ər) *vt.* [OFr. *batre, battre* < VL. < L. *battuere,* to beat; also, in part, freq. of BAT[1], *v.*] **1.** to beat or strike with blow after blow; pound **2.** to injure by pounding, hard wear, or use —*vi.* to pound noisily and repeatedly

bat·ter[2] (bat′ər) *n.* the player whose turn it is to bat in baseball or cricket

bat·ter[3] (bat′ər) *n.* [< OFr., prob. < *batre:* see BATTER[1]] a flowing mixture of flour, milk, eggs, etc. for making cakes, pancakes, etc.

bat·ter·ing ram (bat′ər iŋ ram′) **1.** an ancient military machine having a heavy wooden beam for battering down gates, walls, etc. **2.** any bar, log, etc. used like this to force entrance

bat·ter·y (bat′ər ē, bat′rē) *n., pl.* **-ter·ies** [< Fr. < *battre:* see BATTER[1]] **1.** a battering or beating **2.** a group of similar things arranged, connected, or used together; set or series **3.** *Baseball* the pitcher and the catcher **4.** *Elec.* a connected group of cells (or popularly, a single cell) storing an electrical charge and capable of furnishing a current **5.** *Law* any illegal beating of another person: see ASSAULT AND BATTERY **6.** *Mil. a)* an emplacement or fortification equipped with heavy guns *b)* a set of heavy guns, rockets, etc. *c)* the men who operate such a set: usually the basic unit of artillery

bat·ting (bat′iŋ, bat′'n) *n.* [< BAT[1]] fiber of cotton, wool, or synthetic fiber wadded into sheets and used in bandages, quilts, etc.

batting average 1. a measure of a baseball player's batting effectiveness, figured by dividing the number of safe hits by the number of times at bat **2.** [Colloq.] the average level of competence or success reached in any activity

bat·tle (bat′'l) *n.* [< OFr. < VL. *battalia* < L. < *battuere:* see BATTER[1]] **1.** a large-scale fight between armed forces **2.** armed fighting; combat or war **3.** any fight or struggle; conflict —*vt., vi.* **-tled, -tling** to oppose, fight, or struggle —**give** (or **do**) **battle** to engage in battle; fight —**bat′tler** *n.*

bat·tle-ax, bat·tle-axe (-aks′) *n.* **1.** a heavy ax formerly used as a weapon of war **2.** [Slang] a woman who is harsh, domineering, etc.

battle cruiser a large warship with longer range and greater speed than a battleship, but less heavily armored

battle cry a cry or slogan used to encourage those in a battle, struggle, contest, etc.

bat·tle·dore (bat′'l dôr′) *n.* [< ? Pr. *batedor,* beater] **1.** a paddle or racket used to hit a shuttlecock back and

forth in a game (called **battledore and shuttlecock**) like badminton **2.** this game
battle fatigue *same as* COMBAT FATIGUE
bat·tle·field (bat′'l fēld′) *n.* **1.** the place where a battle is fought or was fought **2.** any area of conflict Also **bat′tle-ground′**
bat·tle·ment (-mənt) *n.* [< OFr. *batailler,* to fortify] **1.** a low wall, as on top of a tower, with open spaces for shooting **2.** an architectural decoration like this —**bat′tle·ment′ed** (-men′tid) *adj.*

BATTLEMENTS

battle royal *pl.* **battles royal** **1.** a fight involving many contestants; free-for-all **2.** a bitterly fought battle **3.** a heated dispute
bat·tle·ship (-ship′) *n.* any of a class of large warships with the biggest guns and very heavy armor: also [Slang] **bat′tle·wag′on**
bat·ty (bat′ē) *adj.* **-ti·er, -ti·est** [< BAT² + -Y²] [Slang] **1.** insane; crazy **2.** odd; eccentric
bau·ble (bô′b'l) *n.* [< OFr. *baubel, belbel,* prob. redupl. of *bel* < L. *bellus,* pretty] a showy but worthless thing; trinket; trifle
Baude·laire (bōd ler′), **(Pierre) Charles** (shärl) 1821–67; Fr. poet & essayist
baulk (bôk) *n., vt., vi. same as* BALK
baux·ite (bôk′sīt, bō′zīt) *n.* [Fr. < (*Les*) *Baux,* town in SE France] the claylike ore from which aluminum is obtained
Ba·var·i·a (bə ver′ē ə) state of S West Germany: cap. Munich —**Ba·var′i·an** *adj., n.*
bawd (bôd) *n.* [< ? OFr. *baud,* gay, licentious (< Frank. *bald,* bold)] [Now Literary] **1.** a person, esp. a woman, who keeps a brothel **2.** a prostitute
bawd·y (bô′dē) *adj.* **bawd′i·er, bawd′i·est** [see prec.] indecent, obscene, etc. —**bawd′i·ly** *adv.* —**bawd′i·ness** *n.*
bawd·y·house (-hous′) *n.* a house of prostitution
bawl (bôl) *vi., vt.* [< ML. *baulare,* to bark & ? ON. *baula,* to low like a cow] **1.** to shout or call out noisily; bellow **2.** to weep loudly —*n.* **1.** an outcry; bellow **2.** a noisy weeping —**bawl out** [Slang] to scold angrily —**bawl′er** *n.*
bay¹ (bā) *n.* [< OFr. < ML. *baia*] a part of a sea or lake, indenting the shoreline; wide inlet
bay² (bā) *n.* [< OFr. *baer* < VL. *batare,* to gape] **1.** *a)* an opening or alcove marked off by columns, etc. *b)* a recess in a wall, as for a window *c) same as* BAY WINDOW **2.** a wing of a building **3.** a compartment or space: cf. BOMB BAY **4.** *same as* SICK BAY
bay³ (bā) *vi.* [< OFr., ult. < VL. *batare,* to gape] to bark in long, deep tones —*vt.* **1.** to bark at **2.** to bring to or hold at bay —*n.* **1.** the sound of baying **2.** the situation of or as of a hunted animal forced to turn and fight —**at bay** **1.** with escape cut off; cornered **2.** held off [the bear kept the hunters *at bay*] —**bring to bay** to force into a situation that makes escape impossible
bay⁴ (bā) *n.* [< OFr. < L. *baca,* berry] **1.** *same as* LAUREL (*n.* 1) **2.** [*pl.*] *a)* a wreath of bay leaves, a classical token of honor given to poets and conquerors *b)* honor; fame
bay⁵ (bā) *adj.* [< OFr. < L. *badius*] reddish-brown: said esp. of horses —*n.* **1.** a horse, etc. of this color **2.** reddish brown
Ba·ya·món (bä yä môn′) city in NE Puerto Rico, near San Juan: pop. 196,000
bay·ber·ry (bā′ber′ē) *n., pl.* **-ries** **1.** *a)* any of several shrubs, as the wax myrtle, having a small, wax-covered, berrylike fruit *b)* this fruit **2.** a tropical American tree yielding an aromatic oil used in bay rum
Bay·ern (bī′ərn) *Ger. name of* BAVARIA
bay leaf the aromatic leaf of the laurel, dried and used as a spice in cooking
bay lynx a wildcat of temperate N. America
bay·o·net (bā′ə nit, -net′; bā′ə net′) *n.* [< Fr. < *Bayonne,* city in France] a detachable, daggerlike blade put on the muzzle end of a rifle, for hand-to-hand fighting —*vt., vi.* **-net′ed** or **-net′ted, -net′ing** or **-net′ting** to stab, prod, or kill with a bayonet
Ba·yonne (bā yōn′) [after a city in SW France] city in NE N.J.: pop. 65,000
bay·ou (bī′o͞o, -ō) *n.* [AmFr. < Choctaw *bayuk,* small stream] in the southern U.S., a marshy inlet or outlet of a lake, river, etc.
bay rum an aromatic liquid formerly obtained from leaves of a bayberry tree, now made of certain oils, water, and alcohol: it is used in medicines and cosmetics
bay window **1.** a window or set of windows jutting out from the wall of a building **2.** [Slang] a large, protruding belly
ba·zaar (bə zär′) *n.* [Per. *bāzār*] **1.** in Oriental countries, a market or street of shops **2.** a shop for selling various kinds of goods **3.** a sale of various articles, usually to raise money for a club, church, etc.
ba·zoo·ka (bə zo͞ok′ə) *n.* [term orig. coined for a comic musical horn] a weapon of metal tubing, for aiming and launching electrically fired, armor-piercing rockets
b.b., bb base on balls
B.B.A. Bachelor of Business Administration
BBC British Broadcasting Corporation
bbl. *pl.* **bbls.** barrel
BB (shot)) [a designation of the size] a size of shot measuring .18 of an inch in diameter, fired from an air rifle (**BB gun**) or shotgun
B.C. **1.** before Christ **2.** British Columbia
bch. *pl.* **bchs.** bunch
bd. *pl.* **bds.** **1.** board **2.** bond **3.** bound
B/D bank draft
B.D. Bachelor of Divinity
bd. ft. board foot (or feet)
bdl. *pl.* **bdls.** bundle
be (bē; *unstressed* bi) *vi.* **was** or **were, been, be′ing** [OE. *beon*] **1.** to exist; live [Caesar *is* no more] **2.** to happen or occur [the party *is* tonight] **3.** to remain or continue [will he *be* here long?] **4.** to come to; belong [peace *be* with you] **5.** to have a place or position [the door *is* on your left] Note: *be* is often used to link its subject to a predicate nominative, adjective, or pronoun and is sometimes equivalent to the mathematical sign (=) (Ex.: he *is* brave, that hat *is* ten dollars, let x *be* y); *be* is also used as an auxiliary: (1) with the past participle of a transitive verb to form the passive voice [he will *be* paid] (2) with the past participle of certain intransitive verbs to form an archaic perfect tense [Christ *is* risen] (3) with the present participle of another verb to express continuation [the motor *is* running] (4) with the present participle or infinitive of another verb to express futurity, possibility, obligation, intention, etc. [he *is* going next week, she *is* to wash the dishes] *Be* is conjugated in the present indicative: (I) *am,* (he, she, it) *is,* (we, you, they) *are;* in the past indicative: (I, he, she, it) *was,* (we, you, they) *were;* archaic forms are (thou) *art, wert, wast;* the present subjunctive is *be,* the past subjunctive *were* —**be off** go away
be- [OE. < *be, bi,* about, near] *a prefix used variously with verbs, nouns, and adjectives to mean:* **1.** around [*besprinkle, beset*] **2.** completely; thoroughly [*bedeck, besmear*] **3.** away [*bereave, betake*] **4.** about [*bethink, bemoan*] **5.** make [*besot, bepretty*] **6.** furnish with; affect by [*befriend, bedizen, becloud*] **7.** covered with; furnished with (to excess) [*bemedaled, bewhiskered*]
Be *Chem.* beryllium
B/E, b.e. bill of exchange
beach (bēch) *n.* [E. dial., orig., pebbles, shingles] **1.** a nearly level stretch of pebbles and sand beside a sea, lake, etc., often washed by high water; sandy shore **2.** an area of shore as for swimmers, sunbathers, etc. —*vt., vi.* to ground (a boat) on a beach —**on the beach** **1.** not aboard a ship; ashore **2.** unemployed
beach·comb·er (-kō′mər) *n.* **1.** a long wave rolling ashore; comber **2.** a man who loafs on beaches or wharves, living on what he can beg or find
beach·head (-hed′) *n.* **1.** a position established by invading troops on an enemy shore **2.** a position secured as a starting point for any action
bea·con (bēk′'n) *n.* [OE. *beacen*] **1.** a signal fire, esp. one on a hill, pole, etc. **2.** any light for warning or guiding **3.** a lighthouse **4.** a radio transmitter that sends out signals for guiding aircraft, as at night **5.** a person or thing that warns, offers guidance, etc. —*vt.* **1.** to light up (darkness, etc.) **2.** to provide or mark with beacons —*vi.* to shine or serve as a beacon
bead (bēd) *n.* [ME. *bede,* prayer bead < OE. *bed* < *biddan,* to pray] **1.** a small, usually round piece of glass, wood, metal, etc., pierced for stringing **2.** [*pl.*] *a)* a string of beads; necklace *b)* a rosary **3.** any small, round object, as the front sight of a rifle **4.** a drop or bubble **5.** foam, as on beer **6.** the inner edge of a rubber tire where it fits on the rim **7.** a narrow, half-round molding —*vt.* **1.** to decorate or string with beads **2.** to string like beads —*vi.* to form a bead or beads —**draw a bead on** to take careful aim at —**say** (or **tell** or **count**) **one's beads** to say prayers with a rosary —**bead′ed** *adj.*
bead·ing (-iŋ) *n.* **1.** beads or decorative work in beads **2.** a molding or edge resembling a row of beads **3.** a narrow, half-round molding **4.** *a)* a narrow trimming of lacelike loops *b)* an openwork trimming through which a ribbon can be run
bea·dle (bē′d'l) *n.* [< OFr. < Frank. *bidal,* messenger]

formerly, a minor parish officer in the Church of England, who kept order in church

beads·man (bēdz′mən) ***n.**, pl.* **-men** [see BEAD] **1.** a person who prays for another's soul, esp. one hired to do so **2.** a person in a poorhouse —**beads′wom′an** ***n.fem.**, pl.* **-wom′en**

bead·y (bē′dē) ***adj.*** **bead′i·er, bead′i·est** **1.** small, round, and glittering like a bead *[*the *beady* eyes of a snake*]* **2.** decorated with beads

bea·gle (bē′g'l) ***n.*** [< ? Fr. *bégueule*, wide-throat] a small hound with a smooth coat, short legs, and drooping ears

BEAGLE (13–15 in. high at shoulder)

beak (bēk) ***n.*** [< OFr. < L. *beccus* < Gaul.] **1.** a bird's bill, esp. the large, sharp, horny bill of a bird of prey **2.** the beaklike mouthpart of various insects, fishes, etc. **3.** the spout of a pitcher **4.** the metal-covered ram projecting from the prow of an ancient warship **5.** [Slang] the nose —**beaked** (bēkt) ***adj.*** —**beak′less** ***adj.*** —**beak′like′** ***adj.***

beak·er (bē′kər) ***n.*** [< ON. *bikarr*, a cup < VL. < LL. < L. *bacar*, wine glass] **1.** a large or ornate cup; goblet **2.** a jarlike container of glass or metal with a lip for pouring, used by chemists, druggists, etc. **3.** its contents or capacity

beam (bēm) ***n.*** [< OE., akin to G. *baum*, a tree] **1.** a long, thick piece of wood, or of metal or stone, esp. one used as a horizontal support for a ceiling **2.** the part of a plow to which the handles, share, etc. are attached **3.** the crossbar of a balance, or the balance itself **4.** any of the heavy, horizontal crosspieces of a ship **5.** a ship's breadth at its widest point **6.** the side of a ship or the direction out sidewise from a ship **7.** a slender shaft of light or other radiation, as of X-rays **8.** a radiant look, smile, etc. **9.** a stream of radio or radar signals sent continuously in one direction as a guide for aircraft or ships —***vt.*** **1.** to give out (shafts of light); radiate **2.** to direct or aim (a radio signal, program, etc.) —***vi.*** **1.** to shine brightly **2.** to smile warmly —**off the beam** **1.** not following a guiding beam, as an airplane **2.** [Colloq.] wrong; incorrect —**on the beam** **1.** at right angles to the ship's keel **2.** following a guiding beam, as an airplane **3.** [Colloq.] working or functioning well; alert, keen, quick, etc. —**beam′ing** ***adj.*** —**beam′ing·ly** ***adv.***

beamed (bēmd) ***adj.*** having exposed beams *[*a *beamed* ceiling*]*

beam-ends (bēm′endz′) ***n.pl.*** the ends of a ship's beams —**on the beam-ends** **1.** tipping so far to the side as to be in danger of overturning **2.** at the end of one's resources, money, etc.

beam·y (-ē) ***adj.*** **beam′i·er, beam′i·est** **1.** sending out beams of light; radiant **2.** beamlike; broad

bean (bēn) ***n.*** [OE. *bean*] **1.** any of various plants of the legume family, with edible, smooth, kidney-shaped seeds **2.** any such seed **3.** a pod with such seeds, eaten as a vegetable when still unripe **4.** any of various beanlike seeds *[*coffee *beans]* **5.** [Slang] the head or brain **6.** [*pl.*] [Slang] even a little amount *[*doesn't know *beans* about music*]* —***vt.*** [Slang] to hit on the head, specif. with a pitched baseball —**full of beans** [Slang] **1.** lively; ebullient **2.** mistaken; in error —**spill the beans** [Colloq.] to divulge secret information —**bean′like′** ***adj.***

bean·bag (bēn′bag′) ***n.*** a small cloth bag filled with beans, and thrown in some games

bean·er·y (bē′nər ē) ***n.**, pl.* **-er·ies** [< baked *beans*, a chief dish] [Colloq.] a cheap restaurant

bean·ie (bē′nē) ***n.*** [Colloq.] any of various kinds of skullcap worn by children, etc.

bean·pole (bēn′pōl′) ***n.*** **1.** a tall pole for bean plants to climb on **2.** [Colloq.] a tall, lean person

bean·stalk (-stôk′) ***n.*** the main stem of a bean plant

bear[1] (ber) ***vt.*** **bore** or archaic **bare, borne** or **born** (see vt. 3), **bear′ing** [OE. *beran*, akin to L. *ferre*, Gr. *pherein*] **1.** to carry; transport **2.** to have or show *[*the letter *bore* his signature*]* **3.** to give birth to: the passive past participle in this sense is **born** when *by* does not follow **4.** to produce or yield *[*fruit-*bearing* trees*]* **5.** to support or sustain **6.** to sustain the burden of *[*to *bear* the cost*]* **7.** to put up with; tolerate *[*to *bear* pain*]* **8.** to call for; require *[*his actions *bear* watching*]* **9.** to carry or conduct (oneself) **10.** to carry over or hold (a sentiment) *[*to *bear* a grudge*]* **11.** to bring and tell (a message, tales, etc.) **12.** to move or push as if carrying *[*the crowd *bore* us along*]* **13.** to give or supply *[*to *bear* witness*]* —***vi.*** **1.** to be productive *[*the tree *bears* well*]* **2.** *a)* to lie or move in a given direction *b)* to point toward (with *on* or *upon*) **3.** to have bearing (*on*); have a relation *[*his story *bears* on the crime*]* **4.** to tolerate; put up patiently (*with*) **5.** to be oppressive; weigh *[*grief *bears* heavily on her*]* —**bear down** **1.** to press or push down **2.** to make a strong effort —**bear down on** **1.** to exert pressure on **2.** to make a strong effort toward accomplishing **3.** to approach —**bear out** to support or confirm —**bear up** to endure, as under a strain —**bring to bear on** (or **upon**) to cause to have an effect on

bear[2] (ber) ***n.**, pl.* **bears, bear:** see PLURAL, II, D, 1 [OE. *bera*] **1.** a large, heavy mammal with shaggy fur and a very short tail, native to temperate and arctic zones **2.** [B-] either of two N constellations, the **Great Bear** and the **Little Bear** **3.** a person who is clumsy, rude, etc. **4.** one who sells stock-market shares, etc. in the expectation of buying them later at a lower price —***adj.*** falling in price *[*a *bear* market*]* —**be a bear for punishment** to be able to withstand rough treatment, hardship, etc. —**bear′like′** ***adj.***

bear·a·ble (-ə b'l) ***adj.*** that can be borne or endured; tolerable —**bear′a·bly** ***adv.***

beard (bird) ***n.*** [OE., akin to G. *bart*] **1.** the hair growing on the lower part of a man's face; whiskers **2.** any beardlike part, as of certain animals **3.** a hairy outgrowth on the head of certain grains, etc.; awn **4.** anything that projects like a beard; barb or hook —***vt.*** **1.** to face or oppose courageously, as if grasping by the beard; defy **2.** to provide with a beard —**beard′ed** ***adj.***

beard·less (bird′lis) ***adj.*** **1.** having no beard **2.** too young to have a beard **3.** young, callow, etc.

Beards·ley (birdz′lē), **Aubrey Vincent** 1872–98; Eng. artist & illustrator

bear·er (ber′ər) ***n.*** **1.** a person or thing that bears, carries, or supports **2.** a plant or tree that bears fruit **3.** a person presenting for payment a check, note, money order, etc. —***adj.*** made out to the bearer *[bearer* bonds*]*

bear·ing (ber′iŋ) ***n.*** **1.** way of carrying and conducting oneself; carriage; manner **2.** a support or supporting part **3.** *a)* the act, power, or period of producing young, fruit, etc. *b)* that which is produced, as a crop **4.** endurance **5.** *a)* [*sometimes pl.*] direction or position with reference to the compass, some known points, etc. *b)* [*pl.*] awareness of one's position or situation *[*to lose one's *bearings]* **6.** relevant meaning; application; relation *[*the evidence has no *bearing* on the case*]* **7.** *Heraldry* any figure in a coat of arms **8.** *Mech.* any part of a machine in or on which another part revolves, slides, etc. —***adj.*** that bears, or supports weight

bear·ish (ber′ish) ***adj.*** **1.** bearlike; rough, surly, etc. **2.** directed toward or causing a lowering of prices in the stock exchange —**bear′ish·ly** ***adv.*** —**bear′ish·ness** ***n.***

bear·skin (ber′skin′) ***n.*** **1.** the pelt or hide of a bear **2.** a rug, coat, etc. made of this

beast (bēst) ***n.*** [< OFr. < L. *bestia*] **1.** orig., any animal except man **2.** any large, four-footed animal **3.** a person who is brutal, gross, vile, etc.

beast·ly (bēst′lē) ***adj.*** **-li·er, -li·est** **1.** of or like a beast; bestial, brutal, etc. **2.** [Colloq.] disagreeable; unpleasant —***adv.*** [Brit. Colloq.] very *[beastly* bad news*]* —**beast′li·ness** ***n.***

beast of burden any animal used for carrying things

beast of prey any animal that hunts and kills other animals for food

beat (bēt) ***vt.*** **beat, beat′en, beat′ing** [OE. *beatan*] **1.** to strike repeatedly; pound **2.** to punish by so striking; flog **3.** to dash repeatedly against *[*waves *beat* the shore*]* **4.** to form (a path, etc.) by repeated treading or riding **5.** to shape by hammering; forge **6.** to mix by stirring or striking repeatedly with a utensil; whip **7.** to move (esp. wings) up and down; flap **8.** to hunt through; search *[*the posse *beat* the countryside*]* **9.** to make or force, as by flailing or pounding *[*to *beat* one's way through a crowd*]* **10.** *a)* to defeat in a contest or struggle *b)* to outdo or surpass *c)* to act, arrive, or finish before **11.** to mark (time) by tapping, etc. **12.** to sound or signal, as by a drumbeat **13.** [Colloq.] to baffle or puzzle **14.** [Colloq.] to cheat or trick **15.** [Slang] to avoid the penalties associated with (a charge, indictment, etc.) —***vi.*** **1.** to strike repeatedly **2.** to move or sound rhythmically; throb, pulsate, etc. **3.** to hunt through woods, etc. for game **4.** to take a beating or stirring *[*this cream doesn't *beat* well*]* **5.** to make a sound by being struck, as a drum **6.** [Colloq.] to win **7.** *Naut.* to progress by tacking into the wind —***n.*** **1.** a beating, as of the heart **2.** any of a series of blows or strokes **3.** a pulsating movement or sound; throb **4.** a habitual route *[*a policeman's *beat]* **5.** *a)* the unit of musical rhythm *[*four *beats* to a measure*]* *b)* the accent in the rhythm of verse or music *c)* the gesture of the hand, baton, etc. used to mark this **6.** *same as* BEATNIK **7.** *Journalism* a publishing of news before rival newspapers; scoop —***adj.*** **1.** [Slang] tired out; exhausted **2.** of or belonging to a group of alienated young persons, esp. of the 1950's, rebelling against conventional attitudes, dress, speech, etc. —**beat about** to hunt or look through or around —**beat back** to force to retreat —**beat down** **1.** to shine with dazzling light and intense heat **2.** to put down; suppress **3.** [Colloq.] to force to a lower price —**beat it!** [Slang] go away! —**beat off** to drive back; repel —**beat up (on)** [Slang] to give a beating to; thrash —**to beat the band** (or **hell, the devil,** etc.) [Slang] vigorously; fast and furiously —**beat′er** *n.*

beat·en (bēt′'n) *adj.* **1.** struck with repeated blows; whipped **2.** shaped by hammering **3.** flattened by treading [a *beaten* path] **4.** *a)* defeated *b)* crushed in spirit by defeat **5.** tired out —**off the beaten track** (or **path**) unusual, unfamiliar, etc.

be·a·tif·ic (bē′ə tif′ik) *adj.* [see BEATIFY] **1.** making blissful or blessed **2.** full of bliss or joy [a *beatific* smile] —**be′a·tif′i·cal·ly** *adv.*

be·at·i·fi·ca·tion (bē at′ə fi kā′shən) *n.* [see ff.] *R.C.Ch.* the process of declaring a certain dead person to be among the blessed in heaven: he is then entitled to public veneration

be·at·i·fy (bē at′ə fī′) *vt.* **-fied′, -fy′ing** [< Fr. < LL. *beatificare* < L. *beatus,* happy + *facere,* to make] **1.** to make blissfully happy **2.** *R.C.Ch.* to pronounce the beatification of by papal decree

beat·ing (bēt′iŋ) *n.* **1.** the act of one that beats **2.** a whipping **3.** a throbbing **4.** a defeat

be·at·i·tude (bē at′ə to͞od′, -tyo͞od′) *n.* [< Fr. < L. < *beatus,* happy] perfect blessedness or happiness —**the Beatitudes** the blessings on the meek, the peacemakers, etc. in the Sermon on the Mount: Matt. 5:3–12

beat·nik (bēt′nik) *n.* [BEAT, *adj.* 2 + Russ. (via. Yid.) *-nik,* equiv. to -ER] a member of the beat group

Be·a·trice (bē′ə tris) [It. < L. *beatrix,* she who makes happy < *beatus,* happy] a feminine name: var. *Beatrix*

beat-up (bēt′up′) *adj.* [Slang] in a worn-out condition; dilapidated, battered, shabby, etc.

beau (bō) *n., pl.* **beaus, beaux** (bōz) [Fr. < *beau,* pretty < L. *bellus,* pretty] the sweetheart of a woman or girl

Beau Brum·mell (brum′əl) **1.** (*George Bryan Brummell*), 1778–1840; Eng. gentleman famous for his fashionable dress and manners **2.** a dandy; fop

Beau·fort scale (bō′fərt) [after Sir Francis *Beaufort* (1774–1857), Brit. naval officer] *Meteorol.* a scale of wind velocities ranging from 0 (calm) to 17 (hurricane)

‡**beau geste** (bō zhest′) *pl.* **beaux gestes** (bō zhest′) [Fr.] **1.** a fine gesture **2.** an act or offer that seems fine, noble, etc., but is empty

beau i·de·al (ī dē′əl) [Fr.] **1.** ideal beauty **2.** the perfect type or conception (*of* something)

beau monde (bō′mänd′) [Fr.] fashionable society

Beau·mont (bō′mänt) [ult. < Fr., lit., beautiful hill] city in SE Tex.: pop. 118,000

beaut (byo͞ot) *n.* [Slang] one that is beautiful or superlative in some way: often used ironically

beau·te·ous (byo͞ot′ē əs) *adj. same as* BEAUTIFUL —**beau′te·ous·ly** *adv.*

beau·ti·cian (byo͞o tish′ən) *n.* a person who does hair styling, manicuring, etc. in a beauty shop

beau·ti·ful (byo͞ot′ə fəl) *adj.* having beauty; very pleasing to the eye, ear, mind, etc. —**beau′ti·ful·ly** *adv.* —**beau′ti·ful·ness** *n.*

beau·ti·fy (byo͞ot′ə fī′) *vt., vi.* **-fied′, -fy′ing** to make or become beautiful or more beautiful —**beau′ti·fi·ca′tion** *n.* —**beau′ti·fi′er** *n.*

beau·ty (byo͞ot′ē) *n., pl.* **-ties** [< OFr. < L. *bellus,* pretty] **1.** the quality attributed to whatever pleases the senses or mind, as by line, color, form, tone, behavior, etc. **2.** a thing having this quality **3.** good looks **4.** a very good-looking woman **5.** any very attractive feature —*adj.* [Slang] best, nicest, etc. [the *beauty* part]

beauty shop (or **salon** or **parlor**) a place where women go for hair styling, manicuring, etc.

beauty spot **1.** a tiny black patch formerly applied by women to the face or back to emphasize whiteness of skin **2.** a natural mark or mole on the skin **3.** any place noted for its beauty

beaux (bōz; *Fr.* bō) *n. alt. pl. of* BEAU

‡**beaux-arts** (bō zär′) *n.pl.* [Fr.] the fine arts

bea·ver[1] (bē′vər) *n.* [OE. *beofor*] **1.** *pl.* **-vers, -ver:** see PLURAL, II, D, 1 *a)* a large rodent with soft, brown fur, webbed hind feet, and a flat, broad tail: it can live on land or in water *b)* its fur **2.** a man's high silk hat **3.** a heavy cloth of felted wool **4.** [Colloq.] a hard-working, conscientious person

bea·ver[2] (bē′vər) *n.* [OFr. *baviere,* ult. < *bave,* saliva] **1.** orig., a piece of armor to protect the mouth and chin **2.** later, the visor of a helmet

BEAVER (32–47 in. long, including tail)

Bea·ver·board (-bôrd′) *a trademark for* artificial board made of wood fiber, used for walls, etc. —*n.* [**b-**] fiberboard of this kind

be·calm (bi käm′) *vt.* **1.** to make calm **2.** to make (a sailing ship) motionless from lack of wind

be·came (bi kām′) *pt. of* BECOME

be·cause (bi kôz′, -kuz′) *conj.* [< ME. *bi,* by + *cause*] for the reason or cause that; since —**because of** by reason of; on account of

‡**bêche-de-mer** (besh də mer′) *n.* [Fr., worm of the sea < Port. *bicho do mar,* sea slug] **1.** *pl.* **bêches-de-mer′** (besh-) *same as* TREPANG **2.** a pidgin English spoken in island areas of the SW Pacific

beck (bek) *n.* [< BECKON] a beckoning gesture of the hand, head, etc. —*vt., vi.* [Archaic] to beckon —**at the beck and call of** at the service of

Beck·et (bek′ət), Saint **Thomas à** 1118?–70; Eng. prelate; archbishop of Canterbury

beck·on (bek′'n) *vi., vt.* [OE. *beacnian* < *beacen,* a beacon] **1.** to call or summon by a gesture **2.** to attract; lure —*n.* a summoning gesture

be·cloud (bi kloud′) *vt.* to cloud over; obscure

be·come (bi kum′) *vi.* **-came′, -come′, -com′ing** [OE. *becuman:* see BE- & COME] **1.** to come to be [to *become* ill] **2.** to grow to be [the tadpole *becomes* a frog] —*vt.* to be right for or suitable to [that hat *becomes* you] —**become of** to happen to; be the fate of

be·com·ing (bi kum′iŋ) *adj.* **1.** that is suitable or appropriate; fit **2.** suitable to the wearer [a *becoming* gown] —**be·com′ing·ly** *adv.*

Bec·que·rel (be krel′), **An·toine Hen·ri** (än twȧn′ än rē′) 1852–1908; Fr. physicist

bed (bed) *n.* [OE.] **1.** a piece of furniture for sleeping or resting on, consisting typically of a bedstead, spring, mattress, and bedding **2.** *same as* BEDSTEAD **3.** any place or thing used for sleeping or reclining, or for sexual intercourse **4.** *a)* a plot of soil where plants are raised *b)* such plants **5.** *a)* the bottom of a river, lake, etc. *b)* a place on the ocean floor where things grow [oyster *bed*] **6.** rock, etc. in which something is embedded **7.** any flat surface used as a base or support **8.** a pile or heap resembling a bed **9.** a geological layer [a *bed* of coal] —*vt.* **bed′ded, bed′ding** **1.** to provide with a sleeping place **2.** to put to bed **3.** to have sexual intercourse with **4.** to embed **5.** *a)* to plant in a bed of earth *b)* to make (earth) into a bed for plants **6.** to arrange in layers —*vi.* **1.** to go to bed; rest **2.** to form in layers —**bed and board** **1.** sleeping accommodations and meals **2.** the married state —**bed down** to prepare and use a sleeping place —**get up on the wrong side of the bed** to be cross or grouchy —**put to bed** **1.** to get (a child, etc.) ready for sleep **2.** [Slang] to get (a newspaper, etc.) ready for the press —**take to one's bed** to go to bed because of illness, etc.

be·daub (bi dôb′) *vt.* **1.** to make daubs on; smear over **2.** to overdecorate

be·daz·zle (bi daz′'l) *vt.* **-zled, -zling** to dazzle thoroughly; bewilder; confuse

bed·bug (bed′bug′) *n.* a small, wingless, reddish-brown, bloodsucking insect that infests beds, etc.

bed·cham·ber (-chām′bər) *n. same as* BEDROOM

bed·clothes (-klōz′, -klō*th*z′) *n.pl.* sheets, blankets, comforters, etc. used on a bed

bed·ding (-iŋ) *n.* **1.** mattresses and bedclothes **2.** straw, hay, etc., used to bed animals **3.** a bottom layer **4.** *Geol.* stratification

be·deck (bi dek′) *vt.* to decorate; adorn

be·dev·il (bi dev′'l) *vt.* **-iled** or **-illed, -il·ing** or **-il·ling** **1.** to plague diabolically; torment **2.** to bewitch **3.** to confuse completely; muddle **4.** to corrupt; spoil —**be·dev′il·ment** *n.*

be·dew (bi do͞o′, -dyo͞o′) *vt.* to make wet with or as if with drops of dew

bed·fast (bed′fast′) *adj. same as* BEDRIDDEN

bed·fel·low (-fel′ō) *n.* **1.** a person who shares one's bed **2.** an associate, ally, etc.

be·dight (bi dīt′) *adj.* [pp. of obs. *bedight* < ME. < *bi-,* BE- + *dighten,* to set in order < OE. *dihtan,* to compose < L. *dictare:* see DICTATE] [Archaic or Poet.] bedecked; arrayed

be·dim (bi dim′) *vt.* **-dimmed′, -dim′ming** to make (the eyes or vision) dim; darken or obscure

be·di·zen (bi dī′z'n, -diz′'n) *vt.* [BE- + DIZEN] to dress in a cheap, showy way —**be·di′zen·ment** *n.*

bed jacket a woman's short, loose upper garment sometimes worn in bed over a nightgown

bed·lam (bed′ləm) *n.* [< *Bedlam,* altered < (St. Mary of) *Bethlehem,* old insane asylum in London] **1.** [Archaic] an insane asylum **2.** any place or condition of noise and confusion —**bed′lam·ite′** (-īt′) *n.*

bed linen bed sheets, pillowcases, etc.

bed of roses [Colloq.] a situation or position of ease and luxury

Bed·ou·in (bed′oo win) ***n.**, pl.* **-ins, -in** [< Fr. < Ar. *badāwīn,* dwellers in the desert] [*also* **b-**] **1.** an Arab of any of the nomadic desert tribes of Arabia, Syria, or N Africa **2.** any wanderer or nomad —***adj.*** of or like the Bedouins
bed·pan (bed′pan′) ***n.*** **1.** *same as* WARMING PAN **2.** a shallow pan for use as a toilet by a person confined to bed
be·drag·gle (bi drag′'l) ***vt.*** **-gled, -gling** to make wet, limp, and dirty, as by dragging through mud —**be·drag′gled** ***adj.***
bed·rid·den (bed′rid′'n) ***adj.*** having to stay in bed, usually for a long period, because of illness, infirmity, etc.: also **bed′rid′**
bed·rock (-räk′) ***n.*** **1.** solid rock beneath the soil and superficial rock **2.** a secure foundation **3.** the very bottom **4.** basic principles
bed·roll (-rōl′) ***n.*** a portable roll of bedding, generally for sleeping outdoors
bed·room (-ro͞om′) ***n.*** a room to sleep in —***adj.*** **1.** dealing with sex or sexual affairs [a *bedroom* farce] **2.** housing those who work days in a nearby metropolis [*bedroom* suburbs]
bed·side (-sīd′) ***n.*** the side of a bed; space beside a bed —***adj.*** **1.** beside a bed **2.** as regards patients [a doctor's *bedside* manner]
bed·sore (-sôr′) ***n.*** a sore on the body of a bedridden person, caused by chafing or pressure
bed·spread (-spred′) ***n.*** a cover spread over the blanket on a bed, mainly for ornament
bed·spring (-spriŋ′) ***n.*** **1.** a framework of springs in a bed to support the mattress **2.** any such spring
bed·stead (-sted′) ***n.*** a framework for supporting the spring and mattress of a bed
bed·straw (-strô′) ***n.*** [from its former use as straw for beds] a small plant of the madder family, with whorled leaves and small, white or colored flowers
bed·time (-tīm′) ***n.*** one's usual time for going to bed
bed-wet·ting (-wet′iŋ) ***n.*** urinating in bed
bee[1] (bē) ***n.*** [OE. *beo*] a four-winged, hairy insect that gathers pollen and nectar: some bees live in organized colonies and make honey —**have a bee in one's bonnet** **1.** to be preoccupied or obsessed by an idea **2.** to be not quite sane
bee[2] (bē) ***n.*** [ult. < OE. *ben,* compulsory service] a meeting of people to work together or to compete [a sewing *bee,* spelling *bee*]
bee·bread (-bred′) ***n.*** a yellowish-brown mixture of pollen and honey, made and eaten by some bees
beech (bēch) ***adj.*** [OE. *boece, bece*] designating a family of trees including the beeches, oaks, and chestnuts —***n.*** **1.** a tree of the beech family, with smooth bark, hard wood, dark-green leaves, and edible nuts **2.** its wood —**beech′en** ***adj.***
Bee·cher (bē′chər), **Henry Ward** 1813–87; U.S. clergyman & lecturer
beech·mast (bēch′mast′) ***n.*** beechnuts, esp. as they lie on the ground: also **beech mast**
beech·nut (-nut′) ***n.*** the small, three-cornered, edible nut of the beech tree
beef (bēf) ***n.**, pl.* **beeves;** also, and for 5 always, **beefs** [< OFr. *boef* < L. *bovis,* gen. of *bos,* ox] **1.** a full-grown ox, cow, bull, or steer, esp. one bred for meat **2.** meat from such an animal; specif., a dressed carcass **3.** such animals collectively **4.** [Colloq.] *a)* human flesh or muscle *b)* strength; brawn **5.** [Slang] a complaint —***vi.*** [Slang] to complain —**beef up** [Colloq.] to strengthen by addition, reinforcement, etc.

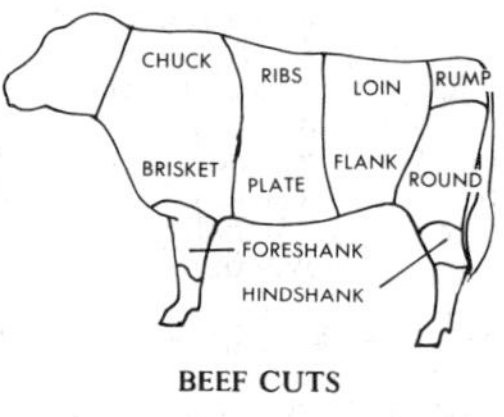

BEEF CUTS

beef cattle cattle bred and fattened for meat
beef·eat·er (-ēt′ər) ***n.*** **1.** an eater of beef, typified as portly, ruddy, etc. **2.** *same as* YEOMAN OF THE GUARD **3.** a guard at the Tower of London **4.** [Slang] an Englishman
beef·steak (-stāk′) ***n.*** a slice of beef, esp. from the loin, cut thick for broiling or frying
beef tea a drink made from beef extract or by boiling lean strips of beef
beef·y (bēf′ē) ***adj.*** **beef′i·er, beef′i·est** fleshy and solid; very muscular; brawny —**beef′i·ness** ***n.***
bee·hive (bē′hīv′) ***n.*** **1.** a box or other shelter for a colony of bees, where they make and store honey **2.** a place of great activity
bee·keep·er (-kēp′ər) ***n.*** a person who keeps bees for producing honey —**bee′keep′ing** ***n.***
bee·line (-līn′) ***n.*** a straight, direct route —**make a beeline for** [Colloq.] to go straight toward
Be·el·ze·bub (bē el′zə bub′) *Bible* the chief devil; Satan: also **Be·el′ze·bul′** (-bool′)
bee moth a moth whose larvae, hatched in beehives, eat the wax of the honeycomb
been (bin, ben; *chiefly Brit.* bēn) *pp. of* BE
beep (bēp) ***n.*** [echoic] **1.** the brief, high-pitched sound of a horn, as on an automobile **2.** a brief, high-pitched electronic signal, used in warning, direction-finding, etc. —***vi., vt.*** to make or cause to make such a sound
beer (bir) ***n.*** [OE. *beor*] **1.** an alcoholic, fermented beverage made from grain, esp. malted barley, and flavored with hops **2.** any of various soft drinks made from root and plant extracts [root *beer*]
Beer·she·ba (bir shē′bə) city in S Israel, in the Negev: pop. 70,000
beer·y (bir′ē) ***adj.*** **beer′i·er, beer′i·est** **1.** of or like beer **2.** showing the effects of drinking beer; drunken, maudlin, etc. —**beer′i·ness** ***n.***
beest·ings (bēs′tiŋz) ***n.pl.*** [*often with sing. v.*] [OE. *bysting* < *beost,* beestings] the first milk of a cow after having a calf
bees·wax (bēz′waks′) ***n.*** wax secreted and used by bees to build their honeycomb: see WAX[1] (sense 1)
beet (bēt) ***n.*** [< OE. < L. *beta*] **1.** a plant with edible leaves and a thick, fleshy, white or red root **2.** this root: some varieties are eaten as a vegetable, others are a source of sugar
Bee·tho·ven (bā′tō vən), **Lud·wig van** (lo͞ot′viH vän) 1770–1827; Ger. composer
bee·tle[1] (bēt′'l) ***n.*** [OE. *bitela* < *bitan,* to bite] an insect with biting mouthparts and hard front wings that cover the membranous hind wings when these are folded
bee·tle[2] (bēt′'l) ***n.*** [OE. *betel,* ult. connected with BEAT] **1.** a heavy, wooden mallet **2.** a household mallet or pestle for mashing or beating —***vt.*** **-tled, -tling** to pound with a beetle
bee·tle[3] (bēt′'l) ***vi.*** **-tled, -tling** [prob. < ff.] to project or jut; overhang —***adj.*** jutting; overhanging: also **bee′tling**
bee·tle-browed (bēt′'l broud′) ***adj.*** [ME. < ? *bitel,* sharp + *brouwe,* BROW] **1.** having bushy or overhanging eyebrows **2.** frowning; scowling
beet sugar sugar extracted from sugar beets
beeves (bēvz) ***n.*** *alt. pl. of* BEEF
be·fall (bi fôl′) ***vi.*** **-fell′, -fall′en, -fall′ing** [< OE. < *be-* + *feallan,* to fall] to come to pass; happen —***vt.*** to happen to [what *befell* them?]
be·fit (bi fit′) ***vt.*** **-fit′ted, -fit′ting** to be suitable or proper for —**be·fit′ting·ly** ***adv.***
be·fog (bi fôg′, -fäg′) ***vt.*** **-fogged′, -fog′ging** **1.** to cover with fog; make foggy **2.** to make obscure or muddled; confuse [to *befog* an issue]
be·fore (bi fôr′) ***adv.*** [< OE. < *be-,* by + *foran,* before] **1.** ahead; in front **2.** in the past; previously [I've seen him *before*] **3.** earlier; sooner [come at ten, not *before*] —***prep.*** **1.** ahead of in time, space, rank, or importance **2.** just in front of [he paused *before* the door] **3.** in the sight, notice, presence, etc. of [to stand *before* a judge] **4.** being considered, judged, or decided by [the bill *before* the assembly] **5.** earlier than [he left *before* noon] **6.** in preference to [death *before* dishonor] —***conj.*** **1.** earlier than the time that [drop in *before* you go] **2.** rather than [I'd die *before* I'd tell]
be·fore·hand (-hand′) ***adv., adj.*** **1.** ahead of time; in advance **2.** in anticipation
be·foul (bi foul′) ***vt.*** to dirty or sully; foul
be·friend (-frend′) ***vt.*** to act as a friend to; help
be·fud·dle (-fud′'l) ***vt.*** **-dled, -dling** **1.** to fuddle or confuse (the mind, a person, etc.) **2.** to stupefy with alcoholic liquor —**be·fud′dle·ment** ***n.***
beg (beg) ***vt.*** **begged, beg′ging** [< Anglo-Fr. < OFr. *begard,* beggar < MDu. *beggaert*] **1.** to ask for as charity [he *begged* a dime] **2.** to ask for earnestly as a kindness or favor —***vi.*** **1.** to ask for alms; be a beggar **2.** to entreat —**beg off** to ask to be released from —**beg the question** **1.** to use an argument that assumes as proved the very thing one is trying to prove **2.** loosely, to evade the issue —**go begging** to be unwanted
be·gan (bi gan′) *pt. of* BEGIN
be·get (bi get′) ***vt.*** **-got′** or archaic **-gat′** (-gat′), **-got′ten** or **-got′, -get′ting** [< OE. *begitan,* to acquire: see BE- & GET] **1.** to be the father of; procreate **2.** to bring into being; produce [tyranny *begets* rebellion] —**be·get′ter** ***n.***
beg·gar (beg′ər) ***n.*** [< OFr. *begard:* see BEG] **1.** a person who begs; esp., one who lives by begging **2.** a very poor person; pauper **3.** a person; fellow [a cute little *beggar*] —***vt.*** **1.** to make a beggar of; make poor **2.** to make seem inadequate or useless [her beauty *beggars* description] —**beg′gar·dom** (-dəm) ***n.***
beg·gar·ly (-lē) ***adj.*** like or fit for a beggar; very poor, inadequate, etc. —**beg′gar·li·ness** ***n.***
beg·gar·y (beg′ər ē) ***n.*** **1.** extreme poverty **2.** the act of begging
be·gin (bi gin′) ***vi.*** **be·gan′, be·gun′, be·gin′ning** [< OE. *beginnan*] **1.** to start doing something; get under way **2.** to come into being; arise **3.** to have a first part [the Bible *begins* with Genesis] **4.** to be or do in the slightest degree [they don't *begin* to compare] —***vt.*** **1.** to cause to start;

commence **2.** to bring into being; originate **3.** to do or be the first part of

be·gin·ner (-ər) ***n.*** **1.** one who begins anything **2.** one just beginning to do or learn a thing; novice

be·gin·ning (-iŋ) ***n.*** **1.** a starting or commencing **2.** the time or place of starting; birth; origin; source **3.** the first part *[the beginning of a book]* **4.** [*usually pl.*] an early stage

be·gird (bi gurd′) ***vt.*** **-girt′** or **-gird′ed, -girt′, -gird′ing** **1.** to bind around; gird **2.** to encircle

be·gone (bi gôn′, -gän′) ***interj., vi.*** (to) be gone; go away; get out

be·gon·ia (bi gōn′yə) ***n.*** [after M. *Bégon* (1638–1710), Fr. governor of the Dominican Republic] a plant with showy flowers and ornamental leaves

be·got (bi gät′) *pt. & alt. pp. of* BEGET

be·got·ten (-′n) *alt. pp. of* BEGET

be·grime (bi grīm′) ***vt.*** **-grimed′, -grim′ing** to cover with grime; make dirty; soil

be·grudge (bi gruj′) ***vt.*** **-grudged′, -grudg′ing** **1.** to feel ill will or resentment at the possession or enjoyment of (something) by another *[to begrudge another's fortune]* **2.** to give with reluctance *[he begrudges her every cent]* **3.** to regard with displeasure —**be·grudg′ing·ly *adv.***

be·guile (bi gīl′) ***vt.*** **-guiled′, -guil′ing** **1.** to mislead by guile; deceive **2.** to deprive (*of* or *out of*) by deceit; cheat **3.** to pass (time) pleasantly; while away *[he beguiled his day with reading]* **4.** to charm or delight —**be·guile′ment *n.*** —**be·guil′er *n.*** —**be·guil′ing·ly *adv.***

be·guine (bi gēn′) ***n.*** [< Fr. *béguin,* infatuation] a native dance of Martinique or its music

be·gum (bē′gəm) ***n.*** [< Hindi *begam,* lady] in India, a Moslem princess or lady of high rank

be·gun (bi gun′) *pp. of* BEGIN

be·half (bi haf′) ***n.*** [< OE. *be,* by + *healf,* side, half] support, interest, side, etc. *[speak in his behalf]* —**in** (or **on**) **behalf of** in the interest of; for —**on behalf of** speaking for; representing

be·have (bi hāv′) ***vt., vi.*** **- haved′, -hav′ing** [see BE- & HAVE] **1.** to conduct (oneself or itself) or act in a specified way **2.** to conduct (oneself) properly; do what is right

be·hav·ior (bi hāv′yər) ***n.*** **1.** the way a person behaves or acts; conduct **2.** an organism's observable responses to stimulation **3.** the way a machine, element, etc. acts or functions —**be·hav′ior·al *adj.*** —**be·hav′ior·al·ly *adv.***

behavioral science any of the sciences, as sociology, psychology, or anthropology, that study human behavior

be·hav·ior·ism (bi hāv′yər iz′m) ***n.*** the doctrine that observed behavior provides the only valid data of psychology: it rejects the concept of mind —**be·hav′ior·ist *n., adj.*** —**be·hav′ior·is′tic *adj.***

be·hav·iour (bi hāv′yər) ***n.*** *Brit. sp. of* BEHAVIOR

be·head (bi hed′) ***vt.*** to cut off the head of

be·held (bi held′) *pt. & pp. of* BEHOLD

be·he·moth (bi hē′məth, bē′ə-) ***n.*** [Heb. *behēmōth,* intens. pl. of *behēmāh,* beast] **1.** *Bible* a huge animal, assumed to be the hippopotamus: Job 40:15–24 **2.** any huge animal or thing

be·hest (bi hest′) ***n.*** [OE. *behæs,* a vow] an order, command, or earnest request

be·hind (bi hīnd′) ***adv.*** [OE. *behindan:* see BE- & HIND[1]] **1.** in or to the rear or back *[walk behind]* **2.** in a former time, place, condition, etc. *[the girl he left behind]* **3.** into a retarded state *[to drop behind in one's studies]* **4.** into arrears *[to fall behind in one's dues]* **5.** slow in time; late —***prep.*** **1.** remaining after *[the sons he left behind him]* **2.** in back of *[sit behind her]* **3.** lower than in rank, achievement, etc. **4.** later than *[behind schedule]* **5.** on the other or farther side of *[behind the hill]* **6.** gone by or ended for *[his schooling is behind him]* **7.** supporting or advocating *[Congress is behind the plan]* **8.** hidden by; not yet revealed *[the story behind the news]* —***adj.*** that follows *[the person behind]* —***n.*** [Colloq.] the buttocks

be·hind·hand (-hand′) ***adv., adj.*** **1.** behind in paying debts, rent, etc. **2.** behind time; late **3.** behind or slow in progress, advancement, etc.

be·hold (bi hōld′) ***vt.*** **-held′, -held′** or archaic **-hold′en, -hold′ing** [OE. *bihealdan,* to hold: see BE- & HOLD[1]] to hold in view; look at; regard —***interj.*** look! see!

be·hold·en (-ən) ***adj.*** obliged to feel grateful; owing thanks; indebted

be·hoof (bi hōōf′) ***n.*** [OE. *behof,* profit] behalf, benefit, interest, advantage, sake, etc.

be·hoove (-hōōv′) ***vt.*** **-hooved′, -hoov′ing** [OE. *behofian,* to need] to be necessary for or incumbent upon *[it behooves you to do this]*

be·hove (-hōv′) ***vt.*** **-hoved′, -hov′ing** *chiefly Brit. var. of* BEHOOVE

beige (bāzh) ***n.*** [Fr.] **1.** a soft, unbleached and undyed, wool fabric **2.** its characteristic sandy color; grayish tan —***adj.*** grayish-tan

be·ing (bē′iŋ) ***n.*** [see BE] **1.** existence; life **2.** basic or essential nature **3.** one that lives or exists, or is assumed to do so *[a human being, a divine being]* —**being as** (or **that**) [Dial. or Colloq.] since; because —**for the time being** for now

Bei·rut (bā rōōt′, bā′rōōt) capital of Lebanon: pop. c. 500,000

be·jab·bers (bi jab′ərz) ***interj.*** [< *by Jesus*] an exclamation used to express surprise, pleasure, anger, etc.: also used as a slang noun of indefinite meaning in **beat** (or **scare**) **the bejabbers out of:** also **be·ja′bers** (-jā′bərz), **be·je′sus** (-jē′zəs)

be·jew·el (bi jōō′əl) ***vt.*** **-eled** or **-elled, -el·ing** or **-el·ling** to decorate with or as with jewels

be·la·bor (-lā′bər) ***vt.*** **1.** to beat severely **2.** to attack verbally **3.** *popularly, same as* LABOR, *vt.*

be·lat·ed (-lāt′id) ***adj.*** late or too late; tardy —**be·lat′ed·ly *adv.*** —**be·lat′ed·ness *n.***

be·lay (-lā′) ***vt., vi.*** **-layed′, -lay′ing** [< OE. < *be-* + *lecgan,* to lay] **1.** to make (a rope) secure by winding around a pin (**belaying pin**), cleat, etc. **2.** [Naut. Colloq.] to hold; stop *[belay there!]* **3.** to secure by a rope

bel can·to (bel′ kän′tō) [It., lit., beautiful song] a style of singing with brilliant vocal display and purity of tone

belch (belch) ***vi., vt.*** [OE. *bealcian*] **1.** to expel (gas) through the mouth from the stomach **2.** to utter (curses, etc.) violently **3.** to throw forth (its contents) violently *[the volcano belched flame]* —***n.*** a belching

bel·dam, bel·dame (bel′dəm) ***n.*** [*bel-* < Fr. *belle* (see BELLE) + DAME] an old woman; esp., a hag

be·lea·guer (bi lē′gər) ***vt.*** [Du. *belegeren* < *legeren,* to camp < *leger,* a camp] **1.** to besiege by encircling, as with an army **2.** to beset; harass

Be·lém (be len′) seaport in NE Brazil: pop. 402,000

Bel·fast (bel′fast) seaport & capital of Northern Ireland: pop. 398,000

bel·fry (bel′frē) ***n.,*** *pl.* **-fries** [altered (after BELL[1]) < OFr. *berfroi* < OHG. < *bergen,* to protect + *frid,* peace] **1.** a bell tower **2.** the part of a steeple that holds the bell or bells —**bel′fried *adj.***

Belg. **1.** Belgian **2.** Belgium

Bel·gium (bel′jəm) kingdom in W Europe, on the North Sea: 11,779 sq. mi.; pop. 9,660,000; cap. Brussels: Fr. name **Bel·gique** (bel zhēk′); Fl. name **Bel·gi·ë** (bel′gē ə) —**Bel′gian *adj., n.***

Bel·grade (bel′grād, -gräd; bel grād′, -gräd′) capital of Yugoslavia, on the Danube: pop. 598,000

Be·li·al (bē′lē əl, bēl′yəl) ***n.*** [< LL. < Heb. *belīya'al,* worthlessness] *Bible* wickedness as an evil force (in the *New Testament,* personified as Satan)

be·lie (bi lī′) ***vt.*** **-lied′, -ly′ing** **1.** to give a false idea of; misrepresent *[his smile belies his anger]* **2.** to leave unfulfilled *[war belied hopes for peace]* **3.** to show to be untrue *[her cruelty belied her kind words]* —**be·li′er *n.***

be·lief (bə lēf′) ***n.*** [ME. < *bi-,* BE- + *-leve* < OE. *geleafa,* belief] **1.** the state of believing; conviction **2.** faith, esp. religious faith **3.** trust or confidence *[I have belief in his ability]* **4.** anything believed or accepted as true; esp., a creed, tenet, etc. **5.** an opinion; expectation *[my belief is that he'll come]*

be·lieve (bə lēv′) ***vt.*** **-lieved′, -liev′ing** [ME. < *bi-,* BE- + *-leven* < OE. *geliefan,* believe] **1.** to take as true, real, etc. **2.** to have confidence in a statement or promise of (another person) **3.** to suppose or think —***vi.*** **1.** to have trust or confidence (*in*) **2.** to have religious faith **3.** to suppose or think —**be·liev′a·bil′i·ty *n.*** —**be·liev′a·ble *adj.*** —**be·liev′a·bly *adv.*** —**be·liev′er *n.***

Be·lin·da (bə lin′də) [< Gmc. *Betlindis* < ?] a feminine name

be·lit·tle (bi lit′'l) ***vt.*** **-tled, -tling** to make seem little, less important, etc.; depreciate —**be·lit′tle·ment *n.***

Be·lize (bə lēz′) self-governing Brit. territory in Central America: 8,867 sq. mi.; pop. 127,000

bell[1] (bel) ***n.*** [OE. *belle*] **1.** a hollow object, usually cuplike and of metal, which rings when struck **2.** the sound made by a bell **3.** anything shaped like a bell, as a flower, the flare of a horn, etc. **4.** *Naut. a)* a bell rung every half hour to mark the periods of the watch *b)* any of these periods —***vt.*** **1.** to attach a bell to **2.** to shape like a bell —***vi.*** to flare out like a bell

bell[2] (bel) ***n., vi., vt.*** [< OE. *bellan*] bellow; roar; bay

Bell (bel), **Alexander Graham** 1847–1922; U.S. inventor of the telephone, born in Scotland

bel·la·don·na (bel′ə dän′ə) *n.* [ModL. < It. *bella donna,* beautiful lady, a folk etym. for ML. *bladona,* nightshade] **1.** a poisonous plant with purplish, bell-shaped flowers and black berries; deadly nightshade: it yields atropine **2.** *same as* ATROPINE

bell-bot·tom (bel′bät′əm) *adj.* designating trousers flaring at the ankles: also **bell′-bot′tomed**

bell·boy (-boi′) *n. same as* BELLMAN (sense 2)

bell buoy a buoy with a warning bell rung by the motion of the waves

Belle (bel) [Fr.: see ff.] a feminine name

belle (bel) *n.* [Fr., fem. of *beau:* see BEAU] a pretty woman or girl; often, one who is the prettiest or most popular [the *belle* of the ball]

belles-let·tres (bel let′rə) *n.pl.* [Fr.] literature as a fine art; fiction, poetry, drama, etc. as distinguished from technical and scientific writings —**bel·let·rist** (bel let′rist) *n.* —**bel′-le·tris′tic** (-lə tris′tik) *adj.*

Belle·vue (bel′vyōō′) [Fr., lit., beautiful view] city in NW Wash.: suburb of Seattle: pop. 74,000

Bell·flow·er (bel′flou′ər) city in SW Calif.: suburb of Los Angeles: pop. 53,000

bell·flow·er (bel′flou′ər) *n.* any of a large genus of plants, with showy, bell-shaped flowers of white, pink, or blue

bell·hop (bel′häp′) *n. same as* BELLMAN (sense 2)

bel·li·cose (bel′ə kōs′) *adj.* [< L. < *bellicus,* of war < *bellum,* war] of a quarrelsome nature; eager to fight; warlike —**bel′li·cose′ly** *adv.* —**bel′li·cos′i·ty** (-käs′ə tē) *n.*

bel·lied (bel′ēd) *adj.* having a belly, esp. of a specified kind [the yellow-*bellied* sapsucker]

bel·lig·er·ence (bə lij′ər əns) *n.* belligerent or aggressively hostile attitude or quality

bel·lig·er·en·cy (-ən sē) *n.* **1.** the state of being at war or of being recognized as a belligerent **2.** *same as* BELLIGERENCE

bel·lig·er·ent (bə lij′ər ənt) *adj.* [< L. prp. of *belligerare* < *bellum,* war + *gerere,* to carry on] **1.** recognized under international law as being at war **2.** of war; of fighting **3.** warlike **4.** showing readiness to fight or quarrel —*n.* a belligerent person or nation —**bel·lig′er·ent·ly** *adv.*

Bel·li·ni (bel lē′nē), **Gio·van·ni** (jô vän′nē) 1430?–1516; Venetian painter

bell jar a bell-shaped container or cover made of glass, used to keep gases, air, moisture, etc. in or out: also **bell glass**

bell·man (bel′mən) *n., pl.* **-men 1.** *same as* TOWN CRIER **2.** a man or boy employed by a hotel, etc. to carry luggage and do errands

bel·low (bel′ō) *vi.* [OE. *bylgan*] **1.** to roar with a reverberating sound, as a bull **2.** to cry out loudly, as in anger or pain —*vt.* to utter loudly or powerfully —*n.* a bellowing sound; roar

Bel·low (bel′ō), **Saul** 1915– ; U.S. novelist

bel·lows (bel′ōz, -əz) *n.sing. & pl.* [ME. *belwes,* orig. pl. of *beli:* see BELLY] **1.** a device that produces a stream of air through a narrow tube when its sides are pumped together: used for blowing fires, in pipe organs, etc. **2.** anything like a bellows, as the folding part of some cameras

bell-shaped curve (bel′shāpt′) a statistical curve, as of probability, which in graphic representation resembles the outline of a cuplike bell standing on its flared lip: also **bell curve**

bell·weth·er (bel′weth′ər) *n.* a male sheep, usually wearing a bell, that leads the flock

bel·ly (bel′ē) *n., pl.* **-lies** [ME. *beli* < OE. *belg,* leather bag, bellows] **1.** the lower front part of the human body between the chest and thighs; abdomen **2.** the underside of an animal's body **3.** the abdominal cavity **4.** the stomach **5.** the deep interior [the *belly* of a ship] **6.** any part, surface, or section that curves outward or bulges —*vt., vi.* **-lied, -ly·ing** to swell out; bulge

bel·ly·ache (-āk′) *n.* pain in the abdomen or bowels —*vi.* **-ached′, -ach′ing** [Slang] to complain —**bel′ly·ach′er** *n.*

bel·ly·band (-band′) *n.* a girth around an animal's belly for keeping a saddle, etc. in place

bel·ly·but·ton (-but″n) *n.* [Colloq.] the navel: also **belly button**

belly dance a dance of eastern Mediterranean origin characterized by a twisting of the abdomen, sinuous hip movements, etc. —**bel′ly-dance′** *vi.* **-danced′, -danc′ing** —**belly dancer**

bel·ly-flop (-fläp′) *vi.* **-flopped′, -flop′ping** [Colloq.] **1.** to dive awkwardly, with the belly striking flat against the water **2.** to throw oneself on a sled, with the belly downward, and coast, as down a hill Also **bel′ly-bump′, bel′ly-whop′, bel′ly-slam′,** etc.

bel·ly·ful (-fool′) *n.* **1.** enough or more than enough to eat **2.** [Slang] all that one can bear

belly laugh [Colloq.] a hearty laugh

Be·lo Ho·ri·zon·te (be′lô rē zôn′te) city in SE Brazil: pop. 693,000

be·long (bi lôŋ′) *vi.* [ME. < *be-,* intens. + OE. *langian,* belong] **1.** to have a proper or fitting place [the book *belongs* on his desk] **2.** to be part of; be related (*to*) **3.** to be a member (with *to*) **4.** to be owned (with *to*) **5.** [Slang] to be the owner (with *to*) [who *belongs* to this hat?]

be·long·ing (-iŋ) *n.* **1.** a thing that belongs to one **2.** [*pl.*] possessions; property **3.** close relationship; affinity [a sense of *belonging*]

be·lov·ed (bi luv′id, -luvd′) *adj.* dearly loved —*n.* a dearly loved person

be·low (bi lō′) *adv., adj.* [see BE- & LOW[1]] **1.** in or to a lower place; beneath **2.** in a lower place on the page or on a later page (of a book, etc.) **3.** in hell **4.** on earth **5.** on or to a lower floor or deck **6.** in or to a lesser rank, function, etc. —*prep.* **1.** lower than, as in position, rank, worth, etc. **2.** unworthy of [it is *below* her to do that]

Bel·shaz·zar (bel shaz′ər) *Bible* the last king of Babylon: Dan. 5

belt (belt) *n.* [OE., ult. < L. *balteus,* a belt] **1.** a band of leather, etc., worn about the waist to hold clothing up, support tools, etc., or as an ornament: see also SAFETY BELT **2.** any encircling thing like this **3.** an endless band for transferring motion from one wheel or pulley to another, or for carrying things **4.** an area or zone with some distinctive feature [the corn *belt*] **5.** an encircling road or route **6.** [Slang] a hard blow; cuff **7.** [Slang] *a)* a drink or big gulp, esp. of liquor *b)* a thrill —*vt.* **1.** to surround or encircle as with a belt **2.** to fasten or attach as with a belt **3.** to hit hard, as with a belt **4.** [Colloq.] to sing (*out*) lustily —**below the belt** unfair(ly); foul —**tighten one's belt** to live more thriftily —**under one's belt** [Colloq.] as part of one's experience [ten years at sea *under his belt*]

belt·ed (bel′tid) *adj.* **1.** wearing a belt, esp. as a mark of distinction **2.** marked by a band or stripe

belt·ing (-tiŋ) *n.* **1.** material for making belts **2.** belts collectively **3.** [Slang] a beating

be·lu·ga (bə lōō′gə) *n., pl.* **-ga, -gas:** see PLURAL, II, D, 2 [< Russ. < *byeli,* white] **1.** a large, white sturgeon of the Black and Caspian seas **2.** a large, white dolphin of northern seas; white whale

be·moan (bi mōn′) *vt., vi.* to moan about or lament (a loss, grief, etc.) [to *bemoan* one's fate]

be·muse (bi myōōz′) *vt.* **-mused′, -mus′ing** [BE- + MUSE] **1.** to muddle, confuse, or stupefy **2.** to plunge in thought; preoccupy —**be·muse′ment** *n.*

bench (bench) *n.* [OE. *benc* (cf. BANK[2])] **1.** a long, hard seat for several persons, with or without a back **2.** the place where judges sit in a court **3.** [*sometimes* **B-**] *a)* the status or office of a judge *b)* judges collectively *c)* a law court **4.** *a)* a seat on which the players on a sports team sit when not on the field *b)* auxiliary players collectively **5.** a stand for exhibiting a dog at a dog show **6.** a strong table on which work with tools is done; worktable —*vt.* **1.** to provide with benches **2.** to place on a bench, esp. an official one **3.** *Sports* to keep (a player) out of a game —**on the bench 1.** presiding in a law court **2.** *Sports* not taking part in the game, as an auxiliary player

bench mark 1. a surveyor's mark made on a permanent landmark for use as a reference point in determining other altitudes **2.** a standard in judging quality, value, etc. Also **bench′mark′** *n.*

bench warrant an order issued by a judge or law court for the arrest of a person

bend[1] (bend) *vt.* **bent** or archaic **bend′ed, bend′ing** [OE. *bendan,* to bind with a string; hence, to bend (a bow)] **1.** to force (an object) into a curved or crooked form, or (*back*) to its original form **2.** to turn from a straight line [to *bend* one's steps from a path] **3.** to make (someone) submit or give in, as to one's will **4.** to turn or direct (one's attention, etc. *to*) **5.** to incline or tend (*to* or *toward*) **6.** *Naut.* to fasten (sails or ropes) into position —*vi.* **1.** to turn or be turned as from a straight line **2.** to yield by curving or crooking, as from pressure **3.** to crook or curve the body; stoop (*over* or *down*) **4.** to give in; yield [he *bent* to her wishes] —*n.* **1.** a bending or being bent **2.** a bending or curving part, as of a river —**bend′a·ble** *adj.*

bend[2] (bend) *n.* [ME. < prec.] any of various knots used in tying ropes —**the bends** [Colloq.] *same as* DECOMPRESSION SICKNESS

bend[3] (bend) *n.* [< OFr. < Goth. *bindan,* to bind] *Heraldry* a band or stripe on a coat of arms, from the upper left to the lower right corner

bend·er (ben′dər) *n.* **1.** a person or thing that bends **2.** [Slang] a drinking bout; spree

bend sinister *Heraldry* a band or stripe on a coat of arms, from the upper right to the lower left corner: a sign of bastardy in the family line

be·neath (bi nēth′) *adv., adj.* [< OE. < *be-* + *neothan,* down] **1.** in a lower place **2.** just below something; underneath —*prep.* **1.** lower than; below **2.** directly under; underneath **3.** inferior to in rank, quality, worth, etc. **4.** unworthy of [it is *beneath* him to cheat]

ben·e·dic·i·te (ben′ə dis′ə tē′; *for n. 2 usually* bā′nā dē′chē tā′) ***interj.*** [L.] bless you! —***n.*** **1.** the invocation of a blessing **2.** [**B-**] a canticle praising God

Ben·e·dict (ben′ə dikt′) [< L. *Benedictus,* blessed] **1.** a masculine name **2.** Saint, 480?–543? A.D.; It. monk: founder of the Benedictine order

ben·e·dict (ben′ə dikt′) ***n.*** [< *Benedick,* a bachelor in Shakespeare's *Much Ado About Nothing*] a newly married man, esp. one who seemed to be a confirmed bachelor

Ben·e·dic·tine (ben′ə dik′tin; *also, and for n. 2 usually,* -tēn) ***adj.*** **1.** of Saint Benedict **2.** designating or of the monastic order based on his teachings —***n.*** **1.** a Benedictine monk or nun **2.** [**b-**] a liqueur, orig. made by Benedictine monks

ben·e·dic·tion (ben′ə dik′shən) ***n.*** [< L. < *bene,* well + *dicere,* to speak] **1.** a blessing **2.** an invocation of divine blessing, esp. ending a religious service **3.** blessedness —**ben′e·dic′to·ry** ***adj.***

ben·e·fac·tion (ben′ə fak′shən, ben′ə fak′shən) ***n.*** [< LL. < L. *benefacere* < *bene,* well + *facere,* to do] **1.** the act of doing good or helping those in need **2.** money or help freely given

ben·e·fac·tor (ben′ə fak′tər) ***n.*** a person who has given help, esp. financial help; patron —**ben′e·fac′tress** (-tris) ***n.fem.***

ben·e·fice (ben′ə fis) ***n.*** [OFr. < L. *beneficium,* a kindness: see BENEFACTION] **1.** an endowed church office providing a living for a vicar, rector, etc. **2.** its income —***vt.*** **-ficed, -fic·ing** to provide with a benefice

be·nef·i·cence (bə nef′ə s′ns) ***n.*** [< L.: see BENEFACTION] **1.** the fact or quality of being kind or doing good **2.** a charitable act or generous gift

be·nef·i·cent (-s′nt) ***adj.*** **1.** showing beneficence; doing good **2.** resulting in benefit Also **be·nef·ic** (bə nef′ik) —**be·nef′i·cent·ly** ***adv.***

ben·e·fi·cial (ben′ə fish′əl) ***adj.*** producing benefits; advantageous; favorable —**ben′e·fi′cial·ly** ***adv.***

ben·e·fi·ci·ar·y (ben′ə fish′ē er′ē, -fish′ər ē) ***adj.*** of or holding a benefice —***n.,*** *pl.* **-ar·ies** **1.** a holder of a benefice **2.** anyone receiving benefit **3.** a person named to receive the income or inheritance from a will, insurance policy, trust, etc.

ben·e·fit (ben′ə fit) ***n.*** [< OFr. < L.: see BENEFACTION] **1.** [Archaic] a charitable act **2.** anything helping to improve conditions; advantage **3.** [*often pl.*] payments made by an insurance company, public agency, etc. as during sickness or retirement **4.** a public performance, dance, etc. whose proceeds go to help a certain person, cause, etc. —***vt.*** **-fit·ed, -fit·ing** to do good to or for; aid —***vi.*** to receive advantage; profit

benefit of clergy **1.** the exemption which the medieval clergy had from trial or punishment except in a church court **2.** the rites or approval of the church *[*marriage without *benefit of clergy]*

be·nev·o·lence (bə nev′ə ləns) ***n.*** [ME. & OFr. < L. < *bene,* well + *volens,* prp. of *velle,* to wish] **1.** an inclination to do good; kindliness **2.** a kindly, charitable act or gift; beneficence

be·nev·o·lent (-lənt) ***adj.*** **1.** doing or inclined to do good; kindly; charitable **2.** characterized by benevolence —**be·nev′o·lent·ly** ***adv.***

Beng. Bengali

Ben·gal (ben gôl′, beŋ-) **1.** region in the NE Indian peninsula, divided (1947) into **East Bengal** (now *Bangladesh*) and **West Bengal** (a state of India) **2.** **Bay of,** part of the Indian Ocean, east of India and west of Burma and the Malay Peninsula —**Ben′ga·lese′** (-gə lēz′) ***adj., n.,*** *pl.* **-lese′**

Ben·gal·i (ben gôl′ē, beŋ-) ***n.*** **1.** a native of Bengal **2.** the Indo-European, Indic language of Bengal —***adj.*** of Bengal, its people, or their language

ben·ga·line (beŋ′gə lēn′, beŋ′gə lēn′) ***n.*** [Fr. < *Bengal*] a heavy, corded cloth of silk, rayon, etc. and either wool or cotton

Ben·gha·zi (ben gä′zē, beŋ-) seaport in Libya & one of its two capitals: pop. 140,000

be·night·ed (bi nīt′id) ***adj.*** **1.** surrounded by darkness or night **2.** intellectually or morally backward; unenlightened —**be·night′ed·ness** ***n.***

be·nign (bi nīn′) ***adj.*** [OFr. < L. < *bene,* well + *genus,* birth] **1.** good-natured; kindly **2.** favorable; beneficial **3.** *Med.* doing little or no harm; not malignant —**be·nign′ly** ***adv.***

be·nig·nant (bi nig′nənt) ***adj.*** [< prec., by analogy with MALIGNANT] **1.** kindly or gracious **2.** favorable; beneficial —**be·nig′nan·cy** ***n.,*** *pl.* **-cies**

be·nig·ni·ty (-nə tē) ***n.,*** *pl.* **-ties** **1.** benignancy; kindliness **2.** a kind act; favor

Be·nin (be nēn′) country in WC Africa, on the Atlantic: 44,696 sq. mi.; pop. 3,112,000

ben·i·son (ben′ə z′n, -s′n) ***n.*** [< OFr. < L.: see BENEDICTION] a blessing; benediction

Ben·ja·min (ben′jə mən) [Heb. *binyāmīn,* lit., son of the right hand; hence, favorite son] **1.** a masculine name: dim. *Ben, Benjie, Benny* **2.** *Bible a)* Jacob's youngest son *b)* the tribe of Israel descended from him

ben·ny (ben′ē) ***n.,*** *pl.* **-nies** [Slang] an amphetamine pill, esp. Benzedrine, used as a stimulant

bent[1] (bent) *pt. and pp. of* BEND[1] —***adj.*** **1.** made curved or crooked; not straight **2.** strongly determined (with *on*) *[*she is *bent* on going*]* **3.** set in a course; bound *[*westward *bent]* —***n.*** **1.** an inclining; tendency **2.** a mental leaning; propensity *[*a *bent* for art*]* —**to** (or **at**) **the top of one's bent** to (or at) the limit of one's ability

bent[2] (bent) ***n.*** [OE. *beonot*] **1.** any of various wiry, low-growing grasses much used for lawns and golf greens: also called **bent′grass′** **2.** the stiff flower stalk of certain grasses

Ben·tham (ben′thəm), **Jeremy** 1748–1832; Eng. philosopher & economist

Ben·tham·ism (-iz′m) ***n.*** the utilitarian philosophy of Jeremy Bentham, which holds that the greatest happiness of the greatest number should be the main goal of society

ben·ton·ite (ben′tə nīt′) ***n.*** [after Fort *Benton,* Montana, where found] a porous clay, formed by the decomposition of volcanic ash

bent·wood (bent′wood′) ***adj.*** designating furniture made of wood permanently bent into various forms by heat, moisture, and pressure

BENTWOOD CHAIR

be·numb (bi num′) ***vt.*** **1.** to make numb **2.** to deaden the mind, will, or feelings of

Ben·ze·drine (ben′zə drēn′) *a trademark for* AMPHETAMINE —***n.*** [**b-**] this drug

ben·zene (ben′zēn, ben zēn′) ***n.*** [BENZ(OIC) + -ENE] a clear, flammable, poisonous liquid, C_6H_6, obtained from coal tar and used as a solvent for fats and in making varnishes, dyes, etc.

benzene ring a structural unit thought to exist in the molecules of benzene and derivatives of benzene, consisting of a ring of six carbon atoms with alternate double bonds between them

ben·zine (ben′zēn, ben zēn′) ***n.*** [BENZ(OIC) + -INE[4]] a colorless, flammable liquid obtained in the fractional distillation of petroleum and used as a motor fuel, a solvent in dry cleaning, etc.

ben·zo·ate (ben′zō āt′) ***n.*** a salt or ester of benzoic acid

ben·zo·caine (ben′zə kān′) ***n.*** [BENZO(IN) + (CO)CAINE] a white, odorless powder, $C_9H_{11}NO_2$, used in ointments as an anesthetic and to protect against sunburn

ben·zo·ic (ben zō′ik) ***adj.*** [BENZO(IN) + -IC] of or derived from benzoin

benzoic acid a white, crystalline organic acid, C_6H_5COOH, used as an antiseptic, preservative, etc.

ben·zo·in (ben′zō in, -zoin) ***n.*** [< Fr. < It. *benzoino* < Ar. *lubān jāwī,* incense of Java] the balsamic resin from certain tropical Asiatic trees, used in medicine, perfumes, etc.

ben·zol (ben′zōl, -zôl) ***n.*** [BENZ(OIN) + -OL[1]] *same as* BENZENE: sometimes, a mixture distilling below 100° C that is 70 percent benzene

Be·o·wulf (bā′ə woolf′) the hero of an Old English folk epic of that name (c. 700 A.D.)

be·queath (bi kwēth′, -kwēth′) ***vt.*** [OE. *becwethan,* to give by will < *be-* + *cwethan,* to say: see QUOTH] **1.** to leave (property) to another by last will and testament **2.** to hand down; pass on —**be·queath′al** (-əl) ***n.***

be·quest (-kwest′) ***n.*** [< *be-* + OE. *cwis* < *cwethan:* see prec.] **1.** a bequeathing **2.** anything bequeathed

be·rate (bi rāt′) ***vt.*** **-rat′ed, -rat′ing** [BE- + RATE[2]] to scold or rebuke severely

Ber·ber (bur′bər) ***n.*** **1.** any of a Moslem people living in N Africa **2.** their language —***adj.*** of the Berbers, their culture, or their language

ber·ceuse (ber sooz′; *Fr.* ber söz′) ***n.,*** *pl.* **-ceus′es** (-sooz′iz; *Fr.* -söz′) [Fr. < *bercer,* to rock] **1.** a lullaby **2.** a piece of instrumental music that has a lulling effect

be·reave (bi rēv′) ***vt.*** **-reaved′** or **-reft′** (-reft′), **-reav′ing** [OE. *bereafian* < *be-* + *reafian,* to rob] **1.** to deprive or rob: now usually in the pp. (**bereft**) *[bereft* of hope*]* **2.** to leave in a sad or lonely state, as by death —**the bereaved** the survivors of a recently deceased person —**be·reave′ment** ***n.***

be·ret (bə rā′) *n.* [< Fr. < Pr. < LL.: see BIRETTA] a flat, round cap of felt, wool, etc.
berg (burg) *n. same as* ICEBERG
ber·ga·mot (bur′gə mät′) *n.* [< Fr. < It. < Turk. *beg-armûdī,* prince's pear] **1.** *a)* a pear-shaped citrus fruit grown in S Europe for its oil, used in perfumery *b)* this oil **2.** any of several aromatic N. American herbs of the mint family
Ber·gen (ber′gən; *E.* bur′-) seaport in SW Norway: pop. 117,000
Berg·son (berg sōn′; *E.* berg′sən), **Hen·ri** (än rē′) 1859–1941; Fr. philosopher —**Berg·so·ni·an** (berg sō′nē ən) *adj., n.* —**Berg′son·ism** *n.*

BERET

ber·i·ber·i (ber′ē ber′ē) *n.* [Singh. *beri,* weakness] a disease caused by lack of thiamine (vitamin B_1) in the diet and characterized by nerve disorders, body swelling, etc.
Ber·ing Sea (ber′iŋ, bir′-) part of the N Pacific Ocean, between NE Siberia & Alaska
Bering Standard Time *see* STANDARD TIME
Bering Strait strait between Siberia & Alaska: average width, c. 50 mi.
Berke·ley (bur′klē) [after ff.] city in Calif., just north of Oakland: pop. 103,000
Berke·ley (bär′klē, bur′-), **George** 1685–1753; Ir. philosopher & bishop —**Berke′le·ian** (-klē ən, bər klē′ən) *adj.*
berke·li·um (bur′klē əm) *n.* [< U. of California at BERKELEY, where first isolated] a radioactive chemical element: symbol, Bk; at. wt., 248 (?); at. no., 97
Berk·shire Hills (burk′shir, -shər) region of wooded hills and mountains in W Mass.: also **Berk′shires**
Ber·lin (bər lin′; *G.* ber lēn′) city in E Germany: capital of Germany (1871–1945): now divided into EAST BERLIN and WEST BERLIN
ber·lin (bər lin′, bur′lin) *n.* [after prec.] **1.** a four-wheeled, closed carriage with a footman's platform behind **2.** [*sometimes* **B-**] a fine, soft wool yarn: also called **Berlin wool**
Ber·li·oz (ber′lē ōz′; *Fr.* ber lyôz′), **(Louis) Hector** 1803–69; Fr. composer
berm, berme (burm) *n.* [Fr. < MDu. *baerm*] a ledge or shoulder, as along the edge of a paved road
Ber·mu·da (bər myōō′də) self-governing Brit. colony on a group of islands in the W Atlantic, c. 580 mi. southeast of N.C.: 20 sq. mi.; pop. 52,000 —**Ber·mu′dan, Ber·mu′di·an** *adj., n.*
Bermuda grass a creeping perennial grass widely grown in warm climates for lawns or pasture
Bermuda onion a large onion with a mild flavor, grown in Texas, California, etc.
Bermuda shorts short trousers reaching just above the knee
Bermuda triangle triangular area in the Atlantic Ocean, bounded by Bermuda, Puerto Rico, and Florida, where ships and aircraft are rumored, since the 1940's, to have disappeared mysteriously
Bern, Berne (burn; *Fr.* bern) capital of Switzerland, in the WC part: pop. 167,000
Ber·nard (bər närd′, bur′nərd; *for 2* ber når′) [Fr. < OHG. *bero,* BEAR[2] + *hart,* bold] **1.** a masculine name: dim. *Bernie* **2. Claude** (klōd), 1813–78; Fr. physiologist
Bernard of Clair·vaux (kler vō′), Saint 1090?–1153; Fr. Cistercian monk & theological writer —**Ber·nard·ine** (bur′nər din, -dēn′) *adj.*
Bern·hardt (burn′härt′; *Fr.* ber når′), **Sarah** (born *Rosine Bernard*) 1844–1923; Fr. actress
Ber·nice (bər nēs′, bur′nis) [< L. < Gr. *Berenikē,* lit., victory-bringing] a feminine name: var. *Berenice*
ber·ret·ta (bə ret′ə) *n. same as* BIRETTA
ber·ry (ber′ē) *n., pl.* **-ries** [OE. *berie*] **1.** any small, juicy, fleshy fruit, as a raspberry, blueberry, etc. **2.** the dry seed or kernel of various plants, as a coffee bean **3.** an egg of a lobster, crayfish, etc. **4.** *Bot.* a fleshy fruit with a soft wall and thin skin, as the tomato, grape, etc. —*vi.* **-ried, -ry·ing** **1.** to bear berries **2.** to pick berries —**ber′ry·like′** *adj.*
ber·serk (bər surk′, -zurk′; bur′sərk) *n.* [ON. *berserkr,* warrior in bearskin < *ber,* a bear + *serkr,* coat] *Norse Legend* a frenzied warrior: also **ber·serk′er** —*adj., adv.* in or into a state of violent or destructive rage or frenzy
berth (burth) *n.* [< base of BEAR[1]] **1.** *Naut. a)* enough space to keep clear of another ship, the shore, etc. *b)* space for anchoring *c)* a place of anchorage **2.** a position, office, job, etc. **3.** *a)* a built-in bed or bunk on a ship, train, etc. *b)* any sleeping place —*vt.* **1.** to put into a berth **2.** to furnish with a berth —*vi.* to come into or occupy a berth —**give a wide berth to** to stay well away from
Ber·tha (bur′thə) [G. < OHG. < *beraht,* shining] a feminine name —*n.* [**b-**] [Fr. *berthe* < *Berthe,* Bertha] a woman's wide collar, often of lace, usually extending over the shoulders
Ber·til·lon system (bur′tə län′; *Fr.* ber tē yōn′) [after A. *Bertillon* (1853–1914), Fr. anthropologist] a system of identifying people through records of measurements, coloring, fingerprints, etc.
Ber·tram (bur′trəm) [G. < OHG. < *beraht,* shining + *hraban,* raven] a masculine name
Ber·trand (-trənd) *var. of* BERTRAM
Ber·wyn (bur′win) [after *Berwyn* Mts., Wales] city in NE Ill., near Chicago: pop. 47,000
ber·yl (ber′əl) *n.* [< OFr. < L. < Gr. *bēryllos*] beryllium aluminum silicate, a very hard, crystalline mineral: emerald and aquamarine are two gem varieties of beryl
be·ryl·li·um (bə ril′ē əm) *n.* [ModL. < prec.] a hard, rare, metallic chemical element: symbol, Be; at. wt., 9.0122; at. no., 4
be·seech (bi sēch′) *vt.* **-sought′** or **-seeched′, -seech′ing** [< OE. *besecan:* see BE- & SEEK] **1.** to ask (someone) earnestly; implore **2.** to ask for earnestly; beg for —**be·seech′ing·ly** *adv.*
be·seem (bi sēm′) *vi.* to be suitable or appropriate (to)
be·set (bi set′) *vt.* **-set′, -set′ting** [< OE. *besettan:* see BE- & SET] **1.** to set thickly with; stud **2.** to attack from all sides; harass or besiege **3.** to surround or hem in —**be·set′ment** *n.*
be·set·ting (-iŋ) *adj.* constantly harassing or attacking [a *besetting* temptation]
be·shrew (bi shrōō′) *vt.* [< ME.: see BE- & SHREW] [Archaic] to curse: used mainly in mild oaths
be·side (bi sīd′) *prep.* [ME.: see BY & SIDE] **1.** by or at the side of; alongside; near **2.** in comparison with [*beside* yours, my share seems small] **3.** in addition to; besides **4.** other than; aside from [*beside* him, who cares?] **5.** not pertinent to [*beside* the point] —*adv.* [Archaic] in addition —**beside oneself** wild with fear, rage, etc.
be·sides (-sīdz′) *adv.* [ME. < prec. + adv. gen. -(*e*)s] **1.** in addition; as well **2.** except for that mentioned; else **3.** moreover; furthermore —*prep.* **1.** in addition to; as well as **2.** other than; except
be·siege (bi sēj′) *vt.* **-sieged′, -sieg′ing** [ME. < *be-* + *segen,* to lay siege to < *sege,* SIEGE] **1.** to hem in with armed forces, esp. for a sustained attack **2.** to close in on; crowd around **3.** to overwhelm or beset [*besieged* with queries] —**be·sieg′er** *n.*
be·smear (bi smir′) *vt.* to smear over; soil
be·smirch (bi smurch′) *vt.* [BE- + SMIRCH] **1.** to make dirty; soil **2.** to bring dishonor to; sully
be·som (bē′zəm) *n.* [< OE. *besma,* broom, rod] **1.** a broom, esp. one made of twigs tied to a handle **2.** *same as* BROOM (*n.* 1)
be·sot (bi sät′) *vt.* **-sot′ted, -sot′ting** **1.** to make a sot of; stupefy, as with alcoholic drink **2.** to make silly or foolish —**be·sot′ted** *adj.*
be·sought (bi sôt′) *alt. pt. and pp. of* BESEECH
be·span·gle (bi spaŋ′g′l) *vt.* **-gled, -gling** to cover with or as with spangles
be·spat·ter (bi spat′ər) *vt.* to spatter, as with mud or slander; soil or sully by spattering
be·speak (bi spēk′) *vt.* **-spoke′** (-spōk′) or archaic **-spake** (-spāk′), **-spo′ken** or **-spoke′, -speak′ing** **1.** to speak for or engage in advance; reserve **2.** to be indicative of; show [a mansion that *bespeaks* wealth] **3.** to foreshadow; point to **4.** [Archaic or Poet.] to speak to; address
be·spec·ta·cled (bi spek′tə k′ld) *adj.* wearing eyeglasses
be·spread (bi spred′) *vt.* **-spread′, -spread′ing** to spread over or cover
be·sprin·kle (bi spriŋ′k′l) *vt.* **-kled, -kling** to sprinkle over (*with* something)
Bess (bes) a feminine name: see ELIZABETH
Bes·sa·ra·bi·a (bes′ə rā′bē ə) region in SW European Russia —**Bes′sa·ra′bi·an** *adj., n.*
Bes·se·mer process (bes′ə mər) [after Sir Henry *Bessemer* (1813–98), Eng. inventor] a method of making steel by blasting air through molten pig iron in a large container (**Bessemer converter**) to burn away the impurities
best (best) *adj. superl. of* GOOD [OE. *betst*] **1.** of the most excellent sort; above all others in worth or ability **2.** most suitable, most desirable, etc. **3.** being almost the whole; largest [the *best* part of an hour] —*adv. superl. of* WELL[2] **1.** in the most excellent or most suitable manner **2.** in the highest degree; most —*n.* **1.** the person or people, thing, condition, action, etc. of the greatest excellence, worth, suitability, etc. **2.** the utmost [to do one's *best*] **3.** one's finest clothes —*vt.* to win out over; defeat or outdo —**all for the best** turning out to be fortunate after all —**as best one can** as well as one can —**at best** **1.** under the most favorable conditions **2.** at most —**at one's best** in one's best mood, form, health, etc. —**get** (or **have**) **the best of** **1.** to outdo or defeat **2.** to outwit —**had best** ought to —**make the best of** to do as well as one can with
be·stead (bi sted′) *adj.* [< ME. < *bi-,* be + *stad,* placed < ON. *staddr,* prp. of *stethja,* to place] [Archaic] situated; placed —*vt.* **-stead′ed, -stead′, -stead′ing** [Archaic] to help; avail
bes·tial (bes′chəl, -tyəl; bēs′-) *adj.* [OFr. < LL. *bestialis*]

1. of beasts **2.** like a beast; brutish, savage, vile, etc. **—bes·ti·al·i·ty** (bes'chē al'ə tē, bēs'-) ***n.**, pl.* **-ties —bes'tial·ly** ***adv.***

bes·tial·ize (bes'chə līz', -tyə-; bēs'-) ***vt.*** **-ized', -iz'ing** to make bestial; brutalize

bes·ti·ar·y (bes'chē er'ē, bēs'-) ***n.**, pl.* **-ar'ies** [< ML. < L. < *bestia,* beast] a type of medieval natural history book with moralistic or religious fables about real and mythical animals

be·stir (bi stʉr') ***vt.*** **-stirred', -stir'ring** to stir to action; exert or busy (oneself)

best man the principal attendant of the bridegroom at a wedding

be·stow (bi stō') ***vt.*** [see BE- & STOW] **1.** to give or present as a gift (often with *on* or *upon*) **2.** to apply; devote **3.** [Archaic] to put or place, as in storage **4.** [Obs.] to give in marriage **—be·stow'al** ***n.***

be·strew (bi stro͞o') ***vt.*** **-strewed', -strewed'** or **-strewn', -strew'ing 1.** to cover over (a surface); strew **2.** to scatter or lie scattered over or about

be·stride (bi strīd') ***vt.*** **-strode'** (-strōd'), **-strid'den** (-strid''n), **-strid'ing 1.** to sit on, mount, or stand over with a leg on each side; straddle **2.** [Archaic] to stride over

best seller a book, phonograph record, etc. currently outselling most others

bet (bet) ***n.*** [prob. < ABET] **1.** an agreement between two persons that the one proved wrong about the outcome of something will do or pay what is stipulated; wager **2.** *a)* the thing or sum thus staked *b)* the thing, contestant, etc. that something is staked on **3.** a person, thing, or action likely to bring about a desired result [he's the best *bet* for the job] —***vt.*** **bet** or **bet'ted, bet'ting 1.** to declare in or as in a bet [I *bet* he'll be late] **2.** to stake (money, etc.) in a bet **3.** to wager with (someone) —***vi.*** to make a bet **—you bet (you)!** [Colloq.] certainly!

be·ta (bāt'ə; *chiefly Brit.* bēt'ə) ***n.*** [L. < Gr. *bēta* < Heb. *bēth,* lit., house; of Phoen. origin] **1.** the second letter of the Greek alphabet (Β, β) **2.** the second of a group or series

beta blocker any of a class of drugs used to control heartbeat, relieve angina pectoris, reduce anxiety, etc. by inhibiting adrenal gland secretions

be·take (bi tāk') ***vt.*** **-took', -tak'en, -tak'ing 1.** to go (used reflexively) [he *betook* himself to his castle] **2.** to direct or devote (oneself)

beta particle an electron or positron ejected at high velocity from the nucleus of an atom undergoing radioactive disintegration

beta ray 1. *same as* BETA PARTICLE **2.** a stream of beta particles

be·ta·tron (bāt'ə trän') ***n.*** [BETA (RAY) + (ELEC)TRON] an electron accelerator that uses a rapidly changing magnetic field to accelerate the particles to high velocities

be·tel (bēt''l) ***n.*** [Port. < Malay *veṭṭilai*] a tropical Asian climbing plant of the pepper family, whose leaf is chewed by some Asians

Be·tel·geuse, Be·tel·geux (bet''l jo͞oz', bēt'-) [< Fr. < Ar. *bayt al jauza,* lit., house of the twins] a very large, red, first-magnitude star, second brightest in the constellation Orion

betel nut the fruit of the betel palm, chewed together with lime and leaves of the betel (plant) by some Asians

betel palm a palm grown in SE Asia

bête noire (bāt' nwär') *pl.* **bêtes noires** (bāt' nwärz') [Fr., lit., black beast] a person or thing feared, disliked, and avoided

beth (bāth, beth; *Heb.* bāt, bās) ***n.*** [Heb. *bēth:* see BETA] the second letter of the Hebrew alphabet

Beth·a·ny (beth'ə nē) ancient town in Palestine, near Jerusalem

Beth·el (beth'əl) ancient town in Palestine, just north of Jerusalem

beth·el (beth'əl) ***n.*** [LL. < Heb. *bēth 'ēl,* house of God] **1.** a holy place **2.** a church or other place of worship for seamen

be·think (bi thiŋk') ***vt.*** **-thought', -think'ing** to bring (oneself) to think of, consider, or recollect; remind (oneself)

Beth·le·hem (beth'lə hem', -lē əm) **1.** ancient town in Judea: birthplace of Jesus **2.** city in E Pa.: pop. 70,000

be·tide (bi tīd') ***vi., vt.*** **-tid'ed, -tid'ing** [< ME. < *be-* + OE. *tidan,* to happen < *tid,* time] to happen (to); befall

be·times (bi tīmz') ***adv.*** [ME. < *bi-,* by + *time,* TIME + adv. gen. -*(e)s*] **1.** early or early enough **2.** [Archaic] promptly or quickly

be·to·ken (bi tō'k'n) ***vt.*** [< ME. < *be-* + *toknen* < OE. *tacnian,* to mark < *tacen,* TOKEN] **1.** to be a token or sign of; show **2.** to show beforehand

be·tray (bi trā') ***vt.*** [< ME. < *be-* + *traien,* betray < OFr. < L. *tradere,* to hand over] **1.** to help the enemy of (one's country, cause, etc.); be a traitor to **2.** to break faith with; fail to uphold [to *betray* a trust] **3.** to lead astray; specif., to seduce and then desert **4.** to reveal unknowingly **5.** to reveal or show signs of **6.** to disclose (secret information, etc.) **—be·tray'al** ***n.*** **—be·tray'er** ***n.***

be·troth (bi trōth', -trôth') ***vt.*** [< ME. < *be-* + *treuthe* < OE. *treowth,* truth] **1.** to promise in marriage **2.** [Archaic] to promise to marry

be·troth·al (-əl) ***n.*** a betrothing or being betrothed; mutual pledge to marry; engagement

be·trothed (-trōthd', -trôtht') ***adj.*** engaged to be married —***n.*** the person to whom one is betrothed

bet·ta (bet'ə) ***n.*** [ModL.] a brightly colored, tropical, freshwater fish of SE Asia: some species are kept in aquariums

bet·ted (bet'id) *alt. pt. and pp. of* BET

bet·ter (bet'ər) ***adj.*** *compar. of* GOOD [< OE. *betera*] **1.** more excellent; above another or others in worth or ability **2.** more suitable, more desirable, etc. **3.** being more than half; larger [the *better* part of an hour] **4.** improved in health or disposition —***adv.*** *compar. of* WELL[2] **1.** in a more excellent or more suitable manner **2.** in a higher degree **3.** more [it took *better* than an hour] —***n.*** **1.** a person superior in authority, position, etc. **2.** the thing, condition, etc. that is more excellent, etc. —***vt.*** **1.** to outdo; surpass **2.** to make better; improve —***vi.*** to become better **—better off** in a better condition **—for the better** to a better condition **—get** (or **have**) **the better of 1.** to outdo **2.** to outwit **—had better** ought to

better half [Slang] one's wife or, less often, one's husband

bet·ter·ment (-mənt) ***n.*** **1.** a making or being made better; improvement **2.** *Law* an improvement, other than repairs, that increases the value of property

bet·tor, bet·ter (bet'ər) ***n.*** a person who bets

be·tween (bi twēn') ***prep.*** [< OE. < *be,* by + *tweon(um),* by twos, in pairs] **1.** in or through the space that separates (two things) **2.** in or of the time, amount, or degree that separates (two things); intermediate to **3.** that connects or relates to [a bond *between* friends] **4.** along a course that connects [a road *between* here and there] **5.** by the joint action of [*between* them they landed the fish] **6.** in or into the combined possession of [they had fifty dollars *between* them] **7.** from one or the other of [choose *between* love and duty] **8.** because of the combined effect of [*between* work and study he has no time left] *Between* is sometimes used of more than two, if the relationship is thought of as individual with each of the others [a treaty *between* four powers] —***adv.*** in an intermediate space, position, or function **—between ourselves** in confidence; as a secret: also **between you and me —in between** in an intermediate position

be·tween·times (-tīmz') ***adv.*** in the intervals: also **between'·whiles'**

be·twixt (bi twikst') ***prep., adv.*** [< OE. *betwix* < *be-* + a form related to *twegen,* TWAIN] between: now archaic except in **betwixt and between,** neither altogether one nor altogether the other

Beu·lah (byo͞o'lə) [Heb. *be 'ūlāh,* married: a Biblical name for the land of Israel] a feminine name

bev, Bev (bev) ***n.**, pl.* **bev, Bev** [B(ILLION) + E(LECTRON-)V(OLTS)] a unit of energy equal to one billion electron-volts

bev·a·tron (bev'ə trän') ***n.*** [< BEV + (CYCLO)TRON] a synchrotron for raising atomic particles to a level of six or more bev

bev·el (bev''l) ***n.*** [prob. < OFr. hyp. *baivel,* dim. < *baif,* gaping: see BAY[2]] **1.** a tool that is a rule with a movable arm, for measuring or marking angles, etc.: also **bevel square 2.** an angle other than a right angle **3.** a sloping edge between parallel surfaces —***adj.*** sloped; beveled —***vt.*** **-eled** or **-elled, -el·ing** or **-el·ling** to cut to an angle other than a right angle —***vi.*** to slope at an angle

bevel gear a gearwheel meshed with another so that their shafts are at an angle

bev·er·age (bev'rij, -ər ij) ***n.*** [< OFr. < *bevre* < L. *bibere,* IMBIBE] any liquid for drinking, esp. other than plain water

Bev·er·ley, Bev·er·ly (bev'ər lē) [< ME. *bever,* BEAVER[1] + *ley,* lea] a feminine name

bev·y (bev'ē) ***n.**, pl.* **bev'ies** [< Anglo-Fr. *bevée* < OFr., a drinking bout < *bevre:* see BEVERAGE] **1.** a group, esp. of girls or women **2.** a flock: now chiefly of quail

BEVEL GEAR

be·wail (bi wāl') ***vt.*** to wail over or complain about; lament; mourn **—be·wail'er** ***n.***

be·ware (bi wer') ***vi., vt.*** **-wared', -war'ing** [prob. < OE. < *be-* + *warian,* to be wary] to be wary or careful (of); be on one's guard (against)

be·wil·der (bi wil'dər) ***vt.*** [BE- + archaic *wilder,* to lose one's way] to confuse hopelessly, as by something complicated; befuddle; puzzle —**be·wil′dered** ***adj.*** —**be·wil′der·ing** ***adj.*** —**be·wil′der·ing·ly** ***adv.*** —**be·wil′der·ment** ***n.***

be·witch (bi wich′) ***vt.*** [< ME. < *be-* + *wicchen* < OE. < *wicca:* see WITCH] **1.** to cast a spell over **2.** to enchant; fascinate; charm —**be·witch′ing** ***adj.*** —**be·witch′ing·ly** ***adv.***

be·witch·ment (-mənt) ***n.*** **1.** power to bewitch **2.** a bewitching or being bewitched **3.** a spell that bewitches Also **be·witch′er·y** (-ər ē), *pl.* **-er·ies**

be·wray (bi rā′) ***vt.*** [< ME. < *be-* + OE. *wregan,* to inform] [Archaic] to divulge; reveal; betray

bey (bā) ***n.*** [Turk. *bey, beg*] **1.** in the Ottoman Empire, the governor of a Turkish province **2.** a Turkish title of respect and former title of rank **3.** the former native ruler of Tunis

be·yond (bi yänd′) ***prep.*** [< OE. < *be-* + *geond,* yonder] **1.** on or to the far side of; farther on than **2.** later than [*beyond* noon] **3.** outside the reach or understanding of [*beyond* help] **4.** more or better than; exceeding [success *beyond* one's hopes] —***adv.*** **1.** farther away **2.** in addition —**the (great) beyond** whatever follows death

bez·el (bez′'l) ***n.*** [< OFr. hyp. *bisel* (Fr. *biseau*), sloping edge] **1.** a sloping surface, as the cutting edge of a chisel **2.** the slanting faces of a cut jewel, esp. those of the upper half **3.** the groove and flange holding a gem or a watch crystal in place

be·zique (bi zēk′) ***n.*** [Fr. *bésigue*] a card game resembling pinochle

bf, b.f. boldface

B/F brought forward

bg. *pl.* **bgs.** bag

bhang (baŋ) ***n.*** [Hindi < Sans. *bhangā,* hemp] **1.** the hemp plant **2.** its dried leaves and flowers, or a preparation, such as hashish, made from these and used for its intoxicating properties

Bha·rat (bu′rut) *Hindu name for* INDIA (sense 2)

B-horizon ***n.*** *see* ABC SOIL

Bhu·tan (bo͞o tän′) country in the Himalayas: c. 18,000 sq. mi.; pop. 750,000 —**Bhu·tan·ese** (bo͞ot′'n ēz′) ***adj., n.,*** *pl.* **-ese′**

bi- (bī) [L. *bi-* < OL. *dui-*] *a prefix meaning:* **1.** having two [*biangular*] **2.** doubly [*biconvex*] **3.** happening every two [*biweekly*] **4.** happening twice during every [*bimonthly*]: in this sense, now usually *semi-* or *half-* **5.** using two or both [*bilabial*] **6.** joining or involving two [*bilateral*] **7.** *Chem.* having twice as many atoms or chemical equivalents for a definite weight of the other constituent of the compound [sodium *bicarbonate*]: in organic compounds, usually replaced by *di-*

Bi *Chem.* bismuth

Bi·a·fra (bē äf′rə) region in E Nigeria: fought an unsuccessful war for independence (1967–70)

bi·an·gu·lar (bī aŋ′gyoo lər) ***adj.*** having two angles

bi·an·nu·al (-an′yoo wəl, -yool) ***adj.*** coming twice a year; semiannual: see also BIENNIAL —**bi·an′nu·al·ly** ***adv.***

bi·as (bī′əs) ***n.,*** *pl.* **bi′as·es** [Fr. *biais,* a slant] **1.** a slanting or diagonal line, cut or sewn across the weave of cloth **2.** a mental leaning; partiality; prejudice; bent —***adj.*** slanting; diagonal —***adv.*** diagonally —***vt.*** **-ased** or **-assed, -as·ing** or **-as·sing** to cause to have a bias; prejudice —**on the bias** diagonally

bi·ax·i·al (bī ak′sē əl) ***adj.*** having two axes, as some crystals —**bi·ax′i·al·ly** ***adv.***

bib (bib) ***n.*** [< L. *bibere,* to drink] **1.** an apronlike cloth tied under a child's chin at meals **2.** the front upper part of an apron or overalls

Bib. **1.** Bible **2.** Biblical

bib and tucker [Colloq.] an outfit of clothes

bibb lettuce (bib) [after J. *Bibb* (1789–1884), Kentucky horticulturist] a kind of lettuce in loose heads of dark-green leaves

bib·cock (bib′käk′) ***n.*** a faucet whose nozzle is bent downward

‡**bi·be·lot** (bē blō′) ***n.*** [Fr. < OFr. < *belbel,* BAUBLE] a small object whose value lies in its beauty or rarity

Bibl., bibl. **1.** Biblical **2.** bibliographical

Bi·ble (bī′b'l) ***n.*** [< OFr. < ML. < Gr. *biblia,* collection of writings, pl. of *biblion,* book < *biblos,* papyrus] **1.** the sacred book of Christianity; Old Testament and New Testament **2.** the Holy Scriptures of Judaism, identical with the Old Testament of Christianity **3.** any collection of writings sacred to a religion [the Koran is the Moslem *Bible*] **4.** [**b-**] any book regarded as authoritative See also AUTHORIZED VERSION, REVISED STANDARD VERSION, DOUAY BIBLE, VULGATE, SEPTUAGINT, APOCRYPHA

Bib·li·cal (bib′li k'l) ***adj.*** [*also* **b-**] **1.** of or in the Bible **2.** in keeping with or according to the Bible; like that in the Bible —**Bib′li·cal·ly** ***adv.***

Bib·li·cist (-sist) ***n.*** **1.** a person who takes the words of the Bible literally **2.** a specialist in Biblical literature —**Bib′li·cism** ***n.***

bib·li·o- [< Gr. *biblion:* see BIBLE] *a combining form meaning:* **1.** book; of books [*bibliophile*] **2.** of the Bible [*bibliomancy*]

bib·li·og·ra·phy (bib′lē äg′rə fē) ***n.,*** *pl.* **-phies** [< Gr.: see BIBLE & -GRAPHY] **1.** the study of the editions, dates, authorship, etc. of books and other writings **2.** a list of writings on a given subject, by a given author, etc. **3.** a list of the books, articles, etc. referred to by an author —**bib′li·og′ra·pher** ***n.*** —**bib′li·o·graph′ic** (-ə graf′ik), **bib′li·o·graph′i·cal** ***adj.*** —**bib′li·o·graph′i·cal·ly** ***adv.***

bib·li·o·man·cy (bib′lē ə man′sē) ***n.*** [BIBLIO- + -MANCY] prediction based on a Bible verse chosen at random

bib·li·o·ma·ni·a (bib′lē ə mā′nē ə, -nyə) ***n.*** [BIBLIO- + -MANIA] a craze for collecting books, esp. rare ones —**bib′li·o·mane′** (-mān′) ***n.*** —**bib′li·o·ma′ni·ac** ***n., adj.***

bib·li·o·phile (bib′lē ə fīl′) ***n.*** [BIBLIO- + -PHILE] **1.** one who loves or admires books, esp. for their style of binding, printing, etc. **2.** a book collector Also **bib′li·o·phil′** (-fil′), **bib·li·oph·i·list** (bib′lē äf′ə list) —**bib′li·o·phil′ic** (-ə fil′ik) ***adj.*** —**bib′li·oph′i·lism** (-äf′ə liz'm), **bib′li·oph′i·ly** (-äf′ə lē) ***n.***

bib·li·o·pole (-pōl′) ***n.*** [< L. < Gr. < *biblion,* a book + *pōlein,* to sell] a bookseller, esp. one dealing in rare works: also **bib·li·op·o·list** (bib′lē äp′ə list) —**bib′li·o·pol′ic** (-ə päl′ik) ***adj.*** —**bib′li·op′o·ly** (-äp′ə lē), **bib′li·op′o·lism** ***n.***

bib·u·lous (bib′yoo ləs) ***adj.*** [< L. < *bibere,* to drink] **1.** highly absorbent **2.** fond of alcoholic liquor —**bib′u·lous·ly** ***adv.*** —**bib′u·lous·ness** ***n.***

bi·cam·er·al (bī kam′ər əl) ***adj.*** [< BI- + L. *camera,* a chamber] made up of or having two legislative chambers —**bi·cam′er·al·ism** ***n.***

bi·car·bon·ate (bī kär′bə nit, -nāt′) ***n.*** an acid salt of carbonic acid containing the radical HCO_3

bicarbonate of soda *same as* SODIUM BICARBONATE

bi·cen·te·nar·y (bī′sen ten′ər ē, bī sen′tə ner′ē) ***adj., n.,*** *pl.* **-nar·ies** *same as* BICENTENNIAL

bi·cen·ten·ni·al (bī′sen ten′ē əl) ***adj.*** **1.** happening once in a period of 200 years **2.** lasting for 200 years —***n.*** a 200th anniversary or its celebration

bi·ceps (bī′seps) ***n.,*** *pl.* **-ceps** or **-ceps·es** [L. < *bis,* two + *caput,* head] **1.** a muscle having two heads, or points of origin; esp., the large muscle in the front of the upper arm or the corresponding muscle at the back of the thigh **2.** strength or muscular development, esp. of the arm

bi·chlo·ride (bī klôr′īd) ***n.*** **1.** a binary compound containing two atoms of chlorine for each atom of another element **2.** *same as* MERCURIC CHLORIDE

bichloride of mercury *same as* MERCURIC CHLORIDE

bi·chro·mate (bī krō′māt) ***n.*** *same as* DICHROMATE

bick·er (bik′ər) ***vi.*** [ME. *bikeren*] **1.** to have a petty quarrel; squabble **2.** to flicker, twinkle, etc. —***n.*** a petty quarrel —**bick′er·er** ***n.***

bi·col·or (bī′kul′ər) ***adj.*** of two colors: also **bi′col′ored**

bi·con·cave (bī′kän kāv′, bī kän′kāv) ***adj.*** concave on both surfaces [a *biconcave* lens]

bi·con·vex (bī′kän veks′, bī kän′veks) ***adj.*** convex on both surfaces [a *biconvex* lens]

bi·cus·pid (bī kus′pid) ***adj.*** [< BI- + L. *cuspis,* pointed end] having two points [a *bicuspid* tooth]: also **bi·cus′pi·date′** (-pi dāt′) —***n.*** any of eight adult teeth with two-pointed crowns

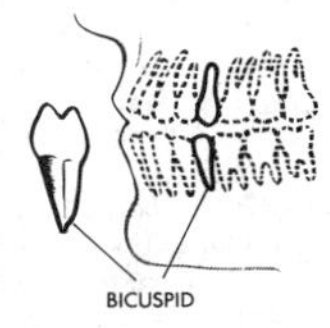
BICUSPID

bi·cy·cle (bī′si k'l) ***n.*** [Fr.: see BI- & CYCLE] a vehicle consisting of a metal frame mounted on two wheels, one behind the other, and equipped with handlebars, a saddlelike seat, and, usually, foot pedals —***vi., vt.*** **-cled, -cling** to ride on a bicycle —**bi′cy·clist, bi′cy·cler** ***n.***

bid (bid) ***vt.*** **bade** or **bid** or archaic **bad, bid′den** or **bid, bid′ding;** for vt. 2, 6, & for vi., the pt. & pp. are always **bid** [< OE. *biddan,* to urge & OE. *beodan,* to command] **1.** to command, ask, or tell **2.** to offer (a certain amount) as the price that one will pay or accept **3.** to declare openly [to *bid* defiance] **4.** to express in greeting or taking leave [to *bid* farewell] **5.** [Archaic or Dial.] to invite **6.** *Card Games* to state (the number of tricks one expects to take) and declare (a suit or no-trump) —***vi.*** to make a bid —***n.*** **1.** a bidding of an amount **2.** the amount bid **3.** a chance to bid **4.** an attempt or try [a *bid* for fame] **5.** [Colloq.] an invitation, esp. to become a member **6.** *Card Games* *a*) the act of bidding *b*) the number of tricks stated *c*) a player's turn to bid —**bid fair** to seem likely —**bid in** at an auction, to bid more than the best offer on one's own property in order to keep it —**bid up** to raise the amount bid —**bid′der** ***n.***

bid·ding (bid′iŋ) ***n.*** **1.** a command or request **2.** an invitation or summons **3.** the bids or the making of bids in a card game or auction

bid·dy (bid′ē) ***n.,*** *pl.* **-dies** **1.** a hen **2.** [Slang] a woman, esp. an elderly, gossipy one

bide (bīd) *vi.* **bode** or **bid′ed, bid′ed, bid′ing** [OE. *bidan*] [Archaic or Dial.] **1.** to stay; continue **2.** to dwell; reside **3.** to wait —*vt.* [Archaic or Dial.] to endure or tolerate —**bide one's time** *pt.* **bid′ed** to wait patiently for an opportunity

bi·den·tate (bī den′tāt) *adj.* having two teeth or toothlike parts

bi·det (bi dā′) *n.* [Fr.] a low, bowl-shaped bathroom fixture with running water, used for bathing the crotch

bi·en·ni·al (bī en′ē əl) *adj.* [< L. < *bis,* twice + *annus,* year + -AL] **1.** happening every two years **2.** lasting for two years —*n.* **1.** a biennial event **2.** *Bot.* a plant that lasts two years, usually producing flowers and seed the second year —**bi·en′ni·al·ly** *adv.*

bier (bir) *n.* [OE. *bær,* a bed] **1.** a portable framework on which a coffin or corpse is placed **2.** a coffin and its supporting platform

Bierce (birs), **Ambrose** 1842–1914?; U.S. writer

biff (bif) *n.* [prob. echoic] [Slang] a blow; strike; hit —*vt.* [Slang] to strike; hit

bi·fid (bī′fid) *adj.* [< L. < *bis,* twice+ *findere,* to cleave] divided into two equal parts by a cleft; forked —**bi·fid′i·ty** (-ə tē) *n.* —**bi′fid·ly** *adv.*

bi·fo·cal (bī fō′k'l, bī′fō′k'l) *adj.* adjusted to two different focal lengths —*n.* a lens with one part ground to adjust the eyes for close focus, and the rest ground for distant focus

bi·fo·cals (bī′fō′k'lz) *n.pl.* a pair of glasses with bifocal lenses

bi·fur·cate (bī′fər kāt′, bī fur′kāt; *for adj. also* -kit) *adj.* [< ML. < L. < *bi-* + *furca,* FORK] having two branches; forked —*vt., vi.* **-cat′ed, -cat′ing** to divide into two branches —**bi′fur·cate′ly** *adv.* —**bi′fur·ca′tion** *n.*

big (big) *adj.* **big′ger, big′gest** [ME.; akin to L. *bucca,* puffed cheek] **1.** *a)* of great size, extent, or capacity; large *b)* great in force or intensity [a *big* wind] **2.** *a)* full-grown *b)* elder [his *big* sister] **3.** *a)* far advanced in pregnancy (*with*) *b)* filled or swelling (*with*) **4.** loud **5.** important or outstanding [to do *big* things] **6.** boastful; extravagant [*big* talk] **7.** generous; noble [a *big* heart] *Big* is much used in combination to form adjectives [*big*-bodied, *big*-souled] —*adv.* [Colloq.] **1.** pompously; boastfully [to talk *big*] **2.** impressively **3.** in a broad way; showing imagination [think *big!*] —**big′ness** *n.*

big·a·my (big′ə mē) *n., pl.* **-mies** [< OFr. < LL. < *bis,* twice + Gr. *gamos,* marriage] the act of marrying a second time while a previous marriage is still legally in effect: when done knowingly, it is a criminal offense —**big′a·mist** *n.* —**big′a·mous** *adj.* —**big′a·mous·ly** *adv.*

Big Apple *nickname for* NEW YORK CITY

big-bang theory a theory of cosmology holding that the expansion of the universe began with a gigantic explosion

Big Ben **1.** the great bell in the Parliament clock tower in London **2.** the clock itself

Big Dipper a dipper-shaped group of stars in the constellation Ursa Major (Great Bear)

big game **1.** large wild animals hunted for sport, as lions, tigers, etc. **2.** the object of any important or dangerous undertaking

big·head (big′hed′) *n.* [Colloq.] conceit; egotism: also **big head**

big·heart·ed (big′här′tid) *adj.* generous or magnanimous —**big′heart′ed·ly** *adv.*

big·horn (-hôrn′) *n., pl.* **-horns′, -horn′**: see PLURAL, II, D, 1 an animal with large horns, esp. a large, wild, shaggy-haired sheep of the Rocky Mountains

big house, the [Slang] a penitentiary

bight (bīt) *n.* [ME. *byht*] **1.** a loop or slack part in a rope **2.** *a)* a curve in a river, coastline, etc. *b)* a bay formed by such a curve —*vt.* to fasten with a bight

big-league (big′lēg′) *adj.* [after the *big* (i.e., major) *leagues* in professional baseball] [Colloq.] of or at the top level in a field of activity

big lie, the **1.** a gross distortion of facts, constantly repeated to make it seem credible **2.** a propaganda technique using this device

big mouth [Slang] a person who talks too much

big·no·ni·a (big nō′nē ə) *n.* [after the Abbé *Bignon,* 18th-c. Fr. librarian] a tropical American vine with trumpet-shaped flowers

big·ot (big′ət) *n.* [Fr. < OFr., a term of insult used of Normans] a narrow-minded person who is intolerant of other creeds, opinions, races, etc. —**big′ot·ed** *adj.* —**big′ot·ed·ly** *adv.* —**big′ot·ry** (-ə trē) *n., pl.* **-ries**

big shot [Slang] an important, influential person: also **big noise, big wheel,** etc.

big stick [< use of term by T. ROOSEVELT] [*also* **B- S-**] a policy of acting or negotiating from a position backed by a show of strength

big time [Slang] **1.** formerly, vaudeville in the top-ranking theatrical circuits **2.** the highest level in any profession, etc. —**big′-time′** *adj.*

big top [Colloq.] **1.** the main tent of a circus **2.** the life or work of circus performers

big tree a giant Sequoia tree related to the redwood and found in the high Sierras

big·wig (big′wig′) *n.* [Colloq.] *same as* BIG SHOT

bi·jou (bē′zhōō) *n., pl.* **-joux** (-zhōōz) [Fr. < Bret. *bizou,* a ring < *biz,* a finger] **1.** a jewel **2.** an exquisite trinket

bi·ju·gate (bī′joo gāt′, bī jōō′git) *adj.* [BI- + JUGATE] having two pairs of leaflets, as some pinnate leaves: also **bi′ju·gous** (-gəs)

bike (bīk) *n., vt., vi.* **biked, bik′ing** [< BICYCLE] [Colloq.] **1.** bicycle **2.** motorcycle

bike·way (-wā′) *n.* a path or lane for bicycle riders only

bi·ki·ni (bi kē′nē) *n.* [< *Bikini,* atoll in the Marshall Islands] an extremely brief two-piece bathing suit for women

bi·la·bi·al (bī lā′bē əl) *adj.* **1.** *same as* BILABIATE **2.** *Phonet.* made by stopping or constricting the airstream with the lips, as the English stops *p* and *b* —*n.* a bilabial sound

bi·la·bi·ate (-bē it, -āt′) *adj.* [BI- + LABIATE] *Bot.* having two lips, as the corolla of some flowers

bi·lat·er·al (bī lat′ər əl) *adj.* [BI- + LATERAL] **1.** of, on, or having two sides, factions, etc. **2.** affecting both sides equally; reciprocal [a *bilateral* trade pact] **3.** symmetrical on both sides of an axis —**bi·lat′er·al·ism** *n.* —**bi·lat′er·al·ly** *adv.*

BIKINI

Bil·ba·o (bil bä′ō) seaport in N Spain: pop. 372,000

bil·ber·ry (bil′ber′ē) *n., pl.* **-ries** [ult. < ON. *bollr,* BALL[1] + *ber,* berry] a N. American blueberry or its fruit

bil·bo (bil′bō) *n., pl.* **-boes** [after BILBAO] **1.** [*pl.*] a long iron bar with shackles, for fettering a prisoner's feet **2.** [Archaic] a sword

bile (bīl) *n.* [Fr. < L. *bilis*] **1.** the bitter, yellow-brown or greenish fluid secreted by the liver and found in the gallbladder: it helps in digestion, esp. of fats **2.** [< ancient belief in bile as the humor causing anger] bad temper; anger

bilge (bilj) *n.* [var. of BULGE] **1.** the bulge of a cask **2.** the rounded, lower part of a ship's hold **3.** stagnant, dirty water that gathers there: also **bilge water** **4.** [Slang] worthless talk or writing; nonsense —*vt., vi.* **bilged, bilg′ing** to break open in the bilge: said of a ship

bil·i·ar·y (bil′ē er′ē, bil′yər ē) *adj.* [Fr. *biliaire*] **1.** of or involving the bile **2.** bile-carrying **3.** bilious

bi·lin·gual (bī liŋ′gwəl) *adj.* [< L. < *bis,* two + *lingua,* tongue] **1.** of or in two languages **2.** capable of using two languages, esp. with equal facility —**bi·lin′gual·ism** *n.* —**bi·lin′gual·ly** *adv.*

bil·ious (bil′yəs) *adj.* **1.** of the bile **2.** having, appearing to have, or resulting from some ailment of the bile or the liver **3.** bad-tempered; cross; irritable —**bil′ious·ly** *adv.* —**bil′ious·ness** *n.*

bilk (bilk) *vt.* [? altered < BALK] **1.** to cheat or swindle; defraud **2.** to get away without paying (a debt, etc.) **3.** to elude —*n.* **1.** a bilking or being bilked **2.** a cheat or swindler —**bilk′er** *n.*

bill[1] (bil) *n.* [< Anglo-L. *billa,* altered < ML. *bulla,* sealed document < L. *bulla,* knob] **1.** a statement of charges for goods or services; invoice **2.** a list, as a menu, theater program, ship's roster, etc. **3.** a poster or handbill, esp. one announcing a circus, show, etc. **4.** the entertainment offered in a theater **5.** a draft of a law proposed to a lawmaking body **6.** a bill of exchange **7.** any promissory note **8.** *a)* a bank note or piece of paper money *b)* [Slang] a hundred dollars or a hundred-dollar bill **9.** *Law* a written declaration of charges filed in a legal action —*vt.* **1.** to make out a bill of (items); list **2.** to present a statement of charges to **3.** *a)* to advertise by bills or posters *b)* to book (a performer or performance) **4.** to post bills or placards throughout (a town, etc.) **5.** to enter on a bill of consignment; book for shipping —**fill the bill** [Colloq.] to meet the requirements —**bill′a·ble** *adj.*

bill[2] (bil) *n.* [OE. *bile*] **1.** the horny jaws of a bird, usually pointed; beak **2.** a beaklike mouthpart, as of a turtle **3.** [Colloq.] the peak or visor of a cap —*vi.* **1.** to touch bills together **2.** to caress lovingly: now only in **bill and coo,** to kiss, talk softly, etc. in a loving way

bill[3] (bil) *n.* [OE. *bill*] **1.** an ancient weapon having a hook-shaped blade with a spike at the back **2.** *same as* BILLHOOK

bill·a·bong (bil′ə bäŋ′) *n.* [native term < *billa,* water + ?] in Australia, **1.** a backwater channel that forms a lagoon or pool **2.** a river branch that reenters the main stream

bill·board (bil′bôrd′) ***n.*** a large signboard, usually outdoors, for advertising posters

bil·let[1] (bil′it) ***n.*** [< Anglo-Fr., dim. of *bille,* BILL[1]] **1.** *a)* a written order to provide lodging for military personnel, as in private buildings *b)* the quarters thus occupied *c)* the sleeping place assigned to a sailor on ship **2.** a position or job —***vt.*** to assign to lodging by billet —***vi.*** to be billeted or quartered

bil·let[2] (bil′it) ***n.*** [OFr. *billette,* dim. of *bille,* tree trunk] **1.** *a)* a short, thick piece of firewood *b)* [Obs.] a wooden club **2.** a small, unfinished metal bar, esp. of iron or steel

bil·let-doux (bil′ē do͞o′; *Fr.* bē ye do͞o′) ***n.,*** *pl.* **bil·lets-doux** (bil′ē do͞oz′; *Fr.* bē ye do͞o′) [Fr., lit., sweet letter] a love letter

bill·fold (bil′fōld′) ***n.*** *same as* WALLET

bill·hook (-ho͝ok′) ***n.*** a tool with a curved or hooked blade at one end, for pruning and cutting

bil·liard (bil′yərd) ***adj.*** of or for billiards —***n.*** a point scored in billiards by a carom

bil·liards (-yərdz) ***n.*** [Fr. *billard;* orig., a cue < *bille:* see BILLET[2]] any of several games played with hard balls on an oblong, cloth-covered table with raised, cushioned edges: a cue is used to hit and move the balls: see also POOL[2]

bill·ing (bil′iŋ) ***n.*** the listing or the order of listing of actors' names on a playbill, marquee, etc.

Bil·lings (bil′iŋz) [after F. *Billings* (1823–90), railroad executive] city in S Mont.: pop. 67,000

bil·lings·gate (bil′iŋz gāt′) ***n.*** [after a fish market in London] foul, vulgar, abusive talk

bil·lion (bil′yən) ***n.*** [Fr. contr. < *bi-,* BI- + *million*] **1.** a thousand millions (1,000,000,000) **2.** formerly, in Great Britain, a million millions (1,000,000,000,000) **3.** an indefinite but very large number —***adj.*** amounting to one billion in number —**bil′lionth *adj., n.***

bil·lion·aire (bil′yə ner′) ***n.*** one whose wealth comes to at least a billion dollars, pounds, etc.

bill of attainder a legislative enactment pronouncing a person guilty, without a trial, of an alleged crime (esp. treason) and inflicting the punishment of death and attainder upon him: prohibited in the U.S. by the Constitution

bill of exchange a written order to pay a certain sum of money to the person named; draft

bill of fare a list of the foods served; menu

bill of goods a shipment of goods sent to an agent for sale —**sell (someone) a bill of goods** [Colloq.] to persuade (someone) by deception or misrepresentation to accept, believe, or do something

bill of health a certificate stating whether there is infectious disease aboard a ship or in the port sailed from —**clean bill of health** **1.** a bill of health certifying the absence of infectious disease **2.** [Colloq.] a good record; favorable report, as after an investigation

bill of lading a contract issued to a shipper by a transportation agency, listing the goods received for shipment and promising their delivery

bill of rights **1.** a list of the rights and freedoms regarded as essential to a people **2.** [**B- R-**] the first ten amendments to the Constitution of the U.S., which guarantee certain rights to the people, as freedom of speech, assembly, and worship

bill of sale a written statement transferring the ownership of something by sale

bil·low (bil′ō) ***n.*** [ON. *bylgja:* see BELLY] **1.** a large wave; great swell of water **2.** any large, swelling mass or surge, as of smoke, sound, etc. —***vi., vt.*** to surge, swell, or cause to swell like or in a billow

bil·low·y (bil′ə wē) ***adj.*** **-low·i·er, -low·i·est** swelling in or as in a billow —**bil′low·i·ness *n.***

bill·post·er (bil′pōs′tər) ***n.*** a person hired to fasten advertisements on walls, billboards, etc.

bil·ly (bil′ē) ***n.,*** *pl.* **-lies** [< BILLET[2]] a club or heavy stick, esp. one carried by a policeman

billy goat a male goat

bi·lo·bate (bī lō′bāt) ***adj.*** having or divided into two lobes: also **bi·lo′bat·ed, bi·lobed′**

bi·man·u·al (bī man′yoo wəl) ***adj.*** using or requiring both hands —**bi·man′u·al·ly *adv.***

bi·met·al (bī′met′'l) ***n.*** a bimetallic substance

bi·me·tal·lic (bī′mə tal′ik) ***adj.*** **1.** containing or using two metals, often two metals bonded together **2.** of or based on bimetallism

bi·met·al·lism (bī met′'l iz'm) ***n.*** **1.** the use of two metals, usually gold and silver, as the monetary standard, with fixed values in relation to each other **2.** the actions or policies supporting this —**bi·met′al·list *n.***

bi·month·ly (bī munth′lē) ***adj., adv.*** **1.** once every two months **2.** twice a month: in this sense, *semimonthly* is the preferred term —***n.,*** *pl.* **-lies** a publication appearing once every two months

bin (bin) ***n.*** [OE., manger, crib] a box or enclosed space, esp. for storing foods or other things —***vt.*** **binned, bin′ning** to store in a bin

bi·na·ry (bī′nər ē) ***adj.*** [< L. < *bini,* two by two < *bis,* double] **1.** made up of two parts or things; twofold; double **2.** designating or of a number system that has 2 as its base **3.** *Chem.* composed of two elements or radicals or of one element and one radical —***n.,*** *pl.* **-ries** **1.** something made up of two parts or things **2.** *same as* BINARY STAR

binary star two stars revolving around a common center of gravity; double star

bi·nate (bī′nāt) ***adj.*** [see BINARY] *Bot.* occurring in pairs *[binate* leaves*]* —**bi′nate·ly *adv.***

bi·na·tion·al (bī nash′ə n'l) ***adj.*** composed of or involving two nations or two nationalities

bin·au·ral (bī nôr′əl, bi-) ***adj.*** [see BI- & AURAL] **1.** having two ears **2.** of or involving the use of both ears **3.** of sound reproduction or transmission using at least two sources of sound to give a stereophonic effect

bind (bīnd) ***vt.*** **bound, bind′ing** [< OE. *bindan*] **1.** to tie together; make fast, as with a rope **2.** to hold or restrain as if tied *[bound* by convention*]* **3.** to gird or encircle with a belt, etc. **4.** to bandage (often with *up*) **5.** to make stick together **6.** to constipate **7.** to strengthen or ornament the edges of by a band, as of tape **8.** to fasten together printed sheets of (a book) and enclose within a cover **9.** to secure or make firm (a bargain, contract, etc.) **10.** to obligate, as by duty **11.** to compel, as by oath or legal restraint **12.** to make an apprentice of (often with *out or over*) **13.** to unite or hold, as by loyalty or love —***vi.*** **1.** to do the act of binding **2.** to grow hard or stiff **3.** to be constricting or restricting **4.** to be obligatory —***n.*** **1.** anything that binds **2.** [Colloq.] a difficult situation —**bind over** to put under bond to appear, as before a law court

bind·er (bīn′dər) ***n.*** **1.** a person who binds; specif., a bookbinder **2.** a thing that binds; specif., *a)* a band, cord, etc. *b)* a substance, as tar, that binds things together *c)* a detachable cover for holding sheets of paper together **3.** a device attached to a reaper, for tying grain in bundles **4.** *Law* a temporary memorandum of a contract, in effect pending execution of the final contract

bind·er·y (bīn′dər ē, -drē) ***n.,*** *pl.* **-er·ies** a place where books are bound

bind·ing (-diŋ) ***n.*** **1.** the action of one that binds **2.** a thing that binds, as *a)* the fastenings on a ski for the boot *b)* a band or bandage *c)* tape used in sewing for strengthening seams, edges, etc. *d)* the covers and backing of a book **3.** a cohesive substance for binding a mixture —***adj.*** that binds; esp., that holds one to an agreement, etc.; obligatory

bind·weed (bīnd′wēd′) ***n.*** any of a number of twining vines related to the morning glory

bine (bīn) ***n.*** [dial. form of BIND] any climbing, twining stem, as of the hop

Bi·net-Si·mon test (bi nā′ sī′mən) [after its Fr. devisers, A. *Binet* (1857–1911) and T. *Simon* (1873–1961)] any of a series of tests seeking to measure intelligence in children: also **Binet test**

binge (binj) ***n.*** [? < dial. *binge,* to soak] [Colloq.] a drunken or unrestrained spree

Bing·ham·ton (biŋ′əm tən) [after W. *Bingham* (1752–1804), land donor] city in SC N.Y.: pop. 56,000

bin·go (biŋ′gō) ***n.*** [< ?] a gambling game, like lotto, usually with many players

bin·na·cle (bin′ə k'l) ***n.*** [formerly *bittacle* < Port. < L. *habitaculum,* dwelling place < *habitare,* to inhabit] the case enclosing a ship's compass

bin·oc·u·lar (bī näk′yə lər; *also, esp. for n.,* bi-) ***adj.*** [< L. *bini,* double + *oculus,* an eye] using, or for the use of, both eyes at the same time —***n.*** [*usually pl.*] a binocular instrument, as field glasses or opera glasses —**bin·oc′u·lar′i·ty** (-lar′ə tē) ***n.*** —**bin·oc′u·lar·ly *adv.***

BINOCULARS

bi·no·mi·al (bī nō′mē əl) ***n.*** [< LL. < *bi-* + Gr. *nomos,* law + -AL] **1.** a mathematical expression consisting of two terms connected by a plus or minus sign **2.** a two-word scientific name of a plant or animal —***adj.*** **1.** composed of two terms **2.** of binomials

bi·o (bī′ō) ***n.,*** *pl.* **bi′os** [Colloq.] a biography, often a very brief one

bi·o- [Gr. < *bios,* life] *a combining form meaning* life, of living things, biological *[biography]*

bi·o·as·tro·nau·tics (bī′ō as′trə nô′tiks) ***n.pl.*** [*with sing. v.*] the science dealing with the effects of space travel upon living organisms

bi·o·chem·is·try (-kem′is trē) ***n.*** the branch of chemistry that deals with plants and animals and their life processes —**bi′o·chem′i·cal *adj.*** —**bi′o·chem′ist *n.***

bi·o·cide (bī′ə sīd′) *n.* [BIO- + -CIDE] any substance that can kill living organisms
bi·o·de·grad·a·ble (bī′ō di grā′də b'l) *adj.* [BIO- + DEGRAD(E) + -ABLE] that can be readily decomposed by biological, esp. bacterial, action, as some detergents
bi·o·en·gi·neer·ing (-en′jə nir′iŋ) *n.* a science dealing with the application of engineering science to problems of biology and medicine
bi·o·feed·back (-fēd′bak′) *n.* a technique of seeking to control emotional states, as anxiety, by training oneself, with the aid of electronic devices, to modify involuntary body functions, as blood pressure
biog. **1.** biographer **2.** biographical **3.** biography
bi·o·gen·e·sis (bī′ō jen′ə sis) *n.* [BIO- + GENESIS] **1.** the principle that living organisms derive only from other similar organisms **2.** such generation of organisms —**bi′o·ge·net′ic** (-jə net′ik), **bi′o·ge·net′i·cal** *adj.*
bi·og·ra·phee (bī äg′rə fē′, bē-) *n.* a person who is the subject of a biography
bi·og·ra·phy (bī äg′rə fē, bē-) *n.* [< Gr.: see BIO- & -GRAPHY] **1.** *pl.* **-phies** an account of a person's life written by another **2.** such writings, collectively, as a branch of literature —**bi·og′ra·pher** *n.* —**bi·o·graph·i·cal** (bī′ə graf′i k'l), **bi′o·graph′ic** *adj.* —**bi′o·graph′i·cal·ly** *adv.*
bi·o·haz·ard (bī′ō haz′ərd) *n.* a danger to life or health, esp. that resulting from biological experimentation
biol. **1.** biological **2.** biologist **3.** biology
bi·o·log·i·cal (bī′ə läj′i k'l) *adj.* **1.** of or connected with biology **2.** of the nature of living matter **3.** used in or produced by practical biology Also **bi′o·log′ic** —*n.* a biological product —**bi′o·log′i·cal·ly** *adv.*
biological warfare the use of disease-spreading microorganisms, toxins, etc. as a weapon of war
bi·ol·o·gy (bī äl′ə jē) *n.* [BIO- + -LOGY] **1.** the science that deals with the origin, history, life processes, structure, etc. of plants and animals: it includes botany, zoology, and their subdivisions **2.** animal and plant life, as of a given area —**bi·ol′o·gist** *n.*
bi·o·med·i·cine (bī′ō med′ə s'n) *n.* a branch of medicine combined with research in biology —**bi′o·med′i·cal** *adj.*
bi·o·met·rics (-met′riks) *n.pl.* [*with sing. v.*] that branch of biology which deals with its data statistically —**bi′o·met′ric, bi′o·met′ri·cal** *adj.* —**bi′o·met′ri·cal·ly** *adv.*
bi·on·ic (bī än′ik) *adj.* **1.** designating an artificial replacement for a bodily part **2.** furnished with such a replacement part or parts, specif. in science fiction, so that strength, abilities, etc. are greatly enhanced
bi·on·ics (bī än′iks) *n.pl.* [*with sing. v.*] [< Gr. *bion,* living + -ICS] the science of designing instruments or systems modeled after living organisms
bi·o·phys·ics (bī′ō fiz′iks) *n.pl.* [*with sing. v.*] the study of biological phenomena in relation to physics —**bi′o·phys′i·cal** *adj.* —**bi′o·phys′i·cist** *n.*
bi·op·sy (bī′äp′sē) *n., pl.* **-sies** [see BIO- & -OPSIS] the removal of bits of living tissue, fluids, etc. from the body for diagnostic examination
bi·o·rhythm (bī′ō rith′'m, -rith′əm) *n.* any of three separate biological cycles in terms of which, according to a theory, a person's physical, emotional, and intellectual energy levels regularly and predictably rise and fall
bi·os·co·py (bī äs′kə pē) *n.* [BIO- + -SCOPY] a medical examination to find out whether life is present
-bi·o·sis (bī ō′sis, bē-) [< Gr. *biōsis,* way of life < *bios,* life] *a combining form meaning* way of living *[symbiosis]*
bi·o·sphere (bī′ə sfir′) *n.* [BIO- + SPHERE] that portion of the earth and its atmosphere containing living organisms
bi·o·tin (bī′ə tin) *n.* [< Gr. *bios,* life + -IN[1]] a bacterial growth factor, $C_{10}H_{16}O_3N_2S$, one of the vitamin B group, found in liver, egg yolk, and yeast
bi·par·ti·san (bī pär′tə z'n, -s'n) *adj.* of or representing two parties —**bi·par′ti·san·ship′** *n.*
bi·par·tite (bī pär′tīt) *adj.* [< L. < *bi-,* two + *partire,* to divide] **1.** having two (corresponding) parts **2.** with two involved **3.** *Bot.* divided in two nearly to the base, as some leaves —**bi·par′tite·ly** *adv.* —**bi′par·ti′tion** (-tish′ən) *n.*
bi·ped (bī′ped) *n.* [< L. < *bi-* + *pedis,* gen. of *pes,* foot] any two-footed animal —*adj.* two-footed: also **bi·ped′al**
bi·pet·al·ous (bī pet′'l əs) *adj.* having two petals
bi·pin·nate (bī pin′āt, -it) *adj.* having pinnate leaflets on stems that grow opposite each other on a main stem
bi·plane (bī′plān′) *n.* an airplane with two sets of wings, one above the other
bi·po·lar (bī pō′lər) *adj.* **1.** of or having two poles **2.** of or involving both of the earth's polar regions **3.** characterized by two opposed opinions, natures, etc. —**bi·po·lar·i·ty** (bī′pō lar′ə tē) *n.*
bi·ra·cial (bī rā′shəl) *adj.* consisting of or involving two races, esp. blacks and whites
birch (burch) *n.* [OE. *beorc*] **1.** a tree having smooth bark easily peeled off in thin sheets, and hard, closegrained wood **2.** this wood **3.** a birch rod or bunch of twigs used for whipping —*vt.* to beat with a birch —*adj.* of birch
bird (burd) *n.* [OE. *bridd,* young bird] **1.** any of a class of warmblooded, two-legged, egg-laying vertebrates with feathers and wings **2.** a small game bird **3.** same as CLAY PIGEON **4.** a shuttlecock **5.** [Slang] a person, esp. a mildly eccentric one **6.** [Slang] a sound of disapproval made by fluttering the lips **7.** [Slang] a rocket or guided missile —*vi.* **1.** to shoot or catch birds **2.** to engage in bird watching —**bird in the hand** something sure because already in one's possession: opposed to **bird in the bush,** something unsure, etc. —**birds of a feather** people with the same characteristics or tastes —**for the birds** [Slang] ridiculous, worthless, etc.
bird·bath (-bath′) *n.* a basinlike garden ornament for birds to bathe in
bird·brain (-brān′) *n.* [Colloq.] a stupid or silly person
bird·call (-kôl′) *n.* **1.** the sound or song of a bird **2.** an imitation of this **3.** a device for imitating bird sounds
bird dog **1.** a dog trained for hunting birds, as a pointer **2.** [Colloq.] a person whose work is searching, as for missing persons, etc.
bird·ie (bur′dē) *n.* **1.** a small bird: child's word **2.** *Golf* a score of one stroke under par for a hole
bird·lime (burd′līm′) *n.* **1.** a sticky substance spread on twigs to catch birds **2.** anything that snares
bird of paradise **1.** any of a number of brightly colored birds found in and near New Guinea **2.** a tropical plant with brilliant orange and blue flowers in a form resembling a bird in flight
bird of passage **1.** any migratory bird **2.** anyone who travels or roams about constantly
bird of prey any bird, as the hawk, owl, etc., that kills and eats mammals and other birds
bird·seed (-sēd′) *n.* seed for feeding caged birds
bird's-eye (burdz′ī′) *n.* a cotton or linen cloth with a woven pattern of small, diamond-shaped figures —*adj.* **1.** *a)* seen from above *b)* general; cursory **2.** having markings like birds' eyes
bird·shot (burd′shät′) *n.* small shot for shooting birds
bird watching the hobby of observing wild birds in their habitat —**bird watcher**
bi·re·frin·gence (bī′ri frin′jəns) *n.* [< BI- + L. prp. of *refringere:* see REFRACT] the splitting of a light ray, generally by a crystal, into two components which travel at different velocities within the crystal —**bi′re·frin′gent** *adj.*
bi·reme (bī′rēm) *n.* [< L. < *bi-* + *remus,* oar] a galley having two rows of oars on each side
bi·ret·ta (bə ret′ə) *n.* [< It. < LL. dim. of L. *birrus,* a hood, cloak] a square cap with three projections and a tassel on top, worn by Roman Catholic clergy

BIRETTA

Bir·ken·head (bur′k'n hed′) seaport in W England, at the mouth of the Mersey River: pop. 142,000
birl (burl) *vt., vi.* [? echoic, after *whirl, purl,* etc.] to revolve (a floating log) by treading
birl·ing (-iŋ) *n.* a competition among loggers in which each tries to keep his balance while revolving a floating log with his feet —**birl′er** *n.*
Bir·ming·ham (bur′miŋ əm *for 1;* -ham′ *for 2*) **1.** city in C England: pop. 1,075,000 **2.** [after prec.] city in NC Ala.: pop. 284,000 (met. area 834,000)
birr (bur) *n., pl.* **birr′otch** (-äch) [Amharic, silver] *see* MONETARY UNITS, table (Ethiopia)
birth (burth) *n.* [< OE. *byrde* < *beran,* to BEAR[1]] **1.** the act of bringing forth offspring **2.** the act of being born **3.** origin or descent *[a Spaniard by birth]* **4.** the beginning of anything **5.** an inherited or natural inclination or talent *[an actor by birth]* —*vi., vt.* [Dial.] to give birth (to) —**give birth to** **1.** to bring forth (offspring) **2.** to be the cause or origin of; originate
birth control control of how many children a woman will have, as by contraception
birth·day (-dā′) *n.* **1.** the day of a person's birth or a thing's beginning **2.** the anniversary of this
birth·mark (-märk′) *n.* a skin blemish present at birth
birth·place (-plās′) *n.* **1.** the place of one's birth **2.** the place where something originated
birth·rate (-rāt′) *n.* the number of births per year per thousand of population in a given group: sometimes other units of time or population are used
birth·right (-rīt′) *n.* the rights that a person has because he was born in a certain family, nation, etc. or because he was the firstborn son

birth·stone (-stōn′) *n.* a precious or semiprecious gem symbolizing the month of one's birth

Bis·cay (bis′kā, -kē), **Bay of** part of the Atlantic, north of Spain & west of France

bis·cuit (bis′kit) *n., pl.* **-cuits, -cuit** [OFr. *bescuit* < ML. < L. *bis,* twice + *coctum,* pp. of *coquere,* to cook] **1.** [Chiefly Brit.] a cracker or cookie **2.** a quick bread baked in small pieces **3.** light brown; tan **4.** pottery after the first firing and before glazing

bi·sect (bī sekt′, bī′sekt) *vt.* [< ML. pp. of *bisecare* < L. *bi-* + *secare,* to cut] **1.** to cut in two **2.** *Geom.* to divide into two equal parts —*vi.* to divide; fork —**bi·sec′tion** *n.* —**bi·sec′tion·al** *adj.* —**bi·sec′tor** *n.*

bi·sex·u·al (bī sek′shoo wəl) *adj.* **1.** of both sexes **2.** having both male and female organs; hermaphroditic **3.** sexually attracted to both sexes —*n.* one that is bisexual —**bi·sex′u·al′i·ty** (-wal′ə tē), **bi·sex′u·al·ism** *n.* —**bi·sex′u·al·ly** *adv.*

bish·op (bish′əp) *n.* [< OE. *bisceop* < LL. < Gr. *episkopos,* overseer < *epi-,* upon + *skopein,* to look] **1.** a highranking Christian clergyman usually supervising a diocese or church district **2.** a chessman that can move only diagonally

bish·op·ric (bish′ə prik) *n.* the district, office, authority, or rank of a bishop

Bis·marck (biz′märk) [after ff.] capital of N.Dak., on the Missouri River: pop. 44,000

Bis·marck (biz′märk), Prince **Otto von** 1815–98; Prussian chancellor of Germany (1871–90)

bis·muth (biz′məth) *n.* [< G. *wismut* < ?] a hard, brittle, metallic chemical element used in low-melting alloys, medical compounds, etc.: symbol, Bi; at. wt., 208.980; at. no., 83

bi·son (bī′s'n, -z'n) *n., pl.* **bi′sons** [Fr. < L. < Gmc. hyp. *wisunt*] any of several four-legged bovine mammals with a shaggy mane, short, curved horns, and a humped back, as the American buffalo

BISON
(5½–6 ft. high at shoulder)

bisque[1] (bisk) *n.* [Fr.] **1.** a rich, thick, creamy soup made from shellfish or from rabbit, fowl, etc. **2.** a thick, strained, creamy vegetable soup

bisque[2] (bisk) *n.* **1.** biscuit ceramic ware left unglazed in the finished state **2.** a red-yellow color

bis·ter, bis·tre (bis′tər) *n.* [Fr. *bistre*] **1.** a yellowish-brown to dark-brown pigment made from the soot of burned wood **2.** a color in this range

bis·tro (bis′trō, bēs′-) *n., pl.* **-tros** [Fr.] a small nightclub or bar

bi·sul·fate (bī sul′fāt) *n.* an acid sulfate; compound containing the monovalent HSO_4– radical

bi·sul·fide (bī sul′fīd) *n.* same as DISULFIDE

bit[1] (bit) *n.* [< OE. *bite,* a bite < *bitan,* to bite] **1.** the metal mouthpiece on a bridle, used for controlling the horse **2.** anything that curbs or controls **3.** the part of a key that actually turns the lock **4.** the cutting part of any tool **5.** a drilling or boring tool for use in a brace, drill press, etc. —*vt.* **bit′ted, bit′ting** to put a bit into the mouth of (a horse)

bit[2] (bit) *n.* [< OE. *bita,* a piece < *bitan,* to bite] **1.** *a)* a small piece or quantity *b)* a limited degree: used with *a* and having adverbial force *[a bit bored] c)* a short time **2.** [Colloq.] an amount equal to 12½ cents: now usually in *two bits, four bits,* etc. **3.** a small part, as in a play —*adj.* very small *[a bit role]* —**bit by bit** little by little; gradually —**do one's bit** to do one's share —**every bit** altogether; entirely

bit[3] (bit) *n.* [*b(inary) (dig)it*] a single character in a binary number system; specif., a unit of information equal to the amount of information obtained by learning which of two equally likely events occurred

bitch (bich) *n.* [< OE. *bicce*] **1.** the female of the dog, wolf, etc. **2.** a bad-tempered, malicious, or promiscuous woman: a coarse term of contempt **3.** [Slang] a complaint —*vi.* [Slang] to complain —**bitch′i·ness** *n.* —**bitch′y** *adj.* **bitch′i·er, bitch′i·est**

bite (bīt) *vt.* **bit** (bit), **bit·ten** (bit′'n) or **bit, bit′ing** [< OE. *bitan*] **1.** to seize or cut with or as with the teeth **2.** to cut into, as with a sharp weapon **3.** to sting, as an insect **4.** to hurt in a sharp, stinging way **5.** to eat into; corrode **6.** to seize or possess *[bitten* by a lust for fame*]* —*vi.* **1.** *a)* to press or snap the teeth (*into, at,* etc.) *b)* to have a tendency to do this **2.** to cause a biting sensation **3.** to press hard; grip *[the tires bit* into the snow*]* **4.** to seize a bait **5.** to be caught, as by a trick —*n.* **1.** the act of biting **2.** biting quality; sting **3.** a wound or sting from biting **4.** *a)* a mouthful *b)* a light meal or snack **5.** a tight hold or grip **6.** the way the upper and lower teeth meet **7.** [Colloq.] an amount cut off or sum deducted —**bite the bullet** to confront a painful situation with fortitude or stoicism —**put the bite on** [Slang] to press for a loan, gift, or bribe of money —**bit′er** *n.*

bit·ing (bīt′iŋ) *adj.* **1.** cutting; sharp **2.** sarcastic —**bit′ing·ly** *adv.*

biting midge a tiny fly which has piercing and sucking mouthparts

bitt (bit) *n.* [< ?] *Naut.* any of the deck posts, usually in pairs, around which ropes or cables are fastened —*vt.* to wind around a bitt

bit·ter (bit′ər) *adj.* [< OE. < base of *bitan,* to bite] **1.** having a sharp, often unpleasant taste; acrid **2.** causing or showing sorrow, pain, etc. **3.** sharp; harsh; piercing **4.** characterized by hatred, resentment, etc. —*adv.* in a bitter way —*n.* **1.** something bitter *[take the bitter* with the sweet*]* **2.** [Brit.] bitter, strongly hopped ale: cf. BITTERS —**bit′ter·ly** *adv.* —**bit′ter·ness** *n.*

bit·tern (bit′ərn) *n., pl.* **-terns, -tern:** see PLURAL, II, D, 1 [< OFr. *butor,* prob. < L. *butio*] a wading bird of the heron family, the male of which has a resounding, thumping call

bit·ter·root (bit′ər ro͞ot′, -root′) *n.* a plant of W N. America having fleshy, edible roots and white or pink flowers

bit·ters (bit′ərz) *n.pl.* a liquor containing bitter herbs, roots, etc. and usually alcohol, used as a tonic and for flavoring in some cocktails

bit·ter·sweet (bit′ər swēt′) *n.* **1.** a N. American woody vine bearing clusters of orange fruits which open to expose the red seeds **2.** an old-world climbing vine of the nightshade family, with purple flowers and poisonous, red berries —*adj.* **1.** both bitter and sweet **2.** pleasant with sad overtones

bi·tu·men (bi to͞o′mən, bī-; -tyo͞o′-) *n.* [L. < Celt.] any of several substances obtained as asphaltic residue in the distillation of coal tar, petroleum, etc., or occurring as natural asphalt —**bi·tu′mi·nize′** (-mə nīz′) *vt.* **-nized′, -niz′ing** —**bi·tu′mi·nous** *adj.*

bituminous coal coal that yields pitch or tar when it burns; soft coal

bi·va·lent (bī vā′lənt, biv′ə-) *adj.* **1.** having two valences **2.** having a valence of two —**bi·va′lence, bi·va′len·cy** *n.*

bi·valve (bī′valv′) *n.* any mollusk having a shell of two parts, or valves, hinged together, as a mussel, clam, etc. —*adj.* having such a shell: also **bi′valved′**

biv·ou·ac (biv′wak, -oo wak′) *n.* [Fr. < OHG. *biwacht,* outpost < *bi-,* by + *wacht,* a guard] a temporary encampment (esp. of soldiers) in the open, with only improvised shelter —*vi.* **-acked, -ack·ing** to encamp in the open

bi·week·ly (bī wēk′lē) *adj., adv.* **1.** once every two weeks **2.** twice a week: in this sense, *semiweekly* is the preferred term —*n., pl.* **-lies** a publication that appears once every two weeks

bi·year·ly (bī yir′lē) *adj., adv.* **1.** once every two years; biennial(ly) **2.** twice a year: in this sense, *semiyearly, semiannual(ly),* or *biannual(ly)* is preferred

bi·zarre (bi zär′) *adj.* [Fr. < It. < Sp. *bizarro,* bold < Basque *bizar,* a beard] **1.** odd in manner, appearance, etc.; grotesque; queer; eccentric **2.** unexpected and unbelievable; fantastic —**bi·zarre′ly** *adv.* —**bi·zarre′ness** *n.*

Bi·zet (bē zā′), **Georges** (zhôrzh) (born *Alexandre César Léopold Bizet*) 1838–75; Fr. composer

Bk *Chem.* berkelium

bk. *pl.* **bks.** **1.** bank **2.** block **3.** book

bkg. banking

bkt. **1.** basket(s) **2.** bracket

bl. **1.** bale(s) **2.** barrel(s) **3.** black

B/L *pl.* **BS/L** bill of lading

B.L. Bachelor of Laws

blab (blab) *vt., vi.* **blabbed, blab′bing** [ME. *blabben:* see ff.] **1.** to give away (a secret) in idle chatter **2.** to chatter; prattle —*n.* **1.** loose chatter; gossip **2.** a person who blabs

blab·ber (-ər) *vt., vi.* [ME. *blabberen,* freq. of *blabben,* of echoic origin] [Dial. or Colloq.] to blab or babble —*n.* a person who blabs: also [Colloq.] **blab′ber·mouth′** (-mouth′)

black (blak) *adj.* [OE. *blæc*] **1.** opposite to white; of the color of coal: see COLOR **2.** having dark-colored skin and hair; esp., Negro **3.** *a)* totally without light; in complete darkness *b)* very dark **4.** without cream, milk, etc.: said of coffee **5.** soiled; dirty **6.** wearing black clothing **7.** evil; wicked **8.** disgraceful **9.** sad; dismal **10.** sullen or angry **11.** without hope *[a black* future*]* **12.** humorous or satirical in a morbid or cynical way *[black* comedy*]* —*n.* **1.** *a)* black color *b)* a black pigment, dye, etc. **2.** black clothes, esp. when worn in mourning **3.** a person with dark-colored skin; esp., a Negro: *black* is now the generally preferred term **4.** complete darkness —*vt., vi.* **1.** to blacken **2.** to polish with blacking —**black out** **1.** to cover (writing, etc.) as with black pencil marks **2.** to cause a blackout in **3.** to lose consciousness —**in the black** operating at a profit —**black′ish** *adj.* —**black′ly** *adv.* —**black′ness** *n.*

black-and-blue (-ən blo͞o′) *adj.* discolored from congestion of blood under the skin, as a bruise

black and white writing or print *[to put an agreement down in black and white]*
black art *same as* BLACK MAGIC
black·ball (-bôl′) ***n.*** a secret ballot or vote against a person or thing —***vt.*** **1.** to vote against; esp., to vote to exclude **2.** to ostracize
black bass (bas) any of various freshwater game fishes of N. America
black bear **1.** the common N. American bear **2.** any of several dark-colored bears of Asia
black belt a black-colored belt awarded to an expert in judo or karate
black·ber·ry (-ber′ē) ***n., pl.*** **-ries** **1.** the fleshy, purple or black, edible fruit of various brambles of the rose family **2.** a bush or vine bearing this fruit
black·bird (-burd′) ***n.*** any of various birds the male of which is almost entirely black, as the red-winged blackbird, English thrush, etc.
black·board (-bôrd′) ***n.*** a smooth, usually dark surface of slate or other material on which to write with chalk
black·bod·y (-bäd′ē) ***n.*** an ideal surface or body that can absorb all radiation striking it
black book a book with the names of those blacklisted
black·cap (-kap′) ***n.*** **1.** a bird with a black crown, as the chickadee **2.** same as BLACK RASPBERRY
black·cock (-käk′) ***n., pl.*** **-cocks′, -cock′**: see PLURAL, II, D, 1 the male of the black grouse
black·damp (-damp′) ***n.*** a suffocating gas, a mixture of carbon dioxide and nitrogen, found in mines
Black Death a deadly disease, probably bubonic plague, which devastated Europe and Asia in the 14th cent.
black·en (blak′'n) ***vi.*** to become black or dark —***vt.*** **1.** to make black; darken **2.** to slander; defame; vilify —**black′en·er** ***n.***
black eye **1.** a discoloration of the skin surrounding an eye, resulting from a sharp blow or contusion **2.** [Colloq.] bad reputation; dishonor
black-eyed pea (blak′īd′) *same as* COWPEA (sense 2)
black-eyed Susan a N. American wildflower with yellow ray flowers about a dark, cone-shaped center
black·face (blak′fās′) ***adj.*** having a black face —***n.*** black makeup used by performers, as in minstrel shows, in gross caricature of Negroes
black flag the flag of piracy, usually with a white skull and crossbones on a black background
Black·foot (-foot′) ***n.*** **1.** *pl.* **-feet′, -foot′** any member of an Indian tribe consisting of three subtribes of Montana, Alberta, and Saskatchewan **2.** their Algonquian language
Black Forest heavily wooded, mountainous region in SW Germany
black grouse a large grouse of Europe and Asia: the male is almost entirely black
black·guard (blag′ərd, -ärd) ***n.*** [BLACK + GUARD] a scoundrel; villain —***adj.*** vulgar, abusive, etc. —***vt.*** to abuse with words; revile —**black′guard·ly** ***adj., adv.***
black·head (blak′hed′) ***n.*** **1.** any of various birds black about the head **2.** a black-tipped plug of dried fatty matter clogging a skin pore
black·heart·ed (-här′tid) ***adj.*** wicked; evil
Black Hills mountainous region in SW S.Dak. & NE Wyo.
black hole a hypothetical body in space, supposed to be an invisible collapsed star so condensed that neither light nor matter can escape its gravitational field
black·ing (-iŋ) ***n.*** a black polish, as for shoes
black·jack (-jak′) ***n.*** [see JACK-] **1.** a small, leathercovered bludgeon with a flexible handle **2.** the card game TWENTY-ONE —***vt.*** **1.** to hit with a blackjack **2.** to coerce
black·list (-list′) ***n.*** a list of censured persons being discriminated against, refused employment, etc. —***vt.*** to put on a blacklist
black lung (disease) a disease of the lungs caused by the continual inhalation of coal dust
black magic magic with an evil purpose; sorcery
black·mail (-māl′) ***n.*** [lit., black rent < OE. *mal,* lawsuit < ON. *mal,* discussion; infl. by OFr. *maille,* a coin] **1.** payment extorted to prevent disclosure of information that could bring disgrace **2.** extortion of such payment —***vt.*** **1.** to get or try to get blackmail from **2.** to coerce (*into* doing something) as by threats —**black′mail′er** ***n.***
black mark an unfavorable item in one's record
black market a place or system for selling goods illegally, esp. in violation of rationing —**black′-mar′ket** ***vt., vi.*** —**black marketeer** (or **marketer**)
Black Muslim a member of a militant Islamic sect of American blacks that advocates racial separation: members of the sect call themselves simply "Muslims"
black nationalism a movement for establishing a separate nation of blacks within the U.S.
black·out (-out′) ***n.*** **1.** the extinguishing of all stage lights to end a play or scene **2.** a concealing of all lights that might be visible to enemy air raiders at night **3.** a temporary loss of electricity in an area because of a failure in its generation or transmission **4.** a temporary loss of consciousness **5.** a loss of memory of an event **6.** suppression or concealment, as of news by censorship
black pepper a hot seasoning made by grinding the whole dried, black berries of the pepper plant
Black·pool (blak′po͞ol′) city in NW England, on the Irish Sea: pop. 148,000
black power political and economic power sought by black Americans in the struggle for civil rights
black raspberry a shrub of the rose family, bearing juicy, purple-black fruits
Black Sea sea surrounded by the European U.S.S.R., Asia Minor, & the Balkan Peninsula
black sheep a person regarded as not so respectable as the rest of his family or group
Black Shirt a member of any fascist organization (specif., of the Italian Fascist party) having a black-shirted uniform: also **Black′shirt′** ***n.***
black·smith (blak′smith′) ***n.*** a smith who works in iron, making and fitting horseshoes, etc.
black·snake (-snāk′) ***n.*** a slender, harmless, black or dark-colored snake of the U.S.
Black·stone (blak′stōn; *Brit.* -stən), Sir **William** 1723–80; Eng. jurist & writer on law
black·strap molasses (blak′strap′) crude, dark molasses
black tea tea withered and fermented before being dried by heating
black·thorn (-thôrn′) ***n.*** **1.** a thorny, white-flowered shrub with blue-black, plumlike fruit; sloe **2.** a walking stick made of its stem
black tie **1.** a black bow tie, properly worn with a tuxedo **2.** a tuxedo and the proper accessories
black·top (blak′täp′) ***n.*** a bituminous mixture, usually asphalt, used as a surface for roads, etc. —***vt.*** **-topped′, -top′ping** to cover with blacktop
black walnut **1.** a tall walnut tree of E N. America **2.** its hard, heavy, dark-brown wood, used in making furniture, etc. **3.** its edible, oily nut
black widow an American spider the female of which has a black body with red markings underneath, and a very poisonous bite: the female sometimes eats its mate
blad·der (blad′ər) ***n.*** [OE. *blædre*] **1.** a bag of membranous tissue in the bodies of many animals, that inflates to receive and contain liquids or gases; esp., the **urinary bladder** in the pelvic cavity, which holds urine flowing from the kidneys **2.** a bag, etc. resembling this **3.** an air sac, as in some water plants —**blad′der·y** ***adj.***
blad·der·wort (-wurt′) ***n.*** a plant growing in or near water and having leaves with bladders on them that trap small insects and crustaceans
blade (blād) ***n.*** [OE. *blæd*] **1.** *a)* the leaf of a plant, esp. of grass *b)* the flat, expanded part of a leaf; lamina **2.** a broad, flat surface, as of an oar **3.** a flat bone *[the shoulder blade]* **4.** the cutting part of a knife, tool, etc. **5.** the metal runner of an ice skate **6.** a sword or a swordsman **7.** a gay, dashing young man **8.** *Phonet.* the flat part of the tongue, behind the tip —***adj.*** designating or of various cuts of meat from the shoulder blade section —**blad′ed** ***adj.***
blah (blä) ***n., interj.*** [Slang] nonsense —***adj.*** [Slang] **1.** unappetizing **2.** dull, lifeless, etc.
blain (blān) ***n.*** [< OE. *blegen*] a pustule or blister
Blake (blāk), **William** 1757–1827; Eng. poet & artist
blam·a·ble, blame·a·ble (blām′ə b'l) ***adj.*** that deserves blame; culpable —**blam′a·bly** ***adv.***
blame (blām) ***vt.*** **blamed, blam′ing** [< OFr. < LL. *blasphemare,* BLASPHEME] **1.** to accuse of being at fault; condemn (*for* something) **2.** to find fault with **3.** to put the responsibility of (an error, fault, etc. *on*) —***n.*** **1.** a blaming; condemnation **2.** responsibility for a fault or wrong **3.** [Archaic] fault —**be to blame** to be blamable —**blame′ful** ***adj.*** —**blame′ful·ly** ***adv.*** —**blame′ful·ness** ***n.*** —**blame′less** ***adj.*** —**blame′less·ly** ***adv.*** —**blame′less·ness** ***n.***
blame·wor·thy (blām′wur′*thē*) ***adj.*** deserving to be blamed —**blame′wor′thi·ness** ***n.***
Blanc (blän), **Mont** (mōn) mountain in E France: highest peak in the Alps: 15,781 ft.
blanch (blanch) ***vt.*** [OFr. *blanchir* < *blanc:* see BLANK] **1.** to make white; bleach **2.** to make pale **3.** to scald (vegetables, almonds, etc.), as for removing the skins —***vi.*** to turn white or pale —**blanch′er** ***n.***

Blanche, Blanch (blanch) [Fr., lit., white, fem. of *blanc:* see BLANK] a feminine name

blanc·mange (blə mänzh′, -mänj′) ***n.*** [Fr. < *blanc*, white + *manger*, to eat] a sweet, molded, jellylike dessert made with starch or gelatin, milk, etc.

bland (bland) ***adj.*** [< L. *blandus*, mild] **1.** pleasantly smooth; agreeable; suave **2.** *a)* mild and soothing; not sharp, harsh, etc. *b)* tasteless, insipid, dull, etc. —**bland′ly** ***adv.*** —**bland′ness** ***n.***

blan·dish (blan′dish) ***vt., vi*** [< OFr. < L. *blandiri*, to flatter < prec.] to flatter or coax in persuading; cajole —**blan′dish·er** ***n.*** —**blan′dish·ment** ***n.***

blank (blaŋk) ***adj.*** [OFr. *blanc*, white < Frank.] **1.** *a)* not written on; not marked [*a blank paper*] *b)* having empty spaces to be filled in **2.** having an empty or vacant look **3.** empty of thought [*a blank mind*] **4.** utter; complete [*a blank denial*] **5.** lacking certain elements or characteristics —***n.*** **1.** an empty space, esp. one to be filled out in a printed form **2.** such a printed form **3.** an empty place or time; void **4.** a piece of metal, etc. to be finished by stamping or marking **5.** a lottery ticket that fails to win **6.** a powder-filled cartridge without a bullet: in full, **blank cartridge** —***vt.*** to hold (an opponent) scoreless in a game —**blank out** to cancel or obscure as by covering over —**draw a blank** [Colloq.] **1.** to be unsuccessful in an attempt **2.** to be unable to remember a particular thing —**blank′ly** ***adv.*** —**blank′ness** ***n.***

blank check a check carrying a signature only and allowing the bearer to fill in any amount

blan·ket (blaŋ′kit) ***n.*** [< OFr. dim. of *blanc*, white] **1.** a large, soft piece of cloth used for warmth, esp. as a bed cover **2.** anything like a blanket [*a blanket of leaves*] —***adj.*** covering a group of conditions or items [*a blanket insurance policy*] —***vt.*** **1.** to cover, as with a blanket **2.** to apply uniformly to: said of rates **3.** to suppress; obscure [*a powerful radio station blankets a weaker one*]

blank verse unrhymed verse; esp., unrhymed verse having five iambic feet per line

blare (bler) ***vt., vi.*** **blared, blar′ing** [ME. *bleren*, to bellow] **1.** to sound out with loud, trumpetlike tones **2.** to exclaim loudly —***n.*** **1.** a loud, brassy sound **2.** harsh brilliance or glare

blar·ney (blär′nē) ***n.*** [see ff.] smooth talk used in flattering or coaxing —***vt., vi.*** **-neyed, -ney·ing** to use blarney (on)

Blarney stone a stone in Blarney Castle in the county of Cork, Ireland, said to impart skill in blarney to those who kiss it

bla·sé (blä zā′, blä′zā) ***adj.*** [Fr., pp. of *blaser*, to satiate] having indulged in pleasure so much as to be unexcited by it; satiated and bored

blas·pheme (blas fēm′, blas′fēm) ***vt.*** **-phemed′, -phem′ing** [< OFr. < LL. < Gr. *blasphēmein*, to speak evil of] **1.** to speak irreverently or profanely of or to (God or sacred things) **2.** to curse or revile —***vi.*** to utter blasphemy —**blas·phem′er** ***n.***

blas·phe·my (blas′fə mē) ***n.***, *pl.* **-mies** [see prec.] **1.** words or action showing disrespect or scorn for God or anything held sacred **2.** any irreverent or disrespectful remark or action —**blas′phe·mous** ***adj.*** —**blas′phe·mous·ly** ***adv.***

blast (blast) ***n.*** [< OE. *blæst*] **1.** a gust of wind; strong rush of air **2.** the sound of a sudden rush of air or gas, as through a trumpet **3.** the steady current of air forced into a blast furnace **4.** an abrupt and damaging influence; blight **5.** *a)* an explosion, as of dynamite *b)* a charge of explosive causing this **6.** [Slang] a gay, hilarious time; esp., a wild party —***vi.*** **1.** to make a loud, harsh sound **2.** to set off explosives, gunfire, etc. **3.** to suffer from a blight —***vt.*** **1.** to damage or destroy by or as if by a blight; wither **2.** to blow up with an explosive; explode **3.** [Colloq.] to criticize sharply **4.** *Sports* to hit (a ball) with great, driving force —**blast off** to take off with explosive force and begin its flight, as a rocket —**(at) full blast** at full speed or capacity —**blast′er** ***n.***

-blast (blast) [< Gr. *blastos*, a sprout] *a combining form meaning* formative, embryonic

blast·ed (blas′tid) ***adj.*** **1.** blighted; withered; destroyed **2.** damned; confounded

blast furnace a smelting furnace into which a blast of air is forced from below for intense heat

blast·off, blast-off (blast′ôf′) ***n.*** the launching of a rocket, space vehicle, etc.

blas·tu·la (blas′choo lə) ***n.***, *pl.* **-las, -lae′** (-lē′) [ModL. dim. < Gr. *blastos*, a germ, sprout] an embryo at the stage of development in which it consists typically of a single layer of cells around a central cavity —**blas′tu·lar** ***adj.***

blat (blat) ***vi.*** **blat′ted, blat′ting** [var. of BLEAT] to bleat —***vt.*** to blurt out —***n.*** a blatting sound

bla·tant (blāt′′nt) ***adj.*** [coined by E. Spenser; prob. < L. *blaterare*, to babble] **1.** disagreeably loud; noisy **2.** glaringly conspicuous or obtrusive —**bla′tan·cy** ***n.***, *pl.* **-cies** —**bla′tant·ly** ***adv.***

blath·er (blath′ər) ***n.*** [ON. *blathr*] foolish talk —***vi., vt.*** to chatter foolishly —**blath′er·er** ***n.***

blath·er·skite (-skīt′) ***n.*** a talkative, foolish person

blaze[1] (blāz) ***n.*** [< OE. *blæse*] **1.** a brilliant burst of flame; strongly burning fire **2.** any very bright light or glare **3.** a sudden or spectacular outburst [*a blaze of oratory*] **4.** a brightness; vivid display —***vi.*** **blazed, blaz′ing** **1.** to burn rapidly or brightly **2.** to give off a strong light; glare **3.** to be deeply stirred, as with anger —**blaze away** to fire a gun rapidly several times

blaze[2] (blāz) ***n.*** [< ON. *blesi*] **1.** a white spot on an animal's face **2.** a mark made on a tree by cutting off a piece of bark —***vt.*** **blazed, blaz′ing** to mark (a tree or trail) with blazes —**blaze a way** (or **path**, etc.) **in** to pioneer in

blaze[3] (blāz) ***vt.*** **blazed, blaz′ing** [ME. *blasen*, to blow < OE. or ON.] to make known publicly

blaz·er (blā′zər) ***n.*** [< BLAZE[1] + -ER] a lightweight sports jacket, often brightly colored or striped

bla·zon (blā′z′n) ***n.*** [OFr. *blason*, a shield] **1.** a coat of arms **2.** showy display —***vt.*** **1.** to make widely known; proclaim (often with *forth*, *out*, or *abroad*) **2.** to describe or portray (coats of arms) **3.** *a)* to portray in colors *b)* to adorn colorfully or showily —**bla′zon·er** ***n.*** —**bla′zon·ment** ***n.*** —**bla′zon·ry** ***n.***, *pl.* **-ries**

bldg. building

bleach (blēch) ***vt., vi.*** [OE. *blæcan* < *blac*, pale] to make or become white or colorless by means of chemicals or by exposure to sunlight —***n.*** **1.** a bleaching **2.** a substance used for bleaching —**bleach′er** ***n.***

bleach·ers (-ərz) ***n.pl.*** [< prec., in reference to the effects of exposure] seats or benches in tiers without a roof, for spectators at sporting events

bleak (blēk) ***adj.*** [< ON. *bleikr*, pale] **1.** exposed to wind and cold; unsheltered **2.** cold and cutting; harsh **3.** not cheerful or hopeful; gloomy —**bleak′ly** ***adv.*** —**bleak′ness** ***n.***

blear (blir) ***adj.*** [< ME. *bleren*, to have watery eyes] **1.** made dim by tears, mucus, etc.: said of eyes **2.** blurred; dim —***vt.*** **1.** to dim (the eyes) with tears, mucus, etc. **2.** to blur

blear·y (-ē) ***adj.*** **blear′i·er, blear′i·est** **1.** dim or blurred **2.** having blurred vision —**blear′i·ly** ***adv.*** —**blear′i·ness** ***n.***

blear·y-eyed (-īd′) ***adj.*** having bleary eyes or blurred vision: also **blear′eyed′**

bleat (blēt) ***vi.*** [< OE. *blætan*] **1.** to make the cry of a sheep, goat, or calf **2.** to make a sound like this cry —***vt.*** to say in a bleating voice —***n.*** a bleating cry or sound —**bleat′er** ***n.***

bleed (blēd) ***vi.*** **bled** (bled), **bleed′ing** [< OE. *bledan* < *blod*, blood] **1.** to emit or lose blood **2.** to suffer wounds or die in a battle or cause **3.** to feel pain, grief, or sympathy; suffer **4.** to ooze sap, juice, etc., as bruised plants **5.** to run together, as dyes in wet cloth **6.** to come through a covering coat of paint —***vt.*** **1.** to draw blood from **2.** to ooze (sap, juice, etc.) **3.** to empty of liquid, air, or gas **4.** to take sap or juice from **5.** [Colloq.] to extort money from

bleed·er (-ər) ***n.*** a person who bleeds profusely; hemophiliac

bleeding heart **1.** a plant with fernlike leaves and drooping clusters of pink, heart-shaped flowers **2.** a person regarded as too sentimental or too liberal in his approach to social problems

bleep (blēp) ***n., vi.*** [echoic] *same as* BEEP —***vt.*** to censor (something said), as in a telecast, by substituting a beep

blem·ish (blem′ish) ***vt.*** [<OFr. *blesmir*, to injure] to mar, as by some flaw or fault —***n.*** **1.** a mark that mars the appearance, as a stain or nick **2.** any flaw, defect, or shortcoming

blench[1] (blench) ***vt., vi.*** [var. of BLANCH] to make or become pale; whiten

blench[2] (blench) ***vi.*** [< OE. *blencan*, to deceive] to shrink back, as in fear; flinch

blend (blend) ***vt.*** **blend′ed** or **blent, blend′ing** [< OE. *blendan* & ON. *blanda*, to mix] **1.** to mix or mingle (varieties of tea, tobacco, etc.) **2.** to mix or fuse thoroughly, so the parts are no longer distinct —***vi.*** **1.** to mix or merge **2.** to shade gradually into each other, as colors **3.** to go well together; harmonize —***n.*** **1.** a blending **2.** a mixture of varieties [*a blend of coffee*] **3.** *Linguis.* a word formed by combining parts of other words (Ex.: *smog*) —**blend′er** ***n.***

blende (blend) ***n.*** [G. < *blenden*, to blind, deceive] sphalerite or any of certain other sulfides

blended whiskey whiskey that is a blend of straight whiskey and neutral spirits or of two or more straight whiskeys

blen·ny (blen′ē) ***n.***, *pl.* **-nies, -ny**: see PLURAL, II, D, 1 [< L. < Gr. < *blenna*, slime] any of a number of small ocean fishes having long dorsal fins and a tapering body covered with a slimy substance —**blen′ni·oid′** (-ē oid′) ***adj.***

bless (bles) ***vt.*** **blessed** or **blest, bless′ing** [< OE. *bletsian*, orig. to consecrate with blood < *blod*, blood] **1.** to make holy; hallow **2.** to ask divine favor for **3.** to favor or endow (*with*) *[blessed* with health*]* **4.** to make happy or prosperous **5.** to praise or glorify **6.** to make the sign of the cross over or upon **7.** to protect from evil, harm, etc. —**bless me** (or **you, him,** etc.)! an exclamation of surprise, dismay, etc.

bless·ed (bles′id; *occas.* blest) ***adj.*** **1.** holy; sacred **2.** blissful; fortunate **3.** of or in eternal bliss: a title applied to one who has been beatified **4.** bringing joy —**bless′ed·ly** ***adv.*** —**bless′ed·ness** ***n.***

bless·ing (-iŋ) ***n.*** **1.** an invocation or benediction **2.** a grace said before or after eating **3.** the gift of divine favor **4.** good wishes or approval **5.** a special benefit or favor

blest (blest) *alt. pt. & pp. of* BLESS —***adj.*** blessed

bleu cheese (blo͞o; *Fr.* blö) [Fr. *bleu,* blue] *same as* BLUE CHEESE

blew (blo͞o) *pt. of* BLOW[1] & BLOW[3]

blight (blīt) ***n.*** [? < ON. *blikja,* turn pale] **1.** any parasite, insect, etc. that destroys or stunts plants **2.** any of several plant diseases, as mildew **3.** anything that destroys, prevents growth, frustrates, etc. —***vt.*** **1.** to wither **2.** to destroy **3.** to frustrate —***vi.*** to suffer blight

blimp (blimp) ***n.*** [echoic coinage] [Colloq.] a small, nonrigid or semirigid airship

blind (blīnd) ***adj.*** [OE.] **1.** without the power of sight; sightless **2.** of or for sightless persons **3.** not able or willing to notice or understand **4.** done without adequate directions or knowledge *[a blind search]* **5.** disregarding evidence, sound logic, etc. *[blind faith]* **6.** reckless; unreasonable **7.** hard to see; hidden *[a blind driveway]* **8.** dense; impenetrable *[a blind hedge]* **9.** closed at one end *[a blind alley]* **10.** not controlled by intelligence *[blind destiny]* **11.** *Aeron.* by the use of instruments only *[blind flying]* **12.** *Archit.* having no opening —***vt.*** **1.** to make sightless **2.** to dazzle **3.** to deprive of the power of insight or judgment **4.** to make dim; obscure **5.** to hide —***n.*** **1.** anything that obscures or prevents sight **2.** *a)* anything that keeps out light, as a window shade *b) same as* VENETIAN BLIND **3.** a place of concealment **4.** a decoy —***adv.*** **1.** blindly **2.** recklessly **3.** sight unseen *[to buy a thing blind]* —**the blind** blind people —**blind′ly** ***adv.*** —**blind′ness** ***n.***

blind date [Colloq.] **1.** a date arranged for a man and a woman previously unacquainted **2.** either of these persons

blind·er (blīn′dər) ***n.*** either of two flaps on a horse's bridle that shut out the side view

blind·fold (blīnd′fōld′) ***vt.*** [altered (after FOLD[1]) < ME. *blindfeld,* struck blind: see BLIND & FELL[2]] to cover the eyes of, as with a cloth —***n.*** something used to cover the eyes —***adj.*** **1.** with the eyes covered **2.** reckless

blind·man's buff (blīnd′manz buf′) [*buff,* contr. < BUFFET[1]] a game in which a blindfolded player has to catch and identify another: also **blind′man's bluff′** (bluf′)

blind spot **1.** the small area, insensitive to light, in the retina of the eye where the optic nerve enters **2.** an area where vision is obscured **3.** a prejudice, or area of ignorance, that one has but is often unaware of

blind trust an arrangement whereby a person, as a public official, in an effort to avoid conflicts of interest places certain personal assets under the control of an independent trustee with the provision that the person is to have no knowledge of how those assets are managed

blink (bliŋk) ***vi.*** [ME. *blenken* (see BLENCH[2])] **1.** to wink quickly one or more times **2.** to flash on and off; twinkle **3.** to look with eyes half shut and winking —***vt.*** to cause (eyes, light, etc.) to wink or blink —***n.*** **1.** a blinking **2.** a glimmer —**blink at** to ignore or condone (a mistake) —**on the blink** [Slang] not working right; out of order

blink·er (-ər) ***n.*** **1.** a flashing warning light at crossings **2.** *same as* BLINDER

blintz (blints) ***n.*** [< Yid. < Russ. < *blin,* pancake] a thin pancake rolled with a filling of cottage cheese, etc.

blip (blip) ***n.*** [echoic of a brief sound] **1.** a luminous image on an oscilloscope **2.** a quick, sharp sound —***vt.*** **blipped, blip′ping** *same as* BLEEP

bliss (blis) ***n.*** [OE. *bliths* < *blithe,* BLITHE] **1.** great joy or happiness **2.** spiritual joy —**bliss′ful** ***adj.*** —**bliss′ful·ly** ***adv.*** —**bliss′ful·ness** ***n.***

blis·ter (blis′tər) ***n.*** [< Du. *bluister* or OFr. *blestre* < ON. *blastr*] **1.** a raised patch of skin filled with watery matter and caused by burning or rubbing **2.** anything resembling a blister —***vt.*** **1.** to raise blisters on **2.** to lash with words —***vi.*** to have or form blisters —**blis′ter·y** ***adj.***

blithe (blīth, blīth) ***adj.*** [OE.] gay; cheerful; carefree —**blithe′ly** ***adv.*** —**blithe′ness** ***n.***

blith·er·ing (blith′ər iŋ) ***adj.*** [*blither,* var. of BLATHER] talking without sense; jabbering

blithe·some (blīth′səm, blīth′-) ***adj.*** blithe; gay —**blithe′some·ly** ***adv.*** —**blithe′some·ness** ***n.***

B.Litt., B.Lit. [L. *Baccalaureus Lit(t)erarum*] Bachelor of Letters (or Literature)

blitz (blits) ***n.*** [< ff.] a sudden, overwhelming attack —***vt.*** to subject to a blitz; overwhelm

blitz·krieg (-krēg′) ***n.*** [G. < *blitz,* lightning + *krieg,* war] **1.** sudden, swift, large-scale offensive warfare intended to win a quick victory **2.** any sudden, overwhelming attack

bliz·zard (bliz′ərd) ***n.*** [dial. *bliz,* violent blow (? akin to G. *blitz,* lightning) + -ARD] a violent storm with driving snow and very cold winds

blk. **1.** black **2.** block **3.** bulk

bloat[1] (blōt) ***vt., vi*** [< ON. *blautr,* soaked] **1.** to swell, as with water or air **2.** to puff up, as with pride

bloat[2] (blōt) ***vt.*** [< ME. *blote,* soft with moisture < ON. *blautr:* see prec.] to cure (herring, etc.) by soaking in salt water and smoking

bloat·er (-ər) ***n.*** a fat herring or mackerel that has been bloated, or cured

blob (bläb) ***n.*** [echoic] **1.** a small drop or mass **2.** something of indefinite form

bloc (bläk) ***n.*** [Fr. & OFr. < LowG. *block,* log] a bipartisan group of legislators, or a group of nations, acting together in some common cause

block (bläk) ***n.*** [< MDu. or OFr. < LowG. *block:* see prec.] **1.** any large, solid piece of wood, stone, or metal **2.** a blocklike stand on which chopping, etc. is done **3.** an auctioneer's platform **4.** a mold upon which hats, etc. are shaped **5.** an obstruction or hindrance **6.** an interruption of a normal body function **7.** a pulley in a frame **8.** a large, hollow building brick **9.** a child's wooden or plastic toy brick **10.** a group of buildings **11.** *a)* a city square *b)* one side of a city square **12.** any number of things regarded as a unit **13.** *Printing* a piece of engraved wood, etc. with a design or picture **14.** *Sports* a legal thwarting of an opponent's play or movement —***vt.*** **1.** to impede the passage or progress of; obstruct **2.** to stand in the way of; hinder **3.** to shape or mold on a block **4.** to strengthen or support with blocks **5.** to sketch with little detail (often with *out*) **6.** *Med.* to deaden (a nerve), esp. by anesthesia **7.** *Sports* to hinder (an opponent or his play) —**on the block** up for sale or auction —**block′age** ***n.***

block·ade (blä kād′) ***n.*** [BLOCK + -ADE] **1.** a shutting off of a port or region by hostile troops or ships to prevent passage **2.** the troops or ships so used **3.** any strategic barrier —***vt.*** **-ad′ed, -ad′ing** to subject to a blockade —**run the blockade** to go through a blockade —**block·ad′er** ***n.***

block and tackle pulley blocks and ropes or cables, used for hoisting large, heavy objects

block·bust·er (bläk′bus′tər) ***n.*** [Colloq.] **1.** a large, highly destructive aerial bomb **2.** a successful, heavily promoted movie, novel, etc.

block·bust·ing (-bus′tiŋ) ***n.*** [Colloq.] the practice of inducing the quick sale of homes by creating fear about a minority group moving into the neighborhood

block·head (-hed′) ***n.*** a stupid person

block·house (-hous′) ***n.*** **1.** formerly, a strong wooden fort with a projecting second story and openings in the walls to shoot from **2.** any building of squared timber or logs **3.** *Mil.* a small structure of concrete for defense or observation

BLOCKHOUSE

block·ish (-ish) ***adj.*** stupid; dull —**block′ish·ly** ***adv.***

block·y (-ē) ***adj.*** **block′i·er, block′i·est** **1.** having contrasting blocks or patches **2.** stocky; chunky —**block′i·ness** ***n.***

Bloem·fon·tein (blo͞om′fän tān′) city in C South Africa: pop. 146,000

bloke (blōk) ***n.*** [< ?] [Chiefly Brit. Slang] a fellow; chap

blond (bländ) ***adj.*** [Fr. < ? Gmc.] **1.** having yellow or yellowish-brown hair, often with fair skin and blue or gray eyes **2.** yellow or yellowish-brown: said of hair **3.** light-colored *[blond furniture]* —***n.*** a blond person —**blond′ness** ***n.***

blonde (bländ) ***adj.*** *same as* BLOND —***n.*** a blond woman or girl

blood (blud) ***n.*** [< OE. *blod*] **1.** *a)* the fluid, usually red, circulating in the heart, arteries, and veins of vertebrates *b)* a similar fluid in invertebrates **2.** the spilling of blood; murder **3.** the essence of life; lifeblood **4.** the sap of a plant **5.** passion, temperament, or disposition **6.** parental heritage; family line; lineage; ancestry **7.** kinship; family relationship **8.** descent from nobility **9.** a descent from purebred stock **10.** a dandy **11.** people, esp. youthful people *[*new *blood* in the firm*]* —**bad blood** anger; hatred —**in cold blood 1.** with cruelty; unfeelingly **2.** dispassionately; deliberately —**make one's blood boil** to make one angry —**make one's blood run cold** to terrify one

blood bank 1. a place where whole blood or plasma is stored for future use in transfusion **2.** any reserve of such blood

blood bath a massacre; slaughter

blood brother 1. a brother by birth **2.** a person bound to one by the ceremony of mingling his blood with one's own —**blood brotherhood**

blood count the number of red corpuscles and white corpuscles in a given volume of blood

blood·cur·dling (-kurd′liŋ) ***adj.*** very frightening

blood·ed (blud′id) ***adj.*** **1.** having (a specified kind of) blood *[*hot-*blooded]* **2.** of fine stock or breed

blood group any of several groups into which human blood is classified

blood·hound (-hound′) ***n.*** any of a breed of large, keen-scented dogs used in tracking fugitives, etc.

blood·less (-ləs) ***adj.*** **1.** without blood **2.** without bloodshed **3.** anemic or pale **4.** having little energy or vitality —**blood′less·ly *adv.*** —**blood′less·ness *n.***

blood·let·ting (-let′iŋ) ***n.*** **1.** the opening of a vein to remove blood; bleeding **2.** *same as* BLOODSHED

blood·mo·bile (-mō bēl′, -mə-) ***n.*** [BLOOD + (AUTO)MOBILE] a traveling unit equipped for collecting blood from donors for blood banks

blood money 1. money paid to a hired killer **2.** money paid as compensation for a murder **3.** money gotten ruthlessly through others' suffering

blood poisoning any of various diseases in which the blood contains microorganisms, their toxins, or other poisonous matter; septicemia

blood pressure the pressure exerted by the blood against the inner walls of the blood vessels

blood pudding a large sausage made of pig's blood and suet, enclosed in a casing

blood·root (-ro͞ot′, -ro͝ot′) ***n.*** a N. American wildflower of the poppy family, with a white flower and a rootstock that yields a red juice

blood·shed (-shed′) ***n.*** the shedding of blood; killing

blood·shot (-shät′) ***adj.*** red because the small blood vessels are swollen or broken: said of an eye

blood·stained (-stānd′) ***adj.*** **1.** soiled or discolored with blood **2.** guilty of murder

blood·stone (-stōn′) ***n.*** a dark-green variety of quartz spotted with red jasper, used as a gem

blood·stream (-strēm′) ***n.*** the blood flowing through the circulatory system of a body

blood·suck·er (-suk′ər) ***n.*** **1.** an animal that sucks blood, esp. a leech **2.** a person who extorts from others all that he can —**blood′suck′ing *adj., n.***

blood·thirst·y (-thur′stē) ***adj.*** eager to kill; murderous

blood type *same as* BLOOD GROUP

blood typing the classification of blood to determine compatible blood groups for transfusion

blood vessel a tube through which the blood circulates in the body; artery, vein, or capillary

blood·y (blud′ē) ***adj.* blood′i·er, blood′i·est 1.** of, like, or containing blood **2.** covered or stained with blood **3.** involving bloodshed **4.** bloodthirsty **5.** [Brit. Slang] cursed; damned: a vulgar usage —***adv.*** [Brit. Slang] very: a vulgar usage —***vt.* blood′ied, blood′y·ing** to cover or stain with blood —**blood′i·ly *adv.*** —**blood′i·ness *n.***

Bloody Mary a drink of vodka with tomato juice

bloom (blo͞om) ***n.*** [< ON. *blomi,* flowers] **1.** a flower; blossom **2.** flowers collectively, as of a plant **3.** the state or time of flowering **4.** the state or time of most health, vigor, etc. **5.** a youthful, healthy glow, as of the cheeks **6.** *a)* the powdery coating on some fruits or leaves *b)* a similar coating, as on new coins —***vi.*** **1.** to bear flowers; blossom **2.** to be in one's prime; flourish **3.** to glow as with health —**bloom′ing *adj.***

bloom·er[1] (blo͞o′mər) ***n.*** **1.** a plant with reference to its blooming *[*an early *bloomer]* **2.** a person in his prime

bloom·er[2] (blo͞o′mər) ***n.*** [after Amelia J. *Bloomer* (1818–94), U.S. feminist who advocated it] **1.** formerly, a woman's costume consisting of a short skirt and loose trousers gathered at the ankles **2.** [*pl.*] *a)* baggy trousers gathered at the knee, formerly worn by women for athletics *b)* an undergarment somewhat like this

Bloom·ing·ton (blo͞o′miŋ tən) [? from abundance of flowering plants orig. found there] city in E Minn., near Minneapolis: pop. 82,000

bloop (blo͞op) ***vt.*** [Slang] *Baseball* **1.** to hit (a ball) as a blooper **2.** to get (a hit) in this way

bloop·er (blo͞op′ər) ***n.*** [echoic of a vulgar noise] [Slang] **1.** a stupid mistake **2.** *Baseball* a ball batted so that it drops between the infield and outfield, usually for a hit

blos·som (bläs′əm) ***n.*** [< OE. *blostma*] **1.** a flower or bloom, esp. of a fruit-bearing plant **2.** a state or time of flowering —***vi.*** **1.** to have or open into blossoms; bloom **2.** to begin to thrive or flourish; develop —**blos′som·y *adj.***

blot (blät) ***n.*** [< ?] **1.** a spot or stain, esp. of ink **2.** anything that spoils or mars something **3.** a moral stain; disgrace —***vt.* blot′ted, blot′ting 1.** to spot; stain **2.** to erase or get rid of *[*memories *blotted* from one's mind*]* **3.** to dry, as with blotting paper —***vi.*** **1.** to make blots **2.** to become blotted **3.** to be absorbent —**blot out 1.** to darken or obscure **2.** to destroy

blotch (bläch) ***n.*** [? extension of BLOT] **1.** a discolored patch or blemish on the skin **2.** any large blot or stain —***vt.*** to mark with blotches —**blotch′y *adj.* blotch′i·er, blotch′i·est**

blot·ter (blät′ər) ***n.*** **1.** a piece of blotting paper **2.** a book for recording events as they occur *[*a police *blotter* is a record of arrests, etc.*]*

blotting paper a thick, soft, absorbent paper used to dry a surface freshly written on in ink

blouse (blous, blouz) ***n.*** [Fr., workman's or peasant's smock] **1.** a loose, shirtlike garment extending to the waist, worn by women and children **2.** the coat or jacket of a military uniform **3.** a sailor's jumper —***vi., vt.* bloused, blous′ing** to gather in and drape at the waistline

blow[1] (blō) ***vi.* blew, blown, blow′ing** [< OE. *blawan*] **1.** to move with some force: said of the wind **2.** to send forth air, as with the mouth **3.** to pant; be breathless **4.** to sound by blowing or being blown **5.** to spout water and air, as whales do **6.** to be carried by the wind *[*the paper *blew* away*]* **7.** to be stormy **8.** to burst suddenly, as a tire, or melt, as a fuse (often with *out*) **9.** to lay eggs: said of flies **10.** [Colloq.] to brag; boast **11.** [Slang] to go away —***vt.*** **1.** to force air from (a bellows, etc.) **2.** to send out (breath, etc.) from the mouth **3.** to force air onto, into, or through **4.** to drive by blowing **5.** *a)* to sound (a wind instrument) by blowing *b)* to make (a sound) by blowing **6.** to shape or form by blown air or gas **7.** to clear by blowing through **8.** to burst by an explosion **9.** to cause (a horse) to pant **10.** to melt (a fuse, etc.) **11.** [Colloq.] to spend (money) freely **12.** [Colloq.] to forget (one's lines) in a show **13.** [Slang] to go away from **14.** [Slang] to bungle and fail in —***n.*** **1.** a blowing **2.** a blast of air **3.** a strong wind; gale —**blow hot and cold** to be favorable toward and then opposed to; vacillate —**blow in** [Slang] to arrive —**blow off** [Colloq.] to give vent to one's feelings, as by loud talking —**blow one's stack** (or **top** or **lid**) [Slang] to lose one's temper —**blow out 1.** to put out or be put out by blowing **2.** to blow (*vi.* 8) **3.** to dispel (itself) after a time: said of a storm —**blow over 1.** to move away, as rain clouds **2.** to be forgotten —**blow up 1.** to fill with air or gas **2.** to explode **3.** to arise and become intense, as a storm **4.** to enlarge (a photograph) **5.** to exaggerate (an incident, etc.) **6.** [Colloq.] to lose one's temper —**blow′er *n.***

blow[2] (blō) ***n.*** [ME. *blowe,* akin to G. *bleuen,* to strike] **1.** a hard hit or stroke, as with the fist **2.** a sudden attack or forcible effort **3.** a sudden calamity or misfortune; shock —**at a** (or **one**) **blow** by one action —**come to blows** to begin fighting

blow[3] (blō) ***vi.* blew, blown, blow′ing** [OE. *blowan*] [Poet.] to bloom; blossom —***n.*** a mass of blossoms

blow·by (-bī′) ***adj.*** designating or of a crankcase device that returns unburned gases to the engine for combustion so as to reduce air pollution

blow-by-blow (-bī′blō′) ***adj.*** told in great detail *[*a *blow-by-blow* description*]*

blow-dry (-drī′) ***vt.* -dried′, -dry′ing** to dry (wet hair) with an electric device (**blow′-dry′er**) that sends out a powerful stream of heated air —***n.*** the act of blow-drying the hair

blow·fish (-fish′) ***n.,*** *pl.* **-fish′, -fish′es:** see FISH *same as* PUFFER (sense 2)

blow·fly (-flī′) ***n.,*** *pl.* **-flies′** [BLOW[1] (*vi.* 9) + FLY[2]] any of various two-winged flies that deposit eggs in meat, open wounds, etc.

blow·gun (-gun′) ***n.*** a long, tubelike weapon through which darts or pellets are blown

blow·hard (-härd′) ***n.*** [Slang] a loudly boastful person

blow·hole (-hōl′) ***n.*** **1.** a nostril in the top of the head of whales, etc., used for breathing **2.** a hole through which gas or air can escape **3.** a hole in the ice to which seals, etc. come for air

blown (blōn) *pp. of* BLOW[1] & BLOW[3] —***adj.*** **1.** swollen or bloated **2.** out of breath, as from exertion **3.** made by blowing or by using a blowpipe, etc.

blow·out (blō′out′) ***n.*** **1.** the bursting of a tire **2.** the melting of an electric fuse **3.** [Slang] a party, banquet, etc.

blow·pipe (-pīp′) *n.* **1.** a tube for forcing air or gas into a flame to increase its heat **2.** a metal tube used in blowing glass **3.** *same as* BLOWGUN

blow·torch (-tôrch′) *n.* a small gasoline torch that shoots out a hot flame intensified by a blast of air: used to melt metal, remove old paint, etc.

blow·up (-up′) *n.* **1.** an explosion **2.** an enlarged photograph **3.** [Colloq.] a hysterical outburst

blow·y (-ē) *adj.* **blow′i·er, blow′i·est** windy

blowz·y (blou′zē) *adj.* **blowz′i·er, blowz′i·est** [< obs. *blouze,* wench] **1.** fat, ruddy, and coarse-looking **2.** slovenly; sloppy Also **blows′y**

BLS Bureau of Labor Statistics

bls. 1. bales **2.** barrels

B.L.S. Bachelor of Library Science

BLT bacon, lettuce, and tomato (sandwich)

blub·ber[1] (blub′ər) *n.* [ME. *blober,* a bubble; prob. echoic] **1.** the fat of the whale and other sea mammals **2.** unsightly fat on the human body —**blub′ber·y** *adj.*

blub·ber[2] (blub′ər) *vi.* [ME. *bloberen,* to bubble (see prec.)] to weep loudly, like a child —*vt.* to say while blubbering —*n.* loud weeping —*adj.* thick or swollen —**blub′ber·er** *n.*

blu·cher (bloo͞′chər, -kər) *n.* [after G. L. von *Blücher* (1742–1819), Prussian field marshal] a kind of shoe in which the upper laps over the vamp, which is of one piece with the tongue

BLUCHER

bludg·eon (bluj′′n) *n.* [? altered < MFr. dim. of *bouge,* a club] a short club with a thick, heavy, or loaded end —*vt., vi.* **1.** to strike with or as with a bludgeon **2.** to bully or coerce

blue (bloo͞) *adj.* [< OFr. *bleu* < Frank. *blao*] **1.** having the color of the clear sky or the deep sea **2.** livid: said of the skin **3.** sad and gloomy; depressed or depressing **4.** puritanical; rigorous **5.** [Colloq.] indecent; risqué —*n.* **1.** the color of the clear sky or the deep sea **2.** any blue pigment or dye **3.** anything colored blue **4.** *a)* [*often* **B-**] one who wears a blue uniform *b)* [*pl.*] a sailor's blue uniform **5.** [*pl.*] [Colloq.] a depressed, unhappy feeling (with *the*) **6.** [*pl., also with sing. v.*] *a)* Negro folk music, or the jazz evolved from it, with minor harmonies, slow tempo, and melancholy words (often with *the*) *b)* a song in this style —*vt.* **blued, blu′ing** or **blue′ing 1.** to make blue **2.** to use bluing on or in —*vi.* to become blue —**once in a blue moon** very seldom —**out of the blue** as if from the sky; unexpectedly —**the blue 1.** the sky **2.** the sea —**blue′ness** *n.*

blue baby a baby born with cyanosis

Blue·beard (-bird′) a legendary character who married and murdered one wife after another

blue·bell (-bel′) *n.* any of various plants with blue, bell-shaped flowers

blue·ber·ry (-ber′ē, -bər ē) *n., pl.* **-ries 1.** a shrub bearing small, edible, blue-black berries with tiny seeds **2.** any of the berries

blue·bird (-burd′) *n.* any of several small N. American songbirds: the male has a blue or bluish back and an orange or reddish breast

blue blood 1. descent from nobility or royalty **2.** a person of such descent; aristocrat: also **blue′blood′** *n.*

blue·bon·net (-bän′it) *n.* **1.** a wildflower with blue blossoms, common in the SW U.S. **2.** [Chiefly Scot.] a cornflower with blue blossoms Also **blue bonnet**

blue book 1. a book listing socially prominent people **2.** a blank booklet with a blue cover in which students write examination answers: also **blue′book′** *n.*

blue·bot·tle (-bät′′l) *n.* **1.** any of several plants with blue, bottle-shaped flowers, as the cornflower, grape hyacinth, etc. **2.** a large blowfly with a steel-blue abdomen

blue cheese a cheese similar to Roquefort, but usually made of cow's milk

blue-chip (-chip′) *adj.* [after the high-value *blue chips* of poker] **1.** designating a high-priced stock with a good record of earnings and price stability **2.** [Colloq.] excellent, valuable, etc.

blue·coat (-kōt′) *n.* a policeman

blue-col·lar (-käl′ər) *adj.* [from the color of many work shirts] designating or of industrial workers, esp. the semiskilled and unskilled

Blue Cross a nonprofit health-insurance organization offering hospitalization, etc. to subscribers

blue·fish (-fish′) *n., pl.* **-fish′, -fish′es:** see FISH a bluish food fish, common along the Atlantic coast of N. America

blue flag any iris with blue flowers

blue fox 1. a mutant of the arctic fox, having bluish or smoky-gray fur **2.** this fur

blue·gill (-gil′) *n.* a bluish, freshwater sunfish

blue·grass (-gras′) *n.* **1.** any of various forage grasses, as **Kentucky bluegrass 2.** [*often* **B-**] Southern string-band folk music

blue gum a large Australian tree, grown extensively in California, with aromatic leaves and a smooth bark that peels off in strips

blue·ing (-iŋ) *n. same as* BLUING

blue·ish (-ish) *adj. same as* BLUISH

blue·jack·et (-jak′it) *n.* an enlisted man in the U.S. or British navy

blue jay a noisy, often crested, American bird with a bluish upper part: also **blue′jay′** *n.*

blue law a puritanical law, esp. one prohibiting certain activities on Sunday

blue·nose (-nōz′) *n.* [Colloq.] a puritanical person

blue-pen·cil (-pen′s′l) *vt.* **-pen′ciled** or **-pen′cilled, -pen′cil·ing** or **-pen′cil·ling** to edit, cross out, etc. with or as with a blue pencil

blue·point (-point′) *n.* [< *Blue Point,* Long Island] a small oyster, usually eaten raw

blue·print (-print′) *n.* **1.** a photographic reproduction in white on a blue background, as of architectural plans **2.** any detailed plan —*vt.* to make a blueprint of

blue-rib·bon (-rib′ən) *adj.* [Colloq.] **1.** outstanding of its kind **2.** specially selected, as a jury

blue ribbon first prize in a competition

Blue Ridge Mountains easternmost range of the Appalachians, extending from S Pa. to N Ga.

blue·stock·ing (-stäk′iŋ) *n.* [from the blue stockings worn at literary meetings in 18th-c. London] a learned, bookish, or pedantic woman

blue streak [Colloq.] anything thought of as like a streak of lightning in speed, vividness, etc.

blu·et (bloo͞′it) *n.* [< Fr. dim. of *bleu,* blue] a small plant having little, pale-blue flowers

blue whale a whalebone whale with a dark blue-gray body: the largest animal that has ever lived

bluff[1] (bluf) *vt., vi.* [prob. < Du. *bluffen,* to baffle] **1.** to mislead by a false, bold front **2.** to frighten by threats that cannot be made good **3.** to manage to get (one's way) by bluffing —*n.* **1.** a bluffing **2.** a person who bluffs: also **bluff′er**

bluff[2] (bluf) *adj.* [< Du. *blaf,* flat] **1.** having a broad, flat front that slopes steeply **2.** having a rough, frank, but affable manner —*n.* a high, steep bank or cliff —**bluff′ly** *adv.*

blu·ing (bloo͞′iŋ) *n.* a blue liquid, powder, etc. used in rinsing white fabrics to prevent yellowing

blu·ish (-ish) *adj.* somewhat blue

blun·der (blun′dər) *vi.* [< ON. *blunda,* to shut the eyes] **1.** to move clumsily or carelessly; flounder; stumble **2.** to make a foolish mistake —*vt.* **1.** to say stupidly or confusedly; blurt (*out*) **2.** to do clumsily or poorly; bungle —*n.* a foolish or stupid mistake —**blun′der·er** *n.* —**blun′der·ing·ly** *adv.*

blun·der·buss (-bus′) *n.* [Du. *donderbus,* thunder box: altered after prec.] **1.** an obsolete short gun with a broad muzzle **2.** a person who blunders

blunt (blunt) *adj.* [< ?] **1.** slow to perceive; dull **2.** having a dull edge or point **3.** plain-spoken and abrupt —*vt.* **1.** to make dull or insensitive **2.** to make less effective —*vi.* to become dull —**blunt′ly** *adv.* —**blunt′ness** *n.*

blur (blur) *vt., vi.* **blurred, blur′ring** [? akin to BLEAR] **1.** to smear or smudge **2.** to make or become less distinct or clear **3.** to dim or dull —*n.* **1.** the state of being blurred **2.** an obscuring stain or blot **3.** anything indistinct to the sight or mind —**blur′ri·ness** *n.* —**blur′ry** *adj.*

blurb (blurb) *n.* [arbitrary coinage (c. 1907) by Gelett Burgess (1866–1951), U.S. humorist] [Colloq.] an advertisement, as on a book jacket, esp. a very laudatory one

blurt (blurt) *vt.* [prob. echoic] to say suddenly, without stopping to think (with *out*)

blush (blush) *vi.* [< OE. *blyscan,* to shine] **1.** to become red in the face from shame, embarrassment, etc. **2.** to be ashamed or embarrassed (*at* or *for*) **3.** to be or become rosy —*n.* **1.** a reddening of the face, as from shame **2.** a rosy color *[*the *blush* of youth*]* —*adj.* rosy *[blush*-pink*]* —**at first blush** at first sight; without further thought —**blush′ful** *adj.* —**blush′ing·ly** *adv.*

blush·er (-ər) *n.* **1.** a person who blushes, esp. one who blushes readily **2.** any of various cosmetic powders, gels, creams, etc. applied to the face to give it color

blus·ter (blus′tər) *vi.* [< or akin to LowG. *blüstern*] **1.** to blow stormily: said of wind **2.** to speak or behave in a noisy, swaggering, or bullying way —*vt.* **1.** to force by blustering **2.** to say noisily and aggressively —*n.* **1.** noisy commotion **2.** noisy swaggering or bullying talk —**blus′ter·er** *n.* —**blus′ter·ing·ly** *adv.* —**blus′ter·y, blus′ter·ous** *adj.*

blvd. boulevard

BM **1.** bench mark **2.** [Colloq.] bowel movement
BMR basal metabolic rate
BO, B.O. **1.** body odor **2.** box office
b.o. **1.** back order **2.** branch office
bo·a (bō′ə) ***n.*** [L.] **1.** any of a number of tropical snakes that crush their prey in their coils, as the anaconda **2.** a woman's long, fluffy scarf, as of feathers
boa constrictor a species of boa that is 10 to 15 feet long
boar (bôr) ***n., pl.*** **boars, boar:** see PLURAL, II, D 1 [OE. *bar*] **1.** an uncastrated male hog or pig **2.** a wild hog of Europe, Africa, and Asia
board (bôrd) ***n.*** [< OE. *bord,* plank & OFr. *bord,* side of a ship] **1.** a long, broad, flat piece of sawed wood ready for use **2.** a flat piece of wood or other material for some special use *[a bulletin board, diving board]* **3.** *a)* a construction material made in thin, flat, rectangular sheets *[fiberboard] b)* pasteboard or stiff paper, often used in book covers **4.** *a)* a table for meals *b)* food served at a table; esp., meals provided regularly for pay **5.** a council table **6.** a group of administrators; council **7.** a stock exchange or its listings **8.** the side of a ship *[overboard]* **9.** a rim or border *[seaboard]* —***vt.*** **1.** to cover or close (*up*) with boards **2.** to provide with meals, or room and meals, regularly for pay **3.** to come onto the deck of (a ship) **4.** to get on (an airplane, bus, etc.) —***vi.*** to receive meals, or room and meals, regularly for pay —**across the board** **1.** *Horse Racing* to win, place, and show: said of betting **2.** including all classes or groups —**go by the board** **1.** to be swept overboard **2.** to be got rid of, lost, etc. —**on board** on or in a ship, aircraft, bus, etc. —**the boards** the stage (of a theater)
board·er (bôr′dər) ***n.*** **1.** one who boards at a boardinghouse, etc. **2.** one who boards a ship, etc.
board foot *pl.* **board feet** a unit of measure of lumber, equal to a board one foot square and one inch thick
board·ing·house (-hous′) ***n.*** a house where meals, or room and meals, can be had for pay: also **boarding house**
boarding school a school providing lodging and meals for the pupils
board of health a local government agency that supervises public health
board·walk (bôrd′wôk′) ***n.*** a walk made of boards, esp. one elevated and placed along a beach
boast (bōst) ***vi.*** [< Anglo-Fr.] **1.** to talk about deeds, abilities, etc. with too much pride and satisfaction; brag **2.** to be vainly proud; exult —***vt.*** **1.** to brag about **2.** to glory in having or doing (something); be proud of —***n.*** **1.** the act of one who boasts **2.** anything boasted of —**boast′er** ***n.*** —**boast′ing·ly** ***adv.***
boast·ful (-fəl) ***adj.*** inclined to brag; boasting —**boast′ful·ly** ***adv.*** —**boast′ful·ness** ***n.***
boat (bōt) ***n.*** [OE. *bat*] **1.** a small, open vessel or watercraft propelled by oars, sails, or engine **2.** a large vessel; ship: landsman's term **3.** a boat-shaped dish *[a gravy boat]* —***vt.*** to lay or carry in the boat *[boat the oars]* —***vi.*** to row, sail, or cruise in a boat —**in the same boat** in the same unfavorable situation —**miss the boat** [Colloq.] to fail to make the most of an opportunity —**rock the boat** [Colloq.] to disturb the status quo —**boat′er** ***n.***
boat·house (bōt′hous′) ***n.*** a building for storing a boat or boats
boat·ing (-iŋ) ***n.*** rowing, sailing, or cruising
boat·load (-lōd′) ***n.*** **1.** all the freight or passengers that a boat can carry or contain **2.** the load carried by a boat
boat·man (-mən) ***n., pl.*** **-men** a man who operates, works on, rents, or sells boats
boat·swain (bō′s'n) ***n.*** a ship's warrant officer or petty officer in charge of the deck crew, the rigging, anchors, etc.
bob[1] (bäb) ***n.*** [ME. *bobbe,* hanging cluster; senses 4 & 5 < the *v.*] **1.** a knoblike weight hanging as at the end of a plumb line **2.** a docked tail, as of a horse **3.** a woman's or girl's short haircut **4.** a quick, jerky motion **5.** a float on a fishing line: now usually **bob′ber** —***vt.*** **bobbed, bob′bing** [ME. *bobben,* to knock against] **1.** to move, esp. up and down, with short, jerky motions **2.** to cut (hair, a tail, etc.) short —***vi.*** **1.** to move with short, jerky motions **2.** to try to catch hanging or floating fruit with the teeth (with *for*) —**bob up** to appear unexpectedly or suddenly
bob[2] (bäb) ***n., pl.*** **bob** [< ? *Bob,* nickname for ROBERT] [Brit. Slang] a shilling
bob·bin (bäb′in) ***n.*** [Fr. *bobine*] a reel or spool for thread or yarn, used in spinning, weaving, machine sewing, etc.
bob·ble (bäb′'l) ***n.*** [< BOB[1], *v.*] **1.** a bobbing, up-and-down movement **2.** [Colloq.] an awkward juggling of a ball in trying to catch it —***vi.*** **-bled, -bling** to move jerkily; bob —***vt.*** [Colloq.] to deal with awkwardly; specif., to make a bobble with (a ball); muff; bungle
bob·by (bäb′ē) ***n., pl.*** **-bies** [after Sir Robert (*Bobby*) Peel (1788–1850), who reorganized the London police force] [Brit. Colloq.] a policeman
bobby pin [from use with *bobbed* hair] a metal hairpin with the sides pressing close together
bobby socks (or **sox**) [< BOB[1] (*vt.* 2)] [Colloq.] girls' socks that reach just above the ankle
bob·cat (bäb′kat′) ***n., pl.*** **-cats′, -cat′:** see PLURAL, II, D, 1 [< its short tail] *same as* BAY LYNX
bob·o·link (bäb′ə liŋk′) ***n.*** [echoic, after its call] a migratory songbird of N. America
bob·sled (-sled′) ***n.*** a long sled with two sets of runners one behind the other, steering apparatus, and brakes: it is ridden by a team of four or two men in races down a prepared run —***vi.*** **-sled′ded, -sled′ding** to ride or race on a bobsled

BOBSLED

bob·stay (-stā′) ***n.*** a rope or chain for tying down a bowsprit to keep it from bobbing
bob·tail (-tāl′) ***n.*** **1.** a tail cut short; docked tail **2.** a horse or dog with a bobtail —***adj.*** **1.** having a bobtail **2.** cut short; abbreviated —***vt.*** **1.** to dock the tail of **2.** to cut short; curtail
bob·white (bäb′hwīt′, -wīt′) ***n., pl.*** **-whites′, -white′:** see PLURAL, II, D, 1 [echoic, after its call] a small N. American quail having markings of brown and white on a gray body
Boc·cac·cio (bō kä′chē ō′; *It.* bô kät′chô), **Gio·van·ni** (jô-vän′nē) 1313–75; It. writer
boc·cie, boc·ce, boc·ci (bäch′ē) ***n.*** [It. *bocce*] an Italian game similar to bowls
bock (bäk) ***n.*** [G. < *bockbier* < *Einbecker bier* < *Einbeck,* Hanover, where first brewed] a dark beer traditionally drunk in the spring: also **bock beer**
bode[1] (bōd) ***vt.*** **bod′ed, bod′ing** [< OE. < *boda,* messenger] to be an omen of; presage —**bode ill** (or **well**) to be a bad (or good) omen
bode[2] (bōd) *alt. pt. of* BIDE
bod·ice (bäd′is) ***n.*** [altered < *bodies,* pl. of *body*] **1.** the upper part of a woman's dress **2.** a kind of vest worn over a blouse or dress by women or girls, usually laced in front
bod·ied (bäd′ēd) ***adj.*** having a body or substance, esp. of a specified kind *[able-bodied]*
bod·i·less (-ē lis) ***adj.*** without a body; having no material substance; incorporeal
bod·i·ly (-'l ē) ***adj.*** of, in, by, or to the body —***adv.*** **1.** in person; in the flesh **2.** as a single body; in entirety
bod·kin (bäd′k'n) ***n.*** [ME. *boidekyn* < ?] **1.** a pointed instrument for making holes in cloth **2.** a long, ornamental hairpin **3.** a thick, blunt needle **4.** [Obs.] a dagger
bod·y (bäd′ē) ***n., pl.*** **bod′ies** [< OE. *bodig,* trunk, orig. sense "cask"] **1.** the whole physical substance of a person, animal, or plant **2.** *a)* the trunk or torso of a man or animal *b)* the part of a garment that covers the trunk **3.** a dead person; corpse **4.** the flesh, as opposed to the spirit **5.** [Colloq.] a person **6.** a group of people or things regarded as a unit *[an advisory body]* **7.** the main or central part of anything **8.** a portion or mass of matter *[a body of water]* **9.** density or consistency, as of a liquid, fabric, etc. **10.** richness of tone or flavor —***vt.*** **bod′ied, bod′y·ing** to give a body or substance to —**body forth** to give shape or form to —**keep body and soul together** to stay alive
body English [cf. ENGLISH (*n.* 3)] a follow-through motion of the body, as after bowling a ball, in a joking effort to control its movement
bod·y·guard (-gärd′) ***n.*** a person or persons, usually armed, assigned to guard someone
body language gestures, unconscious body movements, facial expressions, etc. which serve as nonverbal communication or as accompaniments to speech
body politic the people who collectively constitute a political unit under a government
body stocking a tightfitting garment, usually of one piece, that covers the torso and, sometimes, the legs
bod·y·suit (-so͞ot′) ***n.*** a one-piece, tightfitting, sleeved or sleeveless garment that covers the torso, usually worn with slacks, a skirt, etc.: also **body shirt**
bod·y·surf (-surf′) ***vi.*** to engage in the sport of surfing, lying prone on the wave without the use of a surfboard
Boe·o·tia (bē ō′shə) region in EC Greece: in ancient times, a region dominated by Thebes —**Boe·o′tian** ***adj., n.***
Boer (bôr, boor, bō′ər) ***n.*** [Du. *boer,* peasant: see BOOR] a South African whose ancestors were Dutch colonists
bog (bäg, bôg) ***n.*** [< Gael. & Ir. *bog,* soft, moist] wet, spongy ground; a small marsh or swamp —***vt., vi.*** **bogged, bog′ging** to sink or become stuck in or as in a bog (often with *down*); mire —**bog′gi·ness** ***n.***
bo·gey (bō′gē) ***n., pl.*** **-geys** **1.** *same as* BOGY **2.** [after Colonel *Bogey,* imaginary first-rate golfer] *Golf* par or, now usually, one stroke more than par on a hole —***vt.*** **-geyed, -gey·ing** *Golf* to score one over par on (a hole)
bog·gle (bäg′'l) ***vi.*** **-gled, -gling** [< Scot. *bogle,* specter;

now associated with BUNGLE] **1.** to be startled or frightened (*at*); shy away **2.** to hesitate (*at*); have scruples **3.** to be or become confused —*vt.* **1.** to bungle; botch **2.** to confuse or stagger (the mind) —*n.* a boggling

bo·gie (bō′gē) *n., pl.* **-gies** [< Brit. Dial.] **1.** an undercarriage on a railroad car **2.** any of the wheels supporting the tread of an armored tank

Bo·go·tá (bō′gə tä′) capital of Colombia, in the C part: pop. 2,148,000

bo·gus (bō′gəs) *adj.* [< ?] not genuine; counterfeit

bo·gy (bō′gē, boog′ē) *n., pl.* **-gies** [see BOGGLE] **1.** an imaginary evil spirit; goblin **2.** anything causing great, often needless, fear; bugbear

bo·gy·man, bo·gey·man (bō′gē man′, boog′ē-) *n., pl.* **-men′** (-men′) an imaginary frightful being, esp. one used as a threat in disciplining children

Bo·he·mi·a (bō hē′mē ə) region and former province of W Czechoslovakia: earlier, a kingdom

Bo·he·mi·an (-ən) *n.* **1.** a native or inhabitant of Bohemia **2.** *same as* CZECH (*n.* 2) **3.** a gypsy **4.** [*often* **b-**] an artist, poet, etc. who lives in an unconventional, nonconforming way —*adj.* **1.** of Bohemia, its people, or their language; Czech **2.** [*often* **b-**] like or characteristic of a Bohemian (*n.* 4) —**Bo·he′mi·an·ism** *n.*

Bohr (bôr), **Niels (Henrik David)** (nēlz) 1885–1962; Dan. theoretical physicist

boil[1] (boil) *vi.* [< OFr. < L. < *bulla,* a bubble] **1.** to bubble up and vaporize by being heated **2.** to seethe like boiling liquids **3.** to be agitated, as with rage **4.** to cook in boiling water or other liquid —*vt.* **1.** to heat to the boiling point **2.** to cook or process in boiling water, etc. —*n.* the act or state of boiling —**boil away** to evaporate by boiling —**boil down 1.** to lessen in quantity by boiling **2.** to condense; summarize —**boil over 1.** to come to a boil and spill over the rim **2.** to lose one's temper

boil[2] (boil) *n.* [< OE. *byl*] an inflamed, painful, pus-filled swelling on the skin, caused by infection

boil·er (boi′lər) *n.* **1.** a container in which things are boiled or heated **2.** a tank in which water is turned to steam for heating or power **3.** a tank for heating water and storing it

boil·er·mak·er (-mā′kər) *n.* **1.** a worker who makes or repairs boilers **2.** [Colloq.] a drink of whiskey in beer or with beer as a chaser

boiling point the temperature at which a specified liquid boils: water at sea level boils at 212°F or 100°C

Boi·se (boi′sē, -zē) [< Fr. *boisé,* wooded] capital of Ida.: pop. 102,000: also **Boise City**

bois·ter·ous (bois′tər əs) *adj.* [ME. *boistreous,* crude, coarse < *boistous,* violent] **1.** rough and stormy **2.** *a*) noisy and unruly *b*) loud and exuberant —**bois′ter·ous·ly** *adv.* —**bois′ter·ous·ness** *n.*

bok choy (bäk choi) [Cantonese, white vegetable] a variety of CHINESE CABBAGE

bo·la (bō′lə) *n.* [Sp., a ball < L. *bulla,* a bubble] a throwing weapon made of a long cord or thong with heavy balls at the ends: also **bo′las** (-ləs)

bold (bōld) *adj.* [< OE. *beald*] **1.** daring; fearless **2.** taking liberties; impudent **3.** steep or abrupt **4.** prominent and clear [to write a *bold* hand] —**make bold** to dare (*to*) —**bold′ly** *adv.* —**bold′ness** *n.*

bold·face (bōld′fās′) *n.* a printing type with a heavy, dark face (Ex.: **face**)

bold·faced (-fāst′) *adj.* impudent; forward

bole (bōl) *n.* [ON. *bolr*] a tree trunk

bo·le·ro (bə ler′ō, bō-) *n., pl.* **-ros** [Sp.] **1.** a Spanish dance in 3/4 time **2.** music for this **3.** a sleeveless or sleeved jacket that ends at the waist and is open in front

bo·lí·var (bō lē′vär, bäl′ə vər) *n., pl.* **bo·lí·var·es** (bō′li vä′res), **bo·lí′vars** [after ff.] *see* MONETARY UNITS, table (Venezuela)

Bol·í·var (bäl′ə vər; *Sp.* bô lē′vär), **Si·món** (*Sp.* sē môn′) 1783–1830; S. American general & revolutionary leader

Bo·liv·i·a (bə liv′ē ə) country in WC S. America: 424,000 sq. mi.; pop. 4,804,000; capitals, La Paz & Sucre —**Bo·liv′i·an** *adj., n.*

boll (bōl) *n.* [< OE. *bolla,* a bowl] the roundish seed pod of a plant, esp. of cotton or flax

bol·lix (bäl′iks) *vt.* [< OE. *beallucas,* testicles] [Slang] to bungle or botch (usually with *up*)

boll weevil a small, grayish weevil whose larvae destroy the cotton bolls in which they are hatched

bo·lo (bō′lō) *n., pl.* **-los** [Sp. < native name] a large, single-edged knife used in the Philippines

Bo·lo·gna (bô lô′nyä; *E.* bə lō′nə) city in NC Italy: pop. 485,000 —*n.* [*usually* **b-**] (bə lō′nē, -nyə, -nə) a large, smoked sausage of various meats: also **bologna sausage**

bo·lo tie (bō′lō) [altered from *bola tie:* see BOLA] a man's string tie held together with a slide device

Bol·she·vik (bōl′shə vik′, bäl′-) *n., pl.* **-viks′, Bol′she·vi′ki** (-vē′kē) [Russ. < *bolshe,* the majority] [*also* **b-**] **1.** orig., a member of a majority faction of the Social Democratic Party of Russia, which formed the Communist Party after seizing power in the 1917 Revolution **2.** a Communist, esp. of the Soviet Union **3.** loosely, any radical: hostile usage —*adj.* [*also* **b-**] of or like the Bolsheviks or Bolshevism —**Bol′she·vism** *n.* —**Bol′she·vist** *n., adj.* —**Bol′she·vize′** (-vīz′) *vt.* **-vized′, -viz′ing**

bol·ster (bōl′stər) *n.* [OE.] **1.** a long, narrow cushion or pillow **2.** a soft pad **3.** any bolsterlike object or support —*vt.* to prop up as with a bolster; support or strengthen (often with *up*)

bolt[1] (bōlt) *n.* [OE.] **1.** an arrow with a thick, blunt head, shot from a crossbow **2.** a flash of lightning **3.** a sudden dash or movement **4.** a sliding bar for locking a door, etc. **5.** a similar bar in a lock, moved by a key **6.** a metal rod with a head, threaded and used with a nut to hold parts together **7.** a roll (*of* cloth, paper, etc.) of a given length **8.** a withdrawal from one's party or group **9.** *Firearms* a sliding bar that pushes the cartridge into place and extracts the empty cartridge case after firing —*vt.* **1.** [Archaic] to shoot (an arrow, etc.) **2.** to say suddenly; blurt (*out*) **3.** to swallow (food) hurriedly; gulp down **4.** to fasten as with a bolt **5.** to roll (cloth, etc.) into bolts **6.** to abandon (a party, group, etc.) —*vi.* **1.** to dash or spring away suddenly; dart **2.** to withdraw support from a party, group, etc. —*adv.* straight; erectly [to sit *bolt* upright] —**bolt from the blue** a sudden, unforeseen occurrence, often an unfortunate one —**shoot one's bolt** to exhaust one's capabilities —**bolt′er** *n.*

bolt[2] (bōlt) *vt.* [< OFr. *buleter* < ?] **1.** to sift (flour, grain, etc.) so as to separate and grade **2.** to examine closely —**bolt′er** *n.*

bo·lus (bō′ləs) *n., pl.* **bo′lus·es** [L. < Gr. *bōlos,* a lump] **1.** a small, round lump, as of chewed food **2.** a large pill

bomb (bäm) *n.* [< Fr. < It. < L. < Gr. *bombos,* hollow sound] **1.** a container filled with an explosive, incendiary, or other chemical, for dropping or hurling, or for detonating by a timing mechanism **2.** a sudden, surprising occurrence **3.** an aerosol container **4.** a shielded device containing radioactive material, used in radiotherapy [a cobalt *bomb*] **5.** [Slang] a complete failure: said esp. of a performance or show —*vt.* to attack or destroy with a bomb or bombs —*vi.* [Slang] to have a complete failure

bom·bard (bäm bärd′; *for n.* bäm′bärd) *vt.* [< Fr. < *bombarde,* mortar < *bombe,* BOMB] **1.** to attack with or as with artillery or bombs **2.** to keep attacking with questions, suggestions, etc. **3.** to direct a stream of particles, as neutrons, against —*n.* an early type of cannon, hurling stones —**bom·bard′ment** *n.*

bom·bar·dier (bäm′bə dir′, -bər-) *n.* a person who releases the bombs in a bomber

bom·bast (bäm′bast) *n.* [< OFr. < ML. < *bambax,* cotton < LGr. < Per. *pambak,* cotton] pompous, high-sounding talk or writing

bom·bas·tic (bäm bas′tik) *adj.* using or characterized by high-sounding but unimportant or meaningless language; pompous —**bom·bas′ti·cal·ly** *adv.*

Bom·bay (bäm′bā′) seaport in W India, on the Arabian Sea: pop. 4,152,000

bomb bay a compartment in the fuselage of a bomber that can be opened to drop bombs

bom·ba·zine (bäm′bə zēn′, bäm′bə zēn′) *n.* [< Fr. < ML. < *bambax:* see BOMBAST] a twilled cloth of silk or rayon with worsted, often dyed black

bomb·er (bäm′ər) *n.* **1.** an airplane designed for dropping bombs **2.** a person who uses bombs as for illegal purposes

bomb·proof (bäm′prōōf′) *adj.* capable of withstanding the force of ordinary bombs

bomb·shell (-shel′) *n. same as* BOMB (*n.* 1, 2)

bomb·sight (-sīt′) *n.* an instrument on a bomber for aiming the bombs

bo·na fi·de (bō′nə fīd′, bän′ə; bō′nə fī′dē) [L.] in good faith; without fraud or deceit

bo·nan·za (bə nan′zə, bō-) *n.* [Sp., prosperity, ult. < Gr. *malakia,* a calm at sea] **1.** a rich vein of ore **2.** any source of wealth or profits

Bo·na·parte (bō′nə pärt′; *Fr.* bô nä pärt′) Corsican family including NAPOLEON I & LOUIS NAPOLEON

bon·bon (bän′bän′) *n.* [Fr. *bon,* good] a small piece of candy, esp. one with a creamy filling

bond[1] (bänd) *n.* [ME. *bond, band:* see BAND[1]] **1.** anything that binds, fastens, or unites; specif., glue, solder, etc. **2.** [*pl.*] *a*) fetters; shackles *b*) [Archaic] imprisonment **3.** a binding or uniting force; tie; link **4.** a binding agreement; covenant **5.** the status of goods kept in a warehouse until taxes are paid **6.** *same as* BOND PAPER **7.** *Chem.* the means by which atoms or groups of atoms are combined in molecules **8.** *Finance* an interest-bearing certificate issued by a government or business, promising to pay the holder a specified sum on a specified date **9.** *Law* *a*) a written obligation to pay specified sums, do or not do specified things, etc. *b*) an amount paid as surety or bail *c*) [Archaic] a bondsman —*vt.* **1.** to fasten or unite as with a bond **2.** to furnish a bond, or bail, and thus become a surety for (someone) **3.** to place (goods) under bond **4.** to issue bonds (sense 8) on; mortgage **5.** to put under bonded debt —*vi.* to hold together by or as by a bond —**bottled in bond** bottled and stored in bonded warehouses for the length of time stated on the label, as some whiskey —**bond′a·ble** *adj.* —**bond′er** *n.*

bond[2] (bänd) *n.* [see ff.] [Obs.] a serf or slave —*adj.* in serfdom or slavery

bond·age (bän′dij) *n.* [< Anglo-L. < OE. *bonda* < ON. *bonde* < *bua*, to inhabit] **1.** serfdom; slavery **2.** subjection to some force or influence

bond·ed (-did) *adj.* **1.** subject to or secured by a bond or bonds **2.** placed in a government-certified, or bonded, warehouse pending payment of taxes

bond·hold·er (bänd′hōl′dər) *n.* an owner of bonds issued by a company, government, or person

bond·man (-mən) *n.*, *pl.* **-men** **1.** a feudal serf **2.** a man or boy bondservant —**bond′maid′** *n.fem.* —**bond′wom′an** *n.fem.*, *pl.* **-wom′en**

bond paper a strong, superior stock of paper, esp. of rag pulp, used for documents, letterheads, etc.

bond·ser·vant (-sur′vənt) *n.* **1.** a person bound to service without pay **2.** a slave

bonds·man (bändz′mən) *n.*, *pl.* **-men** **1.** *same as* BONDMAN **2.** a person who takes responsibility for another by furnishing a bond; surety

bone (bōn) *n.* [OE. *ban*] **1.** any of the pieces of hard tissue forming the skeleton of most vertebrate animals **2.** this hard tissue **3.** [*pl.*] *a*) the skeleton *b*) the body **4.** a bonelike substance or part **5.** a thing made of bone, plastic, etc.; specif., *a*) a corset stay *b*) [*pl.*] [Colloq.] dice **6.** [*pl.*] *a*) flat sticks used as clappers in minstrel shows *b*) [*with sing. v.*] an end man in a minstrel show **7.** *same as* BONE WHITE —*vt.* **boned, bon′ing** **1.** to remove the bones from **2.** to put whalebone, etc. into — *vi.* [Slang] to study hard and hurriedly; cram (usually with *up*) —**feel in one's bones** to be certain without any real reason —**have a bone to pick** to have something to quarrel about —**make no bones about** [Colloq.] to make no attempt to hide; admit freely —**bone′like′** *adj.*

bone-dry (bōn′drī′) *adj.* dry as bone; very dry

bone·head (-hed′) *n.* [Slang] a stupid person

bone·less (-lis) *adj.* without bones; specif., with the bones removed

bone meal crushed or finely ground bones, used as feed for stock or as fertilizer

bon·er (bōn′ər) *n.* [Slang] a stupid blunder

bone·set (-set′) *n.* a plant of the composite family, with flat clusters of white flowers: used in folk medicine

bone white any of various shades of grayish-white or yellowish-white

bon·fire (bän′fīr′) *n.* [ME. *banefyre*, bone fire; later, funeral pyre] a large fire built outdoors

bong (bôŋ, bäŋ) *n.* [echoic] a deep, ringing sound, as of a large bell —*vi.* to make this sound

bon·go (bäŋ′gō) *n.*, *pl.* **-gos** [AmSp. < ?] either of a pair of small joined drums, of different pitch, struck with the fingers: in full, **bongo drum**

BONGO DRUMS

bon·ho·mie, bon·hom·mie (bän′ə-mē′; *Fr.* bô nô mē′) *n.* [Fr. < *bon*, good + *homme*, man] good nature; pleasant, affable manner; amiability

bo·ni·to (bə nēt′ō) *n.*, *pl.* **-tos, -toes, -to**: see PLURAL, II, D, 1 [Sp.] any of several saltwater fishes of the mackerel family, related to the tuna

‡**bon jour** (bōn zhōōr′) [Fr.] good day; hello

bon mot (bōn′mō′; *Fr.* bōn mō′) *pl.* **bons mots** (bōn′mōz′; *Fr.* bōn mō′) [Fr., lit., good word] an apt, clever, or witty remark

Bonn (bän) capital of West Germany, on the Rhine: pop. 138,000

bon·net (bän′it) *n.* [OFr. *bonet*] **1.** a flat, brimless cap, worn by men and boys in Scotland **2.** *a*) a hat with a chin ribbon, worn by babies or girls *b*) [Colloq.] any hat for a woman or girl **3.** *short for* WAR BONNET **4.** *a*) a metal covering, as over a fireplace *b*) [Brit.] an automobile hood —*vt.* to put a bonnet on

bon·ny, bon·nie (bän′ē) *adj.* **-ni·er, -ni·est** [< Fr. *bon*, good < L. *bonus*] [Now Chiefly Scot. or Eng. Dial.] **1.** handsome or pretty, with a healthy, cheerful glow **2.** fine; pleasant —**bon′ni·ly** *adv.* —**bon′ni·ness** *n.*

bon·sai (bän sī′) *n.* [Jap., lit., tray arrangement] **1.** the art of dwarfing and shaping trees, shrubs, etc. **2.** *pl.* **bon-sai′** such a tree or shrub

‡**bon soir** (bōn swȧr′) [Fr.] good evening

bo·nus (bō′nəs) *n.*, *pl.* **bo′nus·es** [L., good] anything given or paid in addition to the customary or required amount as an incentive, reward, etc.

bon vi·vant (bän′ vi vänt′; *Fr.* bōn vē vän′) *pl.* **bons vi-vants** (bän′ vi vänts′; *Fr.* bōn vē vän′) [Fr.] one who enjoys good food and other luxuries

bon voy·age (bän′voi äzh′; *Fr.* bōn vwȧ yȧzh′) [Fr.] pleasant journey: a farewell to a traveler

bon·y (bō′nē) *adj.* **bon′i·er, bon′i·est** **1.** of or like bone **2.** having many bones **3.** having protruding bones **4.** thin; emaciated —**bon′i·ness** *n.*

boo (bōō) *interj.*, *n.*, *pl.* **boos** [echoic] a prolonged sound made to show disapproval, scorn, etc., or, more abruptly, to startle —*vi.*, *vt.* **booed, boo′ing** to make this sound (at)

boob (bōōb) *n.* [Slang] a booby; foolish person

boo-boo, boo·boo (bōō′bōō′) *n.*, *pl.* **-boos′** **1.** [Slang] a stupid or foolish mistake **2.** a minor injury or bruise: child's usage

boo·by (bōō′bē) *n.*, *pl.* **-bies** [prob. < Sp. *bobo*, stupid] **1.** a stupid or foolish person **2.** a tropical, diving sea bird related to the gannet **3.** the one doing worst in a game, contest, etc.

booby prize a prize, usually ridiculous, given in fun to whoever has done worst in a game, race, etc.

booby trap **1.** any device for tricking a person unawares **2.** a mine set to be exploded by some action of the unsuspecting victim —**boo′by-trap′** *vt.* **-trapped′, -trap′ping**

boo·dle (bōō′d'l) *n.* [< Du. *boedel*, property] [Slang] **1.** the entire lot; caboodle **2.** something given as a bribe **3.** the loot taken in a robbery

boo·gie-woo·gie (boog′ē woog′ē) *n.* [? echoic of the characteristic "walking" bass] a style of jazz piano playing in which repeated bass figures in 8/8 rhythm accompany the melodic variations

boo·hoo (bōō′hōō′) *vi.* **-hooed′, -hoo′ing** [echoic] to weep noisily —*n.*, *pl.* **-hoos′** noisy weeping

book (book) *n.* [OE. *boc*, pl. *bec*, akin to OE. *bece*, beech: runes were first carved on beech tablets] **1.** *a*) a number of sheets of paper, etc. with writing or printing on them, fastened together along one edge, usually between protective covers *b*) a relatively long literary work, scientific writing, etc. **2.** a main division of a literary work **3.** *a*) a number of blank or ruled sheets or printed forms bound together [*an account book*] *b*) a record or account kept in this **4.** the words of an opera, etc.; libretto **5.** a booklike package, as of matches or tickets **6.** a record of bets, as on horse races **7.** *Bridge*, etc. a specified number of tricks that must be won before scoring can take place —*vt.* **1.** to record in a book; list **2.** to engage (rooms, performers, etc.) ahead of time **3.** to record charges against on a police record —*adj.* in, from, or according to books or accounts —**bring to book** **1.** to force to explain **2.** to reprimand —**by the book** according to the rules —**close the books** *Bookkeeping* to make no further entries —**in one's book** in one's opinion —**keep books** to keep a record of business transactions —**know like a book** to know well or fully —**make book** [Slang] to make or accept bets —**on the books** **1.** recorded **2.** enrolled —**the Book** the Bible —**throw the book at** [Slang] **1.** to place all possible charges against (an accused person) **2.** to give the maximum punishment to —**book′er** *n.*

book·bind·ing (-bīn′diŋ) *n.* the art, trade, or business of binding books —**book′bind′er** *n.* —**book′bind′er·y** *n.*, *pl.* **-er·ies**

book·case (-kās′) *n.* a set of shelves or a cabinet for holding books

book club an organization that sells books, usually at reduced prices, to members who undertake to buy a minimum number of them annually

book·end (-end′) *n.* an ornamental weight or bracket at the end of a row of books to keep them upright

book·ie (-ē) *n.* [Slang] *same as* BOOKMAKER (sense 2)

book·ing (-iŋ) *n.* an engagement, as for a lecture, performance, etc.

book·ish (-ish) *adj.* **1.** of books **2.** inclined to read and study; scholarly **3.** having mere book learning; pedantic; stodgy —**book′ish·ness** *n.*

book·keep·ing (-kēp′iŋ) *n.* the work of keeping a systematic record of business transactions —**book′keep′er** *n.*

book learning knowledge gained from reading or formal education rather than from practical experience: also **book′lore′** (-lôr′) *n.*

book·let (-lit) *n.* a small, often paper-covered book

book·mak·er (-māk′ər) *n.* **1.** a maker of books **2.** a person in the business of taking bets, as on horse races —**book′mak′ing** *n.*

book·mark (-märk′) *n.* anything slipped between the pages of a book to mark a place

book·mo·bile (-mō bēl′, -mə-) ***n.*** [BOOK + (AUTO)MOBILE] a traveling lending library moved from place to place in a truck

Book of Common Prayer the official book of services and prayers used in Anglican churches

book·plate (-plāt′) ***n.*** a label pasted in a book to identify its owner

book·rest (-rest′) ***n.*** *same as* BOOKSTAND (sense 1)

book review an article or talk in which a book is discussed and critically analyzed

book·sell·er (-sel′ər) ***n.*** the owner or manager of a bookstore

book·shelf (-shelf′) ***n., pl.*** **-shelves′** a shelf on which books are kept

book·stack (-stak′) ***n.*** a series of bookshelves, one over the other, as in a library

book·stall (-stôl′) ***n.*** a stand, booth, or counter, often one outdoors, where books are sold

book·stand (-stand′) ***n.*** **1.** a stand for holding a book open before a reader **2.** *same as* BOOKSTALL

book·store (-stôr′) ***n.*** a store where books are sold: also **book′shop′**

book value the value as shown in account books; specif., the value of the capital stock of a business as shown by the excess of assets over liabilities

book·worm (-wurm′) ***n.*** **1.** an insect or insect larva that harms books by feeding on the binding, paste, etc. **2.** one who reads or studies much

boom[1] (bo͞om) ***vi.*** [echoic] to make a deep, hollow, resonant sound —***vt.*** to utter with such a sound —***n.*** a booming sound, as of thunder, heavy guns, etc.

boom[2] (bo͞om) ***n.*** [Du., a tree, beam] **1.** a spar extending from a mast to hold the bottom of a sail outstretched **2.** a long beam extending as from an upright to lift and guide something **3.** a barrier of chains or timbers to keep ships out or to keep floating logs in **4.** *Aeron.* a retractable metal tube for transferring fuel from one plane to another in flight —***vt.*** **1.** to stretch out (sails) with a boom **2.** to place a boom in (a river, etc.) —***vi.*** to sail or move at top speed (usually with *along*) —**lower the boom** [Colloq.] to act forcefully in punishing, criticizing, etc.

boom[3] (bo͞om) ***vi.*** [< ? prec. *vi.*; later associated with BOOM[1]] to increase suddenly or grow swiftly; flourish *[business boomed]* —***vt.*** **1.** to cause to flourish **2.** to promote vigorously —***n.*** a period of business prosperity, etc. —***adj.*** of or resulting from a boom in business *[a boom town]*

boom·er·ang (bo͞om′ə raŋ′) ***n.*** [< Australian native name] **1.** a flat, curved stick that can be thrown so that it will return to the thrower: used as a weapon by Australian aborigines **2.** something that goes contrary to the expectation of its originator and results in his disadvantage or harm —***vi.*** to act as a boomerang

boon[1] (bo͞on) ***n.*** [ON. *bon,* a petition] **1.** a welcome benefit; blessing **2.** [Archaic] a request or favor

boon[2] (bo͞on) ***adj.*** [< OFr. < L. *bonus,* good] **1.** [Archaic or Poet.] kind, generous, pleasant, etc. **2.** merry; convivial: now only in **boon companion**

boon·docks (bo͞on′däks′) ***n.pl.*** [orig. military slang < Tag. *bundok,* mountain] [Colloq.] **1.** a wild, heavily wooded area; wilderness **2.** any remote rural region; hinterland Used with *the*

boon·dog·gle (bo͞on′dôg′'l, -däg′-) ***vi.*** **-gled, -gling** [orig. sense, ornamental leather strap] [Colloq.] to do trifling, pointless work —***n.*** trifling, pointless work or a useless project —**boon′dog′gler** ***n.***

Boone (bo͞on), **Daniel** 1734–1820; Am. frontiersman

boor (boor) ***n.*** [Du. *boer* < MDu. *gheboer,* fellow dweller < *ghe-,* with, CO- + *bouwen,* to cultivate] **1.** orig., a peasant or farm worker **2.** a rude, awkward, or ill-mannered person —**boor′ish** ***adj.*** —**boor′ish·ly** ***adv.*** —**boor′ish·ness** ***n.***

boost (bo͞ost) ***vt.*** [< ?] **1.** to raise by or as by a push from behind or below **2.** to urge others to support; promote **3.** to increase in amount, power, etc. —***n.*** **1.** a push to help a person or thing upward or forward **2.** an act that helps or promotes **3.** an increase in amount, power, etc.

boost·er (bo͞os′tər) ***n.*** **1.** one who boosts; ardent supporter **2.** any device providing added power, thrust, etc. **3.** any of the early stages of a multistage rocket; also, a rocket system that launches a spacecraft, etc.: also **booster rocket**

booster shot (or **injection**) a later injection of a vaccine for maintaining immunity

boot[1] (bo͞ot) ***n.*** [OFr. *bote*] **1.** *a)* a protective covering of leather, rubber, etc. for the foot and part of the leg *b)* an overshoe **2.** a boot-shaped instrument of torture **3.** a patch for the inner surface of an automobile tire **4.** [Brit.] the trunk of an automobile **5.** *a)* a kick *b)* [Colloq.] pleasurable excitement; thrill **6.** [Slang] a navy or marine recruit —***vt.*** **1.** to put boots on **2.** to kick **3.** [Slang] to dismiss **4.** *Baseball* to fumble (a grounder) —**die with one's boots on** to die in action —**lick the boots of** to be servile toward —**the boot** [Slang] dismissal; discharge

boot[2] (bo͞ot) ***n., vt., vi.*** [< OE. *bot,* advantage] [Archaic] profit —**to boot** besides; in addition

boot·black (-blak′) ***n.*** a person whose work is shining shoes and boots

boot camp [Colloq.] a station where navy or marine recruits receive basic training

boot·ee, boot·ie (bo͞ot′ē, bo͞o tē′) ***n.*** **1.** a short boot or light overshoe worn by women and children **2.** a baby's soft, knitted or cloth shoe

Bo·ö·tes (bō ō′tēz) [L. < Gr. *boōtēs,* lit., plowman] a N constellation including the star Arcturus

booth (bo͞oth) ***n., pl.*** **booths** (bo͞o*th*z) [< ON. *buth,* temporary dwelling < *bua,* to dwell, akin to BONDAGE] **1.** a stall for the sale or display of goods, as at a market **2.** a small enclosure for voting at elections **3.** a small structure to house a sentry, public telephone, etc. **4.** a small, partially enclosed compartment with a table and seats, as in some restaurants

Booth (bo͞oth), **1. Edwin (Thomas),** 1833–93; U.S. actor **2. John Wilkes** (wilks), 1838–65; U.S. actor, brother of *prec.:* assassin of Abraham Lincoln **3. William,** 1829–1912; Eng. founder of the Salvation Army

boot·jack (bo͞ot′jak′) ***n.*** a device to grip a boot heel, for helping a person to pull off boots

boot·leg (-leg′) ***vt., vi.*** **-legged′, -leg′ging** [in allusion to concealing objects in the leg of a boot] to make, carry, or sell (esp. liquor) illegally —***adj.*** bootlegged; illegal —***n.*** bootlegged liquor —**boot′leg′ger** ***n.***

boot·less (-lis) ***adj.*** [BOOT[2] + -LESS] useless —**boot′less·ly** ***adv.*** —**boot′less·ness** ***n.***

boot·lick (-lik′) ***vt., vi.*** [Colloq.] to try to gain favor with (someone) by fawning, servility, etc. —**boot′lick′er** ***n.***

boot·strap (-strap′) ***n.*** a strap on a boot for pulling it on —***adj.*** undertaken without others' help *[a bootstrap operation]* —**lift** (or **raise**) **oneself by the** (or **one's own**) **bootstraps** to achieve success by one's own unaided efforts

boo·ty (bo͞ot′ē) ***n., pl.*** **-ties** [< MLowG. *bute;* infl. by BOOT[2]] **1.** spoils of war **2.** any loot **3.** any valuable gain; prize: a humorous usage

booze (bo͞oz) ***vi.*** **boozed, booz′ing** [< Du. *buizen*] [Colloq.] to drink too much alcoholic liquor —***n.*** [Colloq.] alcoholic liquor —**booz′er** ***n.*** —**booz′y** ***adj.*** **-i·er, -i·est**

bop[1] (bäp) ***n., vt.*** **bopped, bop′ping** [echoic] [Slang] hit; punch

bop[2] (bäp) ***n.*** [< earlier *be-bop* < ?] a style of jazz with complex rhythms and harmonies, etc.

bo·rac·ic (bə ras′ik) ***adj.*** *same as* BORIC

bor·age (bôr′ij, bur′-) ***n.*** [< OFr. < ML. < ? *burra,* coarse hair] an annual plant with brilliant blue flowers and hairy leaves

bo·rate (bôr′āt) ***n.*** a salt or ester of boric acid —***vt.*** **-rat·ed, -rat·ing** to treat or mix with borax or boric acid —**bo′rat·ed** ***adj.***

bo·rax (bôr′aks) ***n.*** [< OFr. < ML. < Ar. < Per. *būrah*] a white, crystalline salt, $Na_2B_4O_7$, used as a flux and in glass, soaps, etc.

Bor·deaux (bôr dō′) seaport in SW France: pop. 267,000 —***n.*** red or white wine from the region around Bordeaux

bor·der (bôr′dər) ***n.*** [< OFr. < OHG. *bord,* margin] **1.** an edge or a part near an edge; margin **2.** a dividing line between countries, etc.; frontier **3.** a narrow, ornamental strip along an edge —***vt.*** **1.** to provide with a border **2.** to bound —***adj.*** of, forming, or near a border —**border on** (or **upon**) **1.** to be next to **2.** to be like; be nearly —**bor′dered** ***adj.***

bor·der·land (-land′) ***n.*** **1.** land forming or near a border **2.** a vague, uncertain condition

bor·der·line (-lin′) ***n.*** a boundary —***adj.*** on the boundary of what is acceptable, normal, etc.

bore[1] (bôr) ***vt.*** **bored, bor′ing** [< OE. < *bor,* auger] **1.** to make a hole in or through with a drill, etc. **2.** to make (a hole, tunnel, etc.) as by drilling **3.** to force (one's way), as through a crowd **4.** to weary by being dull or monotonous —***vi.*** to bore a hole or passage —***n.*** **1.** a hole made by or as by boring **2.** *a)* the hollow part of a tube, gun barrel, etc. *b)* its inside diameter; caliber **3.** a tiresome, dull person or thing

bore[2] (bôr) ***n.*** [< ON. *bara,* a billow] a high, abrupt tidal wave in a narrow channel

bore[3] (bôr) *pt. of* BEAR[1]

bo·re·al (bôr′ē əl) ***adj.*** [LL. *borealis* < ff.] **1.** northern **2.** of the northern zone of plant and animal life lying just below the tundra

Bo·re·as (bôr′ē əs) **1.** *Gr. Myth.* the god of the north wind **2.** the north wind personified

bore·dom (bôr′dəm) ***n.*** the condition of being bored or uninterested; ennui
bor·er (bôr′ər) ***n.*** **1.** a tool for boring **2.** an insect or worm that bores holes in trees, fruit, etc.
bore·some (bôr′səm) ***adj.*** boring; tiresome
Bor·glum (bôr′gləm), (**John**) **Gut·zon** (gut′s'n) 1867–1941; U.S. sculptor
bo·ric (bôr′ik) ***adj.*** of or containing boron
boric acid a white, crystalline, weakly acid compound, H_3BO_3, used as a mild antiseptic
Bor·is (bôr′is) [Russ., lit., fight] a masculine name
born (bôrn) *alt. pp. of* BEAR[1] —***adj.*** **1.** brought into life or being **2.** by birth *[*French-*born]* **3.** having certain qualities innately; natural *[*a *born* athlete*]*
born-a·gain (bôrn′ə gen′) ***adj.*** having undergone a spiritual conversion, esp. to evangelical Christianity
borne (bôrn) *alt. pp. of* BEAR[1]
Bor·ne·o (bôr′nē ō) large island in the Malay Archipelago, southwest of the Philippines: the S part is in Indonesia & the N part is composed of Brunei & two states of Malaysia: 288,000 sq. mi.
Bo·ro·din (bôr′ə din; *Russ.* bô′rô dyēn′), **A·lek·san·dr Por·fir·e·vich** (ä′lyik sän′dr′ pôr fir′yi vich) 1833–87; Russ. composer
bo·ron (bôr′än) ***n.*** [< BOR(AX) + *-on* as in (CARB)ON] a nonmetallic chemical element occurring only in combination, as with sodium and oxygen in borax: symbol, B; at. wt., 10.811; at. no., 5
boron carbide a compound of boron and carbon, B_4C, almost as hard as diamond: used as an abrasive and in control rods for nuclear reactors
bor·ough (bur′ō) ***n.*** [< OE. *burg,* town, fortress] **1.** in certain States, a self-governing, incorporated town **2.** any of the five administrative units of New York City **3.** in England *a)* a town with a municipal corporation granted by royal charter *b)* a town that sends representatives to Parliament
bor·row (bär′ō, bôr′ō) ***vt., vi.*** [< OE. *borgian,* to borrow, lend] **1.** to take or receive (something) with the understanding that one will return it or an equivalent **2.** to adopt (something) as one's own *[*to *borrow* a theory*]* **3.** to adopt (a word) from another language **4.** *Arith.* in subtraction, to take from the next higher denomination in the minuend and add to the next lower —**borrow trouble** to worry prematurely —**bor′row·er *n.***
borsch (bôrsh, bôrshch) ***n.*** [Russ. *borshch*] a Russian beet soup, served hot or cold, usually with sour cream: also **borsht** (bôrsht)
bort (bôrt) ***n.*** [< ? OFr. *bourt,* bastard] a poorly crystallized variety of diamond used as an abrasive in industry: also **bortz** (bôrts)
bor·zoi (bôr′zoi) ***n.*** [Russ., swift] any of a breed of large dog with a narrow head, long legs, and silky coat

BORZOI
(28–31 in. high at shoulder)

bos·cage (bäs′kij) ***n.*** [OE. < Frank. *busk,* forest] a natural growth of trees or shrubs
Bosch (bäs, bôs), **Hier·on·y·mus** (hi rän′ə məs) 1450?–1516; Du. painter
bosh (bäsh) ***n., interj.*** [Turk., empty, worthless] [Colloq.] nonsense
bosk (bäsk) ***n.*** [ME. *bosk,* BUSH[1]] a small wooded place; thicket
bosk·y (bäs′kē) ***adj.*** covered with trees or shrubs
bo's'n (bōs′'n) ***n.*** *contracted form of* BOATSWAIN
Bos·ni·a and Her·ce·go·vi·na (bäz′nē ə ənd hert′sə gō vē′nə) republic of Yugoslavia, in the C part: 19,745 sq. mi.; cap. Sarajevo
bos·om (booz′əm, bōō′zəm) ***n.*** [OE. *bosm*] **1.** the human breast; specif., a woman's breasts **2.** a thing thought of as like this *[*the *bosom* of the sea*]* **3.** the breast regarded as the source of feelings **4.** the enclosing space formed by the breast and arms in embracing **5.** the midst *[*in the *bosom* of one's family*]* **6.** the part of a garment that covers the breast —***vt.*** **1.** to embrace **2.** to conceal —***adj.*** close; intimate *[*a *bosom* companion*]*
bos·om·y (-ē) ***adj.*** having large breasts
Bos·po·rus (bäs′pər əs) strait between the Black Sea & Sea of Marmara: also **Bos′pho·rus** (-fər əs)
boss[1] (bôs, bäs) ***n.*** [Du. *baas,* a master] **1.** a person in authority over employees, as an employer or supervisor **2.** a person who controls a political organization: often **political boss** —***vt.*** **1.** to act as boss of **2.** [Colloq.] to order (a person) about; act bossy with —***adj.*** **1.** [Colloq.] chief **2.** [Slang] fine
boss[2] (bôs, bäs) ***n.*** [< OFr. *boce,* a swelling] **1.** a raised part on a flat surface; esp., a decorative knob, stud, etc. **2.** *Mech.* the enlarged part of a shaft —***vt.*** to decorate with knobs, studs, etc.
boss·ism (bôs′iz'm, bäs′-) ***n.*** control by bosses, esp. of a political machine or party
boss·y[1] (bôs′ē, bäs′ē) ***adj.*** **boss′i·er, boss′i·est** [BOSS[1] + -Y[2]] [Colloq.] domineering or dictatorial —**boss′i·ly *adv.*** —**boss′i·ness *n.***
boss·y[2] (-ē) ***n.*** *a pet name for* a cow
Bos·ton (bôs′t'n, bäs′-) [after *Boston,* port in NE England] capital of Mass., on the Atlantic: pop. 563,000 (met. area 2,760,000) —**Bos·to′ni·an** (-tō′nē ən) ***adj., n.***
Boston brown bread a dark, steamed bread made of cornmeal, rye flour, etc. and molasses
Boston fern a fern having pinnately compound leaves of various forms, used as a house plant
Boston ivy a climbing vine of the grape family, with shield-shaped leaves and purple berries: often grown to cover walls
Boston terrier any of a breed of small dog having a smooth, dark coat with white markings
bo·sun (bōs′'n) ***n.*** *same as* BOATSWAIN
Bos·well (bäz′wel, -wəl), **James** 1740–95; Scot. writer: biographer of Samuel Johnson
bot (bät) ***n.*** [< ? Gael. < *boiteag,* maggot] the larva of the botfly
bot. **1.** botanical **2.** botanist **3.** botany
bo·tan·i·cal (bə tan′i k'l) ***adj.*** [< ML. < Gr. < *botanē,* a plant] **1.** of plants and plant life **2.** of or connected with the science of botany Also **bo·tan′ic** —***n.*** a vegetable drug prepared from roots, herbs, etc. —**bo·tan′i·cal·ly *adv.***
bot·a·nize (bät′'n īz′) ***vi.*** **-nized′, -niz′ing** **1.** to gather plants for botanical study **2.** to study plants, esp. in their natural environment —***vt.*** to investigate the plant life of (a region)
bot·a·ny (bät′'n ē) ***n.*** [BOTAN(ICAL) + -Y[3]] **1.** the science, a branch of biology, that deals with plants, their life, structure, growth, etc. **2.** the plant life of an area **3.** the characteristics of a plant or plant group —**bot′a·nist *n.***
Botany Bay bay on the SE coast of Australia: site of a former Brit. penal colony
botch (bäch) ***vt.*** [ME. *bocchen,* to repair < ? Du. *botsen,* to patch] **1.** to repair or patch clumsily **2.** to bungle —***n.*** **1.** a badly patched place or part **2.** a bungled piece of work —**botch′er *n.*** —**botch′y *adj.***
bot·fly (bät′flī′) ***n., pl.*** **-flies′** [see BOT] a fly whose larvae are parasitic in horses, sheep, etc.
both (bōth) ***adj., pron.*** [< OE. *ba tha,* both these] the two (of them) *[both* (birds) sang*]* —***conj., adv.*** together; equally: used correlatively with *and [both* tired *and* sick*]*
both·er (bä*th*′ər) ***vt., vi.*** [prob. Anglo-Ir. for POTHER] **1.** to worry, trouble, annoy, etc. **2.** to bewilder **3.** to concern or trouble (oneself) —***n.*** **1.** worry; trouble **2.** a person who gives trouble —***interj.*** a mild expression of annoyance, irritation, etc.
both·er·a·tion (bä*th*′ə rā′shən) ***n., interj.*** [Colloq.] *same as* BOTHER
both·er·some (bä*th*′ər səm) ***adj.*** causing bother; annoying; troublesome; irksome
Bot·swa·na (bät swä′nə) country in S Africa: a member of the Commonwealth: 222,000 sq. mi.; pop. 629,000
bott (bät) ***n.*** *same as* BOT
Bot·ti·cel·li (bät′ə chel′ē), **San·dro** (sän′drō) (born *Alessandro di Mariano dei Filipepi*) 1445?–1510; It. Renaissance painter
bot·tle (bät′'l) ***n.*** [< OFr. < ML. *butticula,* a bottle < LL. *buttis,* a cask] **1.** a container, esp. for liquids, usually of glass or plastic, with a relatively narrow neck **2.** the amount that a bottle holds **3.** milk from an infant's nursing bottle —***vt.*** **-tled, -tling** **1.** to put into a bottle or bottles **2.** to store under pressure in a cylinder, etc. *[bottled* gas*]* —**bottle up** **1.** to shut in (enemy troops, etc.) **2.** to hold in or suppress (emotions) —**hit the bottle** [Slang] to drink much alcoholic liquor —**bot′tle·ful′ *n., pl.*** **-fuls′** —**bot′tler *n.***
bot·tle·neck (-nek′) ***n.*** **1.** a place, as a narrow road, where traffic is slowed up or halted **2.** any point at which progress is slowed up
bot·tle·nose (-nōz′) ***n.*** a kind of dolphin, gray or greenish, with a bottle-shaped snout
bot·tom (bät′əm) ***n.*** [< OE. *botm, bodan,* ground] **1.** the lowest part **2.** *a)* the lowest or last position *b) Baseball* the second half (*of* an inning) **3.** the part on which something rests; base **4.** the side or end that is underneath **5.** the seat of a chair **6.** the ground beneath a body of water **7.** [*often pl.*] *same as* BOTTOM LAND **8.** *a)* a ship's keel *b)* a ship **9.** [*usually pl.*] pajama trousers **10.** basic meaning or cause; source **11.** stamina **12.** [Colloq.] the buttocks —***adj.*** of, at, or on the bottom; lowest, last, etc. —***vt.*** **1.** to provide (a chair, etc.) with a bottom **2.** to understand; fathom **3.** to place or base (*on* or *upon*) —***vi.*** **1.** to reach the bottom **2.** to be based —**at bottom** fundamentally; actually —**be at the bottom of** to be the real reason for —**bottom out** to level off at a low point, as prices —**bottoms up!** [Colloq.] drink deep!: a toast
bottom land low land through which a river flows, rich in alluvial deposits; flood plain

bot·tom·less (-lis) ***adj.*** **1.** having no bottom **2.** very deep, endless, etc.

bottom line **1.** the bottom line of the earnings report of a company, on which net profit per share of stock is shown **2.** [Colloq.] profits or losses **3.** [Slang] the basic or most important factor, meaning, etc.

bot·u·lism (bäch′ə liz'm) ***n.*** [< G. < L. *botulus,* sausage + *-ismus,* -ISM: from early German cases involving sausages] poisoning resulting from the toxin produced by a certain bacillus sometimes found in foods improperly canned or preserved

bou·clé, bou·cle (bo͞o klā′) ***n.*** [Fr., pp. of *boucler,* to buckle, curl] **1.** a curly yarn that gives a fabric a tufted or knotted texture **2.** fabric made from this yarn

bou·doir (bo͞od′wär) ***n.*** [Fr., lit., pouting room < *bouder,* to pout, sulk] a woman's bedroom, dressing room, or private sitting room

bouf·fant (bo͞o fänt′) ***adj.*** [Fr., prp. of *bouffer,* to puff out] puffed out; full, as some skirts

bou·gain·vil·le·a, bou·gain·vil·lae·a (bo͞o′gən vil′ē ə) ***n.*** [ModL., after L. A. de *Bougainville* (1729–1811), Fr. explorer] a woody tropical vine having flowers with large, showy, purple or red bracts

bough (bou) ***n.*** [OE. *bog,* shoulder, hence branch] a branch of a tree, esp. a main branch

bought (bôt) *pt. & pp. of* BUY —***adj.*** [Dial.] *same as* BOUGHTEN

bought·en (-'n) ***adj.*** [Dial.] bought at a store and not homemade

bouil·la·baisse (bo͞ol′yə bās′; *Fr.* bo͞o yȧ bes′) ***n.*** [Fr. < Pr. < *bouli,* to boil + *abaissa,* to settle] a chowder made with several kinds of fish

bouil·lon (bool′yän, -yən; *Fr.* bo͞o yōn′) ***n.*** [Fr. < *bouillir,* to boil] a clear broth, esp. of beef

Boul·der (bōl′dər) [from the abundance of large rocks there] city in NC Colo.: pop. 77,000

boul·der (bōl′dər) ***n.*** [< ME. *bulderstan* < Scand., as in Sw. *bullersten,* lit., noisy stone] any large rock worn smooth and round by weather and water

Boulder Dam *former name of* HOOVER DAM

boule (bo͞ol) ***n.*** [Fr., ball] **1.** [*usually pl.*] a French game similar to bowls **2.** a gambling game like roulette **3.** a small rounded mass, as of synthetic ruby, produced by the fusion of alumina

boul·e·vard (bool′ə värd′) ***n.*** [Fr. < MDu. *bolwerc,* bulwark] a broad street, often lined with trees, plots of grass, etc.

bounce (bouns) ***vt.*** **bounced, bounc′ing** [akin to Du. *bonzen* & LowG. *bunsen,* to thump] **1.** orig., to bump or thump **2.** to cause to hit against a surface so as to spring back **3.** [Slang] *a)* to put (a person) out by force *b)* to discharge from employment —***vi.*** **1.** to spring back after striking a surface; rebound **2.** to jump; leap [*bounce* out of bed] **3.** [Slang] to be returned to the payee by a bank: said of a worthless check —***n.*** **1.** *a)* a bouncing; rebound *b)* a leap or jump **2.** capacity for bouncing **3.** [Colloq.] energy; zest —**bounce back** [Colloq.] to recover strength, spirits, etc. quickly —**the bounce** [Slang] dismissal or forcible ejection —**bounc′y** ***adj.***

bounc·er (boun′sər) ***n.*** [Slang] a man hired to remove disorderly people from a nightclub, etc.

bounc·ing (-siŋ) ***adj.*** big, healthy, strong, etc.

bouncing Bet (bet) a perennial plant with pinkish flowers

bound[1] (bound) ***vi.*** [Fr. *bondir,* to leap, orig., to echo < LL. < L. *bombus,* a humming (see BOMB)] **1.** to move with a leap or series of leaps **2.** to bounce or rebound, as a ball —***vt.*** to cause to bound or bounce —***n.*** **1.** a jump; leap **2.** a bounce

bound[2] (bound) *pt. & pp. of* BIND —***adj.*** **1.** tied **2.** closely connected **3.** certain; destined [*bound* to win] **4.** obliged [legally *bound* to pay] 5 constipated **6.** provided with a binding, as a book **7.** [Colloq.] determined; resolved —**bound up in** (or **with**) **1.** devoted to **2.** involved in

bound[3] (bound) ***adj.*** [ME. < *boun,* ready < ON. *buinn,* pp. of *bua:* see BONDAGE] ready to go or going; headed [*bound* for home]

bound[4] (bound) ***n.*** [< OFr. < ML. *bodina,* boundary] **1.** a boundary; limit **2.** [*pl.*] a place near or enclosed by a boundary —***vt.*** **1.** to limit; confine **2.** to be a limit or boundary to **3.** to name the boundaries of (a state, etc.) —***vi.*** to have a boundary (*on* another country, etc.) —**out of bounds** **1.** beyond the boundaries or limits **2.** not to be entered or used; forbidden

-bound (bound) *a combining form meaning* going or headed in (a specified direction) [*southbound*]

bound·a·ry (boun′drē, -dər ē) ***n.,*** *pl.* **-ries** [altered after BOUND[4] < ML. *bunnarium*] any line or thing marking a limit; bound; border

bound·en (boun′dən) ***adj.*** [old pp. of BIND] **1.** under obligation **2.** obligatory [*bounden* duty]

bound·er (-dər) ***n.*** [BOUND[1] + -ER] [Chiefly Brit. Colloq.] an ill-mannered fellow; cad

bound·less (bound′lis) ***adj.*** having no bounds; unlimited —**bound′less·ly** ***adv.*** —**bound′less·ness** ***n.***

boun·te·ous (boun′tē əs) ***adj.*** [< OFr. *bontive:* see BOUNTY] *same as* BOUNTIFUL —**boun′te·ous·ly** ***adv.*** —**boun′te·ous·ness** ***n.***

boun·ti·ful (-tə f'l) ***adj.*** **1.** giving freely and graciously; generous **2.** abundant; plentiful —**boun′ti·ful·ly** ***adv.***

boun·ty (-tē) ***n.,*** *pl.* **-ties** [< OFr. < L. < *bonus,* good] **1.** generosity **2.** a generous gift **3.** a reward or premium, as one given by a government for the performance of certain services

bou·quet (bō kā′; *also, & for 2 usually,* bo͞o-) ***n.*** [Fr.] **1.** a bunch of cut flowers **2.** a fragrant smell or aroma, esp. of a wine or brandy

Bour·bon (boor′bən) the ruling family at various times of France, Spain, Naples, Sicily, etc. —***n.*** [*also* **b-**] a political and social reactionary —**Bour′bon·ism** ***n.***

bour·bon (bur′bən, boor′-) ***n.*** [< *Bourbon* County, Ky.] [*sometimes* **B-**] a whiskey made from a mash of at least 51% corn and aged for not less than two years —***adj.*** of or made with such whiskey

bour·geois (boor zhwä′, boor′zhwä) ***n.,*** *pl.* **-geois′** [Fr. < OFr. < ML. < LL. *burgus,* castle] **1.** a shopkeeper **2.** a member of the bourgeoisie **3.** a person whose beliefs, attitudes, etc. are middle-class —***adj.*** of or characteristic of the bourgeoisie; middle-class, conventional, smug, materialistic, etc. —**bour·geoise′** (-zhwäz′) ***n.fem.***

bour·geoi·sie (boor′zhwä zē′) ***n.*** [*with sing. or pl. v.*] **1.** the social class between the aristocracy or very wealthy and the working class; middle class **2.** in Marxist doctrine, capitalists as a social class antithetical to the proletariat

bour·geon (bur′jən) ***n., vt., vi.*** *same as* BURGEON

bourn[1], **bourne**[1] (bôrn, boorn) ***n.*** [OE. *burna,* a stream] a brook or stream

bourn[2], **bourne**[2] (bôrn, boorn) ***n.*** [< Fr. < OFr. < ML. *bodina:* see BOUND[4]] [Archaic] **1.** a limit; boundary **2.** a goal; objective **3.** a domain

Bourne·mouth (bôrn′məth, boorn′-) resort city in S England: pop. 151,000

bour·rée (bo͞o rā′) ***n.*** [Fr. < *bourrir,* to whir] **1.** a lively, 17th-cent. French dance in duple time **2.** music for this

bourse (boors) ***n.*** [Fr., a purse < OFr. < ML. *bursa,* a bag < Gr. *byrsa,* a hide] a stock exchange; specif., [**B-**] the stock exchange of Paris

bout (bout) ***n.*** [for earlier *bought* < ME. *bught*] **1.** a struggle; contest or match **2.** a period of time taken up by some activity, illness, etc.

bou·tique (bo͞o tēk′) ***n.*** [Fr. < Gr. *apothēkē:* see APOTHECARY] a small shop, or a small department in a store, selling fashionable, expensive items

bou·ton·niere, bou·ton·nière (bo͞ot′'n ir′, -yer′) ***n.*** [Fr. *boutonnière,* a buttonhole] a flower or flowers worn in a buttonhole, as of a lapel

bou·var·di·a (bo͞o vär′dē ə) ***n.*** [ModL., after C. *Bouvard,* 17th-c. Fr. physician] a plant of the madder family, having showy flowers often used in brides' bouquets

bou·vi·er des Flan·dres (bo͞o′vē ā′ də flan′dərz) [Fr., cowherd of Flanders] a large, strong dog with a rough, wiry coat: first used in Flanders for herding cattle

bou·zou·ki (bo͞o zo͞o′kē) ***n.*** [< ModGr., prob. < Turk.] a stringed musical instrument of Greece, somewhat like a mandolin

bo·vine (bō′vīn, -vin, -vēn) ***adj.*** [< LL. < L. *bovis,* gen. of *bos,* ox] **1.** of an ox or cow **2.** slow, dull, stupid, stolid, etc. —***n.*** an ox, cow, etc.

bow[1] (bou) ***vi.*** [< OE. *bugan,* to bend] **1.** [Dial.] to bend or stoop **2.** to bend the head or body in respect, greeting, agreement, etc. **3.** to yield, as to authority —***vt.*** **1.** [Dial.] to bend **2.** to bend (the head) in respect, prayer, shame, etc. **3.** to indicate (agreement, thanks, etc.) by bowing **4.** to weigh (*down*); overwhelm —***n.*** a bending of the head or body, as in respect, greeting, etc. —**bow and scrape** to be too polite and ingratiating —**bow out** **1.** to leave or retire formally **2.** (or **in**) to usher out (or in) with a bow —**take a bow** to acknowledge applause, etc. as by bowing

bow[2] (bō) ***n.*** [< OE. *boga* < *bugan,* BOW[1]] **1.** anything curved or bent [*a rainbow*] **2.** a curve; bend **3.** a device for shooting arrows, a flexible, curved strip of wood, etc. with a taut cord connecting the two ends **4.** an archer **5.** a slender stick strung along its length with horsehairs, drawn across the strings of a violin, cello, etc. to play it **6.** *same as* BOWKNOT **7.** either of the sidepieces for the ears on a pair of glasses; temple —***vt., vi.*** **1.** to bend in the shape of a bow **2.** to play (a violin, etc.) with a bow

bow[3] (bou) ***n.*** **[**< LowG. or Scand.**]** **1.** the front part of a ship, etc.; prow **2.** the oarsman nearest the bow —***adj.*** of or near the bow

bowd·ler·ize (boud′lə rīz′, bōd′-) ***vt.*** **-ized′, -iz′ing** **[**after Thomas *Bowdler*, who in 1818 published an expurgated Shakespeare**]** to expurgate —**bowd′ler·ism** ***n.*** —**bowd′ler·i·za′tion** ***n.***

bow·el (bou′əl, boul) ***n.*** **[**< OFr. < ML. < L. *botellus*, dim. of *botulus*, sausage**]** **1.** an intestine, esp. of a human being; gut; entrail: *usually used in pl.* **2.** [*pl.*] the inner part [the *bowels* of the earth] **3.** [*pl.*] [Archaic] tender emotions —***vt.*** **-eled** or **-elled, -el·ing** or **-el·ling** to disembowel —**move one's bowels** to pass waste matter from the large intestine; defecate

bowel movement **1.** the act of defecating **2.** defecated matter; feces

bow·er (bou′ər) ***n.*** **[**< OE. *bur*, a dwelling**]** **1.** a place enclosed as by leafy boughs; arbor **2.** [Archaic] a boudoir —***vt.*** to enclose in a bower —**bow′er·y** ***adj.***

Bow·er·y (bou′ər ē, bou′rē) a street in New York City, a center of cheap hotels, saloons, etc.

bow·fin (bō′fin′) ***n.*** a primitive freshwater fish of E N. America, with a rounded tail fin

bow·ie knife (bo͞o′ē, bō′ē) **[**after Col. J. *Bowie*, Am. frontiersman**]** a long sheath knife with a single edge, orig. carried by frontiersmen

bow·knot (bō′nät′) ***n.*** a decorative knot, usually with two loops, untied by pulling the ends

bowl[1] (bōl) ***n.*** **[**< OE. *bolla***]** **1.** a deep, hollow, rounded dish **2.** a large drinking cup **3.** convivial drinking **4.** a thing or part shaped like a bowl, as the hollowed-out part of a smoking pipe, a hollow land formation, or an amphitheater **5.** the contents of a bowl —**bowl′like′** ***adj.***

bowl[2] (bōl) ***n.*** **[**< OFr. < L. *bulla*, a bubble**]** **1.** a heavy ball used in the game of bowls **2.** a roll of the ball in bowling or bowls —***vi., vt.*** **1.** to roll (a ball) or participate in bowling or bowls **2.** to move or cause to move swiftly and smoothly, as on wheels **3.** *Cricket* to throw (a ball) to the batsman —**bowl over** **1.** to knock over **2.** [Colloq.] to astonish and confuse —**bowl′er** ***n.***

bowl·der (bōl′dər) ***n.*** *same as* BOULDER

bow·leg (bō′leg′) ***n.*** a leg that is bowed or curved outward —**bow′leg′ged** (-leg′id, -legd′) ***adj.***

bowl·er (bōl′ər) ***n.*** **[**< *Bowler*, name of 19th-c. London hat manufacturer**]** [Brit.] a derby hat

bow·line (bō′lin, -līn′) ***n.*** **[**ME. *boueline*, prob. < Scand.**]** **1.** a rope used to keep the sail taut when sailing into the wind **2.** a knot used to tie off a loop: also **bowline knot**

bowl·ing (bōl′iŋ) ***n.*** **1.** a game in which a heavy ball is bowled along a wooden lane (**bowling alley**) in an attempt to knock over wooden pins, now usually ten, set upright at the far end **2.** *same as* BOWLS **3.** the playing of either game

bowls (bōlz) ***n.*** **1.** a game played on a smooth lawn (**bowling green**) with wooden balls which are rolled in an attempt to make them stop near a target ball (the *jack*) **2.** ninepins, tenpins, or skittles

bow·man (bō′mən) ***n.***, *pl.* **-men** an archer

bow·shot (-shät′) ***n.*** the distance an arrow can travel when shot from a bow

bow·sprit (bou′sprit, bō′-) ***n.*** **[**prob. < Du. < *boeg*, BOW[3] + *spriet*, SPRIT**]** a large, tapered spar extending forward from the bow of a sailing vessel

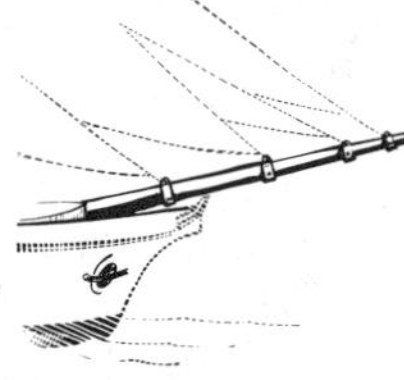

BOWSPRIT

bow·string (bō′striŋ′) ***n.*** a cord stretched from one end of an archer's bow to the other

bow tie (bō) a small necktie tied in a bowknot

box[1] (bäks) ***n.*** **[**OE. < ML. *buxis* < L. < Gr. *pyxos*, boxwood**]** **1.** any of various kinds of containers, usually lidded, made of cardboard, wood, or other stiff material; case; carton **2.** the contents of a box **3.** **[**< the tool *box* under the seat**]** the driver's seat on a coach **4.** any boxlike thing, as *a)* a small, enclosed group of seats in a theater, stadium, etc. *b)* a small booth *c)* a large, enclosed stall, for a horse, etc.: in full, **box stall** *d)* a space for a certain person or group [a jury *box*] **5.** a short newspaper article enclosed in borders **6.** *Baseball* any of the designated areas for the batter, pitcher, catcher, and coaches **7.** *Mech.* a protective casing for a part [a journal *box*] —***vt.*** **1.** to provide with a box **2.** to put into a box —***adj.*** **1.** shaped or made like a box **2.** packaged in a box —**box in** (or **up**) to shut in or keep in —**box the compass** **1.** to name the thirty-two points of the compass in order: compasses were kept in boxes **2.** to make a complete circuit —**in a box** [Colloq.] in difficulty or a dilemma —**box′like′** ***adj.***

box[2] (bäks) ***n.*** **[**< ?**]** a blow struck with the hand or fist, esp. on the ear —***vt.*** **1.** to strike such a blow **2.** to fight in a boxing match with —***vi.*** to fight with the fists; engage in boxing

box[3] (bäks) ***n.*** **[**OE. < L. *buxus* < Gr. *pyxos***]** an evergreen shrub or small tree with small, leathery leaves

box·car (-kär′) ***n.*** a fully enclosed railroad freight car

box elder a fast-growing N. American maple with compound leaves

Box·er (bäk′sər) ***n.*** a member of a Chinese society that led an unsuccessful uprising (the **Boxer Rebellion,** 1900) against foreigners in China

box·er (bäk′sər) ***n.*** **1.** a man who boxes; pugilist; prizefighter **2.** a medium-sized dog with a sturdy body and a smooth, fawn or brindle coat

box·ing (-siŋ) ***n.*** **[**< BOX[2]**]** the skill or sport of fighting with the fists, esp. in padded leather mittens (**boxing gloves**)

box office **1.** a place where admission tickets are sold, as in a theater **2.** [Colloq.] the power of a show or performer to attract an audience

box pleat a double pleat with the under edges folded toward each other

box score a statistical summary of a baseball game, showing the hits, runs, errors, etc.

box seat a seat in a box at a theater, etc.

box turtle a N. American land turtle with a hinged under shell that can be completely closed

box·wood (bäks′wood′) ***n.*** **1.** the wood of the box (shrub or tree) **2.** the box (shrub or tree)

box·y (bäk′sē) ***adj.*** **-i·er, -i·est** like a box, as in squarish form, confining quality, etc.

boy (boi) ***n.*** **[**ME. *boie***]** **1.** a male child from birth to physical maturity **2.** an immature or callow man **3.** any man; fellow: familiar term **4.** a man servant, porter, etc.: a patronizing term **5.** [Colloq.] a son —***interj.*** [Slang] an exclamation of pleasure, surprise, etc.: often **oh, boy!** —**boy′ish** ***adj.*** —**boy′ish·ly** ***adv.*** —**boy′ish·ness** ***n.***

boy·cott (boi′kät) ***vt.*** **[**after Captain C. C. *Boycott*, Irish land agent so treated in 1880**]** **1.** to join together in refusing to deal with, so as to punish, coerce, etc. **2.** to refuse to buy, sell, or use (something) —***n.*** the act of boycotting

boy·friend (boi′frend′) ***n.*** [Colloq.] **1.** a sweetheart, beau, or escort of a girl or woman **2.** a boy who is one's friend

boy·hood (-hood′) ***n.*** **[**see -HOOD**]** **1.** the time or state of being a boy **2.** boys collectively

boy scout a member of the **Boy Scouts,** a worldwide boys' organization that stresses outdoor life and service to others

boy·sen·ber·ry (boi′z'n ber′ē) ***n.***, *pl.* **-ries** **[**after Rudolph *Boysen*, U.S. horticulturist**]** a large, purple berry, a cross of the raspberry, loganberry, and blackberry

bp. **1.** birthplace: also **bpl.** **2.** bishop

B/P, BP, b.p. bills payable

b.p. **1.** below proof **2.** boiling point

Br *Chem.* bromine

Br. **1.** Breton **2.** Britain **3.** British

br. **1.** branch **2.** bronze **3.** brother **4.** brown

B/R, BR, b.r. bills receivable

bra (brä) ***n.*** **[**< BRA(SSIERE)**]** an undergarment worn by women to support and shape the breasts

brace (brās) ***vt.*** **braced, brac′ing** **[**< OFr. < L. *brachia*, pl. of *brachium*, an arm**]** **1.** to tie or bind on firmly **2.** to tighten, esp. by stretching **3.** to strengthen or make firm by supporting the weight of, etc.; prop up **4.** to equip with braces **5.** to make ready for an impact, shock, etc. **6.** to stimulate **7.** to get a firm hold with (the hands or feet) —***n.*** **1.** a couple; pair **2.** a device that clasps or connects; fastener **3.** [*pl.*] [Brit.] suspenders **4.** a device for maintaining tension, as a guy wire **5.** either of the signs { }, used to connect words, lines, or staves of music **6.** a device, as a beam, used as a support, to resist strain, etc.; prop **7.** *a)* any of various devices for supporting a weak or deformed part of the body *b)* [*often pl.*] a device for irregular teeth to force them into proper occlusion **8.** a tool for holding and rotating a drilling bit —**brace up** [Colloq.] to call forth one's courage, etc.

brace and bit a tool for boring, consisting of a removable drill (*bit*) in a rotating handle (*brace*)

brace·let (brās′lit) ***n.*** **[**< OFr. < L. < *brachium*, an arm**]** **1.** an ornamental band or chain worn about the wrist or arm **2.** [Colloq.] a handcuff: *usually used in pl.* —**brace′let·ed** ***adj.***

brac·er (brā′sər) ***n.*** **1.** a person or thing that braces **2.** [Slang] a drink of alcoholic liquor

bra·ce·ro (brə ser′ō) ***n.***, *pl.* **-ros** **[**Sp. < *brazo*, an arm < L. *brachium***]** a Mexican farm laborer brought into the U.S. temporarily for migrant work in harvesting crops

bra·chi·o- **[**< L. < Gr. *brachiōn*, an arm**]** *a combining form meaning* of an arm or the arms [*brachiopod*]: also **bra′chi-**

BRACE AND BIT

bra·chi·o·pod (brā′kē ə päd′, brak′ē-) ***n.*** [prec. + -POD] any of a number of related marine animals with hinged upper and lower shells and two armlike parts with tentacles

bra·chi·um (brā′kē əm, brak′ē-) ***n., pl.*** **-chi·a** (-ə) [L.] **1.** the part of the arm from the shoulder to the elbow **2.** *Biol.* any armlike part —**bra′chi·al** ***adj.***

brach·y- [< Gr. *brachys*, short] *a combining form meaning* short *[brachycephalic]*

brach·y·ce·phal·ic (brak′i sə fal′ik) ***adj.*** [BRACHY- + -CEPHALIC] having a relatively short or broad head: also **brach′y·ceph′a·lous** (-sef′ə ləs): see CEPHALIC INDEX —**brach′y·ceph′a·ly** (-sef′ə lē) ***n.***

brac·ing (brās′iŋ) ***adj.*** invigorating; stimulating —***n.*** **1.** a device that braces **2.** braces

brack·en (brak′′n) ***n.*** [< ON.] **1.** a large, coarse fern, as the brake **2.** a growth of such ferns

brack·et (brak′it) ***n.*** [< Fr. dim. of *brague*, knee pants, ult. < Gaul. *braca*, pants] **1.** an architectural support projecting from a wall **2.** any angle-shaped support, esp. one in the form of a right triangle **3.** a wall shelf held up by brackets **4.** a wall fixture, as for a small electric lamp **5.** either of the signs [ ], used to enclose words, figures, etc. **6.** the part of a classified grouping that falls within specified limits *[*a $5 to $10 price *bracket]* —***vt.*** **1.** to support with brackets **2.** to enclose in brackets **3.** to classify together

brack·ish (brak′ish) ***adj.*** [earlier Scot. *brack* < MDu. *brak*, salty + -ISH] **1.** somewhat salty, as water in some marshes near the sea **2.** having an unpleasant taste; nauseating —**brack′ish·ness** ***n.***

bract (brakt) ***n.*** [L. *bractea*, thin metal plate] a modified leaf, usually small and scalelike, growing at the base of a flower or on its stalk —**brac·te·al** (brak′tē əl) ***adj.*** —**brac′te·ate** (-it) ***adj.***

bract·let (-lit) ***n.*** a secondary bract at the base of a flower: also **brac·te·ole** (brak′tē ōl′)

brad (brad) ***n.*** [ON. *broddr*, a spike] a thin wire nail with a small or off-center head —***vt.*** **brad′ded, brad′ding** to fasten with brads

Brad·ford (brad′fərd) city in N England, in Yorkshire: pop. 294,000

Brad·ford (brad′fərd), **William** 1590–1657; 2d governor of Plymouth Colony

Bra·dy (brā′dē), **Mat·hew B.** (math′yo͞o) 1823?–96; U.S. photographer

brae (brā) ***n.*** [ON. *bra*, eyelid, brow] [Scot.] a sloping bank; hillside

brag (brag) ***vt., vi*** **bragged, brag′ging** [prob. < OFr. *braguer;* ? akin to BRAY] to boast —***n.*** **1.** boastful talk or manner **2.** [Colloq.] anything boasted of; boast **3.** a braggart —**brag′ger** ***n.***

brag·ga·do·ci·o (brag′ə dō′shē ō, -dō′shō) ***n., pl.*** **-os** [coined by Spenser < BRAG + It. ending] **1.** a braggart **2.** noisy boasting or bragging

brag·gart (brag′ərt) ***n.*** [< OFr.: see BRAG] an offensively boastful person —***adj.*** boastful

Bra·he (brä′ə), **Ty·cho** (tü′kō) 1546–1601; Dan. astronomer

Brah·ma (brä′mə; *for n.* brā′-) [Hindi < Sans. *brahman*, worship] *Hinduism* **1.** the supreme essence or spirit of the universe **2.** the chief member of the trinity (Brahma, Vishnu, and Siva) and creator of the universe —***n.*** *same as* BRAHMAN (sense 2)

Brah·man (brä′mən; *for 2* brā′-) ***n., pl.*** **-mans** [see prec.] **1.** a member of the priestly Hindu caste, the highest **2.** a breed of domestic cattle developed from the zebu of India —**Brah·man·ic** (brä man′ik), **Brah·man′i·cal** ***adj.***

Brah·man·ism (-iz'm) ***n.*** the religious doctrines and system of the Brahmans

Brah·min (brä′mən) ***n.*** **1.** *same as* BRAHMAN (sense 1) **2.** a cultured, upper-class person, esp. of New England, regarded as haughty or conservative —**Brah·min·ic** (brä min′ik), **Brah·min′i·cal** ***adj.***

Brah·min·ism (-iz'm) ***n.*** **1.** *same as* BRAHMANISM **2.** the characteristic attitude, etc. of Brahmins

Brahms (brämz), **Jo·han·nes** (yō hän′əs) 1833–97; Ger. composer

braid (brād) ***vt.*** [< OE. *bregdan*, to move quickly] **1.** to interweave three or more strands of (hair, straw, etc.) **2.** to make by such interweaving **3.** to arrange (the hair) in a braid or braids **4.** to trim or bind with braid —***n.*** **1.** a band or strip formed by braiding **2.** a length of braided hair **3.** a woven band of tape, ribbon, etc. used to bind or decorate clothing —**braid′er** ***n.*** —**braid′ing** ***n.***

Braille (brāl) ***n.*** [after L. *Braille* (1809–52), Fr. teacher who devised it] [*also* **b-**] **1.** a system of printing and writing for the blind, using raised dots felt by the fingers **2.** the characters used in this system —***vt.*** **Brailled, Brail′ling** [*also* **b-**] to print or write in such characters

brain (brān) ***n.*** [OE. *brægen*] **1.** the mass of nerve tissue in the cranium of vertebrate animals: it is the center of thought and receives and transmits impulses: cf. GRAY MATTER, WHITE MATTER **2.** *a)* [*often pl.*] intelligence; mental ability *b)* [Colloq.] a person of great intelligence *c)* [Colloq.] the main organizer of a group activity —***vt.*** **1.** to dash out the brains of **2.** [Slang] to hit hard on the head —**beat** (or **rack, cudgel,** etc.) **one's brains** to try hard to remember, understand, etc. —**have on the brain** to be obsessed by

brain·case (-kās′) ***n.*** *same as* BRAINPAN

brain·child (-chīld′) ***n.*** [Colloq.] an idea, plan, etc. regarded as produced by one's mental labor

brain drain [Colloq.] depletion of the intellectual or professional resources of a country, etc., esp. through emigration

brain·less (-lis) ***adj.*** foolish or stupid —**brain′less·ly** ***adv.*** —**brain′less·ness** ***n.***

brain·pan (-pan′) ***n.*** the part of the cranium containing the brain

brain·pow·er (-pou′ər) ***n.*** mental ability

brain·storm (-stôrm′) ***n.*** [Colloq.] a sudden inspiration or idea —***vi.*** to engage in brainstorming

brain·storm·ing (-stôr′miŋ) ***n.*** the unrestrained offering of ideas by all members of a conference to seek solutions to problems

brain trust a group of experts acting as administrative advisers —**brain truster**

brain·wash (-wôsh′, -wäsh′) ***vt.*** [Colloq.] to indoctrinate so intensively and thoroughly as to effect a radical transformation of beliefs

brain wave rhythmic electric impulses given off by nerve centers in the brain during rest

brain·y (-ē) ***adj.*** **brain′i·er, brain′i·est** [Colloq.] intelligent; mentally bright —**brain′i·ness** ***n.***

braise (brāz) ***vt.*** **braised, brais′ing** [Fr. *braiser* < *braise* (< Gmc. *brasa*), live coals] to cook (meat) by browning in fat and then simmering in a covered pan with a little liquid

brake[1] (brāk) ***n.*** [prob. taken as sing. of BRACKEN] a large, coarse fern, a variety of bracken

brake[2] (brāk) ***n.*** [< MLowG. *brake* or ODu. *braeke* < *breken*, to break] **1.** a device for beating flax or hemp so that the fiber can be separated **2.** any device for slowing or stopping the motion of a vehicle or machine, as by causing a block or band to press against a moving part —***vt.*** **braked, brak′ing** **1.** to break up (flax, etc.) into smaller pieces **2.** to slow down or stop as with a brake —***vi.*** **1.** to operate a brake **2.** to be slowed down or stopped by a brake —**brake′less** ***adj.***

brake[3] (brāk) ***n.*** [< or akin to MLowG. *brake*, stumps] a clump of brushwood, briers, etc.

brake[4] (brāk) *archaic pt. of* BREAK

brake band a band with a lining (**brake lining**) of asbestos, fine wire, etc., that creates friction when tightened about the drum of a brake

brake·man (-mən) ***n., pl.*** **-men** a railroad worker who operated the brakes on a train, but is now chiefly an assistant to the conductor

brake shoe a block curved to fit the shape of a wheel and forced against it to act as a brake

bram·ble (bram′b'l) ***n.*** [< OE. *bræmel* < *brom*, broom] **1.** any prickly shrub of the rose family, as the raspberry, blackberry, etc. **2.** any prickly shrub or vine —**bram′bly** ***adj.*** **-bli·er, -bli·est**

bran (bran) ***n.*** [OFr. *bren*] the skin or husk of grains of wheat, rye, oats, etc. separated from the flour, as by sifting

branch (branch) ***n.*** [< OFr. *brance* < LL. *branca*, a paw] **1.** any woody extension from the trunk or main stem, or from a main limb, of a tree or shrub **2.** anything like a branch, as a tine of a deer's antler **3.** any of the streams into which a river may divide or which flow into it **4.** *same as* BRANCH WATER **5.** *a)* a division of a body of learning *b)* a division of a family *c)* a separately located unit of an organization *[*a *branch* of a library*]* —***vi.*** **1.** to put forth or divide into branches; ramify **2.** to come out (*from* the trunk or stem) as a branch —***vt.*** to separate into branches —**branch off** **1.** to separate into branches; fork **2.** to go off in another direction; diverge —**branch out** **1.** to put forth branches **2.** to extend the scope of interests, activities, etc. —**branched** ***adj.*** —**branch′like′** ***adj.***

bran·chi·ae (braŋ′ki ē′) ***n.pl., sing.*** **-chi·a** (-ə) [< L. < Gr. *branchia*, fins] the gills of a fish —**bran′chi·al** ***adj.*** —**bran′chi·ate** (-kē it) ***adj.***

branch water **1.** water from a small stream **2.** water as used for mixing with whiskey, etc.

brand (brand) ***n.*** [< OE., flame, sword < base of *biernan*, *vi.*, to burn] **1.** a stick that is burning or partially burned **2.** *a)* a mark burned on the skin with a hot iron, formerly used to punish and identify criminals, now used on cattle to show ownership *b)* the iron thus used **3.** a mark of disgrace; stigma **4.** *a)* an identifying mark or label on products; trademark *b)* the kind or make of a commodity *[a brand of cigars] c)* a special kind *[a brand of nonsense]* **5.** [Archaic] a sword *—vt.* **1.** to mark with or as with a brand **2.** to mark as disgraceful —**brand′er** *n.*

Bran·deis (bran′dīs), **Louis Dem·bitz** (dem′bits) 1856–1941; U.S. Supreme Court justice

Bran·den·burg (bran′dən burg′; *G.* brän′dən boork′) region in E Germany, surrounding Berlin

bran·dish (bran′dish) *vt.* [< OFr. < Gmc. *brand:* see BRAND] to wave or shake menacingly or exultantly; flourish *—n.* a brandishing of something

brand name the name by which a brand or make of commodity is known —**brand′name′** *adj.*

brand-new (brand′no͞o′, -nyo͞o′) *adj.* [orig., fresh from the fire: see BRAND] **1.** entirely new; recently made **2.** recently acquired

bran·dy (bran′dē) *n., pl.* **-dies** [earlier *brandywine* < Du. *brandewijn,* lit., burnt (i.e., distilled) wine] **1.** an alcoholic liquor distilled from wine **2.** a similar liquor distilled from fermented fruit juice *[cherry brandy] —vt.* **-died, -dy·ing** to flavor, mix, or preserve with brandy

bran·ni·gan (bran′ə gən) *n.* [prob. < surname *Brannigan*] [Slang] a noisy quarrel or fight; brawl

brant (brant) *n., pl.* **brants, brant:** see PLURAL, II, D, 1 [< ?] any of a number of related small, dark wild geese of Europe and N. America

Brant·ford (brant′fərd) city in SE Ontario, Canada: pop. 60,000

Braque (bråk), **Georges** (zhôrzh) 1882–1963; Fr. painter

brash (brash) *adj.* [< ?] **1.** brittle, as some wood **2.** reckless; rash **3.** bold, presumptuous, impudent, etc. —**brash′ly** *adv.* —**brash′ness** *n.*

bra·sier (brā′zhər) *n. same as* BRAZIER

Bra·sil (brä zēl′) *Port. sp. of* BRAZIL

Bra·sí·lia (brä zē′lyä) capital of Brazil, in the EC part: pop. 400,000

brass (bras) *n., pl.* **brass′es:** *see* PLURAL, II, D, 3 [OE. *bræs*] **1.** a yellowish metal that is essentially an alloy of copper and zinc **2.** things made of brass **3.** [*often pl.*] brass-wind musical instruments **4.** [Colloq.] bold impudence **5.** [*often with pl. v.*] [Slang] *a)* military officers of high rank: see BRASS HAT *b)* any high officials *—adj.* made of brass

bras·sard (brə särd′, bras′ärd) *n.* [Fr., ult. < *bras,* an arm] **1.** armor for the upper arm: also **bras·sart** (bras′ärt) **2.** an identifying arm band

brass band a band of esp. brass-wind instruments

brass hat [< the gold braid on the cap] [Slang] **1.** a military officer of high rank **2.** any high official

brass·ie (bras′ē) *n.* [orig. made with a *brass* sole] a golf club with a wooden head, used for long fairway shots: now usually called *number 2 wood*

bras·siere, bras·sière (brə zir′) *n.* [Fr., orig. arm guard < *bras,* an arm] *same as* BRA

brass knuckles linked metal rings or a metal bar with finger holes, worn for rough fighting

brass tacks [Colloq.] basic facts; practical details: usually in **get** (or **come**) **down to brass tacks**

brass·ware (bras′wer′) *n.* articles made of brass

brass winds (windz) musical instruments made of coiled metal tubes and having a cup-shaped mouthpiece —**brass′-wind′** *adj.*

brass·y (-ē) *adj.* **brass′i·er, brass′i·est** **1.** of or decorated with brass **2.** like brass **3.** tawdry **4.** loud and blaring **5.** impudent; brazen —**brass′i·ly** *adv.* —**brass′i·ness** *n.*

brat (brat) *n.* [OE. *bratt,* a cloak < Gael. *bratt,* a cloth, rag < ?] a child, esp. an impudent, unruly child: scornful or playful term —**brat′ti·ness, brat′tish·ness** *n.* —**brat′ty, brat′tish** *adj.*

Bra·ti·sla·va (brä′ti slä′və) city in S Czechoslovakia, on the Danube: pop. 277,000

brat·wurst (brat′wərst; *G.* brät′voorsht) *n.* [G. < OHG. < *brato,* lean meat + *wurst,* sausage] highly seasoned, fresh sausage of veal and pork

bra·va·do (brə vä′dō) *n.* [< Sp. *bravada* < *bravo,* BRAVE] pretended courage or feigned confidence

brave (brāv) *adj.* [Fr. < It. *bravo,* brave, fine, orig., wild, savage < L. *barbarus,* BARBAROUS] **1.** not afraid; having courage; valiant **2.** fine; splendid *[brave new world] —n.* **1.** any brave man **2.** [< 17th-c. NAmFr.] a N. American Indian warrior *—vt.* **braved, brav′ing** **1.** to face with courage **2.** to defy; dare —**brave′ly** *adv.* —**brave′ness** *n.*

brav·er·y (brā′vər ē) *n.* **1.** courage; valor **2.** fine appearance, show, or dress

bra·vo[1] (brä′vō) *interj.* [It.: see BRAVE, *adj.*] well done! very good! excellent! *—n., pl.* **-vos** a shout of "bravo!" —**bra′va** (-vä) *interj., n.fem.*

bra·vo[2] (brä′vō) *n., pl.* **-voes, -vos;** It. **-vi** (-vē) [It.: see BRAVE] a hired killer; assassin

bra·vu·ra (brə vyoor′ə) *n.* [It., spirit < *bravo,* BRAVE] **1.** a display of daring; dash **2.** *Music a)* a brilliant passage or piece that displays the performer's skill and technique *b)* brilliant technique *—adj.* characterized by bravura

braw (brô, brä) *adj.* [< BRAVE] [Scot.] **1.** finely dressed **2.** fine; excellent

brawl (brôl) *vi.* [< ? Du. *brallen,* to boast] to quarrel or fight noisily *—n.* **1.** a noisy quarrel or fight; row **2.** [Slang] a noisy party —**brawl′er** *n.*

brawn (brôn) *n.* [< OFr. *braon,* muscular part < Frank. *brado,* meat, calf (of leg)] **1.** strong, well-developed muscles **2.** muscular strength —**brawn′i·ness** *n.* —**brawn′y** *adj.* **brawn′i·er, brawn′i·est**

bray (brā) *vi.* [< OFr. < VL. *bragire,* to cry out] to make the loud, harsh cry of a donkey, or a sound, esp. a laugh, like this *—vt.* to utter loudly and harshly *—n.* the loud, harsh cry of a donkey, or a sound like this

braze[1] (brāz) *vt.* **brazed, braz′ing** [Fr. *braser,* to solder, var. of *braiser,* BRAISE] to solder with a metal having a high melting point, esp. with an alloy of zinc and copper —**braz′er** *n.*

braze[2] (brāz) *vt.* **brazed, braz′ing** [< OE. *bræsian* < *bræs,* BRASS] **1.** to make of, or coat with, brass **2.** to make hard like brass —**braz′er** *n.*

bra·zen (brā′z'n) *adj.* [OE. *bræsen* < *bræs,* BRASS] **1.** of brass **2.** like brass in color, etc. **3.** showing no shame; bold; impudent **4.** harsh and piercing —**brazen it out** to act boldly as if one need not be ashamed —**bra′zen·ly** *adv.* —**bra′zen·ness** *n.*

bra·zier[1] (brā′zhər) *n.* [Fr. *brasier* < *braise:* see BRAISE] a metal pan, bowl, etc. to hold burning coals or charcoal

bra·zier[2] (brā′zhər) *n.* [see BRASS] a person who works in brass

Bra·zil (brə zil′) country in C & SE S. America: c. 3,287,000 sq. mi.; pop. 90,990,000; cap. Brasília —**Bra·zil′ian** (-yən) *adj., n.*

Brazil nut **1.** a hard-shelled, three-sided, oily, edible seed of a tall S. American tree **2.** this tree, on which the seeds grow clustered in capsules

BRAZIL NUTS

Braz·za·ville (brä′zə vil′) capital of the Congo, on the Congo River: pop. 156,000

breach (brēch) *n.* [< OE. < *brecan,* to break] **1.** orig., a breaking or being broken **2.** a failure to observe a law, a contract, etiquette, public peace, etc. **3.** an opening made by breaking through a wall, defense, etc. **4.** a break in friendly relations *—vt.* to make a breach in; break through

breach of promise a breaking of a promise to marry

bread (bred) *n.* [OE. *bread,* crumb, morsel] **1.** a food baked from a leavened, kneaded dough made with flour or meal, water, yeast, etc. **2.** any baked food like bread but made with a batter *[quick breads]* **3.** food generally **4.** one's livelihood **5.** [Slang] money *—vt.* to cover with bread crumbs before cooking —**bread and butter** one's means of subsistence; livelihood —**break bread** to partake of food; eat —**cast one's bread upon the waters** to do good deeds without expecting something in return —**know which side one's bread is buttered on** to know what is to one's economic interest

bread-and-but·ter (-'n but′ər) *adj.* **1.** of the product, work, etc. basically relied on for earnings **2.** basic, commonplace, everyday, etc. **3.** expressing thanks, as a letter to one's host after a visit

bread·bas·ket (-bas′kit) *n.* **1.** a region supplying much grain **2.** [Slang] the stomach or abdomen

bread·fruit (-fro͞ot′) *n.* **1.** a large, round fruit with a starchy pulp, that is like bread when baked **2.** the tropical tree on which it grows

bread line a line of people waiting to be given food as government relief or private charity

bread·stuff (-stuf′) *n.* **1.** ground grain or flour for making bread **2.** bread

breadth (bredth) *n.* [OE. *brædu* < *brad,* broad + -TH[1]] **1.** the distance from side to side of a thing; width **2.** a piece of a given and regular width *[a breadth of linoleum]* **3.** lack of narrowness *[breadth of knowledge]*

breadth·ways (-wāz′) *adv., adj.* in the direction of the breadth: also **breadth′wise′** (-wīz′)

bread·win·ner (bred′win′ər) *n.* a person who supports dependents by his earnings

break (brāk) *vt.* **broke, bro′ken, break′ing** [OE. *brecan*] **1.** to cause to come apart by force; smash; burst **2.** to cut open the surface of (soil, the skin, etc.) **3.** to cause the failure of by force *[to break a strike]* **4.** to make inoperative by cracking, disrupting, etc. **5.** to make obedient with or as with force **6.** to get rid of (a habit) or to cause to get rid (*of* a habit) **7.** to lower in rank or grade; demote **8.** *a*) to reduce to poverty or bankruptcy *b*) to wreck the health, spirit, etc. of **9.** to surpass (a record) **10.** to violate (a law, agreement, etc.) **11.** to escape from by force [to *break* prison] **12.** to disrupt the order or completeness of [to *break* ranks] **13.** to interrupt (a journey, electric circuit, etc.) **14.** to reduce the force of by interrupting (a fall, etc.) **15.** to bring to a sudden end [to *break* a tie] **16.** to penetrate (silence, darkness, etc.) **17.** to make known; disclose **18.** *a*) to decipher (a code, etc.) *b*) to solve [to *break* a criminal case] **19.** to make (a will) invalid **20.** to prove (an alibi) false **21.** to begin; open **22.** to exchange (a bill or coin) for smaller units —*vi.* **1.** to split into pieces; come apart; burst **2.** to scatter; disperse [*break* and run] **3.** to force one's way (*through*) **4.** to stop associating (*with*) **5.** to become inoperative **6.** to rise, fall, turn, shift, etc. suddenly **7.** to move away suddenly **8.** to begin suddenly to perform, etc. [*break* into song] **9.** to come into being, evidence, or general knowledge [the story *broke*] **10.** *a*) to fall apart slowly; disintegrate *b*) to dash apart, as a wave on the shore **11.** to curve near the plate: said of a pitched baseball **12.** [Colloq.] to happen in a certain way [things were *breaking* badly] —*n.* **1.** a breaking; breach; fracture **2.** *a*) a breaking in, out, or forth *b*) a sudden move; rush; dash **3.** a broken place; separation; crack **4.** a beginning or appearance [*break* of day] **5.** an interruption of something regular **6.** a gap; interval; omission **7.** a breach in friendly relations **8.** a sudden change **9.** an escape, as from prison **10.** a lowering or drop, as of prices **11.** [Colloq.] an improper or untimely action or remark **12.** [Slang] a chance piece of luck, specif. of good luck **13.** *Music* *a*) the point where one register changes to another *b*) a transitional phrase in a piece of jazz music —**break down** **1.** to go out of working order **2.** to give way to tears or emotion **3.** to have a physical or nervous collapse **4.** to analyze —**break in** **1.** to enter forcibly **2.** to interrupt **3.** to train (a beginner) **4.** to work the stiffness out of (new equipment) —**break off** **1.** to stop abruptly **2.** to stop being friendly —**break out** **1.** to begin suddenly **2.** to escape **3.** to become covered with pimples or a rash **4.** to bring out for use [*break out* the gear] —**break up** **1.** to disperse: also, esp. as a command, **break it up** **2.** to take apart **3.** to put a stop to **4.** [Colloq.] to end a relationship **5.** [Colloq.] to distress; upset **6.** [Colloq.] to laugh or make laugh uncontrollably —**break′a·ble** ***adj.***

break·age (-ij) ***n.*** **1.** a breaking **2.** things or quantity broken **3.** loss or damage due to breaking, or the sum allowed for this

break·down (-doun′) ***n.*** **1.** a breaking down; specif., *a*) a failure to function properly *b*) a failure of health *c*) decomposition *d*) a separating into parts; analysis **2.** a lively, shuffling dance

break·er (-ər) ***n.*** a person or thing that breaks; specif., a wave that breaks into foam

break·fast (brek′fəst) ***n.*** the first meal of the day —*vi.* to eat breakfast —*vt.* to give breakfast to —**break′fast·er** ***n.***

break·front (brāk′frunt′) ***adj.*** having a front with a projecting section —*n.* a breakfront cabinet

breaking point the point at which material, or one's endurance, etc., collapses under strain

break·neck (brāk′nek′) ***adj.*** likely to cause an accident; highly dangerous [*breakneck* speed]

break·out (-out′) ***n.*** **1.** a sudden, forceful escape, as from prison **2.** a skin eruption

break·through (-thro͞o′) ***n.*** **1.** the act or place of breaking through against resistance **2.** a strikingly important advance or discovery

break·up (-up′) ***n.*** a breaking up; specif., *a*) a dispersion *b*) a disintegration or decay *c*) a collapse *d*) a stopping or ending

break·wa·ter (-wôt′ər, -wät′-) ***n.*** a barrier to break the impact of waves, as before a harbor

bream (brēm; *also, esp. for 2,* brim) ***n., pl.*** **bream, breams:** see PLURAL, II, D, 2 [< OFr. *bresme* < Frank. *brahsima*] **1.** a European freshwater fish related to the minnows **2.** any of various saltwater fishes **3.** any of various freshwater sunfishes

breast (brest) ***n.*** [OE. *breost*] **1.** either of two milk-secreting glands at the upper, front part of a woman's body **2.** a corresponding gland in other animals **3.** the upper, front part of the body; chest **4.** the part of a garment, etc. that is over the breast **5.** the breast regarded as the center of emotions **6.** anything likened to the breast [the *breast* of the sea] —*vt.* to face, esp. firmly —**beat one's breast** to make an exaggerated display of feeling, as of guilt —**make a clean breast of** to confess (guilt, etc.) fully

breast·bone (-bōn′) ***n.*** *same as* STERNUM

breast-feed (-fēd′) ***vt.*** **-fed′** (-fed′), **-feed′ing** to feed (a baby) milk from the breast; suckle

breast·pin (-pin′) ***n.*** an ornamental pin or brooch worn on a dress, near the throat

breast·plate (-plāt′) ***n.*** a piece of armor for the breast

breast stroke a swimming stroke in which both arms are simultaneously brought out sideways from a position close to the chest

breast·work (-wurk′) ***n.*** a low wall put up quickly as a defense, esp. to protect gunners

breath (breth) ***n.*** [OE. *bræth,* odor, exhalation] **1.** air taken into the lungs and then let out **2.** breathing; respiration **3.** the power to breathe easily **4.** life or spirit **5.** air carrying fragrance or odor **6.** a puff or whiff, as of air; slight breeze **7.** moisture produced by a condensing of the breath, as in cold air **8.** a whisper or murmur **9.** the time taken by a single respiration; moment **10.** a slight pause or rest **11.** a faint hint or indication **12.** *Phonet.* a voiceless exhalation of the airstream, as in pronouncing (s) or (p) —**below** (or **under**) **one's breath** in a whisper or murmur —**catch one's breath** **1.** to gasp or pant **2.** to pause or rest —**in the same breath** almost simultaneously —**out of breath** breathless, as from exertion —**save one's breath** to refrain from talking —**take one's breath away** to thrill

breathe (brē*th*) ***vi., vt.*** **breathed, breath′ing** [< ME. < *breth,* BREATH] **1.** to take (air) into the lungs and let it out again; inhale and exhale **2.** to live **3.** to give out (an odor) **4.** to instill [to *breathe* confidence] **5.** to blow softly **6.** to speak or sing softly; whisper **7.** to give or take time to breathe; rest **8.** to pant or cause to pant, as from exertion —**breathe again** (or **freely**) to have a feeling of relief or reassurance —**breathe one's last** to die —**breath·a·ble** (brē′*th*ə b'l) ***adj.***

breath·er (brē′*th*ər) ***n.*** **1.** one who breathes in a certain way **2.** a small vent, as for releasing moisture **3.** [Colloq.] a pause as for rest

breath·ing (brē′*th*iŋ) ***adj.*** that breathes; living; alive —*n.* **1.** respiration **2.** a single breath or the time taken by this **3.** a pause for rest **4.** the sound of *h* in *hit, hope,* etc.; aspirate

breath·less (breth′lis) ***adj.*** **1.** without breath **2.** no longer breathing; dead **3.** out of breath; gasping **4.** unable to breathe easily because of excitement, fear, etc. **5.** still and heavy, as the air —**breath′less·ly** ***adv.*** —**breath′less·ness** ***n.***

breath·tak·ing (-tāk′iŋ) ***adj.*** **1.** that takes one's breath away **2.** very exciting; thrilling —**breath′tak′ing·ly** ***adv.***

breath·y (-ē) ***adj.*** with too much, audible letting out of breath —**breath′i·ly** ***adv.*** —**breath′i·ness** ***n.***

brec·ci·a (brech′ē ə, bresh′-) ***n.*** [It.] rock consisting of sharp-cornered bits cemented together by sand, clay, or lime

Brecht (breHt; *E.* brekt), **Ber·tolt** (ber′tôlt) 1898–1956; Ger. playwright

bred (bred) *pt. & pp. of* BREED

breech (brēch; *for vt. 1, usually* brich) ***n.*** [< OE. *brec,* pl. of *broc*] **1.** the buttocks; rump **2.** the lower or back part of a thing **3.** the part of a gun behind the barrel —*vt.* **1.** to clothe with breeches **2.** to provide (a gun) with a breech

breech·cloth (-klôth′) ***n.*** a cloth worn about the loins; loincloth: also **breech′clout′** (-klout′)

breech·es (brich′iz) ***n.pl.*** [see BREECH] **1.** trousers reaching to the knees **2.** [Colloq.] any trousers

breeches buoy (brēch′iz, brich′-) a device for rescuing people at sea, consisting of a pair of short canvas breeches suspended from a life preserver that is run along a rope from ship to shore or to another ship

BREECHES

breech·ing (brich′iŋ, brēch′-) ***n.*** a harness strap around a horse's hindquarters

breech·load·er (brēch′lōd′ər) ***n.*** any gun loaded at the breech —**breech′-load′ing** ***adj.***

breed (brēd) ***vt.*** **bred, breed′ing** [< OE. *bredan* < *brod,* a hatching, fetus] **1.** to bring forth (offspring) **2.** to be the source of; produce [ignorance *breeds* prejudice] **3.** to cause to reproduce; raise [to *breed* dogs] **4.** to bring up or train **5.** to produce (fissionable material) in a breeder reactor —*vi.* **1.** to be produced; originate **2.** to reproduce —*n.* **1.** a stock of animals or plants descended from common ancestors **2.** a kind; sort; type —**breed′er** ***n.***

breeder reactor a nuclear reactor that produces more fissionable material than it consumes

breed·ing (-iŋ) ***n.*** **1.** the producing of young **2.** the rearing of young **3.** good upbringing or training **4.** the producing of plants and animals, esp. so as to develop new or better types

breeze (brēz) *n.* [< Fr. *brise,* prob. < EFris. *brisen,* to blow fresh and strong] **1.** a wind, esp. a gentle wind **2.** [Brit. Colloq.] commotion **3.** [Colloq.] a thing easy to do **4.** *Meteorol.* any wind ranging in speed from 4 to 31 miles per hour —*vi.* **breezed, breez′ing** [Slang] to move or go quickly, jauntily, etc. —**in a breeze** [Colloq.] easily —**shoot** (or **bat**) **the breeze** [Slang] to chat idly

breeze·way (-wā′) *n.* a covered passageway, as between a house and garage

breez·y (brē′zē) *adj.* **breez′i·er, breez′i·est 1.** slightly windy **2** lively and carefree *[breezy* talk*]* —**breez′i·ly** *adv.* —**breez′i·ness** *n.*

Bre·men (brem′ən; *G.* brā′mən) port in N West Germany: pop. 604,000

Bren·ner Pass (bren′ər) mountain pass across the Alps at the border between Italy & Austria

Bre·scia (bre′shä) city in N Italy, at the foot of the Alps: pop. 201,000

Bres·lau (bres′lou) *Ger. name of* WROCŁAW

breth·ren (breth′rən, -ərn) *n.pl.* brothers: now chiefly in religious use

Bret·on (bret′'n) *adj.* [Fr., ult. same word as BRITON] of Brittany, its people, or their language —*n.* **1.** a native or inhabitant of Brittany **2.** the Celtic language of the people of Brittany

Breu·ghel (brü′gəl; *occas.* broi′-) *same as* BRUEGEL

breve (brev, brēv) *n.* [It. < L. *brevis,* brief] **1.** a mark (˘) put over a short vowel or short or unstressed syllable **2.** *Music* a note (|o|) equal to two whole notes

bre·vet (brə vet′; *chiefly Brit.* brev′it) *n.* [< OFr., a note < ML. *breve,* letter < L. *brevis,* brief] *Mil.* a commission giving an officer a higher honorary rank without more pay —*adj.* held by brevet —*vt.* **-vet′ted** or **-vet′ed, -vet′ting** or **-vet′ing** to give a brevet to —**bre·vet′cy** *n., pl.* **-cies**

bre·vi·ar·y (brē′vē er′ē, brēv′yər ē) *n., pl.* **-ar′ies** [< ML. *brevarium,* abridgment, ult. < L. *brevis,* brief] *R.C.Ch.* a book of the daily prayers, hymns, etc. prescribed for priests and other clerics

brev·i·ty (brev′ə tē) *n.* [< L. < *brevis,* brief] **1.** briefness of time **2.** conciseness; terseness

brew (bro͞o) *vt.* [< OE. *breowan*] **1.** to make (beer, ale, etc.) from malt and hops by steeping, boiling, and fermenting **2.** to make (tea, coffee, etc.) by steeping or boiling **3.** to plan (mischief, trouble, etc.); plot —*vi.* **1.** to brew beer, ale, etc. **2.** to begin to form: said of a storm, trouble, etc. —*n.* **1.** a brewed beverage **2.** an amount brewed —**brew′er** *n.*

brew·er·y (bro͞o′ər ē) *n., pl.* **-er·ies** an establishment where beer, ale, etc. are brewed

brew·ing (bro͞o′iŋ) *n.* **1.** the preparation of a brew **2.** the amount of brew made at one time

Bri·an (brī′ən) [Celt., ? strong] a masculine name

bri·ar[1] (brī′ər) *n. same as* BRIER[1] —**bri′ar·y** *adj.*

bri·ar[2] (brī′ər) *n.* **1.** *same as* BRIER[2] **2.** a tobacco pipe made of brierroot

bri·ar·root (-ro͞ot′, -root′) *n. same as* BRIERROOT

bri·ar·wood (-wood′) *n. same as* BRIERWOOD

bribe (brīb) *n.* [< OFr., morsel of bread given to beggars < *briber,* to beg] **1.** anything given or promised to induce a person to do something illegal or wrong **2.** anything given or promised as an inducement —*vt.* **bribed, brib′ing 1.** to offer or give a bribe to **2.** to get or influence by bribing —*vi.* to give bribes —**brib′a·ble** *adj.* —**brib′er** *n.*

brib·er·y (brī′bər ē) *n., pl.* **-er·ies** the giving, offering, or taking of bribes

bric-a-brac (brik′ə brak′) *n.* [< Fr. < *à bric et à brac,* by hook or crook] small, rare, or artistic objects, or knickknacks, placed about a room for ornament

brick (brik) *n.* [< MDu. *bricke* & OFr. *brique,* a fragment] **1.** a substance made from clay molded into oblong blocks and baked, used in building, etc. **2.** any of these blocks **3.** bricks collectively **4.** anything shaped like a brick **5.** [Colloq.] a fine fellow —*adj.* **1.** built or paved with brick **2.** like brick *[brick* red*]* —*vt.* to build or pave with brick —**brick up** (or **in**) to wall in with brick

brick·bat (-bat′) *n.* **1.** a piece of brick used as a missile **2.** an unfavorable or critical remark

brick cheese a ripened semihard American cheese shaped like a brick

brick·lay·ing (-lā′iŋ) *n.* the act or work of building with bricks —**brick′lay′er** *n.*

brick red yellowish or brownish red —**brick′-red′** *adj.*

brick·work (-wurk′) *n.* anything built of bricks

brick·yard (-yärd′) *n.* a place where bricks are made or sold

brid·al (brīd′'l) *n.* [< OE. *bryd ealo,* marriage feast < *bryd,* bride + *ealo,* ale] a wedding —*adj.* **1.** of a bride **2.** of a wedding

bridal wreath a cultivated shrub of the rose family, with many small, white double flowers

bride (brīd) *n.* [OE. *bryd*] a woman who has just been married or is about to be married

bride·groom (brīd′gro͞om′, -groom′) *n.* [< OE. *brydguma,* suitor < *bryd,* bride + *guma,* man; altered by folk etym. after GROOM] a man who has just been married or is about to be married

brides·maid (brīdz′mād′) *n.* any of the young women who attend the bride at a wedding

bridge[1] (brij) *n.* [< OE. *brycge*] **1.** a structure built over a river, railroad, etc. to provide a way across for vehicles or pedestrians **2.** a thing that provides connection or contact **3.** *a)* the upper, bony part of the nose *b)* the curved bow of a pair of glasses fitting over the nose **4.** the thin, arched piece over which the strings are stretched on a violin, etc. **5.** a raised platform on a ship for the commanding officer **6.** *Dentistry* a fixed or removable mounting for false teeth, attached to real teeth **7.** *Music* a connecting passage between two sections of a composition —*vt.* **bridged, bridg′ing 1.** to build a bridge on or over **2.** to provide a connection, transition, etc. across or between —**burn one's bridges (behind one)** to commit oneself to a course from which there is no retreat —**bridge′a·ble** *adj.*

bridge[2] (brij) *n.* [earlier *biritch,* "Russian whist," altered after prec.; ? of Russ. origin] any of various card games that developed from whist: see AUCTION BRIDGE, CONTRACT BRIDGE

bridge·head (-hed′) *n.* **1.** a fortified position established by an attacking force on the enemy's side of a bridge, river, etc. **2.** *same as* BEACHHEAD (sense 2)

Bridge·port (brij′pôrt) [after the bridge across a local river] seaport in SW Conn.: pop. 143,000

bridge·work (-wurk′) *n.* a dental bridge or bridges

bri·dle (brīd′'l) *n.* [< OE. < *bregdan,* to pull] **1.** a head harness for guiding a horse: it consists of headstall, bit, and reins **2.** anything that controls or restrains —*vt.* **-dled, -dling 1.** to put a bridle on **2.** to curb as with a bridle —*vi.* **1.** to pull one's head back quickly with the chin drawn in, as in showing anger, scorn, etc. **2.** to take offense (*at*)

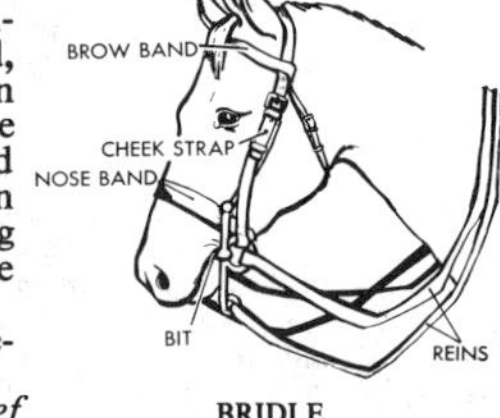

BRIDLE

bridle path a path for horseback riding

brief (brēf) *adj.* [< OFr. *bref* < L. *brevis*] **1.** of short duration or extent **2.** terse; concise **3.** curt or abrupt —*n.* **1.** a summary or abstract **2.** a concise statement of the main points of a law case for use in court **3.** [*pl.*] closefitting, legless underpants —*vt.* **1.** to summarize **2.** to supply with all the pertinent instructions or information **3.** [Brit.] *a)* to furnish with a legal brief *b)* to hire as counsel —**hold a brief for** to argue for or be in favor of —**in brief** in a few words —**brief′ing** *n.* —**brief′ly** *adv.* —**brief′ness** *n.*

brief·case (-kās′) *n.* a flat, flexible case, usually of leather, for carrying papers, etc.

bri·er[1] (brī′ər) *n.* [< OE. *brer*] **1.** any thorny bush, as a bramble, wild rose, etc. **2.** a growth of such bushes —**bri′er·y** *adj.*

bri·er[2] (brī′ər) *n.* [Fr. *bruyère,* white heath] **1.** a heath native to S Europe **2.** its root, or a tobacco pipe made from the root: usually sp. **bri′ar**

bri·er·root (-ro͞ot′, -root′) *n.* the root wood of the brier, or a pipe made of this

bri·er·wood (-wood′) *n. same as* BRIERROOT

brig[1] (brig) *n.* [< BRIGANTINE] a two-masted ship with square sails

brig[2] (brig) *n.* [< ?] **1.** a prison on a U.S. warship **2.** [Mil. Slang] the guardhouse; prison

bri·gade (bri gād′) *n.* [Fr. < It. *brigata,* troop < *brigare,* to contend < *briga,* strife] **1.** a large unit of soldiers **2.** *U.S. Army* a military unit composed of two or more battalions **3.** a group of people organized to function as a unit in some work *[*a fire *brigade]* —*vt.* **-gad′ed, -gad′ing** to organize into a brigade

brig·a·dier (brig′ə dir′) *n.* a brigade commander

brigadier general *pl.* **brigadier generals** *U.S. Mil.* an officer ranking just above a colonel: abbrev. **Brig. Gen.**

brig·and (brig′ənd) *n.* [< OFr. < It. *brigante* < *brigare:* see BRIGADE] a bandit, usually one of a roving band —**brig′and·age** (-ən dij) *n.*

brig·an·tine (brig′ən tēn′) *n.* [< Fr. < It. *brigantino,* pirate vessel: see BRIGAND] a two-masted ship with the foremast square-rigged and a fore-and-aft mainsail

bright (brīt) *adj.* [OE. *bryht,* earlier *beorht*] **1.** shining with light that is radiated or reflected; full of light **2.** clear or brilliant in color or sound; vivid or intense **3.** lively; vivacious; cheerful **4.** mentally quick; clever **5.** *a)* full of happiness or hope *b)* favorable; auspicious **6.** glorious or splendid; illustrious —*adv.* in a bright manner —**bright′ly** *adv.* —**bright′ness** *n.*

bright·en (brīt′'n) *vt., vi.* **1.** to make or become bright or brighter **2.** to gladden; cheer up

Brigh·ton (brīt'n) resort city in S England: pop. 165,000

Bright's disease (brīts) [after R. *Bright* (1789–1858), Eng. physician] chronic nephritis

bril·liance (bril'yəns) *n.* great brightness, radiance, splendor, intelligence, etc.: also **bril'lian·cy**

bril·liant (-yənt) *adj.* [< Fr. prp. of *briller* < It. *brillare,* to sparkle] **1.** shining brightly; sparkling **2.** vivid; intense **3.** very splendid or distinguished **4.** highly intelligent, talented, or skillful —*n.* a gem, esp. a diamond, cut with many facets to increase its sparkle —**bril'liant·ly** *adv.*

brim (brim) *n.* [OE. *brim,* sea] **1.** the topmost edge of a cup, bowl, etc. **2.** a projecting rim or edge, as of a hat —*vt., vi.* **brimmed, brim'ming** to fill or be full to the brim —**brim'·less** *adj.*

brim·ful (brim'fool') *adj.* full to the brim

brim·stone (-stōn') *n.* [< OE. *brynstan:* see BURN[1] & STONE] *same as* SULFUR

brin·dle (brin'd'l) *adj. same as* BRINDLED

brin·dled (-d'ld) *adj.* [prob. < ME. *brended* < *brennen,* to burn] gray or tawny, streaked or spotted with a darker color [a *brindled* cow]

brine (brīn) *n.* [OE.] **1.** water full of salt **2.** *a)* the water of the sea *b)* the sea; ocean —*vt.* **brined, brin'ing** to soak in or treat with brine

bring (briŋ) *vt.* **brought, bring'ing** [OE. *bringan*] **1.** to carry or lead (a person or thing) to the place thought of as "here" or to a place the speaker will be **2.** to cause to be, happen, appear, etc. [war *brings* death] **3.** to lead, persuade, or influence along a course of action or belief **4.** to sell for [to *bring* a high price] **5.** *Law a)* to present in a law court [to *bring* charges] *b)* to advance (evidence, etc.) —**bring about** to make happen; effect —**bring around** (or **round**) **1.** to persuade by arguing, urging, etc. **2.** to bring back to consciousness —**bring forth** **1.** to produce (offspring, fruit, etc.) **2.** to make known; disclose —**bring forward** to introduce; show —**bring in** **1.** to import **2.** to produce (income or revenue) —**bring off** to accomplish —**bring on** to cause to be, happen, or appear —**bring out** **1.** to reveal; make clear **2.** to publish (a book), produce (a play), etc. **3.** to introduce (a girl) formally to society —**bring to** **1.** to revive (an unconscious person) **2.** to cause (a ship) to stop —**bring up** **1.** to take care of during childhood; raise; rear **2.** to introduce, as into discussion **3.** to cough up **4.** to vomit **5.** to stop abruptly

brink (briŋk) *n.* [< MLowG. or Dan., shore, bank] the edge, esp. at the top of a steep place; verge: often used figuratively [at the *brink* of war]

brink·man·ship (briŋk'mən ship') *n.* [BRINK + *-manship,* as in *statesmanship*] the policy of pursuing a hazardous course of action to the brink of catastrophe: also **brinks'man·ship'** (briŋks'-)

brin·y (brīn'ē) *adj.* **brin'i·er, brin'i·est** of or like brine; very salty —**the briny** [Slang] the ocean —**brin'i·ness** *n.*

bri·o (brē'ō) *n.* [It.] animation; vivacity; zest

bri·oche (brē ōsh', -ôsh') *n.* [Fr.] a light, rich roll made with flour, butter, eggs, and yeast

bri·quette, bri·quet (bri ket') *n.* [< Fr. dim. of *brique,* brick] a brick made of compressed coal dust, etc., used for fuel or kindling

Bris·bane (briz'bān, -bən) seaport on the E coast of Australia: pop. 719,000

brisk (brisk) *adj.* [< ? Fr. *brusque,* BRUSQUE] **1.** quick in manner; energetic **2.** cool, dry, and bracing [*brisk* air] **3.** pungent, keen, sharp, etc. [a *brisk* flavor] **4.** active; busy [*brisk* trading] —**brisk'ly** *adv.* —**brisk'ness** *n.*

bris·ket (bris'kit) *n.* [ME. *brusket,* akin to Dan. *bryske*] **1.** the breast of an animal **2.** meat cut from this part

bris·ling (bris'liŋ, briz'-) *n.* [Norw. dial. < older Dan. *bretling*] *same as* SPRAT (sense 1)

bris·tle (bris''l) *n.* [< OE. *byrst*] any short, stiff, prickly hair; esp., any of the hairs of a hog, etc., used for brushes —*vi.* **-tled, -tling** **1.** to become stiff and erect, like bristles **2.** to have the bristles become erect, as in fear **3.** to become tense with fear, anger, etc. **4.** to be thickly covered (*with*) —*vt.* **1.** to make stand up like bristles **2.** to make bristly

bris·tly (bris'lē) *adj.* **-tli·er, -tli·est** **1.** having bristles; rough with bristles **2.** bristlelike; prickly —**bris'tli·ness** *n.*

Bris·tol (bris't'l) **1.** seaport in SW England: pop. 428,000 **2.** [after prec.] city in C Conn.: pop. 57,000

Bristol board [after BRISTOL, England] a fine, smooth pasteboard, used by artists, printers, etc.

Bristol Channel arm of the Atlantic, between S Wales & SW England

Brit (brit) *adj.* [Slang] British —*n.* [Slang] Britisher

Brit. **1.** Britain **2.** Britannia **3.** British

Brit·ain (brit''n) *same as* GREAT BRITAIN

Bri·tan·ni·a (bri tan'yə, -tan'ē ə) **1.** *Roman name for* GREAT BRITAIN (sense 1), esp. the southern part **2.** *same as* BRITISH EMPIRE

britannia metal [*also* **B-**] an alloy of tin, copper, and antimony, used in tableware, like pewter

Bri·tan·nic (bri tan'ik) *adj.* of Britain; British

britch·es (brich'iz) *n.pl.* [Colloq.] *same as* BREECHES (sense 2)

Brit·i·cism (brit'ə siz'm) *n.* a word, phrase, or idiom peculiar to British English: also **Brit'ish·ism**

Brit·ish (brit'ish) *adj.* [< OE. *Bryttisc* < *Bret,* a Celt. inhabitant of Britain < Celt.] **1.** of Great Britain or its people **2.** of the British Commonwealth —*n.* the English language as spoken and written in England —**the British** the people of Great Britain

British Columbia province of SW Canada: 366,255 sq. mi.; pop. 2,467,000; cap. Victoria: abbrev. **B.C.**

British Commonwealth (of Nations) confederation of independent nations, including the United Kingdom and dominions, former colonies, etc. that were once part of the British Empire, united under the British crown: official name, **the Commonwealth**

British Empire formerly, the United Kingdom and British dominions, colonies, etc.

Brit·ish·er (-ər) *n.* a native of Great Britain, esp. an Englishman

British Honduras *former name of* BELIZE

British Isles group of islands consisting of Great Britain, Ireland, & adjacent islands

British thermal unit the quantity of heat required to raise the temperature of one pound of water one degree Fahrenheit

British West Indies Brit. possessions in the West Indies, including the Bahamas, British Virgin Islands, etc.

Brit·on (brit''n) *n.* [< OFr. < L. *Brit(t)o;* of Celt. origin: see BRITISH] **1.** a member of an early Celtic people living in S Britain at the time of the Roman invasion **2.** a native or inhabitant of Great Britain, esp. an Englishman

Brit·ta·ny (brit''n ē) peninsula of NW France

brit·tle (brit''l) *adj.* [< OE. *breotan,* to break] **1.** easily broken or shattered because hard and inflexible **2.** having a sharp, hard quality [*brittle* tones] **3.** stiff and unbending in manner —*n.* a brittle, crunchy candy with nuts in it [peanut *brittle*] —**brit'tle·ly, brit'tly** *adv.* —**brit'tle·ness** *n.*

Br·no (bur'nô) city in C Czechoslovakia: pop. 333,000

bro. *pl.* **bros.** brother

broach (brōch) *n.* [< OFr. < ML. *brocca,* a spike < L. *broccus,* with projecting teeth] **1.** a spit for roasting meat **2.** a tapered bit for enlarging or shaping holes **3.** *same as* BROOCH —*vt.* **1.** to make a hole in so as to let out liquid **2.** to start a discussion of; bring up —**broach'er** *n.*

broad (brôd) *adj.* [< OE. *brad*] **1.** of large extent from side to side; wide **2.** spacious [*broad* prairies] **3.** clear; open; full [*broad* daylight] **4.** plain to the mind; obvious [a *broad* hint] **5.** strongly marked [a *broad* accent] **6.** coarse or ribald [a *broad* joke] **7.** tolerant; liberal [a *broad* view] **8.** wide in range; not limited [a *broad* survey] **9.** main or general; not detailed [in *broad* outline] **10.** *Phonet.* pronounced with the tongue held low and flat in the mouth; open, esp. as the (ä) of *father* —*n.* **1.** the broad part of anything **2.** [Slang] a woman: a vulgar term —**broad'ly** *adv.* —**broad'ness** *n.*

broad·ax, broad·axe (-aks') *n.* an ax with a broad blade, used as a weapon or tool

broad·cast (-kast') *vt.* **-cast'** or, in radio, occas. **-cast'ed, -cast'ing** **1.** to scatter (seed) widely **2.** to spread (information, etc.) widely **3.** to transmit by radio or TV —*vi.* to broadcast radio or TV programs —*adj.* **1.** widely scattered **2.** of, for, or by radio or TV broadcasting —*n.* **1.** a broadcasting **2.** a radio or TV program —*adv.* far and wide —**broad'cast'er** *n.*

Broad Church that part of the Anglican Church holding a doctrinal position between the ritualism and formality of the High Church and the evangelism of the Low Church —**Broad'-Church'** *adj.*

broad·cloth (-klôth') *n.* **1.** a fine, smooth woolen cloth: it originally was made on broad looms **2.** a fine, smooth cotton or silk cloth, used for shirts, pajamas, etc.

broad·en (-'n) *vt., vi.* to make or become broad or broader; widen; expand

broad gauge a width (between the rails of a railroad) greater than standard gauge or width (56 1/2 inches) —**broad'-gauge', broad'-gauged'** *adj.*

broad jump *earlier term for* LONG JUMP

broad·loom (-lōōm') *adj.* woven on a broad loom, as in widths of 6, 9, 12, 15, or 18 feet

broad-mind·ed (-mīn'did) *adj.* tolerant of others' opinions and behavior; not bigoted; liberal —**broad'-mind'ed·ly** *adv.* —**broad'-mind'ed·ness** *n.*

broad·side (-sīd′) ***n.*** **1.** the entire side of a ship above the waterline **2.** *a)* all the guns that can be fired from one side of a ship *b)* their simultaneous firing **3.** an abusive attack in words **4.** a large sheet of paper printed as with advertising and often folded —***adv.*** **1.** with the length turned (*to* an object) **2.** directly in the side **3.** indiscriminately [to level charges *broadside*]

broad-spec·trum (-spek′trəm) ***adj.*** effective against a wide variety of microorganisms

broad·sword (-sôrd′) ***n.*** a sword with a broad blade, for slashing rather than thrusting

broad·tail (-tāl′) ***n.*** **1.** *same as* KARAKUL (sense 1) **2.** the glossy, wavy pelt of the karakul lamb, esp. of one prematurely born

Broad·way (brôd′wā′) street in New York City, the axis of the city's entertainment section

Brob·ding·nag (bräb′diŋ nag′) in Swift's *Gulliver's Travels,* a land of giants —**Brob′ding·nag′i·an** ***adj., n.***

bro·cade (brō kād′) ***n.*** [Sp. *brocado* < It. pp. of *broccare,* to embroider: see BROACH] a rich cloth with a raised design, as of silk, velvet, gold, or silver, woven into it —***vt.*** **-cad′ed, -cad′ing** to weave a raised design into (cloth)

broc·co·li (bräk′ə lē) ***n.*** [It., pl. of *broccolo,* a sprout, dim. of *brocco:* see BROACH] a plant related to the cauliflower but bearing tender shoots with greenish buds, cooked as a vegetable

bro·chette (brō shet′) ***n.*** [Fr., dim. of *broche:* see BROACH] a small spit, as for broiling kebabs

bro·chure (brō shoor′, -shyoor′) ***n.*** [Fr. < *brocher,* to stitch] a pamphlet

Brock·ton (bräk′tən) [after I. *Brock* (1769–1812), Lt. Gov. of Canada] city in E Mass.: pop. 95,000

bro·gan (brō′g'n) ***n.*** [Ir., dim of *brōg*] a heavy work shoe, fitting high on the ankle

brogue[1] (brōg) ***n.*** [prob. < Ir. *barrōg,* a hold, grip (esp. on the tongue)] dialectal pronunciation, esp. that of English as spoken by the Irish

brogue[2] (brōg) ***n.*** [Gael. & Ir. *brōg,* a shoe] **1.** a coarse shoe of untanned leather, formerly worn in Ireland **2.** a man's heavy oxford shoe, usually a kind of blucher with decorative perforations

broil[1] (broil) ***vt.*** [OFr. *bruillir,* prob. by confusion of *bruir,* to burn & *usler,* to singe] **1.** to cook by exposing to direct heat **2.** to expose directly to intense heat —***vi.*** **1.** to become broiled **2.** to become heated or angry —***n.*** a broiling

broil[2] (broil) ***n.*** [ME. *broilen,* to quarrel < OFr. *brouillier,* to dirty] a noisy or violent quarrel; brawl —***vi.*** to take part in a broil

broil·er (broil′ər) ***n.*** **1.** a pan, grill, etc. for broiling **2.** the part of a stove designed for broiling **3.** a young chicken suitable for broiling

broke (brōk) *pt. & archaic pp. of* BREAK —***adj.*** [Colloq.] having no money; bankrupt —**go broke** [Colloq.] to become bankrupt —**go for broke** [Slang] to risk everything in a venture

bro·ken (brō′k'n) *pp. of* BREAK —***adj.*** **1.** splintered, fractured, burst, etc. **2.** not in working condition **3.** violated [a *broken* promise] **4.** disrupted as by divorce [a *broken* home] **5.** sick, weakened, or beaten **6.** bankrupt **7.** not even; interrupted **8.** not complete [*broken* sizes] **9.** imperfectly spoken, esp. with reference to grammar and syntax [*broken* English] **10.** subdued and trained; tamed **11.** [Colloq.] demoted in rank For phrases, see BREAK —**bro′ken·ly** ***adv.*** —**bro′ken·ness** ***n.***

bro·ken-down (-doun′) ***adj.*** **1.** sick or worn out, as by old age or disease **2.** out of order; useless

bro·ken·heart·ed (-här′tid) ***adj.*** crushed by sorrow, grief, or disappointment; inconsolable

bro·ker (brō′kər) ***n.*** [< ONormFr. < OFr. *brochier,* to broach, tap; orig. sense "wine dealer"] **1.** a person hired to act as an agent in making contracts or sales **2.** *same as* STOCKBROKER

bro·ker·age (-ij) ***n.*** **1.** the business of a broker **2.** a broker's fee

bro·mide (brō′mīd) ***n.*** [BROM(INE) + -IDE] **1.** a compound of bromine with another element or with a radical **2.** potassium bromide, KBr, used in medicine as a sedative **3.** a trite saying or remark

bro·mid·ic (brō mid′ik) ***adj.*** [see prec.] using or containing a trite remark or remarks; dull

bro·mine (brō′mēn) ***n.*** [Fr. *brome* < Gr. *brōmos,* stench + -INE[4]] a chemical element, usually a reddish-brown, corrosive liquid volatilizing to form an irritating vapor: symbol, Br; at. wt., 79.909; at. no., 35

bron·chi (bräŋ′kī) ***n.*** *pl. of* BRONCHUS

bron·chi·al (-kē əl) ***adj.*** of the bronchi or bronchioles

bronchial tubes the bronchi and the tubes branching from them

bron·chi·ole (bräŋ′kē ōl′) ***n.*** any of the small subdivisions of the bronchi

bron·chi·tis (bräŋ kīt′əs) ***n.*** [BRONCH(O)- + -ITIS] an inflammation of the mucous lining of the bronchial tubes —**bronchit′ic** (-kit′ik) ***adj.***

bron·cho- [< Gr. *bronchos,* windpipe] *a combining form meaning* having to do with the bronchi [*bronchoscope*] : also, before a vowel, **bronch-**

bron·cho·scope (bräŋ′kə skōp′) ***n.*** [BRONCHO- + -SCOPE] an instrument for examining the bronchi, or for removing foreign bodies from them

bron·chus (bräŋ′kəs) ***n.,*** *pl.* **-chi** (-kī) [ModL. < Gr. *bronchos,* windpipe] either of the two main branches of the trachea, or windpipe

bron·co (bräŋ′kō) ***n.,*** *pl.* **-cos** [MexSp. < Sp., rough] a wild or partially tamed horse or pony of the western U.S.: also sp. **bron′cho,** *pl.* **-chos**

bron·co·bust·er (-bus′tər) ***n.*** [Colloq.] a cowboy who tames broncos —**bron′co·bust′ing** ***n.***

Bron·të (brän′tē) **1. Charlotte,** 1816–55; Eng. novelist **2. Emily Jane,** 1818–48; Eng. novelist: sister of *prec.*

bron·to·sau·rus (brän′tə sôr′əs) ***n.,*** *pl.* **-sau′rus·es, -sau′ri** (-ī) [ModL. < Gr. *brontē,* thunder + -SAURUS] a huge, plant-eating American dinosaur of the Jurassic Period: also **bron′to-saur′** (-sôr′)

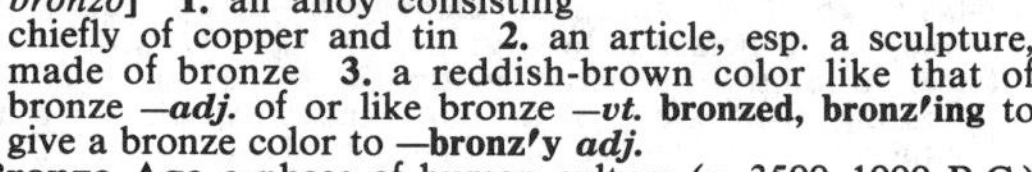
BRONTOSAURUS (to 75 ft. long)

Bronx (bräŋks) [after J. *Bronck,* early settler] N borough of New York City: pop. 1,169,000

Bronx cheer [Slang] a noisy vibration of the lips and extended tongue, as to show derision

bronze (bränz) ***n.*** [Fr. < It. *bronzo*] **1.** an alloy consisting chiefly of copper and tin **2.** an article, esp. a sculpture, made of bronze **3.** a reddish-brown color like that of bronze —***adj.*** of or like bronze —***vt.*** **bronzed, bronz′ing** to give a bronze color to —**bronz′y** ***adj.***

Bronze Age a phase of human culture (c. 3500–1000 B.C.) characterized by bronze tools and weapons

brooch (brōch, brōōch) ***n.*** [see BROACH] a large ornamental pin with a clasp

brood (brōōd) ***n.*** [< OE. *brod*] **1.** a group of birds or fowl hatched at one time and cared for together **2.** all the children in a family **3.** a group of a particular breed or kind —***vt.*** **1.** to sit on and hatch (eggs) **2.** to hover over or protect (offspring, etc.) —***vi.*** **1.** to brood eggs or offspring **2.** to keep thinking about something in a troubled way; worry (often with *on, over,* or *about*) —***adj.*** kept for breeding [a *brood* mare] —**brood′ing·ly** ***adv.***

brood·er (-ər) ***n.*** **1.** one that broods **2.** a heated shelter for raising young fowl

brood·y (-ē) ***adj.*** **brood′i·er, brood′i·est** **1.** ready to brood, as poultry **2.** inclined to dwell moodily on one's own thoughts —**brood′i·ly** ***adv.*** —**brood′i·ness** ***n.***

brook[1] (brook) ***n.*** [OE. *broc*] a small stream, usually not so large as a river

brook[2] (brook) ***vt.*** [OE. *brucan,* to use] to put up with; endure [he will *brook* no interference]

brook·let (-lit) ***n.*** a little brook

Brook·lyn (brook′lən) [< Du.] borough of New York City, on W Long Island: pop. 2,231,000 —**Brook′lyn·ite′** (-lə nīt′) ***n.***

brook trout a mottled trout native to NE N. America, but introduced elsewhere as a game fish

broom (brōōm, broom) ***n.*** [OE. *brom,* brushwood] **1.** a shrub of the legume family, with many, usually yellow, flowers **2.** a bundle of long, stiff fibers or straws (orig. twigs of broom) fastened to a long handle and used for sweeping —***vt.*** to sweep as with a broom

broom·corn (-kôrn′) ***n.*** a cultivated variety of sorghum: the stiff stems of the flower clusters are used in making brooms and brushes

broom·stick (-stik′) ***n.*** the handle of a broom

bros. brothers

broth (brôth) ***n.*** [OE.] a clear, thin soup made by boiling meat, etc. in water

broth·el (brôth′əl, bräth′-) ***n.*** [ME., wretched person < OE. pp. of *breothan,* to go to ruin] a house of prostitution

broth·er (bruth′ər) ***n.,*** *pl.* **broth′ers;** chiefly religious, **breth′ren** [OE. *brothor*] **1.** a male as he is related to the other children of his parents **2.** a close friend who is like a brother **3.** a fellow man **4.** a fellow member of the same race, creed, profession, organization, etc. **5.** a lay member of a men's religious order —***vt.*** to treat or address as a brother

broth·er·hood (-hood′) ***n.*** **1.** the state of being a brother or brothers **2.** an association of men united in a common interest, work, creed, etc.

broth·er-in-law (-in lô′) ***n.,*** *pl.* **broth′ers-in-law′** **1.** the brother of one's husband or wife **2.** the husband of one's sister **3.** the husband of the sister of one's wife or husband

broth·er·ly (-lē) ***adj.*** **1.** of or like a brother **2.** friendly, kind, loyal, etc. —**broth′er·li·ness** ***n.***

brougham (brōōm; brōō′əm, brō′-) *n.* [after Lord *Brougham* (1778–1868), Brit. statesman] **1.** a closed carriage with the driver's seat outside **2.** any of various styles of automobile

BROUGHAM

brought (brôt) *pt. & pp. of* BRING
brow (brou) *n.* [< OE. *bru*] **1.** the eyebrow **2.** the forehead **3.** the facial expression *[an angry brow]* **4.** a projecting edge, as of a cliff
brow·beat (-bēt′) *vt.* **-beat′, -beat′en, -beat′ing** to intimidate with harsh, stern looks and talk
brown (broun) *adj.* [< OE. *brun*] **1.** having the color of chocolate or coffee, a mixture of red, black, and yellow **2.** tanned or dark-skinned —*n.* **1.** a brown color **2.** a brown pigment or dye —*vt., vi.* to make or become brown, as by exposure to sunlight or heat —**do up brown** [Slang] to do completely or perfectly —**brown′ish** *adj.* —**brown′ness** *n.*
Brown, John 1800–59; U.S. abolitionist: hanged for raiding an arsenal at Harpers Ferry (W.Va.)
brown bet·ty (bet′ē) [*also* **b- B-**] a baked apple pudding made with bread crumbs, butter, etc.
brown bread **1.** any bread made of dark flour **2.** *same as* BOSTON BROWN BREAD
brown coal *same as* LIGNITE
Browne (broun) **1. Charles Far·rar** (far′ər), *see* Artemus WARD **2. Sir Thomas,** 1605–82; Eng. physician & writer
Brown·i·an movement (broun′ē ən) [after R. *Brown* (1773–1858), Brit. botanist who described it] the constant, random, zigzag movement of small particles dispersed in a fluid medium, caused by collision with molecules of the fluid
brown·ie (broun′ē) *n.* **1.** a small, helpful, brown elf or goblin in folk tales **2.** [**B-**] a Girl Scout of the youngest group, those seven and eight years old **3.** any of the small bars cut from a flat, rich chocolate cake with nuts in it
Brown·ing (broun′iŋ) **1. Elizabeth Bar·rett** (bar′it), 1806–61; Eng. poet **2. Robert,** 1812–89; Eng. poet: husband of *prec.*
brown·out (-out′) *n.* partial elimination of lights in a city, as during an electric power shortage
brown rice rice that has not been polished
brown shirt **1.** [*often* **B- S-**] a storm trooper in Nazi Germany **2.** any Nazi
brown·stone (-stōn′) *n.* **1.** a reddish-brown sandstone, used for building **2.** a house with a façade of brownstone: also **brownstone front**
brown study [< early sense of BROWN, gloomy] deep absorption in thought; reverie
brown sugar soft sugar prepared so that the crystals retain a brown coating of dark syrup
Browns·ville (brounz′vil) [after a Major *Brown,* killed there] seaport in S Tex.: pop. 85,000
browse (brouz) *n.* [< OFr. < OS. *brustian,* to sprout] **1.** leaves, twigs, and young shoots of trees or shrubs, which animals feed on **2.** the act of browsing —*vt.* **browsed, brows′ing** **1.** to nibble at **2.** to graze on **3.** to examine casually —*vi.* **1.** to nibble at leaves, twigs, etc. **2.** to glance through a book, etc. casually **3.** to look casually over articles for sale —**brows′er** *n.*
Bruce (brōōs) [Scot. < Fr. *Brieuse,* locality in France] **1.** a masculine name **2. Robert (the),** 1274–1329; Scot. patriot &, as *Robert I,* king of Scotland (1306–29)
bru·cel·lo·sis (brōō′sə lō′sis) *n.* [after Sir David *Bruce* (1855–1931), Scot. physician + -OSIS] a disease, esp. in man and cattle, caused by bacteria: see UNDULANT FEVER
Brue·gel, Brue·ghel (brü′gəl; *occas.* broi′-), **Pie·ter** (pē′tər) 1522?–69; Fl. painter
Bru·in (brōō′ən) [Du., brown] [*also* **b-**] *a name for* the bear in fable and folklore
bruise (brōōz) *vt.* **bruised, bruis′ing** [ME. *bruisen* (infl. by OFr. *bruisier,* to break) < OE. *brysan,* to crush] **1.** to injure (body tissue) without breaking the skin but causing discoloration **2.** to injure the surface of (fruit, etc.) **3.** to crush as with a pestle in a mortar **4.** to hurt (the feelings, spirit, etc.) —*vi.* to be or become bruised —*n.* **1.** a bruised area of tissue, of a surface, etc. **2.** an injury to one's feelings, etc.
bruis·er (brōōz′ər) *n.* a strong, pugnacious man; specif., a professional boxer
bruit (brōōt) *vt.* [< OFr. < *bruire,* to rumble, prob. < L. *rugire,* to roar] to spread (*about*) a rumor of
brunch (brunch) *n.* [BR(EAKFAST) + (L)UNCH] [Colloq.] a meal combining breakfast and lunch
Bru·nei (broo nī′) Brit.-protected sultanate on the NW coast of Borneo: 2,226 sq. mi.; pop. 116,000
bru·net (brōō net′) *adj.* [< OFr., dim. of *brun* < OHG. *brun,* brown] **1.** having black or dark-brown hair, often along with dark eyes and a dark complexion **2.** having a dark color: said of hair, eyes, or skin —*n.* a brunet person
bru·nette (-net′) *adj.* [Fr., fem. of prec.] *same as* BRUNET —*n.* a brunette woman or girl
Brun·hild (brōōn′hild) in the *Nibelungenlied,* a queen of Iceland: see also BRÜNNHILDE, BRYNHILD
Brünn·hil·de (broon hil′də; *G.* brün-) in Wagner's *Die Walküre,* a Valkyrie whom Siegfried releases from enchantment: see also BRUNHILD, BRYNHILD
Bru·no (brōō′nō) [OHG. < *brun,* brown] a masculine name
Bruns·wick (brunz′wik) **1.** region in C Germany **2.** city in this region: pop. 229,000
brunt (brunt) *n.* [< ? ON. *bruni,* heat] **1.** the shock (of an attack) or impact (of a blow) **2.** the heaviest or hardest part
brush[1] (brush) *n.* [< OFr. *broce,* bush < VL. *bruscia* < Gmc.] **1.** *same as* BRUSHWOOD **2.** sparsely settled, scrubby country **3.** *a)* a device for cleaning, polishing, painting, etc., having bristles, hairs, or wires fastened into a back, with or without a handle *b)* a device of wires spread from a handle, used as on drums for a swishing effect **4.** the act of brushing **5.** a light, grazing stroke **6.** a bushy tail, esp. that of a fox **7.** [Slang] *same as* BRUSHOFF **8.** *Elec.* a piece or bundle of carbon, copper, etc. used as a conductor between an external circuit and a revolving part —*vt.* **1.** to clean, polish, paint, etc. with a brush **2.** to apply, remove, etc. with a stroke or strokes as of a brush **3.** to touch or graze in passing —*vi.* to graze past something —**brush aside** (or **away**) to dismiss from consideration —**brush off** [Slang] to dismiss or get rid of abruptly —**brush up** **1.** to clean up **2.** to refresh one's memory or skill (often with *on*)
brush[2] (brush) *vi.* [ME. *bruschen* < ?] to move with a rush; hurry —*n.* a short, quick fight or quarrel
brush fire **1.** a fire in brushwood **2.** a flare-up that threatens to intensify unless controlled
brush·off (-ôf′) *n.* [Slang] an abrupt dismissal: esp. in the phrase **give** (or **get**) **the brushoff**
brush·wood (-wood′) *n.* **1.** chopped-off tree branches **2.** a thick growth of small trees and shrubs
brush·y (-ē) *adj.* **brush′i·er, brush′i·est** **1.** rough and bristly **2.** covered with brushwood or underbrush
brusque (brusk) *adj.* [Fr. < It. *brusco* < ML. *bruscus,* brushwood] rough and abrupt in manner or speech; curt: also **brusk** —**brusque′ly** *adv.* —**brusque′ness** *n.*
Brus·sels (brus′′lz) capital of Belgium, in the C part: pop. 1,079,000
Brussels sprouts **1.** a plant of the mustard family that bears miniature cabbagelike heads on an erect stem **2.** these edible heads
bru·tal (brōōt′′l) *adj.* **1.** like a brute; cruel and unfeeling; savage, violent, ruthless, etc. **2.** very harsh *[a brutal winter]* **3.** plain and direct, but disturbing *[brutal facts]* —**bru′tal·ly** *adv.*
bru·tal·i·ty (brōō tal′ə tē) *n.* **1.** the quality of being brutal **2.** *pl.* **-ties** a brutal act
bru·tal·ize (brōōt′′l īz′) *vt.* **-ized′, -iz′ing** **1.** to make brutal **2.** to treat brutally —*vi.* to become brutal —**bru′tal·i·za′tion** *n.*
brute (brōōt) *adj.* [OFr. *brut* < L. *brutus,* irrational] **1.** lacking the ability to reason *[a brute beast]* **2.** lacking consciousness *[the brute force of nature]* **3.** of or like an animal; brutal, cruel, sensual, stupid, etc. —*n.* **1.** an animal **2.** a person who is brutal or stupid, sensual, etc.
brut·ish (brōōt′ish) *adj.* of or like a brute; savage, stupid, sensual, etc. —**brut′ish·ly** *adv.* —**brut′ish·ness** *n.*
Bru·tus (brōōt′əs), **(Marcus Junius)** 85?–42 B.C.; Rom. statesman who helped kill Julius Caesar
Bry·an (brī′ən) **1.** *var. of* BRIAN **2. William Jen·nings** (jen′iŋz), 1860–1925; U.S. politician & orator
Bry·ant (brī′ənt), **William Cul·len** (kul′ən) 1794–1878; U.S. poet & journalist
Bryn·hild (brin′hild) *Norse Legend* a Valkyrie awakened from an enchanted sleep by Sigurd: see also BRUNHILD, BRÜNNHILDE
bry·ol·o·gy (brī äl′ə jē) *n.* [< Gr. *bryon,* moss + -LOGY] the branch of botany dealing with bryophytes —**bry′o·log′i·cal** (-ə läj′i k′l) *adj.* —**bry·ol′o·gist** *n.*
bry·o·ny (brī′ə nē) *n., pl.* **-nies** [< L. < Gr. < *bryein,* to swell] a vine of the gourd family, with large, fleshy roots and greenish flowers
bry·o·phyte (-fīt′) *n.* [< Gr. *bryon,* moss + -PHYTE] any moss or liverwort —**bry′o·phyt′ic** (-fit′ik) *adj.*
Bry·thon·ic (bri thän′ik) *adj., n.* [W., ult. < same word as BRITON] *see* CELTIC
B/s, b/s **1.** bags **2.** bales
B.S. Bachelor of Science
b.s. **1.** balance sheet **2.** bill of sale
B.S.A. Boy Scouts of America

B.Sc. [L. *Baccalaureus Scientiae*] Bachelor of Science
B.S.Ed. Bachelor of Science in Education
Bs/L bills of lading
Bt. Baronet
B.Th., B.T. [L. *Baccalaureus Theologiae*] Bachelor of Theology
btry battery (of artillery)
B.t.u. British thermal unit(s): also **B.T.U., b.t.u., Btu, btu**
bu. 1. bureau 2. bushel(s)
bub·ble (bub′'l) ***n.*** [echoic] **1.** a very thin film of liquid forming a ball around air or gas [*soap bubbles*] **2.** a tiny ball of air or gas in a liquid or solid **3.** anything shaped like a bubble, sphere, or hemisphere **4.** any scheme, etc. that seems plausible but proves to be worthless **5.** the act or sound of bubbling —***vi.*** **-bled, -bling 1.** to rise in bubbles; boil; foam **2.** to make a gurgling sound —***vt.*** to form bubbles in; make bubble —**bubble over 1.** to overflow, as boiling liquid **2.** to be unrestrained in one's enthusiasm, etc. —**bub′bly *adj.***
bubble bath 1. a bath perfumed and softened by a solution, crystals, or powder that forms surface bubbles **2.** such a solution, powder, etc.
bubble gum a kind of chewing gum that can be blown into large bubbles
bu·bo (byo͞o′bō, bo͞o′-) ***n., pl.*** **-boes** [< ML. < Gr. *boubōn*, groin] an inflamed swelling of a lymph gland, esp. in the groin —**bu·bon′ic** (-bän′ik) ***adj.***
bubonic plague a contagious disease characterized by buboes, fever, and delirium: fleas from infected rats are the carriers
buc·cal (buk′'l) ***adj.*** [L. *bucca*, cheek + -AL] **1.** of the cheek or cheeks **2.** of the mouth
buc·ca·neer (buk′ə nir′) ***n.*** [Fr. *boucanier*, user of a *boucan*, native Brazilian grill for roasting meat; orig. applied to Fr. hunters in Haiti] a pirate, or sea robber
Bu·chan·an (byo͞o kan′ən), **James** 1791–1868; 15th president of the U.S. (1857–61)
Bu·cha·rest (bo͞o′kə rest′, byo͞o′-) capital of Romania, in the S part: pop. 1,415,000
Buch·en·wald (bo͞o′k'n wôld′; *G.* bo͞okh′ən vält′) village in C Germany: site of a notorious Nazi concentration camp & extermination center
buck¹ (buk) ***n.*** [< OE. *bucca*, male goat] **1.** *pl.* **bucks, buck:** see PLURAL, II, D, 1 a male deer, goat, etc. **2.** the act of bucking **3.** *same as* BUCKSKIN **4.** [Colloq.] a young man: sometimes a patronizing term —***vi.*** **1.** to rear upward quickly in an attempt to throw off a rider: said of a horse, etc. **2.** to plunge forward with lowered head, as a goat **3.** [Colloq.] to resist something as if plunging against it **4.** [Colloq.] to move jerkily —***vt.*** **1.** to charge against, as in football **2.** to throw by bucking **3.** [Colloq.] to resist stubbornly —***adj.*** **1.** male **2.** of the lowest military rating [*buck* sergeant] —**buck for** [Slang] to work eagerly for (a promotion, etc.) —**buck up** [Colloq.] to cheer up —**buck′er *n.***
buck² (buk) ***n.*** [< Du. *zaagbok*] **1.** a sawbuck; sawhorse **2.** a gymnastic apparatus somewhat like a sawhorse, with a padded top, for vaulting over
buck³ (buk) ***n.*** [prob. < BUCKHORN: a knife with a buckhorn handle was used as a counter] **1.** *Poker* a counter placed before a player as a reminder to deal next, etc. **2.** [Slang] a dollar —**pass the buck** [Colloq.] to seek to make someone else take the blame or responsibility
buck and wing a complicated, fast tap dance
buck·a·roo (buk′ə ro͞o′, buk′ə ro͞o′) ***n., pl.*** **-roos′** [prob. < Gullah *buckra*, white man, altered after Sp. *vaquero*, cowboy] a cowboy
buck·board (buk′bôrd′) ***n.*** [< ?] a four-wheeled, open carriage with the seat carried on a flooring of long, flexible boards whose ends rest directly on the axles

BUCKBOARD

buck·et (buk′it) ***n.*** [< Anglo-Fr. *buket*, dim. of OE. *buc*, pitcher] **1.** a round container with a curved handle, for carrying water, coal, etc.; pail **2.** the amount held by a bucket: also **buck′et·ful′**, *pl.* **-fuls′ 3.** a thing like a bucket, as a scoop on a steam shovel **4.** [Slang] the buttocks —***vt., vi.*** to carry or lift in a bucket —**kick the bucket** [? < obs. *bucket*, beam on which a slaughtered pig was hung] [Slang] to die
bucket seat a single contoured seat whose back can be tipped forward, as in some sports cars
buck·eye (buk′ī′) ***n.*** [BUCK¹ + EYE: from the appearance of the seed] **1.** a tree of the horse-chestnut family, with large, spiny capsules enclosing shiny brown seeds **2.** the seed **3.** [**B-**] [Colloq.] a native or inhabitant of Ohio (the **Buckeye State**)
buck·horn (-hôrn′) ***n.*** the horn of a buck, used for knife handles, etc.
Buck·ing·ham Palace (buk′iŋ əm) the official residence in London of British sovereigns
buck·le¹ (buk′'l) ***n.*** [< OFr. < LL. < L. *buccula*, cheek strap of a helmet, dim. of *bucca*, cheek] **1.** a clasp for fastening a strap, belt, etc. **2.** a clasplike ornament, as for shoes —***vt., vi.*** **-led, -ling** to fasten with a buckle —**buckle down** to apply oneself energetically
buck·le² (buk′'l) ***vt., vi.*** **-led, -ling** [prob. < Du. *bukken*, to bend] to bend, warp, or crumple —***n.*** a bend, bulge, kink, etc. —**buckle under** to give in; yield; submit
buck·ler (buk′lər) ***n.*** [OFr. *bocler* < *bocle*, the boss, in its center] **1.** a small, round shield worn on the arm **2.** any protection or defense
buck·o (buk′ō) ***n., pl.*** **-oes** [< BUCK¹] a bully
buck-pass·er (-pas′ər) ***n.*** [Colloq.] a person who regularly seeks to shift blame or responsibility to someone else —**buck′-pass′ing *n.***
buck·ram (buk′rəm) ***n.*** [< OFr., prob. < *Bokhara*, in Asia Minor] a coarse cloth stiffened with glue or other size, for use in bookbinding, for lining clothes, etc. —***adj.*** of or like buckram
buck·saw (buk′sô′) ***n.*** [see BUCK²] a saw set in a frame and held with both hands in cutting wood
buck·shot (buk′shät′) ***n.*** a large lead shot for shooting deer and other large game
buck·skin (-skin′) ***n.*** **1.** a soft, usually napped, yellowish-gray leather made from the skins of deer or sheep **2.** [*pl.*] clothes or shoes made of buckskin —***adj.*** made of buckskin
buck·thorn (-thôrn′) ***n.*** [BUCK¹ + THORN] **1.** a tree or shrub with small, greenish flowers and purple drupes **2.** any of a genus of trees of the sapodilla family, native to the southern U.S.
buck·tooth (-to͞oth′) ***n., pl.*** **-teeth′** [BUCK¹ + TOOTH] a projecting front tooth —**buck′toothed′ *adj.***
buck·wheat (-hwēt′, -wēt′) ***n.*** [< ME. *bok-* (< OE. *boc-*), BEECH + WHEAT: from the beechnut-shaped seeds] **1.** a plant grown for its black, tetrahedral grains **2.** the grain of this plant, from which a dark flour is made **3.** this flour
bu·col·ic (byo͞o käl′ik) ***adj.*** [< L. < Gr. < *boukolos*, herdsman < *bous*, ox] **1.** of shepherds; pastoral **2.** of country life; rustic —***n.*** a pastoral poem —**bu·col′i·cal·ly *adv.***
bud¹ (bud) ***n.*** [ME. *budde*, seedpod] **1.** *a*) a small swelling on a plant, from which a shoot, cluster of leaves, or flower develops *b*) a partly opened flower **2.** any immature person or thing —***vi.*** **bud′ded, bud′ding 1.** to put forth buds **2.** to begin to develop **3.** to be young, promising, etc. —***vt.*** **1.** to cause to bud **2.** to graft by inserting a bud of (a plant) into the bark of another sort of plant —**nip in the bud** to check at the earliest stage —**bud′der *n.*** —**bud′like′ *adj.***
bud² (bud) ***n.*** [Slang] *short for* BUDDY: used in addressing a man or boy
Bu·da·pest (bo͞o′də pest′) capital of Hungary, on the Danube: pop. 1,990,000
Bud·dha (bo͝od′ə, bo͞o′də) [Sans., the enlightened one] Siddhartha Gautama, a religious philosopher who lived in India 563?–483? B.C. and was the founder of Buddhism
Bud·dhism (bo͝od′iz'm, bo͞o′diz'm) ***n.*** a religion of central and eastern Asia, founded in India by Buddha: it teaches that right living and self-denial will enable the soul to reach Nirvana, a divine state of release from bodily pain and sorrow —**Bud′dhist *n., adj.*** —**Bud′dhis′tic *adj.***
bud·dy (bud′ē) ***n., pl.*** **-dies** [< ? Brit. dial. *butty*, companion] [Colloq.] **1.** a companion; comrade **2.** either of two persons paired off in an arrangement (**buddy system**) for mutual help
budge (buj) ***vt., vi.*** **budged, budg′ing** [Fr. *bouger*, to move, ult. < L. *bulla*: see BOIL¹] **1.** to move even a little **2.** to yield or cause to yield
budg·er·i·gar (buj′ə ri gär′) ***n.*** [native name] an Australian parakeet with a greenish-yellow body and bright blue on the cheeks and tail feathers
budg·et (buj′it) ***n.*** [< OFr. *bougette*, dim. of *bouge*, a bag < L. *bulga*, leather bag] **1.** a collection of items; stock **2.** a plan adjusting expenses to the expected income during a certain period **3.** the estimated cost of living, operating, etc. **4.** the amount of money needed for a specific use —***vt.*** **1.** to put on or in a budget **2.** to plan in detail; schedule [*budget* your time] —***vi.*** to make a budget —**budg′et·ar′y *adj.*** —**budg′et·er *n.***
budg·ie (buj′ē) ***n.*** [Colloq.] *same as* BUDGERIGAR
Bue·na Park (bwā′nə) [Sp. *buena*, good + PARK] city in SW Calif., near Los Angeles: pop. 64,000
Bue·nos Ai·res (bwā′nəs er′ēz, ī′rēz; *Sp.* bwe′nôs ī′res) capital of Argentina, on the Río de la Plata: pop. 2,967,000
buff¹ (buf) ***n.*** [earlier *buffe*, buffalo < It. *bufalo*, BUFFALO] **1.** a heavy, soft, brownish-yellow leather made from the skin of a buffalo or from other animal hides **2.** a military coat made of this leather **3.** a stick, small block, or wheel (**buffing wheel**) covered with leather or cloth, used for cleaning or shining **4.** a dull brownish yellow **5.**

[Colloq.] a devotee; fan *[a jazz buff]* —*adj.* **1.** made of buff **2.** of the color buff —*vt.* to shine with a buff —**in the buff** naked

buff² (buf) *vt.* [OFr. *buffe:* see BUFFET¹] to lessen the force of —*vi.* to serve as a buffer

Buf·fa·lo (buf'ə lō') [transl. of the name of a Seneca Indian who lived there] city in W N.Y., on Lake Erie: pop. 358,000 (met. area 1,241,000)

buf·fa·lo (buf'ə lō') *n., pl.* **-loes', -los', -lo':** see PLURAL, II, D, 1 [It. *bufalo* < LL. < Gr. < *bous,* ox] **1.** any of various wild oxen, sometimes domesticated, as the water buffalo of India, Cape buffalo of Africa, etc. **2.** popularly, the American bison —*vt.* **-loed', -lo'ing** [Slang] to baffle, bluff, or overawe

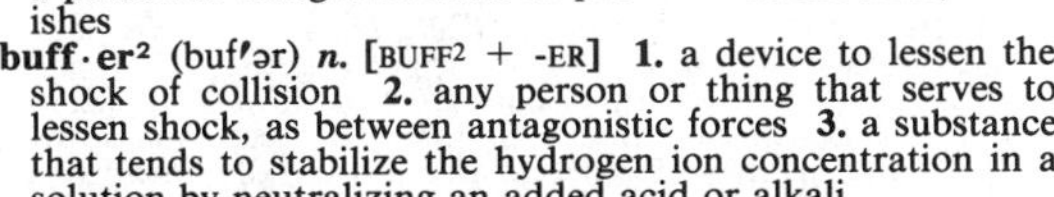

WATER BUFFALO (55–70 in. high at shoulder)

Buffalo Bill *nickname of* William CODY

buffalo grass a low, creeping range grass of the Great Plains, used for forage

buff·er¹ (buf'ər) *n.* [BUFF¹, *v.* + -ER] a person or thing that buffs or polishes

buff·er² (buf'ər) *n.* [BUFF² + -ER] **1.** a device to lessen the shock of collision **2.** any person or thing that serves to lessen shock, as between antagonistic forces **3.** a substance that tends to stabilize the hydrogen ion concentration in a solution by neutralizing an added acid or alkali

buf·fet¹ (buf'it) *n.* [< OFr. < *buffe,* a blow] **1.** a blow with the hand or fist **2.** any blow or shock —*vt.* **1.** to punch or slap **2.** to thrust about **3.** to struggle against —*vi.* to struggle

buf·fet² (bə fā', boo-) *n.* [Fr. < OFr. *buffet,* a bench] **1.** a piece of furniture with drawers and cupboards for dishes, table linen, silver, etc. **2.** a counter where refreshments are served, or a restaurant with such a counter **3.** a meal at which guests serve themselves as from a buffet

‡**buf·fo** (bo͞of'fô; *E.* bo͞o'fō) *n., pl.* **-fi** (-fē) [It., comic: see ff.] an opera singer, generally a bass, in a comic role

buf·foon (bə fo͞on') *n.* [< Fr. < It. < *buffare,* to jest] a person who is always clowning and trying to be funny —**buf·foon'er·y** *n.* —**buf·foon'ish** *adj.*

bug (bug) *n.* [prob. < W. *bwg,* hobgoblin] **1.** any of various insects with sucking mouthparts and with forewings thickened toward the base **2.** any insect or small, insectlike animal, specif. one regarded as a pest **3.** [Colloq.] a germ or virus **4.** [Slang] a tiny microphone hidden to record conversation secretly **5.** [Slang] a defect, as in a machine **6.** [Slang] a hobbyist or devotee —*vt.* **bugged, bug'ging** [Slang] **1.** to hide a microphone in (a room, etc.) for secretly recording conversation **2.** to annoy, anger, etc. —*vi.* [Slang] to bulge or open wide: said of the eyes —**bug off** [Slang] to stop annoying someone and leave

bug·a·boo (bug'ə bo͞o') *n., pl.* **-boos'** a bugbear

bug·bear (-ber') *n.* [BUG + BEAR²] **1.** an imaginary hobgoblin or terror **2.** a cause of needless fear or anxiety

bug-eyed (-īd') *adj.* [Slang] with bulging eyes

bug·gy¹ (bug'ē) *n., pl.* **-gies** [< ?] **1.** a light, one-horse carriage with one seat **2.** *same as* BABY CARRIAGE

bug·gy² (bug'ē) *adj.* **-gi·er, -gi·est** **1.** infested or swarming with bugs **2.** [Slang] mentally ill

bug·house (-hous') *n.* [Slang] an insane asylum —*adj.* [Slang] mentally ill

bu·gle (byo͞o'g'l) *n.* [< OFr. < L. *buculus,* young ox, dim. of *bos,* ox] a brass-wind instrument like a trumpet but smaller, and usually without keys or valves: used chiefly for military calls —*vi., vt.* **-gled, -gling** to call or signal by blowing a bugle —**bu'gler** *n.*

bugs (bugz) *adj.* [Slang] mentally ill

bug·shah (bug'shə, -shô) *n., pl.* **-shah, -shahs** *see* MONETARY UNITS, table (Yemen Arab Rep.)

build (bild) *vt.* **built** or archaic **build'ed, build'ing** [< OE. *byldan* < base of *bold,* a house] **1.** to make, or direct the making of, by putting together materials, parts, etc.; construct **2.** to make a basis for; establish *[to build a theory on facts]* **3.** to create, develop, promote, strengthen, etc. —*vi.* **1.** *a)* to put up buildings *b)* to have a house, etc. built **2.** to grow or intensify —*n.* the way a thing is built or shaped; form or figure *[a stocky build]*

build·er (bil'dər) *n.* **1.** one that builds **2.** a person in the business of constructing buildings

build·ing (-diŋ) *n.* **1.** anything that is built with walls and a roof **2.** the act, process, work, or business of constructing houses, ships, etc.

build·up, build-up (bild'up') *n.* [Colloq.] **1.** favorable publicity or praise **2.** growth or expansion *[a military buildup]*

built-in (bilt'in') *adj.* **1.** made as part of the building *[a built-in bathtub]* **2.** intrinsic; inherent

built-up (-up') *adj.* **1.** made higher, stronger, etc. by the addition of parts **2.** having many buildings on it: said of an area

bulb (bulb) *n.* [< L. < Gr. *bolbos*] **1.** an underground bud that sends down roots and has a very short stem covered with leafy scales, as in a lily, onion, etc. **2.** a corm, tuber, or tuberous root resembling a bulb, as in a crocus **3.** a plant that grows from a bulb **4.** anything shaped like a bulb *[an electric light bulb]* —**bul·bar** (bul'bər) *adj.* —**bulbed** *adj.*

bul·ba·ceous (bəl bā'shəs) *adj. same as* BULBOUS

bul·bous (bul'bəs) *adj.* **1.** of, having, or growing from bulbs **2.** shaped like a bulb

Bul·gar·i·a (bəl ger'ē ə, bool-) country in SE Europe, on the Black Sea, south of Romania: 42,796 sq. mi.; pop. 8,436,000; cap. Sofia —**Bul·gar'i·an, Bul·gar** (bul'gär, bool'-) *adj., n.*

bulge (bulj) *n.* [ME., var. of *bouge:* see BUDGET] **1.** an outward swelling; protuberance **2.** a projecting part **3.** [Colloq.] a sudden increase —*vi., vt.* **bulged, bulg'ing** to swell or bend outward; protrude —**bulg'y** (-ē) *adj.*

bul·gur (wheat) (bool'gər, bul'-) [Turk.] wheat cooked and dried, then coarsely ground: often cooked like pilaf

bulk (bulk) *n.* [ON. *bulki,* a heap, cargo] **1.** size, mass, or volume, esp. if great **2.** the main mass or body; largest part *[the bulk of one's fortune]* **3.** soft, bulky matter that passes through the intestines unabsorbed —*vi.* **1.** to form into a mass **2.** to increase in size, importance, etc. **3.** to have size or importance —*vt.* to cause to bulk; give more bulk to —*adj.* **1.** total; aggregate **2.** not put up in individual packages —**in bulk** **1.** not put up in individual packages **2.** in large amounts

bulk·head (bulk'hed') *n.* [< ON. *balkr,* partition + HEAD] **1.** any of the upright partitions separating parts of a ship, airplane, etc. as for protection against fire or leakage **2.** a wall or embankment for holding back earth, fire, water, etc. **3.** a boxlike structure built over an opening, as at the head of a staircase, elevator shaft, etc.

bulk·y (bul'kē) *adj.* **bulk'i·er, bulk'i·est** **1.** *a)* having great bulk; large; massive *b)* relatively large for its weight **2.** awkwardly large; big and clumsy —**bulk'i·ly** *adv.* —**bulk'i·ness** *n.*

bull¹ (bool) *n.* [< OE. *bula,* a steer] **1.** the adult male of any bovine animal, as the ox, buffalo, etc. **2.** the adult male of certain other large animals, as the elephant, moose, walrus, whale, etc. **3.** a person who buys stocks, etc. expecting, or seeking to bring about, a rise in their prices **4.** a person regarded as like a bull in size, strength, etc. **5.** [Slang] a policeman or detective **6.** [Slang] foolish or insincere talk; nonsense —**[B-]** *same as* TAURUS —*vt.* to make (one's way) with force —*adj.* **1.** male **2.** like a bull in size, strength, etc. **3.** rising in price *[a bull market]* —**shoot the bull** [Slang] to talk idly —**take the bull by the horns** to deal boldly with a danger or difficulty —**bull'ish** *adj.* —**bull'ish·ly** *adv.* —**bull'ish·ness** *n.*

bull² (bool) *n.* [< OFr. < LL. *bulla,* a seal (L., bubble)] an official document or decree from the Pope

bull³ (bool) *n.* [ult. < L. *bulla,* bubble] a mistake in statement that is illogical in a ludicrous way

bull- [< BULL¹] *a combining form meaning:* **1.** of a bull or bulls *[bullfight]* **2.** like a bull or bull's *[bullhead]* **3.** large or male *[bullfrog]*

bull·dog (bool'dôg', -däg') *n.* [BULL- + DOG] a short-haired, square-jawed, heavily built dog noted for its strong, stubborn grip —*adj.* like or characteristic of a bulldog —*vt.* **-dogged', -dog'ging** to throw (a steer) by seizing its horns and twisting its neck

bull·doze (-dōz') *vt.* **-dozed', -doz'ing** [< *bull* (Botany Bay slang), a flogging of 75 lashes + DOSE] **1.** [Colloq.] to force or frighten by threatening; intimidate **2.** to move, make level, dig out, etc. with a bulldozer

bull·doz·er (-dō'zər) *n.* **1.** a person who bulldozes **2.** a tractor with a large, shovellike blade on the front, for pushing or moving earth, debris, etc.

bul·let (bool'it) *n.* [Fr. *boulette,* dim. of *boule,* a ball < L. *bulla:* see BULL²] **1.** a small, shaped piece of lead, metal alloy, etc. to be shot from a firearm **2.** anything like a bullet in shape, action, etc.

bul·le·tin (bool'ət 'n) *n.* [Fr. < It. dim. of LL. *bulla:* see BULL²] **1.** a brief statement of the latest news **2.** a regular publication, as for members of a society —*vt.* to announce in a bulletin

bulletin board a board or wall area on which notices or displays are put up

bul·let·proof (bool'it pro͞of') *adj.* that bullets cannot pierce —*vt.* to make bulletproof

bull·fight (bool′fīt′) ***n.*** a public show in which a bull is first provoked in various ways and then usually killed with a sword by a matador —**bull′fight′er** ***n.*** —**bull′fight′ing** ***n.***

bull·finch (-finch′) ***n.*** [BULL- + FINCH] **1.** a European songbird with a black head and white rump **2.** any of various other small songbirds

bull·frog (-frôg′, -fräg′) ***n.*** [BULL- + FROG] a large N. American frog with a deep, loud croak

bull·head (-hed′) ***n.*** [see BULL-] **1.** any of various N. American freshwater catfishes **2.** any of various similar fishes of fresh or salt waters

bull·head·ed (-hed′id) ***adj.*** blindly stubborn —**bull′head′ed·ly** ***adv.*** —**bull′head′ed·ness** ***n.***

bull·horn (-hôrn′) ***n.*** [BULL- + HORN] a portable electronic voice amplifier

bul·lion (bool′yən) ***n.*** [< Du. < OFr. *billon*, small coin < *bille*, a stick: see BILLET[2]] **1.** gold and silver regarded as raw material **2.** bars of gold or silver, as before coinage

bull-necked (-nekt′) ***adj.*** having a short, thick neck

bull·ock (bool′ək) ***n.*** [< OE. *bulluc*, dim. of *bula:* see BULL[1]] a castrated bull; steer

bull·pen (-pen′) ***n.*** **1.** a fenced enclosure for bulls **2.** [Colloq.] an enclosure in a jail, where prisoners are herded temporarily **3.** *Baseball* an area where relief pitchers practice and warm up

bull·ring (-riŋ′) ***n.*** an arena for bullfighting

Bull Run [< ?] small stream in NE Va.: site of two Union defeats (1861 & 1862) in the Civil War

bull's-eye (boolz′ī′) ***n.*** **1.** a thick, circular glass in a roof, ship's deck, etc., for admitting light **2.** *a)* the central mark of a target *b)* a direct hit **3.** *a)* a convex lens for concentrating light *b)* a lantern with such a lens **4.** a hard, round candy

bull terrier a strong, lean, white dog, developed by crossing the bulldog and the terrier

bull·whip (bool′hwip′, -wip′) ***n.*** [BULL- + WHIP] a long, heavy whip, formerly used by cattle drivers, etc. —***vt.*** **-whipped′, -whip′ping** to whip with a bullwhip

bul·ly[1] (bool′ē) ***n.,*** *pl.* **-lies** [orig., sweetheart < Du. < MHG. *buole* (G. *buhle*), lover; later infl. by BULL[1]] a person who hurts, frightens, or browbeats those who are smaller or weaker —***vt., vi.*** **-lied, -ly·ing** to behave like a bully (toward) —***adj.*** **1.** dashing, hearty, or jolly **2.** [Colloq.] fine; very good —***interj.*** [Colloq.] good! well done!

bul·ly[2] (bool′ē) ***n.*** [< Fr. < *bouillir*, to boil] canned or corned beef: also **bully beef**

bul·ly·rag (-rag′) ***vt.*** **-ragged′, -rag′ging** [see BULLY[1], *vt.* & RAG[2], *vt.*] [Dial. or Colloq.] to bully or intimidate

bul·rush (bool′rush′) ***n.*** [< OE. *bol*, BOLE + *risc*, a rush] **1.** a marsh plant of the sedge family **2.** [Brit.] the cattail **3.** the papyrus or other aquatic plant like a bulrush: cf. Ex. 2:3

bul·wark (bool′wərk, bul′-) ***n.*** [< MDu. *bolwerc:* see BOLE & WORK] **1.** an earthwork or defensive wall; rampart **2.** a defense or protection **3.** [*usually pl.*] a ship's side above the deck —***vt.*** **1.** to provide bulwarks for **2.** to be a bulwark to

bum (bum) ***n.*** [prob. < G. *bummler*, loafer < *bummeln*, to go slowly] [Colloq.] **1.** a vagrant, tramp, beggar, or derelict **2.** any shiftless or irresponsible person **3.** a devotee, as of golf or skiing, who neglects all else —***vi.*** **bummed, bum′ming** [Colloq.] **1.** to live as a bum **2.** to live by sponging on people —***vt.*** [Slang] to get by sponging; cadge —***adj.*** **bum′mer, bum′mest** [Slang] **1.** poor in quality **2.** false or not valid *[a bum steer]* **3.** lame or ailing —**give** (or **get**) **the bum's rush** [Slang] to eject (or be ejected) forcibly —**on the bum** [Colloq.] **1.** living as a vagrant **2.** out of repair; broken —**bum′mer** ***n.***

bum·ble·bee (bum′b'l bē′) ***n.*** [altered (after ME. *bomblen*, to buzz) < ME. *humbul-be*, bumblebee] a large, hairy, yellow-and-black social bee

bum·bling (bum′bliŋ) ***adj.*** [prp. of *bumble*, buzz: see prec.] self-important in a blundering way

bump (bump) ***vt.*** [echoic] **1.** to hit against; collide lightly with **2.** [Slang] to displace, as from a job, plane reservation, etc. —***vi.*** **1.** to collide with a jolt **2.** to move with jolts —***n.*** **1.** a light blow or jolt **2.** a swelling or lump, esp. one caused by a blow —**bump into** [Colloq.] to meet unexpectedly —**bump off** [Slang] to murder

bump·er[1] (bum′pər) ***n.*** a device for absorbing some of the shock of a collision; specif., a metal bar across the front or back of an automobile

bump·er[2] (bum′pər) ***n.*** [prob. < obs. *bombard*, liquor jug, altered after BUMP] **1.** a cup or glass filled to the brim **2.** [Colloq.] anything unusually large of its kind —***adj.*** unusually abundant *[a bumper crop]*

bump·kin (bump′kən, bum′-) ***n.*** [prob. < MDu. *bommekijn*, small cask] an awkward or simple person from the country

bump·tious (bump′shəs) ***adj.*** [prob. < BUMP] disagreeably conceited, arrogant, or forward —**bump′tious·ly** ***adv.*** —**bump′tious·ness** ***n.***

bump·y (bum′pē) ***adj.*** **bump′i·er, bump′i·est** full of bumps; rough —**bump′i·ly** ***adv.*** —**bump′i·ness** ***n.***

bun (bun) ***n.*** [ME. *bunne*, wheat cake, prob. < OFr. *buigne*, a swelling] **1.** a small roll, usually somewhat sweetened and often spiced **2.** hair worn in a roll or knot

bunch (bunch) ***n.*** [ult. < Fl. *boudje*, dim. of *boud*, bundle] **1.** a cluster of things growing together *[a bunch of grapes]* **2.** a collection of things of the same kind fastened, grouped, or thought of together *[a bunch of keys]* **3.** [Colloq.] a group of people —***vt., vi.*** to gather together in a mass or in loose folds, wads, etc. (often with *up*) —**bunch′i·ness** ***n.*** —**bunch′y** ***adj.***

bun·co (buŋ′kō) ***n.,*** *pl.* **-cos** [< Sp. *banca*, card game < It. *banca*, BANK[1]] [Colloq.] a swindle, esp. at a card game; confidence game —***vt.*** **-coed, -co·ing** [Colloq.] to swindle; cheat

bun·combe (buŋ′kəm) ***n.*** [< *Buncombe* county, N.C., whose Congressman (1819–21) regularly made "a speech for Buncombe"] [Colloq.] talk that is empty, insincere, or merely for effect; humbug

bund, Bund (boond; *G.* boont) ***n.,*** *pl.* **bunds;** G. **Bun·de** (bün′də) [G.] **1.** a league or confederation **2.** the German-American Bund, a former pro-Nazi organization in the U.S. —**bund′ist** ***n.***

bun·dle (bun′d'l) ***n.*** [prob. < MDu. *bondel* < *binden*, BIND] **1.** a number of things tied or wrapped together **2.** a package or parcel **3.** a bunch, collection, or group **4.** [Slang] a large amount of money **5.** *same as* VASCULAR BUNDLE —***vt.*** **-dled, -dling** **1.** to make into a bundle; wrap or tie together **2.** to send hastily (*away, off, out,* or *into*) —***vi.*** **1.** to move or go hastily; bustle **2.** to lie in the same bed with one's sweetheart without undressing: a former courting custom, esp. in New England —**bundle up** to put on plenty of warm clothing —**bun′dler** ***n.***

bung (buŋ) ***n.*** [< MDu. *bonge*] **1.** a cork or other stopper for the hole in a barrel, cask, or keg **2.** a bunghole —***vt.*** **1.** to close (a bunghole) with a stopper **2.** to stop up **3.** [Slang] to bruise or damage (with *up*)

bun·ga·low (buŋ′gə lō′) ***n.*** [< Hindi *bānglā*, thatched house, lit., Bengalese] a small house or cottage, usually of one story and an attic

bung·hole (buŋ′hōl′) ***n.*** a hole in a barrel or keg through which liquid can be drawn out

bun·gle (buŋ′g'l) ***vt.*** **-gled, -gling** [< ? Sw. *bangla*, to work ineffectually] to spoil by clumsy work; botch —***vi.*** to do things badly or clumsily —***n.*** **1.** a bungling, or clumsy, act **2.** a bungled piece of work —**bun′gler** ***n.*** —**bun′gling·ly** ***adv.***

bun·ion (bun′yən) ***n.*** [prob. < ME. *boni*, swelling, boil < OFr. *buigne:* see BUN] an inflammation and swelling at the base of the big toe

bunk[1] (buŋk) ***n.*** [prob. < Scand. cognate of BENCH] **1.** a shelflike bed or berth built into or against a wall, as in a ship **2.** [Colloq.] any sleeping place, as a narrow cot —***vi.*** **1.** to sleep in a bunk **2.** [Colloq.] to use a makeshift sleeping place —***vt.*** to provide a sleeping place for

bunk[2] (buŋk) ***n.*** [Slang] *same as* BUNCOMBE

bunk bed a pair of twin beds linked one above the other, often with a detachable ladder

bunk·er (buŋ′kər) ***n.*** [Scot. < ?] **1.** a large bin or tank, as for a ship's fuel **2.** a weapon emplacement of steel and concrete in an underground fortification system **3.** a sand trap or mound of earth serving as an obstacle on a golf course —***vt.*** *Golf* to hit (a ball) into a bunker

Bun·ker Hill (buŋ′kər) hill in Boston, Mass., near which a battle of the American Revolution was fought in 1775

bunk·house (buŋk′hous′) ***n.*** a barracks for ranch hands, migratory farm workers, etc.

bun·ko (buŋ′kō) ***n.,*** *pl.* **-kos,** ***vt.*** **-koed, -ko·ing** *same as* BUNCO

bun·kum (buŋ′kəm) ***n.*** *same as* BUNCOMBE

bun·ny (bun′ē) ***n.,*** *pl.* **-nies** [dim. of dial. *bun*, rabbit] a rabbit: pet name used by children

Bun·sen burner (bun′s'n) [after R. W. *Bunsen*, 19th-c. Ger. chemist] a small, tubular gas burner that produces a hot, blue flame

bunt (bunt) ***vt., vi.*** [< ? base of Bret. *bounta*, to butt] **1.** [Brit. Dial.] to strike or butt with or as with horns **2.** *Baseball* to bat (a pitched ball) lightly without swinging so that it does not go beyond the infield, usually in attempting a sacrifice play —***n.*** **1.** a butt or shove **2.** *Baseball a)* the act of bunting *b)* a bunted ball

bun·ting[1] (bun′tiŋ) ***n.*** [< ? ME. *bonting*, sifting (cloth)] **1.** a thin cloth used in making flags, etc. **2.** flags, or strips of cloth in the colors of the flag, used as decorations **3.** a baby's garment of soft, warm cloth made into a kind of hooded blanket that can be closed

bun·ting[2] (bun′tiŋ) ***n.*** [< ?] any of various small, brightly colored birds having a stout bill

bunt·line (bunt′lin, -līn′) ***n.*** [*bunt*, middle part of a sail + LINE[1]] one of the ropes attached to the foot of a square sail to prevent the sail from bellying when drawn up to be furled

Bun·yan (bun′yən) **1. John,** 1628–88; Eng. writer & preacher **2.** *see* PAUL BUNYAN
Buo·na·par·te (bwô′nä pär′te) *It. sp. of* BONAPARTE
buoy (bo͞o′ē, boi; *for v., usually* boi) ***n.*** [< OFr. *buie,* chain < L. *boia,* fetter: prob. first applied to the chain anchoring the float] **1.** a floating object anchored in water to warn of rocks, shoals, etc. or to mark a channel **2.** *short for* LIFE BUOY —***vt.*** **1.** to mark or provide with a buoy **2.** to keep afloat: usually with *up* **3.** to lift or keep up in spirits; encourage: usually with *up*
buoy·an·cy (boi′ən sē, bo͞o′yən-) ***n.*** [< ff.] **1.** the ability or tendency to float or rise in liquid or air **2.** the power to keep something afloat **3.** lightness of spirit; cheerfulness
buoy·ant (-ənt, -yənt) ***adj.*** [< ? Sp. < *boyar,* to float] having or showing buoyancy —**buoy′ant·ly** ***adv.***
bur (bʉr) ***n.*** [ME. *burre* < Scand.] **1.** the rough, prickly seedcase or fruit of certain plants **2.** a weed or other plant with burs **3.** anything that clings like a bur **4.** *Dentistry* a cutting or drilling bit **5.** *same as* BURR[1] & BURR[2] —***vt.*** **burred, bur′ring** **1.** to remove burs from **2.** to burr
bur. bureau
Bur·bank (bʉr′baŋk) [after Dr. D. *Burbank,* one of the city planners] city in SW Calif.: suburb of Los Angeles: pop. 85,000
Bur·bank (bʉr′baŋk), **Luther** 1849–1926; U.S. horticulturist: bred numerous varieties of plants
bur·ble (bʉr′b'l) ***vi.*** **-bled, -bling** [echoic] **1.** to make a gurgling or bubbling sound **2.** to babble as a child does
bur·bot (bʉr′bət) ***n.,*** *pl.* **-bot, -bots:** see PLURAL, II, D, 2 [< OFr. *borbote,* ult. < L. *barba,* a beard] a freshwater fish of the cod family, with barbels on the nose and chin
bur·den[1] (bʉrd′'n) ***n.*** [< OE. *byrthen* < base of *beran:* see BEAR[1]] **1.** anything that is carried; load **2.** a heavy load, as of work, responsibility, sorrow, etc. **3.** the carrying of loads *[*a beast of *burden]* **4.** the carrying capacity of a ship, or the weight of its cargo —***vt.*** to put a burden on; load; oppress
bur·den[2] (bʉrd′'n) ***n.*** [< OFr. *bourdon,* a humming < ML. *burdo,* DRONE[1], wind instrument] **1.** a chorus or refrain of a song **2.** a repeated, central idea; theme *[*the *burden* of a speech*]*
burden of proof the obligation to prove what is asserted and in dispute
bur·den·some (-səm) ***adj.*** hard to bear; heavy; oppressive —**bur′den·some·ly** ***adv.***
bur·dock (bʉr′däk′) ***n.*** [BUR + DOCK[3]] a plant of the composite family, with large leaves, and purple-flowered heads covered with hooked prickles
bu·reau (byoor′ō) ***n.,*** *pl.* **-reaus, -reaux** (-ōz) [Fr., desk < OFr. *burel,* coarse cloth (as table cover) < LL. *burra,* ragged (woolen) garment] **1.** [Brit.] a desk with drawers for papers **2.** a chest of drawers, often with a mirror, for clothing, etc. **3.** an agency providing specified services for clients *[*a travel *bureau]* **4.** a government department or a subdivision of this
bu·reau·cra·cy (byoo rä′krə sē) ***n.,*** *pl.* **-cies** [< Fr. < *bureau* + *-cratie,* -CRACY] **1.** the administration of government through departments managed by officials following an inflexible routine **2.** the officials collectively **3.** governmental officialism or inflexible routine **4.** concentration of authority in a complex structure of administrative bureaus
bu·reau·crat (byoor′ə krat′) ***n.*** an official in a bureaucracy, esp. one who follows a routine strictly, insisting on proper forms, petty rules, etc. —**bu′reau·crat′ic** ***adj.*** —**bu′reau·crat′i·cal·ly** ***adv.***
bu·reau·cra·tize (byoo rä′krə tīz′) ***vt., vi.*** **-tized′, -tiz′ing** to make or become bureaucratic —**bu·reau′cra·ti·za′tion** ***n.***
bu·rette, bu·ret (byoo ret′) ***n.*** [Fr. < OFr. dim. of *buire,* flagon] a graduated glass tube with a stopcock at the bottom, for measuring small quantities of liquid or gas
burg (bʉrg) ***n.*** [var. of BOROUGH] **1.** orig., a fortified town **2.** [Colloq.] a city, town, or village, esp. one regarded as quiet, unexciting, etc.
-burg (bʉrg) *a suffix meaning* burg or borough *[Vicksburg]* : also **-burgh** *[Pittsburgh]*
bur·geon (bʉr′jən) ***vi.*** [< OFr. < *burjon,* a bud] **1.** to put forth buds, shoots, etc. **2.** to grow or develop rapidly; flourish *[*the *burgeoning* suburbs*]*
-bur·ger (bʉr′gər) [< (HAM)BURGER] *a combining form meaning:* **1.** sandwich of a patty of ground meat, fish, etc. *[turkeyburger]* **2.** hamburger and *[cheeseburger]*
Bur·ger (bʉr′gər), **Warren Earl** 1907– ; U.S. jurist; chief justice of the U.S. (1969–)
bur·gess (bʉr′jis) ***n.*** [OFr. *burgeis:* see BOURGEOIS] a member of the lower house of the legislature of Md. or Va. before the American Revolution
burgh (bʉrg; *Scot.* bu′rə) ***n.*** [Scot. var. of BOROUGH] **1.** [Brit.] a borough **2.** in Scotland, a chartered town
burgh·er (bʉr′gər) ***n.*** an inhabitant of a borough or town; now, esp., a middle-class townsman
bur·glar (bʉr′glər) ***n.*** [< Anglo-L. *burglator,* altered after L. *latro,* thief < OFr. *burgeor,* burglar] a person who commits burglary
bur·glar·i·ous (bər gler′ē əs) ***adj.*** of, given to, or being burglary —**bur·glar′i·ous·ly** ***adv.***
bur·glar·ize (bʉr′glə rīz′) ***vt.*** **-ized′, -iz′ing** [Colloq.] to commit burglary in or upon
bur·gla·ry (bʉr′glər ē) ***n.,*** *pl.* **-ries** [BURGLAR + -Y[4]] **1.** the act of breaking into a house at night to commit theft or other felony **2.** a breaking into any building at any time to commit theft, etc.
bur·gle (bʉr′g'l) ***vt., vi.*** **-gled, -gling** [< BURGLAR] [Colloq.] to commit burglary (in)
bur·go·mas·ter (bʉr′gə mas′tər) ***n.*** [< MDu. < *burg,* town + *meester,* master] the mayor or head magistrate of a city or town in the Netherlands, Flanders, Austria, or Germany
Bur·gun·dy (bʉr′gən dē) region in SE France: formerly a province, duchy, & kingdom of varying extent —***n.*** [*occas.* **b-**] *pl.* **-dies** **1.** a kind of wine, either red or white, made in the Burgundy region **2.** a similar red wine made elsewhere —**Bur·gun·di·an** (bər gun′dē ən) ***adj., n.***
bur·i·al (ber′ē əl) ***n.*** the burying of a dead body; interment —***adj.*** of or connected with burial
burial ground a cemetery; graveyard
bu·rin (byoor′in) ***n.*** [Fr. < It. < Gmc. *boro,* borer] a pointed cutting tool used by engravers or marble workers

BURIN

Burke (bʉrk), **Edmund** 1729–97; Brit. statesman, orator, & writer, born in Ireland
burl (bʉrl) ***n.*** [< OFr. < VL. < LL. *burra:* see BUREAU] **1.** a knot in wool, thread, yarn, etc. that gives a nubby appearance to cloth **2.** a kind of knot on some tree trunks —***vt.*** to finish (cloth) by taking out the burls, etc. —**burled** ***adj.***
bur·lap (bʉr′lap) ***n.*** [< ? ME. *borel,* coarse cloth (< OFr. *burel:* see BUREAU) + *lappa,* LAP[1]] a coarse cloth made of jute or hemp, used for making sacks, etc.
bur·lesque (bər lesk′) ***n.*** [Fr. < It. < *burla,* a jest] **1.** any broadly comic or satirical imitation; parody **2.** (*also, facetiously,* bʉr′li kyo͞o′) a sort of vaudeville characterized by low comedy, striptease acts, etc. —***adj.*** **1.** comically imitating; parodying **2.** of or connected with burlesque (sense 2) —***vt., vi.*** **-lesqued′, -lesqu′ing** to imitate comically or derisively; parody
bur·ley (bʉr′lē) ***n.*** [< ? a proper name] [*also* **B-**] a thin-leaved tobacco grown esp. in Kentucky
bur·ly (bʉr′lē) ***adj.*** **-li·er, -li·est** [ME. *borlich,* excellent, handsome < ? OE. *borlice,* very, excellently] **1.** big and strong; heavy and muscular **2.** rough and hearty in manner —**bur′li·ness** ***n.***
Bur·ma (bʉr′mə) country in SE Asia, on the Indochinese peninsula: 261,789 sq. mi.; pop. 26,980,000; cap. Rangoon —**Bur·mese** (bər mēz′) ***adj., n.,*** *pl.* **-mese′**
burn[1] (bʉrn) ***vt.*** **burned** or **burnt, burn′ing** [< ON. & OE.: ON. *brenna,* to burn, light; OE. *biernan*] **1.** to set on fire or subject to combustion **2.** to destroy by fire **3.** to injure or damage by fire, friction, or acid; scorch, scald, etc. **4.** to consume as fuel **5.** to transform into energy by metabolism **6.** to sunburn **7.** to cauterize **8.** to harden or glaze (bricks, pottery, etc.) by fire; fire **9.** to cause by fire, heat, etc. *[*to *burn* a hole in a coat*]* **10.** to cause a sensation of heat in *[*horseradish *burns* the throat*]* **11.** [Slang] *a)* to cheat, swindle, or rob *b)* to cause to suffer through misplaced trust: usually used in the passive —***vi.*** **1.** to be on fire; flame; blaze **2.** to undergo combustion **3.** to give out light or heat; shine; glow **4.** to be destroyed by fire or heat **5.** to be injured or damaged by or as by fire or heat **6.** to feel hot **7.** to be excited or inflamed, as with anger or desire —***n.*** **1.** an injury caused by fire, heat, wind, etc. **2.** the process or result of burning —**burn down** to burn to the ground —**burn oneself out** to exhaust oneself by too much work or dissipation —**burn up** **1.** to burn completely **2.** [Slang] to make or become angry
burn[2] (bʉrn) ***n.*** [see BOURN[1]] [Scot.] a brook
burn·a·ble (-ə b'l) ***adj.*** that can be burned —***n.*** something, esp. refuse, that can be burned
burn·er (bʉr′nər) ***n.*** **1.** the part of a stove, furnace, etc. from which the flame comes **2.** an apparatus for burning fuel or trash
burn·ing (bʉr′niŋ) ***adj.*** **1.** that burns **2.** intense; critical *[*a *burning* issue*]*

bur·nish (bur′nish) *vt., vi.* [< OFr. *brunir,* to make brown < *brun,* brown] to make or become shiny by rubbing; polish —*n.* a gloss or polish —**bur′nish·er** *n.*

bur·noose, bur·nous (bər no͞os′, bur′no͞os) *n.* [< Fr. < Ar. *burnus,* prob. < Gr. *birros,* a cloak] a long cloak with a hood, worn by Arabs and Moors

Burns (burnz), **Robert** 1759–96; Scot. poet

burn·sides (burn′sīdz′) *n.pl.* [after A. E. *Burnside,* Union general in the Civil War] a style of beard with full side whiskers and mustache, but with the chin clean-shaven

burnt (burnt) *alt. pt. and pp. of* BURN[1]

burnt sienna *see* SIENNA

burnt umber *see* UMBER

burp (burp) *n., vi.* [echoic] [Colloq.] belch —*vt.* to cause (a baby) to relieve itself of stomach gas, as by patting its back

burp gun [echoic] [Mil. Slang] any of various automatic pistols or submachine guns

burr[1] (bur) *n.* [var. of BUR] **1.** a rough edge left on metal, etc. by cutting or drilling **2.** *same as* BUR (senses 1, 2, 3) —*vt.* **1.** to form a rough edge on **2.** to remove burrs from (metal)

burr[2] (bur) *n.* [prob. echoic] **1.** the trilling of *r,* with uvula or tongue *[a Scottish burr]* **2.** a whirring sound —*vi.* **1.** to speak with a burr **2.** to make a whir —*vt.* to pronounce with a burr

Burr (bur), **Aaron** 1756–1836; U.S. political leader: killed Alexander Hamilton in a duel

bur·ro (bur′ō, boor′ō) *n., pl.* **-ros** [Sp. < LL. *burricus,* small horse] [Southwest] a donkey

bur·row (bur′ō, -ə) *n.* [see BOROUGH] **1.** a hole dug in the ground by an animal **2.** any similar hole for shelter, etc. —*vi.* **1.** to make a burrow **2.** to live or hide in or as in a burrow **3.** to delve or search, as if by digging —*vt.* **1.** to make burrows in **2.** to make by burrowing

bur·ry[1] (bur′ē) *adj.* **-ri·er, -ri·est** **1.** full of burs **2.** like a bur or burs; prickly

bur·ry[2] (bur′ē) *adj.* **-ri·er, -ri·est** having a burr in speech

bur·sa (bur′sə) *n., pl.* **-sae** (-sē), **-sas** [ML., a bag < Gr. *byrsa,* a hide] *Anat.* a sac or cavity, esp. one containing a fluid that reduces friction, as between a tendon and bone —**bur′sal** *adj.*

bur·sar (bur′sər) *n.* [ML. *bursarius* < *bursa:* see prec.] a treasurer, as of a college

bur·si·tis (bər sīt′əs) *n.* [< BURSA + -ITIS] inflammation of a bursa

burst (burst) *vi.* **burst, burst′ing** [< OE. *berstan* & ON. *bresta*] **1.** to come apart suddenly and violently; break open or out; explode **2.** to give sudden expression to some feeling; break (*into* tears, laughter, etc.) **3.** to go, come, start, etc. suddenly and with force *[he burst into the room]* **4.** *a)* to be as full or crowded as possible *b)* to be filled (*with* anger, pride, etc.) —*vt.* to cause to burst —*n.* **1.** a bursting; explosion **2.** the result of a bursting; break **3.** a sudden, violent display of feeling **4.** a sudden action; spurt *[a burst of speed]* **5.** a single series of shots from an automatic firearm —**burst′er** *n.*

bur·then (bur′*th*ən) *n., vt. archaic var. of* BURDEN[1]

Bur·ton (bur′tən), Sir **Richard Francis** 1821–90; Eng. writer, translator, & explorer

Bu·run·di (boo roon′dē, -run′-) country in EC Africa, east of Zaire: 10,745 sq. mi.; pop. 3,475,000 —**Bu·run′di·an** *adj., n.*

bur·y (ber′ē) *vt.* **bur′ied, bur′y·ing** [OE. *byrgan,* akin to *beorgan,* conceal] **1.** to put (a dead body) into the earth, a tomb, the sea, etc.; inter **2.** *a)* to hide (something) in the ground *b)* to cover up so as to conceal **3.** to put away *[to bury a feud]* **4.** to get deeply in *[to bury oneself in one's work]*

bus (bus) *n., pl.* **bus′es, bus′ses** [< (OMNI)BUS] **1.** a large motor coach for carrying many passengers, usually along a regular route; omnibus **2.** [Slang] an automobile —*vt.* **bused** or **bussed, bus′ing** or **bus′sing** to transport by bus —*vi.* **1.** to go by bus **2.** to do the work of a busboy

bus. business

bus·boy (-boi′) *n.* a waiter's assistant who clears tables, brings water, etc.

bus·by (buz′bē) *n., pl.* **-bies** [prob. < the name *Busby*] a tall fur hat worn by hussars, British guardsmen, etc.

bush[1] (boosh) *n.* [ME., of WGmc. orig.] **1.** a woody plant having many stems branching out low instead of one main stem; shrub **2.** anything resembling a bush; esp., a thickly furred tail **3.** shrubby woodland or uncleared country —*vi.* to spread out like a bush —**beat around the bush** to talk around a subject without getting to the point

bush[2] (boosh) *n.* [MDu. *busse,* box < ML. *buxis:* see BOX[1]] *same as* BUSHING —*vt.* to fit with a bushing

bushed (boosht) *adj.* [Colloq.] tired; fatigued

bush·el[1] (boosh′'l) *n.* [< OFr. *boissel* < *boisse,* grain measure] **1.** a unit of dry measure for grain, fruit, etc., equal to 4 pecks or 32 quarts **2.** a container holding one bushel **3.** [Colloq.] a large amount Abbrev. **bu.** —**bush′el·bas′ket** *n.*

bush·el[2] (boosh′'l) *vt., vi.* **-eled** or **-elled, -el·ing** or **-el·ling** [< ? G. *bosseln,* to repair] to repair or alter (garments)

Bu·shi·do (bo͞o′shē dō′) *n.* [Jap., way of the warrior] [*also* **b-**] the chivalric code of the samurai of feudal Japan

bush·ing (boosh′iŋ) *n.* [< BUSH[2]] a removable metal sleeve for reducing the effect of friction on a bearing or for decreasing the diameter of a hole

bush league [Slang] *Baseball* a small or second-rate minor league —**bush′-league′** *adj.*

bush leaguer [Slang] **1.** a player in a bush league **2.** any second-rate performer

bush·man (boosh′mən) *n., pl.* **-men** **1.** a person who lives in the Australian bush **2.** a backwoodsman **3.** [**B-**] a member of a nomadic people of SW Africa

bush·mas·ter (-mas′tər) *n.* a large, poisonous snake of Central and South America

bush·rang·er (-rān′jər) *n.* [< BUSH[1] (*n.* 3) + RANGER] **1.** a person who lives in the bush **2.** in Australia, an outlaw who makes the bush his hide-out

bush·whack (-hwak′, -wak′) *vi.* [prob. < BUSH[1] + WHACK] **1.** to beat or cut one's way through bushes **2.** to engage in guerrilla fighting, attacking from ambush —*vt.* to ambush —**bush′whack′er** *n.* —**bush′whack′ing** *n.*

bush·y (boosh′ē) *adj.* **bush′i·er, bush′i·est** **1.** covered or overgrown with bushes **2.** thick and spreading out like a bush —**bush′i·ness** *n.*

bus·i·ly (biz′ə lē) *adv.* in a busy manner

busi·ness (biz′nis) *n.* [OE. *bisignes:* see BUSY & -NESS] **1.** one's work, occupation, or profession **2.** rightful concern or responsibility **3.** a matter, affair, activity, etc. **4.** the buying and selling of goods and services; commerce; trade **5.** a commercial or industrial establishment; store, factory, etc. **6.** action in a drama to take up a pause in dialogue, etc. —*adj.* of or for business —**business is business** sentiment, friendship, etc. cannot be allowed to interfere with profit making —**do business with** **1.** to engage in commerce with **2.** to have dealings with —**give** (or **get**) **the business** [Slang] to subject (or be subjected) to rough treatment, practical joking, etc. —**mean business** [Colloq.] to be in earnest

business college (or **school**) a school offering instruction in secretarial skills, business administration, etc.

busi·ness·like (-līk′) *adj.* efficient, methodical, etc.

busi·ness·man (-man′) *n., pl.* **-men′** (-men′) a man in business, esp. as an owner or executive —**busi′ness·wom′an** *n.fem., pl.* **-wom′en**

bus·ing, bus·sing (bus′iŋ) *n.* the act of transporting children by bus to a school outside of their neighborhood, esp. in order to desegregate the school

bus·kin (bus′kin) *n.* [< ? OFr. < MDu. *brosekin,* small leather boot] **1.** a boot reaching to the calf or knee, worn long ago **2.** *a)* the high, thick-soled, laced boot worn by actors in ancient Greek and Roman tragedy *b)* tragic drama; tragedy —**bus′kined** *adj.*

BUSKINS

bus·man (bus′mən) *n., pl.* **-men** the operator of a bus

busman's holiday a holiday in which one's recreation is very similar to one's daily work

buss (bus) *n., vt., vi.* [? akin to G. dial. (or W. & Gael.) *bus*] [Archaic or Dial.] kiss

bus·ses (bus′iz) *n. alt. pl. of* BUS

bust[1] (bust) *n.* [< Fr. < It. *busto*] **1.** a piece of sculpture representing a person's head, shoulders, and upper chest **2.** a woman's bosom

bust[2] (bust) *vt., vi.* [orig., dial. var. of BURST] [Slang] **1.** to burst or break **2.** to make or become penniless or bankrupt **3.** to demote or become demoted **4.** to tame (esp. broncos) **5.** to hit **6.** to arrest —*n.* [Slang] **1.** a failure **2.** a financial collapse **3.** a punch **4.** a spree **5.** an arrest —**bust′ed** *adj.*

bus·tard (bus′tərd) *n.* [< OFr., ult. < L. *avis tarda,* lit., slow bird] a large, long-legged, old-world game bird

bus·tle[1] (bus′'l) *vi., vt.* **-tled, -tling** [< ME. *busken,* to prepare < ON.] to hurry busily or with much fuss and bother —*n.* busy and noisy activity —**bus′tling·ly** *adv.*

bus·tle[2] (bus′'l) *n.* [late 18th c. < ? G. *buschel,* a bunch, pad] a framework or padding worn at the back by women to puff out the skirt

bus·y (biz′ē) *adj.* **bus′i·er, bus′i·est** [< OE. *bisig*] **1.** occupied; at work; not idle **2.** full of activity **3.** *a)* in use at the moment, as a telephone line *b)* indicating such use *[the busy signal]* **4.** meddlesome **5.** displeasingly crowded with detail, colors, etc. —*vt.* **bus′ied, bus′y·ing** to make or keep busy —**bus′y·ness** *n.*

bus·y·bod·y (-bäd′ē) ***n.***, *pl.* **-bod′ies** one who mixes into other people's affairs; meddler
but (but; *unstressed* bət) ***prep.*** [< OE. *butan*, without < *be*, by + *utan*, out < *ut*, out] **1.** except; save *[*nobody came *but* me*]*: sometimes regarded as a conjunction *[*nobody came *but* I (came)*]* **2.** other than *[*we cannot choose *but* (to) stay*]* —***conj.*** **1.** yet; still; however *[*he is bad, *but* he has some virtues*]* **2.** on the contrary *[*I am old, *but* you are young*]* **3.** unless *[*it never rains *but* it pours*]* **4.** that *[*I don't question *but* you're right*]* **5.** that . . . not *[*I never think of London *but* I think of fog*]* —***adv.*** **1.** only *[*if I had *but* known*]* **2.** merely *[*he is *but* a child*]* **3.** just *[*I heard it *but* now*]* **4.** [Slang] absolutely *[*do it *but* now!*]* —***pron.*** who . . . not; which . . . not *[*not a man *but* felt it*]* —**but for** if it were not for —**but that** **1.** about the fact that *[*I've no doubt *but that* he'll come*]* **2.** that there isn't some chance that *[*we can't be sure *but that* he's right*]* Also [Colloq.] **but what**
bu·ta·di·ene (byo͞o′tə dī′ēn, -dī ēn′) ***n.*** [BUTA(NE) + DI-[1] + -ENE] a hydrocarbon, C_4H_6, used to make buna, a synthetic rubber
bu·tane (byo͞o′tān, byo͞o tān′) ***n.*** [BUT(YL) + -ANE] either of two hydrocarbons in the methane series, with the formula C_4H_{10}, used as a fuel, etc.
bu·ta·nol (byo͞o′tə nōl′, -nōl′) ***n.*** [BUTAN(E) + -OL[1]] *same as* BUTYL ALCOHOL
butch (boochh) ***adj.*** [prob. < *Butch*, nickname for a boy] [Slang] **1.** designating a man's close-cropped haircut **2.** masculine in appearance, manner, etc.; mannish —***n.*** [Slang] a tough or rugged man or boy: chiefly a term of address
butch·er (booch′ər) ***n.*** [< OFr. < *bouc*, he-goat < Frank. *bukk*] **1.** one whose work is killing animals or dressing their carcasses for meat **2.** one who cuts up meat for sale **3.** anyone who kills as if slaughtering animals **4.** one who sells candy, drinks, etc. in theaters, circuses, etc. —***vt.*** **1.** to kill or dress (animals) for meat **2.** to kill brutally or in large numbers; slaughter **3.** to botch; mangle —**butch′er·er** ***n.***
butch·er·bird (-burd′) ***n.*** a shrike which, after killing prey, impales it on thorns
butch·er·y (-ē) ***n.***, *pl.* **-er·ies** **1.** a slaughterhouse **2.** the work or business of a butcher **3.** brutal bloodshed **4.** the act or result of botching
but·ler (but′lər) ***n.*** [< OFr. < *bouteille*, BOTTLE] a manservant, now usually the head servant of a household, in charge of wines, pantry, etc.
But·ler (but′lər) **1. Samuel,** 1612–80; Eng. satirical poet **2. Samuel,** 1835–1902; Eng. novelist
butler's pantry a serving pantry between the kitchen and the dining room
but·ler·y (but′lər ē) ***n.***, *pl.* **-ler·ies** the butler's pantry; buttery
butt[1] (but) ***n.*** [< ? OFr. *bout*, end, or < ? ON. *būtr*, block of wood] **1.** the thick end of anything **2.** a stub or stump, as of a partially smoked cigarette **3.** *a)* [? infl. by Fr. *butte*, mound] a mound of earth behind a target for receiving fired rounds *b)* a target *c)* [*pl.*] a target range **4.** an object of ridicule or criticism **5.** [Slang] a cigarette **6.** [Slang] the buttocks —***vt., vi.*** to join end to end
butt[2] (but) ***vt.*** [< OFr. *buter* (< Frank. *botan*), to thrust against] **1.** to ram with the head **2.** to strike against **3.** to abut on —***vi.*** **1.** to make a butting motion **2.** to project **3.** to abut —***n.*** a thrust with the head or horns —**butt in** (or **into**) [Slang] to mix into (another's business, a conversation, etc.)
butt[3] (but) ***n.*** [< OFr. *botte* < ML. < LL. *bottis*, cask] **1.** a large barrel or cask, as for wine or beer **2.** a measure of liquid capacity equal to 126 gallons or two hogsheads
butte (byo͞ot) ***n.*** [Fr., mound] a steep hill standing alone on a plain, esp. in the W U.S.; small mesa
but·ter (but′ər) ***n.*** [< OE. < L. *butyrum* < Gr. *boutyron* < *bous*, ox, cow + *tyros*, cheese] **1.** the solid, yellowish, edible fat obtained by churning cream or whole milk **2.** a substance somewhat like butter; specif., *a)* any of certain other spreads for bread *[*peanut *butter]* *b)* any of certain vegetable oils that are solid at ordinary temperatures *[*cocoa *butter]* *c)* any of certain metallic chlorides *[butter* of antimony*]* **3.** [Colloq.] flattery —***vt.*** **1.** to spread with butter **2.** [Colloq.] to flatter (often with *up*) —**look as if butter would not melt in one's mouth** to look innocent or demure
butter bean *same as:* **1.** LIMA BEAN **2.** WAX BEAN
but·ter·cup (-kup′) ***n.*** any of a genus of yellow-flowered plants, common in meadows and wet places —***adj.*** designating a large family of plants, including the peony, aconite, larkspur, etc.
but·ter·fat (-fat′) ***n.*** the fatty part of milk, from which butter is made
but·ter·fin·gers (-fiŋ′gərz) ***n.*** one who often fumbles and drops things —**but′ter·fin′gered** ***adj.***
but·ter·fish (-fish′) ***n.***, *pl.* **-fish′**, **-fish′es**: see FISH any of various slippery-coated fishes
but·ter·fly (-flī′) ***n.***, *pl.* **-flies′** [< OE. *buttorfleoge*] **1.** any of a large group of insects active by day, having a sucking mouthpart, slender body, and four broad, usually brightly colored wings **2.** a person, esp. a woman, thought of as flighty, frivolous, etc. —***adj.*** like a butterfly in having parts spread out like wings *[*a *butterfly* chair*]*
butter knife a small, dull-edged knife for cutting or spreading butter
but·ter·milk (-milk′) ***n.*** the sour liquid left after churning butter from milk
but·ter·nut (-nut′) ***n.*** **1.** a species of walnut of E N.America, with compound leaves and hard-shelled nuts **2.** the oily, edible nut of this tree
butternut squash a small, bell-shaped, smooth winter squash, with yellowish flesh
but·ter·scotch (-skäch′) ***n.*** a hard, sticky candy made with brown sugar, butter, etc. —***adj.*** having the flavor of butterscotch
but·ter·y[1] (but′ər ē, but′rē) ***n.***, *pl.* **-ter·ies** [< OFr. < ML. *buteria*: see BUTT[3]] **1.** a storeroom for wine and liquor **2.** a pantry
but·ter·y[2] (but′ər ē) ***adj.*** **1.** like butter **2.** containing or spread with butter **3.** adulatory
but·tock (but′ək) ***n.*** [< OE. *buttuc*, end] **1.** either of the two fleshy, rounded parts at the back of the hips **2.** [*pl.*] the rump
but·ton (but′'n) ***n.*** [OFr. *boton*, a button < *buter*: see BUTT[2]] **1.** any small disk or knob used as a fastening, ornament, etc. on a garment **2.** anything small and shaped like a button; specif., *a)* a small emblem worn in the lapel, etc. *b)* a small knob for operating a doorbell, electric lamp, etc. *c)* a small mushroom **3.** [Slang] the point of the chin **4.** [Slang] [*pl.*] one's full senses *[*to have all of one's *buttons]* —***vt., vi.*** to fasten with buttons —**on the button** [Slang] exactly at the desired point, time, etc. —**but′ton·er** ***n.*** —**but′ton·less** ***adj.***
but·ton-down (-doun′) ***adj.*** designating a collar with points fastened down by small buttons
but·ton·hole (-hōl′) ***n.*** a slit or loop through which a button can be fastened —***vt.*** **-holed′**, **-hol′ing** **1.** to make buttonholes in **2.** to make (a person) listen to one, as if by grasping his coat by a buttonhole —**but′ton·hol′er** ***n.***
but·ton·hook (-hook′) ***n.*** a hook for pulling buttons through buttonholes, as in some shoes
but·ton·wood (-wood′) ***n.*** *same as* PLANE[1]
but·tress (but′ris) ***n.*** [< OFr. < *buter*: see BUTT[2]] **1.** a projecting structure built against a wall to support or reinforce it **2.** a support; prop —***vt.*** **1.** to support or reinforce with a buttress **2.** to prop up; bolster
bu·tut (boo toot′) ***n.***, *pl.* **-tut′** [native term, lit., small] *see* MONETARY UNITS, table (Gambia)
bu·tyl (byo͞ot′'l) ***n.*** [< L. *butyrum* (see BUTTER) + -YL] any of the four isomeric organic radicals C_4H_9
butyl alcohol any of four isomeric alcohols, C_4H_9OH, used as solvents and in organic synthesis
bu·tyr·ic (byo͞o tir′ik) ***adj.*** [< L. *butyrum* (see BUTTER) + -IC] **1.** of or obtained from butter **2.** of or pertaining to butyric acid
butyric acid a fatty acid, $C_3H_7CO_2H$, with a rancid odor, found in butter, etc.
bux·om (buk′səm) ***adj.*** [ME., humble, obedient < base of *bouen*, to BOW[1] + *-sum*, -SOME[1]] healthy, comely, plump, jolly, etc.; specif. now, having a shapely, full-bosomed figure: said of a woman or girl —**bux′om·ly** ***adv.*** —**bux′om·ness** ***n.***
buy (bī) ***vt.*** **bought, buy′ing** [< OE. *bycgan*] **1.** to get by paying money; purchase **2.** to get by any exchange **3.** to be the means of purchasing *[*all that money can *buy]* **4.** to bribe **5.** [Slang] to accept as valid, agreeable, etc. —***vi.*** to buy things; be a buyer —***n.*** **1.** a buying **2.** anything bought or buyable **3.** [Colloq.] a bargain —**buy into** (or **in**) to pay money so as to get shares of, membership in, etc. —**buy off** to bribe —**buy out** to buy all the stock, rights, etc. of —**buy up** to buy all that is available of —**buy′a·ble** ***adj.***
buy·er (-ər) ***n.*** **1.** one who buys; consumer **2.** one whose work is to buy merchandise for a retail store
buzz (buz) ***vi.*** [echoic] **1.** to hum like a bee **2.** to talk excitedly **3.** to gossip **4.** to move with a buzzing sound **5.** to be filled with noisy activity or talk —***vt.*** **1.** to tell (rumors, etc.) in a buzzing manner **2.** to make (wings, etc.) buzz **3.** to fly an airplane low over **4.** to signal with a buzzer **5.** [Colloq.] to telephone —***n.*** **1.** a sound like a bee's hum **2.** a confused sound, as of many voices **3.** noisy activity **4.** a signal on a buzzer **5.** [Colloq.] a tele-

phone call —**buzz about** (or **around**) to scurry about —**buzz off** [Brit. Colloq.] to hurry away

buz·zard (buz′ərd) ***n.*** **[**< OFr. *busart* < *buse* (< L. *buteo*, kind of hawk) + *-art*, -ARD**]** **1.** any of various hawks that are slow and heavy in flight **2.** *same as* TURKEY BUZZARD **3.** a person regarded as mean, grasping, etc.

buzz·er (buz′ər) ***n.*** an electrical device that makes a buzzing sound as a signal

buzz saw a circular saw rotated by machinery

bwa·na (bwä′nə) ***n.*** **[**Swahili < Ar. *abūna*, our father**]** [*often* **B-**] master; sir: native respectful term of address used in parts of Africa

B.W.I. British West Indies

bx. *pl.* **bxs.** box

by (bī) ***prep.*** **[**< OE. *be* (unstressed), *bi* (stressed)**]** **1.** near or beside; at [stand *by* the wall] **2.** *a*) in or during [to travel *by* night] *b*) for a fixed time [to work *by* the hour] *c*) not later than [be back *by* noon] **3.** *a*) via *b*) past; beyond [to march *by* the reviewing stand] *c*) toward [north *by* west] **4.** in behalf of [he did well *by* me] **5.** through the means, work, or operations of [made *by* hand] **6.** *a*) according to [*by* the book] *b*) in [to grow dark *by* degrees] *c*) following in series [march two *by* two] **7.** with the sanction of [*by* your leave] **8.** *a*) in or to the amount or degree of [apples *by* the peck] *b*) and in another dimension [two *by* four] *c*) using (the given number) as multiplier or divisor —***adv.*** **1.** close at hand; near [stand *by*] **2.** away; aside [put money *by*] **3.** past [cars sped *by*] **4.** at someone's place [stop *by*] —***adj., n.*** *same as* BYE —**by and by** after a while —**by and large** considering everything —**by oneself** **1.** alone **2.** unaided —**by the by** incidentally

by- *a prefix meaning:* **1.** close by; near [*bystander*] **2.** secondary [*byproduct*]

by-and-by (bī′'n bī′) ***n.*** a future time

bye (bī) ***n.*** **[**see BY**]** **1.** something incidental **2.** in sports in which competitors are paired, the status of the extra man, who advances to the next round without playing **3.** *Golf* any holes left unplayed at the end of a match —***adj.*** incidental —**by the bye** incidentally

bye-bye (bī′bī′, bī′bī′) ***n., interj.*** goodbye

by-e·lec·tion (bī′i lek′shən) ***n.*** [Chiefly Brit.] a special election between general elections

Bye·lo·rus·sian Soviet Socialist Republic (bye′lō-rush′ən) republic of the U.S.S.R., in the W European part: 80,154 sq. mi.; pop. 8,800,000; cap. Minsk: also **Bye′lo-rus′sia** —**Bye′lo·rus′sian** ***adj., n.***

by·gone (bī′gôn′, -gän′) ***adj.*** gone by; past —***n.*** anything that is gone or past —**let bygones be bygones** to let past offenses be forgotten

by·law (bī′lô′) ***n.*** **[**< ME. < *bi*, town (< ON. *bȳr* < *būa*, to dwell) + *laue*, LAW: meaning infl. by BY**]** any of a set of rules adopted by an organization for governing its own meetings or affairs

by·line (-līn′) ***n.*** a line at the head of a newspaper or magazine article, telling who wrote it

by·pass (-pas′) ***n.*** **1.** a way, path, pipe, channel, etc. between two points that avoids or is auxiliary to the main way; detour **2.** *Elec.* *same as* SHUNT (*n.* 3) —***vt.*** **1.** to go around instead of through **2.** to furnish with a bypass **3.** to ignore, fail to consult, etc.

by·path, by-path (-path′) ***n.*** a side path; byway

by·play (-plā′) ***n.*** action, gestures, etc. going on aside from the main action, as in a play

by·prod·uct, by-prod·uct (-präd′əkt) ***n.*** anything produced, as from residues, in the course of making another thing; secondary product or result

Byrd (burd), **Richard Evelyn** 1888–1957; U.S. polar explorer

by·road (bī′rōd′) ***n.*** a side road; byway

By·ron (bī′rən) **[**< Fr. < *Biron*, district in France**]** **1.** a masculine name **2. George Gordon,** 6th Baron Byron, 1788–1824; Eng. poet

By·ron·ic (bī rän′ik) ***adj.*** of, like, or characteristic of Byron or his writings; romantic, passionate, cynical, ironic, etc. —**By·ron′i·cal·ly** ***adv.***

by·stand·er (bī′stan′dər) ***n.*** a person who stands near but does not participate; onlooker

by·way (bī′wā′) ***n.*** **1.** a path or road that is not a main road, esp. one not used very much **2.** a secondary activity, line of study, etc.

by·word (-wurd′) ***n.*** **1.** a familiar saying; proverb **2.** a person or thing proverbial for some contemptible or ridiculous quality **3.** a favorite or pet word or phrase

By·zan·tine (biz′'n tēn′, -tīn′; bi zan′tin) ***adj.*** **1.** of or like Byzantium or the Byzantine Empire, its culture, etc **2.** of or pertaining to the Orthodox Eastern Church **3.** *Archit.* designating or of a style developed in Byzantium, characterized by domes, round arches, mosaics, etc. —***n.*** a native or inhabitant of Byzantium

Byzantine Empire empire (395–1453) in SE Europe & SW Asia, formed by the division of the Roman Empire: cap. Constantinople

By·zan·ti·um (bi zan′shē əm, -tē əm) *ancient name of* ISTANBUL (until 330 A.D.)

C

C, c (sē) ***n.,*** *pl.* **C's, c's** **1.** the third letter of the English alphabet **2.** a sound of *C* or *c* **3.** *a symbol for* the third in a sequence or group

C (sē) ***n.*** **1.** a Roman numeral for 100 **2.** *Chem.* carbon **3.** *Educ.* a grade indicating average work **4.** *Music* *a*) the first tone in the scale of C major *b*) the scale having this tone as the keynote

C- cargo transport

C, C. **1.** Celsius or centigrade **2.** Central

C. **1.** Catholic **2.** Church **3.** Congress **4.** Corps

C., c. **1.** capacitance **2.** carat **3.** catcher **4.** cathode **5.** cent **6.** center **7.** centimeter **8.** century **9.** *pl.* **CC.** chapter **10.** circa **11.** contralto **12.** copyright **13.** cubic **14.** cycle

Ca *Chem.* calcium

CA California

ca. **1.** cathode **2.** centiare **3.** circa

C.A. **1.** Central America **2.** Confederate Army

Caa·ba (kä′bə) *same as* KAABA

cab (kab) ***n.*** **[**< CABRIOLET**]** **1.** a horse-drawn carriage, esp. one for public hire **2.** *clipped form of* TAXICAB **3.** the place in a locomotive, motor truck, crane, etc. where the operator sits

CAB Civil Aeronautics Board

ca·bal (kə bal′) ***n.*** **[**Fr., intrigue < ML. *cabbala*, CABALA**]** **1.** a small group of persons joined in a secret intrigue; junta **2.** the intrigues of such a group; plot —***vi.*** **-balled′, -bal′-ling** to join in a cabal; plot

cab·a·la (kab′ə lə, kə bäl′ə) ***n.*** **[**< ML. < Heb. *qabbālāh*, received lore < *qābal*, to receive**]** **1.** an occult rabbinical philosophy, based on a mystical interpretation of the Scriptures **2.** any esoteric or secret doctrine; occultism Also sp. **cab′ba·la** —**cab′a·lism** ***n.*** —**cab′a·list** ***n.*** —**cab′a·lis′-tic** ***adj.*** —**cab′a·lis′ti·cal·ly** ***adv.***

ca·bal·le·ro (kab′ə ler′ō, -əl yer′ō; *Sp.* kä′bä lye′rô) ***n.,*** *pl.* **-ros** (-ōz; *Sp.* -rôs) **[**Sp. < LL. < L. *caballus*, horse**]** **1.** a Spanish cavalier **2.** [Southwest] *a*) a horseman *b*) a lady's escort

ca·ba·na (kə bän′ə, -bän′yə; -ban′-) ***n.*** **[**Sp. *cabaña* < LL. *capanna*, hut**]** **1.** a cabin or hut **2.** a small shelter for swimmers at a beach, pool, etc.

cab·a·ret (kab′ə rā′, kab′ə rā′) ***n.*** **[**Fr., pothouse, ult. < OFr. dial.**]** **1.** a restaurant or café with dancing, singing, etc. as entertainment **2.** such entertainment

cab·bage (kab′ij) ***n.*** **[**OFr. *caboche*, ult. < ? L. *caput*, the head**]** a common vegetable of the mustard family, with thick leaves formed into a round, compact head on a short stalk

cabbage butterfly a common white butterfly whose green larvae feed on cabbage and related plants

cabbage palm **1.** any of several palms with terminal buds used as a vegetable: also **cabbage tree** **2.** *see* PALMETTO

cab·driv·er (kab′drīv′ər) ***n.*** a person who drives a cab: also [Colloq.] **cab′by, cab′bie** (-ē), *pl.* **-bies**

cab·in (kab′'n) ***n.*** **[**< OFr. < Pr. < LL. *capanna*, hut**]** **1.** a small house, built simply or crudely **2.** any simple, small structure designed for a brief stay **3.** a private room on a ship, as a bedroom or office **4.** a roofed section of a small boat **5.** an enclosed section for passengers in an aircraft —***vt.*** to confine in or as in a cabin; cramp

cabin boy a boy whose work is to serve and run errands for officers and passengers aboard a ship

cabin cruiser a motorboat with a cabin and the necessary equipment for living on board

cab·i·net (kab′ə nit, kab′nit) ***n.*** [Fr., dim. of *cabine;* origin obscure] **1.** a case with drawers or shelves for holding or storing things **2.** a boxlike enclosure for a record player, radio, television, etc. **3.** formerly, a private council room **4.** [*often* **C-**] a body of official advisers to a president, king, governor, etc.: in the U.S., the heads of certain governmental departments —***adj.*** **1.** of a kind usually kept in a cabinet **2.** of a political cabinet

cab·i·net·mak·er (-māk′ər) ***n.*** a workman who makes fine furniture, etc. —**cab′i·net·mak′ing** ***n.***

cab·i·net·work (-wʉrk′) ***n.*** **1.** articles made by a cabinetmaker **2.** the work or art of a cabinetmaker Also **cab′i·net·ry** (-rē)

ca·ble (kā′b'l) ***n.*** [OFr. < LL. *capulum* < L. *capere,* to take hold] **1.** a thick, heavy rope, now often of wire **2.** a ship's anchor chain **3.** *same as* CABLE LENGTH **4.** a bundle of insulated wires through which an electric current can be passed **5.** *same as* CABLEGRAM —***vt.*** **-bled, -bling** **1.** to fasten with a cable **2.** to transmit by undersea cable **3.** to send a cablegram to —***vi.*** to send a cablegram

CABLES

cable car a car drawn by a moving cable

ca·ble·gram (-gram′) ***n.*** a message sent by undersea cable

cable length a unit of nautical measure variously equal to 720 feet (120 fathoms) or 600 feet (100 fathoms): also **cable's length**

cable railway a street railway on which cars are pulled by a continuously moving underground cable

ca·bob (kə bäb′) ***n.*** *same as* KEBAB

ca·boo·dle (kə bo͞o′d'l) ***n.*** [*ca-*, colloq. intens. prefix + BOODLE] [Colloq.] lot; group [*the whole caboodle*]

ca·boose (kə bo͞os′) ***n.*** [< MDu. *kabuys, kambuis* (< ?), cabin house, ship's galley] **1.** [Brit.] a ship's galley or kitchen **2.** the trainmen's car on a freight train, usually at the rear

Cab·ot (kab′ət), **John** (It. name *Giovanni Caboto*) 1450?–98; It. explorer in the service of England: discovered coast of N. America (1497)

ca·bret·ta (kə bret′ə) ***adj.*** [< Sp. *cabra,* goat + It. dim. suffix *-etta*] designating or of a soft leather made from a special kind of sheepskin

cab·ri·o·let (kab′rē ə lā′, -let′) ***n.*** [Fr., dim. of *cabriole,* a leap < It. *capriola*] **1.** a light, two-wheeled carriage, usually with a hood that folds, drawn by one horse **2.** a former style of automobile like a convertible coupe

cab·stand (kab′stand′) ***n.*** a place where cabs are stationed for hire

ca·ca·o (kə kā′ō, -kä′-) ***n.,*** *pl.* **-ca′os** [Sp. < Nahuatl *cacauatl,* cacao seed] **1.** a tropical American tree, bearing large, elliptical seedpods **2.** the seeds **(cacao beans)** of this tree, from which cocoa and chocolate are made

cac·cia·to·re (kach′ə tôr′ē) ***adj.*** [It., lit., a hunter < pp. of *cacciare,* to hunt] cooked in a casserole with olive oil and tomatoes, onions, spices, etc. [*chicken cacciatore*]

cach·a·lot (kash′ə lät′, -lō′) ***n.*** [Fr. < Sp. < ? Port. *cachola,* big head] *same as* SPERM WHALE

cache (kash) ***n.*** [Fr. < *cacher,* conceal < L. *coactare,* constrain] **1.** a place in which stores of food, supplies, etc. are hidden **2.** a safe place for hiding things **3.** anything so hidden —***vt., vi.*** **cached, cach′ing** to hide or store in a cache

cache·pot (kash′pät, -pō) ***n.*** [Fr., lit., hide-pot < *cacher,* to hide + *pot,* pot] a decorative pot, jar, etc., esp. for house plants: also **cache pot**

ca·chet (ka shā′, kash′ā) ***n.*** [Fr. < *cacher:* see CACHE] **1.** a seal or stamp on an official letter **2.** *a*) a mark indicating genuine or superior quality *b*) prestige **3.** a commemorative design, slogan, etc. stamped on mail

cach·in·nate (kak′ə nāt′) ***vi.*** **-nat′ed, -nat′ing** [< L. pp. of *cachinnare,* prob. echoic] to laugh loudly or too much —**cach′in·na′tion** ***n.***

ca·cique (kə sēk′) ***n.*** [Sp. < native word] **1.** in Spanish America, an Indian chief **2.** in Spanish America and Spain, a local political boss

cack·le (kak′'l) ***vi.*** **-led, -ling** [akin to Du. *kokkelen,* of echoic origin] **1.** to make the shrill, broken, vocal sounds of a hen **2.** to laugh or chatter with similar sounds —***vt.*** to utter in a cackling manner —***n.*** **1.** a cackling **2.** cackling laughter or chatter

cac·o- [< Gr. *kakos,* bad, evil] *a combining form meaning* bad, poor, harsh [*cacography*]: also, before a vowel, **cac-**

ca·cog·ra·phy (kə käg′rə fē) ***n.*** [CACO- + -GRAPHY] **1.** bad handwriting **2.** incorrect spelling —**cac·o·graph·ic** (kak′ə graf′ik) ***adj.***

ca·coph·o·ny (kə käf′ə nē) ***n.,*** *pl.* **-nies** [< ModL. < Gr. < *kakos,* bad + *phōnē,* voice] harsh, jarring sound; dissonance —**ca·coph′o·nous** ***adj.*** —**ca·coph′o·nous·ly** ***adv.***

cac·tus (kak′təs) ***n.,*** *pl.* **-tus·es, -ti** (-tī) [L. < Gr. *kaktos,* kind of thistle] any of various new-world desert plants with fleshy stems, reduced or spinelike leaves, and often showy flowers

cad (kad) ***n.*** [< CADDIE & CADET] a man or boy whose behavior is not gentlemanly

ca·dav·er (kə dav′ər) ***n.*** [L., prob. < *cadere,* to fall] a dead body, esp. of a person; corpse, as for dissection —**ca·dav′er·ic** ***adj.***

ca·dav·er·ous (-ər əs) ***adj.*** of or like a cadaver; esp., pale, ghastly, or gaunt and haggard —**ca·dav′er·ous·ly** ***adv.***

cad·die (kad′ē) ***n.*** [Scot. form of Fr. *cadet*: see CADET] **1.** a person who attends a golf player, carrying his clubs, etc. **2.** a small, wheeled cart —***vi.*** **-died, -dy·ing** to act as a caddie

cad·dis fly (kad′is) [see CADDIS WORM] a small, mothlike insect with two pairs of wings, a soft body, and long legs

cad·dish (kad′ish) ***adj.*** like or characteristic of a cad; ungentlemanly —**cad′dish·ly** ***adv.*** —**cad′dish·ness** ***n.***

cad·dis worm (kad′is) [< OFr. *cadas,* floss silk (with reference to the case)] the wormlike larva of the caddis fly that lives in a case made of twigs, grains of sand, etc. cemented together with its secreted silk: used as bait by anglers

cad·dy[1] (kad′ē) ***n.,*** *pl.* **-dies** [< Malay *kati,* weight equivalent to a little more than a pound] **1.** a small container used for tea **2.** any of various devices for holding or storing certain articles

cad·dy[2] (kad′ē) ***n., vi.*** *same as* CADDIE

-cade (kād) [< (CAVAL)CADE] *a suffix meaning* procession, parade [*motorcade*]

ca·dence (kād′'ns) ***n.*** [ult. < L. prp. of *cadere,* to fall] **1.** fall of the voice in speaking **2.** inflection or modulation in tone **3.** a rhythmic flow of sound **4.** measured movement, as in marching, or the beat of such movement **5.** *Music* the harmonic ending, final trill, etc. of a phrase or movement Also **ca′den·cy** —**ca′denced** ***adj.***

ca·den·za (kə den′zə) ***n.*** [It.: see prec.] **1.** an elaborate, often improvised musical passage played by the solo instrument in a concerto, usually near the end of the first movement **2.** any brilliant flourish in an aria or solo passage

ca·det (kə det′) ***n.*** [Fr. < Gascon *capdet,* chief < Pr. < LL. dim. of L. *caput:* see CAPTAIN] **1.** a younger son or brother **2.** a student at an armed forces academy **3.** a student at a military school **4.** any trainee, as a practice teacher or a junior business associate —**ca·det′ship′** ***n.***

cadge (kaj) ***vt., vi.*** **cadged, cadg′ing** [ME. *caggen,* to tie; ? var. of *cacchen,* to catch] to beg or get by begging; sponge —**cadg′er** ***n.***

ca·di (kä′dē, kā′-) ***n.*** [Ar. *qādi*] a minor Moslem magistrate or judge

Cá·diz (kə diz′, kā′diz; *Sp.* kä *th*ēth′) seaport in SW Spain, on the Atlantic: pop. 133,000

Cad·me·an (kad mē′ən) ***adj.*** of or like Cadmus

Cadmean victory a victory won with great losses to the victors

cad·mi·um (kad′mē əm) ***n.*** [ModL. < L. *cadmia,* zinc ore < Gr. *kadmeia*] a blue-white, malleable, ductile, metallic chemical element occurring in zinc ores: it is used in some alloys, electroplating, etc.: symbol, Cd; at. wt., 112.40; at. no., 48 —**cad′mic** (-mik) ***adj.***

Cad·mus (kad′məs) *Gr. Myth.* a Phoenician prince who killed a dragon and sowed its teeth, from which many armed men rose and fought, five surviving to help him build Thebes

ca·dre (kad′rē) ***n.*** [Fr. < It. < L. *quadrum,* a square] **1.** a framework **2.** an operational unit around which an expanded organization, as a military unit, can be built; nucleus

ca·du·ce·us (kə do͞o′sē əs, -dyo͞o′-) ***n.,*** *pl.* **-ce·i′** (-sē ī′) [L.] **1.** the staff of an ancient herald; esp., the winged staff with two serpents twined about it, carried by Mercury **2.** a staff like this twined with one or two serpents, used as a symbol of the medical profession —**ca·du′ce·an** ***adj.***

cae·cum (sē′kəm) ***n.,*** *pl.* **-ca** (-kə) *same as* CECUM —**cae′cal** ***adj.***

Caed·mon (kad′mən) fl. late 7th cent. A.D.; first Eng. poet whose name is known

Cae·sar (sē′zər) ***n.*** [after ff. < ? L. pp. of *caedere,* to cut] **1.** the title of the Roman emperors from Augustus to Hadrian **2.** any emperor or dictator

Cae·sar (sē′zər), **(Gaius) Julius** 100?–44 B.C.; Roman general & statesman

Cae·sar·e·an, Cae·sar·i·an (si zer′ē ən) ***adj.*** of Julius Caesar or the Caesars —***n.*** *same as* CAESAREAN SECTION

CADUCEUS

Caesarean section [after Julius *Caesar,* supposedly born in this way] [*also* **c- s-**] a surgical operation for

fat, āpe, cär; ten, ēven; is, bīte; gō, hôrn, to͞ol, look; oil, out; up, fʉr; get; joy; yet; chin; she; thin, *th*en; zh, leisure; ŋ, ring; ə for *a* in *ago, e* in *agent, i* in *sanity, o* in *comply, u* in *focus;* ′ as in *able* (ā′b'l); Fr. bál; ë, Fr. coeur; ö, Fr. feu; Fr. mo*n*; ô, Fr. coq; ü, Fr. duc; *r,* Fr. cri; H, G. ich; kh, G. doch; ‡foreign; *hypothetical; < derived from. See inside front cover.

delivering a baby by cutting through the mother's abdominal and uterine walls
cae·si·um (sē′zē əm) ***n.*** *same as* CESIUM
cae·su·ra (si zhoor′ə, -zyoor′ə) ***n.,*** *pl.* **-ras, -rae** (-ē) [L., a cutting < pp. of *caedere,* to cut] **1.** a break or pause in a line of verse: in Greek and Latin verse, the caesura falls within the metrical foot; in English verse, it is usually about the middle of the line **2.** a pause showing rhythmic division of a melody —**cae·su′ral** ***adj.***
ca·fé, ca·fe (ka fā′, kə-) ***n.*** [Fr. < It. *caffè,* COFFEE] **1.** coffee **2.** a coffeehouse **3.** a small restaurant, esp. one serving alcoholic drinks and sometimes providing entertainment **4.** a barroom
‡**ca·fé au lait** (kȧ fā ō lā′) [Fr.] **1.** coffee with an equal part of hot milk **2.** pale brown
café curtains short, straight curtains hung from a rod by sliding rings
‡**ca·fé noir** (kȧ fā nwȧr′) [Fr.] black coffee
caf·e·te·ri·a (kaf′ə tir′ē ə) ***n.*** [AmSp., coffee store] a restaurant in which food is displayed on counters and patrons serve themselves
caf·feine, caf·fein (kaf′ēn, -ē in; ka fēn′) ***n.*** [< G., ult. < It. *caffè,* COFFEE + *-in,* -INE[4]] an alkaloid, $C_8H_{10}N_4O_2$, present in coffee, tea, and kola: it is a stimulant to the heart and central nervous system
caf·tan (kaf′tən, käf tän′) ***n.*** [Turk. *qaftān*] a long-sleeved robe with a girdle, worn in eastern Mediterranean countries
cage (kāj) ***n.*** [OFr. < L *cavea,* hollow place < *cavus,* hollow] **1.** a box or structure of wires, bars, etc. for confining birds or animals **2.** an openwork structure, as some elevator cars **3.** *Baseball* a backstop used in batting practice, etc. **4.** *Basketball* the basket **5.** *Hockey* the network frame that is the goal —***vt.*** **caged, cag′ing** to put or confine, as in a cage
ca·gey, ca·gy (kā′jē) ***adj.*** **ca′gi·er, ca′gi·est** [< ?] [Colloq.] **1.** sly; tricky; cunning **2.** careful not to get caught or fooled —**ca′gi·ly** ***adv.*** —**ca′gi·ness** ***n.***
Ca·glia·ri (kä′lyä rē′) capital of Sardinia; seaport on the S coast: pop. 216,000
Ca·guas (kä′gwäs) city in EC Puerto Rico: pop. 63,000
ca·hoots (kə hoots′) ***n.pl.*** [< ?] [Slang] partnership; league —**go cahoots** [Slang] to share alike —**in cahoots** [Slang] in league: usually applied to questionable dealing
cai·man (kā′mən) ***n.,*** *pl.* **-mans** [Sp. < Carib native name] a reptile of Central or South America similar to the alligator and crocodile
Cain (kān) *Bible* the oldest son of Adam and Eve: he killed his brother Abel: Gen. 4 —***n.*** any murderer —**raise Cain** [Slang] to cause a great commotion or much trouble
ca·ique, ca·ïque (kä ēk′) ***n.*** [Fr. < It. < Turk. *qayiq*] **1.** a light rowboat used on the Bosporus **2.** a sailboat used esp. in the eastern Mediterranean
cairn (kern) ***n.*** [Scot. < Gael. *carn,* an elevation] a conical heap of stones built as a monument or landmark —**cairned** ***adj.***
Cai·ro (kī′rō) capital of Egypt, at the head of the Nile delta: pop. 3,346,000
cais·son (kā′sän, kās′'n) ***n.*** [Fr. < It. < *cassa* < L. *capsa,* a box, CASE[2]] **1.** a chest for holding ammunition **2.** a two-wheeled wagon for transporting ammunition **3.** a watertight enclosure inside which men can do construction work under water **4.** a watertight box for raising sunken ships
caisson disease *same as* DECOMPRESSION SICKNESS
cai·tiff (kāt′if) ***n.*** [OFr. *caitif,* a captive < L. *captivus,* CAPTIVE] a mean, evil, or cowardly person —***adj.*** mean, evil, or cowardly
ca·jole (kə jōl′) ***vt., vi.*** **-joled′, -jol′ing** [< Fr. < ? blend of OFr. *cage,* CAGE + *jaole, gaole,* prison: see JAIL] to coax with flattery and insincere talk; wheedle —**ca·jole′ment, ca·jol′er·y** ***n.*** —**ca·jol′er** ***n.*** —**ca·jol′ing·ly** ***adv.***
Ca·jun, Ca·jan (kā′jən) ***n.*** [< Acadian Fr.] **1.** a native of Louisiana originally descended from Acadian French immigrants: sometimes used contemptuously **2.** the dialect of the Cajuns
cake (kāk) ***n.*** [< ON. *kaka*] **1.** a small, flat mass of dough or batter, or of some hashed food, that is baked or fried **2.** a mixture of flour, eggs, milk, sugar, etc. baked as in a loaf and often covered with icing **3.** a shaped, solid mass, as of soap, ice, etc. **4.** a hard crust or deposit —***vt., vi.*** **caked, cak′ing** to form into a hard mass or a crust —**take the cake** [Slang] to win the prize; excel: ironic usage —**cak′y** ***adj.*** **cak′i·er, cak′i·est**
cakes and ale the good things of life
cake·walk (-wôk′) ***n.*** **1.** an elaborate step or walk formerly performed by Negroes in the South competing for the prize of a cake **2.** a strutting dance developed from this —***vi.*** to do a cakewalk
Cal. **1.** California **2.** large calorie(s)
cal. **1.** calendar **2.** caliber **3.** small calorie(s)
cal·a·bash (kal′ə bash′) ***n.*** [< Fr. < Sp. *calabaza* < ?] **1.** a tropical American tree or its large, gourdlike fruit **2.** *a*) a tropical vine bearing white flowers, or its bottle-shaped gourd *b*) a large smoking pipe made from the neck of this gourd **3.** the dried, hollow shell of a calabash, used as a bowl, cup, etc.
cal·a·boose (kal′ə bo͞os′) ***n.*** [Sp. *calabozo*] [Slang] a prison; jail
ca·la·di·um (kə lā′dē əm) ***n.*** [ModL. < Malay *kélādy,* kind of plant] a tropical American plant of the arum family, with brilliantly colored leaves
Cal·ais (ka lā′, kal′ā) seaport in N France, on the Strait of Dover: pop. 75,000
cal·a·mine (kal′ə mīn′, -min) ***n.*** [Fr. < ML. *calamina* < L. *cadmia:* see CADMIUM] a pink powder consisting of zinc oxide mixed with a little ferric oxide, used in skin lotions and ointments
ca·lam·i·tous (kə lam′ə təs) ***adj.*** bringing or causing calamity —**ca·lam′i·tous·ly** ***adv.*** —**ca·lam′i·tous·ness** ***n.***
ca·lam·i·ty (-tē) ***n.,*** *pl.* **-ties** [< Fr. < L. *calamitas*] **1.** deep trouble or misery **2.** any extreme misfortune; disaster
cal·a·mon·din (kal′ə män′din) ***n.*** [Tag. *kalamunding*] a small, spicy orange of the Philippines
cal·a·mus (kal′ə məs) ***n.,*** *pl.* **-mi′** (-mī′) [L. < Gr. *kalamos,* a reed] **1.** *same as* SWEET FLAG **2.** the quill of a feather
ca·lash (kə lash′) ***n.*** [Fr. *calèche* < G. < Czech *kolésa;* prob. < *kolo,* a wheel] **1.** a light, low-wheeled carriage, usually with a folding top **2.** a folding top of a carriage **3.** a folding hood or bonnet, worn by women in the 18th cent.
cal·ca·ne·us (kal kā′nē əs) ***n.,*** *pl.* **-ne·i′** (-nē ī′) [LL. < L. < *calx,* the heel] the heel bone: also **cal·ca′ne·um** (-əm), *pl.* **-ne·a** (-ə) —**cal·ca′ne·al** ***adj.***
cal·car·e·ous (kal ker′ē əs) ***adj.*** [< L. < *calx,* lime] of, like, or containing calcium carbonate, calcium, or lime —**cal·car′e·ous·ness** ***n.***
cal·ces (kal′sēz) ***n.*** *alt. pl. of* CALX
cal·ci- [< L. *calx* (gen. *calcis*), lime] *a combining form meaning* calcium or lime *[calcify]*
cal·cif·er·ol (kal sif′ə rôl′, -rōl′) ***n.*** [CALCIF(EROUS) + (ERGOST)EROL] vitamin D_2: it is a crystalline alcohol, $C_{28}H_{43}OH$
cal·cif·er·ous (-ər əs) ***adj.*** [CALCI- + -FEROUS] producing or containing calcite
cal·ci·fy (kal′sə fī′) ***vt., vi.*** **-fied′, -fy′ing** [CALCI- + -FY] to change into a hard, stony substance by the deposit of lime or calcium salts —**cal′ci·fi·ca′tion** ***n.***
cal·ci·mine (-mīn′, -min) ***n.*** [< L. *calx,* lime] a white or colored liquid of whiting or zinc white, glue, and water, used as a wash for plastered surfaces —***vt.*** **-mined′, -min′-ing** to cover with calcimine
cal·cine (kal′sīn, kal sīn′) ***vt., vi.*** **-cined, -cin·ing** [< OFr. < ML. *calcinare* (an alchemists' term)] **1.** to change to calx or powder by heat **2.** to burn to ashes or powder —**cal·ci·na·tion** (kal′sə nā′shən) ***n.***
cal·cite (kal′sīt) ***n.*** calcium carbonate, $CaCO_3$, a mineral found as limestone, chalk, and marble
cal·ci·um (kal′sē əm) ***n.*** [ModL. < L. *calx,* lime] a soft, silver-white, metallic chemical element found in limestone, marble, chalk, etc.: symbol, Ca; at. wt., 40.08; at. no., 20
calcium carbide a dark-gray, crystalline compound, CaC_2, used to produce acetylene, etc.
calcium carbonate a white powder or colorless, crystalline compound, $CaCO_3$, found mainly in limestone, marble, and chalk, and in bones, teeth, shells, and plant ash: used in making lime
calcium chloride a white, crystalline compound, $CaCl_2$, used in making ice, for dehydrating, etc.
calcium hydroxide slaked lime, $Ca(OH)_2$, a white, crystalline compound, used in making alkalies, bleaching powder, etc.
calcium oxide a white, soft, caustic solid, CaO, prepared by heating calcium carbonate; lime: used in mortar and plaster, in ceramics, etc.
calcium phosphate any of a number of phosphates of calcium found in bones, teeth, etc.
calc·spar (kalk′spär′) ***n.*** *same as* CALCITE
cal·cu·la·ble (kal′kyə lə b'l) ***adj.*** that can be calculated —**cal′cu·la·bil′i·ty** ***n.*** —**cal′cu·la·bly** ***adv.***
cal·cu·late (kal′kyə lāt′) ***vt.*** **-lat′ed, -lat′ing** [< L. pp. of *calculare,* to reckon < *calculus,* pebble used in counting, dim. of *calx,* limestone] **1.** to determine by using mathematics; compute **2.** to determine by reasoning; estimate **3.** to plan or intend *[a tale calculated to fool us]* **4.** [Colloq.] to think; suppose —***vi.*** **1.** to make a computation **2.** to rely or count (*on*)
cal·cu·lat·ed (-lāt′id) ***adj.*** **1.** undertaken after the probable results have been estimated *[calculated risk]* **2.** deliberately planned *[calculated cruelty]* **3.** apt or likely —**cal′cu·lat′ed·ly** ***adv.***
cal·cu·lat·ing (-iŋ) ***adj.*** shrewd or scheming
cal·cu·la·tion (kal′kyə lā′shən) ***n.*** **1.** a calculating **2.** something deduced by calculating; estimate; plan **3.**

careful planning or forethought, esp. with selfish motives —**cal′cu·la′tive** *adj.*

cal·cu·la·tor (kal′kyə lāt′ər) *n.* **1.** a person who calculates **2.** a machine for doing rapid addition, subtraction, multiplication, and division: also **calculating machine**

cal·cu·lous (kal′kyə ləs) *adj. Med.* caused by or having a calculus or calculi

cal·cu·lus (kal′kyə ləs) *n., pl.* **-li′** (-lī′), **-lus·es** [L.: see CALCULATE] **1.** any abnormal stony mass or deposit formed in the body, as in a kidney **2.** *Math. a)* a method of calculation using symbols *b)* a method of mathematical analysis using the combined methods of DIFFERENTIAL CALCULUS and INTEGRAL CALCULUS

Cal·cut·ta (kal kut′ə) seaport in NE India, in the Ganges delta: pop. 2,927,000

cal·dron (kôl′drən) *n.* [< OFr. < L. *caldaria,* warm bath < *calidus,* warm] a large kettle or boiler

Ca·leb (kā′ləb) [Heb. *kālēb,* lit., dog: hence, faithful] a masculine name

ca·lèche, ca·leche (kə lesh′) *n. same as* CALASH

Cal·e·do·ni·a (kal′ə dōn′yə, -dō′nē ə) [L.] *poet. name for* SCOTLAND —**Cal′e·do′ni·an** *adj., n.*

cal·en·dar (kal′ən dər) *n.* [L. *kalendarium,* account book < *kalendae,* CALENDS] **1.** a system for arranging time into days, weeks, months, and years **2.** a table or chart that shows such an arrangement, usually for a single year **3.** a list or schedule, as of pending court cases —*adj.* that appears on popular calendars [*calendar* art] —*vt.* to enter in a calendar; schedule

calendar year the period of time from Jan. 1 through Dec. 31: distinguished from FISCAL YEAR

cal·en·der (kal′ən dər) *n.* [< Fr. < ML. < L. *cylindrus,* CYLINDER] a machine with rollers between which paper, cloth, etc. is run, as to give it a smooth or glossy finish —*vt.* to process (paper, etc.) in a calender

cal·ends (-əndz) *n.pl.* [*often with sing. v.*] [< L. *kalendae* < *calare,* to proclaim < Gr. *kalein*] the first day of each month in the ancient Roman calendar

ca·len·du·la (kə len′jə lə) *n.* [ModL. < L. *kalendae,* calends: prob. because the plants flower in most months] any of a genus of plants of the composite family, with yellow or orange flowers

ca·les·cent (kə les′′nt) *adj.* [< L. < *calescere,* to grow warm] getting warm or hot —**ca·les′cence** *n.*

calf[1] (kaf) *n., pl.* **calves;** esp. for 3, **calfs** [< OE. *cealf* & ON. *kalfr*] **1.** a young cow or bull **2.** the young of some other large animals, as the elephant, whale, hippopotamus, seal, etc. **3.** leather from the hide of a calf; calfskin **4.** [Colloq.] an awkward or silly youth —**kill the fatted calf** to make a feast of welcome: Luke 15:23

calf[2] (kaf) *n., pl.* **calves** [ON. *kalfi*] the fleshy back part of the leg below the knee

calf's-foot jelly (kafs′foot′) an edible gelatin made by boiling calves' feet

calf·skin (kaf′skin′) *n.* **1.** the skin of a calf **2.** a soft, flexible leather made from this

Cal·ga·ry (kal′gər ē) city in S Alberta, Canada: pop. 470,000

Cal·houn (kal hōōn′), **John Cald·well** (kôld′wel) 1782–1850; U.S. statesman

Ca·li (kä′lē) city in SW Colombia: pop. 638,000

Cal·i·ban (kal′ə ban′) a deformed, savage creature in Shakespeare's *The Tempest*

cal·i·ber, cal·i·bre (kal′ə bər) *n.* [< Fr. & Sp. < *calibo* < Ar. *qālib,* a mold] **1.** the size of a bullet or shell as measured by its diameter **2.** the diameter of the bore of a gun measured in hundredths of an inch or in millimeters **3.** the diameter of the inside of any cylinder **4.** quality or ability

cal·i·brate (-brāt′) *vt.* **-brat′ed, -brat′ing 1.** to determine the caliber of **2.** to fix, check, or correct the scale of (a measuring instrument, as a thermometer) —**cal′i·bra′tion** *n.* —**cal′i·bra′tor** *n.*

cal·i·co (kal′ə kō′) *n., pl.* **-coes′, -cos′** [< *Calicut* (now Kozhikode), city in India where first obtained] any of several kinds of cotton cloth, usually coarse and printed —*adj.* **1.** of calico **2.** spotted like calico [*a calico* cat]

ca·lif (kā′lif, kal′if) *n. same as* CALIPH

Cal·i·for·ni·a (kal′ə fôr′nyə, -nē ə) [Sp., name of a fabled island] **1.** State of the SW U.S., on the Pacific coast: 158,693 sq. mi.; pop. 23,669,000; cap. Sacramento: abbrev. **Calif., CA, Cal. 2. Gulf of,** arm of the Pacific, between Baja California & the Mexican mainland —**Cal′i·for′ni·an** *adj., n.*

cal·i·for·ni·um (kal′ə fôr′nē əm) *n.* [< University of *California*] a radioactive chemical element produced by intense neutron irradiation of plutonium or curium: symbol, Cf; at. wt., 251 (?); at. no., 98

Ca·lig·u·la (kə lig′yoo lə) (born *Gaius Caesar*) 12–41 A.D.; Roman emperor (37–41 A.D.)

cal·i·per (kal′ə pər) *n.* [var. of CALIBER] **1.** [*usually pl.*] an instrument consisting of a pair of movable, curved legs fastened together at one end, used to measure the thickness or diameter of something: there are **inside calipers** and **outside calipers 2.** *same as* CALIPER RULE —*vt., vi.* to measure with calipers

caliper rule a graduated rule with one sliding jaw and one that is stationary

ca·liph (kā′lif, kal′if) *n.* [< OFr. < Ar. *khalīfa*] supreme ruler: the title taken by Mohammed's successors as heads of Islam

cal·iph·ate (kal′ə fāt′, -fit) *n.* the rank, reign, or dominion of a caliph: also **cal′if·ate′**

cal·is·then·ics (kal′əs then′iks) *n.pl.* [< Gr. *kallos,* beauty + *sthenos,* strength] **1.** exercises to develop a strong, trim body; simple gymnastics **2.** [*with sing. v.*] the art of developing bodily strength and gracefulness by such exercises —**cal′is·then′ic, cal′is·then′i·cal** *adj.*

calk[1] (kôk) *vt. same as* CAULK —**calk′er** *n.*

calk[2] (kôk) *n.* [OE. *calc,* shoe < L. *calx,* a heel] **1.** the part of a horseshoe that projects downward to prevent slipping **2.** a metal plate with spurs, fastened to the sole of a shoe to prevent slipping —*vt.* to fasten calks on

call (kôl) *vt.* [< OE. *ceallian* & (or <) ON. *kalla*] **1.** to say or read in a loud tone; shout; announce **2.** to ask to come; summon **3.** to summon to a specific duty, etc. [the army *called* him] **4.** to convoke [to *call* a meeting] **5.** to give or apply a name to [*call* the baby Ann] **6.** to consider or declare to be as specified [I *call* it silly] **7.** to awaken [*call* me at six] **8.** to communicate with by telephone **9.** to give orders for [to *call* a strike] **10.** to stop [game *called* because of rain] **11.** to demand payment of (a loan or bond issue) **12.** to utter directions for (a square dance) **13.** in pool, to describe (the shot one plans to make) **14.** *a) Poker* to require (a player) to show his hand by equaling his bet *b)* to force to account for something said or done *c)* to expose (someone's bluff) by such action —*vi.* **1.** to speak in a loud tone; shout **2.** to utter its characteristic cry, as a bird or animal **3.** to visit for a short while **4.** to telephone **5.** *Poker* to require a player to show his hand by equaling his bet —*n.* **1.** an act or instance of calling **2.** a loud utterance; shout **3.** the distinctive cry of an animal or bird, or a device imitating this **4.** a summons to a meeting, etc. **5.** a signal on a bugle, etc. **6.** an economic demand, as for a product **7.** an inner urging toward a certain action or profession, esp. to be a priest, minister, etc. **8.** power to attract [the *call* of the wild] **9.** need; occasion [no *call* for tears] **10.** an order or demand for payment **11.** a brief visit, esp. a formal or professional visit **12.** *Sports* an official's decision —**call back 1.** to ask or command to come back **2.** to telephone again or in return —**call down 1.** to invoke **2.** [Colloq.] to scold sharply —**call for 1.** to demand **2.** to come and get; stop for —**call forth** to bring into play —**call in 1.** to summon for help or consultation **2.** to take out of circulation, as coin —**call off 1.** to order away **2.** to read aloud in order from a list **3.** to cancel (a scheduled event) —**call on 1.** to visit briefly **2.** to ask (a person) to speak —**call out 1.** to shout **2.** to summon into action —**call time** *Sports* to suspend play temporarily —**call up 1.** to make one remember **2.** to summon, esp. for military duty **3.** to telephone —**on call 1.** available when summoned **2.** payable on demand

cal·la (kal′ə) *n.* [ModL. (named by Linnaeus) < L., a kind of plant] any of several plants of the arum family, with a large spathe surrounding a yellow spadix: also **calla lily**

call·board (kôl′bôrd′) *n. Theater* a bulletin board backstage for posting instructions, etc.

call·boy (-boi′) *n.* **1.** a boy who calls actors when it is time for them to go on the stage **2.** *same as* BELLMAN (sense 2)

call·er (-ər) *n.* **1.** a person or thing that calls **2.** a person who makes a short visit

call girl a prostitute who is called by telephone to assignations

cal·lig·ra·phy (kə lig′rə fē) *n.* [< Gr. < *kallos,* beauty + *graphein,* to write] **1.** beautiful handwriting **2.** handwriting —**cal·lig′ra·pher, cal·lig′ra·phist** *n.* —**cal·li·graph·ic** (kal′ə graf′ik) *adj.*

call·ing (kôl′iŋ) *n.* **1.** the action of one that calls **2.** one's occupation, profession, or trade

calling card a small card with one's name and, sometimes, one's address, used in making visits

Cal·li·o·pe (kə lī′ə pē; *for n., also* kal′ē ōp′) [L. < Gr. *Kalliopē* < *kallos,* beauty + *ops,* voice] *Gr. Myth.* the Muse of eloquence and epic poetry —*n.* [c-] a keyboard instrument like an organ, having a series of steam whistles

cal·li·per (kal′ə pər) *n., vt., vi. same as* CALIPER

cal·lis·then·ics (kal′əs then′iks) *n.pl. same as* CALISTHENICS —**cal′lis·then′ic** *adj.*

call loan a loan that must be repaid on demand

cal·los·i·ty (ka läs′ə tē, kə-) *n.* **1.** the quality or state of being callous, hardened, or unfeeling **2.** *pl.* **-ties** a hardened, thickened place on skin or bark; callus

cal·lous (kal′əs) *adj.* [< L. < *callum,* hard skin] **1.** *a)* having calluses *b)* thick and hardened **2.** lacking pity, mercy, etc.; unfeeling; insensitive —*vt., vi.* to make or become callous —**cal′lous·ly** *adv.* —**cal′lous·ness** *n.*

cal·low (kal′ō) *adj.* [< OE. *calu,* bald] **1.** still lacking the feathers needed for flying **2.** young and inexperienced; immature —**cal′low·ness** *n.*

cal·lus (kal′əs) *n., pl.* **-lus·es** [L., var. of *callum,* hard skin] **1.** a hardened, thickened place on the skin **2.** the hard substance that forms at the break in a fractured bone so as to reunite the parts **3.** a mass of undifferentiated cells that develops over cuts or wounds on plants —*vi., vt.* to develop or cause to develop a callus

calm (käm; *occas.* kälm) *n.* [< OFr. < It. < LL. *cauma,* heat of the day (hence, in It., time to rest: cf. SIESTA) < Gr. *kauma,* heat] **1.** lack of wind or motion; stillness **2.** lack of excitement; tranquillity; serenity —*adj.* **1.** without wind or motion; still; quiet **2.** not excited; tranquil —*vt., vi.* to make or become calm (often with *down*) —**calm′ly** *adv.* —**calm′ness** *n.*

cal·o·mel (kal′ə mel′, -məl) *n.* [Fr. < Gr. *kalos,* beautiful + *melas,* black] mercurous chloride, HgCl, a white, tasteless powder, formerly used as a cathartic, for intestinal worms, etc.

ca·lor·ic (kə lôr′ik, -lär′-) *n.* [< Fr. < L. *calor,* heat] [Archaic] heat —*adj.* **1.** of heat **2.** of or pertaining to calories —**ca·lor′i·cal·ly** *adv.*

cal·o·rie (kal′ə rē) *n.* [Fr. < L. *calor,* heat] **1.** the amount of heat needed to raise the temperature of one gram of water one degree centigrade: also **small calorie** **2.** [*occas.* C-] the amount of heat needed to raise the temperature of one kilogram of water one degree centigrade: also **large calorie** **3.** a unit equal to the large calorie, used for measuring energy produced by food when oxidized in the body Also sp. **cal′o·ry,** *pl.* **-ries**

cal·o·rif·ic (kal′ə rif′ik) *adj.* [< Fr. < L. < *calor,* heat + *facere,* to make] producing heat

cal·o·rim·e·ter (kal′ə rim′ə tər) *n.* [< L. *calor,* heat + -METER] an apparatus for measuring amounts of heat, as in chemical combination, friction, etc.

cal·o·rim·e·try (kal′ə rim′ə trē) *n.* [< L. *calor,* heat + -METRY] measurement of the quantity of heat —**cal·o·ri·met·ric** (kal′ə ri met′rik, kə lôr′ə-), **cal′o·ri·met′ri·cal** *adj.*

cal·u·met (kal′yə met′, kal′yə met′) *n.* [Fr.; ult. < L. *calamus,* a reed] a long-stemmed ceremonial pipe, smoked by N. American Indians as a token of peace

CALUMET

ca·lum·ni·ate (kə lum′nē āt′) *vt., vi.* **-at′ed, -at′ing** [< L. pp. of *calumniari,* to slander < *calumnia,* CALUMNY] to spread false and harmful statements about; slander —**ca·lum′ni·a′tion** *n.* —**ca·lum′ni·a′tor** *n.*

ca·lum·ni·ous (kə lum′nē əs) *adj.* full of calumnies; slanderous —**ca·lum′ni·ous·ly** *adv.*

cal·um·ny (kal′əm nē) *n., pl.* **-nies** [< Fr. < L. *calumnia,* trickery, slander] **1.** a false and malicious statement meant to hurt someone's reputation **2.** the uttering of such a statement; slander

Cal·va·ry (kal′vər ē) [< LL. < L. *calvaria,* skull; transl. of Aram. *gūlgūlthā,* Golgotha, lit., skull] *Bible* the place near Jerusalem where the crucifixion of Jesus took place: Luke 23:33, Matt. 27:33

calve (kav, käv) *vi., vt.* **calved, calv′ing** [< OE. *cealfian*] to give birth to (a calf)

calves (kavz, kävz) *n. pl. of* CALF

Cal·vin (kal′vin) [< ModL. < Fr., prob. < L. *calvus,* bald] **1.** a masculine name **2. John,** (born *Jean Cau(l)vin* or *Chauvin*) 1509–64; Fr. Protestant reformer

Cal·vin·ism (-iz′m) *n.* the theological system of John Calvin and his followers, which emphasizes the doctrines of predestination and salvation solely by God's grace: associated, in practice, with a stern moral code —**Cal′vin·ist** *n., adj.* —**Cal′vin·is′tic, Cal′vin·is′ti·cal** *adj.* —**Cal′vin·is′ti·cal·ly** *adv.*

calx (kalks) *n., pl.* **calx′es, cal·ces** (kal′sēz) [L., small stone, lime] the ashy powder left after a metal or mineral has been calcined

Ca·lyp·so (kə lip′sō) in Homer's *Odyssey,* a sea nymph who kept Odysseus on her island for seven years

ca·lyp·so (kə lip′sō) *adj.* [< ? prec.] designating or of satirical ballads improvised and sung as originally by natives of Trinidad and characterized by wrenched syllabic stress and syncopated rhythms —*n.* a calypso song or calypso music

ca·lyx (kā′liks, kal′iks) *n., pl.* **ca′lyx·es, ca·ly·ces** (kā′lə sēz′, kal′ə-) [L., outer covering, pod < Gr. *kalyx*] **1.** the outer whorl of protective leaves, or sepals, of a flower, usually green **2.** *Zool.* a cuplike part or cavity

cal·zo·ne (kal zō′nē, -zōn′) *n.* [It.] a kind of turnover filled variously with cheese, meat, and vegetables

cam (kam) *n.* [Du. *cam,* orig., comb] a wheel, projection on a wheel, etc. which gives an eccentric or reciprocating motion to another wheel, a shaft, etc., or receives such motion from it

ca·ma·ra·de·rie (käm′ə räd′ər ē, kam′-) *n.* [Fr. < *camarade,* comrade] loyalty and warm, friendly feeling among comrades; comradeship

CAM

cam·a·ril·la (kam′ə ril′ə; *Sp.* kä′mä rēl′yä) *n.* [Sp. dim. of *camara,* chamber < L. *camera,* a vault] a group of secret or confidential advisers; cabal

cam·ass, cam·as (kam′əs) *n.* [Chinook < *chamas,* sweet] any of a genus of N. American plants of the lily family, with sweet, edible bulbs and racemes of bluish flowers

cam·ber (kam′bər) *n.* [OFr., dial. var. of *chambre,* bent < L. *camur,* arched] **1.** a slight convex curve of a surface, as of a road, a beam, etc. **2.** a slight tilt given to each of a pair of automobile wheels by aligning them so that the bottoms are closer together than the tops **3.** *Aeron.* the arching curve of an airfoil from the leading edge to the trailing edge —*vt., vi.* to arch slightly

cam·bi·um (kam′bē əm) *n.* [LL., change] a layer of formative cells between the wood and bark in woody plants: the cells increase by division and differentiate to form new wood and bark

Cam·bo·di·a (kam bō′dē ə) country in the S Indochinese peninsula: 69,884 sq. mi.; pop. 6,701,000; cap. Phnom Penh: official name *Democratic Kampuchea* —**Cam·bo′di·an** *adj., n.*

Cam·bri·a (kam′brē ə) *poet. name for* WALES

Cam·bri·an (-ən) *adj.* **1.** of Cambria; Welsh **2.** designating or of the first geological period in the Paleozoic Era —*n.* a native or inhabitant of Cambria; Welshman —**the Cambrian** the Cambrian Period or its rocks: see GEOLOGY, chart

cam·bric (kām′brik) *n.* [< *Kambryk,* Fl. name of *Cambrai,* city in N France] **1.** a very fine, thin linen **2.** a cotton cloth like this

cambric tea a hot drink of milk, sugar, and water or, often, weak tea

Cam·bridge (kām′brij) **1.** city in EC England: pop. 100,000: site of Cambridge University **2.** city in E Mass., near Boston: pop. 95,000

Cam·den (kam′dən) [after C. Pratt, Earl of *Camden* (1714–94)] city in SW N.J.: pop. 85,000

came (kām) *pt. of* COME

cam·el (kam′'l) *n.* [< OE. or OFr. < L. *camelus* < Gr. *kamēlos* < Heb. *gāmāl* (or) < Egypt. *kamál*] either of two species of large, domesticated, cud-chewing mammals with a humped back, long neck, and large, cushioned feet: capable of storing water in its body tissue, the camel is the common beast of burden in Asian and African deserts: see BACTRIAN CAMEL and DROMEDARY

cam·el·eer (kam′ə lir′) *n.* a camel driver

ca·mel·li·a (kə mēl′yə, -mē′lē ə) *n.* [after G. J. *Kamel* (1661–1706), Jesuit missionary to the Far East] **1.** any of a genus of Asian evergreen trees and shrubs with glossy evergreen leaves and waxy, roselike flowers **2.** the flower

ca·mel·o·pard (kə mel′ə pärd′) *n.* [< LL. < L. < Gr. < *kamēlos,* camel + *pardalis,* leopard: from its camellike neck and leopardlike spots] *early name for the* GIRAFFE

Cam·e·lot (kam′ə lät′) the legendary English town where King Arthur had his court

camel's hair **1.** the hair of the camel **2.** cloth made of this hair, sometimes mixed with wool, etc. —**cam′el's-hair′, cam′el-hair′** *adj.*

camel's-hair brush an artist's small brush, made of hair from a squirrel's tail

Cam·em·bert (cheese) (kam′əm ber′) [from *Camembert,* in Normandy] a soft, creamy, rich cheese

cam·e·o (kam′ē ō′) *n., pl.* **-os′** [< It. < ML. *camaeus* < ?] **1.** a carving in relief on certain stratified gems or shells so that the raised design, often a head in profile, is usually in a layer of different color from its background: opposed to INTAGLIO **2.** a gem, shell, etc. so carved **3.** *a)* a choice bit role, esp. when played by a notable actor *b)* a fine bit of descriptive writing

cam·er·a (kam′ər ə, kam′rə) *n., pl.* **-er·as;** also for 1, **-er·ae′** (-ə rē′) [L., a vault < Gr. *kamara,* vaulted chamber] **1.** a chamber; specif., the private office of a judge **2.** a device for taking photographs, consisting of a closed box containing a sensitized plate or film on which an image is formed when light enters the box through a lens **3.** *TV* that part of the transmitter which consists of a lens and a special cathode-ray tube containing a plate on which the image to be televised is projected for transformation into electrical signals **—in camera** in privacy or secrecy

cam·er·a·man (-man', -mən) *n., pl.* **-men'** (-men', -mən) an operator of a camera, esp. of a motion-picture or television camera

cam·er·a-shy (-shī') *adj.* unwilling to be photographed

Cam·e·roun (kam'ə ro͞on') country in WC Africa, on the Atlantic: 183,000 sq. mi.; pop. 5,562,000: also sp. **Cameroon —Cam'e·roun'i·an** *adj., n.*

Ca·mille (kə mēl') [Fr. < L. *camilla,* virgin of unblemished character] a feminine name: var. **Ca·mil'la** (-mil'ə)

cam·i·sole (kam'ə sōl') *n.* [Fr. < Sp. dim. of *camisa,* shirt: see CHEMISE] **1.** a woman's sleeveless underwaist, orig. a corset cover, now worn under a sheer blouse **2.** a woman's short negligee

cam·o·mile (kam'ə mīl', -mēl') *n. same as* CHAMOMILE

cam·ou·flage (kam'ə fläzh', -fläj') *n.* [Fr. < *camoufler,* to disguise] **1.** the disguising of troops, ships, guns, etc. to conceal them from the enemy, as by the use of paint, nets, leaves, etc. in patterns merging with the background **2.** a disguise or concealment of this kind **3.** any device or action used to conceal or mislead; deception *—vt., vi.* **-flaged', -flag'ing** to disguise or conceal by camouflage **—cam'ou·flag'er** *n.*

camp (kamp) *n.* [< Fr. < It. < L. *campus,* a field] **1.** *a)* a place where tents, huts, barracks, etc. are put up, as for soldiers in training or in bivouac *b)* military life **2.** *a)* a group of people who support or advance a common opinion, cause, etc. *b)* the position taken by such a group **3.** a tent, cabin, etc., or a group of these, used for temporary lodging, as by hunters, fishermen, etc. **4.** a place in the country for vacationers, esp. children, with outdoor recreation, often organized and supervised **5.** the people living in a camp **6.** [Slang] [orig., homosexual jargon] banality, mediocrity, artifice, etc. so extreme as to amuse or have a perversely sophisticated appeal *—adj.* [Slang] characterized by camp (*n.* 6) *—vi.* **1.** to set up a camp **2.** to live or stay in or as if in a camp (often with *out*) *—vt.* to put into a camp **—break camp** to pack up camping equipment and go away **—camp it up** [Slang] to behave in a camp way

cam·paign (kam pān') *n.* [Fr. *campagne,* open country < It. < LL. < L. *campus,* a field] **1.** a series of military operations with a particular objective in a war **2.** a series of organized, planned actions for a particular purpose, as for electing a candidate *—vi.* to participate in, or go on, a campaign **—cam·paign'er** *n.*

cam·pa·ni·le (kam'pə nē'lē) *n., pl.* **-les, -li** (-lē) [It. < LL. *campana,* a bell] a bell tower, esp. one that stands apart from another building

cam·pan·u·la (kam pan'yoo lə) *n.* [ModL. < LL., dim. of *campana,* a bell] any of a genus of plants with bell-shaped flowers; bellflower

camp chair a lightweight folding chair

camp·craft (kamp'kraft') *n.* the art or practice of camping outdoors

cam·pea·chy wood (kam pē'chē) [< *Campeche,* state of SE Mexico] *same as* LOGWOOD (sense 1)

camp·er (kamp'ər) *n.* **1.** a person who vacations at a camp **2.** any of various motor vehicles or trailers equipped for camping out

‡**cam·pe·si·no** (käm'pe sē'nô) *n., pl.* **-nos** (-nôs) [Sp.] a peasant or farm worker

camp·fire (kamp'fīr') *n.* **1.** an outdoor fire at a camp **2.** a social gathering around such a fire

campfire girl a member of the **Camp Fire Girls,** a girls' organization, founded in 1910, to promote activities that build health and character

camp·ground (-ground') *n.* **1.** a place where a camp is set up **2.** a place where a camp meeting or religious revival is held

cam·phor (kam'fər) *n.* [< OFr. < LL. < Ar. < Sans. *karpurah,* camphor tree] a volatile, crystalline substance, $C_{10}H_{16}O$, with a strong characteristic odor, derived chiefly from the wood of an Asian laurel (**camphor tree**): used as a moth repellent, in making cellulose plastics, and in medicine as an irritant, etc. **—cam·phor'ic** (-fôr'ik) *adj.*

cam·phor·ate (kam'fə rāt') *vt.* **-at'ed, -at'ing** to put camphor in or on *[camphorated* oil*]*

camphor ball *same as* MOTHBALL

camphor ice an ointment made of white wax, camphor, spermaceti, and castor oil, used for dry, chapped skin

cam·pi·on (kam'pē ən) *n.* [prob. ult. < L. *campus,* field] any of various flowering plants of the pink family, with white or pink flowers

camp meeting a religious gathering held outdoors or in a tent, etc., usually lasting several days

camp·site (kamp'sīt') *n.* **1.** any site for a temporary camp **2.** an area in a public or private park set aside for camping, often equipped with water, toilets, picnic stoves, etc.

camp·stool (-sto͞ol') *n.* a light folding stool

cam·pus (kam'pəs) *n., pl.* **-pus·es** [L., a field] the grounds, sometimes including the buildings, of a school or college *—adj.* **1.** on or of the campus **2.** of a school or college *[campus* politics*]*

camp·y (kam'pē) *adj.* **camp'i·er, camp'i·est** [Slang] characterized by camp (*n.* 6)

cam·shaft (kam'shaft') *n.* a shaft to which a cam is fastened

can[1] (kan; *as an auxiliary, usually* kən, k'n) *vi. pt.* **could** [< OE. < *cunnan,* to know, be able] **1.** to know how to **2.** to be able to **3.** to be likely to *[can* it be true?*]* **4.** to have the right to **5.** [Colloq.] to be permitted to; may **—can but** can only

can[2] (kan) *n.* [< OE. *canne,* a cup] **1.** a container of various kinds, usually made of metal with a separate cover *[a* milk *can,* a garbage *can]* **2.** a container made of tinned iron or other metal, in which foods or other perishable products are sealed for preservation **3.** the contents of a can; canful **4.** [Slang] *a)* a prison *b)* the buttocks *c)* a toilet *—vt.* **canned, can'ning** **1.** to put up in airtight cans or jars for preservation **2.** [Slang] *a)* to dismiss; discharge *b)* to make a recording of

Can. 1. Canada **2.** Canadian **3.** Canon

Ca·naan (kā'nən) Promised Land of the Israelites, between the Jordan & the Mediterranean

Ca·naan·ite (-īt') *n.* **1.** one of the original inhabitants of Canaan **2.** their Semitic language **—Ca'naan·it'ish** (-īt'ish), **Ca'naan·it'ic** (-it'ik) *adj.*

Canad. Canadian

Can·a·da (kan'ə də) country in N North America: a member of the Commonwealth: 3,852,000 sq. mi.; pop. 20,015,000; cap. Ottawa

Canada balsam a thick, yellow, resinous fluid from the balsam fir

Canada goose a large wild goose of Canada and the northern U.S., gray, with black head and neck

Ca·na·di·an (kə nā'dē ən) *adj.* of Canada or its people *—n.* a native or inhabitant of Canada

Ca·na·di·an·ism (-iz'm) *n.* **1.** a custom, belief, etc. originating in Canada **2.** a word or phrase originating in or peculiar to Canadian English

ca·naille (kə nāl'; *Fr.* kȧ nä'y') *n.* [Fr. < It. *canaglia* < L. *canis,* a dog] the mob; rabble

ca·nal (kə nal') *n.* [< OFr. < L. *canalis,* a channel < *canna,* a reed] **1.** an artificial waterway for transportation or irrigation **2.** *Anat.* a tubular passage or duct *—vt.* **-nalled'** or **-naled', -nal'ling** or **-nal'ing** to build a canal through or across

ca·nal·boat (-bōt') *n.* a long, narrow freight-carrying boat, used on canals: also **canal boat**

can·a·lic·u·lus (kan'ə lik'yoo ləs) *n., pl.* **-li'** (-lī') [L., dim. of *canalis,* a groove] *Anat., Bot., Zool.* a very small groove, as in bone **—can'a·lic'u·late** (-lit, -lāt') *adj.*

ca·nal·i·za·tion (kə nal'ə zā'shən, kan''l ə-) *n.* **1.** a canalizing **2.** a system of canals or channels

ca·nal·ize (kə nal'īz, kan'ə līz') *vt.* **-ized, -iz·ing** **1.** to make a canal through **2.** to change into or make like a canal **3.** to provide an outlet for, esp. by directing into a specific channel

Canal Zone *former name of* the strip of land in Panama that extends 5 miles on either side of the Panama Canal: it was leased to the U.S., which governed it (1904–79)

ca·na·pé (kan'ə pē, -pā') *n.* [Fr.] a small piece of bread or toast or a cracker spread with spiced meat, fish, cheese, etc., served as an appetizer

ca·nard (kə närd') *n.* [Fr., a duck, hoax] a false, malicious report, fabricated as by a newspaper

ca·nar·y (kə ner'ē) *n., pl.* **-nar'ies** [< CANARY ISLANDS] **1.** a small, yellow songbird of the finch family **2.** a light yellow: also **canary yellow** **3.** a sweet wine like madeira, of the Canary Islands

Canary Islands group of Sp. islands in the Atlantic, off the NW coast of Africa

ca·nas·ta (kə nas'tə) *n.* [Sp., basket] a double-deck card game for two to six players

Ca·na·ver·al (kə nav'ər əl), **Cape** [Sp. *cañaveral,* canebrake] cape on the E coast of Fla.: U.S. proving ground for missiles and spacecraft

Can·ber·ra (kan'bər ə) capital of Australia, in the SE part: pop. 92,000

canc. 1. cancel **2.** canceled **3.** cancellation

can·can (kan'kan') *n.* [Fr.] a lively dance with much high kicking performed by women entertainers, orig. in Paris dance halls in the late 19th cent.

can·cel (kan′s'l) ***vt.*** **-celed** or **-celled, -cel·ing** or **-cel·ling** [< Anglo-Fr. < L. *cancellare,* to draw latticelike lines across < *cancer,* lattice] **1.** to cross out with lines or mark over, as in deleting written matter or marking a postage stamp, check, etc. as used **2.** to make invalid; annul **3.** to do away with; abolish, withdraw, etc. *[to cancel an order]* **4.** to neutralize or balance; offset (often with *out*) **5.** *Math.* to remove (a common factor from both terms of a fraction, equivalents on opposite sides of an equation, etc.) —***vi.*** to offset or cancel each other (with *out*) —***n.*** a cancellation —**can′cel·er, can′cel·ler** ***n.***

can·cel·la·tion (kan′sə lā′shən) ***n.*** **1.** the act of canceling **2.** something canceled **3.** the mark showing that something is canceled

can·cer (kan′sər) [< L., a crab; later, malignant tumor] **1.** [C-] a N constellation **2.** [C-] the fourth sign of the zodiac: see ZODIAC, illus. —***n.*** **1.** a malignant new growth, or tumor, anywhere in the body: cancers tend to spread: see also CARCINOMA, SARCOMA **2.** anything bad or harmful that spreads and destroys —**can′cer·ous** ***adj.***

can·de·la (kan dē′lə) ***n.*** [L., candle] *same as* CANDLE (*n.* 3)

can·de·la·brum (kan′də lä′brəm, -lab′rəm, -lā′brəm) ***n.,*** *pl.* **-bra** (-brə), **-brums** [L.: see CHANDELIER] a large branched candlestick: also **can′de·la′bra,** *pl.* **-bras**

can·des·cent (kan des′'nt) ***adj.*** [< L. prp. of *candescere* < *candere,* to shine] glowing; incandescent —**can·des′cence** ***n.***

can·did (kan′did) ***adj.*** [L. *candidus,* white, sincere < *candere:* see prec.] **1.** free from bias; fair; impartial **2.** very honest or frank in speech or writing **3.** unposed and informal *[a candid photograph]* —**can′did·ly** ***adv.*** —**can′did·ness** ***n.***

can·di·da·cy (kan′də də sē) ***n.,*** *pl.* **-cies** the fact or state of being a candidate: also [Brit.] **can′di·da·ture** (-di chər, -dā′chər)

can·di·date (kan′də dāt′, -dit) ***n.*** [L. *candidatus,* white-robed < *candidus* (see CANDID): office seekers in Rome wore white gowns] **1.** a person who seeks, or has been proposed for, an office, an award, etc. **2.** a person or thing apparently destined for a certain end *[a candidate for fame]*

candid camera a camera, usually small, with a fast lens, used to take informal, unposed pictures

can·died (kan′dēd) ***adj.*** **1.** cooked in or with sugar or syrup, esp. to preserve, glaze, or encrust **2.** crystallized into sugar **3.** sugary in expression

can·dle (kan′d'l) ***n.*** [< OE. < L. *candela,* a torch < *candere,* to shine] **1.** a cylinder of tallow or wax with a wick through its center, which gives light when burned **2.** anything like this in form or use **3.** a unit of luminous intensity equal to 1/60 of the luminous intensity of one square centimeter of a blackbody at the temperature of solidification of platinum —***vt.*** **-dled, -dling** to examine (eggs) for freshness, fertilization, etc. by holding in front of a light —**burn the candle at both ends** to work or, esp., play too much so that one's energy is dissipated —**not hold a candle to** to be not nearly so good as —**not worth the candle** not worth doing —**can′dler** ***n.***

can·dle·ber·ry (-ber′ē) ***n.,*** *pl.* **-ries** *same as:* **1.** BAYBERRY (sense 1) **2.** CANDLENUT

can·dle·light (-līt′) ***n.*** **1.** subdued light given by or as by candles **2.** twilight; evening

Can·dle·mas (kan′d'l məs) ***n.*** [< OE.: see CANDLE & MASS] a church feast, Feb. 2, commemorating the purification of the Virgin Mary: candles for sacred uses are blessed then: also **Candlemas Day**

can·dle·nut (kan′d'l nut′) ***n.*** **1.** a tree growing in the Pacific Islands, whose fruit the natives burn as candles **2.** its fruit

can·dle·pow·er (-pou′ər) ***n.*** the luminous intensity of a light source expressed in candles

can·dle·stick (-stik′) ***n.*** a cupped or spiked holder for a candle or candles

can·dor (kan′dər) ***n.*** [L., whiteness, openness < *candere:* see CANDESCENT] **1.** the quality of being fair and unprejudiced **2.** sharp honesty in expressing oneself Also, Brit. sp., **can′dour**

can·dy (kan′dē) ***n.,*** *pl.* **-dies** [< *sugar candy* < OFr. < It. < Ar. < Per. *qand,* cane sugar] **1.** crystallized sugar made by evaporating boiled cane sugar, syrup, etc. **2.** *a)* a sweet food, usually made from sugar or syrup, in small pieces, with flavoring, fruit, chocolate, nuts, etc. added *b)* a piece of such food —***vt.*** **-died, -dy·ing** **1.** to cook in or with sugar or syrup, esp. to preserve, glaze, or encrust **2.** to crystallize into sugar **3.** to sweeten; make pleasant —***vi.*** to become candied (in senses 1 & 2)

can·dy-striped (-strīpt′) ***adj.*** having diagonal, colored stripes like those on a stick of candy

cane (kān) ***n.*** [< OFr. < It. < L. *canna* < Gr. *kanna*] **1.** the slender, jointed, usually flexible stem of any of certain plants, as bamboo, rattan, etc. **2.** any plant with such a stem, as sugar cane, sorghum, etc. **3.** the woody stem of a fruiting plant, as the blackberry **4.** a stick used for flogging **5.** *same as* WALKING STICK (sense 1) **6.** split rattan, used in weaving chair seats, etc. —***vt.*** **caned, can′ing** **1.** to flog with a cane **2.** to make or furnish (chairs, etc.) with cane —**can′er** ***n.***

cane·brake (kān′brāk′) ***n.*** [CANE + BRAKE[3]] a dense growth of cane plants

cane sugar sugar (*sucrose*) from sugar cane

ca·nine (kā′nīn) ***adj.*** [L. *caninus* < *canis,* a dog] **1.** of or like a dog **2.** of the family of animals that includes dogs, wolves, jackals, and foxes —***n.*** **1.** a dog or other canine animal **2.** a sharp-pointed tooth on either side of the upper jaw and lower jaw, between the incisors and the bicuspids: in full, **canine tooth**

Ca·nis Ma·jor (kān′is mā′jər) [L., the Greater Dog] a S constellation southeast of Orion, containing the Dog Star, Sirius

Canis Mi·nor (mī′nər) [L., the Lesser Dog] a N constellation east of Orion, containing the bright star Procyon

can·is·ter (kan′is tər) ***n.*** [< L. *canistrum,* wicker basket < Gr. *kanistron* < *kanna,* a reed] **1.** a small box or can for coffee, tea, etc. **2.** a boxlike vacuum cleaner **3.** the part of a gas mask with chemicals for filtering the air

can·ker (kaŋ′kər) ***n.*** [< OFr. < L. *cancer:* see CANCER] **1.** an ulcerlike sore, esp. in the mouth, that spreads **2.** a disease of plants that causes decay **3.** anything that corrupts —***vt.*** **1.** to attack or infect with canker **2.** to infect or debase with corruption —***vi.*** to become cankered —**can′ker·ous** ***adj.***

can·ker·worm (-wurm′) ***n.*** any of several moth larvae harmful to fruit and shade trees

can·na (kan′ə) ***n.*** [L., a reed] any of a genus of broad-leaved tropical plants, often grown for its striking foliage and brilliant flowers

can·na·bis (kan′ə bis) ***n.*** [L., hemp < Gr. *kannabis*] **1.** *same as* HEMP **2.** the female flowering tops of the hemp

canned (kand) ***adj.*** **1.** preserved in cans or jars **2.** [Slang] *a)* recorded for reproduction, as on radio *[canned commercials]* *b)* prepared for publication in a newspaper chain *[a canned editorial]*

can·nel (coal) (kan′'l) [< ? *candle coal*] a variety of bituminous coal that burns with a bright flame and has a high volatile content

can·nel·lo·ni (kan′ə lō′nē; *It.* kän′nel lô′nē) ***n.*** [It., pl. of *cannellone,* hollow noodle] tubular casings of dough filled with ground meat, baked, and served in a tomato sauce

can·ner·y (kan′ər ē) ***n.,*** *pl.* **-ner·ies** a factory where foods are canned

Cannes (kan, kanz; *Fr.* kån) city in SE France, on the Riviera: pop. 67,000

can·ni·bal (kan′ə b'l) ***n.*** [Sp. *canibal,* a savage (term used by Columbus) < *Caniba,* a cannibal people, prob. < Carib *galibi,* lit., strong men] **1.** a person who eats human flesh **2.** an animal that eats its own kind —***adj.*** of, resembling, or having the habits of, cannibals —**can′ni·bal·ism** ***n.*** —**can′ni·bal·is′tic** ***adj.***

can·ni·bal·ize (-īz′) ***vt., vi.*** **-ized′, -iz′ing** **1.** to strip (old or worn equipment) of parts for use in other units **2.** to take personnel or components from (one organization) for use in building up another **3.** to devour (another of the same kind): used figuratively —**can′ni·bal·i·za′tion** ***n.***

can·ni·kin (kan′ə k'n) ***n.*** [< CAN[2] + -KIN] **1.** a small can; cup **2.** [Dial.] a wooden bucket

can·ning (kan′iŋ) ***n.*** the act, process, or work of putting food in cans or jars for preservation

can·non (kan′ən) ***n.,*** *pl.* **-nons, -non:** see PLURAL, II, D, 4 [< OFr. < It. < L. *canna:* see CANE] **1.** *a)* a large, mounted piece of artillery; sometimes, specif., a large gun with a relatively short barrel, as a howitzer *b)* an automatic gun, now usually of 20-mm. caliber, mounted on an aircraft **2.** *same as* CANNON BONE —***vt., vi.*** to cannonade

can·non·ade (kan′ə nād′) ***n.*** a continuous firing of artillery —***vi., vt.*** **-ad′ed, -ad′ing** to fire artillery (at)

can·non·ball (kan′ən bôl′) ***n.*** **1.** a heavy ball, esp. of iron, formerly used as a projectile in cannon: also **cannon ball** **2.** [Colloq.] a fast express train —***adj.*** [Slang] fast; rapid —***vi.*** [Slang] to move very rapidly

cannon bone the bone between hock or knee and fetlock in a four-legged, hoofed animal

can·non·eer (kan′ə nir′) ***n.*** an artilleryman

cannon fodder soldiers, sailors, etc. thought of as being expended (i.e., killed or maimed) or expendable in war

can·non·ry (kan′ən rē) ***n.,*** *pl.* **-ries** **1.** cannons collectively; artillery **2.** cannon fire

can·not (kan′ät, -ət; kə nät′) can not —**cannot but** have no choice but to; must

can·ny (kan′ē) ***adj.*** **-ni·er, -ni·est** [< CAN[1]] **1.** careful and shrewd in one's actions and dealings; clever and cautious **2.** wise and well-informed **3.** careful with money; thrifty —**can′ni·ly** (-'l ē) ***adv.*** —**can′ni·ness** (-ē nis) ***n.***

ca·noe (kə no͞o′) *n.* [< Sp. *canoa* < the Carib name] a narrow, light boat with its sides meeting in a sharp edge at each end: it is moved by paddles —*vi.* **-noed′, -noe′ing** to paddle, or go in, a canoe —*vt.* to transport by canoe —**ca·noe′ist** *n.*

can·on¹ (kan′ən) *n.* [< OE. & OFr. < L., a rule < Gr. *kanōn,* rod, bar < *kanna:* see CANE] **1.** a law or body of laws of a church **2.** *a)* an established or basic rule, principle, or criterion *[the canons of good taste] b)* a body of rules, principles, criteria, etc. **3.** *a)* a list of books of the Bible officially accepted as genuine *b)* a list of the genuine works of an author *[the Shakespearean canon]* **4.** *a)* [*often* **C-**] *Eccles.* the fundamental part of the Mass, between the Preface and the Communion *b)* a list of recognized saints as in the Roman Catholic Church **5.** *Music* a polyphonic composition in which a melody is repeated at delayed intervals in the same or a related key

can·on² (kan′ən) *n.* [< OE. & OFr. < LL. *canonicus,* one living by the canon: see prec.] **1.** a member of a clerical group living according to a canon, or rule **2.** a clergyman serving in a cathedral or collegiate church

ca·ñon (kan′yən; *Sp.* kä nyôn′) *n. same as* CANYON

ca·non·ic (kə nän′ik) *adj.* **1.** *same as* CANONICAL **2.** of a musical canon

ca·non·i·cal (kə nän′i k′l) *adj.* **1.** of, according to, or ordered by church canon **2.** authoritative; accepted **3.** belonging to the canon of the Bible **4.** of a canon (clergyman) —**ca·non′i·cal·ly** *adv.*

canonical hour any of the seven periods of the day assigned to prayer and worship

ca·non·i·cals (-k′lz) *n.pl.* the clothes prescribed by canon for a clergyman when conducting services

can·on·ic·i·ty (kan′ə nis′ə tē) *n.* the fact or condition of being canonical

can·on·ist (kan′ən ist) *n.* an expert in canon law —**can′on·is′tic** *adj.*

can·on·ize (kan′ə nīz′) *vt.* **-ized′, -iz′ing** [< LL. *canonizare:* see CANON¹ + -IZE] **1.** to declare (a dead person) a saint in formal church procedure **2.** to glorify **3.** to put in the Biblical canon **4.** to give church sanction to —**can′on·i·za′tion** *n.*

canon law the laws governing the ecclesiastical affairs of a Christian church

can·on·ry (kan′ən rē) *n., pl.* **-ries** **1.** the benefice or office of a canon **2.** canons collectively

can·o·py (kan′ə pē) *n., pl.* **-pies** [< ML. < L. < Gr. *kōnōpeion,* bed with mosquito nets, dim. of *kōnōps,* gnat] **1.** a covering of cloth, etc. fastened above a bed, throne, etc. or held on poles over a person or sacred thing **2.** a canvas structure forming a sheltered walk to a building entrance **3.** anything that covers or seems to cover like a canopy, as the sky **4.** the transparent hood over an airplane cockpit **5.** a rooflike projection over a door, pulpit, etc. —*vt.* **-pied, -py·ing** to place or form a canopy over; cover; shelter

canst (kanst; *unstressed* kənst) *archaic 2d pers. sing., pres. indic., of* CAN¹: *used with* thou

cant¹ (kant) *n.* [< L. *cantus:* see CHANT] **1.** whining, singsong speech, esp. as used by beggars **2.** the secret slang of beggars, thieves, etc.; argot **3.** the special words and phrases used by those in a certain sect, occupation, etc.; jargon **4.** insincere, trite talk, esp. when pious or moral —*vi.* to use cant; speak in cant —*adj.* of, or having the nature of, cant —**cant′er** *n.*

cant² (kant) *n.* [< OFr. < LL. < L. *cant(h)us,* tire of a wheel < Celt.] **1.** a corner or outside angle **2.** a slanting surface; beveled edge **3.** a sudden movement that causes tilting, turning, or overturning **4.** the tilt, turn, or slant thus caused —*vt.* **1.** to give a sloping edge to; bevel **2.** to tilt or overturn **3.** to pitch; toss —*vi.* **1.** to tilt or turn over **2.** to slant —*adj.* **1.** with canted sides or corners **2.** slanting

can't (kant) cannot

can·ta·bi·le (kän tä′bi lā′) *adj., adv.* [< It. < L. < *cantare:* see CHANT] *Music* in any easy, flowing manner; songlike —*n.* music in this style

Can·ta·brig·i·an (kan′tə brij′ē ən, -brij′ən) *adj.* [< ML. *Cantabrigia,* Cambridge] of Cambridge, England, or Cambridge University —*n.* **1.** a student or graduate of Cambridge University **2.** any inhabitant of Cambridge, England

can·ta·loupe, can·ta·loup (kan′tə lōp′) *n.* [< Fr. < It. < *Cantalupo,* near Rome, where first grown in Europe] **1.** a muskmelon with a hard, rough rind and sweet, juicy flesh **2.** any muskmelon

can·tan·ker·ous (kan taŋ′kər əs) *adj.* [prob. < ME. *contakour,* a troublemaker (< *contek,* strife, quarrel) + -OUS] bad-tempered; quarrelsome —**can·tan′ker·ous·ly** *adv.* —**can·tan′ker·ous·ness** *n.*

can·ta·ta (kən tät′ə) *n.* [< It. pp. of *cantare:* see CHANT] a musical composition with vocal solos, choruses, etc., telling a story that is sung but not acted

can·teen (kan tēn′) *n.* [< Fr. < It. *cantina,* wine cellar] **1.** *same as* POST EXCHANGE **2.** *a)* a place where refreshments can be obtained, as by employees or visitors *b)* such a place serving as a social center *[a youth canteen]* **3.** a place where cooked food is dispensed to people in distress, as in a disaster area **4.** a small flask for carrying drinking water

can·ter (kan′tər) *n.* [contr. < *Canterbury gallop,* the riding pace of the medieval Canterbury pilgrims] a smooth, easy pace like a moderate gallop —*vi., vt.* to ride or move at a canter

Can·ter·bur·y (kan′tər ber′ē, -bər ē) city in SE England: site of a famous cathedral: pop. 33,000

Canterbury bells a cultivated bellflower with white, pink, or blue, cuplike flowers

cant hook [see CANT²] a pole with a movable hooked arm at or near one end, for catching hold of logs and rolling them

can·thus (kan′thəs) *n., pl.* **-thi** (-thī) [ModL. < Gr. *kanthos*] either corner of the eye, where the eyelids meet

can·ti·cle (kan′ti k′l) *n.* [< L. dim. of *canticum,* song < *cantus*] **1.** a song or chant **2.** a liturgical hymn with words from the Bible

Can·ti·cles (-k′lz) *same as* SONG OF SOLOMON: also (in the Douay Bible) **Canticle of Canticles**

can·ti·le·na (kan′tə lē′nə) *n.* [It. < L., a song < *cantare,* to sing] a smooth, flowing, lyrical passage of vocal, or sometimes instrumental, music

can·ti·le·ver (kan′t′l ē′vər, -ev′ər) *n.* [as if < CANT² + LEVER] **1.** a large bracket or block projecting from a wall to support a balcony, cornice, etc. **2.** a projecting beam or structure supported only at one end, which is anchored as to a pier or wall —*vt.* to support by means of cantilevers —**can′ti·le′vered** *adj.*

CANTILEVER

cantilever bridge a bridge whose span is formed by two cantilevers projecting toward each other

can·til·la·tion (kan′t′l ā′shən) *n.* [< L. *cantillare,* to hum < *cantare:* see CHANT] in Jewish liturgy, a chanting with certain prescribed musical phrases indicated by notations —**can′til·late′** (-āt′) *vt., vi.* **-lat′ed, -lat′ing**

can·ti·na (kan tē′nə) *n.* [Sp.] [Southwest] a saloon or barroom

can·tle (kan′t′l) *n.* [< OFr. < ML. dim. of L. *cantus:* see CANT²] the upward-curving rear part of a saddle

can·to (kan′tō) *n., pl.* **-tos** [It. < L. *cantus:* see CHANT] any of the chapterlike divisions of certain long poems

Can·ton (kan tän′; *for 2* kan′tən) **1.** *former name of* KWANGCHOW **2.** [ult. after prec. sense] city in EC Ohio: pop. 95,000

can·ton (kan′tən, -tän, kan tän′; *for vt. 2* kan tän′, -tōn′) *n.* [Fr. < It. < LL. *cantus,* corner: see CANT²] any of the political divisions of a country or territory; specif., any of the states in the Swiss Republic —*vt.* **1.** to divide into cantons **2.** to assign quarters to (troops, etc.) —**can′ton·al** *adj.* —**can·ton′ment** *n.*

Can·ton·ese (kan′tə nēz′) *adj.* of Canton, China, or its people —*n.* **1.** *pl.* **-ese** a native or inhabitant of Canton **2.** the Chinese dialect spoken in and around Canton

can·tor (kan′tər) *n.* [L., singer < *canere:* see CHANT] **1.** a church choir leader **2.** a singer of liturgical solos in a synagogue, who leads the congregation in prayer —**can·to′ri·al** (-tôr′ē əl) *adj.*

Ca·nuck (kə nuk′) *n., adj.* [< ?] [Colloq.] (a) Canadian; sometimes specif., (a) French Canadian

Ca·nute (kə no͞ot′, -nyo͞ot′) 994?–1035; Dan. king of England (1017–35) & of Denmark (1018–35) & of Norway (1028–35): also called **Canute the Great**

can·vas (kan′vəs) *n.* [< OFr. < It. < L. *cannabis,* hemp] **1.** a closely woven, coarse cloth of hemp, cotton, or linen, used for tents, sails, etc. **2.** a sail or set of sails **3.** *a)* a specially prepared piece of canvas on which an oil painting is made *b)* such a painting **4.** a tent or tents, esp. circus tents **5.** any loosely woven, coarse cloth for embroidery, etc. —**the canvas** the canvas-covered floor of a boxing or wrestling ring —**under canvas** **1.** in tents **2.** with sails unfurled **3.** by means of sails

can·vas·back (-bak′) *n., pl.* **-backs′, -back′** : see PLURAL, II, D,1 a large, N. American wild duck with a brownish-red head and dark back

can·vass (kan′vəs) *vt.* [< *canvas:* ? because used for sifting] **1.** to examine or discuss in detail **2.** to go through (places) or among (people) asking for (votes, opinions, orders, etc.) —*vi.* to try to get votes, orders, etc. —*n.* the act of canvassing, esp. in an attempt to estimate the outcome of an election, sales campaign, etc. —**can′vass·er** ***n.***

can·yon (kan′yən) ***n.*** [Sp. *cañón*, a canyon, tube < L. *canna*, a reed: see CANE] a long, narrow valley between high cliffs, often containing a stream

caou·tchouc (kou cho͞ok′, ko͞o′cho͝ok) ***n.*** [Fr. < obs. Sp. *cauchuc* < Quechua] crude, natural rubber

cap (kap) ***n.*** [OE. *cæppe* < LL. *cappa*, a cloak] **1.** any close-fitting head covering, brimless or visored **2.** *a)* a head covering worn as a mark of occupation, rank, etc. *[a cardinal's cap] b)* a mortarboard (sense 2) **3.** a caplike part or thing; cover or top **4.** *same as* PERCUSSION CAP —***vt.*** **capped, cap′ping** **1.** to put a cap on **2.** to present ceremoniously with a cap, as at a graduation *[to cap a nurse]* **3.** to cover the top or end of *[snow capped the hills]* **4.** to match, surpass, or top **5.** to bring to a high point; climax —**cap the climax** to be or do more than could be expected or believed

CAP, C.A.P. Civil Air Patrol

cap. **1.** capacity **2.** *pl.* **caps.** capital **3.** capitalize

ca·pa·bil·i·ty (kā′pə bil′ə tē) ***n.,*** *pl.* **-ties** **1.** the quality of being capable; practical ability **2.** a capacity for being used or developed **3.** [*pl.*] abilities, features, etc. not yet developed

ca·pa·ble (kā′pə b′l) ***adj.*** [Fr. < LL. *capabilis* < L. *capere*, to take] having ability; able; skilled; competent —**capable of** **1.** admitting of; open to **2.** having the ability or qualities necessary for **3.** able or ready to *[capable of telling a lie]* —**ca′pa·ble·ness** ***n.*** —**ca′pa·bly** ***adv.***

ca·pa·cious (kə pā′shəs) ***adj.*** [< L. *capax* (gen. *capacis*) < *capere*, to take + -OUS] able to contain or hold much; spacious —**ca·pa′cious·ly** ***adv.*** —**ca·pa′cious·ness** ***n.***

ca·pac·i·tance (kə pas′ə təns) ***n.*** [CAPACIT(Y) + -ANCE] *Elec.* the quantity of electric charge that can be stored in a capacitor, expressed, in farads, as the ratio of the charge to the potential difference between the plates —**ca·pac′i·tive** ***adj.***

ca·pac·i·tor (-tər) ***n.*** *Elec.* a device consisting of two or more conducting plates separated by insulating material and used for storing an electric charge; condenser

ca·pac·i·ty (kə pas′ə tē) ***n.,*** *pl.* **-ties** [< OFr. < L. < *capax*: see CAPACIOUS] **1.** the ability to contain, absorb, or receive **2.** the amount of space that can be filled; content or volume **3.** mental ability **4.** aptitude; capability; potentiality **5.** maximum output or producing ability *[operating at capacity]* **6.** position, function, status, etc. *[acting in the capacity of adviser]* **7.** *Elec. same as* CAPACITANCE **8.** *Law* legal authority or competency

cap and bells a fool's cap with little bells on it

cap-a-pie, cap-ā-pie (kap′ə pē′) ***adv.*** [< OFr. < L. *caput*, head + *pes*, foot] from head to foot

ca·par·i·son (kə par′ə s′n) ***n.*** [< Fr. < Pr. *caparasso*, large cloak < ff.] **1.** an ornamented covering for a horse; trappings **2.** clothing, equipment, and ornaments; outfit —***vt.*** to adorn, as with trappings or rich clothing

cape[1] (kāp) ***n.*** [Fr. < Pr. *capa* < LL. *cappa*, mantle, cloak] a sleeveless garment fastened at the neck and hanging over the back and shoulders

cape[2] (kāp) ***n.*** [OFr. < ML. *caput*, headland < L., head] a piece of land projecting into a body of water —**the Cape** *same as* **1.** Cape of GOOD HOPE **2.** Cape COD

Ca·pek (chä′pek), **Ka·rel** (kär′əl) 1890–1938; Czech playwright & novelist

ca·per[1] (kā′pər) ***vi.*** [prob. < CAPRIOLE] to skip about in a playful manner —***n.*** **1.** a gay, playful jump or leap **2.** a wild, foolish prank **3.** [Slang] a criminal act, esp. a robbery —**cut a caper** (or **capers**) **1.** to caper **2.** to play tricks

ca·per[2] (kā′pər) ***n.*** [< L. < Gr. *kapparis*] **1.** a prickly, trailing Mediterranean bush whose green flower buds are pickled and used to flavor sauces, etc. **2.** any of these buds

Ca·pe·tian (kə pē′shən) ***adj.*** the French dynasty (987–1328 A.D.) founded by **Hugh Ca·pet** (kā′pit, kap′it) —***n.*** a member of this dynasty

Cape Town seat of the legislature of South Africa, a seaport on the SW coast: pop. 807,000: also, esp. formerly, **Cape′town′**

Cape Verde country on a group of islands in the Atlantic, west of Cape Verde, Senegal: 1,557 sq. mi.; pop. 294,000

cap·ful (kap′fool′) ***n.,*** *pl.* **-fuls′** as much as the cap of the bottle can hold

ca·pi·as (kā′pē əs, kap′ē-) ***n.*** [< ML. < L., 2d pers. sing., pres. subj., of *capere*, to take] *Law* a writ issued by a court directing an officer to arrest the person named

cap·il·lar·i·ty (kap′ə ler′ə tē) ***n.*** **1.** capillary state **2.** the property of exerting or having capillary attraction **3.** *same as* CAPILLARY ATTRACTION

cap·il·lar·y (kap′ə ler′ē) ***adj.*** [< L. < *capillus*, hair] **1.** of or like a hair; very slender **2.** having a very small bore **3.** in or of capillaries —***n.,*** *pl.* **-lar′ies** **1.** a tube with a very small bore: also **capillary tube** **2.** any of the tiny blood vessels connecting the arteries with the veins

capillary attraction a force that is the resultant of adhesion, cohesion, and surface tension in liquids which are in contact with solids, as in a capillary tube, causing the liquid surface to rise or be depressed in the tube: also **capillary action**

cap·i·tal[1] (kap′ə t′l) ***adj.*** [< OFr. < L. < *caput*, head] **1.** involving or punishable by death *[a capital offense]* **2.** most important or most serious; principal; chief *[a capital virtue]* **3.** being the seat of government *[a capital city]* **4.** of or having to do with capital, or wealth **5.** first-rate; excellent *[a capital idea]* See also CAPITAL LETTER —***n.*** **1.** *same as* CAPITAL LETTER **2.** a city or town that is the official seat of government of a state, nation, etc. **3.** a city where a certain industry, etc. is centered *[the rubber capital]* **4.** money or property owned or used in business by a person, corporation, etc. **5.** an accumulation of such wealth, or its value **6.** wealth used to produce more wealth **7.** any source of benefit **8.** [*often* **C-**] capitalists collectively: distinguished from LABOR —**make capital of** to make the most of; exploit

cap·i·tal[2] (kap′ə t′l) ***n.*** [< OFr. < L. dim. of *caput*, head] the top part of a column or pilaster

CAPITAL

cap·i·tal·ism (-iz′m) ***n.*** **1.** the economic system in which the means of production and distribution are privately owned and operated for profit, originally under fully competitive conditions **2.** the principles, power, etc. of capitalists

cap·i·tal·ist (-ist) ***n.*** **1.** a person who has capital; owner of wealth used in business **2.** an upholder of capitalism —***adj.*** capitalistic

cap·i·tal·is·tic (kap′ə t′l is′tik) ***adj.*** **1.** of or characteristic of capitalists or capitalism **2.** upholding, preferring, or practicing capitalism —**cap′i·tal·is′ti·cal·ly** ***adv.***

cap·i·tal·i·za·tion (-ə zā′shən) ***n.*** **1.** the act or process of converting something into capital **2.** the total capital funds of a corporation, represented by stocks, bonds, undivided profit, etc. **3.** the total value of the stocks and bonds outstanding of a corporation **4.** the act or system of using capital letters in writing and printing

cap·i·tal·ize (kap′ə t′l īz′) ***vt.*** **-ized′, -iz′ing** **1.** to use as capital; convert into capital **2.** to establish the capital stock of (a business firm) at a certain figure **3.** to supply capital to or for (an enterprise) **4.** to print or write (a word or words) in capital letters **5.** to begin (a word) with a capital letter —**capitalize on (something)** to use (something) to one's own advantage

capital letter a large letter of a kind used to begin a sentence or proper name, as A, B, C

cap·i·tal·ly (kap′ə t′l ē) ***adv.*** excellently; very well

capital punishment penalty of death for a crime

capital ship formerly, an armored war vessel carrying guns exceeding a caliber of a specified size

capital stock **1.** the capital of a corporation, divided into negotiable shares **2.** the total par or stated value of the issued shares of stock

cap·i·ta·tion (kap′ə tā′shən) ***n.*** [< LL. < L. *caput*, the head] a tax or fee of so much per head

Cap·i·tol (kap′ə t′l) [< OFr. < L. *Capitolium*, the temple of Jupiter] **1.** the temple of Jupiter in Rome **2.** the building in which the U.S. Congress meets, at Washington, D.C. —***n.*** [*usually* **c-**] the building in which a State legislature meets

Cap·i·to·line (kap′ə t′l īn′) one of the SEVEN HILLS OF ROME —***adj.*** **1.** of this hill **2.** of the temple of Jupiter which stood there

ca·pit·u·late (kə pich′ə lāt′) ***vi.*** **-lat′ed, -lat′ing** [< LL. pp. of *capitulare*, to draw up in chapters] **1.** to give up (*to* an enemy) on prearranged conditions **2.** to give up

ca·pit·u·la·tion (kə pich′ə lā′shən) ***n.*** **1.** a statement of the main parts of a subject **2.** a conditional surrender **3.** a document containing terms of surrender, etc.; treaty

ca·pon (kā′pän, -pən) ***n.*** [< OE. & OFr. < L. *capo*] a castrated rooster fattened for eating —**ca′pon·ize′** (-pə nīz′) ***vt.*** **-ized′, -iz′ing**

ca·pote (kə pōt′) ***n.*** [Fr., dim. of *cape*, CAPE[1]] a long cloak, usually with a hood

Ca·pri (ka prē′, kä′prē) island near the entrance to the Bay of Naples: 5 sq. mi.

ca·pric·ci·o (kə prē′chē ō; *It.* kä prēt′chô) ***n.,*** *pl.* **-ci·os;** It. **-pric′ci** (-chē) [It.: see ff.] **1.** a whim; caprice **2.** a lively musical composition of irregular form

ca·price (kə prēs′) ***n.*** [Fr. < It. *capriccio* < *capo*, head + *riccio*, curl, lit., hedgehog] **1.** a sudden, impulsive change in thought or action; freakish notion; whim **2.** a capricious quality or nature **3.** *Music same as* CAPRICCIO

ca·pri·cious (kə prish′əs) ***adj.*** subject to caprices; erratic; flighty —**ca·pri′cious·ly *adv.*** —**ca·pri′cious·ness *n.***

Cap·ri·corn (kap′rə kôrn′) [< OFr. < L. < *caper*, goat + *cornu*, a horn] **1.** a S constellation **2.** the tenth sign of the zodiac: see ZODIAC, illus.

cap·ri·fi·ca·tion (kap′rə fi kā′shən) ***n.*** [< L. < *caprificare*, to ripen figs by caprification] the pollination of certain cultivated figs by a species of small wasps

cap·ri·ole (kap′rē ōl′) ***n.*** [Fr. < It., ult. < L. *caper*, goat] **1.** a caper; leap **2.** an upward leap made by a horse without going forward —***vi.*** **-oled′, -ol′ing** to make a capriole

caps. capitals (capital letters)

cap·si·cum (kap′sə kəm) ***n.*** [ModL. < L. *capsa*, a box] **1.** any of various red peppers whose pungent, fleshy pods are the chili peppers, cayenne peppers, etc. of commerce **2.** these pods prepared as condiments, or, in medicine, as a gastric stimulant

cap·size (kap′sīz, kap sīz′) ***vt., vi.*** **-sized, -siz·ing** [? < Sp. *cabezar*, lit., to sink by the head] to overturn or upset: said esp. of a boat

cap·stan (kap′stən) ***n.*** [Fr. & Pr. *cabestan* < ? L. < *capere*, to take] an apparatus, mainly on ships, consisting of an upright cylinder around which cables or hawsers are wound, by machinery or by hand, for hoisting anchors, etc.

capstan bar any of the poles inserted in a capstan and used as levers in turning it by hand

cap·stone (-stōn′) ***n.*** the uppermost stone of a structure

CAPSTAN

cap·sule (kap′s'l, -syool) ***n.*** [Fr. < L. dim. of *capsa*, chest] **1.** a small, soluble gelatin container for enclosing a dose of medicine **2.** *a)* an ejectable airplane cockpit *b)* a detachable, closed compartment to hold and protect men, instruments, etc. in a rocket: in full, **space capsule** **3.** *Anat.* a sac or membrane enclosing a part **4.** *Bot.* a case, pod, or fruit containing seeds, spores, or carpels, esp. one that bursts when ripe —***adj.*** in a concise form [a *capsule* biography] —***vt.*** **-suled, -sul·ing** to condense —**cap′su·lar *adj.*** —**cap′su·late′, cap′su·lat′ed *adj.***

cap·sul·ize (-īz′) ***vt.*** **-ized′, -iz′ing** **1.** to enclose in a capsule **2.** to condense

Capt. Captain

cap·tain (kap′tən) ***n.*** [< OFr. < LL. < L. *caput*, the head] **1.** a chief or leader **2.** the head of a group or division; esp., *a)* *U.S. Mil.* an officer ranking above a first lieutenant *b)* *U.S. Navy* an officer ranking above a commander *c)* the commander or master of a ship *d)* the pilot of a commercial airplane *e)* the leader of a team, as in sports *f)* a precinct commander in a police or fire department —***vt.*** to be captain of —**cap′tain·cy** (-sē), *pl.* **-cies, cap′tain·ship′ *n.***

cap·tion (kap′shən) ***n.*** [< OFr. < L. < pp. of *capere*, to take] **1.** a heading, as of a newspaper article, or a legend, as under an illustration **2.** *same as* SUBTITLE (*n.* 2) —***vt.*** to supply a caption for

cap·tious (-shəs) ***adj.*** [< L. *captiosus* < prec.] **1.** made for the sake of argument or faultfinding; sophistical **2.** quick to find fault; quibbling —**cap′tious·ly *adv.*** —**cap′tious·ness *n.***

cap·ti·vate (kap′tə vāt′) ***vt.*** **-vat′ed, -vat′ing** [< LL., ult. < L. *captivus*, CAPTIVE] **1.** orig., to take captive **2.** to capture the attention or affection of; charm —**cap′ti·vat′ing·ly *adv.*** —**cap′ti·va′tion *n.*** —**cap′ti·va′tor *n.***

cap·tive (kap′tiv) ***n.*** [L. *captivus* < pp. of *capere*, to take] a person caught and held, as a prisoner in war, or captivated, as by love —***adj.*** **1.** *a)* taken or held prisoner *b)* unable to act independently *c)* forced to listen, willing or not [a *captive* audience] **2.** captivated **3.** of captivity

cap·tiv·i·ty (kap tiv′ə tē) ***n., pl.*** **-ties** the condition or time of being captive; imprisonment

cap·tor (kap′tər) ***n.*** [L.] a person who captures

cap·ture (kap′chər) ***n.*** [Fr. < L. *captura* < pp. of *capere*, to take] **1.** a taking or being taken by force, surprise, or skill **2.** that which is thus taken **3.** the absorption of a bombarding particle by an atomic nucleus, often causing radiation —***vt.*** **-tured, -tur·ing** **1.** to take or seize by force, surprise, or skill **2.** to represent (something immaterial, etc.) in more or less permanent form [to *capture* her charm on canvas] **3.** to effect the capture of (a subatomic particle)

Cap·u·chin (kap′yoo shin, -chin; kə pyōō′-) ***n.*** [< Fr. < *capuce* (It. *cappuccio*), a cowl] **1.** a monk of a branch of the Franciscan order that adheres strictly to the original rule **2.** [c-] a woman's cloak with a hood **3.** [c-] a new-world monkey with a hoodlike crown of hair

car (kär) ***n.*** [< ONormFr. < LL. < L. *carrus*, two-wheeled chariot < Gaul. *carros*] **1.** any vehicle on wheels **2.** [Poet.] a chariot **3.** a vehicle that moves on rails, as a streetcar **4.** an automobile **5.** an elevator cage **6.** the part of a balloon or airship for carrying people and equipment

ca·ra·bao (kär′ə bou′) ***n., pl.*** **-baos′, -bao′**: see PLURAL, II, D, 1 [Sp. < Malay *karbau*] *same as* WATER BUFFALO

car·a·bi·neer, car·a·bi·nier (kar′ə bə nir′) ***n.*** [Fr. *carabinier*] a cavalryman armed with a carbine

ca·ra·ca·ra (kär′ə kär′ə) ***n.*** [Sp. < Tupi] a large, vulturelike hawk of S. America

Ca·ra·cas (kə räk′əs, -rak′-; *Sp.* kä rä′käs) capital of Venezuela, in the NC part: pop. 1,000,000

car·a·cole (kar′ə kōl′) ***n.*** [Fr. < Wal. < Sp. *caracol*, shell of a snail < Catal. < Fr. *escargot*, snail] a half turn to the right or left made by a horse with a rider —***vi.*** **-coled′, -col′ing** to make a caracole or caracoles

car·a·cul (kar′ə kəl) ***n.*** *same as* KARAKUL

ca·rafe (kə raf′, -räf′) ***n.*** [Fr. < It. *caraffa*, prob. < Ar. *gharafa*, to draw water] a bottle of glass or metal for water, coffee, etc.

car·a·mel (kar′ə m'l, -mel′; kär′m'l) ***n.*** [Fr. < OFr., ult. < L. *canna mellis*, sugar cane] **1.** burnt sugar used to color or flavor food **2.** a chewy candy made from sugar, milk, etc.

car·a·mel·ize (-mə līz′) ***vt., vi.*** **-ized′, -iz′ing** to turn into caramel

car·a·pace (kar′ə pās′) ***n.*** [Fr. < Sp. *carapacho*] an upper case or shell, as of the turtle

car·at (kar′ət) ***n.*** [Fr. < It. < Ar. < Gr. *keration*, carat, dim. of *keras*, horn] **1.** a unit of weight for precious stones, equal to 200 milligrams **2.** *same as* KARAT

Ca·ra·vag·gio (kä′rä väd′jô), (**Michelangelo da**) (born *Michelangelo Merisi*) 1573–1610; It. painter

car·a·van (kar′ə van′) ***n.*** [< Fr. < OFr. < Per. *kārwān*, caravan] **1.** a company of merchants, pilgrims, etc. traveling together for safety, as through a desert **2.** a number of vehicles traveling together **3.** a large covered vehicle for passengers, circus animals, etc.; van

car·a·van·sa·ry (kar′ə van′sə rē) ***n., pl.*** **-ries** [< Fr. < Per. < *kārwān*, caravan + *sarāī*, palace] in the Orient, a kind of inn with a large central court, where caravans stop for the night

car·a·vel (kar′ə vel′) ***n.*** [< Fr. < Port. < LL. < Gr. *karabos*, kind of light ship] a fast, small sailing ship used in the 16th cent.

car·a·way (kar′ə wā′) ***n.*** [< Ar. *karawiyā'* < ? Gr. *karon*, caraway] **1.** an herb with spicy, strong-smelling seeds **2.** the seeds, used to flavor bread, cakes, cheese, etc.

car·bide (kär′bīd) ***n.*** [CARB(O)- + -IDE] a compound of an element, usually a metal, with carbon; esp., calcium carbide

car·bine (kär′bīn, -bēn) ***n.*** [< Fr., ult. < *scarabée*, a beetle] **1.** a rifle with a short barrel **2.** *U.S. Armed Forces* a semiautomatic or automatic .30-caliber rifle

car·bi·neer (kär′bə nir′) ***n.*** *same as* CARABINEER

car·bo- *a combining form meaning* carbon: also, before a vowel, **carb-**

car·bo·hy·drate (kär′bə hī′drāt) ***n.*** [CARBO- + HYDRATE] any of a group of organic compounds, including the sugars and starches, composed of carbon, hydrogen, and oxygen: carbohydrates form an important class of foods

car·bo·lat·ed (kär′bə lāt′id) ***adj.*** containing or treated with carbolic acid

car·bol·ic acid (kär bäl′ik) [CARB(O)- + -OL[1] + -IC] *same as* PHENOL (sense 1)

car·bo·lize (kär′bə līz′) ***vt.*** **-lized′, -liz′ing** [see prec.] to treat or sterilize with phenol

car·bon (kär′bən) ***n.*** [< Fr. < L. *carbo*, coal] **1.** a nonmetallic chemical element found in many inorganic compounds and all organic compounds: diamond and graphite are pure carbon; carbon is also present in coal, coke, etc.: symbol, C; at. wt., 12.01115; at. no., 6: a radioactive isotope (**carbon 14**) is used in biochemical research and in dating archaeological specimens, etc. **2.** a sheet of carbon paper **3.** a copy, as of a letter, made with carbon paper: in full, **carbon copy** **4.** *Elec.* *a)* a stick of carbon used in an arc lamp *b)* a carbon plate or rod used in a battery —***adj.*** of carbon

car·bo·na·ceous (kär′bə nā′shəs) ***adj.*** of, consisting of, or containing carbon

car·bon·ate (kär′bə nit; *also, and for v. always,* -nāt′) ***n.*** a salt or ester of carbonic acid —***vt.*** **-at′ed, -at′ing** **1.** to charge with carbon dioxide [*carbonated* drinks] **2.** to form into a carbonate —**car′bon·a′tion *n.***

fat, āpe, cär; ten, ēven; is, bīte; gō, hôrn, tōōl, look; oil, out; up, fur; get; joy; yet; chin; she; thin, *th*en; zh, leisure; ŋ, ring; ə for *a* in *ago*, *e* in *agent*, *i* in *sanity*, *o* in *comply*, *u* in *focus*; ' as in *able* (ā′b'l); Fr. bál; ë, Fr. coeur; ö, Fr. feu; Fr. mon; ô, Fr. coq; ü, Fr. duc; *r*, Fr. cri; H, G. ich; kh, G. doch; ‡foreign; *hypothetical; < derived from. See inside front cover.

carbon black finely divided carbon produced by the incomplete burning of oil or gas, used esp. in rubber and ink

car·bon-date (kär′bən dāt′) *vt.* **-dat′ed, -dat′ing** to establish the approximate age of (fossils, etc.) by measuring the carbon 14 content

carbon dioxide a colorless, odorless gas, CO_2: it passes out of the lungs in respiration, and is absorbed by plants in photosynthesis

car·bon·ic (kär bän′ik) *adj.* of, containing, or obtained from carbon or carbon dioxide

carbonic acid a weak, colorless acid, H_2CO_3, formed by the solution of carbon dioxide in water

car·bon·if·er·ous (kär′bə nif′ər əs) *adj.* [< CARBON + -FEROUS] **1.** producing or containing carbon or coal **2.** [C-] designating or of a great coal-making period of the Paleozoic Era: the warm, damp climate produced great forests, which later formed rich coal seams —**the Carboniferous 1.** the Carboniferous Period **2.** the rock and coal strata formed then See GEOLOGY, chart

car·bon·ize (kär′bə nīz′) *vt.* **-ized′, -iz′ing 1.** to change into carbon, as by partial burning **2.** to treat, cover, or combine with carbon —*vi.* to become carbonized —**car′bon·i·za′tion** *n.*

carbon monoxide a colorless, odorless, highly poisonous gas, CO, produced by the incomplete combustion of carbon

carbon paper very thin paper coated on one side with a carbon preparation: placed between sheets of paper, it is used to make copies of letters, etc.

carbon tet·ra·chlo·ride (tet′rə klôr′īd) a nonflammable, colorless liquid, CCl_4, used in fire extinguishers, cleaning mixtures, etc.

Car·bo·run·dum (kär′bə run′dəm) [CARB(ON) + (C)ORUNDUM] *a trademark for* a very hard, abrasive substance, esp. a carbide of silicon, used in grindstones, abrasives, etc.

car·boy (kär′boi) *n.* [< Per. *qarābah*] a large glass bottle enclosed in basketwork or in a wooden crate: used as a container for corrosive liquids

car·bun·cle (kär′buŋ k'l) *n.* [< OFr. < L. dim. of *carbo*, coal] **1.** a smooth, convex-cut garnet **2.** a painful, pus-bearing inflammation of the tissue beneath the skin, more severe than a boil and having several openings —**car·bun′cu·lar** (-kyoo lər) *adj.*

car·bu·ret (kär′bə rāt′, -ret′; -byoo-) *vt.* **-ret′ed** or **-ret′ted, -ret′ing** or **-ret′ting** [< obs. *carburet*, carbide] **1.** to combine chemically with carbon **2.** to mix or charge (gas or air) with volatile carbon compounds —**car′bu·re′tion** (-rā′shən) *n.*

car·bu·ret·or (kär′bə rāt′ər, -byoo-) *n.* a device in which air is mixed with gasoline spray to make an explosive mixture in an internal-combustion engine: Brit. sp. **car′bu·ret′tor** (-byoo ret′ər)

car·ca·jou (kär′kə jo͞o′, -zho͞o′) *n.* [CanadFr. < Algonquian] *same as* WOLVERINE

car·cass (kär′kəs) *n.* [< OFr. & Fr. < ?] **1.** the dead body of an animal, often specif. of a slaughtered animal dressed as meat **2.** the human body, living or dead: scornful or humorous usage **3.** the worthless remains of something **4.** a framework or shell Also, Brit. var., **car′case** (-kəs)

car·cin·o·gen (kär sin′ə jən) *n.* [< ff. + -GEN] any substance that produces cancer —**car·ci·no·gen·e·sis** (kär′sə nō jen′ə sis) *n.* —**car′ci·no·gen′ic** *adj.*

car·ci·no·ma (kär′sə nō′mə) *n., pl.* **-mas, -ma·ta** (-mə tə) [L. < Gr. *karkinōma*, cancer < *karkinos*, a crab] a cancerous growth made up of epithelial cells —**car′ci·nom′a·tous** (-näm′ə təs, -nō′mə-) *adj.*

car coat a short overcoat, mid-thigh in length

card[1] (kärd) *n.* [< OFr. < L. *charta* < Gr. *chartēs*, leaf of paper] **1.** a flat, stiff piece of thick paper or thin pasteboard, usually rectangular; specif., *a)* one of a pack of playing cards: see also CARDS *b)* a pasteboard with small articles attached for sale *[a card of thumbtacks] c) same as* CALLING CARD, COMPASS CARD, POST CARD, SCORE CARD *d)* a card bearing a message or greeting *[a birthday card] e)* a card to advertise or announce *f)* a card identifying a person as an agent, member, patron, etc. *g)* any of a series of cards on which information is recorded *[a file card]* **2.** a series of events making up a program, as in boxing **3.** an event or attraction *[a drawing card]* **4.** [Colloq.] a comical person —*vt.* **1.** to provide with a card **2.** to put or list on a card or cards —**card up one's sleeve** a plan or resource kept secret or in reserve —**in (or on) the cards** likely or seemingly destined to happen —**put (or lay) one's cards on the table** to reveal frankly, as one's intentions

card[2] (kärd) *n.* [< Fr. < Pr. < L. *carere*, to card; sp. infl. by L. *carduus*, thistle] **1.** a metal comb or wire brush for raising nap or combing fibers of wool, cotton, etc. **2.** a machine with rollers covered with wire teeth, used to brush, clean, and straighten such fibers —*vt.* to use a card on (fibers) in preparation for spinning —**card′er** *n.* —**card′ing** *n., adj.*

car·da·mom (kär′də məm) *n.* [< L. < Gr. < *kardamon*, cress + *amōmon*, spice plant] **1.** an Asiatic plant with aromatic seeds **2.** its seeds, used in medicine and as a spice Also **car′da·mon** (-mən)

card·board (kärd′bôrd′) *n.* stiff, thick paper, or pasteboard, used for cards, boxes, etc.

card file cards containing data or records, arranged systematically: also **card catalog**

car·di·ac (kär′dē ak′) *adj.* [< Fr. < L. < Gr. < *kardia*, the heart] **1.** of, near, or affecting the heart **2.** relating to the part of the stomach connected with the esophagus —*n.* a person with a heart disorder

Car·diff (kär′dif) seaport in SE Wales, on the Bristol Channel: pop. 287,000

car·di·gan (kär′də gən) *n.* [after 7th Earl of *Cardigan* (1797–1868), Eng. general] a sweater or jacket, usually knitted, that opens down the front: also **cardigan sweater** (or **jacket**)

CARDIGAN

car·di·nal (kärd′'n əl) *adj.* [< OFr. < L. *cardinalis*, chief < *cardo*, hinge] **1.** of main importance; principal; chief **2.** bright-red —*n.* **1.** one of the Roman Catholic officials appointed by the Pope to his council **2.** bright red **3.** a bright-red, crested American songbird: in full, **cardinal bird 4.** *same as* CARDINAL NUMBER —**car′di·nal·ly** *adv.* —**car′di·nal·ship′** *n.*

car·di·nal·ate (-āt′) *n.* the position, dignity, or rank of a cardinal

cardinal flower 1. the bright-red flower of a N. American plant that grows in damp, shady places or in shallow water **2.** this plant

cardinal number any number used in counting or showing how many (e.g., two, forty, 627, etc.): distinguished from ORDINAL NUMBER

cardinal points the four principal points of the compass; north, south, east, and west

cardinal virtues the basic virtues taught in ancient Greek philosophy: justice, prudence, fortitude, and temperance: see also THEOLOGICAL VIRTUES

card index *same as* CARD FILE

car·di·o- [< Gr. *kardia*, heart] *a combining form meaning* of the heart: also, before a vowel, **cardi-**

car·di·o·gram (kär′dē ə gram′) *n. same as* ELECTROCARDIOGRAM —**car′di·o·graph′** (-graf′) *n.* —**car′di·og′ra·phy** (-äg′rə fē) *n.*

car·di·ol·o·gy (kär′dē äl′ə jē) *n.* the branch of medicine dealing with the heart, its functions, and its diseases —**car′di·ol′o·gist** *n.*

car·di·o·vas·cu·lar (kär′dē ō vas′kyoo lər) *adj.* of the heart and the blood vessels as a system

cards (kärdz) *n.pl.* **1.** a game or games played with a deck of cards, as bridge, rummy, poker, etc. **2.** the playing of such games; card playing

card shark [Colloq.] **1.** an expert card player **2.** *same as* CARDSHARP

card·sharp (kärd′shärp′) *n.* [Colloq.] a professional cheater at cards: also **card′sharp′er**

care (ker) *n.* [< OE. *caru*, sorrow] **1.** *a)* worry or concern *b)* a cause of this **2.** close attention or careful heed **3.** a liking or regard *(for)* **4.** charge; protection; custody **5.** something to watch over or attend to —*vi.* **cared, car′ing 1.** to have objection, worry, regret, etc.; mind **2.** to feel concern or interest **3.** to feel love or a liking *(for)* **4.** to look after; provide *(for)* **5.** to wish *(for)*; want —**care of** at the address of —**have a care** to be careful: also **take care** —**take care of 1.** to be responsible for; attend to **2.** to provide for

ca·reen (kə rēn′) *vt.* [< Fr. < It. < L. *carina*, keel] **1.** to cause (a ship) to lean or lie on one side, as for repairs **2.** to cause to lean sideways; tip; tilt —*vi.* **1.** to lean sideways **2.** to lurch from side to side —*n.* a careening

ca·reer (kə rir′) *n.* [Fr. *carrière*, racecourse < It. < *carro*, CAR] **1.** a swift course **2.** one's progress through life or in a particular vocation **3.** a profession or occupation —*adj.* pursuing a normally temporary activity as a lifework *[a career soldier]* —*vi.* to move at full speed; rush wildly —**in full career** at full speed

ca·reer·ist (-ist) *n.* a person interested chiefly in his own professional ambitions, to the neglect of other things —**ca·reer′ism** *n.*

care·free (ker′frē′) *adj.* free from troubles or worry

care·ful (-fəl) *adj.* **1.** acting or working in a thoughtful, painstaking way **2.** cautious or wary **3.** accurately or thoroughly done *[a careful analysis]* —**care′ful·ly** *adv.* —**care′ful·ness** *n.*

care·less (-lis) *adj.* **1.** carefree; untroubled **2.** not paying enough attention; not thinking before one acts or speaks; inconsiderate **3.** done without enough attention, precision, etc. —**care′less·ly** *adv.* —**care′less·ness** *n.*

ca·ress (kə res′) *vt.* [< Fr. < It., ult. < L. *carus*, dear] to touch or stroke lovingly or gently; also, to embrace or kiss —*n.* an affectionate touch or gesture —**ca·ress′er** *n.* —**ca·ress′ing·ly** *adv.* —**ca·res′sive** *adj.* —**ca·res′sive·ly** *adv.*

car·et (kar′it, ker′-) ***n.*** [L., lit., there is lacking] a mark (^) used in writing or in correcting proof, to show where something is to be added

care·tak·er (ker′tāk′ər) ***n.*** a person hired to take care of something, as a house, estate, etc.

care·worn (-wôrn′) ***adj.*** showing the effects of troubles and worry; haggard

car·fare (kär′fer′) ***n.*** the price of a ride on a streetcar, bus, etc.

car·go (kär′gō) ***n.***, *pl.* **-goes, -gos** [< Sp. < *cargar*, to load < VL. *carricare:* see CHARGE] the load of commodities carried by a ship, airplane, truck, etc.; freight

car·hop (kär′häp′) ***n.*** [CAR + (BELL)HOP] one who serves customers in cars at a drive-in restaurant

Car·ib (kar′ib) ***n.*** [< Sp. *caribal*, altered < *canibal*: see CANNIBAL] **1.** a member of an Indian people of the S West Indies and the N coast of S. America **2.** the family of languages of the Caribs —**Car′ib·an** ***adj., n.***

Car·ib·be·an (kar′ə bē′ən, kə rib′ē ən) *same as* CARIBBEAN SEA —***adj.*** **1.** of the Caribs, their language, culture, etc. **2.** of the Caribbean Sea, its islands, etc. —***n.*** *same as* CARIB (sense 1)

Car·ib·be·an Sea (kar′ə bē′ən, kə rib′ē ən) part of the Atlantic, bounded by the West Indies, Central America, & South America

ca·ri·be (kə rē′bā) ***n.*** [AmSp., lit., Carib (see CANNIBAL)] *same as* PIRANHA

car·i·bou (kar′ə bo͞o′) ***n.***, *pl.* **-bous′, -bou′**: see PLURAL, II, D, 1 [CanadFr. < Algonquian name] a large, northern N. American deer

car·i·ca·ture (kar′ə kə chər, -choor′) ***n.*** [Fr. < It. < *caricare*, to load, exaggerate] **1.** a picture or imitation of a person, literary style, etc. that exaggerates certain features or mannerisms for satirical effect **2.** the art of making caricatures **3.** a poor imitation —***vt.*** **-tured, -tur·ing** to depict as in a caricature —**car′i·ca·tur·ist** ***n.***

CARIBOU (40–55 in. high at shoulder)

car·ies (ker′ēz) ***n.*** [L., decay] decay of bones, or, esp., of teeth

car·il·lon (kar′ə län′; *occas.* kə ril′yən) ***n.*** [Fr., chime of (orig. four) bells, ult. < L. *quattuor*, four] **1.** a set of stationary bells, each producing one tone of the chromatic scale **2.** a melody played on such bells **3.** an organ stop producing a carillonlike sound

car·il·lon·neur (kar′ə lə nur′) ***n.*** [Fr.] a carillon player

car·i·ole (kar′ē ōl′) ***n.*** [< Fr. < It. dim. of *carro*, CAR] **1.** a small carriage drawn by one horse **2.** a light, covered cart **3.** [Canad.] a dog sled

car·i·ous (kar′ē əs) ***adj.*** [L. *cariosus*] having caries; decayed —**car′i·os′i·ty** (-äs′ə tē) ***n.***

cark (kärk) ***vt., vi.*** [< ONormFr. var. of OFr. *chargier:* see CHARGE] [Archaic] to worry or be worried —***n.*** [Archaic] distress; anxiety

Carl (kärl) *var. of* CHARLES

carl, carle (kärl) ***n.*** [OE. < ON. *karl*] **1.** [Archaic or Obs.] a peasant, bondman, or villein **2.** [Scot.] a boor **3.** [Scot.] a sturdy fellow

car·load (kär′lōd′) ***n.*** a load that fills a car, esp. a freight car

car·load·ings (-iŋz) ***n.pl.*** the number of railroad carloads shipped within a given period

Car·lot·ta (kär lät′ə) *var. of* CHARLOTTE

Car·lyle (kär līl′, kär′līl), **Thomas** 1795–1881; Brit. writer, born in Scotland

car·ma·gnole (kär′mən yōl′) ***n.*** [Fr., altered < older *carmignole*, kind of cap] **1.** the costume worn by French Revolutionaries (1792) **2.** a song and dance popular during the French Revolution

car·man (kär′mən) ***n.***, *pl.* **-men** (-mən) a streetcar conductor or motorman

Car·mel·ite (kär′mə līt′) ***n.*** a friar or nun of the order of Our Lady of Mount Carmel, founded in Syria about 1160 —***adj.*** of this order

car·min·a·tive (kär min′ə tiv, kär′mə nāt′iv) ***adj.*** [ModL. < L. pp. of *carminare*, to card, cleanse] causing gas to be expelled from the stomach and intestines —***n.*** a carminative medicine

car·mine (kär′min, -mīn) ***n.*** [< Fr. < ML. *carminium* < Ar. *qirmiz*, crimson] **1.** a red or purplish-red pigment obtained mainly from cochnineal **2.** its color —***adj.*** red or purplish-red; crimson

car·nage (kär′nij) ***n.*** [< Fr. < It., ult. < L. *caro* (gen. *carnis*), flesh] bloody and extensive slaughter, esp. in battle; massacre; bloodshed

car·nal (-n'l) ***adj.*** [OFr. < LL. *carnalis* < L. *caro*: see prec.] **1.** in or of the flesh; material or worldly, not spiritual **2.** sensual; sexual —**car·nal·i·ty** (kär nal′ə tē) ***n.***, *pl.* **-ties** —**car′nal·ly** ***adv.***

car·na·tion (kär nā′shən) ***n.*** [Fr. < LL. *carnatio* < *caro:* see CARNAGE] **1.** formerly, rosy pink; now, deep red **2.** a plant of the pink family, with white, pink, or red flowers that smell like cloves

car·nau·ba (kär nô′bə, -nou′-) ***n.*** [Braz. Port. < Tupi native name] a Brazilian palm yielding a hard wax used in polishes, lipsticks, etc.

Car·ne·gie (kär′nə gē′, kär nā′gē), **Andrew** 1835–1919; U.S. industrialist & philanthropist, born in Scotland

car·nel·ian (kär nēl′yən) ***n.*** [altered (after L. *caro:* see CARNAGE) < CORNELIAN] a red variety of chalcedony, used in jewelry

car·ni·val (kär′nə vəl) ***n.*** [< Fr. or It. < ML. < hyp. *carnem levare*, to remove meat] **1.** the period of feasting and revelry just before Lent **2.** a reveling; festivity; merrymaking **3.** a traveling entertainment with rides, games, etc. **4.** a program of contests, etc. *[sports carnival]*

car·ni·vore (-vôr′) ***n.*** [Fr.: see ff.] **1.** any of an order of fanged, flesh-eating mammals, including the dog, wolf, cat, lion, bear, seal, etc.: opposed to HERBIVORE **2.** a plant that ingests insects

car·niv·o·rous (kär niv′ə rəs) ***adj.*** [< L. < *caro* (see CARNAGE) + *vorare*, to eat] **1.** *a)* flesh-eating: opposed to HERBIVOROUS *b)* insect-eating, as certain plants **2.** of the carnivores —**car·niv′o·rous·ly** ***adv.*** —**car·niv′o·rous·ness** ***n.***

car·ny, car·ney, car·nie (kär′nē) ***n.***, *pl.* **-nies** [Slang] **1.** *same as* CARNIVAL (sense 3) **2.** a worker in such a carnival

Car·ol (kar′əl) *var. of:* **1.** CAROLINE **2.** CHARLES

car·ol (kar′əl) ***n.*** [< OFr. < L. < Gr. < *choros*, dance + *aulein*, to play on the flute] a song of joy or praise; esp., a Christmas song —***vi.*** **-oled** or **-olled, -ol·ing** or **-ol·ling** **1.** to sing in joy; warble **2.** to sing carols, esp. Christmas carols, in unison —***vt.*** **1.** to sing (a tune, etc.) **2.** to praise in song —**car′ol·er, car′ol·ler** ***n.***

Car·o·li·na[1] (kar′ə lī′nə) [L. fem. adj. of *Carolus* (see CAROLINE), in honor of CHARLES I] English colony including what is now N.Carolina, S.Carolina, Ga., & N Fla. —**the Carolinas** N.Carolina & S.Carolina

Ca·ro·li·na[2] (kä′rô lē′nä) city in NE Puerto Rico, near San Juan: pop. 95,000

Car·o·line (kar′ə līn′, -lən) [G. & Fr. < It. *Carolina*, fem. < ML. *Carolus*, CHARLES] a feminine name

Caroline Islands group of islands in the W Pacific: see Trust Territory of the PACIFIC ISLANDS

Car·o·lin·i·an (kar′ə lin′ē ən) ***adj.*** of North Carolina or South Carolina —***n.*** a native or inhabitant of North Carolina or South Carolina

Car·o·lyn (kar′ə lin) *var. of* CAROLINE

car·om (kar′əm) ***n.*** [< Fr. < Sp. *carambola*] **1.** *Billiards* a shot in which the cue ball successively hits the two object balls **2.** a hitting and rebounding, as of a ball striking a surface —***vi.*** **1.** to make a carom **2.** to hit and rebound

car·o·tene (kar′ə tēn′) ***n.*** [< L. *carota*, CARROT + -ENE] any of three red or orange-colored isomeric hydrocarbons, $C_{40}H_{56}$, found in carrots and some other vegetables, and changed into vitamin A in the body: also **car′o·tin** (-tin)

ca·rot·e·noid, ca·rot·i·noid (kə rät′'n oid′) ***n.*** any of several red and yellow pigments related to and including carotene —***adj.*** **1.** of or like carotene **2.** of the carotenoids

ca·rot·id (kə rät′id) ***adj.*** [Gr. *karōtides*, the carotids < *karoun*, to plunge into sleep: compression of these arteries causes unconsciousness] designating, of, or near either of the two principal arteries, one on each side of the neck, which convey the blood to the head —***n.*** a carotid artery

ca·rous·al (kə rou′zəl) ***n.*** *same as* CAROUSE

ca·rouse (kə rouz′) ***vi.*** **-roused′, -rous′ing** [< Fr. < G. *gar aus(trinken)*, (to drink) quite out] to drink much alcoholic liquor, esp. along with others having a noisy, merry time —***n.*** a noisy, merry drinking party —**ca·rous′er** ***n.***

car·ou·sel (kar′ə sel′, -zel′) ***n.*** *same as* CARROUSEL

carp[1] (kärp) ***n.***, *pl.* **carp, carps:** see PLURAL, II, D, 2 [OFr. *carpe* < Gmc. *carpa*] **1.** any of a group of edible freshwater fishes living in ponds **2.** any of various similar fishes, as the goldfish

carp[2] (kärp) ***vi.*** [< ON. *karpa*, to brag] to find fault in a petty or nagging way —**carp′er** ***n.***

-carp (kärp) [< Gr. *karpos*, fruit] *a terminal combining form meaning* fruit *[endocarp]*

car·pal (kär′pəl) ***adj.*** [ModL. *carpalis*] of the carpus —***n.*** a bone of the carpus: also **car·pa′le** (-pā′lē), *pl.* **-li·a** (-ə)

Car·pa·thi·an Mountains (kär pā′thē ən) mountain

system in C Europe, extending from S Poland into NE Romania: also **Car·pa′thi·ans**

‡**car·pe di·em** (kär′pe dē′em, dī′-) [L., lit., seize the day] make the most of present opportunities

car·pel (kär′pəl) *n.* [ModL. dim. < Gr. *karpos,* fruit] **1.** a simple pistil, regarded as a single ovule-bearing leaf or modified leaflike structure **2.** any of the segments of a compound pistil —**car′pel·lar′y** (-pə ler′ē) *adj.* —**car′pel·late′** (-pə lāt′) *adj.*

car·pen·ter (kär′pən tər) *n.* [Anglo-Fr. < LL. *carpentarius* < L. *carpentum,* a cart < Gaul.] a workman who builds and repairs wooden articles, buildings, etc. —*vi.* to do a carpenter's work —*vt.* to make or repair as by carpentry

car·pen·try (-trē) *n.* the work or trade of a carpenter

car·pet (kär′pit) *n.* [< OFr. < ML. *carpita,* woolen cloth < L. pp. of *carpere,* to card] **1.** a heavy fabric for covering a floor, stairs, etc., usually in a strip, or several joined strips **2.** anything like a carpet [a *carpet* of snow] —*vt.* to cover as with a carpet —**on the carpet 1.** under consideration **2.** being, or about to be, reprimanded

car·pet·bag (-bag′) *n.* an old-fashioned type of traveling bag, made of carpeting —*vi.* **-bagged′, -bag′ging** to act as a carpetbagger

car·pet·bag·ger (-bag′ər) *n.* a Northern politician or adventurer who went South to take advantage of unsettled conditions after the Civil War: contemptuous term

carpet beetle (or **bug**) a small beetle whose larvae feed on furs and woolens, esp. carpets

car·pet·ing (-iŋ) *n.* carpets or carpet fabric

carpet sweeper a hand-operated device with a revolving brush for sweeping carpets and rugs

-car·pic (kär′pik) *same as* -CARPOUS

carp·ing (kär′piŋ) *adj.* tending to carp, or find fault; captious —**carp′ing·ly** *adv.*

car pool an arrangement by a group to rotate the use of their cars, as for going to work

car·port (kär′pôrt′) *n.* a shelter for an automobile, consisting of a roof extended from the side of a building, sometimes with an additional wall

-car·pous (kär′pəs) [< Gr. *karpos,* fruit] *a terminal combining form meaning* fruited, having fruit

car·pus (kär′pəs) *n., pl.* **-pi** (-pī) [ModL. < Gr. *karpos,* wrist] the wrist, or the wrist bones

car·rack (kar′ək) *n.* [< OFr. < Sp. < Ar. pl. of *qurqūr,* merchant ship] *same as* GALLEON

Car·ra·ra (kə rä′rə; *It.* kär rä′rä) city in NW Italy: a fine, white marble (**Carrara marble**) is quarried in nearby mountains: pop. 67,000

car·rel, car·rell (kar′əl) *n.* [< ML. *carula,* small study in a cloister] a small enclosure in the stack room of a library, for study or reading

car·riage (kar′ij; *for 2, usually* kar′ē ij) *n.* [< Anglo-Fr. < *carier,* CARRY] **1.** a carrying; transportation **2.** the cost of carrying **3.** manner of carrying the head and body; posture **4.** *a)* a four-wheeled passenger vehicle, usually horse-drawn *b) same as* BABY CARRIAGE **5.** a wheeled support [a gun *carriage*] **6.** a moving part (as on a typewriter) for supporting and shifting something

Car·rie (kar′ē) [< CAROLINE] a feminine name

car·ri·er (kar′ē ər) *n.* **1.** a person or thing, as a mailman or a train, that carries something **2.** one in the transportation business **3.** a messenger or porter **4.** something in or on which something else is carried or conducted **5.** *same as* AIRCRAFT CARRIER **6.** a person or animal that carries and transmits disease germs, esp. a person immune to the germs **7.** *Electronics* the steady transmitted wave whose amplitude, frequency, or phase is modulated by the signal

carrier pigeon a homing pigeon trained to carry a written message fastened to its leg

car·ri·ole (kar′ē ōl′) *n. same as* CARIOLE

car·ri·on (kar′ē ən) *n.* [< Anglo-Fr., ult. < L. *caro,* flesh] **1.** the decaying flesh of a dead body **2.** anything very repulsive —*adj.* **1.** of or like carrion **2.** feeding on carrion

carrion crow the common crow of Europe

Car·roll (kar′əl), **Lewis** (pseud. of *Charles Lutwidge Dodgson*) 1832–98; Eng. writer

car·rom (kar′əm) *n., vi. same as* CAROM

car·rot (kar′ət) *n.* [< Fr. < L. < Gr. *karōton*] **1.** a plant of the parsley family with a fleshy, orange-red root, eaten as a vegetable **2.** the root

car·rou·sel (kar′ə sel′, -zel′) *n.* [Fr. < It. dial. *carusiello,* prob. < *carro,* CAR] **1.** *same as* MERRY-GO-ROUND **2.** something that revolves like a merry-go-round, as a revolving tray from which slides are fed into a projector, or a circular conveyor in an airport from which passengers pick up their luggage

car·ry (kar′ē) *vt.* **-ried, -ry·ing** [< Anglo-Fr. *carier* < VL. *carricare:* see CHARGE] **1.** to hold or support while moving **2.** to take from one place to another; transport, as in a vehicle **3.** to hold, and direct the motion of [a pipe *carrying* water] **4.** to lead or impel **5.** to transmit [air *carries* sound] **6.** to transfer or extend [to *carry* a pipe to a sewer] **7.** to transfer (a figure, entry, etc.) from one column, time, etc. to the next **8.** to bear the weight of **9.** to be pregnant with **10.** to have as a quality, consequence, etc. [to *carry* a guarantee] **11.** to keep with one [to *carry* a watch] **12.** to hold or conduct (oneself) in a specified way **13.** to include as part of its contents or program: said of a newspaper, TV station, etc. **14.** to have or keep on a list or register **15.** to capture (a fortress, etc.) **16.** to win over or influence (a group) **17.** *a)* to win (an election, argument, etc.) *b)* to gain a majority of the votes in (a district, state, etc.) **18.** *Commerce a)* to keep in stock *b)* to keep on one's account books, etc. **19.** *Music* to sing the notes of (a melody or part) accurately —*vi.* **1.** to act as a bearer, conductor, etc. **2.** to have or cover a range [his voice *carries* well] **3.** to have an intended effect **4.** to win approval [the motion *carried*] —*n., pl.* **-ries 1.** the range or distance covered by a gun, golf ball, etc. **2.** a portage between two navigable bodies of water **3.** a carrying —**be** (or **get**) **carried away** to be moved to unreasoning enthusiasm —**carry off 1.** to kill [disease *carries off* many] **2.** to win (a prize, etc.) **3.** to handle (a situation), esp. with success —**carry on 1.** to engage in; conduct **2.** to continue as before **3.** [Colloq.] to behave in a wild or childish way **4.** [Colloq.] to engage in an illicit love affair —**carry out 1.** to put (plans, etc.) into practice **2.** to get done; accomplish —**carry over 1.** to have or be remaining **2.** to transfer, hold over for, or extend to another place or later time **3.** to postpone; continue —**carry through 1.** to get done; accomplish **2.** to keep (a person) going; sustain

car·ry·all[1] (-ôl′) *n.* [< Fr. *carriole* (see CARIOLE); sp. infl. by CARRY & ALL] a light, covered carriage with seats for several people

car·ry·all[2] (-ôl′) *n.* a large bag, basket, etc.

carrying charge 1. interest paid on the balance owed in installment buying **2.** the costs associated with property ownership, as taxes, upkeep, etc.

car·ry·ings-on (kar′ē iŋz än′) *n.pl.* [Colloq.] wild, extravagant, or immoral behavior

car·ry-on (kar′ē än′) *adj.* designating lightweight luggage to be carried onto an airplane by a passenger, esp. if small enough to fit under an airplane seat

car·ry·out (kar′ē out′) *adj.* designating a service, as of a restaurant, by which food and beverages may be taken out to be eaten elsewhere

car·ry-o·ver (-ō′vər) *n.* something carried over, as a remainder of crops or goods

car·sick (kär′sik′) *adj.* nauseated from riding in an automobile, bus, etc. —**car′sick′ness** *n.*

Car·son (kär′s'n) [after ff.] city in SW Calif.: suburb of Los Angeles: pop. 81,000

Car·son (kär′s'n), **Kit** (kit) (full name *Christopher Carson*) 1809–68; U.S. frontiersman

Carson City [after prec.] capital of Nev., near Lake Tahoe: pop. 32,000

cart (kärt) *n.* [< ON. *kartr*] **1.** a small, strong, two-wheeled vehicle drawn by a horse, etc. **2.** a small, wheeled vehicle, drawn or pushed by hand —*vt., vi.* to carry or deliver, as in a cart, truck, etc. —**put the cart before the horse** to do things backwards —**cart′er** *n.*

cart·age (kär′tij) *n.* **1.** the act or work of carting **2.** the charges made for carting

carte blanche (kärt′ blänsh′, blänch′) *pl.* **cartes blanches** (kärts′ blänsh′, kärt blän′shəz) [Fr., lit., white (i.e., blank) card] **1.** full authority **2.** freedom to do as one thinks best

car·tel (kär tel′) *n.* [Fr. < It. *cartello,* dim. of *carta,* CARD[1]] **1.** a written challenge, as to a duel **2.** a written agreement between nations at war, esp. as to exchange of prisoners **3.** [G. *kartell* < Fr.] an association of business firms establishing a national or international monopoly

Car·ter (kär′tər), **Jim·my** (jim′ē) (full name *James Earl Carter, Jr.*) 1924– ; 39th president of the U.S. (1977–81)

Car·te·sian (kär tē′zhən) *adj.* [< *Cartesius,* Latinized form of DESCARTES] of Descartes or his philosophical or mathematical ideas —*n.* a follower of Descartes

Cartesian coordinates a pair of numbers that locate a point by its distances from two lines intersecting usually at right angles

Car·thage (kär′thij) ancient city-state in N Africa, founded by the Phoenicians near the site of modern Tunis: destroyed by the Romans, 146 B.C. —**Car′tha·gin′i·an** (-thə jin′ē ən) *adj., n.*

Car·thu·sian (kär thōō′zhən, -thyōō′-) *n.* [< ML. < L. name for Chartreuse] a monk or nun of a very strict order founded at Chartreuse, France, in 1084 —*adj.* of the Carthusians

Car·tier (kȧr tyā′), **Jacques** (zhȧk) 1491–1557; Fr. explorer in North America

car·ti·lage (kärt′'l ij) *n.* [OFr. < L. *cartilago*] **1.** a tough, elastic, whitish tissue forming part of the skeleton; gristle **2.** a part or structure consisting of cartilage

car·ti·lag·i·nous (kärt′'l aj′ə nəs) *adj.* **1.** of or like cartilage **2.** having a skeleton made up mainly of cartilage

cart·load (kärt′lōd′) *n.* as much as a cart holds
car·tog·ra·phy (kär täg′rə fē) *n.* [< ML. *carta* (see CARD[1]) + -GRAPHY] the art or work of making maps or charts —**car·tog′ra·pher** *n.* —**car·to·graph·ic** (kär′tə graf′ik), **car′to·graph′i·cal** *adj.*
car·ton (kärt′′n) *n.* [Fr. < It. *cartone* < *carta:* see CARD[1]] **1.** a cardboard box or container **2.** its full contents
car·toon (kär tōōn′) *n.* [Fr. *carton* < It. *cartone:* see prec.] **1.** a drawing that caricatures, often satirically, some situation or person **2.** a full-size sketch of a design or picture to be copied in a fresco, tapestry, etc. **3.** *a)* a humorous drawing, often with a caption *b) same as* COMIC STRIP **4.** *same as* ANIMATED CARTOON —*vt.* to draw a cartoon of —*vi.* to draw cartoons —**car·toon′ist** *n.*
car·tridge (kär′trij) *n.* [altered < Fr. *cartouche* < It. < *carta:* see CARD[1]] **1.** a cylindrical case of cardboard, metal, etc. containing the charge and primer, and usually the projectile, for a firearm **2.** a small container holding a supply of material for insertion into a larger device **3.** a protected roll of camera film **4.** a replaceable stylus unit in a phonograph pickup
cartridge clip a metal container for cartridges, inserted in certain types of firearms
cart·wheel (kärt′hwēl′, -wēl′) *n.* **1.** a kind of handspring performed sidewise **2.** [Slang] a silver dollar
Ca·ru·so (kə rōō′sō; *It.* kä rōō′zô), **En·ri·co** (en rē′kō) 1873–1921; It. operatic tenor
carve (kärv) *vt.* **carved, carv′ing** [< OE. *ceorfan*] **1.** to make or shape by or as by cutting, chipping, etc. [*carve* a statue, *carve* a career] **2.** to decorate the surface of with cut designs **3.** to divide by cutting; slice —*vi.* **1.** to carve statues or designs **2.** to carve meat —**carv′er** *n.*
car·vel (kär′vəl) *n. same as* CARAVEL
carv·en (kär′v′n) *adj.* [Archaic or Poet.] carved
Car·ver (kär′vər), **George Washington** 1864–1943; U.S. botanist & chemist
carv·ing (kär′viŋ) *n.* **1.** the work or art of a person who carves **2.** a carved figure or design
carving knife a large knife for carving meat, used with a large, two-tined fork (**carving fork**)
car·wash (kär′wôsh′, -wäsh′) *n.* a facility for washing and polishing automobiles
car·y·at·id (kar′ē at′id) *n., pl.* **-ids, -i·des′** (-ə dēz′) [< L. < Gr. *karyatides,* priestesses at Karyai, in Macedonia] a supporting column that has the form of a draped female figure
car·y·o- *same as* KARYO-
ca·sa·ba (kə sä′bə) *n.* [< *Kassaba,* town near Smyrna, Asia Minor] a cultivated melon with a hard, yellow rind and sweet, usually white flesh
Ca·sa·blan·ca (kas′ə blaŋ′kə, kä′sə bläŋ′kə) seaport in NW Morocco: pop. 1,177,000
Ca·sals (kə sälz′, -salz′; *Sp.* kä säls′), **Pa·blo** (päb′lō) 1876–1973; Sp. cellist & composer
Ca·sa·no·va (kas′ə nō′və; *It.* kä′zä nô′vä), **Gio·van·ni (Jacopo)** (jô vän′nē) 1725–98; It. adventurer, noted for his *Memoirs*

CARYATID

cas·bah (käz′bä, kas′-) *n.* [Fr. < Ar. dial. *qaṣba* < Ar. *qaṣaba,* fortress] **1.** in N Africa, a fortress **2.** the old, crowded quarter of a N African city, esp. [C-] of Algiers
cas·cade (kas kād′) *n.* [Fr. < It. *cascata* < L. *cadere,* to fall] **1.** a small, steep waterfall, esp. one of a series **2.** a shower of sparks, or rippling fall of lace, etc. —*vt., vi.* **-cad′ed, -cad′ing** to fall or drop in a cascade
Cascade Range [after cascades on the Columbia River] mountain range extending from N Calif., through Oreg. and Wash., into British Columbia
cas·car·a (kas ker′ə) *n.* [Sp. *cáscara,* bark] **1.** a small buckthorn of the U.S. Pacific coast **2.** a laxative made from its bark: in full, **cascara sa·gra·da** (sə grä′də, -grā′-)
case[1] (kās) *n.* [< OFr. *cas,* an event < L. *casus,* an accident, pp. of *cadere,* to fall] **1.** an example or instance [a *case* of measles] **2.** a person being treated or helped, as by a doctor or social worker **3.** any matter undergoing observation, study, etc. **4.** a statement of the facts, as in a law court **5.** convincing arguments [he has no *case*] **6.** a lawsuit **7.** [Colloq.] a peculiar person **8.** [Colloq.] an infatuation **9.** *Gram. a)* an inflected form taken by a noun, pronoun, or adjective to show syntactic relationship *b)* such relationship —*vt.* **cased, cas′ing** [Slang] to look over carefully, esp. for an intended robbery —**in any case** anyhow —**in case** in the event that —**in case of** in the event of —**in no case** by no means; never
case[2] (kās) *n.* [< ONormFr. *casse* < L. *capsa,* a box < *capere,* to hold] **1.** a container, as a box, sheath, etc. **2.** a protective cover [a *watchcase*] **3.** a full box or its contents **4.** a set or pair [a *case* of pistols] **5.** a frame, as for a window **6.** *Printing* a shallow tray in which type is kept: the **upper case** is for capitals, the **lower case** for small letters —*vt.* **cased, cas′ing 1.** to put in a container **2.** to cover or enclose
ca·se·fy (kā′sə fī′) *vt., vi.* **-fied′, -fy′ing** [< L. *caseus,* CHEESE[1] + -FY] to make or become cheeselike
case·hard·en (kās′här′d′n) *vt.* **1.** *Metallurgy* to form a hard, thin surface on (an iron alloy) **2.** to make callous or unfeeling —**case′hard′ened** *adj.*
case history (or **study**) collected information about an individual or group, for use in sociological, medical, or psychiatric studies
ca·se·in (kā′sē in, kā′sēn) *n.* [< L. *caseus,* CHEESE[1] + -IN[1]] a protein that is one of the chief constituents of milk and the basis of cheese
case knife 1. *same as* SHEATH KNIFE **2.** a table knife
case law law based on previous judicial decisions, or precedents: distinguished from STATUTE LAW
case·load (kās′lōd′) *n.* the number of cases being handled by a court, a social or welfare agency, a caseworker, etc.
case·mate (kās′māt′) *n.* [Fr. < It. < Gr. *chasmata,* pl. of *chasma,* CHASM] a shellproof or armored enclosure with openings for guns, as in a fortress or on a warship —**case′mat′ed** *adj.*
case·ment (kās′mənt) *n.* [< OFr. *encassement,* a frame: see CASE[2]] **1.** a hinged window frame that opens outward: a **casement window** often has two such frames, opening like French doors **2.** a casing; covering —**case′ment·ed** *adj.*
ca·se·ous (kā′sē əs) *adj.* [< L. *caseus,* cheese] of or like cheese
ca·sern, ca·serne (kə zʉrn′) *n.* [< Fr. < Pr. *cazerna,* small hut < LL. *quaterna,* four each < *quattuor,* four] a military barracks in a fortified town
case·work (kās′wʉrk′) *n.* social work in which the worker investigates a case of personal or family maladjustment and gives guidance —**case′work′er** *n.*
cash[1] (kash) *n.* [< Fr. *caisse,* money box < Pr. < L. *capsa:* see CASE[2]] **1.** money that a person actually has; esp., ready money **2.** bills and coins **3.** money, a check, etc. paid at the time of purchase —*vt.* to give or get cash for —*adj.* of, for, or requiring cash [a *cash* sale] —**cash in 1.** to turn into cash **2.** [Slang] to die —**cash in on** to get profit or profitable use from
cash[2] (kash) *n., pl.* **cash** [Port. *caixa* < Tamil *kasu* < Sans. *karṣa*] any of several Chinese or Indian coins of small value
cash-and-car·ry (kash′ən kar′ē) *adj.* with cash payments and no deliveries
cash·book (-bo͝ok′) *n.* a book in which all receipts and payments of money are entered
cash discount a discount allowed a purchaser paying within a specified period
cash·ew (kash′ōō, kə shōō′) *n.* [< Fr. < Port. < Tupi *acajú*] **1.** a tropical tree bearing edible, kidney-shaped nuts **2.** the nut: also **cashew nut**
cash flow the pattern of expenses and income of a company, government, etc. that determines how much cash, if any, is available at any given time
cash·ier[1] (ka shir′) *n.* [< Fr. *caissier*] a person in charge of cash transactions for a bank, store, etc.
cash·ier[2] (ka shir′) *vt.* [< MDu. < OFr. < LL. *cassare* (see QUASH[1]) & L. *quassare* (see QUASH[2])] **1.** to dismiss, esp. in dishonor, from a position of command, trust, etc. **2.** to discard or reject
cashier's check a check drawn by a bank on its own funds and signed by the cashier
cash·mere (kazh′mir, kash′-) *n.* [< *Cashmere,* former sp. of KASHMIR] **1.** a fine carded wool from goats of Kashmir and Tibet **2.** a soft, twilled cloth of this or similar wool **3.** a cashmere shawl, sweater, coat, etc.
cash register a business machine, usually with a money drawer, that registers visibly the amount of each sale
cas·ing (kās′iŋ) *n.* **1.** a protective covering; specif., *a)* a membrane used to encase processed meats *b)* a pneumatic rubber tire exclusive of an inner tube and often of the tread *c)* the steel pipe used to line an oil or gas well **2.** a frame, as of a window or door
ca·si·no (kə sē′nō) *n., pl.* **-nos** [It., dim. of *casa,* house < L., hut] **1.** a room or building for dancing, or, esp., gambling **2.** *same as* CASSINO
cask (kask, käsk) *n.* [< Fr. *casque* < Sp. *casco,* ult. < L. *quassare:* see QUASH[2]] **1.** a barrel of any size, made of staves, esp. one for liquids **2.** the contents of a full cask; barrelful
cas·ket (kas′kit) *n.* [prob. < OFr. dim. of *casse* (see CASE[2])] **1.** a small box or chest, as for valuables **2.** a coffin —*vt.* to put into a casket
Cas·pi·an Sea (kas′pē ən) inland sea between Caucasia and Asiatic U.S.S.R. —**Cas′pi·an** *adj.*

casque (kask) ***n.*** [Fr.: see CASK] a helmet —**casqued** (kaskt) ***adj.***
cas·sa·ba (kə sä′bə) ***n.*** *same as* CASABA
Cas·san·dra (kə san′drə) *Gr. Myth.* Priam's daughter: Apollo gave her prophetic power but decreed no one should believe her prophecies —***n.*** a person whose warnings of misfortune are disregarded
cas·sa·va (kə sä′və) ***n.*** [< Fr. < Sp. < native Indian *casávi*] **1.** any of several tropical American plants with edible starchy roots **2.** a starch taken from the root, used to make bread and tapioca
cas·se·role (kas′ə rōl′) ***n.*** [Fr., dim. of *casse,* a bowl < Pr. < VL. < Gr. dim. of *kyathos,* a bowl] **1.** an earthenware or glass baking dish, often with a cover, in which food can be cooked and served **2.** the food baked in such a dish
cas·sette (ka set′, kə-) ***n.*** [Fr., dim. < ONormFr. *casse,* a CASE[2]] **1.** a case with roll film in it, for loading a camera quickly and easily **2.** a similar case with magnetic tape, for use in a tape recorder
cas·sia (kash′ə) ***n.*** [< L. < Gr. *kasia,* kind of cinnamon < Heb. *qeṣī'āh*] **1.** *a)* the bark (**cassia bark**) of a tree native to SE Asia: used as a source of cinnamon *b)* this tree **2.** *a)* any of a genus of herbs, shrubs, etc. of the legume family, common in tropical countries: the pods (**cassia pods**) of some of these plants have a mildly laxative pulp (**cassia pulp**); from others the drug senna is extracted *b)* cassia pods *c)* cassia pulp
cas·si·mere (kas′ə mir′) ***n.*** [var. of CASHMERE] a woolen cloth, twilled or plain, used for men's suits
cas·si·no (kə sē′nō) ***n.*** [see CASINO] a simple card game for two to four players
Cas·si·o·pe·ia (kas′ē ə pē′ə) **1.** *Gr. Myth.* the mother of Andromeda **2.** a N constellation near Andromeda
Cassiopeia's Chair five stars in the constellation Cassiopeia, supposedly outlining a chair
Cas·si·us (Longinus) (kash′əs, kas′ē əs), **(Gaius)** ?–42 B.C.; Rom. general & conspirator against Caesar
cas·sock (kas′ək) ***n.*** [< Fr. < Per. *kazhāghand,* a jacket < *kazh,* raw silk] a long, closefitting vestment, usually black, worn as an outer garment or under the surplice by clergymen, choristers, etc.
cas·so·war·y (kas′ə wer′ē) ***n.,*** *pl.* **-war′ies** [Malay *kasuārī*] any of a genus of large, flightless birds of Australia and New Guinea, somewhat like the ostrich, but smaller
cast (kast) ***vt.*** **cast, cast′ing** [< ON. *kasta,* to throw] **1.** to throw with force; fling; hurl **2.** to deposit (a ballot or vote) **3.** *a)* to cause to fall or turn; direct [to *cast* one's eyes on a thing] *b)* to give forth [to *cast* light, gloom, etc.] **4.** to throw out or drop (a net, anchor, etc.) at the end of a rope or cable **5.** to throw out (a fly, etc.) at the end of a fishing line **6.** to draw (lots) or shake (dice) out of a container **7.** to throw off; shed [the snake *casts* its skin] **8.** to add up (accounts) **9.** to calculate (a horoscope, tides, etc.) **10.** to formulate **11.** *a)* to form (molten metal, plastic, etc.) by pouring or pressing into a mold *b)* to make by such a method **12.** *a)* to choose actors for (a play or movie) *b)* to select (an actor) for (a role) —***vi.*** **1.** to throw dice **2.** to throw out a fly, etc. on a fishing line —***n.*** **1.** a casting; a throw; specif., *a)* a throw of dice; also, the number thrown *b)* a turn of the eye; glance; look *c)* a throw of a fishing line, net, etc. **2.** a quantity or thing cast in a certain way; specif., *a)* something formed in a mold, as a statue; also, the mold *b)* a mold taken of an object *c)* a plaster form to immobilize a broken arm, leg, etc. *d)* the set of actors in a play or movie **3.** the form in which a thing is cast; specif., *a)* an appearance, as of features *b)* kind; quality *c)* a tinge; shade [a reddish *cast*] *d)* a turn or twist to one side *e)* a slight turning in or out of the eye —**cast about** **1.** to search (*for*) **2.** to devise —**cast aside** (or **away**) to discard —**cast back** to refer to something past —**cast down** **1.** to turn downward **2.** to sadden; discourage —**cast off** **1.** to discard; disown **2.** to set free **3.** to free a ship from a dock, quay, etc., as by releasing the lines **4.** *Knitting* to make the last row of stitches —**cast on** *Knitting* to make the first row of stitches —**cast out** to expel —**cast up** **1.** to throw up **2.** to turn upward **3.** to total **4.** to construct by digging [to *cast up* earthworks]
cas·ta·nets (kas′tə nets′) ***n.pl.*** [< Fr. < Sp. *castañeta,* dim. < L. *castanea,* chestnut: from the shape] a pair of small, hollowed pieces of hard wood, ivory, etc. held in the hand and clicked together in time to music, esp. in Spanish dances
cast·a·way (kas′tə wā′) ***n.*** **1.** a person or thing cast out or off, esp. an outcast **2.** a shipwrecked person —***adj.*** **1.** thrown away; discarded **2.** cast adrift or stranded, as by shipwreck

CASTANETS

caste (kast) ***n.*** [Fr. < Port. *casta,* a breed < L. *castus,* pure] **1.** any of the distinct, hereditary Hindu social classes, each by tradition, but no longer officially, excluded from social dealings with the others **2.** any exclusive social or occupational class or group **3.** rigid class distinction based on birth, wealth, etc., operating as a social system or principle **4.** any of the differentiated types of social insects in a colony —**lose caste** to lose social status or rank
cas·tel·lat·ed (kas′tə lāt′id) ***adj.*** [< ML. < L. *castellum,* CASTLE] built with turrets and battlements, like a castle —**cas′tel·la′tion** ***n.***
cast·er (kas′tər) ***n.*** **1.** a person or thing that casts **2.** *a)* a small bottle or container for serving vinegar, salt, etc. at the table *b)* a stand for holding such containers **3.** a wheel or freely rolling ball set in a frame and attached to each leg, bottom corner, etc. of a piece of furniture, etc. so that it can be moved easily
cas·ti·gate (kas′tə gāt′) ***vt.*** **-gat′ed, -gat′ing** [< L. pp. of *castigare,* to purify, chastise < *castus,* pure] to punish or rebuke severely, esp. by public criticism —**cas′ti·ga′tion** ***n.*** —**cas′ti·ga′tor** ***n.*** —**cas′ti·ga·to′ry** (-gə tôr′ē) ***adj.***
Cas·tile (kas tēl′) region and former kingdom in N and C Spain
Castile soap [< *Castile,* where first made] [*also* **c- s-**] a fine, mild, hard soap made from olive oil and sodium hydroxide
Cas·til·ian (kas til′yən) ***adj.*** of Castile, its people, language, or culture —***n.*** **1.** a native or inhabitant of Castile **2.** the dialect spoken in Castile, now the standard form of Spanish
cast·ing (kas′tiŋ) ***n.*** **1.** the action of one that casts **2.** anything, esp. of metal, that has been cast in a mold **3.** *Zool.* anything thrown off, excreted, etc.
casting vote (or **voice**) the deciding vote cast by the presiding officer in the event of a tie
cast-i·ron (kast′ī′ərn) ***adj.*** **1.** made of cast iron **2.** very hard, rigid, strong, healthy, etc.
cast iron a hard, unmalleable alloy of iron made by casting: it has a high proportion of carbon
cas·tle (kas′'l) ***n.*** [< OE. & Anglo-Fr. < L. *castellum,* dim. of *castrum,* fort] **1.** a large building or group of buildings fortified with thick walls, turrets, and often a moat: castles were strongholds for noblemen in the Middle Ages **2.** any massive dwelling like this **3.** a safe, secure place **4.** *Chess* *same as* ROOK[2] —***vt.*** **-tled, -tling** **1.** to furnish with a castle **2.** *Chess* to move (a king) two squares to either side and then, in the same move, set the castle in the square skipped by the king —***vi.*** *Chess* **1.** to castle a king **2.** to be castled: said of a king
castle in the air an imaginary scheme unlikely to be realized; daydream: also **castle in Spain**
cast·off (kast′ôf′) ***adj.*** thrown away; discarded —***n.*** a person or thing cast off
Cas·tor (kas′tər) **1.** *Gr. & Rom. Myth.* the mortal twin of Pollux **2.** one of the two bright stars in the constellation Gemini
cas·tor[1] (kas′tər) ***n.*** [Fr. < L. < Gr. *kastōr,* beaver] **1.** a strong-smelling, oily substance obtained from the beaver, used in perfumery: also **cas·to′re·um** (-tôr′ē əm) **2.** a hat of beaver or rabbit fur
cas·tor[2] (kas′tər) ***n.*** *same as* CASTER (senses 2 & 3)
cas·tor-oil plant (kas′tər oil′) a tropical plant with large, beanlike seeds (**castor beans**) from which oil (**castor oil**) is extracted: this oil is used as a cathartic and lubricant
cas·trate (kas′trāt) ***vt.*** **-trat·ed, -trat·ing** [< L. *castratus,* pp. of *castrare*] **1.** to remove the testicles of; emasculate; geld **2.** to deprive of real vigor or meaning by mutilation, expurgation, etc.; emasculate —**cas·tra′tion** ***n.***
cast steel steel formed by casting, not by rolling or forging —**cast′-steel′** ***adj.***
cas·u·al (kazh′o͞o wəl) ***adj.*** [< OFr. < LL. *casualis,* by chance < L. *casus,* chance] **1.** happening or governed by chance; not planned [a *casual* visit] **2.** happening, active, etc. at irregular intervals; occasional [a *casual* worker] **3.** slight or superficial [a *casual* acquaintance] **4.** careless or nonchalant **5.** *a)* informal or relaxed [a *casual* atmosphere] *b)* designed for informal occasions or use [*casual* clothes] —***n.*** **1.** one who does something only occasionally or temporarily, esp. a casual worker **2.** [*pl.*] shoes, clothes, etc. for informal occasions **3.** *Mil.* a person temporarily attached to a unit —**cas′u·al·ly** ***adv.*** —**cas′u·al·ness** ***n.***
cas·u·al·ty (kazh′əl tē, -o͞o wəl-) ***n.,*** *pl.* **-ties** [see prec.] **1.** an accident, esp. a fatal one **2.** a member of the armed forces killed, wounded, captured, etc. **3.** anyone hurt or killed in an accident **4.** anything lost, destroyed, or made useless by some unfortunate or unforeseen happening
cas·u·ist (kazh′o͞o wist) ***n.*** [< Fr. < L. *casus,* CASE[1]] a person expert in, or apt to resort to, casuistry —**cas′u·is′tic, cas′u·is′ti·cal** ***adj.*** —**cas′u·is′ti·cal·ly** ***adv.***
cas·u·ist·ry (kazh′o͞o wis trē) ***n.,*** *pl.* **-ries** [prec. + -RY] **1.** the solving of specific cases of right and wrong in conduct by applying general principles of ethics **2.** subtle but misleading or false reasoning, esp. about moral issues; sophistry

‡**ca·sus bel·li** (kā′səs bel′ī) [L.] an event provoking war or used as a pretext to make war

cat (kat) ***n.,*** *pl.* **cats, cat:** see PLURAL, II, D, 1 [OE.] **1.** any of a family of flesh-eating, predacious mammals, including the lion, tiger, leopard, etc.; specif., a small, lithe, soft-furred animal of this family, often kept as a pet or for killing mice **2.** a person regarded as a cat in some way, esp. a woman who makes spiteful remarks **3.** *same as* CAT-O'-NINE-TAILS **4.** a catfish **5.** [C-] *same as* CATERPILLAR (tractor) **6.** [Slang] *a)* a jazz musician or enthusiast *b)* any person, esp. a man **7.** *Naut.* tackle to hoist an anchor to the cathead —***vt.*** **cat′ted, cat′ting** to hoist (an anchor) to the cathead —**let the cat out of the bag** to let a secret be found out

cat. 1. catalog **2.** catechism

cat·a- (kat′ə) [< Gr. *kata,* down] *a prefix meaning:* **1.** down, downward *[catabolism]* **2.** away, completely *[catalysis]* **3.** against *[catapult]* Also, before a vowel, **cat-**

ca·tab·o·lism (kə tab′ə liz′m) ***n.*** [< CATA- + Gr. *ballein,* to throw + -ISM] the process in a plant or animal by which living tissue is changed into waste products of a simpler composition; destructive metabolism: opposed to ANABOLISM —**cat·a·bol·ic** (kat′ə bäl′ik) ***adj.***

ca·tab·o·lize (-līz′) ***vi., vt.*** **-lized′, -liz′ing** to change by catabolism

cat·a·chre·sis (kat′ə krē′sis) ***n.,*** *pl.* **-ses** (-sēz) [L. < Gr. < *kata-,* against + *chrēsthai,* to use] incorrect use of a word or words —**cat′a·chres′tic** (-kres′tik), **cat′a·chres′ti·cal** ***adj.*** —**cat′a·chres′ti·cal·ly** ***adv.***

cat·a·clysm (kat′ə kliz′m) ***n.*** [< L. < Gr. < *kata-,* down + *klyzein,* to wash] **1.** a great flood; deluge **2.** any great upheaval or sudden, violent change, as an earthquake, war, etc. —**cat′a·clys′mic** (-kliz′mik), **cat′a·clys′mal** ***adj.***

cat·a·comb (kat′ə kōm′) ***n.*** [< LL. *catacumba* < L. < *cata* (< Gr. *kata*), by + *tumba,* TOMB] any of a series of galleries in an underground burial place: *usually used in pl.*

cat·a·falque (kat′ə falk′, -fôlk′) ***n.*** [Fr. < It. < L. *cata(*< Gr. *kata*), by + *fala,* a scaffold] a wooden framework, usually draped, on which the body in a coffin awaiting burial lies in state

Cat·a·lan (kat′'l an′, -'l ən) ***adj.*** of Catalonia, its people, or their language —***n.*** **1.** a native or inhabitant of Catalonia **2.** the Romance language of Catalonia, closely akin to Provençal

cat·a·lep·sy (kat′'l ep′sē) ***n.*** [< LL. < Gr. *katalēpsis,* a seizing < *kata-,* down + *lambanein,* to seize] a condition in which consciousness and feeling are suddenly and temporarily lost, and the muscles become rigid: it may occur in epilepsy, schizophrenia, etc. —**cat′a·lep′tic** ***adj., n.***

cat·a·lo (kat′'l ō′) ***n.,*** *pl.* **-loes′, -los′** [CAT(TLE) + (BUFF)ALO] an animal bred by crossing the American buffalo, or bison, with domestic cattle

cat·a·log, cat·a·logue (kat′'l ôg′, -äg′) ***n.*** [Fr. < LL. *catalogus,* list < Gr. < *kata,* down + *legein,* to count] a complete list; esp., *a)* an alphabetical card file, as of the books in a library *b)* a list of things exhibited, articles for sale, school courses offered, etc., usually with comments and illustrations *c)* a book or pamphlet with such a list —***vt., vi.*** **-loged′** or **-logued′, -log′ing** or **-logu′ing 1.** to enter in a catalog **2.** to make a catalog of —**cat′a·log′er** or **cat′a·logu′er, cat′a·log′ist** or **cat′a·logu′ist** ***n.***

Cat·a·lo·ni·a (kat′'l ō′nē ə) region in NE Spain, on the Mediterranean —**Cat′a·lo′ni·an** ***adj., n.***

ca·tal·pa (kə tal′pə) ***n.*** [< AmInd. (Creek) *kutuhlpa*] a tree of America and Asia with large, heart-shaped leaves, showy trumpet-shaped flowers, and slender, beanlike pods

ca·tal·y·sis (kə tal′ə sis) ***n.,*** *pl.* **-ses′** (-sēz′) [Gr. *katalysis,* dissolution < *kata-,* down + *lyein,* to loose] the speeding up or, sometimes, slowing down of the rate of a chemical reaction by the addition of some substance which itself undergoes no permanent chemical change thereby

cat·a·lyst (kat′'l ist) ***n.*** **1.** any substance serving as the agent in catalysis **2.** a person or thing that is a stimulus in producing or hastening results —**cat′a·lyt′ic** ***adj., n.*** —**cat′a·lyt′i·cal·ly** ***adv.***

catalytic converter a device that is part of the exhaust system of an automotive vehicle and contains a chemical catalyst to reduce polluting emissions

cat·a·lyze (kat′'l īz′) ***vt.*** **-lyzed′, -lyz′ing** to change or bring about as a catalyst —**cat′a·lyz′er** ***n.***

cat·a·ma·ran (kat′ə mə ran′) ***n.*** [Tamil *kattumaram* < *kattu,* tie + *maram,* log] **1.** a log raft or float propelled by sails or paddles **2.** a boat with two parallel hulls

cat·a·mount (kat′ə mount′) ***n.*** [< CAT + obs. *a,* of + MOUNT(AIN)] any of various wildcats; esp., *a)* the puma; cougar *b)* the lynx

Ca·ta·nia (kä tä′nyä; *E.* kə tān′yə) seaport on the E coast of Sicily: pop. 407,000

cat·a·pult (kat′ə pult′, -poolt′) ***n.*** [< L. < Gr. *katapeltēs* < *kata-,* down + *pallein,* to hurl] **1.** an ancient military device for throwing or shooting stones, spears, etc. **2.** a slingshot **3.** a mechanism for launching an airplane, rocket, etc., as from a ship's deck —***vt.*** to shoot from or as from a catapult; hurl —***vi.*** to be catapulted; leap

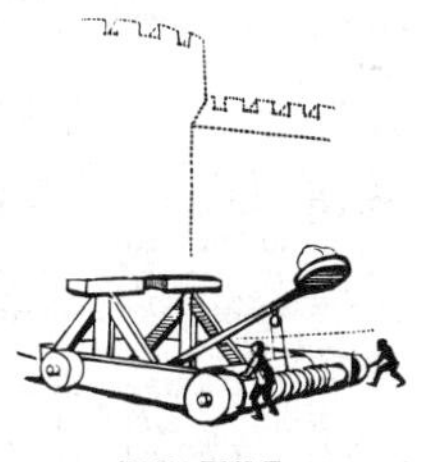
CATAPULT

cat·a·ract (kat′ə rakt′) ***n.*** [< L. *cataracta* < Gr. *kataraktēs* < *kata-,* down + *rhēgnynai,* to break] **1.** a large waterfall **2.** any strong flood or rush of water **3.** *a)* an eye disease in which the crystalline lens or its capsule becomes opaque, causing partial or total blindness *b)* the opaque area

ca·tarrh (kə tär′) ***n.*** [< Fr. < LL. < Gr. < *kata-,* down + *rhein,* to flow] inflammation of a mucous membrane, esp. of the nose or throat, causing an increased flow of mucus: a term not now in use —**ca·tarrh′al, ca·tarrh′ous** ***adj.***

ca·tas·tro·phe (kə tas′trə fē) ***n.*** [< L. < Gr. *katastrophē,* an overthrowing < *kata-,* down + *strephein,* to turn] **1.** the culminating event of a drama, esp. of a tragedy, by which the plot is resolved **2.** a disastrous end **3.** any sudden, great disaster **4.** a total failure —**cat·a·stroph·ic** (kat′ə sträf′ik) ***adj.*** —**cat′a·stroph′i·cal·ly** ***adv.***

cat·a·ton·ic (kat′ə tän′ik) ***adj.*** [< CATA- + Gr. *tonos,* tension] of or in a state of schizophrenia marked esp. by stupor or catalepsy

Ca·taw·ba (kə tô′bə) ***n.*** [after name of a Choctaw Indian tribe] [*often* **c-**] **1.** a reddish grape of the E U.S. **2.** a wine made from this grape

cat·bird (kat′burd′) ***n.*** a slate-gray N. American songbird with a black crown and tail: its call is similar in sound to the mew of a cat

cat·boat (-bōt′) ***n.*** a catrigged sailboat, usually having a centerboard

cat burglar [Slang] a burglar who climbs up to openings in upper stories, roofs, etc. to enter

cat·call (-kôl′) ***n.*** a shrill shout or whistle expressing derision or disapproval, as of a speaker, actor, etc. —***vt., vi.*** to make catcalls (at)

catch (kach, kech) ***vt.*** **caught, catch′ing** [< Anglo-Fr. *cachier* < VL. < L. *captare,* to try to seize < pp. of *capere,* to take] **1.** to seize and hold, as after a chase; capture **2.** to take by or as by a trap, snare, etc. **3.** to deceive; ensnare **4.** to surprise in the act *[*to be *caught* stealing*]* **5.** to hit *[*the blow *caught* him in the eye*]* **6.** to get to in time *[*to *catch* a train*]* **7.** to lay hold of; grab *[*to *catch* a ball*]* **8.** *a)* to get as by chance or quickly *[*to *catch* a glimpse*]* *b)* [Colloq.] to manage to see, hear, etc. *[*to *catch* a newscast*]* **9.** to get as by exposure to others infected *[*to *catch* the mumps*]* **10.** *a)* to understand; apprehend *b)* to show an understanding of by depicting *[*the statue *catches* her beauty*]* **11.** to captivate; charm **12.** to cause to be entangled *[*to *catch* one's heel in a rug*]* **13.** *Baseball* to act as catcher for (a specified pitcher) —***vi.*** **1.** to become held, fastened, or entangled **2.** to take fire or start burning **3.** to take and keep hold, as a lock **4.** to act as a catcher —***n.*** **1.** the act of catching **2.** a thing that catches or holds **3.** the person or thing caught **4.** the amount caught **5.** a person worth catching, esp. as a husband or wife **6.** a snatch, scrap, or bit *[catches* of old tunes*]* **7.** an emotional break in the voice **8.** a simple game of throwing and catching a ball **9.** [Colloq.] a hidden qualification; tricky condition *[*a *catch* in his offer*]* **10.** *Music* a round for three or more voices **11.** *Sports* a catching of a ball in a specified manner —***adj.*** **1.** tricky; deceptive *[*a *catch* question on an exam*]* **2.** attracting or meant to attract attention or interest —**catch as catch can** with any hold, approach, etc.: orig. said of a style of wrestling —**catch at 1.** to try to catch **2.** to reach for eagerly —**catch it** [Colloq.] to receive a scolding or other punishment —**catch on 1.** to understand **2.** to become fashionable, popular, etc. —**catch oneself** to hold oneself back abruptly from saying or doing something —**catch up 1.** to take up suddenly; snatch **2.** to show to be in error **3.** to heckle **4.** to come up even, as by hurrying or by extra work **5.** to fasten in loops —**catch up on** to engage in more (work, sleep, etc.) so as to compensate for earlier neglect

catch·all (-ôl′) ***n.*** a place for holding all sorts of things *[*one drawer was a *catchall]*

catch basin a sievelike device at the entrance to a sewer to catch, or stop, bulky matter

catch·er (-ər) *n.* **1.** one that catches **2.** *Baseball* the player stationed behind home plate, who catches pitched balls not hit away by the batter

catch·fly (-flī′) *n., pl.* **-flies′** *same as* CAMPION

catch·ing (-iŋ) *adj.* **1.** contagious; infectious **2.** attractive; catchy

catch·pen·ny (-pen′ē) *adj.* cheap and flashy; worthless —*n., pl.* **-nies** a catchpenny commodity

catch phrase a phrase that catches or is meant to catch popular attention

catch·up (kech′əp, kach′-) *n. same as* KETCHUP

catch·word (kach′wurd′, kech′-) *n.* **1.** a word placed to catch attention and be a guide, as either of the words at the top of this page **2.** a word or phrase repeated so often that it becomes a slogan

catch·y (-ē) *adj.* **catch′i·er, catch′i·est** **1.** catching attention; arousing interest **2.** easily taken up and remembered *[a catchy tune]* **3.** meant to trick **4.** spasmodic —**catch′i·ness** *n.*

cat·e·chet·i·cal (kat′ə ket′i k'l) *adj.* **1.** of or like a catechism **2.** teaching by questions and answers Also **cat′e·chet′ic** —**cat′e·chet′i·cal·ly** *adv.*

cat·e·chism (kat′ə kiz'm) *n.* [< LL. < Gr. < *katēchizein,* to catechize < *kata-,* thoroughly + *ēchein,* to sound] **1.** a handbook of questions and answers for teaching the principles of a religion **2.** any similar handbook for teaching the fundamentals of a subject **3.** a series of questions; close questioning —**cat′e·chis′mal** *adj.* —**cat′e·chis′tic** (-kis′tik), **cat′e·chis′ti·cal** *adj.*

cat·e·chist (-kist) *n.* a person who catechizes

cat·e·chize (-kīz′) *vt.* **-chized′, -chiz′ing** [see CATECHISM] **1.** to teach (esp. religion) by the use of questions and answers **2.** to question searchingly Also sp. **cat′e·chise′** —**cat′e·chi·za′tion** *n.* —**cat′e·chiz′er** *n.*

cat·e·chu (kat′ə chōō′) *n.* [Malay *kachu*] a water-soluble, astringent substance obtained from several Asiatic trees: used in dyeing, tanning, etc.

cat·e·chu·men (kat′ə kyōō′mən) *n.* [< LL. < Gr. *katēchoumenos:* see CATECHISM] a person being instructed in Christian fundamentals before baptism or confirmation

cat·e·gor·i·cal (kat′ə gôr′i k'l, -gär′-) *adj.* **1.** unqualified; unconditional; absolute; positive: said of a statement, theory, etc. **2.** of, as, or in a category Also **cat′e·gor′ic** —**cat′e·gor′i·cal·ly** *adv.*

cat·e·go·rize (kat′ə gə rīz′) *vt.* **-rized′, -riz′ing** to place in a category —**cat′e·go·ri·za′tion** *n.*

cat·e·go·ry (kat′ə gôr′ē) *n., pl.* **-ries** [< LL. < Gr. < *katēgorein,* to accuse < *kata-,* against + *agoreuein,* to declaim] **1.** a class or division in a scheme of classification **2.** *Logic* any of the basic concepts into which knowledge is classified

cat·e·nate (kat′'n āt′) *vt.* **-nat′ed, -nat′ing** [< L. < *catena,* chain] to form into a chain or series; link —**cat′e·na′tion** *n.*

ca·ter (kā′tər) *vi.* [< OFr. < *achater,* to buy, ult. < L. *ad-,* to + *capere,* to take] **1.** to provide food; act as a caterer **2.** to seek to gratify another's desires (with *to*) —*vt.* to serve as caterer for (a banquet, party, etc.)

cat·er-cor·nered (kat′ē kôr′nərd, kit′-) *adj.* [ME. *cater,* four (ult. < L. *quattuor,* FOUR) + CORNERED] diagonal —*adv.* diagonally Also **cat′er-cor′ner**

ca·ter·er (kāt′ər ər) *n.* one who caters; esp., one whose business is providing food and service as for parties

cat·er·pil·lar (kat′ər pil′ər, kat′ə-) *n.* [< ONormFr. *catepilose* < L. *catta pilosa,* hairy cat] the wormlike larva of various insects, esp. of a butterfly or moth —[**C-**] *a trademark for* a tractor having on each side an endless roller belt over cogged wheels, to move over rough or muddy ground

cat·er·waul (kat′ər wôl′) *vi.* [ME. *cater* (prob. < MDu. *kater,* tomcat) + *w(r)awlen, v.,* prob. echoic] to make a shrill, howling sound like that of a cat; wail; scream —*n.* such a sound

cat·fish (kat′fish′) *n., pl.* **-fish′, -fish′es:** see FISH any of a group of scaleless fishes with long barbels about the mouth

cat·gut (-gut′) *n.* [CAT + GUT: reason for *cat* unc.] a tough thread made from dried intestines, as of sheep, and used for surgical sutures, musical instruments, etc.

cath- (kath) *same as* CATA-: used before an aspirate

Cath. **1.** Catholic **2.** [*also* **c-**] cathedral

ca·thar·sis (kə thär′sis) *n.* [ModL. < Gr. *katharsis* < *katharos,* pure] **1.** purgation, esp. of the bowels **2.** the purifying or relieving of the emotions, esp. by art **3.** *Psychiatry* the relieving of fears, problems, etc. by bringing them to consciousness or giving them expression

ca·thar·tic (-tik) *adj.* of or effecting catharsis; purging: also **ca·thar′ti·cal** —*n.* a medicine for purging the bowels

Ca·thay (ka thā′, kə-) *poet. or archaic name of* CHINA

cat·head (kat′hed′) *n.* a projecting beam near the bow of a ship, to which the anchor is fastened

ca·the·dra (kə thē′drə, kath′i-) *n.* [LL. < L. < Gr. *kathedra* < *kata-,* down + *hedra,* a seat] **1.** the bishop's throne in a cathedral **2.** the episcopal see See EX CATHEDRA

ca·the·dral (kə thē′drəl) *n.* **1.** the main church of a bishop's see, containing the cathedra **2.** loosely, any large, imposing church —*adj.* **1.** of, like, or containing a cathedra **2.** official **3.** of or like a cathedral

Cath·er·ine (kath′rin, -ər in) [Fr. < L. *Catharina* < Gr. *Aikaterinē;* infl. by *katharos,* pure] **1.** a feminine name: dim. *Cathy, Kate, Kit, Kitty* **2. Catherine II** 1729–96; German-born empress of Russia (1762–96): called **Catherine the Great**

cath·e·ter (kath′ə tər) *n.* [LL. < Gr. *kathetēr* < *kata-,* down + *hienai,* to send] a slender tube inserted into a body passage, etc. for passing fluids, making examinations, etc., esp. for draining urine from the bladder

cath·e·ter·ize (-īz′) *vt.* **-ized′, -iz′ing** to insert a catheter into —**cath′e·ter·i·za′tion** *n.*

cath·ode (kath′ōd) *n.* [< Gr. *kathodos,* descent < *kata-,* down + *hodos,* way] **1.** in an electrolytic cell, the negative electrode, from which current flows **2.** in a vacuum tube, the negatively charged electron emitter **3.** the positive terminal of a battery —**ca·thod·ic** (ka thäd′ik) *adj.*

cathode rays streams of electrons projected from the surface of a cathode: cathode rays produce X-rays when they strike solids

cathode-ray tube a vacuum tube in which the electrons can be focused on a fluorescent screen, producing a visible pattern on the exterior face: used as oscilloscopes, television picture tubes, etc.

cath·o·lic (kath′ə lik, kath′lik) *adj.* [L. *catholicus,* universal < Gr. < *kata-,* completely + *holos,* whole] **1.** of general scope or value; all inclusive; universal **2.** broad in sympathies, tastes, etc.; liberal **3.** [*often* **C-**] of the universal Christian church **4.** [**C-**] of the Christian church headed by the Pope; Roman Catholic —*n.* **1.** [*often* **C-**] a member of the universal Christian church **2.** [**C-**] *same as* ROMAN CATHOLIC —**ca·thol·i·cal·ly** (kə thäl′i k'l ē, -ik lē) *adv.*

Ca·thol·i·cism (kə thäl′ə siz'm) *n.* the doctrine, faith, practice, and organization of a Catholic church, esp. of the Roman Catholic Church

cath·o·lic·i·ty (kath′ə lis′ə tē) *n.* **1.** broadness of taste, sympathy, etc.; liberality, as of ideas **2.** universality **3.** [**C-**] Catholicism

ca·thol·i·cize (kə thäl′ə sīz′) *vt., vi.* **-cized′, -ciz′ing** **1.** to make or become catholic **2.** [**C-**] to convert or be converted to Catholicism

cat·i·on (kat′ī′ən) *n.* [coined by Faraday < Gr. < *kata,* down + *ion,* prp. of *ienai,* to go] a positive ion: in electrolysis, cations move toward the cathode —**cat·i·on·ic** (kat′ī än′ik) *adj.*

cat·kin (kat′kin) *n.* [< Du. dim. of *katte,* cat] a drooping, scaly spike of unisexual flowers without petals, as on poplars or walnuts; ament

cat·nap (kat′nap′) *n.* a short, light sleep; doze —*vi.* **-napped′, -nap′ping** to take a catnap

cat·nip (-nip′) *n.* [CAT + *nip* (dial. for *catnip*) < L. *nepeta*] a plant of the mint family, with downy leaves and bluish flowers: cats like its odor

Ca·to (kāt′ō) **1. (Marcus Porcius),** 234–149 B.C.; Rom. statesman: called *the Elder* **2. (Marcus Porcius),** 95–46 B.C.; Rom. statesman & Stoic philosopher: great-grandson of *prec.:* called *the Younger*

cat-o'-nine-tails (kat′ə nīn′tālz′) *n., pl.* **-tails′** a whip made of nine knotted cords attached to a handle, formerly used for flogging

cat rig a rig, esp. of a catboat, consisting of one large sail on a mast well forward in the bow —**cat′rigged′** (-rigd′) *adj.*

CAT scan (kat) [*c(omputerized) a(xial) t(omography)*: tomography is an X-ray technique] **1.** a method for diagnosing disorders of the soft tissues, esp. of the brain: it uses a computerized combination of many X-rays to form an image **2.** the image —**CAT scanner** —**CAT scanning**

cat's cradle a child's game in which a string looped over the fingers is transferred back and forth on the hands of the players to form designs

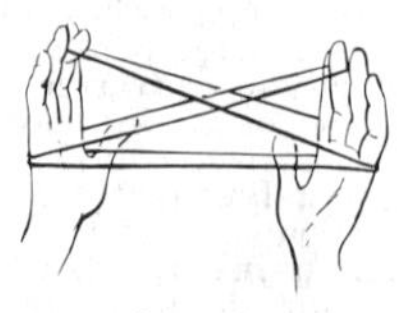

CAT'S CRADLE

cat's-eye (kats′ī′) *n.* any gem, stone, etc. that reflects light in a way suggestive of a cat's eye, as a child's marble, a glass reflector, etc.

Cats·kill Mountains (kat′skil′) [Du., cat stream] mountain range in SE N.Y.: also **Cats′kills′**

cat's-paw (kats′pô′) *n.* **1.** a person used by another to do distasteful or unlawful work; dupe **2.** a light breeze rippling the surface of water

cat·sup (kech′əp, kach′-; kat′səp) *n. same as* KETCHUP

cat·tail (kat′tāl′) *n.* a tall marsh plant with reedlike leaves and long, brown, fuzzy, cylindrical flower spikes

cat·ta·lo (kat′'l ō′) *n., pl.* **-loes′, -los′** *same as* CATALO

cat·tish (kat′ish) ***adj.*** **1.** like a cat; feline **2.** *same as* CATTY —**cat′tish·ly** ***adv.*** —**cat′tish·ness** ***n.***
cat·tle (kat′'l) ***n.*** [< Anglo-Fr. *catel* < ML. *captale,* property < L. < *caput,* the head] **1.** [Archaic] farm animals **2.** domesticated bovine animals collectively; cows, bulls, steers, or oxen **3.** people in the mass: contemptuous term
cat·tle·man (-mən) ***n.,*** *pl.* **-men** a man who tends cattle or raises them for market
cat·ty (kat′ē) ***adj.*** **-ti·er, -ti·est 1.** of or like a cat **2.** spiteful, mean, malicious, etc. —**cat′ti·ly** ***adv.*** —**cat′ti·ness** ***n.***
cat·ty-cor·nered (kat′ē kôr′nərd, kit′-) ***adj., adv.*** *same as* CATER-CORNERED: also **cat′ty-cor′ner**
cat·walk (kat′wôk′) ***n.*** a high, narrow walk, as along the edge of a bridge or over an engine room
Cau·ca·sia (kô kā′zhə) *same as* CAUCASUS (sense 1)
Cau·ca·sian (kô kā′zhən) ***adj.*** **1.** of the Caucasus, its people, their languages, etc. **2.** *same as* CAUCASOID Also **Cau·cas′ic** (-kas′ik) —***n.*** **1.** a native of the Caucasus **2.** *same as* CAUCASOID **3.** the Caucasian languages; Circassian, Georgian, etc.
Cau·ca·soid (kôk′ə soid′) ***adj.*** [from the erroneous notion that the original home of the hypothetical Indo-Europeans was the Caucasus] designating or of one of the major groups of mankind that includes the native peoples of Europe, North Africa, the Near East, India, etc.: loosely called the *white race,* although skin color varies —***n.*** a member of the Caucasoid group
Cau·ca·sus (kô′kə səs) **1.** region in SE European U.S.S.R., between the Black Sea and the Caspian: often called **the Caucasus 2.** mountain range in this region: in full, **Caucasus Mountains**
cau·cus (kôk′əs) ***n.*** [< ? *Caucus* Club, 18th-c. social and political club; ult. < MGr. *kaukos,* drinking cup] a private meeting of leaders or a committee of a political party or faction to decide on policy, candidates, etc., esp. prior to an open meeting —***vi.*** **-cused** or **-cussed, -cus·ing** or **-cussing** to hold, or take part in, a caucus
cau·dal (kôd′'l) ***adj.*** [< L. *cauda,* tail] **1.** of or like a tail **2.** at or near the tail —**cau′dal·ly** ***adv.***
cau·date (kô′dāt) ***adj.*** [< L. *cauda,* tail] having a tail or taillike part: also **cau′dat·ed**
cau·dle (kôd′'l) ***n.*** [< Anglo-Fr., ult. < L. *cal(i)dus,* warm] a warm drink for invalids; esp., a spiced and sugared gruel with wine or ale added
caught (kôt) *pt. & pp. of* CATCH
caul (kôl) ***n.*** [OE. *cawl,* basket, net] a membrane sometimes enveloping the head of a child at birth
caul·dron (kôl′drən) ***n.*** *same as* CALDRON
cau·li·flow·er (kôl′ə flou′ər, käl′-) ***n.*** [< It. *cavolfiore,* after L. *caulis,* cabbage] **1.** a variety of cabbage with a compact white head of fleshy flower stalks **2.** the head of this plant, eaten as a vegetable
cauliflower ear an ear permanently deformed by injuries from repeated blows, as in boxing
cau·lis (kô′lis) ***n.,*** *pl.* **-les** (-lēz) [L., akin to Gr. *kaulos*] *Bot.* the main stem of a plant
caulk (kôk) ***vt.*** [< OFr. < L. *calcare,* to tread < *calx,* a heel] **1.** to make (a boat, etc.) watertight by filling the seams or cracks with oakum, tar, etc. **2.** to stop up (cracks of window frames, etc.) with a filler —**caulk′er** ***n.***
caus·al (kôz′'l) ***adj.*** **1.** of, like, or being a cause **2.** relating to cause and effect **3.** expressing a cause or reason —**caus′al·ly** ***adv.***
cau·sal·i·ty (kô zal′ə tē) ***n.,*** *pl.* **-ties 1.** causal quality or agency **2.** the interrelation or principle of cause and effect
cau·sa·tion (kô zā′shən) ***n.*** **1.** the act of causing **2.** anything producing an effect; cause **3.** causality
caus·a·tive (kôz′ə tiv) ***adj.*** **1.** producing an effect; causing **2.** expressing causation, as the verb *fell* (to cause to fall) —***n.*** a causative word or form —**caus′a·tive·ly** ***adv.***
cause (kôz) ***n.*** [< OFr. (or) < L. *causa*] **1.** anything producing an effect or result **2.** a person or thing that brings about an effect or result **3.** a reason, motive, or ground for some action, feeling, etc.; esp., sufficient reason [*cause* for complaint] **4.** any objective or movement that a person or group is interested in and supports, esp. one involving social reform **5.** *Law* an action or question to be resolved by a court of law —***vt.*** **caused, caus′ing** to be the cause of; bring about; effect —**make common cause with** to join forces with —**caus′a·ble** ***adj.*** —**cause′less** ***adj.***
‡**cause cé·lèb·re** (kōz′ sā leb′r′; *E.* kôz′ sə leb′) [Fr.] a celebrated law case, trial, or controversy
cause of action *Law* the right by which a party seeks a remedy against another in a court of law
cau·se·rie (kō′zə rē′) ***n.*** [Fr. < *causer,* to chat < VL. < L. *causari,* to plead < *causa,* cause] **1.** an informal talk; chat **2.** a short, conversational piece of writing
cause·way (kôz′wā′) ***n.*** [< Brit. dial. *causey,* ult. < L. *calx,* limestone + WAY] **1.** a raised path or road, as across a marsh **2.** a paved way or road; highway
caus·tic (kôs′tik) ***adj.*** [< L. < Gr. *kaustikos* < *kaiein,* to burn] **1.** that can burn or destroy tissue by chemical action; corrosive **2.** cutting or sarcastic in utterance —***n.*** any caustic substance —**caus′ti·cal·ly** ***adv.*** —**caus·tic′i·ty** (-tis′ə tē) ***n.***
caustic potash *same as* POTASSIUM HYDROXIDE
caustic soda *same as* SODIUM HYDROXIDE
cau·ter·ize (kôt′ər īz′) ***vt.*** **-ized′, -iz′ing** [< LL. < Gr. < *kautērion,* branding iron < *kaiein,* to burn] to burn with a hot iron or needle, or with a caustic substance, so as to destroy dead tissue, etc. —**cau′ter·i·za′tion** ***n.***
cau·ter·y (kôt′ər ē) ***n.,*** *pl.* **-ter·ies 1.** an instrument or substance for cauterizing: also **cau′ter·ant 2.** the act of cauterizing
cau·tion (kô′shən) ***n.*** [< L. *cautio* < same base as *cavere,* to be wary] **1.** a warning; admonition **2.** a word, sign, etc. by which warning is given **3.** the act or practice of being cautious; wariness **4.** [Colloq.] a person or thing provoking notice, etc. —***vt.*** to urge to be cautious; warn; admonish
cau·tion·ar·y (-er′ē) ***adj.*** urging caution; warning
cau·tious (kô′shəs) ***adj.*** full of caution; careful to avoid danger; circumspect; wary —**cau′tious·ly** ***adv.*** —**cau′tious·ness** ***n.***
cav·al·cade (kav′'l kād′, kav′'l kād′) ***n.*** [Fr. < It. < *cavalcare,* to ride < VL. < L. *caballus,* horse, nag] **1.** a procession of horsemen or carriages **2.** *a*) any procession *b*) a sequence of events, etc.
cav·a·lier (kav′ə lir′) ***n.*** [Fr. < It. *cavaliere* < LL. < L. *caballus,* horse, nag] **1.** an armed horseman; knight **2.** a gallant gentleman, esp. one serving as a lady's escort **3.** [C-] a partisan of Charles I of England in his struggles with Parliament (1641–49); Royalist —***adj.*** **1.** [C-] of the Cavaliers **2.** *a*) free and easy; gay *b*) casual or indifferent toward matters of some importance *c*) haughty; arrogant; supercilious —**cav′a·lier′ly** ***adv., adj.*** —**cav′a·lier′ness** ***n.***
cav·al·ry (kav′'l rē) ***n.,*** *pl.* **-ries** [< Fr. < It. < *cavaliere:* see CAVALIER] combat troops mounted originally on horses but now often on motorized armored vehicles —**cav′al·ry·man** (-mən) ***n.,*** *pl.* **-men**
cave (kāv) ***n.*** [< OFr. < L. < *cavus,* hollow] a hollow place inside the earth; cavern —***vt.*** **caved, cav′ing** to make a hollow in —***vi.*** [Colloq.] **1.** to cave in **2.** to explore caves —**cave in 1.** to collapse **2.** to make collapse **3.** [Colloq.] to give way; give in; yield —**cav′er** ***n.***
ca·ve·at (kā′vē at′, kav′ē-; kä′vē ät′) ***n.*** [L., let him beware] **1.** *Law* a notice that an interested party files with the proper officers directing them to stop an action until he can be heard **2.** a warning
caveat emp·tor (emp′tôr) [L.] let the buyer beware (i.e., one buys at his own risk)
cave-in (kāv′in′) ***n.*** **1.** a caving in **2.** a place where the ground, a mine, etc. has caved in
cave man **1.** a prehistoric human being of the Stone Age who lived in caves: also **cave dweller 2.** a man who is rough and crudely direct
cav·ern (kav′ərn) ***n.*** [< Fr. < L. *caverna* < *cavus,* hollow] a cave, esp. a large cave —***vt.*** **1.** to enclose in or as in a cavern **2.** to hollow (*out*)
cav·ern·ous (kav′ər nəs) ***adj.*** **1.** full of caverns **2.** full of cavities; porous **3.** like a cavern; deep-set, hollow, etc. —**cav′ern·ous·ly** ***adv.***
cav·i·ar, cav·i·are (kav′ē är′, käv′-; kav′ē är′) ***n.*** [Fr. < It. < Turk. < Per. *khāviyār*] the salted eggs of sturgeon, salmon, etc. eaten as an appetizer
cav·il (kav′'l) ***vi.*** **-iled** or **-illed, -il·ing** or **-il·ling** [< OFr. < L. *cavillari* < *cavilla,* a jest] to object when there is little reason; resort to trivial faultfinding; carp (*at* or *about*) —***n.*** a trivial objection; quibble —**cav′il·er, cav′il·ler** ***n.***
cav·i·ty (kav′ə tē) ***n.,*** *pl.* **-ties** [< Fr. < LL. *cavitas* < L. *cavus,* hollow] **1.** a hole or hollow place, as in a tooth **2.** a natural hollow place within the body [the abdominal *cavity*]
ca·vort (kə vôrt′) ***vi.*** [< ?] **1.** to leap about; prance or caper **2.** to romp about happily; frolic
ca·vy (kā′vē) ***n.,*** *pl.* **-vies** [< Carib *cabiai*] any of several short-tailed S. American rodents, as the guinea pig
caw (kô) ***n.*** [echoic] the harsh, strident cry of a crow or raven —***vi.*** to make this sound
Cax·ton (kak′stən), **William** 1422?–91; 1st Eng. printer
cay (kā, kē) ***n.*** [Sp. *cayo:* see KEY²] a low island, coral reef, or sandbank off a mainland
cay·enne (kī en′, kā-) ***n.*** [< Tupi *kynnha*] a very hot red pepper made from the dried fruit of a pepper plant, esp. of the capsicum: also **cayenne pepper**
cay·man (kā′mən) ***n.,*** *pl.* **-mans** *same as* CAIMAN

Ca·yu·ga (kā yo͞o′gə, kī-) *n.* **1.** *pl.* **-gas, -ga** any member of a tribe of Iroquoian Indians who lived around Cayuga Lake and Seneca Lake in N.Y. **2.** their Iroquoian dialect

Cay·use (kī′o͞os, kī o͞os′) *n., pl.* **-us·es;** for 1 *a,* also **-use** **1.** *a*) a member of a tribe of Oregonian Indians *b*) their language **2.** [**c-**] a small Western horse used by cowboys

CB (sē′bē′) *adj.* [CITIZENS' BAND] designating or having to do with shortwave radio that uses citizens' band frequencies —*n., pl.* **CB's** a shortwave radio using citizens' band frequencies

CBC Canadian Broadcasting Corporation

CBS Columbia Broadcasting System

cc.chapters

cc., c.c. cubic centimeter(s)

C.C., c.c. carbon copy

CCC Commodity Credit Corporation

C clef *Music* a sign on a staff indicating that C is the note on the third line (*alto clef*) or on the fourth line (*tenor clef*)

Cd *Chem.* cadmium

CD, C.D. Civil Defense

CDR, Cdr. Commander

Ce *Chem.* cerium

C.E. **1.** Church of England **2.** Civil Engineer

cease (sēs) *vt., vi.* **ceased, ceas′ing** [< OFr. < L. *cessare* < *cedere,* to yield] to end; stop; discontinue —*n.* a ceasing: chiefly in **without cease**

cease-fire (sēs′fīr′) *n.* a temporary cessation of warfare by mutual agreement of the participants

cease·less (-lis) *adj.* unceasing; continual —**cease′less·ly** *adv.*

Ce·bu (sā bo͞o′) **1.** seaport on an island in the SC Philippines: pop. 310,000 **2.** this island

Ce·cil (sēs′'l, ses′'l) [L. *Caecilius,* prob. < *caecus,* dim-sighted, blind] a masculine name

Ce·cil·ia (sə sēl′yə) [L. < fem. of *Caecilius:* see prec.] a feminine name: var. *Cecile, Cecily*

ce·cro·pi·a moth (si krō′pē ə) [< *Cecrops,* legendary Gr. king] the largest moth of the U.S., having wide wings, each with a crescent-shaped spot

ce·cum (sē′kəm) *n., pl.* **-ca** (-kə) [< L. (*intestinum*) *caecum,* blind (intestine)] the pouch that is the beginning of the large intestine —**ce′cal** *adj.*

ce·dar (sē′dər) *n.* [< OFr. < L. < Gr. *kedros*] **1.** any of certain coniferous trees of the pine family, having durable, fragrant wood, as the **cedar of Lebanon** **2.** any of various trees like this, as the juniper **3.** the wood of any of these —*adj.* of cedar

Cedar Rapids [after the rapids of nearby Cedar River] city in EC Iowa: pop. 110,000

cedar waxwing a brownish-gray, crested American bird, with red, waxlike tips on its secondary wing feathers: also **ce′dar·bird′** *n.*

cede (sēd) *vt.* **ced′ed, ced′ing** [< Fr. < L. *cedere,* to yield] **1.** to give up one's rights in; surrender **2.** to transfer the title or ownership of

ce·di (sā′dē) *n., pl.* **-dis** [< native word *sedie,* cowrie, formerly used as money] *see* MONETARY UNITS, table (Ghana)

ce·dil·la (si dil′ə) *n.* [< Fr. < Sp. *cedilla,* dim. of *zeda* (< Gr. *zēta,* zeta)] a hooklike mark put under *c* in some French words (Ex.: *façade*) to show that it is to be sounded like a voiceless *s*

Ced·ric (sed′rik, sē′drik) [< ? Celt.] a masculine name

ceil (sēl) *vt.* [< OFr. < L. *celare,* to hide; prob. infl. by L. *caelum,* heaven] to build a ceiling in or over

ceil·ing (-iŋ) *n.* [< prec.] **1.** the inside top part of a room, opposite the floor **2.** an upper limit set on anything *[a ceiling* on prices*]* **3.** *Aeron.* *a*) a cloud cover limiting vertical visibility, or the height of its lower surface *b*) the maximum height at which an aircraft can normally fly —**hit the ceiling** [Slang] to lose one's temper

cel·an·dine (sel′ən dīn′, -dēn′) *n.* [< OFr. < L. < Gr. < *chelidōn,* a swallow] **1.** a weedy plant related to the poppy, with yellow flowers **2.** a plant of the buttercup family, with yellow flowers

-cele (sēl) [< Gr. *kēlē*] **1.** *a combining form meaning* tumor, hernia, or swelling **2.** *same as* -COELE

ce·leb (sə leb′) *n. clipped form of* CELEBRITY (sense 2)

Cel·e·bes (sel′ə bēz′, sə lē′bēz) island of Indonesia, east of Borneo: 69,277 sq. mi.

cel·e·brant (sel′ə brənt) *n.* [see ff.] **1.** a person who performs a religious rite, as the priest officiating at Mass **2.** a celebrator

cel·e·brate (-brāt′) *vt.* **-brat′ed, -brat′ing** [< L. pp. of *celebrare,* to frequent, honor < *celeber,* populous] **1.** to perform (a ritual, etc.) publicly and formally; solemnize **2.** to commemorate (an anniversary, etc.) with ceremony or festivity **3.** to honor or praise publicly **4.** to mark (a happy occasion) with a pleasurable activity —*vi.* **1.** to observe a holiday, anniversary, etc. with festivities **2.** to perform a religious ceremony **3.** [Colloq.] to have a good time —**cel′e·bra′tor** *n.* —**ce·leb·ra·to·ry** (sə leb′rə tôr′ē) *adj.*

cel·e·brat·ed (-id) *adj.* famous; renowned

cel·e·bra·tion (sel′ə brā′shən) *n.* **1.** the act or an instance of celebrating **2.** that which is done to celebrate

ce·leb·ri·ty (sə leb′rə tē) *n.* **1.** wide recognition; fame **2.** *pl.* **-ties** a celebrated person

ce·ler·i·ty (sə ler′ə tē) *n.* [< Fr. < L. *celeritas* < *celer,* swift] swiftness in acting or moving; speed

cel·e·ry (sel′ər ē, sel′rē) *n.* [Fr. *céleri* < It. < L. < Gr. *selinon,* parsley] a plant of the parsley family, with long, crisp leafstalks eaten as a vegetable

celery salt a seasoning made of celery seed and salt

ce·les·ta (sə les′tə) *n.* [< Fr. < *céleste,* celestial] a small keyboard instrument with hammers that strike metal plates to make bell-like tones

Ce·leste (sə lest′) [Fr. *Céleste:* see prec.] a feminine name

ce·les·tial (sə les′chəl) *adj.* [OFr. < L. *caelestis* < *caelum,* heaven] **1.** of the heavens, or sky **2.** *a*) of heaven; divine *[celestial* beings*]* *b*) highest; perfect *[celestial* bliss*]* —**ce·les′tial·ly** *adv.*

celestial equator the great circle of the celestial sphere formed by projecting the plane of the earth's equator on the celestial sphere

celestial sphere an imaginary sphere of infinite diameter containing the whole universe and on which all celestial bodies appear to be projected

Cel·ia (sēl′yə) [L. fem. of *Caelius,* name of a Roman clan] a feminine name

ce·li·ac (sē′lē ak′) *adj.* [L. *coeliacus* < Gr. < *koilos,* hollow] of or in the abdominal cavity

cel·i·ba·cy (sel′ə bə sē) *n.* [see ff.] **1.** the state of being unmarried, esp. that of one under a vow not to marry **2.** complete sexual abstinence

cel·i·bate (sel′ə bət, -bāt′) *adj.* [< L. *caelebs,* unmarried] of or in a state of celibacy —*n.* a celibate person

cell (sel) *n.* [< OFr. *celle* < L. *cella*] **1.** a small room or cubicle, as in a convent or prison **2.** a very small hollow, cavity, or enclosed space, as in a honeycomb, or in a plant ovary **3.** any of the smallest organizational units of a group or movement, as of a Communist party **4.** *Biol.* a small unit of protoplasm, usually with a nucleus, cytoplasm, and an enclosing membrane: all plants and animals are made up of one or more cells **5.** *Elec.* a receptacle used either for generating electricity by chemical reactions or for decomposing compounds by electrolysis —**celled** *adj.*

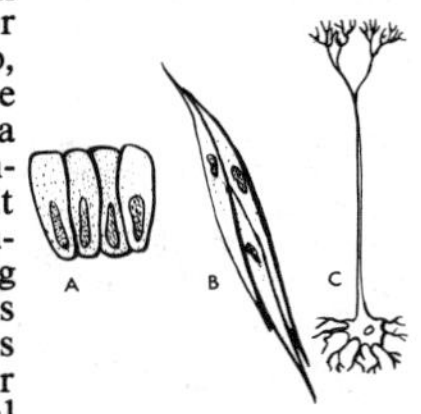

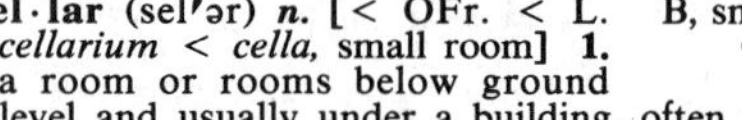

CELLS
(A, epithelial;
B, smooth muscle;
C, nerve)

cel·lar (sel′ər) *n.* [< OFr. < L. *cellarium* < *cella,* small room] **1.** a room or rooms below ground level and usually under a building, often used for storing fuel, wines, provisions, etc. **2.** a stock of wines kept in a cellar —*vt.* to store in a cellar —**the cellar** [Colloq.] the lowest position

cel·lar·age (-ij) *n.* **1.** space of or in a cellar **2.** the fee for storage in a cellar

cel·lar·er (-ər) *n.* a person in charge of a cellar or provisions, as in a monastery

cel·lar·et (sel′ə ret′) *n.* [CELLAR + -ET] a cabinet for bottles of wine or liquor, glasses, etc.

Cel·li·ni (chə lē′nē), **Ben·ve·nu·to** (ben′və no͞o′tō) 1500–71; It. sculptor & goldsmith

cel·lo (chel′ō) *n., pl.* **-los, -li** (-ē) [< VIOLONCELLO] an instrument of the violin family, between the viola and double bass in size and pitch: also sp. **'cel′lo** —**cel′list** *n.*

cel·lo·phane (sel′ə fān′) *n.* [< CELLULOSE + Gr. *phainein,* appear] a thin, transparent material made from cellulose, used as moistureproof wrapping for foods, etc.

cel·lu·lar (sel′yoo lər) *adj.* of, like, or containing a cell or cells —**cel′lu·lar′i·ty** (-lar′ə tē) *n.*

cel·lu·lite (sel′yoo lēt′) *n.* [Fr.] fatty deposits on the hips and thighs: a nonmedical term

Cel·lu·loid (sel′yoo loid′) [CELLUL(OSE) + -OID] *a trademark for* a flammable substance made from pyroxylin and camphor, used for toilet articles, etc. and, formerly, for photographic films —*n.* [**c-**] this substance

cel·lu·lose (sel′yoo lōs′) *n.* [Fr.: see CELLULE & -OSE[1]] the chief substance composing the cell walls or fibers of all plant tissue: used in the manufacture of paper, textiles, explosives, etc. —**cel′lu·los′ic** (-lō′sik) *adj., n.*

cellulose acetate a cellulose resin used in making acetate fiber, plastics, lacquers, etc.

Cel·si·us (sel′sē əs) *adj.* [after A. *Celsius* (1701–44), Swed. astronomer] designating or of a thermometer on which 0° is the freezing point and 100° is the boiling point of water; centigrade: abbrev. **C**

Celt (selt, kelt) *n.* [< Fr. < L. *Celta,* pl. *Celtae* (Gr. *Keltoi*), the Gauls] **1.** a person who speaks Celtic: the Bretons, Irish, Welsh, and Highland Scots are Celts **2.** an ancient Gaul or Briton

Cel·tic (sel′tik, kel′-) *adj.* of the Celts, their languages, culture, etc. —*n.* an Indo-European subfamily of languages with a Goidelic branch (Irish Gaelic, Scottish Gaelic, Manx) in Ireland, the Scottish Highlands, and the Isle of Man, and a Brythonic branch (Welsh, Breton, and the extinct Cornish) in Wales and Brittany

ce·ment (si ment′) *n.* [< OFr. < L. *caementum,* rough stone < *caedere,* to cut] **1.** a powdered substance made of burned lime and clay, mixed with water and sand to make mortar or with water, sand, and gravel to make concrete: the mixture hardens like stone when it dries **2.** any soft substance that fastens things together firmly when it hardens, as glue **3.** a cementlike substance used in dentistry as to fill cavities **4.** anything that joins together or unites; bond **5.** *same as* CEMENTUM —*vt.* **1.** to join or unite as with cement **2.** to cover with cement —*vi.* to become cemented —**ce·men·ta·tion** (sē′men tā′shən) *n.* —**ce·ment′er** *n.* —**ce·ment′like′** *adj.*

ce·men·tum (si men′təm) *n.* [< L.: see prec.] the hard, bony outer tissue of the root of a tooth

cem·e·ter·y (sem′ə ter′ē) *n., pl.* **-ter′ies** [< LL. < Gr. *koimētērion* < *koiman,* to put to sleep] a place for the burial of the dead; graveyard

cen·o·bite (sen′ə bīt′, sē′nə-) *n.* [< LL. *coenobita* < Gr. < *koinos,* common + *bios,* life] a member of a religious order in a monastery or convent —**cen′o·bit′ic** (-bit′ik), **cen′o·bit′i·cal** *adj.* —**cen′o·bit·ism** (-bit iz′m) *n.*

cen·o·taph (sen′ə taf′) *n.* [< Fr. < L. < Gr. < *kenos,* empty + *taphos,* a tomb] a monument honoring a dead person whose body is somewhere else

Ce·no·zo·ic (sē′nə zō′ik, sen′ə-) *adj.* [< Gr. *kainos,* recent + ZO- + -IC] designating or of the geologic era following the Mesozoic and including the present —**the Cenozoic** the Cenozoic Era or its rocks: see GEOLOGY, chart

cen·ser (sen′sər) *n.* [< OFr. < *encens:* see INCENSE[1]] a container in which incense is burned

cen·sor (sen′sər) *n.* [L. < *censere,* to tax, value] **1.** one of two Roman magistrates appointed to take the census and, later, to supervise public morals **2.** an official with the power to examine publications, movies, mail, etc. and to remove or prohibit anything considered obscene, objectionable, etc. —*vt.* to subject (a book, letter, writer, etc.) to censorship —**cen·so·ri·al** (sen sôr′ē əl) *adj.*

cen·so·ri·ous (sen sôr′ē əs) *adj.* [see prec.] inclined to find fault; harshly critical —**cen·so′ri·ous·ly** *adv.* —**cen·so′ri·ous·ness** *n.*

cen·sor·ship (sen′sər ship′) *n.* **1.** the act or a system of censoring **2.** the work or position of a censor

cen·sure (sen′shər) *n.* [L. *censura* < *censor,* CENSOR] **1.** a condemning as wrong; strong disapproval **2.** an official expression of disapproval, specif. as passed by a legislature —*vt.* **-sured, -sur·ing** to express strong disapproval of; condemn as wrong —**cen′sur·a·ble** *adj.* —**cen′sur·er** *n.*

cen·sus (sen′səs) *n.* [L., orig. pp. of *censere:* see CENSOR] **1.** in ancient Rome, a count of the people and evaluation of their property for taxation **2.** an official, usually periodic, count of population and recording of economic status, age, sex, etc.

cent (sent) *n.* [< OFr. < L. *centum,* a hundred] **1.** a 100th part of a dollar, or a coin of this value; penny: symbol, ¢ **2.** a 100th part of a guilder, rand, etc.: see MONETARY UNITS, table

cent. **1.** centigrade **2.** centimeter **3.** century

cen·tare (sen′ter, -tär) *n. same as* CENTIARE

cen·taur (sen′tôr) *n.* [< L. < Gr. *Kentauros*] *Gr. Myth.* any of a race of monsters with a man's head, trunk, and arms, and a horse's body and legs

cen·ta·vo (sen tä′vō) *n., pl.* **-vos** [Sp. < L. *centum,* a hundred] a unit of currency equal to 1/100 of a peso in Mexico, the Philippines, etc. and to 1/100 of a Brazilian cruzeiro, a Portuguese escudo, etc.: see MONETARY UNITS, table

cen·te·nar·i·an (sen′tə ner′ē ən) *adj.* **1.** of 100 years; of a centenary **2.** of a centenarian —*n.* a person at least 100 years old

cen·te·nar·y (sen ten′ər ē, sen′tə ner′ē) *adj.* [< L. < *centum,* a hundred] **1.** of a century, or period of 100 years **2.** of a centennial —*n., pl.* **-nar·ies** **1.** a century; period of 100 years **2.** *same as* CENTENNIAL

cen·ten·ni·al (sen ten′ē əl) *adj.* [< L. *centum,* a hundred + *annus,* year + -AL] **1.** of 100 years **2.** happening once in 100 years **3.** 100 years old **4.** of a 100th anniversary —*n.* a 100th anniversary or its celebration —**cen·ten′ni·al·ly** *adv.*

cen·ter (sen′tər) *n.* [< OFr. < L. *centrum* < Gr. *kentron,* sharp point] **1.** a point equally distant from all points on the circumference of a circle or surface of a sphere **2.** the point around which anything revolves; pivot **3.** a place at which an activity or complex of activities is carried on [a shopping *center*], from which ideas, influences, etc. emanate [Paris, the fashion *center*], or to which many people are attracted [a *center* of interest] **4.** the approximate middle point, place, or part of anything **5.** a group of nerve cells regulating a particular function **6.** in some sports, a player near the center of the line or playing area, who often puts the ball or puck into play **7.** *Mil.* that part of an army between the flanks **8.** [*often* **C-**] *Politics* a position or party between the left (radicals and liberals) and the right (conservatives and reactionaries) —*vt.* **1.** to place in, at, or near the center **2.** to draw or gather to one place —*vi.* to be centered; be concentrated or focused

cen·ter·board (-bôrd′) *n.* a movable, keellike board that is lowered through a slot in the floor of a sailboat to prevent drifting to leeward

cen·ter·fold (-fōld′) *n.* the center facing pages of a magazine, frequently with an extra fold or folds, given over to a photograph, often of a nude young woman or man

center of gravity that point in a body or system around which its weight is evenly distributed or balanced and may be assumed to act

cen·ter·piece (sen′tər pēs′) *n.* an ornament, bowl of flowers, etc. for the center of a table

cen·tes·i·mal (sen tes′ə məl) *adj.* [< L. *centesimus* < *centum,* a hundred] **1.** hundredth **2.** of or divided into hundredths —**cen·tes′i·mal·ly** *adv.*

cen·tes·i·mo (sen tes′ə mō′; *Sp.* -ē mô′; *It.* chen te′sē mô′) *n., pl.* **-mos′** (-mōz′; *Sp.* -môs′); It. **-mi′** (-mē′) [It. & Sp. < L.: see prec.] a unit of currency equal to 1/100th of an Italian lira, a Uruguayan peso, etc.: see MONETARY UNITS, table

cen·ti- [L. < *centum*] *a combining form meaning:* **1.** hundred or hundredfold **2.** a 100th part of

cen·ti·are (sen′tē er′, -är′) *n.* [Fr.: see CENTI- & ARE[2]] a 100th part of an are (unit of land measure)

cen·ti·grade (sen′tə grād′) *adj.* [Fr. < L. *centum,* a hundred + *gradus,* a degree] **1.** consisting of or divided into 100 degrees **2.** *same as* CELSIUS: the preferred term until the international adoption of *Celsius* in 1948

cen·ti·gram (-gram′) *n.* [Fr.: see CENTI- & GRAM[1]] a unit of weight, equal to 1/100 gram: also, chiefly Brit. sp., **cen′ti·gramme′** : abbrev. **cg., cgm.**

cen·ti·li·ter (sen′tə lēt′ər) *n.* [Fr.: see CENTI- & LITER] a unit of capacity, equal to 1/100 liter: also, chiefly Brit. sp., **cen′ti·li′tre:** abbrev. **cl.**

cen·time (sän′tēm; *Fr.* sän tēm′) *n.* [Fr. < L.: see CENTESIMAL] the 100th part of a franc, the Algerian dinar, etc.: see MONETARY UNITS, table

cen·ti·me·ter (sen′tə mēt′ər) *n.* [< Fr.: see CENTI- & METER[1]] a unit of measure, equal to 1/100 meter (.3937 inch): also, chiefly Brit. sp., **cen′ti·me′tre:** abbrev. **cm., c., C., cent.**

cen·ti·me·ter-gram-sec·ond (-gram′sek′ənd) *adj.* designating or of a system of measurement in which the centimeter, gram, and second are used as the units of length, mass, and time, respectively

cen·ti·mo (sen′tə mō′) *n., pl.* **-mos′** [see CENTIME] the 100th part of a Spanish peseta, a Venezuelan bolívar, etc.: see MONETARY UNITS, table

cen·ti·pede (sen′tə pēd′) *n.* [Fr. < L. < *centum,* a hundred + *pes* (gen. *pedis*), a foot] a many-segmented arthropod with a pair of legs to each segment

cen·tral (sen′trəl) *adj.* [L. *centralis*] **1.** in, at, or near the center **2.** of or forming the center **3.** equally distant or accessible from various points **4.** main; basic; principal **5.** of or having to do with a single source that controls all activity in an organization or system **6.** designating or of that part of the nervous system consisting of the brain and spinal cord (of a vertebrate) —*n.* formerly, a telephone exchange, esp. the main one, or the telephone operator —**cen·tral′i·ty** (-tral′ə tē) *n.* —**cen′tral·ly** *adv.*

Central African Republic country in C Africa, south of Chad: 238,224 sq. mi.; pop. 2,370,000

Central America part of N. America between Mexico and S. America —**Central American**

central city the principal municipality of a metropolitan area, surrounded by suburbs; esp., the crowded, industrial, often blighted area

cen·tral·ism (-iz′m) *n.* the principle or system of centralizing power or authority —**cen′tral·ist** *adj., n.*

cen·tral·ize (sen′trə līz′) *vt.* **-ized′, -iz′ing** **1.** to make central; bring to or focus on a center; gather together **2.** to organize under one control —*vi.* to become centralized —**cen′tral·i·za′tion** *n.* —**cen′tral·iz′er** *n.*

Central Powers in World War I, Germany, Austria-Hungary, Turkey, and Bulgaria

Central Standard Time *see* STANDARD TIME

cen·tre (sen′tər) ***n., vt., vi.,*** **-tred, -tring** *chiefly Brit. sp. of* CENTER
cen·tri- *same as* CENTRO-
cen·tric (sen′trik) ***adj.*** **1.** in, at, or near the center; central **2.** of or having a center Also **cen′tri·cal** —**cen′tri·cal·ly** ***adv.*** —**cen·tric′i·ty** (-tris′ə tē) ***n.***
-cen·tric (sen′trik) *a combining form meaning:* **1.** having a center or centers (of a specified kind or number) *[polycentric]* **2.** having (a specified thing) as its center *[geocentric]*
cen·trif·u·gal (sen trif′yə gəl, -ə gəl) ***adj.*** **[**< ModL. < CENTRI- + L. *fugere,* to flee + -AL**]** **1.** moving or tending to move away from a center **2.** using or acted on by centrifugal force —***n.*** a centrifuge —**cen·trif′u·gal·ly** ***adv.***
centrifugal force the force tending to pull a thing outward when it is rotating rapidly around a center
cen·trif·u·gal·ize (-īz′) ***vt.*** **-ized′, -iz′ing** to subject to or as to the action of a centrifuge —**cen·trif′u·gal·i·za′tion** ***n.***
cen·tri·fuge (sen′trə fyo͞oj′) ***n.*** a machine using centrifugal force to separate particles of varying density, as cream from milk —***vt.*** **-fuged′, -fug′ing** to subject to the action of a centrifuge
cen·trip·e·tal (sen trip′ət ′l) ***adj.*** **[**< ModL. < CENTRI- + L. *petere,* to seek + -AL**]** **1.** moving or tending to move toward a center **2.** using or acted on by centripetal force —**cen·trip′e·tal·ly** ***adv.***
centripetal force the force tending to pull a thing inward when it is rotating rapidly around a center
cen·trist (sen′trist) ***n.*** a member of a political party of the center
cen·tro- **[**< L. *centrum,* CENTER**]** *a combining form meaning* center
cen·tro·some (sen′trə sōm′) ***n.*** **[**CENTRO- + -SOME[3]**]** a very small body near the nucleus in most animal cells: it divides in mitosis —**cen′tro·som′ic** (-säm′ik, -sōm′-) ***adj.***
cen·tu·ri·on (sen tyoor′ē ən, -toor′-) ***n.*** **[**< L. *centuria:* see ff.**]** the commanding officer of a Roman century
cen·tu·ry (sen′chər ē) ***n.,*** *pl.* **-ries** **[**L. *centuria* < *centum,* a hundred**]** **1.** any period of 100 years, esp. as reckoned from the beginning of the Christian Era **2.** in ancient Rome *a)* a military unit, originally made up of 100 men *b)* a subdivision of the people made for voting purposes —**cen·tu·ri·al** (sen tyoor′ē əl, -toor′-) ***adj.***
century plant a tropical American agave having fleshy leaves and a tall stalk that bears greenish flowers only once after 10 to 30 years: mistakenly thought to bloom only once a century
ce·phal·ic (sə fal′ik) ***adj.*** **[**< L. < Gr. < *kephalē,* the head**]** **1.** of the head, skull, or cranium **2.** in, on, near, or toward the head —**ce·phal′i·cal·ly** ***adv.***
-ce·phal·ic (sə fal′ik) *a combining form meaning* head or skull *[dolichocephalic]*
cephalic index a measure of the human head computed by dividing its maximum breadth by its maximum length and multiplying by 100
ceph·a·lo- **[**see CEPHALIC**]** *a combining form meaning* the head, skull, or brain: also, before a vowel, **cephal-**
ceph·a·lo·pod (sef′ə lə päd′) ***n.*** **[**prec. + -POD**]** any of a class of mollusks having a distinct head with a beak, and muscular tentacles about the mouth, as the octopus, squid, and cuttlefish
ceph·a·lo·tho·rax (sef′ə lə thôr′aks) ***n.*** the head and thorax united as a single part, in certain crustaceans and arachnids
-ceph·a·lous (sef′əl əs) **[**see CEPHALIC**]** *a combining form meaning* -headed *[microcephalous]*
ce·ram·ic (sə ram′ik) ***adj.*** **[**< Gr. *keramos,* clay, pottery**]** **1.** of pottery, earthenware, tile, porcelain, etc. **2.** of ceramics —***n.*** **1.** [*pl., with sing. v.*] the art or work of making objects of baked clay **2.** such an object —**ce·ram·ist** (sə ram′ist, ser′ə mist), **ce·ram′i·cist** (-ə sist) ***n.***
Cer·ber·us (sur′bər əs) *Gr. & Rom. Myth.* the three-headed dog guarding the gate of Hades
cere (sir) ***n.*** **[**< Fr. < L. < Gr. *kēros,* wax**]** a waxy, fleshy area at the base of the beak of some birds, as the parrot, eagle, etc. —***vt.*** **cered, cer′ing** to wrap in a cerecloth
ce·re·al (sir′ē əl) ***adj.*** **[**< L. *Cerealis,* of Ceres**]** of grain or the grasses producing grain —***n.*** **1.** any grain used for food, as wheat, oats, etc. **2.** any grass producing such grain **3.** food made from grain, esp. breakfast food, as oatmeal
cer·e·bel·lum (ser′ə bel′əm) ***n.,*** *pl.* **-lums, -la** (-ə) [L., dim. of *cerebrum,* the brain**]** the section of the brain behind and below the cerebrum: it is the coordinating center for muscular movement
cer·e·bral (ser′ə brəl, sə rē′-) ***adj.*** of the brain or the cerebrum —**cer·e′bral·ly** ***adv.***
cerebral palsy any of several disorders of the central nervous system resulting from brain damage and characterized by spastic paralysis
cer·e·brate (ser′ə brāt′) ***vi.*** **-brat′ed, -brat′ing** **[**< L. *cerebrum* (see CEREBELLUM) + -ATE[1]**]** to use one's brain; think —**cer′e·bra′tion** ***n.***
cer·e·bro- **[**< L. *cerebrum,* the brain**]** *a combining form meaning* the brain (and); cerebrum (and)
cer·e·bro·spi·nal (ser′ə brō spī′n′l, sə rē′brō-) ***adj.*** of or affecting the brain and the spinal cord
cer·e·brum (ser′ə brəm, sə rē′-) ***n.,*** *pl.* **-brums, -bra** (-brə) **[**L.: see CEREBELLUM**]** the upper, main part of the brain of vertebrate animals, consisting of two equal hemispheres and, in man, controlling conscious and voluntary processes
cere·cloth (sir′klôth′) ***n.*** **[**< *cered cloth:* see CERE**]** cloth treated with wax or a similar substance, formerly used to wrap a dead person for burial
cer·e·ment (ser′ə mənt, sir′mənt) ***n.*** **[**see CERE**]** **1.** a cerecloth; shroud **2.** [*usually pl.*] any burial clothes
cer·e·mo·ni·al (ser′ə mō′nē əl, -nyəl) ***adj.*** of, for, or consisting of ceremony; ritual; formal —***n.*** **1.** an established system of rites or formal actions connected with an occasion; ritual **2.** a rite or ceremony —**cer′e·mo′ni·al·ism** ***n.*** —**cer′e·mo′ni·al·ist** ***n.*** —**cer′e·mo′ni·al·ly** ***adv.***
cer·e·mo·ni·ous (-nē əs, -nyəs) ***adj.*** **1.** ceremonial **2.** full of ceremony **3.** characterized by conventional usages or formality; very polite —**cer′e·mo′ni·ous·ly** ***adv.*** —**cer′e·mo′ni·ous·ness** ***n.***
cer·e·mo·ny (ser′ə mō′nē) ***n.,*** *pl.* **-nies** **[**L. *caerimonia***]** **1.** a formal act or set of formal acts established as proper to a special occasion, such as a wedding, religious rite, etc. **2.** a conventionally courteous act **3.** behavior that follows rigid etiquette **4.** formality or formalities **5.** empty or meaningless formality —**stand on ceremony** to behave with or insist on formality
Ce·res (sir′ēz) **1.** *Rom. Myth.* the goddess of agriculture: identified with the Greek goddess Demeter **2.** the first asteroid discovered (1801)
ce·re·us (sir′ē əs) ***n.*** **[**L., wax taper: from its shape**]** any of various cactuses, esp. night-blooming varieties, of the SW U.S. and Mexico
ce·rise (sə rēs′, -rēz′) ***n., adj.*** **[**Fr.: see CHERRY**]** bright red; cherry red
ce·ri·um (sir′ē əm) ***n.*** **[**after the asteroid *Ceres***]** a gray, metallic chemical element: symbol, Ce; at. wt., 140.12; at. no., 58
ce·ro- **[**< L. < Gr. *kēros,* wax**]** *a combining form meaning* wax
ce·ro·plas·tic (sir′ə plas′tik) ***adj.*** **[**< Gr. < *kēros,* wax + *plassein,* to mold**]** **1.** having to do with wax modeling **2.** modeled in wax
cert. **1.** certificate **2.** certified
cer·tain (surt′′n) ***adj.*** **[**< OFr. < L. *certus,* determined < *cernere,* to decide**]** **1.** fixed, settled, or determined **2.** inevitable **3.** not to be doubted *[*the evidence is *certain]* **4.** reliable; dependable *[*a *certain* cure*]* **5.** controlled; unerring *[*his *certain* aim*]* **6.** sure; positive *[*I'm *certain* he's here*]* **7.** not named or described, though definite *[*a *certain* person*]* **8.** some, but not very much; appreciable *[*to a *certain* extent*]* —**for certain** without doubt
cer·tain·ly (-lē) ***adv.*** beyond a doubt; surely
cer·tain·ty (-tē) ***n.*** **1.** the quality, state, or fact of being certain **2.** *pl.* **-ties** anything certain; definite fact
cer·tes (sur′tēz) ***adv.*** **[**< OFr. < L. *certus,* CERTAIN**]** [Archaic] certainly; verily
cer·tif·i·cate (sər tif′ə kit; *for v.* -kāt′) ***n.*** **[**< OFr. < ML. < LL. pp. of *certificare,* CERTIFY**]** a written or printed statement testifying to a fact, qualification, ownership, etc. —***vt.*** **-cat′ed, -cat′ing** to attest by a certificate; issue a certificate to —**cer·tif′i·ca′tor** ***n.*** —**cer·tif′i·ca·to′ry** (-kə tôr′ē) ***adj.***
cer·ti·fi·ca·tion (sur′tə fi kā′shən) ***n.*** **1.** a certifying or being certified **2.** a certified statement
cer·ti·fied (sur′tə fīd′) ***adj.*** **1.** vouched for; guaranteed **2.** having, or attested to by, a certificate
certified check a check certified by a bank as genuine, on which it guarantees payment
certified mail a postal service which provides a receipt to the sender of first-class mail and a record of its delivery; also, mail sent by this
certified public accountant a public accountant certified by a State examining board after meeting the requirements of State law
cer·ti·fy (sur′tə fī′) ***vt.*** **-fied′, -fy′ing** **[**< OFr. < LL. *certificare* < L. *certus,* CERTAIN + *facere,* to make**]** **1.** to declare (a thing) true, accurate, certain, etc. by formal statement; verify **2.** to declare officially insane **3.** to guarantee; vouch for **4.** to issue a certificate to **5.** [Archaic] to assure; make certain —***vi.*** to testify (*to*) —**cer′ti·fi′a·ble** ***adj.*** —**cer′ti·fi′a·bly** ***adv.*** —**cer′ti·fi′er** ***n.***
cer·ti·o·ra·ri (sur′shē ə rer′ē, -rär′-) ***n.*** [LL., to be made more certain**]** *Law* a writ from a higher court to a lower one, or to a board or official with judicial power, requesting the record of a case for review
cer·ti·tude (sur′tə to͞od′, -tyo͞od′) ***n.*** **[**< OFr. < LL. *certitudo***]** **1.** a feeling absolutely sure **2.** inevitability
ce·ru·le·an (sə ro͞o′lē ən) ***adj.*** **[**< L., prob. < dim. of *caelum,* heaven**]** sky-blue; azure

ce·ru·men (sə ro͞o′mən) ***n.*** [< L. *cera,* wax, after ALBUMEN] *same as* EARWAX
Cer·van·tes (Saavedra) (ther vän′tes; *E.* sər van′tēz), **Miguel de** (mē gel′ *the*) 1547–1616; Sp. writer: author of *Don Quixote*
cer·vi·cal (sur′vi kəl) ***adj.*** of the neck or cervix
cer·vix (sur′viks) ***n.,*** *pl.* **-vi·ces′** (sur′və sēz′, sər vī′-), **-vix·es** [L., the neck] **1.** the neck, esp. the back of the neck **2.** a necklike part, esp. of the uterus
Ce·sar·e·an, Ce·sar·i·an (si zer′ē ən) ***adj., n.*** *same as* CAESAREAN
ce·si·um (sē′zē əm) ***n.*** [ModL., neut. of L. *caesius,* bluish-gray] a soft, silver-white, ductile, metallic chemical element, used in photoelectric cells: symbol, Cs; at. wt., 132.905; at. no., 55
ces·sa·tion (se sā′shən) ***n.*** [< L. < pp. of *cessare,* CEASE] a ceasing, either final or temporary; stop
ces·sion (sesh′ən) ***n.*** [OFr. < L. < pp. of *cedere,* to yield] a ceding or giving up (of rights, territory, etc.) to another
cess·pool (ses′po͞ol′) ***n.*** [< It. *cesso,* privy < L. *secessus,* place of retirement] **1.** a tank or deep hole in the ground to receive drainage or sewage from the sinks, toilets, etc. of a house **2.** a center of moral filth and corruption
ces·tus (ses′təs) ***n.*** [L. *caestus* < *caedere,* to strike] a device of leather straps, sometimes weighted with metal, worn on the hand by boxers in ancient Rome

CESTUS

ce·su·ra (si zhoor′ə, -zyoor′ə) ***n.,*** *pl.* **-ras, -rae** (-ē) *same as* CAESURA
ce·ta·cean (si tā′shən) ***n.*** [L. *cetus,* whale < Gr. *kētos*] any of an order of nearly hairless, fishlike water mammals with paddlelike forelimbs, including whales, porpoises, and dolphins —***adj.*** of the cetaceans: also **ce·ta′ceous** (-shəs)
ce·vi·tam·ic acid (sē′vī tam′ik, -vi-) [< C + VITAM(IN) + -IC] *same as* ASCORBIC ACID
Cey·lon (sə län′, sā-, sī-) country on an island off the SE tip of India: a member of the Commonwealth: 25,332 sq. mi.; pop. 12,240,000; cap. Colombo: official name *Sri Lanka* —**Cey·lo·nese** (sel′ə nēz′) ***adj., n.***
Cé·zanne (sā zän′), **Paul** 1839–1906; Fr. impressionist & postimpressionist painter
Cf *Chem.* californium
cf. [L. *confer*] compare
CG, C.G. Coast Guard
cg, cg., cgm, cgm. centigram(s)
cgs, c.g.s., C.G.S. centimeter-gram-second
Ch. **1.** Chaldean **2.** China **3.** Chinese
Ch., ch. **1.** chain **2.** champion **3.** chapter **4.** child; children **5.** church
cha·conne (shä kôn′) ***n.*** [Fr. < Sp. *chacona*] **1.** a slow, stately dance of 17th- and 18th-cent. Europe **2.** music for this dance, or a musical form based on this dance
Chad (chad) **1.** country in NC Africa, south of Libya: 495,000 sq. mi.; pop. 3,361,000 **2. Lake,** lake at the juncture of the Chad, Niger, and Nigeria borders —**Chad′i·an** ***adj., n.***
chafe (chāf) ***vt.* chafed, chaf′ing** [< OFr. *chaufer,* to warm < L. < *calere,* to be warm + *facere,* to make] **1.** to rub so as to make warm **2.** to wear away by rubbing **3.** to make sore by rubbing **4.** to annoy; irritate —***vi.*** **1.** to rub (*on* or *against*) **2.** to be vexed —***n.*** an injury or irritation caused by rubbing —**chafe at the bit** to be impatient
chaf·er (chāf′ər) ***n.*** [OE. *ceafor*] any of various beetles that feed on plants
chaff (chaf) ***n.*** [OE. *ceaf*] **1.** threshed or winnowed husks of wheat or other grain **2.** anything worthless **3.** good-natured teasing; banter —***vt., vi.*** to tease or ridicule in a good-natured way —**chaff′y** ***adj.*** **chaff′i·er, chaff′i·est**
chaf·fer (chaf′ər) ***vi.*** [< OE. *ceap,* a purchase] [Now Rare] to haggle over price; bargain —**chaf′fer·er** ***n.***
chaf·finch (chaf′finch′) ***n.*** [OE. *ceaffinc:* see CHAFF + FINCH: it eats chaff] a small European songbird, often kept in a cage as a pet
chaf·ing dish (chāf′iŋ) [see CHAFE] a pan with a heating apparatus beneath it, to cook food at the table or to keep food hot
Cha·gall (shä gäl′), **Marc** 1889– ; Russ. painter, esp. in France
cha·grin (shə grin′) ***n.*** [Fr., grief, prob. < OFr. *graignier,* to sorrow < Gmc. *gram,* sorrow] a feeling of embarrassment and distress caused by failure or disappointment —***vt.*** **-grined′, -grin′ing** to cause to feel chagrin
chain (chān) ***n.*** [OFr. *chaine* < L. *catena,* a chain] **1.** a flexible series of joined links, usually of metal **2.** [*pl.*] *a*) bonds, shackles, etc. *b*) captivity; bondage **3.** a chainlike measuring instrument, or its measure of length: a *surveyor's chain* is 66 feet; an *engineer's chain* is 100 feet **4.** a connected series of things or events **5.** a number of stores, restaurants, etc. owned by one company **6.** *Chem.* a linkage of atoms in a molecule —***vt.*** **1.** to fasten or shackle with chains **2.** to hold down, restrain, confine, etc.
chain gang a gang of prisoners chained together, as when working
chain letter a letter to be circulated among many people by being copied and passed to others
chain mail flexible armor made of metal links
chain-re·act (-rē akt′) ***vi.*** to be involved in or subjected to a chain reaction
chain reaction **1.** a self-sustaining series of chemical or nuclear reactions in which the products of the reaction contribute directly to the propagation of the process **2.** any sequence of events, each of which results in the following
chain saw a portable power saw with an endless chain that carries cutting teeth
chain-smoke (-smōk′) ***vt., vi.*** **-smoked′, -smok′ing** to smoke (cigarettes) one right after the other —**chain smoker, chain′-smok′er** ***n.***
chain stitch a fancy stitch in which the loops are connected in a chainlike way, as in crocheting —**chain′-stitch′** ***vt.***
chain store any of a chain of retail stores
chair (cher) ***n.*** [OFr. *chaiere* < L. *cathedra:* see CATHEDRA] **1.** a piece of furniture for one person to sit on, having a back and, usually, four legs **2.** a seat of authority or dignity **3.** the position of a player in an instrumental section of a symphony orchestra **4.** an important or official position, as a professorship **5.** a person who presides over a meeting; chairman **6.** *same as: a*) SEDAN CHAIR *b*) ELECTRIC CHAIR —***vt.*** **1.** to place in a chair; seat **2.** to place in authority **3.** to preside over as chairman —**take the chair** to preside as chairman
chair·lift (-lift′) ***n.*** a line of seats suspended from a power-driven endless cable, used esp. to carry skiers up a slope
chair·man (-mən) ***n.,*** *pl.* **-men** a person who presides at a meeting or heads a committee, board, etc. —***vt.*** **-maned** or **-manned, -man·ing** or **-man·ning** to preside over as chairman —**chair′man·ship′** ***n.*** —**chair′wom′an** ***n.fem.,*** *pl.* **-wom′en**
chair·per·son (-pur′s'n) ***n.*** *same as* CHAIRMAN: used to avoid the masculine implication of *chairman*
chaise (shāz) ***n.*** [Fr., var. of *chaire,* CHAIR] **1.** any of certain lightweight carriages, some with a collapsible top, having two or four wheels **2.** *same as* CHAISE LONGUE
chaise longue (shāz′ lôŋ′; *often also* lounj′—*see next entry*) *pl.* **chaise** (or **chaises**) **longues** (shāz′ lôŋz′; loun′jəz) [Fr., lit., long chair] a couchlike chair with a support for the back and a seat long enough to support the outstretched legs
chaise lounge (lounj) *pl.* **chaise lounges** [by folk etym. < prec.] *same as* CHAISE LONGUE
cha·la·za (kə lā′zə) ***n.,*** *pl.* **-zae** (-zē), **-zas** [ModL. < Gr. *chalaza,* hailstone] either of the spiral bands of dense albumen extending from the yolk toward the lining membrane at each end of a bird's egg
chal·ced·o·ny (kal sed′'n ē, kal′sə dō′nē) ***n.,*** *pl.* **-nies** [< OFr. < LL. < Gr. *chalkēdōn,* a precious stone < ?] a kind of quartz with the luster of wax, variously colored
Chal·de·a, Chal·dae·a (kal dē′ə) **1.** ancient province of Babylonia, at the head of the Persian Gulf **2.** Babylonia: so called during the supremacy of Chaldea (6th cent. B.C.) —**Chal·de′an, Chal·dae′an, Chal·da′ic** (-dā′ik), **Chal′dee** (-dē) ***adj., n.***
cha·let (sha lā′, shal′ē) ***n.*** [Swiss-Fr., prob. ult. < L. *casa,* a house] **1.** a herdsman's hut or cabin in the Swiss Alps **2.** *a*) a type of Swiss house, with balconies and overhanging eaves *b*) any building in this style
chal·ice (chal′is) ***n.*** [OFr. < L. *calix,* a cup] **1.** a cup; goblet **2.** the cup for the wine of Holy Communion **3.** a cup-shaped flower —**chal′iced** ***adj.***
chalk (chôk) ***n.*** [OE. *cealc* < L. *calx,* limestone] **1.** a white or gray limestone that is soft and easily pulverized, composed mainly of minute seashells **2.** any substance like chalk **3.** a piece of chalk, often colored, used for writing on a blackboard, etc. —***adj.*** made or drawn with chalk —***vt.*** **1.** to rub or smear with chalk **2.** to make pale **3.** to write, draw, or mark with chalk —***vi.*** to become chalky or powdery —**chalk out** **1.** to mark out as with chalk **2.** to outline; plan —**chalk up** **1.** to score, get, or achieve **2.** to charge or credit —**walk a chalk line** [Colloq.] to behave with strict propriety —**chalk′i·ness** ***n.*** —**chalk′y** ***adj.*** **chalk′i·er, chalk′i·est**

chal·lenge (chal′ənj) *n.* [< OFr. < L. *calumnia,* CALUMNY] **1.** a demand for identification *[a sentry gave the challenge]* **2.** a calling into question *[a challenge to an assertion]* **3.** a call or dare to take part in a duel, contest, etc. **4.** anything that calls for special effort or dedication **5.** an exception to a vote or to someone's right to vote **6.** *Law* a formal objection or exception to a person chosen as a prospective juror —*vt.* **-lenged, -leng·ing 1.** to call to a halt for identification **2.** *a)* to call to account *b)* to make an objection to; call into question **3.** to call or dare to take part in a duel, contest, etc.; defy **4.** to call for; make demands on *[to challenge the imagination]* **5.** to take exception to (a vote or voter) as not being valid or qualified **6.** to take formal exception to (a prospective juror) —*vi.* to issue or offer a challenge —**chal′lenge·a·ble** *adj.* —**chal′leng·er** *n.*

chal·lis, chal·lie (shal′ē) *n.* [< ?] a soft, lightweight, usually printed fabric of wool, cotton, etc.

cha·lyb·e·ate (kə lib′ē ət, -āt′) *adj.* [< L. *chalybs* < Gr. *chalyps,* steel] **1.** containing salts of iron **2.** tasting like iron —*n.* a chalybeate liquid

cham·ber (chām′bər) *n.* [< OFr. < LL. *camera:* see CAMERA] **1.** a room in a house, esp. a bedroom **2.** [*pl.*] [Brit.] a suite of rooms used by one person **3.** [*pl.*] a judge's office near the courtroom **4.** an assembly hall **5.** a legislative or judicial body or division *[the Chamber of Deputies]* **6.** a council or board *[a chamber of commerce]* **7.** an enclosed space in the body **8.** a compartment; specif., the part of a gun that holds the charge or cartridge —*vt.* to provide a chamber or chambers for —**cham′bered** *adj.*

cham·ber·lain (-lin) *n.* [< OFr. < OHG. < *chamara* (< L. *camera*) + dim. suffix *-linc:* see CAMERA & -LING[1]] **1.** an officer in charge of the household of a ruler or lord; steward **2.** a high official in certain royal courts **3.** [Brit.] a treasurer

cham·ber·maid (-mād′) *n.* a woman whose work is taking care of bedrooms, as in hotels

chamber music music for performance by a small group, as a string quartet, orig. in a small hall

chamber of commerce an association established to further the business interests of its community

chamber pot a portable container kept in a bedroom and used as a toilet

cham·bray (sham′brā) *n.* [var. of CAMBRIC] a smooth fabric of cotton, made by weaving white or unbleached threads across a colored warp

cha·me·le·on (kə mēl′yən, -mē′lē ən) *n.* [< L. < Gr. < *chamai,* on the ground + *leōn,* lion] **1.** any of various lizards that can change the color of their skin **2.** a changeable or fickle person —**cha·me′le·on′ic** (-mē′lē än′ik) *adj.*

CHAMELEON
(to 24 in. long, including tail)

cham·fer (cham′fər) *n.* [< OFr. < Fr. < L. *cantum frangere:* see CANT[2] & FRAGILE] a beveled edge or corner, esp. one cut at a 45° angle —*vt.* **1.** to cut a chamfer on; bevel **2.** to make a groove or fluting in

cham·ois (sham′ē) *n., pl.* **-ois** [Fr. < VL. *camox*] **1.** a small, goatlike antelope of the mountains of Europe and the Caucasus **2.** *a)* a soft leather made from the skin of chamois, or of sheep, deer, goats, etc. *b)* a piece of this leather, used as a polishing cloth: also **cham·my** (sham′ē), *pl.* **-mies** —*adj.* **1.** made of chamois **2.** yellowish-brown —*vt.* **cham′oised** (-ēd), **cham′ois·ing** (-ē iŋ) to polish with a chamois skin

cham·o·mile (kam′ə mīl′, -mēl′) *n.* [< OFr. < L. < Gr. *chamaimēlon* < *chamai,* on the ground + *mēlon,* apple] any of several plants with strong-smelling foliage; esp., a plant whose dried, daisylike flower heads have been used in a medicinal tea

champ[1] (champ) *vt., vi.* [earlier *cham:* prob. echoic] to chew hard and noisily; munch —*n.* the act of champing —**champ at the bit 1.** to bite upon its bit repeatedly and restlessly: said of a horse **2.** to be restless

champ[2] (champ) *n.* [Slang] *same as* CHAMPION

cham·pagne (sham pān′) *n.* **1.** orig., any of various wines produced in Champagne, a region in NE France **2.** now, any effervescent white wine: a symbol of luxury **3.** pale, tawny yellow

Cham·paign (sham pān′) [see ff.] city in EC Ill.: pop. 58,000

cham·paign (sham pān′) *n.* [< OFr. *champaigne:* see CAMPAIGN] a broad plain; flat, open country —*adj.* of or like a champaign

cham·pi·on (cham′pē ən) *n.* [< OFr. < LL. *campio,* gladiator < L. *campus,* a field] **1.** a person who fights for another or for a cause; defender; supporter **2.** a winner of first place in a competition —*adj.* winning first place; excelling over all others —*vt.* to fight for; defend; support

cham·pi·on·ship (-ship′) *n.* **1.** a championing **2.** the position or title of a champion

Cham·plain (sham plān′), **Lake** [after S. de *Champlain,* 17th-c. Fr. explorer] lake between N.Y. and Vt.

Champs É·ly·sées (shän zā lē zā′) [Fr., lit., Elysian fields] famous avenue in Paris

Chan., Chanc. 1. Chancellor **2.** Chancery

chan. channel

chance (chans) *n.* [< OFr. < ML. < L. prp. of *cadere,* to fall] **1.** the happening of events without apparent cause; fortuity; luck **2.** an unpredictable event or accidental happening **3.** a risk or gamble **4.** a ticket in a lottery or raffle **5.** an opportunity *[a chance to go]* **6.** a possibility or probability *[a chance that he will live]* **7.** *Baseball* a fielding opportunity —*adj.* happening by chance; accidental —*vi.* **chanced, chanc′ing 1.** to have the fortune (*to*) **2.** [Archaic] to happen by chance —*vt.* to leave to chance *[let's chance it]* —**by chance** accidentally —**chance on** (or **upon**) to find by chance —**on the (off) chance** relying on the (remote) possibility

chan·cel (chan′s'l) *n.* [< OFr. < LL. < L. *cancelli, pl.,* lattices: see CANCEL] that part of a church around the altar, reserved for the clergy and the choir: it is sometimes set off by a railing

chan·cel·ler·y (chan′sə lə rē, -slə rē) *n., pl.* **-ler·ies 1.** the position of a chancellor **2.** a chancellor's office or the building that houses it **3.** the office of an embassy or consulate Also sp. **chan′cel·lor·y**

chan·cel·lor (-lər) *n.* [< OFr. < LL. *cancellarius,* keeper of the barrier: see CANCEL] **1.** [usually **C-**] any of several high officials in the British government **2.** the title of the president or a high officer in some universities **3.** the prime minister in certain countries **4.** a chief judge of a court of chancery or equity in some States **5.** a high church official —**chan′cel·lor·ship′** *n.*

chance-med·ley (chans′med′lē) *n.* [see CHANCE & MEDDLE] **1.** accidental homicide **2.** haphazard action

chan·cer·y (chan′sər ē) *n., pl.* **-cer·ies** [< OFr. < ML. *cancellaria:* see CHANCELLOR] **1.** a division of the High Court of Justice in England and Wales **2.** a court of equity **3.** equity law **4.** a court of record **5.** *same as* CHANCELLERY (senses 2 & 3) **6.** *R.C.Ch.* the diocesan office in charge of certain documents, secretarial services, etc. for the bishop —**in chancery 1.** in process of litigation in a court of equity **2.** in a helpless situation

chan·cre (shaŋ′kər) *n.* [Fr.: see CANCER] a venereal sore or ulcer; primary lesion of syphilis —**chan′crous** (-krəs) *adj.*

chan·croid (-kroid) *n.* [CHANCR(E) + -OID] a nonsyphilitic venereal ulcer: also called **soft chancre**

chanc·y (chan′sē) *adj.* **chanc′i·er, chanc′i·est** risky; uncertain

chan·de·lier (shan′də lir′) *n.* [Fr. < OFr. < L. *candelabrum* < *candela,* CANDLE] a lighting fixture hanging from a ceiling, with branches for candles, electric bulbs, etc.

chan·dler (chan′dlər) *n.* [< OFr. < L. *candela,* CANDLE] **1.** a maker or seller of candles **2.** a retailer of supplies, equipment, etc. of a certain kind *[ship chandler]* —**chan′·dler·y** (-ē) *n., pl.* **-dler·ies**

Chang·chun (chäŋ′choon′) city in NE China: pop. 1,800,000

change (chānj) *vt.* **changed, chang′ing** [< OFr. < LL. < L. *cambire,* to barter < Celt.] **1.** to put or take (a thing) in place of something else; substitute *[to change one's clothes]* **2.** to exchange *[let's change seats]* **3.** *a)* to make different; alter *b)* to undergo a variation of *[leaves change color]* **4.** to give or receive the equivalent of (a coin or bank note) in currency of lower denominations or in foreign money **5.** to put a fresh covering, as a diaper, on —*vi.* **1.** *a)* to alter; vary *[the scene changes] b)* to undergo alteration or replacement **2.** to become lower in range, as the male voice at puberty **3.** to leave one train, bus, etc. and board another **4.** to put on other clothes **5.** to make an exchange —*n.* **1.** the act or process of substitution, alteration, or variation **2.** variety **3.** something of the same kind but new or fresh **4.** another set of clothes **5.** *a)* money returned as the difference between the purchase price and the larger sum given in payment *b)* a number of coins or bills whose total value equals a single larger coin or bill *c)* small coins **6.** a place where merchants meet to do business; exchange: also **'change 7.** [*usually pl.*] *Bell Ringing* any order in which the bells may be rung —**change off** to take turns —**ring the changes 1.** to ring a set of bells with all possible variations **2.** to do or say a thing in many and various ways —**change′ful** *adj.* —**change′ful·ly** *adv.* —**change′ful·ness** *n.* —**chang′er** *n.*

change·a·ble (chān′jə b'l) *adj.* **1.** that can change or be changed; alterable **2.** having a changing appearance or color —**change′a·bil′i·ty, change′a·ble·ness** *n.* —**change′a·bly** *adv.*

change·less (chānj′lis) *adj.* unchanging; immutable —**change′less·ly** *adv.* —**change′less·ness** *n.*

change·ling (-liŋ) *n.* a child secretly put in the place of another, esp., in folk tales, by fairies

change of life *same as* MENOPAUSE

change·o·ver (-ō′vər) ***n.*** a complete change, as in goods produced, equipment, etc.
change ringing the art of ringing a series of unrepeated changes on a set of bells tuned together
chan·nel (chan′'l) ***n.*** [< OFr.: see CANAL] **1.** the bed of a river, etc. **2.** the deeper part of a river, harbor, etc. **3.** a body of water joining two larger bodies of water **4.** a tubelike passage for liquids **5.** any means of passage or transmission **6.** [*pl.*] the proper or official course of action [to make a request through army *channels]* **7.** a long groove or furrow **8.** a narrow frequency band within which a radio or television transmitting station must keep its signal —***vt.*** **-neled** or **-nelled, -nel·ing** or **-nel·ling** **1.** to make a channel or channels in **2.** to send through or direct into a channel
Channel Islands group of Brit. islands in the English Channel, off the coast of Normandy
‡**chan·son** (shän sōn′; *E.* shan′sən) ***n.,*** *pl.* **-sons′** (-sōn′; *E.* -sənz) [Fr.] a song
chant (chant) ***n.*** [Fr. < L. *cantus,* song < the *v.*] **1.** a song; melody **2.** *a)* a simple liturgical song in which a series of syllables or words is sung to each tone *b)* words, as of a psalm, to be sung in this way **3.** *a)* a singsong way of speaking *b)* anything uttered in this way —***vi.*** [< OFr. < L. *cantare,* freq. of *canere,* to sing] **1.** to sing a chant; intone **2.** to speak monotonously or repetitiously —***vt.*** **1.** to sing **2.** to celebrate in song **3.** to say monotonously **4.** to intone
chan·teuse (shan to͞oz′) ***n.*** [Fr.] a woman singer
chan·tey (shan′tē, chan′tē) ***n.,*** *pl.* **-teys** [< ? Fr.: see CHANT] a song that sailors sing in rhythm with their motions while working: also **chan′ty,** *pl.* **-ties**
chan·ti·cleer (chan′tə klir′) ***n.*** [< OFr.: see CHANT & CLEAR] a rooster: name used in fable and folklore
Cha·nu·kah (khä′no͝o kä′) ***n.*** *same as* HANUKA
cha·os (kā′äs) ***n.*** [L. < Gr. *chaos,* space, chaos (sense 1)] **1.** the disorder of formless matter and infinite space, supposed to have existed before the ordered universe **2.** extreme confusion or disorder
cha·ot·ic (kā ät′ik) ***adj.*** in a state of chaos; in a completely confused or disordered condition —**cha·ot′i·cal·ly** ***adv.***
chap[1] (chäp, chap) ***n.*** [prob. < ME. *cheppe* < ?] *same as* CHOP[2]
chap[2] (chap) ***n.*** [< CHAPMAN] [Colloq.] a man or boy; fellow
chap[3] (chap) ***vt., vi.*** **chapped** or **chapt, chap′ping** [ME. *chappen,* var. of *choppen* (see CHOP[1])] to crack open or roughen, as the skin from exposure to cold —***n.*** a chapped place in the skin
chap. 1. chaplain **2.** chapter
cha·pa·re·jos, cha·pa·ra·jos (chap′ə rā′hōs, shap′-) ***n.pl.*** [MexSp.] [Southwest] *same as* CHAPS[1]
chap·ar·ral (chap′ə ral′, shap′-) ***n.*** [Sp. < *chaparro,* evergreen oak] [Southwest] a thicket of shrubs, thorny bushes, etc., orig. of evergreen oaks
chap·book (chap′bo͝ok′) ***n.*** [< CHAP(MAN): chapmen peddled such books] a small book or pamphlet of poems, ballads, religious tracts, etc.
cha·peau (sha pō′) ***n.,*** *pl.* **-peaus′, -peaux′** (-pōz′) [Fr. < OFr. < VL. *capellus,* dim. of LL. *cappa:* see CAPE[1]] a hat
chap·el (chap′'l) ***n.*** [< OFr. < ML. < VL. (see prec.): orig. sanctuary in which cloak of St. Martin was preserved] **1.** a place of Christian worship smaller than a church **2.** a room or building used as a place of worship, as in a school **3.** a small room in a church, having its own altar **4.** a religious service, as in a chapel **5.** in Great Britain, any place of worship for those who are not members of an established church
chap·er·on, chap·er·one (shap′ə rōn′) ***n.*** [Fr. < OFr., hood (hence, protector) < *chape,* COPE[2]] a person, esp. an older or married woman, who accompanies young unmarried people in public or attends their parties, etc. for propriety or to supervise their behavior —***vt., vi.*** **-oned′, -on′ing** to act as chaperon (to) —**chap′er·on′age** ***n.***
chap·fall·en (chäp′fô′lən, chap′-) ***adj.*** [CHAP[1] + FALLEN] **1.** having the lower jaw hanging down, as from fatigue **2.** disheartened, depressed, or humiliated
chap·lain (chap′lən) ***n.*** [< OFr. < ML.: see CHAPEL] **1.** a clergyman attached to a chapel, as of a royal court **2.** a minister, priest, or rabbi serving in a religious capacity with the armed forces or in a prison, hospital, etc. **3.** a clergyman, or sometimes a layman, appointed to perform religious functions in a public institution, club, etc. —**chap′lain·cy,** *pl.* **-cies, chap′lain·ship′** ***n.***
chap·let (chap′lit) ***n.*** [< OFr. dim. of *chapel* < VL. *capellus:* see CHAPEAU] **1.** a garland for the head **2.** *a)* a string of prayer beads one third the length of a full rosary *b)* the prayers said with such beads **3.** any string of beads —**chap′let·ed** ***adj.***
Chap·lin (chap′lin), Sir **Charles Spencer** 1889–1977; Eng. motion-picture actor & producer
chap·man (chap′mən) ***n.,*** *pl.* **-men** [< OE. < *ceap,* trade + *man*] [Brit.] a peddler; hawker
chaps[1] (chaps, shaps) ***n.pl.*** [< CHAPAREJOS] leather trousers without a seat, worn over ordinary trousers by cowboys to protect their legs
chaps[2] (chäps, chaps) ***n.pl.*** [see CHAP[1]] *same as* CHOPS
chap·ter (chap′tər) ***n.*** [< OFr. *chapitre* < L. CAPITULUM, dim. of *caput,* head] **1.** a main division, as of a book **2.** a thing like a chapter; part; episode **3.** *a)* a formal meeting of canons of a church or of the members of a religious order *b)* the group of such canons, etc. **4.** a local branch of a club, fraternity, etc. —***vt.*** to divide into chapters
char[1] (chär) ***vt., vi.*** **charred, char′ring** [< CHARCOAL] **1.** to burn to charcoal **2.** to scorch —***n.*** anything charred

CHAPS

char[2] (chär) ***n.*** [< CHARWOMAN] [Brit.] a charwoman —***vi.*** **charred, char′ring** [Chiefly Brit.] to work as a charwoman
char[3] (chär) ***n.,*** *pl.* **chars, char:** see PLURAL, II, D, 1 [< Gael. *ceara,* red] any of a genus of trouts with a red belly
char·a·banc, char-à-banc (shar′ə baŋk′, -baŋ′) ***n.*** [Fr., lit., car with bench] [Brit.] a sightseeing bus
char·ac·ter (kar′ik tər) ***n.*** [< OFr. < L. < Gr. *charaktēr,* an engraving instrument < *charattein,* to engrave] **1.** a distinctive mark **2.** any figure, letter, or symbol used in writing and printing **3.** a distinctive trait or quality **4.** nature; kind or sort **5.** the pattern of behavior or personality found in an individual or group **6.** moral strength; self-discipline, fortitude, etc. **7.** *a)* reputation *b)* good reputation **8.** status; position **9.** a personage [great *characters* in history] **10.** a person in a play, novel, etc. **11.** [Colloq.] an odd, eccentric, or noteworthy person **12.** *Biol.* any attribute, as color, shape, etc., caused by the action of one or more genes —**in** (or **out of**) **character** consistent with (or inconsistent with) the role or general character
character actor an actor usually cast in the role of a person with pronounced or eccentric characteristics —**character actress** ***fem.***
char·ac·ter·is·tic (kar′ik tə ris′tik) ***adj.*** of or constituting the special character; typical; distinctive —***n.*** **1.** a distinguishing trait, feature, or quality **2.** the whole number, or integral part, of a logarithm, as 4 in the logarithm 4.7193: cf. MANTISSA —**char′ac·ter·is′ti·cal·ly** ***adv.***
char·ac·ter·ize (kar′ik tə rīz′) ***vt.*** **-ized′, -iz′ing** **1.** to describe or portray the particular traits of **2.** to be the distinctive character of; distinguish —**char′ac·ter·i·za′tion** ***n.***
cha·rade (shə rād′) ***n.*** [Fr. < Pr. *charrada* < *charrar,* to gossip] **1.** [*often pl.*] a game in which a word or phrase to be guessed is acted out in pantomime **2.** a pretense or fiction that can be seen through readily
char·broil, char-broil (chär′broil′) ***vt.*** [CHAR(COAL) + BROIL] to broil over a charcoal fire
char·coal (chär′kōl′) ***n.*** [ME. *char cole,* prob. < *charren,* to turn + *cole,* coal] **1.** a form of carbon produced by partially burning organic matter, as wood, in kilns from which air is excluded **2.** a pencil made of this substance **3.** a drawing made with such a pencil **4.** a very dark gray or brown, almost black —***vt.*** to draw with charcoal
chard (chärd) ***n.*** [Fr. *carde* < L. *carduus,* thistle] a kind of beet whose large leaves and thick stalks are used as food
chare (cher) ***n.*** [OE. *cierr,* a turn, job < *cierran,* to turn] a chore, esp. a household chore —***vi.*** **chared, char′ing** **1.** to do chores **2.** *same as* CHAR[2]
charge (chärj) ***vt.*** **charged, charg′ing** [< OFr. *chargier* < VL. *carricare,* to load < L. *carrus,* car, wagon] **1.** to load or fill with the required material [*charged* with gunpowder] **2.** to saturate with another substance [air *charged* with steam] **3.** to add carbon dioxide to (water, etc.) **4.** to add an electrical charge to (a battery, etc.) **5.** to give as a task, duty, etc. to **6.** to give instructions to or command authoritatively **7.** to accuse of wrongdoing; censure [he *charged* her with negligence] **8.** to make liable for (an error, etc.) **9.** to ask as a price or fee [to *charge* $20 for labor] **10.** to record as a debt against a person or his account [to *charge* a purchase] **11.** to attack vigorously —***vi.*** **1.** to ask payment (*for*) [to *charge* for a service] **2.** to attack vigorously or move forward as if attacking —***n.*** **1.** the amount, as of fuel, gunpowder, etc., used to load or fill something **2.** *a)* the amount of chemical energy stored in a battery and dischargeable as electrical energy *b)* a change from the condition of electrical neutrality by the accumulation of electrons (*negative charge*) or by the loss of elec-

trons (*positive charge*) **3.** [Slang] a thrill **4.** responsibility or duty (*of*) **5.** care or custody (*of*) **6.** a person or thing entrusted to someone's care **7.** instruction or command, esp. instructions given by a judge to a jury **8.** accusation; indictment *[charges* of cruelty*]* **9.** the cost or price of an article, service, etc. **10.** a debt **11.** *same as* CHARGE ACCOUNT **12.** *a)* an attack, as by troops *b)* the signal for this **13.** *Heraldry* a bearing —**charge off 1.** to regard as a loss **2.** to ascribe —**in charge** having the responsibility or control —**charge′a·ble** (chär′jə b'l) *adj.*

charge account an arrangement by which a customer may pay for purchases within a specified future period

char·gé d'af·faires (shär zhā′ də fer′) *pl.* **char·gés d'af·faires** (shär zhāz′ də fer′, shär zhā′ də fer′) [Fr.] **1.** a diplomat substituting for a minister or ambassador **2.** a diplomat ranking below an ambassador or minister

charge plate a metal or plastic plate embossed with the owner's name and address, for stamping his bills when he makes purchases on credit: also **charge card**

charg·er[1] (chär′jər) *n.* **1.** one that charges **2.** a horse ridden in battle or on parade **3.** an apparatus for charging storage batteries

charg·er[2] (chär′jər) *n.* [ME. *chargeour*] [Archaic] a large, flat dish; platter

char·i·ly (cher′ə lē) *adv.* in a chary manner

char·i·ness (-ē nis) *n.* the quality of being chary

char·i·ot (char′ē ət) *n.* [< OFr. < VL. *carricare:* see CHARGE] a horse-drawn, two-wheeled cart used in ancient times for war, racing, etc. —*vt., vi.* to drive or ride in a chariot

CHARIOT

char·i·ot·eer (char′ē ə tir′) *n.* a chariot driver

cha·ris·ma (kə riz′mə) *n., pl.* **-ma·ta** (-mə tə) [< Gr., favor, grace] **1.** *Christian Theol.* a divinely inspired gift or talent, as for prophesying **2.** a special quality of leadership that inspires great popular allegiance Also **char·ism** (kar′iz'm)

char·is·mat·ic (kar′iz mat′ik) *adj.* **1.** having or resulting from charisma **2.** designating or of any religious group or movement that stresses direct divine inspiration —*n.* **1.** a member of a charismatic group or movement **2.** a person who supposedly has some divinely inspired power, as the ability to prophesy

char·i·ta·ble (char′i tə b'l) *adj.* **1.** kind and generous in giving help to those in need **2.** of or for charity **3.** kind and forgiving in judging others —**char′i·ta·bly** *adv.*

char·i·ty (char′ə tē) *n., pl.* **-ties** [< OFr. < L. *caritas,* affection < *carus,* dear] **1.** *Christian Theol.* the love of God for man or of man for his fellow men **2.** an act of good will **3.** benevolence **4.** kindness in judging others **5.** a voluntary giving of money, etc. to those in need **6.** a welfare institution, organization, etc.

cha·ri·va·ri (shə riv′ə rē′, shiv ə rē′, shiv′ə rē) *n.* [Fr. < LL. < Gr. *karēbaria,* heavy head] *same as* SHIVAREE

char·la·tan (shär′lə t'n) *n.* [Fr. < It. *ciarlatano* < LL. *cerretanus,* seller of papal indulgences] one who pretends to have expert knowledge or skill that he does not have; fake —**char′la·tan·ism, char′la·tan·ry,** *pl.* **-ries** *n.*

Char·le·magne (shär′lə mān′) 742–814 A.D.; king of the Franks (768–814); emperor of the Holy Roman Empire (800–814): also called **Charles the Great**

Charles (chärlz) [Fr. < ML. *Carolus* (or) < Gmc. *Karl;* lit., full-grown] **1.** a masculine name: dim. *Charley, Charlie* **2. Charles I** *a)* 1600–49; king of England, Scotland, & Ireland (1625–49) *b) same as* CHARLEMAGNE **3. Charles II** 1630–85; king of England, Scotland, & Ireland (1660–85): son of *Charles I* **4. Charles V** 1500–58; Holy Roman Emperor (1519–56) &, as **Charles I,** king of Spain (1516–56)

Charles's Wain (chärl′ziz) [Brit.] *same as* BIG DIPPER

Charles·ton (chärl′stən) [after CHARLES I of England] **1.** capital of W.Va., in the W part: pop. 64,000 **2.** seaport in S.C.: pop. 70,000 —*n.* [< the seaport] a lively dance in 4/4 time, characterized by a twisting step

char·ley horse (chär′lē) [Colloq.] a cramp in the leg or arm muscles, caused by strain

char·lock (chär′lək) *n.* [OE. *cerlic*] a weed of the mustard family, with yellow flowers

Char·lotte (shär′lət) [Fr., fem. of *Charlot,* dim. of *Charles*] **1.** a feminine name **2.** [after Queen *Charlotte,* wife of GEORGE III] city in S N.C.: pop. 314,000 (met. area 632,000)

char·lotte (shär′lət) *n.* [Fr. < prec.] a dessert made of fruit, gelatin, custard, etc. in a mold lined with strips of bread, cake, etc.

Charlotte A·ma·lie (ə mäl′yə, ə mäl′ē) capital of the Virgin Islands of the U.S.: pop. 12,000

charlotte russe (ro͞os) [Fr., Russian charlotte] a charlotte of whipped cream, custard, etc. in a spongecake mold

Char·lotte·town (shär′lət toun′) capital of Prince Edward Island, Canada: pop. 18,000

charm (chärm) *n.* [< OFr. < L. *carmen,* song, charm] **1.** a chanted word or verse, an action, or an object assumed to have magic power to help or hurt **2.** a trinket on a bracelet, watch chain, etc. **3.** a quality or feature that attracts or delights —*vt.* **1.** to act on as though by magic **2.** to attract or please greatly; fascinate; delight —*vi.* to be charming —**charm′er** *n.*

charm·ing (chärm′iŋ) *adj.* attractive; fascinating; delightful —**charm′ing·ly** *adv.*

char·nel (chär′n'l) *n.* [OFr. < LL. *carnale,* graveyard; neut. of *carnalis,* CARNAL] a building or place where corpses or bones are deposited: in full, **charnel house** —*adj.* of, like, or fit for a charnel

Cha·ron (ker′ən) *Gr. Myth.* the boatman who ferried souls of the dead across the river Styx to Hades

charr (chär) *n., pl.* **charrs, charr:** see PLURAL, II, D, 1 *same as* CHAR[3]

char·ry (chär′ē) *adj.* **-ri·er, -ri·est** like charcoal

chart (chärt) *n.* [OFr. < ML. < L. *charta:* see CARD[1]] **1.** a map, esp. one for marine or air navigation **2.** an outline map on which special information, as on weather, is plotted geographically **3.** *a)* a group of facts set up in the form of a diagram, graph, etc. *b)* such a diagram, graph, etc., or a sheet with diagrams, etc. —*vt.* **1.** to make a chart of **2.** to plan (a course of action) **3.** to show by, on, or as by, a chart —**chart′less** *adj.*

char·ter (chär′tər) *n.* [< OFr. < L. dim. of *charta:* see CARD[1]] **1.** a franchise or written grant of specified rights given by a government or ruler to a person, corporation, etc. **2.** *a)* a document setting forth the aims and principles of a united group, as of nations *b)* a document embodying a city constitution **3.** a document authorizing the organization of a local chapter of a society **4.** the hire or lease of a ship, bus, etc. —*vt.* **1.** to grant a charter to **2.** to hire for exclusive use —**char′ter·er** *n.*

charter member one of the founders or original members of an organization

Char·tres (shär′tr′; *E.* shärt) city in NC France: site of a Gothic cathedral: pop. 31,000

char·treuse (shär tro͞oz′, -tro͞os′; *Fr.* shȧr trëz′) *n.* [Fr., Carthusian] **1.** a yellow, pale-green, or white liqueur made by Carthusian monks **2.** pale, yellowish green

char·wom·an (chär′woom′ən) *n., pl.* **-wom′en** [see CHARE, CHORE] a woman who does cleaning or scrubbing, as in office buildings

char·y (cher′ē, char′ē) *adj.* **char′i·er, char′i·est** [OE. *cearig* < *cearu,* care] **1.** not taking chances; cautious **2.** not giving freely; sparing

Cha·ryb·dis (kə rib′dis) whirlpool off the NE coast of Sicily: see SCYLLA

chase[1] (chās) *vt.* **chased, chas′ing** [< OFr. *chacier, cachier:* see CATCH] **1.** to follow quickly or persistently so as to catch or harm **2.** to run after; follow **3.** to make run away; drive —*vi.* **1.** to go in pursuit **2.** [Colloq.] to go hurriedly; rush —*n.* **1.** a chasing; pursuit **2.** the hunting of game for sport (often with *the*) —**give chase** to chase

chase[2] (chās) *n.* [OFr. *châsse,* a frame, ult. < L. *capsa:* see CASE[2]] **1.** a groove; furrow **2.** a rectangular metal frame in which pages or columns of type are locked —*vt.* **chased, chas′ing** to make a groove or furrow in; indent

chase[3] (chās) *vt.* **chased, chas′ing** [< Fr. *enchâsser,* enshrine] to ornament (metal) by engraving, embossing, etc.

chas·er (chā′sər) *n.* **1.** one that chases or hunts **2.** [Colloq.] a mild drink, as water, taken after or with whiskey

chasm (kaz′'m) *n.* [L. & Gr. *chasma* < Gr. *chainein,* to gape] **1.** a deep crack in the earth's surface; abyss; gorge **2.** any break or gap **3.** a wide divergence of feelings, interests, etc.; rift —**chas′mal** (-m'l), **chas′mic** (-mik) *adj.*

chas·seur (sha sʉr′) *n.* [Fr.] **1.** a hunter **2.** a soldier, esp. one of certain French troops, trained for rapid action **3.** a uniformed attendant

Chas·sid·im (has′i dim; *Heb.* khä sē′-) *n.pl., sing.* **Chas′sid** *same as* HASIDIM —**Chas·sid′ic** *adj.* —**Chas′sid·ism** *n.*

chas·sis (chas′ē, shas′ē) *n., pl.* **-sis** (-ēz) [Fr. *châssis:* see CHASE[2]] **1.** the frame, wheels, etc. of a motor vehicle, but not the body and engine **2.** the frame supporting the body of an airplane **3.** *Radio & TV a)* the framework to which the parts of a receiver, amplifier, etc. are attached *b)* the assembled frame and parts **4.** [Slang] the body; figure

chaste (chāst) *adj.* [OFr. < L. *castus,* pure: see CASTE] **1.** not indulging in unlawful sexual activity; virtuous: said esp. of women **2.** sexually abstinent; celibate **3.** pure; decent; modest **4.** restrained and simple in style —**chaste′ly** *adv.* —**chaste′ness** *n.*

chas·ten (chās′'n) *vt.* [< OFr. < L. *castigare,* to punish < *castus,* pure + *agere,* to lead] **1.** to punish so as to correct; chastise **2.** to restrain from excess; subdue **3.** to refine in style —**chas′ten·er** *n.*

chas·tise (chas tīz′, chas′tīz) *vt.* **-tised′, -tis′ing** [see prec.] **1.** to punish, esp. by beating **2.** to scold or condemn sharply —**chas·tise′ment** *n.* —**chas·tis′er** *n.*

chas·ti·ty (chas′tə tē) *n.* [see CHASTE] the quality or state of being chaste; specif., *a)* virtuousness *b)* sexual abstinence *c)* decency *d)* simplicity of style

chas·u·ble (chaz′yoo b'l, chas′-) *n.* [OFr. < ML. *casubla,* hooded garment] a sleeveless outer vestment worn over the alb by priests at Mass

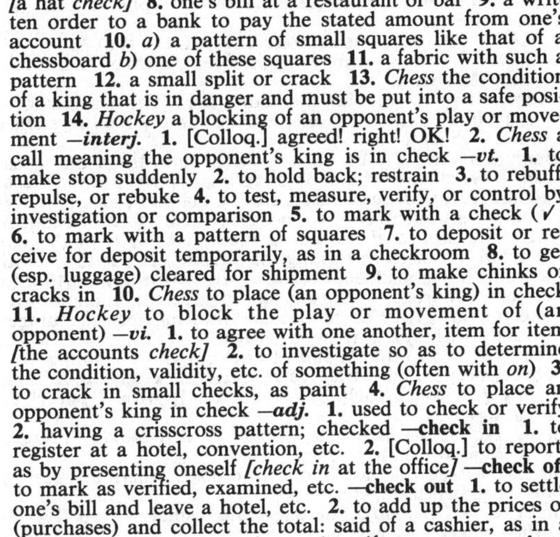
CHASUBLE

chat (chat) *vi.* **chat′ted, chat′ting** [< CHATTER] to talk or converse in a light, easy, informal way —*n.* **1.** a light, easy, informal conversation **2.** any of various birds with a chattering call

châ·teau (sha tō′) *n., pl.* **-teaux′** (-tōz′, -tō′), **-teaus′** [Fr. < OFr. < L. *castellum,* CASTLE] **1.** a French feudal castle **2.** a large country house, esp. in France Also **cha·teau′**

cha·teau·bri·and (shȧ tō brē än′) *n.* [after F. R. de *Chateaubriand* (1768–1848), Fr. statesman] a thick beef fillet from the center of the tenderloin

chat·e·laine (shat′'l ān′) *n.* [Fr., ult. < L. *castellum,* CASTLE] **1.** the mistress of a castle or of any large household **2.** a woman's ornamental chain or clasp, esp. for the waist, with keys, a watch, etc. fastened to it

Chat·ta·noo·ga (chat′ə nōō′gə) [< AmInd.] city in SE Tenn., on the Ga. border: pop. 170,000

chat·tel (chat′'l) *n.* [OFr. *chatel:* see CATTLE] **1.** *a)* a movable item of personal property, as a piece of furniture: in full, **chattel personal** *b)* any interest in real estate less than a freehold: in full, **chattel real** **2.** [Archaic] a slave

chattel mortgage a mortgage on personal property

chat·ter (chat′ər) *vi.* [echoic] **1.** to make short, indistinct sounds in rapid succession, as birds, apes, etc. **2.** to talk fast, incessantly, and foolishly **3.** to click together rapidly, as the teeth do from fright or cold —*vt.* to utter with a chattering sound —*n.* **1.** the act or sound of chattering **2.** rapid, foolish talk —**chat′ter·er** *n.*

chat·ter·box (-bäks′) *n.* an incessant talker

chat·ty (chat′ē) *adj.* **-ti·er, -ti·est** **1.** fond of chatting **2.** light, familiar, and informal: said of talk —**chat′ti·ly** *adv.* —**chat′ti·ness** *n.*

Chau·cer (chô′sər), **Geoffrey** 1340?–1400; Eng. poet: author of *The Canterbury Tales* —**Chau·ce′ri·an** (-sir′ē ən) *adj.*

chauf·feur (shō′fər, shō fʉr′) *n.* [Fr., lit., stoker < *chauffer,* to heat: see CHAFE] a person hired to drive a private automobile for someone else —*vt.* to act as chauffeur to

chaunt (chônt) *n., vt., vi. archaic var. of* CHANT

chau·tau·qua (shə tô′kwə) *n.* [< the summer schools inaugurated at Chautauqua, N.Y., in 1874] an educational and recreational assembly with a program of lectures, etc.

chau·vin·ism (shō′və niz′m) *n.* [< Fr. < N. *Chauvin,* Napoleonic soldier, notorious for his fanatical patriotism] **1.** militant, boastful, and fanatical patriotism **2.** unreasoning devotion to one's race, sex, etc., with contempt for other races, the opposite sex, etc. —**chau′vin·ist** *n., adj.* —**chau′vin·is′tic** *adj.* —**chau′vin·is′ti·cal·ly** *adv.*

chaw (chô) *n. dial. var. of* CHEW (*n.* 2)

cheap (chēp) *adj.* [< *good cheap,* good bargain < OE. *ceap,* a bargain] **1.** low in price; not expensive **2.** charging low prices **3.** spending little **4.** worth more than the price **5.** easily got **6.** of little or no value **7.** contemptible **8.** [Colloq.] stingy; miserly **9.** lowered in buying power or available at low interest rates: said of money —*adv.* at low cost —**cheap′ly** *adv.* —**cheap′ness** *n.*

cheap·en (chēp′'n) *vt., vi.* to make or become cheap or cheaper —**cheap′en·er** *n.*

cheap-jack (-jak′) *n.* [CHEAP + JACK] a peddler of cheap, inferior articles —*adj.* cheap, inferior, base, etc. Also **cheap′-john′** (-jän′)

cheap·skate (-skāt′) *n.* [Slang] a miserly person

cheat (chēt) *n.* [< ME. *eschete:* see ESCHEAT] **1.** a fraud; deception **2.** one who deceives or defrauds others; swindler —*vt.* **1.** to defraud; swindle **2.** to deceive by trickery; fool **3.** to foil or escape by tricks or good luck [to *cheat* death] —*vi.* **1.** to practice fraud or deception **2.** [Slang] to be sexually unfaithful (often with *on*) —**cheat′er** *n.* —**cheat′ing·ly** *adv.*

check (chek) *n.* [OFr. *eschec,* a check at chess < ML. *scaccus* < Per. *shāh,* king] **1.** a sudden stop **2.** any restraint or control of action **3.** one that restrains or controls **4.** a supervision of accuracy, efficiency, etc. **5.** *a)* a test, comparison, etc. to see if something is as it should be *b)* a standard or sample used for this **6.** a mark (✓) to show approval or verification or to call attention to something **7.** an identification token enabling one to re-claim an item [a hat *check*] **8.** one's bill at a restaurant or bar **9.** a written order to a bank to pay the stated amount from one's account **10.** *a)* a pattern of small squares like that of a chessboard *b)* one of these squares **11.** a fabric with such a pattern **12.** a small split or crack **13.** *Chess* the condition of a king that is in danger and must be put into a safe position **14.** *Hockey* a blocking of an opponent's play or movement —*interj.* **1.** [Colloq.] agreed! right! OK! **2.** *Chess* a call meaning the opponent's king is in check —*vt.* **1.** to make stop suddenly **2.** to hold back; restrain **3.** to rebuff, repulse, or rebuke **4.** to test, measure, verify, or control by investigation or comparison **5.** to mark with a check (✓) **6.** to mark with a pattern of squares **7.** to deposit or receive for deposit temporarily, as in a checkroom **8.** to get (esp. luggage) cleared for shipment **9.** to make chinks or cracks in **10.** *Chess* to place (an opponent's king) in check **11.** *Hockey* to block the play or movement of (an opponent) —*vi.* **1.** to agree with one another, item for item [the accounts *check*] **2.** to investigate so as to determine the condition, validity, etc. of something (often with *on*) **3.** to crack in small checks, as paint **4.** *Chess* to place an opponent's king in check —*adj.* **1.** used to check or verify **2.** having a crisscross pattern; checked —**check in** **1.** to register at a hotel, convention, etc. **2.** [Colloq.] to report, as by presenting oneself [*check in* at the office] —**check off** to mark as verified, examined, etc. —**check out** **1.** to settle one's bill and leave a hotel, etc. **2.** to add up the prices of (purchases) and collect the total: said of a cashier, as in a supermarket **3.** to examine and verify or approve **4.** to prove to be accurate, sound, etc. upon examination **5.** [Slang] to die —**check up on** to examine or investigate —**in check** in restraint; under control

check·book (-book′) *n.* a book containing detachable forms for writing checks on a bank

checked (chekt) *adj.* having a pattern of squares

check·er¹ (chek′ər) *n.* [OFr. *eschekier,* a chessboard < *eschec:* see CHECK] **1.** a small square, as on a chessboard **2.** a pattern of such squares **3.** *a)* [*pl., with sing. v.*] a game played on a checkerboard by two players, each with twelve round, flat pieces to move *b)* any of these pieces —*vt.* **1.** to mark off in squares **2.** to break the uniformity of, as with varied features, changes in fortune, etc.

check·er² (chek′ər) *n.* **1.** a person who examines or verifies **2.** a person who checks hats, luggage, etc. **3.** a cashier, as in a supermarket

check·er·ber·ry (-ber′ē) *n., pl.* **-ries** **1.** *same as* WINTERGREEN (sense 1) **2.** the edible, red, berrylike fruit of the wintergreen

check·er·board (-bôrd′) *n.* a board with 64 squares of two alternating colors, used in checkers and chess

check·ered (-ərd) *adj.* **1.** having a pattern of squares **2.** varied in color and shading **3.** marked by diversified features or by varied events, as a career

checking account a bank account against which the depositor can draw checks at any time

check·list (-list′) *n.* a list of things to be checked off or referred to: also **check list**

check·mate (-māt′) *n.* [OFr. *eschec mat,* ult. < Per. *shāh māt,* lit., the king is dead] **1.** *Chess a)* the winning move that checks the opponent's king so that it cannot be put into safety *b)* the king's position after this move **2.** complete defeat, frustration, etc. —*interj. Chess* a call indicating checkmate —*vt.* **-mat′ed, -mat′ing** **1.** to place in checkmate **2.** to defeat completely

check·off (-ôf′) *n.* an arrangement by which dues of trade-union members are withheld from wages and turned over to the union by the employer

check·out (-out′) *n.* **1.** the act or place of checking out purchases, as in a supermarket **2.** the time by which one must check out of a hotel, etc. **3.** a testing, esp. of a machine, as for accuracy Also **check′-out′**

check·point (-point′) *n.* a place where traffic is stopped by authorities, as for inspection

check·rein (-rān′) *n.* a short rein attached to the bridle to keep a horse's head up

check·room (-rōōm′, -room′) *n.* a room in which to check (*vt.* 7) hats, coats, parcels, etc.

check·up (-up′) *n.* an examination or investigation, esp. a general medical examination

Ched·dar (cheese) (ched′ər) [< *Cheddar,* Somersetshire, England, where orig. made] [*often* **c-**] a variety of hard, smooth cheese

cheek (chēk) *n.* [OE. *ceoke,* jaw, jawbone] **1.** either side of the face, below the eye **2.** either of two sides of a thing, as the jaws of a vise: *usually used in pl.* **3.** either of the buttocks **4.** [Colloq.] sauciness; impudence —**cheek by jowl**

close together; intimately —**(with) tongue in cheek** in a humorously ironic or insincere way
cheek·bone (-bōn′) *n.* the bone of the upper cheek, just below the eye
cheek·y (-ē) *adj.* **cheek′i·er, cheek′i·est** [CHEEK + -Y2] [Colloq.] saucy; impudent; insolent —**cheek′i·ly** *adv.* —**cheek′i·ness** *n.*
cheep (chēp) *n.* [echoic] the short, faint, shrill sound of a young bird; peep —*vt., vi.* to make, or utter with, such a sound —**cheep′er** *n.*
cheer (chir) *n.* [< OFr. *chiere* < LL. *cara,* the head < Gr. *kara*] **1.** state of mind or of feeling; spirit: now in **be of good cheer, with good cheer,** etc. **2.** gladness; joy **3.** festive food or entertainment **4.** encouragement **5.** *a)* a shout of welcome, approval, encouragement, etc. *b)* a jingle, etc. shouted in unison in rooting for a team —*vt.* **1.** to fill with joy and hope; gladden; comfort (often with *up*) **2.** to urge on or encourage by cheers **3.** to greet or applaud with cheers —*vi.* **1.** to be or become cheerful; feel encouraged (usually with *up*) **2.** to shout cheers
cheer·ful (-fəl) *adj.* **1.** full of cheer; joyful **2.** filling with cheer; bright and attractive *[a cheerful room]* **3.** willing; ready *[a cheerful helper]* —**cheer′ful·ly** *adv.* —**cheer′ful·ness** *n.*
cheer·i·o (-ē ō′) *interj., n., pl.* **-os′** [Brit. Colloq.] **1.** goodbye **2.** good health: a toast
cheer·lead·er (-lē′dər) *n.* one who leads others in cheering for a football team, etc.
cheer·less (-lis) *adj.* not cheerful; dismal —**cheer′less·ly** *adv.* —**cheer′less·ness** *n.*
cheers (chirz) *interj.* [Chiefly Brit.] good health: a toast
cheer·y (chir′ē) *adj.* **cheer′i·er, cheer′i·est** cheerful —**cheer′i·ly** *adv.* —**cheer′i·ness** *n.*
cheese[1] (chēz) *n.* [OE. *cyse,* akin to L. *caseus*] **1.** a food made from curds of soured milk pressed together to form a solid, variously hardened, ripened, etc. **2.** a shaped mass of this
cheese[2] (chēz) *n.* [Hindi *chīz* (< Per. *čiz*), thing] [Slang] an important person or thing
cheese·burg·er (chēz′bur′gər) *n.* [CHEESE1 + -BURGER] a hamburger topped with melted cheese
cheese·cake (-kāk′) *n.* **1.** a kind of cake made of cottage cheese or cream cheese, eggs, sugar, etc., usually baked with a bottom crust of crumbs **2.** [Slang] display of the figure, esp. the legs, of a pretty girl, as in photographs
cheese·cloth (-klôth′) *n.* [from use as cheese wrapping] a thin cotton cloth with a loose weave
cheese·par·ing (-per′iŋ) *n.* **1.** anything as worthless as a paring of cheese rind **2.** miserly handling of money —*adj.* stingy; miserly
chees·y (-ē) *adj.* **chees′i·er, chees′i·est 1.** like cheese **2.** [Slang] inferior; poor —**chees′i·ness** *n.*
chee·tah (chēt′ə) *n.* [Hindi *chītā* < Sans. *citra,* spotted] a swift, leopardlike animal of Africa and S Asia, with a small head, long legs, and a black-spotted, tawny coat: it can be trained to hunt
chef (shef) *n.* [Fr. < *chef de cuisine,* lit., head of the kitchen: see CHIEF] **1.** a head cook, as in a restaurant **2.** any cook
‡**chef-d'oeu·vre** (she dë′vr′) *n., pl.* **chefs-d'oeu′vre** (she dë′vr′) [Fr., principal work] a masterpiece, as in art or literature
Che·khov (chek′ôf; *Russ.* chekh′ôf), **An·ton (Pavlovich)** (än tôn′) 1860–1904; Russ. dramatist & short-story writer: also sp. **Chekov**
che·la (kē′lə) *n., pl.* **-lae** (-lē) [ModL. < Gr. *chēlē,* claw] a pincerlike claw of a crab, lobster, scorpion, etc.
che·late (kē′lāt) *adj.* resembling or having chelae —*n.* *Chem.* a compound in which a central atom (usually a metal ion) is attached to at least two other atoms by bonds so as to form a ring structure —*vt.* **-lat·ed, -lat·ing** to cause (a metal ion) to react with another molecule to form a chelate —**che·la′tion** *n.*
che·lic·er·a (kə lis′ə rə) *n., pl.* **-er·ae′** (-ə rē′) [ModL. < Gr. *chēlē,* claw + *keras,* horn] either of the first pair of appendages of spiders and other arachnids, used for grasping and crushing
che·lo·ni·an (ki lō′nē ən) *adj.* [< ModL. *Chelonia* < Gr. *chelōnē*] of, like, or being a turtle or tortoise —*n.* a turtle or tortoise
Chel·ya·binsk (chi lyä′binsk) city in the SW R.S.F.S.R., in the S Urals: pop. 851,000
chem. 1. chemical(s) **2.** chemist **3.** chemistry
chem·ic (kem′ik) *adj.* [Now Poet.] chemical
chem·i·cal (kem′i k'l) *adj.* **1.** of or having to do with chemistry **2.** involving the use of chemicals —*n.* any substance used in or obtained by a chemical process —**chem′i·cal·ly** *adv.*
chemical engineering the science or profession of applying chemistry to industrial uses
chemical warfare warfare using poisonous gases, flame throwers, incendiary bombs, etc.
chem·i·lu·mi·nes·cence (kem′i lo͞o′mə nes′'ns) *n.* visible light chemically produced without heat
che·mise (shə mēz′) *n.* [OFr. < VL. *camisia,* shirt < Gaul.] **1.** a woman's undergarment somewhat like a loose, short slip **2.** a straight, loose dress
chem·ist (kem′ist) *n.* [< (AL)CHEMIST] **1.** an expert or specialist in chemistry **2.** [Brit.] a pharmacist, or druggist
chem·is·try (kem′is trē) *n., pl.* **-tries** [prec. + -RY] **1.** the science dealing with the composition and properties of substances, and with the reactions by which substances are produced from or converted into other substances **2.** the application of this to a specified subject or field of activity **3.** the chemical properties, composition, reactions, and uses of a substance **4.** any process of synthesis or analysis similar to that used in chemistry *[the chemistry of wit]*
chem·o- *a combining form meaning* of, with, or by chemicals or chemistry *[chemotherapy]*
chem·o·re·cep·tor (kem′ō ri sep′tər, kē′mō-) *n.* a nerve ending or sense organ responsive to chemical stimuli, as a taste bud —**chem′o·re·cep′tion** *n.*
chem·o·sur·ger·y (-sur′jər ē) *n.* the removal of diseased tissue or abnormal growths by using chemicals
chem·o·ther·a·py (-ther′ə pē) *n.* the prevention or treatment of infection or disease by doses of chemical drugs: also **chem′o·ther′a·peu′tics** (-ther′ə pyo͞ot′iks) —**chem′o·ther′a·peu′tic** *adj.* —**chem′o·ther′a·peu′ti·cal·ly** *adv.* —**chem′o·ther′a·pist** *n.*
chem·ur·gy (kem′ər jē) *n.* [CHEM(O)- + -URGY] the branch of chemistry dealing with the industrial use of organic products, esp. from farms (e.g., the use of soybeans as a base for plastics) —**chem·ur·gic** (kem ur′jik) *adj.*
Cheng·tu (chuŋ′do͞o′) city in SC China: pop. 1,135,000
che·nille (shi nēl′) *n.* [Fr., lit., hairy caterpillar < L. *canicula,* little dog] **1.** a tufted, velvety yarn used for trimming, embroidery, etc. **2.** a fabric filled or woven with this, as for rugs
che·nin blanc (shə nan blän′, shen′in bläŋk′) *[also* **C- B-***]* [Fr.] a light, dry or semisweet white wine
che·ong·sam, che·ong-sam (chē ôŋ′säm′) *n.* [Chin.] a high-necked, closefitting Chinese dress with the skirt slit part way up the sides
Che·ops (kē′äps) *Gr. name of* KHUFU
cheque (chek) *n. Brit. sp. of* CHECK (*n.* 9)
cheq·uer (chek′ər) *n., vt. Brit. sp. of* CHECKER1
Cher·bourg (sher′boorg; *Fr.* sher bo͞or′) seaport in NW France, on the English Channel: pop. 37,000
cher·ish (cher′ish) *vt.* [< OFr. < *cher,* dear < L. *carus*] **1.** to hold dear; feel or show love for **2.** to take good care of; protect; foster *[to cherish one's rights]* **3.** to cling to the idea of
Cher·o·kee (cher′ə kē′) *n.* [prob. < Choctaw *chiluk-ki,* "cave people"] **1.** *pl.* **-kees′, -kee′** a member of a tribe of Iroquoian Indians, most of whom were moved from the SE U.S. to Oklahoma **2.** their Iroquoian language
Cherokee rose an evergreen climbing rose with fragrant, large, white flowers and glossy leaves, native to China but now growing wild in the S U.S.
che·root (shə ro͞ot′) *n.* [< Tamil *churuṭṭu,* a roll] a cigar with both ends cut square
cher·ry (cher′ē) *n., pl.* **-ries** [Anglo-Fr. *cherise* < OFr. < VL. < Gr. *kerasion* < *kerasos,* cherry tree] **1.** a small, fleshy fruit, yellow to dark red, with a smooth, hard pit **2.** any tree of the rose family which bears this fruit, or its wood **3.** the bright-red color of certain cherries —*adj.* **1.** bright-red **2.** of cherry wood **3.** made with cherries
cherry bomb a round, red, powerful firecracker
cher·ry·stone (-stōn′) *n.* a small quahog, a variety of clam: also **cherrystone clam**
chert (churt) *n.* [< ?] a very fine-grained, tough rock composed mainly of silica —**chert′y** (-ē) *adj.*
cher·ub (cher′əb) *n., pl.* **-ubs;** for 1–3 usually **-u·bim** (-ə bim, -yoo bim) or (KJV) **-u·bims** [< LL. < Heb. *kerūbh*] **1.** *Bible* one of certain winged heavenly beings: Ezek. 10 **2.** *Christian Theol.* any of the second order of angels, just below the seraphim **3.** a representation of a cherub, now usually as a chubby, rosy-faced child with wings **4.** a person, esp. a child, with a sweet, innocent face —**che·ru·bic** (chə ro͞o′bik) *adj.* —**che·ru′bi·cal·ly** *adv.*
cher·vil (chur′vəl) *n.* [< OE. < L. < Gr. < *chairein,* to rejoice + *phyllon,* leaf] a plant of the parsley family, with leaves used to flavor soups, etc.
Ches·a·peake (ches′ə pēk′) [see ff.] city in SE Va., at the base of Chesapeake Bay: pop. 114,000
Chesapeake Bay [*Chesapeake* < Algonquian, lit., country on a big river] arm of the Atlantic, extending north into Va. and Md.
Chesh·ire cat (chesh′ir, -ər) a proverbial grinning cat from Cheshire, a county of W England, esp. one described in Lewis Carroll's *Alice's Adventures in Wonderland*
Chesh·van (khesh′vän) *n. same as* HESHVAN
chess (ches) *n.* [< OFr. *esches,* pl. of *eschec:* see CHECK] a game for two, each with 16 pieces moved variously on a

chessboard in alternation, the object being to checkmate the opponent's king

chess·board (-bôrd′) *n.* a board with 64 squares of two alternating colors, for chess and checkers

chess·man (-man′, -mən) *n., pl.* **-men′** (-men′, -mən) any of the pieces used in chess

chess pie [< ?] a dessert made of a custard-like mixture of butter, sugar, eggs, etc., baked in a pie shell

chest (chest) *n.* [< OE. < L. < Gr. *kistē,* a box] **1.** a box with a lid and, often, a lock, for storing or shipping things **2.** a public fund [*community chest*] **3.** *same as* CHEST OF DRAWERS **4.** a cabinet for medicines, toiletries, etc. **5.** *a*) the part of the body enclosed by the ribs; thorax *b*) the outside front of this —**get (something) off one's chest** [Colloq.] to unburden oneself of (some trouble, etc.) by talking about it

chest·ed (-id) *adj.* having a (specified kind of) chest, or thorax [*hollow-chested*]

Ches·ter (ches′tər) [< OE. < L. *castra,* a camp] **1.** a masculine name **2.** [after *Chester,* city in W England] seaport in SE Pa., on the Delaware River: pop. 46,000

Ches·ter·field (ches′tər fēld′), 4th Earl of (*Philip Dormer Stanhope*) 1694–1773; Eng. statesman & writer: called *Lord Chesterfield*

ches·ter·field (ches′tər fēld′) *n.* [after a 19th-c. Earl of *Chesterfield*] **1.** a single-breasted topcoat, usually with a velvet collar **2.** a sofa with upright ends

Chester White [after *Chester* County, Pa.] a variety of large, white hog

chest·nut (ches′nut′, -nət) *n.* [< OFr. < L. < Gr. *kastaneia*] **1.** the smooth-shelled, sweet, edible nut of certain trees of the beech family **2.** one of these trees, or the wood **3.** *same as* HORSE CHESTNUT **4.** reddish brown **5.** a reddish-brown horse **6.** [Colloq.] *a*) an old, stale joke or phrase; cliché *b*) a familiar story, piece of music, etc., repeated too often —*adj.* reddish-brown

chest of drawers a set of drawers within a frame, as for keeping clothing in a bedroom; bureau

chest·y (ches′tē) *adj.* **chest′i·er, chest′i·est** [Colloq.] **1.** having a large chest, or thorax **2.** bosomy **3.** boastful

che·val glass (shə val′) [Fr. *cheval,* horse, support + GLASS] a full-length mirror on swivels in a frame

chev·a·lier (shev′ə lir′; *for 1, often* shə val′yā′) *n.* [see CAVALIER] **1.** a member of the lowest rank of the French Legion of Honor **2.** a cavalier; gallant

Chev·i·ot (chev′ē ət; *also, and for 2 always,* shev′-) *n.* [after the *Cheviot Hills,* between England and Scotland] **1.** any of a breed of sheep with short, dense wool **2.** [*usually* **c-**] *a*) a rough wool fabric in a twill weave *b*) a cotton cloth resembling this

chev·ron (shev′rən) *n.* [< OFr., rafter (from its shape), ult. < L. *capra,* she-goat] a V-shaped bar or bars worn on the sleeve, as of a military uniform, to show rank or service

chev·y (chev′ē) *n., pl.* **chev′ies** [< hunting cry *chivy,* in the ballad of *Chevy Chase*] [Brit.] a hunt; chase —*vt., vi.* **chev′ied, chev′y·ing 1.** [Brit.] to hunt; chase; run about **2.** to worry; fret; chivy

chew (cho͞o) *vt.* [< OE. *ceowan*] **1.** to bite and crush with the teeth **2.** *a*) to think over *b*) to discuss **3.** [Slang] to rebuke severely (often with *out*) —*vi.* **1.** to do chewing **2.** [Colloq.] to chew tobacco —*n.* **1.** a chewing **2.** something chewed or for chewing, as a portion of tobacco —**chew the rag** (or **fat**) [Slang] to converse idly —**chew′er** *n.*

CHEVRON

chew·ing gum (cho͞o′iŋ) chicle or other gummy substance, flavored and sweetened for chewing

che·wink (chi wiŋk′) *n.* [echoic of its note] the eastern towhee of N. America, with the iris of the eye bright red

chew·y (cho͞o′ē) *adj.* **chew′i·er, chew′i·est** needing much chewing —**chew′i·ness** *n.*

Chey·enne[1] (shī en′, -an′) *n.* [Dakota *shaiyena* < *shaia,* to speak unintelligibly] **1.** *pl.* **-ennes′, -enne′** a member of a tribe of Algonquian Indians now of Montana and Oklahoma but originally of Minnesota **2.** their language

Chey·enne[2] (shī an′, -en′) [< prec.] capital of Wyo., in the SE part: pop. 47,000

‡**chez** (shā) *prep.* [Fr.] by; at; at the home of

chg. *pl.* **chgs.** charge

chgd. charged

chi (kī) *n.* [Gr.] the 22d letter of the Greek alphabet (Χ, χ)

Chiang Kai-shek (chaŋ′kī shek′; *Chin.* jyäŋ′-) (born *Chiang Chung-chen*) 1888–1975; Chin. generalissimo & head of government on Taiwan (1950–75)

Chi·an·ti (kē än′tē, -an′-) *n.* [It.] a dry, red wine, orig. made in Tuscany

chi·a·ro·scu·ro (kē är′ə skyoor′ō) *n., pl.* **-ros** [It. < L. *clarus,* clear + *obscurus,* dark] **1.** the treatment of light and shade in a painting, drawing, etc., as to produce an illusion of depth **2.** a style or a painting, etc. emphasizing this

chic (shēk) *n.* [Fr. < MLowG. *schick,* order, skill] smart elegance of style and manner —*adj.* **chic·quer** (shēk′ər), **chic′quest** (-ist) smartly stylish

Chi·ca·go (shə kä′gō, -kô′-) [< Fr. < Algonquian, lit., place of the wild onion] city in NE Ill., on Lake Michigan: pop. 3,005,000 (met. area 7,058,000) —**Chi·ca′go·an** *n.*

chi·cane (shi kān′, chi-) *n.* [Fr. < *chicaner,* to quibble < MLowG. *schikken,* to arrange] *same as* CHICANERY —*vi.* **-caned′, -can′ing** to use chicanery —*vt.* **1.** to trick **2.** to get by chicanery

chi·can·er·y (-ər ē) *n., pl.* **-er·ies 1.** the use of clever but tricky talk or action to deceive, evade, etc. **2.** an instance of this

Chi·ca·no (chi kä′nō) *n., pl.* **-nos** [altered < AmSp. (*Mê*)*jicano,* a Mexican] [*also* **c-**] [Southwest] a U.S. citizen or inhabitant of Mexican descent

chi·chi, chi-chi (shē′shē, chē′chē) *adj.* [Fr.] extremely chic; very elegant or sophisticated, esp. in an affected or showy way —*n.* anything chichi

chick (chik) *n.* [< CHICKEN] **1.** a young chicken **2.** any young bird **3.** a child: term of endearment **4.** [Slang] a young woman

chick·a·dee (chik′ə dē′) *n.* [echoic of its note] any of various small birds closely related to the titmice, with black, gray, and white feathers

chick·a·ree (chik′ə rē′) *n.* [echoic of its cry] a reddish squirrel of the W U.S.

Chick·a·saw (chik′ə sô′) *n.* **1.** *pl.* **-saws′, -saw′** a member of a tribe of Muskogean Indians now of Oklahoma but formerly of Mississippi and Tennessee **2.** their dialect

chick·en (chik′ən) *n.* [< OE. *cycen,* lit., little cock] **1.** a common farm bird raised for its edible eggs or flesh; hen or rooster, esp. a young one **2.** its flesh **3.** any young bird **4.** a young or inexperienced person **5.** [Slang] a timid or cowardly person —*adj.* **1.** of chicken **2.** small and tender [*a chicken lobster*] **3.** [Slang] timid or cowardly —*vi.* [Slang] to lose courage and abandon a plan, action, etc. (usually with *out*) —**count one's chickens before they are hatched** to count on something that may not materialize

chicken feed [Slang] a petty sum of money

chick·en-fried (-frīd′) *adj.* coated with seasoned flour or batter and fried [*chicken-fried steak*]

chicken hawk a hawk preying on barnyard fowl

chick·en-heart·ed (-här′tid) *adj.* timid; cowardly: also **chick′en-liv′ered**

chicken pox an acute, contagious virus disease, usually of young children, with fever and a series of skin eruptions

chicken wire light, pliable wire fencing, used esp. for enclosing chicken coops

chick·pea (chik′pē′) *n.* [for *chich pea,* ult. < L. *cicer,* pea] **1.** a bushy annual plant of the legume family, with short, hairy pods containing usually two seeds **2.** the edible seed

chick·weed (-wēd′) *n.* any of several low-growing plants of the pink family, often found as weeds

chic·le (chik′'l) *n.* [AmSp. < Nahuatl *chictli*] a gumlike substance made from the milky juice of the sapodilla tree, used in making chewing gum

Chic·o·pee (chik′ə pē) [< AmInd., lit., swift river] city in SW Mass.: pop. 55,000

chic·o·ry (chik′ə rē) *n., pl.* **-ries** [< OFr. < L. < Gr. *kichora*] **1.** a weedy plant of the composite family, with blue flowers: the leaves are used for salad **2.** its root, roasted and ground for mixing with coffee or for use as a coffee substitute

chide (chīd) *vt., vi.* **chid′ed** or **chid** (chid), **chid′ed** or **chid** or **chid·den** (chid′'n), **chid′ing** [OE. *cidan*] to scold; now, usually, to reprove mildly —**chid′er** *n.* —**chid′ing·ly** *adv.*

chief (chēf) *n.* [< OFr. < L. *caput,* the head] **1.** the head or leader of a group, organization, etc. **2.** [Archaic] the main part **3.** *Heraldry* the upper third of a shield —*adj.* **1.** highest in rank, office, etc. **2.** main; principal —*adv.* [Archaic] chiefly —**in chief** in the chief position; of highest title or authority

Chief Executive the President of the U.S.

chief justice the presiding judge of a court made up of several judges

chief·ly (-lē) *adv.* **1.** most of all; above all **2.** mainly; mostly —*adj.* of or like a chief

chief·tain (-tən) *n.* [< OFr. < LL. < L. *caput,* the head] a leader, esp. of a clan or tribe —**chief′tain·cy,** *pl.* **-cies, chief′tain·ship′** *n.*

chif·fon (shi fän′, shif′än) *n.* [Fr.,] dim. of *chiffe,* a rag] **1.** a sheer, lightweight fabric of silk, nylon, etc. **2.** [*pl.*] rib-

bons, laces, etc. used as accessories to a woman's dress —*adj.* 1. made of chiffon 2. *Cooking* made light and porous as by adding beaten egg whites
chif·fo·nier, chif·fon·nier (shif'ə nir') *n.* [Fr., orig., ragpicker < prec.] a narrow, high bureau or chest of drawers, often with a mirror
chig·ger (chig'ər) *n.* [of Afr. origin] 1. the tiny, red larva of certain mites, whose bite causes severe itching 2. *same as* CHIGOE
chi·gnon (shēn'yän) *n.* [Fr. < OFr. < L. *catena*, a chain] a knot or coil of hair sometimes worn at the back of the neck by women
chig·oe (chig'ō) *n., pl.* **-oes** (-ōz) [? via Fr. *chique* < WInd. native name] 1. a flea of tropical S. America and Africa: the female burrows into the skin, causing painful sores 2. *same as* CHIGGER
Chi·hua·hua (chi wä'wä) city in NC Mexico: pop. 247,000 —*n.* any of an ancient Mexican breed of very small dog with large, pointed ears
chil·blain (chil'blān') *n.* [CHIL(L) + BLAIN] a painful swelling or sore on the foot or hand, caused by exposure to cold —**chil'blained'** *adj.*
child (chīld) *n., pl.* **chil'dren** [< OE. *cild*, pl. *cildru*] 1. an infant; baby 2. an unborn offspring 3. a boy or girl in the period before puberty 4. a son or daughter 5. a descendant 6. a person like a child; immature or childish adult 7. a person or thing viewed as produced by a certain place, time, source, etc. [*a child* of the Renaissance] —**with child** pregnant —**child'less** *adj.* —**child'less·ness** *n.*
child·bear·ing (-ber'iŋ) *n.* the act of giving birth to children; parturition
child·bed (-bed') *n.* the condition of a woman giving birth to a child
child·birth (-burth') *n.* the act of giving birth to a child; parturition
child·hood (-hood') *n.* the time or state of being a child; period from infancy to puberty
child·ish (-ish) *adj.* 1. of or like a child 2. not fit for an adult; immature; silly —**child'ish·ly** *adv.* —**child'ish·ness** *n.*
child·like (-līk') *adj.* like a child, esp. in being innocent, trusting, etc. —**child'like'ness** *n.*
chil·dren (chil'drən) *n. pl. of* CHILD
child's play (chīldz) anything simple to do
Chil·e (chil'ē; *Sp.* chē'le) country on the SW coast of S. America: 286,397 sq. mi.; pop. 9,566,000; cap. Santiago —**Chil'e·an** *adj., n.*
chil·e (chil'ē) *n. same as* CHILI
chil·e con car·ne (chil'ē kən kär'nē, kän') *same as* CHILI CON CARNE
Chile saltpeter native sodium nitrate
chil·i (chil'ē) *n., pl.* **chil'ies** [MexSp. < Nahuatl *chilli*] 1. the dried pod of red pepper, a very hot seasoning 2. the tropical American plant, of the nightshade family, that bears this pod 3. *same as* CHILI CON CARNE
chil·i con car·ne (chil'ē kən kär'nē, kän') [< MexSp., lit., red pepper with meat] a highly seasoned dish with beef ground or in bits, chilies or chili powder, beans, and often tomatoes
chili powder a powder of dried chili pods, herbs, etc.
chili sauce a spiced sauce of chopped tomatoes, green and red sweet peppers, onions, etc.
chill (chil) *n.* [OE. *ciele*] 1. a feeling of coldness that makes one shiver 2. a moderate coldness 3. a discouraging influence 4. a feeling of sudden fear 5. unfriendliness —*adj. same as* CHILLY —*vi.* 1. to become cool or cold 2. to shiver from cold, fear, etc. —*vt.* 1. to make cool or cold 2. to cause a chill in 3. to check (enthusiasm, etc.) 4. to depress; dispirit 5. *Metallurgy* to harden (metal) on the surface by rapid cooling —**chill'er** *n.* —**chill'ing·ly** *adv.* —**chill'ness** *n.*
chill factor the combined effect of low temperature and high winds on loss of body heat
chil·li (chil'ē) *n., pl.* **-lies** *same as* CHILI
chill·y (chil'ē) *adj.* **chill'i·er, chill'i·est** 1. moderately cold; uncomfortably cool 2. chilling 3. cool in manner; unfriendly 4. depressing; dispiriting —**chill'i·ly** *adv.* —**chill'i·ness** *n.*
Chi·mae·ra (ki mir'ə, kī-) *same as* CHIMERA —*n.* [c-] a chimera
chime[1] (chīm) *n.* [< OFr. < L. *cymbalum*, CYMBAL] 1. [*usually pl.*] *a)* a tuned set of bells or metal tubes *b)* the sounds produced by these 2. a single bell in a clock, etc. 3. harmony; agreement —*vi.* **chimed, chim'ing** 1. to sound as a chime 2. to sound in harmony, as bells 3. to harmonize; agree —*vt.* 1. to ring (a chime or chimes) 2. to indicate (time) by chiming —**chime in** 1. to join in or interrupt, as talk 2. to agree —**chim'er** *n.*
chime[2] (chīm) *n.* [ME. *chimb* < OE. *cimb-* (only in compounds)] the extended rim at each end of a cask or barrel
Chi·me·ra (ki mir'ə, kī-) [< OFr. < L. < Gr. *chimaira*, she-goat] *Gr. Myth.* a fire-breathing monster with a lion's head, goat's body, and serpent's tail —*n.* [c-] 1. any similar unreal monster 2. an impossible or foolish fancy
chi·mer·i·cal (ki mir'i k'l, -mer'-; kī-) *adj.* [see prec.] 1. imaginary; unreal 2. absurd; impossible 3. visionary Also **chi·mer'ic** —**chi·mer'i·cal·ly** *adv.*
chim·ney (chim'nē) *n., pl.* **-neys** [< OFr. < LL. *caminata*, fireplace < L. *caminus* < Gr. *kaminos*, oven] 1. the passage through which smoke escapes from a fire; flue 2. a structure containing a flue and extending above the roof 3. a glass tube around the flame of a lamp, etc. 4. a fissure or vent, as in a cliff or volcano
chimney pot a short pipe on a chimney top to carry the smoke off and increase the draft
chimney swallow 1. *same as* CHIMNEY SWIFT 2. the European barn swallow
chimney sweep a person whose work is cleaning the soot from chimneys
chimney swift a sooty-brown N. American bird resembling the swallow: so called from its habit of making a nest in an unused chimney
chimp (chimp) *n.* [Colloq.] a chimpanzee
chim·pan·zee (chim'pan zē', chim pan'zē) *n.* [< Fr. < Bantu *kampenzi*] an anthropoid ape of Africa, with black hair and large ears: it is smaller than a gorilla and is noted for its intelligence

CHIMPANZEE (35–60 in. high)

chin (chin) *n.* [OE. *cin*] the part of the face below the lower lip; projecting part of the lower jaw —*vt.* **chinned, chin'ning** to pull (oneself) up, while hanging by the hands from a horizontal bar, until the chin is just above the level of the bar —*vi.* 1. to chin oneself 2. [Slang] to chat, gossip, etc. —**keep one's chin up** to bear up bravely —**take it on the chin** [Slang] to suffer defeat, hardship, etc.
Chin. 1. China 2. Chinese
Chi·na (chī'nə) country in E Asia, south and east of the U.S.S.R.: 3,691,000 sq. mi.; pop. 732,000,000; cap. Peking: see also TAIWAN
chi·na (chī'nə) *n.* 1. *a)* porcelain, orig. from China *b)* vitrified ceramic ware like porcelain 2. dishes, etc. of this 3. any earthenware dishes or crockery
chi·na·ber·ry (-ber'ē) *n., pl.* **-ries** 1. a tree, orig. of tropical Asia, bearing yellow, beadlike fruit 2. a tree of Mexico and the SW U.S. with an orange-brown fruit formerly used as soap 3. either fruit
Chi·na·town (-toun') *n.* the Chinese quarter of a city, as in San Francisco
chi·na·ware (-wer') *n. same as* CHINA
chin·ca·pin (chiŋ'kə pin) *n. same as* CHINQUAPIN
chinch (chinch) *n.* [Sp. *chinche*< L. *cimex*, bug] *same as:* 1. BEDBUG 2. CHINCH BUG
chinch bug a small, white-winged, black bug that damages grain plants
chin·chil·la (chin chil'ə) *n.* [Sp., prob. dim. of *chinche:* see CHINCH] 1. a small rodent of the Andes, bred extensively for its fur 2. its expensive, soft, pale-gray fur 3. a heavy, nubby wool cloth
chine (chīn) *n.* [< OFr. *eschine* < Frank. *skina*, small bone, shin bone] 1. the backbone; spine 2. a cut of meat containing part of the backbone 3. a ridge —*vt.* **chined, chin'ing** to cut along or across the backbone of (a meat carcass)
Chi·nese (chī nēz', -nēs'; *for adj., often* chī'nēz') 1. *pl.* **-nese'** a native of China or a person of Chinese descent 2. the standard language of the Chinese; Mandarin 3. any Chinese language —*adj.* of China, its people, etc.
Chinese cabbage any of several vegetables of the mustard family, with long, narrow leaves in loose, cylindrical heads and a cabbagelike taste
Chinese checkers [< ?] a game like checkers for two to six players, using marbles on a board with holes in a star-shaped pattern
Chinese lantern a lantern of brightly colored paper, made so that it can be folded up
Chin·ese-lan·tern plant (-lan'tərn) a perennial herb of the nightshade family, with a bladderlike red calyx
Chinese puzzle any intricate puzzle
Chinese red a brilliant orange-red
chink[1] (chiŋk) *n.* [OE. *cine*] a crack; fissure —*vt.* to close up the chinks in
chink[2] (chiŋk) *n.* [echoic] a sharp, clinking sound, as of coins striking together —*vi., vt.* to make or cause to make a sharp, clinking sound
chin·ka·pin (chiŋ'kə pin) *n. same as* CHINQUAPIN
chi·no (chē'nō, shē'-) *n.* [< ?] 1. a strong, twilled cotton cloth 2. [*pl.*] pants of chino
chin·oise·rie (shin'wäz rē') *n.* [Fr. < *Chinois*, Chinese + *-erie*, -ERY] 1. an ornate decorative style based on Chinese motifs 2. articles, designs, etc. in this style

Chi·nook (chi no͞ok′, -no͝ok′; *for 4, usually* shi-) ***n.*** **1.** *pl.* **-nooks′, -nook′** any of a family of Indian tribes, formerly of the Columbia River valley **2.** their language **3.** *same as* CHINOOK JARGON **4.** [*usually* **c-**] a warm, moist SW wind blowing from the sea onto the coast of the NW U.S. and SW Canada in winter and spring; also, a dry wind blowing down the E slope of the Rocky Mountains: in full, **chinook wind** —**Chi·nook′an** (-ən) ***adj., n.***

Chinook jargon a former pidgin language made up of simple Chinook mixed with English and French

chinook salmon the largest Pacific salmon

chin·qua·pin (chiŋ′kə pin′) ***n.*** **[**of Algonquian origin**]** **1.** the dwarf chestnut tree **2.** a related evergreen tree of the beech family **3.** the edible nut of either of these trees

chintz (chints) ***n.*** **[**earlier a pl. form < Hindi *chhīnt* < Sans. *citra*, spotted, bright**]** a cotton cloth printed in colors and usually glazed

chintz·y (-ē) ***adj.*** **chintz′i·er, chintz′i·est** **1.** like chintz **2.** [Colloq.] cheap, stingy, etc.

chip (chip) ***vt.*** **chipped, chip′ping** **[**< OE. hyp. *cippian***]** **1.** *a)* to break or cut a small piece or thin slice from *b)* to break or cut off (a small piece or pieces) **2.** to shape by cutting or chopping —***vi.*** to break off into small pieces —***n.*** **1.** a small, thin piece of wood, etc. cut or broken off **2.** a place where a small piece has been chipped off **3.** wood, palm leaf, or straw split and woven into hats, etc. **4.** a fragment of dried animal dung, sometimes used for fuel **5.** a worthless thing **6.** a small, round disk used in poker, etc. as a money token; counter **7.** a thin slice or shaving of food *[potato chips]* **8.** *Electronics a)* a semiconductor body for an integrated circuit *b) same as* INTEGRATED CIRCUIT —**chip in** [Colloq.] **1.** to share in giving money or help **2.** to add one's comments —**chip off the old block** a person much like his father —**chip on one's shoulder** [Colloq.] an inclination to fight —**in the chips** [Slang] rich; wealthy —**let the chips fall where they may** whatever the consequences —**when the chips are down** when something is really at stake

chip·munk (-muŋk′) ***n.*** **[**of Algonquian origin**]** a small, striped N. American squirrel: it lives mainly on the ground

chipped beef shavings of dried or smoked beef

Chip·pen·dale (chip′'n dāl′) ***adj.*** **[**after T. *Chippendale* (1718?–79), Eng. cabinetmaker**]** designating or of an 18th-cent. Eng. style of furniture with graceful lines and, often, rococo ornamentation

chip·per (chip′ər) ***adj.*** **[**< N Brit. *kipper***]** [Colloq.] in good spirits; lively

Chip·pe·wa (chip′ə wô′, -wä′, -wə, -wā′) ***n.,*** *pl.* **-was, -wa** *var. of* OJIBWA: also **Chip′pe·way′** (-wā′)

chi·ro- **[**< Gr. *cheir*, the hand**]** *a combining form meaning* hand *[chiromancy]*

chi·rog·ra·phy (kī räg′rə fē) ***n.*** **[**CHIRO- + -GRAPHY**]** handwriting; penmanship —**chi·rog′ra·pher** ***n.*** —**chi·ro·graph·ic** (kī′rə graf′ik), **chi′ro·graph′i·cal** ***adj.***

chi·ro·man·cy (kī′rə man′sē) ***n.*** **[**CHIRO- + -MANCY**]** *same as* PALMISTRY —**chi′ro·man′cer** ***n.***

chi·rop·o·dy (kə räp′ə dē, kī-) ***n.*** **[**CHIRO- + -POD + -Y[3]**]** *same as* PODIATRY —**chi·rop′o·dist** ***n.***

chi·ro·prac·tic (kī′rə prak′tik, kī′rə prak′tik) ***n.*** **[**< CHIRO- + Gr. *praktikos*, practical**]** a method of treating disease by manipulation of the body joints, esp. of the spine —**chi′ro·prac′tor** ***n.***

chirp (churp) ***vi.*** **[**echoic**]** **1.** to make the short, shrill sound of some birds or insects **2.** to speak in a lively, shrill way —***vt.*** to utter in a sharp, shrill tone —***n.*** a short, shrill sound —**chirp′er** ***n.***

chirr (chur) ***n.*** **[**echoic**]** a shrill, trilled sound, as of some insects or birds —***vi.*** to make such a sound

chir·rup (chur′əp, chir′-) ***vi.*** **[**var. of CHIRP**]** to chirp repeatedly —***n.*** a chirruping sound

chis·el (chiz′'l) ***n.*** **[**ONormFr. < VL. < L. pp. of *caedere*, to cut**]** a sharp-edged tool for cutting or shaping wood, stone, or metal —***vi., vt.*** **-eled** or **-elled, -el·ing** or **-el·ling** **1.** to cut or shape with a chisel **2.** [Colloq.] to take advantage of (someone) or get (something) by cheating, sponging, etc. —**chisel in** [Colloq.] to force oneself, uninvited, upon others —**chis′el·er, chis′el·ler** ***n.***

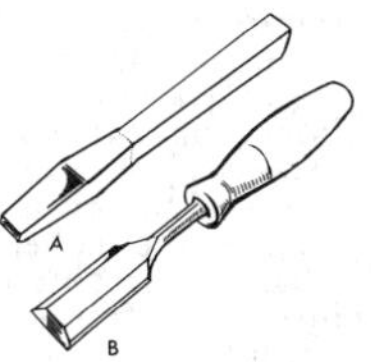

CHISELS (A, cold; B, wood)

chi-square (kī′skwer′) ***n.*** a statistical method used to test whether the classification of data can be ascribed to chance or to some underlying law

chit[1] (chit) ***n.*** **[**ME. *chitte*, prob. var. of *kitte*, for kitten**]** **1.** a child **2.** an immature or childish girl

chit[2] (chit) ***n.*** **[**< Hindi < Sans. *citra*, spotted**]** **1.** [Chiefly Brit.] a memorandum **2.** a voucher of a small sum owed for drink, food, etc.

chit·chat (chit′chat′) ***n.*** **[**< CHAT**]** **1.** light, familiar, informal talk; small talk **2.** gossip

chi·tin (kīt′'n) ***n.*** **[**Fr. *chitine* < Gr.: see CHITON**]** a tough, horny substance forming the outer covering of insects, crustaceans, etc. —**chi′tin·ous** ***adj.***

chit·lins, chit·lings (chit′lənz) ***n.pl.*** *dial. var. of* CHITTERLINGS

chi·ton (kīt′'n, kī′tän) ***n.*** **[**Gr. *chitōn*, garment, tunic < Sem.**]** a loose garment similar to a tunic, worn by both men and women in ancient Greece

chit·ter·lings (chit′lənz; *now chiefly Brit.* chit′ər liŋz) ***n.pl.*** **[**ME. *chiterling* < Gmc. base**]** the small intestines of pigs, used for food

chiv·al·ric (shi val′rik, shiv′'l rik) ***adj.*** **1.** of chivalry **2.** *same as* CHIVALROUS

chiv·al·rous (shiv′'l rəs) ***adj.*** **1.** having the attributes of an ideal knight; gallant, courteous, honorable, etc. **2.** of chivalry; chivalric —**chiv′al·rous·ly** ***adv.*** —**chiv′al·rous·ness** ***n.***

chiv·al·ry (shiv′'l rē) ***n.*** **[**< OFr. *chivalerie* < *chevaler*, a knight: doublet of CAVALRY**]** **1.** a group of knights or gallant gentlemen **2.** the medieval system of knighthood **3.** the noble qualities a knight was supposed to have, such as courage, honor, and a readiness to help the weak and protect women **4.** the demonstration of any of these qualities

chives (chīvz) ***n.pl.*** **[**< OFr. < L. *cepa*, onion**]** *[often with sing. v.]* a plant of the lily family, with small, hollow leaves having a mild onion odor: used to flavor soups, stews, etc.

chiv·y, chiv·vy (chiv′ē) ***n.,*** *pl.* **chiv′ies** or **chiv′vies** *same as* CHEVY —***vt., vi.*** **chiv′ied** or **chiv′vied, chiv′y·ing** or **chiv′vy·ing** **1.** to fret; worry; nag **2.** to manipulate **3.** *same as* CHEVY

chlo·ral (klôr′əl) ***n.*** **[**CHLOR(O)- + AL(COHOL)**]** **1.** a thin, oily, colorless liquid, CCl_3CHO, with a pungent odor, prepared by the action of chlorine on alcohol **2.** *same as* CHLORAL HYDRATE

chloral hydrate a colorless, crystalline compound, $CCl_3{\cdot}CH(OH)_2$, used chiefly as a sedative

chlor·am·phen·i·col (klôr′am fen′ə kôl′, -kōl′) ***n.*** **[**CHLOR(O)- + AM(IDE) + PHE(NO)- + NI(TRO)- + (GLY)COL**]** an antibiotic drug, $C_{11}H_{12}Cl_2N_2O_5$, used against a wide variety of bacterial and rickettsial diseases and against some viruses

chlo·rate (klôr′āt, -it) ***n.*** a salt of chloric acid

chlor·dane (klôr′dān) ***n.*** **[**CHLOR(O)- + (*in*)*dane*, a coal-tar derivative**]** a poisonous, volatile oil, $C_{10}H_6Cl_8$, used as an insecticide: also **chlor′dan** (-dan)

chlo·ric (klôr′ik) ***adj.*** **1.** of or containing chlorine with a higher valence than in corresponding chlorous compounds **2.** designating or of a colorless acid, $HClO_3$, whose salts are chlorates

chlo·ride (-īd) ***n.*** a compound in which chlorine is combined with another element or radical (e.g., a salt of hydrochloric acid)

chloride of lime a white powder, $CaOCl_2$, obtained by treating slaked lime with chlorine and used for disinfecting and bleaching

chlo·ri·nate (klôr′ə nāt′) ***vt.*** **-nat′ed, -nat′ing** to treat or combine (a substance) with chlorine; esp., to pass chlorine into (water or sewage) for purification —**chlo′ri·na′tion** ***n.*** —**chlo′ri·na′tor** ***n.***

chlo·rine (klôr′ēn, -in) ***n.*** **[**CHLOR(O)- + -INE[4]**]** a greenish-yellow, poisonous, gaseous chemical element with a disagreeable odor, used in bleaching, water purification, etc.: symbol, Cl; at. wt., 35.453; at. no., 17

chlo·rite (-īt) ***n.*** a salt of chlorous acid

chlo·ro- **[**< Gr. *chlōros*, pale green**]** *a combining form meaning:* **1.** green *[chlorophyll]* **2.** having chlorine in the molecule *[chloroform]* Also, before a vowel, **chlor-**

chlo·ro·form (klôr′ə fôrm′) ***n.*** **[**see CHLORO- & FORMYL**]** a sweetish, colorless, volatile liquid, $CHCl_3$, used as a general anesthetic and as a solvent —***vt.*** **1.** to anesthetize with chloroform **2.** to kill with chloroform

Chlo·ro·my·ce·tin (klôr′ə mī sēt′'n) **[**CHLORO- + -MYCET(E) + -IN[1]**]** *a trademark for* CHLORAMPHENICOL

chlo·ro·phyll, chlo·ro·phyl (klôr′ə fil′) ***n.*** **[**< Fr. < Gr. *chlōros*, green + *phyllon*, a leaf**]** the green pigment of plants: it is involved in the photosynthetic process —**chlo′ro·phyl′lose** (-ōs), **chlo′ro·phyl′lous** (-əs) ***adj.***

chlo·ro·plast (klôr′ə plast′) ***n.*** **[**CHLORO- + Gr. *plastos*, formed**]** an oval, chlorophyll-bearing body found in the cytoplasm in cells of green plants

chlo·rous (klôr′əs) ***adj.*** **1.** of or containing chlorine with a lower valence than in corresponding chloric compounds

2. designating or of an unstable acid, $HClO_2$, a strong oxidizing agent whose salts are chlorites

chlor·prom·a·zine (klôr präm′ə zēn′) ***n.*** a synthetic drug, $C_{17}H_{19}N_2SCl$, used as a tranquilizer

chlor·tet·ra·cy·cline (-tet′rə sī′klēn, -klin) ***n.*** a yellow antibiotic, $C_{22}H_{23}ClN_2O_8$, used against a wide variety of bacterial and rickettsial infections and certain viruses

chm., chmn. chairman

chock (chäk) ***n.*** [ONormFr. *choque,* a block] **1.** a block or wedge placed under a wheel, barrel, etc. to prevent motion **2.** *Naut.* a block with two hornlike projections curving inward, through which a rope may be run —***vt.*** to provide or wedge fast as with chocks —***adv.*** as close or tight as can be

chock·a·block (-ə bläk′) ***adj.*** **1.** pulled so tight as to have the blocks touching: said of a hoisting tackle **2.** crowded —***adv.*** tightly together

chock-full (chäk′foo͝l′, chuk′-) ***adj.*** as full as possible; filled to capacity

choc·o·late (chôk′lət, chäk′-; -ə lət) ***n.*** [< Fr. < Sp. < Nahuatl *chocolatl*] **1.** a paste, powder, etc. made from cacao seeds that have been roasted and ground **2.** a drink made of chocolate, hot milk or water, and sugar **3.** a candy made of or coated with chocolate **4.** reddish brown —***adj.*** **1.** made of or with chocolate **2.** reddish-brown

Choc·taw (chäk′tô) ***n.*** [< tribal name *Chata* < ?] **1.** *pl.* **-taws, -taw** a member of a tribe of Muskogean Indians originally of the Southeast now living in Oklahoma **2.** their Muskogean dialect

choice (chois) ***n.*** [< OFr. < *choisir,* to choose < Goth. *kausjan,* to taste] **1.** a choosing; selection **2.** the right or power to choose; option **3.** a person or thing chosen **4.** the best part **5.** a variety from which to choose **6.** a supply well chosen **7.** an alternative **8.** care in choosing —***adj.*** **choic′er, choic′est** **1.** of special excellence **2.** carefully chosen —**of choice** that is preferred —**choice′ly** ***adv.*** —**choice′ness** ***n.***

choir (kwīr) ***n.*** [< OFr. *cuer* < ML. *chorus,* choir < L.: see CHORUS] **1.** a group of singers trained to sing together, esp. in a church **2.** the part of a church they occupy **3.** an instrumental section of an orchestra **4.** any organized group

choke (chōk) ***vt.*** **choked, chok′ing** [< OE. *aceocian*] **1.** to prevent from breathing by blocking the windpipe; strangle; suffocate **2.** to block up; obstruct by clogging **3.** to hinder the growth or action of **4.** to fill up **5.** to cut off some air from the carburetor of (a gasoline engine) so as to make a richer gasoline mixture **6.** to hold (a bat, golf club, etc.) toward the middle of the handle —***vi.*** **1.** to be suffocated **2.** to be blocked up; be obstructed —***n.*** **1.** the act or sound of choking **2.** the valve that chokes a carburetor —**choke back** to hold back (feelings, sobs, etc.) —**choke down** to swallow with difficulty —**choke off** to bring to an end; end the growth of —**choke up** **1.** to block up; clog **2.** to fill too full **3.** [Colloq.] to be unable to speak, act efficiently, etc., as because of fear, tension, etc.

choke·bore (-bôr′) ***n.*** **1.** a shotgun bore that tapers toward the muzzle to keep the shot closely bunched **2.** a gun with such a bore

choke·cher·ry (-cher′ē) ***n.,*** *pl.* **-ries** **1.** a N. American wild cherry tree **2.** its astringent fruit

choke·damp (chōk′damp′) ***n.*** *same as* BLACKDAMP

choke-full (chōk′foo͝l′) ***adj.*** *same as* CHOCK-FULL

chok·er (chōk′ər) ***n.*** **1.** a person or thing that chokes **2.** a closely fitting necklace

chok·y (-ē) ***adj.*** **chok′i·er, chok′i·est** **1.** inclined to choke **2.** suffocating; stifling Also sp. **chok′ey**

chol·e- *same as* CHOLO-: also, before a vowel, **chol-**

chol·er (käl′ər) ***n.*** [< OFr. < L. *cholera:* see ff.] **1.** [Obs.] bile: in medieval times yellow bile was considered the source of anger and irritability **2.** [Now Rare] anger or ill humor

chol·er·a (käl′ər ə) ***n.*** [L., jaundice < Gr. *cholera,* nausea < *cholē,* bile] any of several intestinal diseases; esp., ASIATIC CHOLERA —**chol′e·ra′ic** (-ə rā′ik) ***adj.***

chol·er·ic (käl′ər ik, kə ler′ik) ***adj.*** [see CHOLER] showing a quick temper or irascible nature

cho·les·ter·ol (kə les′tə rōl′, -rôl′) ***n.*** [< CHOLE- + Gr. *stereos,* solid + -OL[1]] a crystalline fatty alcohol, $C_{27}H_{45}OH$, found esp. in animal fats, blood, and bile

cho·line (kō′lēn, käl′ēn) ***n.*** [CHOL(O)- + -INE[4]] a viscous liquid, $C_5H_{15}O_2N$, found in many animal and vegetable tissues: a vitamin of the B complex

chol·o- [< Gr. *cholē,* bile] *a combining form meaning* bile

chomp (chämp) ***vt., vi.*** [dial. var. of CHAMP[1]] **1.** to chew hard and noisily **2.** to bite down (*on*) repeatedly and restlessly —***n.*** the act or sound of chomping —**chomp′er** ***n.***

chon (chän) ***n.,*** *pl.* **chon** [Korean, orig., a unit of weight] *see* MONETARY UNITS, table (Korea)

choose (cho͞oz) ***vt.*** **chose, cho′sen** or obs. **chose, choos′ing** [OE. *ceosan*] **1.** to pick out; take as a choice; select **2.** to decide or prefer [to *choose* to remain] —***vi.*** **1.** to make one's selection **2.** to have the desire or wish —**cannot choose but** cannot do otherwise than —**choose up** [Colloq.] to decide on the opposing players, as for a ball game —**choos′er** ***n.***

choos·y, choos·ey (cho͞o′zē) ***adj.*** **choos′i·er, choos′i·est** [Colloq.] very careful or fussy

chop[1] (chäp) ***vt.*** **chopped, chop′ping** [ME. *choppen,* prob. < OFr. *c(h)oper,* to cut] **1.** to cut by blows with an ax or other sharp tool **2.** to cut into small bits **3.** to say in an abrupt way **4.** to hit with a short, sharp stroke —***vi.*** **1.** to make quick, cutting strokes with a sharp tool **2.** to act with a quick, jerky motion —***n.*** **1.** the act of chopping **2.** a short, sharp blow or stroke **3.** a piece chopped off **4.** a slice of lamb, pork, veal, etc. cut from the rib, loin, or shoulder **5.** a short, broken movement of waves

chop[2] (chäp) ***n.*** [var. of CHAP[1]] **1.** a jaw **2.** a cheek See CHOPS

chop[3] (chäp) ***vi.*** **chopped, chop′ping** [OE. *ceapian,* to bargain] to shift or veer suddenly, as the wind; change direction —**chop logic** to argue

chop·fall·en (-fô′lən) ***adj.*** *same as* CHAPFALLEN

chop·house (-hous′) ***n.*** a restaurant that specializes in chops and steaks

Cho·pin (shō′pan; *Fr.* shô pan′), **Fré·dé·ric Fran·çois** (frā dā rēk′ frän swà′) 1810–49; Pol. composer & pianist, in France after 1831

chop·per (chäp′ər) ***n.*** **1.** a person or thing that chops **2.** [*pl.*] [Slang] a set of teeth, esp. false teeth **3.** [Colloq.] a helicopter

chop·py[1] (-ē) ***adj.*** **-pi·er, -pi·est** [< CHOP[3] + -Y[2]] shifting constantly and abruptly, as the wind —**chop′pi·ness** ***n.***

chop·py[2] (-ē) ***adj.*** **-pi·er, -pi·est** [< CHOP[1] + -Y[2]] **1.** rough with short, broken waves, as the sea **2.** making abrupt starts and stops; jerky —**chop′pi·ly** ***adv.*** —**chop′pi·ness** ***n.***

chops (chäps) ***n.pl.*** [see CHAP[1]] **1.** the jaws **2.** the mouth and lower cheeks **3.** [Slang] technical skill, esp. of a jazz or rock musician

chop·sticks (chäp′stiks′) ***n.pl.*** [PidE. for Chin. *k'wai-tsze,* the quick ones] two small sticks held together in one hand and used in some Asian countries to lift food to the mouth

chop su·ey (chäp′ so͞o′ē) [altered < Chin. *tsa-sui,* lit., various pieces] a Chinese-American dish of meat, bean sprouts, celery, mushrooms, etc. cooked together in a sauce and served with rice

cho·ral (kôr′əl) ***adj.*** [Fr.] of, for, sung by, or recited by a choir or chorus —**cho′ral·ly** ***adv.***

cho·rale, cho·ral (kə ral′, kô-) ***n.*** [< G. *choral (gesang),* choral (song)] **1.** a hymn tune **2.** a choral composition based on such a tune **3.** a group of singers; choir

chord[1] (kôrd) ***n.*** [altered (after L. *chorda*) < CORD] **1.** a feeling or emotion thought of as being played on like the string of a harp [to strike a sympathetic *chord*] **2.** *Anat. same as* CORD (sense 5) **3.** *Engineering* a principal horizontal member in a rigid framework, as of a bridge **4.** *Geom.* a straight line joining any two points on an arc, curve, or circumference

C
A
O

CHORDS (AC, AO)

chord[2] (kôrd) ***n.*** [< *cord,* aphetic < ACCORD] *Music* a combination of three or more tones sounded together in harmony —***vi., vt.*** **1.** to harmonize **2.** to play chords on —**chord′al** ***adj.***

chore (chôr) ***n.*** [< OE. *cierr:* see CHARE] **1.** a small routine task; odd job: *often used in pl.* **2.** a hard or unpleasant task

cho·re·a (kô rē′ə) ***n.*** [ModL. < L. < Gr. *choreia,* choral dance] a nervous disorder characterized by jerking movements caused by involuntary muscular contractions; Saint Vitus' dance

chor·e·o·graph (kôr′ē ə graf′) ***vt., vi.*** [< ff.] to design or plan the movements of (a dance, esp. a ballet) —**chor′e·og′ra·pher** (-äg′rə fər) ***n.***

chor·e·og·ra·phy (kôr′ē äg′rə fē) ***n.*** [Gr. *choreia,* dance + -GRAPHY] **1.** dancing, esp. ballet dancing **2.** the arrangement of the movements of a dance **3.** the art of devising dances, esp. ballets —**chor′e·o·graph′ic** (-ə graf′ik) ***adj.*** —**chor′e·o·graph′i·cal·ly** ***adv.***

cho·ric (kôr′ik) ***adj.*** of, for, or like a chorus, esp. in an ancient Greek play

chor·is·ter (kôr′is tər) ***n.*** [< OFr. *cueristre:* see CHOIR] a member of a choir, esp. a boy singer

C-horizon ***n.*** *see* ABC SOIL

cho·roid (kôr′oid) ***adj.*** [< Gr. < *chorion,* leather + *eidos,* form] designating or of certain vascular membranes —***n.*** the dark, vascular membrane between the sclera and retina of the eye Also **cho′ri·oid′** (-ē oid′)

chor·tle (chôr′t′l) ***vi., vt.*** **-tled, -tling** [coined by Lewis Carroll, prob. < CHUCKLE + SNORT] to make, or utter with, a gleeful chuckling or snorting sound —*n.* such a sound —**chor′tler** *n.*

cho·rus (kôr′əs) *n.* [L. < Gr. *choros,* a dance, chorus] **1.** in ancient Greek drama, a group whose singing, dancing, and narration supplement the main action **2.** a group of dancers and singers performing together as in an opera **3.** the part of a drama, song, etc. performed by a chorus **4.** a group trained to sing or speak something together simultaneously **5.** a simultaneous utterance by many [*a chorus* of protest] **6.** music written for group singing **7.** *a*) the refrain of a song following each verse *b*) the main tune, as of a jazz piece, following the introduction —*vt., vi.* to sing, speak, or say in unison —**in chorus** in unison

chorus girl (or **boy**) a woman (or man) singing or dancing in the chorus of a musical show

chose (chōz) *pt. & obs. pp. of* CHOOSE

Cho·sen (chō′sen′) *Jap. name of* KOREA

cho·sen (chō′z′n) *pp. of* CHOOSE —*adj.* picked out by preference; selected

Chou (jō) a Chinese dynasty (1122? to 256? B.C.)

chow (chou) *n.* [< Chin. dial. form akin to Cantonese *kaú,* a dog] **1.** any of a breed of medium-sized dog, originally from China, with a compact, muscular body and thick coat of brown or black: official name **chow chow** **2.** [Slang] food

chow·chow (chou′chou′) *n.* [PidE. < Chin.] chopped pickles in a highly seasoned mustard sauce

chow·der (chou′dər) *n.* [Fr. *chaudière,* a pot < LL. *caldaria:* see CALDRON] a thick soup of onions, potatoes, and salt pork, sometimes corn, tomatoes, etc. and often, specif., clams and milk

chow mein (chou mān′) [Chin. *ch'ao,* to fry + *mien,* flour] a Chinese-American dish consisting of a thick stew of meat, celery, bean sprouts, etc., served with fried noodles and usually soy sauce

Chr. **1.** Christ **2.** Christian **3.** Chronicles

chrism (kriz′'m) *n.* [< OE. < LL. < Gr. *chrisma* < *chriein,* to anoint] consecrated oil used in baptism and other sacraments —**chris′mal** *adj.*

Christ (krīst) [< LL. < Gr. *christos,* the anointed (in NT., MESSIAH) < *chriein,* to anoint] Jesus of Nazareth, regarded by Christians as the Messiah prophesied in the Old Testament

Christ·church (krīst′church′) city on the E coast of South Island, New Zealand: pop. (of urban area) 256,000

chris·ten (kris′'n) *vt.* [OE. *cristnian*] **1.** to take into a Christian church by baptism; baptize **2.** to give a name to at baptism **3.** to give a name to (a ship being launched, etc.) **4.** [Colloq.] to make use of for the first time —**chris′ten·ing** *n.*

Chris·ten·dom (-dəm) *n.* **1.** Christians collectively **2.** those parts of the world where most of the inhabitants profess Christianity

Chris·tian (kris′chən) a masculine name —*n.* [OE. *cristen,* ult. < Gr. *christos:* see CHRIST] **1.** a person professing belief in Jesus as the Christ, or in the religion based on the teachings of Jesus **2.** [Colloq.] a decent, respectable person —*adj.* **1.** of Jesus Christ or his teachings **2.** of or professing the religion based on these teachings **3.** having the qualities demonstrated and taught by Jesus Christ, as love, kindness, etc. **4.** of or representing Christians or Christianity **5.** [Colloq.] humane, decent, etc. —**Chris′tian·ly** *adj., adv.*

Christian Era the era beginning with the year formerly thought to be that of the birth of Jesus Christ (born probably c. 8–4 B.C.)

Chris·ti·a·ni·a (kris′chē an′ē ə, -tē än′-) *former name of* OSLO —*n.* [*also* **c-**] *same as* CHRISTIE

Chris·ti·an·i·ty (kris′chē an′ə tē) *n.* **1.** Christians collectively **2.** the Christian religion **3.** a particular Christian religious system **4.** the state of being a Christian

Chris·tian·ize (kris′chə nīz′) *vt.* **-ized′, -iz′ing** **1.** to convert to Christianity **2.** to cause to conform with Christian character or precepts —**Chris′tian·i·za′tion** *n.* —**Chris′tian·iz′er** *n.*

Christian name the baptismal name or given name, as distinguished from the surname or family name

Christian Science a religion and system of healing founded by Mary Baker Eddy c. 1866: official name, CHURCH OF CHRIST, SCIENTIST —**Christian Scientist**

chris·tie, chris·ty (kris′tē) *n., pl.* **-ties** [< CHRISTIANIA] *Skiing* any of various high-speed turns to change direction, stop, etc., made by shifting weight, with skis usually kept parallel

Chris·tine (kris tēn′) [< LL. fem. of CHRISTIAN] a feminine name: var. *Christina*

Christ·like (krīst′līk′) *adj.* like Jesus Christ, esp. in character or spirit —**Christ′like′ness** *n.*

Christ·ly (-lē) *adj.* of Jesus Christ; Christlike —**Christ′li·ness** *n.*

Christ·mas (kris′məs) *n.* [OE. *Cristesmæsse:* see CHRIST & MASS] **1.** a holiday on Dec. 25 celebrating the birth of Jesus Christ: also **Christmas Day** **2.** *same as* CHRISTMASTIDE

Christmas Eve the evening before Christmas Day

Christ·mas·tide (-tīd′) *n.* Christmas time, from Christmas Eve through New Year's Day or to Epiphany (Jan. 6)

Chris·to·pher (kris′tə fər) [< LL. < Gr. *Christophoros,* lit., bearing Christ] **1.** a masculine name: dim. *Chris* **2.** Saint, 3d cent. A.D.?; patron saint of travelers

chro·mate (krō′māt) *n.* a salt of chromic acid

chro·mat·ic (krō mat′ik) *adj.* [< LL. < Gr. < *chrōma,* color] **1.** of or having color or colors **2.** highly colored **3.** *Music* *a*) using or progressing by semitones [*a chromatic* scale] *b*) using tones not in the key of a work —*n.* *Music* a tone modified by an accidental —**chro·mat′i·cal·ly** *adv.* —**chro·mat′i·cism** (-ə siz'm) *n.*

chro·mat·ics (krō mat′iks) *n.pl.* [*with sing. v.*] the scientific study of colors

chromatic scale the musical scale made up of thirteen successive semitones to the octave

chro·ma·tin (krō′mə tin) *n.* [< Gr. *chrōma* (gen. *chrōmatos*), color + -IN[1]] a protoplasmic substance in the nucleus of living cells that readily takes a deep stain: chromatin forms the chromosomes

chro·ma·to- [< Gr. *chrōma:* see prec.] *a combining form meaning:* **1.** color or pigmentation **2.** chromatin Also, before a vowel, **chromat-**

chrome (krōm) *n.* [Fr. < Gr. *chrōma,* color] **1.** chromium or chromium alloy, esp. as plating **2.** any of certain salts of chromium, used in dyeing and tanning **3.** a chromium pigment —*vt.* **chromed, chrom′ing** **1.** to plate with chromium **2.** to treat with a salt of chromium, as in dyeing

-chrome (krōm) [< Gr. *chrōma,* color] *a suffix meaning:* **1.** color or coloring agent **2.** chromium

chro·mic (krō′mik) *adj.* designating or of compounds containing trivalent chromium

chromic acid an acid, H_2CrO_4, existing only in solution or known in the form of its salts

chro·mi·um (krō′mē əm) *n.* [CHROM(E) + -IUM] a very hard, metallic chemical element with a high resistance to corrosion: symbol, Cr; at. wt., 51.996; at. no., 24

chromium steel a very strong, hard alloy steel containing chromium: also **chrome steel**

chro·mo (krō′mō) *n., pl.* **-mos** a chromolithograph

chro·mo- [< Gr. *chrōma,* color] *a combining form meaning* color or pigment [*chromosome*]: also, before a vowel, **chrom-**

chro·mo·lith·o·graph (krō′mō lith′ə graf′) *n.* a colored picture printed by the lithographic process from a series of stone or metal plates

chro·mo·some (krō′mə sōm′) *n.* [CHROMO- + -SOME[3]] any of the microscopic rod-shaped bodies into which the chromatin of a cell nucleus separates during mitosis: they carry the genes, which convey hereditary characters, and are constant in number for each species —**chro′mo·so′mal** *adj.*

chro·mo·sphere (-sfir′) *n.* [CHROMO- + -SPHERE] the reddish layer of gases around the sun between the photosphere and the corona —**chro′mo·spher′ic** (-sfir′ik, -sfer′-) *adj.*

chro·mous (krō′məs) *adj.* designating or of compounds containing bivalent chromium

Chron. Chronicles

chron. **1.** chronological **2.** chronology

chron·ic (krän′ik) *adj.* [< Fr. < L. < Gr. < *chronos,* time] **1.** lasting a long time or recurring often: said of a disease, and distinguished from ACUTE **2.** having had an ailment for a long time **3.** perpetual; constant [*a chronic* worry] **4.** habitual —*n.* a chronic patient —**chron′i·cal·ly** *adv.*

chron·i·cle (krän′i k'l) *n.* [< Anglo-Fr. < OFr. < L. < Gr. *chronika,* annals: see prec.] **1.** a historical record of events in the order in which they happened **2.** a narrative; history —*vt.* **-cled, -cling** to tell or write the history of; put into a chronicle —**chron′i·cler** (-klər) *n.*

Chron·i·cles (-k'lz) either of two books of the Bible, I and II Chronicles

chro·no- [Gr. < *chronos,* time] *a combining form meaning* time: also, before a vowel, **chron-**

chron·o·graph (krän′ə graf′, krō′nə-) *n.* [CHRONO- + -GRAPH] an instrument for measuring brief, precisely spaced intervals of time, as a stopwatch

chron·o·log·i·cal (krän′ə läj′i k'l) *adj.* **1.** arranged in the order of occurrence **2.** relating to a narrative or history Also **chron′o·log′ic** —**chron′o·log′i·cal·ly** *adv.*

chro·nol·o·gy (krə näl′ə jē) *n., pl.* **-gies** [CHRONO- + -LOGY] **1.** the science of measuring time and of dating events in proper order 2. an arrangement or list of events, dates, etc. in the order of occurrence —**chro·nol′o·gist, chro·nol′o·ger** *n.*

chro·nom·e·ter (-näm′ə tər) *n.* [CHRONO- + -METER] an instrument for measuring time precisely; highly accurate kind of clock or watch —**chron·o·met·ric** (krän′ə met′rik, krō′nə-), **chron′o·met′ri·cal** *adj.* —**chron′o·met′ri·cal·ly** *adv.*

chro·nom·e·try (krə näm′ə trē) *n.* the scientific measurement of time

-chro·ous (krō əs) [Gr. *chrōs, chroos,* color] *a terminal combining form meaning* colored

chrys·a·lid (kris′'l id) *n. same as* CHRYSALIS —*adj.* of a chrysalis

chrys·a·lis (kris′'l əs) *n., pl.* **chry·sal·i·des** (kri sal′ə dēz′), **chrys′a·lis·es** [< L. < Gr. *chrysallis,* golden-colored chrysalis < *chrysos,* gold] 1. the pupa of a butterfly, when it is in a case or cocoon 2. the case or cocoon 3. anything in a formative or undeveloped stage

chrys·an·the·mum (kri san′thə məm) *n.* [L. < Gr. < *chrysos,* gold + *anthemon,* a flower] 1. any of a genus of late-blooming plants of the composite family, cultivated for their showy flowers, in a wide variety of colors 2. the flower

chrys·o·lite (kris′ə līt′) *n.* [< OFr. < L. < Gr. < *chrysos,* gold + *lithos,* stone] *same as* OLIVINE

chrys·o·prase (-prāz′) *n.* [< OFr. < L. < Gr. < *chrysos,* gold + *prason,* leek] a light-green variety of chalcedony sometimes used as a semiprecious stone

chub (chub) *n., pl.* **chubs, chub:** see PLURAL, II, D, 1 [ME. *chubbe*] any of several small, freshwater fishes related to the minnows and carp

chub·by (chub′ē) *adj.* **-bi·er, -bi·est** [< prec.] round and plump —**chub′bi·ness** *n.*

chuck[1] (chuk) *vt.* [< ? Fr. *choquer,* to strike against] 1. to tap or pat gently, esp. under the chin, as a playful gesture 2. to throw with a quick, short movement; toss 3. [Slang] *a)* to discard; get rid of *b)* to quit *c)* to vomit (often with *up*) —*n.* 1. a light tap or squeeze under the chin 2. a toss 3. [Chiefly Western] food

chuck[2] (chuk) *n.* [prob. var. of CHOCK] 1. a cut of beef including the parts around the neck and the shoulder blade 2. a clamplike device, as on a lathe, by which the tool or work is held

CHUCK (of a drill)

chuck-a-luck (chuk′ə luk′) *n.* [< CHUCK[1] + LUCK] a gambling game using three dice: also called **chuck′-luck′**

chuck-full (chuk′fool′) *adj. same as* CHOCK-FULL

chuck·hole (chuk′hōl′) *n.* [< dial. *chock,* a bump + HOLE] a rough hole in a road, made by wear and weathering

chuck·le (chuk′'l) *vi.* **-led, -ling** [prob. < *chuck,* to cluck] 1. to laugh softly in a low tone, as in mild amusement 2. to cluck, as a hen —*n.* a soft, low-toned laugh —**chuck′ler** *n.*

chuck·le·head (-hed′) *n.* [Colloq.] a stupid person

chuck wagon [CHUCK[1], *n.* 3 + WAGON] [Slang] a wagon equipped as a kitchen for feeding cowboys or other outdoor workers

chuff (chuf) *vi., n.* [echoic] *same as* CHUG

chug (chug) *n.* [echoic] any of a series of abrupt, puffing or explosive sounds, as of a locomotive —*vi.* **chugged, chug′ging** to make, or move with, such sounds

chuk·ka (boot) (chuk′ə) [< CHUKKER] a man's ankle-high bootlike shoe, often fleece-lined

chuk·ker, chuk·kar (chuk′ər) *n.* [Hindi *chakar* < Sans. *cakra,* wheel] any of the periods of play, 7 1/2 minutes each, of a polo match

Chu·la Vis·ta (chōō′lə vis′tə) [AmSp., lit., beautiful view] city in SW Calif.: suburb of San Diego: pop. 84,000

chum (chum) *n.* [17th-c. slang; prob. < *chamber* in *chamber mate*] [Colloq.] a close friend —*vi.* **chummed, chum′ming** [Colloq.] to be close friends

chum·my (chum′ē) *adj.* **-mi·er, -mi·est** [Colloq.] intimate; friendly —**chum′mi·ly** *adv.* —**chum′mi·ness** *n.*

chump (chump) *n.* [< ? CHUCK[2] or CHUNK + LUMP[1]] 1. a heavy block of wood 2. a thick, blunt end 3. [Colloq.] a foolish, stupid, or gullible person

Chung·king (chooŋ′kiŋ′; *Chin.* jooŋ′chiŋ′) city in SC China, on the Yangtze: pop. 4,070,000

chunk (chuŋk) *n.* [< ? CHUCK[2]] 1. a short, thick piece, as of meat, wood, etc. 2. a considerable portion 3. a stocky animal, esp. a horse

chunk·y (chuŋ′kē) *adj.* **chunk′i·er, chunk′i·est** 1. short and thick 2. stocky; thickset 3. containing chunks —**chunk′i·ness** *n.*

church (church) *n.* [< OE. *cirice,* ult. < Gr. *kyriakē* (*oikia*), Lord's (house) < *kyros,* supreme power] 1. a building for public worship, esp. one for Christian worship 2. public worship; religious service 3. [*usually* C-] *a)* all Christians collectively *b)* a particular sect or denomination of Christians 4. ecclesiastical government, or its power, as opposed to secular government 5. the profession of the clergy 6. a group of worshipers —*adj.* of a church or of organized Christian worship —**church′less** *adj.*

church·go·er (-gō′ər) *n.* a person who attends church, esp. regularly —**church′go′ing** *n., adj.*

Church·ill (church′chil), Sir **Winston (Leonard Spencer)** 1874–1965; Brit. statesman & writer; prime minister (1940–45; 1951–55)

church·ly (church′lē) *adj.* of, fit for, or belonging to, a church —**church′li·ness** *n.*

church·man (-mən) *n., pl.* **-men** 1. a clergyman 2. a member of a church

Church of Christ, Scientist *see* CHRISTIAN SCIENCE

Church of England the episcopal church of England; Anglican Church: it is an established church with the sovereign as its head

Church of Jesus Christ of Latter-day Saints *see* MORMON

church·ward·en (-wôr′d'n) *n.* a lay officer chosen annually in every parish of the Church of England or of the Protestant Episcopal Church to attend to certain secular matters

church·wom·an (-woom′ən) *n., pl.* **-wom′en** (-wim′in) a woman member of a church

church·yard (-yärd′) *n.* the yard adjoining a church, often used as a place of burial

churl (churl) *n.* [OE. *ceorl,* freeman] 1. a peasant 2. a surly, ill-bred, or miserly person —**churl′ish** *adj.* —**churl′ish·ly** *adv.* —**churl′ish·ness** *n.*

churn (churn) *n.* [OE. *cyrne*] 1. a container or contrivance in which milk or cream is beaten and shaken to form butter 2. unusually strong agitation —*vt.* 1. to beat and shake (milk or cream) in a churn 2. to make (butter) in a churn 3. to stir up vigorously 4. to make (foam, etc.) by stirring vigorously —*vi.* 1. to use a churn in making butter 2. to move as if in a churn; seethe

churr (chur) *n.* a low, trilled or whirring sound made by some birds —*vi.* to make such a sound

chute[1] (shōōt) *n.* [Fr., a fall, ult. < L. *cadere,* to fall] 1. a waterfall or rapids in a river 2. an inclined or vertical trough or passage down which something may slide or be slid or dropped

chute[2] (shōōt) *n. colloq. clipped form of* PARACHUTE —**chut′ist** *n.*

chut·ney (chut′nē) *n., pl.* **-neys** [Hindi *chatnī*] a relish made of fruits, spices, and herbs: also sp. **chut′nee**

chutz·pah, chutz·pa (hoots′pə, khoots′-; -pä) *n.* [Heb.] [Colloq.] shameless audacity; impudence; brass

chyle (kīl) *n.* [< LL. < Gr. *chylos* < *cheein,* to pour] a milky fluid composed of lymph and emulsified fats: it is formed from chyme in the small intestine and is passed into the blood through the thoracic duct —**chy·la·ceous** (kī lā′shəs), **chy′lous** *adj.*

chyme (kīm) *n.* [< LL. < Gr. *chymos,* juice < *cheein,* to pour] the semifluid mass resulting from gastric digestion of food: see CHYLE —**chy′mous** *adj.*

CIA, C.I.A. Central Intelligence Agency

‡**ciao** (chou) *interj.* [It.] an informal expression of greeting or farewell

ci·bo·ri·um (si bôr′ē əm) *n., pl.* **-ri·a** (-ə) [ML. < L., a cup < Gr. *kibōrion,* seed vessel of the Egyptian waterlily, hence, a cup] 1. a canopy covering an altar 2. a covered cup for holding the consecrated wafers of the Eucharist

ci·ca·da (si kā′də, -kä′-) *n., pl.* **-das, -dae** (-dē) [L.] a large flylike insect with transparent wings: the male makes a loud, shrill sound by vibrating a special organ on its underside

cic·a·trix (sik′ə triks) *n., pl.* **ci·cat·ri·ces** (si kat′rə sēz′, sik′ə trī′sēz) [L.] 1. *Med.* the contracted fibrous tissue at the place where a wound has healed; scar 2. *Bot.* the scar left where a branch, leaf, seed, etc. was once attached or where a wound has healed Also **cic′a·trice** (-tris) —**cic′a·tri′cial** (-trish′əl) *adj.*

cic·a·trize (-trīz′) *vt., vi.* **-trized′, -triz′ing** to heal with the formation of a scar —**cic′a·tri·za′tion** *n.*

Cic·er·o (sis′ə rō′) [after ff.] city in NE Ill.: suburb of Chicago: pop. 61,000

Cic·er·o (sis′ə rō′), **(Marcus Tullius)** 106–43 B.C.; Rom. statesman & orator —**Cic′e·ro′ni·an** *adj.*

ci·ce·ro·ne (sis′ə rō′nē; *It.* chē che rô′ne) *n., pl.* **-nes;** It. **-ni** (-nē) [It. < L. *Cicero,* the orator] a well-informed guide for sightseers

Cid (sid; *Sp.* thēth), **the** [Sp. < Ar. *sayyid,* a lord] (born *Rodrigo,* or *Ruy, Díaz de Bivar*) 1040?–99; Sp. hero and soldier of fortune

-cide (sīd) [< Fr. *-cide* or L. *-cida* < L. *caedere,* to kill] *a suffix meaning:* 1. killer *[pesticide]* 2. killing *[genocide]*

ci·der (sī′dər) *n.* [< OFr. < LL. < Gr. *sikera* < Heb. *shēkār,* strong drink] the juice pressed from apples, used as a beverage or for making vinegar: **sweet cider** is unfermented, **hard cider** is fermented

C.I.F., c.i.f. cost, insurance, and freight

ci·gar (si gär′) *n.* [Sp. *cigarro,* prob. < Maya *sicar,* to smoke < *sīć,* tobacco] a compact roll of tobacco leaves for smoking
cig·a·rette, cig·a·ret (sig′ə ret′, sig′ə ret′) *n.* [Fr., dim. of *cigare,* cigar] a small roll of finely cut tobacco wrapped in thin paper for smoking
cig·a·ril·lo (sig′ə ril′ō) *n., pl.* **-los** [Sp., dim. of *cigarro,* CIGAR] a small, thin cigar
cil·i·a (sil′ē ə) *n.pl., sing.* **-i·um** (-əm) [L.] **1.** the eyelashes **2.** *Bot.* small hairlike processes, as on the edges of some leaves **3.** *Zool.* hairlike outgrowths of certain cells, capable of rhythmic beating that can produce locomotion, as in protozoans or small worms —**cil′i·ate** (-it, -āt′), **cil′i·at′ed** *adj.*
cil·i·ar·y (sil′ē er′ē) *adj.* of, like, or having cilia
cim·ba·lom, cym·ba·lom (sim′bə ləm) *n.* [< Hung. < L. *cymbalum,* cymbal] a type of large dulcimer associated with Hungarian folk music
Cim·me·ri·an (si mir′ē ən) *n.* *Class. Myth.* any of a people living in a land of perpetual mist and darkness —*adj.* dark; gloomy
cinch (sinch) *n.* [< Sp. < L. *cingulum,* a girdle < *cingere,* to encircle] **1.** a saddle or pack girth **2.** [Colloq.] a firm grip **3.** [Slang] a sure or easy thing —*vt.* **1.** to gird with a cinch **2.** [Slang] *a)* to get a firm hold on *b)* to make sure of
cin·cho·na (sin kō′nə, siŋ-) *n.* [ModL., after the Countess del *Chinchón,* wife of a 17th-c. Peruv. viceroy, who was treated with the bark] **1.** a tropical S. American tree from the bark of which quinine is obtained **2.** the bitter bark of this tree —**cin·chon′ic** (-kän′ik) *adj.*
cin·cho·nize (sin′kə nīz′) *vt.* **-nized′, -niz′ing** to treat with cinchona, quinine, etc.
Cin·cin·nat·i (sin′sə nat′ē, -ə) [ult. after *Cincinnatus,* Rom. general of 5th c. B.C.] city in SW Ohio, on the Ohio River: pop. 385,000 (met. area 1,392,000)
cinc·ture (siŋk′chər) *n.* [L. *cinctura,* a girdle < *cingere:* see CINCH] **1.** an encircling or girding **2.** anything that encircles, as a belt or girdle —*vt.* **-tured, -tur·ing** to encircle with or as with a cincture
cin·der (sin′dər) *n.* [OE. *sinder*] **1.** slag, as from the smelting of ores **2.** any matter, as coal or wood, burned but not reduced to ashes **3.** a minute piece of such matter **4.** a coal that is still burning but not flaming **5.** [*pl.*] ashes from coal or wood —**cin′der·y** *adj.*
cinder block a building block, usually hollow, made of concrete and fine cinders
Cin·der·el·la (sin′də rel′ə) the title character of a fairy tale, a household drudge who, with the help of a fairy godmother, marries a prince
cin·e·ma (sin′ə mə) *n.* [< CINEMA(TOGRAPH)] [Chiefly Brit.] **1.** a motion picture **2.** a motion-picture theater —**the cinema 1.** the art or business of making motion pictures **2.** motion pictures; the movies —**cin′e·mat′ic** (-mat′ik) *adj.* —**cin′e·mat′i·cal·ly** *adv.*
cin·e·mat·o·graph (sin′ə mat′ə graf′) *n.* [< Fr. < Gr. *kinēma,* motion + *graphein,* to write] [Chiefly Brit.] a motion-picture projector, camera, theater, etc. —*adj.* [Chiefly Brit.] motion-picture
cin·e·ma·tog·ra·pher (sin′ə mə täg′rə fər) *n.* [Chiefly Brit.] a motion-picture cameraman
cin·e·ma·tog·ra·phy (-fē) *n.* the art of photography in making motion pictures —**cin′e·mat′o·graph′ic** (-mat′ə graf′ik), **cin′e·mat′o·graph′i·cal** *adj.* —**cin′e·mat′o·graph′i·cal·ly** *adv.*
‡**cin·é·ma vér·i·té** (sē nā mä′ vā rē tā′) [Fr., lit., truth cinema] a form of documentary film in which a small camera and unobtrusive techniques are used to record scenes as naturally as possible
cin·e·rar·i·a (sin′ə rer′ē ə) *n.* [ModL. < L. < *cinis,* ashes: the leaves have an ash-colored down] a common hothouse plant of the composite family, with heart-shaped leaves and colorful flowers
cin·e·rar·i·um (-ē əm) *n., pl.* **-rar′i·a** (-ə) [L. < *cinis,* ashes] a place to keep the ashes of cremated bodies —**cin′e·rar′y** *adj.*
cin·er·a·tor (sin′ə rāt′ər) *n.* [< CINERARIUM] a furnace for cremation; crematory
cin·na·bar (sin′ə bär′) *n.* [< L. < Gr. *kinnabari* < ? Per. *šangarf*] **1.** mercuric sulfide, HgS, a heavy, bright-red mineral, the principal ore of mercury **2.** artificial mercuric sulfide, used as a red pigment **3.** brilliant red; vermilion
cin·na·mon (sin′ə mən) *n.* [< OFr. < L. < Gr. < Heb. *qinnāmōn*] **1.** the yellowish-brown spice made from the dried inner bark of a laurel tree or shrub native to the East Indies and SE Asia **2.** this bark **3.** any tree or shrub from which it is obtained **4.** yellowish brown —*adj.* **1.** yellowish-brown **2.** made or flavored with cinnamon

cinque·foil (siŋk′foil′) *n.* [< OFr. < It. < L. < *quinque,* five + *folium,* leaf] **1.** a plant of the rose family with a fruit like a dry strawberry: some species have compound leaves with five leaflets **2.** *Archit.* a circular design of five converging arcs

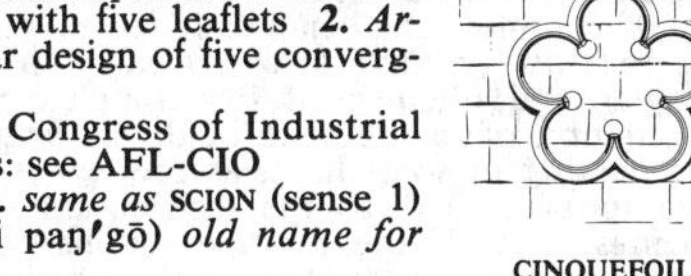
CINQUEFOIL

CIO, C.I.O. Congress of Industrial Organizations: see AFL-CIO
ci·on (sī′ən) *n.* *same as* SCION (sense 1)
Ci·pan·go (si paŋ′gō) *old name for* JAPAN
ci·pher (sī′fər) *n.* [< OFr. < ML. < Ar. *ṣifr,* nothing < *ṣafare,* to be empty] **1.** the symbol 0, indicating a value of naught; zero **2.** a person or thing of no importance or value; nonentity **3.** *a)* a system of secret writing based on a key *b)* a message in such writing *c)* the key to such a system See also CODE **4.** a monogram **5.** an Arabic numeral —*vt., vi.* **1.** [Now Rare] to do, or solve by, arithmetic **2.** to write in cipher, or secret writing
cir., circ. 1. circa **2.** circulation **3.** circumference
cir·ca (sʉr′kə) *prep.* [L.] about: used before an approximate date, figure, etc. [*circa* 1650]
cir·ca·di·an (sər kā′dē ən) *adj.* [coined < L. *circa,* about + acc. sing. of *dies,* day] designating or of certain biological rhythms associated with the 24-hour daily cycles, as, in man, the regular metabolic, glandular, and sleep rhythms
Cir·cas·si·a (sər kash′ə, -kash′ē ə) region of the U.S.S.R., in the NW Caucasus —**Cir·cas′si·an** *adj., n.*
Cir·ce (sʉr′sē) in Homer's *Odyssey,* an enchantress who turned men into swine —**Cir·ce·an** (sər sē′ən, sʉr′sē ən) *adj.*
cir·cle (sʉr′k'l) *n.* [< OFr. < L. *circulus,* dim. of *circus:* see CIRCUS] **1.** a plane figure bounded by a single curved line every point of which is equally distant from the point at the center **2.** the line bounding such a figure; circumference **3.** anything shaped like a circle, as a ring, crown, etc. **4.** the orbit of a heavenly body **5.** a section of seats in a theater, as in a balcony [the dress *circle*] **6.** a complete or recurring series, usually ending as it began; cycle; period **7.** a group of people bound together by common interests; group; coterie **8.** range or extent, as of influence or interest; scope —*vt.* **-cled, -cling 1.** to form a circle around; encompass; surround **2.** to move around, as in a circle —*vi.* to go around in a circle; revolve —**come full circle** to return to an original position or state after going through a series or cycle —**cir′cler** *n.*
cir·clet (sʉr′klit) *n.* **1.** a small circle **2.** a circular band worn as an ornament, esp. on the head
cir·cuit (sʉr′kit) *n.* [OFr. < L. *circuitus* < *circum,* around + *ire,* to go] **1.** the line or the length of the line forming the boundaries of an area **2.** the area bounded **3.** a going around something; course or journey around **4.** *a)* the regular journey through a fixed district of a person performing his duties, as of a circuit court judge *b)* such a district **5.** a chain or group of theaters, resorts, etc. at which plays, movies, entertainers, etc. appear in turn **6.** *Elec. a)* a complete or partial path over which current may flow *b)* a hookup that is connected into this path —*vi.* to go in a circuit —*vt.* to make a circuit about —**cir′cuit·al** *adj.*
circuit breaker a device that automatically interrupts the flow of an electric current
circuit court a State court having original jurisdiction in several counties or a district
cir·cu·i·tous (sər kyōō′ə təs) *adj.* [see CIRCUIT] roundabout; indirect; devious —**cir·cu′i·tous·ly** *adv.* —**cir·cu′i·tous·ness, cir·cu′i·ty** *n., pl.* **-ties**
circuit rider a minister who travels from place to place in his circuit to preach
cir·cuit·ry (sʉr′kə trē) *n.* the scheme, system, or components of an electric circuit
cir·cu·lar (sʉr′kyə lər) *adj.* [L. *circularis*] **1.** in the shape of a circle; round **2.** relating to a circle **3.** moving in a circle or spiral **4.** roundabout; circuitous **5.** intended for circulation among a number of people —*n.* a circular advertisement, letter, etc. —**cir′cu·lar′i·ty** (-ler′ə tē) *n.* —**cir′cu·lar·ly** *adv.*
cir·cu·lar·ize (-lə rīz′) *vt.* **-ized′, -iz′ing 1.** to make circular **2.** to send circulars to **3.** to canvass —**cir′cu·lar·i·za′tion** *n.* —**cir′cu·lar·iz′er** *n.*
circular saw a saw in the form of a disk with a toothed edge, rotated at high speed by a motor
cir·cu·late (sʉr′kyə lāt′) *vi.* **-lat′ed, -lat′ing** [< L. pp. of *circulari,* to form a circle] **1.** to move in a circle or circuit and return to the same point, as the blood **2.** to go from person to person or from place to place; specif., *a)* to move about freely, as air *b)* to move about in society, at a party, meeting, etc. *c)* to be made widely known or felt *d)* to be

distributed to a mass of readers —*vt.* to cause to circulate —**cir′cu·la′tor** *n.* —**cir′cu·la·to′ry** (-lə tôr′ē), **cir′cu·la′tive** (-lā′tiv) *adj.*
circulating library a library from which books can be borrowed, sometimes for a small daily fee
cir·cu·la·tion (sur′kyə lā′shən) *n.* **1.** a circulating or moving around, often specif. in a complete circuit, as of air in ventilating or of blood through the arteries and veins **2.** the passing of something, as money, news, etc., from person to person **3.** *a*) the distribution of newspapers, magazines, etc. *b*) the average number of copies of a magazine or newspaper sold in a given period
cir·cum- [< L. *circum*, around, about] *a prefix meaning* around, about, surrounding, on all sides
cir·cum·am·bi·ent (sur′kəm am′bē ənt) *adj.* [CIRCUM- + AMBIENT] extending all around; surrounding —**cir′cum·am′bi·ence, cir′cum·am′bi·en·cy** *n.*
cir·cum·cise (sur′kəm sīz′) *vt.* **-cised′, -cis′ing** [< OFr. < L. pp. of *circumcidere* < *circum-*, around + *caedere*, to cut] to cut off all or part of the foreskin of —**cir′cum·ci′sion** (-sizh′ən) *n.*
cir·cum·fer·ence (sər kum′fər əns, -frəns) *n.* [< L. prp. of *circumferre* < *circum-*, around + *ferre*, to carry] **1.** the line bounding a circle or other rounded surface or area **2.** the distance measured by this line —**cir·cum′fer·en′tial** (-fə ren′shəl) *adj.* —**cir·cum′fer·en′tial·ly** *adv.*
cir·cum·flex (sur′kəm fleks′) *n.* [< L. pp. of *circumflectere* < *circum-*, around + *flectere*, to bend] a mark (^, ⌒, ~) used over certain vowels in some languages to indicate a specific sound, or as a diacritical mark in some pronunciation systems: also **circumflex accent** —*adj.* **1.** of or marked by a circumflex **2.** bending around; curved —*vt.* **1.** to bend around; curve **2.** to write with a circumflex —**cir′cum·flex′ion** *n.*
cir·cum·flu·ent (sər kum′floo wənt) *adj.* [< L. prp. of *circumfluere* < *circum-*, around + *fluere*, to flow] flowing around; surrounding: also **cir·cum′flu·ous**
cir·cum·fuse (sur′kəm fyōōz′) *vt.* **-fused′, -fus′ing** [< L. pp. of *circumfundere* < *circum-*, around + *fundere*, to pour] **1.** to pour or spread (a fluid) around; diffuse **2.** to surround (*with* a fluid); suffuse (*in*) —**cir′cum·fu′sion** *n.*
cir·cum·lo·cu·tion (-lō kyōō′shən) *n.* [< L.: see CIRCUM- & LOCUTION] a roundabout, indirect, or lengthy way of expressing something —**cir′cum·loc′u·to′ry** (-läk′yə tôr′ē) *adj.*
cir·cum·nav·i·gate (-nav′ə gāt′) *vt.* **-gat′ed, -gat′ing** [< L. pp. of *circumnavigare:* see CIRCUM- & NAVIGATE] to sail or fly around (the earth, an island, etc.) —**cir′cum·nav′i·ga′tion** *n.* —**cir′cum·nav′i·ga′tor** *n.*
cir·cum·scribe (sur′kəm skrīb′, sur′kəm skrīb′) *vt.* **-scribed′, -scrib′ing** [< L. < *circum-*, around + *scribere*, to write] **1.** to trace a line around; encircle **2.** *a*) to limit; confine *b*) to restrict **3.** *Geom. a*) to draw a figure around (another figure) so as to touch it at as many points as possible *b*) to be thus drawn around —**cir′cum·scrib′a·ble** *adj.* —**cir′cum·scrib′er** *n.* —**cir′cum·scrip′tion** (-skrip′shən) *n.*
cir·cum·spect (sur′kəm spekt′) *adj.* [< L. pp. of *circumspicere* < *circum-*, around + *specere*, to look] careful to consider all related circumstances before acting, deciding, etc.; cautious —**cir′cum·spec′tion** *n.* —**cir′cum·spect′ly** *adv.*
cir·cum·stance (-stans′, -stəns) *n.* [< OFr. < L. < *circum-*, around + *stare*, to stand] **1.** a fact or event, esp. one accompanying another, either incidentally or as a determining factor **2.** [*pl.*] conditions affecting a person, esp. financial conditions **3.** chance; luck **4.** ceremony; show [*pomp and circumstance*] **5.** *a*) surrounding detail *b*) fullness of detail —*vt.* **-stanced′, -stanc′ing** to place in certain circumstances —**under no circumstances** under no conditions; never —**under the circumstances** conditions being what they are or were —**cir′cum·stanced′** *adj.*
cir·cum·stan·tial (sur′kəm stan′shəl) *adj.* **1.** having to do with, or depending on, circumstances **2.** incidental **3.** full or complete in detail **4.** ceremonial —**cir′cum·stan′ti·al′i·ty** (-shē al′ə tē) *n., pl.* **-ties** —**cir′cum·stan′tial·ly** *adv.*
circumstantial evidence *Law* evidence offered to prove certain circumstances from which the existence of the fact at issue may be inferred
cir·cum·stan·ti·ate (-stan′shē āt′) *vt.* **-at′ed, -at′ing** to give detailed proof or support of —**cir′cum·stan′ti·a′tion** *n.*
cir·cum·val·late (-val′āt) *vt.* **-lat·ed, -lat·ing** [< L. pp. of *circumvallare* < *circum-*, around + *vallare*, to wall] to surround with or as with a wall or trench —*adj.* surrounded by a wall, trench, etc. —**cir′cum·val·la′tion** *n.*
cir·cum·vent (sur′kəm vent′) *vt.* [< L. pp. of *circumvenire* < *circum-*, around + *venire*, to come] **1.** to surround or circle around **2.** to surround with evils, enmity, etc.; entrap **3.** to get the better of or prevent from happening by craft or ingenuity —**cir′cum·ven′tion** *n.*
cir·cus (sur′kəs) *n.* [L. < or akin to Gr. *kirkos*, a circle] **1.** in ancient Rome, an oval or oblong arena with tiers of seats around it, used for games, races, etc. **2.** a similar arena for a traveling show of acrobats, trained animals, clowns, etc. **3.** such a show or the performance of such a show **4.** [Colloq.] any riotously entertaining person, event, etc.
ci·ré (sə rā′) *adj.* [Fr., lit., waxed, ult. < Gr. *kēros*, wax] having a smooth, glossy finish as by treatment with wax —*n.* a ciré silk, straw, etc.
cir·rho·sis (sə rō′sis) *n.* [ModL. < Gr. *kirrhos*, tawny + -OSIS: after the yellowish color of the diseased liver] a degenerative disease in a bodily organ, esp. the liver, marked by excess formation of connective tissue and the subsequent contraction of the organ —**cir·rhot′ic** (-rät′ik) *adj.*
cir·ri- [< L. *cirrus*] *a combining form meaning* curl, ringlet: also **cir′ro-, cir′rhi-, cir′rho-**
cir·ro·cu·mu·lus (sir′ō kyōō′myə ləs) *n.* a high formation of clouds in small, white puffs, flakes, or streaks
cir·ro·stra·tus (-strāt′əs, -strat′-) *n.* a high formation of clouds in a thin, whitish veil
cir·rus (sir′əs) *n., pl.*, for 1 **-ri** (-ī); for 2 **-rus** [L., a curl] **1.** *a*) a plant tendril *b*) a flexible, threadlike appendage, as a feeler in certain organisms *c*) a cluster of fused cilia as in some infusorians **2.** a high formation of clouds in wispy filaments or feathery tufts
cis- [< L. *cis*, on this side] *a prefix meaning:* **1.** on this side of **2.** subsequent to
cis·al·pine (sis al′pīn, -pin) *adj.* on this (the Roman, or southern) side of the Alps
cis·co (sis′kō) *n., pl.* **-co, -coes, -cos:** see PLURAL, II, D, 2 [< CanadFr. < Algonquian] a fish related to the whitefish, found in the colder lakes of the NE U.S. and of Canada
cis·lu·nar (sis lōō′nər) *adj.* on this side of the moon, between the moon and the earth
Cis·ter·cian (sis tur′shən) *adj.* [< OFr. < ML. *Cistercium* (now *Cîteaux*, France)] designating or of a monastic order following the Benedictine rule strictly —*n.* a Cistercian monk or nun
cis·tern (sis′tərn) *n.* [< OFr. < L. < *cista*, CHEST] **1.** a large receptacle, usually underground, for storing water, esp. rain water **2.** *Anat.* a sac or cavity containing a natural body fluid
cit·a·del (sit′ə d′l, -del′) *n.* [< Fr. < It. dim. of *cittade*, city < L. *civitas*, CITY] **1.** a fortress on a commanding height for defense of a city **2.** a fortified place; stronghold **3.** a place of safety; refuge
ci·ta·tion (sī tā′shən) *n.* [< OFr. < L. pp. of *citare:* see ff.] **1.** a summons to appear before a court of law **2.** a citing; quoting **3.** a passage cited; quotation **4.** a reference to a legal statute, a previous law case, etc. **5.** *a*) official honorable mention for meritorious service in the armed forces *b*) a formal statement honoring a person —**ci′ta·tor** *n.* —**ci·ta·to·ry** (sīt′ə tôr′ē) *adj.*
cite (sīt) *vt.* **cit′ed, cit′ing** [< OFr. < L. *citare*, to summon < *ciere*, to rouse] **1.** to summon to appear before a court of law **2.** to quote (a passage, book, writer, etc.) **3.** to refer to or mention by way of example, proof, etc. **4.** to mention in a citation (sense 5) —**cit′a·ble, cite′a·ble** *adj.*
cith·a·ra (sith′ə rə) *n.* [L. < Gr. *kithara*] an ancient musical instrument somewhat like a lyre
cith·er (sith′ər) *n.* [< Fr. < prec.] *same as* CITTERN: also **cith′ern** (-ərn)
cit·i·fied (sit′i fīd′) *adj.* having the manners, dress, etc. attributed to city people
cit·i·zen (sit′ə zən) *n.* [Anglo-Fr. *citizein* < OFr. < *cite:* see CITY] **1.** formerly, an inhabitant of a town or city **2.** a member of a state or nation who owes allegiance to it by birth or naturalization and is entitled to full civil rights **3.** a civilian, as distinguished from a soldier, policeman, etc.
cit·i·zen·ry (-rē) *n.* all citizens as a group
citizens′ band either of two bands of shortwave radio frequencies for local use at low power by private persons
cit·i·zen·ship (-ship′) *n.* **1.** the status or condition of a citizen, or his duties, rights, and privileges **2.** one's conduct as a citizen
cit·rate (si′trāt, sī′-) *n.* [CITR(US) + -ATE[2]] a salt or ester of citric acid
cit·ric (si′trik) *adj.* [CITR(US) + -IC] **1.** of or from lemons, oranges, or similar fruits **2.** designating or of an acid, $C_6H_8O_7$, obtained from such fruits, used in making dyes, citrates, etc.
cit·ri·cul·ture (-trə kul′chər) *n.* the cultivation of citrus fruits
cit·rine (-trin, -trēn, -trīn) *adj.* [< OFr. < ML. < L. *citrus*, CITRUS] of the yellow color of a lemon —*n.* **1.** lemon yellow **2.** a yellow quartz
cit·ron (-trən) *n.* [Fr., lemon < It. *citrone* < L. *citrus*, CITRUS] **1.** a yellow, thick-skinned fruit resembling a lemon but larger and less acid **2.** the semitropical tree bearing this fruit **3.** the candied rind of this fruit, used in fruitcake, etc.

cit·ron·el·la (si′trə nel′ə) ***n.*** [ModL. < prec.] **1.** a volatile, sharp-smelling oil used in perfume, soap, insect repellents, etc.: also **citronella oil** **2.** a grass of S Asia from which it is derived
cit·rus (si′trəs) ***n.*** [L., citron tree (whence Gr. *kitron*)] **1.** any of a genus of trees and shrubs that bear oranges, lemons, limes, or other such fruit **2.** any such fruit —***adj.*** of these trees or shrubs: also **cit′rous** (-trəs)
cit·tern (sit′ərn) ***n.*** [< CITHER, prob. infl. by ME. *giterne,* GITTERN] a stringed instrument of the guitar family, popular in the 16th & 17th cent.
cit·y (sit′ē) ***n., pl.*** **cit′ies** [< OFr. *cite* < L. *civitas,* orig. citizenship < *civis,* citizen] **1.** a center of population larger or more important than a town or village **2.** in the U.S., an incorporated municipality whose boundaries and powers of self-government are defined by a charter from its State **3.** in Canada, a large urban municipality within a province **4.** all the people of a city —***adj.*** of or in a city
city chicken skewered pieces of pork or veal breaded and cooked by braising or baking
city fathers the important officials of a city
cit·y·fied (sit′i fīd′) ***adj.*** *same as* CITIFIED
city hall **1.** a building housing the offices of a municipal government **2.** a municipal government —**fight city hall** to fight futilely against petty or impersonal bureaucracy
city manager a chief municipal administrator appointed by a city council on a professional basis, with tenure free from public elections
cit·y·scape (sit′ē skāp′) ***n.*** [CITY + (LAND)SCAPE] **1.** a painting, photograph, etc. of a section of a city **2.** a view of a section of a city, esp. of buildings silhouetted against the horizon
cit·y-state (-stāt′) ***n.*** a state made up of an independent city and the territory directly controlled by it, as in ancient Greece
Ciu·dad Juá·rez (syōō *thäth′* hwä′res) city in N Mexico, on the Rio Grande: pop. 522,000
civ. **1.** civil **2.** civilian
civ·et (siv′it) ***n.*** [< Fr. < It. *zibetto* < Ar. *zabād*] **1.** a yellowish substance with a musklike scent, secreted by a gland of the civet cat and used in making some perfumes **2.** the civet cat or its fur
civet cat a catlike, flesh-eating mammal of Africa and S Asia, with spotted, yellowish fur
civ·ic (siv′ik) ***adj.*** [L. *civicus* < *civis:* see CITY] **1.** of a city **2.** of citizens or citizenship —**civ′i·cal·ly** ***adv.***
civ·ics (siv′iks) ***n.pl.*** [*with sing. v.*] the branch of political science dealing with civic affairs and the duties and rights of citizenship
civ·ies (siv′ēz) ***n.pl.*** [Colloq.] *same as* CIVVIES
civ·il (siv′'l) ***adj.*** [OFr. < L. *civilis* < *civis:* see CITY] **1.** of a citizen or citizens [*civil* rights] **2.** of a community of citizens, their government, or their interrelations **3.** civilized **4.** polite or courteous, esp. in a merely formal way **5.** not military or religious [*civil* marriage] **6.** *Law* relating to private rights and legal actions involving these
civil defense a system of warning devices, air-raid or fallout shelters, etc. for defense of a population against enemy attack
civil disobedience nonviolent opposition to a government policy or law by refusing to comply with it, on the grounds of conscience: see also NONCOOPERATION, PASSIVE RESISTANCE
civil engineering the branch of engineering dealing with the design and construction of highways, bridges, harbors, etc. —**civil engineer**
ci·vil·ian (sə vil′yən) ***n.*** [< OFr. < L.: see CIVIL] a person not an active member of the armed forces or of an official force having police power —***adj.*** of or for civilians; nonmilitary
ci·vil·i·ty (-ə tē) ***n., pl.*** **-ties** **1.** politeness, esp. of a merely formal kind **2.** a civil act or utterance
civ·i·li·za·tion (siv′ə lə zā′shən) ***n.*** **1.** a civilizing or becoming civilized **2.** the condition of being civilized; social organization of a high order **3.** the total culture of a people, nation, period, etc. **4.** the countries and peoples considered to have reached a high stage of social and cultural development **5.** intellectual and cultural refinement **6.** the comforts of civilized life
civ·i·lize (siv′ə līz′) ***vt.*** **-lized′, -liz′ing** [< Fr. < L.: see CIVIL & -IZE] **1.** to bring out of a primitive or savage condition and into a state of civilization **2.** to improve in habits or manners; refine —**civ′i·liz′a·ble** ***adj.*** —**civ′i·lized′** ***adj.***
civil law **1.** the body of codified law developed from Roman law **2.** the body of law that an individual nation or state has established for itself **3.** the body of law concerning private rights
civil liberties liberties guaranteed to the individual by law and custom; rights of thinking, speaking, and acting as one likes without hindrance except in the interests of the public welfare
civ·il·ly (siv′'l ē) ***adv.*** **1.** with civility; politely **2.** in relation to civil law, civil rights, etc.
civil marriage a marriage performed by a public official, not by a clergyman
civil rights those rights guaranteed to the individual by the 13th, 14th, 15th, and 19th Amendments to the Constitution
civil service **1.** all those employed in government work except those in the armed forces **2.** any government service in which a position is secured through competitive public examination —**civil servant**
civil war war between different sections or factions of the same nation —**the Civil War** the war between the North (the Union) and the South (the Confederacy) in the U.S. (1861–1865)
civ·vies (siv′ēz) ***n.pl.*** [Colloq.] civilian clothes, as distinguished from a military uniform; mufti
ck. *pl.* **cks.** **1.** cask **2.** check
Cl *Chem.* chlorine
cl. **1.** centiliter(s) **2.** claim **3.** class **4.** clause
clab·ber (klab′ər) ***n.*** [Ir. *clabar*] [Dial.] thickly curdled sour milk —***vi., vt.*** [Dial.] to curdle
clack (klak) ***vi.*** [prob. < ON. *klaka,* of echoic origin] **1.** to make a sudden, sharp sound [high heels *clacking*] **2.** to chatter —***vt.*** to cause to make a sudden, sharp sound —***n.*** **1.** a clacking sound **2.** chatter —**clack′er** ***n.***
clad (klad) *alt. pt. & pp. of* CLOTHE —***adj.*** **1.** clothed; dressed **2.** having a layer of another metal or of an alloy bonded to it [*clad* steel]
clad·ding (-iŋ) ***n.*** [see prec.] **1.** a layer of some metal or alloy bonded to another **2.** the process of bonding such materials
claim (klām) ***vt.*** [< OFr. < L. *clamare,* to cry out] **1.** to demand as rightfully belonging to one; assert one's right to (a title, etc. that should be recognized) **2.** to call for; require; deserve [problems *claiming* our attention] **3.** to assert; maintain —***n.*** **1.** a demand for something rightfully due **2.** a right or title to something **3.** something claimed, as land staked out by a settler **4.** an assertion —**claim′a·ble** ***adj.*** —**claim′er** ***n.***
claim·ant (klā′mənt) ***n.*** one who makes a claim
Claire (kler) [Fr., equiv. of CLARA] a feminine name
clair·voy·ance (kler voi′əns) ***n.*** [Fr. < ff.] **1.** the supposed ability to perceive things that are not in sight or that cannot be seen **2.** keen perception or insight
clair·voy·ant (-ənt) ***adj.*** [Fr. < *clair,* clear + prp. of *voir,* to see] **1.** of or apparently having clairvoyance **2.** having keen insight —***n.*** a clairvoyant person —**clair·voy′ant·ly** ***adv.***
clam (klam) ***n., pl.*** **clams, clam:** see PLURAL, II, D, 1 [< OE. *clamm,* fetter, in reference to the action of the shells] **1.** any of certain hard-shelled, bivalve mollusks living in the shallows of the sea or in fresh water **2.** the soft, edible part of these mollusks **3.** *same as* CLAMSHELL (sense 2) —***vi.*** to dig, or go digging, for clams —**clam up** [Colloq.] to refuse to talk
clam·bake (-bāk′) ***n.*** a picnic at which steamed or baked clams and other foods are served
clam·ber (klam′bər) ***vi., vt.*** [ME. *clambren*] to climb clumsily or with effort, using both hands and feet —***n.*** a hard or clumsy climb —**clam′ber·er** ***n.***
clam·my (klam′ē) ***adj.*** **-mi·er, -mi·est** [prob. < OE. *clam,* clay] unpleasantly moist, cold, and sticky —**clam′mi·ly** ***adv.*** —**clam′mi·ness** ***n.***
clam·or (klam′ər) ***n.*** [< OFr. < L. < *clamare,* to cry out] **1.** a loud outcry; uproar **2.** a strong, insistent public demand or complaint **3.** a loud, sustained noise —***vi.*** to make a clamor; cry out, demand, or complain noisily —***vt.*** to express with clamor Also, Brit. sp., **clam′our** —**clam′or·er** ***n.***
clam·or·ous (-əs) ***adj.*** **1.** loud and confused; noisy **2.** loudly demanding or complaining —**clam′or·ous·ly** ***adv.*** —**clam′or·ous·ness** ***n.***
clamp (klamp) ***n.*** [< MDu. *klampe*] a device for clasping or fastening things together; esp., an appliance with two parts brought together to grip something —***vt.*** **1.** to grip, fasten, or brace with a clamp **2.** to impose forcefully —**clamp down (on)** to become more strict (with)

CLAMP

clam·shell (klam′shel′) ***n.*** **1.** the shell of a clam **2.** a dredging bucket, hinged like the shell of a clam
clan (klan) ***n.*** [Gael. & Ir. *clann,* offspring < L. *planta,* offshoot] **1.** a social group, as in the Scottish Highlands, composed of several fami-

lies descended from a common ancestor **2.** a group of people with interests in common **3.** [Colloq.] family (sense 3)

clan·des·tine (klan des′t'n) ***adj.*** [< Fr. < L. *clandestinus* < *clam,* secret] kept secret or hidden, esp. for some illicit purpose; surreptitious —**clan·des′tine·ly** ***adv.***

clang (klaŋ) ***vi., vt.*** [echoic] to make or cause to make a loud, sharp, ringing sound, as by striking metal —***n.*** a clanging sound or cry

clan·gor (klaŋ′ər) ***n.*** [L. < *clangere,* to clang] a clanging sound, esp. a continued clanging —***vi.*** to make a clangor Also, Brit. sp., **clan′gour** —**clan′gor·ous** ***adj.*** —**clan′gor·ous·ly** ***adv.***

clank (klaŋk) ***n.*** [echoic] a sharp, metallic sound, not so resonant as a clang —***vi.*** to make, or move with, a clank —***vt.*** to cause to clank

clan·nish (klan′ish) ***adj.*** **1.** of a clan **2.** tending to associate closely and to avoid others —**clan′nish·ly** ***adv.*** —**clan′nish·ness** ***n.***

clans·man (klanz′mən) ***n., pl.*** **-men** a member of a clan —**clans′wom′an** ***n.fem., pl.*** **-wom′en**

clap (klap) ***vi.*** **clapped** or archaic **clapt, clap′ping** [OE. *clæppan,* to beat] **1.** to make a sudden, explosive sound, as of two flat surfaces being struck together **2.** to strike the hands together, as in applauding —***vt.*** **1.** to strike together briskly and loudly **2.** to strike with an open hand **3.** to put, move, etc. swiftly *[clapped* into jail*]* **4.** to put together hastily —***n.*** **1.** the sound of clapping **2.** the act of striking the hands together **3.** a sharp slap, as in hearty greeting —**clap eyes on** [Colloq.] to catch sight of; see

clap·board (klab′ərd, klap′bôrd′) ***n.*** [partial transl. of MDu. *klapholt* < *klappen,* to fit + *holt,* wood] a thin board with one edge thicker than the other, used as siding —***vt.*** to cover with clapboards

clap·per (klap′ər) ***n.*** **1.** a person who claps **2.** a thing that makes a clapping noise, as the tongue of a bell or, facetiously, that of a person

clap·trap (-trap′) ***n.*** [CLAP + TRAP[1]] showy, insincere, empty talk, etc. intended only to get applause or attention —***adj.*** showy and cheap

claque (klak) ***n.*** [Fr. < *claquer,* to clap] **1.** a group of people paid to go to a play, opera, etc. and applaud **2.** a group of fawning followers

Clar·a (klar′ə) [< L. fem. of *clarus,* bright] a feminine name: var. *Clare, Clarice, Clarissa*

Clar·ence (klar′əns) [< name of Eng. dukedom of *Clarence*] a masculine name

clar·et (klar′it) ***n.*** [< OFr. dim. of *cler* < L. *clarus,* clear] **1.** a dry red wine, esp. red Bordeaux **2.** purplish red: also **claret red** —***adj.*** purplish-red

clar·i·fy (klar′ə fī′) ***vt., vi.*** **-fied′, -fy′ing** [< OFr. < L. < *clarus,* clear + *facere,* to make] **1.** to make or become clear and free from impurities: said esp. of liquids **2.** to make or become easier to understand *[clarify* your meaning*]* —**clar′i·fi·ca′tion** ***n.*** —**clar′i·fi′er** ***n.***

clar·i·net (klar′ə net′, klar′ə nit) ***n.*** [Fr. *clarinette,* dim. of *clarine,* little bell < ML. *clario:* see ff.] a single-reed, woodwind instrument with a long wooden or metal tube and a flaring bell, played by means of holes and keys —**clar′i·net′ist, clar′i·net′tist** ***n.***

clar·i·on (klar′ē ən) ***n.*** [OFr. < ML. *clario* < L. *clarus,* clear] **1.** a trumpet of the Middle Ages producing clear, sharp, shrill tones **2.** [Poet.] a sound of or like a clarion —***adj.*** clear, sharp, and ringing *[a clarion* call*]* —***vt.*** to announce forcefully or loudly

clar·i·ty (klar′ə tē) ***n.*** [OFr. *clarte* < L. *claritas* < *clarus,* clear] a being clear; clearness

Clark (klärk) [< OFr. & OE.: see CLERK] **1.** a masculine name **2. William,** 1770–1838; Am. explorer: see Meriwether LEWIS

clash (klash) ***vi.*** [echoic] **1.** to collide with a loud, harsh, metallic noise **2.** *a)* to conflict; disagree *b)* to fail to harmonize —***vt.*** to strike together, shut, etc. with a loud, harsh noise —***n.*** **1.** the sound of clashing **2.** *a)* conflict *b)* lack of harmony —**clash′er** ***n.***

clasp (klasp) ***n.*** [ME. *claspe*] **1.** a fastening, as a hook or catch, to hold two things or parts together **2.** a grasping; embrace **3.** a grip of the hand —***vt.*** **1.** to fasten with a clasp **2.** to grasp firmly; embrace **3.** to grip with the hand **4.** to cling to —**clasp′er** ***n.***

class (klas) ***n.*** [< Fr. < L. *classis,* prob. akin to *calare,* to call] **1.** a number of people or things grouped together because of certain likenesses; kind; sort **2.** a group of people of the same social or economic status *[*the middle *class]* **3.** high social rank or caste **4.** the division of society into ranks or castes **5.** *a)* a group of students taught together *b)* a meeting of such a group *c)* a group of students graduating together **6.** grade or quality *[*travel first *class]* **7.** [Slang] excellence, as of style **8.** *Biol.* a group of animals or plants ranking below a phylum and above an order —***vt.*** to put in a class; classify —***vi.*** to be classed —**in a class by itself** (or **oneself**) unique

class. 1. classic; **2.** classical; **3.** classification; **4.** classified

class consciousness an awareness of belonging to a certain economic class in the social order —**class′-con′scious** ***adj.***

clas·sic (klas′ik) ***adj.*** [L. *classicus,* superior < *classis,* CLASS] **1.** of the highest class; being a model of its kind; standard **2.** *a)* of the art, literature, and culture of the ancient Greeks or Romans, or their writers, artists, etc. *b)* derived from their literary and artistic standards **3.** balanced, formal, objective, restrained, regular, etc. **4.** famous as traditional or typical **5.** [Colloq.] simple in style and continuing in fashion: said of an article of apparel —***n.*** **1.** a writer, artist, etc., or a literary or artistic work, recognized as excellent, authoritative, etc. **2.** a famous traditional event **3.** [Colloq.] a suit, dress, etc. that is classic (sense 5) **4.** [Colloq.] an automobile of the period 1925–42 —**the classics** literature regarded as classic (senses 1, 2)

clas·si·cal (-i k'l) ***adj.*** **1.** *same as* CLASSIC (senses 1, 2, 3) **2.** versed in and devoted to Greek and Roman culture, literature, etc. **3.** designating or of music that conforms to certain established standards of form, complexity, musical literacy, etc.: distinguished from POPULAR, ROMANTIC **4.** standard and traditionally authoritative, not new and experimental *[classical* economics*]* —**clas′si·cal′i·ty** (-kal′ə tē), **clas′si·cal·ness,** ***n.*** —**clas′si·cal·ly** ***adv.***

clas·si·cism (klas′ə siz'm) ***n.*** **1.** the aesthetic principles or qualities of ancient Greece and Rome: generally contrasted with ROMANTICISM **2.** adherence to such principles **3.** knowledge of the literature and art of ancient Greece and Rome **4.** a Greek or Latin idiom or expression Also **clas′si·cal·ism** —**clas′si·cist** ***n.***

clas·si·cize (-sīz′) ***vt.*** **-cized′, -ciz′ing** to make classic —***vi.*** to use a classic style

clas·si·fi·ca·tion (klas′ə fi kā′shən) ***n.*** **1.** an arrangement according to some systematic division into classes or groups **2.** such a class or group **3.** *Biol. same as* TAXONOMY —**clas·si·fi·ca·to·ry** (klas′ə fi kā′tər ē, -kə tôr′ē) ***adj.***

classified advertising advertising, as in newspaper columns, under such listings as *help wanted, for sale,* etc.

clas·si·fy (klas′ə fī′) ***vt.*** **-fied′, -fy′ing** **1.** to arrange in classes according to some system or principle **2.** to place in a category **3.** to designate (government documents, etc.) as secret or confidential —**clas′si·fi′a·ble** ***adj.*** —**clas′si·fi′er** ***n.***

class·less (klas′lis) ***adj.*** having no distinct social or economic classes *[a classless* society*]*

class·mate (-māt′) ***n.*** a member of the same class at a school or college

class·room (-ro͞om′) ***n.*** a room in a school or college in which classes are taught

class·y (-ē) ***adj.*** **class′i·er, class′i·est** [Slang] first-class, esp. in style or manner —**class′i·ness** ***n.***

clat·ter (klat′ər) ***vi.*** [ME. *clateren*] **1.** to make, or move with, a rapid succession of loud, sharp noises, as dishes rattling **2.** to chatter noisily —***vt.*** to cause to clatter —***n.*** **1.** a rapid succession of loud, sharp noises **2.** a tumult; hubbub **3.** noisy chatter —**clat′ter·er** ***n.*** —**clat′ter·ing·ly** ***adv.***

Claude (klôd) [Fr. < L. *Claudius,* name of a Roman gens] a masculine name

Clau·di·a (klô′dē ə) [L., fem. of prec.] a feminine name

clause (klôz) ***n.*** [OFr. < ML. *clausa* < L. pp. of *claudere,* to close] **1.** a group of words containing a subject and verb, usually forming part of a compound or complex sentence: cf. MAIN CLAUSE, SUBORDINATE CLAUSE **2.** a particular article, stipulation, or provision in a formal or legal document —**claus′al** ***adj.***

claus·tro·pho·bi·a (klôs′trə fō′bē ə) ***n.*** [< L. *claustrum* (see CLOISTER) + -PHOBIA] an abnormal fear of being in an enclosed or confined place —**claus′tro·pho′bic** ***adj.***

cla·vate (klā′vāt) ***adj.*** [< L. *clava,* a club + -ATE[1]] club-shaped —**cla′vate·ly** ***adv.*** —**cla·va′tion** ***n.***

clave (klāv) *archaic pt. of* CLEAVE[1] & CLEAVE[2]

clav·i·chord (klav′ə kôrd′) ***n.*** [< ML. < L. *clavis,* a key + *chorda,* a string] a stringed musical instrument with a keyboard, predecessor of the piano

clav·i·cle (klav′ə k'l) ***n.*** [< Fr. < L. *clavicula,* dim. of *clavis,* a key] a bone connecting the breastbone with the shoulder blade; collarbone —**cla·vic·u·lar** (kla vik′yoo lər) ***adj.***

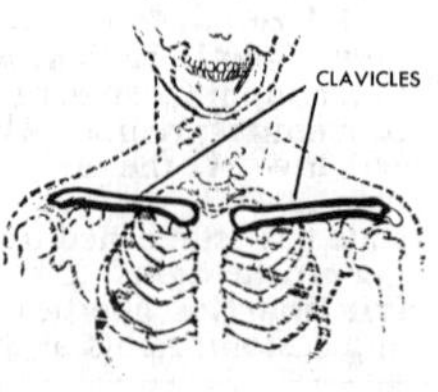

cla·vi·er (klə vir′; *for 1, also* klav′ē ər) ***n.*** [Fr., keyboard < L. *clavis,* a key] **1.** the keyboard of an organ, piano, etc. **2.** any stringed instrument that has a keyboard

claw (klô) ***n.*** [OE. *clawu*] **1.** a sharp, hooked nail on the foot of a bird and of many reptiles and mammals **2.** a foot with such nails **3.** a pincer, or chela, of a lobster, crab, etc. **4.** anything regarded as or resembling a claw, as a hammer (**claw hammer**) with one end forked and curved, used to pull nails —*vt., vi.* to scratch, clutch, pull, dig, or tear with or as with claws —**clawed** *adj.*

clay (klā) *n.* [OE. *clæg*] **1.** a firm, plastic earth, used in the manufacture of bricks, pottery, etc. **2.** *a)* earth *b)* the human body —**clay′ey** *adj.* **clay′i·er, clay′i·est** —**clay′ish** *adj.*

Clay (klā), **Henry** 1777–1852; U.S. statesman

clay·more (klā′môr′) *n.* [Gael. *claidheamhmor,* great sword] **1.** a large, two-edged broadsword formerly used by Scottish Highlanders **2.** a broadsword with a basket hilt worn by Highland regiments

clay pigeon a disk as of baked clay, tossed into the air from a trap as a target in trapshooting

clean (klēn) *adj.* [OE. *clæne*] **1.** free from dirt or impurities; unsoiled; unstained **2.** producing little immediate fallout: said of nuclear weapons **3.** recently laundered; fresh **4.** *a)* morally pure *b)* not obscene or indecent **5.** sportsmanlike **6.** keeping oneself or one's surroundings neat and tidy **7.** shapely or trim *[clean* lines*]* **8.** skillful; deft *[*a *clean* stroke*]* **9.** having no obstructions or flaws; clear **10.** complete; thorough **11.** empty —*adv.* **1.** in a clean manner **2.** completely —*vt.* **1.** to make clean **2.** to remove (dirt, impurities, etc.) **3.** to empty or clear **4.** to prepare (fish, fowl, etc.) for cooking **5.** [Slang] to take away or use up the money, etc. of (often with *out*) —*vi.* to undergo or perform the act of cleaning —**clean out 1.** to empty so as to make clean **2.** to empty —**clean up 1.** to make clean or neat **2.** to get washed, combed, etc. **3.** [Colloq.] to finish **4.** [Slang] to make much profit —**clean up on** [Slang] to defeat; beat —**come clean** [Slang] to confess; tell the truth —**clean′a·ble** *adj.* —**clean′ness** *n.*

clean-cut (-kut′) *adj.* **1.** clearly and sharply outlined **2.** well-formed **3.** distinct; clear **4.** good-looking, trim, neat, etc.

clean·er (-ər) *n.* a person or thing that cleans; specif., *a)* one who dry-cleans *b)* a preparation for removing dirt, stains, etc. —**take to the cleaners** [Slang] to take all the money of, as in gambling

clean·ly[1] (klen′lē) *adj.* **-li·er, -li·est 1.** keeping oneself or one's surroundings clean **2.** always kept clean —**clean′li·ly** *adv.* —**clean′li·ness** *n.*

clean·ly[2] (klēn′lē) *adv.* in a clean manner

cleanse (klenz) *vt.* **cleansed, cleans′ing** [OE. *clænsian*] to make clean, pure, etc.; purge

cleans·er (klen′zər) *n.* a preparation for cleansing, esp. a powder for scouring pots, sinks, etc.

clean·up (klēn′up′) *n.* **1.** a cleaning up **2.** elimination of crime, vice, etc. **3.** [Slang] profit; gain —*adj. Baseball* designating the fourth batter in a team's lineup

clear (klir) *adj.* [< OFr. < L. *clarus*] **1.** free from clouds or mist; bright; light **2.** transparent; not turbid **3.** having no blemishes *[*a *clear* skin*]* **4.** easily seen; sharply defined; distinct **5.** perceiving acutely; keen **6.** serene and calm **7.** not obscure; easily understood **8.** obvious **9.** certain; positive **10.** free from guilt; innocent **11.** free from charges or deductions; net **12.** free from debt or encumbrance **13.** absolute; complete **14.** free from obstruction; open **15.** emptied of freight or cargo —*adv.* **1.** in a clear manner **2.** all the way; completely *[*it sank *clear* to the bottom*]* —*vt.* **1.** to make clear or bright **2.** to free from impurities, muddiness, blemishes, etc. **3.** *a)* to make intelligible or lucid *b)* to decode or decipher **4.** to rid of obstructions; open **5.** to get rid of; remove **6.** to empty or unload **7.** to free (a person or thing) *of* or *from* something **8.** to free from guilt or blame **9.** to pass over, under, by, etc. with space to spare **10.** to discharge (a debt) by paying it **11.** to give or get clearance for **12.** to be passed or approved by **13.** to make (a given amount) as profit; net **14.** *Banking* to pass (a check, etc.) through a clearinghouse —*vi.* **1.** to become clear, unclouded, etc. **2.** to pass away; vanish **3.** to get clearance, as a ship leaving port **4.** *Banking* to exchange checks, etc., and balance accounts, through a clearinghouse —*n.* a clear space —**clear away 1.** to take away so as to leave a cleared space **2.** to go away —**clear off 1.** to clear away **2.** to remove things from (a surface) —**clear out 1.** to clear by emptying **2.** [Colloq.] to depart —**clear the air** (or **atmosphere**) to get rid of emotional tensions, etc. —**clear up 1.** to make or become clear **2.** to make orderly **3.** to explain **4.** to cure or become cured —**in the clear 1.** in the open **2.** [Colloq.] free from suspicion, guilt, etc. —**clear′a·ble** *adj.* —**clear′er** *n.* —**clear′ly** *adv.* —**clear′ness** *n.*

clear·ance (-əns) *n.* **1.** a making clear **2.** the clear space between things, or between a moving object and that which it passes by, through, over, under, etc. **3.** official authorization to see classified documents, work on secret projects, etc. **4.** *Banking* the adjustment of accounts in a clearinghouse **5.** *Naut.* a certificate authorizing a ship to enter or leave port: also called **clearance papers**

clear-cut (-kut′) *adj.* **1.** clearly and sharply outlined **2.** distinct; definite; certain

clear·head·ed (-hed′id) *adj.* having or indicating a clear mind; lucid; unconfused —**clear′head′ed·ly** *adv.* —**clear′-head′ed·ness** *n.*

clear·ing (klir′iŋ) *n.* **1.** a making clear or being cleared **2.** an area of land cleared of trees **3.** *Banking a) same as* CLEARANCE *b)* [*pl.*] the amount of the balances settled in clearance

clear·ing·house (-hous′) *n.* **1.** an office maintained by a group of banks as a center for exchanging checks, balancing accounts, etc. **2.** a central office for getting and giving information, etc.

clear·sight·ed (klir′sīt′id) *adj.* **1.** seeing clearly **2.** understanding or thinking clearly —**clear′sight′ed·ly** *adv.* —**clear′sight′ed·ness** *n.*

clear·sto·ry (-stôr′ē) *n., pl.* **-ries** *same as* CLERESTORY

Clear·wa·ter (klir′wôt′ər, -wät′-) city in WC Fla., on the Gulf of Mexico: suburb of St. Petersburg: pop. 85,000

cleat (klēt) *n.* [< OE. hyp. *cleat,* a lump] **1.** a piece of wood or metal, often wedge-shaped, fastened to something to strengthen it or give secure footing **2.** *Naut.* a small piece of wood or metal with projecting ends on which a rope can be fastened —*vt.* to fasten to or with a cleat

cleav·age (klē′vij) *n.* **1.** a cleaving, splitting, or dividing **2.** the manner in which a thing splits **3.** a cleft; fissure **4.** the hollow between a woman's breasts, as exposed by a low-cut neckline **5.** *Biol.* cell division that transforms the fertilized ovum into the earliest embryonic stage

cleave[1] (klēv) *vt.* **cleaved** or **cleft** or **clove, cleaved** or **cleft** or **clo′ven, cleav′ing** [OE. *cleofan*] **1.** to divide by a blow, as with an ax; split **2.** to pierce **3.** to sever; disunite —*vi.* **1.** to split; separate **2.** to make one's way by or as by cutting —**cleav′a·ble** *adj.*

cleave[2] (klēv) *vi.* **cleaved, cleav′ing** [OE. *cleofian*] **1.** to adhere; cling (*to*) **2.** to be faithful (*to*)

cleav·er (-ər) *n.* a heavy cleaving tool with a broad blade, used by butchers

cleav·ers (-ərz) *n., pl.* **-ers** [< CLEAVE[2]] a plant of the madder family, with stalkless leaves, clusters of small flowers, and prickly stems

clef (klef) *n.* [Fr. < L. *clavis,* a key] a symbol used in music to indicate the pitch of the notes on the staff: there are three clefs: G (treble), F (bass), and C (tenor or alto)

G CLEF F CLEF

C CLEFS

TYPES OF CLEF

cleft[1] (kleft) *n.* [< OE. hyp. *clyft* < *cleofan,* CLEAVE[1]] **1.** an opening made by or as by cleaving; crack; crevice **2.** a hollow between two parts

cleft[2] *alt. pt. & pp. of* CLEAVE[1] —*adj.* split; divided

clem·a·tis (klem′ə tis, klə mat′is) *n.* [L. < Gr. < *klēma,* vine, twig] a perennial plant or woody vine of the buttercup family, with bright-colored flowers

Cle·men·ceau (klā män sō′; *E.* klem′ən sō′), **Georges (Benjamin Eugéne)** (zhôrzh) 1841–1929; Fr. statesman; premier of France (1906–09; 1917–20)

clem·en·cy (klem′ən sē) *n., pl.* **-cies** [< L. < *clemens,* merciful] **1.** forbearance, leniency, or mercy **2.** mildness, as of weather

Clem·ens (klem′ənz), **Samuel Lang·horne** (laŋ′hôrn) (pseud. *Mark Twain*) 1835–1910; U.S. writer & humorist

Clem·ent (klem′ənt) [L. < *clemens,* mild, gentle] a masculine name: dim. *Clem*

clem·ent (klem′ənt) *adj.* [L. *clemens*] **1.** lenient; merciful **2.** mild, as weather —**clem′ent·ly** *adv.*

Clem·en·tine (klem′ən tīn′, -tēn′) [Fr. < L. fem. of CLEMENT] a feminine name

clench (klench) *vt.* [< OE. *-clencan* (in *beclencan*), lit., to make cling] **1.** to clinch, as a nail **2.** to bring together tightly; close (the teeth or fist) firmly **3.** to grip tightly —*n.* **1.** a firm grip **2.** a device that clenches —**clench′er** *n.*

Cle·o·pa·tra (klē′ə pat′rə, -pā′trə, -pä′trə) 69?–30 B.C.; queen of Egypt (51–49; 48–30)

clep·sy·dra (klep′si drə) *n., pl.* **-dras** or **-drae′** (-drē′) [L. < Gr. < *kleptein,* to steal + *hydōr,* water] *same as* WATER CLOCK

clep·to·ma·ni·a (klep′tə mā′nē ə) *n. same as* KLEPTOMANIA

clere·sto·ry (klir′stôr′ē) *n., pl.* **-ries** [< ME. < *cler,* clear

+ *storie,* STORY[2]] **1.** the wall of a church rising above the roofs of the flanking aisles and containing windows for lighting the central part of the structure **2.** any similar windowed wall

cler·gy (klur′jē) ***n.,*** *pl.* **-gies** [< OFr. < LL. *clericus:* see CLERK] ministers, priests, rabbis, etc. collectively

cler·gy·man (-mən) ***n.,*** *pl.* **-men** a member of the clergy; minister, priest, rabbi, etc.

cler·ic (kler′ik) ***n.*** [LL. *clericus:* see CLERK] a clergyman —***adj.*** of a clergyman or the clergy

cler·i·cal (kler′i k′l) ***adj.*** [LL. *clericalis* < *clericus:* see CLERK] **1.** relating to a clergyman or the clergy **2.** relating to office clerks or their work **3.** favoring clericalism —***n.*** **1.** a clergyman **2.** [*pl.*] clergymen's garments **3.** one who favors clericalism —**cler′i·cal·ly** ***adv.***

clerical collar a stiff, white collar buttoned at the back, worn by certain clergymen

cler·i·cal·ism (-iz'm) ***n.*** political influence or power of the clergy —**cler′i·cal·ist** ***n.***

clerk (klurk; *Brit.* klärk) ***n.*** [< OFr. & OE. < LL. *clericus* < Gr. *klērikos,* priest] **1.** a layman who has minor duties in a church **2.** an office worker who keeps records, types letters, does filing, etc. **3.** an official in charge of records, etc. of a court, town, etc. **4.** a hotel employee who keeps the register, assigns guests to rooms, etc. **5.** one who sells in a store; salesclerk **6.** [Archaic] *a)* a clergyman *b)* a scholar —***vi.*** to work as a clerk, esp. a salesclerk —**clerk′ly** ***adj., adv.*** —**clerk′ship′** ***n.***

Cleve·land (klēv′lənd) [after M. *Cleaveland,* 18th-c. Conn. surveyor] city in NE Ohio, on Lake Erie: pop. 574,000 (met. area 1,896,000)

Cleve·land (klēv′lənd), **(Stephen) Gro·ver** (grō′vər) 1837–1908; 22d and 24th president of the U.S. (1885–89; 1893–97)

Cleveland Heights city in NE Ohio: suburb of Cleveland: pop. 56,000

clev·er (klev′ər) ***adj.*** [prob. < EFris. *klüfer* or Norw. *klöver,* skillful] **1.** skillful in doing something; adroit; dexterous **2.** intelligent, quick-witted, witty, facile, etc. **3.** showing quick, sometimes superficial, intelligence *[a clever book]* —**clev′er·ly** ***adv.*** —**clev′er·ness** ***n.***

clev·is (klev′is) ***n.*** [ult. akin to CLEAVE[2]] a U-shaped piece of iron with holes in the ends through which a pin is run to attach one thing to another

clew (klo͞o) ***n.*** [< OE. *cliwen*] **1.** a ball of thread or yarn **2.** something that leads out of a maze or perplexity or helps to solve a problem: usually sp. **clue** **3.** *Naut. a)* a lower corner of a square sail *b)* the lower corner aft of a fore-and-aft sail *c)* a metal loop in the corner of a sail —***vt.*** **1.** to wind (*up*) into a ball **2.** *same as* CLUE —**clew down** (or **up**) to lower (or raise) a sail by the clews

cli·ché (klē shā′) ***n.*** [Fr. < *clicher,* to stereotype] a trite expression or idea

cli·chéd (klē shād′) ***adj.*** **1.** full of clichés *[a dull, cliched style]* **2.** trite; stereotyped *[a clichéd theme]*

click (klik) ***n.*** [echoic] **1.** a slight, sharp sound like that of a door latch snapping into place **2.** a mechanical device, as a catch or pawl, that clicks into position **3.** *Phonet.* a sound made by drawing the breath into the mouth and clicking the tongue —***vi.*** **1.** to make a click **2.** [Colloq.] *a)* to be suddenly comprehensible *b)* to work or get along together successfully *c)* to be a success —***vt.*** to cause to click —**click′er** ***n.***

cli·ent (klī′ənt) ***n.*** [OFr. < L. *cliens,* follower] **1.** a person or company for whom a lawyer, accountant, etc. is acting **2.** a customer —**cli·en·tal** (klī en′t'l) ***adj.***

cli·en·tele (klī′ən tel′; *also, chiefly Brit.,* klē′än-) ***n.*** [< Fr. < L. *clientela*] all one's clients or customers, collectively: also **cli·ent·age** (klī′ən tij)

cliff (klif) ***n.*** [OE. *clif*] a high, steep face of rock, esp. one on a coast; precipice —**cliff′y** ***adj.***

cliff·hang·er, cliff-hang·er (-haŋ′ər) ***n.*** any highly suspenseful story, situation, etc. as in an early type of serialized movie with an episode in which the hero is hanging from a cliff —**cliff′hang′ing, cliff′-hang′ing** ***adj.***

Clif·ton (klif′tən) [< CLIFF + *-ton,* town] **1.** a masculine name **2.** [< its location at the foot of a mountain] city in NE N.J.: pop. 74,000

cli·mac·ter·ic (klī mak′tər ik, klī′mak ter′ik) ***n.*** [< L. < Gr. < *klimax,* ladder] **1.** a period in a person's life when an important physiological change occurs, esp. the menopause **2.** any crucial period —***adj.*** of or resembling a climacteric: also **cli′mac·ter′i·cal**

cli·mac·tic (klī mak′tik) ***adj.*** of or constituting a climax: also **cli·mac′ti·cal** —**cli·mac′ti·cal·ly** ***adv.***

cli·mate (klī′mət) ***n.*** [< OFr. < L. < Gr. *klima,* region] **1.** the prevailing weather conditions of a place, as determined by the temperature and meteorological changes over a period of years **2.** any prevailing conditions affecting life, activity, etc. **3.** a region with certain prevailing weather conditions *[move to a warm climate]* —**cli·mat·ic** (klī mat′ik) ***adj.*** —**cli·mat′i·cal·ly** ***adv.***

cli·ma·tol·o·gy (klī′mə täl′ə jē) ***n.*** the science dealing with climate and climate phenomena —**cli′ma·to·log′i·cal** (-tə läj′i k'l) ***adj.*** —**cli′ma·tol′o·gist** ***n.***

cli·max (klī′maks) ***n.*** [L. < Gr. *klimax,* ladder] **1.** formerly, an arrangement of ideas, images, etc. with the most forceful last **2.** the final, culminating element or event in a series; highest point, as of interest, excitement, etc.; specif., *a)* the decisive turning point of the action, as in drama *b)* an orgasm **3.** *Ecol.* a final, self-perpetuating, local community of plants or animals —***vi., vt.*** to reach, or bring to, a climax

climb (klīm) ***vi., vt.*** **climbed** or archaic **clomb, climb′ing** [OE. *climban*] **1.** to go up by using the feet and often the hands **2.** to rise or ascend gradually; mount **3.** to move (*down, over, along,* etc.) using the hands and feet **4.** *Bot.* to grow upward on by winding around or adhering with tendrils —***n.*** **1.** a climbing; rise; ascent **2.** a thing or place to be climbed —**climb′a·ble** ***adj.***

climb·er (-ər) ***n.*** **1.** one that climbs **2.** *same as* LINEMEN'S CLIMBER: also **climbing iron** **3.** [Colloq.] one who constantly tries to advance himself socially or in business **4.** *Bot.* a climbing plant or vine

clime (klīm) ***n.*** [L. *clima:* see CLIMATE] [Poet.] a region, esp. with reference to its climate

clinch (klinch) ***vt.*** [var. of CLENCH] **1.** to fasten (a nail, bolt, etc. driven through something) by bending or flattening the projecting end **2.** to fasten together by this means **3.** *a)* to settle (an argument, deal, etc.) definitely *b)* to win conclusively —***vi.*** **1.** *Boxing* to grip the opponent's body with the arms **2.** [Slang] to embrace —***n.*** **1.** *a)* a clinching, as with a nail *b)* a clinched nail, bolt, etc. *c)* the part clinched **2.** *Boxing* an act of clinching **3.** [Slang] an embrace

clinch·er (-ər) ***n.*** **1.** a tool for clinching nails **2.** a decisive point, argument, act, etc.

cling (kliŋ) ***vi.*** **clung, cling′ing** [OE. *clingan*] **1.** to hold fast by or as by embracing, entwining, or sticking; adhere **2.** *a)* to be or stay near *b)* to be emotionally attached —**cling′er** ***n.*** —**cling′ing·ly** ***adv.*** —**cling′y** ***adj.***

cling·stone (-stōn′) ***adj.*** having a stone that clings to the fleshy part: said of some peaches —***n.*** a peach of this sort

clin·ic (klin′ik) ***n.*** [L. *clinicus,* physician who attends bedridden persons < Gr. *klinikos,* of a bed < *klinē,* a bed] **1.** the teaching of medicine by examining and treating patients in the presence of students **2.** a class so taught **3.** a place where patients are treated by specialist physicians practicing as a group **4.** a department of a hospital or medical school where outpatients are treated, sometimes free or for a small fee **5.** an organization that offers some kind of advice, treatment, or instruction **6.** a brief, intensive session of group instruction in a specific skill, field of knowledge, etc. *[a basketball clinic]*

clin·i·cal (-i k'l) ***adj.*** **1.** of or connected with a clinic **2.** having to do with the treatment and observation of patients, as distinguished from experimental or laboratory study **3.** scientifically impersonal **4.** austere, antiseptic, etc., like a medical clinic —**clin′i·cal·ly** ***adv.***

clinical thermometer a thermometer with which the body temperature is measured

cli·ni·cian (kli nish′ən) ***n.*** an expert in or practitioner of clinical medicine, psychology, etc.

clink (kliŋk) ***vi., vt.*** [< MDu. *klinken:* echoic] to make or cause to make a slight, sharp sound, as of glasses striking together —***n.*** **1.** such a sound **2.** [< name of an 18th-c. London prison] [Colloq.] a jail; prison

clink·er (-ər) ***n.*** [Du. *klinker,* vitrified brick < *klinken,* to ring] **1.** a hard mass of fused stony matter formed in a furnace, as from impurities in the coal **2.** [Slang] *a)* a mistake; error *b)* a total failure —***vi.*** to form clinkers in burning

cli·nom·e·ter (klī näm′ə tər) ***n.*** [< Gr. < *klinein,* to slope + -METER] an instrument for measuring angles of slope or inclination —**cli·no·met·ric** (klī′nə met′rik), **cli′no·met′ri·cal** ***adj.*** —**cli·nom′e·try** (-ə trē) ***n.***

Clin·ton (klin′t'n) [Eng. place name < ? ME. *clint,* cliff + *tun,* village] a masculine name

Cli·o (klī′ō) [L. < Gr. < *kleos,* fame] *Gr. Myth.* the Muse of history

cli·o·met·rics (klī′ō met′riks) ***n.pl.*** [*with sing. v.*] [< prec. + Gr. *metron,* measure] the use of mathematical and statistical methods, and often of computers, in analyzing historical data —**cli′o·met′ric** ***adj.*** —**cli′o·me·tri′cian** (-mə trish′ən) ***n.***

clip[1] (klip) ***vt.*** **clipped, clip′ping** [< ON. *klippa*] **1.** to cut or cut off as with shears **2.** to cut (an item) out of (a newspaper, etc.) **3.** *a)* to cut short *b)* to shorten by omitting syllables, etc. **4.** to cut the hair of **5.** [Colloq.] to hit with a quick, sharp blow **6.** [Slang] to cheat, esp. by overcharging —***vi.*** **1.** to clip something **2.** to move rapidly —***n.*** **1.** the act of clipping **2.** a thing clipped; specif., *a)* the amount of wool clipped from sheep at one time *b)* a sequence clipped from a movie film **3.** a rapid pace **4.** [Colloq.] a quick, sharp blow **5.** *same as* CLIPPED FORM

clip[2] (klip) *vi., vt.* **clipped, clip′ping** [OE. *clyppan,* to embrace] **1.** to grip tightly; fasten **2.** *Football* to block (an opponent who is not carrying the ball) from behind: an illegal act —*n.* **1.** any device that clips or fastens things together **2.** *same as* CARTRIDGE CLIP **3.** *Football* a clipping

clip·board (-bôrd′) *n.* a portable writing board with a hinged clip at the top to hold papers

clipped form (or **word**) a shortened form of a word, as *pike* (for *turnpike*) or *fan* (for *fanatic*)

clip·per (klip′ər) *n.* [ME. < *clippen,* CLIP[1]] **1.** a person who cuts, trims, etc. **2.** [*usually pl.*] a tool for cutting or trimming **3.** [for sense, cf. CUTTER] a sharp-bowed, narrow-beamed sailing ship built for great speed

CLIPPER SHIP

clip·ping (-iŋ) *n.* **1.** something cut out or trimmed off **2.** an item clipped from a newspaper, magazine, etc.

clique (klēk, klik) *n.* [Fr. < *cliquer,* to make a noise] a small, exclusive circle of people; snobbish or narrow coterie —**cliqu′ish, cliqu′ey, cliqu′y** *adj.* —**cliqu′ish·ly** *adv.* —**cliqu′ish·ness** *n.*

clit·o·ris (klit′ər əs, klīt′-) *n.* [ModL. < Gr. < *kleitys,* hill] a small, sensitive, erectile organ at the upper end of the vulva: it corresponds to the penis in the male —**clit′o·ral** (-ər əl), **cli·tor·ic** (klī tôr′ik) *adj.*

Clive (klīv) [< the surname] **1.** a masculine name **2. Robert,** Baron Clive of Plassey, 1725–74; Brit. soldier & statesman in India

clk. clerk

clo·a·ca (klō ā′kə) *n., pl.* **-cae** (-sē, -kē), **-cas** [L. < *cluere,* to cleanse] **1.** a sewer or cesspool **2.** *Zool.* the cavity into which the intestinal and genitourinary tracts empty in reptiles, birds, amphibians, and many fishes —**clo·a′cal** *adj.*

cloak (klōk) *n.* [< OFr. < ML. *clocca* (see CLOCK[1]), a bell, cloak: so called from its bell-like appearance] **1.** a loose, usually sleeveless outer garment **2.** something that covers or conceals —*vt.* **1.** to cover as with a cloak **2.** to conceal; hide

cloak-and-dag·ger (-ən dag′ər) *adj.* dealing in a melodramatic way with spies and spying

cloak·room (-ro͞om′) *n.* a room where hats, coats, umbrellas, etc. can be left temporarily

clob·ber (kläb′ər) *vt.* [< ?] [Slang] **1.** to beat or hit repeatedly; maul **2.** to defeat decisively

cloche (klōsh) *n.* [Fr. < ML. *clocca:* see ff.] a closefitting, bell-shaped hat for women

clock[1] (kläk) *n.* [ME. *clokke,* orig., clock with bells < ML. *clocca,* bell < Celt.] **1.** a device for measuring and indicating time, as by pointers moving over a dial: clocks, unlike watches, are not carried on one's person **2.** *same as* TIME CLOCK —*vt.* **1.** to measure or record the time of (a race, runner, etc.) with a stopwatch, etc. **2.** to register (an amount, etc.) on a meter —**around the clock** day and night, without stopping

clock[2] (kläk) *n.* [< ? prec., because orig. bell-shaped] a woven or embroidered ornament on the side of a sock or stocking, going up from the ankle —**clocked** *adj.*

clock·like (-līk′) *adj.* as precise or regular as a clock

clock radio a radio with a built-in clock that can be set to turn the radio on or off

clock·wise (-wīz′) *adv., adj.* in the direction in which the hands of a clock rotate

clock·work (-wurk′) *n.* **1.** the mechanism of a clock **2.** any similar mechanism, consisting of springs and geared wheels, as in some mechanical toys —**like clockwork** very regularly and precisely

clod (kläd) *n.* [OE.] **1.** a lump, esp. of earth, clay, loam, etc. **2.** earth; soil **3.** a dull, stupid fellow; dolt —**clod′dish** *adj.* —**clod′dish·ly** *adv.* —**clod′dish·ness** *n.* —**clod′dy** *adj.*

clod·hop·per (-häp′ər) *n.* [CLOD + HOPPER] **1.** a plowman **2.** a clumsy, stupid fellow; lout **3.** a coarse, heavy shoe

clog (kläg) *n.* [ME. *clogge,* a lump of wood] **1.** a weight fastened to an animal's leg to hinder motion **2.** anything that hinders or obstructs **3.** a shoe with a thick, usually wooden sole: light clogs are used in clog dancing **4.** *same as* CLOG DANCE —*vt.* **clogged, clog′ging** **1.** to hinder; impede **2.** to fill with obstructions or with thick, sticky matter; stop up —*vi.* **1.** to become stopped up **2.** to do a clog dance —**clog′gi·ness** *n.* —**clog′gy** *adj.*

clog dance a dance in which clogs are worn to beat out the rhythm —**clog dancer** —**clog dancing**

cloi·son·né (kloi′zə nā′) *adj.* [Fr., lit., partitioned] denoting a kind of enamel work in which the surface decoration is set in hollows formed by thin strips of wire welded to a metal plate in a complex pattern —*n.* cloisonné enamel

clois·ter (klois′tər) *n.* [< OFr. < L. *claustrum,* bolt, place shut in < pp. of *claudere,* to close] **1.** a place of religious seclusion; monastery or convent **2.** monastic life **3.** any place where one may lead a secluded life **4.** a covered walk along the inside walls of a monastery, convent, etc., with a columned opening along one side —*vt.* **1.** to seclude or confine as in a cloister **2.** to furnish with a cloister —**clois′tered** *adj.* —**clois′tral** *adj.*

clomb (klōm) *archaic pt. & pp. of* CLIMB

clomp (klämp) *vi.* to walk heavily or noisily; clump

clone (klōn) *n.* [< Gr. *klōn,* a twig] *Biol.* all the descendants derived asexually from a single individual: also **clon** (klōn, klän)

clonk (kläŋk) *n., vi., vt. same as* CLUNK

clo·nus (klō′nəs) *n.* [ModL. < Gr. *klonos,* turmoil] a series of muscle spasms —**clon·ic** (klän′ik) *adj.* —**clo·nic·i·ty** (klə nis′ə tē) *n.* —**clo′nism** *n.*

clop (kläp) *n.* [echoic] a sharp, clattering sound, like hoofbeats on a pavement —*vi.* **clopped, clop′ping** to make, or move with, such a sound

close[1] (klōs) *adj.* **clos′er, clos′est** [< OFr. *clos,* pp. of *clore:* see ff.] **1.** shut; not open **2.** enclosed or enclosing; shut in **3.** confined or confining [*close* quarters] **4.** carefully guarded [*close* custody] **5.** hidden; secluded **6.** secretive; reserved **7.** miserly; stingy **8.** restricted, as in membership **9.** oppressively warm and stuffy, as stale air **10.** not readily available [credit is *close*] **11.** with little space between; near together **12.** compact; dense [a *close* weave] **13.** fitting tightly **14.** *a*) down or near to the surface [a *close* shave] *b*) nearby [a *close* neighbor] **15.** very near in interests, affection, etc.; intimate [a *close* friend] **16.** varying little from the original [a *close* translation] **17.** strict; thorough; careful [*close* attention] **18.** *a*) concise *b*) accurate; precise **19.** nearly equal or alike [*close* in age] **20.** nearly even [a *close* contest] —*adv.* in a close manner —**close to the wind** *Naut.* heading as closely as possible in the direction from which the wind blows —**close′ly** *adv.* —**close′ness** *n.*

close[2] (klōz) *vt.* **closed, clos′ing** [< OFr. < *clore* < L. *claudere,* to close] **1.** to shut **2.** to block up or stop (an opening, passage, etc.) **3.** to bring together; unite [*close* forces] **4.** to bring to an end; finish **5.** to stop or suspend the operation of (a school, business, etc.) **6.** to complete or make final (a sale, agreement, etc.) —*vi.* **1.** to undergo shutting **2.** to come to an end **3.** to end or suspend operations; specif., in the stock exchange, to show an indicated price level at day's end **4.** to become joined together **5.** to come together **6.** to take hold **7.** to throng closely **8.** to lessen an intervening distance **9.** to come close in order to fight —*n.* **1.** a closing or being closed **2.** the final part; end —**close down** **1.** to shut or stop entirely **2.** to settle down (*on*), as darkness or fog —**close in** to surround, cutting off escape —**close out** to sell out (goods), as in ending a business —**close up** **1.** to draw nearer together **2.** to shut or stop up entirely **3.** to heal, as a wound does —**clos′er** *n.*

close[3] (klōs) *n.* [< OFr. *clos* < L. *clausum,* neut. pp. of *claudere:* see prec.] [Chiefly Brit.] **1.** an enclosed place **2.** enclosed grounds around or beside a building [a cathedral *close*] **3.** a narrow street or passageway

close call (klōs) [Colloq.] a narrow escape from danger: also **close shave**

closed (klōzd) *adj.* **1.** not open; shut **2.** covered over or enclosed **3.** functioning independently **4.** not open to new ideas, discussion, etc. **5.** restricted; exclusive **6.** *Math. a*) of a curve whose ends are joined *b*) of a surface whose plane sections are closed curves **7.** *Phonet.* ending in a consonant sound [a *closed* syllable]

closed chain the structural form of certain molecules, graphically represented as a ring of atoms

closed circuit a system of television transmission by cables to a limited number of receivers on a circuit —**closed′-cir′cuit** *adj.*

closed-end (-end′) *adj.* of an investment company with a fixed number of shares traded on the open market

closed primary *see* DIRECT PRIMARY ELECTION

closed shop a factory, business, etc. operating under a contract with a labor union by which only members of the union may be employed

close·fist·ed (klōs′fis′tid) *adj.* stingy; miserly

close·fit·ting (-fit′iŋ) *adj.* fitting tightly, esp. so as to show the contours of the body

close·hauled (-hôld′) *adj.* with the sails set for heading as nearly as possible into the wind

close·mouthed (-mouthd′, -moutht′) *adj.* not talking much; taciturn: also **close′lipped′** (-lipt′)

close punctuation punctuation characterized by the use of many commas and other marks

clos·et (kläz′it) ***n.*** [OFr., dim. of *clos:* see CLOSE[3]] **1.** a small room or cupboard for clothes, supplies, etc. **2.** a small, private room for reading, consultation, etc. **3.** *same as* WATER CLOSET —***adj.*** private or secret —***vt.*** to shut up in a private room for confidential discussion

closet drama drama written mainly to be read, not staged

close-up (klōs′up′) ***n.*** a photograph, or a movie or TV shot, made at very close range

clo·sure (klō′zhər) ***n.*** [OFr. < L. *clausura* < pp. of *claudere,* CLOSE[2]] **1.** a closing or being closed **2.** a finish; end; conclusion **3.** anything that closes **4.** *same as* CLOTURE —***vt.* -sured, -sur·ing** *same as* CLOTURE

clot (klät) ***n.*** [OE. *clott*] a soft, thickened area or lump formed on or within a liquid *[a blood clot]* —***vt., vi.* clot′ted, clot′ting** to thicken or form into a clot or clots; coagulate

cloth (klôth, kläth) ***n., pl.* cloths** (klô*thz*, klä*thz*; *also* klôths, kläths *for "kinds of cloth"*) [OE. *clath*] **1.** a woven, knitted, or pressed fabric of fibrous material, as cotton, wool, silk, hair, synthetic fibers, etc. **2.** a piece of such fabric for a special use *[tablecloth, washcloth]* —***adj.*** made of cloth —**the cloth 1.** the identifying dress of a profession **2.** the clergy collectively

clothe (klō*th*) ***vt.* clothed** or **clad, cloth′ing** [OE. *clathian* < prec.] **1.** to put clothes on; dress **2.** to provide with clothes **3.** to cover over as if with a garment

clothes (klōz, klō*thz*) ***n.pl.*** [OE. *clathas,* pl. of *clath,* CLOTH] **1.** articles, usually of cloth, to cover the body; apparel; garments **2.** *same as* BEDCLOTHES

clothes·horse (-hôrs′) ***n.*** **1.** a frame on which to hang clothes, etc. for airing or drying **2.** [Slang] one who pays too much attention to his clothes

clothes·line (-līn′) ***n.*** a rope or wire on which clothes, etc. are hung for airing or drying

clothes·pin (-pin′) ***n.*** a small clip, as of wood or plastic, for fastening clothes on a line

clothes·press (-pres′) ***n.*** a closet, wardrobe, or chest in which to keep clothes

clothes tree an upright pole with branching hooks or pegs near the top to hold coats and hats

cloth·ier (klō*th*′yər, klō′*th*ē ər) ***n.*** **1.** a person who makes or sells clothes **2.** a dealer in cloth

cloth·ing (klō′*th*iŋ) ***n.*** **1.** wearing apparel; clothes; garments **2.** a covering

Clo·tho (klō′thō) *Gr. & Rom. Myth.* one of the three Fates, spinner of the thread of human life

clo·ture (klō′chər) ***n.*** [Fr. < OFr. < ML. < L. *clausura:* see CLOSURE] the parliamentary procedure by which debate is closed and the measure put to an immediate vote —***vt.* -tured, -tur·ing** to apply cloture to (a debate, bill, etc.)

cloud (kloud) ***n.*** [OE. *clud,* mass of rock] **1.** a visible mass of condensed water vapor suspended in the atmosphere **2.** a mass of smoke, dust, steam, etc. **3.** a great number of moving things close together *[a cloud of locusts]* **4.** a murkiness or dimness, as in a liquid **5.** a dark marking, as in marble **6.** anything that darkens, obscures, or makes gloomy —***vt.*** **1.** to cover with clouds **2.** to make muddy or foggy **3.** to darken; obscure **4.** to make gloomy or troubled **5.** to sully (a reputation, etc.) —***vi.*** **1.** to become cloudy **2.** to become gloomy or troubled —**in the clouds 1.** high up in the sky **2.** fanciful; impractical **3.** in a reverie or daydream —**under a cloud 1.** under suspicion of wrongdoing **2.** troubled; depressed —**cloud′less *adj.*** —**cloud′less·ly *adv.*** —**cloud′less·ness *n.***

cloud·burst (-burst′) ***n.*** a sudden, very heavy rain

cloud nine [Slang] a state of euphoria

cloud·y (-ē) ***adj.* cloud′i·er, cloud′i·est 1.** covered with clouds; overcast **2.** of or like clouds **3.** streaked, as marble **4.** opaque, muddy, or foggy *[a cloudy liquid]* **5.** obscure; vague **6.** troubled; gloomy —**cloud′i·ly *adv.*** —**cloud′i·ness *n.***

clout (klout) ***n.*** [OE. *clut*] **1.** [Archaic] a piece of cloth **2.** a blow, as with the hand; rap **3.** [Colloq.] *a)* a long hit in baseball *b)* power or influence; esp., political power —***vt.*** **1.** [Colloq.] to strike, as with the hand **2.** [Slang] to hit (a ball) a far distance

clove[1] (klōv) ***n.*** [OFr. *clou* < L. *clavus,* nail: from its shape] **1.** the dried flower bud of a tropical evergreen tree of the myrtle family: it is used as a pungent, fragrant spice **2.** the tree

clove[2] (klōv) ***n.*** [OE. *clufu,* akin to *cleofan,* CLEAVE[1]] a segment of a bulb, as of garlic

clove[3] (klōv) *alt. pt. of* CLEAVE[1]

clo·ven (klō′v'n) *alt. pp. of* CLEAVE[1] —***adj.*** divided; split

cloven foot (or **hoof**) a foot divided by a cleft, as in the ox, deer, and sheep: used as a symbol of the Devil, usually pictured with such hoofs —**clo′ven-foot′ed, clo′ven-hoofed′ *adj.***

clo·ver (klō′vər) ***n.*** [< OE. *clafre*] **1.** any of a genus of low-growing herbs of the legume family, with leaves of three leaflets and small flowers in dense heads **2.** any similar plant: cf. SWEET CLOVER —**in clover** living in ease and luxury

clo·ver·leaf (-lēf′) ***n., pl.* -leafs′** a multiple highway interchange in the form of a four-leaf clover, which, by means of an overpass with curving ramps, permits traffic to move or turn in any of four directions with little interference —***adj.*** in the shape of a leaf of clover

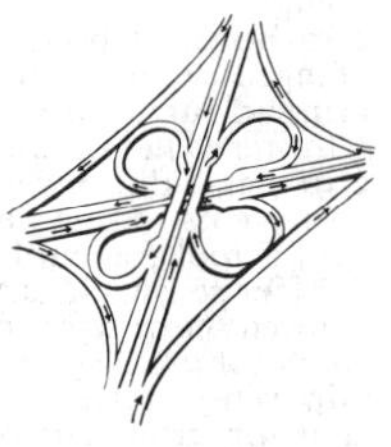
CLOVERLEAF

clown (kloun) ***n.*** [altered < ? Fr. *colon,* farmer < L. *colonus:* see COLONY] **1.** orig., a peasant; rustic **2.** a clumsy, boorish person **3.** a performer who entertains, as in a circus, by antics, jokes, tricks, etc. **4.** a buffoon —***vi.*** **1.** to perform as a clown **2.** to play practical jokes, act silly, etc. —**clown′er·y *n.*** —**clown′ish *adj.*** —**clown′ish·ly *adv.*** —**clown′ish·ness *n.***

cloy (kloi) ***vt., vi.*** [< OFr. *encloyer,* to fasten with a nail, hinder < *clou:* see CLOVE[1]] to surfeit by too much of something, esp. something sweet, rich, etc. —**cloy′ing·ly *adv.***

club (klub) ***n.*** [< ON. *klumba,* mass of something, clump] **1.** *a)* a heavy stick, usually thinner at one end, used as a weapon *b)* anything used to threaten **2.** any stick or bat used to strike a ball in a game *[a golf club]* **3.** *same as* INDIAN CLUB **4.** a group of people associated for a common purpose **5.** the room, building, etc. used by such a group **6.** *same as* NIGHTCLUB **7.** *a)* [*pl.*] a suit of playing cards marked with a black cloverleaf figure (♣) *b)* a card of this suit —***vt.* clubbed, club′bing 1.** to strike as with a club **2.** to unite for a common purpose **3.** to pool (resources, etc.) —***vi.*** to unite or combine for a common purpose

club car a railroad lounge car, usually with a bar

club·foot (-foot′) ***n.*** **1.** a congenital deformity of the foot, often with a clublike appearance; talipes **2.** *pl.* **-feet′** a foot so deformed —**club′foot′ed *adj.***

club·house (-hous′) ***n.*** **1.** a building occupied by a club **2.** a locker room for an athletic team

club·man (-mən, -man′) ***n., pl.* -men** (-mən, -men′) a man who is a member of, or spends much time at, a private club or clubs —**club′wom′an *n.fem., pl.* -wom′en**

club sandwich a sandwich of several layers, often toasted, containing chicken, bacon, lettuce, etc.

club soda *same as* SODA WATER

cluck (kluk) ***vi.*** [< OE. *cloccian:* orig. echoic] to make a low, sharp, clicking sound, as of a hen calling her chickens —***vt.*** to utter with such a sound —***n.*** **1.** the sound of clucking **2.** [Slang] a dull, stupid person; dolt

clue (klo͞o) ***n.*** a clew; esp., a fact, object, etc. that helps solve a mystery or problem —***vt.* clued, clu′ing 1.** to indicate by or as by a clue **2.** [Colloq.] to provide with necessary information (often with *in*)

Cluj (klo͞ozh) city in NW Romania: pop. 191,000

clump (klump) ***n.*** [< Du. *klomp* or LowG. *klump*] **1.** a lump; mass **2.** a cluster, as of trees **3.** the sound of heavy footsteps —***vi.*** **1.** to tramp heavily **2.** to form clumps —***vt.*** **1.** to group together in a cluster **2.** to cause to form clumps —**clump′ish *adj.*** —**clump′y *adj.* clump′i·er, clump′i·est**

clum·sy (klum′zē) ***adj.* -si·er, -si·est** [ME. *clumsid,* numb with cold < ON. base] **1.** lacking grace or skill; awkward **2.** awkwardly shaped or made; ill-constructed **3.** inelegant *[a clumsy style]* —**clum′si·ly *adv.*** —**clum′si·ness *n.***

clung (kluŋ) *pt. & pp. of* CLING

clunk (kluŋk) ***n.*** [echoic] **1.** a dull, metallic sound **2.** [Colloq.] a heavy blow **3.** [Slang] a dull or stupid person —***vi., vt.*** to move or strike with a clunk or clunks

clunk·er (-ər) ***n.*** [Slang] an old machine or automobile in poor repair

clus·ter (klus′tər) ***n.*** [OE. *clyster*] **1.** a number of things of the same sort gathered or growing together; bunch **2.** a number of persons or animals grouped together **3.** *Linguis.* two or more consecutive consonants —***vi., vt.*** to gather or grow in a cluster or clusters —**clus′ter·y *adj.***

clutch[1] (kluch) ***vt.*** [OE. *clyccan,* to clench] **1.** to grasp or snatch with a hand or claw **2.** to grasp or hold eagerly or tightly —***vi.*** to snatch or seize (*at*) —***n.*** **1.** a claw or hand in the act of seizing **2.** [*usually pl.*] power; control **3.** *a)* a clutching *b)* a grasp; grip **4.** *a)* a mechanical device, as in an automobile, for engaging or disengaging the motor *b)* the lever or pedal that operates this **5.** a device for gripping **6.** a woman's small handbag with no handle or strap: also **clutch bag 7.** [Colloq.] an emergency

clutch[2] (kluch) ***n.*** [< ME. *clekken* (< ON. *klekja*), to hatch] **1.** a nest of eggs **2.** a brood of chicks **3.** a cluster of persons, animals, or things

clut·ter (klut′ər) ***n.*** [< CLOT] **1.** a number of things scattered in disorder; jumble **2.** *dial. var. of* CLATTER **3.** the interfering traces on a radarscope caused by hills, buildings, etc. —*vt.* to put into disorder; jumble (often with *up*) —*vi.* [Dial.] to make a clatter —**clut′ter·y** *adj.*

Clyde (klīd) [< ?] a masculine name

Clydes·dale (klīdz′dāl′) *n.* [orig. from *Clydesdale,* Scotland] any of a breed of strong draft horse

clyp·e·ate (klip′ē it, -āt′) *adj.* [< L. < *clypeus,* a shield] *Biol.* **1.** shaped like a round shield **2.** having a shieldlike process Also **clyp′e·at′ed**

clys·ter (klis′tər) *n.* [< L. < Gr. *klystēr* < *klyzein,* to wash] *same as* ENEMA

Cly·tem·nes·tra, Cly·taem·nes·tra (klīt′əm nes′trə) *Gr. Myth.* the wife of Agamemnon: see ELECTRA

Cm *Chem.* curium

cm, cm. centimeter; centimeters

cmdg. commanding

cml. commercial

Cnos·sus (näs′əs) ancient city in N Crete: center of ancient Minoan civilization

C-note (sē′nōt′) *n.* [for CENTURY-note] [Slang] a one-hundred-dollar bill

co- **1.** *a prefix shortened from* COM- *meaning: a)* together with *[cooperation] b)* joint *[co-owner] c)* equally *[coextensive]* **2.** *a prefix meaning* complement of *[cosine]*

Co *Chem.* cobalt

CO Colorado

Co., co. *pl.* **Cos., cos.** **1.** company **2.** county

C/O, c.o. **1.** care of **2.** carried over

C.O., CO **1.** Commanding Officer **2.** conscientious objector

coach (kōch) *n.* [< Fr. < G. < Hung. *kocsi (szekér),* (carriage of) Kócs, village in Hungary] **1.** a large, covered, four-wheeled carriage with an open, raised seat in front for the driver; stagecoach **2.** a railroad passenger car with the lowest-priced seating accommodations **3.** the lowest-priced class of accommodations on some airlines **4.** a bus **5.** an enclosed automobile, usually a two-door sedan **6.** a private tutor who prepares a student as for an examination **7.** an instructor or trainer, as of athletes, singers, etc. **8.** *Sports* a person in charge of a team or of some aspect of team play or practice —*vt.* **1.** to instruct by private tutoring **2.** to instruct and train (athletes, actors, etc.) —*vi.* to act as a coach

coach dog *same as* DALMATIAN

coach·man (-mən) *n., pl.* **-men** the driver of a coach or carriage

co·ad·ju·tor (kō aj′ə tər; *also, and for 2 usually,* kō′ə-jo͞ot′ər) *n.* [< OFr. < L. < *co-,* together + *adjuvare,* to help] **1.** an assistant; helper **2.** a bishop appointed to assist a bishop

co·ag·u·la·ble (kō ag′yoo lə b'l) *adj.* that can be coagulated —**co·ag′u·la·bil′i·ty** *n.*

co·ag·u·late (kō ag′yoo lāt′) *vt.* **-lat′ed, -lat′ing** [< L. pp. of *coagulare* < *coagulum,* coagulating agent < *cogere,* to curdle: see COGENT] to cause (a liquid) to become a soft, semisolid mass; curdle; clot —*vi.* to become coagulated —**co·ag′u·lant** *n.* —**co·ag′u·la′tion** *n.* —**co·ag′u·la′tive** *adj.* —**co·ag′u·la′tor** *n.*

coal (kōl) *n.* [OE. *col,* a live coal, charcoal] **1.** a black, combustible, mineral solid resulting from the partial decomposition of vegetable matter away from air and under high heat and great pressure over millions of years: used as a fuel and in the production of coke and many coal-tar compounds **2.** a piece or, collectively, pieces of this substance **3.** an ember **4.** charcoal —*vt.* to provide with coal —*vi.* to take in a supply of coal —**haul** (or **rake, drag, call**) **over the coals** to criticize sharply; censure —**heap coals of fire on (someone's) head** to cause (someone) to feel remorse by returning good for his evil —**coal′y** *adj.*

coal·er (-ər) *n.* a ship, railroad freight car (also **coal car**), etc. that transports or supplies coal

co·a·lesce (kō′ə les′) *vi.* **-lesced′, -lesc′ing** [< L. *coalescere* < *co-,* together + *alescere,* to grow up] **1.** to grow together **2.** to unite or merge into a single body, group, or mass —**co′a·les′cence** *n.* —**co′a·les′cent** *adj.*

coal gas **1.** a gas produced by the distillation of bituminous coal: used for lighting and heating **2.** a poisonous gas given off by burning coal

co·a·li·tion (kō′ə lish′ən) *n.* [< ML. < LL., orig. pp. of *coalescere:* see COALESCE] **1.** a combination; union **2.** a temporary alliance of political parties, nations, etc. for some specific purpose —**co′a·li′tion·ist** *n.*

coal measures coal beds or strata

coal oil **1.** kerosene **2.** crude petroleum

coal tar a black, thick, opaque liquid obtained by the distillation of bituminous coal: many synthetic compounds have been developed from it, including dyes, medicines, explosives, and perfumes

coam·ing (kō′miŋ) *n.* [< ?] a raised border around a hatchway, etc. to keep out water

coarse (kôrs) *adj.* [var. of COURSE in sense of "ordinary or usual order," as in *of course*] **1.** of inferior or poor quality; common **2.** consisting of rather large particles *[coarse sand]* **3.** not fine in texture, form, etc.; rough *[coarse cloth]* **4.** for rough work or results *[a coarse file]* **5.** lacking in refinement; vulgar *[a coarse joke]* —**coarse′ly** *adv.* —**coarse′ness** *n.*

coarse-grained (-grānd′) *adj.* **1.** having a coarse texture **2.** lacking in refinement; crude

coars·en (-'n) *vt., vi.* to make or become coarse

coast (kōst) *n.* [< OFr. < L. *costa,* a rib, side] **1.** land alongside the sea; seashore **2.** [< CanadFr., hillside, slope] an incline down which a slide is taken **3.** a slide or ride down, as on a sled —*vi.* **1.** to sail near or along a coast **2.** to go down an incline on a sled **3.** to continue in motion on momentum after propelling power has stopped **4.** to let one's past efforts carry one along —*vt.* to sail along or near the coast of —**the Coast** [Colloq.] in the U.S., the Pacific coast —**the coast is clear** there is no apparent danger or hindrance

coast·al (-'l) *adj.* of, at, near, or along a coast

coast·er (kōs′tər) *n.* **1.** a person or thing that coasts **2.** a ship that travels from port to port along a coast **3.** a sled or wagon for coasting **4.** a small tray, mat, disk, etc. placed under a glass or bottle to protect a table or other surface

coaster brake a brake in the hub of the rear wheel of a bicycle, worked by reverse pressure on the pedals: it also permits free coasting

coast guard **1.** a governmental force employed to defend a nation's coasts, prevent smuggling, aid vessels in distress, etc.; specif., [C- G-] such a branch of the U.S. armed forces, normally under the control of the Department of Transportation **2.** a member of a coast guard —**coast guards′-man, coast guard′man,** *pl.* **-men**

coast·land (kōst′land′) *n.* land along a coast

coast·line (-līn′) *n.* the outline of a coast

coast·ward (-wərd) *adj., adv.* toward the coast: also **coast′wards** *adv.*

coast·wise (-wīz′) *adv., adj.* along the coast: also **coast′ways′** (-wāz′) *adv.*

coat (kōt) *n.* [< OFr. < ML. *cot(t)a,* a tunic < Frank. hyp. *kotta,* coarse cloth] **1.** a sleeved outer garment opening down the front, as a suit jacket or an overcoat **2.** the natural covering of an animal, as of skin, fur, wool, etc. **3.** any outer covering, as of a plant **4.** a layer of some substance, as paint, over a surface —*vt.* **1.** to provide or cover with a coat **2.** to cover with a layer of something —**coat′ed** *adj.* —**coat′less** *adj.*

co·a·ti (kō ät′ē) *n., pl.* **-tis** [Tupi < *cua,* a cincture + *tim,* the nose] a small, flesh-eating, tree-dwelling mammal of Mexico and Central and South America, like the raccoon but with a long, flexible snout Also **co·a′ti-mun′di, co·a′ti-mon′di** (-mun′dē)

coat·ing (kōt′iŋ) *n.* **1.** a coat or layer over a surface **2.** cloth for making coats

coat of arms [after Fr. *cotte d'armes,* light garment worn over armor, and blazoned with one's heraldic arms] a group of emblems and figures (heraldic bearings) usually arranged on and around a shield and used as the insignia of a family, etc.

coat of mail *pl.* **coats of mail** a suit of armor made of linked metal rings or overlapping plates

coat·tail (-tāl′) *n.* the back part of a coat below the waist; esp., either half of this part when divided —**ride** (or **hang,** etc.) **on (someone's) coattails** to have one's success dependent on that of someone else

co·au·thor (kō ô′thər) *n.* a joint author

coax (kōks) *vt.* [< obs. slang *coax, cokes,* a fool] **1.** to persuade or urge by soothing words, flattery, etc.; wheedle **2.** to get by coaxing —*vi.* to use gentle persuasion, urging, etc. —**coax′er** *n.* —**coax′ing** *adj., n.* —**coax′ing·ly** *adv.*

co·ax·i·al (kō ak′sē əl) *adj.* [CO- + AXIAL] **1.** having a common axis: also **co·ax′al** **2.** designating a compound loudspeaker consisting of a smaller unit mounted within and connected with a larger one on a common axis **3.** designating a high-frequency transmission cable or line for telephone, telegraph, television, etc.: its outer conductor tube surrounds an insulated, solid or stranded central conductor

cob (käb) *n.* [prob. < LowG.] **1.** [Brit. Dial.] *a)* a lump *b)* a leader; chief **2.** a corncob **3.** a male swan **4.** a short, thickset horse

co·balt (kō′bôlt) *n.* [G. *kobalt* < *kobold,* goblin, demon of the mines] a hard, lustrous, steel-gray, ductile metallic chemical element, used in alloys, inks, paints, etc.: symbol

Co; at. wt., 58.9332; at. no., 27: a radioactive isotope (**cobalt 60**) is used in the treatment of cancer, in research, etc. —**co·bal′tic** ***adj.*** —**co·bal′tous** ***adj.***
cobalt blue **1.** a dark blue pigment made from cobalt and aluminum oxides **2.** dark blue
cob·ble[1] (käb′′l) ***vt.*** **-bled, -bling** [prob. akin to COB] **1.** to mend (shoes, etc.) **2.** to mend or put together clumsily or crudely
cob·ble[2] (käb′′l) ***n.*** [prob. < COB] *same as* COBBLESTONE —***vt.*** **-bled, -bling** to pave with cobblestones
cob·bler[1] (-lər) ***n.*** [of U.S. orig. < ?] **1.** an iced drink of wine, whiskey, or rum, an orange or lemon slice, sugar, etc. **2.** a deep-dish fruit pie
cob·bler[2] (-lər) ***n.*** **1.** a person whose work is mending shoes **2.** [Archaic] a clumsy workman
cob·ble·stone (käb′′l stōn′) ***n.*** [COBBLE[2] + STONE] a rounded stone of a kind formerly much used for paving streets
cob coal coal in large, rounded lumps
co·bel·lig·er·ent (kō′bə lij′ər ənt) ***n.*** a nation associated but not formally allied with another or others in waging war
co·bi·a (kō′bē ə) ***n.*** [< ?] a large, voracious game fish of warm seas
co·bra (kō′brə) ***n.*** [< Port. *cobra* (*de capello*), serpent (of the hood)] a very poisonous snake of Asia and Africa: loose skin around the neck expands into a hood when the snake is excited

INDIAN COBRA (to 6 ft. long)

cob·web (käb′web′) ***n.*** [< ME. *coppe*, spider + WEB] **1.** a web spun by a spider **2.** a single thread of such a web **3.** anything flimsy, gauzy, or ensnaring, like a spider's web —***vt.*** **-webbed′, -web′bing** to cover as with cobwebs —**cob′web′by** ***adj.***
co·ca (kō′kə) ***n.*** [Quechuan *cuca*] **1.** any of certain S. American shrubs, esp. a species whose dried leaves are the source of cocaine and some other alkaloids **2.** these dried leaves
co·caine, co·cain (kō kān′, kō′kān) ***n.*** [COCA + -INE[4]] a crystalline alkaloid, $C_{17}H_{21}NO_4$, obtained from dried coca leaves: it is a narcotic and local anesthetic
-coc·cal (käk′′l) *a combining form meaning* of or produced by a (specified kind of) coccus *[staphylococcal]*: also **-coc′-cic** (-sik)
coc·cus (käk′əs) ***n.,*** *pl.* **coc·ci** (käk′sī) [ModL. < Gr. *kokkos*, a berry] a bacterium of a spherical shape —**coc′-coid** (-oid) ***adj.***
-coc·cus (käk′əs) *a combining form meaning* coccus: used in names of various bacteria *[gonococcus]*
coc·cyx (käk′siks) ***n.,*** *pl.* **coc·cy·ges** (käk sī′jēz) [L. < Gr. *kokkyx*, cuckoo: from its shape like a cuckoo's beak] a small, triangular bone at the lower end of the vertebral column —**coc·cyg′e·al** (-sij′ē əl) ***adj.***
Co·chin (kō′chin′, käch′in) ***n.*** [< ff.] [*also* **c-**] a large domestic fowl with thickly feathered legs: also **Cochin China**
Cochin China, Cochin-China region & former Fr. colony in S Indochina: now part of South Vietnam
coch·i·neal (käch′ə nēl′, käch′ə nēl′) ***n.*** [< Fr. < It. < L. *coccinus*, scarlet-colored < *coccum*, a berry] a red dye made from the dried bodies of female cochineal insects: used, esp. formerly, in coloring foods and cosmetics and as a dye
cochineal insect a scale insect having a brilliant red body fluid and feeding on cactus: found chiefly in Mexico and a source of cochineal
coch·le·a (käk′lē ə) ***n.,*** *pl.* **-le·ae′** (-ē′), **-le·as** [L. < Gr. *kochlias*, snail] the spiral-shaped part of the internal ear, containing the auditory nerve endings —**coch′le·ar** ***adj.***
coch·le·ate (-it, -āt′) ***adj.*** [< L.: see prec.] shaped like a snail shell: also **coch′le·at′ed**
cock[1] (käk) ***n.*** [OE. *coc*] **1.** *a*) the male of the chicken; rooster *b*) the male of certain other birds **2.** a weathercock **3.** a leader or chief **4.** a faucet or valve for regulating the flow of liquid or gas **5.** the hammer of a firearm, or the position of the hammer set for firing **6.** a jaunty, erect position *[*the *cock* of a hat*]* —***vt.*** **1.** to set (a hat, etc.) jauntily on one side **2.** to raise up; erect *[*a dog *cocks* his ears*]* **3.** to turn (the eye or ear) toward something **4.** *a*) to set the hammer of (a gun) in firing position *b*) to set (a tripping device, as for a camera shutter) **5.** to draw back (one's fist, etc.) ready to strike —***vi.*** to assume an upright or tilted position
cock[2] (käk) ***n.*** [ME. *cokke*] a small, cone-shaped pile, as of hay —***vt.*** to pile in cocks
cock·ade (kä kād′) ***n.*** [Fr. *cocarde* < *coq*, a cock] a rosette, knot of ribbon, etc. worn on the hat as a badge —**cock·ad′ed** ***adj.***
cock·a·lo·rum (käk′ə lôr′əm) ***n.*** [pseudo L. extension of COCK[1]] **1.** a little man with an exaggerated idea of his own importance **2.** boastful talk
cock·a·ma·mie (käk′ə mā′mē) ***adj.*** [alteration of DECALCOMANIA] [Slang] of poor quality; inferior
cock-and-bull story (käk′′n bool′) [< Fr. *coq à l'âne*] an absurd, improbable story
cock·a·teel, cock·a·tiel (käk′ə tēl′) ***n.*** [< Du. dim. of *kaketoe*: see ff.] a small, crested, Australian parrot with a long tail and yellow head
cock·a·too (käk′ə to͞o′, käk′ə to͞o′) ***n.,*** *pl.* **-toos′** [Du. *kaketoe* < Malay *kakatua*; prob. echoic] a crested parrot of Australia and the East Indies, with white plumage tinged with yellow or pink
cock·a·trice (käk′ə tris′) ***n.*** [< OFr. < L. *calcare*, to tread < *calx*, the heel] a legendary serpent supposedly hatched from a cock's egg and having power to kill by a look
cock·boat (käk′bōt′) ***n.*** [< ME. < *cok*, ship's boat + *bote*, BOAT] a small boat, esp. one used as a ship's tender
cock·chaf·er (-chāf′ər) ***n.*** [COCK[1] (? because of size) + CHAFER] a large European beetle whose grubs feed on the roots of plants
cock·crow (-krō′) ***n.*** the time when roosters begin to crow; dawn: also **cock′crow′ing**
cocked hat **1.** a three-cornered hat with a turned-up brim **2.** a peaked hat pointed in front and in back —**knock into a cocked hat** [Slang] to damage or spoil completely; ruin
cock·er·el (käk′ər əl, käk′rəl) ***n.*** [dim. of COCK[1]] a young rooster, less than a year old
cock·er (spaniel) (käk′ər) [from its use in hunting woodcock] a small spaniel with a compact body, long, silky hair, and long, drooping ears
cock·eye (käk′ī′) ***n.*** [COCK[1], *vi.* + EYE] a squinting eye
cock·eyed (-īd′) ***adj.*** **1.** cross-eyed **2.** [Slang] *a*) tilted; crooked; awry *b*) silly; foolish *c*) drunk
cock·fight (-fīt′) ***n.*** a fight between gamecocks, usually wearing metal spurs —**cock′fight′ing** ***n.***
cock·horse (-hôrs′) ***n.*** [16th c., toy horse] *same as* ROCKING HORSE or HOBBYHORSE (sense 1)
cock·le[1] (käk′′l) ***n.*** [< OFr. *coquille*, a shell < L. < Gr. < *konchē*, CONCH] **1.** an edible shellfish with two heart-shaped, radially ridged shells **2.** a cockleshell **3.** a wrinkle; pucker —***vi., vt.*** **-led, -ling** to wrinkle; pucker —**cockles of one's heart** one's deepest feelings or emotions
cock·le[2] (käk′′l) ***n.*** [< OE. *coccel*, tares] any of various weeds that grow in grainfields
cock·le·bur (-bur′) ***n.*** a coarse plant of the composite family, bearing burs, that grows as a weed
cock·le·shell (-shel′) ***n.*** **1.** the shell of a cockle **2.** loosely, a scallop shell, etc. **3.** a small boat
cock·ney (käk′nē) ***n.,*** *pl.* **-neys** [ME. *cokenei*, spoiled child; understood as *coken-ey*, lit., cock's egg; ? infl. by Fr. *acoquiné*, idle < *coquin*, rascal] [*often* **C-**] **1.** a native of the East End of London, England, speaking a dialect characterized by loss of initial *h*, use of an intrusive *r*, etc. **2.** this dialect: also **cock′ney·ese′** (-ēz′) —***adj.*** [*often* **C-**] of or like cockneys or their dialect —**cock′ney·ish** ***adj.*** —**cock′ney·ism** ***n.***
cock·pit (käk′pit′) ***n.*** **1.** an enclosed space for cockfighting **2.** in small decked vessels, a sunken space toward the stern used by the steersman, etc. **3.** the space in a small airplane for the pilot and, sometimes, passengers, or in a large airplane for the pilot and copilot or crew
cock·roach (-rōch′) ***n.*** [Sp. *cucaracha*, altered after COCK[1] + ROACH] an insect with long feelers, and a flat, soft body: a common household pest
cocks·comb (käks′kōm′) ***n.*** **1.** the red, fleshy growth on the head of a rooster **2.** *same as* COXCOMB **3.** a plant related to the amaranth, with red or yellow flower heads
cock·sure (käk′shoor′, -shur′) ***adj.*** [COCK[1] (cf. COCKY) + SURE] **1.** absolutely sure **2.** self-confident and overbearing —**cock′sure′ness** ***n.***
cock·swain (käk′s'n, -swān′) ***n.*** *same as* COXSWAIN
cock·tail (-tāl′) ***n.*** [< ?] **1.** an alcoholic drink, usually iced, made of a distilled liquor mixed with a wine, fruit juice, etc. **2.** an appetizer, as fruit juice, diced fruits, or seafood
cock·y (käk′ē) ***adj.*** **cock′i·er, cock′i·est** [COCK[1] + -Y[2]] [Colloq.] jauntily conceited; self-confident in an aggressive or swaggering way —**cock′i·ly** ***adv.*** —**cock′i·ness** ***n.***
co·co (kō′kō) ***n.,*** *pl.* **-cos** [Sp. & Port. < L. *coccum*, a seed < Gr. *kokkos*, a berry] **1.** *same as* COCONUT PALM **2.** its fruit; coconut —***adj.*** made of the fiber from coconut husks
co·coa (kō′kō) ***n.*** [Sp. & Port. *cacao* < Nahuatl *cacauatl*] **1.** powder made from cacao seeds that have been roasted and ground **2.** a drink made by adding sugar and hot water or milk to this powder **3.** a reddish-yellow brown
cocoa butter a yellowish fat prepared from cacao seeds: used in pharmacy and in cosmetics
co·co·nut, co·coa·nut (kō′kə nut′) ***n.*** the fruit of the coconut palm, a thick, brown, oval husk enclosing a layer of edible white meat: the hollow center is filled with a sweet, milky fluid called **coconut milk**
coconut oil oil obtained from the dried meat of coconuts, used for making soap, etc.

coconut palm (or **tree**) a tall tropical palm tree that bears coconuts: also **coco palm**
co·coon (kə ko͞on′) *n.* [< Fr. < Pr. *coucoun*, egg shell, ult. < ML. *coco*, shell] **1.** the silky case which the larvae of certain insects spin about themselves for shelter during the pupa stage **2.** any protective cover like this
cod (käd) *n., pl.* **cod, cods:** see PLURAL, II, D, 2 [ME.] an important food fish, with firm flesh and soft fins, found in northern seas
C.O.D., c.o.d. cash (or collect) on delivery
Cod (käd), **Cape** peninsula in E Mass.
co·da (kō′də) *n.* [It. < L. *cauda*, a tail] *Music* a passage formally ending a composition or section
cod·dle (käd′'l) *vt.* **-dled, -dling** [prob. < CAUDLE] **1.** to cook (esp. eggs) gently in water not quite boiling **2.** to treat tenderly; pamper
code (kōd) *n.* [< OFr. < L. *codex*, wooden tablet for writing, orig., tree trunk] **1.** a body of laws of a nation, city, etc. arranged systematically for easy reference **2.** any set of principles *[a moral code]* **3.** *a)* a set of signals for sending messages, as by telegraph, flags, etc. *b)* any set of signals, as that (**genetic code**) in the chromosomes determining the pattern of growth, etc. **4.** *a)* a system of secret writing, information processing, etc., in which letters, figures, etc. are given certain meanings *b)* the symbols used —*vt.* **cod′ed, cod′ing** to put in the form or symbols of a code —**cod′er** *n.*
co·deine (kō′dēn, -dē in) *n.* [< Gr. *kōdeia*, poppy head + -INE[4]] an alkaloid, $C_{18}H_{21}O_3N{\cdot}H_2O$, derived from opium and resembling morphine: used for the relief of pain and in cough medicines: also **co′dein, co·de·ia** (kō dē′ə)
co·dex (kō′deks) *n., pl.* **co·di·ces** (kō′də sēz′, käd′ə-) [L.: see CODE] **1.** orig., a code, or body of laws **2.** a manuscript volume, esp. of the Scriptures or of a classic text
cod·fish (käd′fish′) *n., pl.* **-fish′, -fish′es:** see FISH *same as* COD
codg·er (käj′ər) *n.* [prob. var. of CADGER] [Colloq.] an eccentric, esp. elderly, fellow
cod·i·cil (käd′i s'l, -sil′) *n.* [< L. dim. of *codex:* see CODE] **1.** *Law* an addition to a will to change, revoke, or add provisions **2.** an appendix or supplement —**cod′i·cil′la·ry** *adj.*
cod·i·fy (käd′ə fī′, kō′də-) *vt.* **-fied′, -fy′ing** [see CODE & -FY] to arrange (laws, etc.) systematically —**cod′i·fi·ca′tion** *n.* —**cod′i·fi′er** *n.*
cod·ling[1] (käd′liŋ) *n., pl.* **-ling, -lings:** see PLURAL, II, D, 2 a young cod
cod·ling[2] (käd′liŋ) *n.* [ult. < Fr. *coeur de lion*, lit., heart of lion] **1.** a variety of elongated apple **2.** a small, unripe apple Also **cod′lin**
codling (or **codlin**) **moth** a small moth whose larva destroys apples, pears, quinces, etc.
cod-liv·er oil (käd′liv′ər) oil obtained from the liver of the cod and related fishes: it is rich in vitamins A and D
Co·dy (kō′dē), **William Frederick** 1846–1917; U.S. plainsman & showman: called *Buffalo Bill*
co·ed, co-ed (kō′ed′) *n.* [Colloq.] a girl attending a coeducational college or university —*adj.* [Colloq.] **1.** coeducational **2.** of a coed
co·ed·u·ca·tion (kō′ej ə kā′shən) *n.* [CO- + EDUCATION] the educational system in which students of both sexes attend classes together —**co′ed·u·ca′tion·al** *adj.* —**co′ed·u·ca′tion·al·ly** *adv.*
co·ef·fi·cient (kō′ə fish′ənt) *n.* [CO- + EFFICIENT] **1.** a factor that contributes to produce a result **2.** *Math.* a number, symbol, etc. used as a multiplier **3.** *Physics* a number, constant for a given substance, used as a multiplier in measuring the change in some property of the substance under given conditions
coe·la·canth (sē′lə kanth′) *n.* [ModL. < Gr. *koilos* (see ff.) + *akantha*, point] any of a group of primitive, almost entirely extinct fishes that were possibly ancestors to land animals
-coele, -coel (sēl) [< Gr. *koilia*, body cavity < *koilos*, hollow] *a combining form meaning* cavity, chamber of the body
coe·len·ter·ate (si len′tə rāt′, -tər it) *n.* [ult. < Gr. *koilos* (see prec.) + *enteron*, intestine] any of a large group of marine animals, as the hydroids, jellyfishes, corals, etc., in which the characteristic structure is a large central cavity with a single opening
coe·li·ac (sē′lē ak′) *adj. same as* CELIAC
coe·lom (sē′ləm) *n.* [< Gr. < *koilos:* see -COELE] the main body cavity of most higher animals, in which the visceral organs are suspended
coe·no- [< Gr. *koinos*, common] *a combining form meaning* common: also, before a vowel, **coen-**
coe·no·bite (sē′nə bīt′, sen′ə-) *n. same as* CENOBITE
co·e·qual (kō ē′kwəl) *adj., n.* equal —**co′e·qual′i·ty** (-i-kwäl′ə tē) *n.* —**co·e′qual·ly** *adv.*
co·erce (kō ʉrs′) *vt.* **-erced′, -erc′ing** [< OFr. < L. *coercere* < *co-*, together + *arcere*, to confine] **1.** to restrain or constrain by force; curb **2.** to force; compel **3.** to enforce —**co·erc′er** *n.* —**co·er′ci·ble** *adj.* —**co·er′ci·bly** *adv.*
co·er·cion (kō ʉr′shən, -zhən) *n.* **1.** the act or power of coercing **2.** government by force
co·er·cive (-siv) *adj.* of coercion or tending to coerce —**co·er′cive·ly** *adv.* —**co·er′cive·ness** *n.*
co·e·val (kō ē′v'l) *adj.* [< LL. < L. *co-*, together + *aevum*, age + -AL] of the same age or period; contemporary —*n.* a contemporary —**co·e′val·ly** *adv.*
co·ex·ec·u·tor (kō′ig zek′yoo tər) *n.* a person acting as executor jointly with another
co·ex·ist (-ig zist′) *vi.* **1.** to exist together, at the same time, or in the same place **2.** to live together without hostility or conflict despite differences, as in political systems —**co′ex·ist′ence** *n.* —**co′ex·ist′ent** *adj.*
co·ex·tend (-ik stend′) *vt., vi.* to extend equally in space or time —**co′ex·ten′sion** *n.* —**co′ex·ten′sive** *adj.* —**co′ex·ten′sive·ly** *adv.*
C. of C. Chamber of Commerce
cof·fee (kôf′ē, käf′ē) *n.* see PLURAL, II, D, 3 [< It. < Turk. *qahwe* < Ar. *qahwa*, orig., wine] **1.** a dark-brown, aromatic drink made by brewing in water the roasted and ground beanlike seeds of a tall tropical shrub of the madder family **2.** these seeds: also **coffee beans** **3.** the shrub **4.** the color of coffee with milk or cream in it; brown
coffee break a brief respite from work when coffee or other refreshment may be taken
cof·fee·cake (-kāk′) *n.* a kind of cake or roll, often nut-filled, coated with icing, etc., to be eaten with coffee or the like
cof·fee·house (-hous′) *n.* a place where coffee and other refreshments are served and people gather for conversation, entertainment, etc.
coffee klatch (or **klatsch**) *same as* KAFFEEKLATSCH
cof·fee·pot (-pät′) *n.* a container with a lid and spout, for making and serving coffee
coffee shop an informal restaurant, as in a hotel, where light refreshments or meals are served
coffee table a low table, usually in a living room, for serving refreshments
cof·fer (kôf′ər, käf′-) *n.* [< OFr. < L. *cophinus:* see COFFIN] **1.** a chest or strongbox for keeping valuables **2.** [*pl.*] a treasury; funds **3.** a decorative sunken panel in a vault, dome, etc. **4.** a cofferdam **5.** a lock in a canal —*vt.* **1.** to enclose in a coffer **2.** to furnish with coffers (*n.* 3)
cof·fer·dam (-dam′) *n.* [prec. + DAM[1]] **1.** a watertight temporary structure in a river, lake, etc. to keep the water from an enclosed area that has been pumped dry so that dams, etc. may be constructed **2.** a watertight box attached to the side of a ship so that repairs can be made below the waterline
cof·fin (kôf′in, käf′-) *n.* [< OFr. < L. *cophinus* < Gr. *kophinos*, basket] the case or box in which a dead person is buried
coffin nail [Old Slang] a cigarette
cog[1] (käg) *n.* [< Scand.] **1.** *a)* any of a series of teeth on the rim of a wheel, for transmitting or receiving motion by fitting between the teeth of another wheel; gear tooth *b)* a cogwheel **2.** [Colloq.] a person thought of as one small part in the working of a business, etc. —**cogged** *adj.*
cog[2] (käg) *n.* [altered (after prec.) < earlier *cock*, to secure] a projection on a beam that fits into a corresponding groove or notch in another beam, making a joint —*vt., vi.* **cogged, cog′ging** to join by a cog or cogs
co·gent (kō′jənt) *adj.* [< L. prp. of *cogere*, to collect < *co-*, together + *agere*, to drive] forceful and to the point, as a reason or argument; compelling —**co′gen·cy** *n.* —**co′gent·ly** *adv.*
cog·i·tate (käj′ə tāt′) *vi., vt.* **-tat′ed, -tat′ing** [< L. pp. of *cogitare*, to ponder] to think seriously and deeply (about); ponder; consider —**cog′i·ta·ble** *adj.* —**cog′i·ta′tion** *n.* —**cog′i·ta′tive** *adj.* —**cog′i·ta′tor** *n.*
co·gnac (kōn′yak, kän′-, kôn′-) *n.* [Fr.] **1.** a French brandy distilled from wine near Cognac, France **2.** loosely, any brandy
cog·nate (käg′nāt) *adj.* [L. *cognatus* < *co-*, together + pp. of *(g)nasci*, to be born] **1.** related by family **2.** derived from a common original form *[French and Italian are cognate languages]* **3.** having the same nature or quality —*n.* **1.** a person related to another through common ancestry **2.** a cognate word, language, or thing —**cog·na′tion** *n.*
cog·ni·tion (käg nish′ən) *n.* [L. *cognito*, knowledge < pp. of *cognoscere* < *co-*, together + *(g)noscere*, to know] **1.**

the process of knowing in the broadest sense, including perception, memory, judgment, etc. **2.** the result of such a process; perception, etc. —**cog·ni′tion·al** ***adj.*** —**cog′ni·tive** ***adj.***

cog·ni·za·ble (käg′ni zə b'l, käg nī′-; *occas.* kän′ə-) ***adj.*** **1.** that can be known or perceived **2.** *Law* within the jurisdiction of a court

cog·ni·zance (käg′nə zəns, kän′ə-) ***n.*** [< OFr. *conoissance*, knowledge < L. *cognoscere:* see COGNITION] **1.** perception or knowledge; esp., the range of knowledge possible through observation **2.** official observation **3.** *Heraldry* a distinguishing crest or mark **4.** *Law a)* a court hearing *b)* the right or power of dealing with a matter judicially —**take cognizance of** to notice or recognize

cog·ni·zant (-zənt) ***adj.*** having cognizance; aware or informed (*of* something)

cog·no·men (käg nō′mən) ***n.,*** *pl.* **-no′mens, -nom′i·na** (-näm′i nə) [L. < *co-*, with + *nomen*, name] **1.** the third or family name of an ancient Roman **2.** any family name; surname **3.** any name; esp., a nickname —**cog·nom′i·nal** (-näm′i n'l) ***adj.***

cog·wheel (käg′hwēl′) ***n.*** a wheel with a rim notched into teeth which mesh with those of another wheel or of a rack to transmit or receive motion

COGWHEELS

co·hab·it (kō hab′it) ***vi.*** [< LL. < L. *co-*, together + *habitare*, to dwell] **1.** to live together as husband and wife, esp. when not legally married **2.** [Archaic] to live together —**co·hab′it·ant** ***n.*** —**co·hab′i·ta′tion** ***n.***

co·heir (kō′er′) ***n.*** a person who inherits jointly with another or others —**co′heir′ess** ***n.fem.***

co·here (kō hir′) ***vi.*** **-hered′, -her′ing** [< L. < *co-*, together + *haerere*, to stick] **1.** to stick together, as parts of a mass **2.** to be connected naturally or logically **3.** to be in accord

co·her·ence (kō hir′əns) ***n.*** **1.** the condition of cohering **2.** the quality of being logically consistent and intelligible Also **co·her′en·cy**

co·her·ent (-ənt) ***adj.*** **1.** sticking together; having cohesion **2.** showing logical consistency or intelligibility —**co·her′ent·ly** ***adv.***

co·he·sion (kō hē′zhən) ***n.*** **1.** the act or condition of cohering; tendency to stick together **2.** *Bot.* the union of like flower parts **3.** *Physics* the force by which the molecules of a substance are held together: distinguished from ADHESION —**co·he′sive** (-hēs′iv) ***adj.*** —**co·he′sive·ly** ***adv.*** —**co·he′sive·ness** ***n.***

co·ho (kō′hō) ***n.,*** *pl.* **-ho, -hos:** see PLURAL, II, D, 2 [< ?] a small Pacific salmon, now a freshwater game fish in N U.S.: also **coho salmon**

co·hort (kō′hôrt) ***n.*** [< L. *cohors*, enclosure, crowd] **1.** an ancient Roman military unit, one tenth of a legion **2.** a band of soldiers **3.** any group or band **4.** an associate, colleague, or supporter

coif (koif; *for n. 2 & vt. 2, usually* kwäf) ***n.*** [< OFr. < LL. *cofea*, a cap, hood] **1.** a cap that fits the head closely, as that once worn under a hood of mail **2.** [< COIFFURE] a style of arranging the hair —***vt.*** **coifed, coif′ing;** also, and for 2 usually, **coiffed, coif′fing** **1.** to cover as with a coif **2.** *a)* to style (the hair) *b)* to give a coiffure to

coif·feur (kwä fur′; *Fr.* kwȧ fër′) ***n.*** [Fr. < *coiffer*, to dress the hair < prec.] a male hairdresser

coif·fure (kwä fyoor′, -fyur′; *Fr.* kwȧ für′) ***n.*** [Fr. < *coiffe*, COIF] **1.** a headdress **2.** a style of arranging the hair —***vt.*** **-fured′, -fur′ing** to coif (sense 2)

coign of vantage (koin) [archaic var. of *coin* (QUOIN)] an advantageous position

coil (koil) ***vt.*** [< OFr. < L. *colligere:* see COLLECT[2]] to wind or gather (rope, etc.) into a circular or spiral form —***vi.*** **1.** to wind around and around **2.** to move in a winding course —***n.*** **1.** anything wound into a series of rings or a spiral **2.** such a series of rings or a spiral **3.** a single turn of a coiled figure **4.** a series of connected pipes in rows or coils **5.** *Elec.* a spiral of wire, etc. used as an inductor, heating element, etc.

coin (koin) ***n.*** [< OFr. < L. *cuneus*, a wedge] **1.** *archaic var. of* QUOIN **2.** *a)* a piece of metal with a distinctive stamp, issued by a government as money *b)* such pieces collectively **3.** [Slang] money —***vt.*** **1.** *a)* to make (coins) by stamping metal *b)* to make (metal) into coins **2.** to invent (a new word or phrase) —***vi.*** to make coins —**coin money** [Colloq.] to earn money rapidly —**coin′er** ***n.***

coin·age (koi′nij) ***n.*** **1.** the act or process of coining **2.** metal money **3.** a system of metal currency **4.** an invented word or expression

co·in·cide (kō′in sīd′) ***vi.*** **-cid′ed, -cid′ing** [< Fr. < ML. < L. *co-*, together + *incidere*, to fall upon] **1.** to take up the same place in space **2.** to occur at the same time **3.** to hold equivalent positions, as on a scale **4.** to be identical; correspond exactly **5.** to be in accord; agree

co·in·ci·dence (kō in′sə dəns) ***n.*** **1.** the fact or condition of coinciding **2.** an accidental and remarkable occurrence of events, ideas, etc. at the same time, with no apparent causal relationship

co·in·ci·dent (-dənt) ***adj.*** **1.** occurring at the same time **2.** in the same position in space at the same time **3.** in agreement; identical [desire *coincident* with need] —**co·in′ci·dent·ly** ***adv.***

co·in·ci·den·tal (kō in′sə den′t'l) ***adj.*** characterized by coincidence —**co·in′ci·den′tal·ly** ***adv.***

coir (koir) ***n.*** [< Port., ult. < Tamil *kayaru*, to be twisted] the prepared fiber of the husks of coconuts, used to make rope, etc.

co·i·tus (kō′it əs, kō ēt′əs) ***n.*** [L. < *co-*, together + *ire*, to go] sexual intercourse: also **co·i·tion** (kō ish′ən) —**co′i·tal** ***adj.***

coke (kōk) ***n.*** [< ME. *colke*, core, charcoal] coal from which most of the gases have been removed by heating: it burns with intense heat and little smoke, and is used as an industrial fuel —***vt., vi.*** **coked, cok′ing** to change into coke

Col. **1.** Colombia **2.** Colonel **3.** Colorado: also **Colo.** **4.** Colossians

col. **1.** collected **2.** collector **3.** college **4.** colony **5.** color(ed) **6.** column

co·la (kō′lə) ***n.*** [< WAfr. name] **1.** an African tree whose nuts yield an extract with caffeine, used in soft drinks and medicine **2.** a sweet, carbonated soft drink flavored with this extract

col·an·der (kul′ən dər, käl′-) ***n.*** [prob. ult. < L. *colare*, to strain < *colum*, strainer] a pan with a perforated bottom to drain off liquids

COLANDER

col·chi·cine (käl′chə sēn′, -ki sin) ***n.*** [< ff. + -INE[4]] a poisonous alkaloid, $C_{22}H_{25}O_6N$, extracted from colchicum, used to treat gout and to produce chromosome doubling in plants

col·chi·cum (-kəm) ***n.*** [L. < Gr. *kolchikon*, plant with a poisonous root] **1.** a plant of the lily family, with crocuslike flowers usually blooming in the fall **2.** its dried seeds or corm

cold (kōld) ***adj.*** [OE. *cald*] **1.** of a temperature much lower than that of the human body; very chilly; frigid **2.** without the proper heat or warmth [this soup is *cold*] **3.** dead **4.** feeling chilled **5.** without warmth of feeling; not cordial [a *cold* personality] **6.** sexually frigid **7.** depressing or saddening [the *cold* truth] **8.** not involving one's feelings; detached [*cold* logic] **9.** designating or having colors that suggest cold, as tones of blue, green, or gray **10.** faint or stale [a *cold* scent] **11.** [Colloq.] with little or no preparation [to enter a game *cold*] **12.** [Slang] completely mastered [the actor had his lines down *cold*] **13.** [Slang] unconscious [knocked *cold*] —***n.*** **1.** *a)* absence of heat; lack of warmth: often thought of as an active force *b)* a low temperature; esp., one below freezing **2.** the sensation produced by a loss or absence of heat **3.** cold weather **4.** an acute inflammation of the mucous membranes of the nose and throat, thought to be caused by a virus and characterized by nasal discharge, malaise, etc. —**catch** (or **take**) **cold** to become ill with a cold —**cold comfort** little or no comfort —**have** (or **get**) **cold feet** [Colloq.] to be (or become) timid or fearful —**in the cold** ignored; neglected —**throw cold water on** to discourage —**cold′ly** ***adv.*** —**cold′ness** ***n.***

cold·blood·ed (-blud′id) ***adj.*** **1.** having a body temperature approximating that of the surrounding air, land, or water, as fishes and reptiles **2.** easily affected by cold **3.** without pity; cruel —**cold′blood′ed·ly** ***adv.*** —**cold′blood′ed·ness** ***n.***

cold chisel a hardened and tempered steel chisel for cutting or chipping cold metal

cold cream a creamy, soothing preparation for softening and cleansing the skin

cold cuts slices of cold meats and, often, cheeses

cold duck [transl. of G. *kalte ente* < ?] a drink made from equal parts of sparkling burgundy and champagne

cold frame an unheated, boxlike, glass-covered structure for protecting young plants

cold front *Meteorol.* the forward edge of a cold air mass advancing into a warmer air mass

cold·heart·ed (-här′tid) ***adj.*** lacking sympathy or kindness; unfeeling —**cold′heart′ed·ly** ***adv.*** —**cold′heart′ed·ness** ***n.***

cold pack a process of canning foodstuffs in which the raw products are placed in jars first and then subjected to heat —**cold′-pack′** ***vt.***

cold shoulder [Colloq.] deliberate indifference; slight or snub: often with *the* —**cold′-shoul′der** ***vt.***

cold sore *same as* HERPES SIMPLEX

cold turkey [Slang] **1.** the abrupt, total withdrawal of drugs from an addict **2.** in a frank, blunt way [to talk *cold* *turkey]* **3.** without preparation *[take a test cold turkey]* **—cold′-tur′key** *adj.*

cold war sharp conflict in diplomacy, economics, etc. between states, without actual warfare

cold wave **1.** a period of weather colder than is normal **2.** a permanent wave in which the hair is set with a liquid preparation instead of heat

cole (kōl) *n.* [OE. *cal* < L. *caulis, colis,* a cabbage] any of various plants of the mustard family, to which cabbage belongs; esp., rape

co·le·op·ter·an (kō′lē äp′tər ən, käl′ē-) *n.* [< Gr. *koleos,* sheath + *pteron,* wing] any of a large group of insects, including beetles and weevils, with the front wings forming a horny covering for the membranous hind wings **—co′le·op′ter·ous** *adj.*

Cole·ridge (kōl′rij, -ər ij), **Samuel Taylor** 1772–1834; Eng. poet & critic

cole·slaw (kōl′slô′) *n.* [< Du. *kool,* cabbage (akin to COLE) + *sla,* for *salade,* salad] a salad made of shredded raw cabbage: also **cole slaw**

co·le·us (kō′lē əs) *n.* [ModL. < Gr. *koleos,* a sheath] a plant of the mint family, with showy, bright-colored leaves

cole·wort (kōl′wurt′) *n.* [COLE + WORT[2]] any cabbage whose leaves do not form a compact head

col·ic (käl′ik) *n.* [< OFr. < L. < Gr. < *kolon,* colon] acute abdominal pain caused by various abnormal conditions in the bowels *—adj.* **1.** of colic **2.** of the colon **—col′ick·y** *adj.*

co·li·form (kō′lə fôrm′, käl′ə-) *adj.* designating, of, or like the aerobic bacillus normally found in the colon: a coliform count is an indicator of fecal contamination of water supplies

Co·lin (kō′lin, käl′in) [prob. < L. *columba,* a dove] a masculine name

col·i·se·um (käl′ə sē′əm) [see COLOSSEUM] [C-] *same as* COLOSSEUM *—n.* a large building or stadium for sports events, shows, etc.

co·li·tis (kō līt′is) *n.* [ModL. < Gr. *kolon,* colon + -ITIS] inflammation of the large intestine

coll. **1.** collect **2.** collection **3.** college

col·lab·o·rate (kə lab′ə rāt′) *vi.* **-rat′ed, -rat′ing** [< L. pp. of *collaborare* < *com-,* with + *laborare,* to work] **1.** to work together, esp. in some literary, artistic, or scientific undertaking **2.** to cooperate with an enemy invader **—col·lab′o·ra′tion** *n.* **—col·lab′o·ra′tive** *adj.* **—col·lab′o·ra′tor** *n.*

col·lab·o·ra·tion·ist (kə lab′ə rā′shən ist) *n.* a person who cooperates with an enemy invader

col·lage (kə läzh′) *n.* [Fr. < *colle,* paste < Gr. *kolla*] **1.** an art form in which bits of objects, as newspaper, cloth, leaves, etc., are pasted together on a surface **2.** a composition so made

col·la·gen (käl′ə jen′) *n.* [< Gr. *kolla,* glue + -GEN] a fibrous protein found in connective tissue, bone, and cartilage **—col′la·gen′ic** *adj.*

col·lapse (kə laps′) *vi.* **-lapsed′, -laps′ing** [< L. pp. of *collabi* < *com-,* together + *labi,* to fall] **1.** to fall down or fall to pieces; cave in **2.** to break down suddenly; fail; give way **3.** *a)* to break down suddenly in health *b)* to fall down, as from a blow or exhaustion *c)* to fall or drop drastically, as in value, force, etc. **4.** to fold or come together compactly *—vt.* to cause to collapse *—n.* the act of collapsing; a falling in or together; failure or breakdown, as in business, health, etc. **—col·laps′i·bil′i·ty** *n.* **—col·laps′i·ble** *adj.*

col·lar (käl′ər) *n.* [< OFr. < L. < *collum,* the neck] **1.** the part of a garment that encircles the neck **2.** a cloth band attached to the neck of a garment **3.** a band of leather or metal for the neck of a dog, cat, etc. **4.** the part of the harness that fits over the neck of a horse **5.** a ring or flange, as on rods or pipes, to prevent sideward motion, connect parts, etc. **6.** a band of contrasting color, etc. on an animal's neck *—vt.* **1.** to put a collar on **2.** to seize by or as by the collar

col·lar·bone (-bōn′) *n.* a slender bone joining the breastbone to the shoulder blade; clavicle

col·lard (käl′ərd) *n.* [contr. < COLEWORT] a kind of kale whose coarse leaves are borne in tufts

collat. collateral

col·late (kä lāt′, kə-; käl′āt) *vt.* **-lat′ed, -lat′ing** [< L. *collatus,* pp. of *conferre* < *com-,* together + *ferre,* to bring] **1.** to compare (texts, data, etc.) critically **2.** *a)* to gather (the sections of a book) together in proper order for binding *b)* to examine (such sections) to see that all pages are present and in proper order **—col·la′tor** *n.*

col·lat·er·al (kə lat′ər əl) *adj.* [< ML. *collateralis* < L. *com-,* together + *lateralis,* LATERAL] **1.** side by side; parallel **2.** accompanying the main thing in a subordinate or corroborative way **3.** of the same ancestors but in a different line **4.** *a)* designating or of security given as a pledge for the fulfillment of an obligation *b)* secured by stocks, bonds, etc. *[a collateral loan] —n.* **1.** a collateral relative **2.** stocks, bonds, etc. used for collateral security **—col·lat′er·al·ly** *adv.*

col·la·tion (kä lā′shən, kə-) *n.* **1.** the act, process, or result of collating **2.** a light meal

col·league (käl′ēg) *n.* [< Fr. < L. *collega* < *com-,* with + *legare,* to appoint as deputy] a fellow worker in the same profession; associate in office

col·lect[1] (kə lekt′) *vt.* [< OFr. < L. *collectus:* see ff.] **1.** to gather together; assemble **2.** to gather (stamps, books, etc.) for a hobby **3.** to call for and receive (money) for (rent, a fund, taxes, bills, etc.) **4.** to regain control of (oneself or one's wits) *—vi.* **1.** to gather; assemble *[a crowd collected]* **2.** to accumulate *[water collects in the basement]* **3.** to collect payments, etc. *—adj., adv.* with payment to be made by the receiver *[to telephone collect]*

col·lect[2] (käl′ekt) *n.* [< OFr., ult. < L. *collectus,* pp. of *colligere* < *com-,* together + *legere,* to gather] [*also* C-] a short prayer used in certain church services

col·lect·ed (kə lek′tid) *adj.* **1.** gathered together; assembled **2.** in control of oneself; calm **—col·lect′ed·ly** *adv.* **—col·lect′ed·ness** *n.*

col·lect·i·ble, col·lect·a·ble (-tə b′l) *adj.* **1.** that can be collected **2.** suitable as a collectible *—n.* any of a class of old things, but not antiques, that people collect as a hobby, usually things of no great intrinsic value

col·lec·tion (-shən) *n.* **1.** the act or process of collecting **2.** things collected *[a collection of stamps]* **3.** a mass or pile; accumulation **4.** money collected, as during a church service

col·lec·tive (-tiv) *adj.* **1.** formed by collecting; gathered into a whole **2.** of or as a group; of or by the individuals in a group acting together *[the collective effort of the students]* **3.** designating or of any enterprise in which people work together as a group, esp. under a system of collectivism *[a collective farm]* **4.** *Gram.* designating a noun which is singular in form but denotes a collection of individuals (e.g., *army, crowd*) *—n.* **1.** *a)* any collective enterprise; specif., a collective farm *b)* the people involved **2.** *Gram.* a collective noun **—col·lec′tive·ly** *adv.* **—col′lec·tiv′i·ty** *n.*

collective bargaining negotiation between organized workers and their employer or employers concerning wages, hours, and working conditions

col·lec·tiv·ism (kə lek′tə viz′m) *n.* the ownership and control of the means of production and distribution by the people collectively **—col·lec′tiv·ist** *n., adj.* **—col·lec′tiv·is′tic** *adj.*

col·lec·tiv·ize (-tə vīz′) *vt.* **-ized′, -iz′ing** to establish or organize under a system of collectivism **—col·lec′ti·vi·za′tion** *n.*

col·lec·tor (kə lek′tər) *n.* a person or thing that collects; specif., *a)* a person whose work is collecting taxes, overdue bills, etc. *b)* a person who collects stamps, books, coins, etc. as a hobby

Col·leen (käl′ēn, kə lēn′) [see ff.] a feminine name

col·leen (käl′ēn, kə lēn′) *n.* [< Ir., dim. of *caile,* girl] [Irish] a girl

col·lege (käl′ij) *n.* [< OFr. < L. *collegium,* a society, guild < *collega,* COLLEAGUE] **1.** an association of individuals having certain powers, duties, etc. *[the electoral college]* **2.** an institution of higher education that grants degrees; specif., *a)* any of the schools of a university granting degrees in any of several specialized courses of study *b)* the undergraduate division of a university, which offers a general four-year course leading to the bachelor's degree **3.** a school offering specialized instruction in some occupation *[a secretarial college]* **4.** the buildings, students, faculty, or administrators of a college

College of Cardinals the cardinals of the Roman Catholic Church, serving as a privy council to the Pope and electing his successor

col·le·gi·al (kə lē′jē əl) *adj.* **1.** with authority shared equally among colleagues **2.** *same as* COLLEGIATE

col·le·gi·al·i·ty (kə lē′jē al′ə tē) *n.* **1.** the sharing of authority among colleagues **2.** *R. C. Ch.* the principle that authority is shared by the Pope and the bishops

col·le·gian (kə lē′jən) *n.* a college student

col·le·giate (-jət, -jē ət) *adj.* of or like a college or college students

collegiate church a church with a chapter of canons although it is not a bishop's see

col·lide (kə līd′) *vi.* **-lid′ed, -lid′ing** [L. *collidere* < *com-,* together + *laedere,* to strike] **1.** to come into violent contact; strike violently against each other; crash **2.** to come into conflict; clash

col·lie (käl′ē) *n.* [< ? *coaly,* from black coat of earlier collies] a large, long-haired dog with a long, narrow head: first bred in Scotland to herd sheep

COLLIE (24–26 in. high at shoulder)

col·lier (käl′yər) *n.* [see COAL & -IER] [Chiefly Brit.] **1.** a coal miner **2.** a ship for carrying coal

col·lier·y (-ē) *n., pl.* **-lier·ies** [Chiefly Brit.] a coal mine and its buildings, equipment, etc.

col·li·mate (käl′ə māt′) *vt.* **-mat′ed, -mat′ing** [< false reading of L. *collineare* < *com-,* with + *lineare,* to make straight < *linea,* a line] **1.** to make (light rays, etc.) parallel **2.** to adjust the line of sight of (a telescope, etc.) —**col′li·ma′tion** *n.*

col·li·ma·tor (-māt′ər) *n.* [see prec.] a small telescope with cross hairs at its focus, fixed to another telescope, surveying instrument, etc. for adjusting the line of sight

Col·lins (käl′inz) *n.* an iced drink made with gin (*Tom Collins*), or vodka, rum, whiskey, etc., mixed with soda water, lime or lemon juice, and sugar

col·li·sion (kə lizh′ən) *n.* **1.** a colliding, or coming together with sudden, violent force **2.** a clash or conflict of opinions, interests, etc.

col·lo·cate (käl′ə kāt′) *vt.* **-cat′ed, -cat′ing** [< L. pp. of *collocare:* see LOCATE] to arrange or place together, esp. side by side —**col′lo·ca′tion** *n.*

col·lo·di·on (kə lō′dē ən) *n.* [< Gr. < *kolla,* glue + *eidos,* form] a highly flammable solution of nitrated cellulose that dries quickly, forming a tough, elastic film: used to protect wounds, in photographic films, etc.

col·logue (kə lōg′) *vi.* **-logued′, -lo′guing** [< Fr. < L.: see COLLOQUY] **1.** to confer privately **2.** [Dial.] to conspire

col·loid (käl′oid) *n.* [< Gr. *kolla,* glue + -OID] a solid, liquid, or gaseous substance made up of insoluble, nondiffusible particles (as single large molecules or masses of smaller molecules) that remain suspended in a medium of different matter —**col·loi′dal** *adj.*

colloq. 1. colloquial(ly) **2.** colloquialism

col·lo·qui·al (kə lō′kwē əl) *adj.* [see COLLOQUY] **1.** having to do with or like conversation **2.** designating or of the words, phrases, and idioms characteristic of informal speech and writing; informal: the label [Colloq.] is used throughout this dictionary in this sense, and does not indicate substandard or illiterate usage —**col·lo′qui·al·ly** *adv.* —**col·lo′qui·al·ness** *n.*

col·lo·qui·al·ism (-iz'm) *n.* **1.** colloquial quality, style, or usage **2.** a colloquial word or expression

col·lo·qui·um (kə lō′kwē əm) *n., pl.* **-qui·a** (-ə), **-qui·ums** [L.: see ff.] an organized conference or seminar on some subject, involving a number of scholars or experts

col·lo·quy (käl′ə kwē) *n., pl.* **-quies** [L. *colloquium,* conversation < *com-,* together + *loqui,* to speak] a conversation, esp. a formal discussion; conference —**col′lo·quist** *n.*

col·lude (kə lo͞od′) *vi.* **-lud′ed, -lud′ing** [< L. < *com-,* with + *ludere,* to play] to act in collusion

col·lu·sion (kə lo͞o′zhən) *n.* [see prec.] a secret agreement for fraudulent or illegal purpose; conspiracy —**col·lu′sive** (-siv) *adj.* —**col·lu′sive·ly** *adv.*

Colo. Colorado

Co·logne (kə lōn′) city in W West Germany, on the Rhine: pop. 854,000

co·logne (kə lōn′) *n. same as* EAU DE COLOGNE

Co·lom·bi·a (kə lum′bē ə; *Sp.* kô lôm′byä) country in NW S. America: 455,335 sq. mi.; pop. 20,463,000; cap. Bogotá —**Co·lom′bi·an** *adj., n.*

Co·lom·bo (kə lum′bō) capital of Ceylon: seaport on the W coast: pop. 512,000

Co·lón (kə lōn′) seaport in Panama, at the Caribbean entrance to the Panama Canal: pop. 64,000

co·lon[1] (kō′lən) *n.* [L. < Gr. *kōlon,* member, limb] a mark of punctuation (:) used before a long quotation, example, series, etc., and after the salutation of a formal letter

co·lon[2] (kō′lən) *n., pl.* **-lons, -la** (-lə) [L. < Gr. *kolon*] that part of the large intestine extending from the cecum to the rectum —**co·lon·ic** (kə län′ik) *adj.*

co·lon[3] (kə lōn′; *Sp.* kô lôn′) *n., pl.* **-lons′,** Sp. **-lon′es** (-lô′nes) [AmSp. *colón* < Sp.*Colón,* COLUMBUS] *see* MONETARY UNITS, table (Costa Rica, El Salvador)

colo·nel (kur′n'l) *n.* [earlier *coronel* < Fr. < It. < *colonna,* (military) column < L. *columna*] **1.** a military officer ranking above a lieutenant colonel **2.** an honorary, nonmilitary title in some southern or western States —**colo′nel·cy** (-sē) *n., pl.* **-cies**

co·lo·ni·al (kə lō′nē əl) *adj.* **1.** of or living in a colony or colonies **2.** [*often* C-] of or characteristic of the thirteen British colonies that became the U.S., or of their period **3.** made up of or having colonies —*n.* an inhabitant of a colony —**co·lo′ni·al·ly** *adv.*

co·lo·ni·al·ism (-iz'm) *n.* the system or policy by which a country maintains foreign colonies, esp. in order to exploit them economically —**co·lo′ni·al·ist** *n., adj.*

col·o·nist (käl′ə nist) *n.* **1.** any of the original settlers of a colony **2.** an inhabitant of a colony

col·o·nize (käl′ə nīz′) *vt., vi.* **-nized′, -niz′ing 1.** to found or establish a colony or colonies (in) **2.** to settle in a colony —**col′o·ni·za′tion** *n.* —**col′o·niz′er** *n.*

col·on·nade (käl′ə nād′) *n.* [Fr. < It. < L. *columna,* column] *Archit.* a series of columns set at regular intervals, usually supporting a roof or series of arches —**col′on·nad′ed** *adj.*

COLONNADE

col·o·ny (käl′ə nē) *n., pl.* **-nies** [< L. < *colonus,* farmer < *colere,* to cultivate] **1.** *a*) a group of people who settle in a distant land but under the jurisdiction of their native land *b*) the region thus settled **2.** a territory distant from the state having jurisdiction over it **3.** [C-] [*pl.*] the thirteen British colonies in N. America that became the U.S. **4.** a community of people of the same nationality or pursuits concentrated in a particular place [an artists' *colony*] **5.** *Bacteriology* a group of similar bacteria growing in a culture medium **6.** *Biol.* a group of similar plants or animals living or growing together **7.** *Zool.* a compound organism of incompletely separated individuals, as in corals

col·o·phon (käl′ə fän′, -fən) *n.* [LL. < Gr. *kolophōn,* summit, top, end] **1.** a note in a book giving facts about its production **2.** the distinctive emblem of the publisher

col·or (kul′ər) *n.* [< OFr. < L. < OL. *colos,* orig., a covering] **1.** the sensation resulting from stimulation of the retina of the eye by light waves **2.** the property of reflecting light of a particular wavelength: the distinct colors of the spectrum are red, orange, yellow, green, blue, indigo, and violet; the *primary colors* of the spectrum are red, green, and blue **3.** any coloring matter; dye; pigment; paint: the *primary colors* (red, yellow, and blue) and *secondary colors* formed from these (green, orange, purple, etc.) are sometimes distinguished from black, white, and gray (*achromatic colors*) **4.** color of the face; esp., a healthy rosiness or a blush **5.** the color of the skin of a Negro or other person not Caucasoid **6.** [*pl.*] a colored badge, costume, etc. that identifies the wearer **7.** [*pl.*] *a*) a flag of a country, regiment, etc. *b*) the armed forces of a country, symbolized by the flag [to serve with the *colors*] **8.** [*pl.*] one's position or opinion [stick to your *colors*] **9.** outward appearance or semblance; plausibility **10.** appearance of truth; justification [the news lent *color* to the rumor] **11.** general nature; character [the *color* of his mind] **12.** vivid quality, as in a personality, literary work, etc. **13.** *Art* the way of using color —*adj. TV, Radio* designating or of a sports commentator who supplies details and analysis between play-by-play accounts of the action —*vt.* **1.** to give color to; paint; stain; dye **2.** to change the color of **3.** to alter or influence, as by distortion [prejudice *colored* his views] —*vi.* **1.** to become colored **2.** to change in color **3.** to blush or flush —**call to the colors 1.** call or order to serve in the armed forces **2.** *Mil.* a bugle call for the daily flag-raising and flag-lowering ceremonies —**change color 1.** to become pale **2.** to blush or flush —**lose color** to become pale —**under color of** under the pretext of —**col′or·er** *n.*

col·or·a·ble (-ə b'l) *adj.* **1.** capable of being colored **2.** apparently plausible, but actually specious; deceptive

Col·o·rad·o (käl′ə rad′ō, -rä′dō) **1.** [after the river] Mountain State of the U.S.: 104,247 sq. mi.; pop. 2,889,000; cap. Denver: abbrev. **Colo., CO 2.** [< Sp. *Río Colorado,* Red River] river flowing from N Colo. southwest into the Gulf of California —**Col′o·rad′an, Col′o·rad′o·an** *adj., n.*

col·o·rad·o (käl′ə rad′ō, -rä′dō) *adj.* [Sp., red] of medium strength and color: said of cigars

Colorado beetle a widely distributed black-and-yellow beetle that is a destructive pest of potatoes and other plants

Colorado Springs city in C Colo.: pop. 215,000

col·or·ant (kul′ər ənt) *n.* [Fr. < prp. of *colorer,* to color] anything used to give color to something; pigment, dye, etc.

col·or·a·tion (kul′ə rā′shən) *n.* **1.** a being colored **2.** the way a thing is colored **3.** the technique of using colors

col·o·ra·tu·ra (kul′ər ə toor′ə, -tyoor′-) *n.* [It. < L. pp. of *colorare,* to color] **1.** brilliant runs, trills, etc., used to display a singer's skill **2.** music containing such ornamentation **3.** a soprano who sings such music: in full, **coloratura soprano**

col·or·blind (kul′ər blīnd′) *adj.* unable to perceive colors or to distinguish between certain colors, as red and green —**col′or·blind′ness** *n.*

col·or·cast (-kast′) *n.* [COLOR + (TELE)CAST] a television broadcast in color —*vt., vi.* **-cast′** or **-cast′ed, -cast′ing** to televise in color

col·ored (kul′ərd) ***adj.*** **1.** having color **2.** of a (specified) color **3.** of a group of mankind other than the Caucasoid; specif., Negro **4.** [C-] in South Africa, of racially mixed parentage: usually **Coloured** **5.** of or having to do with colored persons **6.** altered, distorted, or exaggerated —**the colored** colored persons

col·or·fast (kul′ər fast′) ***adj.*** that will keep its color without fading or running —**col′or·fast′ness** ***n.***

col·or·ful (-fəl) ***adj.*** **1.** full of vivid colors **2.** full of interest or variety; picturesque; vivid —**col′or·ful·ly** ***adv.*** —**col′or·ful·ness** ***n.***

color guard persons escorting the colors (flag)

col·or·ing (kul′ər iŋ) ***n.*** **1.** the act or art of applying colors **2.** anything applied to impart color; pigment, dye, stain, etc. **3.** *same as* COLORATION **4.** skin color **5.** specious or false appearance **6.** alteration or influence

col·or·ist (-ist) ***n.*** **1.** a person who uses colors **2.** an artist skillful in using colors

col·or·less (-lis) ***adj.*** **1.** without color **2.** dull in color; gray or pallid **3.** lacking interest; dull —**col′or·less·ly** ***adv.*** —**col′or·less·ness** ***n.***

color line the barrier of social, political, and economic restrictions imposed on Negroes or other nonwhites

Co·los·sae (kə läs′ē) city in ancient Phrygia, SW Asia Minor —**Co·los′sian** (-läsh′ən) ***adj., n.***

co·los·sal (kə läs′'l) ***adj.*** **1.** like a colossus in size; huge; gigantic **2.** [Colloq.] extraordinary *[a colossal* fool*]* —**co·los′sal·ly** ***adv.***

Col·os·se·um (käl′ə sē′əm) [L., neut. of *colosseus,* gigantic: see COLOSSUS] an amphitheater in Rome, built c. 75–80 A.D.: much of it is still standing —***n.*** [c-] *same as* COLISEUM

Co·los·sians (kə läsh′ənz) a book of the New Testament: an epistle from the Apostle Paul to the Christians of Colossae

co·los·sus (kə läs′əs) ***n., pl.*** **-los′si** (-ī), **-los′sus·es** [L. < Gr. *kolossos*] **1.** a gigantic statue; esp., [C-] that of Apollo set at the entrance to the harbor of Rhodes c. 280 B.C. **2.** any huge or important person or thing

col·our (kul′ər) ***n., vt., vi. Brit. sp. of*** COLOR

-co·lous (kə ləs) [< base of L. *colere,* to inhabit + -OUS] *a combining form meaning* growing (or living) in or among

colt (kōlt) ***n.*** [OE.] **1.** a young horse, donkey, zebra, etc.; specif., a male racehorse four years of age or under **2.** a young, inexperienced person

col·ter (kōl′tər) ***n.*** [< OFr. or OE., both < L. *culter,* plowshare] a blade or disk on a plow, for making vertical cuts in the soil

colt·ish (kōl′tish) ***adj.*** of or like a colt; esp., frisky, frolicsome, etc. —**colt′ish·ly** ***adv.***

colts·foot (kōlts′foot′) ***n., pl.*** **-foots′** a plant of the composite family, with yellow flowers and large leaves suggesting the print of a colt's foot

Co·lum·bi·a (kə lum′bē ə, -byə) [after Christopher COLUMBUS] **1.** [Poet.] the U.S. personified as a woman **2.** capital of S.C.: pop. 99,000 **3.** city in C Mo.: pop. 62,000 **3.** river flowing from SE British Columbia, through Wash., into the Pacific —**Co·lum′bi·an** ***adj.***

col·um·bine (käl′əm bīn′) ***n.*** [OFr. < ML. < L. *columbinus,* dovelike < *columba,* dove] a plant of the buttercup family, with showy, spurred flowers of various colors

Co·lum·bus (kə lum′bəs) [after ff.] **1.** capital of Ohio, in the C part: pop. 565,000 (met. area 1,089,000) **2.** city in W Ga.: pop. 169,000

Co·lum·bus (kə lum′bəs), **Christopher** (It. name *Cristoforo Colombo;* Sp. name *Cristóbal Colón*) 1451?–1506; It. explorer in the service of Spain: discovered America (1492)

Columbus Day a legal holiday in the U.S. commemorating the discovery of America by Columbus in 1492, observed on the second Monday in October

col·umn (käl′əm) ***n.*** [< OFr. < L. *columna*] **1.** a slender upright structure, generally a cylindrical shaft with a base and a capital; pillar: it is usually a supporting or ornamental member in a building **2.** anything like a column in shape or function *[the spinal column]* **3.** a formation of troops, ships, etc. in a file **4.** any of the vertical sections of printed matter lying side by side on a page and separated by a rule or blank space **5.** a series of feature articles under a fixed title in a newspaper or magazine, written by a special writer or devoted to a certain subject —**co·lum·nar** (kə lum′nər), **col′umned** ***adj.***

CAPITAL
SHAFT
BASE

COLUMN

co·lum·ni·a·tion (kə lum′nē ā′shən) ***n.*** the architectural use or arrangement of columns

col·um·nist (käl′əm nist, -ə mist) ***n.*** a person who writes or conducts a column, as in a newspaper

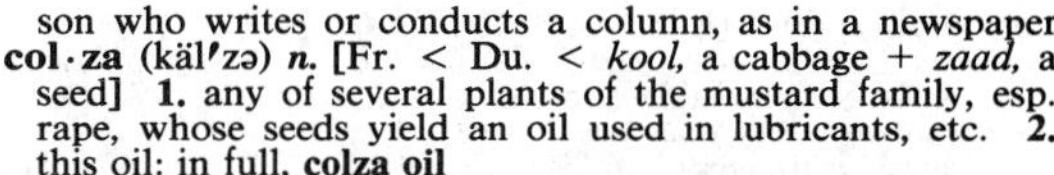

col·za (käl′zə) ***n.*** [Fr. < Du. < *kool,* a cabbage + *zaad,* a seed] **1.** any of several plants of the mustard family, esp. rape, whose seeds yield an oil used in lubricants, etc. **2.** this oil: in full, **colza oil**

com- [L. *com-* < OL. *com* (L. *cum*), with] *a prefix meaning* with or together *[combine]* : also used as an intensive *[command]* : assimilated to **col-** before *l;* **cor-** before *r;* **con-** before *c, d, g, j, n, q, s, t,* and *v;* and **co-** before *h, w,* and all vowels

COM computer-output microfilm (or microfiche)

Com. **1.** Commander **2.** Commission(er) **3.** Committee

com. **1.** commerce **2.** commercial **3.** common **4.** communication

co·ma[1] (kō′mə) ***n.*** [ModL. < Gr. *koma,* deep sleep] **1.** a state of deep and prolonged unconsciousness caused by injury or disease **2.** a condition of stupor or lethargy

co·ma[2] (kō′mə) ***n., pl.*** **-mae** (-mē) [L. < Gr. *komē,* hair] **1.** *Astron.* a globular, cloudlike mass around the nucleus of a comet **2.** *a)* a bunch of branches, as on the top of some palms *b)* a tuft of hairs at the end of certain seeds —**co′mate** (-māt) ***adj.***

co·make (kō′māk′) ***vt.*** **-made′**, **-mak′ing** *same as* COSIGN —**co′mak′er** ***n.***

Co·man·che (kə man′chē) ***n.*** [MexSp. < Ute *komanchi,* stranger] **1.** *pl.* **-ches, -che** any member of a tribe of Uto-Aztecan Indians who ranged from the Platte River to the Mexican border and now live in Oklahoma **2.** their Shoshonean dialect of Uto-Aztecan

co·ma·tose (kō′mə tōs′, käm′ə-) ***adj.*** **1.** of, like, or in a coma or stupor **2.** as if in a coma; torpid

comb (kōm) ***n.*** [OE. *camb*] **1.** a thin strip of hard rubber, plastic, metal, etc. with teeth, passed through the hair to arrange or clean it, or set in the hair to hold it in place **2.** anything like a comb in form or function; specif., *a)* a currycomb *b)* a tool for cleaning and straightening wool, flax, etc. *c)* a red, fleshy outgrowth on the top of the head, as of a rooster *d)* a thing like a rooster's comb in position or appearance, as a helmet crest **3.** a honeycomb —***vt.*** **1.** to clean or arrange with a comb **2.** to remove with or as with a comb; separate (often with *out*) **3.** to search thoroughly; look everywhere in —***vi.*** to roll over; break: said of waves

com·bat (*for v.,* kəm bat′, käm′bat; *for n. & adj.,* käm′bat, kum′-) ***vi.*** **-bat′ed** or **-bat′ted, -bat′ing** or **-bat′ting** [< Fr. < VL. < L. *com-,* with + *battuere,* to beat] to fight, contend, or struggle —***vt.*** to fight or struggle against; oppose; resist, or seek to get rid of —***n.*** **1.** armed fighting; battle **2.** any struggle or conflict; strife —***adj.*** *Mil.* of or for combat

com·bat·ant (käm′bə tənt, kəm bat′'nt) ***adj.*** **1.** fighting **2.** ready or prepared to fight —***n.*** a person who engages in combat; fighter

combat fatigue a neurotic condition characterized by anxiety, irritability, depression, etc., often occurring after prolonged combat in warfare

com·bat·ive (kəm bat′iv, käm′bə tiv) ***adj.*** ready or eager to fight; pugnacious —**com·bat′ive·ly** ***adv.*** —**com·bat′ive·ness** ***n.***

comb·er (kō′mər) ***n.*** **1.** one that combs wool, flax, etc. **2.** a large wave that breaks as on a beach

com·bi·na·tion (käm bə nā′shən) ***n.*** **1.** a combining or being combined **2.** a thing formed by combining **3.** an association of persons, firms, political parties, etc. for a common purpose **4.** the series of numbers or letters used in opening a combination lock **5.** a one-piece undergarment combining an undershirt and drawers **6.** *Math.* any of the various groupings, or subsets, into which a number, or set, of units may be arranged without regard to order —**com′bi·na′tion·al, com′bi·na′tive** ***adj.***

combination lock a lock operated by a dial that is turned to a set series of numbers or letters to work the mechanism that opens it

com·bine (kəm bīn′; *for n. & v. 3,* käm′bīn) ***vt., vi.*** **-bined′**, **-bin′ing** [< OFr. < LL. *combinare* < L. *com-,* together + *bini,* two by two: see BI-] **1.** to come or bring into union; act or mix together; unite; join **2.** to unite to form a chemical compound **3.** to harvest and thresh with a combine —***n.*** **1.** a machine for harvesting and threshing grain **2.** an association of persons, corporations, etc. for commercial or political, often unethical, purposes —**com·bin′a·able** ***adj.*** —**com·bin′er** ***n.***

comb·ings (kō′miŋz) ***n.pl.*** loose hair, wool, etc. removed in combing

combining form a word form that occurs only in compounds or derivatives, and that can combine with other such forms or with affixes to form a word (Ex.: *cardio-* and *-graph* in *cardiograph*)

com·bo (käm′bō) ***n., pl.*** **-bos** [Colloq.] a combination; specif., a small jazz ensemble

fat, āpe, cär, ten, ēven, is, bīte; gō, hôrn, tōōl, look; oil, out; up, fur; get; joy; yet; chin; she; thin, *th*en; zh, leisure; ŋ, ring; ə for *a* in *ago, e* in *agent, i* in *sanity, o* in *comply, u* in *focus;* ′ as in *able* (ā′b'l); Fr. bål; ë, Fr. coeur; ö, Fr. feu; Fr. mo*n*; ô, Fr. coq; ü, Fr. duc; *r,* Fr. cri; H, G. ich; kh, G. doch; ‡foreign; *hypothetical; < derived from. See inside front cover.

com·bus·ti·ble (kəm bus′tə b'l) ***adj.*** [see ff.] **1.** that catches fire and burns easily; flammable **2.** easily aroused; fiery —***n.*** a flammable substance —**com·bus′ti·bil′i·ty** ***n.*** —**com·bus′ti·bly** ***adv.***

com·bus·tion (-chən) ***n.*** [< OFr. < LL. < L. pp. of *comburere* < *com-*, intens. + *urere*, to burn] **1.** the act or process of burning **2.** rapid oxidation accompanied by heat and, usually, light **3.** slow oxidation accompanied by relatively little heat and no light **4.** violent excitement; tumult —**com·bus′tive** (-tiv) ***adj.***

com·bus·tor (-tər) ***n.*** the chamber in a jet engine, gas turbine, etc. in which combustion occurs

Comdr. Commander

Comdt. Commandant

come (kum) ***vi.*** **came, come, com′ing** [OE. *cuman*] **1.** to move from a place thought of as "there" to a place thought of as "here" **2.** to approach by moving toward **3.** to arrive or appear [help will *come*] **4.** to extend; reach **5.** to take place; happen [success *came* to him] **6.** to take form in the mind [her name *came* to him] **7.** to occur in a certain place or order [after 9 *comes* 10] **8.** to become actual; evolve; develop [will peace *come*?] **9.** *a*) to be derived or descended *b*) to be a resident or former resident (with *from*) **10.** to be caused; result **11.** to be due or owed (*to*): used in the participle [to get what is *coming* to one] **12.** to pass as by inheritance **13.** to get to be; become [it *came* loose] **14.** to be available [this dress *comes* in four sizes] **15.** to amount; add up [*to*] —***interj.*** look! see here! stop! —**come about 1.** to happen; occur **2.** to turn about —**come across 1.** to find by chance **2.** [Colloq] to be effective, etc. **3.** [Slang] to give, do, or say what is wanted —**come again?** [Colloq.] what did you say? —**come and get it!** [Colloq.] the meal is ready! —**come around** (or **round**) **1.** to revive; recover **2.** to make a turn **3.** to concede or yield —**come at 1.** to reach; attain **2.** to approach angrily or swiftly —**come back 1.** to return **2.** [Colloq.] to make a comeback —**come between** to estrange; divide —**come by 1.** to get; gain **2.** to pay a visit —**come down** to suffer loss in status, wealth, etc. —**come down on** (or **upon**) to scold; criticize harshly —**come in 1.** to enter **2.** to come into fashion **3.** to finish in a contest [he *came in* fifth] —**come in for** [Colloq.] to get; acquire —**come into 1.** to enter into **2.** to inherit —**come off 1.** to become detached **2.** to occur **3.** [Colloq.] to prove successful, etc. —**come on 1.** to make progress **2.** to find **3.** to appear, make an entrance, etc. —**come on!** [Colloq.] **1.** get started! hurry! **2.** stop behaving like that! —**come one's way** to yield or become agreeable —**come out 1.** to be disclosed **2.** to be offered for public sale, etc. **3.** to make a debut **4.** to end up; turn out —**come out for** to support; endorse —**come out with 1.** to disclose **2.** to say; publish **3.** to offer for public sale, etc. —**come through 1.** to complete or endure something successfully **2.** [Slang] to do or give what is wanted —**come to 1.** to recover consciousness **2.** to anchor —**come up 1.** to arise, as in discussion **2.** to rise, as in status **3.** to be put forward, as for a vote —**come upon** to find —**come up to 1.** to reach to **2.** to equal —**come up with** to propose, produce, find, etc. —**how come?** [Colloq.] how is it that? why?

come·back (kum′bak′) ***n.*** [Colloq.] **1.** a return to a previous state or position, as of success **2.** a witty answer **3.** ground for complaint

co·me·di·an (kə mē′dē ən) ***n.*** **1.** an actor who plays comic parts **2.** an entertainer who tells jokes, sings comic songs, etc. **3.** a person who amuses others by behaving in a comic way

co·me·di·enne (kə mē′dē en′) ***n.*** a woman comedian

com·e·do (käm′ə dō′) ***n.***, *pl.* **com′e·do′nes** (-dō′nēz), **com′e·dos′** [< L. < *comedere:* see COMESTIBLE] *same as* BLACKHEAD (sense 2)

come·down (kum′doun′) ***n.*** a fall to a lower status or position, as of power, wealth, etc.

com·e·dy (käm′ə dē) ***n.***, *pl.* **-dies** [< OFr. < L. < Gr. *kōmōidia* < *kōmos*, festival + *aeidein*, to sing] **1.** orig., a drama or narrative with a happy ending or nontragic theme **2.** *a*) any of various types of play or motion picture with a humorous treatment of characters and situation and a happy ending *b*) the branch of drama having to do with such plays **3.** a novel or any narrative having a comic theme, tone, etc. **4.** the comic element in a literary work, or in life —**cut the comedy** [Slang] to stop joking —**co·me·dic** (kə mē′dik, -med′ik) ***adj.***

comedy of manners a type of comedy satirizing the manners and customs of fashionable society

come-hith·er (kum′hi*th*′ər) ***adj.*** [Colloq.] flirtatious or inviting [a *come-hither* look]

come·ly (kum′lē) ***adj.*** **-li·er, -li·est** [OE. *cymlic* < *cyme*, delicate, orig., feeble] **1.** pleasant to look at; attractive **2.** [Archaic] seemly; proper —**come′li·ness** ***n.***

come-on (kum′än′) ***n.*** [Slang] **1.** an inviting look or gesture **2.** an inducement **3.** a swindler

com·er (-ər) ***n.*** **1.** a person who comes [a contest open to all *comers*] **2.** [Colloq.] a person or thing that shows promise of being a success

co·mes·ti·ble (kə mes′tə b'l) ***adj.*** [Fr. < L. pp. of *comedere* < *com-*, intens. + *edere*, to eat] [Rare] eatable; edible —***n.*** [*usually pl.*] food

com·et (käm′ət) ***n.*** [< OE. < L. *cometa* < Gr. < *komē*, hair] a heavenly body having a starlike nucleus with a luminous mass (*coma*) around it, and, usually, a long, luminous tail: comets move in orbits around the sun —**com′et·ar′y** (-ə ter′ē), **co·met·ic** (kä met′ik) ***adj.***

come·up·pance (kum′up′'ns) ***n.*** [< COME + UP[1] + -ANCE] [Colloq.] deserved punishment; retribution

com·fit (kum′fit, käm′-) ***n.*** [< OFr. < L. *conficere:* see CONFECT] a candy or sweetmeat, as a candied fruit

com·fort (kum′fərt) ***vt.*** [< OFr. < LL. < L. *com-*, intens. + *fortis*, strong] **1.** to soothe in distress or sorrow; console **2.** to give a sense of ease to **3.** *Law* to help; aid —***n.*** **1.** aid; encouragement: now only in **aid and comfort** **2.** relief from distress, grief, etc. **3.** a person or thing that comforts **4.** a state of, or thing that provides, ease and quiet enjoyment **5.** a quilted bed covering —**com′fort·ing** ***adj.*** —**com′fort·ing·ly** ***adv.*** —**com′fort·less** ***adj.***

com·fort·a·ble (kumf′tər b'l, kum′fər tə b'l) ***adj.*** **1.** providing comfort [*comfortable* shoes] **2.** at ease in body or mind; contented **3.** [Colloq.] sufficient to satisfy [a *comfortable* salary] —**com′fort·a·ble·ness** ***n.*** —**com′fort·a·bly** ***adv.***

com·fort·er (kum′fər tər, -fə tər) ***n.*** **1.** a person or thing that comforts **2.** a quilted bed covering —**the Comforter** *Bible* the Holy Spirit: John 14:26

comfort station a public toilet or restroom

com·fy (kum′fē) ***adj.*** **-fi·er, -fi·est** [contr. < COMFORTABLE] [Colloq.] comfortable

com·ic (käm′ik) ***adj.*** [< L. < Gr. *kōmikos*] **1.** of or having to do with comedy **2.** amusing; humorous; funny **3.** of comic strips or cartoons —***n.*** **1.** a comedian **2.** the humorous element in art or life **3.** *a*) *same as* COMIC STRIP or COMIC BOOK *b*) [*pl.*] a section of comic strips, as in a newspaper

com·i·cal (käm′i k'l) ***adj.*** causing amusement; humorous; funny; droll —**com′i·cal′i·ty** (-kal′ə tē), **com′i·cal·ness** ***n.*** —**com′i·cal·ly** ***adv.***

comic book a paper booklet of extended comic strips, sometimes sensational or violent

comic opera opera with humorous situations, a story that ends happily, and some spoken dialogue

comic strip a series of cartoons, as in a newspaper, telling a humorous or adventurous story

Com·in·form (käm′in fôrm′) ***n.*** [< *Com*(*munist*) *Inform*(*ation*)] the Communist Information Bureau, an association of various European Communist parties (1947–56)

com·ing (kum′iŋ) ***adj.*** **1.** approaching; next [this *coming* Tuesday] **2.** showing promise of being successful, etc. [the *coming* thing] —***n.*** arrival; advent

Com·in·tern (käm′in turn′) ***n.*** [< *Com*(*munist*) *Intern*(*ational*)] the international organization (*Third International*) of Communist parties (1919–43)

com·i·ty (käm′ə tē) ***n.***, *pl.* **-ties** [< L. *comitas* < *comis*, polite, kind] **1.** courteous behavior; politeness **2.** agreement among Christian denominations to avoid duplication of churches, missions, etc. in specific areas

comity of nations the respect of peaceful nations for each other's laws and institutions

comm. **1.** commander **2.** commission **3.** committee **4.** commonwealth

com·ma (käm′ə) ***n.*** [L. < Gr. *komma*, clause, that which is cut off < *koptein*, to cut off] **1.** a mark of punctuation (,) used to indicate a slight separation of sentence elements, as in setting off nonrestrictive or parenthetical elements, quotations, items in a series, etc. **2.** a slight pause

comma bacillus the bacillus causing Asiatic cholera

com·mand (kə mand′) ***vt.*** [< OFr. < VL. < L. *com-*, intens. + *mandare:* see MANDATE] **1.** to give an order to; direct with authority **2.** to have authority over; control **3.** to have ready for use [to *command* a large vocabulary] **4.** to deserve and get; require as due [to *command* respect] **5.** to control or overlook from a higher position —***vi.*** to exercise authority; be in control; act as commander —***n.*** **1.** an order; direction; mandate **2.** authority to command **3.** power to control by position **4.** range of view **5.** ability to use; mastery **6.** *a*) a military or naval force, organization, or district, under a specified authority *b*) *same as* AIR COMMAND **7.** the post where the person in command is stationed

com·man·dant (käm′ən dant′, -dänt′) ***n.*** a commanding officer of a fort, service school, etc.

com·man·deer (käm′ən dir′) ***vt.*** [< Du. or Afrik. < Fr. *commander*, to command] **1.** to force into military service **2.** to seize (property) for military or governmental use **3.** [Colloq.] to take forcibly

com·mand·er (kə man′dər) ***n.*** **1.** a person who com-

mands; leader 2. *same as* COMMANDING OFFICER 3. *U.S. Navy* an officer ranking above a lieutenant commander —**com·mand′er·ship′** *n.*
commander in chief *pl.* **commanders in chief** 1. the supreme commander of the armed forces of a nation, as, in the U.S., the President 2. an officer in command of all armed forces in a certain theater of war
commanding officer the officer in command of any of certain military units or installations
com·mand·ment (kə mand′mənt) *n.* an authoritative command or order; mandate; precept; specif., any of the Ten Commandments
com·man·do (kə man′dō) *n., pl.* **-dos, -does** [Afrik. < Port., lit., party commanded] 1. orig., in South Africa, a force of Boer troops 2. *a*) a small raiding force trained to operate inside enemy territory *b*) a member of such a group
command post the field headquarters of a military unit, where the commander directs operations
com·me·dia del·l'ar·te (kôm mā′dyä del lär′te) [It., lit., comedy of art] a type of Italian comedy of the 16th century, having a stereotyped plot, improvised dialogue, and stock characters
‡**comme il faut** (kô mēl fō′) [Fr.] as it should be; proper; fitting
com·mem·o·rate (kə mem′ə rāt′) *vt.* **-rat′ed, -rat′ing** [< L. pp. of *commemorare* < *com-*, intens. + *memorare*, to remind] 1. to honor the memory of, as by a ceremony 2. to serve as a memorial to —**com·mem′o·ra′tion** *n.* —**com·mem′o·ra·tive** (-ər ə tiv, -ə rāt′iv), **com·mem′o·ra·to′ry** *adj.* —**com·mem′o·ra·tive·ly** *adv.* —**com·mem′o·ra′tor** *n.*
com·mence (kə mens′) *vi., vt.* **-menced′, -menc′ing** [< OFr. < L. *com-*, together + *initiare*, to INITIATE] to begin; start; originate —**com·menc′er** *n.*
com·mence·ment (-mənt) *n.* 1. the act or time of commencing; beginning; start 2. the ceremonies at which degrees or diplomas are conferred at a school or college 3. the day this takes place
com·mend (kə mend′) *vt.* [< L. *commendare:* see COMMAND] 1. to put in the care of another; entrust 2. to mention as worthy; recommend 3. to express approval of; praise —**com·mend′a·ble** *adj.* —**com·mend′a·bly** *adv.*
com·men·da·tion (käm′ən dā′shən) *n.* a commending; esp., recommendation or praise
com·mend·a·to·ry (kə men′də tôr′ē) *adj.* 1. expressing praise or approval 2. recommending
com·men·su·ra·ble (kə men′shər ə b′l, -sər-) *adj.* [LL. *commensurabilis* < L. *com-*, together + *mensurare:* see ff.] measurable by the same standard or measure —**com·men′su·ra·bil′i·ty** *n.* —**com·men′su·ra·bly** *adv.*
com·men·su·rate (-shər it, -sər-) *adj.* [< LL. < *com-*, with + pp. of *mensurare*, to measure < L. *mensura*, MEASURE] 1. equal in measure or size; coextensive 2. corresponding in extent or degree; proportionate 3. commensurable —**com·men′su·rate·ly** *adv.* —**com·men′su·ra′tion** (-ā′shən) *n.*
com·ment (käm′ent) *n.* [OFr. < L. < pp. of *comminisci*, to contrive < *com-*, intens. + base of *meminisse*, to remember] 1. a note or notes in explanation or criticism of something written or said; annotation 2. a remark or observation made as in criticism 3. talk; gossip —*vi.* [< OFr. < L. *commentari*, to consider thoroughly] to make a comment or comments (*on* or *upon*); make remarks
com·men·tar·y (käm′ən ter′ē) *n., pl.* **-tar′ies** 1. a series of explanatory notes or annotations 2. a series of remarks or observations 3. something having the force of a comment or remark 4. [*usually pl.*] a memoir —**com′men·tar′i·al** *adj.*
com·men·tate (-tāt′) *vt.* **-tat′ed, -tat′ing** [back-formation from ff.] to give a commentary on —*vi.* to perform as a commentator (sense 2)
com·men·ta·tor (-ər) *n.* 1. a person who gives a commentary 2. a person who reports and analyzes news events, trends, etc., as on radio and TV
com·merce (käm′ərs) *n.* [Fr. < L. *commercium* < *com-*, together + *merx* (gen. *mercis*), merchandise] 1. the buying and selling of goods, as between cities, states, or countries; trade 2. social intercourse 3. [Rare] sexual intercourse
com·mer·cial (kə mur′shəl) *adj.* 1. of or connected with commerce or trade 2. of or having to do with stores, office buildings, etc. 3. of a lower grade, or for use in large quantities in industry 4. *a*) made or done primarily for profit *b*) designed to have wide popular appeal 5. offering training in business skills, etc. 6. *Radio & TV* paid for by sponsors —*n. Radio & TV* a paid advertisement —**com·mer′cial·ly** *adv.*
commercial bank a bank that accepts demand deposits, used as checking accounts
com·mer·cial·ism (-iz'm) *n.* the practices and spirit of commerce or business, esp. in seeking profits —**com·mer′cial·ist** *n.* —**com·mer′cial·is′tic** *adj.*
com·mer·cial·ize (-īz′) *vt.* **-ized′, -iz′ing** 1. to apply commercial or business methods to 2. to make use of or do mainly for profit 3. to imbue with commercialism —**com·mer′cial·i·za′tion** *n.*
commercial paper negotiable instruments, such as promissory notes and bills of exchange
commercial traveler *same as* TRAVELING SALESMAN
Com·mie (käm′ē) *adj., n.* [*sometimes* **c-**] [Colloq.] Communist
com·min·gle (kə miŋ′g'l) *vt., vi.* **-gled, -gling** to mingle together; intermix; blend
com·mi·nute (käm′ə nōōt′, -nyōōt′) *vt.* **-nut′ed, -nut′ing** [< L. pp. of *comminuere* < *com-*, intens. + *minuere*, to make small] to reduce to powder or minute particles; pulverize —**com′mi·nu′tion** *n.*
com·mis·er·ate (kə miz′ə rāt′) *vt.* **-at′ed, -at′ing** [< L. pp. of *commiserari* < *com-*, intens. + *miserari*, to pity] to feel or show sorrow or pity for —*vi.* to condole or sympathize (*with*) —**com·mis′er·a′tion** *n.* —**com·mis′er·a′tive** (-ə rāt′iv, -ər ə tiv) *adj.* —**com·mis′er·a′tive·ly** *adv.*
com·mis·sar (käm′ə sär′) *n.* [< Russ. < ML. *commissarius:* see COMMISSARY] the head of a commissariat (sense 2): since 1946, called *minister*
com·mis·sar·i·at (käm′ə ser′ē ət) *n.* 1. the branch of an army which provides food and supplies for the troops 2. formerly, a government department in the U.S.S.R.: since 1946, called *ministry*
com·mis·sar·y (käm′ə ser′ē) *n., pl.* **-sar′ies** [ML. *commissarius* < L. pp. of *committere:* see COMMIT] 1. a deputy assigned to some duty 2. formerly, an army officer in charge of providing food and supplies 3. a store in a lumber camp, army camp, etc. handling food and supplies 4. a restaurant in a movie or TV studio —**com′mis·sar′i·al** *adj.*
com·mis·sion (kə mish′ən) *n.* [OFr. < ML. < L. pp. of *committere:* see COMMIT] 1. an authorization to perform certain duties or to take on certain powers 2. a document giving such authorization 3. the state of being so authorized 4. authority to act for another 5. that which one is authorized to do for another 6. a committing or perpetration, as of a crime 7. *a*) a group of people officially appointed to perform specified duties *b*) an administrative agency of the government 8. a percentage of the money taken in on sales, allotted to the salesclerk or agent 9. *Mil.* *a*) an official certificate conferring a rank of officer *b*) the rank conferred —*vt.* 1. to give a commission to 2. to authorize; empower 3. to give an order to make or do 4. *Naut.* to put (a vessel) into service —**in** (or **out of**) **commission** 1. in (or not in) use 2. in (or not in) working order
commissioned officer an officer in the armed forces holding rank by a commission
com·mis·sion·er (-ə nər) *n.* 1. a member of a commission (sense 7) 2. an official in charge of a certain government bureau, commission, etc. 3. an official appointed to administer a territory, province, etc.: usually **high commissioner** 4. a man selected to regulate and control a professional sport
com·mit (kə mit′) *vt.* **-mit′ted, -mit′ting** [L. *committere* < *com-*, together + *mittere*, to send] 1. to give in charge or trust; consign [we *commit* his fame to posterity] 2. to put officially in custody or confinement [*committed* to prison] 3. to set apart for some purpose 4. to do or perpetrate (an offense or crime) 5. to bind as by a promise; pledge [*committed* to the struggle] 6. to make known the opinions or views of [to *commit* oneself on an issue] 7. to refer (a bill, etc.) to a committee to be considered —**commit to memory** to learn by heart; memorize —**commit to paper** (or **writing**) to write down —**com·mit′ta·ble** *adj.*
com·mit·ment (-mənt) *n.* 1. a committing or being committed 2. official consignment by court order of a person to prison, to a mental hospital, etc. 3. a pledge or promise Also **com·mit′tal**
com·mit·tee (kə mit′ē) *n.* [< Anglo-Fr. < L. *committere:* see COMMIT] 1. a group of people chosen, as in a legislature or club, to consider or act on some matter 2. a group of people organized to support some cause —**in committee** under consideration by a committee, as a resolution or bill
com·mit·tee·man (-mən) *n., pl.* **-men** 1. a member of a committee 2. a ward or precinct political party leader —**com·mit′tee·wom′an** *n.fem., pl.* **-wom′en**
com·mode (kə mōd′) *n.* [Fr. < L. *commodus*, suitable: see COM- & MODE] 1. a chest of drawers 2. a small, low table with drawers or cabinet space: also **commode table** 3. a

movable washstand **4.** a chair enclosing a chamber pot **5.** a toilet

com·mo·di·ous (kə mō′dē əs) ***adj.*** [ME., convenient: see prec.] spacious; roomy —**com·mo′di·ous·ly** ***adv.*** —**com·mo′di·ous·ness** ***n.***

com·mod·i·ty (kə mäd′ə tē) ***n.,*** *pl.* **-ties** [< OFr. < L. < *commodus:* see COMMODE] **1.** any useful thing **2.** anything bought and sold, as in commerce

com·mo·dore (käm′ə dôr′) ***n.*** [prob. via Du. *kommandeur* < Fr. *commandeur:* see COMMAND] **1.** *U.S. Navy* formerly, an officer ranking above a captain: the rank was temporarily restored in World War II **2.** *Brit. Navy* a title for a captain temporarily heading a squadron or division of a fleet **3.** a courtesy title, as of the president of a yacht club

com·mon (käm′ən) ***adj.*** [< OFr. < L. *communis,* shared by all or many] **1.** belonging equally to, or shared by all **2.** belonging or relating to the community at large; public **3.** widely existing; general; prevalent **4.** notorious *[a common* criminal*]* **5.** familiar; usual **6.** not of the upper classes; of the masses *[the common* people*]* **7.** having no rank *[a common* soldier*]* **8.** below ordinary; inferior **9.** vulgar; low; coarse **10.** *Gram. a)* designating a noun that refers to any of a group or class, as *book, apple, street:* opposed to PROPER *b)* either masculine or feminine *[the* word *child* is of *common* gender*]* **11.** *Math.* belonging equally to two or more quantities *[a common* denominator*]* —***n.*** [*sometimes pl.*] land owned or used by all the inhabitants of a place —**in common** equally with, or shared by, another or all concerned —**com′mon·ly** ***adv.*** —**com′mon·ness** ***n.***

com·mon·al·i·ty (käm′ə nal′ə tē) ***n.*** **1.** the common people **2.** a sharing of common features, etc.

com·mon·al·ty (käm′ən əl tē) ***n.,*** *pl.* **-ties** **1.** the common people **2.** a general body or group **3.** a corporation or its membership

common carrier a person or company in the business of transporting people or goods for a fee

common cold *same as* COLD (*n.* 4)

com·mon·er (-ər) ***n.*** one of the common people

Common Era *same as* CHRISTIAN ERA

common fraction a fraction whose numerator and denominator are both whole numbers

common law the law of a country or state based on custom, usage, and the decisions of law courts: separate from STATUTE LAW and now largely codified

com·mon-law marriage (käm′ən lô′) *Law* a marriage not solemnized by religious or civil ceremony but effected by agreement to live together as husband and wife and by the fact of such cohabitation

common market an association of countries formed to effect a closer economic union; specif., [**C- M-**] the European Economic Community

com·mon·place (-plās′) ***n.*** **1.** a trite or obvious remark; truism; platitude **2.** anything common or ordinary —***adj.*** neither new nor interesting; obvious or ordinary —**com′mon·place′ness** ***n.***

common pleas *Law* in some States, a court having general and original jurisdiction over civil and criminal trials

com·mons (käm′ənz) ***n.pl.*** **1.** the common people **2.** [*often with sing. v.*] [**C-**] *same as* HOUSE OF COMMONS **3.** [*often with sing. v.*] food provided for meals in common for a whole group, or a dining room where such food is served, as at a college

common sense ordinary good sense or sound practical judgment —**com′mon-sense′, com′mon-sen′si·cal** (-sen′si k'l) ***adj.***

common stock ordinary capital stock in a company without a definite dividend rate or the privileges of preferred stock

common time *Music* a meter of four beats to the measure; 4/4 time: also **common measure**

com·mon·weal (käm′ən wēl′) ***n.*** the public good; the general welfare

com·mon·wealth (-welth′) ***n.*** **1.** the people of a nation or state **2.** *a)* a democracy or republic *b)* a federation of states **3.** loosely, any State of the U.S.; strictly, Ky., Mass., Pa., or Va. **4.** a group of people united by common interests —**the Commonwealth** **1.** the government in England under the Cromwells and Parliament (1649–1660) **2.** *same as* BRITISH COMMONWEALTH (OF NATIONS)

com·mo·tion (kə mō′shən) ***n.*** [< L. pp. of *commovere* < *com-,* together + *movere,* to move] **1.** violent motion; turbulence **2.** confusion; bustle

com·mu·nal (käm′yoon ′l, kə myo͞on′′l) ***adj.*** **1.** of a commune or communes **2.** of or belonging to the community; public **3.** designating or of social or economic organization in which there is common ownership of property —**com·mu′nal·ly** ***adv.***

com·mu·nal·ism (-iz'm) ***n.*** **1.** a theory or system of government in which communes or local communities have virtual autonomy within a federated state **2.** communal organization; loosely, socialism —**com·mu′nal·ist** ***n., adj.*** —**com·mu′nal·is′tic** ***adj.***

com·mu·nal·ize (-īz′) ***vt.*** **-ized′, -iz′ing** to make communal —**com·mu′nal·i·za′tion** ***n.***

com·mune[1] (kə myo͞on′; *for n.* käm′yo͞on) ***vi.*** **-muned′, -mun′ing** [< OFr. *comuner,* to share < *comun* (see COMMON)] **1.** *a)* to talk together intimately *b)* to be in close rapport *[to commune* with nature*]* **2.** to receive Holy Communion —***n.*** [Poet.] intimate conversation —**commune with oneself** to ponder

com·mune[2] (käm′yo͞on) ***n.*** [< OFr., ult. < L. *communis,* COMMON] **1.** a community; specif., the smallest administrative district of local government in France, Belgium, and some other European countries **2.** a collective farm, as in China **3.** a small group of people living communally and sharing in work, earnings, etc. —**the Commune** the revolutionary government of Paris from 1792 to 1794 or in 1871

com·mu·ni·ca·ble (kə myo͞o′ni kə b'l) ***adj.*** **1.** that can be communicated, as an idea **2.** that can be transmitted, as a disease —**com·mu′ni·ca·bil′i·ty** ***n.*** —**com·mu′ni·ca·bly** ***adv.***

com·mu·ni·cant (-kənt) ***n.*** a person who receives Holy Communion or belongs to a church celebrating this sacrament

com·mu·ni·cate (-kāt′) ***vt.*** **-cat′ed, -cat′ing** [< L. pp. of *communicare* < *communis,* COMMON] **1.** to pass along; impart; transmit **2.** to make known; give (information, etc.) —***vi.*** **1.** to receive Holy Communion **2.** *a)* to give or exchange information, etc., as by talk, writing, etc. *b)* to have a sympathetic personal relationship **3.** to be connected *[communicating* rooms*]* —**com·mu′ni·ca′tor** ***n.***

com·mu·ni·ca·tion (kə myo͞o′nə kā′shən) ***n.*** **1.** a transmitting **2.** *a)* a giving or exchanging of information, etc. by talk, writing, etc. *b)* the information so given **3.** close, sympathetic relationship **4.** a means of communicating; specif., *a)* [*pl.*] a system for sending and receiving messages, as by telephone or radio *b)* [*pl.*] a system for moving troops and materiel *c)* a passage for getting from one place to another **5.** [*often pl., with sing. v.*] *a)* the art of expressing ideas *b)* the science of transmitting information

com·mu·ni·ca·tive (kə myo͞o′nə kāt′iv, -ni kə tiv) ***adj.*** **1.** giving information readily; talkative **2.** of communication —**com·mu′ni·ca′tive·ly** ***adv.***

com·mun·ion (kə myo͞on′yən) ***n.*** [OFr. < L. < *communis,* COMMON] **1.** a sharing; possession in common **2.** a sharing of one's thoughts and emotions **3.** an intimate relationship with deep understanding **4.** a Christian denomination **5.** [**C-**] a sharing in, or celebrating, of, Holy Communion

com·mu·ni·qué (kə myo͞o′nə kā′; kə myo͞o′nə kā′) ***n.*** [Fr.] an official communication or bulletin

com·mu·nism (käm′yə niz'm) ***n.*** [< Fr.: see COMMON & -ISM] **1.** a theory or system based on the ownership of all property by the community as a whole **2.** [*often* **C-**] *a)* a hypothetical stage of socialism, as formulated by Marx, Engels, Lenin, etc., to be characterized by a classless and stateless society and the equal distribution of economic goods *b)* the form of government in the U.S.S.R., China, etc., professing to be working toward this stage **3.** [*often* **C-**] *a)* a political movement for establishing a communist system *b)* the doctrines, methods, etc. of the Communist parties **4.** loosely, communalism See also SOCIALISM

com·mu·nist (-nist) ***n.*** **1.** an advocate or supporter of communism **2.** [**C-**] a member of a Communist Party —***adj.*** **1.** of, characteristic of, or like communism or communists **2.** advocating or supporting communism **3.** [**C-**] designating or of a political party advocating Communism —**com′mu·nis′tic** ***adj.*** —**com′mu·nis′ti·cal·ly** ***adv.***

com·mu·ni·ty (kə myo͞o′nə tē) ***n.,*** *pl.* **-ties** [< OFr. < L. *communitas* < *communis,* COMMON] **1.** *a)* all the people living in a particular district, city, etc. *b)* the district, city, etc. where they live **2.** a group of people living together as a smaller social unit within a larger one, and having interests, work, etc. in common *[a college community]* **3.** a group of nations associated because of common traditions or for mutual advantage **4.** society; the public **5.** ownership or participation in common **6.** similarity; likeness *[a community* of tastes*]* **7.** friendly association **8.** *Ecology* a group of animals and plants living together and having close interactions

community center a meeting place in a community for cultural, recreational, or social activities

community chest (or **fund**) a fund collected annually in many cities and towns by private contributions for certain local welfare agencies

community college a junior college serving a certain community and supported by it in part

com·mu·nize (käm′yə nīz′) ***vt.*** **-nized′, -niz′ing** **1.** to subject to communal ownership and control **2.** to make communistic —**com′mu·ni·za′tion** ***n.***

com·mu·tate (käm′yə tāt′) ***vt.*** **-tat′ed, -tat′ing** [back-formation < ff.] to change the direction of (an electric current); esp., to change (alternating current) to direct current

com·mu·ta·tion (käm′yə tā′shən) ***n.*** [< OFr. < L. < pp. of *commutare,* COMMUTE] **1.** an exchange; substitution **2.** the substitution of one kind of payment for another **3.** the act of traveling as a commuter **4.** *Elec.* change of the direction of a current by a commutator **5.** *Law* a change of a punishment to one that is less severe —**com·mu·ta·tive** (käm′yə tāt′iv, kə myo͞ot′ə tiv) ***adj.***

com·mu·ta·tor (käm′yə tāt′ər) ***n.*** **1.** a device for commutating an electric current **2.** in a dynamo or motor, a revolving part that collects the current from, or distributes it to, the brushes

com·mute (kə myo͞ot′) ***vt.*** **-mut′ed, -mut′ing** [< L. *commutare* < *com-,* intens. + *mutare,* to change] **1.** to exchange; substitute **2.** to change (an obligation, punishment, etc.) to one that is less severe —***vi.*** **1.** to be a substitute **2.** to travel as a commuter —**com·mut′a·ble** ***adj.***

com·mut·er (-ər) ***n.*** a person who travels regularly, esp. by train, bus, etc., between two points at some distance

Com·o·ros (käm′ə rōs′) country on a group of islands in the Indian Ocean, between Mozambique and Madagascar: formerly a Fr. territory: 700 sq. mi.; pop. 292,000

comp[1] (kämp) ***vi.*** [< ACCOMPANY] [Colloq.] *Jazz* to play an accompaniment: said of a pianist, guitarist, etc.

comp[2] (kämp) ***n.*** [< COMPLIMENTARY] [Slang] a free theater ticket, book, etc. given usually for promotional purposes

comp. **1.** comparative **2.** compare **3.** compiled **4.** composition **5.** compositor **6.** compound

com·pact (kəm pakt′; *also for adj., and for n. always,* käm′pakt) ***adj.*** [< L. pp. of *compingere* < *com-,* together + *pangere,* to fasten] **1.** closely and firmly packed; dense **2.** taking little space **3.** not wordy; terse **4.** composed (*of*) **5.** designating or of a small, economical model of automobile —***vt.*** **1.** to pack or join firmly together **2.** to make by putting together **3.** to condense —***n.*** **1.** a small cosmetic case, usually containing face powder and a mirror **2.** a compact automobile **3.** [< L. pp. of *compacisci,* to agree together] an agreement —**com·pact′ly** ***adv.*** —**com·pact′ness** ***n.***

com·pac·tor (-pak′tər) ***n.*** a device that compresses trash into small bundles for easy disposal

com·pan·ion[1] (kəm pan′yən) ***n.*** [< OFr. < hyp. VL. *companio,* messmate < L. *com-,* with + *panis,* bread] **1.** one who associates with or accompanies another or others; associate; comrade **2.** a person employed to live or travel with another **3.** a thing that matches another in sort, color, etc. —***vt.*** to accompany —**com·pan′ion·ship′** ***n.***

com·pan·ion[2] (kəm pan′yən) ***n.*** [< Du. < OFr. < It. (*camera della*) *compagna,* (room of the) company, crew] *Naut.* **1.** the covering at the head of a companionway **2.** a companionway

com·pan·ion·a·ble (-ə b′l) ***adj.*** having the qualities of a good companion; sociable —**com·pan′ion·a·bil′i·ty** ***n.***

com·pan·ion·ate (-it) ***adj.*** of or characteristic of companions

com·pan·ion·way (-wā′) ***n.*** a stairway leading from the deck of a ship to the cabins or space below

com·pa·ny (kum′pə nē) ***n.,*** *pl.* **-nies** [< OFr. < VL. hyp. *compania,* lit., group sharing bread: see COMPANION[1]] **1.** companionship; society **2.** a group of people; specif., *a*) a group gathered for social purposes *b*) a group associated for some purpose [a business *company*] **3.** the partners who are not named in the title of a firm [John Smith and *Company*] **4.** a guest or guests **5.** one's habitual associates **6.** *Mil.* a body of troops, as of infantry, normally composed of two or more platoons **7.** *Naut.* the whole crew of a ship: in full, **ship's company** —**keep (a person) company** to stay with (a person) and provide companionship —**keep company** **1.** to associate (*with*) **2.** to go together, as a couple intending to marry —**part company** **1.** to stop associating (*with*) **2.** to separate and go in different directions

compar. **1.** comparative **2.** comparison

com·pa·ra·ble (käm′pər ə b′l; *occas.* kəm par′ə b′l) ***adj.*** **1.** that can be compared **2.** worthy of comparison —**com′pa·ra·bil′i·ty, com′pa·ra·ble·ness** ***n.*** —**com′pa·ra·bly** ***adv.***

com·par·a·tive (kəm par′ə tiv) ***adj.*** **1.** that compares; involving comparison as a method [*comparative* linguistics] **2.** relative [*comparative* joy] **3.** *Gram.* designating or of the second degree of comparison of adjectives and adverbs: usually indicated by the suffix *-er* (*harder*) or by the use of *more* (*more beautiful*) —***n.*** *Gram.* **1.** the comparative degree **2.** a word or form in this degree —**com·par′a·tive·ly** ***adv.***

com·pare (kəm per′) ***vt.*** **-pared′, -par′ing** [< OFr. < L. *comparare* < *com-,* with + *par,* equal] **1.** to regard as similar; liken (*to*) **2.** to examine in order to observe similarities or differences (often followed by *with*) **3.** *Gram.* to form the positive, comparative, and superlative degrees of (an adjective or adverb) —***vi.*** **1.** to be worthy of comparison (*with*) **2.** to be regarded as similar —***n.*** [Poet.] comparison —**beyond** (or **past** or **without**) **compare** without equal

com·par·i·son (kəm par′ə s′n) ***n.*** **1.** a comparing or being compared; estimation of similarities and differences **2.** likeness; similarity [no *comparison* between the two] **3.** *Gram.* change in an adjective or adverb to show the positive, comparative, and superlative degrees (Ex.: *long, longer, longest; good, better, best; slowly, more slowly, most slowly*) —**in comparison with** compared with

com·part·ment (kəm pärt′mənt) ***n.*** [< Fr. < It. < LL. < L. *com-,* intens. + *partiri,* to divide < *pars,* a part] **1.** any of the divisions into which a space is partitioned off **2.** a separate section, part, division, or category —***vt.*** *same as* COMPARTMENTALIZE —**com·part′men′tal** (-men′t′l) ***adj.*** —**com·part′ment·ed** ***adj.***

com·part·men·tal·ize (kəm pärt′men′tə līz′) ***vt.*** **-ized′, -iz′ing** to put or separate into detached compartments, divisions, or categories —**com·part′men′tal·i·za′tion** ***n.***

com·pass (kum′pəs) ***vt.*** [< OFr., ult. < L. *com-,* together + *passus,* a step] **1.** to go round **2.** to surround; encircle **3.** to understand; comprehend **4.** to achieve; accomplish **5.** to plot or contrive (something harmful) —***n.*** **1.** [*often pl.*] an instrument consisting of two pivoted legs, used for drawing arcs or circles or for taking measurements: also called **pair of compasses** **2.** a boundary; circumference **3.** an enclosed area **4.** full extent or range; reach; scope; specif., range of tones, as of a voice **5.** an instrument for showing direction, esp. one consisting of a magnetic needle swinging freely on a pivot and pointing to the magnetic north —***adj.*** round; circular or semicircular

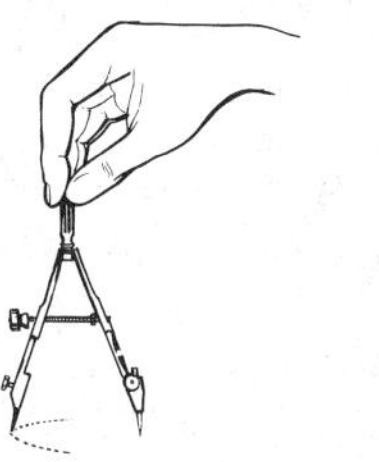

DRAWING COMPASS

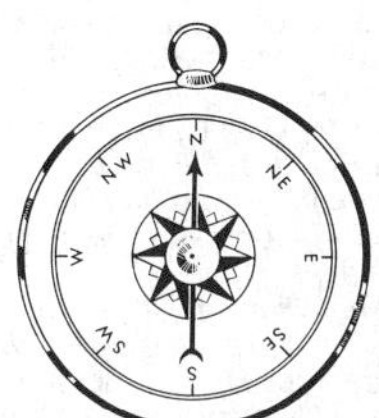

DIRECTIONAL COMPASS

compass card the circular card mounted on a free pivot inside a compass and marked with points of direction and, often, the degrees of the circle

com·pas·sion (kəm pash′ən) ***n.*** [OFr. < LL. *compassio,* ult. < L. *com-,* together + *pati,* to suffer] sorrow for the sufferings or trouble of another, with the urge to help; pity

com·pas·sion·ate (-it; *for v.* -āt′) ***adj.*** feeling or showing compassion; sympathizing deeply —***vt.*** **-at′ed, -at′ing** to pity —**com·pas′sion·ate·ly** ***adv.***

com·pat·i·ble (kəm pat′ə b′l) ***adj.*** [Fr. < LL.: see COMPASSION] **1.** capable of living together harmoniously or getting along well together; in agreement **2.** that can be mixed without adverse effects: said of drugs, etc. **3.** *TV* designating or of a system of color transmission producing satisfactory black and white pictures —**com·pat′i·bil′i·ty, com·pat′i·ble·ness** ***n.*** —**com·pat′i·bly** ***adv.***

com·pa·tri·ot (kəm pā′trē ət: *chiefly Brit.* -pat′rē-) ***n.*** [< Fr. < LL. *compatriota:* see COM- & PATRIOT] **1.** a fellow countryman **2.** a colleague —***adj.*** of the same country

com·peer (käm′pir, kəm pir′) ***n.*** [< OFr. < L. < *com-,* with + *par,* equal] **1.** an equal; peer **2.** a companion; comrade

com·pel (kəm pel′) ***vt.*** **-pelled′, -pel′ling** [< OFr. < L. *compellere* < *com-,* together + *pellere,* to drive] **1.** to force or constrain, as to do something **2.** to get or bring about by force —**com·pel′ler** ***n.*** —**com·pel′ling·ly** ***adv.***

com·pen·di·ous (kəm pen′dē əs) ***adj.*** [L. *compendiosus:* see ff.] containing all the essentials in a brief form; concise but comprehensive —**com·pen′di·ous·ly** ***adv.*** —**com·pen′di·ous·ness** ***n.***

com·pen·di·um (-əm) ***n.,*** *pl.* **-di·ums, -di·a** (-ə) [L., an abridgment < *com-,* together + *pendere,* to weigh] a summary containing the essential information in a brief form; concise but comprehensive treatise

com·pen·sa·ble (kəm pen′sə b′l) ***adj.*** entitling to compensation

com·pen·sate (käm′pən sāt′) ***vt.*** **-sat′ed, -sat′ing** [< L. pp. of *compensare* < *com-,* with + *pensare,* freq. of *pendere,* to weigh] **1.** to make up for; counterbalance in weight, force, etc. **2.** to make equivalent return to; recompense —***vi.*** to make or serve as compensation or amends (*for*) —**com′pen·sa·tive** (käm′pən sāt′iv, kəm pen′sə tiv) ***adj.*** —**com′pen·sa′tor** ***n.*** —**com·pen·sa·to·ry** (kəm pen′sə-tôr′ē) ***adj.***

com·pen·sa·tion (käm′pən sā′shən) ***n.*** **1.** a compensating or being compensated **2.** *a*) anything given as an equivalent, or to make amends for a loss, etc. *b* payment for services; esp., wages **3.** the counterbalancing of a defect by a greater activity or development of some other part, quality, etc. —**com′pen·sa′tion·al** ***adj.***

com·pete (kəm pēt′) ***vi.*** **-pet′ed, -pet′ing** [< L. *competere* < *com-*, together + *petere*, to seek] to enter into or be in rivalry; contend; vie (*in* a contest, etc.)

com·pe·tence (käm′pə təns) ***n.*** [< Fr. < L. < prp. of *competere:* see prec.] **1.** sufficient means for one's needs **2.** ability; fitness; specif., legal capability, power, or jurisdiction Also **com′pe·ten·cy**

com·pe·tent (-tənt) ***adj.*** [< OFr. < L. prp. of *competere:* see COMPETE] **1.** well qualified; capable; fit **2.** sufficient; adequate **3.** *Law* legally qualified or fit —**com′pe·tent·ly** ***adv.***

com·pe·ti·tion (käm′pə tish′ən) ***n.*** **1.** a competing; rivalry **2.** a contest, or match **3.** rivalry in business, as for customers or markets **4.** the person or persons against whom one competes

com·pet·i·tive (kəm pet′ə tiv) ***adj.*** of, involving, or based on competition: also **com·pet′i·to′ry** (-tôr′ē) —**com·pet′i·tive·ly** ***adv.*** —**com·pet′i·tive·ness** ***n.***

com·pet·i·tor (-tər) ***n.*** a person who competes, as a business rival

com·pile (kəm pīl′) ***vt.*** **-piled′, -pil′ing** [< OFr. < L. *compilare* < *com-*, together + *pilare*, to compress] **1.** to gather together (statistics, facts, etc.) in an orderly form **2.** to compose (a book, etc.) of materials gathered from various sources —**com·pi·la·tion** (käm′pə lā′shən) ***n.*** —**com·pil′er** ***n.***

com·pla·cen·cy (kəm plās′′n sē) ***n.*** [< LL. < L.: see ff.] quiet satisfaction; contentment; often, self-satisfaction, or smugness: also **com·pla′cence**

com·pla·cent (-′nt) ***adj.*** [< L. prp. of *complacere* < *com-*, intens. + *placere*, please] **1.** self-satisfied; smug **2.** affable; complaisant —**com·pla′cent·ly** ***adv.***

com·plain (kəm plān′) ***vi.*** [< OFr. < VL. *complangere* < L. *com-*, intens. + *plangere*, to strike (the breast)] **1.** to express pain, displeasure, etc. **2.** to find fault **3.** to make an accusation or a formal charge —**com·plain′er** ***n.*** —**com·plain′ing·ly** ***adv.***

com·plain·ant (-ənt) ***n.*** *Law* one who files a charge or makes the complaint in court; plaintiff

com·plaint (kəm plānt′) ***n.*** **1.** a complaining; utterance of pain, displeasure, annoyance, etc. **2.** a subject or cause for complaining **3.** an illness; ailment **4.** *Law* a formal charge

com·plai·sant (kəm plā′z′nt, -s′nt) ***adj.*** [< Fr. prp. of *complaire* < L. *complacere:* see COMPLACENT] willing to please; affably agreeable; obliging —**com·plai′sance** ***n.*** —**com·plai′sant·ly** ***adv.***

com·plect·ed (kəm plek′tid) ***adj.*** [altered < COMPLEXIONED] [Dial. or Colloq.] *same as* COMPLEXIONED

com·ple·ment (käm′plə mənt; *for v.* -ment′) ***n.*** [L. *complementum* < *complere:* see COMPLETE] **1.** that which completes or brings to perfection **2.** the amount needed to fill or complete **3.** a complete set; entirety **4.** either of two parts that complete each other **5.** *Gram.* a word or words that complete the meaning of the predicate (Ex.: *foreman* in *make him foreman, paid* in *he expects to get paid*) **6.** *Math.* the number of degrees added to an angle or arc to make it equal 90 degrees —***vt.*** to make complete; be a complement to

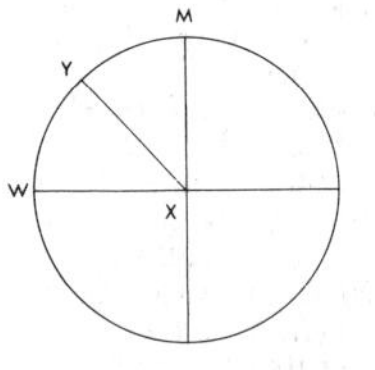

M
Y
W
X

COMPLEMENT
(arc YM, complement of arc WY; angle YXM, complement of angle WXY)

com·ple·men·ta·ry (käm′plə-men′tər ē) ***adj.*** **1.** acting as a complement; completing **2.** mutually making up what is lacking Also **com′ple·men′tal** —**com′ple·men·tar′i·ty** (-ter′ə-tē) ***n.***

complementary angle either of two angles that together form a 90° angle

complementary colors any two colors of the spectrum that combine to form white light

com·plete (kəm plēt′) ***adj.*** [< OFr. < L. pp. of *complere* < *com-*, intens. + *plere*, to fill] **1.** lacking no component part; entire **2.** ended; finished **3.** thorough; absolute —***vt.*** **-plet′ed, -plet′ing** **1.** to end; finish **2.** to make whole, full, or perfect —**com·plete′ly** ***adv.*** —**com·plete′ness** ***n.***

com·ple·tion (kəm plē′shən) ***n.*** **1.** a completing, or finishing **2.** the state of being completed

com·plex (kəm pleks′; *also, and for n. always,* käm′pleks) ***adj.*** [< L. pp. of *complecti* < *com-*, with + *plectere*, to weave] **1.** consisting of two or more related parts **2.** not simple; complicated —***n.*** **1.** a group of related ideas, activities, things, etc. that form, or are viewed as forming, a single whole **2.** *Psychoanalysis* *a*) a group of largely unconscious impulses, ideas, and emotions related to a particular object, activity, etc., strongly influencing the individual's behavior *b*) popularly, an exaggerated dislike or fear —**com·plex′ly** ***adv.*** —**com·plex′ness** ***n.***

complex fraction a fraction with a fraction in its numerator or denominator, or in both

com·plex·ion (kəm plek′shən) ***n.*** [OFr. < L. < *complexus:* see COMPLEX] **1.** one's temperament or disposition **2.** the color, texture, etc. of the skin, esp. of the face **3.** general appearance or nature; character; aspect —**complex′ion·al** ***adj.***

com·plex·ioned (-shənd) ***adj.*** having a (specified) complexion [light-*complexioned*]

com·plex·i·ty (kəm plek′sə tē) ***n.*** **1.** a complex condition or quality **2.** *pl.* **-ties** anything complex or intricate; complication

complex sentence a sentence consisting of a main clause and one or more subordinate clauses

com·pli·ance (kəm plī′əns) ***n.*** **1.** a complying, or giving in to a request, demand, etc. **2.** a tendency to give in readily to others Also **com·pli′an·cy** —**in compliance with** complying with

com·pli·ant (-ənt) ***adj.*** complying; yielding; submissive —**com·pli′ant·ly** ***adv.***

com·pli·cate (käm′plə kāt′) ***vt., vi.*** **-cat′ed, -cat′ing** [< L. pp. of *complicare* < *com-*, together + *plicare*, to fold] to make or become intricate, difficult, or involved

com·pli·cat·ed (-kāt′id) ***adj.*** intricately involved; hard to untangle, solve, analyze, etc. —**com′pli·cat′ed·ly** ***adv.*** —**com′pli·cat′ed·ness** ***n.***

com·pli·ca·tion (käm′plə kā′shən) ***n.*** **1.** a complicating **2.** a complicated condition or structure **3.** a complicating factor, as in the plot of a story **4.** *Med.* a second disease or abnormal condition occurring during the course of a primary disease

com·plic·i·ty (kəm plis′ə tē) ***n.,*** *pl.* **-ties** [< Fr. < L. *complex* (gen. *complicis*): see COMPLEX] the fact or state of being an accomplice in wrongdoing

com·pli·ment (käm′plə mənt; *for v.* -ment′) ***n.*** [Fr. < It., ult. < L. *complere*, to COMPLETE] **1.** a formal act of courtesy **2.** something said in praise **3.** [*pl.*] respects —***vt.*** **1.** to pay a compliment to **2.** to present something to (a person) to show respect

com·pli·men·ta·ry (käm′plə men′tər ē) ***adj.*** **1.** paying or containing a compliment **2.** given free as a courtesy [a *complimentary* ticket] —**com′pli·men·tar′i·ly** (-men ter′ə-lē, -men′tər ə lē) ***adv.***

com·pline, com·plin (käm′plən) ***n.*** [< OFr. < L. *completus:* see COMPLETE] *Eccles.* [*often* **C-**] the last of the seven canonical hours: also **com′plines, com′plins** (-plənz)

com·ply (kəm plī′) ***vi.*** **-plied′, -ply′ing** [< OFr. < L. *complere:* see COMPLETE] to act in accordance (*with* a request, order, rule, etc.) —**com·pli′er** ***n.***

com·po·nent (kəm pō′nənt) ***adj.*** [< L. prp. of *componere:* see COMPOSITE] serving as one of the parts of a whole —***n.*** **1.** an element or ingredient **2.** a main constituent part, as of a hi-fi set

com·port (kəm pôrt′) ***vt.*** [< OFr. < L. *comportare* < *com-*, together + *portare*, to bring] to behave (oneself) in a specified manner —***vi.*** to agree or accord (*with*) —**com·port′ment** ***n.***

com·pose (kəm pōz′) ***vt.*** **-posed′, -pos′ing** [< OFr. *composer* < *com-*, with + *poser*, to place] **1.** to make up; constitute **2.** to put in proper order or form **3.** to create (a musical or literary work) **4.** to adjust or settle [to *compose* differences] **5.** to calm (oneself, one's mind, etc.); allay **6.** *Printing* to set (type) —***vi.*** **1.** to create musical or literary works **2.** to set type

com·posed (-pōzd′) ***adj.*** calm; tranquil; self-possessed —**com·pos′ed·ly** (-pō′zid lē) ***adv.*** —**com·pos′ed·ness** ***n.***

com·pos·er (-pō′zər) ***n.*** a person who composes, esp. one who composes music

com·pos·ite (kəm päz′it) ***adj.*** [< L. pp. of *componere* < *com-*, together + *ponere*, to put] **1.** formed of distinct parts; compound **2.** designating a large family of plants, as the daisy, chrysanthemum, etc., having flower heads composed of dense clusters of small flowers **3.** [**C-**] *Archit.* designating the classic order which combines features of the Ionic and Corinthian capitals —***n.*** **1.** a thing of distinct parts **2.** a composite plant —**com·pos′ite·ly** ***adv.***

composite photograph a photograph made by superimposing one or more photographs on another

com·po·si·tion (käm′pə zish′ən) ***n.*** **1.** a composing; specif., *a*) the art of writing *b*) the creation of musical works **2.** the makeup of a thing or person; constitution **3.** that which is composed; specif., *a)* a mixture of several parts or ingredients *b)* a work of music, literature, or art *c)* an exercise in writing done as schoolwork **4.** an aesthetically unified arrangement of parts **5.** an agreement, or settlement, often by compromise **6.** *Printing* the work of setting type —**com′po·si′tion·al** *adj.*

com·pos·i·tor (kəm päz′ə tər) *n.* a person who sets type; typesetter

com·pos men·tis (käm′pəs men′tis) [L.] *Law* of sound mind; sane

com·post (käm′pōst) *n.* [< OFr. < L.: see COMPOSITE] **1.** a compound **2.** a mixture of decomposing vegetation, manure, etc. for fertilizing soil

com·po·sure (kəm pō′zhər) *n.* [COMPOS(E) + -URE] calmness; tranquillity; self-possession

com·pote (käm′pōt) *n.* [Fr.: see COMPOST] **1.** a dish of fruits stewed in a syrup **2.** a long-stemmed dish for serving candy, fruit, etc.

com·pound[1] (käm pound′, kəm-; *for n. and, usually, for adj.,* käm′pound) *vt.* [< OFr. < L. *componere:* see COMPOSITE] **1.** to mix or combine **2.** to make by combining parts **3.** to settle by mutual agreement **4.** to settle (a debt) by compromise payment **5.** to intensify by adding new elements [to *compound* a problem] **6.** to compute (interest) as compound interest —*vi.* to agree or compromise —*adj.* made up of two or more separate parts or elements —*n.* **1.** a thing formed by the combination of parts **2.** a substance containing two or more elements chemically combined in fixed proportions: distinguished from MIXTURE in that a compound has characteristics different from those of its constituents **3.** a word composed of two or more base morphemes —**compound a felony** (or **crime**) to agree, for payment, not to inform about or prosecute for a felony (or crime)

com·pound[2] (käm′pound) *n.* [Anglo-Ind. < Malay *kampong*] **1.** in the Orient, an enclosed space with a building or group of buildings in it, esp. if occupied by foreigners **2.** any similar space

compound eye an eye made up of numerous simple eyes functioning collectively, as in insects

compound fraction *same as* COMPLEX FRACTION

compound fracture a bone fracture in which broken ends of bone have pierced the skin

compound interest interest paid on both the principal and the accumulated unpaid interest

compound leaf a leaf divided into two or more leaflets with a common leafstalk

compound number a quantity expressed in two or more sorts of related units (Ex.: 4 ft., 7 in.)

compound sentence a sentence consisting of two or more independent, coordinate clauses

com·pre·hend (käm′prə hend′) *vt.* [< L. *comprehendere* < *com-*, with + *prehendere*, to seize] **1.** to grasp mentally; understand **2.** to include; comprise —**com′pre·hend′ing·ly** *adv.*

com·pre·hen·si·ble (-hen′sə b'l) *adj.* that can be comprehended; intelligible —**com′pre·hen′si·bil′i·ty** *n.* —**com′pre·hen′si·bly** *adv.*

com·pre·hen·sion (-hen′shən) *n.* **1.** the fact of including or comprising; inclusiveness **2.** the act of or capacity for understanding

com·pre·hen·sive (-hen′siv) *adj.* **1.** including much; inclusive **2.** able to comprehend fully —**com′pre·hen′sive·ly** *adv.* —**com′pre·hen′sive·ness** *n.*

com·press (kəm pres′; *for n.* käm′pres) *vt.* [< OFr. < LL. < L. pp. of *comprimere* < *com-*, together + *premere*, to press] to press together; make more compact as by pressure —*n.* **1.** a pad of folded cloth, often medicated or wet, for applying pressure, heat, cold, etc. to a part of the body **2.** a machine for compressing cotton bales —**com·pressed′** *adj.* —**com·pres′si·bil′i·ty** *n.* —**com·pres′si·ble** *adj.* —**com·pres′sive** *adj.* —**com·pres′sive·ly** *adv.*

compressed air air held under pressure in a container: its expansive force can operate machines

com·pres·sion (kəm presh′ən) *n.* **1.** a compressing or being compressed **2.** the compressing of a working fluid in an engine, as of the mixture in an internal-combustion engine just before ignition

com·pres·sor (-pres′ər) *n.* **1.** one that compresses **2.** a muscle that compresses a part **3.** a machine for compressing air, gas, etc.

com·prise (-prīz′) *vt.* **-prised′, -pris′ing** [< OFr. pp. of *comprendre:* see COMPREHEND] **1.** to include; contain **2.** to consist of [a nation *comprising* fifty States] **3.** to make up; form [a nation *comprised* of fifty States]: in this sense regarded by some as a loose usage —**com·pris′a·ble** *adj.* —**com·pris′al** *n.*

com·pro·mise (käm′prə mīz′) *n.* [< OFr. < LL. < L. pp. of *compromittere* < *com-*, together + *promittere*, to PROMISE] **1.** a settlement in which each side makes concessions **2.** the result of such a settlement **3.** something midway between two other things **4.** *a)* exposure, as of one's reputation, to danger, suspicion, or disrepute *b)* a weakening, as of one's principles —*vt.* **-mised′, -mis′ing** **1.** to settle by concessions on both sides **2.** to lay open to danger, suspicion, or disrepute **3.** to weaken (one's principles, etc.) —*vi.* to make a compromise —**com′pro·mis′er** *n.*

Comp·ton (kämp′tən) [after G. *Compton,* a founder of the U. of S Cal.] city in SW Calif.: suburb of Los Angeles: pop. 81,000

comp·trol·ler (kən trō′lər) *n.* [altered (after Fr. *compte*, an account) < CONTROLLER] *same as* CONTROLLER (sense 1) —**comp·trol′ler·ship′** *n.*

com·pul·sion (kəm pul′shən) *n.* [< LL. < L. pp. of *compellere*] **1.** a compelling or being compelled; coercion **2.** a driving force **3.** *Psychol.* an irresistible, repeated, irrational impulse to perform some act

com·pul·sive (-siv) *adj.* of, having to do with, or resulting from compulsion —**com·pul′sive·ly** *adv.* —**com·pul′sive·ness** *n.*

com·pul·so·ry (-sər ē) *adj.* **1.** obligatory; required **2.** compelling; coercive —**com·pul′so·ri·ly** *adv.* —**com·pul′so·ri·ness** *n.*

com·punc·tion (kəm puŋk′shən) *n.* [< OFr. < LL. *compunctio*, a pricking (of conscience) < L. *com-*, intens. + *pungere*, to prick] **1.** a sharp feeling of uneasiness brought on by a sense of guilt; remorse **2.** a feeling of slight regret for something done —**com·punc′tious** *adj.* —**com·punc′tious·ly** *adv.*

com·pu·ta·tion (käm′pyoo tā′shən) *n.* **1.** a computing; calculation **2.** a method of computing **3.** a computed amount —**com′pu·ta′tion·al** *adj.*

com·pute (kəm pyōōt′) *vt., vi.* **-put′ed, -put′ing** [L. *computare* < *com-*, with + *putare*, to reckon] to determine (an amount, etc.) by reckoning; calculate —**com·put′a·bil′i·ty** *n.* —**com·put′a·ble** *adj.*

com·put·er (kəm pyōōt′ər) *n.* a person or thing that computes; specif., an electronic machine that performs rapid, often complex calculations or compiles, correlates, and selects data: see also ANALOG COMPUTER, DIGITAL COMPUTER

com·put·er·ize (-īz′) *vt.* **-ized′, -iz′ing** to equip with, or operate, produce, control, etc. by or as if by means of, an electronic computer —**com·put′er·i·za′tion** *n.*

com·rade (käm′rad, -rəd) *n.* [< Fr. < Sp. *camarada*, chamber mate < L. *camera:* see CAMERA] **1.** a friend; close companion **2.** one who shares interests and activities in common with others; associate **3.** [C-] [Colloq.] a Communist —**com′rade·ly** *adj.* —**com′rade·ship′** *n.*

comrade in arms a fellow soldier

com·rade·ry (-rē) *n. same as* CAMARADERIE

‡**comte** (kōnt) *n.* [Fr.] *same as* COUNT[2] —**com·tesse** (kōn-tes′) *n.fem.*

Comte (kōnt; *E.* kōmt), **(Isidore) Au·guste** (ô güst′) 1798–1857; Fr. philosopher: founder of positivism —**Com·ti·an, Com·te·an** (käm′tē ən, kōm′-) *adj.*

con[1] (kän) *adv.* [contr. < L. *contra*, against] against; in opposition [to argue pro and *con*] —*n.* a reason, vote, position, etc. in opposition

con[2] (kän) *vt.* **conned, con′ning** [ME. *connen*, to be able: see CAN[1]] to peruse or learn carefully

con[3] (kän) *vt., n. same as* CONN

con[4] (kän) *adj.* [Slang] confidence [a *con* man] —*vt.* **conned, con′ning** [Slang] **1.** to swindle (a victim) by first gaining his confidence **2.** to trick or fool, esp. by glib, persuasive talk

con[5] (kän) *n.* [Slang] a convict

con. **1.** concerto **2.** conclusion **3.** consolidated

Con·a·kry (kän′ə krē′) capital of Guinea; seaport on the Atlantic: pop. 120,000

con a·mo·re (kän′ə môr′e; *It.* kôn′ä mô′re) [It.] with love; tenderly: a direction in music

con bri·o (kän brē′ō, kōn) [It.] with spirit; spiritedly: a direction in music

con·cat·e·nate (kän kat′'n āt′, kən-) *adj.* [< LL. pp. of *concatenare* < L. < *com-*, together + *catenare* < *catena*, a chain] linked together; connected —*vt.* **-nat′ed, -nat′ing** to link or join, as in a chain

con·cat·e·na·tion (kän kat′'n ā′shən, kən-) *n.* **1.** a linking together or being linked together **2.** a series of things or events regarded as causally connected

con·cave (kän kāv′; *also, and for n. usually,* kän′kāv) *adj.* [< OFr. < L. < *com-*, intens. + *cavus*, hollow] hollow and curved like the inside half of a hollow ball —*n.* a concave surface, line, object, etc. —*vt.* **-caved′, -cav′ing** to make concave —**con·cave′ly** *adv.* —**con·cave′ness** *n.*

con·cav·i·ty (kän kav′ə tē) ***n.*** **1.** the quality or condition of being concave **2.** *pl.* **-ties** a concave surface, line, etc.

con·ca·vo-con·cave (kän kā′vō kän kāv′) ***adj.*** concave on both sides, as some lenses

con·ca·vo-con·vex (-kän veks′) ***adj.*** concave on one side and convex on the other

con·ceal (kən sēl′) ***vt.*** [< OFr. < L. *concelare* < *com-*, together + *celare,* to hide] **1.** to put out of sight; hide **2.** to keep from another's knowledge; keep secret *[to conceal one's amusement]* **—con·ceal′ment** ***n.***

con·cede (kən sēd′) ***vt.*** **-ced′ed, -ced′ing** [L. *concedere* < *com-*, with + *cedere,* to cede] **1.** to admit as true; acknowledge **2.** to admit as certain **3.** to grant as a right **—*vi.*** **1.** to make a concession **2.** to acknowledge defeat in an election **—con·ced′er** ***n.***

con·ceit (kən sēt′) ***n.*** [see CONCEIVE] **1.** orig., an idea **2.** an exaggerated opinion of oneself, one's merits, etc.; vanity **3.** a fanciful or witty expression or notion; often, specif., a strained or bizarre figure of speech **4.** a flight of imagination; fancy

con·ceit·ed (-id) ***adj.*** having an exaggerated opinion of oneself, one's merits, etc.; vain **—con·ceit′ed·ly** ***adv.*** **—con·ceit′ed·ness** ***n.***

con·ceiv·a·ble (kən sē′və b'l) ***adj.*** that can be conceived, understood, imagined, or believed **—con·ceiv′a·bil′i·ty** ***n.*** **—con·ceiv′a·bly** ***adv.***

con·ceive (kən sēv′) ***vt.*** **-ceived′, -ceiv′ing** [< OFr. < L. *concipere,* to receive < *com-*, together + *capere,* to take] **1.** to become pregnant with **2.** to form in the mind **3.** to think; imagine **4.** to understand **5.** to express in words **—*vi.*** **1.** to become pregnant **2.** to form an idea (*of*)

con·cel·e·brate (kän sel′ə brāt′) ***vt.*** **-brat′ed, -brat′ing** [< L. pp. of *concelebrare:* see COM- & CELEBRATE] to celebrate (the Eucharistic liturgy) jointly: said of two or more priests **—con′cel·e·bra′tion** ***n.***

con·cen·ter (kən sen′tər) ***vt., vi.*** [< Fr. < L. *com-*, together + *centrum,* CENTER] to bring or come to a common center; concentrate or converge

con·cen·trate (kän′sən trāt′) ***vt.*** **-trat′ed, -trat′ing** [< prec. + -ATE[1]] **1.** to bring to a common center **2.** to focus (one's thoughts, efforts, etc.) **3.** to increase the strength, density, or intensity of **—*vi.*** **1.** to come to a common center **2.** to fix one's attention (*on* or *upon*) **—*n.*** a substance that has been concentrated **—*adj.*** concentrated **—con′cen·tra′tive** ***adj.*** **—con′cen·tra′tor** ***n.***

con·cen·tra·tion (kän′sən trā′shən) ***n.*** **1.** a concentrating or being concentrated **2.** close or fixed attention **3.** strength or density, as of a solution

concentration camp a prison camp in which political dissidents, members of minority ethnic groups, etc. are confined

con·cen·tric (kən sen′trik) ***adj.*** [< OFr. < ML. < L. *com-*, together + *centrum,* CENTER] having a center in common *[concentric circles]* : also **con·cen′tri·cal** **—con·cen′tri·cal·ly** ***adv.*** **—con·cen·tric·i·ty** (kän′sen tris′ə tē) ***n.***

Con·cep·ción (kən sep′sē ōn′; *Sp.* kôn sep′syôn′) seaport on a river in SC Chile: pop. 202,000

con·cept (kän′sept) ***n.*** [< L. pp. of *concipere:* see CONCEIVE] an idea or thought, esp. a generalized idea of a class of objects; abstract notion

con·cep·tion (kən sep′shən) ***n.*** **1.** a conceiving or being conceived in the womb **2.** an embryo or fetus **3.** the beginning of some process, etc. **4.** the formulation of ideas **5.** a mental impression; concept **6.** an original idea, design, plan, etc. **—con·cep′tion·al** ***adj.*** **—con·cep′tive** ***adj.***

con·cep·tu·al (kən sep′choo wəl) ***adj.*** of conception or concepts **—con·cep′tu·al·ly** ***adv.***

con·cep·tu·al·ize (-īz′) ***vt.*** **-ized′, -iz′ing** to form a concept or idea of; conceive **—con·cep′tu·al·i·za′tion** ***n.***

con·cern (kən surn′) ***vt.*** [< ML. < LL. *concernere* < L. *com-*, with + *cernere,* to sift] **1.** to have a relation to; deal with **2.** to engage or involve; be a proper affair of **3.** to make uneasy or anxious **—*n.*** **1.** a matter of interest or importance to one; affair **2.** interest in or regard for a person or thing **3.** relation; reference **4.** worry; anxiety **5.** a business firm **—as concerns** in regard to **—concern oneself** **1.** to busy oneself (*with, about, over, in* something) **2.** to be worried, anxious, or uneasy

con·cerned (-surnd′) ***adj.*** **1.** involved or interested (often with *in*) **2.** uneasy or anxious

con·cern·ing (-sur′niŋ) ***prep.*** relating to; having to do with; in regard to; about

con·cern·ment (-surn′mənt) ***n.*** [Rare] concern; specif., *a)* an affair; matter *b)* importance *c)* worry

con·cert (kən surt′; *for n. & adj.* kän′sərt) ***vt., vi.*** [Fr. < It. < L. *concertare* < *com-*, with + *certare,* to strive] to arrange by mutual understanding; plan together; devise **—*n.*** **1.** mutual agreement; concord **2.** musical consonance **3.** a program of vocal or instrumental music **—*adj.*** of or for concerts **—in concert** in unison; together

con·cert·ed (kən sur′tid) ***adj.*** **1.** mutually arranged or agreed upon; done together **2.** *Music* arranged in parts **—con·cert′ed·ly** ***adv.***

con·cer·ti·na (kän′sər tē′nə) ***n.*** [CONCERT + -INA: a coinage] a small musical instrument similar to an accordion, with buttons instead of a keyboard

CONCERTINA

con·cert·ize (kän′sər tīz′) ***vi.*** **-ized′, -iz′ing** to perform as a soloist in concerts

con·cert·mas·ter (kän′sərt mas′tər) ***n.*** [transl. of G. *konzertmeister*] the leader of the first violins of a symphony orchestra, often an assistant to the conductor: also **con′cert·meis′ter** (-mīs′-)

con·cer·to (kən cher′tō) ***n.,*** *pl.* **-tos, -ti** (-tē) [It.: see CONCERT] a composition, usually in three movements in symphonic form, for one or more solo instruments and an orchestra

con·ces·sion (kən sesh′ən) ***n.*** **1.** a conceding **2.** a thing conceded; acknowledgment, as of an argument **3.** a privilege granted by a government, company, etc.; esp., *a)* the right to use land *b)* the right to sell food, parking space, etc. on the lessor's premises **—con·ces′sive** (-ses′iv) ***adj.***

con·ces·sion·aire (kən sesh′ə ner′) ***n.*** [Fr. *concessionnaire*] the holder of a concession granted by a government, company, etc.: also **con·ces′sion·er**

con·ces·sion·ar·y (kən sesh′ə ner′ē) ***adj.*** of a concession **—*n.,*** *pl.* **-ar′ies** a concessionaire

conch (käŋk, känch) ***n.,*** *pl.* **conchs** (käŋks), **conch·es** (kän′chəz) [< L. < Gr. *konchē*] **1.** the spiral, one-piece shell of various sea mollusks **2.** such a mollusk, often edible

con·chol·o·gy (käŋ käl′ə jē) ***n.*** [see prec. & -LOGY] the branch of zoology that deals with mollusks and shells **—con·chol′o·gist** ***n.***

con·ci·erge (kän′sē urzh′; *Fr.* kōn syerzh′) ***n.*** [Fr.] **1.** a doorkeeper **2.** a custodian or head porter

con·cil·i·ar (kən sil′ē ər) ***adj.*** [< L. *concilium,* COUNCIL] of, from, or by means of a council

con·cil·i·ate (-āt′) ***vt.*** **-at′ed, -at′ing** [< L. pp. of *conciliare* < *concilium,* COUNCIL] **1.** to win over; make friendly; placate **2.** to gain (regard, good will, etc.) by friendly acts **3.** [Archaic] to reconcile; make consistent **—con·cil′i·a·ble** ***adj.*** **—con·cil′i·a′tion** ***n.*** **—con·cil′i·a′tor** ***n.***

con·cil·i·a·to·ry (-ə tôr′ē) ***adj.*** tending to conciliate or reconcile: also **con·cil′i·a′tive** (-āt′iv)

con·cise (kən sīs′) ***adj.*** [< L. pp. of *concidere* < *com-*, intens. + *caedere,* to cut] brief and to the point; short and clear **—con·cise′ly** ***adv.*** **—con·cise′ness, con·ci′sion** (-sizh′ən) ***n.***

con·clave (kän′klāv, käŋ′-) ***n.*** [OFr. < L., a room, closet < *com-*, with + *clavis,* a key] **1.** *R.C.Ch. a)* the private meeting of the cardinals to elect a pope *b)* the cardinals collectively **2.** any private or secret meeting

con·clude (kən klōōd′) ***vt.*** **-clud′ed, -clud′ing** [< L. *concludere* < *com-*, together + *claudere,* to shut] **1.** to bring to a close; end; finish **2.** to decide by reasoning; infer; deduce **3.** to decide (*to* do something); determine **4.** to settle; come to an agreement about **—*vi.*** **1.** to come to a close; end; finish **2.** to come to an agreement

con·clu·sion (kən klōō′zhən) ***n.*** **1.** the end or last part; as, *a)* the last division of a discourse *b)* the last step in a reasoning process; judgment or opinion formed after thought *c)* the last of a chain of events; outcome **2.** a concluding; final arrangement (*of* a pact, treaty, etc.) **—in conclusion** lastly; in closing

con·clu·sive (-siv) ***adj.*** that settles a question; final; decisive **—con·clu′sive·ly** ***adv.*** **—con·clu′sive·ness** ***n.***

con·coct (kən käkt′, kän-) ***vt.*** [< L. pp. of *concoquere* < *com-*, together + *coquere,* to cook] **1.** to make by combining ingredients **2.** to devise; plan **—con·coct′er** ***n.*** **—con·coc′tion** ***n.*** **—con·coc′tive** ***adj.***

con·com·i·tance (kən käm′ə təns) ***n.*** the fact of being concomitant: also **con·com′i·tan·cy**

con·com·i·tant (-käm′ə tənt) ***adj.*** [< L. prp. of *concomitari* < *com-*, together + *comitari,* to accompany < *comes,* companion] accompanying; attendant **—*n.*** an accompanying or attendant condition, circumstance, or thing **—con·com′i·tant·ly** ***adv.***

Con·cord (kän′kôrd; *for 2 & 3 & n.* käŋ′kərd) [< ?] **1.** city in W Calif., near Oakland: pop. 103,000 **2.** capital of N.H., in the SC part: pop. 30,000 **3.** town in E Mass., near Boston: site of one of the 1st battles of the Revolutionary War: pop. 16,000 **—*n.*** **1.** a large, dark-blue grape: in full, **Concord grape** **2.** a wine made from it

con·cord (kän′kôrd, käŋ′-) ***n.*** [< OFr. < L. < *concors* (gen. *concordis*), of the same mind < *com-*, together + *cor,* heart] **1.** agreement; harmony **2.** *a)* peaceful relations, as between nations *b)* a treaty establishing this **3.** *Gram. same as* AGREEMENT **4.** musical consonance

con·cord·ance (kən kôr′d'ns, kän-) ***n.*** [see CONCORD]

1. agreement; harmony **2.** an alphabetical list of the important words of a book or author, with references to the passages in which they occur

con·cord·ant (-d'nt) ***adj.*** agreeing; consonant; harmonious —**con·cord′ant·ly** ***adv.***

con·cor·dat (-dat) ***n.*** [Fr. < ML. < L. pp. of *concordare,* to agree < *concors:* see CONCORD] **1.** a compact; formal agreement **2.** an agreement between a pope and a government concerning church affairs

con·course (kän′kôrs, käŋ′-) ***n.*** [< OFr. < L. < *concurrere:* see CONCUR] **1.** a coming or flowing together **2.** a crowd; throng **3.** a large open space where crowds gather, as in a park or airport terminal **4.** a broad boulevard

con·crete (kän krēt′; *also, and for n. & vt. 2 usually,* kän′-krēt) ***adj.*** [< L. pp. of *concrescere* < *com-,* together + *crescere,* to grow] **1.** formed into a solid mass; coalesced **2.** having a material, perceptible existence; real; actual **3.** specific, not general or abstract **4.** made of concrete **5.** *Gram.* designating a thing or class of things that can be perceived by the senses; not abstract —***n.*** **1.** a concrete thing, idea, etc. **2.** a building material of sand and gravel bonded with cement into a hard substance: used in making bridges, road surfaces, etc. —***vt.*** **-cret′ed, -cret′ing** **1.** to form into a mass; solidify **2.** to cover with concrete —***vi.*** to solidify —**con·crete′ly** ***adv.*** —**con·crete′ness** ***n.***

con·cre·tion (kän krē′shən) ***n.*** [see prec.] **1.** a solidifying or being solidified **2.** a solidified mass

con·cre·tize (kän′krə tīz′, käŋ′-) ***vt.*** **-tized′, -tiz′ing** to make (something) concrete; make specific

con·cu·bine (käŋ′kyə bīn′, kän′-) ***n.*** [< OFr. < L. < *concumbere* < *com-,* with + *cubare,* to lie down] **1.** a woman who cohabits with a man although not legally married to him **2.** in certain polygamous societies, a secondary wife, of inferior social and legal status —**con·cu·bi·nage** (kän kyo͞o′bə nij) ***n.***

con·cu·pis·cence (kän kyo͞op′ə s'ns) ***n.*** [OFr. < LL. < L. prp. of *concupiscere* < *com-,* intens. + *cupere,* to desire] strong or abnormal desire or appetite, esp. sexual desire; lust —**con·cu′pis·cent** ***adj.***

con·cur (kən kʉr′) ***vi.*** **-curred′, -cur′ring** [< L. *concurrere* < *com-,* together + *currere,* to run] **1.** to occur at the same time; coincide **2.** to act together **3.** to agree (*with*); be in accord (*in* an opinion, etc.)

con·cur·rence (-əns) ***n.*** **1.** a coming or happening together **2.** a combining to bring about something **3.** agreement; accord Also **con·cur′ren·cy**

con·cur·rent (-ənt) ***adj.*** **1.** occurring or existing at the same time **2.** meeting in the same point **3.** acting together **4.** in agreement **5.** *Law* exercised equally over the same area *[concurrent* jurisdiction*]* —**con·cur′rent·ly** ***adv.***

concurrent resolution a resolution passed by one legislative branch and concurred in by the other, without the force of law: cf. JOINT RESOLUTION

con·cuss (kən kus′) ***vt.*** to give a concussion to

con·cus·sion (kən kush′ən) ***n.*** [L. *concussio* < pp. of *concutere* < *com-,* together + *quatere,* to shake] **1.** a violent shaking; agitation; shock, as from impact **2.** *Med.* a condition of impaired functioning, esp. of the brain, as a result of a violent blow or impact —**con·cus′sive** (-kus′iv) ***adj.***

con·demn (kən dem′) ***vt.*** [< OFr. < L. *condemnare* < *com-,* intens. + *damnare,* to harm, condemn] **1.** to disapprove of strongly; censure **2.** *a)* to declare guilty of wrongdoing; convict *b)* to inflict a penalty upon *c)* to doom **3.** to declare (property) legally appropriated for public use **4.** to declare unfit for use or service —**con·dem′na·ble** (-dem′nə b'l, -ə b'l) ***adj.*** —**con·demn′er** ***n.***

con·dem·na·tion (kän′dem nā′shən, -dəm-) ***n.*** **1.** a condemning or being condemned **2.** a cause for condemning —**con·dem·na·to·ry** (kən dem′nə tôr′ē) ***adj.***

con·den·sa·tion (kän′dən sā′shən) ***n.*** **1.** a condensing or being condensed **2.** anything condensed

con·dense (kən dens′) ***vt.*** **-densed′, -dens′ing** [< Fr. < L. < *com-,* intens. + *densus,* dense] **1.** to make more dense or compact; compress **2.** to express in fewer words; make concise; abridge **3.** to change (a substance) to a denser form, as from a gas to a liquid —***vi.*** to become condensed —**con·dens′a·bil′i·ty, con·dens′i·bil′i·ty** ***n.*** —**con·dens′a·ble, con·dens′i·ble** ***adj.***

condensed milk a thick milk made by evaporating part of the water from cow's milk and adding sugar

con·dens·er (kən den′sər) ***n.*** a person or thing that condenses; specif., *a)* an apparatus for liquefying gases or vapors *b)* a lens or series of lenses for concentrating light rays on an area *c)* *Elec. same as* CAPACITOR

con·de·scend (kän′də send′) ***vi.*** [< OFr. < LL. *condescendere* < L. *com-,* together + *descendere,* DESCEND] **1.** to descend voluntarily to the level, regarded as lower, of the person that one is dealing with; deign **2.** to deal with others in a patronizing manner —**con′de·scend′ing** ***adj.*** —**con′de·scen′sion** (-sen′shən), **con′de·scend′ence** ***n.***

con·dign (kən dīn′) ***adj.*** [< OFr. < L. *condignus* < *com-,* intens. + *dignus,* worthy] deserved; suitable: said esp. of punishment —**con·dign′ly** ***adv.***

con·di·ment (kän′də mənt) ***n.*** [< OFr. < L. *condimentum,* a spice < *condire,* to pickle] a seasoning or relish for food, as pepper, mustard, sauces, etc.

con·di·tion (kən dish′ən) ***n.*** [< OFr. < L. *condicio,* agreement < *com-,* together + *dicere,* to speak] **1.** anything required before the performance or completion of something else; provision; stipulation **2.** prerequisite **3.** anything that modifies the nature of something else *[*good business *conditions]* **4.** manner or state of being **5.** *a)* state of health *[*the patient's *condition]* *b)* [Colloq.] an illness; ailment *[*a lung *condition]* **6.** a proper or healthy state *[*athletes out of *condition]* **7.** social position; rank; station **8.** the requirement that a student make up deficiencies in a subject in order to pass it **9.** *Law* a clause in a contract, will, etc. that revokes or modifies a stipulation on certain contingencies —***vt.*** **1.** to set as a requirement; stipulate **2.** to impose a condition or conditions on **3.** to be a condition of; determine **4.** to affect, modify, or influence **5.** to bring into a proper or desired condition **6.** *Psychol. a)* to develop a conditioned reflex or behavior pattern in *b)* to cause to become accustomed (*to*) —**on condition that** provided that —**con·di′tion·er** ***n.***

con·di·tion·al (-'l) ***adj.*** **1.** containing or dependent on a condition; qualified *[*a *conditional* award*]* **2.** expressing a condition *[*a *conditional* clause*]* —***n.*** *Gram.* the mood expressing a condition —**con·di′tion·al′i·ty** (-al′ə tē) ***n.*** —**con·di′tion·al·ly** ***adv.***

conditioned reflex (or **response**) a reflex in which the response (e.g., secretion of saliva in a dog) is occasioned by a secondary stimulus (e.g., the ringing of a bell) repeatedly associated with the primary stimulus (e.g., the sight of meat)

con·do (kän′dō) ***n.,*** *pl.* **-dos, -does** *clipped form of* CONDOMINIUM (sense 2)

con·dole (kən dōl′) ***vi.*** **-doled′, -dol′ing** [< LL. *condolere* < L. *com-,* with + *dolere,* to grieve] to express sympathy; mourn in sympathy —**con·do′la·to′ry** (-dō′lə tôr′ē) ***adj.***

con·do·lence (kən dō′ləns) ***n.*** expression of sympathy with another in grief: also **con·dole′ment**

con·dom (kun′dəm, kän′-) ***n.*** [supposedly after a 17th-c. Brit. colonel] a thin sheath, esp. of rubber, for the penis, used to prevent venereal disease or as a contraceptive

con·do·min·i·um (kän′də min′ē əm) ***n.*** [ModL. < L. *com-,* together + *dominium,* dominion] **1.** joint rule by two or more states **2.** *pl.* **-i·ums, -i·a** (-ə) an apartment building or multiple-unit dwelling in which each tenant holds full title to his unit and joint ownership in the common grounds

con·done (kən dōn′) ***vt.*** **-doned′, -don′ing** [< L. *condonare* < *com-,* intens. + *donare,* to give] to forgive, pardon, or overlook (an offense) —**con·don′a·ble** ***adj.*** —**con·do·na·tion** (kän′dō nā′shən, -də-) ***n.*** —**con·don′er** ***n.***

con·dor (kän′dər) ***n.*** [Sp. < Quechua *cuntur*] **1.** a very large vulture of the S. American Andes, with a bare head and a neck ruff of downy white feathers **2.** a similar vulture of S Calif. **3.** *pl.* **con·dor·es** (kən dô′res) any of various S. American gold coins

CONDOR
(wingspread to 12 ft.)

con·duce (kən do͞os′, -dyo͞os′) ***vi.*** **-duced′, -duc′ing** [< L. *conducere* < *com-,* together + *ducere,* to lead] to tend or lead (*to* an effect); contribute

con·du·cive (-do͞o′siv, -dyo͞o′-) ***adj.*** conducing; tending or leading (*to*) —**con·du′cive·ness** ***n.***

con·duct (kän′dukt′; *for v.* kən dukt′) ***n.*** [< L. pp. of *conducere:* see CONDUCE] **1.** management; handling **2.** the way that one acts; behavior —***vt.*** **1.** to lead; guide; escort **2.** to manage, control, or direct **3.** to direct (an orchestra, choir, etc.) **4.** to behave (oneself) **5.** to be able to transmit *[*copper *conducts* electricity*]* —***vi.*** to act as a conductor —**con·duct′i·bil′i·ty** ***n.*** —**con·duct′i·ble** ***adj.***

con·duct·ance (kən duk′təns) ***n.*** the ability of a component to conduct electricity, measured by the ratio of the current to applied electromotive force

con·duc·tion (kən duk′shən) ***n.*** **1.** a conveying, as of liquid through a channel **2.** the transmission of nerve impulses **3.** *Physics a*) transmission (*of* electricity, heat, etc.) by the passage of energy from particle to particle *b*) *same as* CONDUCTIVITY: see also CONVECTION, RADIATION
con·duc·tive (-tiv) ***adj.*** having conductivity
con·duc·tiv·i·ty (kän′duk tiv′ə tē) ***n.*** the property of conducting heat, electricity, etc.
con·duc·tor (kən duk′tər) ***n.*** **1.** a person who conducts; leader; guide **2.** the director of an orchestra, choir, etc. **3.** one who has charge of the passengers and collects fares on a train, streetcar, or bus **4.** a thing that conducts electricity, heat, etc. —**con·duc·to·ri·al** (kən duk′tôr′ē əl) ***adj.*** —**con·duc′tor·ship′** ***n.*** —**con·duc′tress** ***n.fem.***
con·duit (kän′dit, -do͞o wit) ***n.*** [< OFr. < L. pp. of *conducere:* see CONDUCE] **1.** a pipe or channel for conveying fluids **2.** a tube or protected trough for electric wires
con·dyle (kän′dīl, -dil) ***n.*** [Fr. < L. < Gr. *kondylos,* knuckle] a rounded process at the end of a bone —**con′dy·lar** (-də lər) ***adj.*** —**con′dy·loid** (-də loid) ***adj.***
cone (kōn) ***n.*** [< L. < Gr. *kōnos*] **1.** *a*) a solid with a circle for its base and a curved surface tapering evenly to a point *b*) a surface described by a moving straight line passing through a fixed point and tracing a fixed curve, as a circle or ellipse, at another point **2.** any object shaped like a cone, as a shell of pastry for holding ice cream, the peak of a volcano, etc. **3.** a reproductive structure of certain lower plants, with an elongated central axis bearing overlapping scales, bracts, etc. which produce pollen, spores, or ovules **4.** *Zool.* any of the flask-shaped cells in the retina, sensitive to light and color —***vt.*** **coned, con′ing** to shape like a cone

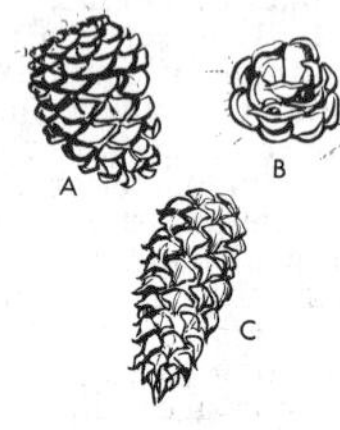

CONES
(A, longleaf pine; B, piñon; C, blue spruce)

Con·es·to·ga wagon (kän′ə stō′gə) [after *Conestoga* Valley, Pa.] a broad-wheeled covered wagon used by American pioneers crossing the prairies
co·ney (kō′nē) ***n.,*** *pl.* **-neys, -nies** [< OFr. < L. *cuniculus,* rabbit] **1.** a rabbit **2.** rabbit fur **3.** *Bible* a small animal, probably the hyrax **4.** *same as* PIKA
Co·ney Island (kō′nē) [< Du. *Konynen Eyland,* rabbit island] beach & amusement park in Brooklyn, N.Y., at the SW end of Long Island
conf. **1.** conference **2.** confessor
con·fab (kän′fab′; *for v., usually* kən fab′) ***n.*** [Colloq.] a confabulation —***vi.*** **-fabbed′, -fab′bing** [Colloq.] to confabulate
con·fab·u·late (kən fab′yə lāt′) ***vi.*** **-lat′ed, -lat′ing** [< L. pp. of *confabulari* < *com-,* together + *fabulari,* to talk: see FABLE] **1.** to talk together informally; chat **2.** to recount fictitious events as if they really occurred —**con·fab′u·la′tion** ***n.***
con·fect (kən fekt′) ***vt.*** [< L. pp. of *conficere* < *com-,* with + *facere,* to make, do] to prepare or make, esp. by mixing or combining
con·fec·tion (kən fek′shən) ***n.*** **1.** a confecting **2.** any candy or other sweet preparation, as ice cream **3.** a frivolous piece of work **4.** a fancy article of women's clothing —**con·fec′tion·ar′y** ***adj.***
con·fec·tion·er (-ər) ***n.*** one whose work or business is making or selling confectionery
confectioners' sugar very fine powdered sugar
con·fec·tion·er·y (-er′ē) ***n.,*** *pl.* **-er′ies** **1.** confections or candy, collectively **2.** the business, work, or shop of a confectioner
con·fed·er·a·cy (kən fed′ər ə sē) ***n.,*** *pl.* **-cies** [see ff.] **1.** people, nations, etc. united for some common purpose **2.** a league or alliance formed by such a union; federation **3.** a conspiracy —**the Confederacy** the league of Southern States that seceded from the U.S. in 1860 & 1861: official name **Confederate States of America**
con·fed·er·ate (kən fed′ər it; *for v.* -ə rāt′) ***adj.*** [< LL. pp. of *confoederare,* to unite by a league < *foedus,* a league] **1.** united in a confederacy or league **2.** [C-] of the Confederacy —***n.*** **1.** a person, group, or state united with another or others for a common purpose; ally **2.** an associate in crime; accomplice **3.** [C-] any Southern supporter of the Confederacy —***vt., vi.*** **-at′ed, -at′ing** to unite in a confederacy; ally
con·fed·er·a·tion (kən fed′ə rā′shən) ***n.*** **1.** a uniting or being united in a league or alliance **2.** nations or states joined in a league, as for common defense —**the Confederation** the United States of America (1781–1789) under the **Articles of Confederation,** the constitution of the 13 original States —**con·fed′er·al** ***adj.*** —**con·fed′er·a′tive** ***adj.***
con·fer (kən fur′) ***vt.*** **-ferred′, -fer′ring** [< L. *conferre* < *com-,* together + *ferre,* to BEAR[1]] to give, grant, or bestow —***vi.*** to have a conference; meet for discussion —**con·fer′ment, con·fer′ral** ***n.*** —**con·fer′ra·ble** ***adj.*** —**con·fer′rer** ***n.***
con·fer·ee (kän′fə rē′) ***n.*** **1.** a participant in a conference **2.** a person on whom an honor, degree, favor, etc. is conferred
con·fer·ence (kän′fər əns, -frəns) ***n.*** **1.** a conversing or consulting on a serious matter **2.** a formal meeting of a group for discussion or consultation, as of committees of legislative branches to reconcile differences between their bills **3.** [*often* **C-**] the governing body of some churches **4.** an association, as of colleges or athletic teams —**con·fer·en·tial** (kän′fə ren′shəl) ***adj.***
con·fess (kən fes′) ***vt.*** [< OFr. < L. pp. of *confiteri* < *com-,* together + *fateri,* to acknowledge] **1.** *a*) to admit (a fault, crime, etc.) *b*) to acknowledge (an opinion, etc.) **2.** to declare one's faith in **3.** *Eccles. a*) to tell (one's sins) to God, in worship service or in private *b*) to hear the confession of (a person): said of a priest —***vi.*** **1.** to admit a fault or crime **2.** *a*) to make one's confession *b*) to hear confessions: said of a priest —**confess to** to admit or admit having —**stand confessed as** to be revealed as
con·fess·ed·ly (-id lē) ***adv.*** admittedly
con·fes·sion (kən fesh′ən) ***n.*** **1.** a confessing; admission of guilt or sin; specif., a confessing of sins in the sacrament of penance **2.** something confessed **3.** *a*) a statement of religious beliefs: in full, **confession of faith** *b*) a church having such a confession; communion
con·fes·sion·al (-'l) ***n.*** a small, enclosed place in a church, where a priest hears confessions —***adj.*** of or for a confession
con·fes·sor (kən fes′ər) ***n.*** **1.** one who confesses **2.** *R.C.Ch.* a male saint who was not a martyr **3.** a priest authorized to hear confessions
con·fet·ti (kən fet′ē) ***n.pl.*** [*with sing. v.*] [It., pl. of *confetto,* sweetmeat: candies were formerly so scattered] bits of colored paper scattered about at carnivals and other celebrations
con·fi·dant (kän′fə dant′, -dänt′; kän′fə dant′, -dänt′) ***n.*** a close, trusted friend to whom one confides personal secrets —**con′fi·dante′** ***n.fem.***
con·fide (kən fīd′) ***vi.*** **-fid′ed, -fid′ing** [L. *confidere* < *com-,* intens. + *fidere,* to trust] to trust (*in* someone), esp. by sharing secrets or discussing private affairs —***vt.*** **1.** to tell or talk about as a secret [to *confide* one's troubles to a friend] **2.** to entrust (a duty, person, etc.) *to* someone —**con·fid′er** ***n.***
con·fi·dence (kän′fə dəns) ***n.*** **1.** firm belief; trust; reliance **2.** certainty; assurance **3.** belief in one's own abilities; self-confidence **4.** a relationship as confidant [take me into your *confidence*] **5.** the belief that another will keep a secret [told in strict *confidence*] **6.** something told as a secret —***adj.*** swindling or used to swindle
confidence game a swindle effected by one (**confidence man**) who first gains the confidence of his victim
con·fi·dent (-dənt) ***adj.*** full of confidence; specif., *a*) assured; certain [*confident* of victory] *b*) sure of oneself; self-confident; bold [a *confident* boy] —***n.*** *same as* CONFIDANT —**con′fi·dent·ly** ***adv.***
con·fi·den·tial (kän′fə den′shəl) ***adj.*** **1.** told in confidence; secret **2.** of or showing confidence **3.** entrusted with private or secret matters [a *confidential* agent] —**con′fi·den′tial·ly** ***adv.***
con·fid·ing (kən fīd′iŋ) ***adj.*** trustful or inclined to trust —**con·fid′ing·ly** ***adv.***
con·fig·u·ra·tion (kən fig′yə rā′shən) ***n.*** [< L. *configurare* < *com-,* together + *figurare:* see FIGURE] **1.** arrangement of parts **2.** form, contour, or structure as determined by the arrangement of parts —**con·fig′u·ra′tion·al** ***adj.*** —**con·fig′u·ra′tive** ***adj.***
con·fine (kən fīn′; *for n.* kän′fīn′) ***n.*** [< OFr. < L. *confinium,* boundary < *com-,* with + *finis,* an end, limit] [*usually pl.*] a boundary or bounded region; border; limit —***vt.*** **-fined′, -fin′ing** **1.** to keep within limits; restrict [to *confine* a talk to ten minutes] **2.** to keep shut up, as in prison, in bed because of illness, indoors, etc. —**be confined** to be undergoing childbirth —**con·fin′a·ble, con·fine′a·ble** ***adj.***
con·fine·ment (kən fīn′mənt) ***n.*** a confining or being confined; specif., *a*) imprisonment *b*) restriction; restraint *c*) childbirth; lying-in
con·firm (kən furm′) ***vt.*** [< OFr. < L. *confirmare* < *com-,* intens. + *firmare* < *firmus,* firm] **1.** to make firm; strengthen; establish **2.** to make valid by formal approval; ratify **3.** to prove the truth or validity of; verify **4.** to cause to undergo religious confirmation —**con·firm′a·ble** ***adj.***
con·fir·ma·tion (kän′fər mā′shən) ***n.*** **1.** a confirming or being confirmed; ratification; verification **2.** something that confirms or proves **3.** *a*) a Christian ceremony admitting a person to full church membership *b*) a Jewish ceremony in which young people reaffirm their belief in Judaism

con·firm·a·to·ry (kən fʉr′mə tôr′ē) ***adj.*** confirming or tending to confirm: also **con·firm′a·tive**

con·firmed (-fʉrmd′) ***adj.*** **1.** firmly established, as in a habit or condition *[a confirmed liar]* **2.** chronic, as a disease **3.** corroborated **4.** having accepted religious confirmation —**con·firm′ed·ly** ***adv.***

con·fis·cate (kän′fə skāt′) ***vt.*** **-cat′ed, -cat′ing** [< L. pp. of *confiscare*, to lay up in a chest < *com-*, together + *fiscus*, money chest, treasury] **1.** to seize (private property) for the public treasury, usually as a penalty **2.** to seize as by authority; appropriate —**con′fis·ca′tion** ***n.*** —**con′fis·ca′tor** ***n.***

con·fis·ca·to·ry (kən fis′kə tôr′ē) ***adj.*** **1.** of, constituting, or effecting confiscation *[a confiscatory tax]* **2.** confiscating

con·fit·e·or (kən fit′ē ôr′) ***n.*** [< LL., I confess] a formal prayer in which sins are confessed

con·fla·gra·tion (kän′flə grā′shən) ***n.*** [< L. < pp. of *conflagrare* < *com-*, intens. + *flagrare*, to burn] a big, destructive fire

con·flict (kən flikt′; *for n.* kän′flikt) ***vi.*** [< L. pp. of *confligere* < *com-*, together + *fligere*, to strike] **1.** orig., to fight **2.** to be antagonistic, incompatible, or contradictory; clash —***n.*** **1.** a fight or struggle **2.** sharp disagreement or opposition, as of interests or ideas **3.** emotional disturbance resulting from opposing impulses —**con·flic′tion** ***n.*** —**con·flic′tive** ***adj.***

conflict of interest a conflict between one's obligation to the public and one's self-interest, as in the case of an elected official who owns stock in a company seeking government contracts

con·flu·ence (kän′flo͞o əns) ***n.*** [OFr. < LL. < L. prp. of *confluere* < *com-*, together + *fluere*, to flow] **1.** a flowing together, esp. of two or more streams **2.** the place where they join, or a stream formed in this way **3.** a coming together as of people; crowd; throng —**con′flu·ent** ***adj.***

con·form (kən fôrm′) ***vt.*** [< OFr. < L. *conformare* < *com-*, together + *formare*, to FORM] **1.** to make the same or similar **2.** to bring into harmony or agreement; adapt —***vi.*** **1.** to be or become the same or similar **2.** to be in accord or agreement **3.** to accept without question customs, traditions, prevailing opinion, etc. —**con·form′er** ***n.*** —**con·form′ism** ***n.*** —**con·form′ist** ***n.***

con·form·a·ble (-fôr′mə b'l) ***adj.*** **1.** that conforms; specif., *a)* similar *b)* in harmony or agreement *c)* suited; adapted **2.** quick to conform; obedient; submissive —**con·form′a·bil′i·ty** ***n.*** —**con·form′a·bly** ***adv.***

con·for·mal (-fôr′m'l) ***adj.*** [< LL. < L.: see CONFORM] designating or of a map projection in which shapes at any point are true, but areas become increasingly exaggerated

con·form·ance (-fôr′məns) ***n.*** *same as* CONFORMITY

con·for·ma·tion (kän′fôr mā′shən) ***n.*** **1.** a symmetrical formation and arrangement of the parts of a thing **2.** the structure or form of a thing as determined by the arrangement of its parts

con·form·i·ty (kən fôr′mə tē) ***n.***, *pl.* **-ties** **1.** the condition or fact of being in harmony or agreement; correspondence; similarity **2.** action in accordance with customs, rules, popular opinion, etc.

con·found (kən found′, kän-; *for 3, usually* kän′-) ***vt.*** [< OFr. < L. *confundere* < *com-*, together + *fundere*, to pour] **1.** to mix up or lump together indiscriminately; confuse **2.** to make feel confused; bewilder **3.** to damn: used as a mild oath **4.** [Archaic] to defeat or destroy

con·found·ed (-id) ***adj.*** **1.** confused; bewildered **2.** damned: a mild oath —**con·found′ed·ly** ***adv.***

con·fra·ter·ni·ty (kän′frə tʉr′nə tē) ***n.***, *pl.* **-ties** [< ML.: see COM- & FRATERNITY] **1.** brotherhood **2.** a group of men associated for some purpose, often religious

con·frere (kän′frer, kōn′-) ***n.*** [OFr. *confrère*] a fellow member or worker; colleague

con·front (kən frunt′) ***vt.*** [Fr. < ML. *confrontare* < L. *com-*, together + *frons*, forehead, front] **1.** to stand or meet face to face **2.** to face or oppose boldly or defiantly **3.** to bring face to face (*with*) *[to confront one with the facts]* —**con·fron·ta·tion** (kän′frən tā′shən), **con·front′al** ***n.***

Con·fu·cian·ism (kən fyo͞o′shən iz'm) ***n.*** the ethical teachings of Confucius, emphasizing devotion to parents, ancestor worship, and the maintenance of justice and peace —**Con·fu′cian·ist** ***n., adj.***

Con·fu·cius (kən fyo͞o′shəs) (L. name of *K'ung Fu-tse*) 551?–479? B.C.; Chin. philosopher & teacher —**Con·fu′cian** (-shən) ***adj. n.***

con·fuse (kən fyo͞oz′) ***vt.*** **-fused′, -fus′ing** [< OFr. < L. pp. of *confundere:* see CONFOUND] **1.** to mix up; jumble together; put into disorder **2.** to mix up mentally; specif., *a)* to bewilder; perplex *b)* to embarrass; disconcert *c)* to fail to distinguish between; mistake the identity of —**con·fus′ed·ly** (-fyo͞oz′id lē) ***adv.*** —**con·fus′ed·ness** ***n.*** —**con·fus′ing** ***adj.*** —**con·fus′ing·ly** ***adv.***

con·fu·sion (kən fyo͞o′zhən) ***n.*** a confusing or being confused; specif., *a)* state of disorder *b)* bewilderment *c)* embarrassment *d)* failure to distinguish between things —**covered with confusion** greatly embarrassed —**con·fu′sion·al** ***adj.***

con·fute (kən fyo͞ot′) ***vt.*** **-fut′ed, -fut′ing** [L. *confutare*] to prove (a person, statement, etc.) to be in error or false; overcome by argument or proof —**con·fu·ta·tion** (kän′fyoo tā′shən) ***n.*** —**con·fu′ta·tive** ***adj.*** —**con·fut′er** ***n.***

Cong. **1.** Congress **2.** Congressional

con·ga (käŋ′gə) ***n.*** [AmSp., ult. < CONGO] **1.** a Latin American dance in which the dancers form a winding line **2.** music for this dance, in 4/4 syncopated time —***vi.*** to dance the conga

con·gé (kän′zhā, -jā′; *Fr.* kōn zhā′) ***n.*** [Fr. < OFr. < L. < *com-*, intens. + *meare*, to go] **1.** a dismissal **2.** permission to leave **3.** a formal farewell

con·geal (kən jēl′) ***vt., vi.*** [< OFr. < L. *congelare* < *com-*, together + *gelare*, to freeze] **1.** to solidify or thicken by cooling or freezing **2.** to thicken; coagulate; jell —**con·geal′a·ble** ***adj.*** —**con·geal′ment** ***n.***

con·gen·er (kän′jə nər) ***n.*** [L. < *com-*, together + *genus* (gen. *generis*), race, kind] a person or thing of the same kind, class, genus, etc. —**con′ge·ner′ic** (-ner′ik), **con·gen·er·ous** (kən jen′ər əs) ***adj.***

con·gen·ial (kən jēn′yəl) ***adj.*** [see COM- & GENIAL] **1.** kindred; compatible **2.** having the same tastes and temperament; sympathetic *[congenial friends]* **3.** suited to one's needs or disposition; agreeable *[congenial work]* —**con·ge′ni·al′i·ty** (-jēn′ē al′ə tē) ***n.*** —**con·gen′ial·ly** ***adv.***

con·gen·i·tal (kən jen′ə t'l) ***adj.*** [< L.: see COM- & GENITAL] **1.** existing as such at birth; resulting from one's prenatal environment *[a congenital disease]* **2.** existing as if inborn; inherent *[a congenital cheerfulness]* —**con·gen′i·tal·ly** ***adv.***

con·ger (eel) (käŋ′gər) [< OFr. < L. < Gr. *gongros*] a large, edible saltwater eel

con·ge·ries (kän′jə rēz′, kän jir′ēz) ***n.***, *pl.* **con′ge·ries′** [see ff.] a collection of things or parts massed together; heap; pile

con·gest (kən jest′) ***vt.*** [< L. pp. of *congerere*, to pile up < *com-*, together + *gerere*, to carry] **1.** to cause too much blood to accumulate in the vessels of (a part of the body) **2.** to fill to excess; overcrowd; clog *[a congested highway]* —***vi.*** to become congested —**con·ges′tion** (-jes′chən) ***n.*** —**con·ges′tive** (-tiv) ***adj.***

con·glom·er·ate (kən gläm′ə rāt′; *for adj. & n.* -ər it) ***vt., vi.*** **-at′ed, -at′ing** [< L. pp. of *conglomerare* < *com-*, together + *glomerare* < *glomus*, a ball] to form or collect into a rounded or compact mass —***adj.*** **1.** formed into a rounded or compact mass; clustered **2.** made up of separate substances collected into a single mass **3.** *Geol.* made up of rock fragments or pebbles cemented together by clay, silica, etc.: also **con·glom′er·at′ic** (-ə rat′ik), **con·glom′er·it′ic** (-ə rit′ik) —***n.*** **1.** a conglomerate mass; cluster **2.** a large corporation formed by merging many diverse companies **3.** *Geol.* a conglomerate rock —**con·glom′er·a′tion** ***n.***

CONGLOMERATE ROCK

Con·go (käŋ′gō) **1.** river in C Africa, flowing through Zaire into the Atlantic **2.** country in WC Africa, west of Zaire: 132,046 sq. mi.; pop. 826,000; cap. Brazzaville **3.** *former name of* ZAIRE —**Con′go·lese′** (-gə lēz′) ***adj., n.***

congo eel (or **snake**) an eellike amphibious animal with two pairs of small, weak legs, of the SE U.S.

con·grat·u·late (kən grach′ə lāt′) ***vt.*** **-lat′ed, -lat′ing** [< L. pp. of *congratulari* < *com-*, together + *gratulari*, to wish joy < *gratus*, agreeable] to express to (a person) one's pleasure at his good fortune, success, etc. —**con·grat′u·la′tor** ***n.*** —**con·grat′u·la·to′ry** (-lə tôr′ē) ***adj.***

con·grat·u·la·tion (kən grach′ə lā′shən) ***n.*** **1.** a congratulating **2.** [*pl.*] expressions of pleasure and good wishes at another's fortune or success

con·gre·gate (käŋ′grə gāt′; *for adj.* -git) ***vt., vi.*** **-gat′ed, -gat′ing** [< L. pp. of *congregare* < *com-*, together + *gregare*, to gather < *grex*, a flock] to gather into a mass or crowd; collect; assemble —***adj.*** **1.** assembled; collected **2.** collective —**con′gre·ga′tive** ***adj.*** —**con′gre·ga′tor** ***n.***

con·gre·ga·tion (käŋ′grə gā′shən) ***n.*** **1.** a congregating or being congregated **2.** a gathering of people or things; assemblage **3.** an assembly of people for religious worship

fat, āpe, cär; ten, ēven; is, bīte; gō, hôrn, to͞ol, look; oil, out; up, fʉr; get; joy; yet; chin; she; thin, *th*en; zh, leisure; ŋ, ring; ə for *a* in *ago*, *e* in *agent*, *i* in *sanity*, *o* in *comply*, *u* in *focus*; ' as in *able* (ā′b'l); Fr. bål; ë, Fr. coeur; ö, Fr. feu; Fr. mo*n*; ô, Fr. coq; ü, Fr. duc; *r*, Fr. cri; H, G. ich; kh, G. doch; ‡foreign; *hypothetical; < derived from. See inside front cover.

4. the members of a particular place of worship **5.** *R.C.Ch.* a religious community not necessarily under solemn vows but bound by a common rule

con·gre·ga·tion·al (-'l) *adj.* **1.** of or like a congregation **2.** [C-] of Congregationalism or Congregationalists

con·gre·ga·tion·al·ism (-'l iz'm) *n.* **1.** a form of church organization in which each local congregation is self-governing **2.** [C-] the faith and form of organization of a Protestant denomination in which each member church is self-governing —**Con'gre·ga'tion·al·ist** *n., adj.*

con·gress (käŋ'grəs) *n.* [< L. pp. of *congredi* < *com-*, together + *gradi,* to walk < *gradus,* a step] **1.** a coming together; meeting **2.** an association or society **3.** an assembly or conference **4.** any of various legislatures, esp. the national legislature of a republic **5.** [C-] *a)* the legislature of the U.S., consisting of the Senate and the House of Representatives *b)* its session *c)* the body of Senators and Representatives during any of the two-year terms of Representatives

con·gres·sion·al (kən gresh'ən 'l) *adj.* **1.** of a congress **2.** [C-] of Congress —**con·gres'sion·al·ly** *adv.*

Congressional district any of the districts into which a State is divided for electing Congressmen

con·gress·man (käŋ'grəs mən) *n., pl.* **-men** [*often* **C-**] a member of Congress, esp. of the House of Representatives —**con'gress·wom'an** *n.fem.* (a former usage)

Con·greve (kän'grēv, käŋ'-), **William** 1670–1729; Eng. Restoration playwright

con·gru·ence (käŋ'groo wəns, kən groo'əns) *n.* [see ff.] **1.** the state or quality of being in agreement; harmony **2.** *Math.* the relation between two numbers each of which, when divided by a third, leaves the same remainder Also **con'gru·en·cy**

con·gru·ent (-wənt, -ənt) *adj.* [< L. prp. of *congruere,* to come together, agree] **1.** in agreement; harmonious **2.** *Geom.* of the same shape and size **3.** *Math.* in congruence [*congruent* numbers] —**con'gru·ent·ly** *adv.*

con·gru·i·ty (kən groo'ə tē) *n., pl.* **-ties** **1.** the condition or fact of being congruous or congruent; specif., *a)* agreement; harmony *b)* appropriateness *c) Geom.* exact coincidence (of two or more figures) **2.** an instance of agreement

con·gru·ous (käŋ'groo wəs) *adj.* **1.** *same as* CONGRUENT **2.** corresponding to what is right, proper, or reasonable; fitting; suitable; appropriate —**con'gru·ous·ly** *adv.* —**con'gru·ous·ness** *n.*

con·ic (kän'ik) *adj. same as* CONICAL —*n. same as* CONIC SECTION

con·i·cal (-i k'l) *adj.* **1.** of a cone **2.** resembling or shaped like a cone —**con'i·cal·ly** *adv.*

conic section a curve, as an ellipse, circle, parabola, or hyperbola, produced by the intersection of a plane with a right circular cone

co·nid·i·um (kə nid'ē əm) *n., pl.* **-i·a** (-ə) [ModL. < Gr. *konis,* dust] a small asexual spore of certain fungi —**co·nid'i·al, co·nid'i·an** *adj.*

co·ni·fer (kän'ə fər, kō'nə-) *n.* [L. < *conus,* a cone + *ferre,* to BEAR[1]] any of an order of cone-bearing trees and shrubs, mostly evergreens, as the pine, spruce, fir, cedar, yew, etc. —**co·nif·er·ous** (kə nif'ər əs) *adj.*

conj. **1.** conjugation **2.** conjunction

con·jec·tur·al (kən jek'chər əl) *adj.* based on or involving conjecture —**con·jec'tur·al·ly** *adv.*

con·jec·ture (kən jek'chər) *n.* [< L. *conjectura* < pp. of *conjicere,* to guess < *com-,* together + *jacere,* to throw] **1.** an inferring, theorizing, or predicting from incomplete evidence; guesswork **2.** an inference, theory, or prediction based on guesswork; guess —*vt., vi.* **-tured, -tur·ing** to arrive at or propose (something) by conjecture; guess —**con·jec'tur·a·ble** *adj.* —**con·jec'tur·er** *n.*

con·join (kən join') *vt., vi.* [< OFr. < L. *conjungere* < *com-,* together + *jungere,* to join] to join together; unite; combine —**con·join'er** *n.*

con·joint (-joint') *adj.* [see prec.] **1.** joined together; united; combined **2.** of or involving two or more in association; joint —**con·joint'ly** *adv.*

con·ju·gal (kän'jə gəl, kən joo'-) *adj.* [< L. < *conjunx,* spouse < *com-,* together + base akin to *jugum,* yoke] of marriage or the relation between husband and wife; matrimonial —**con'ju·gal'i·ty** (-jə gal'ə tē) *n.* —**con'ju·gal·ly** *adv.*

con·ju·gate (kän'jə gət; *also, and for v. always,* -gāt') *adj.* [< L. pp. of *conjugare* < *com-,* together + *jugare,* to join < *jugum,* a yoke] **1.** joined together, esp. in a pair; coupled **2.** *Gram.* derived from the same base and, usually, related in meaning —*n.* a conjugate word —*vt.* **-gat'ed, -gat'ing** **1.** [Archaic] to join together; couple **2.** *Gram.* to inflect (a verb) systematically, according to voice, mood, tense, number, and person —*vi. Gram.* **1.** to conjugate a verb **2.** to be conjugated —**con'ju·ga'tive** *adj.* —**con'ju·ga'tor** *n.*

con·ju·ga·tion (kän'jə gā'shən) *n.* **1.** a conjugating or being conjugated; union **2.** *Gram. a)* a methodical presentation or arrangement of the inflectional forms of a verb *b)* a class of verbs with similar inflectional forms —**con'ju·ga'tion·al** *adj.* —**con'ju·ga'tion·al·ly** *adv.*

con·junc·tion (kən juŋk'shən) *n.* [see CONJOIN] **1.** a joining together or being joined together; union; combination **2.** coincidence **3.** *Astrol., Astron. a)* the apparent closeness of two or more heavenly bodies *b)* the condition of being in the same celestial longitude [planets in *conjunction*] **4.** *Gram.* an uninflected word used to connect words, phrases, clauses, or sentences; connective: conjunctions may be coordinating (e.g., *and, but, or*), subordinating (e.g., *if, when, as, because, though*), or correlative (e.g., *either . . . or, both . . . and*) —**con·junc'tion·al** *adj.* —**con·junc'tion·al·ly** *adv.*

con·junc·ti·va (kän'jəŋk tī'və, kən juŋk'ti və) *n., pl.* **-vas, -vae** (-vē) [< ModL. (*membrana*) *conjunctiva,* connecting (membrane)] the mucous membrane lining the inner surface of the eyelids and covering the front part of the eyeball —**con'junc·ti'val** *adj.*

con·junc·tive (kən juŋk'tiv) *adj.* **1.** serving to join together; connective **2.** united; combined; joint **3.** *Gram.* used as a conjunction [*a conjunctive* adverb] —*n. Gram.* a conjunctive word; esp., a conjunction —**con·junc'tive·ly** *adv.*

con·junc·ti·vi·tis (kən juŋk'tə vīt'is) *n.* [see -ITIS] inflammation of the conjunctiva

con·junc·ture (kən juŋk'chər) *n.* [< ML.: see CONJOIN] **1.** [Rare] a joining or being joined together **2.** a combination of events or circumstances, esp. one creating a critical situation; crisis

con·ju·ra·tion (kän'jə rā'shən) *n.* **1.** a conjuring; invocation **2.** a magic spell; incantation

con·jure (kän'jər, kun'-; *for vt. 1* kən joor') *vi.* **-jured, -jur·ing** [< OFr. < L. *conjurare* < *com-,* together + *jurare,* to swear] **1.** to summon a demon, spirit, etc. by a magic spell **2.** to practice magic —*vt.* **1.** to appeal to or entreat solemnly **2.** to summon (a devil, etc.) by a magic spell —**conjure away** to cause to go away as by magic —**conjure up** **1.** to cause to appear as by magic **2.** to call to mind [the music *conjured up* memories]

con·jur·er, con·ju·ror (kän'jər ər, kun'-; *for 1* kən joor'ər) *n.* **1.** one who solemnly entreats someone **2.** a magician **3.** one skilled in legerdemain

conk (käŋk, kôŋk) *n.* [< CONCH] [Slang] a blow on the head —*vt.* [Slang] to hit on the head —**conk out** [Slang] **1.** to fail suddenly in operation **2.** to become very tired and, usually, fall asleep

con man [Slang] *same as* CONFIDENCE MAN

conn (kän) *vt.* **conned, con'ning** [< OFr. < L. *conducere:* see CONDUCE] *Naut.* to direct the course of (a vessel) —*n.* the act of conning

Conn. Connecticut

con·nect (kə nekt') *vt.* [< L. *connectere* < *com-,* together + *nectere,* to fasten] **1.** to join (two things together, or one thing *with* or *to* another); link; couple **2.** to show or think of as related; associate **3.** to plug into an electrical circuit —*vi.* **1.** to be joined or be related **2.** to meet so that passengers can change to another bus, airplane, etc. **3.** [Colloq.] *Sports* to hit a ball, target, etc. solidly —**con·nec'tor, con·nect'er** *n.*

Con·nect·i·cut (kə net'ə kət) [< Algonquian, lit., place of the long river] New England State of the U.S.: 5,009 sq. mi.; pop. 3,108,000; cap. Hartford: abbrev. **Conn., CT**

connecting rod a rod connecting by reciprocating motion two or more moving parts of a machine, as the crankshaft and a piston of an automobile

con·nec·tion (kə nek'shən) *n.* **1.** a joining or being joined; coupling; union **2.** a thing that joins; means of joining **3.** a relation; association; coherence **4.** *a)* a relative, esp. by marriage *b)* a business associate, friend, etc., esp. an influential one: *usually used in pl.* **5.** [*usually pl.*] the act or means of transferring from one bus, airplane, etc. to another **6.** a group of people associated in politics, business, etc. **7.** *Elec.* a circuit —**in connection with** **1.** together with; in conjunction with **2.** with reference to —**con·nec'tion·al** *adj.*

con·nec·tive (kə nek'tiv) *adj.* connecting or serving to connect —*n.* something that connects, esp. a word that connects words, phrases, or clauses, as a conjunction or relative pronoun —**con·nec'tive·ly** *adv.* —**con·nec·tiv·i·ty** (kän'ek tiv'ə tē) *n.*

connective tissue body tissue that connects and supports other tissues and organs in the body

conn·ing tower (kän'iŋ) [prp. of CONN] **1.** an armored pilothouse on the deck of a warship **2.** on submarines, a low observation tower serving also as an entrance to the interior

con·nip·tion (fit) (kə nip'shən) [pseudo-Latin] [Colloq.] [*often pl.*] a fit of anger, hysteria, etc.

con·niv·ance (kə nī'vəns) *n.* a conniving; esp., passive cooperation, as by consent or pretended ignorance, esp. in wrongdoing

con·nive (kə nīv′) ***vi.*** **-nived′, -niv′ing** [< L. *conivere,* to wink, connive] **1.** to pretend not to see or look (*at* something wrong or evil), thus giving tacit consent or cooperation **2.** *a)* to cooperate secretly (*with* someone), esp. in wrongdoing *b)* to scheme underhandedly —**con·niv′er** ***n.***

con·nois·seur (kän′ə sʉr′, -so͞or′) ***n.*** [< Fr. < OFr. < L. *cognoscere,* to know: see COGNITION] one who has expert knowledge and keen discrimination in some field, esp. in the fine arts

con·no·ta·tion (kän′ə tā′shən) ***n.*** **1.** the act or process of connoting **2.** an idea suggested by or associated with a word, phrase, etc. in addition to its explicit meaning —**con·no·ta·tive** (kän′ə tāt′iv, kə nōt′ə tiv), **con′no·ta′tion·al** ***adj.*** —**con′no·ta′tive·ly** ***adv.***

con·note (kə nōt′) ***vt.*** **-not′ed, -not′ing** [< ML. *connotare* < L. *com-,* together + *notare,* to mark: see NOTE] **1.** to suggest or convey (associations, overtones, etc.) in addition to the explicit, or denoted, meaning **2.** to imply or involve

con·nu·bi·al (kə no͞o′bē əl, -nyo͞o′-) ***adj.*** [< L. < *conubium,* marriage < *com-,* together + *nubere,* to marry] of marriage or the state of being married; conjugal —**con·nu′bi·al′i·ty** (-bē al′ə tē) ***n.*** —**con·nu′bi·al·ly** ***adv.***

co·noid (kō′noid) ***adj.*** cone-shaped: also **co·noi′dal**

con·quer (käŋ′kər) ***vt.*** [< OFr. < VL. *conquarere* < L. *com-,* intens. + *quaerere,* to seek] **1.** to get possession or control of by or as by winning a war **2.** to overcome by physical, mental, or moral force; defeat —***vi.*** to be victorious; win —**con′quer·a·ble** ***adj.*** —**con′quer·or** ***n.***

con·quest (käŋ′kwest, kän′-) ***n.*** [< OFr. < ML. < L. pp. of *conquirere,* to procure] **1.** the act of conquering **2.** something conquered **3.** *a)* a winning of someone's love *b)* one whose love has been won

con·quis·ta·dor (kän kwis′tə dôr′, -kēs′-; käŋ-) ***n.,*** *pl.* **-dors′, -dores′** [Sp., conqueror] any of the Spanish conquerors of Mexico, Peru, or other parts of America in the 16th century

Con·rad (kän′rad) [< G. or Fr. < OHG. < *kuon,* bold, wise + *rat,* counsel] **1.** a masculine name **2. Joseph,** (born *Józef Teodor Konrad Naellecz Korzeniowski*) 1857–1924; Eng. novelist, born in Poland

cons. 1. consolidated **2.** consonant **3.** consulting

cons., Cons. 1. constitution **2.** consul

con·san·guin·e·ous (kän′saŋ gwin′ē əs, -san-) ***adj.*** [see COM- & SANGUINE] having the same ancestor; closely related: also **con·san′guine** (-saŋ′gwin) —**con′san·guin′e·ous·ly** ***adv.*** —**con′san·guin′i·ty** ***n.***

con·science (kän′shəns) ***n.*** [OFr. < L. < prp. of *conscire* < *com-,* with + *scire,* to know] a knowledge or sense of right and wrong, with a compulsion to do right; moral judgment that keeps one from violating one's ethical principles —**in (all) conscience** in fairness —**on one's conscience** causing one to feel guilty —**con′science·less** ***adj.***

conscience money money one pays to relieve one's conscience, as for some former dishonesty

con·sci·en·tious (kän′shē en′shəs, -chəs) ***adj.*** [see CONSCIENCE] **1.** governed by, or done according to, what one knows is right; scrupulous **2.** showing care; painstaking —**con′sci·en′tious·ly** ***adv.*** —**con′sci·en′tious·ness** ***n.***

conscientious objector a person who for reasons of conscience refuses to take part in warfare

con·scious (kän′shəs) ***adj.*** [< L. *conscius* < *conscire:* see CONSCIENCE] **1.** having a feeling or knowledge (with *of* or *that*); aware; cognizant **2.** able to feel and think; in the normal waking state **3.** aware of oneself as a thinking being **4.** *same as* SELF-CONSCIOUS **5.** intentional *[conscious* humor*]* **6.** known to or felt by oneself *[conscious* guilt*]* —**con′scious·ly** ***adv.***

con·scious·ness (-nis) ***n.*** **1.** the state of being conscious; awareness of one's own feelings, what is happening around one, etc. **2.** the totality of one's thoughts, feelings, and impressions; conscious mind

con·script (kən skript′; *for adj. & n.* kän′skript) ***vt.*** [< the *adj.*] **1.** to enroll for compulsory service in the armed forces; draft **2.** to force (labor, capital, etc.) into service for the government —***adj.*** [< L. pp. of *conscribere,* enroll < *com-,* with + *scribere,* to write] conscripted —***n.*** a conscripted person; draftee —**con·scrip′tion** ***n.***

con·se·crate (kän′sə krāt′) ***vt.*** **-crat′ed, -crat′ing** [< L. pp. of *consecrare* < *com-,* together + *sacrare,* to make holy < *sacer,* sacred] **1.** to set apart as holy; make or declare sacred for religious use **2.** to devote entirely; dedicate *[*to *consecrate* one's life to art*]* **3.** to cause to be revered; hallow *[*ground *consecrated* by their martyrdom*]* —**con′se·cra′tion** ***n.*** —**con′se·cra′tor** ***n.***

con·sec·u·tive (kən sek′yə tiv) ***adj.*** [< Fr. < ML. < pp. of L. *consequi:* see CONSEQUENCE] **1.** following in order, without interruption; successive **2.** proceeding from one part or idea to the next in logical order —**con·sec′u·tive·ly** ***adv.*** —**con·sec′u·tive·ness** ***n.***

con·sen·sus (kən sen′səs) ***n.*** [L. < pp. of *consentire:* see ff.] **1.** an opinion held by all or most **2.** general agreement

con·sent (kən sent′) ***vi.*** [< OFr. < L. *consentire* < *com-,* with + *sentire,* to feel] **1.** to agree (*to* do something) **2.** to give permission or approval (*to* something) —***n.*** **1.** permission, approval, or assent **2.** agreement *[*by common *consent]* —**con·sent′er** ***n.***

con·sen·tu·al (kən sen′cho͝o wəl) ***adj.*** involving consent, esp. mutual consent *[consentual* divorce*]*

con·se·quence (kän′sə kwens′, -kwəns) ***n.*** [OFr. < L. < prp. of *consequi* < *com-,* with + *sequi,* to follow] **1.** a result of an action, process, etc.; effect **2.** a logical result or conclusion; inference **3.** importance as a cause *[*a matter of slight *consequence]* **4.** importance in rank *[*a person of *consequence]* —**in consequence (of)** as a result (of) —**take the consequences** to accept the results of one's actions

con·se·quent (-kwent′, -kwənt) ***adj.*** **1.** following as a result; resulting **2.** proceeding in logical sequence —***n.*** anything that follows —**consequent on** (or **upon**) **1.** following as a result of **2.** inferred from

con·se·quen·tial (kän′sə kwen′shəl) ***adj.*** **1.** following as an effect **2.** important —**con′se·quen′ti·al′i·ty** (-shē al′ə tē) ***n.*** —**con′se·quen′tial·ly** ***adv.***

con·se·quent·ly (kän′sə kwent′lē, -kwənt-) ***adv.*** as a result; by logical inference; therefore

con·ser·van·cy (kən sʉr′vən sē) ***n.*** conservation of natural resources —***adj.*** set apart for the protection of natural resources, as a State district

con·ser·va·tion (kän′sər vā′shən) ***n.*** **1.** a conserving; protection from loss, waste, etc. **2.** the official care and protection of natural resources, as forests —**con′ser·va′tion·al** ***adj.*** —**con′ser·va′tion·ist** ***n.***

conservation of energy the principle that energy is never consumed but only changes form, and that the total energy in the universe remains fixed

conservation of matter (or **mass**) the principle that matter is neither created nor destroyed during any physical or chemical change

con·ser·va·tism (kən sʉr′və tiz′m) ***n.*** the principles and practices of a conservative person or party

con·ser·va·tive (-tiv) ***adj.*** **1.** conserving or tending to conserve; preservative **2.** tending to preserve established institutions or methods and to resist or oppose any changes in these **3.** [C-] designating or of the major right-wing political party of Great Britain or of Canada **4.** [C-] designating or of a movement in Judaism moderately adapting religious ritual, etc. to modern conditions **5.** moderate; cautious; safe —***n.*** **1.** a conservative person **2.** [C-] a member of a Conservative party —**con·ser′va·tive·ly** ***adv.*** —**con·ser′va·tive·ness** ***n.***

con·ser·va·toire (kən sʉr′və twär′, -sʉr′və twär′) ***n.*** [Fr.] *same as* CONSERVATORY (*n.* 2)

con·ser·va·tor (kän′sər vāt′ər, kən sʉr′və tər) ***n.*** [see CONSERVE] a protector, guardian, or custodian

con·ser·va·to·ry (kən sʉr′və tôr′ē) ***n.,*** *pl.* **-ries** [see ff.] **1.** a room enclosed in glass, for growing and showing plants **2.** a school, or academy, of music, art, etc.

con·serve (kən sʉrv′; *for n., usually* kän′sərv) ***vt.*** **-served′, -serv′ing** [< OFr. < L. *conservare* < *com-,* with + *servare,* to guard] **1.** to keep from being damaged, lost, or wasted **2.** to make (fruit) into preserves —***n.*** [*often pl.*] a preserve of two or more fruits —**con·serv′a·ble** ***adj.*** —**con·serv′er** ***n.***

con·sid·er (kən sid′ər) ***vt.*** [< OFr. < L. *considerare,* to observe < *com-,* with + *sidus,* a star] **1.** to think about in order to understand or decide; ponder **2.** to keep in mind; take into account **3.** to be thoughtful of (others, their feelings, etc.) **4.** to regard as; think to be *[*I *consider* him an expert*]* —***vi.*** to think carefully; reflect

con·sid·er·a·ble (-ə b'l) ***adj.*** **1.** worth considering; important **2.** much or large —**con·sid′er·a·bly** ***adv.***

con·sid·er·ate (-it) ***adj.*** [see CONSIDER] having or showing regard for others and their feelings; thoughtful —**con·sid′er·ate·ly** ***adv.*** —**con·sid′er·ate·ness** ***n.***

con·sid·er·a·tion (kən sid′ə rā′shən) ***n.*** **1.** the act of considering; deliberation **2.** *a)* thoughtful or sympathetic regard for others *b)* esteem **3.** something considered in making a decision **4.** a thought or opinion produced by considering **5.** a recompense, as for a service rendered; fee; compensation —**in consideration of 1.** because of **2.** in return for —**take into consideration** to keep in mind; take into account —**under consideration** being thought over

con·sid·ered (kən sid′ərd) ***adj.*** arrived at after careful thought

con·sid·er·ing (-ər iŋ) ***prep.*** in view of; taking into account —***adv.*** [Colloq.] all things considered

con·sign (kən sīn′) ***vt.*** [L. *consignare,* to seal < *com-,* together + *signare* < *signum,* a sign] **1.** to hand over; deliver **2.** to put in the care of another; entrust **3.** to assign to an undesirable position or place; relegate **4.** to send or deliver (goods) —**con·sign′a·ble** ***adj.*** —**consign·ee** (kän′sī nē′, kən sī′nē′) ***n.*** —**consign′or, consign′er** ***n.***

con·sign·ment (-mənt) ***n.*** **1.** a consigning or being consigned **2.** something consigned; esp., a shipment of goods sent to an agent for sale or safekeeping

con·sist (kən sist′) ***vi.*** [L. *consistere* < *com-,* together + *sistere,* to stand] **1.** to be formed or composed (*of*) **2.** to be contained or inherent (*in*) as a cause, characteristic, etc. **3.** to exist in harmony (*with*)

con·sis·ten·cy (-ən sē) ***n.,*** *pl.* **-cies** **1.** *a*) firmness or thickness, as of a liquid *b*) degree of this **2.** agreement; harmony **3.** conformity with previous practice or principle Also **con·sis′tence**

con·sis·tent (-ənt) ***adj.*** [see CONSIST] **1.** [Rare] firm; solid **2.** in agreement or harmony; compatible **3.** holding always to the same principles or practice —**con·sis′tent·ly** ***adv.***

con·sis·to·ry (kən sis′tər ē) ***n.,*** *pl.* **-ries** [< OFr. < L. *consistorium,* place of assembly < *consistere:* see CONSIST] **1.** a church council or court, as the papal senate **2.** a session of such a body —**con·sis·to·ri·al** (kän′sis tôr′ē əl) ***adj.***

con·so·la·tion (kän′sə lā′shən) ***n.*** **1.** a consoling or being consoled; solace **2.** a person or thing that consoles

consolation prize a prize given to a contestant who does well but does not win

con·sol·a·to·ry (kən sōl′ə tôr′ē, -säl′-) ***adj.*** consoling or tending to console; comforting

con·sole[1] (kən sōl′) ***vt.*** **-soled′, -sol′ing** [< Fr. < L. *consolari* < *com-,* with + *solari,* to solace] to make feel less sad or disappointed; comfort —**con·sol′a·ble** ***adj.*** —**con·sol′ing·ly** ***adv.***

con·sole[2] (kän′sōl) ***n.*** [Fr.] **1.** an ornamental bracket for supporting a shelf, bust, cornice, etc. **2.** *same as* CONSOLE TABLE **3.** the desklike frame containing the keys, stops, pedals, etc. of an organ **4.** a radio, television, or phonograph cabinet designed to stand on the floor **5.** an instrument panel or unit, containing the controls for operating aircraft, computers, etc.

CONSOLE (of an organ)

console table a small table with legs resembling consoles, placed against a wall

con·sol·i·date (kən säl′ə dāt′) ***vt., vi.*** **-dat′ed, -dat′ing** [< L. pp. of *consolidare* < *com-,* together + *solidare* < *solidus,* solid] **1.** to combine into a single whole; merge; unite **2.** to make or become strong, stable, etc. [the troops *consolidated* their position] **3.** to make or become solid or compact —**con·sol′i·da′tion** ***n.*** —**con·sol′i·da′tor** ***n.***

con·sols (kən sälz′, kän′sälz) ***n.pl.*** [< *consolidated annuities*] British government bonds

con·som·mé (kän′sə mā′) ***n.*** [Fr., orig. pp. of *consommer,* CONSUMMATE, confused with *consumer,* CONSUME] a clear soup made by boiling meat, and sometimes vegetables, in water and straining

con·so·nance (kän′sə nəns) ***n.*** [OFr. < L. < prp. of *consonare* < *com-,* with + *sonare,* to sound < *sonus,* a sound] **1.** harmony or agreement of elements or parts; accord **2.** harmony of musical tones Also **con′so·nan·cy**

con·so·nant (kän′sə nənt) ***adj.*** [see prec.] **1.** in harmony or agreement; in accord **2.** harmonious in tone: opposed to DISSONANT **3.** consonantal —***n.*** **1.** any speech sound produced by obstructing the breath stream in any of various ways, as the sounds of p, t, k, m, l, f, etc. **2.** a letter or symbol representing such a sound —**con′so·nant·ly** ***adv.***

con·so·nan·tal (kän′sə nant′'l) ***adj.*** of, being, or having a consonant or consonants

con·sort (kän′sôrt; *for v.* kən sôrt′) ***n.*** [< OFr. < L. *consors* (gen. *consortis*) < *com-,* with + *sors,* a share] **1.** orig., a partner; companion **2.** a wife or husband; spouse, esp. of a reigning king or queen **3.** a ship that travels along with another —***vi.*** **1.** to keep company; associate **2.** to agree; be in accord —***vt.*** to associate; join

con·sor·ti·um (kən sôr′shē əm) ***n.,*** *pl.* **-ti·a** (-ə) [L., community of goods: see prec.] **1.** an alliance, as of two or more business firms in some venture **2.** an international banking agreement or association

con·spec·tus (kən spek′təs) ***n.*** [L., a view, pp. of *conspicere:* see ff.] **1.** a general view; survey **2.** a summary; synopsis; digest

con·spic·u·ous (kən spik′yoo wəs) ***adj.*** [< L. < *conspicere,* to look at < *com-,* intens. + *specere,* to see] **1.** easy to see or perceive; obvious **2.** attracting attention by being outstanding; striking [*conspicuous* bravery, *conspicuous* folly] —**con·spic′u·ous·ly** ***adv.*** —**con·spic′u·ous·ness** ***n.***

con·spir·a·cy (kən spir′ə sē) ***n.,*** *pl.* **-cies** **1.** a conspiring, esp. in an unlawful or harmful plot **2.** such a plot **3.** the group taking part in such a plot **4.** a combining or working together [the *conspiracy* of events]

con·spir·a·tor (-tər) ***n.*** a person who takes part in a conspiracy —**con·spir·a·to·ri·al** (kən spir′ə tôr′ē əl) ***adj.*** —**con·spir′a·to′ri·al·ly** ***adv.***

con·spire (kən spīr′) ***vi.*** **-spired′, -spir′ing** [< OFr. < L. *conspirare* < *com-,* together + *spirare,* to breathe] **1.** to plan and act together secretly, esp. in order to commit a crime **2.** to combine or work together for any purpose or effect [events *conspired* to ruin him]

con spi·ri·to (kän spir′i tō′) [It.] *Music* with spirit; with vigor

con·sta·ble (kän′stə b'l, kun′-) ***n.*** [< OFr. < LL. *comes stabuli,* lit., count of the stable] **1.** in the Middle Ages, the highest ranking official of a royal household, court, etc. **2.** a peace officer in a town or village **3.** [Chiefly Brit.] a policeman

Con·sta·ble (kun′stə b'l, kän′-), **John** 1776–1837; Eng. landscape painter

con·stab·u·lar·y (kən stab′yə ler′ē) ***n.,*** *pl.* **-ies** **1.** constables, collectively, as of a district **2.** a police force characterized by a military organization —***adj.*** of constables or a constabulary: also **con·stab′u·lar** (-lər)

Con·stance (kän′stəns) [Fr. < L. *Constantia,* lit., constancy] a feminine name

con·stant (kän′stənt) ***adj.*** [< OFr. < L. prp. of *constare* < *com-,* together + *stare,* to stand] **1.** not changing; remaining the same; specif., *a*) remaining firm in purpose; resolute *b*) loyal; faithful *c*) regular; stable; unvarying **2.** going on all the time; continual; persistent [*constant* interruptions] —***n.*** **1.** anything that does not change or vary **2.** *Math., Physics* *a*) a quantity that always has the same value *b*) a quantity or factor assumed to have one value throughout a particular discussion or investigation: symbol, c (or k): opposed to VARIABLE —**con′stan·cy** ***n.*** —**con′stant·ly** ***adv.***

Con·stan·tine I (kän′stən tēn′, -tīn′) 280?–337 A.D.; emperor of Rome (306–337): called *the Great*

Con·stan·ti·no·ple (kän′stan tə nō′p'l) *former name* (330 A.D.–1930) *of* ISTANBUL

con·stel·late (kän′stə lāt′) ***vi., vt.*** **-lat′ed, -lat′ing** to unite in a constellation; cluster

con·stel·la·tion (kän′stə lā′shən) ***n.*** [< OFr. < LL. < L. *com-,* with + pp. of *stellare,* to shine < *stella,* a star] **1.** *a*) an arbitrary group of fixed stars, usually named after some object, animal, or mythological being that they supposedly suggest in outline *b*) the part of the heavens occupied by such a group **2.** any brilliant cluster, gathering, or collection **3.** a group of related ideas, feelings, etc. —**con·stel·la·to·ry** (kən stel′ə tôr′ē) ***adj.***

con·ster·nate (kän′stər nāt′) ***vt.*** **-nat′ed, -nat′ing** to overcome with consternation; dismay

con·ster·na·tion (kän′stər nā′shən) ***n.*** [< L. < *consternare,* to terrify] great fear or shock that makes one feel helpless or bewildered

con·sti·pate (kän′stə pāt′) ***vt.*** **-pat′ed, -pat′ing** [< L. pp. of *constipare* < *com-,* together + *stipare,* to cram] to cause constipation in

con·sti·pa·tion (kän′stə pā′shən) ***n.*** [see prec.] a condition in which the feces are hard and elimination from the bowels is infrequent and difficult

con·stit·u·en·cy (kən stich′oo wən sē) ***n.,*** *pl.* **-cies** [< CONSTITUENT + -CY] **1.** all the people, esp. voters, served by a particular elected official **2.** the district of such a group of voters, etc.

con·stit·u·ent (-oo wənt) ***adj.*** [< L. prp. of *constituere:* see ff.] **1.** necessary in forming a whole; component [a *constituent* part] **2.** that can appoint or elect **3.** authorized to make or revise a constitution or establish a government [a *constituent* assembly] —***n.*** **1.** a person who appoints another as his representative **2.** a member of a constituency **3.** a necessary part or element; component

con·sti·tute (kän′stə tōōt′, -tyōōt′) ***vt.*** **-tut′ed, -tut′ing** [< L. pp. of *constituere* < *com-,* together + *statuere,* to set] **1.** to establish (a law, government, institution, etc.) **2.** to set up (an assembly, proceeding, etc.) in a legal form **3.** to give a certain office or function to [we *constitute* you our spokesman] **4.** to make up; form; compose

con·sti·tu·tion (kän′stə tōō′shən, -tyōō′-) ***n.*** **1.** a constituting; establishment, appointment, or formation **2.** structure; organization; makeup **3.** the physical makeup of a person **4.** *a*) the system of fundamental laws and principles of a government, state, society, etc. *b*) a document in which these are written down; specif., [C-] such a document of the U.S.: it consists of seven articles and twenty-five amendments, and has been the supreme law of the nation since its adoption in 1789

con·sti·tu·tion·al (-əl) ***adj.*** **1.** of or in the constitution of a person or thing; basic; essential **2.** for improving a person's constitution **3.** of or in accordance with the constitution of a nation, society, etc. [*constitutional* rights] **4.** upholding the constitution **—*n.*** a walk or other exercise taken for one's health **—con′sti·tu′tion·al′i·ty** (-shə nal′ə tē) ***n.*** **—con′sti·tu′tion·al·ly** ***adv.***

con·sti·tu·tive (kän′stə tōōt′iv, -tyōōt′-) ***adj.*** **1.** having power to establish, appoint, or enact **2.** making a thing what it is; basic **3.** forming a part (*of*); constituent **—con′sti·tu′tive·ly** ***adv.***

constr. **1.** construction **2.** construed

con·strain (kən strān′) ***vt.*** [< OFr. < L. *constringere* < *com-*, together + *stringere*, to draw tight] **1.** to force into, or hold in, close bounds; confine **2.** to hold back or in by force or strain; restrain **3.** to compel [*constrained* to agree] **—con·strained′** ***adj.*** **—con·strain′ed·ly** (-strā′nid lē) ***adv.***

con·straint (-strānt′) ***n.*** **1.** a constraining or being constrained; specif., *a*) confinement or restriction *b*) compulsion or coercion **2.** forced, unnatural manner

con·strict (kən strikt′) ***vt.*** [< L. pp. of *constringere*: see CONSTRAIN] **1.** to make smaller or narrower by binding, squeezing, etc.; contract **2.** to hold in; limit **—con·stric′tive** ***adj.***

con·stric·tion (-strik′shən) ***n.*** **1.** a constricting or being constricted **2.** a feeling of tightness or pressure, as in the chest **3.** something that constricts **4.** a constricted part

con·stric·tor (-strik′tər) ***n.*** that which constricts; specif., *a*) a muscle that contracts an opening or compresses an organ *b*) a snake that kills by coiling around its prey and squeezing

con·struct (kən strukt′; *for n.* kän′strukt) ***vt.*** [< L. pp. of *construere* < *com-*, together + *struere*, to pile up] **1.** to build, form, or devise by fitting parts or elements together systematically **2.** *Geom.* to draw (a figure) so as to meet the specified requirements **—*n.*** something built or put together systematically **—con·struc′tor, con·struct′er** ***n.***

con·struc·tion (kən struk′shən) ***n.*** **1.** the act or process of constructing **2.** the way in which something is constructed **3.** something constructed; structure; building **4.** an explanation or interpretation, as of a statement **5.** the arrangement and relation of words in a phrase, clause, or sentence **6.** a three-dimensional work of art of various materials **—con·struc′tion·al** ***adj.*** **—con·struc′tion·al·ly** ***adv.***

con·struc·tion·ist (-ist) ***n.*** [see prec., sense 4] a person who interprets a law, document, etc. in a specified way

con·struc·tive (kən struk′tiv) ***adj.*** **1.** helping to construct; leading to improvements [*constructive* criticism] **2.** of construction or structure **3.** inferred or implied by legal or judicial interpretation **—con·struc′tive·ly** ***adv.*** **—con·struc′tive·ness** ***n.***

con·strue (kən strōō′) ***vt.*** **-strued′, -stru′ing** [< L. *construere*: see CONSTRUCT] **1.** to analyze (a sentence, clause, etc.) so as to show its syntactical construction and meaning **2.** to translate **3.** to explain or deduce the meaning of; interpret [her silence was *construed* as agreement] **4.** *Gram.* to combine in syntax [the verb "let," unlike "permit," is *construed* with an infinitive omitting the "to"]

con·sul (kän′s'l) ***n.*** [< OFr. < L. < *consulere*, to deliberate] **1.** either of the two chief magistrates of the ancient Roman republic **2.** any of the three highest officials of the French republic from 1799 to 1804 **3.** a government official appointed to live in a foreign city and serve his country's citizens and business interests there **—con′sul·ar** (-ər) ***adj.*** **—con′sul·ship′** ***n.***

con·sul·ate (-it) ***n.*** **1.** the position, powers, and duties of a consul **2.** the office or residence of a consul **3.** the term of office of a consul **4.** government by consuls; specif., [C-] the government of France from 1799 to 1804

consul general *pl.* **consuls general, consul generals** a consul in a principal commercial city, who supervises other consuls within his district

con·sult (kən sult′) ***vi.*** [L. *consultare* < pp. of *consulere*, to deliberate] to talk things over in order to decide something; confer **—*vt.*** **1.** *a*) to ask the advice of *b*) to refer to, esp. for information **2.** to show regard for; consider [*consult* your own wishes in the matter] **—con·sult′er** ***n.***

con·sult·ant (kən sul′t'nt) ***n.*** **1.** a person who consults with another **2.** an expert called on for professional or technical advice or opinions

con·sul·ta·tion (kän′s'l tā′shən) ***n.*** **1.** the act of consulting **2.** a meeting to discuss, decide, or plan something **—con·sul·ta·tive** (kən sul′tə tiv, kän′s'l tā′-), **con·sul′ta·to′ry** (-tôr′ē) ***adj.***

con·sume (kən sōōm′, -syōōm′) ***vt.*** **-sumed′, -sum′ing** [< OFr. < L. *consumere* < *com-*, together + *sumere*, to take < *sub-*, under + *emere*, to buy] **1.** to destroy, as by fire **2.** to use up; spend or waste (time, energy, money, etc.) **3.** to eat or drink up; devour **4.** to engross or obsess [*consumed* with envy] **—con·sum′a·ble** ***adj.***

con·sum·ed·ly (-id lē) ***adv.*** extremely or excessively

con·sum·er (kən sōō′mər, -syōō′-) ***n.*** a person or thing that consumes; specif., a person who buys goods or services for his own needs and not for resale or to use in the production of other goods for resale: opposed to PRODUCER

con·sum·er·ism (-iz'm) ***n.*** **1.** the movement for consumer protection in connection with defective and unsafe products, misleading business practices, etc. **2.** the consumption of goods and services

con·sum·mate (kən sum′it; *for v.* kän′sə māt′) ***adj.*** [< L. pp. of *consummare*, to sum up < *com-*, together + *summa*, a SUM] **1.** complete or perfect **2.** highly expert [a *consummate* liar] **—*vt.*** **-mat′ed, -mat′ing** **1.** to bring to completion or fulfillment; finish **2.** to make (a marriage) actual by sexual intercourse **—con·sum′mate·ly** ***adv.*** **—con·sum·ma·tive** (kän′sə māt′iv), **con·sum′ma·to′ry** (-ə tôr′ē) ***adj.*** **—con′sum·ma′tor** ***n.***

con·sum·ma·tion (kän′sə mā′shən) ***n.*** **1.** a consummating or being consummated **2.** an end; outcome

con·sump·tion (kən sump′shən) ***n.*** **1.** *a*) a consuming or being consumed; specif., the using up of goods or services *b*) the amount consumed **2.** a disease causing wasting away of the body; esp., tuberculosis of the lungs

con·sump·tive (-tiv) ***adj.*** **1.** consuming or tending to consume; destructive; wasteful **2.** *Med.* of, having, or relating to tuberculosis of the lungs **—*n.*** a person who has tuberculosis of the lungs **—con·sump′tive·ly** ***adv.***

cont. **1.** containing **2.** contents **3.** continent **4.** continue **5.** continued **6.** contra

con·tact (kän′takt) ***n.*** [< L. pp. of *contingere* < *com-*, together + *tangere*, to touch] **1.** the act of touching or meeting **2.** the state or fact of being in touch, communication, or association (*with*) **3.** *a*) an acquaintance, esp. one who is influential *b*) a connection with such a person **4.** *Elec.* *a*) a connection between two conductors in a circuit *b*) a device for opening and closing such a connection **—*vt.*** **1.** to place in contact **2.** to get in touch with **—*vi.*** to be in or come into contact **—*adj.*** of, involving, or relating to contact

contact lens a tiny, thin correctional lens of glass or plastic placed in the fluid over the cornea of the eye

con·ta·gion (kən tā′jən) ***n.*** [L. *contagio*, a touching < *contingere*: see CONTACT] **1.** the spreading of disease by contact **2.** a contagious disease **3.** the causative agent of a communicable disease **4.** *a*) the spreading of an emotion, idea, etc. from person to person *b*) the emotion, idea, etc. so spread

con·ta·gious (-jəs) ***adj.*** [< OFr. < LL. *contagiosus*] **1.** spread by contact: said of diseases **2.** carrying the causative agent of such a disease **3.** spreading from person to person **—con·ta′gious·ly** ***adv.*** **—con·ta′gious·ness** ***n.***

con·tain (kən tān′) ***vt.*** [< OFr. < L. *continere* < *com-*, together + *tenere*, to hold] **1.** to have in it; hold, enclose, or include **2.** to have the capacity for holding **3.** to hold back or within fixed limits; specif., *a*) to restrain (one's feelings, oneself, etc.) *b*) to check the power or expansion of **4.** to be divisible by, esp. without a remainder [10 *contains* 5 and 2] **—con·tain′a·ble** ***adj.***

con·tain·er (-ər) ***n.*** a thing for containing something; box, can, jar, etc.

con·tain·er·ize (-īz′) ***vt.*** **-ized′, -iz′ing** to pack (general cargo) in large, standardized containers for more efficient shipment **—con·tain′er·i·za′tion** ***n.***

con·tain·ment (-mənt) ***n.*** the policy of attempting to prevent the influence of an opposing nation or political system from spreading

con·tam·i·nant (kən tam′ə nənt) ***n.*** a substance that contaminates another substance, the air, water, etc.

con·tam·i·nate (-ə nāt′) ***vt.*** **-nat′ed, -nat′ing** [< L. pp. of *contaminare*, to defile < *contamen*, contact < *com-*, together + base of *tangere*, to touch] to make impure, infected, corrupt, radioactive, etc. by contact with or addition of something; pollute; defile; sully; taint **—con·tam′i·na′tion** ***n.*** **—con·tam′i·na′tive** ***adj.*** **—con·tam′i·na′tor** ***n.***

contd. continued

con·temn (kən tem′) ***vt.*** [< OFr. < L. *contemnere* < *com-*, intens. + *temnere*, to scorn] to treat with contempt; scorn **—con·temn′er, con·tem′nor** (-tem′ər, -tem′nər) ***n.***

con·tem·plate (kän′təm plāt′) ***vt.*** **-plat′ed, -plat′ing** [< L. pp. of *contemplari*, to observe (orig., in augury, to mark out a space for observation) < *com-*, intens. + *templum*, TEMPLE[1]] **1.** to look at intently; gaze at **2.** to think about intently; study carefully; consider **3.** to expect or intend *—vi.* to meditate or muse **—con'tem·pla'tion** *n.* **—con'tem·pla'tor** *n.*

con·tem·pla·tive (kən tem'plə tiv, kän'təm plāt'iv) *adj.* of or inclined to contemplation; thoughtful; meditative *—n.* a member of a religious order dedicated to contemplation **—com·tem'pla·tive·ly** *adv.* **—con·tem'pla·tive·ness** *n.*

con·tem·po·ra·ne·ous (kən tem'pə rā'nē əs) *adj.* [< L. < *com-*, with + *tempus* (gen. *temporis*), time] existing or happening in the same period of time **—con·tem'po·ra·ne'i·ty** (-pər ə nē'ə tē), **con·tem'po·ra'ne·ous·ness** *n.* **—con·tem'po·ra'ne·ous·ly** *adv.*

con·tem·po·rar·y (kən tem'pə rer'ē) *adj.* [< L. *com-*, with + *temporarius* < *tempus,* time] **1.** living or happening in the same period **2.** of about the same age **3.** of or in the style of the present or recent times; modern *—n., pl.* **-ies** a person or thing of the same period or about the same age as another or others

con·tem·po·rize (kən tem'pə rīz') *vt., vi.* **-rized', -riz'ing** to make or become contemporary

con·tempt (kən tempt') *n.* [OFr. < L. pp. of *contemnere:* see CONTEMN] **1.** the feeling of a person toward someone or something he considers worthless or beneath notice; scorn **2.** the condition of being despised or scorned **3.** *Law* a showing disrespect for the dignity of a court (or legislature): in full, **contempt of court** (or **congress,** etc.)

con·tempt·i·ble (kən temp'tə b'l) *adj.* deserving contempt or scorn; despicable **—con·tempt'i·bil'i·ty, con·tempt'i·ble·ness** *n.* **—con·tempt'i·bly** *adv.*

con·temp·tu·ous (kən temp'choo wəs) *adj.* full of contempt; scornful; disdainful **—con·temp'tu·ous·ly** *adv.* **—con·temp'tu·ous·ness** *n.*

con·tend (kən tend') *vi.* [< L. *contendere* < *com-*, together + *tendere,* to stretch] **1.** to strive in combat; fight **2.** to strive in debate; argue **3.** to strive in competition; compete; vie *—vt.* to hold to be a fact; assert **—con·tend'er** *n.*

con·tent[1] (kən tent') *adj.* [< OFr. < L. pp. of *continere:* see CONTAIN] **1.** happy enough with what one has or is; satisfied **2.** willing; assenting *—vt.* to make content; satisfy *—n.* contentment

con·tent[2] (kän'tent) *n.* [< L. pp. of *continere:* see CONTAIN] **1.** [*usually pl.*] *a)* all that is contained in something *b)* all that is dealt with in a writing or speech *[a table of contents]* **2.** *a)* all that is dealt with in an area of study, work of art, discussion, etc. *b)* meaning; substance **3.** the amount contained *[iron with a high carbon content]*

con·tent·ed (kən ten'tid) *adj.* having or showing no desire for something more or different; satisfied **—con·tent'ed·ly** *adv.* **—con·tent'ed·ness** *n.*

con·ten·tion (kən ten'shən) *n.* [see CONTEND] **1.** the act of contending; strife, struggle, controversy dispute, quarrel, etc. **2.** a statement or point that one argues for as true or valid

con·ten·tious (-ten'shəs) *adj.* **1.** quarrelsome **2.** of or characterized by contention **—con·ten'tious·ly** *adv.* **—con·ten'tious·ness** *n.*

con·tent·ment (kən tent'mənt) *n.* the state, quality, or fact of being contented

con·ter·mi·nous (kən tur'mə nəs, kän-) *adj.* [< L. < *com-*, together + *terminus,* an end] **1.** having a common boundary; contiguous **2.** contained within the same boundaries or limits **—con·ter'mi·nous·ly** *adv.*

con·tes·sa (kôn tes'sä) *n.* [It.] *same as* COUNTESS

con·test (kən test'; *for n.* kän'test) *vt.* [< Fr. < L. *contestari* < *com-*, together + *testari,* to bear witness < *testis,* a witness] **1.** to try to disprove or invalidate (something); dispute *[to contest a will]* **2.** to fight for; struggle to win or keep *—vi.* to struggle (*with* or *against*); contend *—n.* **1.** a fight, struggle, or controversy **2.** any race, game, etc. in which individuals or teams compete to determine the winner **—con·test'a·ble** *adj.* **—con·test'er** *n.*

con·test·ant (kən tes'tənt) *n.* [Fr.] **1.** one that competes in a contest **2.** one who contests a claim, decision, etc.

con·text (kän'tekst) *n.* [< L. pp. of *contexere* < *com-*, together + *texere,* to weave] the parts of a sentence, paragraph, etc. next to or surrounding a word or passage and determining its exact meaning **—con·tex·tu·al** (kən teks'choo wəl) *adj.* **—con·tex'tu·al·ly** *adv.*

con·ti·gu·i·ty (kän'tə gyōō'ə tē) *n., pl.* **-ties** the state of being contiguous; nearness or contact

con·tig·u·ous (kən tig'yoo wəs) *adj.* [< L. *contiguus* < base of *contingere:* see CONTACT] **1.** in physical contact; touching along all or most of one side **2.** near, next, or adjacent **—con·tig'u·ous·ly** *adv.* **—con·tig'u·ous·ness** *n.*

con·ti·nence (känt''n əns) *n.* [see ff.] **1.** self-restraint; moderation **2.** self-restraint in sexual activity; esp., total abstinence

con·ti·nent (-ənt) *adj.* [< OFr. < L. prp. of *continere:* see CONTAIN] **1.** self-restrained; temperate **2.** characterized by self-restraint, esp. by total abstinence, in sexual activity *—n.* any of the main large land areas of the earth (Africa, Asia, Australia, Europe, N. America, S. America, and, sometimes, Antarctica) **—the Continent** all of Europe except the British Isles **—con'ti·nent·ly** *adv.*

con·ti·nen·tal (känt''n en't'l) *adj.* **1.** of a continent **2.** [*sometimes* **C-**] European **3.** [**C-**] of the American colonies at the time of the American Revolution *—n.* **1.** [*usually* **C-**] a European **2.** [**C-**] a soldier of the American army during the Revolution **3.** a piece of paper money issued by the Continental Congress: it became almost worthless before the end of the war, hence the phrases **not care** (or **give**), or **not worth, a continental —con'ti·nen'tal·ly** *adv.*

continental breakfast [*also* **C- b-**] a light breakfast, usually of rolls and coffee or tea

Continental Congress either of the two assemblies of representatives from the American colonies during the Revolutionary period: the second issued the Declaration of Independence (1776)

continental drift the hypothetical drifting of continents due to currents in the earth's mantle

continental shelf the submerged, gradually sloping shelf of land that borders a continent and ends in a steep descent (**continental slope**) to the deep ocean

con·tin·gen·cy (kən tin'jən sē) *n., pl.* **-cies** **1.** a contingent quality or condition; esp., dependence on chance or uncertain conditions **2.** a possible, unforeseen, or accidental occurrence **3.** some thing or event which depends on or is incidental to another Also **con·tin'gence**

con·tin·gent (-jənt) *adj.* [< L. prp. of *contingere:* see CONTACT] **1.** that may or may not happen; possible **2.** happening by chance; accidental **3.** unpredictable because dependent on chance **4.** dependent (*on* or *upon* an uncertainty); conditional *—n.* **1.** a chance happening **2.** a share or quota, as of troops, laborers, etc. **3.** a group forming part of a larger group **—con·tin'gent·ly** *adv.*

con·tin·u·al (kən tin'yoo wəl) *adj.* **1.** repeated often; going on in rapid succession **2.** going on uninterruptedly; continuous **—con·tin'u·al·ly** *adv.*

con·tin·u·ance (-yoo wəns) *n.* **1.** the act or process of continuing **2.** the time during which an action or state lasts; duration **3.** the fact of remaining (*in* a place or condition); stay **4.** an unbroken succession **5.** [Rare] a sequel **6.** *Law* postponement or adjournment to a later date

con·tin·u·a·tion (kən tin'yoo wā'shən) *n.* **1.** a keeping up or going on without stopping **2.** a beginning again after an interruption; resumption **3.** a part or thing by which something is continued; extension, sequel, etc.

con·tin·ue (kən tin'yōō, -yoo) *vi.* **-ued, -u·ing** [< OFr. < L. *continuare,* to join < *continere:* see CONTAIN] **1.** to last; endure **2.** to go on in a specified course of action or condition; persist **3.** to go on or extend **4.** to stay **5.** to go on again after an interruption; resume *—vt.* **1.** to go on with; carry on; keep up **2.** to extend **3.** to resume **4.** to cause to remain; retain **5.** *Law* to postpone or adjourn to a later date **—con·tin'u·a·ble** *adj.* **—con·tin'u·er** *n.*

con·ti·nu·i·ty (kän'tə nōō'ə tē, -nyōō'-) *n., pl.* **-ties** **1.** a continuous state or quality **2.** an unbroken, coherent whole **3.** continuous duration **4.** the script or scenario for a motion picture, radio or television program, etc. **5.** a series of comments connecting the parts of a radio or television program

con·tin·u·ous (kən tin'yoo wəs) *adj.* [L. *continuus:* see CONTINUE] going on or extending without interruption or break; unbroken; connected **—con·tin'u·ous·ly** *adv.*

con·tin·u·um (-yoo wəm) *n., pl.* **-u·a** (-wə), **-u·ums** [L.] a continuous whole, quantity, or series

con·tort (kən tôrt') *vt., vi.* [< L. pp. of *contorquere* < *com-*, together + *torquere,* to twist] to twist or wrench out of its usual form into one that is grotesque; distort violently **—con·tor'tion** *n.* **—con·tor'tive** *adj.*

con·tor·tion·ist (kən tôr'shən ist) *n.* a person who can twist his body into unnatural positions

con·tour (kän'toor) *n.* [Fr. < It. < LL. *contornare* < L. *com-*, intens. + *tornare,* to turn: see TURN] the outline of a figure, land, etc. *—vt.* **1.** to represent in contour **2.** to shape or mold to the contour of something *—adj.* **1.** made so as to conform to the shape or outline of something **2.** characterized by the making of furrows along the natural contour lines so as to avoid erosion, as on a hillside *[contour farming]*

contour map a map with lines (**contour lines**) connecting all points of the same elevation

contr. **1.** contract **2.** contraction **3.** contrary

con·tra- [< L. *contra,* against] *a prefix meaning:* **1.** against, opposite, opposed to **2.** lower in musical pitch *[contrabassoon]*

con·tra·band (kän'trə band') *n.* [< Sp. < It. < *contra-*, against + *bando* < VL. *bannum* (akin to BAN[1])] **1.** unlawful or prohibited trade **2.** smuggled goods, illegally imported or

CONTOUR MAP

exported 3. *same as* CONTRABAND OF WAR —*adj.* forbidden by law to be imported or exported —**con'tra·band'ist** *n.*
contraband of war war materiel which, by international law, may be seized by a belligerent when shipped to the other one by a neutral
con·tra·bass (kän'trə bās') *adj.* [see CONTRA- & BASS¹] having its pitch an octave lower than the normal bass —*n.* *same as* DOUBLE BASS —**con'tra·bass'ist** *n.*
con·tra·bas·soon (kän'trə bə soon') *n.* the double bassoon, which is larger than the ordinary bassoon and an octave lower in pitch
con·tra·cep·tion (kän'trə sep'shən) *n.* [CONTRA- + (CON)CEPTION] intentional prevention of the fertilization of the human ovum, as by special devices, drugs, etc. —**con'tra·cep'tive** *adj., n.*
con·tract (kän'trakt *for n. & usually for vt. 1 & vi. 1;* kən trakt' *for v. generally*) *n.* [OFr. < L. pp. of *contrahere* < *com-*, together + *trahere*, to draw] 1. an agreement to do something, esp. a written one enforceable by law 2. a formal agreement of marriage or betrothal 3. a document containing the terms of an agreement 4. *Bridge a)* the number of tricks bid by the highest bidder *b) same as* CONTRACT BRIDGE —*vt.* 1. to enter upon, or undertake, by contract 2. to get, acquire, or incur 3. to reduce in size; draw together; shrink 4. to narrow in scope; restrict 5. *Gram.* to shorten (a word or phrase) by the omission of a letter or sound (*I'm, e'er*) —*vi.* 1. to make a contract 2. to become reduced in size or bulk —**contract out** to assign (a job) by contract —**con·tract'i·bil'i·ty** *n.* —**con·tract'i·ble** *adj.*
con·tract bridge (kän'trakt) a form of auction bridge: only the tricks bid may be counted toward a game
con·trac·tile (kən trak't'l) *adj.* 1. having the power of contracting 2. producing contraction —**con·trac·til·i·ty** (kän'trak til'ə tē) *n.*
con·trac·tion (-shən) *n.* 1. a contracting or being contracted 2. the drawing up and thickening of a muscle in action 3. *Gram. a)* the shortening of a word or phrase *b)* a word form resulting from this (Ex.: *aren't* for *are not*) —**con·trac'tion·al** *adj.* —**con·trac'tive** (-tiv) *adj.*
con·trac·tor (kän'trak tər, kən trak'-) *n.* 1. one of the parties to a contract 2. one, esp. one in the building trades, who contracts to supply certain materials or do certain work for a stipulated sum 3. a muscle that contracts
con·trac·tu·al (kən trak'choo wəl) *adj.* of, or having the nature of, a contract —**con·trac'tu·al·ly** *adv.*
con·tra·dance (kän'trə dans') *n.* *same as* CONTREDANSE
con·tra·dict (kän'trə dikt') *vt.* [< L. pp. of *contradicere* < *contra-*, against + *dicere*, to speak] 1. *a)* to assert the opposite of (a statement) *b)* to deny the statement of (a person) 2. to be contrary or opposed to; go against —**con'tra·dict'a·ble** *adj.* —**con'tra·dic'tor, con'tra·dict'er** *n.*
con·tra·dic·tion (-dik'shən) *n.* 1. a contradicting or being contradicted 2. a statement in opposition to another; denial 3. a condition in which things tend to be contrary to each other; inconsistency; discrepancy
con·tra·dic·to·ry (-dik'tər ē) *adj.* 1. involving a contradiction; inconsistent 2. inclined to contradict or deny Also **con'tra·dic'tive** —**con'tra·dic'to·ri·ly** *adv.* —**con'tra·dic'to·ri·ness** *n.*
con·tra·dis·tinc·tion (-dis tiŋk'shən) *n.* distinction by contrast —**con'tra·dis·tinc'tive** *adj.*
con·tral·to (kən tral'tō) *n., pl.* **-tos, -ti** (-tē) [It.: see CONTRA- & ALTO] 1. the range of the lowest female voice 2. a voice or singer with such range 3. a part for this voice —*adj.* of or for a contralto
con·trap·tion (kən trap'shən) *n.* [< ?] [Colloq.] a contrivance or gadget
con·tra·pun·tal (kän'trə pun't'l) *adj.* [< It. *contrappunto* (see COUNTERPOINT) + -AL] 1. of or characterized by counterpoint 2. according to the principles of counterpoint —**con'tra·pun'tal·ly** *adv.* —**con'tra·pun'tist** *n.*
con·tra·ri·e·ty (kän'trə rī'ə tē) *n.* 1. the condition or quality of being contrary 2. *pl.* **-ties** anything that is contrary; inconsistency
con·trar·i·wise (kän'trer ē wīz'; *for 3, often* kən trer'-) *adv.* 1. on the contrary; from the opposite point of view 2. in the opposite way, order, direction, etc. 3. perversely
con·trar·y (kän'trer ē; *for adj. 4, often* kən trer'ē) *adj.* [< OFr. < L. *contrarius* < *contra*, against] 1. in opposition 2. opposite in nature, order, direction, etc.; altogether different 3. unfavorable [*contrary* winds] 4. inclined to oppose stubbornly; perverse —*n., pl.* **-trar·ies** the opposite; thing that is the opposite of another —*adv.* in a contrary way —**on the contrary** as opposed to what has been said —**to the contrary** to the opposite effect —**con'trar·i·ly** *adv.* —**con'trar·i·ness** *n.*
con·trast (kən trast'; *for n.* kän'trast) *vt.* [< Fr. < It. & VL. < L. *contra*, against + *stare*, to stand] to compare so as to point out the differences; set off against one another —*vi.* to show differences when compared —*n.* 1. a contrasting or being contrasted 2. a difference, esp. a striking difference, between things being compared 3. a person or thing showing differences when compared with another —**con·trast'a·ble** *adj.* —**con·trast'ive** *adj.*
con·tra·vene (kän'trə vēn') *vt.* **-vened', -ven'ing** [< Fr. < LL. < L. *contra*, against + *venire*, to come] 1. to go against; oppose; violate 2. to disagree with; contradict —**con'tra·ven'er** *n.* —**con'tra·ven'tion** (-ven'shən) *n.*
con·tre·danse (kän'trə dans', kōn'trə däns') *n.* [Fr., altered (after *contre*, opposite) < COUNTRY-DANCE] a folk dance with the partners in two facing lines
con·tre·temps (kōn trə tän') *n., pl.* **-temps'** (-tän') [Fr., ult. < OFr. prp. of *contrester*, CONTRAST] an inopportune happening causing embarrassment
con·trib·ute (kən trib'yoot, -yoot) *vt., vi.* **-ut·ed, -ut·ing** [< L. pp. of *contribuere:* see COM- & TRIBUTE] 1. to give jointly with others to a common fund 2. to write (an article, poem, etc.) for a magazine, newspaper, etc. 3. to furnish (ideas, etc.) —**contribute to** to have a share in bringing about —**con·trib'u·tive** *adj.* —**con·trib'u·tor** *n.*
con·tri·bu·tion (kän'trə byoo'shən) *n.* 1. a contributing 2. something contributed 3. [Archaic] a special levy or tax
con·trib·u·to·ry (kən trib'yoo tôr'ē) *adj.* 1. contributing 2. involving a contribution —*n., pl.* **-ries** a person or thing that contributes
con·trite (kən trīt', kän'trīt) *adj.* [OFr. < LL. < L. pp. of *conterere*, to grind < *com-*, together + *terere*, to rub] 1. feeling deep sorrow or remorse for having sinned or done wrong 2. resulting from remorse or guilt —**con·trite'ly** *adv.* —**con·trite'ness, con·tri'tion** (-trish'ən) *n.*
con·triv·ance (kən trī'vəns) *n.* 1. the act, way, or power of contriving 2. something contrived, as an invention, mechanical device, plan, etc.
con·trive (kən trīv') *vt.* **-trived', -triv'ing** [< OFr. *controver*, to find out < VL. *contropare*, to compare] 1. to devise; plan 2. to construct skillfully or ingeniously; fabricate 3. to bring about, as by a scheme —*vi.* to form plans; scheme —**con·triv'a·ble** *adj.* —**con·triv'er** *n.*
con·trived (-trīvd') *adj.* not spontaneous
con·trol (kən trōl') *vt.* **-trolled', -trol'ling** [< Anglo-Fr. < Fr. < ML. *contrarotulus*, a register < L. *contra*, against + *rotulus:* see ROLL] 1. to regulate (financial affairs) 2. to exercise authority over; direct; command 3. to curb; restrain —*n.* 1. power to direct or regulate 2. the condition of being directed; restraint 3. a means of controlling; check 4. a standard of comparison for checking the findings of an experiment 5. [*usually pl.*] an apparatus to regulate a mechanism —**con·trol'la·bil'i·ty** *n.* —**con·trol'la·ble** *adj.*
control experiment an experiment in which one factor after another is varied while the other factors are controlled
con·trol·ler (kən trōl'ər) *n.* 1. a person in charge of expenditures or finances, as in a business, government (usually sp. *comptroller*), etc. 2. a person or device that controls —**con·trol'ler·ship'** *n.*
control tower a tower at an airport, from which air traffic is directed
con·tro·ver·sial (kän'trə vur'shəl) *adj.* of, subject to, or stirring up controversy; debatable —**con'tro·ver'sial·ist** *n.* —**con'tro·ver'sial·ly** *adv.*
con·tro·ver·sy (kän'trə vur'sē) *n., pl.* **-sies** [< L. < *contra*, against + pp. of *vertere*, to turn] 1. a discussion of a question in which opposing opinions clash; debate 2. a quarrel or dispute
con·tro·vert (kän'trə vurt', kän'trə vurt') *vt.* [backformation < prec.] 1. to argue or reason against; dispute 2. to argue about; debate —**con'tro·vert'i·ble** *adj.* —**con'tro·vert'i·bly** *adv.*
con·tu·ma·cious (kän'too mā'shəs, -tyoo-) *adj.* [< ff.] obstinately resisting authority; disobedient
con·tu·ma·cy (kän'too mə sē, -tyoo-; kən too'-) *n., pl.* **-cies** [< L. < *contumax*, stubborn < *com-*, intens. + *tumere*, to swell up] stubborn refusal to submit to authority; disobedience
con·tu·me·ly (kän'too mə lē, -mē'-, -tyoo-; kən too'-) *n., pl.* **-lies** [< OFr. < L. *contumelia*, reproach, prob. akin to prec.] 1. haughty rudeness; humiliating treatment 2. a scornful insult —**con'tu·me'li·ous** (-mē'lē əs) *adj.*
con·tuse (kən tooz', -tyooz') *vt.* **-tused', -tus'ing** [< L. pp. of *contundere* < *com-*, intens. + *tundere*, to beat] to bruise without breaking the skin
con·tu·sion (-too'zhən, -tyoo'-) *n.* a bruise

co·nun·drum (kə nun′drəm) ***n.*** [16th–c. Oxford University L. slang] **1.** a riddle whose answer contains a pun **2.** any puzzling question or problem

con·ur·ba·tion (kän′ər bā′shən) ***n.*** [< CON- + L. *urbs,* city + -ATION] a densely populated urban area, including suburbs and towns around a large city

con·va·lesce (kän′və les′) ***vi.*** **-lesced′, -lesc′ing** [< L. *convalescere* < *com-,* intens. + *valescere* < *valere,* to be strong] to recover gradually from illness; regain health

con·va·les·cence (-les′'ns) ***n.*** [see prec.] **1.** a gradual recovery of health after illness **2.** the period of such recovery —**con′va·les′cent** ***adj., n.***

con·vec·tion (kən vek′shən) ***n.*** [< L. < pp. of *convehere* < *com-,* together + *vehere,* to carry] **1.** a transmitting or conveying **2.** *a)* the movement of parts of a fluid within the fluid because of differences in the density, temperature, etc. of the parts *b)* the transference of heat by such movement —**con·vec′tion·al** ***adj.*** —**con·vec′tive** ***adj.*** —**con·vec′tive·ly** ***adv.*** —**con·vec′tor** ***n.***

con·vene (kən vēn′) ***vi., vt.*** **-vened′, -ven′ing** [< OFr. < L. *convenire* < *com-,* together + *venire,* to come] to assemble for a meeting —**con·ven′er** ***n.***

con·ven·ience (kən vēn′yəns) ***n.*** [< L. < *convenire,* CONVENE] **1.** the quality or condition of being convenient **2.** personal comfort **3.** anything that adds to one's comfort or saves work —**at one's convenience** at a time, place, etc. that suits one

con·ven·ient (-yənt) ***adj.*** **1.** favorable to one's comfort; easy to do, use, or get to; handy **2.** [Colloq.] easily accessible (*to*); near (*to*) —**con·ven′ient·ly** ***adv.***

con·vent (kän′vənt, -vent) ***n.*** [< OFr. < L. *conventus,* assembly, orig. pp. of *convenire,* CONVENE] **1.** a community of nuns or, sometimes, monks, living under strict religious vows **2.** the building or buildings in which they live

con·ven·ti·cle (kən ven′ti k'l) ***n.*** [< OFr. < L. dim. of prec.] **1.** a religious assembly, esp. an illegal or secret one **2.** a place where such an assembly meets

con·ven·tion (kən ven′shən) ***n.*** **1.** an assembly, often periodical, or the delegates to it *[a political convention,* lawyers' *convention]* **2.** *a)* an agreement between persons, nations, etc. *b)* general agreement on the usages and practices of social life **3.** a customary practice, rule, etc.

con·ven·tion·al (-'l) ***adj.*** **1.** having to do with a convention **2.** of, sanctioned by, or growing out of custom or usage; customary **3.** *a)* conforming to accepted rules or standards; formal; not natural, original, or spontaneous *b)* not unusual; ordinary **4.** stylized; conventionalized **5.** nonnuclear *[conventional* weapons*]* —**con·ven′tion·al·ism** ***n.*** —**con·ven′tion·al·ist** ***n.*** —**con·ven′tion·al·ly** ***adv.***

con·ven·tion·al·i·ty (kən ven′shə nal′ə tē) ***n., pl.*** **-ties** **1.** a being conventional **2.** conventional behavior or act **3.** a conventional form, usage, or rule

con·ven·tion·al·ize (kən ven′shən 'l īz′) ***vt.*** **-ized′, -iz′ing** **1.** to make conventional **2.** *Art* to treat in a conventional manner —**con·ven′tion·al·i·za′tion** ***n.***

conventional wisdom the generally accepted belief with regard to some matter, or the set of beliefs held by most people

con·ven·tu·al (kən ven′choo wəl) ***adj.*** of or like a convent —***n.*** a member of a convent

con·verge (kən vurj′) ***vi.*** **-verged′, -verg′ing** [< LL. *convergere* < L. *com-,* together + *vergere,* to turn] to come together or tend to come together at a point —***vt.*** to cause to converge

con·ver·gence (-vur′jəns) ***n.*** **1.** the act, fact, or condition of converging **2.** the point at which things converge Also **con·ver′gen·cy,** ***pl.*** **-cies** —**con·ver′gent** ***adj.***

con·vers·a·ble (kən vur′sə b'l) ***adj.*** **1.** easy to talk to; affable **2.** liking to converse or talk

con·ver·sant (kən vur′s'nt, kän′vər-) ***adj.*** [see CONVERSE[1]] familiar or acquainted (*with*), esp. as a result of study or experience; versed (*in*) —**con·ver′sance, con·ver′san·cy** ***n.*** —**con·ver′sant·ly** ***adv.***

con·ver·sa·tion (kän′vər sā′shən) ***n.*** [see CONVERSE[1]] a talking together; specif., *a)* familiar talk; verbal exchange of ideas, opinions, etc. *b)* an informal conference by representatives of governments, factions, etc.

con·ver·sa·tion·al (-'l) ***adj.*** **1.** of, like, or for conversation **2.** given to conversation; liking to converse —**con′ver·sa′tion·al·ist, con′ver·sa′tion·ist** ***n.***

conversation piece an unusual article of furniture, bric-a-brac, etc. that attracts attention or invites comment

con·verse[1] (kən vurs′; *for n.* kän′vərs) ***vi.*** **-versed′, -vers′ing** [< OFr. < L. *conversari,* to live with, ult. < *convertere:* see CONVERT] to hold a conversation; talk —***n.*** informal talk; conversation —**con·vers′er** ***n.***

con·verse[2] (kän′vərs; *also, for adj.,* kən vurs′) ***adj.*** [< L. pp. of *convertere:* see CONVERT] reversed in position, order, etc.; opposite; contrary —***n.*** a thing related in a converse way; the opposite —**con·verse′ly** ***adv.***

con·ver·sion (kən vur′zhən, -shən) ***n.*** a converting or being converted; specif., a change from lack of faith to religious belief or from one religion to another —**con·ver′sion·al, con·ver′sion·ar′y** ***adj.***

con·vert (kən vurt′; *for n.* kän′vərt) ***vt.*** [< OFr. < L. *convertere* < *com-,* together + *vertere,* to turn] **1.** to change from one form or use to another; transform *[convert* grain into flour*]* **2.** to cause to change from one belief, religion, etc. to another **3.** to exchange for something equal in value **4.** *Finance* to change (a security, currency, etc.) into an equivalent of another form **5.** *Law* to take and use (another's property) unlawfully —***vi.*** **1.** to be converted **2.** *Bowling* to knock down all of the standing pins on the second bowl, scoring a spare **3.** *Football* to score the extra point or points after a touchdown —***n.*** a person converted, as to a religion

con·vert·er (kən vur′tər) ***n.*** a person or thing that converts; specif., *a)* a furnace for converting pig iron into steel *b) Elec.* a device for converting alternating current into direct current: cf. INVERTER *c) Radio & TV* any device for adapting a receiver to added frequencies or modulations Also sp. **con·ver′tor**

converter reactor a nuclear reactor that produces less fissionable material than it consumes

con·vert·i·ble (kən vur′tə b'l) ***adj.*** that can be converted —***n.*** **1.** a thing that can be converted **2.** an automobile with a top that can be folded back —**con·vert′i·bil′i·ty** ***n.***

con·vex (kän veks′, kən-; *also, & for n. usually,* kän′veks) ***adj.*** [< L. *convexus,* pp. of *convehere* < *com-,* together + *vehere,* to bring] curving outward like the surface of a sphere —***n.*** a convex surface, line, object, etc. —**con·vex′i·ty** ***n., pl.*** **-ties** —**con·vex′ly** ***adv.***

con·vex·o-con·cave (kən vek′sō kän kāv′) ***adj.*** convex on one side and concave on the other

A B C

CONVEX LENSES (A, plano-convex; B, convexo-concave; C, convexo-convex)

con·vex·o-con·vex (-kän veks′) ***adj.*** convex on both sides, as some lenses

con·vey (kən vā′) ***vt.*** [< Anglo-Fr. *conveier,* to escort < L. *com-,* together + *via,* way] **1.** to take from one place to another; transport; carry **2.** to serve as a channel or medium for; transmit **3.** to make known; communicate **4.** to transfer, as title to property, to another person —**con·vey′a·ble** ***adj.***

con·vey·ance (-əns) ***n.*** **1.** a conveying **2.** a means of conveying, esp. a vehicle **3.** *a)* the transfer of the ownership of real property from one person to another *b)* a deed —**con·vey′anc·er** ***n.***

con·vey·or, con·vey·er (-ər) ***n.*** one that conveys; esp., a mechanical contrivance, as a continuous chain or belt **(conveyor belt)**

con·vict (kən vikt′; *for n.* kän′vikt) ***vt.*** [< L. pp. of *convincere:* see CONVINCE] **1.** to prove (a person) guilty *[convicted* by the evidence*]* **2.** to judge and find guilty of an offense charged —***n.*** **1.** one found guilty of a crime and sentenced by a court **2.** one serving a sentence in prison

con·vic·tion (kən vik′shən) ***n.*** **1.** a convicting or being convicted **2.** the state or appearance of being convinced, as of the truth of a belief *[to speak with conviction]* **3.** a strong belief —**con·vic′tive** ***adj.*** —**con·vic′tive·ly** ***adv.***

con·vince (kən vins′) ***vt.*** **-vinced′, -vinc′ing** [L. *convincere* < *com-,* intens. + *vincere,* to conquer] to overcome the doubts of; persuade by argument or evidence; make feel sure —**con·vinc′er** ***n.*** —**con·vinc′ing·ly** ***adv.***

con·viv·i·al (kən viv′ē əl) ***adj.*** [< L. < *convivium,* a feast < *com-,* together + *vivere,* to live] **1.** having to do with a feast or festive activity **2.** fond of eating, drinking, and good company; sociable; jovial —**con·viv′i·al·ist** ***n.*** —**con·viv′i·al′i·ty** ***n.*** —**con·viv′i·al·ly** ***adv.***

con·vo·ca·tion (kän′və kā′shən) ***n.*** **1.** a convoking **2.** a group that has been convoked; esp., an ecclesiastical or academic assembly —**con′vo·ca′tion·al** ***adj.***

con·voke (kən vōk′) ***vt.*** **-voked′, -vok′ing** [< Fr. < L. *convocare* < *com-,* together + *vocare,* to call] to call together; summon to assemble; convene —**con·vok′er** ***n.***

con·vo·lute (kän′və lo͞ot′) ***adj.*** [< L. pp. of *convolvere:* see CONVOLVE] rolled up in a spiral with the coils falling one upon the other; coiled —***vt., vi.*** **-lut′ed, -lut′ing** to wind around; coil —**con′vo·lute′ly** ***adv.***

con·vo·lut·ed (-id) ***adj.*** **1.** having convolutions; coiled **2.** involved; intricate; complicated

con·vo·lu·tion (kän′və lo͞o′shən) ***n.*** **1.** a twisting, coiling, or winding together **2.** a convoluted condition **3.** a fold, twist, or coil of something convoluted; specif., any of the irregular folds or ridges on the surface of the brain

con·volve (kən välv′) ***vt., vi.*** **-volved′, -volv′ing** [< L. *convolvere* < *com-,* together + *volvere,* to roll] to roll, coil, or twist together

con·vol·vu·lus (kən väl′vyə ləs) *n., pl.* **-lus·es, -li′** (-lī′) [L., bindweed: see prec.] any of a genus of trailing or twining plants related to the morning glory
con·voy (kän′voi; *also for v.* kən voi′) *vt.* [< OFr. *convoier*, CONVEY] to go along with as an escort, esp. in order to protect —*n.* **1.** the act of convoying **2.** a protecting escort, as for ships or troops **3.** a group of ships, vehicles, etc. traveling together for mutual protection
con·vulse (kən vuls′) *vt.* **-vulsed′, -vuls′ing** [< L. *convulsus*, pp. of *convellere* < *com-*, together + *vellere*, to pluck] **1.** to shake or disturb violently; agitate **2.** to cause convulsions, or spasms, in **3.** to cause to shake with laughter, rage, grief, etc. —**con·vul′sive** *adj.* —**con·vul′sive·ly** *adv.*
con·vul·sion (-vul′shən) *n.* **1.** a violent, involuntary contraction or spasm of the muscles: *often used in pl.* **2.** a violent fit of laughter **3.** any violent disturbance
co·ny (kō′nē) *n., pl.* **-nies** *same as* CONEY
coo (ko͞o) *vi.* [echoic] **1.** to make the soft, murmuring sound of pigeons or doves or a sound like this **2.** to speak gently and lovingly: see BILL[2], *vi.* 2 —*vt.* to express lovingly, as with a coo —*n.* a cooing sound —**coo′ing·ly** *adv.*
cook (kook) *n.* [OE. *coc* < L. < *coquere*, to cook] a person who prepares food for eating —*vt.* **1.** to prepare (food) for eating by boiling, baking, frying, etc. **2.** to subject to heat or a treatment suggestive of this **3.** [Slang] to spoil —*vi.* **1.** to act as a cook **2.** to undergo cooking —**cook up** [Colloq.] to concoct; devise —**what's cooking?** [Slang] what's happening? —**cook′er** *n.*
Cook (kook), **James** 1728–79; Eng. naval officer & explorer: explored Australia, New Zealand, etc.
cook·book (-book′) *n.* a book with recipes and other information about preparing food
cook·er·y (-ər ē) *n.* [Chiefly Brit.] the art, practice, or work of cooking
cook·ie, cook·y (-ē) *n., pl.* **-ies** [prob. Du. *koekje*, dim. of *koek*, a cake] **1.** a small, sweet cake, usually flat **2.** [Slang] a person, esp. one qualified as "tough, smart, etc."
cook·out (-out′) *n.* a meal prepared on an outdoor grill, etc. and eaten outdoors
cool (ko͞ol) *adj.* [OE. *col*] **1.** moderately cold; neither warm nor very cold **2.** tending to reduce discomfort in hot weather *[cool* clothes*]* **3.** *a)* not excited; calm; composed *b)* restrained *[cool jazz]* *c)* [Slang] emotionally uninvolved; dispassionate **4.** showing dislike or indifference **5.** calmly impudent or bold **6.** not suggesting warmth: said of blue-green colors **7.** [Colloq.] without exaggeration *[a cool* thousand dollars*]* **8.** [Slang] pleasing; excellent —*adv.* in a cool manner —*n.* **1.** a cool place, time, thing, etc. **2.** [Slang] cool, dispassionate attitude or manner —*vt., vi.* to make or become cool —**cool off 1.** to calm down **2.** to lose interest or zeal —**play it cool** [Slang] to stay aloof —**cool′ish** *adj.* —**cool′ly** *adv.* —**cool′ness** *n.*
cool·ant (-ənt) *n.* a substance, usually a fluid, used to remove heat as from a nuclear reactor, molten metal, an internal-combustion engine, etc.
cool·er (-ər) *n.* **1.** a device, container, or room for cooling things or keeping them cool **2.** anything that cools **3.** [Slang] a jail
Coo·lidge (ko͞o′lij), **(John) Calvin** 1872–1933; 30th president of the U.S. (1923–29)
coo·lie (ko͞o′lē) *n.* [Hindi *qūlī*, hired servant] **1.** an unskilled native laborer, esp. formerly, in China, India, etc. **2.** any person doing heavy labor for little pay
coon (ko͞on) *n. clipped form of* RACCOON
coon·skin (-skin′) *n.* the skin of a raccoon, used as a fur
coop (ko͞op) *n.* [ult. < L. *cupa*, tub, cask] **1.** a small cage, pen, or building for poultry, etc. **2.** any place of confinement; specif., [Slang] a jail —*vt.* to confine in or as in a coop —**fly the coop** [Slang] to escape, as from a jail
co-op (kō′äp) *n.* [Colloq.] a cooperative
co-op., coop. cooperative
coop·er (ko͞op′ər, koop′-) *n.* [< MDu. < LL. *cuparius* < L. *cupa*, a cask] a person whose work is making or repairing barrels and casks —*vt., vi.* to make or repair (barrels and casks)
Coop·er (ko͞op′ər, koop′-), **James Fen·i·more** (fen′ə môr′) 1789–1851; U.S. novelist
coop·er·age (-ij) *n.* **1.** the work or workshop of a cooper: also **coop′er·y,** *pl.* **-ies 2.** the price for such work
co·op·er·ate, co-op·er·ate (kō äp′ə rāt′) *vi.* **-at′ed, -at′ing** [< LL. pp. of *cooperari* < L. *co-*, with + *operari*, to work < *opus*, work] to act or work together with another or others: also **co·öp′er·ate′** —**co·op′er·a′tor, co-op′er·a′tor** *n.*
co·op·er·a·tion, co-op·er·a·tion (kō äp′ə rā′shən) *n.* **1.** a cooperating; joint effort or operation **2.** the association of a number of people in an enterprise for mutual benefits or profits Also **co·öp′er·a′tion** —**co·op′er·a′tion·ist, co-op′er·a′tion·ist** *n.*
co·op·er·a·tive, co-op·er·a·tive (kō äp′ər ə tiv, -ə rāt′iv; -äp′rə tiv) *adj.* **1.** cooperating or inclined to cooperate **2.** designating or of an organization (as for the production or marketing of goods), an apartment house, store, etc. owned collectively by members who share in its benefits —*n.* a cooperative society, store, etc. Also **co·öp′er·a·tive** —**co·op′er·a·tive·ly, co-op′er·a·tive·ly** *adv.* —**co·op′er·a·tive·ness, co-op′er·a·tive·ness** *n.*
co-opt (kō äpt′) *vt.* [< L. < *co-*, with + *optare*, to choose] **1.** to elect or appoint as an associate **2.** to get (an opponent) to join one's group, accept one's views, etc. Also **co·öpt′** —**co′-op·ta′tion, co-op′tion** *n.* —**co-op′ta·tive, co-op′tive** *adj.*
co·or·di·nate, co-or·di·nate (kō ôr′d'n it; *also, and for v. always,* -də nāt′) *adj.* [< ML. pp. of *coordinare* < L. *co-*, with + *ordinare*, to arrange < *ordo* (gen. *ordinis*), order] **1.** of equal order or importance **2.** of or involving coordination or coordinates **3.** *Gram.* being of equal structural rank *[coordinate* clauses*]* —*n.* **1.** a coordinate person or thing **2.** *Math.* any of two or more magnitudes used to define the position of a point, line, curve, or plane —*vt.* **-nat′ed, -nat′ing 1.** to make coordinate **2.** to bring into proper order or relation; adjust —*vi.* to become coordinate; function harmoniously Also **co·ör′di·nate** —**co·or′di·nate·ly, co-or′di·nate·ly** *adv.* —**co·or′di·na·tive, co-or′di·na·tive** (-nə tiv, -nāt′iv) *adj.* —**co·or′di·na′tor, co-or′di·na′tor** *n.*
coordinating conjunction a conjunction that connects coordinate words, phrases, or clauses (Ex.: *and, but, for, or, nor, yet*)
co·or·di·na·tion, co-or·di·na·tion (kō ôr′d'n ā′shən) *n.* **1.** a coordinating or being coordinated **2.** harmonious action, as of muscles Also **co·ör′di·na′tion**
coot (ko͞ot) *n., pl.* **coots:** also for 1 & 2 **coot:** see PLURAL, II, D, 1 [< ? MDu. *koet*] **1.** a ducklike, freshwater bird of the rail family with unwebbed toes **2.** *same as* SCOTER **3.** [Colloq.] a foolish, stupid, or senile person
coot·ie (-ē) *n.* [Slang] a louse
cop (käp) *vt.* **copped, cop′ping** [< obs. *cap*, to seize; ? ult. < L. *capere*, to take] [Slang] to seize, capture, win, steal, etc. —*n.* [Slang] a policeman —**cop out** [Slang] **1.** to confess to the police **2.** *a)* to back down; renege *b)* to give up; quit
co·pal (kō′pəl, -pal) *n.* [Sp. < Nahuatl *copalli*, resin] a hard resin from tropical trees
co·part·ner (kō pärt′nər) *n.* a partner, or associate —**co-part′ner·ship′** *n.*
cope[1] (kōp) *vi.* **coped, cop′ing** [OFr. *couper*, to strike < *coup*, COUP] **1.** to fight or contend (*with*) successfully or on equal terms **2.** to deal with problems, troubles, etc.
cope[2] (kōp) *n.* [< ML. *capa*, var. of *cappa:* see CAP] **1.** a large, capelike vestment worn by priests at certain ceremonies **2.** anything that covers like a cope, as a canopy —*vt.* **coped, cop′ing** to cover with a cope or coping
cope[3] (kōp) *vt.* **coped, cop′ing** [< COPING] to cut so as to fit against a coping or molding with curves, angles, etc.
Co·pen·hag·en (kō′pən hā′gən, -hä′-) capital of Denmark, on the E coast of Zealand & on an adjacent island: pop. 874,000 (met. area 1,378,000)
Copernican system the theory of Copernicus that the planets revolve around the sun and that the earth rotates
Co·per·ni·cus (kō pur′ni kəs), **Nic·o·la·us** (nik′ə lā′əs) (L. form of *Mikolaj Kopernik*) 1473–1543; Pol. astronomer —**Co·per′ni·can** *adj., n.*
cope·stone (kōp′stōn′) *n.* **1.** the top stone of a wall; stone in a coping **2.** a finishing touch
cop·i·er (käp′ē ər) *n.* **1.** one who copies; imitator, transcriber, etc. **2.** a duplicating machine
co·pi·lot (kō′pī′lət) *n.* the assistant pilot of an aircraft, who aids or relieves the pilot
cop·ing (kō′piŋ) *n.* [< fig. use of COPE[2]] the top layer of a masonry wall, usually sloped
coping saw a saw with a narrow blade in a U-shaped frame, esp. for cutting curved outlines
co·pi·ous (kō′pē əs) *adj.* [< L. < *copia*, abundance] **1.** plentiful; abundant **2.** wordy; profuse or diffuse **3.** full of information —**co′pi·ous·ly** *adv.* —**co′pi·ous·ness** *n.*

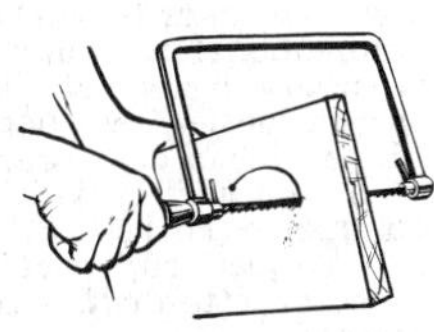
COPING SAW

Cop·land (kōp′lənd), **Aaron** 1900– ; U.S. composer
cop-out (käp′out′) *n.* [Slang] a copping out, as by confessing, backing down, quitting, etc.

cop·per[1] (käp′ər) ***n.*** see PLURAL, II, D, 3 [OE. *coper* < LL. *cuprum*, contr. < *Cyprium (aes)*, Cyprian (metal) < Gr. *Kyprios*, Cyprus, noted for its copper mines] **1.** a reddish-brown, malleable, ductile, metallic element that is an excellent conductor of electricity and heat: symbol, Cu; at. wt., 63.546; at. no., 29 **2.** [Now chiefly Brit.] a copper coin, as a penny **3.** the color of copper; reddish brown —***adj.*** **1.** of copper **2.** reddish-brown —***vt.*** to coat with copper —**cop′per·y** ***adj.***

cop·per[2] (käp′ər) ***n.*** [prob. < COP] [Slang] a policeman

cop·per·as (-əs) ***n.*** [< OFr. < ML. *(aqua) cuprosa*, lit., copper (water)] ferrous sulfate, $FeSO_4 \cdot 7H_2O$, a green, crystalline compound used in dyeing, the making of ink, etc.

cop·per·head (-hed′) ***n.*** **1.** a poisonous N. American pit viper with a copper-colored head **2.** [C-] a Northerner who sympathized with the South during the Civil War: so called in the North

cop·per·plate (-plāt′) ***n.*** **1.** a sheet of copper etched or engraved for printing **2.** a print made from this **3.** copperplate printing or engraving

cop·per·smith (-smith′) ***n.*** a person whose work is making utensils, etc. out of copper

copper sulfate a blue, crystalline substance, $CuSO_4 \cdot 5H_2O$: used in making pigments, batteries, etc.

cop·pice (käp′is) ***n.*** [< OFr. *copeis* < *couper*, to cut: see COUP] *same as* COPSE

co·pra (kō′prə, käp′rə) ***n.*** [Port. < Malayalam < Hindi *khoprā*] dried coconut meat, the source of coconut oil

copse (käps) ***n.*** [< COPPICE] a thicket of small trees or shrubs; coppice

Copt (käpt) ***n.*** **1.** a native of Egypt descended from the ancient inhabitants of that country **2.** a member of the Coptic Church

cop·ter (käp′tər) ***n.*** *shortened form of* HELICOPTER

Cop·tic (käp′tik) ***adj.*** [< ModL. < Ar. *Qufṭ*, the Copts < Gr. *Aigyptios*, Egyptian] **1.** of the Copts, their language, etc. **2.** of the Coptic Church —***n.*** the Afro-Asiatic language of the Copts, derived from ancient Egyptian

Coptic Church the native Christian church of Egypt and of Ethiopia

cop·u·la (käp′yə lə) ***n.***, *pl.* **-las** [L., a link < *co-*, together + OL. *apere*, to join] something that connects or links together; specif., *same as* LINKING VERB —**cop′u·lar** ***adj.***

cop·u·late (-lāt′) ***vi.*** **-lat′ed, -lat′ing** [< L. pp. of *copulare*, to couple < *copula*: see prec.] to have sexual intercourse —**cop′u·la′tion** ***n.*** —**cop′u·la·to′ry** (-lə tôr′ē) ***adj.***

cop·u·la·tive (-lāt′iv, -lə tiv) ***adj.*** **1.** coupling **2.** *Gram.* *a)* connecting coordinate words, phrases, or clauses *b)* involving connected words or clauses *c)* being a copula *[a copulative* verb*]* **3.** of or for copulating —***n.*** a copulative word —**cop′u·la′tive·ly** ***adv.***

cop·y (käp′ē) ***n.***, *pl.* **cop′ies** [< OFr. < ML. *copia*, copious transcript < L. *copia*, plenty] **1.** a thing made just like another; imitation **2.** any of a number of books, magazines, engravings, etc. having the same printed matter **3.** a manuscript or illustration to be set in type or printed **4.** subject matter for a writer **5.** the words of an advertisement —***vt., vi.*** **cop′ied, cop′y·ing** **1.** to make a copy or copies of; reproduce **2.** to imitate

cop·y·book (-book′) ***n.*** a book with models of handwriting, formerly used in teaching penmanship —***adj.*** ordinary; trite *[copybook* maxims*]*

cop·y·cat (-kat′) ***n.*** a person who habitually imitates or mimics: a child's term

copy desk the desk in a newspaper office where copy is edited and headlines are written

cop·y·ist (-ist) ***n.*** **1.** a person who makes written copies; transcriber **2.** a person who imitates

cop·y·read·er (-rē′dər) ***n.*** a person whose work is editing articles or other copy for publication

cop·y·right (-rīt′) ***n.*** [COPY + RIGHT] the exclusive right to the publication, production, or sale of a literary, musical, or artistic work, granted by law for a specified period of time to an author, composer, etc. —***vt.*** to protect (a book, etc.) by copyright —***adj.*** protected by copyright —**cop′y·right′a·ble** ***adj.*** —**cop′y·right′er** ***n.***

cop·y·writ·er (-rīt′ər) ***n.*** a writer of copy for advertising or promotional material

co·quet (kō ket′) ***vi.*** **-quet′ted, -quet′ting** [< Fr. < dim. of *coq*, a rooster: see COCK[1]] **1.** to behave as a coquette; flirt **2.** to trifle or dally (*with* an idea, offer, etc.) —***adj.*** coquettish —**co·quet·ry** (kōk′ə trē, kō ket′rē) ***n.***, *pl.* **-ries**

co·quette (kō ket′) ***n.*** [Fr.: see prec.] a girl or woman flirt —***vi.*** **-quet′ted, -quet′ting** to behave as a coquette; flirt —**co·quet′tish** ***adj.*** —**co·quet′tish·ly** ***adv.*** —**co·quet′tish·ness** ***n.***

co·qui·na (kō kē′nə) ***n.*** [Sp., shellfish < L. *concha*: see CONCH] **1.** a soft, whitish limestone made up of broken seashells and corals **2.** a small saltwater clam

Cor. **1.** Corinthians **2.** Coroner

cor. **1.** corner **2.** cornet **3.** correct **4.** correction **5.** correlative **6.** correspondence

Cor·a (kôr′ə) [L. < Gr. *Korē*, lit., maiden] a feminine name

cor·a·cle (kôr′ə k'l, kär′-) ***n.*** [< W. < *corwg*, orig., leather-covered boat] a small boat of waterproof material stretched over a wooden frame

cor·a·coid (kôr′ə koid′, kär′-) ***adj.*** [< Gr. < *korax*, raven + *eidos*, form] designating or of a bony process extending from the shoulder blade toward the breastbone —***n.*** this bony process

cor·al (kôr′əl, kär′-) ***n.*** [OFr. < L. < Gr. *korallion* < ? Heb. *gōrāl*, pebble] **1.** the hard, stony skeleton of some marine polyps, often in masses forming reefs and atolls in tropical seas **2.** any of such polyps, living singly or in large colonies **3.** a piece of coral **4.** yellowish red or yellowish pink: also **coral red** or **coral pink** —***adj.*** **1.** made of coral **2.** coral-red or coral-pink

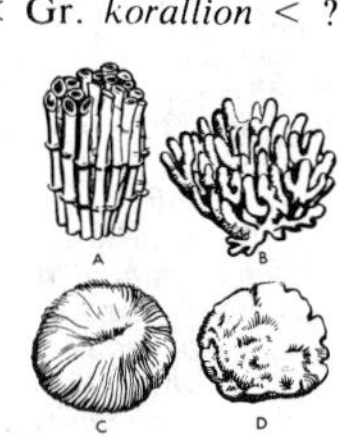

CORAL
(A, organ-pipe; B, reef; C, mushroom; D, Bermuda)

coral reef a reef made up chiefly of coral

cor·al·root (-ro͞ot′, -ro͝ot′) ***n.*** a brownish orchid with corallike rootstocks and no leaves

Coral Sea part of the S Pacific, northeast of Australia & south of the Solomon Islands

coral snake a small, poisonous snake with coral-red, yellow, and black bands around its body, found in the southern U.S.

cor·bel (kôr′bəl) ***n.*** [OFr. < L. *corvus*, raven] a bracket of stone, wood, etc. projecting from a wall to support a cornice, etc. —***vt.*** **-beled** or **-belled, -bel·ing** or **-bel·ling** to provide or support with a corbel or corbels

cor·bie (kôr′bē) ***n.***, *pl.* **-bies** [see prec.] [Scot.] a crow or raven

Corbusier, Le *see* LE CORBUSIER

cord (kôrd) ***n.*** [< OFr. < L. < Gr. *chordē*] **1.** (a) thick string or thin rope **2.** any force acting as a tie or bond **3.** [from cord used in measuring] a measure of wood cut for fuel (128 cubic feet) **4.** *a)* a rib on the surface of a fabric *b)* corduroy *c)* [*pl.*] corduroy trousers **5.** *Anat.* any part like a cord *[*the spinal *cord]*: also CHORD **6.** *Elec.* a slender, insulated cable fitted with a plug or plugs —***vt.*** **1.** to fasten or provide with a cord or cords **2.** to stack (wood) in cords

cord·age (-ij) ***n.*** **1.** cords and ropes collectively, esp. the ropes in a ship's rigging **2.** the amount of wood, in cords, in a given area

cor·date (kôr′dāt) ***adj.*** [< ModL. < L. *cor* (gen. *cordis*), heart] heart-shaped —**cor′date·ly** ***adv.***

cord·ed (kôr′did) ***adj.*** **1.** fastened with cords **2.** made of cords **3.** that looks like a tight cord, as a muscle **4.** having a ribbed surface, as corduroy **5.** stacked in cords, as wood

Cor·del·ia (kôr dēl′yə) [prob. ult. < Celt. *Creiryddlydd*, lit., daughter of the sea] a feminine name

cor·dial (kôr′jəl) ***adj.*** [< ML. < L. *cor* (gen. *cordis*), heart] **1.** [Rare] invigorating **2.** warm and friendly; hearty; sincere —***n.*** **1.** [Rare] a stimulating medicine, food, or drink **2.** an aromatic, alcoholic drink; liqueur —**cor′dial·ly** ***adv.*** —**cor′dial·ness** ***n.***

cor·di·al·i·ty (kôr′jē al′ə tē, kôr jal′-) ***n.*** **1.** a cordial quality; warm, friendly feeling **2.** *pl.* **-ties** a cordial act or remark

cor·dil·le·ra (kôr′dil yer′ə, kôr dil′ər ə) ***n.*** [Sp. < dim. of *cuerda*, rope < L. *chorda*, CORD] a chain of mountains; esp., the principal mountain range of a continent —**cor′dil·le′ran** ***adj.***

cord·ing (kôr′diŋ) ***n.*** the ribbed surface of corded cloth

cord·ite (-dīt) ***n.*** [CORD + -ITE: from its stringiness] a smokeless explosive made of nitroglycerin, guncotton, petroleum jelly, and acetone

cord·less (kôrd′lis) ***adj.*** operated by batteries rather than by current from an outlet

Cor·do·ba (kôr′də bə, -və; *Sp.* kôr′*th*ô bä) **1.** city in NC Argentina: pop. 589,000 **2.** city in S Spain: pop. 220,000

cor·do·ba (kôr′də bə) ***n.*** [after F. F. de *Córdoba*, 16th-cent. Sp. explorer] *see* MONETARY UNITS, table (Nicaragua)

cor·don (kôr′d'n) ***n.*** [Fr., dim. of *corde*: see CORD] **1.** a line or circle of police, ships, etc. stationed around an area to guard it **2.** a cord, ribbon, or braid worn as a decoration or badge —***vt.*** to encircle or shut (*off*) with a cordon

cor·do·van (kôr′də vən) ***adj.*** [< Sp. < CÓRDOBA] made of cordovan —***n.*** **1.** a fine-grained, colored leather, usually of split horsehide **2.** [*pl.*] shoes made of this leather

cor·du·roy (kôr′də roi′) ***n.*** [prob. < CORD + obs. *duroy*, a coarse fabric] **1.** a heavy cotton fabric with a velvety surface, ribbed vertically **2.** [*pl.*] trousers made of this —***adj.*** **1.** made of, or ribbed like, corduroy **2.** made of logs laid crosswise *[a corduroy* road*]*

cord·wood (kôrd′wood′) ***n.*** wood stacked or sold in cords

core (kôr) ***n.*** **[**< OFr., prob. < L. *cor,* heart**]** **1.** the central part of an apple, pear, etc., containing the seeds **2.** the central part of anything **3.** the most important part; essence; pith **4.** in foundry work, that part of a mold forming the interior of a hollow casting **5.** a sample section of the earth's strata from underground, obtained with a hollow drill **6.** the center of a nuclear reactor that contains the fissionable fuel **7.** *Chem.* the nucleus of an atom with its electron shells **8.** *Elec.* a mass of iron inside a wire coil: it increases the magnetic field **—*vt.* cored, cor′ing** to remove the core of **—cor′er *n.***

CORE (kôr) Congress of Racial Equality

co·re·li·gion·ist (kō′ri lij′ə nist) ***n.*** a person of the same religion or religious denomination

co·re·op·sis (kôr′ē äp′sis) ***n.*** [ModL. < Gr. *koris,* bug + *opsis,* appearance: from the shape of the fruit] a plant of the composite family, with showy flowers of yellow, crimson, or maroon

co·re·spond·ent (kō′ri spän′dənt) ***n.*** **[**CO- + RESPONDENT**]** *Law* a person charged with having committed adultery with the wife or husband from whom a divorce is being sought **—co′re·spond′en·cy *n.***

cor·gi (kôr′gē) ***n.*** *same as* WELSH CORGI

co·ri·an·der (kôr′ē an′dər) ***n.*** **[**< OFr. < L. < Gr. *koriandron***]** **1.** a European herb of the parsley family **2.** its strong-smelling, seedlike fruit, used in flavoring food and liqueurs

Cor·inth (kôr′inth, kär′-) ancient city in the NE Peloponnesus, Greece: noted for its luxury

Co·rin·thi·an (kə rin′thē ən) ***adj.*** **1.** of Corinth, its people, or culture **2.** dissolute and loving luxury, as the people of Corinth were said to be **3.** designating or of the most elaborate of the three orders of Greek architecture, distinguished by a bell-shaped capital with a design of acanthus leaves: cf. DORIC, IONIC **—*n.*** a native or inhabitant of Corinth

CORINTHIAN CAPITAL

Co·rin·thi·ans (-ənz) either of two books of the New Testament, epistles from the Apostle Paul to the Christians of Corinth

Cor·i·o·lis force (kô′rē ō′lis) [after G. de *Coriolis,* 19th-c. Fr. mathematician] the apparent force, caused by the earth's rotation, that produces the deflection (**Coriolis effect**) of a moving body to the right in the Northern Hemisphere and to the left in the Southern

Cork (kôrk) seaport in S Ireland: pop. 122,000

cork (kôrk) ***n.*** **[**< Sp. *corcho,* ult. (via ? Ar.) < L. *quercus,* oak**]** **1.** the light, thick, elastic outer bark of an oak tree, the **cork oak,** of the Mediterranean area **2.** a piece of cork; esp., a stopper for a bottle, cask, etc. **3.** any stopper, as one of rubber, etc. **4.** the outer bark of the stems of woody plants **—*adj.*** made of cork **—*vt.*** **1.** to stop with a cork **2.** to restrain; check **3.** to blacken with burnt cork

cork·er (kôr′kər) ***n.*** **1.** a worker or device that corks bottles **2.** [Slang] *a)* a remarkable person or thing *b)* a preposterous lie

cork·ing (-kiŋ) ***adj., adv., interj.*** [Chiefly Brit. Slang] very good; excellent

cork·screw (kôrk′skrōō′) ***n.*** a spiral-shaped device for pulling corks out of bottles **—*adj.*** shaped like a corkscrew **—*vi., vt.*** to move in a spiral; twist

cork·y (kôr′kē) ***adj.* cork′i·er, cork′i·est** **1.** of or like cork **2.** tasting of the cork: said of wine

corm (kôrm) ***n.*** **[**< Gr. *kormos,* a lopped tree trunk < *keirein,* to cut off**]** the fleshy, scaly, underground stem of certain plants, as the gladiolus

cor·mo·rant (kôr′mə rənt) ***n.*** **[**< OFr. < L. < *corvus,* raven + *marinus,* MARINE**]** **1.** a large, voracious, diving bird with webbed toes: used by fishermen in the Orient to catch fish **2.** a greedy person

corn[1] (kôrn) ***n.*** see PLURAL, II, D, 3 [OE.] **1.** a small, hard seed, esp. a seed or grain of a cereal grass; kernel: chiefly in compounds *[peppercorn]* **2.** *a)* a cultivated American cereal plant, with the grain borne on cobs enclosed in husks; maize; Indian corn *b)* its ears or kernels **3.** [Brit.] the seeds of all cereal grasses; grain **4.** the leading cereal crop, as wheat in England or oats in Scotland and Ireland **5.** [Colloq.] corn whiskey **6.** [Slang] ideas, music, etc. considered old-fashioned, trite, sentimental, etc. **—*vt.*** to preserve or pickle (meat, etc.) with salt granules or in brine **—corned *adj.***

corn[2] (kôrn) ***n.*** **[**< OFr. < L. *cornu,* a horn**]** a hard, thick, painful growth of skin, esp. on a toe

corn·ball (-bôl′) ***adj.*** **[**CORN[1], *n.* 6 + (SCREW)BALL**]** [Slang] unsophisticated; corny **—*n.*** [Slang] a person or thing that is corny

Corn Belt NC plains region of the Middle West where much corn and cornfed livestock are raised

corn borer a moth larva that feeds on corn, sorghum, etc.

corn bread a bread made with cornmeal

corn·cob (-käb′) ***n.*** **1.** the woody core of an ear of corn **2.** a tobacco pipe with a bowl made of a hollowed, dried piece of such a core: in full, **corncob pipe**

corn cockle a tall weed of the pink family, with pink flowers, often found in grainfields

cor·ne·a (kôr′nē ə) ***n.*** **[**< ML. < L. *cornea* (*tela*), horny (tissue) < *cornu,* a horn**]** the transparent outer coat of the eyeball, covering the iris and pupil **—cor′ne·al *adj.***

Cor·neille (kôr nā′y′), **Pierre** 1606–84; Fr. dramatist

cor·nel (kôr′n′l, -nel) ***n.*** **[**< OFr. < VL. < L. *cornus***]** any of a genus of shrubs and small trees with very hard wood, including the dogwoods

cor·nel·ian (kôr nēl′yən) ***n.*** **[**< OFr. *corneola,* prob. < VL. *cornea:* see CORNEL**]** *same as* CARNELIAN

cor·ner (kôr′nər) ***n.*** **[**< OFr. < ML. < *cornu,* a horn**]** **1.** the point or place where lines or surfaces join and form an angle **2.** the space within the angle formed at the joining of lines or surfaces **3.** the tip of any angle formed at a street intersection **4.** something used to form, mark, protect, or decorate a corner **5.** a remote or secluded spot **6.** region; quarter *[*every *corner* of America*]* **7.** an awkward position from which escape is difficult **8.** a monopoly acquired on a stock or commodity to raise the price **—*vt.*** **1.** to force into a corner or awkward position, so that escape is difficult **2.** to get a monopoly on (a stock or commodity) **—*vi.*** **1.** to meet at or abut (*on*) a corner: said of buildings, etc. **2.** to turn corners: said of a vehicle **—*adj.*** **1.** at or on a corner **2.** used in a corner **—around the corner** very near or imminent **—cut corners** **1.** to take a direct route by going across corners **2.** to cut down expenses, time, labor, etc. **—cor′nered *adj.***

cor·ner·back (-bak′) ***n.*** *Football* a player of the defensive backfield between the line of scrimmage and the safety men

cor·ner·stone (-stōn′) ***n.*** **1.** a stone laid in the corner of a building, esp. at a ceremony for beginning a building **2.** the basic part; foundation

cor·ner·wise (-wīz′) ***adv.*** **1.** with the corner to the front **2.** from one corner to its opposite; diagonally Also **cor′ner·ways′**

cor·net (kôr net′) ***n.*** **[**< OFr. < L. *cornu,* a horn**]** **1.** a brass-wind musical instrument of the trumpet class **2.** *a)* a cone-shaped paper for holding candy, etc. *b)* a cone-shaped pastry **—cor·net′ist, cor·net′tist *n.***

corn·flakes (kôrn′flāks′) ***n.pl.*** a breakfast cereal of crisp flakes made from hulled corn

corn·flow·er (-flou′ər) ***n.*** a plant of the composite family, with white, pink, or blue flowers

corn·husk·ing (-hus′kiŋ) ***n.*** a gathering of people for husking corn **—corn′husk′er *n.***

cor·nice (kôr′nis) ***n.*** **[**Fr. < It. < L. < Gr. *korōnis,* a wreath**]** **1.** a horizontal molding projecting along the top of a wall, building, etc. **2.** the top part of an entablature **3.** a decorative strip above a window for hiding a curtain rod **—*vt.* -niced, -nic·ing** to top as with a cornice

Cor·nish (kôr′nish) ***adj.*** of Cornwall, its people, or culture **—*n.*** **1.** the Brythonic Celtic language spoken in Cornwall until c. 1800 **2.** *pl.* **Cor′nish** *a)* a British breed of chicken *b)* a breed of chicken crossbred from these and Plymouth Rocks: also **Cornish hen** or **Rock Cornish (hen)**

corn·meal (kôrn′mēl′) ***n.*** meal made from corn (maize)

corn pone [Chiefly Southern] a kind of corn bread baked in small, oval loaves (*pones*)

corn·row (kôrn′rō′) ***n.*** an African hairstyle in which the hair is arranged in an intricate pattern of tight braids separated by wide parts **—*vt.*** to arrange in a cornrow

corn silk the long, silky fibers that hang in a tuft from the husk of an ear of corn

corn·stalk (-stôk′) ***n.*** a stalk of corn (maize)

corn·starch (-stärch′) ***n.*** a starch made from corn and used in cooking and to make corn syrup, etc.

corn syrup a sweet syrup made from cornstarch

cor·nu·co·pi·a (kôr′nə kō′pē ə, -nyōō-) ***n.*** [L. *cornu copiae,* horn of plenty] **1.** a representation in painting, sculpture, etc. of a horn overflowing with fruits, flowers, and grain; horn of plenty **2.** an abundance **3.** any cone-shaped container

CORNUCOPIA

Corn·wall (kôrn′wôl; *chiefly Brit.* -wəl) county at the SW tip of England: 1,357 sq. mi.

Corn·wal·lis (kôrn wôl′is, -wäl′-), **Charles,** 1st Marquis Cornwallis, 1738–1805; Eng. general: a commander of Brit. forces in the Am. Revolution

corn whiskey whiskey made from corn (maize)

corn·y (kôr′nē) *adj.* **corn′i·er, corn′i·est** 1. of corn 2. [Colloq.] unsophisticated, old-fashioned, trite, sentimental, etc. —**corn′i·ness** *n.*

corol., coroll. corollary

co·rol·la (kə räl′ə, -rōl′ə) *n.* [L., dim. of *corona,* CROWN] the petals, or inner floral leaves, of a flower —**cor·ol·late** (kôr′ə lāt′, kär′-), **cor′ol·lat′ed** *adj.*

cor·ol·lar·y (kôr′ə ler′ē, kär′-) *n., pl.* **-lar′ies** [< LL. *corollarium,* a deduction < L., a gift < *corolla:* see prec.] 1. a proposition that follows from another that has been proved 2. an inference or deduction 3. anything that follows as a normal result

co·ro·na (kə rō′nə) *n., pl.* **-nas, -nae** (-nē) [L., CROWN] 1. a crown or something like a crown 2. a long cigar with blunt ends 3. *Anat.* the upper part of a tooth, of a skull, etc. 4. *Astron. a)* the outermost part of the sun's atmosphere, seen during a total eclipse *b)* a ring of colored light seen around a luminous body, as the sun or moon, as a result of diffraction by mist, dust, etc. 5. *Bot.* the cuplike part on the inner side of the corolla of certain flowers, as the daffodil 6. *Elec.* a sometimes visible electric discharge around a conductor at high potential —**cor·o′nal** *adj.*

Co·ro·na·do (kôr′ə nä′dō; *Sp.* kô′rô nä′*th*ô), **Fran·cis·co Vás·quez de** (frän thēs′kô väs′keth *the*) 1510?–54?; Sp. explorer in SW N. America

cor·o·nar·y (kôr′ə ner′ē, kär′-) *adj.* [see CORONA] 1. of, or in the form of, a crown 2. *Anat.* designating or of either of two arteries branching from the aorta and supplying blood directly to the heart muscle —*n., pl.* **-nar′ies** *same as* CORONARY THROMBOSIS

coronary insufficiency inability of the coronary arteries to supply enough blood to the myocardium

coronary thrombosis the formation of an obstructing clot in a coronary artery: also **coronary occlusion**

cor·o·na·tion (kôr′ə nā′shən, kär′-) *n.* [< OFr. < L. pp. of *coronare* < *corona,* CROWN] the act or ceremony of crowning a sovereign

cor·o·ner (kôr′ə nər, kär′-) *n.* [ME., officer of the crown < Anglo-Fr. < L. *corona,* CROWN] a public officer whose chief duty is to determine by inquest before a jury the causes of any deaths not obviously due to natural causes

cor·o·net (kôr′ə net′, kär′-) *n.* [< OFr. dim. of *corone,* CROWN] 1. a small crown worn by princes and others of high rank 2. an ornamental band, as of gold, jewels, or flowers, worn around the head —**cor′o·net′ed, cor′o·net′ted** *adj.*

Co·rot (kə rō′; *Fr.* kô rō′), **Jean Bap·tiste Ca·mille** (zhän bȧ tēst′ kȧ mē′y′) 1796–1875; Fr. painter

corp., corpn. corporation

cor·po·ral[1] (kôr′pər əl) *n.* [< Fr. < It. < *capo,* chief < L. *caput,* the head: sp. infl. by *corps* or ff.] the lowest-ranking noncommissioned officer, just below a sergeant; specif., an enlisted man or woman in the fourth grade in the U.S. Army and Marine Corps: abbrev. **Corp., Cpl** —**cor′po·ral·cy,** *pl.* **-cies, cor′po·ral·ship′** *n.*

cor·po·ral[2] (kôr′pər əl) *adj.* [< L. *corporalis* < *corpus,* body] of the body; bodily —**cor′po·ral′i·ty** (-pə ral′ə tē) *n.* —**cor′po·ral·ly** *adv.*

cor·po·ral[3] (kôr′pə rəl) *n.* [OFr. < ML. *corporalis* (*palla*), body (cloth): see prec.] *Eccles.* a small, linen altar cloth on which the bread and chalice are placed for the Eucharist

corporal punishment punishment inflicted directly on the body, as flogging

cor·po·rate (kôr′pər it) *adj.* [< L. pp. of *corporare,* to make into a body < *corpus,* body] 1. incorporated 2. of a corporation 3. shared by all in a group *[corporate* blame*]* —**cor′po·rate·ly** *adv.*

cor·po·ra·tion (kôr′pə rā′shən) *n.* 1. a group of people who get a charter granting them as a body certain of the legal powers, rights, and liabilities of an individual 2. a group of people, as the mayor and aldermen of an incorporated town, legally authorized to act as an individual —**cor′po·ra·tive** *adj.* —**cor′po·ra′tor** *n.*

cor·po·re·al (kôr pôr′ē əl) *adj.* [< L. < *corpus* (gen. *corporis*), body] 1. of or for the body; bodily 2. material; physical; tangible —**cor·po′re·al′i·ty** (-al′ə tē) *n.* —**cor·po′re·al·ly** *adv.*

corps (kôr) *n., pl.* **corps** (kôrz) [< OFr. *corps, cors* < L. *corpus,* body] 1. a body of people associated in some work, organization, etc. 2. *Mil. a)* a branch of the armed forces with some specialized function *[*Signal *Corps] b)* a tactical subdivision of an army, normally composed of two or more divisions

corpse (kôrps) *n.* [var. of CORPS] 1. a dead body, esp. of a person 2. something lifeless and of no use

corps·man (kôr′mən) *n., pl.* **-men** *same as* AIDMAN

cor·pu·lence (kôr′pyoo ləns) *n.* [OFr. < L. < *corpus,* body] fatness or stoutness of body; obesity: also **cor′pu·len·cy** —**cor′pu·lent** *adj.* —**cor′pu·lent·ly** *adv.*

cor·pus (kôr′pəs) *n., pl.* **cor′po·ra** (-pər ə) [L.] 1. a human or animal body; esp., a dead one: now mainly a facetious usage 2. a complete or comprehensive collection, as of laws or writings of a specified type 3. the main body or substance of anything

Corpus Christ·i (kris′tē) [L., Body of Christ] 1. *R.C.Ch.* a festival celebrated on the Thursday after Trinity Sunday, in honor of the Eucharist 2. city in SE Tex., on the Gulf of Mexico: pop. 232,000

cor·pus·cle (kôr′pəs ′l, -pus′′l) *n.* [< L. dim. of *corpus,* body] 1. a very small particle 2. *Anat.* a protoplasmic particle with a special function; esp., any of the erythrocytes (**red corpuscles**) or leukocytes (**white corpuscles**) that float in the blood, lymph, etc. of vertebrates: also **cor·pus·cule** (kôr pus′kyo͞ol) —**cor·pus′cu·lar** (-kyoo lər) *adj.*

corpus de·lic·ti (di lik′tī) [ModL., lit., body of the crime] 1. the facts constituting or proving a crime 2. loosely, the body of a murder victim

corpus ju·ris (joor′is) [L., body of law] a collection of all the laws of a nation or district

corpus lu·te·um (lo͞o′tē əm) *pl.* **cor·po·ra lu·te·a** (kôr′pər ə lo͞o′tē ə) [ModL., lit., yellow body] a mass of yellow tissue, formed in the ovary after ovulation, that secretes progesterone if fertilization occurs

corr. 1. corrected 2. correspondence

cor·ral (kə ral′) *n.* [Sp. < *corro,* a circle < L. *currere,* to run] an enclosure for holding or capturing horses, cattle, etc.; pen —*vt.* **-ralled′, -ral′ling** 1. to drive into or confine in a corral 2. to surround or capture; round up

cor·rect (kə rekt′) *vt.* [< L. pp. of *corrigere* < *com-,* together + *regere,* to lead straight] 1. to make right; change from wrong to right 2. to mark the errors or faults of 3. to make conform to a standard 4. to scold or punish so as to cause to rectify faults 5. to cure or counteract (a fault, disease, etc.) —*vi.* to make corrections or an adjustment to compensate (*for* an error, etc.) —*adj.* 1. conforming to an established standard; proper 2. conforming to fact or logic; true; accurate; right 3. equal to the required number, amount, etc. —**cor·rect′a·ble** *adj.* —**cor·rect′ly** *adv.* —**cor·rect′ness** *n.* —**cor·rec′tor** *n.*

cor·rec·tion (kə rek′shən) *n.* 1. a correcting or being corrected 2. a change that corrects a mistake; rectification 3. punishment or scolding to correct faults —**cor·rec′tion·al** *adj.*

cor·rec·tive (-tiv) *adj.* tending or meant to correct or improve; remedial —*n.* something corrective; remedy —**cor·rec′tive·ly** *adv.*

Cor·reg·gio (kə rej′ō), (**Antonio Allegri da**) 1494?–1534; It. painter

cor·re·late (kôr′ə lāt′, kär′-) *n.* [*cor-* (see COM-) + L. *relatus:* see RELATE] either of two interrelated things —*adj.* closely and naturally related —*vi.* **-lat′ed, -lat′ing** to be mutually related (*to* or *with*) —*vt.* to bring (a thing) into mutual relation (*with* another); calculate or show the relation between

cor·re·la·tion (kôr′ə lā′shən, kär′-) *n.* [see prec.] 1. a mutual relationship or connection 2. the degree of relative correspondence between two sets of data 3. a correlating or being correlated —**cor′re·la′tion·al** *adj.*

cor·rel·a·tive (kə rel′ə tiv) *adj.* 1. having a mutual relationship; reciprocally dependent 2. *Gram.* expressing mutual relation and used in pairs *[neither . . . nor* are *correlative* conjunctions*]* —*n.* 1. a thing closely related to something else 2. a correlative word —**cor·rel′a·tive·ly** *adv.* —**cor·rel′a·tiv′i·ty** *n.*

cor·re·spond (kôr′ə spänd′, kär′-) *vi.* [< Fr. < ML. *correspondere* < L. *com-,* together + *respondere,* to answer] 1. to be in agreement (*with* something); conform (*to* something); match 2. to be similar, analogous, or equal (*to* something) 3. to communicate (*with* someone) by letters —**cor′re·spond′ing·ly** *adv.*

cor·re·spond·ence (-spän′dəns) *n.* [see prec.] 1. agreement; conformity 2. similarity; analogy 3. *a)* communication by exchange of letters *b)* the letters written or received

correspondence school a school that gives courses of instruction (**correspondence courses**) by mail

cor·re·spond·ent (kôr′ə spän′dənt, kär′-) *adj.* corresponding —*n.* 1. a thing that corresponds 2. a person who exchanges letters with, or writes a letter to, another 3. a person hired as by a newspaper to send news regularly from a distant place

cor·ri·dor (kôr′ə dər, kär′-; -dôr′) *n.* [Fr. < It. < L. *currere,* to run] 1. a long passageway or hall 2. a strip of land providing passage through foreign-held land, as from a country to its seaport

cor·ri·gen·dum (kôr′ə jen′dəm, kär′-) *n., pl.* **-da** (-də) [L., gerundive of *corrigere:* see CORRECT] an error to be corrected in a printed work, or [*pl.*] a list of such errors inserted in the work

cor·ri·gi·ble (kôr′i jə b′l, kär′-) *adj.* [< OFr. < ML. < L. *corrigere:* see CORRECT] capable of being corrected, improved, or reformed —**cor′ri·gi·bil′i·ty** *n.* —**cor′ri·gi·bly** *adv.*

cor·rob·o·rate (kə räb′ə rāt′) *vt.* **-rat′ed, -rat′ing** [< L. pp. of *corroborare* < *com-,* intens. + *roborare* < *robur,*

strength] to confirm; bolster; support —**cor·rob′o·ra′tion** *n.* —**cor·rob′o·ra′tor** *n.*
cor·rob·o·ra·tive (kə räb′ə rāt′iv, -ər ə tiv) *adj.* corroborating; confirmatory: also **cor·rob′o·ra·to′ry** (-ər ə-tôr′ē) —**cor·rob′o·ra′tive·ly** *adv.*
cor·rode (kə rōd′) *vt.* **-rod′ed, -rod′ing** [< OFr. < L. *corrodere* < *com-*, intens. + *rodere*, to gnaw] to eat into or wear away gradually, as by rusting or by the action of chemicals —*vi.* to become corroded —**cor·rod′i·ble** *adj.*
cor·ro·sion (kə rō′zhən) *n.* **1.** a corroding or being corroded **2.** a substance formed by corroding
cor·ro·sive (kə rōs′iv) *adj.* [< OFr. < ML. *corrosivus*] causing corrosion —*n.* something causing corrosion —**cor-ro′sive·ly** *adv.* —**cor·ro′sive·ness** *n.*
corrosive sublimate *same as* MERCURIC CHLORIDE
cor·ru·gate (kôr′ə gāt′, kär′-; -yoo-) *vt., vi.* **-gat′ed, -gat′ing** [< L. pp. of *corrugare* < *com-*, intens. + *rugare*, to wrinkle] to shape into parallel grooves and ridges; make wrinkles in; furrow *[corrugated* iron, *corrugated* paper*]*

CORRUGATED SURFACE

cor·ru·ga·tion (kôr′ə gā′shən, kär′-; -yoo-) *n.* **1.** a corrugating or being corrugated **2.** any ridge or groove of a corrugated surface
cor·rupt (kə rupt′) *adj.* [< L. pp. of *corrumpere*, to ruin < *com-*, together + *rumpere*, to break] **1.** orig., spoiled; rotten **2.** morally debased; evil; depraved **3.** taking bribes **4.** containing alterations, foreign admixtures, or errors *[*a *corrupt* text*]* —*vt., vi.* to make or become corrupt —**cor-rupt′er, cor·rup′tor** *n.* —**cor·rup′tive** *adj.* —**cor·rupt′ly** *adv.* —**cor·rupt′ness** *n.*
cor·rupt·i·ble (kə rup′tə b'l) *adj.* that can be corrupted, esp. morally —**cor·rupt′i·bil′i·ty** *n.* —**cor·rupt′i·bly** *adv.*
cor·rup·tion (kə rup′shən) *n.* **1.** a making, becoming, or being corrupt **2.** depravity **3.** bribery **4.** decay; rottenness **5.** something corrupted
cor·sage (kôr säzh′, -säj′) *n.* [Fr.: see CORPS & -AGE] **1.** the bodice of a dress **2.** a small bouquet for a woman to wear, as at the waist or shoulder
cor·sair (kôr′ser) *n.* [< Fr. < Pr. < It. < L. *cursus*, a COURSE] **1.** a privateer **2.** a pirate **3.** a pirate ship
corse (kôrs) *n.* [Archaic or Poet.] a corpse
corse·let (kôrs′lət; *for 2* kôr′sə let′) *n.* [see ff.] **1.** a medieval piece of body armor: also sp. **cors′let** **2.** a woman's lightweight corset: also sp. **cor′se·lette′**
cor·set (kôr′sit) *n.* [OFr., dim of *cors:* see CORPS] [*sometimes pl.*] a closefitting undergarment, often reinforced with stays, worn, chiefly by women, to give support to or shape the torso —*vt.* to dress in, or fit with, a corset
Cor·si·ca (kôr′si kə) Fr. island in the Mediterranean, north of Sardinia: 3,367 sq. mi.; pop. 270,000; cap. Ajaccio: Fr. name **Corse** (kôrs) —**Cor′si·can** *adj., n.*
cor·tege, cor·tège (kôr tezh′, -tāzh′) *n.* [Fr. < It. *corteggio*, retinue < L. *cohors:* see COURT] **1.** a group of attendants; retinue **2.** a ceremonial procession, as at a funeral
Cor·tés (kôr tez′; *Sp.* kôr tes′), **Her·nan·do** (hər nan′dō) or **Her·nán** (er nän′) 1485–1547; Sp. explorer: conqueror of Mexico: also sp. **Cortez**
cor·tex (kôr′teks) *n., pl.* **-ti·ces′** (-tə sēz′) [L., bark of a tree] **1.** *a)* the outer part of an internal organ, as of the kidney *b)* the outer layer of gray matter over most of the brain **2.** a layer of tissue under the epidermis in plant roots and stems **3.** the bark or rind of a plant —**cor′ti-cal** (-ti k'l) *adj.* —**cor′ti·cal·ly** *adv.*
cor·ti·cate (kôr′ti kit, -kāt′) *adj.* [L. *corticatus* < *cortex*] covered with bark: also **cor′ti·cat′ed, cor′ti·cose′** (-kōs′)
cor·ti·sone (kôrt′ə sōn′, -zōn′) *n.* [< *corticosterone*, a hormone] an adrenal-gland hormone, $C_{21}H_{28}O_5$, used in treating adrenal insufficiency and various inflammatory and allergic diseases
co·run·dum (kə run′dəm) *n.* [Tamil *kurundam* < Sans. *kuruvinda*, ruby] a hard mineral, aluminum oxide, Al_2O_3, used for grinding and polishing: the ruby, sapphire, etc. are precious varieties
cor·us·cate (kôr′əs kāt′, kär′-) *vt.* **-cat′ed, -cat′ing** [< L. pp. of *coruscare* < *coruscus*, vibrating] to emit flashes of light; glitter; sparkle —**co·rus·cant** (kə rus′kənt) *adj.* —**cor′us·ca′tion** *n.*
cor·vette (kôr vet′) *n.* [Fr., prob. ult. < L. *corbita (navis)*, cargo (ship) < *corbis*, basket] **1.** formerly, a sailing warship smaller than a frigate **2.** a small, fast British warship used for antisubmarine and convoy duty
cor·vine (kôr′vīn, -vin) *adj.* [< L. < *corvus*, a raven] of or like a crow or raven
Cor·y·bant (kôr′ə bant′) *n., pl.* **-bants′, Cor′y·ban′tes** (-ban′tēz) **1.** *a) Gr. Myth.* an attendant of the goddess Cybele at her orgiastic revelries *b)* a priest of Cybele **2.** [c-] a reveler —**Cor′y·ban′tic, Cor′y·ban′tian** (-ban′-shən) *adj.*
cor·ymb (kôr′im, -imb; kär′-) *n.* [< Fr. < L. *corymbus*, flower cluster < Gr. *korymbos*] a broad, flat cluster of flowers in which the outer stems are long and those toward the center progressively shorter —**co·rym·bose** (kə rim′-bōs), **co·rym′bous** *adj.* —**co·rym′bose·ly** *adv.*
co·ry·za (kə rī′zə) *n.* [ModL. < LL. < Gr. *koryza*, catarrh] a cold in the head; acute nasal congestion
cos cosine
Cos., cos. **1.** companies **2.** counties
cosec cosecant
co·se·cant (kō sē′kənt, -kant) *n. Trigonometry* the ratio between the hypotenuse and the side opposite a given acute angle in a right triangle
co·sey, co·sie (kō′zē) *adj., n. same as* COZY
co·sign (kō′sīn′) *vt., vi.* **1.** to sign (a promissory note) in addition to the maker, thus becoming responsible for the obligation if the maker should default **2.** to sign jointly —**co′sign′er** *n.*
co·sig·na·to·ry (kō sig′nə tôr′ē) *adj.* signing jointly —*n., pl.* **-ries** one of two or more joint signers
co·sine (kō′sīn) *n. Trigonometry* the ratio between the side adjacent to a given acute angle in a right triangle and the hypotenuse
cos·met·ic (käz met′ik) *adj.* [< Gr. *kosmētikos*, skilled in arranging < *kosmos*, order] **1.** designed to beautify the complexion, hair, etc. **2.** for improving the appearance by correcting deformities, esp. of the face —*n.* any cosmetic preparation for the skin, hair, etc. —**cos·met′i·cal·ly** *adv.*
cos·me·tol·o·gy (käz′mə täl′ə jē) *n.* the work of applying cosmetics to women, as in a beauty shop —**cos′me·tol′o-gist** *n.*
cos·mic (käz′mik) *adj.* [Gr. *kosmikos* < *kosmos*, order] **1.** of the cosmos; relating to the universe as a whole **2.** vast —**cos′mi·cal·ly** *adv.*
cosmic dust small particles falling from interstellar space to the earth
cosmic rays streams of highly penetrating charged particles that bombard the earth from outer space
cos·mo- [see COSMOS] *a combining form meaning* world, universe *[cosmology]*
cos·mog·o·ny (käz mäg′ə nē) *n.* [< Gr. < *kosmos*, universe + *gignesthai*, to produce] **1.** the origin of the universe **2.** *pl.* **-nies** a theory or account of this —**cos′mo-gon′ic** (-mə gän′ik), **cos′mo·gon′i·cal, cos·mog′o·nal** *adj.* —**cos·mog′o·nist** *n.*
cos·mog·ra·phy (-rə fē) *n.* [< LL. < Gr.: see COSMO- & -GRAPHY] the science dealing with the structure of the universe as a whole —**cos·mog′ra·pher** *n.* —**cos′mo·graph′ic** (-mə graf′ik), **cos′mo·graph′i·cal** *adj.* —**cos′mo·graph′i-cal·ly** *adv.*
cos·mol·o·gy (käz mäl′ə jē) *n.* [COSMO- + -LOGY] the study of the universe as a whole and of its form, nature, etc. as a physical system —**cos′mo·log′i·cal** (-mə läj′ə k'l) *adj.* —**cos′mo·log′i·cal·ly** *adv.* —**cos·mol′o·gist** *n.*
cos·mo·naut (käz′mə nôt′, -nät′) *n.* [Russ. *kosmonaut* < *kosmo-*, COSMO- + *-naut* < Gr. *nautēs*, sailor (see NAUTICAL)] *same as* ASTRONAUT
cos·mo·pol·i·tan (käz′mə päl′ə t'n) *adj.* [COSMOPOLIT(E) + -AN] **1.** representative of all or many parts of the world **2.** not bound by local or national prejudices; at home in all countries or places —*n.* a cosmopolitan person —**cos′mo-pol′i·tan·ism** *n.*
cos·mop·o·lite (käz mäp′ə līt′) *n.* [< Gr. < *kosmos*, world + *politēs*, citizen < *polis*, city] **1.** a cosmopolitan person **2.** a plant or animal common to all or most parts of the world
cos·mos (käz′məs; *for 1 & 2 also* -mōs) *n.* [Gr. *kosmos*, universe, harmony] **1.** the universe considered as a harmonious and orderly system **2.** any complete and orderly system **3.** *pl.* **cos′mos** a tropical American plant of the composite family, with white, pink, or purple flower heads
co·spon·sor (kō′spän′sər) *n.* a joint sponsor, as of a proposed piece of legislation —*vt.* to be a cosponsor of —**co′spon′sor·ship′** *n.*
Cos·sack (käs′ak, -ək; kô′sak) *n.* [Russ. *kozak* < Turk.] a member of a people of southern Russia, famous as horsemen —*adj.* of the Cossacks
cos·set (käs′it) *n.* [< ? OE. *cot-sæta*, cot dweller] a pet lamb, or any small pet —*vt.* to make a pet of; pamper
cost (kôst) *vt.* **cost** or, for 2, **cost′ed, cost′ing** [< OFr. < ML. *costare* < L. < *com-*, together + *stare*, to stand] **1.** *a)* to be obtained or obtainable for (a certain price) *b)* to require the expenditure, loss, or experience of **2.** *Business* to estimate the cost of producing (often with *out*) —*n.* **1.** *a)* the amount asked or paid for a thing *b)* the amount

spent in producing a commodity **2.** *a)* the amount of money, effort, etc. required to achieve an end *b)* loss; sacrifice **3.** [*pl.*] *Law* court expenses of a lawsuit —**at all costs** by any means required: also **at any cost**
cos·tal (käs′t'l) *adj.* [Fr. < ML. < L. *costa,* a rib] of or near a rib or the ribs
Cos·ta Me·sa (kōs′tə mā′sə) [Sp., lit., coast plateau] city in SW Calif., near Long Beach: pop. 82,000
Cos·ta Ri·ca (käs′tə rē′kə, kôs′-, kōs′-) country in Central America: 19,575 sq. mi.; pop. 1,685,000; cap. San José —**Cos′ta Ri′can**
cos·ter·mon·ger (käs′tər muŋ′gər, kôs′-) *n.* [< *costard,* a kind of apple + MONGER] [Brit.] a person who sells fruit or vegetables from a cart or street stand: also **cos′ter**
cos·tive (käs′tiv, kôs′-) *adj.* [< OFr. pp. of *costever* < L. *constipare:* see CONSTIPATE] constipated or constipating —**cos′tive·ly** *adv.* —**cos′tive·ness** *n.*
cost·ly (kôst′lē) *adj.* **-li·er, -li·est** **1.** *a)* costing much; expensive; dear *b)* at the cost of great effort, damage, etc. **2.** magnificent; sumptuous —**cost′li·ness** *n.*
cost of living the average cost of the necessities of life, as food, shelter, and clothes
cost-plus (kôst′plus′) *adj.* with the price for goods or services set at the cost of materials, labor, etc. plus a specified amount of profit
cos·tume (käs′to͞om, -tyo͞om) *n.* [< Fr. < It. < L. *consuetudo,* CUSTOM] **1.** *a)* the style of dress typical of a certain period, people, etc. *b)* a set of such clothes as worn in a play or at a masquerade **2.** a set of outer clothes for some occasion, esp. one worn by a woman —*vt.* **-tumed, -tum·ing** to provide with a costume
costume jewelry relatively inexpensive jewelry
cos·tum·er (-ər) *n.* one who makes, sells, or rents costumes, as for masquerades, theaters, etc.: also **cos·tum·ier** (käs to͞om′yər, -tyo͞om′-)
co·sy (kō′zē) *adj.* **-si·er, -si·est** & *n., pl.* **-sies** *same as* COZY —**co′si·ly** *adv.* —**co′si·ness** *n.*
cot[1] (kät) *n.* [Anglo-Ind. < Hindi *khāṭ* < Sans.] a narrow, collapsible bed, as one made of canvas on a folding frame
cot[2] (kät) *n.* [OE.] **1.** [Poet.] a cottage **2.** a cote **3.** a sheath, as for a hurt finger
cot cotangent
co·tan·gent (kō tan′jənt) *n.* *Trigonometry* the ratio between the side adjacent to a given acute angle in a right triangle and the side opposite
cote (kōt) *n.* [ME., COT[2]] **1.** a small shelter for sheep, doves, etc. **2.** [Dial.] a cottage
co·ten·ant (kō ten′ənt) *n.* one of two or more tenants who share a place —**co·ten′an·cy** *n.*
co·te·rie (kōt′ər ē) *n.* [Fr., orig., organization of feudal tenants < OFr. *cotier,* COTTER[1]] a close circle of friends with common interests
co·ter·mi·nous (kō tʉr′mə nəs) *adj. same as* CONTERMINOUS: also **co·ter′mi·nal** —**co·ter′mi·nous·ly** *adv.*
co·til·lion (kō til′yən, kə-) *n.* [Fr. *cotillon,* orig., petticoat < OFr. *cotte,* a COAT] **1.** a dance with many intricate figures and the continual changing of partners **2.** a formal ball, esp. one at which debutantes are presented Also sp. **co·til′lon**
cot·tage (kät′ij) *n.* [< ML. *cotagium* < OFr. *cote* or ME. *cot,* hut] a small house, now often a summer home or any of the separate dwelling units for small groups in certain institutions, etc.
cottage cheese a soft, white cheese made by straining and seasoning the curds of sour milk
cottage pudding cake covered with a sweet sauce
cot·tag·er (-ər) *n.* **1.** a person who lives in a cottage **2.** [Brit.] a farm laborer
cot·ter[1], **cot·tar** (kät′ər) *n.* [< OFr. *cotier* < OE. *cot,* COT[2]] **1.** a cottager **2.** [Scot.] a tenant farmer
cot·ter[2] (kät′ər) *n.* [< ?] **1.** a bolt or wedge put through a slot to hold together parts of machinery **2.** *same as* COTTER PIN
cotter pin a split pin used as a cotter, fastened in place by spreading apart its ends after it is inserted

COTTER PIN

cot·ton (kät′'n) *n.* [< OFr. < Ar. *quṭun*] **1.** the soft, white seed hairs filling the seedpods of various shrubby plants of the mallow family **2.** a plant or plants producing this material **3.** the crop of such plants **4.** thread or cloth made of cotton —*adj.* of cotton —**cotton to** [Colloq.] **1.** to take a liking to **2.** to become aware of (a situation) —**cotton up to** [Colloq.] to try to make friends with —**cot′ton·y** *adj.*
cotton batting thin, pressed layers of fluffy, absorbent cotton, used for surgical dressing, etc.
Cotton Belt region in S and SE U.S. where much cotton is grown
cotton candy a cottony candy consisting of fibers of melted sugar spun into a fluffy mass around a paper cone
cotton flannel a soft, fleecy cotton cloth
cotton gin [see GIN[2]] a machine for separating cotton fibers from the seeds
cotton·mouth (-mouth′) *n.* [from its whitish mouth] *same as* WATER MOCCASIN
cot·ton-pick·ing (-pik′'n) *adj.* [Slang] worthless, damned, hateful, etc.
cot·ton·seed (-sēd′) *n.* the seed of the cotton plant, from which an oil (**cottonseed oil**) is pressed for use in margarine, cooking oil, etc.
cot·ton·tail (-tāl′) *n.* a common American rabbit with a short, fluffy tail
cot·ton·wood (-wood′) *n.* **1.** a poplar that has seeds covered with cottony hairs **2.** its wood
cotton wool raw cotton or cotton batting
cot·y·le·don (kät′'l ēd′'n) *n.* [L. < Gr. < *kotylē,* a cavity] the first single leaf or either of the first pair of leaves produced by the embryo of a flowering plant —**cot′y·le′donous, cot′y·le′don·al** *adj.*
couch (kouch) *n.* [< OFr.: see the *v.*] **1.** an article of furniture on which one may sit or lie down; sofa **2.** any resting place —*vt.* [< OFr. *coucher,* to lie down < L. *collocare* < *com-,* together + *locare,* to place] **1.** to lay as on a couch: now usually used reflexively or in the passive voice **2.** to bring down; esp., to lower (a spear, etc.) to an attacking position **3.** to put in words; express —*vi.* **1.** to lie down on a bed; recline **2.** to lie in hiding or ambush
couch·ant (-ənt) *adj.* [see prec.] *Heraldry* lying down
couch grass (kouch) [var. of QUITCH] a weedy grass that spreads rapidly by its underground stems
cou·gar (ko͞o′gər, -gär) *n., pl.* **-gars, -gar:** see PLURAL, II, D, 1 [< Fr. < Port. *çuçuarana* < Tupi < *suusú,* deer + *rana,* false] a large, tawny-brown animal of the cat family, with a long, slender body
cough (kôf) *vi.* [ME. *coughen*] to expel air suddenly and noisily from the lungs through the glottis —*vt.* to expel by coughing —*n.* **1.** a coughing **2.** a condition, as of the lungs or throat, causing frequent coughing —**cough up** **1.** to bring up (phlegm, etc.) by coughing **2.** [Slang] to hand over (money, etc.) —**cough′er** *n.*
cough drop a small, flavored, medicated tablet for the relief of coughs, hoarseness, etc.
could (kood) *v.* [< OE. *cuthe,* pt. of *cunnan:* see CAN[1]] **1.** *pt. of* CAN[1] **2.** an auxiliary in verbal phrases with present or future sense, generally equivalent to *can* in meaning and use, expressing esp. a shade of doubt or a smaller degree of possibility *[*it *could* be so*]*
could·n't (-'nt) could not
couldst (koodst) *archaic or poetic 2d pers. sing., past indic., of* CAN[1]: *used with* thou
cou·lee (ko͞o′lē) *n.* [Fr. < *couler,* to flow < L. < *colum,* a strainer] **1.** a stream or sheet of lava **2.** [Northwest] a deep gulch or ravine, usually dry in summer
cou·lomb (ko͞o läm′, ko͞o′läm) *n.* [after C. A. de *Coulomb* (1736–1806), Fr. physicist] the meter-kilogram-second unit of electric charge; charge transported through a conductor by a current of one ampere flowing for one second
coul·ter (kōl′tər) *n. same as* COLTER
coun·cil (koun′s'l) *n.* [< OFr. < L. *concilium,* meeting < *com-,* with + *calere,* to call] **1.** a group of people called together for consultation, advice, etc. **2.** a group of people chosen as an administrative or legislative assembly **3.** the legislative body of a city or town **4.** a church assembly to discuss points of doctrine, etc. **5.** any of various organizations or societies
Council Bluffs [scene of councils with Indians by LEWIS & CLARK] city in SW Iowa: pop. 56,000
coun·cil·man (-mən) *n., pl.* **-men** a member of a council, esp. of a city or town —**coun′cil·man′ic** (-man′ik) *adj.*
coun·ci·lor (koun′sə lər) *n.* [< COUNSELOR] a member of a council: also [Chiefly Brit.] **coun′cil·lor** —**coun′ci·lor·ship′** *n.*
coun·sel (koun′s'l) *n.* [< OFr. < L. *consilium*] **1.** a mutual exchange of ideas, opinions, etc.; discussion **2.** *a)* advice resulting from such an exchange *b)* any advice **3.** *a)* a lawyer or group of lawyers giving legal advice or acting for clients *b)* a consultant —*vt.* **-seled** or **-selled, -sel·ing** or **-sel·ling** **1.** to give advice to; advise **2.** to urge the acceptance of (a plan, etc.) —*vi.* to give or take advice —**keep one's own counsel** to keep one's thoughts, plans, etc. to oneself —**take counsel** to consult; exchange advice, opinions, etc.
coun·se·lor, coun·sel·lor (-ər) *n.* **1.** a person who counsels; adviser **2.** a lawyer, esp. one who conducts cases in court: in full, **counselor-at-law** **3.** a group worker in a children's camp —**coun′se·lor·ship′, coun′sel·lor·ship′** *n.*
count[1] (kount) *vt.* [< OFr. < L. *computare,* COMPUTE] **1.** to name numbers in regular order to (a certain number) *[*to *count* five*]* **2.** to add up, one by one, by units or groups, so as to get a total **3.** to check by numbering off; inventory **4.** to take account of; include *[*ten, *counting* you*]* **5.** to believe to be; consider *[*to *count* oneself fortunate*]* —*vi.* **1.** to name numbers or add up items in order **2.** to be tak-

en into account; have importance, value, etc. **3.** to have a specified value (often with *for*) **4.** to rely or depend (*on* or *upon*) —*n.* **1.** a counting, or adding up **2.** the number or a total reached by counting **3.** a reckoning or accounting **4.** *Baseball* the number of balls and strikes that have been pitched to the batter **5.** *Boxing* ten seconds counted to give a fallen boxer time to rise before he loses the match **6.** *Law* any of the charges in an indictment, each of which is sufficient for prosecution —**count in** to include —**count off** to separate into equal divisions by counting —**count out** **1.** to disregard; omit **2.** *Boxing* to declare (a boxer) defeated when he has remained down for a count of ten —**count′a·ble** *adj.*

count[2] (kount) *n.* [< OFr. < L. *comes* (gen. *comitis*), companion < *com-*, with + *ire*, to go] a European nobleman equal in rank to an English earl

count·down (-doun′) *n.* the schedule of operations just before the firing of a rocket, etc.; also, the counting off, in reverse order, of units of time in such a schedule

coun·te·nance (koun′tə nəns) *n.* [< OFr. < L. *continentia*, bearing < *continere*, CONTAIN] **1.** the look on a person's face that shows his nature or feelings **2.** the face; facial features **3.** *a*) a look of approval *b*) approval; support **4.** calm control; composure —*vt.* **-nanced, -nanc·ing** to give support to; approve —**in countenance** calm; composed —**put out of countenance** to disconcert

count·er[1] (koun′tər) *n.* [see COUNT[1]] **1.** a person or thing that counts or keeps count **2.** a small piece of metal, wood, etc., used in some games, esp. for keeping score **3.** an imitation coin, or token **4.** a long table, board, etc., as in a store or kitchen for the display of goods, serving of food, etc. —**over the counter** sold directly, not through a stock exchange —**under the counter** in a surreptitious manner: said of illegal sales

coun·ter[2] (koun′tər) *adv.* [< Fr. < L. *contra*, against] in a contrary direction, manner, etc.; opposite —*adj.* acting in opposition or in an opposite direction —*n.* **1.** the opposite; contrary **2.** an opposing action **3.** a stiff leather piece around the heel of a shoe **4.** the part of a ship's stern between the waterline and the curved part **5.** *Boxing* *a*) a blow given while parrying an opponent's blow *b*) a giving of such a blow —*vt., vi.* **1.** to oppose or check (a person or thing) **2.** to say or do (something) in reply or retaliation **3.** *Boxing* to strike one's opponent while parrying (his blow)

coun·ter- [< Fr. < L. *contra-*, against] *a combining form meaning:* **1.** opposite, contrary to [*counterclockwise*] **2.** in retaliation or return [*counterplot*] **3.** complementary [*counterpart*]

coun·ter·act (koun′tər akt′) *vt.* to act against; neutralize the effect of with opposing action —**coun′ter·ac′tion** *n.* —**coun′ter·ac′tive** *adj., n.*

coun·ter·at·tack (koun′tər ə tak′; *for v., usually* koun′tər ə tak′) *n.* an attack made in opposition to another attack —*vt., vi.* to attack so as to offset the enemy's attack

coun·ter·bal·ance (koun′tər bal′əns; *for v., usually* koun′tər bal′əns) *n.* **1.** a weight used to balance another weight **2.** any force or influence that balances or offsets another —*vt.* **-anced, -anc·ing** to be a counterbalance to; offset

coun·ter·check (koun′tər chek′; *for v., usually* koun′tər-chek′) *n.* **1.** anything that checks, restrains, etc. **2.** a double-check to be sure —*vt.* **1.** to check or counteract **2.** to check again to be sure

counter check a check obtained at a bank by a depositor making a withdrawal

coun·ter·claim (koun′tər klām′; *for v., usually* koun′tər-klām′) *n.* an opposing claim to offset another —*vt., vi.* to make a counterclaim (of) —**coun′ter·claim′ant** *n.*

coun·ter·clock·wise (koun′tər kläk′wīz) *adj., adv.* in a direction opposite to that in which the hands of a clock move

coun·ter·cul·ture (koun′tər kul′chər) *n.* the culture of the young people of the 1960's and 1970's with a life style opposed to the prevailing culture

coun·ter·es·pi·on·age (coun′tər es′pē ə näzh′, -näj′, -nij) *n.* actions to prevent or thwart enemy espionage

coun·ter·feit (koun′tər fit) *adj.* [< OFr. pp. of *contrefaire*, to imitate < *contre-*, counter- + *faire* (< L. *facere*), to make] **1.** made in imitation of something genuine so as to defraud; forged [*counterfeit* money] **2.** pretended; sham; feigned —*n.* **1.** an imitation made to deceive **2.** something so much like something else as to mislead —*vt., vi.* **1.** to make an imitation of (money, pictures, etc.) in order to defraud **2.** to pretend **3.** to resemble (something) closely —**coun′ter·feit′er** *n.*

coun·ter·foil (-foil′) *n.* [COUNTER- + FOIL[2]] the stub of a check, receipt, etc. kept by the issuer as a record

coun·ter·in·sur·gen·cy (koun′tər in sur′jən sē) *n.* military and political action carried on to defeat an insurgency

coun·ter·in·tel·li·gence (-in tel′ə jəns) *n.* actions to counter enemy intelligence or espionage activity, prevent sabotage, etc.

coun·ter·ir·ri·tant (-ir′ə tənt) *n.* anything used to produce a slight irritation to relieve more serious inflammation elsewhere

count·er·man (koun′tər man′, -mən) *n., pl.* **-men′** (-men′, -mən) a man whose work is serving customers at a counter as of a lunchroom

coun·ter·mand (koun′tər mand′; *also, and for n. always,* koun′tər mand′) *vt.* [< OFr. < L. *contra*, against + *mandare:* see MANDATE] **1.** to cancel or revoke (a command or order) **2.** to call back or order back by a contrary order —*n.* a command or order canceling another

coun·ter·march (koun′tər märch′; *for v., also* koun′tər märch′) *n.* a march back or in the opposite direction —*vi., vt.* to march back

coun·ter·move (koun′tər mo͞ov′; *for v., also* koun′tər-mo͞ov′) *n.* a move made in opposition or retaliation —*vi., vt.* **-moved′, -mov′ing** to move in opposition or retaliation

coun·ter·of·fen·sive (koun′tər ə fen′siv) *n.* an attack in force by troops who have been defending a position

coun·ter·pane (koun′tər pān′) *n.* [altered < ME. *countrepoint*, quilt < OFr. < L. *culcita puncta*, pricked (i.e., embroidered) quilt] a bedspread

coun·ter·part (-pärt′) *n.* **1.** a person or thing that corresponds to or closely resembles another **2.** a thing that completes or complements another **3.** a copy or duplicate, as of a lease

coun·ter·plot (koun′tər plät′; *for v., also* koun′tər plät′) *n.* a plot to defeat another plot —*vt., vi.* **-plot′ted, -plot′ting** to plot against (a plot); defeat (a plot) with another

coun·ter·point (-point′) *n.* [< Fr. < It. *contrappunto*, lit., pointed against: see COUNTER- & POINT, *n.*] **1.** a melody accompanying another melody note for note **2.** *a*) the art of adding related but independent melodies to a basic melody, in accordance with the fixed rules of harmony *b*) this kind of composition

coun·ter·poise (-poiz′) *n.* [< ONormFr.: see COUNTER[2] & POISE] **1.** *same as* COUNTERBALANCE **2.** a state of balance or equilibrium —*vt.* **-poised′, -pois′ing** *same as* COUNTERBALANCE

coun·ter·pro·po·sal (-prə pō′z'l) *n.* a proposal in response to one regarded as unsatisfactory

Counter-Reformation the reform movement in the Roman Catholic Church in the 16th cent., following in reaction to the Protestant Reformation

coun·ter·rev·o·lu·tion (koun′tər rev′ə lo͞o′shən) *n.* **1.** a political movement or revolution against a government or social system set up by a previous revolution **2.** a movement to combat revolutionary tendencies —**coun′ter·rev′o·lu′tion·ar′y** *adj., n.* —**coun′ter·rev′o·lu′tion·ist** *n.*

coun·ter·shaft (koun′tər shaft′) *n.* an intermediate shaft that transmits motion from the main shaft of a machine to a working part

coun·ter·sign (koun′tər sīn′; *for v., also* koun′tər sīn′) *n.* **1.** a signature added to a previously signed document for confirmation **2.** *Mil.* a secret word or signal which must be given to a sentry by someone wishing to pass —*vt.* to confirm (a previously signed document) by signing —**coun′ter·sig′na·ture** (-sig′nə chər) *n.*

coun·ter·sink (koun′tər siŋk′; *for v., also* koun′tər siŋk′) *vt.* **-sunk′, -sink′ing** **1.** to enlarge the top part of (a hole in metal, wood, etc.) to make the head of a bolt, screw, etc. fit into it **2.** to sink (a bolt, screw, etc.) into such a hole —*n.* **1.** a tool for countersinking holes **2.** a countersunk hole

coun·ter·spy (-spī′) *n.* a spy in counterespionage

coun·ter·ten·or (-ten′ər) *n.* **1.** the range of the highest mature male voice, above tenor **2.** a voice, singer, or part with such a range

coun·ter·vail (koun′tər vāl′) *vt.* [< OFr. < *contre* (see COUNTER[2]) + *valoir*, to avail < L. *valere*, to be strong] **1.** to make up for; compensate **2.** to counteract; avail against —*vi.* to avail (*against*)

coun·ter·weigh (-wā′) *vt.* *same as* COUNTERBALANCE —**coun′ter·weight′** *n.*

counter word any word freely used as a general term of approval or disapproval without reference to its more exact meaning, as *nice* or *terrible*

count·ess (koun′tis) *n.* **1.** the wife or widow of a count or earl **2.** a noblewoman whose rank is equal to that of a count or earl

count·ing·house (koun′tiŋ hous′) *n.* [Now Rare] an office where a firm keeps accounts, etc.

count·less (kount′lis) ***adj.*** too many to count; innumerable; myriad

coun·tri·fied (kun′tri fīd′) ***adj.*** **1.** rural; rustic **2.** having the appearance, actions, etc. attributed to country people Also sp. **coun′try·fied′**

coun·try (kun′trē) ***n.,*** *pl.* **-tries** [< OFr. < VL. *contrata,* that which is beyond < L. *contra,* opposite] **1.** an area of land; region *[wooded country]* **2.** the whole territory of a nation **3.** the people of a nation **4.** the land of a person's birth or citizenship **5.** land with farms and small towns; rural region —***adj.*** **1.** of, in, or from a rural district **2.** like that of the country; rustic

country club a social club in the outskirts of a city, equipped with a clubhouse, golf course, etc.

coun·try-dance (-dans′) ***n.*** an English folk dance, esp. one in which partners form two facing lines

coun·try·man (-mən) ***n.,*** *pl.* **-men** **1.** a man who lives in the country; rustic **2.** a man of one's own country; compatriot —**coun′try·wom′an** ***n.fem.,*** *pl.* **-wom′en**

country music rural folk music, esp. a commercialized variety deriving from the folk music of the Southern highlands and backwoods

coun·try·seat (-sēt′) ***n.*** a rural mansion or estate

coun·try·side (-sīd′) ***n.*** a rural region or its inhabitants

coun·ty (koun′tē) ***n.,*** *pl.* **-ties** [< OFr. < ML. *comitatus,* jurisdiction of a count < L. *comes:* see COUNT[2]] **1.** a small administrative district; esp., *a)* the largest local administrative subdivision of most States *b)* any of the chief administrative and judicial districts into which Great Britain and Ireland are divided **2.** the people in a county

county agent a government-employed specialist assigned to inform farmers in a county of improved practices in agriculture

county commissioner a member of an elected governing board in the counties of certain States

county seat a town or city that is the seat of government of a county

coup (ko͞o) ***n.,*** *pl.* **coups** (ko͞oz; *Fr.* ko͞o) [Fr. < VL. < L. *colaphus,* a blow < Gr. *kolaphos*] **1.** literally, a blow **2.** a sudden, successful move or action; brilliant stroke **3.** *same as* COUP D'ÉTAT

‡**coup de grâce** (ko͞o də gräs′) [Fr., lit., stroke of mercy] **1.** the blow, shot, etc. that brings death to a sufferer **2.** a finishing stroke

‡**coup de main** (man′) [Fr., lit., stroke of hand] a surprise attack or movement, as in war

‡**coup d'é·tat** (dā tä′) [Fr., lit., stroke of state] a sudden, forceful stroke in politics, esp. the sudden, forcible overthrow of a government

coupe (ko͞op; *orig., but now rarely,* ko͞o pā′) ***n.*** [see ff.] a closed, two-door automobile with a body smaller than that of a sedan

cou·pé (ko͞o pā′) ***n.*** [Fr., pp. of *couper,* to cut] **1.** a closed carriage seating two passengers, with a seat outside for the driver **2.** *same as* COUPE

cou·ple (kup′'l) ***n.*** [< OFr. < L. *copula:* see COPULA] **1.** anything joining two things together; bond; link **2.** two things or persons of the same sort that are somehow associated **3.** a man and a woman who are engaged, married, or partners in a dance, etc. **4.** [Colloq.] a few; several: now often used with adjectival force *[a couple ideas]* —***vt.*** **-pled, -pling** to join together; link; connect —***vi.*** **1.** to come together; unite **2.** to copulate

cou·pler (kup′lər) ***n.*** a person or thing that couples; specif., a pneumatic device for coupling two railroad cars

cou·plet (kup′lit) ***n.*** [Fr. dim.: see COUPLE] **1.** two successive lines of poetry, esp. two of the same length that rhyme **2.** [Rare] a couple

cou·pling (kup′liŋ) ***n.*** **1.** a joining together **2.** a mechanical device for joining parts together **3.** a device for joining railroad cars **4.** a method or device for joining two electric circuits to transfer energy from one to the other

COUPLING

cou·pon (ko͞o′pän, kyo͞o′-) ***n.*** [Fr. < *couper,* to cut] **1.** a detachable printed statement on a bond, specifying the interest due at a given time **2.** a certificate or ticket entitling the holder to a specified right, as reduced purchase price **3.** a part of a printed advertisement for use in ordering goods, etc.

cour·age (kur′ij) ***n.*** [< OFr. < L. *cor,* heart] a willingness to face and deal with danger, trouble, or pain; fearlessness; bravery; valor —**the courage of one's convictions** the courage to do what one thinks is right

cou·ra·geous (kə rā′jəs) ***adj.*** having or showing courage; brave —**cou·ra′geous·ly** ***adv.*** —**cou·ra′geous·ness** ***n.***

Cour·bet (ko͞or be′), **Gus·tave** (güs täv′) 1819–77; Fr. painter

cou·ri·er (koor′ē ər, kur′-) ***n.*** [< OFr., ult. < L. *currere,* to run] a messenger sent in haste or on a regular schedule with important or urgent messages

course (kôrs) ***n.*** [< OFr. *cours* < L. pp. of *currere,* to run] **1.** an onward movement; progress **2.** a way, path, or channel of movement; specif., *same as: a)* [Brit.] RACECOURSE *b)* GOLF COURSE **3.** the direction taken, as by a ship or plane *[a course due south]* **4.** *a)* a regular manner of procedure *[the law must take its course]* *b)* a way of behaving; mode of conduct **5.** *a)* a series of like things in some regular order *b)* a particular succession of events or actions **6.** natural development *[the course of true love]* **7.** a part of a meal served at one time **8.** a horizontal layer, as of bricks, in the face of a building **9.** *Educ. a)* a complete series of studies leading to graduation, a degree, etc. *b)* any of the separate units of instruction in a subject —***vt.*** **coursed, cours′ing** **1.** to pursue **2.** to cause (esp. hunting hounds) to chase **3.** to traverse —***vi.*** **1.** to run or race **2.** to hunt with hounds —**in due course** in the usual or proper sequence (of events) —**in the course of** in the process of; during —**of course** **1.** as is or was to be expected; naturally **2.** certainly —**on** (or **off**) **course** moving (or not moving) in the intended direction

cours·er (kôr′sər) ***n.*** [see prec.] [Poet.] a graceful, spirited, or swift horse

court (kôrt) ***n.*** [OFr. < LL. < L. *cohors:* see COHORT] **1.** an uncovered space wholly or partly surrounded by buildings or walls **2.** a short street, often closed at one end **3.** *a)* an area for playing any of several ball games *b)* a part of such an area **4.** a motel: in full, **motor court** **5.** *a)* the palace of a sovereign *b)* the family, advisers, etc. of a sovereign, as a group *c)* a sovereign and his councilors as a governing body *d)* any formal gathering held by a sovereign **6.** attention paid to someone in order to get something **7.** courtship; wooing **8.** *a)* a person or persons appointed to try law cases, make investigations, etc.; judge or judges *b)* a place where trials are held, investigations made, etc. *c)* a judicial assembly; also, a regular session of such an assembly —***vt.*** **1.** to pay attention to (a person) in order to get something **2.** to try to get the love of; woo **3.** to try to get; seek *[to court favor]* **4.** to make oneself open to *[to court insults]* —***vi.*** to woo —***adj.*** of or fit for a court —**out of court** without a trial —**pay court to** to court, as for favor or love —**court′er** ***n.***

cour·te·ous (kur′tē əs) ***adj.*** [< OFr. *courteis* < *court:* see COURT & -EOUS] polite and gracious; considerate of others; well-mannered—**cour′te·ous·ly** ***adv.*** —**cour′te·ous·ness** ***n.***

cour·te·san (kôr′tə z'n, kur′-) ***n.*** [< Fr. < It. *cortigiana,* court lady < *corte,* COURT] a prostitute; esp., formerly, a mistress of a king, nobleman, etc.: also **cour′te·zan**

cour·te·sy (kur′tə sē) ***n.,*** *pl.* **-sies** [< OFr. *curteisie:* see COURTEOUS] **1.** courteous behavior; gracious politeness **2.** a polite or considerate act or remark **3.** an act or usage intended to honor or compliment *[a title of courtesy]*

courtesy card a card entitling the bearer to special privileges, as at a hotel, bank, etc.

court·house (kôrt′hous′) ***n.*** **1.** a building in which law courts are held **2.** a building that houses the offices of a county government

cour·ti·er (kôr′tē ər, -tyər) ***n.*** **1.** an attendant at a royal court **2.** a person who courts favor by flattery, etc.

court·ly (kôrt′lē) ***adj.*** **-li·er, -li·est** **1.** suitable for a king's court; dignified, elegant, etc. **2.** flattering, esp. in an obsequious or humble way —***adv.*** in a courtly manner —**court′li·ness** ***n.***

court-mar·tial (-mär′shəl) ***n.,*** *pl.* **courts′-mar′tial;** for 2, now often **court′-mar′tials** **1.** a court of personnel in the armed forces to try offenses against military law **2.** a trial by a court-martial —***vt.*** **-tialed** or **-tialled, -tial·ing** or **-tial·ling** to try by a court-martial

court of appeals *[often* **C- A-***]* **1.** a State court to which appeals are taken from the trial courts **2.** any of the Federal appellate courts, between the U.S. district courts and the Supreme Court

Court of St. James [< *St. James Palace,* former royal residence] the British royal court

court plaster [from former use by court ladies for beauty spots] cloth covered with an adhesive material, formerly used to protect minor skin wounds

court·room (kôrt′ro͞om′) ***n.*** a room in which a law court is held

court·ship (-ship′) ***n.*** the act, process, or period of courting, or wooing

court tennis *see* TENNIS

court·yard (-yärd′) ***n.*** a space enclosed by walls, adjoining or in a large building

cous·cous (ko͞os′ko͞os, ko͞os ko͞os′) ***n.*** [Fr. < Berber < Ar. < *kaskasa,* to grind] a N African dish of crushed grain, usually steamed and served with meat

cous·in (kuz′'n) ***n.*** [< OFr. < L. < *com-,* with + *sobrinus,* maternal cousin < *soror,* sister] **1.** the son or daughter of one's uncle or aunt: also **cous′in-ger′man** (-jur′mən), **first** (or **full**) **cousin** **2.** loosely, any relative by blood or marriage **3.** a person thought of as related to another **4.** a title of address used by one sovereign to another or to a nobleman —**cous′in·ly** ***adj., adv.*** —**cous′in·ship′** ***n.***

cou·ture (ko͞o to͞or′) ***n.*** [Fr., sewing < L. pp. of *consuere* < *com-*, together + *suere*, to sew] the work or business of designing new fashions in women's clothes

‡**cou·tu·rier** (ko͞o tü ryā′; *E.* ko͞o to͝or′ē ā′) ***n.*** [Fr.] a man engaged in couture —**cou·tu·rière** (-tü *ryer′*; *E.* -to͝or′ē er′) ***n.fem.***

co·va·lence (kō vā′ləns) ***n.*** the number of pairs of electrons an atom can share with neighboring atoms —**co·va′·lent** ***adj.***

cove (kōv) ***n.*** [< OE. *cofa*, cave, cell] **1.** a sheltered nook or recess, as in cliffs **2.** a small bay or inlet **3.** a small valley **4.** a concave molding **5.** a trough for concealed lighting on a wall near a ceiling —***vt., vi.*** **coved, cov′ing** to curve concavely

cov·en (kuv′ən, kō′vən) ***n.*** [< OFr. < L. *convenire*, CONVENE] a gathering or meeting, esp. of witches

cov·e·nant (kuv′ə nənt) ***n.*** [OFr. < L. *convenire*, CONVENE] **1.** a binding agreement made by two or more individuals, parties, etc. to do or keep from doing a specified thing; compact **2.** *Law* a formal, sealed contract **3.** *Theol.* the promises made by God to man, as recorded in the Bible —***vt., vi.*** to promise by or in a covenant —**cov′e·nan′·tal** (-nan′t'l) ***adj.*** —**cov′e·nant·er, cov′e·nan·tor** (-nan-tər) ***n.***

Cov·en·try (kuv′ən trē, käv′-) city in C England: pop. 335,000 —***n.*** ostracism *[to send someone to Coventry]*

cov·er (kuv′ər) ***vt.*** [< OFr. < L. < *co-*, intens. + *operire*, to hide] **1.** to place something on, over, or in front of **2.** to extend over; overlay **3.** to mate with (a mare): said of a stallion **4.** to clothe **5.** to coat, sprinkle, etc. thickly **6.** to sit on (eggs); brood **7.** to conceal by hiding or screening **8.** to protect as by shielding **9.** to take into account **10.** *a)* to protect against financial loss, or make up for (a loss, etc.), as by insurance *b)* to be sufficient for payment of (a debt, etc.) *c)* to buy stock to replace (shares borrowed from a broker to effect a short sale) **11.** to accept (a bet) **12.** to travel over *[to cover a distance]* **13.** to be responsible for (an area or range of activity) **14.** to deal with *[to cover a subject]* **15.** to point a firearm at **16.** *Journalism* to get news, pictures, etc. of *[to cover a train wreck]* **17.** *Sports* to guard or obstruct (an opponent, position, etc.) —***vi.*** **1.** to spread over a surface, as a liquid **2.** to put on a cap, hat, etc. **3.** to provide an alibi or excuse (*for* another) —***n.*** **1.** anything that covers, as a binding, lid, top, etc. **2.** a protective shelter or a hiding place **3.** a tablecloth and a place setting for one person **4.** *same as* COVER-UP **5.** an envelope, wrapping, etc. for mail —**break cover** to come out of protective shelter —**cover up 1.** to cover entirely **2.** to keep blunders, crimes, etc. from being known —**take cover** to seek protective shelter —**under cover** in secrecy or concealment —**cov′er·er** ***n.***

cov·er·age (-ij) ***n.*** **1.** the amount, extent, etc. covered by something **2.** *Insurance* all the risks covered by an insurance policy

cov·er·all (-ôl′) ***n.*** [*usually pl.*] a one-piece garment with sleeves and legs, worn like overalls

cover charge a fixed charge added to the cost of food and drink, as at a nightclub or restaurant

cover crop a crop, as vetch or clover, grown to protect soil from erosion and to keep it fertile

Cov·er·dale (kuv′ər dāl′), **Miles** 1488–1568; Eng. clergyman & translator of the Bible (1535)

covered wagon a large wagon with an arched cover of canvas, used by American pioneers

cover girl [Colloq.] a girl model whose picture is often put on magazine covers, etc.

cov·er·ing (kuv′ər iŋ) ***n.*** anything that covers

cov·er·let (kuv′ər lit) ***n.*** [< Anglo-Fr. < OFr. *covrir*, COVER + *lit*, a bed < L. *lectus*] **1.** a bedspread **2.** any covering Also [Dial.] **cov′er·lid**

cov·ert (kuv′ərt, kō′vərt) ***adj.*** [OFr., pp. of *covrir*, COVER] concealed, hidden, or disguised —***n.*** **1.** a covered or protected place; shelter **2.** a hiding place for game **3.** any of the small feathers covering the bases of the larger feathers of a bird's wing and tail —**cov′ert·ly** ***adv.*** —**cov′ert·ness** ***n.***

covert (cloth) a smooth, twilled, lightweight cloth, usually of wool, used for suits, topcoats, etc.

cov·er·ture (kuv′ər chər) ***n.*** **1.** a covering **2.** a refuge **3.** a concealment or disguise

cov·er-up (kuv′ər up′) ***n.*** something used for hiding one's real activities, intentions, etc.

cov·et (kuv′it) ***vt., vi.*** [< OFr. < L. *cupiditas*: see CUPIDITY] to want ardently (esp., something that another has) —**cov′et·a·ble** ***adj.*** —**cov′et·er** ***n.***

cov·et·ous (-əs) ***adj.*** greedy; avaricious —**cov′et·ous·ly** ***adv.*** —**cov′et·ous·ness** ***n.***

cov·ey (kuv′ē) ***n., pl.*** **-eys** [< OFr. < *cover*, to hatch < L. *cubare*, to lie down] **1.** a small flock of birds, esp. partridges or quail **2.** a small group of people or, sometimes, things

Cov·ing·ton (kuv′iŋ tən) [after Gen. L. *Covington*, 1768–1813] city in N Ky.: pop. 53,000

cow[1] (kou) ***n., pl.*** **cows;** archaic **kine** (kīn) [OE. *cu*] **1.** the mature female of domestic cattle, valued for its milk, or of certain other animals, as the buffalo, elephant, etc.: the male of such animals is called a *bull* **2.** [Western] any domestic bovine animal, whether a steer, bull, cow, or calf

cow[2] (kou) ***vt.*** [< ON. *kūga*, to subdue] to make timid and submissive by filling with fear or awe

cow·ard (kou′ərd) ***n.*** [< OFr. < *coe* < L. *cauda*, tail] one who lacks courage or suffers from cowardice —***adj.*** cowardly

cow·ard·ice (-is) ***n.*** lack of courage; esp., shamefully excessive fear of danger, difficulty, etc.

cow·ard·ly (-lē) ***adj.*** of or typical of a coward; shamefully fearful —***adv.*** in the manner of a coward —**cow′ard·li·ness** ***n.***

cow·bell (kou′bel′) ***n.*** a bell hung from a cow's neck so she can be found by its clanking

cow·ber·ry (-ber′ē) ***n., pl.*** **-ries** **1.** a low creeping shrub with white or pink flowers and dark-red, acid berries **2.** its berry

cow·bird (-burd′) ***n.*** a small American blackbird often seen near cattle

cow·boy (-boi′) ***n.*** **1.** a ranch worker who rides horseback on his job of herding cattle: also **cow′hand′** **2.** a performer in a rodeo —**cow′girl′** ***n.fem.***

cow·catch·er (-kach′ər, -kech′ər) ***n.*** a metal frame on the front of a locomotive or streetcar to remove obstructions from the tracks

cow·er (kou′ər) ***vi.*** [ME. *couren*, prob. < ON.] **1.** to crouch or huddle up, as from fear **2.** to shrink and tremble, as from someone's anger, threats, or blows; cringe —**cow′er·ing·ly** ***adv.***

cow·herd (kou′hurd′) ***n.*** a tender of grazing cattle

cow·hide (-hīd′) ***n.*** **1.** the hide of a cow **2.** leather made from it **3.** a whip made of this —***vt.*** **-hid′ed, -hid′ing** to flog with a cowhide

cow killer a large, wingless, antlike wasp of the S U.S. that has a vicious sting

cowl (koul) ***n.*** [< OE. < LL. < L. *cucullus*, hood] **1.** *a)* a monk's hood *b)* a monk's cloak with a hood **2.** something shaped like a cowl; esp., *a)* a cover for the top of a chimney, to increase the draft *b)* the top front part of an automobile body, to which the windshield and dashboard are fastened *c)* a cowling —***vt.*** to cover as with a cowl —**cowled** ***adj.***

cow·lick (kou′lik) ***n.*** [< the notion that it looks as if it has been licked by a cow] a tuft of hair on the head that cannot easily be combed flat

cowl·ing (kou′liŋ) ***n.*** [see COWL] a detachable metal covering for an airplane engine, etc.

cow·man (kou′mən) ***n., pl.*** **-men** **1.** the owner or operator of a cattle ranch **2.** a cowherd

co-work·er (kō′wur′kər) ***n.*** a fellow worker

cow·pea (kou′pē′) ***n.*** **1.** a bushlike annual forage plant of the legume family, with seeds in slender pods **2.** its edible seed

Cow·per (ko͞o′pər, ko͞op′ər; *now occas.* kou′pər), **William** 1731–1800; Eng. poet

cow·poke (kou′pōk′) ***n.*** [cf. COWPUNCHER] [Colloq.] a cowboy

cow pony a pony used in herding cattle

cow·pox (kou′päks′) ***n.*** a contagious disease of cows that causes pustules on the udders: smallpox vaccine is made from the virus

cow·punch·er (-pun′chər) ***n.*** [from the prodding of animals in herding] [Colloq.] a cowboy

cow·rie, cow·ry (kou′rē) ***n., pl.*** **-ries** [< Hindi < Sans. *kaparda*] **1.** any of certain gastropods of warm seas, with brightly colored shells **2.** the shell of such a mollusk, esp. of the **money cowrie,** formerly used as currency in parts of Africa and S Asia

cow·shed (kou′shed′) ***n.*** a shelter for cows

cow·slip (-slip′) ***n.*** [< OE., lit., cow dung < *cu*, cow + *slyppe*, paste] **1.** a European primrose with yellow or purple flowers **2.** *same as:* *a)* MARSH MARIGOLD *b)* VIRGINIA COWSLIP

cox (käks) ***n., pl.*** **cox′es** [Colloq.] a coxswain —***vt., vi.*** to be coxswain for (a boat or crew)

cox·a (käk′sə) ***n., pl.*** **cox′ae** (-sē) [L.] **1.** the hip or hip joint **2.** the basal segment of an arthropod leg —**cox′al** ***adj.***

cox·al·gi·a (käk sal′jē ə, -jə) ***n.*** [see prec. & -ALGIA] pain in, or disease of, the hip or hip joint: also **cox′al′gy** (-jē) —**cox·al′gic** ***adj.***

cox·comb (käks′kōm′) ***n.*** [for *cock's comb*] **1.** a cap topped with a notched strip of red cloth like a cock's comb, formerly worn by jesters **2.** a silly, vain, foppish fellow; dandy —**cox·comb·i·cal** (käks kō′mi k'l, -käm′i-) ***adj.*** —**cox·comb′i·cal·ly** ***adv.*** —**cox′comb′ry** (-kōm′rē) ***n.,*** *pl.* **-ries**

cox·swain (käk′s'n, -swān′) ***n.*** [< COCK(BOAT) + SWAIN] **1.** a person in charge of a ship's boat and acting as its steersman **2.** the steersman of a racing shell, calling out the stroke rhythm

coy (koi) ***adj.*** [< OFr. < LL. < L. *quietus*: see QUIET] **1.** bashful; shy **2.** affecting innocence or shyness, esp. playfully or coquettishly **3.** reticent in making a commitment —**coy′ly** ***adv.*** —**coy′ness** ***n.***

coy·o·te (kī ōt′ē, kī′ōt) ***n.,*** *pl.* **coy·o′tes, coy·o′te:** see PLURAL, II, D, 1 [AmSp. < Nahuatl *coyotl*] a small wolf of western N. American prairies

COYOTE
(to 4 ft. long, including tail)

coy·pu (koi′po͞o) ***n.,*** *pl.* **-pus, -pu:** see PLURAL, II, D, 1 [< AmSp. < native name] *same as* NUTRIA

coz (kuz) ***n.*** [Colloq.] cousin

coz·en (kuz′'n) ***vt., vi.*** [< ME. *cosin,* fraud < ?] to cheat, defraud, or deceive —**coz′en·age** ***n.***

co·zy (kō′zē) ***adj.*** **-zi·er, -zi·est** [Scot., prob. < Scand.] warm and comfortable; snug —***n.,*** *pl.* **-zies** a knitted or padded cover to keep a teapot hot —**cozy up to** [Colloq.] to try to ingratiate oneself with —**play it cozy** [Slang] to act cautiously —**co′zi·ly** ***adv.*** —**co′zi·ness** ***n.***

CP Command Post

cp, c.p. candlepower

cp. compare

C.P. **1.** Common Pleas **2.** Common Prayer

c.p. chemically pure

CPA, C.P.A. Certified Public Accountant

cpd. compound

Cpl, Cpl. Corporal

cpm, c.p.m. cycles per minute

CPO, C.P.O. Chief Petty Officer

cps, c.p.s. cycles per second

cpt. counterpoint

CQ amateur radio operators' signal inviting a reply

Cr *Chem.* chromium

cr. **1.** credit **2.** creditor **3.** crown

C.R. Costa Rica

crab[1] (krab) ***n.*** [< OE. *crabba*] **1.** any of various crustaceans with four pairs of legs, one pair of pincers, a flattish shell, and a short, broad abdomen folded under its thorax **2.** any of several similar animals **3.** *same as* CRAB LOUSE **4.** a machine for hoisting heavy weights —[C-] Cancer, the constellation and zodiac sign —***vi.*** **crabbed, crab′bing** to fish for or catch crabs —**catch a crab** *Rowing* to unbalance the boat by a faulty stroke —**crab′ber** ***n.***

crab[2] (krab) ***n.*** [akin ? to Scot. *scrabbe,* Sw. dial. *scrabba,* wild apple] **1.** *same as* CRAB APPLE **2.** a sour-tempered person —***adj.*** of a crab apple —***vi.*** **crabbed, crab′bing** [Colloq.] to complain peevishly —**crab one's act (the deal,** etc.) [Colloq.] to spoil one's scheme (the deal, etc.) —**crab′ber** ***n.***

crab apple **1.** a small, very sour apple, used for jellies, etc. **2.** a tree bearing crab apples: also **crab tree**

crab·bed (krab′id) ***adj.*** [< CRAB (APPLE)] **1.** peevish; cross **2.** hard to understand; intricate **3.** hard to read; illegible —**crab′bed·ly** ***adv.*** —**crab′bed·ness** ***n.***

crab·by (-ē) ***adj.*** **-bi·er, -bi·est** [see prec.] peevish; cross —**crab′bi·ly** ***adv.*** —**crab′bi·ness** ***n.***

crab grass a coarse, weedy annual grass that spreads rapidly because of its freely rooting stems

crab louse a louse, somewhat crablike in shape, infesting the pubic regions, armpits, etc.

crack (krak) ***vi.*** [< OE. *cracian,* to resound] **1.** to make a sudden, sharp breaking noise **2.** to break or split, usually without complete separation of parts **3.** to become rasping or change pitch suddenly, as the voice **4.** [Colloq.] to break down [to *crack* under the strain] —***vt.*** **1.** to cause to make a sharp, sudden noise **2.** to cause to break or split **3.** to destroy or impair **4.** to subject (as petroleum) to cracking: see CRACKING **5.** to hit or strike with a sudden, sharp blow or impact **6.** to manage to solve [to *crack* a code] **7.** [Colloq.] to break open or into **8.** [Slang] to make (a joke) —***n.*** **1.** a sudden, sharp noise **2.** *a)* a break, usually partial *b)* a flaw **3.** a chink; fissure **4.** an abrupt, erratic shift of vocal tone **5.** a moment; instant [the *crack* of dawn] **6.** [Colloq.] a sudden, sharp blow or impact **7.** [Colloq.] an attempt; try **8.** [Slang] a joke or gibe —***adj.*** [Colloq.] excelling in skill; first-rate [*crack* troops] —**crack a smile** [Slang] to relax or unbend enough to smile —**crack down (on)** to become strict or stricter (with) —**cracked up to be** [Colloq.] alleged or believed to be —**crack up** **1.** to crash, as (in) an airplane **2.** [Colloq.] *a)* to break down physically or mentally *b)* to break into a fit of laughter or tears

crack·a·jack (krak′ə jak′) ***adj., n.*** [Slang] *same as* CRACKERJACK

crack·brain (-brān′) ***n.*** a crazy person

crack·brained (-brānd′) ***adj.*** crazy

crack·down (-doun′) ***n.*** a resorting to strict or stricter measures of discipline or punishment

cracked (krakt) ***adj.*** **1.** broken, usually without complete separation of parts **2.** harsh [a *cracked* voice] **3.** [Colloq.] crazy

cracked wheat coarsely milled wheat particles

crack·er (krak′ər) ***n.*** **1.** one that cracks **2.** a firecracker **3.** a little paper roll used as a party favor: it contains candy, etc. and pops open when the ends are pulled **4.** a thin, crisp wafer **5.** *same as* POOR WHITE: contemptuous term

crack·er-bar·rel (-bar′əl) ***adj.*** [< the large barrel of soda crackers formerly found in general stores] [Colloq.] designating or typical of informal discussions by persons gathered at a country store

crack·er·jack (krak′ər jak′) ***adj.*** [extension of CRACK, *adj.* + JACK (nickname)] [Slang] excellent —***n.*** [Slang] an excellent person or thing

crack·ers (krak′ərz) ***adj.*** [altered < CRACKED] [Chiefly Brit. Slang] crazy

crack·ing[1] (krak′iŋ) ***adj.*** [Colloq.] excellent; fine —***adv.*** [Colloq.] very

crack·ing[2] (krak′iŋ) ***n.*** the process of breaking down heavier hydrocarbons, as by heat and pressure, into lighter hydrocarbons, as in producing gasoline

crack·le (krak′'l) ***vi.*** **-led, -ling** [freq. of CRACK] **1.** to make slight, sharp popping sounds, as of dry wood burning **2.** to be bursting with vivacity, etc. **3.** to develop a finely cracked surface —***vt.*** **1.** to crush or break with crackling sounds **2.** to produce a finely cracked surface on —***n.*** **1.** crackling sounds **2.** fine, irregular surface cracks, as on old oil paintings **3.** crackleware

crack·le·ware (krak′'l wer′) ***n.*** pottery, porcelain, etc. with a finely cracked surface

crack·ling (krak′liŋ; *for 2 usually* -lin) ***n.*** **1.** the production of slight, sharp popping sounds **2.** *a)* the browned, crisp rind of roast pork *b)* [*pl.*] crisp bits left when hog fat is rendered

crack·ly (-lē) ***adj.*** that crackles; crackling

crack·pot (-pät′) ***n.*** [Colloq.] a crazy or eccentric person —***adj.*** [Colloq.] crazy or eccentric

crack·up (krak′up′) ***n.*** **1.** a crash, as of an airplane **2.** [Colloq.] a mental or physical collapse

-cra·cy (krə sē) [< Fr. < ML. < Gr. *-kratia* < *kratos,* rule] *a combining form meaning* a (specified) type of government; rule by [*autocracy*]

cra·dle (krā′d'l) ***n.*** [OE. *cradol*] **1.** a baby's small bed, usually on rockers **2.** infancy **3.** the place of a thing's beginning **4.** anything cradlelike; specif., *a)* a framework to hold or lift a boat, etc. being built or repaired *b)* the support for the handset of a telephone (**cradle telephone**) *c)* *Agric.* a frame on a scythe (**cradle scythe**) for laying the grain evenly as it is cut *d)* *Mining* a boxlike device on rockers for washing out gold —***vt.*** **-dled, -dling** **1.** to place, rock, or hold in or as in a cradle **2.** *Mining* to wash (sand) in a cradle

cra·dle·song (-sôŋ′) ***n.*** a lullaby

craft (kraft) ***n.*** [OE. *cræft,* strength, power] **1.** a special skill or art **2.** an occupation requiring this; esp., any manual art **3.** the members of a skilled trade **4.** skill in deceiving; guile **5.** *pl.* **craft** a boat, ship, or aircraft —***vt.*** to make with skill or artistry: usually in pp.

-craft (kraft) [< prec.] *a combining form meaning* the work, skill, or practice of [*handicraft*]

crafts·man (krafts′mən) ***n.,*** *pl.* **-men** **1.** a skilled workman **2.** a skillful artist or one having only technical skill —**crafts′man·ship′** ***n.***

craft union a labor union to which only workers in a certain trade, craft, or occupation can belong: distinguished from INDUSTRIAL UNION

craft·y (kraf′tē) ***adj.*** **craft′i·er, craft′i·est** sly; cunning —**craft′i·ly** ***adv.*** —**craft′i·ness** ***n.***

crag (krag) ***n.*** [< Celt.] a steep, rugged rock rising above others or projecting from a rock mass

crag·gy (-ē) ***adj.*** **-gi·er, -gi·est** having many crags: also **crag′ged** (-id) —**crag′gi·ness** ***n.***

crake (krāk) ***n.,*** *pl.* **crakes, crake:** see PLURAL, II, D, 1 [< ON. *kraka,* crow] any of several rails with long legs and a short bill

cram (kram) ***vt.*** **crammed, cram′ming** [OE. *crammian,* to stuff] **1.** to pack full or too full **2.** to stuff; force **3.** to feed to excess **4.** to prepare (a student) or review (a subject) for an examination in a hurried, intensive way —***vi.***

1. to eat too much or too quickly 2. to study a subject in a hurried, intensive way, for an examination —*n.* 1. a crowded condition 2. a cramming —**cram′mer** *n.*

cramp[1] (kramp) *n.* [< OFr. *crampe,* bent, twisted < Frank.] 1. a sudden, painful, involuntary contraction of a muscle from chill, strain, etc. 2. partial local paralysis, as from excessive use of muscles 3. [*usually pl.*] abdominal spasms and pain —*vt.* to cause a cramp in

cramp[2] (kramp) *n.* [MDu. *krampe,* lit., bent in] 1. a metal bar bent at each end at a right angle, for holding together timbers, etc.: also **cramp iron** 2. a clamp 3. anything that confines or hampers —*vt.* 1. to fasten as with a cramp 2. to confine or hamper 3. to turn (the wheels of a car, etc.) sharply —*adj. same as* CRAMPED —**cramp one's style** [Slang] to hamper one's usual skill, confidence, etc. in doing something

cramped (krampt) *adj.* 1. confined; restricted 2. irregular and crowded, as some handwriting

cramp·fish (kramp′fish′) *n., pl.* **-fish′, -fish′es:** see FISH *same as* ELECTRIC RAY

cram·pon (kram′pän, -pən) *n.* [Fr., akin to CRAMP[2]] 1. either of a pair of iron hooks for raising heavy weights 2. either of a pair of spiked iron plates fastened on shoes to prevent slipping Also **cram·poon** (kram po͞on′)

cran·ber·ry (kran′ber′ē, -bər ē) *n., pl.* **-ries** [< Du. *kranebere,* LowG. *kraanbere,* lit., crane berry] 1. a firm, sour, edible, red berry of an evergreen shrub of the heath family 2. this shrub

crane (krān) *n.* [OE. *cran*] 1. *pl.* **cranes, crane:** see PLURAL, II, D, 1 *a*) a large wading bird with very long legs and neck, and a long, straight bill *b*) popularly, any of various herons or storks 2. a machine for lifting or moving heavy weights by means of a movable projecting arm or a horizontal traveling beam 3. any device with a swinging arm fixed on a vertical axis, as to hold a kettle —*vt., vi.* **craned, cran′ing** 1. to raise or move as by a crane 2. to stretch (the neck) in trying to see over something

Crane (krān) 1. **(Harold) Hart,** 1899–1932; U.S. poet 2. **Stephen,** 1871–1900; U.S. writer

crane fly any of various two-winged, slender flies with very long legs

cranes·bill, crane's-bill (krānz′bil′) *n. a popular name for* GERANIUM (sense 1)

cra·ni·al (krā′nē əl) *adj.* of or from the cranium

cranial nerve any of the pairs of nerves, twelve in man, connected directly with the brain

cra·ni·ate (krā′nē it, -āt′) *adj.* having a cranium, as mammals —*n.* a craniate animal

cra·ni·o- [Gr. *kranio-* < *kranion,* skull] *a combining form meaning* of the head, cranial

cra·ni·ol·o·gy (krā′nē äl′ə jē) *n.* the scientific study of skulls, esp. human skulls

cra·ni·om·e·try (-äm′ə trē) *n.* the science of measuring skulls; cranial measurement

cra·ni·ot·o·my (-ät′ə mē) *n., pl.* **-mies** the surgical operation of opening the skull

cra·ni·um (krā′nē əm) *n., pl.* **-ni·ums, -ni·a** (-ə) [ML. < Gr. *kranion*] 1. the skull 2. the bones forming the enclosure of the brain

crank (kraŋk) *n.* [< OE. *cranc-, as in crancstæf,* yarn comb] 1. a handle or arm at right angles to a shaft of a machine, to transmit or change motion 2. [Colloq.] *a*) an eccentric person *b*) an irritable, complaining person —*vt.* to start or operate by a crank —*vi.* to turn a crank

crank·case (kraŋk′kās′) *n.* the metal casing of the crankshaft of an internal-combustion engine

crank·pin (-pin′) *n.* a cylindrical bar or pin, as part of a crankshaft, to which a connecting rod is attached: also **crank pin**

crank·shaft (-shaft′) *n.* a shaft having one or more cranks for transmitting motion

crank·y (kraŋ′kē) *adj.* **crank′i·er, crank′i·est** 1. out of order; loose 2. irritable; cross 3. queer; eccentric —**crank′i·ly** *adv.* —**crank′i·ness** *n.*

Cran·mer (kran′mər), **Thomas** 1489–1556; Eng. churchman; archbishop of Canterbury

cran·ny (kran′ē) *n., pl.* **-nies** [OFr. *cran* < OIt. < LL. *crena,* a notch] a small, narrow opening; crevice —**cran′nied** (-ēd) *adj.*

Cran·ston (kran′stən) [after S. *Cranston,* 18th-c. colonial governor] city in EC R.I.: pop. 72,000

crap[1] (krap) *n.* [see CRAPS] 1. *same as* CRAPS 2. a losing throw at craps —**crap out** 1. to make a losing throw at craps 2. [Slang] to fail, give up, etc. because of exhaustion, etc.

crap[2] (krap) *n.* [< OFr., ordure] [Vulgar Slang] 1. nonsense, insincerity, etc. 2. trash; junk —**crap′py** *adj.* **-pi·er, -pi·est**

crape (krāp) *n.* [Fr. *crêpe:* see CREPE] 1. *same as* CREPE (sense 1) 2. a piece of black crepe as a sign of mourning

crape·hang·er (-haŋ′ər) *n.* [Slang] a pessimist

crap·pie (krap′ē) *n., pl.* **-pies, -pie:** see PLURAL, II, D, 1 [< ?] a small sunfish of the E and C U.S.

craps (kraps) *n.pl.* [*with sing. v.*] [Fr. *crabs, craps* < obs. E. *crabs,* lowest throw at hazard, two aces] a gambling game played with two dice, in which, for example, a first throw of seven or eleven wins

crap·shoot·er (krap′sho͞ot′ər) *n.* a gambler at craps —**crap′shoot′ing** *n.*

crap·u·lence (krap′yoo ləns) *n.* [see ff.] 1. sickness from excess in drinking or eating 2. gross intemperance, esp. in drinking —**crap′u·lent** *adj.*

crap·u·lous (-ləs) *adj.* [< LL. < L. *crapula,* drunkenness < Gr. *kraipalē,* drunken headache] 1. intemperate, esp. in drinking 2. sick from such intemperance

crash[1] (krash) *vi.* [ME. *crashen,* prob. echoic var. of *craken,* CRACK] 1. to fall, collide, or break with force and with a loud, smashing noise 2. *a*) to make this noise *b*) to move with such a noise 3. to fall and be damaged or destroyed: said of aircraft 4. to collapse, as a business —*vt.* 1. to break into pieces; smash 2. to cause to crash 3. to force or impel with a crashing noise (with *in, out,* etc.) 4. [Colloq.] to get into (a party, etc.) without an invitation, etc. —*n.* 1. a loud, smashing noise 2. a crashing 3. a sudden collapse —*adj.* [Colloq.] using all possible resources, effort, and speed [*a crash* program]

crash[2] (krash) *n.* [prob. < Russ. *krashenina,* colored linen] a coarse cloth of plain, loose weave

crash dive a sudden submergence of a submarine to escape from attack —**crash′-dive′** *vi.* **-dived′, -div′ing**

crash helmet a thickly padded, protective helmet worn by motorcyclists, aviators, etc.

crash·ing (-iŋ) *adj.* [Colloq.] thorough; complete [*a crashing* bore]

crash-land (krash′land′) *vt., vi.* to bring (an airplane) down in a forced landing, with some damage —**crash landing**

crass (kras) *adj.* [L. *crassus,* gross] 1. grossly stupid, dull, or obtuse 2. tasteless, insensitive, materialistic, etc. —**crass′ly** *adv.* —**crass′ness, cras′si·tude′** (-ə to͞od′, -ə tyo͞od′) *n.*

-crat (krat) [< Fr. < Gr. *-kratēs* < *kratos,* rule] *a combining form meaning* participant in or supporter of (a specified kind of) government or ruling body [*democrat, aristocrat*]

crate (krāt) *n.* [L. *cratis,* wickerwork] 1. a box or case made of wood slats, for shipping or storing things 2. [Slang] an old, decrepit automobile or airplane —*vt.* **crat′ed, crat′ing** to pack in a crate —**crat′er** *n.*

cra·ter (krāt′ər) *n.* [L. < Gr. *kratēr*] 1. in ancient Greece, a kind of bowl or jar 2. a bowl-shaped cavity, as at the mouth of a volcano or on the moon 3. any pit like this, as one made by an exploding bomb

craunch (krônch, kränch) *vt., vi., n. same as* CRUNCH

cra·vat (krə vat′) *n.* [< Fr. < *Cravate,* Croat: referring to scarves worn by Croatian soldiers] 1. a neckerchief or scarf 2. a necktie

crave (krāv) *vt.* **craved, crav′ing** [OE. *crafian*] 1. to ask for earnestly; beg 2. to long for; desire strongly 3. to need greatly —*vi.* to have a longing or strong desire (*for*) —**crav′er** *n.*

cra·ven (krā′vən) *adj.* [< OFr. < L. *crepare,* to creak] very cowardly —*n.* a thorough coward —**cra′ven·ly** *adv.* —**cra′ven·ness** *n.*

crav·ing (krā′viŋ) *n.* an intense desire or longing, as for affection or a food, drug, etc.

craw (krô) *n.* [ME. *craue*] 1. the crop of a bird or insect 2. the stomach of any animal —**to stick in the** (or **one's**) **craw** to be unacceptable to one

craw·fish (krô′fish′) *n., pl.* **-fish′, -fish′es:** see FISH *same as* CRAYFISH —*vi.* [Colloq.] to withdraw from a position; back down

crawl[1] (krôl) *vi.* [< ON. *krafla*] 1. to move slowly by drawing the body along the ground, as a worm 2. to go on hands and knees 3. to move slowly 4. to act abjectly servile 5. to swarm (*with* crawling things) 6. to feel as if insects were crawling on the skin —*n.* 1. a crawling; slow movement 2. an overarm swimming stroke, face downward —**crawl′er** *n.*

crawl[2] (krôl) *n.* [WIndDu. *kraal* < Sp. *corral:* see CORRAL] an enclosure made in shallow water for confining fish, turtles, etc.

crawl space a narrow space, as under a roof or floor, allowing access to wiring, plumbing, etc.

crawl·y (krôl′ē) *adj.* **crawl′i·er, crawl′i·est** *same as* CREEPY

cray·fish (krā′fish′) *n., pl.* **-fish′, -fish′es** see FISH [< OFr. *crevice* < OHG.] 1. any of certain small, lobster-shaped freshwater crustaceans 2. *same as* SPINY LOBSTER

cray·on (krā′ən, -än′) ***n.*** [Fr. < *craie*, chalk < L. *creta*] **1.** a small stick of chalk, charcoal, or colored wax, used for drawing, coloring, or writing **2.** a crayon drawing —***vt.*** to draw or color with crayons —**cray′on·ist** ***n.***

craze (krāz) ***vt.*** **crazed, craz′ing** [ME. *crasen*, to crack < Scand.] **1.** to make mentally ill or insane **2.** to produce small cracks in the surface or glaze of (pottery, etc.) —***vi.*** to become finely cracked, as pottery glaze —***n.*** **1.** a mania **2.** a fad **3.** a crack in the glaze of pottery, etc.

cra·zy (krā′zē) ***adj.*** **-zi·er, -zi·est** [< CRAZE] **1.** flawed, cracked, or rickety **2.** mentally unbalanced or insane **3.** [Colloq.] foolish, wild, fantastic, etc. **4.** [Colloq.] very enthusiastic or eager **5.** [Slang] excellent, thrilling, etc. —**cra′zi·ly** ***adv.*** —**cra′zi·ness** ***n.***

crazy bone *same as* FUNNY BONE

crazy quilt a quilt made of pieces of cloth of various colors, patterns, shapes, and sizes

cra·zy·weed (-wēd′) ***n.*** *same as* LOCOWEED

creak (krēk) ***vi., vt.*** [ME. *creken*, akin to CROAK] to make, cause to make, or move with a harsh, shrill, grating, or squeaking sound, as rusted hinges —***n.*** such a sound

creak·y (-ē) ***adj.*** **creak′i·er, creak′i·est** creaking —**creak′i·ly** ***adv.*** —**creak′i·ness** ***n.***

cream (krēm) ***n.*** [OFr. *cresme*, prob. a blend of LL. *chrisma* (see CHRISM) & VL. *crama*, cream] **1.** the oily, yellowish part of milk **2.** any food made of cream or having a creamy consistency **3.** a creamy cosmetic or emulsion **4.** the best part **5.** yellowish white —***adj.*** of, with, or like cream; creamy, cream-colored, etc. —***vi.*** to form cream or a creamy foam —***vt.*** **1.** to take cream from **2.** to add cream to **3.** to cook with cream or a cream sauce **4.** to make creamy by beating, etc. **5.** [Slang] to beat soundly —**cream of** creamed purée of *[cream of* tomato soup*]*

cream cheese a soft, white cheese made of cream or of milk enriched with cream

cream·er (-ər) ***n.*** **1.** a small pitcher for cream **2.** a device for separating cream from milk

cream·er·y (-ər ē) ***n., pl.*** **-er·ies** **1.** a place where milk and cream are pasteurized, separated, and bottled, and butter and cheese are made **2.** a shop where dairy products are sold

cream of tartar a white, acid, crystalline substance, $KHC_4H_4O_6$, used in baking powder

cream puff a round shell of pastry filled with whipped cream or custard

cream sauce a sauce made of butter and flour cooked together with milk or cream

cream soda soda pop, usually colorless, that is flavored with vanilla

cream·y (-ē) ***adj.*** **cream′i·er, cream′i·est** **1.** full of cream **2.** like cream in consistency or color —**cream′i·ness** ***n.***

crease[1] (krēs) ***n.*** [earlier *creaste*, lit., ridge < ME. *creste*, crest < OFr. *creste:* see CREST] **1.** a line, mark, or ridge made by folding and pressing cloth, paper, etc. **2.** a fold or wrinkle *[creases* in a jowl*]* —***vt.*** **1.** to make a crease in **2.** to graze with a bullet —***vi.*** to become creased —**creas′er** ***n.*** —**creas′y** ***adj.***

crease[2] (krēs) ***n.*** *same as* KRIS

cre·ate (krē āt′) ***vt.*** **-at′ed, -at′ing** [< L. pp. of *creare*] **1.** to bring into being; originate, design, invent, etc. **2.** to bring about; cause **3.** to invest with a new rank, function, etc. **4.** *Theater* to be the first to portray (a role)

cre·a·tion (-ā′shən) ***n.*** **1.** a creating or being created **2.** the whole universe **3.** anything created; esp., an original design, etc. —**the Creation** *Theol.* God's creating of the world

cre·a·tive (-āt′iv) ***adj.*** **1.** creating or able to create **2.** productive (*of*) **3.** imaginative and inventive **4.** stimulating the inventive powers —**cre·a′tive·ly** ***adv.*** —**cre·a′tive·ness,** ***n.*** —**cre·a·tiv·i·ty** (krē′ā tiv′ə tē) ***n.***

cre·a·tor (-āt′ər) ***n.*** **1.** one who creates **2.** [C-] God

crea·ture (krē′chər) ***n.*** [< OFr. < L. *creatura*] **1.** anything created, animate or inanimate **2.** a living being; esp., *a)* a domestic animal *b)* a human being: often used patronizingly or contemptuously **3.** one completely dominated by or dependent on another —**crea′tur·al, crea′ture·ly** ***adj.***

crèche (kresh, krāsh) ***n.*** [Fr. < Frank. hyp. *kripja*, crib] **1.** a display of a stable with figures, representing a scene at the birth of Jesus **2.** an institution for foundlings **3.** [Chiefly Brit.] a day nursery

cre·dal (krēd′'l) ***adj.*** of a creed

cre·dence (krēd′'ns) ***n.*** [< OFr. < ML. < L. prp. of *credere:* see CREED] **1.** belief, esp. in another's reports or testimony **2.** credentials: now only in **letter of credence** **3.** *Eccles.* a small side table for the Eucharistic wine, etc.

cre·den·tial (kri den′shəl, -chəl) ***n.*** **1.** that which entitles to credit, confidence, etc. **2.** [*usually pl.*] a letter or certificate showing that one has a right to a certain position or authority

cre·den·za (kri den′zə) ***n.*** [It.] a type of buffet, or sideboard

cred·i·ble (kred′ə b'l) ***adj.*** [< L. < *credere:* see CREED] that can be believed; believable —**cred′i·bil′i·ty, cred′i·ble·ness** ***n.*** —**cred′i·bly** ***adv.***

cred·it (kred′it) ***n.*** [< Fr. < It. < L. pp. of *credere:* see CREED] **1.** belief or trust; confidence **2.** *a)* good reputation *b)* one's influence based on one's reputation **3.** praise to which one is entitled **4.** a source of approval or honor *[a credit* to the team*]* **5.** acknowledgment of work done or help given; specif., [*pl.*] a list of such acknowledgments in a movie, TV show, etc. **6.** *a)* the amount in a bank account, etc. *b)* a sum made available by a bank for withdrawal by someone specified **7.** *Accounting* *a)* acknowledgment of a payment by entry of the amount in an account *b)* the right-hand side of an account, for such entries *c)* an entry, or the sum of entries, there *d)* a deduction from a debt or an addition (as to a bank account) in making an adjustment **8.** *Business* *a)* trust in one's ability to make payments when due *b)* time allowed for payment **9.** *Educ.* *a)* certification of a successfully completed unit or course of study *b)* a unit so certified —***vt.*** **1.** to believe in the truth, reliability, etc. of; trust **2.** to give credit to or deserved commendation for **3.** to give credit in a bank account, etc. **4.** *Accounting* to enter on the credit side **5.** *Educ.* to enter credits on the record of (a student) —**credit one with** to ascribe to one —**do credit to** to bring approval or honor to —**give credit to** **1.** to trust **2.** to commend —**give one credit for** **1.** to commend one for **2.** to believe or recognize that one has —**on credit** with agreement on future payment —**to one's credit** bringing approval or honor to one

cred·it·a·ble (-ə b'l) ***adj.*** **1.** praiseworthy **2.** ascribable (*to*) —**cred′it·a·bil′i·ty, cred′it·a·ble·ness** ***n.*** —**cred′it·a·bly** ***adv.***

credit bureau an agency supplying information on the credit rating of individuals or firms

credit card a card allowing a person to charge bills at certain restaurants, gas stations, etc.

cred·i·tor (-ər) ***n.*** a person who extends credit or to whom money is owed

credit rating the rating of an individual or firm as a credit risk, based on past records of debt repayment, financial status, etc.

credit union a cooperative association for pooling savings of members and making loans to them at a low rate of interest

cre·do (krē′dō, krā′dō) ***n., pl.*** **-dos** [L., I believe: see CREED] **1.** *same as* CREED **2.** [*usually* C-] the Apostles' Creed or the Nicene Creed

cre·du·li·ty (krə do͞o′lə tē, -dyo͞o′-) ***n.*** a tendency to believe too readily

cred·u·lous (krej′oo ləs) ***adj.*** [L. *credulus* < *credere:* see CREED] **1.** tending to believe too readily **2.** resulting from or indicating credulity —**cred′u·lous·ly** ***adv.*** —**cred′u·lous·ness** ***n.***

Cree (krē) ***n.*** [< AmInd.] **1.** *pl.* **Crees, Cree** a member of a tribe of Algonquian Indians of C Canada **2.** the Algonquian language of this tribe

creed (krēd) ***n.*** [< OE. < L. *credo*, lit., I believe < *credere*, to trust] **1.** a brief statement of religious belief, esp. as accepted by a church **2.** any statement of belief, opinions, etc. —**creed′al** ***adj.***

Creek (krēk) ***n.*** [from the many creeks in their territory] **1.** *pl.* **Creeks, Creek** an American Indian of any of several tribes, mainly Muskogean, orig. in SE U.S., now in Oklahoma **2.** their language

creek (krēk, krik) ***n.*** [ME. *creke* < ON. *-kriki*, a winding] **1.** a small stream, somewhat larger than a brook **2.** [Now chiefly Brit.] a narrow inlet or bay —**up the creek** [Slang] in trouble

creel (krēl) ***n.*** [< OFr. *grail:* see GRIDDLE] a wicker basket for fishermen to carry fish caught

CREEL

creep (krēp) ***vi.*** **crept, creep′ing** [OE. *creopan*] **1.** to move along with the body close to the ground, as on hands and knees **2.** to come on or move slowly, gradually, stealthily, etc. **3.** to grow along the ground, etc., as some plants **4.** to change position or shape slightly —***n.*** **1.** a creeping **2.** [Slang] a person regarded as very annoying, etc. —**make one's flesh** (or **skin**) **creep** to make one fearful, etc., as if insects were creeping on one's skin —**the creeps** [Colloq.] a feeling of fear, repugnance, etc.

creep·age (-ij) ***n.*** a gradual creeping movement

creep·er (-ər) ***n.*** **1.** a person, animal, or thing that creeps **2.** a plant whose stem puts out tendrils or rootlets for creeping along a surface **3.** [*pl.*] a baby's one-piece garment, of pants and shirt

creep·y (krēp′ē) ***adj.*** **creep′i·er, creep′i·est** **1.** creeping; moving slowly **2.** having or causing fear or disgust, as if insects were creeping on one's skin —**creep′i·ly** ***adv.*** —**creep′i·ness** ***n.***

creese (krēs) ***n.*** *same as* KRIS

cre·mate (krē′māt, kri māt′) ***vt.*** **-mat·ed, -mat·ing** [< L. pp. of *cremare,* to burn] to burn up; esp., to burn (a dead body) to ashes —**cre·ma′tion** ***n.*** —**cre′ma·tor** ***n.***

cre·ma·to·ry (krē′mə tôr′ē; *chiefly Brit.* krem′ə-) ***n., pl.*** **-ries** **1.** a furnace for cremating **2.** a building with such a furnace in it Also **cre′ma·to′ri·um** (-ē əm), *pl.* **-ri·ums, -ri·a** (-ə) —***adj.*** of or for cremation: also **cre′ma·to′ri·al**

crème (krem, krēm) ***n.*** [Fr.] **1.** cream **2.** a thick liqueur

crème de ca·ca·o (də kə kä′ō, -kā′ō; də kō′kō) [Fr.] a sweet, chocolate-flavored liqueur

crème de menthe (də mänt′, menth′, mint′) [Fr.] a sweet, mint-flavored liqueur, green or colorless

Cre·mo·na (kri mō′nə) ***n.*** any famous violin formerly made in Cremona, Italy, as by Stradivari

cre·nate (krē′nāt) ***adj.*** [< ModL. < VL. *crena,* a notch] having a scalloped edge, as certain leaves: also **cre′nat·ed** —**cre′nate·ly** ***adv.*** —**cre·na′tion** ***n.***

cren·el (kren′'l) ***n.*** [OFr. < VL. *crena,* a notch] an indentation in the top of a battlement or wall: also **cre·nelle** (kri-nel′) —***vt.*** **-eled** or **-elled, -el·ing** or **-el·ling** to crenelate

cren·el·ate, cren·el·late (kren′'l āt′) ***vt.*** **-el·at′ed** or **-el·lat′ed, -el·at′ing** or **-el·lat′ing** to furnish with crenels or with squared notches —**cren′el·a′tion, cren′el·la′tion** ***n.***

Cre·ole, cre·ole (krē′ōl) ***n.*** [< Fr. < Sp. *criollo* < Port. < *criar,* to rear < L. *creare,* to create] **1.** orig., a person of European parentage born in Latin America or the Gulf States **2.** *a*) a descendant of such persons, esp. of French settlers in Louisiana or of Spanish settlers in the Gulf States *b*) a person of mixed Creole and Negro descent **3.** French as spoken by Creoles —***adj.*** **1.** of Creoles or their languages **2.** [*usually* **c-**] made with sautéed tomatoes, green peppers, onions, etc.

cre·o·sol (krē′ə sōl′, -sôl′) ***n.*** [CREOS(OTE) + -OL[1]] a colorless, oily, antiseptic liquid, $C_8H_{10}O_2$, obtained esp. from beech tar

cre·o·sote (krē′ə sōt′) ***n.*** [< Gr. *kreas,* flesh + *sōzein,* to save] a transparent, pungent, oily liquid distilled from wood tar or coal tar: used as an antiseptic and a wood preservative —***vt.*** **-sot′ed, -sot′ing** to treat with creosote

crepe, crêpe (krāp; *for 3, also* krep) ***n.*** [Fr. *crêpe* < L. *crispus:* see CRISP] **1.** a thin, crinkled cloth, as of silk or wool; crape **2.** *same as: a*) CRAPE (sense 2) *b*) CREPE PAPER *c*) CREPE RUBBER **3.** a very thin pancake, generally rolled up or folded with a filling: usually **crêpe**

crepe paper thin paper crinkled like crepe

crepe rubber soft rubber in sheets with a wrinkled surface, used for some shoe soles

crêpes su·zette (krāp′ so͞o zet′; *Fr.* krep sü-) [Fr.] crêpes in a hot, orange-flavored sauce, usually served in flaming brandy

crep·i·tate (krep′ə tāt′) ***vi.*** **-tat′ed, -tat′ing** [< L. pp. of *crepitare,* freq. of *crepare,* to creak] to crackle —**crep′i-tant** ***adj.*** —**crep′i·ta′tion** ***n.***

crept (krept) *pt. & pp. of* CREEP

cre·pus·cu·lar (kri pus′kyoo lər) ***adj.*** [< L. *crepusculum,* twilight < *creper,* dark] of, like, or active at, twilight

cre·scen·do (krə shen′dō) ***adj., adv.*** [It. < L. *crescere:* see ff.] *Music* gradually getting louder: symbol < —***n., pl.*** **-dos** **1.** a gradual increase in loudness or intensity **2.** a passage played crescendo —***vi.*** **-doed, -do·ing** to get louder

cres·cent (kres′'nt) ***n.*** [< OFr. < L. *crescere,* to grow] **1.** the moon in its first or last quarter, when it appears concavo-convex **2.** a figure of or like this **3.** anything of similar shape, as a curved roll **4.** [*also* **C-**] [< the Turkish crescent emblem] Turkish or Moslem power —***adj.*** **1.** [Poet.] increasing; growing **2.** shaped like a crescent —**cres·cen′tic** (krə sen′tik) ***adj.***

cre·sol (krē′sōl, -sôl) ***n.*** [< CREOSOTE + -OL[1]] any of three colorless, oily liquids or solids, C_7H_8O, distilled from coal tar: used in disinfectants, etc.

cress (kres) ***n.*** [OE. *cressa,* lit., ? creeper] a plant of the mustard family, as watercress, with pungent leaves used in salads and as garnishes

cres·set (kres′it) ***n.*** [< OFr.] a metal container for burning oil, wood, etc., used as a torch or lantern

crest (krest) ***n.*** [< OFr. < L. *crista*] **1.** a comb, tuft, etc. on the heads of some animals or birds **2.** a plume or emblem on a helmet **3.** a helmet **4.** a heraldic device above the shield in a coat of arms or used on silverware, note paper, etc. **5.** top; ridge **6.** the highest point or level —***vt.*** **1.** to provide with a crest **2.** to reach the top of —***vi.*** to form or reach a crest —**crest′ed** ***adj.***

crest·fall·en (krest′fôl′ən) ***adj.*** **1.** with drooping crest or bowed head **2.** dejected or humbled

cre·ta·ceous (kri tā′shəs) ***adj.*** [< L. < *creta:* see CRAYON] **1.** of, like, or containing chalk **2.** [**C-**] designating or of the third geological period of the Mesozoic Era —**the Cretaceous** the Cretaceous Period or its rocks: see GEOLOGY, chart

Crete (krēt) Greek island in the E Mediterranean: 3,218 sq. mi.; pop. 483,000 —**Cre′tan** ***adj., n.***

cre·tin (krēt′'n) ***n.*** [< Fr. dial. form of *chrétien,* Christian, hence human being] a person suffering from cretinism —**cre′ti·nous** ***adj.***

cre·tin·ism (-iz'm) ***n.*** [see prec.] a congenital thyroid deficiency with resulting deformity and idiocy

cre·tonne (krē′tän, kri tän′) ***n.*** [Fr. < *Creton,* village in Normandy] a heavy, unglazed, printed cotton or linen cloth, for curtains, etc.

cre·vasse (kri vas′) ***n.*** [Fr. < OFr. *crevace,* CREVICE] **1.** a deep crack or fissure, esp. in a glacier **2.** a break in a levee, as of a river —***vt.*** **-vassed′, -vas′sing** to make crevasses in

crev·ice (krev′is) ***n.*** [< OFr. < L. *crepare,* to creak] a narrow opening caused by a crack or split; fissure; cleft —**crev′iced** ***adj.***

crew[1] (kro͞o) ***n.*** [OFr. *creue,* growth < L. *crescere,* to grow] **1.** a group of people associating or working together or classed together; company, set, gang, etc. **2.** the personnel of a ship, usually excepting the officers, or of an aircraft **3.** a rowing team —***vt., vi.*** to serve (on) as a crew member —**crew′man** (-mən) ***n., pl.*** **-men**

crew[2] (kro͞o) *alt. pt. of* CROW[2] (sense 1)

crew cut a man's style of close-cropped haircut

crew·el (kro͞o′əl) ***n.*** [LME. *crule* < ?] a fine worsted yarn used in fancywork and embroidery —**crew′el·work′** ***n.***

crew neck a round, closefitting neckline

crib (krib) ***n.*** [OE.] **1.** a rack, trough, or box for fodder; manger **2.** a small, crude house or room **3.** a small bed with high sides, for a baby **4.** a framework of bars for support or strengthening **5.** a framework or enclosure for storage **6.** a structure anchored under water, serving as a pier, water intake, etc. **7.** [Colloq.] *a*) a petty theft *b*) a plagiarism *c*) a translation or other aid used, often dishonestly, in doing schoolwork —***vt.*** **cribbed, crib′bing** **1.** to confine **2.** to provide with a crib **3.** [Colloq.] *a*) to steal *b*) to plagiarize —***vi.*** [Colloq.] to do schoolwork dishonestly, as by using a crib —**crib′ber** ***n.***

crib·bage (krib′ij) ***n.*** [< prec. + -AGE] a card game in which the object is to form various combinations that count for points: score is kept on a pegboard

crib biting a habit some horses have of biting the feeding trough and swallowing air —**crib′-bite′** ***vi.*** **-bit′, -bit′ten** or **-bit′, -bit′ing**

crick[1] (krik) ***n.*** [< ? ON.] a painful cramp in the neck, back, etc. —***vt.*** to cause a crick in

crick[2] (krik) ***n.*** [Dial.] *same as* CREEK (sense 1)

crick·et[1] (krik′it) ***n.*** [< OFr. < *criquer,* to creak] **1.** a leaping insect, usually with long antennae, related to the locusts and grasshoppers: the males make a chirping noise with their forewings **2.** a small toy or device pressed to make a clicking sound

crick·et[2] (krik′it) ***n.*** [< OFr.; prob. < MDu. *cricke,* a stick] **1.** an outdoor game played by two teams of eleven men each, in which a ball, bats, and wickets are used **2.** [Colloq.] fair play; sportsmanship —***vi.*** to play cricket —**crick′et·er** ***n.***

crick·et[3] (krik′it) ***n.*** [< ?] a wooden footstool

cried (krīd) *pt. & pp. of* CRY

cri·er (krī′ər) ***n.*** **1.** a person who cries **2.** a person who shouts out news, proclamations, etc.

crime (krīm) ***n.*** [OFr. < L. *crimen,* verdict, offense] **1.** an act committed or omitted in violation of a law; specif., any felony or misdemeanor except a petty violation of a local ordinance **2.** an offense against morality; sin **3.** criminal acts, collectively **4.** [Colloq.] something deplorable; shame

Cri·me·a (krī mē′ə, krə-) peninsula in SW U.S.S.R., extending into the Black Sea —**Cri·me′an** ***adj.***

crim·i·nal (krim′ə n'l) ***adj.*** **1.** having the nature of crime; being a crime **2.** relating to or dealing with crime **3.** guilty of crime **4.** [Colloq.] deplorable —***n.*** a person guilty of, or convicted of, a crime —**crim′i·nal′i·ty** (-ə-nal′ə tē) ***n., pl.*** **-ties** —**crim′i·nal·ly** ***adv.***

criminal conversation *Law* adultery

criminal law law dealing with crime

crim·i·nate (krim′ə nāt′) ***vt.*** **-nat′ed, -nat′ing** [< L. pp. of *criminari* < *crimen:* see CRIME] **1.** to accuse of a crime **2.** to incriminate —**crim′i·na′tion** ***n.*** —**crim′i·na′tive, crim′i·na·to′ry** (-nə tôr′ē) ***adj.*** —**crim′i·na′tor** ***n.***

crim·i·nol·o·gy (krim′ə näl′ə jē) *n.* [< L. *crimen* (gen. *criminis*): see CRIME & -LOGY] the scientific study and investigation of crime —**crim′i·no·log′i·cal** (-nə läj′i k'l) *adj.* —**crim′i·no·log′i·cal·ly** *adv.* —**crim′i·nol′o·gist** *n.*
crimp[1] (krimp) *vt.* [< OE. (*ge*)*crympan*, to curl & MDu. *crimpen*, to wrinkle] **1.** to press into narrow, regular folds; pleat **2.** to make (hair, etc.) wavy or curly **3.** to pinch together **4.** [Colloq.] to hamper —*n.* **1.** a crimping **2.** anything crimped or crimpy **3.** crimpy condition —**put a crimp in** [Colloq.] to hamper —**crimp′er** *n.*
crimp[2] (krimp) *n.* [< prec.] a person who gets men by force or trickery to serve as sailors or soldiers —*vt.* to get (men) thus into such service
crimp·y (krim′pē) *adj.* **crimp′i·er, crimp′i·est** [< CRIMP[1]] curly; wavy; frizzly —**crimp′i·ness** *n.*
crim·son (krim′z'n) *n.* [< ML., ult. < Ar. *qirmiz:* see CARMINE] **1.** deep red **2.** deep-red coloring matter —*adj.* **1.** deep-red **2.** bloody —*vt., vi.* to make or become crimson
cringe (krinj) *vi.* **cringed, cring′ing** [OE. *cringan*, to fall (in battle)] **1.** to draw back, crouch, etc., as when afraid; cower **2.** to act servilely; fawn —*n.* a cringing —**cring′er** *n.*
crin·gle (kriŋ′g'l) *n.* [< ON. *kringla*, circle, or MDu. *kringel*, ring] a small ring or loop of rope or metal on the edge of a sail, for inserting a rope
crin·kle (kriŋ′k'l) *vi., vt.* **-kled, -kling** [OE. *crincan*, var. of *cringan:* see CRINGE] **1.** to be or make full of wrinkles or ripples **2.** to rustle, as paper when crushed —*n.* **1.** a wrinkle, twist, or ripple **2.** a rustling sound —**crin′kly** *adj.* **-kli·er, -kli·est**
cri·noid (krī′noid, krin′oid) *adj.* [< Gr. < *krinon*, lily + *-eidēs*, -OID] **1.** lily-shaped **2.** designating or of a class of marine animals that are flowerlike and anchored by a stalk or that are free-swimming —*n.* such an animal
crin·o·line (krin′'l in) *n.* [Fr. < It. < L. *crinis*, hair + *linum*, thread] **1.** a coarse, stiff, heavily sized cloth, orig. of horsehair and linen, used as lining to stiffen garments **2.** a petticoat of this, to puff out a skirt **3.** *same as* HOOP SKIRT
crip·ple (krip′'l) *n.* [< OE. < base of *creopan*, to creep] a person or animal that is lame or disabled in a way preventing normal movement —*vt.* **-pled, -pling** to lame or disable —**crip′pler** *n.*
cri·sis (krī′sis) *n., pl.* **-ses** (-sēz) [L. < Gr. < *krinein*, to separate] **1.** the turning point in a disease, indicating either imminent recovery or death **2.** a turning point in the course of anything **3.** a time of great danger or trouble
crisp (krisp) *adj.* [OE. < L. *crispus*, curly] **1.** easily broken or crumbled; brittle **2.** fresh and firm, as celery **3.** fresh and tidy, as a uniform **4.** sharp and clear [*a crisp analysis*] **5.** lively, as talk **6.** invigorating [*crisp air*] **7.** closely curled and wiry **8.** rippled; wavy —*n.* something crisp —*vt., vi.* to make or become crisp —**crisp′ly** *adv.* —**crisp′ness** *n.*
crisp·y (kris′pē) *adj.* **crisp′i·er, crisp′i·est** *same as* CRISP —**crisp′i·ness** *n.*
criss·cross (kris′krôs′) *n.* [earlier Christ's cross, for the symbol *X*, abbrev. of Christ] **1.** a mark made of two crossed lines (X) **2.** a pattern of crossed lines **3.** a being confused —*adj.* marked with or moving in crossing lines —*vt., vi.* **1.** to mark with crossing lines **2.** to cross back and forth —*adv.* **1.** crosswise **2.** awry
cri·ter·i·on (krī tir′ē ən) *n., pl.* **-i·a** (-ē ə), **-i·ons** [< Gr. < *kritēs*, judge: see ff.] a standard, rule, or test by which something can be judged
crit·ic (krit′ik) *n.* [< L. < Gr. *kritikos*, orig., able to discern, akin to *krinein:* see CRISIS] **1.** a person who forms and expresses judgments of people or things; specif., one who writes judgments of books, plays, music, etc. professionally **2.** a person given to faultfinding and censure
crit·i·cal (krit′i k'l) *adj.* **1.** tending to find fault; censorious **2.** characterized by careful analysis **3.** of critics or criticism **4.** of or forming a crisis; decisive **5.** dangerous or risky **6.** designating or of supplies subject to increased production and restricted distribution, as in wartime **7.** designating or of the point at which a change of character, property, or condition is effected, or at which a nuclear chain reaction becomes self-sustaining —**crit′i·cal′i·ty** (-kal′ə tē), **crit′i·cal·ness** *n.* —**crit′i·cal·ly** *adv.*
crit·i·cise (krit′ə sīz′) *vi., vt.* **-cised′, -cis′ing** *Brit. sp. of* CRITICIZE—**crit′i cis′er** *n.*
crit·i·cism (krit′ə siz′m) *n.* **1.** the act, art, or principles of criticizing, esp. of criticizing literary or artistic work **2.** a comment, review, article, etc. expressing this **3.** faultfinding; disapproval
crit·i·cize (-sīz′) *vi., vt.* **-cized′, -ciz′ing** **1.** to analyze and judge as a critic **2.** to find fault (with) —**crit′i·ciz′a·ble** *adj.* —**crit′i·ciz′er** *n.*
cri·tique (kri tēk′) *n.* [Fr.] **1.** a critical analysis or evaluation **2.** the art of criticizing
crit·ter, crit·tur (krit′ər) *n. dial. var. of* CREATURE
croak (krōk) *vi.* [< OE. < *crǣcettan*, of echoic origin] **1.** to make a deep, hoarse sound, as that of a frog **2.** to talk dismally; grumble **3.** [Slang] to die —*vt.* **1.** to utter in deep, hoarse tones **2.** [Slang] to kill —*n.* a croaking sound —**croak′y** (-ē) *adj.* **croak′i·er, croak′i·est**
croak·er (-ər) *n.* **1.** an animal or fish that makes croaking sounds **2.** a foreteller of evil; grumbler
Cro·at (krō′at, -ət; krōt) *n.* **1.** a native or inhabitant of Croatia **2.** *same as* CROATIAN (*n.* 2) —*adj. same as* CROATIAN
Cro·a·tia (krō ā′shə) republic of Yugoslavia, in the NW part: 21,830 sq. mi.; cap. Zagreb
Cro·a·tian (-shən) *adj.* of Croatia, its people, language, etc. —*n.* **1.** a Croat **2.** the South Slavic language of the Croats: see SERBO-CROATION
cro·chet (krō shā′) *n.* [Fr., small hook: see CROTCHET] needlework in which loops of thread or yarn are interwoven with a hooked needle (**crochet hook**) —*vi., vt.* **-cheted′** (-shād′), **-chet′ing** to do crochet or make by crochet —**cro·chet′er** *n.*
crock[1] (kräk) *n.* [OE. *crocca*] **1.** an earthenware pot or jar **2.** [Slang] something absurd; nonsense
crock[2] (kräk) *n.* [< ON. *kraki*, bent object] [Slang] anyone or anything worthless or useless, as from age
crocked (kräkt) *adj.* [Slang] drunk; intoxicated
crock·er·y (kräk′ər ē) *n.* [CROCK[1] + -ERY (sense 5)] earthenware pots, jars, dishes, etc.
Crock·ett (kräk′it), **David** (called *Davy Crockett*) 1786–1836; Am. frontiersman & politician
croc·o·dile (kräk′ə dīl′) *n.* [< OFr. < ML. < L. < Gr. *krokodilos* < ? *krokē*, pebble + *drilos*, worm] **1.** a large, flesh-eating, lizardlike reptile of tropical streams, with a thick, horny skin, long tail, and long, narrow head with massive jaws **2.** leather made from a crocodile's hide

CROCODILE
(to 20 ft. long)

crocodile tears insincere tears or a hypocritical show of grief
croc·o·dil·i·an (kräk′ə dil′ē-ən) *adj.* **1.** of or like a crocodile **2.** of a group of reptiles including the crocodile, alligator, cayman, and gavial —*n.* any reptile of this group
cro·cus (krō′kəs) *n., pl.* **cro′cus·es, cro′ci** (-sī) [L. < Gr. *krokos*, saffron, via Sem. ult. < Sans.] any of a genus of spring-blooming plants with fleshy corms and a yellow, purple, or white flower
Croe·sus (krē′səs) fl. 6th cent. B.C.; last king of Lydia (560–546), noted for his great wealth —*n.* a very rich man
croft (krôft) *n.* [OE.] [Brit.] **1.** a small enclosed field **2.** a small farm, esp. one worked by a renter —**croft′er** *n.*
crois·sant (krə sänt′) *n.* [Fr., lit., CRESCENT] a rich, flaky bread roll in the shape of a crescent
‡**croix de guerre** (krwä də ger′) [Fr., cross of war] a French military decoration for bravery
Cro-Ma·gnon (krō mag′nən, -man′yən) *adj.* [after the *Cro-Magnon* cave in SW France, where remains were found] belonging to a prehistoric, Caucasoid type of man, tall and erect, who lived on the European continent —*n.* a member of this group
crom·lech (kräm′lek) *n.* [W. < *crom*, bent + *llech*, flat stone] **1.** *same as* DOLMEN **2.** an ancient monument of monoliths, arranged in a circle around a mound or dolmen
Crom·well (kräm′wel, -wəl) **1. Oliver**, 1599–1658; Eng. revolutionary leader & Protector of the Commonwealth (1653–58) **2. Richard**, 1626–1712; Protector of the Commonwealth (1658–59): son of *prec.*
crone (krōn) *n.* [< Anglo-Fr. *carogne* (cf. CARRION) or via MDu. *kronje*, old ewe] an ugly, withered old woman; hag
Cro·nus (krō′nəs) *Gr. Myth.* a Titan who overthrew his father, Uranus, and was himself overthrown by his son Zeus: identified with the Roman Saturn
cro·ny (krō′nē) *n., pl.* **-nies** [Brit. university slang < ? Gr. *chronios*, long-continued (hence "old friend")] a close companion
crook (krook) *n.* [< ON. *krōkr*, hook] **1.** a hooked, bent, or curved thing or part; hook **2.** *a*) a shepherd's staff *b*) a crosier **3.** a bend or curve **4.** [Colloq.] a swindler or thief —*vt., vi.* **crooked** (krookt), **crook′ing** to bend or curve
crook·ed (krookt; *for 2 & 3* krook′id) *adj.* **1.** having a crook or hook **2.** not straight; bent; curved **3.** dishonest; swindling —**crook′ed·ly** *adv.* —**crook′ed·ness** *n.*
crook·neck (krook′nek′) *n.* a squash with a long, tapering, curved neck
croon (krōōn) *vi., vt.* [< MDu. *cronen*, to growl] **1.** to sing or hum in a low, gentle tone **2.** to sing (popular songs) in a soft, sentimental manner —*n.* a low, gentle singing or humming —**croon′er** *n.*
crop (kräp) *n.* [OE. *croppa*, cluster, flower, crop of bird] **1.** a saclike enlargement of a bird's gullet, in which food is stored before digestion; craw **2.** any agricultural product,

growing or harvested, as wheat, fruit, etc. **3.** the yield of any product in one season or place **4.** a group or collection **5.** the handle or butt of a whip **6.** a short whip with a looped lash, used in horseback riding **7.** hair cut close to the head **8.** an earmark on an animal, made by clipping —***vt.*** **cropped, crop′ping** **1.** to cut off or bite off the tops or ends of **2.** to grow or harvest as a crop **3.** to cut short —***vi.*** **1.** to plant, grow, or bear crops **2.** to feed by grazing —**crop out** (or **up**) **1.** to appear unexpectedly **2.** to appear at the surface, as a rock formation

crop-dust·ing (-dust′iŋ) ***n.*** the spraying of growing crops with pesticides from an airplane —**crop′-dust′** ***vi., vt.*** —**crop′-dust′er** ***n.***

crop·per (-ər) ***n.*** **1.** a person or thing that crops **2.** a sharecropper —**come a cropper** [Colloq.] **1.** to fall heavily or headlong **2.** to fail

crop·pie (kräp′ē) ***n., pl.*** **-pies, -pie:** see PLURAL, II, D, 1 *same as* CRAPPIE

crop rotation a system of growing successive crops that have different food requirements, to prevent soil depletion, break up a disease cycle, etc.

cropt (kräpt) *occas. pt. & pp. of* CROP

cro·quet (krō kā′) ***n.*** [Fr., dial. form of *crochet:* see CROTCHET] an outdoor game in which the players use mallets to drive a wooden ball through a series of hoops placed in the ground

cro·quette (krō ket′) ***n.*** [Fr. < *croquer,* to crunch] a small mass of chopped meat, fish, etc., coated with crumbs and fried in deep fat

cro·sier (krō′zhər) ***n.*** [< OFr. < *croce* < ML. *crocia* < Frank. hyp. *krukja,* crutch] a staff with a crook at the top, carried by or before a bishop or abbot as a symbol of his office

cross (krôs) ***n.*** [< OE. *cros* & ON. *kross,* both < OIr. *cros* < L. *crux* (gen. *crucis*), a cross] **1.** an upright post with a bar across it near the top, on which the ancient Romans fastened convicted persons to die **2.** a representation of a cross, used as a badge, crossroad marker, etc. **3.** a representation of a cross as a symbol of the crucifixion of Jesus, and hence of the Christian religion **4.** any trouble or affliction that one has to bear or that thwarts one **5.** any mark made by intersecting lines or surfaces **6.** such a mark (X) made as a signature by one who cannot write **7.** *a*) a crossing of varieties or breeds; hybridization *b*) the result of such mixing; hybrid **8.** something that combines the qualities of two different things or types **9.** [Slang] a double-cross —***vt.*** **1.** to make the sign of the cross over or upon **2.** to place across or crosswise *[cross* your fingers*]* **3.** to lie or cut across; intersect **4.** to draw a line or lines across **5.** to pass over; go across **6.** to carry or lead across **7.** to extend across *[*the bridge *crosses* a river*]* **8.** to bring into contact, causing electrical interference *[*the wires were *crossed]* **9.** to thwart; oppose **10.** to interbreed (animals or plants); hybridize —***vi.*** **1.** to intersect **2.** to go or extend from one side to the other **3.** to pass each other while moving in opposite directions **4.** to interbreed —***adj.*** **1.** lying or passing across; crossing; transverse **2.** going counter; contrary; opposed **3.** ill-tempered; cranky; irritable **4.** involving reciprocation **5.** of mixed variety or breed; hybrid —***adv.*** crosswise —**cross off** (or **out**) to cancel by or as by drawing lines across —**cross one's mind** to come suddenly or briefly to one's mind —**cross one's palm** to pay one money, esp. as a bribe —**cross one's path** to meet one —**cross up** **1.** to confuse or disorder **2.** to deceive or double-cross —**the Cross** **1.** the cross on which Jesus was put to death **2.** the suffering and death or Atonement of Jesus **3.** Christianity or Christendom —**cross′a·ble** ***adj.*** —**cross′ly** ***adv.*** —**cross′ness** ***n.***

CROSSES (A, Greek; B, Maltese; C, Latin; D, Patriarchal)

cross·bar (krôs′bär′) ***n.*** a bar, line, or stripe placed crosswise —***vt.*** **-barred′, -bar′ring** to furnish with crossbars

cross·beam (-bēm′) ***n.*** a beam placed across another or from one wall to another

cross·bill (-bil′) ***n.*** a finch having a bill with curving points that cross

cross·bones (-bōnz′) ***n.*** *see* SKULL AND CROSSBONES

cross·bow (-bō′) ***n.*** a medieval weapon consisting of a bow set transversely on a wooden stock: the stock was grooved to direct an arrow or stone —**cross′bow′man** ***n., pl.*** **-men**

cross·bred (-bred′, -bred′) ***adj.*** produced by the interbreeding of different varieties or breeds —***n.*** a hybrid; mongrel

cross·breed (-brēd′, -brēd′) ***vt., vi.*** **-bred** (-bred′, -bred′), **-breed′ing** *same as* HYBRIDIZE —***n.*** *same as* HYBRID (sense 1)

cross-coun·try (-kun′trē) ***adj., adv.*** **1.** across open country or fields, not by roads **2.** across a country —***n.*** cross-country footracing

cross·cur·rent (-kʉr′ənt) ***n.*** **1.** a current flowing at an angle to the main current **2.** an opposing opinion, influence, or tendency

cross·cut (-kut′) ***adj.*** **1.** made or used for cutting across *[*a *crosscut* saw*]* **2.** cut across —***n.*** **1.** a cut across **2.** something that cuts across **3.** *Mining* a cutting made across a vein —***vt., vi.*** **-cut′, -cut′ting** to cut across

crosse (krôs) ***n.*** [Fr.: see CROSIER] the pouched racket used in playing lacrosse

cross-ex·am·ine (krôs′ig zam′in) ***vt., vi.*** **-ined, -in·ing** **1.** to question closely **2.** *Law* to question (a witness already questioned by the opposing side) to determine the validity of his testimony —**cross′-ex·am′i·na′tion** ***n.*** —**cross′-ex·am′in·er** ***n.***

cross-eye (krôs′ī′) ***n.*** an abnormal condition in which the eyes are turned toward each other; convergent strabismus —**cross′-eyed′** (-īd′) ***adj.***

cross-fer·ti·lize (-fʉrt′'l īz′) ***vt., vi.*** **-lized′, -liz′ing** to fertilize or be fertilized by pollen from another plant or variety of plant —**cross′-fer′ti·li·za′tion** ***n.***

cross fire **1.** *Mil.* a firing at an objective from two or more positions so that the lines of fire cross **2.** any complex of opposing forces, opinions, etc.

cross-grained (-grānd′) ***adj.*** **1.** having an irregular or transverse grain: said of wood **2.** contrary; perverse; cantankerous

cross·hatch (-hach′) ***vt., vi.*** to shade with two sets of crossing parallel lines

cross·ing (-iŋ) ***n.*** **1.** the act of passing across, thwarting, interbreeding, etc. **2.** an intersection, as of lines, streets, etc. **3.** a place where a street, river, etc. may be crossed

cross-leg·ged (-leg′id, -legd′) ***adj., adv.*** with ankles crossed, or with one leg crossed over the other

cross·patch (-pach′) ***n.*** [CROSS + dial. *patch,* fool] [Colloq.] a cross, bad-tempered person

cross·piece (-pēs′) ***n.*** a piece lying across another

cross-pol·li·nate (krôs′päl′ə nāt′) ***vt., vi.*** **-nat′ed, -nat′ing** to transfer pollen from the anther of (one flower) to the stigma of (another) —**cross′-pol′li·na′tion** ***n.***

cross-pur·pose (krôs′pʉr′pəs) ***n.*** a contrary or conflicting purpose —**at cross-purposes** having a misunderstanding as to each other's purposes

cross-ques·tion (-kwes′chən) ***vt.*** to cross-examine —***n.*** a question asked in cross-examination

cross-re·fer (-ri fʉr′) ***vt., vi.*** **-ferred′, -fer′ring** to refer from one part to another

cross-ref·er·ence (-ref′ər əns, -ref′rəns) ***n.*** a reference from one part of a book, catalog, index, etc. to another part —***vt., vi.*** **-enced, -enc·ing** **1.** to provide (an index, reference book, etc.) with systematic cross-references **2.** *same as* CROSS-REFER

cross·road (-rōd′) ***n.*** **1.** a road that crosses another **2.** a road that connects main roads **3.** [*usually pl.*] *a*) the place where roads intersect *b*) any center of congregation, activity, etc. for a wide area —**at the crossroads** at the point where one must choose between different courses of action

cross·ruff (-ruf′) ***n.*** *Card Games* a sequence of plays in which each of two partners in turn leads a card which the other can trump

cross section **1.** *a*) a cutting through something, esp. at right angles to its axis *b*) a piece so cut off *c*) a drawing of a plane surface as exposed by such a cutting **2.** a sample with enough of each kind to show what the whole is like —**cross′-sec′tion** ***vt.*** —**cross′-sec′tion·al** ***adj.***

cross-stitch (-stich′) ***n.*** **1.** a stitch made by crossing two stitches diagonally in the form of an X **2.** needlework made with this stitch —***vt., vi.*** to sew or embroider with this stitch

cross·tie (-tī′) ***n.*** a beam, rod, etc. placed crosswise to give support; specif., any of the transverse timbers supporting a railroad track

cross-town (-toun′) ***adj.*** going across the main avenues or transportation lines of a city

cross·trees (-trēz′) ***n.pl.*** two short, horizontal bars across a ship's masthead, which spread the rigging that supports the mast

cross·walk (-wôk′) ***n.*** a lane marked off for pedestrians to use in crossing a street

cross·way (-wā′) ***n.*** *same as* CROSSROAD

cross·wise (-wīz′) ***adv.*** so as to cross; across: also **cross′-ways′** (-wāz′)

cross·word puzzle (-wʉrd′) an arrangement of numbered squares to be filled in with words, a letter to each square:

fat, āpe, cär; ten, ēven; is, bīte; gō, hôrn, tōōl, look; oil, out; up, fʉr; get; joy; yet; chin; she; thin, *th*en; zh, leisure; ŋ, ring; ə for *a* in *ago*, *e* in *agent*, *i* in *sanity*, *o* in *comply*, *u* in *focus*; ′ as in *able* (ā′b'l); Fr. bàl; ë, Fr. coeur; ö, Fr. feu; Fr. mo*n*; ô, Fr. coq; ü, Fr. duc; *r*, Fr. cri; H, G. ich; kh, G. doch; ‡foreign; *hypothetical; < derived from. See inside front cover.

numbered synonyms, definitions, etc. are given as clues for the words

crotch (kräch) ***n.*** [ME. *croche,* var. of *crucche,* CRUTCH] **1.** a pole forked on top **2.** a forked place, as where a tree trunk divides into two branches **3.** the place where the legs fork from the human body **4.** the place where the legs of a pair of pants, etc. meet **—crotched** ***adj.***

crotch·et (kräch′it) ***n.*** [OFr. *crochet,* dim. < *croc,* hook] **1.** a peculiar whim or stubborn notion **2.** [Brit.] *same as* QUARTER NOTE

crotch·et·y (-ē) ***adj.*** full of peculiar whims or stubborn notions **—crotch′et·i·ness** ***n.***

cro·ton (krōt′'n) ***n.*** [ModL. < Gr. *kroton*] any of a large, mostly tropical genus of shrubs and trees of the spurge family: one species yields an oil **(croton oil)** formerly used in medicine

Croton bug [< *Croton* Aqueduct in New York City] a small cockroach

crouch (krouch) ***vi.*** [< OFr. *crochir* < *croc,* a hook] **1.** to stoop low with the limbs close to the body, as an animal ready to pounce or cowering **2.** to cringe or bow in a servile manner ***—n.*** the act or position of crouching

croup[1] (kro͞op) ***n.*** [< obs. or dial. *croup,* to speak hoarsely, of echoic origin] an inflammation of the respiratory passages, with labored breathing and hoarse coughing **—croup′y** ***adj.***

croup[2] (kro͞op) ***n.*** [OFr. *croupe* < Frank.] the rump of a horse, etc.

crou·pi·er (kro͞o′pē ā′, -ər) ***n.*** [Fr., orig., one who rides on the croup: see prec.] a person in charge of a gambling table, who rakes in and pays out the money

crou·ton (kro͞o′tän, kro͞o tän′) ***n.*** [< Fr. < *croûte* < L. *crusta:* see CRUST] a small piece of toasted or fried bread, often served in soup or salads

Crow (krō) ***n.*** [transl., via Fr., of their native name, *Absaroke,* crow people] **1.** *pl.* **Crows, Crow** a member of a tribe of Siouan Indians living near the Yellowstone River **2.** their Siouan language

crow[1] (krō) ***n.*** [OE. *crawa*] a large bird with glossy black plumage and a typical harsh call: the raven, rook, and jackdaw are crows **—as the crow flies** in a direct line **—eat crow** [Colloq.] to undergo the humiliation of admitting an error, etc.

crow[2] (krō) ***vi.*** **crowed** or, for 1, chiefly Brit., **crew** (kro͞o), **crowed, crow′ing** [OE. *crawan*] **1.** to make the shrill cry of a rooster **2.** to boast in triumph; exult **3.** to make a sound expressive of well-being or pleasure, as a baby does ***—n.*** a crowing sound

crow·bar (krō′bär′) ***n.*** a long metal bar, chisellike at one end, used as a lever for prying, etc.

crowd[1] (kroud) ***vi.*** [OE. *crudan*] **1.** to press, push, or squeeze **2.** to push one's way (*forward, into,* etc.) **3.** to throng ***—vt.*** **1.** to press, push, or shove **2.** to press closely together; cram **3.** to fill too full **4.** to be or press very near to **5.** [Colloq.] to put (a person) under pressure, as by dunning ***—n.*** **1.** a large number of people or things gathered closely together **2.** the common people; the masses **3.** [Colloq.] a set or clique **—crowd out** to exclude because of insufficient space or time **—crowd′ed** ***adj.***

crowd[2] (kroud) ***n.*** [W. *crwth*] an obsolete Celtic musical instrument somewhat like a violin but with a shallow, broad body

crow·foot (krō′foot′) ***n.,*** *pl.* **-foots′** a plant of the buttercup family, with leaves somewhat resembling a crow's foot

crown (kroun) ***n.*** [< OFr. < L. *corona,* a garland < Gr. *korōnē,* wreath] **1.** a garland or wreath worn on the head as a sign of honor, victory, etc. **2.** a reward or honor given for merit; specif., a sports championship **3.** the emblematic headdress of a monarch **4.** [*often* **C-**] *a)* the power or dominion of a monarch *b)* the monarch as head of the state **5.** anything serving to adorn or honor like a crown **6.** a thing like a crown in shape, position, etc., as the top of the head, of a hat, etc. **7.** *a)* orig., any coin bearing the figure of a crown *b)* a British coin equal to five shillings **8.** the highest point, as of an arch **9.** the highest quality, state, etc. of anything **10.** *a)* the part of a tooth projecting beyond the gum line *b)* an artificial substitute for this **11.** the lowest point of an anchor, between the arms ***—vt.*** **1.** *a)* to put a crown on the head of *b)* to enthrone **2.** to honor or reward as with a crown **3.** to be the crown or highest part of **4.** to put the finishing touch on **5.** to cover (a tooth) with an artificial crown **6.** [Slang] to hit on the head **7.** *Checkers* to make a king of **—crown′er** ***n.***

crown colony a British colony directly under the control of the home government in London

crown glass a very clear optical glass

crown prince the male heir apparent to a throne

crown princess **1.** the wife of a crown prince **2.** a female heir presumptive to a throne

crow's-foot (krōz′foot′) ***n.,*** *pl.* **-feet′** any of the wrinkles that often develop at the outer corners of the eyes: *usually used in pl.*

crow's-nest (-nest′) ***n.*** **1.** a small, partly enclosed platform close to the top of a ship's mast, used by the lookout **2.** any platform like this

CROW'S-NEST

cro·zier (krō′zhər) ***n.*** *same as* CROSIER

cru·ces (kro͞o′sēz) ***n.*** *alt. pl. of* CRUX

cru·cial (kro͞o′shəl) ***adj.*** [Fr. < L. *crux,* CROSS] **1.** of supreme importance; decisive; critical **2.** extremely trying; severe **—cru′cial·ly** ***adv.***

cru·ci·ble (kro͞o′sə b'l) ***n.*** [< ML. *crucibulum,* lamp] **1.** a container made of a heat-resistant substance, as graphite, for melting ores, metals, etc. **2.** a severe test or trial

cru·ci·fix (kro͞o′sə fiks′) ***n.*** [< OFr. or ML., orig. pp. of LL. *crucifigere,* CRUCIFY] **1.** a representation of a cross with the figure of Jesus crucified on it **2.** the cross as a Christian symbol

cru·ci·fix·ion (kro͞o′sə fik′shən) ***n.*** **1.** a crucifying or being crucified **2.** [**C-**] the crucifying of Jesus, or a representation of this in painting, statuary, etc.

cru·ci·form (kro͞o′sə fôrm′) ***adj.*** [< L. *crux,* CROSS + -FORM] cross-shaped **—cru′ci·form′ly** ***adv.***

cru·ci·fy (kro͞o′sə fī′) ***vt.*** **-fied′, -fy′ing** [< OFr. < LL. *crucificare,* for *crucifigere* < L. *crux,* CROSS + *figere,* FIX] **1.** to execute by nailing or binding to a cross and leaving to die of exposure **2.** to torment; torture **—cru′ci·fi′er** ***n.***

crud[1] (krud) ***vt., vi.*** **crud′ded, crud′ding** [ME. *crud:* see CURD] [Dial.] to curdle ***—n.*** [Slang] **1.** any coagulated substance, caked deposit, dregs, filth, etc. **2.** a worthless, disgusting, or contemptible person or thing **—crud′dy** ***adj.*** **-di·er, -di·est**

crud[2] (krud) ***n.*** [< ? W. *cryd,* plague] [Slang] an imaginary or vaguely identified disease or ailment

crude (kro͞od) ***adj.*** [L. *crudus,* raw, rough] **1.** in a raw or natural condition; not refined or processed **2.** lacking grace, taste, etc.; uncultured *[a crude remark]* **3.** not carefully made or done; rough **4.** stark *[crude reality]* **—crude′ly** ***adv.*** **—crude′ness** ***n.***

cru·di·tés (kro͞o′də tā; *Fr.* krü dē tā′) ***n.pl.*** [Fr., lit., something raw] raw vegetables cut up and served as appetizers, usually with a dip

cru·di·ty (kro͞o′də tē) ***n.*** **1.** a crude condition or quality **2.** *pl.* **-ties** a crude remark, etc.

cru·el (kro͞o′əl) ***adj.*** [OFr. < L. *crudelis* < *crudus:* see CRUDE] **1.** enjoying others' suffering; merciless **2.** causing, or of a kind to cause, pain, distress, etc. **—cru′el·ly** ***adv.*** **—cru′el·ness** ***n.***

cru·el·ty (-tē) ***n.*** **1.** the quality of being cruel; inhumanity; hardheartedness **2.** *pl.* **-ties** a cruel action, remark, etc. **3.** *Law* willful mistreatment harmful to life or to health

cru·et (kro͞o′it) ***n.*** [< Anglo-Fr. dim. of OFr. *crue,* earthen pot < Gmc.] a small glass bottle, as for holding vinegar, oil, etc., for the table

cruise (kro͞oz) ***vi.*** **cruised, cruis′ing** [< Du. *kruisen,* to cross < *kruis* < L. *crux,* CROSS] **1.** to sail from place to place, as for pleasure or in search of something **2.** to go or drive about in a similar manner, as a taxi **3.** to move at the most efficient speed for sustained travel ***—vt.*** to sail, journey, or move over or about ***—n.*** the action of cruising; esp., a cruising voyage

cruis·er (-ər) ***n.*** **1.** one that cruises, as an airplane, squad car, etc. **2.** a fast warship somewhat smaller than a battleship and having less armor and fire power **3.** *same as* CABIN CRUISER

crul·ler (krul′ər) ***n.*** [Du. < *krullen,* to curl] a kind of twisted doughnut made with a rich dough

crumb (krum) ***n.*** [OE. *cruma*] **1.** a small piece broken off something, as of bread or cake **2.** any bit or scrap *[crumbs of knowledge]* **3.** the soft, inner part of bread **4.** [Slang] a worthless or despicable person: also **crum′bum′** ***—vt.*** **1.** to clear (a table, etc.) of crumbs **2.** *Cooking* to cover or thicken with crumbs

crum·ble (krum′b'l) ***vt.*** **-bled, -bling** [freq. of prec.] to break into crumbs or small pieces ***—vi.*** to fall to pieces; decay

crum·bly (-blē) ***adj.*** **-bli·er, -bli·est** apt to crumble; easily crumbled **—crum′bli·ness** ***n.***

crumb·y (krum′ē) ***adj.*** **crumb′i·er, crumb′i·est** **1.** full of crumbs **2.** soft, as the inner part of bread **3.** [Slang] *same as* CRUMMY **—crumb′i·ness** ***n.***

crum·my (krum′ē) ***adj.*** **-mi·er, -mi·est** [< CRUM(B) + -Y[2]] [Slang] **1.** dirty, cheap, etc. **2.** inferior, worthless, contemptible, etc. **—crum′mi·ness** ***n.***

crum·pet (krum′pit) ***n.*** [prob. < ME. *crompid* < OE. *crompeht,* flat cake] a batter cake baked on a griddle: it is usually toasted before serving

crum·ple (krum′p'l) ***vt., vi.*** **-pled, -pling** [ME. *crumplen,* var. of *crimplen,* to wrinkle, freq. of *crimpen,* CRIMP[1]] **1.** to crush or become crushed together into wrinkles **2.** to break down; collapse ***—n.*** a crease or wrinkle **—crum′ply** ***adj.***

crunch (krunch) *vi., vt.* [of echoic origin] **1.** to chew with a noisy, crackling sound **2.** to press, grind, tread, etc. with a noisy, crushing sound —*n.* **1.** the act or sound of crunching **2.** [Slang] *a)* a showdown *b)* a tight situation

crunch·y (-ē) *adj.* **crunch′i·er, crunch′i·est** making a crunching sound —**crunch′i·ness** *n.*

crup·per (krup′ər, kroop′-) *n.* [< OFr. *cropiere* < *crope,* rump] **1.** a leather strap attached to a saddle or harness and passed under the horse's tail **2.** a horse's rump; croup

cru·sade (kro͞o sād′) *n.* [< Sp. *cruzada* & Fr. *croisade,* both < ML. pp. of *cruciare,* to mark with a cross < L. *crux,* CROSS] **1.** [*sometimes* C-] any of the military expeditions which Christians undertook from the 11th to the 13th cent. to recover the Holy Land from the Moslems **2.** any church-sanctioned war or expedition like this **3.** vigorous, concerted action for some cause or against some abuse —*vi.* **-sad′ed, -sad′ing** to engage in a crusade —**cru·sad′er** *n.*

cruse (kro͞oz, kro͞os) *n.* [OE. *cruse*] a small container for water, oil, honey, etc.

crush (krush) *vt.* [< OFr. *croisir,* to break < Frank. *krostjan,* to gnash] **1.** to press between opposing forces so as to break or put out of shape; crumple **2.** to grind or pound into small particles **3.** to subdue; overwhelm **4.** to oppress **5.** to extract by pressing or squeezing —*vi.* **1.** to be or become crushed **2.** to crowd (*into,* etc.) —*n.* **1.** a crushing; severe pressure **2.** a crowded mass of people **3.** a drink with fruit juice **4.** [Colloq.] an infatuation —**crush′a·ble** *adj.* —**crush′er** *n.*

Cru·soe (kro͞o′sō), **Robinson** *see* ROBINSON CRUSOE

crust (krust) *n.* [< OFr. *crouste* or < L. *crusta*] **1.** *a)* the hard, outer part of bread *b)* a piece of this *c)* any dry, hard piece of bread **2.** the pastry shell of a pie **3.** any hard surface layer, as of snow, soil, etc. **4.** *same as* SCAB (*n.* 1) **5.** [Slang] audacity; insolence **6.** *Geol.* the solid outer shell of the earth —*vt., vi.* **1.** to cover or become covered with a crust **2.** to harden into a crust —**crus·tal** (krus′t′l) *adj.* —**crust′ed** *adj.*

crus·ta·cean (krus tā′shən) *n.* [< ModL. < *crustaceus,* having a crust < L. *crusta,* crust] any of a class of arthropods, including shrimps, crabs, barnacles, and lobsters, that usually live in water and breathe through gills: they have a hard outer shell and jointed appendages and bodies —*adj.* of crustaceans: also **crus·ta′ceous**

crust·y (krus′tē) *adj.* **crust′i·er, crust′i·est** **1.** having, forming, or resembling a crust **2.** rudely abrupt or surly; bad-tempered —**crust′i·ly** *adv.* —**crust′i·ness** *n.*

crutch (kruch) *n.* [OE. *crycce,* staff] **1.** a staff with a hand grip and a crosspiece on top that fits under the armpit, used by lame people as an aid in walking **2.** anything relied on for support; prop **3.** any device that resembles a crutch —*vt.* to support with or as with a crutch; prop up

crux (kruks) *n., pl.* **crux′es, cru·ces** (kro͞o′sēz) [L., CROSS] **1.** a difficult problem **2.** the essential or deciding point

cru·zei·ro (kro͞o zā′rō; *Port.* kro͞o zā′ro͝o) *n., pl.* **-ros** [Port. < *cruz,* a cross < L. *crux,* CROSS] *see* MONETARY UNITS, table (Brazil)

cry (krī) *vi.* **cried, cry′ing** [OFr. *crier* < L. *quiritare,* to wail] **1.** to make a loud vocal sound or utterance, as for help **2.** to sob and shed tears in expressing sorrow, pain, etc.; weep **3.** *a)* to plead or clamor (*for*) *b)* to show a great need (*for*) [problems *crying* for solution] **4.** to utter its characteristic call: said of an animal —*vt.* **1.** to plead or beg for [to *cry* quarter] **2.** to utter loudly; shout **3.** to call out (wares for sale, etc.) —*n., pl.* **cries** **1.** a loud vocal sound expressing pain, anger, etc. **2.** any loud utterance; shout **3.** an announcement called out publicly **4.** an urgent appeal; plea **5.** popular report; rumor; rallying call **6.** the current opinion or fashion **7.** public outcry **8.** a slogan **9.** a fit of weeping **10.** the characteristic vocal sound of an animal **11.** the baying of hounds in the chase —**a far cry** a great distance or difference —**cry down** to belittle; disparage —**cry one's eyes out** to weep much and bitterly —**cry out** **1.** to shout; yell **2.** to complain loudly —**cry up** to praise highly —**in full cry** in eager pursuit

cry·ba·by (-bā′bē) *n., pl.* **-bies** **1.** a child who cries often or with little cause **2.** a person who complains when he fails to win or get his own way

cry·ing (-iŋ) *adj.* **1.** that cries **2.** demanding immediate notice —**for crying out loud** [Slang] an exclamation of annoyance, surprise, etc.

cry·o- [< Gr. *kryos,* cold] *a combining form meaning* cold or freezing [*cryolite*]

cry·o·gen (krī′ə jən) *n.* [CRYO- + -GEN] a refrigerant

cry·o·gen·ics (krī′ə jen′iks) *n.pl.* [*with sing. v.*] [CRYOGEN + -ICS] the science that deals with the effects of very low temperatures on the properties of matter

cry·o·lite (krī′ə līt′) *n.* [CRYO- + -LITE] a fluoride of sodium and aluminum, Na_3AlF_6, a source of aluminum

cry·on·ics (krī än′iks) *n.pl.* [*with sing. v.*] [CRYO- + *-n-* + -ICS] the practice of freezing a body just after death to preserve it for possible resuscitation, as when a cure is found for the disease that caused death —**cry·on′ic** *adj.*

cry·o·sur·ger·y (krī′ə sur′jə rē) *n.* [CRYO- + SURGERY] surgery in which tissues are destroyed by freezing

crypt (kript) *n.* [< L. < Gr. < *kryptein,* to hide] an underground chamber; esp., a vault under the main floor of a church, used as a burial place

cryp·tic (krip′tik) *adj.* [< LL. < Gr.: see prec.] **1.** having a hidden meaning; mysterious **2.** obscure and curt Also **cryp′ti·cal** —**cryp′ti·cal·ly** *adv.*

cryp·to- *a combining forming meaning:* **1.** secret or hidden **2.** being such secretly Also, before a vowel, **crypt-**

cryp·to·gam (krip′tə gam′) *n.* [< Fr. < Gr. *kryptos,* hidden + *gamos,* marriage] a plant that bears no flowers or seeds but propagates by means of spores, as algae, mosses, ferns, etc. —**cryp′to·gam′ic, cryp·tog′a·mous** (-täg′ə məs) *adj.*

cryp·to·gram (krip′tə gram′) *n.* [CRYPTO- + -GRAM] something written in code or cipher: also **cryp′to·graph′** (-graf′) —**cryp′to·gram′mic** *adj.*

cryp·tog·ra·phy (krip täg′rə fē) *n.* [CRYPTO- + -GRAPHY] **1.** the art of writing or deciphering messages in code **2.** a code system —**cryp·tog′ra·pher, cryp·tog′ra·phist** *n.* —**cryp·to·graph·ic** (krip′tə graf′ik) *adj.* —**cryp′to·graph′i·cal·ly** *adv.*

cryst. **1.** crystalline **2.** crystallized

crys·tal (kris′t′l) *n.* [< OE. & OFr. < L. < Gr. *krystallos,* ice < *kryos,* frost] **1.** *a)* a clear, transparent quartz *b)* a piece of this cut in the form of an ornament **2.** *a)* a very clear, brilliant glass *b)* an article or articles made of such glass, as goblets, bowls, etc. **3.** the transparent covering over the face of a watch **4.** anything clear and transparent like crystal **5.** a solidified form of a substance made up of plane faces in three dimensions in a symmetrical arrangement **6.** *Radio* a piezoelectric material, as quartz, used to produce and control very precisely a desired frequency, as in transmitters, etc. —*adj.* **1.** of or composed of crystal **2.** like crystal; transparent **3.** *Radio* using a crystal

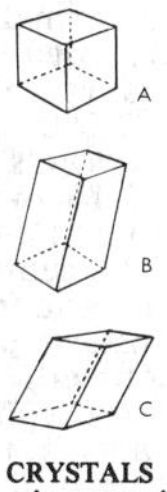

A

B

C

CRYSTALS
(A, isometric;
B, monoclinic;
C, triclinic)

crystal detector *Radio* a semiconductor rectifier used for demodulation

crystal gazing the practice of gazing into a large glass ball (**crystal ball**) and professing to see images, esp. of future events —**crystal gazer**

crys·tal·line (kris′tə lin) *adj.* **1.** consisting or made of crystal or crystals **2.** like crystal; clear and transparent **3.** having the character or structure of a crystal

crystalline lens the lens of the eye, serving to focus light on the retina

crys·tal·lize (kris′tə līz′) *vt.* **-lized′, -liz′ing** **1.** to cause to form crystals **2.** to give a definite form to **3.** to coat with sugar —*vi.* **1.** to become crystalline in form **2.** to take on a definite form —**crys′tal·liz′a·ble** *adj.* —**crys′tal·li·za′tion** *n.*

crys·tal·lo- [< Gr. *krystallos,* CRYSTAL] *a combining form meaning* crystal Also **crys·tall-**

crys·tal·log·ra·phy (kris′tə läg′rə fē) *n.* [prec. + -GRAPHY] the science of the form, structure, properties, and classification of crystals —**crys′tal·lo·graph′ic** (-lə graf′ik), **crys′tal·lo·graph′i·cal** *adj.*

crys·tal·loid (kris′tə loid′) *adj.* **1.** like a crystal **2.** having the nature of a crystalloid —*n.* a substance, usually crystallizable, which, when in solution, readily passes through vegetable and animal membranes —**crys′tal·loi′dal** *adj.*

crystal pickup a piezoelectric vibration pickup, often used on electric phonographs

crystal set an early type of radio receiver with a crystal, instead of an electron tube, detector

Cs *Chem.* cesium

cs. case; cases

C.S. Christian Science

C.S., c.s. **1.** capital stock **2.** civil service

CSC Civil Service Commission

csc cosecant

CST, C.S.T. Central Standard Time

CT Connecticut

ct. **1.** *pl.* **cts.** cent **2.** court

ctn **1.** carton: also **ctn.** **2.** cotangent

ctr. center

cts. **1.** centimes **2.** cents

Cu [L. *cuprum*] *Chem.* copper

cu. cubic

cub (kub) ***n.*** **[**< ? OIr. *cuib*, whelp**]** **1.** the young of certain mammals, as the fox, bear, lion, whale, etc. **2.** an inexperienced or callow person, esp. a novice reporter —**cub′bish** ***adj.*** —**cub′bish·ness** ***n.***

Cu·ba (kyo͞o′bə; *Sp.* ko͞o′bä) island country in the West Indies, south of Fla.: 44,218 sq. mi.; pop. 8,074,000; cap. Havana —**Cu′ban** ***adj., n.***

cub·by·hole (kub′ē hōl′) ***n.*** **[**< Brit. dial. *cub*, little shed + HOLE**]** **1.** a small, enclosed space or room **2.** a pigeonhole

cube (kyo͞ob) ***n.*** **[**Fr. < L. < Gr. *kybos*, a cube, die**]** **1.** a solid with six equal, square sides **2.** anything having more or less this shape *[*an ice *cube]* **3.** the product obtained by multiplying a given number or quantity by its square; third power *[*the *cube* of 3 is 27 (3x3x3)*]* —***vt.*** **cubed, cub′ing** **1.** to raise to the third power **2.** to cut or shape into cubes —**cub′er** ***n.***

cu·beb (kyo͞o′beb) ***n.*** **[**< Fr. < ML. < Ar. *kabāba***]** the spicy berry of an East Indian vine, formerly used medicinally in cigarettes

cube root the number or quantity of which a given number or quantity is the cube *[*the *cube root* of 8 is 2*]*

cu·bic (kyo͞o′bik) ***adj.*** **1.** having the shape of a cube **2.** having three dimensions, or having the volume of a cube whose length, width, and depth each measure the given unit *[*a *cubic* foot*]* **3.** relating to the cubes of numbers or quantities —**cu′bi·cal** (-bi k'l) ***adj.*** —**cu′bi·cal·ly** ***adv.***

cu·bi·cle (kyo͞o′bi k'l) ***n.*** **[**L. *cubiculum* < *cubare*, to lie down**]** **1.** a small sleeping compartment, as in a dormitory **2.** any small compartment

cubic measure a system of measuring volume in cubic units, esp. that in which 1,728 cubic inches = 1 cubic foot and 1,000 cubic millimeters = 1 cubic centimeter: see TABLE OF WEIGHTS AND MEASURES in Supplements

cu·bi·form (kyo͞o′bə fôrm′) ***adj.*** cube-shaped

cub·ism (kyo͞o′biz'm) ***n.*** a movement in art, esp. of the early 20th century, characterized by the use of cubes and other geometric forms in abstract arrangements rather than by a realistic representation of nature —**cub′ist** ***n., adj.*** —**cu·bis′tic** ***adj.***

cu·bit (kyo͞o′bit) ***n.*** **[**< OE. < L. *cubitum*, the elbow, cubit**]** an ancient measure of length, about 18–22 inches; orig., the length of the arm from the end of the middle finger to the elbow

cu·boid (kyo͞o′boid) ***adj.*** cube-shaped: also **cu·boi′dal** —***n.*** a six-sided figure with all faces rectangular

Cub Scout a member of a division of the Boy Scouts for boys eight through ten years old

cuck·old (kuk′'ld) ***n.*** **[**< OFr. *cucuault* < *cucu:* see ff.**]** a man whose wife has committed adultery —***vt.*** to make a cuckold of —**cuck′old·ry** (-rē) ***n.***

cuck·oo (ko͞o′ko͞o′, kook′o͞o) ***n., pl.*** **cuck′oos** **[**< OFr. *coucou, cucu*, echoic of its cry**]** **1.** any of a family of grayish-brown birds with a long, slender body: the European species lays eggs in the nests of other birds, but the American varieties hatch their own young **2.** the call of a cuckoo, which sounds somewhat like its name **3.** an imitation of this **4.** [Slang] a crazy or foolish person —***vi.*** to utter the call of a cuckoo —***vt.*** to repeat continually —***adj.*** [Slang] crazy; silly

cuckoo clock a clock with a toy bird that pops out and cuckoos to mark intervals of time

cuckoo spit (or **spittle**) a froth produced on plants by the nymphs of certain insects

cu·cul·late (kyo͞o′kə lāt′, kyoo kul′it) ***adj.*** **[**< L. *cucullus*, hood**]** shaped like a hood, as the leaves of violets: also **cu′cul·lat′ed**

cu·cum·ber (kyo͞o′kum bər) ***n.*** **[**< OFr. < L. *cucumis* (gen. *cucumeris*)**]** **1.** an annual vine of the gourd family, grown for its edible fruit **2.** the long fruit, with a green rind and firm, white flesh, used in salads or preserved as pickles —**cool as a cucumber** **1.** comfortably cool **2.** calm and self-possessed

cud (kud) ***n.*** **[**OE. *cudu***]** a mouthful of swallowed food regurgitated from the first stomach of cattle and other ruminants and chewed slowly a second time —**chew the cud** to ruminate; ponder

cud·dle (kud′'l) ***vt.*** **-dled, -dling** **[**? < ME. hyp. *couthelen* < *couth*, known, hence comfortable with + *-le*, freq. suffix**]** to hold lovingly and gently in one's arms; embrace and fondle —***vi.*** to lie close and snug; nestle —***n.*** **1.** a cuddling **2.** an embrace; hug —**cud′dle·some** (-səm), **cud′dly** ***adj.*** **-dli·er, -dli·est**

cud·dy (kud′ē) ***n., pl.*** **-dies** **[**< ?**]** **1.** a small cabin on a ship **2.** the cook's galley on a small ship

cudg·el (kuj′əl) ***n.*** **[**OE. *cycgel***]** a short, thick stick or club —***vt.*** **-eled** or **-elled, -el·ing** or **-el·ling** to beat with a cudgel —**cudgel one's brains** to think hard —**take up the cudgels (for)** to come to the defense (of)

cue[1] (kyo͞o) ***n.*** **[**< *q*, *Q* (? for L. *quando*, when) found in 16th-c. plays to mark actors' entrances**]** **1.** a bit of dialogue, action, or music that is a signal for an actor's entrance or speech, or for lights, sound effects, etc. **2.** anything serving as a signal to do something **3.** an indirect suggestion; hint —***vt.*** **cued, cu′ing** or **cue′ing** to give a cue to

cue[2] (kyo͞o) ***n.*** **[**var. of QUEUE**]** **1.** *same as* QUEUE **2.** a long, tapering rod used in billiards, pool, etc. to strike the cue ball **3.** a long, shovellike stick used in shuffleboard to push the disks —***vt.*** **cued, cu′ing** or **cue′ing** **1.** to braid (hair, etc.) **2.** to strike (a cue ball, etc.) with a cue

cue ball the ball, usually white, that a player strikes with his cue in billiards or pool

cuff[1] (kuf) ***n.*** **[**< ME. *cuffe*, glove**]** **1.** a fixed or detachable band or fold at the end of a sleeve **2.** a turned-up fold at the bottom of a trouser leg **3.** a handcuff —***vt.*** to put a cuff on —**off the cuff** [Slang] in an offhand manner —**on the cuff** [Slang] on credit

cuff[2] (kuf) ***vt.*** **[**< ? CUFF[1] (in orig. sense "glove")**]** to strike, esp. with the open hand; slap —***n.*** a slap or blow

cuff link a pair of linked buttons or any similar small device for keeping a shirt cuff closed

‡**cui bo·no** (kwē bō′nō) [L., to whom for a good] **1.** for whose benefit? **2.** to what purpose?

cui·rass (kwi ras′) ***n.*** **[**< Fr. < It. < L. (*vestis*) *coriacea*, leather (clothing) < *corium*, leather**]** **1.** a piece of closefitting armor for protecting the breast and back **2.** the breastplate of such armor —***vt.*** to cover as with a cuirass

cui·ras·sier (kwi′rə sir′) ***n.*** **[**Fr.**]** a cavalryman wearing a cuirass

cui·sine (kwi zēn′) ***n.*** **[**Fr. < LL. *coquina*, kitchen < L. *coquere*, to cook**]** **1.** style of cooking or preparing food **2.** the food prepared, as at a restaurant

cuisse (kwis) ***n.*** **[**< OFr. < L. *coxa*, hip**]** a piece of armor to protect the thigh: also **cuish** (kwish)

cul-de-sac (kul′də sak′, kool′-; *Fr.* küt sȧk′) ***n., pl.*** **cul-de-sacs;** Fr. **culs-de-sac** (küt sȧk′) **[**Fr., lit., bottom of a sack**]** a passage or position with only one outlet; blind alley

-cule (kyo͞ol, kyool) **[**< Fr. or L.**]** *a suffix meaning* small

cu·lex (kyo͞o′leks) ***n.*** **[**L., a gnat**]** any of a large genus of mosquitoes including many of the most common species found in N. America and Europe

cu·li·nar·y (kyo͞o′lə ner′ē, kul′ə-) ***adj.*** **[**< LL. < L. *culina*, kitchen**]** of the kitchen or of cooking

cull (kul) ***vt.*** **[**< OFr. < L. *colligere:* see COLLECT[2]**]** **1.** to pick out; select and gather **2.** to pick over —***n.*** something picked out; esp., something rejected as not being up to standard

culm[1] (kulm) ***n.*** **[**< ME. *colme* < ? OE. *col*, coal**]** waste material from coal screenings or washings

culm[2] (kulm) ***n.*** **[**L. *culmus*, a stem**]** the jointed stem of various grasses, usually hollow —***vi.*** to grow or develop into a culm

cul·mi·nate (kul′mə nāt′) ***vi.*** **-nat′ed, -nat′ing** **[**< ML. pp. of *culminare* < L. *culmen* (gen. *culminis*), peak**]** to reach its highest point or climax —***vt.*** to bring to its climax —**cul′mi·nant** ***adj.***

cul·mi·na·tion (kul′mə nā′shən) ***n.*** **1.** a culminating **2.** the highest point; climax

cu·lotte (koo lät′, kyoo-) ***n.*** **[**Fr. < *cul*, posterior < L. *culus***]** *[often pl.]* trousers made full in the legs to resemble a skirt, worn by women and girls

cul·pa·ble (kul′pə b'l) ***adj.*** **[**< OFr. < L. < *culpa*, fault, blame**]** deserving blame; blameworthy —**cul′pa·bil′i·ty** ***n.*** —**cul′pa·bly** ***adv.***

cul·prit (kul′prit) ***n.*** **[**< Anglo-Fr. *cul.*, contr. for *culpable*, guilty + *prit*, ready (i.e., to prove guilt)**]** **1.** a person accused of a crime or offense, as in a court **2.** a person guilty of a crime or offense; offender

cult (kult) ***n.*** **[**< L. *cultus*, care, orig. pp. of *colere*, to till**]** **1.** a system of religious worship or ritual **2.** *a)* devoted attachment to, or admiration for, a person, principle, etc. *b)* the object of such attachment **3.** a group of followers; sect —**cult′ic** ***adj.*** —**cult′ism** ***n.*** —**cult′ist** ***n.***

cul·ti·va·ble (kul′tə və b'l) ***adj.*** that can be cultivated: also **cul′ti·vat′a·ble** (-vāt′ə b'l) —**cul′ti·va·bil′i·ty** ***n.***

cul·ti·vate (kul′tə vāt′) ***vt.*** **-vat′ed, -vat′ing** **[**< ML. < LL. *cultivus*, tilled < L. *cultus:* see CULT**]** **1.** to prepare and use (land) for growing crops; till **2.** to break up the surface soil around (plants) in order to aerate it, destroy weeds, etc. **3.** to grow (plants or crops) **4.** to develop (plants) by various horticultural techniques **5.** to develop or improve by care, training, etc.; refine *[*to *cultivate* one's mind*]* **6.** to seek to become familiar with —**cul′ti·vat′ed** ***adj.***

cul·ti·va·tion (kul′tə vā′shən) ***n.*** **1.** the act of cultivating (in various senses) **2.** refinement, or culture

cul·ti·va·tor (kul′tə vāt′ər) ***n.*** **1.** one who cultivates **2.** a tool or machine for loosening the earth and destroying weeds around growing plants

cul·tur·al (kul′chər əl) ***adj.*** **1.** of culture **2.** obtained by breeding —**cul′tur·al·ly** ***adv.***

cul·ture (kul′chər) ***n.*** **[**< L. *cultura* < *colere:* see CULT**]** **1.** cultivation of the soil **2.** development or improvement of a particular plant or animal **3.** a growth of bacteria, etc.

in a specially prepared nourishing substance (**culture medium**) **4.** *a)* development, improvement, or refinement of the mind, manners, taste, etc. *b)* the result of this **5.** development or improvement of physical qualities by special training or care *[*body *culture]* **6.** the ideas, customs, skills, arts, etc. of a given people in a given period; civilization —*vt.* **-tured, -tur·ing** to cultivate —**cul′tur·ist** *n.*

cul·tured (-chərd) *adj.* **1.** produced by cultivation **2.** refined in speech, behavior, etc.

cul·tus (kul′təs) *n.* [L.] a religious cult

cul·ver·in (kul′vər in) *n.* [< Fr. < L. *colubra,* a snake] **1.** a musket used in the Middle Ages **2.** a long cannon of the 16th and 17th centuries

cul·vert (kul′vərt) *n.* [< ?] a conduit, esp. a drain, under a road, through an embankment, etc.

CULVERT

cum·ber (kum′bər) *vt.* [< OFr. *encombrer* < *en-* (see EN[1]-) + *combre,* obstruction] **1.** to hinder by obstruction or interference; hamper **2.** to burden in a troublesome way

Cum·ber·land (kum′bər lənd) [after the Duke of *Cumberland* (1721–65), Eng. general] river in S Ky. & N Tenn., flowing west into the Ohio

Cumberland Gap pass in the W Appalachians, at the juncture of the Va., Ky., & Tenn. borders

cum·ber·some (kum′bər səm) *adj.* burdensome; unwieldy; clumsy —**cum′ber·some·ly** *adv.* —**cum′ber·some·ness** *n.*

cum·brance (kum′brəns) *n.* a troublesome burden

cum·brous (-brəs) *adj. same as* CUMBERSOME —**cum′brous·ly** *adv.* —**cum′brous·ness** *n.*

cum·in (kum′in) *n.* [< OFr. < L. < Gr. < Sem., as in Heb. *kammōn,* Ar. *kammūn*] **1.** a small plant of the parsley family **2.** its aromatic fruits, used for flavoring pickles, soups, etc. Also sp. **cum′min**

‡**cum lau·de** (koom lou′de, kum lô′dē) [L.] with praise: phrase used to signify graduation with honors from a college or university

cum·mer·bund (kum′ər bund′) *n.* [Hindi & Per. *kamarband,* loin band] a wide sash worn as a waistband, esp. with men's formal dress

cum·quat (kum′kwät) *n. same as* KUMQUAT

cu·mu·late (kyōōm′yə lāt′) *vt., vi.* **-lat′ed, -lat′ing** [< L. pp. of *cumulare,* to heap up < *cumulus,* a heap] *same as* ACCUMULATE —**cu′mu·la′tion** *n.*

cu·mu·la·tive (kyōōm′yə lāt′iv, -lə tiv) *adj.* [see prec.] increasing in effect, size, quantity, etc. by successive additions; accumulated *[cumulative* interest is interest added to the principal and drawing additional interest*]* —**cu′mu·la′tive·ly** *adv.*

cu·mu·lo·nim·bus (kyōōm′yoo lō nim′bəs) *n.* a towering cloud type, usually producing heavy rain

cu·mu·lus (-yə ləs) *n., pl.* **-li′** (-lī′) [L., a heap] **1.** a heap **2.** a thick cloud type with a dark, horizontal base and upper parts resembling domes —**cu′mu·lous** *adj.*

cu·ne·ate (kyōō′nē it, -āt′) *adj.* [< L. < *cuneus,* a wedge] wedge-shaped; tapering, as some leaves: also **cu′ne·al, cu′ne·at′ed** (-āt′id), **cu′ne·at′ic** (-at′ik)

cu·ne·i·form (kyōō nē′ə fôrm′, kyōō′nē ə-) *adj.* [< L. *cuneus* (see prec.) + -FORM] wedge-shaped; esp., designating the characters used in ancient Assyrian, Babylonian, and Persian inscriptions, or such inscriptions —*n.* cuneiform characters or inscriptions

cun·ning (kun′iŋ) *adj.* [ME. < prp. of *cunnen,* to know: see CAN[1]] **1.** [Now Rare] skillful or clever **2.** skillful in deception; sly; crafty **3.** made or done with skill or ingenuity **4.** pretty in a delicate way; cute —*n.* **1.** [Now Rare] skill **2.** skill in deception; slyness; craftiness —**cun′ning·ly** *adv.* —**cun′ning·ness** *n.*

cup (kup) *n.* [OE. *cuppe* < LL. *cuppa* < L. *cupa,* tub] **1.** a small, bowl-shaped container for beverages, often with a handle **2.** the bowl part of a drinking vessel **3.** a cup and its contents **4.** the amount a cup holds; cupful: see CUPFUL **5.** anything shaped like a cup **6.** an ornamental cup given as a prize **7.** the wine chalice at Communion; also, the wine **8.** one's portion or allotment **9.** something served in a cup **10.** *Golf* the hole in each putting green —*vt.* **cupped, cup′ping 1.** to shape like a cup **2.** to take in or put into a cup **3.** *Med.* to subject to cupping —**in one's cups** drunk —**cup′like′** *adj.*

cup·bear·er (-ber′ər) *n.* a person who fills and serves the wine cups, as in a king's palace

cup·board (kub′ərd) *n.* a closet or cabinet with shelves for holding cups, plates, food, etc.

cup·cake (kup′kāk′) *n.* a little cake for one person, baked in a cup-shaped mold

cup·ful (kup′fool′) *n., pl.* **-fuls′** as much as a cup will hold: a standard measuring cup holds eight ounces

Cu·pid (kyōō′pid) [< OFr. < L. < *cupido,* desire] the Roman god of love, son of Venus: identified with the Greek god Eros —*n.* [c-] a representation of Cupid as a naked, winged cherub with bow and arrow

cu·pid·i·ty (kyōō pid′ə tē) *n.* [< Anglo-Fr. < L. < *cupere,* to desire] strong desire for wealth; greed

cup of tea [Colloq.] a favorite thing, activity, etc. *[*golf isn't his *cup of tea]*

cu·po·la (kyōō′pə lə) *n.* [It. < L. dim. of *cupa,* a tub] **1.** a rounded roof or ceiling **2.** a small dome or similar structure on a roof —**cu′po·laed** (-ləd) *adj.*

cup·ping (kup′iŋ) *n.* the use of a glass cup (**cupping glass**) from which the air has been exhausted, to draw blood to the surface of the skin: used, esp. formerly, in medicine —**cup′per** *n.*

cu·pre·ous (kyōō′prē əs) *adj.* [< L.: see COPPER[1]] of, like, or containing copper

cu·pric (kyōō′prik) *adj.* [CUPR(O)- + -IC] *Chem.* of or containing copper with a valence of two

cu·pro- [< L. *cuprum:* see COPPER[1]] *a combining form meaning* copper (and): also **cu·pri-, cupr-**

cu·pro·nick·el (kyōō′prō nik′'l) *n.* an alloy of copper and nickel, used in condenser tubes, some coins, etc.

cu·prous (kyōō′prəs) *adj.* [CUPR(O)- + -OUS] *Chem.* of or containing copper with a valence of one

cur (kur) *n.* [prob. < ON. *kurra* or MLowG. *korren,* to growl] **1.** a dog of mixed breed; mongrel **2.** a mean, contemptible, or cowardly person

cur. 1. currency **2.** current

cur·a·ble (kyoor′ə b'l) *adj.* that can be cured —**cur′a·bil′i·ty** *n.*

Cu·ra·çao (kyoor′ə sō′, kyoor′ə sou′) largest island of the Netherlands Antilles, off the N coast of Venezuela —*n.* [c-] a liqueur flavored with orange peel

cu·ra·cy (kyoor′ə sē) *n., pl.* **-cies** the position, office, or work of a curate

cu·ra·re, cu·ra·ri (kyoo rä′rē, koo-) *n.* [< Port. or Sp. < native (Tupi) name] **1.** a black, resinous substance prepared from the juices of certain S. American plants, used as an arrow poison by some Indians and in medicine to relax muscles **2.** any of the plants from which this is prepared

cu·rate (kyoor′it) *n.* [< ML. < L. pp. of *curare:* see CURATOR] a clergyman who assists a vicar or rector

cur·a·tive (kyoor′ə tiv) *adj.* curing or having the power to cure —*n.* a thing that cures; remedy

cu·ra·tor (kyoo rāt′ər; kyoor′āt′ər, -ə tər) *n.* [L. < *curare,* take care of < *cura,* care] a person in charge of a museum, library, etc. —**cu·ra·to·ri·al** (kyoor′ə tôr′ē əl) *adj.* —**cu·ra′tor·ship′** *n.*

curb (kurb) *n.* [< OFr. < L. *curvus,* bent] **1.** a chain or strap passed around a horse's lower jaw and attached to the bit, used to check the horse **2.** anything that checks, restrains, or subdues **3.** a raised margin along an edge, to strengthen or confine **4.** the stone or concrete edging forming a gutter along a street **5.** a market dealing in stocks and bonds not listed on the stock exchange —*vt.* **1.** to restrain; check; control **2.** to lead (a dog) to the curb to pass its waste matter **3.** to provide with a curb

curb bit a horse's bit with a curb

curb·ing (-iŋ) *n.* **1.** material for a curb **2.** a curb (sense 4)

curb roof *same as* MANSARD ROOF *or* GAMBREL ROOF

curb·stone (-stōn′) *n.* any of the stones, or a row of stones, making up a curb

cur·cu·li·o (kər kyōō′lē ō′) *n., pl.* **-li·os′** [L., weevil] any of a family of weevils with long snouts: some are harmful to fruit

curd (kurd) *n.* [< ME. *crud,* orig., any coagulated substance] [*often pl.*] the coagulated part of milk, from which cheese is made: it is formed when milk sours and is distinguished from whey, the watery part —*vt., vi.* to curdle —**curd′y** *adj.*

cur·dle (kur′d'l) *vt., vi.* **-dled, -dling** [< CURD + -LE, freq. suffix] to form into curd; coagulate; congeal —**curdle one's blood** to horrify or terrify one

cure (kyoor) *n.* [OFr. < L. *cura,* care] **1.** a healing or being healed **2.** a medicine or treatment for restoring health; remedy **3.** a method or course of treating a disease, ailment, etc. **4.** *same as* CURACY **5.** a process for curing meat, fish, tobacco, etc. —*vt.* **cured, cur′ing 1.** to restore to health or a sound condition; heal **2.** to get rid of (an ailment, evil, etc.) **3.** to get rid of an undesirable condition in (with *of*) *[cured* him of lying*]* **4.** *a)* to preserve (meat, fish, etc.), as by salting or smoking *b)* to process (tobacco, leather, etc.), as by drying or aging —*vi.* **1.** to bring about a cure **2.** to undergo curing, preserving, or processing —**cure′less** ***adj.*** —**cur′er** ***n.***

cu·ré (kyoo rā′) ***n.*** [Fr.] in France, a parish priest

cure-all (kyoor′ôl′) ***n.*** something supposed to cure all ailments or evils; panacea

cu·ret, cu·rette (kyoo ret′) ***n.*** [Fr. < *curer,* to cleanse] a spoon-shaped surgical instrument for the removal of tissue from the walls of body cavities —***vt.*** **-ret′ted, -ret′ting** to clean or scrape with a curet

cu·ret·tage (kyoor′ə täzh′, kyoo ret′ij) ***n.*** [Fr.: see prec.] the process of curetting

cur·few (kʉr′fyōō) ***n.*** [< OFr. *covrefeu* < *covrir,* to COVER + *feu,* fire < L. *focus,* fireplace] **1.** *a)* in the Middle Ages, the ringing of a bell every evening as a signal for people to cover fires, put out lights, and retire *b)* the bell *c)* the time at which it was rung **2.** *a)* a time in the evening set as a deadline beyond which children, etc. may not appear on the streets *b)* the regulation establishing this time

cu·ri·a (kyoor′ē ə) ***n.,*** *pl.* **-ri·ae′** (-ē′) [L.] **1.** a medieval judicial court held in the king's name **2.** [C-] the administrative body of the Roman Catholic Church, consisting of various departments, courts, officials, etc. functioning under the authority of the Pope: in full, **Curia Ro·ma·na** (rō mä′nə, -mā′-) —**cu′ri·al** ***adj.***

Cu·rie (kyoo rē′, kyoor′ē; *Fr.* kü *rē′*), **Marie** (born *Marie Sklodowska*) 1867–1934; Pol. chemist & physicist in France: discoverer, with her husband **Pierre** (1859–1906), of polonium & radium

cu·rie (kyoor′ē, kyoo rē′) ***n.*** [after Marie CURIE] the unit used in measuring radioactivity

cu·ri·o (kyoor′ē ō′) ***n.,*** *pl.* **-os′** [contr. of CURIOSITY] any unusual or rare article

cu·ri·os·i·ty (kyoor′ē äs′ə tē) ***n.,*** *pl.* **-ties** [< OFr. < L. *curiositas* < *curiosus:* see CURIOUS] **1.** a desire to learn or know **2.** a desire to learn about things that do not properly concern one **3.** anything curious, rare, or novel

cu·ri·ous (kyoor′ē əs) ***adj.*** [OFr. < L. *curiosus,* careful] **1.** eager to learn or know **2.** unnecessarily inquisitive; prying **3.** arousing attention or interest because unusual or strange —**cu′ri·ous·ly** ***adv.*** —**cu′ri·ous·ness** ***n.***

cu·ri·um (kyoor′ē əm) ***n.*** [ModL., after Marie & Pierre CURIE] a radioactive chemical element of the actinide series: symbol, Cm; at. wt., 247 (?); at. no., 96

curl (kʉrl) ***vt.*** [ME. *curlen* < *crul,* curly] **1.** to wind (esp. hair) into ringlets or coils **2.** to cause to bend around **3.** to raise the upper corner of (the lip), as in showing scorn —***vi.*** **1.** to become curled **2.** to form, or move in, a spiral or curve **3.** to play the game of curling —***n.*** **1.** a ringlet of hair **2.** anything with a curled shape; coil **3.** a curling or being curled —**curl up 1.** to gather into spirals or curls **2.** to sit or lie with the legs drawn up —**in curl** curled —**curl′er** ***n.***

cur·lew (kʉr′lōō, -lyōō) ***n.,*** *pl.* **-lews, -lew:** see PLURAL, II, D, 1 [< OFr. *corlieu,* of echoic origin] a large, brownish wading bird with long legs

CURLEW (length to 19 in.; wingspread to 33 in.)

curl·i·cue (kʉr′li kyōō′) ***n.*** [< CURLY + CUE²] a fancy curve, flourish, etc., as in a design

curl·ing (kʉr′liŋ) ***n.*** a game played on ice by sliding a heavy disk **(curling stone)** toward a target circle

curling iron (or **irons**) a metal rod heated for curling or waving hair rolled around it

curl·y (kʉr′lē) ***adj.*** **curl′i·er, curl′i·est 1.** curling or tending to curl **2.** having curls **3.** having a wavy grain, as certain woods —**curl′i·ness** ***n.***

cur·mudg·eon (kər muj′ən) ***n.*** [< ?] a surly, ill-mannered person; cantankerous fellow

cur·rant (kʉr′ənt) ***n.*** [< Anglo-Fr. (*raisins de*) *Corauntz,* lit., (raisins of) Corinth] **1.** a small, seedless raisin from the Mediterranean region **2.** *a)* the sour, red, white, or black berry of several species of hardy shrubs, used for jellies and jams *b)* a shrub bearing this fruit

cur·ren·cy (kʉr′ən sē) ***n.,*** *pl.* **-cies** [< L. *currens:* see ff.] **1.** a continual passing from hand to hand; circulation **2.** the money in circulation in any country **3.** common acceptance or use; prevalence

cur·rent (kʉr′ənt) ***adj.*** [< OFr. < L. *currere,* to run] **1.** *a)* now in progress *[*his *current* job*]* *b)* contemporary *[current* fashions*]* *c)* of most recent date *[*the *current* edition*]* **2.** passing from person to person; circulating **3.** commonly used or accepted; prevalent —***n.*** **1.** a flow of water or air in a definite direction **2.** a general tendency or drift; course **3.** *Elec.* the flow or rate of flow of electric charge in a conductor — **cur′rent·ly** ***adv.***

cur·ri·cle (kʉr′i k'l) ***n.*** [< L.: see ff.] a two-wheeled carriage drawn by two horses abreast

cur·ric·u·lum (kə rik′yə ləm) ***n.,*** *pl.* **-u·la** (-lə), **-u·lums** [L., a course, race < *currere,* to run] **1.** a series of studies required, as for graduation **2.** all of the courses, collectively, offered in a school, college, etc., or in a particular subject —**cur·ric′u·lar** ***adj.***

cur·rish (kʉr′ish) ***adj.*** like a cur; mean; ill-bred —**cur′rish·ly** ***adv.***

cur·ry¹ (kʉr′ē) ***vt.*** **-ried, -ry·ing** [< OFr. *correier,* to put in order] **1.** to rub down and clean the coat of (a horse, etc.) with a currycomb or brush **2.** to prepare (tanned leather) by soaking, cleaning, beating, etc. —**curry favor** to try to win favor by flattery, fawning, etc. —**cur′ri·er** ***n.***

cur·ry² (kʉr′ē) ***n.,*** *pl.* **-ries** [Tamil *kari,* sauce] **1.** *same as* CURRY POWDER **2.** a sauce made with curry powder **3.** a kind of stew prepared with curry —***vt.*** **-ried, -ry·ing** to prepare with curry powder

cur·ry·comb (kʉr′ē kōm′) ***n.*** a comb with teeth or ridges, to curry a horse —***vt.*** to curry with this

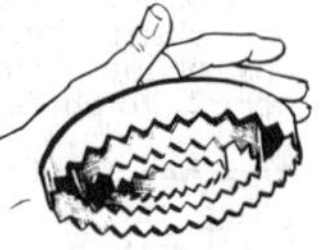

CURRYCOMB

curry powder a seasoning prepared from turmeric and various spices and herbs

curse (kʉrs) ***n.*** [Late OE. *curs, n., cursian, v.*] **1.** a calling on God or the gods to send evil or injury to some person or thing **2.** a profane or blasphemous oath, imprecation, etc. **3.** a thing cursed **4.** evil or injury that seems to come in answer to a curse **5.** any cause of evil or injury —***vt.*** **cursed** or **curst, curs′ing 1.** to call evil or injury down on; damn **2.** to swear at **3.** to bring evil or injury on; afflict —***vi.*** to swear; blaspheme —**be cursed with** to suffer from —**curs′er** ***n.***

curs·ed (kʉr′sid, kʉrst) ***adj.*** **1.** under a curse **2.** deserving to be cursed; specif., *a)* evil; wicked *b)* hateful —**curs′ed·ly** ***adv.*** —**curs′ed·ness** ***n.***

cur·sive (kʉr′siv) ***adj.*** [ML. *cursivus* < L. *cursus:* see COURSE] designating or of writing in which the letters are joined in each word —***n.*** **1.** a cursive character **2.** *Printing* a typeface that looks like handwriting —**cur′sive·ly** ***adv.*** —**cur′sive·ness** ***n.***

cur·so·ry (kʉr′sər ē) ***adj.*** [< L. < *cursor,* runner < *cursus:* see COURSE] hastily, often superficially, done; performed rapidly with little attention to detail —**cur′so·ri·ly** ***adv.*** —**cur′so·ri·ness** ***n.***

curt (kʉrt) ***adj.*** [L. *curtus*] **1.** orig., short or shortened **2.** so brief as to be rude; terse; brusque *[*a *curt* reply*]* —**curt′ly** ***adv.*** —**curt′ness** ***n.***

cur·tail (kər tāl′) ***vt.*** [< OFr. *curtald,* shortened < L. *curtus,* short] to cut short; reduce; abridge —**cur·tail′er** ***n.*** —**cur·tail′ment** ***n.***

cur·tain (kʉr′t'n) ***n.*** [< OFr. < LL. *cortina,* circle of a theater < L. *cohors,* a COURT] **1.** a piece of cloth, etc., often one that can be drawn up or sideways, hung, as at a window, to decorate, cover, or conceal **2.** anything that covers, conceals, or shuts off **3.** *Theater* *a)* the drape at the front of the stage, which is drawn up or aside to reveal the stage *b)* the opening or the closing of the curtain for a play, act, or scene **4.** [*pl.*] [Slang] death; the end —***vt.*** to provide or shut off as with a curtain —**draw** (or **drop**) **the curtain on 1.** to end **2.** to conceal —**lift** (or **raise**) **the curtain on 1.** to begin **2.** to reveal

curtain call 1. a call, usually by continued applause, for the performers to return to the stage **2.** such a return, acknowledging the applause

curtain raiser 1. a short play or skit presented before a longer production **2.** any brief preliminary event

curtain wall an independently supported outer wall bearing only its own weight

Cur·tis (kʉr′tis) [< ONormFr. *curteis,* courteous] a masculine name

curt·sy (kʉrt′sē) ***n.,*** *pl.* **-sies** [var. of COURTESY] a gesture of greeting, respect, etc. made, esp. formerly, by girls and women and characterized by a bending of the knees and a slight lowering of the body —***vi.*** **-sied, -sy·ing** to make a curtsy Also sp. **curt′sey**

cur·va·ceous (kər vā′shəs) ***adj.*** [CURV(E) + -ACEOUS] [Colloq.] having a full, shapely figure: said of a woman

cur·va·ture (kʉr′və chər) ***n.*** **1.** a curving or being curved **2.** a curve; curved part of anything

curve (kʉrv) ***n.*** [L. *curvus,* bent] **1.** a line having no straight part; bend with no angles **2.** a thing or part with the shape of a curve **3.** a curving, or the extent of this **4.** a curved line indicating variations, as in prices **5.** *Baseball* a pitched ball thrown so that it curves before crossing the plate **6.** *Math.* a one-dimensional continuum of points in a space of two or more dimensions —***vt., vi.*** **curved, curv′ing 1.** to form a curve by bending **2.** to move in a curve

cur·vet (kʉr′vit; *for v., usually* kər vet′) ***n.*** [< It. dim. < *corvo* < L. *curvus,* bent] an upward leap by a horse, raising its hind legs just before its forelegs come down again —***vi.*** **-vet′ted** or **-vet′ed, -vet′ting** or **-vet′ing 1.** to make a curvet **2.** to leap; frolic —***vt.*** to cause to curvet

cur·vi·lin·e·ar (kʉr′və lin′ē ər) ***adj.*** consisting of or enclosed by a curved line or lines: also **cur′vi·lin′e·al**

curv·y (kʉr′vē) ***adj.*** **curv′i·er, curv′i·est** **1.** having curves or a curve **2.** [Colloq.] curvaceous

cush·ion (koosh′ən) ***n.*** **[**< OFr. *coissin* < ML. *coxinum* (infl. by L. *coxa*, hip) < L. *culcita***]** **1.** a pillow or pad for sitting or kneeling on, or reclining against **2.** a thing like this in shape or use **3.** anything serving to absorb shock, as air or steam in some machines, the elastic inner rim of a billiard table, or a soft, padded insole **4.** anything that relieves distress, provides comfort, etc. —***vt.*** **1.** to provide with a cushion **2.** to seat or set on a cushion **3.** to absorb (shock or noise) **4.** to act as a cushion as in protecting from injury, relieving distress, etc.

Cush·it·ic (kush it′ik, koosh-) ***adj.*** **[**< *Cush*, son of HAM**]** designating or of a group of languages spoken in Ethiopia and E Africa —***n.*** this group of languages

cush·y (koosh′ē) ***adj.*** **cush′i·er, cush′i·est** **[**orig. Brit. army slang < Hindi *khush*, pleasant < Per.**]** [Slang] easy; comfortable *[*a *cushy* job*]* —**cush′i·ly** ***adv.*** —**cush′i·ness** ***n.***

cusp (kusp) ***n.*** **[**L. *cuspis*, a point**]** **1.** a pointed end; peak **2.** any of the elevations on the chewing surface of a tooth **3.** any triangular fold of a heart valve **4.** either horn of a crescent, as of the moon **5.** *Geom.* a corner point formed by two tangent branches of a curve

cus·pid (kus′pid) ***n.*** a canine tooth: see CANINE

cus·pi·date (kus′pə dāt′) ***adj.*** **1.** having a cusp or cusps **2.** having a short, abrupt point, as some leaves Also **cus′pi·dat′ed**

cus·pi·dor (kus′pə dôr′) ***n.*** **[**< Port. < *cuspir*, to spit < L. < *com-*, intens. + *spuere*, to spit out**]** *same as* SPITTOON

cuss (kus) ***n.*** **[**< CURSE**]** [Colloq.] **1.** a curse **2.** a person or animal regarded as queer or annoying —***vt., vi.*** [Colloq.] to curse —**cuss′ed** (-id) ***adj.*** —**cuss′ed·ly** ***adv.*** —**cuss′ed·ness** ***n.*** —**cuss′er** ***n.***

cus·tard (kus′tərd) ***n.*** **[**< L. *crusta*, a crust**]** **1.** a mixture of eggs, milk, flavoring, and, often, sugar, either boiled or baked **2.** a similar mixture frozen like ice cream: in full, **frozen custard**

cus·tard-ap·ple (-ap′'l) ***n.*** **1.** any of several tropical trees with edible, heart-shaped fruits **2.** the fruit

Cus·ter (kus′tər), **George Armstrong** 1839–76; U.S. army officer: killed in a battle with Sioux Indians

cus·to·di·an (kəs tō′dē ən) ***n.*** **1.** one who has the custody or care of something; keeper **2.** a janitor —**cus·to′di·an·ship′** ***n.***

cus·to·dy (kus′tə dē) ***n.***, *pl.* **-dies** **[**< L. < *custos*, a guard**]** a guarding or keeping safe; care —**in custody** in the keeping of the police; under arrest —**take into custody** to arrest —**cus·to′di·al** (-tō′dē əl) ***adj.***

cus·tom (kus′təm) ***n.*** **[**< OFr. < L. *consuetudo* < *com-*, intens. + *suere*, to be accustomed**]** **1.** a usual practice or habitual way of behaving; habit **2.** *a)* a social convention carried on by tradition *b)* such practices, collectively **3.** [*pl.*] *a)* duties or taxes imposed by a government on imported and, occasionally, exported goods *b)* [*with sing. v.*] the agency in charge of collecting these duties **4.** the regular patronage of a business establishment **5.** *Law* such usage as by common consent and long-established practice has taken on the force of law —***adj.*** **1.** made or done to order or as if to order **2.** making things to order, or dealing in such things

cus·tom·ar·y (kus′tə mer′ē) ***adj.*** **1.** in keeping with custom, or usage; usual; habitual **2.** *Law* holding or held by custom —**cus′tom·ar′i·ly** ***adv.*** —**cus′tom·ar′i·ness** ***n.***

cus·tom-built (kus′təm bilt′) ***adj.*** built to order, according to the customer's specifications

cus·tom·er (kus′tə mər) ***n.*** **[**see CUSTOM**]** **1.** a person who buys, esp. one who patronizes an establishment regularly **2.** [Colloq.] any person with whom one has dealings *[*a rough *customer]*

cus·tom·house (kus′təm hous′) ***n.*** a building or office where customs or duties are paid, and ships cleared for entering or leaving: also **cus′toms·house′**

cus·tom·ize (-īz′) ***vt., vi.*** **-ized′, -iz′ing** **[**CUSTOM + -IZE**]** to make or build according to individual specifications —**cus′tom·iz′er** ***n.***

cus·tom-made (-mād′) ***adj.*** made to order, according to the customer's specifications

cut (kut) ***vt.*** **cut, cut′ting** **[**ME. *cutten***]** **1.** to make an opening in as with a sharp-edged instrument; pierce; gash **2.** to pierce sharply so as to hurt **3.** to hurt the feelings of **4.** to grow (a new tooth making its way through the gum) **5.** to divide into parts with a sharp-edged instrument; sever **6.** to carve (meat) **7.** to fell; hew **8.** to mow or reap **9.** to pass through or across; intersect *[*the path *cuts* the meadow*]* **10.** to divide (a pack of cards) at random before dealing **11.** to stop photographing (a motion-picture scene) **12.** to reduce; lessen; curtail *[*to *cut* salaries*]* **13.** to make shorter by trimming (hair, branches, etc.) **14.** to dilute (alcohol, etc.) **15.** to dissolve the fat globules of *[*lye *cuts* grease*]* **16.** to make or do by or as by cutting; specif., *a)* to make (an opening, clearing, channel, etc.) *b)* to type or otherwise mark (a stencil) for mimeographing *c)* to cut cloth so as to form (a garment) *d)* to perform *[*to *cut* a caper*]* *e)* to hit, drive, or throw (a ball) so that it spins or is deflected *f)* to cause (a wheel) to turn sharply *g)* to edit (movie film) as by deleting scenes *h)* to make a recording of (a speech, music, etc.) on (a phonograph record) **17.** [Colloq.] to pretend not to see or know (a person) **18.** [Colloq.] to stay away from (a school class, etc.) without being excused **19.** [Slang] to stop; discontinue —***vi.*** **1.** to do the work of a sharp-edged instrument; pierce, sever, gash, etc. **2.** to work as a cutter **3.** to take cutting *[*pine *cuts* easily*]* **4.** to use an instrument that cuts **5.** to cause pain by sharp, piercing strokes *[*the wind *cut* through his coat*]* **6.** to swing a bat, etc. (*at* a ball) **7.** to move swiftly **8.** to make a sudden shift to another scene, as in a movie —***adj.*** **1.** that has been cut **2.** made or formed by cutting **3.** reduced; lessened —***n.*** **1.** a cutting or being cut **2.** a stroke or blow with a sharp-edged instrument, whip, etc. **3.** a stroke taken at a ball **4.** an opening, wound, etc. made by a sharp-edged instrument **5.** the omission of a part **6.** a piece or part cut off or out, as from a meat animal **7.** *a)* the amount cut *b)* a reduction; decrease **8.** the shortest way across: usually **short cut** **9.** a passage or channel cut out or worn away **10.** the style in which a thing is cut; fashion *[*a stylish *cut]* **11.** an act, remark, etc. that hurts one's feelings **12.** a block or plate engraved for printing, or the impression made from it **13.** [Colloq.] the act of snubbing or ignoring **14.** [Colloq.] an unauthorized absence from school, etc. **15.** [Slang] a share, as of profits or loot —**a cut above** [Colloq.] somewhat better than —**cut across** to take a shorter course by going straight across —**cut a figure** to attract attention or make a (certain) impression —**cut and dried** **1.** arranged beforehand **2.** lifeless; dull; boring —**cut back** **1.** to make shorter by cutting off the end **2.** to reduce or discontinue (production, etc.) **3.** to go back to earlier narrative events, as in a novel **4.** to change direction suddenly, as a runner in football —**cut dead** [Colloq.] to snub completely —**cut down** **1.** to make fall by cutting **2.** to kill **3.** to reduce; lessen —**cut in** **1.** to move in suddenly **2.** to interrupt **3.** to interrupt a couple dancing in order to dance with one of them **4.** to make a connection, as in an electrical circuit **5.** to give a share to —**cut it fine** [Colloq.] to make exact calculations or distinctions —**cut it out** [Colloq.] to stop what one is doing —**cut loose** [Colloq.] to act without restraint —**cut no ice** [Colloq.] to make no impression —**cut off** **1.** to sever **2.** to stop abruptly **3.** to shut off **4.** to interrupt **5.** to intercept **6.** to disinherit —**cut out** **1.** to remove by cutting **2.** to remove; omit **3.** to eliminate and take the place of (a rival) **4.** to make or form as by cutting **5.** [Colloq.] to discontinue; stop **6.** [Slang] to leave abruptly —**cut out for** suited for —**cut short** to stop abruptly before the end —**cut up** **1.** to cut into pieces **2.** to inflict cuts on **3.** [Colloq.] *a)* to criticize harshly *b)* to cause to be dejected **4.** [Slang] to clown, joke, etc. to attract attention

cu·ta·ne·ous (kyo͞o tā′nē əs) ***adj.*** **[**< ML. < L. *cutis*, the skin**]** of, on, or affecting the skin

cut·a·way (kut′ə wā′) ***n.*** a man's formal daytime coat with the front of the skirt cut so as to curve back to the tails: also **cutaway coat** —***adj.*** designating or of a diagram or model having outer parts cut away so as to show the inside

cut·back (kut′bak′) ***n.*** a cutting back; specif., a reduction, as of production, personnel, etc.

cute (kyo͞ot) ***adj.*** **cut′er, cut′est** **[**< ACUTE**]** [Colloq.] **1.** clever; sharp; shrewd **2.** pretty, esp. in a dainty way **3.** straining for effect; artificial —**cute′ly** ***adv.*** —**cute′ness** ***n.***

cut glass glass, esp. flint glass, shaped or ornamented by grinding and polishing —**cut′-glass′** ***adj.***

cut·i·cle (kyo͞ot′i k'l) ***n.*** **[**L. *cuticula*, skin, dim. < *cutis*, skin**]** **1.** *same as* EPIDERMIS **2.** hardened skin accumulating at the base and sides of a fingernail or toenail **3.** *Zool.* the tough, nonliving outer structure secreted by the epidermis in many invertebrates

cu·tin·i·za·tion (kyo͞ot′'n ə zā′shən) ***n.*** **[**< L. *cutis*, skin**]** a process in which the outermost plant cells become thickened and covered with a varnishlike material **(cutin)**, making them waterproof —**cu′tin·ize′** (-īz′) ***vi., vt.*** **-ized′, -iz′ing**

cu·tis (kyo͞ot′is) ***n.*** **[**L.**]** **1.** the vertebrate skin, including both of its layers, the dermis and the epidermis **2.** the dermis only

cut·lass, cut·las (kut′ləs) ***n.*** [< Fr. < It. < L. < *culter,* a knife] a short, thick, curved sword with a single cutting edge, formerly used esp. by sailors

cut·ler (kut′lər) ***n.*** [< Anglo-Fr. < OFr. < ML. < L. < *culter,* a knife] a person who makes, sells, or repairs knives and other cutting tools

cut·ler·y (kut′lər ē) ***n.*** **1.** the work or business of a cutler **2.** cutting instruments, such as knives and scissors; often, specif., such implements used in preparing food

cut·let (kut′lit) ***n.*** [< Fr. *côtelette* < OFr. dim. of *coste,* a rib < L. *costa*] **1.** a small slice of meat from the ribs or leg, often breaded and fried, etc. **2.** a small, flat croquette of chopped meat or fish

cut·off (kut′ôf′) ***n.*** **1.** the act of cutting off; esp., the limit set for a process, activity, etc. **2.** a road or passage that is a short cut **3.** the act of stopping steam, etc. from entering the cylinder of an engine **4.** any device for cutting off the flow of a fluid, a connection, etc.

cut·out (-out′) ***n.*** **1.** a device for breaking or closing an electric circuit **2.** a device for letting the exhaust gases of an internal-combustion engine pass directly into the air instead of through a muffler **3.** a design to be cut out

cut·o·ver (-ō′vər) ***adj.*** cleared of trees

cut·purse (-purs′) ***n.*** **1.** orig., a thief who cut purses from belts **2.** a pickpocket

cut-rate (-rāt′) ***adj.*** **1.** available at a lower price **2.** offering cut-rate goods or services

cut·ter (kut′ər) ***n.*** **1.** a device for cutting **2.** a person whose work is cutting, as the sections of a garment **3.** a small, swift vessel; specif., *a)* a boat carried by large ships as a communications tender: also **ship's cutter** *b)* an armed sailing vessel, formerly used to pursue smugglers, etc.: also **revenue cutter** *c)* a small, armed, engine-powered ship, used by the Coast Guard: also **Coast Guard cutter** *d)* a single-masted sailboat with two headsails **4.** a small, light sleigh, usually drawn by one horse

cut·throat (kut′thrōt′) ***n.*** a murderer —***adj.*** **1.** murderous **2.** merciless; ruthless

cut·ting (kut′iŋ) ***n.*** **1.** the act of one that cuts **2.** a piece cut off **3.** [Brit.] a newspaper clipping **4.** a shoot cut away from a plant for rooting or grafting —***adj.*** **1.** that cuts; sharp **2.** chilling or piercing **3.** sarcastic; harsh —**cut′ting·ly** ***adv.***

cut·tle·bone (kut′'l bōn′) ***n.*** the internal shell of cuttlefish, used as food for caged birds and, when powdered, as a polishing agent

cut·tle·fish (-fish′) ***n.,*** *pl.* **-fish′, -fish′es:** see FISH [OE. *cudele*] a squidlike sea mollusk with ten sucker-bearing arms and a hard internal shell: when in danger, some cuttlefish eject an inky fluid: also **cuttle**

cut·up (kut′up′) ***n.*** [Colloq.] a person who clowns, plays practical jokes, etc. to attract attention

cut·wa·ter (-wôt′ər, -wät′ər) ***n.*** the fore part of a ship's stem

cut·worm (-wurm′) ***n.*** any of a number of caterpillars that feed on young plants of cabbage, corn, etc., cutting them off at ground level

Cuy·a·ho·ga Falls (kī′ə hō′gə, -hô′-) [< Iroquois name] city in NE Ohio: suburb of Akron: pop. 50,000

Cuz·co (kōōs′kō) city in S Peru: capital of the former Inca empire: pop. 93,000

CWO Chief Warrant Officer

C.W.O., c.w.o. cash with order

cwt. hundredweight

-cy (sē, si) [< OFr. *-cie,* L. *-cia,* Gr. *-kia*] *a suffix meaning:* **1.** quality, condition, state, or fact of being *[hesitancy]* **2.** position, rank, or office of *[curacy]*

cy·a·nate (sī′ə nāt′) ***n.*** a salt of cyanic acid

cy·an·ic (sī an′ik) ***adj.*** **1.** of or containing cyanogen **2.** blue

cyanic acid a colorless, poisonous acid, HOCN

cy·a·nide (sī′ə nīd′, -nid) ***n.*** a compound containing the cyanogen radical, —CN; esp., potassium cyanide, KCN, or sodium cyanide, NaCN, highly poisonous compounds with many industrial uses

cy·an·o·gen (sī an′ə jən) ***n.*** [< Gr. *kyanos,* blue + -GEN] **1.** a colorless, poisonous, flammable gas, C_2N_2 **2.** the univalent radical —CN, in cyanides

cy·a·no·sis (sī′ə nō′sis) ***n.*** [ModL. < Gr. < *kyanos,* blue] a bluish coloration of the skin caused by lack of oxygen in the blood —**cy′a·not′ic** (-nät′ik) ***adj.***

Cyb·e·le (sib′ə lē′) a nature goddess of ancient Asia Minor: identified with the Greek goddess Rhea

cy·ber·na·tion (sī′bər nā′shən) ***n.*** [CYBERN(ETICS) + -ATION] the use of computers in connection with automation —**cy′ber·nate′** ***vt.*** **-nat′ed, -nat′ing**

cy·ber·net·ics (sī′bər net′iks) ***n.pl.*** [*with sing. v.*] [< Gr. *kybernētēs,* helmsman + -ICS] a science dealing with the comparative study of the operations of complex electronic computers and the human nervous system —**cy′ber·net′ic** ***adj.***

cyc. **1.** cyclopedia **2.** cyclopedic

cy·cad (sī′kad) ***n.*** [ModL. *Cycas* < Gr. *kykas,* erroneous pl. of *koïx,* a palm] any of an order of tropical shrubs and trees resembling thick-stemmed palms, with crowns of leathery, fernlike leaves

Cyc·la·des (sik′lə dēz′) group of Greek islands in the S Aegean: 995 sq. mi.

cy·cla·mate (sī′klə māt′, sik′lə-) ***n.*** a complex organic compound with an extremely sweet taste

cyc·la·men (sī′klə mən, sik′lə-) ***n.,*** *pl.* **-mens** [< L. < Gr. *kyklaminos*] a plant of the primrose family, having heart-shaped leaves and white, pink, or red flowers with reflexed petals

cy·cle (sī′k'l) ***n.*** [< LL. *cyclus* < Gr. *kyklos,* a circle] **1.** *a)* a period of time within which a round of regularly recurring events is completed *b)* a complete set or series of such events **2.** a very long period of time; an age **3.** all the traditional poems, songs, etc. connected with a hero or an event **4.** a series of poems or songs on the same theme **5.** a bicycle, tricycle, or motorcycle **6.** *Elec.* one complete period of the reversal of an alternating current —***vi.*** **-cled, -cling** **1.** to occur in cycles; pass through a cycle **2.** to ride a bicycle, tricycle, or motorcycle

cy·clic (sī′klik, sik′lik) ***adj.*** **1.** of, or having the nature of, a cycle; moving or occurring in cycles **2.** *Chem.* arranged in a ring or closed-chain structure: said of atoms Also **cy′cli·cal** —**cy′cli·cal·ly** ***adv.***

cy·clist (sī′klist) ***n.*** a person who rides a bicycle, motorcycle, etc.

cy·cli·zine (sī′klə zēn′) ***n.*** an antihistamine, $C_{18}H_{22}N_2$, used to treat nausea and motion sickness

cy·clo- [< Gr. *kyklos,* a circle] *a combining form meaning* of a circle or wheel, circular: also, before a vowel, **cycl-**

cy·cloid (sī′kloid) ***adj.*** [< Gr. < *kyklos,* a circle + *eidos,* form] circular: also **cy·cloi·dal** (sī kloi′d'l)

cy·clom·e·ter (sī kläm′ə tər) ***n.*** [CYCLO- + -METER] an instrument that records the revolutions of a wheel, for measuring distance traveled

cy·clone (sī′klōn) ***n.*** [< Gr. < *kykloein,* to whirl < *kyklos,* a circle] **1.** loosely, a violent, whirling windstorm; tornado or hurricane **2.** *Meteorol.* a storm with strong winds rotating about a moving center of low atmospheric pressure —**cy·clon·ic** (sī klän′ik) ***adj.*** —**cy·clon′i·cal·ly** ***adv.***

Cy·clo·pe·an (sī′klə pē′ən) ***adj.*** **1.** of the Cyclopes **2.** [c-] huge; gigantic; enormous

cy·clo·pe·di·a, cy·clo·pae·di·a (sī′klə pē′dē ə) ***n.*** *same as* ENCYCLOPEDIA —**cy′clo·pe′dic, cy′clo·pae′dic** ***adj.*** —**cy′clo·pe′dist, cy′clo·pae′dist** ***n.***

Cy·clops (sī′kläps) ***n.,*** *pl.* **Cy·clo·pes** (sī klō′pēz) [L. < Gr. < *kyklos,* a circle + *ōps,* an eye] *Gr. Myth.* any of a race of giants who had only one eye, centered in the forehead

cy·clo·ra·ma (sī′klə ram′ə) ***n.*** [CYCLO- + Gr. *horama,* sight] **1.** a series of large pictures, as of a landscape, put on the wall of a circular room so as to suggest natural perspective to a viewer **2.** a large, curved curtain or screen used as a background for stage sets —**cy′clo·ram′ic** ***adj.***

cy·clo·tron (sī′klə trän′) ***n.*** [CYCLO- + (ELEC)TRON] an apparatus for giving high energy to particles, usually protons and deuterons, so as to produce transmutations or radioactivity in a target element

cyg·net (sig′nət) ***n.*** [dim. < Fr. *cygne,* swan < VL. < Gr. *kyknos,* swan] a young swan

cyl. **1.** cylinder **2.** cylindrical

cyl·in·der (sil′ən dər) ***n.*** [< Fr. < L. < Gr. < *kylindein,* to roll] **1.** *Geom.* a solid figure described by the edge of a rectangle rotated around the parallel edge as axis: the ends of a cylinder are parallel and equal circles **2.** anything, hollow or solid, with the shape of a cylinder; specif., *a)* the turning part of a revolver, containing chambers for cartridges *b)* the chamber in which the piston moves in a reciprocating engine *c)* the barrel of a pump

cy·lin·dri·cal (sə lin′dri k'l) ***adj.*** **1.** having the shape of a cylinder **2.** of a cylinder Also **cy·lin′dric** —**cy·lin′dri·cal′i·ty** (-kal′ə tē) ***n.*** —**cy·lin′dri·cal·ly** ***adv.***

Cym. Cymric

cym·bal (sim′b'l) ***n.*** [< OFr. & OE. < L. < Gr. < *kymbē,* hollow of a vessel] a circular, slightly concave brass plate used as a percussion instrument: it is struck with a drumstick, brush, etc. or used in pairs which are struck together to produce a crashing, ringing sound —**cym′bal·ist** ***n.***

CYMBALS

cym·bid·i·um (sim bid′ē əm) ***n.,*** *pl.* **-i·ums, -i·a** (-ə) [ModL. < L. *cymba,* a boat (< Gr. *kymbē*) + ModL. *-idium,* dim. suffix] any of various tropical Asiatic orchids with sprays of white, pink, yellow, or maroon flowers

cyme (sīm) ***n.*** [< L. < Gr. *kyma,* swelling < *kyein,* to be pregnant] a flat-topped flower clus-

ter in which the central flower blooms first, followed by the outer ones —**cy·mose** (sī′mōs, sī mōs′) ***adj.***
Cym·ric (kim′rik; *occas.* sim′-) ***adj.*** [< W. < *Cymru*, Wales] **1.** of the Celtic people of Wales **2.** of their language —***n.*** Brythonic: see CELTIC
Cym·ry (-rē) ***n.pl.*** the Cymric Celts; the Welsh
cyn·ic (sin′ik) ***n.*** [see ff.] **1.** [C-] a member of a school of ancient Greek philosophers who held virtue to be the only good, and stressed independence from worldly needs and pleasures: they became critical of materialistic social values **2.** a cynical person —***adj.*** **1.** [C-] of or like the Cynics or their doctrines **2.** *same as* CYNICAL
cyn·i·cal (sin′i k'l) ***adj.*** [< L. < Gr. *kynikos*, canine < *kyōn*, dog] **1.** denying the sincerity of people's motives and actions, or the value of living **2.** sarcastic, sneering, etc. **3.** [C-] *same as* CYNIC —**cyn′i·cal·ly** ***adv.*** —**cyn′i·cal·ness** ***n.***
cyn·i·cism (sin′ə siz'm) ***n.*** **1.** [C-] the philosophy of the Cynics **2.** the attitude or beliefs of a cynical person **3.** a cynical remark, idea, or action
cy·no·sure (sī′nə shoor′, sin′ə-) [L. < Gr. *kynosoura*, dog's tail] [C-] *an old name for:* **1.** URSA MINOR **2.** NORTH STAR —***n.*** any person or thing that is a center of attention or interest
Cyn·thi·a (sin′thē ə) [L. < Gr. *Kynthia*, epithet of Artemis] **1.** a feminine name **2.** Artemis, goddess of the moon **3.** the moon personified
cy·pher (sī′fər) ***n., vt., vi. Brit. var. of*** CIPHER
cy·press (sī′prəs) ***n.*** [< OFr. < L. *cupressus* < Gr. *kyparissos*] **1.** any of a group of dark-foliaged, cone-bearing evergreens, native to N. America, Europe, and Asia **2.** any of a number of related trees **3.** the wood of any of these **4.** cypress branches used as a symbol of mourning
cyp·ri·noid (sip′rə noid′) ***adj.*** [< Gr. *kyprinos*, carp + -OID] of or like the fishes of the carp family —***n.*** any of a family of freshwater fishes, including the carps, minnows, dace, etc. Also **cyp′ri·nid** (-nid)
cyp·ri·pe·di·um (sip′rə pē′dē əm) ***n.***, *pl.* **-di·ums, -di·a** (-ə) [ModL. < Gr. *Kypris*, Venus + *podion*, slipper] *same as* LADY-SLIPPER
Cy·prus (sī′prəs) country on an island at the E end of the Mediterranean: a member of the Commonwealth: 3,572 sq. mi.; pop. 630,000; cap. Nicosia —**Cyp·ri·ot** (sip′rē ət) ***adj., n.***
Cy·ril (sir′əl) [< Gr. < *kyrios*, lord] a masculine name
Cy·ril·lic (sə ril′ik) ***adj.*** designating or of the Slavic alphabet attributed to Saint Cyril, 9th-cent. apostle to the Slavs: it is used in Russia, Bulgaria, and other Slavic countries
Cy·rus (sī′rəs) [L. < Gr. < OPer. *Kūrush*] **1.** a masculine name **2.** ?–529 B.C.; king of the Medes & Persians: founded Persian Empire: called *the Great*
cyst (sist) ***n.*** [ModL. *cystis* < Gr. *kystis*, sac] **1.** any of certain saclike structures in plants or animals; specif., such a structure when abnormal and filled with fluid or diseased matter **2.** a protective membrane surrounding certain organisms in a resting stage —**cyst′ic** ***adj.*** —**cyst′oid** ***adj., n.***
-cyst (sist) [see prec.] *a suffix meaning* sac, pouch, bladder *[encyst]*
cys·ti·cer·cus (sis′tə sur′kəs) ***n.***, *pl.* **-cer′ci** (-sī) [ModL. < CYSTI- (see CYSTO-) + Gr. *kerkos*, tail] the larva of certain tapeworms having the head and neck partly enclosed in a cyst
cystic fibrosis a congenital disease of children, characterized by fibrosis and malfunctioning of the pancreas, and frequent respiratory infections
cys·ti·tis (sis tīt′is) ***n.*** [CYST- + -ITIS] an inflammation of the urinary bladder
cys·to- [see CYST] *a combining form meaning* of or like a bladder or sac: also **cyst-, cysti-**
cys·to·scope (sis′tə skōp′) ***n.*** [CYSTO- + -SCOPE] an instrument for visually examining the interior of the urinary bladder —***vt.*** **-scoped′, -scop′ing** to examine with a cystoscope —**cys′to·scop′ic** (-skäp′ik) ***adj.*** —**cys·tos′co·py** (-täs′kə pē) ***n.***
-cyte (sīt) [< Gr. *kytos*, a hollow] *a combining form meaning* a cell *[lymphocyte]*
Cyth·e·re·a (sith′ə rē′ə) *same as* APHRODITE —**Cyth′e·re′an** ***adj.***
cy·to- [see -CYTE] *a combining form meaning* of a cell or cells: also, before a vowel, **cyt-**
cy·to·ge·net·ics (sīt′ō jə net′iks) ***n.pl.*** [*with sing. v.*] the science correlating cytology and genetics with regard to heredity and variation —**cy′to·ge·net′ic, cy′to·ge·net′i·cal** ***adj.*** —**cy′to·ge·net′i·cal·ly** ***adv.*** —**cy′to·ge·net′i·cist** ***n.***
cy·tol·o·gy (sī täl′ə jē) ***n.*** [CYTO- + -LOGY] the branch of biology dealing with the structure, function, pathology, and life history of cells —**cy·to·log·ic** (sīt′ə läj′ik), **cy′to·log′i·cal** ***adj.*** —**cy′to·log′i·cal·ly** ***adv.*** —**cy·tol′o·gist** ***n.***
cy·to·plasm (sīt′ə plaz'm) ***n.*** [CYTO- + -PLASM] the protoplasm of a cell, exclusive of the nucleus: also **cy′to·plast′** —**cy′to·plas′mic** ***adj.***
cy·to·sine (sīt′ə sēn′) ***n.*** [G. *zytosin*] a nitrogenous base, $C_4H_5N_3O$, a constituent of various nucleic acids
C.Z., CZ Canal Zone
czar (zär) ***n.*** [< Russ. < OSlav. via Goth. < L. *Caesar*] **1.** an emperor: title of any of the former emperors of Russia **2.** an absolute ruler; despot —**czar′dom** ***n.*** —**czar′ism** ***n.*** —**czar′ist** ***adj., n.***
czar·das (chär′dəsh, -däsh) ***n.*** [Hung. *csárdás*] **1.** a Hungarian dance with fast and slow sections **2.** music for this dance
czar·e·vitch (zär′ə vich′) ***n.*** [< Russ.] the eldest son of a czar of Russia
cza·ri·na (zä rē′nə) ***n.*** [< G. < Russ. *tsaritsa*] the wife of a czar; empress of Russia: also **cza·rit′za** (-rit′sə)
Czech (chek) ***n.*** **1.** a Bohemian, Moravian, or Silesian Slav of Czechoslovakia **2.** the West Slavic language of the Czechs —***adj.*** of Czechoslovakia, its people, or their language: also **Czech′ish**
Czech·o·slo·vak (chek′ə slō′väk) ***adj.*** of Czechoslovakia or its people —***n.*** a Czech or Slovak living in Czechoslovakia Also **Czech′o·slo·vak′i·an** (-slō vä′kē ən)
Czech·o·slo·va·ki·a (chek′ə slō vä′kē ə) country in C Europe, east of Germany: 49,367 sq. mi.; pop. 14,445,000; cap. Prague

D

D, d (dē) ***n.***, *pl.* **D's, d's** **1.** the fourth letter of the English alphabet **2.** the sound of *D* or *d* **3.** *a symbol for* the fourth in a sequence or group
D (dē) ***n.*** **1.** a Roman numeral for 500 **2.** *Chem.* deuterium **3.** *Educ.* a grade indicating below-average work, or merely passing **4.** *Music a)* the second tone in the ascending scale of C major *b)* the scale having this tone as the keynote **5.** *Physics the symbol for* density
D. **1.** December **2.** Democrat(ic) **3.** Dutch
d. **1.** daughter **2.** day(s) **3.** dead **4.** delete **5.** diameter **6.** died **7.** dose **8.** dyne **9.** [L. *denarius*, pl. *denarii*] penny; pence
'd **1.** *contracted auxiliary form of* had or would *[I'd, they'd]* **2.** *contraction of* -ed *[foster'd]*
D.A. District Attorney
dab[1] (dab) ***vt., vi.*** **dabbed, dab′bing** [ME. *dabben*, to strike] **1.** to touch lightly and quickly **2.** to pat with something soft or moist **3.** to put on (paint, etc.) with light, quick strokes —***n.*** **1.** a light, quick stroke; tap; pat **2.** a bit, esp. of a soft or moist thing *[a* dab *of rouge]* —**dab′ber** ***n.***
dab[2] (dab) ***n.*** [ME. *dabbe* < ?] **1.** any of several flounders of coastal waters **2.** any small flatfish
dab·ble (dab′'l) ***vt.*** **-bled, -bling** [Du. *dabbelen*, freq. of *dabben*, to strike, DAB[1]] **1.** to dip lightly in and out of a liquid **2.** to spatter or splash —***vi.*** **1.** to play in water, as with the hands **2.** to do something superficially (with *in* or *at*) *[to* dabble *in art]* —**dab′bler** ***n.***
dab·chick (dab′chik′) ***n.*** [DAB[1] + CHICK] either of two small grebes of Europe and the Americas
‡da ca·po (dä kä′pô) [It.] *Music* from the beginning: a direction to repeat
Dac·ca (dak′ə, däk′ə) capital of Bangladesh, in the EC part: pop. 557,000
dace (dās) ***n.***, *pl.* **dace, dac′es:** see PLURAL, II, D, 2 [< OFr.

dars < VL. *darsus*] a small freshwater fish of the carp family

‡**da·cha** (dä′chə) ***n.*** [Russ.] a country house or cottage used as a summer home

Da·chau (dä′khou) city in S Germany: site of a Nazi concentration camp & extermination center

dachs·hund (däks′hoond, -hoont; dash′hund) ***n.*** [G. *dachs,* a badger + *hund,* a dog] a small dog of German breed, with a long body and short legs

DACHSHUND (8–10 in. high at shoulder)

Da·cron (dā′krän, dak′rän) [arbitrary coinage, after (NYL)ON] *a trademark for* a synthetic polyester fiber or a washable, wrinkle-resistant fabric made from it —***n.*** [*also* **d-**] this fiber or fabric

dac·tyl (dak′t′l) ***n.*** [< L. < Gr. *daktylos,* a finger or (by analogy with a finger's three joints) a dactyl] a metrical foot of three syllables, the first accented and the others unaccented, as in English verse (Ex.: "táke hĕr ŭp/ téndĕrlў̆") —**dac·tyl′ic** ***adj.***

dad (dad) ***n.*** [< child's cry *dada*] [Colloq.] father: also **dad·dy** (dad′ē), *pl.* **-dies**

da·da (dä′dä, -də) ***n.*** [Fr., lit., hobbyhorse < baby talk] [*also* **D-**] a cult (1916–22) in art and literature characterized by fantastic, abstract, or incongruous creations and by nihilistic satire: also **da′da·ism** —**da′da·ist** ***adj., n.*** —**da′da·is′tic** ***adj.***

dad·dy-long·legs (dad′ē lôŋ′legz′) ***n.,*** *pl.* **-long′legs′** *same as:* **1.** HARVESTMAN (sense 2) **2.** CRANE FLY

da·do (dā′dō) ***n.,*** *pl.* **-does** [< It. < L. *datum,* a die] **1.** the part of a pedestal between the cap and the base **2.** the lower part of the wall of a room if decorated differently from the upper part **3.** *a)* a rectangular groove cut in the side of one board so that another board may be fitted into it *b)* the joint thus made: in full, **dado joint** —***vt.*** **-doed, -do·ing** **1.** to furnish with a dado **2.** to fit into a dado groove

Daed·a·lus (ded′'l əs, dēd′-) *Gr. Myth.* the builder of the Labyrinth in Crete from which, by means of wings he fabricated, he and his son Icarus escaped —**Dae·da·li·an, Dae·da·le·an** (di dāl′yən, -ē ən) ***adj.***

dae·mon (dē′mən) ***n.*** [L. < Gr. *daimōn*] **1.** *Gr. Myth.* any of the secondary divinities ranking below the gods **2.** a guardian spirit **3.** *same as* DEMON —**dae·mon·ic** (di män′ik) ***adj.***

daf·fa·down·dil·ly, daf·fy·down·dil·ly (daf′ə doun dil′ē) ***n.,*** *pl.* **-lies** [Dial.] a daffodil: also **daf′fo·dil′ly, daf′fa·dil′ly,** *pl.* **-lies**

daf·fo·dil (daf′ə dil′) ***n.*** [< ML. < L. < Gr. *asphodelos*] **1.** any of several hardy kinds of narcissus, typically having a single, yellow flower and a large, trumpetlike central crown **2.** the flower

daf·fy (daf′ē) ***adj.*** **-fi·er, -fi·est** [see ff.] [Colloq.] **1.** crazy; foolish; silly **2.** frolicsome in a giddy way —**daf′fi·ness** ***n.***

daft (daft) ***adj.*** [< OE. *(ge)dæfte,* mild, gentle] **1.** silly; foolish **2.** insane; crazy —**daft′ly** ***adv.*** —**daft′ness** ***n.***

da Gam·a (də gam′ə; *Port.* dä gä′mä), **Vas·co** (väs′kō) 1469?–1524; Port. navigator

dag·ger (dag′ər) ***n.*** [< ML. *daggarius*] **1.** a weapon with a short, pointed blade, used for stabbing **2.** *Printing* a reference mark (†) —***vt.*** **1.** to stab with a dagger **2.** to mark with a dagger —**look daggers at** to look at with anger or hatred

Da·gon (dā′gän) [< LL. < LGr. < Heb.] the main god of the ancient Philistines, represented as half man and half fish

da·guerre·o·type (də ger′ə tīp′) ***n.*** [after L. J. M. *Daguerre* (1789–1851), Fr. inventor] **1.** a photograph made by an early method on a plate of chemically treated metal or glass **2.** this method —***vt.*** **-typed′, -typ′ing** to photograph by this method —**da·guerre′o·typ′y** ***n.***

Dag·wood (sandwich) (dag′wood′) [after a character in a comic strip by Chic Young (1901–73)] a tall sandwich with a wide variety of ingredients

dahl·ia (dal′yə, däl′-; *chiefly Brit.* dāl′-) ***n.*** [after A. *Dahl,* 18th-c. Swed. botanist] **1.** a perennial plant of the composite family, with tuberous roots and large, showy flowers **2.** the flower

Da·ho·mey (də hō′mē) *former name of* BENIN

Dail Eir·eann (dôl′er′ən) [Ir. *dāil,* assembly + *Éireann,* gen. of *Éire,* Ireland] the lower house of the legislature of Ireland

dai·ly (dā′lē) ***adj.*** **1.** relating to, done, happening, or published every day or every weekday **2.** calculated by the day [*daily* rate] —***n.,*** *pl.* **-lies** a daily newspaper —***adv.*** every day; day after day

daily double a betting procedure or bet, the success of which depends on choosing both winners in two specified races on the same program

daily dozen [Colloq.] gymnastic setting-up exercises (originally twelve) done daily

dain·ty (dān′tē) ***n.,*** *pl.* **-ties** [< OFr. *deinté,* worth, delicacy < L. *dignitas,* worth, dignity] a choice food; delicacy —***adj.*** **1.** delicious and choice **2.** delicately pretty or lovely **3.** *a)* of or showing delicate and refined taste *b)* overly fastidious; squeamish —**dain′ti·ly** ***adv.*** —**dain′ti·ness** ***n.***

dai·qui·ri (dak′ər ē, dīk′-) ***n.*** [after *Daiquirī,* village in Cuba] a cocktail made of rum, sugar, and lime or lemon juice

dair·y (der′ē) ***n.,*** *pl.* **dair′ies** [ME. *daierie* < *daie,* dairymaid < OE. *dæge,* breadmaker] **1.** a room, building, etc. where milk and cream are kept and butter, cheese, etc. are made **2.** a farm **(dairy farm)** in the business of producing milk and milk products **3.** *a)* a commercial establishment that processes and distributes milk and milk products *b)* a retail store where these are sold —***adj.*** of milk, cream, butter, cheese, etc.

dairy cattle cows raised mainly for their milk

dair·y·ing (-iŋ) ***n.*** the business of producing or selling dairy products

dair·y·maid (-mād′) ***n.*** a girl or woman who milks cows or works in a dairy

dair·y·man (-mən) ***n.,*** *pl.* **-men** a man who works in or for a dairy or who owns a dairy

da·is (dā′is, dī′-) ***n.,*** *pl.* **da′is·es** [< OFr. < ML. *discus,* table < L. *discus,* DISCUS] a platform raised above the floor at one end of a hall or room, as for a speaker's stand, seats of honor, etc.

Dai·sy (dā′zē) [< ff.] a feminine name

dai·sy (dā′zē) ***n.,*** *pl.* **-sies** [< OE. *dæges eage,* lit., day's eye] **1.** a plant of the composite family, bearing flowers with white rays around a yellow disk **2.** any similar member of the composite family **3.** the flower of any of these plants —**push up (the) daisies** [Slang] to be dead and buried

Da·kar (dä kär′, dak′är) capital of Senegal, at the westernmost point of Africa: pop. 474,000

Da·ko·ta[1] (də kō′tə) ***n.*** [< Dakota *dakóta,* allies] **1.** *pl.* **-tas, -ta** a member of a group of Indian tribes (also called *Sioux*) of the northern plains of the U.S. and adjacent S Canada **2.** their Siouan language —***adj.*** **1.** of the Dakota Indians or their language **2.** of North Dakota, South Dakota, or both —**the Dakotas** North Dakota and South Dakota —**Da·ko′tan** ***adj., n.***

Da·ko·ta[2] (də kō′tə) [< prec.] former U.S. territory from which N.Dak. & S.Dak. were formed in 1889

Da·lai La·ma (dä lī′ lä′mə) [Mongol. *dalai,* ocean + *blama:* see LAMA] the traditional high priest of the Lamaist religion: see LAMAISM

da·la·si (da′la sē) ***n.,*** *pl.* **-si** [native term, lit., complete] *see* MONETARY UNITS, table (Gambia)

dale (dāl) ***n.*** [OE. *dæl*] a valley

d'A·lem·bert (dȧ län ber′), **Jean le Rond** (zhän lə rōn′) 1717–83; Fr. philosopher & encyclopedist

Da·li (dä′lē), **Sal·va·dor** (sal′və dôr′) 1904– ; Sp. surrealist painter

Dal·las (dal′əs) [after G. *Dallas* (1792–1864), U.S. vice president (1845–49)] city in NE Tex: pop. 904,000 (met. area, with Fort Worth, 2,964,000)

dal·li·ance (dal′ē əns) ***n.*** the act of dallying; flirting, toying, trifling, etc.

dal·ly (dal′ē) ***vi.*** **-lied, -ly·ing** [< OFr. *dalier,* to converse, trifle] **1.** to make love in a playful way **2.** to deal lightly or carelessly (*with*); trifle; toy **3.** to waste time; loiter —**dally away** to waste (time) in trifling activities

Dal·ma·tia (dal mā′shə) region along the Adriatic coast of Yugoslavia: part of Croatia

Dal·ma·tian (-shən) ***adj.*** of Dalmatia or its people —***n.*** a large, short-haired dog with dark spots on a white coat

‡**dal se·gno** (däl se′nyô) [It.] *Music* from the sign: a direction to return and repeat from the sign (𝄋)

Da·ly City (dā′lē) [after a prominent citizen, J. *Daly*] city in W Calif.: suburb of San Francisco: pop. 79,000

dam[1] (dam) ***n.*** [< Gmc. base seen in ON. *dammr,* to stop up] **1.** a barrier built to hold back flowing water **2.** the water thus kept back **3.** any barrier like a dam —***vt.*** **dammed, dam′ming** **1.** to build a dam in **2.** to keep back or confine as by a dam (usually with *up*)

dam[2] (dam) ***n.*** [ME., var. of *dame,* DAME] **1.** the female parent of any four-legged animal **2.** [Archaic] a mother

dam·age (dam′ij) ***n.*** [OFr. < L. *damnum,* loss, injury] **1.** injury or harm resulting in a loss in soundness, value, etc. **2.** [*pl.*] *Law* money claimed by, or ordered paid to, a person to compensate for injury, loss, etc. that is another's fault **3.** [Colloq.] cost or expense —***vt.*** **-aged, -ag·ing** to do damage to —***vi.*** to incur damage —**dam′age·a·ble** ***adj.***

Dam·a·scene (dam′ə sēn′, dam′ə sēn′) ***adj.*** [L. *Damascenus,* of Damascus] **1.** of Damascus, its people, etc. **2.** [**d-**] of damascening or damask —***n.*** **1.** a native or inhabitant of Damascus **2.** [**d-**] damascened work —***vt.*** **-scened′, -scen′ing** [**d-**] to decorate (steel, etc.) with wavy markings or with inlaid patterns of gold or silver

Da·mas·cus (də mas′kəs) capital of Syria, a very ancient city in the SC part: pop. 530,000

Damascus steel a hard, flexible steel decorated with wavy lines, orig. made in Damascus and used for sword blades: also **damask steel**

dam·ask (dam′əsk) *n.* [< It. < L. *Damascus* (the city)] **1.** a durable, lustrous, reversible fabric as of silk or linen, in figured weave, used for table linen, upholstery, etc. **2.** *a)* *same as* DAMASCUS STEEL *b)* the wavy markings of such steel **3.** deep pink or rose —*adj.* **1.** orig., of or from Damascus **2.** made of damask **3.** like damask **4.** deep-pink or rose —*vt.* **1.** to ornament with flowered designs or wavy lines **2.** to make deep-pink or rose

damask rose a very fragrant rose important as a source of attar of roses

dame (dām) *n.* [OFr. < L. *domina,* lady, fem. of *dominus,* a lord] **1.** orig., a title given to the mistress of a household **2.** a lady **3.** an elderly woman **4.** [D-] in Great Britain *a)* the legal title of the wife of a knight or baronet *b)* the title of a woman who has received an order of knighthood **5.** [Slang] a woman or girl

damn (dam) *vt.* **damned, damn′ing** [< OFr. < L. *damnare,* to condemn < *damnum,* loss] **1.** *a)* to condemn to an unhappy fate; doom *b)* *Theol.* to condemn to endless punishment **2.** to condemn as bad, inferior, etc. **3.** to criticize adversely **4.** to cause the ruin of; make fail **5.** to swear at by saying "damn" —*vi.* to swear or curse; say "damn," etc. —*n.* the saying of "damn" as a curse —*adj., adv.* [Colloq.] *clipped form of* DAMNED —*interj.* an expression of anger, annoyance, disappointment, etc. —**damn with faint praise** to condemn by praising mildly —**not give** (or **care**) **a damn** [Colloq.] not care at all —**not worth a damn** [Colloq.] worthless

dam·na·ble (dam′nə b'l) *adj.* deserving to be damned; outrageous; execrable —**dam′na·bly** *adv.*

dam·na·tion (dam nā′shən) *n.* a damning or being damned —*interj.* an expression of anger, annoyance, etc.

dam·na·to·ry (dam′nə tôr′ē) *adj.* **1.** threatening with damnation; damning **2.** condemning *[damnatory* evidence*]*

damned (damd; *occas.* dam′nid) *adj.* **1.** condemned or deserving condemnation **2.** [Colloq.] deserving cursing; outrageous: now often a mere intensive *[a damned* shame*]* —*adv.* [Colloq.] very *[a damned* good job*]* —**do** (or **try**) **one's damnedest** (or **damndest**) [Colloq.] to do or try one's utmost —**the damned** *Theol.* souls doomed to eternal punishment

Dam·o·cles (dam′ə klēz′) a courtier of ancient Syracuse who, according to legend, was given a lesson in the perils to a ruler's life when the king seated him at a feast under a sword hanging by a hair —**sword of Damocles** any imminent danger

dam·oi·selle, dam·o·sel, dam·o·zel (dam′ə zel′) *n.* [Archaic or Poet.] a damsel

Da·mon and Pyth·i·as (dā′mən ən pith′ē əs) *Classical Legend* friends so devoted to each other that when Pythias, who had been condemned to death, wanted time to arrange his affairs, Damon pledged his life that his friend would return

damp (damp) *n.* [MDu., vapor] **1.** a slight wetness; moisture **2.** any harmful gas in a mine; firedamp, blackdamp, etc. —*adj.* somewhat moist or wet; humid —*vt.* **1.** to make damp; moisten **2.** to reduce or check (energy, action, etc., as fire in a furnace or the vibration of a piano string) —**damp′ish** *adj.* —**damp′ly** *adv.* —**damp′ness** *n.*

damp-dry (-drī′) *vt.* **-dried′, -dry′ing** to dry (laundry) so that some moisture is retained —*adj.* designating or of laundry so treated

damp·en (dam′pən) *vt.* **1.** to make damp; moisten **2.** to deaden, depress, reduce, or lessen —*vi.* to become damp

damp·er (-pər) *n.* [see DAMP] **1.** anything that deadens or depresses **2.** a movable plate or valve in the flue of a stove or furnace, for controlling the draft **3.** a device to check vibration in the strings of a piano, etc. **4.** a device for lessening the oscillation of a magnetic needle, a moving coil, etc.

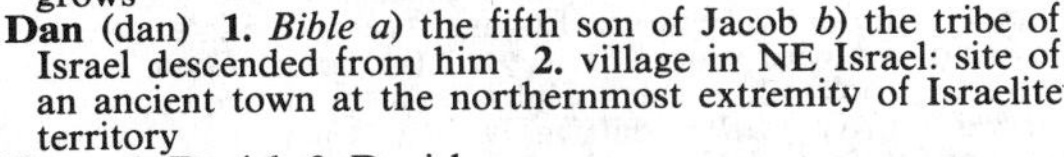
DAMPER

dam·sel (dam′z'l) *n.* [< OFr. *dameisele* < L. *domina:* see DAME] [Archaic or Poet.] a girl; maiden

dam·son (dam′z'n, -s'n) *n.* [< OFr. < L. *Damascenus,* (plum) of Damascus] **1.** a variety of small, purple plum **2.** the tree on which it grows

Dan (dan) **1.** *Bible a)* the fifth son of Jacob *b)* the tribe of Israel descended from him **2.** village in NE Israel: site of an ancient town at the northernmost extremity of Israelite territory

Dan. 1. Daniel **2.** Danish

Da·na·i·des, Da·na·ï·des (də nā′ə dēz′) *n.pl., sing.* **Dan·a·id, Dan·a·ïd** (dan′ē id) *Gr. Myth.* the fifty daughters of Danaus, a king of Argos: forty-nine murdered their husbands at their father's command and were condemned in Hades to keep drawing water with a sieve

Dan·a·us (dan′ē əs) *see* DANAIDES

Dan·bur·y (dan′ber′ē, -bər ē) [after *Danbury,* town in England] city in SW Conn., near Bridgeport: pop. 60,000

dance (dans) *vi.* **danced, danc′ing** [< OFr. *danser*] **1.** to move the body and feet in rhythm, ordinarily to music **2.** to move lightly, rapidly, or gaily about, as leaves in a wind **3.** to bob up and down —*vt.* **1.** to take part in or perform (a dance) **2.** to cause to dance —*n.* **1.** rhythmic movement of the body and feet, ordinarily to music **2.** a particular kind of dance, as the waltz, tango, etc. **3.** the art of dancing **4.** one round of a dance **5.** a party to which people come to dance **6.** a piece of music for dancing **7.** rapid, lively movement —**dance attendance on** to be always near so as to lavish attentions on —**dance to another tune** to alter one's actions or opinions as a result of changed conditions —**danc′er** *n.*

D and C dilatation (of the cervix) and curettage (of the uterus)

dan·de·li·on (dan′də lī′ən, -dē-) *n.* [< OFr. *dent de lion* < L. *dens* (gen. *dentis*), tooth + *de,* of + *leo,* lion] a common weed with jagged leaves, often used as greens, and yellow flowers

dan·der (dan′dər) *n.* [< ?] [Colloq.] anger or temper —**get one's dander up** [Colloq.] to become or make angry; lose, or make lose, one's temper

dan·di·fy (dan′də fī′) *vt.* **-fied′, -fy′ing** to dress up like a dandy —**dan′di·fi·ca′tion** *n.*

dan·dle (dan′d'l) *vt.* **-dled, -dling** [< ? OIt. *dandolare,* to dally] **1.** to dance (a child) up and down on the knee or in the arms **2.** to fondle; pet

dan·druff (dan′drəf) *n.* [< earlier *dandro* (< ?) + dial. *hurf,* scab] little scales or flakes of dead skin formed on the scalp —**dan′druff·y** *adj.*

dan·dy (dan′dē) *n., pl.* **-dies** [Scot. var. of *Andy* < *Andrew* (see MERRY-ANDREW)] **1.** a man overly attentive to his clothes and appearance; fop **2.** [Colloq.] something very good or first-rate —*adj.* **-di·er, -di·est** [Colloq.] very good; first-rate —**dan′dy·ish** *adj.* —**dan′dy·ism** *n.*

Dane (dān) *n.* a native or inhabitant of Denmark

Dane·law, Dane·lagh (-lô′) *n.* the law code enforced in NE England by Danish invaders in the 9th and 10th cent. A.D.; also, this part of England

dan·ger (dān′jər) *n.* [< OFr. < L. < *dominus,* a master] **1.** liability to injury, damage, loss, or pain **2.** a thing that may cause injury, pain, etc.

dan·ger·ous (-əs) *adj.* full of danger; unsafe; perilous —**dan′ger·ous·ly** *adv.* —**dan′ger·ous·ness** *n.*

dan·gle (daŋ′g'l) *vi.* **-gled, -gling** [< Scand.] **1.** to hang swinging loosely **2.** to be a hanger-on; follow (*after*) **3.** *Gram.* to lack clear connection, as one sentence element modifying another *[a dangling* participle*]* —*vt.* to cause to dangle —**dan′gler** *n.*

Dan·iel (dan′yəl) [Heb. *dānī'ēl,* lit., God is my judge] **1.** a masculine name: dim. *Dan* **2.** *Bible a)* a Hebrew prophet whose faith saved him in the lions' den *b)* the book containing his story

Dan·ish (dā′nish) *adj.* of Denmark, the Danes, or their language —*n.* **1.** the language of the Danes **2.** [*also* **d-**] *clipped form of* DANISH PASTRY

Danish pastry [*also* **d- p-**] a rich, flaky pastry of raised dough filled with fruit, cheese, etc. and usually topped with icing

dank (daŋk) *adj.* [ME., akin to ON.] disagreeably damp; moist and chilly —**dank′ly** *adv.* —**dank′ness** *n.*

dan·seuse (dän sooz′; *Fr.* dän söz′) *n., pl.* **-seus′es** (-sooz′əz; *Fr.* -söz′) [Fr.] a girl or woman dancer, esp. a ballet dancer

Dan·te (Alighieri) (dän′tā, -tē; dan′tē; *It.* dän′te) 1265–1321; It. poet: wrote *The Divine Comedy* —**Dan′te·an** *adj., n.* —**Dan·tesque′** (-tesk′) *adj.*

Dan·ube (dan′yo͞ob) river in S Europe, flowing from SW Germany eastward into the Black Sea: c. 1,770 mi. —**Da·nu′bi·an** *adj.*

Dan·zig (dan′sig; *G.* dän′tsiH) *German name of* GDAŃSK

Daph·ne (daf′nē) [L. < Gr. *daphnē,* the laurel tree] **1.** a feminine name **2.** *Gr. Myth.* a nymph who escaped from Apollo by becoming a laurel tree

dap·per (dap′ər) *adj.* [< ? MDu. *dapper,* nimble] **1.** small and active **2.** trim, neat, or smart in appearance —**dap′per·ly** *adv.* —**dap′per·ness** *n.*

dap·ple (dap′'l) *adj.* [< ON. *depill,* a spot < *dapi,* a pool] marked or variegated with spots; mottled: also **dap′pled** —*n.* **1.** a spotted condition **2.** an animal with skin that is spotted —*vt., vi.* **-pled, -pling** to cover or become covered with spots

dap·ple-gray (-grā′) *adj.* gray spotted with darker gray —*n.* a dapple-gray horse

DAR, D.A.R. Daughters of the American Revolution

Dar·by and Joan (där′bē ən jōn′) [< an 18th-cent. song] an old married couple devoted to each other

Dar·da·nelles (där′də nelz′) strait between the Aegean Sea & the Sea of Marmara

dare (der, dar) *vi.* **dared** or archaic **durst** (durst), **dared, dar′-ing;** 3d pers. sing., pres. indic., **dare** or **dares** [< OE. *dear,* 1st pers. sing. of *durran,* to dare] to have enough courage or audacity for some act; be fearless —*vt.* **1.** to have courage for; venture upon **2.** to oppose and defy [he *dared* the wrath of the tyrant] **3.** to test the courage of (someone) with a dare —*n.* a challenge to do a hard, dangerous, or rash thing as a test of courage —**dare say** to think likely or probable; suppose [I *dare say* you're right] —**dar′er** *n.*

dare·dev·il (-dev′'l) *adj.* bold and reckless —*n.* a bold, reckless person —**dare′dev′il·ry, dare′dev′il·try** *n.*

Dar es Sa·laam (där′ es sə läm′) capital of Tanzania, on the Indian Ocean: pop. 373,000

dar·ing (der′iŋ, dar′-) *adj.* having or showing a bold willingness to take risks, etc.; fearless —*n.* bold courage —**dar′-ing·ly** *adv.*

Da·ri·us I (də rī′əs) 550?–486? B.C.; king of Persia (521–486?): called *the Great*

Dar·jee·ling (där jē′liŋ) *n.* a fine variety of tea from Darjeeling, a district in NE India

dark (därk) *adj.* [< OE. *deorc*] **1.** entirely or partly without light **2.** neither giving nor receiving light **3.** giving no performance [this theater is *dark* tonight] **4.** *a)* almost black *b)* not light in color; deep in shade **5.** not fair in complexion; brunet **6.** hidden; secret **7.** not easily understood **8.** gloomy; dismal **9.** angry or sullen **10.** evil; sinister **11.** ignorant; unenlightened —*n.* **1.** the state of being dark **2.** night; nightfall **3.** a dark color or shade —**in the dark** uninformed; ignorant —**keep dark** to keep secret or hidden —**dark′ish** *adj.* —**dark′ly** *adv.* —**dark′ness** *n.*

Dark Ages, dark ages the Middle Ages; esp., the early part from 476 A.D. to the late 10th cent.

dark·en (där′kən) *vt., vi.* to make or become dark or darker —**not darken one's door** (or **doorway**) not come to one's home —**dark′en·er** *n.*

dark horse [Colloq.] **1.** an unexpected, almost unknown winner, as in a horse race **2.** *Politics* a person who gets or may get the nomination unexpectedly, often by a compromise

dark lantern a lantern with a shutter that can hide the light

dark·ling (därk′liŋ) *adv.* [DARK + -LING[2]] [Poet.] in the dark —*adj.* [Poet.] dark, dim, obscure, etc.

dark·room (därk′ro͞om′) *n.* a room from which all actinic rays are excluded, where photographs can be developed

dark·some (-səm) *adj.* [Poet.] **1.** dark; darkish **2.** dismal; gloomy

Dar·ling (där′liŋ) river in SE Australia, flowing southwest into the Murray River

dar·ling (där′liŋ) *n.* [OE. *deorling,* dim. of *deore,* DEAR] **1.** a person much loved by another **2.** a favorite or a lovable person —*adj.* **1.** very dear; beloved **2.** [Colloq.] cute; attractive [a *darling* dress]

darn[1] (därn) *vt., vi.* [< MFr. dial. *darner,* to mend] to mend (cloth, etc.) or repair (a hole in cloth) by sewing a network of stitches across the gap —*n.* a darned place in fabric —**darn′er** *n.*

darn[2] (därn) *vt., vi., n., adj., adv., interj.* [Colloq.] *a euphemism for* DAMN (the curse) —**darned** *adj., adv.*

dar·nel (där′n'l) *n.* [< Fr. dial. *darnelle*] a weedy rye grass often found in grainfields: a certain fungus can make the seeds poisonous

darn·ing (där′niŋ) *n.* **1.** a mending with interlaced stitches **2.** things to be darned

darning needle **1.** a large needle for darning **2.** *same as* DRAGONFLY

Dar·row (dar′ō), **Clarence** 1857–1938; U.S. lawyer

dart (därt) *n.* [< OFr.] **1.** a small, pointed missile for throwing or shooting **2.** anything resembling this **3.** a sudden, quick movement **4.** a short, tapered, stitched fold to make a garment fit more closely **5.** [*pl., with sing. v.*] a game in which a number of darts (sense 1) are thrown at a target —*vt., vi.* **1.** to throw, shoot, send out, etc. suddenly and fast **2.** to move suddenly and fast

dart·er (-ər) *n.* **1.** a thing or animal that darts **2.** a tropical diving bird with a long, pointed bill and a long neck **3.** any of various small, brightly colored freshwater fishes of N. America

dar·tle (därt′'l) *vt., vi.* **-tled, -tling** to dart about

Dart·mouth (därt′məth) city in S Nova Scotia, Canada, near Halifax: pop. 59,000

Dar·von (där′vän) *a trademark for* a pain-killing drug containing aspirin, etc.

Dar·win (där′win), **Charles Robert** 1809–82; Eng. naturalist —**Dar·win′i·an** (-win′ē ən) *adj., n.*

Darwinian theory Darwin's theory of evolution, which holds that all species of plants and animals developed from earlier forms by hereditary transmission of slight variations in successive generations, those forms surviving which are best adapted to the environment (*natural selection*): also called **Dar′win·ism** —**Dar′win·ist** *adj., n.*

dash (dash) *vt.* [< Scand., as in Sw. *daska,* to slap] **1.** to throw so as to break; smash **2.** to strike violently (*against*) **3.** to throw, thrust, etc. (with *away, down,* etc.) **4.** to splash (liquid) on (someone or something) **5.** to mix with a little of another substance **6.** to destroy; frustrate [to *dash* one's hopes] **7.** to depress; discourage **8.** to put to shame; abash **9.** [Colloq.] *a euphemism for* DAMN —*vi.* **1.** to strike violently (*against* or *on*) **2.** to move swiftly; rush —*n.* **1.** the sound of smashing **2.** a bit of something added **3.** a sudden rush **4.** a short, fast run or race **5.** vigor; verve **6.** showy appearance **7.** *short for* DASHBOARD (sense 2) **8.** the mark (—), used in printing and writing to indicate a break in a sentence, a parenthetical element, an omission, etc. **9.** *Telegraphy* a long sound or signal, as in Morse code: cf. DOT —**dash off** **1.** to do, write, etc. hastily **2.** to rush away —**dash′er** *n.*

dash·board (-bôrd′) *n.* **1.** a screen at the front or side of a carriage, boat, etc., for protection against splashing **2.** a panel with instruments and gauges on it, as in an automobile

dash·ing (-iŋ) *adj.* **1.** full of dash or spirit; lively **2.** showy; stylish —**dash′ing·ly** *adv.*

dash light a light to illuminate a dashboard (sense 2)

das·tard (das′tərd) *n.* [ME., prob. < Scand. base] a sneaky, cowardly evildoer

das·tard·ly (-lē) *adj.* [see prec.] mean, sneaky, cowardly, etc. —**das′tard·li·ness** *n.*

das·y·ure (das′ē yoor′) *n.* [< Gr. *dasys,* hairy + *oura,* tail] a small tree-dwelling marsupial of Australia

dat. dative

da·ta (dāt′ə, dat′ə) *n.pl.* [*often with sing. v.*] [L., things given < pp. of *dare,* to give] things known or assumed; facts or figures from which conclusions can be inferred; information: the sing. form is **datum**

data base (or **bank**) a large collection of data in a computer organized so that it can be expanded, updated, and retrieved rapidly for various uses: also **da′ta·base′, da′ta·bank′** *n.*

data processing the recording and handling of information by means of mechanical or electronic equipment

date[1] (dāt) *n.* [< OFr. < L. *data,* as in *data Romae,* etc., lit., given at Rome, etc., formula used in letters for place and date] **1.** a statement on a writing, coin, etc. of when it was made **2.** the time at which a thing happens or is done **3.** the time that anything lasts **4.** the day of the month **5.** *a)* an appointment for a set time; specif., a social engagement with a person of the opposite sex *b)* the person with whom one has such an engagement —*vt.* **dat′ed, dat′ing** **1.** to mark (a letter, etc.) with a date **2.** to find out or give the date of **3.** to assign a date to **4.** *a)* to show or reveal as typical of a certain period or age *b)* to make seem old-fashioned or out of date **5.** to reckon by dates **6.** to have a social engagement with —*vi.* to belong to, or have origin in, a definite period in the past (usually with *from*) —**out of date** no longer in use; old-fashioned —**to date** until now; as yet —**up to date** in or into agreement with the latest facts, ideas, styles, etc. —**dat′a·ble, date′a·ble** *adj.* —**dat′er** *n.*

date[2] (dāt) *n.* [< OFr. < L. < Gr. *daktylos,* a date, lit., a finger] **1.** the sweet, fleshy fruit of a cultivated palm (**date palm**) **2.** the tree itself

date·less (-lis) *adj.* **1.** without a date **2.** without limit or end **3.** too old for its date to be fixed **4.** still good or interesting though old

date·line (-līn′) *n.* **1.** the date and place of writing or issue, as given in a line in a newspaper, a dispatch, etc. **2.** *same as* DATE LINE —*vt.* **-lined′, -lin′ing** to furnish with a dateline

date line an imaginary line drawn north and south through the Pacific Ocean, largely along the 180th meridian: at this line, by international agreement, each calendar day begins at midnight, so that when it is Sunday just west of the line, it is Saturday just east of it

da·tive (dāt′iv) *adj.* [L. *dativus,* of giving < *datus,* pp. of *dare,* to give] designating, of, or in that case of a noun, pronoun, or adjective which expresses the indirect object of a verb and, in many languages, approach toward something —*n.* **1.** the dative case: in English, the dative is expressed by *to* or by word order (Ex.: I gave the book *to him,* I gave *him* the book) **2.** a word or phrase in the dative case —**da·ti·val** (dā tī′v'l) *adj.* —**da′tive·ly** *adv.*

da·tum (dāt′əm, dat′-) *n. sing. of* DATA

dau. daughter

daub (dôb) *vt., vi.* [< OFr. < L. *dealbare,* to whitewash < *de-,* intens. + *albus,* white] **1.** to cover or smear with sticky, soft matter, such as plaster, grease, etc. **2.** to smear on (grease, etc.) **3.** to paint coarsely and unskillfully —*n.* **1.** anything daubed on **2.** a daubing stroke or splash **3.** a poorly painted picture —**daub′er** *n.*

Dau·det (dō dā′), **Al·phonse** (äl fōns′) 1840–97; Fr. novelist

daugh·ter (dôt′ər) *n.* [< OE. *dohtor*] **1.** a girl or woman as she is related to either or both parents: sometimes also used of animals **2.** a female descendant **3.** *a)* a daughter-in-law *b)* a stepdaughter **4.** a female thought of as if in the relation of child to parent *[a daughter* of France*]* **5.** anything thought of as like a daughter in relation to its origin —**daugh′ter·li·ness** *n.* —**daugh′ter·ly** *adj.*

daugh·ter-in-law (-in lô′) *n., pl.* **daugh′ters-in-law′** the wife of one's son

Dau·mier (dō myā′), **Ho·no·ré** (ô nô rā′) 1809–79; Fr. painter & caricaturist

daunt (dônt, dänt) *vt.* [< OFr. < L. < *domare,* to tame] to make afraid or discouraged; intimidate; dishearten

daunt·less (-lis) *adj.* that cannot be daunted or discouraged; fearless —**daunt′less·ly** *adv.* —**daunt′less·ness** *n.*

dau·phin (dô′fin; *Fr.* dō fan′) *n.* [Fr., lit., DOLPHIN: orig. a proper name] the eldest son of the king of France: a title used from 1349 to 1830

Dav·en·port (dav′ən pôrt′) [after Col. G. *Davenport,* 19th-c. fur trader] city in E Iowa, on the Mississippi: pop. 103,000

dav·en·port (dav′ən pôrt′) *n.* [< ?] a large sofa, sometimes one convertible into a bed

Da·vid (dā′vid) [Heb. *dāvīd,* lit., beloved] **1.** a masculine name: dim. *Dave, Davy* **2.** *Bible* the second king of Israel, succeeded by his son Solomon **3.** (dȧ vēd′), **Jacques Louis** (zhȧk lwē), 1748–1825; Fr. painter

da Vin·ci (də vin′chē; *It.* dä vēn′chē), **Le·o·nar·do** (lē′ə när′dō; *It.* le′ô när′dô) 1452–1519; It. painter, sculptor, architect, & scientist

Da·vis (dā′vis), **Jefferson** 1808–89; U.S. statesman; president of the Confederacy (1861–65)

dav·it (dav′it) *n.* [< OFr. dim. of *David*] either of a pair of uprights projecting over the side of a ship for suspending, lowering, or raising a boat

DAVITS

Da·vy (dā′vē), Sir **Humphry** 1778–1829; Eng. chemist

Da·vy Jones (dā′vē jōnz′) the spirit of the sea: humorous name given by sailors

Davy Jones's locker (jōn′ziz, jōnz) the bottom of the sea; grave of those drowned or buried at sea

daw (dô) *n.* [ME. *dawe*] *same as* JACKDAW

daw·dle (dôd′'l) *vi., vt.* **-dled, -dling** [< ?] to waste (time) in trifling or by being slow; loiter (often with *away*) —**daw′dler** *n.*

dawn (dôn) *vi.* [< OE. < *dagian,* to become day < *dæg,* DAY] **1.** to begin to be day; grow light **2.** to begin to appear, develop, etc. **3.** to begin to be understood or felt (usually with *on* or *upon*) *[*the meaning *dawned* on me*]* —*n.* **1.** daybreak **2.** the beginning (*of* something)

day (dā) *n.* [< OE. *dæg*] **1.** *a)* the period of light between sunrise and sunset *b)* daylight *c)* sunshine **2.** *a)* the time (24 hours) that it takes the earth to revolve once on its axis: the civil day is from midnight to midnight *b) Astron.* the time that it takes any celestial body to revolve once on its axis **3.** [*often* **D-**] a particular or specified day *[*Memorial *Day]* **4.** [*also pl.*] a period of time; era *[*the best writer of his *day,* in *days* of old*]* **5.** a time of power, glory, success, etc. *[*he has had his *day]* **6.** the time one works each day *[*an eight-hour *day]* **7.** [*pl.*] one's lifetime *[*to spend one's *days* in study*]* —**call it a day** [Colloq.] to stop working for the day —**day after day** every day —**day by day** each day —**day in, day out** every day —**from day to day 1.** from one day to the next **2.** without particular concern about the future

Day·ak (dī′ak) *n. same as* DYAK

day·bed (dā′bed′) *n.* a couch that can also be used as a bed

day·book (-book′) *n.* **1.** a diary or journal **2.** *Bookkeeping* a book used for recording the transactions of each day as they occur

day·break (-brāk′) *n.* the time in the morning when light first appears; dawn

day care daytime care given to preschool children, as at a day nursery, or to the elderly, as at a social agency or nursing home —**day′-care′** *adj.*

day·dream (-drēm′) *n.* **1.** a pleasant, dreamlike thinking or wishing; reverie **2.** a pleasing but visionary notion —*vi.* to have daydreams —**day′dream′er** *n.*

day laborer an unskilled worker paid by the day

day letter a telegram with a minimum charge for fifty words or fewer, sent in the daytime: it is cheaper but slower than a regular telegram

Day-Lew·is (dā′lo͞o′is), **C(ecil)** 1904–72; Brit. poet & novelist, born in Ireland

day·light (-līt′) *n.* **1.** the light of day; sunlight **2.** dawn; daybreak **3.** daytime **4.** full understanding or knowledge of something hidden or obscure **5.** the approaching end of a task, etc. *[*to see *daylight]* **6.** [*pl.*] [Slang] orig., the eyes; hence, consciousness: often used hyperbolically, as in **scare** (or **beat, knock,** etc.) **the daylights out of**

day·light-sav·ing time (-sā′viŋ) standard time that is one hour later than the standard time for a given zone based on Greenwich time: it is used to give an hour more of daylight at the end of the usual working day

day·long (dā′lôŋ′) *adj., adv.* during the whole day

day nursery a nursery school for the daytime care and training of preschool children, as of working mothers

Day of Atonement *same as* YOM KIPPUR

day room a room for recreation, reading, etc., as in a barracks, institution, or the like

days (dāz) *adv.* on every day or most days

day school 1. a school that has classes only in the daytime **2.** a private school whose students live at home and attend classes daily

day·time (dā′tīm′) *n.* the period of daylight

day-to-day (dā′tə dā′) *adj.* everyday; daily

Day·ton (dāt′'n) [after Gen. E. *Dayton* (1737–1807)] city in SW Ohio: pop. 204,000 (met. area 827,000)

day·work (dā′wurk′) *n.* work done (esp. by a domestic worker) and paid for on a daily basis

daze (dāz) *vt.* **dazed, daz′ing** [< ON. *dasast,* to become weary < *dasi,* tired] **1.** to stun or bewilder, as by a shock or blow **2.** to dazzle —*n.* a dazed condition; bewilderment —**daz′ed·ly** *adv.*

daz·zle (daz′'l) *vt.* **daz′zled, daz′zling** [freq. of DAZE] **1.** to overpower or dim the vision of with very bright light or moving lights **2.** to surprise or overpower with brilliant qualities, display, etc. —*vi.* **1.** to be overpowered by glare **2.** to arouse admiration by brilliant display —*n.* **1.** a dazzling **2.** something that dazzles —**daz′zle·ment** *n.* —**daz′zler** *n.* —**daz′zling·ly** *adv.*

db decibel; decibels

dbl. double

DC, D.C., d.c. direct current

D.C., DC District of Columbia

dd., d/d delivered

D.D. 1. demand draft: also **D/D 2.** [L. *Divinitatis Doctor*] Doctor of Divinity

D-day (dē′dā′) *n.* the day for beginning a military operation; specif., June 6, 1944, the day Allied forces invaded W Europe in World War II

DDD a colorless, crystalline insecticide related to DDT but considered to be less toxic to animals

D.D.S. Doctor of Dental Surgery

DDT a powerful insecticide effective upon contact

de- [< Fr. *dé-* or L. *de* < L. *dis-:* see DIS-] *a prefix meaning:* **1.** away from, off *[derail]* **2.** down *[decline]* **3.** wholly, entirely *[defunct]* **4.** reverse the action of; undo *[defrost, decode]*

dea·con (dēk′'n) *n.* [OE. < LL. < Gr. *diakonos,* servant] **1.** a cleric ranking just below a priest in the Roman Catholic and Anglican churches **2.** in certain other Christian churches, a church officer who helps the minister, esp. in secular matters

dea·con·ess (dēk′'n is) *n.* a woman appointed as an assistant in a church, as for helping with the care of the sick and poor of a parish

de·ac·ti·vate (dē ak′tə vāt′) *vt.* **-vat′ed, -vat′ing 1.** to make (an explosive, chemical, etc.) inactive or inoperative **2.** *Mil.* to place (troops, etc.) on nonactive status —**de·ac′ti·va′tion** *n.*

dead (ded) *adj.* [OE.] **1.** no longer living; having died **2.** without life; inanimate *[dead* stones*]* **3.** deathlike **4.** lacking vitality, interest, variety, warmth, brilliance, etc. **5.** without feeling, motion, or power **6.** *a)* extinguished *b)* extinct *[*a *dead* volcano*]* **7.** slack, stagnant, etc. **8.** no longer resilient **9.** no longer used or significant; obsolete *[dead* languages*]* **10.** barren or unprofitable *[dead* soil*]* **11.** unerring; sure *[*a *dead* shot*]* **12.** exact; precise *[dead* center*]* **13.** complete; absolute *[*a *dead* stop*]* **14.** [Colloq.] very tired; exhausted **15.** *Elec. a)* without current *[*a *dead* line*]* *b)* uncharged *[*a *dead* battery*]* **16.** *Sports* no longer in play *[*a *dead* ball*]* —*n.* the time of greatest darkness, most intense cold, etc. *[*the *dead* of night, the *dead* of winter*]* —*adv.* **1.** completely; absolutely *[dead* right*]* **2.** directly; straight *[dead* ahead*]* —**the dead** those who have died —**dead′ness** *n.*

dead·beat (-bēt′) *n.* [Slang] 1. a person who evades paying his debts, etc. 2. a lazy, idle person
dead·en (ded′'n) *vt.* 1. to lessen the vigor or intensity of 2. to make numb 3. to make soundproof —*vi.* to become as if dead; lose vigor, etc.
dead-end (-end′) *adj.* 1. having only one outlet [a *dead-end* street] 2. giving no opportunity for progress [a *dead-end* plan] 3. [Colloq.] [< *Dead End,* a play (1935) by S. Kingsley] of or characteristic of slums or slum life
dead end 1. an end of a street, etc. that has no regular exit 2. an impasse
dead·eye (-ī′) *n.* 1. a round, flat wooden block with three holes in it for the lanyard, used on a ship to fasten the shrouds 2. [Slang] an accurate marksman
dead·fall (-fôl′) *n.* a trap arranged so that a heavy weight is dropped on the prey
dead·head (-hed′) *n.* 1. a person using a free ticket as to get into a show 2. a vehicle traveling without cargo or passengers 3. [Slang] a boring person —*vt., vi.* to drive (a vehicle) or travel as a deadhead —*adv.* without passengers or cargo
dead heat a race in which two or more contestants reach the finish line at exactly the same time; tie
dead letter 1. a law, practice, etc. no longer enforced or operative but not formally done away with 2. a letter that cannot be delivered or returned, as because incorrectly addressed
dead·line (-līn′) *n.* 1. a boundary which it is forbidden to cross 2. the latest time by which something must be done or completed
dead·lock (-läk′) *n.* 1. a standstill resulting from the action of equal and opposed forces 2. a tie between opponents —*vt., vi.* to bring or come to a deadlock
dead·ly (-lē) *adj.* **-li·er, -li·est** 1. causing or likely to cause death 2. to the death; mortal [*deadly* combat] 3. typical of death [*deadly* pallor] 4. very harmful 5. extreme or excessive [*deadly* silence] 6. oppressively tiresome [a *deadly* bore] 7. perfectly accurate [*deadly* aim] 8. *Theol.* causing spiritual death [*deadly* sins] —*adv.* 1. as if dead [to lie *deadly* still] 2. extremely or excessively [*deadly* serious] —**dead′li·ness** *n.*
deadly nightshade *same as* BELLADONNA (sense 1)
dead march funeral music in slow march tempo
dead·pan (-pan′) *n.* [Slang] an expressionless face, or a person with such a face —*adj., adv.* [Slang] without expression
dead reckoning [< ? *ded* (for *deduced*) *reckoning*] the finding of a ship's position by an estimate based on data recorded in the log, such as the time spent on a specified course, speed, etc., rather than by taking astronomical observations
Dead Sea inland body of salt water between Israel and Jordan: c. 1,290 ft. below sea level
Dead Sea Scrolls scrolls dating from 100? B.C.–70? A.D. discovered since 1947 in caves near the Dead Sea: they contain Jewish Scriptural writings, etc.
dead soldier [Slang] an emptied bottle, as of liquor
dead weight 1. the weight of an inert person or thing 2. the weight of a vehicle without a load
dead·wood (-wood′) *n.* 1. dead wood on trees 2. a useless or burdensome person or thing
deaf (def) *adj.* [OE.] 1. totally or partially unable to hear 2. unwilling to hear or listen [*deaf* to her pleas] —**deaf′ly** *adv.* —**deaf′ness** *n.*
deaf-and-dumb (-'n dum′) *adj.* 1. deaf-mute 2. of or for deaf-mutes Now opprobrious
deaf·en (-'n) *vt.* 1. to make deaf 2. to overwhelm with noise 3. to soundproof with insulation —**deaf′en·ing** *adj., n.* —**deaf′en·ing·ly** *adv.*
deaf-mute (-myōōt′) *n.* a person who is deaf, esp. from birth, and unable to speak: most deaf-mutes, having the necessary vocal organs, can be taught to speak —*adj.* of or being a deaf-mute
deal[1] (dēl) *vt.* **dealt, deal′ing** [OE. *dælan*] 1. to portion out or distribute 2. to give or administer (a blow) —*vi.* 1. to have to do (*with*) [books *dealing* with fish] 2. to act or conduct oneself (followed by *with*) [*deal* fairly with others] 3. to consider or attend to; cope (*with*) [to *deal* with a problem] 4. to do business; trade (*with* or *in*) [to *deal* in hardware] 5. to distribute playing cards to the players —*n.* 1. *a*) the act of distributing playing cards *b*) cards dealt *c*) a player's turn to deal *d*) the playing of one deal of cards 2. a business transaction 3. a bargain or agreement, esp. when secret or underhanded 4. *a*) [Colloq.] behavior or conduct toward another; treatment [a square *deal*] *b*) a particular plan, policy, etc. [the New *Deal*] —**big deal** [Colloq.] a very important or impressive thing —**deal′er** *n.*
deal[2] (dēl) *n.* [OE. *dæl,* a part] an indefinite or considerable amount [a *deal* of trouble] —**a good** (or **great**) **deal** 1. a large amount 2. very much
deal[3] (dēl) *n.* [MDu. *dele*] 1. a fir or pine board 2. fir or pine wood —*adj.* made of deal
deal·er·ship (dēl′ər ship′) *n.* a franchise to market a product in an area, or a distributor holding this
deal·ing (dēl′iŋ) *n.* 1. distribution 2. way of acting toward others 3. [*usually pl.*] transactions or relations, usually of business
dealt (delt) *pt. and pp. of* DEAL[1]
dean (dēn) *n.* [< OFr. < LL. *decanus,* head of ten soldiers or monks < L. *decem,* ten] 1. *a*) the presiding official of a cathedral or collegiate church *b*) *R.C.Ch.* a priest chosen by his bishop to supervise a number of parishes within the diocese 2. a college or university official in charge of a school or faculty, or of the students 3. the senior or preeminent member of a particular group [the *dean* of American poets] —**dean′ship′** *n.*
dean·er·y (dēn′ər ē) *n., pl.* **-er·ies** 1. the rank or authority of a dean 2. the residence of a dean
dean's list a list of students with the highest grades, issued periodically at certain colleges
dear (dir) *adj.* [OE. *deore*] 1. much loved; beloved 2. much valued; esteemed: a polite form of address [*Dear* Sir] 3. *a*) high-priced *b*) charging high prices 4. earnest [our *dearest* wish] —*adv.* 1. with deep affection 2. at a high cost —*n.* a loved or endearing person —*interj.* an expression of surprise, pity, etc. —**dear′ly** *adv.* —**dear′ness** *n.*
Dear·born (dir′bərn, -bôrn′) [after Gen. H. *Dearborn,* U.S. Secretary of War (1801–09)] city in SE Mich.: suburb of Detroit: pop. 91,000
Dearborn Heights city in SE Mich.: suburb of Detroit: pop. 68,000
dearth (durth) *n.* [see DEAR & -TH[1]] 1. scarcity of food; famine 2. any scarcity or lack
dear·y, dear·ie (dir′ē) *n., pl.* **-ies** [Colloq.] dear; darling: now often ironic or humorous
death (deth) *n.* [OE.] 1. the act or fact of dying; permanent ending of life 2. [D-] the personification of death, usually as a skeleton holding a scythe 3. the state of being dead 4. any end resembling dying [the *death* of fascism] 5. any experience thought of as like dying or being dead 6. the cause of death 7. murder or bloodshed —**at death's door** nearly dead —**put to death** to kill; execute —**to death** very much [worried *to death*] —**to the death** 1. to the very end of (a struggle, etc.) 2. always —**death′like′** *adj.*
death·bed (-bed′) *n.* the bed on which a person dies or spends his last hours of life —*adj.* done or made in one's last hours of life [a *deathbed* will]
death·blow (-blō′) *n.* 1. a blow that kills 2. a thing destructive or fatal (*to* something)
death cup a deadly mushroom with a white cap and a cuplike structure around the base of the stalk
death duty [Brit.] *same as* INHERITANCE TAX
death house a cell block or place where prisoners condemned to die are kept until their execution
death·less (-lis) *adj.* that cannot die; immortal —**death′less·ly** *adv.* —**death′less·ness** *n.*
death·ly (-lē) *adj.* 1. causing death; deadly 2. like or characteristic of death —*adv.* 1. in a deathlike way 2. extremely [*deathly* ill]
death mask a cast of a dead person's face
death rate the number of deaths per year per thousand of population: sometimes other units of time or population are used
death row *same as* DEATH HOUSE
death's-head (deths′hed′) *n.* a human skull or a representation of it, symbolizing death
death tax *same as* INHERITANCE TAX
death·trap (deth′trap′) *n.* 1. an unsafe building, vehicle, etc. 2. any very dangerous place or situation
Death Valley dry, hot desert basin in E Calif. & S Nev.: 282 ft. below sea level
death warrant 1. an official order to put a person to death 2. anything that makes inevitable the destruction or end of a person or thing
death·watch (-wäch′, -wôch′) *n.* 1. a vigil kept beside a dead or dying person 2. a guard set over a person soon to be executed
deb (deb) *n.* [Colloq.] *short for* DEBUTANTE
deb. debenture
de·ba·cle (di bäk′'l, -bak′-; dā-) *n.* [< Fr. < *débâcler,* to break up] 1. a breaking up of ice in a river, etc. 2. a rush of debris-filled waters 3. an overwhelming defeat or rout 4. a total, often ludicrous, collapse or failure
de·bar (dē bär′) *vt.* **-barred′, -bar′ring** [< Anglo-Fr.: see DE- & BAR[1]] 1. to exclude (*from* something); bar 2. to prevent or prohibit —**de·bar′ment** *n.*
de·bark (di bärk′) *vt., vi.* [< Fr.: see DE- & BARK[3]] to unload from or leave a ship or aircraft —**de·bar·ka·tion** (dē′bär kā′shən) *n.*
de·base (di bās′) *vt.* **-based′, -bas′ing** [DE- + (A)BASE] to make lower in value, quality, character, dignity, etc.; cheapen —**de·base′ment** *n.* —**de·bas′er** *n.*
de·bate (di bāt′) *vi.* **-bat′ed, -bat′ing** [< OFr. *debatre,* to fight: see DE- & BATTER[1]] 1. to discuss opposing reasons;

argue **2.** to take part in a formal discussion or a debate (*n.* 2) —*vt.* **1.** to dispute about, esp. in a meeting or legislature **2.** to argue (a question) or argue with (a person) formally **3.** to consider reasons for and against (*with* oneself or *in* one's own mind) —*n.* **1.** discussion of opposing reasons; argument **2.** a formal contest of skill in reasoned argument, with two teams taking opposite sides of a specified question **3.** the art or study of formal debate —**de·bat′a·ble** *adj.* —**de·bat′er** *n.*

de·bauch (di bôch′) *vt.* [< Fr. < OFr. *desbaucher,* to seduce] to lead astray morally; corrupt —*vi.* to indulge in debauchery; dissipate —*n.* **1.** debauchery **2.** an orgy —**de·bauch′ed·ly** (-id lē) *adv.* —**de·bauch′er** *n.* —**de·bauch′ment** *n.*

deb·au·chee (di bôch′ē′; deb′ô chē′, -shē′) *n.* one who indulges in debauchery; dissipated person

de·bauch·er·y (di bôch′ər ē) *n., pl.* **-er·ies** **1.** extreme indulgence of one's appetites; dissipation **2.** [*pl.*] orgies **3.** a leading astray morally

de·ben·ture (di ben′chər) *n.* [< ML. < L. *debentur,* there are owing < *debere:* see DEBT] **1.** a voucher acknowledging that a debt is owed by the signer **2.** an interest-bearing bond issued by a corporation or governmental unit, often without security

de·bil·i·tate (di bil′ə tāt′) *vt.* **-tat′ed, -tat′ing** [< L. pp. of *debilitare,* to weaken < *debilis,* weak] to make weak; enervate —**de·bil′i·ta′tion** *n.*

de·bil·i·ty (-tē) *n., pl.* **-ties** [< OFr. < L. *debilitas* < *debilis,* weak] bodily weakness; feebleness

deb·it (deb′it) *n.* [< OFr. < L. *debitum,* what is owing; neut. pp. of *debere:* see DEBT] **1.** an entry on the left-hand side of an account, giving rise to an increase in an asset account or decrease in a liability or net worth account **2.** the total of such entries —*vt.* to enter as a debit or debits

deb·o·nair, deb·o·naire (deb′ə ner′) *adj.* [< OFr. < *de bon aire,* lit., of good breed] **1.** friendly in a cheerful way; genial; affable **2.** carefree in manner; jaunty; sprightly —**deb′o·nair′ly** *adv.*

Deb·o·rah (deb′ə rə, deb′rə) [Heb. *debōrāh,* lit., a bee] **1.** a feminine name: dim. *Debby* **2.** *Bible* a prophetess and judge of Israel: Judg. 4 & 5

de·bouch (di bo͞osh′) *vi.* [< Fr. < *dé-,* DE- + *bouche,* the mouth < L. *bucca,* cheek] **1.** *Mil.* to come forth from a narrow or shut-in place into open country **2.** to come forth; emerge —**de·bouch′ment** *n.*

de·brief (dē brēf′) *vt.* [DE- + BRIEF] to question and instruct (a pilot, emissary, etc.) following a flight or mission —**de·brief′ing** *n.*

de·bris, dé·bris (də brē′; *also, esp. Brit. & Canad.,* de′brē, dā′-) *n.* [Fr. < OFr. *desbrisier,* to break apart] **1.** broken pieces of stone, wood, etc., as after destruction; rubble **2.** bits of rubbish; litter **3.** a heap of rock fragments, as from a glacier

Debs (debz), **Eugene Victor** 1855–1926; U.S. labor leader & Socialist candidate for president

debt (det) *n.* [< OFr. < L. *debitum,* neut. pp. of *debere,* to owe < *de-,* from + *habere,* to have] **1.** something owed by one person to another **2.** an obligation or liability to pay or return something **3.** the condition of owing [*to be in debt*] **4.** *Theol.* a sin

debt of honor a gambling or betting debt

debt·or (-ər) *n.* one that owes a debt

de·bug (dē bug′) *vt.* **-bugged′, -bug′ging** [DE- + BUG] **1.** to remove insects from **2.** [Slang] to find and correct defects, faults, etc. in **3.** [Slang] to find and remove hidden electronic listening devices from (a room, etc.)

de·bunk (di buŋk′) *vt.* [DE- + BUNK[2]] [Colloq.] to expose the false or exaggerated claims, pretensions, glamour, etc. of —**de·bunk′er** *n.*

De·bus·sy (də bü sē′; *E.* deb′yoo sē′, də byo͞o′sē), **(Achille) Claude** 1862–1918; Fr. composer

de·but, dé·but (di byo͞o′, dā-; dā′byo͞o) *n.* [Fr. < *débuter,* to lead off < (*jouer*) *de but,* (to play) for the mark] **1.** the first appearance before the public, as of an actor **2.** the formal introduction of a girl into society **3.** the beginning of a career, course, etc.

deb·u·tante (deb′yoo tänt′, deb′yoo tänt′) *n.* [< Fr. *débutant,* prp. of *débuter,* to make a DEBUT] a girl making a debut, esp. into society

Dec. December

dec. **1.** deceased **2.** decimeter **3.** declension **4.** declination **5.** decrease

dec·a- [< Gr. *deka,* ten] *a combining form meaning* ten [*decagon, decameter*] : also, before a vowel, **dec-**

dec·ade (dek′ād) *n.* [< OFr. < L. < Gr. < *deka,* ten] **1.** a group of ten **2.** a period of ten years

dec·a·dence (dek′ə dəns, di kā′d′ns) *n.* [< Fr. < ML. < prp. of VL. *decadere* < L. *de-,* from + *cadere,* to fall] a process, condition, or period of decline, as in morals, art, literature, etc.; deterioration; decay

dec·a·dent (-dənt) *adj.* in a state of decline; characterized by decadence —*n.* a decadent person, esp. a decadent writer or artist —**dec′a·dent·ly** *adv.*

dec·a·gon (dek′ə gän′) *n.* [see DECA- & -GON] a plane figure with ten sides and ten angles —**de·cag·o·nal** (di kag′ə nəl) *adj.*

dec·a·gram (-gram′) *n.* [see DECA- & GRAM] a measure of weight, equal to 10 grams: also, chiefly Brit., **dec′a·gramme′** (-gram′)

dec·a·he·dron (dek′ə hē′drən) *n., pl.* **-drons, -dra** (-drə) [see DECA- & -HEDRON] a solid figure with ten plane surfaces —**dec′a·he′dral** (-drəl) *adj.*

de·cal (di kal′, dē′kal) *n. same as* DECALCOMANIA

de·cal·ci·fy (dē kal′sə fī′) *vt.* **-fied′, -fy′ing** to remove calcium or lime from (bones, etc.) —**de·cal′ci·fi·ca′tion** *n.* —**de·cal′ci·fi′er** *n.*

de·cal·co·ma·ni·a (di kal′kə mā′nē ə) *n.* [< Fr. < *dé-,* DE- + *calquer,* to copy + *manie,* mania] **1.** the process of transferring decorative pictures or designs from specially prepared paper onto glass, wood, etc. **2.** a picture or design of this kind

dec·a·li·ter (dek′ə lēt′ər) *n.* [see DECA- & LITER] a measure of capacity, equal to 10 liters: also, chiefly Brit., **dec′a·li′tre** (-lēt′ər)

Dec·a·logue, Dec·a·log (dek′ə lôg′, -läg′) *n.* [< LL. < Gr. *dekalogos:* see DECA- & -LOGUE] [*sometimes* **d-**] *same as* TEN COMMANDMENTS

dec·a·me·ter (dek′ə mēt′ər) *n.* [see DECA- & METER[1]] a measure of length, equal to 10 meters: also, chiefly Brit., **dec′a·me′tre** (-mēt′ər)

de·camp (di kamp′) *vi.* [< Fr.: see DE- & CAMP] **1.** to break or leave camp **2.** to go away suddenly and secretly; run away —**de·camp′ment** *n.*

de·cant (di kant′) *vt.* [< Fr. < ML. < L. *de-,* from + *canthus,* rim, edge] to pour off (a liquid) gently without stirring up the sediment —**de·can·ta·tion** (dē′kan tā′shən) *n.*

de·cant·er (-ər) *n.* a decorative glass bottle, used for serving wine, etc.

DECANTER

de·cap·i·tate (di kap′ə tāt′) *vi.* **-tat′ed, -tat′ing** [< Fr. < ML. pp. of *decapitare* < L. *de-,* off + *caput,* the head] to cut off the head of; behead —**de·cap′i·ta′tion** *n.* —**de·cap′i·ta′tor** *n.*

dec·a·pod (dek′ə päd′) *adj.* [see DECA- & -POD] ten-legged —*n.* **1.** any crustacean with ten legs, as a lobster, shrimp, crab, etc. **2.** any cephalopod with ten arms, as a squid —**de·cap·o·dal** (di kap′ə d′l), **de·cap′o·dous** (-dəs) *adj.* —**de·cap′o·dan** (-dən) *adj., n.*

de·car·bon·ate (dē kär′bə nāt′) *vt.* **-at′ed, -at′ing** to remove carbon dioxide or carbonic acid from —**de·car′bon·a′tion** *n.*

de·car·bon·ize (-nīz′) *vt.* **-ized′, -iz′ing** to remove carbon from: also **de·car′bu·rize′** (-bə rīz′, -byo͞o-) **-rized′, -riz′ing** —**de·car′bon·i·za′tion** *n.*

dec·a·syl·la·ble (dek′ə sil′ə b′l) *n.* a line of verse with ten syllables —**dec′a·syl·lab′ic** (-si lab′ik) *adj.*

de·cath·lon (di kath′län, -lən) *n.* [DEC(A)- + Gr. *athlon,* a contest] an athletic contest consisting of ten events in track and field sports: the contestant receiving the highest total of points wins

De·ca·tur (di kāt′ər) [after ff.] city in C Ill.: pop. 94,000

De·ca·tur (di kāt′ər), **Stephen** 1779–1820; U.S. naval officer

de·cay (di kā′) *vi.* [< Anglo-Fr. & OFr. < VL. *decadere:* see DECADENCE] **1.** to lose strength, soundness, prosperity, etc. gradually; deteriorate **2.** to rot —*vt.* to cause to decay —*n.* **1.** a gradual decline; deterioration **2.** a rotting **3.** *a*) rottenness *b*) rotted matter **4.** *a*) the spontaneous disintegration of radioactive atoms with a resulting decrease in their number *b*) the spontaneous disintegration of a particle or nucleus, as a meson, with the formation of a more stable state

de·cease (di sēs′) *n.* [< OFr. < L. *decessus,* pp. of *decedere* < *de-,* from + *cedere,* to go] death —*vi.* **-ceased′, -ceas′ing** to die

de·ceased (di sēst′) *adj.* dead —**the deceased** the dead person or persons

de·ce·dent (di sēd′′nt) *n. Law* a deceased person

de·ceit (di sēt′) *n.* [< OFr. pp. of *deceveir*] **1.** the act of deceiving or lying **2.** a dishonest action or trick; lie **3.** the quality of being deceitful

de·ceit·ful (-fəl) *adj.* **1.** tending to deceive; apt to lie or cheat **2.** intended to deceive; deceptive; false —**de·ceit′ful·ly** *adv.* —**de·ceit′ful·ness** *n.*

de·ceive (di sēv′) *vt.* **-ceived′, -ceiv′ing** [< OFr. *deceveir* < L. *decipere*, to ensnare < *de-*, from + *capere*, to take] to make (a person) believe what is not true; mislead —*vi.* to use deceit —**de·ceiv′a·ble** *adj.* —**de·ceiv′er** *n.* —**de·ceiv′·ing·ly** *adv.*

de·cel·er·ate (dē sel′ə rāt′) *vt., vi.* **-at′ed, -at′ing** [DE- + (AC)CELERATE] to slow down —**de·cel′er·a′tion** *n.* —**de·cel′er·a′tor** *n.*

De·cem·ber (di sem′bər) *n.* [< OFr. < L. < *decem*, ten: the early Romans reckoned from March] the twelfth and last month of the year, having 31 days: abbrev. **Dec., D.**

de·cem·vir (di sem′vər) *n., pl.* **-virs, -vir·i′** (-və rī′) [L. < *decem*, ten + *vir*, a man] a member of a council of ten magistrates in ancient Rome

de·cen·cy (dē′s'n sē) *n., pl.* **-cies** **1.** a being decent; propriety; proper behavior, modesty, good taste, etc. **2.** [*pl.*] socially proper actions **3.** [*pl.*] things needed for a proper standard of living

de·cen·ni·al (di sen′ē əl) *adj.* [< L. *decem*, ten + *annus*, year + -AL] **1.** of or lasting ten years **2.** occurring every ten years —*n.* a tenth anniversary —**de·cen′ni·al·ly** *adv.*

de·cent (dē′s'nt) *adj.* [< L. prp. of *decere*, to befit] **1.** proper and fitting **2.** not immodest; not obscene **3.** conforming to approved social standards; respectable **4.** reasonably good; adequate *[decent* wages*]* **5.** fair and kind **6.** [Colloq.] adequately clothed for propriety —**de′cent·ly** *adv.*

de·cen·tral·ize (dē sen′trə līz′) *vt.* **-ized′, -iz′ing** to break up a concentration of (governmental authority, etc.) in a main center and distribute more widely —**de·cen′tral·i·za′tion** *n.*

de·cep·tion (di sep′shən) *n.* [< OFr. < L. pp. of *decipere*] **1.** a deceiving or being deceived **2.** something that deceives, as an illusion, or is meant to deceive, as a fraud

de·cep·tive (-tiv) *adj.* deceiving or meant to deceive —**de·cep′tive·ly** *adv.* —**de·cep′tive·ness** *n.*

dec·i- [Fr. < L. < *decem*, ten] *a combining form meaning* one tenth *[decigram]*

dec·i·bel (des′ə bel′, -b'l) *n.* [DECI- + *bel* (after A. G. *Bell*)] a numerical expression of the relative loudness of a sound or of the relative power level of an electrical signal

de·cide (di sīd′) *vt.* **-cid′ed, -cid′ing** [< L. *decidere* < *de-*, off + *caedere*, to cut] **1.** to end (a contest, dispute, etc.) by giving one side the victory **2.** to reach a decision about **3.** to cause to reach a decision —*vi.* to arrive at a judgment or decision —**de·cid′a·ble** *adj.* —**de·cid′er** *n.*

de·cid·ed (di sīd′id) *adj.* **1.** definite; clear-cut **2.** unhesitating; determined —**de·cid′ed·ly** *adv.*

de·cid·u·ous (di sij′oo wəs) *adj.* [L. *deciduus* < *de-*, off + *cadere*, to fall] **1.** falling off at a certain season or stage of growth, as some leaves, antlers, etc. **2.** shedding leaves annually: opposed to EVERGREEN —**de·cid′u·ous·ly** *adv.* —**de·cid′u·ous·ness** *n.*

dec·i·gram (des′ə gram′) *n.* [see DECI- & GRAM] a metric weight, equal to 1/10 gram: also, chiefly Brit., **dec′i·gramme′**

dec·i·li·ter (des′ə lēt′ər) *n.* [see DECI- & LITER] a metric measure of volume, equal to 1/10 liter: also, chiefly Brit., **dec′i·li′tre**

de·cil·lion (di sil′yən) *n.* [DEC- + (M)ILLION] **1.** in the U.S. and France, the number written as 1 followed by 33 zeros **2.** in England and Germany, the number written as 1 followed by 60 zeros —*adj.* amounting to one decillion in number

dec·i·mal (des′ə m'l) *adj.* [OFr. < ML. *decimalis* < L. < *decem*, ten] of or based on the number 10; progressing by tens —*n.* a fraction with an unwritten denominator of 10 or some power of ten, indicated by a point (**decimal point**) before the numerator (Ex.: .5 = 5/10): in full, **decimal fraction** —**dec′i·mal·ly** *adv.*

decimal classification a library system of classifying books by use of numbers with decimals

dec·i·mate (des′ə māt′) *vt.* **-mat′ed, -mat′ing** [< L. pp. of *decimare* < *decem*, ten] **1.** orig., to select by lot and kill every tenth one of **2.** to destroy or kill a large part of —**dec′i·ma′tion** *n.* —**dec′i·ma′tor** *n.*

dec·i·me·ter (des′ə mēt′ər) *n.* [see DECI- & METER[1]] a metric measure of length, equal to 1/10 meter: also, chiefly Brit., **dec′i·me′tre**

de·ci·pher (di sī′fər) *vt.* [DE- + CIPHER] **1.** to translate (a message in cipher or code) into ordinary language; decode **2.** to make out the meaning of (ancient inscriptions, a scrawl, etc.) —**de·ci′pher·a·ble** *adj.* —**de·ci′pher·ment** *n.*

de·ci·sion (di sizh′ən) *n.* **1.** the act of deciding something **2.** a judgment or conclusion reached or given **3.** determination; firmness of mind *[*a man of *decision]* **4.** *Boxing* a victory on points instead of by a knockout —**de·ci′sion·al** *adj.*

de·ci·sive (di sī′siv) *adj.* **1.** that settles a dispute, question, etc.; conclusive **2.** critically important; crucial **3.** showing decision or determination —**de·ci′sive·ly** *adv.* —**de·ci′sive·ness** *n.*

dec·i·stere (des′ə stir′) *n.* [see DECI- & STERE] a metric measure of volume, 1/10 cubic meter

deck[1] (dek) *n.* [prob. < MLowG. *verdeck* (< *ver-*, prefix + *decken*, to cover)] **1.** a roof over a section of a ship's hold, serving as a floor **2.** any platform or floor like a ship's deck **3.** a pack of playing cards —*vt.* [Slang] to knock down —**clear the decks** to get ready for action —**hit the deck** [Slang] **1.** to get out of bed **2.** to get ready for action **3.** to throw oneself to the ground, as to avoid injury **4.** to be knocked down —**on deck** [Colloq.] ready; on hand

deck[2] (dek) *vt.* [MDu. *decken*, to cover] **1.** to cover with finery or ornaments; adorn **2.** to furnish (a ship, etc.) with a deck

deck chair a folding chair, usually with a leg rest

-deck·er (dek′ər) *a combining form meaning* having (a specified number of) decks, layers, etc.

deck·hand (dek′hand′) *n.* a common sailor

deck·le edge (dek′'l) [G. dim. of *decke*, a cover] a rough, irregular edge sometimes given to a sheet of paper

de·claim (di klām′) *vi., vt.* [< L. < *de-*, intens. + *clamare*, to shout] **1.** to recite (a speech, poem, etc.) with artificial eloquence **2.** to speak or utter in a pompous way **3.** to deliver a tirade (against) —**de·claim′er** *n.*

dec·la·ma·tion (dek′lə mā′shən) *n.* [< L. *declamatio* < pp. of prec.] **1.** the act or art of declaiming **2.** a speech, poem, etc. that is or can be declaimed —**de·clam·a·to·ry** (di klam′ə tôr′ē) *adj.*

de·clar·a·ble (di klar′ə b'l, -kler′-) *adj.* that can be or must be declared for taxation

dec·la·ra·tion (dek′lə rā′shən) *n.* **1.** the act of declaring; announcement **2.** a thing declared **3.** a formal statement **4.** a statement of taxable goods **5.** the winning bid in a game of bridge

Declaration of Independence a formal statement adopted July 4, 1776, by the Second Continental Congress, declaring the thirteen American colonies free and independent of Great Britain

de·clar·a·tive (di klar′ə tiv, -kler′-) *adj.* making a statement or assertion: also **de·clar′a·to′ry** (-ə tôr′ē) —**de·clar′a·tive·ly** *adv.*

de·clare (di kler′) *vt.* **-clared′, -clar′ing** [< OFr. < L. < *de-*, intens. + *clarare* < *clarus*, clear] **1.** to make clearly known; announce openly, formally, etc. **2.** to show or reveal **3.** to say emphatically **4.** to make a statement of (taxable goods), as at customs **5.** to authorize payment of (a dividend, etc.) **6.** *Card Games* to establish (trump or no-trump) by a successful bid —*vi.* **1.** to make a declaration **2.** to state openly a choice, opinion, etc. (for or against) —**declare oneself** **1.** to state strongly one's opinion **2.** to reveal one's true character, etc. —**I declare!** I am surprised, startled, etc. —**de·clar′er** *n.*

de·clas·si·fy (dē klas′ə fī′) *vt.* **-fied′, -fy′ing** to remove (governmental documents, reports, etc.) from secret or restricted classifications and make available to the public

de·clen·sion (di klen′shən) *n.* [< OFr. < L. < pp. of *declinare*: see DECLINE] **1.** a sloping; descent **2.** a declining; deterioration **3.** *Gram.* *a)* a class of nouns, pronouns, or adjectives having the same or a similar system of inflections to show case *b)* their inflection —**de·clen′sion·al** *adj.*

dec·li·na·tion (dek′lə nā′shən) *n.* **1.** a bending or sloping downward **2.** an oblique variation from a definite direction **3.** the angle formed by a magnetic needle with the line pointing to true north **4.** a polite refusal **5.** *Astron.* the angular distance of a heavenly body north or south from the celestial equator

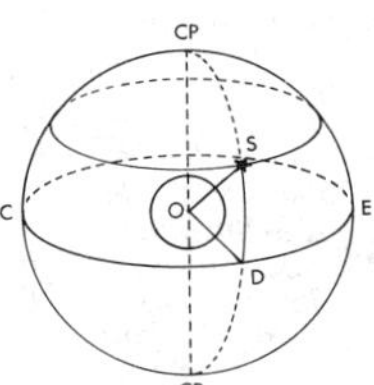

DECLINATION (CP, celestial poles; CE, celestial equator; O, observer, or center of earth; DS, or angle DOS, declination of star S)

de·cline (di klīn′) *vi.* **-clined′, -clin′ing** [< OFr. < L. < *de-*, from + *-clinare*, to bend] **1.** to bend or slope downward or aside **2.** to sink, as the setting sun **3.** to approach the end; wane **4.** to deteriorate; decay **5.** to descend to base or immoral behavior **6.** to refuse to do something —*vt.* **1.** to cause to bend or slope downward or aside **2.** to refuse, esp. politely **3.** *Gram.* to give the inflected forms of (a noun, pronoun, or adjective) —*n.* **1.** a declining; deterioration; decay **2.** a failing of health, etc. **3.** a period of decline **4.** the last part **5.** a wasting disease, esp. tuberculosis of the lungs **6.** a downward slope —**de·clin′a·ble** *adj.* —**de·clin′er** *n.*

de·cliv·i·tous (di kliv′ə təs) *adj.* fairly steep

de·cliv·i·ty (-tē) *n., pl.* **-ties** [< L. < *de-*, down + *clivus*, a slope] a downward slope of the ground

de·coct (di käkt′) *vt.* [< L. pp. of *decoquere* < *de-*, down + *coquere*, to cook] to extract the essence, flavor, etc. of by boiling —**de·coc′tion** *n.*

de·code (dē kōd′) *vt.* **-cod′ed, -cod′ing** to translate (a coded message) into ordinary, understandable language —**de·cod′er** *n.*

dé·col·le·té (dā kal′ə tā′; *Fr.* dā kôl tā′) *adj.* [Fr., ult. < L. *de*, from + *collum*, the neck] **1.** cut low so as to bare the neck and shoulders **2.** wearing a décolleté dress, etc.

de·col·o·ni·za·tion (dē käl′ə nə zā′shən) *n.* a freeing or being freed from colonialism or colonial status —**de·col′o·nize′** (-nīz′) *vt., vi.* **-nized′, -niz′ing**

de·com·pose (dē′kəm pōz′) *vt., vi.* **-posed′, -pos′ing** [< Fr.: see DE- & COMPOSE] **1.** to break up into basic components or parts **2.** to rot —**de′com·pos′a·ble** *adj.* —**de′com·po·si′tion** (-käm pə zish′ən) *n.*

de·com·press (dē′kəm pres′) *vt.* to free from pressure —**de′com·pres′sion** *n.*

decompression sickness a condition caused by the formation of nitrogen bubbles in the blood or body tissues as a result of a sudden lowering of air pressure, resulting in collapse in severe cases

de·con·gest·ant (dē′kən jes′tənt) *n.* a medication that relieves congestion, as in the nasal passages

de·con·tam·i·nate (-tam′ə nāt′) *vt.* **-nat′ed, -nat′ing** to rid of a harmful substance, as radioactive products —**de′con·tam′i·na′tion** *n.*

de·con·trol (-trōl′) *vt.* **-trolled′, -trol′ling** to free from controls —*n.* withdrawal of controls

dé·cor, de·cor (dā kôr′, dā′kôr) *n.* [Fr. < L. < *decere*, to befit] the decorative scheme of a room, stage set, etc.

dec·o·rate (dek′ə rāt′) *vt.* **-rat′ed, -rat′ing** [< L. pp. of *decorare* < *decus*, an ornament] **1.** to adorn; ornament **2.** to plan and arrange the colors, furnishings, etc. of **3.** to paint or wallpaper **4.** to give a medal or similar token of honor to —**dec·o·ra·tive** (dek′ər ə tiv, -ə rāt′iv; dek′rə-) *adj.* —**dec′o·ra·tive·ly** *adv.* —**dec′o·ra·tive·ness** *n.* —**dec′o·ra′tor** *n.*

dec·o·ra·tion (dek′ə rā′shən) *n.* **1.** the act of decorating **2.** anything used for decorating; ornament **3.** a medal, badge, or similar token of honor

Decoration Day *same as* MEMORIAL DAY

dec·or·ous (dek′ər əs, di kôr′əs) *adj.* [L. *decorus*, becoming < *decor*: see DÉCOR] characterized by or showing decorum, good taste, etc. —**dec′o·rous·ly** *adv.*

de·co·rum (di kôr′əm) *n.* [L., neut. of *decorus*: see prec.] **1.** whatever is suitable or proper; propriety **2.** propriety and good taste in behavior, speech, dress, etc. **3.** an act or requirement of polite behavior: *often used in pl.*

de·cou·page, dé·cou·page (dā′ko͞o päzh′) *n.* [Fr., a cutting up] the mounting of decorative paper cutouts on a surface

de·coy (di koi′; *for n. also* dē′koi) *n.* [< Du. *de kooi*, the cage < L. *cavea*, CAGE] **1.** a place into which wild ducks, etc. are lured for capture **2.** an artificial or trained bird or animal used to lure game to a place where it can be shot **3.** a thing or person used to lure into a trap —*vt., vi.* to lure or be lured into a trap, danger, etc.

DECOY

de·crease (di krēs′; *also, & for n. usually,* dē′krēs) *vi., vt.* **-creased′, -creas′ing** [< OFr. < L. < *de-*, from + *crescere*, to grow] to become or cause to become gradually less, smaller, etc.; diminish —*n.* **1.** a decreasing; lessening **2.** amount of decreasing —**on the decrease** decreasing —**de·creas′ing·ly** *adv.*

de·cree (di krē′) *n.* [< OFr. < L. *decretum* < *de-*, from + *cernere*, to see, judge] **1.** an official order or decision, as of a government **2.** something that is or seems to be foreordained —*vt.* **-creed′, -cree′ing** to order, decide, or appoint by decree —*vi.* to issue a decree

de·crep·it (di krep′it) *adj.* [< OFr. < L. < *de-*, intens. + pp. of *crepare*, to creak] broken down or worn out by old age, illness, or long use —**de·crep′it·ly** *adv.*

de·crep·i·tude (di krep′ə to͞od′, -tyo͞od′) *n.* a decrepit condition; feebleness or infirmity

de·cre·scen·do (dē′krə shen′dō, dā′-) *adj., adv.* [It.] *Music* with a gradual decrease in loudness —*n., pl.* **-dos** *Music* **1.** a gradual decrease in loudness: symbol > **2.** a decrescendo passage

de·cre·tal (di krēt′'l) *adj.* [< LL. *decretalis*] of or containing a decree —*n.* **1.** a decree **2.** *R.C.Ch.* a decree issued by the Pope on some matter of ecclesiastical discipline

de·crim·i·nal·ize (dē krim′ə n'l īz′) *vt.* **-ized′, -iz′ing** to eliminate or reduce the legal penalties for (a specified crime) [to *decriminalize* the use of marijuana]

de·cry (di krī′) *vt.* **-cried′, -cry′ing** [< Fr. < OFr. *descrier*: see DE- & CRY] **1.** to speak out against strongly and openly; denounce **2.** to depreciate (money, etc.) officially —**de·cri′al** *n.* —**de·cri′er** *n.*

de·cum·bent (di kum′bənt) *adj.* [< L. prp. of *decumbere* < *de-*, down + *-cumbere*, *cubare*, to recline] **1.** lying down **2.** *Bot.* trailing on the ground and rising at the tip, as some stems —**de·cum′ben·cy** *n.*

ded·i·cate (ded′ə kāt′) *vt.* **-cat′ed, -cat′ing** [< L. pp. of *dedicare* < *de-*, intens. + *dicare*, to proclaim < *dicere*, to speak] **1.** to devote to a sacred purpose **2.** to devote to some work, duty, etc. **3.** to address (a book, artistic performance, etc.) to someone as a sign of honor or affection —**ded′i·ca′tor** *n.*

ded·i·ca·tion (ded′ə kā′shən) *n.* **1.** a dedicating or being dedicated **2.** an inscription, as in a book, dedicating it to someone **3.** wholehearted devotion —**ded′i·ca·to′ry, ded′i·ca′tive** *adj.*

de·duce (di do͞os′, -dyo͞os′) *vt.* **-duced′, -duc′ing** [< L. < *de-*, down + *ducere*, to lead] **1.** to trace the course or derivation of **2.** to infer by logical reasoning; conclude from known facts or general principles —**de·duc′i·ble** *adj.*

de·duct (di dukt′) *vt.* [L. *deductus*, pp. of *deducere*: see prec.] to take away or subtract (a quantity)

de·duct·i·ble (-ə b'l) *adj.* **1.** that can be deducted **2.** that is allowed as a deduction in computing income tax —**de·duct′i·bil′i·ty** *n.*

de·duc·tion (di duk′shən) *n.* **1.** a deducting or being deducted; subtraction **2.** the amount deducted **3.** *Logic* reasoning from the general to the specific, or from a premise to a logical conclusion; also, a conclusion so deduced: opposed to INDUCTION —**de·duc′tive** *adj.* —**de·duc′tive·ly** *adv.*

deed (dēd) *n.* [OE. *ded*, *dæd*] **1.** a thing done; act **2.** a feat of courage, skill, etc. **3.** action; actual performance **4.** *Law* a document under seal which, when delivered, transfers a present interest in property —*vt.* to transfer (property) by such a document —**in deed** in fact; really

deem (dēm) *vt., vi.* [OE. *deman*, to judge < base of *dom*, DOOM] to think, believe, or judge

de·em·pha·size (dē em′fə sīz′) *vt.* **-sized′, -siz′ing** to lessen the importance or prominence of —**de·em′pha·sis** (-sis) *n.*

deep (dēp) *adj.* [OE. *deop*] **1.** extending far downward from the top, inward from the surface, or backward from the front **2.** extending down, back, or in a specified distance [two feet *deep*] **3.** *a)* located far down or back *b)* coming from or going far down or back **4.** hard to understand; abstruse **5.** extremely grave or serious [in *deep* trouble] **6.** strongly felt **7.** intellectually profound **8.** *a)* tricky and sly *b)* carefully guarded [a *deep* secret] **9.** dark and rich [a *deep* red] **10.** absorbed by [*deep* in thought] **11.** *a)* intense *b)* heavy and unbroken [a *deep* sleep] **12.** of low pitch [a *deep* voice] —*n.* **1.** a deep place **2.** the middle part; part that is darkest, etc. [the *deep* of the night] —*adv.* in a deep way; far down, far back, far on, etc. —**go off the deep end** [Colloq.] to become angry or excited —**in deep water** in trouble or difficulty —**the deep** [Poet.] the sea or ocean —**deep′ly** *adv.* —**deep′ness** *n.*

deep-dish pie (-dish′) a pie baked in a deep dish and having only a top crust

deep·en (-'n) *vt., vi.* to make or become deep or deeper

Deep·freeze (-frēz′) *a trademark for* a deep freezer —*n.* [d-] **1.** storage in a deep freezer **2.** a condition of suspended activity —*vt.* [d-] **-froze′** or **-freezed′, -fro′zen** or **-freezed′, -freez′ing** **1.** to subject (foods) to sudden freezing so as to preserve and store **2.** to store in a deep freezer

deep-fry (-frī′) *vt.* **-fried′, -fry′ing** to fry in a deep pan of boiling fat or oil

deep-root·ed (-ro͞ot′id, -root′id) *adj.* **1.** having deep roots **2.** firmly fixed; hard to remove

deep-seat·ed (-sēt′id) *adj.* **1.** placed or originating far beneath the surface **2.** firmly fixed

deep-set (-set′) *adj.* **1.** deeply set **2.** firmly fixed

deer (dir) *n., pl.* **deer**, occas. **deers** [OE. *deor*, wild animal] any of a family of hoofed, cud-chewing animals, including the moose, reindeer, caribou, etc., the males of which usually bear antlers that are shed annually

deer·skin (-skin′) *n.* **1.** the hide of a deer **2.** leather or a garment made from this

de·es·ca·late (dē es′kə lāt′) *vi., vt.* **-lat′ed, -lat′ing** to lessen in scope, magnitude, etc. —**de·es′ca·la′tion** *n.*

def. **1.** defendant **2.** deferred **3.** definite **4.** definition

de·face (di fās′) *vt.* **-faced′, -fac′ing** [< OFr. *desfacier*: see DE- & FACE] to spoil or mar the surface or appearance of —**de·face′ment** *n.* —**de·fac′er** *n.*

de fac·to (di fak′tō, dā) [L.] existing in actual fact though

not by official recognition, etc. [*a de facto* government]: cf. DE JURE
de·fal·cate (di fal′kāt, -fôl′-) *vi.* **-cat·ed, -cat·ing** [< ML. pp. of *defalcare*, to cut off < L. *de-*, from + *falx* (gen. *falcis*), sickle] to steal or misuse funds entrusted to one's care; embezzle —**de·fal·ca·tion** (dē′fal kā′shən, -fôl-) *n.* —**de·fal′ca·tor** *n.*
de·fame (di fām′) *vt.* **-famed′, -fam′ing** [< OFr. or ML. < L. < *dis-*, from + *fama*, FAME] to attack the reputation of; slander or libel —**def·a·ma·tion** (def′ə mā′shən) *n.* —**de·fam·a·to·ry** (di fam′ə tôr′ē) *adj.* —**de·fam′er** *n.*
de·fault (di fôlt′) *n.* [< OFr. *defaute* < L. *de-*, away + *fallere*, to fail, deceive] failure to do or appear as required; specif., *a*) failure to pay money due *b*) failure to appear in court to defend or prosecute a case *c*) failure to take part in or finish a contest —*vi.* **1.** to fail to do or appear as required; specif., *a*) to fail to make payment when due *b*) to fail to appear in court *c*) to fail to take part in or finish a contest **2.** to lose by default —*vt.* **1.** to fail to do, pay, finish, etc. (something) when required **2.** to lose (a contest, etc.) by default —**de·fault′er** *n.*
de·feat (di fēt′) *vt.* [< OFr. < ML. < L. *dis-*, from + *facere*, to do] **1.** to win victory over; overcome; beat **2.** to bring to nothing; frustrate **3.** to make null and void —*n.* a defeating or being defeated
de·feat·ist (-ist) *n.* a person who too readily accepts or expects defeat —*adj.* of or like a defeatist —**de·feat′ism** *n.*
def·e·cate (def′ə kāt′) *vt.* **-cat′ed, -cat′ing** [< L. pp. of *defaecare* < *de-*, from + *faex* (gen. *faecis*), dregs] to remove impurities from; refine —*vi.* **1.** to become free from impurities **2.** to excrete waste matter from the bowels —**def′e·ca′tion** *n.* —**def′e·ca′tor** *n.*
de·fect (dē′fekt; *also, and for v. always,* di fekt′) *n.* [< L. pp. of *deficere*, to fail < *de-*, from + *facere*, to do] **1.** lack of something necessary for completeness; shortcoming **2.** an imperfection; fault; blemish —*vi.* to forsake a party, cause, etc.; desert —**de·fec′tor** *n.*
de·fec·tion (di fek′shən) *n.* **1.** abandonment of loyalty, duty, etc.; desertion **2.** a failure
de·fec·tive (-tiv) *adj.* **1.** having a defect or defects; faulty **2.** *Gram.* lacking some of the usual grammatical forms **3.** subnormal in intelligence —*n.* a person with some bodily or mental defect —**de·fec′tive·ly** *adv.* —**de·fec′tive·ness** *n.*
de·fence (di fens′) *n. Brit. sp. of* DEFENSE
de·fend (di fend′) *vt.* [< OFr. < L. *defendere* < *de-*, away + *fendere*, to strike] **1.** to guard from attack; protect **2.** to support, maintain, or justify **3.** *Law* *a*) to oppose (an action, etc.) *b*) to act as lawyer for (an accused) —*vi.* to make a defense —**de·fend′a·ble** *adj.* —**de·fend′er** *n.*
de·fend·ant (di fen′dənt) *adj.* defending —*n.* *Law* the person sued or accused: opposed to PLAINTIFF
de·fense (di fens′, dē′fens) *n.* [OFr. < LL. < L. pp. of *defendere*] **1.** a defending against attack or danger **2.** a being defended **3.** means of protection **4.** justification or support by speech or writing **5.** self-protection, as by boxing **6.** the side that is defending in any contest **7.** *a*) the arguments of the defendant in contesting a case *b*) the defendant and his lawyer or lawyers, collectively —**de·fense′less** *adj.* —**de·fense′less·ly** *adv.* —**de·fense′less·ness** *n.*
defense mechanism *Psychiatry* any behavior unconsciously used by an individual to protect himself against painful feelings, impulses, etc.
de·fen·si·ble (di fen′sə b'l) *adj.* that can be defended or justified —**de·fen′si·bil′i·ty, de·fen′si·ble·ness** *n.* —**de·fen′si·bly** *adv.*
de·fen·sive (-siv) *adj.* **1.** defending **2.** of or for defense **3.** *Psychol.* feeling under attack and hence quick to justify one's actions —*n.* a position of defense: chiefly in the phrase **on the defensive,** in a position that makes defense necessary —**de·fen′sive·ly** *adv.* —**de·fen′sive·ness** *n.*
de·fer[1] (di fur′) *vt., vi.* **-ferred′, -fer′ring** [< OFr. *differer*: see DIFFER] **1.** to put off; postpone; delay **2.** to postpone the induction of (a person) into compulsory military service —**de·fer′ment, de·fer′ral** *n.* —**de·fer′rer** *n.*
de·fer[2] (di fur′) *vi.* **-ferred′, -fer′ring** [< OFr. < L. < *de-*, down + *ferre*, to bear] to give in or yield to the wish or judgment of another
def·er·ence (def′ər əns) *n.* **1.** a yielding in opinion, judgment, etc. **2.** courteous regard or respect —**in deference to** out of regard for (a person, his wishes, etc.)
def·er·en·tial (def′ə ren′shəl) *adj.* showing deference; very respectful: also **def·er·ent** (def′ər ənt) —**def′er·en′tial·ly** *adv.*
de·fi·ance (di fī′əns) *n.* **1.** a defying; open, bold resistance to authority or opposition **2.** a challenge —**bid defiance to** to defy —**in defiance of** in spite of —**de·fi′ant** *adj.* —**de·fi′ant·ly** *adv.*
de·fib·ril·late (di fib′rə lāt′) *vt.* **-lat′ed, -lat′ing** to stop fibrillation of the heart, as by electric current —**de·fib′ril·la′tion** *n.* —**de·fib′ril·la′tor** *n.*
de·fi·cien·cy (di fish′ən sē) *n.* **1.** the quality or state of being deficient; absence of an essential; incompleteness **2.** *pl.* **-cies** *a*) a shortage *b*) the amount of shortage; deficit
deficiency disease a disease, as rickets, caused by lack of vitamins, minerals, etc. in the diet
de·fi·cient (di fish′ənt) *adj.* [< L. *deficiens*, prp. of *deficere*: see DEFECT] **1.** lacking in some essential; incomplete; defective **2.** inadequate in amount, quality, degree, etc. —*n.* a deficient person or thing —**de·fi′cient·ly** *adv.*
def·i·cit (def′ə sit) *n.* [L., it is lacking < *deficere*, to lack] the amount by which a sum of money is less than the required amount, as an excess of expenditure over income
de·fi·er (di fī′ər) *n.* a person who defies
de·file[1] (di fīl′) *vt.* **-filed′, -fil′ing** [< OFr. *defouler*, to tread underfoot (infl. by OE. *fylan*, make foul)] **1.** to make filthy; pollute **2.** to corrupt **3.** to profane or sully (a person's name, etc.) **4.** [Archaic] to violate the chastity of —**de·file′ment** *n.* —**de·fil′er** *n.*
de·file[2] (di fīl′, dē′fīl) *vi.* **-filed′, -fil′ing** [< Fr. < *dé-* (L. *de*), from + *filer*, to form a line] to march in single file or by files —*n.* **1.** a narrow passage through which troops must defile **2.** any narrow valley or mountain pass
de·fine (di fīn′) *vt.* **-fined′, -fin′ing** [< OFr. < L. *definire*, to limit < *de-*, from + *finis*, boundary] **1.** to determine the boundaries of **2.** to determine the extent and nature of **3.** to state the meaning or meanings of (a word, etc.) —*vi.* to prepare definitions —**de·fin′a·ble** *adj.* —**de·fin′er** *n.*
def·i·nite (def′ə nit) *adj.* [< L. pp. of *definire*: see prec.] **1.** having exact limits **2.** precise and clear in meaning; explicit **3.** certain; positive **4.** *Gram.* limiting or specifying ["the" is the *definite* article] —**def′i·nite·ly** *adv.* —**def′i·nite·ness** *n.*
def·i·ni·tion (def′ə nish′ən) *n.* **1.** a defining or being defined **2.** a statement of the meaning of a word, phrase, etc. **3.** *a*) a putting or being in clear, sharp outline *b*) a making or being definite or explicit **4.** the power of a lens to show (an object) in clear, sharp outline **5.** *Radio & TV* the clearness with which sounds or images are reproduced —**def′i·ni′tion·al** *adj.*
de·fin·i·tive (di fin′ə tiv) *adj.* **1.** decisive; conclusive **2.** most nearly complete and accurate **3.** serving to define precisely **4.** *Biol.* fully developed —**de·fin′i·tive·ly** *adv.* —**de·fin′i·tive·ness** *n.*
de·flate (di flāt′) *vt., vi.* **-flat′ed, -flat′ing** [DE- + (IN)FLATE] **1.** to collapse by letting out air or gas **2.** to make or become smaller or less important **3.** to cause deflation of (currency, prices, etc.) Opposed to INFLATE —**de·fla′tor** *n.*
de·fla·tion (di flā′shən) *n.* **1.** a deflating or being deflated **2.** a lessening of the amount of money in circulation, causing a rise in its value and a fall in prices —**de·fla′tion·ar′y** *adj.*
de·flect (di flekt′) *vt., vi.* [< L. < *de-*, from + *flectere*, to bend] to bend or turn to one side; swerve —**de·flec′tion** or Brit. **de·flex′ion** *n.* —**de·flec′tive** *adj.* —**de·flec′tor** *n.*
de·flow·er (di flou′ər) *vt.* [see DE- & FLOWER] **1.** to make (a woman) no longer a virgin **2.** to ravage or spoil **3.** to remove flowers from (a plant) —**def·lo·ra·tion** (def′lə rā′shən) *n.*
De·foe (di fō′), **Daniel** 1660?–1731; Eng. writer
de·fo·li·ant (dē fō′lē ənt) *n.* a chemical spray that strips growing plants of their leaves
de·fo·li·ate (-āt′) *vt.* **-at′ed, -at′ing** [< LL. pp. of *defoliare* < L. *de-*, from + *folium*, a leaf] **1.** to strip (trees, etc.) of leaves **2.** to use defoliants on —**de·fo′li·a′tion** *n.* —**de·fo′li·a′tor** *n.*
de·for·est (dē fôr′ist, -fär′-) *vt.* to clear (land) of forests or trees —**de·for′est·a′tion** *n.*
De For·est (di fôr′ist, fär′-), **Lee** 1873–1961; U.S. inventor
de·form (di fôrm′) *vt.* [< OFr. < L. < *de-*, from + *forma*, form] **1.** to impair the form or shape of **2.** to make ugly; disfigure **3.** *Physics* to change the shape of by pressure or stress —*vi.* to become deformed —**de·form′a·ble** *adj.* —**de·for·ma·tion** (dē′fôr mā′shən, def′ər-) *n.*
de·formed (di fôrmd′) *adj.* changed as in form or shape, esp. so as to be misshapen, ugly, etc.
de·form·i·ty (di fôr′mə tē) *n., pl.* **-ties** **1.** the condition of being deformed **2.** a deformed or disfigured part of the body **3.** ugliness or depravity **4.** anything deformed or disfigured
de·fraud (di frôd′) *vt.* [< OFr. < L. *defraudare* < *de-*, from + *fraus*, FRAUD] to take or hold back property, rights, etc. from by fraud; cheat —**de·frau·da·tion** (dē′frô dā′shən) *n.*
de·fray (di frā′) *vt.* [< Fr. < OFr., prob. < L. *de*, from + *fractum*, neut. pp. of *frangere*, to break] to pay (the cost or expenses) —**de·fray′a·ble** *adj.* —**de·fray′al, de·fray′ment** *n.*
de·frost (di frôst′) *vt.* **1.** to remove frost or ice from by thawing **2.** to cause (frozen foods) to become unfrozen —*vi.* to become defrosted
de·frost·er (-ər) *n.* a device for melting ice and frost, as on a windshield

deft (deft) *adj.* [see DAFT] skillful in a quick, sure, and easy way —**deft′ly** *adv.* —**deft′ness** *n.*

de·funct (di fuŋkt′) *adj.* [< L. *defunctus,* pp. of *defungi,* to finish, die < *de-,* from, off + *fungi,* to perform] no longer living or existing; dead or extinct

de·fuse (dē fyo͞oz′) *vt.* **-fused′, -fus′ing** **1.** to remove the fuse from (a bomb or the like) **2.** to render harmless

de·fy (di fī′; *also for n.* dē′fī) *vt.* **-fied′, -fy′ing** [< OFr. *defier* < L. *dis-,* from + *fidus,* faithful] **1.** to resist or oppose boldly or openly **2.** to resist completely in a baffling way **3.** to dare (someone) to do or prove something —*n., pl.* **-fies** [Colloq.] a defiance or challenge

De·gas (də gä′), **(Hilaire Germain) Ed·gar** (ed gȧr′) 1834–1917; Fr. painter

de Gaulle (də gôl′; *Fr.* gōl′), **Charles** 1890–1970; Fr. general; president of France (1959–69)

de·gauss (di gous′) *vt.* [DE- + GAUSS] to demagnetize (as a ship) by passing an electric current through a coil along or around the edge in order to neutralize the surrounding magnetic field —**de·gauss′er** *n.*

de·gen·er·a·cy (di jen′ər ə sē) *n.* **1.** the state of being degenerate **2.** degenerate behavior

de·gen·er·ate (-ər it; *for v.* -ə rāt′) *adj.* [L. pp. of *degenerare,* ult. < *de-,* from + *genus,* race] **1.** having sunk below a former or normal condition, etc.; deteriorated **2.** morally corrupt; depraved —*n.* a degenerate person, esp. one who is morally depraved or sexually perverted —*vi.* **-at′ed, -at′ing** **1.** to lose former normal or higher qualities **2.** to become debased morally, culturally, etc. **3.** *Biol.* to undergo degeneration —**de·gen′er·ate·ly** *adv.* —**de·gen′er·ate·ness** *n.* —**de·gen′er·a·tive** *adj.* —**de·gen′er·a·tive·ly** *adv.*

de·gen·er·a·tion (di jen′ə rā′shən) *n.* **1.** the process of degenerating **2.** a degenerate condition **3.** *Biol.* deterioration or loss of a function or structure in the course of evolution **4.** *Med.* deterioration in structure or function of cells, tissues, or organs, as in disease or aging

de·grade (di grād′) *vt.* **-grad′ed, -grad′ing** [< OFr. < LL. *degradare* < L. *de-,* down + *gradus:* see GRADE] **1.** to lower in rank or status; demote **2.** to lower or corrupt in quality, moral character, etc. **3.** to bring into dishonor or contempt **4.** *Chem.* to convert (an organic compound) into a simpler compound **5.** *Geol.* to lower (a land surface) by erosion —**de·grad′a·ble** *adj.* —**deg·ra·da·tion** (deg′rə dā′shən) *n.* —**de·grad′er** *n.*

de·grad·ed (-id) *adj.* disgraced, debased, depraved, etc. —**de·grad′ed·ly** *adv.* —**de·grad′ed·ness** *n.*

de·grad·ing (-iŋ) *adj.* that degrades; debasing —**de·grad′ing·ly** *adv.*

de·gree (di grē′) *n.* [< OFr. < LL. *degradare:* see DEGRADE] **1.** any of the successive steps or stages in a process or series **2.** a step in the direct line of descent **3.** social or official rank **4.** relative condition; manner or respect **5.** extent, amount, or relative intensity *[hungry to a slight degree]* **6.** *Algebra* rank as determined by the sum of a term's exponents *[a^3c^2 and x^5 are each of the fifth degree]* **7.** *Educ.* a rank given by a college or university to a student who has completed a required course of study, or to a distinguished person as an honor **8.** *Gram.* a grade of comparison of adjectives and adverbs *[the superlative degree of "good" is "best"]* **9.** *Law* the seriousness of a crime *[murder in the first degree]* **10.** *Math., Astron., Geog.,* etc. a unit of measure for angles or arcs, 1/360 of the circumference of a circle **11.** *Music a)* a line or space on the staff *b)* an interval between two such lines or spaces **12.** *Physics* a unit of measure on a scale, as for temperature —**by degrees** step by step; gradually —**to a degree** somewhat

de·hisce (di his′) *vi.* **-hisced′, -hisc′ing** [< L. < *de-,* off + *hiscere,* to gape] to burst or split open, as a seedpod —**de·his′cence** *n.* —**de·his′cent** *adj.*

de·horn (dē hôrn′) *vt.* to remove the horns from

de·hu·man·ize (dē hyo͞o′mə nīz′) *vt.* **-ized′, -iz′ing** to deprive of human qualities; make inhuman or machinelike —**de·hu′man·i·za′tion** *n.*

de·hu·mid·i·fy (dē′hyo͞o mid′ə fī′) *vt.* **-fied′, -fy′ing** to remove moisture from (the air, etc.) —**de′hu·mid′i·fi·ca′tion** *n.* —**de′hu·mid′i·fi′er** *n.*

de·hy·drate (dē hī′drāt) *vt.* **-drat·ed, -drat·ing** to remove water from (a compound, body tissues, etc.); dry —*vi.* to lose water; become dry —**de′hy·dra′tion** *n.* —**de·hy′dra·tor** *n.*

de·hy·dro·gen·ate (dē hī′drə jə nāt′) *vt.* **-at′ed, -at′ing** to remove hydrogen from: also **de·hy′dro·gen·ize′** (-nīz′) **-ized′, -iz′ing** —**de·hy′dro·gen·a′tion** *n.*

de-ice (dē īs′) *vt.* **-iced′, -ic′ing** to melt ice from or keep free of ice —**de-ic′er** *n.*

de·i·fy (dē′ə fī′) *vt.* **-fied′, -fy′ing** [< OFr. < LL. < L. *deus,* god + *facere,* to make] **1.** to make a god of; rank among the gods **2.** to look upon or worship as a god —**de·if′ic** (-if′ik) *adj.* —**de′i·fi·ca′tion** (-ə fi kā′shən) *n.* —**de′i·fi′er** *n.*

deign (dān) *vi.* [< OFr. < L. *dignare* < *dignus,* worthy] to think it not beneath one's dignity (*to do* something); condescend

de·ism (dē′iz′m) *n.* [< Fr. < L. *deus,* god] the doctrine that God created the world and its natural laws, but takes no further part in its functioning —**de′ist** *n.* —**de·is′tic, de·is′ti·cal** *adj.* —**de·is′ti·cal·ly** *adv.*

de·i·ty (dē′ə tē) *n., pl.* **-ties** [< OFr. < LL. < L. *deus,* god] **1.** the state of being a god; divine nature **2.** a god or goddess —**the Deity** God

‡**dé·jà vu** (dā zhȧ vü′) [Fr., lit., already seen] *Psychol.* the illusion that one has previously experienced something actually new to one

de·ject (di jekt′) *vt.* [< L. pp. of *dejicere* < *de-,* down + *jacere,* to throw] to dishearten; depress

de·ject·ed (di jek′tid) *adj.* in low spirits; depressed; disheartened —**de·ject′ed·ly** *adv.* —**de·ject′ed·ness** *n.*

de·jec·tion (di jek′shən) *n.* lowness of spirits; depression

de ju·re (di joor′ē, dā) [L.] by right or legal establishment *[de jure government]* : cf. DE FACTO

dek·a- *same as* DECA-: also, before a vowel, **dek-**

del. **1.** delegate **2.** delegation **3.** delete

De·la·croix (də lȧ krwȧ′), **(Ferdinand Victor) Eu·gène** (ö zhen′) 1798–1863; Fr. painter

Del·a·ware (del′ə wer′, -war′) [after Baron *De La Warr,* colonial gov. of Va. (1610–11)] **1.** E State of the U.S., on the Atlantic: 2,057 sq. mi.; pop. 595,000; cap. Dover: abbrev. **Del., DE** **2.** river flowing southward from S N.Y. into the Atlantic —*n.* **1.** *pl.* **-wares′, -ware′** a member of a tribe of Indians who lived in the Delaware River valley **2.** their Algonquian language —**Del′a·war′e·an** *adj., n.*

de·lay (di lā′) *vt.* [< OFr. < *de-,* intens. + *laier,* to leave, let < L. *laxare:* see RELAX] **1.** to put off; postpone **2.** to make late; detain —*vi.* to stop for a while; linger —*n.* **1.** a delaying or being delayed **2.** the period of time for which something is delayed —**de·lay′er** *n.*

de·le (dē′lē) *vt.* **-led, -le·ing** [L., imperative sing. of *delere:* see DELETE] *Printing* to take out (a letter, word, etc.); delete: usually in the imperative and expressed by the mark (₰), indicating the matter to be deleted —*n.* this mark

de·lec·ta·ble (di lek′tə b′l) *adj.* [< L. < *delectare:* see DELIGHT] very pleasing; delightful; now, esp., pleasing to the taste; delicious —**de·lec′ta·bil′i·ty, de·lec′ta·ble·ness** *n.* —**de·lec′ta·bly** *adv.*

de·lec·ta·tion (dē′lek tā′shən, di lek′-) *n.* [OFr. < L. < *delectare:* see DELIGHT] delight; entertainment

del·e·gate (del′ə gāt′; *also for n.* -git) *n.* [< L. pp. of *delegare* < *de-,* from + *legare,* to send] **1.** a person authorized to act for others; representative, as at a convention **2.** a member of a House of Delegates —*vt.* **-gat′ed, -gat′ing** **1.** to send or appoint as a representative or deputy **2.** to entrust (authority, power, etc.) to a person acting as one's representative

del·e·ga·tion (del′ə gā′shən) *n.* **1.** a delegating or being delegated **2.** a body of delegates Also **del·e·ga·cy** (del′ə gə sē) *pl.* **-cies**

de·lete (di lēt′) *vt.* **-let′ed, -let′ing** [< L. *deletus,* pp. of *delere,* to destroy] to take out (a printed or written letter, word, etc.); cross out —**de·le′tion** *n.*

del·e·te·ri·ous (del′ə tir′ē əs) *adj.* [Gr. *dēlētērios* < *dēleisthai,* to injure] harmful to health, well-being, etc.; injurious —**del′e·te′ri·ous·ly** *adv.* —**del′e·te′ri·ous·ness** *n.*

delft·ware (delft′wer′) *n.* **1.** glazed earthenware, usually blue and white, which originated in Delft, a city in W Netherlands **2.** any similar ware Also **delft, delf** (delf)

Del·hi (del′ē) city in N India: pop. 2,062,000: see also NEW DELHI

Del·ia (dēl′yə) [L., fem. of *Delius,* of Delos, a Greek island] a feminine name

de·lib·er·ate (di lib′ər it; *for v.* -āt′) *adj.* [< L. pp. of *deliberare* < *de-,* intens. + *librare,* to weigh < *libra,* a scales] **1.** carefully thought out and formed, or done on purpose **2.** careful in considering; not rash or hasty **3.** unhurried and methodical *[deliberate aim]* —*vi.* **-at′ed, -at′ing** to think or consider carefully and fully; esp., to consider reasons for and against in order to make up one's mind —*vt.* to consider carefully —**de·lib′er·ate·ly** *adv.* —**de·lib′er·ate·ness** *n.* —**de·lib′er·a′tor** *n.*

de·lib·er·a·tion (di lib′ə rā′shən) *n.* **1.** a deliberating, or considering carefully **2.** [*often pl.*] consideration and discussion before reaching a decision **3.** carefulness; slowness

de·lib·er·a·tive (di lib′ə rāt′iv, -ər ə tiv) *adj.* **1.** of or for deliberating *[a deliberative assembly]* **2.** characterized by deliberation —**de·lib′er·a′tive·ly** *adv.* —**de·lib′er·a′tive·ness** *n.*

del·i·ca·cy (del′i kə sē) ***n., pl.*** **-cies 1.** a delicate quality **2.** graceful slightness, softness, etc.; fineness **3.** weakness of constitution or health **4.** a need for careful and deft handling **5.** fineness of feeling or appreciation **6.** fineness of touch, skill, etc. **7.** a fine regard for the feelings of others **8.** a sensitive distaste for what is considered improper or offensive **9.** a choice food

del·i·cate (del′i kit) ***adj.*** [L. *delicatus*, delightful < OL. *delicere:* see DELIGHT] **1.** pleasing in its lightness, mildness, etc. **2.** beautifully fine in texture, workmanship, etc. **3.** slight and subtle **4.** easily damaged, disordered, spoiled, etc. **5.** frail in health **6.** *a)* needing careful handling, tact, etc. [a *delicate* situation] *b)* showing tact, consideration, etc. **7.** finely sensitive [a *delicate* gauge] **8.** finely skilled **9.** having a sensitive distaste for what is considered offensive or improper —**del′i·cate·ly *adv.*** —**del′i·cate·ness *n.***

del·i·ca·tes·sen (del′i kə tes′'n) ***n.*** [G. pl. < Fr. *délicatesse*, delicacy] **1.** prepared cooked meats, smoked fish, cheeses, salads, relishes, etc., collectively **2.** a shop where such foods are sold

de·li·cious (di lish′əs) ***adj.*** [< OFr. < L. < *deliciae*, delight < OL. *delicere:* see DELIGHT] **1.** very enjoyable; delightful **2.** very pleasing to taste or smell —***n.*** **[D-]** a sweet, red winter apple —**de·li′cious·ly *adv.*** —**de·li′cious·ness *n.***

de·light (di līt′) ***vt.*** [< OFr. < L. < OL. *delicere* < *de-*, from + *lacere*, to entice] to give great pleasure to —***vi.*** **1.** to give great pleasure **2.** to be highly pleased —***n.*** **1.** great pleasure **2.** something giving great pleasure —**de·light′ed *adj.*** —**de·light′ed·ly *adv.*** —**de·light′ed·ness *n.***

de·light·ful (-fəl) ***adj.*** giving delight; very pleasing; charming: also [Archaic] **de·light′some** (-səm) —**de·light′ful·ly *adv.*** —**de·light′ful·ness *n.***

De·li·lah (di lī′lə) [Heb. *delīlāh*, lit., delicate] *Bible* the mistress of Samson, who betrayed him to the Philistines: Judg. 16 —***n.*** a seductive, treacherous woman

de·lim·it (di lim′it) ***vt.*** to set the limits or boundaries of: also **de·lim′i·tate′ -tat′ed, -tat′ing** —**de·lim′i·ta′tion *n.*** —**de·lim′i·ta′tive *adj.***

de·lin·e·ate (di lin′ē āt′) ***vt.*** **-at′ed, -at′ing** [< L. < *de-*, from + *linea*, LINE[1]] **1.** to trace the outline of **2.** to draw; depict **3.** to depict in words; describe —**de·lin′e·a′tion *n.*** —**de·lin′e·a′tive *adj.*** —**de·lin′e·a′tor *n.***

de·lin·quen·cy (di liŋ′kwən sē) ***n., pl.*** **-cies 1.** failure or neglect to do what duty or law requires **2.** an overdue debt, tax, etc. **3.** a fault; misdeed **4.** antisocial or illegal behavior, esp. by the young: see JUVENILE DELINQUENCY

de·lin·quent (-kwənt) ***adj.*** [< L. *delinquens*, prp. of *delinquere* < *de-*, from + *linquere*, to leave] **1.** failing or neglecting to do what duty or law requires **2.** overdue [*delinquent* taxes] —***n.*** a delinquent person; esp., a juvenile delinquent —**de·lin′quent·ly *adv.***

del·i·quesce (del′ə kwes′) ***vi.*** **-quesced′, -quesc′ing** [< L. *deliquescere* < *de-*, from + *liquere*, to be liquid] **1.** to melt away **2.** to become liquid by absorbing moisture from the air —**del′i·ques′cence *n.*** —**del′i·ques′cent *adj.***

de·lir·i·ous (di lir′ē əs) ***adj.*** **1.** in a state of delirium **2.** of or caused by delirium **3.** wildly excited —**de·lir′i·ous·ly *adv.*** —**de·lir′i·ous·ness *n.***

de·lir·i·um (-ē əm) ***n., pl.*** **-i·ums, -i·a** (-ə) [L. < *delirare*, to rave, lit., to turn the furrow awry in plowing < *de-*, from + *lira*, a line] **1.** a temporary state of extreme mental excitement, marked by confused speech and hallucinations: it sometimes occurs during a fever, in some forms of insanity, etc. **2.** uncontrollably wild excitement

delirium tre·mens (trē′mənz) [ModL., lit., trembling delirium] a violent delirium resulting chiefly from excessive drinking of alcoholic liquor

De·li·us (dē′lē əs, dēl′yəs), **Frederick** 1862–1934; Eng. composer

de·liv·er (di liv′ər) ***vt.*** [< OFr. < VL. < L. *de-*, from + *liberare*, to free < *liber*, free] **1.** to set free or save from evil, danger, etc. **2.** to assist at the birth of (offspring) **3.** to express in words; utter [to *deliver* a speech] **4.** to hand over; transfer **5.** to distribute [*deliver* the mail] **6.** to strike (a blow) **7.** to throw (a ball, etc.) —***vi.*** to make deliveries, as of merchandise —**be delivered of** to give birth to —**deliver oneself of** to express; utter —**de·liv′er·a·ble *adj.*** —**de·liv′er·er *n.***

de·liv·er·ance (-əns) ***n.*** **1.** a freeing or being freed **2.** an opinion, etc. publicly expressed

de·liv·er·y (-ē) ***n., pl.*** **-er·ies 1.** a handing over; transfer **2.** a distributing, as of mail **3.** a giving birth; childbirth **4.** any giving forth **5.** the act or manner of giving a speech, striking a blow, throwing a ball, etc. **6.** something delivered

dell (del) ***n.*** [OE. *del*] a small, secluded valley or glen, usually a wooded one

de·louse (dē lous′, -louz′) ***vt.*** **-loused′, -lous′ing** to rid of lice —**de·lous′er *n.***

Del·phi (del′fī) ancient city in C Greece, on the slopes of Mount Parnassus

Del·phic (-fik) ***adj.*** **1.** of Delphi **2.** designating or of the oracle of Apollo at Delphi in ancient times Also **Del′phi·an** (-fē ən)

del·phin·i·um (del fin′ē əm) ***n.*** [< Gr. *delphin*, dolphin: its nectary resembles a dolphin] a plant bearing spikes of spurred, irregular flowers, usually blue, on tall stalks: some are poisonous

del·ta (del′tə) ***n.*** [< Gr.] **1.** the fourth letter of the Greek alphabet (Δ, δ) **2.** a deposit of sand and soil, usually triangular, formed at the mouth of some rivers —**del·ta·ic** (del tā′ik) ***adj.***

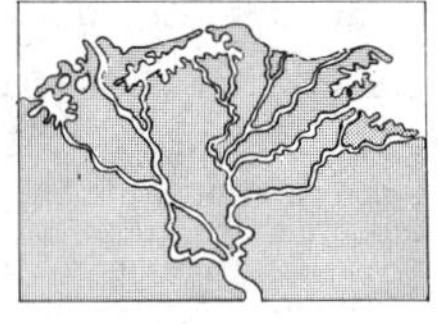

DELTA

delta ray an electron ejected by the passage of a primary ionizing particle through matter

delta wing the triangular shape of certain kinds of jet aircraft —**del′ta-wing′, del′ta-winged′ *adj.***

del·toid (del′toid) ***adj.*** **1.** shaped like a delta; triangular **2.** designating or of a large, triangular muscle of the shoulder —***n.*** the deltoid muscle

de·lude (di lo͞od′) ***vt.*** **-lud′ed, -lud′ing** [< L. < *de-*, from + *ludere*, to play] to mislead; deceive; trick —**de·lud′er *n.***

del·uge (del′yo͞oj) ***n.*** [< OFr. < L. *diluvium* < *dis-*, off + *lavere*, to wash] **1.** a great flood **2.** a heavy rainfall **3.** an overwhelming, floodlike rush of anything —***vt.*** **-uged, -ug·ing 1.** to flood **2.** to overwhelm —**the Deluge** *Bible* the great flood in Noah's time: Gen. 7

de·lu·sion (di lo͞o′zhən) ***n.*** **1.** a deluding or being deluded **2.** a false belief or opinion **3.** *Psychiatry* a false, persistent belief not substantiated by sensory or objective evidence —**de·lu′sion·al *adj.***

de·lu·sive (di lo͞os′iv) ***adj.*** **1.** tending to delude; misleading **2.** unreal Also **de·lu′so·ry** (-lo͞o′sə rē) —**de·lu′sive·ly *adv.*** —**de·lu′sive·ness *n.***

de·luxe (di luks′, -looks′, -lo͞oks′) ***adj.*** [Fr., lit., of luxury] of extra fine quality; luxurious; elegant —***adv.*** in a deluxe manner

delve (delv) ***vi.*** **delved, delv′ing** [OE. *delfan*] **1.** [Archaic] to dig with a spade **2.** to investigate for information; search (*into* books, the past, etc.) —**delv′er *n.***

Dem. 1. Democrat **2.** Democratic

de·mag·net·ize (dē mag′nə tīz′) ***vt.*** **-ized′, -iz′ing** to deprive of magnetism —**de·mag′net·i·za′tion *n.*** —**de·mag′net·iz′er *n.***

dem·a·gog·ic (dem′ə gäj′ik, -gäg′-, -gō′jik) ***adj.*** of, like, or characteristic of a demagogue or demagogy: also **dem′a·gog′i·cal** —**dem′a·gog′i·cal·ly *adv.***

dem·a·gogue, dem·a·gog (dem′ə gäg′, -gôg′) ***n.*** [< Gr. < *dēmos*, the people + *agōgos*, leader < *agein*, to lead] a person who tries to stir up the people by appeals to emotion, prejudice, etc. in order to win them over quickly and so gain power —***vi.*** **-gogued′** or **-goged′, -gogu′ing** or **-gog′ing** to behave as a demagogue

dem·a·gog·y (dem′ə gō′jē, -gäg′ē, -gôg′ē) ***n.*** the methods or practices of a demagogue: also **dem′a·gog′uer·y** (-gäg′ər ē, -gôg′-)

de·mand (di mand′) ***vt.*** [< OFr. < L. < *de-*, from + *mandare*, to entrust: see MANDATE] **1.** to ask for boldly or urgently **2.** to ask for as a right or with authority **3.** to ask to know or be informed of **4.** to require [the work *demands* time] —***vi.*** to make a demand —***n.*** **1.** a demanding **2.** a thing demanded **3.** a strong request **4.** an urgent requirement or claim **5.** *a)* the desire for a commodity along with ability to pay for it *b)* the amount people are ready to buy at a certain price —**in demand** asked for —**on demand** when presented for payment —**de·mand′a·ble *adj.*** —**de·mand′er *n.***

demand deposit *Banking* a deposit that may be withdrawn on demand, without advance notice

de·mand·ing (-iŋ) ***adj.*** making demands on one's patience, energy, etc. —**de·mand′ing·ly *adv.***

de·mar·cate (di mär′kāt, dē′mär kāt′) ***vt.*** **-cat·ed, -cat·ing** [< ff.] **1.** to mark the limits of **2.** to distinguish; separate Also **de·mark′**

de·mar·ca·tion, de·mar·ka·tion (dē′mär kā′shən) ***n.*** [Sp. < *de-* (L. *de*), from + *marcar*, to mark] **1.** the act of setting and marking boundaries **2.** a limit or boundary **3.** a separation

dé·marche (dā märsh′) ***n.*** [Fr.: see DE- & MARCH[1]] a line of action; maneuver, esp. in diplomacy

de·mean[1] (di mēn′) ***vt.*** [DE- + MEAN[2], after DEBASE] to degrade; humble [to *demean* oneself by lying]

de·mean[2] (di mēn′) ***vt.*** [see ff.] to behave or conduct (oneself)

de·mean·or (-ər) ***n.*** [< OFr. < *de-* (L. *de*), from + *mener*, to lead < LL. *minare*, to drive (animals) < L. *minari*, to threaten] outward behavior; conduct; deportment: also, Brit. sp., **de·mean′our**

de·ment·ed (di ment′id) ***adj.*** [< L. < *demens* (gen. *demen-*

tis), mad: see ff.] mentally deranged; insane —**de·ment′ed·ly** *adv.*
de·men·tia (di men′shə) *n.* [L. < *de-*, out from + *mens*, the mind] loss or impairment of mental powers due to organic causes: cf. AMENTIA
dementia prae·cox (prē′käks) [ModL.: see prec. & PRECOCIOUS] *obs. term for* SCHIZOPHRENIA
de·mer·it (di mer′it) *n.* [< OFr. < ML. < L. *demerere*, to deserve well, with intens. prefix *de-* mistaken as negative in ML.] **1.** a fault; defect **2.** a mark recorded against a student, trainee, etc. for poor conduct or work
de·mesne (di mān′, -mēn′) *n.* [OFr. *demeine* < L. *dominium:* see DOMAIN] **1.** *Law* possession (of real estate) in one's own right **2.** the land around a mansion **3.** a region or domain: also used figuratively
De·me·ter (di mēt′ər) *Gr. Myth.* the goddess of agriculture: identified with the Roman goddess Ceres
dem·i- [OFr. < L. < *dis-*, apart + *medius*, middle] *a prefix meaning:* **1.** half *[demisemiquaver]* **2.** less than usual in size, power, etc. *[demigod]*
dem·i·god (dem′ē gäd′) *n.* **1.** *Myth. a)* a minor deity *b)* the offspring of a human being and a god or goddess **2.** a godlike person
dem·i·john (-jän′) *n.* [Fr. *dame-jeanne*] a large bottle of glass or earthenware, with a narrow neck and a wicker casing and handle

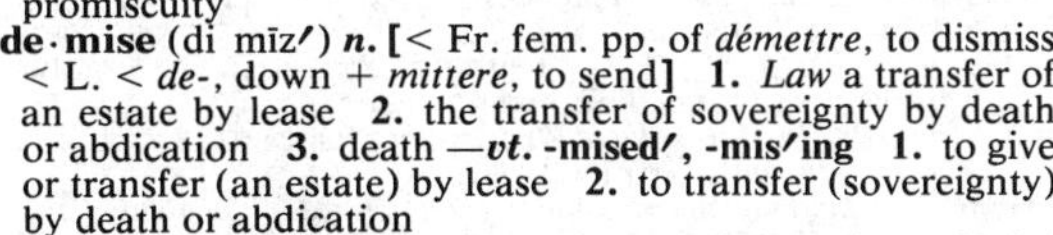
DEMIJOHN

de·mil·i·ta·rize (dē mil′ə tə rīz′) *vt.* **-rized′, -riz′ing** to free from military control or activity, or from militarism —**de·mil′i·ta·ri·za′tion** *n.*
dem·i·mon·daine (dem′ē män dān′) *n.* [Fr.] a woman of the demimonde
dem·i·monde (dem′ē mänd′, dem′ē-mänd′) *n.* [Fr. < *demi-*, DEMI- + *monde* (< L. *mundus*), world] the class of women who have lost social standing because of sexual promiscuity
de·mise (di mīz′) *n.* [< Fr. fem. pp. of *démettre*, to dismiss < L. < *de-*, down + *mittere*, to send] **1.** *Law* a transfer of an estate by lease **2.** the transfer of sovereignty by death or abdication **3.** death —*vt.* **-mised′, -mis′ing 1.** to give or transfer (an estate) by lease **2.** to transfer (sovereignty) by death or abdication
dem·i·sem·i·qua·ver (dem′ē sem′ē kwā′vər) *n.* [Brit.] *same as* THIRTY-SECOND NOTE
dem·i·tasse (dem′ē tas′, -täs′) *n.* [Fr. < *demi-*, DEMI- + *tasse*, a cup] a small cup of or for after-dinner black coffee
de·mob (dē mäb′) *vt.* **-mobbed′, -mob′bing** [Brit. Colloq.] to demobilize
de·mo·bi·lize (dē mō′bə līz′) *vt.* **-lized′, -liz′ing 1.** to disband (troops) **2.** to discharge (a person) from the armed forces —**de·mo′bi·li·za′tion** *n.*
de·moc·ra·cy (di mäk′rə sē) *n., pl.* **-cies** [< Fr. < ML. *democratia* < Gr. < *dēmos*, the people + *kratein*, to rule] **1.** government in which the people hold the ruling power either directly or through elected representatives **2.** a country, state, etc. with such government **3.** majority rule **4.** the principle of equality of rights, opportunity, etc., or the practice of this principle
dem·o·crat (dem′ə krat′) *n.* **1.** a person who believes in and upholds government by the people **2.** a person who believes in and practices the principle of equality of rights, opportunity, etc. **3.** [**D-**] a member of the Democratic Party
dem·o·crat·ic (dem′ə krat′ik) *adj.* **1.** of, belonging to, or upholding (a) democracy **2.** of or for all or most people **3.** treating people of all classes in the same way **4.** [**D-**] of or belonging to the Democratic Party —**dem′o·crat′i·cal·ly** *adv.*
Democratic Party one of the two major political parties in the U.S., since about 1830
de·moc·ra·tize (di mäk′rə tīz′) *vt., vi.* **-tized′, -tiz′ing** to make or become democratic —**de·moc′ra·ti·za′tion** *n.*
de·mod·u·late (dē mäj′oo lāt′) *vt.* **-lat′ed, -lat′ing** to cause to undergo demodulation —**de·mod′u·la′tor** *n.*
de·mod·u·la·tion (dē mäj′oo lā′shən) *n.* *Radio* the recovery, at the receiver, of a signal that has been modulated on a carrier wave
de·mog·ra·phy (di mäg′rə fē) *n.* [< Gr. *dēmos*, the people + -GRAPHY] the statistical science dealing with the distribution, vital statistics, etc. of populations —**de·mog′ra·pher** *n.* —**de·mo·graph·ic** (dē′mə graf′ik, dem′ə-) *adj.* —**de′mo·graph′i·cal·ly** *adv.*
dem·oi·selle (dem′wə zel′) *n.* [Fr.] a damsel
de·mol·ish (di mäl′ish) *vt.* [< Fr. < L. *demoliri*, to destroy < *de-*, down + *moliri*, to build < *moles*, a mass] **1.** to tear down or smash to pieces (a building, etc.) **2.** to destroy; ruin —**de·mol′ish·er** *n.* —**de·mol′ish·ment** *n.*
dem·o·li·tion (dem′ə lish′ən, dē′mə-) *n.* a demolishing or being demolished; often, specif., destruction by explosives
de·mon (dē′mən) *n.* [L. *daemon:* see DAEMON] **1.** *same as* DAEMON **2.** a devil; evil spirit **3.** a person or thing regarded as evil, cruel, etc. **4.** a person who has great energy or skill —**de·mon·ic** (di män′ik) *adj.* —**de·mon′i·cal·ly** *adv.*
de·mon·e·tize (dē män′ə tīz′) *vt.* **-tized′, -tiz′ing 1.** to deprive (currency) of its standard value **2.** to stop using (silver or gold) as a monetary standard —**de·mon′e·ti·za′tion** *n.*
de·mo·ni·ac (di mō′nē ak′) *adj.* **1.** possessed or influenced by a demon **2.** of a demon or demons **3.** like or characteristic of a demon; fiendish Also **de·mo·ni·a·cal** (dē′mə nī′ə k'l) —*n.* a person supposedly possessed by a demon —**de′mo·ni′a·cal·ly** *adv.*
de·mon·ism (dē′mən iz'm) *n.* belief in the existence and powers of demons —**de′mon·ist** *n.*
de·mon·o- *a combining form meaning* demon: also, before a vowel, **demon-**
de·mon·ol·a·try (dē′mə näl′ə trē) *n.* worship of demons —**de′mon·ol′a·ter** *n.*
de·mon·ol·o·gy (-jē) *n.* the study of demons or of beliefs about them —**de′mon·ol′o·gist** *n.*
de·mon·stra·ble (di män′strə b'l, dem′ən-) *adj.* that can be demonstrated, or proved —**de·mon′stra·bil′i·ty** *n.* —**de·mon′stra·bly** *adv.*
dem·on·strate (dem′ən strāt′) *vt.* **-strat′ed, -strat′ing** [< L. pp. of *demonstrare* < *de-*, from + *monstrare*, to show] **1.** to show by reasoning; prove **2.** to explain by using examples, experiments, etc. **3.** to show the operation or working of **4.** to show (feelings) plainly —*vi.* **1.** to show one's feelings or views by taking part in a public meeting, parade, etc. **2.** to show military power
dem·on·stra·tion (dem′ən strā′shən) *n.* **1.** a making evident or proving **2.** an explanation by example, experiment, etc. **3.** a practical showing of how something works or is used **4.** a display or outward show **5.** a public show of opinion, etc., as by a mass meeting **6.** a show of military force
de·mon·stra·tive (di män′strə tiv) *adj.* **1.** giving convincing evidence or proof (usually with *of*) **2.** having to do with demonstration **3.** showing feelings openly and frankly **4.** *Gram.* pointing out *["this" is a demonstrative pronoun]* —**de·mon′stra·tive·ly** *adv.* —**de·mon′stra·tive·ness** *n.*
dem·on·stra·tor (dem′ən strāt′ər) *n.* [L.] one that demonstrates; specif., a person who takes part in a public demonstration
de·mor·al·ize (di môr′ə līz′) *vt.* **-ized′, -iz′ing 1.** [Now Rare] to corrupt the morals of **2.** to lower the morale of **3.** to throw into confusion —**de·mor′al·i·za′tion** *n.* —**de·mor′al·iz′er** *n.*
De·mos·the·nes (di mäs′thə nēz′) 384?–322 B.C.; Athenian orator & statesman
de·mote (di mōt′) *vt.* **-mot′ed, -mot′ing** [DE- + (PRO)MOTE] to reduce to a lower grade; lower in rank —**de·mo′tion** *n.*
de·mot·ic (di mät′ik) *adj.* [< ML. < Gr. < *dēmotes*, one of the people < *dēmos*, the people] **1.** of the people; popular; specif., vernacular (sense 2) **2.** designating or of a simplified system of ancient Egyptian writing
de·mul·cent (di mul′s'nt) *adj.* [< L. prp. of *demulcere* < *de-*, down + *mulcere*, to stroke] soothing —*n.* a medicine or ointment that soothes irritated mucous membrane
de·mur (di mur′) *vi.* **-murred′, -mur′ring** [OFr. *demorer* < L. < *de-*, from + *morari*, to delay < *mora*, a delay] **1.** to be unwilling because of doubts or objections; object **2.** *Law* to enter a demurrer —*n.* **1.** a demurring **2.** an objection raised or exception taken Also **de·mur′ral** *n.*
de·mure (di myoor′) *adj.* [< ME. < *de-* (prob. intens.) + *mur* < OFr. *mëur*, ripe < L. *maturus*, mature] **1.** modest; reserved **2.** affectedly modest or shy; coy —**de·mure′ly** *adv.* —**de·mure′ness** *n.*
de·mur·rage (di mur′ij) *n.* [< OFr. < *demorer:* see DEMUR] **1.** the delaying of a ship, freight car, etc., as by failure to load, unload, or sail within the time allowed **2.** the compensation paid for this
de·mur·rer (-ər) *n.* [OFr. *demorer*, to DEMUR] **1.** a plea for the dismissal of a lawsuit on the grounds that even if the statements of the opposition are true, they do not sustain the claim **2.** an objection; demur **3.** a person who demurs
den (den) *n.* [OE. *denn*] **1.** the cave or other lair of a wild animal **2.** a retreat or headquarters, as of thieves **3.** a small, cozy room where a person can be alone to read, work, etc. —*vi.* **denned, den′ning** to live or hide as in a den
Den. Denmark

de·nar·i·us (di nar′ē əs, -ner′-) *n., pl.* **-nar′i·i′** (-ī′) [< L. < *deni,* by tens < *decem,* ten] **1.** an ancient Roman silver coin, the penny of the New Testament **2.** an ancient Roman gold coin

de·na·tion·al·ize (dē nash′ə n′l īz′) *vt.* **-ized′, -iz′ing 1.** to deprive of national rights or status **2.** to place (a government-controlled industry) under private ownership —**de·na′tion·al·i·za′tion** *n.*

de·nat·u·ral·ize (dē nach′ər ə līz′) *vt.* **-ized′, -iz′ing 1.** to make unnatural **2.** to take citizenship away from —**de·nat′u·ral·i·za′tion** *n.*

de·na·ture (dē nā′chər) *vt.* **-tured, -tur·ing 1.** to change the nature of **2.** to make (alcohol, etc.) unfit for human consumption without spoiling for other uses **3.** to change the composition of (a protein) by heat, acids, etc. —**de·na′tur·a′tion** *n.*

den·drite (den′drīt) *n.* [< Gr. < *dendron:* see ff.] the branched part of a nerve cell that carries impulses toward the cell body —**den·drit′ic** (-drit′ik), **den·drit′i·cal** *adj.* —**den·drit′i·cal·ly** *adv.*

den·dro- [< Gr. *dendron,* a tree] *a combining form meaning* tree: also **dendri-** or, before a vowel, **dendr-**

den·drol·o·gy (den dräl′ə jē) *n.* the scientific study of trees —**den′dro·log′ic** (-drə läj′ik), **den′dro·log′i·cal** *adj.* —**den·drol′o·gist** *n.*

-den·dron (den′drən) [see DENDRO-] *a combining form meaning* tree or treelike structure

den·gue (deŋ′gē, -gā) *n.* [WIndSp. < Swahili *dinga,* a cramp, infl. by Sp. *dengue,* contortion] an infectious tropical disease transmitted by mosquitoes and characterized by severe pain in the joints and back, fever, and rash

de·ni·al (di nī′əl) *n.* **1.** a denying; saying "no" (to a request, etc.) **2.** a statement in opposition to another **3.** a disowning; repudiation *[*the *denial* of one's family*]* **4.** a refusal to believe or accept (a doctrine, etc.) **5.** *same as* SELF-DENIAL

de·nier[1] (den′yər) *n.* [< OFr. < L. *denarius,* DENARIUS] a unit of weight for measuring the fineness of threads of silk, nylon, etc.

de·ni·er[2] (di nī′ər) *n.* a person who denies

den·i·grate (den′ə grāt′) *vt.* **-grat′ed, -grat′ing** [< L. pp. of *denigrare* < *de-,* intens. + *nigrare,* to blacken < *niger,* black] to disparage the character of; defame —**den′i·gra′tion** *n.* —**den′i·gra′tor** *n.*

den·im (den′əm) *n.* [< Fr. *(serge) de Nîmes,* (serge) of Nîmes, Fr. town] a coarse, twilled cotton cloth used for overalls, uniforms, etc.

Den·is (den′is) [Fr. < L. *Dionysius*] a masculine name: also sp. **Den′nis**

den·i·zen (den′i zən) *n.* [< Anglo-Fr. < OFr. *denzein* < *denz,* within < VL. < L. *de intus,* from within] **1.** *a)* an inhabitant *b)* a frequenter of a particular place **2.** an animal, plant, etc. that has become naturalized

Den·mark (den′märk) country in Europe, on the peninsula of Jutland & several nearby islands: 16,615 sq. mi.; pop. 4,870,000; cap. Copenhagen

de·nom·i·nate (di näm′ə nāt′) *vt.* **-nat′ed, -nat′ing** [< L. pp. of *denominare* < *de-,* intens. + *nominare:* see NOMINATE] to give a specified name to; call

de·nom·i·na·tion (di näm′ə nā′shən) *n.* **1.** the act of denominating **2.** a name, esp. of a class of things **3.** a class or kind with a specific name or value *[*coins of different *denominations]* **4.** a religious sect or body

de·nom·i·na·tion·al (-′l) *adj.* of, or under the control of, a religious denomination —**de·nom′i·na′tion·al·ism** *n.* —**de·nom′i·na′tion·al·ly** *adv.*

de·nom·i·na·tive (di näm′ə nə tiv) *adj. Gram.* formed from a noun or adjective stem

de·nom·i·na·tor (-nāt′ər) *n.* [ML.] the term below the line in a fraction, indicating the number of equal parts into which the whole is divided

de·no·ta·tion (dē′nō tā′shən) *n.* **1.** a denoting **2.** the explicit meaning or reference of a word or term: cf. CONNOTATION **3.** an indication or sign

de·note (di nōt′) *vt.* **-not′ed, -not′ing** [< Fr. < L. < *de-,* down + *notare,* to mark < *nota,* NOTE] **1.** to be a sign of; indicate **2.** to signify or refer to explicitly; mean: cf. CONNOTE —**de·not′a·ble** *adj.* —**de·no·ta·tive** (dē′nō tāt′iv) *adj.*

de·noue·ment, dé·noue·ment (dā no͞o′män; *Fr.* dā no͞o män′) *n.* [Fr. < *dé-* (L. *dis-*), out + *nouer,* to tie < L. < *nodus:* see NODE] **1.** the outcome, solution, or unraveling of a plot in a drama, story, etc. **2.** any final revelation or outcome

de·nounce (di nouns′) *vt.* **-nounced′, -nounc′ing** [< OFr. < L. *denuntiare:* see DENUNCIATION] **1.** to accuse publicly; inform against **2.** to condemn strongly as evil **3.** to give formal notice of the ending of (a treaty, armistice, etc.) —**de·nounce′ment** *n.* —**de·nounc′er** *n.*

‡**de no·vo** (dē nō′vō) [L.] once more; anew

dense (dens) *adj.* **dens′er, dens′est** [L. *densus,* compact] **1.** packed tightly together; compact **2.** difficult to get through, penetrate, etc. **3.** stupid **4.** *Photog.* opaque, with good contrast in light and shade: said of a negative —**dense′ly** *adv.* —**dense′ness** *n.*

den·si·ty (den′sə tē) *n., pl.* **-ties 1.** the quality or condition of being dense **2.** quantity or number per unit, as of area *[*the *density* of population*]* **3.** *Physics* the ratio of the mass of an object to its volume

dent (dent) *n.* [ME., var. of DINT] **1.** a slight hollow made in a surface by a blow or pressure **2.** an appreciable effect —*vt.* to make a dent in —*vi.* to become dented

den·tal (den′t'l) *adj.* [ModL. < L. *dens* (gen. *dentis*), a tooth] **1.** of or for the teeth or dentistry **2.** *Phonet.* formed by placing the tip of the tongue against or near the upper front teeth —*n. Phonet.* a dental consonant (th, *th*)

dental floss thin, strong thread for removing food particles from between the teeth

dental hygienist a dentist's assistant, who cleans teeth, takes dental X-rays, etc.

den·tate (den′tāt) *adj.* [< L. < *dens:* see DENTAL] having teeth or toothlike projections; toothed or notched —**den′tate·ly** *adv.* —**den·ta′tion** *n.*

den·ti- [< L. *dens:* see DENTAL] *a combining form meaning* tooth or teeth: also **dento-** or, before a vowel, **dent-**

den·ti·frice (den′tə fris) *n.* [< L. < *dens* (see DENTAL) + *fricare,* to rub] any preparation for cleaning teeth, as a powder, paste, or liquid

den·til (den′til) *n.* [< MFr. < L. *dens:* see DENTAL] *Archit.* any of a series of small rectangular blocks projecting like teeth, as from under a cornice

den·tin (den′tin) *n.* [< L. *dens:* see DENTAL] the hard, calcareous tissue forming the body of a tooth, under the enamel: also **den′tine** (-tēn, -tin)

den·tist (den′tist) *n.* [< Fr. < ML. < L. *dens:* see DENTAL] one whose profession is the care of teeth and surrounding tissues, the replacement of missing teeth with artificial ones, etc.

den·tist·ry (-rē) *n.* the profession or work of a dentist

den·ti·tion (den tish′ən) *n.* [< L. < *dentire,* to cut teeth < *dens:* see DENTAL] **1.** the teething process **2.** the number and kind of teeth and their arrangement

den·ture (den′chər) *n.* [Fr. < L. *dens:* see DENTAL] a fitting for the mouth, with artificial teeth

de·nu·cle·ar·ize (dē no͞o′klē ə rīz′, -nyo͞o′-) *vt.* **-ized′, -iz′ing** to prohibit the possession of nuclear weapons in —**de·nu′cle·ar·i·za′tion** *n.*

de·nu·date (di no͞o′dāt, -nyo͞o′-; den′yoo dāt′) *vt.* **-dat·ed, -dat·ing** [< L. pp. of *denudare* < *de-,* off + *nudare,* to strip] *same as* DENUDE —**de·nu·da·tion** (dē′no͞o dā′shən, -nyo͞o-; den′yoo-) *n.*

de·nude (di no͞od′, -nyo͞od′) *vt.* **-nud′ed, -nud′ing** [see prec.] **1.** to make bare; strip **2.** to destroy all life in (an area) **3.** to lay bare as by erosion

de·nun·ci·ate (di nun′sē āt′) *vt.* **-at′ed, -at′ing** *same as* DENOUNCE —**de·nun′ci·a′tor** *n.*

de·nun·ci·a·tion (di nun′sē ā′shən) *n.* [< L. pp. of *denuntiare* < *de-,* intens. + *nuntiare,* ANNOUNCE] the act of denouncing —**de·nun′ci·a·to′ry** (-ə tôr′ē), **de·nun′ci·a′tive** (-āt′iv) *adj.*

Den·ver (den′vər) [after J. *Denver* (1817–94), gov. of Kans.] capital of Colo., in the NC part: pop. 491,000 (met. area 1,615,000)

de·ny (di nī′) *vt.* **-nied′, -ny′ing** [< OFr. < L. < *de-,* intens. + *negare,* to deny] **1.** to declare (a statement) untrue **2.** to refuse to accept as true or right **3.** to refuse to acknowledge as one's own; repudiate **4.** to refuse access to **5.** to refuse to give **6.** to refuse the request of —**deny oneself** to do without desired things

de·o·dar (dē′ə där′) *n.* [Hindi < Sans. *dēvadāru,* lit., tree of the gods] **1.** a Himalayan cedar with fragrant, light-red wood **2.** the wood

de·o·dor·ant (dē ō′dər ənt) *adj.* that prevents, destroys, or masks undesired odors —*n.* any deodorant preparation, esp. one used on the body

de·o·dor·ize (dē ō′də rīz′) *vt.* **-ized′, -iz′ing** to remove or mask the odor of or in —**de·o′dor·i·za′tion** *n.* —**de·o′dor·iz′er** *n.*

de·ox·i·dize (dē äk′sə dīz′) *vt.* **-dized′, -diz′ing** to remove oxygen, esp. chemically combined oxygen, from —**de·ox′i·diz′er** *n.*

de·ox·y·gen·ate (-jə nāt′) *vt.* **-at′ed, -at′ing** to remove oxygen, esp. free oxygen, from (water, air, etc.)

dé·ox·y·ri·bo·nu·cle·ic acid (dē äk′si rī′bō no͞o klē′ik, -nyo͞o-) an essential component of all living matter and a basic material in the chromosomes of the cell nucleus: it contains the genetic code and transmits the hereditary pattern

dep. 1. department **2.** deposit **3.** deputy

de·part (di pärt′) *vi.* [< OFr. *departir* < VL. < L. < *dis-,* apart + *partire,* to divide < *pars,* a PART] **1.** to go away *(from)*; leave **2.** to set out; start **3.** to die **4.** to turn aside *(from* something) *[*to *depart* from custom*]* —*vt.* to leave: now only in **depart this life,** to die

de·part·ed (-id) ***adj.*** **1.** gone away; past **2.** dead **—the departed** the dead person or persons

de·part·ment (-mənt) ***n.*** [see DEPART] **1.** a separate part or division, as of a government, business, or school **2.** a field of knowledge or activity **3.** an administrative district in France or in certain Latin American countries **—de·part·men·tal** (di pärt′men′t'l, dē′pärt-) ***adj.*** **—de·part′men′·tal·ly** ***adv.***

de·part·men·tal·ize (di pärt′men′tə līz′, dē′pärt-) ***vt.*** **-ized′, -iz′ing** to organize into departments

department store a retail store for the sale of many kinds of goods arranged in departments

de·par·ture (di pär′chər) ***n.*** **1.** a departing, or going away **2.** a starting out, as on a trip or new course of action **3.** a deviation or turning aside (*from* something) **4.** [Archaic] death

de·pend (di pend′) ***vi.*** [< OFr. < L. < *de-*, down + *pendere*, to hang] **1.** to be influenced or determined by something else; be contingent (*on*) **2.** to be sure of; rely (*on*) **3.** to rely (*on*) for support or aid **4.** [Archaic] to hang down

de·pend·a·ble (di pen′də b'l) ***adj.*** that can be depended on; reliable **—de·pend′a·bil′i·ty** ***n.*** **—de·pend′a·bly** ***adv.***

de·pend·ence (-dəns) ***n.*** **1.** the condition or fact of being dependent; specif., *a*) a being influenced or determined by something else *b*) reliance (*on* another) for support or aid *c*) subordination **2.** reliance; trust Also sp. **de·pend′ance**

de·pend·en·cy (-dən sē) ***n.***, *pl.* **-cies** **1.** *same as* DEPENDENCE **2.** something dependent or subordinate **3.** a land or territory geographically distinct from the country governing it

de·pend·ent (-dənt) ***adj.*** **1.** hanging down **2.** influenced or determined by something else **3.** relying (*on* another) for support or aid **4.** subordinate **—*n.*** a person who depends on someone else for support, etc. Also sp., esp. for *n.*, **de·pend′ant**

dependent clause *same as* SUBORDINATE CLAUSE

de·per·son·al·ize (dē pur′s'n ə līz′) ***vt.*** **-ized′, -iz′ing** **1.** to deprive of individuality; treat impersonally **2.** to cause to lose one's sense of personal identity **—de·per′son·al·i·za′tion** ***n.***

de·pict (di pikt′) ***vt.*** [< L. pp. of *depingere* < *de-*, intens. + *pingere*, to paint] **1.** to represent in a drawing, sculpture, etc. **2.** to picture in words; describe **—de·pic′tion** ***n.*** **—de·pic′tor** ***n.***

dep·i·late (dep′ə lāt′) ***vt.*** **-lat′ed, -lat′ing** [< L. pp. of *depilare* < *de-*, from + *pilus*, hair] to remove hair from **—dep′i·la′tion** ***n.***

de·pil·a·to·ry (di pil′ə tôr′ē) ***adj.*** serving to remove unwanted hair **—*n.***, *pl.* **-ries** a depilatory agent, as in cream form

de·plane (dē plān′) ***vi.*** **-planed′, -plan′ing** to get out of an airplane after it lands

de·plete (di plēt′) ***vt.*** **-plet′ed, -plet′ing** [< L. pp. of *deplere* < *de-*, from + *plere*, to fill] **1.** to make less by gradually using up (funds, energy, etc.) **2.** to empty wholly or partly **—de·ple′tion** ***n.***

de·plor·a·ble (di plôr′ə b'l) ***adj.*** **1.** that can or should be deplored; lamentable **2.** very bad; wretched **—de·plor′a·bly** ***adv.***

de·plore (di plôr′) ***vt.*** **-plored′, -plor′ing** [< Fr. < L. < *de-*, intens. + *plorare*, to weep] **1.** to be regretful or sorry about; lament **2.** to regard as unfortunate or wretched

de·ploy (dē ploi′) ***vt., vi.*** [< Fr. < OFr. *desployer* < L. *displicare*, to scatter, unfold: see DISPLAY] *Mil.* **1.** to spread out (troops, etc.) so as to form a wider front **2.** to station or move in accordance with a plan **—de·ploy′ment** ***n.***

de·po·lar·ize (dē pō′lə rīz′) ***vt.*** **-ized′, -iz′ing** to destroy or counteract the polarization of **—de·po′lar·i·za′tion** ***n.***

de·pon·ent (di pō′nənt) ***adj.*** [< L. prp. of *deponere*, to set down: see DEPOSIT] *L. & Gr. Gram.* denoting a verb with a passive voice form and an active meaning **—*n.*** **1.** a deponent verb **2.** *Law* a person who gives written testimony under oath

de·pop·u·late (dē päp′yə lāt′) ***vt.*** **-lat′ed, -lat′ing** to reduce the population of, esp. by violence, pestilence, etc. **—de·pop′u·la′tion** ***n.*** **—de·pop′u·la′tor** ***n.***

de·port (di pôrt′) ***vt.*** [< OFr. < L. < *de-*, from + *portare*, to carry] **1.** to behave (oneself) in a specified way **2.** to carry or send away; specif., to expel (an alien) from a country by official order

de·por·ta·tion (dē′pôr tā′shən) ***n.*** expulsion, as of an undesirable alien, from a country

de·port·ment (di pôrt′mənt) ***n.*** the manner of conducting oneself; behavior

de·pose (di pōz′) ***vt.*** **-posed′, -pos′ing** [< OFr. < *de-* (L. *de*), from + *poser* < L. *pausare*, to cease: confused with L. *deponere:* see ff.] **1.** to remove from office or a position of power, esp. from a throne; oust **2.** *Law* to state under oath but out of court **—*vi.*** to bear witness **—de·pos′al** ***n.***

de·pos·it (di päz′it) ***vt.*** [< L. *depositus*, pp. of *deponere*, to put down < *de-*, down + *ponere*, to put] **1.** to place or entrust, as for safekeeping [to *deposit* money in a bank] **2.** to give as a pledge or partial payment **3.** to put or set down **4.** to leave (sediment, etc.) lying **—*n.*** **1.** something placed for safekeeping; specif., money put in a bank **2.** a pledge or part payment **3.** a depository **4.** something left lying, as sand or clay deposited by the action of wind, water, etc. **—on deposit** placed or entrusted for safekeeping

de·pos·i·tar·y (di päz′ə ter′ē) ***n.***, *pl.* **-tar′ies** **1.** a person, firm, etc. entrusted with something for safekeeping; trustee **2.** a storehouse; depository

dep·o·si·tion (dep′ə zish′ən) ***n.*** **1.** a deposing or being deposed, as from office **2.** a testifying **3.** a depositing or being deposited **4.** something deposited **5.** *Law* the written testimony of a witness, made under oath, to be used in court

de·pos·i·tor (di päz′ə tər) ***n.*** a person who deposits something, esp. money in a bank

de·pos·i·to·ry (di päz′ə tôr′ē) ***n.***, *pl.* **-ries** **1.** a place where things are put for safekeeping; storehouse **2.** a trustee; depositary

de·pot (dē′pō; *military & Brit.* dep′ō) ***n.*** [Fr. *dépôt*, a storehouse < L. *depositum:* see DEPOSIT] **1.** a storehouse; warehouse **2.** a railroad or bus station **3.** *Mil.* *a*) a storage place for supplies *b*) a station for assembling recruits or combat replacements

de·prave (di prāv′) ***vt.*** **-praved′, -prav′ing** [< OFr. < L. < *de-*, intens. + *pravus*, crooked] to make morally bad; corrupt **—dep·ra·va·tion** (dep′rə vā′shən) ***n.*** **—de·praved′** ***adj.*** **—de·prav′er** ***n.***

de·prav·i·ty (di prav′ə tē) ***n.*** **1.** a depraved condition; corruption; wickedness **2.** *pl.* **-ties** a depraved act or practice

dep·re·cate (dep′rə kāt′) ***vt.*** **-cat′ed, -cat′ing** [< L. pp. of *deprecari* < *de-*, off + *precari*, PRAY] **1.** to feel and express disapproval of **2.** to depreciate; belittle **—dep′re·cat′ing·ly** ***adv.*** **—dep′re·ca′tion** ***n.*** **—dep′re·ca′tor n.**

dep·re·ca·to·ry (-kə tôr′ē) ***adj.*** deprecating; disapproving, belittling, etc. Also **dep′re·ca′tive** (-kāt′iv) **—dep′re·ca·to′ri·ly** ***adv.***

de·pre·ci·ate (di prē′shē āt′) ***vt.*** **-at′ed, -at′ing** [< L. pp. of *depretiare* < *de-*, from + *pretiare*, to value < *pretium*, a PRICE] **1.** to reduce in value or price **2.** to belittle; disparage **—*vi.*** to drop in value or price **—de·pre′ci·a·to′ry** (-shē ə tôr′ē, -shə tôr′ē) ***adj.***

de·pre·ci·a·tion (di prē′shē ā′shən) ***n.*** **1.** a decrease in value of property through wear, deterioration, etc. **2.** a decrease in the purchasing power of money **3.** a belittling; disparagement

dep·re·da·tion (dep′rə dā′shən) ***n.*** [< LL. pp. of *depraedari* < L. *de-*, intens. + *praedari*, to plunder < *praeda*, PREY] a robbing, plundering, or laying waste

de·press (di pres′) ***vt.*** [< OFr. < L. *depressus*, pp. of *deprimere* < *de-*, down + *premere*, to PRESS¹] **1.** to press down; lower **2.** to lower in spirits; make gloomy; sadden **3.** to decrease the activity of; weaken **4.** to lower in value, price, or amount **5.** *Music* to lower the pitch of **—de·press′ing** ***adj.*** **—de·press′ing·ly** ***adv.***

de·pres·sant (-ənt) ***adj.*** lowering the rate of muscular or nervous activity **—*n.*** a depressant medicine, drug, etc.; sedative

de·pressed (di prest′) ***adj.*** **1.** pressed down **2.** lowered in position, intensity, amount, etc. **3.** flattened or hollowed, as if pressed down **4.** gloomy; dejected; sad **5.** characterized by widespread unemployment, poverty, etc. [a *depressed* area] **6.** *Bot.* flattened vertically, as if from downward pressure

de·pres·sion (di presh′ən) ***n.*** **1.** a depressing or being depressed **2.** a depressed part or place; hollow or low place **3.** low spirits; dejection **4.** a decrease in force, activity, amount, etc. **5.** a period marked by slackening business activity, much unemployment, falling prices and wages, etc. **6.** *Psychol.* an emotional condition characterized by feelings of hopelessness, inadequacy, etc.

de·pres·sive (di pres′iv) ***adj.*** **1.** tending to depress **2.** characterized by psychological depression **—de·pres′sive·ly** ***adv.*** **—de·pres′sive·ness** ***n.***

de·pres·sor (-ər) ***n.*** **1.** one that depresses **2.** a muscle that draws down a part of the body **3.** an instrument for pressing a protruding part out of the way, as during a medical examination

dep·ri·va·tion (dep′rə vā′shən) ***n.*** a depriving or being deprived

---

fat, āpe, cär; ten, ēven; is, bīte; gō, hôrn, tōōl, look; oil, out; up, fur; get; joy; yet; chin; she; thin, *th*en; zh, leisure; ŋ, ring; ə for *a* in *ago*, *e* in *agent*, *i* in *sanity*, *o* in *comply*, *u* in *focus*; ′ as in *able* (ā′b'l); Fr. bål; ë, Fr. coeur; ö, Fr. feu; Fr. mon; ô, Fr. coq; ü, Fr. duc; *r*, Fr. cri; H, G. ich; kh, G. doch; ‡foreign; *hypothetical; < derived from. See inside front cover.

de·prive (di prīv′) ***vt.*** **-prived′, -priv′ing** [< ML. < L. *de-*, intens. + *privare*, to separate] **1.** to take something away from forcibly; dispossess **2.** to keep from having, using, or enjoying *[deprived of his rights]*

dept. **1.** department **2.** deputy

depth (depth) ***n.*** [ME. *depthe:* see DEEP & -TH¹] **1.** *a)* the distance from the top downward, or from front to back *b)* perspective, as in a painting **2.** the condition of being deep; deepness; specif., *a)* intensity, as of colors, emotion, etc. *b)* profundity of thought *c)* lowness of pitch **3.** the middle part *[the depth of winter]* **4.** [*usually pl.*] the inmost part *[the depths of a wood]* **5.** [*usually pl.*] the deep or deepest part, as of the sea **6.** [*usually pl.*] the extreme degree, as of despair —**in depth** in a thorough way —**out of** (or **beyond**) **one's depth** **1.** in water too deep for one **2.** past one's ability or understanding

depth charge (or **bomb**) an explosive charge that explodes under water: used esp. against submarines

depth perception ability to perceive perspective

depth psychology any system of psychology, as psychoanalysis, dealing with the unconscious

dep·u·ta·tion (dep′yo͝o tā′shən) ***n.*** **1.** a deputing or being deputed **2.** a group of persons, or one person, appointed to represent others; delegation

de·pute (di pyo͞ot′) ***vt.*** **-put′ed, -put′ing** [< OFr. < L. < *de-*, from + *putare*, lit., to cleanse] **1.** to give (authority, etc.) to someone else as deputy **2.** to appoint as one's substitute, agent, etc.

dep·u·tize (dep′yə tīz′) ***vt.*** **-tized′, -tiz′ing** to appoint as deputy —***vi.*** to act as deputy

dep·u·ty (-tē) ***n.***, *pl.* **-ties** [see DEPUTE] **1.** a person appointed to substitute for, or to assist, another **2.** a member of a legislature called a Chamber of Deputies —***adj.*** acting as deputy

De Quin·cey (də kwin′sē), **Thomas** 1785–1859; Eng. essayist & critic

de·rac·i·nate (di ras′ə nāt′) ***vt.*** **-nat′ed, -nat′ing** [< Fr. < *dé-* (L. *dis-*), from + *racine*, a root < LL. < L. *radix*] to pull up by or as by the roots; uproot; eradicate —**de·rac′i·na′tion** ***n.***

de·rail (di rāl′) ***vi., vt.*** to go or cause to go off the rails: said of a train, etc. —**de·rail′ment** ***n.***

de·range (di rānj′) ***vt.*** **-ranged′, -rang′ing** [< Fr. < OFr. < *des-* (L. *dis-*), apart + *rengier:* see RANGE] **1.** to upset the order or working of **2.** to make insane —**de·ranged′** ***adj.*** —**de·range′ment** ***n.***

Der·by (dʉr′bē; *chiefly Brit.* där′bē) city in C England: pop. 221,000 —***n.***, *pl.* **-bies** **1.** an annual race for three-year-old horses at Epsom Downs, begun by the Earl of Derby in 1780 **2.** any similar horse race, esp. the one (**Kentucky Derby**) run in Louisville, Kentucky **3.** [**d-**] a stiff felt hat with a round crown and curved brim

DERBY

de·reg·u·late (dē reg′yə lāt′) ***vt.*** **-lat′ed, -lat′ing** to remove regulations governing —**de·reg′u·la′tion** ***n.***

der·e·lict (der′ə likt′) ***adj.*** [< L. pp. of *derelinquere* < *de-*, intens. + *relinquere:* see RELINQUISH] **1.** deserted by the owner; abandoned **2.** neglectful of duty; negligent —***n.*** **1.** a property abandoned by the owner; esp., a ship deserted at sea **2.** a destitute person with no home or job

der·e·lic·tion (der′ə lik′shən) ***n.*** **1.** an abandoning or being abandoned **2.** a neglect of, or failure in, duty

de·ride (di rīd′) ***vt.*** **-rid′ed, -rid′ing** [< L. < *de-*, down + *ridere*, to laugh] to laugh at in contempt or scorn; ridicule —**de·rid′er** ***n.*** —**de·rid′ing·ly** ***adv.***

‡**de ri·gueur** (də rē gʉr′) [Fr.] **1.** required by etiquette; according to good form **2.** fashionable

de·ri·sion (di rizh′ən) ***n.*** a deriding or being derided; contempt or ridicule

de·ri·sive (di rī′siv) ***adj.*** showing derision: also **de·ri′so·ry** (-sə rē) —**de·ri′sive·ly** ***adv.*** —**de·ri′sive·ness** ***n.***

deriv. **1.** derivation **2.** derivative **3.** derived

der·i·va·tion (der′ə vā′shən) ***n.*** **1.** a deriving or being derived **2.** something derived **3.** *a)* the source or origin of something *b)* the etymology of a word **4.** the forming of words from bases, as by adding affixes

de·riv·a·tive (də riv′ə tiv) ***adj.*** **1.** derived **2.** not original —***n.*** **1.** something derived **2.** a word formed by derivation **3.** *Chem.* a substance derived from another by chemical change **4.** *Math.* the instantaneous rate of change of one variable with respect to another —**de·riv′a·tive·ly** ***adv.***

de·rive (di rīv′) ***vt.*** **-rived′, -riv′ing** [< OFr. < L. *derivare*, to divert a stream < *de-*, from + *rivus*, a stream] **1.** to get or receive (*from* a source) **2.** to deduce or infer **3.** to trace from or to a source; show the derivation of **4.** *Chem.* to obtain (a compound) from another compound by replacing one element with one or more other elements —***vi.*** to come (*from* a source) —**de·riv′a·ble** ***adj.***

-derm (dʉrm) [see ff.] *a suffix meaning* skin or covering *[endoderm]*

der·ma¹ (dʉr′mə) ***n.*** [ModL. < Gr. *derma*, the skin] *same as* DERMIS —**der′mal, der′mic** ***adj.***

der·ma² (dʉr′mə) ***n.*** [< Yid. pl. of *darm*, gut, ult. < OHG. *daram*] beef casing stuffed with bread crumbs, seasoning, etc. and roasted

der·ma·ti·tis (dʉr′mə tīt′is) ***n.*** [ff. + -ITIS] inflammation of the skin

der·ma·to- [Gr. < *derma* (gen. *dermatos*)] *a combining form meaning* skin: also **dermat-, dermo-**

der·ma·tol·o·gy (dʉr′mə täl′ə jē) ***n.*** [DERMATO- + -LOGY] the branch of medicine dealing with the skin and its diseases —**der′ma·to·log′i·cal** (-tə läj′ə k'l) ***adj.*** —**der′ma·tol′o·gist** ***n.***

der·mis (dʉr′mis) ***n.*** [ModL. < LL. *epidermis*, EPIDERMIS] the layer of skin just below the epidermis

der·o·gate (der′ə gāt′) ***vt., vi.*** **-gat′ed, -gat′ing** [< L. pp. of *derogare* < *de-*, from + *rogare*, to ask] **1.** [Archaic] to take away (*from*) so as to impair **2.** to lower (someone) in esteem; disparage —**der′o·ga′tion** ***n.***

de·rog·a·to·ry (di räg′ə tôr′ē) ***adj.*** **1.** tending to lessen or impair **2.** disparaging; belittling Also **de·rog′a·tive** —**de·rog′a·to′ri·ly** ***adv.***

der·rick (der′ik) ***n.*** [orig., a gallows, after T. *Derrick*, 17th-c. London hangman] **1.** a large apparatus with tackle and beams, for lifting and moving heavy objects **2.** a tall, tapering framework, as over an oil well, to support drilling machinery, etc.

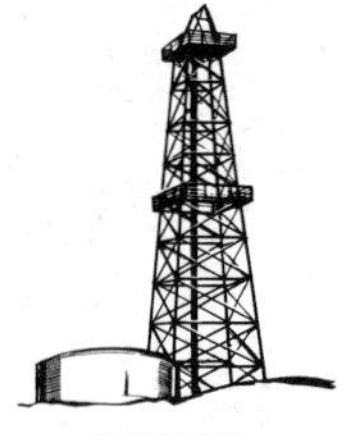

DERRICK (for oil well)

der·ri·ère (der′ē er′) ***n.*** [Fr., back part < LL. < L. *de*, from + *retro*, back] the buttocks

der·ring-do (der′iŋ do͞o′) ***n.*** [ME. *der-ryng*e *do*, daring to do] daring action; reckless courage

der·rin·ger (der′in jər) ***n.*** [after H. *Deringer*, 19th-cent. U.S. gunsmith] a small, short-barreled pistol of large caliber

der·vish (dʉr′vish) ***n.*** [Turk. < Per. *darvēsh*, beggar] a member of any of various Moslem orders dedicated to poverty and chastity: some dervishes practice whirling, howling, etc. as religious acts

de·sal·i·na·tion (dē sal′ə nā′shən) ***n.*** [DE- + SALIN(E) + -ATION] the removal of salt, esp. from sea water to make it drinkable: also **de·sal′i·ni·za′tion** —**de·sal′i·nate′** ***vt.***

des·cant (des′kant; *for vi., also* des kant′) ***n.*** [< Anglo-Fr. < L. *dis-*, apart + *cantus*, song] **1.** *Medieval Music a)* singing in which there is a fixed melody and a subordinate melody added above *b)* this added melody **2.** a comment; discourse —***vi.*** **1.** to discourse (*on* or *upon*) **2.** to sing or play a descant **3.** to sing

Des·cartes (dā kärt′), **Re·né** (rə nā′) 1596–1650; Fr. philosopher & mathematician

de·scend (di send′) ***vi.*** [< OFr. < L. < *de-*, down + *scandere*, to climb] **1.** to move from a higher to a lower place; come or go down **2.** to pass from an earlier to a later time, from greater to less, etc. **3.** to slope downward **4.** to come down (*from* a source) *[he is descended from pioneers]* **5.** to pass by inheritance or heredity **6.** to stoop (*to* some act) **7.** to make a sudden visit or attack (*on* or *upon*) **8.** *Astron.* to move toward the horizon —***vt.*** to move down, down along, or through —**de·scend′er** ***n.*** —**de·scend′i·ble** ***adj.***

de·scend·ant (-ənt) ***adj.*** descending: also **de·scend′ent** —***n.*** **1.** one who is an offspring, however remote, of a certain ancestor, family, group, etc. **2.** something derived from an earlier form

de·scent (di sent′) ***n.*** **1.** a descending; coming or going down **2.** lineage; ancestry **3.** one generation (in a specified lineage) **4.** a downward slope **5.** a way down **6.** a sudden attack (*on* or *upon*) **7.** a decline; fall **8.** a stooping (*to* an act) **9.** *Law* transference (of property) to heirs

de·scribe (di skrīb′) ***vt.*** **-scribed′, -scrib′ing** [< OFr. < L. < *de-*, from + *scribere*, to write] **1.** to tell or write about **2.** to picture in words **3.** to trace the outline of —**de·scrib′a·ble** ***adj.***

de·scrip·tion (di skrip′shən) ***n.*** **1.** the act, process, or technique of describing **2.** a statement or passage that describes **3.** sort or variety *[books of every description]*

de·scrip·tive (-tiv) ***adj.*** of or characterized by description —**de·scrip′tive·ly** ***adv.*** —**de·scrip′tive·ness** ***n.***

de·scry (di skrī′) ***vt.*** **-scried′, -scry′ing** [< OFr. *descrier*, to proclaim < *des-*, from + *crier:* see CRY] **1.** to catch sight of (distant or obscure objects) **2.** to detect

Des·de·mo·na (dez'də mō'nə) *see* OTHELLO

des·e·crate (des'ə krāt') *vt.* **-crat'ed, -crat'ing** [DE- + (CON)SECRATE] to violate the sacredness of; profane —**des'e·crat'er, des'e·cra'tor** *n.* —**des'e·cra'tion** *n.*

de·seg·re·gate (dē seg'rə gāt') *vt., vi.* **-gat'ed, -gat'ing** to abolish racial segregation in (public schools, etc.) —**de·seg're·ga'tion** *n.*

de·sen·si·tize (dē sen'sə tīz') *vt.* **-tized', -tiz'ing** to make insensitive or less sensitive *[desensitized* to an allergen*]* —**de·sen'si·ti·za'tion** *n.* —**de·sen'si·tiz'er** *n.*

de·sert[1] (di zʉrt') *vt.* [< Fr. < LL. *desertare* < L. pp. of *deserere* < *de-*, from + *serere,* to join] **1.** to forsake (someone or something that one ought not to leave); abandon **2.** to leave (one's post, etc.) without permission —*vi.* to leave one's post, etc. without permission and with no intent to return or, in war, to avoid hazardous duty —**de·sert'er** *n.*

des·ert[2] (dez'ərt) *n.* [< OFr. < LL. *desertum,* a desert < L. pp. of *deserere:* see prec.] **1.** an uncultivated region without inhabitants; wilderness **2.** a dry, barren, sandy region —*adj.* **1.** of a desert **2.** wild and uninhabited

de·sert[3] (di zʉrt') *n.* [< OFr. < *deservir,* DESERVE] **1.** the fact of deserving reward or punishment **2.** [*often pl.*] deserved reward or punishment

de·ser·tion (di zʉr'shən) *n.* a deserting or being deserted

de·serve (di zʉrv') *vt.* **-served', -serv'ing** [< OFr. *deservir* < L. < *de-*, intens. + *servire,* to SERVE] to be worthy of (reward, punishment, etc.); merit —*vi.* to be worthy

de·served (-zʉrvd') *adj.* rightfully earned or merited; just —**de·serv'ed·ly** (-zʉr'vid lē) *adv.*

de·serv·ing (-zʉr'viŋ) *adj.* having merit; worthy (*of* help, reward, etc.) —**de·serv'ing·ly** *adv.*

de·sex (dē seks') *vt.* **1.** to remove the sex organs of **2.** to suppress or lessen the sexual characteristics of

des·ic·cant (des'i kənt) *adj.* [see ff.] drying —*n.* a substance used as a drying agent

des·ic·cate (-kāt') *vt.* **-cat'ed, -cat'ing** [< L. pp. of *desiccare* < *de-*, intens. + *siccare* < *siccus,* dry] **1.** to dry completely **2.** to preserve (food) by drying —*vi.* to become completely dry —**des'ic·ca'tion** *n.* —**des'ic·ca'tor** *n.*

de·sid·er·ate (di sid'ə rāt') *vt.* **-at'ed, -at'ing** [< L. pp. of *desiderare:* see DESIRE] to want; need —**de·sid'er·a'tion** *n.*

de·sid·er·a·tum (di sid'ə rāt'əm, -zid'-; -rät'-) *n., pl.* **-ta** (-ə) [L., neut. pp. of *desiderare:* see DESIRE] something needed and wanted

de·sign (di zīn') *vt.* [< L. < *de-*, out + *signare* < *signum,* a mark] **1.** to make preliminary sketches of; plan **2.** to form (plans, etc.) in the mind; contrive **3.** to plan and work out (something) creatively; devise **4.** to plan to do; intend **5.** to intend for some purpose —*vi.* to make original plans, patterns, etc. —*n.* **1.** a plan; scheme; project **2.** purpose; intention; aim **3.** [*pl.*] a secret, usually dishonest or selfish scheme (often with *on* or *upon*) **4.** a plan or sketch to work from; pattern **5.** the art of making designs or patterns **6.** the arrangement of parts, form, color, etc. so as to produce an artistic unit **7.** a finished artistic work or decoration —**by design** purposely

des·ig·nate (dez'ig nāt'; *for adj., also* -nit) *adj.* [see prec.] named for an office, etc. but not yet in it —*vt.* **-nat'ed, -nat'ing** **1.** to point out; indicate; specify **2.** to refer to by a distinguishing name, title, etc.; name **3.** to name for an office or duty —**des'ig·na'tive** *adj.* —**des'ig·na'tor** *n.*

designated hitter *Baseball* a player in the regular batting order who does not play a defensive position, but has been designated to bat in place of the pitcher, whose status is otherwise unaffected

des·ig·na·tion (dez'ig nā'shən) *n.* **1.** a pointing out or marking out **2.** appointment to an office, post, etc. **3.** a distinguishing name, title, etc.

de·sign·ed·ly (di zī'nid lē) *adv.* purposely

de·sign·er (di zī'nər) *n.* a person who designs, or makes original sketches, patterns, etc.

de·sign·ing (-niŋ) *adj.* **1.** that designs or makes plans, patterns, etc. **2.** scheming; crafty —*n.* the art or work of creating designs, patterns, etc.

de·sir·a·ble (di zīr'ə b'l) *adj.* worth having; pleasing, excellent, etc. —**de·sir'a·bil'i·ty** *n.* —**de·sir'a·bly** *adv.*

de·sire (di zīr') *vt.* **-sired', -sir'ing** [< OFr. < L. *desiderare* < *de-*, from + *sidus* (gen. *sideris*), a star] **1.** to wish or long for; crave **2.** to ask for; request **3.** to want sexually —*vi.* to have a desire —*n.* **1.** a strong wish or craving **2.** sexual appetite **3.** a request **4.** anything desired

de·sir·ous (di zīr'əs) *adj.* desiring; characterized by desire

de·sist (di zist') *vi.* [< OFr. < L. < *de-*, from + *sistere,* to cause to stand < *stare,* to stand] to cease (*from* an action); stop —**de·sis'tance** *n.*

desk (desk) *n.* [ML. *desca,* a table, ult. < L. *discus,* DISCUS] **1.** a kind of table with drawers and with a flat or sloping top for writing, etc. **2.** the place in a hotel where guests register, check out, etc.

Des Moines (də moin') [Fr., lit., of the monks] capital of Iowa, in the C part: pop. 191,000

des·o·late (des'ə lit; *for v.* -lāt') *adj.* [< L. pp. of *desolare* < *de-*, intens. + *solare,* to make lonely < *solus,* alone] **1.** lonely; solitary **2.** uninhabited; deserted **3.** made uninhabitable; laid waste **4.** forlorn; wretched —*vt.* **-lat'ed, -lat'ing** **1.** to make desolate; rid of inhabitants **2.** to make uninhabitable; lay waste; devastate **3.** to forsake; abandon **4.** to make forlorn, wretched, etc. —**des'o·late·ly** *adv.* —**des'o·late·ness** *n.*

des·o·la·tion (des'ə lā'shən) *n.* **1.** a making desolate **2.** a desolate condition **3.** lonely grief; misery **4.** loneliness **5.** a desolate place

De So·to (di sōt'ō), **Her·nan·do** (hər nan'dō) 1500?–42; Sp. explorer in America: also **de Soto**

de·spair (di sper') *vi.* [< OFr. < L. < *de-*, without + *sperare,* to hope < *spes,* hope] to lose hope; be without hope (usually with *of*) —*n.* **1.** a despairing; loss of hope **2.** a person or thing causing despair

de·spair·ing (-iŋ) *adj.* feeling or showing despair; hopeless —**de·spair'ing·ly** *adv.*

des·patch (di spach') *vt., n. var. sp. of* DISPATCH

des·per·a·do (des'pə rä'dō, -rā'-) *n., pl.* **-does, -dos** [OSp. < L. *desperare:* see DESPAIR] a dangerous, reckless criminal; bold outlaw

des·per·ate (des'pər it) *adj.* [< L. pp. of *desperare:* see DESPAIR] **1.** rash or violent because of despair **2.** having a very great desire, need, etc. *[desperate* for affection*]* **3.** causing despair; extremely dangerous or serious *[a desperate* illness*]* **4.** extreme; drastic *[in desperate* need*]* —**des'per·ate·ly** *adv.*

des·per·a·tion (des'pə rā'shən) *n.* **1.** the state of being desperate **2.** recklessness caused by despair

des·pi·ca·ble (des'pik ə b'l, di spik'-) *adj.* deserving to be despised; contemptible —**des'pi·ca·bly** *adv.*

de·spise (di spīz') *vt.* **-spised', -spis'ing** [< OFr. < L. *despicere* < *de,* down + *specere,* to look at] **1.** to look down on with contempt and scorn **2.** to regard with extreme dislike

de·spite (di spīt') *n.* [< OFr. < L. pp. of *despicere:* see prec.] **1.** malice; spite **2.** [Archaic] contempt —*prep.* in spite of; notwithstanding

Des Plaines (des plānz') [prob. < Miss. Valley Fr. *plaines,* sugar maples, once growing there] city in NE Ill.: suburb of Chicago: pop. 54,000

de·spoil (di spoil') *vt.* [< OFr. < L. < *de-*, intens. + *spoliare,* to plunder: see SPOIL] to deprive (*of* something) by force; rob; plunder —**de·spoil'er** *n.* —**de·spoil'ment** *n.*

de·spo·li·a·tion (di spō'lē ā'shən) *n.* a despoiling or being despoiled; pillage

de·spond (di spänd') *vi.* [L. *despondere,* to give up < *de,* from + *spondere,* to promise] to lose courage or hope; become disheartened —*n.* despondency: now chiefly in **slough of despond** —**de·spond'ing·ly** *adv.*

de·spond·en·cy (di spän'dən sē) *n.* [see prec.] loss of courage or hope; dejection: also **de·spond'ence**

de·spond·ent (-dənt) *adj.* filled with despondency; dejected —**de·spond'ent·ly** *adv.*

des·pot (des'pət, -pät) *n.* [< OFr. < Gr. *despotēs,* a master] **1.** an absolute ruler; autocrat **2.** anyone in charge who acts like a tyrant

des·pot·ic (de spät'ik) *adj.* of or like a despot; autocratic; tyrannical —**des·pot'i·cal·ly** *adv.*

des·pot·ism (des'pə tiz'm) *n.* **1.** rule by a despot; autocracy **2.** the methods of a despot; tyranny

des·sert (di zʉrt') *n.* [< OFr. < *desservir,* to clear the table < *des-* (L. *de*), from + *servir* < L. *servire,* to serve] **1.** a course of pie, cake, ice cream, etc., served at the end of a meal **2.** [Brit.] uncooked fruit and nuts served after the sweet course

de·sta·bi·lize (dē stā'bə līz') *vt.* **-lized', -liz'ing** to upset the stability of; unbalance

des·ti·na·tion (des'tə nā'shən) *n.* **1.** the end for which something or someone is destined **2.** the place toward which someone or something is going or sent

des·tine (des'tin) *vt.* **-tined, -tin·ing** [< OFr. < L. *destinare,* to secure, fix < *de-*, intens. + base of *stare,* to stand] **1.** to predetermine, as by fate *[he seemed destined* to succeed*]* **2.** to set apart for a certain purpose; intend —**destined for** **1.** bound for **2.** intended for

des·tin·y (des'tə nē) *n., pl.* **-ies** [see prec.] **1.** the seemingly inevitable or necessary succession of events **2.** what will necessarily happen to any person or thing; (one's) fate **3.** that which determines events

des·ti·tute (des′tə to͞ot′, -tyo͞ot′) ***adj.*** [< L. pp. of *destituere,* to forsake < *de-,* down + *statuere,* to set] **1.** not having; lacking (with *of*) *[destitute* of trees*]* **2.** living in complete poverty

des·ti·tu·tion (des′tə to͞o′shən, -tyo͞o′-) ***n.*** the state of being destitute; esp., abject poverty

de·stroy (di stroi′) ***vt.*** [< OFr. < L. < *de-,* down + *struere,* to build] **1.** to tear down; demolish **2.** to spoil completely; ruin **3.** to put an end to **4.** to kill **5.** to neutralize the effect of **6.** to make useless —***vi.*** to bring about destruction

de·stroy·er (-ər) ***n.*** **1.** a person or thing that destroys **2.** a small, fast, heavily armed warship

de·struct (di strukt′, dē′strukt′) ***n.*** [back-formation < DESTRUCTION] the deliberate destruction of a malfunctioning missile, rocket, etc. after its launch —***vi.*** to be automatically destroyed

de·struct·i·ble (di struk′tə b'l) ***adj.*** that can be destroyed —**de·struct′i·bil′i·ty** ***n.***

de·struc·tion (di struk′shən) ***n.*** [< OFr. < L. pp. of *destruere:* see DESTROY] **1.** a destroying or being destroyed **2.** the cause or means of destroying

de·struc·tive (di struk′tiv) ***adj.*** **1.** tending or likely to cause destruction **2.** causing destruction; destroying **3.** merely negative; not helpful *[destructive* criticism*]* —**de·struc′tive·ly** ***adv.*** —**de·struc′tive·ness, de·struc′tiv′i·ty** ***n.***

destructive distillation the decomposition of coal, wood, etc. by heat in the absence of air, and the recovery of the volatile products of the decomposition by condensation or other means

des·ue·tude (des′wi to͞od′, -tyo͞od′) ***n.*** [< L. < pp. of *desuescere* < *de-,* from + *suescere,* to be accustomed] disuse *[*laws fallen into *desuetude]*

de·sul·fur·ize (dē sul′fə rīz′) ***vt.*** **-ized′, -iz′ing** to remove sulfur from: also **de·sul′fur**

des·ul·to·ry (des′'l tôr′ē) ***adj.*** [< L. < *desultor,* vaulter < pp. of *desilire* < *de-,* from + *salire,* to leap] **1.** passing from one thing to another in an aimless way; disconnected; not methodical **2.** lacking direct relevancy; random *[*a *desultory* observation*]* —**des′ul·to′ri·ly** ***adv.*** —**des′ul·to′ri·ness** ***n.***

de·tach (di tach′) ***vt.*** [< Fr. < OFr. < *de-,* off + *estachier,* to ATTACH] **1.** to unfasten or separate and remove; disconnect **2.** to send (troops, ships, etc.) on a special mission —**de·tach′a·bil′i·ty** ***n.*** —**de·tach′a·ble** ***adj.***

de·tached (di tacht′) ***adj.*** **1.** not connected; separate **2.** disinterested; impartial; aloof —**de·tach′ed·ly** (-tach′id lē) ***adv.*** —**de·tach′ed·ness** ***n.***

de·tach·ment (di tach′mənt) ***n.*** **1.** a detaching; separation **2.** *a)* the sending of troops or ships on special service *b)* a unit of troops assigned to some special task **3.** the state of being disinterested, impartial, or aloof

de·tail (di tāl′, dē′tāl) ***n.*** [< Fr. < *dé-* (L. *de*), from + *tailler,* to cut] **1.** a dealing with things item by item **2.** a minute account *[*to go into *detail]* **3.** an item or particular **4.** a small part of a whole structure, design, etc. **5.** *a)* one or more soldiers, sailors, etc. chosen for a particular task *b)* the task itself —***vt.*** **1.** to give the particulars of; tell, item by item **2.** to choose for a particular task *[detail* a man for sentry duty*]* —**in detail** item by item; with particulars —**de·tailed′** ***adj.***

de·tain (di tān′) ***vt.*** [< OFr. < L. < *de-,* off + *tenere,* to hold] **1.** to keep in custody; confine **2.** to keep from going on; hold back —**de·tain′er** ***n.*** —**de·tain′ment** ***n.***

de·tect (di tekt′) ***vt.*** [< L. *detectus,* pp. of *detegere* < *de-,* from + *tegere,* to cover] **1.** to catch or discover, as in a misdeed **2.** to discover (something hidden or not easily noticed) **3.** *Radio same as* DEMODULATE —**de·tect′a·ble, de·tect′i·ble** ***adj.***

de·tec·tion (di tek′shən) ***n.*** **1.** a finding out or being found out **2.** *same as* DEMODULATION

de·tec·tive (-tiv) ***adj.*** **1.** of or for detection **2.** of detectives and their work —***n.*** a person, usually on a police force, whose work is investigating crimes, getting secret information, etc.

de·tec·tor (-tər) ***n.*** **1.** a person or thing that detects **2.** *Radio* a device used in demodulation

de·tent (di tent′, dē′tent) ***n.*** [< Fr.] *Mech.* a part that stops or releases a movement

dé·tente de·tente (dā tänt′) ***n.*** [Fr.] a lessening of tension or hostility, esp. between nations

de·ten·tion (di ten′shən) ***n.*** a detaining or being detained; specif., *a)* a keeping in custody; confinement *b)* an enforced delay

detention home a place where juvenile offenders or delinquents are held in custody, esp. temporarily

de·ter (di tur′) ***vt.*** **-terred′, -ter′ring** [< L. < *de-,* from + *terrere,* to frighten] to keep or discourage (a person) from doing something by instilling fear, anxiety, doubt, etc. —**de·ter′ment** ***n.***

de·terge (di turj′) ***vt.*** **-terged′, -terg′ing** [< L. < *de-,* off + *tergere,* to wipe] to cleanse, as a wound —**de·ter′gen·cy, de·ter′gence** ***n.***

de·ter·gent (di tur′jənt) ***adj.*** [see prec.] cleansing —***n.*** a cleansing substance that is like soap but is made synthetically and not from fats and lye

de·te·ri·o·rate (di tir′ē ə rāt′) ***vt., vi.*** **-rat′ed, -rat′ing** [< LL. pp. of *deteriorare* < L. *deterior,* worse] to make or become worse; depreciate —**de·te′ri·o·ra′tion** ***n.*** —**de·te′ri·o·ra′tive** ***adj.***

de·ter·mi·na·cy (di tur′mi nə sē) ***n.*** **1.** the state or quality of being determinate **2.** the condition of being determined, as in being caused or in having predictable results

de·ter·mi·nant (-nənt) ***adj.*** determining —***n.*** a thing or factor that determines

de·ter·mi·nate (-nit) ***adj.*** [see DETERMINE] **1.** having exact limits; definite; fixed **2.** settled; conclusive **3.** *Bot.* having a flower at the end of the primary axis and of each secondary axis —**de·ter′mi·nate·ly** ***adv.*** —**de·ter′mi·nate·ness** ***n.***

de·ter·mi·na·tion (di tur′mə nā′shən) ***n.*** **1.** a determining or being determined **2.** a firm intention **3.** firmness of purpose

de·ter·mi·na·tive (di tur′mə nā′tiv, -nə tiv) ***adj.*** determining —***n.*** a thing that determines —**de·ter′mi·na′tive·ly** ***adv.*** —**de·ter′mi·na′tive·ness** ***n.***

de·ter·mine (di tur′mən) ***vt.*** **-mined, -min·ing** [< OFr. < L. < *de-,* from + *terminare,* to set bounds < *terminus,* an end] **1.** to set limits to; bound; define **2.** to settle conclusively; decide **3.** to reach a decision about; decide upon **4.** to establish or affect the nature, kind, or quality of *[*genes *determine* heredity*]* **5.** to find out exactly; calculate precisely **6.** to give a definite aim to; direct —***vi.*** **1.** to decide; resolve **2.** *Law* to come to an end —**de·ter′mi·na·ble** ***adj.*** —**de·ter′min·er** ***n.***

de·ter·mined (-mənd) ***adj.*** **1.** having one's mind made up; resolved **2.** resolute; unwavering —**de·ter′mined·ly** ***adv.*** —**de·ter′mined·ness** ***n.***

de·ter·min·ism (-mə niz'm) ***n.*** the doctrine that everything, esp. one's choice of action, is determined by a sequence of causes independent of one's will —**de·ter′min·ist** ***n., adj.*** —**de·ter′min·is′tic** ***adj.***

de·ter·rent (di tur′ənt) ***adj.*** deterring or tending to deter —***n.*** anything that deters; hindrance —**de·ter′rence** ***n.***

de·test (di test′) ***vt.*** [< Fr. < L. *detestari,* to curse by calling the gods to witness < *de-,* down + *testis,* a witness] to dislike intensely; hate; abhor —**de·test′er** ***n.***

de·test·a·ble (di tes′tə b'l) ***adj.*** that is or should be detested; hateful; odious —**de·test′a·bil′i·ty, de·test′a·ble·ness** ***n.*** —**de·test′a·bly** ***adv.***

de·tes·ta·tion (dē′tes tā′shən) ***n.*** **1.** intense dislike or hatred; loathing **2.** a detested person or thing

de·throne (dē thrōn′) ***vt.*** **-throned′, -thron′ing** to remove from a throne; depose —**de·throne′ment** ***n.***

det·o·nate (det′'n āt′) ***vi., vt.*** **-nat′ed, -nat′ing** [< L. pp. of *detonare* < *de-,* intens. + *tonare,* to thunder] to explode noisily —**det′o·na′tion** ***n.***

det·o·na·tor (-āt′ər) ***n.*** **1.** a fuse, percussion cap, etc. for setting off explosives **2.** an explosive

de·tour (dē′toor, di toor′) ***n.*** [< Fr. < *détourner,* to turn aside < OFr. < *des-* (L. *dis-*) + *tourner:* see TURN] **1.** a roundabout way **2.** a route used when the regular route is closed to traffic —***vi., vt.*** to go or cause to go by way of a detour

de·tract (di trakt′) ***vt.*** [< L. pp. of *detrahere* < *de-,* from + *trahere,* to draw] to take or draw away —***vi.*** to take something desirable away (*from*) *[*frowning *detracts* from her beauty*]* —**de·trac′tion** ***n.*** —**de·trac′tive** ***adj.*** —**de·trac′tor** ***n.***

de·train (dē trān′) ***vi., vt.*** to get off or remove from a railroad train —**de·train′ment** ***n.***

det·ri·ment (det′rə mənt) ***n.*** [OFr. < L. *detrimentum,* damage < pp. of *deterere* < *de-,* off + *terere,* to rub] **1.** damage; injury; harm **2.** anything that causes damage or injury —**det′ri·men′tal** (-men′t'l) ***adj.*** —**det′ri·men′tal·ly** ***adv.***

de·tri·tus (di trīt′əs) ***n.*** [L., pp. of *deterere:* see prec.] fragments of rock, etc. produced by disintegration or wearing away; debris

De·troit (di troit′) [< Fr. *détroit,* strait] **1.** river flowing south from Lake St. Clair into Lake Erie **2.** city in SE Mich., on this river: pop. 1,203,000 (met. area 4,344,000)

‡**de trop** (də trō′) [Fr.] too much; superfluous

deuce[1] (do͞os, dyo͞os) ***n.*** [< OFr. < L. acc. of *duo,* two] **1.** a playing card with two spots **2.** the side of a die bearing two spots, or a throw of the dice totaling two **3.** *Tennis* a score of 40 each (or five games each) after which one side must get two successive points (or games) to win the game (or set)

deuce[2] (do͞os, dyo͞os) ***n., interj.*** [< OFr. *dieu* & L. *deus,* God: also infl. by DEUCE[1], in reference to low score at dice] bad luck, the devil, etc.: a mild oath or exclamation of annoyance, surprise, etc.

deu·ced (do͞o′sid, dyo͞o′-; do͞ost, dyo͞ost) ***adj.*** **1.** devilish; confounded **2.** extreme Used in mild oaths —***adv.*** extremely; very: also **deu′ced·ly**

‡**De·us** (dā′oos, dē′əs) [L.] God

Deut. Deuteronomy

deu·te·ri·um (do͞o tir′ē əm, dyo͞o-) ***n.*** [ModL. < Gr. *deuteros,* second] the hydrogen isotope having an atomic weight of 2.0141 and boiling point of −249.7°C; heavy hydrogen: symbol, D

deu·ter·o-, deu·ter- [< Gr. *deuteros,* second] *a combining form meaning* second, secondary

deu·ter·on (do͞ot′ər än′, dyo͞ot′-) ***n.*** the nucleus of an atom of deuterium

Deu·ter·on·o·my (do͞ot′ər än′ə mē, dyo͞ot′-) [< LL. < Gr. < DEUTERO- + *nomos,* law] the fifth book of the Pentateuch in the Bible

deut·sche mark (doi′chə) *pl.* **mark,** Eng. **marks** *see* MONETARY UNITS, table (West Germany)

Deutsch·land (doich′länt′) [G.] *Ger. name of* GERMANY

de·val·ue (dē val′yo͞o) ***vt.*** **-ued, -u·ing** **1.** to lessen the value of **2.** to lower the exchange value of (a currency) in relation to other currencies Also **de·val′u·ate′** (-yoo wāt′) **-at′ed, -at′ing** —**de·val′u·a′tion** ***n.***

dev·as·tate (dev′ə stāt′) ***vt.*** **-tat′ed, -tat′ing** [< L. pp. < *de-,* intens. + *vastare,* to make empty < *vastus,* empty] **1.** to lay waste; make desolate; ravage; destroy **2.** to make helpless —**dev′as·tat′ing·ly** ***adv.*** —**dev′as·ta′tion** ***n.*** —**dev′as·ta′tor** ***n.***

de·vel·op (di vel′əp) ***vt.*** [< Fr. < *dé-* (L. *dis-*), apart + OFr. *voloper,* to wrap] **1.** to cause to become gradually fuller, larger, better, stronger, etc. **2.** to bring (an idea, plan, etc.) into activity or reality **3.** to cause (a bud, etc.) to evolve gradually **4.** to make (housing, highways, etc.) more available or extensive **5.** *Music* to elaborate (a theme) **6.** *Photog.* *a*) to put (an exposed film, plate, or printing paper) in various chemical solutions in order to make the picture visible *b*) to make (a picture) thus **7.** to show or work out by degrees; make known gradually; reveal **8.** to explain more clearly —***vi.*** **1.** to come into being or activity **2.** to become larger, fuller, better, etc.; make progress; grow or evolve **3.** to be disclosed —**de·vel′op·a·ble** ***adj.***

de·vel·op·er (-ər) ***n.*** a person or thing that develops; esp., *Photog.* a chemical used to develop film, plates, etc.

de·vel·op·ment (-mənt) ***n.*** **1.** a developing or being developed **2.** a stage in growth, advancement, etc. **3.** an event or happening **4.** a thing that is developed, as a tract of land with newly built homes, etc. —**de·vel′op·men′tal** (-men′t′l) ***adj.*** —**de·vel′op·men′tal·ly** ***adv.***

de·vi·ant (dē′vē ənt) ***adj.*** [< LL. prp. of *deviare:* see ff.] deviating, esp. from what is considered normal, established, etc. —***n.*** a person whose behavior is deviant —**de′vi·an·cy, de′vi·ance** ***n.***

de·vi·ate (dē′vē āt′; *for adj. & n.* -it) ***vi., vt.*** **-at′ed, -at′ing** [< LL. pp. of *deviare* < *de-,* from + *via,* road] to turn aside (*from* a course, direction, standard, etc.) —***adj.*** *same as* DEVIANT —***n.*** a deviant; esp., one with deviant sexual behavior —**de′vi·a′tor** ***n.***

de·vi·a·tion (dē′vē ā′shən) ***n.*** **1.** a deviating or being deviant, as in behavior, political ideology, etc. **2.** *Statistics* the difference between a particular number in a set and some fixed value, usually the mean —**de′vi·a′tion·ism** ***n.*** —**de′vi·a′tion·ist** ***adj., n.***

de·vice (di vīs′) ***n.*** [< OFr. *devis,* division < *deviser:* see DEVISE] **1.** a thing devised; esp., an underhanded scheme; trick **2.** a mechanical invention or contrivance **3.** something used for artistic effect [*rhetorical devices*] **4.** an ornamental figure or design **5.** a design or emblem on a coat of arms **6.** any motto or emblem —**leave to one's own devices** to allow to do as one wishes

dev·il (dev′'l) ***n.*** [OE. *deofol* < LL. < Gr. *diabolos,* slanderous (in N.T., devil) < *dia-,* across + *ballein,* to throw] **1.** [*often* **D-**] *Theol.* *a*) the chief evil spirit; Satan (with *the*): typically depicted as a man with horns, a tail, and cloven feet *b*) any demon of hell **2.** a wicked or malevolent person **3.** one who is mischievous, reckless, etc. **4.** an unlucky, unhappy person [*that poor devil*] **5.** anything hard to operate, control, etc. **6.** any machine for tearing paper, rags, etc. to bits —***vt.*** **-iled** or **-illed, -il·ing** or **-il·ling** **1.** to prepare (food, often finely chopped) with hot seasoning **2.** to annoy; torment; tease —**a devil of a** an extreme example of a —**between the devil and the deep (blue) sea** between equally unpleasant alternatives —**give the devil his due** to acknowledge the good qualities of even a wicked person —**go to the devil** to fall into bad habits —**play the devil with** [Colloq.] to disturb; upset —**the devil!** [Colloq.] an exclamation of anger, surprise, etc. —**the devil to pay** trouble as a consequence

dev·il·fish (-fish′) ***n.,*** *pl.* **-fish′, -fish′es:** see FISH **1.** a large ray whose pectoral fins are hornlike when rolled up **2.** an octopus

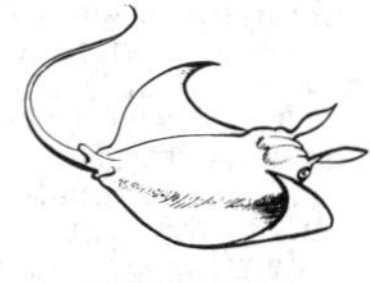

DEVILFISH
(to 20 ft. across)

dev·il·ish (dev′'l ish, dev′lish) ***adj.*** **1.** of, like, or characteristic of a devil; diabolical **2.** mischievous; reckless **3.** [Colloq.] *a*) extremely bad *b*) extreme —***adv.*** [Colloq.] extremely; very —**dev′il·ish·ly** ***adv.*** —**dev′il·ish·ness** ***n.***

dev·il-may-care (dev′'l mā ker′) ***adj.*** reckless or careless; happy-go-lucky

dev·il·ment (dev′'l mənt) ***n.*** **1.** [Archaic] evil behavior **2.** mischief or mischievous action

dev·il·ry (-rē) ***n.,*** *pl.* **-ries** [Chiefly Brit.] **1.** witchcraft **2.** evil behavior **3.** *same as* DEVILTRY

devil's advocate **1.** *R.C.Ch.* an official selected to raise objections in the case of one named for beatification or canonization **2.** one who upholds the wrong side, as for argument's sake

dev·il's-darn·ing-nee·dle (dev′'lz där′niŋ nē′d'l) ***n.*** *same as* DRAGONFLY

dev·il's-food cake (dev′'lz fo͞od′) a rich cake made with chocolate or cocoa and baking soda

Devil's Island Fr. island off the coast of French Guiana: site of a former penal colony

dev·il·try (dev′'l trē) ***n.,*** *pl.* **-tries** **1.** reckless mischief, fun, etc. **2.** *same as* DEVILRY

de·vi·ous (dē′vē əs) ***adj.*** [< L. *devius* < *de-,* off, from + *via,* road] **1.** roundabout; winding **2.** going astray **3.** not straightforward or frank; deceiving —**de′vi·ous·ly** ***adv.*** —**de′vi·ous·ness** ***n.***

de·vise (di vīz′) ***vt., vi.*** **-vised′, -vis′ing** [< OFr. *deviser,* to distribute, direct < L. pp. of *dividere,* to divide] **1.** to work out (something) by thinking; plan; invent **2.** *Law* to bequeath (real property) by will —***n.*** *Law* **1.** a gift of real property by will **2.** a will, or clause in a will, granting such a gift —**de·vis′a·ble** ***adj.*** —**de·vis′al** ***n.*** —**de·vis′er** ***n.***

de·vi·tal·ize (dē vīt′'l īz′) ***vt.*** **-ized′, -iz′ing** to lower in vitality —**de·vi′tal·i·za′tion** ***n.***

de·void (di void′) ***adj.*** [< OFr. < *des-* (L. *dis-*), from + *vuidier:* see VOID] completely without; empty (*of*)

de·voir (də vwär′, dev′wär) ***n.*** [< OFr. < L. *debere,* to owe] **1.** duty **2.** [*pl.*] acts of due respect or courtesy

de·volve (di välv′) ***vt., vi.*** **-volved′, -volv′ing** [< L. < *de-,* down + *volvere,* to roll] to pass (*on*) to another: said of duties, responsibilities, etc. —**dev·o·lu·tion** (dev′ə lo͞o′shən), **de·volve′ment** ***n.***

De·vo·ni·an (di vō′nē ən) ***adj.*** [after *Devonshire,* county in England] *Geol.* designating or of the period after the Silurian in the Paleozoic Era —**the Devonian** the Devonian Period or its rocks: see GEOLOGY, chart

de·vote (di vōt′) ***vt.*** **-vot′ed, -vot′ing** [< L. *devotus,* pp. < *de-,* from + *vovere,* to vow] **1.** to set apart for a special use or service; dedicate **2.** to give up (oneself or one's time, energy, etc.) to some purpose, activity, or person

de·vot·ed (-id) ***adj.*** **1.** dedicated; consecrated **2.** very loving, loyal, or faithful —**de·vot′ed·ly** ***adv.*** —**de·vot′ed·ness** ***n.***

dev·o·tee (dev′ə tē′, -tā′) ***n.*** a person strongly devoted to someone or to something, as a religion

de·vo·tion (di vō′shən) ***n.*** **1.** a devoting or being devoted **2.** piety **3.** religious worship **4.** [*pl.*] prayers **5.** loyalty or deep affection

de·vo·tion·al (-'l) ***adj.*** of or characterized by devotion —***n.*** a brief worship service —**de·vo′tion·al·ly** ***adv.***

de·vour (di vour′) ***vt.*** [< OFr. < L. < *de-,* intens. + *vorare,* to swallow whole] **1.** to eat (up) hungrily or voraciously **2.** to consume; destroy; devastate **3.** to take in greedily with the eyes, ears, or mind [*to devour novels*] **4.** to engross [*devoured by curiosity*] **5.** to swallow up; engulf —**de·vour′er** ***n.***

de·vout (di vout′) ***adj.*** [< OFr. < L. *devotus:* see DEVOTE] **1.** very religious; pious **2.** showing reverence **3.** earnest; sincere; heartfelt —**de·vout′ly** ***adv.*** —**de·vout′ness** ***n.***

dew (do͞o, dyo͞o) ***n.*** [OE. *deaw*] **1.** the moisture that condenses after a warm day and appears during the night in little drops on cool surfaces **2.** anything regarded as refreshing, pure, etc., like dew **3.** any moisture in small drops —***vt.*** [Poet.] to wet as with drops of dew

dew·ber·ry (do͞o′ber′ē, dyo͞o′-) ***n.,*** *pl.* **-ries** **1.** any of various trailing blackberry plants of the rose family **2.** the fruit of any of these plants

dew·claw (-klô′) ***n.*** **1.** a functionless digit on the foot of some animals, as on the inner side of a dog's leg **2.** the claw or hoof on such a digit

dew·drop (-dräp′) ***n.*** a drop of dew

Dew·ey (dōō′ē, dyōō′ē) **1. George,** 1837–1917; U.S. admiral in the Spanish-American War **2. John,** 1859–1952; U.S. philosopher & educator **3. Melvil,** 1851–1931; U.S. librarian: originated **Dewey Decimal System** for book classification in libraries

dew·lap (-lap′) ***n.*** [< ME. < *dew,* prob. dew + *lappe,* a fold < OE. *læppa*] **1.** a loose fold of skin hanging from the throat of cattle and certain other animals **2.** a similar loose fold under the chin of an elderly person —**dew′lapped′** (-lapt′) ***adj.***

DEWLAP

DEW line (dōō, dyōō) [*D(istant) E(arly) W(arning)*] a line of radar stations near the 70th parallel in N. America

dew point the temperature at which dew starts to form or vapor to condense into liquid

dew·y (-ē) ***adj.* dew′i·er, dew′i·est 1.** wet or damp with dew **2.** of dew **3.** [Poet.] dewlike; refreshing, etc. —**dew′i·ly** ***adv.*** —**dew′i·ness** ***n.***

Dex·e·drine (dek′sə drēn′, -drin) [< ff. & EPHEDRINE] *a trademark for* AMPHETAMINE

dex·ter (dek′stər) ***adj.*** [L., right] of or on the right-hand side (on a coat of arms, the left of the viewer)

dex·ter·i·ty (dek ster′ə tē) ***n.*** [< L. < *dexter:* see prec.] **1.** skill in using one's hands or body; adroitness **2.** skill in using one's mind; cleverness

dex·ter·ous (dek′strəs, -stər əs) ***adj.*** [see prec.] **1.** having or showing skill in the use of the hands or body **2.** having or showing mental skill —**dex′ter·ous·ly** ***adv.*** —**dex′ter·ous·ness** ***n.***

dex·tral (dek′strəl) ***adj.*** [< L. *dextra,* right-hand side] **1.** on the right-hand side; right **2.** right-handed —**dex·tral′i·ty** (-stral′ə tē) ***n.*** —**dex′tral·ly** ***adv.***

dex·trin (dek′strin) ***n.*** [< Fr. < L. *dexter,* right: it turns the plane of polarized light to the right] a soluble, gummy substance obtained from starch and used as adhesive, sizing, etc.: also **dex′trine** (-strēn, -strən)

dex·trorse (dek′strôrs) ***adj.*** [< L. < *dexter,* right + *versus,* pp. of *vertere,* to turn] *Bot.* twining upward to the right, as the stem of the hop

dex·trose (dek′strōs) ***n.*** [ult. < L. *dexter:* cf. DEXTRIN] a glucose, $C_6H_{12}O_6$, found in plants and animals

dex·trous (-strəs) ***adj.*** *same as* DEXTEROUS

DF, D/F, D.F. *Radio* direction finder

dg. decigram; decigrams

‡dhar·ma (dur′mə, där′-) ***n.*** [Sans., law] *Hinduism, Buddhism* **1.** cosmic order or law, including the natural and moral principles that apply to all beings and things **2.** observance of this law in one's life

dhow (dou) ***n.*** [Ar. *dāwa*] a single-masted ship with a lateen sail, used along the Indian Ocean coasts

di-[1] [Gr. *di-* < *dis,* twice] *a prefix meaning:* **1.** twice, double, twofold **2.** *Chem.* having two atoms, molecules, radicals, etc. Also **dis-**

di-[2] *same as* DIS-

di-[3] *same as* DIA-

di., dia. diameter

di·a- [< Gr.] *a prefix meaning:* **1.** through, across [*diaphragm, diagonal*] **2.** apart, between [*diagnose*]

di·a·be·tes (dī′ə bēt′is, -ēz) ***n.*** [L. < Gr. *diabētēs,* a siphon < *dia-,* through + *bainein,* to go] any of various diseases characterized by an excessive discharge of urine; esp., DIABETES MELLITUS

diabetes mel·li·tus (mə līt′is) [ModL., lit., honey diabetes] a chronic form of diabetes involving an insulin deficiency and characterized by excess of sugar in the blood and urine, hunger, thirst, etc.

di·a·bet·ic (dī′ə bet′ik) ***adj.*** of or having diabetes —***n.*** a person who has diabetes

di·a·bol·ic (dī′ə bäl′ik) ***adj.*** [< Fr. < LL. < Gr. *diabolos:* see DEVIL] **1.** of the Devil or devils **2.** very wicked or cruel; fiendish Also **di′a·bol′i·cal** —**di′a·bol′i·cal·ly** ***adv.***

di·ac·o·nal (dī ak′ə n'l) ***adj.*** of a deacon or deacons

di·ac·o·nate (-nit) ***n.*** **1.** the rank, office, or tenure of a deacon **2.** a group of deacons

di·a·crit·ic (dī′ə krit′ik) ***adj.*** [Gr. *diakritikos* < *dia-,* across + *krinein,* to separate] *same as* DIACRITICAL —***n.*** *same as* DIACRITICAL MARK

di·a·crit·i·cal (-i k'l) ***adj.*** **1.** serving to distinguish **2.** able to distinguish —**di′a·crit′i·cal·ly** ***adv.***

diacritical mark a mark, as a macron or a cedilla, added to a letter or symbol to show its pronunciation or to distinguish it in some way

di·a·dem (dī′ə dem′, -dəm) ***n.*** [< OFr. < L. < Gr. *diadēma* < *dia-,* through + *dein,* to bind] **1.** a crown **2.** an ornamental cloth headband worn as a crown **3.** royal power or authority —***vt.*** to crown

di·aer·e·sis (dī er′ə sis) ***n., pl.*** **-ses′** (-sēz′) *same as* DIERESIS

diag. **1.** diagonal **2.** diagram

di·ag·nose (dī′əg nōs′, -nōz′) ***vt., vi.*** **-nosed′ -nos′ing** to make a diagnosis of (a disease, etc.)

di·ag·no·sis (dī′əg nō′sis) ***n., pl.*** **-ses** (-sēz) [ModL. < Gr. < *dia-,* between + *gignōskein,* to know] **1.** the act or process of deciding the nature of a diseased condition by examination of the symptoms **2.** a careful analysis of the facts meant to explain something **3.** a decision based on such an examination or analysis —**di′ag·nos′tic** (-näs′tik) ***adj.*** —**di′ag·nos′ti·cal·ly** ***adv.*** —**di′ag·nos·ti′cian** (-näs-tish′ən) ***n.***

di·ag·o·nal (dī ag′ə n'l) ***adj.*** [L. *diagonalis* < Gr. < *dia-,* through + *gōnia,* an angle] **1.** extending slantingly between opposite corners, as of a rectangle **2.** having a slanting direction or slanting markings, lines, etc. —***n.*** **1.** *a*) a diagonal line or plane *b*) *same as* VIRGULE **2.** any diagonal course, row, part, etc. —**di·ag′o·nal·ly** ***adv.***

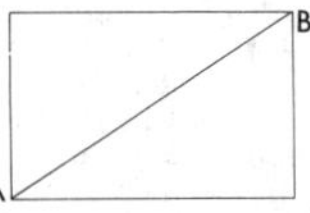

DIAGONAL (AB)

di·a·gram (dī′ə gram′) ***n.*** [Gr. *diagramma* < *dia-,* across + *graphein,* to write] a drawing, plan, or chart that explains a thing, as by outlining its parts and their relationships, workings, etc. —***vt.*** **-gramed′** or **-grammed′, -gram′ing** or **-gram′ming** to make a diagram of —**di′a·gram·mat′ic** (-grə mat′ik), **di′a·gram·mat′i·cal** ***adj.*** —**di′a·gram·mat′i·cal·ly** ***adv.***

di·al (dī′əl, dīl) ***n.*** [< ML. *dialis,* daily < L. *dies,* day] **1.** a sundial **2.** the face of a watch or clock **3.** the face of a meter, gauge, etc. on which a pointer indicates an amount, degree, etc. **4.** a graduated disk or strip on a radio or television set, for tuning in stations or channels **5.** a rotating disk on a telephone, used in making connections automatically —***vt., vi.*** **-aled** or **-alled, -al·ing** or **-al·ling** **1.** to measure, regulate, etc. with a dial **2.** to tune in (a radio station, television channel, program, etc.) **3.** to call on a telephone by using a dial or other automatic device

dial. **1.** dialect(al) **2.** dialectic(al)

di·a·lect (dī′ə lekt′) ***n.*** [< L. < Gr. *dialektos,* discourse < *dia-,* between + *legein,* to talk] **1.** the sum total of local characteristics of speech **2.** any form of speech that differs from a real or imaginary standard speech **3.** the form of a spoken language peculiar to a region, community, social group, occupational group, etc. **4.** any language as a member of a group or family of languages [*English is a West Germanic dialect*] —***adj.*** of or in dialect —**di′a·lec′tal** ***adj.*** —**di′a·lec′tal·ly** ***adv.***

di·a·lec·tic (dī′ə lek′tik) ***n.*** [< OFr. < L. < Gr. < *dialektikos:* see prec.] **1.** [*often pl.*] the art or practice of examining ideas logically, often by question and answer, so as to determine their validity **2.** logical argumentation **3.** [*often pl.*] the method of logic used by Hegel and adapted by Marx to observable social and economic processes —***adj.*** *same as* DIALECTICAL

di·a·lec·ti·cal (-ti k'l) ***adj.*** **1.** of or using dialectic or dialectics **2.** of or characteristic of a dialect; dialectal —**di′a·lec′ti·cal·ly** ***adv.***

dialectical materialism the philosophy stemming from Marx and Engels which applies Hegel's dialectical method to observable social processes

di·a·lec·ti·cian (dī′ə lek tish′ən) ***n.*** **1.** an expert in dialectic; logician **2.** a specialist in dialects

di·a·logue, di·a·log (dī′ə lôg′, -läg′) ***n.*** [OFr. < L. < Gr. *dialogos* < *dialegein:* see DIALECT] **1.** a talking together; conversation **2.** open and frank discussion of ideas, as in seeking mutual understanding **3.** a written work in the form of a conversation **4.** the passages of talk in a play, story, etc. —***vi.*** **-logued′, -logu′ing** to hold a conversation —***vt.*** to express in dialogue —**di·al·o·gist** (dī al′ə jist, dī′ə lôg′ist) ***n.***

Dialogue Mass *R.C.Ch.* a Low Mass at which the congregation, following an earlier custom now revived, makes the responses aloud and in unison

dial tone a low buzzing sound indicating to the user of a dial telephone that the line is open and a number may be dialed

di·al·y·sis (dī al′ə sis) ***n., pl.*** **-ses′** (-sēz′) [L. < Gr. < *dia-,* apart + *lyein,* to loose] the separation of crystalloids from colloids in solution by the greater diffusibility of the smaller molecules through a semipermeable membrane —**di·a·lyt·ic** (dī′ə lit′ik) ***adj.*** —**di′a·lyt′i·cal·ly** ***adv.***

di·a·lyze (dī′ə līz′) ***vt.*** **-lyzed′, -lyz′ing** to apply dialysis to or separate by dialysis —***vi.*** to undergo dialysis —**di′a·lyz′er** ***n.***

diam. diameter

di·a·mag·net·ic (dī′ə mag net′ik) ***adj.*** having diamagnetism —***n.*** a diamagnetic substance, as bismuth or zinc: also **di′a·mag′net**

di·a·mag·net·ism (-mag′nə tiz'm) ***n.*** the property that certain substances have of being repelled by both poles of a magnet

di·a·man·té (dē′ə män tā′, -män′tā) ***adj.*** [Fr.] decorated with rhinestones or other glittering bits of material —***n.*** glittering ornamentation

di·am·e·ter (dī am′ət ər) ***n.*** [< OFr. < ML. < L. < Gr. < *dia-*, through + *metron*, a measure] **1.** a straight line passing through the center of a circle, sphere, etc. from one side to the other **2.** the length of such a line

di·a·met·ri·cal (dī′ə met′ri k'l) ***adj.*** **1.** of or along a diameter **2.** designating an opposite, a difference, etc. that is wholly so [*diametrical* opposites]: also **di′a·met′ric** —**di′a·met′ri·cal·ly** ***adv.***

di·a·mond (dī′mənd, -ə mənd) ***n.*** [< OFr. < ML. *diamas* (gen. *diamantis*) < L. < Gr. *adamas*, ADAMANT, diamond] **1.** a mineral consisting of nearly pure carbon in crystalline form: it is the hardest mineral known and has great brilliance: unflawed stones are cut into precious gems; less perfect forms are used for phonograph-needle tips, cutting tools, abrasives, etc. **2.** a gem cut from this mineral **3.** *a*) a lozenge-shaped plane figure (◊) *b*) a red mark like this on a suit of playing cards *c*) [*pl.*] this suit *d*) a card of this suit **4.** *Baseball* *a*) the infield *b*) the whole playing field —***adj.*** of, like, or set with a diamond —**diamond in the rough** **1.** a diamond in its natural state **2.** a person or thing of fine quality but lacking polish

diamond anniversary the sixtieth, or sometimes seventy-fifth, anniversary: also **diamond jubilee**

di·a·mond·back (-bak′) ***adj.*** having diamond-shaped markings on the back —***n.*** **1.** a large, poisonous rattlesnake native to the S U.S. **2.** an edible turtle found in coastal salt marshes from Cape Cod to Mexico: in full, **diamondback terrapin** **3.** a small, brown and white moth

diamond wedding a sixtieth, or sometimes seventy-fifth, wedding anniversary

Di·an·a (dī an′ə) [ML. < L., ult. < *divus*, divine] **1.** a feminine name: var. *Diane* **2.** *Rom. Myth.* the virgin goddess of the moon and of hunting: identified with the Greek goddess Artemis

di·a·pa·son (dī′ə pāz′'n, -pās′-) ***n.*** [< L. < Gr. contr. < *dia*, through + *pasōn*, gen. pl. of *pas*, all (notes)] **1.** *a*) the entire range of a musical instrument or voice *b*) the entire range of some activity, emotion, etc. **2.** one of the principal stops of an organ covering the instrument's complete range **3.** a swelling burst of harmony

di·a·per (dī′pər, dī′ə pər) ***n.*** [< OFr. *diapre* < ML. *diasprum*, flowered cloth] **1.** *a*) orig., cloth or fabric with a pattern of repeated small figures, such as diamonds *b*) such a pattern, as in art **2.** a soft, absorbent cloth folded and arranged between the legs and around the waist of a baby —***vt.*** **1.** to give a diaper design to **2.** to put a fresh diaper on (a baby)

di·aph·a·nous (dī af′ə nəs) ***adj.*** [< ML. < Gr. < *dia-*, through + *phainein*, to show] **1.** so fine or gauzy in texture as to be transparent or translucent [*diaphanous* cloth] **2.** vague or indistinct —**di·aph′a·nous·ly** ***adv.***

di·a·pho·re·sis (dī′ə fə rē′sis) ***n.*** [LL. < Gr. < *dia-*, through + *pherein*, to bear] perspiration, esp. when profuse —**di′a·pho·ret′ic** (-ret′ik) ***adj., n.***

di·a·phragm (dī′ə fram′) ***n.*** [< LL. < Gr. < *dia-*, through + *phragma*, a fence < *phrassein*, enclose] **1.** the partition of muscles and tendons between the chest cavity and the abdominal cavity; midriff **2.** any separating membrane or device **3.** a device to regulate the amount of light entering a camera lens, etc. **4.** a thin, vibrating disk or cone that produces electrical signals, as in a microphone, or sound waves, as in a loudspeaker —**di′a·phrag·mat′ic** (-frag-mat′ik) ***adj.*** —**di′a·phrag·mat′i·cal·ly** ***adv.***

di·aph·y·sis (dī af′ə sis) ***n., pl.*** **-ses′** (-sēz′) [ModL. < Gr. < *dia-*, through + *phyein*, to produce] the shaft of a long bone —**di·a·phys·e·al, di·a·phys·i·al** (dī′ə fiz′ē əl) ***adj.***

di·a·rist (dī′ə rist) ***n.*** a person who keeps a diary

di·ar·rhe·a, di·ar·rhoe·a (dī′ə rē′ə) ***n.*** [< OFr. & LL. < Gr. < *dia-*, through + *rhein*, to flow] excessive frequency and looseness of bowel movements —**di′ar·rhe′al, di′ar·rhe′ic** ***adj.***

di·a·ry (dī′ə rē) ***n., pl.*** **-ries** [L. *diarium* < *dies*, day] **1.** a daily written record, esp. of the writer's own experiences, thoughts, etc. **2.** a book for this

Di·as·po·ra (dī as′pə rə) ***n.*** [< Gr. < *dia-*, across + *speirein*, to sow] **1.** *a*) the dispersion of the Jews after the Babylonian exile *b*) these Jews **2.** [**d-**] any scattering of people with a common origin, background, beliefs, etc.

di·a·stase (dī′ə stās′) ***n.*** [Fr. < Gr. *diastasis*, separation < *dia-*, apart + *histanai*, to stand] an enzyme, occurring in the seed of grains and malt, that changes starches into maltose and later into dextrose —**di′a·stat′ic** (-stat′ik) ***adj.***

di·as·to·le (dī as′tə lē′) ***n.*** [LL. < Gr. *diastolē*, expansion < *dia-*, apart + *stellein*, to put] the usual rhythmic dilatation of the heart, esp. of the ventricles, during which the chambers fill with blood —**di·a·stol·ic** (dī′ə stäl′ik) ***adj.***

di·as·tro·phism (dī as′trə fiz'm) ***n.*** [< Gr. < *dia-*, aside + *strephein*, to turn + -ISM] the process by which the earth's surface is reshaped by rock movements —**di·a·stroph·ic** (dī′ə sträf′ik) ***adj.***

di·a·ther·my (dī′ə thur′mē) ***n.*** [ModL. < Gr. *dia-*, through + *thermē*, heat] medical treatment in which heat is produced in the tissues beneath the skin by a high-frequency electric current —**di′a·ther′mic** ***adj.***

di·a·tom (dī′ə täm′, -ət əm) ***n.*** [ModL. < Gr. < *dia-*, through + *temnein*, to cut] any of a number of related microscopic algae whose cell walls contain silica: diatoms are a source of food for marine life —**di·a·to·ma·ceous** (dī′ət-ə mā′shəs, dī at′ə-) ***adj.***

di·a·ton·ic (dī′ə tän′ik) ***adj.*** [Fr. < LL. < Gr. *diatonikos*, stretched through (the notes) < *dia-*, through + *teinein*, to stretch] *Music* designating, of, or using any standard major or minor scale of eight tones without the chromatic intervals —**di′a·ton′i·cal·ly** ***adv.***

di·a·tribe (dī′ə trīb′) ***n.*** [Fr. < L. < Gr. *diatribē*, a wearing away < *dia-*, through + *tribein*, to rub] a bitter, abusive criticism or denunciation

di·bas·ic (dī bās′ik) ***adj.*** denoting or of an acid with two hydrogen atoms which may be replaced by basic radicals or atoms to form a salt

dib·ble (dib′'l) ***n.*** [ME. *dibbel*, prob. < *dibben*, to dip] a pointed tool used to make holes in the soil for seeds, bulbs, or young plants: also called **dib′ber** —***vt.*** **-bled, -bling** **1.** to make a hole in (the soil) with a dibble **2.** to plant with a dibble —***vi.*** to use a dibble

DIBBLE

dibs (dibz) ***n.pl.*** [< *dibstone*, a jack in a children's game] [Colloq.] a claim to a share of, or rights in, something wanted —***interj.*** an exclamation announcing such a claim: chiefly a child's term

dice (dīs) ***n.pl., sing.*** **die** or **dice** [ME. *dis*, pl.: see DIE[2]] **1.** small cubes of bone, plastic, etc. marked on each side with from one to six spots and used, usually in pairs, in games of chance **2.** [*with sing. v.*] a gambling game played with dice **3.** any small cubes —***vi.*** **diced, dic′ing** to play or gamble with dice —***vt.*** to cut (vegetables, etc.) into small cubes —**no dice** **1.** no: used in refusing a request **2.** no success, luck, etc. —**dic′er** ***n.***

di·chlo·ride (dī klôr′īd, -id) ***n.*** any chemical compound in which two atoms of chlorine are combined with an element or radical

di·chot·o·my (dī kät′ə mē) ***n., pl.*** **-mies** [< Gr. < *dicha*, in two + *temnein*, to cut] **1.** division into two usually opposed parts or groups **2.** *Biol., Bot.* a dividing or branching into two parts, esp. when repeated —**di·chot′o·mize′** (-mīz′) ***vt.*** **-mized′, -miz′ing** —**di·chot′o·mous** (-məs) ***adj.***

di·chro·mate (dī krō′māt) ***n.*** any salt of dichromic acid

di·chro·mat·ic (dī′krō mat′ik) ***adj.*** [DI-[1] + CHROMATIC] **1.** having two colors **2.** *Biol.* having two varieties of coloration that are independent of sex or age —**di·chro′ma·tism** ***n.***

di·chro·mic (dī krō′mik) ***adj.*** **1.** *same as* DICHROMATIC **2.** *Chem.* designating a hypothetical acid, $H_2Cr_2O_7$, from which dichromates are formed

Dick (dik) [< RICHARD] a masculine name —***n.*** [**d-**] [Slang] a detective

dick·cis·sel (dik sis′'l) ***n.*** [echoic of its cry] an American bunting with a black throat and yellow breast

dick·ens (dik′'nz) ***n., interj.*** [prob. < nickname for RICHARD] [Colloq.] devil; deuce: a mild oath

Dick·ens (dik′'nz), **Charles** (pseud. *Boz*) 1812–70; Eng. novelist —**Dick·en·si·an** (di ken′zē ən) ***adj.***

dick·er (dik′ər) ***vi., vt.*** [< *dicker*, ten, ten hides (as a unit of barter), ult. < L. *decem*, ten] to trade by bargaining, esp. on a small scale; barter; haggle —***n.*** the act of bargaining or haggling

dick·ey (dik′ē) ***n., pl.*** **-eys** [< DICK] **1.** a man's detachable, or false, shirt front **2.** a woman's detachable collar or blouse front **3.** a small bird: also **dickey bird** Also sp. **dick′y,** *pl.* **dick′ies**

DICKEY

Dick·in·son (dik′in s'n), **Emily (Elizabeth)** 1830–86; U.S. poet

di·cli·nous (dī klī′nəs) ***adj.*** [< DI-[1] + Gr. *klinē*, bed + -OUS] *Bot.* having the stamens and pistils in separate flowers —**di·cli·nism** (dī′klī niz'm), **di′cli·ny** (-nē) ***n.***

di·cot·y·le·don (dī′kät 'l ēd′'n, dī-kät′'l-) ***n.*** a flowering plant with two seed leaves (cotyledons) —**di′cot·y·le′don·ous** ***adj.***

di·cou·mar·in (dī ko͞o′mər in) ***n.*** [DI-[1]

+ *coumarin,* a plant extract] a chemical compound, $C_{19}H_{12}O_6$, used as an anticoagulant
dict. 1. dictator 2. dictionary
dic·ta (dik′tə) *n. alt. pl. of* DICTUM
Dic·ta·phone (dik′tə fōn′) [DICTA(TE) + -PHONE] *a trademark for* a machine that records spoken words so that they can be played back later for typed transcripts, etc. —*n.* this machine
dic·tate (dik′tāt; *also for v.* dik tāt′) *vt., vi.* **-tat·ed, -tat·ing** [< L. pp. of *dictare,* freq. of *dicere,* to speak] **1.** to speak or read (something) aloud for someone else to write down **2.** to command expressly **3.** to impose or give (orders) with authority or arbitrarily —*n.* **1.** an authoritative command **2.** a guiding principle *[*the *dictates* of conscience*]*
dic·ta·tion (dik tā′shən) *n.* **1.** the dictating of words for another to write down **2.** the words so spoken or read **3.** the giving of authoritative orders or commands —**dic·ta′tion·al** *adj.*
dic·ta·tor (dik′tāt ər, dik tāt′-) *n.* **1.** a ruler with absolute power and authority, esp. a tyrant or despot **2.** a person who is domineering or arbitrary in giving orders, etc. **3.** one who dictates words for another to write down —**dic·ta′tor·ship′** *n.*
dic·ta·to·ri·al (dik′tə tôr′ē əl) *adj.* of, like, or characteristic of a dictator; autocratic; tyrannical; domineering —**dic′ta·to′ri·al·ly** *adv.*
dic·tion (dik′shən) *n.* [< L. pp. of *dicere,* to say] **1.** manner of expression in words; choice of words **2.** enunciation
dic·tion·ar·y (dik′shə ner′ē) *n., pl.* **-ar′ies** [ML. *dictionarium* < LL. *dictio:* see prec.] **1.** a book of alphabetically listed words in a language, with definitions, etymologies, pronunciations, etc.; lexicon **2.** such a book of words in one language with their equivalents in another **3.** any alphabetically arranged list of words or articles relating to a special subject *[*a medical *dictionary]*
dic·tum (dik′təm) *n., pl.* **-tums, -ta** (-tə) [L., neut. pp. of *dicere,* to speak] a formal statement of fact, opinion, principle, etc.; pronouncement
Di·cu·ma·rol (dī ko͞o′mə rôl′, -kyo͞o′-) *a collective trademark for* DICOUMARIN
did (did) *pt. of* DO[1]
di·dact (dī′dakt) *n.* [< ff.] a didactic person
di·dac·tic (dī dak′tik) *adj.* [Gr. *didaktikos* < *didaskein,* to teach] **1.** used or intended for teaching or instruction **2.** morally instructive **3.** too much inclined to teach others; boringly pedantic or moralistic Also **di·dac′ti·cal** —**di·dac′ti·cal·ly** *adv.* —**di·dac′ti·cism** (-tə siz′m) *n.*
di·dac·tics (-tiks) *n.pl.* [*usually with sing. v.*] the art or science of teaching; pedagogy
did·dle[1] (did′'l) *vi., vt.* **-dled, -dling** [Eng. dial. *duddle, diddle,* to totter] [Colloq.] to move back and forth jerkily; jiggle —**did′dler** *n.*
did·dle[2] (did′'l) *vt., vi.* **-dled, -dling** [ult. < OE. *dyderian,* to fool] [Colloq.] **1.** to cheat or swindle **2.** to waste (time) in trifling —**did′dler** *n.*
Di·de·rot (dē′də rō′; *Fr.* dē drō′), **Denis** 1713–84; Fr. encyclopedist & philosopher
did·n't (did′'nt) did not
Di·do (dī′dō) *Rom. Legend* queen of Carthage, who kills herself when her lover Aeneas leaves her
di·do (dī′dō) *n., pl.* **-does, -dos** [< ?] [Colloq.] a mischievous trick; prank; caper
didst (didst) *archaic 2d pers. sing., past indic., of* DO[1]: *used with* thou
di·dy (dī′dē) *n., pl.* **-dies** [< DIAPER] [Colloq.] a diaper (sense 2)
di·dym·i·um (dī dim′ē əm) *n.* [< Gr. *didymos,* twin] a mixture of two rare-earth elements, formerly considered a single element: symbol, Di
die[1] (dī) *vi.* **died, dy′ing** [ME. *dien* < ON. *deyja*] **1.** to stop living; become dead **2.** to suffer the agony of, or like that of, death **3.** to cease existing or stop functioning; end **4.** to lose force or activity **5.** to fade or wither away **6.** to pine away, as with desire **7.** [Colloq.] to wish intensely; yearn *[*she's *dying* to tell*]* **8.** *Theol.* to suffer spiritual death —**die away** (or **down**) to become weaker and cease gradually —**die back** (or **down**) to wither to the roots or woody part —**die hard** to resist to the last —**die off** to die one by one until all are gone —**die out** to go out of existence
die[2] (dī) *n., pl.,* for 1 **dice** (dīs); for 2 **dies** (dīz) [< OFr. *de* < L. pp. of *dare,* to give] **1.** a small, marked cube used in games of chance: see also DICE **2.** any of various tools or devices for molding, stamping, cutting, or shaping —*vt.* **died, die′ing** to mold, stamp, cut, or shape with a die —**the die is cast** the irrevocable decision has been made
die casting 1. the process of making a casting by forcing molten metal into a metallic mold, or die, under pressure **2.** a casting so made —**die caster**
dief·fen·bach·i·a (dēf′'n bak′ē ə) *n.* [ModL. < E. *Dieffenbach* (19th-c. Ger. botanist)] a tropical plant of the arum family, with large leaves
die-hard, die·hard (dī′härd′) *adj.* extremely stubborn in resistance; unwilling to give in —*n.* a stubborn or resistant person, esp. an extreme conservative
diel·drin (dēl′drin) *n.* a highly toxic, long-lasting insecticide, $C_{12}H_8OCl_6$
di·e·lec·tric (dī′ə lek′trik) *n.* [< DI(A)- + ELECTRIC] a material, as rubber, glass, etc., that does not conduct electricity and that can sustain an electric field: used in capacitors, etc. —*adj.* having the properties or function of a dielectric
di·er·e·sis (dī er′ə sis) *n., pl* **-ses′** (-sēz′) [LL. < Gr. *diairesis,* division < *dia-,* apart + *hairein,* to take] a mark (¨) placed over the second of two consecutive vowels to show that it is pronounced in a separate syllable: now usually replaced by a hyphen (*reënter, re-enter*), or simply omitted (*cooperate, naive*) The mark is also used, as in this dictionary, to show a certain pronunciation of a vowel (ä) —**di·e·ret·ic** (dī′ə ret′ik) *adj.*
die·sel (dē′z'l, -s'l) *n.* [after R. *Diesel* (1858–1913), Ger. inventor] *[often* **D-***]* **1.** a type of internal-combustion engine that burns fuel oil: the ignition is brought about by heat resulting from air compression, instead of by an electric spark as in a gasoline engine: also **diesel engine** (or **motor**) **2.** a locomotive, truck, etc. with such an engine
die·sink·er (dī′siŋ′kər) *n.* a maker of dies used in stamping or shaping —**die′sink′ing** *n.*
‡**Di·es I·rae** (dē′ez ir′ā, dē′ās ir′ē) [L., Day of Wrath] a medieval Latin hymn about Judgment Day, beginning *Dies Irae,* a part of the Requiem Mass
di·e·sis (dī′ə sis) *n., pl.* **-ses′** (-sēz′) [L. < Gr. < *diienai,* to send through] a reference mark (‡) used in printing: also called DOUBLE DAGGER
di·et[1] (dī′ət) *n.* [< OFr. < ML. < L. < Gr. *diaita,* way of life] **1.** *a)* what a person or animal usually eats and drinks; daily fare *b)* figuratively, what a person regularly reads, listens to, does, etc. **2.** a regimen of special or limited food and drink, chosen or prescribed for health or to gain or lose weight —*vi.* to eat special or limited food, esp. for losing weight —**di′et·er** *n.*
di·et[2] (dī′ət) *n.* [< OFr. < ML. < L. *dies,* day] **1.** a formal assembly, as formerly of princes, electors, etc. of the Holy Roman Empire **2.** in some countries, a national or local legislative assembly
di·e·tar·y (dī′ə ter′ē) *n., pl.* **-ies 1.** a system of diet **2.** daily food allowance or ration —*adj.* **1.** of diet **2.** of a dietary
di·e·tet·ic (dī′ə tet′ik) *adj.* of, relating to, or designed for a particular diet of food and drink: also **di′e·tet′i·cal** —**di′e·tet′i·cal·ly** *adv.*
di·e·tet·ics (-iks) *n.pl.* [*with sing. v.*] the study of the kinds and quantities of food needed for health
di·e·ti·tian, di·e·ti·cian (dī′ə tish′ən) *n.* an expert in dietetics; specialist in planning meals or diets
dif- *same as* DIS-: used before *f*
dif·fer (dif′ər) *vi.* [< OFr. < L. *differre* < *dis-,* apart + *ferre,* to bear] **1.** to be unlike; be not the same (often with *from*) **2.** to be of opposite or unlike opinions; disagree
dif·fer·ence (dif′ər əns, dif′rəns) *n.* [see prec.] **1.** condition or quality of being different **2.** the way in which people or things are different **3.** the state of holding a differing opinion; disagreement; also, the point at issue; point of disagreement **4.** a dispute; quarrel **5.** *Math.* the amount by which one quantity is greater or less than another —**make a difference 1.** to have an effect; matter **2.** to change the situation —**split the difference 1.** to share equally what is left over **2.** to make a compromise —**what's the difference?** [Colloq.] what does it matter?
dif·fer·ent (dif′ər ənt, dif′rənt) *adj.* [see DIFFER] **1.** not alike; dissimilar (with *from,* or, esp. colloquially, *than,* and, in Brit. usage, *to*) **2.** not the same; distinct; separate; other **3.** various **4.** unlike most others; unusual —**dif′fer·ent·ly** *adv.*
dif·fer·en·ti·a (dif′ə ren′shē ə, -shə) *n., pl.* **-ti·ae′** (-shi-ē′) a distinguishing characteristic
dif·fer·en·tial (-shəl) *adj.* **1.** of, showing, or depending on a difference **2.** constituting a specific difference; distinguishing **3.** having different effects or making use of differences *[*a *differential* gear*]* **4.** *Math.* of or involving differentials —*n.* **1.** a differentiating amount, degree, factor, etc. *[differentials* in salary*]* **2.** *Math. a)* an infinitesimal difference between two consecutive values of a variable quantity *b)* the derivative of a function multiplied by the increment of the independent variable **3.** *Mech. same as* DIFFERENTIAL GEAR **4.** *Railroading* a difference in rates, as between different routes —**dif′fer·en′tial·ly** *adv.*
differential calculus the branch of higher mathematics which deals with derivatives and their applications
differential gear (or **gearing**) an arrangement of gears connecting two axles in the same line and allowing one axle to turn faster than the other: used in the rear axles of automobiles to permit a difference in axle speeds while turning curves

dif·fer·en·ti·ate (-shē āt′) ***vt.* -at′ed, -at′ing 1.** to constitute a difference in or between **2.** to make unlike **3.** to perceive or express the difference in; distinguish between **4.** *Math.* to work out the differential or derivative of —***vi.* 1.** to become different or differentiated **2.** to perceive or express a difference —**dif′fer·en′ti·a′tion *n.***

dif·fi·cult (dif′i kəlt, -kult′) ***adj.* 1.** hard to do, make, manage, understand, etc. **2.** hard to satisfy, persuade, please, etc. —**dif′fi·cult·ly *adv.***

dif·fi·cul·ty (dif′i kul′tē, -kəl-) ***n.,*** *pl.* **-ties** [< OFr. < L. *difficultas* < *dis-,* not + *facilis,* easy] **1.** the condition or fact of being difficult **2.** something difficult; an obstacle or objection **3.** trouble or distress **4.** a disagreement or quarrel —**in difficulties** in distress, esp. financially

dif·fi·dent (dif′ə dənt) ***adj.*** [< L. prp. of *diffidere* < *dis-,* not + *fidere,* to trust] lacking confidence in oneself; hesitant to assert oneself; timid; shy —**dif′fi·dence *n.*** —**dif′fi·dent·ly *adv.***

dif·fract (di frakt′) ***vt.*** [< L. pp. of *diffringere* < *dis-,* apart + *frangere,* to break] to break into parts; specif., to subject to diffraction

dif·frac·tion (di frak′shən) ***n.* 1.** the breaking up of a ray of light into dark and light bands or into the colors of the spectrum, as when it is deflected at the edge of an opaque object **2.** a similar breaking up of other waves, as of sound or electricity —**dif·frac′tive** (-tiv) ***adj.*** —**dif·frac′tive·ly *adv.***

dif·fuse (di fyo͞os′; *for v.* -fyo͞oz′) ***adj.*** [< L. pp. < *dis-,* apart + *fundere,* to pour] **1.** spread out; not concentrated **2.** using more words than are needed —***vt., vi.* -fused′, -fus′ing 1.** to pour or disperse in every direction; spread or scatter widely **2.** *Physics* to mix by diffusion, as gases, liquids, etc. —**dif·fuse′ly *adv.*** —**dif·fuse′ness *n.*** —**dif·fus′er, dif·fu′sor** (-fyo͞o′zər) ***n.*** —**dif·fus′i·bil′i·ty *n.*** —**dif·fus′i·ble *adj.***

dif·fu·sion (di fyo͞o′zhən) ***n.* 1.** a diffusing or being diffused; specif., *a)* a dissemination, as of news *b)* a scattering of light rays, as by reflection; also, the dispersion and softening of light, as by using frosted glass *c)* an intermingling of the molecules of liquids, gases, etc. **2.** wordiness

dif·fu·sive (-siv) ***adj.* 1.** tending to diffuse **2.** characterized by diffusion **3.** diffuse —**dif·fu′sive·ly *adv.*** —**dif·fu′sive·ness *n.***

dig (dig) ***vt.* dug** or archaic & poet. **digged, dig′ging** [< OFr. *digue,* dike < Du. *dijk*] **1.** to break and turn up or remove (ground, etc.) with a spade or other tool, or with hands, claws, etc. **2.** to make (a hole, cellar, etc.) as by doing this **3.** to get from the ground in this way *[to dig potatoes]* **4.** to find out, as by careful study; unearth (usually with *up* or *out*) *[to dig out the truth]* **5.** to jab or prod **6.** [Slang] *a)* to understand *b)* to approve of or like —***vi.* 1.** to dig the ground **2.** to make a way by or as by digging (*through, into, under*) **3.** [Colloq.] to work or study hard —***n.* 1.** the act of digging **2.** [Colloq.] *a)* a poke, nudge, etc. *b)* a sarcastic comment **3.** an archaeological excavation **4.** [*pl., often with sing. v.*] [Colloq.] living quarters —**dig in 1.** to dig trenches for cover **2.** to entrench oneself **3.** [Colloq.] *a)* to begin to work hard *b)* to begin eating —**dig into** [Colloq.] to work hard at

di·gest (dī′jest; *for v.* di jest′, dī-) ***n.*** [< L. pp. of *digerere,* to separate < *di-,* apart + *gerere,* to bear] **1.** a collection of condensed, systematic information; summary or synopsis, as of legal material **2.** a book, periodical, etc. consisting of such summaries —***vt.* 1.** *a)* to arrange systematically, usually in condensed form *b)* to condense and summarize (a piece of writing) **2.** to change (food), esp. in the stomach and intestines, so that it can be absorbed by the body **3.** to aid the digestion of (food) **4.** to think over and absorb **5.** to soften or dissolve soluble material in, esp. with liquid —***vi.* 1.** to be digested **2.** to digest food —**di·gest′er *n.***

di·gest·i·ble (di jes′tə b′l) ***adj.*** that can be digested —**di·gest′i·bil′i·ty *n.*** —**di·gest′i·bly *adv.***

di·ges·tion (-chən) ***n.* 1.** the act or process of digesting food **2.** the ability to digest food **3.** the absorption of ideas **4.** decomposition of sewage by bacteria

di·ges·tive (-tiv) ***adj.*** of, for, or aiding digestion —***n.*** any substance or drink that aids digestion —**di·ges′tive·ly *adv.*** —**di·ges′tive·ness *n.***

dig·ger (dig′ər) ***n.* 1.** a person or thing that digs **2.** a tool or machine for digging **3.** [**D-**] a member of any of several tribes of Indians in the W U.S. who dug roots for food **4.** *same as* DIGGER WASP **5.** [**D-**] [Slang] an Australian or New Zealander

digger wasp any of various wasps that dig a nest in the ground

dig·gings (dig′iŋz) ***n.pl.* 1.** materials dug out **2.** [*often with sing. v.*] a place where digging or mining is carried on **3.** [Slang] one's lodgings

dight (dīt) ***vt.* dight** or **dight′ed, dight′ing** [< OE. *dihtan,* to arrange < L. *dictare:* see DICTATE] [Archaic or Poet.] **1.** to adorn **2.** to equip

dig·it (dij′it) ***n.*** [L. *digitus,* a finger, toe] **1.** a finger or toe **2.** any numeral from 0 to 9

dig·it·al (-'l) ***adj.* 1.** of, like, or constituting a digit **2.** having digits **3.** performed with the finger **4.** using numbers that are digits to represent all the variables involved in calculation **5.** showing the time, temperature, etc. by a row of digits rather than by numbers on a dial, etc. *[a digital watch]* —***n.* 1.** a finger **2.** a key played with a finger, as on the piano —**dig′it·al·ly *adv.***

digital computer a computer that uses numbers to perform calculations, usually in a binary system

dig·i·tal·is (dij′ə tal′is) ***n.*** [ModL. < L.: see DIGIT: from its flowers] **1.** any of a genus of plants of the figwort family, with long spikes of thimblelike flowers **2.** the dried leaves of the purple foxglove **3.** a medicine made from these leaves, used as a heart stimulant

dig·i·tate (dij′ə tāt′) ***adj.*** [see DIGIT] **1.** having separate fingers or toes **2.** fingerlike **3.** *Bot.* having fingerlike divisions, as some leaves Also **dig′i·tat′ed** —**dig′i·tate′ly *adv.*** —**dig′i·ta′tion *n.***

dig·ni·fied (dig′nə fīd′) ***adj.*** having or showing dignity or stateliness —**dig′ni·fied′ly *adv.***

dig·ni·fy (dig′nə fī′) ***vt.* -fied′, -fy′ing** [< OFr. < ML. < L. *dignus,* worthy + *facere,* to make] to give dignity to; make worthy of esteem; honor; exalt

dig·ni·tar·y (-ter′ē) ***n.,*** *pl.* **-tar′ies** [< L. *dignitas,* dignity + -ARY] a person holding a high, dignified position or office

dig·ni·ty (-tē) ***n.,*** *pl.* **-ties** [< OFr. < L. < *dignus,* worthy] **1.** the quality of being worthy of esteem or honor **2.** high repute; honor **3.** the degree of worth, repute, or honor **4.** a high position, rank, or title **5.** loftiness of appearance or manner; stateliness **6.** proper pride and self-respect

di·graph (dī′graf) ***n.*** [DI-[1] + -GRAPH] a combination of two letters to express a simple sound (Ex.: r*ea*d, *sh*ow, gra*ph*ic) —**di·graph′ic *adj.***

di·gress (dī gres′, di-) ***vi.*** [< L. pp. of *digredi* < *dis-,* apart + *gradi,* to go, step] to depart temporarily from the main subject in talking or writing —**di·gres′sion** (-gresh′ən) ***n.***

di·gres·sive (-gres′iv) ***adj.*** given to digression —**di·gres′sive·ly *adv.*** —**di·gres′sive·ness *n.***

di·he·dral (dī hē′drəl) ***adj.*** [< DI-[1] + Gr. *hedra,* a seat] **1.** having or formed by two intersecting plane faces *[a dihedral angle]* **2.** *a)* inclined to each other at a dihedral angle, as some airplane wings *b)* having such wings —***n.*** a dihedral angle

DIHEDRAL ANGLE (angle formed by planes MWON and MWXY)

Di·jon (dē zhōn′) city in EC France: pop. 145,000

dik-dik (dik′dik′) ***n.*** [< the Ethiopian native name] any of several small antelopes found in E Africa

dike (dīk) ***n.*** [< OE. *dic* & ON. *diki*] **1.** [Brit. Dial.] a ditch or watercourse **2.** an embankment or dam made to prevent flooding as by the sea **3.** a protective barrier **4.** *Geol.* igneous rock solidified as a tabular body in a vertical fissure —***vt.* diked, dik′ing 1.** to protect or enclose with a dike **2.** to drain by a ditch —**dik′er *n.***

Di·lan·tin (Sodium) (di lan′tin, dī-) *a trademark for* a drug, $C_{15}H_{11}N_2O_2Na$, used in the treatment of epileptic attacks —***n.*** [**d-**] this substance

di·lap·i·date (di lap′ə dāt′) ***vi., vt.* -dat′ed, -dat′ing** [< L. pp. of *dilapidare,* to demolish < *dis-,* apart + *lapidare,* to throw stones at < *lapis,* a stone] to become or make partially ruined and in need of repairs —**di·lap′i·dat′ed *adj.*** —**di·lap′i·da′tion *n.***

dil·a·ta·tion (dil′ə tā′shən, dī′lə-) ***n.*** *same as* DILATION

di·late (dī lāt′, di-; dī′lāt) ***vt.* -lat′ed, -lat′ing** [L. *dilatare* < *dis-,* apart + *latus,* wide] to make wider or larger; cause to expand or swell —***vi.* 1.** to become wider or larger; swell **2.** to speak or write in detail (*on* or *upon* a subject) —**di·lat′a·ble *adj.*** —**di·lat′ive *adj.*** —**di·la′tor *n.***

di·la·tion (dī lā′shən, di-) ***n.* 1.** a dilating or being dilated **2.** a dilated part

dil·a·to·ry (dil′ə tôr′ē) ***adj.*** [< LL. < L. < *dilatus,* pp. of *differre,* DEFER[1]] **1.** causing or tending to cause delay **2.** inclined to delay; slow; tardy —**dil′a·to′ri·ly *adv.*** —**dil′a·to′ri·ness *n.***

di·lem·ma (di lem′ə) ***n.*** [LL. < LGr. < *di-,* two + *lēmma,* proposition] an argument or a situation in which one must choose between unpleasant alternatives —**dil·em·mat·ic** (dil′ə mat′ik) ***adj.***

dil·et·tante (dil′ə tänt′, -tän′tē, -tan′tē; dil′ə tänt′) ***n.,*** *pl.* **-tantes′, -tan′ti** (-tän′tē, -tan′tē) [It. < prp. of *dilettare* < L. *delectare,* to delight] **1.** a person who loves the fine arts **2.** a person who dabbles in an art or science in a superficial way —***adj.*** of or characteristic of a dilettante —**dil′et·tant′ish** ***adj.*** —**dil′et·tant′ism, dil′et·tan′te·ism** ***n.***

dil·i·gence[1] (dil′ə jəns) ***n.*** a being diligent; constant, careful effort; perseverance; industry

dil·i·gence[2] (dil′ə jəns; *Fr.* dē lē zhäns′) ***n.*** [Fr.] a public stagecoach, esp. as formerly used in France

dil·i·gent (dil′ə jənt) ***adj.*** [OFr. < L. prp. of *diligere,* to esteem highly < *di-,* apart + *legere,* to choose] **1.** persevering and careful in work; industrious **2.** done with careful, steady effort; painstaking —**dil′i·gent·ly** ***adv.***

dill (dil) ***n.*** [OE. *dile*] **1.** a plant of the parsley family, with bitter seeds and aromatic leaves, used to flavor pickles, etc. **2.** the seeds or leaves

DILL

dill pickle a cucumber pickle flavored with dill

dil·ly (dil′ē) ***n.,*** *pl.* **-lies** [< ? DEL(IGHTFUL) + -Y[1]] [Slang] a surprising or remarkable person or thing

dil·ly·dal·ly (dil′ē dal′ē) ***vi.*** **-lied, -ly·ing** [redupl. form of DALLY] to waste time in hesitation; loiter or dawdle

di·lute (di lo͞ot′, dī-) ***vt.*** **-lut′ed, -lut′·ing** [< L. pp. of *diluere* < *dis-,* off + *-luere* < *lavare,* to wash] **1.** to thin down or weaken by mixing with water or other liquid **2.** to change or weaken (in brilliance, force, effect, etc.) by mixing with something else —***vi.*** to become diluted —***adj.*** diluted —**di·lute′ness** ***n.*** —**di·lut′er, di·lu′·tor** ***n.***

di·lu·tion (-lo͞o′shən) ***n.*** **1.** a diluting or being diluted **2.** something diluted

di·lu·vi·al (di lo͞o′vē əl) ***adj.*** [< LL. < L. *diluvium,* a deluge] of or caused by a flood, esp. the Deluge Also **di·lu′vi·an**

dim (dim) ***adj.*** **dim′mer, dim′mest** [OE. *dimm*] **1.** not bright; somewhat dark; dull **2.** not clear or distinct; lacking definition, strength, etc. **3.** not clearly seen, heard, or understood; vague **4.** not clearly seeing, hearing, or understanding **5.** not likely to turn out well *[dim* prospects*]* —***vt., vi.*** **dimmed, dim′ming** to make or grow dim —***n.*** **1.** [Poet.] dim light; dusk **2.** a dim headlight on an automobile —**take a dim view of** to view skeptically, etc. —**dim′ly** ***adv.*** —**dim′ness** ***n.***

dim., dimin. **1.** diminuendo **2.** diminutive

dime (dīm) ***n.*** [< OFr. < L. *decimus,* a tenth < *decem,* ten] a coin of the U.S. and of Canada equal to ten cents; tenth of a dollar —**a dime a dozen** [Colloq.] very abundant or cheap

di·men·hy·dri·nate (dī′men hī′drə nāt′) ***n.*** a white, crystalline solid, $C_{24}H_{28}ClN_5O_3$, used to control nausea and vomiting, as in motion sickness

dime novel a very cheap, melodramatic novel

di·men·sion (də men′shən) ***n.*** [L. *dimensio* < pp. of *dimetiri* < *dis-,* off + *metiri,* to MEASURE] **1.** any measurable extent, as length, width, depth, etc.: see also FOURTH DIMENSION **2.** [*pl.*] measurements in length and width, and often depth **3.** [*often pl.*] *a)* extent or size *b)* scope or importance —**di·men′sion·al** ***adj.*** —**di·men′sion·al·ly** ***adv.***

dime store *same as* FIVE-AND-TEN-CENT STORE

di·min·ish (də min′ish) ***vt.*** [a blend of ME. *diminuen* (ult. < L. *deminuere,* to make smaller) & *minishen* (ult. < L. *minutus,* MINUTE[2])] **1.** to make, or make seem, smaller; reduce in size, degree, importance, etc. **2.** *Music* to reduce (a minor interval) by a semitone —***vi.*** to become smaller or less —**di·min′ish·a·ble** ***adj.*** —**di·min′ished** ***adj.***

di·min·u·en·do (də min′yoo wen′dō) ***adj., adv., n.,*** *pl.* **-dos** [It. < L. *diminuere,* make smaller] *same as* DECRESCENDO

dim·i·nu·tion (dim′ə nyo͞o′shən, -no͞o′-) ***n.*** a diminishing or being diminished; lessening; decrease

di·min·u·tive (də min′yoo tiv) ***adj.*** **1.** very small; tiny **2.** *Gram.* expressing smallness or diminution *[a diminutive* suffix*]* —***n.*** **1.** a very small person or thing **2.** *a)* a word or name formed from another by the addition of a suffix expressing smallness and, sometimes, endearment or condescension, as *ringlet, Jackie, sonny* *b)* such a suffix —**di·min′u·tive·ly** ***adv.*** —**di·min′u·tive·ness** ***n.***

dim·i·ty (dim′ə tē) ***n.,*** *pl.* **-ties** [< ML. < MGr. *dimitos,* double-threaded < *dis-,* two + *mitos,* a thread] a thin, often corded or patterned cotton cloth, used for curtains, dresses, etc.

dim·mer (dim′ər) ***n.*** **1.** a person that dims **2.** a device for dimming an electric light, as in automobile headlights or theater stage lights

dim·out (-out′) ***n.*** a dimming or reduction of the night lighting in a city, etc., to make it less easily visible, as to enemy aircraft

dim·ple (dim′p′l) ***n.*** [ME. *dimpel*] **1.** a small, natural hollow spot, as on the cheek or chin **2.** any little hollow, as on water —***vt.*** **-pled, -pling** to make dimples in —***vi.*** to show or form dimples

dim·wit (dim′wit′) ***n.*** [Slang] a stupid person; simpleton —**dim′wit′ted** ***adj.*** —**dim′wit′ted·ly** ***adv.*** —**dim′wit′ted·ness** ***n.***

din (din) ***n.*** [OE. *dyne*] a loud, continuous noise; confused clamor or uproar —***vt.*** **dinned, din′ning** **1.** to beset with a din **2.** to repeat insistently or noisily *[*to *din* an idea into one's ears*]* —***vi.*** to make a din

Di·nah (dī′nə) [Heb. *dīnāh,* lit., judged] a feminine name

di·nar (di när′) ***n.*** [< Ar. < L. *denarius:* see DENARIUS] the monetary unit of Algeria, Iraq, Jordan, Libya, Tunisia, etc., and a coin of Iran: see MONETARY UNITS, table

dine (dīn) ***vi.*** **dined, din′ing** [< OFr. *disner,* ult. < L. *dis-,* away + *jejunus,* fasting] to eat dinner —***vt.*** to provide a dinner for, or entertain at dinner —**dine out** to dine away from home

din·er (dī′nər) ***n.*** **1.** a person eating dinner **2.** *same as* DINING CAR **3.** a small restaurant built to look like a dining car

din·ette (dī net′) ***n.*** **1.** an alcove or small, partitioned space used as a dining room **2.** a set of tables and chairs for such a space *[*a 5-piece *dinette]*

ding (diŋ) ***vi.*** [< Scand. (as in ON. *dengja,* to hammer)] **1.** to make a sound like that of a bell; ring **2.** [Colloq.] to speak repetitiously and tiresomely —***vt.*** [Colloq.] to repeat insistently or tiresomely; din —***n.*** the sound of a bell

ding-a-ling, ding·a·ling (diŋ′ə liŋ′) ***n.*** [Slang] a person who seems crazy, silly, eccentric, etc.

ding-dong (-dôŋ′, -däŋ′) ***n.*** [echoic] the sound of a bell struck repeatedly —***adj.*** [Colloq.] vigorously contested —***vi.*** to sound with a ding-dong

din·ghy (diŋ′gē, diŋ′ē) ***n.,*** *pl.* **-ghies** [Hindi *ḍiṅgī*] **1.** orig., a rowboat used on the rivers of India **2.** any small boat used as a tender to a yacht, etc. **3.** a small, undecked, single-masted racing boat **4.** an inflatable life raft Also sp. **din′gey**

din·go (diŋ′gō) ***n.,*** *pl.* **-goes** [native name] the Australian wild dog

ding·us (diŋ′əs) ***n.*** [Du. *dinges* (or G. *dings*), orig. gen. of *ding,* thing] [Colloq.] any device; contrivance; gadget: humorous substitute for a name not known or temporarily forgotten

din·gy (din′jē) ***adj.*** **-gi·er, -gi·est** [orig. dial. var. of DUNGY] **1.** dirty-colored; not bright or clean **2.** dismal; shabby —**din′gi·ly** ***adv.*** —**din′gi·ness** ***n.***

dining car a railroad car equipped to serve meals to passengers

dining room a room where meals are eaten

din·key (diŋ′kē) ***n.,*** *pl.* **-keys** [prob. < ff.] [Colloq.] **1.** a small locomotive for hauling cars, etc. in a railroad yard **2.** a small trolley car

din·ky (diŋ′kē) ***adj.*** **-ki·er, -ki·est** [< Scot. *dink,* trim + -Y[2]] [Colloq.] small and unimportant; of no consequence —***n.,*** *pl.* **-kies** *same as* DINKEY

din·ner (din′ər) ***n.*** [< OFr. *disner,* inf. used as n.: see DINE] **1.** the chief meal of the day, whether eaten in the evening or about noon **2.** a banquet in honor of some person or event **3.** a complete meal at a set price with no course omitted; table d'hôte

dinner jacket a tuxedo jacket

din·ner·ware (-wer′) ***n.*** **1.** plates, cups, saucers, etc., collectively **2.** a set of such dishes

di·no·saur (dī′nə sôr′) ***n.*** [< Gr. *deinos,* terrible + *sauros,* lizard] any of a large group of extinct, four-limbed reptiles of the Mesozoic Era, including some almost 100 ft. long —**di′no·sau′ri·an** ***adj.***

dint (dint) ***n.*** [OE. *dynt,* a blow] **1.** force; exertion: now chiefly in **by dint of** **2.** a dent —***vt.*** **1.** to dent **2.** to drive in with force

dioc. **1.** diocesan **2.** diocese

di·oc·e·san (dī äs′ə s′n) ***adj.*** of a diocese —***n.*** the bishop of a diocese

di·o·cese (dī′ə sis, -sēs′) ***n.*** [< OFr. < L. < Gr. *dioikēsis,* administration < *dioikein,* to keep house < *dia-,* through + *oikos,* a house] the district under a bishop's jurisdiction

di·ode (dī′ōd) ***n.*** [DI-[1] + -ODE] an electron tube or semiconductor device having two terminals and conducting electricity in only one direction

di·oe·cious (dī ē′shəs) ***adj.*** [< DI-[1] + Gr. *oikos,* a house + -OUS] *Biol.* having the male reproductive organs in one individual and the female organs in another —**di·oe′cious·ly** ***adv.*** —**di·oe′cism** (-siz'm) ***n.***

Di·og·e·nes (dī äj′ə nēz′) 412?–323? B.C.; Gr. Cynic philosopher

Di·o·ny·sian (dī′ə nish′ən, -nis′ē ən, -nī′sē ən) ***adj.*** [< DIONYSUS] wild, frenzied, and sensuous

Di·o·ny·si·us (dī′ə nish′əs, -nis′ē əs, -nī′sē əs) 430?–367 B.C.; Gr. tyrant of ancient Syracuse

Di·o·ny·sus, Di·o·ny·sos (dī′ə nī′səs) *Gr. Myth.* the god of wine and revelry; Bacchus

di·op·ter, di·op·tre (dī äp′tər) ***n.*** [< L. < Gr. *dioptra*, leveling instrument < *dia-*, through + base of *opsis*, sight] a unit of measure of the refractive power of a lens, equal to the power of a lens with a focal distance of one meter —**di·op′tral** ***adj.***

di·o·ra·ma (dī′ə ram′ə) ***n.*** [DI(A)- + (PAN)ORAMA] **1.** a picture painted on a set of transparent curtains and looked at through a small opening **2.** a miniature scene depicting three-dimensional figures in a naturalistic setting **3.** a museum display of a preserved or reconstructed specimen, as of wildlife in a simulated habitat

di·ox·ide (dī äk′sīd) ***n.*** an oxide containing two atoms of oxygen per molecule

dip (dip) ***vt.*** **dipped** or, occas., **dipt, dip′ping** [OE. *dyppan*] **1.** to put into liquid for a moment and then quickly take out **2.** to dye in this way **3.** to baptize by immersion **4.** to bathe and clean (sheep or hogs) in disinfectant **5.** to make (a candle) by putting a wick repeatedly in melted tallow or wax **6.** to take out as by scooping up with a container, the hand, etc. **7.** to lower and immediately raise again *[dip* the flag in salute*]* —***vi.*** **1.** to plunge into a liquid and quickly come out **2.** to sink or seem to sink suddenly *[*the sun *dips* into the ocean*]* **3.** to undergo a slight decline *[*sales *dipped* in May*]* **4.** to slope down **5.** to lower a container, the hand, etc. into liquid, a receptacle, etc., esp. in order to take something out: often figurative *[*to *dip* into one's savings*]* **6.** to read or study casually or superficially (with *into*) *[*to *dip* into a book*]* **7.** *Aeron.* to drop suddenly before climbing —***n.*** **1.** a dipping or being dipped **2.** *a)* a brief plunge into a liquid *b)* a brief swim **3.** a liquid into which something is dipped, as for dyeing **4.** whatever is removed by dipping **5.** a candle made by dipping **6.** *a)* a downward slope or inclination or a deviation *b)* the amount of this **7.** a slight hollow **8.** a short downward plunge, as of an airplane **9.** *a)* a sweet liquid sauce for desserts *b)* a thick, creamy sauce into which one dips crackers or other appetizers **10.** [Slang] a pickpocket

diph·the·ri·a (dif thir′ē ə, dip-) ***n.*** [ModL. < Fr. < Gr. *diphthera*, leather < *dephein*, to tan hides] an acute infectious disease caused by a bacterium and characterized by weakness, high fever, and the formation in the air passages of a membrane-like obstruction to breathing —**diph·the′ri·al** ***adj.*** —**diph′the·rit′ic** (-thə rit′ik), **diph·ther′ic** ***adj.***

diph·thong (dif′thôŋ, dip′-) ***n.*** [< LL. < Gr. < *di-*, two + *phthongos*, sound] *Phonet.* a complex vowel sound made by gliding continuously from the position for one vowel to that for another within the same syllable, as (ou) in *down*, (oi) in *boy* —**diph·thon′gal** (-thôŋ′g'l) ***adj.***

diph·thong·ize (-īz′) ***vt.*** **-ized′, -iz′ing** to pronounce (a simple vowel) as a diphthong —***vi.*** to become a diphthong —**diph′thong·i·za′tion** ***n.***

dip·loid (dip′loid) ***adj.*** [< Gr. *diploos*, double + -OID] **1.** twofold or double **2.** *Biol.* having twice the number of chromosomes normally occurring in a mature germ cell: most somatic cells are diploid: see HAPLOID—**dip·loi′dy** (-loi′dē) ***n.***

di·plo·ma (di plō′mə) ***n.*** [L. < Gr. *diplōma*, folded letter < *diploos*, double] **1.** a certificate conferring honors, privileges, etc. **2.** a certificate recording the graduation of a student from a school, college, or university, or conferring a degree

di·plo·ma·cy (di plō′mə sē) ***n.***, *pl.* **-cies** [< Fr.: see ff.] **1.** (skill in) conducting relations between nations **2.** tact in dealing with people

dip·lo·mat (dip′lə mat′) ***n.*** [< Fr., ult. < L. *diploma*, DIPLOMA] **1.** a representative of a government who conducts relations with another government in the interests of his own country **2.** a tactful person Also **di·plo·ma·tist** (di plō′mə tist)

dip·lo·mat·ic (dip′ lə mat′ik) ***n.*** **1.** of or connected with diplomacy **2.** tactful and adroit in dealing with people —**dip′lo·mat′i·cal·ly** ***adv.***

diplomatic immunity exemption from local taxes, court action, etc. in a foreign country, granted to all members of a diplomatic service

di·pole (dī′pōl′) ***n.*** **1.** *Physics* any system having two equal but opposite electric charges or magnetic poles separated by a small distance **2.** an antenna usually separated at the center by an insulator and fed by a balanced transmission line: in full, **dipole antenna** —**di·po′lar** ***adj.***

dip·per (dip′ər) ***n.*** **1.** a person whose work is dipping something in liquid **2.** a container for dipping; esp., a long-handled cup **3.** [**D-**] either of two groups of stars in the shape of a dipper: see BIG DIPPER, LITTLE DIPPER **4.** any of a genus of songbirds, as the water ouzel, which wade and submerge in streams in search of insects, etc. —**dip′per·ful′** ***n.***, *pl.* **-fuls′**

dip·so·ma·ni·a (dip′sə mā′nē ə, -nyə) ***n.*** [ModL. < Gr. *dipsa*, thirst + -MANIA] an abnormal and insatiable craving for alcoholic drink —**dip′so·ma′ni·ac′** (-ak′) ***n.*** —**dip′so·ma·ni′a·cal** (-mə nī′ə k'l) ***adj.***

dip·stick (dip′stik′) ***n.*** a graduated rod for measuring the depth of a substance in its container

dipt (dipt) *occas. pt. & pp. of* DIP

dip·ter·an (dip′tər ən) ***n.*** [see ff.] any of a large order of insects, including the housefly, gnat, etc., having two pair of wings, one pair usually vestigial

dip·ter·ous (-əs) ***adj.*** [<ModL. < Gr. < *di-*, two + *pteron*, a wing] **1.** having two wings or two winglike appendages **2.** of the dipterans

dip·tych (dip′tik) ***n.*** [< LL. < Gr. < *di-*, twice + *ptychē*, a fold] **1.** an ancient writing tablet made up of a hinged pair of wooden or ivory pieces **2.** a picture painted or carved on two hinged tablets

dire (dīr) ***adj.*** **dir′er, dir′est** [L. *dirus*] **1.** arousing terror; dreadful **2.** urgent *[*a *dire* need*]* —**dire′ly** ***adv.*** —**dire′ness** ***n.***

di·rect (di rekt′, dī-) ***adj.*** [< L. pp. of *dirigere*, to lay straight < *dis-*, apart + *regere*, to rule] **1.** by the shortest way; not roundabout; straight *[*a *direct* route*]* **2.** honest and straightforward; frank **3.** with nothing or no one between; immediate *[direct* contact*]* **4.** in an unbroken line of descent; lineal **5.** exact; complete *[*the *direct* opposite*]* **6.** in the exact words of the speaker *[* a *direct* quotation*]* **7.** by action of the people through popular vote instead of through representatives —***vt.*** **1.** to manage the affairs or action of; guide; conduct **2.** to order or command with authority **3.** to turn or point (a person or thing) toward an object or goal; aim; head **4.** to tell (a person) the way to a place **5.** to address (words, etc.) to a specific person or persons **6.** to write the name and address on (a letter, etc.) **7.** *a)* to plan and supervise the action of (a play, motion picture, etc.) or of (the actors, etc.) *b)* to rehearse and conduct the performance of (a choir, band, etc.) —***vi.*** **1.** to give directions **2.** to be a director —***adv.*** directly —**di·rect′ness** ***n.***

direct current an electric current flowing in one direction

di·rec·tion (də rek′shən, dī-) ***n.*** **1.** the act of directing; management; supervision **2.** [*usually pl.*] instructions for doing, using, etc. **3.** an authoritative order or command **4.** the point toward which one faces or line along which one moves or lies **5.** an aspect, way, trend, etc. *[*research in new *directions]*

di·rec·tion·al (-'l) ***adj.*** **1.** of, aimed at, or indicating (a specific) direction **2.** designed for radiating or receiving radio signals most effectively in one or more particular directions *[*a *directional* antenna*]* **3.** designed to pick up or send out sound most efficiently in one direction —**di·rec′tion·al′i·ty** ***n.*** —**di·rec′tion·al·ly** ***adv.***

direction finder a device for finding out the direction from which radio waves or signals are coming

di·rec·tive (də rek′tiv, dī-) ***adj.*** **1.** directing **2.** indicating direction —***n.*** a general instruction or order issued authoritatively

di·rect·ly (-rekt′lē) ***adv.*** **1.** in a direct way or line; straight **2.** with nothing coming between *[directly* responsible*]* **3.** exactly *[directly* opposite*]* **4.** right away —***conj.*** [Chiefly Brit.] as soon as

direct mail mail sent directly to a large number of individuals, promoting a product, institution, etc., and soliciting orders, donations, etc.

direct object the word or words denoting the thing or person that receives the action of a transitive verb (Ex.: *ball* in *he hit the ball*)

di·rec·tor (di rek′tər) ***n.*** a person or thing that directs; specif., *a)* the supervisor of a bureau, school, etc. *b)* a member of a board chosen to direct the affairs of a corporation or institution *c)* a person who directs the production of a play, motion picture, etc. *d) Music* a conductor —**di·rec·to·ri·al** (də rek′tôr′ē əl, dī-) ***adj.*** —**di·rec′tor·ship′** ***n.*** —**di·rec′tress** (-tris) ***n.fem.***

di·rec·tor·ate (-it) ***n.*** **1.** the position of director **2.** a board of directors

di·rec·to·ry (də rek′tə rē, dī-) ***adj.*** directing or advising —***n.***, *pl.* **-ries** **1.** a book of directions **2.** a book listing the names, addresses, etc. of a specific group of persons **3.** a directorate

direct primary election a preliminary election at which candidates for public office are chosen by direct vote of the people instead of by delegates at a convention: in **closed primary elections** voters may vote only for candidates of their party

direct tax a tax levied directly on the person who is to pay it, as an income tax or property tax
dire·ful (dīr′fəl) ***adj.*** dreadful; terrible —**dire′ful·ly *adv.***
dirge (durj) ***n.*** [< L. *dirige* (imper. of *dirigere*, to direct), first word of an antiphon in the Office of the Dead] **1.** a funeral hymn **2.** a slow, sad song, poem, etc. expressing grief or mourning
dir·ham (dir ham′) ***n.*** [Ar. < L. *drachma*, DRACHMA] *see* MONETARY UNITS, table (Morocco, Qatar, United Arab Emirates)
dir·i·gi·ble (dir′i jə b'l, də rij′ə-) ***adj.*** [ML. *dirigibilis:* see DIRECT & -IBLE] that can be directed or steered —***n.*** *same as* AIRSHIP
dirk (durk) ***n.*** [earlier *dork*, *durk* < ?] a short, straight dagger —***vt.*** to stab with a dirk
dirn·dl (durn′d'l) ***n.*** [G., dial. dim. of *dirne*, girl] **1.** a kind of dress with a full skirt, gathered waist, and closefitting bodice **2.** the skirt of such a dress: also **dirndl skirt**
dirt (durt) ***n.*** [ME. < *drit* < ON. *dritr*, excrement] **1.** any unclean matter, as mud, trash, etc.; filth **2.** earth or garden soil **3.** dirtiness, corruption, etc. **4.** obscene writing, speech, etc. **5.** malicious talk or gossip **6.** *Gold Mining* the gravel, soil, etc. from which gold is separated by washing or panning —***adj.*** surfaced with compacted earth [a *dirt* road] —**do one dirt** [Slang] to harm one —**hit the dirt** [Slang] to drop to the ground
dirt-cheap (-chēp′) ***adj.*** [Colloq.] as cheap as dirt; very inexpensive
dirt farmer [Colloq.] a farmer who works his own land
dirt·y (-ē) ***adj.*** **dirt′i·er, dirt′i·est** **1.** soiled or soiling with dirt; unclean **2.** muddy or clouded [a *dirty* green] **3.** obscene; pornographic [*dirty* jokes] **4.** mean; nasty; vile [a *dirty* coward] **5.** unfair; dishonest [a *dirty* player] **6.** producing much fallout: said of nuclear weapons **7.** *Naut.* squally; rough [*dirty* weather] —***vt., vi.*** **dirt′ied, dirt′y·ing** to make or become dirty; soil; stain —**a dirty shame** a very unfortunate circumstance —**dirty linen** (or **wash**) private matters that could cause gossip —**dirty pool** [Slang] unfair or dishonest tactics —**dirt′i·ly *adv.*** —**dirt′i·ness *n.***
Dis (dis) *Rom. Myth.* **1.** the god of the lower world: identified with the Greek Pluto **2.** Hades
dis- [< OFr. or L.; OFr. *des-* < L. *dis-:* cf. DE-] **1.** *a v.-forming prefix meaning:* *a*) away, apart [*dismiss*] *b*) deprive of, expel from [*disbar*] *c*) cause to be the opposite of [*disable*] *d*) fail, cease, refuse to [*dissatisfy*] or do the opposite of [*disjoin*] **2.** *an adj.-forming prefix meaning* not, un-, the opposite of [*dishonest*] **3.** *a n.-forming prefix meaning* opposite of, lack of [*disunion*]
dis·a·bil·i·ty (dis′ə bil′ə tē) ***n., pl.* -ties** **1.** a disabled condition **2.** that which disables, as an illness or injury **3.** a legal disqualification **4.** a limitation or disadvantage
dis·a·ble (dis ā′b'l) ***vt.*** **-bled, -bling** **1.** to make unable, unfit, or ineffective; cripple; incapacitate **2.** to disqualify legally —**dis·a′ble·ment *n.***
dis·a·buse (dis′ə byōōz′) ***vt.*** **-bused′, -bus′ing** to rid of false ideas; undeceive
dis·ad·van·tage (-əd van′tij) ***n.*** **1.** an unfavorable situation or circumstance; drawback; handicap **2.** harm or detriment to one's interests —***vt.*** **-taged, -tag·ing** to act to the disadvantage of —**at a disadvantage** in an unfavorable situation
dis·ad·van·taged (-tijd) ***adj.*** deprived of a decent standard of living, education, etc. by poverty and a lack of opportunity; underprivileged
dis·ad·van·ta·geous (dis ad′vən tā′jəs) ***adj.*** causing disadvantage; unfavorable; adverse —**dis·ad′van·ta′geous·ly *adv.***
dis·af·fect (dis′ə fekt′) ***vt.*** to make unfriendly, discontented, or disloyal, as toward the government —**dis′af·fect′ed *adj.*** —**dis′af·fec′tion *n.***
dis·af·fil·i·ate (-ə fil′ē āt′) ***vt., vi.*** **-at′ed, -at′ing** to end an affiliation (with) —**dis′af·fil′i·a′tion *n.***
dis·a·gree (-ə grē′) ***vi.*** **-greed′, -gree′ing** **1.** to fail to agree; differ **2.** to differ in opinion; often, specif., to quarrel or dispute **3.** to give distress [corn *disagrees* with me]
dis·a·gree·a·ble (-ə b'l) ***adj.*** **1.** not to one's taste; unpleasant; offensive **2.** hard to get along with; quarrelsome —**dis′a·gree′a·ble·ness *n.*** —**dis′a·gree′a·bly *adv.***
dis·a·gree·ment (-mənt) ***n.*** **1.** refusal to agree **2.** failure to agree; difference; discrepancy **3.** difference of opinion **4.** a quarrel or dispute
dis·al·low (dis′ə lou′) ***vt.*** to refuse to allow; reject as invalid or illegal —**dis′al·low′ance *n.***
dis·ap·pear (-ə pir′) ***vi.*** **1.** to cease to be seen; go out of sight **2.** to cease being; become lost or extinct —**dis′ap·pear′ance *n.***
dis·ap·point (-ə point′) ***vt.*** **1.** to fail to satisfy the hopes or expectations of; leave unsatisfied **2.** to frustrate (hopes, etc.) —**dis′ap·point′ing·ly *adv.***
dis·ap·point·ment (-mənt) ***n.*** **1.** a disappointing or being disappointed **2.** a person or thing that disappoints
dis·ap·pro·ba·tion (-ap′rə bā′shən) ***n.*** disapproval
dis·ap·prov·al (-ə prōōv′'l) ***n.*** **1.** failure or refusal to approve **2.** unfavorable opinion
dis·ap·prove (-ə prōōv′) ***vt.*** **-proved′, -prov′ing** **1.** to have or express an unfavorable opinion of **2.** to refuse to approve; reject —***vi.*** to feel or express disapproval (*of*) —**dis′ap·prov′ing·ly *adv.***
dis·arm (dis ärm′) ***vt.*** **1.** to take away weapons or armaments from **2.** to make harmless **3.** to overcome the hostility of —***vi.*** **1.** to lay down arms **2.** to reduce or do away with armed forces and armaments
dis·ar·ma·ment (-är′mə mənt) ***n.*** **1.** the act of disarming **2.** the reduction of armed forces and armaments, as to a limitation set by treaty
dis·arm·ing (-är′miŋ) ***adj.*** removing suspicions, fears, or hostility —**dis·arm′ing·ly *adv.***
dis·ar·range (dis′ə rānj′) ***vt.*** **-ranged′, -rang′ing** to upset the order or arrangement of; make less neat; disorder —**dis′ar·range′ment *n.***
dis·ar·ray (-ə rā′) ***vt.*** **1.** to throw into disorder or confusion; upset **2.** [Archaic] to undress —***n.*** **1.** disorder; confusion **2.** a state of disorderly or insufficient dress
dis·as·sem·ble (-ə sem′b'l) ***vt.*** **-bled, -bling** to take apart —**dis′as·sem′bly *n.***
dis·as·so·ci·ate (-ə sō′shē āt′, -sē-) ***vt.*** **-at′ed, -at′ing** to sever association with; separate; dissociate —**dis′as·so′ci·a′tion *n.***
dis·as·ter (di zas′tər) ***n.*** [< OFr. < It. < L. *dis-* + *astrum* < Gr. *astron*, a star: cf. ILL-STARRED] any happening that causes great harm or damage; serious or sudden misfortune; calamity
dis·as·trous (-trəs) ***adj.*** of the nature of a disaster; causing great harm, damage, grief, etc.; calamitous —**dis·as′trous·ly *adv.***
dis·a·vow (dis′ə vou′) ***vt.*** to deny any knowledge or approval of, or responsibility for; disclaim; disown —**dis′a·vow′al *n.***
dis·band (dis band′) ***vt.*** **1.** to break up (an association or organization) **2.** to dismiss (a military force) from service —***vi.*** to cease to exist as an organization; scatter; disperse —**dis·band′ment *n.***
dis·bar (-bär′) ***vt.*** **-barred′, -bar′ring** to expel (a lawyer) from the bar; deprive of the right to practice law —**dis·bar′ment *n.***
dis·be·lief (dis′bə lēf′) ***n.*** refusal to believe; absence of belief
dis·be·lieve (-lēv′) ***vt.*** **-lieved′, -liev′ing** to reject as untrue —***vi.*** to refuse to believe (*in*) —**dis′be·liev′er *n.***
dis·bur·den (dis bur′d'n) ***vt.*** to relieve of a burden or of anything burdensome
dis·burse (-burs′) ***vt.*** **-bursed′, -burs′ing** [< OFr. *desbourser:* see DIS- & BOURSE] to pay out; expend —**dis·burs′a·ble *adj.*** —**dis·burse′ment *n.*** —**dis·burs′er *n.***
disc (disk) ***n.*** **1.** *same as* DISK **2.** *a*) a phonograph record *b*) a thin, flat, circular plate coated with ferromagnetic particles, on which computer data can be stored **3.** any of the sharp, circular blades on a disc harrow **4.** *Biol.* any disc-shaped part or structure: cf. DISK
disc. **1.** discount **2.** discovered
dis·card (dis kärd′; *for n.* dis′kärd) ***vt.*** [< OFr.: see DIS- & CARD[1]] **1.** *Card Games* *a*) to remove (a card or cards) from the hand dealt *b*) to play (a card not a trump and not in the suit led) **2.** to get rid of as no longer valuable or useful —***vi.*** *Card Games* to make a discard —***n.*** **1.** a discarding or being discarded **2.** something discarded **3.** *Card Games* the card or cards discarded
disc brake a brake, as on an automobile, that causes two friction pads to press on either side of a disc rotating along with the wheel
dis·cern (di surn′, -zurn′) ***vt.*** [< OFr. < L. < *dis-*, apart + *cernere*, to separate] **1.** to recognize as separate or different **2.** to perceive or recognize; make out clearly —***vi.*** to perceive or recognize the difference —**dis·cern′i·ble *adj.*** —**dis·cern′i·bly *adv.***
dis·cern·ing (-iŋ) ***adj.*** having or showing good judgment or understanding —**dis·cern′ing·ly *adv.***
dis·cern·ment (-mənt) ***n.*** **1.** a discerning **2.** keen perception or judgment; insight; acumen
dis·charge (dis chärj′; *for n. usually* dis′chärj) ***vt.*** **-charged′, -charg′ing** [< OFr. < L. *dis-*, from + *carrus*, wagon, CAR] **1.** to relieve of or release from something that burdens or confines; specif., *a*) to remove the cargo of (a ship) *b*) to release the charge of (a gun) *c*) to release (a soldier, jury, etc.) from duty *d*) to dismiss from employment *e*) to release (a prisoner) from jail, (a defendant) from suspicion, (a debtor or bankrupt) from obligations, etc. **2.** to release or remove (that by which one is burdened or confined); specif., *a*) to unload (a cargo) *b*) to shoot (a projectile) **3.** to relieve oneself or itself of (a burden, load, etc.); specif., *a*) to throw off; emit [to *discharge* pus] *b*) to pay (a debt) or perform (a duty) **4.** *Elec.* to remove stored energy from (a battery or capacitor) —***vi.*** **1.** to get

rid of a burden, load, etc. **2.** to be released or thrown off **3.** to go off: said of a gun, etc. **4.** to emit waste matter: said of a wound, etc. *—n.* **1.** a discharging or being discharged **2.** that which discharges, as a legal order for release, a certificate of dismissal from military service, etc. **3.** that which is discharged, as pus from a sore **4.** a flow of electric current across a gap, as in a spark or arc **—dis·charge′a·ble** *adj.* **—dis·charg′er** *n.*

discharge tube a device in which a gas or metal vapor conducting an electric discharge is the source of light

disc harrow a harrow with sharp, revolving circular blades used to break up the soil for sowing

dis·ci·ple (di sī′p'l) *n.* [< OFr. & OE., both < L. *discipulus,* pupil < *dis-,* apart + *capere,* to hold] **1.** a pupil or follower of any teacher or school **2.** an early follower of Jesus, esp. one of the Apostles **—dis·ci′ple·ship′** *n.*

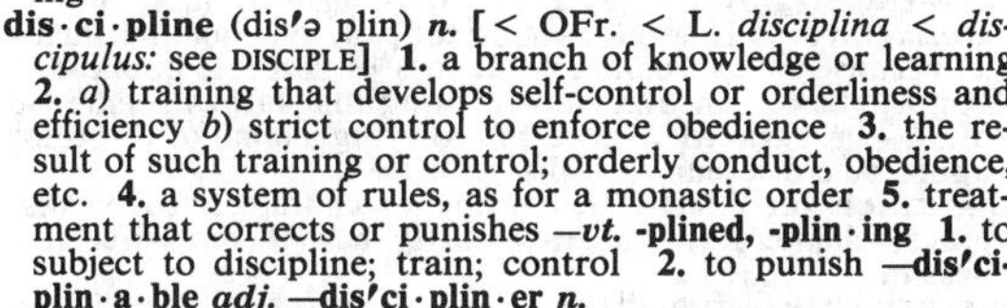
DISC HARROW

dis·ci·pli·nar·i·an (dis′ə pli ner′ē ən) *n.* one who believes in or enforces strict discipline

dis·ci·pli·nar·y (dis′ə pli ner′ē) *adj.* **1.** of or having to do with discipline **2.** that enforces discipline by punishing or correcting

dis·ci·pline (dis′ə plin) *n.* [< OFr. < L. *disciplina* < *discipulus:* see DISCIPLE] **1.** a branch of knowledge or learning **2.** *a)* training that develops self-control or orderliness and efficiency *b)* strict control to enforce obedience **3.** the result of such training or control; orderly conduct, obedience, etc. **4.** a system of rules, as for a monastic order **5.** treatment that corrects or punishes *—vt.* **-plined, -plin·ing 1.** to subject to discipline; train; control **2.** to punish **—dis′ci·plin·a·ble** *adj.* **—dis′ci·plin·er** *n.*

disc jockey a person who conducts a radio program of recorded music or plays recorded music at a disco

dis·claim (dis klām′) *vt.* **1.** to give up any claim to or connection with **2.** to refuse to acknowledge or admit; repudiate *—vi.* to make a disclaimer **—dis·cla·ma·tion** (dis′klə mā′shən) *n.*

dis·claim·er (-ər) *n.* **1.** a disclaiming or renunciation, as of a claim, title, etc. **2.** a disavowing

dis·close (-klōz′) *vt.* **-closed′, -clos′ing 1.** to bring into view; uncover **2.** to reveal; make known **—dis·clos′er** *n.*

dis·clos·ure (-klō′zhər) *n.* **1.** a disclosing or being disclosed **2.** a thing disclosed; revelation

dis·co (dis′kō) *n., pl.* **-cos** [DISCO(THÈQUE)] **1.** a public place for dancing to music played by a disc jockey **2.** such music, with a strong beat and simple lyrics

dis·cob·o·lus (dis käb′ə ləs) *n.* [L. < Gr. < *diskos,* discus + *ballein,* to throw] a discus thrower

dis·cog·ra·phy (dis käg′rə fē) *n., pl.* **-phies** [< L. *discus,* a disk + (BIBLIO)GRAPHY] **1.** the systematic cataloging of phonograph records **2.** a list of the recordings of a particular performer, composer, etc. **—dis·cog′ra·pher** *n.*

dis·coid (dis′koid) *adj.* [< LL. < Gr. < *diskos,* a disk + *eidos,* form] shaped like a disk: also **dis·coi′dal** *—n.* anything shaped like a disk

dis·col·or (dis kul′ər) *vt., vi.* to change in color by fading, streaking, or staining **—dis·col′or·a′tion** *n.*

dis·com·bob·u·late (dis′kəm bäb′yoo lāt′) *vt.* **-lat′ed, -lat′ing** [prob. whimsical alteration of ff.] [Colloq.] to upset the composure of; disconcert

dis·com·fit (dis kum′fit) *vt.* [< OFr. < L. *dis-* + *conficere:* see CONFECT] **1.** orig., to defeat **2.** to frustrate the plans or expectations of **3.** to make uneasy; disconcert **—dis·com′fi·ture** (-fi chər) *n.*

dis·com·fort (dis kum′fərt) *n.* **1.** lack of comfort; uneasiness; inconvenience **2.** anything causing this *—vt.* to cause discomfort to; distress

dis·com·mode (dis′kə mōd′) *vt.* **-mod′ed, -mod′ing** [< DIS- + L. *commodare,* to make suitable] to cause bother to; inconvenience

dis·com·pose (-kəm pōz′) *vt.* **-posed′, -pos′ing 1.** to disturb the calm or poise of; fluster; disconcert **2.** [Now Rare] to disturb the order of; disarrange **—dis′com·po′sure** (-pō′zhər) *n.*

dis·con·cert (-kən surt′) *vt.* **1.** to upset or frustrate (plans, etc.) **2.** to upset the composure of **—dis′con·cert′ing** *adj.* **—dis′con·cert′ing·ly** *adv.*

dis·con·nect (-kə nekt′) *vt.* to break or undo the connection of; separate, detach, unplug, etc. **—dis′con·nec′tion** *n.*

dis·con·nect·ed (-nek′tid) *adj.* **1.** separated, detached, etc. **2.** broken up into unrelated parts; incoherent **—dis′con·nect′ed·ly** *adv.* **—dis′con·nect′ed·ness** *n.*

dis·con·so·late (dis kän′sə lit) *adj.* [< ML. < L.: see DIS- & CONSOLE[1]] **1.** so unhappy that nothing will console; dejected **2.** causing dejection; cheerless **—dis·con′so·late·ly** *adv.* **—dis·con′so·late·ness, dis·con′so·la′tion** (-lā′shən) *n.*

dis·con·tent (dis′kən tent′) *adj. same as* DISCONTENTED *—n.* lack of contentment; dissatisfaction: also **dis′con·tent′ment** *—vt.* to make discontented

dis·con·tent·ed (-id) *adj.* not contented; wanting something more or different **—dis′con·tent′ed·ly** *adv.* **—dis′con·tent′ed·ness** *n.*

dis·con·tin·ue (dis′kən tin′yoo͞) *vt.* **-ued, -u·ing 1.** to stop using, doing, etc.; cease; give up **2.** *Law* to stop (a suit) prior to trial *—vi.* to stop; end **—dis′con·tin′u·ance** (-yoo wəns), **dis′con·tin′u·a′tion** (-yoo wā′shən) *n.*

dis·con·tin·u·ous (-yoo wəs) *adj.* not continuous; broken; intermittent **—dis·con·ti·nu·i·ty** (dis kän′tə no͞o′ə tē, dis′kän-; -nyo͞o′-) *n.* **—dis′con·tin′u·ous·ly** *adv.*

dis·co·phile (dis′kə fīl′) *n.* [< L. *discus,* disk + -PHILE] an expert on, or collector of, phonograph records

dis·cord (dis′kôrd; *for v., usually* dis kôrd′) *n.* [< OFr. < L. < *discors* (gen. *discordis*), discordant < *dis-,* apart + *cor,* heart] **1.** lack of concord; disagreement **2.** a harsh or confused noise, as the sound of battle **3.** *Music* a lack of harmony in tones sounded together; dissonance *—vi.* to disagree; clash

dis·cord·ant (dis kôr′d'nt) *adj.* **1.** not in accord; disagreeing; conflicting **2.** not in harmony; dissonant; clashing **—dis·cord′ance, dis·cord′an·cy** *n.* **—dis·cord′ant·ly** *adv.*

dis·co·thèque (dis′kə tek) *n.* [Fr. < *disque,* record + *bibliothèque,* library] *the full name for* DISCO (*n.* 1.)

dis·count (dis′kount; *for v., also* dis kount′) *n.* [< OFr. < ML. *discomputare:* see DIS- & COMPUTE] **1.** *a)* a reduction from a usual or list price *b)* a deduction from a debt, allowed for prompt or cash payment **2.** the interest deducted in advance by one who lends money on a promissory note, etc. **3.** the rate of interest **(discount rate)** charged for this **4.** a discounting *—vt.* **1.** to pay or receive the value of (a promissory note, etc.), minus the discount (sense 2) **2.** to deduct an amount or percent from (a bill, price, etc.) **3.** to sell at less than the regular price **4.** *a)* to take (a story, etc.) at less than face value, allowing for exaggeration, bias, etc. *b)* to disbelieve or disregard entirely **5.** to reckon with in advance **—at a discount 1.** below the regular price **2.** worth little **—dis′count·a·ble** *adj.*

dis·coun·te·nance (dis koun′tə nəns) *vt.* **-nanced, -nanc·ing 1.** to make ashamed or embarrassed; disconcert **2.** to refuse approval or support to

discount house (or **store**) a retail store that sells goods for less than regular or list prices

dis·cour·age (dis kur′ij) *vt.* **-aged, -ag·ing** [OFr. *descoragier*] **1.** to deprive of courage; dishearten **2.** to advise or persuade (a person) to refrain **3.** to prevent or try to prevent by disapproving *—vi.* to become discouraged **—dis·cour′age·ment** *n.* **—dis·cour′ag·ing** *adj.* **—dis·cour′ag·ing·ly** *adv.*

dis·course (dis′kôrs; *also, and for v. usually,* dis kôrs′) *n.* [< OFr. < L. pp. < *dis-,* from + *currere,* to run] **1.** communication of ideas, information, etc., esp. by talking; conversation **2.** a formal treatment of a subject, in speech or writing **3.** [Archaic] ability to reason *—vi.* **-coursed′, -cours′ing 1.** to converse; talk **2.** to speak or write (*on* or *upon* a subject) formally *—vt.* [Archaic] to utter or tell **—dis·cours′er** *n.*

dis·cour·te·ous (dis kur′tē əs) *adj.* not courteous; impolite; ill-mannered **—dis·cour′te·ous·ly** *adv.* **—dis·cour′te·ous·ness** *n.*

dis·cour·te·sy (-tə sē) *n.* **1.** lack of courtesy; impoliteness; rudeness **2.** *pl.* **-sies** a rude or impolite act or remark

dis·cov·er (dis kuv′ər) *vt.* [< OFr. < LL. *discooperire:* see DIS- & COVER] **1.** to be the first to find, see, or know about **2.** to be the first non-native person to come to or see **3.** to find out; realize **4.** [Archaic] *a)* to reveal *b)* to uncover **—dis·cov′er·a·ble** *adj.* **—dis·cov′er·er** *n.*

dis·cov·er·y (-ər ē) *n., pl.* **-er·ies 1.** a discovering **2.** anything discovered **3.** [Archaic] a revealing **4.** *Law* any disclosure that a defendant is compelled to make

Discovery Day *same as* COLUMBUS DAY

dis·cred·it (dis kred′it) *vt.* **1.** to reject as untrue **2.** to cast doubt on **3.** to damage the reputation of; disgrace *—n.* **1.** loss of belief or trust; doubt **2.** damage to one's reputation; disgrace **3.** something that causes disgrace **—dis·cred′it·a·ble** *adj.* **—dis·cred′it·a·bly** *adv.*

dis·creet (dis krēt′) *adj.* [< OFr. < L. pp. of *discernere:* see DISCERN] careful about what one says or does; prudent; esp., preserving confidences when necessary **—dis·creet′ly** *adv.* **—dis·creet′ness** *n.*

dis·crep·an·cy (dis krep′ən sē) *n., pl.* **-cies** [< OFr. < L. < prp. of *discrepare,* to sound differently < *dis-,* from + *crepare,* to rattle] lack of agreement, or an instance of this;

difference; inconsistency —**dis·crep′ant** *adj.* —**dis·crep′ant·ly** *adv.*

dis·crete (dis krēt′) *adj.* [< L.: see DISCREET] **1.** separate and distinct; not attached to others; unrelated **2.** made up of distinct parts; discontinuous —**dis·crete′ly** *adv.* —**dis·crete′ness** *n.*

dis·cre·tion (dis kresh′ən) *n.* **1.** the freedom or authority to make decisions and choices **2.** the quality of being discreet; prudence —**at one's discretion** as one wishes

dis·cre·tion·ar·y (-er′ē) *adj.* left to one's discretion: also **dis·cre′tion·al**

dis·crim·i·na·ble (dis krim′ə nə b'l) *adj.* that can be discriminated or distinguished

dis·crim·i·nate (dis krim′ə nāt′; *for adj.* -nit) *vt.* **-nat′ed, -nat′ing** [< L. pp. of *discriminare* < *discrimen,* division < *discernere:* see DISCERN] **1.** to constitute a difference between; differentiate **2.** to recognize the difference between; distinguish —*vi.* **1.** to see the difference (*between* things); distinguish **2.** to be discerning **3.** to show partiality (*in favor of*) or prejudice (*against*) —*adj.* distinguishing carefully —**dis·crim′i·nat′ing** *adj.* —**dis·crim′i·na′tive** (-nāt′iv, -nə tiv) *adj.* —**dis·crim′i·na′tor** *n.*

dis·crim·i·na·tion (dis krim′ə nā′shən) *n.* **1.** the act of discriminating, or distinguishing differences **2.** the ability to do this **3.** a showing of partiality or prejudice in treatment; specif., policies directed against the welfare of minority groups

dis·crim·i·na·to·ry (-krim′ə nə tôr′ē) *adj.* **1.** practicing discrimination, or showing prejudice **2.** discriminating, or distinguishing

dis·cur·sive (dis kur′siv) *adj.* [< ML. < L.: see DISCOURSE] **1.** wandering from one topic to another; rambling; digressive **2.** *Philos.* going from premises to conclusions in a series of logical steps —**dis·cur′sive·ly** *adv.* —**dis·cur′sive·ness** *n.*

dis·cus (dis′kəs) *n., pl.* **dis′cus·es, dis·ci** (dis′ī) [L. < Gr. *diskos*] **1.** a heavy disk of metal and wood, orig. often of stone, thrown for distance in competition **2.** such a contest: in full, **discus throw**

dis·cuss (dis kus′) *vt.* [< L. pp. of *discutire* < *dis-,* apart + *quatere,* to shake] to talk or write about; consider and argue the pros and cons of —**dis·cuss′a·ble, dis·cuss′i·ble** *adj.* —**dis·cuss′ant, dis·cuss′er** *n.*

dis·cus·sion (dis kush′ən) *n.* talk or writing in which the pros and cons or various aspects of a subject are considered —**under discussion** being discussed

DISCUS THROWER

dis·dain (dis dān′) *vt.* [< OFr. < L. *dis-,* not + *dignari,* DEIGN] to regard as beneath one's dignity; specif., to refuse or reject with aloof contempt or scorn —*n.* aloof contempt or scorn —**dis·dain′ful** *adj.* —**dis·dain′ful·ly** *adv.* —**dis·dain′ful·ness** *n.*

dis·ease (di zēz′) *n.* [OFr. *desaise* < *des-,* DIS- + *aise,* EASE] **1.** any departure from health; illness in general **2.** a particular destructive process in an organ or organism; specific illness **3.** a harmful condition, as of society —*vt.* **-eased′, -eas′ing** to cause disease in; infect —**dis·eased′** *adj.*

dis·em·bark (dis′im bärk′) *vt.* to unload (passengers or goods) from a ship, aircraft, etc. —*vi.* to go ashore from a ship or leave an aircraft, etc. —**dis·em·bar·ka·tion** (dis′em bär kā′shən) *n.*

dis·em·bar·rass (-im bar′əs) *vt.* to rid or relieve of something embarrassing, annoying, entangling, perplexing, or burdensome

dis·em·bod·y (-im bäd′ē) *vt.* **-bod′ied, -bod′y·ing** to free from bodily existence; make incorporeal —**dis′em·bod′ied** *adj.* —**dis′em·bod′i·ment** *n.*

dis·em·bow·el (-im bou′əl) *vt.* **-eled** or **-elled, -el·ing** or **-el·ling** to take out the bowels, or entrails, of; eviscerate —**dis′em·bow′el·ment** *n.*

dis·em·ployed (-im ploid′) *adj.* out of work, esp. because of lack of training or education, rather than because work is unavailable —**dis′em·ploy′ment** *n.*

dis·en·chant (-in chant′) *vt.* to set free from an enchantment or illusion —**dis′en·chant′ment** *n.*

dis·en·cum·ber (-in kum′bər) *vt.* to relieve of a burden; free from a hindrance or annoyance

dis·en·fran·chise (-in fran′chīz) *vt.* **-chised, -chis·ing** *same as* DISFRANCHISE —**dis′en·fran′chise·ment** *n.*

dis·en·gage (-in gāj′) *vt.* **-gaged′, -gag′ing** to release or loosen from something that binds, holds, entangles, etc.; unfasten; detach —*vi.* to release oneself or itself —**dis′en·gage′ment** *n.*

dis·en·tan·gle (-in taŋ′g'l) *vt.* **-gled, -gling** **1.** to free from something that entangles, confuses, etc.; extricate **2.** to straighten out (anything tangled, confused, etc.); untangle —*vi.* to get free from a tangle —**dis′en·tan′gle·ment** *n.*

dis·e·qui·lib·ri·um (dis ē′kwə lib′rē əm) *n., pl.* **-ri·ums, -ri·a** (-ə) lack or destruction of equilibrium, esp. in the economy

dis·es·tab·lish (dis′ə stab′lish) *vt.* **1.** to deprive of the status of being established **2.** to deprive (a state church) of official sanction and support by the government —**dis′es·tab′lish·ment** *n.*

dis·es·teem (-ə stēm′) *vt.* to hold in low esteem; dislike; slight —*n.* lack of esteem; disfavor

dis·fa·vor (dis fā′vər) *n.* **1.** an unfavorable opinion; dislike; disapproval **2.** the state of being disliked or disapproved of **3.** an unkind act; disservice —*vt.* to regard or treat unfavorably; slight

dis·fig·ure (-fig′yər) *vt.* **-ured, -ur·ing** to hurt the appearance or attractiveness of; deface; mar —**dis·fig′ure·ment, dis·fig′u·ra′tion** *n.*

dis·fran·chise (-fran′chīz) *vt.* **-chised, -chis·ing** **1.** to deprive of the rights of citizenship, esp. of the right to vote **2.** to deprive of a privilege, right, or power —**dis·fran′chise·ment** *n.*

dis·gorge (-gôrj′) *vt., vi.* **-gorged′, -gorg′ing** [< OFr.: see DIS- & GORGE] **1.** to vomit **2.** to give up (something) against one's will **3.** to pour forth (its contents)

dis·grace (-grās′) *n.* [< Fr. < It. < *dis-* (L. *dis-*), not + *grazia,* favor < L. *gratia:* see GRACE] **1.** a being in disfavor as because of bad conduct **2.** loss of respect; public dishonor; shame **3.** a person or thing that brings shame (*to* one) —*vt.* **-graced′, -grac′ing** to bring shame or dishonor upon; be a discredit to —**dis·grac′er** *n.*

dis·grace·ful (-fəl) *adj.* causing or characterized by disgrace; shameful —**dis·grace′ful·ly** *adv.* —**dis·grace′ful·ness** *n.*

dis·grun·tle (-grun′t'l) *vt.* **-tled, -tling** [DIS- + obs. *gruntle,* freq. of GRUNT] to make peevishly discontented —**dis·grun′tle·ment** *n.*

dis·guise (-gīz′) *vt.* **-guised′, -guis′ing** [< OFr.: see DIS- & GUISE] **1.** to make appear, sound, etc. different from usual so as to be unrecognizable **2.** to hide the real nature of —*n.* **1.** any clothes, equipment, manner, etc. used for disguising **2.** the state of being disguised **3.** the act or practice of disguising —**dis·guis′ed·ly** *adv.* —**dis·guis′er** *n.*

dis·gust (-gust′) *n.* [< MFr. < *des-* (see DIS-) + L. *gustus,* taste] a sickening distaste or dislike; deep aversion; repugnance —*vt.* to cause to feel disgust; be sickening or repulsive to —**dis·gust′ed** *adj.* —**dis·gust′ed·ly** *adv.* —**dis·gust′ing** *adj.* —**dis·gust′ing·ly** *adv.*

dish (dish) *n.* [OE. *disc,* dish, ult. < L. *discus,* DISCUS] **1.** *a)* any container, generally shallow and concave, for food *b)* [*pl.*] plates, bowls, cups, etc., collectively **2.** *a)* the food in a dish *b)* a particular kind of food **3.** a dishful **4.** a dish-shaped object or concavity **5.** [Slang] *a)* a pretty girl or woman *b)* a favorite thing: also **dish of tea** —*vt.* **1.** to serve (food) in a dish (usually with *up* or *out*) **2.** to make concave —*vi.* to be or become dish-shaped; cave in —**dish it out** [Slang] to scold, harass, etc.

dis·ha·bille (dis′ə bēl′) *n.* [< Fr. < *dés-* (see DIS-) + *habiller,* to dress] the state of being dressed only partially or in night clothes

dish antenna a radio transmitting or receiving antenna with a dish-shaped reflector

dis·har·mo·ny (dis här′mə nē) *n.* lack of harmony; discord —**dis′har·mo′ni·ous** (-mō′nē əs) *adj.*

dish·cloth (dish′klôth′, -kläth′) *n.* a cloth for washing dishes

dis·heart·en (dis här′t'n) *vt.* to discourage; depress —**dis·heart′en·ing** *adj.* —**dis·heart′en·ing·ly** *adv.* —**dis·heart′en·ment** *n.*

di·shev·el (di shev′'l) *vt.* **-eled** or **-elled, -el·ing** or **-el·ling** [< OFr. < *des-,* DIS- + *chevel,* hair < L. *capillus*] **1.** to cause (hair, clothing, etc.) to become disarranged and untidy; rumple **2.** to cause the hair or clothes of (a person) to become disarranged —**di·shev′eled, di·shev′elled** *adj.* —**di·shev′el·ment** *n.*

dish·ful (dish′fool′) *n., pl.* **-fuls′** as much as a dish holds

dis·hon·est (dis än′ist) *adj.* not honest; lying, cheating, etc. —**dis·hon′est·ly** *adv.*

dis·hon·es·ty (-ist ē) *n.* **1.** the quality of being dishonest **2.** *pl.* **-ties** a dishonest act or statement; fraud, lie, etc.

dis·hon·or (dis än′ər) *n.* **1.** *a)* loss of honor, respect, etc. *b)* state of shame; disgrace **2.** a cause of dishonor; discredit **3.** a refusal or failure to pay a check, draft, etc. —*vt.* **1.** to treat disrespectfully **2.** to disgrace **3.** to refuse or fail to pay (a check, draft, etc.)

dis·hon·or·a·ble (-ə b'l) *adj.* causing or deserving dishonor; shameful; disgraceful —**dis·hon′or·a·ble·ness** *n.* —**dis·hon′or·a·bly** *adv.*

dish·pan (dish′pan′) *n.* a pan in which dishes, cooking utensils, etc. are washed

dish·rag (-rag′) *n. same as* DISHCLOTH

dish towel a towel for drying dishes

dis·il·lu·sion (dis′i lo͞o′zhən) *vt.* **1.** to free from illusion or false ideas **2.** to take away the idealism of and make disappointed, bitter, etc. —*n.* a disillusioning or being disillusioned: also **dis′il·lu′sion·ment**

dis·in·cli·na·tion (dis in′klə nā′shən) *n.* a dislike or unwillingness; aversion; reluctance

dis·in·cline (dis′in klīn′) *vt.* **-clined′, -clin′ing** to make unwilling

dis·in·fect (-in fekt′) *vt.* to destroy the harmful bacteria, viruses, etc. in or on —**dis′in·fec′tion** *n.*

dis·in·fect·ant (-ənt) *adj.* disinfecting —*n.* anything that disinfects

dis·in·fla·tion (-in flā′shən) *n. Econ.* a reduction of price levels, planned to increase purchasing power but control deflation —**dis′in·fla′tion·ar′y** *adj.*

dis·in·gen·u·ous (-in jen′yo͞o wəs) *adj.* not straightforward; not candid; insincere —**dis′in·gen′u·ous·ly** *adv.* —**dis′in·gen′u·ous·ness** *n.*

dis·in·her·it (-in her′it) *vt.* **1.** to deprive of an inheritance or the right to inherit **2.** to deprive of any right or privilege —**dis′in·her′it·ance** *n.*

dis·in·te·grate (dis in′tə grāt′) *vt., vi.* **-grat′ed, -grat′ing** **1.** to separate into parts or fragments; break up **2.** to undergo or cause to undergo a nuclear transformation —**dis·in′te·gra′tion** *n.* —**dis·in′te·gra′tive** *adj.* —**dis·in′te·gra′tor** *n.*

dis·in·ter (dis′in tʉr′) *vt.* **-terred′, -ter′ring** **1.** to remove from a grave, tomb, etc.; dig up; exhume **2.** to bring to light —**dis′in·ter′ment** *n.*

dis·in·ter·est (dis in′trist, -tər ist) *n.* **1.** lack of personal or selfish interest **2.** lack of interest

dis·in·ter·est·ed (-id) *adj.* **1.** not influenced by personal interest or selfish motives; impartial **2.** uninterested: a revival of an obsolete meaning —**dis·in′ter·est·ed·ly** *adv.* —**dis·in′ter·est·ed·ness** *n.*

dis·join (-join′) *vt.* to separate or detach

dis·joint (-joint′) *vt.* **1.** to put out of joint; dislocate **2.** to dismember **3.** to destroy the unity, connections, or orderliness of —*vi.* to come apart at the joints —**dis·joint′ed** *adj.* —**dis·joint′ed·ly** *adv.* —**dis·joint′ed·ness** *n.*

dis·junc·tion (-juŋk′shən) *n.* **1.** a disjoining or being disjoined; separation: also **dis·junc′ture** (-chər) **2.** *a)* the relation between alternatives of a disjunctive proposition *b)* a disjunctive proposition

dis·junc·tive (-tiv) *adj.* **1.** disjoining; separating or causing to separate **2.** *Gram.* indicating a contrast or an alternative between words, clauses, etc. *[*"or" and "but" are *disjunctive* conjunctions*]* **3.** *Logic* presenting alternatives *[*a *disjunctive* proposition*]* —*n.* **1.** *Gram.* a disjunctive conjunction **2.** *Logic* a disjunctive proposition —**dis·junc′tive·ly** *adv.*

disk (disk) *n.* **[**< L. *discus,* DISCUS**]** **1.** any thin, flat, circular thing **2.** anything like this in form *[*the moon's *disk]* **3.** *same as* DISC; specif., *a)* the disk-shaped center of certain composite flowers *b)* a layer of fibrous connective tissue, with some cartilage, occurring between vertebrae

disk flower any of the tubular flowers in the central disk of the flower head of a composite plant

disk harrow *same as* DISC HARROW

disk jockey *same as* DISC JOCKEY

dis·like (dis līk′) *vt.* **-liked′, -lik′ing** to have a feeling of not liking; feel aversion to —*n.* a feeling of not liking; distaste; aversion —**dis·lik′a·ble, dis·like′a·ble** *adj.*

dis·lo·cate (dis′lō kāt′, dis lō′kāt) *vt.* **-cat′ed, -cat′ing** **1.** to put out of place; specif., to displace (a bone) from its proper position at a joint **2.** to disarrange; disrupt —**dis′lo·ca′tion** *n.*

dis·lodge (dis läj′) *vt., vi.* **-lodged′, -lodg′ing** to force or be forced from a position or place where lodged, hiding, etc. —**dis·lodg′ment** *n.*

dis·loy·al (-loi′əl) *adj.* not loyal or faithful; faithless —**dis·loy′al·ly** *adv.*

dis·loy·al·ty (-tē) *n.* **1.** the quality of being disloyal **2.** *pl.* **-ties** a disloyal act

dis·mal (diz′m'l) *adj.* **[**ME., orig. n., evil days < OFr. < ML. *dies mali***]** **1.** causing gloom or misery **2.** dark and gloomy; bleak; dreary **3.** depressed; miserable —**dis′mal·ly** *adv.*

dis·man·tle (dis man′t'l) *vt.* **-tled, -tling** **[**< OFr. *desmanteller:* see DIS- & MANTLE**]** **1.** to strip of covering **2.** to strip (a house, ship, etc.) of furniture, equipment, etc. **3.** to take apart; disassemble —**dis·man′tle·ment** *n.*

dis·may (-mā′) *vt.* **[**< Anglo-Fr. < OFr. *des-,* intens. + *esmayer,* to deprive of power**]** to make discouraged at the prospect of trouble; fill with alarm; daunt —*n.* a loss of courage at the prospect of trouble

dis·mem·ber (-mem′bər) *vt.* **[**< OFr.: see DIS- & MEMBER**]** **1.** to remove the limbs of by cutting or tearing **2.** to pull or cut to pieces; divide up or mutilate —**dis·mem′berment** *n.*

dis·miss (-mis′) *vt.* **[**< ML. pp. of *dismittere,* for L. *dimittere* < *dis-,* from + *mittere,* to send**]** **1.** to send away; cause or allow to leave **2.** to remove or discharge from an office, employment, etc. **3.** to put out of one's mind **4.** *Law* to reject (a claim or action) —**dis·miss′al** *n.* —**dis·miss′i·ble** *adj.*

dis·mount (-mount′) *vi.* to get off, as from a horse or bicycle —*vt.* **1.** to remove (a thing) from its mounting or setting **2.** to cause to dismount **3.** to take apart —*n.* a dismounting

dis·o·be·di·ence (dis′ə bē′dē əns) *n.* refusal to obey; failure to follow commands; insubordination —**dis′o·be′di·ent** *adj.* —**dis′o·be′di·ent·ly** *adv.*

dis·o·bey (dis′ə bā′) *vt., vi.* to refuse or fail to obey

dis·o·blige (-ə blij′) *vt.* **-bliged′, -blig′ing** **1.** to refuse to oblige, or do a favor for **2.** to slight; offend —**dis′o·blig′ing** *adj.* —**dis′o·blig′ing·ly** *adv.*

dis·or·der (dis ôr′dər) *n.* **1.** a lack of order; confusion **2.** a breach of public peace; riot **3.** a disregard of system; irregularity **4.** an upset of normal function; ailment —*vt.* **1.** to throw into disorder; disarrange **2.** to upset the normal functions or health of —**dis·or′dered** *adj.*

dis·or·der·ly (-lē) *adj.* **1.** not orderly; untidy; unsystematic **2.** unruly; riotous **3.** *Law* violating public peace, safety, or order —**dis·or′der·li·ness** *n.*

dis·or·gan·ize (dis ôr′gə nīz′) *vt.* **-ized′, -iz′ing** to break up the order, arrangement, or system of; throw into disorder —**dis·or′gan·i·za′tion** *n.*

dis·o·ri·ent (-ôr′ē ent′) *vt.* **1.** to cause to lose one's bearings **2.** to confuse mentally Also **dis·o′ri·en·tate′** (-ən tāt′) **-tat′ed, -tat′ing** —**dis·o′ri·en·ta′tion** *n.*

dis·own (-ōn′) *vt.* to refuse to acknowledge as one's own; repudiate; cast off

dis·par·age (-par′ij) *vt.* **-aged, -ag·ing** **[**< OFr. *desparagier,* to marry one of inferior rank < *des-* (see DIS-) + *parage,* rank < *per,* PEER[1]**]** **1.** to lower in esteem; discredit **2.** to speak slightingly of; belittle —**dis·par′age·ment** *n.* —**dis·par′ag·ing** *adj.* —**dis·par′ag·ing·ly** *adv.*

dis·pa·rate (dis′pər it) *adj.* **[**< L. pp. of *disparare* < *dis-,* apart, not + *parare,* to make equal < *par,* equal**]** distinct or different in kind; unequal —**dis′pa·rate·ly** *adv.* —**dis′pa·rate·ness** *n.*

dis·par·i·ty (dis par′ə tē) *n., pl.* **-ties** **1.** inequality or difference, as in quality **2.** incongruity

dis·pas·sion·ate (-pash′ən it) *adj.* free from passion, emotion, or bias; calm; impartial —**dis·pas′sion** *n.* —**dis·pas′sion·ate·ly** *adv.*

dis·patch (-pach′) *vt.* **[**< Sp. & It. < OFr. *despeechier,* ult. < L. *dis-,* not + LL. *impedicare,* to entangle < L. < *pes,* a foot**]** **1.** to send off or out promptly on a specific errand or official business; specif., to send out (trains, buses, etc.) according to a schedule **2.** to kill **3.** to finish quickly or promptly —*n.* **1.** a sending out or off **2.** a killing **3.** efficient speed; promptness **4.** a message, esp. an official message **5.** a news story sent to a newspaper, TV station, etc., as by a special reporter or news agency —**dis·patch′er** *n.*

dis·pel (-pel′) *vt.* **-pelled′, -pel′ling** **[**< L. *dispellere* < *dis-,* away + *pellere,* to drive**]** to scatter and drive away; disperse

dis·pen·sa·ble (-pen′sə b'l) *adj.* **1.** that can be dispensed or dealt out **2.** that can be dispensed with —**dis·pen′sa·bil′i·ty** *n.*

dis·pen·sa·ry (-sə rē) *n., pl.* **-ries** a room or place, as in a school or factory, where medicines and first aid are available

dis·pen·sa·tion (dis′pən sā′shən, -pen-) *n.* **1.** a dispensing; distribution **2.** anything distributed **3.** an administrative system; management **4.** a release from an obligation **5.** *R.C.Ch.* an exemption from a specific church law **6.** *Theol.* *a)* the ordering of events under divine authority *b)* any religious system —**dis′pen·sa′tion·al** *adj.*

dis·pen·sa·to·ry (dis pen′sə tôr′ē) *n., pl.* **-ries** a handbook on medicines; pharmacopeia

dis·pense (-pens′) *vt.* **-pensed′, -pens′ing** **[**< OFr. < L. *dispensare* < pp. of *dispendere* < *dis-,* out + *pendere,* to weigh**]** **1.** to give or deal out; distribute **2.** to prepare and give out (medicines, prescriptions, etc.) **3.** to administer *[*to *dispense* the law*]* **4.** to exempt; excuse —**dispense with** **1.** to get rid of **2.** to do without

dis·pen·ser (-pen′sər) *n.* one that dispenses, as a container designed to dispense its contents in handy units or portions

dis·perse (-pʉrs′) *vt.* **-persed′, -pers′ing** **[**< L. pp. of *dispergere* < *dis-,* out + *spargere,* to strew**]** **1.** to break up and scatter in all directions; distribute widely **2.** to dispel (mist, etc.) **3.** to break up (light) into its component colored rays —*vi.* to move in different directions —**dis·per′sal** *n.* —**dis·pers′er** *n.* —**dis·pers′i·ble** *adj.* —**dis·per′sive** (-pur′siv) *adj.*

dis·per·sion (dis pur′zhən, -shən) *n.* **1.** a dispersing or being dispersed **2.** the breaking up of light into component colored rays, as by a prism **3.** a colloidal system with its dispersed particles and the medium in which these are suspended

dis·pir·it (di spir′it) *vt.* to depress; deject —**dis·pir′it·ed** *adj.* —**dis·pir′it·ed·ly** *adv.*

dis·place (dis plās′) *vt.* **-placed′, -plac′ing 1.** to move from its usual or proper place **2.** to discharge **3.** to replace [a ship *displaces* a certain amount of water]

displaced person a person forced from his country, esp. in war, and left homeless elsewhere

dis·place·ment (-mənt) *n.* **1.** a displacing or being displaced **2.** *a*) the weight or volume of a fluid displaced by a floating object; specif., the weight of water displaced by a ship *b*) the volume displaced by a piston

dis·play (-plā′) *vt.* [< OFr. < L. *displicare* < *dis-*, apart + *plicare*, to fold] **1.** to unfold; spread out **2.** to put or spread out to be seen; exhibit **3.** to disclose; reveal —*n.* **1.** a displaying; exhibition **2.** anything displayed; exhibit **3.** showy exhibition; ostentation **4.** *a*) a manifestation [a *display* of courage] *b*) a mere show; sham [a *display* of pity] —*adj.* designating printing types used for headings, advertisements, etc. —**dis·play′er** *n.*

dis·please (-plēz′) *vt., vi.* **-pleased′, -pleas′ing** to fail to please; annoy; offend

dis·pleas·ure (-plezh′ər) *n.* **1.** the fact or feeling of being displeased; dissatisfaction, annoyance, etc. **2.** [Archaic] discomfort, trouble, etc.

dis·port (-pôrt′) *vi.* [< OFr. < *des-* (see DIS-) + *porter* < L. *portare*, to carry] to play; frolic —*vt.* to amuse or divert (oneself)

dis·pos·a·ble (-pō′zə b'l) *adj.* **1.** that can be discarded **2.** that can be disposed as one wishes

dis·pos·al (-pō′z'l) *n.* **1.** a disposing; specif., *a*) arrangement in a particular order *b*) a dealing with matters; settling of affairs *c*) a giving away; transfer *d*) a getting rid of **2.** the power to dispose **3.** *same as* DISPOSER (sense 2) —**at one's disposal** available to be used as one wishes

dis·pose (-pōz′) *vt.* **-posed′, -pos′ing** [< OFr. < L. pp. of *disponere:* see DIS- & POSITION] **1.** to place in a certain order; arrange **2.** to arrange (matters); settle (affairs) **3.** to make willing **4.** to make susceptible or liable —*vi.* to have the power to arrange or settle affairs —**dispose of 1.** to deal with; settle **2.** to give away or sell **3.** to throw away **4.** to eat or drink up

dis·pos·er (-pō′zər) *n.* **1.** one that disposes **2.** a device installed in a sink drain to grind up garbage that is then flushed away

dis·po·si·tion (dis′pə zish′ən) *n.* **1.** proper or orderly arrangement **2.** management or settlement of affairs **3.** a selling, giving away, etc. of something **4.** the power to dispose; control **5.** an inclination or tendency **6.** one's nature or temperament

dis·pos·sess (-pə zes′) *vt.* to deprive of the possession of land, a house, etc.; oust —**dis′pos·ses′sion** (-zesh′ən) *n.* —**dis′pos·ses′sor** *n.*

dis·praise (dis prāz′) *vt.* **-praised′, -prais′ing** to speak of with disapproval; disparage; censure —*n.* a dispraising; blame —**dis·prais′ing·ly** *adv.*

dis·proof (-pro͞of′) *n.* **1.** a disproving; refutation **2.** evidence that disproves

dis·pro·por·tion (dis′prə pôr′shən) *n.* lack of proportion; lack of symmetry —*vt.* to cause to be disproportionate —**dis′pro·por′tion·al** *adj.* —**dis′pro·por′tion·al·ly** *adv.*

dis·pro·por·tion·ate (-it) *adj.* not proportionate; not in proportion —**dis′pro·por′tion·ate·ly** *adv.*

dis·prove (dis pro͞ov′) *vt.* **-proved′, -prov′ing** to prove to be false or in error —**dis·prov′a·ble** *adj.*

dis·pu·ta·ble (dis pyo͞ot′ə b'l, dis′pyo͞ot-) *adj.* that can be disputed; debatable —**dis·pu′ta·bil′i·ty** *n.* —**dis·pu′ta·bly** *adv.*

dis·pu·tant (dis pyo͞ot′'nt, dis′pyoo tənt) *adj.* disputing —*n.* one who disputes, or debates

dis·pu·ta·tion (dis′pyoo tā′shən) *n.* **1.** a disputing; dispute **2.** a debatelike discussion

dis·pu·ta·tious (-shəs) *adj.* inclined to dispute; fond of arguing: also **dis·pu·ta·tive** (dis pyo͞ot′ə tiv) —**dis′pu·ta′tious·ly** *adv.* —**dis′pu·ta′tious·ness** *n.*

dis·pute (dis pyo͞ot′) *vi.* **-put′ed, -put′ing** [< OFr. < L. *disputare* < *dis-*, apart + *putare*, to think] **1.** to argue; debate **2.** to quarrel —*vt.* **1.** to argue or debate (a question) **2.** to question the truth of; doubt **3.** to oppose in any way; resist **4.** to fight for; contest —*n.* **1.** a disputing; argument; debate **2.** a quarrel —**beyond dispute 1.** not open to dispute; settled **2.** indisputably —**in dispute** not settled —**dis·put′er** *n.*

dis·qual·i·fy (-kwäl′ə fī′) *vt.* **-fied′, -fy′ing 1.** to make unfit or unqualified **2.** to make or declare ineligible, as to participate further in a sport, for breaking rules —**dis·qual′i·fi·ca′tion** (-fi kā′shən) *n.*

dis·qui·et (-kwī′ət) *vt.* to make anxious or restless; disturb —*n.* restlessness; anxiety —**dis·qui′et·ing** *adj.* —**dis·qui′et·ing·ly** *adv.*

dis·qui·e·tude (-kwī′ə to͞od′, -tyo͞od′) *n.* a disturbed or uneasy condition; restlessness; anxiety

dis·qui·si·tion (dis′kwə zish′ən) *n.* [< L. < pp. of *disquirere* < *dis-*, apart + *quaerere*, to seek] a formal discussion of some subject; treatise

Dis·rae·li (diz rā′lē), **Benjamin,** 1st Earl of Beaconsfield, 1804–81; Eng. prime minister

dis·re·gard (dis′ri gärd′) *vt.* **1.** to pay little or no attention to **2.** to treat without due respect; slight —*n.* **1.** lack of attention **2.** lack of due regard or respect —**dis′re·gard′ful** *adj.*

dis·re·mem·ber (-ri mem′bər) *vt.* [Dial. or Colloq.] to forget; be unable to remember

dis·re·pair (-ri per′) *n.* the condition of needing repairs; state of neglect; dilapidation

dis·rep·u·ta·ble (dis rep′yoo tə b'l) *adj.* **1.** not reputable; having or causing a bad reputation **2.** not fit to be seen; shabby, dirty, etc. —**dis·rep′u·ta·bly** *adv.*

dis·re·pute (dis′ri pyo͞ot′) *n.* lack or loss of repute; bad reputation; disgrace; disfavor

dis·re·spect (-ri spekt′) *n.* lack of respect or esteem; discourtesy —*vt.* to have or show a lack of respect for —**dis′respect′ful** *adj.* —**dis′re·spect′ful·ly** *adv.* —**dis′re·spect′ful·ness** *n.*

dis·robe (dis rōb′) *vt., vi.* **-robed′, -rob′ing** to undress —**dis·rob′er** *n.*

dis·rupt (-rupt′) *vt., vi.* [< L. pp. of *disrumpere* < *dis-*, apart + *rumpere*, to break] **1.** to break apart; rend asunder **2.** to interrupt the orderly course of (a meeting, etc.) —**dis·rupt′er, dis·rup′tor** *n.* —**dis·rup′tion** *n.* —**dis·rup′tive** *adj.*

dis·sat·is·fac·tion (dis sat′is fak′shən) *n.* the condition of being dissatisfied; discontent

dis·sat·is·fac·to·ry (-tə rē) *adj.* not satisfactory

dis·sat·is·fy (dis sat′is fī′) *vt.* **-fied′, -fy′ing** to fail to satisfy; discontent; displease

dis·sect (di sekt′, dī-) *vt.* [< L. pp. of *dissecare* < *dis-*, apart + *secare*, to cut] **1.** to cut apart piece by piece; separate into parts, as a body for purposes of study **2.** to examine or analyze closely —**dis·sec′tion** *n.* —**dis·sec′tor** *n.*

dis·sect·ed (-id) *adj.* **1.** cut up into parts **2.** *Bot.* consisting of many lobes and segments, as some leaves **3.** *Geol.* cut by erosion into valleys and hills

dis·sem·ble (di sem′b'l) *vt.* **-bled, -bling** [< OFr. < *des-*, DIS- + *sembler* < L. *simulare*, SIMULATE] **1.** to conceal under a false appearance [to *dissemble* fear by smiling] **2.** to make a false show of; feign [to *dissemble* innocence] —*vi.* to conceal the truth, or one's true feelings, motives, etc., by pretense —**dis·sem′blance** *n.* —**dis·sem′bler** *n.*

dis·sem·i·nate (di sem′ə nāt′) *vt.* **-nat′ed, -nat′ing** [< L. pp. of *disseminare* < *dis-*, apart + *seminare*, to sow < *semen*, seed] to scatter far and wide; spread abroad; promulgate widely —**dis·sem′i·na′tion** *n.* —**dis·sem′i·na′tive** *adj.* —**dis·sem′i·na′tor** *n.*

dis·sen·sion (di sen′shən) *n.* a dissenting in opinion; disagreement or, esp., violent quarreling or wrangling

dis·sent (di sent′) *vi.* [< L. *dissentire* < *dis-*, apart + *sentire*, to feel] **1.** to differ in belief or opinion; disagree **2.** to reject the doctrines and forms of an established church —*n.* a dissenting; specif., *a*) a minority opinion in the decision of a law case *b*) religious nonconformity —**dissent′er** *n.* —**dis·sent′ing** *adj.*

dis·sen·tient (di sen′shənt) *adj.* dissenting, esp. from the majority opinion —*n.* one who dissents

dis·ser·ta·tion (dis′ər tā′shən) *n.* [< L. < pp. of *dissertare*, to discuss, freq. of *disserere* < *dis-*, apart + *serere*, to join] a formal and lengthy discourse or treatise; thesis

dis·serv·ice (dis sur′vis) *n.* harmful action; injury

dis·sev·er (di sev′ər) *vt.* **1.** to sever; separate **2.** to divide into parts —*vi.* to separate; disunite —**dis·sev′er·ance, dis·sev′er·ment** *n.*

dis·si·dence (dis′ə dəns) *n.* [< L. < prp. of *dissidere* < *dis-*, apart + *sidere*, to sit] disagreement; dissent —**dis′si·dent** *adj., n.* —**dis′si·dent·ly** *adv.*

dis·sim·i·lar (di sim′ə lər) *adj.* not similar or alike; different —**dis·sim′i·lar′i·ty** *n., pl.* **-ties** —**dis·sim′i·lar·ly** *adv.*

dis·sim·i·la·tion (di sim′ə lā′shən) *n.* **1.** a making or becoming dissimilar **2.** the replacement or disappearance of a phoneme when it recurs in the same word (Ex.: Eng. ma*r*ble < OFr. ma*r*b*r*e)

dis·si·mil·i·tude (dis′si mil′ə to͞od′, -tyo͞od′) *n.* dissimilarity; difference

dis·sim·u·late (di sim′yə lāt′) *vt., vi.* **-lat′ed, -lat′ing** [< L. pp. of *dissimulare:* see DIS- & SIMULATE] to hide (one's feelings, motives, etc.) by pretense; dissemble —**dis·sim′u·la′tion** *n.* —**dis·sim′u·la′tor** *n.*

dis·si·pate (dis′ə pāt′) *vt.* **-pat′ed, -pat′ing** [< L. pp. of *dissipare* < *dis-*, apart + *supare*, to throw] **1.** to scatter; disperse **2.** to drive completely away; make disappear **3.** to waste or squander —*vi.* **1.** to be dispelled; vanish **2.** to indulge in pleasure to the point of harming oneself —**dis′si·pat′er, dis′si·pa′tor** *n.* —**dis′si·pa′tive** *adj.*

dis·si·pat·ed (-id) *adj.* **1.** scattered **2.** squandered or wasted **3.** dissolute; debauched

dis·si·pa·tion (dis′ə pā′shən) *n.* a dissipating or being dissipated; dispersion, squandering, dissoluteness, etc.

dis·so·ci·ate (di sō′shē āt′, -sē-) *vt.* **-at′ed, -at′ing** [< L. pp. of *dissociare* < *dis-*, apart + *sociare*, to join < *socius*, companion] **1.** to break the ties between; sever association with; separate; disunite **2.** to cause to undergo dissociation —*vi.* **1.** to stop associating **2.** to undergo dissociation —**dissociate oneself from** to repudiate any connection with

dis·so·ci·a·tion (di sō′sē ā′shən, -shē-) *n.* **1.** a dissociating or being dissociated **2.** *Chem.* the breaking up of a compound into simpler components **3.** *Psychol.* a split in the individual consciousness in which a group of mental activities functions as a separate unit —**dis·so′ci·a′tive** *adj.*

dis·sol·u·ble (di säl′yoo b'l) *adj.* that can be dissolved —**dis·sol′u·bil′i·ty** *n.*

dis·so·lute (dis′ə lo͞ot′) *adj.* [< L. pp. of *dissolvere:* see DISSOLVE] dissipated and immoral; debauched —**dis′so·lute′ly** *adv.* —**dis′so·lute′ness** *n.*

dis·so·lu·tion (dis′ə lo͞o′shən) *n.* a dissolving or being dissolved; specif., *a*) a breaking up or into parts; disintegration *b*) the termination, as of a business or union *c*) death *d*) the dismissal of an assembly or adjournment of a meeting

dis·solve (di zälv′, -zôlv′) *vt., vi.* **-solved′, -solv′ing** [< L. *dissolvere* < *dis-*, apart + *solvere*, to loosen: see SOLVE] **1.** to make or become liquid; melt **2.** to merge with a liquid; pass or make pass into solution **3.** to break up; decompose **4.** to end as by breaking up; terminate **5.** to disappear or make disappear **6.** *Motion Pictures & TV* to fade or be faded out by means of a lap dissolve —*n. Motion Pictures & TV* *same as* LAP DISSOLVE —**dissolved in tears** weeping —**dis·solv′a·ble** *adj.* —**dis·solv′er** *n.*

dis·so·nance (dis′ə nəns) *n.* [< LL. < L. prp. of *dissonare* < *dis-*, apart + *sonare*, to SOUND[1]] **1.** an inharmonious combination of sounds; discord **2.** any lack of harmony or agreement; incongruity **3.** *Music* a chord that sounds harsh and incomplete

dis·so·nant (-nənt) *adj.* **1.** characterized by or constituting a dissonance **2.** opposing in opinion, temperament, etc.; incompatible —**dis′so·nant·ly** *adv.*

dis·suade (di swād′) *vt.* **-suad′ed, -suad′ing** [L. *dissuadere* < *dis-*, away + *suadere*, to persuade] to turn (a person) aside (*from* a course, etc.) by persuasion or advice —**dis·suad′er** *n.* —**dis·sua′sion** *n.* —**dis·sua′sive** *adj.* —**dis·sua′sive·ly** *adv.*

dis·syl·la·ble (dis′sil′ə b'l) *n. same as* DISYLLABLE —**dis·syl·lab·ic** (dis′si lab′ik) *adj.*

dist. **1.** distance **2.** distinguish **3.** district

dis·taff (dis′taf) *n.* [< OE. < *dis-*, flax + *stæf*, a staff] **1.** a staff on which flax, wool, etc. is wound for use in spinning **2.** woman's work or concerns **3.** woman, or women in general —*adj.* female, or designating the maternal side of a family

DISTAFF

dis·tal (dis′t'l) *adj.* [DIST(ANT) + -AL] *Anat.* farthest from the center or the point of attachment or origin —**dis′tal·ly** *adv.*

dis·tance (dis′təns) *n.* [< OFr. < L. < prp. of *distare* < *dis-*, apart + *stare*, to stand] **1.** the fact or condition of being separated in space or time; remoteness **2.** a space between two points **3.** an interval between two points in time **4.** the length of a line between two points **5.** a remoteness in relationship or in behavior **6.** a remote point in space or time —*vt.* **-tanced, -tanc·ing** to leave behind; outdistance —**go the distance** to last through an activity —**keep at a distance** to treat aloofly —**keep one's distance** to be aloof

dis·tant (-tənt) *adj.* **1.** having a space between; separated **2.** widely separated; far apart in space or time **3.** away [ten miles *distant*] **4.** far apart in relationship [a *distant* cousin] **5.** cool in manner; aloof **6.** from or at a distance **7.** faraway or dreamy [a *distant* look] —**dis′tant·ly** *adv.*

dis·taste (dis tāst′) *n.* dislike or aversion (*for*)

dis·taste·ful (-fəl) *adj.* **1.** unpleasant to taste **2.** causing distaste; unpleasant; disagreeable —**dis·taste′ful·ly** *adv.* —**dis·taste′ful·ness** *n.*

dis·tem·per[1] (dis tem′pər) *vt.* [< OFr. < ML. *distemperare*, to disorder < L. *dis-*, apart + *temperare*, to mix in proportion] to upset the functions of; derange; disorder —*n.* **1.** a mental or physical disorder; disease **2.** an infectious virus disease of young dogs **3.** civil disorder

dis·tem·per[2] (dis tem′pər) *n.* [< OFr. < ML. < L. *dis-*, intens. + *temperare:* see prec.] [Chiefly Brit.] any of various water-based paints, as for walls, etc.

dis·tend (dis tend′) *vt., vi.* [< L. *distendere* < *dis-*, apart + *tendere*, to stretch] **1.** to stretch out **2.** to expand; make or become swollen —**dis·ten′si·ble** *adj.* —**dis·ten′tion, dis·ten′sion** *n.*

dis·tich (dis′tik) *n.* [< L. < Gr. < *di-*, two + *stichos*, a row] two successive lines of verse regarded as a unit; couplet

dis·till, dis·til (dis til′) *vi.* **-tilled′, -till′ing** [< OFr. < L. *destillare* < *de-*, down + *stillare*, to drip < *stilla*, a drop] **1.** to fall in drops; drip **2.** to undergo distillation **3.** to be produced as the essence of something —*vt.* **1.** to let fall in drops **2.** to subject to distillation **3.** to remove, extract, etc. by distillation **4.** to purify, refine, or concentrate as by distillation

dis·til·late (dis′tə lāt′, -t'l it) *n.* **1.** a liquid obtained by distilling **2.** the essence of anything

dis·til·la·tion (dis′tə lā′shən) *n.* **1.** a distilling **2.** the process of heating a mixture to separate the more volatile from the less volatile parts, and condensing the resulting vapor to produce a more nearly pure substance **3.** a distillate

dis·till·er (dis til′ər) *n.* **1.** a person or apparatus that distills **2.** a person, company, etc. in the business of distilling alcoholic liquors

dis·till·er·y (-til′ər ē) *n., pl.* **-er·ies** a place where distilling is carried on

dis·tinct (-tiŋkt′) *adj.* [OFr. < L. pp. of *distinguere:* see DISTINGUISH] **1.** not alike; different **2.** separate; individual **3.** clearly marked off; plain **4.** well-defined; unmistakable —**dis·tinct′ly** *adv.* —**dis·tinct′ness** *n.*

dis·tinc·tion (-tiŋk′shən) *n.* **1.** the act of making or keeping distinct **2.** the condition of being different **3.** a quality, mark, or feature that differentiates **4.** fame; eminence **5.** the quality that makes one seem superior **6.** a mark or sign of honor

dis·tinc·tive (-tiŋk′tiv) *adj.* distinguishing from others; characteristic —**dis·tinc′tive·ly** *adv.* —**dis·tinc′tive·ness** *n.*

dis·tin·gué (dis taŋ gā′) *adj.* [Fr.] having an air of distinction; distinguished: also, sometimes, **dis·tin·guée′** *fem.*

dis·tin·guish (dis tiŋ′gwish) *vt.* [< L. *distinguere* < *dis-*, apart + *-stinguere*, to prick, pierce] **1.** to perceive or show the difference in; differentiate **2.** to characterize **3.** to recognize plainly by any of the senses **4.** to separate and classify **5.** to make famous or eminent —*vi.* to make a distinction (*between* or *among*) —**dis·tin′guish·a·ble** *adj.* —**dis·tin′guish·a·bly** *adv.*

dis·tin·guished (-gwisht) *adj.* **1.** celebrated; famous **2.** having an air of distinction

dis·tort (dis tôrt′) *vt.* [< L. pp. of *distorquere* < *dis-*, intens. + *torquere*, to twist] **1.** to twist out of the usual shape, form, or appearance **2.** to misrepresent; pervert **3.** to modify (a sound, etc.) so as to produce an unfaithful reproduction —**dis·tort′er** *n.* —**dis·tor′tion** *n.*

distr. **1.** distributed **2.** distribution

dis·tract (dis trakt′) *vt.* [< L. pp. of *distrahere* < *dis-*, apart + *trahere*, to draw] **1.** to draw (the mind, etc.) away in another direction; divert **2.** to create conflict and confusion in —**dis·tract′ed** *adj.* —**dis·tract′ed·ly** *adv.* —**dis·tract′i·ble** *adj.* —**dis·tract′ing** *adj.* —**dis·tract′ing·ly** *adv.*

dis·trac·tion (-trak′shən) *n.* **1.** a distracting or being distracted; confusion **2.** anything that distracts; specif., *a*) a cause of mental confusion *b*) anything that gives mental relaxation **3.** great mental distress —**dis·trac′tive** *adj.*

dis·train (dis trān′) *vt., vi.* [< OFr. < ML. *distringere* < L. < *dis-*, apart + *stringere*, to stretch] *Law* to seize and hold (property) as security or indemnity for a debt —**dis·train′a·ble** *adj.* —**dis·train′er, dis·trai′nor** *n.* —**dis·traint′** *n.*

dis·trait (-trā′) *adj.* [< OFr. < L. *distrahere:* see DISTRACT] absent-minded; inattentive

dis·traught (-trôt′) *adj.* [var. of prec.] **1.** very troubled or confused **2.** driven mad; crazed

dis·tress (dis tres′) *vt.* [< OFr. < ML. < L. pp. of *distringere:* see DISTRAIN] **1.** to cause sorrow, misery, or suffering to; pain; trouble **2.** to weaken with strain —*n.* **1.** the state of being distressed; pain, suffering, etc. **2.** anything that distresses; affliction **3.** a state of danger or trouble **4.** *Law* *a*) distraint *b*) the property distrained —**dis·tress′ful** *adj.* —**dis·tress′ful·ly** *adv.* —**dis·tress′ing** *adj.* —**dis·tress′ing·ly** *adv.*

dis·tressed (-trest′) *adj.* **1.** full of distress; troubled, etc. **2.** given an antique appearance, as by having the finish marred *[distressed* walnut*]* 3. designating an area in which there is much poverty, unemployment, etc. 4. designating repossessed goods sold at low prices

dis·trib·ute (dis trib′yoot) *vt.* **-ut·ed, -ut·ing** [< L. pp. of *distribuere* < *dis-*, apart + *tribuere,* to allot] 1. to divide and give out in shares; allot 2. to scatter or spread out, as over a surface 3. to classify 4. to put (things) in various distinct places —**dis·trib′ut·a·ble** *adj.*

dis·tri·bu·tion (dis′trə byōō′shən) *n.* 1. a distributing or being distributed; specif., *a)* apportionment by law (*of* funds, etc.) *b)* the process by which commodities get to consumers *c)* frequency of occurrence or extent of existence 2. anything distributed; portion; share 3. *Statistics* the arrangement of a set of numbers classified according to some property, as frequency, or to some other criterion, as time or location —**dis′tri·bu′tion·al** *adj.*

dis·trib·u·tive (dis trib′yoo tiv) *adj.* 1. distributing or tending to distribute 2. relating to distribution 3. *Gram.* referring to each member of a group regarded individually *[*"each" is a *distributive* word*]* 4. *Math.* of the principle in multiplication that allows the multiplier to be used separately with each term of the multiplicand —*n.* a distributive word —**dis·trib′u·tive·ly** *adv.*

dis·trib·u·tor (-tər) *n.* a person or thing that distributes; specif., *a)* an agent or business firm that distributes goods to consumers or dealers *b)* a device for distributing electric current to spark plugs —**dis·trib′u·tor·ship′** *n.*

dis·trict (dis′trikt) *n.* [Fr. < ML. < L. pp. of *distringere:* see DISTRAIN] 1. a geographical or political division made for a specific purpose *[*a school *district]* 2. any region; part of a country, city, etc. —*vt.* to divide into districts

district attorney a lawyer serving in a specified judicial district as a prosecutor for the State or Federal government in criminal cases

district court 1. the Federal trial court sitting in each district of the U.S. 2. in some States, the court of general jurisdiction in each judicial district

District of Columbia [after Christopher COLUMBUS] Federal district of the U.S., on the Potomac: 69 sq. mi.; pop. 638,000; coextensive with the city of Washington: abbrev. **D.C., DC**

dis·trust (dis trust′) *n.* a lack of trust or of confidence; doubt; suspicion —*vt.* to have no trust or confidence in; doubt; suspect

dis·trust·ful (-fəl) *adj.* distrusting; doubting —**distrustful of** suspicious of —**dis·trust′ful·ly** *adv.*

dis·turb (dis turb′) *vt.* [< OFr. < L. *disturbare* < *dis-*, intens. + *turbare,* to disorder < *turba,* a mob] 1. to break up the quiet or calm of; agitate 2. to make uneasy or anxious 3. to break up the settled order of 4. to break in on; interrupt 5. to inconvenience —**dis·turb′er** *n.*

dis·turb·ance (-əns) *n.* 1. *a)* a disturbing or being disturbed *b)* any departure from normal 2. anything that disturbs 3. commotion; disorder

di·sul·fide (dī sul′fīd) *n.* a chemical compound of two sulfur atoms united with a single radical or with a single atom of an element

dis·un·ion (dis yōōn′yən) *n.* 1. the ending of union; separation 2. lack of unity; discord

dis·u·nite (dis′yoo nīt′) *vt.* **-nit′ed, -nit′ing** to destroy the unity of; separate —*vi.* to become separated or divided —**dis·u′ni·ty** (-yōō′nə tē) *n.*

dis·use (dis yōōz′; *for n.* -yōōs′) *vt.* **-used′, -us′ing** to stop using —*n.* lack of use

di·syl·la·ble (dī sil′ə b′l, di-; dī′sil′-) *n.* [< Fr. < L. < Gr. < *di-*, two + *syllabē,* SYLLABLE] a word of two syllables —**di·syl·lab·ic** (dī′si lab′ik, di′-) *adj.*

ditch (dich) *n.* [OE. *dic*] a long, narrow channel dug into the earth, as a trough for drainage or irrigation —*vt.* 1. to make a ditch in 2. to cause (a car, etc.) to go into a ditch 3. to set (a disabled aircraft) down on water and abandon it 4. [Slang] to get rid of or get away from —*vi.* 1. to dig a ditch 2. to ditch a disabled plane

dith·er (di*th*′ər) *vi.* [prob. akin to ME. *daderen,* DODDER] to be nervously excited or confused —*n.* a nervously excited or confused condition

dith·y·ramb (dith′ə ram′, -ramb′) *n.* [< L. < Gr. *dithyrambos*] 1. in ancient Greece, a wild choric hymn in honor of Dionysus 2. any wildly emotional speech or writing —**dith′y·ram′bic** *adj., n.*

dit·to (dit′ō) *n., pl.* **-tos** [It. < L. *dictum,* a saying: see DICTUM] 1. the same (as something stated above or before) 2. a duplicate 3. *same as* DITTO MARK —*adv.* as said before; likewise —*vt.* **-toed, -to·ing** 1. to duplicate 2. to indicate repetition by ditto marks 3. to repeat

ditto mark a mark (") used in lists or tables to show that the item above is to be repeated

dit·ty (dit′ē) *n., pl.* **-ties** [< OFr. < L. pp. of *dictare:* see DICTATE] a short, simple song

ditty bag (or **box**) [< ? obs. *dutty,* coarse calico, orig. Anglo-Ind.] a small bag (or box) used as by sailors for carrying sewing equipment, toilet articles, etc.

di·u·ret·ic (dī′yoo ret′ik) *adj.* [< LL. < Gr. < *dia-*, through + *ourein,* to urinate] increasing the secretion and flow of urine —*n.* a diuretic drug or other substance —**di′u·ret′i·cal·ly** *adv.*

di·ur·nal (dī ur′n′l) *adj.* [< L. < *diurnus* < *dies,* day] 1. happening each day; daily 2. of or in the daytime: opposed to NOCTURNAL —**di·ur′nal·ly** *adv.*

div. 1. dividend 2. division 3. divorced

di·va (dē′və) *n., pl.* **-vas;** It. **-ve** (-ve) [It. < L., goddess] a prima donna in grand opera

di·va·gate (dī′və gāt′) *vi.* **-gat′ed, -gat′ing** [< LL. < L. *dis-*, from + *vagari,* to wander] 1. to wander about 2. to digress —**di′va·ga′tion** *n.*

di·va·lent (dī vā′lənt) *adj. Chem. same as* BIVALENT

di·van (dī′van, di van′) *n.* [< Turk. *dīwān* < Per.] a large, low couch or sofa, usually without armrests or back

dive (dīv) *vi.* **dived** or **dove, dived, div′ing** [OE. *dyfan*] 1. to plunge headfirst into water 2. to go under water; submerge, as a submarine 3. to plunge the hand or body suddenly into something *[*to *dive* into a foxhole*]* 4. to bring oneself zestfully into something *[*to *dive* into one's work*]* 5. to make a steep, sudden descent, as an airplane —*vt.* to cause to dive; specif., to send (one's airplane) into a dive —*n.* 1. a plunge into water 2. any sudden plunge 3. a sharp descent, as of an airplane 4. [Colloq.] a cheap, disreputable bar, nightclub, etc. —**take a dive** [Slang] to lose a prizefight purposely by pretending to get knocked out

dive bomber an airplane designed to release bombs while diving at a target —**dive′bomb′** *vt., vi.*

div·er (dīv′ər) *n.* one that dives; specif., *a)* one who works or explores under water *b)* any of several diving water birds, esp. the loon

di·verge (də vurj′, dī-) *vi.* **-verged′, -verg′ing** [ML. *divergere* < L. *dis-*, apart + *vergere,* to turn] 1. to branch off or go in different directions from a common point or from each other 2. to take on gradually a different form *[*customs *diverge]* 3. to depart from a given viewpoint, practice; etc.; differ —*vt.* to make diverge

di·ver·gence (-vur′jəns) *n.* 1. a diverging, or branching off 2. a becoming different in form or kind 3. departure from a particular viewpoint, practice, etc. 4. difference of opinion; disagreement Also **di·ver′gen·cy,** *pl.* **-cies** —**di·ver′gent** *adj.* —**di·ver′gent·ly** *adv.*

di·vers (dī′vərz) *adj.* [OFr.: see ff.] several; various

di·verse (dī vurs′, də-; dī′vurs) *adj.* [OFr. < L. pp. of *divertere* < *dis-*, apart + *vertere,* to turn] 1. different; dissimilar 2. varied —**di·verse′ly** *adv.* —**di·verse′ness** *n.*

di·ver·si·fy (də vur′sə fī′) *vt.* **-fied′, -fy′ing** [see prec. & -FY] 1. to make diverse; give variety to; vary 2. to divide up (investments, liabilities, etc.) among different companies, securities, etc. 3. to expand (a business, etc.) by adding different products to the line, etc. —*vi.* to multiply business operations —**di·ver′si·fi·ca′tion** *n.*

di·ver·sion (də vur′zhən, dī-) *n.* 1. a diverting, or turning aside 2. distraction of attention 3. a pastime

di·ver·sion·ar·y (-er′ē) *adj.* serving to divert or distract *[diversionary* military tactics*]*

di·ver·si·ty (də vur′sə tē, dī-) *n., pl.* **-ties** 1. a being diverse; difference 2. variety

di·vert (-vurt′) *vt.* [< OFr. < L. *divertere:* see DIVERSE] 1. to turn aside (*from* a course, direction, etc.); deflect 2. to amuse; entertain

di·ver·tic·u·li·tis (dī′vər tik′yoo līt′əs) *n.* [see -ITIS] inflammation of a diverticulum

di·ver·tic·u·lum (dī′vər tik′yoo ləm) *n., pl.* **-la** (-lə) [L. < *devertere* < *de-*, from + *vertere,* to turn] *Anat.* a normal or abnormal pouch or sac opening out from a tubular organ or main cavity

di·vert·ing (də vurt′iŋ, dī-) *adj.* that diverts; esp., amusing or entertaining —**di·vert′ing·ly** *adv.*

‡**di·ver·tisse·ment** (dē ver tēs män′; *E.* di vurt′is mənt) *n.* [Fr.] 1. a diversion; amusement 2. a short ballet, etc. as an entr'acte

di·vest (də vest′, dī-) *vt.* [altered < earlier *devest,* ult. < L. *devestire* < *dis-*, from + *vestire,* to dress] 1. to strip (*of* clothing, etc.) 2. to deprive or dispossess (*of* rank, rights, etc.) 3. to rid (*of* something) —**di·vest′i·ture** (-ə chər), **di·vest′ment, di·ves′ture** *n.*

di·vide (də vīd′) *vt.* **-vid′ed, -vid′ing** [< L. *dividere*] 1. to separate into parts; split up 2. to separate into groups; classify 3. to make or keep separate as by a partition 4. to give out in shares; apportion 5. to cause to disagree; alienate 6. *Math.* to separate into equal parts by a divisor 7. *Mech.* to mark off the divisions of; graduate —*vi.* 1. to be or become separate; part 2. to disagree 3. to separate into groups in voting on a question 4. to share 5. *Math.* to do division —*n.* a ridge that divides two drainage areas; watershed —**di·vid′a·ble** *adj.*

di·vid·ed (-id) *adj.* 1. *a)* separated into parts *b)* having a median strip separating traffic *[*a *divided* highway*]* *c)* having indentations reaching to the base or midrib, as some leaves 2. disagreeing

div·i·dend (div′ə dend′) ***n.*** [< L.] **1.** the number or quantity to be divided **2.** *a)* a sum of money to be divided among stockholders, creditors, etc. *b)* a single share of this **3.** a bonus

di·vid·er (də vīd′ər) ***n.*** a person or thing that divides; specif., *a)* [*pl.*] an instrument for dividing lines, etc.; compasses *b)* a set of shelves, etc. used to separate a room into distinct areas

div·i·na·tion (div′ə nā′shən) ***n.*** [< L. < pp. of *divinare:* see ff.] **1.** the act or practice of trying to foretell the future or the unknown by occult means **2.** a prophecy; augury **3.** a successful guess —**di·vin·a·to·ry** (də vin′ə tôr′ē) ***adj.***

di·vine (də vīn′) ***adj.*** [< OFr. < L. *divinus* < *divus,* a god] **1.** of or like God or a god **2.** given or inspired by God; holy; sacred **3.** devoted to God; religious **4.** supremely great, good, etc. **5.** [Colloq.] very pleasing, attractive, etc. —***n.*** **1.** a clergyman **2.** a theologian —***vt.* -vined′, -vin′ing** **1.** to prophesy **2.** to guess; conjecture **3.** to find out by intuition —***vi.*** **1.** to engage in divination **2.** to use a divining rod —**di·vine′ly** ***adv.*** —**di·vin′er** ***n.***

Divine Comedy a long narrative poem in Italian, written (c. 1307–1321) by Dante Alighieri

Divine Office the prayers for the canonical hours

divine right of kings the God-given right of kings to rule, as formerly believed

div·ing bell (dīv′iŋ) a large, hollow, air-filled apparatus in which divers can work under water

diving board a springboard projecting over a swimming pool, lake, etc., for use in diving

diving suit a heavy, waterproof garment worn by divers working under water: it has a detachable helmet into which air is pumped through a hose

divining rod a forked stick alleged to reveal hidden water or minerals by dipping downward

di·vin·i·ty (də vin′ə tē) ***n.,*** *pl.* **-ties** **1.** the quality or condition of being divine **2.** a god; deity **3.** the study of religion; theology —**the Divinity** God

di·vis·i·ble (də viz′ə b′l) ***adj.*** that can be divided, esp. without leaving a remainder —**di·vis′i·bil′i·ty** ***n.***

di·vi·sion (də vizh′ən) ***n.*** **1.** a dividing or being divided **2.** a sharing or distribution **3.** a difference of opinion; disagreement **4.** a separation into groups in voting **5.** anything that divides; partition; boundary **6.** anything separated or distinguished from the larger unit of which it is a part; a section, group, rank, segment, etc. **7.** the process of finding how many times a number (the *divisor*) is contained in another (the *dividend*): the answer is the *quotient* **8.** *Mil.* a major tactical or administrative unit under one command; specif., an army unit larger than a regiment and smaller than a corps —**di·vi′sion·al** ***adj.***

division sign (or **mark**) the symbol (÷), indicating that the preceding number is to be divided by the following number (Ex.: 8 ÷ 4 = 2)

di·vi·sive (də vī′siv, -vis′iv) ***adj.*** causing disagreement or dissension —**di·vi′sive·ly** ***adv.*** —**di·vi′sive·ness** ***n.***

di·vi·sor (də vī′zər) ***n.*** [L.] the number or quantity by which the dividend is divided to produce the quotient

di·vorce (də vôrs′) ***n.*** [OFr. < L. *divortium* < *divertere:* see DIVERSE] **1.** legal dissolution of a marriage **2.** any complete separation or disunion —***vt.* -vorced′, -vorc′ing** **1.** to dissolve legally a marriage between **2.** to separate from (one's spouse) by divorce **3.** to separate; disunite —***vi.*** to get a divorce —**di·vorce′ment** ***n.***

di·vor·cé (də vôr′sā′, -sē′; -vôr′sā, -sē) ***n.*** [Fr.] a divorced man

di·vor·cée, di·vor·cee (-vôr′sā′, -sē′; -vôr′sā, -sē) ***n.*** [Fr.] a divorced woman

div·ot (div′ət) ***n.*** [Scot. dial. < ?] *Golf* a lump of turf dislodged in making a stroke

di·vulge (də vulj′) ***vt.* -vulged′, -vulg′ing** [< L. *divulgare* < *dis-,* apart + *vulgare,* to make public < *vulgus,* the common people] to make known; disclose; reveal —**di·vul′gence** (-vul′jəns), **di·vulge′ment** ***n.*** —**di·vulg′er** ***n.***

div·vy (div′ē) ***vt., vi.* -vied, -vy·ing** [< DIVIDE] [Slang] to share; divide (*up*) —***n.*** [Slang] a division

Dix·ie (dik′sē) ***n.*** [< title of song (1859) by D.D. Emmett, ult. < proper name] the Southern States of the U.S., collectively

Dix·ie·land (-land′) ***adj.*** in, of, or like a style of jazz modified by white New Orleans musicians, with a fast, ragtime tempo —***n.*** **1.** the South; Dixie: also **Dixie Land** **2.** Dixieland jazz

diz·en (diz′'n, dī′z'n) ***vt.*** [MDu. *disen,* to put flax on a distaff < LowG. *diesse,* bunch of flax] [Archaic or Poet.] *same as* BEDIZEN

diz·zy (diz′ē) ***adj.* -zi·er, -zi·est** [OE. *dysig,* foolish] **1.** feeling giddy or unsteady **2.** causing or likely to cause giddiness [*dizzy* heights] **3.** confused; bewildered **4.** [Colloq.] silly —***vt.* -zied, -zy·ing** to make dizzy —**diz′zi·ly** ***adv.*** —**diz′zi·ness** ***n.***

D.J., DJ disc jockey

Dji·bou·ti (ji bo͞ot′ē) country in E Africa, on the Gulf of Aden: 8,500 sq. mi.; pop. 180,000

dkg. decagram; decagrams

dkl. decaliter; decaliters

dkm. decameter; decameters

dl, dl. deciliter; deciliters

D layer the lowest layer of the ionosphere

DM, Dm deutsche mark

dm. decimeter; decimeters

DMZ demilitarized zone

DNA deoxyribonucleic acid

Dne·pr (nē′pər; *Russ.* dnye′pər) river in W U.S.S.R., flowing south & southwest into the Black Sea

Dne·pro·pe·trovsk (dnye′prô pye trôfsk′) city in the Ukrainian S.S.R., on the Dnepr: pop. 837,000

Dnes·tr (nēs′tər; *Russ.* dnyes′tər) river in SW U.S.S.R., flowing southeast into the Black Sea

do[1] (do͞o) ***vt.* did, done, do′ing** [OE. *don*] **1.** *a)* to perform (an action, etc.) [*do* great deeds] *b)* to carry out **2.** to bring to completion; finish [dinner has been *done* for an hour] **3.** to bring about; cause [it *does* no harm] **4.** to exert (efforts, etc.) [*do* your best] **5.** to deal with as is required; attend to [*do* the ironing] **6.** to have as one's occupation; work at **7.** to work out; solve [*do* a problem] **8.** to produce (a play, etc.) [we *did* Hamlet] **9.** to play the role of [she *did* Juliet] **10.** to write (a book), compose (a musical score), etc. **11.** *a)* to cover (distance) [to *do* a mile in four minutes] *b)* to move along at a speed of [to *do* 60 miles an hour] **12.** to give; render [*do* honor to the dead] **13.** to be convenient to; suit [this will *do* me very well] **14.** [Colloq.] to cheat; swindle [you've been *done*] **15.** [Colloq.] to serve (a jail term) **16.** [Slang] to take; ingest; use [to *do* drugs] —***vi.*** **1.** to behave [he *does* well when praised] **2.** to be active; work [*do;* don't talk] **3.** to get along; fare [the patient is *doing* well] **4.** to be adequate or suitable [that necktie will *do*] **5.** to take place [anything *doing* tonight?] Auxiliary uses of *do:* **1.** to give emphasis [please *do* stay] **2.** to ask a question [*did* you write?] **3.** to help express negation [*do* not go] **4.** to serve as a substitute verb [love me as I *do* (love) you] **5.** to form inverted constructions after some adverbs [little *did* he realize] —***n.,*** *pl.* **do's** or **dos** **1.** [Colloq.] a party or social event **2.** something to be done —**do by** to act toward or for —**do for** [Colloq.] to ruin; destroy —**do in** [Slang] to kill —**do over** [Colloq.] to redecorate —**do up** [Colloq.] **1.** to clean and prepare (laundry, etc.) **2.** to wrap up; tie up **3.** to arrange (the hair) off the neck and shoulders —**do with** to make use of —**do without** to get along without —**have to do with** **1.** to be related to **2.** to deal with —**make do** to get along with what is available

do[2] (dō) ***n.*** [It.: used instead of earlier *ut:* see GAMUT] *Music* a syllable representing the first or last tone of the diatonic scale

do. ditto

D.O. Doctor of Osteopathy

do·a·ble (do͞o′ə b'l) ***adj.*** that can be done

dob·bin (däb′in) ***n.*** [< *Dobbin,* nickname for ROBERT (sense 1)] a horse, esp. a plodding, patient one

Do·ber·man pin·scher (dō′bər mən pin′shər) [< G.] a breed of large dog, with smooth, dark hair and tan markings

dob·son·fly (däb′s'n flī′) ***n.,*** *pl.* **-flies′** a large insect whose larvae live in water: some males develop huge mandibles

doc (däk) ***n.*** [Slang] doctor: often used as a general term of address like *Mac, Bud, Jack,* etc.

doc. document

doc·ile (däs′'l) ***adj.*** [Fr. < L. *docilis* < *docere,* to teach] **1.** [Now Rare] easy to teach **2.** easy to manage or discipline; tractable —**doc′ile·ly** ***adv.*** —**do·cil·i·ty** (dä sil′ə tē) ***n.***

dock[1] (däk) ***n.*** [< MDu. *docke,* channel < It. *doccia:* see DOUCHE] **1.** a large excavated basin with floodgates, for receiving ships between voyages **2.** *a)* a landing pier; wharf *b)* the water between two piers **3.** a platform at which trucks or freight cars are loaded and unloaded **4.** a building or area for servicing aircraft —***vt.*** **1.** to pilot (a ship) to a dock **2.** to join (vehicles) together in outer space —***vi.*** **1.** to come into a dock **2.** to join up with another vehicle in outer space

dock[2] (däk) ***n.*** [< Fl. *dok,* cage] the place where the accused stands or sits in court

dock[3] (däk) ***n.*** [OE. *docce*] a coarse weed of the buckwheat family, with large leaves

dock[4] (däk) ***n.*** [< OE. *-docca* or ON. *dockr*] **1.** the solid part of an animal's tail **2.** an animal's bobbed tail —***vt.*** **1.** to cut off the end of (a tail); bob **2.** to bob the tail of **3.** to deduct from (wages, etc.) **4.** to deduct from the wages of **5.** to remove part of —**dock′er** ***n.***

dock·age[1] (däk′ij) ***n.*** **1.** docking accommodations **2.** the fee for this **3.** the docking of ships

dock·age[2] (däk′ij) ***n.*** a docking, or cutting off

dock·et (däk′it) ***n.*** [earlier *doggette,* register] **1.** a summary, as of legal decisions **2.** a list of cases to be tried by a law court **3.** any list of things to be done; agenda **4.** a label listing the contents of a package, directions, etc. —***vt.*** **1.** to enter in a docket **2.** to put a docket on; label

dock·side (däk′sīd′) ***n.*** the area alongside a dock

dock·yard (-yärd′) ***n.*** a place with docks, machinery, etc. for repairing or building ships

doc·tor (däk′tər) ***n.*** [< OFr. or < L. *doctor,* teacher < pp. of *docere,* to teach] **1.** orig., a teacher or learned man **2.** a person on whom a university or college has conferred any of several high degrees *[Doctor* of Philosophy*]* **3.** a physician or surgeon (M.D.) **4.** a person licensed to practice any of the healing arts, as an osteopath, dentist, veterinarian, etc. **5.** a witch doctor or medicine man —***vt.*** [Colloq.] **1.** to try to heal; apply medicine to **2.** to repair; mend **3.** to tamper with —***vi.*** [Colloq.] **1.** to practice medicine **2.** to undergo medical treatment, take medicine, etc. —**doc′tor·al** (-əl) ***adj.***

doc·tor·ate (-it) ***n.*** the degree or status of doctor conferred by a university or college

doc·tri·naire (däk′trə ner′) ***n.*** [Fr.] a person who dogmatically tries to apply theories regardless of the practical problems involved —***adj.*** adhering to a doctrine or theory in an unyielding, dogmatic way —**doc′tri·nair′ism** ***n.***

doc·trine (däk′trən) ***n.*** [< L. *doctrina* < *doctor:* see DOCTOR] **1.** something taught; teachings **2.** something taught as the principles of a religion, political party, etc.; tenet or tenets; dogma **3.** a principle of law **4.** a statement of basic policy *[*the Monroe *Doctrine]* —**doc′tri·nal** ***adj.*** —**doc′tri·nal·ly** ***adv.***

doc·u·ment (däk′yə mənt; *for v.* -ment′) ***n.*** [OFr. < L. *documentum,* lesson, proof < *docere,* to teach] **1.** anything printed, written, etc., relied upon to record or prove something **2.** any proof —***vt.*** **1.** to provide (a book, etc.) with documents or supporting references **2.** to prove or support by reference to documents —**doc′u·men′tal** ***adj.***

doc·u·men·ta·ry (däk′yə men′tə rē) ***adj.*** **1.** of, in, supported by, or serving as a document or documents **2.** dramatically showing or analyzing news events, social conditions, etc., with little or no fictionalization —***n.,*** *pl.* **-ries** a documentary film, television show, etc.

doc·u·men·ta·tion (-mən tā′shən, -men-) ***n.*** **1.** the supplying of documents or supporting references **2.** the documents or references supplied **3.** the collecting, abstracting, and coding of printed or written information for future reference

dod·der (däd′ər) ***vi.*** [ME. *daderen*] **1.** to shake or tremble, as from old age **2.** to totter —**dod′der·ing** ***adj.***

do·dec·a- [< Gr. *dōdeka,* twelve] *a prefix meaning* twelve: also, before a vowel, **do·dec-**

do·dec·a·gon (dō dek′ə gän′) ***n.*** [< Gr.: see DODECA- & -GON] a plane figure with twelve angles and twelve sides

do·dec·a·he·dron (dō′dek ə hē′drən) ***n.,*** *pl.* **-drons, -dra** (-drə) [< Gr.: see DODECA- & -HEDRON] a solid figure with twelve plane faces —**do′dec·a·he′dral** ***adj.***

Do·dec·a·nese (dō dek′ə nēz′, -nēs′) group of Greek islands in the Aegean

dodge (däj) ***vi.*** **dodged, dodg′ing** [? akin to Scot. *dod,* to jog] **1.** to move or twist quickly aside, as to avoid a blow **2.** to use tricks or evasions —***vt.*** **1.** to avoid by moving quickly aside **2.** to evade by trickery, cleverness, etc. **3.** to avoid meeting —***n.*** **1.** a dodging **2.** a trick used in evading or cheating —**dodg′y** ***adj.*** **dodg′i·er, dodg′i·est**

dodg·er (-ər) ***n.*** **1.** a person who dodges **2.** a tricky, dishonest person **3.** a small handbill

do·do (dō′dō) ***n.,*** *pl.* **-dos, -does** [Port. *doudo,* lit., foolish, stupid] **1.** a large bird, now extinct, that had rudimentary wings useless for flying: formerly found on Mauritius **2.** an old-fashioned person; fogy

DODO
(2 ft. high)

Doe a name (*John Doe*) used in legal papers, etc. to refer to any person whose name is unknown

doe (dō) ***n.,*** *pl.* **does, doe:** see PLURAL, II, D, 1 [OE. *da*] the female of the deer, or of the antelope, rabbit, or almost any other animal the male of which is called a buck

do·er (do͞o′ər) ***n.*** **1.** a person who does something **2.** a person who gets things done

does (duz) *3d pers. sing., pres. indic., of* DO[1]

doe·skin (dō′skin′) ***n.*** **1.** the skin of a female deer **2.** leather made from this or, now usually, from lambskin **3.** a fine, soft, smooth woolen cloth

does·n't (duz′′nt) does not

do·est (do͞o′ist) *archaic 2d pers. sing., pres. indic., of* DO[1]: *used with* thou

do·eth (-ith) *archaic 3d pers. sing., pres. indic., of* DO[1]: *used with* thou

doff (däf, dôf) ***vt.*** [ME. *doffen* < *don of:* see DO[1] & OFF] **1.** to take off (clothes, etc.); esp., to remove or raise (one's hat) **2.** to put aside or discard

dog (dôg, däg) ***n.,*** *pl.* **dogs, dog:** see PLURAL, II, D, 1 [OE. *docga*] **1.** any of a large group of domesticated animals belonging to the same family as the fox, wolf, jackal, etc. **2.** the male of any of these **3.** a mean, contemptible fellow **4.** a prairie dog, dogfish, or other animal thought to resemble a dog **5.** an andiron **6.** [Colloq.] a boy or man *[*lucky *dog]* **7.** [*pl.*] [Slang] feet **8.** [Slang] *a)* an unattractive or unpopular person *b)* an unsatisfactory thing or unsuccessful venture **9.** [D-] *Astron.* either of the constellations Great Dog or Little Dog **10.** *Mech.* a device for holding or grappling —***vt.*** **dogged, dog′ging** to follow or hunt like a dog —***adv.*** very; completely *[dog-*tired*]* —**a dog's age** [Colloq.] a long time —**a dog's life** a wretched existence —**dog eat dog** ruthless competition —**dog in the manger** a person who keeps others from using something which he cannot or will not use —**go to the dogs** [Colloq.] to deteriorate; degenerate —**put on the dog** [Slang] to make a show of being very elegant, wealthy, etc.

dog biscuit a hard biscuit containing ground bones, meat, etc., for feeding dogs

dog·cart (-kärt′) ***n.*** **1.** a small, light cart drawn by dogs **2.** a small, light, open carriage having two seats arranged back to back

dog·catch·er (-kach′ər) ***n.*** a local official whose work is catching and impounding stray animals

dog days the hot, humid days in July and August

doge (dōj) ***n.*** [It. < L. *dux,* leader] the chief magistrate of either of the former republics of Venice and Genoa

dog·ear (dôg′ir′, däg′-) ***n.*** a turned-down corner of the leaf of a book —***vt.*** to turn down the corner or corners of (a leaf in a book) —**dog′eared′** ***adj.***

dog·face (-fās′) ***n.*** [Slang] an enlisted man in the army, esp. an infantryman

dog·fight (-fīt′) ***n.*** a rough, violent fight, as between dogs; specif., *Mil.* combat as between fighter planes at close quarters

dog·fish (-fish′) ***n.,*** *pl.* **-fish′, -fish′es:** see FISH **1.** any of various small sharks **2.** any of several other fishes, as the bowfin

dog·ged (dôg′id, däg′-) ***adj.*** [see DOG] not giving in readily; persistent; stubborn —**dog′ged·ly** ***adv.*** —**dog′ged·ness** ***n.***

dog·ger·el (-ər əl) ***n.*** [prob. < It. *doga,* barrel stave] trivial, poorly constructed verse, usually of a comic sort; jingle —***adj.*** designating or of such verse Also **dog′grel** (-rəl)

dog·gie bag (dôg′ē, däg′-) a bag supplied to a patron of a restaurant, in which he may place leftovers as to take to his dog

dog·gish (-ish) ***adj.*** of or like a dog —**dog′gish·ly** ***adv.*** —**dog′gish·ness** ***n.***

dog·gone (dôg′gôn′, däg′gän′) ***interj.*** damn! darn! —***vt.*** **-goned′, -gon′ing** [Colloq.] to damn —***n.*** [Colloq.] a damn —***adj.*** [Colloq.] damned: also **dog′goned′**

dog·gy, dog·gie (-ē) ***n.,*** *pl.* **-gies** a little dog: a child's word —***adj.*** **-gi·er, -gi·est** **1.** of or like a dog **2.** [Colloq.] stylish and showy

dog·house (-hous′) ***n.*** a dog's shelter; kennel —**in the doghouse** [Slang] in disfavor

do·gie, do·gy (dō′gē) ***n.*** [< ?] in the western U.S., a stray or motherless calf

dog·leg (dôg′leg′, däg′-) ***n.*** a sharp angle or bend like that formed by a dog's hind leg, as in a golf fairway

dog·ma (dôg′mə, däg′-) ***n.,*** *pl.* **-mas, -ma·ta** (-mə tə) [L. < Gr. < *dokein,* to think] **1.** a doctrine; tenet; belief **2.** doctrines, tenets, or beliefs, collectively **3.** a positive, arrogant assertion of opinion **4.** *Theol.* a doctrine or body of doctrines formally and authoritatively affirmed

dog·mat·ic (dôg mat′ik, däg-) ***adj.*** **1.** of or like dogma **2.** asserted without proof **3.** stating opinion in a positive or arrogant manner: also **dog·mat′i·cal** —**dog·mat′i·cal·ly** ***adv.***

dog·ma·tism (dôg′mə tiz'm, däg′-) ***n.*** dogmatic assertion of opinion, usually without reference to evidence —**dog′ma·tist** ***n.***

dog·ma·tize (-tīz′) ***vi.*** **-tized′, -tiz′ing** to speak or write dogmatically —***vt.*** to formulate or express as dogma —**dog′ma·tiz′er** ***n.***

dog·nap (-nap′) ***vt.*** **-napped′** or **-naped′, -nap′ping** or **-nap′ing** [DOG + (KID)NAP] to steal (a dog), esp. in order to sell it to a medical research laboratory —**dog′nap′per, dog′nap′er** ***n.***

do-good·er (do͞o′goo͝d′ər) ***n.*** [Colloq.] a person who seeks to correct social ills in an idealistic, but usually impractical way —**do′-good′, do′-good′ing *adj.*** —**do′-good′ism *n.***
dog rose a European wild rose with single, pink flowers and hooked spines
dog sled (or **sledge**) a sled (or sledge) drawn by dogs
Dog Star **1.** the brightest star in the constellation Canis Major; Sirius **2.** Procyon
dog tag **1.** an identification tag or license tag for a dog **2.** [Slang] a military identification tag worn about the neck
dog·tooth (dôg′to͞oth′, däg′-) ***n.,*** *pl.* **-teeth′** a canine tooth
dogtooth violet **1.** a small American plant of the lily family, with a yellow or white flower **2.** a European plant with a purple or rose flower Also **dog's-tooth violet**
dog·trot (-trät′) ***n.*** a slow, easy trot
dog·watch (-wäch′, -wôch′) ***n.*** *Naut.* a duty period, either from 4 to 6 P.M. or from 6 to 8 P.M.
dog·wood (-woo͝d′) ***n.*** **1.** a small tree of eastern U.S., with groups of small flowers surrounded by four large white or pink bracts **2.** its hard wood
doi·ly (doi′lē) ***n.,*** *pl.* **-lies** [after name of a 17th-c. London draper] a small mat, as of lace or paper, used to protect or decorate a surface
do·ings (do͞o′iŋz) ***n.pl.*** things done; actions, events, etc.
do-it-your·self (do͞o′it yoor self′) ***n.*** the practice of constructing, repairing, redecorating, etc. by oneself instead of hiring another to do it —***adj.*** of, used for, or engaged in do-it-yourself
dol. *pl.* **dols.** dollar
dol·drums (däl′drəmz, dōl′-) ***n.pl.*** [< ? ME. *dul,* DULL] **1.** low spirits; dull, listless feeling **2.** sluggishness; stagnation **3.** equatorial ocean regions noted for dead calms and light, fluctuating winds
dole[1] (dōl) ***n.*** [OE. *dal*] **1.** a giving out of money or food to those in need **2.** that which is thus given out **3.** anything given out sparingly **4.** a form of payment by a government to the unemployed —***vt.*** **doled, dol′ing** to give sparingly or as a dole —**on the dole** receiving a dole (sense 4)
dole[2] (dōl) ***n.*** [see ff.] [Archaic] sorrow
dole·ful (dōl′fəl) ***adj.*** [< OFr. < VL. < L. *dolere,* to suffer + *-ful,* -FUL] full of sorrow or sadness; mournful —**dole′ful·ly *adv.*** —**dole′ful·ness *n.***
dol·i·cho·ce·phal·ic (däl′i kō′sə fal′ik) ***adj.*** [< Gr. *dolichos,* long + -CEPHALIC] having a relatively long head: also **dol′i·cho·ceph′a·lous** (-sef′ə ləs) : see CEPHALIC INDEX —**dol′i·cho·ceph′a·ly** (-ə lē) ***n.***
doll (däl) ***n.*** [< *Doll,* nickname for DOROTHY] **1.** a child's toy made to resemble a human being **2.** a pretty but silly young woman **3.** a pretty child **4.** [Slang] *a)* any young woman *b)* any lovable person —***vt., vi.*** [Colloq.] to dress stylishly or showily (with *up*)
dol·lar (däl′ər) ***n.*** [< LowG. & Early ModDu. < G. *thaler,* contr. < *Joachimsthaler,* coin made at *Joachimstal,* Bohemia] **1.** the monetary unit of the U.S., equal to 100 cents: symbol, $ **2.** the monetary unit of various other countries, as of Canada, Australia, Ethiopia, etc.: see MONETARY UNITS, table **3.** a monetary unit used only in trade, as the British Hong Kong dollar **4.** a coin or paper bill of the value of a dollar
dollar diplomacy the use of the economic power of a government to promote in other countries the business interests of its corporations, etc.
dollar sign (or **mark**) a symbol, $, for dollar(s)
dol·lop (däl′əp) ***n.*** [< ?] **1.** a soft mass, as of some food **2.** a splash, jigger, etc. of liquid **3.** a small amount
dol·ly (däl′ē) ***n.,*** *pl.* **-lies** **1.** a doll: child's word **2.** any of several kinds of low, flat, wheeled frames or platforms for moving heavy objects —***vi.*** **-lied, -ly·ing** to move a camera on a dolly (*in, out,* etc.) as in televising —***vt.*** to move on a dolly
dol·man sleeve (däl′mən, dōl′-) [< Fr. < Turk. *dolama,* long robe] a kind of sleeve for a woman's coat or dress, tapering from a wide opening at the armhole to a narrow one at the wrist
dol·men (däl′mən, dōl′-) ***n.*** [Fr. < Bret. *taol,* a table + *men,* stone] a prehistoric monument formed by a large, flat stone laid across upright stones
do·lo·mite (dō′lə mīt′, däl′ə-) ***n.*** [after the Fr. geologist *Dolomieu* (1750–1801)] a common rock-forming mineral, $CaMg(CO_3)_2$
do·lor (dō′lər) ***n.*** [< OFr. < L. *dolor* < *dolere,* to suffer] [Poet.] sorrow; grief
Do·lor·es (də lôr′əs) [Sp. < *María de los Dolores,* lit., Mary of the sorrows] a feminine name
do·lor·ous (dō′lər əs, däl′ər-) ***adj.*** **1.** sorrowful or sad; mournful **2.** painful —**do′lor·ous·ly *adv.***
dol·phin (däl′fən, dôl′-) ***n.*** [< OFr. < L. < Gr. *delphis* (gen. *delphinos*)] **1.** any of several water-dwelling mammals, with numerous teeth and often a beaklike snout **2.** either of two swift marine game fishes that change to bright colors out of water

BOTTLE-NOSED DOLPHIN (70–160 in. long)

dolt (dōlt) ***n.*** [prob. < ME. pp. of *dullen,* to dull] a stupid, slow-witted person; blockhead —**dolt′ish *adj.*** —**dolt′ish·ly *adv.*** —**dolt′ish·ness *n.***
-dom (dəm) [OE. *dom,* state] *a suffix meaning:* **1.** the rank, position, or dominion of *[kingdom]* **2.** fact or state of being *[martyrdom]* **3.** a total of all who are *[officialdom]*
dom. **1.** domestic **2.** dominion
do·main (dō mān′, də-) ***n.*** [< MFr. < L. < *dominus,* a lord] **1.** territory under one government or ruler **2.** land belonging to one person; estate **3.** field of activity or influence
dome (dōm) ***n.*** [< Fr. < Pr. < LL. < Gr. *dōma,* housetop, house] **1.** a hemispherical roof or one formed by a series of rounded arches or vaults on a round or many-sided base **2.** any dome-shaped structure **3.** [Slang] the head —***vt.*** **domed, dom′ing** **1.** to cover as with a dome **2.** to form into a dome —***vi.*** to swell out like a dome
do·mes·tic (də mes′tik) ***adj.*** [< OFr. < L. *domesticus* < *domus,* house] **1.** of the home or family *[domestic joys]* **2.** of one's own country or the country referred to **3.** made in the home country; native **4.** domesticated; tame: said of animals **5.** devoted to home and family life —***n.*** a servant for the home, as a maid —**do·mes′ti·cal·ly *adv.***
do·mes·ti·cate (də mes′tə kāt′) ***vt.*** **-cat′ed, -cat′ing** **1.** to accustom to home life; make domestic **2.** *a)* to tame (wild animals) *b)* to adapt (wild plants) to home cultivation **3.** to naturalize (a custom, word, etc.) from another country —***vi.*** to become domestic —**do·mes′ti·ca′tion *n.***
do·mes·tic·i·ty (dō′mes tis′ə tē) ***n.,*** *pl.* **-ties** **1.** home life; family life **2.** devotion to home and family life **3.** [*pl.*] household affairs
domestic science *same as* HOME ECONOMICS
dom·i·cile (däm′ə sīl′, -sil; dō′mə-) ***n.*** [OFr. < L. < *domus,* house] a customary dwelling place; home; residence —***vt.*** **-ciled′, -cil′ing** to establish (oneself or another) in a domicile —**dom′i·cil′i·ar′y** (-sil′ē er′ē) ***adj.***
dom·i·nance (däm′ə nəns) ***n.*** a dominating; being dominant; control; authority: also **dom′i·nan·cy**
dom·i·nant (-nənt) ***adj.*** **1.** dominating; ruling; prevailing **2.** *Genetics* designating or of that one of any pair of allelic characters which, when both are present in the germ plasm, dominates over the other and appears in the organism: opposed to RECESSIVE **3.** *Music* of or based upon the fifth note of a diatonic scale —***n.*** *Music* the fifth note of a diatonic scale —**dom′i·nant·ly *adv.***
dom·i·nate (-nāt′) ***vt., vi.*** **-nat′ed, -nat′ing** [< L. pp. of *dominari,* to rule < *dominus,* a master] **1.** to rule or control by superior power or influence **2.** to tower over; rise high above (the surroundings, etc.) —**dom′i·na′tion *n.*** —**dom′i·na′tive** (-nāt′iv) ***adj.*** —**dom′i·na′tor *n.***
dom·i·neer (däm′ə nir′) ***vi., vt.*** [< Du. < Fr. < L.: see prec.] to rule (*over*) in a harsh or arrogant way; tyrannize
dom·i·neer·ing (-iŋ) ***adj.*** overbearing; tyrannical
Dom·i·nic (däm′ə nik) [L. *Dominicus,* lit., belonging to a lord < *dominus,* a master] **1.** a masculine name **2.** Saint, 1170–1221; Sp. priest: founder of the Dominican order
Dom·i·ni·ca (däm′ə nē′kə, də min′i kə) a country that is an island in the Windward group of the West Indies: 290 sq. mi.; pop. 80,000
Do·min·i·can (də min′i kən) ***adj.*** **1.** of Saint Dominic or of a mendicant order founded by him **2.** of the Dominican Republic —***n.*** **1.** a friar or nun of one of the Dominican orders **2.** a native or inhabitant of the Dominican Republic
Dominican Republic country occupying the E part of Hispaniola, in the West Indies: 18,816 sq. mi.; pop. 4,012,000; cap. Santo Domingo
dom·i·nie (däm′ə nē) ***n.*** [< vocative case (*domine*) of L. *dominus,* a master] **1.** in Scotland, a schoolmaster **2.** [Colloq.] a clergyman
do·min·ion (də min′yən) ***n.*** [< ML. *dominio* < L. *dominus,* a lord] **1.** rule or power to rule; sovereignty **2.** a governed territory or country **3.** [**D-**] formerly, any of certain self-governing member nations of the British Commonwealth of Nations
Dominion Day in Canada, July 1, a legal holiday, the anni-

versary of the proclamation in 1867 of the establishment of the Dominion of Canada

dom·i·no (däm′ə nō′) ***n.,*** *pl.* **-noes′, -nos′** [Fr. & It. < dat. of L. *dominus,* a lord] **1.** a loose cloak with wide sleeves, hood, and mask, worn at masquerades **2.** a small mask for the eyes; half mask **3.** one dressed in such a cloak or mask **4.** a small, oblong piece of wood, etc. marked with dots **5.** [*pl., with sing. v.*] a game played with such pieces

DOMINOES

domino theory the theory that a certain result **(domino effect)** will follow a certain cause like a row of upright dominoes falling if only one is pushed; specif., the theory that if a nation becomes Communist, the nations nearby will also become Communist

Don (dän; *Russ.* dôn) river of the C European R.S.F.S.R., flowing south into the Sea of Azov

don[1] (dän) ***n.*** [Sp. < L. *dominus,* master] **1.** [**D-**] Sir; Mr.: a Spanish title of respect **2.** a Spanish nobleman or gentleman **3.** a distinguished man **4.** [Colloq.] a head, tutor, or fellow of any college of Oxford or Cambridge

don[2] (dän) ***vt.*** **donned, don′ning** [contr. of *do on*] to put on (a garment, etc.)

‡**Do·ña** (dô′nyä) ***n.*** [Sp. < L. *domina,* mistress] **1.** Lady; Madam: a Spanish title of respect **2.** [**d-**] a Spanish lady

Don·ald (dän′′ld) [Ir. *Donghal,* lit., brown stranger (or ? Gael. *Domhnall,* lit., world ruler)] a masculine name: dim. *Don*

do·nate (dō′nāt, dō nāt′) ***vt., vi.*** **-nat·ed, -nat·ing** [prob. back-formation < DONATION] to give or contribute, as to some cause —**do′na·tor *n.***

Do·na·tel·lo (dän′ə tel′ō) (born *Donato di Niccolò di Betto Bardi*) 1386?–1466; It. sculptor

do·na·tion (dō nā′shən) ***n.*** [< L. < pp. of *donare* < *donum,* gift] **1.** the act of donating **2.** a gift or contribution

done (dun) *pp. of* DO[1] —***adj.*** **1.** completed **2.** sufficiently cooked **3.** socially acceptable —**done (for)** [Colloq.] dead, ruined, finished, etc. —**done in** [Colloq.] exhausted

do·nee (dō nē′) ***n.*** one who receives a donation

Do·nets (də nets′; *Russ.* dô nyets′) river in SW European U.S.S.R., flowing into the Don

Do·netsk (dô nyetsk′) city in SE Ukrainian S.S.R., in the Donets River valley: pop. 855,000

dong[1] (dôŋ, däŋ) ***n.*** [echoic] a sound of, or like that of, a large bell

dong[2] (däŋ) ***n.*** *see* MONETARY UNITS, table (Vietnam)

Don·i·zet·ti (dän′ə zet′ē), **Ga·e·ta·no** (gä e tä′nō) 1797–1848; It. composer of operas

don·jon (dun′jən, dän′-) ***n.*** [old sp. of DUNGEON] the heavily fortified inner tower of a castle

Don Ju·an (dän′ jo͞o′ən, dän′ wän′; *Sp.* dôn Hwän′) **1.** *Sp. Legend* a dissolute nobleman and seducer of women **2.** any man who seduces women; libertine

don·key (däŋ′kē, dôŋ′-, duŋ′-) ***n.,*** *pl.* **-keys** [< ? DUNCAN or < ? DUN[1]] **1.** a domesticated ass **2.** a stupid or stubborn person **3.** a small steam engine: in full, **donkey engine**

Don·na (dän′ə) [It. < L. *domina,* mistress] a feminine name —***n.*** (*It.* dôn′nä) **1.** Lady; Madam: an Italian title of respect **2.** [**d-**] an Italian lady

Donne (dun), **John** 1573–1631; Eng. poet

don·nish (dän′ish) ***adj.*** of or like a university don —**don′nish·ly *adv.*** —**don′nish·ness *n.***

don·ny·brook (dän′ē broo͝k′) ***n.*** [< a fair formerly held at *Donnybrook,* Ireland: scene of many fights] [Colloq.] a rough, rowdy fight or free-for-all

do·nor (dō′nər) ***n.*** [< Anglo-Fr. < L. *donator*] **1.** one who donates; giver **2.** one from whom blood for transfusion, tissue for grafting, etc. is taken

Don Qui·xo·te (dän′ kē hōt′ē, dän′ kwik′sət; *Sp.* dôn′kē Hô′te) **1.** a satirical romance by Cervantes **2.** the chivalrous, unrealistic hero of this romance

don't (dōnt) **1.** do not **2.** does not: in this sense now generally considered substandard

do·nut (dō′nut′) ***n.*** *informal sp. for* DOUGHNUT

doo·dad (do͞o′dad′) ***n.*** [fanciful extension of DO[1]] [Colloq.] **1.** a trinket **2.** any small object or device whose name does not readily occur to one

doo·dle (do͞od′′l) ***vi.*** **-dled, -dling** [G. *dudeln,* to play (the bagpipe), hence to trifle] to scribble or draw aimlessly, esp. when the attention is elsewhere —***n.*** a mark, design, etc. made in doodling —**doo′dler *n.***

doo·hick·ey (do͞o′hik′ē) ***n.*** [fanciful extension of DO[1]] [Colloq.] any small object or device whose name is not known or temporarily forgotten

doom (do͞om) ***n.*** [OE. *dom*] **1.** a judgment; esp., a sentence of condemnation **2.** destiny; fate **3.** tragic fate; ruin or death —***vt.*** **1.** to pass judgment on; condemn **2.** to destine to a tragic fate **3.** to ordain as a penalty

dooms·day (do͞omz′dā′) ***n.*** **1.** *same as* JUDGMENT DAY **2.** any day of judgment

door (dôr) ***n.*** [OE. *dor, duru*] **1.** a movable structure for opening or closing an entrance, as to a building, room, closet, etc.: most doors turn on hinges, slide in grooves, or revolve on an axis **2.** the room or building to which a particular door belongs [two *doors* down the hall] **3.** *same as* DOORWAY —**lay at the door of** to blame (a person) for —**out of doors** outdoors —**show (someone) the door** to command (someone) to leave

door·bell (dôr′bel′) ***n.*** a bell rung by someone wishing to enter a building or room

door·jamb (-jam′) ***n.*** a vertical piece of wood, etc. forming the side of a doorway: also **door′post′** (-pōst′)

door·keep·er (-kēp′ər) ***n.*** a person guarding the entrance of a house, hotel, etc.; porter

door·knob (-näb′) ***n.*** a small knob or lever on a door, usually for releasing the latch

door·man (-man′, -mən) ***n.,*** *pl.* **-men** (-men′, -mən) a man whose work is opening the door of a building for those who enter or leave, hailing taxicabs, etc.

door·mat (-mat′) ***n.*** a mat to wipe the shoes on before entering a house, room, etc.

door·nail (-nāl′) ***n.*** a large-headed nail used in studding some doors —**dead as a doornail** dead beyond a doubt

door·plate (-plāt′) ***n.*** a plate on an entrance door, bearing the number, a name, etc.

door prize a prize given by lottery to one or more of those attending some gathering

door·sill (-sil′) ***n.*** a length of wood, masonry, etc. placed beneath a door; threshold

door·step (-step′) ***n.*** a step that leads from an outer door to a path, lawn, etc.

door·stop (-stäp′) ***n.*** any device for controlling or stopping the closing of a door

door-to-door (-tə dôr′) ***adj., adv.*** from one home to the next, calling on each in turn

door·way (-wā′) ***n.*** **1.** an opening in a wall that can be closed by a door **2.** any means of access

door·yard (-yärd′) ***n.*** a yard onto which a door of a house opens

doo·zy (do͞o′zē) ***n.,*** *pl.* **-zies** [< ?] [Slang] anything outstanding of its kind

dope (dōp) ***n.*** [Du. *doop,* sauce < *doopen,* to dip] **1.** any thick liquid or paste used as a lubricant or absorbent **2.** a varnish or filler, as for protecting the cloth covering of airplane wings **3.** any additive, as a food preservative **4.** [Slang] any drug or narcotic, or such drugs collectively **5.** [Slang] a slow-witted or stupid person **6.** [Slang] information, esp. as used for predicting —***vt.*** **doped, dop′ing** **1.** to give dope to **2.** to drug or stupefy **3.** to introduce an adulterant or additive into —**dope out** [Colloq.] to figure out or work out —**dop′er *n.***

dope·ster (dōp′stər) ***n.*** [Colloq.] an analyzer or predictor of trends in politics, sports, etc.

dop·ey, dop·y (dō′pē) ***adj.*** **dop′i·er, dop′i·est** [Slang] **1.** under the influence of a narcotic **2.** lethargic or stupid —**dop′i·ness *n.***

Dor·a (dôr′ə) [dim. of DOROTHEA] a feminine name

Do·ré (dô *rā′*), **(Paul) Gus·tave** (güs tàv′) 1832?–83; Fr. artist

Dor·ic (dôr′ik, där′-) ***adj.*** [< L. < Gr. *Dorikos,* of *Dōris:* see ff. etym.] designating or of the simplest of the classic orders of architecture, distinguished by fluted, heavy columns with simple capitals: cf. CORINTHIAN, IONIC

DORIC CAPITAL

Dor·is (-is) [L. < Gr. *Dōris,* an ancient region of Greece] a feminine name

dorm (dôrm) ***n.*** [Colloq.] *same as* DORMITORY

dor·mant (dôr′mənt) ***adj.*** [OFr. prp. of *dormir* < L. *dormire,* to sleep] **1.** sleeping **2.** as if asleep; quiet; still **3.** inactive, as some animals or plants in winter —**dor′man·cy** (-mən sē) ***n.***

dor·mer (dôr′mər) ***n.*** [< OFr. < L. *dormitorium:* see ff.] **1.** a window set upright in a sloping roof **2.** the roofed projection in which this window is set Also **dormer window**

DORMER

dor·mi·to·ry (dôr′mə tôr′ē) ***n.,*** *pl.* **-ries** [L. *dormitorium* < pp. of *dormire,* to sleep] **1.** a room with sleeping accommodations for a number of people **2.** a building with many rooms that provide sleeping and living accommodations for a number of people, as at a college

dor·mouse (dôr′mous′) ***n.,*** *pl.* **-mice′** (-mīs′) [ME. *dormous* ? altered by folk etym. (after *mous,* MOUSE) < OFr.

dormeuse, sleepy < *dormir:* see DORMANT] a small, old-world rodent that resembles a squirrel

Dor·o·the·a (dôr′ə thē′ə, där′-) [L. < Gr. *Dōrothea,* lit., gift of God < *dōron,* gift + *theos,* God] a feminine name: dim. *Dolly, Dora, Dotty*

Dor·o·thy (dôr′ə thē, där′-) [var. of prec.] a feminine name

dor·sal (dôr′s'l) ***adj.*** [< ML. < L. < *dorsum,* the back] of, on, or near the back —**dor′sal·ly** ***adv.***

Dort·mund (dôrt′moont; *E.* dôrt′mənd) city in W West Germany: pop. 648,000

do·ry (dôr′ē) ***n.,*** *pl.* **-ries** [AmInd. (Central America) *dori,* a dugout] a small, flat-bottomed fishing boat with high sides

dos·age (dōs′ij) ***n.*** **1.** a dosing or being dosed **2.** the system to be followed in taking doses, as of medicine **3.** the amount used in a dose

dose (dōs) ***n.*** [OFr. < ML. < Gr. *dosis,* orig., a giving < *didonai,* to give] **1.** an amount of medicine to be taken at one time or at stated intervals **2.** amount of a punishment or other unpleasant experience undergone at one time **3.** the amount of ionizing radiation delivered to a specified area or body part —***vt.*** **dosed, dos′ing** to give doses of medicine to —***vi.*** to take a dose of medicine

do·sim·e·ter (dō sim′ə tər) ***n.*** [see DOSE & -METER] a device for measuring radiation a person has absorbed

dos·si·er (däs′ē ā′, dôs′-) ***n.*** [Fr. < *dos,* the back: so named because labeled on the back] a collection of documents about some person or matter

dost (dust) *archaic 2d pers. sing., pres. indic., of* DO[1]: *used with* thou (chiefly as an auxiliary)

Dos·to·ev·ski (dôs′tô yef′skē), **Feo·dor (Mikhailovich)** (fyô′dôr) 1821–81; Russ. novelist

dot[1] (dät) ***n.*** [OE. *dott,* head of boil] **1.** a tiny spot, speck, or mark; point; as, *a)* the mark placed above an *i* or *j* *b)* *Music* a point after a note, increasing its time value by one half; also, a point above or below a note to show it is staccato **2.** any small, round spot **3.** a short sound or click in Morse code —***vt.*** **dot′ted, dot′ting 1.** to mark with a dot or dots **2.** to cover as with dots *[trees dotted* the landscape*]* —***vi.*** to make a dot or dots —**dot one's i's and cross one's t's** to be minutely correct —**on the dot** [Colloq.] at the exact time —**dot′ter** ***n.***

dot[2] (dät) ***n.*** [Fr. < L. *dos* (gen. *dotis*) < *dare,* to give] a woman's marriage dowry —**do·tal** (dōt′'l) ***adj.***

dot·age (dōt′ij) ***n.*** [ME. < *doten,* DOTE] **1.** feeble and childish state due to old age; senility **2.** a doting; foolish or excessive affection

dot·ard (-ərd) ***n.*** [ME. < *doten,* DOTE] a foolish and doddering old person

dote (dōt) ***vi.*** **dot′ed, dot′ing** [ME. *doten*] **1.** to be foolish or weak-minded, esp. because of old age **2.** to be excessively or foolishly fond (with *on* or *upon*) —**dot′er** ***n.*** —**dot′ing** ***adj.*** —**dot′ing·ly** ***adv.***

doth (duth) *archaic 3d pers. sing., pres. indic., of* DO[1] (chiefly in auxiliary uses)

dot·ter·el (dät′ər əl) ***n.,*** *pl.* **-els, -el:** see PLURAL, II, D, 1 [< DOTE, because easy to catch] a European and Asian plover with a short bill

dot·tle, dot·tel (dät′'l) ***n.*** [< ME. var. of *dosel,* a plug] the tobacco plug left in the bowl of a pipe after it has been smoked

dot·ty (dät′ē) ***adj.*** **-ti·er, -ti·est 1.** covered with dots; dotted **2.** [Colloq.] feeble; unsteady **3.** [Colloq.] feeble-minded or crazy

Dou·ay Bible (do͞o ā′) [< *Douai,* in France, where it was published in part (1609–10)] an English translation of the Bible from the Vulgate, for Roman Catholics: also **Douay Version**

dou·ble (dub′'l) ***adj.*** [OFr. < L. *duplus,* lit., twofold] **1.** twofold; duplex **2.** having two layers; folded in two **3.** having two of one kind; repeated *[a double* consonant*]* **4.** being of two kinds; dual *[a double* standard*]* **5.** having two meanings; ambiguous **6.** twice as much, as many, as large, etc. **7.** of extra size, value, strength, etc. **8.** made for two *[a double* bed*]* **9.** two-faced; deceiving **10.** having a tone an octave lower *[double* bass*]* **11.** *Bot.* having more than one set of petals —***adv.*** **1.** twofold **2.** two together; in pairs —***n.*** **1.** anything twice as much, as many, or as large as normal **2.** a person or thing looking very much like another; duplicate; counterpart **3.** a stand-in, as in motion pictures **4.** a fold; second ply **5.** a sharp shift of direction **6.** a trick; shift **7.** [*pl.*] a game of tennis, handball, etc. with two players on each side **8.** *Baseball* a hit on which the batter reaches second base **9.** *Bridge a)* the doubling of an opponent's bid *b)* a hand that makes this possible —***vt.*** **-bled, -bling 1.** to make twice as much or many **2.** to fold **3.** to repeat or duplicate **4.** to be the double of **5.** *Baseball a)* to put out (the second runner) in executing a double play *b)* to advance (a runner) by hitting a double **6.** *Bridge* to increase the point value or penalty of (an opponent's bid) **7.** *Naut.* to sail around *[*they *doubled* Cape Horn*]* —***vi.*** **1.** to become double **2.** to turn sharply backward *[*the animal *doubled* on its tracks*]* **3.** to serve as a double **4.** to serve an additional purpose or function **5.** [Colloq.] to double-date **6.** *Baseball* to hit a double —**double back 1.** to fold back **2.** to turn back in the direction from which one came —**double up 1.** to fold completely; clench (one's fist) **2.** to bend over, as in laughter or pain **3.** to share a room, etc. with someone —**on** (or **at**) **the double** [Colloq.] **1.** in double time **2.** quickly —**dou′bler** ***n.***

double agent a spy who infiltrates an enemy espionage organization in order to betray it

dou·ble-bar·reled (-bar′əld) ***adj.*** **1.** having two barrels, as a kind of shotgun **2.** having a double purpose or meaning

double bass (bās) the largest and deepest-toned instrument of the violin family (orig. of the viol family), with a range of approximately three octaves

DOUBLE BASS

double bassoon *same as* CONTRABASSOON

double boiler a utensil consisting of two pans, one of which fits over the other: food is cooked in the upper one by water boiling in the lower

dou·ble-breast·ed (-bres′tid) ***adj.*** overlapping across the breast and having a double row of buttons, as a coat

dou·ble-check (-chek′) ***vt., vi.*** to check again; verify —***n.*** the act of double-checking

double chin a fold of flesh beneath the chin

dou·ble-cross (-krôs′) ***vt.*** [Colloq.] to betray (a person) by doing the opposite of, or intentionally failing to do, what one has promised —**dou′ble-cross′er** ***n.***

double cross [Colloq.] a double-crossing; treachery

double dagger a mark (‡) used in printing and writing to indicate a note or cross-reference

dou·ble-date (-dāt′) ***vi., vt.*** **-dat′ed, -dat′ing** [Colloq.] to go out on a double date (*with*)

double date [Colloq.] a social engagement shared by two couples

dou·ble-deal·ing (-dēl′iŋ) ***n.*** the act of doing the opposite of what one pretends to do; duplicity —**dou′ble-deal′er** ***n.***

dou·ble-deck·er (-dek′ər) ***n.*** **1.** any structure or vehicle with two levels **2.** [Colloq.] a sandwich with two layers of filling

dou·ble-dig·it (-dij′it) ***adj.*** amounting to ten percent or more *[double-digit* inflation*]*

dou·ble-edged (-ejd′) ***adj.*** **1.** having two cutting edges **2.** applicable both ways, as an argument

dou·ble-en·ten·dre (do͞o′blän tän′drə, dub′'l än-) ***n.*** [Fr. (now obs.), double meaning] a word or phrase with two meanings, esp. when one of them is risqué or indecorous

double entry a system of bookkeeping in which each transaction is entered as a debit and a credit

double exposure *Photog.* **1.** the making of two exposures on one film or plate **2.** a photograph resulting from this

dou·ble-faced (dub′'l fāst′) ***adj.*** **1.** having two faces or aspects **2.** hypocritical; insincere

double feature two full-length motion pictures on the same program

dou·ble-head·er (-hed′ər) ***n.*** two games played in succession on the same day

double indemnity a clause in some insurance policies providing for the payment of twice the face value of the contract for accidental death

double jeopardy *Law* the jeopardy in which a defendant is placed by a second prosecution for the same offense: prohibited by the U.S. Constitution

dou·ble-joint·ed (-join′tid) ***adj.*** having joints that permit limbs, fingers, etc. to bend at other than the usual angles

dou·ble-knit (-nit′) ***adj.*** knit with a double stitch, which gives extra thickness to the fabric

dou·ble-park (-pärk′) ***vt., vi.*** to park (a vehicle) parallel to another parked alongside a curb

double play *Baseball* a play in which two players are put out

double pneumonia pneumonia of both lungs

dou·ble-quick (-kwik′) ***adj.*** very quick —***n.*** a very quick marching pace; specif., *same as* DOUBLE TIME (sense 2) —***vi., vt.*** to march at such a pace —***adv.*** at this pace

dou·ble-reed (-rēd′) ***adj.*** designating or of a group of woodwind instruments, as the oboe or bassoon, having two

reeds separated by a narrow opening —*n.* a double-reed instrument
dou·ble-space (-spās′) *vt., vi.* **-spaced′, -spac′ing** to type (copy) so as to leave a full space between lines
double standard a system, code, etc. applied unequally; specif., one that is stricter for women than for men, esp. in matters of sex
dou·blet (dub′lit) *n.* [OFr. dim. of *double,* orig., something folded] **1.** a man's short, closefitting jacket of the 14th to the 16th cent. **2.** either of a pair of similar things **3.** a pair; couple **4.** either of two words that derive ultimately from the same source but have changed in form (e.g., *card, chart*)
double take a delayed reaction to some remark, situation, etc., in which there is first unthinking acceptance and then startled surprise or a second glance as the real meaning strikes one
double talk **1.** ambiguous and deceptive talk **2.** deliberately confusing talk made up of a mixture of real words and meaningless syllables
double time **1.** a rate of payment twice as high as usual, as for overtime on Sundays **2.** a marching cadence of 180 three-foot steps a minute
dou·ble·tree (dub′′l trē′) *n.* [DOUBLE + (SINGLE)TREE] a crossbar on a wagon, plow, etc.
dou·bloon (du blo͞on′) *n.* [< Fr. < Sp. < L. *duplus,* double] an obsolete Spanish gold coin
dou·bly (dub′lē) *adv.* **1.** twice **2.** two at a time
doubt (dout) *vi.* [< OFr. < L. *dubitare*] to be uncertain in opinion or belief; be undecided —*vt.* **1.** to be uncertain about; question **2.** to be inclined to disbelieve **3.** [Archaic] to be fearful of —*n.* **1.** *a)* a lack of conviction; uncertainty *b)* lack of trust **2.** a condition of uncertainty **3.** an unsettled point or matter; difficulty —**beyond** (or **without**) **doubt** certainly —**no doubt** **1.** certainly **2.** probably —**doubt′a·ble** *adj.* —**doubt′er** *n.* —**doubt′ing·ly** *adv.*
doubt·ful (-fəl) *adj.* **1.** in doubt; not definite **2.** uncertain **3.** giving rise to doubt; questionable, as in reputation **4.** feeling doubt; unsettled —**doubt′ful·ly** *adv.* —**doubt′ful·ness** *n.*
doubt·less (-lis) *adj.* [Rare] free from doubt —*adv.* **1.** without doubt; certainly **2.** probably —**doubt′less·ly** *adv.* —**doubt′less·ness** *n.*
douche (do͞osh) *n.* [Fr. < It. *doccia,* shower, orig., conduit, ult. < L. *ductus,* pp. of *ducere,* to lead] **1.** a jet of liquid applied externally or internally to some part of the body **2.** a bath or treatment of this kind **3.** a device for douching —*vt., vi.* **douched, douch′ing** to apply a douche (to)
dough (dō) *n.* [OE. *dag*] **1.** a mixture of flour, liquid, and other ingredients, worked into a soft, thick mass for baking into bread, etc. **2.** any pasty mass like this **3.** [Slang] money
dough·boy (-boi′) *n.* [Colloq.] a U.S. infantryman, esp. of World War I
dough·nut (-nut′) *n.* a small, usually ring-shaped cake, fried in deep fat
dough·ty (dout′ē) *adj.* **-ti·er, -ti·est** [< OE. < *dugan,* to avail] valiant; brave: now used with a consciously archaic flavor —**dough′ti·ly** *adv.* —**dough′ti·ness** *n.*
dough·y (dō′ē) *adj.* **dough′i·er, dough′i·est** of or like dough; soft, pasty, etc. —**dough′i·ness** *n.*
Doug·las (dug′ləs) [< Gael., lit., black stream] **1.** a masculine name: dim. *Doug* **2. Stephen A(rnold),** 1813–61; U.S. politician
Douglas fir (or **spruce, pine, hemlock**) [after David *Douglas,* 19th-c. Scot. botanist in U.S.] a tall evergreen tree of the pine family, found in W N. America and valued for its wood
Doug·lass (dug′ləs), **Frederick** 1817?–95; U.S. Negro leader, journalist, & statesman
dour (door, do͞or, dour) *adj.* [< L. *durus,* hard] **1.** [Scot.] stern; severe **2.** [Scot.] obstinate **3.** sullen; gloomy —**dour′ly** *adv.* —**dour′ness** *n.*
douse[1] (dous) *vt.* **doused, dous′ing** [< ?] **1.** *Naut.* to lower (sails) quickly **2.** [Colloq.] to put out (a light or fire) quickly
douse[2] (dous) *vt.* **doused, dous′ing** [< ? prec.] **1.** to plunge or thrust suddenly into liquid **2.** to drench; pour liquid over —*vi.* to get immersed or drenched —*n.* an immersion or drenching
douse[3] (douz) *vi.* **doused, dous′ing** *same as* DOWSE[2]
dove[1] (duv) *n.* [< ? ON. *dūfa*] **1.** a bird of the pigeon family, with a full-breasted body and short legs: a symbol of peace **2.** an advocate of the use of peaceful measures to solve international conflicts **3.** a person regarded as gentle or innocent —**dov′ish** *adj.*
dove[2] (dōv) *alt. pt. of* DIVE
dove·cote (duv′kōt′, -kät′) *n.* [DOVE[1] + COTE] a small house or box with compartments for nesting pigeons: also **dove′cot′** (-kät′)
Do·ver (dō′vər) **1.** seaport in SE England, on the Strait of Dover: pop. 36,000 **2.** capital of Del.: pop. 24,000 **3. Strait** (or **Straits**) **of,** strait between France and England
dove·tail (duv′tāl′) *n.* **1.** a thing shaped like a dove's tail; specif., a projecting, wedge-shaped part that fits into a corresponding indentation to form a joint **2.** a joint thus formed —*vt.* **1.** to join together by means of dovetails **2.** to piece together (facts, etc.) —*vi.* to fit together closely or logically

DOVETAIL

dow·a·ger (dou′ə jər) *n.* [< OFr. < *douage,* dowry, ult. < L. *dos:* see DOT[2]] **1.** a widow with a title or property derived from her dead husband **2.** an elderly woman of wealth and dignity
dow·dy (dou′dē) *adj.* **-di·er, -di·est** [< ME. *doude,* unattractive woman] not neat or fashionable in dress; shabby —*n., pl.* **-dies** a dowdy woman —**dow′di·ly** *adv.* —**dow′di·ness** *n.* —**dow′dy·ish** *adj.*
dow·el (dou′əl) *n.* [ME. *doule*] a peg or pin of wood, metal, etc., usually fitted into corresponding holes in two pieces to fasten them together —*vt.* **-eled** or **-elled, -el·ing** or **-el·ling** to fasten with dowels

DOWEL

dow·er (dou′ər) *n.* [< OFr. < ML. *dotarium* < L. *dos:* see DOT[2]] **1.** that part of a man's property which his widow inherits for life **2.** a dowry **3.** a natural talent, or endowment —*vt.* **1.** to give a dower to **2.** to endow (*with*)
dow·er·y (-ē) *n., pl.* **-er·ies** *same as* DOWRY
down[1] (doun) *adv.* [< OE. *adune,* from the hill < *a-,* off + *dune,* hill] **1.** from a higher to a lower place **2.** in or on a lower position or level **3.** *a)* in or to a place thought of as lower; often, specif., southward *b)* out of one's hands *[put it down]* **4.** below the horizon **5.** from an earlier to a later period or person **6.** into a low physical or emotional condition **7.** in an inferior position or condition **8.** to a lower amount or bulk **9.** into a tranquil or quiet state **10.** seriously; earnestly *[get down to work]* **11.** completely *[loaded down]* **12.** in cash or when bought *[$5 down]* **13.** in writing; on record *[take down his name]* —*adj.* **1.** directed toward a lower position **2.** in a lower place **3.** gone, brought, pulled, etc. down **4.** dejected; discouraged **5.** prostrate; ill **6.** completed *[four down,* six to *go]* **7.** in cash, as part of the purchase price *[a down payment]* **8.** *Sports a)* no longer in play: said of a football *b)* trailing an opponent by a specified number of points, strokes, etc. *c) Baseball* put out —*prep.* down toward, along, through, into, or upon —*vt.* **1.** *a)* to put, bring, get, throw, or knock down *b)* to defeat, as in a game **2.** to gulp or eat rapidly —*n.* **1.** a downward movement or depressed condition: see phr. UPS AND DOWNS at UP **2.** *Football a)* one of four consecutive plays in which a team, in order to keep possession of the ball, must either score or advance the ball at least ten yards *b)* the declaring of the ball as down, or no longer in play —**down and out** **1.** *Boxing* knocked out **2.** penniless, friendless, ill, etc. —**down on** [Colloq.] hostile to; angry or annoyed with —**down to the ground** thoroughly; completely —**down with!** do away with!
down[2] (doun) *n.* [< ON. *dūnn*] **1.** soft, fine feathers **2.** soft, fine hair or hairy growth
down[3] (doun) *n.* [OE. *dun,* a hill] **1.** an expanse of open, high, grassy land: *usually used in pl.* **2.** [confused with *dune*] [Archaic] a sandy mound formed by the wind
down·beat (-bēt′) *n. Music* a downward stroke made by a conductor to show the first beat of each measure
down·cast (-kast′) *adj.* **1.** directed downward **2.** very unhappy or discouraged; dejected
Down East [Colloq.] New England, esp. Maine: also **down east** —**down′-east′** *adj.* —**down′-east′er** *n.*
down·er (-ər) *n.* [Slang] **1.** any depressant or sedative, as a barbiturate, tranquilizer, etc. **2.** something depressing; esp., a depressing experience
Dow·ney (dou′nē) [after J. *Downey,* gov. of Calif., 1860–62] city in SW Calif.: suburb of Los Angeles: pop. 83,000
down·fall (doun′fôl′) *n.* **1.** *a)* a sudden fall, as from prosperity or power *b)* the cause of such a fall **2.** a sudden, heavy fall, as of snow
down·grade (-grād′) *n.* a downward slope, esp. in a road —*adv., adj.* downhill; downward —*vt.* **-grad′ed, -grad′ing** **1.** to demote to a less skilled job at lower pay **2.** to lower in importance, value, etc. **3.** to belittle —**on the downgrade** losing status, influence, health, etc.; declining
down·heart·ed (-här′tid) *adj.* discouraged; dejected —**down′heart′ed·ly** *adv.*
down·hill (-hil′) *adv.* **1.** toward the bottom of a hill **2.** to a poorer condition, status, etc. —*adj.* **1.** sloping or going downward **2.** of or relating to skiing downhill
Down·ing Street (doun′iŋ) [after Sir G. *Downing* (1623–

84), who owned property there] **1.** street in the West End of London, location of some important government offices **2.** the British government

down·pour (doun′pôr′) ***n.*** a heavy rain

down·range (-rānj′) ***adv., adj.*** along the course away from the launching site

down·right (-rīt′) ***adv.*** thoroughly; utterly —***adj.*** **1.** absolute; thoroughgoing; utter **2.** straightforward; plain; frank

down·spout (-spout′) ***n.*** a vertical pipe for carrying rain water from a roof gutter to ground level

Down's syndrome (dounz) [after J.L.H. *Down* (1828–96), Eng. physician] a congenital disease in which there is mental deficiency and a characteristic broad face, with slanting eyes, etc.

down·stairs (doun′sterz′) ***adv.*** **1.** down the stairs **2.** on or to a lower floor —***adj.*** situated on a lower floor —***n.*** a lower floor or floors

down·state (-stāt′) ***n.*** that part of a State farther to the south —***adj., adv.*** in, to, or from downstate

down·stream (-strēm′) ***adv., adj.*** in the direction of the current of a stream

down·swing (-swiŋ′) ***n.*** a downward trend, as in business: also **down′turn′** (-turn′)

down-to-earth (-tə urth′) ***adj.*** realistic or practical

down·town (-toun′) ***adj., adv.*** of, in, like, to, or toward the lower part or main business section of a city or town —***n.*** the downtown section

down·trod·den (-träd′'n) ***adj.*** **1.** trampled on or down **2.** oppressed; tyrannized over

down under [Colloq.] Australia or New Zealand

down·ward (-wərd) ***adv., adj.*** **1.** toward a lower place, state, etc. **2.** from an earlier to a later time Also **down′wards** ***adv.*** —**down′ward·ly** ***adv.***

down·wind (-wind′) ***adv., adj.*** in the direction in which the wind is blowing or usually blows

down·y (-ē) ***adj.*** **down′i·er, down′i·est** **1.** of or covered with soft, fine feathers or hair **2.** soft and fluffy, like down —**down′i·ness** ***n.***

dow·ry (dou′rē) ***n., pl.*** **-ries** [see DOWER] **1.** the property that a woman brings to her husband at marriage **2.** a natural talent, gift, etc.

dowse[1] (dous) ***vt.*** **dowsed, dows′ing** *same as* DOUSE[1]

dowse[2] (douz) ***vi.*** **dowsed, dows′ing** [< ? ME. *dushen,* to push down] to search for a source of water or minerals with a divining rod **(dowsing rod)** —**dows′er** ***n.***

dox·ol·o·gy (däk säl′ə jē) ***n., pl.*** **-gies** [ML. *doxologia* < Gr. < *doxa,* praise + *-logia,* -LOGY] a hymn of praise to God; specif., *a*) the **greater doxology,** which begins "Glory to God in the highest" *b*) the **lesser doxology,** which begins "Glory to the Father" *c*) a hymn beginning "Praise God from whom all blessings flow"

Doyle (doil), Sir **Arthur Co·nan** (kō′nən) 1859–1930; Eng. writer of *Sherlock Holmes* stories

doz. dozen; dozens

doze (dōz) ***vi.*** **dozed, doz′ing** [prob. < Scand.] to sleep lightly or fitfully; be half asleep —***vt.*** to spend (time) in dozing —***n.*** a light sleep; nap —**doze off** to fall into a light sleep —**doz′er** ***n.***

doz·en (duz′'n) ***n., pl.*** **-ens** or, esp. after a number, **-en** [< OFr. < *douze,* twelve < L. < *duo,* two + *decem,* ten] a set of twelve —**doz′enth** ***adj.***

doz·y (dō′zē) ***adj.*** **doz′i·er, doz′i·est** sleepy; drowsy —**doz′i·ly** ***adv.*** —**doz′i·ness** ***n.***

DP, D.P. displaced person

dpt. **1.** department **2.** deponent

Dr. **1.** Doctor **2.** Drive

dr. **1.** debit **2.** debtor **3.** drachma(s) **4.** dram(s)

drab[1] (drab) ***n.*** [< Fr. *drap,* cloth < VL. *drappus*] a dull yellowish brown —***adj.*** **drab′ber, drab′best** **1.** of a dull yellowish-brown color **2.** dull; monotonous —**drab′ly** ***adv.*** —**drab′ness** ***n.***

drab[2] (drab) ***n.*** [< Celt. as in Ir. *drabog,* slattern] **1.** a slovenly woman **2.** a prostitute —***vi.*** **drabbed, drab′bing** to fornicate with prostitutes

drachm (dram) ***n.*** *same as:* **1.** DRACHMA **2.** DRAM

drach·ma (drak′mə) ***n., pl.*** **-mas, -mae** (-mē), **-mai** (-mī) [L. < Gr. *drachmē,* lit., a handful < *drassesthai,* to grasp] **1.** an ancient Greek silver coin **2.** the monetary unit of modern Greece: see MONETARY UNITS, table

draft (draft) ***n.*** [ME. *draught,* a drawing < OE. *dragan,* DRAW] **1.** *a*) a drawing, as of a vehicle or load *b*) the thing, quantity, or load pulled **2.** *a*) a drawing in of a fish net *b*) the amount of fish caught in one draw **3.** *a*) a drinking *b*) the amount taken at one drink **4.** *a*) a drink; specif., a dose of medicine *b*) [Colloq.] a portion of beer, ale, etc. drawn from a cask **5.** *a*) a drawing into the lungs, as of air *b*) the amount of air, etc. drawn in **6.** a rough sketch of a writing **7.** a plan or drawing of a work to be done **8.** a current of air, as in a room **9.** a device for regulating the current of air in a heating system **10.** a written order from one person, firm, etc., directing the payment of money to another; check **11.** a demand or drain made on something **12.** *a*) the taking of persons for a special purpose, esp. compulsory military service *b*) those so taken **13.** *Naut.* the depth of water that a ship displaces, esp. when loaded **14.** *Sports* a system of allotting to each team in a professional league exclusive rights to certain new players —***vt.*** **1.** to take, as for compulsory military service, by drawing from a group **2.** to draw off or away **3.** to make a preliminary sketch of or working plans for —***adj.*** **1.** used for pulling loads [*draft* animals] **2.** drawn from a cask on order [*draft* beer] **3.** in a preliminary or rough form —**on draft** ready to be drawn directly from the cask —**draft′a·ble** ***adj.*** —**draft′er** ***n.***

draft·ee (draf tē′) ***n.*** a person drafted, esp. for service in the armed forces

drafts·man (drafts′mən) ***n., pl.*** **-men** **1.** a person who draws plans of structures or machinery **2.** a person who draws up legal documents, speeches, etc. **3.** an artist skillful in drawing —**drafts′man·ship′** ***n.***

draft·y (draf′tē) ***adj.*** **draft′i·er, draft′i·est** letting in, having, or exposed to a draft or drafts of air —**draft′i·ly** ***adv.*** —**draft′i·ness** ***n.***

drag (drag) ***vt.*** **dragged, drag′ging** [< OE. *dragan* or ON. *draga:* see DRAW] **1.** to pull, draw, or move with effort, esp. along the ground; haul **2.** to force into some action, etc. **3.** to pull a grapnel, net, etc. over the bottom of (a river, etc.) in searching for something; dredge **4.** to draw a harrow over (land) **5.** to draw (something) out over a period of time —***vi.*** **1.** to be dragged; trail **2.** to lag behind **3.** to move or pass too slowly **4.** to search a body of water with a grapnel, net, etc. **5.** [Slang] to draw (*on*) a cigarette, etc. **6.** [Slang] to participate in a drag race —***n.*** **1.** something dragged along the ground; specif., *a*) a harrow *b*) a heavy sledge or sled **2.** a grapnel, dragnet, etc. **3.** anything that hinders **4.** a dragging **5.** [Slang] influence **6.** [Slang] a puff of a cigarette, etc. **7.** [Slang] street; road [the main *drag*] **8.** [Slang] a dull or boring person, situation, etc. **9.** [Slang] clothing of the opposite sex **10.** *Aeron.* a resisting force exerted on an aircraft, tending to retard its motion —**drag on** (or **out**) to prolong or be prolonged tediously —**drag one's feet** (or **heels**) [Slang] to be uncooperative —**drag′ger** ***n.*** —**drag′gy** ***adj.*** **-gi·er, -gi·est**

drag·gle (drag′'l) ***vt., vi.*** **-gled, -gling** [freq. of DRAG] to make or become wet or dirty by dragging in mud or water

drag·net (-net′) ***n.*** **1.** a net dragged along the bottom of a river, lake, etc. for catching fish **2.** a net for catching small game **3.** an organized system or network for catching criminals, etc.

drag·o·man (drag′ə mən) ***n., pl.*** **-mans, -men** [< OFr. < It. < MGr. *dragomanos* < Ar. *targumān*] in the Near East, an interpreter or guide

drag·on (drag′ən) ***n.*** [< OFr. < L. < Gr. *drakōn* < *derkesthai,* to see] **1.** a mythical monster, usually represented as a large reptile with wings and claws, breathing out fire and smoke **2.** a fierce person, esp. a strict chaperon

drag·on·fly (-flī′) ***n., pl.*** **-flies′** a large, harmless insect having narrow, transparent, net-veined wings: it feeds mostly on flies, etc.

dra·goon (drə gōōn′) ***n.*** [Fr. *dragon:* see DRAGON] a heavily armed cavalryman —***vt.*** **1.** to harass or persecute by dragoons **2.** to force (*into* doing)

drag race a race between automobiles to test their rates of acceleration from a complete stop, specif. between hot-rod cars **(dragsters)** on a short, straight course **(drag strip)** —**drag′-race′** ***vi.*** **-raced′, -rac′ing**

drain (drān) ***vt.*** [< OE. *dreahnian* < base of *dryge,* DRY] **1.** to draw off (liquid) gradually **2.** to draw liquid from gradually [to *drain* a swamp] **3.** to receive the waters of **4.** to drink all the liquid from (a cup, etc.) **5.** to exhaust (strength, emotions, or resources) gradually —***vi.*** **1.** to flow off gradually **2.** to become dry by the drawing or flowing off of liquid **3.** to disappear gradually **4.** to discharge its waters [central Europe *drains* into the Danube] —***n.*** **1.** a channel, pipe, tube, etc. for carrying off water, sewage, pus, etc. **2.** a draining **3.** that which gradually exhausts strength, etc. —**down the drain** lost in a wasteful, heedless way —**drain′er** ***n.***

drain·age (-ij) ***n.*** **1.** the act, process, or method of draining **2.** a system of pipes, etc. for carrying off waste matter **3.** that which is drained off **4.** an area drained, as by a river

drainage basin the land drained by a river system

drain·pipe (-pīp′) ***n.*** a large pipe used to carry off water, sewage, etc.

drake (drāk) *n.* [< WGmc. hyp. *drako,* male] a male duck

Drake (drāk), Sir **Francis** 1540?–96; Eng. admiral, navigator, & buccaneer

dram (dram) *n.* [< OFr. < ML. < L. *drachma:* see DRACHMA] **1.** *Apothecaries' Weight* a unit equal to 1/8 ounce **2.** *Avoirdupois Weight* a unit equal to 1/16 ounce **3.** *same as* FLUID DRAM **4.** a small drink of alcoholic liquor **5.** a small amount of anything

dra·ma (drä′mə, dram′ə) *n.* [LL. < Gr., a deed, drama < *dran,* to do] **1.** a literary composition that tells a story by means of dialogue and action, to be performed by actors; play **2.** the art or profession of writing, acting, or producing plays (often with *the*) **3.** plays collectively **4.** a series of events as interesting, vivid, etc. as a play **5.** the quality of being dramatic

Dram·a·mine (dram′ə mēn′) *a trademark for* DIMENHYDRINATE —*n.* **[d-]** this substance

dra·mat·ic (drə mat′ik) *adj.* **1.** of or connected with drama **2.** *a)* like a play *b)* full of action; vivid, striking, exciting, etc. —**dra·mat′i·cal·ly** *adv.*

dra·mat·ics (-iks) *n.pl.* **1.** [*usually with sing. v.*] the art of performing or producing plays **2.** plays presented by amateurs **3.** dramatic effect

dram·a·tis per·so·nae (dram′ə tis pər sō′nē) [ModL.] the characters in a play

dram·a·tist (dram′ə tist) *n.* a playwright

dram·a·tize (dram′ə tīz′) *vt.* **-tized′, -tiz′ing 1.** to make into a drama; adapt for performance on the stage, screen, etc. **2.** to regard or present in a dramatic manner —*vi.* **1.** to be capable of being dramatized **2.** to dramatize oneself —**dram′a·ti·za′tion** *n.* —**dram′a·tiz′er** *n.*

dram·a·tur·gy (-tʉr′jē) *n.* [< G. < Gr. *dramatourgia* < *drama,* DRAMA + *ergon,* work] the art of writing or producing plays —**dram′a·tur′gic, dram′a·tur′gi·cal** *adj.* —**dram′a·tur′gi·cal·ly** *adv.* —**dram′a·tur′gist, dram′a·turge′** *n.*

drank (draŋk) *pt. & often colloq. pp. of* DRINK

drape (drāp) *vt.* **draped, drap′ing** [< OFr. < *drap,* cloth: see DRAB[1]] **1.** to cover, hang, or decorate as with cloth or clothes in loose folds **2.** to arrange (a garment, cloth, etc.) artistically in folds or hangings —*vi.* to hang or fall in folds —*n.* cloth hanging in loose folds; esp., a drapery: *usually used in pl.*

drap·er (drā′pər) *n.* [Brit.] a dealer in dry goods

drap·er·y (drā′pər ē) *n., pl.* **-er·ies 1.** *a)* hangings, etc. arranged in loose folds *b)* an artistic arrangement of such hangings **2.** [*pl.*] curtains of heavy material

dras·tic (dras′tik) *adj.* [Gr. *drastikos,* active < *dran,* to do] acting with force; having a violent effect; severe; harsh —**dras′ti·cal·ly** *adv.*

draught (draft) *n., vt., adj. now chiefly Brit. sp. of* DRAFT

draughts (drafts) *n.pl.* [Brit.] the game of checkers

draughts·man (-mən) *n., pl.* **-men** *Brit. sp. of* DRAFTSMAN —**draughts′man·ship′** *n.*

draught·y (draf′tē) *adj.* **draught′i·er, draught′i·est** *Brit. sp. of* DRAFTY —**draught′i·ness** *n.*

Dra·vid·i·an (drə vid′ē ən) *n.* **1.** any of a group of intermixed races chiefly in S India and N Ceylon **2.** the family of non-Indo-European languages spoken by these races, including Tamil, Malayalam, etc. —*adj.* of the Dravidians or their languages: also **Dra·vid′ic**

draw (drô) *vt.* **drew, drawn, draw′ing** [< OE. *dragan*] **1.** to make move toward one or along with one; pull; drag **2.** to pull up, down, in, across, back, etc. **3.** to need (a specified depth of water) to float in: said of a ship **4.** to attract; charm **5.** to breathe in; inhale **6.** to bring forth; elicit [*his challenge drew no reply*] **7.** to bring on; provoke [*to draw enemy fire*] **8.** to pull out; extract (a cork, sword, etc.) **9.** *a)* to remove (liquid) by sucking, draining, etc. *b)* to bring up, as water from a well *c)* to cause (liquid) to flow [*to draw a bath, draw blood*] **10.** to disembowel **11.** *a)* to get from some source [*to draw a salary*] *b)* to get or pick at random **12.** to withdraw (money) held in an account **13.** to have accruing to it [*savings draw interest*] **14.** to write (a check or draft) **15.** to reach (a conclusion, etc.); deduce **16.** to bring (a game or contest) to a tie **17.** to stretch tautly or to full length **18.** to distort **19.** to flatten or shape (metal) by die stamping, hammering, etc. **20.** to make (metal) into wire by pulling it through holes **21.** to make (lines, pictures, etc.) as with a pencil, pen, brush, etc. **22.** to describe or formulate in words —*vi.* **1.** to draw something (in various senses of the *vt.*) **2.** to be drawn or have a drawing effect **3.** to come; move [*to draw near*] **4.** to shrink; contract **5.** to allow a draft, as of smoke, to move through **6.** to attract audiences —*n.* **1.** a drawing or being drawn (in various senses) **2.** the result of drawing **3.** a thing drawn **4.** the cards dealt as replacement in draw poker **5.** a tie; stalemate **6.** a thing that attracts interest, audiences, etc. **7.** the movable part of a drawbridge **8.** a gully or ravine that water drains into —**draw away** to move away or ahead —**draw on** (or **nigh**) to approach —**draw out 1.** to extend **2.** to take out; extract **3.** to get (a person) to talk —**draw up 1.** to arrange in order **2.** to compose (a document) in proper form **3.** to stop

draw·back (-bak′) *n.* anything that prevents or lessens full satisfaction; shortcoming

draw·bridge (-brij′) *n.* a bridge that can be raised, lowered, or drawn aside

draw·ee (drô′ē′) *n.* the party that the drawer directs, by a draft, etc., to pay money over to a third party (called *payee*)

draw·er (drô′ər; *for 4* drôr) *n.* **1.** a person or thing that draws **2.** one who draws an order for the payment of money **3.** a draftsman **4.** a sliding box in a table, chest, bureau, etc., that can be drawn out and then pushed back into place

drawers (drôrz) *n.pl. same as* UNDERPANTS

draw·ing (drô′iŋ) *n.* **1.** the act of one that draws; specif., the art of representing something by lines made on a surface with a pencil, pen, etc. **2.** a picture, design, etc. thus made **3.** a lottery

draw·ing card an entertainer, speaker, show, etc. that normally draws a large audience

drawing room [< earlier *withdrawing room,* to which guests withdrew after dinner] **1.** a room where guests are received or entertained; parlor **2.** a private compartment on a railroad sleeping car

draw·knife (drô′nīf′) *n., pl.* **-knives′** (-nīvz′) a knife with a handle at each end: the user draws it toward him in shaving a surface: also **drawing knife, draw′shave′** (-shāv′)

drawl (drôl) *vt., vi.* [prob. freq. of DRAW] to speak slowly, prolonging the vowels —*n.* a slow manner of speech in which vowels are prolonged —**drawl′er** *n.* —**drawl′ing·ly** *adv.*

drawn (drôn) *pp. of* DRAW —*adj.* **1.** pulled out of the sheath **2.** even; tied **3.** eviscerated **4.** tense; haggard

drawn butter melted butter, sometimes thickened and seasoned, used as a sauce

drawn·work (-wʉrk′) *n.* ornamental work done on textiles by pulling out threads to produce a lacelike design

draw poker a form of poker in which each player is dealt five cards face down, and may be dealt replacements for unwanted cards (usually three or fewer)

draw·string (drô′striŋ′) *n.* a string that tightens or closes an opening, as of a bag, when drawn

dray (drā) *n.* [< OE. *dræge,* lit., something drawn < *dragan,* to draw] a low cart with detachable sides, for carrying heavy loads —*vt.* to carry on a dray —*vi.* to drive a dray

dray·age (-ij) *n.* **1.** the hauling of a load by dray **2.** the charge made for this

dray·man (-mən) *n., pl.* **-men** the driver of a dray

dread (dred) *vt.* [OE. *drædan*] to anticipate with great fear, misgiving, or distaste —*n.* **1.** intense fear, esp. of something which may happen **2.** fear mixed with awe **3.** something dreaded —*adj.* **1.** dreaded or dreadful **2.** inspiring awe

dread·ful (-fəl) *adj.* **1.** inspiring dread; terrible or awesome **2.** [Colloq.] very bad, offensive, disagreeable, etc. —**dread′ful·ness** *n.*

dread·ful·ly (-fəl ē) *adv.* **1.** in a dreadful manner **2.** [Colloq.] very; extremely [*dreadfully tired*]

dread·nought, dread·naught (-nôt′, -nät′) *n.* a large, heavily armored battleship with big guns

dream (drēm) *n.* [form < OE. *dream,* joy, music; sense < ON. *draumr,* a dream] **1.** a sequence of sensations, images, thoughts, etc. passing through a sleeping person's mind **2.** a fanciful vision of the conscious mind; daydream; reverie **3.** the state in which such a daydream occurs **4.** a fond hope or aspiration **5.** anything so lovely, transitory, etc. as to seem dreamlike —*vi.* **dreamed** (drēmd, dremt) or **dreamt** (dremt), **dream′ing 1.** to have dreams **2.** to have daydreams **3.** to think (*of*) as at all possible, etc. —*vt.* **1.** *a)* to have (a dream or dreams) *b)* to have a dream of **2.** to spend in dreaming (with *away* or *out*) **3.** to imagine as possible —*adj.* ideal [*her dream house*] —**dream up** [Colloq.] to conceive of or devise —**dream′er** *n.* —**dream′ful** *adj.* —**dream′less** *adj.* —**dream′like′** *adj.*

dream·y (drē′mē) *adj.* **dream′i·er, dream′i·est 1.** filled with dreams **2.** visionary; impractical **3.** like something in a dream; misty, vague, etc. **4.** lulling; soothing [*dreamy music*] **5.** [Slang] delightful —**dream′i·ly** *adv.* —**dream′i·ness** *n.*

drear (drir) *adj.* [Poet.] dreary; melancholy

drear·y (-ē) *adj.* **drear′i·er, drear′i·est** [< OE. *dreorig,* sad, orig., bloody, gory] gloomy; cheerless; depressing; dismal; dull —**drear′i·ly** *adv.* —**drear′i·ness** *n.*

dredge[1] (drej) *n.* [prob. < MDu. *dregge*] **1.** a net attached to a frame, dragged along the bottom of a river, bay, etc. to gather shellfish, etc. **2.** an apparatus for scooping or sucking up mud, sand, etc., as in deepening or clearing channels, harbors, etc. **3.** a barge or other boat with a dredge on it —*vt.* **dredged, dredg′ing 1.** to gather (*up*) with or as with a dredge **2.** to enlarge or clean out (a river channel, harbor, etc.) with a dredge —*vi.* **1.** to use a dredge **2.** to search as with a dredge —**dredg′er** *n.*

dredge² (drej) *vt.* **dredged, dredg′ing** [< ME. *dragge*, sweetmeat, ult. < Gr. *tragēma*, dessert] **1.** to coat (food) with flour or the like, as by sprinkling **2.** to sprinkle (flour, etc.) —**dredg′er** *n.*

dregs (dregz) *n.pl.* [< ON. *dregg*] **1.** the particles that settle at the bottom of a liquid; lees **2.** the most worthless part [*dregs* of society] —**dreg′gi·ness** *n.* —**dreg′gy** *adj.* **-gi·er, -gi·est**

Drei·ser (drī′sər, -zər), **Theodore** (**Herman Albert**) 1871–1945; U.S. novelist

drench (drench) *vt.* [< OE. *drencan*, caus. of *drincan*, to drink] **1.** to make (a horse, cow, etc.) swallow a medicinal liquid **2.** to make wet all over; soak or saturate —*n.* **1.** a large liquid dose, esp. for a sick animal **2.** a drenching; soaking **3.** a solution for soaking

Dres·den (drez′dən) city in SC East Germany, on the Elbe: pop. 500,000 —*n.* a fine porcelain or chinaware made near Dresden —*adj.* designating or of such porcelain or chinaware

dress (dres) *vt.* **dressed** or **drest, dress′ing** [< OFr. *drecier*, to arrange < L. *directus*: see DIRECT] **1.** to put clothes on; clothe **2.** to provide with clothing **3.** to decorate; trim; adorn **4.** to arrange a display in [to *dress* a store window] **5.** to arrange or do up (the hair) **6.** to arrange (troops, etc.) in straight lines **7.** to apply medicines and bandages to (a wound, etc.) **8.** to treat in preparing for use, grooming, etc.; esp., *a*) to clean and draw (a fowl, etc.) *b*) to cultivate (fields or plants) *c*) to smooth or finish (leather, stone, etc.) —*vi.* **1.** to put on or wear clothes **2.** to dress in formal clothes **3.** to get into a straight line —*n.* **1.** clothes; clothing; apparel **2.** the usual outer garment of women, generally of one piece with a skirt **3.** formal clothes **4.** external covering or appearance —*adj.* **1.** of or for dresses [*dress* material] **2.** worn on formal occasions [a *dress* suit] **3.** requiring formal clothes [a *dress* occasion] —**dress down** to scold severely; reprimand —**dress up** to dress in formal clothes, or in clothes more elegant, showy, etc. than usual

dres·sage (drə säzh′) *n.* [Fr., training] exhibition horsemanship in which the horse is controlled by very slight movements of the rider

dress circle a section of seats in a theater or concert hall, usually a mezzanine, where formal dress was orig. customary

dress·er¹ (dres′ər) *n.* **1.** a person who dresses people, as actors in their costumes, or things, as store windows, leather, wounds, etc. **2.** one who dresses elegantly or in a certain way [a fancy *dresser*]

dress·er² (dres′ər) *n.* [< OFr. *dreceur*] **1.** formerly, a table on which food was prepared for serving **2.** a kitchen cupboard **3.** a chest of drawers for clothes, usually with a mirror; bureau

dress·ing (-iŋ) *n.* **1.** the act of one that dresses **2.** that which is used to dress something (as manure applied to soil, bandages applied to a wound, etc.) **3.** a sauce for salads, etc. **4.** a stuffing, as of bread and seasoning, for fowl, etc.

dress·ing-down (-doun′) *n.* a sound scolding

dressing gown a loose robe for wear when one is undressed or lounging

dressing room a room for getting dressed in, esp. backstage in a theater

dressing table a low table with a mirror, for use while putting on cosmetics, grooming the hair, etc.

dress·mak·er (dres′māk′ər) *n.* one who makes women's dresses, suits, etc. to order —*adj.* designating a woman's suit, coat, etc. not cut on severe, mannish lines: cf. TAILORED —**dress′mak′ing** *n.*

dress parade a military parade in dress uniform

dress rehearsal a final rehearsal, as of a play, performed exactly as it is to take place

dress suit a man's formal suit for evening wear

dress·y (-ē) *adj.* **dress′i·er, dress′i·est** **1.** showy in dress or appearance **2.** stylish, elegant, etc. —**dress′i·ly** *adv.* —**dress′i·ness** *n.*

drew (dro͞o) *pt. of* DRAW

Drey·fus (drā′fəs, drī′-; *Fr.* dre füs′), **Alfred** 1859–1935; Fr. army officer convicted of treason and imprisoned but later exonerated when proved to be the victim of anti-Semitism and conspiracy

drib (drib) *vi., vt.* **dribbed, drib′bing** [< DRIP] [Obs.] to fall, or let fall, in driblets —**dribs and drabs** small amounts

drib·ble (-'l) *vi., vt.* **-bled, -bling** [freq. of DRIB] **1.** to flow, or let flow, in drops or driblets; trickle **2.** to come forth or let out a little at a time **3.** to slaver; drool **4.** in certain games, to move (the ball or puck) along by rapid, repeated bounces, short kicks, or light taps —*n.* **1.** a small drop, or a flowing in small drops **2.** a very small amount **3.** the act of dribbling a ball or puck **4.** a drizzling rain —**drib′bler** *n.*

drib·let (-lit) *n.* [dim. of prec.] a small amount

dried (drīd) *pt. & pp. of* DRY

dri·er (drī′ər) *n.* **1.** a substance added to paint, varnish, etc. to make it dry fast **2.** *same as* DRYER —*adj. compar. of* DRY

dri·est (-ist) *adj. superl. of* DRY

drift (drift) *n.* [< OE. *drifan*, to drive] **1.** a being driven or carried along, as by a current of air or water or by circumstances **2.** the course on which something is directed **3.** the deviation of a ship or aircraft from its course, caused by side currents or winds **4.** *a*) a slow ocean current *b*) a gradual shifting *c*) a random course, variation, etc. **5.** a tendency or trend **6.** general meaning; tenor **7.** *a*) something driven, as rain or snow before the wind *b*) a heap of snow, sand, etc. piled up by the wind, or floating matter washed ashore **8.** *Geol.* gravel, boulders, etc. moved and deposited by a glacier or water **9.** *Mining* a horizontal passageway, as along the path of a vein —*vi.* **1.** to be carried along as by a current **2.** to go along aimlessly **3.** to wander about from place to place, etc. **4.** to pile up in heaps by force of wind or water **5.** to move gradually away from a set position —*vt.* **1.** to cause to drift **2.** to cover with drifts —**drift′er** *n.*

drift·age (-ij) *n.* **1.** a drifting **2.** deviation caused by drifting **3.** that which has drifted

drift·wood (-wood′) *n.* wood drifting in the water, or that has been washed ashore

drill¹ (dril) *n.* [Du. *dril* < *drillen*, to bore] **1.** a tool or apparatus for boring holes in wood, metal, etc. **2.** a snail that bores into the shells of oysters and kills them **3.** military or physical training, esp. of a group, as in marching, the manual of arms, or gymnastic exercises **4.** the process of training or teaching by the repetition of an exercise **5.** a single exercise in drilling —*vt.* **1.** to bore (a hole) in (something) with or as with a drill **2.** to train in military or physical exercises **3.** to teach by having do repeated exercises **4.** to instill (ideas, etc. *into*) by repetition **5.** [Colloq.] to cause to move swiftly and directly [he *drilled* the ball past me] **6.** [Slang] to penetrate with bullets —*vi.* **1.** to bore a hole or holes **2.** to engage in military, physical, or mental exercises —**drill′er** *n.*

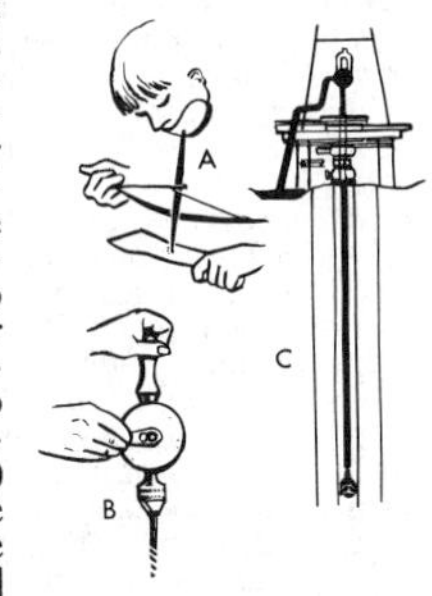

DRILLS
(A, bow; B, hand; C, rotary oil)

drill² (dril) *n.* [< ? prec.] **1.** a furrow in which seeds are planted **2.** a row of planted seeds **3.** a machine for making holes or furrows, dropping seeds into them, and covering them —*vt.* **1.** to sow (seeds) in rows **2.** to plant (a field) in drills

drill³ (dril) *n.* [< earlier *drilling*, ult. < L. < *tri-*, TRI- + *licium*, a thread] a coarse linen or cotton twill, used for work clothes, linings, etc.

drill⁴ (dril) *n.* [< ? Fr. *drill*, a soldier] a bright-cheeked monkey native to W Africa

drill·mas·ter (-mas′tər) *n.* **1.** an instructor in military drill **2.** one who teaches by drilling

drill press a machine tool for drilling holes

dri·ly (drī′lē) *adv. same as* DRYLY

drink (driŋk) *vt.* **drank** or archaic **drunk, drunk** or now colloq. **drank** or archaic **drunk′en, drink′ing** [OE. *drincan*] **1.** to swallow (liquid) **2.** to absorb (liquid or moisture) **3.** to swallow the contents of **4.** to join in (a toast) **5.** to bring (oneself) into a specified condition by drinking **6.** to use (*up*) or spend by drinking alcoholic liquor —*vi.* **1.** to swallow liquid **2.** to absorb anything as if in drinking **3.** to drink alcoholic liquor, etc. to excess —*n.* **1.** any liquid for drinking; beverage **2.** alcoholic liquor **3.** habitual or excessive use of alcoholic liquor —**drink in** to take in eagerly with the senses or with the mind —**drink to** to drink a toast to —**the drink** [Colloq.] a body of water, esp. the ocean —**drink′a·ble** *adj.* —**drink′er** *n.*

drinking fountain a device for providing a jet or flow of drinking water, as in a public place

drip (drip) *vi.* **dripped** or **dript, drip′ping** [OE. *dryppan*] **1.** to fall in drops **2.** to let drops of liquid fall —*vt.* to let fall in drops —*n.* **1.** a falling in drops **2.** liquid falling in drops, or the sound made by this **3.** a projecting part of a sill, etc. that sheds rain water **4.** [Slang] a person regarded as dull, insipid, etc.

drip-dry (-drī′) ***adj.*** designating or of fabrics or garments that dry quickly when hung soaking wet and require little or no ironing —***vi.*** **-dried′, -dry′ing** to launder as a drip-dry fabric does

drip·pings (drip′iŋz) ***n.*** the fat and juices that drip from roasting meat

drip·py (-ē) ***adj.*** **-pi·er, -pi·est 1.** characterized by dripping water, rain, etc. **2.** [Slang] overly sentimental, stupid, etc.

drive (drīv) ***vt.*** **drove, driv′en, driv′ing** [OE. *drifan*] **1.** to force to go; push forward **2.** to force into or from a state or act [he *drove* her mad] **3.** to force to work, usually to excess **4.** *a)* to force as by a blow *b)* to hit or cast (a ball) hard and swiftly **5.** to make penetrate **6.** to produce by penetrating [to *drive* a hole through metal] **7.** to control the movement of (a vehicle) **8.** to transport in a vehicle **9.** to cause to function **10.** to push (a bargain, etc.) through —***vi.*** **1.** to advance violently; dash **2.** to work or try hard **3.** to drive a blow, ball, etc. **4.** to be driven; operate: said of a motor vehicle **5.** to be conveyed in a vehicle **6.** to operate a motor vehicle —***n.*** **1.** a driving **2.** a trip in a vehicle **3.** *a)* a road for automobiles, etc. *b)* a driveway **4.** *a)* a rounding up of animals as for branding *b)* the animals rounded up **5.** a hard, swift blow, thrust, etc. **6.** an organized movement to achieve some purpose; campaign **7.** aggressive vigor; energy; push **8.** that which is urgent, as a basic biological impulse **9.** a collection of logs floating down a river **10.** *a)* the propelling mechanism of a motor vehicle, machine, etc. *b)* that arrangement in an automatic transmission of a motor vehicle allowing forward speeds —**drive at 1.** to aim at **2.** to mean; intend —**drive in 1.** to force in, as by a blow **2.** *Baseball* to cause (a runner) to score or (a run) to be scored, as by getting a hit —**let drive** to hit or aim

drive-in (-in′) ***adj.*** designating or of a restaurant, movie theater, etc. that renders its services to persons who drive up and remain seated in their cars —***n.*** such a restaurant, theater, etc.

driv·el (driv′'l) ***vi.*** **-eled** or **-elled, -el·ing** or **-el·ling** [< OE. *dreflian*] **1.** to let saliva flow from one's mouth; slobber **2.** to speak in a silly or stupid manner —***vt.*** to say in a silly, stupid, or nonsensical manner —***n.*** silly, stupid talk; childish nonsense —**driv′el·er, driv′el·ler** ***n.***

driv·en (driv′'n) *pp. of* DRIVE —***adj.*** moved along and piled up by the wind [*driven* snow]

driv·er (drī′vər) ***n.*** **1.** a person who drives; specif., *a)* one who drives an automobile, etc. *b)* one who herds cattle *c)* one who makes his subordinates work hard **2.** a thing that drives; specif., *a)* a mallet, hammer, etc. *b)* a wooden-headed golf club used in hitting the ball from the tee: also called **number 1 wood** *c)* any machine part that communicates motion —**the driver's seat** the position of control or dominance

drive·way (drīv′wā′) ***n.*** a path for cars, leading from a street to a garage, house, etc.

driz·zle (driz′'l) ***vi., vt.*** **-zled, -zling** [prob. freq. of ME. hyp. *drisnen*, to fall as dew] to rain or let fall in fine, mistlike drops —***n.*** a fine, mistlike rain —**driz′zly** ***adj.***

drogue (drōg) ***n.*** [prob. < Scot. *drug*, DRAG] **1.** *same as* SEA ANCHOR **2.** a funnel-shaped device towed behind an aircraft for its drag effect (also **drogue parachute**), or as a target, etc.

droll (drōl) ***adj.*** [< Fr. < MDu. *drol*, short, stout fellow] amusing in an odd or wry way —**droll′ness** ***n.*** —**drol′ly** ***adv.***

droll·er·y (-ər ē) ***n., pl.*** **-er·ies 1.** a droll act, remark, picture, story, etc. **2.** the act of joking **3.** quaint or wry humor

-drome (drōm) [< Gr. *dromos*, a running] *a suffix meaning* running, racecourse [*hippodrome*]

drom·e·dar·y (dräm′ə der′ē) ***n., pl.*** **-dar′ies** [< OFr. < LL. < L. < Gr. < *dramein*, to run] the one-humped camel, found from N Africa to India and trained for fast riding

drone[1] (drōn) ***n.*** [< OE. *dran*] **1.** a male honeybee, having only a reproductive function and no sting **2.** an idle parasite or loafer **3.** a pilotless airplane directed by remote control —***vi.*** **droned, dron′ing** to live in idleness; loaf

drone[2] (drōn) ***vi.*** **droned, dron′ing** [LME. *dronen* < prec.] **1.** to make a continuous humming sound **2.** to talk on and on in a monotonous way —***vt.*** to utter in a dull, monotonous tone —***n.*** **1.** a continuous humming sound **2.** *a)* a bagpipe *b)* any of the pipes of fixed tone in a bagpipe

drool (drōōl) ***vi.*** [< DRIVEL] **1.** to let saliva flow from one's mouth; drivel **2.** to flow from the mouth, as saliva **3.** [Slang] to speak in a silly or stupid way **4.** [Slang] to be overly enthusiastic, etc. —***vt.*** to let drivel from the mouth —***n.*** saliva running from the mouth

droop (drōōp) ***vi.*** [< ON. *drūpa*] **1.** to sink, hang, or bend down **2.** to lose vitality or strength **3.** to become dejected —***vt.*** to let sink or hang down —***n.*** a drooping

droop·y (-ē) ***adj.*** **droop′i·er, droop′i·est 1.** tending to droop **2.** [Colloq.] tired or dejected —**droop′i·ly** ***adv.*** —**droop′i·ness** ***n.***

drop (dräp) ***n.*** [OE. *dropa*] **1.** a small quantity of liquid that is somewhat spherical, as when falling **2.** a very small quantity of liquid **3.** [*pl.*] liquid medicine taken in drops **4.** a very small quantity of anything **5.** a thing like a drop in shape, size, etc. **6.** a dropping; sudden fall, descent, slump, etc. **7.** *same as* AIRDROP **8.** anything that drops or is used for dropping, as a drop curtain, a trapdoor, a slot for depositing letters, etc. **9.** the distance between a higher and lower level —***vi.*** **dropped** or, occas., **dropt, drop′ping 1.** to fall in drops **2.** to fall; come down **3.** to fall exhausted, wounded, or dead **4.** to pass into a specified state [to *drop* off to sleep] **5.** to come to an end [let the matter *drop*] **6.** to become lower or less, as prices, etc. **7.** to move down with a current of water or air —***vt.*** **1.** to let or make fall; release hold of **2.** to give birth to: said of animals **3.** to utter (a hint, etc.) casually **4.** to send (a letter) **5.** to cause to fall, as by wounding, killing, etc. **6.** *a)* to stop or have done with *b)* to dismiss **7.** to lower or lessen **8.** to make (the voice) less loud **9.** *same as* AIRDROP **10.** to omit (a letter or sound) in a word **11.** [Colloq.] to leave (a person or thing) at a specified place **12.** [Slang] to lose (money or a game) —**at the drop of a hat** immediately —**drop back 1.** to move back; retreat **2.** to be outdistanced: also **drop behind** —**drop in** (or **over, by,** etc.) to pay a casual or unexpected visit —**drop off 1.** to decline; decrease **2.** [Colloq.] to fall asleep —**drop out** to stop being a member or participant

drop cookie a cookie made from batter dropped onto a baking sheet as by teaspoonfuls

drop curtain a theater curtain that is lowered and raised rather than drawn

drop-forge (-fôrj′) ***vt.*** **-forged′, -forg′ing** to pound (heated metal) between dies with a drop hammer or a press —**drop′-forg′er** ***n.***

drop forging a product made by drop-forging

drop hammer 1. a machine for pounding metal into shape, with a heavy weight that is raised and then dropped on the metal **2.** this weight

drop kick *Football* a kick in which the ball is dropped to the ground and kicked just as it rebounds —**drop′-kick′** ***vt., vi.*** —**drop′-kick′er** ***n.***

drop·let (-lit) ***n.*** a very small drop

drop·out (-out′) ***n.*** a person who withdraws from school, esp. high school, before graduating

drop·per (-ər) ***n.*** **1.** a person or thing that drops **2.** a small tube of glass, plastic, etc. with a hollow rubber bulb at one end, used to release a liquid in drops

drop press *same as* DROP HAMMER

drop·sy (dräp′sē) ***n.*** [< OFr. < L. < Gr. *hydrōps* < *hydōr*, water] *an earlier term for* EDEMA —**drop′si·cal** (-si k'l), **drop′sied** ***adj.*** —**drop′si·cal·ly** ***adv.***

dropt (dräpt) *occas. pt. & pp. of* DROP

drosh·ky (dräsh′kē, drôsh′-) ***n., pl.*** **-kies** [Russ. *drozhki*] a low, open, four-wheeled Russian carriage: also **dros′ky** (dräs′-, drôs′-) *pl.* **-kies**

dro·soph·i·la (drə säf′ə lə, drō-) ***n., pl.*** **-lae′** (-lē′) [ModL. < Gr. *drosos*, dew + fem. of *philos*, loving] a tiny fly used in laboratory experiments in heredity; fruit fly

dross (drôs, dräs) ***n.*** [OE. *dros*, dregs] **1.** a scum formed on the surface of molten metal **2.** waste matter; rubbish —**dross′i·ness** ***n.*** —**dross′y** ***adj.*** **dross′i·er, dross′i·est**

drought (drout, drouth) ***n.*** [OE. *drugoth*, dryness < *drugian*, to dry up] **1.** prolonged dry weather; lack of rain **2.** a serious deficiency —**drought′y** ***adj.*** **drought′i·er, drought′i·est**

drouth (drouth, drout) ***n.*** *same as* DROUGHT

drove[1] (drōv) ***n.*** [OE. *draf* < *drifan*, DRIVE] **1.** a number of cattle, sheep, etc. driven or moving as a group; flock; herd **2.** a moving crowd of people

drove[2] (drōv) *pt. of* DRIVE

drov·er (drō′vər) ***n.*** a person who herds droves of animals, esp. to market

drown (droun) ***vi.*** [prob. < var. of ON. *drukna*] to die by suffocation in water or other liquid —***vt.*** **1.** to kill by such suffocation **2.** *a)* to cover with water; flood *b)* to overwhelm **3.** to be so loud as to overcome (another sound): usually with *out* **4.** to get rid of [to *drown* one's sorrow in drink]

drowse (drouz) ***vi.*** **drowsed, drows′ing** [< OE. *drusian*, to become sluggish] to sleep lightly; doze —***vt.*** to spend (time) in drowsing —***n.*** the act or an instance of drowsing; doze

drow·sy (drou′zē) ***adj.*** **-si·er, -si·est 1.** *a)* sleepy or half asleep *b)* making sleepy **2.** brought on by sleepiness **3.** peacefully quiet or inactive —**drow′si·ly** ***adv.*** —**drow′si·ness** ***n.***

drub (drub) ***vt.*** **drubbed, drub′bing** [< ? Turk. *durb* < Ar. *darb*, a beating] **1.** to beat as with a stick; cudgel **2.** to defeat soundly in a fight, contest, etc. —***vi.*** to drum or tap —***n.*** a blow as with a club —**drub′ber** ***n.***

drub·bing (drub′iŋ) ***n.*** a thorough beating or defeat
drudge (druj) ***n.*** **[**prob. < OE. *dreogan*, to suffer**]** a person who does hard, menial, or tedious work —***vi.*** **drudged, drudg′ing** to do such work
drudg·er·y (druj′ər ē) ***n., pl.*** **-er·ies** work that is hard, menial, or tiresome
drug (drug) ***n.*** **[**< OFr. *drogue***]** **1.** any substance used as or in a medicine **2.** a narcotic, hallucinogen, etc., esp. a habit-forming one —***vt.*** **drugged, drug′ging** **1.** to put a harmful drug in (a drink, etc.) **2.** to administer a drug to **3.** to stupefy as with a drug —**drug on the market** something for which there is a plentiful supply but little demand
drug addict a habitual user of narcotics
drug·gist (-ist) ***n.*** **1.** a dealer in drugs, medical equipment, etc. **2.** a person authorized to fill prescriptions; pharmacist **3.** an owner or manager of a drugstore
drug·store (-stôr′) ***n.*** a store where drugs and medical supplies are sold: most drugstores also sell a wide variety of merchandise
dru·id (dro͞o′id) ***n.*** **[**< Fr. < L. *druides*, pl. < Celt.**]** [*often* **D-**] a member of a Celtic religious order in ancient Britain, Ireland, and France —**dru·id′ic, dru·id′i·cal** ***adj.*** —**dru′id·ism** ***n.***
drum (drum) ***n.*** **[**< Du. *trom***]** **1.** a percussion instrument consisting of a hollow cylinder or hemisphere with a membrane stretched tightly over the end or ends **2.** the sound produced by beating a drum, or any sound like this **3.** any drumlike cylindrical object; specif., *a*) a metal cylinder around which cable, etc. is wound in a machine *b*) a barrellike metal container for oil, etc. **4.** any of various fishes that make a drumming sound **5.** *Anat. same as: a*) MIDDLE EAR *b*) EARDRUM —***vi.*** **drummed, drum′ming** **1.** to beat a drum **2.** to beat or tap continually, as with the fingers —***vt.*** **1.** to beat out (a tune, etc.) as on a drum **2.** to beat or tap continually **3.** to assemble by beating a drum **4.** to instill (ideas, facts, etc. *into*) by continued repetition —**beat the drum for** [Colloq.] to try to arouse enthusiasm for —**drum out of** to expel from in disgrace —**drum up** **1.** to summon as by beating a drum **2.** to get (business) by soliciting
drum·beat (-bēt′) ***n.*** a sound made by beating a drum
drum·fish (-fish′) ***n., pl.*** **-fish′, -fish′es** see FISH *same as* DRUM (*n.* 4)
drum·head (-hed′) ***n.*** the membrane stretched over the open end or ends of a drum
drum·lin (-lin) ***n.*** **[**< Ir. *druim*, a ridge + *-lin*, dim. suffix**]** a long ridge formed by glacial drift
drum major a person who leads or precedes a marching band, often twirling a baton and prancing —**drum majorette** ***fem.***
drum·mer (-ər) ***n.*** **1.** a drum player **2.** an animal that makes a drumming sound **3.** [see DRUM, phr. *drum up*] [Colloq.] a traveling salesman
drum·stick (-stik′) ***n.*** **1.** a stick for beating a drum **2.** the lower half of the leg of a cooked fowl
drunk (druŋk) *pp. & archaic pt. of* DRINK —***adj.*** [*usually used in the predicate*] **1.** overcome by alcoholic liquor; intoxicated **2.** overcome by any powerful emotion **3.** [Colloq.] *same as* DRUNKEN (sense 2) —***n.*** [Slang] **1.** a drunken person **2.** a drinking spree
drunk·ard (druŋ′kərd) ***n.*** a person who often gets drunk; inebriate
drunk·en (-kən) *archaic pp. of* DRINK —***adj.*** [*used before the noun*] **1.** intoxicated or habitually intoxicated **2.** caused by or occurring during intoxication —**drunk′en·ly** ***adv.*** —**drunk′en·ness** ***n.***
drupe (dro͞op) ***n.*** **[**< ModL. *drupa* < L. *drupa* (*oliva*), overripe (olive) < Gr. *dryppa*, olive**]** any fruit with a soft, fleshy part around an inner stone that contains the seed, as an apricot, cherry, plum, etc. —**dru·pa·ceous** (dro͞o pā′shəs) ***adj.***

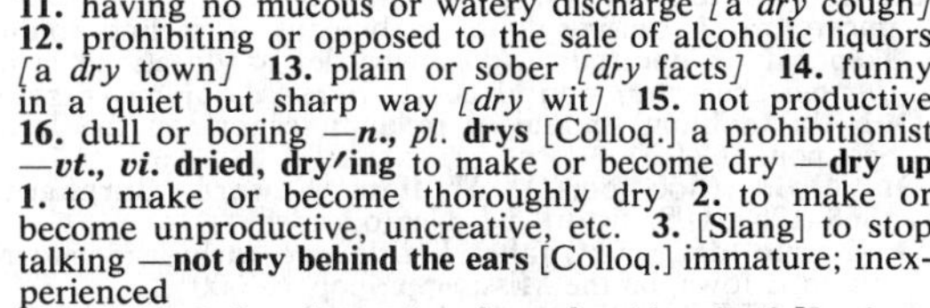

DRUPE (of peach)

drupe·let (-lit) ***n.*** a small drupe: a single blackberry consists of many drupelets
druth·ers (dru*th*′ərz) ***n.*** **[**contr. < *I'd rather*, with sound infl. by OTHER**]** [Dial. or Colloq.] a choice or preference [*if I had my druthers*]
dry (drī) ***adj.*** **dri′er, dri′est** **[**OE. *dryge***]** **1.** not under water [*dry* land] **2.** having no moisture; not wet or damp **3.** not shedding tears **4.** lacking rain [*a dry* summer] **5.** *a*) having lost water or moisture; arid, withered, dehydrated, etc. *b*) empty of water or other liquid **6.** thirsty **7.** not yielding milk [*a dry* cow] **8.** without butter, jam, etc. [*dry* toast] **9.** solid; not liquid **10.** not sweet [*dry* wine] **11.** having no mucous or watery discharge [*a dry* cough] **12.** prohibiting or opposed to the sale of alcoholic liquors [*a dry* town] **13.** plain or sober [*dry* facts] **14.** funny in a quiet but sharp way [*dry* wit] **15.** not productive **16.** dull or boring —***n., pl.*** **drys** [Colloq.] a prohibitionist —***vt., vi.*** **dried, dry′ing** to make or become dry —**dry up** **1.** to make or become thoroughly dry **2.** to make or become unproductive, uncreative, etc. **3.** [Slang] to stop talking —**not dry behind the ears** [Colloq.] immature; inexperienced
dry·ad (drī′əd, -ad) ***n., pl.*** **-ads, -ad·es′** (-ə dēz′) **[**L. *dryas* (gen. *dryadis*) < Gr. < *drys*, an oak, tree**]** [*also* **D-**] *Gr. & Rom. Myth.* any nymph living in a tree; wood nymph
dry battery **1.** an electric battery made up of several connected dry cells **2.** a dry cell
dry cell a voltaic cell containing an absorbent so that its contents cannot spill
dry-clean (drī′klēn′) ***vt.*** to clean (garments, etc.) with some solvent other than water, as naphtha, gasoline, etc. —**dry cleaner** —**dry cleaning**
Dry·den (drīd′'n), **John** 1631–1700; Eng. poet, critic, & playwright
dry-dock (drī′däk′) ***vt., vi.*** to place or go into a dry dock
dry dock a dock from which the water can be emptied, used for building and repairing ships
dry·er (-ər) ***n.*** **1.** a person or thing that dries; specif., an apparatus for drying by heating or blowing air, esp. an appliance for drying clothes **2.** *same as* DRIER
dry-eyed (-īd′) ***adj.*** shedding no tears
dry farming farming in an almost rainless region without irrigation: done by conserving the soil moisture and planting drought-resistant crops —**dry′-farm′** ***vt., vi.*** —**dry farmer**
dry goods cloth, cloth products, thread, etc.
dry ice carbon dioxide solidified and compressed into snowlike cakes, used as a refrigerant
dry·ly (-lē) ***adv.*** in a dry manner; matter-of-factly
dry measure a system of measuring the volume of dry things, as grain, vegetables, etc.; esp., the system in which 2 pints = 1 quart, 8 quarts = 1 peck, and 4 pecks = 1 bushel: see TABLE OF WEIGHTS AND MEASURES in Supplements
dry·ness (-nis) ***n.*** the quality or state of being dry
dry point **1.** a needle for engraving lines on a copper plate without using acid **2.** a print from such a plate **3.** this way of engraving
dry rot **1.** a fungous decay causing seasoned timber to crumble to powder **2.** a similar fungous disease of plants, fruits, etc. —**dry′-rot′** ***vi., vt.*** **-rot′ted, -rot′ting**
dry run **1.** [Mil. Slang] practice in firing without using live ammunition **2.** [Slang] a rehearsal
dry wall **1.** a wall of rocks or stones with no mortar **2.** a wall constructed of wallboard, plasterboard, etc. without using wet plaster —**dry′wall′** ***adj.***
D.S., d.s. [It. *dal segno*] (repeat) from this sign
D.S., D.Sc. Doctor of Science
D.S.C., DSC Distinguished Service Cross
D.S.M., DSM Distinguished Service Medal
D.S.O., DSO Distinguished Service Order
D.S.T., DST Daylight Saving Time
D.T.'s, d.t.'s (dē′tēz′) [Slang] *same as* DELIRIUM TREMENS
Du. **1.** Duke **2.** Dutch
du·al (do͞o′əl, dyo͞o′-) ***adj.*** **[**L. *dualis* < *duo*, two**]** **1.** of two **2.** having or composed of two parts or kinds, like or unlike; double; twofold —***n.*** *Linguis.* **1.** *same as* DUAL NUMBER **2.** a word having dual number —**du·al′i·ty** (-al′ə tē) ***n.*** —**du′al·ly** ***adv.***
du·al·ism (-iz'm) ***n.*** **1.** the state of being dual; duality **2.** any theory or doctrine based on a twofold distinction, as the theory that the world is ultimately composed of mind and matter —**du′al·ist** ***n.*** —**du′al·is′tic** ***adj.*** —**du′al·is′ti·cal·ly** ***adv.***
du·al·ize (-īz′) ***vt.*** **-ized′, -iz′ing** to make, or consider as, dual
dual number in some languages, a grammatical number indicating *two, a pair:* distinguished from *singular* and *plural*
dub[1] (dub) ***vt.*** **dubbed, dub′bing** **[**< OE. *dubbian*, to strike**]** **1.** to confer knighthood on by tapping on the shoulder with a sword **2.** to confer a title, name, or nickname upon **3.** to make smooth, as by hammering, scraping, or rubbing **4.** [Slang] to bungle (a golf stroke, etc.) —***n.*** [Slang] a clumsy, unskillful person —**dub′ber** ***n.***
dub[2] (dub) ***vt.*** **dubbed, dub′bing** **[**contr. < DOUBLE**]** to insert (dialogue, music, etc.) in a film or recording (often with *in*) —***n.*** dialogue, music, etc. so inserted —**dub′ber** ***n.***
du Bar·ry (do͞o bar′ē; *Fr.* dü bä *rē′*) comtesse (born *Marie Jeanne Bécu*) 1743?–93; mistress of Louis XV of France
du·bi·e·ty (do͞o bī′ə tē, dyo͞o-) ***n.*** **[**LL. *dubietas***]** **1.** a being dubious **2.** *pl.* **-ties** a doubtful thing

du·bi·ous (do͞o′bē əs, dyo͞o′-) ***adj.*** [< L. < *dubius,* uncertain] **1.** causing doubt; ambiguous **2.** feeling doubt; skeptical **3.** uncertain [*dubious* battle] **4.** questionable [a *dubious* character] —**du′bi·ous·ly** ***adv.*** —**du′bi·ous·ness** ***n.***

Dub·lin (dub′lən) capital of Ireland; seaport on the Irish Sea: pop. 569,000

Du Bois (do͞o bois′), **William Edward Burghardt** 1868–1963; U.S. historian & Negro leader

Du·buque (də byo͞ok′) [after J. *Dubuque,* early lead miner] city in E Iowa, on the Mississippi: pop. 62,000

du·cal (do͞o′k'l, dyo͞o′-) ***adj.*** [see DUKE] of a duke or dukedom —**du′cal·ly** ***adv.***

duc·at (duk′ət) ***n.*** [OFr. < It. *ducato,* coin with image of a duke < LL. *ducatus:* see DUCHY] **1.** any of several former European coins of gold or silver **2.** [Slang] a ticket

du·ce (do͞o′che) ***n.*** [It. < L. *dux,* leader] chief; leader: title (*Il Duce*) assumed by Benito Mussolini

Du·champ (dü shän′), **Marcel** 1887–1968; U.S. painter, born in France

duch·ess (duch′is) ***n.*** **1.** the wife or widow of a duke **2.** a woman who, like a duke, rules a duchy

duch·y (-ē) ***n., pl.*** **duch′ies** [< OFr. < LL. *ducatus,* military command < L. *dux:* see DUKE] the territory ruled by a duke or duchess; dukedom

duck[1] (duk) ***n.*** [< OE. *duce,* lit., diver < base of ff.] **1.** *pl.* **ducks, duck:** see PLURAL, II, D, 1 a swimming bird with a flat bill, short neck and legs, and webbed feet **2.** a female duck: opposed to DRAKE **3.** the flesh of a duck as food **4.** [Slang] a person [an odd *duck*] —**like water off a duck's back** with no effect or reaction

duck[2] (duk) ***vt., vi.*** [ME. *douken* < hyp. OE. *ducan,* to dive] **1.** to plunge or dip under water for a moment **2.** to lower or move (the head, body, etc.) suddenly, as in avoiding a blow or in hiding **3.** [Colloq.] to avoid (a task, person, etc.) **4.** [Slang] to run (*in* or *out*) —***n.*** a ducking

duck[3] (duk) ***n.*** [Du. *doek*] **1.** a cotton or linen cloth like canvas but finer and lighter in weight **2.** [*pl.*] [Colloq.] trousers made of this cloth

duck[4] (duk) ***n.*** [altered (after DUCK[1]) < *DUKW,* code name] [Mil. Slang] an amphibious motor vehicle

duck·bill (duk′bil′) ***n.*** *same as* PLATYPUS

duck·ling (-liŋ) ***n.*** a young duck

duck·pins (-pinz′) ***n.pl.*** **1.** [*with sing. v.*] a game like bowling or tenpins, played with smaller pins and balls **2.** the pins used

duck soup [Slang] something that is easy to do

duck·weed (-wēd′) ***n.*** a minute flowering plant that floats on ponds and sluggish streams

duck·y (-ē) ***adj.*** **duck′i·er, duck′i·est** [Slang] pleasing, delightful, darling, etc.

duct (dukt) ***n.*** [< ML. < L. *ductus,* pp. of *ducere,* to lead] **1.** a tube or channel through which a fluid moves **2.** a tube in the body for the passage of excretions or secretions [a bile *duct*] **3.** a tubule in plant tissues, conducting resin, etc. **4.** a pipe or conduit enclosing wires —**duct′less** ***adj.***

duc·tile (duk′t'l) ***adj.*** [see prec.] **1.** that can be stretched, drawn, or hammered thin without breaking: said of metals **2.** easily molded; pliant **3.** easily led; tractable —**duc·til′i·ty** (-til′ə tē) ***n.***

ductless gland an endocrine gland

dud (dud) ***n.*** [prob. < Du. *dood,* dead] [Colloq.] **1.** a bomb or shell that fails to explode **2.** a person or thing that fails —***adj.*** [Colloq.] worthless

dude (do͞od) ***n.*** [< ?] **1.** a dandy; fop **2.** [Western Slang] a city fellow or tourist, esp. an Easterner —**dud′ish** ***adj.*** —**dud′ish·ly** ***adv.***

dude ranch a ranch or farm operated as a vacation resort, with horseback riding, etc.

dudg·eon (duj′ən) ***n.*** [prob. < Anglo-Fr. *en digeon,* at the dagger hilt] anger or resentment: now chiefly in **in high dudgeon,** very angry, offended, or resentful

duds (dudz) ***n.pl.*** [prob. < ON. < *dutha,* to wrap up, swathe] [Colloq.] **1.** clothes **2.** belongings

due (do͞o, dyo͞o) ***adj.*** [< OFr. *deu,* pp. of *devoir,* to owe < L. *debere:* see DEBT] **1.** owed or owing as a debt, right, etc.; payable **2.** suitable; proper [*due* respect] **3.** enough; adequate [*due* care] **4.** expected or scheduled to arrive or be ready [the plane is *due* now] —***adv.*** exactly; directly [*due* west] —***n.*** anything due; specif., *a*) deserved recognition *b*) [*pl.*] fees, taxes, or other charges [membership *dues*] —**become** (or **fall**) **due** to become payable as previously arranged —**due to 1.** caused by; resulting from [deaths *due to* cancer] **2.** [Colloq.] because of [*due to* his help, we won the game]

du·el (do͞o′əl, dyo͞o′-) ***n.*** [< ML. < OL. *duellum* (L. *bellum*), war] **1.** a formal, prearranged fight between two persons armed with deadly weapons **2.** any contest suggesting such a fight [a verbal *duel*] —***vi., vt.*** **-eled** or **-elled, -el·ing** or **-el·ling** to fight a duel (with) —**du′el·ist** or **du′el·list, du′el·er** or **du′el·ler** ***n.***

du·en·na (do͞o en′ə, dyo͞o-) ***n.*** [Sp. *dueña* < L. *domina,* mistress] **1.** an elderly woman who has charge of the young unmarried women of a Spanish or Portuguese family **2.** a chaperon or governess

due process (of law) the course of legal proceedings established to protect individual rights

du·et (do͞o et′, dyo͞o-) ***n.*** [< It. < L. *duo,* two] *Music* **1.** a composition for two voices or instruments **2.** the two performers of such a composition

duff (duf) ***n.*** [dial. var. of DOUGH] a thick flour pudding boiled in a cloth bag

duf·fel, duf·fle (duf′'l) ***n.*** [Du. < *Duffel,* town in N Belgium] **1.** a coarse woolen cloth **2.** clothing and equipment carried by a camper, soldier, etc. **3.** *same as* DUFFEL BAG

duffel (or duffle) bag a large, cylindrical cloth bag for carrying clothing and personal belongings

duf·fer (duf′ər) ***n.*** [< thieves' slang *duff,* to fake] [Slang] an incompetent or stupid person; specif., a relatively unskilled golfer

Du·fy (dü fē′), **Ra·oul (Ernest Joseph)** (*r*ä o͞ol′) 1877–1953; Fr. painter

dug[1] (dug) *pt. & pp. of* DIG

dug[2] (dug) ***n.*** [< same base as Dan. *dægge,* to suckle] a nipple, teat, or udder

du·gong (do͞o′gôŋ, -gäŋ) ***n.*** [Malay *dūyung*] a large, whalelike mammal of tropical seas

dug·out (dug′out′) ***n.*** **1.** a boat or canoe hollowed out of a log **2.** a shelter, as in warfare, dug in the ground or in a hillside **3.** a covered shelter near a baseball diamond for the players to sit in

dui·ker (dī′kər) ***n., pl.*** **-kers, -ker:** see PLURAL, II, D, 1 [Du.] any of several small, African antelopes

Duis·burg (düs′boo*r*k) city in W West Germany, on the Rhine: pop. 469,000

duke (do͞ok, dyo͞ok) ***n.*** [< OFr. < L. *dux,* leader < *ducere,* to lead] **1.** the ruler of an independent duchy **2.** a nobleman of the highest hereditary rank below that of a prince —**duke′dom** ***n.***

dukes (do͞oks, dyo͞oks) ***n.pl.*** [< *duke,* short for *Duke of York,* used in 19th-c. E. rhyming slang for *fork,* fingers] [Slang] the fists or hands

dul·cet (dul′sit) ***adj.*** [< OFr. < L. *dulcis,* sweet] soothing or pleasant to hear; melodious

dul·ci·mer (dul′sə mər) ***n.*** [< OFr. < Sp. < L. < *dulce,* sweet + *melos* < Gr. *melos,* a song] **1.** a musical instrument with metal strings, which are struck with two small hammers by the player **2.** a violin-shaped stringed instrument of the southern Appalachians, plucked with a plectrum or a goose quill: also **dul′ci·more′** (-môr′, -mər)

DULCIMER

dull (dul) ***adj.*** [OE. *dol,* stupid] **1.** mentally slow; stupid **2.** lacking sensitivity; unfeeling **3.** physically slow; sluggish **4.** lacking spirit; listless **5.** not active; slack **6.** causing boredom; tedious **7.** not sharp; blunt **8.** not felt keenly [a *dull* headache] **9.** not vivid **10.** not glossy **11.** not distinct; muffled [a *dull* thud] **12.** gloomy; cloudy —***vt., vi.*** to make or become dull —**dull′ish** ***adj.*** —**dull′ness, dul′ness** ***n.*** —**dul′ly** ***adv.***

dull·ard (-ərd) ***n.*** a stupid person

dulse (duls) ***n.*** [Ir. & Gael. *duileasg*] any of several edible marine algae with large, red fronds

Du·luth (də lo͞oth′) [after D. *Du Lhut,* 17th-c. Fr. explorer] city in NE Minn.: pop. 93,000

du·ly (do͞o′lē, dyo͞o′-) ***adv.*** in due manner; specif., *a*) as due; rightfully *b*) when due; at the right time *c*) as required; sufficiently

Du·ma (do͞o′mä) ***n.*** [Russ. < Gmc., as in OE. *dom,* judgment] the parliament of czarist Russia (1905–17)

Du·mas (dü mä′; *E.* do͞o′mä) **1. Alexandre,** 1802–70; Fr. novelist & playwright: called *Dumas père* **2. Alexandre,** 1824–95; Fr. playwright & novelist: son of *prec.:* called *Dumas fils*

dumb (dum) ***adj.*** [OE.] **1.** lacking the power of speech; mute **2.** unwilling to talk; silent **3.** not accompanied by speech **4.** temporarily speechless, as from fear **5.** [G. *dumm*] [Colloq.] stupid; moronic —**dumb′ly** ***adv.*** —**dumb′ness** ***n.***

dumb·bell (dum′bel′) ***n.*** **1.** a device usually used in pairs for muscular exercise: each pair has round weights joined by a short bar **2.** [Slang] a dumb or stupid person

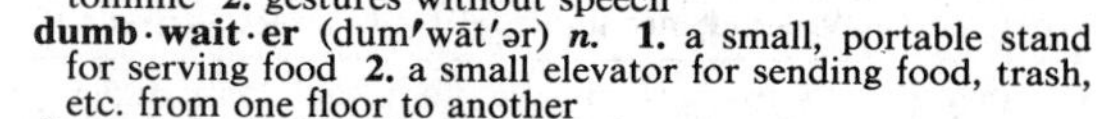

dumb·found, dum·found (dum′found′) ***vt.*** [DUMB + (CON)FOUND] to make speechless by shocking

dumb show 1. formerly, a part of a play done in pantomime **2.** gestures without speech

dumb·wait·er (dum′wāt′ər) ***n.*** **1.** a small, portable stand for serving food **2.** a small elevator for sending food, trash, etc. from one floor to another

dum·dum (bullet) (dum′dum′) [< *Dumdum,* arsenal near

Calcutta, India] a soft-nosed bullet that expands when it hits, inflicting a large wound

dum·my (dum′ē) ***n.***, *pl.* **-mies** **1.** a person unable to talk: a vulgar usage **2.** a figure made in human form, as for displaying clothing, practicing tackling in football, etc. **3.** an imitation or sham **4.** a person secretly acting for another while apparently representing his own interests **5.** [Slang] a stupid person **6.** *Bridge, Whist,* etc. *a)* the declarer's partner, whose hand is exposed on the board and played by the declarer *b)* such a hand **7.** the skeleton copy, as of a book, upon which the format is laid out —***adj.*** **1.** imitation; sham **2.** secretly acting as a front for another **3.** *Bridge,* etc. played with a dummy —**dummy up, -mied, -my·ing** [Slang] to refuse to talk

dump[1] (dump) ***vt.*** [prob. < ON.] **1.** to empty out or unload as in a heap or mass **2.** *a)* to throw away (rubbish, etc.) esp. in or at a dump *b)* to get rid of abruptly or roughly **3.** to sell (a commodity) in a large quantity at a low price, esp. abroad —***vi.*** **1.** to fall in a heap or mass **2.** to unload rubbish **3.** to dump commodities —***n.*** **1.** a rubbish pile or a place for dumping **2.** *Mil.* a temporary storage center, as for ammunition **3.** [Slang] a place that is unpleasant, ugly, etc. —**dump′er** ***n.***

dump[2] (dump) ***n.*** [< ? Du. *domp,* haze] [Obs.] a sad song —**in the dumps** in low spirits; depressed

dump·ling (-liŋ) ***n.*** [< Brit. *dump,* lump + -LING[1]] **1.** a small piece of dough, steamed or boiled and served with meat or soup **2.** a crust of dough filled with fruit and steamed or baked

dump truck a truck that is unloaded by tilting the truck bed backward with the tailgate open

dump·y[1] (dum′pē) ***adj.*** **dump′i·er, dump′i·est** **1.** short and thick; squat **2.** [Slang] ugly, rundown, etc. —**dump′i·ly** ***adv.*** —**dump′i·ness** ***n.***

dump·y[2] (dum′pē) ***adj.*** **dump′i·er, dump′i·est** [see DUMP[2]] melancholy; depressed

dun[1] (dun) ***adj.*** [OE.] dull grayish-brown —***n.*** **1.** a dull grayish brown **2.** a dun horse

dun[2] (dun) ***vt., vi.*** **dunned, dun′ning** [? dial. var. of DIN] to ask (a debtor) repeatedly for payment —***n.*** an insistent demand for payment of a debt

Dun·can (duŋ′kən) [Gael. *Donnchadh,* lit., brown warrior] a masculine name

dunce (duns) ***n.*** [< *Dunsmen* or *Dunces,* followers of DUNS SCOTUS, who were considered foes of new ideas] **1.** a dull, ignorant person **2.** a person slow at learning

dunce cap a cone-shaped hat which children slow at learning were formerly forced to wear in school

Dun·dee (dun dē′) seaport in E Scotland, on the North Sea: pop. 182,000

dun·der·head (dun′dər hed′) ***n.*** [< Du. *donder,* thunder, infl. by BLUNDER] a stupid person; dunce

dune (do͞on, dyo͞on) ***n.*** [Fr. < ODu. *duna*] a rounded hill or ridge of sand heaped up by the wind

dune buggy [from orig. use on sand dunes] a small, light automobile made from a standard, compact chassis and a prefabricated body

Dun·e·din (də nē′d'n) city on the SE coast of South Island, New Zealand: pop. 110,000

dung (duŋ) ***n.*** [OE.] **1.** animal excrement; manure **2.** filth —***vt.*** to spread with dung, as in fertilizing —**dung′y** ***adj.*** **dung′i·er, dung′i·est**

dun·ga·ree (duŋ′gə rē′) ***n.*** [Hindi *dungrī*] **1.** a coarse cotton cloth; specif., blue denim **2.** [*pl.*] work trousers or overalls of this cloth

dun·geon (dun′jən) ***n.*** [< OFr. *donjon*] **1.** *same as* DONJON **2.** a dark, underground cell or prison

dung·hill (duŋ′hil′) ***n.*** **1.** a heap of dung **2.** anything vile or filthy

dunk (duŋk) ***vt.*** [G. *tunken,* to dip < OHG. *dunchôn*] **1.** to dip (bread, cake, etc.) into coffee or other liquid before eating it **2.** to immerse in liquid for a short time

Dun·kirk (dun′kərk) seaport in N France: scene of the evacuation of Allied troops under fire (1940): Fr. name **Dun·kerque** (dön kerk′)

dun·lin (dun′lin) ***n.***, *pl.* **-lins, -lin:** see PLURAL, II, D, 1 [< DUN[1] + -LING[1]] a small sandpiper with a reddish back and a black patch on its belly

dun·nage (dun′ij) ***n.*** [< ML. *dennagium* < ?] **1.** a loose packing of any bulky material put around cargo for protection **2.** personal baggage or belongings

Duns Sco·tus (dunz skōt′əs), **John** 1265?–1308; Scot. scholastic philosopher & theologian

du·o (do͞o′ō, dyo͞o′ō) ***n.***, *pl.* **du′os, du′i** (-ē) [It.] **1.** *same as* DUET (esp. sense 2) **2.** a pair; couple

du·o- [< L. *duo,* two] *a combining form meaning* two, double *[duologue]*

du·o·dec·i·mal (do͞o′ə des′ə m'l, dyo͞o′-) ***adj.*** [< L. *duo,* two + *decem,* ten + -AL] **1.** relating to twelve or twelfths **2.** consisting of or counting by twelves —***n.*** **1.** one twelfth **2.** [*pl.*] *Math.* a system of numeration with twelve as its base

du·o·dec·i·mo (-mō′) ***n.***, *pl.* **-mos′** [< L. *in duodecimo,* in twelve] **1.** a page size (about 5 by 7 1/2 in.), 1/12 of a printer's sheet **2.** a book with pages of this size Also called *twelvemo,* and written *12mo* or *12°* —***adj.*** with pages of this size

du·o·de·num (do͞o′ə dē′nəm, dyo͞o′-; do͞o äd′'n əm) ***n.***, *pl.* **-de′na** (-nə), **-de′nums** [< ML. < L. *duodeni,* twelve each: its length is about twelve fingers' breadth] the first section of the small intestine, between the stomach and the jejunum —**du′o·de′nal** ***adj.***

du·o·logue (do͞o′ə lôg′, -läg′; dyo͞o′-) ***n.*** [DUO- + (MONO)-LOGUE] a conversation between two people

du·op·o·ly (do͞o äp′ə lē, dyo͞o-) ***n.*** [DUO- + (MONO)POLY] control of a commodity or service by only two producers or suppliers

dup. duplicate

dupe (do͞op, dyo͞op) ***n.*** [Fr. < OFr. < L. *upupa,* hoopoe, stupid bird] a person easily tricked or fooled —***vt.*** **duped, dup′ing** to deceive or cheat —**dup′a·ble** ***adj.*** —**dup′er** ***n.*** —**dup′er·y** ***n.***, *pl.* **-er·ies**

du·ple (do͞o′p'l, dyo͞o′-) ***adj.*** [L. *duplus:* see DOUBLE] **1.** double; twofold **2.** *Music* having two (or a multiple of two) beats to the measure *[duple* time*]*

du·plex (do͞o′pleks, dyo͞o′-) ***adj.*** [L. < *duo,* two + *-plex,* -fold, akin to *plaga,* area] **1.** double; twofold **2.** having two units operating in the same way or simultaneously —***n.*** *same as* DUPLEX HOUSE or DUPLEX APARTMENT —**du·plex′i·ty** ***n.***

duplex apartment an apartment with rooms on two floors and a private inner stairway

duplex house a house consisting of two separate family units

du·pli·cate (do͞o′plə kit, dyo͞o′-; *for v.* -kāt′) ***adj.*** [< L. pp. of *duplicare,* to double: see DUPLEX] **1.** double **2.** having two similar parts **3.** corresponding exactly **4.** designating a game of bridge, etc. in which the same hands are played off again by other players to compare scores —***n.*** **1.** an exact copy; replica; facsimile **2.** a counterpart or double **3.** a duplicate game of bridge, etc. —***vt.*** **-cat′ed, -cat′ing** **1.** to make double or twofold **2.** to make an exact copy of **3.** to make, do, or cause to happen again —**in duplicate** in two precisely similar forms —**du′pli·ca·ble, du′pli·cat′a·ble** ***adj.*** —**du′pli·ca′tion** ***n.*** —**du′pli·ca′tive** ***adj.***

duplicating machine a machine for making exact copies of a letter, photograph, drawing, etc.: also **du′pli·ca′tor** ***n.***

du·plic·i·ty (do͞o plis′ə tē, dyo͞o-) ***n.***, *pl.* **-ties** [< OFr. < LL. *duplicitas:* see DUPLEX] hypocritical cunning or deception; double-dealing

du Pont (do͞o pänt′, do͞o′ pänt; dyo͞o) name of a family prominent as U.S. industrialists since 1802

dur·a·ble (door′ə b'l, dyoor′-) ***adj.*** [OFr. < L. < *durare,* to last, harden < *durus,* hard] **1.** lasting in spite of hard wear or frequent use **2.** continuing to exist; stable —***n.*** [*pl.*] *same as* DURABLE GOODS —**du′ra·bil′i·ty** ***n.*** —**du′ra·bly** ***adv.***

durable goods goods usable for a relatively long time, as machinery, cars, or home appliances

du·ral·u·min (doo ral′yoo m'n, dyoo-) ***n.*** [DUR(ABLE) + ALUMIN(UM)] a strong, lightweight alloy of aluminum with copper, manganese, magnesium, and silicon

du·ra ma·ter (door′ə māt′ər, dyoor′-) [ML., lit., hard mother < an Ar. term] the outermost and toughest of the three membranes covering the brain and spinal cord: also **du′ra** ***n.*** —**du′ral** ***adj.***

du·ra·men (doo rā′mən, dyoo-) ***n.*** [L. < *durare:* see DURABLE] *same as* HEARTWOOD

dur·ance (door′əns, dyoor′-) ***n.*** [< OFr. < L. *durans,* prp. of *durare:* see DURABLE] imprisonment: mainly in phrase **in durance vile**

du·ra·tion (doo rā′shən, dyoo-) ***n.*** [< ML. < pp. of L. *durare:* see DURABLE] **1.** continuance in time **2.** the time that a thing continues or lasts

Dur·ban (dur′bən) seaport in Natal, on the E coast of South Africa: pop. 663,000

dur·bar (dur′bär) ***n.*** [Hindi < Per. < *dar,* portal + *bār,* court] **1.** formerly in India or Africa, a reception or audience held by a native prince or British governor **2.** the place where this was held

Dü·rer (dü′rər; *E.* dyoor′ər), **Al·brecht** (äl′breHt) 1471–1528; Ger. painter & wood engraver

du·ress (doo res′, dyoo-; door′is, dyoor′-) ***n.*** [< OFr. < L. *duritia,* hardness < *durus,* hard] **1.** imprisonment **2.** the use of force or threats *[*signed under *duress]*

Dur·ham (dur′əm) [after *Durham* County, England] city in NC N.C.: pop. 101,000 —*n.* one of a breed of short-horned beef cattle, orig. bred in Durham County, England
dur·ing (door′iŋ, dyoor′-) *prep.* [see DURABLE] **1.** throughout the entire time of **2.** at some point in the entire time of; in the course of
Du·roc-Jer·sey (door′äk jur′zē, dyoor′-) *n.* any of a breed of large, red hog: also **Du′roc**
dur·ra (door′ə) *n.* [Ar. *dhurah*] a kind of grain sorghum
durst (durst) *archaic pt. of* DARE
du·rum (wheat) (door′əm, dyoor′-) [L., neut. of *durus,* hard] a hard wheat that yields flour and semolina used in macaroni, spaghetti, etc.
Du·shan·be (do͞o shän′be) capital of the Tadzhik S.S.R., in the W part: pop. 345,000
dusk (dusk) *adj.* [by metathesis < OE. *dox,* dark-colored] [Poet.] dark in color; dusky —*n.* **1.** the dim part of twilight **2.** gloom; dusky quality —*vt., vi.* to make or become dusky or shadowy
dusk·y (dus′kē) *adj.* **dusk′i·er, dusk′i·est** **1.** somewhat dark in color; esp., swarthy **2.** lacking light; dim **3.** gloomy —**dusk′i·ly** *adv.* —**dusk′i·ness** *n.*
Düs·sel·dorf (düs′əl dôrf′) city in W West Germany, on the Rhine: pop. 689,000
dust (dust) *n.* [OE.] **1.** powdery earth or any finely powdered matter **2.** a cloud of such matter **3.** confusion; turmoil **4.** *a)* earth *b)* disintegrated mortal remains **5.** a humble or abject condition **6.** anything worthless **7.** *same as* GOLD DUST —*vt.* **1.** to sprinkle with dust, powder, etc. **2.** to sprinkle (powder, etc.) on **3.** to rid of dust, as by brushing or wiping —*vi.* to remove dust, as from furniture —**bite the dust** to be killed, esp. in battle —**dust off** [Slang] to pitch a baseball deliberately close to (the batter) —**shake the dust off one's feet** to leave with disdain —**throw dust in (someone's) eyes** to deceive (someone) —**dust′less** *adj.*
dust·bin (-bin′) *n.* [Brit.] a container for rubbish
dust bowl a region where eroded topsoil is blown away by winds during droughts
dust·er (-ər) *n.* **1.** a person or thing that dusts; specif., *a)* a brush or cloth for removing dust from furniture, etc. *b)* a device for sprinkling on a powder **2.** a short, loose, lightweight housecoat
dust jacket a detachable paper cover for protecting the binding of a book
dust·man (-mən) *n., pl.* **-men** [Brit.] a man whose work is removing rubbish, ashes, garbage, etc.
dust·pan (-pan′) *n.* a shovellike receptacle into which dust or debris is swept from a floor
dust storm a windstorm that sweeps up clouds of dust when passing over an arid region
dust·y (-ē) *adj.* **dust′i·er, dust′i·est** **1.** covered with or full of dust **2.** like dust; powdery **3.** of the color of dust —**dust′i·ly** *adv.* —**dust′i·ness** *n.*
Dutch (duch) *adj.* [< MDu. *Duutsch,* Dutch, German] **1.** of the Netherlands, its people, language, or culture **2.** of the Pennsylvania Dutch **3.** [Slang] German —*n.* **1.** the language of the Netherlands **2.** [Slang] German —**beat the Dutch** [Colloq.] to be very unusual —**go Dutch** [Colloq.] to have each pay his own expenses —**in Dutch** [Colloq.] in trouble or disfavor —**the Dutch** **1.** the people of the Netherlands **2.** the Pennsylvania Dutch
Dutch bob a haircut with bangs and a straight, even bob that covers the ears
Dutch courage [Colloq.] courage stimulated by drinking alcoholic liquor
Dutch door a door with upper and lower halves that can be opened separately
Dutch East Indies *same as* NETHERLANDS (EAST) INDIES
Dutch elm disease [from its first appearance in the Netherlands] a widespread fungous disease of elms that causes the tree to die
Dutch Guiana *former name of* SURINAME
Dutch·man (-mən) *n., pl.* **-men** **1.** a native or inhabitant of the Netherlands **2.** a Dutch ship **3.** [Slang] a German
Dutch·man's-breech·es (-mənz brich′iz) *n., pl.* **-breech′es** a spring wildflower with pinkish flowers, found in E U.S.

DUTCH DOOR

Dutch oven **1.** a heavy metal pot with a high, arched lid, for cooking pot roasts, etc. **2.** a metal container for roasting meats, etc., with an open side placed toward the fire
Dutch treat [Colloq.] any entertainment, etc. at which each participant pays his own expenses
Dutch uncle [Colloq.] a person who bluntly and sternly lectures or scolds someone else
Dutch West Indies *former name of* NETHERLANDS ANTILLES
du·te·ous (do͞ot′ē əs, dyo͞ot′-) *adj.* dutiful; obedient —**du′te·ous·ly** *adv.* —**du′te·ous·ness** *n.*
du·ti·a·ble (do͞ot′ē ə b'l, dyo͞ot′-) *adj.* necessitating payment of a duty or tax, as imported goods
du·ti·ful (-ə fəl) *adj.* **1.** showing, or resulting from, a sense of duty **2.** obedient —**du′ti·ful·ly** *adv.*
du·ty (do͞ot′ē, dyo͞ot′ē) *n., pl.* **-ties** [< Anglo-Fr. *dueté,* what is due: see DUE & -TY[1]] **1.** obedience or respect to parents, older people, etc. **2.** conduct based on moral or legal obligation **3.** any action required by one's occupation or position **4.** a sense of obligation **5.** service, esp. military service **6.** a payment due to the government, esp. a tax imposed on imports, exports, etc. **7.** service or use: see HEAVY-DUTY —**on** (or **off**) **duty** at (or having time off from) one's work or duty
du·ty-free (-frē′) *adj., adv.* with no payment of a duty or tax required
du·um·vir (do͞o um′vər, dyo͞o-) *n., pl.* **-virs, -vi·ri′** (-və rī′) [L. < *duo,* two + *vir,* a man] either of two magistrates in ancient Rome who held office jointly
du·um·vi·rate (-və rit) *n.* **1.** governmental position held jointly by two men **2.** two such men
du·ve·tyne, du·ve·tyn (do͞o′və tēn′) *n.* [< Fr. < *duvet,* eiderdown] a soft, velvetlike textile, originally made of cotton and silk
D.V.M. Doctor of Veterinary Medicine
Dvo·řák (dvôr′zhäk, -zhak), **An·ton** (än′tôn) 1841–1904; Czech composer
dwarf (dwôrf) *n., pl.* **dwarfs, dwarves** (dwôrvz) [OE. *dweorg*] **1.** a person, animal, or plant much smaller than usual for its species **2.** *Folklore* an ugly little being with supposed magic powers **3.** a star of relatively small mass and low luminosity: in full, **dwarf star** —*vt.* **1.** to stunt the growth of **2.** to make small or insignificant **3.** to make seem small by comparison —*adj.* undersized; stunted —**dwarf′ish** *adj.* —**dwarf′ish·ness** *n.* —**dwarf′ism** *n.*
dwell (dwel) *vi.* **dwelt** or **dwelled, dwell′ing** [OE. *dwellan,* to lead astray, hinder] to make one's home; reside —**dwell on** (or **upon**) to linger over in thought or speech —**dwell′er** *n.*
dwell·ing (-iŋ) *n.* a place to live in; residence; house; abode: also **dwelling place**
DWI, D.W.I. driving while intoxicated
Dwight (dwīt) [a surname < ?] a masculine name
dwin·dle (dwin′d'l) *vi., vt.* **-dled, -dling** [freq. of ME. *dwinen* < OE. *dwinan,* to wither] to become or make smaller or less; diminish; shrink
dwt. [*d*(*enarius*) *w*(*eigh*)*t*] pennyweight(s)
DX, D.X. *Radio* **1.** distance **2.** distant
Dy *Chem.* dysprosium
Dy·ak (dī′ak) *n.* [Malay *dayak,* savage] **1.** a member of an aboriginal people of Borneo **2.** their Indonesian language
dyb·buk (dib′ək) *n.* [Heb. *dibbūq* < *dābhaq,* to cleave] *Jewish Folklore* the spirit of a dead person that enters and possesses the body of a living person
dye (dī) *n.* [OE. *deag*] **1.** color produced in fabric, hair, etc. by saturating it with a coloring agent; tint; hue **2.** any such coloring agent or a solution containing it —*vt.* **dyed, dye′ing** to color as with a dye —*vi.* to take on color in dyeing —**of (the) deepest dye** of the worst sort —**dy′er** *n.*
dyed-in-the-wool (dīd′'n *thə* wool′) *adj.* **1.** dyed before being woven **2.** thoroughgoing; unchanging
dye·ing (dī′iŋ) *n.* the process or work of coloring fabrics, hair, etc. with dyes
dye·stuff (dī′stuf′) *n.* any substance yielding a dye
dy·ing (dī′iŋ) *prp. of* DIE[1] —*adj.* **1.** about to die or come to an end **2.** of or at the time of death —*n.* a ceasing to live or exist; death
dyke (dīk) *n., vt. same as* DIKE
dy·nam·ic (dī nam′ik) *adj.* [< Fr. < Gr. < *dynamis,* power < *dynasthai,* to be able] **1.** relating to energy or physical force in motion: opposed to STATIC **2.** relating to dynamics **3.** energetic; vigorous; forceful **4.** relating to change Also **dy·nam′i·cal** —*n. same as* DYNAMICS (sense 2*a*) —**dy·nam′i·cal·ly** *adv.*
dy·nam·ics (-iks) *n.pl.* [*with sing. v. for 1, 2c, & 3*] **1.** the branch of mechanics dealing with the motions of material bodies under the action of given forces; kinetics **2.** *a)* the various forces, physical, moral, economic, etc., operating in any field *b)* the way such forces operate mutually *c)* the study of such forces **3.** the effect of varying degrees of loudness in musical performance
dy·na·mism (dī′nə miz'm) *n.* **1.** the theory that force or energy is the basic universal principle **2.** a dynamic quality —**dy′na·mis′tic** *adj.*
dy·na·mite (dī′nə mīt′) *n.* [coined (1866–67) by A. NOBEL < Gr. *dynamis:* see DYNAMIC] a powerful explosive made of some absorbent soaked with nitroglycerin —*vt.* **-mit′ed, -mit′ing** to blow up with dynamite —*adj.* [Slang] outstanding; very exciting, effective, etc. —**dy′na·mit′er** *n.*
dy·na·mo (-mō′) *n., pl.* **-mos′** [< *dynamoelectric machine*] **1.** a machine that generates electricity: see GENERATOR **2.** a forceful, dynamic person
dy·na·mo- [< Gr. *dynamis:* see DYNAMIC] *a combining form meaning* power *[dynamoelectric]*
dy·na·mo·e·lec·tric (dī′nə mō i lek′trik) *adj.* having to do with production of electrical energy from mechanical

energy, or the reverse process: also **dy′na·mo·e·lec′tri·cal**

dy·na·mom·e·ter (-mäm′ə tər) ***n.*** an apparatus for measuring force or power, esp. mechanical power —**dy′na·mo·met′ric** (-mō met′rik) ***adj.*** —**dy′na·mom′e·try** ***n.***

dy·na·mo·tor (dī′nə mōt′ər) ***n.*** an electrical machine combining generator and motor, for transforming current from one voltage to another

dy·nast (dī′nast, -nəst) ***n.*** **[**< L. < Gr. < *dynasthai,* to be strong**]** a ruler, esp. a hereditary ruler

dy·nas·ty (dī′nəs tē) ***n., pl.*** **-ties** [see prec.] **1.** a succession of rulers who are members of the same family **2.** the period during which a certain family reigns —**dy·nas·tic** (dī nas′tik), **dy·nas′ti·cal** ***adj.*** —**dy·nas′ti·cal·ly** ***adv.***

dyne (dīn) ***n.*** **[**Fr. < Gr. *dynamis,* power**]** the amount of force that imparts to a mass of one gram an acceleration of one centimeter per second per second

Dy·nel (dī nel′) *a trademark for* a synthetic fiber —***n.*** [**d-**] this fiber or a furlike fabric made from it

dys- **[**Gr.**]** *a prefix meaning* bad, ill, abnormal, impaired, difficult, etc. *[dysfunction]*

dys·en·ter·y (dis′′n ter′ē) ***n.*** **[**< OFr. < L. < Gr. < *dys-,* bad + *entera,* bowels**]** a painful intestinal inflammation characterized by diarrhea with bloody, mucous feces —**dys′en·ter′ic** ***adj.***

dys·func·tion (dis fuŋk′shən) ***n.*** abnormal, impaired, or incomplete functioning, as of a body organ or part —**dys·func′tion·al** ***adj.***

dys·lex·i·a (dis lek′sē ə) ***n.*** **[**ModL. < Gr. *dys-,* bad + *lexis,* speech < *legein,* to speak**]** impairment of the ability to read, often from brain injury or genetic defect —**dys·lex′ic** ***adj.***

dys·pep·si·a (dis pep′shə, -sē ə) ***n.*** **[**L. < Gr. < *dys-,* bad + *pepsis,* cooking < *peptein,* to digest**]** impaired digestion; indigestion: also [Dial.] **dys·pep′sy**

dys·pep·tic (-tik) ***adj.*** **1.** of, causing, or having dyspepsia **2.** gloomy; grouchy —***n.*** a person who has dyspepsia —**dys·pep′ti·cal·ly** ***adv.***

dysp·ne·a (disp′nē ə, disp nē′ə) ***n.*** **[**< L. < Gr. < *dys-,* hard + *pnoē* < *pnein,* to breathe**]** difficult or painful breathing —**dysp·ne′al, dysp·ne′ic** ***adj.***

dys·pro·si·um (dis prō′sē əm, -zē-, -shē-) ***n.*** **[**< Gr. *dysprositos,* difficult of access**]** a chemical element of the rare-earth group: symbol, Dy; at. wt., 162.50; at. no., 66: it is one of the most magnetic of all known substances

dys·tro·phy (dis′trə fē) ***n.*** **[**ModL. *dystrophia:* see DYS- & -TROPHY**]** **1.** faulty nutrition **2.** faulty development, or degeneration: cf. MUSCULAR DYSTROPHY —**dys·tro′phic** (-träf′ik, -trō′fik) ***adj.***

dz. dozen; dozens

E

E, e (ē) ***n., pl.*** **E's, e's** **1.** the fifth letter of the English alphabet **2.** a sound of *E* or *e*

E (ē) ***n.*** **1.** *Educ. a)* a grade indicating below-average work *b)* occas., a grade indicating excellence **2.** *Music a)* the third tone in the ascending scale of C major *b)* the scale having this tone as the keynote

e **1.** *Physics* erg **2.** *Math.* the number used as the base of a system of logarithms, approximately 2.71828: written *e*

e- *a prefix meaning* out, from, etc.: see EX-

E, E., e, e. **1.** east **2.** eastern

E. **1.** Earl **2.** Easter **3.** English

E., e. **1.** earth **2.** engineer(ing) **3.** *Baseball* errors

ea. each

each (ēch) ***adj., pron.*** **[**< OE. *ælc***]** every one of two or more considered separately —***adv.*** apiece *[ten cents each]* —**each other** each one the other; one another: some use *each other* only of two and *one another* of more than two, but in common use no distinction is made *[help each other]*

ea·ger (ē′gər) ***adj.*** **[**< OFr. *aigre* < L. *acer,* sharp, keen**]** feeling or showing keen desire; impatient or anxious to do or get —**ea′ger·ly** ***adv.*** —**ea′ger·ness** ***n.***

ea·gle (ē′g′l) ***n.*** **[**< OFr. *aigle* < L. *aquila***]** **1.** a large, strong, flesh-eating bird of prey having sharp vision and powerful wings **2.** a representation of the eagle as a symbol of a nation, etc.; esp., the national emblem of the U.S. **3.** a former U.S. gold coin worth $10 **4.** *Golf* a score of two below par on any hole

ea·gle-eyed (-īd′) ***adj.*** having keen vision

ea·glet (ē′glit) ***n.*** a young eagle

-e·an (ē′ən) **[**< L. & Gr.**]** *a suffix meaning* of, belonging to, like *[European]*

ear[1] (ir) ***n.*** **[**OE. *eare***]** **1.** the part of the body that perceives sound; organ of hearing **2.** the visible, external part of the ear **3.** the sense of hearing **4.** the ability to recognize slight differences in sound, esp. in musical tones **5.** anything shaped or placed like an ear —**be all ears** to listen attentively or eagerly —**bend someone's ear** [Slang] to talk excessively to someone —**fall on deaf ears** to be ignored or unheeded —**have** (or **keep**) **an ear to the ground** to pay attention to the trends of public opinion —**play by ear** to play (a musical instrument or piece) without the use of notation —**play it by ear** [Colloq.] to act as the situation demands —**turn a deaf ear** to be unwilling to listen or heed

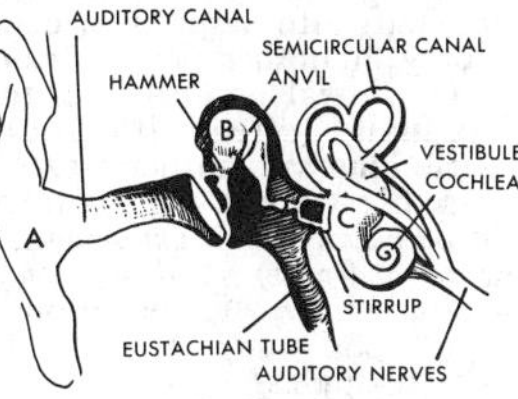

HUMAN EAR
(A, external ear; B, middle ear; C, inner ear)

ear[2] (ir) ***n.*** **[**< OE. *ær***]** the grain-bearing spike of a cereal plant *[an ear of corn]* —***vi.*** to sprout ears

ear·ache (ir′āk′) ***n.*** an ache or pain in the ear

ear·drum (-drum′) ***n.*** *same as:* **1.** TYMPANIC MEMBRANE **2.** MIDDLE EAR

ear·ful (-fool′) ***n.*** [Colloq.] talk listened to that is especially gossipy, scolding, tedious, etc.

Earl, Earle (url) [see ff.] a masculine name

earl (url) ***n.*** **[**OE. *eorl,* warrior, nobleman**]** a British nobleman ranking above a viscount and below a marquess —**earl′dom** ***n.***

ear·lap (ir′lap′) ***n.*** **1.** the ear lobe **2.** the external ear

ear·ly (ur′lē) ***adv., adj.*** **-li·er, -li·est** **[**< OE. < *ær,* before (see ERE) + *-lice* (see -LY[2])**]** **1.** near the beginning of a given period of time or of a series, as of events **2.** before the expected or usual time **3.** in the far distant past **4.** in the near future; before long —**ear′li·ness** ***n.***

early bird [Colloq.] a person who arrives early or gets up early in the morning

Early Modern English English as spoken and written from about 1450 to about 1750

ear·mark (ir′märk′) ***n.*** **1.** an identification mark put on the ear of an animal to show ownership **2.** an identifying mark or feature; sign —***vt.*** **1.** to mark the ears of (livestock) for identification **2.** to set a distinctive mark upon; identify **3.** to reserve or set aside for a special purpose

ear·muffs (-mufs′) ***n.pl.*** cloth or fur coverings for the ears in cold weather

earn (urn) ***vt.*** **[**OE. *earnian,* to gain, lit., to harvest**]** **1.** to receive (salary, wages, etc.) for one's labor or service **2.** to get or deserve as a result of something done **3.** to gain (interest, etc.) as profit **4.** *Baseball* to score (a run not a result of an error) against a pitcher —**earn′er** ***n.***

Ear·nest (ur′nist) [var. of ERNEST] a masculine name

ear·nest[1] (ur′nist) ***adj.*** **[**OE. *eornoste***]** **1.** serious and intense; not joking; zealous and sincere **2.** not petty; important —**in earnest** **1.** serious **2.** in a determined manner —**ear′nest·ly** ***adv.*** —**ear′nest·ness** ***n.***

ear·nest[2] (ur′nist) ***n.*** **[**< OFr. *erres* < L. *arrae,* pl. < Gr. *arrabōn* < Heb. *'ērābōn***]** **1.** money given as a part payment and pledge in binding a bargain: in full, **earnest money** **2.** something given or done as an indication of what is to come; token

earn·ings (ur′niŋz) ***n.pl.*** **1.** wages or other recompense **2.** profits, interest, dividends, etc.

ear·phone (ir′fōn′) ***n.*** a receiver for radio, telephone, etc. held to or put into the ear

fat, āpe, cär; ten, ēven; is, bīte; gō, hôrn, tōōl, look; oil, out; up, fur; get; joy; yet; chin; she; thin, *th*en; zh, leisure; ŋ, ring; ə for *a* in *ago, e* in *agent, i* in *sanity, o* in *comply, u* in *focus;* ' as in *able* (ā′b'l); Fr. bál; ë, Fr. coeur; ö, Fr. feu; Fr. mo*n*; ô, Fr. coq; ü, Fr. duc; *r,* Fr. cri; H, G. ich; kh, G. doch; ‡foreign; *hypothetical; < derived from. See inside front cover.

ear·plug (-plug′) *n.* a plug inserted in the outer ear, as to keep out sound or water

ear·ring (-riŋ′) *n.* a ring or other small ornament for the lobe of the ear

ear·shot (-shät′) *n.* the distance within which a sound, esp. that of the unaided human voice, can be heard

earth (urth) *n.* [OE. *eorthe*] **1.** the planet that we live on: it is the fifth largest planet of the solar system and the third in distance from the sun: diameter, 7,927 mi. **2.** this world, as distinguished from heaven and hell **3.** all the people on the earth **4.** land, as distinguished from sea or sky **5.** soil; ground **6.** [Poet.] *a*) the human body *b*) worldly matters **7.** the hole of a burrowing animal **8.** *Chem.* any of the metallic oxides which are reduced with difficulty, as alumina **9.** *Elec.* [Brit.] *same as* GROUND[1] —*vt.* to cover (*up*) with soil for protection, as seeds or plants —**come back** (or **down**) **to earth** to return to reality —**down to earth** practical; realistic —**on earth** of all things: an intensive [what *on earth* is that?] —**run to earth 1.** to hunt down **2.** to find by search

earth·bound (-bound′) *adj.* **1.** confined to or by the earth or earthly things **2.** headed for the earth

earth·en (ur′thən) *adj.* **1.** made of earth or of baked clay **2.** earthly

earth·en·ware (-wer′) *n.* the coarser sort of containers, tableware, etc. made of baked clay

earth·ly (urth′lē) *adj.* **1.** of the earth; specif., *a*) terrestrial *b*) worldly *c*) temporal or secular **2.** conceivable; possible —**earth′li·ness** *n.*

earth·man (-man′) *n., pl.* **-men′** (-men′) a person on or from the planet earth, as in science fiction

earth·nut (-nut′) *n.* the root, tuber, or underground pod of various plants, as the peanut

earth·quake (-kwāk′) *n.* a shaking of the crust of the earth, caused by underground volcanic forces or by shifting of rock

earth·ward (-wərd) *adv., adj.* toward the earth: also **earth′-wards** *adv.*

earth·work (-wurk′) *n.* **1.** a defensive embankment made by piling up earth **2.** *Engineering* the work of excavating or building embankments

earth·worm (-wurm′) *n.* a round, segmented worm that burrows in the soil

earth·y (ur′thē) *adj.* **earth′i·er, earth′i·est 1.** of or like earth or soil **2.** *a*) coarse; unrefined *b*) simple and natural —**earth′i·ness** *n.*

ear trumpet a trumpet-shaped tube formerly used as a hearing aid by the partially deaf

ear·wax (ir′waks′) *n.* the yellowish, waxlike secretion in the canal of the outer ear; cerumen

ear·wig (-wig′) *n.* [< OE. < *eare,* EAR[1] + *wicga,* beetle, worm] any of an order of insects with short, horny forewings and a pair of forceps at the tail end

ease (ēz) *n.* [< OFr. *aise* < L. *adjacens,* lying nearby: see ADJACENT] **1.** freedom from pain or trouble; comfort **2.** natural, unstrained manner; poise **3.** freedom from difficulty; facility **4.** freedom from poverty; affluence **5.** leisure; relaxation —*vt.* **eased, eas′ing 1.** to free from pain or trouble; comfort **2.** to lessen (pain, anxiety, etc.) **3.** to make easier; facilitate **4.** to reduce the strain or pressure of **5.** to move by careful shifting, etc. —*vi.* **1.** to move or be moved by careful shifting, etc. **2.** to lessen in tension, speed, pain, etc. —**at ease 1.** without pain, anxiety, etc. **2.** *Mil.* relaxed, but keeping silent and staying in place —**take one's ease** to relax in comfort —**ease′ful** *adj.*

ea·sel (ē′z′l) *n.* [< Du. *ezel* (G. *esel*), ass, ult. < L. *asinus,* ASS] an upright frame or tripod to hold an artist's canvas, a picture on display, etc.

ease·ment (ēz′mənt) *n.* **1.** an easing or being eased **2.** a comfort, relief, or convenience **3.** *Law* a right that one may have in another's land, as a right of way

eas·i·ly (ē′z′l ē) *adv.* **1.** in an easy way **2.** by far [*easily* the best] **3.** very likely [it may *easily* rain]

eas·i·ness (ē′zē nis) *n.* the quality or state of being easy to do or get, or of being at ease

east (ēst) *n.* [OE. *east*] **1.** the direction to the right of a person facing north; direction in which sunrise occurs (90° on the compass, opposite west) **2.** a region or district in or toward this direction **3.** [E-] Asia and the nearby islands; the Orient —*adj.* **1.** in, of, to, or toward the east **2.** from the east **3.** [E-] designating the eastern part of a country, etc. —*adv.* in or toward the east —**the East** the eastern part of the U.S., esp. from Maine through Maryland

East Berlin E section of Berlin; capital of East Germany: pop. 1,084,000: cf. BERLIN

east·bound (-bound′) *adj.* going eastward

East China Sea part of the Pacific Ocean east of China and west of Kyushu, Japan

East·er (ēs′tər) *n.* [< OE. < *Eastre,* dawn goddess] **1.** an annual Christian festival celebrating the resurrection of Jesus, held on the first Sunday after the first full moon on or after March 21 **2.** this Sunday: also **Easter Sunday**

Easter egg a colored egg or an egg-shaped candy, etc., used as an Easter gift or ornament

Easter Island [discovered *Easter* day, 1722] Chilean island in the South Pacific, c. 2,000 mi. west of Chile: 64 sq. mi.

east·er·ly (ēs′tər lē) *adj., adv.* **1.** toward the east **2.** from the east

east·ern (-tərn) *adj.* **1.** in, of, or toward the east **2.** from the east **3.** [E-] of or characteristic of the East —**east′ern-most′** (-mōst′) *adj.*

Eastern Church 1. *a*) orig., the Christian Church in E Europe, W Asia, and Egypt *b*) those Churches descended from this Church and in union with Rome but having their own rite (**Eastern Rite**) **2.** *same as* ORTHODOX EASTERN CHURCH

east·ern·er (-ər) *n.* a native or inhabitant of the east, specif. [E-] of the eastern part of the U.S.

Eastern Hemisphere that half of the earth that includes Europe, Africa, Asia, and Australia

Eastern Orthodox Church *same as* ORTHODOX EASTERN CHURCH

Eastern Roman Empire Byzantine Empire, esp. so called until 476 A.D.: cf. WESTERN ROMAN EMPIRE

Eastern Standard Time *see* STANDARD TIME

East·er·tide (ēs′tər tīd′) *n.* the period after Easter, extending in various churches to Ascension Day, Whitsunday, or Trinity Sunday

East Germany E section of Germany, constituting a country in NC Europe: 41,800 sq. mi.; pop. 17,084,000; cap. East Berlin: cf. GERMANY

East Indies 1. Malay Archipelago; esp., the islands of Indonesia **2.** formerly, India, the Indochinese peninsula, the Malay Peninsula, and the Malay Archipelago —**East Indian**

east-north·east (ēst′nôrth′ēst′; *nautical* -nôr′-) *n.* the direction halfway between due east and northeast; 22°30′ north of due east —*adj., adv.* **1.** in or toward this direction **2.** from this direction

East Orange city in NE N.J., adjoining Newark: pop. 77,000

East Prussia former province of NE Germany, on the Baltic Sea: since 1945, in Poland & the U.S.S.R.

East River strait in SE N.Y., separating Manhattan Island from Long Island

east-south·east (ēst′south′ēst′; *nautical* -sou′-) *n.* the direction halfway between due east and southeast; 22°30′ south of due east —*adj., adv.* **1.** in or toward this direction **2.** from this direction

East St. Louis city in SW Ill., on the Mississippi, opposite St. Louis: pop. 55,000

east·ward (ēst′wərd) *adj., adv.* toward the east: also **east′-wards** *adv.* —*n.* an eastward direction, point, or region

east·ward·ly (-lē) *adv., adj.* **1.** toward the east **2.** from the east

eas·y (ē′zē) *adj.* **eas′i·er, eas′i·est** [< OFr. *aisé* < *aise:* see EASE] **1.** that can be done, got, etc. with ease; not difficult **2.** free from trouble, anxiety, pain, etc. **3.** providing comfort or rest **4.** fond of comfort or ease **5.** not stiff or awkward **6.** not strict; lenient **7.** compliant or credulous **8.** *a*) unhurried *b*) gradual —*adv.* [Colloq.] **1.** easily **2.** slowly and carefully —**easy does it** be careful —**go easy on** [Colloq.] **1.** to use with restraint **2.** to deal with leniently —**on easy street** well-to-do —**take it easy** [Colloq.] **1.** to refrain from anger, haste, violence, etc. **2.** to refrain from hard work; relax; rest

easy chair a stuffed or padded armchair

eas·y·go·ing (-gō′iŋ) *adj.* **1.** not hurried or agitated **2.** lenient or lackadaisical

eat (ēt) *vt.* **ate** (āt; *Brit.* et) or archaic & dial. **eat** (et, ēt), **eat·en** (ēt′'n) or archaic **eat** (et, ēt), **eat′ing** [OE. *etan*] **1.** to chew and swallow (food) **2.** to use up or destroy as by eating; consume or ravage (usually with *away* or *up*) **3.** to penetrate and destroy, as acid does; corrode **4.** to make by or as by eating [acid *ate* holes in the cloth] **5.** to bring (oneself) into a specified condition by eating **6.** [Slang] to worry or bother [what's *eating* him?] —*vi.* **1.** to eat food; have a meal or meals **2.** to destroy or use up something gradually (often with *into*) —**eat one's words** to retract something said earlier —**eat′er** *n.*

eat·a·ble (-ə b'l) *adj.* fit to be eaten; edible —*n.* a thing fit to be eaten; food: *usually used in pl.*

eat·er·y (-ər ē) *n., pl.* **-er·ies** [Colloq.] a restaurant

eat·ing (-iŋ) *n.* **1.** the action of one that eats **2.** edible quality of food —*adj.* **1.** that eats **2.** good for eating uncooked [*eating* apples]

eats (ēts) *n.pl.* [Colloq.] food; meals

eau de Co·logne (ō′də kə lōn′) [Fr., lit., water of Cologne] a perfumed toilet water made of alcohol and aromatic oils: usually clipped to *cologne*

eaves (ēvz) *n.pl., sing.* **eave** [orig. sing., OE. *efes*] the lower edge or edges of a roof, usually projecting beyond the sides of a building

eaves·drop (-dräp′) *vi.* **-dropped′, -drop′ping** [prob. back-formation < *eavesdropper,* lit., one who stands under the

eaves to listen] to listen secretly to a private conversation —**eaves′drop′per** *n.*
ebb (eb) *n.* [OE. *ebba*] **1.** the flow of water back toward the sea, as the tide falls **2.** a weakening or lessening; decline —*vi.* **1.** to flow back; recede, as the tide **2.** to weaken or lessen; decline
ebb tide the outgoing or falling tide
eb·on (eb′ən) *adj., n.* [< L. *ebenus* < Gr. *ebenos* < Egypt. *hbnj* (Heb. *hobnim*)] [Poet.] *same as* EBONY
eb·on·ite (-īt′) *n. same as* VULCANITE
eb·on·ize (-īz′) *vt.* **-ized′, -iz′ing** to give a finish to (wood, etc.) like that of ebony
eb·on·y (-ē) *n., pl.* **-on·ies** [< LL. *ebenius* < *ebenus:* see EBON] **1.** the hard, heavy, dark, durable wood of certain tropical trees, used in decorative woodwork, etc. **2.** such a tree —*adj.* **1.** made of ebony **2.** like ebony, esp. in color; dark; black
e·bul·lient (i bool′yənt, -bul′-) *adj.* [< L. prp. of *ebullire* < *e-*, out + *bullire*, to BOIL[1]] **1.** bubbling; boiling **2.** overflowing with enthusiasm, etc.; exuberant —**e·bul′lience, e·bul′lien·cy** *n.* —**e·bul′lient·ly** *adv.*
e·bul·li·tion (eb′ə lish′ən) *n.* **1.** a boiling or bubbling up **2.** a sudden outburst, as of emotion
ec·cen·tric (ik sen′trik) *adj.* [< ML. < LL. < Gr. < *ek-*, out of + *kentron*, CENTER] **1.** not having the same center, as two circles: opposed to CONCENTRIC **2.** not having the axis exactly in the center; off center **3.** not exactly circular in shape or motion **4.** deviating from the norm, as in conduct; odd; unconventional —*n.* **1.** a disk set off center on a shaft in an apparatus for converting circular motion into back-and-forth motion **2.** an eccentric person —**ec·cen′tri·cal·ly** *adv.*
ec·cen·tric·i·ty (ek′sen tris′ə tē, -sən-) *n., pl.* **-ties** **1.** the state, quality, or amount of being eccentric **2.** deviation from the norm; oddity
eccl., eccles. ecclesiastical
Eccles., Eccl. Ecclesiastes
Ec·cle·si·as·tes (i klē′zē as′tēz) [LL. < Gr. (see ff.): transl. of Heb. *qōheleth*, speaker before an assembly] a book of the Bible, written as though by Solomon
ec·cle·si·as·tic (-tik) *adj.* [< LL. < Gr. < *ekklēsia*, assembly, ult. < *ek-*, out + *kalein*, to call] *same as* ECCLESIASTICAL —*n.* a clergyman
ec·cle·si·as·ti·cal (-ti k′l) *adj.* of the church or the clergy —**ec·cle′si·as′ti·cal·ly** *adv.*
Ec·cle·si·as·ti·cus (-ti kəs) [LL.] a book of proverbs in the Apocrypha: abbrev. **Ecclus.**
ECG electrocardiogram
ech·e·lon (esh′ə län′) *n.* [< Fr. < OFr. *eschelle* < L. *scala*, ladder] **1.** a steplike formation of ships, aircraft, or troops **2.** a functional or positional military subdivision **3.** *a)* an organizational level, as of responsibility *b)* persons at such a level —*vt., vi.* to assemble in echelon
e·chid·na (i kid′nə) *n.* [ModL. < L. < Gr. *echidna*, adder] a small, egg-laying, ant-eating Australasian mammal with a long snout and a spiny coat
e·chi·no·derm (i kī′nə durm′, ek′ə-) *n.* [< ModL. < Gr. *echinos*, sea urchin, hedgehog + *derma*, skin] any of a group of marine animals with a hard, spiny skeleton and radial body, as a starfish
ech·o (ek′ō) *n., pl.* **-oes** [< L. < Gr. *ēchō*] **1.** *a)* the repetition of a sound by reflection of sound waves from a surface *b)* a sound so made **2.** *a)* any repetition or imitation of the words, ideas, etc. of another *b)* a person doing this **3.** sympathetic response **4.** a radar wave reflected from an object, appearing as a spot of light on a radarscope —[E-] *Gr. Myth.* a nymph who pined away for Narcissus until only her voice remained —*vi.* **-oed, -o·ing** **1.** to resound with an echo **2.** to be repeated as an echo —*vt.* **1.** to repeat (the words, ideas, etc.) of (another) **2.** to repeat or reflect (sound) from a surface
e·cho·ic (e kō′ik) *adj.* **1.** having the nature of an echo **2.** imitative in sound; onomatopoeic, as a word formed in approximate imitation of some sound (e.g., *clash*) —**ech′o·ism** *n.*
ech·o·lo·ca·tion (ek′ō lō kā′shən) *n.* the determination, as by a bat, of an object's position by emission of sound waves which are reflected back to the sender —**ech′o·lo′cate** *vt., vi.* **-cat·ed, -cat·ing**
echo sounding determination of water depth or of underwater distances by a device (**echo sounder**) that measures the time it takes for a sound wave to be reflected
é·clair (ā kler′, ē-, i-) *n.* [Fr., lit., lightning] a small, oblong pastry shell filled with flavored custard or whipped cream and covered with frosting
é·clat (ā klä′, i-) *n.* [Fr. < *éclater*, to burst (out)] **1.** brilliant success **2.** dazzling display **3.** approval; acclaim **4.** fame; renown
ec·lec·tic (i klek′tik, e-) *adj.* [< Gr. < *ek-*, out + *legein*, to pick] **1.** selecting from various systems, doctrines, or sources **2.** composed of material selected thus —*n.* one who uses eclectic methods —**ec·lec′ti·cal·ly** *adv.* —**ec·lec′ti·cism** (-siz′m) *n.*
e·clipse (i klips′, ē-) *n.* [< OFr. < L. < Gr. *ekleipsis* < *ek-*, out + *leipein*, to leave] **1.** a partial or total obscuring of the sun when the moon comes between it and the earth (**solar eclipse**), or of the moon when the earth's shadow is cast upon it (**lunar eclipse**) **2.** a dimming or extinction, as of fame or glory —*vt.* **e·clipsed′, e·clips′ing** **1.** to cause an eclipse of **2.** to overshadow or surpass

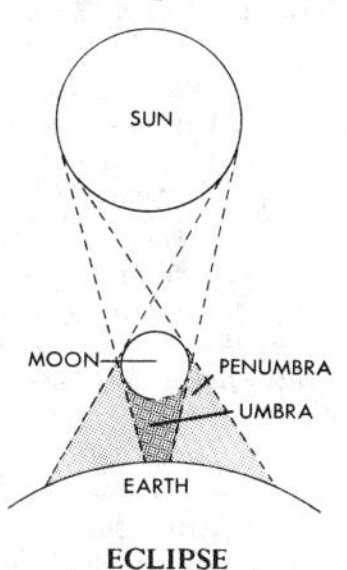

ECLIPSE
(of the sun)

e·clip·tic (i klip′tik, ē-) *n.* **1.** the apparent annual path of the sun on the celestial sphere **2.** a great circle on the celestial sphere formed by the intersection of an infinite plane through the earth's orbit with the celestial sphere —*adj.* of eclipses or the ecliptic
ec·logue (ek′lôg, -läg) *n.* [< Fr. < L. < Gr. < *eklegein:* see ECLECTIC] a short pastoral poem, usually a dialogue between two shepherds
e·co- [< LL. < Gr. < *oikos*, house] *a combining form meaning* environment or habitat [*ecosystem*]
ecol. **1.** ecological **2.** ecology
e·col·o·gy (ē käl′ə jē) *n.* [< G. < Gr. *oikos*, house + *-logia*, -LOGY] the interrelationship of organisms and their environment, or the study of this —**ec·o·log·i·cal** (ek′ə läj′i k′l, ē′kə-), **ec′o·log′ic** *adj.* —**ec′o·log′i·cal·ly** *adv.* —**e·col′o·gist** *n.*
econ. **1.** economic **2.** economics **3.** economy
e·con·o·met·rics (i kän′ə met′riks) *n.pl.* [*with sing. v.*] [< ECONOMY + METER[2] + -ICS] the use of mathematical and statistical methods to verify and develop economic theories —**e·con′o·met′ric** *adj.* —**e·con′o·me·tri′cian** (-mə trish′ən) *n.*
e·co·nom·ic (ē′kə näm′ik, ek′ə-) *adj.* **1.** of the management of the income, expenditures, etc. of a business, community, etc. **2.** of the production, distribution, and consumption of wealth **3.** of economics **4.** of the satisfaction of the material needs of people
e·co·nom·i·cal (-i k′l) *adj.* **1.** not wasting money, time, material, etc.; thrifty or efficient **2.** expressed or done with economy **3.** of economics —**e′co·nom′i·cal·ly** *adv.*
e·co·nom·ics (-iks) *n.pl.* [*with sing. v.*] **1.** the science dealing with the production, distribution, and consumption of wealth and with the various related problems of labor, finance, taxation, etc. **2.** economic factors
e·con·o·mist (i kän′ə mist) *n.* a specialist in economics
e·con·o·mize (-mīz′) *vi.* **-mized′, -miz′ing** to avoid waste or reduce expenses —*vt.* to manage or use with thrift —**e·con′o·miz′er** *n.*
e·con·o·my (-mē) *n., pl.* **-mies** [< L. < Gr. < *oikonomos*, manager < *oikos*, house + *nomos*, managing < *nemein*, to distribute] **1.** management of income, expenditures, etc. **2.** *a)* careful management of wealth, resources, etc.; thrift *b)* restrained or efficient use of one's materials, techniques, etc., as in the arts *c)* an instance of such management or use **3.** an orderly arrangement or management of parts **4.** an economic system of a specified kind, place, era, or condition
e·co·sys·tem (ē′kō sis′təm, ek′ō-) *n.* [ECO- + SYSTEM] a given community of animals, plants, and bacteria and its interrelated physical and chemical environment
ec·ru (ek′rōō, ā′krōō) *adj., n.* [Fr. *écru*, unbleached < OFr. < *es-* (L. *ex-*), intens. + *cru*, raw < L. *crudus*] light tan; beige
ec·sta·sy (ek′stə sē) *n., pl.* **-sies** [< OFr. < LL. < Gr. *ekstasis*, distraction < *ek-*, out + *histanai*, to place] **1.** an overpowering feeling of joy or delight; state of rapture **2.** a trance, as of a religious mystic
ec·stat·ic (ik stat′ik, ek-) *adj.* of, feeling, causing, or caused by ecstasy —**ec·stat′i·cal·ly** *adv.*
ec·to- [ModL. < Gr. *ektos*, outside] *a combining form meaning* outside, external: also, before a vowel, **ect-**
ec·to·derm (ek′tə durm′) *n.* [ECTO- + -DERM] the outer layer of cells of an embryo, from which the skin, hair, etc. develop —**ec′to·der′mal, ec′to·der′mic** *adj.*
ec·to·mor·phic (ek′tə môr′fik) *adj.* [ECTO- + -MORPHIC] designating or of the slender type of human body, in which the structures developed from the ectoderm predominate —**ec′to·morph′** *n.*
-ec·to·my (ek′tə mē) [< Gr. < *ek-*, out + *temnein*, to cut]

combining form meaning a surgical excision of *[appendectomy]*

ec·to·plasm (ek'tə plaz'm) ***n.*** [ECTO- + -PLASM] **1.** the outer cytoplasm of a cell **2.** a vaporous, luminous substance believed by spiritualists to emanate from the medium in a trance —**ec'to·plas'mic** ***adj.***

Ec·ua·dor (ek'wə dôr') country on the NW coast of S. America: 104,506 sq. mi.; pop. 5,840,000; cap. Quito —**Ec'ua·do're·an, Ec'ua·do'ri·an, Ec'ua·dor'an** ***adj., n.***

ec·u·men·i·cal (ek'yoo men'i k'l) ***adj.*** [< LL. < Gr. < *oikoumenē (gē)*, the inhabited (world) < *oikein*, to inhabit < *oikos*, house] **1.** general, or universal; esp., of the Christian church as a whole **2.** *a)* furthering the unity of Christian churches *b)* promoting better understanding among differing religious groups Also **ec'u·men'ic** —**ec'u·men'i·cal·ism** ***n.*** —**ec'u·men'i·cal·ly** ***adv.***

ec·u·men·i·cism (-i siz'm) ***n.*** *same as* ECUMENISM

ec·u·men·ism (ek'yoo mə niz'm, e kyōō'-) ***n.*** **1.** any ecumenical movement **2.** ecumenical principles or practice Also **ec'u·me·nic'i·ty** (-nis'ə tē) —**ec'u·men·ist** ***n.***

ec·ze·ma (ek'sə mə, eg'zə-; ig zē'mə) ***n.*** [ModL. < Gr. < *ek-*, out of + *zein*, to boil] a disorder of the skin in which it becomes inflamed, scaly, and very itchy —**ec·zem·a·tous** (ig zem'ə təs, -zē'mə-) ***adj.***

-ed (id, əd; d, t) [< OE.] **1.** *a suffix used: a)* to form the past tense and past participle of weak verbs *[wanted] b)* to form adjectives from nouns or verbs *[cultured]* or from adjectives ending in *-ate [serrated]* **2.** *a suffix added to nouns, meaning* having *[bearded]*

ed. **1.** edited **2.** *pl.* **eds.** *a)* edition *b)* editor **3.** education

E·dam (cheese) (ē'dəm, -dam) [orig. made in the Du. town of *Edam*] a round, mild, yellow cheese, usually coated with red paraffin

Ed.B. Bachelor of Education

Ed.D. Doctor of Education

Ed·da (ed'ə) [ON.] either of two early Icelandic literary works: *a)* the **Prose,** or **Younger, Edda** (c. 1230), a summary of Norse mythology *b)* the **Poetic,** or **Elder, Edda** (c. 1200), a collection of Old Norse poetry —**Ed·dic** (ed'ik), **Ed·da·ic** (i dā'ik) ***adj.***

ed·dy (ed'ē) ***n.,*** *pl.* **-dies** [prob. < ON. *itha*] **1.** a current of air, water, etc. moving with a circular motion against the main current; little whirlpool or whirlwind **2.** a contrary movement —***vi.*** **-died, -dy·ing** to move in an eddy; whirl

Ed·dy (ed'ē), **Mary Baker** 1821–1910; U.S. founder of Christian Science

e·del·weiss (ā'd'l vīs') ***n.*** [G. < *edel*, noble + *weiss*, white] a small plant of the composite family, native to the high mountains of Europe and C Asia, esp. the Alps, with white, woolly leaves and bracts

e·de·ma (i dē'mə) ***n.,*** *pl.* **-mas, -ma·ta** (-mə tə) [ModL. < Gr. *oidēma*, a swelling] **1.** an abnormal accumulation of fluid in tissues or cavities of the body, causing swelling **2.** a similar swelling in plants —**e·dem·a·tous** (i dem'ə təs, i dē'mə-) ***adj.***

E·den (ē'd'n) [LL. < Heb. *'ēdhen*, lit., delight] *Bible* the garden where Adam and Eve first lived; Paradise —***n.*** any delightful place or state

e·den·tate (ē den'tāt) ***adj.*** [< L. pp. of *edentare*, to make toothless < *e-*, out + *dens*, tooth] **1.** without teeth **2.** of the edentates —***n.*** any of an order of mammals with molars only or no teeth at all, as sloths and anteaters

Ed·gar (ed'gər) [< OE. < *ead*, riches + *gar*, a spear] a masculine name: dim. *Ed*

edge (ej) ***n.*** [OE. *ecg*] **1.** the sharp, cutting part of a blade **2.** sharpness; keenness **3.** a projecting ledge, as of a cliff **4.** the line or part where something begins or ends; border; margin **5.** the line at which two surfaces of a solid meet **6.** the verge or brink, as of a condition **7.** [Colloq.] advantage *[you have the edge on me]* —***vt.*** **edged, edg'ing** **1.** *a)* to put an edge on *b)* to trim the edge of **2.** to make (one's way) sideways **3.** to move gradually or cautiously **4.** [Colloq.] to defeat narrowly (often with *out*) —***vi.*** to move sideways or gradually or cautiously —**on edge** irritable or impatient —**set one's teeth on edge** **1.** to give a sensation of tingling discomfort **2.** to irritate; provoke —**take the edge off** to dull the intensity or pleasure (of) —**edg'er** ***n.***

edge·ways (-wāz') ***adv.*** with the edge foremost; on, by, or toward the edge: also **edge'wise'** (-wīz') —**get a word in edgeways** to manage to say something in a conversation monopolized by others

edg·ing (ej'iŋ) ***n.*** something forming an edge

edg·y (-ē) ***adj.*** **edg'i·er, edg'i·est** **1.** having an edge; sharp **2.** irritable; on edge —**edg'i·ly** ***adv.*** —**edg'i·ness** ***n.***

ed·i·ble (ed'ə b'l) ***adj.*** [LL. *edibilis* < L. *edere*, to eat] fit to be eaten —***n.*** anything fit to be eaten —**ed'i·bil'i·ty** (-bil'ə tē), **ed'i·ble·ness** ***n.***

e·dict (ē'dikt) ***n.*** [< L. pp. of *edicere*, to proclaim < *e-*, out + *dicere*, to say] an official public proclamation issued by authority; decree

ed·i·fice (ed'ə fis) ***n.*** [< OFr. < L. *aedificium*, a building < *aedificare:* see ff.] **1.** a building, esp. a large, imposing one **2.** any complicated organization

ed·i·fy (ed'ə fī') ***vt.*** **-fied', -fy'ing** [< OFr. < L. *aedificare*, to build < *aedes*, a house + *-ficare* < *facere*, to make] to instruct so as to improve morally or spiritually —**ed'i·fi·ca'tion** (-fi kā'shən) ***n.*** —**ed'i·fi'er** ***n.***

Ed·in·burgh (ed''n bur'ə, -ō) capital of Scotland, on the Firth of Forth: pop. 468,000

Ed·i·son (ed'ə s'n), **Thomas Al·va** (al'və) 1847–1931; U.S. inventor

ed·it (ed'it) ***vt., vi.*** [back-formation < EDITOR] **1.** to prepare (an author's works, a manuscript, etc.) for publication by selecting, arranging, revising, etc. **2.** to govern the policy for (a newspaper or periodical) **3.** to prepare (a movie film, video tape, or recording) for presentation by cutting, rearranging, etc. —**edit out** to delete in editing

edit. **1.** edited **2.** edition **3.** editor

E·dith (ē'dith) [< OE. < *ead*, riches + *guth*, battle] a feminine name

e·di·tion (i dish'ən) ***n.*** [< L. *editio*, a publishing < *edere:* see ff.] **1.** the size, style, or form in which a book, etc. is published **2.** *a)* the total number of copies of a book, etc. published at about the same time *b)* one of these copies

ed·i·tor (ed'i tər) ***n.*** [< L. pp. of *edere*, to publish < *e-*, out + *dare*, to give] **1.** a person who edits **2.** the head of a department of a newspaper, magazine, etc. **3.** a device used to edit (sense 3) —**ed'i·tor·ship'** ***n.***

ed·i·to·ri·al (ed'ə tôr'ē əl) ***adj.*** of, by, or characteristic of an editor or editors —***n.*** a statement of opinion in a newspaper, etc. or on radio or TV by an editor, publisher, etc. —**ed'i·to'ri·al·ly** ***adv.***

ed·i·to·ri·al·ist (-ist) ***n.*** an editorial writer

ed·i·to·ri·al·ize (-īz') ***vt., vi.*** **-ized', -iz'ing** **1.** to express editorial opinions about (something) **2.** to express editorial opinions in (an article, etc.) —**ed'i·to'ri·al·i·za'tion** ***n.*** —**ed'i·to'ri·al·iz'er** ***n.***

editor in chief *pl.* **editors in chief** the editor who heads the editorial staff of a publication

Ed·mon·ton (ed'mən tən) capital of Alberta, Canada, in the C part: pop. 461,000

Ed·mund, Ed·mond (ed'mənd) [< OE. < *ead*, riches + *mund*, protection] a masculine name

Ed·na (ed'nə) [Gr. < Heb. *'ēdnāh*, rejuvenation] a feminine name

E·dom (ē'dəm) ancient kingdom in SW Asia, south of the Dead Sea —**E'dom·ite'** (-īt') ***n.***

EDP electronic data processing

ed·u·ca·ble (ej'ə kə b'l) ***adj.*** that can be educated or trained —**ed'u·ca·bil'i·ty** ***n.***

ed·u·cate (ej'ə kāt') ***vt.*** **-cat'ed, -cat'ing** [< L. pp. of *educare*, to train < *educere* < *e-*, out + *ducere*, to lead] **1.** to train, teach, instruct, or develop, esp. by formal schooling **2.** to pay for the schooling of (a person)

ed·u·cat·ed (-kāt'id) ***adj.*** **1.** having, or indicating, education **2.** based on knowledge or experience

ed·u·ca·tion (ej'ə kā'shən) ***n.*** **1.** an educating or a being educated **2.** knowledge, ability, etc. thus developed **3.** a type of formal schooling **4.** study of the methods of teaching and learning —**ed'u·ca'tion·al, ed'u·ca'tive** ***adj.*** —**ed'u·ca'tion·al·ly** ***adv.***

ed·u·ca·tion·ist (-ist) ***n.*** an educator; esp., an authority on educational theory: often a disparaging term: also **ed'u·ca'tion·al·ist**

ed·u·ca·tor (ej'ə kāt'ər) ***n.*** **1.** a person whose work is to educate others; teacher **2.** a specialist in educational methods, theories, etc.

e·duce (i dōōs', ē-; -dyōōs') ***vt.*** **-duced', -duc'ing** [L. *educere:* see EDUCATE] **1.** to draw out; elicit **2.** to deduce —**e·duc'i·ble** ***adj.*** —**e·duc·tion** (i duk'shən, ē-) ***n.***

Ed·ward (ed'wərd) [< OE. < *ead*, riches + *weard*, guardian] **1.** a masculine name **2.** name of eight kings of England in the 13th–16th cent. & in the 20th cent.; specif., **Edward VII** 1841–1910; king (1901–10): son of Queen VICTORIA

Ed·ward·i·an (ed wär'dē ən, -wôr'-) ***adj.*** designating or of the reign of any of the English kings named Edward, specif. of Edward VII

Ed·wards (ed'wərdz), **Jonathan** 1703–58; Am. theologian

Edward the Confessor 1004?–66; king of England (1042–66)

Ed·win (ed'win) [< OE. < *ead*, riches + *wine*, friend] a masculine name

-ee (ē) [< OFr. *-é*, orig. masc. ending of pp. of verbs in *-er*] *a n.-forming suffix designating:* **1.** the recipient of a specified action or benefit *[appointee, mortgagee]* **2.** a person in a specified condition *[absentee, employee]* **3.** a person or thing associated in some way with another *[goatee]*

E.E.C. European Economic Community

EEG electroencephalogram

eel (ēl) ***n.,*** *pl.* **eels, eel:** see PLURAL, II, D, 1 [OE. *æl*] a snakelike fish with a long, slippery body and no pelvic fins —**eel′like′, eel′y** ***adj.***

EEL
(to 5 ft. long)

eel·grass (-gras′) ***n.*** an underwater flowering plant with long, grasslike leaves

eel·pout (-pout′) ***n.,*** *pl.* **-pout′, -pouts′:** see PLURAL, II, D, 2 [OE. *ælepute*] **1.** a saltwater fish resembling the blenny **2.** *same as* BURBOT

eel·worm (-wurm′) ***n.*** any of various nematode worms, either free-living or parasitic on plants

e'en (ēn) ***adv.*** [Poet.] even —***n.*** [Poet. or Dial.] even(ing)

e'er (er, ar) ***adv.*** [Poet.] ever

-eer (ir) [Fr. *-ier* < L. *-arius*] *a suffix used to form:* **1.** *nouns meaning* one that has to do with *[mountaineer]* or one that writes, makes, etc. *[pamphleteer]* **2.** *verbs meaning* to have to do with *[electioneer]*

ee·rie, ee·ry (ir′ē) ***adj.*** **-ri·er, -ri·est** [prob. ult. < OE. *earg,* timid] weird or uncanny, esp. in a frightening way —**ee′ri·ly** ***adv.*** —**ee′ri·ness** ***n.***

ef·face (i fās′, e-) ***vt.*** **-faced′, -fac′ing** [Fr. *effacer* < *e-* (L. *ex,* out) + *face:* see FACE] **1.** to rub out or wipe out; erase *[to efface a memory]* **2.** to make (oneself) inconspicuous —**ef·face′a·ble** ***adj.*** —**ef·face′ment** ***n.*** —**ef·fac′er** ***n.***

ef·fect (ə fekt′, i-) ***n.*** [< OFr. (& L.) < L. pp. of *efficere* < *ex-,* out + *facere,* to do] **1.** anything brought about by a cause or agent; result **2.** the power to produce results; efficacy **3.** influence or action *[a cathartic effect]* **4.** general meaning; purport *[he spoke to this effect]* **5.** *a)* the impression produced, as by artistic design, a way of speaking, acting, etc. *[done for effect]* *b)* something that makes such an impression *[cloud effects]* **6.** the condition or fact of being in force *[a law now in effect]* **7.** [*pl.*] belongings; property *[personal effects]* —***vt.*** to bring about; cause; accomplish —**in effect** **1.** in result; actually **2.** in essence; virtually —**take effect** to begin to produce results; become operative —**ef·fect′er** ***n.***

ef·fec·tive (ə fek′tiv, i-) ***adj.*** **1.** having an effect **2.** producing a desired effect **3.** in effect; operative **4.** actual, not merely theoretical **5.** making a striking impression **6.** equipped and ready for combat —***n.*** a combat-ready soldier, unit, etc. —**ef·fec′tive·ly** ***adv.*** —**ef·fec′tive·ness** ***n.***

ef·fec·tu·al (ə fek′choo wəl, i-) ***adj.*** **1.** producing, or able to produce, the desired effect **2.** having legal force; valid —**ef·fec′tu·al′i·ty** (-wal′ə tē) ***n.*** —**ef·fec′tu·al·ly** ***adv.***

ef·fec·tu·ate (-wāt′) ***vt.*** **-at′ed, -at′ing** to bring about; effect —**ef·fec′tu·a′tion** ***n.***

ef·fem·i·nate (i fem′ə nit) ***adj.*** [< L. pp. of *effeminare* < *ex-,* out + *femina,* woman] having or showing qualities generally attributed to women, as weakness, delicacy, etc.; unmanly —**ef·fem′i·na·cy** (-nə sē) ***n.*** —**ef·fem′i·nate·ly** ***adv.***

ef·fen·di (i fen′dē) ***n.,*** *pl.* **-dis** [< Turk. < ModGr. < Gr. *authentēs,* a master] Sir; Master: former Turkish title of respect

ef·fer·ent (ef′ər ənt) ***adj.*** [< L. prp. of *efferre* < *ex-,* out + *ferre,* to bear] *Physiol.* carrying away from a central part; specif., designating nerves that carry impulses away from a nerve center: opposed to AFFERENT

ef·fer·vesce (ef′ər ves′) ***vi.*** **-vesced′, -vesc′ing** [< L. < *ex-,* out + *fervescere,* to begin to boil < *fervere,* to boil] **1.** to give off gas bubbles, as soda water; bubble **2.** to be lively —**ef′fer·ves′cence** ***n.*** —**ef′fer·ves′cent** ***adj.*** —**ef′fer·ves′cent·ly** ***adv.***

ef·fete (e fēt′, i-) ***adj.*** [L. *effetus,* exhausted by bearing < *ex-,* out + *fetus,* productive] **1.** no longer able to produce; spent and sterile **2.** decadent, soft, etc. —**ef·fete′ly** ***adv.*** —**ef·fete′ness** ***n.***

ef·fi·ca·cious (ef′ə kā′shəs) ***adj.*** [L. *efficax* < *efficere* (see EFFECT) + -OUS] producing or capable of producing the desired effect; effective —**ef′fi·ca′cious·ly** ***adv.*** —**ef′fi·ca′cious·ness** ***n.***

ef·fi·ca·cy (ef′i kə sē) ***n.,*** *pl.* **-cies** [see prec.] power to produce intended results; effectiveness

ef·fi·cien·cy (ə fish′ən sē, i-) ***n.,*** *pl.* **-cies** **1.** ability to produce a desired effect with the least effort or waste; a being efficient **2.** the ratio of effective work to energy used in producing it: said of a machine, etc. **3.** *same as* EFFICIENCY APARTMENT

efficiency apartment a one-room apartment having a kitchenette and a bathroom

ef·fi·cient (-ənt) ***adj.*** [< L. prp. of *efficere:* see EFFECT] **1.** directly producing an effect or result; effective **2.** producing a desired effect with the least effort or waste —**ef·fi′cient·ly** ***adv.***

ef·fi·gy (ef′ə jē) ***n.,*** *pl.* **-gies** [< Fr. < L. *effigies* < *ex-,* out + *fingere,* to form] a statue or other likeness; often, a crude representation of a despised person —**burn** (or **hang**) **in effigy** to burn (or hang) a despised person's effigy in public protest

ef·flo·resce (ef′lô res′, -lə-) ***vi.*** **-resced′, -resc′ing** [< L. < *ex-,* out + *florescere,* to blossom < *flos,* a flower] **1.** to blossom out; flower **2.** *Chem.* *a)* to change from crystals to a powder through loss of the water of crystallization *b)* to develop a powdery crust by evaporation or chemical change

ef·flo·res·cence (-res′'ns) ***n.*** **1.** a flowering **2.** the time of flowering **3.** *Chem.* *a)* an efflorescing *b)* the resulting powder or crust **4.** *Med.* an eruption on the skin; rash —**ef′flo·res′cent** ***adj.***

ef·flu·ence (ef′loo wəns) ***n.*** [< L. prp. of *effluere* < *ex-,* out + *fluere,* to flow] **1.** a flowing out or forth **2.** a thing that flows out or forth; emanation —**ef′flu·ent** ***adj., n.***

ef·flu·vi·um (e flōō′vē əm, i-) ***n.,*** *pl.* **-vi·a** (-ə), **-vi·ums** [L., a flowing out: see prec.] a vaporous or invisible emanation; esp., a disagreeable or foul vapor or odor —**ef·flu′vi·al** ***adj.***

ef·fort (ef′ərt) ***n.*** [Fr. < OFr. < *esforcier,* to make an effort, ult. < L. *ex-,* intens. + *fortis,* strong] **1.** use of energy to do something; physical or mental exertion **2.** a try; attempt **3.** a result of working or trying; achievement —**ef′fort·less** ***adj.*** —**ef′fort·less·ly** ***adv.*** —**ef′fort·less·ness** ***n.***

ef·fron·ter·y (e frun′tər ē, i-) ***n.,*** *pl.* **-ter·ies** [< Fr. < L. *effrons,* shameless, barefaced < *ex-,* from + *frons,* forehead] unashamed boldness; impudence

ef·ful·gence (e ful′jəns, i-) ***n.*** [< L. prp. of *effulgere* < *ex-,* forth + *fulgere,* to shine] great brightness; radiance —**ef·ful′gent** ***adj.***

ef·fuse (e fyōōz′, i-) ***vt., vi.*** **-fused′, -fus′ing** [< L. pp. of *effundere* < *ex-,* out + *fundere,* to pour] to pour, or spread, out or forth

ef·fu·sion (e fyōō′zhən, i-) ***n.*** [see prec.] **1.** a pouring forth **2.** unrestrained expression in words

ef·fu·sive (-siv) ***adj.*** too demonstrative; gushy —**ef·fu′sive·ly** ***adv.*** —**ef·fu′sive·ness** ***n.***

eft (eft) ***n.*** [OE. *efeta*] *same as* NEWT

eft·soon (eft sōōn′) ***adv.*** [OE. < *eft,* again + *sona,* soon] [Archaic] soon after: also **eft·soons′** (-sōōnz′)

Eg. **1.** Egypt **2.** Egyptian **3.** Egyptology

e.g. [L. *exempli gratia*] for example

e·gad (i gad′, ē-) ***interj.*** [prob. < *oh God*] a softened or euphemistic oath

e·gal·i·tar·i·an (i gal′ə ter′ē ən, ē-) ***adj.*** [< Fr. < *égalité,* equality + -IAN] of or for equal rights for all —***n.*** an advocate of equal rights —**e·gal′i·tar′i·an·ism** ***n.***

egg[1] (eg) ***n.*** [ON.] **1.** an oval or round body laid by a female bird, fish, insect, etc. containing within a shell or membrane the germ of a new individual and food for its development **2.** a female reproductive cell; ovum: also called **egg cell** **3.** a hen's egg, raw or cooked **4.** something egglike, esp. in shape **5.** [Slang] a person —**lay an egg** [Slang] to fail, as a performance

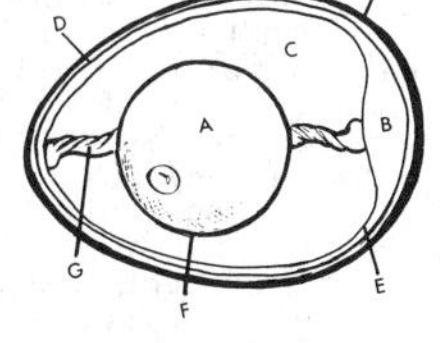

HEN'S EGG
(A, yolk; B, air space; C, white; D, outer shell membrane; E, inner shell membrane; F, chalaza-bearing membrane; G, chalaza; H, shell)

egg[2] (eg) ***vt.*** [< ON. *eggja,* lit., to give edge to < *egg,* edge] to urge or incite (with *on*)

egg·beat·er (-bēt′ər) ***n.*** **1.** a kitchen utensil for beating eggs, etc. **2.** [Slang] a helicopter

egg·head (-hed′) ***n.*** [Slang] an intellectual

egg·nog (-näg′) ***n.*** [EGG[1] + NOG] a drink of beaten eggs, milk, sugar, and nutmeg, often with alcoholic liquor

egg·plant (-plant′) ***n.*** **1.** a plant of the nightshade family, with a large, ovoid, usually purple-skinned fruit eaten as a vegetable **2.** the fruit

egg·shell (-shel′) ***n.*** the shell of an egg; esp., the hard, brittle covering of a bird's egg —***adj.*** **1.** fragile and thin, like an eggshell **2.** yellowish-white

eg·lan·tine (eg′lən tīn′, -tēn′) ***n.*** [< Fr. < OFr. *aiglent* < L. *aculeus,* a sting, dim. of *acus,* a point] a European rose with hooked spines, sweet-scented leaves, and usually pink flowers

e·go (ē′gō; *chiefly Brit.* eg′ō) ***n.,*** *pl.* **e′gos** [L., I] **1.** the self; the individual as aware of himself **2.** egotism; conceit **3.** *Psychoanalysis* the part of the psyche resolving conflicts between the impulses of the id, the demands of the environment, and the standards of the superego

e·go·cen·tric (ē′gō sen′trik; *chiefly Brit.* eg′ō-) ***adj.*** self-centered —***n.*** an egocentric person —**e′go·cen′tri·cal·ly *adv.*** —**e′go·cen·tric′i·ty** (-tris′ə tē) ***n.*** —**e′go·cen′trism *n.***

e·go·ism (ē′gō iz'm; *chiefly Brit.* eg′ō-) ***n.*** **1.** the tendency to be self-centered **2.** self-conceit; egotism **3.** the doctrine that self-interest is the proper goal of all human actions: opposed to ALTRUISM —**e′go·ist *n.*** —**e′go·is′tic, e′go·is′ti·cal *adj.*** —**e′go·is′ti·cal·ly *adv.***

e·go·ma·ni·a (ē′gō mā′nē ə, -mān′yə) ***n.*** abnormally excessive egotism —**e′go·ma′ni·ac′** (-ak′) ***n.*** —**e′go·ma·ni′a·cal** (-mə nī′ə k'l) ***adj.***

e·go·tism (ē′gə tiz'm; *chiefly Brit.* eg′ə-) ***n.*** **1.** constant, excessive reference to oneself in speaking or writing **2.** self-conceit **3.** selfishness *Egotism* is generally considered a more opprobrious term than *egoism* —**e′go·tist *n.*** —**e′go·tis′tic, e′go·tis′ti·cal *adj.*** —**e′go·tis′ti·cal·ly *adv.***

e·gre·gious (i grē′jəs, -jē əs) ***adj.*** [L. *egregius*, apart from the herd, outstanding < *e-*, out + *grex*, a herd] remarkably bad; flagrant [an *egregious* error] —**e·gre′gious·ly *adv.*** —**e·gre′gious·ness *n.***

e·gress (ē′gres) ***n.*** [< L. pp. of *egredi* < *e-*, out + *gradi*, to step, go] **1.** a going out; emergence: also **e·gres·sion** (i gresh′ən) **2.** the right to go out **3.** a way out; exit

e·gret (ē′grit, eg′rit) ***n.*** [< OFr. *aigrette* < Pr. < *aigron*, a heron < Frank.] **1.** *pl.* **-grets, -gret:** see PLURAL, II, D, 1 a heronlike wading bird, usually with long, white plumes, esp. the **American egret** of temperate and tropical America **2.** an aigrette (sense 1)

E·gypt (ē′jipt) country in NE Africa, on the Mediterranean and Red seas: c. 386,000 sq. mi.; pop. 32,501,000; cap. Cairo

Egypt. Egyptian

E·gyp·tian (i jip′shən, ē-) ***adj.*** of Egypt, its people, etc. —***n.*** **1.** a native or inhabitant of Egypt **2.** the language of the ancient Egyptians

E·gyp·tol·o·gy (ē′jip täl′ə jē) ***n.*** the study of ancient Egyptian culture, language, architecture, etc. —**E′gyp·tol′o·gist *n.***

eh (ā, e, en) ***interj.*** a sound expressing: **1.** surprise **2.** doubt or inquiry

EHF extremely high frequency

Ehr·lich (er′lik; *G.* er′liH), **Paul** 1854–1915; Ger. bacteriologist & immunologist

ei·der (ī′dər) ***n.*** [ult. < ON. gen. of *æthr*] **1.** *pl.* **-ders, -der:** see PLURAL, II, D, 1 a large sea duck of northern regions: often **eider duck** **2.** *same as* EIDERDOWN

ei·der·down (-doun′) ***n.*** **1.** the soft, fine breast feathers, or down, of the eider duck, used to stuff quilts, pillows, etc. **2.** a quilt so stuffed

ei·det·ic (ī det′ik) ***adj.*** [< Gr. < *eidos*, what is seen] designating or of unusually vivid or lifelike mental images —**ei·det′i·cal·ly *adv.***

Eif·fel Tower (ī′f'l) [after A. G. *Eiffel* (1832–93), Fr. engineer] tower of iron framework in Paris, built for the 1889 Exposition: 984 ft. high

eight (āt) ***adj.*** [OE. *eahta*] totaling one more than seven —***n.*** **1.** the cardinal number between seven and nine; 8; VIII **2.** anything having eight units or members, or numbered eight, or shaped like 8; specif., an eight-cylinder engine or automobile

eight ball a black ball with the number eight on it, used in playing pool —**behind the eight ball** [Slang] in a very unfavorable position

eight·een (ā′tēn′) ***adj.*** [OE. *eahtatiene*] eight more than ten —***n.*** the cardinal number between seventeen and nineteen; 18; XVIII

eight·eenth (ā′tēnth′) ***adj.*** **1.** preceded by seventeen others in a series; 18th **2.** designating any of the eighteen equal parts of something —***n.*** **1.** the one following the seventeenth **2.** any of the eighteen equal parts of something; 1/18

eight·fold (āt′fōld′) ***adj.*** [see -FOLD] **1.** having eight parts **2.** having eight times as much or as many —***adv.*** eight times as much or as many

eighth (ātth, āth) ***adj.*** **1.** preceded by seven others in a series; 8th **2.** designating any of the eight equal parts of something —***n.*** **1.** the one following the seventh **2.** any of the eight equal parts of something; 1/8 **3.** *Music* the interval of an octave

eighth note *Music* a note having one eighth the duration of a whole note: see NOTE, illus.

eight·i·eth (āt′ē ith) ***adj.*** **1.** preceded by seventy-nine others in a series; 80th **2.** designating any of the eighty equal parts of something —***n.*** **1.** the one following the seventy-ninth **2.** any of the eighty equal parts of something; 1/80

eight·y (āt′ē) ***adj.*** [OE. (*hund*)*eahtatig*] eight times ten —***n.***, *pl.* **eight′ies** the cardinal number between seventy-nine and eighty-one; 80; LXXX —**the eighties** the numbers or years, as of a century, from eighty through eighty-nine

ei·kon (ī′kän) ***n.*** *same as* ICON

Ei·leen (ī lēn′, ā-) [Ir. *Eibhlin*] a feminine name

Eind·ho·ven (īnt′hō′vən) city in S Netherlands: pop. 185,000

Ein·stein (īn′stīn), **Albert** 1879–1955; U.S. physicist, born in Germany: formulated theory of relativity —**Ein·stein′i·an** (-stī′nē ən) ***adj.***

ein·stein·i·um (īn stī′nē əm) ***n.*** [after prec.] a radioactive chemical element produced by irradiating plutonium with neutrons: symbol, Es; at. wt., 252(?); at. no., 99

Eir·e (er′ə) *Gaelic name of* IRELAND (sense 2)

Ei·sen·how·er (ī′z'n hou′ər), **Dwight David** 1890–1969; U.S. general & 34th president of the U.S. (1953–61)

ei·ther (ē′*th*ər, ī′-) ***adj.*** [OE. *æghwæther* < *a* (æ), always (see AYE[1]) + *gehwæther*, each of two (cf. WHETHER)] **1.** one or the other (of two) [use *either* hand] **2.** each (of two) [doors open at *either* end of the room] —***pron.*** one or the other (of two) —***conj.*** a correlative used with *or*, implying a choice of alternatives [*either* go or stay] —***adv.*** **1.** any more than the other; also (after negatives) [if he won't, she won't *either*] **2.** [Colloq.] an intensifier in a negative statement ["It's his. It isn't *either!*"]

e·jac·u·late (i jak′yə lāt′) ***vt., vi.*** **-lat′ed, -lat′ing** [< L. pp. of *ejaculari* < *e-*, out + *jaculari*, to throw < *jaculum*, a dart < *jacere*, to throw] **1.** to eject or discharge (esp. semen) **2.** to utter suddenly and vehemently; exclaim —**e·jac′u·la′tion *n.*** —**e·jac′u·la′tor *n.*** —**e·jac′u·la·to′ry *adj.***

e·ject (i jekt′, ē-) ***vt.*** [< L. pp. of *ejicere* < *e-*, out + *jacere*, to throw] **1.** to throw out; expel; discharge **2.** to drive out; evict —**e·ject′a·ble *adj.*** —**e·jec′tion *n.*** —**e·jec′tive *adj.*** —**e·jec′tor *n.***

eke[1] (ēk) ***vt.*** **eked, ek′ing** [OE. *eacan* & *eacian*] [Archaic or Dial.] to increase —**eke out** **1.** to supplement [to *eke out* one's income with a second job] **2.** to make (a living) with difficulty **3.** to use (a supply) frugally

eke[2] (ēk) ***adv., conj.*** [OE. *eac*] [Archaic] also

EKG electrocardiogram

el (el) ***n.*** **1.** *same as* ELL[1] **2.** [< *el*(*evated*)] [Colloq.] an elevated railway

e·lab·o·rate (i lab′ər it; *for v.* -ə rāt′) ***adj.*** [< L. pp. of *elaborare* < *e-*, out + *laborare* < *labor*, LABOR] **1.** developed in great detail **2.** complicated **3.** painstaking —***vt.*** **-rat′ed, -rat′ing** **1.** to produce by effort **2.** to work out in careful detail **3.** to change (food or substances in the body) into compounds that can be assimilated, etc. —***vi.*** to state something in detail or add more details (usually with *on* or *upon*) —**e·lab′o·rate·ly *adv.*** —**e·lab′o·rate·ness *n.*** —**e·lab′o·ra′tion *n.*** —**e·lab′o·ra′tive *adj.*** —**e·lab′o·ra′tor *n.***

E·laine (i lān′, ē-) [OFr., equiv. of HELEN] a feminine name

E·lam (ē′ləm) ancient kingdom of SW Asia, on the Persian Gulf —**E′lam·ite′** (-īt′) ***adj., n.***

é·lan (ā län′; *Fr.* -län′) ***n.*** [Fr. < *élancer*, to dart] spirited self-assurance; verve; dash

e·land (ē′lənd) ***n.***, *pl.* **e′land, e′lands:** see PLURAL, II, D, 2 [Afrik. < Du., elk] either of two large, oxlike African antelopes with spirally twisted horns

e·lapse (i laps′) ***vi.*** **e·lapsed′, e·laps′ing** [< L. pp. of *elabi* < *e-*, out + *labi*, to glide] to slip by; pass: said of time

e·las·mo·branch (i laz′mə braŋk′, -las′-) ***adj.*** [< ModL. < Gr. *elasmos*, beaten metal + L. *branchia*, gills] of a class of fishes with cartilaginous skeletons, horny scales, and no air bladders —***n.*** any fish of this class, as the shark, ray, etc.

e·las·tic (i las′tik) ***adj.*** [< ModL. < LGr. *elastikos* < Gr. *elaunein*, to drive] **1.** having the property of immediately returning to its original size, shape, or position after being stretched, squeezed, etc.; springy **2.** able to recover easily from dejection, fatigue, etc.; buoyant **3.** readily adaptable to circumstances —***n.*** **1.** *a*) an elastic fabric loosely woven with strands of rubber, etc. running through it *b*) a band, garter, etc. made of this **2.** a rubber band —**e·las′ti·cal·ly *adv.*** —**e·las·tic·i·ty** (i las′tis′ə tē, ē′las-) ***n.***, *pl.* **-ties**

e·las·ti·cize (i las′tə sīz′) ***vt.*** **-cized′, -ciz′ing** to make (fabric) elastic

e·las·to·mer (i las′tə mər) ***n.*** [< ELAST(IC) + (POLY)MER] a rubberlike synthetic polymer, as silicone rubber —**e·las′to·mer′ic** (-mer′ik) ***adj.***

e·late (i lāt′, ē-) ***vt.*** **-lat′ed, -lat′ing** [< L. *elatus*, pp. of *efferre* < *ex-*, out + *ferre*, to bear] to raise the spirits of; make very proud, happy, joyful, etc. —**e·lat′ed·ly *adv.*** —**e·lat′ed·ness *n.***

e·la·tion (i lā′shən, ē-) ***n.*** high spirits

E layer a layer of the ionosphere at an altitude of about 60 miles that can reflect radio waves

El·ba (el′bə) It. island between Corsica & Italy: site of Napoleon's first exile (1814–15)

El·be (el′bə, elb) river flowing from NW Czechoslovakia through Germany into the North Sea

el·bow (el′bō) ***n.*** [OE. *elboga*] **1.** the joint between the upper and lower arm; esp., the outer part of the angle made by a bent arm **2.** anything bent like an elbow, as a pipe fitting —***vt., vi.*** **1.** to shove or jostle with the elbow **2.** to push (one's way) thus —**out at (the) elbows** shabby or poor

elbow grease [Colloq.] vigorous physical effort

ELBOW (sense 2)

el·bow·room (-ro͞om′, -room′) ***n.*** room enough to move or work in; sufficient space

El·brus (el′broos, -bro͞oz), **Mount** mountain of the Caucasus range, in the Georgian S.S.R.: highest peak in Europe, 18,481 ft.: also sp. **El′brus**

El·burz Mountains (el boorz′) mountain range in N Iran, along the Caspian Sea

El Ca·jon (el kə hōn′) [Sp., the box] city in S Calif.: suburb of San Diego: pop. 74,000

eld (eld) ***n.*** [< OE. < base of *ald,* OLD] [Archaic] **1.** old age **2.** ancient times; days of yore

eld·er[1] (el′dər) ***adj.*** [OE. *eldra,* compar. < base of *ald,* OLD] **1.** born or brought forth earlier than another or others; senior; older **2.** of superior rank, validity, etc. **3.** earlier; former —***n.*** **1.** an older person, esp. one with authority in a tribe or community **2.** an ancestor **3.** an officer in an early Christian church **4.** in some Protestant churches, a minister; also, a member of the ruling body —**eld′er·ship′** ***n.***

el·der[2] (el′dər) ***n.*** [OE. *ellern*] a shrub or tree with flat-topped clusters of small white flowers and red or purple berries

el·der·ber·ry (-ber′ē) ***n.,*** *pl.* **-ries** **1.** *same as* ELDER[2] **2.** its berry, or drupe, used in wines, etc.

eld·er·ly (-lē) ***adj.*** somewhat old; approaching old age —**eld′er·li·ness** ***n.***

eld·est (el′dist) ***adj.*** [OE. superl. of *ald,* old] oldest; esp., first-born or oldest surviving

El Do·ra·do, El·do·ra·do (el′də rä′dō, -rā′dō, -rad′ō) *pl.* **-dos** [Sp., the gilded] **1.** a legendary country in S. America, supposed to be rich in gold and jewels **2.** any place that is, or is supposed to be, rich in gold, opportunity, etc.

El·ea·nor (el′ə nər, -nôr′) [var. of HELEN] a feminine name

elec., elect. **1.** electric **2.** electrical **3.** electricity

e·lect (i lekt′) ***adj.*** [< L. pp. of *eligere* < *e-,* out + *legere,* to choose] **1.** chosen; given preference **2.** elected but not yet installed in office *[*the mayor-*elect]* **3.** *Theol.* chosen by God for salvation and eternal life —***n.*** a person who is elect —***vt.*** **1.** to select for some office by voting **2.** to choose; select —***vi.*** to make a choice; choose —**the elect** **1.** persons belonging to a specially privileged group **2.** *Theol.* those who are elect

e·lec·tion (i lek′shən) ***n.*** **1.** a choosing or choice **2.** a choosing or being chosen for office by vote **3.** *Theol.* the selection by God of certain people for salvation and eternal life

e·lec·tion·eer (i lek′shə nir′) ***vi.*** to canvass votes for a candidate, party, etc. in an election —**e·lec′tion·eer′er** ***n.*** —**e·lec′tion·eer′ing** ***n.***

e·lec·tive (i lek′tiv) ***adj.*** **1.** *a)* filled by election *[*an *elective* office*]* *b)* chosen by election **2.** of or based on election **3.** having the power to choose **4.** that may be chosen but is not required; optional —***n.*** an optional course in a school or college curriculum —**e·lec′tive·ly** ***adv.***

e·lec·tor (-tər) ***n.*** **1.** one who elects; specif., a qualified voter **2.** a member of the electoral college **3.** [*usually* **E-**] any of the German princes of the Holy Roman Empire who took part in the election of the emperor —**e·lec′tor·al** ***adj.***

electoral college an assembly elected by the voters to perform the formal duty of electing the president and the vice-president of the United States

e·lec·tor·ate (-tər it) ***n.*** all those qualified to vote in an election

E·lec·tra (i lek′trə) *Gr. Myth.* a daughter of Agamemnon and Clytemnestra: she encouraged her brother, Orestes, to kill their mother and their mother's lover, to avenge Agamemnon's murder

e·lec·tric (i lek′trik) ***adj.*** [ModL. *electricus,* orig., produced from amber by rubbing < ML. < L. *electrum,* amber < Gr. *ēlektron*] **1.** of, charged with, or conducting electricity *[*an *electric* wire*]* **2.** producing, or produced by, electricity *[*an *electric* generator*]* **3.** operated by electricity *[*an *electric* iron*]* **4.** very tense or exciting; electrifying —***n.*** a train, car, etc. operated by electricity

e·lec·tri·cal (-tri k'l) ***adj.*** **1.** *same as* ELECTRIC **2.** connected with the science or use of electricity *[*an *electrical* engineer*]* —**e·lec′tri·cal·ly** ***adv.***

electric chair **1.** an apparatus in the form of a chair, used in electrocuting persons sentenced to death **2.** the death sentence by electrocution

electric eel a large, eel-shaped fish of N S. America, with special organs that can give electric shocks

electric eye *same as* PHOTOELECTRIC CELL

electric field a region at every point within which there is a force on an electric charge

electric guitar a guitar whose tones are transmitted to an amplifier and loudspeaker through an electrical pickup attached to the instrument

e·lec·tri·cian (i lek′trish′ən, ē′lek-) ***n.*** a person whose work is the construction, repair, or installation of electric apparatus

e·lec·tric·i·ty (-tris′ə tē) ***n.*** **1.** a property of certain fundamental particles of all matter, as electrons (negative charges) and protons or positrons (positive charges) that have a force field associated with them and that can be separated by the expenditure of energy: electrical charge can be generated by friction, induction, or chemical change **2.** *a)* an electric current: see CURRENT (*n.* 3) *b)* an electric charge: see CHARGE (*n.* 2) **3.** the branch of physics dealing with electricity **4.** electric current as a public utility for lighting, heating, etc. **5.** strong emotional tension, excitement, etc.

electric needle a slender, pointed electrode used in surgery to cut and cauterize tissue, etc.

electric ray a cartilaginous fish with electric organs that can stun enemies or prey

e·lec·tri·fy (i lek′trə fī′) ***vt.*** **-fied′, -fy′ing** **1.** to charge with electricity **2.** to give an electric shock to **3.** to give a shock of excitement to; thrill **4.** to equip for the use of electricity; provide with electric power —**e·lec′tri·fi′a·ble** ***adj.*** —**e·lec′tri·fi·ca′tion** ***n.*** —**e·lec′tri·fi′er** ***n.***

e·lec·tro (i lek′trō) ***n.,*** *pl.* **-tros** *short for:* **1.** ELECTROTYPE **2.** ELECTROPLATE

e·lec·tro- *a combining form meaning:* **1.** electric *[electromagnet]* **2.** electrically *[electrocute]* **3.** electricity *[electrostatics]*

e·lec·tro·car·di·o·gram (i lek′trō kär′dē ə gram′) ***n.*** a tracing showing the changes in electric potential produced by contractions of the heart

e·lec·tro·car·di·o·graph (-kär′dē ə graf′) ***n.*** an instrument for making an electrocardiogram —**e·lec′tro·car′di·o·graph′ic** ***adj.*** —**e·lec′tro·car′di·og′ra·phy** (-äg′rə fē) ***n.***

e·lec·tro·chem·is·try (-kem′is trē) ***n.*** the science dealing with the use of electrical energy to bring about a chemical reaction or with the generation of electrical energy by chemical action —**e·lec′tro·chem′i·cal** ***adj.*** —**e·lec′tro·chem′i·cal·ly** ***adv.***

e·lec·tro·con·vul·sive therapy (-kən vul′siv) *see* SHOCK THERAPY

e·lec·tro·cute (i lek′trə kyo͞ot′) ***vt.*** **-cut′ed, -cut′ing** [ELECTRO- + (EXE)CUTE] to kill with a charge of electricity; specif., to execute in the electric chair —**e·lec′tro·cu′tion** ***n.***

e·lec·trode (i lek′trōd) ***n.*** [ELECTR(O-) + -ODE] any terminal that conducts an electric current into or away from various conducting substances in a circuit, as the anode or cathode in a battery, or that emits, collects, or controls the flow of electrons in an electron tube, as the cathode, plate, or grid

e·lec·tro·dy·nam·ics (i lek′trō dī nam′iks) ***n.pl.*** [*with sing. v.*] the branch of physics dealing with the phenomena of electric currents and associated magnetic forces —**e·lec′tro·dy·nam′ic** ***adj.***

e·lec·tro·en·ceph·a·lo·gram (-en sef′ə lə gram′) ***n.*** a tracing showing the changes in electric potential produced by the brain

e·lec·tro·en·ceph·a·lo·graph (-en sef′ə lə graf′) ***n.*** an instrument for making electroencephalograms —**e·lec′tro·en·ceph′a·lo·graph′ic** ***adj.*** —**e·lec′tro·en·ceph′a·log′ra·phy** (-ə läg′rə fē) ***n.***

e·lec·trol·y·sis (i lek′träl′ə sis) ***n.*** [ELECTRO- + -LYSIS] **1.** the decomposition of an electrolyte by the action of an electric current passing through it **2.** the removal of unwanted hair from the body by destroying the hair roots with an electrified needle

e·lec·tro·lyte (i lek′trə līt′) ***n.*** [ELECTRO- + -LYTE] any substance which in solution can conduct an electric current by the movement of its dissociated positive and negative ions to the electrodes of opposite charge, where the ions are deposited as a coating, liberated as a gas, etc. —**e·lec′tro·lyt′ic** (-lit′ik) ***adj.*** —**e·lec′tro·lyt′i·cal·ly** ***adv.***

e·lec·tro·lyze (i lek′trə līz′) ***vt.*** **-lyzed′, -lyz′ing** to subject to electrolysis

e·lec·tro·mag·net (i lek′trō mag′nit) ***n.*** a soft iron core surrounded by a coil of wire, that temporarily becomes a magnet when an electric current flows through the wire

e·lec·tro·mag·net·ic (-mag net′ik) ***adj.*** of, produced by, or having to do with electromagnetism or an electromagnet —**e·lec′tro·mag·net′i·cal·ly *adv.***

electromagnetic wave a wave propagated through space or matter by the oscillating electric and magnetic field generated by an oscillating electric charge

e·lec·tro·mag·net·ism (-mag′nə tiz'm) ***n.*** **1.** magnetism produced by an electric current **2.** the branch of physics dealing with the relations between electricity and magnetism

e·lec·trom·e·ter (i lek′träm′ə tər, ē′lek-) ***n.*** a device for detecting or measuring differences of potential by means of electrostatic or mechanical forces

e·lec·tro·mo·tive (i lek′trə mōt′iv) ***adj.*** **1.** producing an electric current through differences in potential **2.** relating to electromotive force

electromotive force the force that causes or tends to cause a current to flow in a circuit, equivalent to the potential difference between the terminals and commonly measured in volts

e·lec·tron (i lek′trän) ***n.*** [arbitrary coinage < ELECTR(IC) + -ON] any of the negatively charged particles that form a part of all atoms: the number of electrons circulating around a nucleus is equal to the number of positive charges on the nucleus

e·lec·tro·neg·a·tive (i lek′trō neg′ə tiv) ***adj.*** **1.** having a negative electrical charge; tending to move to the positive electrode, or anode, in electrolysis **2.** able to attract electrons, esp. in forming a chemical bond

e·lec·tron·ic (i lek′trän′ik, ē′lek-) ***adj.*** **1.** of electrons **2.** operating, produced, or done by the action of electrons or by devices dependent on such action —**e·lec′tron′i·cal·ly *adv.***

electronic data processing data processing by means of electronic equipment, esp. computers

electronic music music in which the sounds are originated or altered by electronic devices, and arranged and recorded on tape for presentation

electronic organ a musical instrument with a console like that of a pipe organ, but producing tones by means of electronic devices instead of pipes

e·lec·tron·ics (-iks) ***n.pl.*** [*with sing. v.*] the science that deals with the behavior and control of electrons in vacuums and gases, and with the use of electron tubes, transistors, etc.

electron microscope an instrument for focusing a beam of electrons, using electric or magnetic fields, to form an enlarged image of an object on a fluorescent screen or photographic plate: it is much more powerful than any optical microscope

electron tube a sealed glass or metal tube completely evacuated or filled with gas at low pressure and having two or more electrodes, used to control the flow of electrons

e·lec·tron-volt (-vōlt′) ***n.*** a unit of energy equal to that attained by an electron falling unimpeded through a potential difference of one volt

e·lec·tro·pho·re·sis (i lek′trō fə rē′sis) ***n.*** [ModL. < ELECTRO- + Gr. *phorēsis* < *pherein*, BEAR[1]] the migration of colloidal particles in an electric field

e·lec·troph·o·rus (i lek′träf′ər əs) ***n.,*** *pl.* **-ri′** (-ī′) [ModL. < ELECTRO- + Gr. *-phoros* < *pherein*, BEAR[1]] an apparatus consisting of a resin disk and a metal plate, for generating static electricity by induction

e·lec·tro·plate (i lek′trə plāt′) ***vt.*** **-plat′ed, -plat′ing** to deposit a coating of metal on by electrolysis —***n.*** anything so plated

e·lec·tro·pos·i·tive (i lek′trə päz′ə tiv) ***adj.*** **1.** having a positive electrical charge; tending to move to the negative electrode, or cathode, in electrolysis **2.** able to give up electrons, esp. in forming a chemical bond

e·lec·tro·scope (i lek′trə skōp′) ***n.*** [ELECTRO- + -SCOPE] an instrument for detecting very small charges of electricity, as by the divergence of electrically charged strips of gold leaf —**e·lec′tro·scop′ic** (-skäp′ik) ***adj.***

GOLD LEAF

ELECTROSCOPE

e·lec·tro·shock therapy (-shäk′) *see* SHOCK THERAPY

e·lec·tro·stat·ics (i lek′trə stat′iks) ***n.pl.*** [*with sing. v.*] the branch of physics dealing with the phenomena accompanying electric charges at rest, or static electricity —**e·lec′tro·stat′ic *adj.*** —**e·lec′tro·stat′i·cal·ly *adv.***

e·lec·tro·ther·a·py (-ther′ə pē) ***n.*** the treatment of disease by means of electricity, as by diathermy —**e·lec′tro·ther′a·pist *n.***

e·lec·tro·type (i lek′trə tīp′) ***n.*** *Printing* **1.** a facsimile plate made by electroplating a wax or plastic impression of the surface to be reproduced **2.** a print made from such a plate **3.** *same as* ELECTROTYPY —***vt., vi.*** **-typed′, -typ′ing** to make an electrotype or electrotypes (of) —**e·lec′tro·typ′er *n.***

e·lec·tro·typ·y (-tīp′ē) ***n.*** the process of making electrotypes

e·lec·trum (i lek′trəm) ***n.*** [L. < Gr. *ēlektron:* see ELECTRIC] a light-yellow alloy of gold and silver

e·lec·tu·ar·y (i lek′choo wer′ē) ***n.,*** *pl.* **-ar′ies** [< LL. < Gr. < *ek-*, out + *leichein*, to lick] a medicine mixed with honey or syrup to form a paste

el·ee·mos·y·nar·y (el′i mäs′ə ner′ē, el′ē ə-) ***adj.*** [< ML. < LL. < Gr. *eleēmosynē*, pity (in NT., alms) < *eleos*, mercy] **1.** of or for charity; charitable **2.** supported by or dependent on charity **3.** given as charity; free

el·e·gance (el′ə gəns) ***n.*** **1.** the quality of being elegant; specif., *a)* dignified richness and grace *b)* polished fastidiousness or refined grace **2.** anything elegant Also, esp. for sense 2, **el′e·gan·cy,** *pl.* **-cies**

el·e·gant (-gənt) ***adj.*** [< Fr. < L. *elegans* < *e-*, out + hyp. *legare*, var. of *legere*, to choose] **1.** characterized by dignified richness and grace, as of design, dress, style, etc.; tastefully luxurious **2.** impressively fastidious or refined in manners and tastes **3.** [Colloq.] excellent; fine —**el′e·gant·ly *adv.***

el·e·gi·ac (el′ə jī′ək, i lē′jē ak′) ***adj.*** **1.** *Gr. & Rom. Prosody* of or composed in dactylic hexameter couplets, the second line having only an accented syllable in the third and sixth feet: the form was used for elegies, etc. **2.** of, like, or fit for an elegy **3.** sad; mournful Also **el′e·gi′a·cal** —***n.*** **1.** an elegiac couplet **2.** [*pl.*] a poem or poems written in such couplets

el·e·gize (el′ə jīz′) ***vi.*** **-gized′, -giz′ing** to write elegies —***vt.*** to lament as in an elegy

el·e·gy (-jē) ***n.,*** *pl.* **-gies** [< Fr. < L. < Gr. *elegeia* < *elegos*, a lament] **1.** a poem or song of lament and praise for the dead **2.** any poem in elegiac verse **3.** a poem, song, etc. in a mournfully contemplative tone —**el′e·gist *n.***

elem. 1. element(s) **2.** elementary

el·e·ment (el′ə mənt) ***n.*** [OFr. < L. *elementum*] **1.** any of the four substances—earth, air, fire, water—formerly believed to constitute all physical matter **2.** the natural or suitable environment, situation, etc. for a person or thing **3.** *a)* a component part or quality, often one that is basic or essential *b)* a constituent group of a specified kind [the criminal *element*] **4.** *Chem.* any substance that cannot be separated into different substances by ordinary chemical methods: all matter is composed of such substances **5.** [*pl.*] *Eccles.* the bread and wine of Communion **6.** *Elec.* the wire coil, etc. that becomes glowing hot, as in an electric oven —**the elements 1.** the first or basic principles; rudiments **2.** wind, rain, etc.; forces of the atmosphere See table of CHEMICAL ELEMENTS on next page

el·e·men·tal (el′ə men′t'l) ***adj.*** **1.** of the four elements (sense 1) **2.** of or like the forces of nature **3.** basic and powerful; primal [hunger is an *elemental* drive] **4.** *same as* ELEMENTARY (sense 2 *a*) **5.** being an essential part or parts **6.** being a chemical element in uncombined form —***n.*** a basic principle: *usually used in pl.* —**el′e·men′tal·ly *adv.***

el·e·men·ta·ry (-tər ē, -trē) ***adj.*** **1.** *same as* ELEMENTAL **2.** *a)* of first principles or fundamentals; introductory; basic *b)* of or having to do with the formal instruction of children in basic subjects —**el′e·men′ta·ri·ly *adv.*** —**el′e·men′ta·ri·ness *n.***

elementary particle a subatomic particle that is capable of independent existence, as a neutron, proton, etc.

elementary school a school of the first six grades (sometimes, first eight grades), where basic subjects are taught

el·e·phant (el′ə fənt) ***n.,*** *pl.* **-phants, -phant:** see PLURAL, II, D, 1 [< L. < Gr. *elephas* (gen. *elephantos*), elephant, ivory] a huge, thick-skinned mammal, the largest of extant four-footed animals, with a long, flexible snout (called a *trunk*) and, usually, two ivory tusks: the **African elephant** has a flatter head and larger ears than the **Asian** (or **Indian**) **elephant**

AFRICAN

INDIAN

ELEPHANTS (shoulder height: African, 10–13 ft.; Indian, 8½–10 ft.)

el·e·phan·ti·a·sis (el′ə fən tī′ə sis) ***n.*** a chronic disease of the skin characterized by the enlargement of the legs or other parts, and by the hardening of the skin: it is caused by obstruction of the lymphatic vessels, esp. by filarial worms

el·e·phan·tine (el′ə fan′tēn, -tīn, -tin) ***adj.*** **1.** of an elephant or elephants **2.** like an elephant in size or gait; huge, heavy, slow, clumsy, etc.

El·eu·sin·i·an (el′yoo sin′ē ən) ***adj.*** [after *Eleusis*, ancient Gr. city near Athens, where celebrated] of the secret

CHEMICAL ELEMENTS

With International Atomic Weights. Carbon at 12 is the standard.

	Symbol	Atomic Number	Atomic Weight
actinium	Ac	89	227(?)
aluminum	Al	13	26.9815
americium	Am	95	243.13
antimony	Sb	51	121.75
argon	Ar	18	39.948
arsenic	As	33	74.9216
astatine	At	85	210(?)
barium	Ba	56	137.34
berkelium	Bk	97	248(?)
beryllium	Be	4	9.0122
bismuth	Bi	83	208.980
boron	B	5	10.811
bromine	Br	35	79.909
cadmium	Cd	48	112.40
calcium	Ca	20	40.08
californium	Cf	98	251(?)
carbon	C	6	12.01115
cerium	Ce	58	140.12
cesium	Cs	55	132.905
chlorine	Cl	17	35.453
chromium	Cr	24	51.996
cobalt	Co	27	58.9332
copper	Cu	29	63.546
curium	Cm	96	247(?)
dysprosium	Dy	66	162.50
einsteinium	Es	99	252(?)
erbium	Er	68	167.28
europium	Eu	63	151.96
fermium	Fm	100	257(?)
fluorine	F	9	18.9984
francium	Fr	87	223(?)
gadolinium	Gd	64	157.25
gallium	Ga	31	69.72
germanium	Ge	32	72.59
gold	Au	79	196.967
hafnium	Hf	72	178.49
helium	He	2	4.0026
holmium	Ho	67	164.930
hydrogen	H	1	1.00797
indium	In	49	114.82
iodine	I	53	126.9044
iridium	Ir	77	192.2
iron	Fe	26	55.847
krypton	Kr	36	83.80
lanthanum	La	57	138.91
lawrencium	Lr	103	256(?)
lead	Pb	82	207.19
lithium	Li	3	6.939
lutetium	Lu	71	174.97
magnesium	Mg	12	24.312
manganese	Mn	25	54.9380
mendelevium	Md	101	258(?)

	Symbol	Atomic Number	Atomic Weight
mercury	Hg	80	200.59
molybdenum	Mo	42	95.94
neodymium	Nd	60	144.24
neon	Ne	10	20.183
neptunium	Np	93	237.00
nickel	Ni	28	58.71
niobium	Nb	41	92.906
nitrogen	N	7	14.0067
nobelium	No	102	255(?)
osmium	Os	76	190.2
oxygen	O	8	15.9994
palladium	Pd	46	106.4
phosphorus	P	15	30.9738
platinum	Pt	78	195.09
plutonium	Pu	94	239.05
polonium	Po	84	210.05
potassium	K	19	39.102
praseodymium	Pr	59	140.907
promethium	Pm	61	145(?)
protactinium	Pa	91	231.10
radium	Ra	88	226.00
radon	Rn	86	222.00
rhenium	Re	75	186.2
rhodium	Rh	45	102.905
rubidium	Rb	37	85.47
ruthenium	Ru	44	101.07
samarium	Sm	62	150.35
scandium	Sc	21	44.956
selenium	Se	34	78.96
silicon	Si	14	28.086
silver	Ag	47	107.868
sodium	Na	11	22.9898
strontium	Sr	38	87.62
sulfur	S	16	32.064
tantalum	Ta	73	180.948
technetium	Tc	43	97(?)
tellurium	Te	52	127.60
terbium	Tb	65	158.924
thallium	Tl	81	204.37
thorium	Th	90	232.038
thulium	Tm	69	168.934
tin	Sn	50	118.69
titanium	Ti	22	47.90
tungsten	W	74	183.85
uranium	U	92	238.03
vanadium	V	23	50.942
xenon	Xe	54	131.30
ytterbium	Yb	70	173.04
yttrium	Y	39	88.905
zinc	Zn	30	65.37
zirconium	Zr	40	91.22

fat, āpe, cär; ten, ēven; is, bīte; gō, hôrn, tōōl, look; oil, out; up, fur; get; joy; yet; chin; she; thin, *th*en; zh, leisure; ŋ, ring; ə for *a* in *ago*, *e* in *agent*, *i* in *sanity*, *o* in *comply*, *u* in *focus*; ' as in *able* (ā'b'l); Fr. bål; **ë**, Fr. coeur; **ö**, Fr. feu; Fr. mo*n*; **ô**, Fr. coq; **ü**, Fr. duc; ***r***, Fr. cri; **H**, G. ich; **kh**, G. doch; ‡foreign; *hypothetical; < derived from. See inside front cover.

religious rites (**Eleusinian mysteries**) anciently celebrated in honor of Demeter and Persephone

elev. elevation

el·e·vate (el′ə vāt′) *vt.* **-vat′ed, -vat′ing** [< L. pp. of *elevare* < *e-*, out + *levare*, to lift < *levis*, light] **1.** to lift up; raise **2.** to raise in rank or position **3.** to raise to a higher intellectual or moral level **4.** to raise the spirits of; elate

el·e·vat·ed (-vāt′id) *adj.* **1.** lifted up; raised; high **2.** exalted; dignified; lofty **3.** high-spirited; exhilarated —*n.* a railway elevated above street level: in full, **elevated railway**

el·e·va·tion (el′ə vā′shən) *n.* **1.** an elevating or being elevated **2.** a high place or position **3.** height above the surface of the earth **4.** dignity; loftiness **5.** a flat scale drawing of the front, rear, or side of a building, etc. **6.** *Astron.* altitude **7.** *Geog.* height above sea level

el·e·va·tor (el′ə vāt′ər) *n.* **1.** a person or thing that raises or lifts up **2.** a cage or car for hoisting or lowering people or things, attached by cables to a machine that moves it in a shaft **3.** a machine, usually consisting of buckets or scoops fastened to an endless belt, for hoisting grain, etc. **4.** a warehouse for storing, hoisting, and discharging grain **5.** a movable airfoil like a horizontal rudder, for making an aircraft go up or down

e·lev·en (i lev′ən) *adj.* [OE. *endleofan*, lit., one left over (ten)] totaling one more than ten —*n.* **1.** the cardinal number between ten and twelve; 11; XI **2.** a football or cricket team

e·lev·enth (-ənth) *adj.* **1.** preceded by ten others in a series; 11th **2.** designating any of the eleven equal parts of something —*n.* **1.** the one following the tenth **2.** any of the eleven equal parts of something; 1/11 —**at the eleventh hour** at the last possible time

elf (elf) *n., pl.* **elves** (elvz) [OE. *ælf*] **1.** *Folklore* a tiny, often prankish fairy **2.** a mischievous, small child or being —**elf′ish** *adj.* —**elf′ish·ly** *adv.* —**elf′ish·ness** *n.* —**elf′like′** *adj.*

elf·in (el′fin) *adj.* of, appropriate to, or like an elf; fairylike —*n.* an elf

elf·lock (elf′läk′) *n.* a tangled, matted lock of hair

El·gar (el′gər, -gär), Sir **Edward (William)** 1857–1934; Eng. composer

El·gin (el′jən) [after *Elgin*, city in Scotland] city in NE Ill., near Chicago: pop. 64,000

El Grec·o (el grek′ō) (born *Domenikos Theotokopoulos*) 1541?–1614?; painter in Italy & Spain, born in Crete

E·li (ē′lī) [Heb. *'ēlī*, lit., high] a masculine name

e·lic·it (i lis′it) *vt.* [< L. pp. of *elicere* < *e-*, out + *lacere*, to entice] **1.** to draw forth; evoke *[to elicit a reply]* **2.** to cause to be revealed *[to elicit facts]* —**e·lic′i·ta′tion** *n.* —**e·lic′i·tor** *n.*

e·lide (i līd′) *vt.* **e·lid′ed, e·lid′ing** [< L. *elidere* < *e-*, out + *laedere*, to strike] **1.** to leave out; suppress; omit **2.** to leave out or slur over (a vowel, syllable, etc.) in pronunciation —**e·lid′i·ble** *adj.*

el·i·gi·ble (el′i jə b′l) *adj.* [< ML. < L. *eligere*: see ELECT] **1.** fit to be chosen; qualified **2.** desirable, esp. for marriage —*n.* an eligible person —**el′i·gi·bil′i·ty** *n.* —**el′i·gi·bly** *adv.*

E·li·jah (i lī′jə) [Heb. *'ēlīyāhū*, lit., Jehovah is God] **1.** a masculine name **2.** a prophet of Israel in the 9th century B.C.: I Kings 17–19; II Kings 2:1–11 Also **E·li·as** (i lī′əs)

e·lim·i·nate (i lim′ə nāt′) *vt.* **-nat′ed, -nat′ing** [< L. pp. of *eliminare* < *e-*, out + *limen*, threshold] **1.** to take out; get rid of **2.** to leave out of consideration; reject; omit **3.** to drop (a person, team, etc. losing a round or match) from further competition **4.** *Algebra* to get rid of (an unknown quantity) by combining equations **5.** *Physiol.* to excrete —**e·lim′i·na′tion** *n.* —**e·lim′i·na′tive** *adj.* —**e·lim′i·na′tor** *n.* —**e·lim′i·na·to′ry** *adj.*

el·int (el′int) *n.* [*el(ectronic) int(elligence)*] the gathering of intelligence by monitoring with electronic equipment from airplanes, ships, satellites, etc.

El·i·ot (el′ē ət, el′yət) [dim. of ELLIS] **1.** a masculine name **2. George**, (pseud. of *Mary Ann Evans*) 1819–80; Eng. novelist **3. T(homas) S(tearns)**, 1888–1965; Brit. poet & critic, born in the U.S.

E·li·sha (i lī′shə) [Heb. *elīshā'*, lit., God is salvation] **1.** a masculine name **2.** *Bible* a prophet of Israel, who succeeded Elijah: II Kings 2

e·li·sion (i lizh′ən) *n.* **1.** the eliding of a vowel, syllable, etc. in pronunciation (Ex.: it's, they'd, we've) **2.** any leaving out of parts

e·lite, é·lite (i lēt′, ā-) *n.* [< Fr., ult. < L. *eligere*: see ELECT] **1.** [*also used with pl. v.*] the group or part of a group selected or regarded as the finest, best, most powerful, etc. **2.** a size of type for typewriters, measuring 12 characters to the inch —*adj.* of, forming, or for an elite

e·lit·ism (-iz'm) *n.* government or control by an elite, or advocacy of such control —**e·lit′ist** *adj., n.*

e·lix·ir (i lik′sər) *n.* [< ML. < Ar. *al-iksīr*, prob. < Gr. *xērion*, powder for drying wounds < *xēros*, dry] **1.** a hypothetical substance sought for by medieval alchemists to change base metals into gold or (in full, **elixir of life**) to prolong life indefinitely **2.** [Rare] the quintessence **3.** a cure-all **4.** a medicine made of drugs in alcoholic solution, usually sweetened

E·liz·a·beth¹ (i liz′ə bəth) [< LL. < Gr. < Heb. *elīsheba'*, lit., God is (my) oath] **1.** a feminine name: dim. *Elsie*; var. *Elisabeth, Eliza* **2. Elizabeth I** 1533–1603; queen of England (1558–1603): daughter of HENRY VIII **3. Elizabeth II** 1926– ; queen of Great Britain & Northern Ireland (1952–): daughter of GEORGE VI

E·liz·a·beth² (i liz′ə bəth) [after wife of Sir G. Carteret, proprietor] city in NE N.J., adjacent to Newark: pop. 106,000

E·liz·a·be·than (i liz′ə bē′thən, -beth′ən) *adj.* of or characteristic of the time when Elizabeth I was queen of England —*n.* an English person, esp. a writer, of the time of Queen Elizabeth I

Elizabethan sonnet *same as* SHAKESPEAREAN SONNET

elk (elk) *n., pl.* **elk, elks**: see PLURAL, II, D, 2 [OE. *eolh*] **1.** a large, mooselike deer of N Europe and Asia, with broad antlers **2.** *same as* WAPITI

ell¹ (el) *n.* something L-shaped; specif., an extension or wing at right angles to the main structure

ell² (el) *n.* [OE. *eln*] a former English measure of length, mainly for cloth, equal to 45 in.

El·la (el′ə) [dim. of ELEANOR] a feminine name

El·len (el′ən) [var. of HELEN] a feminine name

el·lipse (i lips′, ə-) *n., pl.* **-lip′ses** (-lip′siz) [< ModL. < Gr. < *elleipein*, to fall short (of a perfect circle)] *Geom.* the path of a point that moves so that the sum of its distances from two fixed points (called *foci*) is constant

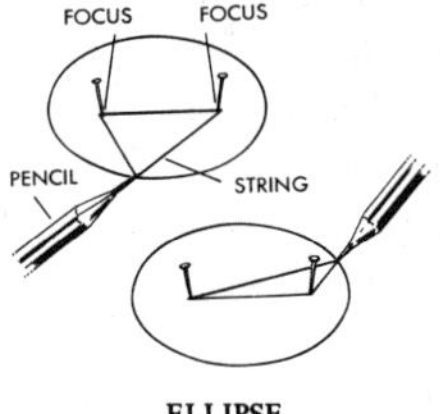

ELLIPSE

el·lip·sis (i lip′sis, ə-) *n., pl.* **-ses** (-sēz) [see prec.] **1.** *Gram.* the omission of a word or words necessary for complete grammatical construction but understood in the context (Ex.: "if possible" for "if it is possible") **2.** *Writing & Printing a)* a mark (. . . or formerly ***) indicating an intentional omission of words or letters, a lapse of time, etc. *b)* the use of such marks

el·lip·soid (-soid) *n. Geom.* a solid whose plane sections are all ellipses or circles —*adj.* shaped like an ellipsoid: also **el·lip′soi′dal**

el·lip·ti·cal (i lip′ti k'l, ə-) *adj.* **1.** of, or having the form of, an ellipse **2.** of or characterized by ellipsis; with a word or words omitted; with incomplete constructions, etc. Also **el·lip′tic** —**el·lip′ti·cal·ly** *adv.*

El·lis (el′is) [var. of ELISHA] **1.** a masculine name **2. (Henry) Have·lock** (hav′läk, -lək), 1859–1939; Eng. psychologist & writer

Ellis Island [after S. *Ellis*, former owner] small island in New York Bay: former examination center for immigrants seeking to enter the U.S.

elm (elm) *n.* [OE.] **1.** a tall, hardy shade tree growing largely in the North Temperate Zone **2.** the hard, heavy wood of this tree

El·mer (el′mər) [< ? OE. < *æthel*, noble or *egil-* (< *ege*, awe) + *mære*, famous] a masculine name

Elm·hurst (elm′hurst′) [after *elm* + *hurst*, grove] city in NE Ill.: suburb of Chicago: pop. 51,000

El Mon·te (el män′tē) [Sp., lit., the thicket] city in SW Calif.: suburb of Los Angeles: pop. 79,000

el·o·cu·tion (el′ə kyōō′shən) *n.* [< L. < pp. of *eloqui*: see ELOQUENT] **1.** style or manner of speaking or reading in public **2.** the art of public speaking or declaiming —**el′o·cu′tion·ar′y** *adj.* —**el′o·cu′tion·ist** *n.*

El·o·ise (el′ə wēz′, el′ə wēz′) [var. of LOUISE] a feminine name

e·lon·gate (i lôŋ′gāt) *vt., vi.* **-gat·ed, -gat·ing** [< LL. pp. of *elongare*, to prolong < L. *e-*, out + *longus*, long] to make or become longer; stretch —*adj.* **1.** lengthened; stretched **2.** *Bot.* long and narrow —**e·lon·ga·tion** (i lôŋ′gā′shən, ē′lôŋ-) *n.*

e·lope (i lōp′, ə-) *vi.* **e·loped′, e·lop′ing** [Anglo-Fr. *aloper*, prob. < ME. < OE. < *a-*, away + *hleapan*, to run] **1.** to run away secretly, esp. in order to get married **2.** to run away; escape —**e·lope′ment** *n.* —**e·lop′er** *n.*

el·o·quence (el′ə kwəns) *n.* **1.** speech or writing that is forceful, fluent, etc. **2.** the art or manner of such speech or writing **3.** persuasive power

el·o·quent (-kwənt) *adj.* [OFr. < L. prp. of *eloqui* < *e-*, out + *loqui*, to speak] **1.** having, or characterized by, eloquence; fluent, forceful, and persuasive **2.** vividly expressive —**el′o·quent·ly** *adv.*

El Pas·o (el pas′ō) [Sp., the ford] city in westernmost Tex., on the Rio Grande: pop. 425,000

El·sa (el′sə) [G. < ?] a feminine name

El Sal·va·dor (el sal′və dôr′; *Sp.* säl′vä *th*ôr′) country in Central America, on the Pacific: 8,260 sq. mi.; pop. 3,390,000; cap. San Salvador

else (els) ***adj.*** [OE. *elles,* adv. gen. of n. base *el-,* other] **1.** different; other *[*somebody *else]* **2.** in addition; more *[*is there anything *else?]* **—*adv.*** **1.** in a different or additional time, place, or manner; otherwise *[*where *else* can I go?*]* **2.** if not *[*study, (or) *else* you will fail*]*

else·where (-hwer′, -wer′) ***adv.*** in or to some other place; somewhere else

El·sie (el′sē) [dim. of ELIZABETH[1]] a feminine name

e·lu·ci·date (i lo͞o′sə dāt′, ə-) ***vt., vi.*** **-dat′ed, -dat′ing** [< LL. pp. of *elucidare* < L. *e-,* out + *lucidus,* clear < *lux,* light] to make clear (esp. something abstruse); explain **—e·lu′ci·da′tion *n.* —e·lu′ci·da′tive *adj.* —e·lu′ci·da′tor *n.***

e·lude (i lo͞od′) ***vt.*** **e·lud′ed, e·lud′ing** [< L. *eludere* < *e-,* out + *ludere,* to play] **1.** to avoid or escape from by quickness, cunning, etc.; evade **2.** to escape detection, notice, or understanding by **—e·lud′er *n.* —e·lu·sion** (i lo͞o′zhən, ə-) ***n.***

El·ul (el′o͝ol) ***n.*** [Heb.] the twelfth month of the Jewish year: see JEWISH CALENDAR

e·lu·sive (i lo͞o′siv) ***adj.*** **1.** tending to elude **2.** hard to grasp or retain mentally; baffling **—e·lu′sive·ly *adv.* —e·lu′sive·ness *n.***

el·ver (el′vər) ***n.*** [for *eelfare,* migration of eels] a young eel

elves (elvz) ***n.*** *pl. of* ELF

El·vi·ra (el vī′rə, -vir′ə) [Sp., prob. < Goth.] a feminine name

elv·ish (el′vish) ***adj.*** of or like an elf **—elv′ish·ly *adv.***

E·lyr·i·a (i lir′ē ə, ə-) [after J. *Ely,* proprietor, & M*aria,* his wife] city in N Ohio, near Cleveland: pop. 58,000

E·ly·si·um (i lizh′ē əm, -liz′-) [L. < Gr.] *Gr. Myth.* the dwelling place of virtuous people after death **—*n.*** any place or condition of ideal bliss or complete happiness; paradise Also **Elysian Fields —E·ly·sian** (i lizh′ən, -ē ən) ***adj.***

em (em) ***n.*** **1.** the letter M, m **2.** *Printing* a square of any type body, used as a unit of measure, as of column width; esp., an em pica, about 1/6 in.

'em (əm, 'm) ***pron.*** [Colloq.] them

e·ma·ci·ate (i mā′shē āt′, -sē-) ***vt.*** **-at′ed, -at′ing** [< L. pp. of *emaciare* < *e-,* out + *macies,* leanness < *macer,* lean] to cause to become abnormally lean; cause to lose much flesh or weight, as by starvation or disease **—e·ma′ci·a′tion *n.***

em·a·nate (em′ə nāt′) ***vi.*** **-nat′ed, -nat′ing** [< L. pp. of *emanare* < *e-,* out + *manare,* to flow] to come forth; issue, as from a source **—*vt.*** [Rare] to send forth; emit

em·a·na·tion (em′ə nā′shən) ***n.*** **1.** an emanating **2.** something that comes forth from a source **3.** *Chem. a)* *same as* RADON *b)* a gas given off by several radioactive substances **—em′a·na′tive *adj.***

e·man·ci·pate (i man′sə pāt′) ***vt.*** **-pat′ed, -pat′ing** [< L. pp. of *emancipare* < *e-,* out + *mancipare,* to deliver up as property, ult. < *manus,* the hand + *capere,* to take] **1.** to set free (a slave, etc.); release from bondage or serfdom **2.** to free from restraint or influence **—e·man′ci·pa′tion *n.* —e·man′ci·pa′tive, e·man′ci·pa·to′ry** (-pə tôr′ē) ***adj.*** **—e·man′ci·pa′tor *n.***

e·mas·cu·late (i mas′kyə lāt′) ***vt.*** **-lat′ed, -lat′ing** [< L. pp. of *emasculare* < *e-,* out + *masculus,* MASCULINE] **1.** to deprive (a male) of the power to reproduce, as by removing the testicles; castrate **2.** to destroy the strength or force of; weaken **—e·mas′cu·la′tion *n.* —e·mas′cu·la′tive, e·mas′cu·la·to′ry** (-lə tôr′ē) ***adj.*** **—e·mas′cu·la′tor *n.***

em·balm (im bäm′) ***vt.*** [< OFr. *embaumer:* see EN- & BALM] **1.** to treat (a dead body) with various chemicals to keep it from decaying rapidly **2.** to preserve in memory **3.** to make fragrant; perfume **—em·balm′er *n.* —em·balm′ment *n.***

em·bank (im baŋk′) ***vt.*** to protect, support, or enclose with a bank of earth, rubble, etc.

em·bank·ment (-mənt) ***n.*** **1.** the act or process of embanking **2.** a bank of earth, rubble, etc. used to keep back water, hold up a roadway, etc.

em·bar·ca·der·o (em bär′kə der′ō) ***n.,*** *pl.* **-der′os** [Sp. < pp. of *embarcar,* EMBARK] a wharf, dock, or pier

em·bar·go (im bär′gō) ***n.,*** *pl.* **-goes** [Sp., ult. < L. *in-,* in, on + ML. *barra,* BAR[1]] **1.** a government order prohibiting the entry or departure of commercial ships at its ports **2.** any restriction, restraint, or prohibition, esp. one imposed on commerce by law **—*vt.*** **-goed, -go·ing** to put an embargo on

em·bark (im bärk′) ***vt.*** [<Fr. < Sp. or OPr. < *em-* (L. *in-*) + L. *barca,* BARK[3]] to put or take (passengers or goods) aboard a ship, airplane, etc. **—*vi.*** **1.** to go aboard a ship, airplane, etc. **2.** to begin a journey **3.** to get started in an enterprise **—em·bar·ka·tion** (em′bär kā′shən), **em·bark′ment *n.***

em·bar·rass (im ber′əs) ***vt.*** [< Fr. < Sp. < It. < *imbarrare,* to impede < *in-* (L. *in-*) + *barra,* BAR[1]] **1.** to cause to feel self-conscious; disconcert **2.** to cause difficulties to; hinder **3.** to cause to be in debt; cause financial difficulties to **4.** to complicate **—em·bar′rass·ing *adj.* —em·bar′rass·ing·ly *adv.* —em·bar′rass·ment *n.***

em·bas·sy (em′bə sē) ***n.,*** *pl.* **-sies** [< MFr. < OIt. < Pr. < hyp. *ambaissa:* see AMBASSADOR] **1.** the position or functions of an ambassador **2.** the official residence or offices of an ambassador **3.** an ambassador and his staff **4.** a person or group sent on an official mission to a foreign government **5.** any important or official mission

em·bat·tle[1] (im bat′'l) ***vt.*** **-tled, -tling** to provide with battlements; build battlements on

em·bat·tle[2] (im bat′'l) ***vt.*** **-tled, -tling** [Rare, except in pp.] to prepare or set in line for battle

em·bay (im bā′) ***vt.*** to shut in; enclose or surround, as in a bay **—em·bay′ment *n.***

em·bed (im bed′) ***vt.*** **-bed′ded, -bed′ding** **1.** to set or fix firmly in a surrounding mass *[*to *embed* tiles in cement*]* **2.** to fix in the mind, memory, etc. **—em·bed′ment *n.***

em·bel·lish (im bel′ish) ***vt.*** [< OFr. *embelir* < *em-* (L. *in*) + *bel* < L. *bellus,* beautiful] **1.** to decorate; ornament; adorn **2.** to improve (a story, etc.) by adding details, often of a fictitious kind; touch up **—em·bel′lish·ment *n.***

em·ber[1] (em′bər) ***n.*** [< OE. *æmerge*] **1.** a glowing piece of coal, wood, etc. from a fire **2.** [*pl.*] the smoldering remains of a fire

em·ber[2] (em′bər) ***adj.*** [< OE. < *ymbryne* < *ymb,* round + *ryne,* a running] [*often* **E-**] designating or of three days (Wednesday, Friday, and Saturday) set aside for prayer and, sometimes, fasting in a specified week of each season of the year: observed in the Roman Catholic Church and certain other churches

em·bez·zle (im bez′'l) ***vt.*** **-zled, -zling** [< Anglo-Fr. < OFr. < *en-* (see EN-) + *besillier,* to destroy] to steal (money, etc. entrusted to one's care); take by fraud for one's own use **—em·bez′zle·ment *n.* —em·bez′zler *n.***

em·bit·ter (-bit′ər) ***vt.*** to cause to have bitter or more bitter feelings **—em·bit′ter·ment *n.***

em·bla·zon (im blā′z'n) ***vt.*** [see BLAZON] **1.** to decorate (*with* coats of arms, etc.) **2.** to display brilliantly; decorate with bright colors **3.** to praise; celebrate **—em·bla′zon·ment *n.***

em·blem (em′bləm) ***n.*** [orig., inlaid work < L. < Gr. *emblēma,* insertion < *en-,* in + *ballein,* to throw] **1.** a visible symbol of a thing, idea, etc.; object that stands for or suggests something else *[*the cross is an *emblem* of Christianity*]* **2.** a sign, badge, or device

em·blem·at·ic (em′blə mat′ik) ***adj.*** of, containing, or serving as an emblem; symbolic: also **em′blem·at′i·cal —em′blem·at′i·cal·ly *adv.***

em·bod·i·ment (im bäd′ē mənt) ***n.*** **1.** an embodying or being embodied **2.** that in which some idea, quality, etc. is embodied *[*she is the *embodiment* of virtue*]*

em·bod·y (-bäd′ē) ***vt.*** **-bod′ied, -bod′y·ing** **1.** to give bodily form to; incarnate **2.** to give definite or visible form to **3.** to bring together into, or make part of, an organized whole; incorporate *[*the latest findings *embodied* in the new book*]*

em·bold·en (-bōl′d'n) ***vt.*** to give courage to; cause to be bold or bolder

em·bo·lism (em′bə liz'm) ***n.*** *Med.* the obstruction of a blood vessel by an embolus

em·bo·lus (-ləs) ***n.,*** *pl.* **-li′** (-lī′) [ModL. < Gr. < *en-,* in + *ballein,* to throw] any foreign matter, as a blood clot or air bubble, carried in the bloodstream **—em·bol′ic** (-bäl′ik) ***adj.***

em·bos·om (im bo͝oz′əm, -bo͞o′zəm) ***vt.*** **1.** to embrace; cherish **2.** to enclose; surround; shelter

em·boss (-bôs′, -bäs′) ***vt.*** [< OFr.: see EN- & BOSS[2]] **1.** to decorate with designs, etc. raised above the surface **2.** to raise (a design, etc.) in relief **—em·boss′er *n.* —em·boss′ment *n.***

em·bou·chure (äm′bo͝o shoor′, äm′bo͝o shoor′) ***n.*** [Fr. < *emboucher,* to put into the mouth < L. *in,* in + *bucca,* the cheek] **1.** the mouth of a river **2.** *Music a)* the mouthpiece of a wind instrument *b)* the method of applying the lips and tongue to the mouthpiece of a wind instrument

em·bow·er (im bou′ər) ***vt.*** to enclose or shelter in or as in a bower

em·brace (-brās′) ***vt.*** **-braced′, -brac′ing** [< OFr. < L. *im-,* in + *brachium,* an arm] **1.** to clasp in the arms lovingly or affectionately; hug **2.** to accept readily *[*to *embrace* an opportunity*]* **3.** to take up or adopt, esp. eagerly or seriously [to *embrace* a new profession] **4.** to encircle; surround **5.** to include; contain —*vi.* to clasp each other in the arms —*n.* an embracing; hug —**em·brace′a·ble** *adj.* —**em·brace′ment** *n.* —**em·brac′er** *n.*

em·bra·sure (im brā′zhər) *n.* [Fr. < obs. *embraser*, to widen an opening] **1.** an opening (for a door, window, etc.) with the sides slanted so that it is wider on the inside than on the outside **2.** an opening, as in a parapet, with the sides slanting outward to increase the angle of fire of a gun

em·bro·cate (em′brō kāt′, -brə-) *vt.* **-cat′ed, -cat′ing** [< LL. pp. of *embrocare*, to foment < L. < Gr. < *en-*, in + *brechein*, to wet] to moisten and rub (a part of the body) with an oil, liniment, etc. —**em′bro·ca′tion** *n.*

em·broi·der (im broi′dər) *vt.* [< OFr. < *en-*, in + *brosder*, to embroider] **1.** to ornament (fabric) with a design in needlework **2.** to make (a design, etc.) on fabric with needlework **3.** to embellish (a story, etc.); exaggerate —*vi.* **1.** to do embroidery **2.** to exaggerate —**em·broi′der·er** *n.*

em·broi·der·y (-ē) *n., pl.* **-der·ies** **1.** the art or work of ornamenting fabric with needlework **2.** embroidered work or fabric **3.** embellishment, as of a story **4.** an unnecessary but attractive addition

em·broil (im broil′) *vt.* [< Fr.: see EN- & BROIL[2]] **1.** to confuse (affairs, etc.); mix up; muddle **2.** to draw into a conflict or fight; involve in trouble —**em·broil′ment** *n.*

em·bry·o (em′brē ō′) *n., pl.* **-os′** [ML. < Gr. *embryon* < *en-*, in + *bryein*, to swell] **1.** an animal in the earliest stages of its development in the uterus: the human organism up to the third month after conception is called an *embryo*, thereafter a *fetus* **2.** *a)* an early or undeveloped stage of something *b)* anything in such a stage **3.** the rudimentary plant contained in a seed —*adj.* embryonic

em·bry·o- *a combining form meaning* embryo, embryonic [*embryology*]

em·bry·ol·o·gy (em′brē äl′ə jē) *n.* [EMBRYO- + -LOGY] the branch of biology dealing with the formation and development of embryos —**em′bry·o·log′ic** (-ə läj′ik), **em′bry·o·log′i·cal** *adj.* —**em′bry·o·log′i·cal·ly** *adv.* —**em′bry·ol′o·gist** *n.*

em·bry·on·ic (-än′ik) *adj.* **1.** of or like an embryo **2.** in an early stage; rudimentary

em·cee (em′sē′) *vt., vi.* **-ceed′, -cee′ing** [< M.C., sense 1] [Colloq.] to act as master of ceremonies (for) —*n.* [Colloq.] a master of ceremonies

e·meer (ə mir′) *n. same as* EMIR —**e·meer′ate** *n.*

e·mend (i mend′) *vt.* [L. *emendare*, to correct < *e-*, out + *mendum*, a fault] to make scholarly corrections or improvements in (a text)

e·men·date (ē′mən dāt′) *vt.* **-dat′ed, -dat′ing** *same as* EMEND —**e·men·da·tion** (ē′mən dā′shən, em′ən-) *n.* —**e′men·da′tor** *n.* —**e·mend·a·to·ry** (i men′də tôr′ē) *adj.*

em·er·ald (em′ər əld, em′rəld) *n.* [< OFr. < VL. *smaraldus* < L. < Gr. *smaragdos*] **1.** a bright-green, transparent precious stone; green variety of beryl **2.** a similar variety of corundum **3.** bright green —*adj.* **1.** bright-green **2.** made of or with an emerald or emeralds **3.** designating or of a cut of gem in a rectangular style used esp. with emeralds

Emerald Isle [< its green landscape] Ireland

e·merge (i murj′) *vi.* **e·merged′, e·merg′ing** [L. *emergere* < *e-*, out + *mergere*, to dip] **1.** to rise as from a fluid **2.** *a)* to come forth into view; become visible *b)* to become apparent or known **3.** to develop as something new, improved, etc. [a strong breed *emerged*] —**e·mer′gence** *n.* —**e·mer′gent** *adj.*

e·mer·gen·cy (i mur′jən sē) *n., pl.* **-cies** [orig. sense, an emerging] a sudden, generally unexpected occurrence or set of circumstances demanding immediate action —*adj.* for use in case of sudden necessity [an *emergency* exit]

e·mer·i·tus (i mer′ə təs) *adj.* [L., pp. of *emereri* < *e-*, out + *mereri*, to serve] retired from active service, usually for age, but retaining one's rank or title [professor *emeritus*]

e·mer·sion (ē mur′zhən, -shən) *n.* an emerging

Em·er·son (em′ər sən), **Ralph Waldo** 1803–82; U.S. essayist, philosopher, & poet

em·er·y (em′ər ē, em′rē) *n.* [< Fr. < OFr. < It. < MGr. *smeri*, for Gr. *smyris*, emery] a dark, impure variety of corundum used in solid, crushed, or powdered form for grinding, polishing, etc.

e·met·ic (i met′ik) *adj.* [< L. < Gr. *emetikos* < *emein*, to vomit] causing vomiting —*n.* an emetic medicine or other substance

E.M.F., e.m.f., EMF, emf electromotive force

-e·mi·a (ēm′ē ə, ēm′yə) [ModL. < Gr. < *haima*, blood] *a suffix meaning* a (specified) condition or disease of the blood [*leukemia*]

em·i·grant (em′ə grənt) *adj.* **1.** emigrating **2.** of emigrants or emigration —*n.* one who emigrates

em·i·grate (-grāt′) *vi.* **-grat′ed, -grat′ing** [< L. pp. of *emigrare* < *e-*, out + *migrare*, to move] to leave one country or region to settle in another —**em′i·gra′tion** *n.*

é·mi·gré, e·mi·gré (em′ə grā′, ā′mə grā′) *n.* [Fr.] **1.** an emigrant **2.** a person forced to flee his country for political reasons

E·mil (ā′m'l, ē′-; em′'l) [G. < Fr. < L. *aemulus:* see EMULATE] a masculine name

Em·i·ly (em′'l ē) [fem. of EMIL] a feminine name: var. *Emilia*

em·i·nence (em′ə nəns) *n.* [< OFr. < L. < prp. of *eminere*, to stand out] **1.** a high or lofty place, thing, etc., as a hill **2.** *a)* superiority in rank, position, etc.; greatness *b)* a person of eminence **3.** [E-] *R.C.Ch.* a title of honor used in speaking to or of a cardinal, preceded by *His* or *Your*

em·i·nent (-nənt) *adj.* [< L.: see prec.] **1.** rising high above others; high; lofty **2.** projecting; prominent **3.** standing high by comparison with others; exalted; distinguished **4.** outstanding; noteworthy —**em′i·nent·ly** *adv.*

eminent domain *Law* the right of a government to take private property for public use, just compensation usually being given to the owner

e·mir (i mir′) *n.* [Ar. *amīr*, commander] **1.** in certain Moslem countries, a ruler, prince, or commander **2.** a title given Mohammed's descendants through his daughter Fatima —**e·mir′ate** (-it, -āt) *n.*

em·is·sar·y (em′ə ser′ē) *n., pl.* **-sar′ies** [< L. < pp. of *emittere:* see EMIT] a person or agent, esp. a secret agent, sent on a specific mission —*adj.* of, or serving as, an emissary or emissaries

e·mis·sion (i mish′ən) *n.* **1.** an emitting; issuance **2.** something emitted; discharge —**e·mis′sive** *adj.*

e·mit (i mit′) *vt.* **e·mit′ted, e·mit′ting** [< L. *emittere* < *e-*, out + *mittere*, to send] **1.** to send out; give forth **2.** to utter (sounds, etc.) **3.** to transmit (a signal) as by radio waves **4.** to give off (electrons) under the influence of heat, etc. —**e·mit′ter** *n.*

Em·ma (em′ə) [G. < *Erma* < names beginning with *Erm-:* see IRMA] a feminine name

Em·man·u·el (i man′yoo wəl) [< Gr. < Heb. *'immānūēl*, lit., God with us] **1.** a masculine name: var. *Emanuel* **2.** the Messiah: see IMMANUEL

Em·my (em′ē) *n., pl.* **-mys** [altered < *Immy*, slang for a kind of TV camera] [Slang] any of the statuettes awarded annually in the U.S. for special achievement in television programming, acting, etc.

EmnE., EMnE. Early Modern English

e·mol·li·ent (i mäl′yənt) *adj.* [< L. prp. of *emollire* < *e-*, out + *mollire*, to soften < *mollis*, soft] softening; soothing —*n.* an emollient preparation, esp. for the surface tissues of the body

e·mol·u·ment (i mäl′yoo mənt) *n.* [< L. < *emolere* < *e-*, out + *molere*, to grind] gain from employment or position; salary, wages, fees, etc.

e·mote (i mōt′) *vi.* **e·mot′ed, e·mot′ing** [< ff., by analogy with DEVOTE] [Colloq.] to express emotion in a showy or theatrical manner

e·mo·tion (i mō′shən) *n.* [Fr. (prob. after *motion*) < L. *emovere* < *e-*, out + *movere*, to move] **1.** strong feeling; excitement **2.** any specific feeling, as love, hate, fear, anger, etc.

e·mo·tion·al (-'l) *adj.* **1.** of emotion or the emotions **2.** showing emotion, esp. strong emotion **3.** easily aroused to emotion **4.** appealing to or arousing the emotions —**e·mo′tion·al·ly** *adv.*

e·mo·tion·al·ism (-'l iz'm) *n.* **1.** the tendency to be emotional **2.** display of emotion **3.** an appeal to emotion, esp. to sway an audience

e·mo·tion·al·ize (-'l īz′) *vt.* **-ized′, -iz′ing** to treat, present, or interpret in an emotional way —**e·mo′tion·al·i·za′tion** *n.*

e·mo·tive (i mōt′iv) *adj.* **1.** expressing or producing emotion **2.** relating to the emotions

Emp. **1.** Emperor **2.** Empire **3.** Empress

em·pan·el (im pan′'l) *vt.* **-eled** or **-elled, -el·ing** or **-el·ling** *same as* IMPANEL

em·pa·thy (em′pə thē) *n.* [< Gr. < *en-*, in + *pathos*, feeling] intellectual or emotional identification with another —**em·path·ic** (im path′ik), **em·pa·thet·ic** (em′pə thet′ik) *adj.*

Em·ped·o·cles (em ped′ə klēz′) 495?–435? B.C.; Gr. philosopher

em·per·or (em′pər ər) *n.* [< OFr. < L. *imperator* < pp. of *imperare*, to command < *in-*, in + *parare*, to set in order] the supreme ruler of an empire

em·pha·sis (em′fə sis) *n., pl.* **-ses′** (-sēz′) [L. < Gr. < *emphainein*, to indicate < *en-*, in + *phainein*, to show] **1.** force of expression, feeling, action, etc. **2.** special stress given to a syllable, word, phrase, etc. in speaking **3.** special attention given to something so as to make it stand out; importance; stress

em·pha·size (-sīz′) *vt.* **-sized′, -siz′ing** to give emphasis, or special force, to; stress

em·phat·ic (im fat′ik) *adj.* **1.** expressed, felt, or done with emphasis **2.** using emphasis in speaking, expressing, etc. **3.** very striking; forcible; definite [an *emphatic* defeat] **4.** *Gram.* designating or of a present tense or past tense in which a form of *do* is used as an auxiliary for emphasis (Ex.: I *do* care) —**em·phat′i·cal·ly** *adv.*

em·phy·se·ma (em′fə sē′mə) *n.* [Gr. < *en-*, in + *physaein*, to blow] abnormal distention of the alveoli, or air cells, of the lungs, accompanied by loss of elasticity in the tissues and impairment in breathing

em·pire (em′pīr; *for adj. usually* äm pir′) *n.* [< OFr. < L. < *imperare:* see EMPEROR] **1.** supreme rule; absolute power or authority **2.** government by an emperor or empress **3.** *a*) a group of states or territories under the sovereignty of an emperor or empress *b*) a state uniting many territories and peoples under one ruler **4.** an extensive social or economic organization under the control of a single person, family, or corporation —*adj.* [E-] of or characteristic of the first French Empire (1804–15) under Napoleon [*Empire* furniture]

em·pir·ic (em pir′ik) *n.* [< L. < Gr. < *empeiria*, experience < *en-*, in + *peira*, a trial] a person who relies solely on practical experience rather than on scientific principles —*adj.* empirical

em·pir·i·cal (-i k'l) *adj.* [see prec.] **1.** relying or based solely on experiment and observation rather than theory [the *empirical* method] **2.** relying or based on practical experience without reference to scientific principles [an *empirical* remedy] —**em·pir′i·cal·ly** *adv.*

em·pir·i·cism (-ə siz'm) *n.* **1.** experimental method; search for knowledge by observation and experiment **2.** *a*) a disregarding of scientific methods and relying solely on experience *b*) quackery **3.** *Philos.* the theory that experience is the only source of knowledge —**em·pir′i·cist** *n.*

em·place (im plās′) *vt.* **-placed′, -plac′ing** to place in position

em·place·ment (-mənt) *n.* **1.** an emplacing; placement **2.** the position in which something is placed; specif., *Mil.* the prepared position from which a heavy gun or guns are fired

em·plane (em plān′) *vi.* **-planed′, -plan′ing** *same as* ENPLANE

em·ploy (im ploi′) *vt.* [< OFr. < L. *implicare*, to enfold: see IMPLY] **1.** to make use of; use **2.** to keep busy or occupied; devote **3.** to provide work and pay for **4.** to engage the services or labor of for pay; hire —*n.* the state of being employed; paid service; employment —**em·ploy′a·ble** *adj.*

em·ploy·ee, em·ploy·e (im ploi′ē, em′ploi ē′) *n.* a person hired by another, or by a business firm, etc., to work for wages or salary

em·ploy·er (im ploi′ər) *n.* one who employs; esp., a person, business firm, etc. that hires one or more persons to work for wages or salary

em·ploy·ment (-mənt) *n.* **1.** an employing or being employed **2.** the thing at which one is employed; work; occupation; job **3.** the number or percentage of persons gainfully employed

em·po·ri·um (em pôr′ē əm) *n., pl.* **-ri·ums, -ri·a** (-ə) [L. < Gr. < *emporos*, traveler < *en-*, in + *poros*, way] **1.** a place of commerce; trading center; marketplace **2.** a large store with a wide variety of things for sale

em·pow·er (im pou′ər) *vt.* **1.** to give power to; authorize **2.** to enable; permit —**em·pow′er·ment** *n.*

em·press (em′pris) *n.* **1.** the wife of an emperor **2.** a woman ruler of an empire

emp·ty (emp′tē) *adj.* **-ti·er, -ti·est** [< OE. *æmettig*, unoccupied < *æmetta*, leisure + *-ig*, -Y²] **1.** containing nothing; having nothing in it **2.** having no one in it; unoccupied [an *empty* house] **3.** worthless; unsatisfying [*empty* pleasures] **4.** meaningless; insincere; vain [*empty* promises] **5.** [Colloq.] hungry —*vt.* **-tied, -ty·ing** **1.** to make empty **2.** to pour out or remove (the contents) of something **3.** to unburden or discharge (oneself or itself) —*vi.* **1.** to become empty **2.** to pour out; discharge —*n., pl.* **-ties** an empty freight car, truck, bottle, etc. —**empty of** lacking; without; devoid of —**emp′ti·ly** *adv.* —**emp′ti·ness** *n.*

emp·ty-hand·ed (-han′did) *adj.* bringing or carrying away nothing

emp·ty-head·ed (-hed′id) *adj.* silly and ignorant

em·pur·ple (im pur′p'l) *vt., vi.* **-pled, -pling** to make or become purple

em·pyr·e·al (em pir′ē əl; em′pī rē′əl, -pə-) *adj.* [< LL. < Gr. *empyrios*, fiery < *en-*, in + *pyr*, a fire] of the empyrean; heavenly; sublime

em·py·re·an (em′pī rē′ən, -pə-; em pir′ē ən) *n.* [see prec. & -AN] **1.** the highest heaven: among the ancients, the sphere of pure light or fire **2.** the sky; the firmament —*adj. same as* EMPYREAL

e·mu (ē′myoo) *n.* [prob. < Port. *ema*, a crane] a large, nonflying Australian bird, similar to the ostrich but somewhat smaller

EMU (to 5 ft. high)

E.M.U., e.m.u., emu electromagnetic units

em·u·late (em′yə lāt′) *vt.* **-lat′ed, -lat′ing** [< L. pp. of *aemulari* < *aemulus*, trying to equal] **1.** to try to equal or surpass **2.** to imitate (a person or thing admired) **3.** to rival successfully —**em′u·la′tion** *n.* —**em′u·la′tive** *adj.* —**em′u·la′tor** *n.*

em·u·lous (em′yə ləs) *adj.* **1.** desirous of equaling or surpassing **2.** characterized or caused by emulation —**em′u·lous·ly** *adv.* —**em′u·lous·ness** *n.*

e·mul·si·fy (i mul′sə fī′) *vt., vi.* **-fied′, -fy′ing** to form into an emulsion —**e·mul′si·fi′a·ble** *adj.* —**e·mul′si·fi·ca′tion** *n.* —**e·mul′si·fi′er** *n.*

e·mul·sion (i mul′shən) *n.* [< ModL. < L. pp. of *emulgere* < *e-*, out + *mulgere*, to milk] a fluid, as milk, formed by the suspension of one liquid in another; specif., *a*) *Pharmacy* a preparation of an oily substance held in suspension in a watery liquid *b*) *Photog.* a suspension of a salt of silver in gelatin or collodion, used to coat plates and film —**e·mul′sive** *adj.*

en (en) *n.* **1.** the letter N, n **2.** *Printing* a space half the width of an em

en- (in, en) [OFr. < L. *in-* < *in*, IN] **1.** *a prefix meaning:* *a*) to put or get into or on [*entrain*] *b*) to cover with [*enrobe*] *c*) to make, cause to be [*endanger, enfeeble*] *d*) in or into [*enclose*] **2.** *a prefix used as an intensifier* [*enliven*] It is assimilated to *em-* before *p, b, m* Many words with *en-* are also spelled *in-* (Ex.: *enquire, inquire*)

-en (ən, 'n) [< OE. suffixes *-nian, -an, -en*] *any of several suffixes:* **1.** *meaning:* *a*) to become or cause to be [*darken, weaken*] *b*) to come to have, cause to have [*strengthen*] **2.** *meaning* made of [*woolen*] **3.** *used to form the pp. of strong verbs* [*risen*] **4.** *used to form plurals* [*children*] **5.** *used to form diminutives* [*chicken*]

en·a·ble (in ā′b'l) *vt.* **-bled, -bling** **1.** to make able; provide with means, opportunity, power, or authority (*to* do something) **2.** to make possible

en·act (in akt′) *vt.* **1.** to make (a bill, etc.) into a law; pass (a law); decree; ordain **2.** to represent or perform in or as in a play; act out —**en·ac′tive** *adj.* —**en·ac′tor** *n.*

en·act·ment (-mənt) *n.* **1.** an enacting or being enacted **2.** something enacted, as a law

en·am·el (i nam′'l) *n.* [see the *v.*] **1.** a glassy, colored, opaque substance fused to surfaces, as of metals, as an ornamental or protective coating **2.** any smooth, hard, glossy coating like enamel **3.** the hard, white, glossy coating of the crown of a tooth **4.** anything enameled **5.** paint or varnish with a smooth, hard, glossy surface when it dries —*vt.* **-eled** or **-elled, -el·ing** or **-el·ling** [< Anglo-Fr. < *en-* (see EN-) + *amayl* < OFr. *esmail*, enamel] **1.** to inlay or cover with enamel **2.** to decorate in various colors, as if with enamel **3.** to form an enamellike surface on —**en·am′el·er, en·am′el·ler, en·am′el·ist, en·am′el·list** *n.*

en·am·el·ware (-wer′) *n.* kitchen utensils, etc. made of enameled metal

en·am·or (in am′ər) *vt.* [< OFr. < *en-*, in + *amour* < L. *amor*, love] to fill with love and desire; charm; captivate: now mainly in the passive voice, with *of* [much *enamored* of her]

en bloc (en bläk′; *Fr.* än blôk′) [Fr., lit., in a block] in one lump; as a whole; all together

enc., encl. enclosure

en·camp (in kamp′) *vi.* to set up a camp —*vt.* **1.** to put in a camp **2.** to form into a camp

en·camp·ment (-mənt) *n.* **1.** an encamping or being encamped **2.** a camp or campsite

en·cap·su·late (in kap′sə lāt′, -syoo-) *vt.* **-lat′ed, -lat′ing** **1.** to enclose in or as if in a capsule **2.** to condense; abridge Also **en·cap′sule** (-s'l, -syool) **-suled, -sul·ing** —**en·cap′su·la′tion** *n.*

en·case (in kās′) *vt.* **-cased′, -cas′ing** **1.** to cover completely; enclose **2.** to put into a case or cases —**en·case′ment** *n.*

en cas·se·role (en cas′ə rōl′; *Fr.* än kȧs rôl′) [Fr.] (baked and served) in a casserole

en·caus·tic (en kôs′tik) *adj.* [< L. < Gr. < *en-*, in + *kaiein*, to burn] done by a process of burning in or applying heat [*encaustic* tile] —*n.* a method of painting in which colors in wax are fused to a surface with hot irons —**en·caus′ti·cal·ly** *adv.*

fat, āpe, cär; ten, ēven; is, bīte; gō, hôrn, tōōl, look; oil, out; up, fur; get; joy; yet; chin; she; thin, *th*en; zh, leisure; ŋ, ring; ə for *a* in *ago*, *e* in *agent*, *i* in *sanity*, *o* in *comply*, *u* in *focus*; ′ as in *able* (ā′b'l); Fr. bål; ë, Fr. coeur; ö, Fr. feu; Fr. mo*n*; ô, Fr. coq; ü, Fr. duc; *r*, Fr. cri; H, G. ich; kh, G. doch; ‡foreign; *hypothetical; < derived from. See inside front cover.

-ence (əns, ’ns) [< OFr. *-ence* & L. *-entia* (see -ENT + -IA)] *a suffix meaning* act, fact, quality, state, result, or degree *[conference, excellence]*

‡**en·ceinte** (än sant′; *E.* än sānt′) *adj.* [Fr., ult. < L. *in-*, not + pp. of *cingere*, to gird] pregnant

en·ceph·a·li·tis (en sef′ə lit′is, en′sef-) *n.* [< ff. + -ITIS] inflammation of the brain —**en·ceph′a·lit′ic** (-lit′ik) *adj.*

en·ceph·a·lo- [< Gr. *enkephalos*, the brain] *a combining form meaning* of the brain: also **en·ceph′al-**

en·ceph·a·lo·gram (en sef′ə lō gram′) *n. clipped form of:* **1.** ELECTROENCEPHALOGRAM **2.** PNEUMOENCEPHALOGRAM

en·ceph·a·lon (-län′) *n., pl.* **-la** (-lə) [ModL. < Gr. < *en-*, in + *kephalē*, the head] *Anat.* the brain —**en·ce·phal·ic** (en′sə fal′ik) *adj.*

en·chain (in chān′) *vt.* **1.** to bind with chains; fetter **2.** to captivate —**en·chain′ment** *n.*

en·chant (in chant′) *vt.* [< OFr. < L. *incantare*, to bewitch: see INCANTATION] **1.** to cast a spell over, as by magic; bewitch **2.** to charm greatly; delight —**en·chant′er** *n.* —**en·chant′ress** *n.fem.*

en·chant·ing (-iŋ) *adj.* **1.** charming; delightful **2.** bewitching; fascinating —**en·chant′ing·ly** *adv.*

en·chant·ment (-mənt) *n.* **1.** an enchanting or being enchanted **2.** a magic spell or charm **3.** something that charms greatly **4.** great delight

en·chase (in chās′) *vt.* **-chased′, -chas′ing** [< OFr. *enchasser:* see CHASE[3]] **1.** to put in a setting **2.** to ornament by engraving, inlaying with gems, etc. **3.** to carve (designs, etc.)

en·chi·la·da (en′chə lä′də) *n.* [AmSp.] a tortilla rolled with meat inside and served with a chili-flavored sauce

en·cir·cle (in sur′k’l) *vt.* **-cled, -cling** **1.** to make a circle around; surround **2.** to move in a circle around —**en·cir′cle·ment** *n.*

en·clave (en′klāv) *n.* [Fr. < OFr. < L. *in*, in + *clavis*, a key] **1.** a territory surrounded by the territory of a foreign country **2.** a minority culture group that exists within a larger group

en·clit·ic (en klit′ik) *adj.* [< LL. < Gr. < *enklinein*, to lean toward] *Gram.* dependent for its stress on the preceding word, often one with which it has combined (Ex.: *man* in *layman*) —*n.* any such word or particle

en·close (in klōz′) *vt.* **-closed′, -clos′ing** **1.** to shut in all around; surround **2.** to insert in an envelope, wrapper, etc., often along with something else **3.** to contain

en·clo·sure (-klō′zhər) *n.* **1.** an enclosing or being enclosed **2.** something that encloses **3.** something enclosed; specif., *a)* an enclosed place *b)* a document, money, etc. enclosed as with a letter

en·code (in kōd′) *vt.* **-cod′ed, -cod′ing** to put (information, etc.) into code —**en·cod′er** *n.*

en·co·mi·ast (en kō′mē ast′) *n.* [< Gr. < *enkōmiazein*, to praise] a person who speaks or writes encomiums; eulogist —**en·co′mi·as′tic** *adj.*

en·co·mi·um (en kō′mē əm) *n., pl.* **-mi·ums, -mi·a** (-ə) [L. < Gr. *enkōmion*, song of praise < *en-*, in + *kōmos*, a revel] a formal expression of high praise; eulogy; panegyric

en·com·pass (in kum′pəs) *vt.* **1.** to shut in all around; surround **2.** to contain; include **3.** to compass or achieve —**en·com′pass·ment** *n.*

en·core (äŋ′kôr, än kôr′) *interj.* [Fr., yet, again] again; once more —*n.* **1.** a demand by the audience, shown by applause, for further performance **2.** the performance or piece performed in answer to such a demand —*vt.* **-cored, -cor·ing** to demand further performance of or by

en·coun·ter (in koun′tər) *vt.* [< OFr. < L. *in*, in + *contra*, against] **1.** to meet unexpectedly; come upon **2.** to meet in conflict or battle **3.** to face (difficulties, trouble, etc.) —*vi.* to meet accidentally or in opposition —*n.* **1.** a direct meeting, as in conflict or battle **2.** an unexpected meeting —*adj.* designating or of a small group meeting to explore personal relationships through an open exchange of intimate feelings, release of inhibitions, etc.

en·cour·age (in kur′ij) *vt.* **-aged, -ag·ing** **1.** to give courage, hope, or confidence to; hearten **2.** to give support to; foster; help —**en·cour′ag·ing** *adj.* —**en·cour′ag·ing·ly** *adv.*

en·cour·age·ment (-mənt) *n.* **1.** an encouraging or being encouraged **2.** something that encourages

en·croach (in krōch′) *vi.* [< OFr. *encrochier*, to seize upon < *en-*, in + *croc*, a hook] **1.** to trespass or intrude (*on* or *upon* the rights, property, etc. of another) **2.** to advance beyond the proper, original, or customary limits —**en·croach′ment** *n.*

en·crust (in krust′) *vt., vi. same as* INCRUST —**en′crus·ta′tion** *n.*

en·cum·ber (in kum′bər) *vt.* [< OFr.: see EN- & CUMBER] **1.** to hold back the motion or action of, as with a burden; hinder **2.** to fill so as to obstruct; block up **3.** to load or weigh down; burden

en·cum·brance (-brəns) *n.* **1.** something that encumbers; hindrance; burden **2.** *Law same as* INCUMBRANCE

-en·cy (ən sē, ’n sē) [L. *-entia*] *a suffix meaning* act, fact, quality, state, result, or degree *[dependency, efficiency]*

ency., encyc., encycl. encyclopedia

en·cyc·li·cal (in sik′li k’l, -sī′kli-) *adj.* [LL. *encyclicus* < Gr. < *en-*, in + *kyklos*, a circle] for general circulation: also **en·cyc′lic** —*n. R.C.Ch.* a letter from the Pope to the bishops, usually dealing with doctrinal matters

en·cy·clo·pe·di·a, en·cy·clo·pae·di·a (in sī′klə pē′dē ə) *n.* [ModL. < Gr. *enkyklopaideia* < *enkyklios*, general + *paideia*, education] a book or set of books giving information on all or many branches of knowledge, or on one of these, generally in articles alphabetically arranged —**en·cy′clo·pe′dic, en·cy′clo·pae′dic** *adj.* —**en·cy′clo·pe′di·cal·ly, en·cy′clo·pae′di·cal·ly** *adv.* —**en·cy′clo·pe′dist, en·cy′clo·pae′dist** *n.*

en·cyst (en sist′) *vt., vi.* to enclose or become enclosed in a cyst, capsule, or sac —**en·cyst′ment, en′cys·ta′tion** (-sis tā′shən) *n.*

end (end) *n.* [OE. *ende*] **1.** a limit or limiting part; boundary **2.** the last part of anything; final point; finish; conclusion **3.** a ceasing to exist; death or destruction **4.** the part at or near either extremity of anything; tip **5.** a purpose; intention; object **6.** an outcome; result; consequence **7.** a piece left over; remnant *[*odds and *ends]* **8.** the reason for being **9.** *Football a)* a player at either end of the line *b)* his position —*vt.* **1.** to bring to an end; finish; stop **2.** to form the end of —*vi.* **1.** to come to an end; terminate: often with *up* **2.** to die —*adj.* at the end; final *[end* product*]* —**ends of the earth** remote regions —**make an end of** **1.** to finish; stop **2.** to do away with —**make (both) ends meet** to keep one's expenses within one's income —**no end** [Colloq.] extremely —**on end** **1.** in an upright position **2.** without interruption *[*for days *on end]* —**put an end to** **1.** to stop **2.** to do away with

en·da·moe·ba (en′də mē′bə) *n.* [see ENDO- & AMOEBA] any of a genus of parasitic amoebas, including the species that causes amoebic dysentery in man: also sp. **en′da·me′ba** —**en′da·moe′bic** *adj.*

en·dan·ger (in dān′jər) *vt.* to expose to danger, harm, or loss; imperil —**en·dan′ger·ment** *n.*

en·dan·gered species (-jərd) a species of animal or plant in danger of becoming extinct

en·dear (in dir′) *vt.* to make dear or beloved

en·dear·ing (-iŋ) *adj.* **1.** that makes dear or well liked **2.** expressing affection *[endearing* tones*]*

en·dear·ment (-mənt) *n.* **1.** warm liking; affection **2.** a word or act expressing affection

en·deav·or (in dev′ər) *vi.* [< *en-* + OFr. *deveir*, duty < L. *debere*, to owe] to make an earnest attempt —*vt.* **1.** [Archaic] to try to achieve **2.** to try (*to* do something) —*n.* an earnest attempt or effort Also, Brit. sp., **en·deav′our**

en·dem·ic (en dem′ik) *adj.* [Fr. < Gr. < *en-*, in + *dēmos*, the people] **1.** native to a particular country, region, etc.: said of plants and animals **2.** restricted to and present in a particular country or locality: said of a disease: also **en·dem′i·cal** —*n.* **1.** an endemic plant or animal **2.** an endemic disease —**en·dem′i·cal·ly** *adv.* —**en·de·mic·i·ty** (en′də mis′ə tē), **en·dem′ism** *n.*

end·ing (en′diŋ) *n.* **1.** *a)* the last part; finish *b)* death **2.** *Gram.* the final letter or letters added to a word base to make a derivative or an inflectional form *[-ed* is the *ending* in *wanted]*

en·dive (en′dīv, än′dēv) *n.* [OFr. < ML. < MGr. < L. *intibus* < Gr. *entybon*] **1.** *a)* a cultivated plant of the composite family, with curled, narrow leaves used in salads *b)* another form of this with wide, smooth leaves **2.** the young leaves of chicory (sense 1) blanched for salads

end·less (end′lis) *adj.* **1.** having no end; going on forever; eternal; infinite **2.** lasting too long *[*an *endless* speech*]* **3.** continual *[endless* interruptions*]* **4.** with the ends joined to form a closed unit that can move continuously over wheels, etc. *[*an *endless* belt*]* —**end′less·ly** *adv.* —**end′less·ness** *n.*

end·most (-mōst′) *adj.* at the end; farthest; last

en·do- [< Gr. *edon*, within] *a combining form meaning* within, inner *[endoderm]* : also, before a vowel, **end-**

en·do·blast (en′də blast′) *n. same as* ENDODERM

en·do·car·di·tis (en′dō kär dīt′is) *n.* [ModL. < ENDO- + Gr. *kardia*, heart + -ITIS] inflammation of the thin membrane lining the heart cavities

en·do·carp (en′də kärp′) *n.* the inner layer of the wall of a ripened ovary or fruit, as the pit around the seed of a plum

en·do·crine (en′də krin, -krīn′, -krēn′) *adj.* [ENDO- + Gr. *krinein*, to separate] **1.** designating or of any gland producing one or more internal secretions that, introduced into the bloodstream, are carried to other parts of the body whose functions they regulate **2.** designating or of such a secretion —*n.* any such gland or its secretion, as the thyroid, adrenal, and pituitary glands

en·do·cri·nol·o·gy (en′dō kri näl′ə jē, -krī-) ***n.*** the branch of medicine dealing with the endocrine glands and the internal secretions of the body —**en′do·cri′no·log′i·cal** (-nə läj′ə k'l) ***adj.*** —**en′do·cri·nol′o·gist** ***n.***

en·do·derm (en′də durm′) ***n.*** the inner layer of cells of the embryo, from which is formed the lining of the digestive tract, of other internal organs, and of certain glands —**en′do·der′mal, en′do·der′mic** ***adj.***

en·dog·a·my (en däg′ə mē) ***n.*** [ENDO- + -GAMY] **1.** the custom of marrying only within one's own tribe, clan, etc.; inbreeding **2.** cross-pollination among flowers of the same plant —**en·dog′a·mous, en·do·gam·ic** (en′də gam′ik) ***adj.***

en·dog·e·nous (en däj′ə nəs) ***adj.*** **1.** developing from within; originating internally **2.** *Biol.* growing or developing from or on the inside —**en·dog′e·nous·ly** ***adv.***

en·do·mor·phic (en′də môr′fik) ***adj.*** [ENDO- + -MORPHIC] designating or of the fleshy or heavy type of human body, in which the structures developed from the endoderm predominate —**en′do·morph′** ***n.***

en·do·plasm (en′də plaz'm) ***n.*** the inner part of the cytoplasm of a cell —**en′do·plas′mic** ***adj.***

end organ any structure at the end of a nerve fibre that either receives a sensation or sends an impulse to a muscle

en·dorse (in dôrs′) ***vt.*** **-dorsed′, -dors′ing** [< OFr. < ML. < L. *in*, on + *dorsum*, the back] **1.** to write on the back of (a document); specif., to sign (one's name) as payee on the back of (a check, etc.) **2.** to give approval to; support; sanction —**en·dors′a·ble** ***adj.*** —**en·dor·see** (in dôr′sē′, en′dôr sē′) ***n.*** —**en·dors′er** ***n.***

en·dorse·ment (-mənt) ***n.*** **1.** an endorsing **2.** something written in endorsing; specif., *a*) the signature of a payee on the back of a check, etc. *b*) a statement endorsing a person, product, etc.

en·do·skel·e·ton (en′də skel′ə t'n) ***n.*** the internal bony, supporting structure in vertebrates

en·do·sperm (en′də spurm′) ***n.*** [ENDO- + SPERM[1]] a tissue which surrounds the developing embryo of a seed and provides food for its growth; albumen —**en′do·sper′mic** ***adj.***

en·dow (in dou′) ***vt.*** [< Anglo-Fr. < OFr. < *en-*, in + *douer* < L. *dotare*, to endow] **1.** to provide with some talent, quality, etc. [*endowed* with courage] **2.** to think of as having some quality or characteristic [to *endow* gods with human traits] **3.** to give money or property so as to provide an income for the support of (a college, hospital, etc.)

en·dow·ment (-mənt) ***n.*** **1.** an endowing **2.** that with which something is endowed; bequest **3.** a gift of nature; talent, ability, etc.

endowment policy an insurance policy by which a stated amount is paid to the insured after the period of time specified in the contract

end product the final result of any series of changes, processes, or chemical reactions

end table a small table placed beside a chair, etc.

en·due (in do͞o′, -dyo͞o′) ***vt.*** **-dued′, -du′ing** [< OFr. < L. *inducere:* see INDUCE] to provide (*with* something); specif., to endow (*with* qualities, talents, etc.)

en·dur·ance (in door′əns, -dyoor′-) ***n.*** **1.** an enduring **2.** ability to last, continue, or remain **3.** ability to stand pain, distress, fatigue, etc.; fortitude **4.** duration

en·dure (in door′, -dyoor′) ***vt.*** **-dured′, -dur′ing** [< OFr. < LL. < L. < *in-*, in + *durare*, to harden < *durus*, hard] **1.** to hold up under (pain, fatigue, etc.); bear **2.** to put up with; tolerate —***vi.*** **1.** to continue in existence; last; remain **2.** to bear pain, etc. without flinching; hold out —**en·dur′a·ble** ***adj.*** —**en·dur′a·bly** ***adv.***

en·dur·ing (-iŋ) ***adj.*** lasting; permanent; durable —**en·dur′ing·ly** ***adv.*** —**en·dur′ing·ness** ***n.***

end·ways (end′wāz′) ***adv.*** **1.** on end; upright **2.** with the end foremost **3.** lengthwise **4.** end to end Also **end′wise′** (-wīz′)

end zone *Football* the area between the goal line and the end boundary **(end line)** ten yards behind it, at each end of the playing field

-ene (ēn) [after L. *-enus*, Gr. *-ēnos*, adj. suffix] *a suffix used:* **1.** *Chem.* to form names for some hydrocarbons [*propylene, benzene*] **2.** to form some commercial names

ENE, E.N.E., e.n.e. east-northeast

en·e·ma (en′ə mə) ***n.*** [LL. < Gr. < *en-*, in + *hienai*, to send] **1.** a liquid injected into the colon through the anus, as a purgative, medicine, etc. **2.** such an injection

en·e·my (en′ə mē) ***n.***, *pl.* **-mies** [< OFr. < L. *inimicus* < *in-*, not + *amicus*, friend] **1.** a person who hates another, and wishes or tries to injure him; foe **2.** *a*) a nation or force hostile to another *b*) troops, fleet, ship, member, etc. of a hostile nation **3.** a person hostile to an idea, cause, etc. **4.** anything injurious or harmful —***adj.*** of an enemy

en·er·get·ic (en′ər jet′ik) ***adj.*** of, having, or showing energy; vigorous; forceful —**en′er·get′i·cal·ly** ***adv.***

en·er·gize (en′ər jīz′) ***vt.*** **-gized′, -giz′ing** **1.** to give energy to; invigorate **2.** *Elec.* to apply a source of voltage or current to (a circuit, etc.) —**en′er·giz′er** ***n.***

en·er·gy (en′ər jē) ***n.***, *pl.* **-gies** [< LL. < Gr. *energeia* < *en-*, in + *ergon*, work] **1.** force of expression **2.** potential forces; capacity for action **3.** effective power **4.** *Physics* the capacity for doing work and overcoming resistance

en·er·vate (en′ər vāt′; *for adj.* i nur′vit) ***vt.*** **-vat′ed, -vat′ing** [< L. pp. of *enervare* < *e-*, out + *nervus*, a nerve, sinew] to deprive of strength, force, vigor, etc.; debilitate —***adj.*** enervated; weakened —**en′er·va′tion** ***n.*** —**en′er·va′tor** ***n.***

‡**en fa·mille** (än fȧ mē′y') [Fr.] **1.** with one's family; at home **2.** in an informal way

‡**en·fant ter·ri·ble** (än fän te rē′bl') [Fr.] **1.** an unmanageable, mischievous child **2.** a person who causes trouble or embarrassment by his imprudent remarks or actions

en·fee·ble (in fē′b'l) ***vt.*** **-bled, -bling** to make feeble —**en·fee′ble·ment** ***n.***

en·fi·lade (en′fə lād′, en′fə lād′) ***n.*** [Fr. < *enfiler*, to thread < *en-* (L. *in*), in + *fil* (L. *filum*), a thread] **1.** gunfire directed from either flank along the length of a line of troops **2.** a placement of troops that makes them vulnerable to such fire —***vt.*** **-lad′ed, -lad′ing** to direct such gunfire at (a column, etc.)

en·fold (in fōld′) ***vt.*** **1.** to wrap in folds; envelop **2.** to embrace —**en·fold′ment** ***n.***

en·force (in fôrs′) ***vt.*** **-forced′, -forc′ing** **1.** to give force to [to *enforce* an argument by analogies] **2.** to bring about or impose by force [to *enforce* one's will on a child] **3.** to compel observance of (a law, etc.) —**en·force′a·ble** ***adj.*** —**en·force′ment** ***n.*** —**en·forc′er** ***n.***

en·fran·chise (in fran′chīz) ***vt.*** **-chised, -chis·ing** **1.** to free from slavery, bondage, etc. **2.** to give a franchise to; specif., to admit to citizenship, esp. to the right to vote —**en·fran′chise·ment** (-chiz mənt, -chīz-) ***n.*** —**en·fran′chis·er** ***n.***

Eng. **1.** England **2.** English

eng. **1.** engineer(ing) **2.** engraved **3.** engraving

en·gage (in gāj′) ***vt.*** **-gaged′, -gag′ing** [< OFr. *engagier:* see EN- & GAGE[1]] **1.** to bind (oneself) by a promise; pledge; specif. (now only in the passive), to bind by a promise of marriage; betroth **2.** to hire; employ **3.** to arrange for the use of; reserve [to *engage* a hotel room] **4.** to draw into; involve, as in conversation **5.** to attract and hold (the attention, etc.) **6.** to keep busy; occupy **7.** to enter into conflict with (the enemy) **8.** to interlock with; mesh together [*engage* the gears] —***vi.*** **1.** to pledge oneself; promise; undertake **2.** to involve oneself; be active [to *engage* in dramatics] **3.** to enter into conflict **4.** to interlock; mesh

en·gaged (-gājd′) ***adj.*** **1.** pledged; esp., pledged in marriage; betrothed **2.** occupied or busy **3.** involved in combat, as troops **4.** attached to or partly set into a wall, etc. [*engaged* columns] **5.** in gear; interlocked; meshed

en·gage·ment (-gāj′mənt) ***n.*** **1.** an engaging or being engaged; specif., *a*) a betrothal *b*) an appointment or commitment *c*) employment or period of employment, esp. in the performing arts *d*) a conflict; battle *e*) [*usually pl.*] financial obligations *f*) state of being in gear **2.** something that engages

en·gag·ing (-gāj′iŋ) ***adj.*** attractive; winning; charming —**en·gag′ing·ly** ***adv.***

‡**en garde** (än gȧrd′) [Fr.] *Fencing* on guard: the opening position in which the fencer is prepared either to attack or defend

En·gels (eŋ′əls), **Frie·drich** (frē′driH) 1820–95; Ger. socialist theoretician (with Karl Marx)

en·gen·der (in jen′dər) ***vt.*** [< OFr. < L. < *in-*, in + *generare*, GENERATE] to bring into being; cause; produce [militarism *engenders* war]

engin. **1.** engineer **2.** engineering

en·gine (en′jən) ***n.*** [< OFr. < L. *ingenium*, genius < *in-*, in & base of *gignere*, to produce] **1.** any machine that uses energy to develop mechanical power; esp., a machine for starting motion in some other machine **2.** a railroad locomotive **3.** any instrument or machine; apparatus [*engines* of torture] **4.** *same as* FIRE ENGINE

en·gi·neer (en′jə nir′) ***n.*** **1.** a person skilled in some branch of engineering [a mechanical *engineer*] **2.** *a*) an operator of engines or technical equipment [a locomotive *engineer*, radio *engineer*] *b*) a specialist in planning or directing operations in some technical field **3.** a skillful or clever manager **4.** *Mil.* a member of that branch of the armed forces concerned with the construction and demolition of bridges, roads, etc. —***vt.*** **1.** to plan, construct, or manage as an engineer **2.** to plan and direct skillfully [to *engineer* a business merger]

en·gi·neer·ing (-iŋ) ***n.*** **1.** *a*) the science concerned with putting scientific knowledge to practical uses, divided into different branches, as civil, electrical, mechanical, or chemical engineering *b*) the planning, designing, construction, or management of machinery, roads, bridges, buildings, waterways, etc. **2.** a maneuvering or managing

Eng·land (iŋ′glənd) **1.** division of the United Kingdom, occupying most of the S part of Great Britain: 50,331 sq. mi.; pop. 47,023,000; cap. London **2.** *same as* UNITED KINGDOM

Eng·lish (iŋ′glish) ***adj.*** **[**OE. *Englisc*, lit., of the Angles**]** **1.** of England, its people, their culture, etc. **2.** of their language —***n.*** **1.** the language of the people of England, the official language of the British Commonwealth, the U.S., Liberia, etc. **2.** the English language of a specific period: see OLD ENGLISH, MIDDLE ENGLISH, MODERN ENGLISH **3.** [*sometimes* **e-**] *Billiards, Bowling*, etc. a spinning motion given to a ball, as by striking it on one side —***vt.*** **1.** to translate into English **2.** to Anglicize (a foreign word) —**the English** the people of England

English Channel arm of the Atlantic, between England & France: 21–150 mi. wide

English horn a double-reed instrument of the woodwind family, similar to the oboe but larger and a fifth lower in pitch

ENGLISH HORN

English ivy *same as* IVY (sense 1)

Eng·lish·man (-mən) ***n.***, *pl.* **-men** a native or inhabitant of England, esp. a man —**Eng′lish·wom′an** ***n.fem.***, *pl.* **-wom′en**

English muffin a large, flat yeast roll, often baked on a griddle, and served split and toasted

English setter any of a breed of setter with a white, long-haired coat with black, yellow, or orange spots

English sonnet *same as* SHAKESPEAREAN SONNET

English sparrow the common sparrow, a small brownish-gray, finchlike bird of European origin

English walnut **1.** an Asiatic walnut tree now grown in Europe and N. America **2.** its nut

en·gorge (in gôrj′) ***vt., vi.*** **-gorged′, -gorg′ing** **1.** to eat gluttonously; gorge; glut **2.** *Med.* to congest with blood or other fluid —**en·gorge′ment** ***n.***

engr. **1.** engineer **2.** engraved **3.** engraver

en·graft (in graft′) ***vt.*** **1.** to graft (a shoot, etc.) from one plant onto another **2.** to establish firmly; implant —**en·graft′ment** ***n.***

en·grave (in grāv′) ***vt.*** **-graved′, -grav′ing** **[**< Fr. < *en-*, in + *graver*, to incise, ult. < Gr. *graphein*, to write**]** **1.** to cut or etch (letters, designs, etc.) in or on (a surface) or into (a metal plate, wooden block, etc. for printing) **2.** to print by means of such a plate, block, etc. **3.** to impress deeply on the mind or memory —**en·grav′er** ***n.***

en·grav·ing (-iŋ) ***n.*** **1.** the act, process, or art of one who engraves **2.** an engraved plate, design, etc. **3.** a print made from an engraved surface

en·gross (in grōs′) ***vt.*** **[**< OFr.: see EN- & GROSS**]** **1.** *a*) to write in the large letters once used for legal documents *b*) to make a final fair copy of (a document) **2.** to express formally or in legal form **3.** to take the entire attention of; occupy wholly; absorb —**en·gross′er** ***n.*** —**en·gross′ing** ***adj., n.*** —**en·gross′ment** ***n.***

en·gulf (in gulf′) ***vt.*** **1.** to swallow up; overwhelm **2.** to plunge, as into a gulf —**en·gulf′ment** ***n.***

en·hance (-hans′) ***vt.*** **-hanced′, -hanc′ing** **[**< Anglo-Fr. < OFr. *enhaucier*, ult. < L. *in*, in + *altus*, high**]** to make greater, as in value, attractiveness, etc.; heighten —***vi.*** to increase, as in value or price —**en·hance′ment** ***n.*** —**en·hanc′er** ***n.***

e·nig·ma (ə nig′mə) ***n.***, *pl.* **-mas** **[**< L. < Gr. *ainigma* < *ainissesthai*, to speak in riddles < *ainos*, tale**]** **1.** a perplexing, usually ambiguous, statement; riddle **2.** a perplexing or baffling matter, person, etc. —**e·nig·mat·ic** (en′ig-mat′ik, ē′nig-), **e′nig·mat′i·cal** ***adj.*** —**e′nig·mat′i·cal·ly** ***adv.***

en·join (in join′) ***vt.*** **[**< OFr. < L. < *in-*, in + *jungere*, to join**]** **1.** to order; enforce *[*to *enjoin* silence*]* **2.** to prohibit, esp. by legal injunction; forbid **3.** to order (someone) to do something, esp. by legal injunction

en·joy (in joi′) ***vt.*** **[**< OFr. *enjoir* < *en-*, in + *joir* < L. *gaudere*, to be glad**]** **1.** to have or experience with joy; get pleasure from; relish **2.** to have the use or benefit of —**enjoy oneself** to have a good time —**en·joy′a·ble** ***adj.*** —**en·joy′a·ble·ness** ***n.*** —**en·joy′a·bly** ***adv.***

en·joy·ment (-mənt) ***n.*** **1.** an enjoying **2.** something enjoyed **3.** pleasure; gratification; joy

en·kin·dle (en kin′d'l) ***vt.*** **-dled, -dling** **1.** to set on fire; make blaze up **2.** to stir up; arouse

enl. **1.** enlarge **2.** enlisted

en·lace (in lās′) ***vt.*** **-laced′, -lac′ing** **1.** to wind about as with a lace; encircle; enfold **2.** to entangle; interlace —**en·lace′ment** ***n.***

en·large (in lärj′) ***vt.*** **-larged′, -larg′ing** **1.** to make larger; increase in size, volume, extent, etc.; expand **2.** *Photog.* to reproduce on a larger scale —***vi.*** **1.** to become larger; increase **2.** to discuss at greater length or in greater detail (with *on* or *upon*) —**en·large′ment** ***n.*** —**en·larg′er** ***n.***

en·light·en (in līt′'n) ***vt.*** **1.** to give the light of knowledge to; free from ignorance, prejudice, or superstition **2.** to give clarification to (a person) as to meanings, intentions, etc.; inform —**en·light′en·er** ***n.***

en·light·en·ment (-mənt) ***n.*** an enlightening or being enlightened —**the Enlightenment** an 18th-cent. European philosophical and social movement characterized by rationalism

en·list (in list′) ***vt.*** **1.** to enroll in some branch of the armed forces **2.** to win the support of **3.** to get (another's help, support, etc.) —***vi.*** **1.** to join some branch of the armed forces **2.** to join or support a cause or movement (with *in*) —**en·list′ee′** ***n.***

enlisted man any man in the armed forces who is not a commissioned officer or warrant officer

en·list·ment (-mənt) ***n.*** **1.** an enlisting or being enlisted **2.** the period for which one enlists

en·liv·en (in lī′v'n) ***vt.*** to make active, vivacious, interesting, or cheerful; liven up or brighten —**en·liv′en·er** ***n.*** —**en·liv′en·ment** ***n.***

en masse (en mas′; *Fr.* än màs′) **[**Fr., lit., in mass**]** in a group; as a whole; all together

en·mesh (en mesh′) ***vt.*** to catch in or as in the meshes of a net; entangle

en·mi·ty (en′mə tē) ***n.***, *pl.* **-ties** **[**< OFr. < L. *inimicus*, ENEMY**]** the bitter attitude or feelings of an enemy or mutual enemies; hostility

en·no·ble (i nō′b'l) ***vt.*** **-bled, -bling** **1.** to raise to the rank of nobleman **2.** to give a noble quality to; dignify —**en·no′ble·ment** ***n.*** —**en·no′bler** ***n.***

en·nui (än′wē; *Fr.* än nwē′) ***n.*** **[**Fr.: see ANNOY**]** weariness and dissatisfaction resulting from inactivity or lack of interest; boredom

e·nor·mi·ty (i nôr′mə tē) ***n.***, *pl.* **-ties** **[**< Fr. < L. < *enormis*, irregular, immense < *e-*, out + *norma*, rule**]** **1.** great wickedness *[*the *enormity* of a crime*]* **2.** a very wicked crime **3.** enormous size or extent: generally considered a loose usage

e·nor·mous (i nôr′məs) ***adj.*** **[**see prec.**]** **1.** very much exceeding the usual size, number, or degree; huge; vast **2.** [Archaic] very wicked; outrageous —**e·nor′mous·ly** ***adv.*** —**e·nor′mous·ness** ***n.***

e·nough (i nuf′) ***adj.*** **[**OE. *genoh***]** as much or as many as necessary, desirable, or tolerable; sufficient —***n.*** the amount or number needed, desired, or allowed —***adv.*** **1.** as much or as often as necessary; sufficiently **2.** fully; quite *[*oddly *enough]* **3.** just adequately; tolerably; fairly *[*he played well *enough]*

e·now (i nou′) ***adj., n., adv.*** [Archaic] enough

en·plane (en plān′) ***vi.*** **-planed′, -plan′ing** to board an airplane

en·quire (in kwīr′) ***vt., vi.*** **-quired′, -quir′ing** *same as* INQUIRE —**en·quir′y** ***n.***, *pl.* **-quir′ies**

en·rage (in rāj′) ***vt.*** **-raged′, -rag′ing** to put into a rage; infuriate —**en·rage′ment** ***n.***

‡en rap·port (än rà pôr′) **[**Fr.**]** in harmony; in sympathy; in accord

en·rapt (in rapt′) ***adj.*** enraptured; rapt

en·rap·ture (-rap′chər) ***vt.*** **-tured, -tur·ing** to fill with great pleasure or delight: also **en·rav′ish**

en·rich (in rich′) ***vt.*** to make rich or richer; specif., *a*) to give more wealth to *b*) to give greater value or effectiveness to *[*to *enrich* a curriculum*]* *c*) to decorate; adorn *d*) to fertilize (soil) *e*) to add vitamins, minerals, etc. to (bread, etc.) for more food value —**en·rich′ment** ***n.***

en·roll, en·rol (in rōl′) ***vt.*** **-rolled′, -roll′ing** **1.** to record in a list **2.** to enlist **3.** to accept as a member —***vi.*** to enroll oneself or become enrolled; register; become a member —**en·roll′ee′** ***n.***

en·roll·ment, en·rol·ment (-mənt) ***n.*** **1.** an enrolling or being enrolled **2.** a list of those enrolled **3.** the number of those enrolled

en route (än ro͞ot′, en) **[**Fr.**]** on or along the way

Ens. Ensign

en·sconce (in skäns′) ***vt.*** **-sconced′, -sconc′ing** **[**EN- + SCONCE[2]**]** **1.** [Now Rare] to hide; conceal; shelter **2.** to place or settle snugly

en·sem·ble (än säm′b'l) ***n.*** **[**Fr. < OFr. < L. < *in-*, in + *simul*, at the same time**]** **1.** all the parts considered as a whole; total effect **2.** a whole costume, esp. of matching or complementary articles of dress **3.** a company of actors, dancers, etc. **4.** *Music* *a*) a small group of musicians performing together *b*) their instruments or voices *c*) the performance together of such a group, or of an orchestra, chorus, etc.

en·shrine (in shrīn′) ***vt.*** **-shrined′, -shrin′ing** **1.** to enclose in or as in a shrine **2.** to hold as sacred; cherish —**en·shrine′ment *n.***

en·shroud (-shroud′) ***vt.*** to cover as if with a shroud; hide; veil; obscure

en·sign (en′sīn; *also, and for 4 always,* -s'n) ***n.*** [< OFr. < L. < *insignia:* see INSIGNIA] **1.** a badge, symbol, or token of office or authority **2.** a flag or banner; specif., a national flag **3.** *Brit. Army* formerly, a commissioned officer who served as standard-bearer **4.** *U.S. Navy* a commissioned officer of the lowest rank, ranking below a lieutenant junior grade —**en′sign·ship′, en′sign·cy *n.***

en·si·lage (en′s'l ij) ***n.*** [Fr.] **1.** the preserving of green fodder by storage in a silo **2.** green fodder so preserved; silage

en·slave (in slāv′) ***vt.*** **-slaved′, -slav′ing** **1.** to put into slavery; make a slave of **2.** to dominate; subjugate —**en·slave′ment *n.*** —**en·slav′er *n.***

en·snare (-sner′) ***vt.*** **-snared′, -snar′ing** to catch in or as in a snare; trap —**en·snare′ment *n.***

en·snarl (-snärl′) ***vt.*** to draw into a snarl or tangle

en·sue (in so͞o′, -syo͞o′) ***vi.*** **-sued′, -su′ing** [< OFr., ult. < L. *insequi* < *in-*, in + *sequi*, to follow] **1.** to come afterward; follow immediately **2.** to happen as a consequence; result

en·sure (in shoor′) ***vt.*** **-sured′, -sur′ing** [< Anglo-Fr. *enseurer:* see EN- & SURE] **1.** to make sure; guarantee **2.** to make safe; protect

-ent (ənt, 'nt) [< OFr. *-ent*, L. *-ens* (gen. *entis*), stem ending of certain present participles] **1.** *a suffix meaning* that has, shows, or does *[insistent]* **2.** *a suffix meaning* a person or thing that *[superintendent, solvent]*

en·tab·la·ture (en tab′lə chər) ***n.*** [MFr. < It. *intavolatura* < *in-*, in + *tavola* < L. *tabula*, TABLE] *Archit.* **1.** a horizontal superstructure supported by columns and composed of architrave, frieze, and cornice **2.** any structure like this

en·tail (in tāl′) ***vt.*** [< ME. < *en-*, in + *taile*, an agreement < OFr. < *taillier*, to cut: see TAILOR] **1.** *Law* to limit the inheritance of (real property) to a specific line or class of heirs **2.** to cause or require as a necessary consequence; necessitate *[the plan entails work]* —***n.*** **1.** an entailing or being entailed **2.** an entailed inheritance **3.** the order of descent for an entailed inheritance —**en·tail′ment *n.***

en·tan·gle (in taŋ′g'l) ***vt.*** **-gled, -gling** **1.** to involve in a tangle; ensnare **2.** to involve in difficulty **3.** to confuse; perplex **4.** to cause to be tangled; complicate —**en·tan′gle·ment *n.***

en·tente (än tänt′) ***n.*** [Fr. < OFr. < *entendre*, to understand] **1.** an understanding or agreement, as between nations **2.** the parties to this

en·ter (en′tər) ***vt.*** [< OFr. *entrer* < L. *intrare* < *intra*, within] **1.** to come or go in or into **2.** to force a way into; penetrate **3.** to put into; insert **4.** to write down in a record, list, etc. **5.** to become a participant in (a contest) **6.** to join; become a member of (a school, club, etc.) **7.** to get (someone) admitted **8.** to start upon; begin (a career, etc.) **9.** to submit *[to enter a protest]* **10.** to register (a ship or cargo) at a customhouse **11.** *Law* to place on record before a court —***vi.*** **1.** to come or go into some place **2.** to pierce; penetrate —**enter into** **1.** to engage in; take part in **2.** to form a part or component of **3.** to deal with; discuss —**enter on** (or **upon**) **1.** to begin; start **2.** to begin to possess or enjoy

en·ter·ic (en ter′ik) ***adj.*** [see ff.] intestinal: also **en·ter·al** (en′tər əl)

en·ter·o- [< Gr. *enteron*, intestine] *a combining form meaning* intestine: also **enter-**

en·ter·prise (en′tər prīz′) ***n.*** [< OFr. < *entreprendre*, to undertake < *entre-* (L. *inter*), in + *prendre* (L. *prehendere*), to take] **1.** an undertaking; project; specif., *a)* a bold, difficult, dangerous, or important undertaking *b)* a business venture or company **2.** willingness to undertake new or risky projects; energy and initiative **3.** active participation in projects —**en′ter·pris′er *n.***

en·ter·pris·ing (-prī′ziŋ) ***adj.*** showing enterprise; full of energy and initiative; venturesome —**en′ter·pris′ing·ly *adv.***

en·ter·tain (en′tər tān′) ***vt.*** [< OFr. *entre* (< L. *inter*), between + *tenir* (L. *tenere*), to hold] **1.** to hold the interest of and give pleasure to; divert; amuse **2.** to give hospitality to; have as a guest **3.** to have in mind; consider, as an idea —***vi.*** to have guests

en·ter·tain·er (-ər) ***n.*** a person who entertains; esp., a popular singer, dancer, comedian, etc.

en·ter·tain·ing (-iŋ) ***adj.*** interesting and pleasurable; amusing —**en′ter·tain′ing·ly *adv.***

en·ter·tain·ment (-mənt) ***n.*** **1.** an entertaining or being entertained **2.** something that entertains; interesting, diverting, or amusing thing; esp., a show or performance

en·thrall, en·thral (in thrôl′) ***vt.*** **-thralled′, -thrall′ing** [see EN- & THRALL] **1.** [Now Rare] to enslave **2.** to hold as if in a spell; captivate; fascinate —**en·thrall′ment, en·thral′ment *n.***

en·throne (-thrōn′) ***vt.*** **-throned′, -thron′ing** **1.** to place on a throne; make a king, etc. of **2.** to accord the highest place to; exalt —**en·throne′ment *n.***

en·thuse (-tho͞oz′, -thyo͞oz′) ***vi.*** **-thused′, -thus′ing** [back-formation < ff.] [Colloq.] to express enthusiasm —***vt.*** [Colloq.] to make enthusiastic

en·thu·si·asm (in tho͞o′zē az'm, -thyo͞o′-) ***n.*** [< Gr. < *enthous*, possessed by a god, inspired < *en-*, in + *theos*, god] **1.** intense or eager interest; zeal; fervor **2.** something arousing this

en·thu·si·ast (-ast′) ***n.*** a person full of enthusiasm; an ardent supporter, a devotee, etc.

en·thu·si·as·tic (in tho͞o′zē as′tik, -thyo͞o′-) ***adj.*** of, having, or showing enthusiasm; ardent —**en·thu′si·as′ti·cal·ly *adv.***

en·tice (in tīs′) ***vt.*** **-ticed′, -tic′ing** [< OFr. *enticier*, to set afire, excite, prob. ult. < L. *in*, in + *titio*, a firebrand] to attract by offering hope of reward or pleasure; tempt —**en·tice′ment *n.*** —**en·tic′er *n.*** —**en·tic′ing·ly *adv.***

en·tire (in tīr′) ***adj.*** [< OFr. *entier* < L. *integer*, untouched, whole] **1.** *a)* not lacking any of the parts; whole *b)* complete; absolute **2.** unbroken; intact **3.** being wholly of one piece **4.** not castrated **5.** *Bot.* having an unbroken margin, as some leaves —**en·tire′ly *adv.*** —**en·tire′ness *n.***

en·tire·ty (-tē) ***n., pl.*** **-ties** **1.** the state or fact of being entire; wholeness; completeness **2.** an entire thing; whole —**in its entirety** as a whole

en·ti·tle (in tīt′'l) ***vt.*** **-tled, -tling** **1.** to give a title or name to **2.** to honor or dignify by a title **3.** to give a right or legal title to

en·ti·ty (en′tə tē) ***n., pl.*** **-ties** [< Fr. or < ML. *entitas* < L. prp. of *esse*, to be] **1.** being; existence **2.** a thing that has definite, individual existence in reality or in the mind

en·to- [ModL. < Gr. *entos*, within] *a combining form meaning* within or inner

entom., entomol. entomology

en·tomb (in to͞om′) ***vt.*** to place in a tomb or grave; bury —**en·tomb′ment *n.***

en·to·mo- [Fr. < Gr. *entoma* (*zōa*), lit., notched animals: cf. INSECT] *a combining form meaning* insect or insects

en·to·mol·o·gy (en′tə mäl′ə jē) ***n.*** [see prec. & -LOGY] the branch of zoology that deals with insects —**en′to·mo·log′i·cal** (-mə läj′i k'l), **en′to·mo·log′ic *adj.*** —**en′to·mo·log′i·cal·ly *adv.*** —**en′to·mol′o·gist *n.***

en·tou·rage (än′too räzh′) ***n.*** [Fr. < *entourer*, to surround] a group of accompanying attendants, assistants, or associates; retinue

en·tr'acte (än trakt′, än′trakt) ***n.*** [Fr. < *entre-*, between + *acte*, an act] **1.** the interval between two acts of a play, opera, etc.; intermission **2.** music, a dance, etc. performed during this interval

en·trails (en′trālz, -trəlz) ***n.pl.*** [< OFr. < ML. *intralia* < L. < *interaneus*, internal < *inter*, between] **1.** the inner organs of men or animals; specif., the intestines; viscera; guts **2.** the inner parts of a thing

en·train (in trān′) ***vt.*** to put aboard a train —***vi.*** to go aboard a train —**en·train′ment *n.***

en·trance[1] (en′trəns) ***n.*** **1.** the act or point of entering **2.** a place for entering; door, gate, etc. **3.** permission or right to enter; admission

en·trance[2] (in trans′) ***vt.*** **-tranced′, -tranc′ing** **1.** to put into a trance **2.** to enchant; charm; enrapture —**en·trance′ment *n.*** —**en·tranc′ing·ly *adv.***

en·trant (en′trənt) ***n.*** a person who enters

en·trap (in trap′) ***vt.*** **-trapped′, -trap′ping** **1.** to catch as in a trap **2.** to trick into difficulty, as into incriminating oneself —**en·trap′ment *n.***

en·treat (-trēt′) ***vt.*** [< Anglo-Fr. < OFr. < *en-*, in + *traiter:* see TREAT] to ask earnestly; beg; beseech; implore —***vi.*** to make an earnest appeal; plead —**en·treat′ing·ly *adv.*** —**en·treat′ment *n.***

en·treat·y (-ē) ***n., pl.*** **-treat′ies** an earnest request; plea

en·tree, en·trée (än′trā; *Fr.* än trā′) ***n.*** [< Fr. < OFr. *entrer*, ENTER] **1.** *a)* the act of entering *b)* the right or freedom to enter, participate, etc.; access **2.** *a)* the main course of a meal *b)* formerly, and still in some countries, a dish served before the roast or between the main courses

en·trench (in trench′) ***vt.*** **1.** to surround or fortify with a trench or trenches **2.** to establish securely *[entrenched in office]* —**en·trench′ment** ***n.***

en·tre·pre·neur (än′trə prə nur′, -noor′, -nyoor′) ***n.*** [Fr. < OFr. *entreprendre:* see ENTERPRISE] a person who organizes and manages a business undertaking, assuming the risk for the sake of profit

en·tro·py (en′trə pē) ***n.*** [G. *entropie,* arbitrary use of Gr. *entropē,* a turning toward] a measure of the amount of energy unavailable for work in a thermodynamic system: entropy keeps increasing and available energy diminishing in a closed system, as the universe

en·trust (in trust′) ***vt.*** **1.** to charge with a trust or duty **2.** to assign the care of; turn over for safekeeping

en·try (en′trē) ***n.,*** *pl.* **-tries** [< OFr. < *entrer,* ENTER] **1.** *a)* the act of entering; entrance *b)* the right or freedom to enter; entree **2.** a way or passage by which to enter; door, hall, etc. **3.** *a)* the recording of an item or note in a list, journal, etc. *b)* an item thus recorded **4.** the registration of a ship or cargo at a customhouse **5.** one entered in a race, competition, etc. **6.** *Law* the taking possession of buildings, land, etc. by entering them

en·twine (in twīn′) ***vt., vi.*** **-twined′, -twin′ing** to twine or twist together or around

e·nu·mer·ate (i nōō′mə rāt′, -nyōō′-) ***vt.*** **-at′ed, -at′ing** [< L. pp. of *enumerare* < *e-,* out + *numerare,* to count < *numerus,* a number] **1.** to determine the number of; count **2.** to name one by one; specify, as in a list —**e·nu′mer·a′tion** ***n.*** —**e·nu′mer·a′tive** ***adj.*** —**e·nu′mer·a′tor** ***n.***

e·nun·ci·ate (i nun′sē āt′, -shē-) ***vt.*** **-at′ed, -at′ing** [< L. pp. of *enuntiare* < *e-,* out + *nuntiare,* ANNOUNCE] **1.** to state definitely **2.** to announce; proclaim **3.** to pronounce (words) —***vi.*** to pronounce words, esp. clearly; articulate —**e·nun′ci·a′tion** ***n.*** —**e·nun′ci·a′tor** ***n.***

en·u·re·sis (en′yoo rē′sis) ***n.*** [ModL. < Gr. *enourein,* to urinate in] inability to control urination; esp., bed-wetting —**en′u·ret′ic** (-ret′ik) ***adj.***

en·vel·op (in vel′əp) ***vt.*** [< OFr. *envoluper:* see EN- & DEVELOP] **1.** to wrap up; cover completely **2.** to surround **3.** to conceal; hide —**en·vel′op·ment** ***n.***

en·ve·lope (en′və lōp′, än′-) ***n.*** [< Fr. < OFr.: see prec.] **1.** a thing that envelops; wrapper; covering **2.** a folded paper container for letters, etc., usually with a gummed flap **3.** the bag that contains the gas in a dirigible or balloon **4.** any enclosing membrane, skin, etc.

en·ven·om (in ven′əm) ***vt.*** **1.** to put venom or poison on or into **2.** to fill with hate; embitter

en·vi·a·ble (en′vē ə b′l) ***adj.*** worthy to be envied or desired —**en′vi·a·ble·ness** ***n.*** —**en′vi·a·bly** ***adv.***

en·vi·ous (-əs) ***adj.*** [< OFr. < L. < *invidia,* ENVY] feeling, showing, or resulting from envy —**en′vi·ous·ly** ***adv.***

en·vi·ron (in vī′rən) ***vt.*** [< OFr. < *environ,* about: see ENVIRONS] to surround; encircle

en·vi·ron·ment (in vī′rən mənt, -ərn mənt) ***n.*** [prec. + -MENT] **1.** surroundings **2.** all the conditions, circumstances, and influences surrounding, and affecting the development of, an organism or group of organisms —**en·vi′ron·men′tal** (-men′t′l) ***adj.*** —**en·vi′ron·men′tal·ly** ***adv.***

en·vi·ron·men·tal·ist (in vī′rən men′t′l ist) ***n.*** a person working to solve environmental problems, such as air and water pollution, the careless use of natural resources, uncontrolled population growth, etc.

en·vi·rons (in vī′rəns, -ərnz; en′vər ənz) ***n.pl.*** [< OFr. < *en-,* in + *viron,* a circuit < *virer,* to turn] **1.** the districts surrounding a city; suburbs or outskirts **2.** vicinity

en·vis·age (en viz′ij) ***vt.*** **-aged, -ag·ing** [< Fr.: see EN- & VISAGE] to form an image of in the mind

en·vi·sion (en vizh′ən) ***vt.*** to imagine (something not yet in existence)

en·voi (en′voi, än′-) ***n.*** [Fr.] **1.** *same as* ENVOY[2] **2.** a remark made in farewell or conclusion

en·voy[1] (en′voi, än′-) ***n.*** [< Fr. < *envoyer,* to send < OFr. < *en-* (L. *in*), in + *voie* (L. *via*), way] **1.** a messenger; agent **2.** an agent sent by a government or ruler to transact diplomatic business: an **envoy extraordinary** ranks just below an ambassador

en·voy[2] (en′voi, än′-) ***n.*** [< OFr. *envoy,* lit., a sending: see prec.] a postscript to a poem, essay, or book, containing a dedication, explanation, etc.

en·vy (en′vē) ***n.,*** *pl.* **-vies** [< OFr. < L. *invidia* < *invidere,* to look askance at < *in-,* upon + *videre,* to look] **1.** a feeling of discontent and ill will because of another's advantages, possessions, etc. **2.** desire for some advantage, quality, etc. that another has **3.** an object of envious feeling —***vt.*** **-vied, -vy·ing** to feel envy toward, at, or because of —**en′vi·er** ***n.*** —**en′vy·ing·ly** ***adv.***

en·wrap (en rap′) ***vt.*** **-wrapped′, -wrap′ping** to wrap; envelop

en·wreathe (-rēth′) ***vt.*** **-wreathed′, -wreath′ing** to encircle with or as with a wreath

en·zyme (en′zīm) ***n.*** [< G. < LGr. *enzymos,* leavened < Gr. *en-,* in + *zymē,* leaven] a proteinlike substance, formed in plant and animal cells, that acts as an organic catalyst in initiating or speeding up specific chemical reactions —**en′zy·mat′ic** (-zī mat′ik, -zi-), **en·zy′mic** ***adj.***

e·o- [< Gr. *ēōs,* dawn] *a prefix meaning* early, early part of a period *[Eocene]*

E·o·cene (ē′ə sēn′) ***adj.*** [EO- + Gr. *kainos,* new] designating or of the second and longest epoch of the Tertiary Period in the Cenozoic Era —**the Eocene** the Eocene Epoch or its rocks: see GEOLOGY, chart

E·o·li·an (ē ō′lē ən) ***adj., n.*** *same as* AEOLIAN

e·o·lith·ic (ē′ə lith′ik) ***adj.*** [EO- + -LITHIC] designating or of the early part of the Stone Age, during which crude stone tools were first used

e·on (ē′ən, ē′än) ***n.*** [LL. < Gr. *aiōn,* an age, lifetime] an extremely long, indefinite period of time

E·os (ē′äs) [see EO-] *Gr. Myth.* the goddess of dawn: identified with the Roman goddess Aurora

e·o·sin (ē′ə sin) ***n.*** [< Gr. *ēōs,* dawn + -IN[1]] a rosecolored dye, $C_{20}H_8O_5Br_4$, used as an industrial pigment and biological stain: also **e′o·sine** (-sin, -sēn′) —**e′o·sin′ic** ***adj.***

-e·ous (ē əs) [< L. *-eus* + -OUS] *a suffix meaning* having the nature of, like *[beauteous]*

EPA Environmental Protection Agency

ep·au·let, ep·au·lette (ep′ə let′) ***n.*** [< Fr. < OFr. < L. *spatula:* see SPATULA] a shoulder ornament, as on military uniforms

e·pee, é·pée (e pā′, ā-) ***n.*** [Fr. < OFr. < L. < Gr. *spathē,* blade] a sword, esp. a thin, pointed sword without a cutting edge, used in fencing —**e·pee′ist, é·pée′ist** ***n.***

Eph. Ephesians: also **Ephes.**

e·phah, e·pha (ē′fə) ***n.*** [< LL. < Heb. *'ēphāh*] an ancient Hebrew dry measure, estimated at from 1/3 bushel to a little over one bushel

EPAULETS

e·phed·rine (i fed′rin) ***n.*** [< ModL. *Ephedra,* genus name of the plants < L. < Gr. *ephedra,* the horsetail] an alkaloid, $C_{10}H_{15}NO$, derived from certain Asiatic plants or synthesized, used to relieve nasal congestion and asthma

e·phem·er·al (i fem′ər əl) ***adj.*** [< Gr. < *epi-,* upon + *hēmera,* a day + -AL] **1.** lasting only one day **2.** short-lived; transitory —***n.*** an ephemeral thing —**e·phem′er·al·ly** ***adv.***

e·phem·er·id (-id) ***n.*** [see prec. & -ID] *same as* MAYFLY

e·phem·er·is (-is) ***n.,*** *pl.* **eph·e·mer·i·des** (ef′ə mer′ə dēz′) [see EPHEMERAL] a table giving the daily positions of a heavenly body for a given period

E·phe·sians (i fē′zhənz) a book of the New Testament: an epistle of the Apostle Paul to the Christians of Ephesus

Eph·e·sus (ef′ə səs) ancient Greek city in W Asia Minor —**E·phe·sian** (i fē′zhən) ***adj., n.***

eph·od (ef′äd, -əd) ***n.*** [< LL. < Heb. < *āphad,* to put on] an outer vestment worn by ancient Jewish priests

eph·or (ef′ôr, -ər) ***n.,*** *pl.* **-ors, -or·i′** (-ə rī′) [< L. < Gr. < *epi-,* over + *horan,* to see] any of a body of five magistrates of ancient Sparta

E·phra·im (ē′frē əm) [LL. < Gr. < Heb. *ephrayim,* lit., very fruitful] **1.** a masculine name **2.** *Bible a)* the younger son of Joseph *b)* the tribe of Israel descended from this son *c)* the kingdom of Israel

ep·i- [< Gr. *epi,* at, on, upon, etc.] *a prefix meaning* on, upon, over, on the outside, anterior, beside *[epiglottis, epidemic, epidermis]* : also **ep-** (before a vowel) and **eph-** (in an aspirated word, as *ephemeral*)

ep·ic (ep′ik) ***n.*** [< L. < Gr. < *epos,* a word, song] **1.** a long narrative poem with a dignified style and certain formalities of structure, about the deeds of a traditional or historical hero or heroes, as the *Iliad* and *Odyssey* **2.** a prose narrative, play, etc. regarded as having the qualities of an epic **3.** a series of events regarded as a proper subject for an epic —***adj.*** of, or having the nature of, an epic; heroic; grand; majestic: also **ep′i·cal** —**ep′i·cal·ly** ***adv.***

ep·i·ca·lyx (ep′ə kā′liks, -kal′iks) ***n.,*** *pl.* **-lyx·es, -ly·ces′** (-lə sēz′) [EPI- + CALYX] a ring of small leaves (called *bracts*) at the base of certain flowers, resembling an extra outer calyx

ep·i·can·thus (-kan′thəs) ***n.*** [EPI- + CANTHUS] a small fold of skin sometimes covering the inner corner of the eye —**ep′i·can′thic** ***adj.***

ep·i·car·di·um (-kär′dē əm) ***n.,*** *pl.* **-di·a** (-ə) [ModL. < EPI- + Gr. *kardia,* heart] the innermost layer of the pericardium —**ep′i·car′di·al** ***adj.***

ep·i·carp (ep′ə kärp′) ***n.*** [EPI- + -CARP] *same as* EXOCARP

ep·i·cene (ep′ə sēn′) ***adj.*** [< L. < Gr. < *epi-*, to + *koinos*, common] belonging to one sex but having characteristics of the other, or of neither —***n.*** an epicene person

ep·i·cen·ter (-sen′tər) ***n.*** **1.** the area of the earth's surface directly above the place of origin, or focus, of an earthquake: also **ep′i·cen′trum** (-trəm), *pl.* **-tra** (-trə) **2.** a focal or central point —**ep′i·cen′tral *adj.***

ep·i·cure (ep′i kyoor′) ***n.*** [< L. < Gr.: see EPICURUS] **1.** a person who enjoys and has a discriminating taste for fine foods and drinks **2.** [Archaic] a person who is especially fond of luxury and sensuous pleasure —**ep′i·cur·ism *n.***

Ep·i·cu·re·an (ep′i kyoo rē′ən, -kyoor′ē ən) ***adj.*** **1.** of Epicurus or his philosophy **2.** [e-] *a)* fond of luxury and sensuous pleasure, esp. that of eating and drinking *b)* suited to or characteristic of an epicure —***n.*** **1.** a follower of Epicurus or his philosophy **2.** [e-] an epicure —**Ep′i·cu·re′an·ism, ep′i·cu·re′an·ism *n.***

Ep·i·cu·rus (ep′ə kyoor′əs) 341?–270 B.C.; Gr. philosopher: he held that the goal of man should be a life of calm pleasure regulated by morality, temperance, serenity, and cultural development

ep·i·dem·ic (ep′ə dem′ik) ***adj.*** [< Fr. < *épidémie* < ML. < Gr. < *epi-*, among + *dēmos*, people] prevalent and spreading rapidly among many individuals in a community at the same time, as a contagious disease: also **ep′i·dem′i·cal** —***n.*** **1.** an epidemic disease **2.** the epidemic spreading of a disease **3.** the rapid, widespread occurrence of a fad, fashion, etc. —**ep′i·dem′i·cal·ly *adv.***

ep·i·der·mis (ep′ə dur′mis) ***n.*** [LL. < Gr. < *epi-*, upon + *derma*, the skin] **1.** the outermost layer of skin in vertebrates **2.** the outermost layer of cells covering seed plants and ferns **3.** any of various other integuments —**ep′i·der′mal, ep′i·der′mic *adj.***

ep·i·der·moid (-dur′moid) ***adj.*** like epidermis: also **ep′i·der·moi′dal**

ep·i·glot·tis (ep′ə glät′is) ***n.*** [see EPI- & GLOTTIS] the thin, triangular, lidlike piece of cartilage that folds back over the opening of the windpipe during swallowing, thus preventing food, etc. from entering the lungs —**ep′i·glot′tal, ep′i·glot′tic *adj.***

PHARYNX
EPIGLOTTIS
LARYNX
ESOPHAGUS
TRACHEA

ep·i·gram (ep′ə gram′) ***n.*** [< OFr. < L. < Gr. *epigramma* < *epi-*, upon + *graphein*, to write] **1.** a short poem with a witty or satirical point **2.** any terse, witty, pointed statement, often with a clever twist in thought (Ex.: "Experience is the name everyone gives to his mistakes") —**ep·i·gram·mat·ic** (ep′i grə mat′ik), **ep′i·gram·mat′i·cal *adj.*** —**ep′i·gram·mat′i·cal·ly *adv.*** —**ep′i·gram′ma·tist *n.***

ep·i·gram·ma·tize (ep′ə gram′ə tīz′) ***vt., vi.*** **-tized′, -tiz′ing** to express (something) epigrammatically; make epigrams (about)

ep·i·graph (ep′ə graf′) ***n.*** [Gr. *epigraphē*, inscription < *epigraphein:* see EPIGRAM] **1.** an inscription on a building, monument, etc. **2.** a motto or quotation at the beginning of a book, chapter, etc.

ep·i·graph·ic (ep′ə graf′ik) ***adj.*** of an epigraph or epigraphy: also **ep′i·graph′i·cal** —**ep′i·graph′i·cal·ly *adv.***

e·pig·ra·phy (i pig′rə fē) ***n.*** [see EPIGRAPH] **1.** inscriptions collectively **2.** the study that deals with deciphering, interpreting, and classifying inscriptions —**e·pig′ra·phist, e·pig′ra·pher *n.***

ep·i·lep·sy (ep′ə lep′sē) ***n.*** [< OFr. < LL. < Gr. *epilēpsia* < *epi-*, upon + *lambanein*, to seize] a chronic disease of the nervous system, characterized by convulsions and, often, unconsciousness

ep·i·lep·tic (ep′ə lep′tik) ***adj.*** of or having epilepsy —***n.*** a person who has epilepsy

ep·i·logue, ep·i·log (ep′ə lôg′, -läg′) ***n.*** [< OFr. < L. < Gr. *epilogos*, conclusion < *epi-*, upon + *legein*, to say] **1.** a closing section of a novel, play, etc., providing further comment **2.** a short speech or poem spoken to the audience by one of the actors at the end of a play **3.** the actor speaking this

ep·i·neph·rine (ep′ə nef′rin, -rēn) ***n.*** [EPI- + NEPHR- + -INE[4]] a hormone secreted by the adrenal gland, that stimulates the heart, increases muscular strength, etc.: it is extracted from animal adrenals or prepared synthetically for therapeutic use

E·piph·a·ny (i pif′ə nē) ***n.***, *pl.* **-nies** [< OFr. < LL. < Gr. *epiphaneia*, appearance < *epi-*, upon + *phainein*, to show] in many Christian churches, a yearly festival (January 6) commemorating both the revealing of Jesus as the Christ to the Gentiles in the persons of the Magi and the baptism of Jesus

ep·i·phyte (ep′ə fīt′) ***n.*** [EPI- + -PHYTE] a nonparasitic plant that grows on another plant, producing its own food by photosynthesis, as certain orchids, mosses, and lichens; air plant —**ep′i·phyt′ic** (-fit′ik) ***adj.*** —**ep′i·phyt′i·cal·ly *adv.***

E·pi·rus (i pī′rəs) ancient kingdom on the Ionian Sea, in what is now S Albania & NW Greece

Epis. Epistle

Epis., Episc. **1.** Episcopal **2.** Episcopalian

e·pis·co·pa·cy (i pis′kə pə sē) ***n.***, *pl.* **-cies** [< LL. < *episcopus*, BISHOP] **1.** church government by bishops **2.** *same as* EPISCOPATE

e·pis·co·pal (-kə pəl) ***adj.*** [see prec.] **1.** of or governed by bishops **2.** [E-] designating or of any of various churches governed by bishops, as the Protestant Episcopal or the Anglican Church —**e·pis′co·pal·ly *adv.***

E·pis·co·pa·li·an (i pis′kə pāl′yən, -pā′lē ən) ***adj.*** *same as* EPISCOPAL —***n.*** a member of the Protestant Episcopal Church —**E·pis′co·pa′li·an·ism *n.***

e·pis·co·pate (i pis′kə pit, -pāt′) ***n.*** **1.** the position, rank, or term of office of a bishop **2.** a bishop's see **3.** bishops collectively

ep·i·sode (ep′ə sōd′) ***n.*** [< Gr. < *epeisodios*, following upon the entrance < *epi-*, upon + *eis-*, into + *hodos*, a way] **1.** any part of a novel, poem, musical composition, etc. that is complete in itself; incident **2.** any event or series of events complete in itself but forming part of a larger one **3.** any installment of a serialized story or drama

ep·i·sod·ic (ep′ə säd′ik) ***adj.*** **1.** of the nature of an episode; incidental **2.** made up of episodes, often not well integrated Also **ep′i·sod′i·cal** —**ep′i·sod′i·cal·ly *adv.***

e·pis·te·mol·o·gy (i pis′tə mäl′ə jē) ***n.***, *pl.* **-gies** [< Gr. *epistēmē*, knowledge + -LOGY] the study or theory of the origin, nature, methods, and limits of knowledge —**e·pis′te·mo·log′i·cal** (-mə läj′i k'l) ***adj.*** —**e·pis′te·mo·log′i·cal·ly *adv.*** —**e·pis′te·mol′o·gist *n.***

e·pis·tle (i pis′'l) ***n.*** [< OFr. < L. < Gr. *epistolē* < *epi-*, to + *stellein*, to send] **1.** a letter, esp. a long, formal, instructive letter: now used humorously **2.** [E-] *a)* any of the letters of the Apostles in the New Testament *b)* a selection from these Epistles, read as part of Mass, Communion, etc. in various churches —**e·pis′tler *n.***

e·pis·to·lar·y (-tə ler′ē) ***adj.*** [see prec.] **1.** of or suitable to letters or letter writing **2.** contained in, conducted by, or made up of letters

ep·i·taph (ep′ə taf′) ***n.*** [< OFr. < L. *epitaphium*, eulogy < Gr. < *epi-*, upon + *taphos*, tomb] an inscription, as on a tomb, in memory of the person buried there —**ep′i·taph′ic, ep′i·taph′i·al *adj.***

ep·i·the·li·um (ep′ə thē′lē əm) ***n.***, *pl.* **-li·ums, -li·a** (-ə) [ModL. < Gr. *epi-*, upon + *thēlē*, nipple] cellular tissue covering surfaces, forming glands, and lining most cavities of the body —**ep′i·the′li·al *adj.***

ep·i·thet (ep′ə thet′, -thət) ***n.*** [< L. < Gr. *epitheton* < *epi-*, on + *tithenai*, to put] **1.** a word or phrase used to characterize some person or thing, often specif. a disparaging one (Ex.: "egghead" for an intellectual) **2.** a descriptive name or title (Ex.: Philip the Fair) —**ep′i·thet′i·cal, ep′i·thet′ic *adj.***

e·pit·o·me (i pit′ə mē) ***n.***, *pl.* **-mes** [L. < Gr. *epitomē*, abridgment < *epi-*, upon + *temnein*, to cut] **1.** a short statement of the main points of a book, report, etc.; abstract; summary **2.** a person or thing that is representative of the characteristics of a whole class

e·pit·o·mize (-mīz′) ***vt.*** **-mized′, -miz′ing** to make or be an epitome of —**e·pit′o·miz′er *n.***

ep·i·zo·ot·ic (ep′ə zō ät′ik) ***adj.*** [< Fr. < Gr. *epi-*, upon + *zōion*, animal] epidemic among animals —***n.*** an epizootic disease

‡**e plu·ri·bus u·num** (ē′ ploor′ə bəs yoo′nəm) [L.] out of many, one: a motto of the U.S.

ep·och (ep′ək; *Brit. & Canad., usually* ē′päk) ***n.*** [< ML. < Gr. *epochē*, a pause < *epi-*, upon + *echein*, to hold] **1.** the beginning of a new and important period in the history of anything *[the first earth satellite marked a new epoch in man's study of the universe]* **2.** a period of time considered in terms of noteworthy events, developments, persons, etc. *[an epoch of social revolution]* **3.** *Astron.* the time at which observations are made, as of the positions of planets or stars **4.** *Geol.* a subdivision of a geologic period *[the Eocene Epoch]* —**ep′och·al *adj.*** —**ep′och·al·ly *adv.***

ep·ode (ep′ōd) ***n.*** [MFr. < L. < Gr. *epōidos*, aftersong < *epi-*, upon + *aeidein*, to sing] the final stanza in certain lyric odes, following the strophe and antistrophe

ep·o·nym (ep′ə nim′) ***n.*** [< Gr. < *epi-*, upon + *onyma*, a name] **1.** a real or mythical person from whose name the

name of a nation, race, etc. is derived *[William Penn is the eponym of Pennsylvania]* **2.** a person whose name has become identified with some period, movement, theory, etc. —**e·pon·y·mous** (i pän′ə məs), **ep′o·nym′ic** (-nim′ik) ***adj.***
ep·ox·y (e päk′sē) ***adj.*** **[**EP(I)- + OXY(GEN)**]** designating or of a compound in which an oxygen atom is joined to two carbon atoms in a chain to form a bridge; specif., designating a tough resin formed by polymerization, used in glues, etc. —***n.,*** *pl.* **-ox·ies** an epoxy resin
ep·si·lon (ep′sə län′, -lən) ***n.*** **[**Gr.**]** the fifth letter of the Greek alphabet (Ε, ϵ)
Ep·som (ep′səm) town in England, near London: site of **Epsom Downs,** where the Derby is run
Epsom salts (or **salt**) **[**< prec.**]** a white, crystalline salt, magnesium sulfate, $MgSO_4 \cdot 7H_2O$, used as a cathartic
Ep·stein (ep′stīn), Sir **Jacob** 1880–1959; Brit. sculptor, born in the U.S.
eq. 1. equal **2.** equation **3.** equivalent
eq·ua·ble (ek′wə b′l, ē′kwə-) ***adj.*** **[**< L. < *aequare,* to make equal < *aequus:* see ff.**] 1.** not varying or fluctuating much; steady; uniform *[an equable temperature]* **2.** even; serene *[an equable temperament]* —**eq′ua·bil′i·ty** ***n.*** —**eq′ua·bly** ***adv.***
e·qual (ē′kwəl) ***adj.*** **[**< L. < *aequus,* plain, even, flat**] 1.** of the same quantity, size, number, value, degree, etc. **2.** having the same rights, ability, rank, etc. **3.** evenly proportioned; being balanced or uniform **4.** having the necessary ability, power, courage, etc. (*to*) *[equal to the challenge]* **5.** [Archaic] fair; just —***n.*** any thing or person that is equal *[to be the equal of another]* —***vt.*** **e′qualed** or **e′qualled, e′qual·ing** or **e′qual·ling 1.** to be equal to; match in value **2.** to do or make something equal to *[to equal a record]*
e·qual·i·tar·i·an (i kwäl′ə ter′ē ən, -kwôl′-) ***adj., n.*** *same as* EGALITARIAN —**e·qual′i·tar′i·an·ism** ***n.***
e·qual·i·ty (i kwäl′ə tē, -kwôl′-) ***n.,*** *pl.* **-ties** state or instance of being equal
e·qual·ize (ē′kwə līz′) ***vt.*** **-ized′, -iz′ing 1.** to make equal **2.** to make uniform —**e′qual·i·za′tion** ***n.*** —**e′qual·iz′er** ***n.***
e·qual·ly (ē′kwə lē) ***adv.*** in an equal manner; to an equal degree; uniformly, impartially, etc.
equal sign (or **mark**) the arithmetical sign (=), indicating equality (Ex.: 2 + 2 = 4)
e·qua·nim·i·ty (ek′wə nim′ə tē, ē′kwə-) ***n.*** **[**< L. < *aequus,* even + *animus,* the mind**]** calmness of mind; evenness of temper; composure
e·quate (i kwāt′) ***vt.*** **e·quat′ed, e·quat′ing [**< L. pp. of *aequare,* to make equal < *aequus,* plain, even**] 1.** *a)* to make equal or equivalent *b)* to treat, regard, or express as equal, equivalent, or closely related **2.** *Math.* to state the equality of; put in the form of an equation —**e·quat′a·ble** ***adj.***
e·qua·tion (i kwā′zhən) ***n.*** **1.** an equating or being equated **2.** a complex whole **3.** a statement of equality between two quantities, as shown by the equal sign (=) *[a quadratic equation]* **4.** an expression in which symbols and formulas are used to represent a chemical reaction (Ex.: $H_2SO_4 + 2NaCl = 2HCl + Na_2SO_4$) —**e·qua′tion·al** ***adj.***
e·qua·tor (i kwāt′ər) ***n.*** **[**< ML. < LL. *aequator* < L. *aequare:* see EQUATE**] 1.** an imaginary circle around the earth, equally distant from the North Pole and the South Pole: it divides the earth into the Northern Hemisphere and the Southern Hemisphere **2.** any circle that divides a sphere, etc. into two equal parts **3.** *same as* CELESTIAL EQUATOR
e·qua·to·ri·al (ē′kwə tôr′ē əl, ek′wə-) ***adj.*** **1.** of or near the earth's equator **2.** of any equator **3.** like or characteristic of conditions near the earth's equator *[equatorial heat]*
Equatorial Guinea country in C Africa, including a mainland section & two islands in the Atlantic: 10,832 sq. mi.; pop. 286,000
eq·uer·ry (ek′wər ē; *also, esp. Brit.,* i kwer′i) ***n.,*** *pl.* **-ries [**altered (after L. *equus,* horse) < Fr. < OFr. *escuerie,* status of a squire**] 1.** formerly, an officer in charge of the horses of a royal or noble household **2.** an officer who is a personal attendant on some member of a royal family
e·ques·tri·an (i kwes′trē ən) ***adj.*** **[**< L. *equestris* < *eques,* horseman < *equus,* a horse**] 1.** of horses, horsemen, or horsemanship **2.** on horseback *[an equestrian statue]* —***n.*** a rider on horseback, as in a circus —**e·ques′tri·an·ism** ***n.*** —**e·ques′tri·enne′** (-trē en′) ***n.fem.***
e·qui- [< L. *aequus,* equal**]** *a combining form meaning* equal, equally *[equidistant]*
e·qui·an·gu·lar (ē′kwə aŋ′gyə lər) ***adj.*** having all angles equal
e·qui·dis·tant (-dis′tənt) ***adj.*** equally distant —**e′qui·dis′tance** ***n.*** —**e′qui·dis′tant·ly** ***adv.***
e·qui·lat·er·al (-lat′ər əl) ***adj.*** **[**< LL. < L. *aequus,* equal + *latus,* side**]** having all sides equal *[an equilateral triangle]* —***n.*** **1.** a figure having equal sides **2.** a side exactly equal to another
e·quil·i·brant (i kwil′ə brənt) ***n.*** **[**< Fr. < L. *aequilibrium,* EQUILIBRIUM**]** *Physics* a force or combination of forces that can balance another
e·quil·i·brate (i kwil′ə brāt′, ē′kwə lī′brāt) ***vt., vi.*** **-brat′ed, -brat′ing** to bring into or be in equilibrium; balance or counterbalance —**e·quil′i·bra′tion** ***n.*** —**e·quil′i·bra′tor** ***n.***
e·qui·lib·ri·um (ē′kwə lib′rē əm) ***n.,*** *pl.* **-ri·ums, -ri·a** (-ə) **[**L. *aequilibrium* < *aequus,* equal + *libra,* a balance**] 1.** a state of balance or equality between opposing forces **2.** a state of balance or adjustment of conflicting desires, interests, etc. **3.** *a)* bodily stability or balance *b)* mental or emotional stability
e·quine (ē′kwīn, ek′wīn) ***adj.*** **[**< L. < *equus,* a horse**]** of, like, or characteristic of a horse —***n.*** a horse
e·qui·noc·tial (ē′kwə näk′shəl) ***adj.*** **1.** relating to either of the equinoxes **2.** occurring at about the time of an equinox *[an equinoctial storm]* **3.** equatorial —***n.*** **1.** *same as* CELESTIAL EQUATOR **2.** an equinoctial storm
equinoctial circle (or **line**) *same as* CELESTIAL EQUATOR
e·qui·nox (ē′kwə näks′) ***n.*** **[**< OFr. < ML. < L. < *aequus,* equal + *nox,* night**] 1.** the time when the sun crosses the equator, making night and day of equal length in all parts of the earth: the **vernal equinox** occurs about March 21, the **autumnal equinox** about September 22 **2.** either of the two points on the celestial equator where the sun crosses it on these dates: also **equinoctial point**
e·quip (i kwip′) ***vt.*** **e·quipped′, e·quip′ping [**< Fr. < OFr. *esquiper,* embark, prob. < OE. < *scip,* a ship; or < ? ON. *skipa,* to arrange**] 1.** to provide with what is needed; outfit **2.** to prepare by training, instruction, etc. —**e·quip′per** ***n.***
eq·ui·page (ek′wə pij) ***n.*** **1.** the equipment of a ship, army, expedition, etc. **2.** a carriage, esp. one with horses and liveried servants
e·quip·ment (i kwip′mənt) ***n.*** **1.** an equipping or being equipped **2.** whatever one is equipped with; supplies, furnishings, apparatus, etc. **3.** one's abilities, knowledge, etc.
eq·ui·poise (ek′wə poiz′, ē′kwə-) ***n.*** **[**EQUI- + POISE**] 1.** equal distribution of weight; state of balance **2.** a weight or force that balances another
eq·ui·se·tum (ek′wə sēt′əm) ***n.,*** *pl.* **-tums, -ta** (-tə) **[**ModL. < L. < *equus,* horse + *saeta,* bristle**]** *same as* HORSETAIL (sense 2)
eq·ui·ta·ble (ek′wit ə b′l) ***adj.*** **1.** characterized by equity; fair; just **2.** *Law a)* having to do with equity, as distinguished from common or statute law *b)* valid in equity —**eq′ui·ta·ble·ness** ***n.*** —**eq′ui·ta·bly** ***adv.***
eq·ui·ta·tion (ek′wə tā′shən) ***n.*** **[**< L. < pp. of *equitare,* to ride < *eques,* horseman**]** the art of riding on horseback; horsemanship
eq·ui·ty (ek′wət ē) ***n.,*** *pl.* **-ties [**< OFr. < L. *aequitas,* equality < *aequus,* equal**] 1.** fairness; impartiality; justice **2.** anything that is fair or equitable **3.** the value of property beyond the total amount owed on it in mortgages, liens, etc. **4.** *Law a)* a system of rules and doctrines, as in the U.S., supplementing common and statute law and superseding such law when it proves inadequate for just settlement *b)* a right or claim recognized in a court of equity
equity capital 1. funds contributed by the owners of a business **2.** assets minus liabilities; net worth
equiv. equivalent
e·quiv·a·lence (i kwiv′ə ləns) ***n.*** the condition of being equivalent; equality of quantity, value, meaning, etc.: also **e·quiv′a·len·cy**
e·quiv·a·lent (-lənt) ***adj.*** **[**< OFr. < LL. < L. *aequus,* equal + *valere,* to be strong**] 1.** equal in quantity, value, force, meaning, etc. **2.** *Chem.* having the same valence **3.** *Geom.* equal in area or volume but not of the same shape —***n.*** **1.** an equivalent thing **2.** *Chem.* the quantity by weight (of a substance) that combines with one gram of hydrogen or eight grams of oxygen —**e·quiv′a·lent·ly** ***adv.***
e·quiv·o·cal (i kwiv′ə k′l) ***adj.*** **[**< LL. *aequivocus* (see ff.) + -AL**] 1.** having two or more meanings; purposely vague or ambiguous *[an equivocal reply]* **2.** uncertain; doubtful *[an equivocal outcome]* **3.** suspicious; questionable *[equivocal conduct]* —**e·quiv′o·cal′i·ty** (-kal′ə tē), **e·quiv′o·cal·ness** ***n.*** —**e·quiv′o·cal·ly** ***adv.***
e·quiv·o·cate (-kāt′) ***vi.*** **-cat′ed, -cat′ing [**< LL. < *aequivocus,* of like sound < L. *aequus,* equal + *vox,* voice**]** to use equivocal terms in order to deceive, mislead, hedge, etc. —**e·quiv′o·ca′tion** ***n.*** —**e·quiv′o·ca′tor** ***n.***
er (*variously* u, ə, ä, *etc.*; ʉr, ər *are spelling pronunciations*) ***interj.*** a conventionalized representation of a sound often made by a speaker when hesitating briefly
-er (ər) *a suffix of various origins and meanings:* **1. [**OE. *-ere***]** *a)* a person having to do with *[hatter]*: see also -IER, -YER *b)* a person living in *[New Yorker]* *c)* a thing or action connected with *[diner]* *d)* a person or thing that *[sprayer, roller]* **2. [**OE. *-ra***]** more: *added to many adjectives and adverbs to form the comparative degree [greater,*

later] **3.** [< Anglo-Fr. inf. suffix] the action of ——ing: *used in legal language [demurrer, waiver]* **4.** [OE. *-rian,* freq. suffix] repeatedly *[flicker]*

Er *Chem.* erbium

e·ra (ir′ə; *now often* er′ə) *n.* [LL. *aera,* era, earlier sense, "counters" < pl. of L. *aes,* brass] **1.** a system of reckoning time by numbering the years from some given date *[the Christian Era]* **2.** an event or date that marks the beginning of a new period in the history of something **3.** a period of time measured from some important occurrence or date **4.** a period of time considered in terms of noteworthy and characteristic events, men, etc. *[an era of progress]* **5.** any of the five main divisions of geologic time *[the Paleozoic Era]* : see also EPOCH, PERIOD, AGE

ERA Equal Rights Amendment

e·ra·di·ate (ē rā′dē āt′) *vi., vt.* **-at′ed, -at′ing** *same as* RADIATE —**e·ra′di·a′tion** *n.*

e·rad·i·cate (i rad′ə kāt′) *vt.* **-cat′ed, -cat′ing** [< L. pp. of *eradicare,* to root out < *e-,* out + *radix,* a root] **1.** to tear out by the roots; uproot **2.** to wipe out; destroy —**e·rad′i·ca·ble** (-kə b′l) *adj.* —**e·rad′i·ca′tion** *n.* —**e·rad′i·ca′tive** *adj.* —**e·rad′i·ca′tor** *n.*

e·rase (i rās′) *vt.* **e·rased′, e·ras′ing** [< L. pp. of *eradere* < *e-,* out + *radere,* to scrape] **1.** to rub, scrape, or wipe out (esp. writing or printing); efface **2.** to remove (something recorded) from (magnetic tape) **3.** to remove any sign of; obliterate, as from the mind **4.** [Slang] to kill —**e·ras′a·ble** *adj.*

e·ras·er (i rā′sər) *n.* a thing that erases; specif., a device made of rubber for erasing ink or pencil marks, or a pad of felt or cloth for removing chalk marks from a blackboard

E·ras·mus (i raz′məs), **Des·i·der·i·us** (des′ə dir′ē əs) (born *Gerhard Gerhards*) 1466?–1536; Du. humanist & scholar —**E·ras′mi·an** (-mē ən) *adj., n.*

e·ra·sure (i rā′shər; *chiefly Brit.* -zhər) *n.* **1.** an erasing **2.** an erased word, mark, etc. **3.** the place where something has been erased

Er·a·to (er′ə tō′) *Gr. Myth.* the Muse of love poetry

er·bi·um (ʉr′bē əm) *n.* [ModL. < *(Ytt)erby,* Sw. town where first found] a metallic chemical element of the rare-earth group: symbol, Er; at. wt., 167.28; at. no., 68

ere (er) *prep.* [< OE. *ær*] [Archaic or Poet.] before (in time) —*conj.* [Archaic or Poet.] **1.** before **2.** rather than

Er·e·bus (er′ə bəs) *Gr. Myth.* the dark place under the earth through which the dead passed before entering Hades

e·rect (i rekt′) *adj.* [< L. *erectus,* pp. of *erigere* < *e-,* up + *regere,* to make straight] **1.** upright; vertical **2.** sticking out or up; bristling; stiff —*vt.* **1.** to raise or construct (a building, etc.) **2.** to set up; cause to arise *[to erect social barriers]* **3.** to set in an upright position; raise **4.** to put together; assemble **5.** [Archaic] to establish; found **6.** *Geom.* to construct or draw (a perpendicular, figure, etc.) upon a base line —**e·rec′tion** *n.* —**e·rect′ly** *adv.* —**e·rect′ness** *n.* —**e·rec′tor** *n.*

e·rec·tile (i rek′t′l; *chiefly Brit.* -tīl′) *adj.* that can become erect: used esp. of tissue that becomes swollen and rigid when filled with blood —**e·rec′til′i·ty** (-til′ə tē) *n.*

ere·long (er′lôŋ′) *adv.* [Archaic or Poet.] before long; soon

er·e·mite (er′ə mīt′) *n.* [< OFr. or LL.: see HERMIT] a religious recluse; hermit —**er′e·mit′ic** (-mit′ik), **er′e·mit′i·cal** *adj.*

e·rep·sin (i rep′sin) *n.* [G. < L. pp. of *eripere* < *e-,* out + *rapere,* to snatch + G. *pepsin,* PEPSIN] an enzyme mixture secreted by the intestine and involved in the breaking down of proteins into their component amino acids

Er·furt (er′foort) city in SW East Germany: pop. 193,000

erg (ʉrg) *n.* [< Gr. *ergon,* work] *Physics* the unit of work or energy in the cgs (metric) system, being the work done by one dyne acting through a distance of one centimeter

er·go (ʉr′gō, er′-) *conj., adv.* [L.] therefore

er·go·nom·ics (ʉr′gə näm′iks) *n.pl.* [*with sing. v.*] [ERG + (EC)ONOMICS] the study of the problems of people in adjusting to their environment; esp., the science that seeks to adapt work or working conditions to suit the worker —**er′go·nom′i·cal** *adj.*

er·gos·ter·ol (ər gäs′tə rōl′) *n.* [< ff. + STEROL] an alcohol, $C_{28}H_{44}O$, formerly prepared from ergot but now chiefly from yeast: when exposed to ultraviolet rays it produces a vitamin (D_2) used to prevent or cure rickets

er·got (ʉr′gət) *n.* [Fr. < OFr. *argot,* a rooster's spur: from the shape of the growth] **1.** a fungous growth that invades the kernels of rye, or of other cereal plants **2.** the disease in which this occurs **3.** an extract of the dried rye fungus, used as a drug to contract blood vessels and smooth muscle tissue

Er·ic (er′ik) [Scand. < ON. *Eirìkr,* lit., honorable ruler] a masculine name

Er·ics·son (er′ik sən), **Leif** (lāf) fl. 1000; Norw. explorer: discovered what is now believed to be part of N. America: son of *ff.* Also sp. **Ericson**

Eric the Red fl. 10th cent.; Norw. explorer: discovered & colonized Greenland

Er·ie¹ (ir′ē) *n., pl.* **Er′ies, Er′ie** [AmFr. < Huron *yĕñresh,* wildcat + *-'e,* at the place of] a member of a tribe of Iroquoian Indians who lived in an area east and southeast of Lake Erie

Er·ie² (ir′ē) [after prec.] **1.** port on Lake Erie, in NW Pa.: pop. 119,000 **2. Lake,** one of the Great Lakes, between Lake Huron & Lake Ontario: 9,914 sq. mi.; 241 mi. long

Erie Canal barge canal between Buffalo, on Lake Erie, and Albany, on the Hudson: completed 1825: now part of the New York State Barge Canal

Er·in (er′in) [OIr.] *poet. name for* IRELAND

E·rin·y·es (i rin′ē ēz′) *n.pl., sing.* **E·rin·ys** (i rin′is, -rī′nis) *Gr. Myth. same as* FURIES

E·ris (ir′is, er′-) *Gr. Myth.* the goddess of strife and discord

ERISA Employee Retirement Income Security Act

Er·i·tre·a (er′ə trē′ə) province of Ethiopia, on the Red Sea: 45,000 sq. mi. —**Er′i·tre′an** *adj., n.*

er·mine (ʉr′mən) *n., pl.* **-mines, -mine:** see PLURAL, II, D, 1 [OFr.; prob. < MHG. < OHG. *harmo,* weasel] **1.** a weasel of northern regions whose fur is brown in summer but white with a black-tipped tail in winter **2.** the soft, white fur of this animal **3.** the position, rank, or functions of some European judges or peers, whose state robe is trimmed with ermine —**er′mined** *adj.*

ERMINE (body 5–10 in. long; tail 1–6 in. long)

erne, ern (ʉrn) *n.* [OE. *earn*] the European white-tailed eagle, which lives near the sea

Er·nest (ʉr′nəst) [< G. < OHG. *Ernust,* lit., resolute < *ernust,* seriousness] a masculine name

Er·nes·tine (ʉr′nəs tēn′) [G., fem. < prec.] a feminine name

e·rode (i rōd′) *vt.* **e·rod′ed, e·rod′ing** [< Fr. < L. < *e-,* out, off + *rodere,* to gnaw] **1.** to eat into; wear away; disintegrate *[acid erodes metal]* **2.** to form by wearing away gradually *[the stream eroded a gully]* **3.** to cause to deteriorate, decay, or vanish —*vi.* to become eroded

e·rog·e·nous (i räj′ə nəs) *adj.* [< Gr. *erōs,* love + -GENOUS] *same as* EROTOGENIC

E·ros (er′äs, ir′-) *Gr. Myth.* the god of love, son of Aphrodite: identified with the Roman god Cupid

e·ro·sion (i rō′zhən) *n.* an eroding or being eroded —**e·ro′sion·al** *adj.* —**e·ro′sive** *adj.*

e·rot·ic (i rät′ik) *adj.* [Gr. *erōtikos* < *erōs* (gen. *erōtos*), love] of, having, or arousing sexual feelings or desires; having to do with sexual love —**e·rot′i·cal·ly** *adv.*

e·rot·i·ca (-i kə) *n.pl.* [*often with sing. v.*] erotic books, pictures, etc.

e·rot·i·cism (-ə siz′m) *n.* **1.** erotic quality or character **2.** sexual excitement or behavior **3.** preoccupation with sex Also, and for 2 now usually, **er·o·tism** (er′ə tiz′m)

e·ro·to·gen·ic (i rät′ə jen′ik; er′ə tə-) *adj.* [*eroto-* (< Gr.), sexual desire + -GENIC] designating or of those areas of the body that are highly sensitive to sexual stimulation

err (ʉr, er) *vi.* [< OFr. *errer* < L. *errare,* to wander] **1.** to be wrong or mistaken; fall into error **2.** to deviate from the established moral code; do wrong

er·rand (er′ənd) *n.* [OE. *ærende,* message] **1.** a short trip to do a definite thing, often for someone else **2.** the thing for which one goes or is sent on a trip

er·rant (er′ənt) *adj.* [OFr., prp. of *errer,* to travel, ult. < L. *iter,* a journey] **1.** roving or wandering, esp. in search of adventure *[a knight-errant]* **2.** *a)* [see ERR] erring *b)* shifting about *[an errant wind]* —**er′rant·ry** *n.*

er·rat·ic (i rat′ik) *adj.* [< OFr. < L. *erraticus* < pp. of *errare,* to wander] **1.** having no fixed course; irregular; random **2.** eccentric; queer —**er·rat′i·cal·ly** *adv.*

er·ra·tum (e rät′əm, -rāt′-, -rat′-) *n., pl.* **-ta** (-ə) [L., neut. pp. of *errare,* to wander] an error in printing or writing

er·ro·ne·ous (ə rō′nē əs, e-) *adj.* containing or based on error; mistaken; wrong —**er·ro′ne·ous·ly** *adv.*

er·ror (er′ər) *n.* [< OFr. < L. *error* < *errare,* to wander] **1.** the state of believing what is untrue or incorrect **2.** a wrong belief; incorrect opinion **3.** something incorrect or wrong; inaccuracy; mistake **4.** transgression; wrongdoing; sin **5.** the amount by which something deviates from what is required or correct **6.** *Baseball* any misplay in fielding a ball which results in a player being safe who should have been out or which permits a runner to advance —**er′ror·less** *adj.*

er·satz (ʉr′zäts, er′-) *n., adj.* [G.] substitute or synthetic: the word usually suggests inferior quality

Erse (urs) ***adj., n.*** [ME. *Erish,* var. of *Irisc,* Irish] *same as* GAELIC, *adj.* 2, *n.* 2

erst (urst) ***adv.*** [OE. *ærest,* superl. of *ær,* ere] [Archaic] formerly —***adj.*** [Obs.] first

erst·while (-hwīl′) ***adv.*** [Archaic] some time ago; formerly —***adj.*** former

e·ruct (i rukt′) ***vt., vi.*** [< L. *eructare* < *e-,* out + *ructare,* to belch] to belch: also **e·ruc′tate** (-tāt) **-tat·ed, -tat·ing** — **e·ruc·ta·tion** (i ruk′tā′shən, ē′ruk-) ***n.***

er·u·dite (er′yoo dīt′, -oo-) ***adj.*** [< L. pp. of *erudire,* to instruct < *e-,* out + *rudis,* RUDE] learned; scholarly —**er′u·dite′ly** ***adv.***

er·u·di·tion (er′yoo dish′ən, -oo-) ***n.*** learning acquired by reading and study; scholarship

e·rupt (i rupt′) ***vi.*** [< L. *eruptus,* pp. of *erumpere* < *e-,* out + *rumpere,* to break] **1.** to burst forth or out, as from some restraint *[the lava erupted,* a riot *erupted]* **2.** to throw forth lava, water, steam, etc., as a volcano **3.** to break out in a rash **4.** to break through the gums, as a new tooth —***vt.*** to cause to burst forth —**e·rupt′i·ble** ***adj.***

e·rup·tion (i rup′shən) ***n.*** **1.** a bursting forth or out **2.** a throwing forth of lava, water, steam, etc. **3.** *Med. a)* a breaking out in a rash *b)* a rash —**e·rup′tive** ***adj.*** —**e·rup′tive·ly** ***adv.***

Er·win (ur′win) [G. < OHG. *hari,* host + *wini,* friend] a masculine name

-er·y (ər ē) [< OFr. *-erie* < LL. *-aria,* or < OFr. *-ier* + *-ie* (L. *-ia*)] *a suffix meaning:* **1.** a place to *[tannery]* **2.** a place for *[nunnery]* **3.** the practice, act, or occupation of *[surgery]* **4.** the product or goods of *[pottery]* **5.** a collection of *[crockery]* **6.** the state or condition of *[drudgery]* **7.** the behavior or qualities of *[tomfoolery]*

er·y·sip·e·las (er′ə sip′'l əs, ir′-) ***n.*** [< L. < Gr. < *erythros,* red + *-pelas* (L. *pellis*), skin] an acute infectious disease of the skin or mucous membranes caused by a streptococcus and characterized by local inflammation and fever

e·ryth·ro- [< Gr. *erythros,* red] *a combining form meaning:* **1.** red *[erythrocyte]* **2.** erythrocyte

e·ryth·ro·cyte (i rith′rə sīt′) ***n.*** [prec. + -CYTE] a red blood corpuscle: it is a very small, circular disk and contains hemoglobin, which carries oxygen to the body tissues —**e·ryth′ro·cyt′ic** (-sit′ik) ***adj.***

e·ryth·ro·my·cin (i rith′rə mī′sin) ***n.*** [< ERYTHRO- + Gr. *mykēs,* fungus + -IN¹] an antibiotic derived from a soil bacterium, used to treat various bacterial diseases

Es *Chem.* einsteinium

-es (iz, əz, z) [variously < OE. *-as, -s*] *a suffix used:* **1.** to form the plural of some nouns, as in *fishes:* see PLURAL **2.** to form the third person singular, present indicative, of verbs, as in (he) *kisses:* cf. -s

E·sau (ē′sô) [L. < Gr. < Heb. *'ēsāw,* lit., hairy] *Bible* the son of Isaac and Rebekah, who sold his birthright to his younger twin brother, Jacob: Gen. 25:21–34, 27

es·ca·drille (es′kə dril′; *Fr.* es kȧ drē′y′) ***n.*** [Fr. < Sp. < *escuadra,* squad] a squadron of airplanes, as in the French armed forces of World War I

es·ca·lade (es′kə lād′, es′kə lād′) ***n.*** [< Fr. < It. < *scalare,* to climb < L. *scala,* ladder] the act of climbing the walls of a fortified place by ladders —***vt.*** **-lad′ed, -lad′ing** to climb (a wall, etc.) or enter (a fortified place) by ladders

es·ca·late (es′kə lāt′) ***vi.*** **-lat′ed, -lat′ing** [back-formation < ff.] **1.** to rise as on an escalator **2.** to expand, as from a limited conflict into a general war **3.** to increase rapidly, as prices —***vt.*** to cause to escalate —**es′ca·la′tion** ***n.***

es·ca·la·tor (-ər) ***n.*** [< ESCALA(DE) + *-tor,* as in (ELEVA)TOR] a moving stairway consisting of treads linked in an endless belt

escalator clause a clause in a contract by which wages, etc. are adjusted to cost of living, etc.

es·cal·lop, es·cal·op (e skäl′əp, -skal′-) ***n., vt.*** [< OFr.: see SCALLOP] *same as* SCALLOP

es·ca·pade (es′kə pād′) ***n.*** [Fr., ult. < ff.] a reckless adventure or prank

es·cape (ə skāp′, e-) ***vi.*** **-caped′, -cap′ing** [< ONormFr. < L. *ex-,* out of + *cappa,* cloak (i.e., leave one's cloak)] **1.** to get free; get away **2.** to avoid an illness, accident, pain, etc. **3.** to flow, drain, or leak away *[gas escaping* from a pipe*]* **4.** to slip away; disappear —***vt.*** **1.** to get away from; flee from **2.** to manage to keep away from; avoid *[to escape* punishment*]* **3.** to come from involuntarily *[a scream escaped* her lips*]* **4.** to slip away from; be missed or forgotten by *[his name escapes* me*]* —***n.*** **1.** an escaping or the state of having escaped **2.** a means of escape **3.** an outward flow or leakage **4.** a temporary mental release from reality —***adj.*** **1.** giving temporary mental release from reality **2.** *a)* making escape possible *[an escape* hatch*]* *b)* giving a basis for evading a claim, responsibility, etc. *[an escape* clause*]* —**es·cap′a·ble** ***adj.*** —**es·cap′er** ***n.***

es·cap·ee (ə skā′pē′, e-) ***n.*** a person who has escaped, esp. from confinement

es·cape·ment (ə skāp′mənt, e-) ***n.*** **1.** [Rare] a means of escape **2.** the part in a clock or watch that controls the speed and regularity of the balance wheel or pendulum, by means of a notched wheel (**escape wheel**), one tooth of which is allowed to escape from the detaining catch at a time **3.** a ratchet mechanism, esp. on a typewriter to regulate the horizontal movement of the carriage

ESCAPEMENT

escape velocity the minimum speed required for a particle, space vehicle, etc. to escape permanently from the gravitational field of a planet, star, etc.

es·cap·ism (ə skāp′iz′m, e-) ***n.*** a tendency to escape from reality, the responsibilities of real life, etc., esp. by unrealistic imaginative activity —**es·cap′ist** ***adj., n.***

es·ca·role (es′kə rōl′) ***n.*** [Fr. < ML. < L. < *esca,* food] *same as* ENDIVE (sense 1)

es·carp·ment (e skärp′mənt) ***n.*** [< Fr.: see SCARP] **1.** a steep slope or cliff formed by erosion or by faulting **2.** ground formed into a steep slope on the exterior of a fortification See also SCARP

-es·cence (es′'ns) *a n.-forming suffix corresponding to the adjective suffix* -ESCENT *[obsolescence]*

-es·cent (es′'nt) [< L. *-escens, -escentis,* prp. ending] *an adj.-forming suffix meaning:* **1.** starting to be; being or becoming *[convalescent]* **2.** giving off or reflecting light, or exhibiting a play of color *[phosphorescent]*

es·cheat (es chēt′) ***n.*** [< OFr. < pp. of *escheoir,* to fall to one's share < VL. < L. *ex-,* out + *cadere,* to fall] *Law* **1.** the reverting of property to the lord of the manor, to the crown, or to the government when there are no legal heirs **2.** property so reverting —***vt., vi.*** to confiscate or revert by escheat —**es·cheat′a·ble** ***adj.***

es·chew (es choo′) ***vt.*** [< Anglo-Fr. < OFr. < OHG. *sciuhan,* to fear] to keep away from (something harmful or disliked); shun —**es·chew′al** ***n.***

es·cort (es′kôrt; *for v.* i skôrt′) ***n.*** [< Fr. < It. < *scorta* < *scorgere,* to lead < L. *ex-,* out + *corrigere,* to CORRECT] **1.** one or more persons (or cars, ships, airplanes, etc.) accompanying another or others to give protection or show honor **2.** a man or boy accompanying a woman or girl, as to a party **3.** accompaniment by an escort —***vt.*** to go with as an escort

es·cri·toire (es′krə twär′) ***n.*** [< OFr. < LL. < pp. of L. *scribere,* to write] a writing desk or table; secretary

es·crow (es′krō; *chiefly Brit.* es krō′) ***n.*** [OFr. *escroue,* scroll] *Law* a written agreement, as a bond or deed, put in the care of a third party until certain conditions are fulfilled —**in escrow** *Law* so put in the care of a third party

es·cu·do (es koo′dō) ***n.,*** *pl.* **-dos** [Sp., a shield < L. *scutum*] **1.** any of several obsolete coins of Spain and Portugal **2.** the monetary unit of Portugal, Cape Verde, and Mozambique: see MONETARY UNITS, table

es·cu·lent (es′kyoo lənt) ***adj.*** [< L. < *esca,* food] fit for food; eatable; edible —***n.*** something fit for food, esp. a vegetable

es·cutch·eon (i skuch′ən) ***n.*** [ONormFr. < L. *scutum,* shield] a shield or shield-shaped surface on which a coat of arms is displayed —**a blot on one's escutcheon** a stain on one's honor

Es·dras (ez′drəs) *Douay Bible name for* EZRA

-ese (ēz, ēs) [< OFr. & It. < L. *-ensis*] *a suffix meaning:* **1.** (a native or inhabitant) of *[Javanese]* **2.** (in) the language or dialect of *[Cantonese]* **3.** (in) the style of *[journalese]*

ESE, E.S.E., e.s.e. east-southeast

Es·fa·hán (es′fä hän′) city in WC Iran: pop. 575,000

Es·ki·mo (es′kə mō′) ***n.*** [< Fr. < Algonquian: lit., eater of raw flesh] **1.** *pl.* **-mos′, -mo′** a member of a group of native N. American people living in Greenland, N Canada and Alaska, and the NE tip of Asia **2.** either of the two languages of the Eskimos —***adj.*** of the Eskimos, their language, or their culture —**Es′ki·mo′an** ***adj.***

Eskimo dog a strong breed of dog with grayish, shaggy fur, used by the Eskimos to pull sleds

e·soph·a·gus (i säf′ə gəs) ***n.,*** *pl.* **-a·gi′** (-jī′) [< OFr. < ML. < Gr. *oisophagos* < *oisein,* fut. inf. of *pherein,* to carry + *phagein,* to eat] the tube through which food passes from the pharynx to the stomach: see EPIGLOTTIS, illus. — **e·soph·a·ge·al** (i säf′ə jē′əl) ***adj.***

es·o·ter·ic (es′ə ter′ik) ***adj.*** [< Gr. < *esōteros,* inner, compar. of *esō,* within] **1.** *a)* understood by only a chosen few, as an inner group of disciples or initiates *b)* beyond the understanding or knowledge of most people; abstruse **2.** confidential; private —**es′o·ter′i·cal·ly** ***adv.***

ESP extrasensory perception

esp., espec. especially

es·pa·drille (es′pə dril′) ***n.*** [Fr. < Sp. *esparto,* ESPARTO] a shoe for casual wear, with a canvas upper and a sole of twisted rope or of rubber, etc.

es·pal·ier (es pal′yər) ***n.*** **[**Fr. < It. *spalliera,* support < *spalla,* the shoulder < L. *spatula:* see SPATULA**]** **1.** a lattice or trellis on which trees and shrubs are trained to grow flat **2.** a plant, tree, etc. so trained —***vt.*** **1.** to train as or on an espalier **2.** to provide with an espalier

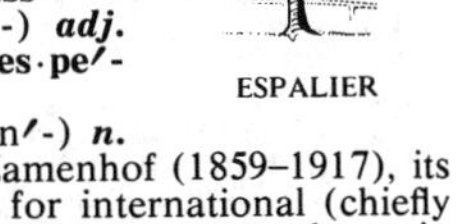

ESPALIER

Es·pa·ña (es pä′nyä) *Sp. name of* SPAIN

es·par·to (es pär′tō) ***n.*** **[**Sp. < L. *spartum* < Gr. *sparton***]** a long, coarse grass of Spain and N Africa, used to make rope, shoes, etc.: also **esparto grass**

es·pe·cial (ə spesh′əl, es pesh′-) ***adj.*** special; particular; exceptional —**es·pe′cial·ly** ***adv.***

Es·pe·ran·to (es′pə rän′tō, -ran′-) ***n.*** **[**after pseudonym of Dr. L. L. Zamenhof (1859–1917), its inventor**]** an artificial language for international (chiefly European) use, based on word bases common to the main European languages

es·pi·al (ə spī′əl, es pī′-) ***n.*** **1.** an espying or being espied; observation **2.** discovery

es·pi·o·nage (es′pē ə näzh′, -nij′) ***n.*** **[**< Fr. < *espion,* a spy < It. *spione* < *spia,* a spy**]** **1.** the act of spying **2.** the use of spies by a government to learn the military secrets of other nations

es·pla·nade (es′plə nād′, -näd′) ***n.*** **[**Fr. < It. < *spianare* < L. *explanare,* to level: see EXPLAIN**]** a level, open space of ground; esp., a public walk or roadway, often along a shore; promenade

es·pous·al (i spou′z'l) ***n.*** **1.** [*often pl.*] *a)* a betrothal ceremony *b)* a wedding **2.** an espousing (of some cause, idea, etc.); advocacy

es·pouse (i spouz′) ***vt.*** **-poused′, -pous′ing** **[**< OFr. < LL. *sponsare* < L. *sponsus:* see SPOUSE**]** **1.** to marry, esp. to take as a wife **2.** to take up, support, or advocate (some cause, idea, etc.) —**es·pous′er** ***n.***

es·pres·so (es pres′ō) ***n.,*** *pl.* **-sos** **[**It. (*caffè*) *espresso,* pressed-out (coffee)**]** coffee prepared in a special machine by forcing steam through finely ground coffee beans

es·prit (es prē′) ***n.*** **[**Fr.**]** **1.** spirit **2.** lively intelligence or wit

es·prit de corps (es prē′ də kôr′) **[**Fr.**]** group spirit; sense of pride, honor, etc. shared by those in the same group or undertaking

es·py (ə spī′, es pī′) ***vt.*** **-pied′, -py′ing** **[**< OFr. *espier:* see SPY**]** to catch sight of; spy

Esq., Esqr. Esquire

-esque (esk) **[**Fr. < It. *-esco***]** *a suffix meaning:* **1.** in the manner or style of *[Romanesque]* **2.** having the quality of *[picturesque]*

Es·qui·mau (es′kə mō′) ***n.,*** *pl.* **-maux′** (-mō′, -mōz′), **-mau′** **[**Fr.**]** *same as* ESKIMO

es·quire (es′kwīr, ə skwīr′) ***n.*** **[**< OFr. < LL. *scutarius,* a shield-bearer < L. *scutum,* a shield**]** **1.** formerly, a candidate for knighthood, acting as attendant for a knight **2.** in England, a member of the gentry ranking just below a knight **3.** [E-] a title of courtesy, usually abbrev. *Esq., Esqr.,* placed after a man's surname

ess (es) ***n.,*** *pl.* **ess′es** **1.** the letter S, s **2.** something shaped like an S

-ess (is, əs; *occas.* es) **[**< OFr. < LL. *-issa* < Gr.**]** *a suffix meaning* female *[lioness]*: as applied to persons (*poetess,* etc.), now often avoided as discriminating

es·say (e sā′; *for n. 1 usually, and for n. 2 always,* es′ā) ***vt.*** **[**< OFr. < LL. < L. *exagium,* a weighing < *ex-,* out of + *agere,* to do**]** to try; attempt —***n.*** **1.** an attempt; trial **2.** a short, personal literary composition of an analytical or interpretive kind —**es·say′er** ***n.***

es·say·ist (es′ā ist) ***n.*** a writer of essays

Es·sen (es′'n) city in W West Germany, in the Ruhr valley: pop. 705,000

es·sence (es′'ns) ***n.*** **[**< OFr. & < L. *essentia* < *esse,* to be**]** **1.** an entity **2.** that which makes something what it is; fundamental nature or most important quality (of something) **3.** *a)* a substance that keeps, in concentrated form, the flavor, fragrance, etc. of the plant, drug, food, etc. from which it is extracted *b)* a solution of such a substance in alcohol *c)* a perfume **4.** *Philos. a)* inward nature; true substance *b)* indispensable conceptual characteristics and relations

Es·sene (es′ēn, ə sēn′) ***n.*** **[**< L. < Gr. *Essēnoi***]** a member of a mystical Jewish sect, existing from the 2d century B.C. to the 2d century A.D.

es·sen·tial (ə sen′shəl) ***adj.*** **1.** of or constituting the essence of something; basic; inherent **2.** absolute; perfect **3.** absolutely necessary; indispensable —***n.*** something necessary, fundamental, or indispensable —**es·sen·ti·al·i·ty** (i sen′shē al′ə tē) ***n.*** —**es·sen′tial·ly** ***adv.*** —**es·sen′tial·ness** ***n.***

es·sen·tial·ism (-iz'm) ***n.*** *Philos.* a theory which stresses essence as opposed to existence

essential oil any volatile oil that gives distinctive odor, flavor, etc. to a plant, flower, or fruit

Es·sex (es′iks), 2d Earl of (*Robert Devereux*) 1566–1601; Eng. soldier & courtier

-est (ist, əst) **[**< OE. *-est, -ost, -ast***]** *a suffix used to form:* **1.** the superlative degree of adjectives and adverbs *[greatest, soonest]* **2.** the archaic 2d pers. sing., pres. indic., of verbs *[goest]*

EST, E.S.T. Eastern Standard Time

est. **1.** established **2.** estimate **3.** estimated

es·tab·lish (ə stab′lish) ***vt.*** **[**< OFr. *establir* < L. < *stabilis,* STABLE[1]**]** **1.** to make stable; settle **2.** to order, ordain, or enact (a law, statute, etc.) permanently **3.** to set up (a nation, business, etc.); found **4.** to cause to be; bring about *[to establish* good relations*]* **5.** to settle in an office, or set up in business or a profession **6.** to make a state institution of (a church) **7.** to cause (a precedent, theory, etc.) to be accepted or recognized **8.** to prove; demonstrate (a case at law) —**es·tab′lish·er** ***n.***

established church the church given exclusive recognition and official support by a government; specif., [E- C-] the Church of England

es·tab·lish·ment (-mənt) ***n.*** **1.** an establishing or being established **2.** a thing established, as a business, military organization, household, etc. —**the Establishment** the ruling inner circle of any nation, institution, etc.

es·tate (ə stāt′) ***n.*** **[**< OFr. *estat,* STATE**]** **1.** *a)* a condition or stage of life *[to come to man's estate]* *b)* status or rank **2.** formerly, any of the three social classes having specific political powers: the clergy (**first estate**), the nobility (**second estate**), and the commons, or bourgeoisie (**third estate**) **3.** property; possessions **4.** landed property; individually owned piece of land containing a residence **5.** *Law a)* the degree, nature, and extent of ownership that one has in land or other property *b)* all the property, real or personal, owned by one

es·teem (ə stēm′) ***vt.*** **[**< OFr. < L. *aestimare,* to value, estimate**]** **1.** to have great regard for; value highly; respect **2.** to hold to be; consider —***n.*** favorable opinion; high regard

Es·tel·la (e stel′ə) **[**Sp. < L. *Stella,* lit., star**]** a feminine name: var. *Estelle*

es·ter (es′tər) ***n.*** **[**G., contr. < *essig,* vinegar + *äther,* ETHER**]** an organic compound, comparable to an inorganic salt, formed by the reaction of an acid and an alcohol, or a phenol: the organic radical of the alcohol or phenol replaces the acid hydrogen of the acid

Es·ther (es′tər) **[**< LL. < Gr. < Heb. *estēr,* prob. < Bab. *Ishtar,* Ishtar**]** **1.** a feminine name **2.** *Bible a)* the Jewish wife of a Persian king: she saved her people from slaughter *b)* the book telling her story: abbrev. **Esth.**

es·thete (es′thēt′) ***n.*** *same as* AESTHETE —**es·thet′ic** (-thet′ik) ***adj.*** —**es·thet′i·cal·ly** ***adv.*** —**es·thet′i·cism** (-ə siz′m) ***n.***

es·thet·ics (es thet′iks) ***n.pl.*** *same as* AESTHETICS

es·ti·ma·ble (es′tə mə b'l) ***adj.*** worthy of esteem —**es′ti·ma·ble·ness** ***n.*** —**es′ti·ma·bly** ***adv.***

es·ti·mate (es′tə māt′; *for n.* -mit) ***vt.*** **-mat′ed, -mat′ing** **[**< L. pp. of *aestimare:* see ESTEEM**]** **1.** to form an opinion about **2.** to determine generally but carefully (size, value, cost, etc.); calculate approximately —***vi.*** to make an estimate —***n.*** **1.** a general calculation of size, value, etc.; esp., an approximate computation of the probable cost of a piece of work made by a person undertaking to do the work **2.** an opinion or judgment —**es′ti·ma′tive** ***adj.*** —**es′ti·ma′tor** ***n.***

es·ti·ma·tion (es′tə mā′shən) ***n.*** **1.** an estimating **2.** an opinion or judgment **3.** esteem; regard

es·ti·val (es′tə v'l, es tī′-) ***adj.*** **[**< L. < *aestivus* < *aestas,* summer**]** of or for summer

es·ti·vate (es′tə vāt′) ***vi.*** **-vat′ed, -vat′ing** **[**< L. pp. of *aestivare* < *aestas,* summer**]** **1.** to spend the summer **2.** to pass the summer in a dormant state, as snails —**es′ti·va′tion** ***n.***

Es·to·ni·a (es tō′nē ə) republic of the U.S.S.R., in NE Europe, on the Baltic Sea: 17,410 sq. mi.; pop. 1,300,000; cap. Tallinn: in full, **Estonian Soviet Socialist Republic** —**Es·to′ni·an** ***adj., n.***

es·top (e stäp′) ***vt.*** **-topped′, -top′ping** **[**< Anglo-Fr. & OFr. < L. *stuppa,* oakum**]** *Law* to stop or prevent (a person) from contradicting a previous statement

es·trange (ə strānj′) ***vt.*** **-tranged′, -trang′ing** **[**OFr. *estranger* < ML. < L. *extraneus,* STRANGE**]** **1.** to remove; keep apart or away **2.** to turn (a person) from an affectionate or friendly attitude to an indifferent, unfriendly, or hostile one; alienate the affections of —**es·trange′ment** *n.*

es·tro·gen (es′trə jən) *n.* [< ESTRUS + -GEN] any of several female sex hormones or similar synthetic compounds —**es′tro·gen′ic** (-jen′ik) *adj.*

estrous cycle the regular female reproductive cycle of most placental mammals that is under hormonal control and includes a period of heat

es·trus (es′trəs, ēs′-) *n.* [ModL. < L. *oestrus* < Gr. *oistros,* frenzy] the periodic sexual excitement, or heat, of most female placental mammals, or the period of this Also **es′trum** (-trəm) —**es′trous** *adj.*

es·tu·ar·y (es′choo wer′ē) *n., pl.* **-ar′ies** [< L. < *aestus,* the tide] an inlet or arm of the sea; esp., the wide mouth of a river, where the tide meets the current —**es′tu·ar′i·al, es′tu·ar·ine** (-in, -īn′) *adj.*

-et (it, ət) [< OFr. *-et,* masc., *-ete* (Fr. *-ette*), fem.] *a suffix added to nouns, meaning* little *[islet]*

e·ta (āt′ə, ēt′ə) *n.* the seventh letter of the Greek alphabet (H, η): it is shown as *ē* in the etymologies of this dictionary

‡é·ta·gère (ā tȧ zher′) *n.* [Fr.] a stand with open shelves like a whatnot, for displaying small art objects, ornaments, etc.

et al. **1.** [L. *et alibi*] and elsewhere **2.** [L. *et alii*] and others

etc. et cetera

et cet·er·a (et set′ər ə, set′rə) [L.] and others; and the like; and the rest; and so forth

et·cet·er·as (-əz, -rəz) *n.pl.* additional things or persons; customary extras

etch (ech) *vt.* [< Du. < G. < MHG. *etzen,* to cause to eat] **1.** to make (a drawing, design, etc.) on metal, glass, etc. by the action of an acid, esp. by coating the surface with wax and letting the acid eat into lines and areas laid bare with a needle **2.** to engrave (a metal plate, glass, etc.) in this way for use in printing such drawings, etc. **3.** to depict or impress sharply and distinctly —*vi.* to make etchings —**etch′er** *n.*

etch·ing (-iŋ) *n.* **1.** an etched plate, drawing, or design **2.** a print made from an etched plate **3.** the art of making such drawings, etc.

e·ter·nal (i tur′n'l) *adj.* [< OFr. < LL. *aeternalis* < L. < *aevum,* an age] **1.** without beginning or end; everlasting **2.** of eternity **3.** forever the same; unchanging *[eternal* truths*]* **4.** never stopping or ending; perpetual *[eternal* rest*]* **5.** seeming never to stop; continual *[eternal* bickering*]* **6.** timeless —**the Eternal** God —**e·ter′nal·ly** *adv.* —**e·ter′nal·ness** *n.*

e·ter·ni·ty (i tur′nə tē) *n., pl.* **-ties** **1.** the quality, state, or fact of being eternal; continuance without end **2.** infinite time; time without beginning or end **3.** a long period of time that seems endless **4.** the endless time after death

e·ter·nize (-nīz) *vt.* **-nized, -niz·ing** **1.** to make eternal **2.** to make famous forever; immortalize Also **e·ter′nal·ize′ -ized′, -iz′ing** —**e·ter′ni·za′tion** *n.*

-eth[1] (əth, ith) *same as* -TH[2] *[fortieth, sixtieth,* etc.*]*

-eth[2] (ith, əth) [< OE. *-(a)th*] archaic ending of the third person singular, present indicative, of verbs *[asketh, bringeth]*: see also -TH[3]

Eth. **1.** Ethiopia **2.** Ethiopian **3.** Ethiopic

E·than (ē′thən) [LL. < Heb. *ēthān,* strength] a masculine name

eth·ane (eth′ān) *n.* [ETH(YL) + -ANE] an odorless, colorless, gaseous hydrocarbon, C_2H_6: it is found in natural gas and used as a fuel, etc.

eth·a·nol (eth′ə nôl′, -nōl′) *n.* [ETHAN(E) + -OL[1]] *same as* ALCOHOL (sense 1)

Eth·el (eth′əl) [< OE. < *æthel,* noble] a feminine name

Eth·el·red II (eth′əl red′) 968–1016; king of England (978–1016): called *the Unready*

eth·ene (eth′ēn) *n. same as* ETHYLENE

e·ther (ē′thər) *n.* [< L. < Gr. *aithēr* < *aithein,* to kindle, burn] **1.** the upper regions of space; clear sky **2.** *Chem.* a volatile, colorless, highly flammable liquid, $(C_2H_5)_2O$: it is used as an anesthetic and a solvent for resins and fats **3.** *Physics* an invisible substance postulated (in older theory) as pervading space and serving as the medium for the transmission of radiant energy, as light waves

e·the·re·al (i thir′ē əl) *adj.* **1.** of or like the ether, or upper regions of space **2.** very light; airy; delicate **3.** heavenly —**e·the′re·al′i·ty** (-al′ə tē), **e·the′re·al·ness** *n.* —**e·the′re·al·ly** *adv.*

e·the·re·al·ize (-ə līz′) *vt.* **-ized′, -iz′ing** to make, or treat as being, ethereal —**e·the′re·al·i·za′tion** *n.*

e·ther·ize (ē′thə rīz′) *vt.* **-ized′, -iz′ing** to anesthetize as by causing to inhale ether fumes —**e′ther·i·za′tion** *n.*

eth·ic (eth′ik) *n.* [see ff.] **1.** ethics or a system of ethics *[the humanist ethic]* **2.** any single element in a system of ethics —*adj. same as* ETHICAL

eth·i·cal (-i k'l) *adj.* [< L. < Gr. *ēthikos* < *ēthos,* character, custom + -AL] **1.** having to do with ethics or morality; of or conforming to moral standards **2.** conforming to professional standards of conduct **3.** designating or of a drug available only on a doctor's prescription —**eth′i·cal′i·ty** (-kal′ə tē), **eth′i·cal·ness** *n.* —**eth′i·cal·ly** *adv.*

eth·ics (eth′iks) *n.pl.* [*with sing. v. in 1 & 2, and occas. 3*] [see prec.] **1.** the study of standards of conduct and moral judgment **2.** a treatise on this study **3.** the system or code of morals of a particular person, religion, group, profession, etc.

E·thi·o·pi·a (ē′thē ō′pē ə) **1.** ancient kingdom in NE Africa, corresponding to modern Sudan & N Ethiopia (sense 2) **2.** country in E Africa, on the Red Sea: 457,000 sq. mi.; pop. 24,769,000; cap. Addis Ababa —**E′thi·o′pi·an** *adj., n.*

E·thi·op·ic (-äp′ik, -ō′pik) *adj.* **1.** *same as* ETHIOPIAN **2.** of the Semitic languages of the Ethiopians —*n.* **1.** the classical Semitic language of Ethiopia, used in the liturgy of the Christian church in Ethiopia **2.** the group of languages spoken by Ethiopians, belonging to the Semitic branch of the Afro-Asiatic language family

eth·nic (eth′nik) *adj.* [< LL. < Gr. *ethnikos,* national < *ethnos,* nation] designating or of any of the basic groups or divisions of mankind or of a heterogeneous population, as distinguished by customs, characteristics, language, etc.; ethnological Also **eth′ni·cal** —*n.* a member of an ethnic group, esp. a member of a minority or nationality group that is part of a larger community —**eth′ni·cal·ly** *adv.*

eth·no- [< Gr. *ethnos,* nation] *a combining form meaning* ethnic group or division; people or peoples *[ethnology]*

eth·no·cen·trism (eth′nə sen′triz'm) *n.* the emotional attitude that one's own ethnic group, nation, or culture is superior to all others —**eth′no·cen′tric** *adj.* —**eth′no·cen′tri·cal·ly** *adv.*

eth·nog·ra·phy (eth näg′rə fē) *n.* the branch of anthropology that deals descriptively with specific cultures, esp. those of nonliterate peoples —**eth·nog′ra·pher** *n.* —**eth′no·graph′ic** (-nə graf′ik), **eth′no·graph′i·cal** *adj.*

eth·nol·o·gy (eth näl′ə jē) *n.* the branch of anthropology that deals with the comparative cultures of various peoples, including their distribution, characteristics, folkways, etc. —**eth·no·log·i·cal** (eth′nə läj′i k'l), **eth′no·log′ic** *adj.* —**eth′no·log′i·cal·ly** *adv.* —**eth·nol′o·gist** *n.*

e·thol·o·gy (e thäl′ə jē, ē-) *n.* [L. *ethologia,* character portrayal < Gr.: see ETHOS & -LOGY] *Biol.* the scientific study of the characteristic behavior patterns of animals —**e·tho·log·i·cal** (eth′ə läj′i k'l, ē′thə-) *adj.* —**e·thol′o·gist** *n.*

e·thos (ē′thäs) *n.* [Gr. *ēthos,* character] the characteristic attitudes, habits, beliefs, etc. of an individual or group

eth·yl (eth′'l) *n.* [ETH(ER) + -YL] the monovalent hydrocarbon radical, C_2H_5, which forms the base of common alcohol, ether, and many other compounds

ethyl alcohol *same as* ALCOHOL (sense 1)

eth·yl·ene (eth′ə lēn′) *n.* [ETHYL + -ENE] a colorless, flammable, gaseous hydrocarbon, C_2H_4, used as a fuel and anesthetic, in hastening the ripening of fruits, and to form polyethylene

ethylene glycol a colorless, viscous alcohol, $C_2H_6O_2$, used as an antifreeze, solvent, in resins, etc.

e·ti·ol·o·gy (ēt′ē äl′ə jē) *n., pl.* **-gies** [< LL. < Gr. < *aitia,* cause + -LOGY] **1.** the assignment of a cause, or the cause assigned *[the etiology* of a folkway*]* **2.** the science of causes or origins **3.** *Med.* the causes of a disease —**e′ti·o·log′ic** (-ə läj′ik), **e′ti·o·log′i·cal** *adj.* —**e′ti·o·log′i·cal·ly** *adv.*

et·i·quette (et′i kət, -ket′) *n.* [Fr. *étiquette,* a ticket] the forms, manners, and ceremonies established by convention as acceptable or required in social relations

Et·na (et′nə) volcanic mountain in E Sicily

E·ton (ēt′'n) town in SC England, near London: site of a private preparatory school for boys (**Eton College**) —**E·to·ni·an** (ē tō′nē ən) *adj., n.*

Eton collar a broad, white linen collar worn with an Eton jacket, or a collar like this

Eton jacket (or **coat**) a black waist-length jacket with broad lapels, left open in front, as that worn by students at Eton

E·tru·ri·a (i troor′ē ə) ancient country in what is now WC Italy

E·trus·can (i trus′kən) *adj.* of Etruria, its people, their language, or culture —*n.* **1.** a native or inhabitant of Etruria **2.** the language of the ancient Etruscans Also **E·tru·ri·an** (i troor′ē ən)

et seq. **1.** [L. *et sequens*] and the following **2.** [L. *et sequentes* or *et sequentia*] and those that follow

Et·ta (et′ə) [dim. of HENRIETTA] a feminine name

-ette (et) [Fr.: see -ET] *a suffix meaning:* **1.** little *[statuette]* **2.** female *[majorette]* **3.** a substitute for *[leatherette]*

é·tude (ā′tōōd, -tyōōd; *Fr.* ā tüd′) *n.* [Fr., STUDY] a musical composition for a solo instrument, designed to give practice in some special point of technique

ETV educational television

ety., etym., etymol. 1. etymological 2. etymology

et·y·mol·o·gy (et′ə mäl′ə jē) ***n.,*** *pl.* **-gies** [< OFr. < L. < Gr. < *etymon,* literal sense of a word, neut. of *etymos,* true + -LOGY] the origin and development of a word, affix, phrase, etc.; the tracing of a word or words back as far as possible, or the branch of linguistics dealing with this —**et′y·mo·log′i·cal** (-mə läj′ə k'l) ***adj.*** —**et′y·mol′o·gist** ***n.*** —**et′y·mol′o·gize′** (-jīz′) ***vt., vi.*** **-gized′, -giz′ing**

eu- [Fr. < Gr.] *a prefix meaning* good, well *[euphemism, eugenic]* : opposed to DYS-, CACO-

Eu *Chem.* europium

eu·ca·lyp·tus (yōō′kə lip′təs) ***n.,*** *pl.* **-tus·es, -ti** (-tī) [ModL. < EU- + Gr. *kalyptos,* covered (from the covering of the buds) < *kalyptein,* to cover] any of a genus of tall, chiefly Australian evergreen trees of the myrtle family, valued for their timber, gum, and oil: also **eu′ca·lypt′**

EUCALYPTUS (tree and leaves)

eucalyptus oil an essential oil from eucalyptus leaves, used as an antiseptic and expectorant

Eu·cha·rist (yōō′kə rist) ***n.*** [< OFr. < LL. < Gr. *eucharistia,* gratitude < *eu-,* well + *charis,* favor] **1.** *same as* HOLY COMMUNION **2.** the consecrated bread and wine used in Holy Communion —**Eu′cha·ris′tic** ***adj.***

eu·chre (yōō′kər) ***n.*** [earlier *yuker, uker* < ?] **1.** a card game for two, three, or four players, played with thirty-two cards **2.** a euchring or being euchred —***vt.*** **-chred, -chring** **1.** to prevent (the trump-declaring opponent at euchre) from taking the required three tricks **2.** [Colloq.] to outwit

Eu·clid[1] (yōō′klid) fl. 300 B.C.; Gr. mathematician: author of a basic work in geometry —**Eu·clid′e·an, Eu·clid′i·an** (-ē ən) ***adj.***

Eu·clid[2] (yōō′klid) [so named (after prec.) by its surveyors] city in NE Ohio: suburb of Cleveland: pop. 60,000

Eu·gene (yōō′jēn; *also, & for sense 2 always,* yōō jēn′) [< Fr. < L. < Gr. < *eugenēs,* well-born] **1.** a masculine name **2.** [after *Eugene* Skinner, early settler] city in W Oreg.: pop. 106,000

Eu·ge·ni·a (yoo jē′nē ə, -jēn′yə) [L., fem. of prec.] a feminine name

eu·gen·ic (yoo jen′ik) ***adj.*** [< Gr.: see EU- & GENESIS] **1.** relating to the bearing of sound offspring **2.** of, relating to, or improved by eugenics —**eu·gen′i·cal·ly** ***adv.***

eu·gen·i·cist (-ə sist) ***n.*** a specialist in or advocate of eugenics: also **eu·gen·ist** (yōō′jə nist, yoo jen′ist)

eu·gen·ics (yoo jen′iks) ***n.pl.*** [*with sing. v.*] the movement devoted to improving the human species by control of hereditary factors in mating

eu·lo·gis·tic (yōō′lə jis′tik) ***adj.*** of or expressing eulogy; praising highly —**eu′lo·gis′ti·cal·ly** ***adv.***

eu·lo·gize (yōō′lə jīz′) ***vt.*** **-gized′, -giz′ing** to praise as in a eulogy —**eu′lo·gist, eu′lo·giz′er** ***n.***

eu·lo·gy (-jē) ***n.,*** *pl.* **-gies** [< ML. < Gr. < *eulegein,* to speak well of] **1.** speech or writing in praise of a person, event, or thing; esp., a funeral oration **2.** high praise

Eu·men·i·des (yoo men′ə dēz′) ***n.pl.*** [L. < Gr. *Eumenidēs,* lit., the gracious ones: a propitiatory euphemism] *same as* FURIES

Eu·nice (yōō′nis) [LL. < Gr. *Eunikē* < *eu-,* well + *nikē,* victory] a feminine name

eu·nuch (yōō′nək) ***n.*** [< L. < Gr. *eunouchos,* bed guardian < *eunē,* bed + *echein,* to keep] a castrated man; esp., one in charge of a harem or employed as a chamberlain in an Oriental palace

eu·pep·si·a (yoo pep′shə, -sē ə) ***n.*** [ModL. < Gr. *eupepsia,* digestibility] good digestion —**eu·pep′tic** ***adj.*** —**eu·pep′ti·cal·ly** ***adv.***

eu·phe·mism (yōō′fə miz'm) ***n.*** [< Gr. < *eu-,* good + *phēmē,* voice < *phanai,* to speak] **1.** the use of a less expressive or direct word or phrase for one considered distasteful or offensive **2.** a word or phrase so substituted (Ex.: *remains* for *corpse*) —**eu′phe·mist** ***n.*** —**eu′phe·mis′tic, eu′phe·mis′ti·cal** ***adj.*** —**eu′phe·mis′ti·cal·ly** ***adv.***

eu·phe·mize (-mīz′) ***vt., vi.*** **-mized′, -miz′ing** to speak or write (of) euphemistically

eu·phon·ic (yoo fän′ik) ***adj.*** **1.** of euphony **2.** *same as* EUPHONIOUS Also **eu·phon′i·cal** —**eu·phon′i·cal·ly** ***adv.***

eu·pho·ni·ous (yoo fō′nē əs) ***adj.*** characterized by euphony; having a pleasant sound; harmonious —**eu·pho′ni·ous·ly** ***adv.*** —**eu·pho′ni·ous·ness** ***n.***

eu·pho·ni·um (-əm) ***n.*** a brass-wind instrument like the baritone but having a more mellow tone

eu·pho·ny (yōō′fə nē) ***n.,*** *pl.* **-nies** [< LL. < Gr. < *eu-,* well + *phōnē,* voice] the quality of having a pleasing sound; pleasant combination of agreeable sounds in spoken words

eu·phor·bi·a (yoo fôr′bē ə) ***n.*** [< L. < *Euphorbus,* physician of 1st cent. A.D.] *same as* SPURGE

eu·pho·ri·a (yoo fôr′ē ə) ***n.*** [ModL. < Gr. < *eu-,* well + *pherein,* to bear] a feeling of well-being or high spirits, specif. *Psychol.* one that seems exaggerated and without cause —**eu·phor′ic** ***adj.***

eu·pho·tic (yoo fōt′ik) ***adj.*** [< EU- + Gr. *phōs* (gen. *phōtos*), a light + -IC] *Ecol.* of or pertaining to the upper portion of a body of water receiving enough light for photosynthesis and plant growth

Eu·phra·tes (yoo frāt′ēz) river flowing from EC Turkey through Syria & Iraq, joining the Tigris to form the Shatt-al-Arab

eu·phu·ism (yōō′fyoo wiz'm) ***n.*** [< *Euphues,* fictitious character in two works by J. LYLY < Gr. *euphyēs,* graceful < *eu-,* well + *phyē,* growth] **1.** an artificial, affected, high-flown style of speaking or writing, esp. such a style of the late 16th cent., characterized by alliteration, balanced sentences, farfetched figures of speech, etc. **2.** an instance of this —**eu′phu·ist** ***n.*** —**eu′phu·is′tic, eu′phu·is′ti·cal** ***adj.***

Eur. **1.** Europe **2.** European

Eur·a·sia (yoo rā′zhə; *chiefly Brit.* -shə) land mass made up of the continents of Europe & Asia

Eur·a·sian (-zhən; *chiefly Brit.* -shən) ***adj.*** **1.** of Eurasia **2.** of mixed European and Asian descent —***n.*** a person with one European parent and one Asian parent, or of mixed European and Asian descent

Eur·a·tom (yoor′ə täm′) European Atomic Energy Community, an agency of the European Economic Community

eu·re·ka (yoo rē′kə) ***interj.*** [Gr. *heurēka*] I have found (it): an exclamation of triumphant achievement

eu·rhyth·mics (yoo rith′miks) ***n.pl.*** *same as* EURYTHMICS —**eu·rhyth′mic** ***adj.*** —**eu·rhyth′my** ***n.***

Eu·rip·i·des (yoo rip′ə dēz′) 479?–406? B.C.; Gr. writer of tragedies —**Eu·rip′i·de′an** (-dē′ən) ***adj.***

Eu·ro- *a combining form meaning* Europe, European *[Eurodollars, Euromart]*

Eu·ro·com·mu·nism (yoor′ə käm′yə niz'm) ***n.*** a form of Communism in Europe stressing the independence of national Communist parties from Soviet Communism, their support of democratic political procedures, etc. —**Eu′ro·com′mu·nist** ***adj., n.***

Eu·ro·mart (yoor′ə märt′) ***n.*** *same as* EUROPEAN ECONOMIC COMMUNITY: also **Eu′ro·mar′ket** (-mär′kit)

Eu·ro·pa (yoo rō′pə) *Gr. Myth.* a Phoenician princess loved by Zeus: disguised as a bull, he carried her off to Crete

Eu·rope (yoor′əp) continent between Asia (or the Ural Mountains) & the Atlantic Ocean: c.3,750,000 sq. mi.; pop. c.637,366,000 —**Eu′ro·pe′an** (-ə pē′ən) ***adj., n.***

European Economic Community the European common market formed in 1958 by Belgium, France, West Germany, Italy, Luxembourg, and the Netherlands: also **European Community**

European plan a system of hotel operation in which the charge to guests covers rooms and service but not meals: distinguished from AMERICAN PLAN

eu·ro·pi·um (yoo rō′pē əm) ***n.*** [ModL. < EUROPE] a chemical element of the rare-earth group: symbol, Eu; at. wt., 151.96; at. no., 63

Eu·ryd·i·ce (yoo rid′ə sē′) *Gr. Myth.* the wife of Orpheus: see ORPHEUS

eu·ryth·mics (yoo rith′miks) ***n.pl.*** [*with sing. v.*] [< L. < Gr. < *eu-,* well + *rhythmos,* RHYTHM] the art of performing various bodily movements in rhythm, usually to musical accompaniment —**eu·ryth′mic, eu·ryth′mi·cal** ***adj.***

Eu·sta·chi·an tube (yoo stā′shən, -shē ən, -kē ən) [after B. *Eustachio* (1520–1574), It. anatomist] a slender tube between the middle ear and the pharynx, which serves to equalize air pressure on both sides of the eardrum

Eu·ter·pe (yoo tur′pē) *Gr. Myth.* the Muse of music and lyric poetry

eu·tha·na·si·a (yōō′thə nā′zhə, -zhē ə) ***n.*** [< Gr. < *eu-,* well + *thanatos,* death] **1.** an easy and painless death **2.** act or method of causing death painlessly to end suffering

eu·then·ics (yoo then′iks) ***n.pl.*** [*with sing. v.*] [< Gr. *euthēnein,* to flourish + -ICS] the movement devoted to improving species and breeds, esp. the human species, by control of environmental factors

eu·troph·ic (-träf′ik, -trō′fik) ***adj.*** [< EU- + Gr. *trophikos* < *trophē,* food] designating or of a lake, pond, etc. rich in mineral and plant nutrients but often deficient in oxygen —**eu′troph·i·ca′tion** ***n.***

Eux·ine Sea (yōōk′sən, -sīn) *ancient name of the* BLACK SEA

ev, EV electron-volt

E·va (ē′və, ev′ə) [var. of EVE] a feminine name

e·vac·u·ate (i vak′yoo wāt′) *vt.* **-at′ed, -at′ing** [< L. pp. of *evacuare* < *e-*, out + *vacuare*, to make empty < *vacuus*, empty] **1.** to make empty; remove the contents of; specif., to remove the air from **2.** to discharge (bodily waste, esp. feces) **3.** to remove (inhabitants, troops, etc.) from (a place or area), as for protective purposes *—vi.* **1.** to withdraw, as from a danger area **2.** to discharge bodily waste **—e·vac′u·a′tion** *n.* **—e·vac′u·a′tive** *adj.* **—e·vac′u·a′tor** *n.* **—e·vac′-u·ee′** *n.*

e·vade (i vād′) *vi.* **e·vad′ed, e·vad′ing** [< Fr. < L. < *e-*, out, from + *vadere*, to go] to be deceitful or clever in avoiding or escaping something *—vt.* **1.** to avoid or escape from by deceit or cleverness **2.** to avoid doing or answering directly *[*to *evade* tax payment*]* **—e·vad′er** *n.*

e·val·u·ate (i val′yoo wāt′) *vt.* **-at′ed, -at′ing** [< Fr. < *é-* (L. *ex-*), out + *valuer*, to VALUE] **1.** to find the value or amount of **2.** to judge or determine the worth or quality of; appraise **—e·val′u·a′tion** *n.* **—e·val′u·a′tive** *adj.*

Ev·an (ev′ən) [W., var. of JOHN] a masculine name

ev·a·nesce (ev′ə nes′) *vi.* **-nesced′, -nesc′ing** [< L. < *e-*, out + *vanescere*, to vanish < *vanus*, empty] to fade from sight like mist or smoke; vanish

ev·a·nes·cent (-nes′'nt) *adj.* tending to fade away; vanishing; fleeting **—ev′a·nes′cence** *n.* **—ev′a·nes′cent·ly** *adv.*

e·van·gel (i van′jəl) *n.* [< OFr. < LL. < L. < Gr. *euangelos*, bringing good news < *eu-*, well + *angelos*, messenger] **1.** the gospel **2.** [E-] any of the four Gospels **3.** an evangelist

e·van·gel·i·cal (ē′van jel′i k'l, ev′ən-) *adj.* **1.** in, of, or according to the Gospels or the New Testament **2.** of those Protestant churches, as the Methodist and Baptist, that emphasize salvation by faith in the atonement of Jesus **3.** *same as* EVANGELISTIC Also **e′van·gel′ic** *—n.* a member of an evangelical church **—e′van·gel′i·cal·ism** *n.* **—e′van-gel′i·cal·ly** *adv.*

e·van·gel·ism (i van′jə liz'm) *n.* **1.** a preaching of, or zealous effort to spread, the gospel, as in revival meetings **2.** any zealous effort in propagandizing for a cause **—e·van′-gel·is′tic** *adj.* **—e·van′gel·is′ti·cal·ly** *adv.*

e·van·gel·ist (-list) *n.* **1.** [E-] any of the four writers of the Gospels; Matthew, Mark, Luke, or John **2.** anyone who evangelizes; esp., a traveling preacher; revivalist

e·van·gel·ize (-līz′) *vt.* **-ized′, -iz′ing** **1.** to preach the gospel to **2.** to convert to Christianity *—vi.* to preach the gospel **—e·van′gel·i·za′tion** *n.*

Ev·ans·ton (ev′ən stən) [after Dr. J. *Evans*, local philanthropist] city in NE Ill.: suburb of Chicago: pop. 74,000

Ev·ans·ville (ev′ənz vil′) [after Gen. R. *Evans*, who served in the War of 1812] city in SW Ind., on the Ohio River: pop. 130,000

e·vap·o·rate (i vap′ə rāt′) *vt.* **-rat′ed, -rat′ing** [< L. pp. of *evaporare* < *e-*, out + *vapor*, vapor] **1.** to change (a liquid or solid) into vapor **2.** to remove moisture from (milk, vegetables, etc.), as by heating, so as to get a concentrated product *—vi.* **1.** to become vapor **2.** to give off vapor **3.** to disappear; vanish **—e·vap′o·ra·bil′i·ty** *n.* **—e·vap′o·ra·ble** *adj.* **—e·vap′o·ra′tion** *n.* **—e·vap′o·ra′tive** *adj.* **—e·vap′o-ra′tor** *n.*

evaporated milk unsweetened milk thickened by evaporation to about half its weight, and then canned: cf. CONDENSED MILK

e·va·sion (i vā′zhən) *n.* **1.** an evading; specif., an avoiding of a duty, question, etc. by deceit or cleverness **2.** a way of doing this; subterfuge

e·va·sive (-siv) *adj.* **1.** tending or seeking to evade; not straightforward; tricky **2.** hard to catch, grasp, etc.; elusive **—e·va′sive·ly** *adv.* **—e·va′sive·ness** *n.*

Eve (ēv) [< LL. < Heb. *ḥawwāh*, lit., ? life] **1.** a feminine name **2.** *Bible* Adam's wife, the first woman: Gen. 3:20

eve (ēv) *n.* [ME., var. of *even* < OE. *æfen*, EVENING] **1.** [Poet.] evening **2.** [*often* E-] the evening or day before a holiday *[*Christmas *Eve]* **3.** the period immediately before some event

Ev·e·line (ev′ə līn′, -lin′) [ONormFr. < *Aveline*, prob. ult. < Gmc.] a feminine name: var. *Evelina*

Ev·e·lyn (ev′ə lin′; *Brit. usually* ēv′lin) [see prec.] a feminine and masculine name

e·ven[1] (ē′vən, -v'n) *adj.* [OE. *efne, efen*] **1.** flat; level; smooth *[even* country*]* **2.** not varying; constant *[*an *even* tempo*]* **3.** calm; tranquil *[*an *even* disposition*]* **4.** in the same plane or line *[even* with the rim*]* **5.** equally balanced **6.** *a)* owing and being owed nothing *b)* with neither a profit nor a loss **7.** revenged for a wrong, insult, etc. **8.** just; fair *[*an *even* exchange*]* **9.** equal or identical in number, quantity, etc. **10.** exactly divisible by two: said of numbers **11.** exact *[*an *even* mile*]* *—adv.* **1.** moreover; however improbable; indeed; fully *[even* a fool could do it*]* **2.** exactly; just *[*it happened *even* as I expected*]* **3.** just as; while *[even* as he spoke, she entered*]* **4.** comparatively; still; yet *[*an *even* worse mistake*]* *—vt., vi.* to make, become, or be even; level (*off*) **—break even** [Colloq.] to finish as neither a winner nor a loser **—even if** despite the fact that; though **—e′ven·ly** *adv.* **—e′ven·ness** *n.*

e·ven[2] (ē′vən) *n.* [see EVE] [Poet.] evening

e·ven·fall (-fôl′) *n.* [Poet.] twilight; dusk

e·ven·hand·ed (-han′did) *adj.* impartial; fair **—e′ven-hand′ed·ly** *adv.* **—e′ven·hand′ed·ness** *n.*

eve·ning (ēv′niŋ) *n.* [< OE. < *æfnian*, to become evening < *æfen*, evening] **1.** the last part of the day and early part of night **2.** in some parts of the South, the period from noon through sunset **3.** the last period, as of life, a career, etc. *—adj.* in, for, or of the evening

evening primrose a plant having yellow flowers that open in the evening

eve·nings (-niŋz) *adv.* during every evening or most evenings

evening star a bright planet, esp. Venus, seen in the western sky soon after sunset

e·ven·song (ē′vən sôŋ′) *n.* **1.** *R.C.Ch.* vespers (see VESPER, sense 2*a)* **2.** *Anglican Ch.* the worship service assigned to the evening

e·ven-ste·ven, e·ven-ste·phen (ē′v'n stē′v'n) *adj.* [rhyming slang < EVEN[1] + STEVEN] [Colloq.] [*often* S-] *same as* EVEN[1] (senses 4–9): also **even steven, even stephen**

e·vent (i vent′) *n.* [OFr. < L. pp. of *evenire*, to happen < *e-*, out + *venire*, to come] **1.** a happening or occurrence, esp. when important **2.** a result; outcome **3.** a particular contest or item in a program of sports **—in any event** no matter what happens; anyhow: also **at all events —in the event of** in case of **—in the event that** if it should happen that

e·ven-tem·pered (ē′vən tem′pərd) *adj.* not quickly angered or excited; placid; calm

e·vent·ful (i vent′fəl) *adj.* **1.** full of outstanding events **2.** having an important outcome **—e·vent′ful·ly** *adv.* **—e·vent′ful·ness** *n.*

e·ven·tide (ē′vən tīd′) *n.* [Archaic] evening

e·ven·tu·al (i ven′choo wəl) *adj.* **1.** [Archaic] depending on events; contingent **2.** happening in the end; ultimate **—e·ven′tu·al·ly** *adv.*

e·ven·tu·al·i·ty (i ven′choo wal′ə tē) *n., pl.* **-ties** a possible event, outcome, or condition; contingency

e·ven·tu·ate (i ven′choo wāt′) *vi.* **-at′ed, -at′ing** to happen in the end; result (often with *in*)

ev·er (ev′ər) *adv.* [< OE. *æfre*] **1.** at all times; always *[*lived happily *ever* after*]* **2.** at any time *[*have you *ever* seen her?*]* **3.** at all; by any chance; in any way *[*how can I *ever* repay you?*]* **4.** [Colloq.] truly; indeed *[*was she *ever* tired!*]* **—ever so** [Colloq.] very **—for ever and a day** always: also **for ever and ever**

Ev·er·est (ev′ər ist, ev′rist), **Mount** peak of the Himalayas, on the border of Nepal & Tibet: highest known mountain in the world: 29,028 ft.

Ev·er·ett (ev′ər it, ev′rit) [< Du. < OFr. < OHG. < *ebur*, wild boar + *harto*, strong] **1.** a masculine name **2.** [after *Everett* Colby, son of a founder] port in NW Wash., near Seattle: pop. 54,000

ev·er·glade (ev′ər glād′) *n.* swampland **—the Everglades** large tract of swampland in S & SE Fla.

ev·er·green (ev′ər grēn′) *adj.* having green leaves throughout the year: opposed to DECIDUOUS *—n.* **1.** an evergreen plant or tree **2.** [*pl.*] the branches and twigs of evergreens, used for decoration

ev·er·last·ing (ev′ər las′tiŋ) *adj.* **1.** lasting forever; eternal **2.** going on for a long time **3.** going on too long; seeming never to stop *—n.* **1.** eternity **2.** *a)* any of various plants whose blossoms keep their color and shape when dried; esp., an annual with pink, lilac, or white flowers *b)* the blossom of such a plant **—the Everlasting** God **—ev′er-last′ing·ly** *adv.*

ev·er·more (-môr′) *adv.* **1.** forever; constantly **2.** [Poet.] for all future time **—for evermore** forever

e·ver·sion (ē vur′zhən, -shən) *n.* an everting or being everted **—e·ver′si·ble** (-sə b'l) *adj.*

e·vert (ē vurt′) *vt.* [L. *evertere* < *e-*, out + *vertere*, to turn] to turn outward or inside out, as an eyelid

ev·er·y (ev′rē; *occas.* -ər ē) *adj.* [< OE. *æfre ælc*, lit., ever each] **1.** each, individually and separately *[every* man among you*]* **2.** the fullest possible; all that there could be *[*he was given *every* chance*]* **3.** each group or interval of (a specified number or time) *[*a pill *every* three hours*]* **—every now and then** from time to time: also [Colloq.] **every so often —every other** each alternate, as the first, third, fifth, etc. **—every which way** [Colloq.] in complete disorder

ev·er·y·bod·y (-bäd′ē, -bud′ē) *pron.* every person; everyone

ev·er·y·day (-dā′) *adj.* **1.** daily *[*one's *everyday* routine*]* **2.** suitable for ordinary days *[everyday* shoes*]* **3.** usual; common *[*an *everyday* occurrence*]*

ev·er·y·one (-wən, -wun′) *pron.* everybody

every one every person or thing of those named *[*remind *every one* of the students*]*

ev·er·y·thing (-thiŋ′) *pron.* **1.** every thing; all **2.** all

things pertinent to a specified matter **3.** the most important thing [money isn't *everything*]
ev·er·y·where (-hwer′, -wer′) ***adv.*** in or to every place
e·vict (i vikt′) ***vt.*** [< L. *evictus*, pp. of *evincere:* see EVINCE] to remove (a tenant) from leased premises by legal procedure, as for failure to pay rent —**e·vic′tion** ***n.***
ev·i·dence (ev′ə dəns) ***n.*** **1.** the condition of being evident **2.** something that makes another thing evident; indication; sign **3.** something that tends to prove **4.** *Law* something presented before a court, as a statement of a witness, an object, etc., which bears on or establishes the point in question —***vt.*** **-denced, -denc·ing 1.** to make evident; indicate; show **2.** to bear witness to; attest —**in evidence** plainly visible or perceptible
ev·i·dent (-dənt, -dent′) ***adj.*** [< OFr. < L. *evidens*, clear < *e-*, from + prp. of *videre*, to see] easy to see or perceive; clear; obvious; plain —**ev′i·dent·ly** ***adv.***
ev·i·den·tial (ev′ə den′shəl) ***adj.*** of, serving as, or providing evidence —**ev′i·den′tial·ly** ***adv.***
e·vil (ē′v'l) ***adj.*** [OE. *yfel*] **1.** *a)* morally bad or wrong; wicked; depraved *b)* resulting from conduct regarded as immoral [an *evil* reputation] **2.** harmful; injurious **3.** offensive **4.** unlucky; disastrous —***n.*** **1.** wickedness; depravity; sin **2.** anything that causes harm, pain, disaster, etc. —**the Evil One** the Devil —**e′vil·ly** ***adv.*** —**e′vil·ness** ***n.***
e·vil·do·er (-do͞o′ər) ***n.*** a person who does evil, esp. habitually —**e′vil·do′ing** ***n.***
evil eye a look which, in superstitious belief, is able to harm or bewitch the one stared at; also, the supposed power to cast such a look: with *the*
e·vil-mind·ed (-mīn′did) ***adj.*** having an evil mind or disposition; specif., *a)* malicious or wicked *b)* inclined to view everything in an evil or obscene way —**e′vil-mind′ed·ly** ***adv.*** —**e′vil-mind′ed·ness** ***n.***
e·vince (i vins′) ***vt.*** **e·vinced′, e·vinc′ing** [< L. < *e-*, intens. + *vincere*, to conquer] to show plainly; make manifest; esp., to show that one has (a specified quality, feeling, etc.) —**e·vin′ci·ble** ***adj.*** —**e·vin′cive** ***adj.***
e·vis·cer·ate (i vis′ə rāt′) ***vt.*** **-at′ed, -at′ing** [< L. pp. of *eviscerare* < *e-*, out + *viscera*, VISCERA] **1.** to remove the entrails from **2.** to deprive of an essential part —**e·vis′cer·a′tion** ***n.***
ev·o·ca·ble (ev′ə kə b'l, i vō′kə b'l) ***adj.*** that can be evoked
ev·o·ca·tion (ev′ə kā′shən, ē′vō-) ***n.*** an evoking —**e·voc·a·tive** (i väk′ə tiv) ***adj.*** —**e·voc′a·tive·ly** ***adv.*** —**e·voc′a·tive·ness** ***n.*** —**ev′o·ca′tor** ***n.***
e·voke (i vōk′) ***vt.*** **e·voked′, e·vok′ing** [< Fr. < L. < *e-*, out + *vocare*, to call < *vox*, the voice] **1.** to conjure up (a spirit, etc.) **2.** to draw forth or elicit (a particular mental image, reaction, etc.) —**e·vok′er** ***n.***
ev·o·lu·tion (ev′ə lo͞o′shən) ***n.*** [< L. pp. of *evolvere:* see EVOLVE] **1.** an unfolding, opening out, or working out; process of development **2.** a result of this; thing evolved **3.** a movement that is part of a series or pattern **4.** a setting free or giving off, as of gas in a chemical reaction **5.** *Biol.* *a)* the development of a species, organism, or organ from its original to its present state *b)* a theory that all species of plants and animals developed from earlier forms: see DARWINIAN THEORY **6.** *Math.* the extracting of a root **7.** *Mil.* any of various maneuvers by which troops, ships, etc. change formation —**ev′o·lu′tion·al** ***adj.*** —**ev′o·lu′tion·al·ly** ***adv.*** —**ev′o·lu′tion·ar′y** ***adj.***
ev·o·lu·tion·ist (-ist) ***n.*** a person who accepts the principles of evolution, esp. in biology —***adj.*** **1.** of the theory of evolution **2.** of evolutionists —**ev′o·lu′tion·ism** ***n.*** —**ev′o·lu′tion·is′tic** ***adj.*** —**ev′o·lu′tion·is′ti·cal·ly** ***adv.***
e·volve (i välv′) ***vt.*** **e·volved′, e·volv′ing** [< L. < *e-*, out + *volvere*, to roll] **1.** to develop by gradual changes; unfold **2.** to set free or give off (gas, heat, etc.) **3.** to produce or change by evolution —***vi.*** **1.** to develop gradually by a process of growth and change **2.** to become disclosed; unfold —**e·volve′ment** ***n.***
Ev·voi·a (ev′ē ə) large Greek island in the Aegean Sea, off the E coast of Greece
ewe (yo͞o; *dial.* yō) ***n.*** [OE. *eowu*] a female sheep
ew·er (yo͞o′ər) ***n.*** [< Anglo-Fr. < OFr. *evier*, ult. < L. *aquarius:* see AQUARIUM] a large water pitcher with a wide mouth
ex (eks) ***prep.*** [L.] without; exclusive of [*ex* interest] —***n.,*** *pl.* **ex′es** [Colloq.] one's divorced husband or wife
ex- [< OFr. or L., akin to Gr. *ex-, exō-*] **1.** *a prefix meaning: a)* from, out [*expel*] *b)* beyond [*excess*] *c)* out of [*expatriate*] *d)* thoroughly [*exterminate*] *e)* upward [*exalt*] It is assimilated to *ef-* before *f; e-* before *b, d, g, l, m, n, r,* and *v;* and, often, *ec-* before *c* or *s* **2.** *a prefix meaning* former, previously [*ex*-president]

EWER

Ex. Exodus
ex. **1.** examined **2.** example **3.** except(ed) **4.** express **5.** extra
ex·ac·er·bate (ig zas′ər bāt′) ***vt.*** **-bat′ed, -bat′ing** [< L. pp. of *exacerbare* < *ex-*, intens. + *acerbus*, harsh, sour] **1.** to make more intense or sharp; aggravate (disease, pain, feelings, etc.) **2.** to irritate —**ex·ac′er·ba′tion** ***n.***
ex·act (ig zakt′) ***adj.*** [< L. pp. of *exigere*, to measure < *ex-*, out + *agere*, to do] **1.** characterized by, requiring, or capable of accuracy of detail; methodical; correct **2.** without variation; precise [an *exact* replica] **3.** being the very (one specified or understood) **4.** strict; severe; rigorous —***vt.*** **1.** to extort (with *from* or *of*) **2.** to demand and get by authority or force (with *from* or *of*) **3.** to make necessary; require —**ex·act′a·ble** ***adj.*** —**ex·act′ness** ***n.*** —**ex·ac′tor, ex·act′er** ***n.***
ex·act·ing (-iŋ) ***adj.*** **1.** making severe demands; not easily satisfied; strict **2.** demanding great care, effort, etc.; arduous —**ex·act′ing·ly** ***adv.*** —**ex·act′ing·ness** ***n.***
ex·ac·tion (ig zak′shən) ***n.*** **1.** an exacting **2.** an extortion **3.** an exacted fee, tax, etc.
ex·ac·ti·tude (ig zak′tə to͞od′, -tyo͞od′) ***n.*** the quality of being exact; precision; accuracy
ex·act·ly (ig zakt′lē) ***adv.*** in an exact manner; accurately; precisely: also used as an affirmative reply, equivalent to "I agree," "quite true"
ex·ag·ger·ate (ig zaj′ə rāt′) ***vt.*** **-at′ed, -at′ing** [< L. pp. of *exaggerare* < *ex-*, out + *aggerare*, to heap up < *agger*, a heap] **1.** to think, speak, or write of as greater than is really so; overstate **2.** to increase or enlarge to an abnormal degree —***vi.*** to give an exaggerated account —**ex·ag′ger·at′ed·ly** ***adv.*** —**ex·ag′ger·a′tion** ***n.*** —**ex·ag′ger·a′tive** ***adj.*** —**ex·ag′ger·a′tor** ***n.***
ex·alt (ig zôlt′) ***vt.*** [< OFr. < LL. *exaltare* < *ex-*, out, up + *altus*, high] to lift up; specif., *a)* to raise in status, dignity, power, wealth, etc. *b)* to praise; glorify; extol *c)* to fill with joy, pride, etc.; elate: used in the passive or in participial form *d)* to heighten or intensify the action or effect of —**ex·alt′ed·ly** ***adv.*** —**ex·alt′er** ***n.***
ex·al·ta·tion (eg′zôl tā′shən) ***n.*** **1.** an exalting or being exalted **2.** elation; rapture
ex·am (ig zam′) ***n.*** [Colloq.] examination
ex·am·i·na·tion (ig zam′ə nā′shən) ***n.*** **1.** an examining or being examined; investigation; inquiry **2.** means or method of examining **3.** a set of questions asked in testing; test —**ex·am′i·na′tion·al** ***adj.*** —**ex·am′i·na·to′ri·al** (-nə tôr′ē əl) ***adj.***
ex·am·ine (ig zam′ən) ***vt.*** **-ined, -in·ing** [< OFr. < L. < *examen*, tongue of a balance, examination] **1.** to look at or into critically or methodically to find out the facts, condition, etc. of; investigate; inspect **2.** to test by questioning to find out the knowledge, skill, etc. of —**ex·am′i·na·ble** ***adj.*** —**ex·am′i·nee′** ***n.*** —**ex·am′in·er, ex·am′i·nant** ***n.***
ex·am·ple (ig zam′p'l) ***n.*** [< OFr. < L. *exemplum* < *eximere*, to take out < *ex-*, out + *emere*, to buy] **1.** something selected to show the nature or character of the rest; sample **2.** a case that serves as a warning or caution **3.** a person or thing to be imitated; model **4.** a problem, as in mathematics, that illustrates a principle or method —***vt.*** **-pled, -pling** [Obs. except in the passive] to exemplify —**set an example** to behave so as to be a pattern or model for others —**without example** having no precedent
ex·as·per·ate (ig zas′pə rāt′) ***vt.*** **-at′ed, -at′ing** [< L. pp. of *exasperare* < *ex-*, out + *asperare*, to roughen < *asper*, rough] to irritate or annoy very much; vex —**ex·as′per·at′ing·ly** ***adv.*** —**ex·as′per·a′tion** ***n.***
Ex·cal·i·bur (eks kal′ə bər) ***n.*** *Arthurian Legend* King Arthur's sword
ex ca·the·dra (eks′ kə thē′drə, kath′i drə) [ModL., lit., from the chair] with the authority that comes from one's rank or office: often used of certain authoritative papal pronouncements on faith or morals
ex·ca·vate (eks′kə vāt′) ***vt.*** **-vat′ed, -vat′ing** [< L. pp. of *excavare* < *ex-*, out + *cavare*, to make hollow < *cavus*, hollow] **1.** to make a hole or cavity in, as by digging; hollow out **2.** to form by hollowing out [to *excavate* a tunnel] **3.** to uncover by digging; unearth **4.** to dig out (earth, soil, etc.) —**ex′ca·va′tion** ***n.*** —**ex′ca·va′tor** ***n.***

EXCAVATION

ex·ceed (ik sēd′) ***vt.*** [< OFr. < L. < *ex-*, out + *cedere*, to go] **1.** to go or be beyond (a limit, measure, etc.) **2.** to be more than or greater than; surpass —*vi.* to surpass others, as in quality or quantity

ex·ceed·ing (-iŋ) ***adj.*** surpassing; extraordinary; extreme —***adv.*** [Archaic] extremely —**ex·ceed′ing·ly** ***adv.***

ex·cel (ik sel′) ***vi., vt.*** **-celled′, -cel′ling** [< OFr. < L. < *ex-*, out of + *-cellere*, to rise] to be better or greater than (another or others)

ex·cel·lence (ek′s'l əns) ***n.*** **1.** the fact or condition of excelling; superiority **2.** something in which a person or thing excels **3.** [E-] *same as* EXCELLENCY

ex·cel·len·cy (-ən sē) ***n.,*** *pl.* **-cies 1.** [E-] a title of honor applied to various persons of high position, as an ambassador, bishop, etc. **2.** *same as* EXCELLENCE

ex·cel·lent (-ənt) ***adj.*** outstandingly good of its kind; of exceptional merit, virtue, etc. —**ex′cel·lent·ly** ***adv.***

ex·cel·si·or (ek sel′sē ôr′; *for n.* ik sel′sē ər) ***adj., interj.*** [L., compar. of *excelsus*, high < *excellere*, EXCEL] higher; always upward —***n.*** long, thin wood shavings used for packing or as stuffing

ex·cept (ik sept′) ***vt.*** [< Fr. < L. < pp. of *excipere* < *ex-*, out + *capere*, to take] to leave out or take out; exclude; omit —***vi.*** to take exception; object —***prep.*** leaving out; other than; but *[*to everyone *except* me*]* —***conj.*** **1.** [Archaic] unless **2.** [Colloq.] were it not that *[*I'd quit *except* I need the money*]* —**except for** if it were not for

ex·cept·ing (-iŋ) ***prep., conj.*** *same as* EXCEPT

ex·cep·tion (ik sep′shən) ***n.*** **1.** an excepting or being excepted; exclusion **2.** anything that is excepted; specif., *a)* a case to which a rule, principle, etc. does not apply *b)* a person or thing different from others of the same class **3.** an objection —**take exception 1.** to object **2.** to resent; feel offended —**ex·cep′tion·less** ***adj.***

ex·cep·tion·a·ble (-ə b'l) ***adj.*** liable or open to exception —**ex·cep′tion·a·bly** ***adv.***

ex·cep·tion·al (-əl) ***adj.*** **1.** being an exception; not ordinary or average; esp., much above average in quality, ability, etc. **2.** *Educ.* needing special attention because mentally gifted or, esp., because mentally or physically handicapped —**ex·cep′tion·al·ly** ***adv.***

ex·cerpt (ik sʉrpt′; *also, and for n. always,* ek′sʉrpt′) ***vt.*** [< L. pp. of *excerpere* < *ex-*, out + *carpere*, to pick] to select or quote (passages from a book, etc.); extract —***n.*** a passage selected or quoted from a book, etc.; extract —**ex·cerp′tion** ***n.***

ex·cess (ik ses′; *also, and for adj. usually,* ek′ses′) ***n.*** [< OFr. < L. pp. of *excedere:* see EXCEED] **1.** action or conduct that goes beyond the usual, reasonable, or lawful limit **2.** intemperance; overindulgence **3.** an amount or quantity greater than is necessary, desirable, etc. **4.** the amount or degree by which one thing exceeds another; surplus —***adj.*** extra or surplus —**in excess of** more than —**to excess** too much

ex·ces·sive (ik ses′iv) ***adj.*** characterized by excess; being too much; immoderate —**ex·ces′sive·ly** ***adv.*** —**ex·ces′sive·ness** ***n.***

ex·change (iks chānj′) ***vt.*** **-changed′, -chang′ing** [< OFr. < VL. hyp. *excambiare:* see EX- & CHANGE] **1.** *a)* to give or transfer (for another thing in return) *b)* to receive or give another thing for (something returned) **2.** to interchange (gifts, etc.) **3.** to give up for a substitute or alternative *[*to *exchange* honor for wealth*]* —***vi.*** **1.** to make an exchange; barter **2.** *Finance* to pass in exchange —***n.*** **1.** a giving or taking of one thing for another; barter **2.** a giving to one another of similar things **3.** the substituting of one thing for another **4.** a thing given or received in exchange **5.** a place for exchanging; esp., a place where trade is carried on by brokers, merchants, etc. *[*a stock *exchange]* **6.** a central office in a telephone system, serving a certain area **7.** *Commerce, Finance* *a)* the payment of debts by negotiable drafts or bills of exchange *b)* a bill of exchange *c)* a fee paid for settling accounts or collecting a draft, bill of exchange, etc. *d)* an exchanging of a sum of money of one country for the equivalent in the money of another country *e)* the rate of exchange; value of one currency in terms of the other —***adj.*** **1.** exchanged **2.** having to do with an exchange —**ex·change′a·bil′i·ty** ***n.*** —**ex·change′a·ble** ***adj.*** —**ex·chang′er** ***n.***

ex·cheq·uer (iks chek′ər, eks′chek ər) ***n.*** [< OFr. *escheki-er:* see CHECKER[1]] **1.** [*often* E-] the British state department in charge of the national revenue **2.** the funds in the British treasury **3.** a treasury **4.** money in one's possession; funds

ex·cis·a·ble (ik sī′zə b'l, ek′sī-) ***adj.*** **1.** subject to an excise tax **2.** that can be cut out

ex·cise[1] (ek′sīz, -sīs; *for v.* ik sīz′) ***n.*** [< MDu. < OFr. *assise:* see ASSIZE] a tax on the manufacture, sale, or consumption of various commodities within a country, as liquor, tobacco, etc.: also **excise tax** —***vt.*** **-cised′, -cis′ing** to put an excise on

ex·cise[2] (ik sīz′) ***vt.*** **-cised′, -cis′ing** [< L. pp. of *excidere* < *ex-*, out + *caedere*, to cut] to remove (a tumor, etc.) by cutting out or away —**ex·ci′sion** (-sizh′ən) ***n.***

ex·cise·man (ik sīz′mən) ***n.,*** *pl.* **-men** (-mən) in Great Britain, an official who collects excises

ex·cit·a·ble (ik sīt′ə b'l) ***adj.*** that is easily excited —**ex·cit′a·bil′i·ty** ***n.*** —**ex·cit′a·bly** ***adv.***

ex·ci·ta·tion (ek′sī tā′shən, -si-) ***n.*** an exciting or being excited (esp. in senses 4, 5, 6)

ex·cite (ik sīt′) ***vt.*** **-cit′ed, -cit′ing** [< OFr. < L. *excitare* < *ex-*, out + pp. of *ciere*, to call] **1.** to put into motion or activity; stir up **2.** to arouse; provoke *[*to *excite* pity*]* **3.** to arouse the feelings and passions of **4.** *Elec.* to supply electric current to, as to produce a magnetic field **5.** *Physics* to raise (a nucleus, atom, etc.) to a higher energy state **6.** *Physiol.* to produce the response of (an organ, tissue, etc.) to a proper stimulus —**ex·cit′a·tive** (-ə tiv), **ex·cit′a·to′ry** (-ə tôr′ē) ***adj.*** —**ex·cit′er, ex·ci′tor** ***n.***

ex·cit·ed (-id) ***adj.*** emotionally aroused; stirred up —**ex·cit′ed·ly** ***adv.***

ex·cite·ment (-mənt) ***n.*** **1.** an exciting or being excited; agitation **2.** something that excites

ex·cit·ing (-iŋ) ***adj.*** causing excitement; stirring, thrilling, etc. —**ex·cit′ing·ly** ***adv.***

ex·claim (iks klām′) ***vi., vt.*** [< Fr. < L. *exclamare* < *ex-*, out + *clamare*, to shout] to cry out; speak or say suddenly and excitedly, as in surprise, anger, etc. —**ex·claim′er** ***n.***

ex·cla·ma·tion (eks′klə mā′shən) ***n.*** **1.** the act of exclaiming **2.** something exclaimed; interjection —**ex·clam·a·to·ry** (iks klam′ə tôr′ē) ***adj.***

exclamation mark (or **point**) a mark (!) used after a word or sentence in writing or printing to express surprise, strong feeling, etc.

ex·clude (iks klo͞od′) ***vt.*** **-clud′ed, -clud′ing** [< L. *excludere* < *ex-*, out + *claudere*, CLOSE[2]] **1.** to refuse to admit, consider, include, etc.; shut out; reject; bar **2.** to put out; force out; expel —**ex·clud′a·ble** ***adj.*** —**ex·clud′er** ***n.***

ex·clu·sion (-klo͞o′zhən) ***n.*** **1.** an excluding or being excluded **2.** a thing excluded —**to the exclusion of** so as to keep out, bar, etc. —**ex·clu′sion·ar′y** ***adj.***

ex·clu·sive (-klo͞o′siv) ***adj.*** **1.** excluding all others; shutting out other considerations, happenings, etc. *[*an *exclusive* interest*]* **2.** excluding all but what is specified **3.** not shared or divided; sole *[*an *exclusive* right*]* **4.** *a)* excluding certain people or groups, as for social or economic reasons *b)* snobbish; undemocratic **5.** dealing only in costly items *[*an *exclusive* shop*]* —**exclusive of** not including or allowing for —**ex·clu′sive·ly** ***adv.*** —**ex·clu′sive·ness** ***n.***

ex·clu·siv·i·ty (eks′klo͞o siv′ə tē) ***n.*** the condition or practice of being exclusive; esp., clannishness or isolationism: also **ex·clu′siv·ism** —**ex·clu′siv·ist** ***n., adj.*** —**ex·clu′siv·is′tic** ***adj.***

ex·com·mu·ni·cate (eks′kə myo͞o′nə kāt′; *for adj. and n., usually* -kit) ***vt.*** **-cat′ed, -cat′ing** to exclude, by ecclesiastical authority, from the sacraments, privileges, etc. of a church; censure by cutting off from communion with a church —***adj.*** excommunicated —***n.*** an excommunicated person —**ex′com·mu′ni·ca′tion** ***n.*** —**ex′com·mu′ni·ca′tive** ***adj.*** —**ex′com·mu′ni·ca′tor** ***n.*** —**ex′com·mu′ni·ca·to′ry** (-kə tôr′ē) ***adj.***

ex·co·ri·ate (ik skôr′ē āt′) ***vt.*** **-at′ed, -at′ing** [< L. pp. of *excoriare* < *ex-*, off + *corium*, the skin] **1.** to strip, scratch, or rub off the skin of **2.** to denounce harshly —**ex·co′ri·a′tion** ***n.***

ex·cre·ment (eks′krə mənt) ***n.*** [< Fr. < L. < *excretus:* see EXCRETE] waste matter from the bowels; feces —**ex′cre·men′tal** (-men′t'l) ***adj.***

ex·cres·cence (iks kres′'ns) ***n.*** [< OFr. < L. < *ex-*, out + *crescere*, to grow] **1.** [Now Rare] a normal outgrowth, as a fingernail **2.** an abnormal or disfiguring outgrowth, as a bunion —**ex·cres′cent** ***adj.***

ex·cres·cen·cy (-'n sē) ***n.*** **1.** the condition of being excrescent **2.** *pl.* **-cies** *same as* EXCRESCENCE

ex·cre·ta (eks krēt′ə) ***n.pl.*** waste matter excreted from the body, esp. sweat or urine —**ex·cre′tal** ***adj.***

ex·crete (iks krēt′) ***vt., vi.*** **-cret′ed, -cret′ing** [< L. *excretus*, pp. of *excernere* < *ex-*, out of + *cernere*, to sift] to separate (waste matter) from the blood or tissue and eliminate from the body —**ex·cre′tion** ***n.*** —**ex·cre′tive** ***adj.***

ex·cre·to·ry (eks′krə tôr′ē) ***adj.*** of or for excreting —***n.,*** *pl.* **-ries** an excretory organ

ex·cru·ci·ate (iks kro͞o′shē āt′) ***vt.*** **-at′ed, -at′ing** [< L. pp. of *excruciare* < *ex-*, intens. + *cruciare*, to crucify < *crux* (gen. *crucis*), a cross] **1.** to cause intense bodily pain to; torture **2.** to subject to mental anguish; torment —**ex·cru′ci·a′tion** ***n.***

ex·cru·ci·at·ing (-āt′iŋ) ***adj.*** **1.** causing intense physical or mental pain **2.** intense or extreme *[excruciating* care*]* —**ex·cru′ci·at′ing·ly** ***adv.***

ex·cul·pate (eks′kəl pāt′, ik skul′pāt) ***vt.*** **-pat′ed, -pat′ing** [< L. *ex*, out + pp. of *culpare*, to blame < *culpa*, fault] to free from blame; declare or prove guiltless —**ex·cul·pa·ble** (ik skul′pə b'l) ***adj.*** —**ex′cul·pa′tion** ***n.*** —**ex·cul′pa·to′ry** ***adj.***

ex·cur·sion (ik skʉr′zhən) ***n.*** [< L. < pp. of *excurrere* <

ex-, out + *currere*, to run] **1.** a short trip or journey, as for pleasure **2.** a round trip (on a train, bus, etc.) at special reduced rates **3.** a group taking such a trip **4.** a deviation or digression **5.** [Obs.] a military sortie; raid —*adj.* of or for an excursion —**ex·cur′sion·ist** *n.*

ex·cur·sive (-siv) *adj.* rambling; desultory; digressive —**ex·cur′sive·ly** *adv.* —**ex·cur′sive·ness** *n.*

ex·cuse (ik skyo͞oz′; *for n.* -skyo͞os′) *vt.* **-cused′, -cus′ing** [< OFr. < L. *excusare* < *ex-*, from + *causa*, a charge] **1.** to try to free (a person) of blame **2.** to try to minimize (a fault); apologize or give reasons for **3.** to disregard (an offense or fault); overlook *[excuse* my rudeness*]* **4.** to release from an obligation, promise, etc. **5.** to permit to leave **6.** to serve as an explanation or justification for; justify; absolve —*n.* **1.** a plea in defense of some action; apology **2.** a release from obligation, duty, etc. **3.** something that excuses; justifying factor **4.** a pretended reason; pretext —**a poor** (or **bad,** etc.) **excuse for** a very inferior example of —**excuse oneself** **1.** to apologize **2.** to ask for permission to leave —**ex·cus′a·ble** *adj.* —**ex·cus′a·bly** *adv.* —**ex·cus′er** *n.*

ex·ec (ig zek′) *n.* [Colloq.] an executive officer

exec. **1.** executive **2.** executor

ex·e·cra·ble (ek′si krə b'l) *adj.* [L. *execrabilis*] abominable; detestable —**ex′e·cra·bly** *adv.*

ex·e·crate (-krāt′) *vt.* **-crat′ed, -crat′ing** [< L. pp. of *execrare*, to curse < *ex-*, out + *sacrare*, to consecrate < *sacer*, sacred] **1.** orig., to call down evil upon; curse **2.** to denounce scathingly **3.** to loathe; detest; abhor —*vi.* to curse —**ex′e·cra′tion** *n.* —**ex′e·cra′tive, ex′e·cra·to′ry** (-krə tôr′ē) *adj.* —**ex′e·cra′tor** *n.*

ex·e·cute (ek′sə kyo͞ot′) *vt.* **-cut′ed, -cut′ing** [< OFr. < L. pp. of *ex(s)equi* < *ex-*, intens. + *sequi*, to follow] **1.** to carry out; do; perform; fulfill **2.** to carry into effect; administer (laws, etc.) **3.** to put to death in accordance with a legally imposed sentence **4.** to create in accordance with an idea, plan, etc. **5.** to perform (a piece of music, etc.) **6.** *Law* to make valid (a deed, contract, etc.) as by signing, sealing, and delivering —**ex′e·cut′a·ble** *adj.* —**ex′e·cut′er** *n.*

ex·e·cu·tion (ek′sə kyo͞o′shən) *n.* **1.** the act of executing; specif., *a)* a carrying out, doing, etc. *b)* a putting to death in accordance with a legally imposed sentence **2.** the manner of doing or producing something, as of performing a piece of music **3.** *Law* a writ, issued by a court, giving authority to put a judgment into effect

ex·e·cu·tion·er (-ər) *n.* a person who carries out the death penalty imposed by a court

ex·ec·u·tive (ig zek′yə tiv) *adj.* **1.** of, capable of, or concerned with, carrying out duties, functions, etc., as in a business **2.** empowered and required to administer (laws, government affairs, etc.) **3.** of managerial personnel or functions —*n.* **1.** a person, group, or branch of government empowered and required to administer the laws and affairs of a nation **2.** a person whose function is to administer or manage affairs, as of a corporation

Executive Mansion **1.** the White House (in Washington, D.C.), official home of the President of the U.S. **2.** the official home of the governor of a State

executive officer *Mil.* an officer who is chief assistant to the commanding officer

ex·ec·u·tor (ek′sə kyo͞ot′ər; *for 2* ig zek′yə tər) *n.* **1.** a person who gets something done or produced **2.** a person appointed by a testator to carry out the provisions in his will —**ex·ec′u·to′ri·al** (-tôr′ē əl), **ex·ec′u·to′ry** *adj.* —**ex·ec′u·trix** (-triks) *n.fem., pl.* **-trix·es, -tri′ces** (-trī′sēz)

ex·e·ge·sis (ek′sə jē′sis) *n., pl.* **-ge′ses** (-sēz) [< Gr. < *ex-*, out + *hēgeisthai*, to guide] analysis or interpretation of a word, literary passage, etc., esp. of the Bible —**ex′e·get′ic** (-jet′ik), **ex′e·get′i·cal** *adj.* —**ex′e·get′i·cal·ly** *adv.*

ex·e·gete (ek′sə jēt′) *n.* an expert in exegesis

ex·em·plar (ig zem′plär, -plər) *n.* [< OFr. < LL. < L. *exemplum*, EXAMPLE] **1.** one that is considered worthy of imitation; model **2.** a typical specimen or example

ex·em·pla·ry (-plə rē) *adj.* **1.** serving as a model or example; worth imitating *[exemplary* behavior*]* **2.** serving as a warning *[exemplary* punishment*]* **3.** serving as a sample; illustrative —**ex·em·pla·ri·ly** (eg′zəm pler′ə lē) *adv.* —**ex·em′pla·ri·ness** *n.*

exemplary damages *Law* damages beyond the actual loss, imposed as a punishment

ex·em·pli·fy (ig zem′plə fī′) *vt.* **-fied′, -fy′ing** [< OFr. < ML. < L. *exemplum*, an example + *facere*, to make] **1.** to show by example; serve as an example of **2.** to make a certified copy of (a document, etc.) under seal —**ex·em′pli·fi·ca′tion** *n.*

ex·empt (ig zempt′) *vt.* [< Anglo-Fr. < L. pp. of *eximere*: see EXAMPLE] to free from a rule or obligation which applies to others; excuse; release —*adj.* not subject to or bound by a rule, obligation, etc. applying to others —*n.* an exempted person —**ex·empt′i·ble** *adj.* —**ex·emp′tion** *n.*

ex·er·cise (ek′sər sīz′) *n.* [< OFr. < L. < pp. of *exercere*, to drive out (farm animals to work) < *ex-*, out + *arcere*, to enclose] **1.** active use or operation *[*the *exercise* of wit*]* **2.** performance (of duties, etc.) **3.** activity for training or developing the body or mind; esp., bodily exertion for the sake of health **4.** a series of movements to strengthen or develop some part of the body **5.** a problem or task to be worked out for developing some technical skill, as in mathematics **6.** [*pl.*] a set program of formal speeches, etc., as at a graduation —*vt.* **-cised′, -cis′ing** **1.** to use; employ *[*to *exercise* self-control*]* **2.** to put (the body, mind, etc.) into use so as to develop or train **3.** to drill (troops) **4.** to engage the attention and energy of, esp. so as to worry, perplex, or harass **5.** to exert or have (influence, control, etc.) —*vi.* to take exercise; do exercises —**ex′er·cis′a·ble** *adj.* —**ex′er·cis′er** *n.*

ex·ert (ig zurt′) *vt.* [< L. < *exserere*, to stretch out < *ex-*, out + *serere*, to join] **1.** to put into action or use *[exert* your will*]* **2.** to apply (oneself) with great energy or effort —**ex·er′tive** *adj.*

ex·er·tion (ig zur′shən) *n.* **1.** the act, fact, or process of exerting **2.** energetic activity; effort

ex·e·unt (ek′sē ənt, -o͝ont) [L.] they (two or more characters) leave the stage: a stage direction

exeunt om·nes (äm′nēz) [L.] all (of the characters who are on stage) leave: a stage direction

ex·fo·li·ate (eks fō′lē āt′) *vt., vi.* **-at′ed, -at′ing** [< LL. pp. of *exfoliare*, to strip of leaves < *ex-*, out + *folium*, a leaf] to cast or come off in flakes, scales, or layers, as skin, bark, etc. —**ex·fo′li·a′tion** *n.* —**ex·fo′li·a′tive** *adj.*

ex·hale (eks hāl′, ek sāl′) *vi.* **-haled′, -hal′ing** [< Fr. < L. *exhalare* < *ex-*, out + *halare*, to breathe] **1.** to breathe forth air **2.** to rise into the air as vapor; evaporate —*vt.* **1.** to breathe forth (air) **2.** to give off (vapor, fumes, etc.) —**ex·ha·la·tion** (eks′hə lā′shən, ek′sə-) *n.*

ex·haust (ig zôst′) *vt.* [< L. pp. of *exhaurire* < *ex-*, out + *haurire*, to draw] **1.** to draw off or let out completely (air, gas, etc.), as from a container **2.** to use up; expend completely **3.** to empty completely; drain *[*to *exhaust* a well*]* **4.** to drain of power, resources, etc. **5.** to tire out; weaken **6.** to deal with or study completely and thoroughly *[*to *exhaust* a subject*]* —*vi.* to be let out, as gas or steam from an engine —*n.* **1.** the withdrawing of air, gas, etc. from a container or enclosure, as by means of a fan or pump **2.** *a)* the discharge of used steam, gas, etc. from the cylinders of an engine at the end of every working stroke of the pistons *b)* the pipe through which such steam, gas, etc. is released **3.** something given off, as fumes from a gasoline engine —**ex·haust′i·bil′i·ty** *n.* —**ex·haust′i·ble** *adj.* —**ex·haust′less** *adj.*

ex·haus·tion (ig zôs′chən) *n.* **1.** an exhausting **2.** the state of being exhausted; esp., *a)* great fatigue or weariness *b)* complete consumption

ex·haus·tive (ig zôs′tiv) *adj.* **1.** exhausting or tending to exhaust **2.** leaving nothing out; covering every detail —**ex·haus′tive·ly** *adv.* —**ex·haus′tive·ness** *n.*

ex·hib·it (ig zib′it) *vt.* [< L. pp. of *exhibere* < *ex-*, out + *habere*, to hold, have] **1.** to show; display **2.** to present to public view **3.** *Law* to present (evidence, etc.) officially to a court —*vi.* to put pictures, wares, etc. on public display —*n.* **1.** a show; display **2.** an object or objects displayed publicly **3.** *Law* an object produced as evidence in a court —**ex·hib′i·tor, ex·hib′it·er** *n.*

ex·hi·bi·tion (ek′sə bish′ən) *n.* **1.** the act or fact of exhibiting **2.** the thing or things exhibited **3.** a public show or display, as of art

ex·hi·bi·tion·ism (-iz'm) *n.* **1.** a tendency to call attention to oneself or show off one's talents, skill, etc. **2.** *Psychol.* a tendency to expose parts of the body that are conventionally concealed —**ex′hi·bi′tion·ist** *n.* —**ex′hi·bi′tion·is′tic** *adj.*

ex·hib·i·tive (ig zib′ə tiv) *adj.* serving or tending to exhibit (usually with *of*)

ex·hil·a·rate (ig zil′ə rāt′) *vt.* **-rat′ed, -rat′ing** [< L. pp. of *exhilarare* < *ex-*, intens. + *hilarare*, to gladden < *hilaris*, glad] **1.** to make merry or lively **2.** to stimulate —**ex·hil′a·ra′tive** *adj.* —**ex·hil′a·ra′tion** *n.*

ex·hort (ig zôrt′) *vt., vi.* [< L. *exhortari* < *ex-*, out + *hortari*, to urge] to urge earnestly by advice, warning, etc.; entreat —**ex·hor·ta·tion** (eg′zôr tā′shən, ek′sər-) *n.* —**ex·hor′ta·to′ry** (-tə tôr′ē), **ex·hor′ta·tive** *adj.* —**ex·hort′er** *n.*

ex·hume (ig zyo͞om′, iks hyo͞om′) *vt.* **-humed′, -hum′ing** [< ML. *exhumare* < L. *ex*, out + *humus*, the ground] **1.** to dig out of the earth; disinter 2. to reveal —**ex·hu·ma·tion** (eks′hyoo mā′shən) *n.*

ex·i·gen·cy (ek′sə jən sē) *n., pl.* **-cies** [see ff.] 1. urgency 2. a situation calling for immediate action or attention 3. [*pl.*] pressing needs; demands [the *exigencies* of a situation] Also **ex′i·gence**

ex·i·gent (ek′sə jənt) *adj.* [< L. prp. of *exigere:* see EXACT] 1. calling for immediate action or attention; urgent 2. requiring more than is reasonable; demanding; exacting —**ex′i·gent·ly** *adv.*

ex·ig·u·ous (eg zig′yoo wəs) *adj.* [< L. < *exigere:* see EXACT] scanty; little; small; meager —**ex·i·gu·i·ty** (ek′sə-gyoo′ə tē) *n.*

ex·ile (eg′zīl, ek′sīl) *n.* [< OFr. < L. *exilium* < *exul,* an exile] 1. a prolonged, often enforced, living away from one's country, community, etc.; banishment, sometimes self-imposed 2. a person in exile —*vt.* **-iled, -il·ing** to force (a person) to leave his country, community, etc.; banish —**ex·il·ic** (ig zil′ik, ik sil′ik) *adj.*

ex·ist (ig zist′) *vi.* [< Fr. < L. *existere* < *ex-,* forth + *sistere,* to cause to stand] 1. to have reality or actual being; be 2. to occur or be present (*in*) 3. to continue being; live —**ex·ist′ent** *adj.*

ex·ist·ence (-əns) *n.* 1. the act of existing; state or fact of being 2. continuance of being; life; living 3. occurrence 4. a manner of existing 5. a being; entity; thing that exists

ex·is·ten·tial (eg′zis ten′shəl, ek′sis-) *adj.* 1. of, based on, or expressing existence 2. of, relating to, or as conceived of in, existentialism

ex·is·ten·tial·ism (-shəl iz′m) *n.* a philosophical and literary movement which holds that man is totally free and responsible for his acts, and that this responsibility causes man's dread and anguish —**ex′is·ten′tial·ist** *n.*

ex·it (eg′zit, ek′sit) *n.* [L. *exitus,* orig. pp. of *exire* < *ex-,* out + *ire,* to go] 1. an actor's departure from the stage 2. a going out; departure 3. a way out 4. [L., 3d pers. sing., pres. indic., of *exire*] he (or she) leaves: a stage direction —*vi.* to leave a place; depart

‡**ex li·bris** (eks lē′bris, lī′-) [L.] 1. from the library of: an inscription on bookplates 2. a bookplate

ex·o- [< Gr. *exō,* without] *a prefix meaning* outside, outer, outer part

ex·o·bi·ol·o·gy (ek′sō bī äl′ə jē) *n.* [EXO- + BIOLOGY] the study of the possible existence of living organisms elsewhere in the universe than on earth —**ex′o·bi′o·log′i·cal** *adj.* —**ex′o·bi·ol′o·gist** *n.*

ex·o·carp (ek′sō kärp′) *n.* [EXO- + -CARP] the outer layer of a ripened ovary or fruit; peel

ex·o·crine (ek′sə krin, -krīn′, -krēn′) *adj.* [EXO- + (ENDO)CRINE] designating or of a gland secreting externally, either directly or through a duct —*n.* any such gland, as a sweat gland, or its secretion

Exod. Exodus

ex·o·dus (ek′sə dəs) *n.* [< LL. < Gr. < *ex-,* out + *hodos,* way] a going out or forth, esp. in a large group —[E-] 1. the departure of the Israelites from Egypt (with *the*) 2. the second book of the Pentateuch, which describes this

ex of·fi·ci·o (eks′ ə fish′ē ō′) [L., lit., from office] by virtue of one's office, or position

ex·og·a·my (ek säg′ə mē) *n.* [EXO- + -GAMY] the custom of marrying only outside one's own tribe, clan, etc.; outbreeding —**ex·og′a·mous, ex·o·gam·ic** (ek′sə gam′ik) *adj.*

ex·og·e·nous (ek säj′ə nəs) *adj.* [EXO- + -GENOUS] 1. developing from without; originating externally 2. *Biol.* of or relating to external factors, as food, light, etc., that have an effect on an organism —**ex·og′e·nous·ly** *adv.*

ex·on·er·ate (ig zän′ə rāt′) *vt.* **-at′ed, -at′ing** [< L. pp. of *exonerare* < *ex-,* out + *onerare,* to load < *onus,* a burden] to free from a charge of guilt; declare or prove blameless —**ex·on′er·a′tion** *n.* —**ex·on′er·a′tive** *adj.* —**ex·on′er·a′tor** *n.*

ex·oph·thal·mos (ek′säf thal′məs) *n.* [< Gr. < *ex-,* out + *ophthalmos,* an eye] abnormal bulging out of the eyeball, caused by disease: also **ex′oph·thal′mus, ex′oph·thal′mi·a** (-mē ə) —**ex′oph·thal′mic** *adj.*

ex·or·bi·tant (ig zôr′bə tənt) *adj.* [< L. prp. of *exorbitare* < *ex-,* out + *orbita,* a track, ORBIT] going beyond what is reasonable, fair, usual, etc., as a price; excessive; extravagant —**ex·or′bi·tance, ex·or′bi·tan·cy** *n.* —**ex·or′bi·tant·ly** *adv.*

ex·or·cise, ex·or·cize (ek′sôr sīz′) *vt.* **-cised′** or **-cized′, -cis′ing** or **-ciz′ing** [< LL. < Gr. < *ex-,* out + *horkizein,* to make one swear < *horkos,* an oath] 1. to drive (an evil spirit) out or away by ritual prayers, incantations, etc. 2. to free from such a spirit —**ex′or·cis′er, ex′or·ciz′er** *n.*

ex·or·cism (-siz′m) *n.* 1. the act of exorcising 2. a formula or ritual used in exorcising —**ex′or·cist** *n.*

ex·or·di·um (ig zôr′dē əm) *n., pl.* **-di·ums, -di·a** (-ə) [< L. < *ex-,* from + *ordiri,* to begin] 1. a beginning 2. the opening part of a speech, treatise, etc.

ex·o·skel·e·ton (ek′sō skel′ə t′n) *n. Zool.* any hard, external supporting structure, as the shell of crustaceans —**ex′o·skel′e·tal** *adj.*

ex·ot·ic (ig zät′ik) *adj.* [< L. < Gr. *exōtikos* < *exō,* outside] 1. foreign; not native 2. strangely beautiful, enticing, etc. —*n.* 1. a foreign or imported thing 2. a plant that is not native —**ex·ot′i·cal·ly** *adv.* —**ex·ot′i·cism** (-ə siz′m) *n.*

exotic dancer a belly dancer, stripteaser, or the like

exp. 1. expenses 2. export 3. express

ex·pand (ik spand′) *vt.* [< L. < *ex-,* out + *pandere,* to spread] 1. to spread out; open out; stretch out; unfold 2. to make greater in size, scope, etc.; enlarge; dilate 3. to enlarge upon (a topic, idea, etc.); develop in detail or fully —*vi.* to spread out, unfold, enlarge, etc. —**ex·pand′er** *n.*

expanded metal sheet metal stretched out in latticelike strips, used as lath for plastering, etc.

ex·panse (ik spans′) *n.* a large, open area or unbroken surface; wide extent; great breadth

ex·pan·si·ble (ik span′sə b′l) *adj.* that can be expanded: also **ex·pand′a·ble** —**ex·pan′si·bil′i·ty** *n.*

ex·pan·sion (ik span′shən) *n.* 1. an expanding or being expanded; enlargement 2. an expanded thing or part 3. the extent or degree of expansion 4. a development or full treatment, as of a topic

ex·pan·sion·ar·y (-er′ē) *adj.* directed toward expansion

ex·pan·sion·ism (-iz′m) *n.* the policy of expanding a nation's territory or its sphere of influence, often at the expense of other nations —**ex·pan′sion·ist** *adj., n.* —**ex·pan′sion·is′tic** *adj.*

ex·pan·sive (ik span′siv) *adj.* 1. tending or being able to expand 2. of, or working by means of, expansion 3. broad; extensive; comprehensive 4. sympathetic; demonstrative [an *expansive* person] —**ex·pan′sive·ly** *adv.* —**ex·pan′sive·ness** *n.*

ex·pa·ti·ate (ik spā′shē āt′) *vi.* **-at′ed, -at′ing** [< L. pp. of *expatiari,* to wander < *ex-,* out + *spatiari,* to walk < *spatium,* space] to speak or write in great detail (*on* or *upon*) —**ex·pa′ti·a′tion** *n.*

ex·pa·tri·ate (eks pā′trē āt′; *for adj. & n., usually* -it) *vt.* **-at′ed, -at′ing** [< ML. pp. of *expatriare* < L. *ex,* out of + *patria,* fatherland < *pater,* father] 1. to exile or banish 2. to withdraw (oneself) from one's native land —*adj.* expatriated —*n.* an expatriated person —**ex·pa′tri·a′tion** *n.*

ex·pect (ik spekt′) *vt.* [< L. < *ex-,* out + *spectare,* to look] 1. to look for as likely to occur or appear; look forward to; anticipate 2. to look for as due, proper, or necessary [to *expect* a reward] 3. [Colloq.] to suppose; presume; guess —**be expecting** [Colloq.] to be pregnant —**ex·pect′a·ble** *adj.*

ex·pect·an·cy (ik spek′tən sē) *n., pl.* **-cies** 1. an expecting or being expected; expectation 2. that which is expected, esp. on a statistical basis [life *expectancy*] Also **expect′ance**

ex·pect·ant (-tənt) *adj.* expecting; specif., *a*) having or showing expectation *b*) waiting, as for a position, the birth of a child, etc. —*n.* a person who expects something —**ex·pect′ant·ly** *adv.*

ex·pec·ta·tion (ek′spek tā′shən) *n.* 1. a looking forward to; anticipation 2. a looking for as due, proper, or necessary 3. a thing looked forward to 4. [*also pl.*] prospect of future success, prosperity, etc. —**in expectation** in the state of being looked for —**ex·pec·ta·tive** (ik spek′tə tiv) *adj.*

ex·pec·to·rant (ik spek′tər ənt) *adj.* causing or easing the bringing up of phlegm, mucus, etc. from the respiratory tract —*n.* an expectorant medicine

ex·pec·to·rate (-tə rāt′) *vt., vi.* **-rat′ed, -rat′ing** [< L. pp. of *expectorare* < *ex-,* out + *pectus* (gen. *pectoris*), breast] 1. to cough up and spit out (phlegm, mucus, etc.) 2. to spit —**ex·pec′to·ra′tion** *n.*

ex·pe·di·en·cy (ik spē′dē ən sē) *n., pl.* **-cies** 1. the quality or state of being expedient; suitability for a given purpose 2. the doing or consideration of what is of use or advantage rather than what is right or just; self-interest 3. an expedient Also **ex·pe′di·ence**

ex·pe·di·ent (-ənt) *adj.* [< OFr. < L. prp. of *expedire:* see ff.] 1. useful for effecting a desired result; suited to the circumstances; convenient 2. based on what is of use or advantage rather than what is right or just; guided by self-interest —*n.* an expedient thing —**ex·pe′di·ent·ly** *adv.*

ex·pe·dite (ek′spə dīt′) *vt.* **-dit′ed, -dit′ing** [< L. pp. of *expedire,* lit., to free one caught by the feet < *ex-,* out + *pes* (gen. *pedis*), foot] 1. to speed up or make easy the progress or action of; facilitate 2. to do quickly

ex·pe·dit·er (-ər) *n.* a person who expedites; esp., one employed, as in industry, to expedite urgent or involved projects

ex·pe·di·tion (ek′spə dish′ən) *n.* [< OFr. < L. < pp. of *expedire:* see EXPEDITE] 1. *a*) a journey, voyage, etc., as for exploration or battle *b*) the people, ships, etc. on such a journey 2. efficient speed; dispatch —**ex′pe·di′tion·ar′y** *adj.*

ex·pe·di·tious (ek′spə dish′əs) ***adj.*** efficient and speedy; prompt —**ex′pe·di′tious·ly *adv.***

ex·pel (ik spel′) ***vt.* -pelled′, -pel′ling** [< L. *expellere* < *ex-*, out + *pellere*, to thrust] **1.** to drive out by force; force out; eject **2.** to dismiss or send away by authority —**ex·pel′la·ble *adj.*** —**ex·pel·lee** (ek′spel ē′) ***n.*** —**ex·pel′ler *n.***

ex·pend (ik spend′) ***vt.*** [< L. *expendere*, to pay out < *ex-*, out + *pendere*, to weigh] **1.** to spend **2.** to consume by using; use up —**ex·pend′er *n.***

ex·pend·a·ble (ik spen′də b'l) ***adj.*** **1.** that can be expended **2.** *Mil.* designating equipment (and hence, men) expected to be used up (or sacrificed) in service —***n.*** a person or thing considered expendable —**ex·pend′a·bil′i·ty *n.*** —**ex·pend′a·bly *adv.***

ex·pend·i·ture (-də chər) ***n.*** **1.** an expending; a spending or using up of money, time, etc. **2.** the amount of money, time, etc. expended

ex·pense (ik spens′) ***n.*** [< Anglo-Fr. < LL. *expensa* (*pecunia*), paid out (money) < L. pp. of *expendere:* see EXPEND] **1.** financial cost; fee **2.** any cost or sacrifice **3.** [*pl.*] *a*) charges met with in doing one's work, etc. *b*) money to pay for these charges **4.** a cause of spending —**at the expense of** with the payment, loss, etc. borne by

expense account **1.** an arrangement whereby certain expenses of an employee related to his work are paid for by his employer **2.** a record of these

ex·pen·sive (ik spen′siv) ***adj.*** requiring or involving much expense; high-priced; dear —**ex·pen′sive·ly *adv.*** —**ex·pen′sive·ness *n.***

ex·pe·ri·ence (ik spir′ē əns) ***n.*** [< OFr. < L. < prp. of *experiri*, to try < *ex-*, out + base as in *peritus*, experienced] **1.** the act of living through an event or events **2.** anything or everything observed or lived through **3.** effect on one of anything or everything that has happened to him **4.** *a*) activity that includes training and personal participation *b*) the period of such activity *c*) knowledge, skill, or practice resulting from this —***vt.* -enced, -enc·ing** to have experience of; undergo

ex·pe·ri·enced (-ənst) ***adj.*** **1.** having had much experience **2.** having learned from experience; made wise, competent, etc. by experience

ex·pe·ri·en·tial (ik spir′ē en′shəl) ***adj.*** of or based on experience —**ex·pe′ri·en′tial·ly *adv.***

ex·per·i·ment (ik sper′ə mənt, -spir′-; *for v., also* -ment′) ***n.*** [< OFr. < L. *experimentum* < *experiri:* see EXPERIENCE] **1.** any action or process undertaken to discover something not yet known or to demonstrate or test something known **2.** the conducting of such tests or trials —***vi.*** to make an experiment —**ex·per′i·ment′er *n.***

ex·per·i·men·tal (ik sper′ə men′t'l, -spir′-) ***adj.*** **1.** of or based on experience rather than on theory or authority **2.** based on, tested by, or having the nature of, experiment **3.** of or used for experiments —**ex·per′i·men′tal·ism *n.*** —**ex·per′i·men′tal·ist *n., adj.*** —**ex·per′i·men′tal·ly *adv.***

ex·per·i·men·ta·tion (ik sper′ə mən tā′shən, -men-) ***n.*** the conducting of experiments

ex·pert (ek′spərt; *also, for adj.*, ik spurt′) ***adj.*** [< OFr. < L. pp. of *experiri:* see EXPERIENCE] **1.** very skillful; having much training and knowledge in some special field **2.** of or from an expert [*an expert* opinion] —***n.*** a person who is very skillful or highly trained and informed in some special field —**ex′pert·ly *adv.*** —**ex′pert·ness *n.***

ex·pert·ise (ek′spər tēz′) ***n.*** [Fr.] the skill, knowledge, judgment, etc. of an expert

ex·pi·ate (ek′spē āt′) ***vt.* -at′ed, -at′ing** [< L. pp. of *expiare* < *ex-*, out + *piare*, to appease < *pius*, devout] **1.** to make amends for (wrongdoing or guilt); atone for **2.** to suffer for —**ex′pi·a·ble** (-ə b'l) ***adj.*** —**ex′pi·a′tion *n.*** —**ex′pi·a′tor *n.***

ex·pi·a·to·ry (ek′spē ə tôr′ē) ***adj.*** that expiates or is meant to expiate

ex·pi·ra·tion (ek′spə rā′shən) ***n.*** **1.** a breathing out, as of air from the lungs **2.** something breathed out **3.** a breathing one's last; dying **4.** a coming to an end; close —**ex·pir·a·to·ry** (ik spīr′ə tôr′ē) ***adj.***

ex·pire (ik spīr′) ***vt.* -pired′, -pir′ing** [< L. *exspirare* < *ex-*, out + *spirare*, to breathe] to breathe out (air from the lungs) —***vi.*** **1.** to breathe out air **2.** to breathe one's last breath; die **3.** to come to an end; terminate

ex·plain (ik splān′) ***vt.*** [< L. < *ex-*, out + *planare*, to make level < *planus*, level] **1.** to make plain or understandable **2.** to give the meaning or interpretation of; expound **3.** to account for; state reasons for —***vi.*** to give an explanation —**explain away** to state reasons for so as to justify —**explain oneself** **1.** to make clear what one means **2.** to give reasons justifying one's conduct —**ex·plain′a·ble *adj.*** —**ex·plain′er *n.***

ex·pla·na·tion (eks′plə nā′shən) ***n.*** **1.** an explaining **2.** something that explains **3.** the interpretation, meaning, etc. given in explaining

ex·plan·a·to·ry (ik splan′ə tôr′ē) ***adj.*** explaining or intended to explain: also **ex·plan′a·tive** (-ə tiv) —**ex·plan′a·to′ri·ly *adv.***

ex·ple·tive (eks′plə tiv) ***n.*** [< LL. < L. pp. of *explere* < *ex-*, out + *plere*, to fill] **1.** an oath or exclamation **2.** a word, phrase, etc. used merely to fill out a sentence or metrical line —***adj.*** used to fill out a sentence, line, etc.: also **ex′ple·to′ry** (-tôr′ē)

ex·pli·ca·ble (eks′pli kə b'l, iks plik′ə b'l) ***adj.*** that can be explained

ex·pli·cate (eks′pli kāt′) ***vt.* -cat′ed, -cat′ing** [< L. pp. of *explicare* < *ex-*, out + *plicare*, to fold] to make clear or explicit (something obscure or implied); explain fully —**ex′pli·ca′tion *n.*** —**ex′pli·ca′tive** (-kāt′iv, ik splik′ə-tiv), **ex′pli·ca·to′ry** (-kə tôr′ē, ik splik′ə-) ***adj.*** —**ex′pli·ca′tor *n.***

ex·plic·it (ik splis′it) ***adj.*** [< ML. < L. pp. of *explicare:* see prec.] **1.** clearly stated or expressed, with nothing implied; definite **2.** saying what is meant, without reservation; outspoken **3.** plain to see —**ex·plic′it·ly *adv.*** —**ex·plic′it·ness *n.***

ex·plode (ik splōd′) ***vt.* -plod′ed, -plod′ing** [orig., to drive off the stage by clapping and hooting < L. *explodere* < *ex-*, off + *plaudere*, to applaud] **1.** to expose as false; discredit [*to explode* a theory] **2.** to make burst with a loud noise **3.** to cause a rapid, violent change in by chemical reaction or by nuclear fission or fusion —***vi.*** **1.** to burst noisily and violently **2.** to break forth noisily [*to explode* with anger] **3.** to increase very rapidly [*an exploding* population] —**ex·plod′a·ble *adj.*** —**ex·plod′er *n.***

ex·ploit (eks′ploit; *also, and for v. usually*, ik sploit′) ***n.*** [< OFr. < L. pp. of *explicare:* see EXPLICATE] an act remarkable for brilliance or daring; bold deed —***vt.*** **1.** to make use of; utilize productively **2.** to make use of or profit from the labor of (others) in an unethical way **3.** to promote or further the sales of (a product, etc.) —**ex·ploit′a·ble *adj.*** —**ex′ploi·ta′tion *n.*** —**ex·ploit′a·tive, ex·ploi′tive *adj.*** —**ex·ploit′er *n.***

ex·plo·ra·tion (eks′plə rā′shən, -plô-) ***n.*** an exploring or being explored —**ex·plor·a·to·ry** (ik splôr′ə tôr′ē), **ex·plor′a·tive** (-tiv) ***adj.***

ex·plore (ik splôr′) ***vt.* -plored′, -plor′ing** [L. *explorare*, to search out < *ex-*, out + *plorare*, to cry out] **1.** to look into closely; investigate **2.** to travel in (a region previously unknown or little known) for discovery **3.** *Med.* to examine (an organ, etc.) by operation, probing, etc., as in order to make a diagnosis —***vi.*** to explore new regions, etc. —**ex·plor′er *n.***

ex·plo·sion (ik splō′zhən) ***n.*** **1.** an exploding; esp., a blowing up; detonation **2.** the noise made by exploding **3.** a noisy outburst **4.** a sudden, rapid, and widespread increase

ex·plo·sive (-siv) ***adj.*** **1.** of, causing, or having the nature of, an explosion **2.** tending to explode; esp., tending to burst forth noisily **3.** *same as* PLOSIVE —***n.*** **1.** a substance that can explode, as gunpowder **2.** *same as* PLOSIVE —**ex·plo′sive·ly *adv.*** —**ex·plo′sive·ness *n.***

ex·po·nent (ik spō′nənt; *for n. 3, usually* ek′spō′nənt) ***adj.*** [< L. prp. of *exponere:* see EXPOUND] explaining, interpreting, or expounding —***n.*** **1.** a person who expounds or promotes (principles, methods, etc.) **2.** a person or thing that is an example or symbol (*of* something) **3.** *Algebra* a small figure or symbol placed at the upper right of another figure or symbol to show how many times the latter is to be multiplied by itself (Ex.: b^2 = b x b) —**ex·po·nen·tial** (eks′pō nen′shəl) ***adj.*** —**ex′po·nen′tial·ly *adv.***

ex·port (ik spôrt′; *also, and for n. & adj. always*, eks′pôrt) ***vt.*** [< L. < *ex-*, out + *portare*, to carry] **1.** to carry or send (goods, etc.) to other countries, esp. for purposes of sale **2.** to carry or send (ideas, culture, etc.) from one place to another —***n.*** **1.** something exported **2.** an exporting Also **ex′por·ta′tion** —***adj.*** of or for exporting or exports —**ex·port′a·ble *adj.*** —**ex·port′er *n.***

ex·pose (ik spōz′) ***vt.* -posed′, -pos′ing** [< OFr. < L. pp. or *exponere:* see EXPOUND] **1.** *a*) to lay open (*to* danger, attack, ridicule, etc.); leave unprotected *b*) to make accessible or subject (*to* an influence or action) **2.** to leave out in the open, as to die **3.** to allow to be seen; reveal; display **4.** *a*) to make (a crime, fraud, etc.) known *b*) to make known the crimes, etc. of **5.** *Photog.* to subject (a sensitized film or plate) to radiation as of light rays —**ex·pos′er *n.***

ex·po·sé (eks′pō zā′) ***n.*** [Fr., pp. of *exposer*, to expose] a public disclosure of a scandal, crime, etc.

ex·po·si·tion (eks′pə zish′ən) ***n.*** [< OFr. < L. pp. of *ex-*

ponere: see EXPOUND] **1.** a setting forth of facts, ideas, etc.; detailed explanation **2.** writing or speaking that sets forth or explains **3.** a large public exhibition or show **4.** the first section of certain musical forms, introducing the main theme or themes

ex·pos·i·tor (ik späz′ə tər) ***n.*** one that expounds or explains

ex·pos·i·to·ry (-ə tôr′ē) ***adj.*** of, like, or containing exposition; explanatory: also **ex·pos′i·tive** (-ə tiv)

ex post fac·to (eks pōst fak′tō) [L., from (the thing) done afterward] done or made afterward, esp. when having retroactive effect

ex·pos·tu·late (ik späs′chə lāt′) ***vi.*** **-lat′ed, -lat′ing** [< L. pp. of *expostulare* < *ex-*, intens. + *postulare*, to demand] to reason with a person earnestly, objecting to his actions or intentions; remonstrate (*with*) —**ex·pos′tu·la′tion** ***n.*** —**ex·pos′tu·la′tor** ***n.*** —**ex·pos′tu·la·to′ry** (-lə tôr′ē) ***adj.***

ex·po·sure (ik spō′zhər) ***n.*** **1.** an exposing or being exposed **2.** a location, as of a house, in relation to the sun, winds, etc. *[an eastern exposure]* **3.** appearance before the public, as on TV, etc. **4.** a being exposed, when helpless, to the elements **5.** *Photog.* *a)* the subjection of a film or plate to light, etc. *b)* a film section for making one picture *c)* the time during which film is exposed

ex·pound (ik spound′) ***vt.*** [< OFr. < L. < *ex-*, out + *ponere*, to put] **1.** to set forth; state in detail **2.** to explain or interpret —**ex·pound′er** ***n.***

ex·press (ik spres′) ***vt.*** [< ML. < L. *expressus*, pp. of *exprimere* < *ex-*, out + *premere:* see PRESS[1]] **1.** to press out or squeeze out (juice, etc.) **2.** to put into words; state **3.** to make known; show *[his face expressed joy]* **4.** to represent in art, music, etc. **5.** to show by a sign; symbolize **6.** to send by express —***adj.*** **1.** *a)* expressed and not implied; explicit *[an express warranty]* *b)* specific *[his express reason for going]* **2.** exact *[the express image of her aunt]* **3.** fast, direct, and making few stops *[an express train]* **4.** *a)* for fast driving *[an express highway]* *b)* having to do with express (*n.* 2) —***adv.*** by express —***n.*** **1.** an express train, bus, elevator, etc. **2.** *a)* a method or service for transporting goods rapidly: express is usually more expensive than freight *b)* the things sent by express **3.** any method or means of swift transmission —**express oneself** **1.** to state one's thoughts **2.** to give expression to one's feelings, imagination, talents, etc. —**ex·press′er** ***n.*** —**ex·press′i·ble** ***adj.***

ex·press·age (-ij) ***n.*** **1.** the carrying of packages, etc. by express **2.** the charge for this

ex·pres·sion (ik spresh′ən) ***n.*** **1.** a pressing out or squeezing out, as of juice **2.** a putting into words **3.** a representing in art, music, etc. **4.** a manner of expressing; esp., eloquence in speaking, etc. **5.** a particular word or phrase *[a trite expression]* **6.** a showing of feeling, character, etc. *[laughter is an expression of joy]* **7.** a look, intonation, etc. that conveys meaning or feeling *[a quizzical expression]* **8.** a symbol or set of symbols expressing some mathematical fact **9.** a showing by a symbol, sign, figures, etc. —**ex·pres′sion·less** ***adj.*** —**ex·pres′sion·less·ly** ***adv.***

ex·pres·sion·ism (-iz'm) ***n.*** an early 20th-cent. movement in art, drama, etc., characterized by distortion of reality and the use of symbols, stylization, etc. to give objective expression to inner experience —**ex·pres′sion·ist** ***adj., n.*** —**ex·pres′sion·is′tic** ***adj.*** —**ex·pres′sion·is′ti·cal·ly** ***adv.***

ex·pres·sive (ik spres′iv) ***adj.*** **1.** of or characterized by expression **2.** that expresses; indicative (*of*) *[a song expressive of joy]* **3.** full of meaning or feeling *[an expressive nod]* —**ex·pres′sive·ly** ***adv.*** —**ex·pres′sive·ness, ex′pres·siv′i·ty** ***n.***

ex·press·ly (-lē) ***adv.*** **1.** plainly; definitely; explicitly **2.** especially; particularly

ex·press·man (-mən) ***n.**, pl.* **-men** a person employed by an express company; esp., a driver of an express truck, who collects and delivers packages

ex·pres·so (ek spres′ō) ***n.*** *same as* ESPRESSO

ex·press·way (ik spres′wā) ***n.*** a divided highway for through traffic, with controlled access and generally with overpasses or underpasses at intersections

ex·pro·pri·ate (eks prō′prē āt′) ***vt.*** **-at′ed, -at′ing** [< ML. pp. of *expropriare* < L. *ex-*, out + *proprius*, one's own] to take (land, property, etc.) from its owner, esp. for public use —**ex·pro′pri·a′tion** ***n.*** —**ex·pro′pri·a′tor** ***n.***

ex·pul·sion (ik spul′shən) ***n.*** an expelling, or forcing out, or the condition of being expelled —**ex·pul′sive** (-siv) ***adj.***

ex·punge (ik spunj′) ***vt.*** **-punged′, -pung′ing** [L. *expungere* < *ex-*, out + *pungere*, to prick] to erase or remove completely; blot out or strike out; delete —**ex·punc′tion** (-spuŋk′shən) ***n.***

ex·pur·gate (eks′pər gāt′) ***vt.*** **-gat′ed, -gat′ing** [< L. pp. of *expurgare* < *ex-*, out + *purgare*, PURGE] to remove passages considered obscene or otherwise objectionable from (a book, etc.) —**ex′pur·ga′tion** ***n.*** —**ex′pur·ga′tor** ***n.*** —**ex·pur′ga·to′ry** ***adj.***

ex·qui·site (eks′kwi zit, ik skwiz′it) ***adj.*** [< L. pp. of *exquirere*, to search out < *ex-*, out + *quaerere*, to ask] **1.** carefully done or elaborately made **2.** very beautiful, esp. in a delicate or carefully wrought way **3.** of highest quality; consummate **4.** highly sensitive; keenly discriminating *[an exquisite ear for music]* **5.** sharply intense; keen *[exquisite pain]* —***n.*** one who makes a great show of being refined and fastidious in his tastes, etc. —**ex′qui·site·ly** ***adv.*** —**ex′qui·site·ness** ***n.***

ext. **1.** extension **2.** exterior **3.** external **4.** extinct **5.** extra **6.** extract

ex·tant (ek′stənt, ik stant′) ***adj.*** [< L. prp. of *exstare* < *ex-*, out + *stare*, to stand] still existing

ex·tem·po·ra·ne·ous (ik stem′pə rā′nē əs) ***adj.*** [< LL.: see EXTEMPORE] **1.** made, done, or spoken without any preparation; offhand **2.** spoken with some preparation but not written out or memorized: cf. IMPROMPTU **3.** speaking without preparation **4.** improvised; makeshift —**ex·tem′po·ra′ne·ous·ly** ***adv.***

ex·tem·po·rar·y (ik stem′pə rer′ē) ***adj.*** *same as* EXTEMPORANEOUS —**ex·tem′po·rar′i·ly** ***adv.*** —**ex·tem′po·rar′i·ness** ***n.***

ex·tem·po·re (-pə rē) ***adv., adj.*** [L. < *ex*, out of + *tempore*, abl. of *tempus*, time] without preparation; offhand *[to speak extempore]*

ex·tem·po·rize (-rīz′) ***vi., vt.*** **-rized′, -riz′ing** **1.** to speak, perform, or compose extempore; improvise **2.** to contrive as a makeshift —**ex·tem′po·ri·za′tion** ***n.*** —**ex·tem′po·riz′er** ***n.***

ex·tend (ik stend′) ***vt.*** [L. *extendere* < *ex-*, out + *tendere*, to stretch] **1.** *a)* to stretch out or draw out *b)* to draw out or lengthen in time or space; prolong **2.** to enlarge in area, scope, influence, etc.; expand; spread **3.** to stretch forth; hold out **4.** to offer; accord; grant **5.** to straighten out (a flexed limb of the body) **6.** to make (oneself) work or try hard **7.** to increase the bulk of (a substance) by adding another, usually cheaper or inferior, substance —***vi.*** **1.** to be extended **2.** to reach or stretch —**ex·tend′ed** ***adj.*** —**ex·tend′er** ***n.***

ex·ten·si·ble (ik sten′sə b'l) ***adj.*** that can be extended: also **ex·tend′i·ble** —**ex·ten′si·bil′i·ty** ***n.***

ex·ten·sion (ik sten′shən) ***n.*** **1.** an extending or being extended **2.** range; extent **3.** a part that forms a continuation or addition **4.** an extra period of time allowed a debtor for making payment **5.** a branch of a university away from the university proper **6.** an extra telephone on the same line as the main telephone **7.** *Physics* that property of a body by which it occupies space —***adj.*** designating a device that extends or can extend something else *[extension ladder, extension cord]* —**ex·ten′sion·al** ***adj.***

ex·ten·sive (-siv) ***adj.*** **1.** of great extent, or area, amount, length, etc.; vast **2.** broad in scope, influence, etc.; far-reaching —**ex·ten′sive·ly** ***adv.*** —**ex·ten′sive·ness** ***n.***

ex·ten·sor (-sər) ***n.*** a muscle that extends or straightens some part of the body, esp. a flexed arm or leg

EXTENSOR

ex·tent (ik stent′) ***n.*** **1.** the space, amount, or degree to which a thing extends; size; length; breadth **2.** range or limits; scope; coverage **3.** an extended space; vast area

ex·ten·u·ate (ik sten′yoo wāt′) ***vt.*** **-at′ed, -at′ing** [< L. pp. of *extenuare* < *ex-*, out + *tenuare*, to make thin < *tenuis*, thin] to lessen or seem to lessen the seriousness of (an offense, guilt, etc.) by giving excuses or serving as an excuse *[extenuating circumstances]* —**ex·ten′u·a′tion** ***n.*** —**ex·ten′u·a·to′ry, ex·ten′u·a′tive** ***adj.***

ex·te·ri·or (ik stir′ē ər) ***adj.*** [L., compar. of *exter(us)*, on the outside: see EXTERNAL] **1.** *a)* on the outside; outer; outermost *b)* for use on the outside *[exterior paint]* **2.** acting or coming from without *[exterior forces]* —***n.*** **1.** an outside or outside surface **2.** an outward appearance **3.** a picture, view, setting, etc. of an outdoor scene —**ex·te′ri·or·ly** ***adv.***

exterior angle any of the four angles formed on the outside of two straight lines by a straight line cutting across them

ex·te·ri·or·ize (-ə rīz′) ***vt.*** **-ized′, -iz′ing** **1.** to give or attribute an external form or objective character to (states of mind, etc.) **2.** *same as* EXTERNALIZE —**ex·te′ri·or·i·za′tion** ***n.***

L C R E A F D T

EXTERIOR ANGLES (CEL, LER, ADT, TDF)

ex·ter·mi·nate (ik stur′mə nāt′) ***vt.*** **-nat′ed, -nat′ing** [< L. pp. of *exterminare*, to drive out, destroy < *ex-*, out + *terminus*, a boundary] to destroy or get rid of entirely, as by killing; wipe out; annihilate —**ex·ter′mi·na′tion** ***n.*** —**ex·ter′mi·na·to′ry, ex·ter′mi·na′tive** ***adj.***

ex·ter·mi·na·tor (-nāt′ər) ***n.*** a person or thing that exterminates; specif., *a)* one whose work is exterminating rats, cockroaches, and other vermin *b)* any preparation for exterminating vermin

ex·ter·nal (ik stur′n'l) ***adj.*** [< L. *externus* < *exter(us)*, on the outside, compar. form < *ex*, out of (see EX-) + -AL] **1.** on the outside; outer; exterior **2.** on, or for use on, the outside of the body *[a medicine for external use only]* **3.** *a)* outwardly visible *b)* existing apart from the mind; material **4.** acting or coming from without **5.** *a)* for outward appearance or show; superficial *b)* not basic or essential **6.** having to do with foreign countries —***n.*** **1.** an outside or outward surface or part **2.** [*pl.*] outward appearance or behavior —**ex·ter·nal·i·ty** (eks′tər nal′ə tē) ***n., pl.*** **-ties** —**ex·ter′nal·ly** ***adv.***

ex·ter·nal·ize (-īz′) ***vt.*** **-ized′, -iz′ing** **1.** to make external; embody **2.** *same as* EXTERIORIZE —**ex·ter′nal·i·za′tion** ***n.***

ex·tinct (ik stiŋkt′) ***adj.*** [< L. pp. of *exstinguere*: see EXTINGUISH] **1.** having died down or burned out **2.** no longer active *[an extinct volcano]* **3.** no longer in existence *[an extinct species]*

ex·tinc·tion (ik stiŋk′shən) ***n.*** **1.** a putting out or being put out, as of a fire **2.** a destroying or being destroyed **3.** the fact or state of being or becoming extinct

ex·tin·guish (ik stiŋ′gwish) ***vt.*** [< L. *exstinguere* < *ex-*, out + *stinguere*, to extinguish] **1.** to put out (a fire, etc.); quench **2.** to put an end to; destroy **3.** to eclipse; obscure —**ex·tin′guish·a·ble** ***adj.*** —**ex·tin′guish·er** ***n.*** —**ex·tin′guish·ment** ***n.***

ex·tir·pate (ek′stər pāt′, ik stur′pāt) ***vt.*** **-pat′ed, -pat′ing** [< L. pp. of *ex(s)tirpare* < *ex-*, out + *stirps*, root] **1.** to pull up by the roots **2.** to destroy completely; abolish —**ex′tir·pa′tion** ***n.*** —**ex′tir·pa′tive** ***adj.*** —**ex′tir·pa′tor** ***n.***

ex·tol, ex·toll (ik stōl′) ***vt.*** **-tolled′, -tol′ling** [< L. *extollere* < *ex-*, up + *tollere*, to raise] to praise highly; laud —**ex·tol′ler** ***n.*** —**ex·tol′ment, ex·toll′ment** ***n.***

ex·tort (ik stôrt′) ***vt.*** [< L. pp. of *extorquere* < *ex-*, out + *torquere*, to twist] to get (money, etc.) by violence, threats, misuse of authority, etc.; exact (*from*) —**ex·tort′er** ***n.*** —**ex·tor′tive** ***adj.***

ex·tor·tion (ik stôr′shən) ***n.*** **1.** an extorting: sometimes applied to the exaction of too high a price **2.** *Law* the offense of an official who extorts **3.** something extorted —**ex·tor′tion·ate, ex·tor′tion·ar′y** ***adj.***

ex·tor·tion·er (-ər) ***n.*** a person guilty of extortion: also **ex·tor′tion·ist**

ex·tra (eks′trə) ***adj.*** [contr. < EXTRAORDINARY; also < L. *extra, adv.*, more than, outside: see ff.] **1.** more, larger, or better than is normal, expected, necessary, etc.; additional **2.** to be paid for by an added charge —***n.*** an extra person or thing; specif., *a)* an additional charge *b)* formerly, a special newspaper edition for important news *c)* an extra benefit or feature *d)* a spare copy *e)* an extra worker *f)* *Motion Pictures* an actor hired by the day to play a minor part —***adv.*** more than usually *[extra hot]*

ex·tra- [L. < *exter(us)*: see EXTERNAL] *a prefix meaning* outside, outside the scope of, beyond, as in the following list:

extrafamilial	**extramarital**
extragovernmental	**extraofficial**
extrajudicial	**extraterrestrial**

ex·tract (ik strakt′; *for n.* eks′trakt) ***vt.*** [< L. pp. of *extrahere* < *ex-*, out + *trahere*, to draw] **1.** to draw out by effort; pull out *[to extract teeth, to extract a promise]* **2.** to separate (metal) from ore **3.** to obtain by pressing, distilling, using a solvent, etc. *[to extract juice from fruit]* **4.** to deduce, derive, or elicit **5.** to copy out or quote (a passage from a book, etc.) **6.** *Math.* to compute (the root of a quantity) —***n.*** something extracted; specif., *a)* a concentrated form of a food, flavoring, etc. *b)* a quotation from a book, etc. —**ex·tract′a·ble, ex·tract′i·ble** ***adj.*** —**ex·trac′tive** ***adj.*** —**ex·trac′tor** ***n.***

ex·trac·tion (ik strak′shən) ***n.*** **1.** an extracting; specif., the extracting of a tooth **2.** origin; lineage; descent **3.** a thing extracted; extract

ex·tra·cur·ric·u·lar (eks′trə kə rik′yə lər) ***adj.*** not part of the required curriculum but under the supervision of the school, as athletics

ex·tra·dite (eks′trə dīt′) ***vt.*** **-dit′ed, -dit′ing** [back-formation < ff.] **1.** to turn over (an alleged criminal, fugitive, etc.) to the jurisdiction of another country, State, etc. **2.** to obtain the extradition of —**ex′tra·dit′a·ble** ***adj.***

ex·tra·di·tion (eks′trə dish′ən) ***n.*** [Fr. < L. *ex*, out + *traditio*, a surrender: see TRADITION] the turning over of an alleged criminal, fugitive, etc. by one country, State, etc. to another

ex·tra·dos (eks′trə däs′, -dōs′; ik strā′däs) ***n.*** [Fr. < L. *extra*, beyond + Fr. *dos* < L. *dorsum*, back] *Archit.* the outside curved surface of an arch

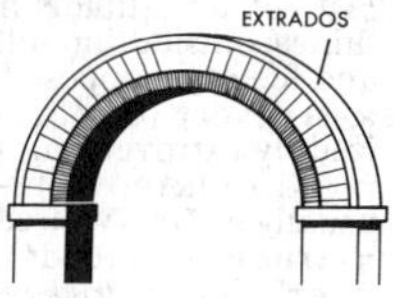

ex·tra·le·gal (eks′trə lē′g'l) ***adj.*** outside of legal control or authority —**ex′tra·le′gal·ly** ***adv.***

ex·tra·mu·ral (-myoor′əl) ***adj.*** [EXTRA- + MURAL] outside the limits of a city, school, university, etc.

ex·tra·ne·ous (ik strā′nē əs) ***adj.*** [< L. *extraneus* < *extra*: see EXTRA-] **1.** coming from outside; foreign **2.** not essential **3.** not pertinent —**ex·tra′ne·ous·ly** ***adv.*** —**ex·tra′ne·ous·ness** ***n.***

ex·traor·di·nar·y (ik strôr′d'n er′ē; *for 3* eks′trə ôr′-) ***adj.*** [< L. < *extra ordinem*, out of the usual order] **1.** not according to the usual custom or regular plan **2.** very unusual; exceptional; remarkable **3.** outside of the regular staff; sent on a special errand *[an envoy extraordinary]* —**ex·traor′di·nar′i·ly** ***adv.*** —**ex·traor′di·nar′i·ness** ***n.***

ex·trap·o·late (ik strap′ə lāt′) ***vt., vi.*** **-lat′ed, -lat′ing** [L. *extra* (see EXTRA-) + (INTER)POLATE] **1.** to estimate (a value, quantity, etc. beyond the known range) on the basis of certain known variables **2.** to arrive at (conclusions) by speculating on the basis of (known facts) —**ex·trap′o·la′tion** ***n.*** —**ex·trap′o·la′tive** ***adj.*** —**ex·trap′o·la′tor** ***n.***

ex·tra·sen·so·ry (eks′trə sen′sər ē) ***adj.*** designating or of perception that seems to occur apart from the normal function of the senses

ex·tra·ter·ri·to·ri·al (-ter′ə tôr′ē əl) ***adj.*** **1.** outside the territorial limits or jurisdiction of the country, State, etc. **2.** of extraterritoriality —**ex′tra·ter′ri·to′ri·al·ly** ***adv.***

ex·tra·ter·ri·to·ri·al·i·ty (-tôr′ē al′ə tē) ***n.*** **1.** freedom from the jurisdiction of a country: a privilege of foreign diplomats, etc. **2.** jurisdiction of a country over its citizens in foreign lands

ex·trav·a·gance (ik strav′ə gəns) ***n.*** **1.** a going beyond reasonable or proper limits; excess **2.** a spending of more than is reasonable or necessary **3.** an instance of excess in spending, behavior, or speech Also **ex·trav′a·gan·cy**, ***pl.*** **-cies**

ex·trav·a·gant (-gənt) ***adj.*** [< Anglo-Fr. < ML. prp. of *extravagari* < L. *extra*, beyond + *vagari*, to wander] **1.** going beyond reasonable limits; excessive or unrestrained **2.** too ornate or showy **3.** costing or spending too much —**ex·trav′a·gant·ly** ***adv.***

ex·trav·a·gan·za (ik strav′ə gan′zə) ***n.*** [< It. *estravaganza*, extravagance] **1.** a literary, musical, or dramatic fantasy characterized by a loose structure and farce **2.** a spectacular, elaborate theatrical show, as some musicals

ex·trav·a·sate (ik strav′ə sāt′) ***vi., vt.*** **-sat′ed, -sat′ing** [L. *extra* (see EXTRA-) + *vas*, a vessel + -ATE[1]] to escape or force to flow into surrounding tissue, as blood, lymph, etc. —**ex·trav′a·sa′tion** ***n.***

ex·tra·ve·hic·u·lar (eks′trə vē hik′yoo lər) ***adj.*** designating or of activity by an astronaut outside a vehicle in space

ex·treme (ik strēm′) ***adj.*** [OFr. < L. *extremus*, superl. of *exterus*, outer: see EXTERNAL] **1.** at the end or outermost point; farthest away **2.** to the greatest or an excessive degree **3.** very unconventional **4.** deviating furthest from a central or moderate view; specif., furthest to the right or left in politics **5.** very severe; drastic —***n.*** **1.** either of two things that are as different or as far as possible from each other **2.** an extreme degree **3.** an extreme act, expedient, etc. **4.** an extreme state **5.** *Math.* the first or last term of a proportion —**go to extremes** to be immoderate in speech or action —**in the extreme** to the utmost degree —**ex·treme′ly** ***adv.*** —**ex·treme′ness** ***n.***

extreme unction *same as* ANOINTING OF THE SICK

ex·trem·ism (ik strēm′iz'm) ***n.*** a being extreme, esp. in politics —**ex·trem′ist** ***adj., n.***

ex·trem·i·ty (ik strem′ə tē) ***n., pl.*** **-ties** **1.** the outermost or utmost point or part; end **2.** the greatest degree **3.** a state of extreme necessity, danger, etc. **4.** the end of life; dying **5.** an extreme measure; strong action: *usually used in pl.* **6.** *a)* a body limb *b)* [*pl.*] the hands and feet

ex·tri·cate (eks′trə kāt′) ***vt.*** **-cat′ed, -cat′ing** [< L. pp. of *extricare* < *ex-*, out + *tricae*, hindrances, vexations] to set free; disentangle (*from* a net, difficulty, embarrassment, etc.) —**ex′tri·ca·bil′i·ty** ***n.*** —**ex′tri·ca·ble** (-kə b'l) ***adj.*** —**ex′tri·ca′tion** ***n.***

ex·trin·sic (ek strin′sik) ***adj.*** [< Fr. < L. *extrinsecus*, from without < *exter*, without + *secus*, following] **1.** not belonging to the real nature of a thing; not inherent **2.** being, coming, or acting from the outside; extraneous —**ex·trin′si·cal·ly** ***adv.***

ex·tro·ver·sion (eks′trə vur′zhən, -shən) ***n.*** **[**< G. < L. *extra-* (see EXTRA-) + ML. *versio*, a turning: see VERSION**]** *Psychol.* an attitude in which a person directs his interest to things outside himself rather than to his own experiences and feelings: opposed to INTROVERSION
ex·tro·vert (eks′trə vurt′) ***n.*** *Psychol.* a person characterized by extroversion; one who is active and expressive: opposed to INTROVERT —***adj.*** characterized by extroversion: usually **ex′tro·vert′ed**
ex·trude (ik strōōd′) ***vt.*** **-trud′ed, -trud′ing [**L. *extrudere* < *ex-*, out + *trudere*, to thrust**]** **1.** to push or force out **2.** to force (metal, plastic, etc.) through a die or very small holes to give it a certain shape —***vi.*** to be extruded; esp., to protrude —**ex·trud′er** ***n.*** —**ex·tru′sion** (-strōō′zhən) ***n.*** —**ex·tru′sive** ***adj.***
ex·u·ber·ance (ig zōō′bər əns, -zyōō′-) ***n.*** **[**< Fr. < L. < prp. of *exuberare* < *ex-*, intens. + *uberare*, to bear abundantly < *uber*, udder**]** **1.** the state or quality of being exuberant; great abundance **2.** an instance of this; esp., action or speech showing high spirits Also **ex·u′ber·an·cy**, *pl.* **-cies**
ex·u·ber·ant (-ənt) ***adj.*** **1.** growing profusely; luxuriant **2.** full of life, vitality, or high spirits **3.** overly elaborate **4.** very great; extreme —**ex·u′ber·ant·ly** ***adv.***
ex·ude (ig zōōd′, -zyōōd′) ***vt., vi.*** **-ud′ed, -ud′ing [**< L. < *ex-*, out + *sudare*, to sweat < *sudor*, sweat**]** **1.** to pass out in drops through pores, an incision, etc.; ooze **2.** to diffuse or seem to radiate *[*to *exude* joy*]* —**ex·u·da·tion** (eks′yə dā′shən) ***n.***
ex·ult (ig zult′) ***vi.*** **[**< Fr. < L. *ex(s)ultare*, to leap for joy < *ex-*, intens. + *saltare*, freq. of *salire*, to leap**]** to rejoice greatly; be jubilant; glory —**ex′ul·ta′tion** ***n.***
ex·ult·ant (-'nt) ***adj.*** exulting; triumphant; jubilant —**ex·ult′ant·ly** ***adv.***
ex·ur·bi·a (eks ur′bē ə) ***n.*** **[**EX- + (SUB)URBIA**]** the small, semirural communities beyond the suburbs, lived in by upper-income people working in the city —**ex·ur′ban** (-bən) ***adj.*** —**ex·ur′ban·ite′** (-bə nīt′) ***n., adj.***
ex·u·vi·ate (ig zōō′vē āt′) ***vt., vi.*** **-at′ed, -at′ing [**< L. *exuere*, to strip off + -ATE[1]**]** to cast off (a skin, shell, etc.); molt —**ex·u′vi·a′tion** ***n.***
-ey (ē, i) *same as* -Y[2]: used esp. after words ending in *y* *[clayey]*
eye (ī) ***n.*** **[**OE. *eage*]** **1.** the organ of sight in man and animals **2.** *a)* the eyeball *b)* the iris **3.** the area around the eye *[*a black *eye]* **4.** [*often pl.*] sight; vision *[*weak *eyes]* **5.** a look; glance **6.** attention; observation **7.** the power of judging, estimating, etc. by eyesight *[*a good *eye* for distances*]* **8.** [*often pl.*] judgment; opinion *[*in the *eyes* of the law*]* **9.** a thing like an eye in shape or function, as a bud of a potato, the hole of a needle, a loop of metal, any primitive, light-sensitive organ, etc. **10.** [Slang] a detective: esp. in **private eye** **11.** *Meteorol.* the calm, low-pressure center (of a hurricane), around which the winds whirl —***vt.*** **eyed, eye′ing** or **ey′ing** to look at; observe —**all eyes** extremely attentive —**an eye for an eye** punishment or retaliation equivalent to the injury suffered —**catch one's eye** to attract one's attention —**easy on the eyes** [Slang] attractive —**feast one's eyes on** to look at with pleasure —**have an eye for** to have a keen appreciation of —**have eyes for** [Colloq.] to be interested in and want —**in the public eye** often brought to public attention —**keep an eye on** to look after; watch —**keep an eye out for** to be watchful for —**keep one's eyes open** (or **peeled** or **skinned**) to be watchful —**lay** (or **set** or **clap**) **eyes on** to see; look at —**make eyes at** to look at flirtatiously; ogle —**my eye!** [Slang] an exclamation of contradiction, astonishment, etc. —**open one's eyes** to make one aware of the facts —**run one's eye over** to glance over —**see eye to eye** to agree completely —**shut one's eyes to** to refuse to see or think about —**with an eye to** paying attention to
eye·ball (-bôl′) ***n.*** the ball-shaped part of the eye, enclosed by the socket and eyelids —***vt., vi.*** [Slang] to examine or observe (something)
eye·brow (-brou′) ***n.*** **1.** the bony arch over each eye **2.** the arch of hair growing on this —**raise** (or **lift**) **an eyebrow** to appear skeptical, etc.
eye-catch·er (-kach′ər) ***n.*** something that especially attracts one's attention —**eye′-catch′ing** ***adj.***
eye·cup (-kup′) ***n.*** a small cup used in applying medicine to the eyes or washing them
eyed (īd) ***adj.*** having eyes (of a specified kind) *[blue-eyed]*
eye·drop·per (ī′dräp′ər) ***n.*** *same as* DROPPER (*n.* 2)
eye·ful (-fool′) ***n.*** **1.** a quantity of something in the eye **2.** a full look at something **3.** [Slang] a person or thing that looks striking or unusual
eye·glass (-glas′) ***n.*** **1.** a lens to help faulty vision; monocle **2.** [*pl.*] a pair of such lenses, usually in a frame; glasses **3.** *same as* EYEPIECE
eye·hole (-hōl′) ***n.*** **1.** the socket for the eyeball **2.** a peephole **3.** *same as* EYELET (sense 1)
eye·lash (-lash′) ***n.*** **1.** any of the hairs on the edge of the eyelid **2.** a fringe of these hairs
eye·less (-lis) ***adj.*** without eyes; blind
eye·let (-lit) ***n.*** **[**< OFr. dim. of *oeil* < L. *oculus*, eye**]** **1.** a small hole for receiving a cord, hook, etc. **2.** a metal ring or short tube for lining such a hole **3.** a small hole edged by stitching in embroidered work **4.** a peephole or loophole —***vt.*** to provide with eyelets
eye·lid (-lid′) ***n.*** either of the two folds of skin that cover and uncover the front of the eyeball
eye liner a cosmetic preparation applied in a thin line on the eyelid at the base of the eyelashes
eye-o·pen·er (-ō′p'n ər) ***n.*** **1.** a surprising piece of news, sudden realization, etc. **2.** [Colloq.] an alcoholic drink, esp. one taken early in the day
eye·piece (-pēs′) ***n.*** in a telescope, microscope, etc., the lens or lenses nearest the viewer's eye
eye shadow a cosmetic preparation, usually green or blue, applied to the upper eyelids
eye·shot (-shät′) ***n.*** range of vision
eye·sight (-sīt′) ***n.*** **1.** the power of seeing; sight; vision **2.** the range of vision
eye·sore (-sôr′) ***n.*** a thing that is unpleasant to look at
eye·spot (-spät′) ***n.*** a small spot of pigment sensitive to light, found in many invertebrates
eye·strain (-strān′) ***n.*** a tired or strained condition of the eye muscles, caused by too much use or an incorrect use of the eyes
eye·tooth (-tōōth′) ***n., pl.*** **-teeth′** a canine tooth of the upper jaw —**cut one's eyeteeth** to become experienced or sophisticated
eye·wash (-wôsh′, -wäsh′) ***n.*** **1.** a lotion for the eyes **2.** [Slang] *a)* nonsense *b)* flattery *c)* something done only to impress an observer
eye·wink (-wiŋk′) ***n.*** **1.** a wink of the eye **2.** an instant
eye·wit·ness (-wit′nis) ***n.*** **1.** a person who sees something happen, as an accident, crime, etc. **2.** a person who testifies to what he has seen
ey·rie, ey·ry (er′ē, ir′-) ***n., pl.*** **-ries** *same as* AERIE
ey·rir (ā′rir) ***n., pl.*** **au·rar** (ou′rär) [Ice. <ON., a coin, unit of weight <L. *aureus*, a gold coin, orig. adj., golden: see AUREATE] *see* MONETARY UNITS, table (Iceland)
E·zek·i·el (i zē′kē əl, -kyəl) **[**< LL. < Gr. < Heb. *yeḥezq'ēl*, lit., God strengthens**]** **1.** a masculine name **2.** *Bible* *a)* a Hebrew prophet of the 6th cent. B.C. *b)* the book containing his prophetic writings: abbrev. **Ezek.**
Ez·ra (ez′rə) [LL. < Heb. *ezrā*, lit., help**]** **1.** a masculine name **2.** *Bible* *a)* a Hebrew scribe, prophet, and religious reformer of the 5th cent. B.C. *b)* the book telling of his life and teachings: abbrev. **Ez., Ezr.**

F

F, f (ef) ***n., pl.*** **F's, f's** **1.** the sixth letter of the English alphabet **2.** the sound of *F* or *f*
F (ef) ***n.*** **1.** *Chem.* fluorine **2.** *Educ.* *a)* a grade indicating failing work *b)* sometimes, a grade indicating fair work **3.** *Music* *a)* the fourth tone in the ascending scale of C major *b)* the scale having this tone as the keynote
F **1.** Fahrenheit **2.** farad **3.** fathom
F/, f/, f:, *f.* f-number
F- fighter (plane)
F. **1.** Fahrenheit **2.** February **3.** Fellow **4.** France **5.** French **6.** Friday
F., f. **1.** farad **2.** farthing **3.** fathom **4.** feminine **5.** fluid **6.** folio(s) **7.** following **8.** *Music* forte **9.** franc(s)
fa (fä) ***n.*** **[**< ML. < *fa(muli)*: see GAMUT**]** *Music* a syllable representing the fourth tone of the diatonic scale
Fa·bi·an (fā′bē ən) ***adj.*** **[**< L. < *Fabius*, Roman general in 2d Punic War**]** **1.** using a cautious strategy of delay and

avoidance of battle **2.** designating or of an English socialist organization (**Fabian Society**) advocating gradual reforms *—n.* a member of the Fabian Society **—Fa′bi·an·ism** ***n.***

fa·ble (fā′b'l) ***n.*** [< OFr. < L. *fabula,* a story < *fari,* to speak] **1.** a fictitious story meant to teach a moral lesson: the characters are usually talking animals **2.** a myth or legend **3.** a falsehood or fiction ***—vi., vt.*** **-bled, -bling** to write or tell (fables, legends, or falsehoods) **—fa′bler *n.***

fa·bled (-b'ld) ***adj.*** **1.** legendary **2.** fictitious

fab·ric (fab′rik) ***n.*** [< MFr. < L. *fabrica,* a workshop < *faber,* a workman] **1.** *a)* anything made of parts put together *b)* the basic structure of anything **2.** the style or plan of construction **3.** any woven, knitted, or felted material

fab·ri·cate (fab′rə kāt′) ***vt.*** **-cat′ed, -cat′ing** [< L. pp. of *fabricari,* to build < *fabrica:* see prec.] **1.** to make, build, construct, etc., esp. by assembling parts; manufacture **2.** to make up (a story, lie, etc.) **—fab′ri·ca′tion *n.* —fab′ri·ca′tor *n.***

Fab·ri·koid (-koid′) [see FABRIC & -OID] *a trademark for* a fabric made to resemble leather

fab·u·list (fab′yoo list) ***n.*** **1.** a person who writes or tells fables **2.** a liar

fab·u·lous (-ləs) ***adj.*** [< L. < *fabula:* see FABLE] **1.** of or like a fable; imaginary; fictitious; legendary **2.** incredible; astounding **3.** [Colloq.] wonderful **—fab′u·lous·ly *adv.* — fab′u·lous·ness *n.***

fa·çade, fa·cade (fə säd′) ***n.*** [Fr. < It. < VL. *facia:* see ff.] **1.** the front of a building **2.** an imposing appearance concealing something shoddy

FAÇADE

face (fās) ***n.*** [< OFr. < VL. *facia* < L. *facies,* the face] **1.** the front of the head; countenance **2.** the expression of the countenance **3.** a surface of a thing; esp., *a)* the main surface or side *b)* the front, upper, or outer surface *c)* any of the surfaces of a crystal **4.** the side or surface that is marked or intended to be seen, as of a clock, playing card, etc. **5.** the appearance; outward aspect **6.** [< Chin. idiom] dignity; self-respect: in **lose** (or **save**) **face** **7.** the topography (of an area) **8.** the functional or striking surface (of a tool, etc.) **9.** [Colloq.] effrontery; audacity **10.** *Typography a)* the printing surface of a letter or plate *b)* the design of type ***—vt.*** **faced, fac′ing 1.** to turn, or have the face turned, toward *[*the house *faces* the park*]* **2.** to meet face to face **3.** to confront with boldness, courage, etc. **4.** to put another material on the surface of **5.** to sew a facing to (a collar, etc.) **6.** to put a smooth surface on (a stone, tool, etc.) **7.** to turn (a card, etc.) with the face up ***—vi.*** **1.** to turn, or have the face turned, toward a specified thing or in a specified direction **2.** *Mil.* to pivot in a specified direction *[*right *face!]* **—face off** *Hockey* to start play with a face-off **—face to face 1.** confronting one another **2.** in the presence of: followed by *with* **—face up to 1.** to confront and resist **2.** to realize and be ready to meet **—in the face of 1.** in the presence of **2.** in spite of **—make a face** to distort the face; grimace **—on the face of it** apparently **—pull** (or **wear**) **a long face** to look sad, glum, disapproving, etc. **—faced *adj.* —face′less *adj.***

face card any king, queen, or jack in a deck of cards

face lifting 1. plastic surgery for removing wrinkles, sagging flesh, etc. from the face **2.** an altering, cleaning, etc., as of the exterior of a building Also **face lift —face′-lift′ *vt.***

face-off (-ôf′) ***n.*** *Hockey* the starting of play by the referee's dropping the puck between two opposing players

face powder a cosmetic powder, as of flesh-colored talc, applied to the face

face-sav·ing (-sā′viŋ) ***adj.*** preserving or intended to preserve one's dignity or self-respect

fac·et (fas′it) ***n.*** [< Fr. dim. of *face:* see FACE] **1.** any of the small, polished plane surfaces of a cut gem **2.** any of the sides or aspects, as of a personality ***—vt.*** **-et·ed** or **-et·ted, -et·ing** or **-et·ting** to cut or make facets on

fa·ce·tious (fə sē′shəs) ***adj.*** [< Fr. < L. < *facetus,* witty] joking or trying to be jocular, esp. at an inappropriate time **—fa·ce′tious·ly *adv.* —fa·ce′tious·ness *n.***

face value 1. the value printed or written on a bill, bond, etc. **2.** the seeming value *[*to take a promise at *face value]*

fa·cial (fā′shəl) ***adj.*** of or for the face *—n.* a cosmetic treatment intended to improve facial appearance **—fa′cial·ly *adv.***

-fa·cient (fā′shənt) [< L. prp. of *facere,* to make] *a suffix meaning* making or causing to become *[liquefacient]*

fa·ci·es (fā′shē ēz′) ***n., pl*** **fa′ci·es′** [L., face] **1.** the general appearance of anything **2.** *Geol.* the characteristics of a rock body, part of a rock body, etc. that differentiate it from others **3.** *Med. a)* the appearance of the face *b)* a surface

fac·ile (fas′'l) ***adj.*** [Fr. < L. *facilis* < *facere,* to make, do] **1.** not hard to do; easy **2.** acting, working, or done quickly and smoothly; fluent; ready **3.** not sincere or profound; superficial **—fac′ile·ly *adv.* —fac′ile·ness *n.***

fa·cil·i·tate (fə sil′ə tāt′) ***vt.*** **-tat′ed, -tat′ing** [< Fr. < It. < L. *facilis* (see prec.) + -ATE¹] to make easy or easier **—fa·cil′i·ta′tion *n.* —fa·cil′i·ta′tive *adj.***

fa·cil·i·ty (fə sil′ə tē) ***n., pl*** **-ties** [< OFr. < L. < *facilis,* FACILE] **1.** ease; absence of difficulty **2.** a ready ability; skill; fluency **3.** [*usually pl.*] the means by which something can be done **4.** a building, room, etc. for some activity

fac·ing (fās′iŋ) ***n.*** **1.** a lining, often decorative, sewn on a collar, cuff, etc. **2.** any material used for this **3.** a covering of contrasting material, as for decorating or protecting a building

fac·sim·i·le (fak sim′ə lē) ***n.*** [L. *fac,* imper. of *facere,* to make + *simile,* like] **1.** (an) exact reproduction or copy **2.** the transmission and reproduction of graphic matter by electrical means, as radio or wire ***—adj.*** of or like a facsimile ***—vt.*** **-led, -le·ing** to make a facsimile of

fact (fakt) ***n.*** [L. *factum,* deed < *facere,* to do] **1.** a deed; act: now esp. "a criminal deed" in **before** (or **after**) **the fact** *[*an accessory *after the fact]* **2.** a thing that has actually happened or is true **3.** the state of things as they are; reality; truth **4.** something said to have occurred or supposed to be true *[*check your *facts]* **—as a matter of fact** in reality; really: also **in fact, in point of fact —the facts of life 1.** basic information about life, esp. about sexual reproduction **2.** the harsh, unpleasant facts one must face in life

fac·tion (fak′shən) ***n.*** [< Fr. < L. *factio,* a making < pp. of *facere,* to do, act] **1.** a group of people in a political party, club, etc. working in a common cause against the main body; clique **2.** partisan conflict within an organization or country; dissension **—fac′tion·al *adj.* —fac′tion·al·ism *n.* —fac′tion·al·ist *n., adj.* —fac′tion·al·ly *adv.***

fac·tious (fak′shəs) ***adj.*** **1.** producing or tending to produce faction, or dissension **2.** produced or characterized by faction **—fac′tious·ly *adv.* —fac′tious·ness *n.***

fac·ti·tious (fak tish′əs) ***adj.*** [< L. < pp. of *facere,* to do] not genuine or spontaneous; forced or artificial **—fac·ti′tious·ly *adv.* —fac·ti′tious·ness *n.***

fac·tor (fak′tər) ***n.*** [< OFr. < L. < pp. of *facere,* to do, make] **1.** a person who carries on business transactions for another; commission merchant **2.** any of the circumstances, conditions, etc. that bring about a result **3.** *Biol. same as* GENE **4.** *Math.* any of two or more quantities which form a product when multiplied together ***—vt.*** *Math.* to resolve into factors: also **fac′tor·ize′** (-tə rīz′) **-ized′, -iz′ing *—vi.*** to act as a factor (sense 1) **—fac′tor·a·ble *adj.* —fac′tor·ship′ *n.***

fac·tor·age (-ij) ***n.*** **1.** the business of a factor **2.** a factor's commission

fac·to·ri·al (fak tôr′ē əl) ***n.*** *Math.* the product of a given series of consecutive whole numbers beginning with 1 *[*the *factorial* of 4 is 1 × 2 × 3 × 4, or 24*]*

fac·to·ry (fak′tə rē, -trē) ***n., pl.*** **-ries** [see FACTOR] a building or buildings in which things are manufactured; manufacturing plant

fac·to·tum (fak tōt′əm) ***n.*** [ModL. < L. *fac,* imper. of *facere,* to do + *totum,* all] a person hired to do all sorts of work; handyman

fac·tu·al (fak′choo wəl) ***adj.*** [FACT + (ACT)UAL] **1.** of or containing facts **2.** having the nature of fact; real; actual **—fac′tu·al·ly *adv.***

fac·ul·ty (fak′'l tē) ***n., pl.*** **-ties** [< OFr. < L. < *facilis:* see FACILE] **1.** formerly, the ability to perform an action **2.** any natural or specialized power of a living organism *[*the *faculty* of speech*]* **3.** special aptitude or skill; knack **4.** all the teachers of a school, college, or university or of one of its divisions **5.** all the members of any profession **6.** an authorization **7.** *Psychol.* any of the powers formerly thought of as composing the mind, such as will, reason, etc.

fad (fad) ***n.*** [< Brit. Midland dial.] a custom, style, etc. that many people are interested in for a short time; craze **— fad′dish *adj.* —fad′dish·ly *adv.* —fad′dish·ness *n.* —fad′dism *n.* —fad′dist *n.***

fade (fād) ***vi.*** **fad′ed, fad′ing** [< OFr. *fader* < *fade,* pale] **1.** to become less distinct; lose color, brilliance, intensity, etc. **2.** to lose freshness or strength; wither; wane **3.** to disappear slowly; die out **4.** to lose braking power: said of brakes ***—vt.*** to cause to fade **—fade in** (or **out**) *Motion Pic-*

tures, Radio & TV to appear (or disappear) gradually or cause to do so; become or make more (or less) distinct
fade-in (-in′) *n. Motion Pictures, Radio & TV* a fading in of a scene or sound
fade-out (-out′) *n. Motion Pictures, Radio & TV* a fading out of a scene or sound
fae·ces (fē′sēz) *n.pl. same as* FECES —**fae′cal** (-k'l) *adj.*
fa·er·ie, fa·er·y (fer′ē; *also, for 1,* fā′ər ē) *n.* [Archaic] **1.** fairyland **2.** *pl.* **-ies** a fairy —*adj.* [Archaic] fairy Also written **faërie, faëry**
Faer·oe Islands (fer′ō) group of Danish islands in the N Atlantic, north of the British Isles
fag[1] (fag) *vi.* **fagged, fag′ging** [< ?] **1.** to work hard and become very tired **2.** [Brit. Colloq.] to serve as a fag or servant —*vt.* to make tired by hard work —*n.* **1.** [Brit. Colloq.] *a)* drudgery *b)* a boy in an English public school who acts as a servant for another boy in a higher form **2.** [Slang] a male homosexual: also **fag′got** (-ət)
fag[2] (fag) *n.* [< ff.] [Old Slang] a cigarette
fag end [< ME. *fagge,* broken thread] **1.** *a)* the last part or coarse end of a piece of cloth *b)* the frayed, untwisted end of a rope **2.** the last and worst part of anything
fag·ot, fag·got (fag′ət) *n.* [< OFr., ult. < Gr. *phakelos,* a bundle] **1.** a bundle of sticks or twigs, esp. for use as fuel **2.** *Metallurgy* a stack of iron or steel pieces to be welded into bars —*vt.* **1.** to form a fagot of **2.** to decorate with fagoting
fag·ot·ing, fag·got·ing (-iŋ) *n.* **1.** a kind of drawnwork or hemstitch with wide spaces **2.** openwork decoration in which the thread is drawn in crisscross or barlike stitches across the open seam

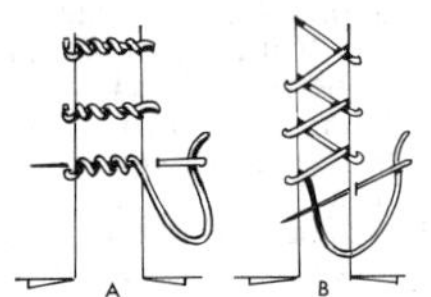

FAGOTING
(A, bar; B, crisscross)

Fah., Fahr. Fahrenheit
Fahr·en·heit (fer′ən hīt′, fär′-) *adj.* [after G. D. *Fahrenheit,* 18th-c. G. physicist] designating or of a thermometer on which 32° is the freezing point and 212° the boiling point of water: abbrev. F
fa·ience (fī äns′, fā-) *n.* [Fr. < *Faenza,* Italy] earthenware having a colorful, opaque glaze
fail (fāl) *vi.* [< OFr. < L. *fallere,* to deceive] **1.** to be lacking or insufficient; fall short; default **2.** to lose power or strength; weaken; die away **3.** to stop functioning **4.** to be unsuccessful in obtaining a desired end **5.** to become bankrupt **6.** *Educ.* to get a grade of failure —*vt.* **1.** to be of no help to; disappoint **2.** to leave; abandon *[his courage failed him]* **3.** to miss, neglect, or omit *[to fail to go]* **4.** *Educ. a)* to give a grade of failure to *b)* to get a grade of failure in —*n.* failure: now only in **without fail,** without failing (to occur, do, etc.) —**fail of** to fail to achieve
fail·ing (-iŋ) *n.* **1.** a failure **2.** a slight fault or defect; weakness —*prep.* without; lacking
faille (fīl, fāl) *n.* [Fr.] a ribbed, soft fabric of silk or rayon
fail-safe (fāl′sāf′) *adj.* [FAIL, *v.* + SAFE, *adj.*] designating an intricate procedure designed to prevent malfunctioning or accidental operation, as of nuclear-armed aircraft
fail·ure (fāl′yər) *n.* [see FAIL] **1.** the act or fact of failing, or falling short, losing strength, breaking down, going bankrupt, not doing or succeeding, etc. **2.** a person or thing that fails **3.** *Educ. a)* a failing to pass *b)* a grade or mark (usually F) indicating a failing to pass
fain (fān) *adj.* [OE. *fægen,* glad] [Archaic] **1.** glad; ready **2.** reluctantly willing **3.** eager —*adv.* [Archaic] gladly or willingly *[he would fain stay]*
faint (fānt) *adj.* [< OFr., orig. pp. of *feindre:* see FEIGN] **1.** without strength; weak; feeble **2.** without courage; timid **3.** done without vigor or enthusiasm **4.** feeling weak and dizzy, as if about to swoon **5.** dim; indistinct **6.** slight *[a faint hope]* —*n.* a condition of temporary loss of consciousness —*vi.* to fall into a faint; swoon —**faint′ish** *adj.* —**faint′ly** *adv.* —**faint′ness** *n.*
faint·heart·ed (-här′tid) *adj.* cowardly; timid —**faint′heart′ed·ly** *adv.* —**faint′heart′ed·ness** *n.*
fair[1] (fer) *adj.* [OE. *fæger*] **1.** beautiful *[a fair maiden]* **2.** unblemished; clean *[a fair name]* **3.** light in color; blond *[fair hair]* **4.** clear and sunny **5.** easy to read; clear *[a fair hand]* **6.** just and honest; impartial; specif., free from discrimination based on race, religion, sex, etc. *[fair housing]* **7.** according to the rules *[a fair blow]* **8.** likely; promising *[in a fair way to benefit]* **9.** pleasant and courteous, often deceptively **10.** favorable; helpful *[a fair wind]* **11.** of moderately good size **12.** neither very bad nor very good; average —*adv.* **1.** in a fair manner *[play fair]* **2.** squarely *[struck fair in the face]* —**fair and square** [Colloq.] with justice and honesty —**fair to middling** [Colloq.] moderately good —**fair′ish** *adj.* —**fair′ness** *n.*
fair[2] (fer) *n.* [< OFr. < ML. < LL. < L. *feriae, pl.,* festivals] **1.** orig., a gathering of people at regular intervals for barter and sale of goods **2.** a carnival where there is entertainment and things are sold, often for charity; bazaar **3.** an exhibition, often regionally competitive **(county fair, state fair)**, of farm, household, and manufactured products, or of international displays **(world's fair)**, with amusement facilities and educational displays; exposition
fair ball *Baseball* a batted ball that first strikes the ground inside the foul line and does not pass the foul line before first or third base
fair game **1.** game that may lawfully be hunted **2.** any legitimate object of attack or pursuit
fair·ground (fer′ground′) *n.* [*often pl.*] an open space where fairs are held
fair-haired (-herd′) *adj.* **1.** having blond hair **2.** [Colloq.] favorite *[mother's fair-haired boy]*
fair·ly (-lē) *adv.* **1.** justly; equitably **2.** moderately; somewhat **3.** clearly; distinctly **4.** completely or really *[his voice fairly rang]*
fair-mind·ed (-mīn′did) *adj.* just; impartial —**fair′-mind′ed·ly** *adv.* —**fair′-mind′ed·ness** *n.*
fair play an abiding by the rules or by decency and honor in sports, business, etc.
fair sex women collectively: used with *the*
fair-spo·ken (-spō′kən) *adj.* speaking or spoken civilly and pleasantly or smoothly and plausibly
fair-trade (-trād′) *adj.* designating or of an agreement whereby a seller is to charge no less than the minimum price set by the manufacturer —*vt.* **-trad′ed, -trad′ing** to sell (a commodity) under a fair-trade agreement
fair·way (-wā′) *n.* **1.** a navigable channel in a river, harbor, etc. **2.** the mowed part of a golf course between a tee and a green
fair-weath·er (-weth′ər) *adj.* **1.** suitable only for fair weather **2.** dependable only in easy circumstances *[fair-weather friends]*
fair·y (fer′ē) *n., pl.* **fair′ies** [< OFr. *faerie* < *fée:* see FAY] **1.** a tiny, graceful imaginary being in human form, supposed to have magic powers **2.** [Slang] a male homosexual —*adj.* **1.** of fairies **2.** like a fairy; graceful; delicate
fair·y·land (-land′) *n.* **1.** the imaginary land where the fairies live **2.** a lovely, enchanting place
fairy tale **1.** a story about fairies, magic deeds, etc. **2.** an unbelievable or untrue story; lie
‡**fait ac·com·pli** (fe tà kōn plē′) [Fr., lit., an accomplished fact] a thing already done, so that opposition or argument is useless
Faith (fāth) [see ff.] a feminine name
faith (fāth) *n.* [< OFr. < L. *fides* < *fidere,* to trust] **1.** unquestioning belief **2.** unquestioning belief in God, religious tenets, etc. **3.** a particular religion **4.** anything believed **5.** complete trust or confidence **6.** loyalty —*interj.* indeed —**bad faith** insincerity; duplicity —**good faith** sincerity; honesty —**in faith** indeed; really
faith cure a trying to cure disease by religious faith, praying, etc.: also **faith healing**
faith·ful (-fəl) *adj.* **1.** keeping faith; loyal **2.** responsible; conscientious **3.** accurate; exact —**the faithful** the true believers or loyal followers —**faith′ful·ly** *adv.* —**faith′ful·ness** *n.*
faith·less (-lis) *adj.* **1.** not keeping faith; dishonest; disloyal **2.** unreliable; undependable —**faith′less·ly** *adv.* —**faith′less·ness** *n.*
fake (fāk) *vt., vi.* **faked, fak′ing** [< ? G. *fegen,* to clean, sweep] to practice deception by giving a false indication or appearance of (something); feign —*n.* anything or anyone not genuine; fraud —*adj.* fraudulent; sham; false —**fak′er** *n.* —**fak′er·y** *n., pl.* **-er·ies**
fa·kir (fə kir′) *n.* [Ar. *faqīr,* lit., poor] **1.** a member of a Moslem holy sect who lives by begging **2.** a Hindu ascetic Also sp. **fa·keer′**
fa·la·fel (fə läf′'l) *n., pl.* **-fel** [Ar. *falāfil*] a patty of ground chickpeas and other vegetables and spices, deep-fried and, usually, served in a pita
Fa·lange (fā′lanj) *n.* [Sp., lit., phalanx] a fascist organization that became the only official political party of Spain under Franco —**Fa·lang′ist** *n.*
fal·cate (fal′kāt) *adj.* [< L. < *falx* (gen. *falcis*), a sickle] sickle-shaped; curved; hooked
fal·chion (fôl′chən, -shən) *n.* [< OFr. < L. *falx:* see prec.] **1.** a medieval sword with a short, broad, slightly curved blade **2.** [Poet.] any sword
fal·con (fal′kən, fôl′-, fô′-) *n.* [< OFr. < LL. *falco* (gen. *falconis*), derived by folk etym. < L. *falx:* see FALCATE] **1.** any hawk trained to hunt and kill small game **2.** a hawklike bird with long, pointed wings and a short, curved, notched beak
fal·con·ry (-rē) *n.* **1.** the art of training falcons to hunt game **2.** the sport of hunting with falcons —**fal′con·er** *n.*
fal·de·ral (fôl′də rôl′, fal′də ral′) *n.* [nonsense syllables] **1.** a showy but worthless trinket **2.** mere nonsense **3.** a refrain in some old songs
Falk·land Islands (fôk′lənd) group of Brit. islands, east of the S tip of S. America

fall (fôl) *vi.* **fell, fall′en, fall′ing** [OE. *feallan*] **1.** to come down by the force of gravity, as when detached, pushed, dropped, etc. *[apples fall from the tree]* **2.** to come down suddenly from a standing or sitting position; tumble **3.** to be wounded or killed in battle **4.** to collapse **5.** to hang down *[hair falling about her shoulders]* **6.** to strike; hit *[to fall wide of the mark]* **7.** to take a downward direction *[land falling away to the sea]* **8.** to become lower in amount, degree, etc.; drop; abate *[prices fell]* **9.** to lose power *[the government fell]* **10.** to lose status, reputation, dignity, etc. **11.** *a)* to do wrong; sin *b)* to lose chastity **12.** to be captured or conquered **13.** to take on a dejected look *[his face fell]* **14.** to become lower in pitch or volume *[her voice fell]* **15.** to take place; occur *[the meeting fell on a Friday]* **16.** to come by lot, inheritance, etc. *[the estate falls to the son]* **17.** to pass into a specified condition; become *[to fall ill]* **18.** to come at a specified place *[the accent falls on the third syllable]* **19.** to be directed by chance *[his eye fell on us]* **20.** to be spoken involuntarily *[an oath fell from his lips]* **21.** to be divided (*into*) *[to fall into two classes]* —*n.* **1.** a dropping; descending **2.** a coming down suddenly from a standing or sitting position **3.** a hanging down, or a part hanging down **4.** a downward direction or slope **5.** a becoming lower or less; reduction in value, price, etc. **6.** a capture; overthrow; ruin **7.** a loss of status, reputation, etc. **8.** something that has fallen *[a fall of leaves]* **9.** autumn **10.** the amount of what has fallen *[a six-inch fall of snow]* **11.** the distance that something falls **12.** [*usually pl., often with sing. v.*] water falling over a cliff, etc.; cascade **13.** a long tress of hair, often synthetic, used by women to fill out their coiffure **14.** *a)* the throwing of an opponent in wrestling on his back so that both shoulders touch the floor *b)* a division of a wrestling match —*adj.* of, for, or in the autumn —**fall (all) over oneself** [Colloq.] to behave in too eager or zealous a manner —**fall away 1.** to take away friendship, support, etc.; desert **2.** to become less in size, strength, etc.; specif., to grow thin and weak —**fall back** to withdraw; give way; retreat —**fall back on** (or **upon**) to turn, or return, to for help —**fall flat** to fail to have the desired effect —**fall for** [Colloq.] **1.** to fall in love with **2.** to be tricked by —**fall in 1.** to agree **2.** *Mil.* to line up in proper formation —**fall off** to become smaller, less, worse, etc. —**fall on** (or **upon**) **1.** to attack **2.** to be the duty of —**fall out 1.** to quarrel **2.** to happen; result **3.** *Mil.* to leave one's place in a formation —**fall through** to come to nothing; fail —**fall to 1.** to begin; start **2.** to start attacking **3.** to start eating —**fall under 1.** to come under (an influence, etc.) **2.** to be classified as —**ride for a fall** to behave in a manner likely to cause one trouble or injury —**the Fall (of Man)** *Christian Theol.* Adam's sin of yielding to temptation in eating the forbidden fruit

fal·la·cious (fə lā′shəs) *adj.* [see ff.] **1.** containing a fallacy **2.** misleading, deceptive, or delusive —**fal·la′cious·ly** *adv.* —**fal·la′cious·ness** *n.*

fal·la·cy (fal′ə sē) *n., pl.* **-cies** [< OFr. < L. < *fallax* (gen. *fallacis*) < *fallere,* to deceive] **1.** aptness to mislead **2.** a false or mistaken idea, opinion, etc.; error **3.** an error in reasoning; specif., *Logic* an argument based on incorrect demonstration, as a vicious circle

fall·en (fôl′ən) *adj.* **1.** having come down; dropped **2.** on the ground; prostrate **3.** degraded **4.** captured; overthrown **5.** ruined **6.** dead

fall guy [Slang] a person left to face the consequences, as of a scheme that has miscarried

fal·li·ble (fal′ə b'l) *adj.* [< ML. < L. *fallere,* to deceive] **1.** liable to be mistaken or deceived **2.** liable to be erroneous or inaccurate —**fal′li·bil′i·ty** *n.* —**fal′li·bly** *adv.*

fall·ing-out (fôl′iŋ out′) *n.* a quarrel

falling sickness *former name for* EPILEPSY

falling star *same as* METEOR (sense 1)

fall-off (fôl′ôf′) *n.* the act or an instance of becoming less or worse; decline

Fal·lo·pi·an tube (fə lō′pē ən) [after G. *Fallopio,* It. anatomist (1523–62)] either of two slender tubes that carry ova from the ovaries to the uterus

fall·out (fôl′out′) *n.* **1.** the descent to earth of radioactive particles, as after a nuclear explosion **2.** these particles **3.** an incidental consequence

fal·low[1] (fal′ō) *n.* [< OE. *fealh*] **1.** land plowed but not seeded for one or more seasons, to kill weeds, enrich the soil, etc. **2.** the plowing of land to be left idle thus —*adj.* **1.** left uncultivated or unplanted **2.** untrained; inactive: said esp. of the mind —*vt.* to leave (land) unplanted after plowing —**lie fallow** to remain uncultivated, unused, etc. for a time —**fal′low·ness** *n.*

fal·low[2] (fal′ō) *adj.* [< OE. *fealo*] pale-yellow

fallow deer a small European deer having a yellowish coat spotted with white in summer

Fall River [transl. of Algonquian name of local river] seaport in SE Mass.: pop. 93,000

false (fôls) *adj.* **fals′er, fals′est** [< OFr. < L. pp. of *fallere,* to deceive] **1.** not true; in error; incorrect; wrong **2.** untruthful; lying **3.** disloyal; unfaithful **4.** deceiving; misleading *[a false scent]* **5.** not real; artificial; counterfeit *[false teeth]* **6.** not properly so named *[false jasmine]* **7.** based on mistaken ideas *[false pride]* **8.** temporary, nonessential, or added on for protection, disguise, etc. *[a false drawer]* **9.** *Music* pitched inaccurately —*adv.* in a false manner —**play (a person) false** to deceive or betray (a person) —**false′ly** *adv.* —**false′ness** *n.*

false arrest *Law* any forceful and unlawful restraint of a person by another

false·heart·ed (-här′tid) *adj.* disloyal; deceitful

false·hood (-hood′) *n.* **1.** lack of accuracy or truth; falsity **2.** the telling of lies; lying **3.** a false statement; lie **4.** a false belief, theory, idea, etc.

false imprisonment *Law* the unlawful arrest or detention of another person

false ribs the five lower ribs on each side of the body: so called because not directly attached to the breastbone

false step 1. a misstep **2.** a social blunder

fal·set·to (fôl set′ō) *n., pl.* **-tos** [It. dim. < L.: see FALSE] **1.** *a)* an artificial way of singing or speaking, in which the voice is placed in a register much higher than that of the natural voice *b)* this voice **2.** a person using falsetto: also **fal·set′tist** —*adj.* of or singing in falsetto —*adv.* in falsetto

fal·si·fy (fôl′sə fī′) *vt.* **-fied′, -fy′ing** [< OFr. < ML. < L. *falsus,* FALSE + *facere,* to make] **1.** to make false; specif., *a)* to give an untrue account of *b)* to alter (a record, etc.) fraudulently **2.** to prove to be unfounded —*vi.* to tell falsehoods; lie —**fal′si·fi·ca′tion** *n.* —**fal′si·fi′er** *n.*

fal·si·ty (-tē) *n., pl.* **-ties 1.** the condition or quality of being false; specif., *a)* incorrectness *b)* dishonesty *c)* deceitfulness *d)* disloyalty **2.** something false; esp., a lie

Fal·staff, Sir John (fôl′staf, -stäf) a fat, jovial, witty knight that is a character in some of Shakespeare's plays —**Fal·staff′i·an** *adj.*

fal·ter (fôl′tər) *vi.* [ME. *faltren,* prob. < ON.] **1.** to move uncertainly or unsteadily; stumble **2.** to stumble in speech; stammer **3.** to act hesitantly; show uncertainty; waver **4.** to lose strength; weaken *[the economy faltered]* —*vt.* to say hesitatingly or timidly —*n.* **1.** a faltering **2.** a faltering sound —**fal′ter·er** *n.* —**fal′ter·ing·ly** *adv.*

fame (fām) *n.* [< OFr. < L. *fama,* fame, akin to *fari,* to speak] **1.** [Archaic] public report; rumor **2.** reputation, esp. for good **3.** the state of being well known or much talked about; renown —*vt.* **famed, fam′ing** [Archaic] to tell about widely; make famous

famed (fāmd) *adj.* much talked about or widely known; famous; renowned (*for* something)

fa·mil·ial (fə mil′yəl) *adj.* of, involving, or common to a family

fa·mil·iar (fə mil′yər) *adj.* [< OFr. < L. < *familia,* FAMILY] **1.** friendly, informal, or intimate **2.** too friendly; unduly intimate or bold **3.** closely acquainted (*with*) *[familiar with the Bible]* **4.** well-known; common *[a familiar sight]* —*n.* **1.** a close friend **2.** in superstitious belief, a spirit acting as servant to a witch —**fa·mil′iar·ly** *adv.*

fa·mil·i·ar·i·ty (fə mil′yar′ə tē, -mil′ē ar′-) *n., pl.* **-ties 1.** intimacy **2.** free and intimate behavior **3.** intimacy that is too bold or unwelcome **4.** a highly intimate act, remark, etc.; specif., a caress **5.** close acquaintance (*with* something)

fa·mil·iar·ize (fə mil′yə rīz′) *vt.* **-ized′, -iz′ing 1.** to make commonly known **2.** to make (another or oneself) accustomed or fully acquainted *[familiarize yourself with the job]* —**fa·mil′iar·i·za′tion** *n.*

fam·i·ly (fam′ə lē, fam′lē) *n., pl.* **-lies** [L. *familia,* household < *famulus,* servant] **1.** orig., all the people living in the same house; household **2.** *a)* a social unit consisting of parents and their children *b)* the children of the same parents **3.** a group of people related by ancestry or marriage; relatives **4.** all those claiming descent from a common ancestor; tribe or clan; lineage **5.** a group of things having a common source or similar features; specif., *a)* *Biol.* a taxonomic category, ranking above a genus and below an order *b)* *Linguis.* a group of languages having a common ancestral language *c)* *Math.* a set of curves, etc. with some shared property —*adj.* of or for a family —**in a family way** [Colloq.] pregnant

family name a surname

family planning *same as* BIRTH CONTROL

family style a way of serving food so that each person at the table helps himself from large dishes

family tree 1. all the ancestors and descendants in a family **2.** a chart showing their relationship

fam·ine (fam′ən) ***n.*** [< OFr., ult. < L. *fames,* hunger] **1.** an acute and general shortage of food, or a period of this **2.** any acute and general shortage **3.** [Archaic] starvation; great hunger

fam·ish (-ish) ***vt., vi.*** [< OFr. < L. *ad,* to + *fames,* hunger] **1.** to make or be very hungry; make or become weak from hunger **2.** [Obs.] to starve to death

fa·mous (fā′məs) ***adj.*** [< L. < *fama,* FAME] **1.** having fame, or celebrity; renowned **2.** [Colloq.] excellent; first-rate **—fa′mous·ly *adv.***

fan[1] (fan) ***n.*** [OE. *fann* < L. *vannus,* basket for winnowing grain] **1.** orig., a device for winnowing grain **2.** any device used to set up a current of air for ventilating or cooling; specif., *a)* any flat surface moved by hand *b)* a folding device of paper, cloth, etc. that opens as a sector of a circle *c)* a motor-driven device with revolving blades **3.** anything in the shape of a fan (sense 2 *b*) ***—vt.* fanned, fan′ning** **1.** to move or agitate (air) as with a fan **2.** to direct a current of air toward with or as with a fan; blow on **3.** to stir up; excite **4.** to blow or drive away with a fan **5.** to spread out into the shape of a fan (*n.* 2 *b*) **6.** to separate (grain) from chaff **7.** [Slang] to fire (a pistol) several times quickly in succession by slapping the hammer back between shots **8.** *Baseball* to strike (a batter) out ***—vi.*** *Baseball* to strike out **—fan out** to scatter or spread out like an open fan **—fan the air** to strike at but fail to hit something **—fan′like′** ***adj.***

fan[2] (fan) ***n.*** [contr. < ff.] [Colloq.] a person enthusiastic about a specified sport, pastime, or performer; devotee *[a baseball fan]*

fa·nat·ic (fə nat′ik) ***adj.*** [< L. < *fanum,* a temple] unreasonably enthusiastic; overly zealous: also **fa·nat′i·cal** ***—n.*** a person whose extreme zeal, piety, etc. goes beyond what is reasonable; zealot **—fa·nat′i·cal·ly *adv.***

fa·nat·i·cism (-ə siz′m) ***n.*** excessive and unreasonable zeal **—fa·nat′i·cize′** (-sīz′) ***vt., vi.*** **-cized′, -ciz′ing**

fan·cied (fan′sēd) ***adj.*** imaginary; imagined

fan·ci·er (fan′sē ər) ***n.*** a person with a special interest in and knowledge of something, particularly plant or animal breeding *[a dog fancier]*

fan·ci·ful (fan′si fəl) ***adj.*** **1.** full of fancy; having or showing a playful imagination *[fanciful costumes]* **2.** not real, practical, etc.; imaginary *[a fanciful tale]* **—fan′ci·ful·ly *adv.* —fan′ci·ful·ness *n.***

fan·cy (fan′sē) ***n., pl.*** **-cies** [contr. < FANTASY] **1.** imagination, now esp. light, whimsical, or capricious imagination **2.** a mental image **3.** an arbitrary idea; notion; caprice; whim **4.** an inclination, liking, or fondness, often temporary *[to take a fancy to someone]* ***—adj.*** **-ci·er, -ci·est** **1.** capricious; whimsical; fanciful **2.** extravagant *[a fancy price]* **3.** not plain; decorated, elaborate, ornamental, etc. *[a fancy necktie]* **4.** of superior skill *[fancy diving]* **5.** of superior quality and therefore more expensive **6.** bred for some special feature ***—vt.*** **-cied, -cy·ing** **1.** to form an idea of; imagine **2.** to have a liking for **3.** to think or suppose **—fancy (that)!** can you imagine (that)! **—fan′ci·less *adj.* —fan′ci·ly *adv.* —fan′ci·ness *n.***

fan·cy-free (-frē′) ***adj.*** **1.** free to fall in love; not married, engaged, etc. **2.** carefree

fan·cy·work (-wurk′) ***n.*** embroidery, crocheting, and other ornamental needlework

fan·dan·go (fan daŋ′gō) ***n., pl.*** **-gos** [Sp.] **1.** a lively Spanish dance in rhythm varying from slow to quick 3/4 time **2.** music for this

fane (fān) ***n.*** [L. *fanum*] [Archaic] a temple or church

fan·fare (fan′fer′) ***n.*** [Fr., prob. < *fanfaron,* braggart] **1.** a loud flourish of trumpets **2.** noisy or showy display

fang (faŋ) ***n.*** [OE. < base of *fon,* to seize] **1.** *a)* one of the long, pointed teeth with which meat-eating animals seize and tear their prey *b)* one of the long, hollow or grooved teeth through which poisonous snakes inject their venom **2.** the pointed part of something **—fanged** (faŋd) ***adj.***

fan·light (fan′līt′) ***n.*** a semicircular window, often with sash bars in a fan-like arrangement, over a door or larger window

fan mail letters of praise or adulation from fans

Fan·nie, Fan·ny (fan′ē) [dim. of FRANCES] a feminine name

fan·tail (fan′tāl′) ***n.*** **1.** a part, tail, or end spread out like an opened fan **2.** *Naut.* the part of the main deck at the stern **3.** *Zool.* a variety of domestic pigeon, a breed of goldfish, etc. with a fanlike tail

fan-tan (fan′tan′) ***n.*** [< Chin. *fan,* number of times + *t'an,* apportion] **1.** a Chinese gambling game **2.** a card game in which the players seek to discard all their cards in proper sequence Also **fan tan**

fan·ta·si·a (fan tā′zhə, -zē ə; fan′tə zē′ə) ***n.*** [It. < L.: see FANTASY] **1.** a musical composition of no fixed form **2.** a medley of familiar tunes

fan·ta·size (fan′tə sīz′) ***vt., vi.*** **-sized′, -siz′ing** [FANTAS(Y) + -IZE] to create or imagine (something) in a fantasy; have daydreams (about) **—fan′ta·sist *n.***

fan·tas·tic (fan tas′tik) ***adj.*** [< OFr. < ML. < LL. < Gr. *phantastikos,* able to present to the mind < *phainein,* to show] **1.** imaginary; unreal *[fantastic terrors]* **2.** grotesque; odd; quaint *[fantastic designs]* **3.** extravagant; capricious; eccentric *[a fantastic plan]* **4.** seemingly impossible; incredible *[fantastic progress]* Also **fan·tas′ti·cal** **—fan·tas′ti·cal·ly *adv.* —fan·tas′ti·cal·ness *n.***

fan·ta·sy (fan′tə sē, -zē) ***n., pl.*** **-sies** [< OFr. < L. < Gr. *phantasia,* appearance < *phainein,* to show] **1.** imagination or fancy; esp., wild, visionary fancy **2.** an unnatural or bizarre mental image **3.** an odd notion; whim; caprice **4.** a highly imaginative poem, play, etc. **5.** *same as* FANTASIA **6.** a daydream or daydreaming, esp. about an unfulfilled desire ***—vt.*** **-sied, -sy·ing** to form fantasies about ***—vi.*** to indulge in fantasies, as by daydreaming

FAO Food and Agriculture Organization (of the UN)

far (fär) ***adj.*** **far′ther, far′thest** [OE. *feorr*] **1.** distant in space or time; not near **2.** extending a long way *[a far journey]* **3.** more distant *[the far side of the room]* **4.** very different in quality or nature *[far from poor]* ***—adv.*** **1.** very distant in space, time, or degree **2.** to or from a great distance in time or position **3.** very much *[far better]* **4.** to a certain distance or degree *[how far did you go?]* ***—n.*** a distant place *[to come from far]* **—as far as** **1.** to the distance, extent, or degree that **2.** [Colloq.] with reference to; as for **—by far** very much: also **far and away** **—far and near** (or **wide**) everywhere **—far be it from me** I would not presume or wish **—far gone** in an advanced state of deterioration **—far out** *same as* FAR-OUT (see below) **—few and far between** scarce; rare **—go far** **1.** to cover much extent; last long **2.** to have a strong tendency **3.** to accomplish much **—in so far as** to the extent or degree that **—so far** up to this place, time, or degree **—so far as** to the extent or point that **—so far, so good** up to this point everything is all right **—far′ness *n.***

far·ad (far′ad, -əd) ***n.*** [after ff.] a unit of capacitance, equal to the amount that permits the storing of one coulomb of charge for each volt of applied potential

Far·a·day (far′ə dā′), **Michael** 1791–1867; Eng. scientist: noted esp. for his work in electricity

far·a·way (fär′ə wā′) ***adj.*** **1.** distant in time or place **2.** dreamy; abstracted *[a faraway look]*

farce (färs) ***n.*** [Fr. < L. *farcire,* to stuff: early farces were used to fill interludes between acts] **1.** an exaggerated comedy based on broadly humorous, highly unlikely situations **2.** broad humor of the kind found in such plays **3.** a ridiculous display, pretense, etc.

far·ci·cal (fär′si k′l) ***adj.*** of, or having the nature of, a farce; absurd, ridiculous, etc. **—far′ci·cal′i·ty** (-kal′ə tē) ***n.*** **—far′ci·cal·ly *adv.***

far·del (fär′d′l) ***n.*** [OFr.] [Archaic] a burden

fare (fer) ***vi.*** **fared, far′ing** [OE. *faran,* to go, wander] **1.** [Poet.] to travel; go **2.** to happen; result *[how did it fare with him?]* **3.** to be in a specified condition; get on *[he fared well on his trip]* **4.** to eat or be given food ***—n.*** **1.** money paid for a trip in a train, taxi, plane, etc. **2.** a passenger who pays a fare **3.** *a)* food *b)* the usual diet

Far East E Asia, including China, Japan, Korea, & Mongolia, &, sometimes, Indochina & Malaya

fare-thee-well (fer′*th*ē wel′) ***n.*** the highest or ultimate degree: usually in the phrase **to a fare-thee-well**

fare·well (fer′wel′; *for adj.* -wel′) ***interj.*** [FARE (imperative) + WELL[2]] goodbye ***—n.*** **1.** parting words; good wishes at parting **2.** a leaving or going away ***—adj.*** parting; last; final *[a farewell gesture]*

far·fel (far′f′l) ***n.*** [Yid. *farfal* < MHG.] noodle dough chopped into small grains, as served in soup

far-fetched (fär′fecht′) ***adj.*** resulting or introduced in a forced, or unnatural, way; strained

far-flung (-fluŋ′) ***adj.*** extending over a wide area

Far·go (fär′gō) [after W. *Fargo* of Wells, Fargo & Co., shippers] city in E N.Dak.: pop. 61,000

fa·ri·na (fə rē′nə) ***n.*** [L. < *far,* kind of grain] flour or meal made from cereal grains (esp. whole wheat), potatoes, nuts, etc., eaten as a cooked cereal

far·i·na·ceous (far′ə nā′shəs) ***adj.*** [see prec.] **1.** containing, consisting of, or made from flour or meal **2.** like meal **3.** containing starch

far·kle·ber·ry (fär′k′l ber′ē) ***n., pl.*** **-ries** [< ?] a shrub or small tree of the southern U.S., with black, inedible berries

farm (färm) ***n.*** [< OFr. < ML. *firma,* fixed payment < *firmare,* to lease < L. *firmus,* steadfast] **1.** the letting out, for a fixed amount, of the privilege to collect and keep taxes **2.** a piece of land (with house, barns, etc.) on which crops or animals are raised; orig., such land let out to tenants **3.** any place where certain things are raised *[a tract of water for raising fish is a fish farm]* **4.** *Baseball* a minor-league team owned by or associated with a major-league team: also **farm club** ***—vt.*** **1.** to cultivate (land) **2.** to collect (taxes) for a fixed amount **3.** to turn over to another for a fee —*vi.* to work on or operate a farm; raise crops or animals on a farm —**farm out** **1.** to rent (land, a business, etc.) for a fixed payment **2.** to send (work) from a shop, office, etc. to workers on the outside **3.** to let out the labor of (a convict, etc.) for a fixed amount **4.** *Baseball* to assign to a farm

farm·er (fär′mər) ***n.*** **1.** a person who earns his living by farming; esp., one who manages or operates a farm **2.** a person who pays for a right, as, formerly, to collect and keep taxes **3.** a person who contracts to do something for a fixed price

farm·hand (färm′hand′) ***n.*** a hired farm laborer

farm·house (-hous′) ***n.*** a house on a farm; esp., the main dwelling house on a farm

farm·ing (fär′miŋ) ***adj.*** of or for agriculture —***n.*** **1.** the business of operating a farm **2.** the letting out to farm of land, revenue, etc.

farm·stead (färm′sted′) ***n.*** the land and buildings of a farm

farm·yard (-yärd′) ***n.*** the yard surrounding or enclosed by the farm buildings

far·o (fer′ō) ***n.*** [Fr. *pharaon* < ? *Pharaoh*] a gambling game in which players bet on the cards to be turned up from the top of the dealer's pack

far-off (fär′ôf′) ***adj.*** distant; remote

fa·rouche (fə ro͞osh′) ***adj.*** [Fr. < OFr., ult. < L. *foras*, out-of-doors] **1.** wild; savage **2.** lacking social grace

far-out (fär′out′) ***adj.*** [Colloq.] very advanced, experimental, or nonconformist; esp., avant-garde

Far·quhar (fär′kwər, -kər), **George** 1678–1707; Brit. playwright, born in Ireland

far·ra·go (fə rā′gō, -rä′-) ***n.***, *pl.* **-goes** [L., mixed fodder, mixture < *far:* see FARINA] a confused mixture; jumble —**far·rag′i·nous** (-raj′ə nəs) ***adj.***

Far·ra·gut (far′ə gət), **David Glasgow** (born *James Glasgow Farragut*) 1801–70; U.S. admiral

far-reach·ing (fär′rēch′iŋ) ***adj.*** having a wide range, extent, influence, or effect

far·ri·er (far′ē ər) ***n.*** [< OFr. < ML. < L. *ferrum*, iron] [Brit.] a blacksmith who shoes horses; also, sometimes, one who treats their diseases —**far′ri·er·y** ***n.***, *pl.* **-er·ies**

far·row (far′ō) ***n.*** [< OE. *fearh*, young pig] a litter of pigs —***vt., vi.*** to give birth to (a litter of pigs)

far·see·ing (fär′sē′iŋ) ***adj.*** *same as* FARSIGHTED (senses 1 & 2)

far·sight·ed (-sīt′id) ***adj.*** **1.** capable of seeing far **2.** prudent in judgment and foresight **3.** having better vision for distant objects than for near ones —**far′sight′ed·ly** ***adv.*** —**far′sight′ed·ness** ***n.***

far·ther (fär′*th*ər) ***adj.*** *compar. of* FAR [ME. *ferther*, var. of *further*, FURTHER] **1.** more distant **2.** additional; further —***adv.*** *compar. of* FAR **1.** at or to a greater distance or more remote point **2.** to a greater degree; further **3.** in addition; further In sense 2 of the *adj.* and senses 2 and 3 of the *adv.*, FURTHER is more commonly used

far·ther·most (-mōst′) ***adj.*** most distant; farthest

far·thest (fär′*th*ist) ***adj.*** *superl. of* FAR [ME. *ferthest:* see FARTHER] most distant —***adv.*** *superl. of* FAR **1.** at or to the greatest distance or most remote point **2.** to the greatest degree

far·thing (fär′*th*iŋ) ***n.*** [OE. *feorthing*, dim. of *feortha*, fourth] **1.** a former small British coin, equal to one fourth of a penny **2.** a thing of little value; the least amount

far·thin·gale (fär′*th*iŋ gāl′) ***n.*** [OFr. *verdugalle* < Sp. < *verdugo*, tree shoot, rod < *verde* < L. *viridis*, green] a hoop skirt worn by women in the 16th and 17th centuries

fas·ces (fas′ēz) ***n.pl.*** [L., pl. of *fascis*, a bundle] a bundle of rods bound about an ax, carried before ancient Roman magistrates as a symbol of authority: later the symbol of Italian fascism

FASCES

fas·ci·a (fash′ē ə, fash′ə) ***n.***, *pl.* **-ci·ae′** (-ē′), **-ci·as** [L., a band] **1.** a flat strip; band **2.** *Anat.* a thin layer of connective tissue —**fas′ci·al** ***adj.***

fas·ci·cle (fas′i k'l) ***n.*** [< OFr. < L. dim. of *fascis:* see FASCES] **1.** a single section of a book published in installments **2.** a small bundle or cluster, as of leaves, stems, etc. —**fas′ci·cled** ***adj.***

fas·cic·u·late (fə sik′yoo lit, -lāt′) ***adj.*** [see prec.] formed of, or growing in, bundles or clusters: also **fas·cic′u·lat′ed** (-lāt′id), **fas·cic′u·lar**

fas·ci·nate (fas′ə nāt′) ***vt.*** **-nat′ed, -nat′ing** [< L. pp. of *fascinare*, to bewitch < *fascinum*, an enchanting] **1.** orig., to put under a spell **2.** to hold motionless, as by inspiring terror **3.** to hold the attention of by being very interesting or delightful; charm —**fas′ci·nat′ing·ly** ***adv.***

fas·ci·na·tion (fas′ə nā′shən) ***n.*** **1.** a fascinating or being fascinated **2.** charm; allure

fas·ci·na·tor (fas′ə nāt′ər) ***n.*** **1.** a person who fascinates **2.** a woman's light scarf, knitted or crocheted: an old-fashioned term

fas·cism (fash′iz'm) ***n.*** [It. *fascismo* < L. *fascis:* see FASCES] **1.** [F-] the doctrines, methods, or movement of the Fascisti **2.** a system of government characterized by dictatorship, belligerent nationalism, racism, militarism, etc.: first instituted in Italy in 1922 **3.** fascist behavior

fas·cist (-ist) ***n.*** **1.** [F-] *a)* a member of the Fascisti *b)* a member of some similar party; Nazi, Falangist, etc. **2.** an adherent of fascism —***adj.*** **1.** [F-] of Fascists or Fascism **2.** of, believing in, or practicing fascism —**fa·scis′tic** (fa shis′tik) ***adj.*** —**fa·scis′ti·cal·ly** ***adv.***

Fa·scis·ti (fa shis′tē) ***n.pl.*** [It., pl. of *fascista*, a Fascist < L. *fascis:* see FASCES] an Italian political organization which seized power and set up a fascist dictatorship (1922–43) under Mussolini

fash·ion (fash′ən) ***n.*** [< OFr. *faceon* < L. *factio:* see FACTION] **1.** the make, form, or shape of a thing **2.** [Now Rare] kind; sort **3.** way; manner **4.** the current style of dress, conduct, etc. **5.** something in the current style **6.** fashionable society [a man of *fashion*] —***vt.*** **1.** to make or form in a certain way; shape **2.** to fit, accommodate (*to*) **3.** [Archaic] to contrive —**after** (or **in**) **a fashion** to some extent, but not very well —**fash′ion·er** ***n.***

fash·ion·a·ble (-ə b'l) ***adj.*** **1.** in fashion; stylish **2.** of, characteristic of, or used by people who follow fashion —***n.*** a fashionable person —**fash′ion·a·ble·ness** ***n.*** —**fash′ion·a·bly** ***adv.***

fashion plate **1.** a picture showing a current style in dress **2.** a fashionably dressed person

fast[1] (fast) ***adj.*** [OE. *fæst*] **1.** firm, fixed, or stuck **2.** firmly fastened or shut **3.** loyal; devoted **4.** that will not fade [*fast* colors] **5.** swift; quick; speedy **6.** permitting swift movement [a *fast* highway] **7.** lasting a short time [a *fast* lunch] **8.** showing a time that is ahead of the correct time [his watch is *fast*] **9.** *a)* reckless; wild [a *fast* crowd] *b)* sexually promiscuous **10.** [Colloq.] glib and deceptive [a *fast* talker] **11.** [Slang] acting, gotten, done, etc. quickly and often dishonestly [out for a *fast* buck] **12.** *Photog.* adapted to very short exposure time **13.** [Dial.] complete; sound [a *fast* sleep] —***adv.*** **1.** firmly; fixedly **2.** thoroughly; soundly [*fast* asleep] **3.** rapidly; swiftly **4.** ahead of time **5.** in a reckless, dissipated way; wildly **6.** [Obs.] close; near [*fast* by the river] —**a fast one** [Slang] a deceptive act [to pull *a fast one*] —**play fast and loose** to behave with duplicity or insincerity

fast[2] (fast) ***vi.*** [OE. *fæstan*] **1.** to abstain from all or certain foods, as in observing a holy day **2.** to eat very little or nothing —***n.*** **1.** the act of fasting **2.** a period of fasting —**break one's fast** to eat food for the first time after fasting

fast·back (-bak′) ***n.*** an automobile contour with an unbroken curve from windshield to rear bumper

fast day a holy day, etc. observed by fasting

fas·ten (fas′'n) ***vt.*** [OE. *fæstnian* < base of *fæst*, FAST[1]] **1.** to join (one thing *to* another); attach **2.** to make secure, as by locking, buttoning, etc. **3.** to hold or direct (the attention, etc.) steadily (*on*) **4.** to cause to be attributed; impute [to *fasten* a crime on someone] **5.** to force (oneself *on* or *upon* another) in an annoying way —***vi.*** **1.** to become attached or joined **2.** to take a firm hold (*on* or *upon*); seize **3.** to concentrate (*on* or *upon*) —**fas′ten·er** ***n.***

fas·ten·ing (-iŋ) ***n.*** anything used to fasten; bolt, clasp, hook, lock, button, etc.

fas·tid·i·ous (fas tid′ē əs, fəs-) ***adj.*** [< L. < *fastidium*, a loathing < *fastus*, disdain + *taedium:* see TEDIUM] **1.** not easy to please; very critical **2.** daintily refined; easily disgusted —**fas·tid′i·ous·ly** ***adv.*** —**fas·tid′i·ous·ness** ***n.***

fast·ness (fast′nis) ***n.*** **1.** the quality or condition of being fast **2.** a secure place; stronghold

fast time *same as* DAYLIGHT-SAVING TIME

fat (fat) ***adj.*** **fat′ter, fat′test** [OE. *fætt*, pp. of *fætan*, to fatten] **1.** containing or full of fat; oily; greasy **2.** *a)* fleshy; plump *b)* too plump; obese **3.** thick; broad **4.** fertile; productive [*fat* land] **5.** profitable; lucrative [a *fat* job] **6.** prosperous **7.** plentiful; ample **8.** stupid; dull **9.** [Slang] large or important [a *fat* role in a play] —***n.*** **1.** any of various solid or semisolid oily or greasy materials found in animal tissue and in plant seeds **2.** fleshiness; corpulence **3.** the richest part of anything **4.** anything unnecessary that can be trimmed away **5.** *Chem.* a class of glyceryl esters of fatty acids, insoluble in water —***vt., vi.*** **fat′ted, fat′ting** to make or become fat: now usually FATTEN —**a fat chance** [Slang] very little or no chance —**chew the fat** [Slang] to talk together; chat —**the fat of the land** the best obtainable; great luxury —**fat′ly** ***adv.*** —**fat′ness** ***n.***

fa·tal (fāt′'l) ***adj.*** [OFr. < L. *fatalis* < *fatum*, FATE] **1.** fateful; decisive [the *fatal* day arrived] **2.** resulting in death **3.** very destructive; most unfortunate **—fa′tal·ly** ***adv.*** **—fa′tal·ness *n.***

fa·tal·ism (-iz′m) ***n.*** **1.** the belief that all events are determined by fate and are hence inevitable **2.** acceptance of every event as inevitable **—fa′tal·ist *n.*** **—fa′tal·is′tic *adj.*** **—fa′tal·is′ti·cal·ly *adv.***

fa·tal·i·ty (fə tal′ə tē, fā-) ***n.,*** *pl.* **-ties** **1.** fate or necessity; subjection to fate **2.** something caused by fate **3.** an inevitable liability to disaster **4.** a fatal quality; deadliness *[*the *fatality* of a disease*]* **5.** a death caused by a disaster, as in an accident, war, etc.

fat·back (fat′bak′) ***n.*** **1.** fat from a hog's back, usually dried and salted in strips **2.** *same as* MENHADEN

fat cat [Slang] a wealthy, influential person

fate (fāt) ***n.*** [< L. *fatum,* oracle < neut. pp. of *fari,* to speak] **1.** the power or agency supposed to determine the outcome of events; destiny **2.** *a)* something supposedly determined by this power *b)* a person's lot or fortune **3.** final outcome **4.** death; destruction **—*vt.*** **fat′ed, fat′ing** to destine: now usually in the passive **—the Fates** *Gr. & Rom. Myth.* the three goddesses who control human destiny and life: see CLOTHO, LACHESIS, and ATROPOS

fat·ed (fāt′id) ***adj.*** **1.** destined **2.** doomed

fate·ful (-fəl) ***adj.*** **1.** prophetic **2.** having important consequences; decisive **3.** controlled as if by fate **4.** bringing death or destruction **—fate′ful·ly *adv.*** **—fate′ful·ness *n.***

fat·head (fat′hed′) ***n.*** [Slang] a stupid person **—fat′head′ed *adj.***

fa·ther (fä′*th*ər) ***n.*** [OE. *fæder*] **1.** a male parent; esp., a man as he is related to his child **2.** *a)* a stepfather *b)* father-in-law **3.** a guardian or protector **4.** [F-] God, or God as the first person of the Trinity **5.** a forefather; ancestor **6.** an originator; founder; inventor **7.** any of the leaders of a city, assembly, etc.: *usually used in the pl.* **8.** [*often* **F-**] *a)* any of the important early Christian religious writers *b)* a Christian priest: used esp. as a title **—*vt.*** **1.** to be the father of; beget **2.** to care for as a father does; protect, rear, etc. **3.** to found, originate, or invent **—fa′ther·hood′ *n.*** **—fa′ther·less *adj.***

father confessor **1.** a priest who hears confessions **2.** a person in whom one habitually confides

father image (or **figure**) a person substituted in one's mind for one's father

fa·ther-in-law (-ən lô′) ***n.,*** *pl.* **fa′thers-in-law′** the father of one's wife or husband

fa·ther·land (-land′) ***n.*** a person's native land or, sometimes, the land of his ancestors

fa·ther·ly (-lē) ***adj.*** of or like a father; kindly; protective **—*adv.*** [Archaic] in a fatherly manner **—fa′ther·li·ness *n.***

Father's Day the third Sunday in June, a day set aside (in the U.S.) in honor of fathers

Father Time time personified as a very old man carrying a scythe and an hourglass

fath·om (fa*th*′əm) ***n.*** [OE. *fæthm,* the two arms outstretched (to measure, etc.)] a nautical unit of depth or length, equal to 6 feet **—*vt.*** **1.** to measure the depth of; sound **2.** to understand thoroughly **—fath′om·a·ble *adj.*** **—fath′om·less *adj.*** **—fath′om·less·ness *n.***

Fa·thom·e·ter (fa*th* äm′ə tər) *a trademark for* a sonar device used to measure depth of oceans, etc. **—*n.*** [**f-**] such a device

fa·tigue (fə tēg′) ***n.*** [Fr. < L. *fatigare,* to weary] **1.** physical or mental exhaustion; weariness **2.** *a)* manual labor or menial duty, other than drill or instruction, assigned to soldiers: in full, **fatigue duty** *b)* [*pl.*] sturdy work clothing worn on fatigue duty: also **fatigue clothes** (or **clothing**) **3.** the tendency of a metal or other material to crack under repeated stress **—*vt., vi.*** **-tigued′, -tigu′ing** **1.** to make or become tired; weary **2.** to subject to or undergo fatigue **—fat′i·ga·bil′i·ty *n.*** **—fat·i·ga·ble** (fat′i gə b′l) ***adj.***

Fat·i·ma (fat′i mə, fät′-; fə tē′mə) 606?–632 A.D.; daughter of Mohammed

fat·ling (fat′liŋ) ***n.*** a calf, lamb, kid, or young pig fattened before being slaughtered

fat·ten (fat′'n) ***vt., vi.*** to make or become fat **—fat′ten·er *n.***

fat·tish (-ish) ***adj.*** somewhat fat

fat·ty (-ē) ***adj.*** **-ti·er, -ti·est** **1.** of or containing fat **2.** very plump **3.** resembling fat; greasy; oily **—*n.*** [Colloq.] a fat person **—fat′ti·ness *n.***

fatty acid **1.** any of a series of saturated organic acids having the general formula $C_nH_{2n+1}COOH$ **2.** any of a number of saturated or unsaturated organic acids usually having an even number of carbon atoms

fa·tu·i·ty (fə to͞o′ə tē, -tyo͞o′-; fa-) ***n.,*** *pl.* **-ties** **1.** complacent stupidity; smug foolishness **2.** a fatuous remark, act, etc. **—fa·tu′i·tous *adj.***

fat·u·ous (fach′oo wəs) ***adj.*** [L. *fatuus,* foolish] **1.** complacently stupid; foolish **2.** [Archaic] illusory **—fat′u·ous·ly *adv.*** **—fat′u·ous·ness *n.***

fau·ces (fô′sēz) ***n.pl.*** [L., throat] the passage leading from the back of the mouth into the pharynx **—fau′cal** (-kəl), **fau′cial** (-shəl) ***adj.***

fau·cet (fô′sit) ***n.*** [< OFr., prob. < *faulser,* to breach, falsify < LL. < L. *falsus,* FALSE] a device with a valve for regulating the flow of a liquid from a pipe, etc.; cock; tap

Faulk′ner (fôk′nər), **William** 1897–1962; U.S. novelist

fault (fôlt) ***n.*** [< OFr. *faulte,* ult. < L. *falsus,* FALSE] **1.** something that mars; flaw; defect **2.** *a)* a misdeed; offense *b)* an error; mistake **3.** responsibility for something wrong; blame *[*it's my *fault* that he's late*]* **4.** *Geol.* a fracture or zone of fractures in rock strata along with displacement of the strata **5.** *Tennis, Squash,* etc. an error in service **—*vt.*** **1.** to find fault with; blame **2.** *Geol.* to cause a fault in **—*vi.*** **1.** to commit a fault in tennis, etc. **2.** *Geol.* to develop a fault **—at fault** guilty of error; deserving blame **—find fault (with)** to seek and point out faults (of) **—to a fault** excessively

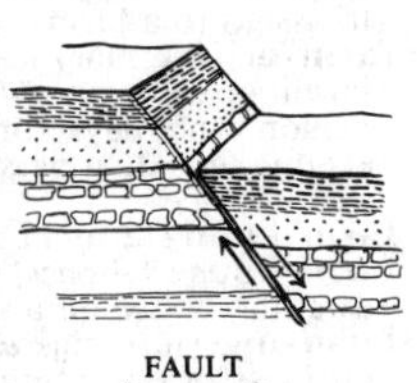

FAULT
(sense 4)

fault·find·ing (-fīn′diŋ) ***n., adj.*** finding fault; calling attention to defects **—fault′find′er *n.***

fault·less (-lis) ***adj.*** without any fault; perfect **—fault′less·ly *adv.*** **—fault′less·ness *n.***

fault·y (-ē) ***adj.*** **fault′i·er, fault′i·est** having a fault or faults; imperfect **—fault′i·ly *adv.*** **—fault′i·ness *n.***

faun (fôn) ***n.*** [< L. < *Faunus,* a Roman nature god] any of a class of minor Roman deities, usually represented as having the body of a man, but the horns, ears, tail, and hind legs of a goat

fau·na (fô′nə) ***n.,*** *pl.* **-nas, -nae** (-nē) [ModL. < LL. *Fauna,* Roman goddess] the animals of a specified region or time **—fau′nal *adj.***

Fau·ré (fô *rā*′), **Gabriel** 1845–1924; Fr. composer

Faust (foust) the hero of a medieval legend, and later literary and operatic works, who sells his soul to the devil to gain knowledge and power: also **Faus′tus** (fôs′təs, fous′-) **—Faust′i·an *adj.***

fau·vism (fō′viz′m) ***n.*** [< Fr. < *fauve,* wild beast] [*often* **F-**] a French form of expressionist painting characterized by bold distortions and strong, pure color **—fauve** (fōv), **fau′vist *n., adj.***

faux pas (fō′ pä′) *pl.* **faux pas** (fō′ päz′) [Fr., lit., false step] a social blunder; error in etiquette

fa·vor (fā′vər) ***n.*** [< OFr. < L. < *favere,* to favor] **1.** friendly regard; good will **2.** unfair partiality; favoritism **3.** a kind or obliging act **4.** a small gift, souvenir, or token **—*vt.*** **1.** to regard with favor; approve or like **2.** to be partial to; prefer unfairly **3.** to support; advocate **4.** to make easier; help *[*rain *favored* his escape*]* **5.** to do a kindness for **6.** to look like; resemble *[*to *favor* one's mother*]* **7.** to use gently; spare *[*to *favor* an injured leg*]* **—find favor** to be pleasing **—in favor of** **1.** approving; supporting **2.** to the advantage of **3.** payable to, as a check **—in one's favor** to one's advantage **—fa′vor·er *n.***

fa·vor·a·ble (-ə b′l) ***adj.*** **1.** approving or commending **2.** helpful or advantageous **3.** pleasing or desirable *[*a *favorable* impression*]* **—fa′vor·a·ble·ness *n.*** **—fa′vor·a·bly *adv.***

fa·vored (fā′vərd) ***adj.*** **1.** treated with favor; specially privileged **2.** having (specified) features *[ill-favored]*

fa·vor·ite (fā′vər it, fāv′rit) ***n.*** **1.** a person or thing regarded with special liking; specif., a person granted special privileges, as by a king, etc. **2.** a contestant regarded as most likely to win **—*adj.*** held in special regard; best liked; preferred

fa·vor·it·ism (-iz′m) ***n.*** **1.** the act of being unfairly partial **2.** the condition of being a favorite

fa·vour (fā′vər) ***n., vt.*** *Brit. var. of* FAVOR

Fawkes (fôks), **Guy** 1570–1606; Eng. conspirator in a plot to blow up the king & Parliament

fawn[1] (fôn) ***vi.*** [< OE. *fagnian* < *fagen,* var. of *fægen,* fain] **1.** to show friendliness by licking hands, wagging its tail, etc.: said of a dog **2.** to cringe and flatter **—fawn′er *n.*** **—fawn′ing·ly *adv.***

fawn[2] (fôn) ***n.*** [< OFr. *faon,* ult. < L. *fetus,* FETUS] **1.** a young deer less than one year old **2.** a pale, yellowish brown **—*adj.*** of this color **—*vi., vt.*** to bring forth (young): said of deer

Fay, Faye (fā) [< ? ME. *faie,* FAY or ? ME. *fei,* faith] a feminine name

fay (fā) ***n.*** [< OFr. < VL. < L. *fatum,* FATE] a fairy

Fay·ette·ville (fā′ət vil′) [after Marquis de (LA)FAYETTE] city in SC N.C.: pop. 60,000

faze (fāz) ***vt.*** **fazed, faz′ing** [< OE. *fesan,* to drive] [Colloq.] to disturb; disconcert

FBI, F.B.I. Federal Bureau of Investigation

FCC, F.C.C. Federal Communications Commission

F clef *same as* BASS CLEF

FDA, F.D.A. Food and Drug Administration

FDIC, F.D.I.C. Federal Deposit Insurance Corporation

Fe [L. *ferrum*] *Chem.* iron

F.E.A., FEA Federal Energy Administration

fe·al·ty (fē′əl tē) ***n., pl.* -ties** [< OFr. *feauté* < L. *fidelitas,* FIDELITY] **1.** the loyalty owed by a vassal to his feudal lord **2.** [Archaic] loyalty
fear (fir) ***n.*** [OE. *fær,* danger] **1.** anxiety and agitation caused by the presence of danger, evil, pain, etc.; fright **2.** awe; reverence **3.** a feeling of uneasiness or apprehension; concern **4.** a cause for fear **—*vt.* 1.** to be afraid of **2.** to feel reverence or awe for **3.** to expect with misgiving [I *fear* I am late] **4.** [Obs.] to frighten **—*vi.* 1.** to feel fear **2.** to be uneasy or anxious **—for fear of** in order to avoid or prevent **—fear′less *adj.* —fear′less·ly *adv.* —fear′less·ness *n.***
fear·ful (-fəl) ***adj.* 1.** causing fear; dreadful **2.** feeling fear; afraid **3.** showing fear [a *fearful* look] **4.** [Colloq.] very bad, great, etc. [a *fearful* liar] **—fear′ful·ly *adv.* —fear′ful·ness *n.***
fear·some (-səm) ***adj.* 1.** causing fear; frightful **2.** frightened; timid **—fear′some·ly *adv.* —fear′some·ness *n.***
fea·si·ble (fē′zə b'l) ***adj.*** [< OFr. < *faire,* to make, do < L. *facere*] **1.** capable of being done or carried out; practicable; possible **2.** within reason; likely; probable **3.** capable of being used successfully; suitable **—fea′si·bil′i·ty** *pl.* **-ties, fea′si·ble·ness *n.* —fea′si·bly *adv.***
feast (fēst) ***n.*** [< OFr. < VL. *festa* < pl. of L. *festum* < *festus,* festal] **1.** a festival; esp., a religious festival **2.** a rich and elaborate meal; banquet **3.** anything that gives pleasure by its abundance or richness **—*vi.* 1.** to eat a rich, elaborate meal **2.** to have a special treat **—*vt.* 1.** to entertain at a feast or banquet **2.** to delight or gratify [to *feast* one's eyes on a sight] **—feast′er *n.***
feat (fēt) ***n.*** [< Anglo-Fr. < OFr. < L. *factum,* a deed < pp. of *facere,* to do] an act or deed showing unusual daring, skill, etc.
feath·er (fe*th*′ər) ***n.*** [OE. *fether*] **1.** *Zool.* any of the growths covering the body of a bird and making up a large part of the wing surface **2.** anything like a feather in appearance, lightness, etc. **3.** [*pl.*] *a*) plumage *b*) attire **4.** class; kind [birds of a *feather*] **—*vt.* 1.** to provide or adorn as with feathers **2.** to give a featheredge to **3.** to join by inserting a wedge-shaped part into a groove **4.** to turn the edge of (the blade of an oar or propeller) toward the line of movement **—*vi.* 1.** to grow feathers **2.** to move, grow, or look like feathers **3.** to feather an oar or propeller **—feather in one's cap** an achievement worthy of pride **—feather one's (own) nest** to provide for one's own comfort or security **—in feather** feathered **—in fine** (or **high** or **good**) **feather** in very good humor, health, or form **—feath′ered *adj.* —feath′er·ing *n.* —feath′er·less *adj.***
feather bed a strong cloth container thickly filled with feathers or down, used as a mattress
feath·er·bed·ding (-bed′iŋ) ***n.*** the practice of limiting output or requiring extra workers, as by union contract, in order to provide more jobs **—feath′er·bed′ *adj., vi., vt.* -bed′ded, -bed′ding**
feath·er·brain (-brān′) ***n.*** a silly, foolish, or frivolous person **—feath′er·brained′ *adj.***
feath·er·edge (-ej′) ***n.*** a very thin edge, easily broken or curled **—*vt.* -edged′, -edg′ing** to give such an edge to
feath·er·stitch (-stich′) ***n.*** an embroidery stitch forming a zigzag line **—*vt., vi.*** to embroider with such a stitch
feath·er·weight (-wāt′) ***n.* 1.** any person or thing of light weight or small size **2.** a boxer who weighs over 118 but not over 126 pounds **3.** a wrestler who weighs over 123 but not over 134 pounds **—*adj.* 1.** of featherweights **2.** light or trivial
feath·er·y (-ē) ***adj.* 1.** covered with or as with feathers **2.** resembling feathers; soft, light, etc. **—feath′er·i·ness *n.***

FEATHER-STITCH

fea·ture (fē′chər) ***n.*** [< OFr. < L. *factura,* a making < pp. of *facere,* to make] **1.** orig., the make, form, or appearance of a person or thing **2.** *a*) [*pl.*] the form or look of the face *b*) any of the parts of the face, as the eyes, nose, mouth, etc. **3.** a distinct or outstanding part or quality of something **4.** a prominently displayed or publicized attraction at an entertainment, sale, etc. **5.** a special story, article, etc. in a newspaper or magazine **6.** a full-length motion picture **—*vt.* -tured, -tur·ing 1.** to give prominence to; make a feature of **2.** to sketch or show the features of **3.** to be a feature of **4.** [Slang] to conceive of **—*vi.*** to have a prominent part **—fea′ture·less *adj.***
fea·tured (-chərd) ***adj.* 1.** having (a specified kind of) facial features [broad-*featured*] **2.** given special prominence as a main attraction
feaze (fēz, fāz) ***vt.* feazed, feaz′ing** *var. of* FAZE
Feb. February
feb·ri- [< L. *febris*] *a combining form meaning* fever [*febrifuge*]
feb·ri·fuge (feb′rə fyo͞oj′) ***n.*** [< Fr.: see FEBRI- & -FUGE] any substance for reducing fever; antipyretic **—*adj.*** reducing fever
fe·brile (fē′brəl, feb′rəl) ***adj.*** [< Fr. < L. *febris,* fever] of or characterized by fever; feverish
Feb·ru·ar·y (feb′rə wer′ē, feb′yoo wer′ē) ***n.*** [L. *Februarius* < *februa,* Roman festival of purification held Feb. 15] the second month of the year, having 28 days (or 29 days in leap years): abbrev. **Feb., F.**
fe·cal (fē′kəl) ***adj.*** of or consisting of feces
fe·ces (fē′sēz) ***n.pl.*** [< L. *faeces,* dregs] waste matter expelled from the bowels; excrement
feck·less (fek′lis) ***adj.*** [Scot. < *feck* (< EFFECT) + -LESS] **1.** weak; ineffective **2.** careless; irresponsible **—feck′less·ly *adv.* —feck′less·ness *n.***
fe·cund (fē′kənd, fek′ənd) ***adj.*** [< OFr. < L. *fecundus,* fruitful] fruitful or fertile; productive **—fe·cun·di·ty** (fi kun′də tē) ***n.***
fe·cun·date (fē′kən dāt′, fek′ən-) ***vt.* -dat′ed, -dat′ing** [< L. pp. of *fecundare* < *fecundus:* see prec.] **1.** to make fecund **2.** to fertilize; impregnate; pollinate **—fe′cun·da′tion *n.***
fed[1] (fed) *pt. & pp. of* FEED **—fed up** [Colloq.] having had enough to become disgusted, bored, etc.
fed[2] (fed) ***n.*** [*often* **F-**] [Slang] a Federal agent or officer
Fed. 1. Federal **2.** Federated **3.** Federation
fed·a·yeen (fed′ä yēn′) ***n.pl.*** [Ar., lit., those who sacrifice themselves] Arab irregulars or guerrillas in the Middle East
fed·er·al (fed′ər əl, fed′rəl) ***adj.*** [< L. *foedus* (gen. *foederis*), a league] **1.** of or formed by a compact; specif., designating or of a union of states, groups, etc. in which each member subordinates its governmental power to a central authority in certain common affairs **2.** designating or of a central government in such a union; specif., [*usually* **F-**] of the central government of the U.S. **3.** [**F-**] of the Federalist Party **4.** [**F-**] of or supporting the U.S. government in the Civil War; Union **—*n.* 1.** [**F-**] a Federalist **2.** [**F-**] a supporter or soldier of the U.S. government in the Civil War **3.** [**F-**] a Federal agent or officer **—fed′er·al·ly *adv.***
Federal Bureau of Investigation a branch of the U.S. Department of Justice whose duty is to investigate violations of Federal laws
Federal Communications Commission a Federal agency which regulates communication by wire and radio, including licensing of radio and TV stations
fed·er·al·ism (-iz'm) ***n.* 1.** the federal principle of government or organization **2.** [**F-**] the principles of the Federalist Party
fed·er·al·ist (-ist) ***n.* 1.** one who believes in or supports federalism **2.** [**F-**] a member or supporter of the Federalist Party **—*adj.* 1.** of or supporting federalism **2.** [**F-**] of or supporting the Federalist Party or its principles Also **fed′er·al·is′tic**
Federalist (or **Federal**) **Party** a political party in the U.S. (1789–1816) which advocated the adoption of the Constitution and the establishment of a strong, centralized government
fed·er·al·ize (fed′ər ə līz′, fed′rə-) ***vt.* -ized′, -iz′ing 1.** to unite (states, etc.) in a federal union **2.** to put under the authority of a federal government **—fed′er·al·i·za′tion *n.***
Federal Reserve Bank any of the twelve district banks of the Federal Reserve System
Federal Reserve note any piece of U.S. paper currency issued by the individual Federal Reserve Banks
Federal Reserve System a centralized banking system in the U.S., with supervisory powers over Federal Reserve Banks and about 6,000 member banks
Federal Trade Commission a Federal agency whose duty is to investigate and stop unfair methods of competition in business, fraudulent advertising, etc.
fed·er·ate (fed′ər it; *for v.* -ə rāt′) ***adj.*** [< L. pp. of *foederare* < *foedus:* see FEDERAL] united by common agreement under a central government or authority **—*vt., vi.* -at′ed, -at′ing** to unite in a federation
fed·er·a·tion (fed′ə rā′shən) ***n.* 1.** the act of uniting or of forming a union of states, groups, etc. by agreement of each member to subordinate its power to a central authority in common affairs **2.** an organization formed thus; a federal union, as of states **—fed′er·a′tive *adj.* —fed′er·a′tive·ly *adv.***
fe·do·ra (fə dôr′ə) ***n.*** [Fr. < *Fédora* (1882), play by V. Sardou, Fr. dramatist] a soft felt hat with the crown creased lengthwise and a curved brim

fee (fē) *n.* [< Anglo-Fr. *fee* & < OE. *feoh,* cattle, property] **1.** orig., a fief **2.** payment asked or given for professional services, admissions, licenses, tuition, etc.; charge **3.** *Law* an inheritance in land: an estate can be held with unrestricted rights of disposition **(fee simple)** or with restrictions as to a specified class of heirs **(fee tail)**

fee·ble (fē′b'l) *adj.* **-bler, -blest** [< OFr. < L. *flebilis,* to be wept over < *flere,* to weep] weak; not strong; specif., *a*) infirm [a *feeble* old man] *b*) without force or effectiveness [a *feeble* light] *c*) easily broken; frail [a *feeble* barrier] **—fee′ble·ness** *n.* **—fee′bly** *adv.*

fee·ble·mind·ed (-mīn′did) *adj.* mentally retarded: term no longer used in psychology **—fee′ble·mind′ed·ly** *adv.* **—fee′ble·mind′ed·ness** *n.*

feed (fēd) *vt.* **fed, feed′ing** [< OE. *fedan* < base of *foda,* food] **1.** to give food to; provide food for **2.** *a*) to provide as food [to *feed* oats to horses] *b*) to serve as food for **3.** to provide something necessary for the growth or existence of; nourish [to *feed* one's anger] **4.** to provide (material to be used up, processed, etc.) [to *feed* coal into a stove] **5.** to provide with material [*feed* the stove] **6.** to provide satisfaction for; gratify [to *feed* one's vanity] *—vi.* **1.** to eat: said chiefly of animals **2.** to flow steadily, as into a machine for use, processing, etc. *—n.* **1.** *a*) food given to animals; fodder *b*) the amount of fodder given at one time **2.** *a*) the material fed into a machine *b*) the part of the machine supplying this material *c*) the supplying of this material **3.** [Colloq.] a meal **—feed on** (or **upon**) to be nourished or gratified by **—off one's feed** [Slang] lacking appetite; somewhat sick **—feed′er** *n.*

feed·back (-bak′) *n.* **1.** *Elec.* the transfer of part of the output back to the input: it may be an unwanted effect or one desired, as to reduce distortion **2.** a process in which the result modifies the factors producing the result

feed bag a bag filled with grain, fastened over a horse's muzzle for feeding

feed·stock (-stäk′) *n.* raw material for industrial processing, as petroleum products for making petrochemicals

feel (fēl) *vt.* **felt, feel′ing** [OE. *felan*] **1.** to touch; examine by touching or handling **2.** to be aware of through physical sensation [to *feel* rain on the face] **3.** *a*) to experience (an emotion or condition) *b*) to be emotionally moved by **4.** to be aware of mentally **5.** to think or believe, often for emotional reasons *—vi.* **1.** to have physical sensation **2.** to appear to be to the senses, esp. to the sense of touch [the water *feels* warm] **3.** to have the indicated effect [it *feels* good to be home] **4.** to search by touching; grope (*for*) **5.** to be aware of being [to *feel* sad] **6.** to be moved to sympathy, pity, etc. (*for*) *—n.* **1.** the act of feeling **2.** the sense of touch **3.** the nature of a thing perceived through touch **4.** an emotional sensation **5.** instinctive ability or appreciation [a *feel* for design] **—feel (a person) out** to try cautiously to find out the opinions of (a person) **—feel like** [Colloq.] to have a desire for **—feel one's way** to move cautiously **—feel up to** [Colloq.] to feel capable of

feel·er (-ər) *n.* **1.** a person or thing that feels **2.** a specialized organ of touch in an animal or insect, as an antenna **3.** a remark, question, offer, etc. made to feel out another

feel·ing (-iŋ) *adj.* sensitive and sympathetic *—n.* **1.** the sense of touch, by which sensations of contact, pressure, temperature, and pain are transmitted through the skin **2.** the ability to experience physical sensation **3.** an awareness; sensation [a *feeling* of pain] **4.** an emotion **5.** [*pl.*] sensitivities; sensibilities [to hurt one's *feelings*] **6.** sympathy or pity **7.** *a*) an opinion or sentiment *b*) a premonition [a *feeling* of doom] **8.** air; atmosphere [the lonely *feeling* of the city] **9.** a natural ability or sensitive appreciation **10.** the emotional quality in a work of art **—feel′ing·ly** *adv.*

feet (fēt) *n. pl. of* FOOT **—have one's feet on the ground** to be practical, realistic, etc. **—on one's feet** firmly established **—sit at the feet of** to be an admiring disciple or pupil of **—stand on one's own feet** to be independent **—sweep** (or **carry) off one's feet** **1.** to fill with enthusiasm **2.** to impress deeply

feign (fān) *vt.* [< OFr. *feindre* < L. *fingere,* to shape] **1.** to make up (a story, excuse, etc.); fabricate **2.** to make a false show of; pretend *—vi.* to pretend; dissemble **—feigned** *adj.* **—feign′er** *n.* **—feign′ing·ly** *adv.*

Fei·ning·er (fī′niŋ ər), **Ly·o·nel (Charles Adrian)** (lī′ə n'l) 1871–1956; U.S. painter

feint (fānt) *n.* [< Fr. pp. of *feindre:* see FEIGN] **1.** a false show; sham **2.** a pretended blow or attack intended to take the opponent off his guard, as in boxing or fencing *—vi., vt.* to deliver (such a blow or attack)

feist·y (fīs′tē) *adj.* **feist′i·er, feist′i·est** [< ME. *fist,* a breaking of wind + -Y[2]] [Colloq. or Dial.] **1.** lively; energetic **2.** quarrelsome; belligerent

feld·spar (feld′spär′, fel′-) *n.* [< G. < *feld,* field + *spat(h),* spar] any of several hard, crystalline minerals made up of aluminum silicates with sodium, potassium, or calcium **—feld·spath′ic** (-spa′thik), **feld·spath′ose** (-spath′ōs) *adj.*

Fe·li·ci·a (fə lish′ē ə) [fem. of FELIX] a feminine name

fe·lic·i·tate (fə lis′ə tāt′) *vt.* **-tat′ed, -tat′ing** [< L. pp. of *felicitare* < *felix,* happy] to wish happiness to **—fe·lic′i·ta′tion** *n.* **—fe·lic′i·ta′tor** *n.*

fe·lic·i·tous (-təs) *adj.* [< ff. + -OUS] **1.** used or expressed in a way suitable to the occasion; appropriate **2.** having the knack of appropriate and pleasing expression **—fe·lic′i·tous·ly** *adv.* **—fe·lic′i·tous·ness** *n.*

fe·lic·i·ty (-tē) *n., pl.* **-ties** [< OFr. < L. < *felix* (gen. *felicis*), happy] **1.** happiness; bliss **2.** anything producing happiness **3.** a quality of appropriate and pleasing expression in writing, speaking, etc. **4.** an apt expression or thought

fe·line (fē′līn) *adj.* [< L. < *felis,* cat] **1.** of a cat or the cat family **2.** catlike; esp., *a*) sly, stealthy, etc. *b*) sleekly graceful *—n.* any animal of the cat family, including the cat, lion, panther, tiger, etc. **—fe′line·ly** *adv.* **—fe′line·ness, fe·lin·i·ty** (fi lin′ə tē) *n.*

Fe·lix (fē′liks) [L., lit., happy] a masculine name

fell[1] (fel) *pt. of* FALL

fell[2] (fel) *vt.* [OE. *fellan*] **1.** to make fall; knock down **2.** to cut down (a tree) **3.** to turn over (the rough edge of a seam) and sew down flat on the underside *—n.* **1.** the trees cut down in one season **2.** a felled seam **—fell′a·ble** *adj.* **—fell′er** *n.*

fell[3] (fel) *adj.* [< OFr. < ML. *fello:* see FELON[1]] **1.** fierce; terrible; cruel **2.** [Archaic] causing death; deadly [a *fell* plague] **—fell′ness** *n.*

fell[4] (fel) *n.* [OE. *fel*] an animal's hide or skin

fell[5] (fel) *n.* [< Scand.] [Brit.] a moor; down

fel·lah (fel′ə) *n., pl.* **fel′lahs;** Ar. **fel·la·heen, fel·la·hin** (fel′ə hēn′) [< Ar. < *falāha,* to plow] a peasant or farm laborer in Egypt or some other countries where Arabic is spoken

fel·loe (fel′ō) *n. same as* FELLY

fel·low (fel′ō, -ə) *n.* [< Late OE. *feolaga,* partner < *feoh* (see FEE) + *laga,* a laying down] **1.** a companion; associate **2.** one of the same class or rank; equal **3.** either of a pair of corresponding things; mate **4.** a graduate student holding a fellowship in a university or college **5.** a member of a learned society **6.** at some British and U.S. universities, a member of the governing body **7.** [Colloq.] *a*) a man or boy *b*) a person; one [a *fellow* must eat] **8.** [Colloq.] a suitor; beau *—adj.* having the same ideas, position, work, etc.; associated [*fellow* workers]

fel·low·ship (-ship′) *n.* **1.** companionship; friendly association **2.** a mutual sharing, as of activity, etc. **3.** a group of people with the same interests **4.** an endowment, or a sum of money paid from it, for the support of a graduate student, scholar, etc. doing advanced study **5.** the rank or position of a fellow in a university or college

fellow traveler a person who espouses the cause of a party without being a member

fel·ly (fel′ē) *n., pl.* **-lies** [OE. *felg*] the rim of a spoked wheel, or a segment of the rim

fel·on[1] (fel′ən) *n.* [< OFr. < ML. *felo,* earlier *fello* < ?] *Law* a person guilty of a major crime; criminal *—adj.* [Poet.] wicked; base

fel·on[2] (fel′ən) *n.* [< ? same base as prec.] a painful, pus-producing infection near the nail of a finger or toe

fe·lo·ni·ous (fə lō′nē əs) *adj.* **1.** [Poet.] wicked; base **2.** *Law* of, like, or constituting a felony **—fe·lo′ni·ous·ly** *adv.* **—fe·lo′ni·ous·ness** *n.*

fel·o·ny (fel′ə nē) *n., pl.* **-nies** [< OFr. < ML. < *felo,* FELON[1]] a major crime, as murder, arson, rape, etc., for which statute provides a greater punishment than for a misdemeanor

fel·spar (fel′spär′) *n. same as* FELDSPAR

felt[1] (felt) *n.* [OE.] **1.** a fabric of wool, often mixed with fur, cotton, rayon, etc., the fibers being worked together by pressure, heat, chemical action, etc.: also **felt′ing** **2.** anything like felt, with a fuzzy, springy surface **3.** anything made of felt *—adj.* made of felt *—vt.* **1.** *a*) to make into felt *b*) to cover with felt **2.** to mat (fibers) together *—vi.* to become matted together

felt[2] (felt) *pt. and pp. of* FEEL

fe·luc·ca (fə luk′ə, -lo͞o′kə) *n.* [< It. *feluca,* prob. < Ar.] a small, narrow ship propelled by oars or lateen sails, used esp. in the Mediterranean

fem. feminine

fe·male (fē′māl) *adj.* [< OFr. < L. dim. of *femina,* a woman] **1.** designating or of the sex that produces ova and bears offspring **2.** of, like, or suitable to members of this sex; feminine **3.** of women or girls **4.** having a hollow part shaped to receive a corresponding inserted part (called *male*): said of electric sockets, etc. **5.** *Bot.* having a pistil and no stamen *—n.* a female person, animal, or plant **—fe′male·ness** *n.*

fem·i·nine (fem′ə nin) *adj.* [< OFr. < L. < *femina,* woman] **1.** of women or girls **2.** having qualities regarded as characteristic of women and girls, as delicacy, etc. **3.** suitable to or characteristic of a woman **4.** effeminate: said of a man **5.** *Gram.* designating or of the gender of words referring to females or things orig. regarded as female **6.** *Prosody* designating or of a rhyme of two or three syllables with only the first stressed (Ex.: danger, stranger) —***n.*** *Gram.* **1.** the feminine gender **2.** a word or form in this gender —**fem′i·nine·ly** ***adv.*** —**fem′i·nin′i·ty, fem′i·nine·ness** ***n.***

fem·i·nism (fem′ə niz′m) ***n.*** **1.** the principle that women should have political, economic, and social rights equal to those of men **2.** the movement to win these rights —**fem′i·nist** ***n., adj.*** —**fem′i·nis′tic** ***adj.***

fem·i·nize (fem′ə nīz′) ***vt., vi.*** **-nized′, -niz′ing** to make or become feminine or effeminate —**fem′i·ni·za′tion** ***n.***

femme (fem; *Fr.* fȧm) ***n.,*** *pl.* **femmes** (femz; *Fr.* fȧm) **[**Fr.**]** [Slang] a woman or wife

fe·mur (fē′mər) ***n.,*** *pl.* **fe′murs, fem·o·ra** (fem′ər ə) **[**ModL. < L., thigh**]** *same as* THIGHBONE —**fem′o·ral** ***adj.***

fen[1] (fen) ***n.*** **[**OE.**]** an area of low, flat, marshy land; swamp; bog —**fen′ny** ***adj.***

fen[2] (fen) ***n.*** *see* MONETARY UNITS, table (China)

fe·na·gle (fə nā′g'l) ***vi., vt.*** **-gled, -gling** *same as* FINAGLE —**fe·na′gler** ***n.***

fence (fens) ***n.*** **[**ME. *fens*, short for *defens*, DEFENSE**]** **1.** a barrier of posts, wire, rails, etc., used as a boundary or means of protection or confinement **2.** the art of self-defense with foil, saber, etc.; fencing **3.** *a)* one who buys and sells stolen goods *b)* a place for such dealings —***vt.*** **fenced, fenc′ing** **1.** to enclose, restrict, etc. with or as with a fence (with *in*, *off*, etc.) **2.** to keep (*out*) by or as by a fence —***vi.*** **1.** to practice the art of fencing **2.** to avoid giving a direct reply; be evasive (*with*) **3.** to buy or sell stolen goods —**mend (one's) fences** to engage in politicking: said esp. of a legislator —**on the fence** not taking one side or the other; uncommitted —**fence′less** ***adj.*** —**fenc′er** ***n.***

fenc·ing (fen′siŋ) ***n.*** **1.** the art of fighting with a foil or other sword **2.** *a)* material for making fences *b)* a system of fences

fend (fend) ***vt.*** **[**ME. *fenden*, short for *defenden*, DEFEND**]** [Archaic] to defend —***vi.*** to resist; parry —**fend for oneself** to get along without help from others —**fend off** to ward off; turn aside

fend·er (fen′dər) ***n.*** anything that fends off or protects something else; specif., *a)* any of the metal frames over the wheels of an automobile or other vehicle to protect against splashing mud, etc. *b)* a device on the front of a streetcar or locomotive to catch or push aside anything on the track *c)* a screen or guard placed in front of a fireplace

fen·es·tra·tion (fen′ə strā′shən) ***n.*** **[**ult. < L. *fenestra*, window**]** **1.** the arrangement of windows and doors in a building **2.** the surgical operation of making an opening into the inner ear in certain cases of otosclerosis

Fe·ni·an (fē′nē ən, fēn′yən) ***n.*** **[**< pl. of Ir. Gael. *Fiann*, the old militia of Ireland**]** a member of a secret Irish revolutionary group formed in New York about 1858 to free Ireland from English rule —***adj.*** of the Fenians —**Fe′ni·an·ism** ***n.***

fen·nel (fen′'l) ***n.*** **[**< OE. < L. *feniculum*, dim. of *fenum*, hay**]** a tall herb of the parsley family, with yellow flowers: its aromatic seeds are used as a seasoning and in medicine

feoff (fef, fēf) ***vt.*** **[**< Anglo-Fr. < OFr. < *fieu*, fief**]** to give or sell a fief to —***n.*** a fief —**feoff′ment** ***n.*** —**feof′for, feoff′er** ***n.***

FEP Fair Employment Practice(s)

-fer (fər) **[**< Fr. or L. < *ferre*, BEAR[1]**]** *a suffix meaning* bearer, producer *[conifer]*

fe·ral (fir′əl) ***adj.*** **[**< L. < *ferus*, fierce + -AL**]** **1.** untamed; wild **2.** savage; brutal

fer-de-lance (fer′də läns′) ***n.*** **[**Fr., iron tip of a lance**]** a large, poisonous pit viper, related to the rattlesnake, found in tropical America

Fer·di·nand (fur′d'n and′) **[**Fr., prob. < Gmc. bases meaning "bold in peace"**]** **1.** a masculine name **2. Ferdinand V** 1452–1516; king of Castile (1474–1504): husband of ISABELLA I

fer·ma·ta (fer mät′ə) ***n.*** **[**It. < *fermare*, to stop**]** **1.** the holding of a tone or rest beyond its written value, at the performer's discretion **2.** the sign (𝄐) or (𝄑) indicating this

fer·ment (fur′ment; *for v.* fər ment′) ***n.*** **[**< OFr. < L. *fermentum* < *fervere*, to boil**]** **1.** a substance or organism causing fermentation, as yeast, bacteria, etc. **2.** *same as* FERMENTATION **3.** a state of excitement or agitation —***vt.*** **1.** to cause fermentation in **2.** to excite; agitate —***vi.*** **1.** to be in the process of fermentation **2.** to be excited or agitated —**fer·ment′a·ble** ***adj.***

fer·men·ta·tion (fur′mən tā′shən, -men-) ***n.*** **1.** the breakdown of complex molecules in organic compounds, caused by a ferment *[*bacteria curdle milk by *fermentation]* **2.** excitement; agitation —**fer·ment·a·tive** (fər men′tə tiv) ***adj.***

Fer·mi (fer′mē), **En·ri·co** (en rē′kō) 1901–54; It. nuclear physicist, in the U.S. after 1938

fer·mi·um (fer′mē əm) ***n.*** **[**after prec.**]** a radioactive chemical element: symbol, Fm; at. wt., 257(?); at. no., 100

fern (furn) ***n.*** **[**OE. *fearn***]** any of a widespread class of nonflowering plants having roots, stems, and fronds, and reproducing by spores instead of by seeds —**fern′y** ***adj.***

fern·er·y (fur′nər ē) ***n.,*** *pl.* **-er·ies** a place where ferns are grown; collection of growing ferns

fe·ro·cious (fə rō′shəs) ***adj.*** **[**< L. *ferox* (gen. *ferocis*) < *ferus*, fierce + -OUS**]** **1.** fierce; savage; violently cruel **2.** [Colloq.] very great *[*a *ferocious* appetite*]* —**fe·ro′cious·ly** ***adv.*** —**fe·ro′cious·ness** ***n.***

fe·roc·i·ty (fə räs′ə tē) ***n.,*** *pl.* **-ties** wild force or cruelty; ferociousness

-fer·ous (fər əs) **[**L. *-fer* < *ferre*, BEAR[1] + -OUS**]** *a suffix meaning* bearing, producing *[coniferous]*

fer·ret (fer′it) ***n.*** **[**< OFr. < LL. dim. of *furo* < L. *fur*, thief**]** a small, weasellike animal, easily tamed and used for hunting rabbits, rats, etc. —***vt.*** **1.** to force out of hiding as with a ferret **2.** to search for persistently and discover (facts, etc.); search (*out*) —***vi.*** **1.** to hunt with ferrets **2.** to search around —**fer′ret·er** ***n.***

fer·ri- *a combining form meaning* containing ferric iron: see FERRO-

fer·ric (fer′ik) ***adj.*** **[**FERR(O)- + -IC**]** **1.** of, containing, or derived from iron **2.** *Chem.* designating or of iron with a valence of three, or compounds containing such iron

Fer·ris wheel (fer′is) **[**after G. *Ferris* (1859–1896), U.S. engineer who invented it**]** a large, upright wheel revolving on a fixed axle and having seats hanging from the frame: used as an amusement ride

fer·ro- **[**< L. *ferrum*, iron**]** *a combining form meaning:* **1.** iron *[ferromagnetic]* **2.** iron and *[ferromanganese]* **3.** containing ferrous iron

fer·ro·con·crete (fer′ō kän′krēt, -kän krēt′) ***n.*** *same as* REINFORCED CONCRETE

fer·ro·mag·net·ic (-mag net′ik) ***adj.*** designating a material, as iron, nickel, or cobalt, having a high magnetic permeability —**fer′ro·mag′net·ism** ***n.***

fer·ro·man·ga·nese (-maŋ′gə nēs′, -nēz′) ***n.*** an alloy of iron and manganese, used for making hard steel

fer·rous (fer′əs) ***adj.*** **[**< L. *ferrum*, iron + -OUS**]** **1.** of, containing, or derived from iron **2.** *Chem.* designating or of iron with a valence of two, or compounds containing it

fer·ru·gi·nous (fə ro͞o′ji nəs) ***adj.*** **[**< L. < *ferrugo*, iron rust < *ferrum*, iron**]** **1.** of, containing, or having the nature of, iron **2.** having the color of iron rust; reddish-brown

fer·rule (fer′əl, -o͞ol) ***n.*** **[**< OFr. < L. *viriola*, dim. of *viriae*, bracelets**]** a metal ring or cap put around the end of a cane, tool handle, etc. to give added strength —***vt.*** **-ruled, -rul·ing** to furnish with a ferrule

fer·ry (fer′ē) ***vt.*** **-ried, -ry·ing** **[**OE. *ferian*, to carry**]** **1.** to take across a river, etc. in a boat **2.** to cross (a river, etc.) on a ferry **3.** to deliver (airplanes) by flying to the destination —***vi.*** to cross a river, etc. by ferry —***n.,*** *pl.* **-ries** **1.** a system for carrying people, cars, etc. across a river, etc. by boat **2.** a boat (**fer′ry·boat′**) used for this, or the place where it docks on either shore **3.** the delivery of airplanes to their destination by flying them —**fer′ry·man** ***n.,*** *pl.* **-men**

fer·tile (fur′t'l; *chiefly Brit.* -tīl) ***adj.*** **[**< OFr. < L. *fertilis* < stem of *ferre*, BEAR[1]**]** **1.** producing abundantly; rich in resources or invention; fruitful **2.** able to produce young, seeds, fruit, etc. **3.** capable of developing into a new individual; fertilized —**fer′tile·ly** ***adv.*** —**fer′tile·ness** ***n.***

fer·til·i·ty (fər til′ə tē) ***n.*** the quality, state, or degree of being fertile; fecundity

fer·til·ize (fur′t'l īz′) ***vt.*** **-ized′, -iz′ing** **1.** to make fertile; make fruitful or productive **2.** to spread fertilizer on **3.** to make (the female reproductive cell or female individual) fruitful by introducing the male germ cell; impregnate —**fer′til·iz′a·ble** ***adj.*** —**fer′til·i·za′tion** ***n.***

fer·til·iz·er (-ī′zər) ***n.*** one that fertilizes; specif., manure, chemicals, etc. put in soil to improve the quality or quantity of plant growth

fer·ule (fer′əl, -o͞ol) ***n.*** **[**L. *ferula*, rod**]** a flat stick or ruler used for punishing children —***vt.*** **-uled, -ul·ing** to strike with a ferule

fer·vent (fur′vənt) ***adj.*** **[**< L. prp. of *fervere*, to glow, boil**]** **1.** hot; burning; glowing **2.** having or showing great warmth of feeling; intensely earnest —**fer′ven·cy** (-vən sē) ***n.*** —**fer′vent·ly** ***adv.***

fer·vid (fur′vəd) ***adj.*** **[**< L. < *fervere:* see prec.**]** **1.** hot; glowing **2.** impassioned; fervent; ardent —**fer′vid·ly** ***adv.*** —**fer′vid·ness** ***n.***

fer·vor (fur′vər) ***n.*** [< OFr. < L. < *fervere:* see FERVENT] **1.** intense heat **2.** great warmth of emotion; ardor; zeal Brit. sp. **fer′vour**

fes·cue (fes′kyo͞o) ***n.*** [< OFr. < L. *festuca,* a straw] a tough grass used for pasture or lawns

fess, fesse (fes) ***n.*** [< OFr. < L. *fascia,* a band] *Heraldry* a horizontal band forming the middle third of an escutcheon

-fest (fest) [< G. *fest,* a celebration < L. *festum,* feast] *an informal combining form meaning* an occasion of much *[fun-fest]*

fes·tal (fes′t'l) ***adj.*** [< L. *festum,* feast] of or like a joyous celebration; festive —**fes′tal·ly** ***adv.***

fes·ter (fes′tər) ***n.*** [< OFr. < L. *fistula,* ulcer] a small sore filled with pus —***vi.*** **1.** to form pus **2.** to cause irritation; rankle **3.** to decay —***vt.*** **1.** to cause pus to form in **2.** to make rankle

fes·ti·val (fes′tə v'l) ***n.*** [< OFr. < ML. < L. *festivus:* see ff.] **1.** a time or day of feasting or celebration **2.** a celebration or series of performances of a certain kind *[a Bach festival]* **3.** merrymaking; festivity —***adj.*** of, for, or fit for a festival

fes·tive (fes′tiv) ***adj.*** [< L. *festivus* < *festum,* feast] of or for a feast or festival; merry; joyous —**fes′tive·ly** ***adv.*** —**fes′tive·ness** ***n.***

fes·tiv·i·ty (fes tiv′ə tē) ***n., pl.*** **-ties** **1.** merrymaking; gaiety **2.** *a)* a festival *b)* [*pl.*] festive proceedings; things done in celebration

fes·toon (fes to͞on′) ***n.*** [< Fr. < It. *festone* < *festa,* feast] **1.** a garland of flowers, leaves, etc. hanging in a loop or curve **2.** any molding or decoration like this —***vt.*** to adorn with, form into, or join by festoons —**fes·toon′er·y** ***n.***

fet·a (cheese) (fet′ə) [< ModGr. < It. *fetta,* a slice, ult. < L. *offa,* a piece] a white, soft cheese made in Greece from ewe's milk or goat's milk

fe·tal (fēt′'l) ***adj.*** of or like a fetus

fetch (fech) ***vt.*** [OE. *feccan*] **1.** to go after and come back with; bring; get **2.** to cause to come; produce **3.** to draw (a breath) or heave (a sigh, groan, etc.) **4.** to bring as a price; sell for **5.** [Colloq.] to attract; charm **6.** [Colloq.] to deliver or deal (a blow, etc.) —***vi.*** to go after things and bring them back —***n.*** **1.** a fetching **2.** a trick; dodge —**fetch up** **1.** [Colloq.] to reach; stop **2.** [Dial.] to raise (a child, pet, etc.)

fetch·ing (-iŋ) ***adj.*** attractive; charming —**fetch′ing·ly** ***adv.***

fete, fête (fāt) ***n.*** [Fr. < OFr.: see FEAST] a festival; entertainment, esp. one held outdoors —***vt.*** **fet′ed** or **fêt′ed, fet′ing** or **fêt′ing** to celebrate or honor with a fete; entertain

fet·id (fet′id, fēt′-) ***adj.*** [< L. *f(o)etidus* < *f(o)etere,* to stink] having a bad smell, as of decay; stinking —**fet′id·ly** ***adv.*** —**fet′id·ness** ***n.***

fet·ish (fet′ish, fēt′-) ***n.*** [< Fr. < Port. *feitiço,* a charm < L. *facticius,* FACTITIOUS] **1.** any object believed by superstitious people to have magical power **2.** any thing or activity to which one is irrationally devoted **3.** *Psychiatry* any nonsexual object that evokes fetishism Also sp. **fet′ich**

fet·ish·ism (-iz'm) ***n.*** **1.** worship of or belief in fetishes **2.** *Psychiatry* an abnormal condition in which erotic feelings are excited by a nonsexual object, as a foot, glove, etc. Also sp. **fet′ich·ism** —**fet′ish·ist** ***n.*** —**fet′ish·is′tic** ***adj.***

fet·lock (fet′läk′) ***n.*** [ME. *fitlok* < MDu. or MLowG.] **1.** a tuft of hair on the back of the leg of a horse, donkey, etc., just above the hoof **2.** the joint or projection bearing this tuft

fet·ter (fet′ər) ***n.*** [OE. *feter* < base of *fot,* foot] **1.** a shackle or chain for the feet **2.** anything that holds in check; restraint —***vt.*** **1.** to bind with fetters; shackle; chain **2.** to hold in check; restrain

fet·tle (fet′'l) ***vt.*** **-tled, -tling** [ME. *fetlen,* to make ready, prob. < OE. *fetel,* belt] [Dial.] to arrange —***n.*** condition of body and mind *[in fine fettle]*

fe·tus (fēt′əs) ***n., pl.*** **-tus·es** [L., a bringing forth] the unborn young of an animal while still in the uterus or egg, esp. in its later stages: cf. EMBRYO

feud[1] (fyo͞od) ***n.*** [OFr. *faide* < Frank. *faida*] a bitter, long-continued, and deadly quarrel, esp. between clans or families —***vi.*** to carry on a feud; quarrel —**feu′dal** ***adj.*** —**feud′ist** ***n.***

feud[2] (fyo͞od) ***n.*** [< ML. *feodum* < OHG. *feho,* cattle + *od,* wealth] land held from a feudal lord in return for service; fief

feu·dal (fyo͞od′'l) ***adj.*** **1.** of a feud (land) **2.** of or like feudalism —**feu′dal·ly** ***adv.***

feu·dal·ism (-iz'm) ***n.*** the economic, political, and social system (**feudal system**) in medieval Europe, in which land, worked by serfs who were bound to it, was held by vassals in exchange for military and other services given to overlords —**feu′dal·ist** ***n.*** —**feu′dal·is′tic** ***adj.***

feu·da·to·ry (fyo͞o′də tôr′ē) ***n., pl.*** **-ries** **1.** a feudal vassal **2.** a feudal estate; fief —***adj.*** **1.** of the feudal relationship between vassal and lord **2.** owing feudal allegiance (*to*)

fe·ver (fē′vər) ***n.*** [< OE. *fefer* & OFr. *fievre,* both < L. *febris*] **1.** a state of abnormally increased body temperature, often accompanied by a quickened pulse, delirium, etc. **2.** any of various diseases characterized by a high fever **3.** a condition of nervousness —***vt.*** to cause fever in —**fe′vered** ***adj.***

fever blister (or **sore**) *same as* HERPES SIMPLEX

fe·ver·few (-fyo͞o′) ***n.*** [< OE., ult. < L. *febris,* fever + *fugia* < *fugare,* to drive away] a bushy plant of the composite family, with small, white heads of flowers

fe·ver·ish (-ish) ***adj.*** **1.** having fever, esp. slight fever **2.** of, like, or caused by fever **3.** causing fever **4.** greatly excited or agitated Also **fe′ver·ous** —**fe′ver·ish·ly** ***adv.*** —**fe′ver·ish·ness** ***n.***

few (fyo͞o) ***adj.*** [OE. *feawe, pl.*] not many; a small number of —***pron., n.*** not many; a small number —**quite a few** [Colloq.] a rather large number —**the few** a small select group —**few′ness** ***n.***

fey (fā) ***adj.*** [OE. *fæge,* fated] **1.** [Archaic or Scot.] *a)* fated to die *b)* highly excited **2.** strange, as in being eccentric, puckish, visionary, etc.

fez (fez) ***n., pl.*** **fez′zes** [Fr. < Turk. < *Fez,* city in Morocco] a conical felt hat, usually red, with a black tassel hanging from its flat crown: formerly the Turkish national headdress of men

FEZ

ff. **1.** folios **2.** following (pages, lines, entry, etc.) **3.** fortissimo

FHA Federal Housing Administration

fi·an·cé (fē′än sā′, fē än′sā) ***n.*** [Fr., pp. of *fiancer* < OFr. *fiance,* a promise] the man to whom a woman is engaged to be married

fi·an·cée (fē′än sā′, fē än′sā) ***n.*** [Fr., fem. pp. of *fiancer:* see prec.] the woman to whom a man is engaged to be married

fi·as·co (fē as′kō) ***n., pl.*** **-coes, -cos** [Fr. < It. *(far) fiasco,* to fail < *fiasco,* bottle] a complete failure; esp., an ambitious project that ends as a ridiculous failure

fi·at (fī′at, -ət) ***n.*** [L., let it be done] **1.** an order issued by legal authority; decree **2.** a sanction; authorization **3.** any arbitrary order

fiat money paper currency made legal tender by law or fiat, although not backed by gold or silver and not necessarily redeemable in coin

fib (fib) ***n.*** [? ult. < *fable*] a lie about something unimportant —***vi.*** **fibbed, fib′bing** to tell such a lie or lies —**fib′ber** ***n.***

fi·ber, fi·bre (fī′bər) ***n.*** [< Fr. < L. *fibra*] **1.** *a)* a slender, threadlike structure that combines with others to form animal or vegetable tissue *b)* the tissue so formed *[muscle fiber]* **2.** *a)* any substance that can be separated into threadlike structures for weaving, etc. *b)* such a threadlike structure **3.** a threadlike root **4.** the texture of something **5.** character or nature *[a man of strong moral fiber]* —**fi′ber·like′** ***adj.***

fi·ber·board (-bôrd′) ***n.*** a flexible boardlike material made from pressed fibers of wood, etc., used in building

Fi·ber·glas (-glas′) *a trademark for* finespun filaments of glass made into textiles, used as insulation, etc. —***n.*** [**f-**] this substance: usually **fiberglass, fiber glass,** or **fiber-glass**

fi·bril (fī′brəl) ***n.*** **1.** a small fiber **2.** a root hair —**fi′bril·lar** (-brə lər), **fi′bril·lar′y** (-brə ler′ē) ***adj.*** —**fi′bril·lose′** (-brə lōs′) ***adj.***

fi·bril·la·tion (fib′rə lā′shən, fī′brə-) ***n.*** [< FIBRIL + -ATION] a rapid series of contractions of the heart, causing weak and irregular heartbeats

fi·brin (fī′brən) ***n.*** [FIBR(E) + -IN[1]] an elastic, threadlike, insoluble protein formed in the clotting of blood —**fi′brinous** ***adj.***

fi·bro- [< L. *fibra,* fiber] *a combining form meaning* of fibrous matter or structure: also, before a vowel, **fibr-**

fi·broid (fī′broid) ***adj.*** [FIBR(O)- + -OID] like, composed of, or forming fibrous tissue *[fibroid tumors]*

fi·bro·sis (fī brō′sis) ***n.*** [FIBR(O)- + -OSIS] an abnormal increase in the amount of fibrous connective tissue in an organ or tissue —**fi·brot′ic** (-brät′ik) ***adj.***

fi·brous (fī′brəs) ***adj.*** **1.** containing or composed of fibers **2.** like fiber

fib·u·la (fib′yoo lə) ***n., pl.*** **-lae′** (-lē′), **-las** [L., a clasp] **1.** the long, thin, outer bone of the human leg below the knee **2.** a similar bone in the hind leg of other animals —**fib′u·lar** ***adj.***

-fic (fik) [< Fr. < *-fique* < L. *-ficus* < *facere,* to make] *a suffix meaning* making, creating *[terrific]*

FICA Federal Insurance Contributions Act

-fi·ca·tion (fi kā′shən) [< Fr. & L., ult. < L. *facere,* to make] *a suffix meaning* a making, creating, causing *[glorification]*

fich·u (fish′o͞o) ***n.*** [Fr.] a three-cornered lace or muslin cape for women, worn with the ends fastened or crossed in front

fick·le (fik′'l) ***adj.*** [OE. *ficol*] changeable or unstable in affection, interest, etc. —**fick′le·ness** ***n.***

fic·tion (fik′shən) ***n.*** [< OFr. < L. *fictio*, a making < pp. of *fingere*, to form, mold] **1.** anything made up or imagined, as a statement, story, etc. **2.** *a)* any literary work portraying imaginary characters and events, as a novel, story, or play *b)* such works collectively **3.** *Law* something accepted as fact for convenience, although not necessarily true —**fic′tion·al, fic′tive** ***adj.*** —**fic′tion·al·ly** ***adv.***

fic·tion·al·ize (-′l īz′) ***vt.*** **-ized′, -iz′ing** to deal with (historical events, etc.) as fiction: also **fic′tion·ize′** —**fic′tion·al·i·za′tion** ***n.***

fic·ti·tious (fik tish′əs) ***adj.*** **1.** of or like fiction; imaginary **2.** not real; pretended **3.** assumed for disguise or deception [a *fictitious* name] —**fic·ti′tious·ly** ***adv.*** —**fic·ti′tious·ness** ***n.***

fid (fid) ***n.*** [< ?] **1.** a hard, tapering pin for separating the strands of rope in splicing **2.** a bar or pin for supporting something; specif., a square bar for supporting a topmast

-fid (fid) [< L. < *findere*, to cleave] *a combining form meaning* split or separated into parts

fid·dle (fid′'l) ***n.*** [OE. *fithele*] any stringed instrument played with a bow, esp. the violin —***vt.*** **-dled, -dling** [Colloq.] to play (a tune) on a fiddle —***vi.*** **1.** [Colloq.] to play on a fiddle **2.** to tamper or tinker (*with*), esp. in a nervous way —**fiddle around** [Colloq.] to pass time aimlessly —**fiddle away** to waste (time) —**fit as a fiddle** in excellent health —**fid′dler** ***n.***

fiddler (crab) a small, burrowing crab, the male of which has one claw much larger than the other

FIDDLER CRAB (width to 1 2/3 in.; length to 1 in.)

fid·dle·stick (fid′'l stik′) ***n.*** **1.** the bow for a fiddle **2.** a trifle; mere nothing

fid·dle·sticks (-stiks′) ***interj.*** nonsense!

fi·del·i·ty (fə del′ə tē, fī-) ***n.,*** *pl.* **-ties** [< OFr. < L. < *fides*, FAITH] **1.** faithful devotion to duty, obligations, or vows **2.** accuracy of a description, translation, sound reproduction, etc.

fidg·et (fij′it) ***n.*** [< ? ON. *fikja*] **1.** a being restless, nervous, or uneasy **2.** a fidgety person —***vi.*** to move about in a restless, nervous, or uneasy way —***vt.*** to make restless or uneasy —**the fidgets** restless, uneasy feelings or movements —**fidg′et·i·ness** ***n.*** —**fidg′et·y** ***adj.***

fi·du·ci·ar·y (fi do͞o′shē er′ē, -shə rē) ***adj.*** [< L. < *fiducia*, trust < *fidere:* see FAITH] **1.** designating or of one who holds something in trust for another [a *fiduciary* guardian for a child] **2.** held in trust [*fiduciary* property] **3.** valuable only because of public confidence: said of certain paper money —***n.,*** *pl.* **-ar′ies** a trustee

fie (fī) ***interj.*** [< OFr., of echoic origin] for shame!: now often used in mock reproach

fief (fēf) ***n.*** [Fr.: see FEE] **1.** under feudalism, heritable land held from a lord in return for service **2.** the right to hold such land

field (fēld) ***n.*** [OE. *feld*] **1.** a wide stretch of open land; plain **2.** a piece of cleared land for raising crops or pasturing livestock **3.** a piece of land for some particular purpose [a landing *field*] **4.** an area of land producing some natural resource [a gold *field*] **5.** any wide, unbroken expanse [a *field* of ice] **6.** *a)* a battlefield *b)* a battle **7.** an area of military operations **8.** *a)* an area where practical work is done, away from the central office, laboratory, etc. *b)* a realm of knowledge or of special work [the *field* of electronics] **9.** an area of observation, as in a microscope **10.** the background, as on a flag or coin **11.** *a)* an area where athletic events are held *b)* the part of such an area, usually inside a closed racing track, where contests in jumping, shot put, pole vault, etc. are held *c)* in baseball, the outfield *d)* all the entrants in a contest **12.** *Physics* a space within which magnetic or electrical lines of force are active: in full, **field of force** —***adj.*** **1.** of, operating in, or held on the field or fields **2.** living or growing in fields —***vt.*** *Baseball*, etc. **1.** to stop or catch or to catch and throw (a ball) in play **2.** to put (a player) into a field position —***vi.*** *Baseball*, etc. to play as a fielder —**play the field** to explore every opportunity —**take** (or **leave**) **the field** to begin (or withdraw from) activity in a game, military operation, etc.

field artillery movable artillery capable of accompanying an army into battle

field corn corn (maize) grown to feed livestock

field day **1.** a day of military exercises and display, or of athletic events **2.** a day of enjoyably exciting events or highly successful activity

field·er (-ər) ***n.*** *Baseball*, etc. a player in the field

field event any of the contests held on the field in a track meet, as the high jump, shot put, etc.

field glass a small, portable, binocular telescope: *usually used in pl.* (**field glasses**)

field goal **1.** *Basketball* a basket toss made from play, scoring two points **2.** *Football* a goal kicked from the field, scoring three points

field hand a hired farm laborer

field hockey *same as* HOCKEY (sense 2)

field house **1.** a building near an athletic field, with lockers, showers, etc. for the athletes' use **2.** a large building for indoor sports events

Field·ing (fēl′diŋ), **Henry** 1707–54; Eng. novelist

field magnet the magnet used to create and maintain the magnetic field in a motor or generator

field marshal in some armies, an officer of the highest rank

field officer a colonel, lieutenant colonel, or major in the army

field·piece (fēld′pēs′) ***n.*** a mobile artillery piece

field-test (-test′) ***vt.*** to test (a device, method, etc.) under actual operating conditions

field·work (-wurk′) ***n.*** **1.** any temporary fortification made by troops in the field **2.** the work of collecting scientific data in the field —**field′work′er** ***n.***

fiend (fēnd) ***n.*** [OE. *feond*] **1.** an evil spirit; devil **2.** an inhumanly wicked or cruel person **3.** [Colloq.] *a)* a person addicted to some activity, habit, etc. [a fresh-air *fiend*] *b)* one who is excellent at some activity [a *fiend* at tennis] —**the Fiend** the Devil —**fiend′like′** ***adj.***

fiend·ish (-ish) ***adj.*** **1.** of or like a fiend; devilish; inhumanly wicked or cruel **2.** extremely vexatious or difficult —**fiend′ish·ly** ***adv.*** —**fiend′ish·ness** ***n.***

fierce (firs) ***adj.*** **fierc′er, fierc′est** [< OFr. < L. *ferus*, wild] **1.** of a violently cruel nature; savage [a *fierce* dog] **2.** violent; uncontrolled [a *fierce* storm] **3.** intensely eager; ardent [a *fierce* effort] **4.** [Colloq.] very distasteful, bad, etc. —**fierce′ly** ***adv.*** —**fierce′ness** ***n.***

fi·er·y (fī′ər ē) ***adj.*** **-er·i·er, -er·i·est** [ME. *firi*] **1.** containing or consisting of fire **2.** like fire; glaring, hot, etc. **3.** characterized by strong emotion; ardent **4.** easily stirred up; excitable [a *fiery* nature] **5.** inflamed [a *fiery* sore] —**fi′er·i·ly** ***adv.*** —**fi′er·i·ness** ***n.***

fi·es·ta (fē es′tə) ***n.*** [Sp. < VL. *festa:* see FEAST] **1.** a religious festival; esp., a saint's day **2.** any gala celebration; holiday

fife (fīf) ***n.*** [< G. < MHG. < OHG. *pfifa*] a small, shrill-toned musical instrument resembling a flute —***vt., vi.*** **fifed, fif′ing** to play on a fife —**fif′er** ***n.***

fif·teen (fif′tēn′) ***adj.*** [OE. *fiftene*] five more than ten —***n.*** the cardinal number between fourteen and sixteen; 15; XV

fif·teenth (-tēnth′) ***adj.*** **1.** preceded by fourteen others in a series; 15th **2.** designating any of the fifteen equal parts of something —***n.*** **1.** the one following the fourteenth **2.** any of the fifteen equal parts of something; 1/15

fifth (fifth) ***adj.*** [< OE. < *fif*, five] **1.** preceded by four others in a series; 5th **2.** designating any of the five equal parts of something —***n.*** **1.** the one following the fourth **2.** any of the five equal parts of something; 1/5 **3.** a fifth of a gallon **4.** *Music* *a)* the fifth tone of an ascending diatonic scale, or a tone four degrees above or below a given tone *b)* the interval between two such tones, or a combination of them —**fifth′ly** ***adv.***

Fifth Amendment the fifth amendment to the U.S. Constitution; specif., the clause protecting a person from being compelled to be a witness against himself

fifth column [orig. (1936) applied to Franco sympathizers inside Madrid, then besieged by four of his columns on the outside] a group of people who give aid and support to the enemy from within their own country —**fifth columnist**

fifth wheel any superfluous person or thing

fif·ti·eth (fif′tē ith) ***adj.*** **1.** preceded by forty-nine others in a series; 50th **2.** designating any of the fifty equal parts of something —***n.*** **1.** the one following the forty-ninth **2.** any of fifty equal parts of something; 1/50

fif·ty (fif′tē) ***adj.*** [OE. *fiftig*] five times ten —***n.,*** *pl.* **-ties** the cardinal number between forty-nine and fifty-one; 50; L —**the fifties** the numbers or years, as of a century, from fifty through fifty-nine

fif·ty-fif·ty (fif′tē fif′tē) ***adj.*** [Colloq.] equal; even —***adv.*** [Colloq.] equally

fig (fig) ***n.*** [< OFr., ult. < L. *ficus*] **1.** a small, hollow, pear-shaped fruit with sweet, seed-filled flesh **2.** a tree bearing this fruit **3.** a trifle [not worth a *fig*]

fig. **1.** figurative(ly) **2.** figure(s)

fig·eat·er (-ēt′ər) ***n.*** a large, green beetle that feeds on ripe fruit: the June bug of the southeastern U.S.

fight (fīt) ***vi.*** **fought, fight′ing** [OE. *feohtan*] **1.** to take part in a physical struggle or battle, specif. in a boxing match **2.** to struggle or work hard in trying to overcome; contend —***vt.*** **1.** to oppose physically, as with fists in boxing or in battle with weapons, etc. **2.** to struggle against or contend with, as by argument **3.** to engage in or carry on (a war, conflict, etc.) **4.** to gain by struggle *[he fought his way up]* **5.** to cause to fight; manage (a boxer, etc.) —*n.* **1.** a physical struggle; battle; combat **2.** any struggle, contest, or quarrel **3.** power or readiness to fight —**fight it out** to fight until one side is defeated —**fight off** to struggle to avoid

fight·er (-ər) *n.* **1.** one that fights or is inclined to fight **2.** a boxer; prizefighter **3.** a small, fast, highly maneuverable airplane for aerial combat

fig·ment (fig′mənt) *n.* [< L. *figmentum* < *fingere*, to make, devise] something merely imagined or made up in the mind

fig·u·ra·tion (fig′yə rā′shən) *n.* **1.** a forming; shaping **2.** form; appearance **3.** a representing by or ornamenting with figures —**fig′u·ra′tion·al** *adj.*

fig·u·ra·tive (fig′yər ə tiv) *adj.* **1.** representing by means of a figure or symbol **2.** not in its usual, literal, or exact sense or reference; metaphorical **3.** containing or using figures of speech —**fig′u·ra·tive·ly** *adv.* —**fig′u·ra·tive·ness** *n.*

fig·ure (fig′yər; *chiefly Brit.* fig′ər) *n.* [< OFr. < L. *figura* < *fingere*, to form] **1.** the outline or shape of something; form **2.** the human form **3.** a person seen or thought of in a specified way *[a great social figure]* **4.** a likeness of a person or thing **5.** an illustration; diagram; picture **6.** an artistic design in fabrics, etc.; pattern **7.** *a)* the symbol for a number *[the figure 5]* *b)* [*pl.*] arithmetic **8.** a sum of money **9.** *Dancing & Skating* a series or pattern of steps or movements **10.** *Geom.* a surface or space bounded on all sides by lines or planes **11.** *Music* a series of consecutive tones or chords forming a distinct group **12.** *Rhetoric same as* FIGURE OF SPEECH —*vt.* **-ured, -ur·ing** **1.** to represent in definite form **2.** to represent mentally; imagine **3.** to ornament with a design **4.** to compute with figures **5.** [Colloq.] to believe, think, decide, etc. —*vi.* **1.** to appear prominently; be conspicuous **2.** to do arithmetic **3.** [Colloq.] to be as expected —**figure in** to add in; include —**figure on** to plan or depend on —**figure out** **1.** to solve; compute **2.** to understand; reason out —**figure up** to add; total —**fig′ur·er** *n.*

fig·ured (-yərd) *adj.* **1.** shaped; formed **2.** having a design or pattern **3.** *Music* with numbers to indicate accompanying chords: said of the bass

fig·ure·head (fig′yər hed′) *n.* **1.** a carved figure on the bow of a ship **2.** a person holding a high position but having no real power or authority

figure of speech an expression, as a metaphor or simile, using words in a nonliteral or unusual sense to add vividness, etc. to what is said

figure skating ice skating in which the performer traces various elaborate figures on the ice

fig·u·rine (fig′yə rēn′) *n.* [Fr. < It. *figurina*] a small sculptured or molded figure; statuette

fig·wort (fig′wurt′) *adj.* designating a large family of plants including the foxglove, snapdragon, etc. —*n.* any of a genus of plants of the figwort family, with square stems and small flowers

Fi·ji (fē′jē) country on a group of islands (**Fiji Islands**) in the SW Pacific, north of New Zealand: a member of the Commonwealth: c.7,000 sq. mi.; pop. 512,000 —**Fi′ji·an** *adj., n.*

fil·a·gree (fil′ə grē′) *n., adj., vt.* **-greed′, -gree′ing** *same as* FILIGREE

fil·a·ment (fil′ə mənt) *n.* [Fr. < ML. < VL. < L. *filum*, a thread] **1.** a very slender thread or threadlike part; specif., *a)* the fine metal wire in a light bulb which is made incandescent by an electric current *b)* the wire cathode of a thermionic tube **2.** *Bot.* the stalk of a stamen bearing the anther —**fil′a·men′ta·ry** (-men′tər ē) *adj.* —**fil′a·men′tous** *adj.*

fi·lar·i·a (fi ler′ē ə) *n., pl.* **fi·lar′i·ae′** (-ē ē′) [ModL. < L. *filum*, a thread] any of several kinds of threadlike parasitic worms that live in the blood and tissues of vertebrate animals —**fi·lar′i·al, fi·lar′i·an** *adj.*

fil·a·ri·a·sis (fil′ə rī′ə sis) *n.* [see prec.] a disease caused by filarial worms transmitted by mosquitoes: the worms cause swelling, esp. in the lower parts of the body

fil·bert (fil′bərt) *n.* [ult. < St. *Philibert*, whose feast came in the nutting season] **1.** the edible nut of a cultivated European hazel tree **2.** a tree bearing this nut **3.** *same as* HAZELNUT

filch (filch) *vt.* [ME. *filchen*] to steal (esp. something small or petty); pilfer —**filch′er** *n.*

file[1] (fīl) *vt.* **filed, fil′ing** [Fr. < OFr. *filer*, to string papers on a thread < VL. *filare*, to spin < L. *filum*, a thread] **1.** to arrange (papers, etc.) in order for future reference **2.** to dispatch (a news story) to a newspaper office **3.** to register (an application, etc.) **4.** to put (a legal document) on public record **5.** to initiate (a legal action) —*vi.* **1.** to move in a line **2.** to register or apply (*for*) —*n.* **1.** a folder, cabinet, etc. for keeping papers in order **2.** an orderly arrangement of papers, cards, etc., as for reference **3.** a line of persons or things, one behind another —**on file** kept as in a file for reference —**file′a·ble** *adj.* —**fil′er** *n.*

file[2] (fīl) *n.* [OE. *feol*] a steel tool with a rough, ridged surface for smoothing or grinding down something —*vt.* **filed, fil′ing** to smooth or grind down with a file —**fil′er** *n.*

file·fish (fīl′fish′) *n., pl.* **-fish′, -fish′es:** see FISH a fish with very small, rough scales

fi·let (fi lā′, fil′ā) *n.* [see FILLET] **1.** a net or lace with a simple pattern on a square mesh background **2.** *same as* FILLET (*n.* 3) —*vt.* **-leted′** (-lād′), **-let′ing** (-lā′iŋ) *same as* FILLET (*vt.* 2)

fi·let mi·gnon (fi lā′ min yōn′, -yän′; *Fr.* fē le mē-nyōn′) [Fr., lit., tiny fillet] a thick, round cut of lean beef tenderloin broiled, usually with mushrooms and bacon

fil·i·al (fil′ē əl, fil′yəl) *adj.* [< LL. < L. *filius*, son, *filia*, daughter] **1.** of, suitable to, or due from a son or daughter *[filial devotion]* **2.** *Genetics* of the indicated generation (i.e., F_1, F_2, etc.) following the parental —**fil′i·al·ly** *adv.*

fil·i·bus·ter (fil′ə bus′tər) *n.* [< Sp. < MDu. *vrijbuiter*, freebooter] **1.** an adventurer who engages in unauthorized warfare against another country; freebooter **2.** a member of a legislative body who obstructs the passage of a bill by making long speeches, introducing irrelevant issues, etc.: also **fil′i·bus′ter·er** **3.** the use of such methods to obstruct a bill —*vi.* **1.** to engage in unauthorized warfare as a freebooter **2.** to engage in a filibuster —*vt.* to obstruct the passage of (a bill) by a filibuster

fil·i·gree (fil′ə grē′) *n.* [< earlier *filigrain* < Fr. < It. < L. *filum*, a thread + *granum*, grain] **1.** lacelike ornamental work of intertwined wire of gold, silver, etc. **2.** any delicate work or design like this —*adj.* like, made of, or made into filigree —*vt.* **-greed′, -gree′ing** to ornament with filigree

fil·ing (fīl′iŋ) *n.* a small piece, as of metal, scraped off with a file: *usually used in pl.*

Fil·i·pine (fil′ə pēn′) *adj. same as* PHILIPPINE

Fil·i·pi·no (fil′ə pē′nō) *n.* [Sp.] **1.** *pl.* **-nos** a native or citizen of the Philippines **2.** *see also* PILIPINO —*adj.* Philippine

fill (fil) *vt.* [OE. *fyllan* < base of *full*, FULL[1]] **1.** *a)* to put as much as possible into; make full *b)* to put a great amount of something into **2.** *a)* to take up or occupy all or nearly all the capacity or extent of *[the crowd filled the room]* *b)* to spread throughout **3.** *a)* to occupy (an office, position, etc.) *b)* to put a person into (an office, position, etc.) **4.** to fulfill (an engagement to perform, etc.) **5.** *a)* to supply the things called for in (an order, prescription, etc.) *b)* to satisfy (a need, requirement, etc.) **6.** to close or plug (holes, cracks, etc.) **7.** to satisfy the hunger or desire of —*vi.* to become full —*n.* **1.** all that is needed to make full **2.** all that is needed to satisfy **3.** anything that fills; esp., earth, gravel, etc. used for filling holes, etc. —**fill in** **1.** to fill with some substance **2.** to complete by supplying (something) **3.** to be a substitute —**fill one in on** [Colloq.] to provide one with additional details about —**fill out** **1.** to make or become rounder, shapelier, etc. **2.** to complete (a document, etc.) by inserting information —**fill up** to make or become completely full

fill·er (fil′ər) *n.* a person or thing that fills; specif., *a)* matter added to increase bulk, solidity, etc. *b)* a preparation used to fill in cracks, etc. *c)* the tobacco inside a cigar *d)* a short, space-filling item in a newspaper *e)* the paper for a loose-leaf notebook

fil·lér (fēl′er) *n., pl.* **-lér, -lérs** *see* MONETARY UNITS, table (Hungary)

fil·let (fil′it; *for n. 3 & vt. 2, usually* fil′ā, fi lā′) *n.* [< OFr. dim. of *fil* < L. *filum*, a thread] **1.** a narrow band worn around the head as to hold the hair in place **2.** a thin strip or band **3.** a boneless, lean piece of meat or fish —*vt.* **1.** to bind or decorate with a band, molding, etc. **2.** to bone and slice (meat or fish)

fill·ing (fil′iŋ) *n.* **1.** a thing used to fill something else; specif., *a)* the metal, plastic, etc. inserted by a dentist into a prepared cavity in a tooth *b)* the foodstuff used in a pastry shell, etc. **2.** the woof in a woven fabric

filling station *same as* SERVICE STATION

fil·lip (fil′əp) *n.* [echoic extension of FLIP[1]] **1.** the snap made by a finger held down by the thumb and then suddenly released **2.** a light tap given in this way **3.** anything that stimulates or livens up —*vt.* **1.** to strike or snap with a fillip **2.** to stimulate or liven up —*vi.* to make a fillip

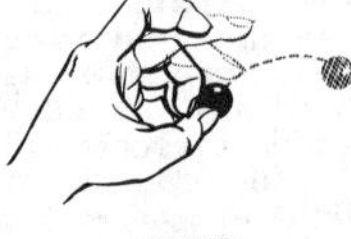
FILLIP

Fill·more (fil′môr), **Mill·ard** (mil′ərd) 1800–74; 13th president of the U.S. (1850–53)

fil·ly (fil′ē) *n., pl.* **-lies** [ON. *fylja*] **1.** a young female horse, specif. one under five years of age **2.** [Colloq.] a vivacious girl

film (film) *n.* [OE. *filmen*] **1.** a fine, thin skin or coating

2. a flexible cellulose material covered with a substance sensitive to light and used in taking photographs or making motion pictures 3. a haze or blur, as over the eyes 4. a motion picture or motion pictures 5. a gauzy web —*vt.* 1. to cover as with a film 2. to take a photograph of 3. to make a motion picture of —*vi.* 1. to become covered with a film 2. *a)* to make a motion picture *b)* to be filmed or suitable for filming —**film′er** *n.*

film·ic (fil′mik) *adj.* of motion pictures or the art of making them

film·strip (film′strip′) *n.* a length of film containing still photographs arranged in sequence for projection separately and used in teaching, etc.

film·y (fil′mē) *adj.* **film′i·er, film′i·est** 1. of or like a film; hazy, gauzy, etc. 2. covered as with a film —**film′i·ly** *adv.* —**film′i·ness** *n.*

fils (fēls, fils) *n., pl.* **fils** [< Ar. < LGr. *phollis,* a small coin] *see* MONETARY UNITS, table (Bahrain, Iraq, Jordan, Kuwait, United Arab Emirates, Yemen)

fil·ter (fil′tər) *n.* [< OFr. < ML. *filtrum, feltrum,* felt (used for filters)] 1. a device for passing a fluid through a porous substance so as to strain out solid particles, impurities, etc. 2. any porous substance so used, as sand, charcoal, etc. 3. *a)* a device that passes electric currents of certain frequencies only *b)* a device that absorbs certain light rays [a color *filter* for a camera lens] —*vt.* 1. to pass (a fluid) through a filter 2. to remove (solid particles, etc.) from a fluid with a filter 3. to act as a filter for —*vi.* 1. to pass through or as if through a filter 2. to pass slowly [the news *filtered* through town]

fil·ter·a·ble (-ə b'l) *adj.* that can be filtered: also **fil′tra·ble** (-trə b'l) —**fil′ter·a·bil′i·ty** *n.*

filterable virus any virus: so called because most viruses can pass through fine filters that bacteria cannot pass through

filter paper porous paper for filtering liquids

filth (filth) *n.* [OE. *fylthe* < base of *ful,* FOUL + -TH[1]] 1. disgustingly offensive dirt, garbage, etc. 2. anything considered grossly indecent or obscene 3. gross moral corruption

filth·y (fil′thē) *adj.* **filth′i·er, filth′i·est** 1. full of filth; disgustingly foul 2. grossly obscene 3. morally corrupt —**filth′i·ly** *adv.* —**filth′i·ness** *n.*

fil·trate (fil′trāt) *vt.* **-trat·ed, -trat·ing** to filter —*n.* a filtered liquid —**fil·tra′tion** *n.*

fin[1] (fin) *n.* [OE. *finn*] 1. any of several winglike, membranous organs on the body of a fish, dolphin, etc., used in swimming and balancing 2. anything like a fin in shape or use, as on an aircraft or boat

fin[2] (fin) *n.* [< Yid. < MHG. < OHG. *fimf,* five] [Slang] a five-dollar bill

fin. 1. finance 2. financial 3. finis

fi·na·gle (fə nā′g'l) *vt.* **-gled, -gling** [< ?] to get or arrange by cleverness, persuasion, etc., or esp. by craftiness or trickery —*vi.* to use craftiness or trickery —**fi·na′gler** *n.*

fi·nal (fī′n'l) *adj.* [< OFr. < L. *finalis* < *finis,* end] 1. of or coming at the end; last; concluding 2. deciding; conclusive [a *final* decree] 3. having to do with the ultimate purpose or end [a *final* cause] —*n.* 1. anything final 2. [*pl.*] the last of a series of contests 3. a final examination

fi·na·le (fə nä′lē, -nal′ē) *n.* [It.] 1. the concluding part of a musical composition or an entertainment 2. the conclusion; end

fi·nal·ist (fī′n'l ist) *n.* a contestant who participates in the final, deciding contest of a series

fi·nal·i·ty (fī nal′ə tē) *n.* 1. the quality or condition of being final, settled, or complete; conclusiveness 2. *pl.* **-ties** anything final

fi·nal·ize (fī′n'l īz′) *vt.* **-ized′, -iz′ing** [FINAL + -IZE] to make final —**fi′nal·i·za′tion** *n.*

fi·nal·ly (-ē) *adv.* 1. at the end; in conclusion 2. decisively; conclusively

fi·nance (fə nans′, fī′nans) *n.* [< OFr. < *finer,* to end, settle accounts < *fin* < L. *finis,* an end] 1. [*pl.*] the money resources, income, etc. of a nation, organization, or person 2. the managing or science of managing money matters —*vt.* **-nanced′, -nanc′ing** to supply or obtain money or credit for

fi·nan·cial (fə nan′shəl, fī-) *adj.* of finance, finances, or financiers —**fi·nan′cial·ly** *adv.*

fin·an·cier (fin′ən sir′) *n.* [Fr.] 1. a person skilled in finance 2. a person who engages in financial operations on a large scale

fin·back (fin′bak′) *n.* a large whalebone whale of the eastern coast of the U.S., with a large dorsal fin

finch (finch) *n.* [OE. *finc*] any of a large group of small songbirds with short beaks, including the bunting, canary, cardinal, and sparrow

find (fīnd) *vt.* **found, find′ing** [OE. *findan*] 1. to happen on; discover by chance 2. to get by searching 3. to get sight or knowledge of; perceive; learn 4. to experience or feel 5. *a)* to recover (something lost) *b)* to recover the use of 6. to consider; think [he *finds* TV boring] 7. to get to; reach [the arrow *found* its mark] 8. to declare after deliberation [to *find* him guilty] 9. to supply; furnish —*vi.* to announce a decision [the jury *found* for the accused] —*n.* 1. a finding 2. something found, esp. something valuable —**find oneself** 1. to learn what one's real talents are and begin to apply them 2. to become aware of being [to *find oneself* tired] —**find out** 1. to discover; learn 2. to learn the true character or identity of

find·er (fīn′dər) *n.* 1. a person or thing that finds 2. a camera device that shows what will appear in the photograph 3. a small telescope attached to, and used to locate objects for closer view with, a larger, more powerful one

‡**fin de siè·cle** (fan̸t sye′kl′) [Fr., end of the century] of or like the last years of the 19th century

find·ing (fīn′diŋ) *n.* 1. the act of one who finds; discovery 2. something found or discovered 3. [*often pl.*] the conclusion reached after consideration of facts, as by a judge, scholar, etc.

fine[1] (fīn) *adj.* **fin′er, fin′est** [< OFr. < ML. *finus,* for L. *finis,* an end] 1. orig., perfected 2. superior in quality, character, ability, etc.; excellent 3. with no impurities; refined 4. containing a specified proportion of pure metal: said of gold or silver 5. clear and bright: said of the weather 6. not heavy, gross, or coarse [*fine* sand] 7. *a)* very thin [*fine* thread] *b)* very small [*fine* print] 8. sharp; keen [a knife with a *fine* edge] 9. discriminating; subtle [*fine* distinctions] 10. having a delicate quality [*fine* china] 11. involving precision [a *fine* adjustment] 12. too elegant; showy [*fine* writing] —*adv.* 1. *same as* FINELY 2. [Colloq.] very well —*vt., vi.* **fined, fin′ing** to make or become fine or finer —**fine′ly** *adv.* —**fine′ness** *n.*

fine[2] (fīn) *n.* [< OFr. *fin* < L. *finis,* an end] a sum of money required to be paid as punishment for an offense —*vt.* **fined, fin′ing** to order to pay a fine —**in fine** 1. in conclusion 2. in brief

fine art any of the art forms that include drawing, painting, sculpture, and ceramics, or, occasionally, architecture, literature, music, dramatic art, or dancing: *usually used in pl.*

fine-drawn (fīn′drôn′) *adj.* 1. drawn out until very fine, as wire 2. very subtle: said of reasoning, arguments, etc.

fine-grained (-grānd′) *adj.* having a fine, smooth grain, as some wood, leather, etc.

fin·er·y (fīn′ər ē) *n., pl.* **-er·ies** showy, gay, elaborate decoration, esp. clothes, jewelry, etc.

fine·spun (fīn′spun′) *adj.* 1. delicate; fragile 2. extremely or overly subtle

fi·nesse (fi nes′) *n.* [Fr. < OFr. *fin,* FINE[1]] 1. adroitness and delicacy of performance 2. the ability to handle delicate and difficult situations diplomatically 3. cunning; skill 4. *Bridge* an attempt to take a trick with a lower card while holding a higher card not in sequence with it —*vt., vi.* **-nessed′, -ness′ing** 1. to manage by or use finesse 2. *Bridge* to make a finesse with (a card)

fine-toothed comb (fīn′tōōtht′) a comb with fine, closely set teeth: also **fine-tooth comb** —**go over with a fine-toothed comb** to examine very thoroughly

fin·ger (fiŋ′gər) *n.* [OE.] 1. any of the five parts at the end of the hand, esp. any of these other than the thumb 2. the part of a glove covering a finger 3. anything like a finger in shape or use 4. a unit of measurement based on the breadth of a finger (about 3/4 inch) or the length of a finger (about 4 1/2 inches) —*vt.* 1. to touch or handle with the fingers 2. to play (an instrument) by using the fingers on strings, keys, etc. —*vi.* to be fingered, as a violin —**have a finger in the pie** to participate —**put one's finger on** to indicate or ascertain exactly

fin·ger·board (-bôrd′) *n.* a strip of hard wood in the neck of a violin, cello, etc., against which the strings are pressed with the fingers to produce the desired tones

fin·gered (fiŋ′gərd) *adj.* having fingers (of a specified kind or number) [thick-*fingered*]

fin·ger·ing (fiŋ′gər iŋ) *n.* 1. a touching with the fingers 2. *Music a)* technique of using the fingers on the strings, keys, etc. to produce tones *b)* directions on a score for using the fingers

fin·ger·ling (-liŋ) *n.* 1. any small object 2. a small fish about the length of a finger

fin·ger·nail (-nāl′) *n.* the horny substance on the upper part of the end joint of a finger

finger painting the process of painting by using the fingers or hand to spread paints (**finger paints**) made of starch, glycerin, and pigments on moistened paper —**fin′ger-paint′** (-pānt′) *vi., vt.*

fin·ger·print (-print′) ***n.*** an impression of the lines and whorls on the inner surface of the end joint of the finger, used to identify a person —***vt.*** to take the fingerprints of

FINGERPRINT

finger tip the tip of a finger —**have at one's finger tips** **1.** to have available for instant use **2.** to be completely familiar with —**to one's** (or **the**) **finger tips** entirely; altogether

fin·i·al (fin′ē əl) ***n.*** [ME., orig. adj., FINAL] a decorative part at the tip of a spire, lamp shade support, etc., or projecting upward from the top of a cabinet, etc.

fin·i·cal (fin′i k'l) ***adj.*** [< FINE[1]] *same as* FINICKY —**fin′i·cal·ly** ***adv.***

fin·ick·y (fin′i kē′) ***adj.*** [see prec.] too particular; overly fastidious; fussy: also **fin′ick·ing, fin′nick·y** —**fin′ick·i·ness** ***n.***

fi·nis (fin′is, fī′nis) ***n.,*** *pl.* **-nis·es** [L.] the end, as of a book; conclusion

fin·ish (fin′ish) ***vt.*** [< OFr. < L. *finire* < *finis*, an end] **1.** *a)* to bring to an end; complete *b)* to come to the end of **2.** to use up; consume entirely **3.** to give final touches to **4.** to give (cloth, wood, etc.) a desired surface effect **5.** *a)* to cause the defeat, death, etc. of *b)* to render worthless, useless, etc. —***vi.*** **1.** to come to an end **2.** to complete something being done —***n.*** **1.** the last part; end **2.** anything used to give a desired surface effect, as varnish, wax, etc. **3.** completeness; perfection **4.** the manner or method of completion **5.** the way in which the surface, as of furniture, is finished **6.** refinement in manners, speech, etc. **7.** defeat, collapse, etc. or that which brings it about **8.** finishing joiner work, as doors, moldings, panels, etc. —**finish off** **1.** to end or complete **2.** to kill or destroy —**finish up** **1.** to end or complete **2.** to consume all of —**finish with** **1.** to end or complete **2.** to end relations with—**fin′ished** ***adj.*** —**fin′ish·er** ***n.***

finishing school a private school for girls that specializes in imparting social poise and polish

fi·nite (fī′nīt) ***adj.*** [< L. *finitus*, pp. of *finire*, FINISH] **1.** having definable limits; not infinite **2.** *Gram.* having limits of person, number, and tense: said of a verb that can be used in a predicate —**fi′nite·ly** ***adv.*** —**fi′nite·ness** ***n.***

fin·i·tude (fin′ə to͞od′, fī′nə-; -tyo͞od′) ***n.*** the state or quality of being finite

fink (fiŋk) ***n.*** [< ?] [Slang] **1.** an informer or strikebreaker **2.** a person regarded as obnoxious

Fin·land (fin′lənd) **1.** country in N Europe, northeast of the Baltic Sea: 130,119 sq. mi.; pop. 4,696,000; cap. Helsinki **2. Gulf of,** arm of the Baltic Sea, between Finland & the U.S.S.R.

Finn (fin) ***n.*** a native or inhabitant of Finland

Finn. Finnish

fin·nan had·die (fin′ən had′ē) [prob. < *Findhorn* (Scot. fishing port) *haddock*] smoked haddock: also **finnan haddock**

Finn·ish (fin′ish) ***adj.*** **1.** of Finland **2.** of the Finns, their language, or culture —***n.*** the Finno-Ugric language of the Finns

Fin·no- *a combining form meaning* Finn, Finnish

Fin·no-U·gric (fin′ō o͞o′grik, -yo͞o′-) ***adj.*** designating or of a subfamily of the Uralic languages spoken in NE Europe, W Siberia, and Hungary: it includes Finnish, Estonian, Hungarian, etc. —***n.*** this subfamily of languages Also **Fin′no-U′gri·an** (-grē ən)

fin·ny (fin′ē) ***adj.*** **1.** *a)* having fins *b)* like a fin **2.** of or being fish

fiord (fyôrd) ***n.*** [< Norw. < ON. *fjörthr*] a narrow inlet of the sea bordered by steep cliffs, esp. in Norway

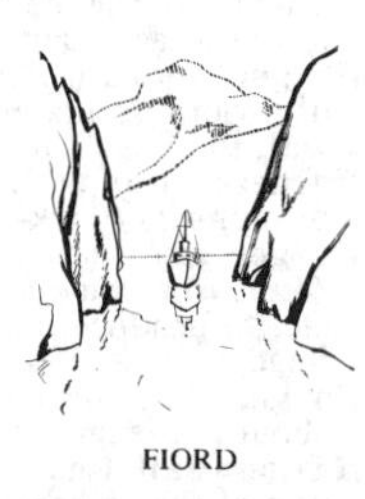
FIORD

fip·ple flute (fip′'l) [< ?] any of a class of vertical flutes, as the recorder, in which a plug (fipple) near the mouthpiece diverts the breath in producing the tones

fir (fur) ***n.*** [< OE. *fyrh*] **1.** a cone-bearing evergreen tree of the pine family **2.** its wood

fire (fīr) ***n.*** [OE. *fyr*] **1.** the heat and light of combustion **2.** something burning, as fuel in a furnace **3.** a destructive burning [*a forest fire*] **4.** anything like fire in heat, brilliance, etc. **5.** torture by burning **6.** extreme distress; tribulation **7.** fever or inflammation **8.** strong feeling; fervor **9.** vivid imagination **10.** *a)* a discharge of firearms or artillery *b)* anything like this in speed and continuity [*a fire of criticism*] —***vt.*** **fired, fir′ing** **1.** to make burn; ignite **2.** to supply with fuel [*to fire a furnace*] **3.** to bake (bricks, pottery, etc.) in a kiln **4.** to dry by heat **5.** to animate, inspire, excite, etc. **6.** to shoot or discharge (a gun, bullet, etc.) **7.** to hurl or direct with force [*to fire questions*] **8.** to dismiss from a job; discharge —***vi.*** **1.** to start burning; flame **2.** to tend a fire **3.** to become excited or aroused **4.** to shoot a firearm **5.** to discharge a projectile —**between two fires** shot at, criticized, etc. from both sides —**catch (on) fire** to begin burning —**fire up** to start a fire, as in a furnace —**miss fire** **1.** to fail to fire, as a gun **2.** to fail in an attempt —**on fire** **1.** burning **2.** greatly excited —**open fire** **1.** to begin to shoot **2.** to begin; start —**play with fire** to do something risky —**set fire to** to make burn; ignite —**take fire** **1.** to begin to burn **2.** to become excited —**under fire** **1.** under attack, as by gunfire **2.** subjected to criticism, etc. —**fir′er** ***n.***

fire·arm (-ärm′) ***n.*** any weapon from which a shot is fired by explosive force; esp., such a weapon small enough to be carried, as a rifle

fire·boat (-bōt′) ***n.*** a boat equipped with firefighting equipment, used along waterfronts

fire·bomb (-bäm′) ***n.*** a bomb intended to start a fire; incendiary bomb —***vt.*** to attack with a firebomb or firebombs

fire·box (-bäks′) ***n.*** the place for the fire in a furnace, etc.

fire·brand (-brand′) ***n.*** **1.** a piece of burning wood **2.** a person who stirs up strife, etc.

fire·break (-brāk′) ***n.*** a strip of land cleared to stop the spread of fire, as in a forest

fire·brick (-brik′) ***n.*** a brick made to withstand great heat, used to line furnaces, etc.

fire·bug (-bug′) ***n.*** [Colloq.] a person who deliberately sets fire to buildings, etc.; pyromaniac

fire·clay (-klā′) ***n.*** a clay that can resist intense heat, used to make firebricks, furnace linings, etc.

fire·crack·er (-krak′ər) ***n.*** a roll of paper that contains an explosive and an attached fuse, set off as a noisemaker at celebrations, etc.

fire·damp (-damp′) ***n.*** a gas, largely methane, formed in coal mines, which is explosive when mixed with a certain proportion of air

fire·dog (-dôg′) ***n.*** *same as* ANDIRON

fire door a door of metal or other fire-resistant material designed to keep a fire from spreading

fire·eat·er (-ēt′ər) ***n.*** **1.** an entertainer who pretends to eat fire **2.** a belligerent person

fire engine **1.** a motor truck equipped to spray water, chemicals, etc. on fires to put them out **2.** loosely, any motor truck for carrying firemen and equipment to a fire

fire escape a stairway, ladder, etc. down an outside wall, for escape from a burning building

fire extinguisher a portable device containing chemicals for spraying on a fire to put it out

fire·fight·er (-fīt′ər) ***n.*** *same as* FIREMAN (sense 1)

fire·fly (-flī′) ***n.,*** *pl.* **-flies′** a winged beetle whose abdomen glows with a luminescent light

fire insurance insurance against loss or damage resulting from fire

fire·light (-līt′) ***n.*** light from an open fire

fire·man (-mən) ***n.,*** *pl.* **-men** **1.** a man whose work is fighting fires **2.** a man who tends a fire in a furnace, locomotive engine, etc. **3.** *U.S. Navy* a nonrated enlisted man whose duties are concerned with the ship's engines, etc. **4.** [Slang] *Baseball* a relief pitcher

Fi·ren·ze (fē ren′dze) *It. name of* FLORENCE, Italy

fire·place (fīr′plās′) ***n.*** a place for a fire, esp. an open place built in a wall, at a chimney base

fire·plug (-plug′) ***n.*** a street hydrant to which a hose can be attached for fighting fires

fire·pow·er (-pou′ər) ***n.*** *Mil.* **1.** the effectiveness of a weapon in terms of the accuracy and volume of its fire **2.** the capacity of a given unit to deliver fire

fire·proof (-pro͞of′) ***adj.*** that does not burn or is not easily destroyed by fire —***vt.*** to make fireproof

fire sale a sale of goods damaged in a fire

fire·side (-sīd′) ***n.*** **1.** the part of a room near a fireplace; hearth **2.** home or home life

fire station the place where fire engines are kept and where firemen stay when on duty: also **fire′house′** (-hous′) ***n.***

fire·storm (-stôrm′) ***n.*** an intense fire over a large area, as one caused by an atomic explosion

fire·trap (-trap′) ***n.*** a building unsafe in case of fire, as because it lacks adequate exits

fire·wa·ter (-wôt′ər, -wät′ər) ***n.*** [prob. transl. of AmInd. term] alcoholic liquor: now humorous

fire·weed (-wēd′) ***n.*** any of various plants that grow readily on cleared or burned-over land

fire·works (-wurks′) ***n.pl.*** **1.** firecrackers, rockets, etc. used, as in celebrations, to produce loud noises or brilliant lighting effects: *sometimes used in sing.* **2.** a display of or as of fireworks

firing line **1.** the line from which gunfire is directed against the enemy **2.** the front position in any kind of activity

fir·kin (fur′kin) ***n.*** [< MDu. dim. of *vierdel*, a fourth] **1.** a small wooden tub for butter, lard, etc. **2.** a measure of capacity equal to 1/4 barrel

firm[1] (fɵrm) *adj.* [< OFr. < L. *firmus*] **1.** not yielding easily under pressure; solid **2.** not moved or shaken easily; fixed; stable **3.** remaining the same; steady *[a firm market]* **4.** resolute; constant *[a firm faith]* **5.** showing determination, strength, etc. *[a firm command]* **6.** formally concluded; definite; final *[a firm contract]* —*vt., vi.* to make or become firm: often with *up* —**firm′ly** *adv.* —**firm′ness** *n.*

firm[2] (fɵrm) *n.* [It. *firma,* signature < L. < *firmus,* FIRM[1]] a business company or partnership

fir·ma·ment (fɵr′mə mənt) *n.* [< OFr. < LL. < L. *firmare,* to strengthen < *firmus,* FIRM[1]] the sky, viewed poetically as a solid arch or vault

first (fɵrst) *adj.* [< OE. *fyrst*] **1.** before any others; 1st: used as the ordinal of ONE **2.** happening or acting before all others; earliest **3.** foremost in rank, quality, importance, etc. **4.** *Music* playing or singing the part highest in pitch or the leading part —*adv.* **1.** *a)* before any other person or thing *b)* before doing anything else **2.** as the first point **3.** for the first time **4.** sooner; preferably —*n.* **1.** the first person, thing, class, place, etc. **2.** the first day of the month **3.** the beginning; start **4.** a first happening or thing of its kind **5.** [*pl.*] the best quality of merchandise **6.** the winning place, as in a race **7.** the first or lowest forward gear ratio of a motor vehicle

first aid emergency treatment for injury or sudden illness, before regular medical care is available —**first′-aid′** *adj.*

first base *Baseball* the base on the pitcher's left, the first of the four bases a runner must touch in succession to score a run —**get to first base** [Slang] get the first stage done

first·born (-bôrn′) *adj.* born first in a family; oldest —*n.* the firstborn child

first-class (-klas′) *adj.* **1.** of the highest class, rank, quality, etc.; excellent **2.** designating or of the most expensive accommodations, as on a ship **3.** designating or of a class of mail consisting of sealed matter and carrying the highest regular postage rates —*adv.* **1.** with the most expensive accommodations **2.** as or by first-class mail

first cousin the son or daughter of one's aunt or uncle

first finger the finger next to the thumb

first·hand (-hand′) *adj., adv.* from the original producer or source; direct

first lady [*often* **F- L-**] the wife of the U.S. president

first lieutenant a U.S. military officer ranking above a second lieutenant

first·ling (-liŋ) *n.* **1.** the first of a kind **2.** the first fruit, produce, offspring, etc.

first·ly (-lē) *adv.* in the first place; first

first mate a merchant ship's officer next in rank below the captain: also **first officer**

first mortgage a mortgage having priority over all other liens on the same property

first offender a person convicted for the first time of an offense against the law

first person that form of a pronoun (as *I* or *we*) or verb (as *do*) which refers to the speaker or speakers

first-rate (-rāt′) *adj.* of the highest class, rank, or quality; excellent —*adv.* [Colloq.] very well

first sergeant *U.S. Army & Marine Corps* the noncommissioned officer, usually a master sergeant, serving as chief assistant to the commander of a company, battery, etc.

first-string (-striŋ′) *adj.* [Colloq.] **1.** *Sports* that is the first choice for regular play at a specified position **2.** first-class; excellent

first water the best quality and purest luster: said of gems, but also used figuratively

firth (fɵrth) *n.* [< ON. *fjörthr*] a narrow arm of the sea; estuary

fis·cal (fis′kəl) *adj.* [Fr. < LL. < L. *fiscus,* money basket] **1.** having to do with the public treasury or revenues **2.** financial —**fis′cal·ly** *adv.*

fiscal year the twelve-month period between settlements of financial accounts: the U.S. government fiscal year legally ends June 30

fish (fish) *n., pl.* **fish;** in referring to different species, **fish′es:** see PLURAL, II, D, 2 [OE. *fisc*] **1.** any of a large group of cold-blooded animals living in water and having backbones, gills for breathing, fins, and, usually, scales **2.** loosely, any animal living in water only, as a crab, oyster, etc. **3.** the flesh of a fish used as food **4.** [Colloq.] a person thought of as like a fish in being easily lured, lacking emotion, etc. —[**F-**] the constellation Pisces —*vi.* **1.** to catch or try to catch fish **2.** to try to get something indirectly or by cunning (often with *for*) —*vt.* **1.** to fish in (a stream, lake, etc.) **2.** to grope for, find, and bring to view *[he fished a coin out of his pocket]* —*adj.* **1.** of fish or fishing **2.** selling fish —**drink like a fish** to drink heavily, esp. alcoholic liquor —**like a fish out of water** in surroundings not suited to one —**neither fish, flesh, nor fowl** not anything definite or recognizable —**other fish to fry** other, more important things to attend to —**fish′a·ble** *adj.* —**fish′like′** *adj.*

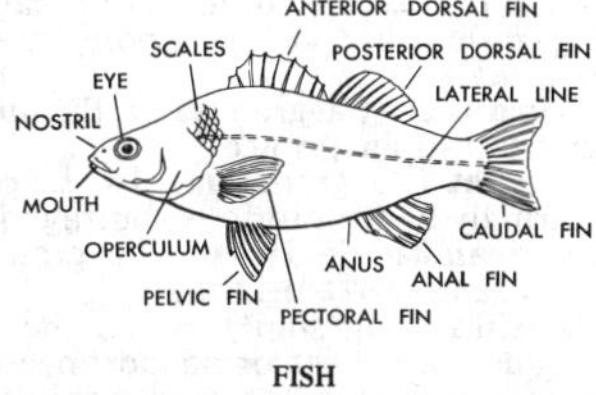

FISH

Fish (fish), **Hamilton** 1808–93; U.S. statesman

fish and chips [Chiefly Brit.] fried fillets of fish served with French fried potatoes

fish·er (fish′ər) *n.* **1.** a fisherman **2.** *pl.* **-ers, -er:** see PLURAL, II, D, 1 a flesh-eating animal of the marten family, like a weasel but larger

fish·er·man (-mən) *n., pl.* **-men** **1.** a person who fishes for sport or for a living **2.** a ship used in fishing

fish·er·y (-ē) *n., pl.* **-er·ies** **1.** the business of catching fish **2.** a place where fish are caught **3.** the legal right to catch fish in certain waters or at certain times **4.** a place where fish are bred

fish-eye lens (fish′ī′) a camera lens designed to record a 180-degree field of vision

fish hawk *same as* OSPREY

fish·hook (-hook′) *n.* a hook, usually barbed, for catching fish

fish·ing (-iŋ) *n.* the catching of fish for sport or for a living

fishing pole a simple device for fishing, consisting of a pole, line, and hook

fishing rod a slender pole with an attached line, hook, and usually a reel, used in fishing

fish joint a joint, as of two railroad rails, held together by fishplates along the sides

fish meal ground, dried fish, used as fertilizer or fodder

fish·mon·ger (-muŋ′gər, -mäŋ′-) *n.* a dealer in fish

fish·plate (-plāt′) *n.* [prob. < Fr. *fiche,* means of fixing] either of a pair of steel plates bolting two rails together lengthwise, as on a railroad

fish story [Colloq.] an exaggerated story

fish·wife (-wīf′) *n., pl.* **-wives′** (-wīvz′) **1.** a woman who sells fish **2.** a coarse, scolding woman

fish·y (-ē) *adj.* **fish′i·er, fish′i·est** **1.** of or full of fish **2.** like a fish in odor, taste, etc. **3.** dull or expressionless *[a fishy stare]* **4.** [Colloq.] questionable; odd *[a fishy story]* —**fish′i·ly** *adv.* —**fish′i·ness** *n.*

fis·sile (fis′'l) *adj.* [< L. < *fissus,* pp. of *findere,* to split] **1.** that can be split **2.** that can undergo fission; fissionable —**fis·sil·i·ty** (fi sil′ə tē) *n.*

fis·sion (fish′ən) *n.* [< L. < *fissus:* see prec.] **1.** a splitting apart; division into parts **2.** *same as* NUCLEAR FISSION **3.** *Biol.* a form of asexual reproduction in which the parent organism divides into two or more parts, each becoming an independent individual —*vi., vt.* to undergo or cause to undergo nuclear fission —**fis′sion·a·ble** *adj.*

fis·sure (fish′ər) *n.* [< OFr. < L. *fissura* < *fissus:* see FISSILE] **1.** a long, narrow, deep cleft or crack **2.** a dividing or breaking into parts —*vt., vi.* **-sured, -sur·ing** to crack or split apart

fist (fist) *n.* [< OE. *fyst*] **1.** a hand with the fingers closed tightly into the palm **2.** [Colloq.] *a)* a hand *b)* the grasp **3.** *Printing* the sign (☞), used to direct special attention to something

fist·ic (fis′tik) *adj.* having to do with boxing; fought with the fists; pugilistic

fist·i·cuffs (fis′ti kufs′) *n.pl.* [< FIST + CUFF[2]] **1.** a fight with the fists **2.** the science of boxing

fis·tu·la (fis′choo lə) *n., pl.* **-las, -lae′** (-lē′) [< OFr. < L., a pipe, ulcer] an abnormal passage from an abscess, cavity, or hollow organ to the skin or to another abscess, cavity, or organ —**fis′tu·lous, fis′tu·lar** *adj.*

fit[1] (fit) *vt.* **fit′ted** or **fit, fit′ted, fit′ting** [ME. *fitten* < ? ON. *fitja,* to knit, tie] **1.** to be suitable or adapted to **2.** to be the proper size, shape, etc. for **3.** *a)* to make or alter so as to fit *b)* to measure (a person) for something that must be fitted **4.** to make suitable or qualified **5.** *a)* to insert, as into a receptacle *b)* to make a place for (with *in* or *into*) **6.** to equip; outfit (often with *out*) —*vi.* **1.** to be suitable or proper **2.** to be in accord or harmony (often with *in* or *into*) **3.** to have the proper size or shape for a particular figure, space, etc. *[his coat fits well]* —*adj.* **fit′ter, fit′test** **1.** adapted, qualified, or suited to some purpose, function, etc. **2.** proper; right **3.** in good physical condition; healthy —*n.* **1.** a fitting or being fitted **2.** the manner of fitting *[a tight fit]* **3.** anything that fits —**fit to be tied** [Colloq.] frustrated or angry —**fit′ly** *adv.* —**fit′ness** *n.*

fit[2] (fit) ***n.*** [OE. *fitt*, conflict] **1.** any sudden, uncontrollable attack *[a fit of coughing]* **2.** a sharp, brief display of feeling *[a fit of anger]* **3.** a temporary burst of activity **4.** *Med.* a seizure in which one loses consciousness or has convulsions or both —**by fits and starts** in an irregular way —**have** (or **throw**) **a fit** [Colloq.] to become very angry or upset

fitch (fich) ***n.*** [< OFr. < MDu. *vitsche*] *same as* POLECAT (sense 1): also **fitch′et** (-it), **fitch′ew** (-o͞o)

fit·ful (fit′fəl) ***adj.*** characterized by intermittent activity, impulses, etc.; spasmodic —**fit′ful·ly** ***adv.*** —**fit′ful·ness** ***n.***

fit·ted (fit′id) ***adj.*** designed to conform to the contours of that which it covers

fit·ter (-ər) ***n.*** **1.** a person who alters or adjusts garments to fit **2.** a person who installs or adjusts machinery, pipes, etc.

fit·ting (-iŋ) ***adj.*** suitable; proper; appropriate —***n.*** **1.** an adjustment or trying on of clothes, etc. for fit **2.** a part used to join, adjust, or adapt other parts, as in a system of pipes **3.** [*pl.*] the fixtures, furnishings, or decorations of a house, automobile, office, etc. —**fit′ting·ly** ***adv.*** —**fit′ting·ness** ***n.***

Fitz·Ger·ald (fits jer′əld), **Edward** (born *Edward Purcell*) 1809–83; Eng. poet & translator of *The Rubáiyát*, a long poem written by OMAR KHAYYÁM: also **Fitzgerald**

Fitz·ger·ald (fits jer′əld), **F(rancis) Scott (Key)** 1896–1940; U.S. author

Fiu·me (fyo͞o′me) *former (It.) name of* RIJEKA

five (fīv) ***adj.*** [< OE. *fif*] totaling one more than four —***n.*** **1.** the cardinal number between four and six; 5; V **2.** anything having five units or members, or numbered five; specif., *a)* a basketball team *b)* [Colloq.] a five-dollar bill

five-and-ten-cent store (-′n ten′sent′) a store that sells a wide variety of inexpensive merchandise: also **five′-and-ten′**, **five′-and-dime′**

five·fold (-fōld′) ***adj.*** [see -FOLD] **1.** having five parts **2.** having five times as much or as many —***adv.*** five times as much or as many

Five Nations a confederation of Iroquoian Indians, including the Mohawks, Oneidas, Onondagas, Cayugas, and Senecas

fix (fiks) ***vt.*** [< L. *fixus*, pp. of *figere*, to fasten] **1.** *a)* to make firm, stable, or secure *b)* to fasten firmly **2.** to set firmly in the mind **3.** to direct steadily *[to fix the eyes on a spot]* **4.** to make rigid **5.** to make permanent or lasting **6.** to establish definitely; set or determine **7.** to set in order; adjust **8.** to repair, mend, etc. **9.** to prepare (food or meals) **10.** [Colloq.] to influence the result or action of (a race, election, etc) by bribery, trickery, etc. **11.** [Colloq.] to revenge oneself on; punish **12.** [Colloq.] to spay or castrate **13.** *Chem.* *a)* to make solid or nonvolatile *b)* to combine (atmospheric nitrogen) in the form of useful compounds, as nitrates, ammonia, etc. **14.** *Photog.* to make (a film, print, etc.) permanent by washing in a chemical solution —***vi.*** **1.** to become fixed, firm, or stable **2.** [Colloq. or Dial.] to prepare or intend *[I'm fixing to go]* —***n.*** **1.** the position of a ship or aircraft determined as from the bearings of two or more known points **2.** [Colloq.] a difficult or awkward situation; predicament **3.** [Slang] *a)* the fixing of the outcome of a contest, situation, etc. *b)* a contest, situation, etc. that has been fixed **4.** [Slang] an injection of a narcotic, as heroin —**fix on** (or **upon**) to choose —**fix up** [Colloq.] **1.** to repair, mend, etc. **2.** to set in order **3.** to make arrangements for —**fix′a·ble** ***adj.*** —**fix′er** ***n.***

fix·ate (fik′sāt) ***vt., vi.*** **-at·ed, -at·ing** **1.** to make or become fixed **2.** *Psychoanalysis* to subject to or undergo fixation

fix·a·tion (fik sā′shən) ***n.*** **1.** a fixing or being fixed, as in chemistry, photography, etc. **2.** popularly, an exaggerated preoccupation; obsession **3.** *Psychoanalysis* attachment to objects of an earlier stage of psychosexual development *[a father fixation]*

fix·a·tive (fik′sə tiv) ***adj.*** that is able or tends to make permanent, prevent fading, etc. —***n.*** a fixative substance, as a mordant

fixed (fikst) ***adj.*** **1.** firmly placed or attached; not movable **2.** established; set **3.** steady; resolute **4.** obsessive *[a fixed idea]* **5.** [Colloq.] supplied with something, specif. money *[comfortably fixed for life]* **6.** [Slang] with the outcome dishonestly prearranged **7.** *Chem.* *a)* nonvolatile *[fixed oils]* *b)* incorporated into a stable compound from its free state, as atmospheric nitrogen —**fix·ed·ly** (fik′sid lē) ***adv.*** —**fix′ed·ness** ***n.***

fixed star a star that appears to keep the same position in relation to other stars

fix·ings (fik′siŋz) ***n.pl.*** [Colloq.] accessories or trimmings *[roast turkey and all the fixings]*

fix·i·ty (-sə tē) ***n.*** **1.** the quality or state of being fixed; steadiness or permanence **2.** *pl.* **-ties** anything fixed

fixt (fikst) *poet. pt. and pp. of* FIX

fix·ture (fiks′chər) ***n.*** [< LL. *fixura* < L. *fixus* (see FIX): form infl. by MIXTURE] **1.** anything firmly in place **2.** any of the firmly attached fittings of a house, store, etc. *[bathroom fixtures]* **3.** a person or thing long-established in a place or job

fizz (fiz) ***n.*** [echoic] **1.** a hissing, sputtering sound, as of an effervescent drink **2.** an effervescent drink —***vi.*** **1.** to make a hissing or bubbling sound **2.** to give off gas bubbles; effervesce

fiz·zle (fiz′'l) ***vi.*** **-zled, -zling** [ME. *fesilen*, to break wind silently] **1.** to make a hissing or sputtering sound **2.** [Colloq.] to fail, esp. after a successful beginning —***n.*** **1.** a hissing or sputtering sound **2.** [Colloq.] a failure

fizz·y (fiz′ē) ***adj.*** **fizz′i·er, fizz′i·est** fizzing; effervescent

fjord (fyôrd) ***n.*** *same as* FIORD

FL Florida

Fl. **1.** Flanders **2.** Flemish

fl. **1.** [L. *floruit*] (he or she) flourished **2.** fluid

Fla. Florida

flab (flab) ***n.*** [back-formation < FLABBY] [Colloq.] soft, sagging flesh

flab·ber·gast (flab′ər gast′) ***vt.*** [< ? ff. + AGHAST] to dumbfound; amaze

flab·by (flab′ē) ***adj.*** **-bi·er, -bi·est** [var. of *flappy* < FLAP] **1.** lacking firmness; limp and soft *[flabby muscles]* **2.** lacking force; weak —**flab′bi·ly** ***adv.*** —**flab′bi·ness** ***n.***

flac·cid (flak′sid, flas′id) ***adj.*** [L. *flaccidus* < *flaccus*, flabby] **1.** soft and limp; flabby **2.** weak; feeble —**flac·cid′i·ty** ***n.*** —**flac′cid·ly** ***adv.***

‡**fla·con** (flȧ kōn′; *E.* flak′'n) ***n.*** [Fr.: see FLAGON] a small bottle with a stopper, as for perfume

flag[1] (flag) ***n.*** [< ? FLAG[4], in obs. sense "to flutter"] **1.** a piece of cloth with colors, patterns, or devices, used as a national or state symbol or as a signal; banner, standard **2.** the tail of a deer **3.** the bushy tail of certain dogs, as setters **4.** *Music* any of the lines extending from a stem, indicating whether the note is an eighth, sixteenth, etc. —***vt.*** **flagged, flag′ging** **1.** to decorate or mark with flags **2.** to signal with or as with a flag; esp., to signal to stop (often with *down*) —**flag′ger** ***n.***

flag[2] (flag) ***n.*** [ON. *flaga*, slab of stone] *same as* FLAGSTONE —***vt.*** **flagged, flag′ging** to pave with flagstones

flag[3] (flag) ***n.*** [ME. *flagge*, akin ? to ff.] **1.** any of various irises, with flowers of blue, purple, white, yellow, etc. **2.** *same as* SWEET FLAG

flag[4] (flag) ***vi.*** **flagged, flag′ging** [< ? ON. *flakka*, to flutter] to lose strength; grow weak or tired

Flag Day June 14, anniversary of the day in 1777 when the U.S. flag was adopted

flag·el·lant (flaj′ə lənt) ***n.*** [see ff.] a person who whips; specif., one who whips himself or has himself whipped as for religious discipline —***adj.*** engaging in flagellation

flag·el·late (flaj′ə lāt′) ***vt.*** **-lat′ed, -lat′ing** [< L. < *flagellare*, to whip < *flagellum*, a whip] to whip; flog —***adj.*** **1.** having a flagellum or flagella: also **flag′el·lat′ed** **2.** shaped like a flagellum —**flag′el·la′tion** ***n.*** —**flag′el·la′tor** ***n.***

fla·gel·lum (flə jel′əm) ***n.***, *pl.* **-la** (-ə), **-lums** [L.: see prec.] **1.** *Biol.* a whiplike part serving as an organ of locomotion in certain cells, bacteria, protozoans, etc. **2.** *Bot.* a threadlike shoot or runner

flag·eo·let (flaj′ə let′) ***n.*** [Fr., dim. of OFr. *flageol*, a flute < L. *flare*, to blow] a small fipple flute similar to the recorder

flag·ging[1] (flag′iŋ) ***adj.*** [prp. of FLAG[4]] weakening or drooping —**flag′ging·ly** ***adv.***

flag·ging[2] (flag′iŋ) ***n.*** flagstones or a pavement made of flagstones

fla·gi·tious (flə jish′əs) ***adj.*** [< L. < *flagitium*, shameful act < *flagitare*, to demand] shamefully wicked; vile and scandalous —**fla·gi′tious·ly** ***adv.*** —**fla·gi′tious·ness** ***n.***

flag·man (flag′mən) ***n.***, *pl.* **-men** a person whose work is signaling with a flag or lantern

flag officer *U.S. Navy* any officer above the rank of captain

flag·on (flag′ən) ***n.*** [< OFr. *flacon* < LL. < *flasca*, flask] **1.** a container for liquids, with a handle, a spout, and, often, a lid **2.** the contents of a flagon

flag·pole (flag′pōl′) ***n.*** a pole on which a flag is flown: also **flag′staff′** (-staf′)

fla·gran·cy (flā′grən sē) ***n.*** the quality or state of being flagrant: also **fla′grance**

fla·grant (flā′grənt) ***adj.*** [< L. prp. of *flagrare*, to blaze] glaringly bad; notorious; outrageous —**fla′grant·ly** ***adv.***

‡**fla·gran·te de·lic·to** (flə gran′tē di lik′tō) [L.] *same as* IN FLAGRANTE DELICTO

flag·ship (flag′ship′) ***n.*** **1.** the ship carrying the commander of a fleet or squadron and displaying his flag **2.** the finest, largest, or newest ship of a steamship line

flag·stone (flag′stōn′) ***n.*** **1.** any hard stone that splits into flat pieces used to pave walks, terraces, etc. **2.** a piece of such stone

flag-wav·ing (flag′wā′viŋ) ***n.*** an emotional appeal calculated to arouse intense patriotic feelings

flail (flāl) ***n.*** [OFr. *flaiel* < L. *flagellum*, a whip] a farm tool having a free-swinging stick attached to a long handle, used to thresh grain by hand —***vt., vi.*** **1.** to thresh with a flail **2.** to beat as with a flail **3.** to move (one's arms) about like flails

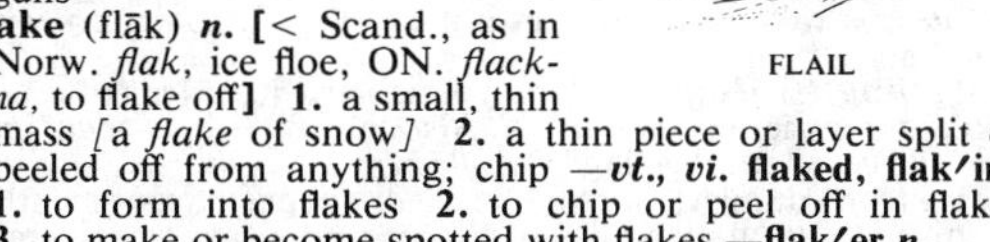
FLAIL

flair (fler) ***n.*** [< OFr. < *flairer*, ult. < L. *fragare*, to smell] **1.** keen, natural discernment **2.** an aptitude; knack **3.** [Colloq.] smartness in style; dash

flak (flak) ***n.*** [G. < *Fl(ieger)-a(bwehr)k(anone)*, antiaircraft gun] the fire of antiaircraft guns

flake (flāk) ***n.*** [< Scand., as in Norw. *flak*, ice floe, ON. *flackna*, to flake off] **1.** a small, thin mass [a *flake* of snow] **2.** a thin piece or layer split or peeled off from anything; chip —***vt., vi.*** **flaked, flak′ing 1.** to form into flakes **2.** to chip or peel off in flakes **3.** to make or become spotted with flakes —**flak′er *n.***

flak·y (flāk′ē) ***adj.*** **flak′i·er, flak′i·est 1.** containing or made up of flakes **2.** breaking easily into flakes **3.** [Slang] very eccentric —**flak′i·ly *adv.*** —**flak′i·ness *n.***

‡flam·bé (flän bā′) ***adj.*** [Fr., lit., flaming] served with a flaming sauce containing brandy, rum, etc.

flam·beau (flam′bō) ***n.***, *pl.* **-beaux** (-bōz), **-beaus** [Fr., dim. of OFr. *flambe*, FLAME] a lighted torch

flam·boy·ant (flam boi′ənt) ***adj.*** [Fr. < OFr. < *flambe*, FLAME] **1.** characterized by flamelike tracery of windows and florid decoration, as late French Gothic architecture **2.** flamelike or brilliant **3.** too showy or ornate —**flam-boy′ance, flam·boy′an·cy *n.*** —**flam·boy′ant·ly *adv.***

flame (flām) ***n.*** [< OFr. < L. < *flamma* < *flagrare*, to burn] **1.** the burning gas of a fire, seen as a flickering light; blaze **2.** a tongue of light rising from a fire **3.** the state of burning with a blaze of light **4.** a thing like a flame in heat, etc. **5.** an intense emotion **6.** a sweetheart: now usually humorous —***vi.*** **flamed, flam′ing 1.** to burst into flame; blaze **2.** to grow red or hot **3.** to become very excited —***vt.*** to treat with flame —**flame up** (or **out**) to burst out in or as in flame

fla·men·co (flə meŋ′kō) ***n.*** [Sp., Flemish < DuFl. *Flaming*, a Fleming] **1.** the energetic, emotional style of dance or music of Spanish gypsies **2.** *pl.* **-cos** a song or dance in this style

flame·out (flām′out′) ***n.*** the ceasing of combustion in a jet engine, due to an abnormal flight condition

flame thrower a military weapon for shooting a stream of flaming gasoline, oil, etc.

flam·ing (flā′miŋ) ***adj.*** **1.** burning with flames; blazing **2.** like a flame in brilliance or heat **3.** ardent; passionate —**flam′ing·ly *adv.***

fla·min·go (flə miŋ′gō) ***n.***, *pl.* **-gos, -goes** [Port. < Sp. *flamenco*, lit., Flemish: infl. by *flama*, FLAME] a tropical wading bird with long legs, a long neck, and bright pink or red feathers

flam·ma·ble (flam′ə b'l) ***adj.*** easily set on fire: term now preferred to INFLAMMABLE in commerce, industry, etc. —**flam′ma·bil′i·ty *n.***

Flan·ders (flan′dərz) region in NW Europe, on the North Sea, including W Belgium & a part of NW France & a part of SW Netherlands

flange (flanj) ***n.*** [< ? ME. *flaunch*, an outer edge of a coat of arms] a projecting rim or collar on a wheel, pipe, etc., to hold it in place, give it strength, or attach it to something else —***vt.*** **flanged, flang′ing** to put a flange on

flank (flaŋk) ***n.*** [< OFr. *flanc*] **1.** the fleshy side of a person or animal between the ribs and the hip **2.** a cut of beef from this part **3.** the side of anything **4.** *Mil.* the right or left side of a formation or force —***adj.*** of or having to do with the flank —***vt.*** **1.** to be at the side of **2.** to place at the side, or on either side, of **3.** *a)* to attack the side of (an enemy unit) *b)* to pass around the side of (an enemy unit) —***vi.*** to be located at the side (with *on* or *upon*)

flank·er (-ər) ***n.*** one that flanks; specif., *Football* an offensive back who takes a position closer to the sidelines than the rest of the team

flan·nel (flan′'l) ***n.*** [< W. *gwlanen* < *gwlan*, wool] **1.** a soft, lightweight, loosely woven woolen cloth **2.** *same as* COTTON FLANNEL **3.** [*pl.*] *a)* trousers, etc. made of light flannel *b)* heavy woolen underwear —**flan′nel·ly *adj.***

flan·nel·ette, flan·nel·et (flan′ə let′) ***n.*** a soft cotton cloth like cotton flannel but lighter

flap (flap) ***n.*** [ME. *flappe* < v. *flappen:* prob. echoic] **1.** anything flat and broad that is attached at one end and hangs loose or covers an opening **2.** the motion or slapping sound of a swinging flap **3.** a hinged section of an airplane wing, used in landing and taking off **4.** [Slang] a commotion; fuss —***vt.*** **flapped, flap′ping 1.** to slap with something flat and broad **2.** to move back and forth or up and down [the bird *flapped* its wings] **3.** to throw, slam, etc. abruptly or noisily —***vi.*** **1.** to move back and forth or up and down, as in the wind; flutter **2.** to fly or try to fly by flapping the wings **3.** [Slang] to become excited or confused —**flap′less *adj.*** —**flap′py *adj.***

flap·jack (flap′jak′) ***n.*** a pancake or griddlecake

flap·per (flap′ər) ***n.*** **1.** one that flaps **2.** [Colloq.] in the 1920's, a young woman considered bold or unconventional in actions and dress

flare (fler) ***vi.*** **flared, flar′ing** [ME. *fleare* < ?] **1.** to blaze up brightly or burn unsteadily **2.** to burst out suddenly in anger, etc. (often with *up* or *out*) **3.** to curve or spread outward, as the bell of a trumpet —***vt.*** to make flare —***n.*** **1.** a bright, brief, unsteady blaze of light **2.** a very bright light used as a distress signal, etc. **3.** a sudden, brief outburst, as of emotion or sound **4.** *a)* a curving outward, as of a skirt *b)* a part that curves or spreads outward **5.** a short-lived outburst of brightness on the sun

flare-up (-up′) ***n.*** a sudden outburst of flame or of anger, trouble, etc.

flar·ing (fler′iŋ) ***adj.*** **1.** blazing brightly for a little while **2.** curving or spreading outward —**flar′ing·ly *adv.***

flash (flash) ***vi.*** [ME. *flaschen*, to splash: echoic] **1.** to send out a sudden, brief light, esp. at intervals **2.** to sparkle or gleam **3.** to speak abruptly, esp. in anger (usually with *out*) **4.** to come or pass swiftly and suddenly —***vt.*** **1.** to send out (light, etc.) in sudden, brief spurts **2.** to cause to flash **3.** to signal with light **4.** to send (news, etc.) swiftly or suddenly **5.** [Colloq.] to show briefly or ostentatiously [to *flash* a roll of money] —***n.*** **1.** *a)* a sudden, brief light *b)* a sudden burst of flame or heat **2.** a brief time; moment **3.** a sudden, brief display [a *flash* of wit] **4.** a brief item of news sent by telegraph or radio **5.** a gaudy display **6.** anything that flashes; specif., [Colloq.] a person adept at something —***adj.*** **1.** happening swiftly or suddenly [a *flash* flood] **2.** working along with a flash of light [a *flash* camera] —**flash in the pan** [orig. of priming in pan of a flintlock] **1.** a sudden, apparently brilliant effort that fails **2.** one that fails after such an effort —**flash′er *n.*** —**flash′-ing·ly *adv.***

flash·back (-bak′) ***n.*** **1.** an interruption in the continuity of a story, play, etc. by the presentation of some earlier episode **2.** such an episode

flash·bulb (-bulb′) ***n.*** *Photog.* an electric light bulb giving a brief, dazzling light

flash·card (-kärd′) ***n.*** any of a set of cards with words, numbers, etc. on them, flashed one by one before a class in a drill

flash·cube (-kyōōb′) ***n.*** a small, rotating cube containing a flashbulb in each of four sides

flash·ing (-iŋ) ***n.*** sheets of metal, etc. used to weatherproof joints, edges, etc., esp. of a roof

flash·light (-līt′) ***n.*** **1.** a portable electric light, usually operated by batteries **2.** a brief, dazzling light for taking photographs at night or indoors

flash point the lowest temperature at which the vapor of a volatile oil will ignite with a flash

flash·y (-ē) ***adj.*** **flash′i·er, flash′i·est 1.** dazzling or bright for a little while **2.** gaudy; showy —**flash′i·ly *adv.*** —**flash′i·ness *n.***

flask (flask) ***n.*** [< ML. *flasco* & OE. *flasce* < LL. < *flasca*] **1.** any small bottle with a narrow neck, used in laboratories, etc. **2.** a small, flat pocket container for liquor, etc.

flat[1] (flat) ***adj.*** **flat′ter, flat′test** [< ON. *flatr*] **1.** having a smooth, level surface **2.** *a)* lying extended at full length *b)* spread out smooth and level **3.** *a)* broad, even, and thin *b)* having a flat heel or no heel [*flat* shoes] **4.** almost straight or level [a *flat* trajectory or flight] **5.** absolute; positive [a *flat* denial] **6.** not fluctuating [a *flat* rate] **7.** having little or no sparkle or taste **8.** monotonous; dull **9.** not clear or full [a *flat* sound] **10.** emptied of air [a *flat* tire] **11.** without gloss [*flat* paint] **12.** *Art* *a)* lacking relief or perspective *b)* uniform in tint **13.** *Music* *a)* below the true or proper pitch *b)* lower in pitch by a half step [D-*flat*] **14.** *Phonet.* designating the vowel *a* sounded with the tongue in a relatively level position, as in *can* —***adv.*** **1.** in a flat manner **2.** in a flat position **3.** *a)* exactly; precisely [ten seconds *flat*] *b)* bluntly; abruptly [she left him *flat*] **4.** *Music* below the true or proper pitch —***n.*** **1.** a flat surface or part [the *flat* of the hand] **2.** an expanse of level land **3.** a low-lying marsh **4.** a shallow; shoal **5.** a shallow box, as for growing seedlings **6.** a piece of theatrical scenery on a flat frame **7.** a deflated tire

8. [*pl.*] flat-heeled shoes 9. *Music* *a*) a note or tone one half step below another *b*) the symbol (♭) indicating such a note —*vt., vi.* **flat′ted, flat′ting** to make or become flat —**fall flat** to arouse no response —**flat′ly** *adv.* —**flat′ness** *n.* —**flat′tish** *adj.*

flat[2] (flat) *n.* [altered < Scot. dial. *flet* (OE. *flet*), a floor of a dwelling] an apartment or suite of rooms on one floor of a building

flat·bed, flat-bed (-bed′) *adj.* designating or of a truck, trailer, etc. having a bed or platform without sides or stakes —*n.* a flatbed truck, trailer, etc.

flat·boat (-bōt′) *n.* a flat-bottomed boat for carrying freight in shallow waters or on rivers

flat·car (-kär′) *n.* a railroad car without sides or a roof, for carrying certain freight

flat·fish (-fish′) *n., pl.* **-fish′, -fish′es:** see FISH a fish with a flat body and both eyes on the uppermost side, as the flounder, halibut, etc.

flat·foot (-foot′) *n.* 1. a condition in which the instep arch of the foot has been flattened 2. [Slang] a policeman

flat-foot·ed (-foot′id) *adj.* 1. having flatfoot 2. [Colloq.] downright and firm —**catch flat-footed** [Colloq.] to take by surprise; catch unprepared —**flat′-foot′ed·ly** *adv.* —**flat′-foot′ed·ness** *n.*

flat·i·ron (-ī′ərn) *n.* an iron for pressing clothes

flat silver silver knives, forks, spoons, etc.

flat·ten (-′n) *vt., vi.* 1. to make or become flat or flatter 2. to make or become prostrate —**flat′ten·er** *n.*

flat·ter (flat′ər) *vt.* [< OFr. *flater,* to smooth < Frank. *flat*] 1. to praise too much or insincerely, as to win favor 2. to try to please, or get the favor of, as by praise 3. to make seem more attractive than is so [his portrait *flatters* him] 4. to make feel pleased or honored —*vi.* to use flattery —**flatter oneself** to be smug or deluded in thinking (*that*) —**flat′ter·er** *n.* —**flat′ter·ing·ly** *adv.*

flat·ter·y (flat′ər ē) *n., pl.* **-ter·ies** 1. a flattering 2. excessive or insincere praise

flat·top (-täp′) *n.* [Slang] something with a flat or level surface, as an aircraft carrier

flat·u·lent (flach′ə lənt, -yoo-) *adj.* [Fr. < ModL. < L. < *flare,* to blow] 1. of, having, or producing gas in the stomach or intestines 2. windy or empty in speech; pompous; pretentious —**flat′u·lence, flat′u·len·cy** *n.* —**flat′u·lent·ly** *adv.*

flat·ware (flat′wer′) *n.* relatively flat tableware; specif., knives, forks, and spoons

flat·work (-wurk′) *n.* sheets, napkins, and other flat pieces that can be pressed in a mangle

flat·worm (-wurm′) *n. same as* PLATYHELMINTH

Flau·bert (flō ber′), **Gus·tave** (güs tàv′) 1821–80; Fr. novelist

flaunt (flônt) *vi.* [prob. < dial. *flant,* to strut coquettishly] 1. to make a gaudy or impudent display 2. to flutter freely —*vt.* to show off proudly or impudently —**flaunt′ing·ly** *adv.*

flau·tist (flôt′ist, flout′-) *n.* [It. *flautista* < *flauto,* flute] *same as* FLUTIST

fla·vin (flā′vin, flav′in) *n.* [< L. *flavus,* yellow + -IN[1]] 1. a complex ketone, $C_{10}H_6N_4O_2$ 2. a natural or synthetic yellow pigment Also **fla′vine** (-vēn, -ēn)

fla·vone (flā′vōn, flav′ōn) *n.* [G. *flavon* < L. *flavus,* yellow] 1. a colorless crystalline compound, $C_{15}H_{10}O_2$: a base for some yellow dyes 2. any derivative of this

fla·vor (flā′vər) *n.* [< OFr. *flaur* < L. *flatare,* freq. of *flare,* to blow] 1. *a*) the combined taste and smell of something *b*) taste in general 2. *same as* FLAVORING 3. characteristic quality —*vt.* to give flavor to —**fla′vor·less** *adj.*

fla·vor·ful (-fəl) *adj.* full of flavor; tasty: also **fla′vor·some** (-səm), **fla′vor·ous** (-əs), **fla′vor·y** (-ē) —**fla′vor·ful·ly** *adv.*

fla·vor·ing (-iŋ) *n.* an essence, extract, etc. added to a food or drink to give it a certain taste

fla·vour (flā′vər) *n., vt. Brit. sp. of* FLAVOR

flaw[1] (flô) *n.* [prob. < Scand.: see FLAKE] 1. a break, scratch, crack, etc. that spoils something; blemish 2. a defect; fault; error —*vt., vi.* to make or become faulty —**flaw′less** *adj.* —**flaw′less·ly** *adv.* —**flaw′less·ness** *n.*

flaw[2] (flô) *n.* [prob. < ON. *flaga,* sudden onset] a sudden, brief gust of wind; squall

flax (flaks) *n.* [OE. *fleax*] 1. any of a certain genus of plants; esp., a slender, erect annual with delicate blue flowers and narrow leaves: the seed (**flax′seed′**) yields linseed oil, and the fibers of the stem are spun into linen thread 2. these fibers

flax·en (-′n) *adj.* 1. of or made of flax 2. like flax in color; pale-yellow: also **flax′y**

flay (flā) *vt.* [OE. *flean*] 1. to strip off the skin or hide of, as by whipping 2. to criticize or scold mercilessly 3. to rob; pillage —**flay′er** *n.*

F layer the highest regular layer of the ionosphere, reflecting high-frequency radio waves

fl. dr. fluid dram; fluid drams

flea (flē) *n.* [< OE. *fleah*] a small, wingless jumping insect that is parasitic and sucks blood

flea·bag (-bag′) *n.* [Slang] a very cheap hotel

flea-bit·ten (-bit′′n) *adj.* 1. bitten by or infested with fleas 2. wretched; shabby

flea market an outdoor bazaar dealing mainly in cheap, secondhand goods

fleck (flek) *n.* [ON. *flekkr*] 1. a spot or small patch of color, etc.; speck 2. a particle; flake —*vt.* to cover or sprinkle with flecks; speckle

flec·tion (flek′shən) *n.* [< L. pp. of *flectere,* to bend] 1. a bending; flexing 2. a bent part 3. *Anat. same as* FLEXION —**flec′tion·al** *adj.*

fled (fled) *pt. & pp. of* FLEE

fledge (flej) *vi.* **fledged, fledg′ing** [< OE. (*un*)*flycge,* (un)fledged] to grow the feathers needed for flying —*vt.* 1. to rear (a young bird) until it can fly 2. to supply with feathers

fledg·ling (flej′liŋ) *n.* 1. a young bird just fledged 2. a young, inexperienced person Also, chiefly Brit., **fledge′ling**

flee (flē) *vi.* **fled, flee′ing** [OE. *fleon*] 1. to run away or escape from danger, pursuit, etc. 2. to pass away swiftly; vanish 3. to go swiftly —*vt.* to run away from; shun —**fle′er** *n.*

fleece (flēs) *n.* [OE. *fleos*] 1. the wool covering a sheep or similar animal 2. the amount of wool cut from a sheep in one shearing 3. a covering like a sheep's 4. a soft, warm napped fabric —*vt.* **fleeced, fleec′ing** 1. to shear fleece from 2. to steal from by fraud; swindle —**fleec′er** *n.*

fleec·y (-ē) *adj.* **fleec′i·er, fleec′i·est** made of, covered with, or like fleece —**fleec′i·ly** *adv.* —**fleec′i·ness** *n.*

fleer (flir) *vi., vt.* [prob. < Scand.] to laugh derisively (at); sneer or jeer (at) —*n.* a derisive grimace, laugh, etc. —**fleer′ing·ly** *adv.*

fleet[1] (flēt) *n.* [OE. *fleot* < *fleotan,* to float] 1. *a*) a number of warships under one command *b*) an entire navy 2. any group of ships, trucks, buses, airplanes, etc. under one control

fleet[2] (flēt) *vi.* [OE. *fleotan:* see prec.] to move swiftly; fly —*adj.* swift; rapid —**fleet′ly** *adv.* —**fleet′ness** *n.*

fleet admiral *U.S. Navy* an admiral of the highest rank, having the insignia of five stars

fleet·ing (flēt′iŋ) *adj.* passing swiftly; not lasting —**fleet′ing·ly** *adv.* —**fleet′ing·ness** *n.*

Flem·ing (flem′iŋ) *n.* [< MDu. *Vlaming*] 1. a native of Flanders 2. a Flemish-speaking Belgian

Flem·ing (flem′iŋ), Sir **Alexander** 1881–1955; Brit. bacteriologist: codiscoverer of penicillin

Flem·ish (-ish) *adj.* of Flanders, the Flemings, or their language —*n.* the West Germanic language of the Flemings —**the Flemish** the people of Flanders

flense (flens) *vt.* **flensed, flens′ing** [< Du. *vlensen* or Dan. *flense*] to cut blubber or skin from (a whale, seal, etc.): also **flench** (flench)

flesh (flesh) *n.* [OE. *flæsc*] 1. *a*) the soft substance of the body (of a person or animal); esp., the muscular tissue *b*) the skin of the body 2. meat; esp., meat other than fish or fowl 3. the pulpy or edible part of fruits and vegetables 4. the human body, as distinguished from the soul 5. human nature, esp. in its sensual aspect 6. all living beings, esp. all mankind 7. kindred: now mainly in **one's (own) flesh and blood,** one's close relatives 8. the typical color of a white person's skin; yellowish pink —*vt.* 1. to incite to bloodshed, etc. by a foretaste 2. to fatten 3. to fill out by adding details, etc. (usually with *out*) —*vi.* to grow fat (usually with *out* or *up*) —**flesh and blood** the human body —**in the flesh** 1. alive 2. in person

flesh-col·ored (-kul′ərd) *adj.* yellowish-pink

flesh·ly (-lē) *adj.* **-li·er, -li·est** 1. of the body 2. sensual 3. *same as* FLESHY —**flesh′li·ness** *n.*

flesh·pot (-pät′) *n.* 1. a pot for cooking meat 2. [*pl.*] *a*) bodily comfort and pleasures; luxuries *b*) a place where such pleasures are provided

flesh·y (-ē) *adj.* **flesh′i·er, flesh′i·est** 1. having much flesh; plump 2. of or like flesh 3. having a firm pulp: said of some fruits —**flesh′i·ness** *n.*

fleur-de-lis (flur′də lē′, -lēs′) *n., pl.* **fleurs-de-lis** (flur′də-lēz′) [< OFr. *flor de lis,* lit., flower of the lily] 1. *same as* IRIS (senses 3 & 4) 2. the coat of arms of the former French royal family 3. *Heraldry* a lilylike emblem Also sp. **fleur-de-lys**

FLEUR-DE-LIS

flew (floo) *pt. of* FLY[1]

flex (fleks) *vt., vi.* [< L. *flexus,* pp. of *flectere,* to bend] 1. to bend (an arm, knee, etc.) 2. to contract (a muscle)

flex·i·ble (flek′sə b′l) *adj.* [< OFr. < L. < *flexus:* see prec.] 1. able to bend without breaking 2. easily persuaded or influenced 3. adjustable to change —**flex′i·bil′i·ty** *n.* —**flex′i·bly** *adv.*

flex·ion (flek′shən) *n.* 1. *same as* FLECTION 2. *Anat.* the bending of a joint or limb by means of the flexor muscles —**flex′ion·al** *adj.*

flex·i·time (fleks′ə tīm′) *n.* a system allowing individual employees some flexibility in choosing the time of their working hours: also **flex′time′** (fleks′-)

flex·or (flek′sər) *n.* [ModL. < L.: see FLEX] a muscle that bends a limb or other part of the body

flex·u·ous (-shoo wəs) *adj.* winding or wavering —**flex′u·os′i·ty** (-wäs′ə tē) *n., pl.* **-ties**

flex·ure (-shər) *n.* **1.** a bending; curving; flexing **2.** a bend; curve; fold —**flex′ur·al** *adj.*

flib·ber·ti·gib·bet (flib′ər tē jib′it) *n.* [< ?] an irresponsible, flighty person

flick[1] (flik) *n.* [echoic, but infl. by FLICKER[1]] **1.** a light, quick stroke, jerk, or snap **2.** a light, snapping sound **3.** a fleck; speck —*vt.* **1.** to strike, remove, etc. with a light, quick stroke **2.** to make such a stroke with (a whip, etc.) —*vi.* to flutter

flick[2] (flik) *n.* [< ff.] [Slang] *same as* MOVIE —**the flicks** [Slang] the movies (see MOVIE)

flick·er[1] (flik′ər) *vi.* [OE. *flicorian*] **1.** to move with a quick, light, wavering motion **2.** to burn or shine unsteadily, as a candle flame —*vt.* to make flicker —*n.* **1.** a flickering **2.** a flame or light that flickers **3.** a quick, passing look or feeling —**flick′er·y** *adj.*

flick·er[2] (flik′ər) *n.* [echoic of its cry] any of several N. American woodpeckers, esp. one with wings of a golden color on the underside

flied (flīd) *pt. & pp. of* FLY[1] (*vi.* 8)

fli·er (flī′ər) *n.* **1.** a thing that flies **2.** an aviator **3.** a bus, train, etc. on a fast schedule **4.** a small handbill **5.** [Colloq.] a reckless gamble or speculation Also, esp. for 2, 3, & 5, **fly′er**

flight[1] (flīt) *n.* [OE. *flyht*] **1.** the act, manner, or power of flying or moving through space **2.** distance flown at one time, as by an airplane, bird, etc. **3.** a group of birds, arrows, etc. flying together **4.** *a)* a formation of military airplanes in flight *b) U.S. Air Force* the smallest tactical unit, a subdivision of a squadron **5.** an airplane scheduled to fly a certain trip **6.** a trip by airplane **7.** a soaring above the ordinary *[a flight* of fancy*]* **8.** a set of stairs, as between floors

flight[2] (flīt) *n.* [< OE. < base of *fleon,* to flee] a fleeing, as from danger —**put to flight** to force to flee —**take (to) flight** to run away; flee

flight·less (-lis) *adj.* not able to fly

flight·y (-ē) *adj.* **flight′i·er, flight′i·est 1.** frivolous or irresponsible **2.** foolish; silly —**flight′i·ly** *adv.* —**flight′i·ness** *n.*

flim·flam (flim′flam′) *n.* [< ?] **1.** nonsense **2.** a sly trick or deception —*vt.* **-flammed′, -flam′ming** [Colloq.] to trick —**flim′flam′mer·y** *n.*

flim·sy (flim′zē) *adj.* **-si·er, -si·est** [< ?] **1.** thin and easily broken or damaged; fragile **2.** weak or inadequate *[a flimsy* excuse*]* —*n.* **1.** a sheet of thin paper **2.** copy written on such paper, as by a reporter —**flim′si·ly** *adv.* —**flim′si·ness** *n.*

flinch (flinch) *vi.* [< OFr. *flenchir*] **1.** to draw back, as from a blow, difficulty, etc. **2.** to wince, as because of pain —*n.* a flinching

flin·ders (flin′dərz) *n.pl.* [< Scand., as in Norw. *flindra,* splinter] splinters or fragments: chiefly in **break** (or **fly**) **into flinders**

fling (fliŋ) *vt.* **flung, fling′ing** [ME. *flingen,* to rush < ON. *flengja,* to whip] **1.** to throw, esp. with force; hurl **2.** to put abruptly or violently *[*to be *flung* into confusion*]* **3.** to move (one's limbs, head, etc.) suddenly or impulsively **4.** to throw (oneself) spiritedly (*into* a task, etc.) **5.** to cast aside —*vi.* to move suddenly and violently; rush —*n.* **1.** a flinging **2.** a brief time of self-indulgence **3.** a spirited dance *[*the Highland *fling]* **4.** [Colloq.] a trial effort; try

Flint (flint) [after nearby *Flint* River, so called from the flint stones in it] city in SE Mich.: pop. 160,000 (met. area 522,000)

flint (flint) *n.* [OE.] **1.** a fine-grained, very hard, siliceous rock that makes sparks when struck with steel **2.** a piece of this stone, used to start a fire, for primitive tools, etc. **3.** anything like flint in hardness, use, etc. *[*a heart of *flint,* a lighter *flint* of iron-cerium alloy*]*

flint glass a hard, bright lead-oxide glass, used for lenses, crystal, etc.

flint·lock (-läk′) *n.* **1.** a gunlock using a flint in the hammer to strike sparks to ignite the powder **2.** an old-fashioned gun with such a lock

flint·y (flin′tē) *adj.* **flint′i·er, flint′i·est 1.** of or containing flint **2.** like flint; very hard or firm —**flint′i·ness** *n.*

flip[1] (flip) *vt.* **flipped, flip′ping** [echoic] **1.** to move with a quick jerk **2.** to snap (a coin) into the air with the thumb, as in betting on which side will land uppermost **3.** to turn (a card, etc.) over quickly —*vi.* **1.** to make a quick, light stroke or move; snap **2.** to flip a coin **3.** to do a flip **4.** [Slang] to lose self-control from excitement, anger, etc.: also **flip one's lid** (or **wig**) —*n.* **1.** a flipping; snap, toss, etc. **2.** a somersault in the air

flip[2] (flip) *n.* [prob. < prec.] a sweetened mixed drink of wine or liquor with egg, spices, etc.

flip[3] (flip) *adj.* **flip′per, flip′pest** [contr. < FLIPPANT] [Colloq.] flippant; saucy; impertinent

flip-flop (flip′fläp′) *n.* **1.** an acrobatic spring backward from feet to hands to feet **2.** an abrupt change, as to the opposite opinion **3.** a flapping noise **4.** *Electronics* a circuit with two stable states, switching from one to the other on signal —*vi.* **-flopped′, -flop′ping** to do a flip-flop

flip·pan·cy (flip′ən sē) *n.* **1.** a being flippant **2.** *pl.* **-cies** a flippant act or remark

flip·pant (-ənt) *adj.* [Early ModE., nimble, prob. < FLIP[1]] frivolous and disrespectful; saucy —**flip′pant·ly** *adv.*

flip·per (-ər) *n.* [< FLIP[1]] **1.** a broad, flat limb, as of a seal, adapted for swimming **2.** a paddlelike rubber piece worn on each foot as a help in swimming and skin diving **3.** [Slang] a hand

flip side [Colloq.] the reverse side (of a phonograph recording), esp. the less important side

flirt (flurt) *vt.* [< ? OFr. *fleureter,* lit., move from flower to flower < *fleur,* FLOWER] to move quickly back and forth —*vi.* **1.** to move jerkily **2.** to woo someone lightly or frivolously **3.** to toy, as with an idea —*n.* **1.** a flirting movement **2.** a person who plays at love —**flirt′y** *adj.*

flir·ta·tion (flər tā′shən) *n.* a flirting, or playing at love

flir·ta·tious (-shəs) *adj.* flirting or inclined to flirt —**flir·ta′tious·ly** *adv.* —**flir·ta′tious·ness** *n.*

flit (flit) *vi.* **flit′ted, flit′ting** [< ON. *flytja*] to pass or fly lightly and rapidly; dart; flutter —*n.* a flitting —**flit′ter** *n.*

flitch (flich) *n.* [OE. *flicce*] the cured and salted side of a hog; side of bacon —*vt.* to cut into flitches

flit·ter (flit′ər) *vi., vt.* [freq. of FLIT] [Chiefly Dial.] *same as* FLUTTER

fliv·ver (fliv′ər) *n.* [< ?] [Old Slang] a small, cheap automobile, esp. an old one

float (flōt) *n.* [OE. *flota* < *fleotan,* to float] **1.** anything staying, or making something else stay, on or at a liquid's surface; specif., *a)* a fishing-line cork *b)* a floating, valve-controlling ball, etc. that regulates liquid level, as in a tank *c)* a buoyant device on an aircraft for landing on water **2.** a platform on wheels that carries a display or exhibit in a parade **3.** a cold beverage with ice cream floating in it —*vi.* **1.** to stay on or at a liquid's surface **2.** to drift gently on water, in air, etc. **3.** to move about vaguely and without purpose —*vt.* **1.** to make float **2.** to flood **3.** *a)* to put into circulation *[float* a bond issue*]* *b)* to establish or start (a business, etc.) **4.** to arrange for (a loan)

float·a·tion (flō tā′shən) *n. same as* FLOTATION

float·er (flōt′ər) *n.* **1.** one that floats **2.** a person who illegally votes at several polling places **3.** a person who changes his place of residence or work frequently **4.** an insurance policy covering movable property wherever it is at the time of loss

float·ing (-iŋ) *adj.* **1.** that floats **2.** not fixed; moving about **3.** *Finance a)* designating an unfunded, short-time debt *b)* not permanently invested *[floating* capital*]* **4.** *Mech.* designating or of suspension that reduces vibration **5.** *Med.* displaced and more movable *[a floating* kidney*]*

floating ribs the eleventh and twelfth pairs of ribs, not attached to the breastbone or to other ribs but only to the vertebrae

floc·cu·late (fläk′yoo lāt′) *vt., vi.* **-lat′ed, -lat′ing** to collect (clouds, precipitates, etc.) into small, flocculent masses —**floc′cu·la′tion** *n.*

floc·cu·lent (-lənt) *adj.* [< L. *floccus,* flock of wool + -ULENT] woolly; fluffy —**floc′cu·lence** *n.*

flock[1] (fläk) *n.* [OE. *flocc,* a troop] **1.** a group of certain animals, as goats or sheep, or of birds, living, feeding, etc. together **2.** any group, esp. a large one, as of church members —*vi.* to assemble or travel in a flock

flock[2] (fläk) *n.* [< OFr. < L. *floccus*] **1.** a small tuft of wool, cotton, etc. **2.** wool or cotton waste used to stuff furniture, etc. **3.** tiny fibers put on wallpaper, etc. to form a velvety surface or design Also sp. **floc** —**flock′y** *adj.*

flock·ing (-iŋ) *n.* **1.** *same as* FLOCK[2] (sense 3) **2.** a material or surface with flock on it

floe (flō) *n.* [prob. < Norw. *flo,* layer] *same as* ICE FLOE

flog (fläg, flôg) *vt.* **flogged, flog′ging** [? cant abbrev. of L. *flagellare,* to whip] **1.** to beat with a stick, whip, etc. **2.** [Brit. Slang] to sell, esp. illegally —**flog′ger** *n.*

flood (flud) *n.* [OE. *flod*] **1.** an overflowing of water on an area normally dry; deluge **2.** the flowing in of water from the sea as the tide rises 3. a great flow or outpouring, as of words 4. [Archaic] a large body of water —*vt.* 1. to cover or fill with or as with a flood; inundate [rain *flooded* the earth, music *flooded* the room] 2. to put much or too much liquid on or in —*vi.* 1. to rise, flow, or gush out in or as in a flood 2. to become flooded —**the Flood** *Bible* the great flood in Noah's time: Gen. 7

flood·gate (-gāt′) *n.* 1. a gate in a stream or canal, to control water height and flow 2. anything like this in controlling an outburst

flood·light (-līt′) *n.* 1. a lamp that casts a broad beam of bright light 2. such light —*vt.* **-light′ed** or **-lit′**, **-light′ing** to illuminate by a floodlight

flood tide the incoming or rising tide

floor (flôr) *n.* [OE. *flor*] 1. the inside bottom surface of a room 2. any bottom surface [the ocean *floor*] 3. the platform of a bridge, pier, etc. 4. a level or story in a building 5. *a*) the part of a legislative chamber, stock exchange, etc. occupied by members *b*) the members as a group 6. the right to speak in an assembly 7. a lower limit set on anything —*vt.* 1. to cover or furnish with a floor 2. to knock down 3. [Colloq.] *a*) to defeat *b*) to make unable to act, as by shocking, amazing, confusing, etc. 4. [Colloq.] to press (a car accelerator) to the floor

floor·age (-ij) *n.* the area of a floor: also **floor space**

floor·board (-bôrd′) *n.* 1. a board in a floor 2. the floor of an automobile, etc.

floor exercise *Gymnastics* any of several exercises, as cart wheels, performed without apparatus

floor·ing (-iŋ) *n.* 1. a floor 2. floors collectively 3. material for making a floor

floor leader a member of a legislature chosen by his political party to direct its actions on the floor

floor plan a scale drawing of the layout of rooms, halls, etc. on one floor of a building

floor show a show presenting singers, dancers, etc. in a restaurant, nightclub, etc.

floor·walk·er (-wôk′ər) *n.* formerly, a department store employee supervising sales, etc.: now usually **floor** (or **sales) manager**

floo·zy, floo·zie (flo͞o′zē) *n., pl.* **-zies** [Slang] a loose, disreputable woman: also sp. **floo′sy, floo′sie**

flop (fläp) *vt.* **flopped, flop′ping** [var. of FLAP] to flap or throw noisily and clumsily —*vi.* 1. *a*) to move or flap around loosely or clumsily *b*) to fall or drop thus 2. [Colloq.] to be a failure —*n.* 1. the act or sound of flopping 2. [Colloq.] a failure —*adv.* with a flop —**flop′per** *n.*

flop·house (-hous′) *n.* [Colloq.] a very cheap hotel frequented chiefly by vagrants

flop·py (-ē) *adj.* **-pi·er, -pi·est** [Colloq.] tending to flop —**flop′pi·ly** *adv.* —**flop′pi·ness** *n.*

floppy disk (or **disc**) a small, flexible, relatively inexpensive computer disc for storing data

Flo·ra (flôr′ə) [L. < *flos*, a FLOWER] 1. a feminine name 2. *Rom. Myth.* the goddess of flowers —*n.* [**f-**] *pl.* **-ras, -rae** (-ē) the plants of a specified region or time

flo·ral (flôr′əl) *adj.* of, made of, or like flowers

Flor·ence (flôr′əns, flär′-) [Fr. < L. *Florentia*, lit., a blooming < *flos*, a FLOWER] 1. a feminine name 2. city in Tuscany, C Italy: pop. 455,000

Flor·en·tine (flôr′ən tēn′) *adj.* of Florence, Italy, or its people, art, etc. —*n.* a native or inhabitant of Florence

flo·res·cence (flô res′'ns, flə-) *n.* [< L. prp. of *florescere* < *florere*, to bloom < *flos*, FLOWER] a blooming or flowering —**flo·res′cent** *adj.*

flo·ret (flôr′it) *n.* [< OFr. dim. of *flor* < L. *flos*, FLOWER] 1. a small flower 2. any of the small flowers making up the head of a composite plant

flo·ri·cul·ture (flôr′ə kul′chər) *n.* the cultivation of flowers —**flo′ri·cul′tur·al** *adj.* —**flo′ri·cul′tur·ist** *n.*

flor·id (flôr′id, flär′-) *adj.* [L. *floridus* < *flos*, FLOWER] 1. flushed with red: said of the complexion 2. showy; ornate —**flo·rid·i·ty** (flô rid′ə tē, flə-), **flor′id·ness** *n.* —**flor′id·ly** *adv.*

Flor·i·da (flôr′ə də, flär′-) [Sp. < L. < *flos*, FLOWER] 1. SE State of the U.S., mostly on a peninsula between the Atlantic & the Gulf of Mexico: 58,560 sq. mi.; pop. 9,740,000; cap. Tallahassee: abbrev. **Fla., FL** 2. **Straits of,** strait between the S tip of Fla. & Cuba —**Flo·rid·i·an** (flô rid′ē ən), **Flor′i·dan** *adj., n.*

flor·in (flôr′in, flär′-) *n.* [< OFr. < It. < L. *flos*, FLOWER: the figure of a lily was stamped on the original coins] 1. a gold coin of medieval Florence 2. any of various European or South African silver or gold coins

Flo·ris·sant (flôr′ə sənt) [Fr., flourishing] city in E Mo.: suburb of St. Louis: pop. 55,000

flo·rist (flôr′ist, flär′-) *n.* [< L. *flos*, FLOWER] a person who cultivates or sells flowers

flo·ris·tic (flô ris′tik) *adj.* of flowers or flora

floss (flôs, fläs) *n.* [prob. < Fr. < L. *floccus*, FLOCK²] 1. the rough silk covering a silkworm's cocoon 2. short, downy waste fibers of silk 3. a soft thread or yarn, as of silk (**floss silk**) or linen (**linen floss**), used in embroidery 4. a soft, silky substance resembling floss, as in milkweed pods 5. *same as* DENTAL FLOSS —*vt., vi.* to clean (the teeth) with dental floss

floss·y (-ē) *adj.* **floss′i·er, floss′i·est** 1. of or like floss; downy; fluffy 2. [Slang] elegant and showy

flo·ta·tion (flō tā′shən) *n.* a floating; specif., the starting or financing of a business, etc., as by selling an entire issue of bonds

flo·til·la (flō til′ə) *n.* [Sp., dim. of *flota*, a fleet] 1. a small fleet, or a fleet of small ships 2. *U.S. Navy* a unit consisting of two or more squadrons

flot·sam (flät′səm) *n.* [< OFr. < MDu. *vloten* (or OE. *flotian*), to float] the wreckage of a ship or its cargo floating at sea: chiefly in **flotsam and jetsam,** *a*) such wreckage or cargo either floating or washed ashore *b*) miscellaneous trifles *c*) transient, unemployed people

flounce¹ (flouns) *vi.* **flounced, flounc′ing** [prob. < Scand.] to move with quick, flinging motions of the body, as in anger —*n.* the act of flouncing

flounce² (flouns) *n.* [earlier *frounce* < OFr. < *froncir*, to wrinkle] a wide, ornamental ruffle, as on a skirt —*vt.* **flounced, flounc′ing** to trim with a flounce or flounces —**flounc′y** *adj.*

floun·der¹ (floun′dər) *vi.* [? var. of FOUNDER¹] 1. to struggle or plunge about awkwardly, as in deep mud 2. to speak or act in an awkward, confused way —*n.* a floundering

floun·der² (floun′dər) *n., pl.* **-ders, -der:** see PLURAL, II, D, 1 [< Scand.] any of a large group of flatfishes caught for food, as the halibut

flour (flour) *n.* [var. of FLOWER, after Fr. *fleur de farine*, lit., flower (i.e., best) of meal] 1. a fine, powdery substance produced by grinding and sifting grain or certain roots, etc. 2. any finely powdered substance —*vt.* 1. to put flour on or in 2. to make into flour —**flour′y** *adj.*

flour·ish (flur′ish) *vi.* [< OFr. *florir*, to blossom, ult. < L. *flos*, FLOWER] 1. to grow vigorously; thrive; prosper 2. to be at the peak of development, activity, etc. 3. to make showy, wavy motions 4. [Now Rare] to perform a fanfare —*vt.* to brandish (a sword, hat, etc.) —*n.* 1. anything done in a showy way 2. a brandishing 3. a decorative line or lines in writing 4. a fanfare —**flour′ish·er** *n.* —**flour′ish·ing** *adj.* —**flour′ish·ing·ly** *adv.*

flout (flout) *vt., vi.* [prob. < ME. *flouten*, to play the flute] to show scorn or contempt (for) —*n.* a flouting —**flout′er** *n.* —**flout′ing·ly** *adv.*

flow (flō) *vi.* [OE. *flowan*] 1. to move as a liquid does 2. to stream 3. to move gently and smoothly; glide 4. to pour out 5. to be derived; proceed 6. to hang loose or in waves [*flowing* hair] 7. to rise, as the tide 8. to be plentiful —*vt.* to flood —*n.* 1. a flowing, or the manner or rate of this 2. anything that flows; stream or current 3. a continuous production

flow chart a diagram showing the progress of work through a sequence of operations

flow·er (flou′ər, flour) *n.* [< OFr. < L. *flos* (gen. *floris*), a flower] 1. *a*) the structure of many plants that produces seeds, typically with brightly colored petals and leaflike sepals; blossom; bloom *b*) the reproductive structure of any plant 2. a plant cultivated for its blossoms 3. the best or finest part or example 4. the best period of a person or thing 5. something decorative; esp., a figure of speech 6. [*pl.*] *Chem.* a powder made from condensed vapors —*vi.* 1. to produce flowers or blossoms; bloom 2. to reach the best period —*vt.* to decorate with flowers or floral patterns —**in flower** in a state of flowering —**flow′er·less** *adj.* —**flow′er·like′** *adj.*

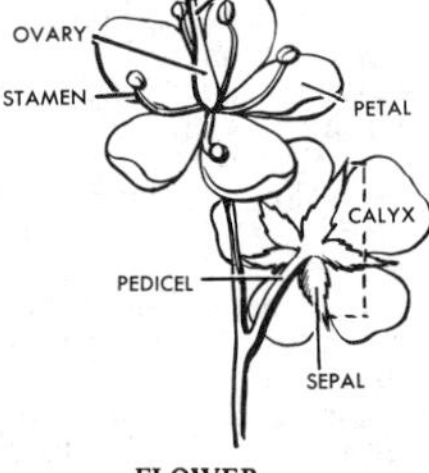

FLOWER

flow·ered (flou′ərd) *adj.* 1. bearing or containing flowers 2. having a floral design

flow·er·et (-ər it) *n. same as* FLORET

flow·er·ing (-ər iŋ) *adj.* 1. having flowers; in bloom 2. bearing showy or profuse flowers

flowering crab a small apple tree bearing many large, rose-red to light-pink flowers

flow·er·pot (-pät′) *n.* a container, usually made of porous clay, in which to grow plants

flow·er·y (-ē) *adj.* **-er·i·er, -er·i·est** 1. covered or decorated with flowers 2. of or like flowers 3. full of figurative and ornate expressions and fine words —**flow′er·i·ly** *adv.* —**flow′er·i·ness** *n.*

flown (flōn) *pp. of* FLY¹

Floyd (floid) [var. of LLOYD] a masculine name

fl. oz. fluid ounce; fluid ounces

flt. flight

flu (flo͞o) *n.* **1.** *a shortened form for* INFLUENZA **2.** popularly, any of various respiratory or intestinal infections caused by a virus
flub (flub) *vt., vi.* **flubbed, flub′bing** [? < FL(OP) + (D)UB[1]] [Colloq.] to botch (a job, chance, etc.); bungle —*n.* [Colloq.] a mistake or blunder
fluc·tu·ate (fluk′cho͞o wāt′) *vi.* **-at′ed, -at′ing** [< L. pp. of *fluctuare* < *fluctus,* a wave] **1.** to move back and forth or up and down **2.** to vary irregularly —*vt.* to cause to fluctuate —**fluc′tu·ant** *adj.* —**fluc′tu·a′tion** *n.*
flue (flo͞o) *n.* [< ? OFr. *fluie,* a flowing] **1.** a tube or shaft for the passage of smoke, hot air, etc., as in a chimney **2.** *a) same as* FLUE PIPE *b)* the opening for air in a flue pipe
flu·ent (flo͞o′ənt) *adj.* [< L. prp. of *fluere,* to flow] **1.** flowing smoothly and easily **2.** able to write or speak easily, smoothly, and expressively —**flu′en·cy** *n.* —**flu′ent·ly** *adv.*
flue pipe an organ pipe whose tone is produced by an air current striking a narrow side opening
fluff (fluf) *n.* [? blend of *flue,* downy mass + PUFF] **1.** soft, light down **2.** a loose, soft, downy mass, as of dust **3.** any light or trivial matter or talk **4.** *Theater, Radio, TV* an error in speaking a line —*vt.* **1.** to shake or pat until loose, soft, and light **2.** *Theater, Radio, TV* to make an error in speaking (one's lines, etc.) **3.** to botch; bungle —*vi.* **1.** to become fluffy **2.** to make an error
fluff·y (-ē) *adj.* **fluff′i·er, fluff′i·est** **1.** soft and light like fluff; feathery **2.** covered with fluff —**fluff′i·ness** *n.*
flu·id (flo͞o′id) *adj.* [L. *fluidus* < *fluere,* to flow] **1.** that can flow; not solid **2.** of a fluid **3.** not settled or fixed *[fluid plans]* **4.** moving gracefully; flowing **5.** available for investment or as cash *[fluid assets]* —*n.* any substance that can flow; liquid or gas —**flu·id·ic** (flo͞o wid′ik) *adj.* —**flu·id′i·ty, flu′id·ness** *n.* —**flu′id·ly** *adv.*
fluid dram (or **drachm**) a liquid measure equal to 1/8 fluid ounce
fluid ounce a liquid measure equal to 1/16 pint, or 29.57 ml.: also **flu′id·ounce′** *n.*
fluke[1] (flo͞ok) *n.* [OE. *floc*] **1.** any of several flatfishes, esp. flounders **2.** a flatworm parasitic in internal organs of vertebrates
fluke[2] (flo͞ok) *n.* [prob. < prec.] **1.** the triangular, pointed end of an anchor arm, by which the anchor catches in the ground **2.** a barb or barbed head of an arrow, harpoon, etc. **3.** either of the two lobes of a whale's tail
fluke[3] (flo͞ok) *n.* [< ?] **1.** [Old Slang] a lucky stroke in billiards, etc. **2.** [Colloq.] a lucky or unlucky outcome —*vt.* **fluked, fluk′ing** [Colloq.] to hit or get by a fluke
fluk·y (flo͞o′kē) *adj.* **fluk′i·er, fluk′i·est** [< prec.] [Colloq.] **1.** resulting from chance **2.** uncertain —**fluk′i·ness** *n.*
flume (flo͞om) *n.* [< OFr. < L. *flumen,* river < *fluere,* to flow] **1.** an inclined chute or trough for carrying water to furnish power, transport logs, etc. **2.** a narrow gorge with a stream running through it —*vt.* **flumed, flum′ing** to send (logs, etc.) down a flume
flum·mer·y (flum′ər ē) *n., pl.* **-mer·ies** [W. *llymru,* soured oatmeal] **1.** any soft, easily eaten food, as custard **2.** meaningless flattery or silly talk
flung (fluŋ) *pt. & pp. of* FLING
flunk (fluŋk) *vt.* [19th-c. college slang < ?] [Colloq.] **1.** to fail in (schoolwork) **2.** to give a grade of *failure* to (a student) —*vi.* [Colloq.] to fail, esp. in schoolwork —*n.* [Colloq.] a grade of *failure* —**flunk out** [Colloq.] to send or be sent away from school or college because of failure
flun·ky (fluŋ′kē) *n., pl.* **-kies** [orig. Scot. < ? Fr. *flanquer,* to flank] **1.** one who obeys superiors in a servile way **2.** one having minor or menial tasks Also sp. **flun′key** —**flun′ky·ism** *n.*
flu·or (flo͞o′ər, -ôr) *n.* [ModL. < L. *flux* < *fluere,* to flow] *same as* FLUORITE
flu·o·resce (flo͞o′ə res′; flo͝o res′, flô-) *vi.* **-resced′, -resc′ing** to show or undergo fluorescence
flu·o·res·cence (-′ns) *n.* [< FLUOR (SPAR) + -ESCENCE] **1.** the property of a substance, as fluorite, of producing light when acted upon by radiant energy, as ultraviolet rays or X-rays **2.** production of such light **3.** light so produced —**flu′o·res′cent** *adj.*
fluorescent lamp (or **tube**) a glass tube coated inside with a fluorescent substance giving off light (**fluorescent light**) when mercury vapor in the tube is acted upon by electrons from the cathode
fluor·i·date (flôr′ə dāt′, flo͝or′-) *vt.* **-dat′ed, -dat′ing** to add fluorides to (a water supply) so as to reduce the incidence of tooth decay —**fluor′i·da′tion** *n.*
flu·o·ride (flo͝or′īd, flôr′-; flo͞o′ə rīd′) *n.* a compound of fluorine and another element or radical
fluor·i·nate (flôr′ə nāt′, flo͝or′-) *vt.* **-nat′ed, -nat′ing** **1.** to treat, or cause to combine, with fluorine **2.** *same as* FLUORIDATE —**fluor′i·na′tion** *n.*
flu·o·rine (flo͝or′ēn, flôr′-; flo͞o′ə rēn′, -rin) *n.* [< FLUOR + -INE[4]] a corrosive, poisonous, pale greenish-yellow, gaseous chemical element, the most reactive nonmetallic element known, forming fluorides with almost all elements: symbol, F; at. wt., 18.9984; at. no., 9
flu·o·rite (flo͝or′īt, flôr′-; flo͞o′ə rīt′) *n.* [< FLUOR(O)- + -ITE] calcium fluoride, CaF_2, a transparent, crystalline mineral of various colors: it is the principal source of fluorine and is used as a flux, in glassmaking, etc.
flu·o·ro- *a combining form meaning:* **1.** fluorine **2.** fluorescence Also, before a vowel, **flu·or-**
flu·o·ro·car·bon (flo͝or′ə kär′bən, flôr′-; flo͞o′ər ə-, -ə-rō′-) *n.* any of a class of inert organic compounds containing carbon, fluorine, and sometimes hydrogen: used as lubricants, plastics, etc.
flu·o·rom·e·ter (flo͝o räm′ə tər, flo͞o′ə-) *n.* an instrument for measuring the wavelength and intensity of fluorescence —**flu·o·ro·met·ric** (flo͝or′ə met′rik, flo͞o′ər ə-) *adj.* —**flu·o·rom′e·try** *n.*
fluor·o·scope (flo͝or′ə skōp′, flôr′-) *n.* [FLUORO- + -SCOPE] a machine for examining internal structures by viewing the shadows cast on a fluorescent screen by objects through which X-rays are directed —*vt.* **-scoped′, -scop′ing** to examine with a fluoroscope —**fluor′o·scop′ic** (-skäp′ik) *adj.* —**fluor′o·scop′i·cal·ly** *adv.*
flu·o·ros·co·py (flo͝o räs′kə pē, flo͞o′ə-) *n.* examination by fluoroscope —**flu·o·ros′co·pist** *n.*
fluor spar *same as* FLUORITE: also **flu′or·spar′** *n.*
flur·ry (flʉr′ē) *n., pl.* **-ries** [< ?] **1.** a sudden, brief rush of wind or fall of snow **2.** a sudden confusion or commotion **3.** a spurt of increased trading and price fluctuation in the stock market —*vt.* **-ried, -ry·ing** to confuse; agitate —*vi.* to move in a quick, flustered way
flush[1] (flush) *vi.* [blend of FLASH & ME. *flusschen,* to fly up suddenly] **1.** to flow and spread suddenly **2.** to blush or glow **3.** to become cleaned or emptied with a sudden flow of water, etc. **4.** to start up from cover: said of birds —*vt.* **1.** to make flow **2.** to clean or empty with a sudden flow of water, etc. **3.** to make blush or glow **4.** to excite; exhilarate *[flushed* with victory*]* **5.** to drive (game birds) from cover **6.** to make level or even —*n.* **1.** a sudden, rapid flow, as of water **2.** a sudden, vigorous growth *[*the first *flush* of youth*]* **3.** sudden excitement or exhilaration **4.** a blush or glow **5.** a sudden feeling of heat, as in a fever —*adj.* **1.** well supplied, esp. with money **2.** abundant **3.** ruddy **4.** *a)* making an even line or plane *b)* even with a margin or edge **5.** direct; full *[*a blow *flush* in the face*]* —*adv.* **1.** so as to be level or in alignment **2.** directly; squarely
flush[2] (flush) *n.* [Fr. *flux:* see FLUX] a hand of cards all in the same suit
flus·ter (flus′tər) *vt., vi.* [prob. < Scand.] to get confused or nervous —*n.* a flustered state
flute (flo͞ot) *n.* [< OFr. < Pr. *fläut* < ?] **1.** *a)* a high-pitched wind instrument consisting of a long, slender tube with finger holes and keys, played by blowing across a hole near one end *b)* any similar instrument, as the recorder **2.** an ornamental groove —*vt., vi.* **flut′ed, flut′ing** **1.** to sing, speak, etc. in a flutelike tone **2.** to play on the flute **3.** to make ornamental grooves (in)
flut·ing (-iŋ) *n.* **1.** a series of ornamental grooves, as in a column **2.** the act of one that flutes
flut·ist (-ist) *n.* a flute player; flautist
flut·ter (flut′ər) *vi.* [OE. *flotorian,* freq. of *flotian* < base of *fleotan,* to float] **1.** to flap the wings rapidly **2.** to wave or vibrate rapidly and irregularly *[*a flag *fluttering* in the wind*]* **3.** to move with quick vibrations, flaps, etc. **4.** to tremble; quiver **5.** to move about in a restless, fussy way —*vt.* **1.** to make flutter **2.** to excite or confuse —*n.* **1.** a fluttering **2.** a state of excitement or confusion —**flut′ter·er** *n.* —**flut′ter·y** *adj*
flut·y (flo͞ot′ē) *adj.* **flut′i·er, flut′i·est** flutelike in tone; soft, clear, and high-pitched
flu·vi·al (flo͞o′vē əl) *adj.* [< L. < *fluvius,* a river < *fluere,* to flow] of, found in, or produced by a river
flux (fluks) *n.* [OFr. < L. *fluxus* < pp. of *fluere,* to flow] **1.** a flowing or flow **2.** a coming in of the tide **3.** continual change **4.** any abnormal discharge of fluid matter from the body **5.** *a)* a substance used to help fuse metals together, as in soldering *b)* a substance used, as in smelting, to fuse with undesired matter in forming a more fluid slag **6.** *Physics* the rate of flow of energy, fluids, etc. over a surface —*vt.* **1.** to make fluid **2.** to fuse (metals)
fly[1] (flī) *vi.* **flew, flown, fly′ing** [OE. *fleogan*] **1.** to move through the air by using wings, as a bird **2.** to travel through the air in an aircraft **3.** to be propelled through

the air or through space, as a missile **4.** to operate an aircraft **5.** to wave or float in the air, as a flag or kite **6.** to move or go swiftly **7.** to flee **8. flied, fly′ing** *Baseball* to hit a fly —*vt.* **1.** *a)* to cause to float in the air *b)* to display (a flag) as from a pole **2.** to operate (an aircraft) **3.** to travel over in an aircraft **4.** to carry in an aircraft **5.** to flee from or avoid —*n., pl.* **flies 1.** a flap concealing the zipper, buttons, etc. in a garment **2.** a flap serving as a tent door **3.** the length of a flag from the staff outward **4.** *same as: a)* FLYWHEEL *b)* FLYLEAF **5.** *Baseball* a ball batted high, esp. within the foul lines **6.** [*pl.*] *Theater* the space behind and above the proscenium arch —**fly at** to attack by or as by springing toward —**fly out** *Baseball* to be put out by hitting a fly that is caught —**let fly (at) 1.** to shoot or throw (at) **2.** to unleash a verbal attack (at) —**on the fly 1.** while in flight **2.** [Colloq.] while in a hurry

fly[2] (flī) *n., pl.* **flies** [OE. *fleoge*] **1.** *a) same as* HOUSEFLY *b)* any of a large group of insects with two transparent wings, as the housefly and gnat *c)* any of several four-winged insects, as the mayfly **2.** a hooked lure for fishing, made to resemble an insect

fly·a·ble (-ə b'l) *adj.* suitable or ready for flying [*flyable* weather, a *flyable* airplane]

fly ash airborne bits of unburnable ash

fly·blown (-blōn′) *adj.* **1.** full of flies' eggs or larvae **2.** spoiled; tainted **3.** [Colloq.] shabby; dingy

fly·by, fly-by (-bī′) *n., pl.* **-bies′** a flight past a given point by an aircraft or spacecraft

fly-by-night (-bī nīt′) *adj.* not trustworthy, esp. financially —*n.* a fly-by-night person

fly-cast (-kast′) *vi.* **-cast′, -cast′ing** to fish by casting artificial flies

fly·catch·er (-kach′ər) *n.* any of various small birds, as the pewee, that catch insects in flight

fly·er (-ər) *n. same as* FLIER

fly·ing (-iŋ) *adj.* **1.** that flies or can fly **2.** moving as if flying; fast **3.** hasty and brief **4.** of or for aircraft or aviators **5.** organized to act quickly —*n.* the action of one that flies

flying boat an airplane with a hull that permits it to land on and take off from water

flying bridge *Naut.* a small structure over the main bridge, from which a vessel may be conned

flying buttress a buttress connected with a wall by an arch, serving to resist outward pressure

flying colors 1. flags flying in the air **2.** notable victory or success

flying fish any of a number of chiefly warm-water sea fishes with winglike pectoral fins that enable them to glide through the air

flying gurnard a marine fish with winglike pectoral fins for gliding short distances in the air

flying jib a small, triangular sail in front of the jib

flying saucer *same as* UFO

flying squirrel any of a number of squirrels with winglike folds of skin attached to the legs and body that enable them to make gliding leaps

FLYING BUTTRESS

fly·leaf (flī′lēf′) *n., pl.* **-leaves′** (-lēvz′) a blank leaf at the beginning or end of a book

fly·pa·per (-pā′pər) *n.* a sticky or poisonous paper set out to catch or kill flies

fly·speck (-spek′) *n.* **1.** a speck of fly excrement **2.** any tiny spot **3.** a petty or insignificant error or flaw —*vt.* to make flyspecks on

fly·trap (-trap′) *n.* **1.** any device for catching flies **2.** a plant that catches insects

fly·way (-wā′) *n.* a flying route of migratory birds

fly·weight (-wāt′) *n.* a boxer who weighs 112 pounds or less —*adj.* of flyweights

fly·wheel (-hwēl′) *n.* a heavy wheel attached to a machine so as to regulate its speed and motion

Fm *Chem.* fermium

FM frequency modulation

fm. 1. fathom **2.** from

f-num·ber (ef′num′bər) *n. Photog.* the ratio of a lens diameter to its focal length: the lower the f-number, the shorter the exposure required

fo. folio

foal (fōl) *n.* [OE. *fola*] a young horse, mule, donkey, etc.; colt or filly —*vt., vi.* to give birth to (a foal)

foam (fōm) *n.* [OE. *fam*] **1.** the whitish mass of bubbles formed on or in liquids by agitation, fermentation, etc. **2.** something like foam, as frothy saliva **3.** a rigid or spongy cellular mass made by gas bubbles dispersed in liquid rubber, plastic, etc. —*vi.* to produce foam; froth —*vt.* to cause to foam —**foam at the mouth** to be very angry; rage —**foam′less** *adj.*

foam rubber rubber treated to form a firm, spongy foam, used in seats, mattresses, etc.

foam·y (-ē) *adj.* **foam′i·er, foam′i·est 1.** foaming or covered with foam **2.** of or like foam —**foam′i·ly** *adv.* —**foam′i·ness** *n.*

fob[1] (fäb) *n.* [prob. < dial. G. *fuppe,* a pocket] **1.** a watch pocket in the front of a man's trousers **2.** a short ribbon or chain hanging from a watch in such a pocket, often with an ornament at the end **3.** such an ornament

fob[2] (fäb) *vt.* **fobbed, fob′bing** [< ME. *fobben,* to cheat] [Obs.] to cheat or deceive —**fob off 1.** to trick or put off (a person) with second-rate articles, lies, excuses, etc. **2.** to get rid of (something worthless) by deceit or trickery

F.O.B., f.o.b. free on board

fo·cal (fō′k'l) *adj.* of or at a focus —**fo′cal·ly** *adv.*

fo·cal·ize (fō′kə līz′) *vt., vi.* **-ized′, -iz′ing** to adjust or come to a focus —**fo′cal·i·za′tion** *n.*

focal length the distance from the optical center of a lens to the point where the light rays converge; length of the focus: also **focal distance**

fo'c's'le (fōk′s'l) *n. phonetic spelling of* FORECASTLE

fo·cus (fō′kəs) *n., pl.* **fo′cus·es, fo′ci** (-sī) [ModL. < L., hearth] **1.** the point where rays of light, heat, etc. or waves of sound come together, or from which they spread or seem to spread; specif., the point where rays of light reflected by a mirror or refracted by a lens meet **2.** *same as* FOCAL LENGTH **3.** adjustment of focal length to make a clear image **4.** any center of activity, attention, etc. **5.** a part of the body where an infection is most active **6.** *Math.* *a)* either of the two fixed points used in determining an ellipse *b)* any analogous point for a parabola or hyperbola —*vt.* **-cused** or **-cussed, -cus·ing** or **-cus·sing 1.** to bring into focus **2.** to adjust the focal length of (the eye, a lens, etc.) so as to make a clear image **3.** to concentrate [*focus* one's attention] —*vi.* to come to a focus —**in focus** clear; distinct —**out of focus** indistinct; blurred —**fo′cus·er** *n.*

fod·der (fäd′ər) *n.* [OE. *fodor* < *foda,* food] coarse food for cattle, horses, etc., as cornstalks, hay, and straw —*vt.* to feed with fodder

foe (fō) *n.* [OE. *fah,* hostile, (*ge*)*fah,* enemy] *same as* ENEMY (in all senses)

foe·man (fō′mən) *n., pl.* **-men** [Archaic] a foe

foe·tid (fet′id, fēt′-) *adj. same as* FETID

foe·tus (fēt′əs) *n. same as* FETUS —**foe′tal** *adj.*

fog (fôg, fäg) *n.* [prob. < Scand.] **1.** a large mass of water vapor condensed to fine particles, just above the earth's surface **2.** a similar mass of smoke, dust, etc. obscuring the atmosphere **3.** a vaporized liquid, as insecticide, widely dispersed **4.** a state of mental confusion **5.** a blur on a photograph or film —*vi.* **fogged, fog′ging 1.** to become covered by fog **2.** to be or become blurred or dimmed —*vt.* **1.** to cover with fog **2.** to blur or dim **3.** to confuse

fog bank a dense mass of fog

fog·gy (-ē) *adj.* **-gi·er, -gi·est 1.** full of fog **2.** dim; blurred **3.** confused; perplexed —**fog′gi·ly** *adv.* —**fog′gi·ness** *n.*

fog·horn (-hôrn′) *n.* a horn blown to give warning to ships in a fog

fo·gy (fō′gē) *n., pl.* **-gies** [< ?] a person who is old-fashioned or highly conservative: also **fo′gey,** *pl.* **-geys** —**fo′gy·ish** *adj.* —**fo′gy·ism** *n.*

foi·ble (foi′b'l) *n.* [obs. form of Fr. *faible,* FEEBLE] a small weakness in character; frailty

foil[1] (foil) *vt.* [< OFr. *fuler,* to trample on] to keep from being successful; thwart; frustrate

foil[2] (foil) *n.* [< OFr. < VL. < L. *folium,* a leaf] **1.** a leaflike, rounded space or design, as in windows, etc. in Gothic architecture **2.** a very thin sheet, leaf, or coating of metal **3.** a thin leaf of polished metal put under an inferior or artificial gem to give it brilliance **4.** one that sets off or enhances another by contrast **5.** [etym. unc.] *a)* a long, thin fencing sword with a button on the point to prevent injury *b)* [*pl.*] the art or sport of fencing with foils —*vt.* **1.** to cover or back with foil **2.** to decorate (windows, etc.) with foils

foist (foist) *vt.* [prob. < dial. Du. *vuisten,* to hide in the hand < *vuist,* a fist] **1.** to put in slyly or surreptitiously **2.** to impose by fraud; palm off

fol. 1. folio **2.** following

fold[1] (fōld) *vt.* [OE. *faldan*] **1.** to bend or press (something) so that one part is over another **2.** to draw together and intertwine [to *fold* the arms] **3.** to draw (wings) close to the body **4.** to clasp in the arms; embrace **5.** to wrap up; envelop —*vi.* **1.** to be or become folded **2.** [Colloq.] *a)* to fail; be forced to close, as a business *b)* to succumb, as to exhaustion —*n.* **1.** a folded part or layer **2.** a mark, hollow, or crease made by folding **3.** *Geol.* a rock layer folded by pressure —**fold in** *Cooking* to blend (an ingredient) into a mixture, using gentle, cutting strokes

fold[2] (fōld) *n.* [OE. *fald*] **1.** a pen in which to keep sheep **2.** a flock of sheep **3.** a group or organization with common aims, faith, etc., as a church —*vt.* to keep or confine in a pen

-fold (fōld) [OE. *-feald*] *a suffix meaning:* **1.** having (a specified number of) parts *[tenfold]* **2.** (a specified number of) times as many or as much

fold·a·way (fōld′ə wā′) ***adj.*** that can be folded for easy storage *[a foldaway cot]*

fold·er (fōl′dər) ***n.*** **1.** a person or thing that folds **2.** a sheet of heavy paper folded as a holder for papers **3.** an unstitched, folded booklet

fol·de·rol (fäl′də räl′, fôl′də rôl′) ***n.*** *same as* FALDERAL

folding door a door with hinged leaves or accordion pleats that can be folded back

fo·li·a·ceous (fō′lē ā′shəs) ***adj.*** [< L. < *folium,* a leaf] **1.** of or like the leaf of a plant **2.** having leaves **3.** consisting of thin layers

fo·li·age (fō′lē ij) ***n.*** [< OFr. < VL. *folia* < L. *folium,* a leaf] **1.** leaves, as of a plant or tree **2.** a decoration consisting of a representation of leaves, branches, flowers, etc.

fo·li·ate (fō′lē āt′; *for adj., usually* -it) ***vt.*** **-at′ed, -at′ing** [L. *foliatus,* leafy < *folium,* a leaf] to divide into thin layers —***vi.*** **1.** to separate into layers **2.** to send out leaves —***adj.*** having or covered with leaves

fo·li·a·tion (fō′lē ā′shən) ***n.*** **1.** a growing of or developing into a leaf or leaves **2.** the state of being in leaf **3.** the way leaves are arranged in the bud **4.** the act of beating metal into layers **5.** a leaflike decoration

fo·lic acid (fō′lik) [< L. *folium,* a leaf + -IC] a crystalline substance, $C_{19}H_{19}N_7O_6$, one of the vitamin B group, found in green leaves, etc. and used esp. in treating certain anemias

fo·li·o (fō′lē ō′) ***n.,*** *pl.* **-li·os′** [L. abl. of *folium,* a leaf] **1.** a large sheet of paper folded once, so that it forms two leaves, or four pages, of a book, etc. **2.** a book (the largest regular size), now often 12 by 15 inches, made of sheets so folded **3.** a leaf of a book, etc. numbered on only one side **4.** the number of a page in a book, etc. —***adj.*** of the size of a folio —**in folio** in the form of a folio

folk (fōk) ***n.,*** *pl.* **folk, folks** [OE. *folc*] **1.** *a)* a people; nation; ethnic group *b)* the common people of such a group: with *the* **2.** [*pl.*] people in general; persons *[folks don't agree]* —***adj.*** of or having to do with the common people —**(one's) folks** [Colloq.] (one's) family

folk dance **1.** a traditional dance of the common people of a country **2.** music for this

folk etymology the change that occurs in the form of a word so as to give it an apparent connection with some other word, as *coleslaw* becomes *cold slaw*

folk·lore (fōk′lôr′) ***n.*** **1.** the traditional beliefs, legends, sayings, etc. of a people **2.** the study of these —**folk′lor′ic** ***adj.*** —**folk′lor′ist** ***n.***

folk medicine the treatment of disease, including the use of herbs, as practiced by the common people over many years

folk music music made and handed down among the common people

folk-rock (-räk′) ***n.*** music with a rock-and-roll beat combined with words in a folk-song style

folk song **1.** a song made and handed down among the common people **2.** a song composed in imitation of such a song —**folk singer**

folk·sy (-sē) ***adj.*** **-si·er, -si·est** [Colloq.] friendly or sociable in a simple and direct or overly familiar manner —**folk′si·ly** ***adv.*** —**folk′si·ness** ***n.***

folk tale (or **story**) a story, often legendary, made and handed down orally among the common people

folk·way (-wā′) ***n.*** any way of thinking, behaving, etc. characteristic of a certain social group

fol·li·cle (fäl′i k′l) ***n.*** [ModL. *folliculus* < L., a small bag, dim. of *follis,* bellows] **1.** *Anat.* any small sac, cavity, or gland for excretion or secretion *[a hair follicle]* **2.** *Bot.* a dry, one-celled seed capsule, opening along one side, as a milkweed pod —**fol·li·cu·lar** (fə lik′yoo lər) ***adj.*** —**fol·lic′u·late** (-lit, -lāt′), **fol·lic′u·lat′ed** ***adj.***

follicle-stimulating hormone a pituitary hormone that stimulates growth of ova and sperm

fol·low (fäl′ō) ***vt.*** [< OE. *folgian*] **1.** to come or go after **2.** to chase; pursue **3.** to go along *[follow the road]* **4.** to come after in time, in a series, etc. **5.** to take the place of in rank, position, etc. **6.** to take up; engage in (a trade, etc.) **7.** to result from **8.** to take as a model; imitate **9.** to accept the authority of; obey **10.** to listen to, watch, or observe closely **11.** to understand the continuity or logic of —***vi.*** **1.** to come, go, or happen after something else in place, sequence, or time **2.** to result —***n.*** the act of following —**follow out** to carry out fully —**follow through** to continue and complete a stroke or action —**follow up** **1.** to follow closely and persistently **2.** to carry out fully **3.** to make more effective by doing something more

fol·low·er (fäl′ə wər) ***n.*** one that follows; specif., *a)* a person who follows another's belief or teachings; disciple *b)* a servant or attendant

fol·low·ing (-ə wiŋ) ***adj.*** that follows; next after —***n.*** a group of followers or adherents —***prep.*** after *[following dinner he went home]* —**the following** **1.** the one or ones to be mentioned immediately **2.** what follows

fol·low-through (-ō thro͞o′) ***n.*** **1.** the act or manner of continuing the swing or stroke of a club, racket, etc. after striking or releasing the ball, etc. **2.** the completing of an undertaking

fol·low-up (-up′) ***adj.*** following as a review, addition, etc. —***n.*** **1.** a follow-up thing or event **2.** a following up, as with follow-up letters, visits, etc.

fol·ly (fäl′ē) ***n.,*** *pl.* **-lies** [< OFr. < *fol:* see FOOL] **1.** a lack of sense or rational conduct; foolishness **2.** any foolish action or belief **3.** any foolish but expensive undertaking

fo·ment (fō ment′) ***vt.*** [< OFr. < LL. *fomentare* < L. < *fovere,* to keep warm] **1.** to treat with warm water, medicated lotions, etc. **2.** to stir up; incite *[to foment a riot]* —**fo′men·ta′tion** ***n.***

fond (fänd) ***adj.*** [< ME. *fonned,* pp. of *fonnen,* to be foolish] **1.** [Now Rare] foolishly naive **2.** tender and affectionate, sometimes in a foolish way **3.** greatly cherished —**fond of** having a liking for —**fond′ly** ***adv.*** —**fond′ness** ***n.***

fon·dant (fän′dənt) ***n.*** [Fr. < prp. of *fondre,* to melt] a soft, creamy candy made of sugar, used esp. as a filling for other candies

fon·dle (fän′d′l) ***vt.*** **-dled, -dling** [freq. of obs. *fond, v.*] to stroke lovingly; caress —**fon′dler** ***n.***

fon·due, fon·du (fän do͞o′, fän′do͞o) ***n.*** [Fr. < pp. of *fondre,* to melt] **1.** cheese melted in wine, used as a dip for cubes of bread **2.** any of various dishes, as hot oil into which cubes of meat are dipped for cooking **3.** cheese soufflé with bread crumbs

font[1] (fänt) ***n.*** [OE. < L. *fons,* FOUNTAIN] **1.** a bowl to hold baptismal water **2.** a basin for holy water; stoup **3.** [Poet.] a fountain or spring **4.** any source —**font′al** ***adj.***

font[2] (fänt) ***n.*** [Fr. *fonte* < OFr. *fondre:* see FOUND[3]] *Printing* a complete assortment of type in one size and style

fon·ta·nel, fon·ta·nelle (fän′tə nel′) ***n.*** [ME. *fontinel,* a hollow < OFr. dim. of *fontaine,* FOUNTAIN] any of the soft, boneless areas in the skull of a baby, later closed over when bone forms

FONTANELS

food (fo͞od) ***n.*** [OE. *foda*] **1.** any substance taken into and assimilated by a plant or animal to keep it alive and enable it to grow; nourishment **2.** solid substances of this sort: distinguished from *drink* **3.** a specified kind of food **4.** anything that nourishes or stimulates *[food for thought]*

food chain *Ecol.* a sequence (as grass, rabbit, fox) in which each member feeds on the one below

food cycle *Ecol.* all the individual food chains in a community: also **food web**

food poisoning **1.** sickness from eating food contaminated by bacteria **2.** poisoning from naturally poisonous foods or from chemical contaminants in food

food stamp any of the Federal stamps allotted to unemployed or low-income persons for use in buying food

food·stuff (-stuf′) ***n.*** any material made into or used as food

fool (fo͞ol) ***n.*** [< OFr. *fol* < LL. < L. *follis,* windbag] **1.** a silly person; simpleton **2.** a man formerly kept by a nobleman or king to entertain as a clown; jester **3.** a victim of a trick; dupe —***adj.*** [Colloq.] foolish —***vi.*** **1.** to act like a fool; be silly **2.** to joke **3.** [Colloq.] to meddle (*with*) —***vt.*** to trick; deceive; dupe —**be no** (or **nobody's**) **fool** to be shrewd and capable —**fool around** [Colloq.] to trifle —**fool away** [Colloq.] to squander —**play the fool** to clown

fool·har·dy (-här′dē) ***adj.*** **-di·er, -di·est** foolishly daring; rash —**fool′har′di·ly** ***adv.*** —**fool′har′di·ness** ***n.***

fool·ish (-ish) ***adj.*** **1.** without good sense; silly; unwise **2.** *a)* absurd *b)* abashed; embarrassed —**fool′ish·ly** ***adv.*** —**fool′ish·ness** ***n.***

fool·proof (-pro͞of′) ***adj.*** so harmless, simple, or indestructible as not to be mishandled, damaged, etc. even by a fool

fools·cap (fo͞olz′kap′) ***n.*** **1.** [from former watermark] a size of writing paper: in the U.S., 13 by 16 inches **2.** *same as* FOOL'S CAP

fool's cap a jester's cap with bells

fool's gold iron pyrites or copper pyrites, like gold in color

foot (foot) ***n.,*** *pl.* **feet:** see also sense 6 [OE. *fot*] **1.** the end part of the leg, on which a person or animal stands or moves 2. the base or bottom [the *foot* of a page] 3. the last of a series 4. the end, as of a bed, toward which the feet are directed 5. the part of a stocking, etc. covering the foot 6. a measure of length, equal to 12 inches (an average length of the human foot): symbol, ′ (e.g., 10′): abbrev. **ft.** (sing. & pl.): pl. often **foot** following a number [a six-*foot* man] 7. [Brit.] infantry 8. a group of syllables serving as a unit of meter in verse —***vi.*** 1. to dance 2. to walk —***vt.*** 1. to walk, dance, or run on, over, or through 2. to make the foot of (a stocking, etc.) 3. to add (a column of figures) and set down a total 4. [Colloq.] to pay (costs, etc.) [to *foot* the bill] —**foot it** [Colloq.] to dance, walk, or run —**of foot** in walking or running [swift *of foot*] —**on foot** 1. walking or running 2. in process —**put one's best foot forward** [Colloq.] 1. to do one's best 2. to try to appear at one's best —**put one's foot down** [Colloq.] to act decisively —**put one's foot in it** (or **in one's mouth**) [Colloq.] to make an embarrassing blunder —**under foot** 1. on the floor, etc. 2. in the way —**foot′less** ***adj.***

foot·age (foot′ij) ***n.*** length expressed in feet

foot-and-mouth disease (foot′'n mouth′) an acute, contagious disease of cattle, deer, etc. characterized by fever and blisters in the mouth and around the hoofs

foot·ball (-bôl′) ***n.*** [ME. *foteballe*] 1. any of several field games played with an inflated leather ball by two teams, the object being to get the ball across the opponents' goal: in U.S. & Canadian football, the players may kick, throw, or run with the ball, and may run ahead of it for interference, forward passes, etc.: cf. SOCCER, RUGBY 2. the elliptical or (for soccer) round ball used in playing these games

foot·board (-bôrd′) ***n.*** 1. a board or small platform for supporting the feet or for standing on 2. a vertical piece across the foot of a bed

foot·bridge (-brij′) ***n.*** a narrow bridge for pedestrians

foot-can·dle (-kan′d'l) ***n.*** a unit for measuring illumination: it is equal to the amount of direct light thrown by one candle (*n.* 3) on a square foot of surface one foot away

foot·ed (-id) ***adj.*** having a foot or feet, esp. of a specified number or kind [four-*footed*]

-foot·er (-ər) *a combining form meaning* a person or thing (a specified number of) feet tall, high, long, etc. [six-*footer*]

foot·fall (-fôl′) ***n.*** the sound of a footstep

foot·hill (-hil′) ***n.*** a low hill at or near the foot of a mountain or mountain range

foot·hold (-hōld′) ***n.*** 1. a place to put a foot down securely, as in climbing 2. a secure position

foot·ing (-iŋ) ***n.*** 1. a secure placing of the feet 2. *a*) the condition of a surface for walking, running, etc. *b*) a secure place to put the feet 3. a secure position or basis 4. a basis for relationship [a friendly *footing*] 5. *a*) the adding of a column of figures *b*) the sum obtained 6. a projecting base under a column, wall, etc.: also **foot′er**

foot·lights (-līts′) ***n.pl.*** a row of lights along the front of a stage at the actors' foot level —**the footlights** the theater, or acting as a profession

foot·loose (-lōōs′) ***adj.*** free to go wherever one likes or do as one likes

foot·man (-mən) ***n.***, *pl.* **-men** a male servant who assists the butler in a household

foot·note (-nōt′) ***n.*** a note of comment or reference at the bottom of a page —***vt.*** **-not′ed, -not′ing** to add such a note or notes to

foot·pad (-pad′) ***n.*** [see PAD[3]] a highway robber or holdup man who travels on foot

foot·path (-path′) ***n.*** a narrow path for pedestrians

foot-pound (-pound′) ***n.*** a unit of energy, equal to the amount of energy required to raise a weight of one pound a distance of one foot

foot-pound-sec·ond (-pound′sek′ənd) ***adj.*** designating or of a system of measurement using the foot, pound, and second as the units of length, mass, and time, respectively

foot·print (-print′) ***n.*** a mark left by a foot

foot·race (-rās′) ***n.*** a race run on foot

foot·rest (-rest′) ***n.*** a support to rest the feet on

foot·sie, foot·sy (-sē) ***n.***, *pl.* **-sies** the foot: a child's term —**play footsie (with)** 1. to touch feet or legs (with) in a caressing way, as under the table 2. to flirt or have surreptitious dealings (with)

foot soldier a soldier on foot; infantryman

foot·sore (-sôr′) ***adj.*** having sore or tender feet, as from much walking

foot·step (-step′) ***n.*** 1. the distance covered in a step 2. the sound of a step; footfall 3. a footprint 4. a step in a stairway —**follow in (someone's) footsteps** to follow (someone's) example, vocation, etc.

foot·stool (-stōōl′) ***n.*** a low stool for supporting the feet of a seated person

foot·wear (-wer′) ***n.*** shoes, boots, slippers, etc.

foot·work (-wurk′) ***n.*** the act or manner of moving the feet, as in walking, boxing, dancing, etc.

foo·zle (fōō′z'l) ***vt., vi.*** **-zled, -zling** [< ? G. *fuseln*, to bungle] to make or do (something) awkwardly; esp., to bungle (a golf stroke) —***n.*** the act or an instance of foozling —**foo′zler** ***n.***

fop (fäp) ***n.*** [ME. *foppe*, a fool, prob. < MDu. or MLowG.] a vain, affected man who pays too much attention to his clothes, appearance, etc.; dandy —**fop′per·y** ***n.***, *pl.* **-per·ies** —**fop′pish** ***adj.*** —**fop′pish·ly** ***adv.*** —**fop′pish·ness** ***n.***

for (fôr; *unstressed* fər) ***prep.*** [OE.] 1. in place of [to use coats *for* blankets] 2. in the interest of [his agent acted *for* him] 3. in defense of; in favor of 4. in honor of [to give a banquet *for* a notable] 5. with the aim or purpose of [to carry a gun *for* protection] 6. with the purpose of going to [to leave *for* home] 7. in order to be, become, get, have, keep, etc. [to walk *for* exercise] 8. in search of [looking *for* berries] 9. meant to be received by a specified person or thing, or to be used in a specified way [flowers *for* a girl, money *for* paying bills] 10. suitable to [a room *for* sleeping] 11. with regard to [need *for* improvement, an ear *for* music] 12. as being [to know *for* a fact] 13. considering the nature of [cool *for* July] 14. because of [to cry *for* pain] 15. in spite of [stupid *for* all her learning] 16. in proportion to [a dollar tax *for* every four earned] 17. to the amount of [a bill *for* $50] 18. at the price of [sold *for* $10] 19. to the length, duration, etc. of; throughout [to work *for* an hour] 20. at (a specified time) [a date *for* two o'clock] —***conj.*** because; seeing that [comfort him *for* he is sad] —**for (one) to** that (one) will, should, must, etc. [a book *for* you *to* read] —**O! for** I wish that I had

for- [OE., replacing *fer-*] *an Old English and Middle English prefix meaning:* 1. away, apart, off, etc. [*forbid, forget, forgo*] 2. very much [*forlorn*]

for·age (fôr′ij, fär′-) ***n.*** [< OFr. < Frank. *fodr*, food] 1. food for domestic animals; fodder 2. a search for food or provisions —***vi.*** **-aged, -ag·ing** 1. to search for food or provisions 2. to search for what one needs or wants —***vt.*** 1. to get or take food or provisions from 2. to provide with forage; feed 3. to get by foraging —**for′ag·er** ***n.***

fo·ra·men (fô rā′mən, fə-) ***n.***, *pl.* **-ram′i·na** (-ram′ə nə), **-ra′mens** [L. < *forare*, to bore] a small opening, esp. in a bone or in a plant ovule —**fo·ram′i·nal** (-ram′ə n'l), **fo·ram′i·nate** (-nit) ***adj.***

for·a·min·i·fer (fôr′ə min′ə fər, fär′-) ***n.***, *pl.* **fo·ram·i·nif·er·a** (fə ram′ə nif′ər ə) [< L. *foramen*: see prec. & -FER] any of a group of small, one-celled sea animals with calcareous shells full of tiny holes through which slender filaments project —**fo·ram′i·nif′er·al, fo·ram′i·nif′er·ous** ***adj.***

for·as·much (fôr′əz much′) ***conj.*** inasmuch (*as*)

for·ay (fôr′ā) ***vt., vi.*** [< OFr. < *forrer*, to forage] to raid for spoils; plunder —***n.*** a sudden attack or raid, as for spoils

for·bade, for·bad (fər bad′, fôr-) *pt. of* FORBID

for·bear[1] (fôr ber′, fər-) ***vt.*** **-bore′** or archaic **-bare′, -borne′, -bear′ing** [< OE.: see FOR- & BEAR[1]] to refrain from; avoid (doing, saying, etc.) —***vi.*** 1. to refrain or abstain 2. to control oneself —**for·bear′er** ***n.*** —**for·bear′ing·ly** ***adv.***

for·bear[2] (fôr′ber′) ***n.*** *same as* FOREBEAR

for·bear·ance (fôr ber′əns, fər-) ***n.*** 1. the act of forbearing 2. self-control; patient restraint

for·bid (fər bid′, fôr-) ***vt.*** **-bade′** or **-bad′, -bid′den** or archaic **-bid′, -bid′ding** [< OE.: see FOR- & BID] 1. to rule against; prohibit 2. to command to stay away from; bar from 3. to make impossible; prevent —**for·bid′dance** ***n.*** —**for·bid′den** ***adj.***

for·bid·ding (-iŋ) ***adj.*** looking dangerous, threatening, or disagreeable; repellent —**for·bid′ding·ly** ***adv.***

for·bore (fôr bôr′, fər-) *pt. of* FORBEAR[1]

for·borne (-bôrn′) *pp. of* FORBEAR[1]

force (fôrs) ***n.*** [OFr. < LL. < L. *fortis*, strong] 1. strength; energy; power 2. impetus [the *force* of a blow] 3. physical power or coercion exerted against a person or thing 4. *a*) the power to control, persuade, etc.; effectiveness *b*) a person or thing having influence, power, etc. [a *force* for good] 5. *a*) military, naval, or air power *b*) [*pl.*] the collective armed strength, as of a nation *c*) any organized group of soldiers, sailors, etc. 6. any group of people organized for some activity [a sales *force*] 7. *Law* binding power; validity 8. *Physics* the cause, or agent, that puts an object at rest into motion or alters the motion of a moving object —***vt.*** **forced, forc′ing** 1. to cause to do something by force; compel 2. to rape (a woman) 3. *a*) to break open, into, or through by force *b*) to overpower or capture in this way 4. to take by force; wrest; extort 5. to drive as by force; push; impel 6. to impose as by force (with *on* or *upon*) 7. to effect or produce as by force [to *force* a smile] 8. to strain [to *force* one's voice] 9. to cause (plants, fruit, etc.) to develop faster by artificial means 10. *Baseball* *a*) to cause (a base runner) to be put out by a force-out: said of a batter *b*) to cause (a runner) to score or (a run) to be scored by walking the batter with the bases full (often with *in*) 11. *Card Games* to cause (an opponent) to play (a particular card) or (one's partner) to make (a particular bid) —**in force** **1.** in full strength **2.** in effect; valid —**force′a·ble** *adj.* —**force′less** *adj.* —**forc′er** *n.*

forced (fôrst) *adj.* **1.** done or brought about by force; compulsory *[forced* labor*]* **2.** produced by unusual effort; strained *[a forced* smile*]* **3.** due to an emergency *[a forced* landing*]* **4.** at a pace faster than usual *[a forced* march*]*

force-feed (fôrs′fēd′) *vt.* **-fed′, -feed′ing** to feed as by a tube through the throat to the stomach

force·ful (-fəl) *adj.* full of force; powerful, vigorous, effective, etc. —**force′ful·ly** *adv.* —**force′ful·ness** *n.*

force·meat (-mēt′) *n.* [< *farce meat* < *farce* (obs.), to stuff] meat chopped up and seasoned, usually for stuffing

force-out (-out′) *n. Baseball* an out that results when a base runner is forced from a base by a teammate's hit

for·ceps (fôr′səps) *n., pl.* **for′ceps** [L., orig., smith's tongs < *formus,* hot + *capere,* to take] small tongs or pincers for grasping, compressing, and pulling, used esp. by surgeons and dentists

FORCEPS (A, fine bent; B, scissors)

force pump a pump with a valveless plunger for forcing a liquid through a pipe under pressure

for·ci·ble (fôr′sə b′l) *adj.* **1.** done or effected by force **2.** having force; forceful —**for′ci·ble·ness** *n.* —**for′ci·bly** *adv.*

ford (fôrd) *n.* [OE.] a shallow place in a stream, river, etc. that can be crossed by wading, on horseback, in a car, etc. —*vt.* to cross (a stream) in this way —**ford′a·ble** *adj.*

Ford (fôrd) **1. Gerald R(udolph),** 1913– ; 38th president of the U.S. (1974–77) **2. Henry,** 1863–1947; U.S. automobile manufacturer

for·done (fôr dun′) *adj.* [Archaic] completely exhausted

fore (fôr) *adv.* [OE.] at, in, or toward the front: now only of a ship —*adj.* situated in front —*n.* the front thing or part —*interj. Golf* a shout warning those ahead that one is about to hit the ball —**to the fore** **1.** to the front; into view **2.** available **3.** still active

'fore (fôr) *prep.* [Poet.] before

fore- [OE.: see FORE] *a prefix meaning:* **1.** before in time, place, order, or rank *[forenoon, foreman]* **2.** the front part of *[forearm]*

fore-and-aft (fôr′'n aft′) *adj. Naut.* from the bow to the stern; lengthwise or set lengthwise

fore and aft *Naut.* **1.** from the bow to the stern; lengthwise or set lengthwise **2.** at, in, or toward both the bow and the stern

fore·arm[1] (fôr′ärm′) *n.* the part of the arm between the elbow and the wrist

fore·arm[2] (fôr ärm′) *vt.* to arm in advance; prepare beforehand for any difficulty

fore·bear (fôr′ber′) *n.* [< FORE + BE + -ER] an ancestor

fore·bode (fôr bōd′) *vt., vi.* **-bod′ed, -bod′ing** [< OE.: see FORE- & BODE[1]] **1.** to foretell; predict (esp. something bad or harmful) **2.** to have a presentiment of (something bad or harmful) —**fore·bod′er** *n.* —**fore·bod′ing** *n., adj.* —**fore·bod′ing·ly** *adv.*

fore·brain (fôr′brān′) *n.* the front part of the brain

fore·cast (fôr′kast′; *for v., also occas.* fôr kast′) *vt.* **-cast′** or **-cast′ed, -cast′ing** **1.** to estimate in advance; predict (weather, etc.) **2.** to serve as a prediction or prophecy of —*vi.* to make a forecast —*n.* a prediction —**fore′cast′er** *n.*

fore·cas·tle (fōk′s'l; fôr′kas′'l *is a sp. pronun.) n.* [FORE + CASTLE] **1.** the upper deck of a ship in front of the foremast **2.** the front part of a merchant ship, where the sailors' quarters are located

fore·close (fôr klōz′) *vt.* **-closed′, -clos′ing** [< OFr. pp. of *forclore,* to exclude < *fors,* outside + *clore,* CLOSE[2]] **1.** to shut out; exclude; bar **2.** to take away the right to redeem (a mortgage, etc.) —*vi.* to foreclose a mortgage, etc. —**fore·clos′a·ble** *adj.* —**fore·clo′sure** (-klō′zhər) *n.*

fore·doom (fôr do͞om′) *vt.* to doom in advance; condemn beforehand

fore·fa·ther (fôr′fä′*th*ər) *n.* an ancestor

fore·fin·ger (-fiŋ′gər) *n.* the finger nearest the thumb; index finger; first finger

fore·foot (-fo͝ot′) *n., pl.* **-feet′** either of the front feet of an animal with four or more feet

fore·front (-frunt′) *n.* **1.** the extreme front **2.** the position of most activity, importance, etc.

fore·gath·er (fôr ga*th*′ər) *vi. same as* FORGATHER

fore·go[1] (fôr gō′) *vt., vi.* **-went′, -gone′, -go′ing** [OE. *foregan*] to go before in place, time, or degree

fore·go[2] (fôr gō′) *vt. same as* FORGO

fore·go·ing (fôr′gō′iŋ) *adj.* previously said, written, etc. —**the foregoing** **1.** the one or ones previously mentioned **2.** what has already been said or written

fore·gone (fôr gôn′) *adj.* **1.** that has gone before; previous **2.** *a)* previously determined *b)* inevitable or unavoidable: said of a conclusion

fore·ground (fôr′ground′) *n.* **1.** the part of a scene, picture, etc. nearest the viewer **2.** the most noticeable or conspicuous position

fore·hand (-hand′) *n.* a kind of stroke, as in tennis, made with the arm extended and the palm of the hand turned forward —*adj.* **1.** foremost; front **2.** done or performed as with a forehand —*adv.* with a forehand

fore·hand·ed (fôr han′did) *adj.* **1.** making provision for the future; thrifty; prudent **2.** prosperous; well-off **3.** *same as* FOREHAND (*adj.* 2) —**fore·hand′ed·ly** *adv.* —**fore·hand′ed·ness** *n.*

fore·head (fôr′id, fär′-; fôr′hed, fär′-) *n.* the part of the face between the eyebrows and the hairline

for·eign (fôr′in, fär′-) *adj.* [< OFr. *forain* < LL. < L. *foras,* out-of-doors] **1.** situated outside one's own country, locality, etc. **2.** of, from, or characteristic of another country *[a foreign* language*]* **3.** concerning the relations of one country to another *[foreign* affairs*]* **4.** *a)* not characteristic *b)* not pertinent **5.** not normally belonging *[foreign* matter in the eye*]* —**for′eign·ness** *n.*

for·eign-born (-bôrn′) *adj.* born in some other country —**the foreign-born** immigrants of a country

for·eign·er (-ər) *n.* a person from another country, thought of as an outsider; alien

foreign office in some countries, the office of government in charge of foreign affairs

fore·know (fôr nō′) *vt.* **-knew′, -known′, -know′ing** to know beforehand —**fore·know′a·ble** *adj.* —**fore·knowl·edge** (fôr′näl′ij) *n.*

fore·land (fôr′lənd) *n.* a headland; promontory

fore·leg (-leg′) *n.* either of the front legs of an animal with four or more legs

fore·limb (-lim′) *n.* a front limb, as an arm, foreleg, wing, or flipper

fore·lock (-läk′) *n.* a lock of hair growing just above the forehead

fore·man (-mən) *n., pl.* **-men** [orig., foremost man, leader] **1.** the chairman of a jury **2.** a man in charge of a department or group of workers in a factory, etc. —**fore′man·ship′** *n.*

fore·mast (fôr′mast′, -məst) *n.* the mast nearest the bow of a ship

fore·most (-mōst′) *adj.* [< OE. superl. of *forma,* superl. of *fore,* fore] **1.** first in place or time **2.** first in rank or importance —*adv.* first

fore·named (-nāmd′) *adj.* named or mentioned before

fore·noon (fôr′no͞on′) *n.* the time from sunrise to noon; morning —*adj.* of or in the forenoon

fo·ren·sic (fə ren′sik) *adj.* [< L. *forensis,* public < *forum,* marketplace] of, characteristic of, or suitable for a law court, public debate, or formal argument —*n.* [*pl.*] debate or formal argumentation —**fo·ren′si·cal·ly** *adv.*

forensic medicine *same as* MEDICAL JURISPRUDENCE

fore·or·dain (fôr′ôr dān′) *vt.* to ordain beforehand —**fore′or·di·na′tion** (-d'n ā′shən) *n.*

fore·paw (fôr′pô′) *n.* an animal's front paw

fore·quar·ter (-kwôr′tər) *n.* **1.** the front half of a side of beef or the like **2.** [*pl.*] the front quarters of a horse, etc., including the forelegs

fore·run (fôr run′) *vt.* **-ran′, -run′, -run′ning** [Rare] **1.** to run before; precede **2.** to be a sign of (a thing to follow) **3.** to forestall

fore·run·ner (fôr′run′ər, fôr run′ər) *n.* **1.** a messenger sent before or going before; herald **2.** a sign that tells or warns of something to follow **3.** *a)* a predecessor *b)* an ancestor

fore·sail (fôr′sāl′, -səl) *n.* **1.** the lowest sail on the foremast of a square-rigged ship **2.** the main triangular sail on the foremast of a fore-and-aft-rigged ship

fore·see (fôr sē′) *vt.* **-saw′, -seen′, -see′ing** to see or know beforehand —**fore·see′a·ble** *adj.* —**fore·se′er** *n.*

fore·shad·ow (-shad′ō) *vt.* to indicate or suggest beforehand; presage —**fore·shad′ow·er** *n.*

fore·shank (fôr′shaŋk′) *n.* **1.** the upper part of the front legs of cattle **2.** meat from this part

fore·sheet (-shēt′) *n.* **1.** one of the ropes used to trim a foresail **2.** [*pl.*] the space forward in an open boat

fore·shock (-shäk′) *n.* a minor earthquake preceding a greater one at or near the same place

fore·shore (-shôr′) *n.* the part of a shore between highwater mark and low-water mark

fore·short·en (fôr shôr′t'n) ***vt.*** *Drawing, Painting,* etc. to represent some lines of (an object) as shorter than they actually are in order to give the illusion of proper relative size

fore·show (-shō′) ***vt.* -showed′, -shown′** or **-showed′, -show′ing** to show or indicate beforehand

fore·sight (fôr′sīt′) ***n.*** **1.** *a)* a foreseeing *b)* the power to foresee **2.** a looking forward **3.** prudent regard or provision for the future —**fore′sight′ed *adj.*** —**fore′sight′ed·ly *adv.*** —**fore′sight′ed·ness *n.***

fore·skin (-skin′) ***n.*** the fold of skin that covers the end of the penis; prepuce

FORESHORTENED ARM

for·est (fôr′ist, fär′-) ***n.*** [OFr. < ML. (*silva*) *forestis,* as if (wood) unenclosed (< L. *foris,* out-of-doors), but prob. (wood) under court control (< L. *forum,* court)] a thick growth of trees and underbrush covering an extensive tract of land; large woods —***adj.*** of or in a forest —***vt.*** to cover with trees or woods —**for′est·ed *adj.***

fore·stall (fôr stôl′) ***vt.*** [OE. *foresteall,* ambush: see FORE & STALL[2]] **1.** to prevent by doing something ahead of time **2.** to act in advance of; anticipate —**fore·stall′er *n.*** —**fore·stall′ment *n.***

for·est·a·tion (fôr′is tā′shən, fär′-) ***n.*** the planting or care of forests

fore·stay (fôr′stā′) ***n.*** a rope or cable reaching from the head of a ship's foremast to the bowsprit, for supporting the foremast

for·est·er (fôr′is tər, fär′-) ***n.*** **1.** a person trained in forestry or charged with the care of a forest **2.** a person or animal that lives in a forest

for·est·ry (-trē) ***n.*** **1.** [Rare] forest land **2.** the science of planting and taking care of forests **3.** systematic forest management for the production of timber, conservation, etc.

fore·taste (fôr′tāst′; *for v.* fôr tāst′) ***n.*** a taste or sample of what can be expected —***vt.* -tast′ed, -tast′ing** [Rare] to taste beforehand

fore·tell (fôr tel′) ***vt.* -told′, -tell′ing** to tell or indicate beforehand; predict —**fore·tell′er *n.***

fore·thought (fôr′thôt′) ***n.*** **1.** a thinking or planning beforehand **2.** foresight; prudence —**fore′thought′ful *adj.*** —**fore′thought′ful·ly *adv.***

fore·to·ken (fôr′tō′kən; *for v.* fôr tō′kən) ***n.*** a prophetic sign; omen —***vt.*** to foreshadow

fore·top (fôr′täp′, -təp) ***n.*** the platform at the top of a ship's foremast

fore-top·gal·lant (fôr′täp gal′ənt, fôr′tə-) ***adj.*** designating or of the mast, sail, yard, etc. just above the fore-topmast

fore-top·mast (fôr täp′mast′, -məst) ***n.*** the section of mast extending above the foremast

fore-top·sail (-sāl′, -s'l) ***n.*** a sail set on the fore-topmast, above the foresail

for·ev·er (fər ev′ər, fôr-) ***adv.*** **1.** for eternity; for always; endlessly **2.** at all times; always Also **for·ev′er·more′** (-môr′)

fore·warn (fôr wôrn′) ***vt.*** to warn beforehand

fore·wing (fôr′wiŋ′) ***n.*** either of the front pair of wings in most insects

fore·word (-wurd′, -wərd) ***n.*** an introductory remark, preface, or prefatory note

for·feit (fôr′fit) ***n.*** [< OFr. < *forfaire,* to transgress, ult. < L. *foris,* beyond + *facere,* to do] **1.** something that one has to give up because of some crime, fault, or neglect; fine; penalty **2.** the act of forfeiting —***adj.*** lost or taken away as a forfeit —***vt.*** to lose or be deprived of as a forfeit —**for′feit·a·ble *adj.*** —**for′feit·er *n.***

for·fei·ture (fôr′fə chər) ***n.*** **1.** a forfeiting **2.** anything forfeited; penalty or fine

for·gath·er (fôr gath′ər) ***vi.*** **1.** to come together **2.** to meet by chance **3.** to be friendly (*with*)

for·gave (fər gāv′, fôr-) *pt. of* FORGIVE

forge[1] (fôrj) ***n.*** [< OFr. < L. *fabrica,* workshop < *faber,* workman] **1.** a furnace for heating metal to be wrought **2.** a place where metal is heated and hammered or wrought into shape; smithy **3.** a place where wrought iron is made, as from iron ore —***vt.* forged, forg′ing** **1.** to shape (metal) by blows or pressure, usually after heating **2.** to form; shape; produce **3.** to imitate for purposes of deception or fraud; esp., to counterfeit (a check, etc.) —***vi.*** **1.** to work at a forge **2.** to commit forgery —**forg′er *n.***

forge[2] (fôrj) ***vt., vi.* forged, forg′ing** [prob. altered < FORCE] **1.** to move forward steadily, as if against difficulties **2.** to move in a sudden spurt Often with *ahead*

for·ger·y (fôr′jər ē) ***n.,*** *pl.* **-ger·ies** **1.** the act or legal offense of forging documents, signatures, works of art, etc. to deceive **2.** anything forged

for·get (fər get′, fôr-) ***vt.* -got′** or archaic **-gat′** (-gat′), **-got′ten** or **-got′, -get′ting** [OE. *forgietan*] **1.** to lose (facts, etc.) from the mind; be unable to remember **2.** to overlook or neglect, either unintentionally or intentionally —***vi.*** to forget things —**forget it** don't trouble to think about it —**forget oneself** **1.** to think only of others **2.** to behave in an improper or unseemly manner —**for·get′ta·ble *adj.*** —**for·get′ter *n.***

for·get·ful (-f'l) ***adj.*** **1.** apt to forget; having a poor memory **2.** negligent **3.** [Poet.] causing to forget —**for·get′ful·ly *adv.*** —**for·get′ful·ness *n.***

for·get-me-not (-mē nät′) ***n.*** a marsh plant with clusters of small blue, white, or pink flowers

for·give (fər giv′, fôr-) ***vt.* -gave′, -giv′en, -giv′ing** [OE. *forgiefan*] **1.** to give up resentment against or the desire to punish; pardon **2.** to overlook (an offense) **3.** to cancel (a debt) —***vi.*** to show forgiveness —**for·giv′a·ble *adj.*** —**for·giv′er *n.***

for·give·ness (-nis) ***n.*** **1.** a forgiving; pardon **2.** inclination to forgive

for·giv·ing (-iŋ) ***adj.*** that forgives; inclined to forgive —**for·giv′ing·ly *adv.*** —**for·giv′ing·ness *n.***

for·go (fôr gō′) ***vt.* -went′, -gone′, -go′ing** [OE. *forgan*] to do without; abstain from —**for·go′er *n.***

for·got (fər gät′, fôr-) *pt. & alt. pp. of* FORGET

for·got·ten (-'n) *pp. of* FORGET

for·int (fôr′int) ***n.*** *see* MONETARY UNITS, table (Hungary)

fork (fôrk) ***n.*** [OE. *forca* & Anglo-Fr. *forque,* both < L. *furca,* hayfork] **1.** an instrument with a handle and two or more prongs, used as an eating utensil or, in much larger form, for pitching hay, etc. **2.** something resembling a fork in shape: cf. TUNING FORK **3.** a division into branches; bifurcation **4.** the point where a river, road, etc. is divided into branches **5.** any of these branches —***vi.*** to divide into branches —***vt.*** **1.** to make into the form of a fork **2.** to pick up, spear, or pitch with a fork —**fork over** (or **out, up**) [Colloq.] to pay out; hand over —**fork′ful′ *n.,*** *pl.* **-fuls′**

forked (fôrkt) ***adj.*** **1.** having a fork or forks; cleft *[forked lightning]* **2.** having prongs *[five-forked]* Also **fork′y -i·er, -i·est**

forked tongue [prob. transl. of AmInd. expression] lying or deceitful talk *[to speak with a forked tongue]*

fork·lift (fôrk′lift′) ***n.*** a device, often on a truck (**forklift truck**), for lifting, stacking, etc. heavy objects: its projecting prongs are slid under the load and raised or lowered

for·lorn (fər lôrn′, fôr-) ***adj.*** [< OE. pp. of *forleosan,* to lose utterly] **1.** abandoned or deserted **2.** wretched; miserable; pitiful **3.** without hope; desperate **4.** bereft (*of*) —**for·lorn′ly *adv.*** —**for·lorn′ness *n.***

form (fôrm) ***n.*** [< OFr. < L. *forma*] **1.** the shape, outline, or configuration of anything; structure **2.** *a)* the body or figure of a person or animal *b)* a model of a human figure used as a clothes dummy **3.** anything used to give shape to something else; mold, as for poured concrete **4.** the mode of existence a thing has or takes *[water in the form of vapor]* **5.** arrangement; esp., orderly arrangement, often of a specified kind **6.** a way of doing something *[one's golf form]* **7.** a customary way of acting or behaving; ceremony; formality **8.** a fixed order of words; formula **9.** a printed document with blank spaces to be filled in **10.** a particular kind, type, species, or variety **11.** a condition of mind or body *[a boxer in good form]* **12.** *a)* a chart giving information about horses in a race *b)* what can be expected, based on past performances *[to react according to form]* **13.** a long, wooden bench, as formerly in a schoolroom **14.** a grade or class in school in some private and British schools **15.** *Gram.* any of the different appearances of a word in changes of inflection, spelling, etc. *["am" is a form of "be"]* **16.** *Printing* the type, plates, etc. locked in a frame for printing —***vt.*** **1.** to shape; fashion; make, as in some particular way **2.** to train; instruct **3.** to develop (habits) **4.** to think of; conceive **5.** to organize into *[to form a club]* **6.** to make up; constitute —***vi.*** **1.** to be formed **2.** to come into being; take form **3.** to take a specific form —**good** (or **bad**) **form** conduct in (or not in) accord with social custom

-form (fôrm) [< OFr. < L. *-formis* < *forma,* form] *a suffix meaning:* **1.** having the form of *[cuneiform]* **2.** having (a specified number of) forms *[multiform]*

for·mal (fôr′məl) ***adj.*** [L. *formalis*] **1.** of external form or structure, rather than nature or content **2.** according to fixed customs, rules, etc. **3.** *a)* appearing to be suitable, correct, etc. but not really so *b)* stiff in manner **4.** *a)* designed for wear at ceremonies, etc. *[formal dress]* *b)* requiring such clothes *[a formal dance]* **5.** done or made in orderly, regular fashion; methodical **6.** rigidly symmetrical *[a formal garden]* **7.** done or made according to the forms that make explicit, definite, etc. *[a formal contract]* **8.** designating education in schools, colleges, etc. **9.** designating or of that level of language usage characterized by expanded vocabulary, complete syntactical constructions, complex sentences, etc.: distinguished from COLLOQUIAL —***n.*** **1.** a formal dance or ball **2.** a woman's evening dress —**go formal** [Colloq.] to go dressed in evening clothes —**for′mal·ly** ***adv.***

form·al·de·hyde (fôr mal′də hīd′, fər-) ***n.*** [FORM(IC) + ALDEHYDE] a colorless, pungent gas, HCHO, used in solution as a disinfectant and preservative

for·mal·ism (fôr′məl iz′m) ***n.*** strict attention to outward forms and customs, as in art or religion —**for′mal·ist** ***n., adj.*** —**for′mal·is′tic** ***adj.***

for·mal·i·ty (fôr mal′ə tē) ***n.,*** *pl.* **-ties** **1.** a being formal; specif., *a)* an observing of prescribed customs, rules, ceremonies, etc.; propriety *b)* careful or too careful attention to order, regularity, or convention; stiffness **2.** a formal or conventional act or requirement; ceremony or form

for·mal·ize (fôr′mə līz′) ***vt.*** **-ized′, -iz′ing** **1.** to give definite form to **2.** to make formal **3.** to make official, valid, etc. —**for′mal·i·za′tion** ***n.***

for·mat (fôr′mat) ***n.*** [G. < L. pp. of *formare,* to form] **1.** the shape, size, and general makeup of a book, magazine, etc. **2.** general arrangement, as of a television program

for·ma·tion (fôr mā′shən) ***n.*** **1.** a forming or being formed **2.** a thing formed **3.** the way in which something is formed or arranged; structure **4.** an arrangement or positioning, as of troops, ships, a football team, etc. **5.** *Ecol.* the major unit of vegetation, as the prairie, tundra, etc. **6.** *Geol.* a rock unit having some common character, as origin

form·a·tive (fôr′mə tiv) ***adj.*** **1.** helping to shape, develop, or mold *[a formative* influence*]* **2.** of formation or development *[*one's *formative* years*]* **3.** *Linguis.* serving to form words, as an affix

form class *Linguis.* a class made up of words having a distinctive position in constructions and certain formal features in common

for·mer[1] (fôr′mər) ***adj.*** [ME. *formere,* compar. of *forme,* first < OE. *forma:* see FOREMOST] **1.** preceding in time; earlier; past **2.** first mentioned of two: opposed to LATTER: often a noun (with *the*)

form·er[2] (fôr′mər) ***n.*** a person or thing that forms

for·mer·ly (fôr′mər lē) ***adv.*** at or in a former or earlier time; in the past

for·mic (fôr′mik) ***adj.*** [< L. *formica,* an ant] **1.** of ants **2.** designating or of a colorless acid, HCOOH, found in ants, spiders, nettles, etc.

For·mi·ca (fôr mī′kə) [arbitrary coinage] *a trademark for* a laminated, heat-resistant plastic used for table tops, etc.

for·mi·da·ble (fôr′mə də b′l) ***adj.*** [OFr. < L. < *formidare,* to dread] **1.** causing fear or dread **2.** hard to handle or overcome **3.** awe-inspiring in size, excellence, etc. —**for′mi·da·bil′i·ty, for′mi·da·ble·ness** ***n.*** —**for′mi·da·bly** ***adv.***

form·less (fôrm′lis) ***adj.*** having no regular form or plan —**form′less·ly** ***adv.*** —**form′less·ness** ***n.***

form letter one of a number of duplicated letters, with the date, address, etc. filled in separately

For·mo·sa (fôr mō′sə, -zə) *former (Portuguese) name of* TAIWAN —**For·mo′san** ***adj., n.***

for·mu·la (fôr′myə lə) ***n.,*** *pl.* **-las, -lae′** (-lē′) [L., dim. of *forma,* form] **1.** a fixed form of words, esp. one that is used only as a conventional expression *[*"Very truly yours" is a *formula]* **2.** a rule or method for doing something, esp. when conventional and used or repeated without thought **3.** an exact statement of religious faith or doctrine **4.** *a)* a prescription for a medicine, a baby's food, etc. *b)* something, esp. fortified milk for a baby, prepared from a prescription **5.** a set of algebraic symbols expressing a mathematical fact, rule, etc. **6.** *Chem.* an expression of the composition, as of a compound, by a combination of symbols and figures —***adj.*** designating or of any of various classes of racing car designed to conform to a particular set of specifications governing size, weight, etc.

for·mu·lar·ize (-lə rīz′) ***vt.*** **-ized′, -iz′ing** *same as* FORMULATE (sense 1)

for·mu·lar·y (fôr′myə ler′ē) ***n.,*** *pl.* **-lar′ies** **1.** a collection of formulas or prescribed forms, as of prayers **2.** a formula **3.** *Pharmacy* a list of medicines with their formulas —***adj.*** of formulas

for·mu·late (-lāt′) ***vt.*** **-lat′ed, -lat′ing** **1.** to express in or reduce to a formula **2.** to express (a theory, plan, etc.) in a systematic way —**for′mu·la′tion** ***n.*** —**for′mu·la′tor** ***n.***

for·mu·lize (-līz′) ***vt.*** **-lized′, -liz′ing** *same as* FORMULATE (sense 1)

for·ni·cate (fôr′nə kāt′) ***vi.*** **-cat′ed, -cat′ing** [< LL. pp. of *fornicari* < L. *fornix* (gen. *fornicis*), a brothel] to commit fornication —**for′ni·ca′tor** ***n.***

for·ni·ca·tion (fôr′nə kā′shən) ***n.*** **1.** voluntary sexual intercourse between unmarried persons **2.** *Bible* any unlawful sexual intercourse

for·sake (fər sāk′, fôr-) ***vt.*** **-sook′** (-so͝ok′), **-sak′en, -sak′ing** [< OE. < *for-,* FOR- + *sacan,* to strive < *sacu:* see SAKE[1]] **1.** to give up; renounce (a habit, idea, etc.) **2.** to leave; abandon

for·sak·en (-sā′kən) ***adj.*** abandoned; desolate

for·sooth (fər so͞oth′, fôr-) ***adv.*** [OE. *forsoth*] [Archaic] in truth; no doubt; indeed

For·ster (fôr′stər), **E(dward) M(organ)** 1879–1970; Eng. novelist

for·swear (fôr swer′) ***vt.*** **-swore′** (-swôr′), **-sworn′, -swear′ing** **1.** to swear or promise earnestly to give up **2.** to deny earnestly or on oath —***vi.*** to swear falsely; commit perjury —**forswear oneself** to perjure oneself

for·syth·i·a (fər sith′ē ə, fôr-) ***n.*** [ModL., after W. *Forsyth,* 18th-c. Eng. botanist] a shrub of the olive family with yellow, bell-shaped flowers, which appear in early spring before the leaves

fort (fôrt) ***n.*** [OFr. < L. *fortis,* strong] **1.** a fortified place or building for military defense **2.** a permanent army post

For·ta·le·za (fôr′tə lā′zə) seaport in NE Brazil, on the Atlantic: pop. 515,000

forte[1] (fôrt) ***n.*** [< OFr.: see FORT] that which one does particularly well; one's strong point

for·te[2] (fôr′tā, -tē) ***adj., adv.*** [It. < L. *fortis,* strong] *Music* loud: a direction to the performer —***n.*** a forte note or passage

Forth (fôrth) river in SE Scotland, flowing through a long estuary **(Firth of Forth)** into the North Sea

forth (fôrth) ***adv.*** [OE.] **1.** forward; onward **2.** out into view, as from hiding —**and so forth** and so on: equivalent to *etc.*

forth·com·ing (fôrth′kum′iŋ) ***adj.*** **1.** about to appear; approaching **2.** ready when needed *[*help was not *forthcoming]* —***n.*** a coming forth; approach

forth·right (-rīt′) ***adj.*** straightforward; direct; frank —***adv.*** straight forward; directly onward —**forth′right′ly** ***adv.*** —**forth′right′ness** ***n.***

forth·with (fôrth′with′, -*with*′) ***adv.*** immediately

for·ti·eth (fôr′tē ith) ***adj.*** **1.** preceded by thirty-nine others in a series; 40th **2.** designating any of the forty equal parts of something —***n.*** **1.** the one following the thirty-ninth **2.** any of the forty equal parts of something; 1/40

for·ti·fi·ca·tion (fôr′tə fi kā′shən) ***n.*** **1.** the act or science of fortifying **2.** a fort or defensive earthwork, wall, etc. **3.** a fortified place

for·ti·fy (fôr′tə fī′) ***vt.*** **-fied′, -fy′ing** [< OFr. < LL. *fortificare* < L. *fortis,* strong + *facere,* to make] **1.** to strengthen physically, emotionally, etc. **2.** to strengthen against attack, as by building forts, walls, etc. **3.** to support; corroborate (an argument, etc.) **4.** to strengthen (wine, etc.) by adding alcohol **5.** to add vitamins, minerals, etc. to (milk, etc.) so as to increase the food value —***vi.*** to build military defenses —**for′ti·fi′a·ble** ***adj.***

for·tis·si·mo (fôr tis′ə mō′) ***adj., adv.*** [It., superl. of *forte,* FORTE[2]] *Music* very loud: a direction to the performer —***n.,*** *pl.* **-mos′, -mi′** (-mē′) a fortissimo note or passage

for·ti·tude (fôr′tə to͞od′, -tyo͞od′) ***n.*** [< L. < *fortis,* strong] patient endurance of misfortune, pain, etc.; firm courage —**for′ti·tu′di·nous** ***adj.***

Fort Knox [see KNOXVILLE] military reservation in N Ky., near Louisville: site of U.S. gold bullion depository

Fort Lau·der·dale (lô′dər dāl′) [after Maj. Wm. *Lauderdale*] city on the SE coast of Fla.: pop. 153,000 (met. area 1,006,000)

fort·night (fôrt′nīt′) ***n.*** [< OE., lit., fourteen nights] [Chiefly Brit.] two weeks

fort·night·ly (-lē) ***adv., adj.*** [Chiefly Brit.] (happening or appearing) once every fortnight, or at two-week intervals —***n.,*** *pl.* **-lies** a periodical issued at two-week intervals

for·tress (fôr′trəs) ***n.*** [< OFr., ult. < L. *fortis,* strong] a fortified place; fort: often used figuratively —***vt.*** to protect by a fortress

Fort Smith [after Gen. T. *Smith,* d. 1865] city in W Ark., on the Arkansas River: pop. 71,000

for·tu·i·tous (fôr to͞o′ə təs, -tyo͞o′-) ***adj.*** [< L. < *fors* (gen. *fortis*), luck] **1.** happening by chance; accidental **2.** bringing, or happening by, good luck; fortunate —**for·tu′i·tous·ly** ***adv.*** —**for·tu′i·tous·ness** ***n.***

for·tu·i·ty (-tē) ***n.,*** *pl.* **-ties** [< L. (see prec.) + -ITY] **1.** a being fortuitous **2.** chance or chance occurrence

for·tu·nate (fôr′chə nit) ***adj.*** [< L. pp. of *fortunare* < *fortuna,* FORTUNE] **1.** having good luck; lucky **2.** bringing, or coming by, good luck; favorable —**for′tu·nate·ly** ***adv.*** —**for′tu·nate·ness** ***n.***

for·tune (fôr′chən) ***n.*** [OFr. < L. *fortuna* < *fors* (gen. *fortis*), luck] **1.** the supposed power that brings good or bad to people; luck; chance; fate: often personified **2.** what happens to one; one's lot, esp. future lot, good or bad *[*to tell one's *fortune]* **3.** good luck; success **4.** wealth; riches —**for′tune·less** ***adj.***

fortune cookie a hollow Chinese cookie with a slip of paper inside predicting the future

fortune hunter a person who tries to become rich, esp. by marrying a rich person

for·tune·tell·er (-tel′ər) *n.* a person who professes to foretell events in other people's lives —**for′tune·tell′ing** *n., adj.*

Fort Wayne [after Anthony WAYNE] city in NE Ind.: pop. 172,000

Fort Worth [after Wm. *Worth* (1794–1849)] city in N Tex.: pop. 385,000: see DALLAS

for·ty (fôr′tē) *adj.* [OE. *feowertig*] four times ten —*n., pl.* **-ties** the cardinal number between thirty-nine and forty-one; 40; XL —**the forties** the numbers or years, as of a century, from forty through forty-nine

for·ty-nin·er (fôr′tē nī′nər) *n.* [*also* **F- N-**] [Colloq.] a participant in the 1849 California gold rush

forty winks [Colloq.] a short sleep; nap

fo·rum (fôr′əm) *n., pl.* **-rums, -ra** (-ə) [L.] **1.** the public square or marketplace of an ancient Roman city, where legal and political business was conducted **2.** a law court; tribunal **3.** *a)* an assembly or program for the discussion of public matters *b)* an opportunity for open discussion —**the Forum** the forum of ancient Rome

for·ward (fôr′wərd) *adj.* [OE. *foreweard*] **1.** at, toward, or of the front **2.** advanced; specif., *a)* mentally advanced *b)* advanced socially, politically, etc. **3.** onward; advancing **4.** ready or eager; prompt **5.** too bold; presumptuous **6.** of or for the future [*forward* buying] —*adv.* **1.** toward the front; ahead **2.** toward the future [to look *forward*] **3.** into view or prominence —*n. Basketball, Hockey,* etc. any of the players in a front position —*vt.* **1.** to promote **2.** to send; transmit; dispatch **3.** to send on to another address [to *forward* mail] —**for′ward·er** *n.* —**for′ward·ly** *adv.* —**for′ward·ness** *n.*

forward pass *Football* a pass from behind the line of scrimmage to a teammate in a forward position

for·wards (-wərdz) *adv. same as* FORWARD

for·went (fôr went′) *pt. of* FORGO

fos·sa (fäs′ə) *n., pl.* **-sae** (-ē) [ModL. < L., a ditch] *Anat.* a cavity, pit, or small hollow —**fos′sate** (-āt) *adj.*

fosse, foss (fôs, fäs) *n.* [< OFr. < L. *fossa,* ditch] a ditch or moat, esp. in fortifications

fos·sil (fäs′'l, fôs′-) *n.* [< Fr. < L. *fossilis,* dug up < pp. of *fodere,* to dig up] **1.** any hardened remains or traces of plant or animal life of some previous geological age, preserved in the earth's crust **2.** anything like a fossil **3.** a person who has outmoded, fixed ideas —*adj.* **1.** of, like, or forming a fossil **2.** dug from the earth [coal is a *fossil* fuel] **3.** antiquated —**fos′sil·like′** *adj.*

fos·sil·if·er·ous (fäs′ə lif′ər əs, fôs′-) *adj.* [< FOSSIL + -FEROUS] containing fossils

fos·sil·ize (fäs′ə līz′, fôs′-) *vt.* **-ized′, -iz′ing** **1.** to change into a fossil; petrify **2.** to make out of date, rigid, or incapable of change —*vi.* to become fossilized —**fos′sil·i·za′tion** *n.*

fos·ter (fôs′tər, fäs′-) *vt.* [OE. *fostrian,* to nourish < base of *foda,* food] **1.** to bring up with care; rear **2.** to help to develop; promote [to *foster* discontent] **3.** to cherish [to *foster* a hope] —*adj.* **1.** having the standing of a specified member of the family but not by birth or adoption [a *foster* child] **2.** of or relating to the care of such a person [*foster* home] —**fos′ter·er** *n.*

Fos·ter (fôs′tər, fäs′-), **Stephen Collins** 1826–64; U.S. composer of songs

fought (fôt) *pt. & pp. of* FIGHT

foul (foul) *adj.* [OE. *ful*] **1.** stinking; loathsome [a *foul* odor] **2.** extremely dirty; disgustingly filthy **3.** full of dirt or foreign objects [a *foul* pipe] **4.** rotten: said of food **5.** not decent; obscene [*foul* language] **6.** wicked; abominable **7.** stormy; unfavorable [*foul* weather] **8.** tangled; caught [a *foul* rope] **9.** not according to the rules of a game; unfair **10.** treacherous; dishonest **11.** [Colloq.] unpleasant, disagreeable, etc. **12.** *Baseball* not fair: see FOUL BALL, FOUL LINE **13.** *Printing* marked for errors or changes [*foul* copy] —*adv.* in a foul way —*n.* anything foul; specif., *a)* a collision of boats, contestants, etc. *b)* an infraction of rules, as of a game *c) Baseball same as* FOUL BALL —*vt.* **1.** to make foul; dirty; soil **2.** to dishonor or disgrace **3.** to obstruct; fill up [grease *fouls* sink drains] **4.** to cover (a ship's bottom) with impeding growths **5.** to entangle; catch [a rope *fouled* in the shrouds] **6.** to collide with **7.** to make a foul against, as in a game **8.** *Baseball* to bat (the ball) so that it falls outside the foul lines —*vi.* **1.** to be or become fouled (in various senses) **2.** to break the rules of a game **3.** *Baseball* to hit a foul ball —**foul out** **1.** *Baseball* to be put out by the catch of a foul ball **2.** *Basketball* to be disqualified for a certain number of personal fouls —**foul up** [Colloq.] to entangle or bungle —**run** (or **fall** or **go**) **foul of** **1.** to collide with and become tangled in **2.** to get into trouble with —**foul′ly** *adv.* —**foul′ness** *n.*

fou·lard (fo͞o lärd′) *n.* [Fr.] **1.** a lightweight material of silk, rayon, or sometimes cotton **2.** a necktie, scarf, etc. of this material

foul ball *Baseball* a batted ball that is not a fair ball: see FAIR BALL

foul line **1.** *Baseball* either of the lines extending from home plate through the outside corners of first base or third base and onward along the outfield **2.** *Basketball* the line from which a player makes throws granted to him when he is fouled **3.** *Tennis, Bowling,* etc. any of various lines bounding the playing area, beyond which the ball must not be hit, the player must not go, etc.

foul play **1.** unfair play; action that breaks the rules of the game **2.** treacherous action or violence

found[1] (found) *pt. & pp. of* FIND

found[2] (found) *vt.* [< OFr. < L. < *fundus,* bottom] **1.** to set for support; base [a statement *founded* on facts] **2.** to begin to build or organize; establish [to *found* a college] —*vi.* [Rare] to be based (*on* or *upon*)

found[3] (found) *vt.* [< OFr. < L. *fundere,* to pour] **1.** to melt and pour (metal) into a mold **2.** to make by pouring molten metal into a mold; cast

foun·da·tion (foun dā′shən) *n.* **1.** a founding or being founded; establishment **2.** *a)* a fund or endowment to maintain a hospital, charity, research, etc. *b)* the organization administering such a fund **3.** the base on which something rests; specif., the supporting part of a wall, house, etc. **4.** basis **5.** a woman's corset or girdle: also **foundation garment** **6.** a cosmetic cream, liquid, etc. over which other makeup is applied —**foun·da′tion·al** *adj.*

foun·der[1] (foun′dər) *vi.* [< OFr. < L. *fundus:* see FOUND[2]] **1.** to stumble, fall, or go lame **2.** to become stuck as in soft ground **3.** to fill with water and sink: said of a ship **4.** to break down; collapse; fail —*vt.* to cause to founder

found·er[2] (foun′dər) *n.* a person who founds, or establishes

found·er[3] (foun′dər) *n.* a person who founds metals

found·ling (found′liŋ) *n.* an infant of unknown parents that has been found abandoned

found·ry (foun′drē) *n., pl.* **-ries** **1.** the act or work of founding metals; casting **2.** metal castings **3.** a place where metal is cast

fount (fount) *n.* [< OFr. < L. *fons,* FOUNTAIN] **1.** [Poet.] a fountain or spring **2.** a source

foun·tain (foun′t'n) *n.* [< OFr. < LL. *fontana* < L. < *fons* (gen. *fontis*), spring] **1.** a natural spring of water **2.** a source or origin of anything **3.** *a)* an artificial spring, jet, or flow of water *b)* the basin, pipes, etc. where this flows *c) same as* DRINKING FOUNTAIN *d) same as* SODA FOUNTAIN **4.** a container or reservoir, as for ink, oil, etc.

foun·tain·head (-hed′) *n.* **1.** a spring that is the source of a stream **2.** the original or main source of anything

fountain pen a pen which is fed ink from a supply in a reservoir or cartridge

four (fôr) *adj.* [OE. *feower*] totaling one more than three —*n.* **1.** the cardinal number between three and five; 4; IV **2.** anything having four units or members, or numbered four —**on all fours** **1.** on all four feet **2.** on hands and knees (or feet)

four-flush (fôr′flush′) *vi.* **1.** *Stud Poker* to bluff when one holds four cards of the same suit (**four flush**) instead of the five in a true flush **2.** [Colloq.] to bluff —**four′-flush′er** *n.*

four·fold (-fōld′) *adj.* [see -FOLD] **1.** having four parts **2.** having four times as much or as many —*adv.* four times as much or as many

four-foot·ed (-foot′id) *adj.* having four feet

Four-H club, 4-H club (fôr′āch′) a rural youth organization offering instruction in scientific agriculture and home economics

four hundred [*also* **F- H-**] the exclusive social set of a particular place (preceded by *the*)

four-in-hand (-in hand′) *n.* **1.** *a)* a team of four horses driven by one man *b)* a coach drawn by such a team **2.** a necktie tied in a slipknot with the ends left hanging —*adj.* of a four-in-hand

four-o'clock (-ə kläk′) *n.* a garden plant with long-tubed, variously colored flowers that generally open in the late afternoon

four-post·er (-pōs′tər) *n.* a bedstead with tall corner posts often supporting a canopy or curtains

four·score (-skôr′) *adj., n.* four times twenty; eighty

four·some (-səm) *n.* **1.** a group of four people **2.** *Golf* a game involving four players

four·square (-skwer′) *adj.* **1.** perfectly square **2.** unyielding; firm **3.** frank; forthright —*adv.* **1.** in a square form **2.** forthrightly

four·teen (-tēn′) *adj.* [OE. *feowertyne*] four more than ten —*n.* the cardinal number between thirteen and fifteen; 14; XIV

four·teenth (-tēnth′) *adj.* **1.** preceded by thirteen others in a series; 14th **2.** designating any of the fourteen equal parts of something —*n.* **1.** the one following the thirteenth **2.** any of the fourteen equal parts of something; 1/14

fourth (fôrth) *adj.* [< OE.] **1.** preceded by three others in a series; 4th **2.** designating any of the four equal parts of something *—n.* **1.** the one following the third **2.** any of the four equal parts of something; 1/4 **3.** the fourth forward gear ratio of a motor vehicle **4.** *Music a)* the fourth tone of an ascending diatonic scale, or a tone three degrees above or below a given tone *b)* the interval between two such tones, or a combination of them **—fourth′ly** *adv.*

fourth dimension a dimension in addition to those of length, width, and depth: in the theory of relativity, time is regarded as this dimension **—fourth′-di·men′sion·al** *adj.*

fourth estate [cf. ESTATE (sense 2)] [*often* **F- E-**] journalism or journalists

Fourth of July *see* INDEPENDENCE DAY

fourth world [*often* **F- W-**] the poorest, most underdeveloped countries of the third world

fowl (foul) *n., pl.* **fowls, fowl:** see PLURAL, II, D, 1 [OE. *fugol*] **1.** any bird: used in combination [wild*fowl*] **2.** any of the larger domestic birds used as food, as the chicken, duck, turkey, etc. **3.** the flesh of any of these birds used for food *—vi.* to hunt wild birds for food or sport **—fowl′er** *n.* **—fowl′ing** *n., adj.*

fowling piece a shotgun for hunting wild fowl

fox (fäks) *n., pl.* **fox′es, fox:** see PLURAL, II, D, 1 [OE.] **1.** a small, wild, flesh-eating mammal of the dog family, with a bushy tail: thought of as sly and crafty **2.** its fur, commonly reddish-brown or gray **3.** a sly, crafty person *—vt.* **1.** to stain (book leaves, prints, etc.) with brownish discolorations **2.** to trick by slyness or craftiness **3.** to bewilder or baffle **—foxed** *adj.*

fox fire the luminescence of decaying wood and plant remains, caused by various fungi

FOX (average length 42 in., including tail)

fox·glove (fäks′gluv′) *n.* [OE. *foxes glofa*] *same as* DIGITALIS (sense 1)

fox·hole (-hōl′) *n.* a hole dug in the ground as a temporary protection for one or two soldiers against enemy gunfire or tanks

fox·hound (-hound′) *n.* a strong, swift hound with a keen scent, bred and trained to hunt foxes

fox·tail (-tāl′) *n.* **1.** the tail of a fox **2.** a grass having spikes bearing spikelets interspersed with stiff bristles

fox terrier a small, active terrier with a smooth or wire-haired coat, formerly trained to drive foxes out of hiding

fox trot **1.** a horse gait that is a shuffling half-walk, half-trot **2.** *a)* a dance for couples in 4/4 time with a variety of steps, both fast and slow *b)* the music for such a dance **—fox′-trot′** *vi.* **-trot′ted, -trot′ting**

fox·y (fäk′sē) *adj.* **fox′i·er, fox′i·est** **1.** foxlike; crafty; sly **2.** covered with brownish stains **3.** [Slang] attractive, stylish, etc.; specif., sexually attractive: used esp. of women **—fox′i·ly** *adv.* **—fox′i·ness** *n.*

foy·er (foi′ər, foi′ā, foi yā′) *n.* [Fr. < ML. < L. *focus,* hearth] an entrance hall or a lobby, as in a theater or hotel

F.P., f.p., fp foot-pound; foot-pounds

f.p., fp, fp. freezing point

FPO *U.S. Navy* Fleet Post Office

fps, f.p.s. **1.** feet per second **2.** foot-pound-second

Fr *Chem.* francium

Fr. **1.** Father **2.** France **3.** French **4.** Friday

fr. franc; francs

Fra (frä) *n.* [It., abbrev. of *frate* < L. *frater*] brother: title given to an Italian friar or monk

fra·cas (frā′kəs, frak′əs) *n.* [Fr. < It. < *fracassare,* to smash] a noisy fight or loud quarrel; brawl

frac·tion (frak′shən) *n.* [< L. < pp. of *frangere,* to break] **1.** a small part, amount, etc.; portion; fragment **2.** *Chem.* a part separated, as by distillation, from a mixture, at its particular boiling point, etc. **3.** *Math. a)* an indicated quotient of two whole numbers, as 1/2, 13/4 *b)* any quantity expressed in terms of a numerator and denominator, as 2x/xy **—frac′tion·al** *adj.* **—frac′tion·al·ly** *adv.*

frac·tion·ate (-āt′) *vt.* **-at′ed, -at′ing** **1.** to separate into fractions, or parts **2.** *Chem.* to separate into fractions by distillation, etc. **—frac′tion·a′tion** *n.*

frac·tious (frak′shəs) *adj.* [prob. < *fraction,* (obs.) discord + -OUS] **1.** unruly; rebellious; refractory **2.** peevish; irritable; cross **—frac′tious·ly** *adv.* **—frac′tious·ness** *n.*

frac·ture (frak′chər) *n.* [< OFr. < L. *fractura* < pp. of *frangere,* to break] **1.** a breaking or being broken **2.** a break, crack, or split **3.** a break in a bone or, occasionally, a tear in a cartilage **4.** the texture of the broken surface of a mineral *—vt., vi.* **-tured, -tur·ing** **1.** to break, crack, or split **2.** to disrupt **—frac′tur·al** *adj.*

frae (frā) *prep.* [Scot.] from

frag·ile (fraj′'l; *chiefly Brit. & Canad.,* -īl) *adj.* [< OFr. < L. *fragilis* < *frangere,* to break] easily broken, damaged, or destroyed; frail; delicate **—fra·gil·i·ty** (frə jil′ə tē) *n.*

frag·ment (frag′mənt; *for v. also* frag ment′) *n.* [< L. < *frangere,* to break] **1.** a part broken away; broken piece **2.** a detached or incomplete part [a *fragment* of a novel] *—vt., vi.* to break into fragments **—frag′ment·ed** *adj.*

frag·men·tar·y (frag′mən ter′ē) *adj.* consisting of fragments or bits; not complete; disconnected: also **frag·men′tal** (-men′təl) **—frag′men·tar′i·ly** *adv.*

frag·men·tate (-tāt′) *vt., vi.* **-tat′ed, -tat′ing** to break into fragments **—frag′men·ta′tion** *n.*

fra·grance (frā′grəns) *n.* a fragrant smell; pleasant odor

fra·grant (frā′grənt) *adj.* [< L. prp. of *fragrare,* to emit a (sweet) smell] having a pleasant odor; sweet-smelling **—fra′grant·ly** *adv.*

fraid·y-cat (frā′dē kat′) *n.* [< AFRAID + CAT] [Colloq.] a person easily frightened: a child's term

frail (frāl) *adj.* [< OFr. < L. *fragilis,* FRAGILE] **1.** easily broken, damaged, or destroyed; fragile; delicate **2.** slender and delicate; not robust; weak **3.** easily tempted to do wrong; morally weak *—n.* [Slang] a woman or girl **—frail′ly** *adv.* **—frail′ness** *n.*

frail·ty (frāl′tē) *n.* **1.** the condition of being frail; weakness; esp., moral weakness **2.** *pl.* **-ties** any fault or failing arising from such weaknesses

frame (frām) *vt.* **framed, fram′ing** [prob. < ON. *frami,* profit, benefit; some senses < OE. *framian,* to be helpful] **1.** to shape or form according to a pattern; design [to *frame* a constitution] **2.** to put together the parts of; construct **3.** to put into words; compose; devise **4.** to adjust; fit [a tax *framed* to benefit a few] **5.** to enclose (a picture, mirror, etc.) in a border **6.** [Colloq.] to falsify evidence, testimony, etc. beforehand so as to make (an innocent person) appear guilty *—n.* **1.** *a)* formerly, anything made of parts fitted together according to a design *b)* body structure in general; build **2.** skeletal or basic, supporting structure; framework, as of a house **3.** the framework supporting the chassis of a motor vehicle **4.** the structural case or border into which a window, door, etc. is set **5.** a border, often ornamental, surrounding a picture, etc. **6.** [*pl.*] the framework for a pair of eyeglasses **7.** any of certain machines built in or on a framework **8.** the way that anything is constructed or put together; form **9.** setting or background circumstances **10.** mood; temper [a bad *frame* of mind] **11.** an established order or system **12.** [Colloq.] the act of framing (sense 6) **13.** [Colloq.] *Baseball* an inning **14.** *Bowling,* etc. any of the divisions of a game **15.** *Motion Pictures* each of the small exposures composing a strip of film **16.** *Pool same as* RACK[1] (*n.* 2) *—adj.* having a wooden framework, usually covered with boards [a *frame* house] **—fram′er** *n.*

frame of reference **1.** *Math.* the fixed points, lines, or planes from which coordinates are measured **2.** the set of ideas, facts, or circumstances within which something exists

frame-up (-up′) *n.* [Colloq.] **1.** a falsifying of evidence, testimony, etc. to make an innocent person seem guilty **2.** a surreptitious, underhanded arrangement or scheme made beforehand

frame·work (-wurk′) *n.* **1.** a structure to hold together or to support something built or stretched over or around it [the *framework* of a house] **2.** a basic structure, arrangement, or system **3.** *same as* FRAME OF REFERENCE

franc (fraŋk) *n.* [Fr. < L. *Francorum rex,* king of the French, device on the coin in 1360] **1.** the monetary unit and a coin of France, Belgium, Switzerland, and Luxembourg **2.** the monetary unit of various other countries **3.** a unit of money in Morocco See MONETARY UNITS, table

France (frans, fräns) country in W Europe, on the Atlantic & the Mediterranean: 212,821 sq. mi.; pop. 50,620,000; cap. Paris

France (frans, fräns), **A·na·tole** (an′ə tōl′) (pseud. of *Jacques Anatole François Thibault*) 1844–1924; Fr. writer

Fran·ces (fran′sis) [< OFr. fem. of FRANCIS] a feminine name: dim. *Fran*

fran·chise (fran′chīz) *n.* [< OFr. < *franc,* free: see FRANK] **1.** *a)* any special right or privilege granted by a government, as to operate a public utility, etc. *b)* the jurisdiction over which this extends **2.** the right to vote; suffrage **3.** the right to market a product or provide a service in an area, as granted by a manufacturer or company *—vt.* **-chised, -chis·ing** to grant a franchise to

Fran·cis (fran′sis) [< OFr. < ML. *Franciscus* < LL. *Francus:* see FRANK] a masculine name

Fran·cis·can (fran sis′kən) *adj.* of Saint Francis of Assisi or the religious order founded by him in 1209 *—n.* any member of this order

Francis of As·si·si (ə sēs′ē), Saint (born *Giovanni Bernardone*) 1181?–1226; It. preacher: founder of the Franciscan Order

fran·ci·um (fran′sē əm) *n.* [ModL. < FRANCE] a radioactive, metallic chemical element of the alkali group: symbol, Fr; at. wt., 223(?); at. no., 87

Franck (fränk), **Cé·sar (Auguste)** (sā zȧr′) 1822–90; Fr. composer, born in Belgium

Fran·co (fraŋ′kō; *Sp.* fräŋ′kô), **Fran·cis·co** (fran sis′kō; *Sp.* frän thēs′kô) 1892–1975; Sp. general & chief of state; dictator of Spain (1939–75)

Fran·co- [ML. < LL. *Francus,* a Frank] *a combining form meaning:* **1.** Frankish **2.** of France or the French **3.** France and; the French and *[Franco-*German*]*

fran·gi·ble (fran′jə b'l) *adj.* [< OFr. < ML. < L. *frangere,* to break] breakable; fragile —**fran′gi·bil′i·ty** *n.*

fran·gi·pan·i (fran′jə pan′ē, -pän′ē) *n., pl.* **-pan′i, -pan′is** [It. < Marquis *Frangipani* (16th-c. It. nobleman)] **1.** any of several tropical American shrubs and trees with large, fragrant flowers **2.** a perfume obtained from this flower **3.** a pastry made with ground almonds

Frank (fraŋk) [dim. of FRANCIS] a masculine name —*n.* [< OE. & OFr. < LL. *Francus:* see ff.] **1.** a member of the Germanic tribes that established the Frankish Empire, which, at its height (9th cent. A.D.), extended over what is now France, Germany, and Italy **2.** any western European: term used in the Near East

frank (fraŋk) *adj.* [< OFr. *franc,* free < ML. < LL. *Francus,* a Frank, hence free man] **1.** open and honest in expressing what one thinks or feels; candid **2.** free from disguise or guile; clearly evident —*vt.* **1.** to send (mail) free of postage, as by virtue of an official position **2.** to mark (mail) so that it can be sent free —*n.* **1.** the privilege of sending mail free **2.** a mark or signature on mail indicating this privilege **3.** any piece of mail sent free in this way —**frank′ly** *adv.* —**frank′ness** *n.*

Frank. Frankish

Frank·en·stein (fraŋ′kən stīn′) **1.** the title character in a novel (1818) by Mary Shelley: he creates a monster that destroys him **2.** popularly, the monster —*n.* anything that becomes dangerous to its creator

Frank·fort (fraŋk′fərt) [after S. *Frank,* a pioneer killed there] capital of Ky.: pop. 26,000

Frank·furt (fraŋk′fərt; *G.* fräŋk′foort) city in C West Germany, on the Main River: pop. 662,000: also **Frankfurt am Main**

frank·furt·er, frank·fort·er (fraŋk′fər tər) *n.* [G., after FRANKFURT (AM MAIN)] a smoked sausage of beef or beef and pork, etc.; wiener: also [Colloq.] **frank**

frank·in·cense (fraŋ′kən sens′) *n.* [< OFr.: see FRANK & INCENSE[1]] a gum resin from various Arabian and NE African trees, burned as incense

Frank·ish (fraŋ′kish) *adj.* of the Franks, their language, or culture —*n.* the West Germanic language of the Franks

Frank·lin (fraŋk′lin) [< Anglo-Fr. < ML. < LL. *Francus:* see FRANK] **1.** a masculine name **2. Benjamin,** 1706–90; Am. statesman, scientist, & writer

frank·lin (fraŋk′lin) *n.* [< Anglo-Fr. < ML. < *francus:* see FRANK] in England in the 14th and 15th cent., a landowner of free but not noble birth, ranking just below the gentry

Franklin stove a cast-iron heating stove, invented by Benjamin Franklin

fran·tic (fran′tik) *adj.* [see PHRENETIC] **1.** wild with anger, pain, worry, etc.; frenzied **2.** marked by frenzy *[frantic* efforts*]* —**fran′ti·cal·ly** or [Rare] **fran′tic·ly** *adv.*

frap·pé (fra pā′) *adj.* [Fr., pp. of *frapper,* to strike] partly frozen; iced; cooled —*n.* **1.** a dessert made of partly frozen beverages, fruit juices, etc. **2.** a drink made of some beverage poured over shaved ice **3.** [Eastern] a milkshake Also, esp. for *n.* 3, **frappe** (frap)

FRANKLIN STOVE

frat (frat) *n.* [Colloq.] a fraternity, as at a college

fra·ter·nal (frə tʉr′n'l) *adj.* [< ML. < L. *fraternus* < *frater,* a brother] **1.** of or characteristic of brothers; brotherly **2.** of or like a fraternal order or a fraternity **3.** designating twins, of the same or different sex, developed from separately fertilized ova —**fra·ter′nal·ism** *n.* —**fra·ter′nal·ly** *adv.*

fraternal order (or **society, association**) a society, often secret, organized for fellowship or for work toward a common goal

fra·ter·ni·ty (frə tʉr′nə tē) *n., pl.* **-ties** **1.** fraternal relationship or spirit; brotherliness **2.** a group of men joined together by common interests, for fellowship, etc.; specif., a Greek-letter college organization **3.** a group of people with the same beliefs, work, etc. *[*the medical *fraternity]*

frat·er·nize (frat′ər nīz′) *vi.* **-nized′, -niz′ing** to associate in a brotherly manner; be on friendly terms —**frat′er·ni·za′tion** *n.*

frat·ri·cide (frat′rə sīd′) *n.* [Fr. < LL. *fratricidium* < L. < *frater,* brother + *caedere,* to kill] **1.** *a)* the act of killing one's own brother or sister *b)* the act of killing relatives or fellow-countrymen, as in a civil war **2.** a person who kills his brother or sister —**frat′ri·ci′dal** (-sīd′'l) *adj.*

‡**Frau** (frou) *n., pl.* **Frau′en** (-ən) [G.] a married woman; wife: used in Germany as a title corresponding to *Mrs.*

fraud (frôd) *n.* [< OFr. < L. *fraus* (gen. *fraudis*)] **1.** deceit; trickery; cheating **2.** an intentional deception or dishonesty; trick **3.** a person who is not what he pretends to be

fraud·u·lent (frô′jə lənt) *adj.* **1.** acting with fraud; deceitful **2.** based on or characterized by fraud **3.** done or obtained by fraud —**fraud′u·lence, fraud′u·len·cy** *n.* —**fraud′u·lent·ly** *adv.*

fraught (frôt) *adj.* [< MDu. < *vracht,* a load] filled, charged, or loaded (*with*) *[*a life *fraught* with hardship*]*

‡**Fräu·lein** (froi′līn; *E.* froi′-, frou′-) *n., pl.* **-lein,** E. **-leins** [G.] an unmarried woman: used in Germany as a title corresponding to *Miss*

fray[1] (frā) *n.* [< AFFRAY] a noisy quarrel or fight; brawl

fray[2] (frā) *vt., vi.* [< OFr. < L. *fricare,* to rub] **1.** to make or become worn, ragged, etc. by rubbing **2.** to make or become weakened or strained

fraz·zle (fraz′'l) *vt., vi.* **-zled, -zling** [Brit. dial. & U.S., prob. < dial. *fazle*] [Colloq.] **1.** to wear to tatters; fray **2.** to make or become physically or emotionally exhausted —*n.* [Colloq.] the state of being frazzled

freak (frēk) *n.* [< ? OE. *frician,* to dance] **1.** *a)* a sudden fancy; odd notion; whim *b)* an unusual happening **2.** any abnormal animal, person, or plant; monstrosity **3.** [Slang] *a)* a user of a specified narcotic, hallucinogen, etc. *[*an acid *freak] b)* a devotee or buff *[*a rock *freak] c) same as* HIPPIE —*adj.* oddly different from what is normal; queer —**freak (out)** [Slang] **1.** to experience in an extreme way the mental reactions, hallucinations, etc. induced by a psychedelic drug **2.** to make or become very excited, distressed, disorganized, etc. —**freak′ish, freak′y** *adj.* —**freak′ish·ly** *adv.* —**freak′ish·ness** *n.*

freck·le (frek′'l) *n.* [< Scand.] a small, brownish spot on the skin, esp. as a result of exposure to the sun —*vt.* **-led, -ling** to cause freckles to appear on —*vi.* to become spotted with freckles —**freck′led, freck′ly** *adj.*

Fred·er·i·ca (fred′ə rē′kə, fred rē′kə) [fem. of ff.] a feminine name

Fred·er·ick (fred′rik, -ər ik) [< Fr. < G. < OHG. *Fridurih,* "peaceful ruler"] a masculine name: dim. *Fred;* var. *Frederic, Fredrick, Fredric*

Frederick the Great 1712–86; king of Prussia (1740–86): also **Frederick II**

Fred·er·ic·ton (fred′ə rik tən) capital of New Brunswick, Canada: pop. 45,000

free (frē) *adj.* **fre′er, fre′est** [OE. *freo*] **1.** *a)* not under the control or power of another; able to act or think without arbitrary restriction; having liberty; independent *b)* characterized by or resulting from liberty **2.** having, or existing under, a government that does not impose arbitrary restrictions on the right to speak, assemble, petition, vote, etc. **3.** able to move in any direction; not held; loose **4.** not held or confined by a court, the police, etc. **5.** not burdened by obligations, debts, discomforts, etc.; unhindered *[free* from pain*]* **6.** at liberty; allowed *[free* to leave*]* **7.** not confined to the usual rules or conventions *[free* verse*]* **8.** not literal; not exact *[*a *free* translation*]* **9.** not busy or in use **10.** not constrained or stilted *[*a *free* gait*]* **11.** *a)* generous; lavish *[*a *free* spender*] b)* profuse; copious **12.** frank; straightforward **13.** too frank or familiar in speech, action, etc.; forward **14.** with no charge or cost *[*a *free* ticket*]* **15.** exempt from certain impositions, as taxes or duties **16.** clear of obstructions; open *[*a *free* road ahead*]* **17.** open to all *[*a *free* market*]* **18.** not fastened *[*the *free* end of a rope*]* **19.** not united; not combined *[free* oxygen*]* —*adv.* **1.** without cost or payment **2.** in a free manner —*vt.* **freed, free′ing** to make free; specif., *a)* to release from bondage or arbitrary power, obligation, etc. *b)* to clear of obstruction, etc.; disengage —**free and easy** informal; unceremonious —**free from** (or **of**) lacking; without —**make free with** **1.** to use freely **2.** to take liberties with —**set free** to release; liberate —**with a free hand** with generosity; lavishly —**free′ly** *adv.* —**free′ness** *n.*

free agent an athlete eligible to play a professional sport who is free to sign a contract with any team with which he can work out an agreement

free·bie (frē′bē) *n., pl.* **-bies** [Slang] something given or gotten free of charge, as a complimentary theater ticket

free·board (-bôrd′) *n.* the height of a ship's side from the main deck or gunwale to the waterline

free·boot·er (-bōōt′ər) *n.* [< Du. < *vrij,* free + *buit,* plunder] a pirate; buccaneer —**free′boot′** *vi.*

free·born (-bôrn′) ***adj.*** **1.** born free, not in slavery **2.** of or fit for a person so born

free city a city that is an autonomous state

freed·man (frēd′mən) ***n., pl.*** **-men** a man legally freed from slavery or bondage

free·dom (frē′dəm) ***n.*** **1.** the state or quality of being free; esp., *a)* exemption or liberation from the control of some other person or some arbitrary power; liberty; independence *b)* exemption from arbitrary restrictions on a specified civil right; civil or political liberty *[freedom* of speech*]* *c)* exemption or immunity from a specified obligation, discomfort, etc. *[freedom* from want*]* *d)* a being able to act, move, use, etc. without hindrance *e)* ease of movement or performance; facility *f)* a being free from the usual rules, conventions, etc. *g)* frankness or easiness of manner; sometimes, an excessive frankness or familiarity **2.** a right or privilege

free enterprise the economic doctrine of permitting private industry to operate under freely competitive conditions with a minimum of governmental control

free fall the unchecked fall of a body through the air; specif., the part of a parachutist's jump before the parachute is opened

free flight the flight of a rocket after the fuel supply has been used up or shut off —**free′-flight′** ***adj.***

free-for-all (frē′fər ôl′) ***n.*** a disorganized, general fight; brawl —***adj.*** open to anyone

free-form (-fôrm′) ***adj.*** **1.** having an irregular, usually curvilinear form or outline **2.** unconventional, unrestrained, etc. in style, form, etc.

free·hand (-hand′) ***adj.*** drawn by hand without the use of instruments, measurements, etc.

free·hand·ed (-han′did) ***adj.*** generous; liberal

free·hold (-hōld′) ***n.*** **1.** an estate in land held for life or with the right to pass it on through inheritance **2.** the holding of an estate in this way —***adj.*** of or held by freehold —**free′hold′er** ***n.***

free-lance (-lans′) ***adj.*** of or acting as a free lance —***vi.*** **-lanced′, -lanc′ing** to work as a free lance

free lance **1.** a medieval soldier who sold his services to any state or army **2.** one who acts according to his principles and is not influenced by any group **3.** a writer, artist, etc. not under contract, who sells his services to individual buyers: also **free′-lanc′er** ***n.***

free-liv·ing (-liv′iŋ) ***adj.*** **1.** freely indulging one's appetites, desires, etc. **2.** *Biol.* not parasitic or symbiotic —**free liver**

free·load·er (-lō′dər) ***n.*** [Colloq.] a person who habitually imposes on others for free food, lodging, etc.

free·man (-mən) ***n., pl.*** **-men** **1.** a person not in slavery or bondage **2.** a person who has full civil and political rights; citizen

free market any market where trade can be carried on without restrictions as to price, etc.

Free·ma·son (frē′mās′'n) ***n.*** a member of an international secret society having as its principles brotherliness, charity, and mutual aid; Mason

Free·ma·son·ry (-rē) ***n.*** **1.** the principles, rituals, etc. of Freemasons **2.** the Freemasons **3.** **[f-]** a natural sympathy and understanding among persons with similar experiences

free on board delivered (by the seller) aboard the train, ship, etc. at the point of shipment, without charge

free·si·a (frē′zhē ə, -zhə, -zē ə) ***n.*** [ModL., after F. *Freese,* 19th-c. Ger. physician] a South African bulbous plant with fragrant, funnel-shaped flowers

free silver the free coinage of silver, esp. at a fixed ratio to the gold coined in the same period

Free-Soil (frē′soil′) ***adj.*** [*also* **f- s-**] opposed to the extension of slavery into U.S. Territories before the Civil War —**Free′-Soil′er** ***n.***

free-spo·ken (-spō′k'n) ***adj.*** frank; outspoken

free-stand·ing (-stan′diŋ) ***adj.*** resting on its own support, without attachment

free·stone (-stōn′) ***n.*** **1.** a stone, esp. sandstone or limestone, that can be cut easily without splitting **2.** *a)* a peach, plum, etc. in which the pit does not cling to the pulp of the ripened fruit *b)* such a pit —***adj.*** having such a pit

free·think·er (-thiŋ′kər) ***n.*** a person who forms his opinions about religion independently of tradition, authority, or established belief —**free′think′ing** ***n., adj.*** —**free thought**

free trade trade conducted without quotas on imports or exports, protective tariffs, etc.

free verse poetry not following regular metrical, rhyming, or stanzaic forms

free·way (-wā′) ***n.*** **1.** an expressway with interchanges for fully controlled access **2.** a highway without toll charges

free·will (-wil′) ***adj.*** voluntary; spontaneous

free will **1.** freedom of the will to choose a course of action without external coercion; freedom of choice **2.** the doctrine that people have such freedom

freeze (frēz) ***vi.*** **froze, fro′zen, freez′ing** [OE. *freosan*] **1.** to be formed into ice; be hardened by cold **2.** to become covered or clogged with ice **3.** to be or become very cold **4.** to become attached by freezing **5.** to die or be damaged by exposure to cold **6.** to become motionless or fixed **7.** to be made momentarily unable to move, act, or speak through fright, etc. **8.** to become formal or unfriendly **9.** *Mech.* to stick or become tight as a result of expansion of parts from overheating or inadequate lubrication —***vt.*** **1.** to cause to form into ice; harden or solidify by cold **2.** to cover or clog with ice **3.** to make very cold **4.** to remove sensation from, as with a local anesthetic **5.** to preserve (food) by rapid refrigeration **6.** to make fixed or attached by freezing **7.** to kill or damage by exposure to cold **8.** to make or keep motionless or stiff **9.** to discourage as by cool behavior **10.** to make formal or unfriendly **11.** *a)* to fix (prices, wages, an employee, etc.) at a given level or place by authoritative regulation *b)* to make (funds, assets, etc.) unavailable to the owners —***n.*** **1.** a freezing or being frozen **2.** a period of cold, freezing weather —**freeze (on) to** [Colloq.] to hold fast to —**freeze out** **1.** to die out through freezing, as plants **2.** [Colloq.] to force out by a cold manner, competition, etc. —**freeze over** to become covered with ice —**freez′a·ble** ***adj.***

freeze-dry (frēz′drī′) ***vt.*** **-dried′, -dry′ing** to subject (food, vaccines, etc.) to quick-freezing followed by drying under high vacuum at a low temperature —**freeze′-dry′er** ***n.***

freez·er (-ər) ***n.*** **1.** a refrigerator, compartment, or room for freezing and storing frozen foods **2.** a hand-cranked or electrically operated device for making ice cream

freez·ing point the temperature at which a liquid freezes: for water, it is 32°F or 0°C

freight (frāt) ***n.*** [< MDu. *vracht,* a load] **1.** a method or service for transporting goods by water, land, or air: freight is usually cheaper but slower than express **2.** the cost for such transportation **3.** the goods transported; cargo **4.** *same as* FREIGHT TRAIN **5.** any load or burden —***vt.*** **1.** to load with freight **2.** to load; burden **3.** to transport as by freight

freight·age (-ij) ***n.*** **1.** the charge for transporting goods **2.** freight; cargo **3.** the transportation of goods

freight car a railroad car for transporting freight

freight·er (-ər) ***n.*** a ship or aircraft for carrying freight

freight train a railroad train of freight cars

Fre·mont (frē′mänt) [after J. C. *Frémont* (1813–90), U.S. politician, general, & explorer] city in W Calif.: suburb of Oakland: pop. 132,000

French (french) ***adj.*** of France, its people, their language, or culture —***n.*** the Romance language of the French —**the French** the people of France —**French′man** (-mən) ***n., pl.*** **-men** —**French′wom′an** ***n., pl.*** **-wom′en**

French Canadian a Canadian of French ancestry

French chalk a very soft chalk used for marking lines on cloth or removing grease spots

French Community political union comprising France, its overseas departments & territories, & six fully independent countries that are former French colonies

French cuff a double cuff turned back on itself and fastened with a link

French doors two adjoining doors with glass panes from top to bottom, hinged at opposite sides of a doorway and opening in the middle

French dressing a salad dressing made of vinegar, oil, and various seasonings

French fry [*often* **f- f-**] to fry in very hot, deep fat until crisp: French fried potatoes (colloquially, **French fries**) are first cut lengthwise into strips

French Guiana French possession in NE S. America

French horn a brass-wind instrument with a long, coiled tube ending in a wide, flaring bell

French·i·fy (-ə fī′) ***vt., vi.*** **-fied′, -fy′ing** to make or become French or like the French in customs, ideas, manners, etc.

French leave an unauthorized or unceremonious departure; act of leaving secretly or in haste

French Revolution the revolution of the people against the monarchy in France: it began in 1789, resulted in the establishment of a republic, and ended in 1799 with the Consulate

French toast sliced bread dipped in a batter of egg and milk and then fried

FRENCH HORN

French windows a pair of casement windows designed like French doors and usually extending to the floor

fre·net·ic (frə net′ik) *adj.* [see PHRENETIC] frantic; frenzied: also **fre·net′i·cal** —**fre·net′i·cal·ly** *adv.*

fre·num (frē′nəm) *n., pl.* **-nums, -na** (-nə) [L., lit., a bridle] a fold of skin or mucous membrane that checks the movements of an organ, as the fold under the tongue

fren·zy (fren′zē) *n., pl.* **-zies** [< OFr. < ML. < L. *phrenesis,* ult. < Gr. *phrenitis,* madness < *phrēn,* mind] wild outburst of feeling or action; brief delirium that is almost insanity —*vt.* **-zied, -zy·ing** to make frantic; drive mad —**fren′zied** *adj.* —**fren′zied·ly** *adv.*

freq. 1. frequent 2. frequentative

fre·quen·cy (frē′kwən sē) *n., pl.* **-cies** 1. frequent occurrence 2. the number of times any event, value, characteristic, etc. is repeated in a given period or group 3. *Physics* the number of periodic oscillations, vibrations, or waves per unit of time: now usually expressed in hertz

frequency modulation 1. the variation of the instantaneous frequency of a carrier wave in accordance with the signal to be transmitted 2. the system of radio broadcasting that uses this

fre·quent (frē′kwənt; *for v., usually* frē kwent′) *adj.* [< OFr. < L. *frequens,* crowded] 1. occurring often; happening repeatedly at brief intervals 2. constant; habitual —*vt.* to go to constantly; be at or in habitually —**fre′quen·ta′tion** *n.* —**fre·quent′er** *n.* —**fre′quent·ly** *adv.*

fre·quen·ta·tive (frē kwen′tə tiv, frē′kwən-) *adj. Gram.* expressing frequent and repeated action —*n. Gram.* a frequentative verb: *sparkle* is a frequentative of *spark*

fres·co (fres′kō) *n., pl.* **-coes, -cos** [It., fresh < OHG. *frisc*] 1. the art of painting with water colors on wet plaster 2. a painting or design so made —*vt.* to paint in fresco

fresh[1] (fresh) *adj.* [< OE. *fersc,* altered after OFr. *fres, fresche*] 1. recently made, obtained, or grown *[fresh* coffee*]* 2. not salted, preserved, etc. 3. not spoiled or stale 4. not tired; vigorous; lively 5. not worn, soiled, etc.; bright; clean 6. youthful or healthy in appearance 7. not known before; new; recent 8. additional; further *[*a *fresh* start*]* 9. inexperienced; unaccustomed 10. having just arrived 11. original and stimulating *[fresh* ideas*]* 12. cool and refreshing *[*a *fresh* spring day*]* 13. brisk; strong: said of the wind 14. not salt: said of water 15. giving milk because having borne a calf: said of a cow —*adv.* in a fresh manner —**fresh out of** [Slang] having just sold or used up —**fresh′ly** *adv.* —**fresh′ness** *n.*

fresh[2] (fresh) *adj.* [< G. *frech,* bold] [Slang] saucy; impudent —**fresh′ly** *adv.* —**fresh′ness** *n.*

fresh·en (fresh′ən) *vt., vi.* to make or become fresh —**freshen up** to bathe oneself, change into fresh clothes, etc. —**fresh′en·er** *n.*

fresh·et (-it) *n.* 1. a rush of fresh water flowing into the sea 2. a flooding of a stream because of melting snow or heavy rain

fresh·man (-mən) *n., pl.* **-men** 1. a beginner; novice 2. a student in the ninth grade in high school, or one in the first year of college —*adj.* of or for first-year students

fresh·wa·ter (-wôt′ər, -wät′ər) *adj.* 1. of or living in water that is not salty 2. *a)* sailing only on inland waters, not on the sea *b)* unskilled 3. *a)* inland *b)* somewhat provincial, obscure, etc.

Fres·no (frez′nō) [< Sp. *fresno,* ash tree] city in C Calif.: pop. 218,000 (met. area 507,000)

fret[1] (fret) *vt.* **fret′ted, fret′ting** [OE. *fretan,* to eat up] 1. to wear away by gnawing, rubbing, corroding, etc. 2. to make by wearing away 3. to make rough; disturb 4. to irritate; vex; worry —*vi.* 1. to gnaw (*into, on,* or *upon*) 2. to become corroded, worn, etc. 3. to become rough or disturbed 4. to be irritated, vexed, etc.; worry —*n.* irritation; worry —**fret′ter** *n.*

fret[2] (fret) *n.* [prob. merging of OFr. *frete,* interlaced work & OE. *frætwa,* ornament] an ornamental pattern of straight bars joining one another at right angles to form a design —*vt.* **fret′ted, fret′ting** to ornament with a fret

fret[3] (fret) *n.* [OFr. *frette,* a band] any of the lateral ridges across the fingerboard of a banjo, guitar, etc. to regulate the fingering —*vt.* **fret′ted, fret′ting** to furnish with frets

FRETS

fret·ful (fret′fəl) *adj.* tending to fret; peevish —**fret′ful·ly** *adv.* —**fret′ful·ness** *n.*

fret·work (fret′wʉrk′) *n.* decorative openwork

Freud (froid), **Sigmund** 1856–1939; Austrian physician & neurologist: founder of psychoanalysis

Freud·i·an (froi′dē ən) *adj.* of or according to Freud or his theories —*n.* a follower of Freud or his theories of psychoanalysis —**Freud′i·an·ism** *n.*

Fri. Friday

fri·a·ble (frī′ə b'l) *adj.* [Fr. < L. *friabilis* < *friare,* to rub] easily crumbled into powder —**fri′a·bil′i·ty, fri′a·ble·ness** *n.*

fri·ar (frī′ər) *n.* [< OFr. *frere* < L. *frater,* brother] *R.C.Ch.* a member of any of several mendicant orders; esp., an Augustinian, Carmelite, Dominican, or Franciscan —**fri′ar·ly** *adj.*

fri·ar·y (-ē) *n., pl.* **-ar·ies** 1. a monastery where friars live 2. a brotherhood of friars

fric·as·see (frik′ə sē′, frik′ə sē′) *n.* [< Fr. < *fricasser,* to cut up and fry] meat cut into pieces, stewed or fried, and served in its own gravy —*vt.* **-seed′, -see′ing** to prepare as a fricassee

fric·a·tive (frik′ə tiv) *adj.* [< L. pp. of *fricare* (see FRICTION) + -IVE] pronounced by forcing the breath through a narrow slit formed at some point in the mouth, as *f, v, z* —*n.* a fricative consonant

fric·tion (frik′shən) *n.* [Fr. < L. < pp. of *fricare,* to rub] 1. a rubbing, esp. of one object against another 2. conflict because of differences of opinion, temperament, etc. 3. the resistance to motion of moving surfaces that touch —**fric′tion·al** *adj.* —**fric′tion·al·ly** *adv.*

friction tape a moisture-resistant adhesive tape, esp. for insulating exposed electric wires

Fri·day (frī′dē, -dā) *n.* [OE. *frigedæg,* lit., day of the goddess Frig: see FRIGG] 1. the sixth day of the week 2. [after the devoted servant of ROBINSON CRUSOE] a faithful follower or efficient helper: usually **man** (or **girl**) **Friday**

Fri·days (-dēz, -dāz) *adv.* on or during every Friday

fried (frīd) *pt. & pp. of* FRY[1]

Frie·da (frē′də) [G. < OHG. *fridu,* peace] a feminine name

fried·cake (frīd′kāk′) *n.* a small cake fried in deep fat; doughnut or cruller

friend (frend) *n.* [OE. *freond*] 1. a person whom one knows well and is fond of; close acquaintance 2. a person on the same side in a struggle; ally 3. a supporter or sympathizer *[*a *friend* of labor*]* 4. something thought of as like a friend 5. [F-] a member of the Society of Friends; Quaker —**make** (or **be**) **friends with** to become (or be) a friend of —**friend′less** *adj.* —**friend′less·ness** *n.*

friend·ly (-lē) *adj.* **-li·er, -li·est** 1. like, characteristic of, or suitable for a friend or friendship; kindly 2. not hostile; amicable 3. supporting; favorable *[*a *friendly* wind*]* 4. ready to be a friend —*adv.* in a friendly manner —**friend′li·ly** *adv.* —**friend′li·ness** *n.*

friend·ship (-ship′) *n.* 1. the state of being friends 2. friendly feeling or attitude

fri·er (frī′ər) *n. same as* FRYER

frieze[1] (frēz) *n.* [< Fr. < ML. *frisium* < ? Frank.] 1. a decoration forming an ornamental band around a room, mantel, etc. 2. a horizontal band, often decorated with sculpture, between the architrave and cornice of a building

frieze[2] (frēz) *n.* [< OFr. < MDu.] a heavy wool cloth with a shaggy, uncut nap on one side

frig·ate (frig′it) *n.* [< Fr. < It. *fregata*] 1. a fast, medium-sized sailing warship of the 18th and early 19th cent. 2. a U.S. warship larger than a destroyer and smaller than a light cruiser

frigate bird a large, long-winged, tropical sea bird that robs other birds of their prey

Frigg (frig) [ON.] *Norse Myth.* the wife of Odin

fright (frīt) *n.* [OE. *fyrhto, fryhto*] 1. sudden fear or terror; alarm 2. an ugly, ridiculous, or startling person or thing —*vt.* [Rare] to frighten

fright·en (-'n) *vt.* 1. to cause to feel fright; make suddenly afraid; scare 2. to force (*away, out,* or *off*) or bring (*into* a specified condition) by frightening —*vi.* to become suddenly afraid —**fright′en·ing·ly** *adv.*

fright·ful (-fəl) *adj.* 1. causing fright; alarming 2. shocking; terrible 3. [Colloq.] *a)* unpleasant; annoying *b)* great *[*in a *frightful* hurry*]* —**fright′ful·ly** *adv.* —**fright′ful·ness** *n.*

frig·id (frij′id) *adj.* [< L. < *frigus,* coldness] 1. extremely cold 2. without warmth of feeling or manner; stiff and formal 3. habitually unaroused sexually: said of a woman —**fri·gid·i·ty** (frə jid′ə tē), **frig′id·ness** *n.* —**frig′id·ly** *adv.*

Frigid Zone either of two zones of the earth (**North Frigid Zone** & **South Frigid Zone**) between the polar circles and the poles

fri·jol (frē′hōl) *n., pl.* **fri·jo′les** (fri′hōlz, frē hō′lēz) [Sp. *frijol, fréjol*] a bean, esp. the kidney bean, used for food in Mexico and the SW U.S.: also **fri·jo·le** (frē hō′lē)

frill (fril) *n.* [< ?] 1. a fringe of hair or feathers around the neck of a bird or animal 2. any unnecessary ornament; thing added only for show 3. a ruffle —*vt.* to decorate with a frill —**frill′y** *adj.* **frill′i·er, frill′i·est**

fringe (frinj) *n.* [< OFr. < L. *frimbria*] 1. a border or trimming of cords or threads, hanging loose or in bunches 2. anything like this *[*a *fringe* of whiskers*]* 3. an outer edge; border; margin 4. a part considered to be peripheral, extreme, or minor *[*the lunatic *fringe* of a political party*]* 5. *same as* FRINGE BENEFIT —*vt.* **fringed, fring′ing** 1. to decorate with or as with fringe **2.** to be a fringe for; line *[*trees *fringed* the lawn*]* —*adj.* **1.** at the outer edge *[*a *fringe* area*]* **2.** additional *[fringe* benefits*]* **3.** less important —**fring′y** *adj.* **fring′i·er, fring′i·est**

fringe benefit an employee's benefit other than wages or salary, such as a pension or insurance

frip·per·y (frip′ər ē) *n., pl.* **-per·ies** [< Fr. < OFr. < *frepe,* a rag] **1.** cheap, gaudy clothes **2.** showy display in dress, manners, speech, etc.

Fris·bee (friz′bē) [< "Mother *Frisbie's*" cookie jar lids] *a trademark for* a plastic disk tossed back and forth in a game —*n.* **[f-]** such a disk

Fris·co (fris′kō) [Colloq.] *nickname for* SAN FRANCISCO: not a local usage

fri·sé (fri zā′) *n.* [Fr. < *friser,* to curl] a type of upholstery fabric with a thick pile of loops, some of which are sometimes cut to form a design

Fri·sian (frizh′ən, frē′zhən) *adj.* of the Frisian Islands, N Netherlands, their people, or their language —*n.* **1.** a native or inhabitant of the Frisian Islands or N Netherlands **2.** the West Germanic language of the Frisians

Frisian Islands island chain in the North Sea, extending along the coast of the N Netherlands, N West Germany, & SW Denmark

frisk (frisk) *n.* [OFr. *frisque* < OHG. *frisc*] **1.** a frolic; gambol **2.** [Slang] the act of frisking a person —*vt.* [Slang] to search (a person) for concealed weapons, etc. by passing the hands quickly over his clothing —*vi.* to frolic; gambol

frisk·y (-ē) *adj.* **frisk′i·er, frisk′i·est** lively; frolicsome —**frisk′i·ly** *adv.* —**frisk′i·ness** *n.*

frith (frith) *n. var. of* FIRTH

frit·il·lar·y (frit′'l er′ē) *n., pl.* **-lar′ies** [ModL. < L. *fritillus,* dice box: from markings on the petals or wings] **1.** a plant of the lily family, with nodding, bell-shaped flowers **2.** any of a group of butterflies with spotted wings

frit·ter[1] (frit′ər) *n.* [< ? OFr. < L. *fractura:* see FRACTURE] [Rare] a small piece —*vt.* **1.** [Rare] to break into small pieces **2.** to waste (money, time, etc.) bit by bit on petty things —**frit′ter·er** *n.*

frit·ter[2] (frit′ər) *n.* [< OFr., ult. < L. pp. of *frigere,* to fry] a small cake of fried batter, usually containing corn, fruit, etc.

fri·vol·i·ty (fri väl′ə tē) *n.* **1.** a frivolous quality **2.** *pl.* **-ties** a frivolous act or thing

friv·o·lous (friv′ə ləs) *adj.* [L. *frivolus*] **1.** trifling; trivial **2.** not properly serious or sensible; silly and light-minded —**friv′o·lous·ly** *adv.* —**friv′o·lous·ness** *n.*

frizz, friz (friz) *vt., vi.* **frizzed, friz′zing** [Fr. *friser*] to form into small, tight curls —*n.* hair, etc. that is frizzed

friz·zle[1] (friz′'l) *vt., vi.* **-zled, -zling** [echoic alteration of FRY[1]] **1.** to make or cause to make a sputtering, hissing noise, as in frying; sizzle **2.** to make or become crisp by broiling or frying

friz·zle[2] (friz′'l) *vt., vi.* **-zled, -zling** [freq. of FRIZZ] to frizz; crimp —*n.* a small, tight curl

friz·zly (-lē) *adj.* **-zli·er, -zli·est** full of or covered with small, tight curls: also **friz′zy, -zi·er, -zi·est**

fro (frō) *adv.* [< ON. *frā*] backward; back: now only in *to and fro:* see under TO —*prep.* [Scot.] from

frock (fräk) *n.* [OFr. *froc* (or ML. *froccus*) < OFrank.] **1.** a robe worn by friars, monks, etc. **2.** any of various other garments; specif., *a)* a smock *b)* a dress *c) same as* FROCK COAT —*vt.* **1.** to clothe in a frock **2.** to ordain as a priest

frock coat a man's double-breasted dress coat with a full skirt reaching to the knees, worn chiefly in the 19th cent.

frog (frôg, fräg) *n.* [OE. *frogga*] **1.** a tailless, leaping, four-legged amphibian with a smooth skin and webbed feet: most species, when grown, can live either in water or on land **2.** a horny pad in the sole of a horse's foot **3.** a corded or braided loop used as a fastener or decoration on clothing **4.** a device on railroad tracks for keeping cars on the proper rails at intersections or switches **5.** a device placed in a bowl, vase, etc. to hold the stems of flowers —**frog in the throat** a hoarseness due to throat irritation

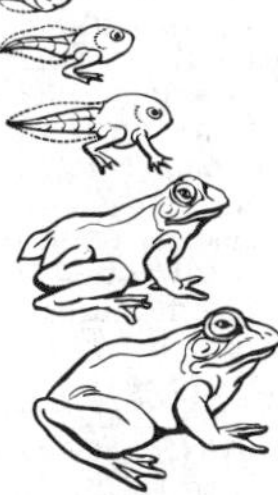
METAMORPHOSIS OF FROG

frog·gy (-ē) *adj.* **-gi·er, -gi·est** **1.** of or like a frog **2.** full of frogs

frog·man (-man′) *n., pl.* **-men** (-mən) a person trained and equipped, as with scuba gear, for underwater demolition, exploration, etc.

frog spit (or **spittle**) **1.** *same as* CUCKOO SPIT **2.** mats of filamentous algae floating on ponds

Frois·sart (frwȧ sȧr′; *E.* froi′särt), **Jean** (zhän) 1337?–1410?; Fr. chronicler & poet

frol·ic (fräl′ik) *adj.* [< Du. < MDu. *vrō,* merry] [Archaic] full of fun and pranks; merry —*n.* **1.** a playful trick; prank **2.** a lively party or game **3.** merriment; fun —*vi.* **-icked, -ick·ing** **1.** to make merry; have fun **2.** to play or romp about in a happy, carefree way —**frol′ick·er** *n.*

frol·ic·some (-səm) *adj.* full of gaiety or high spirits; playful; merry: also **frol′ick·y**

from (frum, främ; *unstressed* frəm) *prep.* [OE. *from, fram*] **1.** beginning at *[*to walk *from* the door*]* **2.** starting with *[from* noon to midnight*]* **3.** out of *[*he took a comb *from* his pocket*]* **4.** with (a person or thing) as the maker, speaker, source, etc. *[*facts learned *from* reading*]* **5.** at a place not near to *[*keep away *from* me*]* **6.** out of the whole of or alliance with *[*take two *from* four*]* **7.** out of the possibility or use of *[*kept *from* going*]* **8.** out of the possession or control of *[*released *from* jail*]* **9.** as not being like *[*to tell one *from* another*]* **10.** by reason of; because of *[*to tremble *from* fear*]*

frond (fränd) *n.* [L. *frons* (gen. *frondis*), leafy branch] **1.** a leaf; specif., *a)* the leaf of a fern *b)* the leaf of a palm **2.** the leaflike part, or shoot, of a lichen, seaweed, etc. —**frond′ed** *adj.*

front (frunt) *n.* [< OFr. < L. *frons* (gen. *frontis*), forehead] **1.** outward, often assumed, attitude, behavior, or appearance *[*to put on a bold *front]* **2.** the part of something that faces forward; most important side **3.** the first part; beginning **4.** the place or position directly before a person or thing **5.** a forward or leading position or situation **6.** the first available bellhop, as in a hotel **7.** the land bordering a lake, ocean, street, etc. **8.** the advanced area of contact between opposing sides in warfare; combat zone **9.** a specified area of activity *[*the home *front]* **10.** a broad movement in which different groups are united for the achievement of common political or social aims **11.** a person who serves as a public representative of a business, group, etc., as because of his prestige **12.** a person or group used to cover the activity or objectives of another really in control **13.** a stiff shirt bosom, worn with formal clothes **14.** a face of a building; esp., the face with the principal entrance **15.** *Meteorol.* the boundary between two masses of air that are different, as in density —*adj.* **1.** at, to, in, on, or of the front **2.** *Phonet.* articulated toward the front of the mouth, as *i* in *bid* or *e* in *met* —*vt.* **1.** to face; be opposite to **2.** to be before in place **3.** to meet; confront **4.** to defy; oppose **5.** to supply or be a front to —*vi.* **1.** to face in a certain direction **2.** to be a front (senses 11 & 12) (with *for*) —**in front of** before; ahead of

front·age (-ij) *n.* **1.** the front part of a building **2.** the direction toward which this faces **3.** the land between the front edge of a building and the street **4.** *a)* the front boundary line of a lot facing the street *b)* the length of this line **5.** land bordering a street, river, lake, etc.

fron·tal (-'l) *adj.* **1.** of, in, on, at, or against the front **2.** of or for the forehead —*n.* the bone forming the forehead: in full, **frontal bone** —**fron′tal·ly** *adv.*

fron·tier (frun tir′) *n.* [< OFr. < *front:* see FRONT] **1.** the border between two countries **2.** that part of a settled country which lies next to an unexplored region **3.** any new or incompletely investigated field or area of learning, etc. *[*the *frontiers* of medicine*]* —*adj.* of, on, or near a frontier

fron·tiers·man (-tirz′mən) *n., pl.* **-men** a man who lives on the frontier

fron·tis·piece (frun′tis pēs′) *n.* [OFr. < LL. *frontispicium,* front view < L. *frons,* FRONT + *specere,* to look] **1.** an illustration facing the first page or title page of a book or division of a book **2.** *Archit. a)* the main façade *b)* a pediment over a door, window, etc.

front·let (frunt′lit) *n.* [< OFr., ult. < L. *frons,* FRONT] a phylactery worn on the forehead

front office the management or administration, as of a company

front-page (frunt′pāj′) *adj.* fit to be printed on the front page of a newspaper; important

front-run·ner (-run′ər) *n.* **1.** one who is leading in a race or competition **2.** one that runs best when in the lead

frost (frôst, fräst) *n.* [OE. < *freosan,* to freeze] **1.** a freezing or being frozen **2.** a temperature low enough to cause freezing **3.** frozen dew or vapor; hoarfrost **4.** coolness of action, feeling, manner, etc. —*vt.* **1.** to cover with frost **2.** to damage or kill by freezing **3.** to cover with frosting **4.** to give a frostlike surface to (glass)

Frost (frôst, fräst), **Robert (Lee)** 1874–1963; U.S. poet

frost·bite (-bīt′) *vt.* **-bit′, -bit′ten, -bit′ing** to injure the tissues of (a part of the body) by exposure to intense cold —*n.* tissue damage caused by such exposure

frost·ing (-iŋ) ***n.*** **1.** a mixture of sugar, butter, eggs, etc. for covering a cake; icing **2.** a dull, frostlike finish on glass, metal, etc.
frost·y (-ē) ***adj.*** **frost′i·er, frost′i·est** **1.** cold enough to produce frost; freezing **2.** covered as with frost **3.** cold in manner or feeling; unfriendly —**frost′i·ly** ***adv.*** —**frost′i·ness** ***n.***
froth (frôth, fräth) ***n.*** [ON. *frotha*] **1.** foam **2.** foaming saliva caused by disease or great excitement **3.** light, trifling, or worthless talk, ideas, etc. —***vt.*** **1.** to cause to foam **2.** to cover with foam **3.** to spill forth as foam —***vi.*** to foam
froth·y (-ē) ***adj.*** **froth′i·er, froth′i·est** **1.** foamy **2.** light; trifling; worthless —**froth′i·ly** ***adv.*** —**froth′i·ness** ***n.***
frou·frou (fro͞o′fro͞o′) ***n.*** [Fr.; echoic] **1.** a rustling or swishing, as of a skirt **2.** [Colloq.] excessive ornateness or affected elegance
fro·ward (frō′ərd, -wərd) ***adj.*** [ME., unruly: see FRO & -WARD] not easily controlled; stubbornly willful —**fro′ward·ly** ***adv.*** —**fro′ward·ness** ***n.***
frown (froun) ***vi.*** [< OFr. < *froigne*, sullen face < Gaul.] **1.** to contract the brows, as in displeasure or concentrated thought **2.** to show displeasure or disapproval (with *on* or *upon*) —***vt.*** to express (disapproval, etc.) by frowning —***n.*** **1.** a contracting of the brows in sternness, thought, etc. **2.** any expression of displeasure or disapproval —**frown′er** ***n.*** —**frown′ing·ly** ***adv.***
frow·zy (frou′zē) ***adj.*** **-zi·er, -zi·est** [< ?] **1.** [Rare] bad-smelling **2.** dirty and untidy; slovenly Also sp. **frow′sy** —**frow′zi·ly** ***adv.*** —**frow′zi·ness** ***n.***
froze (frōz) *pt. of* FREEZE
fro·zen (-'n) *pp. of* FREEZE —***adj.*** **1.** turned into or covered with ice **2.** damaged or killed by freezing **3.** having heavy frosts and extreme cold [the *frozen* north] **4.** preserved by freezing, as food **5.** as if turned into ice [*frozen* with terror] **6.** without warmth or affection **7.** arbitrarily kept at a fixed level or in a fixed position **8.** not readily converted into cash [*frozen* assets]
frozen custard a food like ice cream, but with less butterfat content and a looser consistency
frt. freight
fruc·ti·fy (fruk′tə fī′) ***vi., vt.*** **-fied′, -fy′ing** [< OFr. < L. *fructificare*: see FRUIT & -FY] to bear or cause to bear fruit —**fruc′ti·fi·ca′tion** ***n.***
fruc·tose (fruk′tōs, fro͝ok′-) ***n.*** [< L. *fructus*, FRUIT + -OSE[1]] a crystalline sugar, $C_6H_{12}O_6$, found in sweet fruits and in honey; fruit sugar; levulose
fru·gal (fro͞o′g'l) ***adj.*** [L. *frugalis* < *frugi*, fit for food < *frux* (gen. *frugis*), fruits] **1.** not wasteful; thrifty **2.** not costly; inexpensive or meager [a *frugal* meal] —**fru·gal′i·ty** (-gal′ə tē) ***n.***, *pl.* **-ties** —**fru′gal·ly** ***adv.***
fruit (fro͞ot) ***n.*** see PLURAL, II, D, 3 [OFr. < L. *fructus* < pp. of *frui*, to enjoy] **1.** any plant product, as grain, flax, vegetables, etc.: *usually used in pl.* **2.** a sweet and edible plant structure, consisting of a fruit (sense 5), usually eaten raw or as a dessert **3.** the result or product of any action [the *fruit* of labor] **4.** [Archaic] offspring **5.** *Bot.* the mature ovary of a flowering plant, along with its contents, as the whole peach, pea pod, etc. —***vi., vt.*** to bear or cause to bear fruit
fruit·age (-ij) ***n.*** **1.** the bearing of fruit **2.** a crop of fruit **3.** a result; product; consequence
fruit·cake (-kāk′) ***n.*** a rich cake containing nuts, preserved fruit, citron, spices, etc.
fruit fly **1.** a small fly whose larvae feed on fruits and vegetables **2.** *same as* DROSOPHILA
fruit·ful (-fəl) ***adj.*** **1.** bearing much fruit **2.** producing much; productive; prolific **3.** producing results; profitable —**fruit′ful·ly** ***adv.*** —**fruit′ful·ness** ***n.***
fru·i·tion (fro͞o ish′ən) ***n.*** [OFr. < LL. < *frui*: see FRUIT] **1.** the pleasure of using or possessing **2.** the bearing of fruit **3.** fulfillment; realization
fruit·less (fro͞ot′lis) ***adj.*** **1.** without results; unsuccessful; vain **2.** bearing no fruit; sterile —**fruit′less·ly** ***adv.*** —**fruit′less·ness** ***n.***
fruit sugar *same as* FRUCTOSE
fruit tree a tree that bears edible fruit
fruit·wood (-wood′) ***n.*** the wood of any of various fruit trees, used in furniture, paneling, etc.
fruit·y (fro͞ot′ē) ***adj.*** **fruit′i·er, fruit′i·est** **1.** like fruit in taste or smell **2.** rich or mellow in tone [a *fruity* voice] **3.** [Slang] crazy —**fruit′i·ly** ***adv.*** —**fruit′i·ness** ***n.***
frump (frump) ***n.*** [< Du. *frompelen* < *rompelen*, to rumple] a dowdy, unattractive woman —**frump′ish** ***adj.*** —**frump′y** ***adj.*** **frump′i·er, frump′i·est**
Frun·ze (fro͞on′ze) capital of the Kirghiz S.S.R., in the SC part: pop. 416,000
frus·trate (frus′trāt) ***vt.*** **-trat·ed, -trat·ing** [< L. pp. of *frustrare* < *frustra*, in vain] **1.** to cause to have no effect; nullify [to *frustrate* plans] **2.** to keep from an objective; foil [to *frustrate* a foe] **3.** *Psychol.* to keep from gratifying certain desires —***vi.*** to become frustrated —**frus·tra′tion** ***n.***
frus·tum (frus′təm) ***n.***, *pl.* **-tums, -ta** (-tə) [L., a piece, bit] the solid figure formed when the top of a cone or pyramid is cut off by a plane parallel to the base

FRUSTUM

fry[1] (frī) ***vt., vi.*** **fried, fry′ing** [< OFr. < L. *frigere*, to fry] **1.** to cook or be cooked, usually in hot fat or oil, over direct heat **2.** [Slang] to electrocute or be electrocuted —***n.***, *pl.* **fries** **1.** a fried food; esp., [*pl.*] fried potatoes **2.** a social gathering where food is fried and eaten
fry[2] (frī) ***n.***, *pl.* **fry** [prob. a merging of ON. *frjo*, seed, with Anglo-Fr. *frei*, spawn] **1.** young fish **2.** small adult fish, esp. in large groups **3.** offspring —**small fry** **1.** children **2.** trivial people or things
fry·er (frī′ər) ***n.*** **1.** one that fries; specif., a utensil for frying foods **2.** food to be fried, esp. a young, tender chicken
f-stop (ef′stäp′) ***n.*** any of the settings for the f-number of a camera
ft. **1.** foot; feet **2.** fort
FTC Federal Trade Commission
fth., fthm. fathom
fuch·sia (fyo͞o′shə) ***n.*** [ModL., after L. *Fuchs*, 16th-c. G. botanist] **1.** a shrubby plant with drooping pink, red, or purple flowers **2.** purplish red —***adj.*** purplish-red
fud·dle (fud′'l) ***vt.*** **-dled, -dling** [akin ? to G. dial. *fuddeln*, to swindle] to confuse or stupefy as with alcoholic liquor —***n.*** a fuddled condition
fud·dy-dud·dy (fud′ē dud′ē) ***n.***, *pl.* **-dies** [prob. based on dial. *fud*, buttocks] [Slang] **1.** a fussy, critical person **2.** an old-fashioned person
fudge (fuj) ***n.*** [? echoic] **1.** empty talk; nonsense **2.** [< ?] a soft candy made of butter, milk, sugar, flavoring, etc. —***vt.*** **fudged, fudg′ing** to make dishonestly or carelessly; fake —***vi.*** **1.** to refuse to commit oneself **2.** to cheat
fu·el (fyo͞o′əl, fyo͞ol) ***n.*** [< OFr. *fouaille*, ult. < L. *focus*, fireplace] **1.** coal, oil, gas, wood, etc. burned to supply heat or power **2.** fissionable material, as in a nuclear reactor **3.** anything that maintains or intensifies strong feeling, etc. —***vt.*** **-eled** or **-elled, -el·ing** or **-el·ling** to supply with fuel —***vi.*** to get fuel —**fu′el·er, fu′el·ler** ***n.***
fuel cell any of various devices that convert chemical energy directly into electrical energy
fuel oil any oil used for fuel
-fuge (fyo͞oj) [Fr. < L. *fugere*, to flee] *a suffix meaning* something that drives away [*vermifuge*]
fu·gi·tive (fyo͞o′jə tiv) ***adj.*** [< OFr. < L. pp. of *fugere*, to flee] **1.** fleeing or having fled, as from danger, justice, etc. **2.** passing quickly; fleeting; evanescent **3.** on matters of temporary interest [*fugitive* essays] **4.** roaming; shifting —***n.*** **1.** a person who flees or has fled from danger, justice, etc. **2.** a fleeting or elusive thing —**fu′gi·tive·ly** ***adv.***
fugue (fyo͞og) ***n.*** [Fr. < It. < L. < *fugere*, to flee] a musical composition in which a subject is announced by one voice and then developed contrapuntally by each of usually two or three other voices —**fu′gal** ***adj.*** —**fugu′ist** ***n.***
‡**Füh·rer, Fueh·rer** (fü′rər; *E.* fyo͞or′ər) ***n.*** [G. < *führen*, to lead] leader: title used by A. Hitler
Fu·ji (fo͞o′jē) extinct volcano on Honshu island, Japan, near Tokyo: also **Fu′ji·ya′ma** (-yä′mə)
-ful (fəl, f'l; *for 4, usually* fool) [OE. < *full*, FULL[1]] *a suffix meaning:* **1.** full of, characterized by, having [*joyful*] **2.** having the qualities of [*masterful*] **3.** able or tending to [*helpful*] **4.** *pl.* **-fuls** the quantity that fills [*handful*]
ful·crum (fool′krəm, ful′-) ***n.***, *pl.* **-crums, -cra** (-krə) [L., akin to *fulcire*, to prop] **1.** the support or point of support on which a lever turns in raising or moving something **2.** a means of exerting influence, pressure, etc.

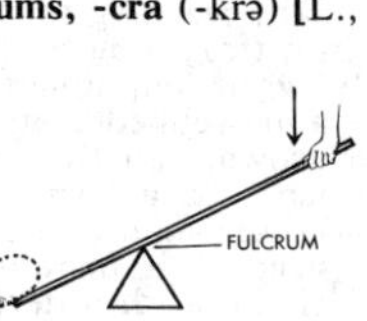

ful·fill, ful·fil (fool fil′) ***vt.*** **-filled′, -fill′ing** [OE. *fullfyllan*] **1.** to carry out (something promised, predicted, etc.); cause to be or happen **2.** to do (something required); obey **3.** to satisfy (a condition) **4.** to bring to an end; complete —**fulfill oneself** to realize completely one's ambitions, potentialities, etc. —**ful·fill′er** ***n.*** —**ful·fill′ment, ful·fil′ment** ***n.***
ful·gent (ful′jənt, fool′-) ***adj.*** [< L. prp. of *fulgere*, to flash] [Now Rare] very bright; radiant
full[1] (fool) ***adj.*** [OE.] **1.** having in it all there is space for; filled [a *full* jar] **2.** *a*) having eaten all that one wants *b*) having had more than one can stand (*of*) **3.** occupying all of a given space [a *full* load] **4.** well supplied or provided (with *of*) [a tank *full* of gas] **5.** filling the required number, measure, etc.; complete [a *full* dozen] **6.** thorough; absolute [come to a *full* stop] **7.** having reached the greatest development, size, etc. [a *full* moon] **8.** having the same parents [*full* brothers] **9.** having clearness, volume, and depth [a *full* tone] **10.** of the highest rank [a *full* professor] **11.** plump; round [a *full* face] **12.** with loose,

wide folds; ample *[a full skirt]* **13.** deeply affected, engrossed, etc. *—n.* the greatest amount, extent, number, etc. *—adv.* **1.** completely *[a full-grown boy]* **2.** directly *[struck full in the face]* **3.** very *[full well]* *—vt.* to make (a skirt, etc.) with loose folds *—vi.* to become full: said of the moon **—in full 1.** to, for, or with the full amount, value, etc. **2.** not abbreviated or condensed

full[2] (fo͞ol) *vt., vi.* [< OFr., ult. < L. *fullo,* cloth fuller] to shrink and thicken (cloth, esp. of wool) with moisture, heat, and pressure

full·back (-bak′) *n. Football* a member of the offensive backfield, traditionally the back farthest behind the line

full-blood·ed (-blud′id) *adj.* **1.** of unmixed breed or race; purebred: also **full′-blood′** **2.** vigorous; lusty **3.** genuine **4.** rich and full

full-blown (-blōn′) *adj.* **1.** in full bloom; open: said of flowers **2.** fully developed; mature

full-bod·ied (-bäd′ēd) *adj.* having much strength, flavor, substance, etc.

full dress formal clothes for important occasions; esp., formal evening clothes **—full′-dress′** *adj.*

full·er (fo͞ol′ər) *n.* one whose work is to full cloth

full·er's earth (fo͞ol′ərz) a highly absorbent clay used to remove grease from cloth in fulling, to clarify oils, etc.

Ful·ler·ton (fo͞ol′ər tən) [after G. *Fullerton,* a founder] city in SW Calif.: suburb of Los Angeles: pop. 102,000

full-fash·ioned (fo͞ol′fash′′nd) *adj.* knitted to conform to body contours, as hosiery or sweaters

full-fledged (-flejd′) *adj.* completely developed or trained; of full rank or status

full house a poker hand containing three of a kind and a pair, as three jacks and two fives

full moon the phase of the moon when its entire illuminated hemisphere is seen as a full disk

full nelson *see* NELSON

full·ness, ful·ness (-nis) *n.* the quality or state of being full

full sail 1. with every sail set **2.** with maximum speed and energy

full-scale (-skāl′) *adj.* **1.** according to the original or standard scale *[a full-scale drawing]* **2.** to the utmost limit, degree, etc. *[full-scale war]*

full-time (-tīm′) *adj.* on a complete regular schedule

full time as a full-time employee, student, etc. *[to work full time]*

full·y (-ē) *adv.* **1.** to the full; completely; entirely **2.** abundantly; amply **3.** at least *[fully two hours later]*

ful·mi·nate (ful′mə nāt′) *vi.* **-nat′ed, -nat′ing** [< L. pp. of *fulminare* < *fulmen,* lightning] **1.** to explode with violence; detonate **2.** to shout forth denunciations, decrees, etc. *—vt.* **1.** to cause to explode **2.** to shout forth (denunciations, etc.) *—n.* any of certain highly explosive compounds used in detonators and percussion caps **—ful′mi·nant** *adj.* **—ful′mi·na′tion** *n.* **—ful′mi·na′tor** *n.*

ful·some (fo͞ol′səm, ful′-) *adj.* [ME. < *ful,* FULL[1] + *-som,* -SOME[1], but infl. by *ful,* foul] disgusting or offensive, esp. because excessive or insincere *[fulsome praise]* **—ful′some·ly** *adv.* **—ful′some·ness** *n.*

Ful·ton (fo͞ol′t'n), **Robert** 1765–1815; U.S. inventor & engineer: designer of the 1st commercially successful U.S. steamboat

fum·ble (fum′b'l) *vi., vt.* **-bled, -bling** [prob. < ON. *famla,* to grope] **1.** to grope clumsily **2.** to handle (a thing) clumsily; bungle **3.** to lose one's grasp on (a football, etc.) while trying to catch or hold it **4.** to make (one's way) as by groping *—n.* the act or fact of fumbling **—fum′bler** *n.* **—fum′bling·ly** *adv.*

fume (fyo͞om) *n.* [< OFr. < L. *fumus*] [*often pl.*] a gas, smoke, or vapor, esp. if offensive or suffocating *—vi.* **fumed, fum′ing 1.** to give off fumes **2.** to rise up or pass off in fumes **3.** to show, or give way to, anger, annoyance, etc. *—vt.* **1.** to expose to fumes **2.** to give off as fumes

fu·mi·gant (fyo͞o′mə gənt) *n.* any substance used in fumigating

fu·mi·gate (-gāt′) *vt.* **-gat′ed, -gat′ing** [< L. pp. of *fumigare* < *fumus,* smoke + *agere,* to make] to expose to the action of fumes, esp. in order to disinfect or kill the vermin in **—fu′mi·ga′tion** *n.* **—fu′mi·ga′tor** *n.*

fum·y (fyo͞o′mē) *adj.* **fum′i·er, fum′i·est** full of or producing fumes; vaporous

fun (fun) *n.* [< ME. *fonne,* a fool, or *fonnen,* to be foolish < ?] **1.** *a)* lively, gay play or playfulness; amusement, sport, recreation, etc. *b)* enjoyment or pleasure **2.** a source of amusement; amusing person or thing *—adj.* [Colloq.] intended for pleasure and amusement *[a fun gift]* *—vi.* **funned, fun′ning** [Colloq.] to make fun; play or joke **—for** (or **in**) **fun** playfully; not seriously **—like fun** [Slang] by no means; not at all **—make fun of** to mock laughingly; ridicule

func·tion (fuŋk′shən) *n.* [OFr. < L. *functio* < pp. of *fungi,* to perform] **1.** the normal or characteristic action of anything; esp., any of the specialized actions of an organ or part of an animal or plant **2.** a special duty or performance required in the course of work or activity **3.** a formal ceremony or social occasion **4.** a thing that depends on and varies with something else **5.** *Math.* a quantity whose value depends on that of another quantity or quantities *—vi.* **1.** to act in a required manner; work **2.** to have a function; be used (*as*)

func·tion·al (-əl) *adj.* **1.** of a function or functions **2.** *a)* performing a function *b)* intended to be useful **3.** *Med.* affecting a function of some organ without apparent structural or organic changes *[a functional disease]* **—func′tion·al·ly** *adv.*

func·tion·al·ism (-əl iz'm) *n.* emphasis on adapting the structure of anything to its function **—func′tion·al·ist** *n., adj.* **—func′tion·al·is′tic** *adj.*

func·tion·ar·y (-er′ē) *n., pl.* **-ar′ies** a person who performs a certain function; esp., an official

fund (fund) *n.* [L. *fundus,* bottom, land] **1.** a supply that can be drawn on; stock; store *[a fund of good humor]* **2.** *a)* a sum of money set aside for a particular purpose *b)* an organization to administer it *c)* [*pl.*] ready money *—vt.* **1.** to provide money to pay the interest on (a debt) **2.** to put or convert into a long-term debt that bears interest **3.** to put in a fund; accumulate **4.** to provide for with a fund

fun·da·ment (fun′də mənt) *n.* [< OFr. < L. < *fundus:* see prec.] **1.** the buttocks **2.** the anus

fun·da·men·tal (fun′də men′t'l) *adj.* [< ML. < L. *fundamentum:* see prec.] **1.** of or forming a foundation or basis; basic; essential **2.** primary; original **3.** most important; chief **4.** *Music a)* designating or of the lowest, or root, tone of a chord *b)* designating or of the prime or main tone of a harmonic series *—n.* **1.** a principle, law, etc. serving as a basis; essential part **2.** *Music* the fundamental tone of a chord or harmonic series **—fun′da·men′tal·ly** *adv.*

fun·da·men·tal·ism (-iz'm) *n.* [*sometimes* **F-**] **1.** religious beliefs based on a literal interpretation of the Bible and regarded as fundamental to Christian faith **2.** among some American Protestants, the movement based on these beliefs **—fun′da·men′tal·ist** *n., adj.*

fundamental particle *same as* ELEMENTARY PARTICLE

Fun·dy (fun′dē), **Bay of** arm of the Atlantic, between New Brunswick & Nova Scotia, Canada

fu·ner·al (fyo͞o′nər əl) *adj.* [< LL. < L. *funus* (gen. *funeris*), a funeral] of or for a funeral *—n.* **1.** the ceremonies connected with burial or cremation of the dead **2.** the procession accompanying the body to the place of burial or cremation

funeral director the manager of a funeral home

funeral home (or **parlor**) a business establishment where the bodies of the dead are prepared for burial or cremation and where funeral services can be held

fu·ne·re·al (fyoo nir′ē əl) *adj.* suitable for a funeral; sad and solemn; gloomy **—fu·ne′re·al·ly** *adv.*

fun·gi·cide (fun′jə sīd′, fuŋ′gə-) *n.* [< FUNGUS & -CIDE] any substance that kills fungi **—fun′gi·ci′dal** *adj.*

fun·goid (fuŋ′goid) *adj.* like or characteristic of a fungus *—n.* a fungus

fun·gous (-gəs) *adj.* of, like, or caused by fungi

fun·gus (fuŋ′gəs) *n., pl.* **fun·gi** (fun′jī, fuŋ′gī), **fun′gus·es** [L., prob. < Gr. *spongos,* a sponge] **1.** any of a group of thallophytes, including molds, mildews, mushrooms, rusts, and smut, that lack chlorophyll, true roots, stems, and leaves and reproduce by means of spores **2.** something that grows suddenly and rapidly like a fungus *—adj.* of, like, or caused by a fungus

fu·nic·u·lar (fyoo nik′yoo lər) *adj.* [< L. *funiculus,* dim. of *funis,* a rope] of or worked by a rope or cable *—n.* a mountain railway on which counterbalanced cars ascend and descend by cables: also **funicular railway**

funk[1] (fuŋk) *n.* [< ? Fl. *fonck,* dismay] [Colloq.] **1.** a cowering through fear; panic **2.** a low, depressed mood: also **blue funk** *—vi.* [Colloq.] to be in a funk or panic *—vt.* [Colloq.] **1.** to be afraid of **2.** to shrink from in fear 3. to frighten

funk[2] (fuŋk) *n.* [cf. FUNKY[2]] **1.** a musty odor, as of moldy tobacco **2.** funky jazz

fun·ky[1] (fuŋ′kē) *adj.* **-ki·er, -ki·est** in a funk, or panic

fun·ky[2] (fuŋ′kē) *adj.* **-ki·er, -ki·est** [orig. Negro argot, earthy < obs. *funk,* smell, smoke] *Jazz* having an earthy quality or style derived from early blues **—fun′ki·ness** *n.*

fun·nel (fun′'l) *n.* [< Pr. < L. (*in*)*fundibulum* < *in-,* in + *fundere,* to pour] **1.** a slender tube with a wide, cone-shaped mouth, for pouring liquids and powders into containers with small openings **2.** anything shaped like a funnel **3.** *a)* a cylindrical smokestack, as of a steamship *b)* a chimney or flue —*vi., vt.* **-neled** or **-nelled, -nel·ing** or **-nel·ling** **1.** to move or pour through a funnel **2.** to move into a central channel or place

fun·ny (fun′ē) *adj.* **-ni·er, -ni·est** **1.** causing laughter; amusing; humorous **2.** [Colloq.] *a)* strange; queer *b)* deceptive or tricky —*n., pl.* **-nies** [Colloq.] *same as* COMIC STRIP: *usually in pl.* —**fun′ni·ly** *adv.* —**fun′ni·ness** *n.*

funny bone [prob. a pun on *humerus* (hence "humorous")] **1.** a place on the elbow where the ulnar nerve passes close to the surface: a sharp impact at this place causes a strange, tingling sensation in the arm **2.** inclination to laughter

fur (fur) *n.* [< OFr. < *fuerre*, a sheath < Frank. *fodr*] **1.** the soft, thick hair covering the body of many mammals **2.** a skin bearing such hair, processed for making garments **3.** any garment made of such skins **4.** any fuzzy coating, as diseased matter on the tongue in illness —*adj.* of fur —*vt.* **furred, fur′ring** **1.** to line, cover, or trim with fur **2.** to coat with a furry deposit **3.** to make level with furring strips —*vi.* to become furred with a deposit —**make the fur fly** **1.** to cause dissension or fighting **2.** to work busily

fur·be·low (fur′bə lō′) *n.* [var. of Fr. *falbala*] **1.** a flounce or ruffle **2.** [*usually pl.*] showy trimming —*vt.* to decorate as with furbelows

fur·bish (fur′bish) *vt.* [< OFr. *forbir* < WGmc.] **1.** to brighten by rubbing or scouring; burnish **2.** to make usable again; renovate —**fur′bish·er** *n.*

fur·cate (fur′kāt; *for adj., also* -kit) *adj.* [< ML. < L. *furca*, a fork] forked —*vi.* **-cat·ed, -cat·ing** to branch; fork —**fur′cate·ly** *adv.* —**fur·ca′tion** *n.*

Fu·ries (fyoor′ēz) *Gr. & Rom. Myth.* three female spirits who punished doers of unavenged crimes

fu·ri·ous (fyoor′ē əs) *adj.* [< OFr. < L. *furiosus*] **1.** full of fury or wild rage **2.** violently overpowering **3.** very great; intense [*furious* speed] —**fu′ri·ous·ly** *adv.* —**fu′ri·ous·ness** *n.*

furl (furl) *vt.* [< OFr. *ferlier* < *fermlier*, to tie up < *ferm*, FIRM[1] + *lier*, to tie] to roll up tightly and make secure, as a flag to a staff —*vi.* to become curled or rolled up —*n.* **1.** a roll or coil of something furled **2.** a furling or being furled

fur·long (fur′lôŋ) *n.* [< OE. < *furh*, a furrow + *lang*, LONG[1]] a measure of distance equal to 1/8 of a mile, or 220 yards

fur·lough (fur′lō) *n.* [< Du. *verlof*] a leave of absence; esp., a leave granted to military enlisted personnel —*vt.* **1.** to grant a furlough to **2.** to lay off (employees), esp. temporarily

fur·nace (fur′nəs) *n.* [< OFr. < L. *fornax* < *fornus*, oven] **1.** an enclosed structure in which heat is produced for heating a building, reducing ores and metals, etc. **2.** any extremely hot place

fur·nish (fur′nish) *vt.* [< OFr. < *furnir* < OFrank.] **1.** to equip with whatever is necessary; esp., to put furniture into (a room, apartment, etc.) **2.** to supply; provide —**fur′nish·er** *n.*

fur·nish·ings (-iŋz) *n.pl.* **1.** the furniture, carpets, etc. for a room, apartment, etc. **2.** articles of dress; things to wear [men's *furnishings*]

fur·ni·ture (fur′ni chər) *n.* [Fr. *fourniture* < *fournir*, FURNISH] **1.** the movable things in a room, etc. which equip it for living, as chairs, beds, etc. **2.** the necessary equipment of a ship, trade, etc.

fu·ror (fyoor′ôr) *n.* [< OFr. *fureur* < L. *furor*] **1.** fury; rage **2.** *a)* widespread enthusiasm; craze *b)* a commotion or uproar Also for 2, **fu′rore** (-ôr)

furred (furd) *adj.* **1.** made, trimmed, or lined with fur **2.** having fur **3.** wearing fur **4.** having a furry coating, as the tongue **5.** made level with furring strips

fur·ri·er (fur′ē ər) *n.* **1.** a dealer in furs **2.** one who processes furs or makes and repairs fur garments —**fur′ri·er·y** *n., pl.* **-er·ies**

fur·ring (fur′iŋ) *n.* **1.** the act of trimming, lining, etc. with fur **2.** fur so used **3.** a furry coating, as on the tongue **4.** *a)* the leveling of a floor, wall, etc. with thin strips of wood or metal before adding boards or plaster *b)* the strips (in full, **furring strips**) so used

fur·row (fur′ō) *n.* [OE. *furh*] **1.** a narrow groove made in the ground by a plow **2.** anything like this, as a wrinkle on the face —*vt.* to make furrows in —*vi.* **1.** to make furrows **2.** to become wrinkled

fur·ry (fur′ē) *adj.* **-ri·er, -ri·est** **1.** of, like, or made of fur **2.** covered with or wearing fur **3.** having a furlike coating —**fur′ri·ness** *n.*

fur·ther (fur′thər) *adj. alt. compar. of* FAR [OE. *furthra*] **1.** additional; more **2.** more distant; farther —*adv. alt. compar. of* FAR **1.** to a greater degree or extent **2.** in addition; moreover **3.** at or to a greater distance in space or time In sense 2 of the *adj.* and sense 3 of the *adv.*, FARTHER is more commonly used —*vt.* [< OE. *fyrthrian* < *furthra*] to give aid to; promote —**fur′ther·er** *n.*

fur·ther·ance (-əns) *n.* a furthering, or helping forward; advancement; promotion

fur·ther·more (-môr′) *adv.* besides; moreover; in addition

fur·ther·most (-mōst′) *adj.* most distant; furthest

fur·thest (fur′thist) *adj. alt. superl. of* FAR [ME., formed as superl. on analogy of *further*] most distant; farthest —*adv. alt. superl. of* FAR **1.** at or to the greatest distance in space or time **2.** to the greatest degree or extent; most

fur·tive (fur′tiv) *adj.* [< Fr. < L. *furtivus*, stolen < *fur*, thief] done or acting in a stealthy manner; sneaky —**fur′tive·ly** *adv.* —**fur′tive·ness** *n.*

fu·ry (fyoor′ē) *n., pl.* **-ries** [< OFr. < L. *furia* < *furere*, to rage] **1.** *a)* violent anger; wild rage *b)* a fit of this **2.** violence; vehemence; fierceness **3.** a violent, vengeful person **4.** [F-] any of the Furies —**like fury** [Colloq.] violently, swiftly, etc.

furze (furz) *n.* [OE. *fyrs*] a prickly evergreen shrub with yellow flowers, esp. on wastelands

fuse[1] (fyo͞oz) *vt., vi.* **fused, fus′ing** [< L. pp. of *fundere*, to shed] **1.** to melt or to join by melting, as metals **2.** to unite or blend together

fuse[2] (fyo͞oz) *n.* [< It. < L. *fusus*, hollow spindle] **1.** a tube or wick filled with combustible material for setting off an explosive charge **2.** *same as* FUZE[2] (*n.* 2) **3.** *Elec.* a strip of easily melted metal placed in a circuit as a safeguard: if the current becomes too strong, the metal melts, thus breaking the circuit —*vt.* **fused, fus′ing** to connect a fuse to —**blow a fuse** **1.** to cause an electrical fuse to melt **2.** [Colloq.] to become very angry

fu·see (fyo͞o zē′) *n.* [Fr. *fusée*, rocket < ML. < L. *fusus*: see prec.] **1.** formerly, a friction match with a large head **2.** a colored flare used as a signal by railroaders, truck drivers, etc.

fu·se·lage (fyo͞o′sə läzh′, -läj′, -lij; -zə-) *n.* [Fr. < *fuselé*, tapering] the body of an airplane, exclusive of the wings, tail, and engines

fu·sel oil (fyo͞o′z'l, -s'l) [G. *fusel*, inferior liquor] an oily, acrid, poisonous liquid occurring in insufficiently distilled alcoholic products

Fu·shun (fo͞o′sho͞on′) city in NE China: pop. 1,019,000

fu·si·ble (fyo͞o′zə b'l) *adj.* that can be fused or easily melted —**fu′si·bil′i·ty** *n.* —**fu′si·bly** *adv.*

fu·si·form (fyo͞o′zə fôrm′) *adj.* [< L. *fusus*, a spindle + -FORM] shaped like a spindle

fu·sil (fyo͞o′z'l) *n.* [Fr., orig., steel for striking sparks < ML. < L. *focus*, hearth] a light flintlock musket

fu·sil·ier, fu·sil·eer (fyo͞o′zə lir′) *n.* formerly, a soldier armed with a fusil: the term *Fusiliers* is still applied to certain British regiments

fu·sil·lade (fyo͞o′sə lād′, -läd′; -zə-) *n.* [Fr. < *fusiller*, to shoot: see FUSIL] **1.** a simultaneous discharge of many firearms **2.** something like this [a *fusillade* of questions] —*vt.* **-lad′ed, -lad′ing** to shoot down or attack with a fusillade

fu·sion (fyo͞o′zhən) *n.* **1.** a fusing or melting together **2.** a blending; coalition [a *fusion* of political parties] **3.** anything made by fusing **4.** *same as* NUCLEAR FUSION

fu·sion·ism (-iz'm) *n.* the promoting of coalition, esp. of political parties —**fu′sion·ist** *n., adj.*

fuss (fus) *n.* [prob. echoic] **1.** a flurry of nervous, excited activity; bustle **2.** nervousness, agitation, etc. **3.** [Colloq.] a quarrel **4.** [Colloq.] a showy display of delight, etc. —*vi.* **1.** to cause or make a fuss **2.** to bustle about or worry over trifles **3.** to whine or fret, as a baby —*vt.* [Colloq.] to bother unnecessarily

fuss·budg·et (-buj′it) *n.* [FUSS + BUDGET, prob. in sense "bag"] [Colloq.] a fussy person

fuss·y (fus′ē) *adj.* **fuss′i·er, fuss′i·est** **1.** bustling about or worrying over trifles **2.** hard to please **3.** whining or fretting, as a baby **4.** showing or needing careful attention **5.** full of unnecessary details —**fuss′i·ly** *adv.* —**fuss′i·ness** *n.*

fus·tian (fus′chən) *n.* [< OFr. < ML. < L. *fustis*, wooden stick] **1.** orig., a coarse cloth of cotton and linen **2.** now, cotton corduroy or velveteen **3.** pompous, pretentious talk or writing —*adj.* **1.** made of fustian **2.** pompous; pretentious

fus·ty (fus′tē) *adj.* **fus′ti·er, fus′ti·est** [< *fust*, a musty smell < Early ModE., a cask < OFr., tree trunk] **1.** smelling stale or stuffy; musty; moldy **2.** old-fashioned —**fus′ti·ly** *adv.* —**fus′ti·ness** *n.*

fut. future

fu·tile (fyo͞ot′'l; *chiefly Brit. & Canad.*, fyo͞o′tīl) *adj.* [Fr. < L. *futilis*, lit., that easily pours out, hence worthless < *fundere*, to pour] **1.** *a)* useless; vain; hopeless *b)* ineffective **2.** trifling or unimportant —**fu′tile·ly** *adv.* —**fu·til·i·ty** (fyoo til′ə tē), *pl.* **-ties, fu′tile·ness** *n.*

fut·tock (fut′ək) *n.* [< ? pronun. of *foot hook*] any of the curved timbers forming the ribs of a wooden ship

fu·ture (fyo͞o′chər) *adj.* [< OFr. < L. *futurus*, used as fut. part. of *esse*, to be] **1.** that is to be or come **2.** indicating time to come [the *future* tense of a verb] —*n.* **1.** the time that is to come **2.** what will happen; what is going to be **3.** prospective condition; chance to be successful [he has a great *future* in law] **4.** [*usually pl.*] a contract for a com-

modity bought or sold for delivery at a later date 5. *Gram.* *a*) the future tense *b*) a verb form in this tense
future perfect 1. a tense indicating an action or state as completed in relation to a specified time in the future 2. a verb form in this tense (Ex.: will have gone)
future shock a sudden awareness of one's inaccurate evaluation of the future and the resulting inability to cope with the rapid and myriad changes of modern society
fu·tur·ism (-iz'm) ***n.*** a movement in the arts shortly before World War I which opposed traditionalism and stressed the dynamic movement and violence of the machine age —**fu′tur·ist** ***n., adj.***
fu·tur·is·tic (fyo͞o′chər is′tik) ***adj.*** of or having to do with the future or futurism —**fu′tur·is′ti·cal·ly** ***adv.***
fu·tu·ri·ty (fyoo toor′ə tē, -tyoor′-, -choor′-) ***n., pl.*** **-ties** 1. *a*) the future *b*) a future condition or event 2. the quality of being future 3. a horse race in which entries are made far ahead of time: in full, **futurity race**
fuze[1] (fyo͞oz) ***vt., vi.*** **fuzed, fuz′ing** *same as* FUSE[1]
fuze[2] (fyo͞oz) ***n.*** 1. *same as* FUSE[2] (*n.* 1) 2. any of various devices for detonating a bomb, projectile, etc. —***vt.*** **fuzed, fuz′ing** to connect a fuze to
fu·zee (fyo͞o zē′) ***n.*** *same as* FUSEE
fuzz (fuz) ***n.*** [< ? Du. *voos*, or back-formation < FUZZY] very loose, light particles of down, wool, etc.; fine hairs or fibers *[*the *fuzz* on a peach*]* —***vi., vt.*** 1. to cover or become covered with fuzz 2. to make or become fuzzy —**the fuzz** [< ? FUSSY (sense 2)] [Slang] a policeman or the police
fuzz·y (-ē) ***adj.*** **fuzz′i·er, fuzz′i·est** [prob. < LowG. *fussig*, spongy] 1. of, like, or covered with fuzz 2. not clear, distinct, or precise; blurred —**fuzz′i·ly** ***adv.*** —**fuzz′i·ness** ***n.***
-fy (fī) [< OFr. *-fier* < L. *-ficare* < *facere*, to make, do] *a suffix meaning:* 1. to make; cause to be *[liquefy]* 2. to cause to have; imbue with *[glorify]* 3. to become *[putrefy]*
FYI for your information

G

G, g (jē) ***n., pl.*** **G's, g's** 1. the seventh letter of the English alphabet 2. a sound of *G* or *g* 3. *Physics* *a*) gravity *b*) acceleration of gravity or a unit of acceleration equal to it, used to measure the force on a body undergoing acceleration
G (jē) ***n.*** 1. [< G(RAND), *n.* 2] [Slang] one thousand dollars 2. *Educ.* a grade meaning *good* 3. *Music* *a*) the fifth tone in the ascending scale of C major *b*) the scale having this tone as the keynote
G general audience: a motion-picture rating meaning that the film is considered suitable for persons of all ages
G. German
G., g. 1. *Elec.* conductance 2. gauge 3. gram(s) 4. guilder(s) 5. guinea(s) 6. gulf
Ga *Chem.* gallium
Ga., GA Georgia
gab (gab) ***vi.*** **gabbed, gab′bing** [< ON. *gabba*, to mock] [Colloq.] to talk much or idly; chatter —***n.*** [Colloq.] idle talk; chatter —**gift of (the) gab** [Colloq.] the ability to speak glibly —**gab′ber** ***n.***
gab·ar·dine (gab′ər dēn′, gab′ər dēn′) ***n.*** [var. of GABERDINE] 1. a twilled cloth of wool, cotton, rayon, etc., with a fine, diagonal weave, used for suits, coats, dresses, etc. 2. a garment made of this cloth 3. *same as* GABERDINE
gab·ble (gab′'l) ***vi.*** **-bled, -bling** [freq. of GAB] 1. to talk rapidly and incoherently; jabber 2. to utter rapid sounds, as a goose —***vt.*** to utter rapidly and incoherently —***n.*** rapid, incoherent talk or meaningless utterance —**gab′bler** ***n.***
gab·by (-ē) ***adj.*** **-bi·er, -bi·est** [Colloq.] inclined to chatter; talkative —**gab′bi·ness** ***n.***
gab·er·dine (gab′ər dēn′, gab′ər dēn′) ***n.*** [< OFr. *gaverdine*, kind of cloak < ? MHG. *walvart*, pilgrimage] 1. a loose coat of coarse cloth worn in the Middle Ages, esp. by Jews 2. *chiefly Brit. sp. of* GABARDINE
gab·fest (gab′fest′) ***n.*** [GAB + -FEST] [Colloq.] 1. an informal gathering of people to talk or gab 2. their talk
ga·bi·on (gā′bē ən) ***n.*** [Fr. < It. < *gabbia*, cage < L. *cavea*: see CAGE] 1. a cylinder of wicker filled with earth or stones, formerly used in building fortifications 2. a similar cylinder of metal, used in building dams, dikes, etc.
ga·ble (gā′b'l) ***n.*** [< OFr. < Gmc., as in ON. *gafl*, gable] 1. *a*) the triangular wall enclosed by the sloping ends of a ridged roof *b*) popularly, the whole section formed by these 2. an end wall having a gable at the top 3. a triangular decorative feature, as over a door —***vt.*** **-bled, -bling** to put gables on

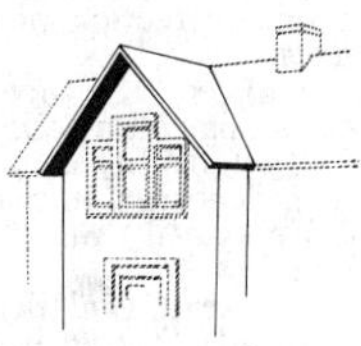
GABLE (sense 1)

gable roof a roof forming a gable at each end
Ga·bon (gȧ bōn′) country on the W coast of Africa: 103,089 sq. mi.; pop. 480,000 —**Gab·on·ese** (gab′ə nēz′) ***adj., n., pl.*** **-ese′**
Ga·bri·el (gā′brē əl) [Heb. *gabhrī'ēl*, lit., God is (my) strength] 1. a masculine name: dim. *Gabe* 2. *Bible* an archangel, the herald of good news
Gad (gad) ***interj.*** [euphemism for GOD] [*also* **g-**] a mild oath or expression of surprise, etc.
gad[1] (gad) ***vi.*** **gad′ded, gad′ding** [? a back-formation < OE. *gædeling*, companion] to wander about in a restless way, as in seeking amusement —***n.*** a gadding: chiefly in **on the gad** —**gad′der** ***n.***
gad[2] (gad) ***n.*** [ON. *gaddr*] *same as* GOAD
gad·a·bout (gad′ə bout′) ***n.*** [Colloq.] a person who gads about; restless seeker after fun, excitement, etc. —***adj.*** fond of gadding
gad·fly (-flī′) ***n., pl.*** **-flies′** [GAD[2] + FLY[2]] 1. a large fly that bites livestock 2. a person who annoys or rouses others
gadg·et (gaj′it) ***n.*** [< ?] 1. any small mechanical contrivance 2. any small object
gadg·e·teer (gaj′ə tir′) ***n.*** a person who contrives, or delights in, gadgets
gadg·et·ry (gaj′ət rē) ***n.*** 1. gadgets collectively 2. preoccupation with mere gadgets
gad·o·lin·i·um (gad′'l in′ē əm) ***n.*** [ModL., after J. *Gadolin* (1760–1852), Finn. chemist] a metallic chemical element of the rare-earth group: symbol, Gd; at. wt., 157.25; at. no., 64
Gads·den (gadz′dən) [after J. *Gadsden* (1788–1858), U.S. diplomat] city in NE Ala.: pop. 54,000
gad·wall (gad′wôl) ***n., pl.*** **-walls, -wall:** see PLURAL, II, D, 1 [< ?] a grayish-brown wild duck of the N freshwater regions of America
Gae·a (jē′ə) [Gr. *Gaia* < *gē*, earth] *Gr. Myth.* the earth personified as a goddess
Gael (gāl) ***n.*** [contr. < Gael. *Gaidheal*] a Celt of Scotland, Ireland, or the Isle of Man; esp., a Celt of the Scottish Highlands
Gael·ic (-ik) ***adj.*** 1. of the Gaels 2. of the Goidelic subbranch of the Celtic family of languages; of Scottish or Irish Gaelic —***n.*** one of the Goidelic languages; esp., Scottish or Irish Gaelic: abbrev. **Gael.**
gaff (gaf) ***n.*** [< OFr. < Pr. *gaf* or Sp. *gafa* < ?] 1. a large, strong hook on a pole, or a barbed spear, for landing large fish 2. a sharp metal spur fastened to the leg of a gamecock 3. a spar or pole supporting a fore-and-aft sail 4. [Slang] any secret device for cheating —***vt.*** to strike or land (a fish) with a gaff —**stand the gaff** [Slang] to bear up well under difficulties, punishment, etc.
gaffe (gaf) ***n.*** [Fr.] a blunder; faux pas
gaf·fer (gaf′ər) ***n.*** [altered < GODFATHER] an old man: now usually humorous
gag (gag) ***vt.*** **gagged, gag′ging** [echoic] 1. to cause to retch or choke 2. to cover or stuff the mouth of, so as to keep from talking, crying out, etc. 3. to keep from speaking or expressing oneself freely, as by intimidation 4. to prevent or limit speech in (a legislative body) —***vi.*** to retch or choke —***n.*** 1. something put into or over the mouth to prevent talking, etc. 2. any restraint of free speech 3. *a*) a comi-

cal remark or act, as on the stage; joke *b)* a practical joke —**gag′ger** *n.*

gage¹ (gāj) *n.* [< OFr., a pledge, pawn < Gmc.] **1.** something pledged to insure that an obligation will be fulfilled; security **2.** a pledge to appear and fight, as a glove thrown down by a challenging knight **3.** a challenge —*vt.* **gaged, gag′ing** [Archaic] to offer as or bind by a pledge

gage² (gāj) *n., vt. same as* GAUGE

gag·gle (gag′'l) *n.* [< ME. *gagelen,* to cackle] **1.** a flock of geese **2.** any group or cluster of persons or things

gag·man (-man′) *n., pl.* **-men′** (-men′) a man who devises jokes, bits of comic business, etc., as for entertainers

gai·e·ty (gā′ə tē) *n., pl.* **-ties** **1.** the state or quality of being gay; cheerfulness **2.** merrymaking; festivity **3.** finery; showy brightness

Gail (gāl) [dim. of ABIGAIL] a feminine name

gai·ly (gā′lē) *adv.* in a gay manner; specif., *a)* happily; merrily *b)* brightly; with bright display

gain (gān) *n.* [< OFr. < *gaaignier,* to earn] **1.** an increase; addition; specif., *a)* [*often pl.*] an increase in wealth, earnings, etc.; profit *b)* an increase in advantage; improvement **2.** the act of getting something; acquisition **3.** *Electronics a)* an increase in signal strength *b)* the ratio of output to input —*vt.* **1.** to get by labor; earn **2.** to get by effort or merit; win **3.** to attract [*to gain one's interest*] **4.** to get as an addition, profit, or advantage **5.** to make an increase in [*to gain speed*] **6.** to go faster by [*my watch gained two minutes*] **7.** to get to; reach —*vi.* **1.** to make progress; improve or advance, as in health **2.** to acquire profit **3.** to become heavier **4.** to be fast: said of a clock, etc. —**gain on 1.** to draw nearer to (an opponent in a race, etc.) **2.** to make more progress than (a competitor) —**gain over** to win over to one's side

gain·er (gā′nər) *n.* **1.** a person or thing that gains **2.** a fancy dive in which the diver faces forward and does a backward somersault in the air

Gaines·ville (gānz′vil) [after Gen. E. *Gaines* (1777–1849)] city in NC Fla.: pop. 81,000

gain·ful (gān′f'l) *adj.* producing gain; profitable —**gain′ful·ly** *adv.* —**gain′ful·ness** *n.*

gain·ly (gān′lē) *adj.* **-li·er, -li·est** [< ON. *gegn,* straight, fit] shapely and graceful —**gain′li·ness** *n.*

gain·say (gān′sā′) *vt.* **-said′** (-sed′, -sād′), **-say′ing** [< OE. *gegn,* against + *seggan,* SAY] **1.** to deny **2.** to contradict **3.** to speak or act against; oppose —*n.* a gainsaying —**gain′say′er** *n.*

Gains·bor·ough (gānz′bur′ō, -bər ə), **Thomas** 1727–88; Eng. painter

'gainst, gainst (genst, gānst) *prep. poet. clip of* AGAINST

gait (gāt) *n.* [< ON. *gata,* path] **1.** manner of walking or running **2.** any of various foot movements of a horse, as a trot, canter, etc. —*vt.* to train (a horse) to certain gaits —**gait′ed** *adj.*

gai·ter (gāt′ər) *n.* [altered (after prec.) < Fr. *guêtre*] **1.** a cloth or leather covering for the instep and ankle and, sometimes, the calf of the leg; spat or legging **2.** a shoe with elastic sides and no lacing **3.** a high overshoe with a cloth upper

gal (gal) *n.* [Colloq.] a girl

Gal. Galatians

gal. gallon; gallons

ga·la (gā′lə, gal′ə) *n.* [It. < OFr. *gale,* enjoyment] a festive occasion; festival; celebration —*adj.* festive, or suitable for a festive occasion

ga·lac·tic (gə lak′tik) *adj.* [Gr. *galaktikos,* milky < *gala,* milk] **1.** of or obtained from milk **2.** *Astron.* of the Milky Way or some other galaxy

Gal·a·had (gal′ə had′) in Arthurian legend, a knight who was successful in the quest for the Holy Grail because of his purity and noble spirit

gal·an·tine (gal′ən tēn′) *n.* [< OFr. < ML. *galatina,* jelly < L. pp. of *gelare,* CONGEAL] a mold of boned, seasoned, boiled white meat, as chicken or veal, chilled and served in its own jelly

Ga·lá·pa·gos Islands (gə lä′pə gōs′) group of islands in the Pacific on the equator, belonging to Ecuador: 3,028 sq. mi.

Gal·a·te·a (gal′ə tē′ə) *see* PYGMALION

Ga·la·tia (gə lā′shə) ancient kingdom in C Asia Minor, made a Roman province c.25 B.C. —**Ga·la′tian** *adj., n.*

Ga·la·tians (-shənz) the Epistle to the Galatians, a book of the New Testament written by the Apostle Paul

gal·ax·y (gal′ək sē) [< LL. *galaxias* < Gr. < *gala,* milk] [*often* **G-**] *same as* MILKY WAY —*n., pl.* **-ax·ies** **1.** any of innumerable vast groupings of stars **2.** an assembly of illustrious people

gale (gāl) *n.* [< ?] **1.** a strong wind; specif., *Meteorol.* one ranging in speed from 32 to 63 miles an hour **2.** an outburst [*a gale of laughter*]

Ga·len (gā′lən) (L. name *Claudius Galenus*) 130?–200? A.D.; Gr. physician & writer on philosophy —**Ga·len·ic** (gə len′ik), **Ga·len′i·cal** *adj.*

ga·le·na (gə lē′nə) *n.* [L., lead ore] native lead sulfide, PbS, a lustrous, lead-gray mineral: it is the principal ore of lead: also **ga·le′nite** (-nīt)

Ga·li·cia (gə lish′ə, -ē ə) **1.** region of SE Poland & the NW Ukrainian S.S.R. **2.** region & former kingdom in NW Spain —**Ga·li′cian** *adj., n.*

Gal·i·le·an¹ (gal′ə lē′ən) *adj.* of Galilee or its people —*n.* a native or inhabitant of Galilee —**the Galilean** Jesus

Gal·i·le·an² (gal′ə lē′ən) *adj.* of Galileo

Gal·i·lee (gal′ə lē′) **1.** region of N Israel **2. Sea of,** lake of NE Israel, on the Syria border

Gal·i·le·o (gal′ə lē′ō, -lā′-) (born *Galileo Galilei*) 1564–1642; It. astronomer & physicist

gal·i·ot (gal′ē ət) *n. same as* GALLIOT

gall¹ (gôl) *n.* [OE. *galla*] **1.** bile, the bitter, greenish fluid secreted by the liver and stored in the gallbladder **2.** something bitter or distasteful **3.** bitter feeling **4.** [Colloq.] impudence; audacity

gall² (gôl) *n.* [OE. *gealla* < L. *galla:* see ff.] **1.** a sore on the skin, esp. of a horse's back, caused by chafing **2.** irritation or annoyance, or a cause of this —*vt.* **1.** to make sore by rubbing; chafe **2.** to irritate; annoy; vex

gall³ (gôl) *n.* [< OFr. < L. *galla,* gallnut] a tumor on plant tissue caused by stimulation by fungi, insects, or bacteria: galls formed on oak trees have a high tannic acid content

gal·lant (gal′ənt; *for adj. 4 & n., usually* gə lant′; *for v., always* gə lant′) *adj.* [< OFr. prp. of *galer,* to rejoice < *gale:* see GALA] **1.** showy and gay in dress or appearance **2.** stately; imposing **3.** brave and noble **4.** polite and attentive to women —*n.* [Now Rare] **1.** a high-spirited, stylish man **2.** a man attentive and polite to women **3.** a lover —*vt., vi.* [Now Rare] to court (a woman) —**gal′lant·ly** *adv.*

gal·lant·ry (gal′ən trē) *n., pl.* **-ries** **1.** nobility of behavior or spirit; heroic courage **2.** the courtly manner of a gallant **3.** an act or speech characteristic of a gallant **4.** amorous intrigue

gall·blad·der (gôl′blad′ər) *n.* a membranous sac attached to the liver, in which excess gall, or bile, is stored

gal·le·ass (gal′ē as′, -əs) *n.* [< Fr. < OFr. < It. < ML. *galea:* see GALLEY] a large, three-masted vessel having sails and oars and carrying heavy guns: used on the Mediterranean in the 16th and 17th cent.

gal·le·on (gal′ē ən) *n.* [Sp. *galeón* < ML. *galea:* see GALLEY] a large Spanish warship and trader of the 15th and 16th cent., with three or four decks at the stern

GALLEON

gal·ler·y (gal′ə rē) *n., pl.* **-ler·ies** [< Fr. < ML. *galeria*] **1.** *a)* a covered walk open at one side or having the roof supported by pillars *b)* [Chiefly South] a veranda or porch **2.** a long, narrow balcony on the outside of a building **3.** a platform at the stern of an early sailing ship **4.** *a)* a platform or projecting upper floor in a church, theater, etc.; esp., the highest of a series of such platforms in a theater, with the cheapest seats *b)* the people occupying these seats *c)* a group of spectators, as at a sporting event **5.** a long, narrow corridor or room **6.** a room, building, or establishment for showing or selling art works **7.** a room or establishment used as a photographer's studio, for shooting at targets, etc. **8.** an underground passage, as one used in mining —*vt.* **-ler·ied, -ler·y·ing** to furnish with a gallery —**play to the gallery** to try to win the approval of the public, esp. in a showy way

gal·ley (gal′ē) *n., pl.* **-leys** [< OFr. < ML. *galea,* < MGr. *galaia,* a kind of ship] **1.** a long, low, usually single-decked ship propelled by oars and sails, used in ancient and medieval times **2.** a ship's kitchen **3.** *Printing a)* a shallow, oblong tray for holding composed type to be put into a form *b) same as* GALLEY PROOF

galley proof printer's proof taken from type in a galley to permit correction of errors before the type is made up in pages

galley slave **1.** a slave or convict sentenced or compelled to pull an oar on a galley **2.** a drudge

gall·fly (gôl′flī′) *n., pl.* **-flies′** a fly whose eggs cause galls when deposited in plant stems

Gal·lic (gal′ik) *adj.* **1.** of ancient Gaul or its people **2.** French

gal·lic acid (gal′ik) [< Fr. *galle,* GALL³] an acid, $C_7H_6O_5 \cdot H_2O$, prepared from nutgalls, tannin, etc. and used in photography and the manufacture of inks, dyes, etc.

Gal·li·cism, gal·li·cism (gal′ə siz'm) *n.* a French idiom, expression, custom, trait, etc.

Gal·li·cize, gal·li·cize (-sīz′) *vt., vi.* **-cized′, -ciz′ing** to make or become French or like the French in thought, language, etc.

gal·li·mau·fry (gal′ə mô′frē) *n., pl.* **-fries** [Fr. *galimafrée*]

1. orig., a hash made of meat scraps 2. a hodgepodge; jumble

gal·li·na·cean (gal′ə nā′shən) ***adj.*** *same as* GALLINACEOUS —***n.*** any gallinaceous bird

gal·li·na·ceous (-shəs) ***adj.*** [< L. < *gallina*, hen < *gallus*, a cock] of, or having the nature of, an order of birds that nest on the ground, including poultry, pheasants, grouse, etc.

gall·ing (gôl′iŋ) ***adj.*** that galls; very annoying; vexing —**gall′ing·ly** ***adv.***

gal·li·nule (gal′ə nyo͞ol′, -no͞ol′) ***n.*** [ModL. < L. dim. of *gallina:* see GALLINACEOUS] any of various marsh birds that both swim and wade

gal·li·ot (gal′ē ət) ***n.*** [< OFr. dim. of *galie* < ML. *galea*, GALLEY] **1.** a small, swift galley with sails and oars **2.** a light Dutch merchant ship with a single mast

Gal·lip·o·li Peninsula (gə lip′ə lē) peninsula in S European Turkey, forming the NW shore of the Dardanelles

gal·li·pot (gal′ə pät′) ***n.*** [see GALLEY & POT] a small pot or jar of glazed earthenware, esp. one used by druggists as a container for medicine

gal·li·um (gal′ē əm) ***n.*** [ModL. < L. *Gallia*, Gaul; also a pun on L. *gallus*, a cock, transl. of *Lecoq* (de Boisbaudran), its 19th-c. Fr. discoverer] a soft, bluish-white, metallic chemical element with a low melting point, used as a substitute for mercury: symbol, Ga; at. wt., 69.72; at. no., 31

gal·li·vant (gal′ə vant′) ***vi.*** [arbitrary elaboration of GALLANT] **1.** orig., to gad about with members of the opposite sex **2.** to go about in search of amusement or excitement —**gal′li·vant′er** ***n.***

gall·nut (gôl′nut′) ***n.*** a nutlike gall, esp. on oaks

Gal·lo- (gal′ō) [L. < *Gallus*, a Gaul] *a combining form meaning:* **1.** French **2.** French and

gal·lon (gal′ən) ***n.*** [< ONormFr. *galon* < ML. *galo*, gallon, jug] **1.** a liquid measure, equal to 4 quarts (231 cubic inches): the British imperial gallon equals 277.42 cubic inches **2.** a dry measure, equal to 1/8 bushel Abbrev. **gal.**

gal·lon·age (-ij) ***n.*** amount or capacity in gallons

gal·loon (gə lo͞on′) ***n.*** [< Fr. < *galonner*, to braid] a braid, as of cotton, silk, or metal thread, used for trimming or binding

gal·lop (gal′əp) ***vi.*** [< OFr. *galoper* < Frank.] **1.** to go at a gallop **2.** to move or act very fast; hurry —***vt.*** to cause to gallop —***n.*** **1.** the fastest gait of a horse, etc., consisting of a succession of leaping strides with all the feet off the ground at one time **2.** a ride on a galloping animal **3.** any fast pace, speedy action, etc. —**gal′lop·er** ***n.***

gal·lows (gal′ōz) ***n., pl.*** **-lows·es, -lows** [OE. *galga*] **1.** an upright frame with a crossbeam and a rope, for hanging condemned persons **2.** any structure like this **3.** the death sentence by hanging

gallows bird [Colloq.] a person who deserves hanging

gallows humor morbid or cynical humor

gall·stone (gôl′stōn′) ***n.*** a small, solid mass sometimes formed in the gallbladder or bile duct

gal·lus·es (gal′əs iz) ***n.pl.*** [< *gallus*, dial. var. of GALLOWS] [Colloq.] suspenders; braces

gall wasp any of various small insects whose larvae produce galls in plants

gal·op (gal′əp) ***n.*** [Fr.: see GALLOP] **1.** a lively round dance in 2/4 time **2.** music for this —***vi.*** to dance a galop

ga·lore (gə lôr′) ***adv.*** [Ir. *go leōr*, enough] in abundance; plentifully *[*to attract crowds *galore]*

ga·losh, ga·loshe (gə läsh′) ***n.*** [< OFr. *galoche*, prob. < LL. *gallicula*, small shoe] an overshoe, esp. a high overshoe of rubber and fabric

Gals·wor·thy (gôlz′wur′*th*ē, galz′-), **John** 1867–1933; Eng. novelist & playwright

Gal·ton (gôl′t′n), Sir **Francis** 1822–1911; Eng. scientist & writer: pioneer in eugenics

Gal·va·ni (gal vä′nē), **Lu·i·gi** (lo͞o wē′jē) 1737–98; It. physiologist & physicist

gal·van·ic (gal van′ik) ***adj.*** [< ff.] **1.** of, caused by, or producing an electric current, esp. from a battery **2.** stimulating or stimulated as if by electric shock; startling —**gal·van′i·cal·ly** ***adv.***

gal·va·nism (gal′və niz′m) ***n.*** [< Fr. < It.: after L. GALVANI] **1.** electricity produced by chemical action **2.** electrical current used in therapy

gal·va·nize (gal′və nīz′) ***vt.*** **-nized′, -niz′ing** **1.** to apply an electric current to **2.** to stimulate as if by electric shock; excite **3.** to plate (metal) with zinc —**gal′va·ni·za′tion** ***n.***

gal·va·no- *a combining form meaning* galvanic, galvanism

gal·va·nom·e·ter (gal′və näm′ə tər) ***n.*** an instrument for detecting and measuring a small electric current —**gal′va·no·met′ric** (-nō met′rik) ***adj.*** —**gal′va·nom′e·try** (-trē) ***n.***

Gal·ves·ton (gal′vis tən) [after B. de *Gálvez*, 18th-c. gov. of La.] seaport in SE Tex.: pop. 62,000

gam (gam) ***n.*** [< dial. Fr. *gambe* < ML. *gamba* < Gr. *kampē*, a joint] [Slang] a leg; often, specif., a woman's shapely leg

Gama, Vasco da *see* DA GAMA

Gam·bi·a (gam′bē ə) country on the W coast of Africa, surrounded on three sides by Senegal: a member of the Commonwealth: c.4,000 sq. mi.; pop. 357,000

gam·bit (gam′bit) ***n.*** [Fr. < OFr. < Sp. *gambito*, a tripping < It. < ML. *gamba:* see GAM] **1.** *Chess* an opening in which a pawn or other piece is sacrificed to get an advantage in position **2.** a maneuver or action intended to gain an advantage

gam·ble (gam′b′l) ***vi.*** **-bled, -bling** [OE. *gamenian*, to play] **1.** to play games of chance for money, etc. **2.** to take a risk in order to gain some advantage —***vt.*** to bet; wager —***n.*** an act or undertaking involving risk of a loss —**gamble away** to squander or lose in gambling —**gam′bler** ***n.***

gam·boge (gam bōj′, -bo͞ozh′) ***n.*** [ModL. *gambogium* < CAMBODIA] a gum resin obtained from a tropical Asian tree, used as a yellow pigment and as a cathartic

gam·bol (gam′b′l) ***n.*** [< Fr. < Pr. < It. *gambata*, a kick < *gamba:* see GAM & GAMBIT] a jumping and skipping about in play; frolic —***vi.*** **-boled** or **-bolled, -bol·ing** or **-bol·ling** to jump and skip about in play; frolic

gam·brel (gam′brəl) ***n.*** [ONormFr. < OFr. *gambe:* see GAM] **1.** the hock of a horse or similar animal **2.** *same as* GAMBREL ROOF

gambrel roof a roof with two slopes on each side, the lower steeper than the upper

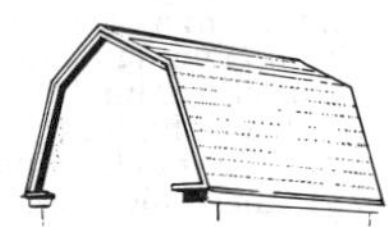

GAMBREL ROOF

game[1] (gām) ***n.*** [OE. < *gamen*] **1.** any form of play; amusement; recreation; sport **2.** *a*) any specific amusement or sport involving competition under specific rules *b*) a single contest in such a competition *c*) a subdivision of a contest, as in a set of tennis **3.** the number of points required for winning **4.** a victory; win **5.** a set of equipment for a competitive amusement *[*to sell toys and *games]* **6.** a way or quality of playing *[*to play a good *game]* **7.** any test of skill, endurance, etc. **8.** a project; scheme *[*to see through another's *game]* **9.** *a*) wild birds or animals hunted for sport or food *b*) their flesh used as food **10.** any object of pursuit or attack: usually in **fair game** **11.** [Colloq.] a business or vocation, esp. a risky one —***vi.*** **gamed, gam′ing** to play cards, etc. for stakes; gamble —***adj.*** **1.** designating or of wild birds or animals hunted for sport or food **2. gam′er, gam′est** *a*) plucky; courageous *b*) having enough spirit; ready (*for* something) —**ahead of the game** [Colloq.] in the position of winning —**make game of** to make fun of; ridicule —**off one's game** performing poorly —**play the game** [Colloq.] to follow the rules; behave as fairness or custom requires —**the game is up** failure is certain —**game′ly** ***adv.*** —**game′ness** ***n.***

game[2] (gām) ***adj.*** [< ?] [Colloq.] lame or injured: said esp. of a leg

game·cock (gām′käk′) ***n.*** a specially bred rooster trained for cockfighting

game fish any fish regularly caught for sport

game·keep·er (-kēp′ər) ***n.*** a person employed to breed and take care of game birds and animals on State farms or private estates

game laws laws regulating hunting and fishing in order to preserve game

games·man·ship (gāmz′mən ship′) ***n.*** [< GAME[1] & (SPORT)SMANSHIP] skill in using ploys to gain a victory or advantage over another person

game·some (gām′səm) ***adj.*** playful; frolicsome —**game′some·ly** ***adv.*** —**game′some·ness** ***n.***

game·ster (-stər) ***n.*** a gambler

gam·ete (gam′ēt, ga mēt′) ***n.*** [ModL. < Gr. *gametē*, a wife < *gamein*, to marry < *gamos:* see GAMO-] a reproductive cell that can unite with another gamete to form the cell (*zygote*) that develops into a new individual —**ga·met·ic** (gə met′ik) ***adj.***

game theory a method of using mathematical analysis to select the best strategy so as to minimize one's maximum losses or maximize one's minimum winnings in a game, war, business competition, etc.

ga·me·to- *a combining form meaning* gamete

ga·me·to·phyte (gə mēt′ə fīt′) ***n.*** in plants characterized by alternation of generations, the individual or generation that reproduces by eggs and sperms —**ga·me′to·phyt′ic** (-fit′ik) ***adj.***

gam·in (gam′ən) ***n.*** [Fr.] **1.** a neglected child left to roam the streets **2.** a girl with a roguish, saucy charm

gam·ing (gā′miŋ) ***n.*** the practice of gambling

gam·ma (gam′ə) ***n.*** [Gr.] **1.** the third letter of the Greek alphabet (Γ, γ) **2.** the third of a group or series
gamma globulin that fraction of blood serum which contains most antibodies: used in the temporary prevention of measles, hepatitis, etc.
gamma ray **1.** an electromagnetic radiation emitted by the nucleus of a radioactive substance: similar to an X-ray, but shorter in wavelength **2.** a stream of such radiation
gam·mer (gam′ər) ***n.*** [altered < GODMOTHER] an old woman: now usually contemptuous or humorous
gam·mon[1] (gam′ən) ***n.*** [< ONormFr. < *gambe:* see GAM] **1.** the bottom end of a side of bacon **2.** a smoked or cured ham or side of bacon
gam·mon[2] (gam′ən) ***n.*** [< ME. var. of *gamen:* see GAME[1]] *Backgammon* a victory in which the winner gets rid of all his men before his opponent gets rid of any —***vt.*** to defeat by scoring a gammon
gam·mon[3] (gam′ən) ***n., interj.*** [< ?] [Brit. Colloq.] deceitful talk; humbug —***vt., vi.*** [Brit. Colloq.] **1.** to talk humbug (to) **2.** to deceive
gam·o- [< Gr. *gamos,* marriage] *a combining form meaning:* **1.** sexually united **2.** joined or united
gam·o·pet·al·ous (gam′ə pet′'l əs) ***adj.*** having the petals united so as to form a tubelike corolla
-ga·mous (gə məs) [< Gr. *gamos* (see GAMO-) + -OUS] *a combining form meaning* marrying, uniting sexually *[polygamous]*
gam·ut (gam′ət) ***n.*** [ML. *gamma ut* < *gamma,* the lowest note of the medieval scale < Gr. *gamma,* GAMMA + *ut* < L. *ut,* that, in a medieval song whose phrases began on successive ascending major tones: *Ut* queant laxis *Re*sonare fibris, *Mi*ra gestorum *Fa*muli tuorum, *Sol*ve polluti *La*bii reatum, *S*ancte *I*ohannes] **1.** *a)* the entire series of recognized notes in modern music *b)* any complete musical scale, esp. the major scale **2.** the entire range or extent, as of emotions
gam·y (gā′mē) ***adj.*** **gam′i·er, gam′i·est** **1.** having a strong, tangy flavor like that of cooked game **2.** strong in smell or taste **3.** game; plucky **4.** risqué or racy —**gam′i·ly** ***adv.*** —**gam′i·ness** ***n.***
-ga·my (gə mē) [< Gr. *gamos:* see GAMO-] *a combining form meaning* marriage, sexual union *[polygamy]*
gan·der (gan′dər) ***n.*** [OE. *gan(d)ra*] **1.** a male goose **2.** a stupid or silly fellow **3.** [Slang] a look: chiefly in the phrase **take a gander**
Gan·dhi (gän′dē, gan′-), **Mo·han·das K(aramchand)** (mō-hän′dəs) 1869–1948; Hindu nationalist leader & social reformer: called *Mahatma Gandhi* —**Gan′dhi·an** ***adj.***
gang[1] (gaŋ) ***n.*** [OE. < base of *gangan* (see ff.)] **1.** a group of people associated together in some way; specif., *a)* a group of workers directed by a foreman *b)* an organized group of criminals *c)* a group of youths from one neighborhood banded together; often, specif., a band of juvenile delinquents **2.** a set of tools, machines, etc. designed to work together —***vi.*** to form, or be associated in, a gang (with *up*) —***vt.*** [Colloq.] to attack as a gang —**gang up on** [Colloq.] to attack as a group
gang[2] (gaŋ) ***vi.*** [OE. *gangan,* to go] [Scot.] to go or walk
Gan·ges (gan′jēz) river in N India & Bangladesh, flowing from the Himalayas into the Bay of Bengal
gan·gling (gaŋ′gliŋ) ***adj.*** [? < dial. *gangrel,* "lanky person"] tall, thin, and awkward; of loose, lanky build: also **gan′gly**
gan·gli·on (gaŋ′glē ən) ***n.,*** *pl.* **-gli·a** (-ə), **-gli·ons** [LL. < Gr. *ganglion,* tumor] **1.** a mass of nerve cells serving as a center from which nerve impulses are transmitted **2.** a center of force, energy, etc. —**gan′gli·on′ic** (-än′ik) ***adj.***
gang·plank (gaŋ′plaŋk′) ***n.*** a narrow, movable platform by which to board or leave a ship
gan·grene (gaŋ′grēn, gaŋ grēn′) ***n.*** [< Fr. < L. *gangraena* < Gr. < *gran,* to gnaw] decay of tissue in a part of the body when the blood supply is obstructed by injury, disease, etc. —**gan′gre·nous** (-grə nəs) ***adj.***
gang·ster (gaŋ′stər) ***n.*** a member of a gang of criminals —**gang′ster·ism** ***n.***
gang·way (gaŋ′wā′) ***n.*** [OE. *gangweg*] a passageway; specif., *a)* an opening in a ship's side for freight or passengers *b) same as* GANGPLANK —***interj.*** make room! clear the way!
gan·net (gan′it) ***n.,*** *pl.* **-nets, -net:** see PLURAL, II, D, 1 [OE. *ganot*] any of several large sea birds; esp., a white, goose-like, web-footed bird that breeds on cliffs along the N Atlantic coast
gan·oid (gan′oid) ***adj.*** [< Fr. < Gr. *ganos,* brightness + *-eidēs,* -OID] of a group of fishes covered by rows of hard, glossy scales or plates, including the sturgeons and gars —***n.*** a ganoid fish
gant·let[1] (gônt′lit, gant′-) ***n.*** [< Sw. *gatlopp,* a run down a lane < *gata,* lane + *lopp,* a run] **1.** a former military punishment in which the offender ran between two rows of men who struck him with clubs, etc. as he passed **2.** a series of troubles or difficulties Now spelled equally **gaunt′let** —**run the gantlet** **1.** to be punished by means of the gantlet **2.** to proceed while under attack from both sides, as by criticism or gossip
gant·let[2] (gônt′lit, gänt′-) ***n.*** *same as* GAUNTLET[1]
gan·try (gan′trē) ***n.,*** *pl.* **-tries** [< OFr. < L. *canterius,* beast of burden < Gr. < *kanthōn*] **1.** a frame for holding barrels horizontally **2.** a framework that spans a distance, as one on wheels that carries a traveling crane **3.** a wheeled framework with a crane, platforms at different levels, etc. used to position and service a rocket at its launching site
Gan·y·mede (gan′ə mēd) *Gr. Myth.* a beautiful youth who was cupbearer to the gods
gaol (jāl) ***n.*** *Brit. sp. of* JAIL —**gaol′er** ***n.***
gap (gap) ***n.*** [ON. < *gapa,* to yawn, GAPE] **1.** a hole or opening made by breaking or parting; breach **2.** a mountain pass or ravine **3.** an interruption of continuity in space or time **4.** a disparity between ideas, natures, etc. **5.** *same as* SPARK GAP —***vi.*** **gapped, gap′ping** to come apart; open
gape (gāp) ***vi.*** **gaped, gap′ing** [< ON. *gapa*] **1.** to open the mouth wide, as in yawning **2.** to stare with the mouth open, as in wonder **3.** to open wide, as a chasm —***n.*** **1.** an open-mouthed stare **2.** a yawn **3.** a wide opening **4.** *Zool.* the measure of the widest possible opening of a mouth or beak —**the gapes** **1.** a disease of poultry and birds, characterized by gaping **2.** a fit of yawning —**gap′er** ***n.*** —**gap′ing·ly** ***adv.***
gar (gär) ***n.,*** *pl.* **gar, gars:** see PLURAL, II, D, 2 [contr. < GARFISH] any of a group of freshwater ganoid fishes with elongated bodies, long beaklike snouts, and many sharp teeth
G.A.R. Grand Army of the Republic
ga·rage (gə räzh′, -räj′; *Brit.* gar′äzh) ***n.*** [Fr. < *garer,* to protect] **1.** a closed shelter for automobiles **2.** a business establishment where automobiles are repaired, stored, etc. —***vt.*** **-raged′, -rag′ing** to put or keep in a garage
Gar·and rifle (gar′ənd, gə rand′) [after J. C. *Garand,* U.S. inventor of it, c. 1930] a semiautomatic rapid-firing, .30-caliber rifle
garb (gärb) ***n.*** [< OFr. < It. *garbo,* elegance, prob. ult. < Gr. < *kalos,* beautiful + *poiein,* to make] **1.** clothing; manner or style of dress **2.** external form, covering, or appearance —***vt.*** to clothe
gar·bage (gär′bij) ***n.*** [ME., entrails of fowls] **1.** spoiled or waste food, as from a kitchen, that is thrown away **2.** worthless or offensive matter
gar·ble (gär′b'l) ***vt.*** **-bled, -bling** [< It. < *garbello,* a sieve < Ar. < *ghirbāl* < L. dim. *cribellum,* a small sieve] **1.** to select, suppress, distort, etc. parts of (a story, etc.) in telling, so as to mislead or misrepresent **2.** to confuse or mix up (a story, etc.) unintentionally —***n.*** the act or result of garbling —**gar′bler** ***n.***
‡**gar·çon** (gȧr sōn′) ***n.,*** *pl.* **-çons′** (-sōn′) [Fr.] **1.** a boy or young man **2.** a waiter or servant
gar·den (gär′d'n) ***n.*** [< ONormFr. *gardin* < Frank.] **1.** a piece of ground, usually close to a house, for the growing of fruits, flowers, or vegetables **2.** an area of fertile, well-cultivated land: also **garden spot** **3.** [*often pl.*] a parklike place for public enjoyment, sometimes having special displays of animals or plants —***vi.*** to work in or take care of a garden, lawn, etc. —***vt.*** to make a garden of —***adj.*** **1.** of, for, or grown in a garden **2.** ordinary; commonplace *[a garden variety of poet]* —**lead (someone) down the garden path** to mislead or deceive (someone) —**gar′den·er** ***n.***
Garden Grove city in SW Calif.: suburb of Los Angeles: pop. 123,000
gar·de·ni·a (gär dēn′yə, -dē′nē ə) ***n.*** [ModL., after A. *Garden,* 18th-c. Am. botanist] any of a genus of plants with glossy leaves and fragrant, white or yellow, waxy flowers
Gar·field (gär′fēld), **James A(bram)** 1831–81; 20th president of the U.S. (1881): assassinated
gar·fish (gär′fish′) ***n.,*** *pl.* **-fish′, -fish′es:** see FISH [< ME. *gare,* spear (OE. *gar*) + *fish,* fish] *same as* GAR
Gar·gan·tu·a (gär gan′choo wə) a giant king with an enormous appetite in Rabelais' *Gargantua and Pantagruel* —**Gar·gan′tu·an, gar·gan′tu·an** ***adj.***
gar·gle (gär′g'l) ***vt., vi.*** **-gled, -gling** [< Fr. < *gargouille,* throat, spout] to rinse (the throat) with a liquid kept in motion by the slow expulsion of air from the lungs —***n.*** **1.** a liquid used for gargling **2.** a gargling sound
gar·goyle (gär′goil) ***n.*** [< OFr. *gargouille:* see prec.] **1.** a waterspout, usually in the form of a carved fantastic creature, projecting from the gutter of a building **2.** a person with grotesque features

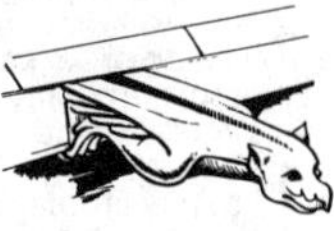
GARGOYLE

Gar·i·bal·di (gar′ə bôl′dē; *It.* gä rē-bäl′dē), **Giu·sep·pe** (jōō zep′pe) 1807–82; It. patriot & general: leader in movement to unify Italy
gar·ish (ger′ish) ***adj.*** [prob. < ME. *gauren,* to stare] too bright or gaudy; showy —**gar′ish·ly** ***adv.*** —**gar′ish·ness** ***n.***

gar·land (gär′lənd) ***n.*** [< OFr. *garlande*] a wreath of flowers, leaves, etc. —***vt.*** to form into or decorate with garlands

Gar·land (gär′lənd) [after A. *Garland,* U.S. attorney general (1885–89)] city in NE Tex.: suburb of Dallas: pop. 139,000

gar·lic (gär′lik) ***n.*** [< OE. < *gar,* a spear + *leac,* a leek] **1.** a bulbous plant of the lily family **2.** its strong-smelling bulb, made up of small sections called cloves, used as a seasoning —**gar′lick·y** ***adj.***

gar·ment (gär′mənt) ***n.*** [< OFr. *garnement* < *garnir:* see GARNISH] any article of clothing —***vt.*** to clothe

gar·ner (gär′nər) ***n.*** [< OFr. < L. *granarium* < *granum,* GRAIN] **1.** a granary **2.** a store of something —***vt.*** **1.** to gather up and store **2.** to get or earn **3.** to collect

gar·net (gär′nit) ***n.*** [< OFr. < ML. *granatus* < *granatum,* garnet, lit., POMEGRANATE] **1.** any of a group of hard silicate minerals, chiefly crystalline: red varieties are used as gems **2.** a deep red

gar·nish (gär′nish) ***vt.*** [< OFr. *garnir,* to furnish, protect < Gmc.] **1.** to decorate; adorn; trim **2.** to decorate (food) with something that adds color or flavor **3.** *Law* to bring garnishment proceedings against —***n.*** **1.** a decoration; ornament **2.** something used to garnish food, as parsley

gar·nish·ee (gär′nə shē′) ***n.*** *Law* a person served with a garnishment —***vt.*** **-eed′, -ee′ing** *Law* **1.** to attach (a debtor's property, wages, etc.) by the authority of a court, so that it can be used to pay the debt **2.** to serve with a garnishment

gar·nish·ment (gär′nish mənt) ***n.*** **1.** a decoration; embellishment **2.** *Law* a notice ordering a person not to dispose of a defendant's property or money in his possession pending settlement of the lawsuit

gar·ni·ture (gär′ni chər) ***n.*** garnish; decoration

gar·pike (gär′pīk′) ***n.*** *same as* GAR

gar·ret (gar′it) ***n.*** [ME. *garite,* a watchtower, loft < OFr. < *garir,* to watch < Frank.] the space or rooms just below the sloping roof of a house; attic

gar·ri·son (gar′ə s′n) ***n.*** [< OFr. < *garir* (see GARRET)] **1.** troops stationed in a fort **2.** a military post or station —***vt.*** **1.** to station troops in (a fortified place) for its defense **2.** to place (troops) on duty in a garrison

Gar·ri·son (gar′ə s′n), **William Lloyd** 1805–79; U.S. editor, lecturer, & abolitionist leader

gar·rote (gə rät′, -rōt′) ***n.*** [Sp., orig., a stick used to wind a cord < OFr. < Frank.] **1.** *a)* a method of execution, as formerly in Spain, by strangling with an iron collar *b)* the iron collar so used **2.** *a)* a cord, length of wire, etc. for strangling a person in a surprise attack *b)* a disabling by strangling in this way —***vt.*** **-rot′ed** or **-rot′ted, -rot′ing** or **-rot′ting** **1.** to execute or attack with a garrote or by strangling **2.** to disable by strangling, as in an attack for robbery Also sp. **ga·rotte′, gar·rotte′** —**gar·rot′er** ***n.***

gar·ru·lous (gar′ə ləs, gar′yoo-) ***adj.*** [< L. < *garrire,* to chatter] talking much or too much, esp. about unimportant things; loquacious —**gar·ru·li·ty** (gə ro͞o′lə tē), **gar′ru·lous·ness** ***n.*** —**gar′ru·lous·ly** ***adv.***

gar·ter (gär′tər) ***n.*** [< ONormFr. *gartier* < OFr. *garet,* the back of the knee < Celt.] **1.** an elastic band, or a fastener suspended from a band, girdle, etc., for holding a stocking or sock in position **2.** [G-] *a)* the badge of the Order of the Garter, the highest order of British knighthood *b)* the order itself —***vt.*** to fasten with a garter

garter belt a wide belt, usually of elastic fabric, with garters suspended from it, worn by women

garter snake any of various small, harmless, striped snakes common in N. America

Gar·y (ger′ē, gar′ē) [< OE. hyp. *Garwig,* lit., spear (of) battle < *gar,* spear + *wig,* battle] **1.** a masculine name **2.** [after E. *Gary* (1846–1927), U.S. industrialist] city in NW Ind., on Lake Michigan: pop. 152,000 (met. area 639,000)

gas (gas) ***n.*** [ModL., coined by the Belgian chemist, Van Helmont (1577–1644), after Paracelsus' use of Gr. *chaos,* CHAOS, to mean "air"] **1.** the fluid form of a substance in which it can expand indefinitely; form that is neither liquid nor solid; vapor **2.** any mixture of flammable gases used for lighting, heating, or cooking **3.** any gas used as an anesthetic **4.** any substance dispersed through the atmosphere, as in war, to act as a poison, irritant, or asphyxiant **5.** gaseous matter formed in the stomach, bowels, etc. **6.** [Colloq.] *a) short for* GASOLINE *b)* the accelerator in an automobile, etc. **7.** [Slang] *a)* idle or boastful talk *b)* a person or thing that is very pleasing, exciting, etc. **8.** *Mining* a mixture of firedamp with air that explodes if ignited —***vt.*** **gassed, gas′sing** **1.** to supply with gas **2.** to subject to the action of gas **3.** to injure or kill by gas, as in war **4.** [Slang] to thrill, delight, etc. —***vi.*** [Slang] to talk idly or boastfully —***adj.*** of or using gas

gas chamber a room in which people are put to be killed with poison gas

Gas·con (gas′kən) ***adj.*** **1.** of Gascony or its people, reputed to be boastful **2.** [g-] boastful —***n.*** **1.** a native of Gascony **2.** [g-] a boaster

gas·con·ade (gas′kə nād′) ***n.*** [see prec. & -ADE] boastful or blustering talk —***vi.*** **-ad′ed, -ad′ing** to boast or bluster

Gas·co·ny (gas′kə nē) region on the SW coast of France: Fr. name, **Gas·cogne** (gȧs kôn′y′)

gas·e·ous (gas′ē əs, gas′yəs) ***adj.*** **1.** of, like, or in the form of gas **2.** [Colloq.] *same as* GASSY (sense 1) —**gas′e·ous·ness** ***n.***

gas fitter a person whose work is installing and repairing gas pipes and fixtures

gash (gash) ***vt.*** [< OFr. *garser,* ult. < Gr. *charassein,* to sharpen, cut] to make a long, deep cut in; slash —***n.*** a long, deep cut

gas·i·fy (gas′ə fī′) ***vt., vi.*** **-fied′, -fy′ing** to change into gas —**gas′i·fi·ca′tion** ***n.***

gas jet **1.** a flame of illuminating gas **2.** a nozzle or burner at the end of a gas fixture

gas·ket (gas′kit) ***n.*** [prob. < OFr. *garcette,* small cord] **1.** a piece or ring of rubber, metal, etc. placed around a piston or joint to make it leakproof **2.** *Naut.* a rope or cord by which a furled sail is tied to the yard

gas·light (gas′līt′) ***n.*** **1.** the light produced by burning illuminating gas **2.** a gas jet or burner —***adj.*** of or characteristic of the period of gaslight illumination *[gaslight melodrama]*

gas mantle a mantle (*n.* 3) for a gas burner

gas mask a filtering device worn over the face to protect against breathing in poisonous gases

gas·o·hol (gas′ə hôl) ***n.*** a mixture of gasoline and alcohol, usually 90 percent unleaded gasoline and 10 percent ethyl alcohol, used as a motor fuel

gas·o·line, gas·o·lene (gas′ə lēn′, gas′ə lēn′) ***n.*** [GAS + -OL(E) + -INE[4], -ENE] a volatile, highly flammable, colorless liquid produced by the distillation of petroleum and used chiefly as a fuel in internal-combustion engines

gas·om·e·ter (gas äm′ə tər) ***n.*** **1.** a container for holding and measuring gas **2.** a tank for gas

gasp (gasp) ***vi.*** [< ON. *geispa,* to yawn] to inhale suddenly, as in surprise, or breathe with effort, as in choking —***vt.*** to say with gasps —***n.*** a gasping; catching of the breath with difficulty

Gas·pé Peninsula (gas pā′) peninsula in S Quebec, Canada, extending into the Gulf of St. Lawrence

gas station *same as* SERVICE STATION (sense 2)

gas·sy (gas′ē) ***adj.*** **-si·er, -si·est** **1.** full of, containing, or producing gas; esp., flatulent **2.** like gas **3.** [Colloq.] full of talk —**gas′si·ness** ***n.***

gas·tric (gas′trik) ***adj.*** [GASTR(O)- + -IC] of, in, or near the stomach

gastric juice the acid digestive fluid produced by glands in the mucous membrane lining the stomach: it contains enzymes and hydrochloric acid

gastric ulcer an ulcer of the stomach lining

gas·tri·tis (gas trīt′is) ***n.*** [GASTR(O)- + -ITIS] inflammation of the stomach, esp. of the stomach lining

gas·tro- [< Gr. *gastēr,* the stomach] *a combining form meaning* the stomach (and): also **gastr-**

gas·tro·en·ter·i·tis (gas′trō en′tə rīt′is) ***n.*** [< GASTRO- + ENTER(O)- + -ITIS] an inflammation of the stomach and the intestines

gas·tro·in·tes·ti·nal (-in tes′tə n′l) ***adj.*** of the stomach and the intestines

gas·tro·nome (gas′trə nōm′) ***n.*** a person who enjoys and has a discriminating taste for foods: also **gas·tron′o·mer** (-trän′ə mər), **gas·tron′o·mist**

gas·tron·o·my (gas trän′ə mē) ***n.*** [< Fr. < Gr. < *gastēr,* the stomach + *nomos,* a rule] the art of good eating —**gas′tro·nom′ic** (-trə näm′ik), **gas′tro·nom′i·cal** ***adj.*** —**gas′tro·nom′i·cal·ly** ***adv.***

gas·tro·pod (gas′trə päd′) ***n.*** [< ModL. < GASTRO- + -POD] any of a large class of mollusks having a single, straight or spiral shell, as snails, limpets, etc., or no shell, as certain slugs: most gastropods move by means of a broad, muscular, ventral foot

gas·tru·la (gas′troo lə) ***n., pl.*** **-lae′** (-lē′), **-las** [ModL. dim. < Gr. *gastēr,* the stomach] an embryo in an early stage of development, consisting of a sac with two layers, the ectoderm and endoderm

gat (gat) *archaic pt. of* GET

gate (gāt) ***n.*** [< OE. *geat*] **1.** a movable structure, esp. one that swings on hinges, controlling entrance or exit through an opening in a fence or wall **2.** an opening for passage through a fence or wall, with or without such a structure; gateway **3.** any means of entrance or exit **4.** a movable barrier, as at a railroad crossing **5.** a structure controlling the flow of water, as in a pipe, canal, etc. **6.** *a)* the total amount of admission money paid by spectators to a performance or exhibition *b)* the total number of such spectators **7.** *Electronics* a circuit that passes signals only when certain input conditions are satisfied —**get the gate** [Slang] to be dismissed or rejected —**give (someone) the gate** to dismiss or reject (someone)

gate·fold (gāt′fōld′) ***n.*** a page larger than the others in a magazine or book, bound so that it can be folded out

gate·house (-hous′) ***n.*** a house beside or over a gateway, used as a porter's lodge, etc.

gate·keep·er (-kē′pər) ***n.*** a person in charge of a gate to control passage through it: also **gate′man,** *pl.* **-men**

gate·leg table (-leg′) a table with drop leaves supported by gatelike legs that swing back to let the leaves drop: also **gate′legged′ table**

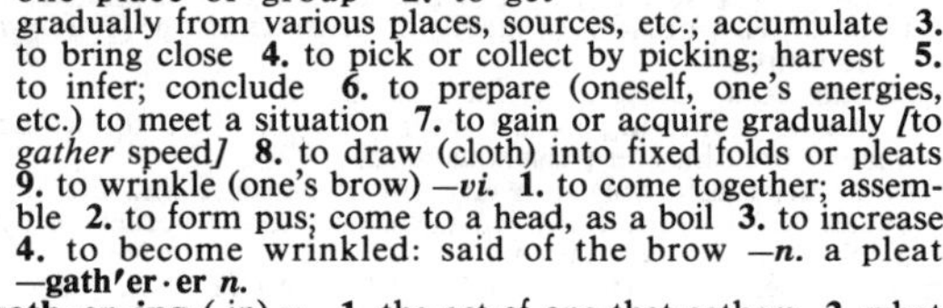
GATELEG TABLE

gate·post (-pōst′) ***n.*** the post on which a gate is hung or to which it is fastened when closed

gate·way (-wā′) ***n.*** **1.** an entrance in a fence, wall, etc. fitted with a gate **2.** a means of access

gath·er (ga*th*′ər) ***vt.*** [< OE. *gad(e)rian*] **1.** to bring together in one place or group **2.** to get gradually from various places, sources, etc.; accumulate **3.** to bring close **4.** to pick or collect by picking; harvest **5.** to infer; conclude **6.** to prepare (oneself, one's energies, etc.) to meet a situation **7.** to gain or acquire gradually *[to gather speed]* **8.** to draw (cloth) into fixed folds or pleats **9.** to wrinkle (one's brow) —***vi.*** **1.** to come together; assemble **2.** to form pus; come to a head, as a boil **3.** to increase **4.** to become wrinkled: said of the brow —***n.*** a pleat —**gath′er·er *n.***

gath·er·ing (-iŋ) ***n.*** **1.** the act of one that gathers **2.** what is gathered; specif., *a)* a meeting; crowd *b)* a series of pleats **3.** a boil or abscess

Gat·ling gun (gat′liŋ) [after R. J. *Gatling,* 19th-c. U.S. inventor] an early kind of machine gun having a rotating cluster of barrels around an axis

gauche (gōsh) ***adj.*** [Fr. < MFr. *gauchir,* to become warped, ult. < Frank.] lacking social grace; awkward; tactless —**gauche′ly *adv.*** —**gauche′ness *n.***

gau·che·rie (gō′shə rē′) ***n.*** [see prec.] **1.** awkwardness; tactlessness **2.** a gauche act or expression

gau·cho (gou′chō) ***n.,*** *pl.* **-chos** [AmSp.] a cowboy of mixed Indian and Spanish ancestry, living on the S. American pampas

gaud (gôd) ***n.*** [ME. *gaude,* a trinket, prob. ult. < L. *gaudium,* joy] a cheap, showy ornament

gaud·y (gôd′ē) ***adj.*** **gaud′i·er, gaud′i·est** [prec. + -Y[2]] bright and showy, but in bad taste; cheaply ornate —**gaud′i·ly *adv.*** —**gaud′i·ness *n.***

gauge (gāj) ***n.*** [< ONormFr. *gaugier,* to gauge] **1.** a standard measure or scale of measurement **2.** dimensions, capacity, thickness, etc. **3.** any device for measuring something, as the thickness of wire, steam pressure, etc. **4.** any means of estimating **5.** the distance between the rails of a railway: cf. STANDARD GAUGE, BROAD GAUGE, NARROW GAUGE **6.** the distance between parallel wheels at opposite ends of an axle **7.** the size of the bore of a shotgun expressed in terms of the number per pound of round lead balls of a diameter equal to that of the bore **8.** the thickness of sheet metal, diameter of wire, etc. **9.** the fineness of a machine-knitted fabric expressed in terms of the number of loops per 1½ inches —***vt.*** **gauged, gaug′ing** **1.** to measure accurately by means of a gauge **2.** to measure the size, amount, or capacity of **3.** to estimate; judge **4.** to make conform with a standard —**gauge′a·ble *adj.*** —**gaug′er *n.***

WIRE GAUGE

Gau·guin (gō gan′), **(Eugène Henri) Paul** (pôl) 1848–1903; Fr. painter, in Tahiti after 1891

Gaul (gôl) ancient division of the Roman Empire, including what is now mainly France & Belgium **(Transalpine Gaul)** and N Italy **(Cisalpine Gaul)** —***n.*** **1.** any of the Celtic-speaking people of Gaul **2.** a Frenchman

Gaul·ish (-ish) ***adj.*** of Gaul or the Gauls —***n.*** the Celtic language spoken in ancient Gaul

gaunt (gônt) ***adj.*** [ME. *gawnte, gant* < ?] **1.** thin and bony; hollow-eyed and haggard, as from great hunger or age **2.** looking grim, forbidding, or desolate —**gaunt′ly *adv.*** —**gaunt′ness *n.***

gaunt·let[1] (gônt′lit, gänt′-) ***n.*** [< OFr. dim. of *gant,* a glove < Frank.] **1.** a medieval glove, usually of leather covered with metal plates, worn to protect the hand in combat **2.** a long glove with a flaring cuff, or this cuff, covering the lower part of the arm —**take up the gauntlet** to accept a challenge —**throw down the gauntlet** to challenge, as to combat —**gaunt′let·ed *adj.***

gaunt·let[2] (gônt′lit, gänt′-) ***n.*** *same as* GANTLET[1]

gauss (gous) ***n.*** [after K. *Gauss* (1777–1855), Ger. scientist] *Elec.* a cgs unit used in measuring magnetic induction or magnetic flux density

gauze (gôz) ***n.*** [Fr. *gaze,* prob. < Sp. < Ar. *ḳazz,* raw silk < Per.] **1.** any very thin, transparent, loosely woven material, as of cotton or silk **2.** a thin mist

gauz·y (gôz′ē) ***adj.*** **gauz′i·er, gauz′i·est** thin, light, and transparent, like gauze; diaphanous —**gauz′i·ness *n.***

gave (gāv) *pt. of* GIVE

gav·el (gav′′l) ***n.*** [< Scot. *gable,* a tool < OE. *gafol*] a small mallet rapped on the table by a chairman, judge, etc. to call for attention or silence

ga·vi·al (gā′vē əl) ***n.*** [Fr. < Hindi *ghaṛiyāl*] a large crocodile of India, with a very long snout

ga·votte (gə vät′) ***n.*** [Fr. < Pr. *gavoto,* dance of the *Gavots,* an Alpine people] **1.** a 17th-cent. dance like the minuet, but livelier **2.** the music for this, in 4/4 time Also sp. **ga·vot′**

Ga·wain (gä′win, -wān) [Fr.] *Arthurian Legend* a knight of the Round Table, nephew of King Arthur

gawk (gôk) ***n.*** [prob. dial. var. of *gowk,* a simpleton] a clumsy, stupid fellow; simpleton —***vi.*** to stare in a stupid way —**gawk′ish *adj.***

gawk·y (gô′kē) ***adj.*** **gawk′i·er, gawk′i·est** [prob. < prec.] awkward; clumsy; ungainly —**gawk′i·ly *adv.*** —**gawk′i·ness *n.***

gay (gā) ***adj.*** [< OFr.] **1.** joyous and lively; merry **2.** bright; brilliant *[gay colors]* **3.** given to social pleasures *[a gay life]* **4.** wanton; licentious *[a gay dog]* **5.** homosexual —***n.*** a homosexual; esp., a male homosexual —**gay′ness *n.***

Gay (gā), **John** 1685–1732; Eng. poet & playwright

gay·e·ty (gā′ə tē) ***n.,*** *pl.* **-ties** *same as* GAIETY

gay·ly (gā′lē) ***adv.*** *same as* GAILY

gaze (gāz) ***vi.*** **gazed, gaz′ing** [< Scand.] to look intently and steadily; stare, as in wonder —***n.*** a steady look —**gaz′er *n.***

ga·ze·bo (gə zē′bō, -zā′-) ***n.,*** *pl.* **-bos, -boes** [< ?] a turret, balcony, or summerhouse with an extensive view

ga·zelle (gə zel′) ***n.,*** *pl.* **-zelles′, -zelle′:** see PLURAL, II, D, 1 [Fr. < Ar. *ghazāl*] any of various small, swift, graceful antelopes of Africa, the Near East, and Asia, with horns that twist back in a spiral and large, lustrous eyes

ga·zette (gə zet′) ***n.*** [Fr. < It. *gazzetta* < dial. *gazeta,* a small coin, price of a newspaper] **1.** a newspaper **2.** in England, any of various official publications containing announcements and bulletins —***vt.*** **-zet′ted, -zet′ting** [Chiefly Brit.] to announce or list in a gazette

gaz·et·teer (gaz′ə tir′) ***n.*** **1.** [Archaic] a person who writes for a gazette **2.** a dictionary or index of geographical names

gaz·pa·cho (gäz pä′chō) ***n.*** [Sp.] a Spanish soup made with tomatoes, chopped cucumbers, onions, oil, vinegar, etc. and served cold

G.B. Great Britain

GCA *Aeron.* ground control approach

G clef *same as* TREBLE CLEF

GCT, G.C.T. Greenwich civil time

Gd *Chem.* gadolinium

Gdansk (g′dänsk′) seaport in N Poland, on the Baltic Sea: pop. 330,000: Ger. name, DANZIG

Ge *Chem.* germanium

gear (gir) ***n.*** [prob. < ON. *gervi,* preparation] **1.** clothing; apparel **2.** apparatus or equipment for some particular task, as a workman's tools, a harness, etc. **3.** *a)* a toothed wheel, disk, etc. designed to mesh with another or with the thread of a worm *b)* [*often pl.*] a system of two or more gears meshed together so that the motion of one is passed on to the others *c)* a specific adjustment of such a system: in motor-vehicle transmissions, *high gear* provides greatest speed and *low gear* greatest power *d)* any part of a mechanism performing a specific function *[the steering gear]* —***vt.*** **1.** to furnish with gear; harness **2.** to adapt (one thing) so as to conform with another *[to gear production to demand]* **3.** *a)* to connect by gears *b)* to furnish with gears —***vi.*** to be in, or come into, proper adjustment or working order —**in** (or **out of**) **gear** **1.** (not) connected to the motor **2.** (not) in proper adjustment or working order —**shift gears** **1.** to change from one gear arrangement to another **2.** to change one's method or approach

GEARS

gear·box (-bäks′) ***n.*** the unit consisting of the transmission gears in a transmission system

gear·ing (-iŋ) ***n.*** **1.** the act or manner of fitting a machine with gears **2.** a system of gears or other parts for transmitting motion

gear·shift (-shift′) ***n.*** a device for connecting or disconnecting any of a number of sets of transmission gears to a motor, etc.

gear·wheel (-hwēl′, -wēl′) ***n.*** a toothed wheel in a system of gears; cogwheel

geck·o (gek′ō) ***n.,*** *pl.* **-os, -oes** [Malay *gekok,* echoic of its cry] a soft-skinned, insect-eating, tropical lizard with suction pads on its feet

gee[1] (jē) ***interj., n.*** [Early ModE. < ?] a word of command to a horse, ox, etc. meaning "turn to the right!" **—*vt., vi.*** **geed, gee′ing** to turn to the right Opposed to HAW[2]

gee[2] (jē) ***interj.*** [euphemistic contr. < JE(SUS)] [Slang] an exclamation of surprise, wonder, etc.

geese (gēs) ***n.*** *pl. of* GOOSE

gee·zer (gē′zər) ***n.*** [< dial. *guiser,* a mummer < GUISE] [Slang] an eccentric old man

Ge·hen·na (gi hen′ə) [< Heb. *gēhinnōm*] *Bible* the valley of Hinnom, near Jerusalem, where refuse was burned: translated in the New Testament as "hell" **—*n.*** any place of torment

Gei·ger counter (gī′gər) [after H. *Geiger* (1882–1945), Ger. physicist] an instrument for detecting and counting ionizing particles: a refined version (**Geiger-Müller counter**) with an amplifying system is used for detecting and measuring radioactivity

gei·sha (gā′shə) ***n.,*** *pl.* **-sha, -shas** [Jap.] a Japanese girl trained in singing, dancing, etc., to serve as a hired companion to men

gel (jel) ***n.*** [< ff.] a jellylike substance formed by the coagulation of a colloidal solution into a solid phase **—*vi.*** **gelled, gel′ling** to form a gel

gel·a·tin, gel·a·tine (jel′ət ′n) ***n.*** [< Fr. < It. < *gelata,* a jelly < pp. of L. *gelare,* to freeze] **1.** the tasteless, odorless, brittle substance extracted by boiling bones, hoofs, etc.; also, a similar vegetable substance: gelatin dissolves in hot water, forming a jellylike substance when cool, and is used in various foods, photographic film, etc. **2.** something, as a jelly, made with gelatin

ge·lat·i·nize (jə lat′′n īz′, jel′ət ′n īz′) ***vt.*** **-nized′, -niz′ing** **1.** to change into gelatin or gelatinous matter **2.** *Photog.* to coat with gelatin **—*vi.*** to be changed into gelatin or gelatinous matter **—ge·lat′i·ni·za′tion *n.***

ge·lat·i·nous (jə lat′′n əs) ***adj.*** **1.** of or containing gelatin **2.** like gelatin or jelly; viscous **—ge·lat′i·nous·ly *adv.*** **—ge·lat′i·nous·ness *n.***

geld (geld) ***vt.*** **geld′ed** or **gelt, geld′ing** [< ON. *gelda* < *geldr,* barren] **1.** to castrate (esp. a horse) **2.** to deprive of essential vigor; weaken

geld·ing (gel′diŋ) ***n.*** a gelded animal; esp., a castrated horse

gel·id (jel′id) ***adj.*** [L. *gelidus* < *gelu,* frost] extremely cold; icy **—ge·lid·i·ty** (jə lid′ə tē) ***n.***

Gel·sen·kir·chen (gel′zən kir′Hən) city in W West Germany, in the Ruhr valley: pop. 356,000

gem (jem) ***n.*** [< OFr. < L. *gemma,* a bud, gem] **1.** a precious or, occas., semiprecious stone, cut and polished for use as a jewel **2.** a highly valued person or thing **3.** a kind of muffin **—*vt.*** **gemmed, gem′ming** to adorn or set with or as with gems

A B C D

CUTS OF GEM (A, marquise; B, emerald; C, round; D, pear-shaped)

gem·i·nate (jem′ə nāt′) ***adj.*** [< L. pp. of *geminare,* to double < *geminus,* a twin] growing or combined in pairs; coupled **—*vt.*** **-nat′ed, -nat′ing** to arrange in pairs; double **—*vi.*** to become doubled or paired **—gem′i·na′tion *n.***

Gem·i·ni (jem′ə nī′, -nē′) [L., twins] **1.** a N constellation containing the stars Castor and Pollux, represented as twins seated **2.** the third sign of the zodiac: see ZODIAC, illus.

gem·ma (jem′ə) ***n.,*** *pl.* **-mae** (-ē) [L.: cf. GEM] *Biol.* a budlike outgrowth which becomes detached and develops into a new organism

gem·mate (jem′āt) ***adj.*** [< L. pp. of *gemmare* < *gemma,* a bud] having, or reproducing by, gemmae **—*vi.*** **-mat·ed, -mat·ing** to have, or reproduce by, gemmae; bud **—gem·ma′tion *n.***

gem·mule (jem′yōōl) ***n.*** *Biol.* a small gemma

gems·bok (gemz′bäk′) ***n.,*** *pl.* **-bok′, -boks′:** see PLURAL, II, D, 2 [Afrik. < G. < *gemse* < VL. *camox,* CHAMOIS + *bock,* a buck] a large antelope of S Africa, with long, straight horns and a tufted tail

gem·stone (jem′stōn′) ***n.*** any mineral that can be used as a gem when cut and polished

-gen (jən, jen) [< Fr. < Gr. < base of *gignesthai,* to be born] *a suffix meaning:* **1.** something that produces *[oxygen, estrogen]* **2.** something produced (in a specified way) *[zymogen]*

Gen. **1.** General **2.** Genesis

gen. **1.** gender **2.** general **3.** genitive

gen·darme (zhän′därm; *Fr.* zhän dȧrm′) ***n.,*** *pl.* **-darmes** (-därmz; *Fr.* -dȧrm′) [Fr., ult. < L. *gens,* a people + *de,* of + *arma,* arms] **1.** in France, Belgium, etc., a soldier serving as an armed policeman **2.** any policeman: a humorous usage

gen·dar·me·rie (zhän där′mə rē; *Fr.* zhän dȧr mə rē′) ***n.*** [Fr.] gendarmes collectively: also **gen·dar′mer·y**

gen·der (jen′dər) ***n.*** [< OFr. *gendre* < L. *genus,* origin, kind] **1.** *Gram. a)* the classification by which nouns, pronouns, adjectives, etc. are variously grouped and inflected as masculine, feminine, or neuter: in English, only some nouns and the third person singular pronouns are distinguished according to gender *b)* any one of such groupings **2.** [Colloq.] sex

gene (jēn) ***n.*** [< G. *gen* < *pangen* (< Gr. *pan-,* PAN- + *-gen,* -GEN)] *Genetics* any of the units occurring at specific points on the chromosomes, by which hereditary characters are transmitted and determined: see DEOXYRIBONUCLEIC ACID (DNA)

ge·ne·al·o·gy (jē′nē äl′ə jē, -al′ə jē) ***n.,*** *pl.* **-gies** [< OFr. < LL. < Gr. < *genea,* race, stock + *-logia,* -LOGY] **1.** a chart or recorded history of the ancestry or descent of a person or family **2.** the study of family descent **3.** descent from an ancestor; pedigree; lineage **—ge′ne·a·log′i·cal** (-ə läj′i k′l, jen′ē-) ***adj.*** **—ge′ne·a·log′i·cal·ly *adv.*** **—ge′ne·al′o·gist *n.***

gen·er·a (jen′ər ə) ***n.*** *pl. of* GENUS

gen·er·al (jen′ər əl, jen′rəl) ***adj.*** [< OFr. < L. *generalis* < *genus* (gen. *generis*), kind, class] **1.** of, for, or from the whole or all; not particular or specialized *[a general anesthetic]* **2.** of, for, or applying to a whole genus, kind, class, order, or race *[the general classifications of matter]* **3.** existing or occurring extensively; widespread *[a general unrest]* **4.** most common; usual *[the general spelling of a word]* **5.** concerned with the main or overall features; lacking in details **6.** not precise; vague *[to speak in general terms]* **7.** highest in rank *[an attorney general]* **—*n.*** **1.** the main or overall fact, idea, etc. **2.** the head of a religious order **3.** any of various military officers ranking above a colonel; specif., *a) U.S. Army & U.S. Air Force* an officer ranking below a GENERAL OF THE ARMY (or AIR FORCE) and above a LIEUTENANT GENERAL *b) U.S. Marine Corps* an officer of the highest rank **—in general** **1.** in the main; usually **2.** without specific details **—gen′er·al·ness *n.***

general assembly **1.** in some States of the U.S., the legislative assembly **2.** [G- A-] the legislative assembly of the United Nations

General Court the legislature of New Hampshire or Massachusetts

general election **1.** an election to choose from among candidates previously nominated **2.** a nationwide or Statewide election

gen·er·al·is·si·mo (jen′ər ə lis′ə mō′, jen′rə-) ***n.,*** *pl.* **-mos′** [It., superl. of *generale,* GENERAL] in certain countries, **1.** the commander in chief of all the armed forces **2.** the commanding officer of several armies in the field

gen·er·al·i·ty (jen′ə ral′ə tē) ***n.,*** *pl.* **-ties** **1.** the condition or quality of being general **2.** a general or nonspecific statement, expression, etc. **3.** the bulk; main body

gen·er·al·i·za·tion (jen′ər ə li zā′shən, jen′rəl i-) ***n.*** **1.** the act or process of generalizing **2.** a general idea, statement, etc. resulting from this

gen·er·al·ize (jen′ər ə līz′, jen′rə-) ***vt.*** **-ized′, -iz′ing** to make general; esp., *a)* to state in terms of a general law *b)* to infer or derive (a general law or precept) from (particular instances) *c)* to emphasize the general character rather than specific details of *d)* to cause to be widely known or used **—*vi.*** **1.** to formulate general principles from particulars **2.** to talk in generalities **3.** to become general or spread throughout an area

gen·er·al·ly (-lē; *also* jen′ər lē) ***adv.*** **1.** widely; popularly; extensively **2.** in most instances; usually **3.** in a general way; not specifically

general officer *Mil.* any officer above a colonel in rank

general of the army (or **air force**) the highest rank in the U.S. Army (or U.S. Air Force), having the insignia of five stars

general practitioner a practicing physician who does not specialize in any particular field of medicine

gen·er·al-pur·pose (-pur′pəs) ***adj.*** having a variety of uses; suitable for general use

gen·er·al·ship (-ship′) ***n.*** **1.** *a)* the rank, tenure, or authority of a general *b)* the military skill of a general **2.** highly skillful leadership

---

fat, āpe, cär; ten, ēven; is, bīte; gō, hôrn, tōōl, look; oil, out; up, fur; get; joy; yet; chin; she; thin, *th*en; zh, leisure; ŋ, ring; ə for *a* in *ago, e* in *agent, i* in *sanity, o* in *comply, u* in *focus;* ′ as in *able* (ā′b′l); Fr. bȧl; ë, Fr. coeur; ö, Fr. feu; Fr. mo*n*; ô, Fr. coq; ü, Fr. duc; *r,* Fr. cri; H, G. ich; kh, G. doch; ‡foreign; *hypothetical; < derived from. See inside front cover.

general staff *Mil.* a group of officers who assist the commander in planning and supervising operations

gen·er·ate (jen′ə rāt′) *vt.* **-at′ed, -at′ing** [< L. pp. of *generare* < *genus,* race, kind] **1.** to produce (offspring); beget **2.** to bring into being; cause to be **3.** to originate or produce by a physical or chemical process **4.** *Math.* to trace out or form (a line, plane, figure, or solid) by the motion of a point, line, or plane

gen·er·a·tion (jen′ə rā′shən) *n.* **1.** the act or process of producing offspring **2.** a bringing into being; production **3.** a single stage in the succession of descent [*father and son are two generations*] **4.** the average period (about thirty years) between the birth of successive generations **5.** *a*) all the people born at about the same time *b*) a group of such people having something in common **6.** *Math.* the generating of a line, figure, etc. **—gen′er·a′tion·al** *adj.*

gen·er·a·tive (jen′ər ə tiv, -ə rāt′iv) *adj.* of, or having the power of, generation or production **—gen′er·a′tive·ly** *adv.* **—gen′er·a′tive·ness** *n.*

gen·er·a·tor (jen′ə rāt′ər) *n.* a person or thing that generates; specif., *a*) a machine for producing gas or steam *b*) a machine for changing mechanical energy into electrical energy; dynamo

gen·er·a·trix (jen′ə rā′triks) *n., pl.* **-er·a·tri′ces** (-ər ə-trī′sēz, -ə rā′trə sēz′) *Math.* a point, line, or plane whose motion generates a line, plane, figure, or solid

ge·ner·ic (jə ner′ik) *adj.* [< ML.: see GENUS & -IC] **1.** of, applied to, or referring to a whole kind, class, or group; inclusive or general **2.** that is not a trademark **3.** *Biol.* of or characteristic of a genus **—ge·ner′i·cal·ly** *adv.*

gen·er·os·i·ty (jen′ə räs′ə tē) *n.* **1.** the quality of being generous; specif., *a*) magnanimity *b*) unselfishness **2.** *pl.* **-ties** a generous act

gen·er·ous (jen′ər əs) *adj.* [L. *generosus,* of noble birth, excellent < *genus:* see GENUS] **1.** noble-minded; gracious; magnanimous **2.** willing to give or share; unselfish **3.** large; ample [*generous portions*] **4.** full-flavored and strong: said of wine **—gen′er·ous·ly** *adv.* **—gen′er·ous·ness** *n.*

gen·e·sis (jen′ə sis) *n., pl.* **-ses′** (-sēz′) [< OE. & LL. < L. < Gr. < *gignesthai,* to be born] a beginning; origin —[G-] the first book of the Bible, giving an account of the Creation

-gen·e·sis (jen′ə sis) *a combining form meaning* origination, creation, evolution (of something specified)

gen·et (jen′ət) *n. same as* JENNET

ge·net·ic (jə net′ik) *adj.* [< GENESIS] **1.** of the genesis, or origin, of something **2.** of genetics Also **ge·net′i·cal** **—ge·net′i·cal·ly** *adv.*

genetic code the order in which four chemical constituents are arranged in DNA molecules for transmitting genetic information to the cells

ge·net·ics (-iks) *n.pl.* [*with sing. v.*] [< GENETIC] the branch of biology that deals with heredity and variation in similar or related animals and plants **—ge·net′i·cist** (-ə sist) *n.*

Ge·ne·va (jə nē′və) **1.** city in Switzerland, on Lake Geneva: pop. 171,000 **2. Lake (of),** lake in SW Switzerland, on the border of France

Geneva Convention an international agreement signed at Geneva in 1864, establishing a code, later revised, for the care and protection in wartime of the sick, wounded, and prisoners of war

Gen·e·vieve (jen′ə vēv′) [Fr. < LL. *Genovefa* < ? Celt.] a feminine name

Gen·ghis Khan (geŋ′gis kän′, jeŋ′-) (born *Temuchin*) 1162?–1227; Mongol conqueror of C Asia

ge·nial (jēn′yəl, jē′nē əl) *adj.* [L. *genialis,* of birth < *genius,* GENIUS] **1.** promoting life and growth; warm and mild [*a genial climate*] **2.** cheerful, friendly, and sympathetic; amiable **—ge·ni·al·i·ty** (jē′nē al′ə tē, jēn yal′-) *n.* **—ge′nial·ly** *adv.*

-gen·ic (jen′ik) *a combining form:* **1.** *used to form adjectives corresponding to nouns ending in* -GEN *or* -GENY [*phylogenic*] **2.** *meaning* suitable to [*photogenic*]

ge·nie (jē′nē) *n.* [Fr. *génie*] *same as* JINNI

gen·i·tal (jen′ə t′l) *adj.* [< OFr. < L. *genitalis* < pp. of *genere, gignere,* to beget] **1.** of reproduction or the sexual organs **2.** *Psychoanalysis* of an early stage of psychosexual development focusing on the genital organs

gen·i·tals (-t′lz) *n.pl.* [< prec.] the reproductive organs; esp., the external sex organs: also **gen′i·ta′li·a** (-tāl′yə, -tā′lē ə)

gen·i·tive (jen′ə tiv) *adj.* [< OFr. < L. (*casus*) *genitivus,* lit., case of origin] designating, of, or in a case, as in Latin, shown by grammatical inflection or by analytical construction and typically expressing possession, source, etc. **—*n.*** **1.** the genitive case **2.** a word or construction in the genitive case **—gen′i·ti′val** (-tī′v′l) *adj.* **—gen′i·ti′val·ly** *adv.*

gen·i·to·u·ri·nar·y (jen′ə tō yoor′ə ner′ē) *adj.* designating or of the genital and urinary organs together

ge·nius (jēn′yəs, jē′nē əs) *n., pl.* **ge′nius·es** for 3, 4, 5; **ge·ni·i** (jē′nē ī′) for 1 & 2 [L., guardian spirit < base of *genere, gignere,* to produce] **1.** *a*) [*often* **G-**] the guardian spirit of a person, place, etc. *b*) either of two spirits, one good and one evil, supposed to influence one's destiny *c*) a person considered as having strong influence over another **2.** *same as* JINNI **3.** particular character or spirit of a nation, place, age, etc. **4.** a great natural ability or strong inclination (*for*) **5.** *a*) great mental and inventive ability *b*) a person having this *c*) popularly, any person with a very high intelligence quotient

Gen·o·a (jen′ə wə) seaport in NW Italy, on the Ligurian Sea: pop. 844,000: It. name, **Ge·no·va** (je′nô vä′) **—Gen′o·ese′** (-wēz′) *adj., n., pl.* **-ese′**

gen·o·cide (jen′ə sīd′) *n.* [< Gr. *genos,* race, kind + -CIDE] the systematic killing of, or a program of action intended to destroy, a whole national or ethnic group **—gen′o·ci′dal** (-sī′d′l) *adj.*

-gen·ous (jə nəs) [-GEN + -OUS] *a suffix meaning:* **1.** producing, generating [*nitrogenous*] **2.** produced by, generated in [*autogenous*]

gen·re (zhän′rə; *Fr.* zhän′r′) *n.* [Fr. < L. *genus:* see GENUS] **1.** a kind, or type, as of works of literature, art, etc. **2.** *same as* GENRE PAINTING

genre painting painting in which subjects from everyday life are treated realistically

gens (jenz) *n., pl.* **gen·tes** (jen′tēz) [L. < *gignere,* to beget] **1.** in ancient Rome, a clan united by descent through the male line from a common ancestor **2.** any tribe or clan

gent (jent) *n.* [Colloq.] a gentleman; man

gen·teel (jen tēl′) *adj.* [< Fr. *gentil* < L. *gentilis:* see GENTLE] **1.** formerly, elegant or fashionable **2.** excessively or affectedly refined, polite, etc. **—gen·teel′ly** *adv.* **—gen·teel′ness** *n.*

gen·tian (jen′shən) *n.* [< OFr. < L. *gentiana*] **1.** any of a large genus of plants with blue, white, red, or yellow flowers **2.** the bitter root of the yellow gentian

gen·tile (jen′tīl) *n.* [< Fr. *gentil* & L. *gentilis,* of the same gens, or clan] [*also* **G-**] **1.** any person not a Jew; specif., a Christian **2.** formerly, among Christians, a heathen or pagan **3.** among Mormons, any person not a Mormon **—*adj.*** [*also* **G-**] **1.** not Jewish **2.** heathen; pagan **3.** not Mormon

gen·til·i·ty (jen til′ə tē) *n., pl.* **-ties** [< OFr. < L. < *gentilis:* see ff.] **1.** the condition of belonging by birth to the upper classes **2.** the quality of being genteel

gen·tle (jent′'l) *adj.* **-tler, -tlest** [< OFr. < L. *gentilis,* of the same clan < *gens,* GENS] **1.** of the upper classes or polite society **2.** like or suitable to polite society; refined, courteous, etc. **3.** [Archaic] noble; chivalrous [*a gentle knight*] **4.** generous; kind **5.** easily handled; tame [*a gentle dog*] **6.** kindly; patient [*a gentle disposition*] **7.** not violent or harsh [*a gentle tap*] **8.** gradual [*a gentle slope*] **—*vt.*** **-tled, -tling** **1.** to tame or train (a horse) **2.** to calm as by stroking **—gen′tle·ness** *n.* **—gen′tly** *adv.*

gen·tle·folk (-fōk′) *n.pl.* people of high social standing: also **gen′tle·folks′**

gen·tle·man (-mən) *n., pl.* **-men** **1.** *a*) orig., a man born into a family of high social standing *b*) any man of independent means who does not work for a living **2.** a courteous, gracious man **3.** a valet: chiefly in **gentleman's gentleman** **4.** any man: polite term, as (chiefly in pl.) of address

gen·tle·man-farm·er (-fär′mər) *n., pl.* **gen′tle·men-farm′ers** a wealthy man who owns and manages a farm as an avocation

gen·tle·man·ly (-lē) *adj.* of, characteristic of, or fit for a gentleman; well-mannered: also **gen′tle·man·like′** **—gen′tle·man·li·ness** *n.*

gentlemen's (or **gentleman's**) **agreement** an unwritten agreement secured only by the parties' pledge of honor and not legally binding

gen·tle·wom·an (jent′'l woom′ən) *n., pl.* **-wom′en** **1.** orig., a woman born into a family of high social standing; lady **2.** a courteous, gracious, considerate woman **3.** formerly, a woman in attendance on a lady of rank

gen·try (jen′trē) *n.* [< OFr. *genterise,* ult. < L. *gentilis:* see GENTLE] **1.** people of high social standing; esp., in Great Britain, the class of landowning people ranking just below the nobility **2.** people of a particular class or group

gen·u·flect (jen′yə flekt′) *vi.* [< ML. < L. *genu,* the knee + *flectere,* to bend] **1.** to bend the knee, as in reverence or worship **2.** to act submissively **—gen′u·flec′tion,** chiefly Brit. **gen′u·flex′ion** (-flek′shən) *n.* **—gen′u·flec′tor** *n.*

gen·u·ine (jen′yoo wən) *adj.* [L. *genuinus* < base of *gignere,* to be born] **1.** of the original stock; purebred **2.** really being what it is said to be; true; authentic **3.** sincere and frank; honest **—gen′u·ine·ly** *adv.* **—gen′u·ine·ness** *n.*

ge·nus (jē′nəs) *n., pl.* **gen·er·a** (jen′ər ə), sometimes **ge′nus·es** [L., birth, origin, race, kind] **1.** a class; kind; sort **2.** *Biol.* a classification of plants or animals with common distinguishing characteristics: a genus is the main subdivision of a family and includes one or more species; the genus name is capitalized, the species name is not (Ex.: *Homo sapiens,* modern man) **3.** *Logic* a class of things made up of subordinate classes, or species

-gen·y (jə nē) [< Gr.: see -GEN] *a suffix meaning* origin, production, development *[phylogeny]*

ge·o- [Gr. *geō-* < *gaia, gē,* the earth] *a combining form meaning:* **1.** earth, of the earth *[geocentric]* **2.** geographical *[geopolitics]*

ge·o·cen·tric (jē'ō sen'trik) *adj.* [prec. + CENTRIC] **1.** measured or viewed as from the center of the earth **2.** having or regarding the earth as a center Also **ge'o·cen'tri·cal** —**ge'o·cen'tri·cal·ly** *adv.*

ge·o·des·ic (jē'ə des'ik, -dē'sik) *adj.* **1.** *same as* GEODETIC (sense 1) **2.** designating the shortest line between two points on a surface, esp. a curved surface —*n.* a geodesic line

ge·od·e·sy (jē äd'ə sē) *n.* [< Gr. < *gē,* the earth + *daiein,* to divide] the branch of applied mathematics concerned with measuring, or determining the shape of, the earth or a large part of its surface, or with locating exactly points on its surface —**ge·od'e·sist** *n.*

ge·o·det·ic (jē'ə det'ik) *adj.* **1.** of or determined by geodesy **2.** *same as* GEODESIC (sense 2) Also **ge'o·det'i·cal** —**ge'o·det'i·cal·ly** *adv.*

Geof·frey (jef'rē) [< OFr. *Geoffroi* < Gmc.: 2d element < Gmc. hyp. *frithu,* peace] a masculine name

geog. 1. geographic(al) **2.** geography

ge·o·graph·i·cal (jē'ə graf'i k'l) *adj.* **1.** of or according to geography **2.** with reference to the geography of a particular region Also **ge'o·graph'ic** —**ge'o·graph'i·cal·ly** *adv.*

ge·og·ra·phy (jē äg'rə fē) *n., pl.* **-phies** [< L. < Gr. < *geō-,* GEO- + *graphein,* to write] **1.** the science dealing with the surface of the earth, its division into continents and countries, and the climate, plants, animals, natural resources, people, and industries of the various divisions **2.** the physical features of a region or place **3.** a book about geography —**ge·og'ra·pher** *n.*

geol. 1. geologic(al) **2.** geologist **3.** geology

ge·o·log·ic (jē'ə läj'ik) *adj.* of or according to geology: also **ge'o·log'i·cal** —**ge'o·log'i·cal·ly** *adv.*

ge·ol·o·gy (jē äl'ə jē) *n., pl.* **-gies** [< ML.: see GEO- & -LOGY] **1.** the science dealing with the physical nature of the earth, including the structure and development of its crust and interior, types of rocks, fossil forms, etc. **2.** the structure of the earth's crust in a given region or place **3.** a book about geology —**ge·ol'o·gist** *n.*

geom. 1. geometric(al) **2.** geometry

ge·o·met·ric (jē'ə met'rik) *adj.* **1.** of or according to geometry **2.** characterized by straight lines, triangles, circles, etc., as a pattern Also **ge'o·met'ri·cal** —**ge'o·met'ri·cal·ly** *adv.*

geometric progression a sequence of terms in which the ratio of each term to the preceding one is the same throughout (Ex.: 1, 2, 4, 8, etc.)

ge·om·e·trid (jē äm'ə trid) *n.* [< ModL. < L. < Gr. < *geōmetrein:* see ff.] any of a family of moths whose larvae move by looping the body

ge·om·e·try (jē äm'ə trē) *n., pl.* **-tries** [< OFr. < L. < Gr. *geōmetrein* < *gē,* earth + *metrein,* to measure] **1.** the branch of mathematics that deals with points, lines, surfaces, and solids, and examines their properties, measurement, and mutual relations in space **2.** a book about geometry —**ge·om'e·tri'cian** (-trish'ən), **ge·om'e·ter** *n.*

ge·o·phys·ics (jē'ō fiz'iks) *n.pl.* [*with sing. v.*] the science that deals with weather, winds, tides, etc. and their effect on the earth —**ge'o·phys'i·cal** *adj.* —**ge'o·phys'i·cist** *n.*

ge·o·pol·i·tics (jē'ō päl'ə tiks) *n.pl.* [*with sing. v.*] [< G. *geopolitik*] **1.** the interrelationship of politics and geography, or the study of this **2.** any program or policy, as for expansion, based on this —**ge'o·po·lit'i·cal** (-pə lit'i k'l) *adj.* —**ge'o·po·lit'i·cal·ly** *adv.* —**ge'o·pol'i·ti'cian** *n.*

George (jôrj) [< Fr. < LL. < Gr. < *geōrgos,* husbandman, lit., earthworker] **1.** a masculine name **2.** name of several kings of Great Britain & Ireland; specif., *a)* **George II** 1683–1760; king (1727–60) *b)* **George III** 1738–1820; king (1760–1820) *c)* **George V** 1865–1936; king (1910–36) **3. George VI** 1895–1952; king of Great Britain & Northern Ireland (1936–52) **4.** Saint, d. 303? A.D.; patron saint of England **5. Henry,** 1839–97; U.S. political economist; advocate of single tax —**by George!** an exclamation of mild surprise, determination, etc.

geor·gette (jôr jet') *n.* [after *Georgette* de la Plante, Parisian modiste] a kind of thin crepe fabric, used for dresses, etc.: also **georgette crepe**

Geor·gia (jôr'jə) **1.** [< GEORGE] a feminine name: var. *Georgiana* **2.** [after GEORGE II] Southern State of the SE U.S.: 58,876 sq. mi.; pop. 5,464,000; cap. Atlanta: abbrev. **Ga., GA 3.** republic of the U.S.S.R., on the Black Sea: 26,900 sq. mi.; pop. 4,700,000; cap. Tbilisi: in full, **Georgian Soviet Socialist Republic**

Geor·gian (jôr'jən) *adj.* **1.** of the reigns of George I, II, III, and IV of England (1714–1830) **2.** of the Georgian S.S.R., its people, language, or culture **3.** of the State of Georgia —*n.* **1.** *a)* a native or inhabitant of the Georgian S.S.R. *b)* the South Caucasian language of the Georgians **2.** a native or inhabitant of the State of Georgia

ge·o·stat·ics (jē'ō stat'iks, jē'ə-) *n.pl.* [*with sing. v.*] [< GEO- + STATIC] the branch of physics dealing with the mechanics of the equilibrium of forces in rigid bodies

ge·ot·ro·pism (jē ät'rə piz'm) *n.* [GEO- + -TROPISM] movement or growth in response to the force of gravity, either downward, as of plant roots (**positive geotropism**), or upward, as of stems (**negative geotropism**) —**ge·o·trop·ic** (jē'ə träp'ik) *adj.*

Ger. 1. German **2.** Germany

ger. 1. gerund **2.** gerundive

Ger·ald (jer'əld) [< OFr. < OHG. < *ger,* spear + base of *waldan,* to rule] a masculine name: feminine **Ger'al·dine'** (-əl dēn', -din)

ge·ra·ni·um (jə rā'nē əm, -rān'yəm) *n.* [L. < Gr. *geranion,* cranesbill: its seed capsule is beaked] **1.** a plant with showy pink or purple flowers and leaves with many lobes **2.** a pelargonium

Ger·ard (jə rärd') [< OFr. < OHG. < *ger,* spear + *hart,* hard] a masculine name

ger·fal·con (jʉr'fal'k'n, -fôl'-, -fô'-) *n. same as* GYRFALCON

ger·i·at·rics (jer'ē at'riks) *n.pl.* [*with sing. v.*] [< Gr. *gēras,* old age + -IATRICS] the branch of medicine that deals with the diseases and hygiene of old age —**ger'i·at'ric** *adj.* —**ger'i·a·tri'cian** (-ə trish'ən), **ger'i·at'rist** *n.*

germ (jʉrm) *n.* [< OFr. < L. *germen,* a sprout, bud] **1.** the rudimentary form from which a new organism is developed; seed, bud, etc. **2.** any microscopic organism, esp. one of the bacteria, that can cause disease **3.** that from which something can develop *[the* germ *of an idea]* —**germ'less** *adj.*

Ger·man (jʉr'mən) *adj.* [< L. *Germanus,* prob. < Celt.] of Germany, its people, language, or culture —*n.* **1.** a native or inhabitant of Germany **2.** the German language now spoken chiefly in Germany, Austria, and Switzerland, technically called *New High German* **3.** [**g-**] *a)* a cotillion (sense 1) *b)* a party at which the german is danced

ger·man (jʉr'mən) *adj.* [< OFr. < L. *germanus,* akin to *germen,* GERM] closely related: now chiefly in compounds, meaning: *a)* having the same parents *[a brother-german] b)* being a first cousin *[a cousin-german]*

ger·man·der (jər man'dər) *n.* [< OFr. < ML. *germandra,* < Gr. < *chamai,* on the ground + *drys,* tree] any of a genus of plants of the mint family, with spikes of flowers that lack an upper lip

ger·mane (jər mān') *adj.* [var. of GERMAN] truly relevant; pertinent; to the point

Ger·man·ic (jər man'ik) *adj.* **1.** of Germany or the Germans; German **2.** designating or of the original language of the German peoples or the languages descended from it; Teutonic —*n.* **1.** the original language of the Germanic peoples: now called **Proto-Germanic 2.** a principal branch of the Indo-European family of languages, comprising this language and the languages descended from it, including Norwegian, Icelandic, Swedish, Danish (all *North Germanic*), German, Dutch, Flemish, Frisian, English (all *West Germanic*), the extinct Gothic (*East Germanic*), etc.

ger·ma·ni·um (jər mā'nē əm) *n.* [ModL. < L. *Germania,* Germany] a rare, grayish-white, metallic chemical element that can be a semiconductor: symbol, Ge; at. wt., 72.59; at. no., 32

Ger·man·ize (jʉr'mə nīz') *vt., vi.* **-ized', -iz'ing** to make or become German in character, thought, language, etc. —**Ger'man·i·za'tion** *n.*

German measles *same as* RUBELLA

Ger·man·o- *a combining form meaning* German, of Germany, or of the Germans

German shepherd dog a breed of dog wolflike in form and size, used in police work, as a guide for the blind, etc.: also **(German) police dog**

German silver *same as* NICKEL SILVER

Ger·ma·ny (jʉr'mə nē) former country in NC Europe, on the North & Baltic seas: divided (1945) into EAST GERMANY and WEST GERMANY

germ cell a cell from which a new organism can develop; egg or sperm cell

ger·mi·cide (jʉr'mə sīd') *n.* [< GERM + -CIDE] anything used to destroy germs —**ger'mi·ci'dal** *adj.*

ger·mi·nal (jʉr'mə n'l) *adj.* **1.** of, like, or characteristic

Geologic Time Chart

MAIN DIVISIONS OF GEOLOGIC TIME			
ERAS	PERIODS or SYSTEMS	Epochs or Series	PRINCIPAL PHYSICAL & BIOLOGICAL FEATURES
CENOZOIC	QUATERNARY	Recent 12,000*	Glaciers restricted to Antarctica and Greenland; development and spread of modern human culture.
		Pleistocene 600,000	Great glaciers covered much of N North America & NW Europe; appearance of modern man late in Pleistocene.
	TERTIARY	Pliocene 10,000,000	W North America uplifted; continued development of mammals; first possible apelike men appeared in Africa.
		Miocene 25,000,000	Renewed uplift of Rockies & other mountains; mammals began to acquire present-day characters; dogs, solid-hoofed horses, manlike apes appeared.
		Oligocene 35,000,000	Many older types of mammals became extinct; mastodons, first monkeys, and apes appeared.
		Eocene 55,000,000	Mountains raised in Rockies, Andes, Alps, & Himalayas; expansion of early mammals; primitive horses appeared.
		Paleocene 65,000,000	Great development of primitive mammals.
MESOZOIC	CRETACEOUS 135,000,000		Rocky Mountains began to rise; dinosaurs reached maximum development & then became extinct; mammals small & very primitive.
	JURASSIC 180,000,000		Sierra Nevada Mountains uplifted; conifers & cycads dominant among plants; primitive birds appeared.
	TRIASSIC 230,000,000		Modern corals appeared & some insects of present-day types; great expansion of reptiles including earliest dinosaurs.
PALEOZOIC	PERMIAN 280,000,000		Trees of coal-forming forests declined; ferns abundant; conifers present; trilobites became extinct; reptiles surpassed amphibians.
	CARBONIFEROUS: PENNSYLVANIAN 310,000,000		Mountains grew along E coast of North America & in C Europe; great coal-forming swamp forests flourished in N Hemisphere; seed-bearing ferns abundant; cockroaches & first reptiles appeared.
	CARBONIFEROUS: MISSISSIPPIAN 345,000,000		Land plants became diversified; crinoids achieved greatest development; sharks of relatively modern types appeared; land animals little known.
	DEVONIAN 405,000,000		Land plants evolved rapidly, large trees appeared; brachiopods reached maximum development; many kinds of primitive fishes; first sharks, insects, & amphibians appeared.
	SILURIAN 425,000,000		Great mountains formed in NW Europe; first small land plants appeared; shelled cephalopods abundant; trilobites began decline; first jawed fish appeared.
	ORDOVICIAN 500,000,000		Much limestone deposited in shallow seas; great expansion among marine invertebrate animals; first primitive jawless fish appeared.
	CAMBRIAN 600,000,000		Shallow seas covered parts of continents; abundant record of marine life, esp. trilobites & brachiopods; other fossils rare.
PRECAMBRIAN	LATE PRECAMBRIAN** 2,000,000,000		Metamorphosed sedimentary rocks and granite formed; first evidence of life, calcareous algae & invertebrates.
	EARLY PRECAMBRIAN** 4,500,000,000		Crust formed on molten earth; crystalline rocks much disturbed; history unknown.

*Figures indicate approximate number of years since the beginning of each division.

** Regarded as separate eras.

of germs or germ cells **2.** in the first stage of growth or development —**ger′mi·nal·ly** ***adv.***

ger·mi·nate (-nāt′) ***vi., vt.*** **-nat′ed, -nat′ing** [< L. pp. of *germinare* < *germen*, GERM] **1.** to sprout or cause to sprout, as from a seed **2.** to start developing or growing —**ger′mi·na′tion** ***n.*** —**ger′mi·na′tive** ***adj.*** —**ger′mi·na′tor** ***n.***

Ger·mis·ton (jur′mis tən) city in S Transvaal, South Africa: pop. 214,000

germ plasm the reproductive cells of an organism, particularly that part of the cells involved in heredity

germ warfare the deliberate contamination of enemy territory with disease germs in warfare

ger·on·tol·o·gy (jer′ən täl′ə jē) ***n.*** [< Gr. < *gerōn*, old man + -LOGY] the scientific study of the process of aging and of the problems of aged people —**ge·ron·to·log·i·cal** (jə rän′tə läj′i k′l) ***adj.*** —**ger′on·tol′o·gist** ***n.***

-ger·ous (jər əs) [L. *-ger* < *gerere*, to bear + -OUS] *a suffix meaning* producing or bearing

ger·ry·man·der (jer′i man′dər, ger′-) ***vt.*** [< E. *Gerry*, governor of Mass. when the method was employed (1812) + SALAMANDER (the shape of the redistricted Essex County)] **1.** to divide (a voting area) so as to give one political party a majority in as many districts as possible **2.** to manipulate unfairly so as to gain advantage —***vi.*** to engage in gerrymandering —***n.*** the act or result of gerrymandering —**ger′ry·man′der·er** ***n.***

Ger·trude (gur′trood) [Fr. < G. < OHG. < *ger*, spear + *trut*, dear] a feminine name: dim. *Gert, Gertie*

ger·und (jer′ənd) ***n.*** [< LL. < L. *gerundus* < *gerere*, to do or carry out] *Gram.* a verbal noun ending in *-ing*, that is used like a noun but is able, like a verb, to take an object or an adverbial modifier (Ex.: *playing* in "Playing golf is his only exercise") —**ge·run·di·al** (jə run′dē əl) ***adj.***

ge·run·dive (jə run′div) ***n.*** [< LL. < prec.] **1.** a Latin verbal adjective with a typical gerund stem form, used as a future passive participle expressing duty, necessity, fitness, etc. **2.** a similar form in any language —**ger·un·di·val** (jer′ən dī′vəl) ***adj.***

gest, geste (jest) ***n.*** [< OFr. < L. *gesta*, deeds, pl. pp. of *gerere*, to do, act] **1.** [Archaic] an adventure; exploit **2.** a romantic story of adventure, esp. a medieval tale in verse

Ge·stalt psychology (gə shtält′, -stält′, -stôlt′) [G., lit., shape, form] a school of psychology, orig. German, based on the idea that the response of an individual in a given situation is a response to the whole situation, not to its components

Ge·sta·po (gə stä′pō; *G.* gə shtä′-) ***n.*** [< G. *Ge(heime) Sta(ats)po(lizei)*, secret state police] the secret police force of the German Nazi state

ges·tate (jes′tāt) ***vt.*** **-tat·ed, -tat·ing** [< L. pp. of *gestare*, freq. of *gerere*, to bear] to carry in the uterus during pregnancy —**ges·ta′tion** ***n.***

ges·tic·u·late (jes tik′yə lāt′) ***vi.*** **-lat′ed, -lat′ing** [< L. pp. of *gesticulari*, to gesture, ult. < pp. of *gerere*, to bear, do] to make or use gestures, esp. with the hands or arms, as in adding force to one's speech —***vt.*** to express by gesticulating —**ges·tic′u·la′tive** ***adj.*** —**ges·tic′u·la′tor** ***n.***

ges·tic·u·la·tion (jes tik′yə lā′shən) ***n.*** **1.** a gesticulating **2.** a gesture, esp. an energetic one —**ges·tic′u·la·to′ry** (-lə tôr′ē) ***adj.***

ges·ture (jes′chər) ***n.*** [< ML. < L. pp. of *gerere*, to bear, do] **1.** a movement of the body, or of part of the body, to express or emphasize ideas, emotions, etc. **2.** anything said or done to convey a state of mind or intention, sometimes something said or done only for effect —***vi.*** **-tured, -tur·ing** to make or use gestures —***vt.*** to express with gestures —**ges′tur·al** ***adj.*** —**ges′tur·er** ***n.***

get (get) ***vt.*** **got** or archaic & dial. **gat, got** or **got′ten, get′ting** [< ON. *geta*] **1.** to come into the state of having; receive, win, gain, obtain, acquire, etc. **2.** to reach; arrive at [to *get* home early] **3.** to set up communication with, as by radio [to *get* Paris] **4.** to go and bring [*get* your books] **5.** to catch; capture; gain hold of **6.** to learn; commit to memory **7.** to persuade (a person) to do something [*get* him to leave] **8.** to cause to act in a certain way [*get* the door to shut properly] **9.** to cause to be or arrive [he *got* his hands dirty, he *got* it there on time] **10.** to be sentenced to [he *got* ten years] **11.** to prepare [to *get* lunch] **12.** to give birth to; beget: usually said of animals **13.** [Colloq.] to be obliged to; feel a necessity to (with *have* or *has*) [he's *got* to pass] **14.** [Colloq.] to own; possess (with *have* or *has*) [he's *got* red hair] **15.** [Colloq.] to be or become the master of; esp., *a*) to overpower [his illness finally *got* him] *b*) to puzzle; baffle [this problem *gets* me] *c*) to take into custody, wound, or kill *d*) *Baseball*, etc. to put (an opponent) out **16.** [Colloq.] to strike; hit [the blow *got* him in the eye] **17.** [Colloq.] to catch the meaning or import of; understand **18.** [Slang] to cause an emotional response in; irritate, please, thrill, etc. [her singing *gets* me] **19.** [Slang] to notice [*get* the look on his face] —***vi.*** **1.** to come or arrive [to *get* to work on time] **2.** to come to be (doing something); come to be (in a situation, condition, etc.) [he *got* caught in the rain] **3.** to contrive [to *get* to do something] **4.** [Colloq.] to leave at once *Get* is used as an auxiliary for emphasis in passive construction [we *got* beaten] —***n.*** **1.** the young of an animal; offspring **2.** a begetting —**get about** **1.** to move from place to place **2.** to go to many social events, places, etc. **3.** to circulate widely, as news —**get across** [Colloq.] **1.** to explain convincingly **2.** to succeed, as in making oneself understood —**get after** [Colloq.] **1.** to pursue or attack **2.** to goad persistently —**get along** *see phrase under* ALONG —**get around** **1.** to get about (in all senses) **2.** to circumvent **3.** to influence or gain favor with by cajoling, flattery, etc. —**get around to** **1.** to find occasion for **2.** to get started on after a delay —**get away** **1.** to go away; leave **2.** to escape **3.** to start —**get away with** [Slang] to succeed in doing or taking without being discovered or punished —**get back** **1.** to return **2.** to recover **3.** [Slang] to get revenge (usually with *at*) —**get by** **1.** to be fairly acceptable **2.** [Colloq.] to succeed without being discovered or punished **3.** [Colloq.] to survive; manage —**get down to** to begin to consider or act on —**get in** **1.** to enter; join **2.** to arrive **3.** to put in —**get off** **1.** to come off, down, or out of **2.** to leave; go away **3.** to take off **4.** to escape **5.** to help to escape punishment **6.** to start, as in a race **7.** to utter (a joke, retort, etc.) **8.** to have time off —**get on** **1.** to go on or into **2.** to put on **3.** to proceed **4.** to grow older **5.** to succeed **6.** to agree —**get out** **1.** to go out **2.** to go away **3.** to take out **4.** to become no longer a secret **5.** to publish —**get over** **1.** to recover from **2.** to forget or overlook —**get somewhere** to succeed —**get through** **1.** to finish **2.** to manage to survive **3.** to push through **4.** to make oneself clear (*to*) —**get to** [Colloq.] **1.** to succeed in reaching **2.** to influence, as by bribery: also **get at** —**get together** **1.** to bring or come together; assemble **2.** [Colloq.] to reach an agreement —**get up** **1.** to rise (from a chair, from sleep, etc.) **2.** to contrive; organize **3.** to dress elaborately **4.** to advance; make progress —**get′ta·ble, get′a·ble** ***adj.*** —**get′ter** ***n.***

get·a·way (get′ə wā′) ***n.*** **1.** the act of starting, as in a race **2.** the act of escaping, as from police

Geth·sem·a·ne (geth sem′ə nē) *Bible* a garden outside of Jerusalem, scene of the agony, betrayal, and arrest of Jesus: Matt. 26:36

get-to·geth·er (get′tə ge*th*′ər) ***n.*** an informal social gathering or meeting

Get·tys·burg (get′iz burg′) [after J. *Gettys*, its 18th-c. founder] town in S Pa.: site of a crucial battle (July, 1863) of the Civil War: pop. 7,000

get-up (get′up′) ***n.*** [Colloq.] **1.** general arrangement or composition **2.** costume; outfit; dress **3.** driving ambition; energy: also **get′-up′-and-go′**

gew·gaw (gyoo′gô, goo′-) ***n.*** [ME. *giuegoue, gugaw* < ?] something showy but useless; trinket

gey·ser (gī′zər, -sər; *Brit.* gā′-) ***n.*** [Ice. *Geysir*, a hot spring in Iceland, lit., gusher < ON. *gjosa*, to gush] a spring from which columns of boiling water and steam gush into the air at intervals

Gha·na (gä′nə) country in W Africa, on the Atlantic: a member of the Commonwealth: 91,843 sq. mi.; pop. 8,600,000; cap. Accra —**Gha·na·ian** (gä′nē ən, -nā-) ***adj., n.***

ghast·ly (gast′lē) ***adj.*** **-li·er, -li·est** [< OE. < *gast*, spirit, ghost] **1.** horrible; frightful **2.** ghostlike; pale **3.** [Colloq.] very unpleasant —***adv.*** in a ghastly manner —**ghast′li·ness** ***n.***

ghat, ghaut (gôt, gät) ***n.*** [Hindi *ghāṭ*] in India, **1.** a mountain pass **2.** a flight of steps leading down to a river landing for ritual bathers

ghee (gē) ***n.*** [Hindi *ghī*] in India, a liquid butter specially made from cow's milk or buffalo milk

Ghent (gent) city in NW Belgium: pop. 156,000

gher·kin (gur′kin) ***n.*** [< Du. or LowG. *gurken*, ult. < Per. *angārah*] **1.** a variety of cucumber bearing small, prickly fruit, used for pickles **2.** the immature fruit of the cucumber when pickled

ghet·to (get′ō) ***n.,*** *pl.* **-tos, -toes** [It., lit., foundry, ult. < L. *jactare*, to cast: the former Jewish quarter on a foundry site in Venice] **1.** in certain European cities, a section to which Jews were formerly restricted **2.** any section of a city in which many members of some minority group live, or to which they are restricted by discrimination

Ghib·el·line (gib′ə lin, -lēn′) ***n.*** any member of a political party in medieval Italy that supported the authority of the German emperors in Italy

Ghi·ber·ti (gē ber′tē), **Lo·ren·zo** (lô ren′tsô) (born *Lorenzo di Cione di Ser Buonaccorso*) 1378–1455; Florentine sculptor, painter, & worker in metals

ghost (gōst) ***n.*** [OE. *gast*] **1.** orig., the spirit or soul: now only in **give up the ghost** (to die) and in HOLY GHOST **2.** the supposed disembodied spirit of a dead person, conceived of as appearing to the living as a pale, shadowy apparition **3.** a haunting memory **4.** a faint semblance; slight trace *[*not a *ghost* of a chance*]* **5.** [Colloq.] *same as* GHOSTWRITER **6.** *Optics & TV* an unwanted secondary image or bright spot *—vi.* [Colloq.] to work as a ghostwriter *—vt.* **1.** to haunt **2.** [Colloq.] to be the ghostwriter of **—ghost′like′** ***adj.*** **—ghost′li·ness** ***n.*** **—ghost′ly** ***adj.***

ghost town the remains of a town that has been permanently abandoned, esp. for economic reasons

ghost·writ·er (-rīt′ər) ***n.*** a person who writes speeches, articles, etc. for another who professes to be the author **—ghost′write′** *vt., vi.* **-wrote′, -writ′ten, -writ′ing**

ghoul (go͞ol) ***n.*** [Ar. *ghūl,* demon < *ghāla,* to seize] **1.** *Oriental Folklore* an evil spirit that robs graves and feeds on the dead **2.** a robber of graves **3.** one who enjoys things that disgust or trouble most people **—ghoul′ish** ***adj.*** **—ghoul′ish·ly** ***adv.*** **—ghoul′ish·ness** ***n.***

GHQ, G.H.Q. General Headquarters

GI (jē′ī′) ***adj.*** **1.** *Mil.* government issue: designating clothing, equipment, etc. issued to military personnel **2.** [Colloq.] *a)* of or characteristic of the U.S. armed forces *[*a *GI* haircut*]* *b)* strict in following or enforcing military regulations *c)* of or for veterans of the U.S. armed forces ***—n.,*** *pl.* **GI's, GIs** [Colloq.] any member of the U.S. armed forces; esp., an enlisted soldier *—vt., vi.* **GI'd, GI'ing** [Mil. Slang] to clean up for official inspection

GI, G.I., g.i. gastrointestinal

gi. gill (unit of measure); gills

gi·ant (jī′ənt) ***n.*** [< ONormFr. < VL. < L. *gigas* < Gr.] **1.** any imaginary being of human form but of superhuman size and strength **2.** a person or thing of great size, intellect, etc. *—adj.* of great size, strength, etc. **—gi′ant·ess** ***n.fem.***

gi·ant·ism (-iz'm) ***n.*** abnormally great growth of the body, due to excessive production of growth hormone by the pituitary gland

giant panda a large, black-and-white, bearlike mammal of China and Tibet

giaour (jour) ***n.*** [< Turk. < Per. *gabr* < Ar. *kāfir,* infidel] in Moslem usage, a non-Moslem; esp., a Christian

gib·ber (jib′ər) *vi., vt.* [echoic] to speak or utter rapidly and incoherently; chatter ***—n.*** unintelligible chatter; gibberish

gib·ber·ish (jib′ər ish; *Brit.* gib′-) ***n.*** rapid and incoherent talk; unintelligible chatter; jargon

GIANT PANDA (4 ft. high at shoulder)

gib·bet (jib′it) ***n.*** [< OFr. dim. < Frank. *gibb,* forked stick] **1.** a gallows **2.** a structure like a gallows, from which bodies of criminals already executed were hung and exposed to public scorn ***—vt.*** **1.** to execute by hanging **2.** to hang on a gibbet **3.** to expose to public scorn

gib·bon (gib′ən) ***n.*** [Fr.] a small, slender, long-armed ape of India, S China, and the East Indies, that lives in trees

Gib·bon (gib′ən), **Edward** 1737–94; Eng. historian

gib·bous (gib′əs) ***adj.*** [< L. *gibbosus* < *gibba,* a hump] **1.** rounded and bulging **2.** designating the moon or a planet when more than half, but not all, of the disk is illuminated **3.** humpbacked **—gib·bos·i·ty** (gi bäs′ə tē) ***n.*** **—gib′bous·ly** ***adv.***

gibe (jīb) *vi., vt.* **gibed, gib′ing** [< ? OFr. *giber,* to handle roughly] to jeer, or taunt; scoff (at) ***—n.*** a jeer; taunt; scoff **—gib′er** ***n.***

gib·let (jib′lit) ***n.*** [< OFr. *gibelet,* stew made of game] any of the parts of a fowl, as the heart, gizzard, neck, etc., usually cooked separately

GIBBON (18 1/2-25 in. long, head & body)

Gi·bral·tar (ji brôl′tər) **1.** Brit. territory on a small peninsula at the S tip of Spain, including a port & naval base: it consists mostly of a rocky hill **(Rock of Gibraltar) 2. Strait of,** strait between Spain & Morocco, joining the Mediterranean & the Atlantic ***—n.*** any strong fortification; unassailable fortress

gid·dy (gid′ē) ***adj.*** **-di·er, -di·est** [OE. *gydig,* insane, prob. < base of *god,* a god (i.e., "possessed by a god")] **1.** having a whirling, dazed sensation; dizzy **2.** causing such a sensation **3.** whirling **4.** *a)* inconstant; fickle *b)* frivolous; flighty *—vt., vi.* **-died, -dy·ing** to make or become giddy **—gid′di·ly** ***adv.*** **—gid′di·ness** ***n.***

Gide (zhēd), **An·dré (Paul Guillaume)** (än drā′) 1869–1951; Fr. novelist, critic, etc.

Gid·e·on (gid′ē ən) [Heb. *gidh'ōn,* lit., hewer] **1.** a masculine name **2.** *Bible* a judge of Israel and a leader in the defeat of the Midianites

gie (gē) *vt., vi.* **gied** or **gae, gi·en** (gē′ən), **gie′ing** [Scot. & Brit. Dial.] to give

gift (gift) ***n.*** [OE., wedding gift (< *giefan,* to give) & < ON. *gipt,* gift] **1.** something given to show friendship, affection, etc.; present **2.** the act, power, or right of giving **3.** a natural ability; talent *[*a *gift* for language*]* ***—vt.*** to present with or as a gift

gift·ed (-id) ***adj.*** **1.** having a natural ability; talented **2.** having superior intelligence

gift of tongues *same as* GLOSSOLALIA

gift-wrap (-rap′) *vt.* **-wrapped′, -wrap′ping** to wrap as a gift, with decorative paper, ribbon, etc.

gig^1 (gig) ***n.*** [prob. < Scand.] **1.** a light, two-wheeled, open carriage drawn by one horse **2.** a long, light ship's boat *—vi.* **gigged, gig′ging** to travel in a gig

gig^2 (gig) ***n.*** [contr. < *fizgig* < Sp. *fisga,* kind of harpoon] a fish spear *—vt., vi.* **gigged, gig′ging** to spear or jab with or as with a gig

gig^3 (gig) ***n.*** [< ?] [Slang] a demerit ***—vi.*** **gigged, gig′ging** [Slang] to give a gig to

gig^4 (gig) ***n.*** [< ?] [Slang] **1.** a job to play or sing jazz, rock, etc. **2.** any stint of work

gi·ga- (jig′ə) [< Gr. *gigas,* giant] *a combining form meaning* one billion *[gigahertz]*

gi·gan·tic (jī gan′tik) ***adj.*** [see GIANT] **1.** of, like, or fit for a giant **2.** very big; huge; enormous; immense **—gi·gan′ti·cal·ly** ***adv.***

gi·gan·tism (jī gan′tiz'm, jī′gan-) ***n.*** [see GIANT] **1.** the state of being gigantic **2.** *same as* GIANTISM

gig·gle (gig′'l) ***vi.*** **-gled, -gling** [prob. < Du. *giggelen*] to laugh with uncontrollable, rapid, high-pitched sounds, suggestive of foolishness, nervousness, etc.; titter ***—n.*** such a laugh **—gig′gler** ***n.*** **—gig′gly** ***adj.*** **-gli·er, -gli·est**

gig·o·lo (jig′ə lō) ***n.,*** *pl.* **-los** [Fr.] a man paid by a woman to be her escort

gig·ot (jig′ət, zhē gō′) ***n.*** [Fr. < OFr., dim. < MHG. *giga,* a fiddle] **1.** a leg of mutton, lamb, veal, etc. **2.** a leg-of-mutton sleeve

Gi·la monster (hē′lə) [< the *Gila* River, Arizona] a stout, poisonous lizard covered with beadlike scales in alternating rings of black and orange: found in deserts of SW U.S. and in Mexico

Gil·bert (gil′bərt) [< OFr. < OHG. < *willo,* will + *beraht,* bright] **1.** a masculine name: dim. *Gil* **2.** Sir **William Schwenck** (shweŋk), 1836–1911; Eng. librettist: collaborated with A. SULLIVAN in writing comic operas **—Gil·ber′ti·an** (-bur′tē ən) ***adj.***

gild^1 (gild) *vt.* **gild′ed** or **gilt, gild′ing** [OE. *gyldan* < base of *gold,* gold] **1.** *a)* to overlay with a thin layer of gold *b)* to coat with a gold color **2.** to make appear bright and attractive **3.** to make (something) seem more attractive or valuable than it is **—gild′er** ***n.***

gild^2 (gild) ***n.*** *same as* GUILD

gild·ing (gil′diŋ) ***n.*** **1.** the art or process of applying gold leaf or a substance like gold to a surface **2.** the substance so applied

Gil·e·ad (gil′ē əd) mountainous region of ancient Palestine, east of the Jordan

gill^1 (gil) ***n.*** [prob. < Anglo-N.] **1.** the organ for breathing of most animals that live in water, as fish, lobsters, clams, etc. **2.** [*pl.*] *a)* the wattle of a fowl *b)* the jowl of a person **3.** a thin, leaflike, radiating plate on the undersurface of a mushroom **—gilled** ***adj.***

gill^2 (jil) ***n.*** [< OFr. < LL. *gillo,* cooling vessel] a liquid measure, equal to 1/4 pint

gil·lie, gil·ly (gil′ē) ***n.,*** *pl.* **-lies** [Scot. < Gael. *gille,* boy, page] **1.** in the Scottish Highlands, a sportsman's attendant **2.** a male servant

gil·li·flow·er (jil′ē flou′ər) ***n.*** [OFr. *gilofre* < LL. < Gr. < *karyon,* nut + *phyllon,* leaf] any of several plants with clove-scented flowers, as the clove pink: also sp. **gil′ly·flow′er**

gilt (gilt) *alt. pt. & pp. of* GILD^1 ***—adj.*** overlaid with gilding *—n. same as* GILDING

gilt-edged (-ejd′) ***adj.*** **1.** having gilded edges **2.** of the highest quality or value *[gilt-edged* securities*]* Also **gilt′-edge′**

gim·bals (gim′b'lz, jim′-) ***n.pl.*** [*with sing. v.*] [< L. *gemellus,* dim. of *geminus,* twin] a pair of rings pivoted in axes at right angles to each other so that one is free to swing within the other: a ship's compass will keep a horizontal position when suspended in gimbals **—gim′baled** ***adj.***

gim·crack (jim′krak′) ***adj.*** [altered < ME. *gibbecrak,* an ornament] showy but cheap and useless ***—n.*** a cheap, showy, useless thing; knickknack **—gim′crack′er·y** ***n.***

gim·let (gim′lit) ***n.*** [< OFr. < MDu. dim. of *wimmel*, wimble] a small boring tool with a handle at right angles to a shaft with a spiral, pointed cutting edge —***vt.*** to make a hole in as with a gimlet

GIMLET

gim·let-eyed (-īd′) ***adj.*** having a piercing glance

gim·mick (gim′ik) ***n.*** [< ? GIMCRACK] **1.** [Colloq.] *a*) a secret device for controlling a game of chance at a carnival, etc. *b*) any trick or secret device **2.** [Slang] *a*) an attention-getting, superficial feature for promoting a product, etc. *b*) any clever little gadget or ruse —***vt.*** [Colloq.] to add gimmicks to (often with *up*) —**gim′mick·ry, gim′mick·er·y *n.*** —**gim′mick·y *adj.***

gimp[1] (gimp) ***n.*** [< ? Du.] a ribbonlike braided fabric, used to trim garments, furniture, etc.

gimp[2] (gimp) ***n.*** [< ?] [Colloq.] **1.** a lame person **2.** a limp —***vi.*** to limp —**gimp′y *adj.***

gin[1] (jin) ***n.*** [< *geneva* < Du. *genever* < OFr. < L. *juniperus*, juniper] **1.** a strong alcoholic liquor distilled from grain and usually flavored with juniper berries **2.** [Slang] any alcoholic liquor

gin[2] (jin) ***n.*** [< OFr., contr. < *engin*, ENGINE] **1.** a snare or trap, as for game **2.** *same as* COTTON GIN —***vt.* ginned, gin′ning 1.** to catch in a trap **2.** to remove seeds from (cotton) with a gin —**gin′ner *n.***

gin[3] (gin) ***vt., vi.* gan, gin′ning** [ME. *ginnen* < OE. *beginnan*, to begin] [Archaic] to begin

gin[4] (jin) ***n.*** *same as* GIN RUMMY —***vi.* ginned, gin′ning** to win in gin rummy with no unmatched cards left in one's hand

gin·ger (jin′jər) ***n.*** [< OE. & OFr., both < ML. < L. *zingiber* < Gr. < Pali] **1.** an Asiatic plant grown for its aromatic rootstalk, used as a spice and in medicine **2.** the rootstalk, or the spice made from it **3.** a reddish-brown color **4.** [Colloq.] vigor; spirit —**gin′ger·y *adj.***

ginger ale a carbonated, sweet soft drink flavored with ginger

ginger beer a drink like ginger ale but with a stronger flavor

gin·ger·bread (-bred′) ***n.*** [ME. *ginge bred* < *gingebras*, preserved ginger < OFr.] **1.** a cake flavored with ginger and molasses **2.** showy ornamentation, as fancy carvings on gables, etc. —***adj.*** cheap and showy: also **gin′ger·bread′y**

gin·ger·ly (-lē) ***adv.*** very carefully or cautiously —***adj.*** very careful; cautious —**gin′ger·li·ness *n.***

gin·ger·snap (-snap′) ***n.*** a crisp, spicy cookie flavored with ginger and molasses

ging·ham (giŋ′əm) ***n.*** [< Du. or Fr., ult. < Malay *ginggang*, striped (cloth)] a cotton cloth, usually woven in stripes, checks, or plaids

gin·gi·vi·tis (jin′jə vīt′əs) ***n.*** [ModL. < L. *gingiva*, the gum + -ITIS] inflammation of the gums

gink (giŋk) ***n.*** [? < dial. *gink*, a trick] [Slang] a man or boy, esp. one regarded as odd

gink·go (giŋ′kō) ***n., pl.* gink′goes** [Jap. *ginkyo* < Chin.] an Asiatic tree with fan-shaped leaves and yellow seeds enclosing an edible kernel: also **ging′ko,** *pl.* **ging′koes**

gin rummy a variety of the card game rummy: a hand which totals no more than ten points in unmatched cards and has been exposed wins unless the opponent has fewer points or an equal number

gin·seng (jin′seŋ) ***n.*** [Chin. *jen shen*] **1.** a perennial plant with a thick, forked, aromatic root: some species are found in China and N. America **2.** the root of this plant, used medicinally

Gior·gio·ne (jôr jô′ne), **Il** (ēl) (born *Giorgio Barbarelli*) 1478?–1510; Venetian painter

Giot·to (di Bondone) (jôt′tô; *E.* jät′ō) 1266?–1337; Florentine painter & architect

gip (jip) ***n., vt., vi.*** *same as* GYP

gip·sy (jip′sē) ***n.*** *same as* GYPSY

gi·raffe (jə raf′) ***n., pl.* -raffes′, -raffe′:** see PLURAL, II, D, 1 [Fr. < It. *giraffa* < Ar. *zarāfa*] a large, cud-chewing animal of Africa, with a very long neck and legs: the tallest of existing animals

gird (gurd) ***vt.* gird′ed** or **girt, gird′ing** [OE. *gyrdan*] **1.** to encircle or fasten with a belt or band **2.** to encircle; enclose **3.** to equip or endow **4.** to prepare (oneself) for action

gird·er (gur′dər) ***n.*** [prec. + -ER] a large beam of timber or steel, for supporting the joists of a floor, a framework, etc.

gir·dle (gur′d′l) ***n.*** [OE. *gyrdel*] **1.** a belt or sash for the waist **2.** anything that surrounds or encircles **3.** a woman's elasticized undergarment for supporting the waist and hips **4.** the rim of a cut gem **5.** a ring made by removing the bark around the trunk of a tree —***vt.* -dled, -dling 1.** to surround or bind, as with a girdle **2.** to encircle **3.** to cut a ring of bark from (a tree) —**gir′dler *n.***

girl (gurl) ***n.*** [ME. *girle, gurle*, youngster] **1.** a female child **2.** a young, unmarried woman **3.** a female servant **4.** [Colloq.] a woman of any age **5.** [Colloq.] a sweetheart —**girl′ish *adj.*** —**girl′ish·ly *adv.*** —**girl′ish·ness *n.***

girl·friend (-frend′) ***n.*** [Colloq.] **1.** a sweetheart of a boy or man **2.** a girl who is one's friend

girl·hood (-hood′) ***n.*** **1.** the state or time of being a girl **2.** girls collectively

girl·ie, girl·y (gur′lē) ***n., pl.* girl′ies** [Slang] a girl or woman

girl scout a member of the **Girl Scouts,** a U.S. organization founded in 1912 (as **Girl Guides**) to provide character-building activities for girls

girt[1] (gurt) *alt. pt. & pp. of* GIRD

girt[2] (gurt) ***vt.*** [var. of GIRD] **1.** to gird; girdle **2.** to fasten with a girth

girth (gurth) ***n.*** [< ON. *gjörth*] **1.** a band put around the belly of a horse, etc. to hold a saddle or pack **2.** the circumference, as of a tree trunk or person's waist —***vt.*** **1.** to encircle **2.** to bind with a girth —***vi.*** to measure in girth

gis·mo (giz′mō) ***n., pl.* -mos** [Slang] *same as* GIZMO

gist (jist) ***n.*** [< OFr. *giste*, point at issue < *gesir*, to lie < L. *jacere*] the essence or main point, as of an article or argument

git·tern (git′ərn) ***n.*** [< OFr. *guiterne*, altered < OSp. *guittarra:* see GUITAR] an obsolete, guitarlike musical instrument with wire strings

give (giv) ***vt.* gave, giv′en, giv′ing** [OE. *giefan*, infl. by ON. *gefa*] **1.** to turn over the control of without cost or exchange; make a gift of **2.** to hand or pass over to be cared for [he *gave* the porter his bag] **3.** to sell (goods, services, etc.) for a price or pay (a price) for goods, services, etc. **4.** to relay [*give* my regards] **5.** to cause to have; impart **6.** to confer (a title, position, etc.) **7.** to act as host of (a party, etc.) **8.** to produce; supply [cows *give* milk] **9.** *a*) to sacrifice [he *gave* his life for his country] *b*) to devote fully [he *gives* all his time to his work] **10.** to concede; yield **11.** to show; exhibit **12.** to offer; proffer **13.** to perform [to *give* a concert] **14.** to make (a gesture, movement, etc.) [to *give* a leap] **15.** to utter (words, etc.); state [*give* a reply] **16.** to inflict (punishment, etc.) —***vi.*** **1.** to make gifts **2.** to bend, sink, move, etc. from force or pressure **3.** to be resilient **4.** to provide a view of or access to [the window *gives* on the park] **5.** [Colloq.] to happen: chiefly in **what gives?** —***n.*** **1.** a bending, sinking, moving, etc. under pressure **2.** resiliency —**give and take** to exchange on an even basis —**give away 1.** to make a gift of **2.** to present (the bride) ritually to the bridegroom **3.** [Colloq.] to reveal; expose —**give back** to return —**give forth** (or **off**) to send forth; emit —**give in 1.** to hand in **2.** to yield —**give it to** [Colloq.] to beat or scold —**give out 1.** to emit **2.** to make public **3.** to distribute **4.** to become worn out or used up —**give to understand** (or **believe,** etc.) to cause to understand (or believe, etc.) —**give up 1.** to hand over; relinquish **2.** to stop; cease **3.** to admit failure and stop trying **4.** to lose hope for **5.** to devote wholly —**giv′er *n.***

give-and-take (-′n tāk′) ***n.*** **1.** a mutual yielding and conceding **2.** a fair and equal exchange of remarks or retorts

give·a·way (-ə wā′) ***n.*** [Colloq.] **1.** an unintentional revelation or betrayal **2.** something given free or sold cheap to attract customers, etc. **3.** the disposal of public property for private profit **4.** *Radio & TV* a program in which prizes are given to contestants

giv·en (giv′′n) *pp. of* GIVE —***adj.*** **1.** bestowed; presented **2.** accustomed; inclined [*given* to lying] **3.** stated; specified **4.** assumed; granted **5.** issued; executed [*given* under his seal as mayor]

given name the first name of a person, as distinguished from the surname

Gi·za (gē′zə) city in N Egypt, near Cairo, on the Nile: pop. 250,000

giz·mo (giz′mō) ***n., pl.* -mos** [< ?] [Slang] **1.** any gadget or contrivance **2.** a gimmick

giz·zard (giz′ərd) ***n.*** [< OFr. *gisier* < L. *gigeria*, pl., cooked entrails of poultry] **1.** the second stomach of a bird: it has thick, muscular walls and a tough lining for grinding food **2.** [Colloq.] the stomach: humorous usage

Gk. Greek

gla·brous (glā′brəs) ***adj.*** [< L. *glaber*, bald] without hair, down, or fuzz; bald —**gla′brous·ness *n.***

gla·cé (gla sā′) ***adj.*** [Fr., pp. of *glacer*, to freeze < L. < *glacies*, ice] **1.** having a smooth, glossy surface **2.** candied or glazed, as fruits —***vt.* -céed′, -cé′ing** to glaze (fruits, etc.)

gla·cial (glā′shəl) ***adj.*** [< L. < *glacies*, ice] **1.** of ice or glaciers **2.** of or produced by a glacial epoch **3.** freezing;

frigid 4. cold and unfriendly 5. as slow as the movement of a glacier 6. having an icelike appearance —**gla′cial·ly** *adv.*

glacial epoch any extent of geologic time when large parts of the earth were covered with glaciers; specif., the Pleistocene Epoch, when a large part of the Northern Hemisphere was intermittently covered with glaciers; ice age

gla·ci·ate (glā′shē āt′, -sē-) *vt.* **-at′ed, -at′ing** 1. *a)* to cover over with ice or a glacier *b)* to form into ice; freeze 2. to expose to or change by glacial action —**gla′ci·a′tion** *n.*

gla·cier (glā′shər) *n.* [Fr. < VL. < L. *glacies,* ice] a large mass of ice and snow that forms in areas where the rate of snowfall exceeds the melting rate: it moves slowly down a mountain, along a valley, etc. until it melts or breaks away

gla·cis (glā′sis, glas′is) *n., pl.* **-cis** (-sēz), **-cis·es** (-sis əz) [Fr. < OFr. *glacier,* to slip < *glace,* ice] 1. a gradual slope 2. an embankment sloping down from a fortification

glad[1] (glad) *adj.* **glad′der, glad′dest** [OE. *glæd*] 1. happy; pleased 2. causing pleasure or joy; making happy 3. very willing *[*I'm *glad* to help*]* 4. bright or beautiful —*vt., vi.* **glad′ded, glad′ding** [Archaic] to gladden —**glad′ly** *adv.* —**glad′ness** *n.*

glad[2] (glad) *n.* [Colloq.] *same as* GLADIOLUS

glad·den (-'n) *vt., vi.* to make or become glad

glade (glād) *n.* [ME., prob. < *glad,* GLAD[1]] 1. an open space in a wood or forest 2. an everglade

glad hand [Slang] a cordial, eager, or effusive welcome —**glad′-hand′** *vt., vi.* —**glad′-hand′er** *n.*

glad·i·a·tor (glad′ē āt′ər) *n.* [L. < *gladius,* sword] 1. in ancient Rome, a man who fought other men or animals in an arena as a public show: gladiators were slaves, captives, or paid performers 2. any person involved in a public controversy or fight —**glad′i·a·to′ri·al** (-ə tôr′ē əl) *adj.*

glad·i·o·lus (glad′ē ō′ləs; *occas.* glə dī′ə ləs) *n., pl.* **-lus·es, -li** (-lī) [ModL. < L. dim. of *gladius,* sword] a plant with swordlike leaves and tall spikes of funnel-shaped flowers in various colors: also **glad′i·o′la** (-lə)

glad·some (glad′səm) *adj.* joyful or cheerful —**glad′some·ly** *adv.* —**glad′some·ness** *n.*

Glad·stone (glad′stōn; *Brit.* -stən), **William Ew·art** (yo͞o′ərt) 1809–98; English prime minister

Glad·stone (bag) (glad′stōn; *Brit.* -stən) [after prec.] a traveling bag hinged so that it can open flat into two compartments of equal size

Glad·ys (glad′is) [W. *Gwladys,* prob. < L. *Claudis:* see CLAUDIA] a feminine name

glair (gler) *n.* [< OFr. < L. *clarus,* clear] 1. raw white of egg, used in sizing or glazing 2. a size or glaze made from this 3. any sticky matter resembling raw egg white —*vt.* to cover with glair —**glair′y** *adj.*

glaive (glāv) *n.* [< OFr. < L. *gladius,* sword] [Archaic] a sword; esp., a broadsword

glam·or·ize (glam′ə rīz′) *vt.* **-ized′, -iz′ing** to make glamorous —**glam′or·i·za′tion** *n.*

glam·or·ous, glam·our·ous (-ər əs) *adj.* full of glamour; fascinating; alluring —**glam′or·ous·ly** *adv.*

glam·our, glam·or (glam′ər) *n.* [Scot. var. of *grammar* in sense of *gramarye,* magic] 1. orig., a magic spell or charm 2. seemingly mysterious and elusive fascination or allure, as of some person, scene, etc.; bewitching charm

glance (glans) *vi.* **glanced, glanc′ing** [prob. a blend < OFr. *glacier,* to slip + *guenchir,* to elude] 1. to strike obliquely and go off at an angle 2. to make an indirect or passing reference 3. to flash or gleam 4. to take a quick look —*vt.* to cause to strike (a surface) at an angle and be deflected —*n.* 1. a glancing off; deflected impact 2. a flash or gleam 3. a quick look

gland (gland) *n.* [< Fr. < OFr. < L. *glandula,* tonsil, dim. of *glans* (gen. *glandis*), acorn] 1. any organ that separates certain elements from the blood and secretes them in a form for the body to use (as an adrenal, a ductless gland, secretes epinephrine) or throw off (as a kidney, a gland with ducts, secretes urine) 2. loosely, any structure like a gland in appearance, etc. *[*lymph *glands]*

glan·ders (glan′dərz) *n.pl.* [*with sing. v.*] [OFr. *glandres,* lit., glands] a contagious disease of horses, mules, etc. characterized by fever, swelling of glands beneath the jaw, nasal inflammation, etc.

glan·du·lar (glan′jə lər) *adj.* 1. of, like, or having a gland or glands 2. derived from or affected by glands —**glan′du·lar·ly** *adv.*

glandular fever *same as* INFECTIOUS MONONUCLEOSIS

glan·dule (glan′jo͞ol) *n.* [Fr.] a small gland

glans (glanz) *n., pl.* **glan·des** (glan′dēz) [L., lit., acorn] 1. the head, or end, of the penis: in full, **glans penis** 2. the corresponding part of the clitoris

glare[1] (gler) *vi.* **glared, glar′ing** [ME. *glaren* < or akin to MDu. *glaren,* to gleam & OE. *glær,* amber] 1. to shine with a steady, dazzling light 2. to be too bright or showy 3. to stare fiercely or angrily —*vt.* to express with a glare —*n.* 1. a steady, dazzling light 2. a too bright or dazzling display 3. a fierce or angry stare

glare[2] (gler) *n.* [prob. < prec.] a smooth, bright, glassy surface, as of ice —*adj.* smooth, bright, and glassy

glar·ing (-iŋ) *adj.* 1. dazzlingly bright 2. too bright and showy 3. staring fiercely 4. flagrant *[*a *glaring* mistake*]* —**glar′ing·ly** *adv.*

glar·y (-ē) *adj.* **glar′i·er, glar′i·est** shining with a too bright light —**glar′i·ness** *n.*

Glas·gow (glas′kō, glaz′gō) seaport in SC Scotland: pop. 961,000 —**Glas·we·gi·an** (glas wē′jən, -jē ən) *adj., n.*

glass (glas) *n.* [OE. *glæs*] 1. a hard, brittle substance, usually transparent, made by fusing silicates with soda or potash, lime, and, sometimes, metallic oxides 2. *same as* GLASSWARE 3. *a)* an article made of glass, as a drinking container, mirror, telescope, barometer, etc. *b)* [*pl.*] eyeglasses *c)* [*pl.*] binoculars 4. the quantity contained in a drinking glass —*vt.* 1. to put in glass jars for preserving 2. to mirror; reflect 3. to equip with glass; glaze 4. to make glassy —*vi.* to become glassy —*adj.* of, made of, or like glass —**glass in** to enclose with glass panes

glass blowing the art or process of shaping molten glass by blowing air into a mass of it at the end of a tube —**glass blower**

glass·ful (-fo͝ol′) *n., pl.* **glass′fuls′** the amount that will fill a glass

glass·house (-hous′) *n. Brit. var. of* GREENHOUSE

glass·ine (gla sēn′) *n.* [GLASS + -INE[1]] a thin, tough paper used for the windows on envelopes, etc.

glass snake a legless lizard found in the S U.S.: so called because its tail breaks off easily

glass·ware (glas′wer′) *n.* articles made of glass

glass wool fine fibers of glass intertwined in a woolly mass, used in filters and as insulation

glass·wort (-wurt′) *n.* a fleshy plant of the goosefoot family, found in saline coastal or desert areas

glass·y (-ē) *adj.* **glass′i·er, glass′i·est** 1. like glass, as in smoothness or transparency 2. expressionless or lifeless *[*a *glassy* stare*]* —**glass′i·ly** *adv.* —**glass′i·ness** *n.*

glau·co·ma (glô kō′mə, glou-) *n.* [L. < Gr. < *glaukos:* see ff. & -OMA] a disease of the eye marked by increased pressure in the eyeball: it leads to a gradual loss of sight —**glau·co′ma·tous** *adj.*

glau·cous (glô′kəs) *adj.* [< L. < Gr. *glaukos,* orig., gleaming] 1. bluish-green or yellowish-green 2. *Bot.* covered with a whitish bloom that can be rubbed off, as grapes, plums, etc.

glaze (glāz) *vt.* **glazed, glaz′ing** [ME. *glasen* < *glas,* GLASS] 1. to fit (windows, etc.) with glass 2. to give a hard, glossy finish or coating to; specif., *a)* to overlay (pottery, etc.) with a substance that gives a glassy finish when fused *b)* to cover (foods) with a coating of sugar syrup, etc. 3. to cover with a thin layer of ice —*vi.* 1. to become glassy or glossy 2. to form a glaze —*n.* 1. *a)* a glassy finish, as on pottery *b)* any substance used to form this 2. a film or coating —**glaz′er** *n.*

gla·zier (glā′zhər) *n.* a person whose work is fitting glass in windows, etc. —**gla′zier·y** *n.*

glaz·ing (-ziŋ) *n.* 1. the work of a glazier 2. a glass set or to be set in frames 3. a glaze or the application of a glaze

gleam (glēm) *n.* [OE. *glæm*] 1. a flash or beam of light 2. a faint light 3. a reflected brightness, as from a polished surface 4. a brief, faint manifestation, as of hope, etc. —*vi.* 1. to shine with a gleam 2. to be manifested briefly; appear suddenly —**gleam′y** *adj.*

glean (glēn) *vt., vi.* [< OFr. < VL. *glennare* < Celt.] 1. to collect (grain left by reapers) from (a field) 2. to collect (facts, etc.) bit by bit from (a source) —**glean′er** *n.*

glean·ings (-iŋz) *n.pl.* that which is gleaned

glebe (glēb) *n.* [< L. *gleba,* clod] 1. church land forming part or all of a benefice 2. [Poet.] soil; earth; land; field

glee (glē) *n.* [OE. *gleo*] 1. lively joy; merriment 2. a part song for three or more voices, usually unaccompanied

glee club a group formed to sing part songs

glee·ful (-fəl) *adj.* full of glee; merry: also **glee′some** —**glee′ful·ly** *adv.* —**glee′ful·ness** *n.*

glen (glen) *n.* [< ScotGael. hyp. *glenn* (now *gleann*)] a narrow, secluded valley

Glen·dale (glen′dāl) [GLEN + DALE] city in SW Calif.: suburb of Los Angeles: pop. 139,000

Glen·gar·ry (glen gar′ē) *n., pl.* **-ries** [< *Glengarry,* valley in Scotland] [*sometimes* **g-**] a Scottish cap for men, creased lengthwise across the top and often having short ribbons at the back: also **Glengarry bonnet** (or **cap**)

Glenn, Glen (glen) [Celt.: see GLEN] a masculine name

glib (glib) *adj.* **glib′ber, glib′best** [orig., slippery < or akin to Du. *glibberig,* slippery] 1. done in a smooth, offhand way 2. speaking or spoken in a smooth, fluent manner, often in a way too smooth and easy to be convincing —**glib′ly** *adv.* —**glib′ness** *n.*

glide (glīd) *vi.* **glid′ed, glid′ing** [OE. *glidan*] 1. to flow or move smoothly and easily 2. to pass gradually and almost unnoticed, as time 3. *Aeron. a)* to fly in a glider *b)* to descend at a normal angle without engine power 4. *Music,*

Phonet. to make a glide —*vt.* to cause to glide —*n.* **1.** the act of gliding **2.** a small disk or ball attached under furniture legs, etc. to allow easy sliding **3.** *Music* loosely, a slur **4.** *Phonet.* an intermediate sound made when the speech organs change from the position for one sound to another

glid·er (glīd′ər) *n.* **1.** a person or thing that glides **2.** an aircraft like an airplane except that it has no engine and is carried along by air currents **3.** a porch seat suspended in an upright frame so that it can glide back and forth

glim·mer (glim′ər) *vi.* [< base of OE. *glæm,* gleam] **1.** to give a faint, flickering light **2.** to appear or be seen faintly —*n.* **1.** a faint, flickering light **2.** a faint manifestation

glim·mer·ing (-iŋ) *n. same as* GLIMMER

glimpse (glimps) *vt.* **glimpsed, glimps′ing** [see GLIMMER] to catch a brief, quick view of, as in passing —*vi.* to look quickly; glance (*at*) —*n.* **1.** a flash **2.** a faint, fleeting appearance; slight trace **3.** a brief, quick view

glint (glint) *vi.* [prob. < Scand.] to gleam; flash —*n.* a gleam, flash, or glitter

glis·sade (gli säd′, -sād′) *n.* [Fr. < *glisser,* to slide] **1.** an intentional slide by a mountain climber down a steep, snow-covered slope **2.** *Ballet* a gliding step —*vi.* **-sad′ed, -sad′ing** to make a glissade

glis·san·do (gli sän′dō) *n., pl.* **-di** (-dē), **-dos** [as if It. prp., equiv. to Fr. *glissant,* prp. of *glisser,* to slide] *Music* a sliding effect achieved by sounding a series of adjacent tones in rapid succession —*adj., adv.* (performed) with such an effect

glis·ten (glis′'n) *vi.* [OE. *glisnian*] to shine or sparkle with reflected light, as a wet or polished surface —*n.* a glistening

glis·ter (glis′tər) *vi., n. archaic var. of* GLISTEN

glit·ter (glit′ər) *vi.* [prob. < ON. *glitra*] **1.** to shine with a sparkling light **2.** to be brilliant, showy, or attractive —*n.* **1.** a bright, sparkling light **2.** showy brilliance or attractiveness **3.** bits of glittering material —**glit′ter·y** *adj.*

glitz·y (glit′sē) *adj.* **glitz′i·er, glitz′i·est** [prob. via Yid. < G. *glitzern,* to glitter] [Slang] **1.** having glitter; sparkling; glittery **2.** attracting attention in an ornate or gaudy way; showy; pretentious

gloam·ing (glō′miŋ) *n.* [OE. *glomung* < *glom,* twilight] evening dusk; twilight

gloat (glōt) *vi.* [prob. < ON. *glotta,* to grin scornfully] to gaze or think with malicious pleasure —*n.* the act of gloating —**gloat′er** *n.*

glob (gläb) *n.* [prob. contr. < GLOBULE, after BLOB] a rounded mass or lump, as of a semisolid

glob·al (glō′b'l) *adj.* **1.** globe-shaped **2.** worldwide *[global war]* **3.** complete —**glob′al·ly** *adv.*

glob·al·ism (-iz'm) *n.* a policy, outlook, etc. that is worldwide in scope —**glob′al·ist** *n., adj.*

globe (glōb) *n.* [< L. *globus,* a ball] **1.** any round, ball-shaped thing; sphere; specif., *a)* the earth *b)* a spherical model of the earth **2.** anything shaped like a globe, as a rounded glass cover for a lamp —*vt., vi.* **globed, glob′ing** to form or gather into a globe —**glo·bate** (glō′bāt) *adj.*

globe·fish (-fish′) *n., pl.* **-fish′, -fish′es:** see FISH any of several tropical fishes that can puff themselves into a globular form

globe-trot·ter (-trät′ər) *n.* a person who travels widely about the world, esp. for pleasure or sightseeing

glo·boid (glō′boid) *adj.* shaped somewhat like a globe or ball —*n.* anything globoid

glo·bose (-bōs) *adj.* [L. *globosus*] *same as* GLOBOID: also **glo′bous** (-bəs) —**glo′bose·ly** *adv.*

glob·u·lar (gläb′yə lər) *adj.* **1.** shaped like a globe or ball; spherical **2.** made up of globules

glob·ule (-yo͞ol) *n.* [Fr. < L. dim. of *globus,* a ball] a tiny ball or globe; esp., a drop of liquid

glob·u·lin (-yə lin) *n.* [GLOBUL(E) + -IN[1]] any of a group of proteins in animal and vegetable tissue

glock·en·spiel (gläk′ən spēl′, -shpēl′) *n.* [G. < *glocke,* a bell + *spiel,* play] a percussion instrument with flat metal bars set in a frame, that produce bell-like tones of the scale when struck with small hammers

GLOCKENSPIEL

glom (gläm) *vt.* **glommed, glom′ming** [< Scot. dial.] [Slang] **1.** to seize **2.** to steal **3.** to look over —**glom onto** [Slang] to take and hold; get

glom·er·ate (gläm′ər it) *adj.* [< L. pp. of *glomerare* < *glomus,* a ball] formed into a rounded mass; clustered —**glom′er·a′tion** *n.*

gloom (glo͞om) *vi.* [prob. < Scand.] **1.** to be or look morose or dejected **2.** to be or become dark, dim, or dismal —*vt.* to make dark, dismal, dejected, etc. —*n.* **1.** darkness; dimness; obscurity **2.** deep sadness; dejection

gloom·y (-ē) *adj.* **gloom′i·er, gloom′i·est** **1.** overspread with or enveloped in darkness or dimness **2.** melancholy or sullen **3.** causing gloom; depressing —**gloom′i·ly** *adv.* —**gloom′i·ness** *n.*

glop (gläp) *n.* [< ? GL(UE) + (SL)OP] [Slang] any soft, gluey substance, thick liquid, etc.

Glo·ri·a (glôr′ē ə) [L., glory] a feminine name —*n.* **1.** either of the Latin hymns beginning *Gloria in Excelsis Deo* (glory be to God on high) or *Gloria Patri* (glory be to the Father) **2.** the music for either

glo·ri·fy (glôr′ə fī′) *vt.* **-fied′, -fy′ing** [< OFr. < LL. < L. *gloria,* glory + *facere,* to make] **1.** to make glorious; give glory to **2.** to exalt in worship **3.** to honor; extol **4.** to make seem better, larger, finer, etc. —**glo′ri·fi·ca′tion** *n.* —**glo′ri·fi′er** *n.*

glo·ri·ous (glôr′ē əs) *adj.* **1.** full of glory; illustrious **2.** giving glory **3.** receiving or deserving glory **4.** splendid; magnificent **5.** [Colloq.] very delightful or enjoyable —**glo′ri·ous·ly** *adv.* —**glo′ri·ous·ness** *n.*

glo·ry (glôr′ē) *n., pl.* **-ries** [< OFr. < L. *gloria*] **1.** *a)* great honor and admiration *b)* anything bringing this **2.** worshipful adoration **3.** the condition of highest achievement, prosperity, etc. **4.** splendor; magnificence **5.** heaven or the bliss of heaven **6.** *same as* HALO (*n.* 1 & 2) —*vi.* **-ried, -ry·ing** to be very proud; exult (with *in*) —**gone to glory** dead —**in one's glory** at one's best, happiest, etc.

gloss[1] (glôs, gläs) *n.* [prob. < Scand.] **1.** the luster of a smooth, polished surface; sheen **2.** a deceptively pleasant outward appearance, as in manners or speech —*vt.* **1.** to make lustrous **2.** to cover up (an error, fault, etc.) by minimizing (often with *over*) —*vi.* to become shiny

gloss[2] (glôs, gläs) *n.* [< OFr. or < ML. < L. < Gr. *glōssa,* the tongue] **1.** a translation inserted between the lines of a text **2.** a note of comment or explanation, as in a footnote **3.** a glossary —*vt.* **1.** to furnish (a text) with glosses **2.** to interpret falsely —*vi.* to annotate —**gloss′er** *n.*

glos·sa·ry (gläs′ə rē, glôs′-) *n., pl.* **-ries** [< L. < *glossa* < Gr. *glōssa,* the tongue] a list of difficult, technical, or foreign terms with definitions or translations, as for a particular author, subject, book, etc. —**glos·sar·i·al** (glä ser′ē əl) *adj.* —**glos′sar·ist** *n.*

glos·so·la·li·a (gläs′ə lā′lē ə, glôs′-) *n.* [ModL., ult. < Gr. *glōssa,* tongue + *lalein,* to speak] an ecstatic utterance of unintelligible speechlike sounds, regarded as caused by religious ecstasy

gloss·y (glôs′ē, gläs′-) *adj.* **gloss′i·er, gloss′i·est** **1.** having a smooth, shiny appearance or finish **2.** specious —*n., pl.* **gloss′ies** **1.** a photographic print with a glossy surface **2.** [Colloq.] a magazine printed on glossy paper —**gloss′i·ly** *adv.* —**gloss′i·ness** *n.*

glot·tal (glät′'l) *adj.* of or produced in or at the glottis

glot·tis (glät′is) *n., pl.* **-tis·es, -ti·des′** (-ə dēz′) [ModL. < Gr. < *glōtta,* var. of *glōssa,* the tongue] the opening between the vocal cords in the larynx

glove (gluv) *n.* [< OE. *glof* & ON. *glofi*] **1.** a covering for the hand, with a separate sheath for each finger and the thumb **2.** *Sports a)* a baseball player's mitt *b)* a padded mitten worn by boxers: usually **boxing glove** —*vt.* **gloved, glov′ing** **1.** to supply with gloves **2.** to cover as with a glove **3.** *Baseball* to catch (a ball) with a glove

glov·er (-ər) *n.* one who makes or sells gloves

glow (glō) *vi.* [OE. *glowan*] **1.** to give off a bright light as a result of great heat; be incandescent or red-hot **2.** to give out a steady, even light without flame **3.** to be or feel hot **4.** to radiate health **5.** to be elated or enlivened by emotion **6.** to be bright with color —*n.* **1.** a light given off as the result of great heat **2.** steady, even light without flame or blaze **3.** brilliance of color **4.** brightness of skin color; flush **5.** a sensation of warmth and well-being **6.** warmth of emotion —**glow′ing** *adj.* —**glow′ing·ly** *adv.*

glow·er (glou′ər) *vi.* [prob. < ON.] to stare with sullen anger; scowl —*n.* a sullen, angry stare; scowl —**glow′er·ing** *adj.* —**glow′er·ing·ly** *adv.*

glow·worm (glō′wurm′) *n.* a wingless insect or insect larva that gives off a luminescent light; esp., the wingless female or the larva of the firefly

glox·in·i·a (gläk sin′ē ə) *n.* [ModL., after B. P. *Gloxin,* 18th-c. Ger. botanist] a cultivated tropical plant with bell-shaped flowers of various colors

gloze (glōz) *vt.* **glozed, gloz′ing** [< OFr. < *glose:* see GLOSS[2]] to explain away; gloss (often with *over*)

glu·cose (glo͞o′kōs) *n.* [Fr. < Gr. *gleûkos,* sweet wine, sweetness] a crystalline sugar, $C_6H_{12}O_6$, occurring naturally in fruits, honey, etc.: the commercial form is prepared

as a sweet syrup by hydrolyzing starch in the presence of dilute acids
glu·co·side (glo͞o′kə sīd′) ***n.*** **[**GLUCOS(E) + -IDE**]** any glycoside having glucose as its sugar constituent —**glu′co·sid′ic** (-sid′ik) ***adj.***
glue (glo͞o) ***n.*** **[**< OFr. *glu*, birdlime < LL. *glus*, glue**]** **1.** a sticky, viscous substance made from animal skins, bones, hoofs, etc. by boiling, etc. and used to stick things together **2.** any similar adhesive made from casein, resin, etc. —***vt.*** **glued, glu′ing** to make stick as with glue —**glu′er** ***n.***
glue·y (-ē) ***adj.*** **glu′i·er, glu′i·est** **1.** like glue; sticky **2.** covered with or full of glue
glum (glum) ***adj.*** **glum′mer, glum′mest** **[**prob. < ME. var. of *gloum(b)en*, to look morose**]** gloomy; sullen; morose —**glum′ly** ***adv.*** —**glum′ness** ***n.***
glume (glo͞om) ***n.*** **[**ModL. *gluma* < L., husk**]** either of the two empty bracts at the base of a grass spikelet, etc.
glut (glut) ***vi.*** **glut′ted, glut′ting** **[**< OFr. *gloter*, to swallow < L. *gluttire***]** to eat like a glutton —***vt.*** **1.** to feed, fill, etc. to excess; surfeit **2.** to flood (the market) with certain goods so that the supply is greater than the demand —***n.*** **1.** a glutting or being glutted **2.** a supply of certain goods that is greater than the demand
glu·ten (glo͞ot′'n) ***n.*** **[**L., glue**]** a gray, sticky substance found in wheat and other grain, the protein part of flour and bread —**glu′ten·ous** ***adj.***
glu·te·us (glo͞o tē′əs, glo͞ot′ē-) ***n.,*** *pl.* **-te′i** (-ī) **[**ModL. < Gr. *gloutos*, rump**]** any of the three muscles forming each of the buttocks —**glu·te′al** ***adj.***
glu·ti·nous (glo͞ot′'n əs) ***adj.*** **[**< L. < *gluten*, glue**]** gluey; sticky —**glu′ti·nous·ly** ***adv.***
glut·ton (glut′'n) ***n.*** **[**< OFr. < L. *gluto* < *glutire*, to devour**]** **1.** a person who greedily eats too much **2.** a person with a great capacity for something **3.** a furry, northern animal related to the marten: the American variety is the WOLVERINE —**glut′ton·ize** ***vt., vi.*** **-ized′, -iz′ing**
glut·ton·ous (-əs) ***adj.*** inclined to eat too much and greedily —**glut′ton·ous·ly** ***adv.***
glut·ton·y (-ē) ***n.,*** *pl.* **-ton·ies** the habit or act of eating too much
glyc·er·ide (glis′ər īd′) ***n.*** an ester of glycerol
glyc·er·in (glis′ər in, glis′rin) ***n.*** **[**< Fr. < Gr. *glykeros*, sweet**]** *popular and commercial term for* GLYCEROL: also sp. **glyc′er·ine**
glyc·er·ol (glis′ər ōl′, -ôl′) ***n.*** **[**< prec. + -OL[1]**]** an odorless, colorless, syrupy liquid, $C_3H_8O_3$, prepared by the hydrolysis of fats and oils: used as a solvent, skin lotion, etc., and in explosives, etc.
gly·co- **[**< Gr. < *glykys*, sweet**]** *a combining form meaning* glycerol, sugar, glycogen: also, before a vowel, **glyc-**
gly·co·gen (glī′kə jən) ***n.*** **[**prec. + -GEN**]** a partially soluble, starchlike substance, $(C_6H_{10}O_5)_x$, produced in animal tissues, esp. in the liver and muscles, and changed into a simple sugar as the body needs it —**gly′co·gen′ic** (-jen′ik) ***adj.***
gly·col (glī′kôl, -kōl) ***n.*** **[**GLYC(ERIN) + -OL[1]**]** **1.** *same as* ETHYLENE GLYCOL **2.** any of a group of alcohols of which ethylene glycol is the type
gly·co·side (glī′kə sīd′) ***n.*** **[**Fr. < *glycose* (for GLUCOSE) + *-ide*, -IDE**]** any of a group of sugar derivatives, widely distributed in plants, which on hydrolysis yield a sugar and one or more other substances —**gly′co·sid′ic** (-sid′ik) ***adj.***
gm. gram(s)
G-man (jē′man′) ***n.,*** *pl.* **G′-men′** (-men′) **[**associated with *g(overnment) man*, but prob. < *G* division of the Dublin Police**]** [Colloq.] an agent of the Federal Bureau of Investigation
Gmc. Germanic
gnarl (närl) ***n.*** **[**back-formation < ff.**]** a knot on the trunk or branch of a tree —***vt., vi.*** to make or become knotted or twisted
gnarled (närld) ***adj.*** **[**ult.< ME. *knur*, a knot**]** knotty and twisted *[*a *gnarled* tree, *gnarled* hands*]*: also **gnarl′y**
gnash (nash) ***vt., vi.*** **[**ME. *gnasten*, prob. < ON.**]** to grind or strike (the teeth) together, as in anger or pain —***n.*** the act of gnashing
gnat (nat) ***n.*** **[**OE. *gnæt***]** **1.** any of a number of small, two-winged insects some of which can bite or sting **2.** [Brit.] a mosquito —**gnat′ty** ***adj.***
gnaw (nô) ***vt.*** **gnawed, gnawed** or, rarely, **gnawn, gnaw′ing** **[**OE. *gnagen***]** **1.** to bite and wear away bit by bit **2.** to make by gnawing **3.** to consume; corrode **4.** to torment, as by constant pain, fear, etc. —***vi.*** **1.** to bite repeatedly (*on, at,* etc.) **2.** to have a gnawing effect
gnaw·ing (-iŋ) ***n.*** **1.** a sensation of dull, constant pain or suffering **2.** [*pl.*] pangs, as of hunger
gneiss (nīs) ***n.*** **[**< G. < OHG. *gneisto*, a spark**]** a coarse-grained, granitelike rock formed of layers of feldspar, quartz, mica, etc. —**gneiss′ic** ***adj.***
gnome (nōm) ***n.*** **[**Fr., ult. < Gr. *gnōmē*, thought**]** *Folklore* a dwarf supposed to dwell in the earth and guard its treasures —**gnom′ish** ***adj.***
gno·mic (nō′mik) ***adj.*** **[**< Gr. *gnōmikos* < *gnōmē*, thought**]** wise and pithy; full of aphorisms
gno·mon (nō′män) ***n.*** **[**L. < Gr. < base of *gignōskein*, to know**]** a column, pin on a sundial, etc. that casts a shadow indicating the time of day
-gnomy **[**Gr. *-gnōmia* < *gnōmē*, thought**]** *a combining form meaning* art of judging or determining *[physiognomy]*
-gnosis **[**see ff.**]** *a combining form meaning* knowledge, recognition *[diagnosis]*
gnos·tic (näs′tik) ***adj.*** **[**< Gr. *gnōstikos* < *gnōsis*, knowledge**]** **1.** of or having knowledge **2.** [G-] of the Gnostics or Gnosticism —***n.*** [G-] a believer in Gnosticism
Gnos·ti·cism (näs′tə siz'm) ***n.*** a system of belief combining ideas derived from Greek philosophy, Oriental mysticism, and, ultimately, Christianity
GNP gross national product
gnu (no͞o, nyo͞o) ***n.,*** *pl.* **gnus, gnu:** see PLURAL, II, D, 1 **[**< the native (Bushman) name**]** a large African antelope with an oxlike head and horns and a horselike mane and tail; wildebeest

GNU (40–50 in. high at shoulder)

go (gō) ***vi.*** **went, gone, go′ing** **[**OE. *gan***]** **1.** to move along; travel; proceed **2.** to be in operation; work *[*the clock won't *go]* **3.** to gesture, act, or make sounds as specified or shown **4.** to take a particular course, line of action, etc.; proceed **5.** to result; turn out *[*the war *went* badly*]* **6.** to pass: said of time **7.** to pass from person to person, as a rumor **8.** to be in a certain state *[*he *goes* in rags*]* **9.** to become; turn *[*to *go* mad*]* **10.** to be expressed, sung, etc. *[*as the saying *goes]* **11.** to be in harmony; fit in **12.** to put oneself *[*to *go* to some trouble*]* **13.** to tend; help *[*facts that *go* to prove a case*]* **14.** to have force, acceptance, etc. **15.** to leave; depart **16.** to pass away *[*the pain is *gone]* **17.** to die **18.** to be removed or eliminated **19.** to break away *[*the mast *went* in the storm*]* **20.** to fail; give way *[*his eyesight is *going]* **21.** to be given *[*the prize *goes* to you*]* **22.** to be sold *[*it *went* for $10*]* **23.** to extend to or along a specified place or time; reach **24.** to turn to, enter, or participate in a certain activity, occupation, etc. *[*to *go* to college*]* **25.** to pass (*through*), fit (*into*), etc. **26.** to be a divisor (*into*) **27.** to endure; last **28.** to continue (unpunished, unrewarded, etc.) **29.** to have a regular place *[*pencils *go* on the desk*]* —***vt.*** **1.** to travel or proceed along *[*he's *going* my way*]* **2.** to bet **3.** [Colloq.] to tolerate *[*I can't *go* him*]* **4.** [Colloq.] to furnish (bail) **5.** [Colloq.] to be willing to pay, bid, etc. (a specified sum) —***n.,*** *pl.* **goes** **1.** the act of going **2.** a success **3.** [Colloq.] animation; energy **4.** [Colloq.] a state of affairs **5.** [Colloq.] an agreement, or bargain *[*is it a *go?]* **6.** [Colloq.] a try; attempt —***adj.*** [Slang: orig. astronaut's jargon] functioning properly or ready to go —**as people** (or **things**) **go** in comparison with how other people (or things) are —**go about** **1.** to be busy at; do **2.** to circulate **3.** *Naut.* to tack; change direction —**go after** [Colloq.] to try to catch or get —**go against** to be or act in opposition to —**go along** **1.** to continue **2.** to agree **3.** to accompany —**go around** **1.** to surround **2.** to be enough to provide a share for each **3.** to circulate —**go at** to attack or work at —**go back on** [Colloq.] **1.** to betray **2.** to break (a promise, etc.) —**go beyond** to exceed —**go by** **1.** to pass **2.** to be guided by **3.** to be known or referred to by (the name of) —**go down** **1.** to sink; set **2.** to suffer defeat **3.** to be perpetuated, as in history —**go for** **1.** to be taken as **2.** to try to get **3.** to support **4.** [Colloq.] to attack **5.** [Colloq.] to be attracted by —**go hard with** to cause trouble to —**go in for** [Colloq.] to engage or indulge in —**go into** **1.** to inquire into **2.** to take up as a study or occupation —**go in with** to share obligations with; join —**go it** [Colloq.] to carry on; proceed *[*to *go it* alone*]* —**go off** **1.** to leave, esp. suddenly **2.** to explode **3.** to happen —**go on** **1.** to continue **2.** to behave **3.** to happen —**go out** **1.** to be extinguished, become outdated, etc. **2.** to attend social affairs, the theater, etc. **3.** to go on strike **4.** to try out (*for*) —**go over** **1.** to examine thoroughly **2.** to do again **3.** to review **4.** [Colloq.] to be successful —**go some** [Colloq.] to do or achieve quite a lot —**go through** **1.** to perform thoroughly **2.** to endure; experience **3.** to search **4.** to get acceptance **5.** to spend —**go through with** to complete —**go together** **1.** to harmonize **2.** [Colloq.] to be sweethearts —**go under** to fail, as in business —**go up** to rise in price, etc.; increase —**go with** [Colloq.] to be a sweetheart of —**go without** to do without —**let go** **1.** to let escape **2.** to release one's hold **3.** to give up; abandon **4.** to dismiss from a job —**let oneself go** to be unrestrained in emotion, action, etc. —**no go** [Colloq.] not possible; no use —**on the go** [Colloq.] in constant motion or action —**to go** [Colloq.] **1.** to be taken out: said of food in a restaurant **2.** left to complete, etc. —**what goes?** [Slang] what's happening?

goad (gōd) ***n.*** [OE. *gad*] **1.** a sharp-pointed stick for driving oxen **2.** any driving impulse; spur —***vt.*** to drive as with a goad; prod into action

go-a·head (gō′ə hed′) ***n.*** permission or a signal to proceed: usually with *the*

goal (gōl) ***n.*** [ME. *gol,* boundary] **1.** the place where a race, trip, etc. is ended **2.** an end that one strives to attain; aim **3.** in certain games, *a)* the line, net, etc. over or into which the ball or puck must go to score *b)* the act of so scoring *c)* the score made

goal·keep·er (-kēp′ər) ***n.*** in certain games, a player stationed at a goal to prevent the ball or puck from crossing or entering it: also **goal′ie** (-ē), **goal′tend′er**

goat (gōt) ***n.*** [OE. *gat*] **1.** *pl.* **goats, goat:** see PLURAL, II, D, 1 *a)* a cud-chewing mammal with hollow horns, related to the sheep *b)* *same as* ROCKY MOUNTAIN GOAT **2.** a lecherous man **3.** [Colloq.] a scapegoat —[**G-**] the constellation Capricorn —**get one's goat** [Colloq.] to annoy or anger one —**goat′ish** ***adj.*** —**goat′ish·ly** ***adv.***

goat·ee (gō tē′) ***n.*** a pointed beard on a man's chin

goat·herd (gōt′hurd′) ***n.*** one who herds goats

goat·skin (-skin′) ***n.*** **1.** the skin of a goat **2.** leather made from this **3.** a container for wine, water, etc., made of this leather

goat·suck·er (-suk′ər) ***n.*** a large-mouthed, nocturnal bird that feeds on insects, as the whippoorwill

gob[1] (gäb) ***n.*** [< OFr. *gobe,* prob. < *gobet:* see GOBBET] **1.** a lump or mass, as of something soft **2.** [*pl.*] [Colloq.] a large quantity or amount

gob[2] (gäb) ***n.*** [< ?] [Slang] a sailor in the U.S. Navy

gob·bet (gäb′it) ***n.*** [OFr. *gobet,* mouthful, prob. < Gaul.] [Archaic] **1.** a fragment or bit, esp. of raw flesh **2.** a lump; chunk **3.** a mouthful

gob·ble[1] (gäb′'l) ***n.*** [echoic, var. of GABBLE] the characteristic throaty sound made by a male turkey —***vi.*** **-bled, -bling** to make this sound

gob·ble[2] (gäb′'l) ***vt., vi.*** **-bled, -bling** [prob. < OFr. *gober,* to swallow < *gobe,* mouthful, GOB[1]] **1.** to eat quickly and greedily **2.** to snatch (*up*)

gob·ble·dy·gook (gäb′'l dē gook′) ***n.*** [Slang] pompous and wordy talk or writing: also **gob′ble·de·gook′**

gob·bler (gäb′lər) ***n.*** a male turkey

Gob·e·lin (gäb′ə lin, gō′bə-; *Fr.* gô blan′) ***adj.*** of or like a kind of tapestry made at the Gobelin works in Paris —***n.*** Gobelin tapestry

go-be·tween (gō′bi twēn′) ***n.*** one who deals with each of two sides in making arrangements between them; intermediary

Go·bi (gō′bē) large desert plateau in E Asia, chiefly in Mongolia

gob·let (gäb′lit) ***n.*** [< OFr. < *gobel* < ? Bret. *gob*] **1.** orig., a cup without handles **2.** a drinking glass with a base and stem

gob·lin (gäb′lin) ***n.*** [< OFr. < ML. *gobelinus,* ult. < ? Gr. *kobalos,* sprite] *Folklore* an evil or mischievous sprite, ugly or misshapen in form

go·by (gō′bē) ***n.,*** *pl.* **-bies, -by:** see PLURAL, II, D, 1 [L. *gobio,* gudgeon < Gr. *kōbios*] any of a group of small, spiny-finned fishes: the ventral fins are sometimes modified into a suction disk

go-by (gō′bī′) ***n.*** [Colloq.] a passing by; esp., an intentional disregard or slight: chiefly in **give** (or **get**) **the go-by,** to slight (or be slighted)

go-cart (-kärt′) ***n.*** **1.** a framework on casters, to support a child learning to walk **2.** a small, low baby carriage **3.** *same as* KART (sense 2)

god (gäd, gôd) ***n.*** [OE.] **1.** any of various beings conceived of as supernatural, immortal, and having power over people and nature; deity, esp. a male one **2.** an idol **3.** a person or thing deified or excessively honored —[**G-**] in monotheistic religions, the creator and ruler of the universe, eternal, infinite, all-powerful, and all-knowing

god·child (gäd′chīld′) ***n.,*** *pl.* **-chil′dren** the person for whom a godparent is sponsor

god·daugh·ter (gäd′dôt′ər) ***n.*** a female godchild

god·dess (gäd′is) ***n.*** **1.** a female god **2.** a woman greatly admired, as for her beauty

god·fa·ther (gäd′fä′*th*ər) ***n.*** a male godparent

God-fear·ing (-fir′iŋ) ***adj.*** [*occas.* **g-**] **1.** fearing God **2.** devout; pious

God·for·sak·en (-fər sā′kən) ***adj.*** [*occas.* **g-**] **1.** depraved; wicked **2.** desolate; forlorn

God·frey (gäd′frē) [< OFr. < OHG. < *god,* God + *fridu,* peace, lit., peace (of) God] a masculine name

God-giv·en (gäd′giv′ən) ***adj.*** [*occas.* **g-**] **1.** given by God **2.** very welcome; opportune

god·head (-hed′) ***n.*** **1.** godhood **2.** [**G-**] God

god·hood (-hood′) ***n.*** the state or quality of being a god; divinity

Go·di·va (gə dī′və) a legendary 11th-cent. noblewoman of Coventry who, on the dare of her husband, rode naked through the streets on horseback so that he would abolish a heavy tax

god·less (gäd′lis) ***adj.*** **1.** denying the existence of God or a god; irreligious **2.** impious; wicked —**god′less·ness** ***n.***

god·like (-līk′) ***adj.*** like or suitable to God or a god; divine

god·ly (-lē) ***adj.*** **-li·er, -li·est** **1.** divine **2.** pious; devout; religious —**god′li·ness** ***n.***

god·moth·er (-mu*th*′ər) ***n.*** a female godparent

god·par·ent (gäd′per′ənt, -par′-) ***n.*** a person who sponsors a child, as at baptism, and assumes responsibility for its faith; godmother or godfather

god·send (gäd′send′) ***n.*** anything unexpected and needed that comes at the opportune moment, as if sent by God

god·son (-sun′) ***n.*** a male godchild

God·speed (-spēd′) ***n.*** [contr. of *God speed you*] success; good fortune: a wish for a person starting on a trip

God·win Austen (gäd′win) mountain in N Jammu & Kashmir, near the Chinese border: second highest mountain in the world: 28,250 ft.

god·wit (gäd′wit) ***n.*** [? echoic] a brownish wading bird, with a long bill that curves up

go·er (gō′ər) ***n.*** one that goes

Goe·the (gö′tə; *also Anglicized to* gur′tə, gāt′ə), **Jo·hann Wolf·gang von** (yō′hän vôlf′gäŋ fôn) 1749–1832; Ger. poet & dramatist

go·fer, go-fer (gō′fər) ***n.*** [from being asked to *go for* whatever is needed] [Slang] an employee who performs minor or menial tasks such as running errands

go-get·ter (gō′get′ər) ***n.*** [Colloq.] an enterprising and aggressive person

gog·gle (gäg′'l) ***vi.*** **-gled, -gling** [ME. *gogelen*] **1.** *a)* to stare with bulging eyes *b)* to roll the eyes **2.** *a)* to bulge in a stare *b)* to roll: said of the eyes —***n.*** **1.** a staring with bulging eyes **2.** [*pl.*] large spectacles, esp. those fitted with side guards to protect the eyes against dust, wind, etc. —***adj.*** bulging: said of the eyes —**gog′gle-eyed′** (-īd′) ***adj.***

Gogh, Vincent van *see* VAN GOGH

go-go (gō′gō′) ***adj.*** [< Fr. *à gogo,* in plenty, ad lib.] **1.** of rock-and-roll dancing or cafés, etc. featuring it **2.** [Slang] lively, energetic, etc.

Go·gol (gô′gôl; *E.* gō′gəl), **Ni·ko·lai Va·sil·ie·vich** (nē′kô lī′ vä sēl′yə vich) 1809–52; Russ. novelist & dramatist

Goi·del·ic (goi del′ik) ***adj.*** [< OIr. *Góidel*] **1.** of the Gaels **2.** designating or of their languages —***n.*** the subbranch of Celtic languages that includes Irish Gaelic, Scottish Gaelic, and Manx

go·ing (gō′iŋ) ***n.*** **1.** the act of one who goes **2.** a departure **3.** the condition of the ground or land as it affects traveling **4.** circumstances affecting progress —***adj.*** **1.** moving; running; working **2.** operating successfully *[a going concern]* **3.** in existence or available *[the best bet going]* **4.** current *[the going rate]* —**be going to** to be intending to; will or shall —**get going** [Colloq.] to start —**get one going** [Slang] to make one excited, angry, etc. —**going on** [Colloq.] nearing or nearly (a specified age or time)

go·ing-o·ver (-ō′vər) ***n.*** [Colloq.] **1.** an inspection, esp. a thorough one **2.** a severe scolding or beating

go·ings-on (gō′iŋz än′) ***n.pl.*** [Colloq.] actions or events, esp. when regarded with disapproval

goi·ter, goi·tre (goit′ər) ***n.*** [< Fr., ult. < L. *guttur,* throat] an enlarged thyroid gland, often visible as a swelling in the front of the neck —**goi·trous** (goi′trəs) ***adj.***

gold (gōld) ***n.*** [OE.] **1.** a heavy, yellow, metallic chemical element that is highly ductile and malleable: it is a precious metal and is used in coins, jewelry, alloys, etc.: symbol, Au; at. wt., 196.967; at. no., 79 **2.** *a)* gold coin *b)* money; riches **3.** the bright yellow color of gold **4.** a thing regarded as having the value, brilliance, etc. of gold —***adj.*** **1.** of, made of, or like gold **2.** having the color of gold

gold·brick (-brik′) ***n.*** **1.** [Colloq.] anything worthless passed off as genuine or valuable **2.** [Mil. Slang] one who avoids work; shirker: also **gold′brick′er** —***vi.*** [Mil. Slang] to shirk; loaf

gold digger [Slang] a woman who tries to get money and gifts from her men friends

gold dust gold in very small bits or as a powder

gold·en (gōl′d'n) ***adj.*** **1.** of, containing, or yielding gold **2.** bright-yellow, like gold **3.** precious; excellent **4.**

prosperous and joyful **5.** auspicious **6.** richly mellow, as a voice **7.** marking the 50th anniversary *[a golden* jubilee*]* —**gold′en·ly** *adv.* —**gold′en·ness** *n.*
Golden Age **1.** *Gr. & Rom. Myth.* an early age in which people were ideally happy, innocent, etc. **2.** [g- a-] a period of great progress, culture, etc. **3.** [*also* g- a-] of or for golden agers
golden ag·er (āj′ər) [Colloq.] [*also* G- A-] an elderly person, esp. one 65 or older and retired
gold·en·eye (gōl′d'n ī′) *n., pl.* **-eyes′**, **-eye′**: see PLURAL, II, D, 1 a swift, diving wild duck of N. America and the Old World, with yellow eyes and a dark-green back
Golden Fleece *Gr. Myth.* the fleece of gold guarded by a dragon until captured by Jason
Golden Gate strait between San Francisco Bay & the Pacific
golden mean the safe, prudent way between extremes; moderation
golden retriever any of a breed of hunting dog with a thick, golden coat
gold·en·rod (-räd′) *n.* a N. American plant of the composite family, typically with long, branching stalks bearing clusters of small, yellow flower heads through late summer and fall
golden rule the precept that one should behave toward others as he would want others to behave toward him: see Matt. 7:12; Luke 6:31
golden wedding a 50th wedding anniversary
gold-filled (gōld′fild′) *adj.* made of a base metal overlaid with gold
gold·finch (-finch′) *n.* [OE. *goldfinc*] **1.** a European songbird with yellow-streaked wings **2.** any of several small American finches, esp. one the male of which has a yellow body and black markings on the wings
gold·fish (-fish′) *n., pl.* **-fish′**, **-fish′es**: see FISH a small, golden-yellow or orange fish of the carp family, often kept in fishbowls
gold foil gold beaten into thin sheets slightly thicker than gold leaf —**gold′-foil′** *adj.*
gold leaf gold beaten into very thin sheets, used for gilding —**gold′-leaf′** *adj.*
gold plate tableware made of gold
gold rush a rush of people to territory where gold has recently been discovered
gold·smith (-smith′) *n.* a skilled worker who makes articles of gold
Gold·smith (gōld′smith′), **Oliver** 1728–74; Brit. poet, playwright, & novelist, born in Ireland
gold standard a monetary standard in which the basic currency unit is made equal to and redeemable by a specified quantity of gold
golf (gôlf, gälf) *n.* [< ? Scot. *gowf*, to strike] an outdoor game played on a golf course with a small, hard ball and a set of clubs, the object being to hit the ball into each of 9 or 18 holes in turn, with the fewest possible strokes —*vi.* to play golf —**golf′er** *n.*
golf club **1.** any of a set of clubs used in golf: each has a wooden or metal head and a long, slender shaft **2.** an organization operating a golf course, clubhouse, etc.
golf course (or **links**) a tract of land for playing golf, with tees, fairways, greens, etc.
Gol·go·tha (gäl′gə thə) [see CALVARY] the place where Jesus was crucified; Calvary
Go·li·ath (gə lī′əth) *Bible* the Philistine giant killed by David with a stone from a sling
gol·ly (gäl′ē) *interj.* an exclamation of surprise, etc.: a euphemism for *God*
go·losh, go·loshe (gə läsh′) *n. Brit. var. of* GALOSH
Go·mor·rah, Go·mor·rha (gə môr′ə) *see* SODOM
Gom·pers (gäm′pərz), **Samuel** 1850–1924; U.S. labor leader, born in England
-gon (gän, gən) [< Gr. < *gōnia*, an angle] *a combining form meaning* a figure having (a specified number of) angles *[pentagon]*
go·nad (gō′nad; *occas.* gän′ad) *n.* [< ModL. < Gr. *gonē*, a seed] an animal organ producing reproductive cells; ovary or testis —**go·nad′al** *adj.*
gon·do·la (gän′də lə, gän dō′lə) *n.* [It. (Venetian) < ?] **1.** a long, narrow boat with a high, pointed prow and stern, propelled by a pole or one oar on the canals of Venice **2.** a flat-bottomed river barge **3.** a railroad freight car with low sides and no top: also **gondola car** **4.** the car of an airship or balloon **5.** a car suspended from and moved along a cable, for holding passengers

GONDOLA

gon·do·lier (gän′də lir′) *n.* a man who rows or poles a gondola
gone (gôn, gän) *pp. of* GO —*adj.* **1.** moved away **2.** ruined **3.** lost **4.** dead **5.** faint; weak **6.** used up; consumed **7.** ago; past **8.** [Slang] *a)* excellent *b)* enraptured *c)* pregnant —**far gone** **1.** deeply involved **2.** very tired —**gone on** [Colloq.] in love with
gon·er (gôn′ər, gän′-) *n.* [Colloq.] one beyond help or seemingly sure to die soon, be ruined, etc.
gon·fa·lon (gän′fə lən, -län′) *n.* [Fr. < OFr. < Frank. < *gund*, a battle + *fano*, banner] a flag hanging from a crosspiece instead of on an upright staff, usually ending in streamers
gong (gôŋ, gäŋ) *n.* [Malay *guṅ*: echoic] **1.** a slightly convex metallic disk that gives a loud, resonant tone when struck **2.** a saucer-shaped bell with such a tone
-go·ni·um (gō′nē əm) [ModL. < Gr. *gonos*, seed] *a combining form meaning* a cell or structure in which reproductive cells are formed *[sporogonium]*
gon·o·coc·cus (gän′ə käk′əs) *n., pl.* **-coc′ci** (-käk′sī) [ModL. < Gr. *gonos*, a seed + COCCUS] the microorganism that causes gonorrhea
gon·or·rhe·a, gon·or·rhoe·a (-rē′ə) *n.* [< LL. < Gr. < *gonos*, a seed, semen + *rheein*, to flow] a venereal disease marked by inflammation of the mucous membrane of the genitourinary tract and a discharge of mucus and pus —**gon′or·rhe′al, gon′or·rhoe′al** *adj.*
-go·ny (gə nē) [< L. < Gr. < base of *gignesthai*, to be born] *a combining form meaning* something generated, produced, descended, etc. *[cosmogony]*
goo (go͞o) *n.* [Slang] **1.** anything sticky, as glue **2.** anything sticky and sweet **3.** sentimentality
goo·ber (go͞o′bər) *n.* [< native Afr. name *nguba*] [Chiefly South] a peanut
good (go͝od) *adj.* **bet′ter, best** [OE. *god*] **1.** *a)* suitable to a purpose; efficient *[a good* lamp*]* *b)* beneficial *[good* exercise*]* **2.** unspoiled *[good* eggs*]* **3.** valid; genuine; real *[good* money*]* **4.** healthy *[good* eyesight*]* **5.** financially sound *[a good* investment*]* **6.** honorable; worthy *[one's good* name*]* **7.** enjoyable, happy, etc. *[a good* life*]* **8.** dependable; reliable *[good* advice*]* **9.** thorough *[did a good* job*]* **10.** *a)* above average *[a good* novel*]* *b)* not for everyday use; best *[her good* china*]* **11.** adequate; satisfying *[a good* meal*]* **12.** morally sound or excellent; specif., *a)* virtuous *b)* pious *c)* kind, generous, etc. *d)* well-behaved; dutiful **13.** proper; correct *[good* manners*]* **14.** able; skilled *[a good* swimmer*]* **15.** loyal or conforming *[a good* Democrat*]* **16.** considerable *[a good* many*]* **17.** full; complete *[a good* six hours*]* —*n.* something good; specif., *a)* worth; virtue; merit *[the good* in a man*]* *b)* benefit; advantage *[for the good* of all*]* *c)* something desirable or desired See also GOODS —*interj.* an exclamation of satisfaction, pleasure, etc. —*adv.* well, fully, etc.: variously regarded as substandard, dialectal, or colloquial —**as good as** virtually; nearly —**for good (and all)** for always; permanently —**good and** [Colloq.] very or altogether —**good for** **1.** able to endure or be used for (a period of time) **2.** worth **3.** able to pay or give **4.** sure to result in *[good for* a laugh*]* —**make good** **1.** to repay or replace **2.** to fulfill **3.** to succeed in doing; accomplish **4.** to be successful **5.** to prove —**no good** useless or worthless —**the good** **1.** those who are good **2.** what is morally good —**to the good** as a profit or advantage
Good Book the Bible (usually with *the*)
good·bye, good-bye (go͝od′bī′) *interj., n., pl.* **-byes′** [contr. of *God be with ye*] farewell: term used in parting: also **good′by′, good′-by′**
good day a salutation of greeting or farewell
good-for-nothing (go͝od′fər nuth′iŋ) *adj.* useless or worthless —*n.* such a person
Good Friday the Friday before Easter Sunday, commemorating the crucifixion of Jesus
good-heart·ed (-här′tid) *adj.* kind and generous —**good′-heart′ed·ly** *adv.* —**good′-heart′ed·ness** *n.*
Good Hope, Cape of **1.** cape at the SW tip of Africa **2.** province of South Africa, in the southernmost part
good humor a cheerful, agreeable, or pleasant mood —**good′-hu′mored** *adj.* —**good′-hu′mored·ly** *adv.*
good·ish (-ish) *adj.* fairly good or fairly large
good looks attractive appearance; esp., pleasing facial features —**good′-look′ing** *adj.*
good·ly (-lē) *adj.* **-li·er, -li·est** **1.** of attractive appearance **2.** of good quality; fine **3.** rather large; ample —**good′-li·ness** *n.*
good·man (-mən) *n., pl.* **-men** [Archaic] **1.** a husband or master of a household **2.** a title like *Mr.*, for a man ranking below a gentleman
good morning a salutation of greeting or farewell used in the morning
good nature a pleasant, agreeable, or kindly disposition —**good′-na′tured** *adj.* —**good′-na′tured·ly** *adv.*
good·ness (-nis) *n.* **1.** the state or quality of being good; specif., *a)* virtue; excellence *b)* kindness; generosity **2.** the best part —*interj.* an exclamation of surprise

good night a salutation of parting or farewell used at night
goods (good͝z) ***n.pl.*** **1.** movable personal property **2.** merchandise; wares **3.** fabric; cloth **4.** [Brit.] freight —**deliver the goods** [Colloq.] to do or produce the thing required —**get** (or **have) the goods on** [Slang] to discover (or know) something incriminating about —**the goods** [Slang] what is required or genuine
good Samaritan one who pities and unselfishly helps another or others: Luke 10:30–37
Good Shepherd *an epithet for* JESUS: John 10:11
good-sized (good͝′sīzd′) ***adj.*** big or fairly big
good-tem·pered (-tem′pərd) ***adj.*** not easily angered or annoyed —**good′-tem′pered·ly** ***adv.***
good turn a good deed; friendly, helpful act
good·wife (-wīf′) ***n.,*** *pl.* **-wives′** (-wīvz′) [Archaic] **1.** a wife or mistress of a household **2.** a title like *Mrs.*, for a woman ranking below a lady
good will **1.** a friendly or kindly attitude **2.** cheerful consent; willingness **3.** the value of a business in patronage, reputation, etc., over and beyond its tangible assets Also **good′will′** ***n.***
good·y[1] (-ē) ***n.,*** *pl.* **good′ies** [Colloq.] **1.** something good to eat, as a candy **2.** *same as* GOODY-GOODY —***adj.*** [Colloq.] *same as* GOODY-GOODY —***interj.*** a child's exclamation of delight
good·y[2] (-ē) ***n.,*** *pl.* **good′ies** [< GOODWIFE] [Archaic] a woman, esp. an old woman or a housewife, of lowly social status: used as a title with the surname
Good·year (good͝′yir′), **Charles** 1800–60; U.S. inventor of the process of vulcanizing rubber
good·y-good·y (good͝′ē good͝′ē) ***adj.*** [Colloq.] moral or pious in a smug, showy way —***n.*** [Colloq.] a goody-goody person
goo·ey (gōō′ē) ***adj.*** **goo′i·er, goo′i·est** [Slang] **1.** sticky **2.** sticky and sweet **3.** sentimental
goof (gōōf) ***n.*** [prob. ult. < It. *goffo*, clumsy] [Slang] **1.** a stupid or silly person **2.** a mistake; blunder —***vi.*** [Slang] **1.** to err, blunder, fail, etc. **2.** to waste time, shirk duty, etc. (with *off*)
goof·y (-ē) ***adj.*** **goof′i·er, goof′i·est** [Slang] like or characteristic of a goof; stupid or silly —**goof′i·ly** ***adv.*** —**goof′i·ness** ***n.***
gook (good͝k, gōōk) ***n.*** [GOO + (GUN)K] [Slang] any sticky, greasy, or slimy substance
goon (gōōn) ***n.*** [Slang] **1.** [< ? GUN] a ruffian or thug **2.** [after a comic-strip character of E.C. Segar, 20th-c. U.S. cartoonist] a person who is awkward, grotesque, stupid, etc.
goo·ney bird (gōō′nē) [< *gooney*, sailors' name for the albatross] an albatross of a black-footed species: also **goo′ny bird**
goop (gōōp) ***n.*** [GOO + (SOU)P] [Slang] any sticky, semiliquid substance —**goop′y** ***adj.*** **-i·er, -i·est**
goose (gōōs) ***n.,*** *pl.* **geese**; for 4 & 5 **goos′es** [OE. *gos*] **1.** a long-necked, web-footed, wild or domestic bird that is like a duck but larger, esp. the female **2.** its flesh, used for food **3.** a silly person **4.** a tailor's pressing iron, with a long, curved handle **5.** [Slang] a sudden, playful prod in the backside —***vt.*** **goosed, goos′ing** [Slang] **1.** to prod suddenly and playfully in the backside so as to startle **2.** to feed gasoline to (an engine) in irregular spurts **3.** to prod or stir into action —**cook one's goose** [Colloq.] to spoil one's chances, hopes, etc.
goose·ber·ry (gōōs′ber′ē, -bə rē; gōōz′-) ***n.,*** *pl.* **-ries** **1.** a small, round, sour berry used in preserves, etc. **2.** the shrub it grows on
goose egg [Slang] **1.** a zero **2.** a large swelling or lump, esp. one caused by a blow
goose flesh a roughened condition of the skin in which the papillae are raised, caused by cold, fear, etc.: also **goose bumps** (or **pimples** or **skin**)
goose·foot (gōōs′foot͝′) ***adj.*** designating a family of plants including spinach and beets —***n.,*** *pl.* **-foots′** any of a genus of plants of this family, with small, green flowers and, often, fleshy foliage
goose·neck (-nek′) ***n.*** any of various mechanical devices shaped like a goose's neck, as a flexible rod for supporting a desk lamp
goose step a parade marching step in which the legs are raised high and kept rigidly unbent —**goose′-step′** ***vi.*** **-stepped′, -step′ping**
GOP, G.O.P. Grand Old Party (Republican Party)
go·pher (gō′fər) ***n.*** [< ? Fr. *gaufre*, honeycomb: from its burrowing] **1.** a burrowing rodent, about the size of a large rat, with wide cheek pouches: also **pocket gopher** **2.** a striped ground squirrel of N. American prairies, related to the chipmunk
Gor·di·an knot (gôr′dē ən) *Gr. Legend* a knot tied by King Gordius of Phrygia, to be undone only by the future master of Asia: Alexander the Great, failing to untie it, cut the knot with his sword —**cut the Gordian knot** to find a quick, bold solution for a problem
Gor·don (gôr′d'n) [Scot. < surname *Gordon*] **1.** a masculine name **2. Charles George,** 1833–85; Brit. general in China, Egypt, & Sudan
gore[1] (gôr) ***n.*** [OE. *gor*, dung, filth] blood shed from a wound; esp., clotted blood
gore[2] (gôr) ***vt.*** **gored, gor′ing** [< OE. *gar*, a spear] to pierce as with a horn or tusk
gore[3] (gôr) ***n.*** [OE. *gara*, corner < base of *gar*, a spear] a tapering piece of cloth in a skirt, sail, etc. to give it fullness —***vt.*** **gored, gor′ing** to make or insert a gore or gores in
gorge (gôrj) ***n.*** [< OFr., throat, ult. < L. *gurges*, whirlpool] **1.** the throat or gullet **2.** the maw or stomach, or food filling it **3.** a deep, narrow pass between steep heights **4.** a mass, as of ice, blocking a passage —***vi., vt.*** **gorged, gorg′ing** to stuff (oneself) with food; glut —**make one's gorge rise** to make one disgusted, angry, etc.
gor·geous (gôr′jəs) ***adj.*** [< OFr. *gorgias*, beautiful] **1.** brilliantly colored; resplendent **2.** [Slang] beautiful, wonderful, delightful, etc. —**gor′geous·ly** ***adv.*** —**gor′geous·ness** ***n.***
gor·get (gôr′jit) ***n.*** [< OFr. < *gorge:* see GORGE] **1.** a piece of armor to protect the throat **2.** a collar **3.** a patch of color on a bird's throat
Gor·gon (gôr′gən) ***n.*** **1.** *Gr. Myth.* any of three sisters with snakes for hair, so horrible that the beholder was turned to stone **2.** [**g-**] any ugly, terrifying, or repulsive woman
Gor·gon·zo·la (gôr′gən zō′lə) ***n.*** [< *Gorgonzola*, town in Italy] a white Italian pressed cheese with veins of blue-green mold and a strong flavor
go·ril·la (gə ril′ə) ***n.*** [< Gr. *gorillai* < an ancient W. African name] **1.** the largest and most powerful manlike ape, native to the jungles of equatorial Africa **2.** [Slang] *a*) a person regarded as like a gorilla in appearance, strength, etc. *b*) a gangster; thug

GORILLA
(50–70 in. high)

Gor·ki, Gor·kiy, Gor·ky (gôr′kē) city in E European R.S.F.S.R., on the Volga: pop. 1,139,000
Gor·ki (gôr′kē), **Max·im** (mak′sim) (pseud. of *Aleksei Maximovich Peshkov*) 1868–1936; Russ. novelist & playwright: also sp. **Gorky**
gor·mand (gôr′mənd) ***n.*** *same as* GOURMAND
gor·mand·ize (gôr′mən dīz′) ***vi., vt.*** **-ized′, -iz′ing** [< Fr. *gourmandise*, gluttony] to eat or devour like a glutton —**gor′mand·iz′er** ***n.***
gorse (gôrs) ***n.*** [OE. *gorst*] furze —**gors′y** ***adj.***
gor·y (gôr′ē) ***adj.*** **gor′i·er, gor′i·est** **1.** covered with gore; bloody **2.** full of bloodshed or killing —**gor′i·ly** ***adv.*** —**gor′i·ness** ***n.***
gosh (gäsh) ***interj.*** an exclamation of surprise, wonder, etc.: a euphemism for *God*
gos·hawk (gäs′hôk′) ***n.*** [< OE.: see GOOSE & HAWK[1]] a large, swift hawk with short wings
Go·shen (gō′shən) *Bible* the fertile land assigned to the Israelites in Egypt: Gen. 45:10 —***n.*** a land of plenty
gos·ling (gäz′liŋ) ***n.*** [< ON.] a young goose
gos·pel (gäs′p'l) ***n.*** [OE. *gödspel*, lit., good news] **1.** [*often* **G-**] *a*) the teachings of Jesus and the Apostles *b*) the history of the life and teachings of Jesus **2.** [**G-**] *a*) any of the first four books of the New Testament (*Matthew, Mark, Luke,* or *John*) *b*) an excerpt from any of these, read in a religious service **3.** anything regarded as the absolute truth: also **gospel truth** **4.** any doctrine or rule widely or ardently maintained **5.** a style of folk singing originally associated with evangelistic revival meetings —***adj.*** of (the) gospel or evangelism
gos·sa·mer (gäs′ə mər) ***n.*** [ME. *gosesomer*, lit., goose summer: the period in fall when geese are in season] **1.** a filmy cobweb in the air or on bushes or grass **2.** a very thin, soft, filmy cloth **3.** anything like gossamer —***adj.*** light, thin, and filmy: also **gos′sa·mer·y** (-mər ē)
gos·sip (gäs′əp) ***n.*** [< Late OE. *godsibbe*, godparent: see GOD & SIB] **1.** [Obs. or Dial.] *a*) a godparent *b*) a close friend **2.** one who chatters or repeats idle talk and rumors, esp. about others' private affairs **3.** *a*) such talk or rumors *b*) chatter —***vi.*** to indulge in idle talk or rumors about others —**gos′sip·er** ***n.*** —**gos′sip·y** ***adj.***
got (gät) *pt. & alt. pp. of* GET
Gö·te·borg (yö′tə bôr′y′) seaport in SW Sweden, on the Kattegat: pop. 445,000

Goth (gäth, gôth) ***n.*** **[**< LL. < Gr. *Gothoi*, pl.**]** **1.** a member of a Germanic people that invaded and conquered most of the Roman Empire in the 3d–5th cent. A.D. **2.** an uncouth, uncivilized person

Goth., goth. Gothic

Goth·am (gäth′əm, gō′thəm; *for 1, Brit.* gät′-) **1.** a village near Nottingham, England, whose inhabitants were, according to legend, very foolish **2.** *nickname for* NEW YORK CITY —**Goth′am·ite′** (-īt′) ***n.***

Goth·ic (gäth′ik) ***adj.*** **1.** of the Goths or their language **2.** designating or of a style of architecture developed in W Europe from the 12th to 16th cent., characterized by flying buttresses, pointed arches, etc. **3.** [*sometimes* **g-**] *a)* medieval *b)* not classical *c)* barbarous **4.** of a style of literature using a medieval or macabre setting, atmosphere, etc., to suggest horror and mystery —***n.*** **1.** the East Germanic language of the Goths **2.** Gothic style, esp. in architecture **3.** *Printing* [*often* **g-**] a plain type with straight lines of uniform width and no serifs —**Goth′i·cal·ly** ***adv.***

Gothic arch a pointed arch

Got·land (gät′lənd; *Sw.* gôt′-) Swed. island in the Baltic, off the SE coast of Sweden

got·ten (gät′'n) *alt. pp. of* GET

gouache (gwäsh) ***n.*** **[**Fr. < It. *guazzo*, water color < L. < *aqua*, water**]** **1.** a way of painting with opaque water colors mixed with gum **2.** such a pigment **3.** a painting made with such pigments

Gou·da (cheese) (gou′də, gōō′-) **[**< *Gouda*, city in Netherlands**]** a mild, semisoft to hard cheese, usually coated with red wax

gouge (gouj) ***n.*** **[**< OFr. < VL. *gubia*, for LL. *gulbia* < Celt.**]** **1.** a chisel with a curved, hollowed blade, for cutting grooves or holes in wood **2.** *a)* a gouging *b)* the groove or hole **3.** [Colloq.] extortion or swindle —***vt.*** **gouged, goug′ing** **1.** to make grooves or holes in as with a gouge **2.** to scoop or dig out **3.** in fighting, to push one's thumb into the eye of **4.** [Colloq.] to cheat out of money, etc.; also, to overcharge —**goug′er** ***n.***

gou·lash (gōō′läsh, -lash) ***n.*** **[**< G. < Hung. *gulyás*, herdsman, hence herdsman's food**]** a stew of beef or veal and vegetables, seasoned with paprika, etc.: also **Hungarian goulash**

Gould (gōōld), **Jay** 1836–92; U.S. financier

Gou·nod (gōō nō′; *E.* gōō′nō), **Charles (François)** (shärl) 1818–93; Fr. composer

gou·ra·mi (goor′ə mē, goo rä′mē) ***n.***, *pl.* **-mis, -mi:** see PLURAL, II, D, 1 **[**Malay *gurami*]** **1.** a food fish of SE Asia, that builds a nest **2.** any of a number of related fishes, mostly brightly colored, that are often kept in aquariums

gourd (gôrd, goord) ***adj.*** **[**< OFr. < L. *cucurbita***]** designating a family of plants that includes the squash, melon, pumpkin, etc. —***n.*** **1.** any trailing or climbing plant of this family **2.** *a) same as* CALABASH (sense 2*a*) *b)* the ornamental, inedible fruit of certain related plants **3.** the dried, hollowed-out shell of such a fruit, used as a drinking cup, dipper, etc.

gourde (goord) ***n.*** **[**Fr. < L. *gurdus*, heavy**]** *see* MONETARY UNITS, table (Haiti)

gour·mand (goor′mənd, goor mänd′) ***n.*** **[**< OFr.**]** **1.** a person who likes to indulge in good food and drink, sometimes to excess **2.** *same as* GOURMET

gour·met (goor′mā; *Fr.* gōōr me′) ***n.*** **[**Fr. < OFr. *gourmet*, wine taster**]** a person who likes and is an excellent judge of fine foods and drinks; epicure

gout (gout) ***n.*** **[**< OFr. < L. *gutta*, a drop**]** **1.** a disease marked by deposits of uric acid salts in tissues and joints, esp. of the feet and hands, with swelling and great pain, esp. in the big toe **2.** a spurt, splash, etc. —**gout′i·ly** ***adv.*** —**gout′i·ness** ***n.*** —**gout′y** ***adj.*** **gout′i·er, gout′i·est**

gov., Gov. **1.** government **2.** governor

gov·ern (guv′ərn) ***vt.*** **[**< OFr. < L. *gubernare* < Gr. *kybernan*, to steer**]** **1.** to exercise authority over; rule, control, manage, etc. **2.** to influence the action or conduct of; guide **3.** to hold in check; curb **4.** to regulate the speed of **5.** to be a rule or law for **6.** *Gram.* *a)* to require (a word) to be in a particular case or mood *b)* to require (a particular case or mood) —***vi.*** to govern someone or something; rule —**gov′ern·a·ble** ***adj.***

gov·ern·ance (-ər nəns) ***n.*** control or rule

gov·ern·ess (-ər nəs) ***n.*** a woman employed in a private home to train and teach the children

gov·ern·ment (guv′ər mənt, -ərn mənt) ***n.*** **1.** *a)* the exercise of authority over a state, district, group, etc.; control; rule *b)* the right, function, or power of governing **2.** *a)* a system of ruling, controlling, etc. *b)* an established system of political administration by which a nation, state, etc. is governed *c)* the study of such systems **3.** all the people that administer the affairs of a nation, state, institution, etc. **4.** [*often* **G-**] the executive or administrative branch of government of a particular nation **5.** *Gram.* the influence of a word over the case or mood of another —**gov′ern·men′tal** ***adj.*** —**gov′ern·men′tal·ly** ***adv.***

gov·er·nor (guv′ə nər, -ər nər) ***n.*** **1.** a person who governs; esp., *a)* one appointed to govern a dependency, province, etc. *b)* the elected head of any State of the U.S. *c)* one of the group directing an organization or institution **2.** a device automatically controlling the speed of an engine or motor as by regulating fuel intake **3.** [Brit. Colloq.] a person with authority; esp., one's father or employer —**gov′er·nor·ship′** ***n.***

governor general *pl.* **governors general, governor generals** a governor with deputy governors under him, as in the British Commonwealth: also, Brit., **gov′er·nor-gen′er·al** ***n.***, *pl.* **gov′er·nors-gen′er·al**

govt., Govt. government

gown (goun) ***n.*** **[**< OFr. < LL. *gunna*]** **1.** a woman's long, usually formal dress **2.** a dressing gown **3.** a nightgown, nightshirt, etc. **4.** a surgeon's smock **5.** a long, flowing robe worn traditionally by certain officials, clergymen, professors, etc. **6.** the members of a college, etc. collectively —***vt.*** to dress in a gown

Goy·a (y Lucientes) (gô′yä), **Fran·cis·co Jo·sé de** (frän thēs′kô hô se′ *th*e) 1746–1828; Sp. painter

G.P., g.p. general practitioner

GPO, G.P.O. Government Printing Office

Gr. **1.** Grecian **2.** Greece **3.** Greek

gr. **1.** grade **2.** grain(s) **3.** gram(s) **4.** gravity **5.** great **6.** gross

grab (grab) ***vt.*** **grabbed, grab′bing** **[**prob. < MDu., MLowG. *grabben*]** **1.** to seize or snatch suddenly **2.** to get possession of by unscrupulous methods **3.** [Slang] to impress (one) greatly —***vi.*** to grab or try to grab something (often with *for, at,* etc.) —***n.*** **1.** a grabbing **2.** something grabbed **3.** a device for clutching something to be hoisted —**up for grabs** [Slang] available to the highest bidder, the most aggressive person, etc. —**grab′ber** ***n.***

grab bag a container holding wrapped or bagged articles sold unseen at a fixed price

grab·by (-ē) ***adj.*** **-bi·er, -bi·est** avaricious

Grace (grās) **[**see ff.**]** a feminine name

grace (grās) ***n.*** **[**< OFr. < L. *gratia*, pleasing quality < *gratus*, pleasing**]** **1.** beauty or charm of form, movement, or expression **2.** an attractive quality, feature, manner, etc. **3.** *a)* a sense of what is right and proper; decency *b)* thoughtfulness toward others **4.** good will; favor **5.** [Archaic] mercy **6.** a delay granted beyond the date set for the performance or payment of an obligation **7.** a short prayer of blessing or thanks for a meal **8.** [**G-**] a title of respect in speaking to or of an archbishop, duke, or duchess **9.** *Music* [*pl.*] ornamental notes or effects, collectively **10.** *Theol.* *a)* the unmerited love and favor of God toward man *b)* divine influence acting in man to make him pure and good *c)* the condition of a person thus influenced *d)* a special virtue given to a person by God —***vt.*** **graced, grac′ing** **1.** to give or add grace or graces to **2.** to honor; dignify **3.** *Music* to add a grace note or notes to —**in the good** (or **bad**) **graces of** in favor (or disfavor) with —**with good** (or **bad**) **grace** in a willing (or unwilling) way

grace·ful (-f'l) ***adj.*** having grace (sense 1) —**grace′ful·ly** ***adv.*** —**grace′ful·ness** ***n.***

grace·less (-lis) ***adj.*** **1.** lacking any sense of what is right or proper **2.** clumsy or inelegant —**grace′less·ly** ***adv.*** —**grace′less·ness** ***n.***

grace note *Music* a merely ornamental note

Grac·es (grā′siz) *Gr. Myth.* three sister goddesses who controlled pleasure, charm, elegance, and beauty in human life and in nature

gra·cious (grā′shəs) ***adj.*** **1.** having or showing kindness, courtesy, charm, etc. **2.** merciful; compassionate **3.** polite to those held to be inferiors **4.** marked by the taste, ease, etc. associated with prosperity, education, etc. [*gracious* living] —***interj.*** an expression of surprise —**gra′cious·ly** ***adv.*** —**gra′cious·ness** ***n.***

grack·le (grak′'l) ***n.*** **[**L. *graculus*, jackdaw**]** any of several American blackbirds that are somewhat smaller than a crow

grad (grad) ***n.*** [Colloq.] a graduate

grad. **1.** graduate **2.** graduated

gra·date (grā′dāt) ***vt., vi.*** **-dat·ed, -dat·ing** **[**backformation < ff.**]** to change, etc. by gradation; shade into one another, as colors

gra·da·tion (grā dā′shən) ***n.*** **[**Fr. < L. *gradatio* < *gradus*: see ff.**]** **1.** a forming or arranging in grades, stages, or steps **2.** a gradual change by steps or stages **3.** a shading of one tone or color into another **4.** a step, stage, or degree in a graded series **5.** *same as* ABLAUT —**gra·da′tion·al** ***adj.*** —**gra·da′tion·al·ly** ***adv.***

grade (grād) ***n.*** **[**Fr. < L. *gradus*, a step < *gradi*, to step**]** **1.** any of the stages in a systematic progression **2.** *a)* a degree in a scale of quality, rank, etc. *b)* any of the official ranks or ratings of officers or enlisted men *c)* an accepted standard or level [up to *grade*] *d)* a group of the same rank, merit, etc. **3.** *a)* the degree of rise or descent of a slope, as of a road *b)* the slope itself **4.** a division in a school curriculum, usually equal to one year **5.** a mark or rating on an examination, in a school course, etc. *—vt.* **grad′ed, grad′ing 1.** to classify by grades of quality, rank, etc.; sort **2.** to give a grade (sense 5) to **3.** to gradate **4.** to make (ground) level or slope (ground) evenly for a roadway, etc. *—vi.* **1.** to be of a certain grade **2.** to change by gradation **—make the grade 1.** to get to the top of a steep incline **2.** to overcome obstacles and succeed

-grade (grād) [< L. *gradi,* to walk] *a combining form meaning* walking or moving *[plantigrade]*

grade crossing a place where two railroads or a railroad and roadway intersect on the same level

grad·er (grā′dər) *n.* **1.** a person or thing that grades **2.** a pupil in a specified grade at school

grade school *same as* ELEMENTARY SCHOOL

gra·di·ent (grā′dē ənt, -dyənt) *adj.* [< L. prp. of *gradi,* to step] ascending or descending with a uniform slope *—n.* **1.** *a)* a slope, as of a road *b)* the degree of such slope **2.** *Physics* the rate of change of temperature, pressure, etc.

grad·u·al (graj′oo wəl) *adj.* [< ML. < L. *gradus:* see GRADE] taking place little by little, not sharply or suddenly *—n. Eccles.* **1.** a set of verses, esp. from the Psalms, following the Epistle at Mass **2.** a book containing these and other sung parts of the Mass **—grad′u·al·ly** *adv.* **—grad′u·al·ness** *n.*

grad·u·al·ism (-iz'm) *n.* the principle of seeking only gradual social or political change **—grad′u·al·ist** *n., adj.* **—grad′u·al·is′tic** *adj.*

grad·u·ate (graj′oo wit; *for v., and occas. for n.,* -wāt′) *n.* [< ML. pp. of *graduare,* to graduate < L. *gradus:* see GRADE] **1.** a person who has completed a course of study at a school or college and has received a degree or diploma **2.** a container marked off for measuring the contents *—vt.* **-at′ed, -at′ing 1.** to give a degree or diploma to upon completion of a course of study **2.** to mark with degrees for measuring **3.** to grade by size, quality, etc. *—vi.* **1.** to become a graduate of a school, etc. **2.** to change, esp. advance, by degrees *—adj.* **1.** graduated from a school, college, etc. **2.** of or for studies leading to degrees above the bachelor's **—grad′u·a′tor** *n.*

grad·u·a·tion (graj′oo wā′shən) *n.* **1.** *a)* a graduating or being graduated from a school or college *b)* the ceremony connected with this; commencement **2.** *a)* a marking with degrees for measuring *b)* a degree or the degrees marked **3.** a grading by size, quality, etc.

Grae·cism (grē′siz'm) *n. same as* GRECISM

Grae·co- *same as* GRECO-

graf·fi·to (grə fēt′ō) *n., pl.* **-fi′ti** (-ē) [It., a scribbling] an inscription or drawing scratched or scribbled on a wall, etc. in a public place

graft (graft) *n.* [< OFr. *graffe* < L. < Gr. *grapheion,* stylus: from resemblance of the scion to a pointed pencil] **1.** *a)* a shoot or bud of a plant or tree inserted into the stem or trunk of another for continued growth as a permanent part *b)* the inserting of such a shoot, etc. or the place of insertion *c)* a tree or plant with such an insertion **2.** a joining of one thing to another as if by grafting **3.** *a)* a taking advantage of one's position to gain money, etc. dishonestly, as in politics *b)* anything so gained **4.** *Surgery a)* a piece of skin, bone, etc. transplanted from one body, or place on a body, to another, where it grows permanently *b)* such a transplanting *—vt.* **1.** *a)* to insert (a shoot or bud) as a graft *b)* to insert a graft of (one plant) in another *c)* to produce (a fruit, flower, etc.) by a graft **2.** to join as if by grafting **3.** *Surgery* to transplant as a graft *—vi.* **1.** to be grafted **2.** to make a graft **3.** to obtain money, etc. by graft **—graft′age** *n.* **—graft′er** *n.*

gra·ham (grā′əm) *adj.* [after S. *Graham* (1794–1851), U.S. dietary reformer] designating or made of finely ground whole-wheat flour *[graham* crackers*]*

Grail (grāl) [< OFr. *graal* < ML. *gradalis,* cup < ?] *Medieval Legend* the cup or platter used by Jesus at the Last Supper and the receptacle of drops of blood from Jesus' body at the Crucifixion: also called **Holy Grail**

grain (grān) *n.* [< OFr. < L. *granum*] **1.** a small, hard seed or seedlike fruit, esp. of a cereal plant, as wheat, rice, corn, etc. **2.** cereal seeds or cereal plants **3.** a tiny, solid particle, as of salt or sand **4.** a tiny bit *[a grain* of sense*]* **5.** the smallest unit in the system of weights of the U.S. and Great Britain, equal to 0.0648 gram **6.** *a)* the arrangement of fibers, layers, or particles of wood, leather, etc. *b)* the markings or texture due to this **7.** the side of leather from which the hair has been removed **8.** disposition; nature *—vt.* **1.** to form into grains; granulate **2.** to paint or finish in imitation of the grain of wood, marble, etc. **3.** to put a finish on the grain surface of (leather) *—vi.* to form grains **—against the** (or **one's**) **grain** contrary to one's feelings, nature, etc.

grain alcohol ethyl alcohol, esp. when made from grain

grain·y (-ē) *adj.* **grain′i·er, grain′i·est 1.** having a well-defined grain, as wood **2.** coarsely textured; granular **—grain′i·ness** *n.*

gram (gram) *n.* [< Fr. < LL. < Gr. *gramma,* a small weight, lit., what is written < *graphein,* to write] the basic unit of weight in the metric system, about 1/28 oz.

-gram (gram) [< Gr.: see prec.] *a combining form meaning:* **1.** something written or recorded *[telegram]* **2.** grams or part of a gram *[kilogram, milligram]*

gram. 1. grammar **2.** grammatical

gram·mar (gram′ər) *n.* [< OFr. < L. < Gr. *grammatikē (technē),* (art) of grammar, learning < *gramma:* see GRAM] **1.** language study dealing with word forms (*morphology*), word order in sentences (*syntax*), and now often language sounds (*phonology*) **2.** the system of word forms and word order of a given language at a given time **3.** a body of rules for speaking or writing a given language **4.** a book or treatise on grammar **5.** one's manner of speaking or writing as judged by how it conforms to the rules of grammar

gram·mar·i·an (grə mer′ē ən) *n.* a specialist or expert in grammar

grammar school 1. *earlier name for* ELEMENTARY SCHOOL **2.** in England, a secondary school

gram·mat·i·cal (grə mat′i k'l) *adj.* **1.** of or according to grammar **2.** conforming to the rules of grammar **—grammat′i·cal·ly** *adv.* **—gram·mat′i·cal·ness** *n.*

gramme (gram) *n. alt. sp. of* GRAM

gram molecule *same as* MOLE[4]: also **gram-mo·lec·u·lar weight** (gram′mə lek′yoo lər)

Gram·my (gram′ē) *n., pl.* **-mys, -mies** [< ff.] any of the annual awards in the U.S. for special achievement in the recording industry, as for the best recordings

gram·o·phone (gram′ə fōn′) *n.* [arbitrary inversion of PHONOGRAPH] [Chiefly Brit.] a phonograph

gram·pus (gram′pəs) *n., pl.* **-pus·es** [< OFr. *graspeis* < L. *crassus,* fat + *piscis,* fish] any of a genus of small, black, fierce whales related to the dolphins

Gra·na·da (grə nä′də; *Sp.* grä nä′*th*ä) **1.** former Moorish kingdom in S Spain **2.** city in S Spain: pop. 164,000

gran·a·ry (gran′ər ē, grā′nər ē) *n., pl.* **-ries** [< L. < *granum,* grain] **1.** a building for storing threshed grain **2.** a region producing much grain

grand (grand) *adj.* [OFr. < L. *grandis,* large] **1.** higher in rank or status than others with the same title **2.** most important; main *[the grand* ballroom*]* **3.** imposing in size, beauty, and extent **4.** marked by splendor and display **5.** distinguished; illustrious **6.** self-important; pretentious **7.** lofty and dignified, as in style **8.** overall *[the grand* total*]* **9.** [Colloq.] excellent, delightful, etc. *—n.* **1.** a grand piano **2.** [Slang] a thousand dollars **—grand′ly** *adv.* **—grand′ness** *n.*

grand- *a combining form meaning* of the generation older (or younger) than *[grandfather, grandson]*

gran·dam (gran′dam, -dəm) *n.* [< Anglo-Fr.: see GRAND & DAME] [Archaic] **1.** a grandmother **2.** an old woman Also sp. **gran′dame**

Grand Army of the Republic an association (1866–1949) of Union veterans of the Civil War

grand·aunt (grand′ant′) *n. same as* GREAT-AUNT

Grand Banks (or **Bank**) large shoal in the Atlantic, southeast of Newfoundland: noted fishing grounds

Grand Canyon deep gorge of the Colorado River, in NW Ariz.: over 200 mi. long; 1 mi. deep

grand·child (gran′chīld′) *n., pl.* **-chil′dren** a child of one's son or daughter

Grand Cou·lee (kōō′lē) dam on the Columbia River, NE Wash.: 500 ft. high

grand·dad, grand-dad (gran′dad′) *n.* [Colloq.] grandfather

grand·daugh·ter (-dôt′ər) *n.* a daughter of one's son or daughter

grand duchess 1. the wife or widow of a grand duke **2.** a woman who has the rank of a grand duke and rules a grand duchy **3.** in czarist Russia, a royal princess

grand duchy the territory or a country ruled by a grand duke or a grand duchess

grand duke 1. the sovereign ruler of a grand duchy, ranking just below a king **2.** in czarist Russia, a royal prince

grande dame (gränd däm) [Fr., great lady] a woman, esp. an older one, of great dignity or prestige

gran·dee (gran dē′) *n.* [Sp. & Port. *grande:* see GRAND] **1.** a Spanish or Portuguese nobleman of the highest rank **2.** a man of high rank

gran·deur (gran′jər, -joor) *n.* [Fr. < *grand:* see GRAND] **1.** splendor; magnificence **2.** moral and intellectual greatness; nobility

grand·fa·ther (gran′fä′*th*ər, grand′-) ***n.*** **1.** the father of one's father or mother **2.** a forefather
grand·fa·ther·ly (-lē) ***adj.*** **1.** of a grandfather **2.** having the conventional characteristics of a grandfather; kindly, indulgent, etc.
gran·dil·o·quent (gran dil′ə kwənt) ***adj.*** [< L. < *grandis,* grand + *loqui,* to speak] using high-flown, pompous, bombastic words and expressions —**gran·dil′o·quence** ***n.*** —**gran·dil′o·quent·ly** ***adv.***
gran·di·ose (gran′dē ōs′) ***adj.*** [Fr. < It. < L. *grandis,* great] **1.** having grandeur; imposing; impressive **2.** pompous and showy —**gran′di·ose′ly** ***adv.*** —**gran′di·os′i·ty** (-äs′ə tē) ***n.***
grand jury a jury that investigates accusations against persons charged with crime and indicts them for trial if there is sufficient evidence
Grand Lama *same as* DALAI LAMA
grand larceny *see* LARCENY
grand·ma (gran′mä, gra′mä) ***n.*** [Colloq.] grandmother
grand·moth·er (gran′mu*th*′ər, grand′-, gra′-) ***n.*** **1.** the mother of one's father or mother **2.** a female ancestor; ancestress
grand·moth·er·ly (-lē) ***adj.*** **1.** of a grandmother **2.** having the conventional characteristics of a grandmother; kindly, indulgent, etc.
grand·neph·ew (gran′nef′yo͞o, grand′-; *chiefly Brit.* -nev′yo͞o) ***n.*** the grandson of one's brother or sister
grand·niece (-nēs′) ***n.*** the granddaughter of one's brother or sister
grand opera opera, generally on a serious theme, in which the whole text is set to music
grand·pa (gran′pä, grand′-, gram′-) ***n.*** [Colloq.] grandfather
grand·par·ent (-per′ənt) ***n.*** a grandfather or grandmother
grand piano a large piano with strings set horizontally in a harp-shaped case
Grand Prairie city in NE Tex.: suburb of Dallas: pop. 71,000
Grand Rapids [after the *rapids* on the *Grand* River] city in SW Mich.: pop. 182,000 (met. area 601,000)
grand·sire (gran′sīr′, grand′-) ***n.*** [Archaic] **1.** a grandfather **2.** a male ancestor **3.** an old man
grand slam **1.** *Baseball* (designating) a home run hit when the bases are loaded: also **grand′-slam′mer** ***n.*** **2.** *Bridge* the winning of all the tricks in a deal
grand·son (gran′sun′, grand′-) ***n.*** a son of one's son or daughter
grand·stand (-stand′) ***n.*** the main seating structure for spectators at a sporting event, etc. —***vi.*** [Colloq.] to make an unnecessarily showy play (**grandstand play**), as in baseball, to get applause
grand tour a tour of continental Europe
grand·un·cle (grand′uŋ′k'l) ***n.*** *same as* GREAT-UNCLE
grange (grānj) ***n.*** [< Anglo-Fr. < ML. *granica* < L. *granum,* grain] **1.** a farm with its dwelling house, barns, etc. **2.** **[G-]** *a)* the Patrons of Husbandry, an association of farmers organized in the U.S. in 1867 for mutual welfare and advancement *b)* any of its local lodges
grang·er (-ər) ***n.*** **1.** a farmer **2.** **[G-]** a member of the Grange —**grang′er·ism** ***n.***
gran·ite (gran′it) ***n.*** [< It. *granito,* grained, ult. < L. *granum,* grain] a very hard, crystalline, plutonic rock consisting chiefly of feldspar and quartz —**gra·nit·ic** (grə nit′ik, gra-) ***adj.***
gran·ite·ware (-wer′) ***n.*** a variety of ironware coated with a hard, grained enamel
gran·ny, gran·nie (gran′ē) ***n.,*** *pl.* **-nies** [Colloq.] **1.** a grandmother **2.** an old woman **3.** a fussy, exacting person **4.** *same as* GRANNY KNOT
granny knot a knot like a square knot but with the ends crossed the wrong way, forming an awkward, insecure knot: also **granny's knot**
grant (grant) ***vt.*** [< OFr. *craanter,* to promise, ult. < L. prp. of *credere,* to believe] **1.** to give (what is requested, as permission, etc.); assent to **2.** *a)* to give formally or according to legal procedure *b)* to transfer (property) by a deed **3.** to admit as true without proof; concede —***n.*** **1.** a granting **2.** something granted, as property, a right, money, etc. —**take for granted** to accept as a matter of course —**grant′a·ble** ***adj.*** —**grant′er,** *Law* **grant′or** ***n.***
Grant (grant), Ulysses **Simp·son** (simp′sən) (born *Hiram Ulysses Grant*) 1822–85; 18th president of the U.S. (1869–77); commander of Union forces in the Civil War
grant·ee (grant ē′) ***n.*** *Law* a person to whom a grant is made
grant-in-aid (grant′in ād′) ***n.,*** *pl.* **grants′-in-aid′** a grant of funds, as by a foundation, to support a specific program or project
gran·u·lar (gran′yə lər) ***adj.*** **1.** containing or consisting of grains or granules **2.** like grains or granules **3.** having a grainy surface —**gran′u·lar′i·ty** (-ler′ə tē) ***n.*** —**gran′u·lar·ly** ***adv.***
gran·u·late (-lāt′) ***vt., vi.*** **-lat′ed, -lat′ing** **1.** to form into grains or granules **2.** to make or become rough on the surface by the development of granules —**gran′u·la′tion** ***n.*** —**gran′u·la′tive** ***adj.*** —**gran′u·la′tor, gran′u·lat′er** ***n.***
gran·ule (gran′yo͞ol) ***n.*** [< LL. *granulum,* dim. of L. *granum,* a grain] **1.** a small grain **2.** a small, grainlike particle or spot
grape (grāp) ***n.*** [< OFr. *grape,* bunch of grapes < *graper,* to gather with a hook < Frank. *krappo,* hook] **1.** a small, round, smooth-skinned, juicy berry, growing in clusters on woody vines and eaten raw, used to make wine or dried to make raisins **2.** a grapevine **3.** a dark purplish red **4.** *same as* GRAPESHOT
grape·fruit (-fro͞ot′) ***n.*** **1.** a large, round, edible citrus fruit with a pale-yellow rind and a somewhat sour, juicy pulp **2.** the tree it grows on
grape·shot (-shät′) ***n.*** a cluster of small iron balls formerly fired as a cannon charge
grape sugar *same as* DEXTROSE
grape·vine (-vīn′) ***n.*** **1.** a woody vine bearing grapes **2.** a secret means of spreading information: in full, **grapevine telegraph** **3.** a rumor
graph (graf) ***n.*** [short for *graphic formula*] **1.** a diagram, or a visual representation, as a broken line, that shows the relationship between certain sets of numbers **2.** *Math. a)* a picture showing the values taken on by a function *b)* a diagram consisting of nodes and links and representing logical relationships or sequences of events —***vt.*** to represent by a graph

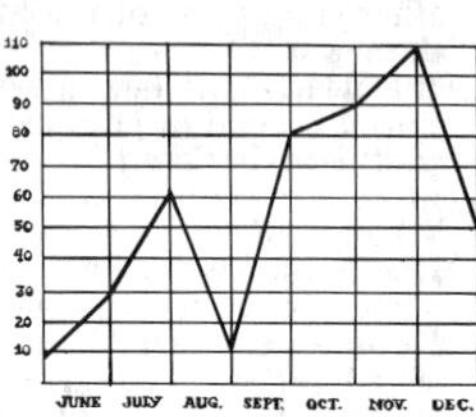

GRAPH

-graph (graf) [Gr. *-graphos* < *graphein,* to write] *a combining form meaning:* **1.** something that writes or records *[telegraph]* **2.** something written *[monograph]*
-gra·pher (grə fər) *a combining form meaning* a person who writes, records, makes copies, etc. *[telegrapher, stenographer]*
graph·ic (graf′ik) ***adj.*** [< L. < Gr. *graphikos* < *graphein,* to write] **1.** described in realistic detail; vivid **2.** of the GRAPHIC ARTS **3.** *a)* of or expressed in handwriting *b)* written or inscribed **4.** shown by graphs or diagrams Also **graph′i·cal** —**graph′i·cal·ly** ***adv.*** —**graph′ic·ness** ***n.***
-graph·ic (graf′ik) *a combining form used to form adjectives corresponding to nouns ending in* -GRAPH: also **-graph′i·cal**
graphic arts **1.** any form of visual artistic representation, esp. painting, drawing, etc. **2.** those arts in which impressions are printed from various kinds of blocks, plates, etc., as etching, lithography, offset, etc.
graph·ite (graf′īt) ***n.*** [G. *graphit* < Gr. *graphein,* to write] a soft, black, lustrous form of carbon found in nature and used for lead in pencils, for lubricants, electrodes, etc. —**gra·phit·ic** (gra fit′ik) ***adj.***
graph·ol·o·gy (gra fäl′ə jē) ***n.*** [< Fr. < Gr. *graphein,* to write + -LOGY] the study of handwriting, esp. as a clue to character, aptitudes, etc. —**graph·ol′o·gist** ***n.***
graph paper paper with small ruled squares on which to make graphs, diagrams, etc.
-gra·phy (grə fē) [< L. < Gr. < *graphein,* to write] *a combining form meaning:* **1.** a process or method of writing, or graphically representing *[lithography]* **2.** a descriptive science *[geography]*
grap·nel (grap′n'l) ***n.*** [< OFr. *grapil* < Pr. < *grapa* < Frank. *krappo:* see GRAPE] **1.** a small anchor with several flukes **2.** an iron bar with claws at one end for grasping and holding things
grap·ple (grap′'l) ***n.*** [OFr. *grapil:* see prec.] **1.** *same as* GRAPNEL (sense 2) **2.** a device consisting of two or more hinged, movable iron prongs for grasping and moving heavy objects **3.** a coming to grips —***vt.*** **grap′pled, grap′pling** to grip and hold; seize —***vi.*** **1.** to use a grapnel (sense 2) **2.** to struggle in hand-to-hand combat **3.** to struggle or try to cope (*with*) —**grap′pler** ***n.***

GRAPNEL

grappling iron (or **hook**) *same as* GRAPNEL (sense 2): also **grap′pling** ***n.***
grap·y (grā′pē) ***adj.*** of or like grapes
grasp (grasp) ***vt.*** [ME. *graspen,* prob. < MLowG.] **1.** to take hold of firmly as with the hand; grip **2.** to take hold of eagerly; seize **3.** to understand; comprehend —***vi.*** **1.** to try to seize (with *at*) **2.** to accept eagerly (with *at*) —***n.*** **1.** the act of grasping **2.** control; possession **3.** the power to hold or seize **4.** comprehension —**grasp′a·ble** ***adj.*** —**grasp′er** ***n.***
grasp·ing (-iŋ) ***adj.*** **1.** that grasps **2.** eager for gain; avaricious —**grasp′ing·ly** ***adv.***

grass (gras) ***n.*** [OE. *gærs, græs*] **1.** any of a family of plants with long, narrow leaves, jointed stems, and seedlike fruit, as wheat, rye, oats, sugar cane, etc. **2.** any of various green plants with long, narrow leaves that are eaten by grazing animals **3.** ground covered with grass; pasture land or lawn **4.** [Slang] marijuana —***vt.*** **1.** to put (animals) out to pasture or graze **2.** to grow grass over **3.** to lay (textiles, etc.) on the grass for bleaching —***vi.*** to become covered with grass —**grass′like′** ***adj.***

grass·hop·per (-häp′ər) ***n.*** **1.** any of a group of plant-eating insects with two pairs of wings and powerful hind legs adapted for jumping **2.** *Mil. Slang* a small, light airplane for scouting, etc.

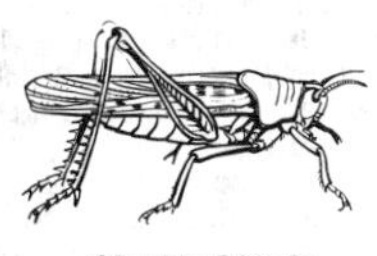

GRASSHOPPER (1 ¼ in. long)

grass·land (-land′) ***n.*** **1.** land with grass growing on it, used for grazing; pasture land **2.** prairie

grass roots [Colloq.] **1.** the common people, thought of in relation to their attitudes on political issues **2.** the basic source or support, as of a movement —**grass′-roots′** ***adj.***

grass widow a woman divorced or otherwise separated from her husband —**grass widower**

grass·y (-ē) ***adj.*** **grass′i·er, grass′i·est** **1.** of or consisting of grass **2.** covered with grass **3.** green like growing grass —**grass′i·ness** ***n.***

grate[1] (grāt) ***vt.*** **grat′ed, grat′ing** [< OFr. *grater* < Frank.] **1.** to grind into particles by scraping **2.** to rub against (an object) with a harsh, scraping sound **3.** to grind (the teeth) together with a rasping sound **4.** to irritate; annoy —***vi.*** **1.** to grind or rub with a rasping sound **2.** to make a harsh or rasping sound **3.** to cause irritation or annoyance —**grat′er** ***n.***

grate[2] (grāt) ***n.*** [< ML. < L. *cratis*, a hurdle] **1.** *same as* GRATING[1] **2.** a frame of metal bars for holding fuel in a fireplace, etc. **3.** a fireplace —***vt.*** **grat′ed, grat′ing** to provide with a grate or grates

grate·ful (grāt′fəl) ***adj.*** [obs. *grate* (< L. *gratus*), pleasing + -FUL] **1.** feeling or expressing gratitude; thankful **2.** causing gratitude; welcome —**grate′ful·ly** ***adv.*** —**grate′ful·ness** ***n.***

grat·i·fy (grat′ə fī′) ***vt.*** **-fied′, -fy′ing** [< Fr. < L. *gratificare* < *gratus*, pleasing + *-ficare*, -FY] **1.** to give pleasure or satisfaction to **2.** to indulge; humor —**grat′i·fi·ca′tion** ***n.*** —**grat′i·fi′er** ***n.***

grat·ing[1] (grāt′iŋ) ***n.*** a framework of parallel or latticed bars set in a window, door, etc.

grat·ing[2] (grāt′iŋ) ***adj.*** **1.** harsh and rasping **2.** irritating or annoying —**grat′ing·ly** ***adv.***

gra·tis (grat′is, grāt′-) ***adv., adj.*** [L. < *gratia*, a favor] without charge or payment; free

grat·i·tude (grat′ə to͞od′, -tyo͞od′) ***n.*** [Fr. < ML. < L. *gratus*, thankful] a feeling of thankful appreciation for favors received; thankfulness

gra·tu·i·tous (grə to͞o′ə təs, -tyo͞o′-) ***adj.*** [< L. < *gratus*, pleasing] **1.** *a)* given or received without charge; free *b)* granted without obligation **2.** without cause or justification; uncalled-for —**gra·tu′i·tous·ly** ***adv.*** —**gra·tu′i·tous·ness** ***n.***

gra·tu·i·ty (grə to͞o′ə tē, -tyo͞o′-) ***n.***, *pl.* **-ties** [see prec.] a gift of money, etc., esp. one given for a service rendered; tip

gra·va·men (grə vā′mən) ***n.***, *pl.* **-mens, gra·vam′i·na** (-vam′ə nə) [LL. < L. < *gravis*, heavy] **1.** a grievance **2.** *Law* the gist of an accusation

grave[1] (grāv) ***adj.*** [Fr. < L. *gravis*, heavy] **1.** important; weighty **2.** threatening; ominous *[a grave illness]* **3.** solemn or sedate **4.** somber; dull **5.** low or deep in pitch —***n.*** *same as* GRAVE ACCENT —**grave′ly** ***adv.*** —**grave′ness** ***n.***

grave[2] (grāv) ***n.*** [OE. *græf* < *grafan*, to dig] **1.** *a)* a hole in the ground in which to bury a dead body *b)* any place of burial; tomb **2.** final end or death —***vt.*** **graved, grav′en** or **graved, grav′ing** **1.** to carve out; sculpture **2.** [Archaic] to engrave; incise **3.** to impress or fix sharply and clearly —**grav′er** ***n.***

grave accent a mark (`) used to indicate: **1.** in French, the quality of an open *e* (è), as in *chère* **2.** full pronunciation of a syllable normally elided, as in *lovèd* **3.** secondary stress, as in *týpewrìter*

grave·clothes (grāv′klōz′, -klōthz′) ***n.pl.*** the clothes in which a dead body is buried

grave·dig·ger (-dig′ər) ***n.*** a person whose work is digging graves

grav·el (grav′'l) ***n.*** [< OFr. dim. of *grave*, coarse sand, beach] **1.** a loose mixture of pebbles and rock fragments coarser than sand **2.** *Med.* a deposit of small concretions in the kidneys, gallbladder, or urinary bladder —***vt.*** **-eled** or **-elled, -el·ing** or **-el·ling** **1.** to cover (a walk, etc.) with gravel **2.** to perplex **3.** [Colloq.] to annoy

grav·el·ly (-ē) ***adj.*** **1.** full of, like, or consisting of gravel **2.** sounding harsh *[a gravelly voice]*

grav·en (grāv′'n) *alt. pp. of* GRAVE[2]

graven image an idol made from stone, wood, etc.

grave·side (grāv′sīd′) ***n.*** the area alongside a grave —***adj.*** being, or taking place, beside a grave

grave·stone (-stōn′) ***n.*** an engraved stone marking a grave; tombstone

grave·yard (-yärd′) ***n.*** a burial ground; cemetery

graveyard shift [Colloq.] a work shift that starts during the night, usually at midnight

grav·i·tate (grav′ə tāt′) ***vi.*** **-tat′ed, -tat′ing** **1.** to move or tend to move in accordance with the force of gravity **2.** to be attracted or tend to move (*toward*) —**grav′i·ta′tive** ***adj.***

grav·i·ta·tion (grav′ə tā′shən) ***n.*** **1.** the act, process, or fact of gravitating **2.** *Physics* *a)* the force by which every mass or particle of matter attracts and is attracted by every other mass or particle of matter *b)* the tendency of these masses or particles to move toward each other —**grav′i·ta′tion·al** ***adj.*** —**grav′i·ta′tion·al·ly** ***adv.***

grav·i·ty (grav′ə tē) ***n.***, *pl.* **-ties** [< L. < *gravis*, heavy] **1.** the state or condition of being grave; esp., *a)* solemnity or sedateness; earnestness *b)* danger or threat *c)* seriousness **2.** weight; heaviness *[specific gravity]* **3.** lowness of musical pitch **4.** gravitation; esp., the force that tends to draw all bodies in the earth's sphere toward the center of the earth

gra·vure (grə vyoor′, grā′vyoor) ***n.*** [Fr. < *graver*, to carve < Frank.] **1.** *a)* any process that makes or uses intaglio printing plates *b)* a plate or print so made **2.** *clipped form of:* *a)* PHOTOGRAVURE *b)* ROTOGRAVURE

gra·vy (grā′vē) ***n.***, *pl.* **-vies** [? a misreading of OFr. *grané* < ? *grain*, cooking ingredients] **1.** the juice given off by meat in cooking **2.** a sauce made with this juice and flour, seasoning, etc. **3.** [Slang] *a)* money easily obtained *b)* any extra benefit

gravy boat a boat-shaped dish for serving gravy

gray (grā) ***adj.*** [< OE. *græg*] **1.** of the color gray **2.** *a)* darkish; dull *b)* dreary; dismal **3.** *a)* having hair that is gray *b)* old **4.** dressed in gray **5.** designating a vague, intermediate area, as between morality and immorality —***n.*** **1.** a color made by mixing black and white **2.** a gray animal or thing **3.** [*often* **G-**] a person dressed in a gray uniform —***vt., vi.*** to make or become gray —**gray′ly** ***adv.*** —**gray′ness** ***n.***

Gray (grā), **Thomas** 1716–71; Eng. poet

gray·beard (-bird′) ***n.*** an old man

gray·hound (-hound′) ***n.*** *same as* GREYHOUND

gray·ish (-ish) ***adj.*** somewhat gray

gray·lag (-lag′) ***n.*** [short for *gray lag goose:* from its color and its late migration] the European wild gray goose

gray·ling (-liŋ) ***n.***, *pl.* **-ling, -lings:** see PLURAL, II, D, 2 [GRAY + -LING[1]: from the color] **1.** a freshwater game fish related to the salmon **2.** any of several varieties of gray or brown butterfly

gray matter **1.** grayish nerve tissue of the brain and spinal cord, consisting of nerve cells and some nerve fibers **2.** [Colloq.] intelligence

gray squirrel a large, gray squirrel with a bushy tail, native to E N. America

gray wolf a large, gray wolf that hunts in packs and was formerly common in the northern part of the Northern Hemisphere

Graz (gräts) city in SE Austria: pop. 237,000

graze[1] (grāz) ***vt.*** **grazed, graz′ing** [OE. *grasian* < *græs*, grass] **1.** to feed on (growing grass, herbage, etc.) **2.** to put livestock to feed on (a pasture, etc.) **3.** to cause (livestock) to graze **4.** to be pasture for —***vi.*** to feed on growing grass, etc. —**graz′er** ***n.***

graze[2] (grāz) ***vt.*** **grazed, graz′ing** [prob. < prec. in sense "to come close to the grass"] **1.** to touch or rub lightly in passing **2.** to scrape or scratch in passing *[the shot grazed him]* —***vi.*** to scrape, touch, or rub lightly against something in passing —***n.*** a grazing, or a scratch or scrape caused by it

gra·zier (grā′zhər; *Brit.* -zyər) ***n.*** [Chiefly Brit.] a person who grazes beef cattle for sale

graz·ing (grā′ziŋ) ***n.*** land to graze on; pasture

Gr. Brit., Gr. Br. Great Britain

grease (grēs; *for v. also* grēz) ***n.*** [< OFr., ult. < L. *crassus*, fat] **1.** melted animal fat **2.** any thick, oily substance or lubricant —***vt.*** **greased, greas′ing** **1.** to smear or lubricate with grease **2.** to bribe or tip: chiefly in **grease the palm** (or **hand**) **of** —**greas′er** ***n.***

grease·paint (-pānt′) ***n.*** a mixture of grease and coloring matter used by performers in making up

grease·wood (-wood′) *n.* a thorny plant of desert regions in the W U.S., with fleshy leaves

greas·y (grē′sē, -zē) *adj.* **greas′i·er, greas′i·est** **1.** smeared or soiled with grease **2.** containing grease, esp. much grease **3.** like grease; oily; slippery —**greas′i·ly** *adv.* —**greas′i·ness** *n.*

great (grāt) *adj.* [OE. *great*] **1.** of much more than ordinary size, extent, number, etc. *[*the *Great* Lakes, a *great* company*]* **2.** much above the ordinary or average in some quality or degree; esp., *a)* existing in a high degree; intense *[great* pain*]* *b)* very much of a *[*a *great* reader*]* *c)* eminent; distinguished; superior *[*a *great* playwright*]* *d)* very impressive or imposing *[great* ceremony*]* *e)* having or showing nobility of mind, purpose, etc. *[*a *great* man*]* **3.** of most importance; main; chief *[*the *great* seal*]* **4.** designating a relationship one generation removed *[great-*grandmother*]* **5.** [Colloq.] clever; skillful *[great* at tennis*]* **6.** [Colloq.] excellent, splendid, fine, etc. —*adv.* [Colloq.] very well —*n.* a great or distinguished person: *usually used in pl.* —**great on** [Colloq.] enthusiastic about —**great′ly** *adv.* —**great′ness** *n.*

great-aunt (-ant′) *n.* a sister of any of one's grandparents; grandaunt

Great Barrier Reef coral reef off the NE coast of Queensland, Australia

Great Bear the constellation URSA MAJOR

Great Bear Lake lake in Northwest Territories, NW Canada

Great Britain **1.** principal island of the United Kingdom, including England, Scotland, & Wales **2.** popularly, the United Kingdom

great calorie *same as* CALORIE (sense 2)

great circle any circle described on the surface of the earth or other sphere by a plane which passes through the center of the sphere: the shortest course between any two points on the earth's surface lies along a great circle passing through these points

great·coat (grāt′kōt′) *n.* a heavy overcoat

Great Dane any of a breed of large, powerful dog with short, smooth hair

Great Divide a principal mountain watershed; specif., the main ridge of the Rocky Mountains

great·en (grāt′'n) *vt., vi.* to make or become great or greater

Greater Antilles group of islands in the West Indies, made up of the N & W Antilles, including Cuba, Jamaica, Hispaniola, & Puerto Rico

Great Falls city in WC Mont., on the Missouri River: pop. 57,000

great-grand·child (grāt′gran′chīld′) *n., pl.* **-chil′dren** a child of any of one's grandchildren —**great′-grand′daugh′-ter** *n.* —**great′-grand′son′** *n.*

great-grand·par·ent (-gran′per′ənt) *n.* a parent of any of one's grandparents —**great′-grand′fa′ther** *n.* —**great′-grand′moth′er** *n.*

great-great- *a combining form used with nouns of relationship to indicate* two degrees of removal *[great-great-*grandparent*]*

great gross twelve gross

great·heart·ed (-här′tid) *adj.* **1.** brave; fearless; courageous **2.** generous; unselfish

Great Lakes chain of freshwater lakes in EC N. America; Lakes Superior, Michigan, Huron, Erie, & Ontario

Great Mogul **1.** the title of the ruler of the Mongol empire in India in the 16th cent. **2.** [**g- m-**] a person of importance

great-neph·ew (-nef′yōō; *chiefly Brit.* -nev′-) *n.* a grandson of one's brother or sister; grandnephew —**great′-niece′** (-nēs′) *n.fem.*

Great Plains sloping region of valleys & plains in WC N. America, east of the base of the Rockies

Great Salt Lake shallow saltwater lake in NW Utah

great seal the chief seal of a nation, state, etc., with which official papers are stamped

Great Slave Lake lake in Northwest Territories, NW Canada

Great Smoky Mountains mountain range of the Appalachians, along the Tenn.–N.C. border

great-un·cle (-uŋ′k'l) *n.* a brother of any of one's grandparents; granduncle

Great Wall of China stone & earth wall across N China: built (3d cent. B.C.) as a defense against invaders

greaves (grēvz) *n.pl.* [< OFr. pl. of *greve,* shin] armor for the legs from the ankle to the knee

grebe (grēb) *n., pl.* **grebes, grebe:** see PLURAL, II, D, 1 [Fr. *grèbe*] any of a family of diving and swimming birds related to the loons, with partially webbed feet, and legs set far back on the body

Gre·cian (grē′shən) *adj. same as* GREEK (sense 1) —*n.* a Greek

Gre·cism (grē′siz'm) *n.* **1.** an idiom of the Greek language **2.** the spirit of Greek culture **3.** imitation of Greek style in the arts

Gre·cize (grē′sīz) *vt.* **-cized, -ciz·ing** to make Greek; give a Greek form to —*vi.* to imitate the Greeks in language, manner, etc.

Greco, El *see* EL GRECO

Gre·co- *a combining form meaning:* **1.** Greek or Greeks **2.** Greek and or Greece and

Gre·co-Ro·man (grē′kō rō′mən) *adj.* of or influenced by both Greece and Rome

Greece (grēs) country in the S Balkan Peninsula, including islands in the Aegean, Ionian, & Mediterranean seas: 50,534 sq. mi.; pop. 8,835,000; cap. Athens: in ancient times, the region was comprised of many small monarchies & republics

greed (grēd) *n.* [back-formation < ff.] excessive desire for getting or having, esp. wealth; avarice

greed·y (-ē) *adj.* **greed′i·er, greed′i·est** [OE. *grædig*] **1.** wanting or taking all that one can get; desiring more than one needs or deserves; avaricious **2.** having too strong a desire for food and drink; gluttonous **3.** intensely eager —**greed′i·ly** *adv.* —**greed′i·ness** *n.*

Greek (grēk) *n.* **1.** a native or inhabitant of ancient or modern Greece **2.** the branch of the Indo-European language family consisting of the dialects of Greece, ancient or modern —*adj.* **1.** of ancient or modern Greece, its people, language, or culture **2.** designating, of, or using the rite of the Orthodox Eastern Church —**be Greek to one** to be incomprehensible to one

Greek fire an incendiary material used in ancient warfare, described as able to burn in water

Greek (Orthodox) Church **1.** the established church of Greece, an autonomous part of the Orthodox Eastern Church **2.** *popular name for* ORTHODOX EASTERN CHURCH Also **Greek Church**

Gree·ley (grē′lē), **Horace** 1811–72; U.S. journalist & political leader

green (grēn) *adj.* [OE. *grene*] **1.** of the color that is characteristic of growing grass **2.** overspread with green foliage *[*a *green* field*]* **3.** keeping the green grass of summer; snowless *[*a *green* December*]* **4.** sickly or bilious, as from illness, fear, etc. **5.** not mature; unripe **6.** not trained; inexperienced **7.** easily led or deceived; naive **8.** not dried, seasoned, or cured **9.** fresh; new **10.** flourishing; vigorous **11.** [Colloq.] jealous —*n.* **1.** the color of growing grass; color between blue and yellow in the spectrum **2.** any green pigment or dye **3.** anything colored green, as clothing **4.** [*pl.*] green leaves, branches, etc., used for ornamentation **5.** [*pl.*] green leafy plants or vegetables, as spinach, lettuce, etc. **6.** an area of smooth turf set aside for special purposes *[*a village *green]* **7.** *Golf* a putting green —*vt., vi.* to make or become green —**green with envy** very envious —**the Green** Ireland's national color —**green′ish** *adj.* —**green′ly** *adv.* —**green′ness** *n.*

green·back (-bak′) *n.* any piece of U.S. paper money printed in green ink on the back

Green Bay [transl. of Fr. *Baie Verte,* Green Bay, arm of Lake Michigan on which city is located] city in NE Wis.: pop. 88,000

green bean the edible, immature green pod of the kidney bean

green·bri·er (-brī′ər) *n. same as* CAT BRIER

green corn young ears of sweet corn, in the milky stage, roasted or boiled for eating

green·er·y (grēn′ər ē) *n., pl.* **-er·ies** **1.** green vegetation; verdure **2.** greens: see GREEN (*n.* 4) **3.** a greenhouse

green-eyed (-īd′) *adj.* **1.** having green eyes **2.** very jealous

green·gage (-gāj′) *n.* [after Sir William *Gage,* who introduced it into England, c. 1725] a large plum with golden-green skin and flesh

green·gro·cer (-grō′sər) *n.* [Brit.] a retail dealer in fresh vegetables and fruit —**green′gro′cer·y** *n.*

green·horn (-hôrn′) *n.* [orig. with reference to a young animal with immature horns] an inexperienced person; beginner; novice

green·house (-hous′) *n.* a building made mainly of glass, with heat and humidity regulated for growing plants; hothouse

green·ing (-iŋ) *n.* any of various apples having greenish-yellow skins when ripe

Green·land (grēn′lənd) [< ON.: orig. so called to attract settlers] self-governing island northeast of N. America, under Danish protection: the world's largest island: 840,000 sq. mi.; pop. 40,000

green light [after the green ("go") signal of a traffic light] [Colloq.] permission or authorization to proceed with some undertaking: usually in **give** (or **get**) **the green light**

Green Mountains range of the Appalachians, extending the length of Vermont

green onion an immature onion with a long stalk and green leaves, eaten raw; scallion

green pepper the green, immature fruit of the sweet red pepper, eaten as a vegetable

green·room (-rōōm′, -room′) *n.* a waiting room in some theaters, for use by performers when they are offstage

Greens·bor·o (grēnz′bur′ō) [after N. *Greene,* Am. general in Revolutionary War] city in north central N.C.: pop. 156,000
green-stick fracture (grēn′stik′) a partial fracture in which the bone is broken on only one side
green·sward (-swôrd′) *n.* green, grassy ground
green tea tea prepared from leaves not fermented before drying
green turtle a large, edible sea turtle with an olive-colored shell
Green·ville (grēn′vil) [see GREENSBORO] city in NW S.C.: pop. 58,000
Green·wich (mean) time (gren′ich; *chiefly Brit.* grin′ij) mean solar time of the prime meridian, which passes through Greenwich, a borough of London: used as the basis for standard time
Green·wich Village (gren′ich) section of New York City: noted as a center for artists, writers, etc.
green·wood (grēn′wood′) *n.* a forest in leaf
greet (grēt) *vt.* [OE. *gretan*] **1.** to address with expressions of friendliness, respect, etc., as in meeting or by letter; hail; welcome **2.** to meet, receive, or acknowledge (a person, event, etc.) in a specified way [he was *greeted* by a rifle shot] **3.** to come or appear to; meet [a roaring sound *greeted* his ears] —**greet′er** *n.*
greet·ing (grēt′iŋ) *n.* **1.** the act or words of a person who greets; salutation; welcome **2.** [*often pl.*] a message of regards from someone absent
greeting card a decorated card bearing a greeting for some occasion, as a birthday
gre·gar·i·ous (grə ger′ē əs) *adj.* [< L. < *grex* (gen. *gregis*), a flock] **1.** living in herds or flocks **2.** fond of the company of others; sociable **3.** having to do with a herd, flock, or crowd **4.** *Bot.* growing in clusters —**gre·gar′i·ous·ly** *adv.* —**gre·gar′i·ous·ness** *n.*
Gre·go·ri·an (grə gôr′ē ən) *adj.* of or relating to Pope Gregory I or Pope Gregory XIII
Gregorian calendar a corrected form of the Julian calendar, introduced by Pope Gregory XIII in 1582 and now used in most countries of the world
Gregorian chant the ritual plainsong of the Roman Catholic Church, introduced under Pope Gregory I: it is unaccompanied and not divided into measures
Greg·o·ry (greg′ər ē) [< LL. < Gr. *Grēgorios,* lit., vigilant, hence, watchman] **1.** a masculine name: dim. *Greg* **2.** **Gregory I, Saint** 540?–604 A.D.; Pope (590–604): called *the Great* **3.** **Gregory XIII** 1502–85; Pope (1572–85): see GREGORIAN CALENDAR
greige (grāzh) *n.* [Fr. *grège,* raw (silk)] a color blending gray and beige —*adj.* grayish-beige
grem·lin (grem′lən) *n.* [prob. < Dan. hyp. *græmling,* imp, dim. of obs. *gram,* a devil] an imaginary small creature humorously blamed when things fail to work
Gre·na·da (grə nā′də) country consisting of the southernmost island of the Windward group of the West Indies, and a chain of nearby islands: 133 sq. mi.; pop. 95,000
gre·nade (grə nād′) *n.* [Fr. < OFr., pomegranate, ult. < L. *granatus,* having seeds < *granum,* a seed] **1.** a small bomb detonated by a fuse and thrown by hand or fired from a rifle **2.** a glass container thrown to break on impact and disperse chemicals inside: used to spread tear gas, etc.
gren·a·dier (gren′ə dir′) *n.* [Fr. < *grenade*] **1.** orig., an infantryman who threw grenades **2.** a member of a special regiment or corps, as the British Grenadier Guards
gren·a·dine¹ (gren′ə dēn′, gren′ə dēn′) *n.* [Fr. < *grenade,* pomegranate] a syrup made from pomegranate juice, used for flavoring drinks, etc.
gren·a·dine² (gren′ə dēn′, gren′ə dēn′) *n.* [Fr.] a thin, loosely woven cloth, used for dresses, etc.
Gre·no·ble (grə nō′b′l; *Fr.* grə nô′bl′) city in SE France, in the Alps: pop. 162,000
Gret·na Green (gret′nə) **1.** border village in S Scotland, where, formerly, many eloping English couples went to be married **2.** any similar village
grew (grōō) *pt. of* GROW
grey (grā) *adj., n., vt., vi. Brit. sp. of* GRAY
grey·hound (grā′hound′) *n.* [OE. *grighund*] any of a breed of tall, slender, swift hound with a narrow, pointed head and a smooth coat

GREYHOUND (28 in. high at shoulder)

grid (grid) *n.* [short for GRIDIRON] **1.** a framework of parallel bars; gridiron; grating **2.** a network of crossing parallel lines, as on graph paper **3.** a metallic plate in a storage cell for conducting the electric current **4.** an electrode, usually a wire spiral or mesh, for controlling the passage of electrons or ions in an electron tube —*adj.* [Slang] of football
grid·der (grid′ər) *n.* [< GRID, *adj.* & GRIDIRON] [Slang] a football player
grid·dle (grid′'l) *n.* [< Anglo-Fr. *gridil* < OFr. *graïl* < L. < *craticula,* gridiron < *cratis,* wickerwork] a flat, metal plate or pan for cooking pancakes, etc. —*vt.* **-dled, -dling** to cook on a griddle
grid·dle·cake (-kāk′) *n.* a thin, flat batter cake cooked on a griddle; pancake
grid·i·ron (grid′ī′ərn) *n.* [ME. *gredirne,* folk etym. on *irne* (see IRON) < *gredire,* var. of *gredil:* see GRIDDLE] **1.** a framework of metal bars or wires on which to broil meat or fish; grill **2.** any framework resembling a gridiron **3.** a football field
grief (grēf) *n.* [< OFr. < *grever:* see GRIEVE] **1.** intense emotional suffering caused by loss, disaster, etc.; acute sorrow; deep sadness **2.** a cause or the subject of such suffering —**come to grief** to fail or be ruined
grief-strick·en (-strik′'n) *adj.* stricken with grief; keenly distressed; sorrowful
Grieg (grēg; *Norw.* grig), **Ed·vard (Hagerup)** (ed′värd; *Norw.* ed′värt) 1843–1907; Norw. composer
griev·ance (grē′vəns) *n.* **1.** a circumstance thought to be unjust or injurious and ground for complaint or resentment **2.** complaint or resentment, or a statement expressing this, against a real or imagined wrong
grieve (grēv) *vt.* **grieved, griev′ing** [OFr. *grever* < L. *gravare,* to burden < *gravis,* heavy] to cause to feel grief; afflict with deep sorrow or distress —*vi.* to feel deep sorrow or distress; mourn; lament —**griev′er** *n.*
griev·ous (grē′vəs) *adj.* **1.** causing grief **2.** showing or full of grief **3.** causing suffering; severe **4.** deplorable; atrocious [a *grievous* crime] —**griev′ous·ly** *adv.* —**griev′ous·ness** *n.*
grif·fin (grif′ən) *n.* [< OFr. < OHG. or It. *grifo,* both < L. *gryphus* < Gr. < *grypos,* hooked] a mythical animal, part eagle and part lion: also sp. **griffon**
Grif·fith (grif′ith) [W. *Gruffydd*] **1.** a masculine name **2.** **D(avid) (Lewelyn) W(ark),** 1875–1948; U.S. motion-picture director
grift·er (grif′tər) *n.* [prob. altered < *grafter*] [Slang] a petty swindler, as an operator of a dishonest gambling device at a carnival —**grift** *vi., vt., n.*
grill¹ (gril) *n.* [Fr. *gril* < OFr. *graïl:* see GRIDDLE] **1.** a gridiron (sense 1) **2.** a large griddle **3.** grilled food **4.** *short for* GRILLROOM —*vt.* **1.** to cook on a grill **2.** to torture by applying heat **3.** to question relentlessly —*vi.* to be subjected to grilling —**grilled** *adj.* —**grill′er** *n.*
grill² (gril) *n. same as* GRILLE
grille (gril) *n.* [Fr. < OFr. *graïlle:* see GRIDDLE] an open grating of wrought iron, wood, etc., forming a screen to a door, window, or other opening, or used as a divider —**grilled** *adj.*
grill·room (gril′rōōm′) *n.* a restaurant that makes a specialty of grilled foods
grill·work (-wurk′) *n.* a grille, or something worked into the form of a grille
grilse (grils) *n., pl.* **grilse, grils′es:** see PLURAL, II, D, 2 [<? OFr. dim. of *gris,* gray] a young salmon on its first return from the sea to fresh water
grim (grim) *adj.* **grim′mer, grim′mest** [OE. *grimm*] **1.** fierce; cruel; savage **2.** hard and unyielding; relentless; stern **3.** appearing stern, forbidding, harsh, etc. **4.** repellent; uninviting; ghastly —**grim′ly** *adv.* —**grim′ness** *n.*
gri·mace (gri mās′, grim′əs) *n.* [Fr. < OFr. *grimuche,* prob. < Frank.] a distortion of the face, as in expressing pain, contempt, etc., or a wry look —*vi.* **-maced′, -mac′ing** to make grimaces —**gri·mac′er** *n.*
gri·mal·kin (gri mal′kin, -môl′-) *n.* [earlier *gray malkin* (cat)] **1.** a cat; esp., an old female cat **2.** a malicious old woman
grime (grīm) *n.* [prob. < Fl. *grijm*] sooty dirt rubbed into or covering a surface, as of the skin —*vt.* **grimed, grim′ing** to make very dirty or grimy
Grimm (grim), **Ja·kob (Ludwig Karl)** (yä′kôp), 1785–1863 & **Wil·helm (Karl)** (vil′helm), 1786–1859; Ger. brother philologists & collaborators in the collection of fairy tales
grim·y (grī′mē) *adj.* **grim′i·er, grim′i·est** covered with grime; very dirty —**grim′i·ly** *adv.* —**grim′i·ness** *n.*
grin (grin) *vi.* **grinned, grin′ning** [OE. *grennian*] **1.** to smile broadly **2.** to draw back the lips and show the teeth in pain, scorn, etc. —*vt.* to express by grinning —*n.* the act or look of one who grins —**grin′ner** *n.* —**grin′ning·ly** *adv.*
grind (grīnd) *vt.* **ground, grind′ing** [OE. *grindan*] **1.** to crush into bits or fine particles between two hard surfaces; pulverize **2.** to afflict with cruelty, hardship, etc.; oppress **3.** to sharpen, shape, or smooth by friction **4.** to press

down or rub together harshly or gratingly *[to grind one's teeth]* **5.** to operate by turning the crank of *[to grind a coffee mill]* **6.** to produce as by grinding —***vi.*** **1.** to perform the act of grinding something **2.** to undergo grinding **3.** to grate **4.** [Colloq.] to work or study hard and steadily —***n.*** **1.** a grinding **2.** the degree of fineness of something ground into particles **3.** long, difficult work or study **4.** [Colloq.] a student who studies very hard —**grind out** to produce by steady or laborious effort —**grind′ing·ly** ***adv.***

grind·er (grīn′dər) ***n.*** **1.** a person or thing that grinds; specif., *a)* any of various machines for crushing or sharpening *b)* a molar tooth *c)* [*pl.*] [Colloq.] the teeth **2.** *same as* HERO SANDWICH

grind·stone (grīnd′stōn′) ***n.*** a revolving stone disk for sharpening tools or shaping and polishing things —**keep** (or **have** or **put**) **one's nose to the grindstone** to work hard and steadily

grip (grip) ***n.*** [< OE. *gripa,* handful < *gripan,* to seize] **1.** a secure grasp; firm hold, as with the hand, teeth, etc. **2.** any special manner of clasping hands, as between members of a secret society **3.** the power of grasping firmly **4.** mental grasp **5.** firm control; mastery **6.** a mechanical contrivance for clutching or grasping **7.** the part by which something is grasped; handle **8.** a small traveling bag or satchel **9.** *Sports* the manner of holding a bat, golf club, etc. —***vt.*** **gripped** or **gript, grip′ping 1.** to take firmly and hold fast with the hand, teeth, etc. **2.** to give a grip (*n.* 2) to **3.** to fasten or join firmly (*to*) **4.** *a)* to get and hold the attention of *b)* to have a strong emotional impact on —***vi.*** to get a grip —**come to grips** to struggle or try to cope (*with*) —**grip′per** ***n.***

gripe (grīp) ***vt.*** **griped, grip′ing** [OE. *gripan,* to seize] **1.** formerly, *a)* to grasp; clutch *b)* to distress; afflict **2.** to cause sudden, sharp pain in the bowels of **3.** [Slang] to annoy; irritate —***vi.*** **1.** to feel sharp pains in the bowels **2.** [Slang] to complain —***n.*** **1.** distress; affliction **2.** a sudden, sharp pain in the bowels: *usually used in pl.* **3.** [Slang] a complaint **4.** [Archaic] *a)* a grasping *b)* control —**grip′er** ***n.***

grippe (grip) ***n.*** [Fr., lit., a seizure < *gripper* < Frank.] *earlier term for* INFLUENZA

gript (gript) *alt. pt. & pp. of* GRIP

Gri·sel·da (gri zel′də, -sel′-) *Medieval Tales* a heroine famous for her patience

gri·sette (gri zet′) ***n.*** [Fr., orig., gray woolen dress cloth < *gris,* gray] a French working girl

gris·ly (griz′lē) ***adj.*** **-li·er, -li·est** [OE. *grislic*] terrifying; ghastly —**gris′li·ness** ***n.***

grist (grist) ***n.*** [OE.] grain that is to be or has been ground; esp., a batch of such grain —**grist to** (or **for**) **one's mill** anything one can use profitably

gris·tle (gris′'l) ***n.*** [OE.] cartilage, now esp. as found in meat —**gris′tli·ness** ***n.*** —**gris·tly** (gris′lē) ***adj.***

grist·mill (grist′mil′) ***n.*** a mill for grinding grain, esp. for individual customers

grit (grit) ***n.*** [OE. *greot*] **1.** rough, hard particles of sand, stone, etc. **2.** a sandstone with sharp grains **3.** stubborn courage; pluck —***vt.*** **grit′ted, grit′ting** to grind (the teeth) in anger or determination —***vi.*** to make a grating sound

grits (grits) ***n.pl.*** [< OE. *grytte*] wheat or corn coarsely ground; esp., [South] fine hominy

grit·ty (grit′ē) ***adj.*** **-ti·er, -ti·est 1.** of, like, or containing grit; sandy **2.** brave; plucky —**grit′ti·ly** ***adv.*** —**grit′ti·ness** ***n.***

griz·zle (griz′'l) ***n.*** [< OFr. < *gris,* gray] **1.** [Archaic] gray hair **2.** gray —***vt., vi.*** **-zled, -zling** to make or become gray —***adj.*** [Archaic] gray

griz·zled (griz′'ld) ***adj.*** **1.** gray or streaked with gray **2.** having gray hair

griz·zly (-lē) ***adj.*** **-zli·er, -zli·est** grayish; grizzled —***n.,*** *pl.* **-zlies** *short for* GRIZZLY BEAR

grizzly bear a large, ferocious bear of western N. America, with brown, gray, or yellow fur

groan (grōn) ***vi.*** [OE. *granian*] **1.** to utter a deep sound expressing pain, distress, or disapproval **2.** to make a creaking sound, as from great strain **3.** to be so weighed down as to groan —***vt.*** to utter with a groan or groans —***n.*** a sound made in groaning —**groan′er** ***n.*** —**groan′ing·ly** ***adv.***

groat (grōt) ***n.*** [< MDu. or < MLowG. *grote*] **1.** an obsolete English silver coin worth fourpence **2.** a trifling sum

groats (grōts) ***n.pl.*** [< OE. *grotan,* pl.] any grain that is hulled, or hulled and coarsely cracked

gro·cer (grō′sər) ***n.*** [< OFr. *grossier* < *gros,* GROSS] a storekeeper who sells food and various household supplies

gro·cer·y (grō′sər ē) ***n.,*** *pl.* **-cer·ies 1.** a grocer's store **2.** [*pl.*] the food and supplies sold by a grocer

grog (gräg) ***n.*** [after *Old Grog,* nickname of E. Vernon (1684–1757), Brit. admiral] any alcoholic liquor, as rum, esp. when diluted with water

grog·gy (-ē) ***adj.*** **-gi·er, -gi·est** [< GROG + -Y[2]] **1.** orig., drunk; intoxicated **2.** shaky or dizzy —**grog′gi·ly** ***adv.*** —**grog′gi·ness** ***n.***

groin (groin) ***n.*** [prob. < OE. *grynde,* abyss] **1.** the hollow or fold where the abdomen joins either thigh **2.** *Archit.* the sharp, curved edge at the junction of two intersecting vaults, or the rib covering it —***vt.*** to build with a groin

GROIN

grok (gräk) ***vt., vi.*** **grokked, grok′king** [coined 1961 by R. A. Heinlein] [Slang] to have empathy (*with*)

grom·met (gräm′it, grum′-) ***n.*** [< obs. Fr. *gromette,* a curb] **1.** a ring of rope or metal used to fasten the edge of a sail to its stay, hold an oar in place, etc. **2.** an eyelet of metal, plastic, etc.

Gro·ning·en (grō′niŋ ən; *Du.* khrō′niŋ ən) city in the N Netherlands: pop. 157,000

groom (groom, groom) ***n.*** [ME. *grom,* boy < ?] **1.** a man or boy whose work is tending horses **2.** any of various officials of the British Royal household **3.** *same as* BRIDEGROOM **4.** [Archaic] a manservant —***vt.*** **1.** to clean and curry (a horse, dog, etc.) **2.** to make neat and tidy **3.** to train for a particular purpose *[to groom a man for political office]*

grooms·man (groomz′mən, groomz′-) ***n.,*** *pl.* **-men** a man who attends a bridegroom at the wedding

groove (groov) ***n.*** [< ON. *grof,* a pit] **1.** a long, narrow furrow cut in a surface with a tool **2.** any channel or rut cut or worn in a surface **3.** a habitual way of doing something; settled routine **4.** [Slang] an exciting or stimulating person, place, experience, etc. —***vt.*** **grooved, groov′ing** to make a groove or grooves in —***vi.*** [Slang] to have understanding, appreciation, enjoyment, etc. in a relaxed, unthinking way (usually with *on* or *with*) —**in the groove** [Slang] performing or performed with smooth, effortless skill: orig. of jazz

groov·y (groo′vē) ***adj.*** **groov′i·er, groov′i·est** [< phrase *in the groove:* see prec.] [Slang] very pleasing

grope (grōp) ***vi.*** **groped, grop′ing** [OE. *grapian,* to seize] to feel or search about blindly or uncertainly —***vt.*** to seek or find (one's way) by groping —***n.*** a groping —**grop′er** ***n.*** —**grop′ing·ly** ***adv.***

Gro·pi·us (grō′pē əs), **Walter** 1883–1969; Ger. architect, in the U.S. after 1937

gros·beak (grōs′bēk′) ***n.*** [< Fr.: see GROSS & BEAK] any of various finchlike birds, with a thick, strong, conical bill

gro·schen (grō′shən) ***n.,*** *pl.* **-schen** [G., ult. < ML. (*denarius*) *grossus,* lit., thick (denarius)] *see* MONETARY UNITS, table (Austria)

gros·grain (grō′grān′) ***n.*** [Fr. < OFr. *gros,* coarse + *grain,* GRAIN] a closely woven silk or rayon fabric with crosswise ribbing, used for ribbons, etc.

gross (grōs) ***adj.*** [< OFr. < LL. *grossus,* thick] **1.** big or fat and coarse-looking; corpulent **2.** flagrant; very bad **3.** dense; thick **4.** *a)* lacking fineness, as in texture *b)* lacking specific details **5.** insensitive or unrefined **6.** vulgar; obscene *[gross language]* **7.** total; entire; with no deductions: opposed to NET[2] *[gross income]* —***n.*** **1.** *pl.* **gross′es** overall total, as of income, before deductions **2.** *pl.* **gross** twelve dozen —***vt., vi.*** [Colloq.] to earn (a specified total amount) before expenses are deducted —**in the gross 1.** in bulk; as a whole **2.** wholesale: also **by the gross** —**gross′ly** ***adv.*** —**gross′ness** ***n.***

gross national product the total value of a nation's annual output of goods and services

gross ton a unit of weight, equal to 2,240 pounds

gross weight the total weight of a commodity, including the packaging or container

grosz (grôsh) ***n.,*** *pl.* **grosz′y** (-ē) [Pol.] *see* MONETARY UNITS, table (Poland)

gro·tesque (grō tesk′) ***adj.*** [Fr. < It. < *grotta,* a grotto: from designs in Roman caves] **1.** in or of a style of painting, sculpture, etc. in which forms of persons and animals are intermingled with foliage, etc. in a fantastic or bizarre design **2.** characterized by distortions or incongruities in appearance, shape, etc.; bizarre **3.** ludicrously eccentric; absurd —***n.*** **1.** a grotesque painting, sculpture, design, etc. **2.** a grotesque thing or quality —**gro·tesque′ly** ***adv.*** —**gro·tesque′ness** ***n.***

grot·to (grät′ō) ***n.,*** *pl.* **-toes, -tos** [< It. < ML. *grupta* < VL. < L. *crypta,* crypt] **1.** a cave **2.** a cavelike summerhouse, shrine, etc.

grouch (grouch) ***vi.*** [< ME. *grucchen:* see GRUDGE] to grumble or complain in a sulky way —***n.*** **1.** a person who grouches continually **2.** a grumbling or sulky mood **3.** a complaint

grouch·y (-ē) ***adj.*** **grouch′i·er, grouch′i·est** in a grouch; grumbling; sulky —**grouch′i·ly** ***adv.*** —**grouch′i·ness** ***n.***

ground[1] (ground) ***n.*** [OE. *grund,* bottom] **1.** *a)* orig., the lowest part or bottom of anything *b)* the bottom of a body of water 2. the solid surface of the earth 3. the soil of the earth; earth; land 4. *a)* a particular piece of land [a hunting *ground*] *b)* [*pl.*] land surrounding or attached to a building; esp., the lawns, gardens, etc. of an estate 5. any particular area of reference, discussion, etc.; subject [arguments covering the same *ground*] 6. [*often pl.*] basis; foundation 7. [*often pl.*] the logical basis of a conclusion, action, etc.; valid reason or cause 8. the underlying, often primed, surface of a painting, colored pattern, etc. 9. [*pl.*] the particles that settle to the bottom of a liquid; dregs [coffee *grounds*] 10. *Elec.* the connection of an electrical conductor with the ground —***adj.*** 1. of, on, or near the ground 2. growing or living in or on the ground —***vt.*** 1. to set on, or cause to touch, the ground 2. to cause (a ship, etc.) to run aground 3. to found on a firm basis; establish 4. to base (a claim, argument, etc.) on something specified 5. to instruct (a person) in the elements or first principles of 6. to provide with a background 7. to keep (an aircraft or pilot) from flying 8. *Elec.* to connect (a conductor) with the ground —***vi.*** 1. to strike the bottom or run ashore: said of a ship 2. *Baseball* *a)* to hit a grounder *b)* to be put out on a grounder (usually with *out*) —**break ground** 1. to dig; excavate 2. to plow 3. to start any undertaking —**cover ground** 1. to move or traverse a certain distance 2. to make a certain amount of progress —**cut the ground from under one** (or **one's feet**) to deprive one of effective defense or argument —**from the ground up** completely; thoroughly —**gain ground** 1. to move forward 2. to make progress 3. to gain in strength, popularity, etc. —**get off the ground** to get (something) started; begin to make progress —**give ground** to withdraw under attack; yield —**hold** (or **stand**) **one's ground** to keep one's position against opposition —**lose ground** 1. to drop back; fall behind 2. to lose in strength, popularity, etc. —**run into the ground** [Colloq.] to overdo (a thing) —**shift one's ground** to change one's argument or defense

ground[2] (ground) *pt. & pp. of* GRIND

ground control personnel, electronic equipment, etc. on the ground for guiding aircraft or spacecraft in takeoff, flight, and landing operations

ground cover ivy, myrtle, etc. used instead of grass for covering the ground

ground crew a group of people in charge of the maintenance and repair of aircraft

ground·er (groun′dər) ***n.*** *Baseball*, etc. a batted ball that strikes the ground almost immediately and rolls or bounces along: also **ground ball**

ground floor that floor of a building which is on or near the ground level; first floor —**in on the ground floor** [Colloq.] in at the beginning of an enterprise and thus in an advantageous position

ground glass 1. glass whose surface has been ground so that it diffuses light and is not transparent 2. glass ground into fine particles

ground·hog (ground′hôg′, -häg′) ***n.*** [prob. transl. of Du. *aardvark*, AARDVARK] *same as* WOODCHUCK

Groundhog Day February 2, when, according to legend, if the groundhog sees his shadow, he returns to his hole for six more weeks of winter weather

ground·less (-lis) ***adj.*** without reason or cause —**ground′less·ly** ***adv.*** —**ground′less·ness** ***n.***

ground·ling (-liŋ) ***n.*** 1. *a)* a fish that lives close to the bottom of the water *b)* an animal that lives on or in the ground *c)* a plant that grows close to the ground 2. [orig. of spectators in a theater pit] a person lacking critical taste

ground·nut (-nut′) ***n.*** 1. any of various plants with edible tubers or tuberlike parts, as the peanut 2. the edible tuber or tuberlike part

ground plan 1. *same as* FLOOR PLAN 2. a first or basic plan

ground rule 1. *Baseball* any of a set of rules adapted to playing conditions in a specific ballpark 2. any of a set of rules governing a specific activity

ground·sel (ground′s'l, groun′-) ***n.*** [< OE., ? < *gund*, pus + *swelgan*, to swallow: from use in poultices] any of a group of plants of the composite family, with usually yellow, rayed flower heads

ground·sill (ground′sil) ***n.*** the bottom horizontal timber in a framework: also **ground′sel** (-s'l)

grounds·keep·er (groundz′kē′pər) ***n.*** a person who tends the grounds of a playing field, estate, cemetery, etc.: also **ground′keep′er**

ground squirrel any of various small, burrowing animals related to tree squirrels and chipmunks

ground·swell (ground′swel′) ***n.*** 1. a violent swelling or rolling of the ocean, caused by a distant storm or earthquake 2. a rapidly growing wave of public opinion, etc. Also **ground swell**

ground water water found underground in porous rock strata and soils, as in a spring

ground wire a wire acting as a conductor from an electric circuit, antenna, etc. to the ground

ground·work (-wurk′) ***n.*** a foundation; basis

ground zero the surface area directly below or above the point of detonation of a nuclear bomb

group (grōōp) ***n.*** [< Fr. < It. *gruppo*] 1. a number of persons or things gathered together and forming a unit; cluster; band 2. a collection of objects or figures forming a design, as in a work of art 3. a number of persons or things classified together because of common characteristics, interests, etc. 4. *Chem. same as* RADICAL 5. *U.S. Air Force* a unit under the command of a colonel 6. *U.S. Mil.* a unit made up of two or more battalions or squadrons —***vt., vi.*** to form into a group or groups —***adj.*** of or involving a group

group·er (grōōp′ər) ***n.***, *pl.* **-ers, -er:** see PLURAL, II, D, 1 [Port. *garoupa*] any of several large fishes found in warm seas

group·ie (grōōp′ē) ***n.*** [Colloq.] a girl fan of rock groups or other popular personalities, who follows them about, often in the hope of achieving sexual intimacy

group work social work in which the worker helps individuals develop through cultural and recreational group activities —**group worker**

grouse[1] (grous) ***n.***, *pl.* **grouse** [Early ModE. < ?] any of a number of game birds with a round, plump body, as the ruffed grouse, sage hen, etc.

grouse[2] (grous) ***vi.*** **groused, grous′ing** [orig. Brit. army slang < ?] [Colloq.] to complain; grumble —***n.*** [Colloq.] a complaint —**grous′er** ***n.***

grout (grout) ***n.*** [OE. *grut*] 1. a thin mortar used to fill chinks, as between tiles 2. a fine plaster for finishing surfaces —***vt.*** to fill or finish with grout —**grout′er** ***n.***

grove (grōv) ***n.*** [< OE. *graf*] 1. a small wood or group of trees without undergrowth 2. a group of trees planted to bear fruit, nuts, etc.; orchard

grov·el (gruv′'l, gräv′-) ***vi.*** **-eled** or **-elled, -el·ing** or **-el·ling** [< earlier *grovelling, adv.*, face downward < ON.] 1. to lie prone or crawl in a prostrate position, esp. abjectly 2. to behave humbly or abjectly 3. to wallow in what is low or contemptible —**grov′el·er, grov′el·ler** ***n.***

grow (grō) ***vi.*** **grew, grown, grow′ing** [OE. *growan*] 1. to come into being or be produced naturally; spring up 2. to exist as living vegetation; thrive [cactus *grows* in sand] 3. to increase in size and develop toward maturity 4. to increase in size, quantity, or degree 5. to come to be; become [to *grow* weary] 6. to become attached or united by growth —***vt.*** 1. to cause to grow; raise; cultivate 2. to cover with a growth: used in the passive 3. to allow to grow [to *grow* a beard] 4. to cause to be or to exist; develop —**grow into** to grow or develop so as to be or to fit [a boy *grows into* a man; he *grew into* his job] —**grow on** to become gradually more acceptable, likable, etc. —**grow out of** 1. to develop from 2. to outgrow —**grow up** to reach maturity; become adult —**grow′er** ***n.***

growl (groul) ***vi.*** [< ? OFr. < MDu. *grollen*, to be noisy] 1. to make a low, rumbling, menacing sound in the throat, as a dog does 2. to complain angrily —***vt.*** to express by growling —***n.*** the act or sound of growling —**growl′er** ***n.*** —**growl′ing·ly** ***adv.***

grown (grōn) *pp. of* GROW —***adj.*** 1. having completed its growth; mature 2. covered with a growth 3. cultivated as specified [home-*grown*]

grown-up (grōn′up′; *for n.* -up′) ***adj.*** 1. adult 2. of or for adults —***n.*** an adult: also **grown′up′**

growth (grōth) ***n.*** 1. a growing or developing 2. degree or extent of increase in size, weight, power, etc. 3. something that grows or has grown [a thick *growth* of grass] 4. an outgrowth or offshoot 5. a tumor or other abnormal mass of tissue in or on the body

grub (grub) ***vi.*** **grubbed, grub′bing** [ME. *grubben*] 1. to dig in the ground 2. to work hard, esp. at menial or tedious jobs; drudge —***vt.*** 1. to clear (ground) of roots and stumps by digging them up 2. to dig up as by the roots; uproot —***n.*** 1. the short, fat, wormlike larva of an insect, esp. of a beetle 2. a drudge 3. [Slang] food —**grub′ber** ***n.***

grub·by (-ē) ***adj.*** **-bi·er, -bi·est** 1. infested with grubs 2. dirty; messy; untidy 3. inferior, mean, etc. —**grub′bi·ly** ***adv.*** —**grub′bi·ness** ***n.***

grub·stake (-stāk′) ***n.*** [GRUB, *n.* 3 + STAKE] [Colloq.] 1. money or supplies advanced to a prospector in return for a share in his findings 2. money advanced for any enterprise —***vt.*** [Colloq.] **-staked′, -stak′ing** to provide with a grubstake —**grub′stak′er** ***n.***

grudge (gruj) ***vt.*** **grudged, grudg′ing** [OFr. *grouchier*] **1.** to envy (someone) because of his possession or enjoyment of (something) **2.** to give with reluctance —***n.*** a strong feeling of hostility or ill will against someone over a grievance —**grudg′er** ***n.*** —**grudg′ing·ly** ***adv.***

gru·el (gro͞o′əl, gro͞ol) ***n.*** [OFr., coarse meal] thin, easily digested broth made by cooking meal in water or milk

gru·el·ing, gru·el·ling (-iŋ) ***adj.*** [prp. of obs. v. *gruel*, to punish] extremely trying; exhausting

grue·some (gro͞o′səm) ***adj.*** [< dial. *grue*, to shudder + -SOME[1]] causing horror or loathing; grisly —**grue′some·ly** ***adv.*** —**grue′some·ness** ***n.***

gruff (gruf) ***adj.*** [< Early ModDu. *grof*] **1.** rough or surly in manner or speech; rude **2.** harsh and throaty; hoarse —**gruff′ly** ***adv.*** —**gruff′ness** ***n.***

grum·ble (grum′b'l) ***vi.*** **-bled, -bling** [prob. < Du. *grommelen*] **1.** to make low, unintelligible sounds in the throat **2.** to mutter or complain in a surly way **3.** to rumble —***vt.*** to express by grumbling —***n.*** a grumbling, esp. in complaint —**grum′bler** ***n.*** —**grum′bling·ly** ***adv.*** —**grum′bly** ***adj.***

grump (grump) ***n.*** [prob. echoic] **1.** [*often pl.*] a fit of bad humor **2.** a grumpy person —***vi.*** to complain and grumble

grump·y (grum′pē) ***adj.*** **grump′i·er, grump′i·est** [prec. + -Y[2]] grouchy; peevish; bad-tempered: also **grump′ish** —**grump′i·ly** ***adv.*** —**grump′i·ness** ***n.***

Grun·dy, Mrs. (grun′dē) [a prudish busybody referred to in an 18th-c. play] a personification of conventional social disapproval, prudishness, narrow-mindedness, etc. —**Grun′dy·ism** ***n.***

grun·ion (grun′yən) ***n.***, *pl.* **-ion, -ions:** see PLURAL, II, D, 2 [prob. < Sp.] a sardine-shaped fish of the California coast

grunt (grunt) ***vi.*** [OE. *grunnettan*, freq. of *grunian*, to grunt] **1.** to make the short, deep, hoarse sound of a hog **2.** to make a sound like this, as in annoyance —***vt.*** to express by grunting —***n.*** **1.** the sound of grunting **2.** a saltwater fish that grunts when removed from water **3.** [Slang] a U.S. infantryman in Vietnam —**grunt′er** ***n.***

Gru·yère (cheese) (gro͞o yer′, grē-) [< *Gruyère*, Switzerland] a light-yellow Swiss cheese, rich in butterfat, or an American cheese like this

gr. wt. gross weight

gryph·on (grif′ən) ***n.*** *same as* GRIFFIN

G.S., g.s. **1.** general secretary **2.** ground speed

GSA, G.S.A. **1.** General Services Administration **2.** Girl Scouts of America

G-string (jē′striŋ′) ***n.*** **1.** a narrow loincloth **2.** a similar band, worn by striptease dancers

G-suit (-so͞ot′) ***n.*** [*G* for *gravity*] a garment for pilots or astronauts, pressurized to counteract the effects of rapid acceleration or deceleration

GT gross ton

gt. **1.** [L. *gutta*] *pl.* **gtt.** *Pharmacy* a drop **2.** great

Gt. Brit., Gt. Br. Great Britain

gtd. guaranteed

GU, g.u. genitourinary

gua·ca·mo·le (gwä′kə mō′lā) ***n.*** [AmSp. < Nahuatl] a thick sauce or dip of seasoned, puréed avocados

Gua·da·la·ja·ra (gwä′d'l ə här′ə; *Sp.* gwä′*th*ä lä hä′rä) city in W Mexico: pop. 1,352,000

Gua·de·loupe (gwä′də lo͞op′) French possession consisting of two large islands and five smaller ones in the Leeward group of the West Indies

guai·a·cum (gwī′ə kəm) ***n.*** [ModL. < genus name] **1.** *a*) any of several tropical American trees with purplish flowers and hard, durable wood *b*) this wood **2.** a greenish-brown resin from certain of these trees, used in medicine, in varnishes, etc.

Guam (gwäm) largest of the Mariana Islands, in the W Pacific: a possession of the U.S.: 209 sq. mi.; pop. 87,000; cap. Agaña

gua·na·co (gwə nä′kō) ***n.***, *pl.* **-cos, -co:** see PLURAL, II, D, 1 [Sp. < Quechua *huanacu*] a woolly, reddish-brown, wild animal of the Andes, related to the camel and llama

GUANACO (4 ft. high at shoulder)

gua·nine (gwä′nēn) ***n.*** [< ff. + -INE[4]] an organic base, $C_5H_5N_5O$, that is in deoxyribonucleic acid and is found in all plant and animal tissues

gua·no (gwä′nō) ***n.***, *pl.* **-nos** [Sp. < Quechua *huanu*, dung] **1.** the manure of sea birds, found especially on islands off the coast of Peru: it is used as a fertilizer **2.** any fertilizer resembling this

guar. guaranteed

Gua·ra·ní (gwä′rä nē′) ***n.*** [*Guaraní*, lit., warrior] **1.** *pl.* **-nís′, -ní′** a member of a tribe of S. American Indians who lived east of the Paraguay River **2.** their language **3.** [g-] *pl.* **-nís′** *see* MONETARY UNITS, table (Paraguay)

guar·an·tee (gar′ən tē′, gär′-) ***n.*** [altered < GUARANTY] **1.** *same as* GUARANTY (*n.* 1 & 3) **2.** *a*) a pledge that something will be replaced if it is not as represented *b*) a positive assurance that something will be done in the manner specified **3.** a guarantor **4.** one who receives a guaranty **5.** something that promises the happening of some event [*the dark clouds were a guarantee of rain*] —***vt.*** **-teed′, -tee′ing** **1.** to give a guarantee or guaranty for **2.** to promise [*I guarantee to be there*]

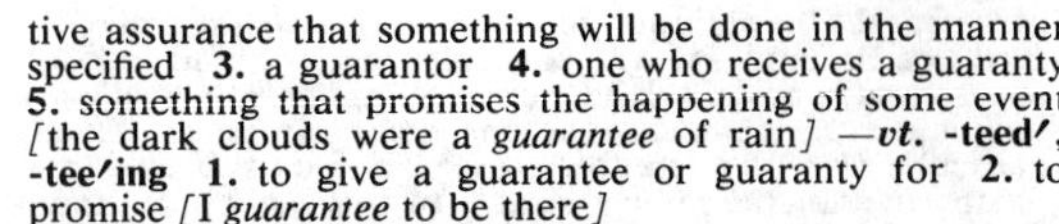

guar·an·tor (gar′ən tôr′, -tər; gär′-) ***n.*** one who makes or gives a guaranty or guarantee

guar·an·ty (-tē) ***n.***, *pl.* **-ties** [< OFr. < *garant*, a warrant < Frank.] **1.** a pledge by which a person promises to pay another's debt or fulfill another's obligation if the other fails to do so **2.** an agreement that secures the existence or maintenance of something **3.** something given or held as security **4.** a guarantor —***vt.*** **-tied, -ty·ing** *same as* GUARANTEE

guard (gärd) ***vt.*** [< the *n.*] **1.** to watch over and protect; defend; shield **2.** *a*) to keep from escape or trouble *b*) to hold in check; control; restrain *c*) *Sports* to keep (an opponent) from making a gain or scoring; also, to cover (a goal or area) in defensive play —***vi.*** **1.** to keep watch (*against*) **2.** to act as a guard —***n.*** [< OFr. < *garder*, to protect < Gmc.] **1.** the act or duty of guarding; defense; protection **2.** a posture of defense, as in boxing, fencing, etc. **3.** any device that protects against injury or loss **4.** a person or group that guards; specif., *a*) a sentinel or sentry *b*) a railway brakeman or gateman *c*) a person who guards prisoners *d*) [*pl.*] a special unit of troops assigned to the British royal household *e*) a military unit with a ceremonial function [*a color guard*] **5.** *Basketball* either of the two players whose function is to set up offensive plays **6.** *Football* either of two players on offense, left and right of the center —**mount guard** to go on sentry duty —**off (one's) guard** not alert for defense —**on (one's) guard** alert for defense —**stand guard** to do sentry duty —**guard′er** ***n.***

guard·ed (-id) ***adj.*** **1.** kept safe; watched over and protected; defended **2.** held in check; supervised **3.** cautious; noncommittal —**guard′ed·ly** ***adv.*** —**guard′ed·ness** ***n.***

guard·house (-hous′) ***n.*** *Mil.* **1.** a building used by the members of a guard when not walking a post **2.** a building where personnel are confined for minor offenses or while awaiting court-martial

guard·i·an (-ē ən) ***n.*** **1.** a person who guards or takes care of another person, property, etc. **2.** a person legally placed in charge of the affairs of a minor or of someone incapable of managing his own affairs —***adj.*** protecting —**guard′i·an·ship′** ***n.***

guard·room (-ro͞om′) ***n.*** *Mil.* a room used by the members of a guard when not walking a post

guards·man (gärdz′mən) ***n.***, *pl.* **-men** a member of a National Guard or of any military guard

Gua·te·ma·la (gwä′tə mä′lə) **1.** country in Central America, south & east of Mexico: 42,042 sq. mi.; pop. 5,014,000 **2.** its capital: pop. 577,000: also **Guatemala City** —**Gua′te·ma′lan** ***adj.***, ***n.***

gua·va (gwä′və) ***n.*** [Sp. *guayaba* < native name in Brazil] **1.** any of several tropical American plants, esp. a tree bearing a yellowish, edible fruit **2.** the fruit, used for jelly, preserves, etc.

Guay·a·quil (gwī′ä kēl′) seaport in W Ecuador: pop. 680,000

Guay·na·bo (gwī nä′bô, -vô) city in NE Puerto Rico, near San Juan: pop. 54,000

gua·yu·le (gwä yo͞o′lē) ***n.*** [AmSp. < Nahuatl *quauhitl*, plant + *olli*, gum] **1.** a small shrub of N Mexico, Texas, etc. **2.** rubber **(guayule rubber)** obtained from it

gu·ber·na·to·ri·al (go͞o′bər nə tôr′ē əl) ***adj.*** [L. *gubernator*, governor < *gubernare*, to steer] of a governor or his office

gudg·eon (guj′ən) ***n.*** [< OFr. < L. *gobio* < Gr. *kōbios*] **1.** a small, European freshwater fish, easily caught, and used for bait **2.** a goby or killifish **3.** a person easily cheated or tricked; dupe —***vt.*** to cheat; trick; dupe

Guelph[1], **Guelf** (gwelf) ***n.*** any member of a political party in medieval Italy supporting the Pope

Guelph[2] (gwelf) city in SE Ontario, Canada: pop. 51,000

guer·don (gʉr′d'n) ***n.***, ***vt.*** [< OFr., ult. < OHG. *widar*, back + *lōn*, reward] [Archaic] reward

Guern·sey (gʉrn′zē) one of the Channel Islands —***n.***, *pl.* **-seys** any of a breed of dairy cattle, originally from this island, usually fawn-colored with white markings

guer·ril·la, gue·ril·la (gə ril′ə) ***n.*** [Sp. dim. of *guerra*, war < OHG.] any member of a small defensive force of irregular soldiers, usually volunteers, making surprise raids, esp. behind the lines of an invading enemy army —***adj.*** of or by guerrillas

guess (ges) ***vt.***, ***vi.*** [prob. < MDu. *gessen*] **1.** to form a judgment or estimate of (something) without actual knowledge or enough facts for certainty; conjecture; surmise **2.** to judge correctly by doing this **3.** to think or suppose [*I guess I can do it*] —***n.*** **1.** a guessing **2.** something guessed; conjecture; surmise —**guess′er** ***n.***

guess·work (-wurk′) ***n.*** **1.** the act of guessing **2.** a judgment, result, etc. arrived at by guessing

guest (gest) ***n.*** [ON. *gestr*] **1.** *a)* a person entertained at the home of another; visitor *b)* a person entertained by another acting as host at a restaurant, theater, etc. **2.** any paying customer of a hotel, restaurant, etc. **3.** a person receiving the hospitality of a club, institution, etc. of which he is not a member **4.** a person who appears on a program by special invitation **5.** an organism, as an insect, that lives on or in the abode of another —***adj.*** **1.** for guests **2.** performing by special invitation *[a guest artist]* —***vt.*** to entertain as a guest —***vi.*** to be, or perform as, a guest

guff (guf) ***n.*** [echoic] [Slang] **1.** foolish talk; nonsense **2.** brash or insolent talk

guf·faw (gə fô′) ***n.*** [echoic] a loud, coarse burst of laughter —***vi.*** to laugh in this way

Gui·a·na (gē an′ə, -än′ə) region in N S. America, including Guyana, Surinam, & French Guiana

guid·ance (gīd′ns) ***n.*** **1.** the act of guiding; direction; leadership **2.** something that guides **3.** advice or assistance, as that given to students by counselors **4.** the process of directing the course of a spacecraft, missile, etc.

guide (gīd) ***vt.*** **guid′ed, guid′ing** [OFr. *guider*, var. of *guier* < Frank.] **1.** to point out the way for; conduct; lead **2.** to direct the course of (a vehicle, implement, etc.) **3.** to direct in (policies, actions, work, etc.); manage; regulate —***vi.*** to act as a guide —***n.*** a person or thing that guides; specif., *a)* one who leads others on a trip or tour *b)* one who directs, or serves as the model for, another in his conduct, career, etc. *c)* a part that controls the motion of other parts *d)* a guidebook *e)* a book of basic instruction in some subject; handbook *[a guide to mathematics]* —**guid′a·ble *adj.***

guide·book (-book′) ***n.*** a book containing directions and information for tourists

guided missile a military missile whose course is controlled by radio signals, radar devices, etc.

guide dog a dog trained to lead a blind person

guide·line (-līn′) ***n.*** a standard or principle by which to determine a policy or action: also **guide line**

guide·post (-pōst′) ***n.*** **1.** a post, as at a roadside, with a sign and directions for travelers **2.** anything that serves as a guide, standard, etc.

gui·don (gīd′'n, gī′dän) ***n.*** [Fr. < It. *guidone*] **1.** the identification flag of a military unit **2.** the soldier carrying it

guild (gild) ***n.*** [< OE. *gyld* and ON. *gildi*, both < base seen in OE. *gieldan*, to pay] **1.** in medieval times, a union of men in the same craft or trade to uphold standards and protect the members **2.** any association for mutual aid and the promotion of common interests

guil·der (gil′dər) ***n.*** [< ME. < MDu.: see GULDEN] **1.** the monetary unit and a coin of the Netherlands and Surinam: see MONETARY UNITS, table

guild·hall (gild′hôl′) ***n.*** **1.** a hall where a guild meets **2.** a town hall

guilds·man (gildz′mən) ***n.***, *pl.* **-men** (-mən) a member of a guild

guile (gīl) ***n.*** [OFr. *guile*, prob. < Frank. *wigila*, guile] slyness and cunning in dealing with others; craftiness —**guile′less *adj.*** —**guile′less·ly *adv.*** —**guile′less·ness *n.***

guile·ful (-fəl) ***adj.*** full of guile; deceitful; tricky —**guile′ful·ly *adv.*** —**guile′ful·ness *n.***

guil·le·mot (gil′ə mät′) ***n.*** [Fr., dim. of *Guillaume*, William] any of various narrow-billed, northern diving birds

guil·lo·tine (gil′ə tēn′; *for v.* gil′ə tēn′) ***n.*** [Fr., after J. I. *Guillotin* (1738–1814), who advocated its use] an instrument for beheading by means of a heavy blade dropped between two grooved uprights —***vt.*** **-tined′, -tin′ing** to behead with a guillotine

GUILLOTINE

guilt (gilt) ***n.*** [OE. *gylt*, a sin] **1.** *a)* the act or state of having done a wrong or committed an offense *b)* a feeling of self-reproach resulting from a belief that one has done something wrong or immoral **2.** conduct involving guilt; crime; sin

guilt·less (-lis) ***adj.*** **1.** free from guilt; innocent **2.** having no knowledge or experience (with *of*) —**guilt′less·ly *adv.*** —**guilt′less·ness *n.***

guilt·y (gil′tē) ***adj.*** **guilt′i·er, guilt′i·est** **1.** having guilt; deserving blame or punishment **2.** having one's guilt proved **3.** showing or conscious of guilt *[a guilty look]* **4.** of or involving guilt or a sense of guilt *[a guilty conscience]* —**guilt′i·ly *adv.*** —**guilt′i·ness *n.***

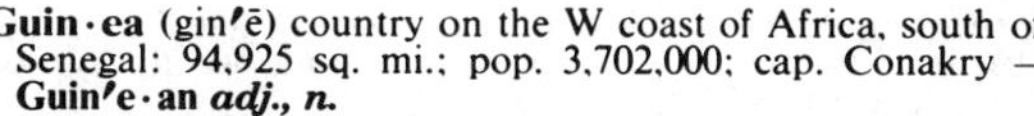

Guin·ea (gin′ē) country on the W coast of Africa, south of Senegal: 94,925 sq. mi.; pop. 3,702,000; cap. Conakry —**Guin′e·an *adj.*, *n.***

guin·ea (gin′ē) ***n.*** **1.** [first coined of gold from *Guinea*] a former English gold coin, last minted in 1813, equal to 21 shillings **2.** the sum of 21 English shillings

Guin·ea-Bis·sau (-bi sou′) country in W Africa, on the coast between Guinea & Senegal: formerly a Port. territory: 15,505 sq. mi.; pop. 487,000

guinea fowl [orig. imported from *Guinea*] a domestic fowl with a featherless head, rounded body, and dark feathers spotted with white

guinea hen **1.** a female guinea fowl **2.** any guinea fowl

guinea pig [prob. orig. brought to England by ships plying between England, *Guinea*, and S. America] **1.** a small, fat mammal of the rat family, with short ears and no external tail, used in biological experiments **2.** any person or thing used in an experiment or test

Guin·e·vere (gwin′ə vir′) *Arthurian Legend* the wife of King Arthur and mistress of Sir Lancelot Also **Guin′e·ver′** (-vir′, -vər)

guise (gīz) ***n.*** [OFr. < OHG. *wisa*, manner] **1.** manner of dress; garb **2.** outward aspect; semblance **3.** a false appearance; pretense *[under the guise of friendship]*

gui·tar (gi tär′) ***n.*** [< Fr. < Sp. *guitarra* < Ar. < Gr. *kithara*, lyre] a musical instrument related to the lute but having a flat back and usually six strings that are plucked or strummed with the fingers or a plectrum —**gui·tar′ist *n.***

gulch (gulch) ***n.*** [prob. < dial. *gulch*, to swallow greedily] a steep-walled valley cut by a swift stream; narrow ravine

gul·den (gool′dən) ***n.***, *pl.* **-dens, -den** [MDu. *gulden* (*florijn*), golden (florin)] *same as* GUILDER

gulf (gulf) ***n.*** [< OFr. < It. *golfo*: ult. < Gr. *kolpos*, bosom] **1.** a large area of ocean, larger than a bay, reaching into land **2.** a wide, deep chasm or abyss **3.** a wide or impassable gap or separation —***vt.*** to swallow up; engulf

Gulf States States on the Gulf of Mexico; Fla., Ala., Miss., La., & Tex.

Gulf Stream warm ocean current flowing from the Gulf of Mexico along the E coast of the U.S., turning east at the Grand Banks toward Europe

gull[1] (gul) ***n.***, *pl.* **gulls, gull:** see PLURAL, II, D, 1 [< Celt.] a water bird with large wings, webbed feet, and white and gray feathers

gull[2] (gul) ***n.*** [prob. < ME. *golle*, silly fellow, lit., unfledged bird < ?] a person easily tricked; dupe —***vt.*** to cheat; trick

Gul·lah (gul′ə) ***n.*** [< ? *Gola* (*Gula*) or < ? *Ngola*, tribal groups in Africa] **1.** any of a group of Negroes living in coastal S. Carolina and Georgia and esp. on the nearby sea islands **2.** their English dialect

gul·let (gul′ət) ***n.*** [OFr. *goulet* < L. *gula*, throat] **1.** the tube leading from the mouth to the stomach; esophagus **2.** the throat or neck

gul·li·ble (gul′ə b'l) ***adj.*** easily tricked; credulous —**gul′li·bil′i·ty *n.*** —**gul′li·bly *adv.***

gul·ly (gul′ē) ***n.***, *pl.* **-lies** [altered < ME. *golet*, water channel, orig., gullet: see GULLET] a channel worn by running water; small, narrow ravine —***vt.*** **-lied, -ly·ing** to make a gully in

gulp (gulp) ***vt.*** [prob. < Du. *gulpen*, to gulp] **1.** to swallow hastily, greedily, or in large amounts **2.** to choke back as if swallowing —***vi.*** to catch the breath as in swallowing —***n.*** **1.** the act of gulping **2.** the amount swallowed at one time —**gulp′er *n.*** —**gulp′ing·ly *adv.***

gum[1] (gum) ***n.*** [< OFr. < L. *gumma* < Egypt. *kemai*] **1.** a sticky, colloidal carbohydrate found in certain trees and plants, which dries into a brittle mass that dissolves or swells in water **2.** any similar plant secretion, as resin **3.** any plant gum processed for use in industry, art, etc. **4.** *a)* an adhesive, as on the back of a postage stamp *b)* any of various sticky substances or deposits **5.** *same as: a)* GUM TREE *b)* GUMWOOD **6.** *same as* CHEWING GUM —***vt.*** **gummed, gum′ming** to coat, unite, or stiffen with gum —***vi.*** **1.** to secrete or form gum **2.** to become sticky or clogged —**gum up** [Slang] to put out of working order

gum[2] (gum) ***n.*** [OE. *goma*] [*often pl.*] the firm flesh surrounding the base of the teeth —***vt.*** **gummed, gum′ming** to chew with toothless gums

gum ammoniac *same as* AMMONIAC

gum arabic a gum obtained from several African acacias, used in medicine and candy, for stabilizing emulsions, etc.

gum·bo (gum′bō) ***n.*** [< Bantu name for okra] **1.** *same as* OKRA **2.** a soup thickened with unripe okra pods **3.** a fine, silty soil of the Western prairies, which becomes sticky and nonporous when wet: also **gumbo soil**

gum·boil (gum′boil′) ***n.*** an abscess on the gum

gum·drop (-dräp′) ***n.*** a small, firm piece of jellylike candy, made of sweetened gum arabic or gelatin, usually colored and flavored

gum·my (gum′ē) ***adj.*** **-mi·er, -mi·est** **1.** having the nature of gum; sticky **2.** covered with or containing gum **3.** yielding gum —**gum′mi·ness** ***n.***

gump·tion (gump′shən) ***n.*** [< Scot. dial.] [Colloq.] **1.** orig., common sense **2.** courage and initiative; enterprise and boldness: the current sense

gum resin a mixture of gum and resin, given off by certain trees and plants

gum·shoe (gum′sho͞o′) ***n.*** **1.** orig., *a*) a rubber overshoe *b*) [*pl.*] sneakers **2.** [Slang] a detective

gum tree any of various trees that yield gum, as the sour gum, sweet gum, eucalyptus, etc.

gum·wood (-wood′) ***n.*** the wood of a gum tree

gun (gun) ***n.*** [< ON. *Gunnhildr*, fem. name (< *gunnr*, war + *hildr*, battle)] **1.** a weapon consisting of a metal tube from which a projectile is discharged by the force of an explosive; specif., *a*) technically, a heavy weapon, as a cannon, etc. *b*) a rifle *c*) popularly, a pistol or revolver **2.** any similar device not discharged by an explosive *[an air gun]* **3.** a discharge of a gun in signaling or saluting **4.** anything like a gun in shape or use **5.** [Slang] *same as* GUNMAN (sense 1) —***vi.*** **gunned, gun′ning** to shoot or hunt with a gun —***vt.*** **1.** [Colloq.] to shoot (a person) **2.** [Slang] to advance the throttle of (an engine) so as to increase the speed —**give it the gun** [Slang] to cause something to start or gain speed —**gun for 1.** to hunt for with a gun **2.** [Slang] to seek —**jump the gun** [Slang] to begin before the signal to start, or before the proper time —**stick to one's guns** to be firm under attack

gun·boat (-bōt′) ***n.*** a small armed ship of shallow draft, used to patrol rivers, etc.

gun·cot·ton (-kät′'n) ***n.*** nitrocellulose in a highly nitrated form, used as an explosive

gun·fight (-fīt′) ***n.*** a fight between persons using pistols or revolvers —**gun′fight′er** ***n.***

gun·fire (-fīr′) ***n.*** the firing of a gun or guns

gung-ho (guŋ′hō′) ***adj.*** [Chin., lit., work together] overly enthusiastic, enterprising, etc.

gunk (guŋk) ***n.*** [< ? G(OO) + (J)UNK[1]] [Slang] any oily or thick, messy substance —**gunk′y** ***adj.***

gun·lock (gun′läk′) ***n.*** in some guns, the mechanism by which the charge is set off

gun·man (-mən) ***n.***, *pl.* **-men** **1.** a man armed with a gun, esp. an armed gangster or hired killer **2.** a man skilled in the use of a gun

gun·met·al (-met′'l) ***n.*** **1.** a kind of bronze formerly used for making cannons; also, any metal or alloy treated to resemble this **2.** the dark gray color (**gunmetal gray**) of tarnished gunmetal —***adj.*** dark gray

gun·nel[1] (gun′'l) ***n.*** [< ?] a small, slimy fish resembling the blenny, found in the N Atlantic

gun·nel[2] (gun′'l) ***n.*** *same as* GUNWALE

gun·ner (gun′ər) ***n.*** **1.** a soldier, sailor, etc. who helps fire artillery **2.** a naval warrant officer in charge of a ship's guns **3.** a hunter with a gun

gun·ner·y (-ē) ***n.*** **1.** heavy guns **2.** the science of making and using heavy guns and projectiles

gunnery sergeant a noncommissioned Marine Corps officer ranking above a staff sergeant

gun·ny (gun′ē) ***n.***, *pl.* **-nies** [< Hindi < Sans. *gōnī*, a sack] **1.** a coarse, heavy fabric of jute or hemp, used for sacks **2.** *same as* GUNNYSACK

gun·ny·sack (-sak′) ***n.*** a sack made of gunny

gun·play (gun′plā′) ***n.*** an exchange of gunshots, as between gunmen and police

gun·point (-point′) ***n.*** the muzzle of a gun —**at gunpoint** under threat of being shot with a gun

gun·pow·der (-pou′dər) ***n.*** an explosive powder, esp. a mixture of sulfur, saltpeter, and charcoal, used in cartridges, shells, etc., for blasting, etc.

gun·run·ning (-run′iŋ) ***n.*** the smuggling of guns and ammunition into a country —**gun′run′ner** ***n.***

gun·shot (-shät′) ***n.*** **1.** shot fired from a gun **2.** the range of a gun —***adj.*** caused by a shot from a gun

gun·smith (-smith′) ***n.*** a person who makes or repairs small guns

gun·stock (-stäk′) ***n.*** the wooden handle or butt to which the barrel of a gun is attached

gun·wale (gun′'l) ***n.*** [first applied to bulwarks supporting a ship's guns] the upper edge of the side of a ship or boat

gup·py (gup′ē) ***n.***, *pl.* **-pies** [after R. *Guppy*, of Trinidad] a tiny, brightly colored tropical fish

gur·gle (gʉr′g'l) ***vi.*** **-gled, -gling** [prob. echoic] **1.** to flow with a bubbling or rippling sound **2.** to make such a sound in the throat —***vt.*** to utter with a gurgle —***n.*** the act or sound of gurgling

gur·nard (gʉr′nərd) ***n.***, *pl.* **-nards, -nard:** see PLURAL, II, D, 1 [< OFr. < *grogner*, to grunt] *same as* FLYING GURNARD

gu·ru (goor′o͞o, goo ro͞o′) ***n.*** [Hindi < Sans. *guru-ḥ*, venerable] **1.** in Hinduism, one's spiritual adviser **2.** a leader with devoted followers

gush (gush) ***vi.*** [prob. akin to ON. *gjosa*, to gush] **1.** to flow out suddenly and plentifully **2.** to have a sudden, plentiful flow of blood, tears, etc. **3.** to express exaggerated enthusiasm or feeling —***vt.*** to cause to flow out suddenly and plentifully —***n.*** **1.** a sudden, plentiful outflow **2.** gushing talk or writing —**gush′ing·ly** ***adv.***

gush·er (-ər) ***n.*** **1.** a person who gushes **2.** an oil well from which oil spouts without being pumped

gush·y (-ē) ***adj.*** **gush′i·er, gush′i·est** characterized by gush (*n.* 2) —**gush′i·ly** ***adv.*** —**gush′i·ness** ***n.***

gus·set (gus′it) ***n.*** [< OFr. *gousset*] **1.** a triangular or diamond-shaped piece inserted in a garment, glove, etc. to make it stronger or roomier **2.** a triangular metal brace for reinforcing a corner or angle —***vt.*** to furnish with a gusset

GUSSET

gus·sie, gus·sy (gus′ē) ***vt., vi.*** **-sied, -sy·ing** [< *Gussie*, nickname for AUGUSTA] [Slang] to dress (*up*) or decorate in a fine or showy way

gust (gust) ***n.*** [< ON. *gustr* < *gjosa*, to gush] **1.** a sudden, strong rush of air or wind **2.** a sudden outburst of rain, laughter, rage, etc. —***vi.*** to blow in gusts

gus·ta·to·ry (gus′tə tôr′ē) ***adj.*** of or having to do with tasting or the sense of taste: also **gus′ta·tive**

gus·to (gus′tō) ***n.*** [It. & Sp. < L. *gustus*, taste] **1.** taste; liking **2.** zest; relish **3.** great vigor

gust·y (gus′tē) ***adj.*** **gust′i·er, gust′i·est** characterized by gusts of air or wind, or by sudden outbursts —**gust′i·ly** ***adv.*** —**gust′i·ness** ***n.***

gut (gut) ***n.*** [OE. *guttas*, pl. < base of *geotan*, to pour] **1.** *a*) [*pl.*] the bowels; entrails *b*) the stomach or belly Regarded as an indelicate usage **2.** all or part of the alimentary canal, esp. the intestine **3.** tough cord made from animal intestines, used for violin strings, surgical sutures, etc. **4.** a narrow passage or gully **5.** [*pl.*] [Colloq.] the basic or inner parts **6.** [*pl.*] [Slang] *a*) daring, courage, etc. *b*) impudence; effrontery *c*) power or force —***vt.*** **gut′ted, gut′ting** **1.** to remove the intestines from; eviscerate **2.** to destroy the interior of, as by fire —***adj.*** [Slang] **1.** urgent and basic *[gut* issues in politics*]* **2.** easy; simple *[a gut* course in college*]*

Gu·ten·berg (go͞ot′'n bʉrg′), **Jo·hann** (yō′hän) (born *Johannes Gensfleisch*) 1400?–68; Ger. printer: reputedly the first European to print with movable type

gut·less (gut′lis) ***adj.*** [Slang] lacking courage

guts·y (gut′sē) ***adj.*** **guts′i·er, guts′i·est** [Slang] full of guts; courageous, forceful, etc.

gut·ta-per·cha (gut′ə pʉr′chə) ***n.*** [< Malay < *gĕtah*, gum + *pĕrchah*, tree from which it is obtained] a rubberlike gum produced from the latex of various SE Asian trees, used in insulation, dentistry, etc.

gut·ter (gut′ər) ***n.*** [< OFr. < L. *gutta*, a drop] **1.** a trough along or under the eaves of a roof, to carry off rain water **2.** any narrow channel, as along the side of a road or street to carry off water **3.** the adjoining inner margins of two facing pages in a book, etc. —***vt.*** to furnish with gutters —***vi.*** **1.** to flow in a stream **2.** to melt rapidly so that the wax runs down in channels: said of a candle

gut·ter·snipe (-snīp′) ***n.*** a child living in the slums, for the most part in the streets: contemptuous term

gut·tur·al (gut′ər əl) ***adj.*** [< L. *guttur*, throat] **1.** of the throat **2.** loosely, produced in the throat; harsh, rasping, etc.: said of sounds **3.** formed with the back of the tongue close to or against the soft palate, as the *k* in *keen* —***n.*** a guttural sound —**gut′tur·al·ly** ***adv.*** —**gut′tur·al·ness** ***n.***

Guy (gī) [Fr., lit., leader] a masculine name

guy[1] (gī) ***n.*** [< OFr. < *guier*, to GUIDE] a rope, chain, etc. attached to something to steady or guide it —***vt.*** to guide or steady with a guy

guy[2] (gī) ***n.*** [after Guy FAWKES] **1.** a person who looks odd **2.** [Slang] *a*) a man or boy; fellow *b*) any person —***vt.*** to make fun of; ridicule

Guy·a·na (gī an′ə, -än′ə) country in NE S. America, on the Atlantic: a member of the Commonwealth: 83,000 sq. mi.; pop. 763,000 —**Guy′a·nese′** (-ə nēz′) ***adj., n.***, *pl.* **-nese′**

guz·zle (guz′'l) ***vi., vt.*** **-zled, -zling** [< ? OFr. < *gosier*, throat] to drink greedily or immoderately —**guz′zler** ***n.***

Gwen·do·len, Gwen·do·line, Gwen·do·lyn (gwen′d'l-ən) [< Celt.; first element prob. W. *gwen*, white] a feminine name: dim. *Gwen*

gybe (jīb) ***n., vi., vt.*** **gybed, gyb′ing** *same as* JIBE[1]

gym (jim) ***n.*** [Colloq.] *same as:* **1.** GYMNASIUM **2.** PHYSICAL EDUCATION

gym·na·si·um (jim nā′zē əm) ***n.**, pl.* **-si·ums, -si·a** (-ə) [L. < Gr. *gymnasion*, ult. < *gymnos*, naked] **1.** a room or building equipped for physical training and athletic sports **2.** [G-] (gim nä′zē ʊom) in Germany and some other European countries, a secondary school for students preparing to enter a university
gym·nast (jim′nast) ***n.*** an expert in gymnastics
gym·nas·tic (jim nas′tik) ***adj.*** [< L. < Gr.: see GYMNASIUM] of or having to do with gymnastics: also **gym·nas′ti·cal —gym·nas′ti·cal·ly *adv.***
gym·nas·tics (-tiks) ***n.pl.*** exercises that develop and train the body and the muscles
gym·no- [< Gr. *gymnos*, naked] *a combining form meaning* naked, stripped, bare: also **gymn-**
gym·no·sperm (jim′nə spurm′) ***n.*** [< ModL. < Gr.: see prec. & -SPERM] any of a large class of seed plants having the ovules borne on open scales, usually in cones, as pines and cedars **—gym′no·sper′mous** (-spur′məs) ***adj.*** **— gym′no·sper′my** (-spur′mē) ***n.***
gym shoe *same as* SNEAKER (sense 2)
gyn·e·co- [< Gr. < *gynē*, a woman] *a combining form meaning* woman, female: also **gynec-**
gyn·e·col·o·gy (gī′nə käl′ə jē, jin′ə-, jī′nə-) ***n.*** [prec. + -LOGY] the branch of medicine dealing with the specific functions, diseases, etc. of women **—gyn′e·co·log′ic** (-kə läj′ik), **gyn′e·co·log′i·cal *adj.* —gyn′e·col′o·gist *n.***
gy·noe·ci·um (ji nē′sē əm, jī-, gī-) ***n.**, pl.* **-ci·a** (-ə) [ModL. < L., ult. < Gr. *gynē*, a woman + *oikos*, house] the female organ or organs of a flower; pistil or pistils: also sp. **gyn·ae·ce·um** (jī′nə sē′əm) *pl.* **-ce′a** (-ə) or **gy·ne′ci·um,** *pl.* **-ci·a** (-ə)
gyn·o·phore (jin′ə fôr′, jī′nə-, gī′nə-) ***n.*** [< Gr. *gynē*, woman + -PHORE] a stalk bearing the gynoecium above the petals and stamens
-gyn·ous (ji nəs) [< ModL. < Gr. < *gynē*, a woman] *a combining form meaning:* **1.** woman or female *[polygynous]* **2.** having female organs or pistils as specified *[androgynous]*
-gyn·y (ji nē) *a combining form used to form nouns from adjectives ending in* -GYNOUS
gyp (jip) ***n.*** [prob. < GYPSY] [Colloq.] **1.** an act of cheating; swindle **2.** a swindler: also **gyp′per, gyp′ster —*vt., vi.* gypped, gyp′ping** [Colloq.] to swindle; cheat
gyp·soph·i·la (jip säf′ə lə) ***n.*** [ModL.: see GYPSUM & -PHIL(E)] any of a genus of plants of the pink family, bearing clusters of small white or pink flowers with a delicate fragrance, as baby's breath
gyp·sum (jip′səm) ***n.*** [L. < Gr. *gypsos*, chalk < Sem.] a hydrated sulfate of calcium, $CaSO_4 \cdot 2H_2O$, occurring naturally in sedimentary rocks and used for making plaster of Paris, in treating soil, etc.
Gyp·sy (jip′sē) ***n.**, pl.* **-sies** [< *Egipcien*, Egyptian: orig. thought to have come from Egypt] **1.** [*also* **g-**] a member of a wandering Caucasoid people with dark skin and black hair, believed to have originated in India: they are known throughout the world as musicians, fortunetellers, etc. **2.** *same as* ROMANY (sense 2) **3.** [**g-**] a person whose appearance or habits are like those of a Gypsy **—*adj.*** of or like a Gypsy or Gypsies
gypsy moth a European moth, brownish or white, now common in the E U.S.: its larvae feed on leaves, damaging trees and plants
gy·rate (jī′rāt) ***vi.*** **-rat·ed, -rat·ing** [< L. pp. of *gyrare*, to turn, ult. < Gr. *gyros*, a circle] to move in a circular or spiral path; rotate or revolve on an axis; whirl **—*adj.*** spiral, coiled, or circular **—gy·ra′tion *n.* —gy′ra′tor *n.***
gyre (jīr) ***n.*** [< L. < Gr. *gyros*, a circle] [Chiefly Poet.] **1.** a circular or spiral motion; whirl **2.** a circular or spiral form; ring or vortex **—*vi., vt.* gyred, gyr′ing** [Chiefly Poet.] to whirl
gyr·fal·con (jur′fal′kən, -fôl′-, -fô′-) ***n.*** [< OFr. *girfaucon* < Frank.] a large, fierce, strong falcon of the Arctic
gy·ro (jī′rō) ***n.**, pl.* **-ros** *short for:* **1.** GYROSCOPE **2.** GYROCOMPASS
gy·ro- [< Gr. *gyros*, a circle] *a combining form meaning:* **1.** gyrating *[gyroscope]* **2.** gyroscope *[gyrocompass]* Also, before a vowel, **gyr-**
gy·ro·com·pass (-kum′pəs) ***n.*** a compass consisting of a motor-operated gyroscope whose rotating axis points to the geographic north pole instead of to the magnetic pole
gy·ro·scope (-skōp′) ***n.*** [GYRO- + -SCOPE] a wheel mounted in a ring so that its axis is free to turn in any direction: when the wheel is spun rapidly, it will keep its original plane of rotation no matter which way the ring is turned **—gy′ro·scop′ic** (-skäp′ik) ***adj.*** **—gy′ro·scop′i·cal·ly *adv.***
gy·ro·sta·bi·liz·er (jī′rō stā′bə lī′zər) ***n.*** a device consisting of a gyroscope spinning in a vertical plane, used to stabilize the side-to-side rolling of a ship
gyve (jīv) ***n., vt.*** **gyved, gyv′ing** [< Anglo-Fr. *gyves*, pl.] [Archaic or Poet.] fetter; shackle

GYROSCOPE

H

H, h (āch) ***n.**, pl.* **H's, h's** **1.** the eighth letter of the English alphabet **2.** the sound of *H* or *h*
H (āch) ***n.*** **1.** *Chem. the symbol for* hydrogen **2.** *Physics the symbol for* henry **3.** [Slang] heroin **—*adj.*** shaped like *H*
H., h. **1.** harbor **2.** hard(ness) **3.** height **4.** high **5.** *Baseball* hits **6.** hour(s) **7.** husband
ha (hä) ***interj.*** [echoic] an exclamation variously expressing surprise, anger, triumph, etc. **—*n.*** the sound of this exclamation or of a laugh
Haar·lem (här′ləm) city in NW Netherlands: pop. 173,000
Ha·bak·kuk (hab′ə kuk, hə bak′ək) *Bible* **1.** a Hebrew prophet of the 7th cent. B.C. **2.** the book containing his prophecies: abbrev. **Hab.** Also, in the Douay Bible, **Ha′ba·cuc**
Ha·ba·na (ä bä′nä), **(La)** *Sp. name of* HAVANA
ha·be·as cor·pus (hā′bē əs kôr′pəs) [L., (that) you have the body] *Law* a writ requiring that a detained person be brought before a court to decide the legality of his detention or imprisonment
hab·er·dash·er (hab′ər dash′ər, hab′ə-) ***n.*** [prob. < Anglo-Fr. *hapertas*, kind of cloth] **1.** a person who sells men's furnishings, such as hats, shirts, gloves, etc. **2.** [Brit.] a dealer in various small articles, such as ribbons, thread, etc.
hab·er·dash·er·y (-ē) ***n.**, pl.* **-er·ies** **1.** things sold by a haberdasher **2.** a haberdasher's shop
hab·er·geon (hab′ər jən) ***n.*** [OFr. *haubergeon*, dim. of *hauberc*, hauberk] **1.** a short, high-necked jacket of mail **2.** *same as* HAUBERK
ha·bil·i·ment (hə bil′ə mənt) ***n.*** [< MFr. < *habiller*, to clothe] **1.** [*usually pl.*] clothing; dress **2.** [*pl.*] furnishings or equipment; trappings
ha·bil·i·tate (-tāt′) ***vt.*** **-tat′ed, -tat′ing** [< ML. pp. of *habilitare*, to make suitable] **1.** to clothe; equip; outfit **2.** to educate or train (the handicapped, the disadvantaged, etc.) to function better in society **—ha·bil′i·ta′tion *n.* —ha·bil′i·ta′tive *adj.***
hab·it (hab′it) ***n.*** [OFr. < L. *habitus* < pp. of *habere*, to have] **1.** a distinctive religious costume **2.** a costume for certain occasions *[a riding habit]* **3.** characteristic or usual way of being, doing, growing, etc.; character, tendency, disposition, etc. **4.** *a)* a thing done often and, hence, easily; practice; custom *b)* an acquired pattern of action that is automatic and thus difficult to break **5.** an addiction, esp. to narcotics **—*vt.*** to dress
hab·it·a·ble (-ə b′l) ***adj.*** fit to be lived in **—hab′it·a·bil′i·ty *n.* —hab′it·a·bly *adv.***
hab·it·ant (-ənt) ***n.*** [Fr. < L. prp. of *habitare*, to inhabit] an inhabitant; resident
hab·i·tat (hab′ə tat′) ***n.*** [L., it inhabits] **1.** native environment **2.** the place where a person or thing is ordinarily found
hab·i·ta·tion (hab′ə tā′shən) ***n.*** **1.** an inhabiting; occupancy **2.** a place in which to live; dwelling; home **3.** a colony or settlement

hab·it-form·ing (hab′it fôr′miŋ) ***adj.*** resulting in the formation of a habit or in addiction

ha·bit·u·al (hə bich′oo wəl) ***adj.*** **1.** done by habit or fixed as a habit; customary **2.** being or doing a certain thing by habit; steady *[a habitual smoker]* **3.** much seen, done, or used; usual; frequent —**ha·bit′u·al·ly** ***adv.*** —**ha·bit′u·al·ness** ***n.***

ha·bit·u·ate (-oo wāt′) ***vt.*** **-at′ed, -at′ing** [< LL., ult. < L. *habitus:* see HABIT] to make used (*to*); accustom; familiarize —**ha·bit′u·a′tion** ***n.***

hab·i·tude (hab′ə to͞od′, -tyo͞od′) ***n.*** **1.** habitual condition of mind or body; disposition **2.** custom

ha·bit·u·é (hə bich′oo wā′) ***n.*** [Fr.] a person who frequents a certain place or places

Habs·burg (häps′boorkh) *same as* HAPSBURG

ha·ci·en·da (hä′sē en′də, has′ē-) ***n.*** [Sp. < L. *facienda,* things to be done < *facere,* to do] in Spanish America, **1.** a large estate, ranch, etc. **2.** the main dwelling on any of these

hack[1] (hak) ***vt.*** [OE. *haccian*] **1.** *a)* to chop or cut roughly or irregularly *b)* to shape, trim, etc. thus **2.** to break up (land) with a hoe, etc. **3.** [Slang] to deal with successfully —***vi.*** **1.** to make rough or irregular cuts **2.** to give harsh, dry coughs —***n.*** **1.** a tool for hacking; ax, hoe, etc. **2.** a slash, gash, or notch **3.** a harsh, dry cough —**hack it** [Slang] to make a success of some undertaking, deal with a situation, etc. —**hack′er** ***n.***

hack[2] (hak) ***n.*** [contr. < HACKNEY] **1.** a horse for hire **2.** a saddle horse **3.** an old, worn-out horse **4.** a person hired to do routine writing **5.** a devoted, unquestioning worker for a political party **6.** a carriage or coach for hire **7.** [Colloq.] *a)* a taxicab *b)* a cabdriver —***vt.*** **1.** to employ as a hack **2.** to hire out (a horse, etc.) **3.** to wear out by constant use —***vi.*** [Colloq.] to drive a taxicab —***adj.*** **1.** employed as a hack **2.** done by a hack **3.** stale; trite

hack·a·more (hak′ə môr′) ***n.*** [altered < Sp. *jaquima,* halter < Ar. *shakīma*] [Western] a rope or rawhide halter, used in breaking horses

hack·ber·ry (hak′ber′ē) ***n.,*** *pl.* **-ries** [< Scand.] **1.** an American tree with a small fruit resembling a cherry **2.** its fruit or its wood

hack·le[1] (hak′'l) ***n.*** [ME. *hechele,* prob. infl. by dial. *hackle,* bird's plumage < OE. *hacele*] **1.** a comb for separating the fibers of flax, hemp, etc. **2.** any of the long, slender feathers at the neck of a rooster, pigeon, etc. **3.** *Fishing a)* a tuft of feathers from a rooster's neck, used in making artificial flies *b)* such a fly **4.** [*pl.*] the bristling hairs on a dog's neck and back —***vt.*** **-led, -ling** to separate the fibers of (flax, hemp, etc.) with a hackle —**get one's hackles up** to become tense with anger; bristle

hack·le[2] (hak′'l) ***vt., vi.*** **-led, -ling** [freq. of HACK[1]] to cut roughly; hack; mangle

hack·ma·tack (hak′mə tak′) ***n.*** [AmInd. (Algonquian)] *same as* TAMARACK

hack·ney (hak′nē) ***n.,*** *pl.* **-neys** [< ME. < *Hackeney* (now *Hackney*), an English village] **1.** a horse for ordinary driving or riding **2.** a carriage for hire

hack·neyed (-nēd′) ***adj.*** made trite by overuse

hack·saw (hak′sô′) ***n.*** a saw for cutting metal, consisting of a narrow, fine-toothed blade held in a frame: also **hack saw**

HACKSAW

had (had; *unstressed* həd, əd) *pt. & pp. of* HAVE: also used to indicate preference or necessity, with certain words and phrases, such as *rather, better, as well* (Ex.: I *had* better leave)

had·dock (had′ək) ***n.,*** *pl.* **-dock, -docks:** see PLURAL, II, D, 2 [< ? OFr. *hadot*] a food fish related to the cod, found off the coasts of Europe and N. America

Ha·des (hā′dēz) **1.** *Gr. Myth. a)* the home of the dead, beneath the earth *b)* the ruler of the underworld **2.** the resting place of the dead: used in some New Testament translations —***n.*** [*often* **h-**] [Colloq.] hell: a euphemism

had·n't (had′'nt) had not

Ha·dri·an (hā′drē ən) (L. name *Publius Aelius Hadrianus*) 76–138 A.D.; Roman emperor (117–138)

hadst (hadst) *archaic 2d pers. sing., past indic., of* HAVE: *used with* thou

Haeck·el (hek′əl), **Ernst Hein·rich** (ernst hīn′riH) 1834–1919; Ger. biologist & philosopher

haemat-, haemato-, haemo- *see* HEMATO-, HEMO-

hae·mo·glo·bin (hē′mə glō′bin, hem′ə-) ***n.*** *same as* HEMOGLOBIN

haf·ni·um (haf′nē əm) ***n.*** [ModL. < L. *Hafnia,* Roman name of Copenhagen] a metallic chemical element found with zirconium and somewhat resembling it: symbol, Hf; at. wt., 178.49; at. no., 72

haft (haft) ***n.*** [OE. *hæft*] a handle or hilt of a knife, ax, etc.

hag (hag) ***n.*** [< OE. *hægtes* < *haga,* a hedge] **1.** a witch **2.** an ugly, often vicious old woman —**hag′gish** ***adj.***

Hag. Haggai

Ha·gar (hā′gər) *Bible* a concubine of Abraham and slave of his wife Sarah

Ha·gen (hä′gən) city in W West Germany, in the Ruhr valley: pop. 200,000

hag·fish (hag′fish′) ***n.,*** *pl.* **-fish′, -fish′es:** see FISH [HAG + FISH] a small, eellike saltwater fish with a round, sucking mouth and horny teeth, with which it bores into other fish and devours them

Hag·ga·da, Hag·ga·dah (hä gä dä′; *E.* hə gä′də) ***n.,*** *pl.* **-ga·dot′** (-dōt′) [Heb. *haggādāh* < *higgid,* to tell] **1.** *a)* [*often* **h-**] in the *Talmud,* an anecdote that explains some point of law *b)* the part of the Talmud devoted to such narratives **2.** the narrative of the Exodus read at the Seder during Passover —**hag·gad·ic** (hə gad′ik, -gä′dik) ***adj.***

Hag·ga·i (hag′ē ī′, hag′ī) *Bible* **1.** a Hebrew prophet who lived c. 500 B.C. **2.** the book attributed to him

hag·gard (hag′ərd) ***adj.*** [MFr. *hagard,* untamed] having a wild, wasted, worn look, as from grief or illness —**hag′gard·ly** ***adv.*** —**hag′gard·ness** ***n.***

hag·gis (hag′is) ***n.*** [ME. *hagas,* kind of pudding] a Scottish dish made of the lungs, heart, etc. of a sheep or calf, mixed with suet, seasoning, and oatmeal and boiled in the animal's stomach

hag·gle (hag′'l) ***vt.*** **-gled, -gling** [freq. of Scot. *hag,* to chop, cut] to hack; mangle —***vi.*** to argue about terms, price, etc.; wrangle —***n.*** a haggling —**hag′gler** ***n.***

hag·i·o- [< Gr. *hagios,* holy] *a prefix meaning* saintly, sacred: also, before a vowel, **hag·i-**

hag·i·ol·o·gy (hag′ē äl′ə jē, hā′jē-) ***n.,*** *pl.* **-gies** [prec. + -LOGY] **1.** literature about saints' lives and legends, sacred writings, etc. **2.** a list of saints —**hag′i·o·log′ic** (-ə läj′ik), **hag′i·o·log′i·cal** ***adj.*** —**hag′i·ol′o·gist** ***n.***

hag·rid·den (hag′rid′'n) ***adj.*** obsessed or harassed, as by fears

Hague (hāg), **The** city in W Netherlands; seat of the government (cf. AMSTERDAM): pop. 576,000

hah (hä) ***interj., n.*** *same as* HA

Hai·fa (hī′fə) seaport in NW Israel: pop. 210,000

hai·ku (hī′ko͞o) ***n.*** [Jap.] **1.** a Japanese verse form of three unrhymed lines of 5, 7, and 5 syllables respectively, usually on some subject in nature **2.** *pl.* **-ku** a poem in this form

hail[1] (hāl) ***vt.*** [< ON. < *heill,* whole, sound] **1.** to welcome, greet, etc. as with cheers; acclaim **2.** to salute as *[they hailed him their leader]* **3.** to call out to, as in summoning *[to hail a taxi]* —***vi.*** *Naut.* to call out or signal to a ship —***n.*** **1.** a hailing or greeting **2.** the distance that a shout will carry *[within hail]* —***interj.*** an exclamation of tribute, greeting, etc. —**hail fellow well met** very friendly to everyone —**hail from** to come from (one's birthplace, etc.)

hail[2] (hāl) ***n.*** [OE. *hægel*] **1.** small, rounded pieces of ice that sometimes fall during thunderstorms; hailstones **2.** a falling, showering, etc. of or like hail *[a hail of bullets]* —***vi.*** to pour down hail *[it is hailing]* —***vt.*** to shower, hurl, etc. violently like hail (often with *on* or *upon*) *[to hail curses on someone]*

Hai·le Se·las·sie (hī′lē sə las′ē, -läs′ē) (born *Tafari Makonnen*) 1891–1975; emperor of Ethiopia (1930–74)

hail·stone (hāl′stōn′) ***n.*** a pellet of hail

hail·storm (-stôrm′) ***n.*** a storm with hail

Hai·phong (hī′fäŋ′) seaport in N Vietnam: pop. 369,000

hair (her) ***n.*** [OE. *hær*] **1.** any of the fine, threadlike outgrowths from the skin of an animal or human being **2.** a growth of these; esp., the growth covering the human head or the skin of most mammals **3.** an extremely small space, degree, etc. **4.** a threadlike growth on a plant —***adj.*** **1.** made of or with hair **2.** for the care of the hair *[hair tonic]* —**get in one's hair** [Slang] to annoy one —**let one's hair down** [Slang] to be very informal, relaxed, etc. —**make one's hair stand on end** to horrify one —**split hairs** to make petty distinctions; quibble —**to a hair** exactly; perfectly —**hair′less** ***adj.*** —**hair′less·ness** ***n.*** —**hair′like′** ***adj.***

hair·breadth (-bredth′) ***n.*** an extremely small space or amount —***adj.*** very narrow; close Also **hairs′breadth′**

hair·cloth (-klôth′) ***n.*** cloth woven from horsehair, camel's hair, etc.: used esp. for upholstery

hair·cut (-kut′) ***n.*** **1.** a cutting of the hair of the head **2.** the style in which the hair is cut —**hair′cut′ter** ***n.***

hair·do (-do͞o′) ***n.,*** *pl.* **-dos′** the style in which (a woman's) hair is arranged; coiffure

hair·dress·er (-dres′ər) ***n.*** a person whose work is dressing (women's) hair —**hair′dress′ing** ***n., adj.***

hair·line (-līn′) ***n.*** **1.** a very thin line or stripe **2.** the outline of the hair on the head, esp. above the forehead

hair·net (-net′) ***n.*** a net or fine-meshed cap for keeping the hair in place

hair·piece (-pēs′) ***n.*** a toupee or wig

hair·pin (-pin′) ***n.*** a small, usually U-shaped, piece of wire, shell, etc., for keeping the hair in place —***adj.*** U-shaped [*a hairpin* turn]

hair-rais·ing (-rā′ziŋ) ***adj.*** [Colloq.] causing the hair to stand on end; terrifying —**hair′-rais′er *n.***

hair shirt a shirt or girdle of haircloth, worn for self-punishment by religious ascetics

hair·split·ting (-split′iŋ) ***adj., n.*** making petty distinctions; quibbling —**hair′split′ter *n.***

hair·spring (-spriŋ′) ***n.*** a very slender, hairlike coil that controls the regular movement of the balance wheel in a watch or clock

hair trigger a trigger so delicately adjusted that slight pressure on it discharges the firearm

hair·y (-ē) ***adj.*** **hair′i·er, hair′i·est 1.** covered with hair **2.** of or like hair **3.** [Slang] difficult, distressing, etc. —**hair′i·ness *n.***

Hai·ti (hāt′ē) country occupying the W portion of the island of Hispaniola, West Indies: 10,714 sq. mi.; pop. 4,768,000; cap. Port-au-Prince —**Hai·tian** (hā′shən, hāt′ē ən) ***adj., n.***

hajj (haj) ***n.*** [Ar. *ḥajj* < *ḥajji,* to go on a pilgrimage] the pilgrimage to Mecca that every Moslem is expected to make at least once

haj·ji, haj·i (haj′ē) ***n.*** [< Ar., pilgrim: see prec.] a Moslem who has made a pilgrimage to Mecca

hake (hāk) ***n., pl.*** **hake, hakes:** see PLURAL, II, D, 2 [prob. < ON. *haki,* a hook (from shape of the jaw)] any of various marine food fishes related to the cod, as the **silver hake**

ha·kim[1] (hä kēm′) ***n.*** [Ar. *ḥakīm,* wise, learned] in Moslem regions, a doctor; physician

ha·kim[2] (hä′kēm, -kim) ***n.*** [Ar. *ḥākim,* governor] in Moslem regions, a ruler, judge, or governor

Hak·luyt (hak′lo͞ot), **Richard** 1552?–1616; Eng. geographer & chronicler of explorations & discoveries

hal·berd (hal′bərd) ***n.*** [ult. < MHG. *helmbarte* < *helm,* handle + *barte,* an ax] a combination spear and battle-ax used in the 15th and 16th cent.: also **hal′bert** (-bərt) —**hal′berd·ier′** (-bər dir′) ***n.***

hal·cy·on (hal′sē ən) ***n.*** [< L. < Gr. *alkyōn,* kingfisher] a legendary bird, identified with the kingfisher, supposed to have a peaceful, calming influence on the sea at the time of the winter solstice —***adj.*** **1.** of the halcyon **2.** tranquil, happy, idyllic, etc.: esp. in phrase **halcyon days**

hale[1] (hāl) ***adj.*** **hal′er, hal′est** [OE. *hal*] strong and healthy

hale[2] (hāl) ***vt.*** **haled, hal′ing** [< OFr. *haler,* prob. < ODu. *halen: see* HAUL] to force (one) to go [*haled* him into court]

Hale (hāl), **Nathan** 1755–76; Am. soldier in the Revolutionary War: hanged by the British as a spy

hal·er (häl′ər) ***n., pl.*** **-er·u′** (-ə ro͞o′), **-ers** [Czech, ult. < MHG. *Haller* (*pfenninc*), (penny of) Hall, a Ger. coin made at Hall, Swabia] *see* MONETARY UNITS, table (Czechoslovakia)

half (haf) ***n., pl.*** **halves** [OE. *healf*] **1.** either of the two equal, or almost equal, parts of something **2.** a half hour [*half* past one] **3.** *Basketball, Football,* etc. either of the two equal periods of the game, between which the players rest —***adj.*** **1.** *a*) being either of the two equal parts *b*) being about a half of the amount, length, etc. **2.** incomplete; partial —***adv.*** **1.** to an extent approximately or exactly fifty percent of the whole **2.** [Colloq.] to some extent [to be *half* convinced] **3.** [Colloq.] by any means; at all: used with *not* [not *half* bad] —**by half** considerably; very much —**in half** into halves —**not the half of** only a small part of

half-and-half (haf′′n haf′) ***n.*** something that is half one thing and half another; esp., *a*) a mixture of equal parts of milk and cream *b*) [Chiefly Brit.] a mixture of equal parts of porter and ale, beer and stout, etc. —***adj.*** combining two things equally —***adv.*** in two equal parts

half·back (-bak′) ***n.*** *Football* either of two players whose position is behind the line of scrimmage together with the fullback and the quarterback

half-baked (-bākt′) ***adj.*** **1.** only partly baked **2.** not completely planned or thought out **3.** having or showing little intelligence and experience

half-blood (-blud′) ***n.*** **1.** a person related to another through one parent only **2.** *same as* HALF-BREED —***adj.*** *same as* HALF-BLOODED

half blood 1. kinship through one parent only [sisters of the *half blood*] **2.** *same as* HALF-BLOODED

half-blood·ed (-blud′id) ***adj.*** **1.** related through one parent only **2.** born of parents of different races

half boot a boot reaching halfway up the lower leg

half-breed (-brēd′) ***n.*** a person whose parents are of different races —***adj.*** *same as* HALF-BLOODED Sometimes regarded as a contemptuous term

half brother a brother through one parent only

half-caste (-kast′) ***n.*** a half-breed; esp., an offspring of one European parent and one Asiatic parent —***adj.*** of a half-caste

half cock the halfway position of the hammer of a firearm, when the trigger is locked —**go off half-cocked 1.** to go off too soon: said of a firearm **2.** to speak or act thoughtlessly or too hastily: also **go off at half cock** —**half′-cocked′ *adj.***

half dollar a coin of the U.S. and Canada, worth 50 cents

half gainer a fancy dive in which the diver, facing forward, does a back flip in the air so as to enter the water headfirst, facing the board

half·heart·ed (-här′tid) ***adj.*** with little enthusiasm, determination, interest, etc. —**half′heart′ed·ly *adv.***

half hitch a knot made by passing the end of the rope around the rope and then through the loop thus made

half-hour (-our′) ***n.*** **1.** half of an hour; thirty minutes **2.** the point thirty minutes after any given hour —***adj.*** **1.** lasting for thirty minutes **2.** occurring every thirty minutes —**half′-hour′ly *adj., adv.***

half-life (-līf′) ***n.*** the period required for the disintegration of half of the atoms in a sample of some radioactive substance: also **half life**

half-mast (-mast′) ***n.*** the position of a flag lowered about halfway down its staff, as in public mourning —***vt.*** to hang (a flag) at half-mast

half-moon (-mo͞on′) ***n.*** **1.** the moon when only half its disk is clearly seen **2.** anything shaped like a half-moon or crescent

half nelson *see* NELSON

half note *Music* a note having one half the duration of a whole note: see NOTE, illus.

half·pen·ny (hā′pə nē, hāp′nē) ***n., pl.*** **-pence** (-pens), **-pennies** a former British coin equal to half a penny —***adj.*** worth a halfpenny, or very little

half pint 1. a liquid or dry measure equal to 1/4 quart **2.** [Slang] a small person

half sister a sister through one parent only

half size any of a series of sizes in women's garments for short-waisted, mature figures

half-sole (haf′sōl′) ***vt.*** **-soled′, -sol′ing** to repair (shoes or boots) by attaching new half soles

half sole a sole (of a shoe or boot) from the arch to the toe

half step 1. *Mil.* a short marching step of fifteen inches (in double time, eighteen inches) **2.** *Music same as* SEMITONE

half-tim·bered (-tim′bərd) ***adj.*** *Archit.* made of a wooden framework having the spaces filled with plaster, brick, etc.

half time the rest period between halves of a football game, basketball game, etc.

half·tone (-tōn′) ***n.*** **1.** *Art* a tone or shading between light and dark **2.** *Music same as* SEMITONE **3.** *Photoengraving a*) a technique of shadings by dots produced by photographing the object from behind a fine screen *b*) a photoengraving so made

half·track (-trak′) ***n.*** an army truck, armored vehicle, etc. with tractor treads instead of rear wheels, but with a pair of wheels in front

half·way (-wā′) ***adj.*** **1.** equally distant between two points, states, etc. **2.** incomplete; partial —***adv.*** **1.** half the distance; to the midway point **2.** incompletely; partially —**meet halfway** to be willing to compromise with

halfway house a place where persons are aided in readjusting to society following imprisonment, hospitalization, etc.

half-wit (-wit′) ***n.*** a stupid, silly, or imbecilic person; fool; dolt —**half′-wit′ted *adj.***

hal·i·but (hal′ə bət) ***n., pl.*** **-but, -buts:** see PLURAL, II, D, 2 [< ME. < *hali,* holy + *butt,* a flounder: because eaten on holidays] a large, edible flatfish found in northern seas, esp. the **Atlantic halibut:** they sometimes weigh hundreds of pounds

Hal·i·car·nas·sus (hal′ə kär nas′əs) ancient city in SW Asia Minor, on the Aegean

hal·ide (hal′īd, hā′līd) ***n.*** [HAL(OGEN) + -IDE] *Chem.* a compound of a halogen with another element or a radical —***adj.*** *same as* HALOID

Hal·i·fax (hal′ə faks′) capital of Nova Scotia; seaport on the Atlantic: pop. 118,000

hal·ite (hal′īt, hā′līt) ***n.*** [< Gr. *hals,* salt + -ITE] native sodium chloride; rock salt

hal·i·to·sis (hal′ə tō′sis) ***n.*** [ModL. < L. *halitus,* breath + -OSIS] bad-smelling breath

hall (hôl) ***n.*** [OE. *heall* < base of *helan,* to cover] **1.** the dwelling of a baron, squire, etc. **2.** [*sometimes* **H-**] a building containing public offices or the headquarters of an organization **3.** a large public or semipublic room or auditorium for gatherings, entertainments, etc. **4.** [*sometimes*

H-] a college dormitory, classroom building, etc. **5.** a passageway or room between the entrance and the interior of a building **6.** a passageway or corridor onto which rooms open

Hal·le (häl′ə; *E.* hal′ē) city in SC East Germany: pop. 266,000

hal·le·lu·jah, hal·le·lu·iah (hal′ə lo͞o′yə) *interj.* [< LL. < Gr. < Heb. < *hallelū,* praise + *yāh,* Jehovah] praise (ye) the Lord! *—n.* an exclamation or hymn of praise to God

Hal·ley's comet (hal′ēz) a comet, last seen in 1910, whose periodic reappearance (c. 75 years) was predicted by Edmund Halley (1656–1742), Eng. astronomer

hal·liard (hal′yərd) *n. same as* HALYARD

hall·mark (hôl′märk′) *n.* **1.** an official mark stamped on British gold and silver articles orig. at Goldsmiths' Hall in London, as a guarantee of genuineness **2.** any mark or symbol of genuineness or high quality *—vt.* to put a hallmark on

hal·lo, hal·loa (hə lō′) *interj., n., vi., vt. same as* HALLOO

hal·loo (hə lo͞o′) *vi., vt.* **-looed′, -loo′ing** **1.** to call out in order to attract the attention of (a person) **2.** to urge on (hounds) by shouting **3.** to shout *—interj., n.* a shout or call

hal·low (hal′ō) *vt.* [OE. *halgian* < *halig,* holy] **1.** to make holy or sacred; consecrate **2.** to regard as holy; honor as sacred

hal·lowed (hal′ōd; *in poetry or liturgy, often* hal′ə wid) *adj.* **1.** made holy or sacred **2.** honored as holy

Hal·low·een, Hal·low·e'en (hal′ə wēn′, häl′-) *n.* [contr. < *all hallow even*] the evening of October 31, which is followed by All Saints' Day

hall tree a clothes tree, esp. one in an entrance hall

hal·lu·ci·nate (hə lo͞o′sə nāt′) *vi., vt.* **-nat′ed, -nat′ing** [< L. pp. of *hallucinari,* to wander mentally] to have or cause to have hallucinations

hal·lu·ci·na·tion (hə lo͞o′sə nā′shən) *n.* **1.** the apparent perception of sights, sounds, etc. that are not actually present **2.** the imaginary thing apparently seen, heard, etc. **—hal·lu′ci·na′tive, hal·lu′ci·na·to′ry** (-nə tôr′ē) *adj.*

hal·lu·ci·no·gen (hə lo͞o′sə nə jen, hal′yoo sin′ə jen) *n.* a drug or other substance that produces hallucinations **—hal·lu′ci·no·gen′ic** *adj.*

hall·way (hôl′wā′) *n.* **1.** a passageway or room between the entrance and the interior of a building **2.** a passageway; corridor; hall

ha·lo (hā′lō) *n., pl.* **-los, -loes** [< L. < Gr. *halōs,* circular threshing floor, halo around the sun < *halein,* to grind] **1.** a ring of light that seems to encircle the sun, moon, etc. **2.** a symbolic ring or disk of light shown around the head of a saint, etc. **3.** the glory with which a famed, revered, or idealized person or thing is invested *—vt.* **-loed, -lo·ing** to encircle with a halo

hal·o·gen (hal′ə jən) *n.* [< Gr. *hals* (gen. *halos*), salt + -GEN] any of the five very active, nonmetallic chemical elements, fluorine, chlorine, bromine, astatine, and iodine **—ha·log·e·nous** (ha läj′ə nəs) *adj.*

hal·o·gen·ate (-jə nāt′) *vt.* **-at′ed, -at′ing** to treat or combine with a halogen **—hal′o·gen·a′tion** *n.*

hal·oid (hal′oid, hā′loid) *adj.* [< Gr. *hals,* salt + -OID] of or like a halide *—n. same as* HALIDE

Hals (häls), **Frans** (fräns) 1580?–1666; Du. painter

halt[1] (hôlt) *n.* [< Fr. < G. < *halten,* to hold] a stop, esp. a temporary one, as in marching *—vi., vt.* to come or bring to a halt **—call a halt** to order a stop

halt[2] (hôlt) *vi.* [< OE. *healtian* < *healt,* adj.] **1.** [Archaic] to limp **2.** to be uncertain; hesitate [*to halt* in one's speech] **3.** to have defects in flow, as of rhythm or logic *—adj.* limping; lame *—n.* [Archaic] a lameness **—the halt** those who are lame **—halt′ing·ly** *adv.*

hal·ter (hôl′tər) *n.* [OE. *hælftre*] **1.** a rope, strap, etc. for tying or leading an animal **2.** a rope for hanging a person; noose **3.** a woman's garment for covering the breast, held up by a loop around the neck *—vt.* to put a halter on (an animal)

hal·vah, hal·va (häl vä′) *n.* [Turk. *helwa* < Ar. *ḥalwa*] a Turkish confection made of ground sesame seeds and nuts mixed with honey, etc.

halve (hav) *vt.* **halved, halv′ing** **1.** to divide into two equal parts **2.** to share equally (*with* someone) **3.** to reduce to half **4.** *Golf* to play (a hole, match, etc.) in the same number of strokes as one's opponent

halves (havz) *n. pl. of* HALF **—by halves** **1.** halfway; imperfectly **2.** halfheartedly **—go halves** to share expenses, etc. equally

hal·yard (hal′yərd) *n.* [< ME. *halier* < *halien* (see HALE[2])] a rope or tackle for raising or lowering a flag, sail, etc.

Ham (ham) *Bible* Noah's second son

ham (ham) *n.* [OE. *hamm*] **1.** the part of the leg behind the knee **2.** *a)* the back of the thigh *b)* the thigh and the buttock together **3.** the hock or hind leg of a four-legged animal **4.** the upper part of a hog's hind leg, salted, smoked, etc. **5.** [Colloq.] an amateur radio operator **6.** [Slang] an incompetent actor or performer, esp. one who overacts *—vi., vt.* **hammed, ham′ming** [Slang] to act with exaggeration; overact: often in **ham it up**

Ha·man (hā′mən) *Bible* a Persian official who sought the destruction of the Jews but was hanged from his own gallows: Esth. 7

Ham·burg (ham′bərg; *G.* häm′boorkh) seaport in N West Germany, on the Elbe: pop. 1,833,000

ham·burg·er (ham′bur′gər) *n.* [earlier *Hamburg steak,* after HAMBURG] **1.** ground beef **2.** a fried, broiled, or baked patty of such meat, often eaten as a sandwich in a round bun Also **ham′burg**

hame (hām) *n.* [< MDu., horse collar] either of the two rigid pieces along the sides of a horse's collar, to which the traces are attached

Ham·il·ton (ham′əl t′n) **1.** city & port in SE Ontario, Canada, on Lake Ontario: pop. 312,000 **2.** [after A. HAMILTON] city in SW Ohio: pop. 63,000 **3.** capital of Bermuda: pop. 3,000

Ham·il·ton (ham′əl t′n), **Alexander** 1757–1804; Am. statesman; 1st secretary of the U.S. treasury (1789–95) **—Ham′il·to′ni·an** (-tō′nē ən) *adj., n.*

Ham·ite (ham′īt) *n.* **1.** a person regarded as descended from Ham **2.** a member of any of several usually dark-skinned peoples of N and E Africa, including the Egyptians, Berbers, etc.

Ham·it·ic (ha mit′ik, hə-) *adj.* **1.** of Ham or the Hamites **2.** designating or of a group of African languages, including ancient Egyptian, Berber, and Cushitic

Ham·let (ham′lit) **1.** a famous tragedy by Shakespeare (c. 1602) **2.** the hero of this play

ham·let (ham′lit) *n.* [< OFr. dim. of *hamel,* itself dim. of LowG. *hamm,* enclosed area] a very small village

ham·mer (ham′ər) *n.* [OE. *hamor*] **1.** a tool for pounding, usually consisting of a metal head and a handle **2.** a thing like this tool in shape or use; specif., *a)* the mechanism that strikes the firing pin or cap in a firearm *b)* any of the felted mallets that strike against the strings of a piano *c)* a power tool for pounding **3.** the malleus, one of the bones of the middle ear **4.** an auctioneer's gavel **5.** *Sports* a heavy metal ball attached to a wire and thrown for distance in a field event (**hammer throw**) *—vt.* **1.** to strike repeatedly as with a hammer **2.** to make or fasten with a hammer **3.** to drive, force, or shape as with hammer blows *—vi.* to strike repeated blows as with a hammer **—hammer (away) at** **1.** to work energetically at **2.** to keep emphasizing **—hammer out** **1.** to shape or flatten by hammering **2.** to take out by hammering **3.** to develop or work out by careful thought or repeated effort **—ham′mer·er** *n.* **—ham′mer·like′** *adj.*

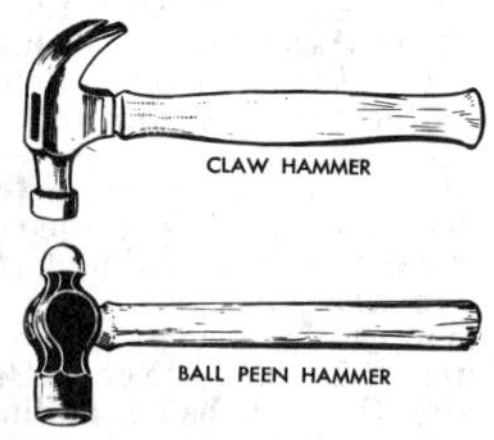

TYPES OF HAMMER

ham·mer·head (-hed′) *n.* a medium-sized shark that has a mallet-shaped head

ham·mer·lock (-läk′) *n.* a wrestling hold in which one arm of the opponent is twisted upward behind his back

ham·mer·toe (-tō′) *n.* **1.** a condition in which the first joint of a toe is permanently bent downward, resulting in a clawlike deformity **2.** such a toe

ham·mock (ham′ək) *n.* [Sp. *hamaca* < native WInd. name] a length of netting, canvas, etc. swung from ropes at both ends and used as a bed or couch

Ham·mond (ham′ənd) [after G. *Hammond,* local meatpacker] city in NW Ind., near Chicago: pop. 94,000

Ham·mu·ra·bi (hä′moo rä′bē, ham′ə-) fl. 18th cent. B.C.; king of Babylon: a famous code of laws is attributed to him

ham·my (ham′ē) *adj.* **-mi·er, -mi·est** [Slang] like or characteristic of a ham (actor); overacting

ham·per[1] (ham′pər) *vt.* [ME. *hampren*] to hinder; impede; encumber

ham·per[2] (ham′pər) *n.* [< OFr. < *hanap,* a cup < Frank.] a large basket, usually with a cover

Hamp·ton (hamp′tən) [after a town in England] seaport in SE Va., on Hampton Roads: pop. 123,000

Hampton Roads [see prec. & ROAD (sense 4)] channel in SE Va., linking the James River estuary with Chesapeake Bay

ham·ster (ham′stər) *n.* [G.] a ratlike animal with large cheek pouches: it is often used in scientific experiments or kept as a pet

ham·string (ham′striŋ′) *n.* **1.** one of the tendons at the back of the human knee **2.** the great tendon at the back of the hock in a four-legged animal *—vt.* **-strung′, -string′ing** **1.** to disable by cutting a hamstring **2.** to make powerless or ineffective

Han·cock (han′käk), **John** 1737–93; Am. statesman; 1st signer of the Declaration of Independence

hand (hand) ***n.*** [OE.] **1.** the part of the human arm below the wrist, used for grasping **2.** the corresponding part in apes, monkeys, etc. **3.** a side, direction, or position indicated by a hand *[at one's right hand]* **4.** possession or care *[the papers are in my hands]* **5.** control; power *[to strengthen one's hand]* **6.** an active part; share *[take a hand in this work]* **7.** *a)* a handshake, as a pledge *b)* a promise to marry **8.** skill; ability *[a master's hand]* **9.** *a)* handwriting *b)* a signature **10.** a clapping of hands; applause *[they gave the singer a hand]* **11.** assistance; help *[to lend a hand]* **12.** a person whose chief work is with his hands, as a sailor, farm laborer, etc. **13.** a person regarded as having some special skill *[quite a hand at sewing]* **14.** a person (or, sometimes, thing) from or through which something comes; source *[to get a story at second hand]* **15.** anything like a hand, as the pointer on a clock **16.** the breadth of a hand, about 4 inches **17.** *Card Games a)* the cards held by a player at one time *b)* a player *c)* a round of play —***adj.*** of, for, made by, or controlled by the hand —***vt.*** **1.** to give as with the hand; transfer **2.** to help, conduct, steady, etc. with the hand *[to hand a lady into her car]* —**(at) first hand** from the original source —**at hand 1.** near; close by **2.** immediately available —**(at) second hand 1.** not from the original source **2.** previously used —**at the hand** (or **hands**) **of** through the action of —**by hand** not by machines but with the hands —**change hands** to pass from one owner to another —**from hand to mouth** with just enough for immediate needs —**hand down 1.** to bequeath **2.** to announce (a verdict, etc.) —**hand in** to give; submit —**hand in hand 1.** holding one another's hand **2.** together —**hand it to** [Slang] to give deserved credit to —**hand on** to pass along; transmit —**hand out** to distribute —**hand over** to give up; deliver —**hand over fist** [Colloq.] easily and in large amounts —**hands down** without effort; easily —**hands off!** don't touch! don't interfere! —**hand to hand** at close quarters: said of fighting —**have one's hands full** to be extremely busy —**in hand 1.** in order or control **2.** in possession **3.** in process —**lay hands on 1.** to attack physically **2.** to seize; take **3.** to touch with the hands in blessing, etc. —**off one's hands** no longer in one's care —**on every hand** on all sides —**on hand 1.** near **2.** available **3.** present —**on one's hands** in one's care —**on the one hand** from one point of view —**on the other hand** from the opposed point of view —**out of hand 1.** out of control **2.** immediately **3.** over and done with —**show** (or **tip**) **one's hand** to disclose one's intentions —**take in hand 1.** to take control of **2.** to handle; treat **3.** to try; attempt —**to hand 1.** near; accessible **2.** in one's possession —**turn** (or **put**) **one's hand to** to undertake; work at —**wash one's hands of** to refuse to go on with or take responsibility for —**with a high hand** with arrogance —**with clean hands** without guilt —**hand′less** ***adj.***

hand- *a combining form meaning* of, with, by, or for a hand or hands *[handclasp, handcuff]*

hand·bag (hand′bag′) ***n.*** **1.** a small container for money, toilet articles, keys, etc., carried by women; purse **2.** a small suitcase or valise

hand·ball (-bôl′) ***n.*** **1.** a game in which players bat a small ball against a wall or walls with the hand **2.** the small rubber ball

hand·bar·row (-bar′ō) ***n.*** a frame carried by two people, each holding a pair of handles attached at either end

hand·bill (-bil′) ***n.*** a small printed notice, advertisement, etc. to be passed out by hand

hand·book (-book′) ***n.*** **1.** a compact reference book on some subject; manual **2.** a guidebook

hand·breadth (-bredth′, -bretth′) ***n.*** the breadth of the human palm, about 4 inches

hand·cart (-kärt′) ***n.*** a small cart, often with only two wheels, pulled or pushed by hand

hand·clasp (-klasp′) ***n.*** a clasping of each other's hand in greeting, farewell, etc.

hand·craft (-kraft′) ***n.*** *same as* HANDICRAFT —***vt.*** to make by hand with skill —**hand′craft′ed** ***adj.***

hand·cuff (-kuf′) ***n.*** either of a pair of connected metal rings that can be locked about the wrists, as in fastening a prisoner to a policeman: *usually used in pl.* —***vt.*** **1.** to put handcuffs on; manacle **2.** to hinder the activities of

hand·ed (han′did) ***adj.*** **1.** having, or for use by one having, a specified handedness *[right-handed]* **2.** having or using a specified number of hands *[two-handed]* **3.** involving (a specified number of) players *[three-handed pinochle]*

hand·ed·ness (-nis) ***n.*** ability in using one hand more skillfully than the other

Han·del (han′d'l), **George Frederick** (born *Georg Friedrich Händel*) 1685–1759; Eng. composer, born in Germany

hand·ful (hand′fool′) ***n.,*** *pl.* **-fuls′ 1.** as much or as many as the hand will hold **2.** a few; not many **3.** [Colloq.] someone or something hard to manage

hand·gun (-gun′) ***n.*** any firearm that is held and fired with one hand, as a pistol

hand·i·cap (han′dē kap′) ***n.*** [orig. a game in which forfeits were drawn from a cap < *hand in cap*] **1.** *a)* a race or other competition in which difficulties are imposed on the superior contestants, or advantages given to the inferior, to make their chances of winning equal *b)* such a difficulty or advantage **2.** something that hampers one; disadvantage —***vt.*** **-capped′, -cap′ping 1.** to give a handicap to **2.** to cause to be at a disadvantage; hinder —**the handicapped** those who are physically disabled or mentally retarded —**hand′i·cap′per** ***n.***

hand·i·craft (han′dē kraft′) ***n.*** [OE. *handcræft*] **1.** skill with the hands **2.** an occupation or art calling for such skill, as weaving —**hand′i·crafts′man** ***n.,*** *pl.* **-men**

hand·i·work (-wurk′) ***n.*** **1.** *same as* HANDWORK **2.** anything made or done by a particular person

hand·ker·chief (haŋ′kər chif, -chēf′) ***n.,*** *pl.* **-chiefs** (-chifs, -chēfs′, -chivz, -chēvz′) **1.** a small, square piece of cloth for wiping the nose, eyes, or face, or worn for ornament **2.** a kerchief

han·dle (han′d'l) ***n.*** [OE. < *hand,* HAND] **1.** that part of a utensil, tool, etc. which is to be held, turned, etc. with the hand **2.** a thing like a handle **3.** [Colloq.] a person's name, nickname, or title —***vt.*** **-dled, -dling 1.** to touch, lift, etc. with the hand or hands **2.** to operate or use with the hands **3.** to manage, control, etc. **4.** to deal with *[to handle a problem tactfully]* **5.** to sell or deal in **6.** to behave toward; treat —***vi.*** to respond to control *[the car handles well]* —**fly off the handle** [Colloq.] to become violently angry or excited —**get a handle on** [Colloq.] to find a means of dealing with, understanding, etc.

han·dle·bar (-bär′) ***n.*** **1.** [*often pl.*] a curved metal bar with handles on the ends, for steering a bicycle, etc. **2.** [Colloq.] a mustache with long curved ends: in full, **handlebar mustache**

han·dler (han′dlər) ***n.*** a person or thing that handles; specif., *a)* a boxer's trainer and second *b)* a person who trains and manages an animal

hand·made (hand′mād′) ***adj.*** made by hand, not by machine

hand·maid·en (-mād′'n) ***n.*** **1.** [Archaic] a woman or girl servant **2.** that which accompanies in a useful but subordinate capacity Also **hand′maid′**

hand-me-down (-mē doun′) ***n.*** [Colloq.] a used article of clothing, etc. which is passed along to someone else —***adj.*** [Colloq.] **1.** used; secondhand **2.** ready-made and cheap

hand organ a barrel organ played by turning a crank by hand

hand·out (hand′out′) ***n.*** **1.** a gift of food, clothing, etc., as to a beggar or tramp **2.** a leaflet, statement, etc. handed out as for publicity

hand·pick (-pik′) ***vt.*** **1.** to pick (fruit or vegetables) by hand **2.** to choose with care or for a special purpose —**hand′picked′** ***adj.***

hand·rail (-rāl′) ***n.*** a rail serving as a guard or hand support, as along a stairway

hand·saw (-sô′) ***n.*** a saw used with one hand

hand's-breadth (handz′bredth′, -bretth′) ***n.*** *same as* HANDBREADTH

hand·sel (han′s'l, hant′-) ***n.*** [< ON. *handsal,* sealing of a bargain by a handclasp] a present for good luck, as at the new year or on the launching of a new business —***vt.*** **-seled** or **-selled, -sel·ing** or **-sel·ling** to give a handsel to

hand·set (hand′set′) ***n.*** a telephone mouthpiece and receiver in a single unit, held in one hand

HANDSET

hand·shake (-shāk′) ***n.*** a gripping of each other's hand in greeting, agreement, etc.

hand·some (han′səm) ***adj.*** [orig., easily handled < ME.: see HAND & -SOME[1]] **1.** large; considerable *[a handsome sum]* **2.** generous; gracious *[a handsome gesture]* **3.** good-looking; of pleasing appearance, esp. in a manly or dignified way —**hand′some·ly** ***adv.*** —**hand′some·ness** ***n.***

hand·spring (hand′spriŋ′) ***n.*** a tumbling feat in which the performer turns over in midair with one or both hands touching the ground

hand-to-hand (han′tə hand′) ***adj.*** in close contact; at close quarters: said of fighting

hand-to-mouth (-mouth′) ***adj.*** barely subsisting

hand·work (hand′wʉrk′) ***n.*** work done or made by hand, not by machine —**hand′worked′** ***adj.***

hand·writ·ing (-rīt′iŋ) ***n.*** **1.** writing done by hand, with pen, pencil, chalk, etc. **2.** a style or form of such writing —**hand′writ′ten** (-rit′'n) ***adj.***

hand·y (han′dē) ***adj.*** **hand′i·er, hand′i·est** **1.** close at hand; easily reached **2.** easily used; convenient **3.** clever with the hands; deft —**hand′i·ly** ***adv.*** —**hand′i·ness** ***n.***

han·dy·man (-man′) ***n.,*** *pl.* **-men′** a man who does odd jobs

hang (haŋ) ***vt.*** **hung, hang′ing;** for vt. 3 & vi. 4 **hanged** is preferred pt. & pp. [OE. *hangian*] **1.** to attach to something above with no support from below; suspend **2.** to attach so as to permit free motion *[to hang a door on its hinges]* **3.** to put to death by suspending from a rope about the neck **4.** to fasten (pictures, etc.) to a wall **5.** to ornament or cover *[to hang a room with pictures]* **6.** to paste (wallpaper) to walls **7.** to deadlock (a jury) by one's vote **8.** to fix (something) *on* a person or thing —***vi.*** **1.** to be suspended **2.** to swing, as on a hinge **3.** to drape, as cloth, a coat, etc. **4.** to die by hanging **5.** to droop; bend **6.** to be doubtful; hesitate **7.** to have one's pictures exhibited at a museum, etc. —***n.*** the way that a thing hangs —**get** (or **have**) **the hang of** **1.** to learn (or have) the knack of **2.** to understand the significance or idea of —**hang around** (or **about**) **1.** to cluster around **2.** [Colloq.] to loiter around —**hang back** (or **off**) to be reluctant to advance —**hang fire** to be unsettled or undecided —**hang on** **1.** to keep hold **2.** to persevere **3.** to depend on **4.** to listen attentively to —**hang out** **1.** to lean out **2.** to display, as by suspending **3.** [Slang] to spend much time —**hang over** to project, hover, or loom over —**hang together** **1.** to stick together **2.** to make sense, as a story —**hang up** **1.** to put on a hanger, hook, etc. **2.** to end a telephone conversation by replacing the receiver **3.** to delay or suspend the progress of —**not care** (or **give**) **a hang about** to not care the least bit about

hang·ar (haŋ′ər) ***n.*** [Fr., a shed] a repair shed or shelter for aircraft

Hang·chow (haŋ′chʊu′; *Chin.* häŋ′jō′) river & canal port in E China: pop. 784,000

hang·dog (haŋ′dôg′) ***adj.*** **1.** contemptible, sneaking, or abject **2.** ashamed and cringing *[a hangdog expression]*

hang·er (haŋ′ər) ***n.*** **1.** a person who hangs things *[a paperhanger]* **2.** a thing that hangs **3.** a thing on which objects, as garments, are hung

hang·er-on (-än′) ***n.,*** *pl.* **hang′ers-on′** a follower or dependent; specif., *a)* one who attaches himself to another, to some group, etc. although not wanted *b)* a sycophant

hang gliding the sport of gliding through the air while hanging suspended by a harness from a large type of kite (**hang glider**)

hang·ing (haŋ′iŋ) ***adj.*** **1.** suspended **2.** leaning over **3.** located on a steep slope **4.** deserving or imposing the death penalty —***n.*** **1.** a suspending or being suspended **2.** a putting to death by hanging **3.** something hung, as a drapery, tapestry, etc.

hang·man (-mən) ***n.,*** *pl.* **-men** an executioner who hangs convicted criminals

hang·nail (-nāl′) ***n.*** [altered < ME. *angnail* < OE. *angnægl,* a corn] a bit of torn skin hanging at the side or base of a fingernail

hang·out (-ʊut′) ***n.*** [Slang] a place frequented by some person or group

hang·o·ver (-ō′vər) ***n.*** **1.** something remaining from a previous time or state; a survival **2.** headache, nausea, etc. occurring as an aftereffect of drinking much alcoholic liquor

hang-up (-up′) ***n.*** [Slang] an emotional problem that cannot easily be resolved

hank (haŋk) ***n.*** [prob. < Scand.] **1.** a loop or coil of something flexible **2.** a standard length of coiled thread or yarn

hank·er (haŋ′kər) ***vi.*** [prob. < Du. or LowG.] to crave or long (followed by *after, for,* or an infinitive) —**hank′er·er** ***n.*** —**hank′er·ing** ***n.***

han·kie, han·ky (haŋ′kē) ***n.,*** *pl.* **-kies** [Colloq.] a handkerchief

han·ky-pan·ky (haŋ′kē paŋ′kē) ***n.*** [altered < HOCUS-POCUS] [Colloq.] trickery or deception

Han·nah, Han·na (han′ə) [var. of ANNA] a feminine name

Han·ni·bal (han′ə b'l) 247?–183? B.C.; Carthaginian general: crossed the Alps to invade Italy in 218 B.C.

Ha·noi (hä noi′, ha-) capital of Vietnam, in the N part: pop. 644,000

Han·o·ver[1] (han′ō vər) ruling family of England (1714–1901): founded by George I, orig. Elector of a territory which included the city of Hanover —**Han′o·ve′ri·an** (-vir′ē ən) ***adj., n.***

Han·o·ver[2] (han′ō vər) city in N West Germany: pop. 527,000 Ger. name **Han·no·ver** (hä nō′vər, -fər)

hanse (hans) ***n.*** [ult. < OHG. *hansa,* band of men] a medieval guild of merchants: also **han·sa** (han′sə) —**the Hanse** a medieval league of free towns in N Germany and adjoining countries, for economic advancement and protection: also **Hanseatic League**

Han·se·at·ic (han′sē at′ik) ***adj.*** of the Hanse

han·sel (han′s'l) ***n.*** *same as* HANDSEL

Han·sen's disease (han′s'nz, hän′-) [after A. *Hansen* (1841–1912), Norw. physician] *same as* LEPROSY

han·som (cab) (han′səm) [after J. A. *Hansom* (1803–1882), Eng. inventor] a two-wheeled covered carriage for two passengers, pulled by one horse: the driver's seat is above and behind the cab

Ha·nu·ka (khä′noo kä′, -kə; hä′-) ***n.*** [Heb. *ḥanūkkāh,* dedication] a Jewish festival in early winter commemorating the rededication of the Temple by the Maccabees in 165 B.C.: also **Ha′nuk·kah′, Ha′nuk·ka′**

hap (hap) ***n.*** [< ON. *happ*] chance; luck —***vi.*** **happed, hap′ping** to occur by chance; happen

hap·haz·ard (hap′haz′ərd) ***n.*** [prec. + HAZARD] mere chance; accident —***adj.*** not planned; casual —***adv.*** by chance —**hap′haz′ard·ly** ***adv.*** —**hap′haz′ard·ness** ***n.***

hap·less (hap′lis) ***adj.*** unfortunate; unlucky —**hap′less·ly** ***adv.*** —**hap′less·ness** ***n.***

hap·loid (hap′loid) ***adj.*** [< Gr. *haploos,* single + -OID] *Biol.* having the full number of chromosomes normally occurring in the mature germ cell: see DIPLOID —**hap′loi′dy** (-loi′dē) ***n.***

hap·ly (hap′lē) ***adv.*** [Archaic] by chance

hap·pen (hap′'n) ***vi.*** [ME. *happenen:* see HAP & -EN] **1.** to take place; occur **2.** to be or occur by chance **3.** to have the luck or occasion; chance *[I happened to see it]* **4.** to come by chance (*along, by, in,* etc.) —**happen on** (or **upon**) to meet or find by chance —**happen to** to be done to or be the fate of; befall

hap·pen·ing (-iŋ) ***n.*** something that happens; occurrence; incident; event

hap·pen·stance (-stans′) ***n.*** [HAPPEN + (CIRCUM)STANCE] [Colloq.] chance occurrence

hap·py (hap′ē) ***adj.*** **-pi·er, -pi·est** [ME. *happi* < HAP] **1.** favored by circumstances; lucky; fortunate **2.** having, showing, or causing a feeling of pleasure, joy, etc. **3.** suitable and clever; apt; felicitous *[a happy suggestion]* —**hap′pi·ly** ***adv.*** —**hap′pi·ness** ***n.***

hap·py-go-luck·y (-gō luk′ē) ***adj.*** easygoing; trusting to luck —***adv.*** haphazardly; by chance

Haps·burg (haps′bʉrg′; *G.* häps′boorkh) ruling family of Austria, Austria-Hungary, Spain, & the Holy Roman Empire at various times from 1278 to 1918

ha·ra-ki·ri (här′ə kir′ē, har′ə-; *popularly* her′ē ker′ē) ***n.*** [Jap. *hara,* belly + *kiri,* a cutting] ritual suicide by disembowelment: it was practiced by high-ranking Japanese to avoid facing disgrace

ha·rangue (hə raŋ′) ***n.*** [< OFr. *arenge* < OIt. < *aringo,* site for public assemblies < Goth.] a long, blustering or scolding speech; tirade —***vi., vt.*** **-rangued′, -rangu′ing** to speak or address in a harangue —**ha·rangu′er** ***n.***

har·ass (hə ras′, har′əs) ***vt.*** [Fr. *harasser* < OFr. *harer,* to set a dog on < Frank.] **1.** to trouble, worry, or torment, as with cares, debts, etc. **2.** to trouble by repeated raids or attacks, etc.; harry —**har·ass′er** ***n.*** —**har·ass′ment** ***n.***

Har·bin (här′bin) city in NE China: pop. 1,552,000

har·bin·ger (här′bin jər) ***n.*** [OFr. *herbergeor,* provider of lodging < *herberge,* a shelter < Frank.] a person or thing that comes before to announce or indicate what follows

har·bor (här′bər) ***n.*** [< OE. < *here,* army + *beorg,* a shelter] **1.** a place of refuge, safety, etc.; shelter **2.** a protected inlet of a sea, lake, etc., for anchoring ships; port —***vt.*** **1.** to serve as, or provide, a place of protection to; shelter or house **2.** to hold in the mind; cling to *[to harbor a grudge]* —***vi.*** to take shelter, as in a harbor —**har′bor·er** ***n.***

har·bor·age (-ij) ***n.*** a shelter for ships

harbor master the official in charge of enforcing the regulations governing the use of a harbor

har·bour (här′bər) ***n., vt., vi.*** *Brit. sp. of* HARBOR

hard (härd) ***adj.*** [OE. *heard*] **1.** not easily pierced or crushed; firm to the touch; solid and compact **2.** having firm muscles; vigorous and robust **3.** powerful; violent *[a hard blow]* **4.** demanding great effort or labor; difficult; specif., *a)* difficult to do *[hard work]* *b)* difficult to understand or explain *[a hard question]* *c)* firmly fastened or tied *[a hard knot]* **5.** not easily moved; unfeeling *[a hard heart]* **6.** practical and shrewd *[a hard customer]* **7.** *a)* firm or definite, esp. in an aggressive way *[a hard line in foreign policy]* *b)* undeniable or actual *[hard facts]* **8.** causing pain or discomfort; specif., *a)* difficult to endure *[a hard life]* *b)* harsh; severe; stern *[a hard master]* **9.** sharp or too sharp *[hard outlines, a hard red]* **10.** having in solution mineral salts that interfere with the lathering of soap: said of water **11.** energetic and persistent *[a hard worker]* **12.** *a)* alcoholic *[hard cider]* *b)* strongly alcoholic *[hard* liquor*]* **13.** [Colloq.] designating any drug, as heroin, that is addictive and potentially very damaging to the body or mind **14.** popularly, designating the letter *c* sounded as in *can* or the letter *g* sounded as in *gun* **15.** *Commerce* high and stable: said of a market, prices, etc. —***adv.*** **1.** energetically and persistently *[*work *hard]* **2.** with strength, violence, or severity *[*hit *hard]* **3.** with difficulty *[hard*-earned*]* **4.** so as to withstand much wear, use, etc. *[hard*-wearing clothes*]* **5.** firmly; tightly *[*hold on *hard]* **6.** close; near *[*we live *hard* by*]* **7.** so as to be or make firm or solid *[*to freeze *hard]* **8.** with vigor and to the fullest extent *[*turn *hard* right*]* —**be hard on 1.** to treat severely **2.** to be difficult or unpleasant for —**hard and fast** invariable; strict —**hard of hearing** partially deaf —**hard put to it** having considerable difficulty —**hard up** [Colloq.] in great need of something, esp. money —**hard′ness** ***n.***

hard·back (-bak′) ***n.*** a hard-cover book

hard-bit·ten (-bit′′n) ***adj.*** stubborn; tough; enduring; dogged *[hard-bitten* soldiers*]*

hard·board (-bôrd′) ***n.*** a boardlike material made in sheets by subjecting fibers from wood chips to pressure and heat

hard-boiled (-boild′) ***adj.*** **1.** cooked in boiling water until both the white and the yolk solidify: said of an egg **2.** [Colloq.] not affected by sentiment, pity, etc.; callous

hard coal *same as* ANTHRACITE

hard-core (-kôr′) ***adj.*** **1.** constituting or of a hard core **2.** absolute; complete; thorough

hard core the firm, unyielding, or unchanging central part or group

hard-cov·er (-kuv′ər) ***adj.*** designating any book bound in a relatively stiff cover: also **hard′-bound′** (-bound′) See also PAPERBACK

hard·en (här′d′n) ***vt., vi.*** to make or become hard (in various senses) —**hard′en·er** ***n.***

hard·ened (-d′nd) ***adj.*** **1.** made hard or harder **2.** confirmed or inveterate in a callous way

hard·fist·ed (härd′fis′tid) ***adj.*** stingy; miserly

hard·goods (-good z′) ***n.pl.*** durable goods, such as automobiles, furniture, etc.: also **hard goods**

hard hat 1. a protective helmet worn by construction workers, etc. **2.** [Slang] such a worker

hard·head·ed (-hed′id) ***adj.*** **1.** shrewd and unsentimental; practical **2.** stubborn —**hard′head′ed·ly** ***adv.*** —**hard′head′ed·ness** ***n.***

hard·heart·ed (-här′tid) ***adj.*** unfeeling; pitiless —**hard′heart′ed·ly** ***adv.*** —**hard′heart′ed·ness** ***n.***

har·di·hood (här′dē hood′) ***n.*** boldness, daring, fortitude, vigor, etc.

Har·ding (här′diŋ), **Warren Ga·ma·li·el** (gə mā′lē əl) 1865–1923; 29th president of the U.S. (1921–23)

hard landing a landing, as of a rocket on the moon, made at such a high speed as to destroy the equipment

hard·ly (härd′lē) ***adv.*** **1.** with difficulty **2.** severely; harshly **3.** only just; scarcely: often used ironically to mean "not at all" *[hardly* the person to ask*]* **4.** probably not; not likely

hard maple *same as* SUGAR MAPLE

hard-nosed (-nōzd′) ***adj.*** [Slang] **1.** tough; stubborn **2.** shrewd and practical —**hard′nose′** ***n.***

hard palate the bony part of the roof of the mouth

hard·pan (-pan′) ***n.*** **1.** a layer of hard, clayey soil **2.** solid, unplowed ground **3.** the hard, underlying part of anything; solid foundation

hard sauce a creamy mixture of butter, sugar, and flavoring, served with plum pudding, etc.

hard sell high-pressure salesmanship —**hard′-sell′** ***adj.***

hard-shell (-shel′) ***adj.*** **1.** having a hard shell: also **hard′-shelled′** **2.** [Colloq.] strict; strait-laced; uncompromising, esp. in religious matters

hard·ship (-ship′) ***n.*** **1.** hard circumstances of life **2.** a thing hard to bear

hard·tack (-tak′) ***n.*** [HARD + *tack* (food)] unleavened bread made in very hard, large wafers: traditionally a part of army and navy rations

hard·top (-täp′) ***n.*** an automobile like a convertible in having no post between the front and rear windows, but with a metal top that cannot fold back

hard·ware (-wer′) ***n.*** **1.** articles made of metal, as tools, nails, fittings, utensils, etc. **2.** heavy military equipment or its parts **3.** *a)* apparatus used for controlling spacecraft, etc. *b)* the mechanical, magnetic, and electronic design, structure, and devices of a computer: cf. SOFTWARE

hard·wood (-wood′) ***n.*** **1.** any tough, heavy timber with a compact texture **2.** *Forestry* wood other than that from a needle-bearing conifer **3.** a tree yielding hardwood

har·dy (här′dē) ***adj.*** **-di·er, -di·est** [< OFr. pp. of *hardir,* to make bold < Frank.] **1.** bold and resolute; daring **2.** too bold; rash **3.** able to withstand fatigue, privation, etc.; vigorous **4.** able to survive the winter without special care: said of plants —**har′di·ly** ***adv.*** —**har′di·ness** ***n.***

Har·dy (här′dē), **Thomas** 1840–1928; Eng. novelist & poet

hare (her) ***n., pl.*** **hares, hare:** see PLURAL, II, D, 1 [OE. *hara*] a swift mammal related to the rabbit, with long ears, soft fur, a cleft upper lip, a short tail, and long, powerful hind legs; specif., one whose young are furry at birth

hare·bell (-bel′) ***n.*** a slender, delicate perennial, with clusters of blue, bell-shaped flowers

hare·brained (-brānd′) ***adj.*** having or showing little sense; reckless, flighty, giddy, rash, etc.

Ha·re Krishna (hä′rē) [< Hindi *Hari,* a name for Vishnu + KRISHNA] **1.** a cult based on some Vedic beliefs and devoted to Vishnu, founded (1966) in the U.S. **2.** a member of this cult

hare·lip (-lip′) ***n.*** **1.** a congenital deformity consisting of a harelike cleft of the lip **2.** a lip with such a deformity —**hare′lipped′** ***adj.***

ha·rem (her′əm, har′-) ***n.*** [Ar. *ḥarīm,* lit., prohibited (place)] **1.** that part of a Moslem's household in which the women live **2.** the wives, concubines, women servants, etc. in a harem **3.** a number of female animals, as of fur seals, who mate and lodge with one male Also **ha·reem** (hä rēm′)

har·i·cot (har′ə kō′) ***n.*** [Fr., ult. < ? Nahuatl *ayecotli,* bean] [Chiefly Brit.] **1.** *same as* KIDNEY BEAN **2.** the pod or seed of other edible beans

ha·ri-ka·ri (her′ē ker′ē, hä′rē kä′rē) ***n.*** *same as* HARA-KIRI

hark (härk) ***vi.*** [< ? OE. *heorcnian,* to hearken] to listen carefully: usually in the imperative —**hark back** to go back; revert

hark·en (här′k′n) ***vi., vt.*** *same as* HEARKEN

Har·lem (här′ləm) [var. of HAARLEM] section of New York City, in N Manhattan

Har·le·quin (här′lə kwin, -kin) [< Fr. < OFr. *hierlekin,* demon] a traditional comic character in pantomime, who wears a mask and gay, spangled, diamond-patterned tights of many colors —***n.*** **[h-]** a clown; buffoon —***adj.*** **[h-]** **1.** comic; ludicrous **2.** of many colors; colorful

HARLEQUIN

har·lot (här′lət) ***n.*** [OFr., rogue] a prostitute

har·lot·ry (-rē) ***n.*** **1.** prostitution **2.** prostitutes, collectively

harm (härm) ***n.*** [OE. *hearm*] **1.** hurt; injury; damage **2.** moral wrong; evil —***vt.*** to do harm to; hurt, damage, etc. —**harm′er** ***n.***

harm·ful (-fəl) ***adj.*** causing or able to cause harm; hurtful —**harm′ful·ly** ***adv.*** —**harm′ful·ness** ***n.***

harm·less (-lis) ***adj.*** causing no harm; inoffensive —**harm′less·ly** ***adv.*** —**harm′less·ness** ***n.***

har·mon·ic (här män′ik) ***adj.*** **1.** harmonious in feeling or effect; agreeing **2.** *Music a)* of or in harmony *b)* pertaining to an overtone —***n.*** **1.** *same as* OVERTONE (sense 1) **2.** *Elec.* an alternating-current voltage or current or a component of this, whose frequency is some integral multiple of a fundamental frequency —**har·mon′i·cal·ly** ***adv.***

har·mon·i·ca (-i kə) ***n.*** [L.: see HARMONY] a small wind instrument played with the mouth; mouth organ: it has a series of graduated metal reeds that vibrate and produce tones when air is blown or sucked across them

har·mon·ics (-iks) ***n.pl.*** [*with sing. v.*] the physical science dealing with musical sounds

har·mo·ni·ous (här mō′nē əs) ***adj.*** [< Fr.: see HARMONY] **1.** having parts combined in a proportionate, orderly, or pleasing way **2.** having similar feelings, ideas, interests, etc. **3.** having musical tones combined for a pleasing effect —**har·mo′ni·ous·ly** ***adv.*** —**har·mo′ni·ous·ness** ***n.***

har·mo·nist (här′mə nist) ***n.*** a musician expert in harmony

har·mo·ni·um (här mō′nē əm) ***n.*** [< Fr.: see HARMONY] a small kind of reed organ

har·mo·nize (här′mə nīz′) ***vi.*** **-nized′, -niz′ing** **1.** to be in harmony; accord; agree **2.** to sing in harmony —***vt.*** **1.** to make harmonious; bring into agreement **2.** to add chords to (a melody) so as to form a harmony —**har′mo·ni·za′tion** ***n.*** —**har′mo·niz′er** ***n.***

har·mo·ny (här′mə nē) ***n., pl.*** **-nies** [< OFr. < L. < Gr. *harmonia* < *harmos,* a fitting] **1.** a combination of parts into a pleasing or orderly whole **2.** agreement in feeling, action, ideas, etc.; peaceable or friendly relations **3.** a state of agreement or orderly arrangement as to color, shape, etc. **4.** agreeable sounds; music **5.** *Music a)* the sounding together of two or more tones, esp. when satisfying to the ear *b)* structure in terms of the arrangement, modulation, etc. of chords *c)* the study of this structure

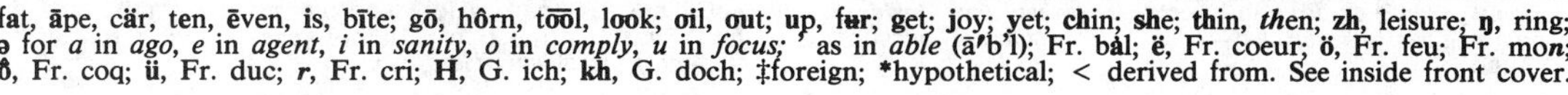

fat, āpe, cär, ten, ēven, is, bīte; gō, hôrn, tōōl, look; oil, out; up, fur; get; joy; yet; chin; she; thin, *th*en; zh, leisure; ŋ, ring; ə for *a* in *ago, e* in *agent, i* in *sanity, o* in *comply, u* in *focus;* ′ as in *able* (ā′b′l); Fr. bál; ë, Fr. coeur; ö, Fr. feu; Fr. mo*n*; ô, Fr. coq; ü, Fr. duc; *r,* Fr. cri; H, G. ich; kh, G. doch; ‡foreign; *hypothetical; < derived from. See inside front cover.

har·ness (här′nis) *n.* [< OFr. *harneis,* armor < ON.] **1.** orig., armor for a man or horse **2.** the leather straps and metal pieces by which a horse, mule, etc. is fastened to a vehicle, plow, or load **3.** any trappings or gear similar to this *—vt.* **1.** to put harness on (a horse, etc.) **2.** to control so as to use the power of *[*to *harness* one's energy*]* **—in harness** in or at one's routine work

harness race a horse race between either trotters or pacers, each pulling a sulky and driver

Har·old (har′əld) [OE. *Hereweald* & *Harald* < ON. *Haraldr,* lit., leader of the army] **1.** a masculine name **2.** Harold II 1022?–66; 1st Saxon king of England (1066): killed in the Battle of Hastings

harp (härp) *n.* [OE. *hearpe*] **1.** a musical instrument with strings stretched across an open, triangular frame, held upright and played by plucking with the fingers **2.** a harp-shaped object or implement *—vi.* **1.** to play a harp **2.** to persist in talking or writing tediously or continuously (*on* or *upon* something) **—harp′er** *n.*

harp·ist (här′pist) *n.* a harp player

har·poon (här po͞on′) *n.* [< MDu. < MFr. < *harper,* to claw < ON. *harpa,* to squeeze] a barbed spear with a line attached to it, used for spearing whales or other large sea animals *—vt.* to strike or kill with a harpoon **—har·poon′er** *n.*

harp·si·chord (härp′si kôrd′) *n.* [< obs. Fr. or < It.: see HARP & CORD] a stringed musical instrument with a keyboard, predecessor of the piano: the strings are plucked by leather or quill points by pressing the keys **—harp′si·chord′ist** *n.*

Har·py (här′pē) *n., pl.* **-pies** [< MFr. < L. < Gr. < *harpazein,* to seize] **1.** *Gr. Myth.* any of several hideous, winged monsters with the head and trunk of a woman and the tail, legs, and talons of a bird **2.** [**h-**] a greedy or grasping person

har·que·bus (här′kwi bəs) *n.* [< Fr., ult. < Du. *haak,* hook + *bus,* a gun] an early type of portable gun

har·ri·dan (har′i d'n) *n.* [prob. < Fr. *haridelle,* worn-out horse] a disreputable, shrewish old woman

har·ri·er[1] (har′ē ər) *n.* [< HARE + -IER] **1.** a dog like the English foxhound, used for hunting hares and rabbits **2.** a cross-country runner

har·ri·er[2] (har′ē ər) *n.* **1.** one who harries **2.** a hawk that preys on small mammals, reptiles, etc.

Har·ri·et (har′ē it) [fem. dim. of HARRY] a feminine name: var. *Harriot*

Har·ris (har′is), **Joel Chan·dler** (chan′dlər) 1848–1908; U.S. writer, esp. of the *Uncle Remus* stories

Har·ris·burg (har′is burg′) [after John *Harris,* Jr., the founder] capital of Pa., on the Susquehanna: pop. 53,000

Har·ri·son (har′ə s'n) **1. Benjamin,** 1833–1901; 23d president of the U.S. (1889–93): grandson of *ff.* **2. William Henry,** 1773–1841; 9th president of the U.S. (1841)

har·row (har′ō) *n.* [prob. < ON. *harfr*] a heavy frame with spikes or sharp-edged disks, drawn by a horse or tractor and used for breaking up and leveling plowed ground, covering seeds, etc. *—vt.* **1.** to draw a harrow over (land) **2.** to cause mental distress to; torment; vex *—vi.* to take harrowing *[*ground that *harrows* well*]* **—har′row·er** *n.* **—har′row·ing** *adj.* **—har′row·ing·ly** *adv.*

har·rumph (hə rumpf′: *conventionalized pronun.*) *vi.* [echoic] **1.** to clear one's throat, esp. in a studied, pompous way **2.** to protest in a pompous or self-righteous way *—n.* a harrumphing

Har·ry (har′ē) [< HENRY] a masculine name

har·ry (har′ē) *vt.* **-ried, -ry·ing** [< OE. *hergian* < base of *here,* army] **1.** to raid and ravage or rob; plunder **2.** to torment; harass **3.** to force along

harsh (härsh) *adj.* [ME. *harsk*] **1.** unpleasantly sharp or rough to the ear, eye, taste, or touch; grating, glaring, bitter, coarse, etc. **2.** unpleasantly crude or abrupt **3.** rough, crude, or forbidding in appearance **4.** excessively severe; cruel or unfeeling **—harsh′ly** *adv.* **—harsh′ness** *n.*

hart (härt) *n., pl.* **harts, hart:** see PLURAL, II, D, 1 [OE. *heorot*] a male of the European red deer, esp. after its fifth year; stag

Harte (härt), **Bret** (bret) (born *Francis Brett Hart*) 1836–1902; U.S. writer, esp. of short stories

har·te·beest (här′tə bēst′, härt′bēst′) *n., pl.* **-beests′, -beest′:** see PLURAL, II, D, 1 [obs. Afrik. < *harte,* hart + *beest,* beast] a large, swift South African antelope having long horns curved backward at the tips

Hart·ford (härt′fərd) [after *Hertford*shire, county in England] capital of Conn., in the C part: pop. 136,000 (met. area 726,000)

harts·horn (härts′hôrn′) *n.* **1.** a hart's horn **2.** [Now Rare] ammonium carbonate, used in smelling salts: orig. obtained from deer's antlers

har·um-scar·um (her′əm sker′əm) *adj.* [< ? HARE + SCARE + 'EM] acting or done in a reckless or rash way *—adv.* in a harum-scarum manner *—n.* a harum-scarum person or action

ha·rus·pex (hə rus′peks, har′əs peks) *n., pl.* **-rus′pi·ces′** (-pə sēz′) [L.] a soothsayer in ancient Rome who professed to foretell the future by interpreting the entrails of sacrificial animals **—ha·rus′pi·cal** (-pi k'l) *adj.*

har·vest (här′vist) *n.* [OE. *hærfest*] **1.** the time of the year when grain, fruit, vegetables, etc. are reaped and gathered in **2.** a season's yield of grain, fruit, etc.; crop **3.** the gathering in of a crop **4.** the outcome of any effort *—vt., vi.* **1.** to gather in (a crop, etc.) **2.** to gather the crop from (a field) **3.** to get (something) as the result of an action or effort **—har′vest·a·ble** *adj.*

har·vest·er (-ər) *n.* **1.** a person who gathers in a crop of grain, fruit, etc. **2.** any of various farm machines for harvesting crops

har·vest·man (-mən) *n., pl.* **-men** **1.** a man who harvests **2.** a spiderlike animal with long, thin legs and a short, broad, segmented abdomen

harvest moon the full moon at or about the time of the autumnal equinox, September 22 or 23

Har·vey (här′vē) [< Fr. < OHG. *Herewig,* lit., army battle] **1.** a masculine name **2. William,** 1578–1657; Eng. physician: discovered the circulation of the blood

Harz (Mountains) (härts) mountain range in C Germany: highest peak, 3,747 ft.

has (haz; *unstressed* həz, əz) *3d pers. sing., pres. indic., of* HAVE

has-been (haz′bin′) *n.* [Colloq.] a person or thing whose popularity or effectiveness is past

ha·sen·pfef·fer (häs′'n fef′ər) *n.* [G. < *hase,* rabbit + *pfeffer,* pepper] a German dish of rabbit meat marinated in vinegar and stewed in the marinade

hash[1] (hash) *vt.* [Fr. *hacher,* to chop] **1.** to chop (meat or vegetables) into small pieces for cooking **2.** [Colloq.] to make a mess of; bungle *—n.* **1.** a chopped mixture of cooked meat and vegetables, usually baked or browned **2.** a mixture or rehash **3.** a hodgepodge; muddle **—hash out** [Colloq.] to settle by prolonged discussion **—hash over** [Colloq.] to discuss at length **—settle one's hash** [Colloq.] to overcome or subdue one

hash[2] (hash) *n.* [Slang] hashish

hash house [Slang] a cheap restaurant

hash·ish (hash′ēsh, -ish) *n.* [Ar. *ḥashīsh,* dried hemp] a drug formed from the resin contained in the flowering tops of Indian hemp, chewed or smoked for its intoxicating or euphoric effects: also **hash′eesh** (-ēsh)

hash mark [Mil. Slang] *same as* SERVICE STRIPE

Has·i·dim (has′ə dim; *Heb.* khä sē′dim) *n.pl., sing.* **Has·id** (has′id; *Heb.* khä′sid) [< Heb. *ḥāsid,* a pious person] a sect of Jewish mystics, orig. in 18th-cent. Poland, that emphasizes joyful worship **—Ha·sid·ic** (ha sid′ik) *adj.*

has·n't (haz′'nt) has not

hasp (hasp) *n.* [OE. *hæpse*] a hinged metal fastening for a door, window, lid, etc.; esp., a metal piece fitted over a staple and fastened by a bolt or padlock

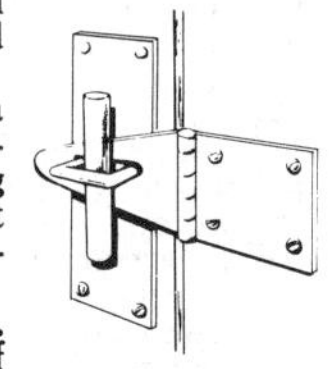

HASP

has·sle (has′'l) *n.* [< ?] [Colloq.] **1.** a heated argument; squabble **2.** a troublesome situation *—vi.* **-sled, -sling** [Colloq.] to have a heated argument *—vt.* [Colloq.] to cause trouble or difficulty for; harass

has·sock (has′ək) *n.* [OE. *hassuc*] **1.** [Now Rare] a thick clump or tuft of grass **2.** a firmly stuffed cushion used as a footstool or seat

hast (hast; *unstressed* həst, əst) *archaic 2d pers. sing., pres. indic., of* HAVE: *used with* thou

has·tate (has′tāt) *adj.* [< L. < *hasta,* a spear] having a triangular shape, as some leaves

haste (hāst) *n.* [OFr. *haste* < Frank.] **1.** quickness of motion; hurrying **2.** careless or reckless hurrying *[haste* makes waste*]* **3.** necessity for hurrying; urgency *—vt., vi.* **hast′ed, hast′ing** [Rare] *same as* HASTEN **—in haste** **1.** in a hurry **2.** in too great a hurry **—make haste** to hasten

has·ten (hās′'n) *vt.* to cause to be or come faster; speed up *—vi.* to move swiftly; hurry

Has·tings (hās′tiŋz) city in SE England, on the English Channel: nearby is the site of the decisive battle of the Norman Conquest

hast·y (hās′tē) *adj.* **hast′i·er, hast′i·est** **1.** done or made with haste; hurried **2.** done or made too quickly and with too little thought; rash *[a hasty* decision*]* **3.** short-tempered or impetuous **4.** showing irritation or impatience *[hasty* words*]* **—hast′i·ly** *adv.* **—hast′i·ness** *n.*

hasty pudding **1.** mush made of cornmeal **2.** [Brit.] mush made of flour or oatmeal

hat (hat) *n.* [OE. *hætt*] a covering for the head, usually with a brim and crown *—vt.* **hat′ted, hat′ting** to cover or provide with a hat **—pass the hat** to take up a collection **—take one's hat off to** to salute or congratulate **—talk through one's hat** [Colloq.] to talk nonsense **—under one's hat** [Colloq.] secret **—hat′less** *adj.*

hat·band (-band′) *n.* a band of cloth around the crown of a hat, just above the brim

hat·box (-bäks′) *n.* a box or case for carrying or storing a hat or hats

hatch[1] (hach) *vt.* [ME. *hacchen*] **1.** *a)* to bring forth (young) from an egg or eggs by applying warmth *b)* to bring forth young from (an egg or eggs) **2.** to bring (a plan, idea, etc.) into existence; esp., to plot *—vi.* **1.** to bring forth young: said of eggs **2.** to come forth from the egg *—n.* **1.** the process of hatching **2.** the brood hatched **—hatch′er** *n.*

hatch[2] (hach) *n.* [OE. *hæcc,* a grating] **1.** the lower half of a door, gate, etc. that has two separately movable halves **2.** *same as* HATCHWAY **3.** a covering for a ship's hatchway, or a lid or trapdoor for a hatchway in a building

hatch[3] (hach) *vt.* [< OFr. < *hache,* an ax] to mark or engrave with fine, crossed or parallel lines so as to indicate shading *—n.* any of these lines

hatch·back (-bak′) *n.* [HATCH[2] + BACK] an automobile body with a rear that swings up, providing a wide opening into a storage area

hatch·el (hach′əl) *n., vt.* **-eled** or **-elled, -el·ing** or **-el·ling** *same as* HACKLE[1]

hatch·er·y (hach′ər ē) *n., pl.* **-er·ies** a place for hatching eggs, esp. those of fish or poultry

hatch·et (hach′it) *n.* [< OFr. dim. of *hache,* an ax] **1.** a small ax with a short handle, for use with one hand **2.** *same as* TOMAHAWK **—bury the hatchet** to stop fighting; make peace

SHINGLING HATCHET

CLAW HATCHET

TYPES OF HATCHET

hatchet man [Colloq.] **1.** a man hired to commit murder **2.** any person assigned by another to carry out disagreeable or unscrupulous tasks

hatch·ing (hach′iŋ) *n.* [HATCH[3] + -ING] **1.** the drawing or engraving of fine, parallel or crossed lines to show shading **2.** such lines

hatch·way (-wā′) *n.* **1.** a covered opening in a ship's deck **2.** a similar opening in the floor or roof of a building

hate (hāt) *vt.* **hat′ed, hat′ing** [OE. *hatian*] **1.** to have strong dislike or ill will for; despise **2.** to dislike or wish to avoid; shrink from *[to hate arguments] —vi.* to feel hatred *—n.* **1.** a strong feeling of dislike or ill will; hatred **2.** a person or thing hated **—hate′a·ble, hat′a·ble** *adj.* **—hat′er** *n.*

hate·ful (-fəl) *adj.* **1.** [Now Rare] feeling or showing hate; malevolent **2.** causing or deserving hate; odious **—hate′ful·ly** *adv.* **—hate′ful·ness** *n.*

hate·mon·ger (-muŋ′gər, -mäŋ′-) *n.* a propagandist who seeks to provoke hatred and prejudice

hath (hath) *archaic 3d pers. sing., pres. indic., of* HAVE

hat·rack (hat′rak′) *n.* a rack, set of pegs or hooks, etc. to hold hats

ha·tred (hā′trid) *n.* [ME. < *hate,* hate + *-red* < OE. *ræden,* state] strong dislike or ill will

hat·ter (hat′ər) *n.* one who makes or sells hats

Hat·ter·as (hat′ər əs), **Cape** [< AmInd. tribal name] cape on an island of N.C., in the Atlantic

hau·ber·geon (hô′bər jən) *n. obs. var. of* HABERGEON

hau·berk (hô′bərk) *n.* [< OFr., ult. < Frank. *hals,* the neck + *bergan,* to protect] a medieval coat of armor, usually of chain mail

haugh·ty (hôt′ē) *adj.* **-ti·er, -ti·est** [< OFr. *haut,* high < L. *altus* + -Y[2]] **1.** having or showing great pride in oneself and contempt or scorn for others **2.** [Archaic] lofty; noble **—haugh′ti·ly** *adv.* **—haugh′ti·ness** *n.*

haul (hôl) *vt.* [< OFr. *haler,* to draw < ODu. *halen,* to fetch] **1.** to move by pulling or drawing; tug; drag **2.** to transport by wagon, truck, etc. *[to haul coal]* **3.** *same as* HALE[2] **4.** *Naut.* to change the course of (a ship) by setting the sails *—vi.* **1.** to pull; tug **2.** to shift direction: said of the wind **3.** *Naut.* to change the course of a ship by trimming sail *—n.* **1.** the act of hauling; pull; tug **2.** *a)* the amount of fish taken in a single pull of a net *b)* [Colloq.] the amount gained, won, earned, etc. at one time **3.** the distance or route covered in transporting or traveling **4.** a load transported **—haul off** [Colloq.] to draw the arm back before hitting **—haul up** **1.** to sail nearer the direction of the wind **2.** to come to rest; stop **—in** (or **over**) **the long haul** over a long period of time **—haul′er** *n.*

haul·age (-ij) *n.* **1.** the act or process of hauling **2.** the charge made for hauling, as by a railroad

haunch (hônch, hänch) *n.* [< OFr. *hanche* < Gmc.] **1.** the part of the body including the hip, buttock, and thickest part of the thigh; hindquarter **2.** an animal's loin and leg together

haunt (hônt, hänt; *for n. 2, usually* hant) *vt.* [< OFr. *hanter,* to frequent] **1.** to visit (a place) often or continually **2.** to seek the company or companionship of; run after **3.** to recur repeatedly to *[memories haunted her]* **4.** to fill the atmosphere of; pervade *[a house haunted by sorrow] —n.* **1.** a place often visited or frequented *[to make the library one's haunt]* **2.** [Dial.] a ghost

haunt·ed (-id) *adj.* supposedly frequented by ghosts

haunt·ing (-iŋ) *adj.* often recurring to the mind *[a haunting melody]* **—haunt′ing·ly** *adv.*

haut·boy (hō′boi′, ō′-) *n.* [< Fr. < *haut,* high + *bois,* wood] *earlier name for* OBOE

‡haute cou·ture (ōt ko͞o tür′) [Fr., lit., high sewing] the leading designers and creators of new fashions in women's clothing, or their creations

hau·teur (hō tʉr′; *Fr.* ō tër′) *n.* [Fr. < *haut,* high, proud] disdainful pride; haughtiness; snobbery

‡haut monde (ō mōnd′) [Fr.] high society

Ha·van·a (hə van′ə) capital of Cuba, on the Gulf of Mexico: pop. 788,000 *—n.* **1.** a cigar made in Cuba or of Cuban tobacco **2.** Cuban tobacco

have (hav; həv, əv; *before "to"* haf) *vt.* **had, hav′ing** [OE. *habban*] **1.** to hold; own; possess *[to have wealth]* **2.** to possess as a part, characteristic, etc. *[the week has seven days]* **3.** to be afflicted with *[to have a cold]* **4.** to experience; undergo *[have a good time]* **5.** to understand or know *[to have a little Spanish]* **6.** to hold or keep in the mind *[to have an idea]* **7.** to declare or state *[so gossip has it]* **8.** *a)* to get, take, or obtain *[have a look at it] b)* to eat or drink *[have some tea]* **9.** to bear or beget (offspring) **10.** to perform; engage in *[to have an argument]* **11.** *a)* to cause to *[have him sing] b)* to cause to be *[have it fixed]* **12.** to be in a certain relation to *[to have a wife]* **13.** to feel and show *[have pity on her]* **14.** to permit; tolerate *[I won't have this noise]* **15.** [Colloq.] *a)* to hold at a disadvantage *[I had my opponent now] b)* to deceive; cheat *[they were had in that business deal]* *Have* is used as an auxiliary to form phrases expressing completed action, as in the perfect tenses (Ex.: I *had* left), and with infinitives to express obligation or necessity (Ex.: we *have* to go) *Have got* often replaces *have* *Have* is conjugated in the present indicative: (I) *have,* (he, she, it) *has,* (we, you, they) *have;* in the past indicative (I, he, she, it, we, you, they) *had* Archaic forms are: (thou) *hast, hadst,* (he, she, it) *hath —n.* a person or nation with relatively much wealth or rich resources **—have at** to attack; strike **—have done** to stop; finish **—have had it** [Slang] to be defeated, disgusted, etc. or no longer popular, useful, etc. **—have it good** [Colloq.] to be well-off **—have it out** to settle a disagreement by fighting or discussion **—have on** to be wearing **—have to be** [Colloq.] to be unquestionably

ha·ven (hā′vən) *n.* [OE. *hæfen*] **1.** a port; harbor **2.** any sheltered, safe place; refuge *—vt.* to provide a haven for

have-not (hav′nät′) *n.* a person or nation with little or no wealth or resources

have·n't (hav′′nt) have not

hav·er·sack (hav′ər sak′) *n.* [< Fr. < G. *habersack,* lit., sack of oats] a canvas bag for rations, worn over one shoulder, as by soldiers and hikers

hav·oc (hav′ək) *n.* [< Anglo-Fr. < OFr. *havot,* plunder] great destruction and devastation **—cry havoc** **1.** orig., to give (an army) the signal for pillaging **2.** to warn of great danger **—play havoc with** to devastate; destroy; ruin

Havre, Le *see* LE HAVRE

haw[1] (hô) *n.* [OE. *haga*] **1.** the berry of the hawthorn **2.** *same as* HAWTHORN

haw[2] (hô) *interj., n.* [< ?] a word of command to a horse, ox, etc., meaning "turn to the left!" *—vt., vi.* to turn to the left Opposed to GEE[1]

haw[3] (hô) *vi.* [echoic] to hesitate in speaking; falter: usually in HEM AND HAW (see HEM[2]) *—n.* a conventionalized expression of sound often made by a speaker when hesitating briefly

Haw. Hawaiian

Ha·wai·i (hə wä′ē, -yē, -yə) [Haw. < ?] **1.** a State of the U.S., consisting of a group of islands **(Hawaiian Islands)** in the North Pacific: 6,424 sq. mi.; pop. 965,000; cap. Honolulu: abbrev. **HI** **2.** largest of the islands of Hawaii

Ha·wai·ian (-yən) *adj.* of Hawaii, its people, language, etc. *—n.* **1.** a native or inhabitant of Hawaii; specif., a native of Polynesian descent **2.** the Polynesian language of the Hawaiians

hawk[1] (hôk) *n.* [OE. *hafoc*] **1.** any of a group of birds of prey characterized by short, rounded wings, a long tail and legs, and a hooked beak and claws: hawks include the falcons, buzzards, harriers, kites, and caracaras, but not vultures and eagles **2.** an advocate of all-out war or of the provocation of open hostilities *—vi.* to hunt birds with the help of hawks *—vt.* to prey on as a hawk does **—hawk′er** *n.* **—hawk′ing** *n.* **—hawk′ish** *adj.* **—hawk′like′** *adj.*

hawk² (hôk) *vt., vi.* [< HAWKER] to advertise or peddle (goods) in the street by shouting

hawk³ (hôk) *vi.* [echoic] to clear the throat audibly —*vt.* to bring up (phlegm) by coughing —*n.* an audible clearing of the throat

hawk·er (hôk′ər) *n.* [ult. < MLowG. *hoken,* to peddle] a person who hawks goods in the street

hawk-eyed (-īd′) *adj.* keen-sighted like a hawk

hawk·moth (-môth′) *n.* a moth with a thick, tapering body, slender wings, and a long feeding tube used for sucking the nectar of flowers

hawks·bill (turtle) (hôwks′bil′) a medium-sized turtle of warm seas, having a hawklike beak and a shell from which tortoise shell is obtained

hawk·weed (hôk′wēd′) *n.* a plant of the composite family, with yellow or scarlet ray flowers

hawse (hôz) *n.* [< ON. *hals,* the neck] **1.** that part of the bow of a ship containing the hawseholes **2.** *same as* HAWSEHOLE **3.** the space between the bow of a ship and the anchors

hawse·hole (-hōl′) *n.* any of the holes in a ship's bow through which a hawser or cable is passed

haw·ser (hô′zər) *n.* [< Anglo-Fr. < OFr. *haucier,* ult. < L. *altus,* high] a large rope or small cable, by which a ship is anchored, moored, or towed

haw·thorn (hô′thôrn′) *n.* [< OE. < *haga,* hedge + *thorn*] a thorny shrub or small tree of the rose family, with flowers of white, pink, or red, and small, red fruits (*haws*) resembling miniature apples

Haw·thorne (hô′thôrn′) [after ff.] city in SW Calif.: suburb of Los Angeles: pop. 56,000

Haw·thorne (hô′thôrn′), **Nathaniel** 1804–64; U.S. novelist & short-story writer

hay (hā) *n.* [OE. *hieg*] **1.** grass, alfalfa, clover, etc. cut and dried for use as fodder **2.** [Slang] bed —*vi.* to mow grass, alfalfa, etc. and spread it out to dry —**hit the hay** [Slang] to go to bed to sleep —**make hay while the sun shines** to make the most of an opportunity

hay·cock (-käk′) *n.* a small, conical heap of hay drying in a field

Hay·dn (hīd′'n), **Franz Jo·seph** (fränts yō′zef) 1732–1809; Austrian composer

Hayes (hāz), **Ruth·er·ford B(irchard)** (ruth′ər fərd) 1822–93; 19th president of the U.S. (1877–81)

hay fever an acute inflammation of the eyes and upper respiratory tract: it is an allergic reaction, caused by the pollen of some grasses and trees

hay·field (hā′fēld′) *n.* a field of grass, alfalfa, etc. to be made into hay

hay·loft (-lôft′) *n.* a loft, or upper story, in a barn or stable, for storing hay

hay·mak·er (-mā′kər) *n.* **1.** a person who cuts hay and spreads it out to dry **2.** [Slang] a powerful blow with the fist

hay·mow (-mou′) *n.* **1.** a pile of hay in a barn **2.** *same as* HAYLOFT

hay·ride (-rīd′) *n.* a pleasure ride taken by a group in a wagon partly filled with hay

hay·seed (-sēd′) *n.* **1.** grass seed shaken from mown hay **2.** [Old Slang] a rustic; yokel

hay·stack (-stak′) *n.* a large heap of hay piled up outdoors: also **hay′rick′** (-rik′)

Hay·ward (hā′wərd) [after W. *Hayward,* local postmaster] city in W Calif.: suburb of Oakland: pop. 94,000

hay·wire (hā′wīr′) *n.* wire for tying up bales of hay —*adj.* [Slang] **1.** out of order; confused **2.** crazy: usually in **go haywire,** to become crazy

haz·ard (haz′ərd) *n.* [OFr. *hasard,* game of dice < Ar. *az-zahr*] **1.** an early game of chance played with dice **2.** chance **3.** risk; peril; danger **4.** an obstacle on a golf course —*vt.* to risk or venture

haz·ard·ous (-əs) *adj.* risky; dangerous —**haz′ard·ous·ly** *adv.* —**haz′ard·ous·ness** *n.*

haze¹ (hāz) *n.* [prob. < HAZY] **1.** a thin vapor of fog, smoke, dust, etc. in the air **2.** slight confusion or vagueness of mind —*vi., vt.* **hazed, haz′ing** to make or become hazy (often with *over*)

haze² (hāz) *vt.* **hazed, haz′ing** [< ? OFr. *haser,* to irritate] to initiate or discipline (fellow students) by forcing to do humiliating or painful things

Ha·zel (hā′z'l) [Heb. *ḥazā'ēl,* lit., God sees] a feminine name

ha·zel (hā′z'l) *n.* [OE. *hæsel*] **1.** a shrub or tree related to the birch, bearing edible nuts **2.** *same as* HAZELNUT **3.** a light brown —*adj.* **1.** of the hazel tree **2.** light-brown: hazel eyes are usually flecked with green or gray —**ha′zel·ly** *adj.*

ha·zel·nut (-nut′) *n.* the small, edible, roundish nut of the hazel; filbert

Haz·litt (haz′lit), **William** 1778–1830; Eng. essayist

ha·zy (hā′zē) *adj.* **-zi·er, -zi·est** [prob. < OE. *hasu,* dusky] **1.** characterized by haze; somewhat foggy or smoky **2.** vague, obscure, or indefinite [*hazy* thinking] —**ha′zi·ly** *adv.* —**ha′zi·ness** *n.*

Hb *the symbol for* hemoglobin

hb *Football* halfback

H-bomb (āch′bäm′) *n. same as* HYDROGEN BOMB

hd. head

hdqrs. headquarters

he (hē; *unstressed* hi, ē, i) *pron. for pl. see* THEY [OE.] **1.** the man, boy, or male animal previously mentioned **2.** the person; the one; anyone [*he* who laughs last laughs best] *He* is the nominative case form of the masculine third personal pronoun —*n., pl.* **hes** a man, boy, or male animal

He *Chem.* helium

head (hed) *n.* [OE. *heafod*] **1.** the top part of the body in man, the apes, etc., or the front part in most other animals: in higher animals it is a bony structure containing the brain, and including the eyes, ears, nose, and mouth **2.** the head as the seat of reason, memory, and imagination; mind; intelligence [to use one's *head*] **3.** a person [dinner at five dollars a *head*] **4.** *pl.* **head** the head as a unit of counting [fifty *head* of cattle] **5.** the obverse of a coin, usually showing a head: often **heads** **6.** the highest or uppermost part or thing; top; specif., *a*) the top of a page, column, etc. *b*) a topic of a section, chapter, etc. *c*) a headline *d*) froth floating on newly poured effervescent beverages *e*) that end of a cask or barrel which is uppermost **7.** the foremost part of a thing; front; specif., *a*) a part associated with the human head [the *head* of a bed] *b*) the front part of a ship; bow *c*) *Naut.* a toilet, or lavatory *d*) the front position, as of a column of marching men *e*) either end of something **8.** the projecting part of something; specif., *a*) the part designed for holding, striking, etc. [the *head* of a pin] *b*) a headland *c*) a projecting place, as in a boil, where pus is about to break through *d*) the part of a tape recorder that records or plays back the magnetic signals on the tape **9.** the membrane stretched across the end of a drum, tambourine, etc. **10.** the source of a river, stream, etc. **11.** a source of water kept at some height to supply a mill, etc. **12.** the pressure in an enclosed fluid, as steam **13.** a position of leadership or honor [the *head* of the class] **14.** the person in charge; leader, ruler, director, etc. **15.** a headmaster **16.** *Bot. a*) a dense, flattened cluster of flowers, as in the dandelion *b*) a large, compact bud [a *head* of cabbage] **17.** *Music* the rounded part of a note, at the end of the stem **18.** [Slang] a habitual user of marijuana, LSD, etc. —*adj.* **1.** of or having to do with the head **2.** most important; principal; first **3.** to be found at the top or front **4.** striking against the front [*head* current] —*vt.* **1.** to be chief of or in charge of **2.** to lead; precede **3.** to supply (a pin, etc.) with a head **4.** [Rare] to behead **5.** to trim the higher part from (a tree or plant); poll **6.** to cause to go in a specified direction —*vi.* **1.** to grow or come to a head **2.** to set out; travel [to *head* eastward] —**by a head** by a small margin —**come to a head** **1.** to be about to suppurate, as a boil **2.** to culminate —**give one his head** to let one do as he likes —**go to one's head** **1.** to confuse or intoxicate one **2.** to make one vain —**hang** (or **hide**) **one's head** to lower one's head or conceal one's face as in shame —**head off** to get ahead of and intercept —**head over heels** **1.** deeply; completely **2.** hurriedly; recklessly —**heads up!** [Colloq.] look out! be careful! —**keep** (or **lose**) **one's head** to keep (or lose) one's poise, self-control, etc. —**make head** to go forward; advance —**make head or tail of** to understand: usually in the negative —**on** (or **upon**) **one's head** as one's responsibility or misfortune —**out of** (or **off**) **one's head** [Colloq.] **1.** crazy **2.** delirious; raving —**over one's head** **1.** too difficult to understand **2.** to a higher authority —**put** (or **lay**) **heads together** to consult or scheme together —**take it into one's head** to conceive the notion, plan, or intention —**turn one's head** **1.** to make one dizzy **2.** to make one vain or overconfident

-head (hed) *same as* -HOOD [*godhead*]

head·ache (hed′āk′) *n.* **1.** a continuous pain in the head **2.** [Colloq.] a cause of worry, trouble, etc.

head·board (-bôrd′) *n.* a board or frame that forms the head of a bed, etc.

head·cheese (-chēz′) *n.* a loaf of jellied, seasoned meat made from the head and feet of hogs

head·dress (-dres′) *n.* **1.** a covering or decoration for the head **2.** a style of arranging the hair

head·ed (-id) *adj.* **1.** formed into a head, as cabbage **2.** having a heading

-head·ed (-id) *a combining form meaning:* **1.** having a (specified kind of) head [*clearheaded*] **2.** having (a specified number of) heads [two-*headed*]

head·er (-ər) *n.* **1.** a person or device that puts heads on pins, nails, rivets, etc. **2.** a machine that takes off the heads of grain and loads them into a truck **3.** [Colloq.] a headlong fall or dive **4.** a wooden beam placed between two long beams with the ends of short beams resting against it **5.** a brick or stone laid against the thickness of a wall with the short end exposed in the wall face

head·first (-furst′) ***adv.*** **1.** with the head in front; headlong **2.** in a reckless way; rashly; impetuously Also **head′fore′-most′** (-fôr′mōst′)

head·gear (-gir′) ***n.*** **1.** a covering for the head; hat, cap, etc. **2.** the harness for the head of a horse, mule, etc.

head·hunt·er (-hun′tər) ***n.*** a member of any of certain primitive tribes who remove the heads of slain enemies and preserve them as trophies —**head′hunt′ing *n.***

head·ing (-iŋ) ***n.*** **1.** something forming or used to form the head, top, edge, or front; specif., an inscription at the top of a chapter, page, etc., giving the title, topic, etc. **2.** a topic or category **3.** the direction in which a ship, plane, etc. is moving: usually expressed as a compass reading

head·land (-lənd) ***n.*** a point of land reaching out into the water; esp., a promontory

head·less (-lis) ***adj.*** **1.** without a head **2.** without a leader **3.** stupid; foolish

head·light (-līt′) ***n.*** a light with a reflector and lens, at the front of an automobile, locomotive, etc.: also **head′lamp′**

head·line (-līn′) ***n.*** **1.** a line at the top of a page, giving the running title, page number, etc. **2.** a line or lines at the top of a newspaper article, giving its topic **3.** an important news item —***vt.* -lined′, -lin′ing** **1.** to provide with a headline **2.** to give featured billing to

head·lin·er (-lī′nər) ***n.*** a featured entertainer

head·long (-lôŋ′) ***adv.*** [< ME. *hedelinge(s)* < *hede,* head + *-linge,* adv. suffix] **1.** with the head first; headfirst **2.** with uncontrolled speed and force **3.** recklessly; rashly; impetuously —***adj.*** **1.** having the head first **2.** moving with uncontrolled speed and force **3.** reckless; impetuous

head·man (hed′mən, -man′) ***n.,*** *pl.* **-men** (-mən, -men′) a leader, chief, or overseer

head·mas·ter (-mas′tər) ***n.*** in some, esp. private, schools, the man who is the principal —**head′mas′ter·ship′** ***n.*** —**head′mis′tress** (-mis′tris) ***n.***

head·most (-mōst′) ***adj.*** in the lead; foremost

head-on (-än′) ***adj., adv.*** **1.** with the head or front foremost *[a head-on* collision*]* **2.** directly or in direct opposition *[*meet problems *head-on]*

head·phone (-fōn′) ***n.*** a telephone or radio receiver held to the ear by a band over the head

head·piece (-pēs′) ***n.*** **1.** a protective covering for the head, as a helmet **2.** the mind; intellect

head·pin (-pin′) ***n.*** the pin at the front of a triangle of bowling pins

head·quar·ters (-kwôr′tərz) ***n.pl.*** [*often with sing. v.*] **1.** the main office, or center of operations, of one in command, as in an army or police force **2.** the main office in any organization —**head′quar′ter *vt.***

head·rest (-rest′) ***n.*** a support for the head, as on a dentist's chair

head·room (-ro͞om′) ***n.*** space or clearance overhead, as in a doorway or tunnel

head·set (-set′) ***n.*** an earphone or earphones, often with a mouthpiece transmitter attached

head·ship (-ship′) ***n.*** the position or authority of a chief or leader; leadership; command

heads·man (hedz′mən) ***n.,*** *pl.* **-men** an executioner who beheads those condemned to die

head·stall (hed′stôl′) ***n.*** the part of a bridle or halter that fits over a horse's head

head start an early start or other advantage given to or taken by a contestant or competitor

HEADSET

head·stock (-stäk′) ***n.*** the part of a lathe supporting the spindle

head·stone (-stōn′) ***n.*** **1.** [Rare] a cornerstone **2.** a stone marker placed at the head of a grave

head·stream (-strēm′) ***n.*** a stream forming the source of another and larger stream

head·strong (-strôŋ′) ***adj.*** **1.** determined not to follow orders, advice, etc. but to do as one pleases; self-willed **2.** showing such determination *[headstrong* desire*]*

head·wait·er (-wāt′ər) ***n.*** a supervisor of waiters, often in charge of table reservations

head·wa·ters (-wôt′ərz, -wät′-) ***n.pl.*** the small streams that are the sources of a river

head·way (-wā′) ***n.*** **1.** forward motion **2.** progress in work, etc. **3.** *same as* HEADROOM **4.** the difference in time or miles between two vehicles traveling the same route

head wind a wind blowing in the direction directly opposite the course of a ship or aircraft

head·work (hed′wurk′) ***n.*** mental effort; thought

head·y (-ē) ***adj.*** **head′i·er, head′i·est** **1.** impetuous; rash; willful **2.** tending to affect the senses; intoxicating —**head′i·ly** ***adv.*** —**head′i·ness *n.***

heal (hēl) ***vt.*** [OE. *hælan* < *hal,* sound, healthy] **1.** to make well or healthy again **2.** *a)* to cure (a disease) *b)* to cause (a wound, sore, etc.) to become closed or scarred **3.** to free from grief, troubles, evil, etc. **4.** to remedy (grief, troubles, etc.) —***vi.*** **1.** to become well or healthy again; be cured **2.** to become closed or scarred: said of a wound —**heal′er *n.***

health (helth) ***n.*** [OE. *hælth* < *hal,* sound, healthy + -TH[1]] **1.** physical and mental well-being; freedom from disease, etc. **2.** condition of body or mind *[*good *health]* **3.** a wish for a person's health and happiness, as in drinking a toast **4.** soundness or vitality, as of a society or culture

health food food considered to be especially healthful; often, specif., such food when organically grown and free of chemical additives

health·ful (-fəl) ***adj.*** **1.** helping to produce or maintain health; wholesome **2.** [Rare] *same as* HEALTHY —**health′ful·ly** ***adv.*** —**health′ful·ness *n.***

health·y (hel′thē) ***adj.*** **health′i·er, health′i·est** **1.** having good health **2.** showing or resulting from good health *[a healthy* appetite*]* **3.** *same as* HEALTHFUL **4.** [Colloq.] large, vigorous, etc. *[a healthy* yell*]* —**health′i·ly** ***adv.*** —**health′i·ness *n.***

heap (hēp) ***n.*** [OE. *heap,* a troop, band] **1.** a pile or mass of things jumbled together **2.** [Colloq.] a large amount **3.** [Slang] an old automobile —***vt.*** **1.** to make a heap of **2.** to give in large amounts *[*to *heap* gifts on one*]* **3.** to fill (a plate, etc.) full or to overflowing —***vi.*** to accumulate or rise in a heap or pile

hear (hir) ***vt.*** **heard** (hurd), **hear′ing** [OE. *hieran*] **1.** to perceive or sense (sounds) by the ear **2.** to listen to and consider; specif., *a)* to listen to carefully or officially *[*to *hear* a child's lesson*]* *b)* to conduct a hearing of (a law case, etc.); try *c)* to consent to; grant *[hear* my plea*]* **3.** to be informed of; be told —***vi.*** **1.** to be able to hear sounds **2.** to listen **3.** to be told (*of* or *about*) —**hear from** to get a letter, telegram, etc. from —**hear! hear!** well said! —**not hear of** to forbid or refuse to consider —**hear′er *n.***

hear·ing (-iŋ) ***n.*** **1.** the act or process of perceiving sounds **2.** the sense by which sounds are perceived **3.** opportunity to speak, sing, etc.; audience **4.** a court appearance before a judge, other than a trial **5.** a formal meeting of an official body for hearing and gathering testimony, etc. **6.** the distance a sound will carry *[*within *hearing]*

hearing aid a small, battery-powered electronic device worn to compensate for hearing loss

heark·en (här′kən) ***vi.*** [OE. *heorcnian* < *hieran,* to hear] to pay careful attention; listen carefully

hear·say (hir′sā′) ***n.*** something one has heard but does not know to be true; rumor; gossip —***adj.*** based on hearsay

hearse (hurs) ***n.*** [< OFr. < L. *hirpex,* a harrow] a vehicle used in a funeral for carrying the corpse

heart (härt) ***n.*** [OE. *heorte*] **1.** the hollow, muscular organ that circulates the blood by alternate dilation and contraction **2.** any place or part centrally located like the heart *[hearts* of celery, the *heart* of the city*]* **3.** the central, vital, or main part; essence; core **4.** the human heart considered as the center of emotions, personality attributes, etc.; specif., *a)* inmost thought and feeling *[*to know in one's *heart]* *b)* one's emotional nature; disposition *[*to have a kind *heart]* *c)* any of various humane feelings; love, sympathy, etc. *d)* mood; feeling *[*to have a heavy *heart]* *e)* spirit or courage *[*to lose *heart]* **5.** a loved one **6.** a conventionalized design of a heart, shaped like this: ♡ **7.** *a)* any of a suit of playing cards marked with such symbols in red *b)* [*pl.*] this suit of cards *c)* [*pl.*] a card game in which the object is to avoid getting hearts in the tricks taken —**after one's own heart** that pleases one perfectly —**at heart** in one's innermost nature —**break one's heart** to overwhelm one with grief or disappointment —**by heart** by or from memorization —**change of heart** a change of mind, affections, etc. —**eat one's heart out** to brood over some frustra-

HUMAN HEART
(A, right atrium; B, left atrium; C, myocardium; D, right ventricle; E, inferior vena cava; F, pulmonary veins; G, pulmonary artery; H, superior vena cava; I, aorta; J, pulmonary artery; K, pulmonary veins; L, left ventricle)

tion or in regret —**have one's heart in one's mouth** (or **boots**) to be full of fear or nervous anticipation —**have one's heart in the right place** to be well-meaning —**heart and soul** with all one's effort, enthusiasm, etc. —**lose one's heart (to)** to fall in love (with) —**set one's heart on** to have a fixed desire for —**take heart** to cheer up —**take to heart** **1.** to consider seriously **2.** to be troubled by —**to one's heart's content** as much as one desires —**wear one's heart on one's sleeve** to show one's feelings plainly —**with all one's heart** with complete sincerity, devotion, etc.

heart·ache (-āk′) ***n.*** sorrow or grief

heart·beat (-bēt′) ***n.*** one pulsation, or full contraction and dilation, of the heart

heart block defective transmission of impulses regulating the heartbeat

heart·break (-brāk′) ***n.*** overwhelming sorrow, grief, or disappointment —**heart′break′ing** ***adj.*** —**heart′bro′ken** ***adj.***

heart·burn (-burn′) ***n.*** a burning sensation beneath the breastbone resulting from a spastic backflow of acid stomach contents into the esophagus

heart·ed (-id) ***adj.*** having a (specified kind of) heart: used in compounds *[stouthearted]*

heart·en (-'n) ***vt.*** to cheer up; encourage

heart failure the inability of the heart to pump enough blood through the body

heart·felt (-felt′) ***adj.*** with or expressive of deep feeling; sincere

hearth (härth) ***n.*** [OE. *heorth*] **1.** the stone or brick floor of a fireplace **2.** *a)* the fireside *b)* the home **3.** the lowest part of a blast furnace, where the molten metal settles, or the floor of a furnace on which the ore or metal rests for exposure to the flame

hearth·stone (-stōn′) ***n.*** **1.** the stone forming a hearth **2.** the home, or home life

heart·i·ly (härt′'l ē) ***adv.*** **1.** in a sincere, cordial way **2.** with enthusiasm **3.** with zestful appetite **4.** completely; very

heart·i·ness (-ē nis) ***n.*** a being hearty

heart·less (-lis) ***adj.*** lacking kindness; hard and pitiless —**heart′less·ly** ***adv.*** —**heart′less·ness** ***n.***

heart-rend·ing (-ren′diŋ) ***adj.*** causing much grief or mental anguish —**heart′-rend′ing·ly** ***adv.***

hearts·ease, heart's-ease (härts′ēz′) ***n.*** **1.** peace of mind **2.** *same as* WILD PANSY

heart·sick (härt′sik′) ***adj.*** sick at heart; extremely unhappy or despondent: also **heart′sore′** (-sôr′)

heart-strick·en (-strik′'n) ***adj.*** deeply grieved or greatly dismayed: also **heart′-struck′** (-struk′)

heart·strings (-striŋz′) ***n.pl.*** [orig. tendons or nerves formerly believed to brace and sustain the heart] deepest feelings or affections

heart·throb (-thräb′) ***n.*** **1.** *same as* HEARTBEAT **2.** [Old Slang] one's sweetheart

heart-to-heart (-tə härt′) ***adj.*** intimate and candid

heart·warm·ing (-wôr′miŋ) ***adj.*** such as to kindle a warm glow of genial feelings

heart·wood (-wood′) ***n.*** the hard wood at the core of a tree trunk: cf. SAPWOOD

heart·y (-ē) ***adj.*** **heart′i·er, heart′i·est** [see HEART & -Y²] **1.** extremely warm and friendly; most cordial **2.** enthusiastic; wholehearted *[hearty support]* **3.** strongly felt or expressed *[a hearty dislike]* **4.** strong and healthy **5.** *a)* nourishing and plentiful *[a hearty meal]* *b)* liking plenty of food *[a hearty eater]* —***n.***, *pl.* **heart′ies** [Archaic] a comrade; esp., a fellow sailor (usually preceded by *my*)

heat (hēt) ***n.*** [OE. *hætu*] **1.** the quality of being hot; hotness: in physics, heat is considered a form of energy whose effect is produced by the accelerated vibration of molecules **2.** *a)* much hotness; great warmth *b)* *same as* FEVER **3.** degree of hotness or warmth **4.** a feeling of hotness or warmth **5.** hot weather or climate **6.** the warming of a room, house, etc., as by a furnace **7.** appearance as an indication of hotness *[blue heat in metals]* **8.** *a)* strong feeling; excitement, ardor, anger, etc. *b)* the period or condition of such feeling *[in the heat of battle]* **9.** a single effort, bout, or trial; esp., a preliminary round of a race, etc. **10.** *a)* sexual excitement *b)* the period of this in animals; esp., the estrus of females **11.** *Metallurgy* a single heating, as of metal, in a furnace or forge **12.** [Slang] *a)* coercion *b)* great pressure, as in criminal investigation —***vt., vi.*** **1.** to make or become warm or hot **2.** to make or become excited

heat·ed (hēt′id) ***adj.*** **1.** hot **2.** vehement, impassioned, or angry —**heat′ed·ly** ***adv.***

heat·er (-ər) ***n.*** a stove, furnace, radiator, etc. for heating a room, car, water, etc.

heat exchanger any device for transferring heat to a cooler medium from a warmer one

heat exhaustion a mild form of heatstroke, characterized by faintness, dizziness, heavy sweating, etc.

heath (hēth) ***n.*** [OE. *hæth*] **1.** a tract of open wasteland, esp. in the British Isles, covered with heather, low shrubs, etc. **2.** any of various shrubs and plants that grow on heaths, as heather —***adj.*** designating a family of woody plants, including the blueberry, cranberry, azalea, etc.

heath·bird (-burd′) ***n.*** *same as* BLACK GROUSE

hea·then (hē′thən) ***n.***, *pl.* **-thens, -then** [OE. *hæthen*] **1.** orig., a member of any people not worshiping the God of Israel **2.** anyone not a Jew, Christian, or Moslem **3.** a person regarded as uncivilized, irreligious, etc. —***adj.*** **1.** of heathens; pagan **2.** irreligious, uncivilized, etc. —**hea′then·dom** ***n.*** —**hea′then·ish** ***adj.*** —**hea′then·ism** ***n.***

hea·then·ize (-īz′) ***vt., vi.*** **-ized′, -iz′ing** to make or become heathen

heath·er (heth′ər) ***n.*** [altered (after HEATH) < ME. *haddyr*] a low-growing plant of the heath family, common in the British Isles, with stalks of small, bell-shaped, purplish-pink flowers —***adj.*** like heather in color or appearance —**heath′er·y** ***adj.***

HEATHER

heat lightning lightning without thunder, seen near the horizon, esp. on hot summer evenings

heat prostration *same as* HEAT EXHAUSTION

heat pump a device for cooling an enclosed space by pumping hot air out, and for warming it by extracting heat from outdoor air or some other source and pumping it in

heat rash *same as* PRICKLY HEAT

heat·stroke (hēt′strōk′) ***n.*** a condition resulting from excessive exposure to intense heat, characterized by high fever and collapse

heat wave **1.** unusually hot weather, resulting from a slowly moving air mass of relatively high temperature **2.** a period of such weather

heaume (hōm) ***n.*** [Fr. < OFr. *helme:* see HELMET] a heavy helmet worn in the Middle Ages

heave (hēv) ***vt.*** **heaved** or (esp. *Naut.*) **hove, heav′ing** [< OE. *hebban*] **1.** to raise or lift, esp. with effort **2.** to lift in this way and throw **3.** to make rise or swell **4.** to utter (a sigh, etc.) with great effort **5.** *Naut.* *a)* to raise, haul, etc. by pulling with a rope or cable *b)* to move (a ship) in a specified manner or direction —***vi.*** **1.** to swell up; bulge out **2.** to rise and fall rhythmically **3.** *a)* to retch or vomit *b)* to pant; breathe hard; gasp **4.** *Naut.* *a)* to tug or haul (*on* or *at* a cable, rope, etc.) *b)* to proceed; move *[a ship hove into sight]* —***n.*** the act or effort of heaving —**heave ho!** pull hard! —**heave to** **1.** *Naut.* to stop forward movement **2.** to stop —**heav′er** ***n.***

heav·en (hev′'n) ***n.*** [OE. *heofon*] **1.** [*usually pl.*] the space surrounding the earth; firmament **2.** *Theol.* *a)* [*often* **H-**] the place where God is and where the blessed go after death *b)* [**H-**] God; Providence **3.** *a)* any place of great beauty and pleasure *b)* a state of great happiness —**move heaven and earth** to do all that can be done

heav·en·ly (-lē) ***adj.*** **1.** of or in the heavens *[the sun is a heavenly body]* **2.** *a)* causing or marked by great happiness, beauty, etc. *b)* [Colloq.] very pleasing, attractive, etc. **3.** *Theol.* of or in heaven; holy; divine —**heav′en·li·ness** ***n.***

heav·en·ward (-wərd) ***adv., adj.*** toward heaven: also **heav′en·wards** ***adv.***

heaves (hēvz) ***n.pl.*** [*with sing. v.*] a respiratory disease of horses, marked by coughing, heaving of the flanks, etc.

Heav·i·side layer (hev′ē sīd′) [after O. *Heaviside* (1850–1925), Eng. physicist] *same as* E LAYER

heav·y (hev′ē) ***adj.*** **heav′i·er, heav′i·est** [OE. *hefig* < base of *hebban*, to heave + *-ig*, -Y²] **1.** hard to lift or move because of great weight; weighty **2.** of concentrated weight for the size **3.** above the usual or a defined weight **4.** larger, greater, rougher, more intense, etc. than usual *[a heavy blow, a heavy vote, a heavy sea, heavy thunder, heavy features]* **5.** being such to an unusual extent *[a heavy drinker]* **6.** serious; grave *[a heavy responsibility]* **7.** hard to endure *[heavy demands]* **8.** hard to do or manage *[heavy work]* **9.** hard to bear *[heavy sorrow]* **10.** sorrowful *[a heavy heart]* **11.** burdened with sleep or fatigue *[heavy eyelids]* **12.** hard to digest *[a heavy meal]* **13.** not leavened properly *[a heavy cake]* **14.** clinging; penetrating *[a heavy odor]* **15.** cloudy; gloomy *[a heavy sky]* **16.** tedious; dull **17.** clumsy; awkward *[a heavy gait]* **18.** steeply inclined *[a heavy grade]* **19.** designating any large, basic industry that uses massive machinery **20.** heavily armed **21.** *Chem.* designating an isotope of greater atomic weight than the normal or most abundant isotope **22.** *Theater* serious, tragic, or villainous —***adv.*** heavily *[heavy-laden]* —***n.***, *pl.* **heav′ies** **1.** something heavy **2.** *Theater* *a)* a serious, tragic, or villainous role *b)* an actor who plays such roles —**hang heavy (on one's hands)** to pass slowly; drag: said of time

—**heavy with child** pregnant —**heav′i·ly** ***adv.*** —**heav′i·ness** ***n.***
heav·y-du·ty (-do͞ot′ē, -dyo͞ot′ē) ***adj.*** made to withstand great strain, bad weather, etc.
heav·y-hand·ed (-han′did) ***adj.*** **1.** clumsy or tactless **2.** cruel; tyrannical —**heav′y-hand′ed·ly** ***adv.*** —**heav′y-hand′ed·ness** ***n.***
heav·y-heart·ed (-här′tid) ***adj.*** sad; depressed —**heav′y-heart′ed·ly** ***adv.*** —**heav′y-heart′ed·ness** ***n.***
heavy hydrogen *same as* DEUTERIUM
heav·y·set (-set′) ***adj.*** stout or stocky in build
heavy spar *same as* BARITE
heavy water water composed of isotopes of hydrogen of atomic weight greater than one or of oxygen greater than 16, or of both; esp., deuterium oxide
heav·y·weight (-wāt′) ***n.*** **1.** a person or animal weighing much more than average **2.** a boxer or wrestler who weighs over 175 pounds **3.** [Colloq.] a very intelligent or important person
Heb. **1.** Hebrew **2.** Hebrews
heb·dom·a·dal (heb däm′ə dəl) ***adj.*** [< L. < Gr. *hebdomas,* seven (days) < *hepta,* seven] weekly —**heb·dom′a·dal·ly** ***adv.***
He·be (hē′bē) *Gr. Myth.* the goddess of youth: she was a cupbearer to the gods
He·bra·ic (hi brā′ik) ***adj.*** of or characteristic of the Hebrews, their language, culture, etc.; Hebrew —**He·bra′i·cal·ly** ***adv.***
He·bra·ism (hē′bri iz'm, -brā-) ***n.*** **1.** a Hebrew idiom, custom, etc. **2.** the characteristic ethical system, moral attitude, etc. of the Hebrews —**He′bra·ist** ***n.*** —**He′bra·is′tic** ***adj.***
He·brew (hē′bro͞o) ***n.*** [< OFr., ult. < Heb. *'ibhri,* lit., one from across (the river)] **1.** any member of a group of Semitic peoples tracing descent from Abraham, Isaac, and Jacob; specif., an Israelite: in modern, but not recent, usage interchangeable with *Jew* **2.** *a*) the ancient Semitic language of the Israelites, in which most of the Old Testament was written *b*) its modern form, the official language of Israel —***adj.*** **1.** of Hebrew or the Hebrews **2.** *same as* JEWISH
Hebrew calendar *same as* JEWISH CALENDAR
He·brews (-bro͞oz) *Bible* the Epistle to the Hebrews, a book of the New Testament
Heb·ri·des (heb′rə dēz′) Scottish island group off W Scotland —**Heb′ri·de′an** (-dē′ən) ***adj., n.***
Hec·a·te (hek′ə tē; *occas.* hek′it) *Gr. Myth.* a goddess of the moon, earth, and underworld, later regarded as the goddess of sorcery
hec·a·tomb (hek′ə tōm′, -to͞om′) ***n.*** [< L. < Gr. < *hekaton,* a hundred + *bous,* ox] **1.** in ancient Greece, the mass slaughter of 100 cattle as an offering to the gods **2.** any large-scale slaughter
heck (hek) ***interj., n.*** [Colloq.] *a euphemism for* HELL
heck·le (hek′'l) ***vt.*** **-led, -ling** [ME. < *hechele:* see HACKLE¹] to annoy or harass (a speaker, etc.) by interrupting with questions or taunts —**heck′ler** ***n.***
hec·tare (hek′ter) ***n.*** [Fr.: see HECTO- & ARE²] a metric measure of surface, equal to 10,000 square meters (100 ares or 2.471 acres)
hec·tic (hek′tik) ***adj.*** [< OFr. < LL. < Gr. *hektikos,* habitual] **1.** of or characteristic of a wasting disease, as tuberculosis, or the fever accompanying this **2.** feverish or flushed **3.** full of confusion, rush, excitement, etc. —**hec′ti·cal·ly** ***adv.***
hec·to- [Fr. < Gr. *hekaton,* a hundred] *a combining form meaning* a hundred
hec·to·gram (hek′tə gram′) ***n.*** [< Fr.: see prec. & GRAM] a metric measure of weight, equal to 100 grams (3.527 ounces)
hec·to·graph (-graf′) ***n.*** [< G. < *hekto-,* HECTO- + *-graph,* -GRAPH] a duplicating device by which written or typed matter is transferred to a sheet of gelatin, from which many copies can be taken —***vt.*** to duplicate by means of a hectograph
Hec·tor (hek′tər) *Gr. Myth.* a Trojan hero killed by Achilles: he was Priam's son
hec·tor (hek′tər) ***n.*** [< prec.] a swaggering fellow; bully —***vt., vi.*** to browbeat; bully
Hec·u·ba (hek′yoo bə) *Gr. Myth.* wife of Priam and mother of Hector, Paris, and Cassandra
he'd (hēd) **1.** he had **2.** he would
hedge (hej) ***n.*** [OE. *hecg*] **1.** a row of closely planted shrubs, bushes, etc. forming a boundary or fence **2.** any fence or barrier **3.** the act of hedging —***adj.*** **1.** of, in, or near a hedge **2.** low, disreputable, etc. —***vt.*** **hedged, hedg′ing** **1.** to place a hedge around or along **2.** to hinder or guard as with a barrier; hem in **3.** to try to avoid loss in (a bet, risk, etc.) by making counterbalancing bets, etc. —***vi.*** to refuse to commit oneself; avoid direct answers —**hedg′er** ***n.***
hedge·hog (hej′hôg′, -häg′) ***n.*** **1.** a small, insect-eating, old-world mammal, with sharp spines on the back, which bristle and form a defense when the animal curls up **2.** the American porcupine
hedge·hop (-häp′) ***vi.*** **-hopped′, -hop′ping** [Colloq.] to fly an airplane very close to the ground, as for spraying insecticide —**hedge′hop′per** ***n.***
hedge·row (-rō′) ***n.*** a row of shrubs, bushes, etc., forming a hedge
he·do·nism (hēd′'n iz'm) ***n.*** [< Gr. *hēdonē,* pleasure] **1.** the doctrine that pleasure or happiness is the principal good and the proper aim of action **2.** pleasure-seeking as a way of life —**he′do·nist** ***n.*** —**he′do·nis′tic** ***adj.*** —**he′do·nis′ti·cal·ly** ***adv.***
-he·dral (hē′drəl) *a combining form used to form adjectives from nouns ending in* -HEDRON
-he·dron (hē′drən) [< Gr. < *hedra,* a side, base] *a combining form meaning* a geometric figure or crystal with (a specified number of) surfaces
heed (hēd) ***vt., vi.*** [OE. *hedan*] to pay close attention (to); take careful notice (of) —***n.*** close attention; careful notice —**heed′ful** ***adj.*** —**heed′ful·ly** ***adv.***
heed·less (-lis) ***adj.*** not taking heed; careless; unmindful —**heed′less·ly** ***adv.*** —**heed′less·ness** ***n.***
hee·haw (hē′hô′) ***n., vi.*** [echoic] *same as* BRAY
heel¹ (hēl) ***n.*** [OE. *hela*] **1.** the back part of the human foot, under the ankle **2.** the corresponding part of the hind foot of an animal **3.** that part of a stocking, etc. which covers the heel **4.** the built-up part of a shoe, supporting the heel **5.** anything like the human heel in location, shape, or function, as the end of a loaf of bread **6.** [Colloq.] a despicable person; cad —***vt.*** **1.** to furnish with a heel **2.** to follow closely at the rear of **3.** to touch or drive forward as with the heel **4.** [Colloq.] to provide (a person) with money —***vi.*** to follow along at the heels of someone —**at heel** just behind —**cool one's heels** [Colloq.] to be kept waiting for some time —**down at the heel(s)** **1.** with the heels of one's shoes worn down **2.** shabby; seedy —**kick up one's heels** to have fun —**on** (or **upon**) **the heels of** close behind —**out at the heel(s)** **1.** having holes in the heels of one's shoes or socks **2.** shabby; seedy —**take to one's heels** to run away: also **show one's heels** —**to heel** **1.** just behind **2.** under control —**turn on one's heel** to turn around abruptly —**heel′less** ***adj.***
heel² (hēl) ***vi.*** [OE. *hieldan*] to lean to one side; list: said esp. of a ship —***vt.*** to make (a ship) list —***n.*** the act or extent of heeling
heeled (hēld) ***adj.*** [Colloq.] **1.** having money **2.** armed, esp. with a gun
heel·er (hē′lər) ***n.*** **1.** one that heels **2.** [Colloq.] *same as* WARD HEELER
heel·tap (hēl′tap′) ***n.*** **1.** a layer of leather, etc. serving as a lift in the heel of a shoe **2.** a bit of liquor left in a glass after drinking
heft (heft) ***n.*** [< base of HEAVE] [Colloq.] **1.** weight; heaviness **2.** importance; influence —***vt.*** [Colloq.] **1.** to lift or heave **2.** to estimate the weight of by lifting —***vi.*** [Colloq.] to weigh
heft·y (hef′tē) ***adj.*** **heft′i·er, heft′i·est** [Colloq.] **1.** weighty; heavy **2.** large and powerful **3.** big or fairly big —**heft′i·ly** ***adv.*** —**heft′i·ness** ***n.***
He·gel (hā′gəl), **Ge·org Wil·helm Frie·drich** (gā ôrkh′ vil′helm frē′driH) 1770–1831; Ger. philosopher —**He·ge′li·an** (-gā′lē ən, hi jē′-) ***adj., n.*** —**He·ge′li·an·ism** ***n.***
he·gem·o·ny (hi jem′ə nē; hej′ə mō′nē) ***n., pl.*** **-nies** [< Gr. < *hēgemōn,* leader] leadership or dominance, esp. of one nation over others
he·gi·ra (hi jī′rə, hej′ər ə) ***n.*** [ML. < Ar. *hijrah,* lit., flight] **1.** [*often* **H-**] the forced journey of Mohammed from Mecca to Medina in 622 A.D.: the Moslem era dates from this event **2.** any journey for safety or as an escape; flight
Hei·del·berg (hīd′'l burg′; *G.* hī′dəl berkh′) city in SW West Germany: site of a famous university (founded 1386): pop. 122,000
heif·er (hef′ər) ***n.*** [OE. *heahfore*] a young cow that has not borne a calf
heigh (hī, hā) ***interj.*** an exclamation to attract notice, show pleasure, express surprise, etc.
heigh-ho (-hō′) ***interj.*** an exclamation of mild surprise, boredom, fatigue, etc.
height (hīt, *occas. colloq.* hītth) ***n.*** [OE. *heihthu* < *heah,* high] **1.** the topmost point of anything **2.** the highest limit or degree; extreme **3.** the distance from the bottom to the top **4.** elevation or distance above a given level, as above the surface of the earth or sea; altitude **5.** a relatively great

distance above a given level or from bottom to top **6.** [*often pl.*] a high place; eminence

height·en (hīt'n) ***vt., vi.*** **1.** to bring or come to a higher position **2.** to make or become larger, greater, etc.; increase —**height'en·er** ***n.***

Hei·ne (hī'nə), **Hein·rich** (hīn'riH) 1797–1856; Ger. poet & essayist

hei·nous (hā'nəs) ***adj.*** [< OFr. < *haine,* hatred < Frank.] outrageously evil or wicked; abominable —**hei'nous·ly** ***adv.*** —**hei'nous·ness** ***n.***

heir (er) ***n.*** [< OFr. < L. *heres*] **1.** a person who inherits or is entitled to inherit another's property or title upon the other's death **2.** a person who appears to get some trait from a predecessor or to carry on in his tradition —**heir'dom, heir'ship'** ***n.***

heir apparent *pl.* **heirs apparent** the heir whose right to a certain property or title cannot be denied if he outlives the ancestor

heir·ess (-is) ***n.*** a woman or girl who is an heir, esp. to great wealth

heir·loom (-lōōm') ***n.*** [HEIR + LOOM[1]] **1.** a piece of personal property that goes to an heir **2.** any treasured possession handed down from generation to generation

heir presumptive *pl.* **heirs presumptive** an heir whose right to a certain property or title will be lost if someone more closely related is born before the ancestor dies

heist (hīst) ***n.*** [< HOIST] [Slang] a robbery or holdup —***vt.*** **1.** [Slang] to rob or steal **2.** *dial. var. of* HOIST —**heist'er** ***n.***

He·jaz (he jaz', hē-; -jäz') district of NW Saudi Arabia: formerly a kingdom: c. 150,000 sq. mi.

he·ji·ra (hi jī'rə, hej'ər ə) ***n.*** *same as* HEGIRA

Hek·a·te (hek'ə tē) *same as* HECATE

hek·to- *same as* HECTO-

held (held) *pt. & pp. of* HOLD[1]

Hel·en (hel'ən) [< OFr. < L. < Gr. *Helenē,* lit., torch] a feminine name

Hel·e·na (hel'i nə; *also, for 1,* hə lē'nə) **1.** [var. of prec.] a feminine name **2.** [prob. ult. after *Helena* (?–338 A.D.), mother of CONSTANTINE I] capital of Mont.: pop. 24,000

Helen of Troy *Gr. Legend* the beautiful wife of Menelaus, king of Sparta: the Trojan War was started because Paris abducted her and took her to Troy

hel·i·cal (hel'i kəl, hē'lə-) ***adj.*** of, or having the form of, a helix; spiral —**hel'i·cal·ly** ***adv.***

hel·i·ces (hel'ə sēz', hē'lə-) ***n.*** *alt. pl. of* HELIX

hel·i·coid (hel'ə koid', hē'lə-) ***adj.*** [< Gr. < *helix,* a spiral + *eidos,* form] shaped like a spiral; coiled: also **hel'i·coi'dal** —***n.*** *Geom.* a spiral or screw-shaped surface

Hel·i·con (hel'ə kän', -kən) mountain group in SC Greece: in Greek mythology, the home of the Muses —***n.*** [prob. < Gr. *helix,* a spiral: from the shape] [**h-**] a brass-wind instrument, similar to a bass tuba

hel·i·cop·ter (hel'ə käp'tər, hē'lə-) ***n.*** [< Fr. < Gr. *helix,* a spiral + *pteron,* wing] a kind of aircraft moved in any direction, or kept hovering, by large, rotary blades (*rotors*) mounted horizontally —***vi., vt.*** to travel or convey by helicopter

he·li·o- [L. < Gr. < *hēlios,* the sun] *a combining form meaning* the sun, bright, radiant: also **heli-**

he·li·o·cen·tric (hē'lē ō sen'trik) ***adj.*** [HELIO- + -CENTRIC] **1.** calculated from, or viewed as from, the center of the sun **2.** having or regarding the sun as the center

he·li·o·graph (hē'lē ə graf') ***n.*** [HELIO- + -GRAPH] a device for sending a message (**heliogram**) or signaling by flashing the sun's rays from a mirror —***vt., vi.*** to signal or communicate by heliograph —**he'li·og'ra·pher** (-äg'rə fər) ***n.*** —**he'li·o·graph'ic** ***adj.*** —**he'li·og'ra·phy** ***n.***

He·li·os (hē'lē äs') *Gr. Myth.* the sun god

he·li·o·trope (hē'lē ə trōp', hēl'yə-) ***n.*** [< Fr. < L. < Gr. < *hēlios* (see HELIO-) + *trepein,* to turn] **1.** formerly, a sunflower **2.** a plant with fragrant clusters of small, white or reddish-purple flowers **3.** reddish purple **4.** *same as* BLOODSTONE —***adj.*** reddish-purple

he·li·ot·ro·pism (hē'lē ät'rə piz'm) ***n.*** the tendency of certain plants or other organisms to turn toward or from light, esp. sunlight —**he'li·o·trop'ic** (-ə träp'ik) ***adj.*** —**he'li·o·trop'i·cal·ly** ***adv.***

hel·i·port (hel'ə pôrt') ***n.*** [HELI(COPTER) + (AIR)PORT] a flat place where helicopters land and take off

he·li·um (hē'lē əm) ***n.*** [ModL. < Gr. *hēlios,* the sun] one of the chemical elements, a very light, inert, colorless gas: it is used for inflating balloons, etc.: symbol, He; at. wt., 4.0026; at. no., 2

he·lix (hē'liks) ***n.,*** *pl.* **-lix·es, -li·ces'** (hel'ə sēz', hē'lə-) [L. < Gr., a spiral < *helissein,* to turn around] **1.** any spiral, either lying in a single plane or, esp., moving around a cone, cylinder, etc. as a screw thread does **2.** the folded rim of cartilage around the outer ear **3.** *Archit.* an ornamental spiral

hell (hel) ***n.*** [OE. *hel* < base of *helan,* to hide] **1.** *Bible* the place where the spirits of the dead are **2.** [*often* **H-**] *a*) *Christianity* the place to which sinners and unbelievers go after death for punishment *b*) those in hell *c*) the powers of evil or darkness **3.** any place or condition of evil, pain, cruelty, etc. **4.** [Colloq.] *a*) any very disagreeable experience *b*) devilishness [*full of hell*] —***vi.*** [Slang] to live or act in a reckless or dissolute way (often with *around*) —***interj.*** an exclamation of irritation, anger, emphasis, etc.: regarded as profanity —**be hell on** [Slang] **1.** to be very difficult or painful for **2.** to be very strict with **3.** to be very damaging to —**catch** (or **get**) **hell** [Slang] to receive a severe scolding, punishment, etc. —**for the hell of it** [Slang] for no serious reason

he'll (hēl; *unstressed* hil, il) **1.** he will **2.** he shall

hell·bend·er (hel'ben'dər) ***n.*** a large, edible salamander, found esp. in the Ohio valley

hell·bent (-bent') ***adj.*** [Slang] **1.** firmly or recklessly determined **2.** moving fast or recklessly

hell·cat (-kat') ***n.*** **1.** a witch **2.** an evil, spiteful, bad-tempered woman

hell·div·er (-dī'vər) ***n.*** the American dabchick

hel·le·bore (hel'ə bôr') ***n.*** [< OFr. < L. < Gr. *helleboros,* orig. prob. "plant eaten by fawns"] **1.** any of a group of winter-blooming plants of the buttercup family, with flowers shaped like buttercups but of various colors **2.** any of a group of plants of the lily family **3.** the poisonous rhizomes of certain of these plants that have been used in medicine

Hel·lene (hel'ēn) ***n.*** [< Gr.] a Greek

Hel·len·ic (hə len'ik, he-) ***adj.*** **1.** of the Hellenes; Greek **2.** of the history, language, or culture of the ancient Greeks from the late 8th century B.C. to the death of Alexander the Great (323 B.C.) —***n.*** the language of ancient Greece

Hel·len·ism (hel'ən iz'm) ***n.*** **1.** a Greek phrase, idiom, or custom **2.** the character, thought, culture, or ethics of ancient Greece **3.** adoption of the Greek language, customs, etc. —**Hel'len·ist** ***n.***

Hel·len·is·tic (hel'ə nis'tik) ***adj.*** **1.** of or characteristic of Hellenism **2.** of Greek history, culture, etc. after the death of Alexander the Great (323 B.C.) —**Hel'len·is'ti·cal·ly** ***adv.***

Hel·len·ize (hel'ə nīz') ***vt., vi.*** **-ized', -iz'ing** to make or become Greek, as in customs, ideals, etc. —**Hel'len·i·za'tion** ***n.*** —**Hel'len·iz'er** ***n.***

Hel·les·pont (hel'əs pänt') *ancient name of the* DARDANELLES

hell·fire (hel'fīr') ***n.*** the fire or torment of hell

hel·lion (hel'yən) ***n.*** [Colloq.] a person fond of deviltry; mischievous troublemaker

hell·ish (hel'ish) ***adj.*** **1.** of, from, or like hell **2.** devilish; fiendish **3.** [Colloq.] very unpleasant; detestable —**hell'ish·ly** ***adv.*** —**hell'ish·ness** ***n.***

hel·lo (he lō', hə lō', hel'ō) ***interj.*** [var. of HOLLO] an exclamation *a*) of greeting or of response, as in telephoning *b*) to attract attention *c*) of surprise —***n.,*** *pl.* **-los** a saying of "hello" —***vi., vt.*** **-loed', -lo'ing** to say "hello" (to)

helm[1] (helm) ***n., vt.*** [OE.] *archaic var. of* HELMET

helm[2] (helm) ***n.*** [OE. *helma*] **1.** the wheel or tiller or, with the rudder, etc., all the gear by which a ship is steered **2.** the control or leadership, as of an organization —***vt.*** to guide; steer

hel·met (hel'mət) ***n.*** [OFr., dim. of *helme,* helmet < Frank.] **1.** a hard, protective head covering, variously designed for use in combat, certain sports, diving, etc. **2.** something like such a head covering in appearance or function —***vt.*** to equip with a helmet —**hel'met·ed** ***adj.***

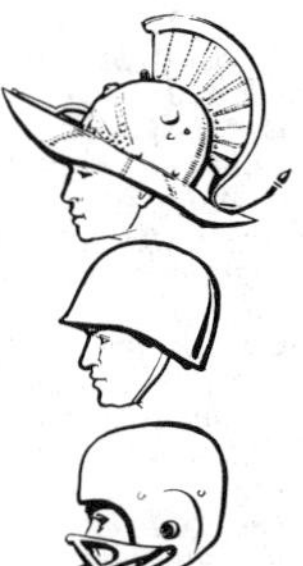
HELMETS

hel·minth (hel'minth) ***n.*** [Gr. *helmins* (gen. *helminthos*)] a worm or wormlike animal; esp., a parasite of the intestine, as the tapeworm, hookworm, or roundworm —**hel·min·thic** (hel min'thik) ***adj.***

helms·man (helmz'mən) ***n.,*** *pl.* **-men** the man at the helm; person who steers a ship

Hé·lo·ïse (ā lô ēz'; *E.* hel'ə wēz') 1101?–64?; mistress &, later, wife of her teacher, Pierre ABÉLARD

Hel·ot (hel'ət, hē'lət) ***n.*** [< L. < Gr. *Heilōtes,* serfs] **1.** a member of the lowest class of serfs in ancient Sparta **2.** [**h-**] any serf or slave —**hel'ot·ism** ***n.*** —**hel'ot·ry** ***n.***

help (help) ***vt.*** [OE. *helpan*] **1.** to make things easier or better for (a person); aid; assist; specif., *a*) to give (one in need) relief, money, etc. *b*) to share the labor of [*help us lift this*] *c*) to aid in getting (*up, down, in, to, into, out of,* etc.) **2.** to make it easier for (something) to exist, happen, improve, etc.; promote **3.** to remedy; relieve [*this will help your cough*] **4.** *a*) to keep from; avoid [*she can't help crying*] *b*) to stop, prevent, change, etc. [*faults that can't be helped*] **5.** to serve or wait on (a customer, etc.) —***vi.*** **1.** to give assistance; be useful or beneficial **2.** to act as a waiter, clerk, etc. —*n.* **1.** a helping; aid; assistance **2.** relief; remedy **3.** *a*) a hired helper, as a servant, farmhand, etc. *b*) hired helpers; employees —**cannot help but** to be compelled or obliged to —**cannot help oneself** to be the victim of circumstances, a habit, etc. —**help oneself to** **1.** to serve oneself with (food, etc.) **2.** to steal —**help out** to help in getting or doing something —**so help me (God)** as God is my witness: used in oaths —**help′er** *n.*

help·ful (-fəl) *adj.* giving help; useful —**help′ful·ly** *adv.* —**help′ful·ness** *n.*

help·ing (-iŋ) *n.* **1.** a giving of aid; assisting **2.** a portion of food served to one person

help·less (-lis) *adj.* **1.** not able to help oneself; weak **2.** lacking help or protection **3.** incompetent; ineffective —**help′less·ly** *adv.* —**help′less·ness** *n.*

help·mate (-māt′) *n.* [altered < ff.] a helpful companion; specif., a wife or husband

help·meet (-mēt′) *n.* [misreading of "an *help meet* for him" (Gen. 2:18)] *same as* HELPMATE

Hel·sin·ki (hel′siŋ kē) capital of Finland; seaport on the Gulf of Finland: pop. 527,000

hel·ter-skel·ter (hel′tər skel′tər) *adv.* [arbitrary formation] in haste and confusion; in a disorderly, hurried manner —*adj.* hurried and confused; disorderly —*n.* anything helter-skelter

helve (helv) *n.* [OE. *helfe*] the handle of a tool, esp. of an ax or hatchet —*vt.* **helved, helv′ing** to put a helve on

Hel·ve·tia (hel vē′shə) *Latin name of* SWITZERLAND —**Hel·ve′tian** *adj., n.*

hem[1] (hem) *n.* [OE.] **1.** the border on a garment or piece of cloth, usually made by folding the edge and sewing it down **2.** any border or edge —*vt.* **hemmed, hem′ming** to fold back the edge of and sew down —**hem in** (or **around** or **about**) **1.** to encircle; surround **2.** to confine or restrain —**hem′mer** *n.*

hem[2] (hem; *conventionalized pronun.*) *interj., n.* the sound made in clearing the throat —*vi.* **hemmed, hem′ming** **1.** to make this sound, as to get attention or show doubt **2.** to grope about in speech, seeking the right words: usually in **hem and haw**

he-man (hē′man′) *n.* [Colloq.] a strong, virile man

hem·a·tite (hem′ə tīt′, hē′mə-) *n.* [< L. < Gr. *haimatitēs*, bloodlike < *haima*, blood] native ferric oxide, Fe_2O_3, an important iron ore, brownish red or black —**hem′a·tit′ic** (-tit′ik) *adj.*

hem·a·to- [< Gr. *haima* (gen. *haimatos*), blood] *a combining form meaning* blood: also **hemat-**

hem·a·to·crit (hi mat′ə krit′) *n.* [< HEMATO- + Gr. *kritēs*, a judge] **1.** a centrifuge for measuring the relative volumes of blood cells and fluid in blood **2.** the proportion of blood cells to a volume of blood so measured: also **hematocrit reading**

he·ma·tol·o·gy (hē′mə täl′ə jē, hem′ə-) *n.* the study of blood and its diseases —**he′ma·to·log′ic** (-tə läj′ik), **he′ma·to·log′i·cal** *adj.* —**he′ma·tol′o·gist** *n.*

he·ma·to·ma (-tō′mə) *n., pl.* **-mas, -ma·ta** (-tə) [ModL.: see HEMAT(O)- & -OMA] a local swelling or tumor filled with bloody fluid

hem·er·a·lo·pi·a (hem′ər ə lō′pē ə) *n.* [ModL. < Gr. < *hēmera*, day + *alaos*, blind + *ōps*, eye + -IA] an eye defect in which vision is reduced in bright light —**hem′er·a·lop′ic** (-läp′ik) *adj.*

hem·i- [Gr. *hēmi-*] *a prefix meaning* half

hem·i·dem·i·sem·i·qua·ver (hem′ē dem′ē sem′ē-kwā′vər) *n.* [Brit.] *same as* SIXTY-FOURTH NOTE

Hem·ing·way (hem′iŋ wā′), **Ernest (Miller)** 1899–1961; U.S. novelist & short-story writer

he·mip·ter·an (hi mip′tər ən) *n.* [< ModL.: see HEMI- & PTERO-] any of a group of insects, including bedbugs, lice, aphids, etc., with piercing and sucking mouthparts —**he·mip′ter·ous** *adj.*

hem·i·sphere (hem′ə sfir′) *n.* [< L. < Gr.: see HEMI- & SPHERE] **1.** half of a sphere or globe **2.** *a*) any of the halves of the earth: the Northern, Southern, Eastern, or Western Hemisphere *b*) a model or map of any of these halves —**hem′i·spher′i·cal** (-sfer′i kəl), **hem′i·spher′ic** *adj.* —**hem′i·spher′i·cal·ly** *adv.*

hem·i·stich (hem′i stik′) *n.* [< L. < Gr. < *hēmi-*, half + *stichos*, a line] **1.** half a line of verse, esp. as divided by the caesura **2.** a metrically short line of verse

hem·line (hem′līn′) *n.* the bottom edge of a dress, coat, etc., where the edge meets the leg

hem·lock (hem′läk) *n.* [OE. *hymlic*] **1.** *a*) a poisonous European plant of the parsley family, with small white flowers: also **poison hemlock** *b*) a poison made from this plant **2.** *a*) an evergreen tree of the pine family, with short, flat needles: the bark is used in tanning *b*) the wood of this tree

he·mo- [< Gr. < *haima*, blood] *a combining form meaning* blood [*hemoglobin*]: also **hem-**

he·mo·cy·tom·e·ter (hē′mō sī täm′ə tər, hem′ō-) *n.* [HEMO- + CYTO- + -METER] a device for counting the number of cells in a sample of blood

he·mo·glo·bin (hē′mə glō′bin, hem′ə-; hē′mə glō′bin, hem′ə-) *n.* [contr. < *haematoglobulin*: see HEMATO- & GLOBULIN] the red coloring matter of the red blood corpuscles: it carries oxygen from the lungs to the tissues, and carbon dioxide from the tissues to the lungs —**he′mo·glo′bin·ous** *adj.*

he·mol·y·sis (hi mäl′ə sis) *n.* [HEMO- + -LYSIS] the destruction of red corpuscles with liberation of hemoglobin into the surrounding fluid —**he·mo·lyt·ic** (hē′mə lit′ik, hem′ə-) *adj.*

he·mo·phil·i·a (hē′mə fil′ē ə, hem′ə-; -fil′yə) *n.* [ModL.: see HEMO-, -PHILE, & -IA] a hereditary condition in which one of the normal blood-clotting factors is absent, causing prolonged bleeding from even minor cuts —**he′mo·phil′i·ac** (-fil′ē ak, -fil′yak) *n.*

hem·or·rhage (hem′ər ij, hem′rij) *n.* [< Fr. < L. < Gr. < *haima*, blood + *rhēgnynai*, to break] the escape of large quantities of blood from a blood vessel; heavy bleeding —*vi.* **-rhaged, -rhag·ing** to have a hemorrhage —**hem′or·rhag′ic** (-ə raj′ik) *adj.*

hem·or·rhoid (hem′ə roid′, hem′roid) *n.* [< L. < Gr. < *haima*, blood + *rhein*, to flow] a painful swelling of a vein in the region of the anus, often with bleeding: *usually used in pl.* —**hem′or·rhoid′al** *adj.*

he·mo·stat (hē′mə stat′, hem′ə-) *n.* [HEMO- + -STAT] anything used to stop bleeding; specif., a clamplike instrument used in surgery

hemp (hemp) *n.* [OE. *hænep*] **1.** *a*) a tall Asiatic plant having tough fiber in its stem *b*) the fiber, used to make rope, sailcloth, etc. *c*) a substance, such as marijuana, hashish, etc., made from the leaves and flowers of this plant **2.** *a*) any of various plants yielding a hemplike fiber, as sisal *b*) this fiber —**hemp′en** *adj.*

hem·stitch (hem′stich′) *n.* **1.** an ornamental stitch, used esp. at a hem, made by pulling out several parallel threads and tying the cross threads into small bunches **2.** decorative needlework done with this stitch —*vt.* to put hemstitches on —**hem′stitch′er** *n.* —**hem′stitch′ing** *n.*

HEMSTITCH

hen (hen) *n.* [< OE. *henn*, fem. of *hana*, rooster] **1.** the female of the chicken (the domestic fowl) **2.** the female of various other birds

hen·bane (-bān′) *n.* a coarse, hairy, foul-smelling, poisonous plant of the nightshade family, used in medicine

hence (hens) *adv.* [< OE. *heonan*, from here + -(*e*)*s*, adv. gen. suffix] **1.** from this place; away [*go hence*] **2.** *a*) from this time [*a year hence*] *b*) thereafter; subsequently **3.** from this life **4.** for this reason; therefore —*interj.* [Archaic] go away! —**hence with** [Archaic] away with!

hence·forth (-fôrth′) *adv.* from this time on: also **hence′for′ward**

hench·man (hench′mən) *n., pl.* **-men** [OE. *hengest*, male horse + *-man*: orig. sense prob. "groom"] **1.** a trusted helper or follower **2.** a political underling who seeks to advance himself **3.** any of the followers of a criminal gang leader

hen·e·quen (hen′ə kin) *n.* [< Sp. < native Yucatan name] **1.** a tropical American agave, cultivated for the hard fiber of the leaves **2.** the fiber, similar to the related sisal, used for rope, twine, rugs, etc.

hen·house (hen′hous′) *n.* a shelter for poultry

hen·na (hen′ə) *n.* [Ar. *ḥinnā′*] **1.** *a*) an old-world plant with white or red flowers *b*) a dye extracted from its leaves, often used to tint the hair auburn **2.** reddish brown —*adj.* reddish-brown —*vt.* **-naed, -na·ing** to tint with henna

hen·ner·y (hen′ər ē) *n., pl.* **-ner·ies** a place where poultry is kept or raised

hen·peck (hen′pek′) *vt.* to nag and domineer over (one's husband) —**hen′pecked′** *adj.*

Hen·ri·et·ta (hen′rē et′ə) [< Fr. fem. dim. of *Henri*, HENRY] a feminine name

Hen·ry (hen′rē) [< Fr. < G. < OHG. *Haganrih*, lit., ruler of an enclosure & *Heimerich*, lit., home ruler] **1.** a masculine name **2. Henry IV** *a*) 1367–1413; king of England (1399–1413); 1st Lancastrian king *b*) 1553–1610; king of France (1589–1610); 1st Bourbon king **3. Henry V** 1387–1422; king of England (1413–22) **4. Henry VI** 1421–71; king of England (1422–61; 1470–71) **5. Henry VIII** 1491–

1547; king of England (1509–47): established the Church of England **6. O.,** (pseud. of *William Sydney Porter*) 1862–1910; U.S. short-story writer **7. Patrick,** 1736–99; Am. patriot, statesman, & orator

hen·ry (hen′rē) ***n.,*** *pl.* **-rys, -ries** [after J. *Henry* (1797–1878), U.S. physicist] *Elec.* the unit of inductance, equal to the inductance of a circuit in which the variation of current at the rate of one ampere per second induces an electromotive force of one volt

hep (hep) ***adj.*** [< ?] [Slang] *earlier form of* HIP³

he·pat·ic (hi pat′ik) ***adj.*** [< L. < Gr. < *hēpar,* the liver] **1.** of or affecting the liver **2.** like the liver in color or shape

he·pat·i·ca (-i kə) ***n.*** [ModL. (see prec.): it has liver-shaped leaves] a small plant of the buttercup family, with spring flowers of white, pink, blue, or purple

hep·a·ti·tis (hep′ə tīt′is) ***n.*** [ModL. < Gr. *hēpar* (gen. *hepatos*), liver + -ITIS] inflammation of the liver

He·phaes·tus (hi fes′təs) *Gr. Myth.* the god of fire and forge: identified with the Roman god Vulcan

Hep·ple·white (hep′'l hwīt′) ***adj.*** [after G. *Hepplewhite* (?–1786), Eng. cabinetmaker] designating or of a style of furniture with graceful curves

hep·ta- [< Gr. *hepta,* seven] *a combining form meaning* seven: also, before a vowel, **hept-**

hep·ta·chlor (hep′tə klôr′) ***n.*** an insecticide, $C_{10}H_7Cl_7$, similar to chlordane

hep·ta·gon (hep′tə gän′) ***n.*** [< Gr.: see HEPTA- & -GON] a plane figure with seven angles and seven sides —**hep·tag′o·nal** (-tag′ə n'l) ***adj.***

hep·tam·e·ter (hep tam′ə tər) ***n.*** [HEPTA- + -METER] a line of verse with seven metrical feet

hep·tane (hep′tān) ***n.*** [HEPT(A)- + -ANE] a flammable, colorless liquid, C_7H_{16}, used as a standard in octane rating, etc.

hep·tar·chy (hep′tär kē) ***n.,*** *pl.* **-chies** **1.** government by seven rulers **2.** a group of seven allied kingdoms, specif. [**the H-**] in Anglo-Saxon England before the 9th century

her (hʉr; *unstressed* ər) ***pron.*** [OE. *hire*] *objective case of* SHE: also used colloquially as a predicate complement with a linking verb (Ex.: that's *her*) —***possessive pronominal adj.*** of, belonging to, made, or done by her

her. heraldry

He·ra (hir′ə) *Gr. Myth.* the wife of Zeus, queen of the gods, and goddess of marriage: identified with the Roman goddess Juno

Her·a·cli·tus (her′ə klīt′əs) fl. about 500 B.C.; Gr. philosopher

Her·a·kles, Her·a·cles (her′ə klēz′) *same as* HERCULES

her·ald (her′əld) ***n.*** [< OFr. *heralt* < Frank.] **1.** formerly, an official who made proclamations, carried state messages, took charge of tournaments, etc. **2.** in England, an official in charge of genealogies, heraldic arms, etc. **3.** a person who announces significant news **4.** a person or thing that presages what is to follow; forerunner; harbinger —***vt.*** **1.** to announce, foretell, etc. **2.** to publicize

he·ral·dic (hə ral′dik) ***adj.*** of heraldry or heralds

her·ald·ry (her′əl drē) ***n.,*** *pl.* **-ries** **1.** the art or science having to do with coats of arms, genealogies, etc. **2.** heraldic devices **3.** heraldic ceremony or pomp

herb (ʉrb, hʉrb) ***n.*** [< OFr. < L. *herba*] **1.** any seed plant whose stem withers away annually, as distinguished from a tree or shrub whose woody stem lives from year to year **2.** any plant used as a medicine, seasoning, or flavoring, as mint, thyme, basil, or sage **3.** grass; herbage —**herb′like′** ***adj.*** —**herb′y** ***adj.***

her·ba·ceous (hər bā′shəs, ər-) ***adj.*** **1.** of or like an herb **2.** like a green leaf in texture, color, etc.

herb·age (ʉr′bij, hʉr′-) ***n.*** **1.** herbs collectively, esp. those used as pasturage; grass **2.** the green foliage and juicy stems of herbs

herb·al (hʉr′b'l, ʉr′-) ***adj.*** of herbs —***n.*** formerly, a book about herbs or plants

herb·al·ist (-ist) ***n.*** **1.** orig., a botanist **2.** a person who grows, collects, or deals in herbs

her·bar·i·um (hər ber′ē əm, ər-) ***n.,*** *pl.* **-i·ums, -i·a** (-ə) [LL. < L. *herba,* herb] **1.** a collection of dried plants used for botanical study **2.** a room, building, etc. for keeping such a collection

Her·bert (hʉr′bərt) [OE. *Herebeorht,* lit., bright army] **1.** a masculine name: dim. *Herb* **2. George,** 1593–1633; Eng. poet **3. Victor,** 1859–1924; U.S. composer & conductor, born in Ireland

her·bi·cide (hʉr′bə sīd′, ʉr′-) ***n.*** [< L. *herba,* herb + -CIDE] any chemical substance used to destroy plants, esp. weeds —**her′bi·ci′dal** ***adj.***

her·bi·vore (-vôr′) ***n.*** [Fr.] a herbivorous animal

her·biv·o·rous (hər biv′ər əs) ***adj.*** [< L. *herba,* herb + -VOROUS] feeding chiefly on grass or other plants

Her·ce·go·vi·na (hert′sə gō vē′nə) former independent duchy: now, with Bosnia, a republic of Yugoslavia: see BOSNIA AND HERCEGOVINA

Her·cu·le·an (hʉr′kyə lē′ən, hər kyōō′lē ən) ***adj.*** **1.** of Hercules **2.** [*usually* **h-**] *a*) having the great size and strength of Hercules *b*) calling for great strength, size, or courage, as a task

Her·cu·les (hʉr′kyə lēz′) **1.** *Class. Myth.* a son of Zeus, renowned for feats of strength, esp. twelve labors imposed on him **2.** a large N constellation —***n.*** [**h-**] any very large, strong man

herd¹ (hʉrd) ***n.*** [OE. *heord*] **1.** a number of cattle or other large animals feeding, living, or being driven together **2.** a crowd **3.** the common people; masses: contemptuous term —***vt., vi.*** to form into or move as a herd, group, crowd, etc.

herd² (hʉrd) ***n.*** [OE. *hierde*] a herdsman: now chiefly in combination [*cowherd*] —***vt.*** to tend or drive as a herdsman —**ride herd on** **1.** to control a moving herd of (cattle) from horseback **2.** to keep a close watch or control over —**herd′er** ***n.***

herds·man (hʉrdz′mən) ***n.,*** *pl.* **-men** a person who keeps or tends a herd

here (hir) ***adv.*** [OE. *her*] **1.** at or in this place: often used as an intensive [*John here is a good player*] **2.** toward, to, or into this place [*come here*] **3.** at this point in action, speech, etc.; now **4.** in earthly life —***interj.*** an exclamation used to call attention, answer a roll call, etc. —***n.*** this place or point —**here and there** in, at, or to various places —**here goes!** an exclamation used when the speaker is about to do something daring, disagreeable, etc. —**neither here nor there** beside the point; irrelevant

here·a·bout (hir′ə bout′) ***adv.*** in this general vicinity: about or near here: also **here′a·bouts′**

here·af·ter (hir af′tər) ***adv.*** **1.** from now on; in the future **2.** following this, as in a writing **3.** in the state or life after death —***n.*** **1.** the future **2.** the state or life after death

here·at (hir at′) ***adv.*** **1.** at this time; when this occurred **2.** at this; for this reason

here·by (hir′bī′) ***adv.*** by this means

he·red·i·ta·ble (hə red′i tə b'l) ***adj.*** *same as* HERITABLE —**he·red′i·ta·bil′i·ty** ***n.***

he·red·i·tar·y (hə red′ə ter′ē) ***adj.*** [< L. < *hereditas:* see ff.] **1.** *a*) of, or passed down by, inheritance from an ancestor *b*) having title, etc. by inheritance **2.** of, or passed down by, heredity **3.** being such because of attitudes, beliefs, etc. passed down through generations —**he·red′i·tar′i·ly** ***adv.*** —**he·red′i·tar′i·ness** ***n.***

he·red·i·ty (hə red′ə tē) ***n.,*** *pl.* **-ties** [< Fr. < L. *hereditas,* heirship < *heres,* heir] **1.** the transmission of characteristics from parents to offspring by means of genes in the chromosomes **2.** all the characteristics that one inherits genetically

Her·e·ford (hʉr′fərd, her′ə-) ***n.*** [orig. bred in *Herefordshire,* England] any of a breed of beef cattle having a white face and a red body with white markings

here·in (hir in′) ***adv.*** **1.** in here **2.** in this writing **3.** in this matter, detail, etc.

here·in·a·bove (hir′in ə buv′) ***adv.*** in the preceding part (of this document, speech, etc.): also **here′in·be·fore′**

here·in·af·ter (-af′tər) ***adv.*** in the following part (of this document, speech, etc.): also **here′in·be·low′**

here·in·to (hir in′tōō) ***adv.*** **1.** into this place **2.** into this matter, condition, etc.

here·of (-uv′) ***adv.*** **1.** of this **2.** concerning this

here·on (-än′) ***adv.*** *same as* HEREUPON

here's (hirz) here is

here's to! here's a toast to! I wish joy, etc. to!

her·e·sy (her′ə sē) ***n.,*** *pl.* **-sies** [< OFr. < L. < Gr. *hairesis,* a selection, sect < *hairein,* to take] **1.** *a*) a religious belief opposed to the orthodox doctrines of a church; esp., such a belief denounced by the church *b*) rejection of a belief that is part of church dogma **2.** any opinion opposed to established views or doctrines **3.** the holding of any such belief or opinion

her·e·tic (her′ə tik) ***n.*** a person who professes a heresy; esp., a church member who holds beliefs opposed to church dogma —***adj.*** *same as* HERETICAL

he·ret·i·cal (hə ret′i k'l) ***adj.*** **1.** of heresy or heretics **2.** characterized by, or having the nature of, heresy —**he·ret′i·cal·ly** ***adv.***

here·to (hir tōō′) ***adv.*** to this (document, etc.) [*attached hereto*]: also **here·un′to**

here·to·fore (hir′tə fôr′, hir′tə fôr′) ***adv.*** up to now; until the present; before this

here·un·der (hir un′dər) ***adv.*** **1.** under or below this (in a document, etc.) **2.** under the terms stated here

here·up·on (hir′ə pän′, hir′ə pän′) ***adv.*** **1.** immediately following this **2.** concerning this

here·with (hir with′, -*with*′) ***adv.*** **1.** along with this **2.** by this method or means

her·it·a·ble (her′it ə b'l) ***adj.*** **1.** that can be inherited **2.** that can inherit —**her′it·a·bil′i·ty** ***n.***

her·it·age (her′ət ij) ***n.*** [OFr. < LL. < L. *hereditas:* see HEREDITY] **1.** property that is or can be inherited **2.** *a*) something handed down from one's ancestors or the past, as a characteristic, a culture, tradition, etc. *b)* birthright

Her·man (hʉr′mən) [< G. < OHG. *Hariman* < *heri*, army + *man*, man] a masculine name

her·maph·ro·dite (hər maf′rə dīt′) ***n.*** [< L. < Gr. < *Hermaphroditos*, son of Hermes and Aphrodite, united in a single body with a nymph] **1.** a person or animal with the sexual organs of both the male and the female **2.** a plant having stamens and pistils in the same flower **3.** *short for* HERMAPHRODITE BRIG —**her·maph′ro·dit′ism, her·maph′ro·dism** ***n.***

hermaphrodite brig a ship with a square-rigged foremast and a fore-and-aft-rigged mainmast

her·maph·ro·dit·ic (-dit′ik) ***adj.*** of or like a hermaphrodite: also **her·maph′ro·dit′i·cal** —**her·maph′ro·dit′i·cal·ly** ***adv.***

Her·mes (hʉr′mēz) *Gr. Myth.* a god who served as messenger of the other gods: identified with the Roman god Mercury and pictured with winged shoes and hat, carrying a caduceus

her·met·ic (hər met′ik) ***adj.*** [< ModL. < L. < Gr. *Hermēs* (reputed founder of alchemy)] airtight: also **her·met′i·cal** —**her·met′i·cal·ly** ***adv.***

her·mit (hʉr′mit) ***n.*** [< OFr. < LL. < LGr. < Gr. *erēmitēs* < *erēmos*, solitary] a person who lives by himself in a secluded spot, often from religious motives; recluse —**her·mit′ic, her·mit′i·cal** ***adj.*** —**her·mit′i·cal·ly** ***adv.*** —**her′·mit·like′** ***adj.***

her·mit·age (-ij) ***n.*** **1.** the place where a hermit lives **2.** a place where a person can live away from other people; secluded retreat

hermit crab any of various soft-bellied crabs that live in the empty shells of certain mollusks, as snails

her·ni·a (hʉr′nē ə) ***n.***, *pl.* **-ni·as, -ni·ae′** (-ē′) [L.] the protrusion of all or part of an organ, esp. a part of the intestine, through a tear in the wall of the surrounding structure; rupture —**her′ni·al** ***adj.***

He·ro (hir′ō) *Gr. Legend* a priestess of Aphrodite: her lover, Leander, swam the Hellespont every night to be with her

he·ro (hir′ō, hē′rō) ***n.***, *pl.* **-roes** [< L. < Gr. *hērōs*] **1.** *Myth. & Legend* a man of great strength and courage, favored by the gods and in part descended from them **2.** any man admired for his courage, nobility, or exploits **3.** any man regarded as an ideal or model **4.** the central, usually sympathetic, male character in a novel, play, poem, etc. **5.** a central figure who played an admirable role in any important event or period **6.** *same as* HERO SANDWICH

Her·od (her′əd) Edomite family of ancient Palestine, including, esp., **1. Herod (the Great)** 73?–4 B.C.; king of Judea (37–4) **2. Herod A·grip·pa (I)** (ə grip′ə) 10? B.C.–44 A.D.; king of Judea (37–44): grandson of *prec.* **3. Herod Agrippa (II)** 27?–100? A.D.; king of Judea (53–100): son of *prec.* **4. Herod An·ti·pas** (an′ti pas′) ?–40? A.D.; ruler of Galilee (4? B.C.–39 A.D.): son of *Herod the Great*

He·rod·o·tus (hə räd′ə təs) 485?–425? B.C.; Gr. historian: called the *Father of History*

he·ro·ic (hi rō′ik) ***adj.*** **1.** like or characteristic of a hero or his deeds *[heroic* conduct*]* **2.** of, about, or characterized by heroes and their deeds; epic *[*a *heroic* poem*]* **3.** exalted; eloquent *[heroic* words*]* **4.** exceptionally daring and risky *[heroic* measures*]* **5.** *Art* somewhat larger than life-size *[*a *heroic* statue*]* Also **he·ro′i·cal** —***n.*** **1.** *a)* a heroic poem *b)* [*pl.*] *same as* HEROIC VERSE **2.** [*pl.*] extravagant or melodramatic talk or action, meant to seem heroic —**he·ro′i·cal·ly** ***adv.***

heroic couplet a pair of rhymed lines in iambic pentameter

heroic verse the verse form in which epic poetry is traditionally written, as iambic pentameter

her·o·in (her′ə win) ***n.*** [G., orig. a trademark] a very powerful, habit-forming narcotic, a derivative of morphine

her·o·ine (her′ə win) ***n.*** a girl or woman hero in life or literature

her·o·ism (-wiz′m) ***n.*** the qualities and actions of a hero or heroine; great bravery, nobility, etc.

her·on (her′ən) ***n.***, *pl.* **-ons, -on:** see PLURAL, II, D, 1 [< OFr. *hairon* < Frank.] any of a group of wading birds with a long neck, long legs, and a long, tapered bill

her·on·ry (-rē) ***n.***, *pl.* **-ries** a place where many herons gather to breed

hero sandwich a large roll sliced lengthwise and filled with cold meats, cheese, vegetables, etc.

hero worship great or exaggerated admiration for heroes —**he′ro-wor′ship** ***vt.*** —**he′ro-wor′ship·er** ***n.***

her·pes (hʉr′pēz) ***n.*** [L. < Gr. < *herpein*, to creep] a virus disease characterized by the eruption of small blisters on the skin and mucous membranes —**her·pet·ic** (hər pet′ik) ***adj.***

herpes simplex a form of herpes principally involving the mouth, lips, and face

herpes zos·ter (zäs′tər) [Gr. *zōstēr*, a girdle] a viral infection of certain sensory nerves, causing pain and an eruption of blisters along the course of the affected nerve; shingles

her·pe·tol·o·gy (hʉr′pə täl′ə jē) ***n.*** [< Gr. *herpeton*, reptile + -LOGY] the branch of zoology having to do with the study of reptiles and amphibians —**her′pe·to·log′ic** (-tə läj′ik), **her′pe·to·log′i·cal** ***adj.*** —**her′pe·tol′o·gist** ***n.***

‡**Herr** (her) ***n.***, *pl.* **Her′ren** (-ən) in Germany, a man; gentleman: also used as a title corresponding to *Mr.* or *Sir*

Her·rick (her′ik), **Robert** 1591–1674; Eng. poet

her·ring (her′iŋ) ***n.***, *pl.* **-rings, -ring:** see PLURAL, II, D, 1 [OE. *hæring*] **1.** a small food fish of the N Atlantic: eaten cooked, dried, salted, or smoked: the young are canned as sardines **2.** loosely, the sprat, pilchard, etc.

her·ring·bone (-bōn′) ***n.*** **1.** the spine of a herring, with the ribs extending from opposite sides in rows of parallel, slanting lines **2.** a pattern with such a design or anything having such a pattern —***adj.*** having the pattern of a herringbone —***vi., vt.*** **-boned′, -bon′ing** to stitch, weave, arrange, etc. in a herringbone pattern

hers (hʉrz) ***pron.*** that or those belonging to her: used without a following noun *[*that book is *hers, hers* are better*]*: also used after *of* to indicate possession *[*a friend of *hers]*

Her·schel (hʉr′shəl) **1.** Sir **John Frederick William,** 1792–1871; Eng. astronomer & physicist: son of *ff.* **2.** Sir **William,** (born *Friedrich Wilhelm Herschel*) 1738–1822; Eng. astronomer, born in Germany

her·self (hər self′) ***pron.*** a form of the 3d pers. sing., fem. pronoun, used: *a)* as an intensive *[*she went *herself]* *b)* as a reflexive *[*she hurt *herself]* *c)* as a quasi-noun meaning "her real or true self" *[*she is not *herself* today*]*

hertz (hʉrts) ***n.***, *pl.* **hertz** [see ff.] the international unit of frequency, equal to one cycle per second

Hertz·i·an waves (hʉrt′sē ən, hert′-) [after H. R. *Hertz* (1857–1894), Ger. physicist] *[sometimes* **h-***]* radio waves or other electromagnetic radiation resulting from the oscillations of electricity in a conductor

Herzegovina *same as* HERCEGOVINA

he's (hēz) **1.** he is **2.** he has

Hesh·van (khesh vän′; *E.* hesh′vən) ***n.*** [Heb.] the second month of the Jewish year: see JEWISH CALENDAR

hes·i·tan·cy (hez′ə tən sē) ***n.***, *pl.* **-cies** hesitation or indecision; doubt: also **hes′i·tance**

hes·i·tant (-tənt) ***adj.*** hesitating or undecided; doubtful —**hes′i·tant·ly** ***adv.***

hes·i·tate (-tāt′) ***vi.*** **-tat′ed, -tat′ing** [< L. pp. of *haesitare*, intens. of *haerere*, to stick] **1.** to stop in indecision; pause or delay in acting or deciding **2.** to pause; stop momentarily **3.** to be reluctant *[*I *hesitate* to ask*]* **4.** to pause continually in speaking; stammer —**hes′i·tat′er, hes′i·ta′tor** ***n.*** —**hes′i·tat′ing·ly** ***adv.***

hes·i·ta·tion (hez′ə tā′shən) ***n.*** a hesitating; specif., *a)* indecision *b)* reluctance *c)* halting speech *d)* a pausing —**hes′i·ta′tive** ***adj.*** —**hes′i·ta′tive·ly** ***adv.***

Hes·per·i·des (hes per′ə dēz′) ***n.pl.*** **1.** *sing.* **Hes·per·id** (hes′pər id) *Gr. Myth.* the nymphs who guarded the golden apples given as a wedding gift by Gaea to Hera **2.** the garden where the apples grew

Hes·per·us (hes′pər əs) ***n.*** [L.] the evening star, esp. Venus: also **Hes′per**

Hesse (hes, hes′i) former region in WC Germany, now a state of West Germany

Hes·sian (hesh′ən) ***adj.*** of Hesse or its people —***n.*** **1.** a native or inhabitant of Hesse **2.** any of the Hessian mercenaries who fought for the British in the Revolutionary War

Hessian fly a small, two-winged fly whose larvae destroy wheat crops

hest (hest) ***n.*** [< OE. *hæs*, command < *hatan*, to call] [Archaic] behest; order

Hes·ter, Hes·ther (hes′tər) [var. of ESTHER] a feminine name

he·tae·ra (hi tir′ə) ***n.***, *pl.* **-rae** (-ē), **-ras** [< Gr. < *hetairos*, companion] in ancient Greece, a courtesan: also **he·tai′ra** (-tī′rə), *pl.* **-rai** (-rī)

het·er·o- [< Gr. < *heteros*, the other (of two)] *a combining form meaning* other, another, different *[heterosexual]*: opposed to HOMO-: also **heter-**

het·er·o·cy·clic (het′ər ō sī′klik, -sik′lik) ***adj.*** designating or of a cyclic molecular arrangement of atoms of carbon and other elements

het·er·o·dox (het′ər ə däks′) ***adj.*** [< Gr. < *hetero-*, HETERO- + *doxa*, opinion] departing from or opposed to the usual beliefs or established doctrines, esp. in religion; unorthodox

het·er·o·dox·y (-däk′sē) ***n.***, *pl.* **-dox′ies** **1.** the quality or fact of being heterodox **2.** a heterodox belief or doctrine

het·er·o·dyne (-dīn′) ***adj.*** [HETERO- + DYNE] designating or of the combination of two different radio frequencies to produce beats with new frequencies —*vi.* **-dyned′, -dyn′ing** to combine two different frequencies so as to produce such beats

het·er·o·ge·ne·ous (het′ər ə jē′nē əs, het′rə-; -jēn′yəs) ***adj.*** [< ML. < Gr. < *hetero-*, HETERO- + *genos*, a kind] **1.** differing or opposite in structure, quality, etc.; dissimilar **2.** composed of unrelated or unlike elements or parts; varied; miscellaneous **—het′er·o·ge·ne′i·ty** (-jə nē′ə tē) ***n.,*** *pl.* **-ties —het′er·o·ge′ne·ous·ly** ***adv.*** **—het′er·o·ge′ne·ous·ness** ***n.***

het·er·o·nym (het′ər ə nim′) ***n.*** [< Gr. < *hetero-*, HETERO- + *onyma*, name] a word with the same spelling as another but with a different meaning and pronunciation (Ex.: *tear*, a drop from the eye; *tear*, to rip) **—het′er·on′y·mous** (-än′ə məs) ***adj.***

het·er·o·sex·u·al (het′ər ə sek′shoo wəl) ***adj.*** **1.** of or characterized by sexual desire for those of the opposite sex **2.** *Biol.* of different sexes —*n.* a heterosexual individual **—het′er·o·sex′u·al′i·ty** (-wal′ə tē) ***n.***

het·man (het′mən) ***n.,*** *pl.* **-mans** [Pol. < G. < *haupt*, head + *mann*, man] a Cossack chief

het up (het) [*het*, dial. pt. & pp. of *heat*] [Slang] excited or angry

HEW (Dept. of) Health, Education, and Welfare

hew (hyōō) ***vt.*** **hewed, hewed** or **hewn, hew′ing** [OE. *heawan*] **1.** to chop or cut with an ax, knife, etc. **2.** to make or shape by or as by cutting or chopping with an ax, etc. **3.** to chop *down* (a tree) with an ax —*vi.* **1.** to make cutting or chopping blows with an ax, knife, etc. **2.** to adhere (*to* a line, principle, etc.) **—hew′er** ***n.***

hex (heks) ***n.*** [< G. *hexe* < OHG.] **1.** [Dial.] a witch or sorcerer **2.** *a)* a sign, spell, etc. supposed to bring bad luck *b)* a jinx —*vt.* to cause to have bad luck; jinx

hex·a- [< Gr. *hex*, six] *a combining form meaning* six *[hexagram]* : also, before a vowel, **hex-**

hex·a·chlo·ro·phene (hek′sə klôr′ə fēn′) ***n.*** [< HEXA- + CHLORO- + PHENOL] a white powder, $C_{13}Cl_6H_6O_2$, used, esp. formerly, in deodorants, soaps, etc. to kill bacteria

hex·a·gon (hek′sə gän′) ***n.*** [< L. < Gr. < *hex*, six + *gōnia*, a corner, angle] a plane figure with six angles and six sides **—hex·ag′o·nal** (-sag′ə n′l) ***adj.*** **—hex·ag′o·nal·ly** ***adv.***

hex·a·gram (hek′sə gram′) ***n.*** [HEXA- + -GRAM] a six-pointed star formed by extending all sides of a regular hexagon to points of intersection

hex·a·he·dron (hek′sə hē′drən) ***n.,*** *pl.* **-drons, -dra** (-drə) [see HEXA- & -HEDRON] a solid figure with six plane surfaces **—hex′a·he′dral** ***adj.***

hex·am·e·ter (hek sam′ə tər) ***n.*** [< L. < Gr.: see HEXA- & METER[1]] **1.** a line of verse containing six metrical feet **2.** verse consisting of hexameters —*adj.* having six metrical feet

hex·a·pod (hek′sə päd′) ***n.*** [see HEXA- & -POD] an insect (sense 1) —*adj.* having six legs, as a true insect: also **hex·ap·o·dous** (hek sap′ə dəs)

hey (hā) ***interj.*** [ME. *hei*, echoic formation] an exclamation used to attract attention, express surprise, etc., or in asking a question

hey·day (hā′dā′) ***n.*** the time of greatest health, vigor, success, prosperity, etc.; prime

Hez·e·ki·ah (hez′ə kī′ə) *Bible* a king of Judah: II Kings 18–20

Hf *Chem.* hafnium

HF, H.F., hf, h.f. high frequency

hf. half

Hg [L. *hydrargyrum*] *Chem.* mercury

HG., H.G. High German

hg. hectogram; hectograms

hgt. height

H.H. **1.** His (or Her) Highness **2.** His Holiness

hhd. hogshead

HI Hawaii

hi (hī) ***interj.*** [ME. *hy*, var. of *hei*, HEY] an exclamation of greeting

Hi·a·le·ah (hī′ə lē′ə) [< ? Seminole-Creek *haiyakpo hili*, lit., pretty prairie] city in SE Fla.: suburb of Miami: pop. 145,000

hi·a·tus (hī āt′əs) ***n.,*** *pl.* **-tus·es, -tus** [L., pp. of *hiare*, to gape] **1.** a break or gap where a part is missing or lost **2.** any gap **3.** a slight pause in pronunciation between two successive vowel sounds, as between the *e's* in *reentry*

Hi·a·wa·tha (hī′ə wô′thə, hē′-; -wä′-) the Indian hero of *The Song of Hiawatha*, a long narrative poem (1855) by Longfellow

hi·ba·chi (hi bä′chē) ***n.,*** *pl.* **-chis** [Jap. < *hi*, fire + *bachi*, bowl] a charcoal-burning brazier and grill of Japanese design

hi·ber·nal (hī bur′nəl) ***adj.*** [< L. < *hibernus*: see ff.] of winter; wintry

hi·ber·nate (hī′bər nāt′) ***vi.*** **-nat′ed, -nat′ing** [< L. pp. of *hibernare* < *hibernus*, wintry] to spend the winter in a dormant state **—hi′ber·na′tion** ***n.*** **—hi′ber·na′tor** ***n.***

Hi·ber·ni·a (hī bur′nē ə) [L.] *poet. name of* IRELAND **—Hi·ber′ni·an** ***adj., n.***

hi·bis·cus (hī bis′kəs, hi-) ***n.*** [< L. *hibiscus*] a plant, shrub, or small tree related to the mallow, with large, colorful flowers

hic·cup (hik′əp) ***n.*** [altered < Early ModE. *hikop, hicket*, of echoic orig.: sp. infl. by association with COUGH] **1.** a sudden, involuntary contraction of the diaphragm that closes the glottis at the moment of breathing, making a sharp, quick sound **2.** [*pl.*] a condition of repeated contractions of this kind —*vi.* **-cuped** or **-cupped, -cup·ing** or **-cup·ping** to make a hiccup —*vt.* to utter with a hiccup Also **hic·cough** (hik′əp)

‡**hic ja·cet** (hik′ jā′sit) [L.] **1.** here lies: inscribed on tombstones **2.** an epitaph

hick (hik) ***n.*** [altered < RICHARD] [Colloq.] an awkward, unsophisticated person regarded as typical of rural areas: somewhat contemptuous term —*adj.* [Colloq.] of or like a hick

hick·o·ry (hik′ər ē, hik′rē) ***n.,*** *pl.* **-ries** [< AmInd. *pawcohiccora*, product made from the nuts] **1.** a N. American tree related to the walnut, with smooth-shelled, edible nuts **2.** its hard, tough wood **3.** its nut: also **hickory nut**

HICKORY
(leaf, nut & tree)

hi·dal·go (hi dal′gō) ***n.,*** *pl.* **-gos** [Sp., contr. of *hijo de algo*, son of something] a Spanish nobleman of secondary rank, below that of a grandee

hid·den (hid′'n) *alt. pp. of* HIDE[1] —*adj.* concealed; secret

hide[1] (hīd) ***vt.*** **hid, hid′den** or **hid, hid′ing** [OE. *hydan*] **1.** to put or keep out of sight; secrete; conceal **2.** to keep secret **3.** to keep from being seen by covering up, obscuring, etc. **4.** to turn away *[to hide* one's head in shame*]* —*vi.* **1.** to be concealed **2.** to conceal oneself **—hid′er** ***n.***

hide[2] (hīd) ***n.*** [OE. *hid*] **1.** an animal skin or pelt, either raw or tanned **2.** [Colloq.] the skin of a person —*vt.* **hid′ed, hid′ing** [Colloq.] to beat; flog **—neither hide nor hair** nothing whatsoever

hide-and-seek (hīd′'n sēk′) ***n.*** a children's game in which one player tries to find the other players, who have hidden: also **hide′-and-go-seek′**

hide·a·way (hīd′ə wā′) ***n.*** [Colloq.] a place where one can hide, be secluded, etc.

hide·bound (-bound′) ***adj.*** **1.** having the hide tight over the body structure, as an emaciated cow **2.** obstinately conservative and narrow-minded

hid·e·ous (hid′ē əs) ***adj.*** [< Anglo-Fr. < OFr. < *hide*, fright] horrible; very ugly or revolting; dreadful **—hid′e·ous·ly** ***adv.*** **—hid′e·ous·ness** ***n.***

hide-out (hīd′out′) ***n.*** [Colloq.] a hiding place

hid·ing[1] (hīd′iŋ) ***n.*** **1.** *a)* the act of one that hides *b)* the condition of being hidden: usually in the phrase **in hiding** **2.** a place to hide

hid·ing[2] (hīd′iŋ) ***n.*** [Colloq.] a severe beating

hie (hī) ***vi., vt.*** **hied, hie′ing** or **hy′ing** [OE. *higian*] to hurry or hasten: usually reflexive

hi·er·arch (hī′ə rärk′, hī′rärk) ***n.*** [< ML. < Gr. < *hieros*, sacred + *archos*, ruler] a chief priest

hi·er·ar·chy (-rär′kē) ***n.,*** *pl.* **-chies** [< OFr. < ML.: see prec.] **1.** a system of church government by priests or other clergy in graded ranks **2.** the group of officials in such a system **3.** a group of persons or things arranged in order of rank, grade, etc. **—hi′er·ar′chi·cal, hi′er·ar′chic, hi′er·ar′chal** ***adj.*** **—hi′er·ar′chi·cal·ly** ***adv.***

hi·er·at·ic (hī′ə rat′ik) ***adj.*** [< L. < Gr. *hieratikos* < *hieros*, sacred] **1.** of or used by priests; priestly **2.** designating or of the abridged form of cursive hieroglyphic writing once used by Egyptian priests Also **hi′er·at′i·cal —hi′er·at′i·cal·ly** ***adv.***

hi·er·o·glyph (hī′ər ə glif′, hī′rə-) ***n.*** *same as* HIEROGLYPHIC

hi·er·o·glyph·ic (hī′ər ə glif′ik, hī′rə-) ***adj.*** [< Fr. < LL. < Gr. < *hieros*, sacred + *glyphein*, to carve] **1.** of, like, or written in hieroglyphics **2.** hard to read or understand Also **hi′er·o·glyph′i·cal** —*n.* **1.** a picture or symbol representing a word, syllable, or sound, used by the ancient Egyptians and others **2.** [*usually pl.*] a method of writing using hieroglyphics **3.** a symbol, sign, etc. hard to understand **4.** [*pl.*] writing hard to decipher **—hi′er·o·glyph′i·cal·ly** ***adv.***

hi-fi (hī′fī′) ***n.*** **1.** *same as* HIGH FIDELITY **2.** a radio, phonograph, etc. having high fidelity —*adj.* of or having high fidelity of sound reproduction

hig·gle (hig′'l) ***vi.*** **-gled, -gling** *same as* HAGGLE **—hig′gler** ***n.***

hig·gle·dy-pig·gle·dy (hig′'l dē pig′'l dē) ***adv.*** [redupl., prob. after PIG] in disorder; in jumbled confusion —*adj.* disorderly; jumbled; confused

high (hī) ***adj.*** [OE. *heah*] **1.** of more than normal height;

lofty; tall: not used of persons **2.** extending upward a (specified) distance **3.** situated far above the ground or other level **4.** reaching to or done from a height *[a high* jump, a *high* dive*]* **5.** above others in rank, position, quality, character, etc.; superior **6.** grave; very serious *[high* treason*]* **7.** greatly developed; complex: usually in the comparative *[higher* mathematics*]* **8.** main; principal; chief *[a high* priest*]* **9.** greater in size, amount, degree, power, etc. than usual *[high* prices*]* **10.** advanced to its acme or fullness *[high* noon*]* **11.** expensive; costly **12.** luxurious and extravagant *[high* living*]* **13.** haughty; overbearing **14.** raised or acute in pitch; sharp; shrill **15.** slightly tainted; strong-smelling: said of meat, esp. game **16.** extremely formal in matters of ceremony, doctrine, etc. **17.** excited; elated *[high* spirits*]* **18.** far from the equator *[a high* latitude*]* **19.** designating or of that gear ratio of a motor vehicle transmission which produces the highest speed **20.** [Slang] *a)* drunk; intoxicated *b)* under the influence of a drug **21.** *Phonet.* produced with the tongue held in a relatively elevated position: said of a vowel, as (ē) *—adv.* **1.** in a high manner **2.** in or to a high level, degree, rank, etc. *—n.* **1.** a high level, place, etc. **2.** an area of high barometric pressure **3.** high gear (see *adj.* 19) **4.** [Slang] a condition of euphoria induced as by drugs **—high and dry** stranded **—high and low** everywhere **—high and mighty** [Colloq.] arrogant; haughty **—high on** [Colloq.] enthusiastic about **—on high 1.** high above **2.** in heaven

high·ball (-bôl′) *n.* **1.** liquor, usually whiskey, served with water, soda water, ginger ale, etc. and ice **2.** a railroad signal meaning "go ahead" *—vi.* [Slang] to go very fast

high·born (-bôrn′) *adj.* of noble birth

high·boy (-boi′) *n.* a high chest of drawers mounted on legs

high·bred (-bred′) *adj.* showing good breeding; cultivated

high·brow (-brou′) *n.* [Colloq.] a person who is or tries to be intellectual *—adj.* [Colloq.] of or for a highbrow

High Church that party of the Anglican Church which emphasizes the importance of the priesthood and of traditional rituals and doctrines **—High′-Church′** *adj.* **—High′-Church′man** *n., pl.* **-men**

high comedy comedy reflecting the life of the upper social classes, characterized by a witty, sardonic treatment

HIGHBOY

high commissioner 1. the chief representative of the British government to one of the Commonwealth countries or from one of these countries to the British government **2.** the chief officer of a commission

high·er-up (hī′ər up′) *n.* [Colloq.] a person of higher rank or position

high·fa·lu·tin, high·fa·lu·ting (hī′fə lo͞ot′′n) *adj.* [Colloq.] ridiculously pretentious or pompous

high fidelity in radio, sound recording, etc., a nearly exact reproduction of a wide range of sound frequencies, from about 20 to 20,000 hertz

high·fli·er, high·fly·er (-flī′ər) *n.* **1.** a person or thing that flies high **2.** a person who acts or talks in an extravagant manner **—high′fly′ing** *adj.*

high-flown (-flōn′) *adj.* **1.** extravagantly ambitious **2.** high-sounding but meaningless; bombastic

high frequency any radio frequency between 3 and 30 megahertz

High German 1. the West Germanic dialects spoken in C and S Germany: distinguished from LOW GERMAN **2.** the official and literary form of the German language, technically called *New High German:* see also OLD HIGH GERMAN, MIDDLE HIGH GERMAN

high-grade (-grād′) *adj.* of superior quality

high·hand·ed (-han′did) *adj.* acting or done in an overbearing or arbitrary manner **—high′hand′ed·ly** *adv.* **—high′hand′ed·ness** *n.*

high-hat (-hat′) *adj.* [Slang] snobbish and aloof *—n.* [Slang] a snob *—vt.* **-hat′ted, -hat′ting** [Slang] to snub

High Holidays the period encompassing Rosh Hashana and Yom Kippur in the Jewish calendar

high·jack (-jak′) *vt.* [Colloq.] *same as* HIJACK

high jump a track and field event in which the contestants jump for height over a horizontal bar

high·land (-lənd) *n.* a region higher than adjacent land and containing many hills or mountains *—adj.* of, in, or from such a region **—the Highlands** mountainous region occupying nearly all of N Scotland **—high′land·er, High′land·er** *n.*

Highland fling a lively dance of the Highlands

high life the luxurious way of life of fashionable society

high·light (-līt′) *n.* **1.** *a)* a part on which light is brightest *b)* a part of a painting, etc. on which light is represented as brightest *c)* the representation or effect of such light in a painting, etc. Also **high light 2.** the most important or interesting part, scene, etc. *—vt.* **1.** to give a highlight or highlights to **2.** to give prominence to **3.** to be the most outstanding in

high·ly (-lē) *adv.* **1.** in a high office or rank **2.** very much **3.** favorably **4.** at a high wage, salary, etc.

High Mass *R.C.Ch.* a sung Mass, usually celebrated with the complete ritual, at which the celebrant is assisted by a deacon and subdeacon: also **Solemn (High) Mass**

high-mind·ed (-mīn′did) *adj.* **1.** [Obs.] haughty **2.** having or showing high ideals, principles, etc. **—high′-mind′ed·ly** *adv.* **—high′-mind′ed·ness** *n.*

high·ness (-nis) *n.* **1.** the quality or state of being high; height **2. [H-]** a title used in speaking to or of a member of a royal family (with *His, Her,* or *Your*)

high-pitched (-picht′) *adj.* **1.** high in pitch; shrill **2.** exalted **3.** agitated **4.** steep in slope

High Point [after its location, the highest point on the N.C. Railroad] city in C N.C.: pop. 64,000

high-pow·ered (-pou′ərd) *adj.* very powerful

high-pres·sure (-presh′ər) *adj.* **1.** *a)* having, using, or withstanding relatively high pressure *b)* having a high barometric pressure **2.** using forcefully persuasive or insistent methods or arguments *—vt.* **-sured, -sur·ing** [Colloq.] to urge with such methods or arguments

high priest a chief priest; specif., the chief priest of the ancient Jewish priesthood

high-proof (-pro͞of′) *adj.* high in alcohol content

high-rise (-rīz′) *adj.* designating or of a tall apartment house, office building, etc. of many stories *—n.* a high-rise building

high·road (-rōd′) *n.* **1.** [Chiefly Brit.] a main road; highway **2.** an easy or direct way

high roller [from rolling the dice in gambling] [Slang] **1.** a person who gambles for very high stakes **2.** a person who spends or invests money freely or recklessly

high school a secondary school that usually includes grades 10, 11, and 12, and sometimes grade 9 **—high′-school′** *adj.*

high seas open ocean waters outside the territorial limits of any single nation

high-sound·ing (-soun′diŋ) *adj.* sounding pretentious or impressive

high-spir·it·ed (-spir′i tid) *adj.* **1.** having or showing a courageous or noble spirit **2.** spirited; fiery **3.** gay; lively

high-strung (-struŋ′) *adj.* nervous and tense

high-tech·nol·o·gy (-tek näl′ə jē) *adj.* of or involving industries and businesses engaged in highly specialized, complex technology, as in electronics

high-ten·sion (hī′ten′shən) *adj.* having, carrying, or operating under a high voltage

high-test (-test′) *adj.* **1.** passing severe tests **2.** vaporizing at a low temperature: said of gasoline

high tide 1. the highest level to which the tide rises **2.** the time when the tide is at this level **3.** any culminating point or time

high time 1. none too soon **2.** [Slang] a gay, exciting time: also **high old time**

high-toned (-tōnd′) *adj.* **1.** [Now Rare] high in tone or pitch **2.** characterized by dignity, high principles, etc. **3.** [Colloq.] of or imitating the manners, attitudes, etc. of the upper classes

high treason treason against the ruler or government

high water 1. *same as* HIGH TIDE **2.** the highest level reached by a body of water

high-wa·ter mark (hī′wôt′ər, -wät′ər) **1.** the highest level reached by a body of water **2.** the mark left after high water has receded **3.** a culminating point; highest point

high·way (-wā′) *n.* **1.** a public road **2.** a main road; thoroughfare **3.** a direct way

high·way·man (-wā mən) *n., pl.* **-men** formerly, a man who robbed travelers on a highway

hi·jack (hī′jak′) *vt.* [prob. *hi* (for HIGH) + JACK, *v.*] [Colloq.] **1.** to steal (goods in transit, a truck and its contents, etc.) from (a person) by force **2.** to swindle, as by the use of force **3.** to force the pilot of (an aircraft) to fly to a nonscheduled landing point **—hi′jack′er** *n.*

hike (hīk) *vi.* **hiked, hik′ing** [< dial. *heik*] **1.** to take a long, vigorous walk; tramp or march **2.** to move up out of place *—vt.* [Colloq.] **1.** to pull up; hoist **2.** to raise (prices, etc.) *—n.* **1.** a long, vigorous walk **2.** [Colloq.] a moving upward; rise **—hik′er** *n.*

hi·lar·i·ous (hi ler′ē əs, hī-; -lar′-) *adj.* [< L. < Gr. *hilaros,* cheerful] **1.** noisily merry; boisterous and gay **2.** provoking laughter; funny **—hi·lar′i·ous·ly** *adv.*

hi·lar·i·ty (-ə tē) *n.* the state or quality of being hilarious

Hil·da (hil′də) [G. < Gmc. hyp. *hild-*, war] a feminine name

hill (hil) ***n.*** [OE. *hyll*] **1.** a natural raised part of the earth's surface, often rounded, smaller than a mountain **2.** a small pile, heap, or mound *[*an *anthill]* **3.** *a)* a small mound of soil heaped over and around plant roots *b)* the plant or plants rooted in such a mound —***vt.*** **1.** to shape into or like a hill **2.** to cover with a hill (sense 3*a*) —**over the hill** [Colloq.] **1.** absent without permission; AWOL **2.** in one's decline —**hill′er** ***n.***

hill·bil·ly (hil′bil′ē) ***n., pl.*** **-lies** [HILL + *Billy*, dim. of WILLIAM] [Colloq.] a person who lives in or comes from the mountains or backwoods, esp. of the South: somewhat contemptuous term —***adj.*** [Colloq.] of or characteristic of hillbillies

Hil·lel (hil′el, -əl) 60? B.C.–10? A.D.; Jewish rabbi & scholar in Jerusalem

hill·ock (hil′ək) ***n.*** a small hill; mound —**hill′ock·y** ***adj.***

hill·side (hil′sīd′) ***n.*** the side or slope of a hill

hill·top (-täp′) ***n.*** the top of a hill

hill·y (-ē) ***adj.*** **hill′i·er, hill′i·est** **1.** full of hills **2.** like a hill; steep —**hill′i·ness** ***n.***

hilt (hilt) ***n.*** [OE.] the handle of a sword, dagger, tool, etc. —**(up) to the hilt** thoroughly; entirely

hi·lum (hī′ləm) ***n., pl.*** **hi′la** (-lə) [ModL. < L., little thing] *Bot.* a scar on a seed, marking the place where it was attached to the seed stalk

him (him; *unstressed* im, əm) ***pron.*** [OE.] *objective case of* HE: also used colloquially as a predicate complement with a linking verb (Ex.: that's *him*)

Hi·ma·la·yas (him′ə lā′əz, hi mäl′yəz) mountain system in SC Asia, along the India-Tibet border: highest peak, Mt. Everest: also **Himalaya Mountains** —**Hi′ma·la′yan** ***adj., n.***

him·self (him self′) ***pron.*** a form of the 3d pers. sing., masc. pronoun, used: *a)* as an intensive *[*he went *himself] b)* as a reflexive *[*he hurt *himself] c)* as a quasi-noun meaning "his real or true self" *[*he is not *himself* today*] d)* [Irish] as a subject *[himself* will have his tea now*]*

hind[1] (hīnd) ***adj.*** **hind′er, hind′most′** or **hind′er·most′** [prob. < HINDER[2]] back; rear; posterior

hind[2] (hīnd) ***n., pl.*** **hinds, hind:** see PLURAL, II, D, 1 [OE.] the female of the red deer, in and after its third year

hind[3] (hīnd) ***n.*** [OE. *hina, higna*] **1.** in N England and Scotland, a skilled farm worker or servant **2.** [Archaic] a simple peasant; rustic

hind·brain (-brān′) ***n.*** the hindmost of the three primary divisions of the vertebrate brain

Hin·de·mith (hin′də məth; *G.* -mit), **Paul** 1895–1963; U.S. composer, born in Germany

hin·der[1] (hin′dər) ***vt.*** [OE. *hindrian*] **1.** to keep back; restrain; prevent; stop **2.** to make difficult for; thwart; frustrate —***vi.*** to be a hindrance

hind·er[2] (hīn′dər) ***adj.*** [OE. *hinder, adv.*, behind: now felt as compar. of HIND[1]] hind; rear; posterior

Hin·di (hin′dē) ***adj.*** [Hindi *hindī* < *Hind:* see HINDU] of or associated with northern India —***n.*** an Indo-Iranian language, the main, now official, language of India

hind·most (hīnd′mōst′) ***adj.*** *superl. of* HIND[1]; farthest back; last: also **hind′er·most′** (hīn′dər-)

Hin·doo (hin′do͞o) ***adj., n., pl.*** **-doos** *same as* HINDU

hind·quar·ter (hīnd′kwôr′tər) ***n.*** **1.** a hind leg and loin of a carcass of veal, beef, lamb, etc. **2.** [*pl.*] the hind part of a four-legged animal

hin·drance (hin′drəns) ***n.*** **1.** the act of hindering **2.** any person or thing that hinders; obstacle

hind·sight (hīnd′sīt′) ***n.*** an understanding, after the event, of what should have been done

Hin·du (hin′do͞o) ***n.*** [< Per. < *Hind*, India, ult. < Sans. *sindhu*, river, the Indus] **1.** any of the peoples of India that speak an Indic language **2.** a follower of Hinduism **3.** popularly, any native of India —***adj.*** **1.** of the Hindus, their language, etc. **2.** of Hinduism

Hin·du·ism (hin′doo wiz′m) ***n.*** the religion and social system of the Hindus

Hindu Kush (ko͞osh) mountain range in SW Asia, mostly in Afghanistan: highest peak, 25,230 ft.

Hin·du·stan (hin′doo stan′, -stän′) **1.** region in N India, where Hindi is spoken **2.** the entire Indian peninsula **3.** the republic of India

Hin·du·sta·ni (-stan′ē, -stä′nē) ***n.*** the most important dialect of Western Hindi, used as a trade language in N India —***adj.*** **1.** of Hindustan or its people **2.** of Hindustani

hinge (hinj) ***n.*** [< ME. *hengen*, to hang] **1.** a joint, etc. on which a door, gate, lid, etc. swings **2.** a natural joint, as of the bivalve shell of a clam or oyster **3.** anything on which matters turn or depend —***vt.*** **hinged, hing′ing** to equip with or attach by a hinge —***vi.*** to be contingent; depend (*on*)

hin·ny (hin′ē) ***n., pl.*** **-nies** [L. *hinnus* < Gr. *innos*] the offspring of a male horse and a female donkey: cf. MULE[1]

hint (hint) ***n.*** [< OE. *henten*, to seize] **1.** a slight indication of a fact, wish, etc.; indirect suggestion or reference **2.** a very small amount or degree; trace —***vt., vi.*** to give a hint (of) —**hint at** to suggest indirectly; intimate —**take a hint** to perceive and act on a hint —**hint′er** ***n.***

hin·ter·land (hin′tər land′) ***n.*** [G. < *hinter*, back + *land*, land] **1.** the land or district behind that bordering on a coast or river **2.** an area far from big cities and towns; back country

hip[1] (hip) ***n.*** [OE. *hype*] **1.** *a)* the part of the body surrounding and including the joint formed by each thighbone and pelvis *b) same as* HIP JOINT **2.** the angle formed by the meeting of two sloping sides of a roof —***vt.*** **hipped, hip′ping** to make (a roof) with such an angle

hip[2] (hip) ***n.*** [OE. *heope*] the fleshy fruit of the rose: it is rich in vitamin C

hip[3] (hip) ***adj.*** **hip′per, hip′pest** [< ? *hep*] [Slang] **1.** *a)* sophisticated; knowing; aware *b)* fashionable; stylish **2.** of or associated with hipsters or hippies —**get** (or **be**) **hip to** [Slang] to become (or be) informed or knowledgeable about —**hip′ness** ***n.***

hip·bone (hip′bōn′) ***n.*** **1.** *same as: a)* INNOMINATE BONE *b)* ILIUM **2.** the neck of the femur

hip joint the junction between the thighbone and its socket in the pelvis

hipped[1] (hipt) ***adj.*** **1.** having hips of a specified kind *[*broad-*hipped]* **2.** *Archit.* having a hip or hips *[*a *hipped* roof*]*

hipped[2] (hipt) ***adj.*** [< HYP(OCHONDRIA)] [Colloq.] having a great interest; obsessed (with *on*)

hip·pie (hip′ē) ***n.*** [< HIP[3] + -IE] [Slang] a young person alienated from conventional society, who has turned to mysticism, drugs, communal living, etc.

hip·po (hip′ō) ***n., pl.*** **-pos** [Colloq.] a hippopotamus

Hip·poc·ra·tes (hi päk′rə tēz′) 460?–370? B.C.; Gr. physician: called the *Father of Medicine* —**Hip·po·crat·ic** (hip′ə krat′ik) ***adj.***

Hippocratic oath the oath, attributed to Hippocrates, generally taken by medical graduates: it sets forth an ethical code for the medical profession

hip·po·drome (hip′ə drōm′) ***n.*** [< Fr. < L. < Gr. < *hippos*, a horse + *dromos*, a course] **1.** in ancient Greece and Rome, an oval course for horse races and chariot races, surrounded by tiers of seats **2.** an arena or building for a circus, etc.

hip·po·pot·a·mus (hip′ə pät′ə məs) ***n., pl.*** **-mus·es, -mi** (-mī′), **-mus:** see PLURAL, II, D, 1 [L. < Gr. < *hippos*, a horse + *potamos*, river] a large, plant-eating mammal with a heavy, thick-skinned, almost hairless body and short legs: it lives chiefly in or near rivers in Africa

hip·py[1] (hip′ē) ***n., pl.*** **-pies** [Slang] *same as* HIPPIE

hip·py[2] (hip′ē) ***adj.*** [Colloq.] having large hips *[*she has a tendency to be *hippy]*

hip roof a roof with sloping ends and sides

hip·ster (hip′stər) ***n.*** [Slang] **1.** a hip person **2.** a beatnik: term of the 1950's and early 1960's

Hi·ram (hī′rəm) [Heb. *ḥīrām*, prob. < *'aḥīrām*, exalted brother] a masculine name: dim. *Hi*

hir·cine (hʉr′sīn, -sin) ***adj.*** [< L. < *hircus*, goat] of or like a goat, esp. in odor

hire (hīr) ***n.*** [OE. *hyr*] **1.** the amount paid for the services of a person or the use of a thing **2.** a hiring or being hired —***vt.*** **hired, hir′ing** **1.** to get the services of (a person) or the use of (a thing) in return for payment; employ or engage **2.** to give the use of (a thing) or the services of (oneself or another) for payment (often with *out*) —**for hire** available for work or use, for payment: also **on hire** —**hire out** to work for payment —**hir′a·ble, hire′a·ble** ***adj.*** —**hir′er** ***n.***

hire·ling (-liŋ) ***n.*** [see HIRE & -LING[1]] a person who will follow anyone's orders for pay; mercenary

Hi·ro·hi·to (hir′ō hē′tō) 1901– ; emperor of Japan (1926–)

Hi·ro·shi·ma (hir′ə shē′mə) seaport in SW Honshu, Japan: largely destroyed (Aug. 6, 1945) by a U.S. atomic bomb, the first ever used in warfare: pop. 504,000

hir·sute (hʉr′so͞ot, hir′-; hər so͞ot′) ***adj.*** [L. *hirsutus*] hairy; shaggy; bristly —**hir′sute·ness** ***n.***

his (hiz) ***pron.*** [OE.] that or those belonging to him: used without a following noun *[*that book is *his, his* are better*]*: also used after *of* to indicate possession *[*a friend of *his]* —***possessive pronominal adj.*** of, belonging to, or done by him

His·pa·ni·a (his pä′nē ə, -pā′-) **1.** *Latin name of the* IBERIAN PENINSULA **2.** *poet. name of* SPAIN

His·pan·ic (his pan′ik) ***adj.*** Spanish or Spanish and Portuguese —**His·pan′i·cism** (-ə siz′m) ***n.***

His·pan·io·la (his′pən yō′lə) island in the West Indies, between Cuba & Puerto Rico, divided between Haiti & the Dominican Republic

hiss (his) ***vi.*** [echoic] **1.** to make a sound like that of a prolonged *s*, as of a goose, snake, escaping steam, etc. **2.** to show dislike or disapproval by hissing —***vt.*** **1.** to say or

indicate by hissing **2.** to condemn, force, or drive by hissing —*n.* the act or sound of hissing —**hiss'er** *n.*
hist (st; hist) *interj.* be quiet! listen!
hist. **1.** historian **2.** historical **3.** history
his·ta·mine (his'tə mēn', -mən) *n.* [see HISTO- & AMINE] an amine, $C_5H_9N_3$, released by the tissues in allergic reactions: it dilates blood vessels, stimulates gastric secretion, etc. —**his'ta·min'ic** (-min'ik) *adj.*
his·to- [< Gr. *histos,* a loom, web] *a combining form meaning* tissue *[histology]* : also **hist-**
his·tol·o·gy (his täl'ə jē) *n.* [prec. + -LOGY] the branch of biology concerned with the microscopic study of the structure of tissues —**his·to·log·ic** (his'tə läj'ik), **his'to·log'i·cal** *adj.* —**his'to·log'i·cal·ly** *adv.* —**his·tol'o·gist** *n.*
his·to·ri·an (his tôr'ē ən) *n.* **1.** a writer of history **2.** an authority on or specialist in history
his·tor·ic (his tôr'ik, -tär'-) *adj.* historical; esp., famous in history
his·tor·i·cal (-i k'l) *adj.* **1.** of or concerned with history as a science *[*the *historical* method*]* **2.** providing evidence for a fact of history *[*a *historical* document*]* **3.** based on people or events of the past *[*a *historical* novel*]* **4.** established by history; factual **5.** in chronological order **6.** famous in history: now usually HISTORIC —**his·tor'i·cal·ly** *adv.* —**his·tor'i·cal·ness** *n.*
historical present the present tense used in telling about past events: also **historic present**
his·to·ric·i·ty (his'tə ris'ə tē) *n.* the condition of having actually occurred in history
his·to·ri·og·ra·pher (his tôr'ē äg'rə fər) *n.* [< LL. < Gr. < *historia,* history + *graphein,* to write] a historian; esp., one appointed to write the history of some institution, country, etc. —**his·to'ri·o·graph'ic** (-ə graf'ik), **his·to'ri·o·graph'i·cal** *adj.* —**his·to'ri·og'ra·phy** *n.*
his·to·ry (his'tə rē, his'trē) *n., pl.* **-ries** [< L. < Gr. *historia* < *histōr,* learned] **1.** an account of what has happened; narrative **2.** *a)* what has happened in the life of a people, country, institution, etc. *b)* a systematic account of this **3.** all recorded events of the past **4.** the branch of knowledge that deals systematically with the recording, analyzing, and correlating of past events **5.** a known or recorded past *[*this coat has a *history]* —**make history** to be or do something important enough to be recorded
his·tri·on·ic (his'trē än'ik) *adj.* [< LL. < L. *histrio,* actor] **1.** of, or having the nature of, acting or actors **2.** overacted or overacting; artificial —**his'tri·on'i·cal·ly** *adv.*
his·tri·on·ics (-iks) *n.pl.* [*sometimes with sing. v.*] **1.** theatricals; dramatics **2.** an artificial or affected manner, display of emotion, etc.
hit (hit) *vt.* **hit, hit'ting** [OE. *hittan* < ON. *hitta,* to meet with] **1.** to come against, usually with force; strike *[*the car *hit* the tree*]* **2.** to give a blow to; strike **3.** to strike by throwing or shooting a missile *[*to *hit* the target*]* **4.** to cause to bump or strike, as in falling, moving, etc. **5.** to affect strongly or adversely *[*a town *hit* hard by floods*]* **6.** to come upon by accident or after search *[*to *hit* the right answer*]* **7.** to reach; attain *[*stocks *hit* a new high*]* **8.** *same as* STRIKE, *vt.* 9, 10, 11 **9.** [Slang] to apply oneself to steadily or frequently *[*to *hit* the books*]* **10.** [Slang] to demand or require of *[*he *hit* me for a loan*]* **11.** *Baseball* to get (a specified base hit) —*vi.* **1.** to give a blow or blows; strike **2.** to attack suddenly **3.** to knock, bump, or strike **4.** to come by accident or after search (with *on* or *upon*) **5.** to ignite the combustible mixture in its cylinders: said of an internal-combustion engine **6.** *Baseball* to get a base hit —*n.* **1.** a blow that strikes its mark **2.** a collision **3.** an effectively witty or sarcastic remark **4.** a stroke of good fortune **5.** a successful and popular song, book, play, etc. **6.** *Baseball same as* BASE HIT —**hit it off** to get along well together —**hit or miss** in a haphazard or aimless way —**hit the road** [Slang] to leave; go away —**hit'ter** *n.*
hit-and-run (-'n run') *adj.* hitting and then fleeing *[*a *hit-and-run* driver*]*
hitch (hich) *vi.* [ME. *hicchen,* to move jerkily < ?] **1.** to move jerkily; limp; hobble **2.** to become fastened or caught **3.** [Slang] to hitchhike —*vt.* **1.** to move, pull, or shift with jerks **2.** to fasten with a hook, knot, etc. **3.** [Colloq.] to marry: usually in the passive **4.** [Slang] to hitchhike —*n.* **1.** a short, sudden movement or pull; tug; jerk **2.** a hobble; limp **3.** a hindrance; obstacle **4.** a catching or fastening; catch **5.** [Slang] a period of time served, as of military service **6.** *Naut.* a kind of knot easy to undo —**without a hitch** smoothly and successfully
hitch·hike (-hīk') *vi.* **-hiked', -hik'ing** to travel by asking for rides from motorists along the way —*vt.* to get (a ride) or make (one's way) by hitchhiking —**hitch'hik'er** *n.*
hith·er (hith'ər) *adv.* [OE. *hider*] to this place; here —*adj.* on or toward this side; nearer
hith·er·most (-mōst') *adj.* nearest
hith·er·to (-to͞o', hith'ər to͞o') *adv.* until this time; to now
Hit·ler (hit'lər), **Adolf** 1889–1945; Nazi dictator of Germany (1933–45), born in Austria
Hit·ler·ism (-iz'm) *n.* the fascist program, ideas, and methods of Hitler and the Nazis —**Hit'ler·ite'** (-īt') *n., adj.*
hit man [< underworld slang *hit,* murder] [Slang] a man paid to kill someone; hired murderer
hit-skip (hit'skip') *adj. same as* HIT-AND-RUN
Hit·tite (hit'īt) *n.* **1.** any of an ancient people of Asia Minor and Syria (fl. 1700–700 B.C.) **2.** the language of the Hittites —*adj.* of the Hittites, their language, or culture
hive (hīv) *n.* [OE. *hyf*] **1.** a box or other shelter for a colony of domestic bees; beehive **2.** a colony of bees living in a hive **3.** a crowd of busy, active people **4.** a place with many busy people —*vt.* **hived, hiv'ing** **1.** to gather (bees) into a hive **2.** to store up (honey) in a hive —*vi.* **1.** to enter a hive **2.** to live together as in a hive —**hive'like'** *adj.*
hives (hīvz) *n.* [orig. Scot. dial.] an allergic skin condition characterized by the appearance of intensely itching wheals
H.M. **1.** Her Majesty **2.** His Majesty
H.M.S. **1.** His (or Her) Majesty's Service **2.** His (or Her) Majesty's Ship or Steamer
ho (hō) *interj.* an exclamation of surprise, derision, etc.: also used to get attention *[*land *ho!]*
Ho *Chem.* holmium
hoar (hôr) *adj.* [OE. *har*] *same as* HOARY
hoard (hôrd) *n.* [OE. *hord*] a supply stored up and hidden or kept in reserve —*vi.* to store away money, goods, etc. —*vt.* to accumulate and store away —**hoard'er** *n.* —**hoard'ing** *n.*
hoard·ing (hôr'diŋ) *n.* [< OFr. < Frank. *hurda,* a pen, fold] [Brit.] **1.** a temporary wooden fence around a site of building construction or repair **2.** a billboard
hoar·frost (hôr'frôst') *n.* white, frozen dew on the ground, leaves, etc.; rime
hoar·hound (-hound') *n. same as* HOREHOUND
hoarse (hôrs) *adj.* **hoars'er, hoars'est** [OE. *has*] **1.** sounding harsh and grating, rough and husky, etc. **2.** having a rough, husky voice —**hoarse'ly** *adv.* —**hoarse'ness** *n.*
hoars·en (-'n) *vt., vi.* to make or become hoarse
hoar·y (hôr'ē) *adj.* **hoar'i·er, hoar'i·est** **1.** white, gray, or grayish-white **2.** having white or gray hair because very old **3.** very old; ancient —**hoar'i·ly** *adv.* —**hoar'i·ness** *n.*
hoax (hōks) *n.* [< ? HOCUS] a trick or fraud, esp. one meant as a practical joke —*vt.* to deceive with a hoax —**hoax'er** *n.*
hob[1] (häb) *n.* [? var. of HUB] **1.** a projecting ledge at the back or side of a fireplace, for keeping a kettle, pan, etc. warm **2.** a peg used as a target in quoits, etc.
hob[2] (häb) *n.* [old form of *Rob,* for *Robin* Goodfellow, elf of English folklore] an elf; goblin —**play** (or **raise**) **hob with** to make trouble for
Ho·bart (hō'bərt, -bärt) capital of Tasmania, on the SE coast: pop. 53,000 (with suburbs, 119,000)
Hobbes (häbz), **Thomas** 1588–1679; Eng. social philosopher
hob·ble (häb''l) *vi.* **-bled, -bling** [ME. *hobelen* < base of *hoppen,* HOP[1] + freq. suffix] **1.** to go unsteadily, haltingly, etc. **2.** to walk lamely; limp —*vt.* **1.** to cause to limp **2.** to hamper the movement of (a horse, etc.) by tying two legs together **3.** to hinder —*n.* **1.** a halting walk; limp **2.** a rope, strap, etc. used to hobble a horse —**hob'bler** *n.*
hob·by (häb'ē) *n., pl.* **-bies** [ME. *hoby* < ? Du. *hobben,* to move back and forth] **1.** a hobbyhorse **2.** something that a person likes to work at, collect, etc. in his spare time —**hob'by·ist** *n.*
hob·by·horse (-hôrs') *n.* **1.** a toy consisting of a horse's head on a stick that one pretends to ride **2.** *same as* ROCKING HORSE
hob·gob·lin (häb'gäb'lin) *n.* [HOB[2] + GOBLIN] **1.** an elf; goblin **2.** a bogy; bugbear
hob·nail (-nāl') *n.* [HOB[1], sense 2 + NAIL] a short nail with a broad head, put on the soles of heavy shoes to prevent wear or slipping —*vt.* to put hobnails on —**hob'nailed'** *adj.*
hob·nob (-näb') *vi.* **-nobbed', -nob'bing** [< ME. *habben,* to have + *nabben,* not to have, esp. with reference to alternation in drinking] to be on close terms (*with*); associate in a familiar way
ho·bo (hō'bō) *n., pl.* **-bos, -boes** **1.** esp. formerly, a migratory worker **2.** a vagrant; tramp

HOBNAILS

Hob·son's choice (häb'sənz) [after T. *Hobson* (1544?–1631), Eng. liveryman, who let horses in strict order according to their position near the door] a choice of taking what is offered or nothing

Ho Chi Minh (hō′ chē′ min′) 1890?–1969; president of North Vietnam (1954–69)

hock[1] (häk) ***n.*** [OE. *hoh,* the heel] the joint bending backward in the hind leg of a horse, ox, etc., but corresponding to the human ankle —***vt.*** to disable by cutting the tendons of the hock

hock[2] (häk) ***n.*** [< *Hochheimer* < *Hochheim,* Germany] [Chiefly Brit.] a white Rhine wine

hock[3] (häk) ***vt., n.*** [< Du. *hok,* prison, (slang) debt] [Slang] *same as* PAWN[1]

hock·ey (häk′ē) ***n.*** [prob. < OFr. *hoquet,* bent stick] **1.** a team game played on ice, in which the players, using curved sticks (**hockey sticks**) and wearing skates, try to drive a rubber disk (*puck*) into their opponents' goal **2.** a similar game played on foot on a field with a small ball instead of a puck

hock·shop (häk′shäp′) ***n.*** [Slang] a pawnshop

ho·cus (hō′kəs) ***vt.*** **-cused** or **-cussed, -cus·ing** or **-cus·sing** [contr. < ff.] **1.** to play a trick on; dupe **2.** to drug **3.** to put drugs in (a drink)

ho·cus-po·cus (-pō′kəs) ***n.*** [imitation L.] **1.** meaningless words used as a formula by conjurers **2.** sleight of hand; legerdemain **3.** trickery; deception —***vt., vi.*** **-cused** or **-cussed, -cus·ing** or **-cus·sing** [Colloq.] to trick; dupe

hod (häd) ***n.*** [prob. < MDu. *hodde*] **1.** a long-handled wooden trough, used for carrying bricks, mortar, etc. on the shoulder **2.** a coal scuttle

hodge·podge (häj′päj′) ***n.*** [< OFr. *hochepot,* stew < *hocher,* to shake + *pot,* POT] any jumbled mixture; mess

Hodg·kin's disease (häj′kinz) [after Dr. T. *Hodgkin* (1798–1866)] a disease characterized by progressive enlargement of the lymph nodes

hoe (hō) ***n.*** [< OFr. *houe* < OHG. < *houwan,* to hew] a tool with a thin, flat blade set across the end of a long handle, used for weeding, loosening soil, etc. —***vt., vi.*** **hoed, hoe′ing** to dig, cultivate, weed, etc. with a hoe —**ho′er** ***n.***

A B C D

TYPES OF HOE (A, nursery; B, weeding; C, garden; D, serrated)

hoe·down (-doun) ***n.*** [infl. by BREAKDOWN, sense 2] **1.** a lively dance, often a square dance **2.** music for this **3.** a party at which hoedowns are danced

hog (hôg, häg) ***n.,*** *pl.* **hogs, hog:** see PLURAL, II, D, 1 [OE. *hogg*] **1.** a pig; esp., a full-grown pig of more than 120 lbs. raised for its meat **2.** [Colloq.] a selfish, greedy, or filthy person —***vt.*** **hogged, hog′ging** [Slang] to take all of or an unfair share of —**go (the) whole hog** [Slang] to go all the way —**high on** (or **off**) **the hog** [Colloq.] in a luxurious or costly way

ho·gan (hō′gôn, -gän) ***n.*** [Navaho *qoghan,* house] the typical dwelling of the Navaho Indians, built of earth walls supported by timbers

Ho·garth (hō′gärth), **William** 1697–1764; Eng. painter & engraver

hog·back (hôg′bak, häg′-) ***n.*** a ridge with a sharp crest and abruptly sloping sides

hog·gish (hôg′ish, häg′-) ***adj.*** like a hog; very selfish, greedy, coarse, or filthy —**hog′gish·ly** ***adv.*** —**hog′gish·ness** ***n.***

hog·nose snake (hôg′nōz′, häg′-) any of several small, harmless N. American snakes with a flat snout: also **hog′nosed′ snake**

hogs·head (hôgz′hed′, hägz′-) ***n.*** [ME. *hoggeshede,* lit., hog's head] **1.** a large barrel or cask holding from 63 to 140 gallons **2.** any of various liquid measures, esp. one equal to 63 gallons

hog·tie (hôg′tī′, häg′-) ***vt.*** **-tied′, -ty′ing** or **-tie′ing** **1.** to tie the four feet or the hands and feet of **2.** [Colloq.] to make incapable of effective action

hog·wash (-wôsh′, -wäsh′) ***n.*** **1.** refuse fed to hogs; swill **2.** useless or insincere talk, writing, etc.

Hoh·en·zol·lern (hō′ən tsôl′ərn; *E.* -zäl′ərn) ruling family of Prussia (1701–1918) & of Germany (1871–1918)

hoi pol·loi (hoi′ pə loi′) [Gr., the many] the common people; the masses: usually patronizing

hoist (hoist) ***vt.*** [< earlier *hyce* < Du. *hijschen* & LowG. *hissen*] to raise aloft; lift, esp. by means of a pulley, crane, etc. —***n.*** **1.** a hoisting **2.** an apparatus for raising heavy things

hoi·ty-toi·ty (hoit′ē toit′ē) ***adj.*** [< obs. *hoit,* to be noisily mirthful] haughty or petulant

hoke (hōk) ***vt.*** **hoked, hok′ing** [< HOKUM] [Slang] to treat in an overly sentimental or showily or falsely contrived way: usually with *up* —***n.*** [Slang] *same as* HOKUM —**hok′ey** ***adj.***

Hok·kai·do (hō kī′dō) one of the four main islands of Japan, north of Honshu: 30,364 sq. mi.

ho·kum (hōk′əm) ***n.*** [altered < HOCUS(-POCUS)] [Slang] **1.** crudely comic or mawkishly sentimental elements in a play, story, etc., used to gain an immediate emotional response **2.** nonsense; humbug

Hol·bein (hōl′bīn), **Hans** (häns) **1.** 1460?–1524; Ger. painter: called *the Elder* **2.** 1497?–1543; Ger. painter in England: son of *prec.:* called *the Younger*

hold[1] (hōld) ***vt.*** **held, hold′ing;** archaic pp. **hold′en** [OE. *haldan*] **1.** to take and keep with the hands, arms, or other means; grasp; clutch **2.** to keep from going away; not let escape [to *hold* a prisoner] **3.** to keep in a certain position or condition [*hold* your head up] **4.** to restrain or control; specif., *a)* to keep from falling; support *b)* to keep from acting [*hold* your tongue] *c)* to get and keep control of [to *hold* our attention] *d)* to maintain [to *hold* a course] *e)* to keep (a room, etc.) for use later **5.** to have and keep as one's own; own; occupy [he *holds* the office of mayor] **6.** to have or conduct together; specif., to carry on (a meeting, conversation, etc.) **7.** to have room for; contain [this can *holds* a pint] **8.** to have or keep in the mind **9.** to regard; consider [to *hold* a statement to be untrue] **10.** *Law a)* to decide; decree *b)* to possess by legal title [to *hold* a mortgage] **11.** *Music* to prolong (a tone or rest) —***vi.*** **1.** to retain a hold, firm contact, etc. [*hold* tight] **2.** to go on being firm, loyal, etc. [he *held* to his resolve] **3.** to remain unbroken or unyielding [the rope *held*] **4.** to be true or valid [a rule which still *holds*] **5.** to keep up; continue [the wind *held* steady] **6.** to halt: usually in the imperative —***n.*** **1.** a grasping or seizing; grip; specif., a way of gripping an opponent in wrestling **2.** a thing to hold on by **3.** a controlling force; restraining authority [to have a *hold* over someone] **4.** an order to make a temporary halt or delay **5.** an order reserving something **6.** [Archaic] a stronghold **7.** *Music same as* FERMATA —**catch hold of** to seize; grasp —**get hold of** **1.** to seize; grasp **2.** to acquire —**hold back** **1.** to restrain **2.** to refrain **3.** to retain —**hold down** **1.** to restrain **2.** [Colloq.] to have and keep (a job) —**hold forth** **1.** to preach; lecture **2.** to offer —**hold in** **1.** to keep in or back **2.** to control oneself —**hold off** **1.** to keep at a distance **2.** to keep from attacking or doing something —**hold on** **1.** to retain one's hold **2.** to persist **3.** [Colloq.] stop! wait! —**hold one's own** to persist in spite of obstacles —**hold out** **1.** to last; endure **2.** to stand firm **3.** to offer **4.** [Colloq.] to refuse to give (what is to be given) —**hold out for** [Colloq.] to stand firm in demanding —**hold over** **1.** to postpone consideration of or action on **2.** to keep or stay for an additional period —**hold up** **1.** to prop up **2.** to show **3.** to last; endure **4.** to stop; delay **5.** to stop forcibly and rob —**hold with** **1.** to agree with **2.** to approve of —**lay** (or **take**) **hold of** **1.** to seize; grasp **2.** to get control of

hold[2] (hōld) ***n.*** [altered < HOLE or < MDu. < *hol*] an area below the decks, as in a ship, for carrying cargo

hold·er (hōl′dər) ***n.*** **1.** a person who holds; specif., one who is legally entitled to payment of a bill, note, or check **2.** a device for holding something

hold·fast (-fast′) ***n.*** a specialized organ or part by which certain animals and plants attach themselves to an object

hold·ing (-iŋ) ***n.*** **1.** land, esp. a farm, rented from another **2.** [*usually pl.*] property owned, esp. stocks or bonds

holding company a corporation organized to hold bonds or stocks of other corporations, which it usually controls

hold·out (-out′) ***n.*** a player in a professional sport who delays signing his contract because he wants better terms

hold·o·ver (-ō′vər) ***n.*** [Colloq.] a person or thing staying on from a previous period

hold·up (-up′) ***n.*** **1.** a stoppage; delay **2.** the act of stopping forcibly and robbing

hole (hōl) ***n.*** [OE. *hol*] **1.** a hollow place; cavity [a *hole* in the ground, a swimming *hole*] **2.** an animal's burrow or lair; den **3.** a small, dingy, squalid place **4.** *a)* an opening in or through anything; gap *b)* a tear or rent, as in a garment **5.** a flaw; fault; defect [*holes* in an argument] **6.** [Colloq.] an embarrassing situation; predicament **7.** *Golf a)* a cylindrical cup sunk into a green, into which the ball is to be hit *b)* any of the sections of a course, including the tee, fairway, and green **8.** *Physics* an energy state in which a particle is missing, esp. when the energy levels above and below are occupied —***vt.*** **holed, hol′ing** to put or drive into a hole —**hole in one** *Golf* the act of getting the ball into the hole on the shot from the tee —**hole up** [Colloq.] **1.** to hibernate, usually in a hole **2.** to shut oneself in —**in the hole** [Colloq.] financially embarrassed or behind —**pick holes in** to pick out errors or flaws in —**hole′y** ***adj.***

hol·i·day (häl′ə dā′) ***n.*** **1.** a religious festival: see HOLY DAY **2.** a day of freedom from labor; day for leisure and recreation **3.** [*often pl.*] [Chiefly Brit.] a vacation **4.** a day set aside, as by law, for the suspension of business, in commemoration of some event —***adj.*** of or suited to a holiday; joyous; gay

ho·li·er-than-thou (hō′lē ər *th*ən *th*ou′) ***adj.*** annoyingly sanctimonious or self-righteous

ho·li·ly (hō′lə lē) ***adv.*** in a holy manner

ho·li·ness (-lē nis) ***n.*** **1.** a being holy **2.** [**H-**] a title of the Pope (with *His* or *Your*)

Hol·ins·hed (häl′inz hed′, -in shed′), **Raphael** ?–1580?; Eng. chronicler

Hol·land (häl′ənd) *same as the* NETHERLANDS —**Hol′land·er** ***n.***

hol·land (häl′ənd) ***n.*** [< prec., where first made] a linen or cotton cloth used for clothing, window shades, etc.

hol·lan·daise sauce (häl′ən dāz′) [Fr., of Holland] a creamy sauce, as for vegetables, made of butter, egg yolks, lemon juice, etc.

hol·ler (häl′ər) ***vi., vt., n.*** [altered < HOLLO] [Colloq.] shout or yell

hol·lo (häl′ō, hə lō′) ***interj., n., pl.*** **-los** **1.** a shout or call, as to attract a person's attention or to urge on hounds in hunting **2.** a shout of greeting or surprise —***vi., vt.*** **-loed, -lo·ing** **1.** to shout (at) so as to attract attention **2.** to urge on (hounds) by calling out "hollo" **3.** to shout, in greeting or surprise

hol·low (häl′ō) ***adj.*** [OE. *holh*] **1.** having a cavity within it; not solid **2.** shaped like a cup or bowl; concave **3.** deeply set; sunken *[hollow cheeks]* **4.** empty or worthless *[hollow praise]* **5.** hungry **6.** deep-toned and muffled, as though resounding from something hollow —***adv.*** in a hollow manner —***n.*** **1.** a hollow place; cavity; hole **2.** a valley —***vt., vi.*** to make or become hollow —**beat all hollow** [Colloq.] to outdo or surpass by far —**hollow out** to make by hollowing —**hol′low·ly** ***adv.*** —**hol′low·ness** ***n.***

hol·lo·ware (häl′ō wer′) ***n.*** serving pieces and table accessories, esp. of silver, that are relatively hollow or concave: also **hol′low-ware′**

hol·ly (häl′ē) ***n., pl.*** **-lies** [OE. *holegn*] **1.** a small tree or shrub with glossy, sharp-pointed leaves and bright-red berries **2.** the leaves and berries, used as Christmas ornaments

hol·ly·hock (häl′ē häk′) ***n.*** [< OE. *halig,* holy + *hoc,* mallow] **1.** a tall, biennial plant of the mallow family, with a hairy stem and large, showy flowers of various colors **2.** its flower

HOLLYHOCK

Hol·ly·wood (häl′ē wood′) [HOLLY + WOOD] **1.** section of Los Angeles, once the site of many U.S. motion-picture studios; hence, the U.S. motion-picture industry or its life, etc. **2.** city on the SE coast of Fla., near Miami: pop. 117,000

Hollywood bed a bed consisting of a mattress on a box spring that rests on a metal frame or has attached legs: it sometimes has a headboard

holm (hōm) ***n.*** *same as* HOLM OAK

Holmes (hōmz, hōlmz), **Oliver Wendell** **1.** 1809–94; U.S. writer & physician **2.** 1841–1935; associate justice, U.S. Supreme Court (1902–32): son of *prec.*

hol·mi·um (hōl′mē əm) ***n.*** [ModL. < *Holmia,* Latinized form of *Stockholm*] a metallic chemical element of the rare-earth group: symbol, Ho; at. wt., 164.930; at. no., 67

holm oak [< OE. *holegn,* holly] **1.** a south European evergreen oak with hollylike leaves **2.** its wood

hol·o- [Fr. < L. < Gr. *holos,* whole] *a combining form meaning* whole, entire *[holography]*

hol·o·caust (häl′ə kôst′, hō′lə-) ***n.*** [< OFr. < LL. < Gr. < *holos,* whole + *kaustos,* burnt: see CAUSTIC] great destruction of life, esp. by fire —**the Holocaust** the destruction of millions of Jews by the Nazis

hol·o·gram (-gram′) ***n.*** a photographic plate containing the record of the interference pattern produced by means of holography

hol·o·graph (-graf′) ***adj.*** [< Fr. < LL. < LGr. < Gr. *holos,* whole + *graphein,* to write] written entirely in the handwriting of the person under whose name it appears —***n.*** a holograph document, letter, etc. —**hol′o·graph′ic** ***adj.***

ho·log·ra·phy (hə läg′rə fē) ***n.*** [HOLO- + -GRAPHY] a method used to produce three-dimensional images by laser light and to record on a photographic plate the interference patterns from which an image can be reconstructed

holp (hōlp) *archaic pt. & obs. pp. of* HELP

Hol·stein (hōl′stēn, -stīn) ***n.*** [after SCHLESWIG-HOLSTEIN, where orig. bred] any of a breed of large, black-and-white dairy cattle: also **Hol′stein-Frie′sian** (-frē′zhən)

hol·ster (hōl′stər) ***n.*** [Du.] a pistol case, usually of leather and attached to a belt or saddle

ho·ly (hō′lē) ***adj.*** **-li·er, -li·est** [OE. *halig* < base of *hal,* sound, whole] [*often* **H-**] **1.** dedicated to religious use; consecrated; sacred **2.** spiritually pure; sinless; saintly **3.** regarded with or deserving deep respect or reverence **4.** [Slang] very much of a *[a holy terror]* —***n., pl.*** **-lies** a holy thing or place

Holy Communion any of various Christian rites in which bread and wine are consecrated and received as the body and blood of Jesus or as symbols of them

holy day a day consecrated to religious observances or to a religious festival

Holy Father a title of the Pope

Holy Ghost the third person of the Trinity

Holy Grail *see* GRAIL

Holy Land *same as* PALESTINE (sense 1)

Holy Mother Mary, mother of Jesus

holy of holies **1.** the innermost part of the Jewish tabernacle and Temple, where the ark of the covenant was kept **2.** any most sacred place

Hol·yoke (hōl′yōk) [after E. *Holyoke,* 18th-c. pres. of Harvard U.] city in SW Mass.: pop. 50,000

holy orders **1.** the sacrament or rite of ordination **2.** the position of being an ordained Christian minister or priest **3.** ranks or grades of the Christian ministry; specif., *a) R.C.Ch. same as* MAJOR ORDERS or, sometimes, MINOR ORDERS *b) Anglican Ch.* bishops, priests, and deacons

Holy Roman Empire empire of WC Europe, comprising the German-speaking peoples & N Italy: begun in 800 A.D. or, in another view, in 962, it lasted until 1806

Holy Scripture (or **Scriptures**) *see* BIBLE

Holy See the position, authority, or court of the Pope; Apostolic See

Holy Spirit the spirit of God; specif., third person of the Trinity

ho·ly·stone (hō′lē stōn′) ***n.*** [< ?] a flat piece of sandstone for scouring a ship's wooden decks —***vt.*** **-stoned′, -ston′ing** to scour with a holystone

Holy Synod the administrative council of any branch of the Orthodox Eastern Church

Holy Week the week before Easter

Holy Writ the Bible

hom·age (häm′ij, äm′-) ***n.*** [< OFr. < ML. *hominaticum* < L. *homo,* a man] **1.** orig., *a)* a public avowal of allegiance by a vassal to his lord *b)* an act done or thing given to show the relationship between lord and vassal **2.** anything given or done to show reverence, honor, etc.: usually with *do* or *pay [to pay homage to a hero]*

hom·bre (äm′brā, -brē) ***n.*** [Sp. < L. *homo,* a man] [Slang] a man; fellow

hom·burg (häm′bərg) ***n.*** [< *Homburg,* Prussia] a man's felt hat with a crown dented front to back and a stiff, slightly curved brim

home (hōm) ***n.*** [OE. *ham*] **1.** the place where a person (or family) lives; one's dwelling place **2.** the city, state, or country where one was born or reared **3.** a place where one likes to be; restful or congenial place **4.** the members of a family as a unit; a household and its affairs **5.** an institution for the care of orphans, the aged, etc. **6.** the natural environment of an animal, plant, etc. **7.** the place of origin, development, etc. *[Paris is the home of fashion]* **8.** in many games, the base or goal; esp., the home plate in baseball —***adj.*** **1.** of one's home or country; domestic **2.** of or at the center of operations *[home office]* **3.** played in the city, at the school, etc. where the team originates —***adv.*** **1.** at, to, or in the direction of home **2.** to the point aimed at **3.** to the heart of a matter; closely —***vi.*** **homed, hom′ing** **1.** to go to one's home **2.** to have a home —**at home** **1.** in one's own house, city, or country **2.** as if in one's own home; comfortable; at ease **3.** willing to receive visitors —**bring (something) home to** to impress upon or make clear to —**home (in) on** to be directed as by radar to (a destination) —**home′less** ***adj.*** —**home′like′** ***adj.***

home·bod·y (-bäd′ē) ***n., pl.*** **-bod′ies** a person whose interests and activities focus on the home

home-brew (-brōō′) ***n.*** an alcoholic beverage, esp. beer, made at home

home·com·ing (-kum′iŋ) ***n.*** in many colleges, an annual celebration attended by alumni

home economics the science and art of homemaking, including nutrition, budgeting, etc.

home·land (-land′) ***n.*** the country in which one was born or makes one's home

home·ly (-lē) ***adj.*** **-li·er, -li·est** **1.** characteristic of or suitable for home or home life; plain or simple *[homely virtues]* **2.** not elegant; crude **3.** not good-looking; plain or unattractive —**home′li·ness** ***n.***

home·made (-mād′) ***adj.*** **1.** made at home **2.** as if made at home; esp., plain, simple, or crude

home·mak·er (-māk′ər) ***n.*** a person who manages a home; esp., a housewife —**home′mak′ing** ***n.***

ho·me·o- [Gr. *homoio-* < *homos,* same] *a combining form meaning* like, the same, similar

ho·me·op·a·thy (hō′mē äp′ə thē) ***n.*** [< G.: see prec. & -PATHY] a system of medical treatment based on the theory that certain diseases can be cured with small doses of drugs which in a healthy person and in large doses would produce symptoms like those of the disease: opposed to ALLOPATHY —**ho′me·o·path′** (-ə path′), **ho′me·op′a·thist** ***n.*** —**ho′me·o·path′ic** (-ə path′ik) ***adj.***

ho·me·o·sta·sis (hō′mē ō stā′sis) ***n.*** [ModL.: see HOMEO- & STASIS] the tendency to maintain, or the maintenance of, stability or equilibrium within an organism, social group, etc. —**ho′me·o·stat′ic** (-stat′ik) ***adj.***

home·own·er (hōm′ō′nər) ***n.*** a person who owns the house he lives in

home plate *Baseball* the slab that the batter stands beside, across which the pitcher must throw the ball for a strike

Ho·mer (hō′mər) [< L. < Gr. < *homēros,* a pledge, hostage, one led, hence blind] **1.** a masculine name **2.** c. 8th cent. B.C.; semilegendary Gr. epic poet: reputed author of the *Iliad* & the *Odyssey* **3. Wins·low** (winz′lō), 1836–1910; U.S. painter

hom·er (hō′mər) ***n.*** [Colloq.] *same as* HOME RUN —***vi.*** [Colloq.] to hit a home run

Ho·mer·ic (hō mer′ik) ***adj.*** of, like, or characteristic of the poet Homer, his poems, or the Greek civilization that they describe (c. 1200–800 B.C.)

home·room (hōm′ro͞om′) ***n.*** the room where a class in school meets daily to be checked for attendance, receive school bulletins, etc.: also **home room**

home rule the administration of the affairs of a country, colony, city, etc. granted to the citizens who live in it by a superior governing authority

home run *Baseball* a safe hit that allows the batter to touch all bases and score a run

home·sick (-sik′) ***adj.*** longing for home —**home′sick′ness** ***n.***

home·spun (-spun′) ***n.*** **1.** cloth made of yarn spun at home **2.** coarse, loosely woven cloth like this —***adj.*** **1.** spun at home **2.** made of homespun **3.** plain; homely *[homespun virtues]*

home·stead (-sted′) ***n.*** **1.** a place where a family makes its home, including the land, house, and outbuildings **2.** a 160-acre tract of public land granted by the U.S. government to a settler to develop as a farm —***vi.*** to become a settler on a homestead —**home′stead′er** ***n.***

home·stretch (-strech′) ***n.*** **1.** the part of a race track between the last turn and the finish line **2.** the final part of any undertaking

home·ward (hōm′wərd) ***adv., adj.*** toward home: also **home′wards** ***adv.***

home·work (-wurk′) ***n.*** **1.** work done at home **2.** schoolwork to be done outside the classroom **3.** study or research in preparation for some project, activity, etc.: usually in **do one's homework**

home·y (-ē) ***adj.*** **hom′i·er, hom′i·est** having qualities usually associated with home; comfortable, familiar, etc.

hom·i·cide (häm′ə sīd′, hō′mə-) ***n.*** [< OFr. < LL. < L. < *homo,* a man + *caedere,* to cut, kill] **1.** any killing of one human being by another **2.** a person who kills another —**hom′i·ci′dal** ***adj.***

hom·i·let·ics (häm′ə let′iks) ***n.pl.*** [*with sing. v.*] [< LL. < Gr. < *homilein,* to converse < *homilos:* see ff.] the art of writing and preaching sermons —**hom′i·let′ic** ***adj.***

hom·i·ly (häm′ə lē) ***n.,*** *pl.* **-lies** [< OFr. < LL. *homilia* < Gr. < *homilos,* assembly, prob. < *homou,* together + *ilē,* a crowd] **1.** a sermon, esp. one about something in the Bible **2.** a solemn, moralizing talk or writing —**hom′i·list** ***n.***

hom·ing (hō′miŋ) ***adj.*** **1.** homeward bound **2.** having to do with guidance to a goal, target, etc.

homing pigeon a pigeon trained to find its way home from distant places

hom·i·nid (häm′ə nid) ***n.*** [< ModL. *Hominidae* (family name)] any form of man, extinct or living

hom·i·noid (-noid′) ***n.*** [< ModL. *Hominoidea* (superfamily name)] any form of man or the great apes, extinct or living —***adj.*** manlike

hom·i·ny (häm′ə nē) ***n.*** [contr. < *rockahominy* < Algonquian] dry corn with the hull and germ removed and often coarsely ground (**hominy grits**): it is boiled for food

ho·mo (hō′mō) ***n.,*** *pl.* **hom·in·es** (häm′ə nēz′) [L., a man] any of a genus of primates including modern man (*Homo sapiens*) and extinct species of man

ho·mo- [< Gr. < *homos,* same] *a combining form meaning* same, equal, like

ho·mo·ge·ne·ous (hō′mə jē′nē əs, häm′ə-) ***adj.*** [< ML. < Gr. < *homos,* same + *genos,* a race, kind] **1.** the same in structure, quality, etc.; similar or identical **2.** composed of similar or identical parts; uniform —**ho′mo·ge·ne′i·ty** (-jə nē′ə tē) ***n.*** —**ho′mo·ge′ne·ous·ly** ***adv.***

ho·mog·e·nize (hə mäj′ə nīz′) ***vt.*** **-nized′, -niz′ing** **1.** to make homogeneous **2.** to make more uniform throughout; specif., to process (milk) so that the fat particles are so finely divided and emulsified that the cream does not separate on standing —**ho·mog′e·ni·za′tion** ***n.***

hom·o·graph (häm′ə graf′, hō′mə-) ***n.*** [HOMO- + -GRAPH] a word with the same spelling as another but with a different meaning and origin (Ex.: *bow,* the front part of a ship, *bow,* to bend) —**hom′o·graph′ic** ***adj.***

ho·mol·o·gize (hō mäl′ə jīz′, hə-) ***vt.*** **-gized′, -giz′ing** **1.** to make homologous **2.** to demonstrate homology in —***vi.*** to be homologous

ho·mol·o·gous (-ə gəs) ***adj.*** [< Gr. < *homos,* same + *legein,* to say] **1.** matching in structure, position, character, etc. **2.** *Biol.* corresponding in structure and origin, as the wing of a bat and the foreleg of a mouse

ho·mol·o·gy (hō mäl′ə jē, hə-) ***n.,*** *pl.* **-gies** **1.** the quality or state of being homologous **2.** a homologous correspondence or relationship

ho·mol·o·sine projection (hə mäl′ə sin, hō-; -sīn′) [< Gr. *homalos,* even, level + SINE] a map of the earth's surface with the land areas shown in their proper relative size and form, with a minimum of distortion

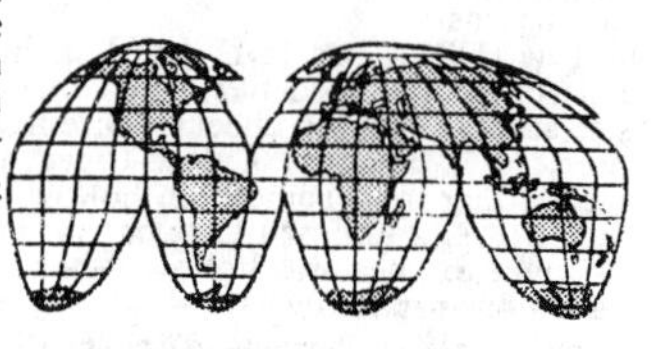

HOMOLOSINE PROJECTION

ho·mo·mor·phism (hō′mə môr′fiz′m, häm′ə-) ***n.*** [HOMO- + -MORPH + -ISM] **1.** similarity in form **2.** *Biol.* resemblance or similarity, without actual relationship, in structure or origin Also **ho′mo·mor′phy** —**ho′mo·mor′phic, ho′mo·mor′phous** ***adj.***

hom·o·nym (häm′ə nim, hō′mə-) ***n.*** [< Fr. < L. < Gr. < *homos,* same + *onyma,* name] a word with the same pronunciation as another but with a different meaning, origin, and, usually, spelling (Ex.: *bore* and *boar*) —**ho·mon·y·mous** (hō män′ə məs), **hom′o·nym′ic** ***adj.***

hom·o·phone (häm′ə fōn′) ***n.*** [< Gr. < *homos,* same + *phōnē,* a sound] **1.** any of two or more letters or groups of letters having the same pronunciation (Ex.: *c* in *civil* and *s* in *song*) **2.** *same as* HOMONYM

hom·o·phon·ic (häm′ə fän′ik, hō′mə-) ***adj.*** [< Gr.: see prec.] **1.** *Music* having a single part, or voice, carrying the melody **2.** of, or having the nature of, a homonym —**ho·moph·o·ny** (hō mäf′ə nē) ***n.,*** *pl.* **-nies**

ho·mop·ter·ous (hō mäp′tər əs) ***adj.*** [HOMO- + -PTEROUS] belonging to an order of insects with sucking mouthparts and two pairs of membranous wings of uniform thickness throughout, as aphids, cicadas, etc.

Ho·mo sa·pi·ens (hō′mō sā′pē enz′, hō′mō sap′ē ənz) [ModL.: see HOMO & SAPIENT] modern man; mankind; human being: the only living species of the genus *Homo*

ho·mo·sex·u·al (hō′mə sek′sho͞o wəl) ***adj.*** of or having sexual desire for those of the same sex as oneself —***n.*** a homosexual person —**ho′mo·sex′u·al′i·ty** (-wal′ə tē) ***n.*** —**ho′mo·sex′u·al·ly** ***adv.***

ho·mun·cu·lus (hō muŋ′kyo͞o ləs) ***n.,*** *pl.* **-li′** (-lī′) [L., dim. of *homo,* man] a little man; dwarf

hom·y (hō′mē) ***adj.*** **hom′i·er, hom′i·est** *same as* HOMEY

Hon., hon. **1.** honorable **2.** honorary

Hon·du·ras (hän do͝or′əs, -dyo͝or′-) country in Central America, north of Nicaragua: 43,227 sq. mi.; pop. 2,495,000; cap. Tegucigalpa —**Hon·du′ran** ***adj., n.***

hone (hōn) ***n.*** [< OE. *han,* a stone] a whetstone used to sharpen cutting tools, esp. razors —***vt.*** **honed, hon′ing** to sharpen as with a hone

hon·est (än′əst) ***adj.*** [< OFr. < L. *honestus* < *honor,* honor] **1.** that will not lie, cheat, or steal; trustworthy; truthful **2.** *a)* showing fairness and sincerity *[an honest effort]* *b)* gained by fair methods *[an honest living]* **3.** being what it seems; genuine *[to give honest measure]* **4.** frank and open *[an honest face]* **5.** [Archaic] chaste —***adv.*** [Colloq.] honestly; truly: an intensive

hon·est·ly (-lē) ***adv.*** **1.** in an honest manner **2.** truly; really: an intensive *[honestly, it is so]*

hon·es·ty (än′əs tē) ***n.*** the state or quality of being honest; specif., *a)* a being truthful, trustworthy, or upright *b)* sincerity; straightforwardness

hon·ey (hun′ē) ***n.,*** *pl.* **-eys** [OE. *hunig*] **1.** a thick, sweet, syrupy substance that bees make as food from the nectar of flowers **2.** sweet quality; sweetness **3.** sweet one; darling **4.** [Colloq.] something pleasing or excellent of its kind —***adj.*** **1.** of or like honey **2.** sweet; dear —***vt.*** **-eyed** or **-ied, -ey·ing** **1.** to make sweet as with honey **2.** to flatter

hon·ey·bee (-bē′) ***n.*** a bee that makes honey

hon·ey·comb (-kōm′) ***n.*** **1.** the structure of six-sided wax cells made by bees to hold their honey, eggs, etc. **2.** anything like this —*vt.* **1.** to fill with holes like a honeycomb; riddle **2.** to permeate or undermine *[honeycombed* with intrigue*]* —*adj.* of, like, or patterned after a honeycomb: also **hon′ey·combed′**

hon·ey·dew (-do͞o′, -dyo͞o′) *n.* **1.** a sweet fluid exuded from various plants **2.** a sweet substance secreted by some juice-sucking plant insects **3.** *short for* HONEYDEW MELON

honeydew melon a variety of melon with a smooth, whitish rind and sweet, greenish flesh

hon·eyed (hun′ēd) *adj.* **1.** sweetened, covered, or filled with honey **2.** sweet as honey; flattering or affectionate *[honeyed* words*]*

honey locust a N. American tree of the legume family, with strong, thorny branches, featherlike foliage, and large, twisted pods

hon·ey·moon (hun′ē mo͞on′) *n.* [as if < HONEY + MOON, but ? folk-etym. for ON. *hjūnōttsmānathr,* lit., wedding-night month] **1.** formerly, the first month of marriage **2.** the vacation spent together by a newly married couple **3.** a brief period of apparent agreement —*vi.* to have or spend a honeymoon —**hon′ey·moon′er** *n.*

hon·ey·suck·le (-suk′'l) *n.* **1.** any of a genus of largely woody plants with small, fragrant flowers of red, yellow, or white **2.** any of several similar plants

Hong Kong (häŋ′ käŋ′, hôŋ′ kôŋ′) Brit. crown colony consisting of a small area on the SE coast of China & several offshore islands: also **Hong′kong′**

hon·ied (hun′ēd) *adj. same as* HONEYED

honk (hôŋk, häŋk) *n.* [echoic] **1.** the call of a wild goose **2.** any similar sound, as of an automobile horn —*vi., vt.* to make or cause to make such a sound —**honk′er** *n.*

hon·ky-tonk (hôŋ′kē tôŋk′, häŋ′kē täŋk′) *n.* [< ?] [Slang] a cheap, disreputable cabaret or nightclub

Hon·o·lu·lu (hän′ə lo͞o′lo͞o, hō′nə-) [Haw., lit., sheltered bay] capital of Hawaii; seaport on Oahu: pop. 365,000 (met. area 763,000)

hon·or (än′ər) *n.* [< OFr. < L. *honor, honos*] **1.** high regard or great respect given or received; esp., *a)* glory; fame; renown *b)* good reputation; credit **2.** a keen sense of right and wrong; adherence to principles considered right *[*to behave with *honor]* **3.** chastity; purity **4.** high rank or position; distinction *[*the great *honor* of the presidency*]* **5.** [**H-**] a title given to certain officials, as judges (preceded by *His, Her,* or *Your*) **6.** something done or given as a token of respect; specif., *a)* a social courtesy *[*may I have the *honor* of this dance?*] b)* [*pl.*] public ceremonies of respect *[*funeral *honors] c)* [*pl.*] special distinction given to students for high academic achievement; also, an advanced course of study for exceptional students **7.** one that brings respect and fame to a school, country, etc. **8.** *Bridge a)* any of the five highest cards in a suit *b)* [*pl.*] the four or five highest cards of the trump suit *c)* [*pl.*] in a no-trump hand, the aces **9.** *Golf* the privilege of driving first from the tee —*vt.* **1.** to respect greatly; regard highly **2.** to treat with deference and courtesy **3.** to worship (a deity) **4.** to do something in honor of **5.** to accept and pay when due *[*to *honor* a check*]* —*adj.* of or showing honor *[honor* roll*]* —**do honor to 1.** to show great respect for **2.** to bring honor to —**do the honors** to act as host or hostess, esp. by making introductions, serving at table, etc. —**on** (or **upon**) **one's honor** staking one's good name on one's truthfulness or reliability

hon·or·a·ble (-ə b'l) *adj.* **1.** worthy of being honored; specif., *a)* of, or having a position of, high rank or worth: used as a title of courtesy *b)* noble; illustrious *c)* of good reputation; respectable **2.** having or showing a sense of right and wrong; upright **3.** bringing honor *[honorable* mention*]* **4.** accompanied with marks of respect *[*an *honorable* burial*]* —**hon′or·a·bly** *adv.*

honorable mention a citation of honor, esp. to one who was not a winner, as in a competition

hon·o·ra·ri·um (än′ə rer′ē əm) *n., pl.* **-ri·ums, -ri·a** (-ə) [L. *honorarium* (*donum*), honorary (gift)] a payment as to a professional person for services on which no fee is set

hon·or·ar·y (än′ə rer′ē) *adj.* [L. *honorarius,* of or conferring honor] **1.** given as an honor only *[*an *honorary* degree*]* **2.** *a)* designating an office held as an honor only, without service or pay *b)* holding such an office —**hon′or·ar′i·ly** *adv.*

hon·or·if·ic (än′ə rif′ik) *adj.* [< L. < *honor* + *facere,* to make] conferring honor; showing respect *[*an *honorific* title*]* —**hon′or·if′i·cal·ly** *adv.*

honor system in some schools, prisons, etc., a system whereby individuals are trusted to obey rules, do their work, take tests, etc. without direct supervision

hon·our (än′ər) *n., vt., adj. Brit. var. of* HONOR

Hon·shu (hän′sho͞o′) largest of the islands forming Japan: 88,946 sq. mi.

hooch (ho͞och) *n.* [< Alaskan Ind. *hoochinoo,* crude alcoholic liquor] [Slang] alcoholic liquor, esp. when made or obtained surreptitiously

hood[1] (hood) *n.* [OE. *hod*] **1.** a covering for the head and neck, worn separately or as part of a robe or cloak **2.** anything like a hood in shape or use; specif., *a)* the metal cover over the engine of an automobile *b) Falconry* the covering for a falcon's head when it is not chasing game —*vt.* to cover as with a hood —**hood′ed** *adj.* —**hood′less** *adj.*

hood[2] (hood, ho͞od) *n.* [Slang] *short for* HOODLUM

-hood (hood) [< OE. *had,* order, condition, rank] *a suffix meaning:* **1.** state, quality, condition *[childhood]* **2.** the whole group of (a specified class, profession, etc.) *[priesthood]*

Hood, Robin *see* ROBIN HOOD

hood·lum (ho͞od′ləm) *n.* [prob. < G. dial. *hudilump,* wretch] a wild, lawless person, often a member of a gang of criminals —**hood′lum·ism** *n.*

hoo·doo (ho͞o′do͞o) *n., pl.* **-doos** [var. of VOODOO] **1.** *same as* VOODOO **2.** [Colloq.] *a)* a person or thing that causes bad luck *b)* bad luck —*vt.* [Colloq.] to bring bad luck to

hood·wink (hood′wiŋk′) *vt.* [HOOD[1] + WINK] **1.** orig., to blindfold **2.** to deceive; trick; dupe

hoo·ey (ho͞o′ē) *interj., n.* [echoic] [Slang] nonsense; bunk

hoof (hoof, ho͞of) *n., pl.* **hoofs, hooves** (hoovz, ho͞ovz) [OE. *hof*] the horny covering on the feet of cattle, deer, horses, etc., or the entire foot —*vt., vi.* [Colloq.] to walk (often with *it*) —**on the hoof** not butchered; alive —**hoofed** *adj.* —**hoof′less** *adj.*

hoof-and-mouth disease (-'n mouth′) *same as* FOOT-AND-MOUTH DISEASE

hoof·beat (-bēt′) *n.* the sound made by the hoof of an animal when it runs, walks, etc.

hoof·er (hoof′ər, ho͞of′-) *n.* [Slang] a professional dancer, esp. a tap dancer, soft-shoe dancer, etc.

hook (hook) *n.* [< OE. *hoc*] **1.** a curved or bent piece of metal, wood, etc. used to catch, hold, or pull something; specif., *a)* a curved piece of wire with a barbed end, for catching fish *b)* a curved piece used to hang things on, etc. *[*a coat *hook] c)* a small metal catch inserted in a loop, or eye, to fasten clothes together **2.** a curved metal implement for cutting grain, etc. **3.** something shaped like a hook, as a curving headland or cape **4.** *a)* the path of a hit or thrown ball that curves away to the left from a right-handed player or to the right from a left-handed player *b)* a ball that follows such a path **5.** *Boxing* a short blow delivered with the arm bent at the elbow **6.** *Music same as* FLAG[1] (sense 4) —*vt.* **1.** to fasten as with a hook **2.** to take hold of or catch as with a hook **3.** to shape into a hook **4.** to make (a rug) by drawing strips of cloth or yarn through a canvas or burlap backing with a hook **5.** to hit or throw (a ball) in a hook (*n.* 4*a*) **6.** [Colloq.] to steal; snatch **7.** *Boxing* to hit with a hook —*vi.* **1.** to curve as a hook does **2.** to be fastened with a hook or hooks **3.** to be caught by a hook —**by hook or by crook** by any means, honest or dishonest —**hook up 1.** to connect or attach with a hook or hooks **2.** to arrange and connect the parts of (a radio, etc.) —**off the hook** [Colloq.] out of trouble, freed from an obligation, etc. —**on one's own hook** [Colloq.] by oneself, without help from others

hook·ah, hook·a (hook′ə) *n.* [Ar. *ḥuqqah*] an Oriental tobacco pipe with a long, flexible tube by means of which the smoke is drawn through water in a vase or bowl and cooled

HOOKAH

hooked (hookt) *adj.* **1.** curved like a hook **2.** having a hook or hooks **3.** made with a hook *[*a *hooked* rug*]* **4.** [Slang] addicted as to the use of a drug (often with *on*) **5.** [Slang] married

hook·er (hook′ər) *n.* **1.** one that hooks **2.** [Slang] a drink of whiskey **3.** [Slang] a prostitute

hook·up (-up′) *n.* **1.** the arrangement and connection of parts, circuits, etc., as in (a) radio **2.** [Colloq.] a connection or alliance

hook·worm (-wurm′) *n.* any of a number of small, parasitic roundworms with hooks around the mouth, infesting the small intestine and causing a disorder (**hookworm disease**) characterized by anemia, weakness, and abdominal pain

hook·y (hook′ē) *n. see* PLAY HOOKY

hoo·li·gan (ho͞o′li gən) *n.* [< ? *Hooligan* (or *Houlihan*), an Irish family in London] [Slang] a hoodlum, esp. a young one —**hoo′li·gan·ism** *n.*

hoop (ho͞op) *n.* [OE. *hop*] **1.** a circular band or ring for holding together the staves of a barrel, cask, etc. **2.** anything like a hoop; specif., *a)* any of the rings forming the framework of a hoop skirt *b)* *Basketball* the metal rim of the basket *c)* *Croquet* same as WICKET

hoop·la (ho͞op′lä) ***n.*** [Colloq.] **1.** great excitement **2.** showy publicity; ballyhoo

hoo·poe (ho͞o′po͞o) ***n.*** [< Fr. *huppe* < L. *upupa*, prob. echoic] a European bird with a long, curved bill and an erectile crest

hoop skirt a skirt worn over a framework of hoops, or rings, to make it spread out

hoo·ray (hoo rā′, hə-, ho͞o-) ***interj., n., vi., vt.*** *same as* HURRAH

hoose·gow, hoos·gow (ho͞os′gou) ***n.*** [< Sp. *juzgado*, court of justice, ult. < L. *judex*, JUDGE] [Slang] a jail

Hoo·sier (ho͞o′zhər) ***n.*** [prob. < dial. *hoozer*, something big] [Colloq.] a native or inhabitant of Indiana

hoot (ho͞ot) ***vi.*** [orig. echoic] **1.** to utter its characteristic hollow sound: said of an owl **2.** to utter a sound like this **3.** to shout, esp. in scorn or disapproval —***vt.*** **1.** to express (scorn, disapproval, etc.) by hooting **2.** to express scorn or disapproval of by hooting **3.** to chase away by hooting *[*to *hoot* an actor off the stage*]* —***n.*** **1.** the sound that an owl makes **2.** any sound like this **3.** a shout of scorn or disapproval **4.** the least bit; whit *[*not worth a *hoot]* —**hoot′er** ***n.***

hoot·en·an·ny (ho͞ot′'n an′ē) ***n.,*** *pl.* **-nies** [a fanciful coinage] a meeting of folk singers, as for public entertainment

Hoo·ver (ho͞o′vər) **1. Herbert Clark,** 1874–1964; 31st president of the U.S. (1929–33) **2. J(ohn) Edgar,** 1895–1972; director of the FBI (1924–72)

Hoover Dam [after Pres. HOOVER] dam on the Colorado River, on the Ariz.-Nev. border

hooves (hoovz, ho͞ovz) ***n.*** *alt. pl. of* HOOF

hop[1] (häp) ***vi.*** **hopped, hop′ping** [OE. *hoppian*] **1.** to make a short leap or leaps on one foot **2.** to move by leaping or springing on both (or all) feet at once, as a bird, frog, etc. **3.** [Colloq.] *a)* to go or move briskly *b)* to take a short, quick trip (with *up, down,* or *over*) —***vt.*** **1.** to jump over *[*to *hop* a fence*]* **2.** to get aboard *[*to *hop* a train*]* —***n.*** **1.** a hopping **2.** a bounce, as of a baseball **3.** [Colloq.] a dance, esp. an informal one **4.** [Colloq.] a short flight in an airplane —**hop on** (or **all over**) [Slang] to scold; reprimand

hop[2] (häp) ***n.*** [< MDu. *hoppe*] **1.** a twining vine with the female flowers borne in small cones **2.** [*pl.*] the dried ripe cones, used for flavoring beer, ale, etc. —***vt.*** **hopped, hop′ping** to flavor with hops —**hop up** [Slang] **1.** to stimulate by or as by a drug **2.** to supercharge (an automobile engine, etc.)

Hope (hōp) [< ff.] a feminine name

hope (hōp) ***n.*** [OE. *hopa*] **1.** a feeling that what is wanted will happen **2.** the thing that one has a hope for **3.** a reason for hope **4.** a person or thing on which one may base some hope **5.** [Archaic] trust; reliance —***vt.*** **hoped, hop′ing** **1.** to want and expect **2.** to want very much —***vi.*** **1.** to have hope (*for*) **2.** [Archaic] to trust or rely —**hope against hope** to continue having hope though it seems baseless —**hop′er** ***n.***

hope chest a chest in which a young woman hoping to get married collects linen, clothing, etc.

hope·ful (-fəl) ***adj.*** **1.** feeling or showing hope **2.** inspiring or giving hope —***n.*** a person who hopes, or seems likely, to succeed —**hope′ful·ness** ***n.***

hope·ful·ly (-ē) ***adv.*** **1.** in a hopeful manner **2.** it is to be hoped (that) *[hopefully* we will win*]*: regarded by some as a loose usage

hope·less (-lis) ***adj.*** **1.** without hope **2.** allowing no hope *[*a *hopeless* situation*]* **3.** impossible to solve, deal with, etc. —**hope′less·ly** ***adv.*** —**hope′less·ness** ***n.***

Ho·pi (hō′pē) ***n.*** [Hopi *Hópitu*, lit., good] **1.** *pl.* **-pis, -pi** a member of a Pueblo tribe of Indians in NE Arizona **2.** their language

hop·lite (häp′līt) ***n.*** [< Gr. < *hoplon*, a tool] a heavily armed foot soldier of ancient Greece

hop·per (häp′ər) ***n.*** **1.** a person or thing that hops **2.** any hopping insect **3.** a container from which the contents can be emptied slowly and evenly *[*the *hopper* of an automatic coal stoker*]*

hop·sack·ing (häp′sak′iŋ) ***n.*** [lit., sacking for hops] **1.** a coarse material for bags **2.** a fabric somewhat simulating this, used for suits, etc. Also **hop′sack′**

hop·scotch (häp′skäch′) ***n.*** [HOP[1] + SCOTCH] a children's game in which each player hops from one compartment to another of a figure drawn on the ground

Hor·ace (hôr′is, här′-) [< L.: see ff.] **1.** a masculine name **2.** (L. name *Quintus Horatius Flaccus*) 65–8 B.C.; Roman poet: known for his odes —**Ho·ra·tian** (hə-rā′shən, hô-) ***adj.***

Ho·ra·ti·o (hə rā′shō, -shē ō; hô-) [< L. *Horatius*, name of a Roman gens] a masculine name

horde (hôrd) ***n.*** [< Fr. < G. < Pol. *horda* < Turk. *ordū*] **1.** a nomadic tribe or clan of Mongols **2.** a large, moving crowd; swarm —***vi.*** **hord′ed, hord′ing** to form or gather in a horde

hore·hound (hôr′hound′) ***n.*** [< OE. < *har*, white + *hune*, horehound] **1.** a bitter plant of the mint family, with white, downy leaves **2.** a bitter juice extracted from its leaves **3.** cough medicine or candy made with this juice

ho·ri·zon (hə rī′z'n) ***n.*** [< OFr. < L. < Gr. *horizōn* (*kyklos*), the bounding (circle)] **1.** the line where the sky seems to meet the earth: called **visible** or **apparent horizon** **2.** [*usually pl.*] the limit of one's experience, interest, knowledge, etc.

hor·i·zon·tal (hôr′ə zän′t'l, här′-) ***adj.*** **1.** *a)* parallel to the plane of the horizon; not vertical *b)* placed or acting in a horizontal direction **2.** flat and even; level **3.** at, or made up of elements at, the same level or status *[*a *horizontal* union*]* —***n.*** a horizontal line, plane, etc. —**hor′i·zon·tal′i·ty** (-tal′ə tē) ***n.*** —**hor′i·zon′tal·ly** ***adv.***

horizontal union *same as* CRAFT UNION

hor·mone (hôr′mōn) ***n.*** [< Gr. < *horman*, to excite < *hormē*, impulse] **1.** a substance formed in some organ of the body, as the adrenal glands, pituitary, etc., and carried to another organ or tissue, where it has a specific effect: often prepared synthetically **2.** a similar substance in plants —**hor·mo′nal** (-mō′n'l), **hor·mon·ic** (-män′ik) ***adj.***

horn (hôrn) ***n.*** [OE.] **1.** *a)* a hard, permanent projection of bone or keratin, that grows on the head of cattle, sheep, etc. *b)* the antler of a deer, shed annually **2.** anything that protrudes from the head of an animal, as a tentacle of a snail **3.** the substance that horns are made of **4.** a container made by hollowing out a horn **5.** a cornucopia **6.** anything shaped like a horn; specif., *a)* a peninsula or cape *b)* either end of a crescent *c)* a projection above the pommel of a cowboy's saddle **7.** *a)* an instrument made of horn and sounded by blowing *b)* any brass-wind instrument; specif., the French horn; also, *Jazz* any wind instrument *c)* a device sounded to give a warning *[*a *foghorn]* *d)* a horn-shaped loudspeaker —***vt.*** **1.** to strike or gore with the horns **2.** to furnish with horns —***adj.*** made of horn —**blow one's own horn** [Colloq.] to boast —**horn in (on)** [Colloq.] to meddle (in) —**lock horns** to have a conflict —**pull** (or **draw** or **haul**) **in one's horns** **1.** to hold oneself back **2.** to withdraw; recant —**horned** ***adj.*** —**horn′less** ***adj.*** —**horn′like′** ***adj.***

Horn, Cape southernmost point of S. America, on an island (**Horn Island**) in Tierra del Fuego, Chile

horn·bill (-bil′) ***n.*** any of a family of large, tropical, old-world birds with a huge, curved bill

horn·blende (-blend′) ***n.*** [G.: see HORN & BLENDE] a black, rock-forming mineral, a type of amphibole common in some granitic rocks

horn·book (-book′) ***n.*** **1.** a parchment sheet with the alphabet, numbers, etc. on it, mounted on a small board under a thin, clear plate of horn: formerly a child's primer **2.** an elementary treatise

horned pout *same as* BULLHEAD: also **horn′pout′** ***n.***

horned toad any of several small, scaly lizards of the New World that eat insects and have short tails and hornlike spines

horned viper a poisonous N African snake with a hornlike spine above each eye

hor·net (hôr′nit) ***n.*** [OE. *hyrnet*] any of several large, yellow-and-black social wasps

horn of plenty *same as* CORNUCOPIA

horn·pipe (hôrn′pīp′) ***n.*** **1.** an obsolete wind instrument with a bell and mouthpiece made of horn **2.** a lively dance formerly popular with sailors **3.** music for this

horn·y (hôr′nē) ***adj.*** **horn′i·er, horn′i·est** **1.** of, like, or made of horn **2.** having horns **3.** toughened and calloused **4.** [Slang] lustful —**horn′i·ness** ***n.***

ho·ro·loge (hôr′ə lōj′, här′-) ***n.*** [< OFr. < L. < Gr. < *hōra*, hour + *legein*, to tell] a timepiece; clock, hourglass, sundial, etc.

ho·rol·o·gist (hô räl′ə jist) ***n.*** an expert in horology; maker of or dealer in timepieces: also **ho·rol′o·ger**

ho·rol·o·gy (hô räl′ə jē) ***n.*** [< Gr. *hōra*, hour + -LOGY] the science or art of measuring time or making timepieces —**hor·o·log·ic** (hôr′ə läj′ik, här′-), **hor′o·log′i·cal** ***adj.***

hor·o·scope (hôr′ə skōp′, här′-) ***n.*** [Fr. < L. < Gr. < *hōra*, hour + *skopos*, watcher] **1.** the position of the planets and stars with relation to one another at a given time, esp. at a person's birth, regarded in astrology as determining his destiny **2.** a chart of the zodiacal signs and the positions of the planets, etc. by which astrologers profess to tell a person's future —**hor′o·scop′ic** (-skäp′ik) ***adj.*** —**ho·ros·co·py** (hô räs′kə pē) ***n.***

hor·ren·dous (hô ren′dəs, hə-) ***adj.*** [L. *horrendus* < prp. of *horrere*, to bristle] horrible; frightful —**hor·ren′dous·ly** ***adv.***

hor·ri·ble (hôr′ə b'l, här′-) ***adj.*** [< OFr. < L. < *horrere*: see prec.] **1.** causing a feeling of horror; terrible; dreadful **2.** [Colloq.] very bad, ugly, unpleasant, etc. —**hor′ri·bly** ***adv.***

hor·rid (hôr′id, här′-) ***adj.*** **1.** causing a feeling of horror; terrible; revolting **2.** very bad, ugly, unpleasant, etc. —**hor′rid·ly** ***adv.*** —**hor′rid·ness** ***n.***

hor·ri·fy (hôr′ə fī′, här′-) ***vt.*** **-fied′, -fy′ing 1.** to cause to feel horror **2.** [Colloq.] to shock or disgust —**hor′ri·fi·ca′tion** ***n.***

hor·ror (hôr′ər, här′-) ***n.*** [< OFr. < L. *horror* < *horrere*, to bristle, be afraid] **1.** the strong feeling caused by something frightful or shocking; terror and repugnance **2.** strong dislike or aversion **3.** the quality of causing horror **4.** something that causes horror **5.** [Colloq.] something very bad, ugly, disagreeable, etc. —***adj.*** intended to cause horror [*horror* movies] —**the horrors** [Colloq.] a fit of extreme nervousness, panic, etc.

‡**hors de com·bat** (ôr′ də kōn bȧ′) [Fr., out of combat] put out of action; disabled

hors d'oeu·vre (ôr′durv′, -duv′; *Fr.* ôr dö′vr′) *pl.* **hors′ d'oeuvres′** (durvz′, duvz′); Fr. **hors d'oeu′vre** [Fr., lit., outside of work] an appetizer, as olives, anchovies, canapés, etc., served usually at the beginning of a meal

horse (hôrs) ***n.***, *pl.* **hors′es, horse:** see PLURAL, II, D, 1 [OE. *hors*] **1.** a large, strong animal with four legs, solid hoofs, and flowing mane and tail, long ago domesticated for drawing loads, carrying riders, etc. **2.** the full-grown male of the horse **3.** a frame on legs to support something [a *sawhorse*] **4.** *slang for: a*) HORSEPOWER *b*) HEROIN **5.** *Gym.* a padded block on legs, used for jumping or vaulting **6.** *Mil.* [*with pl. v.*] mounted troops; cavalry —***vt.*** **horsed, hors′ing 1.** to supply with a horse or horses; put on horseback **2.** [Colloq.] to shove; push **3.** [Slang] to subject to horseplay —***vi.*** to mount or go on horseback —***adj.*** **1.** of a horse or horses **2.** mounted on horses **3.** large, strong, or coarse of its kind [*horseradish*] —**from the horse's mouth** [Colloq.] from the original or authoritative source of information —**hold one's horses** [Slang] to curb one's impatience —**horse around** [Slang] to engage in horseplay —**horse of another** (or **a different**) **color** an entirely different matter —**on one's high horse** [Colloq.] acting in an arrogant or disdainful manner —**to horse!** mount your horse!

HORSE (sense 5)

horse·back (-bak′) ***n.*** the back of a horse —***adv.*** on horseback

horse·car (-kär′) ***n.*** **1.** a streetcar drawn by horses **2.** a car for transporting horses

horse chestnut 1. *a*) a tree with large, palmately compound leaves, clusters of white flowers, and glossy brown seeds *b*) its seed **2.** any of various related shrubs or trees —**horse′-chest′nut** ***adj.***

horse·flesh (-flesh′) ***n.*** **1.** the flesh of the horse, esp. as food **2.** horses collectively

horse·fly (-flī′) ***n.***, *pl.* **-flies′** any of various large flies, the female of which sucks the blood of horses, cattle, etc.

horse·hair (-her′) ***n.*** **1.** hair from the mane or tail of a horse **2.** a stiff fabric made from this hair; haircloth —***adj.*** **1.** of horsehair **2.** covered or stuffed with horsehair

horse·hide (-hīd′) ***n.*** **1.** the hide of a horse **2.** leather made from this

horse latitudes either of two belts of calms, light winds, and high barometric pressure, at c. 30°–35° N. and S. latitude

horse·laugh (-laf′) ***n.*** a loud, boisterous, usually derisive laugh; guffaw

horse·less (-lis) ***adj.*** **1.** without a horse **2.** self-propelled [a *horseless* carriage]

horse·man (-mən) ***n.***, *pl.* **-men 1.** a man who rides on horseback **2.** a man skilled in the riding or care of horses —**horse′man·ship′** ***n.***

horse opera [Slang] a motion picture or play about cowboys, rustlers, etc., esp. in the W U.S.

horse pistol a large pistol formerly carried by horsemen

horse·play (-plā′) ***n.*** rough, boisterous fun

horse·pow·er (-pou′ər) ***n.*** a unit for measuring the power of motors or engines, equal to 746 watts or to a rate of 33,000 foot-pounds per minute

horse·rad·ish (-rad′ish) ***n.*** **1.** a plant of the mustard family, grown for its pungent, white root **2.** a relish made by grating this root

horse sense [Colloq.] ordinary common sense

horse·shoe (hôr′shōō′, hôrs′-) ***n.*** **1.** a flat, U-shaped, protective metal plate nailed to a horse's hoof **2.** anything shaped like this **3.** [*pl.*] a game in which the players toss horseshoes in an attempt to encircle a stake or come as close to it as possible —***vt.*** **-shoed′, -shoe′ing** to fit with a horseshoe or horseshoes —**horse′sho′er** ***n.***

horseshoe crab a sea arthropod shaped like the base of a horse's foot and having a long, spinelike tail

horse·tail (hôrs′tāl′) ***n.*** **1.** a horse's tail **2.** a rushlike plant with hollow, jointed stems and scalelike leaves

horse trade any bargaining marked by shrewd calculation —**horse′-trade′** ***vi.*** **-trad′ed, -trad′ing** —**horse′-trad′er** ***n.***

horse·whip (-hwip′, -wip′) ***n.*** a whip for driving or managing horses —***vt.*** **-whipped′, -whip′ping** to lash with a horsewhip

horse·wom·an (-woom′ən) ***n.***, *pl.* **-wom′en 1.** a woman who rides on horseback **2.** a woman skilled in the riding or care of horses

hors·y (hôr′sē) ***adj.*** **hors′i·er, hors′i·est 1.** of, like, or suggesting a horse; esp., having large features and a big body that looks strong but awkward **2.** of, like, or characteristic of people who are fond of horses, fox hunting, or horse racing Also **hors′ey** —**hors′i·ly** ***adv.*** —**hors′i·ness** ***n.***

hort. 1. horticultural **2.** horticulture

hor·ta·to·ry (hôr′tə tôr′ē) ***adj.*** [< LL. < L. pp. of *hortari*, freq. of *horiri*, to urge] **1.** encouraging or urging to good deeds **2.** exhorting; giving advice Also **hor′ta·tive**

Hor·tense (hôr tens′, hôr′tens) [Fr. < L. < *hortensius*, of a garden] a feminine name

hor·ti·cul·ture (hôr′tə kul′chər) ***n.*** [< L. *hortus*, a garden + *cultura*, culture] the art or science of growing flowers, fruits, vegetables, etc. —**hor′ti·cul′tur·al** ***adj.*** —**hor′ti·cul′tur·ist** ***n.***

Hos. Hosea

ho·san·na (hō zan′ə) ***n.***, ***interj.*** [< OE. < LL. < Gr. *hōsanna* < Heb. *hōshī'āh nnā*, lit., save, we pray] an exclamation of praise to God

hose (hōz) ***n.***, *pl.* **hose** or, for 3, usually **hos′es** [OE. *hosa*] **1.** orig., a man's tightfitting outer garment covering the hips, legs, and feet **2.** [*pl.*] *a*) stockings *b*) socks **3.** [prob. infl. by Du. *hoos*, water pipe] a flexible pipe or tube, used to convey fluids, esp. water from a hydrant —***vt.*** **hosed, hos′ing 1.** to water with a hose **2.** [Slang] to beat as with a hose

Ho·se·a (hō zā′ə, -zē′ə) *Bible* **1.** a Hebrew prophet of the 8th cent. B.C. **2.** the book containing his writings

ho·sen (hō′z'n) ***n.*** *archaic pl. of* HOSE (*n.* 1 & 2)

ho·sier (hō′zhər) ***n.*** [Chiefly Brit.] a person who makes or sells hosiery

ho·sier·y (-ē) ***n.*** **1.** hose; stockings and socks **2.** [Chiefly Brit.] similar knitted or woven goods

hos·pice (häs′pis) ***n.*** [Fr. < L. < *hospes*, host, guest] a place of shelter for travelers, esp. such a shelter maintained by monks

hos·pi·ta·ble (häs′pi tə b'l, häs pit′ə-) ***adj.*** [MFr. < ML. < L. < *hospes*: see prec.] **1.** showing or characterized by friendliness, kindness, and solicitude toward guests **2.** favoring health, growth, etc. [a *hospitable* climate] **3.** receptive or open, as to new ideas —**hos′pi·ta·bly** ***adv.***

hos·pi·tal (häs′pi t'l) ***n.*** [< OFr. < LL. *hospitale*, inn < L. < *hospes*: see HOSPICE] an institution where the ill or injured may receive medical or surgical treatment, nursing care, lodging, etc.

hos·pi·tal·i·ty (häs′pə tal′ə tē) ***n.***, *pl.* **-ties** the act, practice, or quality of being hospitable

hospitalization insurance insurance providing hospitalization for the subscriber and, usually, members of his immediate family

hos·pi·tal·ize (häs′pi t'l īz′) ***vt.*** **-ized′, -iz′ing** to send to, put in, or admit to a hospital —**hos′pi·tal·i·za′tion** ***n.***

host¹ (hōst) ***n.*** [< OFr. < ML. < L. *hostia*, animal sacrificed] a wafer of the Eucharist; esp., [H-] a consecrated wafer

host² (hōst) ***n.*** [< OFr. < L. *hospes*: see HOSPICE] **1.** a man who entertains guests in his own home or at his own expense **2.** a man who keeps an inn or hotel **3.** any organism on or in which another (called a *parasite*) lives —***vi.***, ***vt.*** to act as host or hostess (to)

host³ (hōst) ***n.*** [< OFr. < ML. < L. *hostis*, army] **1.** an army **2.** a multitude; great number

hos·tage (häs′tij) ***n.*** [< OFr. < *hoste*: see HOST²] a person given as a pledge, or taken prisoner as by an enemy, until certain conditions are met

hos·tel (häs′t'l) ***n.*** [see HOSPITAL] an inn; hostelry; specif., *same as* YOUTH HOSTEL

hos·tel·er (-ər) ***n.*** **1.** [Archaic] an innkeeper **2.** a traveler who stops at youth hostels

hos·tel·ry (-rē) ***n.***, *pl.* **-ries** an inn; hotel

host·ess (hōs′tis) ***n.*** **1.** a woman who entertains guests in her own home or at her own expense; often, the wife of a host **2.** *a*) a stewardess, as on an airplane *b*) a woman employed in a restaurant to supervise waitresses, seating, etc. *c*) a woman who serves as paid partner at a public dance hall

hos·tile (häs′t'l; *chiefly Brit.* -tīl) ***adj.*** [< L. < *hostis*, enemy] **1.** of or characteristic of an enemy **2.** unfriendly; antagonistic **3.** not hospitable; adverse —**hos′tile·ly *adv.***

hos·til·i·ty (häs til′ə tē) ***n.**, pl.* **-ties 1.** a feeling of enmity, ill will, unfriendliness, etc. **2.** *a*) an expression of enmity and ill will; hostile act *b*) [*pl.*] acts of war; warfare

hos·tler (häs′lər, äs′-) ***n.*** [contr. of HOSTELER] one who takes care of horses at an inn, stable, etc.

hot (hät) ***adj.* hot′ter, hot′test** [OE. *hat*] **1.** *a*) having a high temperature, esp. one that is higher than that of the human body *b*) having a relatively or abnormally high temperature **2.** producing a burning sensation [*hot* pepper] **3.** full of or characterized by any intense feeling or activity, as *a*) impetuous; excitable [*a hot* temper] *b*) violent; angry [*hot* words] *c*) full of enthusiasm; eagerly intent *d*) lustful *e*) very controversial **4.** following closely [*hot* pursuit] **5.** as if heated by friction; specif., *a*) electrically charged [*a hot* wire] *b*) highly radioactive **6.** designating or of a color that suggests heat, as intense red **7.** [Colloq.] that has not yet lost heat, freshness, etc.; specif., *a*) recent; new [*hot* news] *b*) clear; strong [*a hot* scent] *c*) recent and from an inside source [*a hot* tip] **8.** [Slang] *a*) recently stolen *b*) sought by the police **9.** [Slang] excellent, good, etc. **10.** *Jazz* designating or of music or playing having exciting rhythmic and tonal effects, improvisation, etc. —***adv.*** in a hot manner —**hot up** [Slang] to heat or warm up —**make it hot for** [Colloq.] to make things uncomfortable for —**hot′ly *adv.*** —**hot′ness *n.***

hot air [Slang] empty or pretentious talk

hot·bed (-bed′) ***n.*** **1.** a bed of earth covered with glass and heated by manure, for forcing plants **2.** any place that fosters rapid growth

hot-blood·ed (-blud′id) ***adj.*** easily excited; excitable, ardent, passionate, reckless, etc.

hot·box (-bäks′) ***n.*** an overheated bearing on an axle or shaft

hot cake *same as* GRIDDLECAKE —**sell like hot cakes** [Colloq.] to be sold rapidly in large quantities

hot cell a shielded enclosure used in handling radioactive materials by remote control

hot cross bun a bun marked with a cross of frosting, eaten esp. during Lent

hot dog [Colloq.] a wiener, esp. one served in a soft roll

ho·tel (hō tel′) ***n.*** [< Fr. < OFr. *hostel*, HOSTEL] an establishment providing lodging, and often meals, for travelers, semipermanent guests, etc.

ho·tel·ier (hō′tel yā′, -tə lir′) ***n.*** [Fr.] an owner or manager of a hotel

hot·foot (hät′fʊt′) ***adv.*** [Colloq.] in great haste —***vi.*** [Colloq.] to hurry; hasten —***n.**, pl.* **-foots′** the prank of secretly inserting and lighting a match between the sole and upper of a victim's shoe

hot·head (-hed′) ***n.*** a hotheaded person

hot·head·ed (-hed′id) ***adj.*** **1.** quick-tempered **2.** hasty; impetuous —**hot′head′ed·ly *adv.*** —**hot′head′ed·ness *n.***

hot·house (-hous′) ***n.*** a heated building for growing plants; greenhouse —***adj.*** **1.** grown in a hothouse **2.** needing careful treatment; delicate

hot line a telephone or telegraph line for direct, instant communication as in a crisis, esp. between heads of state

hot pepper any of various pungent peppers

hot plate a small gas or electric stove for cooking

hot rod [Slang] **1.** an old automobile adjusted or rebuilt for quick acceleration and high speed **2.** a driver of hot rods: also **hot rod·der** (räd′ər)

hot spring a spring whose water is above 98° F. (36.7° C)

hot-tem·pered (-tem′pərd) ***adj.*** having a fiery temper; easily made angry

Hot·ten·tot (hät′'n tät′) ***n.*** [Afrik.: echoic origin] **1.** a member of a nomadic pastoral people of SW Africa **2.** their language —***adj.*** of the Hottentots or their language

hot war actual warfare: opposed to COLD WAR

hot water [Colloq.] trouble: preceded by *in* or *into*

Hou·din·i (ho͞o dē′nē), **Harry** (born *Ehrich Weiss*) 1874–1926; U.S. stage magician

hound (hound) ***n.*** [OE. *hund*, a dog] **1.** any of several breeds of hunting dogs with long, drooping ears and short hair **2.** any dog **3.** a contemptible person **4.** [Slang] a devotee or fan —***vt.*** **1.** to hunt or chase with or as with hounds [to *hound* a debtor] **2.** to urge on; incite to pursuit —**follow the** (or **ride to**) **hounds** to hunt (a fox, etc.) on horseback with hounds

hounds·tooth check (houndz′to͞oth′) a pattern of irregular broken checks, used in woven material

hour (our) ***n.*** [< OFr. < L. < Gr. *hōra*, hour, time] **1.** a division of time, one of the twenty-four parts of a day; sixty minutes **2.** a point or period of time; specif., *a*) a fixed point or period of time for a particular activity, etc. [the dinner *hour*] *b*) [*pl.*] a period fixed for work, etc. [office *hours*] *c*) [*pl.*] the usual times for getting up or going to bed [to keep late *hours*] **3.** the time of day as indicated by a timepiece **4.** a measure of distance set by the time it takes to travel it **5.** *Astron.* 1/24 of a SIDEREAL DAY **6.** *Eccles. a*) *same as* CANONICAL HOUR *b*) the prayers said at a canonical hour **7.** *Educ.* a class session of about an hour: regarded as a unit of academic credit —**after hours** after the regular hours for business, school, etc. —**hour after hour** every hour —**of the hour** prominent at this time —**the small** (or **wee**) **hours** the hours just after midnight

hour·glass (-glas′) ***n.*** an instrument for measuring time by the trickling of sand, mercury, etc. from one glass bulb to another below it: the shift of contents takes one hour

HOURGLASS

hou·ri (hoor′ē, hou′rē) ***n.**, pl.* **-ris** [Fr. < Per. *hūri* < Ar., ult. < *hawira*, to be dark-eyed] a beautiful nymph of the Moslem Paradise

hour·ly (our′lē) ***adj.*** **1.** done or happening every hour or during an hour **2.** reckoned by the hour [*hourly* wage] **3.** continual —***adv.*** **1.** at or during every hour **2.** at any hour **3.** continually

house (hous; *for v.* houz) ***n.**, pl.* **hous·es** (hou′ziz) [OE. *hus*] **1.** a building for human beings to live in; specif., *a*) the building or part of a building occupied by one family *b*) a building where a group of people live as a unit [a fraternity *house*] **2.** the people who live in a house; family; household **3.** a family as including kin, ancestors, and descendants, esp. a royal family [the *House* of Tudor] **4.** something regarded as a house, in providing shelter; specif., *a*) the habitation of an animal, as the shell of a mollusk *b*) a building where things are kept or stored **5.** *a*) a theater *b*) the audience in a theater **6.** *a*) a place of business *b*) a business firm **7.** the management of a gambling establishment **8.** [*often* **H-**] *a*) the building or rooms where a legislative assembly meets *b*) a legislative assembly **9.** *Astrol.* any of the twelve parts into which the heavens are divided —***vt.* housed** (houzd), **hous′ing 1.** to provide a house or lodgings for **2.** to store in a house **3.** to cover, shelter, etc. as if by putting in a house —***vi.*** **1.** to take shelter **2.** to reside; live —**keep house** to take care of the affairs of a home —**on the house** given free, at the expense of the establishment —**set** (or **put**) **one's house in order** to put one's affairs in order

house·boat (-bōt′) ***n.*** a large, flat-bottomed boat designed for use as a dwelling place

house·break (-brāk′) ***vt.*** **-broke′, -bro′ken, -break′ing** to make housebroken

house·break·ing (-brāk′iŋ) ***n.*** the act of breaking into another's house to commit theft or some other felony —**house′break′er *n.***

house·bro·ken (-brōk′ən) ***adj.*** trained to live in a house (i.e., to void outdoors or in a special place): said of a dog, cat, etc.

house·clean·ing (-klēn′iŋ) ***n.*** **1.** the cleaning of the furniture, floors, etc. of a house **2.** a getting rid of unwanted things —**house′clean′ *vi., vt.***

house·coat (-kōt′) ***n.*** a woman's long, loose garment for casual wear at home

house·dress (-dres′) ***n.*** any fairly cheap dress, as of printed cotton, worn at home for housework

house·fly (-flī′) ***n.**, pl.* **-flies′** a two-winged fly found in and around houses: it feeds on garbage, manure, and food

house·ful (-fool′) ***n.*** as much or as many as a house will hold or provide room for [a *houseful* of guests]

house·hold (-hōld′) ***n.*** **1.** all those living in one house; family, or family and servants **2.** the home and its affairs —***adj.*** **1.** of a household **2.** ordinary

house·hold·er (-hōl′dər) ***n.*** **1.** one who owns or maintains a house **2.** the head of a household

household word a very familiar word or saying

house·keep·er (-kēp′ər) ***n.*** a woman who manages a home, esp. one hired to do so —**house′keep′ing *n.***

house·lights (-līts′) ***n.pl.*** lights that illuminate the part of a theater where the audience sits

house·maid (-mād′) ***n.*** a girl or woman servant who does housework

housemaid's knee an inflammation of the saclike cavity covering the kneecap

house·moth·er (-mu*th*′ər) ***n.*** a woman in charge of a dormitory, sorority house, etc., often as housekeeper

House of Burgesses the lower branch of the colonial legislature of Virginia

house of cards any flimsy structure, plan, etc.

House of Commons the lower branch of the legislature of Great Britain or Canada

house of correction a place of short-term confinement for persons convicted of minor offenses

House of Delegates the lower branch of the legislature of Maryland, Virginia, or West Virginia
House of Lords the upper branch of the legislature of Great Britain, made up of the nobility and high-ranking clergy
House of Representatives the lower branch of the legislature of the U.S., certain other countries, and most of the States of the U.S.
house organ a periodical published by a business firm for its employees, affiliates, etc.
house party the entertainment of guests overnight or over a period of a few days in a home
house physician a resident physician of a hospital, hotel, etc.: also **house doctor**
house-rais·ing (-rā'ziŋ) *n.* a gathering of the members of a rural community to help a neighbor build his house or its framework
house·top (-täp') *n.* the top of a house; roof —**from the housetops** publicly and widely
house·warm·ing (-wôr'miŋ) *n.* a party given by or for someone moving into a new home
house·wife (-wīf'; *for 2, usually* huz'if) *n., pl.* **-wives'** (-wīvz'; *for 2, usually* huz'ivz) **1.** a woman, esp. a married woman, who manages a household **2.** a small sewing kit —**house'wife'ly** *adj., adv.* —**house'wif'er·y** *n.*
house·work (-wurk') *n.* the work involved in housekeeping, such as cleaning, cooking, etc.
hous·ing[1] (hou'ziŋ) *n.* **1.** the act of providing shelter or lodging **2.** shelter or lodging, as in houses, apartments, etc. **3.** houses collectively **4.** a shelter; covering **5.** *Mech.* a frame, box, etc. for containing some part
hous·ing[2] (hou'ziŋ) *n.* [< OFr. *houce* < Frank.] an ornamental covering draped over a horse
Hous·man (hous'mən), **A(lfred) E(dward)** 1859–1936; Eng. poet & classical scholar
Hous·ton (hyōōs'tən) [after ff.] city in SE Tex.: pop. 1,594,000 (met. area 2,891,000)
Hous·ton (hyōōs'tən), **Samuel** 1793–1863; U.S. general & statesman; president of the Republic of Texas (1836–38; 1841–44)
hove (hōv) *alt. pt. & pp. of* HEAVE
hov·el (huv''l, häv'-) *n.* [ME. < ?] **1.** a low, open shed for sheltering animals, storing equipment, etc. **2.** any small, miserable dwelling; hut —*vt.* **-eled** or **-elled, -el·ing** or **-el·ling** to shelter in a hovel
hov·er (huv'ər, häv'-) *vi.* [< ME. freq. of *hoven,* to stay] **1.** to stay suspended or flutter in the air near one place **2.** to linger or wait close by, esp. in a protective way **3.** to be in an uncertain condition; waver —*n.* a hovering —**hov'er·er** *n.*
how (hou) *adv.* [OE. *hu*] **1.** in what manner or way **2.** in what state or condition **3.** for what reason; why **4.** by what name **5.** with what meaning **6.** to what extent, degree, amount, etc. **7.** at what price **8.** [Colloq.] what: usually a request to repeat something said *How* is also used in exclamations and as an intensive —*n.* the way of doing; manner; method —**how about** what is your thought concerning? —**how now?** what is the meaning of this? —**how so?** how is it so?
How·ard (hou'ərd) [< the surname *Howard*] a masculine name
how·be·it (hou bē'it) *adv.* [Archaic] however it may be; nevertheless
how·dah (hou'də) *n.* [Anglo-Ind. < Hindi < Ar. *haudaj*] a canopied seat for riding on the back of an elephant or camel
how·dy (hou'dē) *interj.* [contr. < *how do you (do)?*] [Dial. or Colloq.] an expression of greeting
Howe (hou), **E·li·as** (i lī'əs) 1819–67; U.S. inventor of a sewing machine
How·ells (hou'əlz), **William Dean** (dēn) 1837–1920; U.S. novelist, critic, & editor
how·ev·er (hou ev'ər) *adv.* **1.** no matter how; in whatever manner **2.** to whatever degree or extent **3.** by what means: intensive of HOW **4.** nevertheless; yet: often used as a conjunctive adverb Also [Poet.] **how·e'er'** (-er')
how·itz·er (hou'it sər) *n.* [< Du. < Early ModG. < Czech *haufnice,* orig., a sling] a short cannon, firing shells in a relatively high trajectory
howl (houl) *vi.* [ME. *houlen* < echoic base] **1.** to utter the long, wailing cry of wolves, dogs, etc. **2.** to utter a similar cry of pain, anger, etc. **3.** to make a sound like this *[the wind howls]* **4.** to shout or laugh in scorn, mirth, etc. —*vt.* **1.** to utter with a howl **2.** to drive or effect by howling —*n.* **1.** the long, wailing cry of a wolf, dog, etc. **2.** any similar sound **3.** [Colloq.] something hilarious —**howl down** to drown out with shouts of scorn, etc.
howl·er (houl'ər) *n.* **1.** a person or thing that howls **2.** [Colloq.] a ludicrous blunder
howl·ing (-iŋ) *adj.* **1.** that howls **2.** mournful; dreary **3.** [Slang] great *[a howling success]* —**howl'ing·ly** *adv.*
How·rah (hou'rə) city in NE India, in the Ganges delta, near Calcutta: pop. 513,000
how·so·ev·er (hou'sō ev'ər) *adv.* **1.** to whatever degree or extent **2.** by whatever means
hoy·den (hoid''n) *n.* [< ? Du. *heiden,* heathen] a bold, boisterous girl; tomboy —*adj.* bold and boisterous; tomboyish —*vi.* to behave like a hoyden —**hoy'den·ish** *adj.*
Hoyle (hoil) *n.* a book of rules and instructions for card games, orig. compiled by Edmond Hoyle (1672–1769) —**according to Hoyle** according to the rules and regulations; in a fair way
HP, H.P., hp, h.p. 1. high pressure **2.** horsepower
HQ, H.Q., hq, h.q. headquarters
hr. *pl.* **hrs.** hour; hours
H.R. House of Representatives
h.r., hr, HR home run
H.R.H. His (or Her) Royal Highness
H.S., h.s. high school
HT high tension
ht. 1. heat **2.** *pl.* **hts.** height
hua·ra·ches (hə rä'chēz) *n.pl.* [MexSp.] flat sandals with straps or woven strips for uppers
hub (hub) *n.* [? akin to HOB[1]] **1.** the center part of a wheel, etc. **2.** a center of interest, importance, or activity —**the Hub** Boston
hub·bub (hub'ub') *n.* [prob. < Celt.] a confused sound of many voices; uproar; tumult
hub·by (hub'ē) *n., pl.* **-bies** [Colloq.] a husband
hub·cap (hub'kap') *n.* a tightfitting metal cap for the hub of a wheel, esp. of a car
Hu·bert (hyōō'bərt) [Fr. < OHG. < *hugu,* mind, spirit + *beraht,* bright] a masculine name
hu·bris (hyōō'bris) *n.* [Gr. *hybris*] wanton insolence or arrogance resulting from excessive pride or from passion —**hu·bris'tic** *adj.*
huck·a·back (huk'ə bak') *n.* [< ?] a coarse linen or cotton cloth with a rough surface, used for toweling: also **huck**
huck·le·ber·ry (huk''l ber'ē) *n., pl.* **-ries** [prob. altered < *hurtleberry,* WHORTLEBERRY] **1.** a shrub of the heath family having dark-blue berries with ten large seeds **2.** the fruit of this shrub
huck·ster (huk'stər) *n.* [< MDu. *hoekster* < *hoeken,* to peddle] **1.** a peddler, esp. of fruits, vegetables, etc. **2.** an aggressive or haggling merchant **3.** [Colloq.] a person engaged in advertising or promotion —*vt.* to sell or advertise, esp. in an aggressive way —**huck'ster·ism** *n.*
HUD (Dept. of) Housing and Urban Development
hud·dle (hud''l) *vi.* **-dled, -dling** [? var. of ME. *hoderen,* to cover up] **1.** to crowd close together, as cows do in a storm **2.** to draw or hunch oneself up, as from cold **3.** [Colloq.] to hold a private, informal conference **4.** *Football* to gather in a huddle —*vt.* **1.** to crowd close together **2.** to hunch or draw (oneself) up **3.** to do, put, or make hastily and carelessly **4.** to push in a hurried manner —*n.* **1.** a confused crowd or heap **2.** confusion; jumble **3.** [Colloq.] a private, informal conference **4.** *Football* a grouping of a team behind the line of scrimmage to receive signals before a play
Hud·son (hud's'n) [after ff.] river in E N.Y., flowing southward into the Atlantic at New York City
Hud·son (hud's'n), **Henry** ?–1611; Eng. explorer, esp. of the waters about NE N. America
Hudson Bay inland sea in NE Canada; arm of the Atlantic
Hudson seal muskrat fur treated to resemble seal
hue[1] (hyōō) *n.* [OE. *heow*] **1.** color; esp., the distinctive characteristics of a given color **2.** a particular shade or tint of a given color —**hued** *adj.*
hue[2] (hyōō) *n.* [< OFr. *hu,* a warning cry] a shouting; outcry: now only in **hue and cry,** meaning: *a)* orig., a loud shout or cry by those pursuing a felon *b)* any loud outcry or clamor
huff (huf) *vt.* [prob. echoic] to make angry; offend —*vi.* **1.** to blow; puff **2.** to become angry —*n.* a condition of smoldering anger or resentment
huff·y (-ē) *adj.* **huff'i·er, huff'i·est 1.** easily offended; touchy **2.** angered or offended —**huff'i·ly** *adv.* —**huff'i·ness** *n.*
hug (hug) *vt.* **hugged, hug'ging** [prob. < ON. *hugga,* to comfort] **1.** to put the arms around and hold closely, esp. affectionately **2.** to squeeze tightly with the forelegs, as a bear does **3.** to cling to (a belief, opinion, etc.) **4.** to keep close to *[the bus hugged the curb]* —*vi.* to embrace one another closely —*n.* **1.** a close, fond embrace **2.** a tight hold with the arms, as in wrestling **3.** a bear's squeeze

huge (hyo͞oj, yo͞oj) *adj.* [OFr. *ahuge*] very large; gigantic; immense —**huge′ly** *adv.* —**huge′ness** *n.*

hug·ger·mug·ger (hug′ər mug′ər) *n.* [prob. based on ME. *mokeren,* to conceal] a confusion; muddle; jumble —*adj.* confused; muddled —*adv.* in a confused or jumbled manner

Hugh (hyo͞o) [< OFr. < OHG. *Hugo,* prob. < *hugu,* heart, mind] a masculine name

Hughes (hyo͞oz), **Charles Ev·ans** (ev′ənz) 1862–1948; U.S. jurist; chief justice of the U.S. (1930–41)

Hu·go (hyo͞o′gō) **1.** [var. of HUGH] a masculine name **2.** (*also Fr.* ü gō′) **Vic·tor Ma·rie** (vēk tôr′ mȧ rē′) 1802–85; Fr. poet, novelist, & playwright

Hu·gue·not (hyo͞o′gə nät′) *n.* [MFr. < G. *eidgenosse,* confederate] any French Protestant of the 16th or 17th century

huh (hu, hu*n*) *interj.* an exclamation used to express contempt, surprise, etc., or to ask a question

hu·la (ho͞o′lə) *n.* [Haw.] a native Hawaiian dance marked by flowing gestures: also **hu′la-hu′la**

hulk (hulk) *n.* [OE. *hulc*] **1.** a big, unwieldy ship **2.** the body of a ship, esp. if old and dismantled **3.** a deserted wreck or ruins **4.** a big, clumsy person or thing —*vi.* to loom bulkily

hulk·ing (hul′kiŋ) *adj.* large, heavy, and often unwieldy or clumsy: also **hulk′y** (-kē)

Hull (hul) **1.** seaport in NE England: pop. 295,000: officially *Kingston upon Hull* **2.** city in SW Quebec, Canada, near Ottawa: pop. 60,000

hull¹ (hul) *n.* [OE. *hulu*] **1.** the outer covering of a seed or fruit, as the husk of grain, shell of nuts, etc. **2.** the calyx of some fruits, as the strawberry **3.** any outer covering —*vt.* to take the hull or hulls off —**hull′er** *n.*

hull² (hul) *n.* [special use of prec., prob. infl. by Du. *hol,* ship's hold] **1.** the frame or body of a ship, excluding the masts, sails, rigging, superstructure, etc. **2.** *a)* the main body of an airship *b)* the frame or main body of a flying boat, amphibian, hydrofoil, etc. —*vt.* to pierce the hull of (a ship) with a torpedo, etc.

hul·la·ba·loo (hul′ə bə lo͞o′) *n.* [echoic, based on ff.] a clamor or hubbub

hul·lo (hə lō′) *interj., n., vt., vi. same as:* **1.** HOLLO **2.** HELLO

hum¹ (hum) *vi.* **hummed, hum′ming** [echoic] **1.** to make the low, murmuring sound of a bee, a motor, etc. **2.** to sing with the lips closed, not producing words **3.** to give forth a confused, droning sound [the room *hummed* with voices] **4.** [Colloq.] to be full of activity —*vt.* **1.** to sing (a tune, etc.) with the lips closed **2.** to produce an effect on by humming [to *hum* a child to sleep] —*n.* the act or sound of humming —**hum′mer** *n.*

hum² (həm: *conventionalized pronun.*) *interj., n. same as:* **1.** HEM² **2.** HUMPH —*vi.* **hummed, hum′ming** *same as* HEM²

hu·man (hyo͞o′mən, yo͞o′-) *adj.* [< OFr. < L. *humanus*] **1.** of, belonging to, or typical of mankind [the *human* race] **2.** consisting of or produced by men [*human* society] **3.** having or showing qualities characteristic of people [*human* values] —*n.* a person: the phrase **human being** is still preferred by some —**hu′man·ness** *n.*

hu·mane (hyo͞o mān′, hyoo-, yo͞o-) *adj.* [earlier var. of prec.] **1.** kind, tender, merciful, sympathetic, etc. **2.** civilizing; humanizing [*humane* learning] —**hu·mane′ly** *adv.* —**hu·mane′ness** *n.*

hu·man·ism (hyo͞o′mə niz′m, yo͞o′-) *n.* **1.** the quality of being human; human nature **2.** any system of thought or action based on the nature, dignity, and ideals of man; specif., a rationalist movement that holds that man can be ethical, find self-fulfillment, etc. without recourse to supernaturalism **3.** the study of the humanities **4.** [H-] the intellectual and cultural secular movement that stemmed from the study of classical Greek and Roman culture in the Middle Ages and helped give rise to the Renaissance —**hu′man·ist** *n., adj.* —**hu′man·is′tic** *adj.* —**hu′man·is′ti·cal·ly** *adv.*

hu·man·i·tar·i·an (hyo͞o man′ə ter′ē ən, hyoo-, yo͞o-) *n.* a person devoted to promoting the welfare of humanity; philanthropist —*adj.* helping humanity —**hu·man′i·tar′i·an·ism** *n.*

hu·man·i·ty (hyo͞o man′ə tē, hyoo-, yo͞o-) *n., pl.* **-ties** **1.** the fact or quality of being human; human nature **2.** the human race; mankind; people **3.** the fact or quality of being humane; kindness, mercy, sympathy, etc. —**the humanities** **1.** languages and literature, esp. classical Greek and Latin **2.** the branches of learning concerned with human thought and relations; esp., literature, philosophy, the fine arts, history, etc.

hu·man·ize (hyo͞o′mə nīz′, yo͞o′-) *vt., vi.* **-ized′, -iz′ing** **1.** to make or become human **2.** to make or become humane —**hu′man·i·za′tion** *n.* —**hu′man·iz′er** *n.*

hu·man·kind (hyo͞o′mən kīnd′, yo͞o′-) *n.* the human race; mankind; people

hu·man·ly (-lē) *adv.* **1.** in a human manner **2.** by human means **3.** from a human viewpoint

hu·man·oid (-oid′) *adj.* nearly human —*n.* a nearly human creature; specif., *a)* any of the earliest ancestors of modern man *b)* in science fiction, a reasoning creature of another planet

hum·ble (hum′b'l, um′-) *adj.* **-bler, -blest** [OFr. < L. *humilis,* low, akin to *humus,* earth] **1.** having or showing a consciousness of one's defects or shortcomings; not proud **2.** low in condition or rank; lowly; unpretentious —*vt.* **-bled, -bling** **1.** to lower in condition or rank; abase **2.** to make modest or humble in mind —**hum′ble·ness** *n.* —**hum′bler** *n.* —**hum′bly** *adv.*

humble pie [< *umbles,* entrails of a deer < OFr. *nombles* < L. < *lumbus,* loin] formerly, a pie made of the inner parts of a deer, served to the servants after a hunt —**eat humble pie** to undergo humiliation, as by admitting one's error

hum·bug (hum′bug′) *n.* [< ?] **1.** *a)* a fraud; sham *b)* misleading or empty talk **2.** a person who is not what he claims to be **3.** a spirit of trickery, deception, etc. —*vt.* **-bugged′, -bug′ging** to dupe; deceive; hoax —*interj.* nonsense! —**hum′bug′ger** *n.* —**hum′bug′ger·y** *n.*

hum·ding·er (hum′diŋ′ər) *n.* [Slang] a person or thing considered excellent of its kind

hum·drum (hum′drum′) *adj.* lacking variety; dull; monotonous —*n.* humdrum talk, routine, etc.

Hume (hyo͞om), **David** 1711–76; Scot. philosopher & historian

hu·mec·tant (hyo͞o mek′tənt) *n.* [< L. prp. of *humectare,* ult. < *umere,* to be moist] a substance, as glycerol, added or applied to another to help it retain moisture

hu·mer·us (hyo͞o′mər əs) *n., pl.* **-mer·i′** (-ī′) [L. *humerus, umerus,* the upper arm] the bone of the upper arm or forelimb, from the shoulder to the elbow —**hu′mer·al** *adj.*

hu·mid (hyo͞o′mid, yo͞o′-) *adj.* [< Fr. < L. *humidus,* ult. < *umere,* to be moist] full of water vapor; damp; moist —**hu′mid·ly** *adv.*

hu·mid·i·fy (hyo͞o mid′ə fī′, yo͞o-) *vt.* **-fied′, -fy′ing** to make humid; moisten; dampen —**hu·mid′i·fi·ca′tion** *n.* —**hu·mid′i·fi′er** *n.*

hu·mid·i·ty (-tē) *n., pl.* **-ties** **1.** moistness; dampness **2.** the amount of moisture in the air —**relative humidity** the ratio of the amount of moisture in the air to the maximum amount that the air could contain at the same temperature, stated as a percentage

hu·mi·dor (hyo͞o′mə dôr′, yo͞o′-) *n.* a jar, case, etc. with a device for keeping tobacco, etc. moist

hu·mil·i·ate (hyo͞o mil′ē āt′, hyoo-, yo͞o-) *vt.* **-at′ed, -at′ing** [< L. pp. of *humiliare* < L. *humilis,* HUMBLE] to hurt the pride or dignity of by causing to seem foolish, etc.; mortify —**hu·mil′i·a′tion** *n.*

hu·mil·i·ty (hyo͞o mil′ə tē) *n.* [< OFr. < L. *humilitas*] the state or quality of being humble; absence of pride

hum·ming·bird (hum′iŋ burd′) *n.* any of a family of very small, brightly colored birds with a long, slender bill and narrow wings that vibrate rapidly, with a humming sound

hum·mock (hum′ək) *n.* [orig. naut. < ?] **1.** a low, rounded hill; knoll **2.** a ridge or rise in an ice field **3.** a tract of wooded land, higher than a surrounding marshy area

hu·mon·gous (hyo͞o mäŋ′gəs, -muŋ′-) *adj.* [? blend of HUGE, MONSTROUS, & TREMENDOUS] [Slang] very large or great

hu·mor (hyo͞o′mər, yo͞o′-) *n.* [< OFr. < L. *humor, umor,* moisture, fluid] **1.** formerly, any of the four fluids (**cardinal humors**) considered responsible for one's health and disposition; blood, phlegm, choler (yellow bile), or melancholy (black bile) **2.** *a)* a person's temperament *b)* a mood; state of mind **3.** whim; fancy; caprice **4.** comic or amusing quality **5.** *a)* the ability to appreciate or express what is funny, amusing, or ludicrous *b)* the expression of this in speech, writing, or action **6.** any fluid or fluidlike substance of the body [the aqueous *humor*] —*vt.* **1.** to comply with the mood or whim of (another); indulge **2.** to adapt oneself to —**out of humor** cross; disagreeable —**hu′mor·less** *adj.*

hu·mor·esque (hyo͞o′mə resk′) *n.* [G. *humoreske*] a light, fanciful or playful musical composition

hu·mor·ist (hyo͞o′mər ist, yo͞o′-) *n.* **1.** a person with a good sense of humor **2.** a professional writer or teller of amusing stories, jokes, etc.

hu·mor·ous (-əs) *adj.* having or expressing humor; funny; amusing; comical —**hu′mor·ous·ly** *adv.*

hu·mour (hyo͞o′mər, yo͞o′-) *n., vt. Brit. sp. of* HUMOR

hump (hump) *n.* [< or akin to LowG. *humpe,* thick piece] **1.** a rounded, protruding lump, as the fleshy mass on the back of a camel: in man, a hump is caused by a deformity of the spine **2.** a hummock; mound —*vt.* to hunch; arch [the cat *humped* its back] —*vi.* [Slang] **1.** to exert oneself **2.** to hurry —**over the hump** [Colloq.] over the worst part —**humped** *adj.* —**hump′y** *adj.* **-i·er, -i·est**

hump·back (-bak′) *n.* **1.** a humped, deformed back **2.** a person having a humped back; hunchback **3.** a large whale having long flippers and a dorsal fin resembling a hump-back —**hump′backed′** *adj.*

humph (humf: *conventionalized pronun.*) *interj., n.* a snorting or grunting sound expressing doubt, surprise, disdain, disgust, etc.
Hum·phrey (hum′frē) [OE. *Hunfrith,* lit., strength in peace] a masculine name: also sp. **Hum′phry**
Hump·ty Dump·ty (hump′tē dump′tē) the personification of an egg in an old nursery rhyme
hu·mus (hyōō′məs, yōō′-) *n.* [L., earth] the brown or black organic part of the soil, resulting from the partial decay of plant and animal matter
Hun (hun) *n.* **1.** a member of a warlike Asiatic people who invaded eastern and central Europe in the 4th and 5th centuries A.D. **2.** [*often* **h-**] any savage or destructive person; vandal
hunch (hunch) *vt.* [< ?] to draw (one's body, etc.) up so as to form a hump *—vi.* **1.** to push oneself forward jerkily **2.** to sit or stand with the back arched *—n.* **1.** a hump **2.** a chunk; hunk **3.** [Colloq.] a premonition or suspicion
hunch·back (-bak′) *n. same as* HUMPBACK (senses 1, 2) **—hunch′backed′** *adj.*
hun·dred (hun′drid, -dərd) *n.* [OE.] **1.** the cardinal number next above ninety-nine; ten times ten; 100; C **2.** a division of an English county *—adj.* ten times ten
hun·dred·fold (-fōld′) *adj.* [see -FOLD] having a hundred times as much or as many *—adv.* a hundred times as much or as many
hun·dredth (hun′dridth) *adj.* **1.** preceded by ninety-nine others in a series; 100th **2.** designating any of the hundred equal parts of something *—n.* **1.** the one following the ninety-ninth **2.** any of the hundred equal parts of something; 1/100
hun·dred·weight (hun′drid wāt′, -dərd-) *n.* a unit of weight equal to 100 pounds in the U.S. and 112 pounds in England: abbrev. **cwt.**
hung (huŋ) *pt. & pp. of* HANG **—hung up (on)** [Slang] **1.** emotionally disturbed (by) **2.** baffled, frustrated, etc. (by) **3.** addicted (to); obsessed (by)
Hung. 1. Hungarian **2.** Hungary
Hun·gar·i·an (huŋ ger′ē ən) *adj.* of Hungary, its people, their language, or culture *—n.* **1.** a native or inhabitant of Hungary **2.** the Finno-Ugric language of the Hungarians; Magyar
Hun·ga·ry (huŋ′gər ē) country in SC Europe: 35,919 sq. mi.; pop. 10,331,000; cap. Budapest
hun·ger (huŋ′gər) *n.* [OE. *hungor*] **1.** *a)* the discomfort, pain, or weakness caused by a need for food *b)* famine; starvation **2.** a need or appetite for food **3.** any strong desire; craving *—vi.* **1.** to be hungry **2.** to crave; long (with *for* or *after*)
hunger strike a refusal, as of a prisoner, to eat until certain demands are granted
hun·gry (huŋ′grē) *adj.* **-gri·er, -gri·est 1.** feeling or showing hunger; specif., *a)* wanting or needing food *b)* craving; eager *[hungry* for praise*]* **2.** not fertile; barren: said of soil **—hun′gri·ly** *adv.* **—hun′gri·ness** *n.*
hunk (huŋk) *n.* [Fl. *hunke,* hunk] [Colloq.] a large piece, lump, or slice of bread, meat, etc.
hun·ker (huŋ′kər) *vi.* [prob. < or akin to ON. *hokra,* to creep] to settle down on one's haunches; squat or crouch *—n.* [*pl.*] haunches
hun·ky-do·ry (huŋ′kē dôr′ē) *adj.* [Slang] all right; satisfactory; fine
hunt (hunt) *vt.* [OE. *huntian*] **1.** to go out to kill or catch (game) for food or sport **2.** to search carefully for; try to find **3.** *a)* to chase; drive *b)* to hound; harry **4.** *a)* to go through (a woods, etc.) in pursuit of game *b)* to search (a place) carefully **5.** to use (dogs or horses) in chasing game *—vi.* **1.** to go out after game **2.** to search; seek *—n.* **1.** a hunting **2.** a group of people who hunt together **3.** a district covered in hunting **4.** a search
Hunt (hunt) **1. (James Henry) Leigh** (lē), 1784–1859; Eng. poet, critic, & essayist **2. (William) Hol·man** (hōl′mən), 1827–1910; Eng. painter
hunt·er (-ər) *n.* **1.** a person who hunts **2.** a horse or dog trained for hunting
hunt·ing (-iŋ) *n.* the act of a person or animal that hunts *—adj.* of or for hunting
Hun·ting·ton (hun′tiŋ tən) [after C.P. *Huntington* (1821–1900), its founder] city in W W.Va., on the Ohio: pop. 64,000
Huntington Beach [after H. *Huntington,* U.S. railroad executive] city in SW Calif.: suburb of Los Angeles: pop. 171,000
hunt·ress (hun′tris) *n.* a woman who hunts
hunts·man (hunts′mən) *n., pl.* **-men 1.** a hunter **2.** the manager of a hunt
Hunts·ville (hunts′vil′) [after J. *Hunt,* its 1st settler (1805)] city in N Ala.: pop. 143,000

hur·dle (hʉr′d'l) *n.* [OE. *hyrdel*] **1.** [Brit.] a portable frame of interlaced twigs, etc., used as a temporary fence **2.** any of a series of framelike barriers over which horses or runners must leap in a race (the **hurdles**) **3.** a difficulty to be overcome; obstacle *—vt.* **-dled, -dling 1.** to fence off with hurdles **2.** to jump over (a barrier), as in a race **3.** to overcome (an obstacle) **—hur′dler** *n.*

HURDLES

hur·dy-gur·dy (hʉr′dē gʉr′dē) *n., pl.* **-gur′dies** [prob. echoic] **1.** an early, lutelike instrument played by turning a crank **2.** *same as* BARREL ORGAN
hurl (hʉrl) *vt.* [prob. < ON.] **1.** to throw with force or violence **2.** to cast down; overthrow **3.** to utter vehemently **4.** [Colloq.] *Baseball* to pitch *—vi.* **1.** to throw or fling something **2.** to rush *—n.* a violent throw **—hurl′er** *n.*
hurl·y-burl·y (hʉr′lē bʉr′lē) *n., pl.* **-burl′ies** a turmoil; uproar *—adj.* disorderly and confused
Hu·ron (hyoor′ən, -än) *n.* [Fr., ruffian] **1.** *pl.* **-rons, -ron** a member of a confederation of Indian tribes that lived east of Lake Huron and now live in Oklahoma and Quebec **2.** their Iroquoian language
Huron, Lake second largest of the Great Lakes, between Mich. & Ontario, Canada: 24,328 sq. mi.; 247 mi. long
hur·rah (hə rô′, -rä′) *interj.* [ult. echoic] a shout of joy, approval, etc. *—n.* **1.** a shouting of "hurrah" **2.** excitement, commotion, etc. *—vi., vt.* to cheer; shout "hurrah" (for) Also **hur·ray′** (-rā′)
hur·ri·cane (hʉr′ə kān′, -kən) *n.* [< Sp. < WInd. *huracan*] a violent tropical cyclone with winds of 73 or more miles per hour, often with torrential rains, and originating usually in the West Indies
hurricane lamp 1. an oil lamp or candlestick with a tall glass chimney to keep the flame from being blown out **2.** an electric lamp in imitation of this
hur·ried (hʉr′ēd) *adj.* in a hurry; rushed or rushing **—hur′ried·ly** *adv.* **—hur′ried·ness** *n.*
hur·ry (hʉr′ē) *vt.* **-ried, -ry·ing** [prob. akin to HURL] **1.** to move, send, or carry with haste **2.** to cause to occur or be done more rapidly or too rapidly **3.** to urge or cause to act soon or too soon *—vi.* to move or act with haste *—n.* **1.** a rush; urgency **2.** eagerness to do, act, go, etc. quickly **—hur′ri·er** *n.*
hur·ry-scur·ry, hur·ry-skur·ry (-skʉr′ē) *n.* a disorderly confusion *—vi.* **-ried, -ry·ing** to hurry and scurry about *—adj.* hurried and confused *—adv.* in a hurried, confused manner
hurt (hʉrt) *vt.* **hurt, hurt′ing** [OFr. *hurter,* to push, hit, prob. < Frank.] **1.** to cause pain or injury to; wound **2.** to harm or damage in any way **3.** to offend or distress *—vi.* **1.** to cause injury, damage, or pain **2.** to give or have the sensation of pain; be sore *—n.* **1.** a pain or injury **2.** harm or damage **3.** something that wounds the feelings *—adj.* damaged *[hurt* books*]* **—hurt′er** *n.*
hurt·ful (-fəl) *adj.* causing hurt; harmful **—hurt′ful·ly** *adv.* **—hurt′ful·ness** *n.*
hur·tle (hʉrt′'l) *vi.* **-tled, -tling** [< freq. of ME. *hurten,* HURT] **1.** orig., to crash; collide **2.** to move swiftly and with great force *—vt.* to throw, shoot, or fling with great force; hurl
hus·band (huz′bənd) *n.* [Late OE. *husbonda* < ON. < *hūs,* house + *bondi,* freeholder] a married man *—vt.* to manage economically; conserve
hus·band·man (-mən) *n., pl.* **-men** [Archaic] a farmer
hus·band·ry (huz′bən drē) *n.* **1.** orig., management of domestic affairs, resources, etc. **2.** careful, thrifty management **3.** farming
hush (hush) *vt.* [< ME. < *huscht,* quiet] **1.** to make quiet or silent **2.** to soothe; lull *—vi.* to be or become quiet or silent *—n.* quiet; silence *—interj.* an exclamation calling for silence **—hush up 1.** to keep quiet **2.** to keep secret; suppress
hush-hush (hush′hush′) *adj.* [Colloq.] very secret; most confidential
hush money money paid to a person to keep him from telling something
hush puppy [< ?] in the southern U.S., a small, fried ball of cornmeal dough
husk (husk) *n.* [prob. < MDu. *huuskijn,* dim. of *huus,* a house] **1.** the dry outer covering of various fruits or seeds, as of an ear of corn **2.** the dry, rough, or useless outside covering of anything *—vt.* to remove the husk from **—husk′er** *n.*
husk·ing (bee) (hus′kiŋ) *same as* CORNHUSKING

hus·ky¹ (hus′kē) ***n.,*** *pl.* **-kies** [altered < ? ESKIMO] [*sometimes* **H-**] a hardy dog used for pulling sleds in the Arctic
husk·y² (hus′kē) ***adj.*** **husk′i·er, husk′i·est** **1.** *a)* full of or consisting of husks *b)* like a husk **2.** sounding deep and hoarse **3.** big and strong; robust —***n.,*** *pl.* **husk′ies** a husky person —**husk′i·ly** ***adv.*** —**husk′i·ness** ***n.***
Huss (hus), **John** 1369?–1415; Bohemian religious reformer & martyr, burned as a heretic: Czech name **Jan Hus** (yän hoos) —**Huss′ite** (-īt) ***n., adj.***
hus·sar (hoo zär′, hə-) ***n.*** [< Hung. < Serb. *husar* < L. *cursus:* see CORSAIR] a member of any European regiment of light-armed cavalry, usually with brilliant dress uniforms
hus·sy (huz′ē, hus′-) ***n.,*** *pl.* **-sies** [contr. < ME. *huswife,* housewife] **1.** a woman, esp. one of low morals **2.** a bold, saucy girl; minx
hus·tings (hus′tiŋz) ***n.pl.*** [*usually with sing. v.*] [OE. < ON. < *hūs,* a house + *thing,* assembly] **1.** the proceedings at an election **2.** the route followed by a political campaigner
hus·tle (hus′'l) ***vt.*** **-tled, -tling** [Du. *hutseln,* to shake up] **1.** to push about; jostle in a rude, rough manner **2.** to force in a rough, hurried manner *[he hustled them into the bus]* **3.** [Colloq.] to hurry (a person, a job, etc.) **4.** [Slang] to get, victimize, etc. by aggressive tactics —***vi.*** **1.** to move hurriedly **2.** [Colloq.] to work or act rapidly or energetically **3.** [Slang] *a)* to obtain money by aggressive or dishonest means *b)* to work as a prostitute —***n.*** **1.** a hustling **2.** [Colloq.] energetic action; drive —**hus′tler** ***n.***
hut (hut) ***n.*** [< Fr. < MHG. < OHG. *hutta*] a little house or cabin of the plainest or crudest kind —***vt., vi.*** **hut′ted, hut′ting** to shelter or be sheltered in or as in a hut
hutch (huch) ***n.*** [OFr. *huche,* bin < ML. *hutica,* a chest] **1.** a bin, chest, or box for storage **2.** a china cabinet with open shelves on top **3.** a pen or coop for small animals **4.** a hut
Hux·ley (huks′lē) **1. Al·dous (Leonard)** (ôl′dəs), 1894–1963; Eng. novelist & essayist **2.** Sir **Julian (Sorrell)**, 1887–1975; Eng. biologist & writer: brother of *prec.* **3. Thomas Henry,** 1825–95; Eng. biologist & writer: grandfather of *Aldous & Julian*
huz·zah, huz·za (hə zä′) ***interj., n., vi., vt.*** [echoic] *former var. of* HURRAH
H.V., HV, h.v., hv high voltage
Hwang Ho (hwäŋ′ hō′) river in N China, flowing from Tibet into the Yellow Sea: c. 2,900 mi.
hwy. highway
hy·a·cinth (hī′ə sinth′) ***n.*** [< L. < Gr. *hyakinthos*] **1.** *a)* among the ancients, a blue gem *b)* a reddish-orange or brownish gem **2.** a plant of the lily family, with spikes of fragrant, bell-shaped flowers **3.** a bluish purple —**hy′a·cin′thine** (-sin′thin, -thīn) ***adj.***
hy·ae·na (hī ē′nə) ***n.*** *same as* HYENA
hy·a·line (hī′ə lin, -līn′) ***adj.*** [< LL. < Gr. < *hyalos,* glass] transparent as glass; glassy: also **hy′a·loid′** (-loid′) —***n.*** anything transparent or glassy
hy·a·lite (hī′ə līt′) ***n.*** [< Gr. *hyalos,* glass + -ITE] a colorless variety of opal
hy·brid (hī′brid) ***n.*** [L. *hybrida,* offspring of mixed parentage] **1.** the offspring of two animals or plants of different species, etc. **2.** anything of mixed origin, unlike parts, etc. **3.** *Linguis.* a word made up of elements from different languages —***adj.*** of, or having the nature of, a hybrid —**hy′brid·ism, hy·brid′i·ty** ***n.***
hy·brid·ize (hī′brə dīz′) ***vi., vt.*** **-ized′, -iz′ing** to produce or cause to produce hybrids; crossbreed —**hy′brid·i·za′tion** ***n.*** —**hy′brid·iz′er** ***n.***
Hyde Park (hīd) **1.** public park in London **2.** village in SE N.Y.: site of the estate & burial place of F.D. Roosevelt
Hy·der·a·bad (hī′dər ə bad′, -bäd′; hī′drə-) city in SC India: pop. 1,119,000
hydr- *same as* HYDRO-: used before vowels
Hy·dra (hī′drə) [< OFr. *ydre* < L. < Gr. *hydra,* water serpent] *Gr. Myth.* the nine-headed serpent slain by Hercules: each head grew back double when cut off —***n.,*** *pl.* **-dras, -drae** (-drē) [**h-**] **1.** any persistent or ever-increasing evil **2.** a small freshwater polyp with a soft, tubelike body and a mouth surrounded by tentacles
hy·dran·ge·a (hī drān′jə, -dran′-; -jē ə) ***n.*** [ModL. < HYDR- + Gr. *angeion,* vessel] a shrubby plant, with opposite leaves and large, showy clusters of white, blue, or pink flowers
hy·drant (hī′drənt) ***n.*** [< Gr. *hydōr,* water] **1.** a large discharge pipe with a valve for drawing water from a water main; fireplug **2.** [Dial.] a faucet
hy·drate (hī′drāt) ***n.*** [HYDR- + -ATE¹] a compound formed by the chemical combination of water and some other substance *[plaster of Paris,* $2CaSO_4 \cdot H_2O$, *is a hydrate]* —***vi., vt.*** **-drat·ed, -drat·ing** **1.** to become or cause to become a hydrate **2.** to combine with water —**hy·dra′tion** ***n.*** —**hy′dra·tor** ***n.***
hy·drau·lic (hī drô′lik, -drä′-) ***adj.*** [< Fr. < L. < Gr. *hydraulikos;* ult. < *hydōr,* water + *aulos,* tube] **1.** of hydraulics **2.** operated by the movement and pressure of liquid, esp. of a liquid forced through an aperture, etc. *[hydraulic brakes]* **3.** setting or hardening under water *[hydraulic mortar]* —**hy·drau′li·cal·ly** ***adv.***

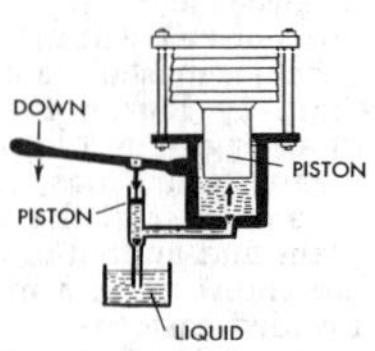

HYDRAULIC PRESS

hydraulic ram a device to move a flowing liquid up by using the momentum of the flowing liquid
hy·drau·lics (-liks) ***n.pl.*** [*with sing. v.*] the branch of physics having to do with the mechanical properties of water and other liquids in motion and their application in engineering
hy·dra·zine (hī′drə zēn′, -zin) ***n.*** [HYDR- + AZ(O) + -INE⁴] a colorless liquid base, NH_2NH_2, used as a jet and rocket fuel
hy·dric (hī′drik) ***adj.*** [HYDR- + -IC] of or containing hydrogen
hy·dride (hī′drīd) ***n.*** [HYDR- + -IDE] a compound of hydrogen with another element or a radical
hy·dro- [< Gr. *hydōr,* water] *a combining form meaning:* **1.** water *[hydrometer]* **2.** containing hydrogen *[hydrocyanic]*
hy·dro·car·bon (hī′drə kär′bən) ***n.*** any compound, as benzene, containing only hydrogen and carbon
hy·dro·ceph·a·lus (hī′drə sef′ə ləs) ***n.*** [ModL. < Gr. < *hydōr,* water + *kephalē,* head] a condition characterized by an abnormal amount of fluid in the cranium, causing enlargement of the head: also **hy′dro·ceph′a·ly** (-lē) —**hy′dro·ce·phal′ic** (-sə fal′ik) ***adj., n.*** —**hy′dro·ceph′a·lous** ***adj.***
hy·dro·chlo·ric acid (hī′drə klôr′ik) [HYDRO- + CHLORIC] a strong, corrosive acid, HCl, that is a solution of the gas hydrogen chloride in water
hy·dro·cy·an·ic acid (-sī an′ik) [HYDRO- + CYANIC] a weak, highly poisonous acid, HCN, a colorless liquid with the odor of bitter almonds
hy·dro·dy·nam·ics (-dī nam′iks) ***n.pl.*** [*with sing. v.*] the branch of physics dealing with the motion and action of water and other liquids —**hy′dro·dy·nam′ic** ***adj.*** —**hy′dro·dy·nam′i·cal·ly** ***adv.***
hy·dro·e·lec·tric (-i lek′trik) ***adj.*** producing, or relating to the production of, electricity by water power —**hy′dro·e·lec′tric′i·ty** ***n.***
hy·dro·fluor·ic acid (hī′drə flôr′ik, -floor′-) [HYDRO- + FLUOR(INE) + -IC] an acid, HF, existing as a colorless, fuming, corrosive liquid: it is used in etching glass
hy·dro·foil (hī′drə foil′) ***n.*** [HYDRO- + (AIR)FOIL] **1.** a winglike structure on the hull of some watercraft: at high speeds the craft skims along on the hydrofoils **2.** a craft with hydrofoils
hy·dro·gen (hī′drə jən) ***n.*** [< Fr.: see HYDRO- & -GEN] a flammable, colorless, odorless, gaseous chemical element, the lightest of all known substances: symbol, H; at. wt., 1.00797; at. no., 1 —**hy·drog·e·nous** (hī dräj′ə nəs) ***adj.***
hy·dro·gen·ate (hī′drə jə nāt′, hī dräj′ə-) ***vt.*** **-at′ed, -at′ing** to combine or treat with hydrogen, as in making a solid fat of oil —**hy′dro·gen·a′tion** ***n.***
hydrogen bomb a highly destructive nuclear bomb, in which the atoms of heavy isotopes of hydrogen are fused by explosion of a nuclear-fission unit in the bomb
hydrogen ion the positively charged ion in all acids: symbol, H^+
hydrogen peroxide an unstable liquid, H_2O_2, often used, diluted, as a bleach or disinfectant, and in more concentrated form as a rocket fuel
hydrogen sulfide a gaseous compound, H_2S, with the characteristic odor of rotten eggs
hy·drog·ra·phy (hī dräg′rə fē) ***n.*** [< Fr.: see HYDRO- & -GRAPHY] the study, description, and mapping of oceans, lakes, and rivers —**hy·drog′ra·pher** ***n.*** —**hy·dro·graph·ic** (hī′drə graf′ik), **hy′dro·graph′i·cal** ***adj.***
hy·droid (hī′droid) ***adj.*** [HYDR(A) + -OID] **1.** like a hydra or polyp **2.** of or related to the group of hydrozoans of which the hydra is a member —***n.*** any member of a group of hydrozoans, mostly marine, typically consisting of polyps
hy·drol·y·sis (hī dräl′ə sis) ***n.,*** *pl.* **-ses′** (-sēz′) [HYDRO- + -LYSIS] the breaking up of a substance, often in the presence of a catalyst, into other substances by reaction with water, as a starch into glucose, natural fats into glycerol and fatty acids, etc. —**hy·dro·lyt·ic** (hī′drə lit′ik) ***adj.***
hy·dro·lyte (hī′drə līt′) ***n.*** any substance undergoing hydrolysis
hy·dro·lyze (-līz′) ***vt., vi.*** **-lyzed′, -lyz′ing** to undergo or cause to undergo hydrolysis —**hy′dro·lyz′a·ble** ***adj.***
hy·drom·e·ter (hī dräm′ə tər) ***n.*** [HYDRO- + -METER] an instrument consisting of a graduated, weighted tube, used

for measuring the specific gravity of liquids —**hy·dro·met·ric** (hī′drə met′rik), **hy′dro·met′ri·cal** ***adj.*** —**hy·drom′e·try** ***n.***
hy·drop·a·thy (hī dräp′ə thē) ***n.*** [HYDRO- + -PATHY] a system of treating all diseases by the external or internal use of water —**hy·dro·path·ic** (hī′drə path′ik) ***adj.*** —**hy·drop′a·thist** ***n.***
hy·dro·pho·bi·a (hī′drə fō′bē ə) ***n.*** [LL. < Gr.: see HYDRO- & -PHOBIA] **1.** an abnormal fear of water **2.** [from the symptomatic inability to swallow liquids] *same as* RABIES —**hy′dro·pho′bic** ***adj.***
hy·dro·phyte (hī′drə fīt′) ***n.*** [HYDRO- + -PHYTE] any plant growing only in water or very wet earth —**hy′dro·phyt′ic** (-fit′ik) ***adj.***
hy·dro·plane (-plān′) ***n.*** [HYDRO- + PLANE[4]] **1.** a small, light motorboat with hydrofoils or with a flat bottom that can skim along the water at high speeds **2.** *same as* SEAPLANE —***vi.*** **-planed′**, **-plan′ing** to drive or ride in a hydroplane
hy·dro·pon·ics (hī′drə pän′iks) ***n.pl.*** [*with sing. v.*] [< HYDRO- + Gr. *ponos*, labor + -ICS] the cultivation of plants in solutions, or moist inert material, containing minerals, instead of in soil —**hy′dro·pon′ic** ***adj.*** —**hy′dro·pon′i·cal·ly** ***adv.***
hy·dro·pow·er (hī′drə pou′ər) ***n.*** hydroelectric power
hy·dro·sphere (-sfir′) ***n.*** [HYDRO- + -SPHERE] **1.** all the water on the surface of the earth **2.** the moisture in the atmosphere surrounding the earth
hy·dro·stat·ics (hī′drə stat′iks) ***n.pl.*** [*with sing. v.*] [< Fr.: see HYDRO- & STATIC] the branch of physics having to do with the pressure and equilibrium of water and other liquids —**hy′dro·stat′ic**, **hy′dro·stat′i·cal** ***adj.*** —**hy′dro·stat′i·cal·ly** ***adv.***
hy·dro·ther·a·peu·tics (hī′drō ther′ə pyōōt′iks) ***n.pl.*** [*with sing. v.*] *same as* HYDROTHERAPY —**hy′dro·ther′a·peu′tic** ***adj.***
hy·dro·ther·a·py (-ther′ə pē) ***n.*** [HYDRO- + THERAPY] the treatment of disease, esp. in physical therapy, by the use of baths, compresses, etc.
hy·drot·ro·pism (hī drät′rə piz′m) ***n.*** [HYDRO- + -TROPISM] movement or growth, as of a plant root, in response to the stimulus of moisture —**hy·dro·trop·ic** (hī′drə-träp′ik) ***adj.***
hy·drous (hī′drəs) ***adj.*** [HYDR- + -OUS] containing water, as certain chemical compounds
hy·drox·ide (hī dräk′sīd) ***n.*** [HYDR- + OXIDE] a compound consisting of an element or radical combined with the hydroxyl radical (OH)
hy·drox·yl (-sil) ***n.*** the monovalent radical OH, present in all hydroxides
hy·dro·zo·an (hī′drə zō′ən) ***adj.*** [< HYDRA + ZO(O)- + -AN] of a class of coelenterate animals having a saclike body and a mouth that opens directly into the body cavity —***n.*** any animal of this class, as a hydra, hydroid, etc.
hy·e·na (hī ē′nə) ***n.*** [< L. < Gr. *hyaina* < *hys*, a hog] a wolflike animal of Africa and Asia, with a characteristic shrill cry: hyenas feed on carrion and are thought of as cowardly
Hy·ge·ia (hī jē′ə) *Gr. Myth.* the goddess of health
hy·giene (hī′jēn) ***n.*** [< Fr. < Gr. *hygieinē* < *hygiēs*, healthy] **1.** the science of health and its maintenance; system of principles for preserving health and preventing disease **2.** hygienic practices
hy·gi·en·ic (hī′jē en′ik, -jē′nik, -jen′ik) ***adj.*** **1.** of hygiene or health **2.** promoting health; sanitary —**hy′gi·en′i·cal·ly** ***adv.***
hy·gi·en·ics (-iks) ***n.pl.*** [*with sing. v.*] the science of health; hygiene
hy·gi·en·ist (hī′jē ə nist, -jē nist; hī jē′nist) ***n.*** an expert in hygiene
hy·gro- [< Gr. *hygros*, wet] *a combining form meaning* wet, moisture: also, before a vowel, **hygr-**
hy·grom·e·ter (hī gräm′ə tər) ***n.*** [< Fr.: see prec. & -METER] any of various instruments for measuring moisture in the air —**hy·gro·met·ric** (hī′grə met′rik) ***adj.*** —**hy·grom′e·try** (-trē) ***n.***
hy·gro·scope (hī′grə skōp′) ***n.*** [HYGRO- + -SCOPE] an instrument that indicates, without actually measuring, changes in atmospheric humidity
hy·gro·scop·ic (hī′grə skäp′ik) ***adj.*** **1.** *a*) absorbing moisture from the air *b*) changed by the absorption of moisture **2.** of or according to a hygroscope —**hy′gro·scop′i·cal·ly** ***adv.***
hy·ing (hī′iŋ) *alt. prp. of* HIE
hy·la (hī′lə) ***n.*** [< Gr. *hylē*, wood] *same as* TREE FROG
Hy·men (hī′mən) *Gr. Myth.* the god of marriage —***n.*** [h-] [Poet.] **1.** marriage **2.** a wedding song
hy·men (hī′mən) ***n.*** [Gr. *hymēn*, membrane] the thin membrane that usually closes part of the opening of the vagina in a virgin —**hy′men·al** ***adj.***
hy·me·ne·al (hī′mə nē′əl) ***adj.*** [see HYMEN] of marriage —***n.*** [Poet.] a wedding song
hy·me·nop·ter·an (hī′mə näp′tər ən) ***n.*** [< Gr. < *hymēn*, membrane + *pteron*, a wing + -AN] any of a large order of insects, including wasps, bees, ants, etc., which have a sucking mouth and four membranous wings —**hy′me·nop′ter·ous** ***adj.***
hymn (him) ***n.*** [< OE. & OFr. < LL. < Gr. *hymnos*] **1.** a song in praise or honor of God, a god, or gods **2.** any song of praise —***vt.*** to praise in a hymn —***vi.*** to sing a hymn —**hym′nist** (-nist) ***n.***
hym·nal (him′nəl) ***n.*** a collection of religious hymns: also **hymn′book′** —***adj.*** of hymns
hym·no·dy (-nə dē) ***n.*** [< ML. < Gr.: see HYMN & ODE] **1.** the singing of hymns **2.** hymns collectively **3.** *same as* HYMNOLOGY —**hym′no·dist** ***n.***
hym·nol·o·gy (him näl′ə jē) ***n.*** [< ML. < Gr.: see HYMN & -LOGY] **1.** the study of hymns, their history, use, etc. **2.** the composition of hymns **3.** *same as* HYMNODY (sense 2) —**hym·nol′o·gist** ***n.***
hy·oid (hī′oid) ***adj.*** [< Fr. < ModL. < Gr. *hyoeidēs*, shaped like the letter *υ* (upsilon) < *hy*, upsilon + *eidos*, form] designating or of a U-shaped bone at the base of the tongue —***n.*** a hyoid bone
hyp. **1.** hypotenuse **2.** hypothesis **3.** hypothetical
hype (hīp) ***vt.*** **hyped**, **hyp′ing** [< HYPODERMIC] [Slang] to stimulate, excite, etc. artificially by or as by the injection of a drug: usually with *up*
hy·per- [Gr. < *hyper*, over, above] *a prefix meaning* over, above, more than normal, excessive [*hypercritical*]
hy·per·a·cid·i·ty (hī′pər ə sid′ə tē) ***n.*** excessive acidity, as of the gastric juice —**hy′per·ac′id** (-as′id) ***adj.***
hy·per·ac·tive (-ak′tiv) ***adj.*** extremely or abnormally active —**hy′per·ac·tiv′i·ty** (-tiv′ə tē) ***n.***
hy·per·bo·la (hī pur′bə lə) ***n.***, *pl.* **-las**, occas. **-lae′** (-lē′) [ModL. < Gr. *hyperbolē* < *hyper-*, over + *ballein*, to throw] a curve formed by the section of a cone cut by a plane more steeply inclined to the base than to the side of the cone

HYPERBOLA

hy·per·bo·le (-bə lē) ***n.*** [L. < Gr.: see prec.] exaggeration for effect, not meant to be taken literally (Ex.: He's as strong as an ox)
hy·per·bol·ic (hī′pər bäl′ik) ***adj.*** **1.** of, having the nature of, or using hyperbole; exaggerated or exaggerating **2.** of, or having the form of, a hyperbola Also **hy′per·bol′i·cal** —**hy′per·bol′i·cal·ly** ***adv.***
hy·per·bo·lize (hī pur′bə līz′) ***vt., vi.*** **-lized′**, **-liz′ing** to express with or use hyperbole
hy·per·bo·re·an (hī′pər bôr′ē ən, -bə rē′ən) ***adj.*** [< LL. < L. < Gr. *hyperboreos*, beyond the north wind] **1.** of the far north **2.** very cold —***n.*** [H-] *Gr. Myth.* an inhabitant of a region of sunshine and eternal spring, beyond the north wind
hy·per·crit·i·cal (-krit′i k′l) ***adj.*** too critical —**hy′per·crit′i·cal·ly** ***adv.*** —**hy′per·crit′i·cism** ***n.***
hy·per·gly·ce·mi·a (-glī sē′mē ə) ***n.*** [ModL. < HYPER- + Gr. *glykys*, sweet + -EMIA] an abnormally high concentration of sugar in the blood
Hy·pe·ri·on (hī pir′ē ən) *Gr. Myth.* **1.** a Titan, father of the sun god Helios **2.** Helios himself
hy·per·me·tro·pi·a (hī′pər mi trō′pē ə) ***n.*** [ModL. < Gr. *hypermetros*, excessive + *-ōpia*, -OPIA] farsightedness; abnormal vision in which distant objects are seen more clearly than near ones —**hy′per·me·trop′ic** (-träp′ik) ***adj.***
hy·per·o·pi·a (-ō′pē ə) ***n.*** *same as* HYPERMETROPIA —**hy′per·op′ic** (-äp′ik) ***adj.***
hy·per·sen·si·tive (-sen′sə tiv) ***adj.*** abnormally or excessively sensitive —**hy′per·sen′si·tiv′i·ty** ***n.***
hy·per·son·ic (-sän′ik) ***adj.*** designating, of, or moving at a speed equal to about five times the speed of sound or greater: see SONIC
hy·per·ten·sion (-ten′shən) ***n.*** abnormally high blood pressure, or a disease of which this is the chief sign —**hy′per·ten′sive** ***adj., n.***
hy·per·thy·roid·ism (-thī′roid iz′m) ***n.*** **1.** excessive activity of the thyroid gland **2.** the disorder caused by this, characterized by nervousness, a rapid pulse, etc. —**hy′per·thy′roid** ***adj., n.***
hy·per·tro·phy (hī pur′trə fē) ***n.*** [ModL.: see HYPER- & -TROPHY] an abnormal increase in the size of an organ or tissue —***vi., vt.*** **-phied**, **-phy·ing** to undergo or cause to undergo hypertrophy —**hy·per·troph·ic** (hī′pər träf′ik) ***adj.***
hy·per·ven·ti·la·tion (hī′pər ven′t′l ā′shən) ***n.*** very rap-

id or deep breathing that overoxygenates the blood, causing dizziness, fainting, etc. —**hy′per·ven′ti·late′** *vi., vt.* **-lat′ed, -lat′ing**

hy·pha (hī′fə) ***n.,*** *pl.* **-phae** (-fē) [ModL. < Gr. *hyphē*, a web] any of the threadlike parts making up the mycelium of a fungus —**hy′phal** ***adj.***

hy·phen (hī′f′n) ***n.*** [LL. < Gr. < *hypo-*, under + *hen*, neut. acc. of *heis*, one] a mark (-) used between the parts of a compound word or the syllables of a divided word, as at the end of a line —***vt.*** *same as* HYPHENATE

hy·phen·ate (-āt′) ***vt.*** **-at′ed, -at′ing 1.** to connect by a hyphen **2.** to write or print with a hyphen —***adj.*** hyphenated —**hy′phen·a′tion** ***n.***

hyp·no- [< Gr. *hypnos*, sleep] *a combining form meaning:* **1.** sleep **2.** hypnotism

hyp·noid (hip′noid) ***adj.*** resembling sleep or hypnosis: also **hyp·noid′al**

hyp·nol·o·gy (hip näl′ə jē) ***n.*** [HYPNO- + -LOGY] the science dealing with sleep and hypnotism

hyp·no·sis (hip nō′sis) ***n.,*** *pl.* **-ses** (-sēz) [ModL.: see HYPNO- & -OSIS] **1.** a sleeplike condition psychically induced, usually by another person, in which the subject is in a state of altered consciousness and responds, with certain limitations, to the suggestions of the hypnotist **2.** *same as* HYPNOTISM

hyp·not·ic (hip nät′ik) ***adj.*** [< Fr. < LL. < Gr. *hypnōtikos*, tending to sleep < *hypnos*, sleep] **1.** causing sleep; soporific **2.** of, like, or inducing hypnosis **3.** easily hypnotized —***n.*** **1.** any agent causing sleep **2.** a hypnotized person or one easily hypnotized —**hyp·not′i·cal·ly** ***adv.***

hyp·no·tism (hip′nə tiz′m) ***n.*** **1.** the act or practice of inducing hypnosis **2.** the science of hypnosis —**hyp′no·tist** ***n.***

hyp·no·tize (-tīz′) ***vt.*** **-tized′, -tiz′ing 1.** to induce hypnosis in **2.** to spellbind by or as if by hypnotism —**hyp′no·tiz′a·ble** ***adj.***

hy·po[1] (hī′pō) ***n.,*** *pl.* **-pos** (-pōz) *short for:* **1.** HYPODERMIC **2.** HYPOCHONDRIAC

hy·po[2] (hī′pō) ***n.*** [contr. < HYPOSULFITE] *same as* SODIUM THIOSULFATE

hy·po- [Gr. < *hypo*, less than] *a prefix meaning:* **1.** under, beneath *[hypodermic]* **2.** less than, deficient in *[hypothyroid]* **3.** *Chem.* having a lower state of oxidation

hy·po·chlo·rite (hī′pə klôr′īt) ***n.*** any salt of hypochlorous acid

hy·po·chlo·rous acid (-klôr′əs) [HYPO- + CHLOROUS] an unstable acid, $HClO$, known only in solution and used as a bleach and oxidizer

hy·po·chon·dri·a (hī′pə kän′drē ə) ***n.*** [ModL. < LL., pl., abdomen (supposed seat of this condition) < Gr. < *hypo-*, under + *chondros*, cartilage of the sternum] abnormal anxiety over one's health, often with imaginary illnesses and severe melancholy

hy·po·chon·dri·ac (-ak′) ***adj.*** of or having hypochondria: also **hy′po·chon·dri′a·cal** (-kən drī′ə k′l) —***n.*** a person who has hypochondria —**hy′po·chon·dri′a·cal·ly** ***adv.***

hy·po·chon·dri·a·sis (-kən drī′ə sis) ***n.*** *same as* HYPOCHONDRIA: term preferred in medicine

hy·po·cot·yl (hī′pə kät′'l) ***n.*** [HYPO- + COTYL(EDON)] the part of the axis, or stem, below the cotyledons in the embryo of a plant —**hy′po·cot′y·lous** ***adj.***

hy·poc·ri·sy (hi päk′rə sē) ***n.,*** *pl.* **-sies** [< OFr. < L. < Gr. *hypokrisis*, acting a part, ult. < *hypo-*, under + *krinesthai*, to dispute] a pretending to be what one is not, or to feel what one does not feel; esp., a pretense of virtue, piety, etc.

hyp·o·crite (hip′ə krit) ***n.*** [< OFr. < L. *hypocrita*, an actor: see prec.] a person who pretends to be better than he really is, or to be pious, virtuous, etc. without really being so —**hyp′o·crit′i·cal** (-krit′i k′l) ***adj.*** —**hyp′o·crit′i·cal·ly** ***adv.***

hy·po·der·mic (hī′pə dʉr′mik) ***adj.*** [HYPO- + DERM(A)[1] + -IC] **1.** of the parts under the skin **2.** injected under the skin —***n.*** *same as:* **1.** HYPODERMIC INJECTION **2.** HYPODERMIC SYRINGE —**hy′po·der′mi·cal·ly** ***adv.***

hypodermic injection the injection of a medicine or drug under the skin

hypodermic syringe a piston syringe as of glass, attached to a hollow metal needle **(hypodermic needle)**, used for giving hypodermic injections

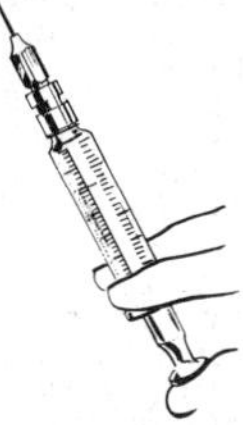

HYPODERMIC SYRINGE

hy·po·der·mis (-mis) ***n.*** [ModL.: see HYPO- & DERMIS] **1.** *Bot.* a specialized layer of cells, as for support or water storage, just beneath the epidermis of a plant **2.** *Zool.* an epidermis secreting an overlying cuticle, as in arthropods and annelids

hy·po·phos·phate (hī′pə fäs′fāt) ***n.*** a salt or ester of hypophosphoric acid

hy·po·phos·phite (-fäs′fīt) ***n.*** a salt or ester of hypophosphorous acid

hy·po·phos·phor·ic acid (-fäs fôr′ik) an acid, $H_4P_2O_6$, obtained when phosphorus is slowly oxidized in moist air

hy·po·phos·pho·rous acid (-fäs′fər əs, -fäs fôr′əs) a monobasic acid of phosphorus, H_3PO_2: it is a strong reducing agent

hy·poph·y·sis (hī päf′ə sis) ***n.,*** *pl.* **-ses′** (-sēz′) [Gr., undergrowth] *same as* PITUITARY GLAND

hy·po·sul·fite (hī′pə sul′fīt) ***n.*** **1.** any salt of hyposulfurous acid **2.** *a popular but erroneous var. of* SODIUM THIOSULFATE

hy·po·sul·fu·rous acid (-səl fyoor′əs) an unstable acid, $H_2S_2O_4$, which has strong reducing properties

hy·po·ten·sion (-ten′shən) ***n.*** abnormally low blood pressure —**hy′po·ten′sive** ***adj.***

hy·pot·e·nuse (hī pät′'n o͞os′, -yo͞os′) ***n.*** [< L. < Gr. *hypoteinousa*, lit., subtending < *hypo-*, under + *teinein*, to stretch] the side of a right-angled triangle opposite the right angle: also **hy·poth′e·nuse** (hī-päth′-)

HYPOTENUSE SIDE BASE

hy·po·thal·a·mus (hī′pə thal′ə məs) ***n.,*** *pl.* **-mi′** (-mī′) [ModL.: see HYPO- & THALAMUS] the part of the brain that forms the floor of the third ventricle and regulates many body functions, as temperature —**hy′po·tha·lam′ic** (-thə lam′ik) ***adj.***

hy·poth·e·cate (hī päth′ə kāt′) ***vt.*** **-cat′ed, -cat′ing** [< ML. pp. of *hypothecare*, ult. < Gr. *hypotithenai*, to pledge] **1.** to pledge (property) to another as security; mortgage **2.** *same as* HYPOTHESIZE —**hy·poth′e·ca′tion** ***n.*** —**hy·poth′e·ca′tor** ***n.***

hy·poth·e·sis (hī päth′ə sis, hi-) ***n.,*** *pl.* **-ses′** (-sēz′) [Gr. < *hypo-*, under + *tithenai*, to place] an unproved theory, proposition, etc. tentatively accepted to explain certain facts or **(working hypothesis)** to provide a basis for further investigation, argument, etc.

hy·poth·e·size (-sīz′) ***vi.*** **-sized′, -siz′ing** to make a hypothesis —***vt.*** to assume; suppose

hy·po·thet·i·cal (hī′pə thet′i k′l) ***adj.*** **1.** based on or involving a hypothesis; assumed; supposed **2.** given to the use of hypotheses *[a hypothetical mind]* **3.** *Logic* conditional *[a hypothetical proposition]* Also **hy′po·thet′ic** —**hy′po·thet′i·cal·ly** ***adv.***

hy·po·thy·roid·ism (hī′pō thī′roid iz′m) ***n.*** **1.** deficient activity of the thyroid gland **2.** the disorder resulting from this, characterized by a retarded rate of metabolism, sluggishness, puffiness, etc. —**hy′po·thy′roid** ***adj., n.***

hy·rax (hī′raks) ***n.,*** *pl.* **-rax·es, -ra·ces′** (-rə sēz′) [Gr., shrew mouse] a small, hoofed mammal of Africa and SW Asia, that feeds on plants

hys·sop (his′əp) ***n.*** [< OFr. < L. < Gr. *hyssōpos* < Heb. *ēzōbh*] **1.** a fragrant, blue-flowered plant of the mint family, used in folk medicine as a tonic, stimulant, etc. **2.** *Bible* a plant whose twigs were used for sprinkling in certain ancient Jewish rites

hys·ter·ec·to·my (his′tə rek′tə mē) ***n.,*** *pl.* **-mies** [< Gr. *hystera*, uterus + -ECTOMY] surgical removal of all or part of the uterus

hys·ter·e·sis (his′tə rē′sis) ***n.*** [Gr., a deficiency] *Physics* a lag of effect, as in magnetization, when the forces acting on a body are changed

hys·te·ri·a (his tir′ē ə, -ter′-) ***n.*** [ModL. < ff. + -IA] **1.** a psychiatric condition characterized by excitability, sensory and motor disturbances, or the unconscious simulation of organic disorders **2.** any outbreak of wild, uncontrolled excitement, such as fits of laughing and crying

hys·ter·ic (his ter′ik) ***adj.*** [< L. < Gr. *hysterikos*, suffering in the womb < *hystera*, uterus: the ancients thought of hysteria as a woman's disorder caused by disturbances of the uterus] *same as* HYSTERICAL —***n.*** **1.** [*usually pl., occas. with sing. v.*] a hysterical fit **2.** a person subject to hysteria

hys·ter·i·cal (-i k′l) ***adj.*** [prec. + -AL] **1.** of, like, or characteristic of hysteria **2.** extremely comical **3.** having or subject to hysteria

Hz, hz hertz

I

I, i (ī) ***n.,*** *pl.* **I's, i's** **1.** the ninth letter of the English alphabet **2.** a sound of *I* or *i*
I[1] (ī) ***n.*** **1.** a Roman numeral for 1 **2.** *Chem.* iodine —***adj.*** shaped like *I*
I[2] (ī) ***pron.*** *for pl. see* WE **[**OE. *ic***]** the person speaking or writing: *I* is the nominative case form of the first personal singular pronoun —***n.,*** *pl.* **I's** the ego
i (ī) ***n.*** **1.** a Roman numeral for 1 *[page iii]* **2.** *Math. the symbol for* $\sqrt{-1}$, the square root of −1
I., i. **1.** island(s) **2.** isle(s)
-i·a (ē ə, yə) **[**L. & Gr.**]** *a suffix used in:* **1.** names of certain diseases *[pneumonia]* **2.** names of some plants and animals *[zinnia]*
Ia., IA Iowa
I·a·go (ē ä′gō) the villain in Shakespeare's *Othello*
-i·al (ē əl, yəl, əl) **[**L. *-ialis, -iale***]** *same as* -AL (senses 1, 2) *[racial, centennial]*
i·amb (ī′amb, -am) ***n.*** **[**< Fr. < L. < Gr. *iambos***]** a metrical foot of two syllables, the first unaccented and the other accented, as in English verse (Ex.: "Tŏ bé,|ŏr nót|tŏ bé")
i·am·bic (ī am′bik) ***adj.*** of or made up of iambs —***n.*** **1.** an iamb **2.** an iambic verse
i·am·bus (-bəs) ***n.,*** *pl.* **-bus·es, -bi** (-bī) **[**L.**]** *same as* IAMB
-i·an (ē ən, yən, ən) **[**< L. *-ianus***]** *same as* -AN *[Indian, reptilian, Grecian]*
-i·an·a (ē an′ə) *same as* -ANA
-i·a·sis (ī′ə sis) **[**< Gr. *-iasis***]** *a combining form meaning* diseased condition *[psoriasis]*
-i·at·rics (ē at′riks) **[**< Gr. < *iatros,* physician**]** *a combining form meaning* treatment of disease *[pediatrics]*
i·at·ro·gen·ic (ī at′rə jen′ik) ***adj.*** **[**< Gr. *iatros,* physician + -GENIC**]** caused by a physician's words or actions: said esp. of imagined symptoms
-i·a·try (ī′ə trē) **[**< Gr. *iatreia,* healing**]** *a combining form meaning* medical treatment *[psychiatry]*
I·ba·dan (ē bä′dän) city in SW Nigeria: pop. 600,000
I·be·ri·a (ī bir′ē ə) peninsula in SW Europe, comprising Spain & Portugal: often called **Iberian Peninsula** —**I·be′ri·an** ***adj., n.***
i·bex (ī′beks) ***n.,*** *pl.* **i′bex·es, i·bi·ces** (ib′ə sēz′, ī′bə-), **i′bex:** see PLURAL, II, D, 1 **[**L.**]** any of certain wild goats of Europe, Asia, or Africa: the male has large, backward-curved horns
ibid. **[**L. *ibidem***]** in the same place: used in citing again the book, page, etc. cited just before
-i·bil·i·ty (ə bil′ə tē) *pl.* **-ties** **[**< L. *-ibilitas***]** *a suffix used to form nouns from adjectives ending in* -IBLE *[sensibility]*
i·bis (ī′bis) ***n.,*** *pl.* **i′bis·es, i′bis:** see PLURAL, II, D, 1 **[**L. < Gr. < Egypt. *hīb***]** a large wading bird related to the herons, with long legs and a long, curved bill, as the sacred ibis of the Nile
-i·ble (i b′l, ə b′l) **[**L. *-ibilis***]** *same as* -ABLE *[legible]*
Ib·sen (ib′s′n), **Hen·rik** (hen′rik) 1828–1906; Norw. playwright & poet
-ic (ik) **[**< Fr. *-ique* or L. *-icus* or Gr. *-ikos***]** **1.** *a suffix forming adjectives, meaning: a*) of, having to do with *[volcanic] b*) like, having the nature of *[angelic] c*) produced by, caused by *[photographic] d*) producing, causing *[psychedelic] e*) consisting of, containing *[dactylic] f*) having, affected by *[lethargic] g*) *Chem.* of or derived from *[citric]*; also, of a higher valence than the compound ending in *-ous [nitric]* **2.** *a suffix forming nouns, meaning* a person or thing having the nature of, affected by, belonging to, producing, etc. *[paraplegic, cynic, hypnotic]*
-i·cal (i k′l, ə k′l) **[**< LL. < *-icus,* -IC + *-alis,* -AL**]** *same as* -IC: adjectives formed with *-ical* sometimes have differentiated meanings (e.g., *historical, economical*) beyond those of the corresponding *-ic* forms
Ic·a·rus (ik′ə rəs) *Gr. Myth.* the son of Daedalus: using wings made by Daedalus, Icarus flew so high that the sun's heat melted the wax in them and he fell to his death —**I·car·i·an** (i ker′ē ən, ī-) ***adj.***
ICBM intercontinental ballistic missile
ICC, I.C.C. Interstate Commerce Commission
ice (īs) ***n.*** **[**OE. *is***]** **1.** water frozen solid by cold **2.** a piece, layer, or sheet of this **3.** anything like frozen water in appearance, etc. **4.** coldness in manner or attitude **5.** a frozen dessert, usually of water, fruit juice, and sugar **6.** icing **7.** [Slang] diamonds —***vt.*** **iced, ic′ing** **1.** to change into ice; freeze **2.** to cover with ice **3.** to cool by putting ice on, in, or around **4.** to cover with icing —***vi.*** to freeze (often with *up* or *over*) —**break the ice** **1.** to make a start by getting over initial difficulties **2.** to make a start toward getting better acquainted —**cut no ice** [Colloq.] to have no effect —**on ice** [Slang] **1.** in readiness or reserve **2.** in abeyance **3.** with success assured —**on thin ice** [Colloq.] in a risky situation
-ice (is, əs) **[**< OFr. *-ice* < L. *-itius***]** *a suffix meaning* condition or quality of *[justice]*
Ice. **1.** Iceland **2.** Icelandic
ice age *same as* GLACIAL EPOCH
ice bag a bag, as of rubber, for holding ice, applied to the body to reduce a swelling, ease pain, etc.
ice·berg (īs′burg′) ***n.*** **[**prob. via Du. *ijsberg,* lit., ice mountain < Scand.**]** a great mass of ice broken off from a glacier and floating in the sea
iceberg lettuce a variety of lettuce with crisp leaves tightly folded into a round, compact head
ice·boat (-bōt′) ***n.*** **1.** a light, boatlike frame, often triangular, equipped with runners and driven over ice by a sail, propeller, or jet engine **2.** *same as* ICEBREAKER (sense 1)
ice·bound (-bound′) ***adj.*** **1.** held fast by ice, as a boat **2.** made inaccessible by ice, as a port
ice·box (-bäks′) ***n.*** a cabinet with ice in it for keeping foods, etc. cold; also, any refrigerator
ice·break·er (-brā′kər) ***n.*** **1.** a sturdy ship for breaking a channel through ice **2.** anything lessening formality
ice·cap (-kap′) ***n.*** a mass of glacial ice that spreads slowly out from a center
ice-cold (īs′kōld′) ***adj.*** very cold
ice cream **[**orig., *iced cream***]** a sweet, creamy frozen food made from variously flavored cream and milk products and often containing gelatin, eggs, fruits, etc. —**ice′-cream′** ***adj.***
ice field **1.** *same as* ICECAP **2.** an extensive area of floating sea ice
ice floe **1.** *same as* ICE FIELD (sense 2) **2.** a single piece, large or small, of floating sea ice
ice hockey *same as* HOCKEY (sense 1)
Ice·land (īs′lənd) island country in the North Atlantic, southeast of Greenland: 39,768 sq. mi.; pop. 204,000; cap. Reykjavik —**Ice′land·er** ***n.***
Ice·lan·dic (īs lan′dik) ***adj.*** of Iceland, its people, their language, or culture —***n.*** the N. Germanic language of the Icelanders
ice·man (īs′man′, -mən) ***n.,*** *pl.* **-men′** (-men′, -mən) a person who sells or delivers ice
ice milk a frozen dessert like ice cream, but with a lower butterfat content
ice pack **1.** a large, floating expanse of ice masses frozen together **2.** an ice bag, folded cloth, etc. filled with crushed ice and applied to the body, as to reduce a swelling or ease pain
ice pick a sharply pointed metal tool used to chop ice into small pieces
ice sheet a thick layer of ice covering an extensive area for a long period, as in the ice age
ice shelf a thick mass of glacial ice along a polar shore, often protruding out to sea for many miles
ice skate a skate for skating on ice: see SKATE[1] (sense 1) —**ice′-skate′** ***vi.*** **-skat′ed, -skat′ing** —**ice skater**
ich·neu·mon (ik nyo͞o′mən, -no͞o′-) ***n.*** **[**L. < Gr. *ichneumōn,* lit., tracker < *ichnos,* a track**]** **1.** the Egyptian species of mongoose **2.** *same as* ICHNEUMON FLY
ichneumon fly a hymenopteran insect whose larvae live as parasites in or on other insect larvae: also **ichneumon wasp**
i·chor (ī′kôr, -kər) ***n.*** **[**Gr. *ichōr***]** **1.** *Gr. Myth.* the fluid flowing instead of blood in the veins of the gods **2.** a watery discharge from a wound or sore —**i′chor·ous** (-kər əs) ***adj.***

ich·thy·o- [< Gr. < *ichthys,* a fish] *a combining form meaning* fish, like a fish: also **ichthy-**

ich·thy·ol·o·gy (ik'thē äl'ə jē) *n.* [< ModL.: see ICHTHYO- & -LOGY] the branch of zoology dealing with fishes —**ich'-thy·o·log'i·cal** (-ə läj'i k'l), **ich'thy·o·log'ic** *adj.* —**ich'-thy·ol'o·gist** *n.*

ich·thy·o·saur (ik'thē ə sôr') *n.* [< ModL. < ICHTHYO- + Gr. *sauros,* lizard] a prehistoric marine reptile, now extinct, which had a fishlike body, four paddle-shaped flippers, and a dolphinlike head —**ich'thy·o·sau'ri·an** (-sôr'ē ən) *adj.*

-i·cian (ish'ən) [< Fr.: see -IC & -IAN] *a suffix meaning* a person engaged in, practicing, or specializing in *[mortician]*

i·ci·cle (ī'si k'l) *n.* [< OE. < *is,* ice + *gicel,* piece of ice] a hanging piece of ice, formed by the freezing of dripping water —**i'ci·cled** *adj.*

ic·ing (ī'siŋ) *n.* a mixture, as of sugar, butter, flavoring, etc., for covering a cake or pastries; frosting

ick·y (ik'ē) *adj.* **ick'i·er, ick'i·est** [baby talk for STICKY] [Slang] **1.** unpleasantly sticky **2.** cloyingly sentimental **3.** very distasteful; disgusting —**ick'i·ness** *n.*

i·con (ī'kän) *n.* [L. < Gr. *eikōn,* an image] **1.** an image **2.** *Orthodox Eastern Ch.* an image or picture of Jesus, Mary, a saint, etc., venerated as sacred —**i·con·ic** (ī kän'ik) *adj.*

i·con·o- [< Gr. *eikōn,* an image] *a combining form meaning* image, figure: also **icon-**

i·con·o·clast (ī kän'ə klast') *n.* [< ML. < MGr. < Gr. *eikōn,* an image + *klaein,* to break] **1.** anyone opposed to the religious use of images **2.** a person who attacks or ridicules traditional or venerated institutions or ideas —**i·con'-o·clasm** *n.* —**i·con'o·clas'tic** *adj.* —**i·con'o·clas'ti·cal·ly** *adv.*

i·con·o·scope (-skōp') *n.* [ICONO- + -SCOPE] an early form of television camera tube

-ics (iks) [-IC + -S (*pl.*)] *a pl. suffix meaning:* **1.** [*usually with sing. v.*] *a*) art, science, study *[economics]* *b*) arrangement, system *[statistics]* **2.** [*usually with pl. v.*] *a*) activities, practices *[histrionics]* *b*) qualities, properties *[atmospherics]*

ic·tus (ik'təs) *n., pl.* **-tus·es, -tus** [< L. < pp. of *icere,* to hit] **1.** rhythmical or metrical stress, or accent **2.** *Med.* a stroke or sudden attack

i·cy (ī'sē) *adj.* **i'ci·er, i'ci·est** **1.** having much ice; full of or covered with ice **2.** of ice **3.** like ice; slippery or very cold **4.** cold in manner; unfriendly —**i'ci·ly** *adv.* —**i'ci·ness** *n.*

id (id) *n.* [ModL. < L., it] *Psychoanalysis* that part of the psyche which is the reservoir of the instinctual drives, dominated by the pleasure principle and irrational wishing

-id (id, əd) [ult. < L. or Gr.] *a suffix meaning:* **1.** a thing belonging to or connected with *[Aeneid, arachnid]* **2.** *Chem. same as* -IDE

ID, I.D. identification —*n.* (ī'dē'), *pl.* **ID's, I.D.'s** a card (**ID card**) or document that identifies a person, proves his age, etc.

id. [L. *idem*] the same

I'd (īd) **1.** I had **2.** I would **3.** I should

I·da (ī'də) [ML. < OHG.: akin ? to ON. *Ithunn,* goddess of youth] a feminine name

Ida. Idaho

-i·dae (i dē') [ModL.] *a suffix used to form the name of* a zoological family *[Canidae* (the dog family)*]*

I·da·ho (ī'də hō') [< AmInd. tribal name] Mountain State of the NW U.S.: 83,557 sq. mi.; pop. 944,000; cap. Boise: abbrev. **Ida., ID** —**I'da·ho'an** *adj., n.*

-ide (īd; *occas.* id) [< (OX)IDE] *a suffix added to part of the name of* the nonmetallic or electronegative element or radical in a binary compound *[sodium chloride] or used in forming the name of* a class of compounds *[glycoside]*

i·de·a (ī dē'ə) *n.* [L. < Gr. *idea,* appearance of a thing] **1.** a thought; mental conception or image; notion **2.** an opinion or belief **3.** a plan; scheme; intention **4.** a hazy perception; vague impression; inkling **5.** meaning or significance **6.** *Philos.* according to Plato, a model or archetype of which all real things are but imperfect imitations

i·de·al (ī dē'əl; *also, esp. for adj. 2 & 4 and for n.,* ī dēl') *adj.* [< Fr. < LL. < L. *idea:* see prec.] **1.** existing as an idea; being a model or archetype **2.** thought of as perfect; exactly as one would wish **3.** identifying or illustrating an idea or conception **4.** existing only in the mind as an image or concept; imaginary **5.** *Philos.* of idealism —*n.* **1.** a conception of something in its most excellent form **2.** a perfect model or standard **3.** a goal or principle

i·de·al·ism (ī dē'əl iz'm) *n.* **1.** behavior or thought based on a conception of things as one thinks they should be **2.** the representation of idealized persons or things in art or literature **3.** a striving to achieve one's ideals **4.** *Philos.* any theory which holds that things exist only as ideas in the mind or that things are really imperfect imitations of unchanging models or forms having independent existence apart from the material world: cf. MATERIALISM

i·de·al·ist (-ist) *n.* **1.** *a*) a person whose behavior or thought is based on ideals *b*) a visionary or impractical dreamer **2.** an adherent or practitioner of idealism in art, literature, or philosophy —*adj. same as* IDEALISTIC

i·de·al·is·tic (ī'dē ə lis'tik, ī dē'ə-) *adj.* **1.** of or characteristic of an idealist **2.** of, characterized by, or based on idealism —**i'de·al·is'ti·cal·ly** *adv.*

i·de·al·ize (ī dē'ə līz') *vt.* **-ized', -iz'ing** to make ideal; regard or show as perfect or more nearly perfect than is true —*vi.* to represent things in the manner of an idealist —**i·de'al·i·za'tion** *n.* —**i·de'al·iz'er** *n.*

i·de·al·ly (ī dē'əl ē) *adv.* **1.** in an ideal manner; perfectly **2.** in theory

i·de·ate (ī'dē āt', ī dē'āt) *vt., vi.* **-at'ed, -at'ing** to form an idea (of) —**i'de·a'tion** *n.* —**i'de·a'tion·al** *adj.* —**i'de·a'-tion·al·ly** *adv.*

‡**i·dée fixe** (ē dā fēks') [Fr.] a fixed idea; obsession

‡**i·dem** (ī'dem, ē'-) *pron.* [L.] the same as that previously mentioned

i·den·ti·cal (ī den'ti k'l) *adj.* [< ML. < LL. *identitas* (see IDENTITY) + -AL] **1.** the very same **2.** exactly alike **3.** designating twins, always of the same sex, developed from a single fertilized ovum and very much alike in appearance —**i·den'ti·cal·ly** *adv.*

i·den·ti·fi·ca·tion (ī den'tə fi kā'shən, i-) *n.* **1.** an identifying or being identified **2.** anything by which a person or thing can be identified **3.** *Psychoanalysis* a mainly unconscious process by which a person thinks, feels, and acts in a way which resembles his image of another person important to him

i·den·ti·fy (ī den'tə fī', i-) *vt.* **-fied', -fy'ing** **1.** to make identical; treat as the same **2.** to show to be the very person or thing known, described, or claimed **3.** to connect or associate closely **4.** *Psychoanalysis* to make identification of (oneself) with someone else —*vi.* to understand and share another's feelings; sympathize (*with*) —**i·den'ti·fi'a·ble** *adj.* —**i·den'ti·fi'er** *n.*

i·den·ti·ty (-tē) *n., pl.* **-ties** [< Fr. < LL. *identitas* < L. *idem,* the same] **1.** the condition or fact of being the same or exactly alike; sameness **2.** *a*) the condition or fact of being a specific person or thing; individuality *b*) the condition of being the same as a person or thing described or claimed

identity crisis [coined by E. Erikson (1902–), U.S. psychoanalyst] the condition of being uncertain of one's feelings about oneself, esp. with regard to character, goals, and origins, occurring esp. in adolescence

id·e·o- [< Fr. *ideo-* or < Gr. *idea*] *a combining form meaning* idea *[ideology]*

id·e·o·gram (id'ē ə gram', ī'dē-) *n.* [prec. + -GRAM] **1.** a graphic symbol representing an object or idea without expressing the sounds that form its name **2.** a symbol representing an idea rather than a word (Ex.: 5, +, ÷) Also **id'-e·o·graph'**

id·e·o·graph·ic (id'ē ə graf'ik) *adj.* of, or having the nature of, an ideogram: also **id'e·o·graph'i·cal** —**id'e·o-graph'i·cal·ly** *adv.*

i·de·o·log·i·cal (ī'dē ə läj'i k'l, id'ē ə-) *adj.* of or concerned with ideology: also **i'de·o·log'ic** —**i'de·o·log'i-cal·ly** *adv.*

i·de·ol·o·gy (ī'dē äl'ə jē, id'ē-) *n., pl.* **-gies** [< Fr.: see IDEO- & -LOGY] **1.** the study of ideas, their nature and source **2.** thinking of an idealistic, abstract, or impractical nature **3.** the doctrines, opinions, or way of thinking of an individual, class, etc.; specif., the ideas on which a political, economic, or social system is based —**i'de·ol'o·gist** *n.*

ides (īdz) *n.pl.* [*often with sing. v.*] [Fr. < L. *idus*] in the ancient Roman calendar, the 15th day of March, May, July, or October, or the 13th of the other months

‡**id est** (id est) [L.] that is (to say)

id·i·o·cy (id'ē ə sē) *n., pl.* **-cies** **1.** the state of being an idiot **2.** great foolishness or stupidity

id·i·om (id'ē əm) *n.* [< Fr. & LL. < Gr. < *idios,* one's own] **1.** the language or dialect of a people, region, etc. **2.** the usual way in which the words of a particular language are joined together to express thought **3.** an accepted phrase or expression having a meaning different from the literal **4.** the style of expression characteristic of an individual **5.** a characteristic style, as in art or music

id·i·o·mat·ic (id'ē ō mat'ik) *adj.* **1.** characteristic of a particular language **2.** using or having many idioms **3.** of, or having the nature of, an idiom or idioms —**id'i·o·mat'i-cal·ly** *adv.*

id·i·o·syn·cra·sy (id'ē ə siŋ'krə sē, -sin'-) *n., pl.* **-sies** [< Gr. < *idio-,* one's own + *synkrasis,* mixture < *syn-,* together + *kerannynai,* to mix] **1.** the temperament peculiar to a person or group **2.** any personal peculiarity, mannerism, reaction, etc. —**id'i·o·syn·crat'ic** (-sin krat'ik) *adj.* —**id'i·o·syn·crat'i·cal·ly** *adv.*

id·i·ot (id'ē ət) *n.* [OFr. < L. < Gr. *idiōtēs,* ignorant person < *idios,* one's own] **1.** a person having severe mental retardation: an obsolescent term: see MENTAL RETARDATION **2.** a very foolish or stupid person

id·i·ot·ic (id'ē ät'ik) *adj.* of or like an idiot; very foolish or stupid —**id'i·ot'i·cal·ly** *adv.*

i·dle (ī'd'l) *adj.* **i'dler, i'dlest** [OE. *idel,* empty] **1.** *a*) worthless; useless *[idle* talk*]* *b)* futile; pointless *[*an *idle* wish*]* **2.** baseless; unfounded *[idle* rumors*]* **3.** *a)* unemployed *[idle* men*]* *b)* not in use *[idle* machines*]* **4.** lazy —***vi.* i′dled, i′dling** **1.** to move slowly or aimlessly **2.** to be unemployed or inactive **3.** to operate without transmitting any power, esp. with disengaged gears —***vt.*** **1.** to waste; squander *[idling* away one's youth*]* **2.** to make (a motor, etc.) idle **3.** to make inactive or unemployed — **i′dle·ness** ***n.*** —**i′dly** ***adv.***

i·dler (īd′lər) ***n.*** **1.** one who loafs **2.** *a)* a gearwheel placed between two others to transfer motion from one to the other without changing their direction or speed: also **idler gear** (or **wheel**), **idle wheel** *b)* a pulley guiding a belt or taking up slack: also **idler pulley**

IDLE WHEEL

i·dol (ī′d′l) ***n.*** **[**< OFr. < L. < Gr. *eidōlon*, an image < *eidos*, form**]** **1.** an image of a god, used as an object of worship **2.** an object of excessive devotion or admiration

i·dol·a·ter (ī däl′ə tər) ***n.*** **[**< OFr. < LL. < LGr. < *eidōlon* (see prec.) + *latris*, servant**]** **1.** a worshiper of idols **2.** a devoted admirer; adorer —**i·dol′a·tress** (-tris) ***n.fem.***

i·dol·a·trize (-trīz′) ***vt., vi.* -trized′, -triz′ing** to worship as an idolater

i·dol·a·trous (-trəs) ***adj.*** **1.** of, or having the nature of, idolatry **2.** worshiping idols **3.** having or showing excessive admiration or devotion —**i·dol′a·trous·ly** ***adv.*** — **i·dol′a·trous·ness** ***n.***

i·dol·a·try (-trē) ***n.***, *pl.* **-tries** **1.** worship of idols **2.** excessive devotion or reverence

i·dol·ize (ī′d′l īz′) ***vt.* -ized′, -iz′ing** **1.** to make an idol of **2.** to love or admire excessively —***vi.*** to worship idols — **i′dol·i·za′tion** ***n.*** —**i′dol·iz′er** ***n.***

i·dyll, i·dyl (ī′d′l; *Brit. often* id′′l) ***n.*** **[**< L. < Gr. dim. of *eidos*, a form, image**]** **1.** a short poem or prose work describing a simple, pleasant scene of rural or pastoral life **2.** a scene or incident suitable for such a work —**i·dyl′lic** ***adj.*** —**i·dyl′li·cal·ly** ***adv.*** —**i′dyll·ist** ***n.***

-ie (ē) **[**earlier form of -Y[1]**]** *a suffix meaning:* **1.** small, little *[doggie]*: often used to express affection **2.** one that is as specified *[softie]*

IE, I.E. Indo-European

i.e. [L. *id est*] that is (to say)

-i·er (ir, ər, ē′ər, yər) **[**< OFr. < L. *-arius***]** *a suffix meaning* a person concerned with (a specified action or thing) *[bombardier, furrier]*

if (if) ***conj.*** **[**OE. *gif***]** **1.** on condition that; in case that *[if* I come, I'll see him*]* **2.** granting that *[if* he was there, I didn't see him*]* **3.** whether *[*ask him *if* he knows her*]* *If* is also used in exclamations expressing: *a)* a wish *[if* I had only known!*]* *b)* surprise, annoyance, etc. *[if* that isn't the limit!*]* —***n.*** **1.** a supposition **2.** a condition *[*an idea filled with *ifs]* —**as if** as the situation would be if; as though

if·fy (if′ē) ***adj.*** [Colloq.] full of uncertainty

IFR Instrument Flight Rules

ig·loo (ig′lo͞o) ***n.***, *pl.* **-loos** **[**Esk. *igdlu*, snow house**]** an Eskimo house or hut, usually dome-shaped and built of blocks of packed snow

Ig·na·tius (of) Loy·o·la (ig nā′shəs loi ō′lə), Saint (born *Iñigo López de Recalde*) 1491–1556; Sp. priest: founder of the Jesuit order

ig·ne·ous (ig′nē əs) ***adj.*** **[**< L. < *ignis*, a fire**]** **1.** of, like, or containing fire **2.** formed by volcanic action or intense heat *[igneous* rock*]*

ig·nis fat·u·us (ig′nis fach′o͞o wəs) *pl.* **ig·nes fat·u·i** (ig′nēz fach′o͞o wī′) [ML. < L. *ignis*, a fire + *fatuus*, foolish] **1.** a light seen at night moving over swamps, etc., probably caused by a combustion of marsh gas: popularly called *will-o'-the-wisp, jack-o'-lantern* **2.** a deceptive hope, goal, or influence; delusion

ig·nite (ig nīt′) ***vt., vi.* -nit′ed, -nit′ing** **[**< L. pp. of *ignire* < *ignis*, a fire**]** **1.** to start burning **2.** to get excited —**ig·nit′a·ble, ig·nit′i·ble** ***adj.*** —**ig·nit′er, ig·ni′tor** ***n.***

ig·ni·tion (ig nish′ən) ***n.*** **1.** an igniting or means of igniting **2.** in an internal-combustion engine, *a)* the igniting of the explosive mixture in the cylinder *b)* the device or system for doing this

ig·no·ble (ig nō′b′l) ***adj.*** [MFr. < L. < *in-*, not + *nobilis*, known] not noble in character or quality; dishonorable; base; mean —**ig·no′ble·ness** ***n.*** —**ig·no′bly** ***adv.***

ig·no·min·i·ous (ig′nə min′ē əs) ***adj.*** **1.** shameful; disgraceful **2.** despicable **3.** degrading —**ig′no·min′i·ous·ly** ***adv.*** —**ig′no·min′i·ous·ness** ***n.***

ig·no·min·y (ig′nə min′ē) ***n.***, *pl.* **-min′ies** **[**< Fr. < L. *ignominia* < *in-*, without + *nomen*, name**]** **1.** loss of one's reputation; shame and dishonor **2.** disgraceful or shameful quality or action

ig·no·ra·mus (ig′nə rā′məs, -ram′əs) ***n.***, *pl.* **-mus·es** **[**< the name of a lawyer in a 17th-c. play; L., lit., we ignore (a legal term)**]** an ignorant person

ig·no·rance (ig′nər əns) ***n.*** the condition or quality of being ignorant; lack of knowledge

ig·no·rant (-ənt) ***adj.*** **[**< OFr. < L. prp. of *ignorare:* see ff.**]** **1.** lacking knowledge, education, or experience **2.** caused by or showing lack of these **3.** unaware *(of)* —**ig′no·rant·ly** ***adv.***

ig·nore (ig nôr′) ***vt.* -nored′, -nor′ing** **[**< Fr. < L. *ignorare* < *in-*, not + base of *gnarus*, knowing**]** to disregard deliberately; pay no attention to; refuse to consider —**ig·nor′er** ***n.***

I·go·rot (ig′ə rōt′, ē′gə-) ***n.*** **1.** *pl.* **-rots′, -rot′** a member of a Malayan people of Luzon, in the Philippines **2.** their Indonesian language

i·gua·na (i gwä′nə) ***n.*** [Sp. < S. AmInd. *iuana*] a large, harmless, tropical American lizard with spines from neck to tail

LAND IGUANA (to 5 ft. long)

IHP, I.H.P., ihp., i.h.p. indicated horsepower

IHS a contraction misread from the Greek word ΙΗΣΟΥΣ, Jesus, used as a symbol or monogram

IJs·sel·meer (ī′səl mer′) freshwater lake in N & C Netherlands: formerly part of the Zuider Zee

i·kon (ī′kän) ***n.*** *var. of* ICON

il- *see* IN-[1], IN-[2]

IL Illinois

-ile (il, əl, ′l; *also, chiefly Brit.* īl) **[**< Fr. *-il, -ile* < L. *-ilis***]** *a suffix meaning* of, having to do with, that can be, like, suitable for *[docile, missile]*: sometimes **-il** *[civil]*

il·e·i·tis (il′ē īt′is) ***n.*** inflammation of the ileum

il·e·um (il′ē əm) ***n.***, *pl.* **il′e·a** (-ə) [ModL. < L., flank, groin (var. of *ilium*)] the lowest part of the small intestine —**il′e·ac′** (-ak′), **il′e·al** (-əl) ***adj.***

i·lex (ī′leks) ***n.*** [L.] *same as:* **1.** HOLLY **2.** HOLM OAK

Il·i·ad (il′ē əd) **[**< L. < Gr. < *Ilios*, Troy**]** a long Greek epic poem, ascribed to Homer, about the final part of the Trojan War

-il·i·ty (il′ə tē) *pl.* **-ties** *a suffix used in nouns formed from adjectives ending in* -ILE, -IL *[imbecility, civility]*

Il·i·um (il′ē əm) *Latin name for* TROY (sense 1)

il·i·um (il′ē əm) ***n.***, *pl.* **il′i·a** (-ə) [ModL.: see ILEUM] the flat, uppermost section of the innominate bone —**il′i·ac′** (-ak′) ***adj.***

ilk (ilk) ***adj.*** [Scot. dial. < OE. *ilca*, same] [Obs.] same; like —***n.*** kind; sort: only in **of that** (or **his, her,** etc.) **ilk**: a misunderstanding of the orig. Scottish phrase meaning "of the same name"

ill (il) ***adj.* worse, worst** **[**< ON. *illr***]** **1.** *a)* morally bad *[ill* repute*]* *b)* adverse *[ill* fortune*]* *c)* not kind or friendly *[ill* will*]* *d)* unfavorable *[*an *ill* omen*]* **2.** not healthy, normal, or well; sick **3.** faulty; improper —***n.*** anything causing harm, trouble, pain, etc.; evil —***adv.* worse, worst** **1.** in an ill way; specif., *a)* badly *b)* unkindly **2.** with difficulty; scarcely *[*he can *ill* afford it*]* —**ill at ease** uneasy; uncomfortable

I'll (īl) **1.** I shall **2.** I will

Ill. Illinois

ill. **1.** illustrated **2.** illustration

ill-ad·vised (il′əd vīzd′) ***adj.*** showing or resulting from a lack of sound advice or proper consideration; unwise — **ill′-ad·vis′ed·ly** (-vī′zid lē) ***adv.***

ill-bred (-bred′) ***adj.*** badly brought up; rude

ill-con·sid·ered (-kən sid′ərd) ***adj.*** not properly considered; not suitable or wise

ill-dis·posed (-dis pōzd′) ***adj.*** **1.** having a bad disposition; malicious or malevolent **2.** unfriendly or unfavorable *(toward)*

il·le·gal (i lē′gəl) ***adj.*** not lawful; against the law or against the rules —**il·le·gal·i·ty** (il′ē gal′ə tē) ***n.***, *pl.* **-ties** —**il·le′gal·ly** ***adv.***

il·leg·i·ble (i lej′ə b′l) ***adj.*** difficult or impossible to read because badly written or printed, faded, etc. —**il·leg′i·bil′i·ty** ***n.*** —**il·leg′i·bly** ***adv.***

il·le·git·i·mate (il′ə jit′ə mit) ***adj.*** **1.** born of parents not married to each other **2.** incorrectly deduced **3.** not lawful **4.** unsanctioned —**il′le·git′i·ma·cy** (-mə sē) ***n.***, *pl.* **-cies** —**il′le·git′i·mate·ly** ***adv.***

ill-fat·ed (il′fāt′id) ***adj.*** **1.** having or sure to have an evil fate or unlucky end **2.** unlucky

ill-fa·vored (-fā′vərd) ***adj.*** **1.** unpleasant or ugly in appearance **2.** offensive

ill-found·ed (-foun′did) *adj.* not supported by facts or sound reasons
ill-got·ten (-gät′'n) *adj.* obtained by evil, unlawful, or dishonest means *[ill-gotten* gains*]*
ill humor a disagreeable, cross, or sullen mood or state of mind —**ill′-hu′mored** *adj.* —**ill′-hu′mored·ly** *adv.*
il·lib·er·al (i lib′ər əl) *adj.* **1.** [Archaic] without culture; unrefined **2.** intolerant; narrow-minded **3.** miserly; stingy —**il·lib′er·al′i·ty** (-ə ral′ə tē) *n.* —**il·lib′er·al·ly** *adv.*
il·lic·it (i lis′it) *adj.* not allowed by law, custom, etc.; unlawful —**il·lic′it·ly** *adv.* —**il·lic′it·ness** *n.*
il·lim·it·a·ble (i lim′it ə b'l) *adj.* without limit or bounds —**il·lim′it·a·bil′i·ty, il·lim′it·a·ble·ness** *n.* —**il·lim′it·a·bly** *adv.*
Il·li·nois[1] (il′ə noi′; *occas.* -noiz′) *n.* [Fr. < Illinois *ileniwe,* man] **1.** *pl.* **-nois′** a member of a tribe or confederacy of Indians who lived in N Illinois, S Wisconsin, and parts of Iowa and Missouri **2.** their Algonquian dialect
Il·li·nois[2] (il′ə noi′; *occas.* -noiz′) [< prec.] Middle Western State of the U.S.: 56,400 sq. mi.; pop. 11,418,000; cap. Springfield: abbrev. **Ill., IL** —**Il′li·nois′an** (-noi′ən, -noiz′ən) *adj., n.*
il·lit·er·a·cy (i lit′ər ə sē) *n.* **1.** the state of being illiterate **2.** *pl.* **-cies** a mistake (in writing or speaking) suggesting poor education
il·lit·er·ate (-it) *adj.* **1.** ignorant; uneducated; esp., not knowing how to read or write **2.** having or showing limited knowledge, experience, or culture **3.** violating accepted usage in language —*n.* an illiterate person —**il·lit′er·ate·ly** *adv.*
ill-man·nered (il′man′ərd) *adj.* rude; impolite
ill nature an unpleasant, disagreeable disposition —**ill′-na′tured** *adj.* —**ill′-na′tured·ly** *adv.*
ill·ness (-nis) *n.* the condition of being ill; sickness; disease
il·log·ic (i läj′ik) *n.* lack of logic
il·log·i·cal (-i k'l) *adj.* not logical; using or based on faulty reasoning —**il·log′i·cal′i·ty** (-i kal′ə tē), **il·log′i·cal·ness** *n.* —**il·log′i·cal·ly** *adv.*
ill-spent (il′spent′) *adj.* misspent; wasted
ill-starred (-stärd′) *adj.* unlucky; doomed
ill-tem·pered (-tem′pərd) *adj.* bad-tempered
ill-timed (-tīmd′) *adj.* coming or done at the wrong time; inopportune
ill-treat (il′trēt′) *vt.* to treat unkindly, cruelly, or unfairly; abuse —**ill′-treat′ment** *n.*
il·lu·mi·nance (i lo͞o′mə nəns) *n. same as* ILLUMINATION (sense 2)
il·lu·mi·nant (-nənt) *adj.* giving light; illuminating —*n.* something that gives light
il·lu·mi·nate (-nāt′) *vt.* **-nat′ed, -nat′ing** [< L. pp. of *illuminare* < *in-,* in + *luminare,* to light < *lumen,* a light] **1.** *a)* to give light to; light up *b)* to brighten; animate **2.** *a)* to make clear; explain *b)* to inform; enlighten **3.** to make famous **4.** to decorate with lights **5.** to decorate (an initial letter, a page border, etc.) with designs of gold, bright colors, etc. —**il·lu′mi·na·ble** *adj.* —**il·lu′mi·na′tive** *adj.* —**il·lu′mi·na′tor** *n.*
il·lu·mi·na·tion (i lo͞o′mə nā′shən) *n.* **1.** an illuminating or being illuminated **2.** the intensity of light per unit of area **3.** the designs used in illuminating manuscripts
il·lu·mine (i lo͞o′min) *vt.* **-mined, -min·ing** *same as* ILLUMINATE —**il·lu′mi·na·ble** *adj.*
illus., illust. 1. illustrated **2.** illustration
ill-us·age (il′yo͞o′sij, -zij) *n.* unfair, unkind, or cruel treatment; abuse: also **ill usage**
ill-use (-yo͞oz′; *for n.* -yo͞os′) *vt.* **-used′, -us′ing** to subject to ill-usage —*n. same as* ILL-USAGE
il·lu·sion (i lo͞o′zhən) *n.* [< OFr. < L. < pp. of *illudere,* to mock] **1.** a false idea or conception **2.** an unreal or misleading appearance or image **3.** a false perception or interpretation of what one sees **4.** a hallucination —**il·lu′sion·al, il·lu′sion·ar′y** *adj.*
il·lu·sion·ist (-ist) *n.* an entertainer who performs sleight-of-hand tricks
il·lu·sive (i lo͞o′siv) *adj.* illusory; unreal —**il·lu′sive·ly** *adv.* —**il·lu′sive·ness** *n.*
il·lu·so·ry (-sər ē) *adj.* producing, based on, or having the nature of, illusion; deceptive; unreal —**il·lu′so·ri·ly** *adv.* —**il·lu′so·ri·ness** *n.*
il·lus·trate (il′ə strāt′, i lus′trāt) *vt.* **-trat′ed, -trat′ing** [< L. pp. of *illustrare* < *in-,* in + *lustrare,* to illuminate] **1.** to make clear or explain, as by examples or comparisons **2.** *a)* to furnish (books, etc.) with explanatory or decorative drawings, pictures, etc. *b)* to explain or decorate: said of pictures, etc. —*vi.* to illustrate something —**il′lus·tra′tor** *n.*
il·lus·tra·tion (il′ə strā′shən) *n.* **1.** an illustrating or being illustrated **2.** an explanatory example, story, etc. **3.** an explanatory or decorative picture, diagram, etc. —**il′lus·tra′tion·al** *adj.*
il·lus·tra·tive (i lus′trə tiv, il′ə strāt′iv) *adj.* serving to illustrate —**il·lus′tra·tive·ly** *adv.*
il·lus·tri·ous (i lus′trē əs) *adj.* [< L. *illustris,* bright] very distinguished; famous; eminent —**il·lus′tri·ous·ly** *adv.* —**il·lus′tri·ous·ness** *n.*
ill will unfriendly feeling; hostility; hate
il·ly (il′lē) *adv.* [Now Dial.] badly; ill
Il·lyr·i·a (i lir′ē ə) ancient region along the E coast of the Adriatic —**Il·lyr′i·an** *adj., n.*
ILO, I.L.O. International Labor Organization
ILS instrument landing system
I'm (īm) I am
im- *see* IN-[1], IN-[2]
im·age (im′ij) *n.* [OFr. < L. < *imago* < base of *imitari,* to imitate] **1.** a representation of a person or thing, drawn, painted, etc.; esp., a statue **2.** the visual impression of something produced by a mirror, lens, etc. **3.** a copy; counterpart; likeness **4.** *a)* a mental picture of something; conception *b)* the public conception of a person, product, etc., often created by publicity **5.** a type; embodiment *[*the *image* of laziness*]* **6.** a figure of speech, esp. a metaphor or simile —*vt.* **-aged, -ag·ing 1.** to portray; delineate **2.** to reflect; mirror **3.** to picture in the mind **4.** to typify **5.** to describe vividly
im·age·ry (im′ij rē, -ər ē) *n., pl.* **-ries 1.** mental images **2.** descriptions and figures of speech
i·mag·i·na·ble (i maj′ə nə b'l) *adj.* that can be imagined —**i·mag′i·na·bly** *adv.*
i·mag·i·nar·y (i maj′ə ner′ē) *adj.* existing only in the imagination; unreal —**i·mag′i·nar′i·ly** *adv.* —**i·mag′i·nar′i·ness** *n.*
i·mag·i·na·tion (i maj′ə nā′shən) *n.* **1.** *a)* the act or power of forming mental images of what is not actually present *b)* the act or power of creating mental images of what has never been actually experienced, or of creating new images or ideas by combining previous experiences **2.** anything imagined **3.** a foolish notion **4.** responsiveness to the imaginative creations of others **5.** resourcefulness in dealing with new or unusual experiences
i·mag·i·na·tive (i maj′ə nə tiv, -nāt′iv) *adj.* **1.** having, using, or showing imagination **2.** given to imagining **3.** of or resulting from imagination —**i·mag′i·na·tive·ly** *adv.* —**i·mag′i·na·tive·ness** *n.*
i·mag·ine (i maj′in) *vt., vi.* **-ined, -in·ing** [< OFr. < L. *imaginari* < *imago,* an IMAGE] **1.** to make a mental image (of); conceive in the mind **2.** to suppose; guess; think —*interj.* an exclamation of surprise
im·ag·ism (im′ə jiz′m) *n.* a movement in modern poetry (c. 1909–1917) using precise, concrete images, free verse, and suggestion —**im′ag·ist** *n., adj.* —**im′ag·is′tic** *adj.*
i·ma·go (i mā′gō) *n., pl.* **-goes, -gos, i·mag·i·nes** (i maj′ə nēz′) [ModL. < L., an IMAGE] an insect in its final, adult, reproductive stage
i·mam (i mäm′) *n.* [Ar. *imām*] **1.** the prayer leader in a Moslem mosque **2.** [*often* **I-**] title for a Moslem ruler
im·bal·ance (im bal′əns) *n.* lack of balance
im·be·cile (im′bə s'l) *n.* [< Fr. < L. *imbecilis,* feeble] **1.** a person having moderate mental retardation: obsolescent term: see MENTAL RETARDATION **2.** a very foolish or stupid person —*adj.* very foolish or stupid: also **im′be·cil′ic** (-sil′ik)
im·be·cil·i·ty (im′bə sil′ə tē) *n., pl.* **-ties 1.** the state of being an imbecile **2.** great foolishness or stupidity **3.** an imbecile act or remark
im·bed (im bed′) *vt. same as* EMBED
im·bibe (im bīb′) *vt.* **-bibed′, -bib′ing** [< L. *imbibere* < *in-,* in + *bibere,* to drink] **1.** *a)* to drink (esp. alcoholic liquor) *b)* to take in with the senses or mind; drink in **2.** to absorb (moisture) —*vi.* to drink, esp. alcoholic liquor —**im·bib′er** *n.*
im·bri·cate (im′brə kit; *also, and for v. always,* -kāt′) *adj.* [< LL. pp. of *imbricare,* to cover with tiles < L. *imbrex,* gutter tile < *imber,* rain] **1.** overlapping evenly, as tiles or fish scales **2.** ornamented as with overlapping scales —*vt., vi.* **-cat′ed, -cat′ing** to make or be imbricate —**im′bri·cate·ly** *adv.* —**im′bri·ca′tion** *n.*
im·bro·glio (im brōl′yō) *n., pl.* **-glios** [It. < *imbrogliare,* to embroil] **1.** an involved and confusing situation **2.** a confused misunderstanding or disagreement
im·brue (im bro͞o′) *vt.* **-brued′, -bru′ing** [< OFr., ult. < L. *imbibere:* see IMBIBE] to wet, soak, or stain, esp. with blood —**im·brue′ment** *n.*
im·bue (im byo͞o′) *vt.* **-bued′, -bu′ing** [< L. *imbuere*] **1.** [Rare] to saturate **2.** to fill with color; dye **3.** to permeate or inspire (*with* principles, ideas, emotions, etc.)
imit. 1. imitation **2.** imitative
im·i·tate (im′ə tāt′) *vt.* **-tat′ed, -tat′ing** [< L. pp. of *imitari,* to imitate] **1.** to follow the example of **2.** to act the same as; mimic **3.** to copy the form, color, etc. of **4.** to be like in appearance; resemble —**im′i·ta·ble** (-tə b'l) *adj.* —**im′i·ta′tor** *n.*
im·i·ta·tion (im′ə tā′shən) *n.* **1.** an imitating **2.** the result or product of imitating —*adj.* made to resemble something that is usually superior or genuine *[imitation* leather*]*

im·i·ta·tive (im′ə tāt′iv) ***adj.*** **1.** formed from a model **2.** given to imitating **3.** not genuine **4.** sounding like the thing signified, as the word *clang* —**im′i·ta′tive·ly** ***adv.*** —**im′i·ta′tive·ness** ***n.***

im·mac·u·late (i mak′yə lit) ***adj.*** [< L. < *in-*, not + pp. of *maculare*, to soil < *macula*, a spot] **1.** perfectly clean; spotless **2.** without flaw **3.** pure; innocent; sinless —**im·mac′u·late·ly** ***adv.*** —**im·mac′u·late·ness, im·mac′u·la·cy** (-lə sē) ***n.***

Immaculate Conception *R.C.Ch.* the doctrine that the Virgin Mary was from the moment of conception free from original sin

im·ma·nent (im′ə nənt) ***adj.*** [< LL. prp. of *immanere* < *in-*, in + *manere*, to remain] **1.** living, remaining, or operating within; inherent **2.** present throughout the universe: said of God —**im′ma·nence, im′ma·nen·cy** ***n.*** —**im′ma·nent·ly** ***adv.***

Im·man·u·el (i man′yoo wəl) **1.** [var. of EMMANUEL] a masculine name **2.** a name given by Isaiah to the Messiah of his prophecy (Isa. 7:14), often applied to Jesus (Matt. 1:23)

im·ma·te·ri·al (im′ə tir′ē əl) ***adj.*** **1.** not consisting of matter; spiritual **2.** that does not matter; not pertinent; unimportant —**im′ma·te′ri·al′i·ty** (-al′ə tē) ***n.***, *pl.* **-ties** —**im′ma·te′ri·al·ly** ***adv.***

im·ma·ture (im′ə toor′, -choor′, -tyoor′) ***adj.*** **1.** not mature or ripe; not completely grown or developed **2.** not finished or perfected —**im′ma·ture′ly** ***adv.*** —**im′ma·tu′ri·ty, im′ma·ture′ness** ***n.***

im·meas·ur·a·ble (i mezh′ər ə b'l) ***adj.*** not measurable; boundless —**im·meas′ur·a·bil′i·ty, im·meas′ur·a·ble·ness** ***n.*** —**im·meas′ur·a·bly** ***adv.***

im·me·di·a·cy (i mē′dē ə sē) ***n.*** the quality or condition of being immediate

im·me·di·ate (i mē′dē it) ***adj.*** [< LL.: see IN-[2] & MEDIATE] having nothing coming between; with no intermediary; specif., *a*) not separated in space; in direct contact; closest; also, close by *b*) not separated in time; without delay *c*) of the present *d*) next in order, succession, etc.; also, directly or closely related *e*) directly affecting; direct

im·me·di·ate·ly (-lē) ***adv.*** in an immediate manner; specif., *a*) without intervening agency or cause *b*) without delay; at once —***conj.*** [Chiefly Brit.] as soon as [*go immediately he comes*]

im·me·mo·ri·al (im′ə môr′ē əl) ***adj.*** back beyond memory or record —**im′me·mo′ri·al·ly** ***adv.***

im·mense (i mens′) ***adj.*** [Fr. < L. < *in-*, not + pp. of *metiri*, to measure] **1.** very large; vast; huge **2.** [Slang] very good; excellent —**im·mense′ly** ***adv.*** —**im·mense′ness** ***n.***

im·men·si·ty (i men′sə tē) ***n.***, *pl.* **-ties** **1.** great size or extent **2.** infinite space or being

im·merge (i murj′) ***vi.*** **-merged′, -merg′ing** [see ff.] to plunge, as into a liquid

im·merse (i murs′) ***vt.*** **-mersed′, -mers′ing** [< L. pp. of *immergere*, to plunge: see IN-[1] & MERGE] **1.** to plunge or dip into or as if into a liquid **2.** to baptize by dipping under water **3.** to absorb deeply; engross —**im·mers′i·ble** ***adj.*** —**im·mer′sion** ***n.***

immersion heater an electric coil or rod that heats water while directly immersed in it

im·mi·grant (im′ə grənt) ***n.*** one that immigrates —***adj.*** immigrating

im·mi·grate (-grāt′) ***vi.*** **-grat′ed, -grat′ing** [< L. pp. of *immigrare*: see IN-[1] & MIGRATE] to come into a new country or region, esp. in order to settle there: opposed to EMIGRATE —**im′mi·gra′tion** ***n.***

im·mi·nence (im′ə nəns) ***n.*** **1.** a being imminent: also **im′mi·nen·cy** **2.** something imminent

im·mi·nent (-nənt) ***adj.*** [< L. prp. of *imminere* < *in-*, in + *minere*, to project] likely to happen soon: said of danger, evil, etc. —**im′mi·nent·ly** ***adv.***

im·mis·ci·ble (i mis′ə b'l) ***adj.*** [< IN-[2] + MISCIBLE] that cannot be mixed, as oil and water —**im·mis′ci·bil′i·ty** ***n.***

im·mo·bile (i mō′b'l, -bēl, -bīl) ***adj.*** not movable or moving; stable; motionless —**im′mo·bil′i·ty** ***n.***

im·mo·bi·lize (i mō′bə līz′) ***vt.*** **-lized′, -liz′ing** **1.** to make immobile **2.** to prevent the movement of (a limb or joint) with splints or a cast —**im·mo′bi·li·za′tion** ***n.***

im·mod·er·ate (i mäd′ər it) ***adj.*** not moderate; without restraint; excessive —**im·mod′er·ate·ly** ***adv.*** —**im·mod′er·a′tion, im·mod′er·ate·ness, im·mod′er·a·cy** (-ə sē) ***n.***

im·mod·est (i mäd′ist) ***adj.*** not modest; specif., *a*) indecent; improper *b*) bold; forward —**im·mod′est·ly** ***adv.*** —**im·mod′es·ty** ***n.***

im·mo·late (im′ə lāt′) ***vt.*** **-lat′ed, -lat′ing** [< L. pp. of *immolare*, to sprinkle with sacrificial meal < *in-*, on + *mola*, meal] to sacrifice; esp., to kill as a sacrifice —**im′mo·la′tion** ***n.*** —**im′mo·la′tor** ***n.***

im·mor·al (i môr′əl, -mär′-) ***adj.*** not in conformity with accepted principles of right behavior; wicked; sometimes, specif., unchaste; lewd —**im·mor′al·ly** ***adv.***

im·mo·ral·i·ty (im′ə ral′ə tē, im′ô-) ***n.*** **1.** the state or quality of being immoral **2.** immoral behavior **3.** *pl.* **-ties** an immoral act or practice

im·mor·tal (i môr′t'l) ***adj.*** **1.** not mortal; living or lasting forever **2.** of immortal beings or immortality **3.** lasting a long time; enduring **4.** having lasting fame —***n.*** an immortal being; specif., *a*) [*pl.*] the ancient Greek or Roman gods *b*) a person of lasting fame —**im′mor·tal′i·ty** (-tal′ə tē) ***n.*** —**im·mor′tal·ly** ***adv.***

im·mor·tal·ize (i môr′tə līz′) ***vt.*** **-ized′, -iz′ing** to make immortal; esp., to give lasting fame to —**im·mor′tal·i·za′tion** ***n.*** —**im·mor′tal·iz′er** ***n.***

im·mor·telle (im′ôr tel′) ***n.*** [Fr. fem. of *immortel*, undying] *same as* EVERLASTING (*n.* 2)

im·mov·a·ble (i moo̅v′ə b'l) ***adj.*** **1.** that cannot be moved; firmly fixed **2.** motionless; stationary **3.** unyielding; steadfast **4.** unemotional; impassive —***n.*** [*pl.*] *Law* immovable objects or property, as land, buildings, etc. —**im·mov′a·bil′i·ty, im·mov′a·ble·ness** ***n.*** —**im·mov′a·bly** ***adv.***

im·mune (i myo̅o̅n′) ***adj.*** [< L. *immunis*, exempt < *in-*, without + *munia*, duties] having immunity; specif., *a*) exempt from or protected against something disagreeable or harmful *b*) not susceptible to a specified disease because having the specific antibodies

immune body *same as* ANTIBODY

im·mu·ni·ty (i myo̅o̅n′ə tē) ***n.***, *pl.* **-ties** **1.** exemption or freedom from something burdensome or otherwise unpleasant **2.** resistance to or protection against a specified disease

im·mu·nize (im′yə nīz′) ***vt.*** **-nized′, -niz′ing** to give immunity to —**im′mu·ni·za′tion** ***n.***

im·mu·no·gen·ic (im′yoo nō jen′ik) ***adj.*** producing immunity —**im′mu·no·gen′i·cal·ly** ***adv.***

im·mu·nol·o·gy (im′yoo näl′ə jē) ***n.*** the branch of medicine dealing with immunity to disease or with allergic reactions, etc. —**im′mu·no·log′i·cal** (-nə läj′i k'l), **im′mu·no·log′ic** ***adj.*** —**im′mu·no·log′i·cal·ly** ***adv.*** —**im′mu·nol′o·gist** ***n.***

im·mure (i myoor′) ***vt.*** **-mured′, -mur′ing** [< OFr. < ML. *immurare* < L. *im-*, in + *murus*, a wall] to shut up as within walls —**im·mure′ment** ***n.***

im·mu·ta·ble (i myo̅o̅t′ə b'l) ***adj.*** never changing or varying; unchangeable —**im·mu′ta·bil′i·ty, im·mu′ta·ble·ness** ***n.*** —**im·mu′ta·bly** ***adv.***

imp (imp) ***n.*** [< OE., ult. < Gr. *emphyta*, scion < *em-*, in + *phyton*, a plant] **1.** a young demon **2.** a mischievous child

imp. **1.** imperative **2.** imperfect **3.** imperial **4.** impersonal **5.** import **6.** importer **7.** imprimatur

im·pact (im pakt′; *for n.* im′pakt) ***vt.*** [< L. pp. of *impingere*, to press firmly together] to force tightly together; wedge —***n.*** **1.** a striking together; collision **2.** the force of a collision; shock **3.** the power of an event, idea, etc. to produce changes, move feelings, etc. —**im·pac′tion** ***n.***

im·pact·ed (im pak′tid) ***adj.*** **1.** firmly lodged in the jaw: said of a tooth unable to erupt **2.** densely populated

IMPACTED TOOTH

im·pair (im per′) ***vt.*** [< OFr., ult. < L. *in-*, intens. + *pejor*, worse] to make worse, less, weaker, etc.; damage; reduce —**im·pair′ment** ***n.***

im·pa·la (im pä′lə, -pal′ə) ***n.***, *pl.* **-la, -las**: see PLURAL, II, D, 2 [Zulu] a medium-sized, reddish antelope of C and S Africa

im·pale (im pāl′) ***vt.*** **-paled′, -pal′ing** [< Fr. < ML. *impalare* < L. *in-*, on + *palus*, a pole] **1.** to pierce through with, or fix on, something pointed **2.** to torture by fixing on a stake **3.** to make helpless, as if fixed on a stake [*impaled by her glance*] —**im·pale′ment** ***n.***

im·pal·pa·ble (im pal′pə b'l) ***adj.*** **1.** not perceptible to the touch **2.** too slight or subtle to be grasped easily by the mind —**im·pal′pa·bil′i·ty** ***n.*** —**im·pal′pa·bly** ***adv.***

im·pan·el (im pan′'l) ***vt.*** **-eled** or **-elled, -el·ing** or **-el·ling** **1.** to enter the name or names of on a jury list **2.** to choose (a jury) from such a list —**im·pan′el·ment** ***n.***

im·part (im pärt′) ***vt.*** [< OFr. < L. *impartire*: see IN-[1] & PART] **1.** to give a share or portion of; give **2.** to tell; reveal —**im·part′a·ble** ***adj.*** —**im′par·ta′tion** ***n.*** —**im·part′er** ***n.***

im·par·tial (im pär′shəl) ***adj.*** favoring no one side or party more than another; fair —**im·par′ti·al′i·ty** (-shē al′ə tē) ***n.*** —**im·par′tial·ly** ***adv.***

im·pass·a·ble (im pas′ə b'l) ***adj.*** that cannot be passed, crossed, or traveled over —**im·pass′a·bil′i·ty** ***n.*** —**im·pass′a·bly** ***adv.***

im·passe (im′pas, im pas′) ***n.*** [Fr.] **1.** a passage open only at one end; blind alley **2.** a situation offering no escape; deadlock

im·pas·si·ble (im pas′ə b'l) ***adj.*** [< OFr. < LL. < L. *im-*, not + *passibilis* < *pati*, to suffer] **1.** that cannot feel pain **2.** that cannot be injured **3.** that cannot be moved emotionally —**im·pas′si·bil′i·ty** ***n.*** —**im·pas′si·bly** ***adv.***

im·pas·sioned (im pash′ənd) ***adj.*** filled with passion; passionate; fiery; ardent —**im·pas′sioned·ly** ***adv.***

im·pas·sive (im pas′iv) ***adj.*** **1.** not feeling pain; insensible **2.** not feeling or showing emotion; placid; calm —**im·pas′sive·ly** ***adv.*** —**im·pas·siv·i·ty** (im′pə siv′ə tē) ***n.***

im·pas·to (im päs′tō) ***n.*** [< It. *impastare*, to paste over] painting with the paint laid on thickly

im·pa·tience (im pā′shəns) ***n.*** lack of patience; specif., *a*) annoyance because of delay, opposition, etc. *b*) restless eagerness to do something, etc.

im·pa·ti·ens (im pā′shē enz′, -shənz) ***n.*** [ModL. < L.: see ff.] a plant with spurred flowers and pods that burst and scatter their seeds when ripe

im·pa·tient (im pā′shənt) ***adj.*** feeling or showing impatience —**im·pa′tient·ly** ***adv.***

im·peach (im pēch′) ***vt.*** [< OFr. < LL. *impedicare*, to entangle < L. *in-*, in + *pedica*, a fetter < *pes*, foot] **1.** to challenge or discredit (a person's honor, etc.) **2.** to challenge the practices or honesty of; esp., to bring (a public official) before the proper tribunal on a charge of wrongdoing —**im·peach′a·bil′i·ty** ***n.*** —**im·peach′a·ble** ***adj.*** —**im·peach′ment** ***n.***

im·pec·ca·ble (im pek′ə b'l) ***adj.*** [< L. < *in-*, not + *peccare*, to sin] **1.** not liable to sin or wrongdoing **2.** without defect or error; flawless —**im·pec′ca·bil′i·ty** ***n.*** —**im·pec′ca·bly** ***adv.***

im·pe·cu·ni·ous (im′pi kyōō′nē əs) ***adj.*** [< IN-² + obs. *pecunious*, wealthy < OFr. < L. < *pecunia*, money] having no money; penniless —**im′pe·cu′ni·os′i·ty** (-äs′ə tē), **im′pe·cu′ni·ous·ness** ***n.*** —**im′pe·cu′ni·ous·ly** ***adv.***

im·ped·ance (im pēd′'ns) ***n.*** [IMPED(E) + -ANCE] the total opposition (a combination of resistance and reactance) offered by an electric circuit to the flow of an alternating current of a single frequency: it is measured in ohms

im·pede (im pēd′) ***vt.*** **-ped′ed, -ped′ing** [< L. *impedire* < *in-*, in + *pes* (gen. *pedis*), foot] to bar or hinder the progress of; obstruct or delay —**im·ped′er** ***n.***

im·ped·i·ment (im ped′ə mənt) ***n.*** [< L. *impedimentum*, hindrance] anything that impedes; specif., a speech defect; lisp, stammer, etc.

im·ped·i·men·ta (im ped′ə men′tə) ***n.pl.*** [L., pl.: see prec.] things hindering progress, as on a trip; esp., baggage, supplies, etc.

im·pel (im pel′) ***vt.*** **-pelled′, -pel′ling** [L. *impellere* < *in-*, on + *pellere*, to drive] **1.** to push, drive, or move forward; propel **2.** to force, compel, or urge —**im·pel′lent** ***adj., n.***

im·pend (im pend′) ***vi.*** [L. *impendere* < *in-*, in + *pendere*, to hang] to be about to happen; threaten

im·pen·e·tra·ble (im pen′i trə b'l) ***adj.*** **1.** that cannot be penetrated or passed through **2.** that cannot be solved or understood; unfathomable **3.** unreceptive to ideas, influences, etc. —**im·pen′e·tra·bil′i·ty** ***n.*** —**im·pen′e·tra·bly** ***adv.***

im·pen·i·tent (im pen′ə tənt) ***adj.*** without regret, shame, or remorse; unrepentant —***n.*** an impenitent person —**im·pen′i·tence, im·pen′i·ten·cy** ***n.*** —**im·pen′i·tent·ly** ***adv.***

imper. imperative

im·per·a·tive (im per′ə tiv) ***adj.*** [< LL. < pp. of L. *imperare*, to order] **1.** of or indicating power or authority; commanding [an *imperative* gesture] **2.** absolutely necessary; urgent **3.** *Gram.* designating or of a verb mood expressing a command, request, etc. —***n.*** **1.** a compelling rule, duty, etc. **2.** a command **3.** *Gram.* *a*) the imperative mood *b*) a verb in this mood —**im·per′a·tive·ly** ***adv.*** —**im·per′a·tive·ness** ***n.***

im·pe·ra·tor (im′pə rāt′ər, -rät′-; -ôr) ***n.*** [L. < pp. of *imperare*, to command] in ancient Rome, a title of honor for generals and, later, emperors —**im·per·a·to·ri·al** (im-pir′ə tôr′ē əl) ***adj.***

im·per·cep·ti·ble (im′pər sep′tə b'l) ***adj.*** not easily perceived by the senses or mind; very slight, gradual, subtle, etc. —**im′per·cep′ti·bil′i·ty** ***n.*** —**im′per·cep′ti·bly** ***adv.***

im·per·cep·tive (-tiv) ***adj.*** not perceiving; lacking perception: also **im′per·cip′i·ent** (-sip′ē ənt) —**im′per·cep′tive·ness** ***n.***

imperf. **1.** imperfect **2.** imperforate

im·per·fect (im pur′fikt) ***adj.*** **1.** not finished or complete; lacking in something **2.** not perfect; having a defect or error **3.** in the grammar of certain inflected languages, designating or of a verb tense indicating an incomplete or continuous past action or state: in English, "was writing" is a form like the imperfect tense —***n.*** *Gram.* **1.** the imperfect tense **2.** a verb in this tense —**im·per′fect·ly** ***adv.*** —**im·per′fect·ness** ***n.***

im·per·fec·tion (im′pər fek′shən) ***n.*** **1.** a being imperfect **2.** a shortcoming; defect; blemish

im·per·fo·rate (im pur′fər it, -fə rāt′) ***adj.*** **1.** having no holes or openings **2.** having a straight edge without perforations: said of a postage stamp Also **im·per′fo·rat′ed** —***n.*** an imperforate stamp —**im·per′fo·ra′tion** ***n.***

im·pe·ri·al (im pir′ē əl) ***adj.*** [< OFr. < L. < *imperium*, empire] **1.** of an empire **2.** of a country having control over other countries or colonies **3.** of, or having the rank of, an emperor or empress **4.** having supreme authority **5.** majestic; august **6.** of great size or superior quality **7.** *a*) of the British Commonwealth *b*) of a system of weights and measures, formerly official in Great Britain, in which the gallon equals 277.42 cubic inches —***n.*** **1.** a size of writing paper (23 x 31 in.) **2.** a pointed tuft of beard on the lower lip and chin —**im·pe′ri·al·ly** ***adv.***

im·pe·ri·al·ism (-iz′m) ***n.*** **1.** imperial state, authority, or government **2.** the policy and practice of forming and maintaining an empire by conquest, colonization, economic or political domination, etc. —**im·pe′ri·al·ist** ***n., adj.*** —**im·pe′ri·al·is′tic** ***adj.*** —**im·pe′ri·al·is′ti·cal·ly** ***adv.***

Imperial Valley irrigated agricultural region in S Calif. & NW Mexico, reclaimed from the desert

im·per·il (im per′əl) ***vt.*** **-iled** or **-illed, -il·ing** or **-il·ling** to put in peril —**im·per′il·ment** ***n.***

im·pe·ri·ous (im pir′ē əs) ***adj.*** [< L. < *imperium*, empire] **1.** arrogant; domineering **2.** urgent —**im·pe′ri·ous·ly** ***adv.*** —**im·pe′ri·ous·ness** ***n.***

im·per·ish·a·ble (im per′ish ə b'l) ***adj.*** that will not die or decay; indestructible; immortal —**im·per′ish·a·bil′i·ty** ***n.*** —**im·per′ish·a·bly** ***adv.***

im·per·ma·nent (im pur′mə nənt) ***adj.*** not permanent; not lasting; temporary —**im·per′ma·nence, im·per′ma·nen·cy** ***n.*** —**im·per′ma·nent·ly** ***adv.***

im·per·me·a·ble (im pur′mē ə b'l) ***adj.*** not permeable; not permitting passage, esp. of fluids —**im·per′me·a·bil′i·ty** ***n.*** —**im·per′me·a·bly** ***adv.***

im·per·son·al (im pur′s'n əl) ***adj.*** **1.** not personal; specif., *a*) without reference to any particular person [an *impersonal* comment] *b*) not existing as a person [an *impersonal* force] **2.** *Gram.* *a*) designating or of a verb occurring only in the third person singular (Ex.: "it is snowing") *b*) indefinite: said of a pronoun —***n.*** an impersonal verb or pronoun —**im·per′son·al′i·ty** (-al′ə tē) ***n.*** —**im·per′son·al·ly** ***adv.***

im·per·son·al·ize (-ə līz′) ***vt.*** **-ized′, -iz′ing** to make impersonal

im·per·son·ate (im pur′sə nāt′) ***vt.*** **-at′ed, -at′ing** **1.** [Now Rare] to personify; embody **2.** to act the part of **3.** *a*) to mimic (a person) for purposes of entertainment *b*) to pretend to be (an officer, etc.) with fraudulent intent —**im·per′son·a′tion** ***n.*** —**im·per′son·a′tor** ***n.***

im·per·ti·nence (im pur′t'n əns) ***n.*** **1.** the quality or fact of being impertinent; specif., *a*) irrelevance *b*) insolence **2.** an impertinent act, remark, etc. Also **im·per′ti·nen·cy**, *pl.* **-cies**

im·per·ti·nent (-ənt) ***adj.*** **1.** not pertinent; irrelevant **2.** insolent —**im·per′ti·nent·ly** ***adv.***

im·per·turb·a·ble (im′pər tur′bə b'l) ***adj.*** that cannot be perturbed or excited; impassive —**im′per·turb′a·bil′i·ty** ***n.*** —**im′per·turb′a·bly** ***adv.***

im·per·vi·ous (im pur′vē əs) ***adj.*** **1.** not pervious; impermeable **2.** not affected by (with *to*) —**im·per′vi·ous·ly** ***adv.*** —**im·per′vi·ous·ness** ***n.***

im·pe·ti·go (im′pə tī′gō) ***n.*** [L. < *impetere*: see IMPETUS] a skin disease with eruption of pustules; esp., a contagious disease of this kind

im·pet·u·os·i·ty (im pech′oo wäs′ə tē, im′pech-) ***n.*** **1.** the quality of being impetuous **2.** *pl.* **-ties** an impetuous action or feeling

im·pet·u·ous (im pech′oo wəs) ***adj.*** [< OFr. < LL. < L. *impetus*: see ff.] **1.** moving with great force or violence; rushing **2.** acting or done suddenly with little thought; rash; impulsive —**im·pet′u·ous·ly** ***adv.*** —**im·pet′u·ous·ness** ***n.***

im·pe·tus (im′pə təs) ***n.***, *pl.* **-tus·es** [L. < *impetere*, to attack < *in-*, in + *petere*, to rush at] **1.** the force with which a body moves against resistance, resulting from its mass and initial velocity **2.** a stimulus to action; incentive

im·pi·e·ty (im pī′ə tē) ***n.*** **1.** lack of piety, esp. toward God **2.** *pl.* **-ties** an impious act or remark

im·pinge (im pinj′) ***vi.*** **-pinged′, -ping′ing** [L. *impingere* < *in-*, in + *pangere*, to strike] **1.** *a*) to strike or hit (*on, upon*, or *against*) *b*) to touch (*on* or *upon*) **2.** to make inroads or encroach (*on* or *upon*) —**im·pinge′ment** ***n.*** —**im·ping′er** ***n.***

im·pi·ous (im′pē əs) ***adj.*** not pious; specif., lacking reverence for God —**im′pi·ous·ly** ***adv.*** —**im′pi·ous·ness** ***n.***

imp·ish (im′pish) ***adj.*** of or like an imp; mischievous —**imp′ish·ly** ***adv.*** —**imp′ish·ness** ***n.***

im·plac·a·ble (im plak′ə b'l, -plā′kə-) ***adj.*** not placable; that cannot be appeased or pacified —**im·plac′a·bil′i·ty** ***n.*** —**im·plac′a·bly** ***adv.***

im·plant (im plant′; *for n.* im′plant′) ***vt.*** **1.** to plant firmly; embed **2.** to fix firmly in the mind; instill **3.** *Med.* to insert (an organ, tissue, etc.) within the body —***n.*** *Med.* an implanted organ, etc. —**im′plan·ta′tion** (-plan tā′shən) ***n.***

im·plau·si·ble (im plô′zə b'l) ***adj.*** not plausible —**im·plau′si·bil′i·ty** ***n.***, *pl.* **-ties** —**im·plau′si·bly** ***adv.***

im·ple·ment (im′plə mənt; *for v.* -ment′) ***n.*** [< LL. *implementum*, a filling up < L. *implere* < *in-*, in + *plere*, to fill] **1.** any tool, instrument, utensil, etc. used or needed in a given activity **2.** a means to an end —***vt.*** **1.** to carry into effect **2.** to provide the means for accomplishing **3.** to provide with implements —**im′ple·men′tal** ***adj.*** —**im′ple·men·ta′tion** (-mən tā′shən) ***n.***

im·pli·cate (im′plə kāt′) ***vt.*** **-cat′ed, -cat′ing** [< L. pp. of *implicare:* see IMPLY] **1.** to cause to be involved in or associated with a crime, fault, etc. **2.** to imply —**im′pli·ca′tion** ***n.*** —**im′pli·ca′tive** ***adj.*** —**im′pli·ca′tive·ly** ***adv.***

im·plic·it (im plis′it) ***adj.*** [< L. pp. of *implicare:* see IMPLY] **1.** suggested or to be understood though not plainly expressed; implied: distinguished from EXPLICIT **2.** necessarily or naturally involved though not plainly apparent or expressed; inherent **3.** without reservation or doubt; absolute —**im·plic′it·ly** ***adv.*** —**im·plic′it·ness** ***n.***

im·plied (im plīd′) ***adj.*** involved, suggested, or understood without being directly expressed

im·plode (im plōd′) ***vt., vi.*** **-plod′ed, -plod′ing** [< IN-[1] + (EX)PLODE] to burst inward —**im·plo′sion** (-plō′zhən) ***n.***

im·plore (im plôr′) ***vt.*** **-plored′, -plor′ing** [< L. *implorare* < *in-*, intens. + *plorare*, to cry out] **1.** to ask earnestly for; beseech **2.** to beg (a person) to do something —**im·plor′ing·ly** ***adv.***

im·ply (im plī′) ***vt.*** **-plied′, -ply′ing** [< OFr. < L. *implicare*, to involve < *in-*, in + *plicare*, to fold] **1.** to have as a necessary part, condition, or effect [war *implies* killing] **2.** to indicate indirectly; hint; suggest [he *implied* that we cheat]

im·po·lite (im′pə līt′) ***adj.*** not polite; discourteous; rude —**im′po·lite′ly** ***adv.*** —**im′po·lite′ness** ***n.***

im·pol·i·tic (im päl′ə tik) ***adj.*** not politic; unwise; injudicious —**im·pol′i·tic·ly** ***adv.***

im·pon·der·a·ble (im pän′dər ə b'l) ***adj.*** [< LL.: see IN-[2] & PONDER] **1.** that cannot be weighed or measured **2.** that cannot be conclusively determined or explained —***n.*** anything imponderable —**im·pon′der·a·bil′i·ty** ***n.*** —**im·pon′der·a·bly** ***adv.***

im·port (im pôrt′; *also, and for n. always,* im′pôrt) ***vt.*** [< L. *importare* < *in-*, in + *portare*, to carry] **1.** *a)* to bring in from the outside *b)* to bring (goods) from another country, esp. for selling **2.** to mean; signify —***vi.*** to be of importance; matter —***n.*** **1.** the importing of goods **2.** something imported **3.** meaning **4.** importance —**im·port′a·ble** ***adj.*** —**im·port′er** ***n.***

im·por·tance (im pôr′t'ns) ***n.*** the state or quality of being important; significance; consequence

im·por·tant (-t'nt) ***adj.*** [Fr. < OIt. < ML. prp. of *importare:* see IMPORT] **1.** meaning a great deal; having much significance or consequence **2.** having, or acting as if having, power, authority, high position, etc. —**im·por′tant·ly** ***adv.***

im·por·ta·tion (im′pôr tā′shən) ***n.*** **1.** an importing or being imported **2.** something imported

im·por·tu·nate (im pôr′chə nit) ***adj.*** urgent or annoyingly persistent in asking or demanding —**im·por′tu·nate·ly** ***adv.*** —**im·por′tu·nate·ness** ***n.***

im·por·tune (im′pôr to͞on′, -tyo͞on′; im pôr′chən) ***vt.*** **-tuned′, -tun′ing** [< Fr. < OFr. < L. *importunus*, troublesome < *in-*, not + *(op)portunus:* see OPPORTUNE] to trouble with requests or demands; entreat persistently —***vi.*** to be importunate —**im′por·tune′ly** ***adv.*** —**im′por·tun′er** ***n.***

im·por·tu·ni·ty (-to͞on′ə tē, -tyo͞on′-) ***n.***, *pl.* **-ties** an importuning or being importunate

im·pose (im pōz′) ***vt.*** **-posed′, -pos′ing** [< Fr. < L. *imponere* < *in-*, on + *ponere*, to place] **1.** to place (a burden, tax, etc. *on* or *upon*) **2.** to force (oneself) on another **3.** to pass off by deception; foist **4.** to arrange (pages of type) in a frame for printing —**impose on** (or **upon**) **1.** to put to some trouble or use unfairly for one's own benefit **2.** to cheat or defraud —**im·pos′er** ***n.***

im·pos·ing (im pō′ziŋ) ***adj.*** impressive in size, dignity, etc. —**im·pos′ing·ly** ***adv.***

im·po·si·tion (im′pə zish′ən) ***n.*** **1.** an imposing or imposing on; specif., a taking advantage of friendship, etc. **2.** something imposed; specif., *a)* a tax, fine, etc. *b)* an unjust burden or requirement *c)* a deception; fraud

im·pos·si·bil·i·ty (im päs′ə bil′ə tē) ***n.*** **1.** the fact or quality of being impossible **2.** *pl.* **-ties** something that is impossible

im·pos·si·ble (im päs′ə b'l) ***adj.*** not possible; specif,, *a)* not capable of being, being done, or happening *b)* not capable of being endured, used, agreed to, etc. because disagreeable or unsuitable —**im·pos′si·bly** ***adv.***

im·post[1] (im′pōst) ***n.*** [OFr. < ML. < L. *impositus*, pp. of *imponere:* see IMPOSE] **1.** a tax; esp., a duty on imported goods **2.** the weight assigned to a horse in a handicap race

im·post[2] (im′pōst) ***n.*** [ult. < L.: see prec.] the top part of a pillar, pier, etc. supporting an arch

im·pos·tor (im päs′tər) ***n.*** [see IMPOSE] a person who deceives or cheats others, esp. by pretending to be someone or something that he is not

im·pos·ture (-chər) ***n.*** the act or practice of an impostor; fraud; deception

im·po·tence (im′pə təns) ***n.*** the quality or condition of being impotent: also **im′po·ten·cy**

im·po·tent (-tənt) ***adj.*** [see IN-[2] & POTENT] **1.** lacking physical strength **2.** ineffective, powerless, or helpless **3.** unable to engage in sexual intercourse, esp. because of an inability to have an erection —**im′po·tent·ly** ***adv.***

im·pound (im pound′) ***vt.*** **1.** to shut up (an animal) in a pound **2.** to take and hold (evidence, etc.) in legal custody **3.** to gather and enclose (water) for irrigation, etc. —**im·pound′ment** ***n.***

im·pov·er·ish (im päv′ər ish, -päv′rish) ***vt.*** [< OFr. < *em-* (< L. *in-*, in) + *povre* (< L. *pauper*, poor)] **1.** to make poor **2.** to deprive of strength, resources, etc. —**im·pov′er·ish·ment** ***n.***

im·prac·ti·ca·ble (im prak′ti kə b'l) ***adj.*** **1.** not capable of being carried out in practice [an *impracticable* plan] **2.** not capable of being used [an *impracticable* road] —**im·prac′ti·ca·bil′i·ty, im·prac′ti·ca·ble·ness** ***n.*** —**im·prac′ti·ca·bly** ***adv.***

im·prac·ti·cal (im prak′tə k'l) ***adj.*** not practical; specif., *a)* not workable or useful *b)* not handling practical matters well *c)* idealistic —**im·prac′ti·cal′i·ty, im·prac′ti·cal·ness** ***n.***

im·pre·cate (im′prə kāt′) ***vt.*** **-cat′ed, -cat′ing** [< L. pp. of *imprecari* < *in-*, on + *precari*, to PRAY] to pray for or invoke (evil, a curse, etc.) —**im′pre·ca′tion** ***n.*** —**im′pre·ca′tor** ***n.*** —**im′pre·ca·to′ry** ***adj.***

im·pre·cise (im′pri sīs′) ***adj.*** not precise or definite —**im′pre·cise′ly** ***adv.*** —**im′pre·ci′sion** ***n.***

im·preg·na·ble[1] (im preg′nə b'l) ***adj.*** [< OFr.: see IN-[2] & PREGNABLE] **1.** not capable of being captured or entered by force **2.** unshakable; firm —**im·preg′na·bil′i·ty** ***n.*** —**im·preg′na·bly** ***adv.***

im·preg·na·ble[2] (im preg′nə b'l) ***adj.*** [IMPREGN(ATE) + -ABLE] that can be impregnated

im·preg·nate (im preg′nāt; *for adj.* -nit) ***vt.*** **-nat·ed, -nat·ing** [< LL. pp. of *impraegnare*, to make pregnant < L. *in-*, in + *praegnans*, PREGNANT] **1.** to fertilize **2.** to make pregnant **3.** to fill or saturate **4.** to imbue (*with* ideas, feelings, etc.) —***adj.*** impregnated —**im′preg·na′tion** ***n.*** —**im·preg′na·tor** ***n.***

im·pre·sa·ri·o (im′prə sär′ē ō, -ser′-) ***n.***, *pl.* **-ri·os** [It. < *impresa*, enterprise, ult. < L. *in-*, in + *prehendere*, to take, grasp] the organizer or manager of an opera company, concert series, etc.

im·pre·scrip·ti·ble (im′pri skrip′tə b'l) ***adj.*** that cannot rightfully be taken away or revoked; inviolable —**im′pre·scrip′ti·bly** ***adv.***

im·press[1] (im pres′) ***vt.*** [< IN-[1] + PRESS[2]] **1.** to force (men) into public service, esp. into a navy **2.** to levy or seize for public use —**im·press′ment** ***n.***

im·press[2] (im pres′; *for n.* im′pres) ***vt.*** [< L. pp. of *imprimere:* see IN-[1] & PRESS[1]] **1.** to use pressure on so as to leave a mark **2.** to mark by using pressure; stamp; imprint **3.** *a)* to affect strongly the mind or emotions of *b)* to arouse the interest or approval of **4.** to fix in the memory —***n.*** **1.** an impressing **2.** any mark, imprint, etc.; stamp **3.** a quality or effect produced by some strong influence —**im·press′i·bil′i·ty** ***n.*** —**im·press′i·ble** ***adj.*** —**im·press′i·bly** ***adv.***

im·pres·sion (im presh′ən) ***n.*** **1.** an impressing **2.** *a)* a mark, imprint, etc. made by physical pressure *b)* an effect produced on the mind or senses *c)* the effect produced by any effort or activity [cleaning made no *impression* on the stain] **3.** a vague notion **4.** an amusing impersonation **5.** *Printing* *a)* a printed copy *b)* all the copies printed at one time from a set of type or plates —**im·pres′sion·al** ***adj.***

im·pres·sion·a·ble (-ə b'l) ***adj.*** easily affected by impressions; capable of being influenced; sensitive —**im·pres′sion·a·bil′i·ty** ***n.*** —**im·pres′sion·a·bly** ***adv.***

im·pres·sion·ism (-iz'm) ***n.*** a theory and school of art whose chief aim is to capture an impression of a subject, esp. to reproduce the play of light on surfaces: the term has been extended to literature and music which seeks to convey moods and impressions —**im·pres′sion·ist** ***n., adj.*** —**im-pres′sion·is′tic** ***adj.*** —**im·pres′sion·is′ti·cal·ly** ***adv.***

im·pres·sive (im pres′iv) ***adj.*** impressing or tending to impress the mind or emotions; striking, imposing, etc. —**im-pres′sive·ly** ***adv.***

im·pri·ma·tur (im′pri mät′ər, -māt′-) ***n.*** [ModL., let it be printed (see ff.)] **1.** license or permission to publish or print a book, article, etc.; specif., *R.C.Ch.* such permission granted by an ecclesiastical censor **2.** any sanction or approval

im·print (im print′; *for n.* im′print) ***vt.*** [< OFr. < L. *imprimere* < *in-*, on + *premere*, to PRESS[1]] **1.** to mark by pressing or stamping; impress **2.** to press [to *imprint* a kiss on the cheek] **3.** to fix in the memory —***n.*** **1.** a mark made by imprinting **2.** a lasting effect or characteristic result **3.** a publisher's note, as on the title page of a book, giving his name, the place of publication, etc.

im·print·ing (im print′iŋ) ***n.*** *Psychol.* a learning mechanism of very young animals by which an initial stimulus establishes an irreversible behavior pattern with reference to the same stimulus in the future

im·pris·on (im priz′'n) ***vt.*** **1.** to put or keep in prison; jail **2.** to restrict, limit, or confine in any way —**im-pris′on·ment** ***n.***

im·prob·a·ble (im präb′ə b'l) ***adj.*** not probable; unlikely to happen or be true —**im′prob·a·bil′i·ty** ***n.***, *pl.* **-ties** —**im-prob′a·bly** ***adv.***

im·promp·tu (im prämp′to͞o, -tyo͞o) ***adj., adv.*** [Fr. < L. *in promptu*, in readiness: see PROMPT] without preparation or advance thought; offhand —***n.*** an impromptu speech, performance, etc.

im·prop·er (im präp′ər) ***adj.*** **1.** not proper or suitable; poorly adapted; unfit **2.** not in accordance with the truth, fact, etc.; incorrect **3.** not in good taste; indecent; indecorous **4.** not normal or regular —**im·prop′er·ly** ***adv.*** —**im·prop′er·ness** ***n.***

improper fraction a fraction in which the denominator is less than the numerator (Ex.: 5/3)

im·pro·pri·e·ty (im′prə prī′ə tē) ***n.***, *pl.* **-ties** **1.** the quality of being improper **2.** improper action or behavior **3.** an improper use of a word (Ex.: "borrow" for "lend")

im·prove (im pro͞ov′) ***vt.*** **-proved′, -prov′ing** [< Anglo-Fr. < *en-*, in + *prou*, gain < LL. < L. *prodesse*, to be of advantage] **1.** to use (time, etc.) profitably **2.** to make better **3.** to make (land or structures) more valuable by cultivation, construction, etc. —***vi.*** to become better —**improve on** (or **upon**) to do or make better than —**im·prov′a·bil′i·ty** ***n.*** —**im·prov′a·ble** ***adj.*** —**im·prov′er** ***n.***

im·prove·ment (-mənt) ***n.*** **1.** an improving or being improved; esp., *a)* betterment *b)* an increase in value *c)* profitable use **2.** *a)* an addition or change that improves something or adds to its value *b)* a person or thing representing a higher degree of excellence

im·prov·i·dent (im präv′ə dənt) ***adj.*** failing to provide for the future; lacking foresight or thrift —**im·prov′i·dence** ***n.*** —**im·prov′i·dent·ly** ***adv.***

im·pro·vise (im′prə vīz′) ***vt., vi.*** **-vised′, -vis′ing** [< Fr. < It. < *improvisso*, unprepared < L. < *in-*, not + pp. of *providere*, to foresee, PROVIDE] **1.** to compose and simultaneously perform without any preparation; extemporize **2.** to make, provide, or do with whatever is at hand —**im·prov-i·sa·tion** (im präv′ə zā′shən, im′prə vi-) ***n.*** —**im·prov′i-sa′tion·al** ***adj.*** —**im′pro·vis′er, im′pro·vi′sor, im·prov′i-sa′tor** ***n.***

im·pru·dent (im pro͞od′'nt) ***adj.*** not prudent; without thought of the consequences; rash; indiscreet —**im·pru′-dence** ***n.*** —**im·pru′dent·ly** ***adv.***

im·pu·dence (im′pyoo dəns) ***n.*** **1.** the quality of being impudent **2.** impudent speech or behavior: also **im′pu-den·cy**, *pl.* **-cies**

im·pu·dent (-dənt) ***adj.*** [< Fr. < L. < *in-*, not + prp. of *pudere*, to feel shame] **1.** orig., immodest; shameless **2.** shamelessly bold; disrespectful; insolent —**im′pu·dent-ly** ***adv.***

im·pugn (im pyo͞on′) ***vt.*** [< OFr. < L. < *in-*, against + *pugnare*, to fight] to attack by argument or criticism; oppose or challenge as false or questionable —**im·pugn′a-ble** ***adj.*** —**im·pug·na·tion** (im′pəg nā′shən) ***n.*** —**im-pugn′er** ***n.***

im·pulse (im′puls) ***n.*** [< L. pp. of *impellere*, IMPEL] **1.** *a)* an impelling, or driving forward with sudden force *b)* an impelling force; push; impetus *c)* the motion or effect caused by such a force **2.** *a)* incitement to action arising from a state of mind or an external stimulus *b)* a sudden inclination to act, without conscious thought **3.** *Elec.* a momentary surge in one direction of voltage or current **4.** *Physiol.* a stimulus transmitted in a muscle or nerve, which causes or inhibits activity

im·pul·sion (im pul′shən) ***n.*** **1.** an impelling or being impelled **2.** an impelling force; impetus

im·pul·sive (-siv) ***adj.*** **1.** impelling; driving forward **2.** *a)* acting or likely to act on impulse *b)* resulting from impulse [an *impulsive* remark] —**im·pul′sive·ly** ***adv.*** —**im-pul′sive·ness** ***n.***

im·pu·ni·ty (im pyo͞o′nə tē) ***n.*** [< Fr. < L. < *impunis* < *in-*, without + *poena*, punishment] exemption from punishment, penalty, or harm

im·pure (im pyoor′) ***adj.*** not pure; specif., *a)* unclean; dirty *b)* unclean according to religious ritual *c)* immoral; obscene *d)* mixed with foreign matter; adulterated *e)* mixed so as to lack purity in color, style, etc. *f)* not idiomatic or grammatical —**im·pure′ly** ***adv.*** —**im·pure′-ness** ***n.***

im·pu·ri·ty (-pyoor′ə tē) ***n.*** **1.** a being impure **2.** *pl.* **-ties** an impure thing or element

im·pute (im pyo͞ot′) ***vt.*** **-put′ed, -put′ing** [< OFr. < L. < *in-*, to + *putare*, to estimate, think] to attribute (esp. a fault or misconduct) to another; charge with; ascribe —**im-put′a·bil′i·ty** ***n.*** —**im·put′a·ble** ***adj.*** —**im′pu·ta′tion** ***n.*** —**im·put′a·tive** ***adj.***

in (in, ən, 'n) ***prep.*** [OE.] **1.** contained or enclosed by; inside [*in* the room] **2.** wearing [a lady *in* red] **3.** during the course of [done *in* a day] **4.** at or near the end of [return *in* an hour] **5.** perceptible to (one of the senses) [*in* sight] **6.** out of a group of [one *in* ten] **7.** amidst; surrounded by [*in* a storm] **8.** affected by; having [*in* trouble] **9.** employed at or occupied by [*in* business, *in* a search for truth] **10.** with regard to; as concerns [weak *in* faith, *in* my opinion] **11.** with; by; using [to paint *in* oil, speak *in* French] **12.** made of [done *in* wood] **13.** because of; for [to cry *in* pain] **14.** by way of [*in* recompense] **15.** belonging to [not *in* his nature] **16.** into [come *in* the house] *In* expresses inclusion with relation to space, place, time, state, circumstances, manner, quality, a class, etc. —***adv.*** **1.** from a point outside to one inside **2.** so as to be contained by a certain space, condition, or position **3.** so as to be agreeing or involved [he fell *in* with our plans] **4.** so as to form a part [mix *in* the cream] —***adj.*** **1.** that is successful or in power [the *in* group] **2.** inner; inside **3.** ingoing [the *in* door] **4.** gathered, counted, etc. [the votes are *in*] **5.** [Colloq.] currently smart, popular, etc. [an *in* joke] —***n.*** **1.** a person, group, etc. in power, office, etc.: *usually used in pl.* **2.** [Colloq.] special influence, favor, etc. —**have it in for** [Colloq.] to hold a grudge against —**in for** certain to have or get (usually an unpleasant experience) —**in on** having a share or part of —**ins and outs** all the parts, details, and intricacies —**in that** because; since —**in with** associated with as a friend, partner, etc.

in-[1] [< the prep. IN; also < OE. & MFr. *in-* or OFr. *en-* < L. *in-* < *in*] *a prefix meaning* in, into, within, on, toward [*inbreed, induct*]: also used as an intensive in some words of Latin origin [*inflame*] and assimilated to *il-* before *l* [*illuminate*], *ir-* before *r* [*irrigate*], and *im-* before *m, p,* and *b*

in-[2] [< OFr. & ML. < L. *in-*] *a prefix meaning* no, not, without, non- [*inhumane*]: assimilated to *il-* before *l* [*illegal*], *ir-* before *r* [*irregular*], and *im-* before *m, p,* and *b*

-in[1] (in) [see -INE[4]] a suffix used in forming the names of various compounds [*albumin, streptomycin*]

-in[2] (in) a combining form used in terms formed by analogy with SIT-IN [*teach-in*]

In *Chem.* indium

IN Indiana

in. inch; inches

-i·na (ē′nə) [L.] *a suffix used to form* feminine names, titles, etc. [*Christina, czarina*]

in·a·bil·i·ty (in′ə bil′ə tē) ***n.*** a being unable; lack of ability, capacity, means, or power

in ab·sen·ti·a (in əb sen′shə, ab sen′shē ə) [L., lit., in absence] although not present

in·ac·ces·si·ble (in′ək ses′ə b'l) ***adj.*** not accessible; specif., *a)* impossible to reach or enter *b)* that cannot be seen, talked to, etc. *c)* not obtainable —**in′ac·ces′si·bil′i-ty** ***n.*** —**in′ac·ces′si·bly** ***adv.***

in·ac·cu·ra·cy (in ak′yər ə sē) ***n.*** **1.** lack of accuracy **2.** *pl.* **-cies** an error; mistake

in·ac·cu·rate (-yər it) ***adj.*** not accurate; not correct; not exact; in error —**in·ac′cu·rate·ly** ***adv.***

in·ac·tion (in ak′shən) ***n.*** absence of action or motion; inertness or idleness

in·ac·ti·vate (-tə vāt′) ***vt.*** **-vat′ed, -vat′ing** **1.** to make inactive **2.** *Chem.* to destroy the activity of (a substance), as by heat —**in·ac′ti·va′tion** ***n.***

in·ac·tive (-tiv) ***adj.*** **1.** not active or moving; inert **2.** idle; sluggish **3.** not functioning **4.** not in active service in the armed forces —**in·ac′tive·ly** ***adv.*** —**in′ac·tiv′i·ty** ***n.***

in·ad·e·quate (in ad′ə kwət) ***adj.*** not adequate; not sufficient —**in·ad′e·qua·cy** *pl.* **-cies, in·ad′e·quate·ness** ***n.*** —**in·ad′e·quate·ly** ***adv.***

in·ad·mis·si·ble (in′əd mis′ə b'l) ***adj.*** not admissible;

not to be allowed, granted, etc. —**in′ad·mis′si·bil′i·ty** ***n.*** —**in′ad·mis′si·bly** ***adv.***
in·ad·vert·ence (in′əd vʉr′təns) ***n.*** **1.** a being inadvertent **2.** an instance of this; oversight; mistake Also **in′ad·vert′en·cy,** *pl.* **-cies**
in·ad·vert·ent (-tənt) ***adj.*** **1.** not attentive or observant **2.** due to oversight; unintentional —**in′ad·vert′ent·ly** ***adv.***
in·ad·vis·a·ble (in′əd vī′zə b′l) ***adj.*** not advisable; not wise or prudent —**in′ad·vis′a·bil′i·ty** ***n.***
in·al·ien·a·ble (in āl′yən ə b′l) ***adj.*** that may not be taken away or transferred *[inalienable* rights*]* —**in·al′ien·a·bil′i·ty** ***n.*** —**in·al′ien·a·bly** ***adv.***
in·am·o·ra·ta (in am′ə rät′ə, in′am-) ***n.*** **[**It. < *innamorare,* to fall in love**]** a woman in relation to the man who is her lover; sweetheart or mistress
in·ane (in ān′) ***adj.*** **[**L. *inanis***]** **1.** empty **2.** lacking sense; silly; foolish —**in·ane′ly** ***adv.***
in·an·i·mate (in an′ə mit) ***adj.*** **1.** not animate; without life **2.** not animated; dull —**in·an′i·mate·ly** ***adv.*** —**in·an′i·mate·ness** ***n.***
in·an·i·ty (in an′ə tē) ***n.*** **1.** a being inane; specif., *a)* emptiness *b)* silliness **2.** *pl.* **-ties** something inane; senseless or silly act, remark, etc.
in·ap·pli·ca·ble (in ap′li kə b′l) ***adj.*** not applicable; not suitable; inappropriate —**in′ap·pli·ca·bil′i·ty** ***n.*** —**in·ap′pli·ca·bly** ***adv.***
in·ap·po·site (in ap′ə zit) ***adj.*** not apposite; irrelevant —**in·ap′po·site·ly** ***adv.***
in·ap·pre·ci·a·ble (in′ə prē′shə b′l, -shē ə-) ***adj.*** too small to be observed or have any value; negligible —**in′ap·pre′ci·a·bly** ***adv.***
in·ap·pro·pri·ate (in′ə prō′prē it) ***adj.*** not appropriate; not suitable, fitting, or proper —**in′ap·pro′pri·ate·ly** ***adv.*** —**in′ap·pro′pri·ate·ness** ***n.***
in·apt (in apt′) ***adj.*** **1.** not apt; inappropriate **2.** lacking skill or aptitude; inept —**in·apt′i·tude′** (-ap′tə to͞od′, -tyo͞od′) ***n.*** —**in·apt′ly** ***adv.*** —**in·apt′ness** ***n.***
in·ar·tic·u·late (in′är tik′yə lit) ***adj.*** **1.** produced without the articulation of normal speech *[*an *inarticulate* cry*]* **2.** *a)* unable to speak; mute *b)* not able to speak coherently or effectively **3.** *Zool.* without joints, hinges, etc. —**in′ar·tic′u·late·ly** ***adv.*** —**in′ar·tic′u·late·ness** ***n.***
in·ar·tis·tic (in′är tis′tik) ***adj.*** not artistic; lacking artistic taste —**in′ar·tis′ti·cal·ly** ***adv.***
in·as·much as (in′əz much′əz) **1.** seeing that; since; because **2.** to the extent that
in·at·ten·tion (in′ə ten′shən) ***n.*** failure to pay attention; heedlessness; negligence
in·at·ten·tive (-tiv) ***adj.*** not attentive; heedless —**in′at·ten′tive·ly** ***adv.*** —**in′at·ten′tive·ness** ***n.***
in·au·di·ble (in ô′də b′l) ***adj.*** not audible; that cannot be heard —**in′au·di·bil′i·ty** ***n.*** —**in·au′di·bly** ***adv.***
in·au·gu·ral (in ô′gyə rəl, -gə rəl) ***adj.*** **[**Fr.**]** **1.** of an inauguration, or ceremonial induction into office **2.** that begins a series —***n.*** an inaugural ceremony or address
in·au·gu·rate (-rāt′) ***vt.*** **-rat′ed, -rat′ing** **[**< L. pp. of *inaugurare,* to practice augury**]** **1.** to induct into office with a formal ceremony **2.** to make a formal beginning of **3.** to celebrate formally the first public use of —**in·au′gu·ra′tion** ***n.*** —**in·au′gu·ra′tor** ***n.***
in·aus·pi·cious (in′ô spish′əs) ***adj.*** not auspicious; unfavorable; unlucky; ill-omened —**in′aus·pi′cious·ly** ***adv.*** —**in′aus·pi′cious·ness** ***n.***
in·board (in′bôrd′) ***adv., adj.*** **[**< *in board:* see BOARD**]** **1.** inside the hull or bulwarks of a ship or boat **2.** close or closer to the fuselage or hull of an aircraft —***n.*** **1.** a marine motor mounted inboard **2.** a boat with such a motor
in·board-out·board (-out′bôrd′) ***adj.*** designating or of a power unit for small watercraft that has an inboard motor connected by a drive shaft to a propeller at the stern —***n.*** a boat thus powered
in·born (in′bôrn′) ***adj.*** present in the organism at birth; innate; natural
in·bound (-bound′) ***adj.*** traveling or going inward
in·bred (in′bred′) ***adj.*** **1.** innate or deeply instilled **2.** resulting from inbreeding
in·breed (in′brēd′) ***vt.*** **-bred′, -breed′ing** to breed by continual mating of individuals of the same or closely related stocks —***vi.*** **1.** to engage in such breeding **2.** to become too refined, effete, etc. from moving in too narrow a social range
inc. **1.** inclosure **2.** including **3.** inclusive **4.** incorporated **5.** increase
In·ca (iŋ′kə) ***n.*** any member of a group of Indian tribes that dominated ancient Peru until the Spanish conquest: the Incas had a highly developed civilization —**In′can** ***adj.***
in·cal·cu·la·ble (in kal′kyə lə b′l) ***adj.*** **1.** that cannot be calculated; too great or too many to be counted **2.** unpredictable; uncertain —**in·cal′cu·la·bil′i·ty** ***n.*** —**in·cal′cu·la·bly** ***adv.***
in·can·desce (in′kən des′) ***vi., vt.*** **-desced′, -desc′ing** to become or make incandescent
in·can·des·cent (-des′′nt) ***adj.*** **[**< L.: see IN-[1] & CANDESCENT**]** **1.** glowing with intense heat; red-hot or, esp., white-hot **2.** very bright; shining brilliantly —**in′can·des′cence** ***n.*** —**in′can·des′cent·ly** ***adv.***
incandescent lamp a lamp in which the light is produced by a filament contained in a vacuum and heated to incandescence by an electric current
in·can·ta·tion (in′kan tā′shən) ***n.*** **[**OFr. < LL. < L. pp. of *incantare,* enchant < *in-,* IN-[1] + *cantare,* to chant**]** **1.** the chanting of special words or a formula in magic spells or rites **2.** words or a formula so chanted —**in′can·ta′tion·al** ***adj.*** —**in·can′ta·to′ry** (-kan′tə tôr′ē) ***adj.***

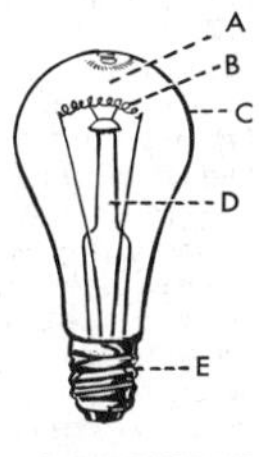

INCANDESCENT LAMP
(A, inert gas filling; B, coiled tungsten wire filament; C, glass envelope; D, glass support; E, metal base)

in·ca·pa·ble (in kā′pə b′l) ***adj.*** not capable; lacking the necessary ability, competence, qualifications, etc. —**incapable of** **1.** not allowing or admitting; not able to accept or experience *[incapable* of change*]* **2.** lacking the ability or fitness for **3.** not legally qualified for —**in′ca·pa·bil′i·ty, in·ca′pa·ble·ness** ***n.*** —**in·ca′pa·bly** ***adv.***
in·ca·pac·i·tate (in′kə pas′ə tāt′) ***vt.*** **-tat′ed, -tat′ing** **1.** to make unable or unfit; esp., to make incapable of normal activity; disable **2.** *Law* to disqualify —**in′ca·pac′i·ta′tion** ***n.***
in·ca·pac·i·ty (in′kə pas′ə tē) ***n.,*** *pl.* **-ties** **1.** lack of capacity, power, or fitness; disability **2.** legal ineligibility
in·car·cer·ate (in kär′sə rāt′) ***vt.*** **-at′ed, -at′ing** **[**< ML. pp. of *incarcerare* < L. *in,* in + *carcer,* prison**]** **1.** to imprison; jail **2.** to confine —**in·car′cer·a′tion** ***n.*** —**in·car′cer·a′tor** ***n.***
in·car·na·dine (in kär′nə dīn′, -din, -dēn′) ***adj.*** **[**< Fr. < It. *incarnatino* < LL. *incarnatus:* see ff.**]** **1.** flesh-colored; pink **2.** red; esp., blood-red —***n.*** the color of either flesh or blood —***vt.*** **-dined′, -din′ing** to make incarnadine
in·car·nate (in kär′nit; *also, and for v. always,* -nāt) ***adj.*** **[**< LL. *incarnatus,* pp. of *incarnari,* to become flesh < L. *in-,* in + *caro,* flesh**]** endowed with a human body; personified *[*evil *incarnate]* —***vt.*** **-nat·ed, -nat·ing** **1.** to give bodily form to; embody **2.** to give actual form to; make real **3.** to be the type or embodiment of
in·car·na·tion (in′kär nā′shən) ***n.*** **[**see prec.**]** **1.** endowment with a human body **2.** **[I-]** the taking on of human form and nature by Jesus as the Son of God **3.** any person or animal serving as the embodiment of a god or spirit **4.** any person or thing serving as the embodiment of a quality or concept
in·case (in kās′) ***vt.*** **-cased′, -cas′ing** *same as* ENCASE —**in·case′ment** ***n.***
in·cau·tion (in kô′shən) ***n.*** lack of caution
in·cau·tious (-shəs) ***adj.*** not cautious; not careful or prudent; reckless; rash —**in·cau′tious·ly** ***adv.*** —**in·cau′tious·ness** ***n.***
in·cen·di·ar·y (in sen′dē er′ē) ***adj.*** **[**< L. < *incendium,* a fire < *incendere:* see ff.**]** **1.** relating to the willful destruction of property by fire **2.** designed to cause fires, as certain bombs **3.** willfully stirring up strife, riot, etc. —***n.,*** *pl.* **-ar′ies** **1.** a person who willfully destroys property by fire **2.** a person who willfully stirs up strife, riot, etc. **3.** an incendiary bomb, substance, etc. —**in·cen′di·a·rism** (-ə riz′m) ***n.***
in·cense[1] (in′sens) ***n.*** **[**< OFr. < LL. < L. pp. of *incendere,* to inflame < *in-,* in + *candere,* to burn**]** **1.** *a)* any substance burned for its pleasant odor *b)* the odor or smoke so produced **2.** any pleasant odor **3.** pleasing attention or praise —***vt.*** **-censed, -cens·ing** **1.** to make fragrant with incense **2.** to burn or offer incense to —***vi.*** to burn incense
in·cense[2] (in sens′) ***vt.*** **-censed′, -cens′ing** **[**< OFr. < L. pp. of *incendere:* see prec.**]** to make very angry; enrage —**in·cense′ment** ***n.***
in·cen·tive (in sen′tiv) ***adj.*** **[**< LL. *incentivum* < L. < *in-,* on + *canere,* to sing**]** stimulating to action; encouraging; motivating —***n.*** a stimulus; motive
in·cep·tion (in sep′shən) ***n.*** **[**< L. < pp. of *incipere:* see INCIPIENT**]** a beginning; start; commencement
in·cep·tive (-tiv) ***adj.*** **[**< OFr. < LL. < L. pp. of *incipere:* see INCIPIENT**]** **1.** beginning; introductory **2.** *Gram.* expressing the beginning of an action —***n.*** an inceptive verb —**in·cep′tive·ly** ***adv.***
in·cer·ti·tude (in sʉr′tə to͞od′, -tyo͞od′) ***n.*** **[**Fr. < ML.:

see IN-[2] + CERTITUDE] **1.** an uncertain state of mind; doubt **2.** insecurity

in·ces·sant (in ses′'nt) ***adj.*** [< LL. < L. *in-*, not + prp. of *cessare*, to CEASE] never ceasing; continuing or repeated endlessly; constant —**in·ces′san·cy** ***n.*** —**in·ces′sant·ly** ***adv.***

in·cest (in′sest) ***n.*** [< L. < *in-*, not + *castus*, chaste] sexual intercourse between persons too closely related to marry legally

in·ces·tu·ous (in ses′choo wəs) ***adj.*** **1.** guilty of incest **2.** of, or having the nature of, incest —**in·ces′tu·ous·ly** ***adv.*** —**in·ces′tu·ous·ness** ***n.***

inch (inch) ***n.*** [OE. *ynce* < L. *uncia*, a twelfth, OUNCE[1]] **1.** a measure of length equal to 1/12 foot: symbol, " (e.g., 10"): abbrev. **in.** (sing. & pl.) **2.** a fall (of rain, snow, etc.) that would cover a surface to the depth of one inch **3.** a very small amount, degree, or distance —***vt., vi.*** to move by degrees; move very slowly —**every inch** in all respects; thoroughly —**inch by inch** gradually; slowly: also **by inches** —**within an inch of** very close to; almost to —**within an inch of one's life** almost to one's death

inch·meal (inch′mēl′) ***adv.*** [prec. + MEAL[1]] gradually; inch by inch: also **by inchmeal**

in·cho·ate (in kō′it) ***adj.*** [< L. pp. of *inchoare*, *incohare*, to begin, orig. "hitch up" < *in-*, in + *cohum*, a strap from plow to yoke] **1.** just begun; in the early stages **2.** not yet clearly formed; disordered —**in·cho′ate·ly** ***adv.*** —**in·cho′ate·ness** ***n.*** —**in′cho·a′tion** (-ā′shən) ***n.***

in·cho·a·tive (-ə tiv) ***adj., n.*** *Gram.* *same as* INCEPTIVE

inch·worm (inch′wurm′) ***n.*** *same as* MEASURING WORM

in·ci·dence (in′si dəns) ***n.*** **1.** the act, fact, or manner of falling upon or influencing **2.** the degree or range of occurrence or effect; extent of influence See also ANGLE OF INCIDENCE

in·ci·dent (-dənt) ***adj.*** [< OFr. < ML. < prp. of L. *incidere* < *in-*, on + *cadere*, to fall] **1.** likely to happen in connection with; incidental (*to*) [the cares *incident* to parenthood] **2.** falling upon or affecting [*incident* rays] —***n.*** **1.** something that happens; occurrence **2.** a minor event or episode, esp. one in a novel, play, etc. **3.** an apparently minor conflict, etc. that may have serious results

in·ci·den·tal (in′si den′t'l) ***adj.*** **1.** happening or likely to happen in connection with something more important; casual **2.** secondary or minor —***n.*** **1.** something incidental **2.** [*pl.*] miscellaneous items

in·ci·den·tal·ly (-dent′lē, den′t'l ē) ***adv.*** **1.** in an incidental manner **2.** by the way

in·cin·er·ate (in sin′ə rāt′) ***vt., vi.*** **-at′ed, -at′ing** [< ML. pp. of *incinerare* < L. *in*, to + *cinis*, ashes] to burn to ashes; burn up —**in·cin′er·a′tion** ***n.***

in·cin·er·a·tor (-rāt′ər) ***n.*** a furnace or other device for incinerating trash

in·cip·i·ent (in sip′ē ənt) ***adj.*** [< L. prp. of *incipere*, to begin < *in-*, on + *capere*, to take] just beginning to exist or to come to notice [an *incipient* illness] —**in·cip′i·ence, in·cip′i·en·cy** ***n.*** —**in·cip′i·ent·ly** ***adv.***

in·cise (in sīz′) ***vt.*** **-cised′, -cis′ing** [< Fr. < L. pp. of *incidere* < *in-*, into + *caedere*, to cut] to cut into with a sharp tool; specif., to engrave or carve —**in·cised′** ***adj.***

in·ci·sion (-sizh′ən) ***n.*** **1.** the act or result of incising; cut **2.** incisive quality **3.** *Surgery* a cut made into a tissue or organ

in·ci·sive (in sī′siv) ***adj.*** **1.** cutting into **2.** sharp; keen; penetrating; acute [an *incisive* mind] —**in·ci′sive·ly** ***adv.*** —**in·ci′sive·ness** ***n.***

in·ci·sor (in sī′zər) ***n.*** any of the front cutting teeth between the canines in either jaw

in·cite (in sīt′) ***vt.*** **-cit′ed, -cit′ing** [< OFr. < L. < *in-*, in, on + *citare*, to arouse] to urge to action; stir up; rouse —**in·cite′ment, in·ci·ta·tion** (in′sī tā′shən, -si-) ***n.*** —**in·cit′er** ***n.***

in·ci·vil·i·ty (in′sə vil′ə tē) ***n.*** [see IN-[2] & CIVIL] **1.** a lack of courtesy or politeness; rudeness **2.** *pl.* **-ties** a rude or discourteous act

incl. **1.** inclosure **2.** including **3.** inclusive

in·clem·ent (in klem′ənt) ***adj.*** [< L.: see IN-[2] & CLEMENT] **1.** rough; severe; stormy **2.** lacking mercy or leniency; harsh —**in·clem′en·cy** ***n.***, *pl.* **-cies** —**in·clem′ent·ly** ***adv.***

in·cli·na·tion (in′klə nā′shən) ***n.*** **1.** an inclining, leaning, bowing, etc. **2.** a slope; slant **3.** the extent or degree of incline from the horizontal or vertical **4.** the angle made by two lines or planes **5.** *a*) a particular bent of mind; tendency *b*) a liking or preference —**in′cli·na′tion·al** ***adj.***

in·cline (in klīn′; *for n., usually* in′klīn) ***vi.*** **-clined′, -clin′ing** [< OFr. < L. < *in-*, on + *clinare*, to lean] **1.** to lean; slope; slant **2.** to bow the body or head **3.** to have a tendency **4.** to have a preference or liking —***vt.*** **1.** to cause to lean, slope, etc. **2.** to bend or bow (the body or head) **3.** to make willing; influence —***n.*** an inclined plane or surface; slope; grade —**incline one's ear** to listen willingly —**in·clin′a·ble** ***adj.*** —**in·clined′** ***adj.*** —**in·clin′er** ***n.***

inclined plane a plane surface set at any angle other than a right angle against a horizontal surface

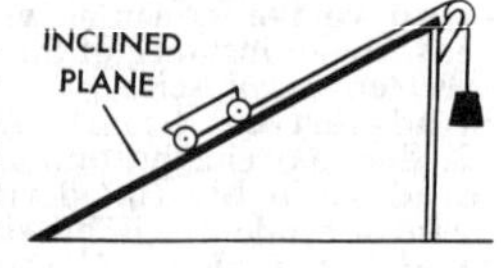

in·cli·nom·e·ter (in′klə näm′ə tər) ***n.*** [< INCLINE + -METER] **1.** *same as* CLINOMETER **2.** an instrument that measures the inclination of an axis of an aircraft or ship in relation to the horizontal

in·close (in klōz′) ***vt.*** **-closed′, -clos′ing** *same as* ENCLOSE —**in·clo′sure** (-klō′zhər) ***n.***

in·clude (in klo͞od′) ***vt.*** **-clud′ed, -clud′ing** [< L. < *in-*, in + *claudere*, to close] **1.** to shut up or in; enclose **2.** to have as part of a whole; contain; comprise **3.** to take into account; put in a total, category, etc. —**in·clud′a·ble, in·clud′i·ble** ***adj.***

in·clu·sion (in klo͞o′zhən) ***n.*** **1.** an including or being included **2.** something included

in·clu·sive (in klo͞o′siv) ***adj.*** **1.** including or tending to include; esp., taking everything into account **2.** including the terms, limits, or extremes mentioned [the first to the tenth *inclusive*] —**inclusive of** including —**in·clu′sive·ly** ***adv.*** —**in·clu′sive·ness** ***n.***

incog. incognito

in·cog·ni·to (in′käg nēt′ō, in käg′ni tō) ***adv., adj.*** [It. < L. < *in-*, not + pp. of *cognoscere*, to know] with true identity unrevealed or disguised; under an assumed name, rank, etc. —***n.***, *pl.* **-tos** **1.** a person who is incognito **2.** *a*) the state of being incognito *b*) the disguise assumed —**in′cog·ni′ta** (-ə, -tə) ***adj., n.fem.***, *pl.* **-tas**

in·co·her·ence (in′kō hir′əns) ***n.*** **1.** a being incoherent **2.** incoherent speech, thought, etc. Also **in′co·her′en·cy**, *pl.* **-cies**

in·co·her·ent (-ənt) ***adj.*** not coherent; specif., *a*) lacking cohesion; not sticking together *b*) not logically connected; disjointed *c*) characterized by incoherent speech, thought, etc. —**in′co·her′ent·ly** ***adv.***

in·com·bus·ti·ble (in′kəm bus′tə b'l) ***adj.*** not combustible; that cannot be burned —***n.*** an incombustible substance —**in′com·bus′ti·bil′i·ty** ***n.***

in·come (in′kum′) ***n.*** the money or other gain received, esp. in a given period, by an individual, corporation, etc. for labor or services, or from property, investments, etc.

income tax a tax on net income or on that part of income which exceeds a certain amount

in·com·ing (in′kum′iŋ) ***adj.*** coming in or about to come in —***n.*** a coming in

in·com·men·su·ra·ble (in′kə men′shər ə b'l, -sər-) ***adj.*** **1.** that cannot be measured or compared by the same standard or measure **2.** not worthy of comparison **3.** having no common divisor —***n.*** an incommensurable thing, quantity, etc. —**in′com·men′su·ra·bil′i·ty** ***n.*** —**in′com·men′su·ra·bly** ***adv.***

in·com·men·su·rate (-it) ***adj.*** not commensurate; specif., *a*) not proportionate; not adequate *b*) *same as* INCOMMENSURABLE (sense 1) —**in′com·men′su·rate·ly** ***adv.***

in·com·mode (in′kə mōd′) ***vt.*** **-mod′ed, -mod′ing** [< Fr. < L. < *in-*, not + *commodus*, convenient] to inconvenience; put to some trouble; bother

in·com·mo·di·ous (-mō′dē əs) ***adj.*** **1.** causing inconvenience; uncomfortable **2.** inconveniently small, narrow, etc. —**in′com·mo′di·ous·ly** ***adv.*** —**in′com·mo′di·ous·ness** ***n.***

in·com·mu·ni·ca·ble (in′kə myo͞o′ni kə b'l) ***adj.*** that cannot be communicated or told —**in′com·mu′ni·ca·bil′i·ty** ***n.*** —**in′com·mu′ni·ca·bly** ***adv.***

in·com·mu·ni·ca·do (in′kə myo͞o′nə kä′dō) ***adj.*** [Sp.] unable or not allowed to communicate

in·com·pa·ra·ble (in käm′pər ə b'l; *occas.* in′kəm par′ə b'l) ***adj.*** that cannot be compared; specif., *a*) having no basis of comparison; incommensurable *b*) beyond comparison; unequaled; matchless [*incomparable* skill] —**in·com′pa·ra·bil′i·ty** ***n.*** —**in·com′pa·ra·bly** ***adv.***

in·com·pat·i·ble (in′kəm pat′ə b'l) ***adj.*** **1.** not compatible; not able to exist in harmony; not going, or getting along, well together **2.** logically contradictory **3.** not suitable for being used together: said of certain drugs or medicines —***n.*** an incompatible person or thing —**in′com·pat′i·bil′i·ty** ***n.***, *pl.* **-ties** —**in′com·pat′i·bly** ***adv.***

in·com·pe·tent (in käm′pə tənt) ***adj.*** **1.** without adequate ability, knowledge, fitness, etc. **2.** not legally qualified —***n.*** an incompetent person; esp., one who is mentally retarded —**in·com′pe·tence, in·com′pe·ten·cy** ***n.*** —**in·com′pe·tent·ly** ***adv.***

in·com·plete (in′kəm plēt′) ***adj.*** **1.** lacking a part or parts **2.** unfinished; not concluded **3.** not perfect; not thorough —**in′com·plete′ly** ***adv.*** —**in′com·plete′ness, in′com·ple′tion** ***n.***

in·com·pre·hen·si·ble (in′käm pri hen′sə b'l, in käm′-) ***adj.*** not comprehensible; that cannot be understood —**in′com·pre·hen′si·bil′i·ty** ***n.*** —**in′com·pre·hen′si·bly** ***adv.***

in·com·press·i·ble (in′kəm pres′ə b'l) ***adj.*** that cannot be compressed —**in′com·press′i·bil′i·ty** ***n.***

in·con·ceiv·a·ble (in′kən sē′və b'l) ***adj.*** that cannot be conceived; that cannot be thought of, imagined, etc. —**in′con·ceiv′a·bil′i·ty, in′con·ceiv′a·ble·ness** ***n.*** —**in′con·ceiv′a·bly** ***adv.***

in·con·clu·sive (in′kən kl͞oo′siv) ***adj.*** not conclusive or final; not leading to a definite result —**in′con·clu′sive·ly** ***adv.*** —**in′con·clu′sive·ness** ***n.***

in·con·gru·i·ty (in′kən gr͞oo′ə tē) ***n.*** **1.** a being incongruous; specif., *a)* lack of harmony or agreement *b)* lack of fitness or appropriateness **2.** *pl.* **-ties** something incongruous

in·con·gru·ous (in käŋ′groo wəs) ***adj.*** not congruous; specif., *a)* lacking harmony or agreement *b)* having inharmonious parts, elements, etc. *c)* unsuitable; inappropriate —**in·con′gru·ous·ly** ***adv.*** —**in·con′gru·ous·ness** ***n.***

in·con·se·quent (in kän′sə kwent′, -kwənt) ***adj.*** not consequent; specif., *a)* not following as a result *b)* not following as a logical inference; irrelevant *c)* not proceeding in logical sequence —**in·con′se·quence′** ***n.*** —**in·con′se·quent′ly** ***adv.***

in·con·se·quen·tial (in kän′sə kwen′shəl) ***adj.*** **1.** inconsequent; illogical **2.** of no consequence; unimportant —***n.*** something inconsequential —**in′con·se·quen′ti·al′i·ty** (-shē al′ə tē) ***n.*** —**in·con′se·quen′tial·ly** ***adv.***

in·con·sid·er·a·ble (in′kən sid′ər ə b'l) ***adj.*** not worth consideration; trivial; small —**in′con·sid′er·a·ble·ness** ***n.*** —**in′con·sid′er·a·bly** ***adv.***

in·con·sid·er·ate (-it) ***adj.*** without thought or consideration for others; thoughtless —**in′con·sid′er·ate·ly** ***adv.*** —**in′con·sid′er·ate·ness, in′con·sid′er·a′tion** (-ə rā′shən) ***n.***

in·con·sis·ten·cy (in′kən sis′tən sē) ***n.*** **1.** a being inconsistent **2.** *pl.* **-cies** an inconsistent act, remark, etc. Also **in′con·sis′tence**

in·con·sis·tent (-tənt) ***adj.*** not consistent; specif., *a)* not in agreement or harmony; incompatible *b)* not uniform; self-contradictory *[inconsistent testimony]* *c)* not holding to the same principles or practice; changeable —**in′con·sis′tent·ly** ***adv.***

in·con·sol·a·ble (in′kən sōl′ə b'l) ***adj.*** that cannot be consoled —**in′con·sol′a·bil′i·ty, in′con·sol′a·ble·ness** ***n.*** —**in′con·sol′a·bly** ***adv.***

in·con·so·nant (in kän′sə nənt) ***adj.*** not consonant; not in harmony or agreement —**in·con′so·nance** ***n.*** —**in·con′so·nant·ly** ***adv.***

in·con·spic·u·ous (in′kən spik′yoo wəs) ***adj.*** not conspicuous; attracting little attention —**in′con·spic′u·ous·ly** ***adv.*** —**in′con·spic′u·ous·ness** ***n.***

in·con·stant (in kän′stənt) ***adj.*** not constant; changeable; specif., *a)* not remaining firm in mind or purpose *b)* fickle *c)* not uniform; irregular —**in·con′stan·cy** ***n.*** —**in·con′stant·ly** ***adv.***

in·con·test·a·ble (in′kən tes′tə b'l) ***adj.*** not to be contested; unquestionable —**in′con·test′a·bil′i·ty** ***n.*** —**in′con·test′a·bly** ***adv.***

in·con·ti·nent (in känt′'n ənt) ***adj.*** [< OFr. < L.: see IN-[2] & CONTINENT] **1.** *a)* without self-restraint, esp. in regard to sexual activity *b)* unrestrained **2.** incapable of containing, holding, etc. **3.** unable to restrain a natural discharge, as of urine —**in·con′ti·nence** ***n.*** —**in·con′ti·nent·ly** ***adv.***

in·con·tro·vert·i·ble (in′kän trə vʉr′tə b'l, in kän′-) ***adj.*** that cannot be controverted; not disputable or debatable; undeniable —**in′con·tro·vert′i·bil′i·ty** ***n.*** —**in′con·tro·vert′i·bly** ***adv.***

in·con·ven·ience (in′kən vēn′yəns) ***n.*** **1.** a being inconvenient; lack of comfort, ease, etc. **2.** anything inconvenient Also **in′con·ven′ien·cy,** *pl.* **-cies** —***vt.*** **-ienced, -ienc·ing** to cause inconvenience to; trouble; bother

in·con·ven·ient (-yənt) ***adj.*** not convenient; not favorable to one's comfort; causing trouble, bother, etc. —**in′con·ven′ient·ly** ***adv.***

in·con·vert·i·ble (in′kən vʉr′tə b'l) ***adj.*** that cannot be converted; that cannot be changed or exchanged —**in′con·vert′i·bil′i·ty** ***n.***

in·cor·po·rate (in kôr′pər it; *for v.* -pə rāt′) ***adj.*** [< LL.: see IN-[1] & CORPORATE] combined, merged, or incorporated —***vt.*** **-rat′ed, -rat′ing** **1.** to combine with something already formed; embody **2.** to bring together into a single whole; merge **3.** to admit into association as a member **4.** to form into a corporation **5.** to give material form to —***vi.*** **1.** to unite or combine into a single whole **2.** to form a corporation —**in·cor′po·ra′tion** ***n.*** —**in·cor′po·ra′tive** ***adj.*** —**in·cor′po·ra′tor** ***n.***

in·cor·po·re·al (in′kôr pôr′ē əl) ***adj.*** not corporeal; without material body or substance —**in′cor·po′re·al·ly** ***adv.***

in·cor·rect (in′kə rekt′) ***adj.*** not correct; specif., *a)* improper *b)* untrue; inaccurate; wrong; faulty —**in′cor·rect′ly** ***adv.*** —**in′cor·rect′ness** ***n.***

in·cor·ri·gi·ble (in kôr′i jə b'l, -kär′-) ***adj.*** not corrigible; that cannot be corrected, improved, or reformed, esp. because firmly set, as a habit, or because set in bad habits, as a child —***n.*** an incorrigible person —**in·cor′ri·gi·bil′i·ty, in·cor′ri·gi·ble·ness** ***n.*** —**in·cor′ri·gi·bly** ***adv.***

in·cor·rupt (in′kə rupt′) ***adj.*** not corrupt; sound, pure, upright, honest, etc. —**in′cor·rupt′ly** ***adv.*** —**in′cor·rupt′ness** ***n.***

in·cor·rupt·i·ble (-rup′tə b'l) ***adj.*** that cannot be corrupted, esp. morally —**in′cor·rupt′i·bil′i·ty** ***n.*** —**in′cor·rupt′i·bly** ***adv.***

incr. **1.** increase **2.** increased **3.** increasing

in·crease (in krēs′; *also, and for n. always,* in′krēs) ***vi.*** **-creased′, -creas′ing** [< OFr. < L. < *in-*, in + *crescere*, to grow] **1.** to become greater in size, amount, etc.; grow **2.** to become greater in numbers by producing offspring; multiply —***vt.*** to cause to become greater in size, amount, etc. —***n.*** **1.** an increasing or becoming increased **2.** the result or amount of an increasing —**on the increase** increasing —**in·creas′a·ble** ***adj.*** —**in·creas′er** ***n.***

in·creas·ing·ly (in krēs′iŋ lē) ***adv.*** more and more; to an ever-increasing degree

in·cred·i·ble (in kred′ə b'l) ***adj.*** **1.** not credible; unbelievable **2.** so great, unusual, etc. as to seem impossible —**in·cred′i·bil′i·ty** ***n.*** —**in·cred′i·bly** ***adv.***

in·cre·du·li·ty (in′krə d͞oo′lə tē, -dy͞oo′-) ***n.*** unwillingness or inability to believe; doubt

in·cred·u·lous (in krej′oo ləs) ***adj.*** **1.** unwilling or unable to believe; doubting **2.** showing doubt or disbelief —**in·cred′u·lous·ly** ***adv.***

in·cre·ment (in′krə mənt, iŋ′-) ***n.*** **1.** a becoming greater or larger; increase; gain **2.** amount of increase *[an annual increment of $300 in salary]* —**in′cre·men′tal** (-men′t'l) ***adj.***

in·crim·i·nate (in krim′ə nāt′) ***vt.*** **-nat′ed, -nat′ing** [< ML.: see IN-[1] & CRIMINATE] **1.** to charge with a crime; accuse **2.** to involve in, or make appear guilty of, a crime or fault —**in·crim′i·na′tion** ***n.*** —**in·crim′i·na·to′ry** ***adj.***

in·crust (in krust′) ***vt.*** **1.** to cover as with a crust **2.** to decorate, as with gems —***vi.*** to form a crust —**in′crus·ta′tion** ***n.***

in·cu·bate (iŋ′kyə bāt′, in-) ***vt.*** **-bat′ed, -bat′ing** [< L. pp. of *incubare* < *in-*, on + *cubare*, to lie] **1.** to sit on and hatch (eggs) **2.** to keep (eggs, embryos, etc.) in a favorable environment for hatching or developing **3.** to develop, as by thought or planning —***vi.*** to undergo incubation

in·cu·ba·tion (iŋ′kyə bā′shən, in′-) ***n.*** **1.** an incubating or being incubated **2.** the phase in the development of a disease between the infection and the first appearance of symptoms —**in′cu·ba′tion·al** ***adj.*** —**in′cu·ba′tive** ***adj.***

in·cu·ba·tor (iŋ′kyə bāt′ər, in′-) ***n.*** a person or thing that incubates; specif., *a)* an artificially heated container for hatching eggs *b)* a similar apparatus in which premature babies are kept for a period *c)* an apparatus for developing bacterial cultures

in·cu·bus (iŋ′kyə bəs, in′-) ***n.,*** *pl.* **-bus·es, -bi′** (-bī′) [< LL., nightmare (in ML., a demon) < L. *incubare:* see INCUBATE] **1.** a spirit or demon thought in medieval times to lie on sleeping women **2.** a nightmare **3.** an oppressive burden

in·cul·cate (in kul′kāt, in′kul kāt′) ***vt.*** **-cat·ed, -cat·ing** [< L. pp. of *inculcare* < *in-*, in + *calcare*, to trample underfoot < *calx*, a heel] to impress upon the mind by repetition or persistent urging —**in′cul·ca′tion** ***n.*** —**in·cul′ca·tor** ***n.***

in·cul·pate (in kul′pāt, in′kul pāt′) ***vt.*** **-pat·ed, -pat·ing** [< ML. pp. of *inculpare* < L. *in*, on + *culpa*, a fault, blame] *same as* INCRIMINATE —**in′cul·pa′tion** ***n.*** —**in·cul′pa·to′ry** ***adj.***

in·cum·ben·cy (in kum′bən sē) ***n.,*** *pl.* **-cies** **1.** a duty or obligation **2.** *a)* the holding and administering of a position *b)* tenure of office

in·cum·bent (-bənt) ***adj.*** [< L. prp. of *incumbere* < *in-*, on + *cubare*, to lie down] **1.** lying, resting, or pressing with its weight on something else **2.** currently in office —***n.*** the holder of an office or benefice —**incumbent on** (or **upon**) resting upon as a duty or obligation

in·cum·ber (in kum′bər) ***vt.*** *same as* ENCUMBER

in·cum·brance (-brəns) ***n.*** **1.** *Law* a lien, claim, mortgage, etc. on property **2.** *same as* ENCUMBRANCE

in·cu·nab·u·la (in′kyoo nab′yə lə) ***n.pl.,*** *sing.* **-u·lum** (-ləm) [< L. < *in-*, in + *cunabula*, neut. pl., a cradle] **1.** the very first stages of anything; beginnings **2.** early printed books; esp., books printed before 1500 —**in′cu·nab′u·lar** ***adj.***

in·cur (in kʉr′) *vt.* **-curred′, -cur′ring** [< L. < *in-*, in + *currere*, to run] **1.** to acquire (something undesirable) [*to incur* a debt] **2.** to bring upon oneself through one's own actions
in·cur·a·ble (in kyoor′ə b'l) *adj.* not curable; that cannot be remedied or corrected —*n.* a person having an incurable disease —**in·cur′a·bil′i·ty** *n.* —**in·cur′a·bly** *adv.*
in·cu·ri·ous (in kyoor′ē əs) *adj.* not curious; uninterested; indifferent —**in·cu·ri·os·i·ty** (in′kyoor ē äs′ə tē), **in·cu′ri·ous·ness** *n.* —**in·cu′ri·ous·ly** *adv.*
in·cur·sion (in kʉr′zhən; *chiefly Brit.* -shən) *n.* [< L. *incursio* < *incurrere*: see INCUR] **1.** a running in; inroad **2.** a sudden, brief invasion or raid —**in·cur′sive** *adj.*
in·curve (in kʉrv′; *for n.* in′kʉrv′) *vt., vi.* **-curved′, -curv′ing** to curve inward —*n. Baseball same as* SCREWBALL
in·cus (iŋ′kəs) *n., pl.* **in·cu·des** (in kyo͞o′dēz) [ModL. < L., anvil] the central one of the three small bones in the middle ear: also called *anvil*
Ind. **1.** India **2.** Indian **3.** Indiana **4.** Indies
ind. **1.** independent **2.** index **3.** industrial
in·debt·ed (in det′id) *adj.* **1.** in debt **2.** obliged; owing gratitude
in·debt·ed·ness (-nis) *n.* **1.** a being indebted **2.** the amount owed; all one's debts
in·de·cen·cy (in dē′s'n sē) *n.* **1.** a being indecent **2.** *pl.* **-cies** an indecent act, statement, etc.
in·de·cent (-s'nt) *adj.* not decent; specif., *a*) not proper and fitting; unseemly *b*) morally offensive; obscene —**in·de′cent·ly** *adv.*
in·de·ci·pher·a·ble (in′di sī′fər ə b'l) *adj.* that cannot be deciphered; illegible —**in′de·ci′pher·a·bil′i·ty** *n.*
in·de·ci·sion (in′di sizh′ən) *n.* inability to decide or a tendency to change the mind frequently
in·de·ci·sive (-sī′siv) *adj.* **1.** not decisive **2.** showing indecision; hesitating or vacillating —**in′de·ci′sive·ly** *adv.* —**in′de·ci′sive·ness** *n.*
in·de·clin·a·ble (in′di klīn′ə b'l) *adj. Gram.* having no case inflections; not declinable
in·dec·o·rous (in dek′ər əs; *occas.* in′di kôr′əs) *adj.* lacking decorum, good taste, etc. —**in·dec′o·rous·ly** *adv.* —**in·dec′o·rous·ness** *n.*
in·de·co·rum (in′di kôr′əm) *n.* **1.** lack of decorum **2.** indecorous conduct, speech, etc.
in·deed (in dēd′) *adv.* [see IN, *prep.* & DEED] certainly; truly; admittedly —*interj.* an exclamation of surprise, doubt, sarcasm, etc.
indef. indefinite
in·de·fat·i·ga·ble (in′di fat′i gə b'l) *adj.* [< MFr. < L. < *in-*, not + *defatigare*, to tire out: see DE- & FATIGUE] that cannot be tired out; untiring —**in′de·fat′i·ga·bil′i·ty** *n.* —**in′de·fat′i·ga·bly** *adv.*
in·de·fea·si·ble (in′di fē′zə b'l) *adj.* that cannot be undone or made void —**in′de·fea′si·bil′i·ty** *n.* —**in′de·fea′si·bly** *adv.*
in·de·fen·si·ble (in′di fen′sə b'l) *adj.* **1.** that cannot be defended **2.** that cannot be justified —**in′de·fen′si·bil′i·ty** *n.* —**in′de·fen′si·bly** *adv.*
in·de·fin·a·ble (-fīn′ə b'l) *adj.* that cannot be defined —**in′de·fin′a·bil′i·ty** *n.* —**in′de·fin′a·bly** *adv.*
in·def·i·nite (in def′ə nit) *adj.* not definite; specif., *a*) having no exact limits *b*) not precise in meaning; vague *c*) not clear in outline; blurred *d*) not sure; uncertain *e*) *Gram.* not limiting or specifying [*a* and *an* are *indefinite* articles, *any* is an *indefinite* pronoun] —**in·def′i·nite·ly** *adv.* —**in·def′i·nite·ness** *n.*
in·de·his·cent (in′di his′'nt) *adj.* not dehiscent; not opening at maturity to discharge its seeds —**in′de·his′cence** *n.*
in·del·i·ble (in del′ə b'l) *adj.* [< L., ult. < *in-*, not + *delere*, to destroy] **1.** that cannot be erased, blotted out, eliminated, etc.; permanent **2.** leaving an indelible mark [*indelible* ink] —**in·del′i·bil′i·ty** *n.* —**in·del′i·bly** *adv.*
in·del·i·ca·cy (in del′i kə sē) *n.* **1.** a being indelicate **2.** *pl.* **-cies** something indelicate
in·del·i·cate (-kit) *adj.* not delicate; coarse; esp., lacking propriety or modesty —**in·del′i·cate·ly** *adv.* —**in·del′i·cate·ness** *n.*
in·dem·ni·fy (in dem′nə fī′) *vt.* **-fied′, -fy′ing** [< L. *indemnis*, unhurt < *in-*, not + *damnum*, hurt + -FY] **1.** to protect against loss, damage, etc.; insure **2.** *a*) to repay for loss or damage *b*) to make good (a loss) —**in·dem′ni·fi·ca′tion** *n.* —**in·dem′ni·fi′er** *n.*
in·dem·ni·ty (-tē) *n., pl.* **-ties** **1.** protection or insurance against loss, damage, etc. **2.** legal exemption from penalties incurred by one's actions **3.** repayment for loss, damage, etc.
in·dent[1] (in dent′; *for n., usually* in′dent) *vt.* [< OFr. < ML. < L. *in*, in + *dens*, tooth] **1.** *a*) to cut toothlike points into (an edge or border); notch; also, to join by mating notches *b*) to make jagged in outline **2.** to bind (a servant or apprentice) by indenture **3.** to space (the first line of a paragraph, etc.) in from the regular margin —*vi.* **1.** to form or be marked by notches, points, or a jagged border **2.** to space in from the margin —*n.* **1.** a notch or cut in an edge **2.** an indenture **3.** an indented line, paragraph, etc.
in·dent[2] (in dent′; *for n., usually* in′dent) *vt.* [IN-[1] + DENT] **1.** to make a dent in **2.** to press (a mark, etc.) in —*n.* a dent, or slight hollow
in·den·ta·tion (in′den tā′shən) *n.* **1.** an indenting or being indented **2.** a notch, cut, or inlet on a coastline, etc. **3.** a dent, or slight hollow **4.** an indention; space in from a margin
in·den·tion (in den′shən) *n.* **1.** a spacing in from the margin **2.** an empty or blank space left by this **3.** *a*) a dent *b*) the making of a dent
in·den·ture (in den′chər) *n.* [< INDENT[1]: orig., duplicates of a contract had correspondingly jagged edges for identification] **1.** a written contract or agreement **2.** [*often pl.*] a contract binding a person to work for another, as an apprentice to a master —*vt.* **-tured, -tur·ing** to bind by indenture
In·de·pend·ence (in′di pen′dəns) [after A. JACKSON, alluding to his *independence* of character] city in W Mo.: suburb of Kansas City: pop. 112,000
in·de·pend·ence (in′di pen′dəns) *n.* a being independent; freedom from the control of another
Independence Day the Fourth of July, the anniversary of the adoption of the Declaration of Independence on July 4, 1776
in·de·pend·en·cy (-dən sē) *n., pl.* **-cies** **1.** *same as* INDEPENDENCE **2.** an independent nation, etc.
in·de·pend·ent (-dənt) *adj.* **1.** free from the influence or control of others; specif., *a*) free from the rule of another; self-governing *b*) free from persuasion or bias; objective *c*) self-confident; self-reliant *d*) not adhering to any political party [*an independent* voter] *e*) not connected with others; separate [*an independent* grocer] **2.** *a*) not depending on another, esp. for financial support *b*) designating, of, or having an income large enough to enable one to live without working **3.** [I-] of or having to do with Independents —*n.* a person who is independent in thinking, action, etc.; specif., [*often* **I-**] a voter not an adherent of any political party —**independent of** apart from; regardless of —**in′de·pend′ent·ly** *adv.*
independent clause *Gram. same as* MAIN CLAUSE
independent variable *Math.* a quantity whose value may be determined freely without reference to other variables
in-depth (in′depth′) *adj.* carefully worked out, detailed, thorough, etc. [*an in-depth* study]
in·de·scrib·a·ble (in′di skrī′bə b'l) *adj.* that cannot be described; beyond the power of description —**in′de·scrib′a·bil′i·ty** *n.* —**in′de·scrib′a·bly** *adv.*
in·de·struct·i·ble (in′di struk′tə b'l) *adj.* that cannot be destroyed —**in′de·struct′i·bil′i·ty** *n.* —**in′de·struct′i·bly** *adv.*
in·de·ter·mi·na·ble (in′di tʉr′mi nə b'l) *adj.* not determinable; specif., *a*) that cannot be decided *b*) that cannot be ascertained —**in′de·ter′mi·na·ble·ness** *n.* —**in′de·ter′mi·na·bly** *adv.*
in·de·ter·mi·nate (-nit) *adj.* not determinate; specif., *a*) inexact in its limits, nature, etc.; indefinite; vague *b*) not yet settled; inconclusive —**in′de·ter′mi·na·cy, in′de·ter′mi·nate·ness** *n.* —**in′de·ter′mi·nate·ly** *adv.*
in·de·ter·mi·na·tion (in′di tʉr′mə nā′shən) *n.* **1.** lack of determination **2.** the state or quality of being indeterminate
in·dex (in′deks) *n., pl.* **-dex·es, -di·ces′** (-də sēz′) [L. < *indicare*, INDICATE] **1.** *short for* INDEX FINGER **2.** a pointer, as the needle on a dial **3.** an indication or sign [performance is an *index* of ability] **4.** *a*) an alphabetical list of names, subjects, etc. together with the page numbers where they appear in the text, usually placed at the end of a publication *b*) *short for* THUMB INDEX *c*) a catalog [a library *index*] **5.** *a*) the relation or ratio of one amount or dimension to another, or the formula expressing this relation *b*) a number used to measure changes in prices, wages, etc.: it shows percentage variation from an arbitrary standard: in full, **index number** **6.** [I-] *R.C.Ch.* formerly, a list of books forbidden to be read **7.** *Math.* *a*) an exponent (sense 3) *b*) a number or symbol placed above and to the left of a radical **8.** *Printing* a sign (☞) calling special attention to certain information —*vt.* **1.** *a*) to make an index of or for *b*) to include in an index *c*) to supply with a thumb index **2.** to indicate —**in′dex·er** *n.* —**in·dex′i·cal** *adj.*
index finger the finger next to the thumb
In·di·a (in′dē ə) **1.** region in S Asia, south of the Himalayas, including a large peninsula between the Arabian Sea & the Bay of Bengal **2.** republic in C & S India: member of the Commonwealth: 1,177,000 sq. mi.; pop. 536,984,000; cap. New Delhi
India ink **1.** a black pigment of lampblack mixed with a gelatinous substance and dried into cakes or sticks **2.** a liquid ink made from this

In·di·an (in′dē ən) ***adj.*** **1.** of India or the East Indies, their people, or culture **2.** of any of the aboriginal peoples (**American Indians**) of N. America, S. America, or the West Indies, or of their cultures **3.** of a type used or made by Indians —***n.*** **1.** a native of India or the East Indies **2.** a member of any of the aboriginal peoples of N. America, S. America, or the West Indies **3.** popularly, any of the languages spoken by American Indians

In·di·an·a (in′dē an′ə) [ModL., "land of the Indians"] Middle Western State of the U.S.: 36,291 sq. mi.; pop. 5,490,000; cap. Indianapolis: abbrev. **Ind., IN** —**In′di·an′i·an** ***adj., n.***

Indian agent a U.S. or Canadian official representing the government in dealings with American Indians, as on reservations

In·di·an·ap·o·lis (in′dē ə nap′ə lis) [INDIANA + Gr. *polis,* city] capital of Indiana, in the C part: pop. 701,000 (met. area 1,162,000)

Indian club a club of wood, metal, etc. shaped like a tenpin and swung in the hand for exercise

INDIAN CLUB

Indian corn *same as* CORN[1] (sense 2)

Indian file *same as* SINGLE FILE

Indian giver [Colloq.] a person who gives something and then asks for it back

Indian meal meal made from corn (maize); cornmeal

Indian Ocean ocean south of Asia, between Africa & Australia

Indian pipe a leafless, fleshy, white plant of the heath family, native to N Hemisphere forests, bearing a single, nodding, white flower

Indian pudding a cornmeal pudding made with milk, molasses, etc.

Indian summer a period of mild, warm, hazy weather following the first frosts of late autumn

Indian tobacco a poisonous annual plant, common in the E U.S., with light blue flowers in spikes

India paper a thin, strong, opaque printing paper, used for some Bibles, dictionaries, etc.

India (or **india**) **rubber** crude, natural rubber obtained from latex —**In′di·a-rub′ber** ***adj.***

In·dic (in′dik) ***adj.*** **1.** of India **2.** designating or of a subgroup of the Indo-Iranian branch of the Indo-European language family, including many of the languages of India, Pakistan, etc.

indic. indicative

in·di·cate (in′də kāt′) ***vt.*** **-cat′ed, -cat′ing** [< L. pp. of *indicare* < *in-,* in + *dicare,* to declare] **1.** to direct attention to; point out **2.** to be or give a sign of; signify *[fever indicates illness]* **3.** to show the need for; call for; make necessary **4.** to show or point out as a cause, treatment, or outcome: said of a disease, etc. **5.** to state briefly

in·di·ca·tion (in′də kā′shən) ***n.*** **1.** an indicating **2.** something that indicates, or shows; sign **3.** something that is indicated as necessary **4.** the amount or degree registered by an indicator

in·dic·a·tive (in dik′ə tiv) ***adj.*** **1.** giving an indication or intimation; signifying: also **in·dic·a·to·ry** (in dik′ə tôr′ē, in′dik-) **2.** designating or of that mood of a verb used to express an act, state, or occurrence as actual, or to ask a question of fact —***n.*** **1.** the indicative mood **2.** a verb in this mood —**in·dic′a·tive·ly** ***adv.***

in·di·ca·tor (in′də kāt′ər) ***n.*** **1.** a person or thing that indicates; specif., any device, as a gauge, dial, register, or pointer, that measures something **2.** any substance used to indicate acidity or alkalinity, the beginning or end of a chemical reaction, etc., by changes in color

in·di·ces (in′də sēz′) ***n.*** *alt. pl. of* INDEX

in·di·ci·a (in dish′ē ə, -dish′ə) ***n.pl.*** [L., ult. < *index:* see INDEX] marks or tokens; esp., printed markings on mail in place of stamps or cancellations

in·dict (in dīt′) ***vt.*** [< Anglo-L. *indictare,* ult. < L. *in,* against + *dictare:* see DICTATE] to charge with the commission of a crime; esp., to make formal accusation against on the basis of positive legal evidence —**in·dict′a·ble** ***adj.*** —**in·dict′er, in·dict′or** ***n.***

in·dict·ment (in dīt′mənt) ***n.*** **1.** an indicting or being indicted **2.** a charge; specif., a formal accusation charging someone with a crime, presented by a grand jury to the court

In·dies (in′dēz) **1.** *same as: a)* EAST INDIES (sense 1) *b)* WEST INDIES **2.** formerly, *same as* EAST INDIES (sense 2)

in·dif·fer·ence (in dif′ər əns, in dif′rəns) ***n.*** a being indifferent; specif., *a)* lack of concern or interest *b)* lack of importance or meaning

in·dif·fer·ent (-ənt, -rənt) ***adj.*** **1.** having or showing no preference; neutral **2.** having or showing no interest, concern, etc.; uninterested or unmoved **3.** of no importance **4.** not particularly good or bad, large or small, etc.; average **5.** not really good **6.** neutral in quality, as a chemical or magnet; inactive —**in·dif′fer·ent·ly** ***adv.***

in·di·gence (in′di jəns) ***n.*** the condition of being indigent: also **in′di·gen·cy**

in·dig·e·nous (in dij′ə nəs) ***adj.*** [< LL. < L. *indigena* < OL. *indu,* in + *gignere,* to be born] **1.** existing, growing, or produced naturally in a region or country; native (*to*) **2.** innate; inborn —**in·dig′e·nous·ly** ***adv.*** —**in·dig′e·nous·ness** ***n.***

in·di·gent (in′di jənt) ***adj.*** [OFr. < L. prp. of *indigere,* to be in need < OL. *indu,* in + *egere,* to need] poor; needy —***n.*** an indigent person —**in′di·gent·ly** ***adv.***

in·di·gest·i·ble (in′di jes′tə b′l, -dī-) ***adj.*** not digestible; not easily digested —**in′di·gest′i·bil′i·ty** ***n.***

in·di·ges·tion (-jes′chən, -jesh′-) ***n.*** **1.** inability to digest, or difficulty in digesting, food **2.** the discomfort caused by this

in·dig·nant (in dig′nənt) ***adj.*** [< L. prp. of *indignari,* to consider unworthy, ult. < *in-,* not + *dignus,* worthy] feeling or expressing indignation —**in·dig′nant·ly** ***adv.***

in·dig·na·tion (in′dig nā′shən) ***n.*** anger or scorn that is a reaction to injustice or meanness

in·dig·ni·ty (in dig′nə tē) ***n., pl.*** **-ties** something that humiliates, insults, or injures the dignity or self-respect; affront

in·di·go (in′di gō′) ***n., pl.*** **-gos′, -goes′** [Sp. < L. *indicum* < Gr. < *Indikos,* Indian < *India,* India] **1.** a blue dye obtained from certain plants or made synthetically **2.** a plant of the legume family that yields indigo **3.** a deep violet blue: also **indigo blue** —***adj.*** of a deep violet-blue: also **in′di·go′blue′**

indigo bunting (or **bird**) a small finch of the E U.S.: the male is indigo, the female brown

in·di·rect (in′di rekt′, -dī-) ***adj.*** not direct; specif., *a)* not straight; roundabout *b)* not straight to the point or object *[an indirect reply] c)* not straightforward; dishonest *[indirect dealing] d)* not immediate; secondary *[an indirect result]* —**in′di·rect′ly** ***adv.*** —**in′di·rect′ness** ***n.***

indirect discourse statement of the speaker but not in his exact words (Ex.: she said that she would go)

in·di·rec·tion (-rek′shən) ***n.*** **1.** roundabout act, procedure, or means **2.** deceit; dishonesty **3.** lack of direction or purpose

indirect lighting lighting reflected, as from a ceiling, wall panel, etc., or diffused so as to avoid glare

indirect object *Gram.* the person or thing indirectly affected by the action of the verb, i.e., the one to which something is given or for which something is done (Ex.: *him* in "do *him* a favor")

indirect tax a tax on manufactured goods, imports, etc. paid indirectly when included in the price

in·dis·cern·i·ble (in′di sʉr′nə b′l, -zʉr′-) ***adj.*** that cannot be discerned; imperceptible —**in′dis·cern′i·bly** ***adv.***

in·dis·creet (in′dis krēt′) ***adj.*** not discreet; lacking prudence; unwise —**in′dis·creet′ly** ***adv.*** —**in′dis·creet′ness** ***n.***

in·dis·cre·tion (in′dis kresh′ən) ***n.*** **1.** lack of discretion **2.** an indiscreet act or remark

in·dis·crim·i·nate (in′dis krim′ə nit) ***adj.*** **1.** not based on careful selection; random or promiscuous **2.** not discriminating; not making careful choices or distinctions —**in′dis·crim′i·nate·ly** ***adv.*** —**in′dis·crim′i·nate·ness, in′dis·crim′i·na′tion** ***n.***

in·dis·pen·sa·ble (in′dis pen′sə b′l) ***adj.*** **1.** that cannot be dispensed with or neglected **2.** absolutely necessary or required —***n.*** an indispensable person or thing —**in′dis·pen′sa·bil′i·ty** ***n.*** —**in′dis·pen′sa·bly** ***adv.***

in·dis·pose (in′dis pōz′) ***vt.*** **-posed′, -pos′ing** **1.** to make unfit or unable **2.** to make unwilling or disinclined **3.** to make slightly ill

in·dis·posed (-pōzd′) ***adj.*** **1.** slightly ill **2.** unwilling; disinclined

in·dis·po·si·tion (in′dis pə zish′ən) ***n.*** **1.** a slight illness **2.** unwillingness; disinclination

in·dis·pu·ta·ble (in′dis pyo͞ot′ə b′l, in dis′pyo͞o tə-) ***adj.*** that cannot be disputed; unquestionable —**in′dis·pu′ta·bil′i·ty** ***n.*** —**in′dis·pu′ta·bly** ***adv.***

in·dis·sol·u·ble (in′di säl′yoo b′l) ***adj.*** that cannot be dissolved, decomposed, or destroyed; firm; lasting —**in′dis·sol′u·bil′i·ty** ***n.*** —**in′dis·sol′u·bly** ***adv.***

in·dis·tinct (in′dis tiŋkt′) ***adj.*** not distinct; specif., *a)* not seen, heard, or perceived clearly; obscure *b)* not separate or separable; not plainly defined —**in′dis·tinct′ly** ***adv.*** —**in′dis·tinct′ness** ***n.***

in·dis·tin·guish·a·ble (-tiŋ′gwish ə b′l) ***adj.*** that cannot be distinguished or recognized as different or separate —**in′dis·tin′guish·a·bly** ***adv.***

in·dite (in dīt′) ***vt.*** **-dit′ed, -dit′ing** [< OFr., ult. < L.: see

INDICT] to put in writing; compose and write —**in·dite′ment** *n.* —**in·dit′er** *n.*
in·di·um (in′dē əm) *n.* [ModL. < L. *indicum*, indigo: from its spectrum] a rare metallic chemical element, soft, ductile, and silver-white: symbol, In; at. wt., 114.82; at. no., 49
in·di·vid·u·al (in′di vij′oo wəl, -vij′əl) *adj.* [< ML. < L. *individuus*, not divisible] **1.** existing as a separate thing or being; single; particular **2.** of, for, or by a single person or thing **3.** of or characteristic of a single person or thing **4.** unique or striking *[an individual style]* —*n.* **1.** a single thing, being, or organism, esp. as a member of a class, etc. **2.** a person
in·di·vid·u·al·ism (-iz'm) *n.* **1.** individual character; individuality **2.** the doctrine of unrestricted individual freedom in economic enterprise **3.** the doctrine that the state exists to serve the individual **4.** the doctrine that self-interest is the proper goal of all human actions; egoism **5.** *a)* action based on any such doctrine *b)* the leading of one's life in one's own way without conforming to conventions —**in′di·vid′u·al·ist** *n., adj.* —**in′di·vid′u·al·is′tic** *adj.*
in·di·vid·u·al·i·ty (in′di vij′oo wal′ə tē) *n., pl.* **-ties** **1.** *a)* the sum of the characteristics that set one person or thing apart; individual character *b)* personal identity; personality **2.** separate existence **3.** an individual
in·di·vid·u·al·ize (-vij′oo wə līz′, -vij′oo līz′) *vt.* **-ized′, -iz′ing** **1.** to make individual; mark as different from others **2.** to make suitable for a particular individual **3.** to consider individually —**in′di·vid′u·al·i·za′tion** *n.*
in·di·vid·u·al·ly (-vij′oo wəl ē, -vij′əl ē) *adv.* **1.** one at a time; separately **2.** as an individual; personally **3.** in a way showing individual characteristics; distinctively
in·di·vis·i·ble (in′di viz′ə b'l) *adj.* **1.** that cannot be divided **2.** *Math.* that cannot be divided without leaving a remainder —*n.* anything indivisible —**in′di·vis′i·bil′i·ty** *n.* —**in′di·vis′i·bly** *adv.*
In·do·chi·na (in′dō chī′nə) **1.** large peninsula south of China, including Burma, Thailand, Indochina (sense 2), & Malaya **2.** E part of this peninsula, consisting of Laos, Cambodia, & Vietnam Also sp. **Indo-China, Indo China**
In·do·chi·nese, In·do-Chi·nese (-chī nēz′) *adj.* of Indochina, its Mongoloid people, their language, or their culture —*n., pl.* **-nese′** a native or inhabitant of Indochina
in·doc·tri·nate (in däk′trə nāt′) *vt.* **-nat′ed, -nat′ing** [prob. < OFr. *endoctriner:* see IN-[1] & DOCTRINE] **1.** to instruct in doctrines, theories, or beliefs, as of a sect **2.** to instruct; teach —**in·doc′tri·na′tion** *n.* —**in·doc′tri·na′tor** *n.*
In·do-Eu·ro·pe·an (in′dō yoor′ə pē′ən) *adj.* designating or of a family of languages that includes most of those spoken in Europe and many of those spoken in southwestern Asia and India —*n.* **1.** this family of languages, including the Indo-Iranian, Greek, Italic, Germanic, and Slavic languages **2.** the hypothetical language from which these languages are thought to have descended
In·do-I·ra·ni·an (-i rā′nē ən) *adj.* designating or of a subfamily of the Indo-European language family that includes Indic and Iranian
in·do·lent (in′də lənt) *adj.* [< LL. < L. *in-*, not + prp. of *dolere*, to feel pain] disliking or avoiding work; idle; lazy —**in′do·lence** *n.* —**in′do·lent·ly** *adv.*
in·dom·i·ta·ble (in däm′it ə b'l) *adj.* [< LL. < L. < *in-*, not + pp. of *domitare*, intens. < *domare*, to tame] not easily discouraged or defeated; unyielding —**in·dom′i·ta·bil′i·ty, in·dom′i·ta·ble·ness** *n.* —**in·dom′i·ta·bly** *adv.*
In·do·ne·sia (in′də nē′zhə, -shə) republic in the Malay Archipelago, consisting of Java, Sumatra, most of Borneo, Celebes, West Irian, & many smaller islands: 736,510 sq. mi.; pop. 113,721,000; cap. Jakarta
In·do·ne·sian (-zhən, -shən) *adj.* **1.** of Indonesia, its people, etc. **2.** designating or of a large group of Malayo-Polynesian languages spoken in Indonesia, the Philippines, Java, etc. —*n.* **1.** a member of a light-brown people of Indonesia, the Philippines, Java, etc. **2.** an inhabitant of Indonesia **3.** the Indonesian languages **4.** the official Malay language of Indonesia
in·door (in′dôr′) *adj.* **1.** of the inside of a house or building **2.** living, belonging, or carried on within a house or building
in·doors (in′dôrz′) *adv.* in or into a house or other building
in·dorse (in dôrs′) *vt.* **-dorsed′, -dors′ing** *same as* ENDORSE
In·dra (in′drə) [Sans.] the chief god of the early Hindu religion, a god associated with rain and thunder
in·du·bi·ta·ble (in dōō′bi tə b'l, -dyōō′-) *adj.* that cannot be doubted; unquestionable —**in·du′bi·ta·bly** *adv.*
in·duce (in dōōs′, -dyōōs′) *vt.* **-duced′, -duc′ing** [< L. *inducere* < *in-*, in + *ducere*, to lead] **1.** to lead on to some action, condition, etc.; persuade **2.** to bring on; cause *[to induce vomiting with an emetic]* **3.** to draw (a general rule or conclusion) from particular facts **4.** *Physics* to bring about (an electric or magnetic effect) in a body by exposing it to the influence of a field of force —**in·duc′er** *n.* —**in·duc′i·ble** *adj.*
in·duce·ment (-mənt) *n.* **1.** an inducing or being induced **2.** anything that induces; motive
in·duct (in dukt′) *vt.* [< L. pp. of *inducere:* see INDUCE] **1.** formerly, to bring or lead in **2.** to place formally in an official position **3.** *a)* to initiate into a society *b)* to provide with knowledge of something not open to all *c)* to enroll (esp. a draftee) into the armed forces
in·duct·ance (-duk′təns) *n.* the property of an electric circuit by which a varying current in it induces voltages in the same circuit or in one nearby
in·duct·ee (in duk′tē′) *n.* a person inducted or being inducted, esp. into the armed forces
in·duc·tile (in duk′t'l) *adj.* not ductile, malleable, or pliant —**in′duc·til′i·ty** (-til′ə tē) *n.*
in·duc·tion (in duk′shən) *n.* **1.** an inducting or being inducted; installation **2.** a bringing forward of separate facts or instances, esp. so as to prove a general statement **3.** *Logic* reasoning from particular facts to a general conclusion; also, a conclusion so reached: opposed to DEDUCTION **4.** *Physics* the act or process by which an electric or magnetic effect is produced in an electrical conductor or magnetizable body when it is exposed to the influence of a field of force
induction coil an apparatus made up of two magnetically coupled coils in a circuit in which interruptions of the direct-current supply to one coil produce an alternating current of high potential in the other
induction heating the heating of a conducting material by means of electric current induced by an alternating magnetic field
in·duc·tive (in duk′tiv) *adj.* **1.** of or using logical induction *[inductive reasoning]* **2.** produced by induction **3.** of inductance or electrical or magnetic induction —**in·duc′tive·ly** *adv.*
in·duc·tor (-tər) *n.* a person or thing that inducts; specif., a device designed to introduce inductance into an electric circuit
in·due (in dōō′, -dyōō′) *vt.* **-dued′, -du′ing** *same as* ENDUE
in·dulge (in dulj′) *vt.* **-dulged′, -dulg′ing** [L. *indulgere*, to be kind to] **1.** to yield to or satisfy (a desire); give oneself up to *[to indulge a craving for sweets]* **2.** to gratify the wishes of; humor —*vi.* to give way to one's own desires; indulge oneself (*in* something) —**in·dulg′er** *n.*
in·dul·gence (in dul′jəns) *n.* **1.** an indulging or being indulgent **2.** a thing indulged in **3.** a giving way to one's desires **4.** a favor or privilege **5.** *R.C.Ch.* a remission of temporal or purgatorial punishment still due for a sin after the guilt has been forgiven
in·dul·gent (-jənt) *adj.* indulging or inclined to indulge; kind or lenient, often to excess —**in·dul′gent·ly** *adv.*
in·du·rate (in′doo rāt′, -dyoo-) *vt.* **-rat′ed, -rat′ing** [< L. pp. of *indurare* < *in-*, in + *durare*, to harden] **1.** to make hard; harden **2.** to make callous or unfeeling **3.** to cause to be firmly established —*vi.* to become indurated —*adj.* **1.** hardened **2.** callous or unfeeling —**in′du·ra′tion** *n.* —**in′du·ra′tive** *adj.*
In·dus (in′dəs) river in S Asia, flowing from SW Tibet into the Arabian Sea: c.1,900 mi.
in·dus·tri·al (in dus′trē əl) *adj.* **1.** having the nature of or characterized by industries **2.** of, connected with, or resulting from industries **3.** working in industries **4.** of or concerned with people working in industries **5.** for use by industries: said of products —**in·dus′tri·al·ly** *adv.*
industrial arts the mechanical and technical skills used in industry, esp. as taught in schools
in·dus·tri·al·ism (in dus′trē əl iz'm) *n.* social and economic organization characterized by large industries, machine production, concentration of workers in cities, etc.
in·dus·tri·al·ist (-əl ist) *n.* a person who owns or manages an industrial enterprise
in·dus·tri·al·ize (-ə līz′) *vt.* **-ized′, -iz′ing** **1.** to develop industrialism in **2.** to organize as an industry —*vi.* to become industrial —**in·dus′tri·al·i·za′tion** *n.*
industrial park an area zoned for industrial and business use, usually on the outskirts of a city
industrial relations relations between industrial employers and their employees
Industrial Revolution [*often* **i- r-**] the great social and economic changes due to the introduction of machine and power tools and large-scale industrial production: it began in England about 1760
industrial union a labor union to which all workers in a given industry may belong, regardless of occupation or trade: cf. CRAFT UNION
in·dus·tri·ous (in dus′trē əs) *adj.* characterized by earnest, steady effort; hard-working —**in·dus′tri·ous·ly** *adv.* —**in·dus′tri·ous·ness** *n.*
in·dus·try (in′dəs trē) *n., pl.* **-tries** [< MFr. < L. *industria* < *industrius*, active] **1.** earnest, steady effort; diligence in work **2.** systematic work **3.** *a)* any particular branch of productive, esp. manufacturing, enterprise *[the paper industry]*; also, all such enterprises collectively *b)* any large-

scale business activity [the TV *industry*] **4.** the owners and managers of industry

in·dwell (in dwel′) ***vi., vt.*** **-dwelt′, -dwell′ing** to dwell (in); reside (within) —**in′dwell′er** ***n.***

-ine[1] (īn, in, ēn, ən) [< Fr. < L. *-inus*] *a suffix meaning* of, having the nature of, like [*divine, marine, crystalline*]

-ine[2] (in, ən, īn, ēn) [< L. < Gr. *-inē*] *a suffix used to form feminine nouns* [*heroine*]

-ine[3] (in, ən) [Fr. < L. *-ina*] *a suffix used to form certain abstract nouns* [*medicine, doctrine*]

-ine[4] (ēn, in, īn, ən) [arbitrary use of L. *-inus*] *a suffix used to form certain commercial names* [*Vaseline*] *or the chemical names of* *a*) halogens [*iodine*] *b*) alkaloids or nitrogen bases [*morphine*]

in·e·bri·ate (in ē′brē āt′; *for adj. & n., usually* -it) ***vt.*** **-at′ed, -at′ing** [< L. pp. of *inebriare*, ult. < *in-*, intens. + *ebrius*, drunk] **1.** to make drunk; intoxicate **2.** to excite; exhilarate —***adj.*** drunk; intoxicated —***n.*** a drunken person, esp. a drunkard —**in·e′bri·at′ed** ***adj.*** —**in·e′bri·a′tion** ***n.***

in·e·bri·e·ty (in′ē brī′ə tē) ***n.*** drunkenness

in·ed·i·ble (in ed′ə b′l) ***adj.*** not edible; not fit to be eaten —**in′ed·i·bil′i·ty** ***n.***

in·ed·u·ca·ble (in ej′ə kə b′l) ***adj.*** thought to be incapable of being educated

in·ef·fa·ble (in ef′ə b′l) ***adj.*** [< MFr. < L. < *in-*, not + *effabilis*, utterable < *ex-*, out + *fari*, to speak] **1.** too overwhelming to be expressed in words **2.** too sacred to be spoken —**in′ef·fa·bil′i·ty, in·ef′fa·ble·ness** ***n.*** —**in·ef′fa·bly** ***adv.***

in·ef·face·a·ble (in′i fās′ə b′l) ***adj.*** that cannot be effaced; impossible to wipe out —**in′ef·face′a·bil′i·ty** ***n.*** —**in′ef·face′a·bly** ***adv.***

in·ef·fec·tive (in′i fek′tiv) ***adj.*** **1.** not effective; not producing the desired effect **2.** not capable of performing satisfactorily; incompetent; inefficient —**in′ef·fec′tive·ly** ***adv.*** —**in′ef·fec′tive·ness** ***n.***

in·ef·fec·tu·al (-choo wəl) ***adj.*** not effectual; not producing or not able to produce the desired effect —**in′ef·fec′tu·al′i·ty** (-wal′ə tē), **in′ef·fec′tu·al·ness** ***n.*** —**in′ef·fec′tu·al·ly** ***adv.***

in·ef·fi·ca·cious (in′ef ə kā′shəs) ***adj.*** not efficacious; unable to produce the desired effect [an *inefficacious* medicine] —**in′ef·fi·ca′cious·ly** ***adv.*** —**in′ef·fi·ca′cious·ness** ***n.***

in·ef·fi·ca·cy (in ef′i kə sē) ***n.*** lack of efficacy; inability to produce the desired effect

in·ef·fi·cient (in′ə fish′ənt) ***adj.*** not efficient; specif., *a*) not producing the desired effect with a minimum use of energy, time, etc. *b*) lacking the necessary ability; incapable —**in′ef·fi′cien·cy** ***n.*** —**in′ef·fi′cient·ly** ***adv.***

in·e·las·tic (in′i las′tik) ***adj.*** not elastic; inflexible, rigid, unyielding, unadaptable, etc. —**in′e·las·tic′i·ty** (-las tis′ə tē) ***n.***

in·el·e·gance (in el′ə gəns) ***n.*** **1.** lack of elegance **2.** something inelegant Also **in·el′e·gan·cy,** *pl.* **-cies**

in·el·e·gant (-gənt) ***adj.*** not elegant; lacking refinement, good taste, grace, etc.; coarse; crude —**in·el′e·gant·ly** ***adv.***

in·el·i·gi·ble (in el′i jə b′l) ***adj.*** not eligible; not qualified under the rules —***n.*** an ineligible person —**in·el′i·gi·bil′i·ty** ***n.*** —**in·el′i·gi·bly** ***adv.***

in·e·luc·ta·ble (in′i luk′tə b′l) ***adj.*** [< L. < *in-*, not + *eluctabilis*, resistible < *eluctari*, to struggle] not to be avoided or escaped; inevitable —**in′e·luc′ta·bil′i·ty** ***n.*** —**in′e·luc′ta·bly** ***adv.***

in·ept (in ept′) ***adj.*** [< Fr. < L. < *in-*, not + *aptus*, fit] **1.** unsuitable; unfit **2.** wrong in a foolish and awkward way [*inept* praise] **3.** clumsy or bungling; inefficient —**in·ept′ly** ***adv.*** —**in·ept′ness** ***n.***

in·ept·i·tude (in ep′tə to͞od′, -tyo͞od′) ***n.*** **1.** the quality or condition of being inept **2.** an inept act, remark, etc.

in·e·qual·i·ty (in′i kwäl′ə tē, -kwôl′-) ***n., pl.*** **-ties** **1.** a being unequal; lack of equality **2.** an instance of this; specif., *a*) a difference in size, amount, quality, rank, etc. *b*) an unevenness in surface *c*) a lack of proper proportion; unequal distribution **3.** *Math.* *a*) the relation between two unequal quantities *b*) an expression of this

in·eq·ui·ta·ble (in ek′wit ə b′l) ***adj.*** not equitable; unfair; unjust —**in·eq′ui·ta·bly** ***adv.***

in·eq·ui·ty (in ek′wət ē) ***n.*** **1.** lack of justice; unfairness **2.** *pl.* **-ties** an instance of this

in·e·rad·i·ca·ble (in′i rad′ə kə b′l) ***adj.*** that cannot be eradicated —**in′e·rad′i·ca·bly** ***adv.***

in·ert (in ʉrt′) ***adj.*** [< L. < *in-*, not + *ars*, ART[1]] **1.** without power to move or act **2.** inactive; dull; slow **3.** having few or no active properties [an *inert* gas] —**in·ert′ly** ***adv.*** —**in·ert′ness** ***n.***

in·er·tia (in ʉr′shə) ***n.*** [see prec.] **1.** *Physics* the tendency of matter to remain at rest (or to keep moving in the same direction) unless affected by an outside force **2.** a tendency to remain fixed, inactive, unchanging, etc. —**in·er′tial** ***adj.***

inertial guidance (or **navigation**) the guidance (or navigation) of an aircraft, spacecraft, etc. along a preassigned course by means of self-contained, automatic instruments that utilize the laws of inertia

in·es·cap·a·ble (in′ə skāp′ə b′l) ***adj.*** that cannot be escaped or avoided; inevitable —**in′es·cap′a·bly** ***adv.***

in·es·ti·ma·ble (in es′tə mə b′l) ***adj.*** too great or valuable to be properly measured or estimated —**in·es′ti·ma·bly** ***adv.***

in·ev·i·ta·ble (in ev′ə tə b′l) ***adj.*** [< L. < *in-*, not + *evitabilis*, avoidable] that cannot be avoided; certain to happen —**in·ev′i·ta·bil′i·ty** ***n.*** —**in·ev′i·ta·bly** ***adv.***

in·ex·act (in′ig zakt′) ***adj.*** not exact; not accurate —**in′ex·act′ly** ***adv.*** —**in′ex·act′ness** ***n.***

in·ex·cus·a·ble (in′ik skyo͞o′zə b′l) ***adj.*** that cannot or should not be excused; unjustifiable —**in′ex·cus′a·bil′i·ty** ***n.*** —**in′ex·cus′a·bly** ***adv.***

in·ex·haust·i·ble (in′ig zôs′tə b′l) ***adj.*** that cannot be exhausted; specif., *a*) that cannot be used up or emptied *b*) tireless —**in′ex·haust′i·bil′i·ty** ***n.*** —**in′ex·haust′i·bly** ***adv.***

in·ex·o·ra·ble (in ek′sər ə b′l) ***adj.*** [< L. < *in-*, not + *exorare*, to move by entreaty] **1.** that cannot be influenced by entreaty; unrelenting **2.** that cannot be altered, checked, etc. [*inexorable* fate] —**in·ex′o·ra·bil′i·ty** ***n.*** —**in·ex′o·ra·bly** ***adv.***

in·ex·pe·di·ent (in′ik spē′dē ənt) ***adj.*** not expedient; not suitable or practicable; unwise —**in′ex·pe′di·en·cy, in′ex·pe′di·ence** ***n.*** —**in′ex·pe′di·ent·ly** ***adv.***

in·ex·pen·sive (in′ik spen′siv) ***adj.*** not expensive; costing relatively little; cheap —**in′ex·pen′sive·ly** ***adv.*** —**in′ex·pen′sive·ness** ***n.***

in·ex·pe·ri·ence (in′ik spir′ē əns) ***n.*** lack of experience or of the knowledge or skill resulting from experience —**in′ex·pe′ri·enced** ***adj.***

in·ex·pert (in ek′spərt, in′ik spʉrt′) ***adj.*** not expert; unskillful; amateurish —**in·ex′pert·ly** ***adv.*** —**in·ex′pert·ness** ***n.***

in·ex·pi·a·ble (in ek′spē ə b′l) ***adj.*** that cannot be expiated or atoned for [an *inexpiable* sin]

in·ex·pli·ca·ble (in eks′pli kə b′l, in′iks plik′ə b′l) ***adj.*** not explicable; that cannot be explained or understood —**in·ex′pli·ca·bil′i·ty** ***n.*** —**in·ex′pli·ca·bly** ***adv.***

in·ex·press·i·ble (in′ik spres′ə b′l) ***adj.*** that cannot be expressed; indescribable or unutterable —**in′ex·press′i·bil′i·ty** ***n.*** —**in′ex·press′i·bly** ***adv.***

in·ex·pres·sive (in′ik spres′iv) ***adj.*** not expressive; lacking meaning or expression —**in′ex·pres′sive·ly** ***adv.***

‡in ex·ten·so (in ik sten′sō) [L.] at full length

in·ex·tin·guish·a·ble (in′ik stiŋ′gwish ə b′l) ***adj.*** not extinguishable; that cannot be put out or stopped —**in′ex·tin′guish·a·bly** ***adv.***

‡in ex·tre·mis (in′ ik strē′mis) [L., in extremity] at the point of death

in·ex·tri·ca·ble (in eks′tri kə b′l, in′ik strik′ə b′l) ***adj.*** **1.** that one cannot extricate himself from **2.** that cannot be disentangled or untied **3.** insolvable —**in·ex′tri·ca·bil′i·ty** ***n.*** —**in·ex′tri·ca·bly** ***adv.***

I·nez (ī′niz, ī′nez′, ī nez′) [Sp. *Iñez*] a feminine name

inf. **1.** [L. *infra*] below **2.** infantry: also **Inf.** **3.** infinitive **4.** information

in·fal·li·ble (in fal′ə b′l) ***adj.*** [< ML.: see IN-[2] & FALLIBLE] **1.** incapable of error; never wrong **2.** not liable to fail, go wrong, etc.; reliable **3.** *R.C.Ch.* incapable of error in setting forth doctrine on faith and morals —**in·fal′li·bil′i·ty** ***n.*** —**in·fal′li·bly** ***adv.***

in·fa·mous (in′fə məs) ***adj.*** **1.** having a very bad reputation; notorious **2.** causing or deserving a bad reputation —**in′fa·mous·ly** ***adv.***

in·fa·my (-mē) ***n., pl.*** **-mies** [< OFr. < L.: see IN-[2] & FAMOUS] **1.** very bad reputation; disgrace; dishonor **2.** the quality of being infamous; great wickedness **3.** an infamous act

in·fan·cy (in′fən sē) ***n., pl.*** **-cies** **1.** the state or period of being an infant; babyhood **2.** the beginning or earliest stage of anything **3.** *Law* the state of being a minor; period before the age of legal majority, usually twenty-one

in·fant (in′fənt) ***n.*** [< OFr. < L., ult. < *in-*, not + prp. of *fari*, to speak] **1.** a very young child; baby **2.** *Law* a minor —***adj.*** **1.** of or for infants or infancy **2.** in a very early stage

in·fan·ta (in fan′tə, -fän′-) ***n.*** [Sp. & Port., fem. of *infante*: see ff.] **1.** any daughter of a king of Spain or Portugal **2.** the wife of an infante

in·fan·te (-tā) ***n.*** [Sp. & Port. < L.: see INFANT] any son of a king of Spain or Portugal, except the heir to the throne

in·fan·ti·cide (in fan′tə sīd′) ***n.*** [Fr. < LL.: see INFANT & -CIDE] **1.** the murder of a baby **2.** a person guilty of this

in·fan·tile (in′fən tīl′, -til) ***adj.*** **1.** of infants or infancy **2.** like or characteristic of an infant; babyish **3.** in the earliest stage of development

infantile paralysis *same as* POLIOMYELITIS

in·fan·ti·lism (in′fən t'l iz'm, in fan′-) ***n.*** immature or childish behavior; specif., *Psychol.* an abnormal state in which such behavior persists into adult life

in·fan·tine (in′fən tin′, -tin) ***adj.*** infantile

in·fan·try (in′fən trē) ***n.,*** *pl.* **-tries** [< Fr. < It. < *infante*, child, knight's page, foot soldier] **1.** foot soldiers collectively; esp., that branch of an army consisting of soldiers trained and equipped to fight chiefly on foot **2.** [**I-**] a (designated) infantry regiment

in·fan·try·man (-mən) ***n.,*** *pl.* **-men** (-mən) a soldier in the infantry

in·fat·u·ate (in fach′oo wāt′) ***vt.*** **-at′ed, -at′ing** [< L. pp. of *infatuare* < *in-*, intens. + *fatuus*, foolish] **1.** to make foolish **2.** to inspire with foolish or shallow love —***adj.*** infatuated —***n.*** a person who is infatuated —**in·fat′u·a′tion** ***n.***

in·fat·u·at·ed (-id) ***adj.*** **1.** foolish **2.** completely carried away by foolish or shallow love

in·fect (in fekt′) ***vt.*** [< MFr. < L. pp. of *inficere*, to stain < *in-*, in + *facere*, to make] **1.** to contaminate with a disease-producing organism **2.** to cause to become diseased by bringing into contact with such an organism **3.** to invade (an individual, organ, tissue, etc.) **4.** to imbue with one's feelings or beliefs —**in·fec′tor** ***n.***

in·fec·tion (in fek′shən) ***n.*** **1.** an infecting; specif., *a*) a causing to become diseased *b*) an affecting with one's feelings or beliefs **2.** a being infected, esp. by bacteria, viruses, etc. **3.** something that results from infecting or being infected; specif., a disease resulting from infection (sense 2) **4.** anything that infects

in·fec·tious (-shəs) ***adj.*** **1.** likely to cause infection **2.** designating a disease that can be communicated by infection (sense 2) **3.** tending to spread to others *[an infectious laugh]* —**in·fec′tious·ly** ***adv.*** —**in·fec′tious·ness** ***n.***

infectious hepatitis a viral disease causing inflammation of the liver

infectious mononucleosis an acute disease, esp. of young people, characterized by fever, swollen lymph nodes, etc.

in·fec·tive (in fek′tiv) ***adj.*** likely to cause infection —**in·fec′tive·ness, in′fec·tiv′i·ty** ***n.***

in·fe·lic·i·tous (in′fə lis′ə təs) ***adj.*** not felicitous; unfortunate or unsuitable —**in′fe·lic′i·tous·ly** ***adv.***

in·fe·lic·i·ty (-tē) ***n.*** **1.** a being infelicitous **2.** *pl.* **-ties** something infelicitous; unsuitable or inapt remark, action, etc.

in·fer (in fʉr′) ***vt.*** **-ferred′, -fer′ring** [< L. *inferre* < *in-*, in + *ferre*, to bring] **1.** to conclude by reasoning from something known or assumed **2.** *a*) to lead to as a conclusion; indicate *b*) to indicate indirectly; imply: sometimes regarded as a loose usage —***vi.*** to draw inferences —**in·fer′a·ble** ***adj.*** —**in·fer′a·bly** ***adv.*** —**in·fer′rer** ***n.***

in·fer·ence (in′fər əns) ***n.*** **1.** an inferring; specif., the deriving of a conclusion by induction or deduction **2.** something inferred; conclusion

in·fer·en·tial (in′fə ren′shəl) ***adj.*** of or based on inference —**in′fer·en′tial·ly** ***adv.***

in·fe·ri·or (in fir′ē ər) ***adj.*** [L., compar. of *inferus*, low] **1.** lower in space; placed lower down **2.** lower in order, status, rank, etc. **3.** lower in quality or value than (with *to*) **4.** poor in quality; below average —***n.*** an inferior person or thing —**in·fe′ri·or′i·ty** (-ôr′ə tē, -är′-) ***n.***

inferiority complex **1.** *Psychol.* a neurotic condition resulting from various feelings of inferiority or inadequacy, often manifested through overcompensation in excessive aggressiveness, etc. **2.** popularly, any feeling of inferiority, inadequacy, etc.

in·fer·nal (in fʉr′n'l) ***adj.*** [< OFr. < LL. *infernalis*, ult. < L. *inferus*: see INFERIOR] **1.** *a*) of the ancient mythological world of the dead *b*) of hell **2.** hellish; fiendish **3.** [Colloq.] hateful; outrageous —**in·fer′nal·ly** ***adv.***

infernal machine *earlier name for* a booby trap or time bomb

in·fer·no (in fʉr′nō) ***n.,*** *pl.* **-nos** [It. < L.: see INFERNAL] hell or any place suggesting hell

in·fer·tile (in fʉr′t'l) ***adj.*** not fertile; barren; sterile —**in·fer·til·i·ty** (in′fər til′ə tē) ***n.***

in·fest (in fest′) ***vt.*** [< Fr. < L. < *infestus*, hostile] **1.** to overrun or swarm about in large numbers, usually so as to be harmful or bothersome **2.** to be parasitic in or on —**in′fes·ta′tion** ***n.***

in·fi·del (in′fə d'l) ***n.*** [< MFr. < L. < *in-*, not + *fidelis*, faithful] **1.** a person who does not believe in a particular, esp. the prevailing, religion **2.** a person who holds no religious belief —***adj.*** **1.** that is an infidel; unbelieving **2.** of infidels

in·fi·del·i·ty (in′fə del′ə tē) ***n.,*** *pl.* **-ties** **1.** the fact or state of being an infidel **2.** unfaithfulness or disloyalty to another; esp., sexual unfaithfulness of a husband or wife; adultery **3.** an unfaithful or disloyal act

in·field (in′fēld′) ***n.*** **1.** *a*) the area enclosed by the four base lines on a baseball field *b*) the infielders collectively, or the area they cover **2.** the area inside a race track or running track

in·field·er (-ər) ***n.*** *Baseball* a player whose position is in the infield; shortstop, first baseman, second baseman, or third baseman

in·fight·ing (in′fīt′iŋ) ***n.*** **1.** fighting, esp. boxing, at close range **2.** intense competition or conflict, often personal, as between political opponents or within an organization —**in′fight′er** ***n.***

in·fil·trate (in fil′trāt, in′fil trāt′) ***vi., vt.*** **-trat·ed, -trat·ing** **1.** to pass into or through (a substance), as in filtering **2.** to pass, or cause (individual troops) to pass, through weak places in the enemy's lines **3.** to penetrate, or cause to penetrate, (a region or group) gradually or stealthily, so as to gain influence or control —***n.*** something that infiltrates —**in′fil·tra′tion** ***n.*** —**in′fil·tra′tive** ***adj.*** —**in′fil·tra′tor** ***n.***

infin. infinitive

in·fi·nite (in′fə nit) ***adj.*** [< L.: see IN-[2] & FINITE] **1.** lacking limits or bounds; extending beyond measure or comprehension; endless **2.** very great; vast; immense **3.** *Math.* indefinitely large; greater than any finite number —***n.*** something infinite —**the Infinite (Being)** God —**in′fi·nite·ly** ***adv.*** —**in′fi·nite·ness** ***n.***

in·fin·i·tes·i·mal (in′fin ə tes′ə məl, in fin′-) ***adj.*** [< ModL. < L. *infinitus*, infinite (patterned after *centesimus*, hundredth)] too small to be measured; infinitely small —***n.*** an infinitesimal quantity —**in′fin·i·tes′i·mal·ly** ***adv.***

in·fin·i·tive (in fin′ə tiv) ***adj.*** [< LL. < L. *infinitus* (*modus*), lit., unlimited (mood)] *Gram.* of or connected with an infinitive —***n.*** *Gram.* the form of the verb which expresses existence or action without reference to person, number, or tense: usually following the marker *to* (*to go*) or another verb form (*let him try*) —**in·fin′i·ti′val** (-tī′vəl) ***adj.***

in·fin·i·tude (-to͞od′, -tyo͞od′) ***n.*** **1.** a being infinite **2.** an infinite quantity or extent

in·fin·i·ty (-tē) ***n.,*** *pl.* **-ties** **1.** the quality of being infinite **2.** endless or unlimited space, time, distance, amount, etc. **3.** an indefinitely large number or amount

in·firm (in fʉrm′) ***adj.*** **1.** not firm or strong physically; weak; feeble **2.** not firm in mind or purpose; vacillating **3.** not stable; frail; shaky, as a structure **4.** not secure or valid —**in·firm′ly** ***adv.*** —**in·firm′ness** ***n.***

in·fir·ma·ry (in fʉr′mə rē) ***n.,*** *pl.* **-ries** a place for the care of the sick, injured, or infirm; esp., a building or room, as in a school, that serves as a hospital or dispensary

in·fir·mi·ty (-mə tē) ***n.*** **1.** a being infirm; feebleness; weakness **2.** *pl.* **-ties** *a*) a physical weakness or defect *b*) a moral weakness

in·fix (in fiks′; *also, and for n. always*, in′fiks′) ***vt.*** **1.** to fasten or set firmly in or on **2.** to fix firmly in the mind; instill **3.** to place (an infix) within the body of a word —***n.*** *Linguis.* a bound morpheme added within a word that has no affixes or within that part of a word to which affixes are added

‡in fla·gran·te de·lic·to (in flə gran′tē di lik′tō) [L.] in the very act of committing the offense

in·flame (in flām′) ***vt.*** **-flamed′, -flam′ing** [< OFr. < L.: see IN-[1] & FLAME] **1.** to set on fire **2.** to arouse passion, desire, or violence in; excite intensely **3.** to increase the intensity of (passion, desire, etc.) **4.** to cause inflammation in (some organ or tissue) —***vi.*** **1.** to become roused, excited, etc. **2.** to catch fire **3.** to become hot, feverish, sore, etc. —**in·flam′er** ***n.***

in·flam·ma·ble (in flam′ə b'l) ***adj.*** **1.** *same as* FLAMMABLE **2.** easily excited —***n.*** anything flammable —**in·flam′ma·bil′i·ty** ***n.*** —**in·flam′ma·bly** ***adv.***

in·flam·ma·tion (in′flə mā′shən) ***n.*** **1.** an inflaming or being inflamed **2.** a condition of some part of the body in reaction to injury, infection, etc., characterized by redness, pain, heat, and swelling

in·flam·ma·to·ry (in flam′ə tôr′ē) ***adj.*** **1.** rousing or likely to rouse excitement, anger, violence, etc. **2.** *Med.* of or characterized by inflammation

in·flate (in flāt′) ***vt.*** **-flat′ed, -flat′ing** [< L. pp. of *inflare* < *in-*, in + *flare*, to blow] **1.** to blow full or swell out as with air or gas **2.** to raise in spirits; make proud **3.** to increase or raise beyond what is normal; specif., to cause inflation of (money, credit, etc.) —***vi.*** to become inflated —**in·flat′a·ble** ***adj.*** —**in·flat′er, in·fla′tor** ***n.***

in·fla·tion (in flā′shən) ***n.*** **1.** an inflating or being inflated **2.** an increase in the amount of money in circulation, resulting in a fall in its value and a rise in prices —**in·fla′tion·ar′y** ***adj.***

in·fla·tion·ism (-iz'm) ***n.*** advocacy or promotion of monetary inflation —**in·fla′tion·ist** ***adj., n.***

in·flect (in flekt′) *vt.* [< L. *inflectere* < *in-,* in + *flectere,* to bend] **1.** to turn, bend, or curve **2.** to vary the tone or pitch of (the voice) **3.** *Gram.* to change the form of (a word) by inflection, as in conjugating or declining —*vi.* to be changed by inflection —**in·flec′tive** *adj.*

in·flec·tion (in flek′shən) *n.* **1.** a turn, bend, or curve **2.** a change in tone or pitch of the voice **3.** *Gram. a)* the change of form by which some words indicate certain grammatical relationships, as number, case, gender, tense, etc. *b)* an inflected form *c)* an inflectional element

in·flec·tion·al (-′l) *adj.* of, having, or showing grammatical inflection —**in·flec′tion·al·ly** *adv.*

in·flex·i·ble (in flek′sə b′l) *adj.* not flexible; specif., *a)* that cannot be bent or curved; rigid *b)* firm in mind or purpose; stubborn *c)* that cannot be changed; unalterable —**in·flex′i·bil′i·ty, in·flex′i·ble·ness** *n.* —**in·flex′i·bly** *adv.*

in·flict (in flikt′) *vt.* [< L. pp. of *infligere* < *in-,* against + *fligere,* to strike] **1.** to cause (pain, wounds, etc.) as by striking **2.** to impose (a punishment, disagreeable task, etc. *on* or *upon*) —**in·flict′er, in·flic′tor** *n.* —**in·flic′tive** *adj.*

in·flic·tion (in flik′shən) *n.* **1.** an inflicting **2.** something inflicted, as punishment

in-flight (in′flīt′) *adj.* done, occurring, shown, etc. while an aircraft is in flight

in·flo·res·cence (in′flô res′′ns, -flə-) *n.* [< ModL. < LL.: see IN-[1] & FLORESCENCE] *Bot.* **1.** the producing of blossoms; flowering **2.** the arrangement of flowers on a stem or axis **3.** a flower cluster on a common axis **4.** flowers collectively —**in′flo·res′cent** *adj.*

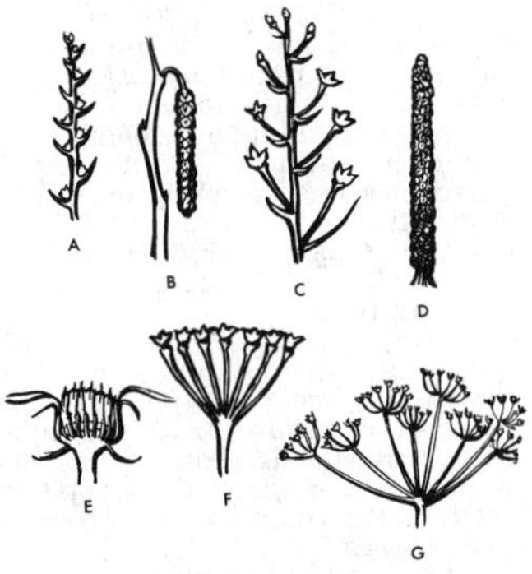

TYPES OF INFLORESCENCE
(A, spike; B, catkin; C, raceme; D, spadix; E, head with disk flowers and ray flowers; F, umbel; G, compound umbel)

in·flow (in′flō′) *n.* **1.** a flowing in or into **2.** anything that flows in

in·flu·ence (in′flo͞o wəns) *n.* [< OFr. < ML. < L. prp. of *influere* < *in-,* in + *fluere,* to flow] **1.** *a)* the power of persons or things to affect others *b)* the effect of such power **2.** the ability to produce effects indirectly by means of power based on wealth, high position, etc. **3.** one that has influence —*vt.* **-enced, -enc·ing** to have influence on; affect the nature, behavior, or thought of

in·flu·en·tial (in′flo͞o wen′shəl) *adj.* having or exerting influence, esp. great influence; powerful —**in′flu·en′tial·ly** *adv.*

in·flu·en·za (in′flo͞o wen′zə) *n.* [It., lit., an influence (because attributed to astrological influences)] an acute, contagious, infectious disease, caused by a virus and characterized by inflammation of the respiratory tract, fever, and muscular pain —**in′flu·en′zal** *adj.*

in·flux (in′fluks′) *n.* [Fr. < LL. pp. of *influere:* see INFLUENCE] **1.** a flowing in or continual coming in; inflow **2.** the point where a river joins another body of water

in·fold (in fōld′) *vt. same as* ENFOLD

in·form (in fôrm′) *vt.* [< OFr. < L.: see IN-[1] & FORM] **1.** *a)* to give character to *b)* to inspire; animate **2.** to give knowledge of something to; tell —*vi.* **1.** to give information **2.** to give information laying blame or accusation upon another

in·for·mal (in fôr′məl) *adj.* not formal; specif., *a)* not according to fixed customs, rules, etc. *b)* casual, easy, unceremonious, or relaxed *c)* for everyday use or casual wear *d)* not requiring formal dress *e) same as* COLLOQUIAL —**in·for′mal·ly** *adv.*

in·for·mal·i·ty (in′fôr mal′ə tē) *n.* **1.** a being informal **2.** *pl.* **-ties** an informal act

in·form·ant (in fôr′mənt) *n.* a person who gives, or serves as a source of, information

in·for·ma·tion (in′fər mā′shən) *n.* **1.** an informing or being informed; esp., a telling or being told **2.** news; word **3.** knowledge acquired in any manner; facts; data **4.** a person or agency answering questions as a service to others **5.** any data stored in a computer **6.** *Law* an accusation of a criminal offense made by a public officer, rather than by a grand jury indictment —**in′for·ma′tion·al** *adj.*

in·form·a·tive (in fôr′mə tiv) *adj.* giving information; instructive —**in·form′a·tive·ly** *adv.*

in·formed (in fôrmd′) *adj.* having much information, knowledge, or education

in·form·er (in fôr′mər) *n.* a person who informs; esp., one who secretly accuses, or gives evidence against, another, often for a reward

in·fra- [< L. *infra,* below] *a prefix meaning* below, beneath *[infrared]*

in·frac·tion (in frak′shən) *n.* [< L. < pp. of *infringere:* see INFRINGE] a violation of a law, pact, etc.

in·fra dig (in′frə dig′) [< L. *infra dig(nitatem)*] [Colloq.] beneath one's dignity

in·fran·gi·ble (in fran′jə b′l) *adj.* **1.** that cannot be broken or separated **2.** that cannot be violated or infringed —**in·fran′gi·bil′i·ty, in·fran′gi·ble·ness** *n.* —**in·fran′gi·bly** *adv.*

in·fra·red (in′frə red′) *adj.* designating or of those invisible rays just beyond the red of the visible spectrum: their waves are longer than those of the spectrum colors and give off penetrating heat

in·fra·son·ic (-sän′ik) *adj.* designating or of a frequency of sound below the range audible to the human ear

in·fra·struc·ture (in′frə struk′chər) *n.* the basic facilities on which a city, state, etc. depends, as roads or schools —**in′fra·struc′tur·al** *adj.*

in·fre·quent (in frē′kwənt) *adj.* not frequent; happening seldom; rare —**in·fre′quen·cy, in·fre′quence** *n.* —**in·fre′quent·ly** *adv.*

in·fringe (in frinj′) *vt.* **-fringed′, -fring′ing** [L. *infringere* < *in-,* in + *frangere,* to break] to break (a law or agreement); violate —**infringe on** (or **upon**) to break in on; encroach on (the rights, etc. of others) —**in·fringe′ment** *n.* —**in·fring′er** *n.*

in·fu·ri·ate (in fyoor′ē āt′) *vt.* **-at′ed, -at′ing** [< ML. pp. of *infuriare* < L. *in-,* in + *furia,* rage] to cause to become very angry; enrage —**in·fu′ri·at′ing·ly** *adv.* —**in·fu′ri·a′tion** *n.*

in·fuse (in fyo͞oz′) *vt.* **-fused′, -fus′ing** [< L. pp. of *infundere* < *in-,* in + *fundere,* to pour] **1.** to instill or impart (qualities, etc.) **2.** to imbue or inspire (*with* a quality, feeling, etc.) **3.** to steep or soak (tea leaves, etc.) so as to extract flavor or other qualities —**in·fus′er** *n.*

in·fu·si·ble (in fyo͞o′zə b′l) *adj.* that cannot be fused or melted —**in·fu′si·bil′i·ty, in·fu′si·ble·ness** *n.*

in·fu·sion (in fyo͞o′zhən) *n.* **1.** an infusing **2.** something infused **3.** the liquid extract that results from steeping a substance in water

in·fu·so·ri·an (in′fyoo sôr′ē ən) *n.* [< ModL.: from their occurrence in infusions] any of certain protozoans having cilia that permit free movement —*adj.* of these protozoans: also **in′fu·so′ri·al**

-ing (iŋ) **1.** [< OE. *-ende*] *a suffix used to form the present participle [hearing]* **2.** [< OE. *-ung*] *a suffix used to form verbal nouns meaning: a)* the act or an instance of *[talking] b)* something produced by the action of *[painting] c)* something that does the action of *[a head covering] d)* material used for *[carpeting]* **3.** [< OE.] *a suffix, sometimes with diminutive force, meaning* one of a specified kind *[farthing]*

in·gen·ious (in jēn′yəs) *adj.* [< MFr. < L. < *ingenium,* ability < *in-,* in + *gignere,* to produce] **1.** clever, resourceful, and inventive **2.** cleverly or originally made or done —**in·gen′ious·ly** *adv.* —**in·gen′ious·ness** *n.*

in·gé·nue (an′zhə no͞o′, -jə-; *Fr.* an zhā nü′) *n., pl.* **-nues′** (-no͞oz′; *Fr.* -nü′) [< Fr. < L. *ingenuus,* INGENUOUS] **1.** an innocent, inexperienced, unworldly young woman **2.** *Theater a)* the role of such a character *b)* an actress playing such a role

in·ge·nu·i·ty (in′jə no͞o′ə tē, -nyo͞o′-) *n.* [< L. < *ingenuus* (see ff.): associated with INGENIOUS] a being ingenious; cleverness, originality, etc.

in·gen·u·ous (in jen′yoo wəs) *adj.* [< L. *ingenuus* < *in-,* in + *gignere,* to produce] **1.** frank; open; candid **2.** simple; artless; naive —**in·gen′u·ous·ly** *adv.* —**in·gen′u·ous·ness** *n.*

in·gest (in jest′) *vt.* [< L. pp. of *ingerere* < *in-,* into + *gerere,* to carry] to take (food, drugs, etc.) into the body, as by swallowing or absorbing —**in·ges′tion** *n.* —**in·ges′tive** *adj.*

in·gle (iŋ′g′l) *n.* [Scot. < Gael. *aingeal,* fire] [Brit. Dial.] **1.** a fire or blaze **2.** a fireplace

in·gle·nook (-nook′) *n.* [Chiefly Brit.] a corner by a fireplace: also **ingle nook**

In·gle·wood (iŋ′g′l wood′) [after the home town in Canada of the owner of the site] city in SW Calif.: suburb of Los Angeles: pop. 94,000

in·glo·ri·ous (in glôr′ē əs) *adj.* **1.** not giving or deserving glory; shameful; disgraceful **2.** [Now Rare] without

glory; not famous —**in·glo′ri·ous·ly** *adv.* —**in·glo′ri·ous·ness** *n.*
in·go·ing (in′gō′iŋ) *adj.* going in; entering
in·got (iŋ′gət) *n.* [< MFr. *lingot* (with faulty separation of *l*-) < OPr.] a mass of metal cast into a bar or other convenient shape
in·graft (in graft′) *vt. same as* ENGRAFT
in·grained (in grānd′, in′grānd) *adj.* **1.** worked into the fiber; firmly fixed or established **2.** inveterate; thoroughgoing *[*an *ingrained* liar*]*
in·grate (in′grāt) *n.* [< OFr. < L. < *in*-, not + *gratus*, grateful] an ungrateful person
in·gra·ti·ate (in grā′shē āt′) *vt.* **-at′ed, -at′ing** [< L. < *in*, in + *gratia*, favor] to bring (oneself) into another's favor or good graces —**in·gra′ti·at′ing·ly** *adv.* —**in·gra′ti·a′tion** *n.*
in·grat·i·tude (in grat′ə tōōd′, -tyōōd′) *n.* lack of gratitude; ungratefulness
in·gre·di·ent (in grē′dē ənt) *n.* [< L. prp. of *ingredi:* see INGRESS] **1.** any of the things that a mixture is made of **2.** a component part of anything
In·gres (an′gr′), **Jean Au·guste Do·mi·nique** (zhän ô·güst′dô mē nēk′) 1780–1867; Fr. painter
in·gress (in′gres) *n.* [< L. pp. of *ingredi*, to enter < *in*-, into + *gradi*, to go] **1.** the act of entering: also **in·gres′sion** (-gresh′ən) **2.** the right to enter **3.** an entrance —**in·gres′sive** *adj.*
Ing·rid (iŋ′grid) [< Scand.; ult. < ON. *Ingvi*, name of a Gmc. god + *rida*, ride] a feminine name
in·grow·ing (in′grō′iŋ) *adj.* growing within, inward, or into; esp., growing into the flesh
in·grown (-grōn′) *adj.* grown within, inward, or into; esp., grown into the flesh, as a toenail
in·gui·nal (iŋ′gwə n′l) *adj.* [< L. < *inguen*, the groin] of or near the groin
in·gulf (in gulf′) *vt. same as* ENGULF
in·hab·it (in hab′it) *vt.* [< OFr. < L. *inhabitare* < *in*-, in + *habitare*, to dwell] to live in (a region, house, etc.); occupy —**in·hab′it·a·bil′i·ty** *n.* —**in·hab′it·a·ble** *adj.* —**in·hab′i·ta′tion** *n.* —**in·hab′it·er** *n.*
in·hab·it·ant (-i tənt) *n.* a person or animal that inhabits some specified region, house, etc.
in·hal·ant (in hāl′ənt) *adj.* used in inhalation —*n.* a medicine to be inhaled as a vapor
in·ha·la·tor (in′hə lāt′ər) *n.* **1.** an apparatus for administering medicinal vapors in inhalation **2.** *same as* RESPIRATOR (sense 2)
in·hale (in hāl′) *vt., vi.* **-haled′, -hal′ing** [L. *inhalare* < *in*-, in + *halare*, to breathe] to breathe in; draw (air, vapor, smoke, etc.) into the lungs —**in·ha·la·tion** (in′hə lā′shən) *n.*
in·hal·er (-ər) *n.* **1.** a person who inhales **2.** *same as: a)* RESPIRATOR (sense 1) *b)* INHALATOR (sense 1)
in·har·mon·ic (in′här män′ik) *adj.* not harmonic; discordant
in·har·mo·ni·ous (-mō′nē əs) *adj.* not harmonious; discordant, in conflict, etc. —**in′har·mo′ni·ous·ly** *adv.* —**in′har·mo′ni·ous·ness** *n.*
in·here (in hir′) *vi.* **-hered′, -her′ing** [< L. < *in*-, in + *haerere*, to stick] to be inherent; exist as a quality, characteristic, or right (*in*)
in·her·ent (in hir′ənt) *adj.* [see prec.] existing in someone or something as a natural and inseparable quality or right; inborn —**in·her′ence, in·her′en·cy** *n., pl.* **-cies** —**in·her′ent·ly** *adv.*
in·her·it (in her′it) *vt.* [< OFr. < LL., ult. < L. *in*, in + *heres*, heir] **1.** to receive (property, etc.) by or as if by inheritance or bequest from a predecessor **2.** to have (certain characteristics) by heredity —*vi.* to receive an inheritance —**in·her′i·tor** *n.* —**in·her′i·tress** (-i tris) *n.fem.*
in·her·it·a·ble (-ə b′l) *adj.* **1.** capable of inheriting; having the rights of an heir **2.** that can be inherited —**in·her′it·a·bil′i·ty, in·her′it·a·ble·ness** *n.*
in·her·it·ance (-əns) *n.* **1.** the action of inheriting **2.** something inherited or to be inherited; legacy; bequest **3.** right to inherit **4.** anything received as if by inheritance **5.** any characteristic passed on by heredity
inheritance tax a tax on inherited property
in·hib·it (in hib′it) *vt.* [< L. pp. of *inhibere*, to curb < *in*-, in + *habere*, to hold] to hold back or keep from some action, feeling, etc. —**in·hib′i·tive, in·hib′i·to′ry** (-i tôr′ē) *adj.* —**in·hib′i·tor, in·hib′it·er** *n.*
in·hi·bi·tion (in′hi bish′ən, in′ə-) *n.* **1.** an inhibiting or being inhibited **2.** a mental or psychological process that restrains an action, emotion, or thought
in·hos·pi·ta·ble (in häs′pi tə b′l, in′häs pit′ə b′l) *adj.* **1.** not hospitable **2.** not offering protection, shelter, etc.; barren; forbidding —**in·hos′pi·ta·ble·ness** *n.* —**in·hos′pi·ta·bly** *adv.*
in·hos·pi·tal·i·ty (in′häs pi tal′ə tē, in häs′-) *n.* lack of hospitality; inhospitable treatment
in·hu·man (in hyōō′mən, -yōō′-) *adj.* not human; esp., not having normal human characteristics; unfeeling, cruel, etc. —**in·hu′man·ly** *adv.*
in·hu·mane (in′hyōō mān′, -yoo-) *adj.* not humane; unmoved by the suffering of others; cruel, brutal, unkind, etc. —**in′hu·mane′ly** *adv.*
in·hu·man·i·ty (-man′ə tē) *n.* **1.** a being inhuman or inhumane **2.** *pl.* **-ties** an inhuman or inhumane act or remark
in·im·i·cal (in im′i k′l) *adj.* [< LL. < L. *inimicus*, ENEMY] **1.** hostile; unfriendly **2.** in opposition; adverse —**in·im′i·cal·ly** *adv.*
in·im·i·ta·ble (in im′ə tə b′l) *adj.* that cannot be imitated or matched; too good to be equaled or copied —**in·im′i·ta·bil′i·ty, in·im′i·ta·ble·ness** *n.* —**in·im′i·ta·bly** *adv.*
in·iq·ui·tous (in ik′wə təs) *adj.* showing iniquity; wicked; unjust —**in·iq′ui·tous·ly** *adv.* —**in·iq′ui·tous·ness** *n.*
in·iq·ui·ty (-wə tē) *n.* [< OFr. < L. < *iniquus*, unequal < *in*-, not + *aequus*, equal] **1.** lack of righteousness or justice; wickedness **2.** *pl.* **-ties** a wicked, unjust, or unrighteous act
in·i·tial (i nish′əl) *adj.* [< Fr. < L. *initialis*, ult. < *in*-, in + *ire*, to go] having to do with or occurring at the beginning —*n.* a capital, or upper-case, letter; specif., the first letter of a name —*vt.* **-tialed** or **-tialled, -tial·ing** or **-tial·ling** to mark or sign with an initial or initials
in·i·tial·ly (-ē) *adv.* at the beginning; first
in·i·ti·ate (i nish′ē āt′; *for adj. & n., usually* -it) *vt.* **-at′ed, -at′ing** [< L. pp. of *initiare:* see INITIAL] **1.** to bring into practice or use **2.** to teach the fundamentals of some subject to **3.** to admit as a member into a fraternity, club, etc., esp. with a special or secret ceremony —*adj.* initiated —*n.* a person who has recently been, or is about to be, initiated —**in·i′ti·a′tor** *n.*
in·i·ti·a·tion (i nish′ē ā′shən) *n.* **1.** an initiating or being initiated **2.** the ceremony by which one is initiated into a fraternity, etc.
in·i·ti·a·tive (i nish′ē ə tiv, -nish′ə-) *adj.* of, or having the nature of, initiation —*n.* **1.** the action of taking the first step or move **2.** the characteristic of originating new ideas or methods **3.** *a)* the right of a legislature to introduce new legislation *b)* the right of a group of citizens to introduce a matter for legislation to the legislature or directly to the voters *c)* the procedure for this
in·i·ti·a·to·ry (-tôr′ē) *adj.* **1.** beginning; introductory **2.** of or used in an initiation
in·ject (in jekt′) *vt.* [< L. pp. of *injicere* < *in*-, in + *jacere*, to throw] **1.** to force or drive (a fluid) into some passage or cavity or into some part of the body by means of a syringe, etc. **2.** to fill by injection **3.** to introduce (a missing quality, etc.) **4.** to interject (a remark, etc.) —**in·ject′a·ble** *adj.* —**in·jec′tion** *n.* —**in·jec′tor** *n.*
in·ju·di·cious (in′jōō dish′əs) *adj.* not judicious; showing poor judgment; not discreet or wise —**in′ju·di′cious·ly** *adv.* —**in′ju·di′cious·ness** *n.*
in·junc·tion (in juŋk′shən) *n.* [< LL. < pp. of *injungere*, ENJOIN] **1.** an enjoining; command **2.** an order **3.** a writ or order from a court prohibiting a person or group from carrying out a given action, or ordering a given action to be done —**in·junc′tive** *adj.*
in·jure (in′jər) *vt.* **-jured, -jur·ing** [see INJURY] **1.** to do physical harm to; hurt **2.** to offend (one's feelings, etc.) **3.** to weaken (a reputation, etc.) **4.** to be unjust to —**in′jur·er** *n.*
in·ju·ri·ous (in joor′ē əs) *adj.* **1.** injuring or likely to injure; harmful **2.** offensive or abusive —**in·ju′ri·ous·ly** *adv.* —**in·ju′ri·ous·ness** *n.*
in·ju·ry (in′jər ē) *n., pl.* **-ries** [< L. *injuria*, ult. < *in*-, not + *jus* (gen. *juris*), right] **1.** physical harm to a person, etc. **2.** an injurious act; injustice, as in injuring a person's feelings or rights, a reputation, etc.
in·jus·tice (in jus′tis) *n.* **1.** the quality of being unjust or unfair **2.** an unjust act; injury
ink (iŋk) *n.* [OFr. *enque* < LL. < Gr. *enkauston*, red ink < *enkaiein*, to burn in] **1.** a colored liquid used for writing, etc. **2.** a sticky, colored paste used in printing **3.** a dark, liquid secretion squirted out by cuttlefish, etc. for protection —*vt.* **1.** to cover with ink **2.** to mark or color with ink (often with *in*) —**ink′er** *n.* —**ink′like′** *adj.*
ink·blot (-blät′) *n.* any of a group of irregular blots of ink, used as in the Rorschach test
ink·horn (-hôrn′) *n.* a small container made of horn, etc., formerly used to hold ink
ink·ling (iŋk′liŋ) *n.* **1.** an indirect suggestion; hint **2.** a vague idea or notion
ink·stand (iŋk′stand′) *n.* **1.** a small stand holding an inkwell, pens, etc. **2.** *same as* INKWELL
ink·well (iŋk′wel) *n.* a container for holding ink, usually set in a desk, inkstand, etc.
ink·y (iŋ′kē) *adj.* **ink′i·er, ink′i·est** **1.** like ink in color; dark; black **2.** colored, marked, or covered with ink —**ink′i·ness** *n.*

in·laid (in′lād′, in lād′) ***adj.*** **1.** set in pieces into a surface of another material so as to form a smooth surface **2.** decorated with such a surface

in·land (in′lənd; *for n. & adv., usually* -land′) ***adj.*** **1.** of, located in, or confined to the interior of a country or region; away from the coast or border **2.** [Brit.] within a country; domestic —***n.*** inland areas —***adv.*** into or toward the interior

in-law (in′lô′) ***n.*** [< (MOTHER-)IN-LAW, etc.] [Colloq.] a relative by marriage

INLAID WOOD

in·lay (in′lā′; *for v., also* in lā′) ***vt.*** **-laid′, -lay′ing 1.** *a*) to set (pieces of wood, metal, etc.) into, and level with, a surface to make a design *b*) to decorate thus **2.** to add extra silverplating to —***n.***, *pl.* **-lays′ 1.** inlaid decoration or material **2.** a filling for a tooth made from a mold and cemented into the cavity —**in′lay′er** ***n.***

in·let (in′let, -lit) ***n.*** **1.** *a*) a narrow strip of water extending into a body of land from a river, lake, ocean, etc. *b*) a narrow strip of water between islands **2.** an entrance, as to a culvert

‡in lo·co pa·ren·tis (in lō′kō pə ren′tis) [L.] in the place of a parent

in·ly (in′lē) ***adv.*** [Poet.] **1.** inwardly **2.** intimately

in·mate (in′māt′) ***n.*** [IN-[1] + MATE[1]] a person living with others in the same building, now esp. one confined with others in a prison, etc.

‡in me·di·as res (in mā′dē äs rās′) [L., lit., into the midst of things] in the middle of the action

in me·mo·ri·am (in mə môr′ē əm) [L.] in memory (of)

in-mi·grant (in′mī′grənt) ***adj.*** coming in from another region of the country —***n.*** an in-migrant person

in·most (in′mōst′) ***adj.*** **1.** located farthest within **2.** most intimate or secret [*inmost* thoughts]

inn (in) ***n.*** [OE.] **1.** an establishment providing food and lodging for travelers; hotel **2.** a restaurant or tavern Now chiefly in the names of such places

in·nards (in′ərdz) ***n.pl.*** [< INWARD(S)] [Dial. or Colloq.] the internal organs of the body; viscera

in·nate (i nāt′, in′āt) ***adj.*** [< L. pp. of *innasci* < *in-*, in + *nasci*, to be born] **1.** existing naturally rather than acquired [*innate* talent] **2.** existing as an inherent attribute [the *innate* humor of a situation] —**in·nate′ly** ***adv.*** —**in·nate′ness** ***n.***

in·ner (in′ər) ***adj.*** **1.** located farther within; interior **2.** of the mind or spirit **3.** more intimate or secret [the *inner* emotions]

inner city the sections of a large city in or near its center, esp. when crowded or blighted

Inner Mongolia region in NE China, south & southeast of the Mongolian People's Republic

in·ner·most (in′ər mōst′) ***adj.*** **1.** located farthest within **2.** most intimate or secret

In·ness (in′is), **George** 1825–94; U.S. painter

in·ning (in′iŋ) ***n.*** [OE. *innung*, a getting in] **1.** *Baseball & (pl.) Cricket a*) the period of play in which a team has a turn at bat *b*) a numbered round of play in which both teams have a turn at bat **2.** [*often pl.*] the period of, or opportunity for, action, exercise of authority, etc.

inn·keep·er (in′kē′pər) ***n.*** the proprietor of an inn

in·no·cence (in′ə səns) ***n.*** **1.** a being innocent; specif., *a*) freedom from sin or guilt *b*) guilelessness; simplicity *c*) naiveté *d*) harmlessness *e*) ignorance: also **in′no·cen·cy 2.** *same as* BLUET

In·no·cent (in′ə sənt) any of 13 popes, including **1. Innocent I,** Saint ?–417 A.D.; Pope (401–417) **2. Innocent III** 1161?–1216; Pope (1198–1216) **3. Innocent IV** ?–1254; Pope (1243–54) **4. Innocent XI** 1611–89; Pope (1676–89)

in·no·cent (in′ə sənt) ***adj.*** [< OFr. < L. < *in-*, not + prp. of *nocere*, to do wrong to] **1.** free from sin, evil, or guilt; specif., *a*) doing or thinking nothing morally wrong; pure *b*) not guilty of a specific crime or offense *c*) free from harmful effect or cause **2.** *a*) knowing no evil *b*) without guile or cunning; artless *c*) naive *d*) ignorant **3.** totally lacking (with *of*) —***n.*** **1.** a person knowing no evil or sin, as a child **2.** a very naive person —**in′no·cent·ly** ***adv.***

in·noc·u·ous (i näk′yoo wəs) ***adj.*** [< L. < *in-*, not + *nocuus*, harmful < *nocere*, to harm] **1.** that does not injure or harm; harmless **2.** not controversial or offensive; dull and uninspiring —**in·noc′u·ous·ly** ***adv.***

in·nom·i·nate bone (i näm′ə nit) [< LL. *innominatus*, unnamed + BONE] either of two large, irregular bones of the pelvis, each formed of the ilium, ischium, and pubis; hipbone

in·no·vate (in′ə vāt′) ***vi.*** **-vat′ed, -vat′ing** [< L. pp. of *innovare* < *in-*, in + *novare*, to alter < *novus*, new] to introduce new methods, devices, etc. —***vt.*** to bring in as an innovation —**in′no·va′tive** ***adj.*** —**in′no·va′tor** ***n.***

in·no·va·tion (in′ə vā′shən) ***n.*** **1.** an innovating **2.** something newly introduced; new method, practice, device, etc. —**in′no·va′tion·al** ***adj.***

in·nu·en·do (in′yoo wen′dō) ***n.***, *pl.* **-does, -dos** [L., abl. of gerund of *innuere*, to nod to, hint] an indirect remark, gesture, or reference, usually implying something derogatory; insinuation

in·nu·mer·a·ble (i no͞o′mər ə b'l, -nyo͞o′-) ***adj.*** too numerous to be counted; countless —**in·nu′mer·a·bil′i·ty, in·nu′mer·a·ble·ness** ***n.*** —**in·nu′mer·a·bly** ***adv.***

in·oc·u·late (i näk′yoo lāt′) ***vt.*** **-lat′ed, -lat′ing** [< L. pp. of *inoculare*, to engraft a bud < *in-*, in + *oculus*, an eye, bud] **1.** to inject a serum, vaccine, etc. into (a living organism), esp. in order to create immunity **2.** to implant microorganisms into (soil, a culture medium, etc.) to develop a culture, fix nitrogen, etc. **3.** to imbue with ideas, etc. —**in·oc′u·la·bil′i·ty** ***n.*** —**in·oc′u·la·ble** ***adj.*** —**in·oc′u·la′tion** ***n.*** —**in·oc′u·la′tive** ***adj.*** —**in·oc′u·la′tor** ***n.***

in·of·fen·sive (in′ə fen′siv) ***adj.*** not offensive; unobjectionable; causing no harm or annoyance —**in′of·fen′sive·ly** ***adv.*** —**in′of·fen′sive·ness** ***n.***

in·op·er·a·ble (in äp′ər ə b'l) ***adj.*** not operable; specif., *a*) not practicable *b*) that will not practicably allow of surgical operation

in·op·er·a·tive (-ər ə tiv, -ə rāt′iv) ***adj.*** not operative; without effect —**in·op′er·a·tive·ness** ***n.***

in·op·por·tune (in äp′ər to͞on′, -tyo͞on′) ***adj.*** not opportune; coming or happening at a poor time; not appropriate —**in·op′por·tune′ly** ***adv.*** —**in·op′por·tune′ness** ***n.***

in·or·di·nate (in ôr′d'n it) ***adj.*** [< L.: see IN-[2] & ORDINATE] **1.** disordered; not regulated **2.** lacking restraint or moderation; excessive —**in·or′di·nate·ly** ***adv.*** —**in·or′di·nate·ness** ***n.***

in·or·gan·ic (in′ôr gan′ik) ***adj.*** not organic; specif., *a*) designating or composed of matter that is not animal or vegetable; not living *b*) not like an organism in structure *c*) designating or of any chemical compound not organic *d*) designating or of the branch of chemistry dealing with these compounds —**in′or·gan′i·cal·ly** ***adv.***

in·o·si·tol (i nō′sə tōl′, -tôl′) ***n.*** [< Gr. *is* (gen. *inos*), muscle + -IT(E) + -OL[1]] a sweet crystalline alcohol, $C_6H_6(OH)_6$, esp. the form found in the vitamin B complex that apparently promotes growth: also **in·o·site** (in′ə sīt′)

‡in per·pe·tu·um (in′ pər pech′oo wəm) [L.] forever

in·put (in′poot) ***n.*** what is put in; specif., *a*) the amount of money, material, effort, etc. put into a project or process *b*) electric current or power put into a circuit, machine, etc. *c*) information fed into a computer, etc.

in·quest (in′kwest) ***n.*** [< OFr. < VL. pp. of hyp. *inquaerere*: see INQUIRE] **1.** a judicial inquiry, as a coroner's investigation of a death **2.** the jury or group holding such an inquiry **3.** the verdict of such an inquiry

in·qui·e·tude (in kwī′ə to͞od′, -tyo͞od′) ***n.*** restlessness; uneasiness

in·quire (in kwīr′) ***vi.*** **-quired′, -quir′ing** [< OFr. < LL. hyp. *inquaerere*, for L. *inquirere* < *in*, into + *quaerere*, to seek] **1.** to ask a question or questions **2.** to carry out an examination or investigation (usually with *into*) —***vt.*** to seek information about [to *inquire* the way] —**inquire after** to pay respects by asking about the health of —**in·quir′er** ***n.*** —**in·quir′ing·ly** ***adv.***

in·quir·y (in′kwə rē, -kwī′-; in kwīr′ē) ***n.***, *pl.* **-quir·ies 1.** the act of inquiring **2.** an investigation or examination **3.** a question; query

in·qui·si·tion (in′kwə zish′ən) ***n.*** **1.** an inquiring; investigation **2.** [I-] *R.C.Ch. a*) formerly, the general tribunal established to discover and suppress heresy and heretics *b*) the activities of this tribunal **3.** *a*) any harsh or arbitrary suppression of dissent or nonconformity *b*) any relentless questioning **4.** *Law* an inquest or any judicial inquiry —**in′qui·si′tion·al** ***adj.***

in·quis·i·tive (in kwiz′ə tiv) ***adj.*** **1.** inclined to ask many questions or seek information **2.** unnecessarily curious; meddlesome; prying —**in·quis′i·tive·ly** ***adv.*** —**in·quis′i·tive·ness** ***n.***

in·quis·i·tor (-tər) ***n.*** **1.** an official whose work is making an inquisition **2.** any harsh or prying questioner **3.** [I-] an official of the Inquisition

in·quis·i·to·ri·al (in kwiz′ə tôr′ē əl) ***adj.*** **1.** of, or having the nature of, an inquisitor or an inquisition **2.** inquisitive —**in·quis′i·to′ri·al·ly** ***adv.***

in re (in rē, rā) [L.] in the matter (of); concerning

I.N.R.I. [L. *Iesus Nazarenus, Rex Iudaeorum*] Jesus of Nazareth, King of the Jews

in·road (in′rōd′) ***n.*** **1.** a sudden invasion or raid **2.** [*usually pl.*] any injurious encroachment
in·rush (-rush′) ***n.*** a rushing in; inflow; influx
ins. **1.** inches **2.** insulated **3.** insurance
in·sane (in sān′) ***adj.*** **1.** not sane; mentally ill or deranged; mad: cf. INSANITY **2.** of or for insane people [an *insane* asylum] **3.** very foolish; senseless —**in·sane′ly** ***adv.***
in·san·i·tar·y (in san′ə ter′ē) ***adj.*** not sanitary; unhealthful
in·san·i·ty (in san′ə tē) ***n.,*** *pl.* **-ties** **1.** the state of being insane; mental illness or derangement: a term used formally in law but not in psychiatry **2.** great folly; extreme senselessness
in·sa·ti·a·ble (in sā′shə b'l, -shē ə-) ***adj.*** constantly wanting more; that cannot be satisfied; very greedy —**in·sa′ti·a·bil′i·ty** ***n.*** —**in·sa′ti·a·bly** ***adv.***
in·sa·ti·ate (-shē it) ***adj.*** not satiated; insatiable —**in·sa′ti·ate·ly** ***adv.*** —**in·sa′ti·ate·ness** ***n.***
in·scribe (in skrīb′) ***vt.*** **-scribed′, -scrib′ing** [< L.: see IN-[1] & SCRIBE] **1.** *a)* to mark or engrave (words, symbols, etc.) on some surface *b)* to write on, mark, or engrave (a surface) **2.** to add the name of (someone) to a list; enroll **3.** *a)* to dedicate (a book, etc.) informally *b)* to write a short, signed message in (a book, etc. one is presenting as a gift) **4.** to fix or impress deeply in the mind, memory, etc. **5.** *Geom.* to draw (a figure) inside another figure so that their boundaries touch at as many points as possible —**in·scrib′a·ble** ***adj.*** —**in·scrib′er** ***n.***
in·scrip·tion (in skrip′shən) ***n.*** **1.** an inscribing **2.** something inscribed or engraved, as on a coin or monument **3.** *a)* an informal dedication in a book, etc. *b)* a short, signed message written in a book, etc. one is presenting as a gift —**in·scrip′tive, in·scrip′tion·al** ***adj.***
in·scru·ta·ble (in skrōōt′ə b'l) ***adj.*** [< LL. < L. *in-*, not + *scrutari*, to examine] that cannot be easily understood; completely obscure or mysterious; enigmatic —**in·scru′ta·bil′i·ty, in·scru′ta·ble·ness** ***n.*** —**in·scru′ta·bly** ***adv.***
in·seam (in′sēm′) ***n.*** the inner seam from the crotch to the bottom of a trouser leg
in·sect (in′sekt) ***n.*** [< L. *insectum* (*animale*), lit., notched (animal): from the segmented bodies] **1.** any of a large class of small arthropod animals, including beetles, bees, flies, wasps, etc., having, in the adult state, a head, thorax, and abdomen, three pairs of legs, and, usually, two pairs of membranous wings **2.** popularly, any of a group of small animals, usually wingless, including spiders, centipedes, ticks, mites, etc.
in·sec·ti·cide (in sek′tə sīd′) ***n.*** any substance used to kill insects —**in·sec′ti·ci′dal** ***adj.***
in·sec·ti·vore (in sek′tə vôr′) ***n.*** [< ModL.: see INSECT & -VOROUS] **1.** any of an order of insect-eating mammals, including moles, shrews, hedgehogs, etc. **2.** any animal or plant that feeds on insects —**in·sec·tiv·o·rous** (in′sek tiv′ər əs) ***adj.***
in·se·cure (in′si kyoor′) ***adj.*** not secure; specif., *a)* not safe from danger *b)* not confident; filled with anxieties *c)* not firm or dependable —**in′se·cure′ly** ***adv.*** —**in′se·cu′ri·ty** ***n.,*** *pl.* **-ties**
in·sem·i·nate (in sem′ə nāt′) ***vt.*** **-nat′ed, -nat′ing** [< L. pp. of *inseminare* < *in-*, in + *seminare*, to sow < *semen*, seed] **1.** to sow seeds in; esp., to impregnate with semen **2.** to implant (ideas, etc.) in (the mind, etc.) —**in·sem′i·na′tion** ***n.***
in·sen·sate (in sen′sāt, -sit) ***adj.*** **1.** lacking sensation; inanimate **2.** without sense or reason; stupid **3.** without feeling for others; insensitive —**in·sen′sate·ly** ***adv.***
in·sen·si·ble (in sen′sə b'l) ***adj.*** **1.** lacking sensation; unable to perceive with the senses **2.** having lost sensation; unconscious **3.** not recognizing or realizing; unaware; indifferent **4.** so small or slight as to be virtually imperceptible —**in·sen′si·bil′i·ty** ***n.*** —**in·sen′si·bly** ***adv.***
in·sen·si·tive (-tiv) ***adj.*** not sensitive; having little or no reaction (*to*) —**in·sen′si·tive·ly** ***adv.*** —**in·sen′si·tiv′i·ty, in·sen′si·tive·ness** ***n.***
in·sen·ti·ent (in sen′shē ənt, -shənt) ***adj.*** not sentient; without life, consciousness, or perception —**in·sen′ti·ence** ***n.***
in·sep·a·ra·ble (in sep′ər ə b'l) ***adj.*** that cannot be separated or parted —***n.*** [*pl.*] inseparable persons or things —**in·sep′a·ra·bil′i·ty, in·sep′a·ra·ble·ness** ***n.*** —**in·sep′a·ra·bly** ***adv.***
in·sert (in sʉrt′; *for n.* in′sərt) ***vt.*** [< L. pp. of *inserere* < *in-*, in + *serere*, to join] to put or fit (something) into something else; set in —***n.*** anything inserted or for insertion; esp., an extra leaf or section inserted in a newspaper, etc. —**in·sert′er** ***n.***
in·ser·tion (in sʉr′shən) ***n.*** **1.** an inserting or being inserted **2.** something inserted; specif., *a)* a piece of lace or embroidery that can be set into a piece of cloth for ornamentation *b)* a single placement of an advertisement, as in a newspaper
in-ser·vice (in′sʉr′vis) ***adj.*** designating or of training given to employees in connection with their work to help them develop skills, etc.
in·set (in set′; *also, and for n. always,* in′set) ***vt.*** **-set′, -set′ting** to set into something; insert —***n.*** something set in; insert
in·shore (in′shôr′, in shôr′) ***adv., adj.*** **1.** in toward the shore **2.** near the shore —**inshore of** nearer than (something else) to the shore
in·side (in′sīd′, -sīd′; *for prep. & adv., usually* in′sīd′) ***n.*** **1.** the part within; inner side, surface, or part **2.** the part closest to something implied, as the part of a sidewalk closest to the buildings **3.** [*pl.*] [Colloq.] the internal organs of the body; viscera —***adj.*** **1.** on or in the inside; internal **2.** working or used indoors **3.** known only to insiders; secret or private [the *inside* story] —***adv.*** **1.** on or to the inside; within **2.** indoors —***prep.*** inside of; in; within —**inside of** within the space or time of —**inside out** **1.** with the inside where the outside should be; reversed **2.** [Colloq.] thoroughly; completely —**on the inside** **1.** in a position of confidence, special advantage or favor, etc. **2.** in one's inner thoughts or feelings
inside job [Colloq.] a crime committed by, or with the aid of, a person employed or trusted by the victim
in·sid·er (in sī′dər) ***n.*** **1.** a person inside a given place or group **2.** a person having or likely to have secret or confidential information
in·sid·i·ous (in sid′ē əs) ***adj.*** [< L. < *insidiae*, an ambush < *in-*, in + *sedere*, to sit] **1.** characterized by treachery or slyness; crafty **2.** more dangerous than seems evident [an *insidious* disease] —**in·sid′i·ous·ly** ***adv.*** —**in·sid′i·ous·ness** ***n.***
in·sight (in′sīt′) ***n.*** **1.** the ability to see and understand clearly the inner nature of things, esp. by intuition **2.** a clear understanding of the inner nature of some specific thing —**in′sight′ful** ***adj.***
in·sig·ni·a (in sig′nē ə) ***n.pl.*** (*in sense 1*), ***n.sing.*** (*in sense 2*) [< L., pl. of *insigne*, ult. < *in-*, in + *signum*, a mark] **1.** *sing.* **in·sig′ne** (-nē) badges, emblems, etc., as of rank or membership **2.** *pl.* **in·sig′ni·as** such a badge, emblem, etc.
in·sig·nif·i·cant (in′sig nif′ə kənt) ***adj.*** **1.** having little or no meaning **2.** having little or no importance; trivial **3.** small; unimposing **4.** low in position, character, etc. —**in′sig·nif′i·cance, in′sig·nif′i·can·cy** ***n.*** —**in′sig·nif′i·cant·ly** ***adv.***
in·sin·cere (in′sin sir′) ***adj.*** not sincere; deceptive or hypocritical —**in′sin·cere′ly** ***adv.***
in·sin·cer·i·ty (-ser′ə tē) ***n.*** **1.** a being insincere **2.** *pl.* **-ties** an insincere act, remark, etc.
in·sin·u·ate (in sin′yoo wāt′) ***vt.*** **-at′ed, -at′ing** [< L. pp. of *insinuare* < *in-*, in + *sinus*, curved surface] **1.** to introduce or work into gradually, indirectly, and artfully **2.** to hint indirectly; imply —***vi.*** to make insinuations —**in·sin′u·at′ing·ly** ***adv.*** —**in·sin′u·a′tive** ***adj.*** —**in·sin′u·a′tor** ***n.***
in·sin·u·a·tion (in sin′yoo wā′shən) ***n.*** **1.** an insinuating **2.** something insinuated; specif., *a)* a sly hint *b)* an act or remark intended to win favor
in·sip·id (in sip′id) ***adj.*** [< Fr. < LL. < L. *in-*, not + *sapidus*, savory < *sapere*, to taste] **1.** without flavor; tasteless **2.** not exciting; dull; lifeless —**in′si·pid′i·ty, in·sip′id·ness** ***n.*** —**in·sip′id·ly** ***adv.***
in·sist (in sist′) ***vi.*** [< MFr. < L. *insistere* < *in-*, in + *sistere*, to stand] to take and maintain a stand or make a firm demand (often with *on* or *upon*) —***vt.*** **1.** to demand strongly **2.** to declare firmly —**in·sist′er** ***n.*** —**in·sist′ing·ly** ***adv.***
in·sist·ent (in sis′tənt) ***adj.*** **1.** insisting or demanding; persistent in demands or assertions **2.** compelling the attention [an *insistent* rhythm] —**in·sist′ence, in·sist′en·cy** ***n.*** —**in·sist′ent·ly** ***adv.***
‡**in si·tu** (in sī′tōō) [L.] in position
in·snare (in sner′) ***vt.*** **-snared′, -snar′ing** *same as* ENSNARE
in·so·bri·e·ty (in′sə brī′ə tē, -sō-) ***n.*** lack of sobriety; intemperance, esp. in drinking
in·so·far (in′sə fär′, -sō-) ***adv.*** to such a degree or extent (usually with *as*)
in·sole (in′sōl′) ***n.*** **1.** the inside sole of a shoe **2.** an extra, removable inside sole for comfort
in·so·lent (in′sə lənt) ***adj.*** [< L. < *in-*, not + prp. of *solere*, to be accustomed] **1.** boldly disrespectful in speech or behavior; impertinent; impudent **2.** [Now Rare] overbearing —**in′so·lence** ***n.*** —**in′so·lent·ly** ***adv.***
INSOLE
in·sol·u·ble (in säl′yoo b'l) ***adj.*** **1.** that cannot be solved; unsolvable **2.** that cannot be dissolved; not soluble —**in·sol′u·bil′i·ty, in·sol′u·ble·ness** ***n.*** —**in·sol′u·bly** ***adv.***
in·solv·a·ble (in säl′və b'l) ***adj.*** not solvable
in·sol·vent (in säl′vənt) ***adj.*** **1.** not solvent; unable to

pay debts; bankrupt 2. not enough to pay all debts 3. of insolvents —*n.* an insolvent person —**in·sol′ven·cy** *n., pl.* **-cies**

in·som·ni·a (in säm′nē ə) *n.* [< L. < *in-,* without + *somnus,* sleep] abnormally prolonged inability to sleep, esp. when chronic —**in·som′ni·ac′** (-ak′) *n., adj.*

in·so·much (in′sō much′, -sə-) *adv.* 1. to such a degree or extent; so (with *that*) 2. inasmuch (*as*)

in·sou·ci·ant (in so͞o′sē ənt) *adj.* [Fr.] calm and unbothered; carefree; indifferent —**in·sou′ci·ance** (-əns) *n.* —**in·sou′ci·ant·ly** *adv.*

in·spect (in spekt′) *vt.* [< L. pp. of *inspicere* < *in-,* at + *specere,* to look] 1. to look at carefully; examine critically 2. to examine or review (troops, etc.) officially —**in·spec′tive** *adj.*

in·spec·tion (in spek′shən) *n.* 1. careful examination 2. official examination, as of troops

in·spec·tor (in spek′tər) *n.* 1. one who inspects; official examiner 2. an officer on a police force, ranking next below a superintendent or police chief —**in·spec′to·ral, in′spec·to′ri·al** (-tôr′ē əl) *adj.* —**in·spec′tor·ship′** *n.*

in·spi·ra·tion (in′spə rā′shən) *n.* 1. a breathing in; inhaling 2. an inspiring or being inspired mentally or emotionally 3. *a*) any stimulus to creative thought or action *b*) an inspired idea, action, etc. 4. a prompting of something written or said 5. *Theol.* a divine influence upon human beings —**in′spi·ra′tion·al** *adj.* —**in′spi·ra′tion·al·ly** *adv.*

in·spire (in spīr′) *vt.* **-spired′, -spir′ing** [< OFr. < L. *inspirare* < *in-,* in + *spirare,* to breathe] 1. to draw (air) into the lungs; inhale 2. to influence, stimulate, or impel, as to some creative or effective effort 3. to guide or motivate by divine influence 4. to arouse (a thought or feeling) *[*kindness *inspires* love*]* 5. to affect with a specified feeling *[*praise *inspires* us with confidence*]* 6. to cause to be written or said —*vi.* 1. to inhale 2. to give inspiration —**in·spir′a·ble** *adj.* —**in·spir′er** *n.* —**in·spir′ing·ly** *adv.*

in·spir·it (in spir′it) *vt.* to put spirit into; cheer; hearten

in·spis·sate (in spis′āt, in′spə sāt′) *vt., vi.* **-sat·ed, -sat·ing** [< LL., ult. < L. *in-,* in + *spissus,* thick] to thicken by evaporation; condense —**in′spis·sa′tion** *n.* —**in′spis·sa′tor** *n.*

Inst. 1. Institute 2. Institution

inst. 1. instant (*adj.* 2) 2. instrumental

in·sta·bil·i·ty (in′stə bil′ə tē) *n.* unstable condition; lack of firmness, steadiness, etc.

in·sta·ble (in stā′b′l) *adj. same as* UNSTABLE

in·stall, in·stal (in stôl′) *vt.* **-stalled′, -stall′ing** [< ML. < *in-,* in + *stallum* < OHG. *stal,* a place] 1. to place in an office, rank, etc. with formality 2. to establish in a place or condition *[*to *install* oneself in a seat*]* 3. to fix in position for use *[*to *install* new fixtures*]* —**in·stall′er** *n.*

in·stal·la·tion (in′stə lā′shən) *n.* 1. an installing or being installed 2. apparatus, etc. installed *[*a heating *installation]* 3. any military post, camp, base, etc.

in·stall·ment, in·stal·ment[1] (in stôl′mənt) *n.* [< earlier *estall,* to arrange payments for < OFr. < OHG. *stal:* see INSTALL] 1. any of the parts of a debt or other sum of money to be paid at regular times over a specified period 2. any of several parts, as of a serial story, appearing at intervals

in·stall·ment, in·stal·ment[2] (in stôl′mənt) *n.* an installing or being installed; installation

installment plan a system by which debts, as for purchased articles, are paid in installments

in·stance (in′stəns) *n.* [OFr. < L. *instantia,* a being present < *instans:* see ff.] 1. an example; case; illustration 2. a step in proceeding; occasion *[*in the first *instance]* —*vt.* **-stanced, -stanc·ing** 1. to exemplify 2. to use as an example; cite —**at the instance of** at the suggestion of —**for instance** as an example

in·stant (in′stənt) *adj.* [< MFr. < L. *instans,* prp. of *instare* < *in-,* upon + *stare,* to stand] 1. urgent; pressing 2. of the current month *[*your letter of the 13th *instant]* 3. soon to happen; imminent 4. without delay; immediate 5. designating a food or beverage in readily soluble, concentrated, or precooked form, that can be prepared quickly —*adv.* [Poet.] at once —*n.* 1. a moment 2. a particular moment —**the instant** as soon as

in·stan·ta·ne·ous (in′stən tā′nē əs, -tān′yəs) *adj.* 1. done, made, or happening in an instant 2. done or made without delay; immediate —**in′stan·ta′ne·ous·ly** *adv.* —**in′stan·ta′ne·ous·ness** *n.*

in·stan·ter (in stan′tər) *adv.* [L., pressingly] immediately

in·stant·ly (in′stənt lē) *adv.* 1. in an instant; without delay; immediately 2. [Archaic] urgently; pressingly —*conj.* as soon as; the instant that

instant replay the immediate reshowing of an action or play on videotape, as in sports, often in slow motion

in·state (in stāt′) *vt.* **-stat′ed, -stat′ing** to put in a particular status, position, or rank; install —**in·state′ment** *n.*

in·stead (in sted′) *adv.* [IN + STEAD] in place of the person or thing mentioned *[*to feel like crying and laugh *instead]* —**instead of** in place of

in·step (in′step′) *n.* 1. the upper part of the arch of the foot, between the ankle and the toes 2. the part of a shoe or stocking covering this

in·sti·gate (in′stə gāt′) *vt.* **-gat′ed, -gat′ing** [< L. pp. of *instigare,* to incite] 1. to urge on or incite to some action 2. to cause by inciting *[*to *instigate* a rebellion*]* —**in′sti·ga′tion** *n.* —**in′sti·ga′tive** *adj.* —**in′sti·ga′tor** *n.*

in·still, in·stil (in stil′) *vt.* **-stilled′, -still′ing** [< MFr. < L. *instillare,* ult. < *in-,* in + *stilla,* a drop] 1. to put in drop by drop 2. to put (an idea, feeling, etc.) *in* or *into* gradually —**in′stil·la′tion** *n.* —**in·still′er** *n.* —**in·still′ment, in·stil′ment** *n.*

in·stinct (in′stiŋkt; *for adj.* in stiŋkt′) *n.* [< L. pp. of *instinguere,* to impel] 1. (an) inborn tendency to behave in a way characteristic of a species; natural, unacquired response to stimuli *[*suckling is an *instinct* in mammals*]* 2. a natural or acquired tendency or talent; knack; gift *[*an *instinct* for doing the right thing*]* —*adj.* filled or charged (*with*) *[*a look *instinct* with pity*]* —**in·stinc·tu·al** (in stiŋk′cho͞o wəl) *adj.*

in·stinc·tive (in stiŋk′tiv) *adj.* 1. of, or having the nature of, instinct 2. prompted or done by instinct —**in·stinc′tive·ly** *adv.*

in·sti·tute (in′stə to͞ot′, -tyo͞ot′) *vt.* **-tut′ed, -tut′ing** [< L. pp. of *instituere* < *in-,* in + *statuere,* to set up] 1. to set up; establish; found 2. to start; initiate *[*to *institute* a search*]* 3. to install in office —*n.* something instituted; specif., *a*) an established principle, law, or custom *b*) an organization for the promotion or teaching of art, science, research, etc. *c*) a school specializing in art, music, technical subjects, etc. *d*) *same as* INSTITUTION (sense 3) —**in′sti·tut′er, in′sti·tu′tor** *n.*

in·sti·tu·tion (in′stə to͞o′shən, -tyo͞o′-) *n.* 1. an instituting or being instituted; establishment 2. an established law, custom, practice, etc. 3. *a*) an organization having a social, educational, or religious purpose, as a school, church, reformatory, etc. *b*) the building housing it 4. [Colloq.] a well-established person or thing

in·sti·tu·tion·al (-'l) *adj.* 1. of, or having the nature of, an institution 2. of or to institutions, rather than individuals 3. of advertising intended primarily to gain prestige rather than immediate sales —**in′sti·tu′tion·al·ly** *adv.*

in·sti·tu·tion·al·ize (-īz′) *vt.* **-ized′, -iz′ing** 1. to make into an institution 2. to make institutional 3. to place in an institution, as for treatment —**in′sti·tu′tion·al·i·za′tion** *n.*

instr. 1. instructor 2. instrument

in·struct (in strukt′) *vt.* [< L. pp. of *instruere,* to erect < *in-,* in + *struere,* to pile up] 1. to communicate knowledge to; teach 2. to inform or guide *[*the judge *instructs* the jury*]* 3. to order or direct

in·struc·tion (in struk′shən) *n.* 1. an instructing; education 2. *a*) knowledge, information, etc. given or taught *b*) a lesson or rule 3. *a*) a command or order *b*) *[pl.]* directions —**in·struc′tion·al** *adj.*

in·struc·tive (-tiv) *adj.* serving to instruct; giving knowledge or information —**in·struc′tive·ly** *adv.* —**in·struc′tive·ness** *n.*

in·struc·tor (-tər) *n.* 1. a teacher 2. a college teacher ranking below an assistant professor —**in·struc′tor·ship′** *n.* —**in·struc′tress** *n.fem.*

in·stru·ment (in′strə mənt) *n.* [< OFr. < L. *instrumentum* < *instruere:* see INSTRUCT] 1. *a*) a thing by means of which something is done; means *b*) a person used by another to bring something about 2. a tool or implement 3. a device for indicating or measuring conditions, performance, etc., or, sometimes, for controlling operations, esp. in aircraft 4. any of various devices producing musical sound 5. *Law* a document, as a deed, contract, etc. —*vt.* to provide with instruments

in·stru·men·tal (in′strə men′t'l) *adj.* 1. serving as a means; helpful (*in* bringing something about) 2. of or performed with an instrument or tool 3. of, performed on, or written for a musical instrument or instruments —**in′stru·men′tal·ly** *adv.*

in·stru·men·tal·ist (-men′t'l ist) *n.* a person who performs on a musical instrument

in·stru·men·tal·i·ty (-men tal′ə tē) *n., pl.* **-ties** 1. a being instrumental 2. a means or agency

in·stru·men·ta·tion (-tā′shən) *n.* 1. the arrangement of music for instruments **2.** a using or equipping with instruments, esp. scientific instruments **3.** the instruments used **4.** *same as* INSTRUMENTALITY

instrument panel (or **board**) a panel or board with instruments, gauges, etc. mounted on it, as in an automobile or airplane

in·sub·or·di·nate (in′sə bôr′d'n it) ***adj.*** not submitting to authority; disobedient —***n.*** an insubordinate person —**in′sub·or′di·nate·ly** ***adv.*** —**in′sub·or′di·na′tion** ***n.***

in·sub·stan·tial (in′səb stan′shəl) ***adj.*** not substantial; specif., *a)* not real; imaginary *b)* not solid or firm —**in′sub·stan′ti·al′i·ty** (-shē al′ə tē) ***n.***

in·suf·fer·a·ble (in suf′ər ə b'l) ***adj.*** not sufferable; intolerable; unbearable —**in·suf′fer·a·bly** ***adv.***

in·suf·fi·cien·cy (in′sə fish′ən sē) ***n.,*** *pl.* **-cies** **1.** lack of sufficiency; deficiency; inadequacy **2.** inability of an organ, etc. to function normally

in·suf·fi·cient (-ənt) ***adj.*** not sufficient; inadequate —**in′suf·fi′cient·ly** ***adv.***

in·su·lar (in′sə lər, -syoo-) ***adj.*** [< L. < *insula,* island] **1.** of, or in the form of, an island **2.** living or situated on an island **3.** like an island **4.** of or like islanders, esp. when regarded as narrow-minded, illiberal, etc. —**in′su·lar′i·ty** (-lar′ə tē), **in′su·lar·ism** ***n.*** —**in′su·lar·ly** ***adv.***

in·su·late (-lāt′) ***vt.*** **-lat′ed, -lat′ing** [< L. *insulatus,* made like an island < *insula,* island] **1.** to set apart; detach from the rest; isolate **2.** to separate or cover with a nonconducting material in order to prevent the passage or leakage of electricity, heat, sound, etc.

in·su·la·tion (in′sə lā′shən, -syoo-) ***n.*** **1.** an insulating or being insulated **2.** any material used to insulate

in·su·la·tor (in′sə lāt′ər, -syoo-) ***n.*** anything that insulates; esp., a device of glass or porcelain for insulating electric wires

in·su·lin (in′sə lin, -syoo-) ***n.*** [< L. *insula,* island + -IN[1]: referring to islands of special tissue in the pancreas] **1.** a secretion of the pancreas, which helps the body use sugar and other carbohydrates **2.** an extract from the pancreas of sheep, oxen, etc., used hypodermically in the treatment of diabetes mellitus

COMMON GLASS
PETTICOAT
PORCELAIN
HIGH TENSION

INSULATORS

in·sult (in sult′; *for n.* in′sult) ***vt.*** [< MFr. < L. *insultare* < *in-,* in, on + *saltare,* freq. of *salire,* to leap] to treat or speak to with scorn, insolence, or disrespect —***n.*** **1.** an insulting act, remark, etc. **2.** *Med.* injury to tissues or organs —**in·sult′er** ***n.*** —**in·sult′ing** ***adj.*** —**in·sult′ing·ly** ***adv.***

in·su·per·a·ble (in sōō′pər ə b'l, -syōō′-) ***adj.*** not superable; that cannot be overcome or passed over; insurmountable —**in·su′per·a·bil′i·ty** ***n.*** —**in·su′per·a·bly** ***adv.***

in·sup·port·a·ble (in′sə pôrt′ə b'l) ***adj.*** not supportable; specif., *a)* intolerable *b)* incapable of being upheld —**in′sup·port′a·bly** ***adv.***

in·sur·ance (in shoor′əns) ***n.*** **1.** an insuring or being insured against loss by fire, accident, death, etc. **2.** *a)* a contract (**insurance policy**) whereby the insurer guarantees the insured that a certain sum will be paid for a specified loss *b)* the premium specified for such a contract **3.** the amount for which life, property, etc. is insured **4.** the business of insuring against loss

in·sure (in shoor′) ***vt.*** **-sured′, -sur′ing** [see ENSURE] **1.** to take out or issue insurance on (something or someone) **2.** *same as* ENSURE —***vi.*** to give or take out insurance —**in·sur′a·bil′i·ty** ***n.*** —**in·sur′a·ble** ***adj.***

in·sured (in shoord′) ***n.*** a person whose life, property, etc. is insured against loss

in·sur·er (in shoor′ər) ***n.*** a person or company that insures others against loss or damage

in·sur·gence (in sur′jəns) ***n.*** a rising in revolt; insurrection: also **in·sur′gen·cy**

in·sur·gent (-jənt) ***adj.*** [< L. prp. of *insurgere* < *in-,* upon + *surgere,* to rise: see SURGE] rising up against established authority —***n.*** one engaged in insurgent activity —**in·sur′gent·ly** ***adv.***

in·sur·mount·a·ble (in′sər moun′tə b'l) ***adj.*** not surmountable; that cannot be overcome —**in′sur·mount′a·bil′i·ty** ***n.*** —**in′sur·mount′a·bly** ***adv.***

in·sur·rec·tion (in′sə rek′shən) ***n.*** [< MFr. < LL. < pp. of L. *insurgere:* see INSURGENT] a rising up against established authority; rebellion; revolt —**in′sur·rec′tion·al** ***adj.*** —**in′sur·rec′tion·ar′y** ***adj., n.,*** *pl.* **-ar′ies** —**in′sur·rec′tion·ist** ***n.***

in·sus·cep·ti·ble (in′sə sep′tə b'l) ***adj.*** not susceptible (*to* or *of*); not easily affected or influenced —**in′sus·cep′ti·bil′i·ty** ***n.*** —**in′sus·cep′ti·bly** ***adv.***

int. **1.** interest **2.** interior **3.** internal **4.** international **5.** intransitive

in·tact (in takt′) ***adj.*** [< L. < *in-,* not + *tactus,* pp. of *tangere,* to touch] with nothing missing or injured; kept or left whole —**in·tact′ness** ***n.***

in·tagl·io (in tal′yō, -täl′-) ***n.,*** *pl.* **-ios** [It. < *in-,* in + *tagliare,* to cut < LL. *taliare:* see TAILOR] **1.** a design or figure carved or engraved below the surface **2.** a gem or stone ornamented in this way **3.** the art of making such designs or figures —***vt.*** **-ioed, -io·ing** to carve, etc. in intaglio

in·take (in′tāk′) ***n.*** **1.** a taking in **2.** the amount or thing taken in **3.** the place at which a fluid is taken into a pipe, channel, etc.

in·tan·gi·ble (in tan′jə b'l) ***adj.*** not tangible; specif., *a)* that cannot be touched *b)* representing value that is neither intrinsic nor material [good will is an *intangible* asset] *c)* hard to define or grasp —***n.*** something intangible —**in·tan′gi·bil′i·ty** ***n.,*** *pl.* **-ties** —**in·tan′gi·bly** ***adv.***

in·te·ger (in′tə jər) ***n.*** [L., untouched, whole] **1.** anything complete in itself; whole **2.** any whole number or zero: distinguished from FRACTION

in·te·gral (in′tə grəl; *also, exc. for adj. 4,* in teg′rəl) ***adj.*** [< prec.] **1.** necessary for completeness; essential **2.** whole or complete **3.** made up of parts forming a whole **4.** *Math.* of or having to do with integers; not fractional —***n.*** a whole —**in′te·gral′i·ty** (-gral′ə tē) ***n.*** —**in′te·gral·ly** ***adv.***

integral calculus the branch of higher mathematics dealing with the process (*integration*) of finding the quantity or function of which a given quantity or function is the differential

in·te·grate (-grāt′) ***vt.*** **-grat′ed, -grat′ing** [< L. pp. of *integrare* < *integer,* whole] **1.** to make whole or complete **2.** to bring (parts) together into a whole; unify **3.** to indicate the sum or total of **4.** to remove legal and social barriers imposing segregation upon (racial groups) or in (schools, etc.) —***vi.*** to become integrated —**in′te·gra′tion** ***n.*** —**in′te·gra′tive** ***adj.*** —**in′te·gra′tor** ***n.***

integrated circuit an electronic circuit containing interconnected amplifying devices formed on a single body, or chip, of semiconductor material

in·te·gra·tion·ist (-grā′shən ist) ***n.*** one who advocates integration, esp. of racial groups —***adj.*** believing in or advocating integration

in·teg·ri·ty (in teg′rə tē) ***n.*** [see INTEGER] **1.** a being complete; wholeness **2.** unimpaired condition; soundness **3.** uprightness, honesty, and sincerity

in·teg·u·ment (in teg′yoo mənt) ***n.*** [< L. < *in-,* upon + *tegere,* to cover] an outer covering, as of the body or of a plant; skin, shell, hide, etc. —**in·teg′u·men′ta·ry** ***adj.***

in·tel·lect (in′t'l ekt′) ***n.*** [< L. < pp. of *intellegere,* to understand < *inter-,* between + *legere,* to choose] **1.** the ability to reason or understand **2.** great mental ability; high intelligence **3.** *a)* a mind or intelligence *b)* a person of high intelligence

in·tel·lec·tu·al (in′t'l ek′choo wəl) ***adj.*** **1.** of, pertaining to, or appealing to the intellect **2.** *a)* requiring or involving the intellect *b)* inclined toward intellectual activities **3.** showing high intelligence —***n.*** a person having intellectual tastes or work —**in′tel·lec′tu·al′i·ty** (-choo wal′ə tē) ***n.*** —**in′tel·lec′tu·al·ly** ***adv.***

in·tel·lec·tu·al·ism (-iz'm) ***n.*** a being intellectual; devotion to intellectual pursuits —**in′tel·lec′tu·al·ist** ***n.*** —**in′tel·lec′tu·al·is′tic** ***adj.***

in·tel·li·gence (in tel′ə jəns) ***n.*** [< OFr. < L. *intelligentia* < prp. of *intelligere:* see INTELLECT] **1.** *a)* the ability to learn or understand from experience; mental ability *b)* the ability to respond successfully to a new situation *c)* any degree of cleverness, shrewdness, etc. **2.** news or information **3.** *a)* the gathering of secret information, as for military purposes *b)* the persons or agency employed at this **4.** an intelligent being

intelligence quotient a number indicating a person's level of intelligence: it is the mental age (as shown by intelligence tests) multiplied by 100 and divided by the chronological age

intelligence test a series of problems intended to test the intelligence of an individual

in·tel·li·gent (-jənt) ***adj.*** **1.** having or using intelligence **2.** having or showing high intelligence; bright, clever, wise, etc. **3.** [Archaic] aware (*of* something) —**in·tel′li·gent·ly** ***adv.***

in·tel·li·gent·si·a (in tel′ə jent′sē ə, -gent′-) ***n.pl.*** [*also with sing. v.*] [< Russ. < L.: see INTELLIGENCE] the people regarded as, or regarding themselves as, the educated class; intellectuals collectively

in·tel·li·gi·ble (in tel′i jə b'l) ***adj.*** [< L. < *intelligere:* see INTELLECT] that can be understood; clear; comprehensible —**in·tel′li·gi·bil′i·ty** ***n.*** —**in·tel′li·gi·bly** ***adv.***

in·tem·per·ance (in tem′pər əns) ***n.*** **1.** a lack of temperance or restraint; immoderation **2.** excessive drinking of alcoholic liquor

in·tem·per·ate (-it) ***adj.*** **1.** not temperate; specif., *a)* not moderate; excessive *b)* severe or violent [an *intemper-*

ate wind*]* **2.** drinking too much alcoholic liquor —**in·tem′per·ate·ly** ***adv.***

in·tend (in tend′) ***vt.*** [< OFr. < L. *intendere,* to aim at < *in-,* at + *tendere,* to stretch] **1.** to have in mind as a purpose; plan; purpose **2.** to mean (something) to be or be used (*for*); design; destine **3.** to mean or signify —***vi.*** to have a purpose or intention —**in·tend′er** ***n.***

in·tend·ant (in ten′dənt) ***n.*** [Fr. < L. prp. of *intendere:* see INTEND] a director, manager of a public business, superintendent, etc.

in·tend·ed (-did) ***adj.*** **1.** meant; planned; purposed **2.** prospective; future —***n.*** [Colloq.] the person whom one has agreed to marry

intens. 1. intensified **2.** intensifier **3.** intensive

in·tense (in tens′) ***adj.*** [< MFr. < L. pp. of *intendere:* see INTEND] **1.** occurring or existing in a high degree; very strong *[*an *intense* light*]* **2.** strained to the utmost; earnest *[intense* thought*]* **3.** having or showing strong emotion, great seriousness, etc. **4.** characterized by much action, emotion, etc. —**in·tense′ly** ***adv.*** —**in·tense′ness** ***n.***

in·ten·si·fy (in ten′sə fī′) ***vt., vi.*** **-fied′, -fy′ing** to make or become intense or more intense; increase; strengthen —**in·ten′si·fi·ca′tion** ***n.*** —**in·ten′si·fi′er** ***n.***

in·ten·si·ty (in ten′sə tē) ***n., pl.*** **-ties** **1.** a being intense; specif., *a)* extreme degree of anything *b)* great energy or vehemence, as of emotion **2.** relative strength, magnitude, etc. **3.** the degree of purity of color; saturation **4.** *Physics* the amount of force or energy of heat, light, sound, etc. per unit area, volume, etc.

in·ten·sive (-siv) ***adj.*** **1.** of or characterized by intensity; thorough; exhaustive **2.** designating very attentive hospital care given to patients, as after surgery **3.** *Agric.* designating a system of farming which aims at the increase of crop yield per unit area **4.** *Gram.* giving force or emphasis (Ex.: "very" in "the very same man") —***n.*** **1.** anything that intensifies **2.** an intensive word, prefix, etc. —**in·ten′sive·ly** ***adv.*** —**in·ten′sive·ness** ***n.***

in·tent (in tent′) ***adj.*** [< L. pp. of *intendere:* see INTEND] **1.** firmly directed; earnest **2.** *a)* having the attention firmly fixed; engrossed *b)* strongly resolved *[intent* on going*]* —***n.*** **1.** an intending **2.** something intended; specif., *a)* a purpose; aim *b)* meaning or import **3.** *Law* one's mental attitude at the time of doing an act —**to all intents and purposes** in almost every respect —**in·tent′ly** ***adv.*** —**in·tent′ness** ***n.***

in·ten·tion (in ten′shən) ***n.*** **1.** an intending; determination to do a specified thing or act in a specified way **2.** *a)* anything intended; aim or purpose *b)* [*pl.*] purpose in regard to marriage

in·ten·tion·al (-shən 'l) ***adj.*** **1.** having to do with intention **2.** done purposely; intended —**in·ten′tion·al·ly** ***adv.***

in·ter (in tʉr′) ***vt.*** **-terred′, -ter′ring** [< OFr. < L. *in,* in + *terra,* earth] to put (a dead body) into a grave or tomb

in·ter- [L. < *inter, prep.*] *a combining form meaning:* **1.** between or among *[interstate]* **2.** with or on each other (or one another), together, mutual, reciprocal, mutually, or reciprocally *[interact]*

in·ter·act (in′tər akt′) ***vi.*** to act on one another —**in′ter·ac′tion** ***n.*** —**in′ter·ac′tive** ***adj.***

‡in·ter a·li·a (in′tər ā′lē ə) [L.] among other things

in·ter·breed (in′tər brēd′) ***vt., vi.*** **-bred′, -breed′ing** *same as* HYBRIDIZE

in·ter·ca·lar·y (in tʉr′kə ler′ē) ***adj.*** [< L.: see ff.] added to the calendar: said of an extra day, month, etc. inserted in a calendar year to make it correspond to the solar year

in·ter·ca·late (-lāt′) ***vt.*** **-lat′ed, -lat′ing** [< L. pp. of *intercalare,* to insert < *inter-,* between + *calare,* to call] **1.** to insert (a day, month, etc.) in the calendar **2.** to interpolate or insert —**in·ter′ca·la′tion** ***n.***

in·ter·cede (in′tər sēd′) ***vi.*** **-ced′ed, -ced′ing** [< L. < *inter-,* between + *cedere,* to go] **1.** to plead in behalf of another or others **2.** to intervene for the purpose of producing agreement; mediate —**in′ter·ced′er** ***n.***

in·ter·cel·lu·lar (-sel′yoo lər) ***adj.*** located between or among cells

in·ter·cept (in′tər sept′; *for n.* in′tər sept′) ***vt.*** [< L. pp. of *intercipere* < *inter-,* between + *capere,* to take] **1.** to seize, stop, or interrupt on the way; cut off *[*to *intercept* a message*]* **2.** *Math.* to mark off between two points, lines, or planes —***n.*** **1.** *Math.* the part of a line, plane, etc. intercepted **2.** *Mil.* the intercepting of enemy aircraft, missiles, etc. —**in′ter·cep′tion** ***n.*** —**in′ter·cep′tive** ***adj.*** —**in′ter·cep′tor, in′ter·cept′er** ***n.***

in·ter·ces·sion (in′tər sesh′ən) ***n.*** an interceding; mediation, pleading, or prayer in behalf of another or others

in·ter·ces·sor (in′tər ses′ər, in′tər ses′ər) ***n.*** a person who intercedes —**in′ter·ces′so·ry** ***adj.***

in·ter·change (in′tər chānj′; *for n.* in′tər chānj′) ***vt.*** **-changed′, -chang′ing** **1.** to give and take mutually; exchange *[*to *interchange* ideas*]* **2.** to put (each of two things) in the other's place **3.** to alternate *[*to *interchange* work with play*]* —***vi.*** to change places with each other —***n.*** **1.** an interchanging **2.** a place on a freeway where traffic can enter or depart, usually by means of a cloverleaf

in·ter·change·a·ble (in′tər chān′jə b'l) ***adj.*** that can be interchanged, esp. in position or use —**in′ter·change′a·bil′i·ty** ***n.*** —**in′ter·change′a·bly** ***adv.***

in·ter·col·le·gi·ate (-kə lē′jət, -jē ət) ***adj.*** between or among colleges and universities

in·ter·com (in′tər käm′) ***n.*** a radio or telephone intercommunication system, as between rooms of a building

in·ter·com·mu·ni·cate (in′tər kə myōō′nə kāt′) ***vt., vi.*** **-cat′ed, -cat′ing** to communicate with or to each other or one another —**in′ter·com·mu′ni·ca′tion** ***n.***

in·ter·con·nect (-kə nekt′) ***vt., vi.*** to connect with one another —**in′ter·con·nec′tion** ***n.***

in·ter·cos·tal (-käs′t'l) ***adj.*** [see INTER- & COSTAL] between the ribs —**in′ter·cos′tal·ly** ***adv.***

in·ter·course (in′tər kôrs′) ***n.*** [< OFr. < L.: see INTER- & COURSE] **1.** communication or dealings between or among people, countries, etc.; interchange of products, services, ideas, etc. **2.** the sexual joining of two individuals; copulation: in full, **sexual intercourse**

in·ter·de·nom·i·na·tion·al (in′tər di näm′ə nā′shən 'l) ***adj.*** between, among, shared by, or involving different religious denominations

in·ter·de·part·men·tal (-di pärt′men′t'l) ***adj.*** between or among departments

in·ter·de·pend·ence (-di pen′dəns) ***n.*** dependence on each other; mutual dependence: also **in′ter·de·pend′en·cy** —**in′ter·de·pend′ent** ***adj.*** —**in′ter·de·pend′ent·ly** ***adv.***

in·ter·dict (in′tər dikt′; *for n.* in′tər dikt′) ***vt.*** [< OFr. < L. pp. of *interdicere,* to forbid < *inter-,* between + *dicere,* to speak] **1.** to prohibit (an action); forbid with authority **2.** to restrain from doing or using something **3.** to hinder (the enemy) or isolate (an area, etc.) by bombing, etc. **4.** *R.C.Ch.* to exclude (a person, parish, etc.) from certain acts or privileges —***n.*** an official prohibition or restraint; specif., *R.C.Ch.* an interdicting of a person, parish, etc. —**in′ter·dic′tion** ***n.*** —**in′ter·dic′to·ry, in′ter·dic′tive** ***adj.***

in·ter·dis·ci·pli·nar·y (-dis′ə pli ner′ē) ***adj.*** involving two or more disciplines, or branches of learning

in·ter·est (in′trist, in′tər ist; *for v. also* -tə rest′) ***n.*** [< ML. *interesse,* compensation < L. < *inter-,* between + *esse,* to be: altered after OFr. *interest* < L., it interests] **1.** a right or claim to something **2.** *a)* a share or participation in something *b)* anything in which one participates or has a share **3.** [*often pl.*] advantage; welfare; benefit **4.** [*usually pl.*] a group of people having a common concern or dominant power in some industry, occupation, cause, etc. *[*the steel *interests]* **5.** *a)* a feeling of intentness, concern, or curiosity about something *b)* the power of causing this feeling *c)* something causing this feeling **6.** importance; consequence *[*a matter of little *interest]* **7.** *a)* money paid for the use of money *b)* the rate of such payment, expressed as a percentage per unit of time **8.** an increase over what is owed *[*to repay kindness with *interest]* —***vt.*** **1.** to cause to have an interest (*in*) **2.** to excite the attention or curiosity of —**in the interest** (or **interests**) **of** for the sake of

in·ter·est·ed (-id) ***adj.*** **1.** having an interest or share **2.** influenced by personal interest; prejudiced **3.** feeling or showing interest, or curiosity —**in′ter·est·ed·ly** ***adv.***

in·ter·est·ing (-iŋ) ***adj.*** exciting interest, curiosity, or attention —**in′ter·est·ing·ly** ***adv.***

in·ter·face (in′tər fās′) ***n.*** **1.** a plane forming the common boundary between two parts of matter or space **2.** a point or means of interaction between two systems, disciplines, groups, etc. —***vt., vi.*** **-faced′, -fac′ing** to interconnect with another system, discipline, group, etc.

in·ter·faith (in′tər fāth′) ***adj.*** between or involving persons adhering to different religions

in·ter·fere (in′tər fir′) ***vi.*** **-fered′, -fer′ing** [< OFr. < *entre-,* INTER- + *férir* < L. *ferire,* to strike] **1.** to come into collision or opposition; clash; conflict **2.** to come between for some purpose; intervene **3.** *Sports* to be guilty of interference **4.** *Physics* to affect each other by interference: said of vibrating waves —**interfere with** to hinder; prevent —**in′ter·fer′er** ***n.*** —**in′ter·fer′ing·ly** ***adv.***

in·ter·fer·ence (-fir′əns) ***n.*** **1.** an interfering **2.** something that interferes **3.** *a)* *Football* the legal blocking of opposing players in order to clear the way for the ball carrier *b) Sports* the illegal hindering of an opposing player **4.** *Physics* the mutual action of two waves of vibration, as of sound, light, etc., in reinforcing or neutralizing each other **5.** *Radio & TV* static, unwanted signals, etc., producing a distortion of sounds or images

in·ter·fer·on (-fir′än) ***n.*** [INTERFER(E) + *-on,* arbitrary suffix] a cellular protein produced by the body to inhibit growth of an infecting virus

in·ter·fold (-fōld′) ***vt., vi.*** to fold together or inside one another

in·ter·fuse (-fyo͞oz′) ***vt.*** **-fused′, -fus′ing 1.** to combine by mixing, blending, or fusing together **2.** to spread itself through; pervade —***vi.*** to fuse; blend —**in′ter·fu′sion *n.***

in·ter·group (in′tər gro͞op′) ***adj.*** between or involving different social, ethnic, or racial groups

in·ter·im (in′tər im) ***n.*** [L., meanwhile < *inter,* between] the period of time between; meantime —***adj.*** temporary; provisional *[*an *interim* council*]*

in·te·ri·or (in tir′ē ər) ***adj.*** [< MFr. < L., compar. of *inter,* between] **1.** situated within; inner **2.** away from the coast, border, etc.; inland **3.** of the domestic affairs of a country **4.** private —***n.*** **1.** the interior part of anything; specif., *a)* the inside of a room or building *b)* the inland part of a country or region *c)* the inner nature of a person or thing **2.** the domestic affairs of a country *[*the U.S. Department of the *Interior]* —**in·te′ri·or′i·ty** (-ôr′ə tē) ***n.*** —**in·te′ri·or·ly *adv.***

interior angle any of the four angles formed on the inside of two straight lines by a straight line cutting across them: cf. EXTERIOR ANGLE

interior decoration the decorating and furnishing of the interior of a room, house, etc.

in·te·ri·or·ize (-īz′) ***vt.*** **-ized′, -iz′ing** to make (a concept, value, etc.) part of one's inner nature

interj. interjection

in·ter·ject (in′tər jekt′) ***vt.*** [< L. pp. of *interjicere* < *inter-,* between + *jacere,* to throw] to throw in between; insert; interpose —**in′ter·jec′tor *n.***

in·ter·jec·tion (-jek′shən) ***n.*** **1.** an interjecting **2.** something interjected, as a word or phrase **3.** *Gram.* an exclamatory word or phrase (Ex.: ah! well!) —**in′ter·jec′tion·al, in′ter·jec′to·ry *adj.***

in·ter·lace (-lās′) ***vt., vi.*** **-laced′, -lac′ing** [< OFr.: see INTER- & LACE] **1.** to unite by passing over and under each other; weave together **2.** to connect intricately —**in′ter·lace′ment *n.***

in·ter·lard (-lärd′) ***vt.*** [< Fr.: see INTER- & LARD] **1.** to intersperse; diversify *[*to *interlard* a lecture with quotations*]* **2.** to be intermixed in

in·ter·lay (-lā′) ***vt.*** **-laid′** (-lād′), **-lay′ing** to lay or put between or among —**in′ter·lay′er *n.***

in·ter·leaf (in′tər lēf′) ***n., pl.*** **-leaves′** (-lēvz′) a leaf, usually blank, bound between the other leaves of a book, for notes, etc. —**in′ter·leave′** (-lēv′) ***vt.*** **-leaved′, -leav′ing**

in·ter·line[1] (in′tər līn′) ***vt.*** **-lined′, -lin′ing** to write or print (something) between the lines of (a text, document, etc.) —**in′ter·lin′e·a′tion** (-lin′ē ā′shən) ***n.***

in·ter·line[2] (in′tər līn′) ***vt.*** **-lined′, -lin′ing** to put a lining between the outer material and the ordinary lining of (a garment)

in·ter·lin·e·ar (in′tər lin′ē ər) ***adj.*** **1.** written or printed between the lines **2.** having the same text in different languages printed in alternate lines Also **in′ter·lin′e·al**

in·ter·lin·ing (in′tər lī′niŋ) ***n.*** a lining between the outer cloth and the ordinary lining

in·ter·link (in′tər liŋk′) ***vt.*** to link together

in·ter·lock (-läk′) ***vt., vi.*** to lock together; join with one another —***n.*** a being interlocked

interlocking directorates boards of directors having some members in common, so that their corporations are more or less under the same control

in·ter·loc·u·tor (-läk′yə tər; *for 2, often* -läk′ə tər) ***n.*** [< L. pp. < *inter,* between + *loqui,* to talk] **1.** a person taking part in a conversation **2.** the master of ceremonies in a minstrel show

in·ter·loc·u·to·ry (-läk′yə tôr′ē) ***adj.*** **1.** of, having the nature of, or occurring in dialogue; conversational **2.** *Law* pronounced during the course of a suit, pending final decision

in·ter·lop·er (in′tər lō′pər) ***n.*** [prob. < INTER- + LOPE] a person who meddles in others' affairs

in·ter·lude (in′tər lo͞od′) ***n.*** [< OFr. < ML. < L. *inter,* between + *ludus,* play] **1.** a short, humorous play formerly presented between the parts of a miracle play or morality play **2.** any performance between the acts of a play **3.** music played between the parts of a song, play, etc. **4.** anything that fills time between two events

in·ter·mar·ry (in′tər mar′ē) ***vi.*** **-ried, -ry·ing** to become connected by marriage: said of persons of different races, religions, etc. —**in′ter·mar′riage *n.***

in·ter·med·dle (-med′'l) ***vi.*** **-dled, -dling** to meddle in the affairs of others —**in′ter·med′dler *n.***

in·ter·me·di·ar·y (-mē′dē er′ē) ***adj.*** **1.** acting between two persons; acting as a mediator **2.** intermediate —***n., pl.*** **-ar′ies** a go-between; mediator

in·ter·me·di·ate (-mē′dē it; *for v.* -āt′) ***adj.*** [< ML. < L. < *inter-,* between + *medius,* middle] being or happening between; in the middle —***n.*** **1.** anything intermediate **2.** *same as* INTERMEDIARY —***vi.*** **-at′ed, -at′ing** to act as an intermediary; mediate —**in′ter·me′di·ate·ly *adv.*** —**in′ter·me′di·ate·ness, in′ter·me′di·a·cy** (-ə sē) ***n.*** —**in′ter·me′di·a′tion *n.*** —**in′ter·me′di·a′tor *n.***

in·ter·ment (in tur′mənt) ***n.*** an interring; burial

in·ter·mez·zo (in′tər met′sō, -med′zō) ***n., pl.*** **-zos, -zi** (-sē, -zē) [It.] **1.** a short, light musical entertainment between the acts of a play or opera **2.** *Music a)* a short movement connecting the main parts of a composition *b)* any of certain short works similar to this

in·ter·mi·na·ble (in tur′mi nə b'l) ***adj.*** not terminable; lasting, or seeming to last, forever; endless —**in·ter′mi·na·bly *adv.***

in·ter·min·gle (in′tər miŋ′g'l) ***vt., vi.*** **-gled, -gling** to mix together; mingle; blend

in·ter·mis·sion (-mish′ən) ***n.*** **1.** an intermitting or being intermitted; interruption **2.** an interval of time between periods of activity; pause, as between acts of a play

in·ter·mit (-mit′) ***vt., vi.*** **-mit′ted, -mit′ting** [< L. < *inter-,* between + *mittere,* to send] to stop for a time; cease at intervals

in·ter·mit·tent (-mit′'nt) ***adj.*** stopping and starting again at intervals; periodic —**in′ter·mit′tence *n.*** —**in′ter·mit′tent·ly *adv.***

in·ter·mix (-miks′) ***vt., vi.*** to mix together; blend —**in′ter·mix′ture *n.***

in·tern (in′tərn; *for vt. usually* in turn′) ***n.*** [< Fr. < L. *internus,* internal] **1.** a doctor serving as an assistant resident in a hospital, generally just after graduation from medical school **2.** an apprentice teacher, journalist, etc. —***vi.*** to serve as an intern —***vt.*** to detain and confine within a country or a definite area *[*to *intern* aliens in time of war*]* —**in·tern′ment *n.***

in·ter·nal (in tur′n'l) ***adj.*** [< ML. < L. *internus*] **1.** of or on the inside; inner **2.** to be taken inside the body *[internal* remedies*]* **3.** of or belonging to the inner nature of a thing; intrinsic *[internal* evidence*]* **4.** of or belonging to a person's inner nature or mind; subjective **5.** domestic; nonforeign *[internal* revenue*]* —**in′ter·nal′i·ty** (-nal′ə tē) ***n.*** —**in·ter′nal·ly *adv.***

in·ter·nal-com·bus·tion engine (-kəm bus′chən) an engine, as in an automobile, in which the power is produced by the combustion of a fuel-and-air mixture within the cylinders

in·ter·nal·ize (in tur′n'l īz′) ***vt.*** **-ized′, -iz′ing** to make internal; specif., to make (others' ideas, values, etc.) a part of one's own patterns of thinking —**in·ter′nal·i·za′tion *n.***

internal medicine the branch of medicine dealing with the diagnosis and nonsurgical treatment of diseases

internal revenue governmental income from taxes on income, profits, luxuries, etc.

in·ter·na·tion·al (in′tər nash′ən 'l) ***adj.*** **1.** between or among nations *[*an *international* treaty*]* **2.** concerned with the relations between nations *[*an *international* court*]* **3.** for the use of all nations *[international* waters*]* **4.** of, for, or by people in various nations —***n.*** an international organization; esp., [**I-**] any of several international socialist organizations in existence variously from 1864 on —**in′ter·na′tion·al′i·ty *n.*** —**in′ter·na′tion·al·ly *adv.***

international date line *same as* DATE LINE

in·ter·na·tion·al·ism (in′tər nash′ən 'l iz'm) ***n.*** the principle of international cooperation for the common good —**in′ter·na′tion·al·ist *n.***

in·ter·na·tion·al·ize (-īz′) ***vt.*** **-ized′, -iz′ing** to make international; bring under international control —**in′ter·na′tion·al·i·za′tion *n.***

International Phonetic Alphabet a set of phonetic symbols for international use: each symbol represents a single sound, whether the sound occurs in only one language or in more than one

in·terne (in′tərn) ***n.*** *same as* INTERN

in·ter·ne·cine (in′tər nē′sin, -sīn; -nes′'n) ***adj.*** [< L. < *inter-,* between + *necare,* to kill] mutually destructive or harmful *[internecine* warfare*]*

in·tern·ee (in′tər nē′) ***n.*** a person interned as a prisoner of war or enemy alien

in·ter·nist (in′tər nist, in tur′nist) ***n.*** a doctor who specializes in internal medicine

in·tern·ship (in′tərn ship′) ***n.*** **1.** the position of an intern **2.** the period of service as an intern

in·ter·of·fice (in′tər ôf′is, -äf′-) ***adj.*** between or among the offices within an organization

in·ter·pel·late (in′tər pel′āt, in tur′pə lāt′) ***vt.*** **-lat·ed, -lat·ing** [< L. pp. of *interpellare,* to interrupt < *inter-,* between + *pellere,* to drive] to ask (a cabinet minister, etc.) formally for an explanation of his action or policy: a form of political challenge in some national legislatures —**in′ter·pel′lant** ***adj., n.*** —**in′ter·pel·la′tion** ***n.***

in·ter·pen·e·trate (-pen′ə trāt′) ***vt.*** **-trat′ed, -trat′ing** to penetrate thoroughly; permeate —***vi.*** to penetrate mutually —**in′ter·pen′e·tra′tion** ***n.***

in·ter·per·son·al (-pʉr′sə n'l) ***adj.*** **1.** between persons **2.** of or involving relations between persons —**in′ter·per′son·al·ly** ***adv.***

in·ter·phone (in′tər fōn′) ***n.*** an intercom telephone system, as between office departments

in·ter·plan·e·tar·y (in′tər plan′ə ter′ē) ***adj.*** **1.** between planets **2.** within the solar system but outside the atmosphere of any planet or the sun

in·ter·play (in′tər plā′) ***n.*** action, effect, or influence on each other or one another; interaction

in·ter·po·late (in tʉr′pə lāt′) ***vt.*** **-lat′ed, -lat′ing** [< L. < *inter-*, between + *polire*, to polish] **1.** to change (a book, text, etc.) by putting in new words, subject matter, etc. **2.** to insert between or among others [to *interpolate* a remark] **3.** *Math.* to estimate a missing value by taking an average of known values at neighboring points —***vi.*** to make interpolations —**in·ter′po·lat′er, in·ter′po·la′tor** ***n.*** —**in·ter′po·la′tion** ***n.*** —**in·ter′po·la′tive** ***adj.***

in·ter·pose (in′tər pōz′) ***vt.*** **-posed′, -pos′ing** **1.** to place between; insert **2.** to introduce by way of intervention **3.** to put in as an interruption —***vi.*** **1.** to be or come between **2.** to intervene **3.** to interrupt —**in′ter·pos′al** ***n.*** —**in′ter·pos′er** ***n.*** —**in′ter·po·si′tion** (-pə zish′ən) ***n.***

in·ter·pret (in tʉr′prit) ***vt.*** [< MFr. < L. *interpretari* < *interpres*, negotiator] **1.** to explain the meaning of; clarify **2.** to translate (oral remarks) **3.** to have one's own understanding of; construe [to *interpret* a laugh as derisive] **4.** to bring out the meaning of; esp., to give one's own conception of, as in performing a play —***vi.*** to act as an interpreter; translate —**in·ter′pret·a·ble** ***adj.*** —**in·ter′pre·tive, in·ter′pre·ta′tive** ***adj.***

in·ter·pre·ta·tion (in tʉr′prə tā′shən) ***n.*** **1.** the act or result of interpreting; explanation, translation, etc. **2.** the expression of a person's conception of a work of art, subject, etc. through acting, writing, etc. —**in·ter′pre·ta′tion·al** ***adj.***

in·ter·pret·er (in tʉr′prə tər) ***n.*** a person who interprets; specif., a person whose work is translating a foreign language orally

in·ter·ra·cial (in′tər rā′shəl) ***adj.*** between, among, or for persons of different races

in·ter·reg·num (-reg′nəm) ***n.***, *pl.* **-reg′nums, -reg′na** (-nə) [L. < *inter-*, between + *regnum*, a REIGN] **1.** an interval between two successive reigns, when the country has no sovereign **2.** any period without the usual ruler, governor, etc. **3.** any break in a series or in a continuity

in·ter·re·late (-ri lāt′) ***vt., vi.*** **-lat′ed, -lat′ing** to make, be, or become mutually related —**in′ter·re·la′tion** ***n.*** —**in′ter·re·la′tion·ship′** ***n.***

in·ter·ro·gate (in ter′ə gāt′) ***vt.*** **-gat′ed, -gat′ing** [< L. pp. of *interrogare* < *inter-*, between + *rogare*, to ask] to ask questions of formally in examining [to *interrogate* a witness] —***vi.*** to ask questions —**in·ter′ro·ga′tor** ***n.***

in·ter·ro·ga·tion (in ter′ə gā′shən) ***n.*** **1.** an interrogating or being interrogated; examination **2.** a question —**in·ter′ro·ga′tion·al** ***adj.***

interrogation mark (or **point**) *same as* QUESTION MARK

in·ter·rog·a·tive (in′tə räg′ə tiv) ***adj.*** asking, or having the form of, a question —***n.*** an interrogative word, element, etc. (Ex.: what? where?) —**in′ter·rog′a·tive·ly** ***adv.***

in·ter·rog·a·to·ry (-ə tôr′ē) ***adj.*** expressing a question —***n.***, *pl.* **-ries** a formal set of questions —**in′ter·rog′a·to′ri·ly** ***adv.***

in·ter·rupt (in′tə rupt′) ***vt.*** [< L. pp. of *interrumpere* < *inter-*, between + *rumpere*, to break] **1.** *a)* to break into (a discussion, etc.) *b)* to break in upon (a person) while he is speaking, working, etc. **2.** to make a break in the continuity of; obstruct —***vi.*** to make an interruption —**in′ter·rupt′er** ***n.*** —**in′ter·rup′tive** ***adj.***

in·ter·rup·tion (in′tə rup′shən) ***n.*** **1.** an interrupting or being interrupted **2.** anything that interrupts **3.** an intermission

in·ter·scho·las·tic (in′tər skə las′tik) ***adj.*** between or among schools [an *interscholastic* debate]

in·ter·sect (in′tər sekt′) ***vt.*** [< L. pp. of *intersecare* < *inter-*, between + *secare*, to cut] to divide into two parts by passing through or across —***vi.*** to cross each other

in·ter·sec·tion (-sek′shən) ***n.*** **1.** an intersecting **2.** a place of intersecting; specif., *a)* the point or line where two lines or surfaces meet or cross *b)* the place where two streets cross

in·ter·sec·tion·al (-'l) ***adj.*** **1.** of or forming an intersection **2.** between sections or regions

in·ter·sperse (in′tər spʉrs′) ***vt.*** **-spersed′, -spers′ing** [< L. pp. of *interspergere* < *inter-*, among + *spargere*, to scatter] **1.** to scatter among other things; put here and there **2.** to decorate or diversify with things scattered here and there —**in′ter·sper′sion** (-spʉr′zhən, -shən) ***n.***

in·ter·state (in′tər stāt′) ***adj.*** between states of a federal government [*interstate* commerce]

in·ter·stel·lar (in′tər stel′ər) ***adj.*** [INTER- + STELLAR] between or among the stars

in·ter·stice (in tʉr′stis) ***n.***, *pl.* **-stic·es** (-stis iz, -stə sēz′) [Fr. < LL. < *inter-*, between + *sistere*, to set < *stare*, to stand] a small space between things or parts; crevice; crack —**in·ter·sti·tial** (in′tər stish′əl) ***adj.*** —**in′ter·sti′tial·ly** ***adv.***

in·ter·twine (in′tər twīn′) ***vt., vi.*** **-twined′, -twin′ing** to twine together; intertwist

in·ter·twist (-twist′) ***vt., vi.*** to twist together

in·ter·ur·ban (-ʉr′bən) ***adj.*** [INTER- + URBAN] between cities or towns —***n.*** an interurban railway

in·ter·val (in′tər v'l) ***n.*** [< OFr. < L. < *inter-*, between + *vallum*, a WALL] **1.** a space between two things **2.** a period of time between two events **3.** the extent of difference between two qualities, conditions, etc. **4.** *Music* the difference in pitch between two tones —**at intervals** **1.** now and then **2.** here and there —**in′ter·val′lic** (-val′ik) ***adj.***

in·ter·vene (in′tər vēn′) ***vi.*** **-vened′, -ven′ing** [< L. < *inter-*, between + *venire*, to come] **1.** to come or be between **2.** to occur between two events, etc. **3.** to come or be in between as something irrelevant **4.** to come between as an influencing force —**in′ter·ven′er,** *Law* **in′ter·ve′nor** ***n.*** —**in′ter·ven′ient** (-yənt) ***adj., n.***

in·ter·ven·tion (in′tər ven′shən) ***n.*** **1.** an intervening **2.** any interference in the affairs of others, esp. of one state in the affairs of another —**in′ter·ven′tion·ist** ***n., adj.***

in·ter·view (in′tər vyōō′) ***n.*** [< Fr.: see INTER- & VIEW] **1.** a meeting of people face to face, as for evaluating a job applicant **2.** *a)* a meeting in which a person is asked about his views, activities, etc., as by a reporter *b)* a published account of this —***vt.*** to have an interview with —**in′ter·view·ee′** ***n.*** —**in′ter·view′er** ***n.***

in·ter·weave (in′tər wēv′) ***vt., vi.*** **-wove′, -wo′ven, -weav′ing** **1.** to weave together; interlace **2.** to connect closely; intermingle

in·tes·tate (in tes′tāt, -tit) ***adj.*** [< L. < *in-*, not + pp. of *testari*, to make a will] **1.** having made no will **2.** not disposed of by a will —***n.*** a person who has died intestate —**in·tes′ta·cy** (-tə sē) ***n.***

in·tes·tin·al (in tes′ti n'l) ***adj.*** of or in the intestines —**in·tes′tin·al·ly** ***adv.***

in·tes·tine (in tes′tin) ***adj.*** [< L. *intestinus* < *intus*, within] internal, with regard to a country or community; domestic —***n.*** [*usually pl.*] the lower part of the alimentary canal, extending from the stomach to the anus and consisting of a convoluted upper part (**small intestine**) and a lower part of greater diameter (**large intestine**); bowel(s)

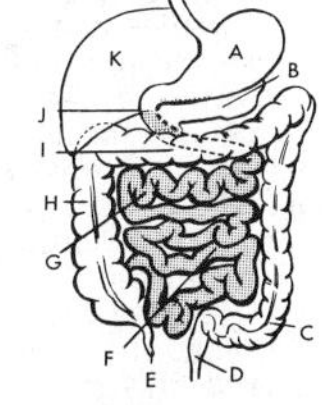

INTESTINES (A, stomach; B, pancreas; C, descending colon; D, rectum; E, appendix; F, ileum; G, jejunum; H, ascending colon; I, transverse colon; J, duodenum; K, liver)

in·thrall, in·thral (in thrôl′) ***vt.*** **-thralled′, -thrall′ing** *same as* ENTHRALL

in·ti·ma·cy (in′tə mə sē) ***n.***, *pl.* **-cies** **1.** a being intimate; familiarity **2.** an intimate act; esp., [*usually pl.*] illicit sexual intercourse

in·ti·mate (in′tə mit; *for v.* -māt′) ***adj.*** [< Fr. < L. *intimus*, superl. of *intus*, within] **1.** fundamental; essential [the *intimate* structure of the atom] **2.** most private or personal [one's *intimate* feelings] **3.** closely associated; very familiar [an *intimate* friend] **4.** suggesting privacy, romance, etc. [an *intimate* nightclub] **5.** *a)* resulting from careful study *b)* very close [*intimate* kinship] **6.** having illicit sexual relations —***n.*** an intimate friend or companion —***vt.*** **-mat′ed, -mat′ing** [< L. pp. of *intimare*, to announce < *intimus*] to hint or imply —**in′ti·mate·ly** ***adv.*** —**in′ti·mate·ness** ***n.*** —**in′ti·ma′tion** (-mā′shən) ***n.***

in·tim·i·date (in tim′ə dāt′) ***vt.*** **-dat′ed, -dat′ing** [< ML. pp. of *intimidare* < L. *in-*, in + *timidus*, afraid] **1.** to make timid; make afraid **2.** to force or deter with threats; cow —**in·tim′i·da′tion** ***n.*** —**in·tim′i·da′tor** ***n.***

in·ti·tle (in tīt′'l) ***vt.*** **-tled, -tling** *same as* ENTITLE

intl. international

in·to (in′tōō, -too, -tə) ***prep.*** [OE.] **1.** to the inside of; toward and within [*into* a house] **2.** advancing to the midst of (a period of time) [dancing far *into* the night] **3.** to the form, substance, etc. of [divided *into* parts] **4.** so as to strike [to bump *into* a door] **5.** to the work, activity, etc. of [to go *into* teaching]

in·tol·er·a·ble (in täl′ər ə b'l) ***adj.*** not tolerable; unbearable; too severe, painful, etc. to be endured —**in·tol′er·a·bil′i·ty, in·tol′er·a·ble·ness** ***n.*** —**in·tol′er·a·bly** ***adv.***

in·tol·er·ance (in täl′ər əns) ***n.*** **1.** lack of tolerance, esp. of others' opinions, beliefs, etc.; bigotry **2.** a sensitivity to some food, medicine, etc.

in·tol·er·ant (-ənt) ***adj.*** not tolerant; unwilling to tolerate others' opinions, beliefs, etc. or persons of other races, background, etc.; bigoted —**intolerant of** not able or willing to tolerate —**in·tol′er·ant·ly** ***adv.*** —**in·tol′er·ant·ness** ***n.***

in·to·na·tion (in′tə nā′shən) ***n.*** **1.** an intoning **2.** the manner of singing or playing tones with regard to accuracy of pitch **3.** variations in pitch in speaking that affect the meaning **4.** the manner of applying final pitch to a spoken sentence or phrase [a question ending with a rising *intonation*] —**in′to·na′tion·al** ***adj.***

in·tone (in tōn′) ***vt.*** **-toned′, -ton′ing** [< OFr. < ML.: see IN-[1] & TONE] **1.** to utter or recite in a singing tone or in prolonged monotones; chant **2.** to give a particular intonation to —***vi.*** to speak or recite in a singing tone or in prolonged monotones; chant —**in·ton′er** ***n.***

in to·to (in tō′tō) [L.] as a whole; entirely

in·tox·i·cant (in täk′sə kənt) ***n.*** something that intoxicates; esp., alcoholic liquor —***adj.*** intoxicating

in·tox·i·cate (-kāt′) ***vt.*** **-cat′ed, -cat′ing** [< ML. pp. of *intoxicare*, to poison, ult. < L. *in-*, in + *toxicum*, a poison: see TOXIC] **1.** to make drunk **2.** to excite to a point beyond self-control **3.** *Med.* to poison

in·tox·i·ca·tion (in täk′sə kā′shən) ***n.*** **1.** a making or becoming drunk **2.** a feeling of wild excitement; frenzy **3.** *Med.* a poisoning or becoming poisoned

intr. intransitive

in·tra- [L. < *intra*, within] *a combining form meaning* within, inside of [*intramural*]

in·trac·ta·ble (in trak′tə b'l) ***adj.*** not tractable; specif., *a*) hard to manage; unruly or stubborn *b*) hard to work, cure, etc. —**in·trac′ta·bil′i·ty, in·trac′ta·ble·ness** ***n.*** —**in·trac′ta·bly** ***adv.***

in·tra·dos (in′trə däs′, -dōs′; in trā′dōs) ***n.*** [Fr. < L. *intra*, within + Fr. *dos* < L. *dorsum*, the back] the inside curve or surface of an arch or vault

in·tra·mu·ral (in′trə myoor′əl) ***adj.*** [INTRA- + MURAL] within the walls or limits of a city, college, etc. [*intramural* athletics] —**in′tra·mu′ral·ly** ***adv.***

in·tra·mus·cu·lar (-mus′kyə lər) ***adj.*** located or injected within the muscle —**in′tra·mus′cu·lar·ly** ***adv.***

intrans. intransitive

in·tran·si·gent (in tran′sə jənt) ***adj.*** [< Fr. < Sp. < L. *in-*, IN-[2] + prp. of *transigere*, to settle] refusing to compromise, be reconciled, etc. —***n.*** one who is intransigent, esp. in politics —**in·tran′si·gence, in·tran′si·gen·cy** ***n.*** —**in·tran′si·gent·ly** ***adv.***

in·tran·si·tive (in tran′sə tiv) ***adj.*** not transitive; designating a verb that does not require a direct object to complete its meaning —***n.*** an intransitive verb —**in·tran′si·tive·ly** ***adv.***

in·tra·state (in′trə stāt′) ***adj.*** within a state; esp., within a State of the U.S.

in·tra·u·ter·ine (-yōōt′ər in, -yōō′tə rīn′) ***adj.*** within the uterus

intrauterine (contraceptive) device any of various devices, as a coil or loop of plastic, inserted in the uterus as a contraceptive

in·tra·ve·nous (-vē′nəs) ***adj.*** [INTRA- + VENOUS] in, or directly into, a vein or veins [an *intravenous* injection] —**in′tra·ve′nous·ly** ***adv.***

in·trench (in trench′) ***vt., vi.*** *same as* ENTRENCH

in·trep·id (in trep′id) ***adj.*** [< L. < *in-*, not + *trepidus*, alarmed] unafraid; bold; fearless; very brave —**in′tre·pid′i·ty** (-trə pid′ə tē), **in·trep′id·ness** ***n.*** —**in·trep′id·ly** ***adv.***

Int. Rev. internal revenue

in·tri·ca·cy (in′tri kə sē) ***n.*** **1.** an intricate quality or state; complexity **2.** *pl.* **-cies** something intricate; involved matter, etc.

in·tri·cate (in′tri kit) ***adj.*** [< L. pp. of *intricare*, to entangle < *in-*, in + *tricae*, perplexities] **1.** hard to follow or understand because full of puzzling parts, details, or relationships [an *intricate* problem] **2.** full of elaborate detail —**in′tri·cate·ly** ***adv.*** —**in′tri·cate·ness** ***n.***

in·trigue (in trēg′; *for n., also* in′trēg) ***vi.*** **-trigued′, -trigu′ing** [< Fr. < It. < L. *intricare*: see prec.] **1.** to carry on a secret love affair **2.** to plot or scheme secretly or underhandedly —***vt.*** **1.** to get by secret or underhanded plotting **2.** to excite the interest or curiosity of [movies *intrigue* her] —***n.*** **1.** secret or underhanded plotting **2.** a secret or underhanded plot or scheme **3.** a secret love affair —**in·trigu′er** ***n.*** —**in·trigu′ing·ly** ***adv.***

in·trin·sic (in trin′sik, -zik) ***adj.*** [< MFr. < LL. *intrinsecus*, inward < L. < *intra-*, within + *secus*, close] belonging to the real nature of a thing; essential; inherent: also **intrin′si·cal** —**in·trin′si·cal·ly** ***adv.*** —**in·trin′si·cal·ness** ***n.***

in·tro- [L. < *intro*, on the inside] *a combining form meaning* into, within, inward [*introvert*]

introd., intro. **1.** introduction **2.** introductory

in·tro·duce (in′trə dōōs′, -dyōōs′) ***vt.*** **-duced′, -duc′ing** [< L. < *intro-*, within + *ducere*, to lead] **1.** to lead or bring in **2.** to put in; insert [to *introduce* a drain into a wound] **3.** to add as a new feature [*introduce* some humor into the play] **4.** to bring into use, knowledge, or fashion [space science has *introduced* many new words] **5.** *a*) to make acquainted; present (*to*) [*introduce* me to her] *b*) to present (a person) to society *c*) to give knowledge or experience of [they *introduced* him to music] **6.** to bring forward [*introduce* a bill into Congress] **7.** to start; begin [to *introduce* a talk with a joke] —**in′tro·duc′er** ***n.*** —**in′tro·duc′i·ble** ***adj.***

in·tro·duc·tion (-duk′shən) ***n.*** **1.** an introducing or being introduced **2.** anything brought into use, knowledge, or fashion **3.** anything that introduces; specif., *a*) the preliminary section of a book, speech, etc. *b*) a preliminary guide or text *c*) an opening section of music **4.** the formal presentation of one person to another, to society, etc.

in·tro·duc·to·ry (-duk′tər ē) ***adj.*** used as an introduction; preliminary: also **in′tro·duc′tive** —**in′tro·duc′to·ri·ly** ***adv.***

in·tro·it (in trō′it; in′trō it, -troit) ***n.*** [< MFr. < L. *introitus*, an entrance, ult. < *intro-*, within + *ire*, to go] **1.** a psalm or hymn at the opening of a Christian worship service **2.** [I-] *R.C.Ch.* the first variable part of the Mass, consisting of a few psalm verses followed by the *Gloria Patri* and then repeated

in·tro·spec·tion (in′trə spek′shən) ***n.*** [< L. < pp. of *introspicere*, ult. < *intro-*, within + *specere*, to look] a looking into one's own mind, feelings, etc. —**in′tro·spec′tive** ***adj.*** —**in′tro·spec′tive·ly** ***adv.***

in·tro·ver·sion (-vur′zhən, -shən) ***n.*** [see ff.] *Psychol.* an attitude in which a person directs his interest to his own experiences and feelings rather than upon external objects or other persons: opposed to EXTROVERSION —**in′tro·ver′sive** ***adj.***

in·tro·vert (in′trə vurt′; *for v., also* in′trə vurt′) ***vt.*** [< L. *intro*, within + *vertere*, to turn] **1.** to direct (one's interest, mind, etc.) upon oneself **2.** to bend (something) inward —***vi.*** to become introverted —***n.*** *Psychol.* a person characterized by introversion: opposed to EXTROVERT —***adj.*** characterized by introversion: usually **in′tro·vert′ed**

in·trude (in trōōd′) ***vt.*** **-trud′ed, -trud′ing** [< L. < *in-*, in + *trudere*, to thrust] **1.** to push or force (something *in* or *upon*) **2.** to force (oneself) upon others without being asked or welcomed **3.** *Geol.* to force (liquid magma, etc.) into or between solid rocks —***vi.*** to intrude oneself —**in·trud′er** ***n.***

in·tru·sion (in trōō′zhən) ***n.*** **1.** an intruding **2.** *Geol.* *a*) the invasion of liquid magma, etc. into or between solid rock *b*) intrusive rock

in·tru·sive (-siv) ***adj.*** **1.** intruding **2.** *Geol.* formed by intruding —**in·tru′sive·ly** ***adv.*** —**in·tru′sive·ness** ***n.***

in·trust (in trust′) ***vt.*** *same as* ENTRUST

in·tu·it (in tōō′it, -tyōō′-) ***vt., vi.*** to know or learn by intuition —**in·tu′it·a·ble** ***adj.***

in·tu·i·tion (in′too wish′ən, -tyoo-) ***n.*** [LL. < L. pp. of *intueri* < *in-*, in + *tueri*, to look at] **1.** *a*) the direct knowing or learning of something without conscious reasoning *b*) the ability to do this **2.** something known or learned in this way —**in′tu·i′tion·al** ***adj.*** —**in′tu·i′tion·al·ly** ***adv.***

in·tu·i·tive (in tōō′i tiv, -tyōō′-) ***adj.*** **1.** having to do with, having, or perceiving by intuition **2.** perceived by intuition [an *intuitive* truth] —**in·tu′i·tive·ly** ***adv.*** —**in·tu′i·tive·ness** ***n.***

in·un·date (in′ən dāt′) ***vt.*** **-dat′ed, -dat′ing** [< L. pp. of *inundare* < *in-*, in + *undare*, to flood < *unda*, a wave] to cover as with a flood; deluge; flood —**in·un·dant** (in un′dənt) ***adj.*** —**in′un·da′tion** ***n.*** —**in′un·da′tor** ***n.*** —**in·un′da·to′ry** (-də tôr′ē) ***adj.***

in·ure (in yoor′) ***vt.*** **-ured′, -ur′ing** [< ME. *in*, in + *ure*, practice, work < OFr. *ovre* < L. *opera*, a work] to make accustomed to something difficult, painful, etc. —***vi.*** to come into use or take effect —**in·ure′ment** ***n.***

inv. **1.** invented **2.** inventor **3.** invoice

‡in va·cu·o (in vak′yōō ō′) [L.] in a vacuum

in·vade (in vād′) ***vt.*** **-vad′ed, -vad′ing** [< L. < *in-*, in + *vadere*, to go] **1.** to enter forcibly, as to conquer **2.** to crowd into; throng [tourists *invading* the beaches] **3.** to intrude upon; violate [he *invaded* my privacy] **4.** to spread through with harmful effects [disease *invades* tissue] —***vi.*** to make an invasion —**in·vad′er** ***n.***

in·va·lid[1] (in′və lid) ***adj.*** [< Fr. < L.: see IN-[2] + VALID] **1.** not well; weak and sickly **2.** of or for invalids [an *in-*

valid home*]* —*n.* a weak, sickly person; esp., one who is chronically ill or disabled —*vt.* **1.** to disable or weaken **2.** ⌊Chiefly Brit.⌋ to remove (a soldier, sailor, etc.) from active duty because of injury or illness —**in′va·lid·ism** *n.*

in·val·id[2] (in val′id) *adj.* not valid; having no force; null or void —**in·va·lid·i·ty** (in′və lid′ə tē) *n.* —**in·val′id·ly** *adv.*

in·val·i·date (in val′ə dāt′) *vt.* **-dat′ed, -dat′ing** to make invalid; deprive of legal force —**in·val′i·da′tion** *n.* —**in·val′i·da′tor** *n.*

in·val·u·a·ble (in val′yoo wə b'l, -yə b'l) *adj.* too valuable to be measured; priceless —**in·val′u·a·ble·ness** *n.* —**in·val′u·a·bly** *adv.*

in·var·i·a·ble (in ver′ē ə b'l) *adj.* not variable; unchanging; constant; uniform —**in·var′i·a·bil′i·ty, in·var′i·a·ble·ness** *n.* —**in·var′i·a·bly** *adv.*

in·va·sion (in vā′zhən) *n.* an invading; specif., *a)* an entering or being entered by an attacking military force *b)* an intruding upon others *c)* the onset, as of a disease —**in·va′sive** *adj.*

in·vec·tive (in vek′tiv) *adj.* [< MFr. < LL. < L. pp. of *invehere:* see ff.] inveighing; vituperative —*n.* **1.** a violent verbal attack; insults, curses, etc. **2.** an abusive term; insult, curse, etc.—**in·vec′tive·ly** *adv.* —**in·vec′tive·ness** *n.*

in·veigh (in vā′) *vi.* [< L. *invehi*, to attack < *invehere* < *in-*, in + *vehere*, to carry] to make a violent verbal attack; talk or write bitterly (*against*); rail —**in·veigh′er** *n.*

in·vei·gle (in vē′g'l, -vā′-) *vt.* **-gled, -gling** [< MFr. *aveugler*, to blind < L. *ab*, from + *oculus*, an eye] to lead on with deception; entice or trick into doing something, etc. —**in·vei′gle·ment** *n.* —**in·vei′gler** *n.*

in·vent (in vent′) *vt.* [< L. pp. of *invenire* < *in-*, on + *venire*, to come] **1.** to think up; devise in the mind *[*to *invent* excuses*]* **2.** to think out or produce (a new device, etc.); devise for the first time

in·ven·tion (in ven′shən) *n.* **1.** an inventing or being invented **2.** the power of inventing; ingenuity **3.** something invented; specif., *a)* something thought up; esp., a falsehood *b)* a new device or contrivance **4.** *Music* a short composition developing a motif in counterpoint

in·ven·tive (-tiv) *adj.* **1.** of or characterized by invention **2.** skilled in inventing; creative —**in·ven′tive·ly** *adv.* —**in·ven′tive·ness** *n.*

in·ven·tor (-tər) *n.* a person who invents; esp., one who devises a new contrivance, method, etc.

in·ven·to·ry (in′vən tôr′ē) *n., pl.* **-ries** [< ML. < LL. < L. pp. of *invenire:* see INVENT] **1.** an itemized list of goods, property, etc., as of a business, often prepared annually **2.** the store of goods, etc. for such listing; stock **3.** any detailed list **4.** the act of making such a list —*vt.* **-ried, -ry·ing** **1.** to make an inventory of **2.** to place on an inventory —**take inventory** **1.** to make an inventory of stock on hand **2.** to make an appraisal, as of one's situation —**in′ven·to′ri·al** *adj.* —**in′ven·to′ri·al·ly** *adv.*

In·ver·ness (in′vər nes′) *n.* [after county in Scotland] ⌊*often* **i-**⌋ **1.** an overcoat with a long, removable cape **2.** the cape: also **Inverness cape**

in·verse (in vurs′, in′vurs′) *adj.* inverted; reversed in order or relation; directly opposite *[*an *inverse* ratio*]* —*n.* any inverse thing; direct opposite —**in·verse′ly** *adv.*

in·ver·sion (in vur′zhən, -shən) *n.* **1.** an inverting or being inverted **2.** something inverted; reversal **3.** *Gram. & Rhetoric* a reversal of the normal order of words in a sentence (Ex.: "said he" for "he said") **4.** *Math.* an interchange of the terms of a ratio **5.** *Meteorol.* an atmospheric condition in which a layer of warm air traps cooler air near the surface of the earth, preventing the normal rising of surface air **6.** *Music* the reversal of the position of the tones in an interval or chord, as by raising the lower tone by an octave —**in·ver′sive** *adj.*

in·vert (in vurt′; *for n.* in′vurt′) *vt.* [< L. < *in-*, to + *vertere*, to turn] **1.** to turn upside down **2.** to change to the direct opposite; reverse the order, position, direction, etc. of **3.** to subject to inversion —*n.* anything inverted —**in·vert′i·ble** *adj.*

in·ver·te·brate (in vur′tə brit, -brāt′) *adj.* **1.** not vertebrate; having no backbone, or spinal column **2.** of invertebrates —*n.* any animal without a backbone; any animal other than a fish, amphibian, reptile, bird, or mammal

in·vert·er (in vur′tər) *n.* *Elec.* a device for changing direct current into alternating current

in·vest (in vest′) *vt.* [< L. < *in-*, in + *vestire*, to clothe < *vestis*, clothing] **1.** to clothe; array **2.** *a)* to cover or surround as with a garment *[*fog *invests* the city*]* *b)* to endow with qualities, attributes, etc. **3.** to install in office with ceremony **4.** to furnish with power, privilege, or authority **5.** to put (money) into business, stocks, bonds, etc. for the purpose of obtaining a profit **6.** to spend (time, effort, etc.) with the expectation of some satisfaction **7.** *Mil.* to besiege (a town, port, etc.) —*vi.* to invest money —**in·ves′tor** *n.*

in·ves·ti·gate (in ves′tə gāt′) *vt.* **-gat′ed, -gat′ing** [< L. pp. of *investigare*, to trace out, ult. < *vestigium*, a track] to search into; inquire into systematically —*vi.* to make an investigation —**in·ves′ti·ga·ble** (-gə b'l) *adj.* —**in·ves′ti·ga′tive, in·ves′ti·ga·to′ry** (-gə tôr′ē) *adj.* —**in·ves′ti·ga′tor** *n.*

in·ves·ti·ga·tion (in ves′tə gā′shən) *n.* **1.** an investigating or being investigated **2.** a careful examination or inquiry —**in·ves′ti·ga′tion·al** *adj.*

in·ves·ti·ture (in ves′tə chər) *n.* **1.** a formal investing with an office, power, authority, etc. **2.** anything that clothes or covers

in·vest·ment (in vest′mənt) *n.* **1.** an investing or being invested **2.** an outer covering **3.** *same as* INVESTITURE (sense 1) **4.** *a)* the investing of money *b)* the amount of money invested *c)* anything in which money is or may be invested

in·vet·er·ate (in vet′ər it) *adj.* [< L. pp. of *inveterare*, to age < *in-*, in + *vetus*, old] **1.** firmly established over a long period; deep-rooted **2.** settled in a habit, practice, prejudice, etc.; habitual —**in·vet′er·a·cy** *n.* —**in·vet′er·ate·ly** *adv.*

in·vid·i·ous (in vid′ē əs) *adj.* [< L. < *invidia*, ENVY] **1.** such as to excite ill will or envy; giving offense **2.** giving offense by discriminating unfairly *[invidious* comparisons*]* —**in·vid′i·ous·ly** *adv.* —**in·vid′i·ous·ness** *n.*

in·vig·or·ate (in vig′ə rāt′) *vt.* **-at′ed, -at′ing** [IN-[1] + VIGOR + -ATE[1]] to give vigor to; fill with energy; enliven —**in·vig′or·a′tion** *n.* —**in·vig′or·a′tive** *adj.* —**in·vig′or·a′tor** *n.*

in·vin·ci·ble (in vin′sə b'l) *adj.* [< MFr. < L.: see IN-[2] & VINCIBLE] that cannot be overcome; unconquerable —**in·vin′ci·bil′i·ty, in·vin′ci·ble·ness** *n.* —**in·vin′ci·bly** *adv.*

in·vi·o·la·ble (in vī′ə lə b'l) *adj.* **1.** not to be violated; not to be profaned or injured; sacred *[*an *inviolable* promise*]* **2.** that cannot be violated; indestructible —**in·vi′o·la·bil′i·ty** *n.* —**in·vi′o·la·bly** *adv.*

in·vi·o·late (in vī′ə lit, -lāt′) *adj.* not violated; kept sacred or unbroken —**in·vi′o·la·cy** (-lə sē), **in·vi′o·late·ness** *n.* —**in·vi′o·late·ly** *adv.*

in·vis·i·ble (in viz′ə b'l) *adj.* **1.** not visible; that cannot be seen **2.** out of sight **3.** imperceptible **4.** kept hidden *[invisible* assets*]* —*n.* an invisible thing or being —**the Invisible** **1.** God **2.** the unseen world —**in·vis′i·bil′i·ty, in·vis′i·ble·ness** *n.* —**in·vis′i·bly** *adv.*

in·vi·ta·tion (in′və tā′shən) *n.* **1.** an inviting to come somewhere or do something **2.** the message or note used in inviting

in·vi·ta·tion·al (-'l) *adj.* participated in only by those invited *[*an *invitational* art exhibit*]*

in·vite (in vīt′; *for n.* in′vīt) *vt.* **-vit′ed, -vit′ing** [< Fr. < L. *invitare*] **1.** to ask courteously to come somewhere or do something **2.** to make a request for *[*to *invite* questions*]* **3.** to give occasion for *[*action that *invites* scandal*]* **4.** to tempt; entice —*n.* ⌊Colloq.⌋ an invitation

in·vit·ing (-vīt′iŋ) *adj.* tempting; enticing

in·vo·ca·tion (in′və kā′shən) *n.* **1.** an invoking of God, the Muses, etc. for blessing, help, etc. **2.** a formal prayer used in invoking, as at the beginning of a church service **3.** *a)* a conjuring of evil spirits *b)* an incantation —**in′vo·ca′tion·al** *adj.* —**in·voc′a·to′ry** (-väk′ə tôr′ē) *adj.*

in·voice (in′vois) *n.* [prob. orig. pl. of ME. *envoie*, a message: see ENVOY[1]] **1.** an itemized list of goods shipped to a buyer, stating quantities, prices, shipping charges, etc. **2.** a shipment of invoiced goods —*vt.* **-voiced, -voic·ing** to present an invoice for or to

in·voke (in vōk′) *vt.* **-voked′, -vok′ing** [< MFr. < L. < *in-*, on + *vocare*, to call] **1.** to call on (God, the Muses, etc.) for blessing, help, etc. **2.** to put into use (a law, penalty, etc.) as pertinent **3.** to call forth; cause **4.** to summon (evil spirits) by incantation; conjure **5.** to ask solemnly for; implore —**in·vok′er** *n.*

in·vo·lu·cre (in′və lo͞o′kər) *n.* [Fr. < L. *involucrum*, wrapper < *involvere*, INVOLVE] *Bot.* a ring of bracts at the base of a flower, flower cluster, or fruit —**in′vo·lu′cral** (-krəl) *adj.*

in·vol·un·tar·y (in väl′ən ter′ē) *adj.* not voluntary; specif., *a)* not done of one's own free will *b)* unintentional; accidental *c)* not consciously controlled *[*sneezing is *involuntary]* —**in·vol′un·tar′i·ly** *adv.* —**in·vol′un·tar′i·ness** *n.*

in·vo·lute (in′və lo͞ot′) *adj.* [L. *involutus*, pp. of *involvere*, INVOLVE] **1.** intricate; involved **2.** rolled up or curled in a spiral; having the whorls wound closely *[involute* shells*]*

3. *Bot.* rolled inward at the edges *[involute* leaves*]* —*vi.* **-lut'ed, -lut'ing** to become involute or undergo involution
in·vo·lu·tion (in'və lo͞o'shən) ***n.*** **1.** an involving or being involved; entanglement **2.** something involved; complication; intricacy —**in'vo·lu'tion·al** ***adj.*** —**in'vo·lu'tion·ar'y** ***adj.***
in·volve (in välv') ***vt.*** **-volved', -volv'ing** [< L. < *in-*, in + *volvere*, to roll] **1.** orig., to enfold or envelop **2.** to make intricate or complicated **3.** to entangle in difficulty, danger, etc.; implicate **4.** to draw or hold within itself; include *[*a riot *involving* thousands*]* **5.** to include by necessity; entail; require *[*saving money *involves* thrift*]* **6.** to relate to or affect *[*his honor is *involved]* **7.** to make busy; occupy *[involved* in research*]* —**in·volve'ment** ***n.***
in·vul·ner·a·ble (in vul'nər ə b'l) ***adj.*** **1.** that cannot be wounded or injured **2.** proof against attack —**in·vul'ner·a·bil'i·ty** ***n.*** —**in·vul'ner·a·bly** ***adv.***
in·ward (in'wərd) ***adj.*** **1.** situated within; internal **2.** mental or spiritual **3.** directed toward the inside *[*the *inward* pull of a centrifuge*]* —***n.*** **1.** the inside **2.** *[pl.]* the entrails —***adv.*** **1.** toward the inside or center **2.** into the mind or spirit Also **in'wards** ***adv.***
in·ward·ly (-lē) ***adv.*** **1.** in or on the inside; internally **2.** in the mind or spirit **3.** toward the inside or center
in·ward·ness (-nis) ***n.*** **1.** the inner nature or meaning **2.** spirituality **3.** introspection
in·weave (in wēv') ***vt.*** **-wove', -wo'ven** or **-wove', -weav'ing** to weave in
in·wrap (in rap') ***vt.*** **-wrapped', -wrap'ping** *same as* ENWRAP
in·wrought (in rôt') ***adj.*** **1.** worked or woven into a fabric: said of a pattern, etc. **2.** closely blended with other things
I·o (ī'ō) *Gr. Myth.* a maiden loved by Zeus and changed into a heifer by Hera
Io *Chem.* ionium
i·o·dide (ī'ə dīd') ***n.*** a compound of iodine with another element or with a radical
i·o·dine (ī'ə dīn', -din; *Brit. & among chemists,* -dēn') ***n.*** [Fr. *iode* (< Gr. *iōdēs,* violetlike < *ion,* a violet + *eidos,* a form) + -INE[4]] **1.** a nonmetallic chemical element of the halogen family, consisting of grayish-black crystals that volatilize into a violet-colored vapor: used as an antiseptic, in photography, etc.: symbol, I; at. wt., 126.9044; at. no., 53: a radioactive isotope (**iodine 131**) is used in medical diagnosis and therapy **2.** tincture of iodine, used as an antiseptic
i·o·dize (ī'ə dīz') ***vt.*** **-dized', -diz'ing** to treat with iodine or an iodide
iodized salt common table salt to which a small amount of sodium iodide or potassium iodide has been added
i·o·do·form (ī ō'də fôrm') ***n.*** *[iodo-* (< Fr. *iode,* IODINE) + FORM(IC)] a yellowish, crystalline compound of iodine, CHI_3, used as an antiseptic in surgical dressings
i·on (ī'ən, -än) ***n.*** [< Gr. *iōn,* prp. of *ienai,* to go] an electrically charged atom or group of atoms, the electrical charge of which results when a neutral atom or group of atoms loses or gains one or more electrons: such loss (resulting in a CATION), or gain (resulting in an ANION), occurs during electrolysis, by the action of certain forms of radiant energy, etc. —**i·on·ic** (ī än'ik) ***adj.***
-ion [< Fr. < L. *-io* (gen. *-ionis*)] *a suffix meaning* the act, condition, or result of *[translation, correction]*
I·o·ni·a (ī ō'nē ə) ancient region along the W coast of Asia Minor, colonized by the Greeks in the 11th cent. B.C. —**I·o'ni·an** ***adj., n.***
Ionian Sea section of the Mediterranean, between Greece, Sicily, & the S Italian peninsula
I·on·ic (ī än'ik) ***adj.*** **1.** of Ionia or its people **2.** designating or of that one of the three orders of Greek architecture distinguished by ornamental scrolls on the capitals: cf. CORINTHIAN, DORIC

IONIC CAPITAL

i·o·ni·um (ī ō'nē əm) ***n.*** [ION + ModL. ending *-ium*] a radioactive isotope of thorium
i·on·ize (ī'ə nīz') ***vt., vi.*** **-ized', -iz'ing** to change or be changed into ions; dissociate into ions, as a salt dissolved in water, or become electrically charged, as a gas under radiation —**i'on·i·za'tion** ***n.*** —**i'on·iz'er** ***n.***
i·on·o·sphere (ī än'ə sfir') ***n.*** the outer part of the earth's atmosphere, with changing layers characterized by an appreciable electron and ion content —**i·on'o·spher'ic** ***adj.***
i·o·ta (ī ōt'ə) ***n.*** **1.** the ninth letter of the Greek alphabet (Ι, ι) **2.** a very small quantity; jot
IOU, I.O.U. (ī'ō'yo͞o') **1.** I owe you **2.** a signed note bearing these letters, acknowledging a debt
-ious (ē əs, yəs, əs) [see -OUS] *a suffix used to form adjectives corresponding to nouns that end in* -ION *[rebellious] or meaning* having, characterized by *[furious]*
I·o·wa (ī'ə wə; *occas.* -wā') [after an Indian tribe in the area, prob. < AmInd. *Ayuba,* lit., sleepy ones] Middle Western State of the U.S.: 56,290 sq. mi.; pop. 2,913,000; cap. Des Moines: abbrev. **Ia., IA** —**I'o·wan** ***adj., n.***
IPA International Phonetic Alphabet
ip·e·cac (ip'ə kak') ***n.*** [< Port. < Tupi] **1.** a tropical S. American plant of the madder family **2.** the dried roots of this plant **3.** an emetic made from the dried roots Also **ip·e·cac·u·an·ha** (ip'ə kak'yoo wan'ə)
Iph·i·ge·ni·a (if'ə jə nī'ə) *Gr. Myth.* a daughter of Agamemnon, offered by him as a sacrifice to Artemis
‡**ip·se dix·it** (ip'sē dik'sit) [L., he himself has said (it)] a dogmatic statement
ip·so fac·to (ip'sō fak'tō) [L.] by that very fact
IQ, I.Q. intelligence quotient
ir- *see* IN-[1] & IN-[2]
Ir *Chem.* iridium
IR, ir, i-r infrared
Ir. **1.** Ireland **2.** Irish
I·ra (ī'rə) [Heb. *'īrā,* lit., watchful] a masculine name
IRA, I.R.A. a retirement plan in which a worker may invest a limited amount of earnings, as in mutual funds, that is tax-free until retirement
I.R.A., IRA Irish Republican Army
I·ran (i ran', ī-; ē rän') country in SW Asia, between the Caspian Sea & the Persian Gulf: 636,000 sq. mi.; pop. 28,237,000; cap. Tehran
Iran. Iranian
I·ra·ni·an (i rā'nē ən, ī-) ***adj.*** of Iran, its people, their language, or culture —***n.*** **1.** one of the people of Iran; Persian **2.** a subbranch of the Indo-European family of languages, including Persian
I·raq (i räk', -rak'; ē-) country in SW Asia, at the head of the Persian Gulf: 171,599 sq. mi.; pop. 9,431,000; cap. Baghdad: also sp. **Irak**
I·ra·qi (i rä'kē, -rak'ē) ***n.*** **1.** *pl.* **-qis** a native or inhabitant of Iraq **2.** the Arabic dialect spoken in Iraq —***adj.*** of Iraq, its people, their language, or culture
i·ras·ci·ble (i ras'ə b'l, ī-) ***adj.*** [< MFr. < LL. < L. *irasci:* see ff.] easily angered; quick-tempered —**i·ras'ci·bil'i·ty, i·ras'ci·ble·ness** ***n.*** —**i·ras'ci·bly** ***adv.***
i·rate (ī rāt', ī'rāt) ***adj.*** [L. *iratus* < *irasci,* to be angry < *ira,* ire] angry; wrathful; incensed —**i·rate'ly** ***adv.*** —**i·rate'ness** ***n.***
IRBM intermediate range ballistic missile
ire (īr) ***n.*** [< OFr. < L. *ira*] anger; wrath —**ire'ful** ***adj.*** —**ire'ful·ly** ***adv.*** —**ire'ful·ness** ***n.***
Ire. Ireland
Ire·land (īr'lənd) **1.** island of the British Isles, west of Great Britain **2.** republic comprising the S provinces of this island & three counties of Ulster province: 27,136 sq. mi.; pop. 2,921,000; cap. Dublin Cf. NORTHERN IRELAND
I·rene (ī rēn') [< Fr. < L. < Gr. *Eirēnē,* lit., peace] a feminine name
ir·i·des·cent (ir'ə des''nt) ***adj.*** [< L. *iris* (< Gr. *iris*), rainbow + -ESCENT] having or showing shifting changes in color or an interplay of rainbowlike colors —**ir'i·des'cence** ***n.*** —**ir'i·des'cent·ly** ***adv.***
i·rid·i·um (i rid'ē əm, ī-) ***n.*** [ModL. < L. *iris* (< Gr. *iris*), rainbow: from the changing color of some of its salts] a white, heavy, brittle, metallic chemical element found in platinum ores: alloys of iridium are used for pen points and bearings of watches: symbol, Ir; at. wt., 192.2; at. no., 77
I·ris (ī'ris) [L. < Gr. *Iris:* see ff.] **1.** a feminine name **2.** *Gr. Myth.* the goddess of the rainbow and a messenger of the gods
i·ris (ī'ris) ***n., pl.*** **i'ris·es, ir·i·des** (ir'ə dēz', ī'rə-) [L. < Gr. *iris,* rainbow] **1.** a rainbow **2.** the round, pigmented membrane surrounding the pupil of the eye **3.** a plant with sword-shaped leaves and showy flowers composed of three petals and three drooping sepals **4.** the flower of this plant

IRIS

I·rish (ī'rish) ***adj.*** of Ireland, its people, their language, or culture —***n.*** **1.** *same as* IRISH GAELIC **2.** the English dialect of Ireland —**the Irish** the people of Ireland —**I'rish·man** ***n., pl.*** **-men** —**I'rish·wom'an** ***n.fem., pl.*** **-wom'en**
Irish bull *same as* BULL[3]
Irish Gaelic the Celtic language of Ireland
Irish potato the common white potato
Irish Sea arm of the Atlantic between Ireland & Great Britain
Irish setter any of a breed of setter with a coat of long, silky, reddish-brown hair
Irish stew a stew of meat, potatoes, onions, etc.
Irish terrier any of a breed of small, lean dog with a wiry, reddish coat
Irish wolfhound any of a breed of very large, heavy, powerful dog with a rough coat
irk (urk) ***vt.*** [ME. *irken,* to be weary of] to annoy, disgust, irritate, tire out, etc.

irk·some (-səm) ***adj.*** that tends to irk; tiresome or annoying —**irk′some·ly** ***adv.*** —**irk′some·ness** ***n.***

Ir·kutsk (ir ko͞otsk′) city in S Asiatic R.S.F.S.R., near Lake Baikal: pop. 428,000

Ir·ma (ʉr′mə) [G., orig. contr. of names beginning with *Irm-* < OHG. *Irmin*, name of a Gmc. god of war] a feminine name

i·ron (ī′ərn) ***n.*** see PLURAL, II, D, 3 [< OE. *iren, isern, isen* < Gmc.] **1.** a white, malleable, ductile, metallic chemical element: it is the most common and important of all metals: symbol, Fe; at. wt., 55.847; at. no., 26 **2.** any tool, device, etc. made of iron, as *a*) a device with a handle and flat undersurface, used, when heated, for pressing clothes or cloth *b*) a rodlike device with a brand at one end, heated for branding cattle: in full, **branding iron** **3.** [*pl.*] iron shackles or chains **4.** firm strength; power **5.** *Golf* any of a set of numbered clubs with metal heads **6.** a medicine containing iron —***adj.*** **1.** of or consisting of iron **2.** like iron, as *a*) firm [*an iron will*] *b*) strong **3.** cruel; merciless —***vt.*** **1.** to furnish or cover with iron **2.** to press (clothes or cloth) with a hot iron —***vi.*** to iron clothes or cloth —**have many** (or **several,** etc.) **irons in the fire** to be engaged in many (or several, etc.) activities —**iron out** to smooth out; eliminate —**strike while the iron is hot** to act at the opportune time

Iron Age a phase of human culture (in Europe, c. 1000 B.C.–100 A.D.) characterized by the introduction and development of iron tools and weapons

i·ron·bound (-bound′) ***adj.*** **1.** bound with iron **2.** hard; rigid; unyielding; inflexible **3.** edged with rocks or cliffs, as a coast

i·ron·clad (-klad′) ***adj.*** **1.** covered or protected with iron **2.** difficult to change or break [*an ironclad lease*] —***n.*** formerly, a warship armored with thick iron plates

iron curtain **1.** a barrier of secrecy and censorship regarded as isolating the Soviet Union and other countries in its sphere **2.** any similar barrier

iron hand firm, rigorous, severe control —**i′ron·hand′ed** ***adj.***

i·ron·i·cal (ī rän′i k′l) ***adj.*** [< L. < Gr. < *eirōneia* (see IRONY) + -AL] **1.** meaning the contrary of what is expressed **2.** using or tending to use irony **3.** directly opposite to what might be expected Also **i·ron′ic** —**i·ron′i·cal·ly** ***adv.***

ironing board (or **table**) a cloth-covered board or stand on which clothes are ironed

iron lung a large metal respirator enclosing all of the body but the head, used for maintaining artificial respiration

i·ron·mon·ger (ī′ərn muŋ′gər, -mäŋ′-) ***n.*** [Brit.] a dealer in hardware —**i′ron·mon′ger·y** ***n.***

iron pyrites *same as* PYRITE

I·ron·sides (-sīdz′) **1.** *nickname of* Oliver CROMWELL **2.** *a*) his regiment *b*) his whole army —***n.pl.*** [i-] [*with sing. v.*] *same as* IRONCLAD

i·ron·stone (-stōn′) ***n.*** a hard variety of white ceramic ware

i·ron·ware (-wer′) ***n.*** things made of iron

i·ron·weed (-wēd′) ***n.*** a plant of the composite family, with clusters of tubular, purple flowers

i·ron·wood (-wood′) ***n.*** **1.** any of various trees with extremely hard wood **2.** the wood

i·ron·work (-wʉrk′) ***n.*** articles or parts made of iron —**i′ron·work′er** ***n.***

i·ron·works (-wʉrks′) ***n.pl.*** [*often with sing. v.*] a place where iron is smelted or heavy iron goods are made

i·ro·ny (ī′rən ē, ī′ər nē) ***n., pl.*** **-nies** [< Fr. < L. < Gr. *eirōneia* < *eirōn*, dissembler in speech < *eirein*, to speak] **1.** expression in which the intended meaning of the words is the direct opposite of their usual sense [*the irony of calling a stupid plan "clever"*] **2.** a set of circumstances or a result that is the opposite of what might be expected [*an irony that the firehouse burned*]

Ir·o·quoi·an (ir′ə kwoi′ən) ***adj.*** of an important linguistic family of N. American Indians, including speakers of Huron, Cherokee, Mohawk, etc. —***n.*** **1.** a member of an Iroquoian tribe **2.** the Iroquoian languages collectively

Ir·o·quois (ir′ə kwoi′) ***n.*** [Fr. < Algonquian *Irinakoiw*, lit., real adders] **1.** *pl.* **-quois′** (-kwoi′, -kwoiz′) a member of a confederation of Iroquoian Indian tribes that lived in W and N New York and in adjacent Canada: see FIVE NATIONS **2.** the Iroquoian language family —***adj.*** of the Iroquois

ir·ra·di·ate (i rā′dē āt′; *for adj., usually* -it) ***vt.*** **-at′ed, -at′ing** [< L. pp. of *irradiare*: see IN-[1] & RADIATE] **1.** to shine upon; light up; make bright **2.** to enlighten **3.** to radiate; diffuse **4.** to expose to or treat by exposing to X-rays, ultraviolet rays, etc. —***vi.*** to emit rays; shine —***adj.*** irradiated —**ir·ra′di·ance, ir·ra′di·an·cy** ***n.*** —**ir·ra′di·ant** ***adj.*** —**ir·ra′di·a′tion** ***n.*** —**ir·ra′di·a′tive** ***adj.*** —**ir·ra′di·a′tor** ***n.***

ir·ra·tion·al (i rash′ən ′l) ***adj.*** **1.** lacking the power to reason **2.** senseless; unreasonable; absurd **3.** *Math.* designating a real number not expressible as an integer or a quotient of two integers —**ir·ra′tion·al′i·ty** (-ə nal′ə tē) ***n., pl.*** **-ties** —**ir·ra′tion·al·ly** ***adv.***

Ir·ra·wad·dy (ir′ə wä′dē, -wô′-) river flowing from N Burma south into the Indian Ocean

ir·re·claim·a·ble (ir′i klā′mə b′l) ***adj.*** that cannot be reclaimed —**ir′re·claim′a·bil′i·ty** ***n.*** —**ir′re·claim′a·bly** ***adv.***

ir·rec·on·cil·a·ble (i rek′ən sīl′ə b′l, i rek′ən sīl′-) ***adj.*** that cannot be reconciled; that cannot be brought into agreement; incompatible —***n.*** one who is irreconcilable and refuses to compromise —**ir·rec′on·cil′a·bil′i·ty** ***n.*** —**ir·rec′on·cil′a·bly** ***adv.***

ir·re·cov·er·a·ble (ir′i kuv′ər ə b′l) ***adj.*** that cannot be recovered, rectified, or remedied; irretrievable —**ir′re·cov′er·a·bly** ***adv.***

ir·re·deem·a·ble (ir′i dēm′ə b′l) ***adj.*** **1.** that cannot be bought back **2.** that cannot be converted into coin, as certain kinds of paper money **3.** that cannot be changed or reformed —**ir′re·deem′a·bly** ***adv.***

ir·re·den·tist (ir′i den′tist) ***n.*** [< It. < (*Italia*) *irredenta*, unredeemed (Italy)] a person who advocates a policy of recovering territory formerly a part of his country; specif., [*usually* **I-**] a member of an Italian political party, after 1878, with such a policy —**ir′re·den′tism** ***n.***

ir·re·duc·i·ble (ir′i do͞os′ə b′l, -dyo͞os′-) ***adj.*** that cannot be reduced —**ir′re·duc′i·bil′i·ty** ***n.*** —**ir′re·duc′i·bly** ***adv.***

ir·ref·ra·ga·ble (i ref′rə gə b′l) ***adj.*** [< LL. < L. *in-*, IN-[2] + *refragari*, to oppose] that cannot be refuted; indisputable —**ir·ref′ra·ga·bil′i·ty** ***n.*** —**ir·ref′ra·ga·bly** ***adv.***

ir·ref·u·ta·ble (i ref′yoo tə b′l, ir′i fyo͞ot′ə b′l) ***adj.*** that cannot be refuted or disproved —**ir·ref′u·ta·bil′i·ty** ***n.*** —**ir·ref′u·ta·bly** ***adv.***

irreg. **1.** irregular **2.** irregularly

ir·re·gard·less (ir′i gärd′lis) ***adj., adv.*** *a substandard or humorous redundancy for* REGARDLESS

ir·reg·u·lar (i reg′yə lər) ***adj.*** **1.** not conforming to established rule, method, usage, standard, etc.; out of the ordinary **2.** immoral; lawless; disorderly **3.** not straight or even; not symmetrical; not uniform in shape, design, etc. **4.** uneven in occurrence; variable **5.** having minor flaws: said of merchandise **6.** *Gram.* not inflected in the usual way [*go is an irregular verb*] **7.** *Mil.* not belonging to the regularly established army —***n.*** a person or thing that is irregular —**ir·reg′u·lar′i·ty** ***n., pl.*** **-ties** —**ir·reg′u·lar·ly** ***adv.***

ir·rel·e·vant (i rel′ə vənt) ***adj.*** not relevant; not pertinent; not to the point —**ir·rel′e·vance, ir·rel′e·van·cy** ***n., pl.*** **-cies** —**ir·rel′e·vant·ly** ***adv.***

ir·re·li·gious (ir′i lij′əs) ***adj.*** **1.** not religious **2.** indifferent or hostile to religion **3.** profane; impious —**ir′re·li′gion** ***n.*** —**ir′re·li′gion·ist** ***n.*** —**ir′re·li′gious·ly** ***adv.***

ir·re·me·di·a·ble (ir′i mē′dē ə b′l) ***adj.*** that cannot be remedied; incurable —**ir′re·me′di·a·ble·ness** ***n.*** —**ir′re·me′di·a·bly** ***adv.***

ir·re·mis·si·ble (-mis′ə b′l) ***adj.*** not remissible; specif., *a*) that cannot be excused or pardoned *b*) that cannot be shirked —**ir′re·mis′si·bly** ***adv.***

ir·re·mov·a·ble (-mo͞o′və b′l) ***adj.*** not removable —**ir′re·mov′a·bil′i·ty** ***n.*** —**ir′re·mov′a·bly** ***adv.***

ir·rep·a·ra·ble (i rep′ər ə b′l) ***adj.*** not reparable; that cannot be repaired, mended, remedied, etc. —**ir·rep′a·ra·bil′i·ty** ***n.*** —**ir·rep′a·ra·bly** ***adv.***

ir·re·place·a·ble (ir′i plās′ə b′l) ***adj.*** not replaceable

ir·re·press·i·ble (-pres′ə b′l) ***adj.*** that cannot be repressed or restrained —**ir′re·press′i·bil′i·ty** ***n.*** —**ir′re·press′i·bly** ***adv.***

ir·re·proach·a·ble (-prō′chə b′l) ***adj.*** blameless; faultless —**ir′re·proach′a·bil′i·ty, ir′re·proach′a·ble·ness** ***n.*** —**ir′re·proach′a·bly** ***adv.***

ir·re·sist·i·ble (-zis′tə b′l) ***adj.*** that cannot be resisted; too strong, fascinating, etc. to be withstood —**ir′re·sist′i·bil′i·ty, ir′re·sist′i·ble·ness** ***n.*** —**ir′re·sist′i·bly** ***adv.***

ir·res·o·lute (i rez′ə lo͞ot′) ***adj.*** not resolute; wavering in decision or purpose —**ir·res′o·lute′ly** ***adv.*** —**ir·res′o·lute′ness** ***n.*** —**ir·res′o·lu′tion** ***n.***

ir·re·spec·tive (ir′i spek′tiv) ***adj.*** [Rare] showing disregard for persons or consequences —**irrespective of** regardless of —**ir′re·spec′tive·ly** ***adv.***

ir·re·spon·si·ble (ir′i spän′sə b′l) ***adj.*** not responsible; specif., *a*) not accountable for actions *b*) showing the lack of a sense of responsibility —***n.*** an irresponsible person —**ir′re·spon′si·bil′i·ty, ir′re·spon′si·ble·ness** ***n.*** —**ir′re·spon′si·bly** ***adv.***

ir·re·spon·sive (-siv) ***adj.*** not responsive —**ir′re·spon′sive·ness** ***n.***

ir·re·triev·a·ble (-trēv′ə b'l) *adj.* that cannot be retrieved, recovered, restored, or recalled —**ir′re·triev′a·bil′i·ty** *n.* —**ir′re·triev′a·bly** *adv.*
ir·rev·er·ence (i rev′ər əns) *n.* **1.** lack of reverence **2.** an act or statement showing this —**ir·rev′er·ent** *adj.* —**ir·rev′er·ent·ly** *adv.*
ir·re·vers·i·ble (ir′i vur′sə b'l) *adj.* not reversible; specif., *a)* that cannot be repealed or annulled *b)* that cannot be run backward, etc. —**ir′re·vers′i·bil′i·ty** *n.* —**ir′re·vers′i·bly** *adv.*
ir·rev·o·ca·ble (i rev′ə kə b'l) *adj.* that cannot be revoked or undone —**ir·rev′o·ca·bil′i·ty, ir·rev′o·ca·ble·ness** *n.* —**ir·rev′o·ca·bly** *adv.*
ir·ri·ga·ble (ir′i gə b'l) *adj.* that can be irrigated
ir·ri·gate (ir′ə gāt′) *vt.* **-gat′ed, -gat′ing** [< L. pp. of *irrigare* < *in-,* in + *rigare,* to water] **1.** to supply (land) with water by means of artificial ditches, etc. **2.** *Med.* to wash out (a cavity, wound, etc.) with water or other fluid —**ir′ri·ga′tion** *n.* —**ir′ri·ga′tive** *adj.* —**ir′ri·ga′tor** *n.*
ir·ri·ta·ble (ir′i tə b'l) *adj.* **1.** easily annoyed or provoked; impatient **2.** *Med.* excessively or pathologically sensitive to a stimulus **3.** *Physiol.* able to respond to a stimulus —**ir′ri·ta·bil′i·ty, ir′ri·ta·ble·ness** *n.* —**ir′ri·ta·bly** *adv.*
ir·ri·tant (-tənt) *adj.* causing irritation —*n.* something causing irritation —**ir′ri·tan·cy** *n.*
ir·ri·tate (-tāt′) *vt.* **-tat′ed, -tat′ing** [< L. pp. of *irritare,* to excite] **1.** to provoke to impatience or anger; annoy **2.** to make (a part of the body) inflamed or sore **3.** *Physiol.* to excite (an organ, muscle, etc.) to a characteristic action by a stimulus —**ir′ri·ta′tive** *adj.*
ir·ri·ta·tion (ir′ə tā′shən) *n.* **1.** an irritating or being irritated **2.** something that irritates **3.** *Med.* an excessive response to stimulation in an organ or part; specif., a sore or inflamed condition
ir·rupt (i rupt′) *vi.* [< L. pp. of *irrumpere* < *in-,* in + *rumpere,* to break] **1.** to burst violently (*into*) **2.** *Ecol.* to increase abruptly in size of population —**ir·rup′tion** *n.* —**ir·rup′tive** *adj.*
IRS, I.R.S. Internal Revenue Service
Ir·tysh (ir tish′) river in C Asia, flowing from NW China northwestward into the Ob River
Ir·ving[1] (ur′viŋ) [north Brit. surname, prob. orig. a place name] **1.** a masculine name **2. Washington,** 1783–1859; U.S. writer
Ir·ving[2] (ur′viŋ) [prob. an arbitrary selection] city in NE Tex.: suburb of Dallas: pop. 110,000
Ir·win (ur′win) [var. of ERWIN] a masculine name
is (iz) [OE.] *3d pers. sing., pres. indic., of* BE
is. 1. island(s) **2.** isle(s)
Isa., Is. Isaiah
I·saac (ī′zək) [< LL. < Gr. < Heb. *yitshāq,* lit., laughter] **1.** a masculine name **2.** *Bible* one of the patriarchs, son of Abraham and Sarah, and father of Jacob and Esau: Gen. 21:3
Is·a·bel (iz′ə bel′) [Sp., prob. altered < *Elizabeth*] a feminine name: var. *Isabelle, Isabella*
Is·a·bel·la (iz′ə bel′ə) [It.] **1.** a feminine name **2. Isabella I** 1451–1504; wife of Ferdinand V & queen of Castile (1474–1504): gave help to Columbus in his expedition
Is·a·dor·a (iz′ə dôr′ə) [fem. of ISIDORE] a feminine name
i·sa·go·ge (ī′sə gō′jē) *n.* [L. < Gr., ult. < *eis-,* into + *agein,* to lead] an introduction, as to a branch of study —**i′sa·gog′ic** (-gäj′ik) *adj.*
I·sa·iah (ī zā′ə; *chiefly Brit.* -zī′-) [< LL. < Gr. < Heb. *yĕsha 'yah,* lit., God is salvation] **1.** a masculine name **2.** *Bible a)* a Hebrew prophet of the 8th cent. B.C. *b)* the book containing his teachings Also, in the Douay Bible, **I·sa′ias** (-əs)
Is·car·i·ot (is ker′ē ət) *see* JUDAS
is·che·mi·a (is kē′mē ə) *n.* [ModL. < Gr. < *ischein,* to hold + *haima,* blood] a lack of blood supply in an organ or tissue —**is·che′mic** *adj.*
is·chi·um (is′kē əm) *n., pl.* **-chi·a** (-ə) [L. < Gr. *ischion,* hip] the lowermost of the three sections of the hipbone
-ise (īz) *chiefly Brit. var. of* -IZE
I·seult (i sōōlt′) [Fr.] *same as* ISOLDE
-ish (ish) **1.** [OE. *-isc*] *a suffix meaning: a)* of or belonging to (a specified people) *[Spanish] b)* like or characteristic of *[devilish] c)* tending to, verging on *[bookish, knavish] d)* somewhat, rather *[tallish] e)* [Colloq.] approximately, about *[thirtyish]* **2.** [< OFr.] *a suffix found in verbs of French origin [finish]*
Ish·ma·el (ish′mē əl, -mā-) [< LL. < Heb. *yishmā'ēl,* lit., God hears] *Bible* the son of Abraham and Hagar: he and his mother were made outcasts: Gen. 21:9–21 —*n.* an outcast
Ish·ma·el·ite (-ə līt′) *n.* **1.** a descendant of Ishmael, the traditional progenitor of Arab peoples **2.** an outcast —**Ish′ma·el·it′ish** *adj.*
Ish·tar (ish′tär) the Babylonian and Assyrian goddess of love and fertility
Is·i·dore, Is·i·dor (iz′ə dôr′) [ult. < Gr. *Isidōros,* lit., gift of Isis] a masculine name: var. *Isadore, Isador*
i·sin·glass (ī′z'n glas′, -ziŋ-) *n.* [prob. < MDu. < *huizen,* sturgeon + *blas,* bladder] **1.** a form of gelatin prepared from fish bladders, used as a clarifying agent and adhesive **2.** mica, esp. in thin sheets
I·sis (ī′sis) the Egyptian goddess of fertility, sister and wife of Osiris
isl. *pl.* **isls. 1.** island **2.** isle
Is·lam (is′läm, iz′-; -ləm, -lam; is läm′) *n.* [Ar. *islām,* lit., submission (to God's will)] **1.** the Moslem religion, a monotheistic religion in which the supreme deity is Allah and the founder and chief prophet is Mohammed **2.** Moslems collectively **3.** all the lands in which the Moslem religion predominates —**Is·lam′ic** (-lam′-, -läm′-), **Is′lam·it′ic** (-lə mit′ik) *adj.* —**Is′lam·ism** *n.* —**Is′lam·ite′** (-lə mīt′) *n.*
Is·lam·a·bad (is läm′ə bäd′) capital of Pakistan, in the NE part, near Rawalpindi: pop. 50,000
Is·lam·ize (is′lə mīz′, iz′-) *vt., vi.* **-ized′, -iz′ing** to subject or adapt to Islam —**Is′lam·i·za′tion** *n.*
is·land (ī′lənd) *n.* [< ME. *iland* (respelled after unrelated ISLE) < OE. *igland,* lit., island land & *ealand,* lit., water land] **1.** a land mass not as large as a continent, surrounded by water **2.** anything like an island in position or isolation **3.** *Anat.* a cluster of cells differing from surrounding tissue in formation, etc. —*vt.* **1.** to make into or like an island **2.** to intersperse as with islands
is·land·er (-ər) *n.* a native or inhabitant of an island
isle (īl) *n.* [< OFr. < ML. < L. *insula*] an island, esp. a small one —*vt.* **isled, isl′ing** *same as* ISLAND —*vi.* to live on an isle
is·let (ī′lit) *n.* a very small island
islets (or **islands**) **of Lang·er·hans** (läŋ′ər häns′) [after P. *Langerhans* (1847–88), G. histologist] irregular groups of endocrine cells in the pancreas: they produce insulin
ism (iz'm) *n.* a doctrine, theory, system, etc., esp. one whose name ends in *-ism*
-ism (iz'm; iz əm) [< OFr. & < L. *-isma* (< Gr. *-isma*) & *-ismus* (< Gr. *-ismos*)] *a suffix meaning:* **1.** the act, practice, or result of *[terrorism]* **2.** the condition of being *[pauperism]* **3.** conduct or qualities characteristic of *[patriotism]* **4.** the doctrine, school, or theory of *[socialism]* **5.** devotion to *[nationalism]* **6.** an instance, example, or peculiarity of *[witticism]* **7.** an abnormal condition caused by *[alcoholism]*
is·n't (iz′'nt) is not
i·so- [< Gr. *isos,* equal] *a combining form meaning* equal, similar, alike, identical: also **is-**
i·so·bar (ī′sə bär′) *n.* [< prec. + Gr. *baros,* weight] **1.** a line on a map connecting points on the earth's surface having equal barometric pressure **2.** any of two or more forms of an atom having the same atomic weight but different atomic numbers —**i′so·bar′ic** (-bar′ik) *adj.*

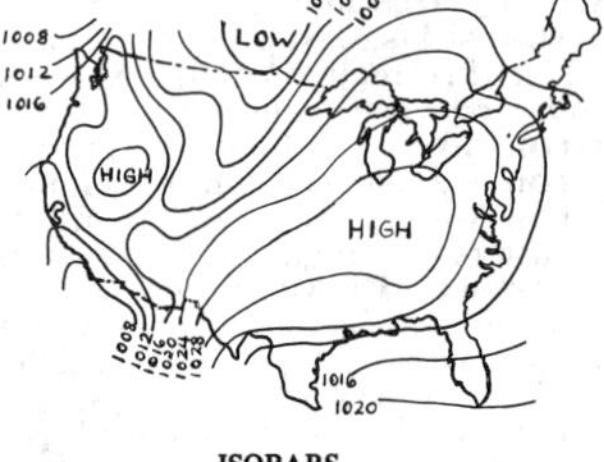

ISOBARS

i·soch·ro·nal (ī säk′rə n'l) *adj.* [< ModL. < Gr. < *isos,* equal + *chronos,* time + -AL] **1.** equal in length of time **2.** occurring at equal intervals of time Also **i·soch′ro·nous** —**i·soch′ro·nism** *n.*
i·so·cline (ī′sə klīn′) *n.* [< ISO- + Gr. *klinein,* to slope] an anticline or syncline so compressed that the strata on both sides of the axis dip with equal inclination in the same direction —**i′so·cli′nal, i′so·clin′ic** (-klin′ik) *adj.* —**i′so·cli′nal·ly** *adv.*
i·so·gon·ic (ī′sə gän′ik) *adj.* [ISO- + -GON + -IC] **1.** of or having equal angles **2.** connecting or showing points on the earth's surface having the same magnetic declination —*n.* an isogonic line
i·so·late (ī′sə lāt′, is′ə-; *for n., usually* -lit) *vt.* **-lat′ed, -lat′ing** [back-formation < *isolated* < It. < *isola* (< L. *insula*), island] **1.** to set apart from others; place alone **2.** *Chem.* to separate (an element or compound) in pure form from another compound or mixture **3.** *Med.* to place (a patient with a contagious disease) apart from others to prevent the spread of infection —*n.* a person or group that is set apart —**i′so·la·ble** (-lə b'l) *adj.* —**i′so·la′tion** *n.* —**i′so·la′tor** *n.*
i·so·la·tion·ist (ī′sə lā′shən ist, is′ə-) *n.* a person who advocates isolation; specif., one who opposes the involvement of his country in international agreements, etc. —*adj.* of isolationists or their policy —**i′so·la′tion·ism** *n.*
I·sol·de (i sōl′də, i sōld′) *see* TRISTRAM
i·so·mer (ī′sə mər) *n.* [< Gr. < *isos,* equal + *meros,* a part] **1.** any of two or more chemical compounds with the

same elements in the same proportion by weight but differing in properties because of differences in the structure of their molecules **2.** *Physics* any of two or more nuclei possessing the same number of neutrons and protons, but having different radioactive properties —**i′so·mer′ic** (-mer′ik) ***adj.*** —**i·som·er·ism** (ī säm′ər iz'm) ***n.***

i·som·er·ous (ī säm′ər əs) ***adj.*** [see ISOMER] *Bot.* having the same number of parts in each whorl

i·so·met·ric (ī′sə met′rik) ***adj.*** [< Gr. < *isos*, equal + *metron*, a measure + -IC] **1.** of or having equality of measure: also **i′so·met′ri·cal** **2.** of isometrics —***n.*** [*pl.*] a method of physical exercise in which one set of muscles is briefly tensed in opposition to another set of muscles or to an immovable object —**i′so·met′ri·cal·ly** ***adv.***

i·so·mor·phic (-môr′fik) ***adj.*** [ISO- + -MORPHIC] having similar or identical structure or form: also **i′so·mor′phous** (-fəs) —**i′so·mor′phism** ***n.***

i·so·prene (ī′sə prēn′) ***n.*** [< ISO- + PR(OPYL) + -ENE] a colorless, volatile liquid, C_5H_8, used in making synthetic rubber, resins, etc.

i·sos·ce·les (ī säs′ə lēz′) ***adj.*** [LL. < Gr. *isoskelēs* < *isos*, equal + *skelos*, a leg] designating a triangle with two equal sides

i·so·therm (ī′sə thurm′) ***n.*** [< Fr. < *iso-*, ISO- + Gr. *thermē*, heat] a line on a map connecting points on the earth's surface having the same mean temperature or the same temperature at a given time

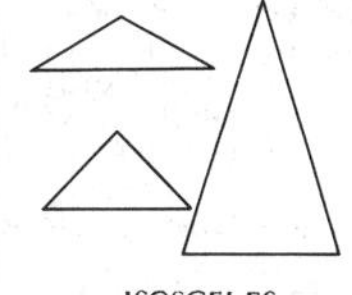

ISOSCELES TRIANGLES

i·so·ther·mal (ī′sə thur′m'l) ***adj.*** **1.** of or indicating equality or constancy of temperature **2.** of isotherms —***n.*** *same as* ISOTHERM —**i′so·ther′mal·ly** ***adv.***

i·so·ton·ic (-tän′ik) ***adj.*** [< Gr. < *isos*, equal + *tonos*, a stretching + -IC] **1.** having equal tension **2.** designating or of a salt solution having the same osmotic pressure as blood —**i′so·ton′i·cal·ly** ***adv.*** —**i′so·to·nic′i·ty** (-tō nis′ə tē) ***n.***

i·so·tope (ī′sə tōp′) ***n.*** [< ISO- + Gr. *topos*, place] any of two or more forms of an element having the same or very closely related chemical properties and the same atomic number but different atomic weights [*uranium isotopes* U 235, U 238, U 239] —**i′so·top′ic** (-täp′ik, -tō′pik) ***adj.***

i·so·trop·ic (ī′sə träp′ik, -trō′pik) ***adj.*** [ISO- + -TROPIC] having physical properties, as conductivity, elasticity, etc., that are the same regardless of the direction of measurement: also **i·sot·ro·pous** (ī sät′rə pəs) —**i·sot′ro·py** (-pē) ***n.***

Is·ra·el (iz′rē əl, -rā-) [< OFr. < LL. < Gr. < Heb. *yisrā'ēl*, lit., contender with God] **1.** a masculine name **2.** *Bible* Jacob: so named after wrestling with the angel: Gen. 32:28 **3.** the Jewish people, as descendants of Jacob **4.** ancient land of the Hebrews, at the SE end of the Mediterranean **5.** kingdom in the N part of this region **6.** country between the Mediterranean Sea & the country of Jordan: a Jewish state: 7,992 sq. mi.; pop. 2,899,000; cap. Jerusalem

Is·rae·li (iz rā′lē) ***adj.*** of modern Israel or its people —***n.***, *pl.* **-lis, -li** a native or inhabitant of modern Israel

Is·ra·el·ite (iz′rē ə līt′, -rā-) ***n.*** any of the people of ancient Israel or their descendants; Jew; Hebrew —***adj.*** of ancient Israel or the Israelites; Jewish: also **Is′ra·el·it′ish** (-līt′ish), **Is′ra·el·it′ic** (-lit′ik)

is·sei (ē′sā) ***n.***, *pl.* **-sei, -seis** [Jap., lit., 1st generation] [*also* **I-**] a Japanese who emigrated to the U.S. between 1907 and 1952

is·su·ance (ish′oo wəns) ***n.*** an issuing; issue

is·sue (ish′ōō; *chiefly Brit.* is′yōō) ***n.*** [< OFr. pp. of *isser*, to go out < L. *exire* < *ex-*, out + *ire*, to go] **1.** an outgoing; outflow **2.** a place or means of going out; exit; outlet **3.** a result; consequence **4.** offspring; a child or children **5.** profits, as from property; proceeds **6.** a point or matter under dispute **7.** a sending or giving out **8.** all that is put forth and circulated at one time [*the May issue of a magazine, an issue of bonds*] **9.** *Med.* a discharge of blood, pus, etc. —***vi.*** **-sued, -su·ing** **1.** to go, pass, or flow out; emerge **2.** to be descended; be born **3.** to be derived or result (*from* a cause) **4.** to end or result (*in* an effect) **5.** to come as revenue **6.** to be published; be put forth and circulated —***vt.*** **1.** to let out; discharge **2.** to give or deal out [*to issue supplies*] **3.** to publish; put forth publicly or officially [*to issue bonds, periodicals, an edict, etc.*] —**at** (or **in**) **issue** in dispute; still to be decided —**join issue** to meet in conflict, argument, etc. —**take issue** to disagree —**is′su·a·ble** ***adj.*** —**is′su·er** ***n.***

-ist (ist, əst) [< OFr. < L. < Gr. *-istēs*] *a suffix meaning:* **1.** a person who does, makes, or practices [*moralist, satirist*] **2.** a person skilled in or occupied with [*druggist, violinist*] **3.** an adherent of [*anarchist*]

Is·tan·bul (is′tan bool′, -tän-; -bōōl′; *Turk.* is täm′bōōl) seaport in NW Turkey, on the Bosporus: pop. 1,751,000 (met. area 2,150,000)

isth·mi·an (is′mē ən) ***adj.*** **1.** of an isthmus **2.** [**I-**] *a)* of the Isthmus of Panama *b)* of the Isthmus of Corinth —***n.*** a native or inhabitant of an isthmus

isth·mus (is′məs) ***n.***, *pl.* **-mus·es, -mi** (-mī) [L. < Gr. *isthmos*, a neck] a narrow strip of land having water at each side and connecting two larger bodies of land

-is·tic (is′tik) [< MFr. < L. < Gr. *-istikos*, or in Eng. < -IST + -IC] *a suffix used to form adjectives from nouns ending in* -ISM *and* -IST [*realistic, artistic*]: also **-is′ti·cal**

is·tle (ist′lē) ***n.*** [< AmSp. < Nahuatl *ichtli*] a fiber obtained from certain tropical American plants, used for baskets, etc.

it (it) ***pron.*** *for pl. see* THEY [OE. *hit*] the animal or thing under discussion *It* is used as: *a)* the subject of an impersonal verb [*it is snowing*] *b)* the grammatical subject of a clause of which the actual subject is a following clause, etc. [*it is settled that he will go*] *c)* an object of indefinite sense [*to lord it over someone*] *d)* the antecedent to a relative pronoun from which it is separated by a predicate [*it is your car that I want*] *e)* a reference to something indefinite but understood [*it's all right, no harm was done*] *f)* [Colloq.] an emphatic predicate pronoun referring to the person, thing, situation, etc. which is considered ultimate, final, or perfect [*zero hour is here; this is it*] —***n.*** the player, as in the game of tag, who must do some specific thing —**with it** [Slang] alert, informed, or hip

It., Ital. **1.** Italian **2.** Italic **3.** Italy

ital. italic (type)

‡**I·tal·ia** (ē täl′yä) *It. name of* ITALY

I·tal·ian (i tal′yən) ***adj.*** of Italy, its people, their language, etc. —***n.*** **1.** a native or inhabitant of Italy **2.** the Romance language of the Italians

I·tal·ic (i tal′ik) ***adj.*** **1.** of ancient Italy, its people, etc. **2.** designating or of the subfamily of the Indo-European languages that includes Latin and the Romance languages —***n.*** the Italic languages collectively

i·tal·ic (i tal′ik, ī-) ***adj.*** [< its first use in an *Italian* edition of Virgil] designating or of a type in which the characters slant upward to the right, used variously, as to emphasize words [*this is italic type*] —***n.*** [*usually pl., sometimes with sing. v.*] italic type or print

i·tal·i·cize (i tal′ə sīz′) ***vt.*** **-cized′, -ciz′ing** **1.** to print in italics **2.** to underscore (copy) to indicate it is to be printed in italics —**i·tal′i·ci·za′tion** ***n.***

It·a·ly (it′'l ē) country in S Europe, mostly on a peninsula & including Sicily & Sardinia: 116,304 sq. mi.; pop. 54,388,000; cap. Rome

itch (ich) ***vi.*** [OE. *giccan*] **1.** to feel an irritating sensation on the skin, with the desire to scratch **2.** to have a restless desire —***vt.*** **1.** to make itch **2.** to irritate or annoy —***n.*** **1.** an itching on the skin **2.** a restless desire; hankering [*an itch to travel*] —**the itch** any of various skin disorders accompanied by severe irritation of the skin; specif., SCABIES

itch·y (-ē) ***adj.*** **itch′i·er, itch′i·est** like, feeling, or causing an itch —**itch′i·ly** ***adv.*** —**itch′i·ness** ***n.***

-ite (īt) [< OFr. or L. < Gr. *-itēs*] *a suffix meaning:* **1.** a native or inhabitant of [*Brooklynite*] **2.** a descendant from [*Israelite*] **3.** an adherent or member of [*laborite*] **4.** a commercially manufactured product [*dynamite*] **5.** a fossil [*trilobite*] **6.** a salt or ester of an acid whose name ends in *-ous* [*nitrite*] **7.** a (specified) mineral or rock [*anthracite*]

i·tem (īt′əm) ***adv.*** [< L. < *ita*, so, thus] also: used before each article in a series being enumerated —***n.*** **1.** an article; unit; separate thing **2.** a bit of news or information

i·tem·ize (-īz′) ***vt.*** **-ized′, -iz′ing** to specify the items of; set down by items [*itemize the bill*] —**i′tem·i·za′tion** ***n.***

it·er·ate (it′ə rāt′) ***vt.*** **-at′ed, -at′ing** [< L. pp. of *iterare* < *iterum*, again] to utter or do again or repeatedly —**it′er·ant** (-ər ənt) ***adj.*** —**it′er·a′tion** ***n.*** —**it′er·a′tive** ***adj.***

Ith·a·ca (ith′ə kə) Gr. island off the W coast of Greece: legendary home of Odysseus

i·tin·er·an·cy (ī tin′ər ən sē, i-) ***n.*** **1.** an itinerating or being itinerant **2.** official work requiring constant travel from place to place or frequent change of residence Also **i·tin′er·a·cy** (-ə sē)

i·tin·er·ant (-ənt) ***adj.*** [< LL. prp. of *itinerari*, to travel < L. *iter*, a walk] traveling from place to place or on a circuit —***n.*** a person who travels from place to place —**i·tin′er·ant·ly** ***adv.***

i·tin·er·ar·y (ī tin′ə rer′ē, i-) ***adj.*** [see prec.] of traveling, journeys, routes, or roads —***n.***, *pl.* **-ar′ies** **1.** a route

fat, āpe, cär; ten, ēven; is, bīte; gō, hôrn, tōōl, look; oil, out; up, fur; get; joy; yet; chin; she; thin, *th*en; zh, leisure; ŋ, ring; ə for *a* in *ago*, *e* in *agent*, *i* in *sanity*, *o* in *comply*, *u* in *focus*; ' as in *able* (ā′b'l); Fr. bál; ë, Fr. coeur; ö, Fr. feu; Fr. mo*n*; ô, Fr. coq; ü, Fr. duc; *r*, Fr. cri; H, G. ich; kh, G. doch; ‡foreign; *hypothetical; < derived from. See inside front cover.

2. a record of a journey 3. a guidebook for travelers 4. a detailed plan or outline for a proposed journey

i·tin·er·ate (-rāt′) ***vi.*** **-at′ed, -at′ing** [< LL. pp. of *itinerari:* see ITINERANT] to travel from place to place or on a circuit —**i·tin′er·a′tion** ***n.***

-i·tion (ish′ən) [< Fr. *-ition* or L. *-itio* (gen. *-itionis*)] *var. of* -ATION *[nutrition]*

-i·tious (ish′əs) [L. *-icius, -itius*] *a suffix that is used to form adjectives from nouns ending in* -ITION *and that means* of, having the nature of, characterized by *[nutritious]*

-i·tis (īt′əs, -is) [ModL. < L. < Gr. *-itis*] *a suffix meaning* inflammatory disease or inflammation of (a specified part or organ) *[sinusitis]*

it'll (it′'l) **1.** it will **2.** it shall

its (its) ***pron.*** that or those belonging to it —***possessive pronominal adj.*** of, belonging to, or done by it

it's (its) **1.** it is **2.** it has

it·self (it self′) ***pron.*** a form of the 3d pers. sing., neuter pronoun, used: *a)* as an intensive *[the work itself is easy]* *b)* as a reflexive *[the dog bit itself]* *c)* as a quasi-noun meaning "its real, true, or actual self" *[the bird is not itself today]*

it·ty-bit·ty (it′ē bit′ē) ***adj.*** [alteration < *little bit*] [Colloq.] very small; tiny Also **it·sy-bit·sy** (it′sē bit′sē)

-i·ty (ə tē, i-) [< OFr. *-ité* < L. *-itas*] *a suffix meaning* state, condition *[chastity, possibility]*

IU, I.U. international unit(s)

IUD intrauterine (contraceptive) device: also **IUCD**

i.v. **1.** initial velocity **2.** intravenous(ly)

I·van (ī′vən; *Russ.* i vän′) [Russ. < Gr.: see JOHN] **1.** a masculine name **2. Ivan III** 1440–1505; grand duke of Muscovy (1462–1505): called *the Great* **3. Ivan IV** 1530–84; grand duke of Muscovy (1533–84) & 1st czar of Russia (1547–84): called *the Terrible*

I·va·no·vo (ē vä′nô vô) city in C European R.S.F.S.R.: pop. 415,000

I've (īv) I have

-ive (iv) [< Fr. *-if,* fem. *-ive* < L. *-ivus*] *a suffix meaning:* **1.** of, relating to, having the nature of *[substantive]* **2.** tending to *[creative]*

Ives (īvz), **Charles Edward** 1874–1954; U.S. composer

i·vied (ī′vēd) ***adj.*** covered or overgrown with ivy

i·vo·ry (ī′vər ē, īv′rē) ***n., pl.*** **-ries** [< OFr. < L. < *ebur* < Egypt. *āb, ābu,* elephant] **1.** the hard, white substance forming the tusks of elephants, walruses, etc. **2.** any substance like ivory **3.** the color of ivory; creamy white **4.** a tusk of an elephant, etc. **5.** [*pl.*] things made of or suggesting ivory; specif., [Slang] *a)* piano keys *b)* teeth *c)* dice —***adj.*** **1.** of or like ivory **2.** creamy-white

Ivory Coast country on the WC coast of Africa: 124,500 sq. mi.; pop. 3,750,000; cap. Abidjan

ivory nut *same as* VEGETABLE IVORY

ivory tower figuratively, a place of mental withdrawal from reality and action

I·vy (ī′vē) [< ff.] a feminine name

i·vy (ī′vē) ***n., pl.*** **i′vies** [OE. *ifig*] **1.** a climbing vine with a woody stem and evergreen leaves; English ivy **2.** any of various similar plants, as ground ivy, poison ivy, etc.

Ivy League [< the ivy-covered buildings] a group of colleges in the NE U.S. forming a league for intercollegiate sports: often used to describe the traditional fashions, attitudes, etc. associated with their students

I.W.W., IWW Industrial Workers of the World

Ix·i·on (ik sī′ən) *Gr. Myth.* a Thessalian king who was bound to a revolving wheel in Tartarus because he sought the love of Hera

ix·tle (iks′tlē, is′-) ***n.*** *same as* ISTLE

I·yar (ē yär′, ē′yär) ***n.*** [Heb.] the eighth month of the Jewish year: see JEWISH CALENDAR

-i·za·tion (ə zā′shən, ī-) *a suffix used to form nouns from verbs ending in* -IZE *[realization]*

-ize (īz) [< OFr. < LL. < Gr. *-izein*] *a suffix meaning:* **1.** to cause to be or become; make *[democratize]* **2.** to become or become like *[crystallize]* **3.** to treat or combine with *[oxidize]* **4.** to engage in; act in a specified way *[soliloquize, theorize]*

Iz·mir (iz mir′) seaport in W Turkey, on the Aegean Sea: pop. 412,000

iz·zard (iz′ərd) ***n.*** [var. of ZED] [Archaic or Dial.] the letter Z

J

J, j (jā) ***n., pl.*** **J's, j's** **1.** the tenth letter of the English alphabet **2.** the sound of *J* or *j*

j *Physics a symbol for* joule

J. **1.** Journal **2.** Judge **3.** Justice

Ja. January

J.A. Judge Advocate

jab (jab) ***vt., vi.*** **jabbed, jab′bing** [< ME. *jobben,* to peck] **1.** to poke or thrust, as with a sharp instrument **2.** to punch with short, straight blows —***n.*** a quick thrust, blow, or punch

jab·ber (jab′ər) ***vi., vt.*** [prob. echoic] to speak or say quickly, incoherently, or nonsensically; chatter —***n.*** fast, incoherent, nonsensical talk —**jab′ber·er** ***n.***

ja·bot (zha bō′, ja-) ***n.*** [Fr., bird's crop] a trimming or frill, as of lace, attached to the neck or front of a blouse, bodice, or shirt

jac·a·ran·da (jak′ə ran′də) ***n.*** [ModL. < Port. < Tupi] a tropical American tree with finely divided foliage and large clusters of lavender flowers

ja·cinth (jā′sinth, jas′inth) ***n.*** [< OFr. < L. *hyacinthus:* see HYACINTH] **1.** *same as* HYACINTH (sense 1 *b*) **2.** a reddish-orange color

jack (jak) [< OFr. < LL. *Jacobus,* JACOB] [**J-**] *a nickname for* JOHN —***n., pl.*** for 5, 6, 7 **jacks, jack:** see PLURAL, II, D, 1 [< nickname] **1.** [*often* **J-**] *a)* a man or boy; fellow *b)* a sailor **2.** *same as* BOOTJACK **3.** a fruit-flavored alcoholic drink, as applejack **4.** *a)* any of various devices used to lift or hoist something heavy a short distance *[hydraulic jack, automobile jack]* *b)* a device for turning a spit in roasting **5.** a male donkey **6.** *short for* JACK RABBIT **7.** any of various fishes, as the pickerel, pike, etc. **8.** [Old Slang] money **9.** *Elec.* a plug-in receptacle used to make electric contact **10.** *Games* *a)* a playing card with a page boy's picture on it; knave *b)* any of the small pebbles or six-pronged metal pieces used in playing jacks: see JACKS *c)* in the game of bowls, the target ball **11.** *Naut.* a small flag flown on a ship's bow as a signal or to show nationality —***vt.*** to raise by means of a jack —***adj.*** male: of some animals —**every man jack** everyone —**jack up** **1.** to raise by means of a jack **2.** [Colloq.] to raise (prices, salaries, etc.) **3.** [Colloq.] to encourage to perform one's duty

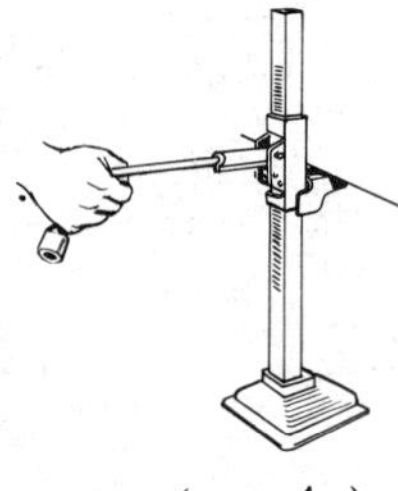

JACK (sense 4 *a*)

jack- [see prec.] *a combining form meaning:* **1.** male *[jackass]* **2.** large or strong *[jackboot]* **3.** boy; fellow: used in hyphenated compounds *[jack-in-the-box]*

jack·al (jak′əl, -ôl) ***n., pl.*** **-als, -al:** see PLURAL, II, D, 1 [< Turk. < Per. *shagāl* < Sans.] **1.** a yellowish-gray, meat-eating wild dog of Asia and N Africa, smaller than the wolf **2.** one who does dishonest or humiliating tasks for another

jack·a·napes (jak′ə nāps′) ***n.*** [< nickname of a 15th-c. Duke of Suffolk] **1.** formerly, a monkey **2.** a conceited, insolent fellow; saucy rascal

jack·ass (jak′as′) ***n.*** [JACK- + ASS] **1.** a male donkey **2.** a stupid or foolish person; nitwit

jack·boot (-bo͞ot′) ***n.*** [JACK- + BOOT[1]] a heavy, sturdy military boot that reaches above the knee

jack·daw (-dô′) ***n.*** [JACK- + DAW] **1.** a European black bird related to the crow, but smaller **2.** *same as* GRACKLE

jack·et (jak′it) ***n.*** [< OFr. dim. of *jaque* < Sp. *jaco,* coat < Ar. *shakk*] **1.** a short coat **2.** an outer covering; specif., *a)* *same as* DUST JACKET *b)* a cardboard holder for a phonograph record *c)* the insulating casing on a boiler, etc. *d)* the skin of a potato, etc. —***vt.*** **1.** to put a jacket, or coat, on **2.** to cover with a casing, wrapper, etc.

Jack Frost frost or cold weather personified

jack·ham·mer (-ham′ər) ***n.*** [JACK- + HAMMER] a portable type of pneumatic hammer, used for drilling rock, brick, etc.

jack-in-the-box (jak′in *th*ə bäks′) ***n., pl.*** **-box′es** a toy consisting of a box from which a little figure on a spring jumps up when the lid is lifted: also **jack′-in-a-box′**

jack-in-the-pul·pit (-pool′pit) *n., pl.* **-pits** an American plant of the arum family, with a flower spike partly arched over by a hoodlike covering

JACK-IN-THE-PULPIT

Jack Ketch (kech) [Brit.] an official hangman

jack·knife (jak′nīf′) *n., pl.* **-knives′** (-nīvz′) [JACK- + KNIFE] **1.** a large pocketknife **2.** a dive in which the diver keeps his knees unbent, touches his feet with his hands, and then straightens out just before plunging into the water —*vi.* **-knifed′, -knif′ing 1.** to bend at the middle as in a jackknife dive **2.** to turn on the hitch so as to form a sharp angle with each other: said of a vehicle and its trailer

jack·leg (-leg′) *adj.* not properly trained or qualified —*n.* a jackleg person or thing

jack-of-all-trades (jak′əv ôl′trādz′) *n., pl.* **jacks′-** [see JACK-, 3] [*often* **J-**] a person who can do many kinds of work acceptably; handyman

jack-o'-lan·tern (jak′ə lan′tərn) *n., pl.* **-terns 1.** a shifting, elusive light seen over marshes at night; will-o'-the-wisp **2.** a hollow pumpkin, real or artificial, cut to look like a face and used as a lantern

jack pine a pine of Canada and the N U.S., having short needles and many woody cones

jack·pot (jak′pät′) *n.* [JACK, *n.* 10 *a* + POT] **1.** cumulative stakes in a poker game, played for only when some player has a pair of jacks or better to open **2.** any cumulative stakes, as in a slot machine —**hit the jackpot** [Slang] **1.** to win the jackpot **2.** to attain the highest success

jack rabbit [JACK(ASS) + RABBIT: from its long ears] a large hare of W N. America, with long ears and strong hind legs

jacks (jaks) *n.pl.* [< JACKSTONE] [*with sing. v.*] a children's game in which pebbles or small, six-pronged metal pieces are tossed and picked up in various ways, esp. while bouncing a small ball

jack·screw (jak′skrōō′) *n.* [JACK- + SCREW] a machine for raising heavy things a short distance, operated by turning a screw

Jack·son (jak′s'n) [after A. JACKSON] capital of Miss., in the SW part: pop. 203,000

Jack·son (jak′s'n) **1. Andrew,** 1767–1845; 7th president of the U.S. (1829–37) **2. Thomas Jonathan,** (nickname *Stonewall Jackson*) 1824–63; Confederate general in the Civil War

Jack·son·ville (jak′s'n vil′) [after A. JACKSON] port in NE Fla.: pop. 541,000 (met. area 736,000)

jack·stone (jak′stōn′) *n.* [for dial. *checkstone* < *check,* pebble] **1.** *same as* JACK (*n.* 10 *b*) **2.** [*pl., with sing. v.*] *same as* JACKS

jack·straw (-strô′) *n.* [JACK- + STRAW] a narrow strip of wood, plastic, etc. used in a game (**jackstraws**) played by tossing a number of such strips into a jumbled heap and trying to remove them one at a time without moving any of the others

Ja·cob (jā′kəb) [< LL. < Gr. < Heb. *ja'aqob,* lit., seizing by the heel] **1.** a masculine name: dim. *Jake* **2.** *Bible* a son of Isaac and father of the founders of the twelve tribes of Israel: Gen. 25–50

Jac·o·be·an (jak′ə bē′ən) *adj.* [< *Jacobus,* Latinized form of *James*] **1.** of James I of England **2.** of the period in England when he was king (1603–25) —*n.* a poet, diplomat, etc. of this period

Jac·o·bin (jak′ə bin) *n.* [< the Church of St. *Jacques* in Paris, the society's meeting place] **1.** any member of a society of radical democrats in France during the Revolution of 1789 **2.** a political radical —*adj.* of the Jacobins: also **Jac′o·bin′ic, Jac′o·bin′i·cal —Jac′o·bin·ism** *n.*

Jac·o·bite (jak′ə bīt′) *n.* [cf. JACOBEAN] a supporter of James II of England after his abdication, or of his descendants' claims to the throne —**Jac′o·bit′ic** (-bit′ik), **Jac′o·bit′i·cal** *adj.*

Jacob's ladder 1. *Bible* the ladder to heaven that Jacob saw in a dream: Gen. 28:12 **2.** a ladder made of rope, wire, etc., used on ships

Jac·quard (jə kärd′) *n.* [after the Fr. inventor, J. M. *Jacquard* (1752–1834)] a loom (**Jacquard loom**) having an endless belt of cards punched with holes arranged to produce a figured weave (**Jacquard weave**)

Jac·que·line (jak′wə lin, jak′ə-) [Fr., fem. of *Jacques,* JACK] a feminine name: dim. *Jacky*

Jacques-Car·tier (zhäk kȧr tyā′; *E.* zhak′kär tyā′) city in S Quebec, near Montreal: pop. 53,000

jade¹ (jād) *n.* [Fr. < Sp. < *piedra de ijada,* stone of the side: from the notion that it cured pains in the side] **1.** a hard stone, usually green, used in jewelry, carvings, etc. **2.** a green color of medium hue —*adj.* **1.** made of jade **2.** green like jade

jade² (jād) *n.* [< ON. *jalda,* a mare < Finn.] **1.** a horse, esp. a worn-out, worthless one **2.** a loose or disreputable woman **3.** [Now Rare] a saucy young woman —*vt., vi.* **jad′ed, jad′ing** to make or become tired, weary, or worn-out —**jad′ish** *adj.*

jad·ed (jā′did) *adj.* **1.** tired; worn-out; wearied **2.** satiated —**jad′ed·ly** *adv.* —**jad′ed·ness** *n.*

jae·ger (yā′gər) *n.* [< G. *jäger,* huntsman] any of several sea birds which force other, weaker birds to leave or give up their prey

Jaf·fa (yä′fə, jaf′ə) *see* TEL-AVIV-JAFFA

jag¹ (jag) *n.* [ME. *jagge*] **1.** a sharp, toothlike projection **2.** [Archaic] a notch or pointed tear, as in cloth —*vt.* **jagged, jag′ging 1.** to notch or pink (cloth, etc.) **2.** to tear raggedly

jag² (jag) *n.* [< ?] [Slang] **1.** an intoxicated condition due to liquor or drugs **2.** a drunken spree **3.** a period of uncontrolled activity [*a crying jag*]

jag·ged (jag′id) *adj.* having sharp projecting points; ragged or notched —**jag′ged·ly** *adv.* —**jag′ged·ness** *n.*

jag·uar (jag′wär, -yoo wär′) *n., pl.* **-uars, -uar:** see PLURAL, II, D, 1 [Port. < Tupi] a large cat, yellowish with black spots, found from SW U.S. to Argentina: it is similar to the leopard, but larger

Jah·veh, Jah·ve, Jah·weh, Jah·we (yä′ve) *same as* JEHOVAH

jai a·lai (hī′lī′, hī′ə lī′) [Sp. < Basque *jai,* celebration + *alai,* merry] a Latin American game like handball, played with a curved basket fastened to the arm, for catching and hurling the ball

jail (jāl) *n.* [< OFr. *gaole* < LL. *caveola,* dim. of L. *cavea,* a cage] **1.** a building for confining those awaiting trial or convicted of minor offenses **2.** imprisonment —*vt.* to put or keep in jail

jail·bird (-burd′) *n.* [Colloq.] **1.** a prisoner in a jail **2.** a person often put in jail

jail·break (-brāk′) *n.* a breaking out of jail

jail·er, jail·or (-ər) *n.* a person in charge of a jail or of prisoners

Jain (jīn) *n.* [< Hindi *Jaina* < Sans. *jina,* saint] a believer in Jainism —*adj.* of the Jains or their religion Also **Jai·na** (jī′nə), **Jain′ist**

Jain·ism (jīn′iz'm) *n.* a Hindu religion founded in the 6th cent. B.C.: it emphasizes asceticism and reverence for all living things

Jai·pur (jī′poor) city in NW India: pop. 403,000

Ja·kar·ta (jə kär′tə) capital of Indonesia, on the NW coast of Java: pop. c.4,500,000

jal·ap (jal′əp) *n.* [Fr. < Sp. < *Jalapa,* city in Mexico] **1.** the dried root of a Mexican plant, formerly used as a purgative **2.** the plant

ja·lop·y (jə läp′ē) *n., pl.* **-lop′ies** [< ?] [Slang] an old, ramshackle automobile

jal·ou·sie (jal′ə sē′) *n.* [Fr. < OFr. *gelosie,* jealousy (see JEALOUS)] a window, shade, or door formed of adjustable, horizontal slats of wood, metal, or glass, for regulating the air or light entering

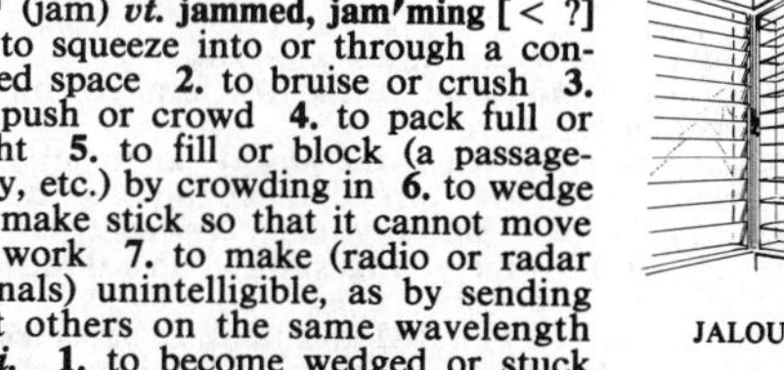
JALOUSIES

jam¹ (jam) *vt.* **jammed, jam′ming** [< ?] **1.** to squeeze into or through a confined space **2.** to bruise or crush **3.** to push or crowd **4.** to pack full or tight **5.** to fill or block (a passageway, etc.) by crowding in **6.** to wedge or make stick so that it cannot move or work **7.** to make (radio or radar signals) unintelligible, as by sending out others on the same wavelength —*vi.* **1.** to become wedged or stuck fast, esp. so as to become unworkable **2.** to push against one another in a confined space **3.** [Slang] *Jazz* to improvise —*n.* **1.** a jamming or being jammed **2.** a group of persons or things blocking a passageway, etc. [*a traffic jam*] **3.** [Colloq.] a difficult situation

jam² (jam) *n.* [< ? prec.] a food made by boiling fruit with sugar to a thick mixture

Ja·mai·ca (jə mā′kə) country on an island of the West Indies, south of Cuba: a member of the Commonwealth: 4,411 sq. mi.; pop. 1,972,000; cap. Kingston —**Ja·mai′can** *adj., n.*

jamb (jam) *n.* [< OFr. *jambe* < LL. *gamba,* a leg] a side post of an opening for a door, window, etc.

jam·ba·lay·a (jum′bə lī′ə) *n.* [AmFr. < ModPr. *jambalaia*] a Creole stew made of rice and shrimp, oysters, crabs, ham, chicken, etc.

jam·bo·ree (jam′bə rē′) ***n.*** [< ?] **1.** [Colloq.] *a)* a boisterous party or revel *b)* a gathering with planned entertainment **2.** a national or international assembly of boy scouts
James[1] (jāmz) [< OFr. < LL. *Jacomus,* later form of *Jacobus,* JACOB] **1.** a masculine name **2.** *Bible a)* either of two Christian apostles *b)* a brother of Jesus; also, a book of the New Testament sometimes attributed to him **3. James I** 1566–1625; king of England (1603–25) **4. James II** 1633–1701; king of England (1685–88): deposed: son of CHARLES I **5. Henry,** 1843–1916; U.S. novelist, in England **6. Jesse (Woodson),** 1847–82; U.S. outlaw **7. William,** 1842–1910; U.S. psychologist & philosopher: brother of *Henry*
James[2] (jāmz) river in Va., flowing from the W part southeast into Chesapeake Bay
James·town (jāmz′toun′) [after JAMES I] colonial settlement (1607) at the mouth of the James River
Jam·mu and Kashmir (jum′o͞o) state of N India, control of which is disputed by Pakistan
jam·packed (jam′pakt′) ***adj.*** tightly packed
jam session an informal gathering of jazz musicians to play improvisations
Jan. January
Jane (jān) [var. of JOANNA] a feminine name —***n.*** [j-] [Slang] a girl or woman
Jan·et (jan′it) [dim. of prec.] a feminine name
jan·gle (jaŋ′g'l) ***vi.*** **-gled, -gling** [< OFr. *jangler*] **1.** to make a harsh, inharmonious sound, as of a bell out of tune **2.** to quarrel noisily —***vt.*** **1.** to utter in a harsh, inharmonious manner **2.** to cause to make a harsh sound **3.** to irritate very much [to *jangle* one's nerves] —***n.*** **1.** noisy talk or arguing **2.** a harsh sound —**jan′gler** ***n.***
Jan·ice (jan′is) [< JANE, JANET] a feminine name
jan·i·tor (jan′i tər) ***n.*** [L., doorkeeper < *janua,* door] the custodian of a building, who does routine maintenance —**jan′i·to′ri·al** (-ə tôr′ē əl) ***adj.***
jan·i·zar·y (jan′ə zer′ē) ***n.,*** *pl.* **-zar′ies** [< Fr. < It. < Turk. < *yeni,* new + *cheri,* soldiery] [*often* **J-**] **1.** a Turkish soldier, orig. one in the former sultan's guard **2.** any very loyal supporter Also **jan′is·sar′y** (-ser′ē)
Jan·u·ar·y (jan′yo͞o wer′ē) ***n.,*** *pl.* **-ar′ies** [< L. *Januarius* (*mensis*), (the month) of Janus] the first month of the year, having 31 days: abbrev. **Jan., Ja.**
Ja·nus (jā′nəs) *Rom. Myth.* the god who was guardian of portals and patron of beginnings and endings: his head is shown with two faces, one in front, the other at the back
Jap. 1. Japan **2.** Japanese
Ja·pan (jə pan′) island country off the E coast of Asia, including Hokkaido, Honshu, Kyushu, Shikoku, & many smaller islands: 142,726 sq. mi.; pop. 102,833,000; cap. Tokyo
ja·pan (jə pan′) ***n.*** [orig. from Japan] **1.** a varnish giving a hard, glossy finish **2.** a liquid used as a paint drier **3.** objects decorated and varnished in the Japanese style —***vt.*** **-panned′, -pan′ning** to varnish with japan
Jap·a·nese (jap′ə nēz′) ***adj.*** of Japan, its people, language, culture, etc. —***n.*** **1.** *pl.* **-nese′** a native of Japan **2.** the language of Japan
Japanese beetle a shiny, green-and-brown beetle, orig. from Japan, which eats leaves, fruits, and grasses, and is damaging to crops
Japanese lantern *same as* CHINESE LANTERN
Japanese quince a spiny plant of the rose family, with pink or red flowers and green fruit
jape (jāp) ***vi.*** **japed, jap′ing** [ME. *japen*] **1.** to joke; jest **2.** to play tricks —***vt.*** [Now Rare] to make fun of —***n.*** **1.** a joke or jest **2.** a trick —**jap′er·y** ***n.,*** *pl.* **-er·ies**
Ja·pheth (jā′fith) *Bible* the youngest of Noah's three sons: Gen. 5:32
ja·pon·i·ca (jə pän′i kə) ***n.*** [ModL., fem. of *Japonicus,* of Japan < *Japonia,* Japan < Fr. *Japon*] *a popular name for* JAPANESE QUINCE, CAMELLIA, etc.
jar[1] (jär) ***vi.*** **jarred, jar′ring** [ult. echoic] **1.** to make a harsh sound; grate **2.** to have a harsh, irritating effect (*on* one) **3.** to vibrate from a sudden impact **4.** to clash, disagree, or quarrel —***vt.*** **1.** to make vibrate by sudden impact **2.** to cause to give a harsh or discordant sound **3.** to jolt or shock —***n.*** **1.** a harsh, grating sound **2.** a vibration due to a sudden impact **3.** a jolt or shock **4.** a sharp clash or quarrel
jar[2] (jär) ***n.*** [Fr. *jarre* < OPr. or Sp. < Ar. *jarrah,* earthen water container] **1.** a container made of glass, stone, or earthenware, with a large opening and no spout **2.** as much as a jar will hold: also **jar′ful′**
jar·di·niere (jär′d'n ir′; *Fr.* zhȧr dē nyer′) ***n.*** [< Fr. < *jardin,* a garden] **1.** an ornamental bowl, pot, or stand for flowers or plants **2.** a garnish for meats, of several vegetables cooked separately
jar·gon (jär′gən) ***n.*** [MFr., a chattering] **1.** incoherent speech; gibberish **2.** a language or dialect that seems incomprehensible or outlandish to one **3.** a hybrid language or dialect; esp., pidgin **4.** the specialized vocabulary and idioms of those in the same work, profession, etc., as of sports writers: see SLANG —**jar′gon·is′tic** ***adj.***
Jas. James
jas·mine, jas·min (jaz′min; *chiefly Brit.* jas′-) ***n.*** [< Fr. < Ar. < Per. *yāsamīn*] **1.** a tropical and subtropical plant of the olive family, with fragrant flowers of yellow, red, or white **2.** any of several other similar plants with fragrant flowers
Ja·son (jās′'n) [< L. *Iāson* < Gr., lit., healer] **1.** a masculine name **2.** *Gr. Myth.* a prince who led the Argonauts and got the Golden Fleece
jas·per (jas′pər) ***n.*** [< MFr. < L. < Gr. *iaspis*] **1.** an opaque variety of colored quartz, usually reddish, yellow, or brown **2.** *Bible* a precious stone, probably an opaque green quartz
ja·to, JA·TO (jā′tō) ***n.*** [*j*(*et*)-*a*(*ssisted*) *t*(*ake*)*o*(*ff*)] an airplane takeoff assisted by small, solid-propellant rockets
jaun·dice (jôn′dis, jän′-) ***n.*** [< OFr. *jaunisse,* ult. < L. *galbinus,* greenish yellow < *galbus,* yellow] **1.** *a)* a condition in which the eyeballs, skin, and urine become abnormally yellow as a result of bile pigments in the blood *b)* popularly, a disease causing this, as hepatitis **2.** bitterness or prejudice caused by jealousy, envy, etc. —***vt.*** **-diced, -dicing 1.** to cause to have jaundice **2.** to make bitter or prejudiced through jealousy, envy, etc.
jaunt (jônt, jänt) ***vi.*** [< ?] to take a short trip for pleasure —***n.*** such a trip; excursion
jaun·ty (-ē) ***adj.*** **-ti·er, -ti·est** [< Fr. *gentil,* genteel] **1.** in fashion; chic **2.** gay and carefree; sprightly —**jaun′ti·ly** ***adv.*** —**jaun′ti·ness** ***n.***
Jav. Javanese
Ja·va (jä′və, jav′ə) large island of Indonesia, southeast of Sumatra: 48,842 sq. mi. —***n.*** **1.** a coffee grown on Java and nearby islands **2.** [*often* **j-**] [Slang] any coffee
Java man a type of primitive man (*Homo erectus erectus*) known from fossil remains found in Java
Jav·a·nese (jav′ə nēz′) ***adj.*** of Java, its people, etc. —***n.*** **1.** *pl.* **-nese′** a native or inhabitant of Java **2.** the Indonesian language of Java
jav·e·lin (jav′lin, jav′ə lin) ***n.*** [MFr. *javeline,* fem. dim. < *javelot,* a spear] **1.** a light spear for throwing **2.** a pointed wooden or metal shaft, about 8½ ft. long, thrown for distance as a field event (**javelin throw**) in track and field meets
jaw (jô) ***n.*** [< ? OFr. *joue,* cheek] **1.** either of the two bony parts that hold the teeth and frame the mouth **2.** either of two parts that open and close to grip or crush something, as in a monkey wrench or vise **3.** [*pl.*] *a)* the mouth *b)* the entrance of a canyon, valley, etc. **4.** [Slang] talk; esp., abusive or boring talk —***vi.*** [Slang] to talk, esp. in a boring or abusive way —***vt.*** [Slang] to scold or reprove
jaw·bone (-bōn′) ***n.*** a bone of a jaw, esp. of the lower jaw —***vt., vi.*** **-boned′, -bon′ing** to attempt to persuade by using the influence of one's high office or position
jaw·break·er (-brā′kər) ***n.*** **1.** a machine with jaws for crushing rocks, ore, etc. **2.** a hard, usually round candy **3.** [Slang] a word that is hard to pronounce
jay (jā) ***n.*** [< OFr. *gai* < LL. *gaius,* a jay] **1.** any of several birds of the crow family **2.** *same as* BLUE JAY **3.** [Colloq.] a stupid or foolish person
Jay (jā), **John** 1745–1829; Am. statesman & jurist: 1st chief justice of the U.S. (1789–95)
Jay·hawk·er (jā′hô′kər) ***n.*** [Colloq.] *a nickname for* a Kansan: also **Jay′hawk′**
jay·walk (jā′wôk′) ***vi.*** [JAY, 3 + WALK] [Colloq.] to walk in or across a street carelessly without obeying traffic rules and signals —**jay′walk′er** ***n.*** —**jay′walk′ing** ***n.***
jazz (jaz) ***n.*** [< ? Creole patois *jass,* sexual term] **1.** a kind of music characterized by syncopation, rubato, melodic variations, and unusual tonal effects on the saxophone, clarinet, trumpet, trombone, etc. **2.** loosely, any popular dance music **3.** [Slang] remarks, acts, etc. regarded as hypocritical, tiresome, etc. —***adj.*** of, in, or like jazz —***vt.*** **1.** to play or arrange as jazz **2.** [Slang] to enliven or embellish (usually with *up*) —**jazz′i·ly** ***adv.*** —**jazz′i·ness** ***n.*** —**jazz′y** ***adj.*** **-i·er, -i·est**
jazz·man (jaz′man′) ***n.,*** *pl.* **-men′** (-men′) a jazz musician
jct. junction
JD juvenile delinquency (or delinquent)
Je. June
jeal·ous (jel′əs) ***adj.*** [< OFr. *gelos* < ML. *zelosus:* see ZEAL] **1.** very watchful or careful in guarding or keeping [*jealous* of one's rights] **2.** *a)* resentfully suspicious, as of a rival [a husband *jealous* of other men] *b)* resentfully envious *c)* resulting from such feelings [a *jealous* rage] **3.** [Now Rare] requiring exclusive loyalty [a *jealous* God] —**jeal′ous·ly** ***adv.*** —**jeal′ous·ness** ***n.***
jeal·ous·y (-ē) ***n.,*** *pl.* **-ous·ies 1.** the quality or condition of being jealous **2.** an instance of this; jealous feeling
Jean (jēn) **1.** [Fr., equiv. of JOHN] a masculine name **2.** [var. of JOANNA] a feminine name

jean (jēn) ***n.*** [< OFr. *Janne* < ML. < L. *Genua,* Genoa] **1.** a durable, twilled cotton cloth, used for work clothes and casual wear **2.** [*pl.*] trousers of this material, often blue, or of denim

Jeanne (jēn) [var. of JOANNA] a feminine name

Jeanne d'Arc (zhän därk) *see* JOAN OF ARC

Jean·nette (jə net′) [dim. of JEANNE] a feminine name

Jeans (jēnz), Sir **James (Hopwood)** 1877–1946; Eng. physicist, astronomer, & writer

jee (jē) ***interj., n., vt., vi.*** *same as* GEE[1]

jeep (jēp) ***n.*** [after a creature in a comic strip by E. C. Segar (1894–1938)] a small, rugged, military automotive vehicle with a 1/4-ton capacity and a four-wheel drive **—[J-]** *a trademark for* a similar vehicle for civilian use

jee·pers (jē′pərz) ***interj.*** [altered < JESUS] a mild exclamation of surprise, etc.

jeer (jir) ***vt., vi.*** [< ? CHEER] to make fun of (a person or thing) in a rude, sarcastic manner; mock; scoff (at) **—*n.*** a jeering remark; sarcastic or derisive comment **—jeer′er *n.*** **—jeer′ing·ly *adv.***

Jef·fer·son (jef′ər s′n), **Thomas** 1743–1826; Am. statesman; 3d president of the U.S. (1801–09): drew up the Declaration of Independence **—Jef′fer·so′ni·an** (-sō′nē ən) ***adj., n.***

Jefferson City [after T. JEFFERSON] capital of Mo., on the Missouri: pop. 34,000

Jeff·rey (jef′rē) [var. of GEOFFREY] a masculine name: dim. *Jeff*

Je·hosh·a·phat (ji häs′ə fat′, -häsh′-) *Bible* a king of Judah in the 9th cent. B.C.: II Chr. 17 ff.

Je·ho·vah (ji hō′və) [transliteration of Heb. sacred name for God] God; (the) Lord

Jehovah's Witnesses a proselytizing Christian sect founded by Charles T. Russell (1852–1916)

je·hu (jē′ho͞o, -hyo͞o) ***n.*** [< *Jehu* in the Bible: II Kings 9] [Colloq.] a fast, reckless driver

je·june (ji jo͞on′) ***adj.*** [L. *jejunus,* empty] **1.** not nourishing **2.** not interesting or satisfying; dull **3.** not mature; childish **—je·june′ly *adv.*** **—je·june′ness *n.***

je·ju·num (ji jo͞o′nəm) ***n., pl.*** **-na** (-nə) [< L.: see JEJUNE] the middle part of the small intestine, between the duodenum and the ileum **—je·ju′nal *adj.***

jell (jel) ***vi., vt.*** [back-formation < JELLY] **1.** to become or make into jelly **2.** [Colloq.] to take or give definite form; crystallize *[the plans didn't jell]* **—*n.*** [Dial.] *same as* JELLY

jel·li·fy (jel′ə fī′) ***vt., vi.*** **-fied′, -fy′ing** to change into jelly **—jel′li·fi·ca′tion *n.***

jel·ly (jel′ē) ***n., pl.*** **-lies** [< OFr. pp. of *geler* < L. *gelare,* to freeze] **1.** a soft, partially transparent, gelatinous food resulting from the cooling of fruit juice boiled with sugar, or of meat juice cooked down **2.** any substance like this **—*vt.*** **-lied, -ly·ing 1.** to make into jelly **2.** to coat, fill, or serve with jelly **—*vi.*** to become jelly **—jel′ly·like′ *adj.***

jel·ly·bean (-bēn′) ***n.*** a small, bean-shaped, gelatinous candy with a colored sugar coating

jel·ly·fish (-fish′) ***n., pl.*** **-fish′, -fish′es:** see FISH **1.** an invertebrate sea animal with a body made up largely of jellylike substance and shaped like an umbrella: it has long, hanging tentacles with stinging cells on them **2.** [Colloq.] a weak-willed person

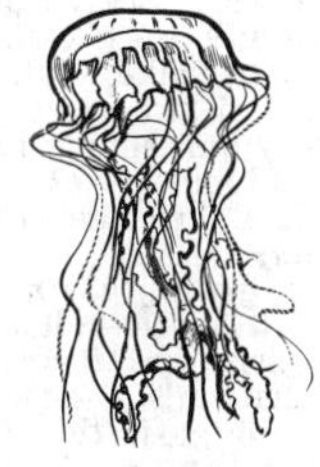

JELLYFISH (to 16 in. long)

jel·ly·roll (-rōl′) ***n.*** a thin sheet of spongecake spread with jelly and rolled so as to form layers

Jen·ghiz Khan (jeŋ′gis) *same as* GENGHIS KHAN

Jen·ner (jen′ər), **Edward** 1749–1823; Eng. physician: introduced vaccination

jen·net (jen′it) ***n.*** [< MFr. < Sp. *jinete,* horseman < Ar. *Zenāta,* a tribe of Barbary] any of a breed of small Spanish horses

Jen·ni·fer (jen′i fər) [altered < GUINEVERE] a feminine name

Jen·ny (jen′ē) [dim. of JANE] a feminine name

jen·ny (jen′ē) ***n., pl.*** **-nies** [< prec.] **1.** *short for* SPINNING JENNY **2.** *a)* the female of some birds *[a jenny wren]* *b)* a female donkey

jeop·ard·ize (jep′ər dīz′) ***vt.*** **-ized′, -iz′ing** to put in jeopardy; risk loss, failure, etc. of; endanger

jeop·ard·y (-dē) ***n., pl.*** **-ard·ies** [< OFr. *jeu parti,* lit., a game with even chances, ult. < L. *jocus,* a game + pp. of *partire,* to divide] **1.** great danger; peril **2.** *Law* the situation of an accused person on trial for a crime

Jer. Jeremiah

jer·bo·a (jər bō′ə) ***n.*** [Ar. *yarbū′*] any of various small, nocturnal, leaping rodents of N Africa and Asia, with very long hind legs

jer·e·mi·ad (jer′ə mī′əd) ***n.*** a lamentation or tale of woe: in allusion to the *Lamentations of Jeremiah*

Jer·e·mi·ah (-ə) [< LL. < Gr. < Heb. *yirmeyāh,* lit., the Lord loosens (i.e., from the womb)] **1.** a masculine name: var. *Jeremy* **2.** *Bible a)* a Hebrew prophet of the 7th and 6th cent. B.C. *b)* the book containing his warnings and prophecies Also, in the Douay Bible, **Jer′e·mi′as** (-əs)

Jer·i·cho (jer′ə kō′) city in W Jordan: site of an ancient city whose walls (*Bible,* Josh. 6) were miraculously destroyed when trumpets were sounded

jerk[1] (jurk) ***vt.*** [< ?] **1.** to pull, twist, push, or throw with a sudden, sharp movement **2.** [Colloq.] to make and serve (ice cream sodas) **—*vi.*** **1.** to move with a jerk or in jerks **2.** to twitch **—*n.*** **1.** a sharp, abrupt pull, twist, push, etc. **2.** a sudden muscular contraction caused by a reflex action **3.** [Slang] a person regarded as stupid, foolish, etc.

jerk[2] (jurk) ***vt.*** [altered (after prec.) < JERKY[2]] to preserve (meat) by slicing into strips and drying in the sun **—*n.*** *same as* JERKY[2]

jer·kin (jur′kin) ***n.*** [< ?] a closefitting, sleeveless jacket of a kind worn in the 16th and 17th cent.

jerk·wa·ter (jurk′wôt′ər, -wät′-) ***n.*** [JERK[1] + WATER] a train on an early branch railroad **—*adj.*** [Colloq.] small, unimportant, etc. *[a jerkwater town]*

jerk·y[1] (-ē) ***adj.*** **jerk′i·er, jerk′i·est 1.** characterized by jerks; making sudden starts and stops; spasmodic **2.** [Slang] stupid, dull, foolish, etc. **—jerk′i·ly *adv.***

jer·ky[2] (jur′kē) ***n.*** [< Sp. *charqui* < Quechua] meat, esp. beef, that has been preserved by being sliced into strips and dried in the sun

Je·rome (jə rōm′) [Fr. < L. < Gr. < *hieros,* holy + *onyma,* name] **1.** a masculine name: dim. *Jerry* **2.** Saint, (born *Eusebius Hieronymus Sophronius*) 340?–420 A.D.; monk & church scholar: author of the Vulgate

jer·ry·built (jer′ē bilt′) ***adj.*** [prob. < name *Jerry,* infl. by JURY[2]] built poorly, of cheap materials

Jer·sey (jur′zē) largest of the Channel Islands **—*n., pl.*** **-seys 1.** any of a breed of small, reddish-brown dairy cattle, originally from Jersey **2.** [j-] *a)* a soft, elastic, knitted cloth *b)* any closefitting, knitted upper garment

Jersey City city in NE N.J., across the Hudson from New York: pop. 224,000 (met. area 555,000)

Je·ru·sa·lem (jə ro͞o′sə ləm) capital of Israel (sense 6), in the C part: pop. 266,000

Jerusalem artichoke [altered (after prec.) < It. *girasole,* sunflower] **1.** a tall N. American sunflower with edible potatolike tubers **2.** such a tuber

jess (jes) ***n.*** [< OFr. *gets,* pl. < L. *jactus,* a casting] a strap for a falcon's leg, with a ring for attaching a leash **—*vt.*** to fasten jesses on

jes·sa·mine (jes′ə min) ***n.*** *same as* JASMINE

Jes·se (jes′ē) [Heb. *yīshai*] **1.** a masculine name: dim. *Jess* **2.** *Bible* the father of David: I Sam. 16

Jes·si·ca (jes′i kə) a feminine name: var. *Jessie*

jest (jest) ***n.*** [OFr. *geste,* an exploit < L. pp. of *gerere,* to perform] **1.** a mocking remark; gibe; taunt **2.** a joke or humorous remark **3.** mere fun; joking *[said in jest]* **4.** something to be laughed at or joked about **—*vi.*** **1.** to jeer; mock **2.** to be playful in speech and actions; joke

jest·er (-ər) ***n.*** one who jests; esp., a professional fool employed by a medieval ruler to amuse him

Je·su (jē′zo͞o, -so͞o; jā′-) *archaic var. of* JESUS

Jes·u·it (jezh′oo wit, jez′-; -yoo-) ***n.*** a member of the Society of Jesus, a Roman Catholic religious order for men founded by Ignatius Loyola in 1534

Je·sus (jē′zəs) [LL. *Iesus* < Gr. *Iēsous* < Heb. *yēshū'a,* contr. of *yĕhōshu'a,* help of Jehovah] c. 8–4 B.C.–29? A.D. (see CHRISTIAN ERA): founder of the Christian religion: also called **Jesus Christ, Jesus of Nazareth:** see also CHRIST

jet[1] (jet) ***vt., vi.*** **jet′ted, jet′ting** [< MFr. *jeter,* ult. < L. *jactare,* freq. of *jacere,* to throw] **1.** to spout, gush, or shoot out in a stream **2.** to travel or convey by jet airplane **—*n.*** **1.** a stream of liquid or gas emitted or forced out, as from a spout **2.** a spout or nozzle for emitting a jet **3.** a jet-propelled airplane: in full, **jet (air) plane —*adj.*** **1.** jet-propelled **2.** of jet propulsion or jet-propelled aircraft *[the jet age]*

jet[2] (jet) ***n.*** [< OFr. < L. < Gr. *gagatēs,* jet < *Gagas,* town in Asia Minor] **1.** a hard, black variety of lignite: sometimes used in jewelry **2.** a deep, lustrous black **—*adj.*** **1.** made of jet **2.** black like jet

jet-black (-blak′) ***adj.*** glossy black, like jet

jet·lin·er (-lī′nər) ***n.*** a commercial jet aircraft for carrying passengers

jet·port (-pôrt′) ***n.*** an airport with long runways, for use by jet airplanes

jet·pro·pelled (-prə peld′) ***adj.*** driven by jet propulsion
jet propulsion a method of propelling airplanes, boats, etc. by the reaction caused when gases are emitted under pressure through a rear vent or vents
jet·sam (jet′səm) ***n.*** **[**var. of JETTISON**]** **1.** that part of the cargo thrown overboard to lighten a ship in danger: cf. FLOTSAM **2.** such discarded cargo washed ashore **3.** discarded things
jet stream **1.** any of several bands of high-velocity winds moving from west to east around the earth at altitudes of from 8 to 10 mi. **2.** the stream of exhaust from a rocket engine
jet·ti·son (jet′ə s'n, -z'n) ***n.*** **[**< Anglo-Fr. < OFr. *getaison* < L. < *jactare,* to throw**]** **1.** a throwing overboard of goods to lighten a ship, airplane, etc. in an emergency **2.** *same as* JETSAM —***vt.*** **1.** to throw (goods) overboard **2.** to discard (something)
jet·ty (jet′ē) ***n., pl.*** **-ties** **[**< OFr. *jetée,* orig. pp. of *jeter:* see JET[1]**]** **1.** a kind of wall built out into the water to restrain currents, protect a harbor, etc. **2.** a landing pier **3.** a projecting part of a building —***vi.*** **-tied, -ty·ing** to project, or jut out
Jew (jo͞o) ***n.*** **[**< OFr. < L. *Judaeus* < Gr. < Heb. *yehūdī,* member of the tribe of Judah**]** **1.** a person descended, or regarded as descended, from the ancient Hebrews **2.** a person whose religion is Judaism
jew·el (jo͞o′əl) ***n.*** **[**< OFr. *joel* < *jeu,* a trifle < L. *jocus,* a joke**]** **1.** a valuable ring, necklace, etc., esp. one set with gems **2.** a precious stone; gem **3.** any person or thing that is very precious or valuable **4.** a small gem or gemlike bit used as one of the bearings in a watch —***vt.*** **-eled** or **-elled, -el·ing** or **-el·ling** to decorate or set with jewels
jew·el·er, jew·el·ler (-ər) ***n.*** a person who makes, deals in, or repairs jewelry, watches, etc.
jew·el·ry (jo͞o′əl rē) ***n.*** jewels collectively: Brit. sp. **jew′el·ler·y**
jew·el·weed (-wēd′) ***n.*** any of a group of plants bearing yellow or orange-yellow flowers and seedpods that split at the touch when ripe
Jew·ess (jo͞o′is) ***n.*** a Jewish woman or girl: term avoided by those who regard the *-ess* suffix as patronizing or discriminatory
jew·fish (-fish′) ***n., pl.*** **-fish′, -fish′es:** see FISH any of several large fish found in warm seas, as a grouper found off Florida
Jew·ish (-ish) ***adj.*** of or having to do with Jews or Judaism —***n.*** [Colloq.] *same as* YIDDISH —**Jew′ish·ness *n.***
Jewish calendar a calendar used by the Jews in calculating holidays, etc., based on the lunar month and reckoned from 3761 B.C., the traditional date of the Creation

Months of the Jewish Calendar

1. **Tishri** (30 days)	7. **Nisan** (30 days)
2. **Heshvan** (29 or 30 days)	8. **Iyar** (29 days)
3. **Kislev** (29 or 30 days)	9. **Sivan** (30 days)
4. **Tebet** (29 days)	10. **Tammuz** (29 days)
5. **Shebat** (30 days)	11. **Ab** (30 days)
6. **Adar** (29 or 30 days)	12. **Elul** (29 days)

N.B. About once every three years an extra month, **Veadar** or **Adar Sheni** (29 days), falls between *Adar* and *Nisan. Tishri* begins in late September or early October
Jew·ry (jo͞o′rē) ***n., pl.*** **-ries** **1.** formerly, a district inhabited by Jews; ghetto **2.** Jewish people collectively *[*American *Jewry]*
jew's-harp, jews'-harp (jo͞oz′härp′) ***n.*** a small musical instrument consisting of a lyre-shaped metal frame held between the teeth and played by plucking a projecting bent piece with the finger

JEW'S-HARP

Jez·e·bel (jez′ə bel′, -b'l) **[**Heb.**]** *Bible* the wicked woman who married Ahab, king of Israel —***n.*** [*also* **j-**] any shameless, wicked woman
jg, j.g. junior grade: designation of the lower rank of lieutenant in the U.S. Navy
jib[1] (jib) ***n.*** **[**prob. < GIBBET**]** **1.** the projecting arm of a crane **2.** the boom of a derrick
jib[2] (jib) ***vi., vt.*** **jibbed, jib′bing** **[**< Dan. *gibbe,* to jibe**]** *Naut.* to jibe; shift —***n.*** a triangular sail projecting ahead of the foremast —**cut of one's jib** [Colloq.] one's appearance
jib[3] (jib) ***vi.*** **jibbed, jib′bing** **[**prob. < prec.**]** **1.** to stop and refuse to go forward; balk **2.** to start or shy (*at* something) —***n.*** an animal that jibs, as a horse —**jib′ber *n.***
jib boom a spar fixed to and extending beyond the bowsprit of a ship: the jib is attached to it
jibe[1] (jīb) ***vi.*** **jibed, jib′ing** **[**< Du. *gijpen***]** **1.** to shift from one side of a ship to the other, as a fore-and-aft sail when the course is changed in a following wind **2.** to change the course of a ship so that the sails shift thus **3.** [Colloq.] to be in harmony, agreement, or accord —***vt.*** *Naut.* to cause to jibe —***n.*** a shift of sail or boom from one side of a ship to another
jibe[2] (jīb) ***vi., vt., n.*** *same as* GIBE —**jib′er *n.***
Jid·da, Jid·dah (jid′ə) seaport in Saudi Arabia, on the Red Sea: pop. c.300,000
jif·fy (jif′ē) ***n., pl.*** **-fies** **[**< ?**]** [Colloq.] a very short time; instant *[*done in a *jiffy]:* also **jiff**
jig (jig) ***n.*** **[**prob. < MFr. *giguer,* to dance < *gigue,* a fiddle**]** **1.** *a)* a fast, gay, springy dance, usually in triple time *b)* the music for such a dance **2.** any of various fishing lures that are jiggled up and down in the water **3.** any of several mechanical devices operated in a jerky manner, as a sieve for separating ores, a drill, etc. **4.** a device used as a guide for a tool or as a template —***vi., vt.*** **jigged, jig′ging** **1.** to dance (a jig) **2.** to move jerkily up and down or to and fro —**the jig is up** [Slang] all chances for success are gone: said of a risky or improper activity
jig·ger[1] (jig′ər) ***n.*** **[**prob. of Afr. origin**]** *same as* CHIGGER
jig·ger[2] (jig′ər) ***n.*** **1.** one who jigs **2.** *a)* a small glass used to measure liquor, containing usually 1½ fluid ounces *b)* the quantity of liquor in a jigger **3.** any device or contraption whose name does not occur to one; gadget **4.** *same as* JIG (*n.* 2) **5.** *Mech.* any of several devices that operate with a jerky, up-and-down motion **6.** *Naut. a)* a small tackle *b)* a small sail *c) same as* JIGGER MAST
jigger mast a mast in the stern of a ship
jig·gle (jig′'l) ***vt., vi.*** **-gled, -gling** **[**freq. of *jig, v.***]** to move in a succession of quick, slight jerks; rock lightly —***n.*** a jiggling movement
jig·gly (jig′lē) ***adj.*** moving or tending to move with a jiggle; unsteady
jig·saw (jig′sô′) ***n.*** a saw with a narrow blade set in a frame, that moves with an up-and-down motion for cutting along curved or irregular lines, as in scrollwork: also **jig saw** —***vt.*** to cut or form with a jigsaw

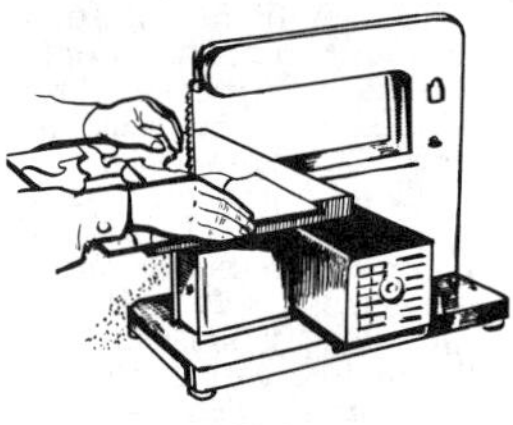

JIGSAW

jigsaw puzzle a puzzle made by cutting up a picture into pieces of irregular shape, which must be put together again to re-form the picture
Jill (jil) **[**< proper name *Gillian* < L. *Juliana***]** a feminine name —***n.*** [*often* **j-**] [Now Rare] a girl or woman; esp., a sweetheart
jilt (jilt) ***n.*** **[**< *jillet,* dim. of prec.**]** a woman who rejects a lover or suitor after accepting or encouraging him —***vt.*** to reject or cast off (a previously accepted lover or sweetheart)
Jim (jim) *a nickname for* JAMES
Jim Crow **[**name of an early Negro minstrel song**]** [*also* **j- c-**] [Colloq.] discrimination against or segregation of Negroes —**Jim′-Crow′ *vt., adj.*** —**Jim Crow′ism**
jim·my (jim′ē) ***n., pl.*** **-mies** **[**< dim. of JAMES**]** a short crowbar, used by burglars to pry open windows, etc. —***vt.*** **-mied, -my·ing** to pry open with a jimmy or similar tool
jim·son weed (jim′s'n) **[**< JAMESTOWN, Va.**]** a poisonous annual weed of the nightshade family, with foul-smelling leaves, prickly fruit, and trumpet-shaped flowers
jin·gle (jiŋ′g'l) ***vi.*** **-gled, -gling** **[**ME. *gingelen,* prob. echoic**]** **1.** to make light, ringing sounds, as small bells or bits of metal striking together; tinkle **2.** to have obvious, easy rhythm, simple repetitions of sound, etc., as some poetry and music —***vt.*** to cause to jingle —***n.*** **1.** a jingling sound **2.** a verse that jingles *[*advertising *jingles]* —**jin′gly** (-glē) ***adj.***
jin·go (jiŋ′gō) ***n., pl.*** **-goes** **[**< phr. *by jingo* in a patriotic Brit. music-hall song (1878)**]** one who boasts of his patriotism and favors an aggressive, warlike foreign policy; chauvinist —***adj.*** of jingoes —**jin′go·ism *n.*** —**jin′go·ist *n.*** —**jin′go·is′tic *adj.*** —**jin′go·is′ti·cal·ly *adv.***
jinn (jin) ***n.*** *pl. of* JINNI: popularly regarded as a singular, with the pl. **jinns**
jin·ni (ji nē′, jin′ē) ***n., pl.*** **jinn** **[**< Ar.**]** *Moslem Legend* a supernatural being that can take human or animal form and influence human affairs
jin·rik·i·sha (jin rik′shô, -shä) ***n.*** **[**< Jap. < *jin,* a man + *riki,* power + *sha,* carriage**]** a small, two-wheeled carriage with a hood, pulled by one or two men, esp. formerly in the Orient: also sp. **jin·rick′sha, jin·rik′sha**
jinx (jiŋks) ***n.*** **[**< L. *iynx* < Gr. *iynx,* the wryneck (bird used in black magic)**]** [Colloq.] **1.** a person or thing supposed to bring bad luck **2.** a spell of bad luck —***vt.*** [Colloq.] to bring bad luck to
jit·ney (jit′nē) ***n., pl.*** **-neys** **[**c. 1903 < ? Fr. *jeton,* a token**]** **1.** [Old Slang] a five-cent coin; nickel **2.** a small bus or car that carries passengers for a low fare, originally five cents
jit·ter (jit′ər) ***vi.*** **[**? echoic**]** [Colloq.] to be nervous; have the jitters; fidget —**the jitters** [Colloq.] a very uneasy, nervous feeling; the fidgets —**jit′ter·y *adj.***
jit·ter·bug (-bug′) ***n.*** **[**prec. + BUG**]** **1.** a dance for couples, esp. in the early 1940's, involving fast, acrobatic movements to swing music **2.** a dancer of the jitterbug —***vi.*** **-bugged′, -bug′ging** to dance the jitterbug

jiu·jit·su, jiu·jut·su (jo͞o jit′so͞o) ***n.*** *var. of* JUJITSU
jive (jīv) ***vt.*** **jived, jiv′ing** [altered < JIBE2] [Slang] to use jive, or nonsense talk, in speaking to, esp. in an effort to mislead —***n.*** **1.** [Slang] foolish, exaggerated, or insincere talk **2.** *former term* (c. 1930–45) *for* JAZZ *or* SWING
Jl. July
jo (jō) ***n.,*** *pl.* **joes** [var. of JOY] [Scot.] a sweetheart
Joan (jōn, jō′ən) [var. of ff.] a feminine name
Jo·an·na (jō an′ə) [ML., fem. of *Johannes:* see JOHN] a feminine name: var. *Joanne, Johanna*
Joan of Arc (ärk), Saint (Fr. name *Jeanne d'Arc*) 1412–31; Fr. heroine: defeated the English at Orléans (1429): burned at the stake for witchcraft: called the *Maid of Orléans*
Job (jōb) *Bible* **1.** a man who endured much suffering but did not lose his faith in God **2.** the book telling of him
job (jäb) ***n.*** [< ?] **1.** a specific piece of work, as in one's trade, or done by agreement for pay **2.** a task; chore; duty **3.** the thing or material being worked on or the resulting product **4.** a position of employment; work **5.** [Colloq.] a criminal act or deed, as a theft, etc. **6.** [Colloq.] any happening, affair, matter, object, etc. —***adj.*** hired or done by the job —***vi.*** **jobbed, job′bing 1.** to do odd jobs **2.** to act as a jobber or broker **3.** [Chiefly Brit.] to engage in jobbery —***vt.*** **1.** to buy and sell (goods) as a wholesaler **2.** to let or sublet (work, contracts, etc.) —**odd jobs** miscellaneous pieces of work —**on the job 1.** while working at one's job **2.** [Slang] attentive to one's task or duty —**job′less** ***adj.***
job·ber (jäb′ər) ***n.*** **1.** a wholesaler; middleman **2.** a person who works by the job or who does piecework
job·ber·y (-ər ē, -rē) ***n.*** [Chiefly Brit.] the carrying on of public business dishonestly for private gain
Job Corps a U.S. government program for training underprivileged youth for employment
job·hold·er (-hōl′dər) ***n.*** a person who has a steady job; specif., a government employee
job lot 1. an assortment of goods for sale as one quantity **2.** any random assortment
Jo·cas·ta (jō kas′tə) *Gr. Myth.* the queen who unwittingly married her own son, Oedipus
jock (jäk) ***n.*** *clip for:* **1.** JOCKEY **2.** JOCKSTRAP
jock·ey (jäk′ē) ***n.,*** *pl.* **-eys** [< Scot. dim. of JACK1] **1.** a person whose work is riding horses in races **2.** [Slang] the operator of a specified vehicle, machine, etc. —***vt., vi.*** **-eyed, -ey·ing 1.** to ride (a horse) in a race **2.** to cheat; swindle **3.** to maneuver for position or advantage **4.** [Slang] to be the operator, pilot, etc. (of)
jock·strap (jäk′strap′) ***n.*** [*jock,* penis + STRAP] **1.** an elastic belt with a pouch to support the genitals, worn by men **2.** [Slang] an athlete
jo·cose (jō kōs′, jə-) ***adj.*** [< L. < *jocus,* a joke] joking or playful; humorous —**jo·cose′ly** ***adv.*** —**jo·cos′i·ty** (-käs′ə tē) *pl.* **-ties, jo·cose′ness** ***n.***
joc·u·lar (jäk′yə lər) ***adj.*** [< L. dim. of *jocus,* a joke] **1.** joking; full of fun **2.** said as a joke —**joc′u·lar′i·ty** (-lar′ə tē) ***n.,*** *pl.* **-ties** —**joc′u·lar·ly** ***adv.***
joc·und (jäk′ənd, jō′kənd) ***adj.*** [< OFr. < LL. < L. *jucundus,* pleasant < *juvare,* to help] cheerful; genial; gay —**jo·cun·di·ty** (jō kun′də tē) ***n.,*** *pl.* **-ties** —**joc′und·ly** ***adv.***
jodh·pur (jäd′pər) ***n.*** [after *Jodhpur,* former state in India] **1.** [*pl.*] riding breeches made loose and full above the knees and tight from knees to ankles **2.** an ankle-high boot, often with an adjustable buckle and strap
Joe (jō) *a nickname for* JOSEPH —***n.*** [Slang] **1.** [*often* **j-**] fellow; guy **2.** [**j-**] coffee
Jo·el (jō′əl) [< LL. < Gr. < Heb. *yō'ēl,* lit., the Lord is God] **1.** a masculine name **2.** *Bible a*) a Hebrew prophet of about 400 B.C. *b*) the book of his preachings
jog1 (jäg) ***vt.*** **jogged, jog′ging** [ME. *joggen,* to spur] **1.** *a*) to give a little shake or jerk to *b*) to nudge **2.** to shake up or revive (a person's memory) **3.** to cause to jog —***vi.*** to move along at a slow, steady, jolting pace or trot —***n.*** **1.** a little shake or nudge **2.** a slow, steady, jolting motion or trot —**jog′ger** ***n.***
jog2 (jäg) ***n.*** [var. of JAG1] **1.** a projecting or notched part, esp. one at right angles, in a surface or line **2.** a sharp, temporary change of direction —***vi.*** **jogged, jog′ging** to form or make a jog
jog·ging (jäg′iŋ) ***n.*** the practice of trotting at a slow, steady pace for some distance as a form of exercise
jog·gle1 (jäg′'l) ***vt., vi.*** **-gled, -gling** [freq. of JOG1] to shake or jolt slightly —***n.*** a slight jolt
jog·gle2 (jäg′'l) ***n.*** [< JOG2] **1.** a joint made by putting a notch in one surface and a projection in the other to fit into it **2.** the notch or projection —***vt.*** **-gled, -gling** to join by joggles
Jo·han·nes·burg (jō han′is burg′, yō hän′-) city in the Transvaal, South Africa: pop. 1,295,000
John (jän) [< OFr. < ML. *Johannes* < LL. < Gr. < Heb. contr. of *yehōḥānān,* lit., Yahweh is gracious] **1.** a masculine name: dim. *Johnnie, Johnny* **2.** 1167?–1216; king of England (1199–1216): forced to sign the Magna Charta (1215) **3.** *Bible a*) a Christian apostle, credited with having written the fourth Gospel, the three Epistles of John, and Revelation: called *the Evangelist* and *the Divine b*) the fourth book of the New Testament *c*) *same as* JOHN THE BAPTIST **4. John XXIII** 1881–1963; Pope (1958–63)
john (jän) ***n.*** [Slang] a toilet
John Barleycorn corn liquor, etc., personified
John Bull England, or an Englishman, personified
John Doe *see* DOE
John Hancock [Colloq.] one's signature
john·ny·cake (jän′ē kāk′) ***n.*** [< Eng. dial. *jannock,* bread of oatmeal] corn bread baked on a griddle
John·ny-jump-up (-jump′up′) ***n.*** **1.** *same as a*) WILD PANSY *b*) DAFFODIL **2.** any of various American violets
John Paul I 1912–1978; Pope (1978)
John Paul II 1920– ; Pope (1978–)
John·son (jän′s'n) **1. Andrew,** 1808–75; 17th president of the U.S. (1865–69) **2. Lyn·don Baines** (lin′dən bānz), 1908–73; 36th president of the U.S. (1963–69) **3. Samuel,** 1709–84; Eng. lexicographer, writer, & critic: known as *Dr. Johnson*
Johns·town (jänz′toun′) [after J. *Johns,* local landowner] city in SW Pa.: site of a disastrous flood (1889): pop. 35,000
John the Baptist *Bible* the forerunner and baptizer of Jesus: Matt. 3
Jo·hore (jə hôr′) state of Malaya, at the tip of the Malay Peninsula
‡**joie de vi·vre** (zhwȧd vē′vr′) [Fr.] joy of living
join (join) ***vt.*** [< OFr. *joindre* < L. *jungere*] **1.** to bring together; connect; combine **2.** to make into one; unite [*join* forces, *joined* in wedlock] **3.** to become a part or member of (a club, etc.) **4.** to go to and combine with [the path *joins* the highway] **5.** to enter into the company of; accompany [*join* us soon] **6.** [Colloq.] to adjoin —***vi.*** **1.** to come together; meet **2.** to enter into association or become a member: often with *up* **3.** to participate (*in* a conversation, singing, etc.) —***n.*** a place of joining, as a seam in a coat —**join battle** to start fighting
join·er (-ər) ***n.*** **1.** a person or thing that joins **2.** a workman who finishes interior woodwork, as doors or molding **3.** [Colloq.] a person given to joining various organizations
join·er·y (-ər ē) ***n.*** the work or skill of a joiner
joint (joint) ***n.*** [< OFr. < L. pp. of *jungere,* to join] **1.** a place where, or way in which, two things or parts are joined **2.** one of the parts of a jointed whole **3.** a large cut of meat with the bones still in it, as for a roast **4.** [Slang] *a*) a cheap bar, restaurant, etc. *b*) any building, etc. **5.** [Slang] a marijuana cigarette **6.** *Anat.* a place or part where two bones, etc. are joined, usually so that they can move **7.** *Bot.* a point where a branch or leaf grows out of the stem —***adj.*** **1.** common to two or more as to ownership or action [*joint* property] **2.** sharing with someone else [*a joint* owner] —***vt.*** **1.** to fasten together by a joint or joints **2.** to give a joint or joints to **3.** to cut (meat) into joints —**out of joint 1.** not in place at the joint; dislocated **2.** disordered —**joint′ed** ***adj.*** —**joint′er** ***n.***
joint·ly (-lē) ***adv.*** in common; together
joint resolution a resolution passed by a legislature with two houses: it becomes a law if signed by the chief executive or passed over his veto
joint return a single income tax return filed by a married couple, combining their incomes
joint-stock company (-stäk′) a business firm owned by the stockholders in shares which each may sell or transfer independently
join·ture (join′chər) ***n.*** [< OFr. < L. < *jungere,* to join] *Law* **1.** an arrangement by which a husband grants real property to his wife for her use after his death **2.** the property thus settled
joist (joist) ***n.*** [< OFr. *giste,* a bed; ult. < L. *jacere,* to lie] any of the parallel beams that hold up the planks of a floor or the laths of a ceiling —***vt.*** to provide with joists
joke (jōk) ***n.*** [L. *jocus*] **1.** anything said or done to arouse laughter; a funny anecdote or amusing trick **2.** a thing done or said merely in fun **3.** a person or thing to be laughed at —***vi.*** **joked, jok′ing 1.** to tell or play jokes **2.** to say or do something as a joke; jest —***vt.*** to bring to a specified condition by joking —**jok′ing·ly** ***adv.***

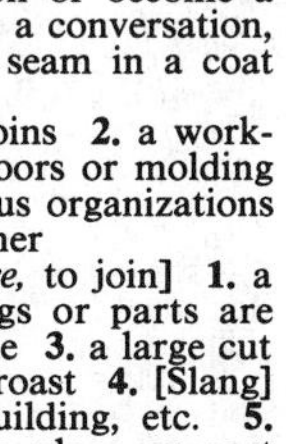

JOISTS

jok·er (jō′kər) ***n.*** **1.** a person who jokes **2.** a hidden provision put into a law, legal document, etc. to make it different from what it seems to be **3.** any hidden, unsuspected difficulty **4.** an extra playing card used in some games

Jo·li·et (jō′lē et′, jō′lē et′) [after L. *Joliet*, 17th-c. Fr.-Canad. explorer] city in NE Ill.: pop. 78,000

jol·li·fy (jäl′ə fī′) *vt., vi.* **-fied′, -fy′ing** [Colloq.] to make or be jolly or merry **—jol′li·fi·ca′tion** *n.*

jol·li·ty (-ə tē) *n.* a being jolly; fun; gaiety

jol·ly (jäl′ē) *adj.* **-li·er, -li·est** [< OFr. *joli*, joyful; prob. < ON. *jol*, YULE] **1.** full of high spirits and good humor **2.** [Colloq.] enjoyable; pleasant **—*adv.*** [Brit. Colloq.] very; altogether **—*vt., vi.*** **-lied, -ly·ing** [Colloq.] **1.** to try to make (a person) feel good or agreeable by coaxing, flattering, etc. (often with *along*) **2.** to make fun of (someone) **—jol′li·ly** ***adv.*** **—jol′li·ness** *n.*

jolly (boat) [< MDu. *jolle*, yawl] a ship's small boat

Jolly Roger a black flag of pirates, with white skull and crossbones

jolt (jōlt) *vt.* [earlier *jot*, to jog, orig. echoic: prob. infl. by *jowl*, to strike] **1.** to shake up or jar, as with a bumpy ride or sharp blow **2.** to shock or surprise **—*vi.*** to move along in a bumpy, jerky manner **—*n.*** **1.** a sudden jerk, bump, etc., as from a blow **2.** a shock or surprise **—jolt′er** *n.* **—jolt′ing·ly** ***adv.*** **—jolt′y** ***adj.***

Jo·nah (jō′nə) [< LL. < Gr. < Heb. *yōnāh*, lit., a dove] **1.** a masculine name: var. *Jonas* **2.** *Bible a)* a Hebrew prophet: thrown overboard in a storm, he was swallowed by a big fish, but later was cast up unharmed *b)* the book telling Jonah's story Also, esp. in the Douay Bible, **Jo′nas** (-nəs) **—*n.*** any person said to bring bad luck by his presence

Jon·a·than (jän′ə thən) [< Heb. < *yehōnāthān*, lit., Yahweh has given] **1.** a masculine name **2.** *Bible* Saul's oldest son, a close friend of David: I Sam. 18–20 **—*n.*** a late fall variety of apple

Jones (jōnz) **1. In·i·go** (in′i gō′), 1573–1652; Eng. architect & stage designer **2. John Paul,** (born *John Paul*) 1747–92; Am. naval officer in the Revolutionary War, born in Scotland

jon·gleur (jäŋ′glər; *Fr.* zhōn glër′) *n.* [Fr. < OFr. *jogleor*, juggler: see JUGGLE] a wandering minstrel in medieval France and England

jon·quil (jäŋ′kwəl, jän′-) *n.* [< Fr. < Sp. dim. *junquillo* < L. *juncus*, a rush] **1.** a species of narcissus having relatively small yellow flowers and long, slender leaves **2.** its bulb or flower

Jon·son (jän′s′n), **Ben** 1572?–1637; Eng. dramatist & poet **—Jon·so′ni·an** (-sō′nē ən) ***adj.***

Jor·dan (jôr′d′n) **1.** river in the Near East, flowing into the Dead Sea **2.** country in the Near East, east of Israel: 37,300 sq. mi.; pop. 2,133,000; cap. Amman **—Jor·da′ni·an** (-dā′nē ən) ***adj., n.***

Jordan almond [prob. < OFr. *jardin*, garden] a variety of large Spanish almond used in candies

Jo·seph (jō′zəf, -səf) [LL. < Gr. < Heb. *yōsēph*, lit., may he add] **1.** a masculine name **2.** *Bible a)* Jacob's eleventh son, who was sold into slavery in Egypt by his jealous brothers but became a high official there: Gen. 37, 39–41 *b)* the husband of Mary, mother of Jesus: Matt. 1:18–25

Jo·se·phine (jō′zə fēn, -sə-) [< Fr. fem. of prec.] **1.** a feminine name: dim. *Jo, Josie* **2.** 1763–1814; wife of Napoleon (1796–1809) & empress of France (1804–09)

Jo·se·phus (jō sē′fəs), **(Flavius)** 37–95? A.D.; Jewish historian

josh (jäsh) *vt., vi.* [< ?] [Colloq.] to ridicule in a good-humored way; tease jokingly; banter **—josh′er** *n.* **—josh′ing·ly** ***adv.***

Josh·u·a (jäsh′oo wə) [Heb. *yehōshūʻa*, lit., help of Jehovah] **1.** a masculine name **2.** *Bible a)* Moses' successor, and leader of the Israelites into the Promised Land *b)* the book telling about him: also, in the Douay Bible, **Jos·u·e** (jäs′yoo wē′)

joss (jäs) *n.* [PidE. < Port. *deos* < L. *deus*, a god] a figure of a Chinese god

joss house a Chinese temple

joss stick a thin stick of dried, fragrant wood dust, burned by the Chinese as incense

jos·tle (jäs′'l) *vt., vi.* **-tled, -tling** [earlier *justle*, freq.: see JOUST] **1.** to bump or push, as in a crowd; shove roughly **2.** to contend (*with* someone *for* something) **—*n.*** a jostling **—jos′tler** *n.*

jot (jät) *n.* [< L. < Gr. *iōta*, the letter *i*, the smallest letter] a trifling amount; the smallest bit **—*vt.*** **jot′ted, jot′ting** to make a brief note of (usually with *down*) **—jot′ter** *n.*

jo·ta (hō′tə) *n.* [Sp. < OSp. < *sotar*, to dance] a Spanish dance in 3/4 time performed by a man and woman to the rhythm of castanets

jot·ting (jät′iŋ) *n.* a short note jotted down

joule (jo͞ol, joul) *n.* [after J. P. *Joule*, 19th.-c. Eng. physicist] *Physics* a unit of work or energy equal to 10,000,000 ergs

jounce (jouns) *n., vt., vi.* **jounced, jounc′ing** [< ?] jolt or bounce **—jounc′y** ***adj.***

jour·nal (jʉr′n'l) *n.* [< OFr., lit., daily < L. *diurnalis* < *dies*, day] **1.** a daily record of happenings, as a diary **2.** a record of the transactions of a legislature, club, etc. **3.** a ship's logbook **4.** a newspaper, magazine, etc. **5.** *Bookkeeping* a book of original entry for recording every transaction with an indication of its proper account **6.** *Mech.* the part of a rotatory axle or shaft that turns in a bearing

journal box *Mech.* a housing for a journal

jour·nal·ese (jʉr′n'l ēz′) *n.* a style of writing characteristic of many newspapers, magazines, etc.; facile style, with many clichés

jour·nal·ism (jʉr′n'l iz'm) *n.* **1.** the work of gathering, writing, and publishing or disseminating news, as through newspapers, etc. or by radio and TV **2.** newspapers and magazines collectively

jour·nal·ist (-ist) *n.* a person whose occupation is journalism; reporter, news editor, etc. **—jour′nal·is′tic** ***adj.*** **—jour′nal·is′ti·cal·ly** ***adv.***

jour·ney (jʉr′nē) *n., pl.* **-neys** [< OFr. *journee* < LL. < L. *diurnus*, daily: see JOURNAL] a traveling from one place to another; trip **—*vi.*** **-neyed, -ney·ing** to go on a trip; travel

jour·ney·man (-mən) *n., pl.* **-men** [ME. < *journee*, day's work + *man*] **1.** formerly, a worker qualified to work at his trade, after serving his apprenticeship **2.** now, a worker who has learned his trade **3.** an experienced craftsman of average ability

joust (joust, just, jo͞ost) *n.* [< OFr. < *juster* < L. *juxta*, beside] **1.** a combat with lances between two knights on horseback **2.** [*pl.*] a tournament **—*vi.*** to engage in a joust **—joust′er** *n.*

Jove (jōv) *same as* JUPITER **—by Jove!** an exclamation of astonishment, emphasis, etc. **—Jo·vi·an** (jō′vē ən) ***adj.***

jo·vi·al (jō′vē əl, -vyəl) *adj.* [Fr. < LL. *Jovialis*, of Jupiter < L. *Jovis*: see prec.] full of hearty, playful good humor; genial and gay **—jo′vi·al′i·ty** (-al′ə tē) *n.* **—jo′vi·al·ly** ***adv.***

jowl[1] (joul, jōl) *n.* [< OE. *ceafl*, jaw] **1.** a jaw; esp., the lower jaw with the chin and cheeks **2.** the cheek **3.** the meat of a hog's cheek

jowl[2] (joul, jōl) *n.* [< OE. *ceole*, throat] [*often pl.*] the fleshy, hanging part under the lower jaw **—jowl′y** ***adj.***

joy (joi) *n.* [< OFr. *joie* < LL. < L. *gaudium*, joy] **1.** a very glad feeling; happiness; delight **2.** anything causing this **3.** the expression of such feeling **—*vi.*** to be full of joy

Joyce (jois) [< L. fem. of *jocosus*, merry] **1.** a feminine name **2. James (Augustine Aloysius),** 1882–1941; Ir. novelist & poet **—Joyc·e·an** (jois′ē ən) ***adj.***

joy·ful (joi′fəl) *adj.* feeling, expressing, or causing joy; glad; happy **—joy′ful·ly** ***adv.*** **—joy′ful·ness** *n.*

joy·less (-lis) *adj.* without joy; unhappy; sad **—joy′less·ly** ***adv.*** **—joy′less·ness** *n.*

joy·ous (-əs) *adj.* full of joy; happy; gay; glad **—joy′ous·ly** ***adv.*** **—joy′ous·ness** *n.*

joy ride [Colloq.] an automobile ride merely for pleasure, often with reckless speed and, sometimes, in a stolen car **—joy rider —joy riding**

J.P. justice of the peace

Jpn. 1. Japan **2.** Japanese

Jr., jr. junior

Ju. June

ju·bi·lant (jo͞o′b'l ənt) *adj.* [L. *jubilans*, prp. of *jubilare*: see ff.] joyful and triumphant; elated **—ju′bi·lance** *n.* **—ju′bi·lant·ly** ***adv.***

ju·bi·late (jo͞o′bə lāt′) *vi.* **-lat′ed, -lat′ing** [< L. pp. of *jubilare*, to shout for joy < *jubilum*, wild shout] to rejoice, as in triumph; exult

ju·bi·la·tion (jo͞o′bə lā′shən) *n.* **1.** a jubilating **2.** a happy celebration, as of victory

ju·bi·lee (jo͞o′bə lē′, jo͞o′bə lē′) *n.* [< OFr. < LL. < Gr. < Heb. *yōbēl*, a ram's horn (trumpet): infl. by L. *jubilum*, wild shout] **1.** *Jewish History* a celebration held every fifty years in which all bondmen were freed, mortgaged lands restored to the owners, etc.: Lev. 25:8–17 **2.** a 50th or 25th anniversary **3.** a time or occasion of rejoicing **4.** jubilation; rejoicing **5.** *R.C.Ch.* a year proclaimed as a solemn time for gaining a plenary indulgence

Ju·dah (jo͞o′də) [Heb. *yehūdhāh* < ?] **1.** a masculine name **2.** *Bible a)* the fourth son of Jacob *b)* the tribe descended from him **3.** the kingdom in the S part of ancient Palestine formed by the tribes of Judah and Benjamin

Ju·da·ic (jo͞o dā′ik) *adj.* of the Jews or Judaism; Jewish **—Ju·da′i·cal·ly** ***adv.***

Ju·da·ism (jo͞o′də iz'm, -dē-) *n.* **1.** the Jewish religion, a monotheistic religion based on the laws and teachings of the Holy Scripture and the Talmud **2.** observance of Jewish morality, traditions, etc. **—Ju′da·ist** *n.* **—Ju′da·is′tic** ***adj.***

Ju·da·ize (-īz′) *vi., vt.* **-ized′, -iz′ing** to conform to, or make conform to, Judaism **—Ju′da·i·za′tion** *n.*

Ju·das (jo͞o′dəs) [var. of JUDAH] **1.** Judas Iscariot, the disciple who betrayed Jesus **2.** *same as* JUDE (sense 1) **—*n.*** a traitor or betrayer

Judas tree a tree of the legume family, with clusters of rose-pink flowers
Jude (jo͞od) *Bible* **1.** a Christian apostle: also called *Judas* (not Iscariot) **2.** *a*) a book of the New Testament, the Epistle of Jude *b*) its author
Ju·de·a (jo͞o dē′ə) ancient region of S Palestine: it corresponded roughly to the Biblical Judah: also sp. **Judaea** —**Ju·de′an** ***adj., n.***
Ju·de·o- (jo͞o dē′ō, -dā′-) *a combining form meaning:* **1.** Judaic; Jewish **2.** Jewish and *[Judeo-*Christian*]*
Judg. Judges
judge (juj) ***n.*** [< OFr. < L. *judex* < *jus*, law + *dicere*, to say] **1.** a public official with authority to hear and decide cases in a court of law **2.** a person designated to determine the winner, settle a controversy, etc. **3.** a person qualified to decide on the relative worth of anything *[*a good *judge* of music*]* **4.** any of the governing leaders of the ancient Israelites before the time of the kings —***vt., vi.*** **judged, judg′ing** **1.** to hear and pass judgment (*on*) in a court of law **2.** to determine the winner of (a contest) or settle (a controversy) **3.** to form an opinion about **4.** to criticize or censure **5.** to think or suppose **6.** *Jewish History* to govern —**judg′er** ***n.*** —**judge′ship′** ***n.***
judge advocate *pl.* **judge advocates** a military legal officer; esp., an officer designated to act as prosecutor at a court-martial
Judg·es (juj′iz) a book of the Bible telling the history of the Jews from the death of Joshua to the birth of Samuel
judg·ment (juj′mənt) ***n.*** **1.** a judging; deciding **2.** a legal decision; order or sentence given by a judge or law court **3.** a debt resulting from a court order **4.** an opinion or estimate **5.** criticism or censure **6.** power of comparing and deciding; understanding **7.** [J-] *short for* LAST JUDGMENT Also sp. **judge′ment** —**judg·men′tal** (-men′t'l) ***adj.***
Judgment Day *Theol.* the time of God's final judgment of all people; end of the world
ju·di·ca·to·ry (jo͞o′di kə tôr′ē) ***adj.*** [< LL. < L. pp. of *judicare*, to judge < *judex*, a JUDGE] having to do with administering justice; judging —***n.,*** *pl.* **-ries** **1.** a court of law; tribunal **2.** law courts collectively
ju·di·ca·ture (-chər) ***n.*** **1.** the administering of justice **2.** the position, functions, or legal power of a judge **3.** the extent of legal power of a judge or court of law **4.** a court of law **5.** judges or courts of law collectively
ju·di·cial (jo͞o dish′əl) ***adj.*** [< OFr. < L. *judicialis* < *judex*, a JUDGE] **1.** of judges, law courts, or their functions **2.** allowed, enforced, or set by order of a judge or law court **3.** like or befitting a judge **4.** fair; unbiased —**ju·di′cial·ly** ***adv.***
ju·di·ci·ar·y (jo͞o dish′ē er′ē, -dish′ər ē) ***adj.*** of judges, law courts, or their functions —***n.,*** *pl.* **-ar′ies** **1.** the part of government that administers justice **2.** a system of law courts **3.** judges collectively
ju·di·cious (-dish′əs) ***adj.*** [< Fr. < L. *judicium*, judgment < *judex*, a JUDGE] having, applying, or showing sound judgment; wise and careful —**ju·di′cious·ly** ***adv.*** —**ju·di′cious·ness** ***n.***
Ju·dith (jo͞o′dith) [LL. < Gr. < Heb. *yehūdhīth*, woman of Judah] **1.** a feminine name: dim. *Judy* **2.** *a*) a book of the Apocrypha and the Douay Bible *b*) the Jewish heroine told about in this book
ju·do (jo͞o′dō) ***n.*** [Jap. < *jū*, soft + *dō*, art] a form of jujitsu, esp. as a means of self-defense
jug (jug) ***n.*** [a pet form of JUDITH or JOAN] **1.** *a*) a container for liquids, with a small opening and a handle *b*) the contents of a jug **2.** [Slang] a jail —***vt.*** **jugged, jug′ging** **1.** to put into a jug **2.** to stew in a covered earthenware container **3.** [Slang] to jail —**jug′ful** (-fool) ***n.***
ju·gate (jo͞o′gāt, -git) ***adj.*** [< L. pp. of *jugare*, to yoke < *jugum*, a yoke] *Biol.* paired or connected
Jug·ger·naut (jug′ər nôt′) ***n.*** [< Hindi < Sans. < *jagat*, world + *nātha*, lord] **1.** an incarnation of the Hindu god Vishnu: his worshipers reputedly threw themselves to be crushed under the wheels of a large car carrying his idol **2.** [*usually* **j-**] *a*) anything that exacts blind devotion *b*) any terrible, irresistible force
jug·gle (jug′'l) ***vt.*** **-gled, -gling** [< OFr. *jogler* < L. *joculari*, to joke < *jocus*, a joke] **1.** to perform skillful tricks of sleight of hand with (balls, knives, etc.) **2.** to make awkward attempts to catch or hold (a ball, etc.) **3.** to use trickery on to deceive or cheat *[*to *juggle* figures to show a profit*]* —***vi.*** to toss up a number of balls, knives, etc. and keep them continuously in the air —***n.*** **1.** a juggling **2.** a clever trick or deception —**jug·gler** (jug′lər) ***n.*** —**jug′gler·y** ***n.,*** *pl.* **-gler·ies**
Ju·go·sla·vi·a (yo͞o′gō slä′vē ə) *same as* YUGOSLAVIA —**Ju′go·slav′** ***adj., n.*** —**Ju′go·sla′vi·an** ***adj., n.*** —**Ju′go·slav′ic** ***adj.***
jug·u·lar (jug′yoo lər, jo͞og′-) ***adj.*** [< LL. < L. *jugulum*, collarbone < *jugum*, a yoke] **1.** of the neck or throat **2.** of a jugular vein —***n.*** either of two large veins in the neck carrying blood back from the head to the heart: in full, **jugular vein**
juice (jo͞os) ***n.*** [< OFr. < L. *jus*] **1.** the liquid part of a plant, fruit, or vegetable **2.** a liquid in or from animal tissue *[*gastric *juice]* **3.** [Colloq.] energy; vitality **4.** [Slang] *a*) electricity *b*) gasoline, oil, or any liquid fuel **5.** [Slang] alcoholic liquor —***vt.*** **juiced, juic′ing** to extract juice from —**juice up** to add power, vigor, excitement, etc. to —**juice′less** ***adj.*** —**juic′er** ***n.***
juic·y (jo͞o′sē) ***adj.*** **juic′i·er, juic′i·est** **1.** full of juice; succulent **2.** [Colloq.] full of interest; piquant; spicy **3.** [Colloq.] highly profitable —**juic′i·ly** ***adv.*** —**juic′i·ness** ***n.***
ju·jit·su (jo͞o jit′so͞o) ***n.*** [< Jap. < *jū*, soft + *jutsu*, art] a Japanese system of wrestling in which the strength and weight of an opponent are used against him: also **ju·jut·su** (-jit′so͞o, -jut′-)
ju·jube (jo͞o′jo͞ob; *for 3, often* jo͞o′jo͞o bē′) ***n.*** [Fr. < ML. < L. *zizyphum* < Gr. *zizyphon*] **1.** the edible, datelike fruit of a tree or shrub growing in warm climates **2.** this tree or shrub **3.** a lozenge of gelatinous, fruit-flavored candy
juke·box (jo͞ok′bäks′) ***n.*** [Gullah *juke*, wicked (as in *jukehouse*, house of prostitution), WAfr. orig.] a coin-operated electric phonograph: a record is chosen by pushing a button: also **juke box**
ju·lep (jo͞o′ləp) ***n.*** [< MFr. < Ar. < Per. < *gul*, rose + *āb*, water] *same as* MINT JULEP
Jul·ia (jo͞ol′yə) [L., fem. of JULIUS] a feminine name: var. *Julie*
Jul·ian (jo͞ol′yən) [< L. < *Julius:* see JULIUS] a masculine name —***adj.*** of Julius Caesar
Julian calendar the calendar introduced by Julius Caesar in 46 B.C., in which the ordinary year had 365 days and every fourth year (leap year) had 366 days: replaced by the Gregorian calendar
ju·li·enne (jo͞o′lē en′; *Fr.* zhü lyen′) ***n.*** [Fr., origin obscure] a clear soup containing vegetables cut into strips or bits —***adj.*** *Cooking* cut into strips: said of vegetables
Ju·li·et (jo͞ol′yət, -ē ət, jo͞o′lē et′) [< Fr. < L. *Julia*] **1.** a feminine name **2.** the heroine of Shakespeare's tragedy *Romeo and Juliet*
Jul·ius (jo͞ol′yəs) [L., name of a Roman gens] a masculine name
Julius Caesar *see* Julius CAESAR
Ju·ly (joo lī′, jo͞o-, jə-) ***n.,*** *pl.* **-lies′** [< Anglo-Fr. < L. < *mensis Julius*, the month of Julius (Caesar)] the seventh month of the year, having 31 days: abbrev. **Jul., Jl., Jy.**
jum·ble (jum′b'l) ***vt.*** **-bled, -bling** [? blend of JUMP + TUMBLE] **1.** to mix in a confused, disorderly heap **2.** to confuse mentally —***vi.*** to be jumbled —***n.*** **1.** a confused mixture or heap **2.** a muddle
jum·bo (jum′bō) ***n.,*** *pl.* **-bos** [< Gullah *jamba*, elephant; infl. by P. T. BARNUM's use of it for his elephant, *Jumbo*] a very large person, animal, or thing —***adj.*** very large
Jum·na (jum′nə) river in N India, flowing from the Himalayas southwest into the Ganges
jump (jump) ***vi.*** [< ?] **1.** to move oneself suddenly from the ground, etc. by using the leg muscles; leap; spring **2.** to jerk; bob; bounce **3.** to leap from an aircraft, using a parachute **4.** to act or react eagerly (often with *at*) **5.** to pass suddenly as from one topic to another **6.** to rise suddenly, as prices **7.** [Slang] to be lively and animated **8.** *Bridge* to make an unnecessarily high bid (**jump bid**) to increase the previous bid **9.** *Checkers* to move a piece over an opponent's piece, thus capturing it —***vt.*** **1.** *a*) to leap over *b*) to skip over **2.** to cause to leap *[*to *jump* a horse over a fence*]* **3.** to advance (a person) by bypassing others **4.** to leap upon; spring aboard **5.** to cause (prices, etc.) to rise suddenly **6.** [Colloq.] to attack suddenly **7.** [Colloq.] to react to prematurely, in anticipation **8.** [Slang] to leave suddenly *[*to *jump* town*]* **9.** *Checkers* to capture (an opponent's piece) —***n.*** **1.** a jumping; leap **2.** a distance jumped **3.** a descent from an aircraft by parachute **4.** a thing to be jumped over **5.** a sudden transition **6.** a sudden rise, as in prices **7.** a sudden, nervous start or jerk; twitch **8.** *Athletics* a contest in jumping **9.** *Checkers* a move by which an opponent's piece is captured —**get** (or **have**) **the jump on** [Slang] to get (or have) an advantage over —**jump a claim** to seize land claimed by someone else —**jump bail** to forfeit one's bail by running away —**jump on** (or **all over**) [Slang] to scold; censure —**jump the track** to go suddenly off the rails —**on the jump** [Colloq.] very busy
jump·er[1] (jum′pər) ***n.*** **1.** a person, animal, or thing that jumps **2.** a short wire used to make a temporary electrical connection

jump·er² (jum′pər) ***n.*** [< dial. *jump,* short coat, prob. < Fr. *jupe* < Sp. < Ar. *jubbah,* undergarment] **1.** a loose jacket or blouse, worn as to protect clothing or as part of a sailor's outfit **2.** a sleeveless dress worn over a blouse or sweater **3.** [*pl.*] rompers: see ROMPER (sense 2)

JUMPER

jumping bean the seed of a Mexican plant, which is made to jump or roll about by the movements of a moth larva inside it

jumping jack a child's toy consisting of a little jointed figure made to jump about by pulling a string

jump suit **1.** a coverall worn by paratroops, etc. **2.** any one-piece garment like this

jump·y (jum′pē) ***adj.*** **jump′i·er, jump′i·est** **1.** moving in jumps, jerks, etc. **2.** easily startled; apprehensive —**jump′i·ly** ***adv.*** —**jump′i·ness** ***n.***

Jun., jun. junior

jun·co (juŋ′kō) ***n.,*** *pl.* **-cos** [< ModL. < Sp. < L. *juncus,* a rush] a sparrowlike bird of North and Central America, with a gray or black head

junc·tion (juŋk′shən) ***n.*** [< L. < *jungere,* to join] **1.** a joining or being joined **2.** a place or point of joining or crossing, as of highways or railroads **3.** the region separating two kinds of semiconductor material —**junc′tion·al** ***adj.***

junc·ture (-chər) ***n.*** [< L.: see prec.] **1.** a joining or being joined **2.** a point or line of joining or connection; joint **3.** a point of time **4.** a crisis **5.** a state of affairs **6.** *Linguis.* the transition marking the boundary between one speech sound and the next

June (jo͞on) [< L. *Junius,* name of a Roman gens] a feminine name —***n.*** [< OFr. < L. < *mensis Junius,* the month of JUNO] the sixth month of the year, having 30 days

Ju·neau (jo͞o′nō) [after J. *Juneau,* a prospector] capital of Alas., on the SE coast: pop. 20,000

June·ber·ry (jo͞on′ber′ē, -bər ē) ***n.,*** *pl.* **-ries** **1.** any of various N. American shrubs and trees of the rose family, with white flowers and purple-black fruits **2.** the fruit

June bug **1.** a large, scarabaeid beetle appearing in May or June in the N U.S.: also **June beetle** **2.** *same as* FIGEATER

Jung (yooŋ), **Carl G(ustav)** 1875–1961; Swiss psychologist & psychiatrist —**Jung′i·an** ***adj., n.***

Jung·frau (yooŋ′frou′) mountain in the Alps of S Switzerland

jun·gle (juŋ′g'l) ***n.*** [< Hindi < Sans. *jaṅgala,* desert] **1.** land with a dense growth of trees, vines, etc., as in the tropics, usually inhabited by predatory animals **2.** any tangled growth **3.** [Slang] a hobos' camp **4.** [Slang] a place where people compete ruthlessly —**jun′gly** ***adj.***

jun·ior (jo͞on′yər) ***adj.*** [< L. compar. of *juvenis,* young] **1.** the younger: written *Jr.* after the name of a son who bears the same name as his father **2.** of more recent position or lower status *[a junior* partner*]* **3.** of later date **4.** made up of younger members **5.** relating to juniors in a high school or college —***n.*** **1.** a younger person **2.** a person of lower standing or rank **3.** a student in the next-to-last year of a high school or college —**one's junior** a person younger than oneself

junior college a school offering courses two years beyond the high school level

junior high school a school intermediate between elementary school and senior high school: it usually includes the 7th, 8th, and 9th grades

Junior League an organization of young society women with leisure to do volunteer welfare work —**Junior Leaguer**

junior varsity a team that represents a school, college, etc. in a secondary level of competition

ju·ni·per (jo͞o′nə pər) ***n.*** [L. *juniperus*] a small evergreen shrub or tree with scalelike foliage and berrylike cones

junk¹ (juŋk) ***n.*** [< ? Port. *junco,* a reed < L. *juncus*] **1.** orig., old rope used for making oakum, mats, etc. **2.** old metal, paper, rags, etc. **3.** [Colloq.] useless stuff; rubbish **4.** [Slang] a narcotic drug; esp., heroin —***vt.*** [Colloq.] to throw away or sell as junk; discard —**junk′y** ***adj.***

junk² (juŋk) ***n.*** [Sp. & Port. *junco* < Jav. *joṅ*] a Chinese flat-bottomed ship

JUNK

Jun·ker (yooŋ′kər) ***n.*** [G. < MHG. < OHG. *jung,* young + *herro,* lord] a German of the militaristic, land-owning class; Prussian aristocrat

jun·ket (juŋ′kit) ***n.*** [ult. < L. *juncus,* a rush: orig. sold in reed baskets] **1.** formerly, curds with cream **2.** milk sweetened, flavored, and thickened into curd with rennet **3.** a feast or picnic **4.** an excursion for pleasure **5.** an excursion by an official, paid for with public funds —***vi.*** to go on a junket —***vt.*** to entertain at a feast —**jun′ket·eer′** (-kə tir′), **jun′ket·er** ***n.***

junk food any of various snack foods processed as with chemical additives and of low nutritional value

junk·ie, junk·y (juŋ′kē) ***n.,*** *pl.* **junk′ies** [Slang] **1.** a narcotics addict, esp. one addicted to heroin **2.** a person who is addicted to a specified interest, activity, food, etc. *[a TV junkie]*

junk mail advertisements, requests for aid, etc. mailed impersonally to a large number of people

junk·man (juŋk′man′) ***n.,*** *pl.* **-men′** (-men′) a dealer in old metal, paper, rags, etc.

junk·yard (-yärd′) ***n.*** a place where old cars are junked or where old metal, etc. is kept, sorted, and sold

Ju·no (jo͞o′nō) [L.] *Rom. Myth.* wife of Jupiter; queen of the gods and goddess of marriage: identified with the Greek goddess Hera

jun·ta (hoon′tə, jun′-) ***n.*** [Sp. < L. pp. of *jungere,* to join] **1.** a Spanish or Latin American legislature or council **2.** a group of political intriguers; also, a group of military men in power after a coup d'état: also **jun·to** (jun′tō), *pl.* **-tos**

Ju·pi·ter (jo͞o′pə tər) [L.] **1.** the chief Roman god: identified with the Greek god Zeus **2.** the largest planet of the solar system and the fifth in distance from the sun: diameter, c.88,000 mi.

Ju·ra Mountains (joor′ə) mountain range along the border of France & Switzerland

Ju·ras·sic (joo ras′ik) ***adj.*** [Fr. *jurassique* < *Jura* (Mountains)] designating or of the second period of the Mesozoic Era, following the Triassic —**the Jurassic** the Jurassic Period or its rocks: see GEOLOGY, chart

ju·rid·i·cal (joo rid′i k'l) ***adj.*** [< L. < *jus,* law + *dicere,* to declare + -AL] of judicial proceedings, or of law

ju·ris·dic·tion (joor′is dik′shən) ***n.*** [< OFr. < L. < *jus,* law + *dictio* < *dicere,* to declare] **1.** the administering of justice; authority to hear and decide cases **2.** authority or power in general **3.** the range of authority —**ju′ris·dic′tion·al** ***adj.*** —**ju′ris·dic′tion·al·ly** ***adv.***

ju·ris·pru·dence (-pro͞o′d'ns) ***n.*** [< L. < *jus,* law + *prudentia,* a foreseeing] **1.** the science or philosophy of law **2.** a part or division of law —**ju′ris·pru·den′tial** (-den′shəl) ***adj.*** —**ju′ris·pru·den′tial·ly** ***adv.***

ju·rist (joor′ist) ***n.*** [< MFr. < ML. < L. *jus,* law] **1.** an expert in law; writer on law **2.** a judge

ju·ris·tic (joo ris′tik) ***adj.*** of jurists or jurisprudence; relating to law —**ju·ris′ti·cal·ly** ***adv.***

ju·ror (joor′ər) ***n.*** **1.** a member of a jury **2.** a person taking an oath, as of allegiance

ju·ry¹ (joor′ē) ***n.,*** *pl.* **-ries** [< OFr. < ML. < L. *jurare,* to swear < *jus,* law] **1.** a group of people sworn to hear evidence in a law case and to give a decision **2.** a group selected to decide the winners in a contest

ju·ry² (joor′ē) ***adj.*** [< ?] *Naut.* for temporary use; makeshift *[a jury* mast*]*

just¹ (just) ***adj.*** [< OFr. < L. *justus,* lawful < *jus,* law] **1.** right or fair *[a just* decision*]* **2.** righteous; upright *[a just* man*]* **3.** deserved; merited *[just* praise*]* **4.** lawful **5.** proper, fitting, etc. **6.** well-founded *[a just* suspicion*]* **7.** correct or true **8.** accurate; exact —***adv.*** **1.** precisely; exactly *[just* one o'clock*]* **2.** almost at the point of *[just* leaving*]* **3.** only *[just* a taste*]* **4.** barely *[just* missed the train*]* **5.** a very short time ago *[just* left the room*]* **6.** immediately *[just* to my right*]* **7.** [Colloq.] quite; really *[*feeling *just* fine*]* —**just now** a moment ago —**just the same** [Colloq.] nevertheless —**just′ness** ***n.***

just² (just) ***n., vi.*** *same as* JOUST

jus·tice (jus′tis) ***n.*** **1.** a being righteous **2.** fairness **3.** a being correct **4.** sound reason; rightfulness **5.** reward or penalty as deserved **6.** the use of authority to uphold what is right, just, or lawful **7.** the administration of law **8.** *same as: a)* JUDGE *b)* JUSTICE OF THE PEACE —**bring to justice** to cause (a wrongdoer) to be tried in court and duly punished —**do justice to** **1.** to treat fitly or fairly **2.** to enjoy properly —**do oneself justice** to do something in a manner worthy of one's abilities —**jus′tice·ship′** ***n.***

justice of the peace a local magistrate, authorized to decide minor cases, perform marriages, etc.

jus·ti·fi·a·ble (jus′tə fī′ə b'l, jus′tə fī′ə b'l) ***adj.*** that can be justified or defended as correct —**jus′ti·fi′a·bly** ***adv.***

jus·ti·fi·ca·tion (jus′tə fi kā′shən) ***n.*** **1.** a justifying or being justified **2.** a fact that justifies

justification by faith *Theol.* the act by which a sinner is freed through faith from the penalty of his sin and is accepted by God as righteous

jus·ti·fy (jus′tə fī′) ***vt.*** **-fied′, -fy′ing** [< OFr. < LL., ult. < L. *justus,* just + *facere,* to make] **1.** to show to be just, right, or reasonable **2.** *Theol.* to free from blame **3.** to supply good grounds for **4.** to space (type) to make the lines correct in length —***vi.*** *Law* to show an adequate reason for something done —**jus′ti·fi′er** ***n.***

Jus·tin·i·an I (jəs tin′ē ən) (L. name *Flavius Ancius Justinianus*) 483–565 A.D.; Byzantine emperor (527–565): known for the codification of Roman law (**Justinian code**): called *the Great*

just·ly (just′lē) ***adv.*** **1.** in a just manner **2.** rightly **3.** deservedly

jut (jut) ***vi., vt.*** **jut′ted, jut′ting** [prob. var. of JET¹] to stick out; project —***n.*** a part that juts

Jute (jo͞ot) ***n.*** a member of any of several early Germanic tribes in Jutland: Jutes settled in SE England in the 5th cent. A.D. —**Jut′ish** ***adj.***

jute (jo͞ot) ***n.*** [Hindi *jhuto* < Sans. *jūṭa,* matted hair] **1.** a strong fiber used for making burlap, sacks, rope, etc. **2.** either of two East Indian plants yielding this fiber

Jut·land (jut′lənd) peninsula of N Europe, forming the mainland of Denmark

Ju·ve·nal (jo͞o′və n'l) (L. name *Decimus Junius Juvenalis*) 60?–140? A.D.; Rom. satirical poet

ju·ven·ile (jo͞o′və n'l, -nīl′) ***adj.*** [< L. < *juvenis,* young] **1.** *a)* young; youthful *b)* immature; childish **2.** of, characteristic of, or suitable for children or young persons —***n.*** **1.** a young person; child or youth **2.** an actor who plays youthful roles **3.** a book for children **4.** *Biol.* an immature animal or plant —**ju′ve·nil′i·ty** (-nil′ə tē) ***n.***

juvenile court a law court for cases involving children under a specified age, usually 18

juvenile delinquency behavior by minors of not more than a specified age, usually 18, that is antisocial or unlawful —**juvenile delinquent**

jux·ta·pose (juk′stə pōz′) ***vt.*** **-posed′, -pos′ing** [< Fr. < *juxta-* (< L. *juxta,* near) + *poser,* POSE¹] to put side by side or close together —**jux′ta·po·si′tion** ***n.***

Jy. July

Jyl·land (yül′län) *Dan. name of* JUTLAND

K

K, k (kā) ***n., pl.*** **K's, k's** **1.** the eleventh letter of the English alphabet **2.** the sound of *K* or *k*

K **1.** karat (carat) **2.** *Physics* Kelvin **3.** *Chess* king **4.** knit **5.** [ModL. *kalium*] *Chem.* potassium

K., k. **1.** *Elec.* capacity **2.** karat (carat) **3.** *Physics* Kelvin **4.** kilo **5.** knight

K2 (kā′to͞o′) *same as* GODWIN AUSTEN

Kaa·ba (kä′bə, kä′ə bə) [Ar. *ka'bah,* lit., square building < *ka'b,* a cube] the sacred Moslem shrine at Mecca, toward which believers turn when praying: it contains a black stone supposedly given to Abraham by the angel Gabriel

kab·a·la, kab·ba·la (kab′ə lə, kə bä′lə) ***n.*** *same as* CABALA

ka·bob (kə bäb′) ***n.*** *same as* KEBAB

Ka·bu·ki (kä bo͞o′kē, kə-) ***n.*** [Jap. < *kabu,* music and dancing + *ki,* spirit] [*also* **k-**] a form of Japanese drama with formalized pantomime, dance, and song, and with male actors in all roles

Ka·bul (kä′bool) capital of Afghanistan, in the NE part: pop. 456,000

ka·di (kä′dē, kā′-) ***n.*** *same as* CADI

kaf·fee·klatsch (kä′fā kläch′, kô′fē klach′) ***n.*** [G.] [*also* **K-**] an informal gathering, as of housewives during the day, to drink coffee and chat: also **kaffee klatsch**

Kaf·fir (kaf′ər) ***n.*** [Ar. *kāfir,* infidel < prp. of *kafara,* to be skeptical] **1.** a member of any of several Bantu-speaking tribes in South Africa **2.** [**k-**] *same as* KAFIR

kaf·fi·yeh (kä fē′yə) ***n.*** [< Ar.] a headdress of draped cotton cloth worn by Arabs

kaf·ir (kaf′ər) ***n.*** [Ar. *kāfir:* see KAFFIR] **1.** a grain sorghum grown in dry regions for grain and fodder **2.** [**K-**] *same as* KAFFIR

Kaf·ka (käf′kə), **Franz** (fränts) 1883–1924; Austrian writer, born in Prague

kaf·tan (kaf′tən, käf tän′) ***n.*** *same as* CAFTAN

kai·ak (kī′ak) ***n.*** *same as* KAYAK

kai·ser (kī′zər) ***n.*** [Gmc. borrowing < L. *Caesar*] emperor: the title [**K-**] of the rulers of the Holy Roman Empire (962–1806), of Austria (1804–1918), and of Germany (1871–1918)

Kal·a·ma·zoo (kal′ə mə zo͞o′) [< Fr. < Ojibwa < ?] city in SW Mich.: pop. 80,000

kale (kāl) ***n.*** [Scot. var. of COLE] a hardy, nonheading cabbage with loose, spreading, curled leaves

ka·lei·do·scope (kə lī′də skōp′) ***n.*** [< Gr. *kalos,* beautiful + *eidos,* form + -SCOPE] **1.** a small tube containing loose bits of colored glass, plastic, etc. reflected by mirrors so that various symmetrical patterns appear when the tube is rotated **2.** anything that constantly changes —**ka·lei′do·scop′ic** (-skäp′ik) ***adj.*** —**ka·lei′do·scop′i·cal·ly** ***adv.***

kal·ends (kal′əndz) ***n.pl.*** *same as* CALENDS

Ka·le·va·la (kä′lə vä′lä) [Finn., lit., land of heroes] a Finnish epic poem

Ka·li (kä′lē) a Hindu goddess viewed both as destroying life and giving it

Ka·li·man·tan (kä′lē män′tän) S part of the island of Borneo, belonging to Indonesia

Kal·muck, Kal·muk (kal′muk) ***n.*** **1.** a member of a group of Mongol peoples living chiefly in the NE Caucasus and N Sinkiang **2.** their western Mongolic language

kal·so·mine (kal′sə mīn′, -min) ***n., vt.*** **-mined′, -min′ing** *same as* CALCIMINE

Ka·ma·su·tra (kä′mə so͞o′trə) [Sans. < *kāma,* love + *sūtra,* manual] a Hindu love manual written in the 8th cent.: also **Kama Sutra**

Kam·chat·ka (käm chät′kä; *E.* kam chat′kə) peninsula in NE Siberia, between the Sea of Okhotsk & the Bering Sea

kam·pong (käm′pôŋ′) ***n.*** [Malay] a small Malay village or cluster of native huts

Kam·pu·che·a (kam′poo chē′ə), **Democratic** *official name of* CAMBODIA

Ka·nak·a (kə nak′ə, kan′ə kə) ***n.*** [Haw., man] **1.** a Hawaiian **2.** a native of the South Sea Islands

Kan·din·sky (kan din′skē), **Was·si·ly** (vas′ə lē) 1866–1944; Russ. painter in Germany & France

kan·ga·roo (kaŋ′gə ro͞o′) ***n., pl.*** **-roos′, -roo′:** see PLURAL, II, D, 1 [said (by James COOK) to be native name] a leaping, plant-eating mammal native to Australia and neighboring islands, with short forelegs, strong, large hind legs, and a long, thick tail: the female has a pouch in front, in which she carries her young

kangaroo court [Colloq.] an unauthorized, irregular court illegally passing and executing judgment, as among frontiersmen or prison inmates

kangaroo rat a small, jumping, mouselike rodent of desert regions in the SW U.S. and Mexico

Kan·pur (kän′poor) city in N India, on the Ganges: pop. 895,000

Kan·sas (kan′zəs) [Fr. < Siouan tribal name] **1.** Middle Western State of the U.S.: 82,264 sq. mi.; pop. 2,363,000; cap. Topeka: abbrev. **Kans., KS** **2.** river in NE Kans., flowing east into the Missouri —**Kan′san** ***adj., n.***

Kansas City **1.** city in W Mo., on the Missouri River: pop. 448,000 **2.** adjoining city in Kans., on the Missouri & Kansas rivers: pop. 161,000 (Both are in a single met. area, pop. 1,322,000)

Kant (kant; *G.* känt), **Immanuel** 1724–1804; Ger. philosopher —**Kant′i·an** ***adj., n.***

ka·o·lin (kā′ə lin) ***n.*** [Fr. < Chin. *kao-ling,* name of hill where found] a fine white clay used in making porcelain

ka·on (kā′än) ***n.*** [*ka* (the letter K) + (MES)ON] any of four mesons having a mass approximately 970 times that of an electron

ka·pok (kā′päk) ***n.*** [Malay *kapoq*] the silky fibers around the seeds of a tropical tree: used for stuffing mattresses, sleeping bags, etc.

kap·pa (kap′ə) ***n.*** [Gr.] the tenth letter of the Greek alphabet (Κ, κ)

Ka·ra·chi (kə rä′chē) seaport in Pakistan, on the Arabian Sea: pop. 3,060,000

Ka·ra·gan·da (kä′rə gän′də) city in EC Kazakh S.S.R.: pop. 505,000

Ka·ra·ko·ram (kä′rä kôr′əm, kar′ə-) NW range of the Himalayas, in India, near the Chinese border

kar·a·kul (kar′ə kəl) ***n.*** [< *Kara Kul,* lake in SC U.S.S.R.] **1.** a broad-tailed sheep of C Asia **2.** *same as* BROADTAIL (sense 2)

kar·at (kar′ət) ***n.*** [var. of CARAT] one 24th part (of pure gold) *[14-karat gold is 14 parts pure gold and 10 parts alloy]*

ka·ra·te (kə rät′ē) ***n.*** **[**Jap. < *kara*, empty + *te*, hand**]** a Japanese system of self-defense in which blows are struck with the side of the open hand

Ka·re·li·a (kə rēl′yə; *Russ.* kä re̅′lē ä) division of the R.S.F.S.R., east of Finland —**Ka·re′li·an** ***adj., n.***

Kar·en (kar′ən) **[**Scand. var. of CATHERINE**]** a feminine name

Karl (kärl) **[**var. of CARL**]** a masculine name

Karl-Marx-Stadt (kärl′märks′shtät′) city in S East Germany: pop. 295,000

Karls·ruh·e (kärls′ro͞o ə; *E.* kärlz′ro͞o ə) city in SW West Germany, on the Rhine: pop. 253,000

kar·ma (kär′mə, kʉr′-) ***n.*** **[**Sans., a deed, fate**]** *Buddhism & Hinduism* a person's actions in one reincarnation thought of as determining his fate in the next

Kar·nak (kär′nak) village in S Egypt, on the Nile: site of ancient Thebes

kart (kärt) ***n.*** **[**altered < CART**]** **1.** any of various small vehicles **2.** a small, flat, 4-wheeled, motorized vehicle for one person, used in racing **(karting)**

kar·y·o- **[**ModL. < Gr. *karyon*, a nut, kernel**]** *a combining form meaning:* **1.** nut, kernel **2.** *Biol.* the nucleus of a cell

kas·bah (käz′bä) ***n.*** *same as* CASBAH

Kash·mir (kash′mir) region in SE Asia, between Afghanistan & Tibet: part of Jammu & Kashmir: see JAMMU AND KASHMIR —**Kash·mir′i·an** ***adj., n.***

kash·rut, kash·ruth (käsh ro͞ot′, käsh′ro͝ot) ***n.*** the dietary regulations of Judaism: see KOSHER

Kas·sel (käs′əl) city in C West Germany: pop. 212,000

kat·a- *same as* CATA-: also, before a vowel, **kat-**

Kath·ar·ine, Kath·er·ine (kath′ər in, kath′rin) **[**see CATHERINE**]** a feminine name: dim. *Kate, Kay*

Kath·leen (kath′lēn, kath lēn′) **[**Ir. var. of CATHERINE**]** a feminine name

Kat·man·du (kät′män do͞o′) capital of Nepal, in the C part: pop. 195,000: also sp. **Kath′man·du′**

Ka·to·wi·ce (kä′tô vē′tse) city in S Poland: pop. 290,000

Kat·te·gat (kat′i gat′) strait between SW Sweden & E Jutland, Denmark

ka·ty·did (kāt′ē did′) ***n.*** **[**echoic of shrill sound made by the males**]** a large, green tree insect resembling the grasshopper

Kau·nas (kou′näs) city in SC Lithuanian S.S.R.: pop. 292,000

kau·ri (kou′rē) ***n.*** **[**Maori**]** **1.** a tall pine tree of New Zealand **2.** its wood **3.** a resin **(kauri resin, kauri gum)** from this tree, used in varnishes, etc.

Ka·wa·sa·ki (kä′wä sä′kē) city in C Honshu, Japan, between Tokyo & Yokohama: pop. 855,000

kay·ak (kī′ak) ***n.*** **[**Esk.**]** an Eskimo canoe made of skins completely covering a wooden frame except for an opening for the paddler

kay·o (kā′ō′) ***vt.*** **-oed′, -o′ing** **[**< KO**]** [Slang] *Boxing* to knock out —***n.*** [Slang] *Boxing* a knockout

Ka·zakh Soviet Socialist Republic (kä zäk′) republic of the U.S.S.R., in W Asia: 1,048,000 sq. mi.; pop. 12,700,000; cap. Alma-Ata: also **Ka·zakh·stan** (kä′zäk-stän′)

KAYAK

Ka·zan (kä zän′; *Russ.* kȧ zän′y′) city in W R.S.F.S.R., on the Volga: pop. 837,000

ka·zoo (kə zo͞o′) ***n.*** **[**echoic**]** a toy musical instrument consisting of a small, open tube with a top hole covered by a membrane that vibrates to give a buzzing quality to tones hummed through the tube

kc, kc. kilocycle; kilocycles

K.C. **1.** King's Counsel **2.** Knight(s) of Columbus

kcal. kilocalorie; kilocalories

Kčs koruna; korunas

ke·a (kā′ə, kē′ə) ***n.*** **[**Maori**]** a large, green parrot of New Zealand that sometimes kills sheep by tearing at their backs to eat the kidney fat

Keats (kēts), **John** 1795–1821; Eng. poet

ke·bab (kə bäb′) ***n.*** **[**Ar. *kabāb***]** **1.** [*often pl.*] a dish consisting of small pieces of marinated meat broiled or roasted on a skewer, often with alternating pieces of onion, tomato, etc. **2.** a piece of such meat

Kech·ua (kech′wä) ***n.*** *same as* QUECHUA —**Kech′uan** ***adj., n.***

kedge (kej) ***vt., vi.*** **kedged, kedg′ing** **[**ME. *caggen*, to fasten < ?**]** to move (a ship) by hauling on a rope fastened to an anchor dropped at some distance —***n.*** a light anchor, esp. for such use: also **kedge anchor**

keel (kēl) ***n.*** **[**< ON. *kjǫlr***]** **1.** the chief timber or steel piece along the entire length of the bottom of a ship or boat **2.** anything like a ship's keel in position, appearance, etc. —***vt., vi.*** to turn over on its side so as to turn up the keel —**keel over** **1.** to turn over; upset **2.** to fall in a faint, etc. —**on an even keel** upright and level, steady, stable, etc.

keel·haul (-hôl′) ***vt.*** to haul (a person) under the keel of a ship as a punishment

keel·son (kel′s'n, kēl′-) ***n.*** **[**prob. via Du. *kolsem* < Dan. < *kjøl*, KEEL + *sville*, sill**]** a beam or set of timbers or metal plates fastened inside a ship's hull along the keel for added strength

keen[1] (kēn) ***adj.*** **[**OE. *cene*, wise**]** **1.** having a sharp edge or point **2.** sharp in force; piercing [a *keen* wind] **3.** sharp and quick in seeing, hearing, thinking, etc.; acute **4.** eager; enthusiastic **5.** strong or intense, as a desire **6.** [Slang] good, fine, excellent, etc. —**keen′ly** ***adv.*** —**keen′ness** ***n.***

keen[2] (kēn) ***n.*** **[**< Ir. < *caoinim*, I wail**]** [Irish] a wailing for the dead; dirge —***vt., vi.*** [Irish] to lament or wail for (the dead)

keep (kēp) ***vt.*** **kept, keep′ing** **[**< OE. *cepan*, to behold, lay hold of**]** **1.** to observe with due ceremony; celebrate [*keep* the Sabbath] **2.** to fulfill (a promise, etc.) **3.** to follow (a routine, diet, etc.) **4.** to go on maintaining [*keep* pace] **5.** to protect; guard; defend **6.** to watch over; take care of; tend **7.** to raise (livestock) **8.** to maintain in good order or condition; preserve **9.** to provide for; support **10.** to supply with food or lodging for pay [to *keep* boarders] **11.** to have in one's service or for one's use [to *keep* servants] **12.** to make regular entries in, detailing transactions, happenings, etc. [to *keep* books, a diary, etc.] **13.** to carry on; conduct; manage **14.** to make stay in a specified condition, position, etc. [to *keep* an engine running] **15.** to hold for future use or a long time **16.** to have regularly in stock for sale **17.** to hold in custody **18.** to detain **19.** to restrain from action **20.** to withhold **21.** to conceal (a secret) **22.** to continue to have or hold; not lose or give up **23.** to stay in or at (a path, course, or place) —***vi.*** **1.** to stay in a specified condition, position, etc. **2.** to continue; go on; persevere (often with *on*) **3.** to hold oneself back; refrain [to *keep* from telling someone] **4.** to stay fresh; not spoil; last **5.** to require no immediate attention [a task that will *keep*] —***n.*** **1.** orig., care, charge, or custody **2.** *a*) a donjon *b*) a fort; castle **3.** food and shelter; support; livelihood —**for keeps** [Colloq.] **1.** with the winner keeping what he wins **2.** forever —**keep at** to continue doing; persist in —**keep to 1.** to persevere in **2.** to adhere to **3.** to remain in —**keep to oneself** **1.** to avoid others **2.** to refrain from telling —**keep up** **1.** to maintain in good condition **2.** to continue **3.** to maintain the pace **4.** to remain informed about (with *on* or *with*)

keep·er (-ər) ***n.*** a person or thing that keeps; specif., *a*) a guard, as of prisoners, animals, etc. *b*) a guardian or protector *c*) a caretaker

keep·ing (-iŋ) ***n.*** **1.** observance (of a rule, holiday, etc.) **2.** care; charge **3.** maintenance or means of this; keep **4.** reservation for future use; preservation —**in keeping with** in conformity or accord with

keep·sake (-sāk′) ***n.*** something kept, or to be kept, in memory of the giver; memento

keg (keg) ***n.*** **[**< or akin to ON. *kaggi*, keg**]** **1.** a small barrel, usually of less than ten gallons **2.** a unit of weight for nails, equal to 100 lbs.

keg·ler (keg′lər) ***n.*** **[**G. < *kegel*, (nine)pin**]** [Colloq.] a person who bowls; bowler

keis·ter, kees·ter (kēs′tər) ***n.*** **[**prob. via Yid. < MHG. *kiste*, a chest, ult. < L.**]** [Slang] **1.** a satchel, suitcase, etc. **2.** the buttocks; rump

Kel·ler (kel′ər), **Helen Adams** 1880–1968; U.S. writer & lecturer: blind & deaf from infancy, she was taught to speak & read

Kel·ly (green) (kel′ē) [*also* **k-**] a bright, yellowish green

ke·loid (kē′loid) ***n.*** **[**< Fr. < Gr. *chēlē*, claw + *-oeidēs*, -OID**]** an excessive growth of scar tissue on the skin —**ke·loi′dal** ***adj.***

kelp (kelp) ***n.*** **[**ME. *culp***]** **1.** any of various large, coarse, brown seaweeds **2.** ashes of seaweed, from which iodine is obtained

kel·pie, kel·py (kel′pē) ***n.***, *pl.* **-pies** **[**Scot. < ? Gael. *calpa*, colt**]** *Gaelic Folklore* a water spirit, supposed to take the form of a horse and drown people

kel·son (kel′s'n) ***n.*** *same as* KEELSON

Kelt (kelt) ***n.*** *same as* CELT —**Kelt′ic** ***adj., n.***

kel·ter (kel′tər) ***n.*** [Colloq.] *same as* KILTER

Kel·vin (kel′vin) ***adj.*** designating, of, or according to the Kelvin scale

Kelvin scale **[**after 1st Baron *Kelvin*, 19th-c. Brit. physicist**]** *Physics* a scale of temperature measured in degrees Celsius from absolute zero (−273.15°C)

Ke·mal A·ta·turk (ke mäl′ ät ä tʉrk′) 1881–1938; 1st president of Turkey: also called **Mus·ta·fa Kemal** (mo͞os′-tä fä) & **Kemal Pasha**

Kem·pis (kem′pis), **Thomas à** (born *Thomas Hamerken* or *Hammerlein*) 1380?–1471; Ger. monk & scholar

ken (ken) *vt., vi.* **kenned, ken′ning** [OE. *cennan,* lit., to cause to know] [Scot.] to know (*of* or *about*) *—n.* range of knowledge; understanding

Ken·ne·dy (ken′ə dē), **Cape** [after ff.] *former name* (1963–73) *of* Cape CANAVERAL

Ken·ne·dy (ken′ə dē), **John Fitzgerald** 1917–63; 35th president of the U.S. (1961–63): assassinated

ken·nel (ken′'l) *n.* [< OFr. *chenil* < L. *canis,* a dog] **1.** a doghouse **2.** [*often pl.*] a place where dogs are bred or kept **3.** a pack of dogs *—vt.* **-neled** or **-nelled, -nel·ing** or **-nel·ling** to place or keep in a kennel *—vi.* to live or take shelter in a kennel

Ken·neth (ken′ith) [Scot. < Gael. *Caioneach,* lit., handsome] a masculine name: dim. *Ken*

ke·no (kē′nō) *n.* [< Fr. *quine,* five winning numbers < L.] a gambling game resembling lotto

Ke·no·sha (ki nō′shə) [< Fr. < Algonquian *kinōzhan,* lit., pickerel] city in SW Wis., on Lake Michigan: pop. 78,000

Kent (kent) county of SE England, on the English Channel: formerly an Anglo-Saxon kingdom

Ken·tuck·y (kən tuk′ē, ken-) [< Iroquoian, level land] EC State of the U.S.: 40,395 sq. mi.: pop. 3,661,000; cap. Frankfort: abbrev. **Ky., KY —Ken·tuck′i·an** *adj., n.*

Ken·ya (ken′yə, kēn′-) country in EC Africa, on the Indian Ocean: a member of the Commonwealth: 224,960 sq. mi.; pop. 10,890,000; cap. Nairobi **—Ken′yan** *adj., n.*

Ke·ogh plan (kē′ō) [after E. J. *Keogh* (1907–), U.S. congressman] a retirement plan like an IRA but for self-employed persons and certain groups of employees

kep·i (kep′ē, kā′pē) *n., pl.* **kep′is** [Fr. *képi* < G. dial. *käppi,* dim. of *kappe,* a CAP] a visored cap with a flat, round top, worn by French soldiers

Kep·ler (kep′lər), **Jo·hann** (yō′hän) 1571–1630; Ger. astronomer & mathematician

kept (kept) *pt. & pp. of* KEEP *—adj.* maintained as a mistress [*a kept* woman]

ker·a·tin (ker′ət ′n) *n.* [< Gr. *keras* (gen. *keratos*), horn + -IN[1]] a tough, fibrous, insoluble protein, the principal matter of hair, nails, horn, etc.

kerb (kurb) *n. Brit. sp. of* CURB (*n.* 4)

ker·chief (kur′chif) *n.* [< OFr. *covrechef* < *covrir,* to cover + *chef,* the head] **1.** a piece of cloth worn over the head or around the neck **2.** a handkerchief

kerf (kurf) *n.* [OE. *cyrf* < *ceorfan,* to CARVE] the cut made by a saw *—vt.* to make a kerf in

ker·mes (kur′mēz) *n.* [< Fr. < Ar. & Per. *qirmiz,* crimson] **1.** the dried bodies of certain Mediterranean insects, used to make a purple-red dye **2.** the dye

ker·mis, ker·mess (kur′mis) *n.* [< Du. < *kerk,* a church + *mis,* MASS] **1.** in the Netherlands, Belgium, etc., an outdoor fair or carnival **2.** any similar fair or entertainment, usually for charity

kern (kurn) *n.* [Fr. *carne,* a hinge < OFr. < L. *cardo*] that part of the face of a letter of type which projects beyond the body

ker·nel (kur′n'l) *n.* [OE. *cyrnel,* dim. of *corn,* seed] **1.** a grain or seed, as of corn, wheat, etc. **2.** the inner, softer part of a nut, fruit pit, etc. **3.** the central, most important part of something; essence *—vt.* **-neled** or **-nelled, -nel·ing** or **-nel·ling** to enclose as a kernel

ker·o·sene (ker′ə sēn′, ker′ə sēn′) *n.* [Gr. *kēros,* wax + -ENE] a thin oil distilled from petroleum or shale oil, used as a fuel, solvent, etc.: also, esp. in science and industry, sp. **kerosine**

ker·sey (kur′zē) *n., pl.* **-seys** [< *Kersey,* village in England] a coarse, lightweight woolen cloth, usually ribbed and with a cotton warp

kes·trel (kes′trəl) *n.* [OFr. *cresserelle:* origin echoic] a small, brown-and-gray European falcon that can hover in the air against the wind

ketch (kech) *n.* [< ME. *cacchen,* to catch: orig. used of fishing vessels] a fore-and-aft rigged sailing vessel with a mainmast toward the bow and a relatively tall mizzenmast, forward of the rudderpost, toward the stern: distinguished from YAWL

ketch·up (kech′əp) *n.* [Malay *kēchap,* a fish sauce < Chin. *ke-tsiap*] a sauce for meat, fish, etc.; esp., a thick sauce **(tomato ketchup)** made of tomatoes flavored with onion, salt, sugar, and spice

ke·tone (kē′tōn) *n.* [G. *keton,* var. of Fr. *acétone:* see ACETONE] an organic chemical compound containing the bivalent radical CO in combination with two hydrocarbon radicals

Ket·ter·ing (ket′ər iŋ) [after C. *Kettering,* 1876–1958, U.S. inventor] city in SW Ohio: suburb of Dayton: pop. 61,000

ket·tle (ket′'l) *n.* [ON. *ketill* < L. dim. of *catinus,* bowl] **1.** a metal container for boiling or cooking things; pot **2.** a teakettle **3.** a kettledrum

ket·tle·drum (-drum′) *n.* a percussion instrument consisting of a hollow hemisphere and a parchment top that can be tightened or loosened to change the pitch; timpano

KETTLEDRUMS

kettle of fish a difficult situation

kev, Kev (kev) *n., pl.* **kev, Kev** [K(ILO-)E(LECTRON-)V(OLTS)] a unit of energy equal to one thousand (10^3) electron-volts

key[1] (kē) *n., pl.* **keys** [OE. *cæge*] **1.** an instrument, usually of metal, for moving the bolt of a lock and thus locking or unlocking something **2.** anything like this; specif., *a*) a device to turn a bolt, etc. [*a skate key*] *b*) a pin, bolt, etc. put into a hole or space to hold parts together *c*) any of the levers, or the disks, etc. connected to them, pressed down to operate a piano, clarinet, typewriter, etc. *d*) a device for opening or closing an electric circuit **3.** a place so located as to give control of a region **4.** a thing that explains or solves, as a book of answers **5.** a controlling or essential person or thing **6.** tone of voice; pitch **7.** tone of thought or expression [*in a cheerful key*] **8.** *Music* a system of notes forming a given scale; tonality *—adj.* controlling; essential; important *—vt.* **keyed, key′ing 1.** to fasten or lock with a key **2.** to furnish with a key **3.** to set the tone or pitch of **4.** to bring into harmony **—key up** to make tense or excited

key[2] (kē) *n., pl.* **keys** [Sp. *cayo*] a reef or low island

key[3] (kē) *n.* [< Sp. pron. of 1st syllable of *kilogramo,* kilogram] [Slang] a kilogram as of marijuana

Key (kē), **Francis Scott** 1779–1843; U.S. lawyer: wrote "The Star-Spangled Banner"

key·board (kē′bôrd′) *n.* **1.** the row(s) of keys of a piano, typewriter, etc. **2.** an electronic piano as in a rock or jazz group *—vt., vi.* to set (type) using a keyboard typesetting machine

key·board·ist (-ist) *n.* a performer on a keyboard

keyed (kēd) *adj.* **1.** having keys, as some musical instruments **2.** pitched in a specified key **3.** made appropriate

key·hole (kē′hōl′) *n.* an opening (in a lock) into which a key is inserted

Keynes (kānz), **John May·nard** (mā′nərd), 1st Baron Keynes, 1883–1946; Eng. economist **—Keynes′i·an** *adj., n.*

key·note (kē′nōt′) *n.* **1.** the lowest, basic note or tone of a musical scale **2.** the basic idea or ruling principle, as of a speech, policy, etc. *—vt.* **-not′ed, -not′ing 1.** to give the keynote of **2.** to give the keynote speech at **—key′not′er** *n.*

keynote speech (or **address**) a speech, as at a convention, setting forth the main line of policy

key punch a keyboard machine that records data by punching holes in cards, later fed into machines for sorting, etc.

key ring a metal ring for holding keys

key signature *Music* one or more sharps or flats after the clef on the staff, showing the key

key·stone (-stōn′) *n.* **1.** the central, topmost stone of an arch **2.** a main or supporting part or principle

KEYSTONE

Key West westernmost island of a chain of islands **(Florida Keys)** off the S tip of Fla.

kg, kg. 1. keg(s) **2.** kilogram(s)

KGB, K.G.B. [Russ. *K*(*omitet*) *G*(*osudarstvennoye*) *B*(*ezopastnosti*), Committee of State Security] the security police, or intelligence agency, of the Soviet Union

Kha·cha·tu·ri·an (kach′ə toor′ē ən; *Russ.* khä′chä too ryän′), **A·ram** (ar′əm) 1903?–1978; Russ. composer

kha·ki (kak′ē, kä′kē) *adj.* [< Hindi < Per. *khāk,* dust] **1.** dull yellowish-brown **2.** made of khaki (cloth) *—n., pl.* **-kis 1.** a dull yellowish brown **2.** strong, twilled cloth of this color **3.** [*often pl.*] a khaki uniform or pants

khan[1] (kän, kan) *n.* [< Turki *khān,* lord, prince] **1.** a title of Turkish, Tatar, and Mongol rulers in the Middle Ages **2.** a title of honor in Iran, Afghanistan, etc. **—khan′ate** (-āt) *n.*

khan[2] (kän, kan) *n.* [Ar. *khān*] in Turkey and other Eastern countries, an inn or caravansary

Khar·kov (kär′kôf; *Russ.* khär′kôf) city in NE Ukrainian S.S.R.: pop. 1,148,000

Khar·toum (kär toom′) capital of Sudan, on the Nile: pop. 185,000 (met. area 490,000)

Khayyám, Omar *see* OMAR KHAYYÁM

khe·dive (kə dēv′) *n.* [< Fr. < Per. *khidīw,* prince] the title of the Turkish viceroys of Egypt (1867–1914)

Khrush·chev (kroos′chev, -chôf; *Russ.* khroosh′chyôf), **Ni·ki·ta (Sergeyevich)** (ni kē′tä) 1894–1971; premier of the U.S.S.R. (1958–64)

fat, āpe, cär, ten, ēven, is, bīte; gō, hôrn, tōōl, look; oil, out; up, fur; get; joy; yet; chin; she; thin, *th*en; zh, leisure; ŋ, ring; ə for *a* in *ago, e* in *agent, i* in *sanity, o* in *comply, u* in *focus;* ′ as in *able* (ā′b'l); Fr. bål; ë, Fr. coeur; ö, Fr. feu; Fr. mon; ô, Fr. coq; ü, Fr. duc; *r,* Fr. cri; H, G. ich; kh, G. doch; ‡foreign; *hypothetical; < derived from. See inside front cover.

Khu·fu (ko͞o′fo͞o) fl. c. 2650 B.C.; king of Egypt: builder of the Great Pyramid near Gîza

Khy·ber Pass (kī′bər) mountain pass in the Hindu Kush, between Afghanistan & Pakistan

kHz kilohertz

Ki. Kings

kib·ble (kib′'l) ***vt.*** **-bled, -bling** [< ?] to grind into coarse bits —***n.*** kibbled food for dogs, etc.

kib·butz (ki bo͞ots′, -boots′) ***n.,*** *pl.* **kib·but·zim** (kē′bo͞o-tsēm′) [ModHeb.] an Israeli collective settlement, esp. a collective farm

kib·itz (kib′its) ***vi.*** [Colloq.] to act as a kibitzer

kib·itz·er (-ər) ***n.*** [Yid. < colloq. G. *kiebitzen* < *kiebitz,* meddlesome onlooker] [Colloq.] **1.** an onlooker at a card game, etc., esp. one who volunteers advice **2.** a giver of unwanted advice

ki·bosh (kī′bäsh) ***n.*** [< ? Yid.] [Slang] orig., nonsense —**put the kibosh on** to squelch; veto

kick (kik) ***vi.*** [ME. *kiken* < ?] **1.** to strike out with the foot or feet **2.** to spring back suddenly, as a gun when fired; recoil **3.** [Colloq.] to object; complain **4.** *Football* to kick the ball —***vt.*** **1.** to strike suddenly with the foot or feet **2.** to drive (a ball, etc.) in this way **3.** to make (one's way) by kicking **4.** to score (a goal or point in football) by kicking **5.** [Slang] *a*) to stop taking (a narcotic drug) *b*) to get rid of (a habit) —***n.*** **1.** a blow with the foot **2.** a kicking **3.** [Colloq.] an objection; complaint **4.** [Colloq.] a stimulating effect, as of alcoholic liquor **5.** [Colloq.] [*often pl.*] pleasure; thrill **6.** *Football* *a*) a kicking of the ball *b*) the kicked ball —**kick around** (or **about**) [Colloq.] **1.** to treat roughly **2.** to move from place to place **3.** to lie about unnoticed **4.** to think about or discuss —**kick back 1.** [Colloq.] to recoil suddenly and unexpectedly **2.** [Slang] to give back (part of one's pay, etc.) —**kick in** [Slang] to pay (one's share) —**kick off 1.** to put a football into play with a place kick **2.** to start (a campaign, etc.) **3.** [Slang] to die —**kick on** [Colloq.] **1.** to turn on (a switch, etc.) **2.** to begin operating —**kick out** [Colloq.] to get rid of; expel —**kick up** [Colloq.] to cause (trouble, etc.) —**on** (or **off**) **a kick** [Slang] currently (or no longer) enthusiastic about an activity

kick·back (-bak′) ***n.*** **1.** [Colloq.] a sharp reaction **2.** [Slang] *a*) a giving back of part of one's pay, etc. *b*) the money returned

kick·er (-ər) ***n.*** **1.** one that kicks **2.** [Slang] *a*) a surprise ending *b*) a hidden difficulty

kick·off (-ôf′) ***n.*** **1.** the act of kicking off in football **2.** the start of a campaign, etc.

kick·shaw (kik′shô′) ***n.*** [< Fr. *quelque chose,* something] **1.** a fancy food or dish; delicacy **2.** a trinket; trifle; gewgaw Also **kick′shaws′** (-shôz′)

kick·stand (kik′stand′) ***n.*** a short metal bar fastened to a bicycle or motorcycle: when kicked down it holds the stationary cycle upright

kid (kid) ***n.*** [prob. < Anglo-N.] **1.** a young goat **2.** its flesh, used as food **3.** leather from the skin of young goats, used for gloves, shoes, etc. **4.** [Colloq.] a child or young person —***adj.*** **1.** made of kidskin **2.** [Colloq.] younger [my *kid* sister] —***vt., vi.*** **kid′ded, kid′ding** [Colloq.] to deceive, fool, or tease playfully —**kid′der** ***n.*** —**kid′like′, kid′dish** ***adj.***

Kidd (kid), Captain (**William**) 1645?–1701; Brit. privateer & pirate, born in Scotland: hanged

kid·dy, kid·die (kid′ē) ***n.,*** *pl.* **-dies** [dim. of KID] [Colloq.] a child

kid gloves soft, smooth gloves made of kidskin —**handle with kid gloves** [Colloq.] to treat with care, tact, etc.

kid·nap (-nap′) ***vt.*** **-napped′** or **-naped′, -nap′ping** or **-nap′ing** [KID + dial. *nap,* NAB] **1.** to steal (a child) **2.** to seize and hold (a person) against his will, by force or fraud, often for ransom —**kid′nap′per, kid′nap′er** ***n.***

kid·ney (kid′nē) ***n.,*** *pl.* **-neys** [ME. *kidenei* < ?] **1.** either of a pair of glandular organs in vertebrates, which separate waste products from the blood and excrete them as urine **2.** an animal kidney, used as food **3.** *a*) temperament *b*) kind; sort

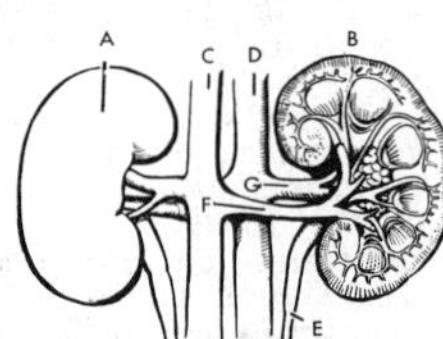

KIDNEYS
(A, right kidney; B, left kidney; C, vena cava; D, aorta; E, ureter; F, renal vein; G, renal artery; left kidney shown in cross section)

kidney bean the kidney-shaped seed of the common garden bean of the legume family

kidney stone a hard mineral deposit formed in the kidney from phosphates, urates, etc.

kid·skin (kid′skin′) ***n.*** leather from the skin of young goats, used for gloves, shoes, etc.

Kiel (kēl) seaport in N West Germany, on a canal (**Kiel Canal**) connecting the North Sea & the Baltic Sea: pop. 270,000

kiel·ba·sa (kēl bä′sə) ***n.,*** *pl.* **-si** (-sē), **-sas** [Pol.] a smoked Polish sausage spiced with garlic

Kier·ke·gaard (kir′kə gärd′; *Dan.* kir′kə gôr), **Sø·ren** (**Aabye**) (sö′rən) 1813–55; Dan. philosopher & theologian

Ki·ev (kē′ef; *E.* kē ev′, kē′ev) capital of the Ukrainian S.S.R., on the Dnepr: pop. 1,476,000

kil. kilometer; kilometers

Kil·i·man·ja·ro (kil′ə män jä′rō) mountain in NE Tanzania, near the Kenya border: highest mountain in Africa: 19,340 ft.

kill[1] (kil) ***vt.*** [ME. *killen* < ? OE. *cwellan*] **1.** to cause the death of; make die **2.** *a*) to destroy the vital or active qualities of *b*) to destroy; put an end to **3.** to defeat or veto (legislation) **4.** to spend (time) on trivial matters **5.** to stop (an engine, etc.), turn off (a light, etc.), or muffle (sound) **6.** to prevent publication of (a newspaper story) **7.** to spoil the effect of: said of colors, etc. **8.** [Colloq.] to overcome with laughter, chagrin, etc. **9.** [Colloq.] to make feel great pain or exhaustion **10.** [Slang] to drink the last, or all, of (a bottle of liquor, etc.) —***vi.*** **1.** to destroy life **2.** to be killed [plants that *kill* easily] —***n.*** **1.** an act of killing **2.** an animal or animals killed **3.** an enemy plane, ship, etc. destroyed

kill[2] (kil) ***n.*** [< Du. < MDu. *kille*] a stream; channel; creek: used esp. in place names

kill·deer (kil′dir′) ***n.,*** *pl.* **-deers′, -deer′:** see PLURAL, II, D, 1 [echoic of its cry] a small, N. American bird of the plover family, with a high, piercing cry: also **kill′dee′** (-dē′)

kill·er (kil′ər) ***n.*** **1.** a person, animal, or thing that kills, esp. habitually **2.** *same as* KILLER WHALE

killer whale any of several fierce, grayish to black, small whales that hunt in large packs and prey on large fish, seals, and other whales

kil·li·fish (kil′ē fish′) ***n.,*** *pl.* **-fish′, -fish′es:** see FISH [< KILL[2] + -IE + FISH] any of several minnowlike freshwater fishes used in mosquito control and as bait: also **kil′lie** (-ē), *pl.* **-lies**

kill·ing (kil′iŋ) ***adj.*** **1.** causing death; deadly **2.** exhausting **3.** [Colloq.] very comical —***n.*** **1.** slaughter; murder **2.** [Colloq.] a sudden, great profit or success —**kill′ing·ly** ***adv.***

kill-joy (-joi′) ***n.*** a person who destroys or lessens other people's enjoyment: also **kill′joy′**

kiln (kil, kiln) ***n.*** [< OE. *cylne* < L. *culina,* cookstove] a furnace or oven for drying, burning, or baking something, as bricks, pottery, or grain —***vt.*** to dry, burn, or bake in a kiln

kiln-dry (-drī′) ***vt.*** **-dried′, -dry′ing** to dry in a kiln

ki·lo (kē′lō, kil′ō) ***n.,*** *pl.* **-los** [Fr.] *short for:* **1.** KILOGRAM **2.** KILOMETER

kil·o- [Fr. < Gr. *chilioi,* thousand] *a combining form meaning* a thousand [*kilogram*]

kilo. **1.** kilogram **2.** kilometer

kil·o·bar (kil′ə bär′) ***n.*** [see KILO- & BAR[2]] a metric unit of pressure equal to 1,000 bars

kil·o·cal·o·rie (kil′ə kal′ər ē) ***n.*** 1,000 calories; great calorie

kil·o·cy·cle (-sī′k'l) ***n.*** *former name for* KILOHERTZ

kil·o·gram (-gram′) ***n.*** a unit of weight and mass, equal to 1,000 grams (2.2046 lb.): also, chiefly Brit., **kil′o·gramme′**

kil·o·hertz (-hurts′) ***n.,*** *pl.* **-hertz′** 1,000 hertz

kil·o·li·ter (-lēt′ər) ***n.*** a unit of capacity, equal to 1,000 liters, or one cubic meter (264.18 gal., or 1.308 cu. yd.): also, chiefly Brit., **kil′o·li′tre**

ki·lo·me·ter (ki läm′ə tər, kil′ə mēt′ər) ***n.*** a unit of length or distance, equal to 1,000 meters (3,280.8 ft., or about 5/8 mi.): also, chiefly Brit., **ki·lo′me·tre** —**kil·o·met·ric** (kil′ə met′rik) ***adj.***

kil·o·ton (kil′ə tun′) ***n.*** the explosive force of 1,000 tons of TNT

kil·o·volt (-vōlt′) ***n.*** 1,000 volts

kil·o·watt (-wät′) ***n.*** a unit of electrical power, equal to 1,000 watts

kil·o·watt-hour (-our′) ***n.*** a unit of electrical energy or work, equal to that done by one kilowatt acting for one hour

kilt (kilt) ***vt.*** [ME. *kilten,* prob. < Scand.] **1.** [Scot.] to tuck up (a skirt, etc.) **2.** to pleat **3.** to provide a kilt for —***n.*** a pleated skirt reaching to the knees; esp., the tartan skirt worn sometimes by men of the Scottish Highlands

KILT

kil·ter (kil′tər) ***n.*** [< ?] [Colloq.] good condition; proper order: now chiefly in **out of kilter**

Kim·ber·ley (kim′bər lē) city in N Cape of Good Hope province, South Africa: diamond-mining center: pop. 95,000

ki·mo·no (kə mō′nə, -nō) ***n.,*** *pl.* **-nos** [Jap.] **1.** a loose outer garment with short, wide sleeves and a sash, a traditional costume of Japanese men and women **2.** a woman's dressing gown like this

kin (kin) *n.* [< OE. *cynn*] relatives; family; kindred —*adj.* related, as by blood —**(near) of kin** (closely) related

-kin (kin) [< MDu. *-ken, -kijn,* dim. suffix] *a suffix meaning* little [*lambkin*]

kind (kīnd) *n.* [< OE. *cynd*] **1.** [Archaic] *a)* origin *b)* nature *c)* manner **2.** a natural group or division [the rodent *kind*] **3.** essential character **4.** sort; class —*adj.* **1.** sympathetic, friendly, gentle, generous, etc. **2.** cordial [*kind* regards] —**in kind** **1.** in goods or produce instead of money **2.** with something like that received —**kind of** [Colloq.] somewhat; rather —**of a kind** **1.** of the same kind; alike **2.** mediocre or inferior

kin·der·gar·ten (kin′dər gär′t'n) *n.* [G., lit., garden of children] a school or class for children, usually four to six years old, preparing them for first grade by games, music, simple handicraft, etc. —**kin′der·gart′ner, kin′der·gar′ten·er** *n.*

kind·heart·ed (kīnd′här′tid) *adj.* having or resulting from a kind heart; sympathetic; kindly —**kind′heart′ed·ly** *adv.* —**kind′heart′ed·ness** *n.*

kin·dle (kin′d'l) *vt.* **-dled, -dling** [ME. *kindlen,* freq. < ON. *kynda*] **1.** to set on fire; ignite **2.** to start (a fire) **3.** to excite (interest, feelings, etc.) **4.** to make bright —*vi.* **1.** to catch fire **2.** to become excited —**kin′dler** *n.*

kin·dling (kin′dliŋ) *n.* bits of dry wood or other easily lighted material for starting a fire

kind·ly (kīnd′lē) *adj.* **-li·er, -li·est** **1.** kind; gracious; benign **2.** agreeable; pleasant [a *kindly* climate] —*adv.* **1.** in a kind, gracious way **2.** agreeably **3.** please [*kindly* reply] —**take kindly to** **1.** to be naturally attracted to **2.** to accept willingly —**kind′li·ness** *n.*

kind·ness (-nis) *n.* **1.** the state, quality, or habit of being kind **2.** kind act or treatment

kin·dred (kin′drid) *n.* [< OE. *cynn,* kin + *ræden,* condition] **1.** formerly, family relationship **2.** relatives or family; kin —*adj.* of like nature

kine (kīn) *n.pl.* [ME. *kin* < *cou* (< OE. *cy,* pl. of *cu,* COW[1]) + *-(e)n*] [Archaic] cows; cattle

kin·e·mat·ics (kin′ə mat′iks) *n.pl.* [*with sing. v.*] [< Fr. < Gr. *kinēma,* motion < *kinein,* to move + -ICS] the branch of mechanics dealing with abstract motion, without reference to force or mass —**kin′e·mat′ic, kin′e·mat′i·cal** *adj.*

kin·e·scope (kin′ə skōp′) *n.* [< Gr. < *kinein,* to move + -SCOPE] **1.** a cathode-ray tube used in television receivers, etc. for picture display **2.** a motion-picture record of such display

ki·ne·sics (ki nē′siks, kī-) *n.pl.* [*with sing. v.*] [< Gr. *kinēsis,* motion + -ICS] the study of bodily movements, facial expressions, etc. as ways of communication —**ki·ne′sic** *adj.*

kin·es·the·si·a (kin′is thē′zhə, -zhē ə) *n.* [ModL. < Gr. *kinein,* to move + *aisthēsis,* perception] the sensation of position, movement, etc. of bodily parts, perceived through nerve end organs in muscles, tendons, and joints: also **kin′es·the′sis** (-sis) —**kin′es·thet′ic** (-thet′ik) *adj.*

ki·net·ic (ki net′ik) *adj.* [Gr. *kinētikos* < *kinein,* to move] **1.** of or resulting from motion **2.** energetic or dynamic

kinetic art sculpture or assemblage involving the use of moving parts, sounds, shifting lights, etc.

ki·net·ics (ki net′iks) *n.pl.* [*with sing. v.*] *same as* DYNAMICS (sense 1)

kin·folk (kin′fōk′) *n.pl.* family; relatives; kin; kindred: also **kin′folks′**

king (kiŋ) *n.* [OE. *cyning*] **1.** the male ruler of a monarchy; male monarch, limited or absolute **2.** *a)* a man who is supreme in some field [an oil *king*] *b)* something supreme in its class **3.** a playing card with a picture of a king on it **4.** *Checkers* a piece crowned upon reaching the opponent's base and hence movable backward and forward **5.** *Chess* the chief piece, movable one square in any direction: see CHECKMATE —*adj.* chief (in size, importance, etc.)

King (kiŋ), **Martin Luther, Jr.** 1929–68; U.S. clergyman & civil rights leader

king·bird (-burd′) *n.* any of several American flycatchers

king·bolt (-bōlt′) *n.* a vertical bolt connecting the front axle of a wagon, etc., or the truck of a railroad car, with the body, to allow pivoting

king crab **1.** *same as* HORSESHOE CRAB **2.** any of various very large crabs

king·dom (-dəm) *n.* [OE. *cyningdom:* see KING & -DOM] **1.** a government or country headed by a king or queen; monarchy **2.** a realm; domain [the *kingdom* of poetry] **3.** any of the three great divisions of things in nature (the animal, vegetable, and mineral kingdoms)

king·fish (-fish′) *n.* **1.** *pl.* **-fish′, -fish′es:** see FISH any of various large food fishes of the Atlantic or Pacific coast **2.** [Colloq.] a person holding absolute power in some group or place

king·fish·er (-fish′ər) *n.* a bright-colored bird with a large, crested head, a large, strong beak, and a short tail

King James Version *same as* AUTHORIZED VERSION

King Lear (lir) **1.** a tragedy by Shakespeare **2.** its main character, a legendary British king

king·ly (kiŋ′lē) *adj.* **-li·er, -li·est** of, like, or fit for a king; royal; regal; noble —*adv.* [Archaic] in the manner of a king —**king′li·ness** *n.*

king·mak·er (-mā′kər) *n.* a politically powerful person who manages to get candidates into high office

king·pin (-pin′) *n.* **1.** *same as* KINGBOLT **2.** the headpin or center pin in bowling, etc. **3.** [Colloq.] the main or essential person or thing

king post *Carpentry* a vertical supporting post between the apex of a triangular truss and the base, or tie beam

Kings (kiŋz) **1.** either of two books of the Bible (I Kings, II Kings) about the reigns of the Jewish kings after David **2.** any of four books of the Douay Bible including I & II Samuel and I & II Kings

king salmon *same as* CHINOOK SALMON

king's (or **queen's**) **English , the** standard (esp. British) English

king·ship (kiŋ′ship′) *n.* **1.** the position, rank, or dignity of a king **2.** the rule of a king

king-size (-sīz′) *adj.* [Colloq.] bigger than normal [a *king-size* bed]: also **king′-sized′**

king snake any of several large, harmless snakes of C and S North America: they eat mice, etc.

Kings·ton (kiŋz′tən, kiŋ′stən) **1.** seaport & capital of Jamaica: pop. 123,000 (met. area 422,000) **2.** port in SE Ontario, Canada: pop. 59,000

kink (kiŋk) *n.* [< Scand.] **1.** a short twist, curl, or bend in a rope, hair, etc. **2.** a painful cramp, as in the neck **3.** an eccentricity; quirk **4.** a difficulty or defect, as in a plan —*vi., vt.* to form or cause to form a kink

kin·ka·jou (kiŋ′kə jo͞o′) *n.* [Fr., *quincajou,* a misapplication of AmInd. name, whence CARCAJOU] a nocturnal, tree-dwelling, raccoonlike mammal of Central and South America, with large eyes and a long, prehensile tail

kink·y (kiŋ′kē) *adj.* **kink′i·er, kink′i·est** **1.** full of kinks; tightly curled [*kinky* hair] **2.** [Slang] weird, bizarre, etc.; specif., sexually abnormal —**kink′i·ness** *n.*

kins·folk (kinz′fōk′) *n.pl. var. of* KINFOLK

Kin·sha·sa (kēn shä′sä) capital of Zaire, in the W part: pop. 902,000

kin·ship (kin′ship′) *n.* **1.** family relationship **2.** relationship; close connection

kins·man (kinz′mən) *n., pl.* **-men** a relative; esp., a male relative —**kins′wom′an** (-woom′ən) *n.fem., pl.* **-wom′en**

ki·osk (kē′äsk, kē äsk′) *n.* [< Fr. < Turk. < Per. *kūshk,* palace] **1.** in Turkey and Persia, an open summerhouse or pavilion **2.** a somewhat similar small structure open at one or more sides, used as a newsstand, bandstand, etc.

kip[1] (kip) *n.* [prob. < Du.] the untanned hide of a calf, lamb, or other young or small animal

kip[2] (kip) *n., pl.* **kips, kip** [Thai] *see* MONETARY UNITS, table (Laos)

kip[3] (kip) *n.* [KI(LO) + P(OUND)[1]] a unit of weight equal to 1,000 pounds

Kip·ling (kip′liŋ), **(Joseph) Rud·yard** (rud′yərd) 1865–1936; Eng. writer, born in India

kip·per (kip′ər) *vt.* [< ? the *n.*] to cure (herring, salmon, etc.) by salting and drying or smoking —*n.* [OE. *cypera*] **1.** a male salmon or sea trout during or shortly after the spawning season **2.** a kippered herring, salmon, etc.

Kir·ghiz (kir gēz′) *n.* **1.** *pl.* **-ghiz′, -ghiz′es** a member of a Mongolian people of SC Asia **2.** their Turkic language Also sp. **Kir·giz′**

Kirghiz (or **Kirgiz**) **Soviet Socialist Republic** republic of the U.S.S.R., in SC Asia: 76,460 sq. mi.; pop. 2,800,000; cap. Frunze: also **Kir·ghi′zia** (-gē′zhə, -zhē ə) —**Kir·ghi′zian** *adj., n.*

Kir·i·bati (kir′ə bas′) country consisting principally of three groups of atolls in the WC Pacific: a member of the Commonwealth: 264 sq. mi.; pop. 58,000

kirk (kurk; *Scot.* kirk) *n.* [ME. *kirke* < OE. *cirice,* CHURCH] [Scot. & North Eng.] a church

kir·mess (kur′mis) *n. var. of* KERMIS

kir·tle (kur′t'l) *n.* [OE. *cyrtel,* ult. < L. *curtus,* short + *-el,* dim. suffix] [Archaic] **1.** a man's tunic or coat **2.** a woman's dress or skirt

Ki·shi·nev (ki shi nyôf′; *E.* kish′i nef′) capital of the Moldavian S.S.R.; pop. 317,000

Kis·lev (kis′lef) *n.* [Heb.] the third month of the Jewish year: see JEWISH CALENDAR

kis·met (kiz′met, kis′-) ***n.*** [< Turk. < Ar. *qismah,* a portion, fate] fate; destiny

kiss (kis) ***vt.*** [OE. *cyssan*] **1.** to touch or caress with the lips in affection, greeting, etc. **2.** to touch lightly —***vi.*** to kiss each other —***n.*** **1.** a kissing **2.** any of various candies —**kiss goodbye** **1.** to kiss in leaving **2.** [Colloq.] to give up all hope of gaining or regaining —**kiss′a·ble** ***adj.***

kiss·er (-ər) ***n.*** **1.** a person who kisses **2.** [Slang] *a)* the mouth or lips *b)* the face

kit (kit) ***n.*** [prob. < MDu. *kitte,* a wooden tub] **1.** personal equipment, esp. as packed for travel **2.** a set of tools, articles for special use, parts to be assembled, etc. **3.** a container for such equipment, tools, etc. **4.** [Colloq.] lot; collection: now chiefly in **the whole kit and caboodle,** everybody or everything

Ki·ta·kyu·shu (kē′tä kyōō′shōō) seaport on the N coast of Kyushu, Japan: pop. 1,042,000

kitch·en (kich′ən) ***n.*** [< OE. *cycene* < VL. < LL. *coquina* < L. *coquere,* to cook] **1.** a room or place for preparing and cooking food; also, the equipment used **2.** a staff that cooks and serves food

Kitch·e·ner (kich′ə nər) city in SE Ontario, Canada: pop. 132,000

Kitch·e·ner (kich′ə nər), **Horatio Herbert,** 1st Earl, Kitchener of Khartoum, 1850–1916; Brit. military officer & statesman, born in Ireland

kitch·en·ette (kich′ə net′) ***n.*** a small, compact kitchen

kitchen midden [transl. of Dan. *kökkenmödding*] a mound of shells, animal bones, etc. marking the site of a prehistoric settlement

kitchen police **1.** soldiers detailed to assist the cooks in an army kitchen **2.** this duty

kitch·en·ware (kich′ən wer′) ***n.*** kitchen utensils

kite (kīt) ***n.*** [OE. *cyta*] **1.** a bird of the hawk family, with long, pointed wings and, usually, a forked tail **2.** a light wooden frame covered with paper or cloth, to be flown in the wind at the end of a string **3.** [*pl.*] the highest sails of a ship **4.** a bad check or the like used to raise money or maintain credit temporarily —***vi.*** **kit′ed, kit′ing** **1.** [Colloq.] *a)* to fly like a kite *b)* to move lightly and rapidly **2.** to get money or credit by using bad checks, etc. —***vt.*** to issue (a bad check, etc.) as a kite

kith (kith) ***n.*** [OE. *cyth* < base of *cuth,* known: see UNCOUTH] friends, acquaintances, or neighbors: now only in **kith and kin,** friends, acquaintances, and relatives; also, often, relatives, or kin

kitsch (kich) ***n.*** [G., gaudy trash < dial. *kitschen,* to smear] pretentious but shallow art, writing, etc., designed for popular appeal —**kitsch′y** ***adj.***

kit·ten (kit′'n) ***n.*** [< OFr. var. of *chaton,* dim. of *chat,* cat] a young cat

kit·ten·ish (-ish) ***adj.*** like a kitten; playful; frisky; often, playfully coy —**kit′ten·ish·ly** ***adv.*** —**kit′ten·ish·ness** ***n.***

kit·ti·wake (kit′i wāk′) ***n.,*** *pl.* **-wakes′, -wake′**: see PLURAL, II, D, 1 [echoic of its cry] any of several sea gulls of the Arctic and North Atlantic

Kit·ty (kit′ē) [dim. of CATHERINE] a feminine name

kit·ty[1] (kit′ē) ***n.,*** *pl.* **-ties** **1.** a kitten **2.** *a pet name for* a cat of any age

kit·ty[2] (kit′ē) ***n.,*** *pl.* **-ties** [prob. < KIT] **1.** in poker, etc., *a)* the stakes or pot *b)* a pool from the winnings, to pay for refreshments, etc. **2.** any money pooled for some special use

kit·ty-cor·nered (kit′ē kôr′nərd) ***adj., adv.*** *same as* CATER-CORNERED: also **kit′ty-cor′ner**

Kitty Hawk [< AmInd.] village on an offshore island of N.C., near where the first controlled & sustained airplane flight was made by Orville & Wilbur Wright in 1903

Ki·wa·nis (kə wä′nis) ***n.*** [said to be < AmInd. *keewanis,* to make (oneself) known] an international club of business and professional men —**Ki·wa′ni·an** (-nē ən) ***adj., n.***

ki·wi (kē′wē) ***n.,*** *pl.* **-wis** [Maori: echoic of its cry] a tailless New Zealand bird with undeveloped wings, hairlike feathers, and a long, slender bill

KJV, K.J.V. King James Version (of the Bible)

K.K.K., KKK Ku Klux Klan

kl, kl. kiloliter; kiloliters

Klan (klan) ***n.*** *short for* KU KLUX KLAN —**Klans′man** ***n.,*** *pl.* **-men**

klatch, klatsch (kläch, klach) ***n.*** [G. *klatsch,* gossip] [Colloq.] an informal gathering, as to chat

Klax·on (klak′s'n) *a trademark for* a kind of electric horn with a loud, shrill sound —***n.*** **[k-]** such a horn

Klee (klā), **Paul** 1879–1940; Swiss abstract painter

Klee·nex (klē′neks) *a trademark for* soft tissue paper used as a handkerchief, etc. —***n.*** [*occas.* **k-**] a piece of such paper

klep·to·ma·ni·a (klep′tə mā′nē ə) ***n.*** [ModL. < Gr. *kleptēs,* thief + -MANIA] an abnormal, persistent impulse to steal —**klep′to·ma′ni·ac′** (-ak′) ***n.***

klieg light (klēg) [after A. & J. *Kliegl,* 20th-c. U.S. inventors] a very bright, hot arc light used to light motion-picture sets: also sp. **kleig**

Klon·dike (klän′dīk) gold-mining region along a tributary (**Klondike River**) of the Yukon River, in W Yukon Territory, Canada

klys·tron (klīs′trən, klis′-; -trän) ***n.*** [< Gr. < *klyzein,* to wash + (ELEC)TRON] an electron tube used as an oscillator, amplifier, etc. in ultrahigh frequency circuits to modify the velocity of an electron stream

km, km. kilometer; kilometers

knack (nak) ***n.*** [ME. *knak,* sharp blow] **1.** a clever way of doing something **2.** ability to do something easily

knack·wurst (näk′wurst′; *G.* knäk′voorsht′) ***n.*** [G.] a thick, highly seasoned sausage

knap·sack (nap′sak′) ***n.*** [Du. *knapzak* < *knappen,* to eat + *zak,* a sack] a leather or canvas bag or case worn on the back, as by hikers, for carrying equipment or supplies

knave (nāv) ***n.*** [OE. *cnafa,* boy] **1.** [Archaic] *a)* a male servant *b)* a man of humble status **2.** a tricky rascal; rogue **3.** a jack (the playing card)

knav·er·y (nāv′ər ē) ***n.,*** *pl.* **-er·ies** behavior or an act characteristic of a knave; rascality

knav·ish (-ish) ***adj.*** like a knave; esp., dishonest; tricky —**knav′ish·ly** ***adv.*** —**knav′ish·ness** ***n.***

knead (nēd) ***vt.*** [OE. *cnedan*] **1.** to work (dough, clay, etc.) into a pliable mass by pressing and squeezing, usually with the hands **2.** to massage with similar movements **3.** to make or form as by kneading —**knead′er** ***n.***

knee (nē) ***n.*** [OE. *cneow*] **1.** the joint between the thigh and the lower part of the human leg **2.** any similar or corresponding joint, as in an animal's forelimb **3.** anything like a knee, esp. like a bent knee **4.** the part of a stocking, trouser leg, etc. covering the knee —***vt.*** **kneed, knee′ing** to hit or touch with the knee

knee·cap (-kap′) ***n.*** a movable bone at the front of the human knee; patella: also **knee′pan′** (-pan′)

knee-deep (-dēp′) ***adj.*** **1.** sunk to the knees, as in water **2.** so deep as to reach the knees

knee-jerk (-jurk′) ***adj.*** [< the reflex when the kneecap is tapped] [Colloq.] designating or characterized by an automatic, predictable response [*a knee-jerk* bigot]

kneel (nēl) ***vi.*** **knelt** or **kneeled, kneel′ing** [OE. *cneowlian* < *cneow,* knee] to bend or rest on a knee or the knees —**kneel′er** ***n.***

knee·pad (nē′pad′) ***n.*** a pad worn to protect the knee, as by a basketball player

knell (nel) ***vi.*** [OE. *cnyllan*] **1.** to ring in a slow, solemn way; toll **2.** to sound ominously or mournfully —***vt.*** to call or announce as by a knell —***n.*** **1.** the sound of a tolling bell **2.** an omen of death, failure, etc.

knelt (nelt) *alt. pt. and pp. of* KNEEL

knew (nōō, nyōō) *pt. of* KNOW

Knick·er·bock·er (nik′ər bäk′ər) ***n.*** [< Diedrich *Knickerbocker,* fictitious Du. author of Washington Irving's *History of New York*] **1.** a descendant of the early Dutch settlers of New York **2.** any New Yorker **3.** **[k-]** [*pl.*] short, loose trousers gathered just below the knees; knickers

knick·ers (nik′ərz) ***n.pl.*** [contr. < prec.] **1.** knickerbockers **2.** [Chiefly Brit.] a woman's underpants

knick·knack (nik′nak′) ***n.*** [redupl. of KNACK] a small ornamental article or contrivance

knife (nīf) ***n.,*** *pl.* **knives** [OE. *cnif*] **1.** a cutting or stabbing instrument with a sharp blade, single-edged or double-edged, set in a handle **2.** a cutting blade, as in a machine —***vt.*** **knifed, knif′ing** **1.** to cut or stab with a knife **2.** [Colloq.] to hurt, defeat, etc. by treachery —***vi.*** to pass into or through something quickly, like a sharp knife —**under the knife** [Colloq.] under surgery —**knife′like′** ***adj.***

knight (nīt) ***n.*** [OE. *cniht,* boy] **1.** in the Middle Ages, *a)* a military attendant of the king or other feudal superior, typically holding land in fief *b)* later, a man of high birth who after serving as page and squire was formally raised to honorable military rank and pledged to chivalrous conduct **2.** in Great Britain, a man who for some achievement is given honorary nonhereditary rank next below a baronet, entitling him to use *Sir* before his given name **3.** [*usually* **K-**] a member of any society that officially calls its members *knights* **4.** [Poet.] a lady's devoted champion or attendant **5.** *Chess* a piece typically shaped like a horse's head —***vt.*** to make (a man) a knight

knight-er·rant (-er′ənt) ***n.,*** *pl.* **knights′-er′rant** **1.** a medieval knight wandering in search of adventure **2.** a chivalrous or quixotic person —**knight′-er′rant·ry** (-er′ən trē) ***n.,*** *pl.* **-ries**

knight·hood (-hood′) ***n.*** **1.** the rank or vocation of a knight **2.** knightly conduct **3.** knights

knight·ly (-lē) ***adj.*** **1.** of or like a knight; chivalrous, brave, etc. **2.** consisting of knights —**knight′li·ness** ***n.***

Knights of Columbus an international fraternal society of Roman Catholic men

Knight Templar *pl.* **Knights Templars** for 1, **Knights Templar** for 2 **1.** a member of a military and religious order established among the Crusaders c. 1118 **2.** a member of a certain order of Masons

knit (nit) *vt., vi.* **knit′ted** or **knit, knit′ting** [OE. *cnyttan* < base of *cnotta,* a knot] **1.** to make (cloth or clothing) by looping yarn or thread together with special needles **2.** to form into cloth in this way **3.** to join closely and firmly **4.** to draw (the brows) together —*n.* cloth or a garment made by knitting —**knit′ter** *n.*

knit·ting (-iŋ) *n.* **1.** the action of a person or thing that knits **2.** knitted work

knitting needle an eyeless, long needle used in pairs, etc. in knitting by hand

knit·wear (-wer′) *n.* knitted clothing

knives (nīvz) *n. pl. of* KNIFE

knob (näb) *n.* [< or akin to MLowG. *knobbe,* a knot, bud, etc.] **1.** a rounded lump or protuberance **2.** a handle, usually round, of a door, drawer, etc. **3.** a rounded hill or mountain —**knobbed** *adj.*

knob·by (näb′ē) *adj.* **-bi·er, -bi·est** **1.** covered with knobs **2.** like a knob —**knob′bi·ness** *n.*

knock (näk) *vi.* [OE. *cnocian*] **1.** to strike a blow, as with the fist; esp., to rap on a door **2.** to bump; collide **3.** to make a thumping or rattling noise, as an engine **4.** [Colloq.] to find fault —*vt.* **1.** to hit; strike **2.** to make by hitting or striking *[to knock a hole in the wall]* **3.** [Colloq.] to find fault with —*n.* **1.** a knocking **2.** a sharp blow; rap, as on a door **3.** a thumping or rattling noise, as in an engine **4.** [Colloq.] an adverse criticism **5.** [Colloq.] a misfortune or trouble —**knock about** (or **around**) [Colloq.] **1.** to wander about; roam **2.** to treat roughly —**knock back** [Colloq.] to gulp down (an alcoholic drink) —**knock down** **1.** to strike down **2.** to take apart **3.** to indicate the sale of at an auction **4.** [Slang] to earn as pay —**knock it off!** [Slang] quit it! specif., stop talking! —**knock off** **1.** [Colloq.] to stop working **2.** [Colloq.] to deduct **3.** [Colloq.] to do **4.** [Slang] to kill, overcome, etc. —**knock (oneself) out** to exert oneself as to point of exhaustion —**knock out** **1.** *Boxing* to score a knockout over **2.** to make unconscious or exhausted **3.** to defeat, destroy, etc. **4.** [Colloq.] to do; make; specif., to compose, write, etc., esp. casually or hastily —**knock together** to make or compose hastily or crudely —**knock up** **1.** [Brit. Colloq.] *a)* to exhaust *b)* to wake (someone) as by knocking at the door **2.** [Slang] to make pregnant

knock·a·bout (-ə bout′) *n.* **1.** a small, one-masted yacht with a mainsail, jib, and centerboard or keel, but no bowsprit **2.** something for knockabout use —*adj.* **1.** rough; noisy; boisterous **2.** made or suitable for rough use

knock·down (-doun′) *adj.* **1.** that knocks down; overwhelming **2.** made so as to be easily taken apart *[a knockdown table]* —*n.* **1.** a knocking down; felling **2.** a blow that knocks down

knock·er (-ər) *n.* one that knocks; specif., a small metal ring, knob, etc. on a door, for knocking

knock-knee (-nē′) *n.* a condition in which the legs curve inward at the knees —**knock′-kneed′** *adj.*

knock·out (-out′) *adj.* that knocks out, as a blow —*n.* **1.** a knocking out or being knocked out **2.** *a)* a blow that knocks out *b) Boxing* a victory won when the opponent is knocked down and cannot rise before an official count of ten **3.** [Slang] a very attractive or striking person or thing

knockout drops [Slang] a drug put into a drink to cause the drinker to become unconscious

knock·wurst (näk′wurst′) *n. same as* KNACKWURST

knoll (nōl) *n.* [OE. *cnoll*] a hillock; mound

Knos·sos (näs′əs) *same as* CNOSSUS

knot (nät) *n.* [OE. *cnotta*] **1.** a lump or knob in a thread, cord, etc., as formed by a tangle drawn tight **2.** a fastening made by intertwining or tying together pieces of string, rope, etc. **3.** an ornamental bow of ribbon or twist of braid **4.** a small group or cluster **5.** something that ties closely or intricately; esp., the bond of marriage **6.** a problem; difficulty **7.** a knotlike part, as in a tense muscle; specif., *a)* a hard lump on a tree where a branch grows out *b)* a cross section of such a lump, appearing cross-grained in a board *c)* a joint on a plant stem where leaves grow out **8.** *Naut.* a unit of speed of one nautical mile (6,076.12 feet) an hour *[a speed of 10 knots]* —*vt.* **knot′ted, knot′ting** **1.** to tie or intertwine in or with a knot **2.** to tie closely or intricately; entangle —*vi.* **1.** to form a knot or knots **2.** to make knots for fringe —**tie the knot** [Colloq.] to get married —**knot′ted** *adj.* —**knot′ter** *n.*

knot·grass (nät′gras′) *n.* a common weed with slender stems and narrow leaves: also **knot′weed′** (-wēd′)

knot·hole (-hōl′) *n.* a hole in a board, etc. where a knot has fallen out

knot·ty (-ē) *adj.* **-ti·er, -ti·est** **1.** full of knots *[a knotty board]* **2.** hard to solve; puzzling *[a knotty problem]* —**knot′ti·ness** *n.*

knout (nout) *n.* [Russ. *knut* < Sw., a knot] a leather whip formerly used in Russia to flog criminals

know (nō) *vt.* **knew, known, know′ing** [OE. *cnawan*] **1.** to be well informed about *[to know the facts]* **2.** to be aware of; have perceived or learned *[to know that one is loved]* **3.** to have securely in the memory *[the actor knows his lines]* **4.** to be acquainted or familiar with **5.** to have understanding of or skill in as a result of study or experience *[to know music]* **6.** to recognize *[I'd know that face anywhere]* **7.** to recognize as distinct; distinguish *[to know right from wrong]* **8.** [Archaic] to have sexual intercourse with —*vi.* **1.** to have knowledge **2.** to be sure, informed, or aware —**in the know** [Colloq.] having confidential information —**know′a·ble** *adj.* —**know′er** *n.*

know-how (-hou′) *n.* [Colloq.] knowledge of how to do something well; technical skill

know·ing (-iŋ) *adj.* **1.** having knowledge or information **2.** shrewd; clever **3.** implying shrewd understanding or secret knowledge *[a knowing look]* **4.** deliberate —**know′ing·ly** *adv.* —**know′ing·ness** *n.*

knowl·edge (näl′ij) *n.* **1.** the act, fact, or state of knowing **2.** acquaintance with facts; range of information, awareness, or understanding **3.** what is known; learning; enlightenment **4.** the body of facts, principles, etc. accumulated by mankind —**to (the best of) one's knowledge** as far as one knows; within the range of one's information

knowl·edge·a·ble (-ə b'l) *adj.* having or showing knowledge or intelligence —**knowl′edge·a·bil′i·ty, knowl′edge·a·ble·ness** *n.* —**knowl′edge·a·bly** *adv.*

known (nōn) *pp. of* KNOW

know-noth·ing (nō′nuth′iŋ) *n.* **1.** an ignoramus **2.** **[K- N-]** a member of a U.S. secret political party in the 1850's with a program of excluding from public office anyone not a native-born American

Knox (näks), **John** 1505?–72; Scot. Protestant clergyman & religious reformer

Knox·ville (näks′vil) [after Gen. H. *Knox* (1750–1806), 1st secretary of war] city in E Tenn., on the Tennessee River: pop. 183,000

knuck·le (nuk′'l) *n.* [< or akin to MDu. & MLowG. *knokel,* little bone] **1.** a joint of the finger; esp., the joint connecting a finger to the rest of the hand **2.** the knee or hock joint of a pig or other animal, used as food **3.** [*pl.*] *same as* BRASS KNUCKLES —*vt.* **-led, -ling** to strike, press, or touch with the knuckles —**knuckle down** **1.** to rest the knuckles on the ground in shooting a marble **2.** to work energetically or seriously —**knuckle under** to yield; give in

knuck·le·head (-hed′) *n.* [Colloq.] a stupid person

knurl (nurl) *n.* [prob. blend of ME. *knur,* a knot + GNARL] **1.** a knot, knob, nodule, etc. **2.** any of a series of small beads or ridges, as along the edge of a coin —*vt.* to make knurls on —**knurled** *adj.*

knurl·y (-ē) *adj.* **knurl′i·er, knurl′i·est** full of knurls, as wood; gnarled

Knut (k′noot) *same as* CANUTE

KO (kā′ō′) *vt.* **KO'd, KO'ing** [Slang] *Boxing* to knock out —*n., pl.* **KO's** [Slang] *Boxing* a knockout Also **K.O., k.o.**

ko·a·la (kō ä′lə) *n.* [< the native name] an Australian, tree-dwelling marsupial animal with thick, gray fur: it feeds on eucalyptus leaves and buds

KOALA (27–35 in. long)

Ko·be (kō′bā′; *E.* kō′bē) seaport on the S coast of Honshu, Japan: pop. 1,217,000

Ko·ben·havn (kö′b'n houn′) *Dan. name of* COPENHAGEN

kob·o (käb′ō) *n., pl.* **kob′o** [native name of a former coin] see MONETARY UNITS, table (Nigeria)

Koch (kōk; *G.* kôkh), **Robert** 1843–1910; Ger. bacteriologist & physician

ko·di·ak bear (kō′dē ak′) a very large, brown bear found on Kodiak Island and in adjacent areas

Ko·di·ak Island (kō′dē ak′) [< Russ. < ? native name meaning "island"] island off the SW coast of Alas., in the State of Alas.

Koh·i·noor, Koh-i-noor (kō′ə noor′) [< Per.] a famous large Indian diamond, now one of the British crown jewels

kohl (kōl) *n.* [Ar. *kuhl*] a cosmetic preparation used, esp. in Eastern countries, for eye makeup

kohl·ra·bi (kōl′rä′bē, kōl′rä′bē) *n., pl.* **-bies** [G. < It., pl. of *cavolo rapa,* cole rape: cf. COLE & RAPE[2]] a garden vegetable related to the cabbage, with an edible bulbous stem

ko·la (kō′lə) ***n.*** *same as* COLA
kola nut the seed of the cola
ko·lin·sky (kə lin′skē, kō-) ***n.,*** *pl.* **-skies** [< Russ. < *Kola,* Russian district] **1.** any of several weasels of Asia **2.** the golden-brown fur of such a weasel
Köln (köln) *Ger. name of* COLOGNE
Kol Nid·re (kōl nē′drā, nid′rə) [Aram. *kōl nidhrē,* lit., all our vows] **1.** the prayer of atonement recited in synagogues at the opening of Yom Kippur eve services **2.** the music for this
koo·doo (ko͞o′do͞o) ***n.,*** *pl.* **-doos, -doo:** see PLURAL, II, D, 1 *same as* KUDU
kook (ko͝ok) ***n.*** [< ? *cuckoo*] [Slang] a person regarded as silly, eccentric, crazy, etc. —**kook′y, kook′ie** ***adj.*** **kook′i·er, kook′i·est**
ko·peck, ko·pek (kō′pek) ***n.*** [< Russ. < *kopye,* a lance] a monetary unit, and a coin, equal to 1/100 of a ruble: see MONETARY UNITS, table (U.S.S.R.)
Ko·ran (kō ran′, -rän′; kô-, kə-) ***n.*** [Ar. *qur'ān,* lit., book, reading < *qara'a,* to read] the sacred book of the Moslems: its contents are reported revelations made to Mohammed by Allah —**Ko·ran′ic** ***adj.***
Ko·re·a (kô rē′ə, kō-) peninsula in E Asia, extending south from NE China: divided (1948) into two countries: *a)* **North Korea,** occupying the N half of the peninsula, 47,255 sq. mi., pop. 11,568,000, cap. Pyongyang, and *b)* **South Korea,** occupying the S half, 38,030 sq. mi., pop. 31,738,000, cap. Seoul
Ko·re·an (-ən) ***adj.*** of Korea, its people, etc. —***n.*** **1.** a native of Korea **2.** the language of the Koreans
ko·ru·na (kō ro͞o′nä) ***n.,*** *pl.* **ko·ru′nas, ko·run′** [Czech < L. *corona,* a crown] *see* MONETARY UNITS, table (Czechoslovakia)
Kos·ci·us·ko (käs′ē us′kō; *Pol.* kôsh cho͞osh′kô), **Thad·de·us** (thad′ē əs) (born *Tadeusz Kościuszko*) 1746–1817; Pol. patriot & general: served in the Am. army in the American Revolution
ko·sher (kō′shər; *for v., usually* käsh′ər) ***adj.*** [Heb. *kāshēr,* fit, proper] **1.** *Judaism a)* clean or fit to eat according to the dietary laws: Lev. 11 *b)* dealing in such food **2.** [Slang] all right, proper, etc. —***n.*** kosher food —***vt.*** to make kosher
Kos·suth (käs′o͞oth; *Hung.* kô′sho͝ot), **Louis** (Hung. name *Lajos Kossuth*) 1802–94; Hung. patriot & statesman
kow·tow (kou′tou′, kō′-) ***n.*** [Chin. *k'o-t'ou,* lit., knock head] the act of kneeling and touching the ground with the forehead to show great deference, submissive respect, homage, etc. —***vi.*** **1.** to make a kowtow **2.** to show submissive respect (*to*)
KP, K.P. kitchen police
Kr *Chem.* krypton
kraal (kräl, krôl) ***n.*** [Afrik. < Port. *curral,* pen for cattle] **1.** a village of South African natives, usually surrounded by a stockade **2.** a fenced enclosure for cattle or sheep in South Africa
krait (krīt) ***n.*** [Hindi *karait*] a very poisonous, yellow-banded snake, found in SC and SE Asia
Kra·ków (kra′kou′; *Pol.* krä′ko͝of) city in S Poland, on the Vistula: pop. 535,000
Kras·no·dar (kräs′nô där′) city in SW R.S.F.S.R., in the N Caucasus: pop. 420,000
Kras·no·yarsk (kräs′nô yärsk′) city in C R.S.F.S.R., in NC Asia: pop. 592,000
Kre·feld (krā′felt) city in W West Germany, on the Rhine: pop. 224,000
Kreis·ler (krīs′lər), **Fritz** (frits) 1875–1962; U.S. violinist & composer, born in Austria
krem·lin (krem′lin) ***n.*** [Fr. < Russ. *kreml'*] in Russia, the citadel of a city —**the Kremlin 1.** the citadel of Moscow, formerly housing government offices of the Soviet Union **2.** the government of the Soviet Union
krim·mer (krim′ər) ***n.*** [G. < *Krim,* Crimea] a grayish, tightly curled fur made from the pelts of Crimean lambs
kris (krēs) ***n.*** [Malay *kerīs*] a Malay dagger with a wavy blade; creese
Krish·na (krish′nə) an important Hindu god, an incarnation of Vishnu —**Krish′na·ism** ***n.***
Kriss Krin·gle (kris′ kriŋ′g'l) [< G. < *Christ,* Christ + *kindl,* dim. of *kind,* child] *same as* SANTA CLAUS
Kri·voi Rog (kri voi′ rôk′) city in SC Ukrainian S.S.R.: pop. 523,000
kro·na (krō′nə; *Sw.* kro͞o′nə) ***n.,*** *pl.* **-nor** (-nôr) [Sw. < L. *corona,* crown] *see* MONETARY UNITS, table (Sweden)
kró·na (krō′nə) ***n.,*** *pl.* **-nur** (-nər) [Ice. < ML. *corona,* a crown] *see* MONETARY UNITS, table (Iceland)
kro·ne (krō′nə) ***n.,*** *pl.* **-ner** (-nər) [Dan. < L. *corona,* crown] *see* MONETARY UNITS, table (Denmark, Norway)
Kru·ger (kro͞o′gər), **Paul** (born *Stephanus Johannes Paulus Kruger*) 1825–1904; South African statesman
krul·ler (krul′ər) ***n.*** *same as* CRULLER
Krupp (krup; *G.* kro͝op) family of Ger. steel & munitions manufacturers in the 19th & 20th cent.
kryp·ton (krip′tän) ***n.*** [< Gr. neut. of *kryptos,* hidden < *kryptein,* to hide] a rare, inert, gaseous chemical element present in very small quantities in air: symbol, Kr; at. wt., 83.80; at. no., 36
KS Kansas
Kt *Chess* knight
kt. 1. karat **2.** kiloton(s)
Kua·la Lum·pur (kwä′lə lo͝om po͝or′) city in the SW Malay Peninsula; capital of Malaysia: pop. c.400,000
Ku·blai Khan (ko͞o′blī kän′, -blə) 1216?–94; Mongol emperor of China (1260?–94): founder of the Mongol dynasty: grandson of GENGHIS KHAN
ku·chen (ko͞o′kən, -khən) ***n.*** [G., cake] a coffeecake made of yeast dough and often frosted or filled with raisins, nuts, etc.
ku·dos (ko͞o′däs, -dōs; kyo͞o′-) ***n.*** [Gr. *kydos,* glory] praise for an achievement; glory; fame
ku·du (ko͞o′do͞o) ***n.,*** *pl.* **-dus, -du:** see PLURAL, II, D, 1 [Hottentot] a large, grayish-brown African antelope with long, twisted horns
Kui·by·shev (kwē′bi shef′) city in SW R.S.F.S.R., on the Volga: pop. 1,014,000
Ku Klux (ko͞o′kluks′, kyo͞o′) [< Gr. *kyklos,* a circle] **1.** *short for* KU KLUX KLAN **2.** a member of the Ku Klux Klan: also **Ku Klux′er**
Ku Klux Klan (klan) [prec. + *klan,* arbitrary sp. for CLAN] **1.** a secret society of white men founded in the S States after the Civil War to reestablish and maintain white supremacy **2.** a U.S. secret, terrorist society organized in 1915: it is anti-Negro, anti-Semitic, anti-Catholic, etc.
ku·lak (ko͞o läk′) ***n.*** [Russ., lit., fist < Estonian] a well-to-do farmer in Russia who profited from the labor of poorer peasants and who opposed the Soviet collectivization of the land
ku·miss (ko͞o′mis) ***n.*** [G. < Russ. < Tatar *kumiz*] mare's or camel's milk fermented and used as a drink by Tatar nomads of Asia
küm·mel (kim′'l; *G.* küm′əl) ***n.*** [G., caraway < OHG. *kumil* < L. *cuminum:* see CUMIN] a colorless liqueur flavored with caraway seeds, anise, cumin, etc.
kum·quat (kum′kwät, -kwôt) ***n.*** [< Chin. *chin-chü,* golden orange] **1.** a small, orange-colored, oval fruit, with a sour pulp and a sweet rind, used in preserves **2.** a tree that bears this fruit
kung fu (ko͝oŋ′ fo͞o′, go͝oŋ′) [< Chin.] a Chinese system of self-defense, like karate but emphasizing circular rather than linear movements
Kuo·min·tang (kwō′min taŋ′; *Chin.* gwō′min′däŋ′) [Chin.] nationalist political party of China, organized chiefly by Sun Yat-sen in 1911 and afterward controlled and led by Chiang Kai-shek
Kurd (kurd, ko͝ord) ***n.*** [Turk. & Ar.] any of a nomadic Moslem people living chiefly in Kurdistan —**Kurd′ish** ***adj., n.***
Kur·dis·tan (kur′di stan′, ko͝or′-; -stän′) region occupying SE Turkey, N Iraq, & NW Iran
Ku·ril (or **Ku·rile**) **Islands** (ko͞o′ril, ko͞o rēl′) chain of islands of the U.S.S.R., between N Hokkaido, Japan, and Kamchatka Peninsula
Kush·it·ic (kush it′ik) ***adj., n.*** *same as* CUSHITIC
Ku·wait (ko͞o wāt′, -wīt′) independent Arab state in E Arabia, on the NW coast of the Persian Gulf: 6,000 sq. mi.; pop. 555,000
kw. kilowatt; kilowatts
kwa·cha (kwä′chä) ***n.,*** *pl.* **-cha** [native term, lit., dawn] *see* MONETARY UNITS, table (Malawi, Zambia)
Kwang·chow (kwäŋ′chō′; *Chin.* gwäŋ′jō′) port in SE China: pop. 2,200,000; also sp. **Kwangchou**
kwa·shi·or·kor (kwä′shē ôr′kôr) ***n.*** [< name in Ghana] a severe disease of young children, caused by chronic deficiency of protein and calories and characterized by stunted growth, edema, etc.
kwh, K.W.H., kw.-hr., kw-hr kilowatt-hour
Ky., KY Kentucky
ky·ak (kī′ak) ***n.*** *same as* KAYAK
kyat (kyät) ***n.*** [Burmese] *see* MONETARY UNITS, table (Burma)
Kym·ric (kim′rik) ***adj., n.*** *same as* CYMRIC
Kym·ry, Kym·ri (-rē) ***n.pl.*** *same as* CYMRY
Kyo·to (kyô′tô′; *E.* kē ōt′ō) city in S Honshu, Japan: pop. 1,365,000
Kyu·shu (kyo͞o′sho͞o′) one of the four main islands of Japan, south of Honshu: 16,223 sq. mi.

L

L, l (el) ***n., pl.* L's, l's** **1.** the twelfth letter of the English alphabet **2.** the sound of *L* or *l*
L (el) ***n., pl.* L's** **1.** an object shaped like L; esp., an extension of a building that gives the whole a shape resembling L **2.** a Roman numeral for 50 —***adj.*** shaped like L
L. **1.** Latin **2.** Licentiate
L., l. **1.** lake **2.** latitude **3.** law **4.** leaf **5.** league **6.** left **7.** length **8.** *pl.* **LL., ll.** line **9.** link **10.** lira; lire **11.** liter **12.** low **13.** [L. *libra*, pl. *librae*] pound(s)
la[1] (lä, lô) ***interj.*** [Dial. or Archaic] an exclamation of surprise or emphasis
la[2] (lä) ***n.*** [see GAMUT] *Music* a syllable representing the sixth tone of the diatonic scale
La *Chem.* lanthanum
La., LA Louisiana
L.A. [Colloq.] Los Angeles
lab (lab) ***n.*** [Colloq.] a laboratory
la·bel (lā′b'l) ***n.*** [OFr., a rag, strip < Gmc.] **1.** a card, strip of paper, etc. marked and attached to an object to indicate its nature, contents, ownership, destination, etc. **2.** a descriptive word or phrase applied to a person, group, etc. as a convenient generalized classification **3.** an identifying brand of a company —***vt.*** **-beled** or **-belled, -bel·ing** or **-bel·ling** **1.** to attach a label to **2.** to classify as; call; describe —**la′bel·er, la′bel·ler** ***n.***
la·bi·a (lā′bē ə) ***n.*** *pl. of* LABIUM
la·bi·al (-əl) ***adj.*** [< ML. < L. *labium*, a lip] **1.** of the labia, or lips **2.** *Phonet.* formed mainly with the lips: said esp. of *b*, *m*, and *p* —***n.*** a labial sound —**la′bi·al·ly** ***adv.***
la·bi·ate (lā′bē āt′, -it) ***adj.*** [< L. *labium*, a lip] **1.** formed or functioning like a lip **2.** having a lip or lips **3.** *Bot.* having the calyx or corolla so divided that one part overlaps the other like a lip
la·bile (lā′b'l, -bīl) ***adj.*** [< L. < *labi*, to slip] liable to change; unstable —**la·bil′i·ty** ***n.***
la·bi·o·den·tal (lā′bē ō den′t'l) ***adj.*** [< L. *labium*, a lip + DENTAL] *Phonet.* formed with the lower lip against the upper teeth, as the sounds of *f* and *v* —***n.*** a labiodental sound
la·bi·um (lā′bē əm) ***n., pl.*** **-bi·a** (-ə) [L., a lip] *Anat., Bot.*, etc. a lip or liplike organ; specif., [*pl.*] the outer folds of skin (**labia majora**) or the inner folds of mucous membrane (**labia minora**) of the vulva
la·bor (lā′bər) ***n.*** [< OFr. < L. *labor*] **1.** physical or mental exertion; work; toil **2.** a specific task **3.** *a*) all wage-earning workers as a group: distinguished from CAPITAL[1] or MANAGEMENT *b*) all manual workers whose work is characterized largely by physical exertion **4.** labor unions collectively **5.** [L-] *same as* LABOR PARTY **6.** the work accomplished by workers collectively **7.** *Med.* the process of giving birth to a child —***vi.*** [< OFr. < L. *laborare* < the *n.*] **1.** to work; toil **2.** to work hard **3.** to move slowly and with difficulty [*the car labored up the hill*] **4.** to be burdened (with *under*) [*to labor under a delusion*] **5.** to undergo, and suffer the pains of, childbirth —***vt.*** to develop in too great detail [*to labor a point*]
lab·o·ra·to·ry (lab′rə tôr′ē, -ər ə tôr′ē; *Brit.* lə bär′ə tər ē, -ə trē) ***n., pl.*** **-ries** [< ML. < L.: see LABOR, *vi.*] **1.** a room or building for scientific experimentation or research **2.** a place for preparing chemicals, drugs, etc. **3.** a place where theories, methods, etc., as in education, are tested, demonstrated, etc. —***adj.*** of or performed in, or as in, a laboratory
Labor Day in the U.S. & Canada, the first Monday in September, a legal holiday in honor of labor
la·bored (lā′bərd) ***adj.*** made or done with great effort; not easy and natural; strained
la·bor·er (lā′bər ər) ***n.*** one who labors; esp., a wage-earning worker whose work is characterized largely by physical exertion
la·bo·ri·ous (lə bôr′ē əs) ***adj.*** **1.** involving or calling for much hard work; difficult **2.** industrious; hard-working —**la·bo′ri·ous·ly** ***adv.*** —**la·bo′ri·ous·ness** ***n.***
la·bor·ite (lā′bə rīt′) ***n.*** **1.** a member or supporter of a labor party **2.** [L-] a member or supporter of the British Labor Party: Brit. sp. **La′bour·ite′**
labor party **1.** a political party organized to protect and further the rights of workers, or one dominated by organized labor **2.** [L- P-] such a party in Great Britain: Brit. sp. **Labour Party**
la·bor-sav·ing (lā′bər sā′viŋ) ***adj.*** eliminating or lessening physical labor [*labor-saving appliances*]
labor union an association of workers to promote and protect the welfare, interests, and rights of its members, mainly by collective bargaining
la·bour (lā′bər) ***n., vi., vt.*** *Brit. sp. of* LABOR
Lab·ra·dor (lab′rə dôr′) **1.** region along the E coast of Canada, constituting the mainland part of the province of Newfoundland **2.** large peninsula occupied by this region & most of Quebec
Labrador retriever any of a breed of medium-sized hunting dog used in retrieving game, having a black, brown, or yellow coat of short, thick hair
la·bur·num (lə bur′nəm) ***n.*** [L.] a small, poisonous tree or shrub of the legume family, with drooping racemes of yellow flowers
lab·y·rinth (lab′ə rinth′) ***n.*** [< L. < Gr. *labyrinthos*] **1.** a structure containing an intricate network of winding passages hard to follow without losing one's way; maze; specif., [L-] *Gr. Myth.* such a structure built for King Minos, to house the Minotaur **2.** a complicated, perplexing arrangement, condition, etc. **3.** *Anat.* the inner ear

LABYRINTH

lab·y·rin·thine (lab′ə rin′thin, -thēn) ***adj.*** of, constituting, or like a labyrinth; intricate: also **lab′y·rin′thi·an** (-thē ən), **lab′y·rin′thic**
lac (lak) ***n.*** [< Hindi < Sans. *lākṣā*] **1.** a resinous substance secreted on various trees in S Asia by certain scale insects: when melted, strained, and rehardened, it forms shellac **2.** *same as* LAKH
lace (lās) ***n.*** [OFr. *laz* < L. *laqueus*, a noose] **1.** a string, ribbon, etc. used to draw together and fasten the parts of a shoe, corset, etc. **2.** braid of gold or silver, as for trimming uniforms **3.** a fine netting or openwork fabric of linen, silk, etc., woven in ornamental designs —***vt.*** **laced, lac′ing** **1.** to draw the ends of (a garment, shoe, etc.) together and fasten with a lace **2.** to compress the waist of by lacing a corset, etc. **3.** to pass (a cord, etc.) in and out *through* eyelets, fabric, etc. **4.** to weave together; intertwine **5.** to ornament with lace **6.** to streak, as with color; intersperse **7.** to thrash; beat **8.** to add a dash of alcoholic liquor to (a beverage) —***vi.*** **1.** to be fastened with a lace [*these shoes lace*] **2.** [Colloq.] to attack physically or verbally (with *into*)
lac·er·ate (las′ə rāt′; *also for adj.* -ər it) ***vt.*** **-at′ed, -at′ing** [< L. pp. of *lacerare* < *lacer*, mangled] **1.** to tear jaggedly; mangle **2.** to hurt (one's feelings, etc.) deeply —***adj.*** **1.** torn; mangled **2.** *Bot.* having jagged edges
lac·er·a·tion (las′ə rā′shən) ***n.*** **1.** a lacerating **2.** the result of lacerating; jagged tear or wound
lace·wing (lās′wiŋ′) ***n.*** any of a large group of insects with four delicate, gauzy wings
lace·work (-wurk′) ***n.*** lace, or any openwork decoration like lace
lach·es (lach′iz) ***n.*** [OFr. *laschesse*, ult. < L. *laxus*, lax] *Law* failure to do the required thing at the proper time; inexcusable delay
Lach·e·sis (lak′ə sis) *Gr. & Rom. Myth.* that one of the three Fates who determines the span of life
lach·ry·mal (lak′rə məl) ***adj.*** [< ML. < L. *lacrima*, TEAR[2]] **1.** of, characterized by, or producing tears **2.** *same as* LACRIMAL (sense 1)
lach·ry·ma·to·ry (-mə tôr′ē) ***adj.*** of, causing, or producing tears
lach·ry·mose (-mōs′) ***adj.*** [< L. < *lacrima*, TEAR[2]] **1.** inclined to shed many tears; tearful **2.** causing tears; sad —**lach′ry·mose′ly** ***adv.***

lac·ing (lās′iŋ) ***n.*** **1.** the act of a person who laces **2.** a thrashing; beating **3.** a cord or lace, as a shoelace **4.** gold or silver braid used to trim a uniform, etc.

lack (lak) ***n.*** [< or akin to MLowG., MDu. *lak*] **1.** the fact or condition of not having enough; shortage; deficiency **2.** the fact or condition of not having any; complete absence **3.** the thing that is lacking or needed —***vi.*** **1.** to be wanting or missing **2.** *a)* to be short (with *in* or *for*) *b)* to be in need —***vt.*** **1.** to be deficient in or entirely without **2.** to fall short by *[lacking* one ounce of being a pound*]*

lack·a·dai·si·cal (lak′ə dā′zi k′l) ***adj.*** [ult. < *alack the day*] showing lack of interest or spirit; listless; languid —**lack′a·dai′si·cal·ly *adv.***

lack·ey (lak′ē) ***n.,*** *pl.* **-eys** [< Fr. < Sp. *lacayo*] **1.** a male servant of low rank, usually in uniform; footman **2.** a servile follower; toady

lack·lus·ter (lak′lus′tər) ***adj.*** lacking brightness; dull *[lackluster* eyes*]* Also, chiefly Brit. sp., **lack′lus′tre**

La·co·ni·a (lə kō′nē ə) ancient region on the S coast of the Peloponnesus, dominated by the city of Sparta

la·con·ic (lə kän′ik) ***adj.*** [< L. < Gr. < *Lakōn,* a Laconian, Spartan] brief or terse in speech or expression; using few words —**la·con′i·cal·ly *adv.***

lac·quer (lak′ər) ***n.*** [< Fr. < Port. < *laca,* gum lac] **1.** a coating substance of natural or synthetic resins, nitrocellulose, etc. dissolved in a solvent that evaporates rapidly leaving a tough, adherent film: pigments are often added to form **lacquer enamels** **2.** a natural resin varnish obtained from certain trees in China and Japan, or woodenware (in full, **lac′quer·ware′**, **lac′quer·work′**) coated with it —***vt.*** to coat with or as with lacquer —**lac′quer·er *n.***

lac·ri·mal (lak′rə məl) ***adj.*** **1.** *Anat.* designating, of, or near the glands that secrete tears **2.** *same as* LACHRYMAL (sense 1)

lac·ri·ma·tion (lak′rə mā′shən) ***n.*** [< L. < pp. of *lacrimare,* to weep < *lacrima,* TEAR[2]] normal or excessive secretion or shedding of tears

la·crosse (lə krôs′, -kräs′) ***n.*** [CanadFr. < Fr. *la,* the + *crosse,* a crutch] a ball game in which two teams of ten men each, using long-handled, pouched rackets, try to advance a small rubber ball across the field into the opponents' goal

LACROSSE

La Crosse (lə krôs′, kräs′) [< prec.] city in W Wis., on the Mississippi: pop. 51,000

lac·tate (lak′tāt) ***vi.*** **-tat·ed, -tat·ing** [< L. pp. of *lactare* < *lac* (see LACTO-)] to secrete milk —***n.*** any salt or ester of lactic acid

lac·ta·tion (lak tā′shən) ***n.*** **1.** the secretion of milk by a mammary gland **2.** the period during which milk is secreted **3.** the suckling of young

lac·te·al (lak′tē əl) ***adj.*** [< L. *lacteus* < *lac* (see LACTO-) + -AL] **1.** of or like milk; milky **2.** containing or carrying chyle, the milky fluid that is a product of digestion —***n.*** any of the lymphatic vessels that carry chyle from the small intestine to the blood

lac·tic (lak′tik) ***adj.*** [< Fr.: see LACTO- & -IC] of or obtained from milk

lactic acid a yellowish or clear, syrupy organic acid, $C_3H_6O_3$, produced by the fermentation of lactose when milk sours

lac·to- [< L. *lac* (gen. *lactis*), milk] *a combining form meaning:* **1.** milk **2.** *Chem.* lactic acid or lactate Also, before a vowel, **lact-**

lac·tose (lak′tōs) ***n.*** [LACT(O)- + -OSE[1]] a white, crystalline sugar, $C_{12}H_{22}O_{11}$, found in milk and used in infant foods, medicine, etc.

la·cu·na (lə kyo͞o′nə) ***n.,*** *pl.* **-nas, -nae** (-nē) [L., a ditch < *lacus,* lake] **1.** a space where something has been omitted or has come out; missing part; gap; hiatus **2.** *Anat., Biol.* any of the very small cavities in bone that are filled with bone cells —**la·cu′nar** (-nər), **la·cu′nal *adj.***

lac·y (lā′sē) ***adj.*** **lac′i·er, lac′i·est** **1.** of lace **2.** like lace; having a delicate open pattern —**lac′i·ly *adv.*** —**lac′i·ness *n.***

lad (lad) ***n.*** [ME. *ladde*] **1.** a boy or youth **2.** [Colloq.] any man; fellow: familiar term

lad·der (lad′ər) ***n.*** [OE. *hlæder*] **1.** a framework of two parallel sidepieces connected by rungs or crosspieces on which a person steps in climbing up or down **2.** anything by means of which a person climbs or rises *[*the *ladder* of success*]* **3.** [Chiefly Brit.] a run as in a stocking

lad·die (lad′ē) ***n.*** [Chiefly Scot.] a young lad

lade (lād) ***vt., vi.*** **lad′ed, lad′ed** or **lad′en, lad′ing** [OE. *hladan*] **1.** to load **2.** to bail; ladle

lad·en (lād′'n) *alt. pp. of* LADE —***adj.*** **1.** loaded **2.** burdened; afflicted *[laden* with sorrow*]*

la-di-da, la-de-da (lä′dē dä′) ***adj.*** [Colloq.] affected in speech, manners, etc.; pretentiously refined

Ladies' Day a special day on which women may attend a particular event, as a baseball game, free or at reduced cost

lad·ing (lā′diŋ) ***n.*** **1.** the act of one that lades **2.** a load; cargo; freight

la·dle (lā′d'l) ***n.*** [OE. *hlædel* < *hladan,* to draw water] a long-handled, cuplike spoon for dipping out liquids —***vt.*** **-dled, -dling** **1.** to dip out with or as with a ladle **2.** to carry in a ladle —**la′dle·ful′** ***n.,*** *pl.* **-fuls′** —**la′dler *n.***

La·do·ga (lä′dô gä), **Lake** lake in NW R.S.F.S.R., near the border of Finland: c.7,000 sq. mi.

la·dy (lā′dē) ***n.,*** *pl.* **-dies** [OE. *hlæfdige* < *hlaf,* loaf + base of *dæge,* kneader] **1.** a woman with the rights, rule, or authority of a lord **2.** *a)* a woman of high social position *b)* a woman who is polite, refined, and well-mannered **3.** any woman **4.** **[L-]** the Virgin Mary (usually with *Our*) **5.** **[L-]** in Great Britain, the title given to women of certain ranks —***adj.*** female *[*a *lady* barber*]*

la·dy·bug (-bug′) ***n.*** a small, roundish beetle with a spotted back, that feeds chiefly on insect pests and their eggs: also **la′dy·bird′ (beetle)**, **lady beetle**

Lady Day *Brit. name for* ANNUNCIATION (sense 2 *b*)

la·dy·fin·ger (-fiŋ′gər) ***n.*** a small spongecake shaped somewhat like a finger

la·dy-in-wait·ing (-in wāt′iŋ) ***n.,*** *pl.* **la′dies-in-wait′ing** a woman attending, or waiting upon, a queen or princess

la·dy·like (-līk′) ***adj.*** like or suitable for a lady; refined

la·dy·love (-luv′) ***n.*** a sweetheart

la·dy·ship (-ship′) ***n.*** the rank or position of a lady: used in speaking to or of a woman having the title of *Lady,* always preceded by *your* or *her*

la·dy-slip·per (-slip′ər) ***n.*** any of certain orchids whose flowers somewhat resemble a slipper: also **la′dy's-slip′per**

LADY-SLIPPER

la·e·trile (lā′ə tril′) ***n.*** [*lae*(*vo-rotatory glycosidic ni*)*trile*] any of several organic compounds obtained from various related plant substances, as apricot kernels and almond seeds, and claimed to be effective in treating cancers

La·fa·yette (laf′i yet′, lä′fi-, lə fā′it) [after ff.] city in SC La.: pop. 82,000

La·fa·yette (lä′fi yet′, laf′i-; *Fr.* lȧ fȧ yet′), marquis **de** 1757–1834; Fr. general & statesman: served in Am. army in the American Revolution

La Fol·lette (lə fäl′it), **Robert Marion** 1855–1925; U.S. legislator & Progressive Party leader

La Fon·taine (lȧ fōn ten′; *E.* lə fän tān′), **Jean de** (zhän də) 1621–95; Fr. poet & writer of fables

lag (lag) ***vi.*** **lagged, lag′ging** [? akin to MDan. *lakke,* to go slowly] **1.** *a)* to fall, move, or stay behind; loiter *b)* to be retarded in motion, development, etc. **2.** to wane; flag —***n.*** **1.** a falling behind or being retarded in motion, development, etc. **2.** the amount of such falling behind —**lag′ger *n.***

lag bolt *same as* LAG SCREW

la·ger (beer) (lä′gər) [G. *lagerbier,* lit., storehouse beer] a beer which is stored for several months for aging after it has been brewed

lag·gard (lag′ərd) ***n.*** [< LAG + -ARD] a slow person, esp. one who is always falling behind —***adj.*** slow or late in doing things; falling behind —**lag′gard·ly *adv., adj.*** —**lag′gard·ness *n.***

la·gniappe, la·gnappe (lan yap′, lan′yap) ***n.*** [Creole < Fr. *la,* the + Sp. *ñapa,* lagniappe < Quechua *yapa*] **1.** [Chiefly South] a small gift given to a customer with a purchase **2.** a gratuity

la·goon (lə go͞on′) ***n.*** [< Fr. *lagune* & It. *laguna* < L. *lacuna,* lake] **1.** a shallow lake or pond, esp. one connected with a larger body of water **2.** the water enclosed by a circular coral reef **3.** shallow salt water separated from the sea by dunes

La·gos (lā′gäs, -gəs) capital of Nigeria; seaport on the Atlantic: pop. 665,000

lag screw a wood screw with a boltlike head

lah-di-dah, lah-de-dah (lä′dē dä′) ***adj.*** *same as* LA-DI-DA

La·hore (lə hôr′, lä-) city in NE Pakistan: pop. 1,296,000

la·ic (lā′ik) ***adj.*** [< LL. *laicus* < Gr. < *laos,* the people] of the laity; secular; lay: also **la′i·cal** —***n.*** a layman

la·i·cize (lā′ə sīz′) ***vt.*** **-cized′, -ciz′ing** [LAIC + -IZE] to turn over to laymen; secularize

laid (lād) *pt. & pp. of* LAY[1]

laid-back (-bak′) ***adj.*** [Slang] relaxed, restrained, easygoing, etc.; not frenetic or hurried

lain (lān) *pp. of* LIE[1]

lair (ler) ***n.*** [OE. *leger*] the den or cave of a wild animal

laird (lerd; *Scot.* lārd) ***n.*** [Scot. form of LORD] in Scotland, a landowner, esp. a wealthy one

lais·sez faire (les′ā fer′, lez′-) [Fr., let (people) do (as they please)] noninterference; specif., the policy of letting the owners of industry and business operate without governmental regulation or control: also sp. **lais′ser faire′** —**lais′-sez-faire′** *adj.*

la·i·ty (lā′ət ē) *n., pl.* **-ties** [< LAY[3]] **1.** all the people not included among the clergy; laymen collectively **2.** all the people not belonging to any given profession

lake[1] (lāk) *n.* [OE. *lacu* & OFr. *lac,* both < L. *lacus,* lake] **1.** a large, inland body of water, usually fresh water **2.** a pool of oil or other liquid

lake[2] (lāk) *n.* [see LAC] **1.** *a)* a dark-red pigment prepared from cochineal *b)* its color **2.** an insoluble coloring compound precipitated from a solution of a dye by adding a metallic salt

Lake Charles [after *Charles* Sallier, an early settler] city in SW La.: pop. 75,000

Lake District (or **Country**) lake & mountain region in NW England: home of Wordsworth, Coleridge, & Southey (the **Lake poets**)

lake dwelling a dwelling built on wooden piles rising above the surface of a lake, esp. in prehistoric times —**lake dweller**

lak·er (lā′kər) *n.* **1.** a fish, esp. a trout, found in lakes **2.** a lake ship, esp. one on the Great Lakes

lake trout a large, gray game fish of deep, cold lakes of the N U.S. and Canada

Lake·wood (lāk′wood) **1.** city in NC Colo.: suburb of Denver: pop. 113,000 **2.** city in SW Calif.: suburb of Los Angeles: pop. 75,000 **3.** city in NE Ohio: suburb of Cleveland: pop. 62,000

lakh (lak) *n.* [< Hindi (see LAC): prob. in reference to the abundance of the insects] in India and Pakistan, **1.** the sum of 100,000: said of rupees **2.** any indefinitely large number

lal·ly·gag (läl′ē gag′) *vi.* **-gagged′, -gag′ging** [Colloq.] *same as* LOLLYGAG

lam[1] (lam) *vt., vi.* **lammed, lam′ming** [< Scand., as in ON. *lemja*] [Slang] to beat; thrash; flog

lam[2] (lam) *n.* [< ? prec.] [Slang] headlong flight, usually to escape arrest or punishment: used in phrase **on the lam** —*vi.* **lammed, lam′ming** [Slang] to flee; escape —**take it on the lam** [Slang] to flee; escape

Lam. Lamentations

la·ma (lä′mə) *n.* [Tibetan *blama*] a priest or monk in Lamaism: cf. DALAI LAMA

La·ma·ism (lä′mə iz′m) *n.* a form of Buddhism practiced in Tibet and Mongolia, characterized by elaborate ritual and a strong hierarchal organization —**La′ma·ist** *adj., n.* —**La′ma·is′tic** *adj.*

La·marck (là märk′; *E.* lə märk′), chevalier **de** 1744–1829; Fr. naturalist who advanced the evolutionary theory that acquired characters can be inherited (see ACQUIRED CHARACTER) —**La·marck′i·an** *adj., n.* —**La·marck′ism** *n.*

la·ma·ser·y (lä′mə ser′ē) *n., pl.* **-ser′ies** [< Fr.] a monastery of lamas

lamb (lam) *n.* [OE.] **1.** a young sheep **2.** its flesh used as food **3.** lambskin **4.** a gentle or innocent person, esp. a child **5.** a dear **6.** a person easily tricked or outwitted —*vi.* to give birth: said of a ewe —**the Lamb** Jesus —**lamb′like′** *adj.*

Lamb (lam), **Charles** 1775–1834; Eng. essayist & critic

lam·baste (lam bāst′, -bast′) *vt.* **-bast′ed, -bast′ing** [LAM[1] + BASTE[3]] [Colloq.] **1.** to beat soundly; thrash **2.** to scold or criticize severely Also sp. **lam·bast′**

lamb·da (lam′də) *n.* the eleventh letter of the Greek alphabet (Λ, λ)

lam·bent (lam′bənt) *adj.* [< L. prp. of *lambere,* to lick] **1.** playing lightly over a surface; flickering **2.** softly glowing **3.** light and graceful *[lambent wit]* —**lam′ben·cy** *n.*

lamb·kin (lam′kin) *n.* **1.** a little lamb **2.** a child or young person: a term of affection

Lamb of God Jesus: John 1:29, 36

lamb·skin (lam′skin′) *n.* **1.** the skin of a lamb, esp. with the fleece left on it **2.** leather or parchment made from the skin of a lamb

lamb's-quar·ters (lamz′kwôr′tərz) *n.* an annual weed of the goosefoot family, with mealy leaves sometimes used for greens

lame (lām) *adj.* [OE. *lama*] **1.** crippled; esp., having an injured leg or foot that makes one limp **2.** stiff and very painful *[a lame back]* **3.** poor, weak, ineffectual, etc. *[a lame excuse]* —*vt.* **lamed, lam′ing** to make lame —**lame′ly** *adv.* —**lame′ness** *n.*

la·mé (la mā′) *n.* [Fr., laminated < *lame,* metal plate] a cloth interwoven with metallic threads

lame·brain (lām′brān′) *n.* [Colloq.] a slow-witted or stupid person —**lame′brained′** *adj.*

lame duck **1.** a disabled, ineffectual, or helpless person or thing **2.** an elected official whose term extends beyond the time of the election at which he was not reelected

la·mel·la (lə mel′ə) *n., pl.* **-lae** (-ē), **-las** [L., dim. of LAMINA] *Biol.* a thin, platelike part, layer, organ, or structure —**la·mel′lar, lam·el·late** (lam′ə lāt′, lə mel′āt) *adj.* —**la·mel′lar·ly** *adv.*

la·mel·li·branch (lə mel′i braŋk′) *n.* [see prec. & BRANCHIAE] any of a class of mollusks, including the clams, oysters, etc., having platelike gills and bivalve shells

la·ment (lə ment′) *vi.* [< Fr. < L. < *lamentum,* a wailing] to feel or express deep sorrow; mourn; grieve —*vt.* **1.** to mourn or grieve for **2.** to regret deeply —*n.* **1.** a lamentation; wail **2.** a song, poem, etc. mourning a loss, death, etc.; elegy or dirge —**la·ment′er** *n.* —**la·ment′ing·ly** *adv.*

lam·en·ta·ble (lam′ən tə b′l, lə men′tə b′l) *adj.* to be lamented; regrettable; distressing —**lam′en·ta·bly** *adv.*

lam·en·ta·tion (lam′ən tā′shən) *n.* a lamenting

Lam·en·ta·tions (-shənz) a book of the Bible attributed to Jeremiah

la·ment·ed (lə men′tid) *adj.* mourned for: usually said of someone dead —**la·ment′ed·ly** *adv.*

lam·i·na (lam′ə nə) *n., pl.* **-nae′** (-nē′), **-nas** [L.] **1.** a thin flake, scale, or layer **2.** the flat, expanded part of a leaf —**lam′i·nar** (-nər), **lam′i·nal** *adj.*

lam·i·nate (lam′ə nāt′; *for adj. & n. usually* -nit) *vt.* **-nat′ed, -nat′ing** **1.** to form or press into a thin sheet or layer **2.** to separate into thin layers **3.** to cover with or bond to thin layers, as of clear plastic **4.** to make by building up in layers —*vi.* to split into thin layers —*adj. same as* LAMINATED —*n.* something made by laminating —**lam′i·na·ble** (-nə b′l) *adj.* —**lam′i·na′tion** *n.* —**lam′i·na′tor** *n.*

lam·i·nat·ed (-nāt′id) *adj.* composed of or built in thin sheets or layers, as of fabric, wood, plastic, etc., that have been bonded or pressed together

lamp (lamp) *n.* [< OFr. < VL. *lampade,* ult. < Gr. *lampein,* to shine] **1.** a container with a wick for burning oil, alcohol, etc. to produce light or heat **2.** any device for producing light or therapeutic rays, as a gas jet with a mantle, an electric light bulb, or an ultraviolet bulb **3.** a holder, stand, or base for such a device

lamp·black (-blak′) *n.* fine soot produced by the incomplete combustion of oils and other forms of carbon: used as a pigment in paint, ink, etc.

lam·per eel (lam′pər) *same as* LAMPREY

lam·poon (lam pōōn′) *n.* [< Fr. < *lampons,* let us drink (refrain in a drinking song)] a piece of strongly satirical writing, usually attacking or ridiculing someone —*vt.* to attack or ridicule in a lampoon —**lam·poon′er, lam·poon′ist** *n.* —**lam·poon′er·y** *n.*

lamp·post (lamp′pōst′, lamp′-) *n.* a post supporting a street lamp

lam·prey (lam′prē) *n., pl.* **-preys** [< OFr. < ML. *lampreda*] an eellike parasitic fish with a funnel-shaped, jawless, sucking mouth: it preys on other fish

la·nai (lä nī′, la-) *n.* [Haw.] a veranda or open-sided living room of a kind found in Hawaii

Lan·cas·ter[1] (laŋ′kəs tər) ruling family of England (1399–1461) —**Lan·cas′tri·an** (-kas′trē ən) *adj., n.*

Lan·cas·ter[2] (laŋ′kas′tər) [ult. < prec.] city in SE Pa.: pop. 55,000

lance (lans) *n.* [OFr. < L. *lancea*] **1.** a thrusting weapon consisting of a long wooden shaft with a sharp metal head **2.** a lancer **3.** any sharp instrument like a lance, as a fish spear **4.** a surgical lancet —*vt.* **lanced, lanc′ing** **1.** to attack or pierce with a lance **2.** to cut open as with a lancet

lance corporal **1.** *Brit. Army* a private acting temporarily as a corporal **2.** *U.S. Marine Corps* an enlisted man ranking below a corporal and above a private first class

lance·let (lans′lit) *n.* [LANCE + -LET] a small, invertebrate, fishlike sea animal closely related to the vertebrates; amphioxus

Lan·ce·lot (lan′sə lät′, -lət) *Arthurian Legend* the bravest and most celebrated of the Knights of the Round Table: he was Guinevere's lover

lan·ce·o·late (lan′sē ə lāt′, -lit) *adj.* [< LL. < *lanceola,* little lance] narrow and tapering like the head of a lance, as certain leaves

lanc·er (lan′sər) *n.* a cavalry soldier armed with a lance or a member of a cavalry regiment originally armed with lances

lanc·ers (-sərz) *n.pl.* [*with sing. v.*] [< prec.] **1.** a 19th-cent. quadrille **2.** music for this

lance sergeant *Brit. Army* a corporal acting temporarily as a sergeant

lan·cet (lan′sit) *n.* [< OFr. dim. of *lance,* LANCE] **1.** a small, pointed surgical knife, usually two-edged, used for making small incisions, skin punctures, etc. **2.** *same as: a)* LANCET ARCH *b)* LANCET WINDOW

lancet arch a narrow, sharply pointed arch

lancet window a narrow, sharply pointed window without tracery, set in a lancet arch

lance·wood (lans′wood′) *n.* **1.** a tough, elastic wood used for fishing rods, billiard cues, etc. **2.** a tropical tree yielding such wood
land (land) *n.* [OE.] **1.** the solid part of the earth's surface not covered by water **2.** *a)* a country, region, etc. *b)* a country's people **3.** ground or soil *[rich land, high land]* **4.** ground considered as property *[to invest in land]* **5.** rural regions *[to return to the land]* **6.** *Econ.* natural resources —*vt.* **1.** to put or set on shore from a ship **2.** to bring into or end up in a particular place or condition *[a fight landed him in jail]* **3.** to set (an aircraft) down on land or water **4.** to catch *[to land a fish]* **5.** [Colloq.] to get or win *[to land a job]* **6.** [Colloq.] to deliver (a blow) —*vi.* **1.** to leave a ship and go on shore **2.** to come to a port or to shore: said of a ship **3.** to arrive at a specified place **4.** to alight or come to rest, as after a flight, jump, or fall —**land on** [Colloq.] to scold or criticize severely
lan·dau (lan′dou, -dô) *n.* [< *Landau,* German town where orig. made] **1.** a four-wheeled carriage with the top in two sections, either of which can be lowered independently **2.** a former style of automobile with a top whose back could be folded down
land contract a contract in which a purchaser of real estate, upon making an initial payment, agrees to pay set amounts at specified intervals until the total purchase price is paid, at which time the seller transfers his interest in the property
land·ed (lan′did) *adj.* **1.** owning land *[landed gentry]* **2.** consisting of land or real estate *[a landed estate]*
land·fall (land′fôl′) *n.* **1.** a sighting of land from a ship at sea **2.** the land sighted **3.** a landing by ship or airplane
land·fill (-fil′) *n.* **1.** the disposal of garbage, rubbish, etc. by burying it in the ground **2.** the site or fill used
land grant a grant of public land by the government for a railroad, State college, etc.
land·grave (-grāv′) *n.* [< G. < *land,* land + *graf,* a count] **1.** in medieval Germany, a count having jurisdiction over a specified territory **2.** later, the title of certain German princes
land·hold·er (-hōl′dər) *n.* an owner or occupant of land —**land′hold′ing** *adj., n.*
land·ing (lan′diŋ) *n.* **1.** the act of coming to shore or putting ashore **2.** the place where a ship is unloaded or loaded **3.** a platform at the end of a flight of stairs **4.** the act of alighting, as after a flight, jump, or fall
landing craft naval craft designed to bring troops and equipment close to shore
landing field a field with a smooth surface to enable airplanes to land and take off easily
landing gear the undercarriage of an aircraft, including wheels, pontoons, etc.
landing net a baglike net attached to a long handle, for taking a hooked fish from the water
landing strip *same as* AIRSTRIP
land·la·dy (land′lā′dē) *n., pl.* **-dies** a woman landlord
land·less (-lis) *adj.* not owning land
land·locked (-läkt′) *adj.* **1.** entirely or almost entirely surrounded by land, as a bay or a country **2.** cut off from the sea and confined to fresh water *[landlocked salmon]*
land·lord (-lôrd′) *n.* **1.** a person, esp. a man, who rents or leases land, houses, etc. to others **2.** a man who keeps a rooming house, inn, etc.
land·lub·ber (-lub′ər) *n.* a person who has had little experience at sea, and is therefore awkward aboard a ship: a sailor's term of contempt
land·mark (-märk′) *n.* **1.** any fixed object used to mark the boundary of a piece of land **2.** any prominent feature of the landscape, as a tree, identifying a particular locality **3.** an event, discovery, etc. considered as a high point or turning point in the development of something
land·mass (-mas′) *n.* a very large area of land; esp., a continent
land mine an explosive charge hidden under the surface of the ground and detonated by pressure upon it
land office a government office that handles and records the sales and transfers of public lands —**land′-of′fice business** [Colloq.] a booming business
Land of Promise *same as* PROMISED LAND
land·own·er (land′ō′nər) *n.* one who owns land —**land′own′er·ship′** *n.* —**land′own′ing** *adj., n.*
land reform the redistribution of agricultural land by breaking up large landholdings and apportioning shares to small farmers, peasants, etc.
land·scape (-skāp′) *n.* [< Du. < *land,* land + *-schap,* -SHIP] **1.** a picture representing natural, inland scenery **2.** an expanse of natural scenery seen in one view —*vt.* **-scaped′, -scap′ing** to change the natural features of (a plot of ground) so as to make it more attractive, as by adding lawns, bushes, trees, etc. —**land′scap′er** *n.*
landscape architecture the art or profession of planning or changing the natural scenery of a place for a desired effect —**landscape architect**
landscape gardening the art or work of arranging lawns, trees, etc. on a plot of ground to make it more attractive —**landscape gardener**
land·scap·ist (-skāp′ist) *n.* a painter of landscapes
land·slide (-slīd′) *n.* **1.** the sliding of a mass of rocks or earth down a hillside or slope **2.** the mass sliding down **3.** an overwhelming majority of votes for a candidate, party, etc. in an election
land·slip (-slip′) *n.* [Chiefly Brit.] *same as* LANDSLIDE (senses 1 & 2)
lands·man (landz′mən) *n., pl.* **-men** **1.** a person who lives on land: distinguished from SEAMAN **2.** [partly via Yid. < MHG.] a fellow countryman
land·ward (land′wərd) *adv.* toward the land: also **land′wards** —*adj.* situated or facing toward the land
lane (lān) *n.* [OE. *lanu*] **1.** a narrow way between hedges, walls, etc.; narrow country road or city street **2.** any narrow way, as an opening in a crowd **3.** *same as: a)* AIR LANE *b)* SEA LANE **4.** a marked strip of road wide enough for a single line of cars, etc. **5.** any of the parallel courses marked off for contestants in a race **6.** *Bowling* a long, narrow strip of highly polished wood, along which the balls are rolled; alley
lang. language
Lang·er (laŋ′ər), **Susanne K(atherina)** (born *Susanne Katherina Knauth*) 1895– ; U.S. philosopher
Lang·ley (laŋ′lē), **Samuel Pier·pont** (pir′pänt) 1834–1906; U.S. astronomer & pioneer in airplane construction
lang·syne (laŋ′sīn′, -zīn′) *adv.* [Scot. < *lang,* LONG[1] + *syne,* since] [Scot.] long ago —*n.* [Scot.] the long ago; bygone days Also **lang syne**
lan·guage (laŋ′gwij) *n.* [< OFr. < *langue,* tongue < L. *lingua*] **1.** *a)* human speech *b)* the ability to communicate by human speech *c)* the vocal sounds used in speech, or the written symbols for them **2.** *a)* any means of communicating, as gestures, animal sounds, etc. *b)* a special set of symbols, rules, etc. used for transmitting information, as in a computer **3.** all the vocal sounds, words, and ways of combining them common to a particular nation, tribe, etc. **4.** the special words, phrases, and style of expression of a particular group, writer, etc. *[the language of teen-agers]* **5.** the study of language or languages; linguistics
lan·guid (laŋ′gwid) *adj.* [< Fr. < L. < *languere,* to be faint] **1.** without vigor or vitality; drooping; weak **2.** without interest or spirit; listless **3.** sluggish; slow —**lan′guid·ly** *adv.* —**lan′guid·ness** *n.*
lan·guish (-gwish) *vi.* [< OFr. < L. < *languere:* see prec.] **1.** to lose vigor or vitality; become weak; droop **2.** to live under distressing conditions *[to languish in poverty]* **3.** to become slack or dull *[his interest languished]* **4.** to suffer with longing; pine **5.** to put on a sentimental or wistful air —**lan′guish·er** *n.* —**lan′guish·ing** *adj.* —**lan′guish·ing·ly** *adv.* —**lan′guish·ment** *n.*
lan·guor (laŋ′gər) *n.* [< OFr. < L. < *languere:* see LANGUID] **1.** a lack of vigor or vitality; weakness **2.** a lack of interest or spirit; listlessness **3.** tenderness of mood or feeling **4.** the condition of being still, sluggish, or dull —**lan′guor·ous** *adj.* —**lan′guor·ous·ly** *adv.* —**lan′guor·ous·ness** *n.*
lan·gur (luŋ′goor′) *n.* [< Hindi < Sans. *lāṅgūlin,* lit., having a tail] any of certain monkeys of SE Asia, with a long tail and a chin tuft
lan·iard (lan′yərd) *n. same as* LANYARD
La·nier (lə nir′), **Sidney** 1842–81; U.S. poet
lank (laŋk) *adj.* [OE. *hlanc*] **1.** long and slender; lean **2.** straight and limp; not curly: said of hair —**lank′ly** *adv.* —**lank′ness** *n.*
lank·y (laŋ′kē) *adj.* **lank′i·er, lank′i·est** awkwardly tall and lean or long and slender —**lank′i·ly** *adv.* —**lank′i·ness** *n.*
lan·o·lin (lan′'l in) *n.* [< L. *lana,* wool + *oleum,* oil + -IN[1]] a fatty substance obtained from sheep wool and used in ointments, cosmetics, etc.: also **lan′o·line** (-in, -ēn)
Lan·sing (lan′siŋ) [after J. *Lansing* (1751–1829), U.S. jurist] capital of Mich.: pop. 130,000
lan·tern (lan′tərn) *n.* [< OFr. < L. *lanterna* < Gr. *lamptēr* < *lampein,* to shine] **1.** a transparent case for holding a light and protecting it from wind and weather **2.** the room containing the lamp at the top of a lighthouse **3.** an open or windowed structure on the roof of a building, in a tower, etc. to admit light and air
lantern jaw **1.** a projecting lower jaw **2.** [*pl.*] long, thin jaws, with sunken cheeks, that give the face a gaunt look —**lan′tern-jawed′** *adj.*
lantern slide a photographic slide for projection, as, originally, by a magic lantern
lan·tha·nide series (lan′thə nīd′) [< ff.] the rare-earth group of chemical elements from element 57 (lanthanum) through element 71 (lutetium)
lan·tha·num (-nəm) *n.* [ModL. < Gr. *lanthanein,* to be concealed] a silvery, metallic chemical element of the rare-earth group: symbol, La; at. wt., 138.91; at. no., 57

lan·yard (lan′yərd) ***n.*** [< MFr. *laniere* < OFr. < *lasne*, noose: altered after YARD[1]] **1.** a short rope used on board ship for holding or fastening something **2.** a cord used by sailors, etc. to hang a knife, whistle, etc. around the neck **3.** a cord for firing certain types of cannon

La·oc·o·ön (lā äk′ə wän′) *Gr. Legend* a Trojan priest who, with his two sons, was destroyed by two huge sea serpents after he had warned against the wooden horse

La·os (lä′ōs, lous) country in the NW part of the Indochinese peninsula: 91,429 sq. mi.; pop. 2,893,000; cap. Vientiane —**La·o·tian** (lā ō′shən) ***adj., n.***

Lao-tse (lou′dzu′) 604? B.C.–?; Chin. philosopher: reputed founder of Taoism: also sp. **Lao-tzu, Lao-tsze**

lap[1] (lap) ***n.*** [OE. *læppa*] **1.** [Now Rare] the loose lower part of a garment, which may be folded over **2.** *a)* the front part from the waist to the knees of a person in a sitting position *b)* the part of the clothing covering this **3.** that in which one is cared for, sheltered, etc. **4.** *a)* an overlapping part *b)* such overlapping *c)* amount or place of this **5.** one complete circuit around a race track **6.** a lapping —***vt.* lapped, lap′ping 1.** to fold (*over* or *on*) **2.** to wrap; enfold **3.** to hold as in the lap; envelop **4.** to place partly upon something else [to *lap* one board over another] **5.** to lie partly upon; overlap [one board *laps* the other] **6.** to get a lap ahead of (an opponent) in a race —***vi.* 1.** to lie partly on something or on one another; overlap **2.** to extend beyond something in space or time (with *over*) —**drop** (or **dump,** etc.) **into someone's lap** to cause to be someone's responsibility

lap[2] (lap) ***vi., vt.* lapped, lap′ping** [OE. *lapian*] **1.** to drink (a liquid) by dipping it up with the tongue as a dog does **2.** to move or strike gently with a light splash: said of waves, etc. —***n.* 1.** a lapping **2.** the sound of lapping —**lap up 1.** to take up (liquid) by lapping **2.** [Colloq.] to take in eagerly —**lap′per *n.***

La Paz (lä päs′; *E.* lə päz′) city in W Bolivia: seat of government (cf. SUCRE): pop. 482,000

lap dissolve *Motion Pictures & TV* a dissolving view in which a new scene is blended in with a scene being faded out, as by lapping two exposures on one film

lap dog a pet dog small enough to hold in the lap

la·pel (lə pel′) ***n.*** [dim. of LAP[1]] either of the front parts of a coat folded back and forming a continuation of the collar

lap·ful (lap′fool′) ***n., pl.* -fuls′** as much as a lap can hold

lap·i·dar·y (lap′ə der′ē) ***n., pl.* -dar′ies** [< LL. *lapidarius* < L. < *lapis*, a stone] a workman who cuts, polishes, and engraves precious stones —***adj.* 1.** of or connected with the art of cutting and engraving precious stones **2.** like an inscription on a monument; short, precise, and elegant

lap·in (lap′in) ***n.*** [Fr., rabbit] rabbit fur, generally dyed in imitation of more valuable skins

lap·is laz·u·li (lap′is laz′yoo lī′, lazh′-; -lē′) [ModL. < L. *lapis*, a stone + ML. gen. of *lazulus*, azure < Ar.: see AZURE] an azure-blue, opaque, semiprecious stone

lap joint a joint made by overlapping parts: also **lapped joint** —**lap′-joint′ *vt.***

La·place (lȧ plȧs′), marquis **Pierre Si·mon de** (pyer sē mōn′ də) 1749–1827; Fr. mathematician & astronomer

LAP JOINT

Lap·land (lap′land′) region of N Europe, including the N parts of Scandinavia & Finland & a NW section of the U.S.S.R., inhabited by the Lapps

La Pla·ta (lä plä′tä) seaport in E Argentina, on the Río de la Plata: pop. 337,000

Lapp (lap) ***n.* 1.** a member of a Mongoloid people living in Lapland: also **Lap′land′er 2.** their Finno-Ugric language: also **Lap′pish**

lap·pet (lap′it) ***n.*** [dim. of LAP[1]] a small fold or flap, as of a garment or as of flesh

lap robe a heavy blanket, fur wrap, etc. laid over the lap and legs for warmth, as when watching outdoor sports

lapse (laps) ***n.*** [L. *lapsus*, a fall < pp. of *labi*, to slip] **1.** a slip or small error [a *lapse* of memory] **2.** *a)* a falling away from a moral standard; moral slip *b)* a falling or slipping into a lower or worse condition, esp. for a short time **3.** a passing away, as of time **4.** *Law* the termination of a right or privilege through disuse, failure of some contingency, or failure to meet stated obligations —***vi.* lapsed, laps′ing 1.** to slip into a specified state [to *lapse* into a coma] **2.** to slip or deviate from a higher standard or fall into former erroneous ways; backslide **3.** to pass away: said of time **4.** to come to an end; stop [his subscription *lapsed*] **5.** to become forfeit or void because of failure to pay the premium at the stipulated time: said of an insurance policy —**laps′a·ble, laps′i·ble *adj.***

lap·wing (lap′wiŋ′) ***n.*** [altered by folk etym. < OE. *hleapewince* < *hleapan*, to leap + *wince* < *wincian*, WINK] an old-world crested plover noted for its irregular, wavering flight

lar·board (lär′bərd, -bôrd′) ***n.*** [< OE. *hladan*, to lade + *bord*, side] the left-hand side of a ship as one faces forward; port —***adj.*** on or of this side Now largely replaced by PORT[4]

lar·ce·ny (lär′sə nē) ***n., pl.* -nies** [< Anglo-Fr. < OFr. < L. < *latrocinari*, to rob < *latro*, robber] *Law* the unlawful taking away of another's property with the intention of depriving him of it; theft: sometimes differentiated as **grand larceny** (more than a stated amount varying in States from $25 to $60) and **petit,** or **petty, larceny** (less than this amount) —**lar′ce·nist *n.*** —**lar′ce·nous *adj.***

larch (lärch) ***n.*** [< G. < L. *larix*] **1.** a tree of the pine family, found throughout the N Hemisphere, bearing cones and needlelike leaves that are shed annually **2.** the tough wood of this tree

lard (lärd) ***n.*** [< OFr. < L. *lardum*] the fat of hogs, melted down and clarified —***vt.* 1.** to smear with lard or other fat; grease **2.** to put strips of fat pork, bacon, etc. on (meat or poultry) before cooking **3.** to add to; embellish [a talk *larded* with jokes] —**lard′y *adj.* -i·er, -i·est**

lard·er (lär′dər) ***n.*** [< OFr. *lardier* < ML. < L. *lardum*, lard] **1.** a place where the food supplies of a household are kept; pantry **2.** a supply of food

La·re·do (lə rā′dō) [after *Laredo*, town in Spain] city in S Tex., on the Rio Grande: pop. 91,000

lar·es (ler′ēz, lā′rēz) ***n.pl., sing.* lar** (lär) [L.] in ancient Rome, guardian ancestral spirits

lares and penates 1. the household gods of the ancient Romans **2.** the treasured belongings of a family or household

large (lärj) ***adj.* larg′er, larg′est** [OFr. < L. *largus*] **1.** big; great; specif., *a)* taking up much space; bulky *b)* enclosing much space; spacious [a *large* office] *c)* of great extent or amount [a *large* sum] **2.** big as compared with others of its kind **3.** operating on a big scale [a *large* manufacturer] —***adv.*** in a large way [to write *large*] —**at large 1.** free; not confined **2.** fully; in complete detail **3.** in general; taken altogether **4.** representing an entire State or area rather than only a subdivision [a congressman *at large*] —**large′ness *n.***

large·heart·ed (-här′tid) ***adj.*** generous; kindly

large·ly (-lē) ***adv.* 1.** much; in great amounts **2.** for the most part; mainly

large-scale (-skāl′) ***adj.* 1.** drawn to a large scale: said of a map, etc. **2.** of wide scope; extensive [*large-scale* business operations]

lar·gess, lar·gesse (lär jes′, lär′jis) ***n.*** [OFr. < *large*, LARGE] **1.** generous giving **2.** a gift or gifts generously given

lar·ghet·to (lär get′ō) ***adj., adv.*** [It. < *largo*: see LARGO] *Music* relatively slow, but faster than largo —***n., pl.* -tos** a larghetto movement or passage

larg·ish (lär′jish) ***adj.*** rather large

lar·go (lär′gō) ***adj., adv.*** [It., large, slow < L. *largus*, large] *Music* slow and stately —***n., pl.* -gos** a largo movement or passage

lar·i·at (lar′ē it) ***n.*** [Sp. *la reata*, the rope] **1.** a rope used for tethering grazing horses, etc. **2.** *same as* LASSO —***vt.*** to tie or catch with a lariat

lark[1] (lärk) ***n.*** [OE. *læwerce*] **1.** any of a large family of chiefly old-world songbirds; esp., the skylark **2.** any of various similar birds, as the meadowlark

lark[2] (lärk) ***vi.*** [? altered after prec. < dial. *lake* < ME. *laike*, to play] to play or frolic —***n.*** a frolic or spree —**lark′ish, lark′y *adj.***

lark·spur (lärk′spur′) ***n.*** *a common name for* DELPHINIUM

La Roche·fou·cauld (lȧ rôsh fōō kō′), duc **Fran·çois de** (frän swȧ′ də) 1613–80; Fr. moralist & writer of maxims

La·rousse (lȧ rōōs′), **Pierre A·tha·nase** (pyer ȧ tȧ näz′) 1817–75; Fr. lexicographer

lar·rup (lar′əp) ***vt.*** [akin to or < Du. *larpen*] [Colloq.] to whip; flog; beat

lar·va (lär′və) ***n., pl.* -vae** (-vē), **-vas** [L., ghost] the early, free-living, immature form of any animal that changes structurally when it becomes an adult [the caterpillar is the *larva* of the butterfly] —**lar′val *adj.***

la·ryn·ge·al (lə rin′jē əl) ***adj.* 1.** of, in, or near the larynx **2.** used for treating the larynx

lar·yn·gi·tis (lar′ən jīt′əs) ***n.*** [ff. + -ITIS] inflammation of the larynx, often with a temporary loss of voice —**lar′yn·git′ic** (-jit′ik) ***adj.***

la·ryn·go- [< Gr.] *a combining form meaning:* **1.** the larynx **2.** laryngeal and Also **laryng-**

la·ryn·go·scope (lə riŋ′gə skōp′) ***n.*** [prec. + -SCOPE] an instrument for examining the larynx —**lar·yn·gos·co·py** (lar′iŋ gäs′kə pē) ***n.***

lar·ynx (lar′iŋks) *n., pl.* **lar′ynx·es, la·ryn·ges** (lə rin′jēz) [< Gr. *larynx*] **1.** the structure of muscle and cartilage at the upper end of the human trachea, containing the vocal cords and serving as the organ of voice: see EPIGLOTTIS, illus. **2.** a similar structure in other animals

la·sa·gna (lə zän′yə) *n.* [It., the noodle < L. *lasanum* (< Gr. *lasanon*), a pot] a dish of wide, flat noodles baked in layers with cheese, tomato sauce, and ground meat

La Salle (lȧ sȧl′; *E.* lə sal′), sieur **Ro·bert Cave·lier de** (rô ber′ kȧv lyā′ də) 1643–87; Fr. explorer in N. America

las·car (las′kər) *n.* [< Hindi < Per. *lashkar* < Ar. *al-'askar,* army] an Oriental sailor, esp. one who is a native of India

las·civ·i·ous (lə siv′ē əs) *adj.* [< ML. < L. < *lascivus,* wanton] **1.** characterized by or expressing lust or lewdness; wanton **2.** tending to excite lust —**las·civ′i·ous·ly** *adv.* —**las·civ′i·ous·ness** *n.*

lase (lāz) *vi.* **lased, las′ing** to emit laser light

la·ser (lā′zər) *n.* [*l(ight) a(mplification by) s(timulated) e(mission of) r(adiation)*] a device that amplifies focused light waves and concentrates them in a narrow, very intense beam

lash[1] (lash) *n.* [ME. *lassche* < ?] **1.** a whip, esp. the flexible striking part **2.** a stroke as with a whip **3.** an eyelash —*vt.* **1.** to strike or drive as with a lash; flog **2.** to swing quickly or angrily; switch [the cat *lashed* her tail] **3.** to strike with great force [waves *lashed* the cliffs] **4.** to attack violently in words; censure or rebuke **5.** to incite by appealing to the emotions —*vi.* **1.** to move quickly or violently; switch **2.** to make strokes as with a whip —**lash out 1.** to strike out violently **2.** to speak angrily —**lash′er** *n.*

lash[2] (lash) *vt.* [< OFr. *lachier:* see LACE] to fasten or tie with a rope, etc.

lash·ing[1] (-iŋ) *n.* **1.** a whipping **2.** a strong rebuke

lash·ing[2] (-iŋ) *n.* **1.** the act of fastening or tying with a rope, etc. **2.** a rope, etc. so used

lash-up (lash′up′) *n.* [Colloq.] an improvised contrivance

Las Pal·mas (läs päl′məs) seaport, & largest city, in the Canary Islands: pop. 244,000

lass (las) *n.* [ME. *lasse,* prob. < ON.] **1.** a young woman; girl **2.** a sweetheart

las·sie (las′ē) *n.* [dim. of prec.] [Scot.] **1.** a young girl **2.** a sweetheart

las·si·tude (las′ə to͞od′, -tyo͞od′) *n.* [Fr. < L. < *lassus,* faint] a state or feeling of being tired and listless; weariness; languor

las·so (las′ō, -o͞o) *n., pl.* **-sos, -soes** [Sp. *lazo* < L. *laqueus,* noose] a long rope with a sliding noose at one end, used to catch cattle or horses —*vt.* **-soed, -so·ing** to catch with a lasso —**las′so·er** *n.*

last[1] (last) *adj. alt. superl. of* LATE [< OE. *latost,* superl. of *læt:* see LATE] **1.** being or coming after all others in place or time; furthest from the first; final **2.** only remaining **3.** most recent [*last* month] **4.** least likely [the *last* person to suspect] **5.** utmost; greatest **6.** lowest in rank, as a prize **7.** newest [the *last* thing in hats] **8.** conclusive [the *last* word in scientific research] **9.** individual: a redundant intensive [eat every *last* bite] —*adv.* **1.** after all others; at the end **2.** most recently **3.** finally —*n.* **1.** someone or something which comes last [the *last* of the kings] **2.** end [friends to the *last*] —**at (long) last** finally —**see the last of** to see for the last time

last[2] (last) *vi.* [< OE. *læstan*] **1.** to remain in existence or operation; continue; endure **2.** to remain in good condition **3.** to continue unconsumed, unspent, etc.; be enough (for) [food to *last* (for) a month] —*vt.* to continue or endure throughout: often with *out* [doubtful whether he can *last* (out) the year] —**last′er** *n.*

last[3] (last) *n.* [OE. *læste* < *last,* footstep] a form shaped like a foot, on which shoes are made or repaired —*vt.* to form with a last —**stick to one's last 1.** to keep to one's own work **2.** to mind one's own business —**last′er** *n.*

last-ditch (-dich′) *adj.* made, done, etc. in a final, often desperate effort to resist or oppose

Las·tex (las′teks) [< (E)LAS(TIC) + TEX(TILE)] *a trademark for* a fine, round rubber thread wound with cotton, silk, etc. and woven, etc. into cloth

last·ing (las′tiŋ) *adj.* that lasts a long time; enduring; durable [a *lasting* peace] —**last′ing·ly** *adv.* —**last′ing·ness** *n.*

Last Judgment *Theol.* the final judgment of mankind at the end of the world

last·ly (last′lē) *adv.* in conclusion; finally

last rites 1. final rites for a dead person **2.** sacraments administered to a dying person

last straw [from the last straw that broke the camel's back in the fable] the last of a sequence of troubles or annoyances that results in a breakdown, loss of patience, etc.

Last Supper the last supper eaten by Jesus with his disciples before the Crucifixion

last word 1. *a)* the final word or speech, regarded as settling the argument *b)* final authority **2.** something regarded as perfect **3.** [Colloq.] the very latest style

Las Ve·gas (läs vā′gəs) [Sp., the plains or meadows] city in SE Nev.: pop. 165,000

Lat. Latin

lat. latitude

La·ta·ki·a (lat′ə kē′ə) *n.* [< *Latakia,* a seaport in Syria] a fine grade of Turkish smoking tobacco

latch (lach) *n.* [OE. *læccan,* to catch] **1.** a fastening for a door or gate consisting of a bar that falls into a notch on the doorjamb or gatepost: now often used of a spring lock on a door **2.** a fastening for a window, etc. —*vt., vi.* to fasten with a latch —**latch onto** [Colloq.] to get or obtain —**on the latch** fastened by the latch but not bolted

latch·key (-kē′) *n.* a key for drawing back or unfastening the latch of a door

latch·string (-striŋ′) *n.* a cord fastened to a latch so that it can be raised from the outside

late (lāt) *adj.* **lat′er** or **lat′ter, lat′est** or **last** [OE. *læt*] **1.** happening, coming, etc. after the usual or expected time; tardy **2.** *a)* happening, continuing, etc. far on in the day, night, year, etc. [a *late* party] *b)* far advanced in a period, development, etc. [the *late* Middle Ages] **3.** recent [a *late* news bulletin] **4.** having been so recently but not now **5.** having recently died —*adv.* **lat′er, lat′est** or **last 1.** after the usual or expected time **2.** at or until an advanced time of the day, night, year, etc. **3.** toward the end of a period, development, etc. **4.** recently [as *late* as yesterday] —**of late** lately —**late′ness** *n.*

la·teen (la tēn′, lə-) *adj.* [< Fr. < (*voile*) *latine,* Latin (sail)] **1.** designating or of a triangular sail attached to a long yard suspended from a short mast: used chiefly on Mediterranean vessels **2.** having such a sail —*n.* a vessel with such a sail

LATEEN SAIL

Late Greek the Greek language of the period after classical Greek, seen chiefly in writings from c.200 to c.600 A.D.

Late Latin the Latin language of the period after classical Latin, seen chiefly in writings from c.200 to c.600 A.D.

late·ly (lāt′lē) *adv.* recently; a short while ago

la·tent (lāt′'nt) *adj.* [< L. prp. of *latere,* to lurk] lying hidden and undeveloped within a person or thing; concealed, dormant, etc. [a *latent* talent] —**la′ten·cy** *n.* —**la′tent·ly** *adv.*

lat·er (lāt′ər) *adj. alt. compar. of* LATE —*adv. compar. of* LATE at a later time; subsequently —**later on** subsequently

lat·er·al (lat′ər əl) *adj.* [< L. < *latus* (gen. *lateris*), a side] of, at, from, or toward the side; sideways [*lateral* movement] —*n.* **1.** any lateral part, growth, etc. **2.** *Football short for* LATERAL PASS —**lat′er·al·ly** *adv.*

lateral pass *Football* a short pass parallel to the goal line or in a slightly backward direction

lat·est (lāt′ist) *alt. superl. of* LATE —**at the latest** no later than (the time specified) —**the latest** the most recent thing, development, etc.

la·tex (lā′teks) *n., pl.* **lat·i·ces** (lat′ə sēz′), **la′tex·es** [L., a fluid] **1.** a milky liquid in certain plants and trees, as the rubber tree, milkweed, etc.: used esp. as the basis of rubber **2.** an emulsion in water of particles of synthetic rubber or plastic: used in rubber goods, adhesives, paints, etc.

lath (lath) *n., pl.* **laths** (la*thz,* laths) [OE. *lætt*] **1.** any of the thin, narrow strips of wood used in building lattices or nailed to two-by-fours, rafters, etc. as a groundwork for plastering, tiling, etc. **2.** any framework for plaster, as wire screening or expanded metal **3.** laths collectively —*vt.* to cover with laths

lathe (lā*th*) *n.* [prob. < MDu. *lade*] a machine for shaping an article of wood, metal, etc. by holding and turning it rapidly against the edge of a cutting tool —*vt.* **lathed, lath′ing** to shape on a lathe

lath·er (la*th*′ər) *n.* [OE. *leathor,* washing soda or soap] **1.** the foam formed by soap or other detergent in water **2.** foamy sweat, as on a race horse **3.** [Slang] an agitated state —*vt.* to cover with lather —*vi.* to form, or become covered with, lather —**lath′er·y** *adj.*

lath·ing (lath′iŋ) *n.* **1.** laths collectively, esp. when used as a base for plaster **2.** the putting up of laths on walls, etc. Also **lath′work′** (-wurk′)

Lat·in (lat′'n) *adj.* **1.** of ancient Latium or its people **2.** of ancient Rome or its people **3.** of or in the language of ancient Latium and ancient Rome **4.** designating or of the languages derived from Latin, the peoples who speak them, their countries, etc. —*n.* **1.** a native or inhabitant of ancient Latium or ancient Rome **2.** the Italic language of ancient Latium and ancient Rome **3.** a person, as a Spaniard or Italian, whose language is derived from Latin

Latin America that part of the Western Hemisphere, south of the U.S., where Spanish, Portuguese, & French are official languages —**Latin American**

Lat·in·ate (-āt′) ***adj.*** of, derived from, or similar to Latin: also **La·tin·ic** (la tin′ik)
Latin Church *same as* ROMAN CATHOLIC CHURCH
Lat·in·ism (-iz'm) ***n.*** a Latin idiom or expression, used in another language
Lat·in·ist (-ist) ***n.*** a scholar in Latin
Lat·in·ize (-īz′) ***vt.*** **-ized′, -iz′ing 1.** to translate into Latin **2.** to give Latin form or characteristics to —***vi.*** to use Latin expressions, forms, etc. —**Lat′in·i·za′tion** ***n.*** —**Lat′in·iz′er** ***n.***
Latin Quarter [transl. of Fr. *Quartier Latin*] a section of Paris, south of the Seine, where many artists and students live
Latin Rite the Latin liturgy used in the Roman Catholic Church
lat·ish (lāt′ish) ***adj., adv.*** somewhat late
lat·i·tude (lat′ə to͞od′, -tyo͞od′) ***n.*** [OFr. < L. *latitudo* < *latus*, wide] **1.** extent; scope; range of applicability **2.** freedom from narrow restrictions **3.** *Geog. a)* angular distance, measured in degrees, north or south from the equator *b)* a place or region in relation to its latitude —**lat′i·tu′di·nal** ***adj.*** —**lat′i·tu′di·nal·ly** ***adv.***
lat·i·tu·di·nar·i·an (lat′ə to͞od′'n er′ē ən, -tyo͞od′-) ***adj.*** [see prec. & -ARIAN] liberal in one's views; permitting free thought, esp. in religious matters —***n.*** one who is very liberal in his views and, in religion, cares little about particular creeds and forms —**lat′i·tu′di·nar′i·an·ism** ***n.***
La·ti·um (lā′shē əm) ancient country on the central coast of Italy, southeast of Rome
la·trine (lə trēn′) ***n.*** [Fr. < L. *latrina* < *lavare*, to wash] a toilet, privy, etc. for the use of a large number of people, as in an army camp
-la·try (lə trē) [< Gr. < *latreia*, service] *a combining form meaning* worship of or excessive devotion to *[idolatry]*
lat·ter (lat′ər) ***adj.*** *alt. compar. of* LATE [OE. *lætra*, compar. of *læt*, late] **1.** *a)* later; more recent *b)* nearer the end or close *[the latter part of May]* **2.** last mentioned of two: opposed to FORMER[1]: often a noun (with *the*)
lat·ter-day (-dā′) ***adj.*** of recent or present time
Lat·ter-day Saint *see* MORMON
lat·ter·ly (lat′ər lē) ***adv.*** lately; recently
lat·tice (lat′is) ***n.*** [OFr. *lattis* < MHG. *latte*, a lath] **1.** an openwork structure of crossed strips of wood, metal, etc. used as a screen, support, etc. **2.** a door, shutter, trellis, etc. formed of such a structure **3.** *Physics* a three-dimensional pattern of points in space, as of atoms in a solid or crystal —***vt.*** **-ticed, -tic·ing 1.** to arrange like a lattice **2.** to furnish with a lattice
lat·tice·work (-wurk′) ***n.*** **1.** a lattice **2.** lattices collectively Also **lat′tic·ing**

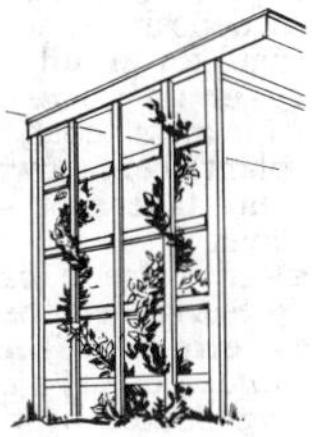

LATTICE

Lat·vi·a (lat′vē ə) republic of the U.S.S.R., in NE Europe, on the Baltic Sea: 24,594 sq. mi.; pop. 2,300,000; cap. Riga: in full, **Latvian Soviet Socialist Republic** —**Lat′vi·an** ***adj., n.***
laud (lôd) ***n.*** [< OFr. < ML. *laudes*, pl. < L. *laus*, praise] **1.** praise **2.** any song of praise **3.** [*pl.*] *Eccles.* [*often* **L-**] the service of dawn which constitutes the second (or, together with matins, the first) of the canonical hours and includes psalms of praise to God —***vt.*** to praise; extol
laud·a·ble (-ə b'l) ***adj.*** worthy of being lauded; praiseworthy —**laud′a·bil′i·ty, laud′a·ble·ness** ***n.*** —**laud′a·bly** ***adv.***
laud·a·num (lôd′'n əm) ***n.*** [ModL., altered use of ML. var. of L. *ladanum*, mastic] **1.** formerly, any of various opium preparations **2.** a solution of opium in alcohol
lau·da·tion (lô dā′shən) ***n.*** a lauding or being lauded; praise; commendation
laud·a·to·ry (lôd′ə tôr′ē) ***adj.*** expressing praise; eulogistic: also **laud′a·tive**
laugh (laf) ***vi.*** [OE. *hleahhan*] **1.** to make the vocal sounds and facial movements that express mirth, amusement, ridicule, etc. **2.** to feel or suggest joyousness —***vt.*** **1.** to express with laughter **2.** to cause to be by means of laughter *[to laugh oneself hoarse]* —***n.*** **1.** the act or sound of laughing **2.** anything that provokes or is fit to provoke laughter **3.** [*pl.*] [Colloq.] mere diversion or pleasure —**have the last laugh** to win after apparent defeat —**laugh at 1.** to be amused by **2.** to make fun of **3.** to be indifferent to or contemptuous of —**laugh off** to scorn, avoid, or reject by laughter or ridicule —**laugh out of** (or **on**) **the other** (or **wrong**) **side of the mouth** to change from joy to sorrow, from amusement to annoyance, etc. —**no laughing matter** a serious matter —**laugh′er** ***n.***
laugh·a·ble (-ə b'l) ***adj.*** of such a nature as to cause laughter; amusing or ridiculous —**laugh′a·ble·ness** ***n.*** —**laugh′a·bly** ***adv.***
laugh·ing (-iŋ) ***adj.*** **1.** that laughs or seems to laugh *[a laughing brook]* **2.** uttered with laughter —***n.*** laughter —**laugh′ing·ly** ***adv.***
laughing gas nitrous oxide used as an anesthetic: it may cause laughter and exhilaration
laugh·ing·stock (laf′iŋ stäk′) ***n.*** a person or thing made the object of ridicule
laugh·ter (laf′tər) ***n.*** **1.** the action or sound of laughing **2.** an indication of amusement *[with laughter in her eyes]*
launch[1] (lônch, länch) ***vt.*** [< OFr. *lanchier* < LL. < L. *lancea*, LANCE] **1.** to hurl, discharge, or send off (a weapon, blow, rocket, etc.) **2.** to cause (a newly built vessel) to slide into the water; set afloat **3.** to set in operation; start *[to launch an attack]* **4.** to start (a person) on some course —***vi.*** **1.** to put to sea (often with *out* or *forth*) **2.** to start on some new course or enterprise (often with *out* or *forth*) **3.** to throw oneself (*into*) with vigor; plunge *[to launch into a tirade]* —***n.*** the act or process of launching a ship, spacecraft, etc. —***adj.*** designating or of facilities, sites, etc. used in launching spacecraft or missiles —**launch′er** ***n.***
launch[2] (lônch, länch) ***n.*** [Sp. or Port. *lancha* < ?] **1.** formerly, the largest boat carried by a warship **2.** an open, or partly enclosed, motorboat
launch pad the platform from which a rocket, guided missile, etc. is launched: also **launching pad**
laun·der (lôn′dər, län′-) ***vt.*** [< OFr. < ML. < LL. *lavandaria*, things to be washed < L. < *lavare*, to wash] to wash, or wash and iron, (clothes, etc.) —***vi.*** **1.** to withstand washing *[this fabric launders well]* **2.** to do laundry —**laun′der·er** ***n.***
Laun·der·ette (lôn′də ret′, län′-) *a service mark for* a self-service laundry —***n.*** [**l-**] such a laundry
laun·dress (lôn′dris, län′-) ***n.*** a woman whose work is washing clothes, ironing, etc.
Laun·dro·mat (lôn′drə mat′, län′-) [< a trademark for an automatic washing machine] *a service mark for* a self-service laundry —***n.*** [**l-**] such a laundry
laun·dry (lôn′drē, län′-) ***n.***, *pl.* **-dries 1.** a laundering **2.** a place where laundering is done **3.** clothes, etc. laundered or to be laundered
laun·dry·man (-mən) ***n.***, *pl.* **-men** a man who works for a laundry, esp. one who collects and delivers laundry
laun·dry·wom·an (-wo͝om′ən) ***n.***, *pl.* **-wom′en** *same as* LAUNDRESS
Lau·ra (lôr′ə) [fem. of LAURENCE] a feminine name
lau·re·ate (lôr′ē it) ***adj.*** [< L. < *laurea* (*corona*), laurel (wreath) < *laurus*, laurel] **1.** crowned with a laurel wreath as a mark of honor **2.** honored —***n.*** **1.** one on whom honor is conferred **2.** *same as* POET LAUREATE —**lau′re·ate·ship′** ***n.***
lau·rel (lôr′əl, lär′-) ***n.*** [< OFr. < L. *laurus*] **1.** an evergreen tree or shrub, native to S Europe, with large, glossy, aromatic leaves **2.** the foliage of this tree, esp. as woven into wreaths such as those used by the ancient Greeks to crown victors in contests **3.** [*pl.*] *a)* fame; honor *b)* victory **4.** a tree or shrub resembling the true laurel, as the mountain laurel —***vt.*** **-reled** or **-relled, -rel·ing** or **-rel·ling 1.** to crown with laurel **2.** to honor —**look to one's laurels** to beware of having one's achievements surpassed —**rest on one's laurels** to be satisfied with what one has already achieved
Lau·rence (lôr′əns, lär′-) [L. *Laurentius*, prob. < *laurus*, laurel] a masculine name
Lau·ren·tian Mountains (lô ren′shən) mountain range in S Quebec, Canada, extending along the St. Lawrence River valley
Lau·sanne (lō zan′) city in W Switzerland, on Lake Geneva: pop. 137,000
la·va (lä′və, lav′ə) ***n.*** [It. < dial. *lave* < L. *labes*, a fall < *labi*, to slide] **1.** melted rock issuing from a volcano **2.** such rock when cool and solid
La·val (lə val′) city in SW Quebec, near Montreal: pop. 196,000: also **Ville de La·val** (vēl də lȧ vȧl′)
lav·a·liere, lav·a·lier (lav′ə lir′, lä′və-) ***n.*** [Fr. *lavallière*, kind of tie] an ornament hanging from a chain, worn around the neck
lav·a·to·ry (lav′ə tôr′ē) ***n.***, *pl.* **-ries** [LL. *lavatorium* < L. *lavare*, to wash] **1.** a washbowl **2.** a room equipped with a washbowl, flush toilet, etc.
lave (lāv) ***vt., vi.*** **laved, lav′ing** [< OE. *lafian* & OFr. *laver*, both < L. *lavare*, to wash] [Poet.] to wash or bathe
lav·en·der (lav′ən dər) ***n.*** [< Anglo-Fr. < ML. *lavandria* < L. *lavare*, to wash] **1.** a fragrant European plant of the mint family, having spikes of pale-purplish flowers and yielding an aromatic oil (**oil of lavender**) **2.** the dried flow-

ers, leaves, and stalks of this plant, used to perfume clothes, linens, etc. **3.** a pale purple *—adj.* pale-purple

la·ver (lā′vər) *n.* [< OFr. < L. < *lavare,* to wash] [Archaic] a large basin to wash in

lav·ish (lav′ish) *adj.* [< MFr. < OFr. *lavasse,* torrent of rain, prob. < *laver* < L. *lavare,* to wash] **1.** very generous or liberal in giving or spending, often extravagantly so **2.** more than enough; very abundant *[lavish* entertainment*]* *—vt.* to give or spend liberally **—lav′ish·ly** *adv.* **—lav′ish·ness** *n.*

La·voi·sier (là vwà zyā′; *E.* lə vwä′zē ā′), **An·toine Lau·rent** (än twàn′ lô rän′) 1743–94; Fr. pioneer in chemistry

law (lô) *n.* [OE. *lagu* < Anglo-N.] **1.** *a)* all the rules of conduct established and enforced by the authority, legislation, or custom of a given community or other group *b)* any one of such rules **2.** the condition existing when obedience to such rules is general *[*to establish *law* and order*]* **3.** the branch of knowledge dealing with such rules; jurisprudence **4.** the system of courts in which such rules are referred to in securing justice *[*to resort to *law]* **5.** all such rules dealing with a particular activity *[*business *law]* **6.** common law, as distinguished from equity **7.** the profession of lawyers, judges, etc. (often with *the*) **8.** *a)* a sequence of events in nature or in human activities occurring with unvarying uniformity under the same conditions: often **law of nature** *b)* the formulation in words of such a sequence **9.** any rule or principle expected to be observed *[*the *laws* of health*]* **10.** *Eccles.* a divine commandment **11.** *Math., Logic,* etc. a general principle to which all applicable cases must conform *[*the *laws* of exponents*]* **—go to law** to take a dispute to a law court for settlement **—lay down the law 1.** to give orders in an authoritative manner **2.** to give a scolding (*to*) **—read law** to study to become a lawyer **—the Law 1.** the Mosaic law, or the part of the Hebrew Scriptures containing it; specif., the Pentateuch **2.** [l-] [Colloq.] a policeman or the police

law-a·bid·ing (lô′ə bīd′iŋ) *adj.* obeying the law

law·break·er (-brā′kər) *n.* a person who violates the law **—law′break′ing** *adj., n.*

law court a court for administering justice under the law

law·ful (-fəl) *adj.* **1.** in conformity with the law; permitted by law *[*a *lawful* act*]* **2.** recognized by law; just *[lawful* debts*]* **—law′ful·ly** *adv.* **—law′ful·ness** *n.*

law·giv·er (-giv′ər) *n.* one who draws up or enacts a code of laws for a nation or people; lawmaker; legislator **—law′giv′ing** *n., adj.*

law·less (-lis) *adj.* **1.** without law; not regulated by the authority of law *[*a *lawless* city*]* **2.** not in conformity with law; illegal *[lawless* practices*]* **3.** not obeying the law; unruly **—law′less·ly** *adv.* **—law′less·ness** *n.*

law·mak·er (-mā′kər) *n.* one who makes or helps to make laws; esp., a legislator **—law′mak′ing** *adj., n.*

law·man (-man′) *n., pl.* **-men′** (-men′) a law officer; esp., a marshal, sheriff, etc.

lawn[1] (lôn) *n.* [< OFr. < Bret. *lann,* country] land covered with grass kept closely mowed, esp. around a house **—lawn′y** *adj.*

lawn[2] (lôn) *n.* [< *Laon,* city in France, where made] a fine, sheer cloth of linen or cotton, used for blouses, curtains, etc. **—lawn′y** *adj.*

lawn mower a hand-propelled or power-driven machine for cutting the grass of a lawn

lawn tennis *see* TENNIS

Law·rence[1] (lôr′əns, lär′-) **1.** a masculine name: see LAURENCE **2. D(avid) H(erbert),** 1885–1930; Eng. novelist & poet **3. T(homas) E(dward),** (changed name, 1927, to *Thomas Edward Shaw*) 1888–1935; Brit. adventurer & writer: called **Lawrence of Arabia**

Law·rence[2] (lôr′əns, lär′-) [after A. *Lawrence* (1814–86) of Boston] city in NE Mass.: pop. 63,000

law·ren·ci·um (lô ren′sē əm, lä-) *n.* [after E. O. *Lawrence,* 20th-c. U.S. physicist] a radioactive chemical element produced by nuclear bombardment of californium: symbol, Lr; at. wt., 256 (?); at. no., 103

law·suit (lô′so͞ot′) *n.* a suit at law between private parties; case before a civil court

Law·ton (lôt′'n) [after Gen. H. W. *Lawton* (1843–99)] city in SW Okla.: pop. 80,000

law·yer (lô′yər) *n.* a person whose profession is advising others in matters of law or representing them in lawsuits

lax (laks) *adj.* [L. *laxus*] **1.** loose; slack; not rigid or tight **2.** not strict or exact; careless *[lax* morals*]* **—lax′ly** *adv.* **—lax′ness** *n.*

lax·a·tive (lak′sə tiv) *adj.* [< OFr. < ML. *laxativus* < LL. < pp. of L. *laxare* < *laxus,* loose] tending to make lax; specif., making the bowels loose and relieving constipation *—n.* any laxative medicine

lax·i·ty (lak′sə tē) *n.* lax quality or condition

lay[1] (lā) *vt.* **laid, lay′ing** [OE. *lecgan* < pt. base of OE. *licgan,* to LIE[1]] **1.** to cause to fall with force; knock down *[*one punch *laid* him low*]* **2.** to place or put so as to rest, lie, etc.; deposit (with *on, in,* etc.) *[lay* the pen on the desk*]* **3.** *a)* to put down (bricks, carpeting, etc.) in the correct way for a specific purpose *b)* to situate in a particular place *[*the scene is *laid* in France*]* **4.** to place; put; set *[*to *lay* emphasis on accuracy*]* **5.** to produce and deposit (an egg or eggs) **6.** *a)* to cause to settle *[*to *lay* the dust*]* *b)* to allay, overcome, or appease *[*to *lay* one's fears*]* **7.** to smooth down *[*to *lay* the nap of cloth*]* **8.** to stake as a bet; wager **9.** to impose (a tax, penalty, etc. *on* or *upon*) **10.** to work out; devise *[*to *lay* plans*]* **11.** to set (a table) with silverware, plates, etc. **12.** to present or assert *[*to *lay* claim to property*]* **13.** to attribute; charge; impute *[*to *lay* the blame on Tom*]* *—vi.* **1.** to lay an egg or eggs **2.** to lie; recline: a dialectal or substandard usage **3.** *Naut.* to go; proceed *[*all hands *lay* aft to the fantail*]* *—n.* the way in which something is situated or arranged *[*the *lay* of the land*]* **—lay aside** to set aside for the future; save: also **lay away, lay by —lay down 1.** to sacrifice (one's life) **2.** to declare emphatically **3.** to store away, as wine in a cellar **—lay for** [Colloq.] to be waiting to attack **—lay in** to get and store away **—lay into** [Slang] to attack with blows or words **—lay it on (thick)** [Colloq.] **1.** to exaggerate **2.** to flatter effusively **—lay off 1.** to discharge (an employee), esp. temporarily **2.** to mark off the boundaries of **3.** [Slang] to cease **—lay on 1.** to spread on **2.** to attack with force **—lay oneself open** to expose oneself to attack, blame, etc. **—lay open 1.** to cut open **2.** to expose **—lay out 1.** to spend **2.** to arrange according to a plan **3.** to spread out (clothes, equipment, etc.) **4.** to make (a dead body) ready for burial **5.** [Slang] to scold (someone) **—lay over** to stop a while in a place before going on **—lay to 1.** to attribute to **2.** to apply oneself with vigor **—lay up 1.** to store for future use **2.** to disable; confine to bed or the sickroom

lay[2] (lā) *pt. of* LIE[1]

lay[3] (lā) *adj.* [< OFr. < LL. *laicus* < Gr. < *lāos,* the people] **1.** of the laity, or ordinary people, as distinguished from the clergy **2.** not belonging to or connected with a given profession *[*a legal handbook for *lay* readers*]*

lay[4] (lā) *n.* [OFr. *lai*] **1.** a short poem, esp. a narrative poem, for singing **2.** [Archaic or Poet.] a song or melody

lay·a·bout (lā′ə bout′) *n.* [Chiefly Brit. Colloq.] a lazy idler or loafer; bum

lay analyst a psychoanalyst who is not a medical doctor

lay·a·way (plan) (lā′ə wā′) a method of buying by making a deposit on something which is delivered only after it is paid for in full

lay·er (lā′ər) *n.* **1.** a person or thing that lays **2.** a single thickness, coat, fold, or stratum **3.** a shoot (of a living plant) bent down and partly covered with earth so that it may take root *—vt., vi.* to grow (a plant) by means of a layer

layer cake a cake of two or more layers, with icing, preserves, etc. between them

lay·ette (lā et′) *n.* [Fr., dim. of *laie,* drawer < Fl. < MDu. *lade,* a chest] a complete outfit for a newborn baby, including clothes, bedding, etc.

lay figure [earlier *layman* < Du. < MDu. *led,* limb + *man,* man] **1.** an artist's jointed model of the human form, on which drapery is arranged **2.** a person who is a mere puppet or a nonentity

lay·man (lā′mən) *n., pl.* **-men** [LAY[3] + MAN] **1.** a member of the laity; person not a clergyman **2.** a person not belonging to or skilled in a given profession

lay·off (lā′ôf′) *n.* the act of laying off; esp., temporary unemployment, or the period of this

lay of the land 1. the arrangement of the natural features of an area **2.** the existing state of affairs Also **lie of the land**

lay·out (lā′out′) *n.* **1.** the act of laying something out **2.** the manner in which anything is laid out; arrangement; specif., the plan or makeup of a newspaper, page, advertisement, etc. **3.** the thing laid out **4.** an outfit or set **5.** [Colloq.] a residence, factory, etc., esp. when large

lay·o·ver (-ō′vər) *n.* a stopping for a while in some place during a journey

la·zar (laz′ər, lā′zər) *n.* [< ML. *lazarus,* leper < LL. < Gr. *Lazaros,* LAZARUS] [Rare] a poor, diseased, esp. leprous person

laz·a·ret·to (laz′ə ret′ō) *n., pl.* **-tos** [It. < Santa Madonna di *Nazaret,* Venetian church used as a plague hospital; initial *l-* after *lazzaro,* leper] formerly, a public hospital for poor people having contagious diseases, esp. for lepers: also **laz′a·ret′, laz′a·rette′** (-ret′)

Laz·a·rus (laz′ə rəs) *Bible* **1.** the brother of Mary and Martha, raised from the dead by Jesus: John 11 **2.** the diseased beggar in Jesus' parable: Luke 16:19–31

laze (lāz) *vi.* **lazed, laz′ing** to be lazy or idle *—vt.* to spend (time, etc.) in idleness

la·zy (lā′zē) *adj.* **-zi·er, -zi·est** [prob. < MLowG. or MDu.] **1.** not eager or willing to work or exert oneself; indolent; slothful **2.** slow and heavy; sluggish *[*a *lazy* river*]* *—vi., vt.* **-zied, -zy·ing** *same as* LAZE **—la′zi·ly** *adv.* **—la′ziness** *n.*

la·zy·bones (-bōnz′) *n.* [Colloq.] a lazy person
Lazy Susan a revolving tray with sections for relishes, condiments, etc.
lb. [L. *libra,* pl. *librae*] pound; pounds
lbs. pounds
L/C, l/c letter of credit
l.c. **1.** [L. *loco citato*] in the place cited **2.** *Printing* lower case
LCD [*l(iquid)-c(rystal) d(isplay)*] a device for alphanumeric displays, as on digital watches, with a sealed-in liquid crystal activated by an external light source
L.C.D., l.c.d. least (or lowest) common denominator
L.C.M., l.c.m. least (or lowest) common multiple
LDC less developed country
lea (lē) *n.* [OE. *leah*] [Chiefly Poet.] a meadow, grassy field, or pasture; grassland
leach (lēch) *vt.* [prob. < OE. *leccan,* to water] **1.** to cause (a liquid) to filter down through some material **2.** to wash (wood ashes, etc.) with a filtering liquid **3.** to extract (a soluble substance) from some material *[lye is leached from wood ashes]* —*vi.* **1.** to lose soluble matter through a filtering liquid **2.** to dissolve and be washed away —*n.* **1.** a leaching **2.** a sievelike container used in leaching —**leach′a·ble** *adj.* —**leach′er** *n.*
lead[1] (lēd) *vt.* **led, lead′ing** [OE. *lǣdan*] **1.** *a)* to direct the course of by going before or along with; conduct; guide *b)* to mark the way for *[lights to lead you there]* **2.** to guide by physical contact, pulling a rope, etc. *[to lead a horse]* **3.** to conduct (water, steam, rope, etc.) in a certain direction, channel, etc. **4.** to direct by influence, etc. to a course of action or thought; cause; prompt **5.** to be the head or leader of (an expedition, orchestra, etc.) **6.** *a)* to be at the head of *[to lead one's class]* *b)* to be ahead of by a specified margin **7.** to live; spend *[to lead a hard life]* **8.** *Card Games* to begin the play with (a card or suit) —*vi.* **1.** to show the way by going before or along; act as guide **2.** to submit to being led: said esp. of a horse **3.** to be or form a way (*to, from, under,* etc.); go **4.** to come, or bring one, as a result (with *to*) *[one thing led to another]* **5.** to be or go first **6.** *Boxing* to aim a first blow **7.** *Card Games* to play the first card —*n.* **1.** leadership **2.** example *[follow his lead]* **3.** *a)* first or front place; precedence *b)* the amount or distance ahead *[to hold a safe lead]* **4.** *same as* LEASH **5.** anything that leads, as a clue **6.** *Baseball* a position taken by a base runner away from his base in the direction of the next **7.** *Boxing* a blow used in leading **8.** *Card Games* the right of playing first, or the card or suit played **9.** *Elec.* a wire carrying current from one point to another in a circuit **10.** *Journalism* the opening paragraph of a news story **11.** *Mining* a stratum of ore **12.** *Music* the main melody in a harmonic composition **13.** *Theater a)* a main role *b)* an actor or actress playing such a role —*adj.* acting as leader *[the lead horse]* —**lead off** to begin —**lead on 1.** to conduct further **2.** to lure —**lead up to 1.** to prepare the way for **2.** to approach (a subject, etc.) in an indirect way
lead[2] (led) *n.* [OE.] **1.** a heavy, soft, malleable, bluish-gray metallic chemical element used for piping and in numerous alloys: symbol, Pb; at. wt., 207.19; at. no., 82 **2.** anything made of this metal; specif., *a)* a weight for sounding depths at sea, etc. *b) Printing* a thin strip of type metal inserted to increase the space between lines of type **3.** bullets **4.** a thin stick of graphite, used in pencils —*adj.* made of or containing lead —*vt.* **1.** to cover, line, or weight with lead **2.** *Printing* to increase the space between (lines of type) by inserting leads
lead·en (led′'n) *adj.* **1.** made of lead **2.** having the heaviness of lead; hard to move **3.** sluggish; dull **4.** depressed; gloomy **5.** of a dull gray —**lead′en·ly** *adv.*
lead·er (lē′dər) *n.* **1.** a person or thing that leads; guiding head **2.** a horse harnessed before all others or in the foremost span **3.** a pipe for carrying fluid **4.** a tendon **5.** a section of blank film or recording tape at the beginning of a reel **6.** a featured, low-priced article of trade **7.** *Bot.* the central stem of a plant **8.** *Fishing* a short piece of catgut, etc. attaching the hook, lure, etc. to the fish line **9.** *Music a)* a conductor, esp. of a band *b)* the main performer, as in a vocal section **10.** [*pl.*] *Printing* dots, dashes, etc. in a line, used to direct the eye across the page —**lead′er·less** *adj.* —**lead′er·ship′** *n.*
lead glass (led) glass that contains lead oxide
lead-in (lēd′in′) *n.* **1.** the wire leading from an aerial or antenna to a receiver or transmitter **2.** an introduction —*adj.* that is a lead-in
lead·ing[1] (led′iŋ) *n.* **1.** a covering or being covered with lead **2.** strips or sheets of lead
lead·ing[2] (lē′diŋ) *n.* guidance; direction —*adj.* **1.** that leads; guiding **2.** principal; chief **3.** playing the lead in a play, motion picture, etc.
lead·ing edge (lē′diŋ) *Aeron.* the front edge of a propeller blade or airfoil
lead·ing light (lē′diŋ) an important or influential member of a club, community, etc.
lead·ing question (lē′diŋ) a question put in such a way as to suggest the answer sought
lead·off (lēd′ôf′) *n.* the first in a series of actions, moves, etc. or in a baseball lineup
lead pencil (led) a pencil consisting of a slender stick of graphite encased in wood, etc.
lead poisoning (led) an acute or chronic poisoning caused by the absorption of lead into the body
lead tetraethyl *same as* TETRAETHYL LEAD
lead time (lēd) the period of time from the decision to make a product to its actual production
leaf (lēf) *n., pl.* **leaves** [OE. *leaf*] **1.** any of the flat, thin, expanded organs, usually green, growing from the stem of a plant **2.** popularly, *a)* the blade of a leaf *b)* a petal **3.** leaves collectively *[choice tobacco leaf]* **4.** a sheet of paper with a page on each side **5.** *a)* a thin sheet of metal *b)* such sheets collectively *[gold leaf]* **6.** *a)* a hinged section of a table top *b)* a board inserted into a table top to increase its surface **7.** a flat, hinged or movable part of a folding door, shutter, etc. —*vi.* **1.** to bear leaves (often with *out*) **2.** to turn the pages of a book, etc. (with *through*) —*vt.* to turn the pages of —**in leaf** with foliage —**take a leaf from someone's book** to follow someone's example —**turn over a new leaf** to start anew —**leaf′less** *adj.* —**leaf′like′** *adj.*
leaf·age (-ij) *n.* leaves collectively; foliage
leaf bud a bud from which only stems and leaves develop
leaf hopper an insect that leaps from one plant to another, sucking the juices and often transmitting plant diseases
leaf lard a high-grade lard, made from the heavily layered fat (**leaf fat**) around the kidneys of a hog
leaf·let (-lit) *n.* **1.** one of the divisions of a compound leaf **2.** a small or young leaf **3.** a separate sheet of printed matter, often folded but not stitched
leaf·stalk (-stôk′) *n.* the slender portion of a leaf, which supports the blade and is attached to the stem
leaf·y (lē′fē) *adj.* **leaf′i·er, leaf′i·est** **1.** of, consisting of, or like a leaf or leaves **2.** having many leaves **3.** having broad leaves, as spinach —**leaf′i·ness** *n.*
league[1] (lēg) *n.* [< OFr. < It. *liga* < *legare* < L. *ligare,* to bind] **1.** a covenant made by nations, groups, or individuals for promoting common interests, etc. **2.** an association or alliance formed by such a covenant **3.** *Sports* a group of teams organized to compete against one another **4.** [Colloq.] a division according to grade or quality —*vt., vi.* **leagued, leagu′ing** to form into a league —**in league** allied —**leagu′er** *n.*
league[2] (lēg) *n.* [< OFr. < LL. *leuga,* Gallic mile < Celt.] a measure of distance varying in different times and countries, usually about 3 miles in English-speaking countries
League of Nations an association of nations (1920–46) to promote international cooperation and peace: it was succeeded by the United Nations
Le·ah (lē′ə) [? Heb. *lēʼāh,* gazelle, or ? *lāʼāh,* to tire, weary] **1.** a feminine name **2.** *Bible* the elder of the sisters who were wives of Jacob: Gen. 29:13–30
leak (lēk) *vi.* [< ON. *leka,* to drip] **1.** to let a fluid substance out or in accidentally *[the boat leaks]* **2.** to enter or escape in this way, as a fluid (often with *in* or *out*) **3.** to become known little by little *[the truth leaked out]* —*vt.* **1.** to allow to leak **2.** to allow to become known —*n.* **1.** an accidental hole or crack that lets something out or in **2.** any means of escape for something that ought not to be let out, lost, etc. **3.** leakage **4.** a disclosure, supposedly accidental but actually intentional: in full, **news leak** **5.** *a)* a loss of electrical charge through faulty insulation *b)* the point where this occurs
leak·age (-ij) *n.* **1.** an act or instance of leaking; leak **2.** something that leaks in or out **3.** the amount that leaks in or out
leak·y (lē′kē) *adj.* **leak′i·er, leak′i·est** having a leak or leaks —**leak′i·ness** *n.*
leal (lēl) *adj.* [< OFr. < L. *legalis:* see LEGAL] [Archaic or Scot.] loyal; true —**leal′ly** *adv.*
lean[1] (lēn) *vi.* **leaned** or **leant, lean′ing** [OE. *hlinian*] **1.** to bend or deviate from an upright position; stand at a slant; incline **2.** to bend the body so as to rest part of one's weight upon something *[he leaned on the desk]* **3.** to depend for aid, etc.; rely (*on* or *upon*) **4.** to have a particular mental inclination; tend (*toward* or *to*) —*vt.* to cause to lean —*n.* an inclination; slant —**lean′er** *n.*
lean[2] (lēn) *adj.* [OE. *hlæne*] **1.** with little flesh or fat; thin; spare **2.** containing little or no fat: said of meat **3.** lacking in richness, profit, etc.; meager —*n.* meat containing little or no fat —**lean′ly** *adv.* —**lean′ness** *n.*

Le·an·der (lē an′dər) *Gr. Legend* the lover of Hero: see HERO

lean·ing (lē′niŋ) *n.* **1.** the act of a person or thing that leans **2.** tendency; inclination

leant (lent) *alt. pt. & pp. of* LEAN[1]

lean-to (lēn′to͞o′) *n., pl.* **lean′-tos′** **1.** a shed with a sloping roof resting against trees, etc. **2.** a structure whose sloping roof abuts a wall or building

leap (lēp) *vi.* **leaped** or **leapt** (lept, lēpt), **leap′ing** [OE. *hleapan*] **1.** to jump; spring **2.** to move suddenly or swiftly, as if by jumping; bound **3.** to accept eagerly something offered (with *at*) —*vt.* **1.** to pass over by a jump **2.** to cause to leap [*to leap* a horse over a wall] —*n.* **1.** a jump; spring **2.** the distance covered in a jump **3.** a place that is, or is to be, leaped over or from —**by leaps and bounds** very rapidly —**leap in the dark** a risky act whose consequences cannot be foreseen —**leap′er** *n.*

leap·frog (-frôg′, -fräg′) *n.* a game in which each player in turn jumps over the bent back of each of the other players —*vi.* **-frogged′**, **-frog′ging** **1.** to skip (*over*) **2.** to progress in jumps or stages —*vt.* to jump or skip over

leap year a year of 366 days, occurring every fourth year: the additional day is February 29: a leap year is a year whose number is exactly divisible by four, or, in the case of century years, by 400

Lear (lir) **1.** *see* KING LEAR **2.** Edward, 1812–88; Eng. humorist

learn (lurn) *vt.* **learned** or **learnt** (lurnt), **learn′ing** [OE. *leornian*] **1.** to get knowledge of (a subject) or skill in (an art, trade, etc.) by study, experience, etc. **2.** to come to know [*to learn* what happened] **3.** to come to know how [*to learn* to swim] **4.** to memorize **5.** to acquire as a habit or attitude **6.** [Dial.] to teach —*vi.* **1.** to gain knowledge or skill **2.** to be informed; hear (*of* or *about*) —**learn′a·ble** *adj.* —**learn′er** *n.*

learn·ed (lur′nid; *for 3* lurnd) *adj.* **1.** having or showing much learning; erudite **2.** of or characterized by study and learning **3.** acquired by study, experience, etc. [*a learned* response] —**learn′ed·ly** *adv.* —**learn′ed·ness** *n.*

learn·ing (lur′niŋ) *n.* **1.** the acquiring of knowledge or skill **2.** acquired knowledge or skill

lease (lēs) *n.* [< Anglo-Fr. *les* < OFr. < L. *laxare,* to loosen < *laxus,* loose] a contract by which a landlord gives to a tenant the use of lands, buildings, etc. for a specified time and for fixed payments; also, the period of time specified —*vt.* **leased, leas′ing** **1.** to give by a lease; let **2.** to get by a lease —**new lease on life** another chance to lead a happy life, be successful, etc. because of a new turn of events —**leas′a·ble** *adj.* —**leas′er** *n.*

leash (lēsh) *n.* [< OFr. < L. *laxa,* fem. of *laxus,* loose] a cord, strap, etc. by which a dog or other animal is held in check —*vt.* **1.** to put a leash on **2.** to control as by a leash —**hold in leash** to control —**strain at the leash** to be impatient to be free

least (lēst) *adj. alt. superl. of* LITTLE [< OE. *læsest, læst,* superl. of *læssa,* LESS] smallest in size, degree, importance, etc. —*adv.* in the smallest degree —*n.* the smallest in size, amount, importance, etc. —**at (the) least** **1.** with no less **2.** at any rate —**not in the least** not at all

least common denominator the least common multiple of the denominators of two or more fractions

least common multiple the smallest positive whole number that is exactly divisible by two or more given whole numbers [the *least common multiple* of 4, 5, and 10 is 20]

least·wise (-wīz′) *adv.* [Colloq.] at least; anyway Also [Chiefly Dial.] **least′ways′** (-wāz′)

leath·er (leth′ər) *n.* [OE. *lether-*] **1.** animal skin prepared for use by removing the hair and tanning **2.** any article made of this —*adj.* of or made of leather —*vt.* [Colloq.] to whip with a leather strap

Leath·er·ette (leth′ə ret′) *a trademark for* imitation leather made of paper or cloth —*n.* [l-] such imitation leather

leath·ern (leth′ərn) *adj.* made of or like leather

leath·er·neck (leth′ər nek′) *n.* [from the leather-lined collar, formerly part of the Marine uniform] [Slang] a U.S. Marine

leath·er·y (-ē) *adj.* like leather; tough and flexible —**leath′er·i·ness** *n.*

leave[1] (lēv) *vt.* **left, leav′ing** [OE. *læfan,* lit., to let remain] **1.** to allow to remain [*leave* some cake for me] **2.** to make, place, etc., and cause to remain behind one [to *leave* footprints] **3.** to have remaining after one [the deceased *leaves* a widow] **4.** to bequeath **5.** to entrust (with *to* or *up to*) [to *leave* a decision to another] **6.** to give as a remainder [ten minus two *leaves* eight] **7.** to go away from **8.** to cause to be in a certain condition [the flood *left* them homeless] **9.** to abandon; forsake **10.** to stop living in, working for, or belonging to **11.** [Dial.] to let or allow [*leave* us go now] —*vi.* to go away or set out —**leave off** **1.** to stop; cease **2.** to stop doing or using —**leave out** **1.** to omit **2.** to fail to consider —**leave (someone) alone** to refrain from bothering (someone) —**leav′er** *n.*

leave[2] (lēv) *n.* [OE. *leaf*] **1.** permission **2.** *a)* permission to be absent from duty or work *b)* the period for which this is granted —**by your leave** with your permission —**on leave** absent from duty with permission —**take leave of** to say goodbye to —**take one's leave** to depart

leave[3] (lēv) *vi.* **leaved, leav′ing** [see LEAF] to put forth, or bear, leaves; leaf

leaved (lēvd) *adj.* having leaves [*narrow-leaved*]

leav·en (lev′'n) *n.* [< OFr. < L. *levamen,* alleviation < *levare,* to raise] **1.** a small piece of fermenting dough used for producing fermentation in a fresh batch of dough **2.** *same as* LEAVENING —*vt.* **1.** to make (batter or dough) rise with a leavening agent **2.** to spread through, causing a gradual change

leav·en·ing (-iŋ) *n.* **1.** a substance, such as yeast, used to make batter or dough rise by the formation of gas: also **leavening agent** **2.** any influence working on something to bring about a gradual change

Leav·en·worth (lev′'n wurth′) [after U.S. Army Col. H. *Leavenworth* (1783–1834)] city in NE Kans.: site of a Federal prison: pop. 34,000

leave of absence a leave from work or duty, esp. for a long time; also, the period of time

leaves (lēvz) *n. pl. of* LEAF

leave-tak·ing (lēv′tāk′iŋ) *n.* the act of taking leave, or saying goodbye

leav·ings (-iŋz) *n.pl.* leftovers, remnants, refuse, etc.

Leb·a·non (leb′ə nən) country in SW Asia, on the Mediterranean: c.4,000 sq. mi.; pop. 2,367,000; cap. Beirut —**Leb′a·nese′** (-nēz′) *adj., n., pl.* **-nese′**

lech·er (lech′ər) *n.* [< OFr. < *lechier,* to be a debauchee, lit., lick] a lewd, grossly sensual man

lech·er·ous (-əs) *adj.* lustful; lewd —**lech′er·ous·ly** *adv.* —**lech′er·ous·ness** *n.*

lech·er·y (-ē) *n., pl.* **-er·ies** gross sensuality

lec·i·thin (les′ə thin) *n.* [< Gr. *lekithos,* yolk of an egg + -IN[1]] a fatty compound found in nerve tissue, blood, egg yolk, and some vegetables: used in medicines, foods, cosmetics, etc.

Le Cor·bu·sier (lə kôr bü zyā′) (pseud. of *Charles-Édouard Jeanneret-Gris*) 1887–1965; Swiss architect in France

lec·tern (lek′tərn) *n.* [< OFr. < ML. *lectrum* < L. pp. of *legere,* to read] **1.** a reading desk in a church; esp., such a desk from which a part of the Scriptures is read during the service **2.** a stand for holding the notes, speech, etc., as of a lecturer

LECTERN

lec·ture (lek′chər) *n.* [< ML. *lectura* < pp. of *legere,* to read] **1.** an informative talk given before an audience, class, etc., and usually prepared beforehand **2.** a lengthy scolding —*vi.* **-tured, -tur·ing** to give a lecture —*vt.* to give a lecture to —**lec′tur·er** *n.* —**lec′ture·ship′** *n.*

led (led) *pt. & pp. of* LEAD[1]

LED [*l*(*ight-*)*e*(*mitting*) *d*(*iode*)] a semiconductor diode that emits light when voltage is applied: used in lamps, digital watches, etc.

Le·da (lē′də) *Gr. Myth.* the mother of Clytemnestra and Castor and Pollux and (by Zeus, who visited her in the form of a swan) of Helen of Troy

ledge (lej) *n.* [prob. < ME. *leggen:* see ff.] **1.** a shelf **2.** a projecting ridge of rocks **3.** *Mining* a vein

ledg·er (lej′ər) *n.* [prob. < ME. *leggen,* to lay, or *liggen,* to lie] *Bookkeeping* the book of final entry, in which a record of debits, credits, and all money transactions is kept

ledger line *same as* LEGER LINE

Lee (lē) **1.** [var. of LEIGH] a masculine or feminine name **2. Henry,** 1756–1818; Am. general in the Revolutionary War: called *Light-Horse Harry Lee* **3. Robert E(dward),** 1807–70; Confederate commander in chief: son of *Henry*

lee (lē) *n.* [OE. *hleo,* shelter] **1.** shelter; protection **2.** a sheltered place, esp. one on the side away from the wind **3.** *Naut.* the side or part away from the wind —*adj.* of or on the side away from the wind

leech[1] (lēch) *n.* [OE. *læce*] **1.** formerly, a physician **2.** any of a number of annelid worms with suckers, living in water or wet earth: one bloodsucking species was formerly used to bleed patients **3.** a person who is a parasite —*vt.* **1.** to bleed with leeches **2.** to drain dry —*vi.* to act as a parasite

LEECH (to 3 in. long)

leech[2] (lēch) *n.* [LME. *lyche*] the free or outside edge of a sail

Leeds (lēdz) city in Yorkshire, N England: pop. 506,000

leek (lēk) *n.* [OE. *leac*] an onionlike vegetable having a bulb with a cylindrical stem, and broad leaves

leer (lir) *n.* [OE. *hleor*] a sly, sidelong look showing salaciousness, malicious triumph, etc. —*vi.* to look with a leer —**leer′ing·ly** *adv.*

leer·y (lir′ē) ***adj.*** **leer′i·er, leer′i·est** wary; suspicious

lees (lēz) ***n.pl.*** **[**< OFr. < ML. *lia*] dregs or sediment, as of wine

lee·ward (lē′wərd; *naut.* lo͞o′ərd) ***adj.*** in the direction toward which the wind blows; of the lee side: opposed to WINDWARD —***n.*** the lee part or side —***adv.*** toward the lee

Lee·ward Islands (lē′wərd) N group of islands in the Lesser Antilles of the West Indies

lee·way (lē′wā′) ***n.*** **1.** the leeward drift of a ship or aircraft from the true course **2.** [Colloq.] *a*) margin of time, money, etc. *b*) room for freedom of action

left[1] (left) ***adj.*** **[**OE. *lyft*, weak**]** **1.** *a*) designating or of that side of one's body which is toward the west when one faces north, the side of the less-used hand in most people *b*) designating or of the corresponding side of anything *c*) closer to the left side of a person directly facing the thing mentioned **2.** of the bank of a river on the left of a person facing downstream **3.** of the political left; radical or liberal —***n.*** **1.** *a*) all or part of the left side *b*) a direction or location on the left side *c*) a turn toward the left side **2.** *Boxing* *a*) the left hand *b*) a blow delivered with the left hand **3.** [*often* **L-**] *Politics* a radical or liberal position, party, etc. (often with *the*): from the location of their seats in some European legislatures —***adv.*** on or toward the left hand or left side

left[2] (left) *pt. & pp. of* LEAVE[1]

left-hand (left′hand′) ***adj.*** **1.** on or directed toward the left **2.** of, for, or with the left hand

left-hand·ed (-han′did) ***adj.*** **1.** using the left hand more skillfully than the right **2.** done with the left hand **3.** clumsy; awkward **4.** designating an insincere or ambiguous compliment **5.** made for use with the left hand **6.** turning from right to left —***adv.*** with the left hand *[*to write *left-handed]* —**left′-hand′ed·ly** ***adv.*** —**left′-hand′ed·ness** ***n.*** —**left′-hand′er** ***n.***

left·ist (-ist) ***n.*** a person whose political position is radical or liberal; member of the left —***adj.*** radical or liberal —**left′ism** ***n.***

left·o·ver (-ō′vər) ***n.*** something left over, as from a meal —***adj.*** remaining unused, etc.

left·ward (-wərd) ***adv., adj.*** on or toward the left: also **left′wards** ***adv.***

left wing the more radical or liberal section of a political party, group, etc. —**left′-wing′** ***adj.*** —**left′-wing′er** ***n.***

left·y (lef′tē) ***n.,*** *pl.* **left′ies** [Slang] a left-handed person: often used as a nickname

leg (leg) ***n.*** **[**< ON. *leggr*] **1.** one of the parts of the body by means of which animals stand and walk: in human beings, either of the two lower limbs **2.** a cut of meat consisting of the leg **3.** the part of a garment covering the leg **4.** anything resembling a leg in shape or use, as one of the supports of a piece of furniture **5.** any of the stages of a course or journey **6.** *Math.* either of the sides of a triangle other than its base or, in a right-angled triangle, its hypotenuse —***vi.*** **legged, leg′ging** [Colloq.] to walk or run: used chiefly in the phr. **leg it** —**get up on one's hind legs** [Colloq.] to become assertive, aggressive, etc. —**not have a leg to stand on** [Colloq.] to have absolutely no defense, excuse, etc. —**on one's** (or **its**) **last legs** [Colloq.] not far from death, breakdown, etc. —**pull someone's leg** [Colloq.] to make fun of or fool someone —**shake a leg** [Slang] to hurry —**stretch one's legs** to walk, esp. after sitting a long time —**leg′less** ***adj.***

leg. **1.** legal **2.** legislative **3.** legislature

leg·a·cy (leg′ə sē) ***n.,*** *pl.* **-cies** **[**< OFr. *legacie* < ML. < L. *legatus:* see LEGATE**]** **1.** money or property left to someone by a will **2.** anything handed down from, or as from, an ancestor

le·gal (lē′gəl) ***adj.*** **[**< MFr. < L. *legalis* < *lex* (gen. *legis*), law**]** **1.** of, based on, or authorized by law **2.** permitted by law *[*a *legal* act*]* **3.** that can be enforced in a court of law **4.** of or applicable to lawyers *[legal* ethics*]* **5.** in terms of the law *[*a *legal* offense*]* —**le′gal·ly** ***adv.***

le·gal·ese (lē′gə lēz′) ***n.*** the special vocabulary of legal forms, documents, etc., often thought of by the layman as incomprehensible

legal holiday a holiday set by statute

le·gal·ism (lē′gəl iz′m) ***n.*** strict, often too strict and literal, adherence to law —**le′gal·ist** ***n.*** —**le′gal·is′tic** ***adj.***

le·gal·i·ty (li gal′ə tē) ***n.,*** *pl.* **-ties** quality, condition, or instance of being legal or lawful

le·gal·ize (lē′gə līz′) ***vt.*** **-ized′, -iz′ing** to make legal or lawful —**le′gal·i·za′tion** ***n.***

legal tender money that may be legally offered in payment of an obligation and that a creditor must accept

leg·ate (leg′it) ***n.*** **[**< OFr. < L. pp. of *legare*, to send as ambassador < *lex*, law**]** an envoy or ambassador, esp. one officially representing the Pope —**leg′ate·ship′** ***n.***

leg·a·tee (leg′ə tē′) ***n.*** one to whom a legacy is bequeathed

le·ga·tion (li gā′shən) ***n.*** **1.** a diplomatic minister and his staff, representing their government in a foreign country and ranking just below an embassy **2.** their headquarters

le·ga·to (li gät′ō) ***adj., adv.*** **[**It., pp. of *legare* < L. *ligare*, to tie**]** *Music* in a smooth, even style, with no noticeable interruption between the notes

leg·end (lej′ənd) ***n.*** **[**< OFr. < ML. *legenda*, things to be read < L. neut. pl. gerundive of *legere*, to read**]** **1.** *a*) a story handed down for generations and popularly believed to have a historical basis: cf. MYTH *b*) all such stories belonging to a particular group of people **2.** *a*) a notable person much talked about in his own time *b*) the stories of his exploits **3.** an inscription on a coin, medal, etc. **4.** a descriptive title, key, etc., as under an illustration

leg·end·ar·y (lej′ən der′ē) ***adj.*** of, based on, or presented in legends; traditional

leg·end·ry (-drē) ***n.*** legends collectively

leg·er·de·main (lej′ər di mān′) ***n.*** **[**< MFr. *leger de main*, lit., light of hand**]** **1.** sleight of hand; tricks of a stage magician **2.** trickery; deceit

leg·er line (lej′ər) **[**altered < *ledger line***]** *Music* a short line written above or below the staff, for notes beyond the range of the staff

leg·ged (leg′id, legd) ***adj.*** having (a specified number or kind of) legs *[*long-*legged]*

leg·ging (leg′iŋ, -ən) ***n.*** a covering of canvas, leather, etc. for protecting the leg below the knee

leg·gy (leg′ē) ***adj.*** **-gi·er, -gi·est** **1.** having long and awkward legs *[*a *leggy* colt*]* **2.** [Colloq.] having long, well-shaped legs —**leg′gi·ness** ***n.***

Leg·horn (leg′hôrn, leg′ərn) city in Tuscany, W Italy: pop. 172,000 —***n.*** **[**after prec.**]** **1.** [*sometimes* **l-**] any of a breed of small chicken, orig. developed in the Mediterranean region **2.** [**l-**] *a*) a plaiting made of an Italian wheat straw *b*) a broad-brimmed hat of this straw

leg·i·ble (lej′ə b′l) ***adj.*** **[**< LL. *legibilis* < *legere*, to read**]** **1.** that can be read or deciphered **2.** that can be read easily —**leg′i·bil′i·ty** ***n.*** —**leg′i·bly** ***adv.***

le·gion (lē′jən) ***n.*** **[**< OFr. < L. *legio* < *legere*, to select**]** **1.** *Rom. History* a military division varying at times from 3,000 to 6,000 foot soldiers, with additional cavalrymen **2.** a large group of soldiers; army **3.** a large number; multitude

le·gion·ar·y (-er′ē) ***adj.*** of or constituting a legion —***n.,*** *pl.* **-ar′ies** a member of a legion

le·gion·naire (lē′jə ner′) ***n.*** **[**< Fr. < L.**]** a member of a legion

leg·is·late (lej′is lāt′) ***vi.*** **-lat′ed, -lat′ing** **[**< LEGISLATOR**]** to make or pass a law or laws —***vt.*** to cause to be, become, go, etc. by making laws

leg·is·la·tion (lej′is lā′shən) ***n.*** **[**< LL. < L. *lex* (gen. *legis*), law + *latio*, a proposing < pp. of *ferre*, to BEAR[1]**]** **1.** the making of a law or laws **2.** the law or laws made

leg·is·la·tive (lej′is lāt′iv) ***adj.*** **1.** of legislation **2.** of a legislature or its members **3.** having the power to make laws *[*a *legislative* assembly*]* **4.** enforced by legislation —***n.*** a legislature —**leg′is·la′tive·ly** ***adv.***

leg·is·la·tor (-lāt′ər) ***n.*** **[**< L.: see LEGISLATION**]** a member of a legislative assembly; lawmaker

leg·is·la·ture (-lā′chər) ***n.*** a body of persons given the responsibility and power to make laws for a country, State, etc.

le·git (lə jit′) ***n.*** [Slang] the legitimate theater, drama, etc. —***adj.*** [Slang] legitimate

le·git·i·ma·cy (lə jit′ə mə sē) ***n.*** a being legitimate

le·git·i·mate (-mit; *for v.* -māt′) ***adj.*** **[**< ML. pp. of *legitimare*, to make lawful, ult. < L. *lex*, law**]** **1.** born of parents legally married to each other **2.** *a*) lawful *b*) conforming to the law **3.** ruling by the rights of heredity *[*a *legitimate* king*]* **4.** *a*) logically correct *[*a *legitimate* inference*]* *b*) justifiable or justified **5.** conforming to established rules, standards, etc. **6.** *Theater* designating or of stage plays, as distinguished from motion pictures, vaudeville, etc. —***vt.*** **-mat′ed, -mat′ing** *same as* LEGITIMIZE —**le·git′i·mate·ly** ***adv.*** —**le·git′i·ma′tion** ***n.***

le·git·i·ma·tize (lə jit′ə mə tīz′) ***vt.*** **-tized′, -tiz′ing** *same as* LEGITIMIZE

le·git·i·mist (-mist) ***n.*** a supporter of legitimate authority or, esp., of claims to monarchy based on the rights of heredity —**le·git′i·mism** ***n.***

le·git·i·mize (-mīz′) ***vt.*** **-mized′, -miz′ing** **1.** to make or declare legitimate **2.** to make seem just, right, or reasonable —**le·git′i·mi·za′tion** ***n.***

leg·man (leg′man′) ***n.,*** *pl.* **-men′** a newspaperman who gathers information at the scene of events or at various sources

leg-of-mut·ton (leg′ə mut′'n, -əv-) ***adj.*** shaped like a leg of mutton: said of a sleeve that puffs out toward the shoulder, etc.

leg·room (leg′ro͞om′) ***n.*** adequate space for the legs while seated, as in a car

leg·ume (leg′yo͞om, li gyo͞om′) ***n.*** [< Fr. < L. *legumen* < *legere*, to gather] **1.** any of a large family of plants, including the peas, beans, clovers, etc., with fruit that is a pod splitting along two sutures: many legumes are nitrogen-fixing **2.** the pod or seed of some members of this family, used for food

le·gu·mi·nous (li gyo͞o′min əs) ***adj.*** **1.** of, having the nature of, or bearing legumes **2.** of the family of plants to which peas and beans belong

leg·work (leg′wurk′) ***n.*** [Colloq.] travel away from the center of work as a routine part of a job, as of a legman

Le Ha·vre (lə häv′rə; *Fr.* lə ȧ′vr′) seaport in NW France, on the English Channel: pop. 200,000

lei (lā, lā′ē) ***n.***, *pl.* **leis** [Haw.] in Hawaii, a wreath of flowers and leaves

Leib·niz (līp′nits), Baron **Gott·fried Wil·helm von** (gôt′frēt vil′helm fôn) 1646–1716; Ger. philosopher & mathematician: also sp. **Leibnitz**

Leices·ter (les′tər) city in C England: pop. 280,000

Leicester, Earl of (*Robert Dudley*) 1532–88; Eng. courtier & general: favorite of Elizabeth I

Lei·den (līd′'n) city in W Netherlands: pop. 103,000

Leigh (lē) [< surname *Leigh* < OE. *leah*, LEA] a masculine or feminine name

Leip·zig (līp′sig, -sik; *G.* līp′tsiH) city in SC East Germany: pop. 592,000

lei·sure (lē′zhər, lezh′ər) ***n.*** [< OFr. < L. *licere*, to be permitted] free, unoccupied time that can be used for rest, recreation, etc. —***adj.*** **1.** free and unoccupied; spare [*leisure* time] **2.** having much leisure [the *leisure* class] —**at leisure 1.** having free time **2.** with no hurry **3.** not occupied or engaged —**at one's leisure** when one has the time or opportunity —**lei′sured** ***adj.***

lei·sure·ly (-lē) ***adj.*** without haste; slow —***adv.*** in an unhurried manner —**lei′sure·li·ness** ***n.***

leit·mo·tif, leit·mo·tiv (līt′mō tēf′) ***n.*** [< G. < *leiten*, to lead + *motiv*, MOTIVE] **1.** a short musical phrase representing and recurring with a given character, situation, etc. as in Wagner's operas **2.** a dominant theme or underlying pattern

lek (lek) ***n.*** *see* MONETARY UNITS, table (Albania)

lem·an (lem′ən, lē′mən) ***n.*** [ME. *lemman* < *lef*, dear (see LIEF) + man] [Archaic] a sweetheart or lover (man or woman); esp., a mistress

Le·man (lē′mən), **Lake** *same as* Lake GENEVA: Fr. name **Lac Lé·man** (lȧk lā män′)

lem·ming (lem′iŋ) ***n.***, *pl.* **-mings, -ming:** see PLURAL, II, D, 1 [Dan. < ON.] a small arctic rodent resembling the mouse but having a short tail and fur-covered feet

lem·on (lem′ən) ***n.*** [< MFr. < Ar. *laimūn* < Per. *līmūn*] **1.** a small, edible citrus fruit with a pale-yellow rind and a juicy, sour pulp **2.** the small, spiny, semitropical tree bearing this fruit **3.** pale yellow **4.** [Slang] *a*) something that is defective *b*) an inadequate person —***adj.*** **1.** pale-yellow **2.** made with or flavored like lemon —**lem′on·y** ***adj.***

lem·on·ade (lem′ə nād′) ***n.*** a drink made of lemon juice and water, usually sweetened

lem·pi·ra (lem pir′ə) ***n.***, *pl.* **-ras** [AmSp., after *Lempira*, native chief] *see* MONETARY UNITS, table (Honduras)

le·mur (lē′mər) ***n.*** [< L. *lemures*, ghosts] a small primate related to the monkey, with large eyes and soft, woolly fur: found mainly in the old-world tropics and active mostly at night

Le·na (lē′nə; *also, for 2, Russ.* lye′nä) **1.** [dim. of HELEN] a feminine name **2.** river in EC R.S.F.S.R., flowing northeast into the Arctic Ocean

lend (lend) ***vt.*** **lent, lend′ing** [OE. *lænan* < *læn*, a loan] **1.** to let another use or have (a thing) temporarily **2.** to let out (money) at interest **3.** to give; impart [to *lend* an air of mystery] —***vi.*** to make a loan or loans —**lend itself** (or **oneself**) **to** to be useful for or open to —**lend′er** ***n.***

lending library a library from which books may be borrowed, usually for a daily fee

lend-lease (-lēs′) ***n.*** in World War II, material aid in the form of munitions, tools, food, etc. granted to foreign countries whose defense was deemed vital to the defense of the U.S. —**lend′-lease′** ***vt.*** **-leased′, -leas′ing**

length (leŋkth, leŋth) ***n.*** [OE. *lengthu* < base of *lang*, long + -TH[1]] **1.** the measure of how long a thing is from end to end; the greatest dimension of anything **2.** extent in space or time **3.** a long stretch or extent **4.** the state or fact of being long **5.** a piece of a certain length [a *length* of pipe] **6.** a unit of measure consisting of the length of an object or animal in a race [the boat won by two *lengths*] —**at full length** completely extended —**at length 1.** finally **2.** in full —**go to any length** (or **great lengths**) to do whatever is necessary

length·en (-'n) ***vt., vi.*** to make or become longer —**length′en·er** ***n.***

length·wise (-wīz′) ***adv., adj.*** in the direction of the length: also **length′ways′** (-wāz′)

length·y (-ē) ***adj.*** **length′i·er, length′i·est** long; esp., too long —**length′i·ly** ***adv.*** —**length′i·ness** ***n.***

le·ni·ent (lē′ni ənt, lēn′yənt) ***adj.*** [< L. prp. of *lenire*, to soften < *lenis*, soft] not harsh or severe in disciplining, judging, etc.; mild; merciful —**le′ni·en·cy,** *pl.* **-cies, le′ni·ence** ***n.*** —**le′ni·ent·ly** ***adv.***

Len·in (len′in; *Russ.* lye′nyin), **V(ladimir) I(lyich)** (orig. surname *Ulyanov:* also called *Nikolai Lenin*) 1870–1924; Russ. Communist revolutionary leader; premier of the U.S.S.R. (1917–24)

Len·in·grad (len′in grad′; *Russ.* lye′nin grät′) seaport in NW R.S.F.S.R., on the Gulf of Finland: pop. 3,752,000

Len·in·ism (len′in iz'm) ***n.*** the communist theories and policies of Lenin, including his theory of the dictatorship of the proletariat —**Len′in·ist** ***n., adj.***

len·i·tive (len′ə tiv) ***adj.*** [< ML. < L. pp. of *lenire*, to soften] soothing or assuaging; lessening pain —***n.*** a lenitive medicine, etc.

len·i·ty (-tē) ***n.*** [< OFr. < L. < *lenis*, mild: see LENIENT] **1.** a being lenient; mildness; gentleness **2.** *pl.* **-ties** a lenient act

Le·nore (lə nôr′) [var. of ELEANOR] a feminine name

lens (lenz) ***n.*** [L., lentil: a double-convex lens is shaped like the seed] **1.** *a*) a piece of glass, or other transparent substance, with two curved surfaces, or one plane and one curved, bringing together or spreading rays of light passing through it: lenses are used in optical instruments *b*) a combination of two or more lenses **2.** a transparent biconvex body of the eye: it focuses upon the retina light rays entering the pupil

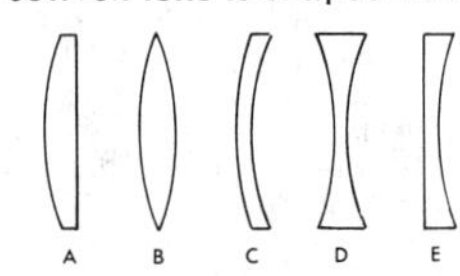

LENS
(A, plano-convex; B, double-convex; C, divergent meniscus; D, double-concave; E, plano-concave)

Lent (lent) ***n.*** [OE. *lengten*, the spring < *lang*, long: because the spring days lengthen] the period of forty weekdays from Ash Wednesday to Easter, observed variously in Christian churches by fasting and penitence

lent (lent) *pt. & pp. of* LEND

-lent (lənt) [L. *-lentus*, -ful] *a suffix meaning* full of, characterized by [*virulent, fraudulent*]

Lent·en (lent′'n) ***adj.*** [*also* **l-**] of, connected with, or suitable for Lent

len·til (lent′'l) ***n.*** [< OFr. < L. *lenticula*, dim. of *lens*, lentil] **1.** an old-world leguminous plant with small, edible seeds shaped like double-convex lenses **2.** the seed of this plant

len·to (len′tō) ***adv., adj.*** [It. < L. *lentus*, slow] *Music* slow —***n.***, *pl.* **-tos** a lento passage or movement

Le·o (lē′ō) [L.: see LION] **1.** a masculine name: var. *Leon* **2.** a N constellation between Cancer and Virgo **3.** the fifth sign of the zodiac: see ZODIAC, illus. **4. Leo I,** Saint 400?–461 A.D.; Pope (440–461): called *the Great* **5. Leo XIII** 1810–1903; Pope (1878–1903)

Le·ón (le ôn′) region in NW Spain: formerly a kingdom

Le·o·na (lē ō′nə) [< LEO] a feminine name

Leon·ard (len′ərd) [< Fr. < OFr. < OHG. < *lewo*, lion + *hart*, strong] a masculine name

le·one (lē ōn′) ***n.*** *see* MONETARY UNITS, table (Sierra Leone)

Le·o·nids (lē′ə nidz) ***n.pl.*** a shower of meteors visible yearly about November 15, appearing to radiate from the constellation Leo: also **Le·on·i·des** (lē än′ə dēz′)

le·o·nine (lē′ə nīn′) ***adj.*** [< OFr. < L. < *leo*, LION] of, characteristic of, or like a lion

leop·ard (lep′ərd) ***n.***, *pl.* **-ards, -ard:** see PLURAL, II, D, 1 [< OFr. < LL. < Gr. *leopardos* < *leōn*, lion + *pardos*, panther] **1.** a large, ferocious animal of the cat family, with a black-spotted tawny coat, found in Africa and Asia **2.** *same as* JAGUAR —**leop′ard·ess** ***n.fem.***

Le·o·pold (lē′ə pōld′) [G. < OHG. < *liut*, people + *balt*, strong] a masculine name

Lé·o·pold·ville (lē′ə pōld vil′, lā′-) *former name of* KINSHASA

le·o·tard (lē′ə tärd′) ***n.*** [after J. *Léotard*, 19th-c. Fr. aerialist] a one-piece, tightfitting garment for the torso, worn by acrobats, dancers, etc.

lep·er (lep′ər) ***n.*** [< OFr. < L. < Gr. < *lepros*, rough, scaly < *lepein*, to peel] **1.** a person having leprosy **2.** a person to be shunned

lep·i·dop·ter·an (lep′ə däp′tər ən) ***n.*** [< ModL. < Gr. *lepis*, a scale + -PTER(OUS) + -AN] any of a large order of insects, including the butterflies and moths, characterized by two pairs of broad, membranous wings covered with very fine scales —**lep′i·dop′ter·ous** ***adj.***

lep·re·chaun (lep′rə kôn′, -kän′) ***n.*** [Ir. *lupracān* < OIr. < *lu*, little + dim. of *corp* (< L. *corpus*), body] *Irish Folklore* a fairy in the form of a little old man who can reveal a buried crock of gold to anyone who catches him

lep·ro·sy (lep′rə sē) ***n.*** [see LEPER] a chronic, infectious disease caused by a bacterium that attacks the skin, flesh, nerves, etc.: it is characterized by ulcers, white scaly scabs, deformities, and wasting of body parts

lep·rous (-rəs) ***adj.*** **1.** of or like leprosy **2.** having leprosy

-lep·sy (lep′sē) [< Gr. *-lēpsia* < *lēpsis*, an attack] *a combining form meaning* a fit, attack, seizure *[catalepsy]*: also **-lep′si·a**

lep·ton (lep′tän) ***n., pl.*** **-ta** (-tə) [Gr. < *leptos*, thin, small < *lepein*, to peel] *see* MONETARY UNITS, table (Greece)

Le·roy (lə roi′, lē′roi) [< Fr. *le roi*, the king] a masculine name

les·bi·an (lez′bē ən) ***adj.*** [in allusion to Sappho and her followers, in Lesbos] [*sometimes* **L-**] of homosexuality between women —***n.*** [*sometimes* **L-**] a homosexual woman —**les′bi·an·ism** ***n.***

Les·bos (lez′bäs, -bəs) Gr. island in the Aegean, off the coast of Asia Minor

lese maj·es·ty (lēz′ maj′is tē) [< Fr. < L. fem. of *laesus*, pp. of *laedere*, to hurt + *majestas*, majesty] **1.** a crime against the sovereign; treason **2.** any insolence toward one to whom deference is due

le·sion (lē′zhən) ***n.*** [< MFr. < L. *laesio* < pp. of *laedere*, to harm] **1.** an injury; hurt **2.** an injury, sore, etc. in an organ or tissue of the body resulting in impairment or loss of function

Les·lie (les′lē, lez′-) [ult. < *less lee* (*lea*), i.e., smaller meadow] a masculine or feminine name

Le·sot·ho (le sut′hō, -sō′thō) country in SE Africa, surrounded by South Africa: a member of the Commonwealth: 11,716 sq. mi.; pop. 997,000

less (les) ***adj.*** *alt. compar. of* LITTLE [OE. *læs, læssa*] not so much, so many, so great, etc.; smaller; fewer —***adv.*** *compar. of* LITTLE not so much; to a smaller extent —***n.*** a smaller amount —***prep.*** minus *[$5,000 less taxes]* —**less and less** decreasingly —**no less a person than** a person of no lower importance, rank, etc. than

-less (lis, ləs) [OE. *-leas* < *leas*, free] *a suffix meaning:* **1.** without, lacking *[valueless]* **2.** that does not *[tireless]* **3.** that cannot be *[dauntless]*

les·see (les ē′) ***n.*** [see LEASE] a person to whom property is leased; tenant

less·en (les′'n) ***vt.*** **1.** to make less; decrease **2.** [Archaic] to disparage —***vi.*** to become less

less·er (les′ər) ***adj.*** *alt. compar. of* LITTLE [LESS + -ER] smaller, less, or less important —***adv.*** less

Lesser Antilles group of islands in the West Indies, southeast of Puerto Rico, including the Leeward Islands & the Windward Islands

lesser panda a reddish, raccoonlike mammal of the Himalayan region

les·son (les′'n) ***n.*** [< OFr. *leçon* < L. < pp. of *legere*, to read] **1.** something to be learned; specif., *a)* an exercise that a student is to prepare or learn *b)* something that needs to be learned for one's safety, etc. *c)* [*pl.*] course of instruction *[music lessons]* **2.** a selection from the Bible, read as part of a church service **3.** a rebuke; reproof

les·sor (les′ôr, les ôr′) ***n.*** [Anglo-Fr. < *lesser:* see LEASE] one who gives a lease; landlord

lest (lest) ***conj.*** [< OE. < *thy læs the*, lit., by the less that] **1.** for fear that; in case *[speak low lest you be overheard]* **2.** that: used after expressions denoting fear *[afraid lest he should fall]*

Les·ter (les′tər) [< LEICESTER] a masculine name

let[1] (let) ***vt.*** **let** or obs. **let′ted, let′ting** [OE. *lætan*, to leave behind] **1.** to leave; abandon: now only in **let alone** (or **let be**), to refrain from bothering, etc. **2.** *a)* to rent; hire out *b)* to assign (a contract) **3.** to allow or cause to escape *[to let blood]* **4.** to allow to pass, come, or go *[let me in]* **5.** to allow; permit *[let me help]* **6.** to cause to: usually with *know* or *hear [let me hear from you]* **7.** to suppose; assume When used in commands, suggestions, or dares, *let* serves as an auxiliary *[let us go]* —***vi.*** to be rented or leased *[house to let]* —**let down** **1.** to lower **2.** to slow up **3.** to disappoint —**let off** **1.** to give forth (steam, etc.) **2.** to deal leniently with —**let on** [Colloq.] **1.** to indicate one's awareness of a fact **2.** to pretend —**let out** **1.** to release **2.** to rent out **3.** to reveal (a secret, etc.) **4.** to make a garment larger by reducing (the hem, etc.) **5.** to dismiss or be dismissed, as school —**let up** **1.** to relax **2.** to cease

let[2] (let) ***vt.*** **let′ted** or **let, let′ting** [OE. *lettan*, lit., to make late] [Archaic] to hinder; obstruct —***n.*** **1.** an obstacle or impediment: used in **without let or hindrance** **2.** in tennis, etc., an interference with the course of the ball in some specific way, making it necessary to play the point over again

-let (lit, lət) [< MFr. *-el* (< L. *-ellus*) + *-et*, both dim. suffixes] *a suffix meaning:* **1.** small *[ringlet]* **2.** a small object worn as a band on *[anklet]*

let·down (let′doun′) ***n.*** **1.** a slowing up or feeling of dejection, as after great excitement, effort, etc. **2.** a disappointment or disillusionment

le·thal (lē′thəl) ***adj.*** [L. *let(h)alis* < *letum*, death] **1.** causing or capable of causing death; fatal or deadly **2.** of or suggestive of death —**le·thal′i·ty** (-thal′ə tē) ***n.*** —**le′thal·ly** ***adv.***

le·thar·gic (li thär′jik) ***adj.*** **1.** of or producing lethargy **2.** abnormally drowsy or dull, sluggish, etc. —**le·thar′gi·cal·ly** ***adv.***

leth·ar·gize (leth′ər jīz′) ***vt.*** **-gized′, -giz′ing** to make lethargic

leth·ar·gy (leth′ər jē) ***n., pl.*** **-gies** [< OFr. < LL. < Gr. < *lēthargos*, forgetful < *lēthē* (see ff.) + *argos*, idle < *a-*, not + *ergon*, work] **1.** a condition of abnormal drowsiness or torpor **2.** a great lack of energy; sluggishness, apathy, etc.

Le·the (lē′thē) [L. < Gr. *lēthē*, oblivion] *Gr. & Rom. Myth.* the river of forgetfulness, in Hades, whose water produced loss of memory in those who drank of it —***n.*** oblivion; forgetfulness —**Le·the·an** (lē thē′ən) ***adj.***

let's (lets) let us

Lett (let) ***n.*** **1.** a member of a people living in Latvia and adjacent Baltic regions **2.** *same as* LETTISH

let·ter (let′ər) ***n.*** [< OFr. < L. *littera*] **1.** any of the characters of the alphabet, theoretically representing a speech sound **2.** a written or printed message, usually sent by mail **3.** [*usually pl.*] an official document authorizing someone or something **4.** [*pl.*] *a)* literature generally *b)* learning; knowledge **5.** literal meaning; exact wording **6.** the first letter of the name of a school or college, awarded and worn for superior performance in sports, etc. —***vt.*** **1.** to mark with letters *[to letter a poster]* **2.** to set down in hand-printed letters —***vi.*** **1.** to make hand-printed letters **2.** [Colloq.] to earn a school letter —**to the letter** just as written or directed —**let′ter·er** ***n.***

letter carrier *same as* MAIL CARRIER

let·tered (let′ərd) ***adj.*** **1.** able to read and write **2.** very well educated **3.** inscribed with letters

let·ter·head (let′ər hed′) ***n.*** **1.** the name, address, etc. of a person or firm printed as a heading on sheets of letter paper **2.** such a sheet

let·ter·ing (-iŋ) ***n.*** **1.** the process of putting letters on something by inscribing, printing, etc. **2.** the letters so made

let·ter·man (-man′) ***n., pl.*** **-men′** (-men′) a student who has won a school letter

letter of credit a letter from a bank asking that the holder of the letter be allowed to draw specified sums of money from other banks or agencies

let·ter-per·fect (-pur′fikt) ***adj.*** **1.** correct in every respect **2.** knowing one's lesson, theatrical role, etc. perfectly

let·ter·press (-pres′) ***n.*** **1.** *a)* the method of printing from raised surfaces, as set type *b)* matter printed by this method **2.** [Chiefly Brit.] reading matter, as distinguished from illustrations

letters (or **letter**) **of marque** formerly, a government document authorizing an individual to arm a ship and capture enemy merchant ships: also **letters** (or **letter**) **of marque and reprisal**

letters patent a document granting a patent

Let·tish (let′ish) ***adj.*** of the Letts or their language —***n.*** the Baltic language of the Letts; Latvian

let·tuce (let′is) ***n.*** [< OFr. < L. *lactuca* < *lac*, milk: from its milky juice] **1.** a hardy, annual composite plant, grown for its crisp, succulent, green leaves **2.** the leaves, much used for salads **3.** [Slang] paper money

let·up (let′up′) ***n.*** [< phr. *let up*] [Colloq.] **1.** a slackening or lessening **2.** a stop or pause

le·u (le′oo) ***n., pl.*** **lei** (lā) [Romanian < L. *leo*, lion] *see* MONETARY UNITS, table (Romania)

leu·ke·mi·a (lōō kē′mē ə) ***n.*** [ModL.: see ff. + -EMIA] any of a group of diseases of the blood-forming organs, resulting in an abnormal increase in the production of leukocytes: also sp. **leu·kae′mi·a** —**leu·ke′mic** (-mik) ***adj.*** —**leu·ke′moid** (-moid) ***adj.***

leu·ko- [< Gr. *leukos*, white] *a combining form meaning* white or colorless: also, before a vowel, **leuk-**

leu·ko·cyte (lōō′kə sīt′) ***n.*** [see prec. & -CYTE] any of the small, colorless cells in the blood, lymph, and tissues, which are important in the body's defenses against infection; white blood corpuscle —**leu′ko·cyt′ic** (-sit′ik) ***adj.***

lev (lef) ***n., pl.*** **le·va** (le′və) [Bulg., ult. < Gr. *leōn*, lion] *see* MONETARY UNITS, table (Bulgaria)

Lev. Leviticus

Le·vant (lə vant′) [< Fr. < It. *levante* (< L. prp. of *levare,* to raise), applied to the East, where the sun "rises"] region on the E Mediterranean, including all countries bordering the sea between Greece & Egypt —*n.* [l-] *same as* LEVANT MOROCCO —**Lev·an·tine** (lev′ən tīn′, -tēn′; lə van′-tin) *adj., n.*

Levant morocco a fine morocco leather with a large, irregular grain, used esp. in bookbinding

le·va·tor (lə vāt′ər) *n., pl.* **lev·a·to·res** (lev′ə tôr′ēz), **le·va′tors** [ModL. < pp. of L. *levare,* to raise] a muscle that raises a limb or other part of the body

lev·ee[1] (lev′ē) *n.* [< Fr. pp. of *lever,* to raise < L. *levare*] **1.** an embankment built alongside a river to prevent high water from flooding bordering land **2.** a quay **3.** a low ridge of earth around a field to be irrigated —*vt.* **lev′eed, lev′ee·ing** to build a levee along

lev·ee[2] (lev′ē; lə vē′, -vā′) *n.* [< Fr. < *se lever,* to rise: see prec.] formerly, a morning reception held by a sovereign or person of high rank upon arising

lev·el (lev′'l) *n.* [< OFr. < L. *libella,* dim. of *libra,* a balance] **1.** an instrument for determining whether a surface is evenly horizontal **2.** *a*) a horizontal plane or line; esp., such a plane as a basis for measuring elevation [sea *level*] *b*) the height of such a plane **3.** a horizontal area **4.** the same horizontal plane [the seats are on a *level*] **5.** normal position or proper place [water seeks its *level*] **6.** position, rank, degree of concentration, etc. in a scale of values [*levels* of income] —*adj.* **1.** perfectly flat and even **2.** not sloping **3.** even in height (*with*) **4.** even with the top of the container [a *level* teaspoonful] **5.** *a*) equal in importance, rank, degree, etc. *b*) conforming to a specified level [high-*level* talks] *c*) equally advanced in development *d*) uniform in tone, color, pitch, volume, rate, etc. **6.** *a*) well-balanced; equable *b*) calm or steady **7.** [Slang] honest —*vt.* **-eled** or **-elled, -el·ing** or **-el·ling 1.** to make level, even, flat, equal (as in rank), etc. **2.** to knock to the ground; demolish **3.** to raise (a gun, etc.) for firing **4.** to aim or direct —*vi.* **1.** to aim a gun, etc. (*at*) **2.** to bring people or things to an equal rank, condition, etc. (usually with *down* or *up*) **3.** [Slang] to be frank (*with* someone) —**level off 1.** to give a flat, horizontal surface to **2.** *Aeron.* to come or bring to a horizontal line of flight: also **level out 3.** to become stable or constant —**one's level best** [Colloq.] the best one can do —**on the level** [Slang] honest(ly) and fair(ly) —**lev′el·er, lev′el·ler** *n.* —**lev′el·ly** *adv.* —**lev′el·ness** *n.*

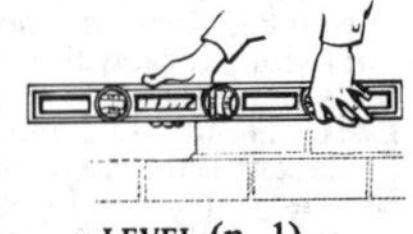
LEVEL (n. 1)

lev·el·head·ed (-hed′id) *adj.* having or showing an even temper and sound judgment —**lev′el·head′ed·ly** *adv.* —**lev′el·head′ed·ness** *n.*

lev·er (lev′ər, lē′vər) *n.* [< OFr. < *lever,* to raise < L. *levare* < *levis,* LIGHT[2]] **1.** a bar used as a pry **2.** a means to an end **3.** *Mech.* a device consisting of a bar turning about a fixed point, the fulcrum, using power or force applied at a second point to lift or sustain a weight at a third point; hence, any handle, etc. used to operate something —*vt.* to move, lift, etc. with a lever —*vi.* to use a lever

LEVERS

lev·er·age (-ij) *n.* **1.** the action of a lever **2.** the mechanical power resulting from this **3.** increased means of accomplishing some purpose

lev·er·et (lev′ər it) *n.* [< MFr. dim. of *levre* < L. *lepus,* hare] a hare during its first year

Le·vi (lē′vī) *Bible* the third son of Jacob and Leah: see also LEVITE

le·vi·a·than (lə vī′ə thən) *n.* [LL. < Heb. *liwyāthān*] **1.** *Bible* a sea monster, thought of as a reptile or a whale **2.** anything huge or very powerful

lev·i·er (lev′ē ər) *n.* one who levies taxes, etc.

Le·vi's (lē′vīz) [after *Levi* Strauss, the U.S. maker] *a trademark for* closefitting trousers of heavy denim, reinforced at the seams, etc. with small copper rivets —*n.pl.* such trousers: usually written **le′vis**

lev·i·tate (lev′ə tāt′) *vt.* **-tat′ed, -tat′ing** [< L. *levis,* LIGHT[2] by analogy with GRAVITATE] to cause to rise and float in the air —*vi.* to rise and float in the air

lev·i·ta·tion (lev′ə tā′shən) *n.* **1.** a levitating or being levitated **2.** the illusion of raising and keeping a heavy body in the air with little or no support

Le·vite (lē′vīt) *n.* *Bible* any member of the tribe of Levi, chosen to assist the priests in the Temple

Le·vit·i·cal (lə vit′i k'l) *adj.* **1.** of the Levites **2.** of Leviticus or its laws

Le·vit·i·cus (-kəs) the third book of the Bible, containing the laws relating to priests and Levites

lev·i·ty (lev′ə tē) *n., pl.* **-ties** [< OFr. < L. *levitas* < *levis,* LIGHT[2]] **1.** [Rare] buoyancy **2.** lightness of disposition, conduct, etc.; esp., improper gaiety; frivolity **3.** fickleness

lev·u·lose (lev′yoo lōs′) *n.* *same as* FRUCTOSE

lev·y (lev′ē) *n., pl.* **lev′ies** [< MFr. fem. pp. of *lever:* see LEVER] **1.** an imposing and collecting of a tax, fine, etc. **2.** the amount levied **3.** *a*) the enlistment, usually compulsory, of personnel, as for military service *b*) a group so enlisted —*vt.* **lev′ied, lev′y·ing 1.** to impose or collect (a tax, fine, etc.) **2.** to enlist (troops) for military service, usually by force **3.** to wage (war) —*vi.* **1.** to make a levy **2.** *Law* to seize property to satisfy a judgment

lewd (lo͞od) *adj.* [OE. *lǣwede,* lay, unlearned] showing, or intended to excite, lust or sexual desire, esp. in an offensive way —**lewd′ly** *adv.* —**lewd′ness** *n.*

Lew·is (lo͞o′is) **1.** [see LOUIS] a masculine name: dim. *Lew* **2. John L(lewellyn),** 1880–1969; U.S. labor leader **3. Mer·i·weth·er** (mer′ē weth′ər), 1774–1809; Am. explorer, with William Clark, of the Northwest **4. Sinclair,** 1885–1951; U.S. novelist

lew·is·ite (lo͞o′ə sīt′) *n.* [after W.L. *Lewis* (1878–1943), U.S. chemist] a pale-yellow, odorless, arsenical compound, $ClCH\text{-}CHAsCl_2$, used as a blistering poison gas

‡**lex** (leks) *n., pl.* **le·ges** (lē′jēz, lā′gās) [L.] law

lex·i·cog·ra·pher (lek′sə käg′rə fər) *n.* [< LGr. < Gr. *lexikon,* LEXICON + *graphein,* to write] a person who writes or compiles a dictionary

lex·i·cog·ra·phy (-fē) *n.* [see prec.] the act, art, or work of writing or compiling a dictionary —**lex·i·co·graph·ic** (lek′si kə graf′ik), **lex′i·co·graph′i·cal** *adj.*

lex·i·con (lek′si kən, -kän′) *n.* [Gr. *lexikon* < *lexis,* a word < *legein,* to say] **1.** a dictionary, esp. of an ancient language **2.** the special vocabulary of a particular author, field of study, etc.

Lex·ing·ton (lek′siŋ tən) **1.** [after ff.] city in NC Ky.: coextensive with Fayette county with which it constitutes a metropolitan government **(Lexington-Fayette)**: pop. 204,000 **2.** [after the 2d Baron of *Lexington* (1661–1723)] suburb of Boston, in E Mass.: with Concord, site of one of the 1st battles of the Revolutionary War: pop. 29,000

Ley·den jar (or **vial**) (līd′'n) [< LEIDEN, where invented] a condenser for static electricity, consisting of a glass jar with a coat of tinfoil outside and inside and a metallic rod connecting with the inner lining and passing through the lid

Ley·te (lāt′ē) island of the EC Philippines, between Luzon & Mindanao

LF, L.F., lf, l.f. low frequency

lf., lf 1. *Baseball* left field (or fielder) **2.** lightface

LG., L.G. Low German

LGr., L.Gr. Late Greek

l.h., L.H., LH left hand

Lha·sa (lä′sə) capital of Tibet: pop. 70,000

Li *Chem.* lithium

L.I. Long Island

li·a·bil·i·ty (lī′ə bil′ə tē) *n., pl.* **-ties 1.** the state of being liable **2.** anything for which a person is liable **3.** [*pl.*] *Accounting* all the entries on a balance sheet showing the debts of a person or business, as accounts and notes payable **4.** something that works to one's disadvantage

li·a·ble (lī′ə b'l; *also, esp. for 3,* lī′b'l) *adj.* [prob. via Anglo-Fr. < OFr. *lier* < L. *ligare,* to bind] **1.** legally bound, as to make good a loss; responsible **2.** likely to have, suffer from, etc.; subject to [*liable* to heart attacks] **3.** likely (*to* do, have, get, etc. something unpleasant or unwanted) [*liable* to cause hard feelings]

li·ai·son (lē′ə zän′, -zōn′; lē ā′zän; *occas.* lā′ə zän′; *for 3,* lē′ə zōn′; *Fr.* lye zōn′) *n.* [Fr. < OFr. < L. < *ligare,* to bind] **1.** a connecting of the parts of a whole, as of military units, in order to bring about proper coordination of activities **2.** an illicit love affair **3.** in spoken French, the linking of words by pronouncing the final consonant of one word as though it were the initial consonant of the following word, as in the phrase *chez elle* (pronounced shā zel′)

li·a·na (lē än′ə, -an′ə) *n.* [NormFr. *liane,* ult. < L. *viburnum,* wayfaring tree] any luxuriantly growing, woody, tropical vine that roots in the ground and climbs, as around tree trunks: also **li·ane′** (-än′, -an′)

li·ar (lī′ər) *n.* a person who tells lies

lib (lib) *n.* *clipped form of* LIBERATION

lib. 1. [L. *liber*] book **2.** librarian **3.** library

li·ba·tion (lī bā′shən) *n.* [< L. *libatio* < *libare,* to pour out] **1.** the ritual of pouring out wine or oil upon the ground as a sacrifice to a god **2.** the liquid so poured out **3.** an alcoholic drink: used humorously —**li·ba′tion·al** *adj.*

li·bel (lī′b'l) *n.* [OFr. < L. *libellus,* dim. of *liber,* a book] **1.** any false and malicious written or printed statement, or any sign, picture, etc., tending to injure a person's reputation unjustly **2.** the act of publishing such a thing **3.** anything that gives an unflattering or damaging picture of the subject it is dealing with —*vt.* **-beled** or **-belled, -bel·ing** or **-bel·ling 1.** to publish or make a libel against **2.** to give an unflattering or damaging picture of —**li′bel·er, li′bel·ler** *n.*

li·bel·ous, li·bel·lous (-əs) ***adj.*** **1.** of or involving a libel **2.** given to writing and publishing libels; defamatory —**li′bel·ous·ly, li′bel·lous·ly** ***adv.***
lib·er·al (lib′ər əl, lib′rəl) ***adj.*** [OFr. < L. *liberalis* < *liber,* free] **1.** orig., suitable for a freeman; not restricted: now only in LIBERAL ARTS, LIBERAL EDUCATION, etc. **2.** giving freely; generous **3.** ample; abundant *[a liberal reward]* **4.** not restricted to the literal meaning *[a liberal interpretation of the Bible]* **5.** broad-minded **6.** favoring reform or progress, as in religion, education, etc.; specif., favoring political reforms tending toward democracy **7.** [L-] designating or of a political party upholding liberal principles, as in England or Canada —***n.*** **1.** a person favoring liberalism **2.** [L-] a member of a liberal political party —**lib′er·al·ly** ***adv.*** —**lib′er·al·ness** ***n.***
liberal arts the subjects of an academic college course, including literature, philosophy, languages, history, etc., as distinguished from professional or technical subjects
liberal education an education mainly in the liberal arts, providing a broad cultural background
lib·er·al·ism (-iz′m) ***n.*** the quality or state of being liberal, esp. in politics or religion
lib·er·al·i·ty (lib′ə ral′ə tē) ***n., pl.*** **-ties** the quality or state of being liberal; specif., *a)* generosity *b)* tolerance; broad-mindedness
lib·er·al·ize (lib′ər ə līz′, lib′rə-) ***vt., vi.*** **-ized′, -iz′ing** to make or become liberal —**lib′er·al·i·za′tion** ***n.*** —**lib′er·al·iz′er** ***n.***
lib·er·ate (lib′ə rāt′) ***vt.*** **-at′ed, -at′ing** [< L. pp. of *liberare,* to free < *liber,* free] **1.** to release from slavery, enemy occupation, etc. **2.** [Slang] to steal or loot, esp. from a defeated enemy in wartime **3.** *Chem.* to free from combination in a compound —**lib′er·a′tion** ***n.*** —**lib′er·a′tor** ***n.***
Li·ber·i·a (lī bir′ē ə) country on the W coast of Africa: founded by freed slaves from the U.S.: 43,000 sq. mi.; pop. 1,200,000; cap. Monrovia —**Li·ber′i·an** ***adj., n.***
lib·er·tar·i·an (lib′ər ter′ē ən) ***n.*** a person who advocates full civil liberties —***adj.*** of or upholding such liberties —**lib′er·tar′i·an·ism** ***n.***
lib·er·tine (lib′ər tēn′, -tin) ***n.*** [< L. < *libertus,* freedman < *liber,* free] a man who leads an unrestrained, sexually immoral life; rake —***adj.*** licentious —**lib′er·tin·ism, lib′er·tin·age** ***n.***
lib·er·ty (lib′ər tē) ***n., pl.*** **-ties** [< OFr. < L. *libertas* < *liber,* free] **1.** freedom from slavery, captivity, or any other form of arbitrary control **2.** the sum of rights possessed in common by the people of a community, state, etc.: see also CIVIL LIBERTIES **3.** a particular right, franchise, freedom, etc. **4.** a too free, too familiar, or impertinent action or attitude **5.** the limits within which a certain amount of freedom may be exercised *[to have the liberty of the third floor]* **6.** *U.S. Navy* permission given to an enlisted person to be absent from duty for a period of 72 hours or less **7.** *Philos.* freedom to choose —**at liberty 1.** not confined; free **2.** allowed (to do or say something) **3.** not busy or in use —**take liberties 1.** to be too familiar or impertinent in action or speech **2.** to deal (*with* facts, etc.) in a distorting way
Liberty Bell the bell of Independence Hall in Philadelphia, rung on July 8, 1776, to proclaim the independence of the U.S.
li·bid·i·nous (li bid′'n əs) ***adj.*** [see ff.] full of or characterized by lust; lewd; lascivious —**li·bid′i·nous·ly** ***adv.*** —**li·bid′i·nous·ness** ***n.***
li·bi·do (li bē′dō, -bī′-) ***n.*** [L., desire, wantonness < *libet,* it pleases] **1.** the sexual urge or instinct **2.** *Psychoanalysis* energy of the psyche associated with the positive, loving instincts —**li·bid′i·nal** (-bid′'n əl) ***adj.*** —**li·bid′i·nal·ly** ***adv.***
Li·bra (lī′brə, lē′-) [L., a balance] **1.** a S constellation between Virgo and Scorpio **2.** the seventh sign of the zodiac: see ZODIAC, illus.
li·bra (lī′brə) ***n., pl.*** **-brae** (-brē) [L.] pound
li·brar·i·an (lī brer′ē ən) ***n.*** **1.** a person in charge of a library **2.** a library worker trained in library science —**li·brar′i·an·ship′** ***n.***
li·brar·y (lī′brer′ē, -brə rē) ***n., pl.*** **-brar′ies** [< OFr. < *libraire,* copyist < L. < *liber,* a book] **1.** a room or building where a collection of books, periodicals, etc. is kept for reading or reference **2.** a public or private institution in charge of the care and circulation of such a collection **3.** a collection of books, periodicals, etc.
library science the study of library organization and management
li·bret·tist (li bret′ist) ***n.*** a writer of librettos
li·bret·to (li bret′ō) ***n., pl.*** **-tos, -ti** (-ē) [It., dim. of *libro,* a book < L. *liber*] **1.** the words, or text, of an opera, oratorio, etc. **2.** a book containing these words
Lib·ri·um (lib′rē əm) *a trademark for* a tranquilizing drug
Lib·y·a (lib′ē ə) **1.** ancient Greek & Roman name of N Africa, west of Egypt **2.** country in N Africa, on the Mediterranean: 679,359 sq. mi.; pop. 1,869,000; caps. Benghazi & Tripoli —**Lib′y·an** ***adj., n.***
lice (līs) ***n.*** *pl. of* LOUSE
li·cense (līs′'ns) ***n.*** [< OFr. < L. *licentia* < prp. of *licere,* to be permitted] **1.** formal or legal permission to do something specified *[license to marry, hunt, etc.]* **2.** a document, tag, etc. indicating that such permission has been granted **3.** *a)* freedom to deviate from strict conduct, rule, or practice *[poetic license]* *b)* an instance of this **4.** excessive, undisciplined freedom, constituting an abuse of liberty Also, Brit. sp., **licence** —***vt.*** **-censed, -cens·ing** to give license or a license to or for; permit formally —**li′cens·a·ble** ***adj.***
li·cen·see (līs′'n sē′) ***n.*** a person to whom a license is granted
li·cens·er (līs′'n sər) ***n.*** a person with authority to grant licenses: also sp., *Law,* **li′cen·sor**
li·cen·ti·ate (lī sen′shē it, -āt′) ***n.*** **1.** a person licensed to practice a specified profession **2.** in certain European and Canadian universities, an academic degree between that of bachelor and that of doctor —**li·cen′ti·ate·ship′** ***n.***
li·cen·tious (lī sen′shəs) ***adj.*** [< L. < *licentia:* see LICENSE] **1.** [Rare] disregarding accepted rules and standards **2.** morally unrestrained, esp. in sexual activity; lascivious —**li·cen′tious·ly** ***adv.*** —**li·cen′tious·ness** ***n.***
li·chee (lē′chē′) ***n.*** *same as* LITCHI
li·chen (lī′kən) ***n.*** [L. < Gr., prob. < *leichein,* to lick] any of a large group of small plants composed of a fungus and an alga growing in close association to form a dual plant, commonly adhering in colored patches to rock, wood, soil, etc. —**li′chen·ous, li′chen·ose′** (-ōs′) ***adj.***
licht (likht) ***adj., adv., n., vi., vt.*** *Scot. var. of* LIGHT
lic·it (lis′it) ***adj.*** [< L. pp. of *licere,* to be permitted] permitted; lawful —**lic′it·ly** ***adv.*** —**lic′it·ness** ***n.***
lick (lik) ***vt.*** [OE. *liccian*] **1.** to pass the tongue over *[to lick one's lips]* **2.** to bring into a certain condition by passing the tongue over *[to lick one's fingers clean]* **3.** to pass lightly over like a tongue *[flames licking the logs]* **4.** [Colloq.] *a)* to whip; thrash *b)* to vanquish —***vi.*** to move lightly and quickly, as a flame —***n.*** **1.** the act of licking with the tongue **2.** a small quantity; bit **3.** *short for* SALT LICK **4.** [Colloq.] *a)* a sharp blow *b)* a short, rapid burst of activity *c)* a fast pace; clip **5.** [Slang] a phrase of jazz music, esp. an interpolated improvisation **6.** [*often pl.*] [Slang] chance; turn *[to get one's licks in]* —**lick and a promise** a hasty, superficial effort —**lick into shape** [Colloq.] to bring into proper condition —**lick one's chops** to anticipate eagerly —**lick up** to consume as by licking
lick·er·ish (lik′ər ish) ***adj.*** [< Anglo-Fr. form of OFr. *lecheros*] [Archaic] **1.** lecherous; lustful; lewd **2.** greedy or eager, esp. to eat or taste
lick·e·ty-split (lik′ə tē split′) ***adv.*** [fanciful formation based on LICK, *n.* 4 *c*] [Colloq.] at great speed
lick·spit·tle (lik′spit′'l) ***n.*** a servile flatterer; toady
lic·o·rice (lik′ər ish, -is; lik′rish) ***n.*** [< OFr. < LL. *liquiritia,* ult. < Gr. *glykys,* sweet + *rhiza,* root] **1.** a European plant of the legume family **2.** its dried root or the black flavoring extract made from this **3.** candy flavored with or as with this extract
lic·tor (lik′tər) ***n.*** [L.] a minor Roman official who carried the fasces and cleared the way for the chief magistrates
lid (lid) ***n.*** [OE. *hlid*] **1.** a movable cover, as for a box, pot, etc. **2.** *short for* EYELID **3.** [Colloq.] a curb or restraint **4.** [Slang] a cap, hat, etc. —**lid′ded** ***adj.*** —**lid′less** ***adj.***
lie[1] (lī) ***vi.*** **lay, lain, ly′ing** [OE. *licgan*] **1.** to be or put oneself in a reclining position along a relatively horizontal surface (often with *down*) **2.** to rest on a support in a more or less horizontal position: said of inanimate things **3.** to be or remain in a specified condition *[motives that lie hidden]* **4.** to be situated *[Canada lies to the north]* **5.** to extend *[the road that lies before us]* **6.** to be; exist *[the love that lies in her eyes]* **7.** to be buried or entombed **8.** [Archaic] to stay overnight or for a short while **9.** [Archaic] to have sexual intercourse (*with*) —***n.*** **1.** the way in which something is situated or arranged; lay **2.** an animal's lair —**lie down on the job** [Colloq.] to put forth less than one's best efforts —**lie in** to be in confinement for childbirth —**lie off** *Naut.* to stay at a distance from shore or another ship —**lie over** to stay and wait until some future time —**lie to** *Naut.* to lie stationary with the head to the wind: said of a ship —**li′er** ***n.***
lie[2] (lī) ***vi.*** **lied, ly′ing** [OE. *leogan*] **1.** to make a statement or statements that one knows to be false, esp. with intent to

deceive **2.** to give a false impression —***vt.*** to bring, put, accomplish, etc. by lying *[*to *lie* oneself into office*]* —***n.*** **1.** a thing said or done in lying; falsehood **2.** anything that gives or is meant to give a false impression —**give the lie to 1.** to charge with telling a lie **2.** to prove to be false

Liech·ten·stein (lēH′tən shtīn′) country in WC Europe, on the Rhine: 61 sq. mi.; pop. 21,000

lied (lēd; *G.* lēt) ***n., pl.*** **lied′er** (lē′dər; *G.* -dər) **[G.]** a German song, esp. one of a lyrical, often popular, character

Lie·der·kranz (lē′dər krants′) [G., lit., garland of songs] *a trademark for* a soft cheese having a strong odor and flavor

lie detector a polygraph used on persons suspected of lying to record the physiological changes assumed to occur when the subject lies in answering questions

lief (lēf) ***adj.*** **[**OE. *leof***]** [Archaic or Obs.] **1.** dear; beloved **2.** willing —***adv.*** willingly; gladly: only in **would** (or **had**) **as lief,** etc.

Li·ège (lē āzh′; *Fr.* lyezh) city in E Belgium, on the Meuse: pop. 152,000

liege (lēj) ***adj.*** **[**< OFr., prob. < Frank. base but infl. by L. *ligare,* to bind**]** **1.** *Feudal Law a)* entitled to the service and allegiance of his vassals *[*a *liege* lord*]* *b)* bound to give service and allegiance to the lord *[liege* subjects*]* **2.** loyal; faithful —***n.*** *Feudal Law* **1.** a lord or sovereign **2.** a subject or vassal

liege·man (-mən) ***n., pl.*** **-men 1.** a vassal **2.** a loyal follower Also **liege man**

li·en (lēn, lē′ən) ***n.*** **[**Fr. < L. *ligamen,* a band < *ligare,* to bind**]** *Law* a claim on the property of another as security for the payment of a debt

lieu (lo͞o) ***n.*** **[**OFr. < L. *locus,* place**]** place: now chiefly in **in lieu of,** in place of; instead of

lieu·ten·ant (lo͞o ten′ənt; *Brit. & Canad. army* lef ten′-) ***n.*** **[**< MFr. < *lieu,* place + *tenant,* holding < L. *tenere,* to hold**]** **1.** one who acts for a superior, as during the latter's absence **2.** an officer ranking below a captain, as in a police department **3.** *U.S. Mil.* an officer ranking below a captain: see also FIRST LIEUTENANT, SECOND LIEUTENANT **4.** *U.S. Navy* an officer ranking just above a lieutenant junior grade Abbrev. **Lieut., Lt.** —**lieu·ten′an·cy** (-ən sē) ***n., pl.*** **-cies**

lieutenant colonel *U.S. Mil.* an officer ranking above a major

lieutenant commander *U.S. Navy* an officer ranking above a lieutenant

lieutenant general *U.S. Mil.* an officer ranking above a major general

lieutenant governor 1. an elected official of a State who ranks below and substitutes for the governor in case of the latter's absence or death **2.** the official head of government of a Canadian province, appointed by the governor general: also **lieu·ten′ant-gov′er·nor *n.***

lieutenant junior grade *U.S. Navy* an officer ranking above an ensign

life (līf) ***n., pl.*** **lives** **[**OE. *lif***]** **1.** that property of plants and animals (ending at death and distinguishing them from inorganic matter) which makes it possible for them to take in food, get energy from it, grow, etc. **2.** the state of possessing this property *[*brought back to *life]* **3.** a living being, esp. a human being *[*the *lives* lost in wars*]* **4.** living things collectively *[*plant *life]* **5.** the time a person or thing is alive, or a specific portion of such time *[*his early *life]* **6.** a sentence of imprisonment for the rest of one's life **7.** one's manner of living *[*a *life* of ease*]* **8.** the people and activities of a given time, or in a given setting or class *[*military *life,* low *life]* **9.** human existence and activity *[*to learn from *life]* **10.** *a)* an individual's lifetime experiences *b)* an account of this **11.** the existence of the soul *[*eternal *life]* **12.** something essential to the continued existence of something else *[*freedom of speech is the *life* of democracy*]* **13.** the source of vigor or liveliness *[*the *life* of the party*]* **14.** vigor; liveliness **15.** the period of flourishing, usefulness, functioning, etc. *[*fads have a short *life]* **16.** representation in art from living models *[*a class in *life]* **17.** [Colloq.] another chance *[*to get a *life]* —***adj.*** of, in, or for life —**as large** (or **big**) **as life 1.** life-size **2.** in actual fact —**for dear life** with a desperate intensity —**for life 1.** for the duration of one's life **2.** in order to save one's life —**from life** from a living model —**see life** to have a wide variety of experiences —**take life** to kill —**take one's (own) life** to commit suicide —**to the life** like the living original; exactly —**true to life** true to reality

life belt a life preserver in the form of a belt

life·blood (-blud′) ***n.*** **1.** the blood necessary to life **2.** a vital element or animating influence

life·boat (-bōt′) ***n.*** any of the small boats carried by a ship for use if the ship must be abandoned

life buoy *same as* LIFE PRESERVER

life expectancy the number of years that an individual of a given age may expect on the average to live, as projected in statistical tables

life-giv·ing (-giv′iŋ) ***adj.*** **1.** that gives or can give life **2.** refreshing —**life′-giv′er *n.***

life·guard (-gärd′) ***n.*** an expert swimmer employed at a beach, a pool, etc. to prevent drownings

life insurance insurance in which a stipulated sum is paid to the beneficiary or beneficiaries at the death of the insured, or to the insured when he reaches a specified age

life jacket (or **vest**) a life preserver in the form of a sleeveless jacket or vest

life·less (-lis) ***adj.*** **1.** without life; specif., *a)* inanimate *b)* dead **2.** dull; listless —**life′less·ly *adv.*** —**life′less·ness *n.***

life·like (-līk′) ***adj.*** **1.** resembling actual life **2.** closely resembling a real person or thing

life·line (-līn′) ***n.*** **1.** a rope for saving life, as one thrown to a person in the water **2.** the rope used to raise or lower a diver **3.** a commercial route or transport line of vital importance

life·long (-lôŋ′) ***adj.*** lasting or not changing during one's whole life *[*a *lifelong* love*]*

life net a strong net used by firemen, etc. as to catch people jumping from a burning building

life preserver a buoyant device for saving a person from drowning by keeping his body afloat, as a ring or sleeveless jacket of canvas-covered cork

LIFE PRESERVER

lif·er (līf′ər) ***n.*** [Slang] a person sentenced to imprisonment for life

life raft a small, inflatable raft or boat

life·sav·er (-sā′vər) ***n.*** **1.** a person or thing that saves people from drowning, as a lifeguard **2.** [Colloq.] a person or thing that is of great timely help —**life′sav′ing *adj., n.***

life-size (-sīz′) ***adj.*** of the same size as the person or thing represented: said of a picture, sculpture, etc.: also **life′-sized′**

life span 1. *same as* LIFETIME **2.** the longest period of time that a typical individual can be expected to live

life style one's way of life as typified by one's activities, attitudes, possessions, etc.

life·time (-tīm′) ***n.*** the length of time that someone lives, or that something lasts, functions, etc. —***adj.*** lasting for such a period *[*a *lifetime* job*]*

life·work (-wurk′) ***n.*** the work or task to which a person devotes his life; chief work in life

lift (lift) ***vt.*** **[**< ON. *lypta* < *lopt,* air**]** **1.** to bring up to a higher position; raise **2.** to pick up and move or set *[lift* the box down from the shelf*]* **3.** to hold up **4.** to raise in rank, condition, spirits, etc.; elevate; exalt **5.** to pay off (a mortgage, debt, etc.) **6.** to end (a blockade, siege, etc.) by withdrawing forces **7.** to revoke or rescind (a ban or order) **8.** to subject to FACE LIFTING **9.** [Colloq.] to plagiarize *[*to *lift* a passage from another writer*]* —***vi.*** **1.** to exert strength in raising or trying to raise something **2.** to rise and vanish; be dispelled *[*the fog *lifted]* **3.** to become raised; go up —***n.*** **1.** a lifting, raising, or rising **2.** the amount lifted **3.** the distance through which something is lifted **4.** lifting force, power, or influence **5.** elevation of spirits or mood **6.** elevated position or carriage, as of the neck, head, etc. **7.** a ride in the direction one is going **8.** help of any kind **9.** a rise in the ground **10.** the means by which something is lifted; specif., *a)* any layer of leather in the heel of a shoe *b)* [Brit.] an elevator *c)* a device used to transport people up or down a slope —**lift′er *n.***

lift·off (-ôf′) ***n.*** the vertical thrust and rise of a spacecraft, missile, etc. as it is launched

lig·a·ment (lig′ə mənt) ***n.*** **[**< L. < *ligare,* to bind**]** **1.** a bond or tie **2.** *Anat.* a band of tough tissue connecting bones or holding organs in place

li·gate (lī′gāt) ***vt.*** **-gat·ed, -gat·ing** to tie with a ligature, as a bleeding artery —**li·ga′tion *n.***

lig·a·ture (lig′ə chər) ***n.*** **[**< MFr. < LL. < pp. of L. *ligare,* to bind**]** **1.** a tying or binding together **2.** a thing used for this; tie, bond, etc. **3.** a written or printed character containing two or more letters united, as æ, *fl, th* **4.** *Music a)* a curved line indicating a slur *b)* the notes slurred **5.** *Surgery* a thread or wire used to tie up an artery, etc. —***vt.*** **-tured, -tur·ing** to tie or bind together with a ligature

li·ger (lī′gər) ***n.*** **[**LI(ON) + (TI)GER**]** the offspring of a male lion and a female tiger

light[1] (līt) ***n.*** **[**OE. *leoht***]** **1.** *a)* the form of electromagnetic radiation that acts upon the retina of the eye, optic nerve, etc., making sight possible: the speed of light is 186,000 miles per second *b)* a similar form of radiant energy not acting on the normal retina, as ultraviolet and infrared radiation **2.** the sensation that light stimulates in the organs of sight **3.** brightness; illumination, often of a specified kind **4.** a source of light, as the sun, a lamp, etc. **5.** *same as* TRAFFIC LIGHT **6.** the light from the sun; daylight or dawn **7.** a thing by means of which something can be started burning *[*a *light* for a cigar*]* **8.** the means by which light is let in; window **9.** knowledge or information; enlightenment [to shed *light* on the past] **10.** spiritual inspiration **11.** public knowledge or view **12.** the way in which something is seen; aspect [presented in a favorable *light*] **13.** facial expression [a *light* of recognition in his eyes] **14.** an outstanding figure [one of the shining *lights* of the school] —***adj.*** **1.** having light; bright **2.** pale in color; whitish; fair —***adv.*** palely [a *light* blue color] —***vt.*** **light′ed** or **lit, light′ing 1.** to set on fire; ignite [to *light* a bonfire] **2.** to cause to give off light [to *light* a lamp] **3.** to furnish with light [lamps *light* the streets] **4.** to brighten; animate **5.** to show the way to by giving light —***vi.*** **1.** to catch fire **2.** to be lighted; brighten (usually with *up*) —**according to one's lights** as one's opinions, information, or standards may direct —**in the light of** considering —**see the light (of day) 1.** to come into existence **2.** to come into public view **3.** to understand

light[2] (līt) ***adj.*** [OE. *leoht*] **1.** having little weight; not heavy **2.** having little weight for its size **3.** below the usual or defined weight [a *light* coin] **4.** less than usual or normal in amount, extent, force, intensity, etc.; specif., *a*) striking with little force [a *light* blow] *b*) of less than the usual quantity or density [a *light* rain] *c*) not coarse, massive, etc.; graceful [*light* tracery] *d*) soft, muted, or muffled [a *light* sound] *e*) not prolonged or intense [*light* applause] **5.** of little importance; not serious [*light* conversation] **6.** easy to bear; not burdensome [a *light* tax] **7.** easy to do; not difficult [*light* work] **8.** gay; happy; buoyant [*light* spirits] **9.** flighty; frivolous; capricious **10.** loose in morals; wanton **11.** dizzy; giddy **12.** of an amusing or nonserious nature [*light* reading] **13.** containing little alcohol [*light* wine] **14.** *a*) not as full as usual [a *light* meal] *b*) easy to digest **15.** well leavened; soft and spongy [a *light* cake] **16.** loose in consistency; porous [*light* sand] **17.** moving with ease and nimbleness [*light* on one's feet] **18.** carrying little weight **19.** unstressed or slightly stressed: said of syllables **20.** designating or of industry equipped with relatively light machinery and producing small products **21.** designating, of, or equipped with light weapons, armor, etc. —***adv.*** lightly —***vi.*** **light′ed** or **lit, light′ing 1.** [Now Dial.] to dismount; alight **2.** to come to rest after traveling through the air [ducks *lighting* on the pond] **3.** to come or happen (*on* or *upon*) by chance **4.** to strike suddenly, as a blow —**light in the head 1.** dizzy **2.** simple; foolish —**light into** [Colloq.] **1.** to attack **2.** to scold —**light out** [Colloq.] to depart suddenly —**make light of** to treat as unimportant —**light′ish** ***adj.***

light air a wind speed of 1 to 3 miles per hour

light breeze a wind speed of 4 to 7 miles per hour

light·en[1] (-'n) ***vt.*** **1.** to make light; illuminate **2.** to make light or pale —***vi.*** **1.** to become light; grow brighter **2.** to shine brightly; flash **3.** to give off flashes of lightning —**light′en·er** ***n.***

light·en[2] (-'n) ***vt.*** **1.** *a*) to make lighter in weight *b*) to reduce the load of **2.** to make less severe, harsh, etc. **3.** to make more cheerful —***vi.*** **1.** to become lighter in weight **2.** to become more cheerful —**light′en·er** ***n.***

light·er[1] (-ər) ***n.*** a person or thing that lights something or starts it burning

light·er[2] (-ər) ***n.*** [< MDu. < *lichten,* to make light < *licht,* LIGHT[2]] an open barge used to load or unload larger ships lying offshore —***vt., vi.*** to transport in a lighter

light·er·age (-ər ij) ***n.*** **1.** the loading or unloading of a ship by means of a lighter **2.** the charge for this

light·face (līt′fās′) ***n.*** *Printing* type having thin, light lines —***adj.*** having thin, light lines: also **light′faced′**

light-fin·gered (-fiŋ′gərd) ***adj.*** skillful at stealing, esp. by picking pockets

light-foot·ed (-foot′id) ***adj.*** stepping lightly and gracefully: also [Poet.] **light′-foot′** —**light′-foot′ed·ly** ***adv.***

light-hand·ed (-han′did) ***adj.*** **1.** having a light, delicate touch **2.** having little to carry

light·head·ed (-hed′id) ***adj.*** **1.** mentally confused or feeling giddy; dizzy **2.** flighty; frivolous —**light′head′ed·ly** ***adv.*** —**light′head′ed·ness** ***n.***

light·heart·ed (-här′tid) ***adj.*** free from care; gay —**light′heart′ed·ly** ***adv.*** —**light′heart′ed·ness** ***n.***

light heavyweight a boxer or wrestler between a middleweight and heavyweight (in boxing, 161–175 pounds)

light·house (-hous′) ***n.*** a tower located at some place important or dangerous to navigation: it has a very bright light at the top, and often foghorns, sirens, etc., by which ships are guided and warned

light·ing (-iŋ) ***n.*** **1.** a giving light or being lighted; illumination; ignition **2.** the distribution of light and shade, as in a painting **3.** the art or manner of arranging stage lights

light·ly (-lē) ***adv.*** **1.** with little weight or pressure; gently **2.** to a small degree or amount [to spend *lightly*] **3.** nimbly; deftly **4.** cheerfully; merrily **5.** with indifference or neglect **6.** with little or no reason **7.** with little or no punishment [to let someone off *lightly*]

light-mind·ed (-mīn′did) ***adj.*** not serious; frivolous —**light′-mind′ed·ly** ***adv.*** —**light′-mind′ed·ness** ***n.***

light·ness[1] (-nis) ***n.*** **1.** the quality or intensity of lighting; brightness **2.** *a*) paleness *b*) the relative amount of light reflected by an object

light·ness[2] (-nis) ***n.*** **1.** the state of being light, not heavy **2.** mildness, nimbleness, delicacy, cheerfulness, lack of seriousness, etc.

light·ning (-niŋ) ***n.*** [< ME. *lightnen,* to LIGHTEN[1]] **1.** a flash of light in the sky caused by the discharge of atmospheric electricity from one cloud to another or between a cloud and the earth **2.** such a discharge of electricity —***vi.*** to give off such a discharge —***adj.*** like lightning

lightning bug (or **beetle**) *same as* FIREFLY

lightning rod a pointed metal rod placed high on a building, etc. and grounded to divert lightning from the structure

light opera a short, amusing musical play

lights (līts) ***n.pl.*** [from their light weight] [Dial.] the lungs of animals, used as food

light·ship (līt′ship′) ***n.*** a ship moored in a place dangerous to navigation and bearing lights, foghorns, sirens, etc. to warn or guide pilots

light·some (-səm) ***adj.*** **1.** nimble, graceful, or lively **2.** lighthearted; gay **3.** frivolous

light·weight (-wāt′) ***n.*** **1.** one below normal weight **2.** a boxer or wrestler between a featherweight and a welterweight (in boxing, 127–135 pounds) **3.** [Colloq.] a person of limited influence, intelligence, etc. —***adj.*** **1.** light in weight **2.** not serious

light-year (-yir′) ***n.*** *Astron.* a unit of distance equal to the distance that light travels in a vacuum in one year, approximately 6 trillion miles

lig·ne·ous (lig′nē əs) ***adj.*** [< L. *ligneus* < *lignum,* wood] of, or having the nature of, wood; woody

lig·nite (lig′nīt) ***n.*** [< Fr.: see LIGNEOUS & -ITE] a soft, brownish-black coal in which the texture of the original wood can still be seen —**lig·nit′ic** (-nit′ik) ***adj.***

lig·num vi·tae (lig′nəm vīt′ē) [ModL. < L., wood of life] **1.** *same as* GUAIACUM (sense 1) **2.** *commercial name for* the very hard wood of the guaiacum

Li·gu·ri·a (li gyoor′ē ə) region of NW Italy, on an arm (**Ligurian Sea**) of the Mediterranean: chief city, Genoa —**Li·gu′ri·an** ***adj., n.***

lik·a·ble (līk′ə b'l) ***adj.*** having qualities that inspire liking; attractive, genial, etc. —**lik′a·ble·ness, lik′a·bil′i·ty** ***n.***

like[1] (līk) ***adj.*** [OE. *gelic*] **1.** having almost or exactly the same characteristics; similar; equal [a cup of sugar and a *like* amount of flour] **2.** [Dial.] likely —***adv.*** [Colloq.] likely [*like* as not, he is already there] —***prep.*** **1.** similar to; resembling [she is *like* a bird] **2.** similarly to [she sings *like* a bird] **3.** characteristic of [not *like* her to cry] **4.** in the mood for; desirous of [to feel *like* sleeping] **5.** indicative of [it looks *like* a clear day tomorrow] **6.** as for example [fruit, *like* pears, for dessert] *Like* was originally an adjective in senses 1, 3, 4, 5, and an adverb in sense 2, and is still considered so by some grammarians —***conj.*** [Colloq.] **1.** as [it was just *like* you said] **2.** as if [it looks *like* he is late] —***n.*** a person or thing regarded as the equal or counterpart of another or of the person or thing being discussed [did you ever see the *like* of it?] —***vt.*** **liked, lik′ing** [Obs.] to liken —***vi.*** [Dial.] to be about (*to* have done something) *Like* is also used without meaning or syntactical function, as in hip talk [it's *like* hot] —**and the like** and others of the same kind —**like anything** [Colloq.] very much —**like blazes** (or **crazy, the devil, mad,** etc.) [Colloq.] with furious energy, speed, etc. —**nothing like** not at all like —**something like** almost like; about —**the like** (or **likes**) **of** [Colloq.] any person or thing like

like[2] (līk) ***vi.*** **liked, lik′ing** [OE. *lician*] to be so inclined; choose [leave whenever you *like*] —***vt.*** **1.** to be pleased with; have a preference for; enjoy **2.** to want or wish [I would *like* to go] —***n.*** [*pl.*] preferences or tastes —**lik′er** ***n.***

-like (līk) [see LIKE[1]] *a suffix meaning* like, characteristic of, suitable for [*doglike, homelike*]

like·a·ble (līk′ə b'l) ***adj.*** *same as* LIKABLE

like·li·hood (līk′lē hood′) ***n.*** (a) probability

like·ly (līk′lē) ***adj.*** **-li·er, -li·est** [prob. < OE. *geliclic* or < ? cognate ON. *likligr*] **1.** credible; probable [a *likely* cause] **2.** reasonably to be expected [it is *likely* to rain] **3.** suitable [a *likely* man for the job] **4.** promising [a *likely* lad] —***adv.*** probably [he will very *likely* go]

like-mind·ed (līk′mīn′did) *adj.* having the same ideas, tastes, etc.; agreeing mentally —**like′-mind′ed·ly** *adv.* —**like′-mind′ed·ness** *n.*

lik·en (-′n) *vt.* to represent or describe as being like, or similar; compare

like·ness (-nis) *n.* **1.** the state or quality of being like; similarity **2.** (the same) form or shape [Zeus took on the *likeness* of a bull] **3.** something that is like; copy, facsimile, portrait, etc.

like·wise (-wīz′) *adv.* [short for *in like wise*] **1.** in the same manner **2.** also; too; moreover

lik·ing (lī′kiŋ) *n.* **1.** fondness; affection **2.** preference; taste; pleasure [not to my *liking*]

li·ku·ta (lē ko͞o′tä) *n., pl.* **ma·ku′ta** (mä-) *see* MONETARY UNITS, table (Zaire)

li·lac (lī′lək, -läk, -lak) *n.* [Fr. < Ar. < Per. *nīlak,* bluish < *nīl,* indigo] **1.** a shrub or tree of the olive family, with large clusters of tiny, fragrant flowers ranging in color from white to lavender or crimson **2.** the flower cluster of this plant **3.** a pale-purple color —*adj.* pale-purple

li·lan·gen·i (li′läŋ gen′i) *n., pl.* **em′a·lan·gen·i** (em′ə-) [native name, royal] *see* MONETARY UNITS, table (Swaziland)

Lil·i·an, Lil·li·an (lil′ē ən) [prob. < L. *lilium,* lily] a feminine name: dim. *Lil, Lily, Lilly*

Lille (lēl) city in N France: pop. 191,000

Lil·li·put (lil′ə put′, -pət) in Swift's *Gulliver's Travels,* a land inhabited by tiny people

Lil·li·pu·tian (lil′ə pyo͞o′shən) *adj.* **1.** of Lilliput or its people **2.** very small; tiny **3.** narrow-minded —*n.* **1.** an inhabitant of Lilliput **2.** a very small person **3.** a narrow-minded person

lilt (lilt) *vt., vi.* [ME. *lilten*] to sing, speak, or play with a light, graceful rhythm —*n.* **1.** a gay song or tune with a swingy rhythm **2.** a light, swingy, and graceful rhythm or movement —**lilt′ing** *adj.* —**lilt′ing·ly** *adv.*

lil·y (lil′ē) *n., pl.* **lil′ies** [< OE. < L. *lilium*] **1.** any of a large genus of plants of the lily family, grown from a bulb and having typically trumpet-shaped flowers, white or colored **2.** the flower or the bulb of any of these **3.** any of several similar plants, as the waterlily **4.** the fleur-de-lis, as in the royal arms of France —*adj.* **1.** designating a family of plants including the lilies, tulips, onions, etc. **2.** like a lily, as in whiteness, delicacy, purity, etc. —**gild the lily** to attempt vain improvements on something that is already excellent or perfect

lil·y-liv·ered (lil′ē liv′ərd) *adj.* cowardly; timid

lily of the valley *pl.* **lilies of the valley** a plant of the lily family which has a single pair of oblong leaves and a single raceme of very fragrant, small, white, bell-shaped flowers

LILY OF THE VALLEY

lil·y-white (-hwīt′, -wīt′) *adj.* **1.** white as a lily **2.** innocent and pure: often used sarcastically **3.** practicing discrimination against, or segregation of, nonwhites, esp. Negroes

Li·ma (lē′mə; *for 2,* lī′-) **1.** capital of Peru, in the WC part: pop. 1,795,000 **2.** [after prec.] city in W Ohio: pop. 47,000

li·ma bean (lī′mə) [after LIMA, Peru] [*also* **L-** **b-**] **1.** a bean plant with creamy flowers and broad pods **2.** its broad, flat, nutritious seed

limb[1] (lim) *n.* [OE. *lim*] **1.** an arm, leg, or wing **2.** a large branch of a tree **3.** a part that projects like an arm or leg **4.** a person or thing regarded as a part or agent —**out on a limb** [Colloq.] in a precarious position or situation —**limb′less** *adj.*

limb[2] (lim) *n.* [< Fr. < ML. < L. *limbus,* edge] a border or edge; specif., *Astron.* the apparent outer edge of a heavenly body

limbed (limd) *adj.* having (a specified number or kind of) limbs [*four-limbed*]

lim·ber[1] (lim′bər) *adj.* [< ? LIMB[1]] **1.** easily bent; flexible **2.** able to bend the body easily; lithe —*vt.* to make limber —*vi.* to make oneself limber, as by exercises (usually with *up*) —**lim′ber·ness** *n.*

lim·ber[2] (lim′bər) *n.* [< ?] the two-wheeled, detachable front part of a gun carriage —*vt., vi.* to attach the limber to (a gun carriage)

lim·bo (lim′bō) *n., pl.* **-bos** [< L. (*in*) *limbo,* (in or on) the border] **1.** [*often* **L-**] in some Christian theologies, a region bordering on hell, the abode after death of unbaptized children and righteous people who lived before Jesus **2.** a place or condition of oblivion or neglect **3.** an indeterminate state midway between two others

Lim·bur·ger (cheese) (lim′bər gər) [< *Limburg,* a Belgian province] a semisoft cheese of whole milk, with a strong odor: also **Lim′burg (cheese)**

lime[1] (līm) *n.* [OE. *lim*] **1.** *short for* BIRDLIME **2.** a white substance, calcium oxide, CaO, obtained by the action of heat on limestone, shells, etc. and used in making mortar and cement and in neutralizing acid soil —*vt.* **limed, lim′ing** **1.** to cement **2.** to smear with birdlime **3.** to catch with birdlime **4.** to treat with lime

lime[2] (līm) *n.* [Fr. < Pr. < Ar. *līma:* cf. LEMON] **1.** a small, lemon-shaped, greenish-yellow citrus fruit with a juicy, sour pulp **2.** the small, semitropical tree that it grows on —*adj.* **1.** made with or of limes **2.** having a flavor like that of limes

lime[3] (līm) *n.* [< earlier *line* < ME. *lind:* see LINDEN] *same as* LINDEN

lime·ade (līm′ād′) *n.* a drink of lime juice and water, usually sweetened

lime·kiln (līm′kil′, -kiln′) *n.* a furnace in which limestone, shells, etc. are burned to make lime

lime·light (-līt′) *n.* **1.** a brilliant light created by the incandescence of lime, formerly used in theaters to throw an intense beam of light upon a particular part of the stage, an actor, etc. **2.** a prominent or conspicuous position before the public

lim·er·ick (lim′ər ik, lim′rik) *n.* [prob. < Ir. refrain containing the name *Limerick,* a county of Ireland] a rhymed, nonsense poem of five anapestic lines

lime·stone (līm′stōn′) *n.* rock consisting mainly of calcium carbonate, from which building stones, lime, etc. are made: cf. MARBLE

lime·wa·ter (-wôt′ər, -wät′ər) *n.* a solution of calcium hydroxide in water, used to neutralize acids

lim·ey (lī′mē) *n.* [from the LIME[2] juice formerly served to British sailors to prevent scurvy] [Slang] **1.** an English sailor or, sometimes, soldier **2.** any Englishman —*adj.* [Slang] British

lim·it (lim′it) *n.* [< OFr. < L. *limes* (gen. *limitis*)] **1.** the point, line, or edge where something ends or must end; boundary **2.** [*pl.*] bounds **3.** the greatest amount allowed [a catch of ten trout is the *limit,* a ten-cent *limit* on raising a bet in poker] —*vt.* to set a limit to; restrict; curb —**the limit** [Colloq.] any person or thing regarded as unbearable, remarkable, etc. to an extreme degree —**lim′it·a·ble** *adj.* —**lim′it·er** *n.*

lim·i·ta·tion (lim′ə tā′shən) *n.* **1.** a limiting or being limited **2.** qualification; restriction **3.** *Law* a period of time, fixed by statute, during which legal action can be brought, as for settling a claim —**lim′i·ta′tive** *adj.*

lim·it·ed (lim′it id) *adj.* **1.** *a)* confined within bounds; restricted *b)* narrow in scope **2.** making a restricted number of stops, and often charging extra fare: said of a train, bus, etc. **3.** exercising governmental powers under constitutional restrictions [a *limited* monarch] **4.** [Chiefly Brit.] restricting the liability of each partner or shareholder to the amount of his actual investment [a *limited* company] —*n.* a limited train, bus, etc. —**lim′it·ed·ly** *adv.* —**lim′it·ed·ness** *n.*

lim·it·ing (-iŋ) *adj. Gram.* designating or of any of a class of adjectives that limit or restrict the words modified (Ex.: *several, four,* etc.)

lim·it·less (-lis) *adj.* without limits; unbounded; vast —**lim′it·less·ly** *adv.* —**lim′it·less·ness** *n.*

limn (lim) *vt.* **limned, limn·ing** (lim′iŋ, -niŋ) [< OFr. *enluminer* < L. *illuminare,* to make light] **1.** to paint or draw **2.** to portray in words; describe —**limn·er** (lim′ər, -nər) *n.*

Li·moges (lē mōzh′; *Fr.* lē môzh′) city in WC France: pop. 133,000 —*n.* fine porcelain made there: also **Limoges ware**

lim·ou·sine (lim′ə zēn′, lim′ə zēn′) *n.* [Fr., lit., a hood] **1.** any large, luxurious sedan, esp. one driven by a chauffeur **2.** a buslike sedan used to carry passengers to or from an airport, etc.

limp[1] (limp) *vi.* [< a sense of OE. *limpan,* to befall] **1.** to walk with or as with a lame leg **2.** to move jerkily, laboriously, etc. —*n.* a halt or lameness in walking —**limp′er** *n.* —**limp′ing·ly** *adv.*

limp[2] (limp) *adj.* [< base of prec.] **1.** lacking stiffness; drooping, wilted, etc. **2.** lacking firmness or vigor —**limp′ly** *adv.* —**limp′ness** *n.*

limp·et (lim′pit) *n.* [< OE. < ML. *lempreda*] a mollusk which clings to rocks, timbers, etc. by means of a thick, fleshy foot

lim·pid (lim′pid) *adj.* [< Fr. < L. *limpidus* < OL. *limpa,* water] **1.** perfectly clear; transparent [*limpid* waters] **2.** clear and simple [*limpid* prose] —**lim·pid′i·ty, lim′pid·ness** *n.* —**lim′pid·ly** *adv.*

lim·y (lī′mē) *adj.* **lim′i·er, lim′i·est** **1.** covered with, consisting of, or like birdlime; sticky **2.** of, like, or containing lime —**lim′i·ness** *n.*

lin·age (lī′nij) *n.* **1.** the number of written or printed lines on a page **2.** payment based on the number of lines produced by a writer

linch·pin (linch′pin′) *n.* [< OE. *lynis,* linchpin] **1.** a pin that goes through the end of an axle outside the wheel to keep the wheel from coming off **2.** anything serving to hold together the parts of a whole

Lin·coln (liŋ′kən) [after Pres. LINCOLN] capital of Nebr., in the SE part: pop. 172,000

Lin·coln (liŋ′kən), **Abraham** 1809–65; 16th president of the U.S. (1861–65): assassinated —**Lin·coln·i·an** (liŋ kō′nē ən) *adj.*

Lind (lind), **Jenny** (born *Johanna Maria Lind*) 1820–87; Swed. soprano

Lin·da (lin′də) [dim. of BELINDA] a feminine name

Lind·bergh (lind′bərg, lin′-), **Charles Augustus** 1902–74; U.S. aviator

lin·den (lin′dən) ***n.*** [ME., *adj.* < OE. *lind,* linden] a tree with dense, heart-shaped leaves

line[1] (līn) ***n.*** [merging of OE. *line,* a cord, with OFr. *ligne* (both < L. *linea,* lit., linen thread < *linum,* flax)] **1.** *a)* a cord, rope, wire, or string *b)* a fine, strong cord with a hook, used in fishing *c)* a cord, steel tape, etc. used in measuring or leveling **2.** a wire or system of wires connecting stations in a telephone or telegraph system **3.** any wire, pipe, etc., or system of these, for conducting gas, water, electricity, etc. **4.** a very thin, threadlike mark; specif., *a)* a long, thin mark made by a pencil, pen, chalk, knife, etc. *b)* a thin crease in the palm or on the face **5.** a border or boundary *[*the State *line]* **6.** a limit; demarcation **7.** outline; contour **8.** [*usually pl.*] a plan of making or doing **9.** a row or series of persons or things; specif., a row of written or printed characters across a page or column **10.** *same as* LINEAGE[1] **11.** the descendants of a common ancestor or of a particular breed **12.** *a)* a transportation system consisting of regular trips by buses, ships, etc. between points *b)* a company operating such a system *c)* one branch of such a system *d)* a single track of a railroad **13.** the course or direction anything moving takes *[*the *line* of fire*]* **14.** course of conduct, action, explanation, etc. **15.** a person's trade or occupation, or the things he deals in *[*what's his *line?]* **16.** a stock of goods of a particular quality, quantity, variety, etc. **17.** *a)* the field of one's special knowledge or interest *b)* a source or piece of information *[*a *line* on a bargain*]* **18.** a short letter, note, or card *[*drop me a *line]* **19.** a verse of poetry **20.** [*pl.*] all the speeches of any one character in a play **21.** [Colloq.] flattering talk that is insincere **22.** *Football* the players arranged in a row even with the ball at the start of each play, or those directly opposite them **23.** *Geog.* an imaginary circle of the earth or of the celestial sphere, as the equator **24.** *Math.* *a)* the path of a moving point *b)* such a path when considered perfectly straight **25.** *Mil.* *a)* a formation of ships, troops, etc. abreast of each other *b)* the area or position in closest contact with the enemy during combat *c)* the troops in this area *d)* the combatant branches of the army as distinguished from the supporting branches and the staff **26.** *Music* any of the long parallel marks forming the staff —***vt.*** **lined, lin′ing 1.** to mark with lines **2.** to trace with or as with lines **3.** to bring into alignment (often with *up*) **4.** to form a line along **5.** to place objects along the edge of **6.** *Baseball* to hit as a line drive —***vi.*** **1.** to form a line (usually with *up*) **2.** *Baseball* to hit a line drive —**all along the line 1.** everywhere **2.** at every turn of events —**bring** (or **come, get) into line** to bring (or come) into alignment —**down the line** completely; entirely —**draw the** (or **a) line** to set a limit —**get a line on** [Colloq.] to find out about —**hold the line** to stand firm —**in** (or **out of) line** in (or not in) alignment, agreement, or conformity —**in line for** being considered for —**lay** (or **put) it on the line 1.** to pay up **2.** to speak frankly and in detail —**line out** *Baseball* to be put out by hitting a line drive that is caught by a fielder —**line up** to bring into or take a specified position —**on a line** in the same plane; level —**read between the lines** to discover a hidden meaning or purpose in something written, said, or done —**lin′a·ble, line′a·ble** ***adj.***

line[2] (līn) ***vt.*** **lined, lin′ing** [< OE. *lin,* ult. < or akin to L. *linum,* flax] **1.** to put a layer or lining of a different material on the inside of **2.** to be used as a lining in **3.** to fill; stuff: now chiefly in **line one's pockets,** to make money, esp. greedily or unethically

lin·e·age[1] (lin′ē ij) ***n.*** [< OFr. *lignage* < *ligne:* see LINE[1]] **1.** direct descent from an ancestor **2.** ancestry; family; stock **3.** *same as* LINE[1] (*n.* 11)

line·age[2] (lī′nij) ***n.*** *same as* LINAGE

lin·e·al (lin′ē əl) ***adj.*** **1.** in the direct line of descent from an ancestor **2.** hereditary **3.** of or composed of lines; linear —**lin′e·al·ly** ***adv.***

lin·e·a·ment (lin′ē ə mənt) ***n.*** [< L. *lineamentum* < *linea,* LINE[1]] **1.** any of the features of the body, usually of the face, esp. with regard to its outline **2.** a distinctive feature *Usually used in pl.*

lin·e·ar (lin′ē ər) ***adj.*** **1.** of or relating to a line or lines **2.** made of or using lines **3.** extended in a line **4.** designating or of a style of art in which line is emphasized **5.** having an effect directly proportional to its cause **6.** *Algebra* of the first degree —**lin′e·ar′i·ty** (-ē ar′ə tē) ***n.*** —**lin′e·ar·ly** ***adv.***

linear measure 1. measurement of length **2.** a system of measuring length, esp. the system in which 12 inches = 1 foot or that in which 100 centimeters = 1 meter: see TABLE OF WEIGHTS AND MEASURES in Supplements

line·back·er (līn′bak′ər) ***n.*** *Football* any player on defense stationed directly behind the line

line drawing a drawing done entirely in lines, from which a cut (**line cut**) can be photoengraved for printing

line drive *Baseball* a hard-hit ball that travels close to, and nearly parallel with, the ground

line·man (līn′mən) ***n.,*** *pl.* **-men 1.** a man who carries a surveying line, tape, etc. **2.** a man whose work is setting up and repairing telephone, telegraph, or electric power lines **3.** *Football* one of the players in the line

linemen's climber a device with sharp spikes, fastened to the shoe or strapped to the leg to aid in climbing telephone poles, etc.

lin·en (lin′ən) ***n.*** see PLURAL, II, D, 3 [OE. < *lin,* flax] **1.** thread or cloth made of flax **2.** [*often pl.*] things made of linen, or of cotton, etc., as tablecloths, sheets, etc. —***adj.*** **1.** spun from flax *[linen* thread*]* **2.** made of linen

line of fire 1. the course of a bullet, shell, etc. **2.** a position open to attack of any kind

line of force a line in a field of electrical or magnetic force that indicates the direction taken by the force at any point

line of scrimmage *Football* an imaginary line, parallel to the goal lines, on which the ball rests at the start of each play

lin·er[1] (lī′nər) ***n.*** **1.** a person or thing that traces lines **2.** a steamship, passenger airplane, etc. in regular service for a specific line **3.** *same as* LINE DRIVE **4.** a cosmetic applied in a fine line, as along the eyelid

lin·er[2] (lī′nər) ***n.*** **1.** a person who makes or attaches linings **2.** a lining **3.** the jacket of a long-playing record

lines·man (līnz′mən) ***n.,*** *pl.* **-men 1.** *same as* LINEMAN **2.** *Football* an official who measures and marks the gains or losses in ground **3.** *Tennis* an official who reports whether the ball is inside or outside the lines he is assigned to watch

line·up (līn′up′) ***n.*** an arrangement of persons or things in or as in a line; specif., *a)* a group of suspected criminals lined up by the police for identification *b) Football, Baseball,* etc. the list of a team's players arranged according to playing position, order at bat, etc.

ling[1] (liŋ) ***n.,*** *pl.* **ling, lings:** see PLURAL, II, D, 2 [akin to MDu. *lange,* ON. *langa*] an edible fish related to the cod, found in the North Atlantic

ling[2] (liŋ) ***n.*** [ON. *lyng*] *same as* HEATHER

-ling[1] (liŋ) [OE.] *a suffix added to nouns, meaning:* **1.** small *[duckling]* **2.** having a connection, esp. of an unimportant or contemptible kind, with the specified thing *[hireling]*

-ling[2] (liŋ) [OE.] [Archaic or Dial.] *a suffix meaning* extent or condition *[darkling]*

ling. linguistics

lin·ger (liŋ′gər) ***vi.*** [< North ME. freq. of *lengen,* to delay < OE. < base of *lang,* LONG[1]] **1.** to continue to stay, esp. through reluctance to leave **2.** to continue to live although very close to death **3.** to be unnecessarily slow in doing something; loiter —**lin′ger·er** ***n.*** —**lin′ger·ing** ***adj.*** —**lin′ger·ing·ly** ***adv.***

lin·ge·rie (län′zhə rā′, -rē′; lan′-; -jə-) ***n.*** [Fr.] women's underwear and night clothes of silk, nylon, lace, etc.

lin·go (liŋ′gō) ***n.,*** *pl.* **-goes** [Pr. < L. *lingua,* tongue] language; esp., a dialect, jargon, or special vocabulary that one is not familiar with: a humorous or disparaging term

lin·gua fran·ca (liŋ′gwə fraŋ′kə) *pl.* **lin′gua fran′cas, lin·guae fran·cae** (liŋ′gwē fran′sē) [It., lit., Frankish language] **1.** a hybrid language of Italian, Spanish, French, Greek, Arabic, and Turkish elements, spoken in certain Mediterranean ports **2.** any hybrid language used for communication between different peoples, as pidgin English

lin·gual (liŋ′gwəl) ***adj.*** [< ML. < L. *lingua,* the tongue] **1.** of the tongue **2.** of language or languages **3.** articulated with the tongue —***n.*** *Phonet.* a lingual sound, as *l* or *t* —**lin′gual·ly** ***adv.***

lin·gui·ne (liŋ gwē′nē) ***n.*** [< It. pl. of *linguina,* dim. of *lingua,* tongue] a kind of pasta like spaghetti but flat, often served with seafood

lin·guist (liŋ′gwist) ***n.*** [< L. *lingua,* the tongue + -IST] **1.** a specialist in linguistics **2.** *same as* POLYGLOT (sense 1)

lin·guis·tic (liŋ gwis′tik) ***adj.*** **1.** of language **2.** of linguistics —**lin·guis′ti·cal·ly** ***adv.***

linguistic atlas an atlas charting the geographical distribution of linguistic forms and usages

lin·guis·tics (liŋ gwis′tiks) ***n.pl.*** [*with sing. v.*] **1.** the science of language, including phonology, morphology, syntax, and semantics: often **general linguistics 2.** the study of the structure, development, etc. of a particular language

lin·i·ment (lin′ə mənt) ***n.*** [< LL. < L. *linere*, to smear] a medicated liquid to be rubbed on the skin to soothe sore, sprained, or inflamed areas

lin·ing (lī′niŋ) ***n.*** [see LINE[2]] the material covering an inner surface

link[1] (liŋk) ***n.*** [< Scand.] **1.** any of the series of rings or loops making up a chain **2.** *a)* a section of something resembling a chain *[a link of sausage]* *b)* an element in a series of circumstances *[a weak link in the evidence]* **3.** anything serving to connect or tie *[a link with the past]* **4.** one division (1/100) of a surveyor's chain, equal to 7.92 in. **5.** *Chem. same as* BOND[1] —***vt., vi.*** to join together with a link or links —**link′er** ***n.***

link[2] (liŋk) ***n.*** [prob. < ML. < L. *lychnus*, a light] a torch made of tow and pitch

link·age (liŋ′kij) ***n.*** **1.** a linking or being linked **2.** a series or system of links

linking verb a verb that functions chiefly as a connection between a subject and a predicate complement (Ex.: *be, seem, become*, etc.); copula

links (liŋks) ***n.pl.*** [OE. *hlinc*, a slope] *same as* GOLF COURSE

link·up (liŋk′up′) ***n.*** a joining together of two objects, factions, interests, etc.

Lin·nae·an, Lin·ne·an (li nē′ən) ***adj.*** [after C. *Linnaeus*, 18th-c. Swed. botanist] designating or of a system of classifying plants and animals by using a double name, the first word naming the genus, and the second the species

lin·net (lin′it) ***n.*** [OFr. *linette* < *lin* (< L. *linum*), flax: the bird feeds on flaxseed] a small finch found in Europe, Asia, and Africa

li·no·cut (lī′nə kut′) ***n.*** [< ff. + CUT] **1.** a design cut into the surface of a linoleum block **2.** a print made from this

li·no·le·um (li nō′lē əm) ***n.*** [coined < L. *linum*, flax + *oleum*, oil] a hard, washable floor covering made of a mixture of ground cork, ground wood, and oxidized linseed oil with a canvas backing

Lin·o·type (līn′ə tīp′) [< *line of type*] *a trademark for* a typesetting machine that casts an entire line of type in one bar, or slug —***n.*** [*often* **l-**] **1.** a machine of this kind **2.** matter set in this way —***vt., vi.*** [**l-**] **-typed′, -typ′ing** to set (matter) with this machine —**lin′o·typ′ist, lin′o·typ′er** ***n.***

lin·seed (lin′sēd′) ***n.*** [OE. *linsæd*] the seed of flax

linseed oil a yellowish oil extracted from flaxseed, used in oil paints, etc.

lin·sey-wool·sey (lin′zē wool′zē) ***n.***, *pl.* **-wool′seys** [ME. < *lin*, flax + *wolle*, wool] a coarse cloth made of linen (or cotton) and wool: also **lin′sey**

lint (lint) ***n.*** [prob. < *lin*, linen] **1.** scraped and softened linen formerly used as a dressing for wounds **2.** bits of thread, ravelings, or fluff from cloth or yarn —***vi.*** to give off lint —**lint′less** ***adj.*** —**lint′y** ***adj.*** **lint′i·er, lint′i·est**

lin·tel (lin′t'l) ***n.*** [OFr., ult. < L. *limen*, threshold] the horizontal crosspiece over a door, window, etc., carrying the weight of the structure above it

lin·ters (lin′tərz) ***n.pl.*** the short, fuzzy fibers clinging to cotton seeds after ginning, used in making cotton batting, etc.

lin·y (lī′nē) ***adj.*** **lin′i·er, lin′i·est** **1.** like a line; thin **2.** marked with lines

Linz (lints) city in N Austria: pop. 196,000

li·on (lī′ən) ***n.***, *pl.* **li′ons, li′on:** see PLURAL, II, D, 1 [OFr. < L. *leo* (gen. *leonis*) < Gr. *leōn*] **1.** a large, powerful mammal of the cat family, found in Africa and SW Asia, with a tawny coat, a tufted tail, and, in the adult male, a shaggy mane **2.** a person of great courage or strength **3.** a celebrity —**li′on·ess** ***n.fem.***

li·on·heart·ed (lī′ən här′tid) ***adj.*** very brave

li·on·ize (lī′ə nīz′) ***vt.*** **-ized′, -iz′ing** to treat as a celebrity —**li′on·i·za′tion** ***n.*** —**li′on·iz′er** ***n.***

lion's share the biggest and best portion

lip (lip) ***n.*** [OE. *lippa*] **1.** either of the two fleshy folds forming the edges of the mouth **2.** anything like a lip, as in structure or in being an edge or rim; specif., *a)* the projecting rim of a pitcher, cup, etc. *b)* the mouthpiece of a wind instrument *c) same as* LABIUM **3.** [Slang] insolent talk —***vt.*** **lipped, lip′ping** **1.** to touch with the lips; specif., to place the lips in the proper position for playing (a wind instrument) **2.** to utter softly —***adj.*** **1.** formed with a lip or the lips; labial **2.** from the lips only; spoken, but insincere —**bite one's lips** to keep back one's anger, annoyance, etc. —**hang on the lips of** to listen to with close attention —**keep a stiff upper lip** [Colloq.] to avoid becoming frightened or discouraged —**lip′less** ***adj.***

li·pase (lī′pās, lip′ās) ***n.*** [< ff. + -ASE] an enzyme that aids in digestion by hydrolizing fats into fatty acids and glycerol

lip·o- [< Gr. *lipos*, fat] *a combining form meaning* of or like fat, fatty: also, before a vowel, **lip-**

li·poid (lip′oid, lī′poid) ***adj.*** [LIP(O)- + -OID] *Biochem., Chem.* resembling fat: also **li·poi′dal**

lipped (lipt) ***adj.*** having a lip or lips: often in compounds *[tight-lipped]*

lip·py (lip′ē) ***adj.*** **-pi·er, -pi·est** [Slang] impudent, brash, or insolent —**lip′pi·ness** ***n.***

lip-read (lip′rēd′) ***vt., vi.*** **-read′** (-red′), **-read′ing** to recognize (a speaker's words) by lip reading —**lip reader**

lip reading the act or skill of recognizing a speaker's words by watching the movement of his lips: it is taught esp. to the deaf

lip·stick (-stik′) ***n.*** a small stick of cosmetic paste, set in a case, for coloring the lips

liq. **1.** liquid **2.** liquor

liq·ue·fa·cient (lik′wə fā′shənt) ***n.*** [< L.: see LIQUEFY] something that causes liquefaction

liq·ue·fac·tion (-fak′shən) ***n.*** a liquefying or being liquefied

liq·ue·fy (lik′wə fī′) ***vt., vi.*** **-fied′, -fy′ing** [< Fr. < L. < *liquere*, to be liquid + *facere*, to make] to change into a liquid —**liq′ue·fi′a·ble** ***adj.*** —**liq′ue·fi′er** ***n.***

li·ques·cent (li kwes′'nt) ***adj.*** [< L. prp. of *liquescere* < *liquere*, to be liquid] becoming liquid; melting —**li·ques′cence** ***n.***

li·queur (li kur′) ***n.*** [Fr.] any of certain sweet, syrupy alcoholic liquors, variously flavored

liq·uid (lik′wid) ***adj.*** [< OFr. < L. *liquidus* < *liquere*, to be liquid] **1.** readily flowing; fluid; specif., that can move freely, unlike a solid, but does not expand indefinitely like a gas **2.** clear; limpid *[liquid eyes]* **3.** flowing smoothly and gracefully *[liquid verse]* **4.** readily convertible into cash *[liquid assets]* **5.** without friction and like a vowel, as the consonants *l* and *r* —***n.*** a liquid substance —**liq·uid′i·ty, liq′uid·ness** ***n.*** —**liq′uid·ly** ***adv.***

liquid air air brought to a liquid state by being subjected to great pressure and then cooled by its own expansion

liq·ui·date (lik′wə dāt′) ***vt.*** **-dat′ed, -dat′ing** [< ML. pp. of *liquidare*, to make clear < L. *liquidus*, liquid] **1.** to settle the amount of (indebtedness, damages, etc.) **2.** to settle the accounts of (a bankrupt business, etc.) by apportioning assets and debts **3.** to pay or settle (a debt) **4.** to convert (holdings or assets) into cash **5.** to dispose of or get rid of, as by killing —***vi.*** to liquidate debts, accounts, etc. —**liq′ui·da′tion** ***n.*** —**liq′ui·da′tor** ***n.***

liq·uid·ize (lik′wə dīz′) ***vt.*** **-ized′, -iz′ing** to cause to have a liquid quality

liquid measure **1.** the measurement of liquids **2.** a system of measuring liquids; esp., the system in which 2 pints = 1 quart, 4 quarts = 1 gallon, etc.: see TABLE OF WEIGHTS AND MEASURES in Supplements

liquid oxygen a light-bluish liquid boiling at −183°C, produced by fractionation of liquid air

liq·uor (lik′ər) ***n.*** [< OFr. *licor* < L. *liquor*] **1.** any liquid or juice **2.** an alcoholic drink, esp. one made by distillation, as whiskey or rum —***vt., vi.*** [Colloq.] to drink or cause to drink alcoholic liquor, esp. to the point of intoxication

li·ra (lir′ə) ***n.***, *pl.* **-re** (-ā), for 2 **-ras** [It. < L. *libra*, a balance] the monetary unit of **1.** Italy **2.** Turkey See MONETARY UNITS, table

Lis·bon (liz′bən) capital, & a seaport, of Portugal: pop. 826,000 (met. area 1,450,000): Port. name **Lis·bo·a** (lēzh-bô′ə)

lisle (līl) ***n.*** [< *Lisle*, earlier sp. of LILLE, France] **1.** a fine, hard, extra-strong cotton thread: in full, **lisle thread** **2.** a fabric, or stockings, gloves, etc., knit or woven of lisle —***adj.*** made of lisle

lisp (lisp) ***vi.*** [< OE. < *wlisp*, a lisping] **1.** to substitute the sounds (th) and (*th*) for the sounds of *s* and *z* **2.** to speak imperfectly or like a child —***vt.*** to utter with a lisp —***n.*** **1.** the act or speech defect of lisping **2.** the sound of lisping —**lisp′er** ***n.*** —**lisp′ing·ly** ***adv.***

lis·some, lis·som (lis′əm) ***adj.*** [altered < *lithesome*] moving gracefully or with ease and lightness; lithe, limber, agile, etc. —**lis′some·ly, lis′som·ly** ***adv.*** —**lis′some·ness, lis′som·ness** ***n.***

list[1] (list) ***n.*** [merging of OE. *liste* & Anglo-Fr. *liste* < OFr. < Gmc.] **1.** formerly, a narrow strip or border; specif., *a)* a strip of cloth *b)* a stripe of color *c)* a boundary **2.** the selvage of cloth **3.** a series of names, words, numbers, etc. set forth in order; catalog, roll, etc. **4.** *same as* LIST PRICE See also LISTS —***vt.*** **1.** formerly, to edge with, or arrange in, stripes or bands **2.** *a)* to set forth (a series of names, items, etc.) in order *b)* to enter in a list, directory, catalog, etc. —***vi.*** to be listed for sale, as in a catalog (at the price specified) —**list′er** ***n.*** —**list′ing** ***n.***

list[2] (list) ***vt.*** [OE. *lystan* < base of *lust*, desire] [Archaic] to be pleasing to; suit —***vi.*** [Archaic] to wish; like; choose

list[3] (list) ***vt., vi.*** [prob. specialized use of prec.] to tilt to one side, as a ship —***n.*** a tilting or inclining to one side

list[4] (list) ***vt., vi.*** [OE. *hlystan* < base of *hlyst*, hearing] [Archaic] to listen (to)

lis·ten (lis′'n) ***vi.*** [OE. *hlysnan:* for base see prec.] **1.** to make a conscious effort to hear; attend closely, so as to hear **2.** to give heed; take advice —***n.*** the act of listening —**listen in** **1.** to listen to others' conversation; esp., to eavesdrop **2.** to listen to a broadcast —**lis′ten·er** ***n.***

list·er (lis′tər) *n.* [< LIST[1] + -ER] a plow with a double moldboard, which heaps earth on both sides of the furrow
Lis·ter (lis′tər), **Joseph** 1827–1912; Eng. surgeon: introduced antiseptic surgery
list·less (list′lis) *adj.* [LIST[2] + -LESS] having or showing no interest in what is going on, as because of illness, weariness, dejection, etc.; spiritless; languid —**list′less·ly** *adv.* —**list′less·ness** *n.*
list price retail price as given in a list or catalog, discounted in sales to dealers, etc.
lists (lists) *n.pl.* [ME. *listes,* specialized use of *liste,* strip, border] **1.** *a)* the high fence enclosing an area where knights held tournaments *b)* this area itself or the tournament held there **2.** any place or realm of combat, conflict, etc. —**enter the lists** to enter a contest or struggle
Liszt (list), **Franz** (fränts) 1811–86; Hung. composer & pianist
lit (lit) *alt. pt. & pp. of* LIGHT
lit. 1. liter(s) **2.** literal **3.** literally **4.** literary **5.** literature
lit·a·ny (lit′'n ē) *n., pl.* **-nies** [< OFr. < LL. < Gr. *litaneia* < *litē,* a request] **1.** a form of prayer in which the clergy and the congregation take part alternately, with recitation of supplications and fixed responses **2.** any dreary recital
li·tchi (lē′chē′) *n.* [Chin. *li-chih*] **1.** a Chinese evergreen tree **2.** the dried or preserved fruit of this tree (**litchi nut**), with a single seed, a sweet, edible pulp, and a rough, brown, papery shell
-lite (līt) [Fr., for *-lithe:* see -LITH] *a combining form meaning* stone: used in the names of minerals, rocks, and fossils *[chrysolite]*
li·ter (lēt′ər) *n.* [Fr. *litre* < ML. < Gr. *litra,* a pound] the basic unit of capacity in the metric system, equal to 1 cubic decimeter (1.0567 liquid quarts or .908 dry quart)
lit·er·a·cy (lit′ər ə sē) *n.* the state or quality of being literate; ability to read and write
lit·er·al (lit′ər əl) *adj.* [< MFr. < LL. *litteralis* < L. *littera,* a letter] **1.** following the exact words of the original *[a literal* translation*]* **2.** based on the actual words in their ordinary meaning; in a basic or strict sense *[the literal* meaning of a passage*]* **3.** habitually interpreting statements or words according to their actual denotation; matter-of-fact *[a literal* mind*]* **4.** real; not going beyond the actual facts *[the literal* truth*]* : often used intensively to mean "virtual" —**lit′er·al′i·ty** (-ə ral′ə tē) *n., pl.* **-ties** —**lit′er·al·ly** *adv.* —**lit′er·al·ness** *n.*
lit·er·al·ism (-iz'm) *n.* **1.** the tendency to take words, statements, etc. in their literal sense **2.** thoroughgoing realism in art —**lit′er·al·ist** *n.* —**lit′er·al·is′tic** *adj.*
lit·er·al·ize (-ə līz′) *vt.* **-ized′, -iz′ing** to interpret literally
lit·er·ar·y (lit′ə rer′ē) *adj.* **1.** *a)* of or dealing with literature *b)* of or having to do with books *[literary* agents*]* **2.** of the relatively formal language of literature **3.** *a)* versed in literature *b)* making literature a profession
lit·er·ate (lit′ər it) *adj.* [< L. < *littera,* a letter] **1.** able to read and write **2.** having or showing extensive learning or culture —*n.* a literate person —**lit′er·ate·ly** *adv.*
lit·e·ra·ti (lit′ə rät′ē, -rā′tī) *n.pl.* [It. < L.] men of letters; scholarly or learned people
‡**lit·e·ra·tim** (-rāt′im, -rät′-) *adv.* [ML. < L. *littera,* a letter] letter for letter; literally
lit·er·a·ture (lit′ər ə chər, lit′rə choor′) *n.* [< OFr. < L. *litteratura* < *littera,* a letter] **1.** the profession of an author **2.** *a)* all the writings of a particular time, country, etc., esp. those of an imaginative or critical character valued for excellence of form and expression *[American literature] b)* all the writings on a particular subject **3.** [Colloq.] printed matter of any kind
-lith (lith) [Fr. *-lithe* < Gr. *lithos,* stone] *a combining form meaning* stone *[monolith]*
Lith. 1. Lithuania **2.** Lithuanian
lith., litho., lithog. 1. lithograph **2.** lithography
lith·arge (lith′ärj, li thärj′) *n.* [< OFr. < L. < Gr. *lithargyros* < *lithos,* a stone + *argyros,* silver] an oxide of lead, PbO, used in storage batteries, paints, etc.
lithe (līth) *adj.* **lith′er, lith′est** [OE. *lithe,* soft, mild] bending easily; supple; limber: also **lithe′some** (-səm) —**lithe′ly** *adv.* —**lithe′ness** *n.*
lith·i·a (lith′ē ə) *n.* [ModL. < Gr. *lithos,* stone] lithium oxide, Li_2O, a white, crystalline compound
-lith·ic (lith′ik) *a combining form meaning* of a (specified) stage in the use of stone *[neolithic]*
lith·i·um (lith′ē əm) *n.* [ModL. < LITHIA] a soft, silver-white, metallic chemical element, the lightest known metal: symbol, Li; at. wt., 6.939; at. no., 3
lithium carbonate a white, powdery salt, Li_2CO_3, used in the manufacture of glass, dyes, etc. and in psychiatry to treat manic-depressive disorders
lith·o (lith′ō) *n., pl.* **-os;** *vt., vi.* **-oed, -o·ing** *clipped form of* LITHOGRAPH
lith·o- [< Gr. *lithos,* a stone] *a combining form meaning* stone, rock: also, before a vowel, **lith-**
lith·o·graph (lith′ə graf′) *n.* a print made by lithography —*vi., vt.* to make (prints or copies) by lithography —**li·thog·ra·pher** (li thäg′rə fər) *n.*
li·thog·ra·phy (li thäg′rə fē) *n.* [LITHO- + -GRAPHY] the art or process of printing from a flat stone or metal plate: the design is put on the surface with a greasy material, and then water and printing ink are successively applied; the greasy parts, which repel water, absorb the ink, but the wet parts do not —**lith·o·graph·ic** (lith′ə graf′ik) *adj.* —**lith′o·graph′i·cal·ly** *adv.*
lith·o·sphere (lith′ə sfir′) *n.* [LITHO- + SPHERE] the solid, rocky part of the earth; earth's crust
li·thot·o·my (li thät′ə mē) *n., pl.* **-mies** [< LL. < Gr.: see LITHO- & -TOMY] the surgical removal of a stone from the bladder
Lith·u·a·ni·a (lith′oo wā′nē ə) republic of the U.S.S.R., in NE Europe, on the Baltic Sea: 25,170 sq. mi.; pop. 3,100,000; cap. Vilnius: in full, **Lithuanian Soviet Socialist Republic** —**Lith′u·a′ni·an** *adj., n.*
lit·i·ga·ble (lit′i gə b'l) *adj.* that gives cause for litigation, or a lawsuit; actionable
lit·i·gant (lit′ə gənt) *n.* a party to a lawsuit
lit·i·gate (-gāt′) *vt.* **-gat′ed, -gat′ing** [< L. pp. of *litigare* < *lis* (gen. *litis*), dispute + *agere,* to do] to contest in a lawsuit —*vi.* to carry on a lawsuit —**lit′i·ga′tor** *n.*
lit·i·ga·tion (lit′ə gā′shən) *n.* **1.** the carrying on of a lawsuit **2.** a lawsuit
li·ti·gious (li tij′əs) *adj.* **1.** *a)* given to carrying on litigations *b)* quarrelsome **2.** disputable at law **3.** of lawsuits —**li·ti′gious·ly** *adv.* —**li·ti′gious·ness** *n.*
lit·mus (lit′məs) *n.* [ON. *litmose,* lichen used in dyeing < *litr,* color + *mosi,* moss] a purple coloring matter obtained from various lichens: it turns blue in bases and red in acids
litmus paper absorbent paper treated with litmus and used as an acid-base indicator
li·tre (lēt′ər) *n. chiefly Brit. sp. of* LITER
Litt.D. [L. *Lit(t)erarum Doctor*] Doctor of Letters; Doctor of Literature
lit·ter (lit′ər) *n.* [< OFr. *litiere* < ML. < L. *lectus,* a couch] **1.** a framework having long horizontal shafts near the bottom and enclosing a couch on which a person can be carried **2.** a stretcher for carrying the sick or wounded **3.** straw, hay, etc. used as bedding for animals, as a covering for plants, etc. **4.** the young borne at one time by a dog, cat, etc. **5.** things lying about in disorder; esp., bits of scattered rubbish **6.** untidiness; disorder —*vt.* **1.** to bring forth (a number of young) at one time: said of certain animals **2.** to make messy with things scattered about **3.** to scatter about carelessly —*vi.* to bear a litter of young
lit·té·ra·teur (lit′ər ə tur′) *n.* [Fr.] a literary man; man of letters: also written **litterateur**
lit·ter·bug (lit′ər bug′) *n.* a person who litters a public place with trash, garbage, etc.
lit·tle (lit′'l) *adj.* **lit′tler** or **less** or **less′er, lit′tlest** or **least** [OE. *lytel*] **1.** small in size; not big, large, or great **2.** small in amount, number, or degree **3.** short in duration or distance; brief **4.** small in importance or power *[the rights of the little* man*]* **5.** small in force, intensity, etc.; weak **6.** trivial; trifling **7.** lacking in breadth of vision; narrow-minded *[a little* mind*]* **8.** young: said of children or animals *Little* is sometimes used to express endearment *[bless your little* heart*]* —*adv.* **less, least 1.** in a small degree; only slightly; not much **2.** not in the least *[he little* suspects the plot*]* —*n.* **1.** *a)* a small amount, degree, etc. *b)* not much *[little* was done*]* **2.** a short time or distance —**little by little** gradually —**make little of** to treat as unimportant —**not a little** very much; very —**lit′tle·ness** *n.*
Little America five operational bases established by U.S. expeditions on the Ross Ice Shelf, Antarctica
Little Bear the constellation URSA MINOR
Little Dipper a dipper-shaped group of stars in the constellation Ursa Minor
Little League a league of baseball teams for youngsters
Little Rock [after a rocky cape in the river] capital of Ark., on the Arkansas River: pop. 158,000
little slam *Bridge* the winning of all but one trick
little theater 1. a small theater, as of a college, art group, etc., usually noncommercial and amateur **2.** drama produced by such theaters
lit·to·ral (lit′ər əl) *adj.* [L. *litoralis* < *litus* (gen. *litoris*), seashore] of, on, or along the shore —*n.* the region along the shore
li·tur·gi·cal (li tur′jə k'l) *adj.* **1.** of or constituting a liturgy **2.** used in or using a liturgy —**li·tur′gi·cal·ly** *adv.*

lit·ur·gy (lit′ər jē) *n., pl.* **-gies** [< Fr. < ML. < Gr. *leitourgia,* public service, ult. < *leōs,* people + *ergon,* work] **1.** prescribed forms or ritual for public worship in any of various religions **2.** the Eucharistic service

liv·a·ble (liv′ə b'l) *adj.* **1.** fit or pleasant to live in, as a house **2.** that can be lived through; endurable Also sp. **liveable** —**liv′a·bil′i·ty, liv′a·ble·ness** *n.*

live[1] (liv) *vi.* **lived, liv′ing** [OE. *libban*] **1.** to be alive; have life **2.** *a)* to remain alive *b)* to endure **3.** *a)* to pass one's life in a specified manner *[*to *live* happily*]* *b)* to conduct one's life *[*to *live* by a strict moral code*]* **4.** to enjoy a full and varied life **5.** *a)* to maintain life *[*to *live* on a pension*]* *b)* to be dependent for a living (with *off*) **6.** to feed; subsist *[*to *live* on fruits and nuts*]* **7.** to make one's dwelling; reside —*vt.* **1.** to carry out in one's life *[*to *live* one's faith*]* **2.** to spend; pass *[*to *live* a useful life*]* —**live down** to live in such a way as to wipe out the shame of (some fault, misdeed, etc.) —**live high** (or **well**) to live in luxury —**live in** to sleep at the place where one is in domestic service —**live it up** [Slang] to indulge in pleasures, extravagances, etc. that one usually forgoes —**live up to** to act according to (ideals, promises, etc.) —**live with** to bear; endure

live[2] (līv) *adj.* [< ALIVE] **1.** having life; not dead **2.** of the living state or living beings **3.** having positive qualities, as of warmth, vigor, vitality, brilliance, etc. *[*a *live* organization*]* **4.** of immediate or present interest *[*a *live* issue*]* **5.** *a)* still burning or glowing *[*a *live* spark*]* *b)* not extinct *[*a *live* volcano*]* **6.** unexploded *[*a *live* shell*]* **7.** unused; unexpended *[live* steam*]* **8.** carrying electrical current *[*a *live* wire*]* **9.** *a)* involving a performance in person, not one on film, tape, etc.; transmitted during the actual performance *b)* recorded at a public performance **10.** *Mech.* imparting motion or power

-lived (līvd; *occas.* livd) [see LIFE & -ED] *a combining form meaning* having (a specified kind or duration of) life *[*short-*lived]*

live·li·hood (līv′lē hood′) *n.* [OE. *liflad* < *lif,* life + *-lad,* course] means of supporting life; subsistence

live·long (liv′lôŋ′) *adj.* [ME. *lefe longe,* lit., lief long (cf. LIEF), phr. in which *lief* is merely intens.] long or tediously long in passing; whole; entire *[*the *livelong* day*]*

live·ly (līv′lē) *adj.* **-li·er, -li·est** [OE. *liflic*] **1.** full of life; active; vigorous **2.** full of spirit; exciting; animated *[*a *lively* debate*]* **3.** gay; cheerful **4.** moving quickly and lightly, as a dance **5.** vivid; keen *[lively* colors*]* **6.** bounding back with great resilience *[*a *lively* ball*]* —*adv.* in a lively manner —**live′li·ness** *n.*

liv·en (lī′vən) *vt., vi.* to make or become lively; cheer (*up*)

live oak **1.** *a)* an evergreen oak of the SE U.S. *b)* an oak of California **2.** the hard wood of these trees

liv·er[1] (liv′ər) *n.* [OE. *lifer*] **1.** the largest glandular organ in vertebrate animals: it secretes bile and has an important function in metabolism **2.** the liver of cattle, fowl, etc. used as food

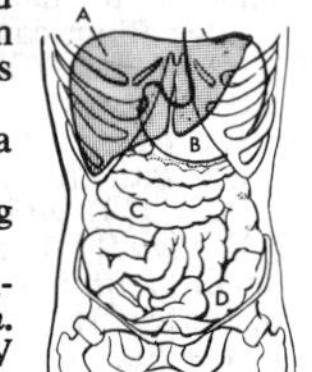

LIVER (A, liver; B, stomach; C, small intestine; D, large intestine)

liv·er[2] (liv′ər) *n.* a person who lives (in a specified way or place) *[*a clean *liver]*

liv·er·ied (liv′ər ēd, liv′rēd) *adj.* wearing a livery

liv·er·ish (liv′ər ish) *adj.* [Colloq.] **1.** bilious **2.** peevish; cross —**liv′er·ish·ness** *n.*

Liv·er·pool (liv′ər po͞ol′) seaport in NW England: pop. 688,000 —**Liv′er·pud′li·an** (-pud′lē ən) *adj., n.*

liver spot a brownish spot on the skin, formerly attributed to faulty functioning of the liver

liv·er·wort (liv′ər wurt′) *n.* any of a class of plants, often forming dense, green mosslike mats on rocks, soil, etc. in moist places

liv·er·wurst (-wurst′) *n.* [LIVER[1] + G. *wurst,* sausage] a sausage containing ground liver: also **liver sausage**

liv·er·y (liv′ər ē, liv′rē) *n., pl.* **-er·ies** [< OFr. *livree,* gift of clothes to a servant < *livrer,* to deliver < L. *liberare,* to free] **1.** an identifying uniform such as is worn by servants or those in some particular group, trade, etc. **2.** the people wearing such uniforms **3.** characteristic dress or appearance **4.** *a)* the keeping and feeding of horses for a fixed charge *b)* the keeping of horses, vehicles, or both, for hire *c)* a stable providing these services: also **livery stable**

liv·er·y·man (-mən) *n., pl.* **-men** a person who owns or works in a livery stable

lives (līvz) *n. pl. of* LIFE

live·stock (līv′stäk′) *n.* domestic animals kept for use on a farm or raised for sale and profit

live wire **1.** a wire carrying an electric current **2.** [Colloq.] an energetic and enterprising person

liv·id (liv′id) *adj.* [< Fr. < L. *lividus*] **1.** discolored by a bruise; black-and-blue **2.** grayish-blue; lead-colored *[livid* with rage*]* : sometimes taken to mean pale, white, or red —**li·vid·i·ty** (li vid′ə tē), **liv′id·ness** *n.*

liv·ing (liv′iŋ) *adj.* **1.** alive; having life **2.** in active operation or use *[*a *living* institution*]* **3.** of persons alive *[*within *living* memory*]* **4.** in its natural state or place, or having its natural force, etc. *[*hewn from the *living* rock*]* **5.** still spoken and undergoing changes *[*a *living* language*]* **6.** true to reality; lifelike *[*the *living* image*]* **7.** of life or the sustaining of life *[living* conditions*]* **8.** suited for social and recreational activities in a house *[*the *living* area*]* **9.** presented in person before a live audience *[living* theater*]* **10.** very *[*the *living* daylights*]* —*n.* **1.** the state of being alive **2.** the means of sustaining life; livelihood **3.** manner of existence *[*the standard of *living]* **4.** in England, a church benefice —**the living** those that are still alive

living death a life of unrelieved misery

living room a room in a home, with sofas, chairs, etc., used for socializing, entertaining, etc.

Liv·ing·stone (liv′iŋ stən), **David** 1813–73; Scot. missionary & explorer in Africa

living wage a wage sufficient to maintain a person and that person's family in reasonable comfort

living will a document, legal in some States, directing that all measures to support life be ended if the signer should be dying of an incurable condition

Li·vo·ni·a (li vō′nē ə) [after *Livonia,* former Russian province] city in SE Mich.: suburb of Detroit: pop. 105,000

Li·vor·no (lē vôr′nô) *It. name of* LEGHORN

Liv·y (liv′ē) (L. name *Titus Livius*) 59 B.C.–17 A.D.; Rom. historian

liz·ard (liz′ərd) *n.* [< OFr. *lesard* < L. *lacerta*] **1.** any of a group of reptiles with a long slender body and tail, a scaly skin, and four legs (sometimes vestigial), as the gecko, chameleon, and iguana **2.** loosely, any of various similar animals, as alligators or salamanders

Lju·blja·na (lyo͞o′blyä nä) city in Slovenia, NW Yugoslavia: pop. 157,000

'll *contraction of* will or shall *[I'll* go*]*

LL., L.L. Late Latin

ll., ll lines

lla·ma (lä′mə) *n., pl.* **-mas, -ma:** see PLURAL, II, D, 1 [Sp. < Quechua] a S. American animal related to the camel but smaller and without humps: it is used as a beast of burden and for its wool, flesh, and milk

lla·no (lä′nō; *Sp.* lyä′nô) *n., pl.* **-nos** (-nōz; *Sp.* -nôs) [Sp. < L. *planus,* plain] a grassy plain in the Southwest and in Spanish America

LL.B. [L. *Legum Baccalaureus*] Bachelor of Laws

LL.D. [L. *Legum Doctor*] Doctor of Laws

Llew·el·lyn (loo wel′ən) [W. *Llewelyn,* lit., prob., lionlike] a masculine name

Lloyd (loid) [W. *Llwyd,* lit., gray] a masculine name

Lloyd George, David 1863–1945; Brit. statesman; prime minister (1916–22)

lo (lō) *interj.* [OE. *la*] look! see!

loach (lōch) *n.* [< OFr. *loche*] a small, old-world, freshwater fish with barbels around the mouth

load (lōd) *n.* [OE. *lad,* a course, way] **1.** something carried or to be carried at one time; burden **2.** the amount that can be carried: a measure of weight or quantity varying with the type of conveyance *[*a *carload* of coal*]* **3.** something carried with difficulty; specif., *a)* a heavy burden or weight *b)* a great mental burden *[*a *load* off one's mind*]* **4.** the weight that a structure bears or the stresses that are put upon it **5.** a single charge, as of powder and bullets, for a firearm **6.** the amount of work carried by a person or a group *[*the class *load* of a teacher*]* **7.** [*often pl.*] [Colloq.] a great amount or number *[loads* of friends*]* **8.** *Elec.* the amount of power delivered by a generator, motor, etc. or carried by a circuit **9.** *Mech.* the external resistance offered to an engine by the machine that it is operating —*vt.* **1.** to put something to be carried into or upon; fill with a load *[*to *load* a truck*]* **2.** to put into or upon a carrier *[*to *load* coal*]* **3.** to burden; oppress **4.** to supply in abundance *[*to *load* one with honors, *loaded* with money*]* **5.** to put ammunition into (a gun or firearm), film into (a camera), etc. **6.** to weight (dice) unevenly for fraudulent use **7.** to add extra costs, a filler, etc. to **8.** to phrase (a question, etc.) so as to elicit a desired response **9.** *Baseball* to have or cause to have runners on (all bases) —*vi.* **1.** to put in or receive a charge, cartridge, etc. **2.** to put on or take on passengers, goods, etc. —**get a load of** [Slang] **1.** to listen to or hear **2.** to look at or see —**have a load on** [Slang] to be intoxicated —**load′ed** *adj.* —**load′er** *n.* —**load′ing** *n.*

load·star (lōd′stär′) *n. same as* LODESTAR

load·stone (lōd′stōn′) *n. same as* LODESTONE

loaf[1] (lōf) *n., pl.* **loaves** (lōvz) [OE. *hlaf*] **1.** a portion of bread baked in one piece, commonly of oblong shape **2.** any mass of food shaped somewhat like a loaf of bread and baked *[*a salmon *loaf]*

loaf[2] (lōf) *vi.* [prob. < ff.] to spend time idly; loiter or lounge about; idle, dawdle, etc. —*vt.* to spend (time) idly (often with *away*)

loaf·er (-ər) *n.* [prob. < G. *landlaüfer,* a vagabond] a person who loafs —[L-] *a trademark for* a moccasinlike sport shoe; also, [l-] a shoe like this

loam (lōm) ***n.*** [OE. *lam*] **1.** a rich soil of clay, sand, and organic matter **2.** popularly, any rich, dark soil —***vt.*** to fill or top with loam —**loam′y** ***adj.***

loan (lōn) ***n.*** [< ON. *lān*] **1.** the act of lending **2.** something lent; esp., a sum of money lent, often at interest —***vt., vi.*** to lend —**on loan** lent for temporary use or service

loan·er (-ər) ***n.*** **1.** one who loans **2.** a car, radio, etc. lent in place of one left for repair

loan shark [Colloq.] a person who lends money at exorbitant or illegal rates of interest

loan·word (-wurd′) ***n.*** [after G. *lehnwort*] a word of one language taken into another and naturalized (Ex.: KINDERGARTEN < G.)

loath (lōth) ***adj.*** [OE. *lath*, hostile] unwilling; reluctant [to be *loath* to depart] —**nothing loath** willing(ly)

loathe (lō*th*) ***vt.*** **loathed, loath′ing** [OE. *lathian*, to be hateful] to feel intense dislike or disgust for; abhor; detest —**loath′er** ***n.***

loath·ing (lō*th*′iŋ) ***n.*** intense dislike, disgust, or hatred; abhorrence

loath·ly[1] (lōth′lē) ***adv.*** [Rare] unwillingly

loath·ly[2] (lō*th*′lē) ***adj.*** *rare var. of* LOATHSOME

loath·some (lō*th*′səm, lōth′-) ***adj.*** causing loathing; disgusting —**loath′some·ly** ***adv.*** —**loath′some·ness** ***n.***

loaves (lōvz) ***n.*** *pl. of* LOAF[1]

lob (läb) ***n.*** [ME. *lobbe-*, lit., "heavy, thick"] *Tennis* a stroke in which the ball is sent high into the air, dropping into the back of the opponent's court —***vt.*** **lobbed, lob′bing** to send (a ball) in a lob —***vi.*** **1.** to move heavily and clumsily **2.** to lob a ball —**lob′ber** ***n.***

lo·bar (lō′bər, -bär) ***adj.*** of a lobe or lobes

lo·bate (-bāt) ***adj.*** having or formed into a lobe or lobes —**lo′bate·ly** ***adv.***

lo·ba·tion (lō bā′shən) ***n.*** **1.** the condition of having lobes **2.** the process of forming lobes **3.** a lobe

lob·by (läb′ē) ***n.***, *pl.* **-bies** [LL. *lobia:* see LODGE] **1.** a hall or large anteroom, as a waiting room of a hotel, theater, etc. **2.** a group of lobbyists —***vi.*** **-bied, -by·ing** to act as a lobbyist —***vt.*** to get or try to get legislators to vote for or against (a measure) by lobbying

lob·by·ist (-ist) ***n.*** a person, acting for a special interest group, who tries to influence the voting on legislation or the decisions of government administrators —**lob′by·ism** ***n.***

lobe (lōb) ***n.*** [Fr. < LL. < Gr. *lobos*] a rounded projecting part; specif., *a*) the fleshy lower end of the human ear *b*) any of the main divisions of an organ [a *lobe* of the brain, lung, or liver] *c*) any of the rounded divisions of the leaves of certain trees —**lobed** ***adj.***

lo·be·li·a (lō bēl′yə, -bē′lē ə) ***n.*** [ModL., after Matthias de *L'Obel* (1538–1616), Fl. botanist] any of a genus of plants with white, blue, or red flowers of very irregular shape

lob·lol·ly (läb′läl′ē) ***n.***, *pl.* **-lies** [prob. < dial. *lob*, to boil + dial. *lolly*, broth] **1.** a common pine of the SE U.S., having long needles **2.** the wood of this tree: also **loblolly pine**

lo·bo (lō′bō) ***n.*** [Sp. < L. *lupus*] *same as* GRAY WOLF

lo·bot·o·my (lō bät′ə mē) ***n.***, *pl.* **-mies** [< LOBE + -TOMY] a surgical operation in which a lobe of the brain is cut into or across

lob·ster (läb′stər) ***n.***, *pl.* **-sters, -ster:** see PLURAL, II, D, 1 [OE. *lopustre* < *loppe*, spider (from external resemblance) + *-estre:* see -STER] **1.** a large, edible sea crustacean with compound eyes, long antennae, and five pairs of legs, the first pair of which are modified into large pincers **2.** any similar crustacean, as the spiny lobster **3.** the flesh of these animals used as food

LOBSTER (to 24 in. long)

lobster tail a tail of a lobster (sense 2), or its flesh used as food, often broiled in the shell

lob·ule (läb′yo͞ol) ***n.*** **1.** a small lobe **2.** a subdivision of a lobe —**lob′u·lar** (-yoo lər) ***adj.*** —**lob′u·late′** (-lāt′) ***adj.***

lo·cal (lō′k'l) ***adj.*** [OFr. < LL. *localis* < L. *locus*, a place] **1.** relating to place **2.** of, characteristic of, or confined to a particular place or district [items of *local* interest] **3.** not broad; narrow [*local* outlook] **4.** of or for a particular part of the body **5.** making all stops along its run [a *local* bus] —***n.*** **1.** a local train, bus, etc. **2.** a newspaper item of local interest only **3.** a chapter or branch, as of a labor union —**lo′cal·ly** ***adv.***

local color behavior, speech, etc. characteristic of a certain region or time, introduced into a novel, play, etc. to supply realism

lo·cale (lō kal′) ***n.*** [Fr. *local*] a place or locality, esp. with reference to events, etc. connected with it, often as a setting for a story, etc.

lo·cal·ism (lō′k'l iz'm) ***n.*** **1.** a local custom **2.** a word, meaning, expression, pronunciation, etc. peculiar to one locality **3.** provincialism

lo·cal·i·ty (lō kal′ə tē) ***n.***, *pl.* **-ties** **1.** position with regard to surrounding objects, landmarks, etc. **2.** a place; district

lo·cal·ize (lō′kə līz′) ***vt.*** **-ized′, -iz′ing** to make local; limit, confine, or trace to a particular place, area, or locality —**lo′cal·iz′a·ble** ***adj.*** —**lo′cal·i·za′tion** ***n.***

local option the right to decide by a vote of the residents whether something, esp. the sale of liquor, shall be permitted in their locality

lo·cate (lō′kāt, lō kāt′) ***vt.*** **-cat·ed, -cat·ing** [< L. pp. of *locare* < *locus*, a place] **1.** to designate the site of (a mining claim, etc.) **2.** to establish in a certain place [offices *located* downtown] **3.** to discover the position of after a search [to *locate* a lost object] **4.** to show the position of [to *locate* Guam on a map] **5.** to assign to a particular place, etc. —***vi.*** [Colloq.] to settle [to *locate* in Boston] —**lo′cat·er, lo′ca·tor** ***n.***

lo·ca·tion (lō kā′shən) ***n.*** **1.** a locating or being located **2.** position; place; situation **3.** an area marked off for a specific purpose **4.** *Motion Pictures* an outdoor set or setting, away from the studio, where scenes are photographed: chiefly in **on location** —**lo·ca′tion·al** ***adj.***

loc·a·tive (läk′ə tiv) ***adj.*** [< L. pp. of *locare:* see LOCATE] *Linguis.* expressing place at which or in which —***n.*** **1.** the locative case (in Latin, Greek, etc.) **2.** a word in this case

loc. cit. [L. *loco citato*] in the place cited

loch (läk, läkh) ***n.*** [< Gael. & OIr.] [Scot.] **1.** a lake **2.** an arm of the sea, esp. when narrow and nearly surrounded by land

lo·ci (lō′sī) ***n.*** *pl. of* LOCUS

lock[1] (läk) ***n.*** [OE. *loc*, a bolt, enclosure] **1.** a mechanical device for fastening a door, strongbox, etc. by means of a key or combination **2.** anything that fastens something else and prevents it from operating **3.** a locking together; jam **4.** an enclosed part of a canal, waterway, etc. equipped with gates so that the level of the water can be changed to raise or lower boats from one level to another **5.** the mechanism of a firearm used to explode the ammunition charge **6.** *same as* AIR LOCK **7.** *Wrestling* a hold in which a part of the opponent's body is firmly gripped —***vt.*** **1.** to fasten (a door, trunk, etc.) by means of a lock **2.** to shut (*up, in,* or *out*); confine [*locked* in jail] **3.** to fit closely; link [we *locked* arms] **4.** to embrace tightly **5.** to jam together so as to make immovable [*locked* gears] **6.** to put in a fixed position **7.** to move (a ship) through a lock —***vi.*** **1.** to become locked **2.** to intertwine or interlock —**lock out** to keep (workers) from a place of employment in seeking to force terms upon them —**lock, stock, and barrel** [Colloq.] completely

lock[2] (läk) ***n.*** [OE. *loc*] **1.** a curl, tress, or ringlet of hair **2.** [*pl.*] [Poet.] the hair of the head **3.** a tuft of wool, cotton, etc.

Locke (läk), **John** 1632–1704; Eng. philosopher

lock·er (läk′ər) ***n.*** **1.** a person or thing that locks **2.** a chest, closet, drawer, etc. which can be locked, esp. one for individual use **3.** a large freezer compartment, as one rented in a cold-storage plant

locker room a room equipped with lockers

lock·et (läk′it) ***n.*** [< OFr. *locquet*, dim. of *loc*, a latch < Frank.] a small, hinged ornamental case of gold, silver, etc., for holding a picture, lock of hair, etc.: it is usually worn on a necklace

lock·jaw (läk′jô′) ***n.*** [short for earlier *locked jaw*] *same as* TETANUS

lock·out (-out′) ***n.*** the locking out of workers by an employer

lock·smith (-smith′) ***n.*** a person whose work is making or repairing locks and keys

lock step a way of marching in very close file

lock·up (-up′) ***n.*** a jail

lo·co (lō′kō) ***n.*** [MexSp. < Sp., mad < L. *ulucus*, owl] [Western] *same as:* **1.** LOCOWEED **2.** LOCO DISEASE —***vt.*** **-coed, -co·ing** to poison with locoweed —***adj.*** [Slang] crazy; demented

lo·co- [< L. *locus*, a place] *a combining form meaning* from place to place [*locomotion*]

‡**lo·co ci·ta·to** (lō′kō sī tāt′ō) [L.] in the place cited or quoted

loco disease a nervous disease of horses, sheep, and cattle, caused by locoweed poisoning: also **lo′co·ism** ***n.***

lo·co·mo·tion (lō′kə mō′shən) ***n.*** [LOCO- + MOTION] motion, or the power of moving, from one place to another

lo·co·mo·tive (-mōt′iv) ***adj.*** **1.** of locomotion **2.** moving or capable of moving from one place to another **3.** designating or of engines that move under their own power *[locomotive* design*]* **—*n.*** an engine that can move about by its own power; esp., an electric, steam, or diesel engine on wheels, designed to push or pull a railroad train
lo·co·mo·tor (lō′kə mōt′ər) ***n.*** a person or thing with power of locomotion **—*adj.*** of locomotion
locomotor ataxia *same as* TABES DORSALIS
lo·co·weed (lō′kō wēd′) ***n.*** any of several plants of the legume family, which are common in western N. America and cause loco disease
lo·cus (lō′kəs) ***n.,*** *pl.* **lo·ci** (-sī) **[L.]** **1.** a place **2.** *Math.* a line, plane, etc. every point of which satisfies a given condition
lo·cust (lō′kəst) ***n.*** **[< L.** *locusta***]** **1.** any of various large grasshoppers; specif., a migratory grasshopper often traveling in great swarms destroying vegetation **2.** *same as* SEVENTEEN-YEAR LOCUST **3.** *a)* a spiny tree of the legume family, native to eastern and central U.S. and having racemes of fragrant white flowers *b)* the yellowish, hard wood of this tree **4.** *same as* HONEY LOCUST

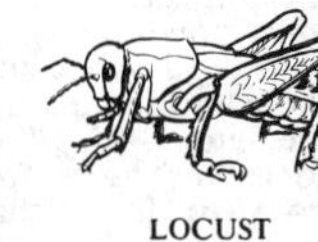
LOCUST
(to 2 in. long)

lo·cu·tion (lō kyōō′shən) ***n.*** **[< L.** *locutio* < pp. of *loqui*, to speak**]** **1.** a word, phrase, or expression **2.** a particular style of speech
lode (lōd) ***n.*** **[**var. of LOAD (< OE. *lad,* course)**]** *Mining* **1.** a vein containing metallic ore and filling a fissure in rock **2.** any deposit of ore separated from the adjoining rock **3.** any rich source
lo·den (lō′d′n) ***adj.*** **[**G. < MHG. < OHG. *lodo,* coarse cloth**]** **1.** designating or of a fulled, waterproof wool cloth, used for coats **2.** of a dark, olive green often used for this cloth
lode·star (lōd′stär′) ***n.*** **[**see LODE & STAR**]** **1.** a star by which one directs his course; esp., the North Star **2.** a guiding principle or ideal
lode·stone (-stōn′) ***n.*** **1.** a strongly magnetic variety of the mineral magnetite **2.** something that attracts as with magnetic force
lodge (läj) ***n.*** **[<** OFr. *loge,* arbor < LL. *lobia* < Gmc.**]** **1.** *a)* a small house for special or seasonal use *[*a hunting *lodge]* *b)* a resort hotel or motel **2.** *a)* the meeting place of a local chapter, as of a fraternal organization *b)* such a local chapter **3.** the den of certain animals, esp. beavers **4.** *a)* the hut or tent of an American Indian *b)* those who live in it **—*vt.* lodged, lodg′ing** **1.** to house, esp. temporarily **2.** to rent rooms to **3.** to deposit for safekeeping **4.** to place or land by shooting, thrusting, etc. (with *in*) **5.** to bring (a complaint, etc.) before legal authorities **6.** to confer (powers) upon (with *in*) **—*vi.*** **1.** to live in a certain place for a time **2.** to live (*with* another or *in* his home) as a paying guest **3.** to come to rest and remain firmly fixed (*in*)
lodg·er (läj′ər) ***n.*** a person or thing that lodges; esp., one who rents a room in another's home
lodg·ing (-iŋ) ***n.*** **1.** a place to live in, esp. temporarily **2.** [*pl.*] a room or rooms rented in a private home
lodging house *same as* ROOMING HOUSE
lodg·ment (-mənt) ***n.*** **1.** a lodging or being lodged **2.** a lodging place **3.** an accumulation of deposited material Also sp. **lodge′ment**
Łódź (looj) city in C Poland: pop. 749,000
lo·ess (les, lō′es) ***n.*** **[**G. *löss* < *lösch,* loose**]** a fine-grained, yellowish-brown, extremely fertile loam deposited by the wind **—lo·ess′i·al *adj.***
loft (lôft, läft) ***n.*** **[**OE. < ON. *lopt,* upper room, sky**]** **1.** *a)* an attic or atticlike space just below the roof of a house, barn, etc. *b)* an upper story of a warehouse or factory **2.** a gallery *[*the choir *loft* in a church*]* **3.** *a)* the slope given to the face of a golf club to aid in hitting the ball in a high curve *b)* the height of a ball hit in a high curve **—*vt.*** **1.** to store in a loft **2.** *a)* to hit or throw (a golf ball, baseball, etc.) into the air in a high curve *b)* to throw (a bowling ball) so that it strikes the alley sharply some distance past the foul line **—*vi.*** to loft a ball **—loft′er *n.***
loft·y (lôf′tē) ***adj.* loft′i·er, loft′i·est** **1.** very high *[*a *lofty* mountain*]* **2.** elevated; noble; grand **3.** haughty; too proud; arrogant **—loft′i·ly *adv.* —loft′i·ness *n.***
log¹ (lôg, läg) ***n.*** **[**ME. *logge,* prob. < or akin to ON. *lāg,* felled tree**]** **1.** a section of the trunk or of a large branch of a felled tree **2.** a device (orig. a quadrant of wood) for measuring the speed of a ship: see also LOG CHIP **3.** a daily record of a ship's speed, progress, etc. and of the events in its voyage; logbook **4.** *a)* a similar record of an aircraft's flight *b)* a record of a pilot's flying time, experience, etc. **5.** any record of progress or occurrences **—*adj.*** made of a log or logs **—*vt.* logged, log′ging** **1.** to saw (trees) into logs **2.** to cut down the trees of (a region) **3.** to enter or record in a log **4.** to sail or fly (a specified distance) **—*vi.*** to cut down trees and transport the logs to a sawmill
log² (lôg, läg) ***n.*** *clipped form of* LOGARITHM
-log *same as* -LOGUE
Lo·gan (lō′gən), **Mount** mountain in SW Yukon, Canada: highest mountain in Canada: 19,850 ft.
lo·gan·ber·ry (lō′gən ber′ē) ***n.,*** *pl.* **-ries** **[**after J. H. *Logan* (1841–1928), U.S. horticulturist**]** **1.** a hybrid bramble developed from the blackberry and the red raspberry **2.** its purplish-red fruit
log·a·rithm (lôg′ə rith′m, läg′-) ***n.*** **[**ModL. < Gr. *logos,* a ratio + *arithmos,* number**]** *Math.* the exponent of the power to which a fixed number (the *base*) must be raised in order to produce a given number (the *antilogarithm*): logarithms are normally computed to the base of 10 and are used for shortening mathematical calculations **—log′a·rith′mic *adj.* —log′a·rith′mi·cal·ly *adv.***
log·book (lôg′book′, läg′-) ***n.*** *same as* LOG¹ (senses 3, 4, & 5)
log chip a flat piece of wood attached to a line (**log line**) and reel (**log reel**) and thrown into the water to measure a ship's rate of speed
loge (lōzh) ***n.*** **[**Fr.: see LODGE**]** **1.** a box in a theater **2.** the forward section of a balcony in a theater
log·ger (lôg′ər, läg′-) ***n.*** a person whose work is logging; lumberjack
log·ger·head (lôg′ər hed′, läg′-) ***n.*** **[**dial. *logger,* block of wood (< LOG¹) + HEAD**]** **1.** a sea turtle of the Atlantic with a large head: also **loggerhead turtle** **2.** [Dial.] a stupid fellow **—at loggerheads** in disagreement; quarreling
log·gi·a (lä′jē ə, lä′jə; lô′-; *It.* lôd′jä) ***n.,*** *pl.* **-gi·as;** It. **log′gie** (-je) **[**It.: see LODGE**]** an arcaded or roofed gallery built into or projecting from the side of a building, often one overlooking an open court

LOGGIA

log·ging (lôg′iŋ, läg′-) ***n.*** the occupation of cutting down trees, cutting them into logs, and transporting them to the sawmill
log·ic (läj′ik) ***n.*** **[<** OFr. < L. < Gr. *logikē* (*technē*), logical (art) < *logos,* word, speech, thought**]** **1.** the science of correct reasoning, dealing with relationships among propositions **2.** a book on this science **3.** correct reasoning; valid induction or deduction **4.** way of reasoning *[*poor *logic]* **5.** necessary connection or outcome, as of events **6.** the systematized interconnections in an electronic digital computer
log·i·cal (läj′i k′l) ***adj.*** **1.** of or used in the science of logic **2.** according to the principles of logic, or correct reasoning **3.** necessary or expected because of what has gone before **4.** using correct reasoning **—log′i·cal′i·ty** (-kal′ə tē), **log′i·cal·ness *n.* —log′i·cal·ly *adv.***
-log·i·cal (läj′i k′l) *a suffix used to form adjectives from nouns ending in* -LOGY *[biological]*: also **-log·ic**
lo·gi·cian (lō jish′ən) ***n.*** an expert in logic
lo·gis·tics (lō jis′tiks) ***n.pl.*** [*with sing. v.*] **[<** Fr. < *logis,* lodgings < *loger,* to quarter**]** the branch of military science having to do with procuring, maintaining, and transporting materiel, personnel, and facilities **—lo·gis′tic, lo·gis′ti·cal *adj.* —lo·gis′ti·cal·ly *adv.***
log·jam (lôg′jam′, läg′-) ***n.*** **1.** logs jammed together in a stream **2.** an accumulation of many items to deal with
log·roll (lôg′rōl′, läg′-) ***vi.*** to take part in logrolling **—*vt.*** to get passage of (a bill) by logrolling **—log′roll′er *n.***
log·roll·ing (-rōl′iŋ) ***n.*** **1.** the act of rolling logs away, as by a group clearing land **2.** mutual aid, esp. among politicians, as by voting for each other's bills **3.** *same as* BIRLING
-logue (lôg, läg) **[**Fr. < L. < Gr. < *logos:* see LOGIC**]** *a combining form meaning:* **1.** a (specified kind of) speaking or writing *[monologue]* **2.** a student or scholar
log·wood (lôg′wood′, läg′-) ***n.*** **[**so named from being imported in logs**]** **1.** the hard, brownish-red wood of a Central American and West Indian tree: it yields a dye used as a stain **2.** this tree or dye
lo·gy (lō′gē) ***adj.* -gi·er, -gi·est** **[<** ? Du. *log,* heavy, dull**]** [Colloq.] dull or sluggish, as from overeating **—lo′gi·ness *n.***
-lo·gy (lə jē) **[**ult. < Gr. < *logos:* see LOGIC**]** *a combining form meaning:* **1.** a (specified kind of) speaking *[eulogy]* **2.** science, doctrine, or theory of *[biology, theology]*
Lo·hen·grin (lō′ən grin′) *Ger. Legend* a knight of the Holy Grail, son of Parsifal
loin (loin) ***n.*** **[<** OFr. *loigne,* ult. < L. *lumbus***]** **1.** [*usually pl.*] the lower part of the back on either side of the backbone between the hipbones and the ribs **2.** the front part of the hindquarters of beef, lamb, veal, etc. with the flank removed **3.** [*pl.*] the hips and the lower abdomen regarded as a part of the body to be clothed or as the region of strength and procreative power **—gird (up) one's loins** to prepare to do something difficult

loin·cloth (-klôth′, -kläth′) *n.* a cloth worn about the loins, as by some tribes in warm climates
Loire (lwȧr) river flowing from S France north & west into the Bay of Biscay
Lo·is (lō′is) [LL. < Gr. *Lōis*] a feminine name
loi·ter (loit′ər) *vi.* [< MDu. *loteren*] **1.** to spend time idly (often with *about*); linger **2.** to move slowly and lazily, with frequent pauses —*vt.* to spend (time) idly —**loi′ter·er** *n.*
Lo·ki (lō′kē) *Norse Myth.* the god who constantly created discord and mischief
loll (läl) *vi.* [< MDu. *lollen*] **1.** to lean or lounge about in a lazy manner **2.** to hang in a relaxed manner; droop —*vt.* to let droop —**loll′er** *n.*
lol·la·pa·loo·za, lol·la·pa·loo·sa (läl′ə pə lo͞o′zə) *n.* [< ?] [Slang] something very striking or exceptional: also **lol-lypalooza,** etc.
Lol·lard (läl′ərd) *n.* [< MDu. *lollaerd,* lit., a mutterer (of prayers)] any of the followers of John Wycliffe in 14th- and 15th-cent. England
lol·li·pop, lol·ly·pop (läl′ē päp′) *n.* [prob. < dial. *lolly,* the tongue + *pop*] a piece of hard candy fixed to the end of a small stick; sucker
lol·lop (läl′əp) *vi.* [extended < LOLL, prob. after GALLOP] [Chiefly Brit.] **1.** to lounge about; loll **2.** to move in a clumsy or relaxed, bobbing way
lol·ly (läl′ē) *n., pl.* **-lies** [contr. < *lollypop:* see LOLLIPOP] [Brit. Slang] **1.** money **2.** a piece of hard candy
lol·ly·gag (läl′ē gag′) *vi.* **-gagged′, -gag′ging** [< ?] [Colloq.] to waste time in trifling activity
Lom·bard (läm′bərd, lum′-; -bärd) *n.* **1.** a native or inhabitant of Lombardy **2.** one of a Germanic tribe that settled in the Po Valley —*adj.* of Lombardy or the Lombards: also **Lom·bar′dic**
Lom·bar·dy (läm′bər dē, lum′-) region of N Italy, on the border of Switzerland: chief city, Milan
Lombardy poplar a tall, slender poplar with upward curving branches
Lo·mond (lō′mənd), **Loch** lake in WC Scotland
Lon·don (lun′dən) **1.** administrative county in SE England, consisting of the City of London & 28 metropolitan boroughs; capital of England, the United Kingdom, & the Brit. Commonwealth **2.** this county with its suburbs: pop. 11,025,000: called *Greater London* **3.** city in SE Ontario, Canada: pop. 240,000 **4. City of,** historic center of the county of London: pop. 4,800 —**Lon′don·er** *n.*
Lon·don (lun′dən), **Jack** 1876–1916; U.S. writer
London broil a boneless cut of beef, as of the flank, that is marinated, then broiled, and served in thin slices
Lon·don·der·ry (lun′dən der′ē) seaport in NW Northern Ireland: pop. 56,000
lone (lōn) *adj.* [< ALONE] **1.** by oneself; solitary **2.** lonesome **3.** unmarried or widowed **4.** *a)* isolated *b)* unfrequented —**lone′ness** *n.*
lone·ly (-lē) *adj.* **-li·er, -li·est** **1.** alone; solitary **2.** *a)* isolated *b)* unfrequented **3.** unhappy at being alone; longing for friends, etc. **4.** causing such a feeling —**lone′li·ly** *adv.* —**lone′li·ness** *n.*
lon·er (lō′nər) *n.* [Colloq.] one who avoids the company of others
lone·some (lōn′səm) *adj.* **1.** having or causing a lonely feeling **2.** unfrequented; desolate —*n.* [Colloq.] self [*all by my lonesome*] —**lone′some·ly** *adv.* —**lone′some·ness** *n.*
long[1] (lôŋ) *adj.* [OE. *long, lang*] **1.** measuring much from one end or point to the other in space or time **2.** of a specified extent in length [*a foot long*] **3.** of greater than usual or standard length, quantity, etc. [*a long ton, a long list*] **4.** overextended in length **5.** tedious; slow **6.** extending to what is distant in space or time; far-reaching [*a long view of the matter*] **7.** large; big [*long odds, a long chance*] **8.** well supplied [*long on excuses*] **9.** holding a supply of a commodity or security in anticipation of a rise in price **10.** requiring a relatively long time to pronounce: said of a speech sound —*adv.* **1.** for a long time **2.** for the duration of [*all day long*] **3.** at a much earlier or a much later time [*to stay long after midnight*] —*n.* **1.** a variation of a clothing size longer than average for that size **2.** a signal, syllable, etc. of long duration **3.** a long time [*it won't take long*] —**as** (or **so**) **long as** **1.** during the time that **2.** seeing that; since **3.** provided that —**before long** soon —**the long and (the) short of** the whole story of in a few words
long[2] (lôŋ) *vi.* [OE. *langian*] to feel a strong yearning; wish earnestly [*to long to go home*]
long. longitude
Long Beach seaport in SW Calif., on the Pacific: pop. 361,000
long·boat (lôŋ′bōt′) *n.* the largest boat carried on a merchant sailing ship
long·bow (-bō′) *n.* a large bow drawn by hand and shooting a long, feathered arrow: cf. CROSSBOW
long·cloth (-klôth′, -kläth′) *n.* a soft cotton fabric of fine quality
long distance a telephone service or system for calls to distant places —**long′-dis′tance** *adj., adv.*
long division the process of dividing one number by another and putting the steps down in full
long-drawn (-drôn′) *adj.* continuing for a long time; prolonged: also **long′-drawn′-out′**
lon·gev·i·ty (län jev′ə tē, lôn-) *n.* [< L. < *longus,* long + *aevum,* age] **1.** *a)* great span of life *b)* length of life **2.** length of service
long face a glum, disconsolate look —**long′-faced′** *adj.*
Long·fel·low (lôŋ′fel′ō), **Henry Wads·worth** (wädz′wurth′) 1807–82; U.S. poet
long green *slang term for* PAPER MONEY
long·hair (lôŋ′her′) *adj.* [Colloq.] designating or of intellectuals or their tastes; specif., preferring classical music to jazz or popular tunes: also **long′haired′** —*n.* [Colloq.] **1.** an intellectual; specif., a longhair musician **2.** *same as* HIPPIE
long·hand (-hand′) *n.* ordinary handwriting, with the words written out in full
long-head·ed, long·head·ed (-hed′id) *adj.* **1.** having a long head **2.** having much foresight; shrewd —**long′-head′ed·ly** *adv.* —**long′-head′ed·ness** *n.*
long·horn (-hôrn′) *n.* any of a breed of long-horned cattle formerly raised in great numbers in the Southwest
long house a communal home or council hall among the Iroquois and other Indian tribes
long·ing (-iŋ) *n.* strong desire; yearning —*adj.* feeling or showing a yearning —**long′ing·ly** *adv.*
long·ish (-ish) *adj.* somewhat long
Long Island island in SE N.Y., between Long Island Sound & the Atlantic: pop. 6,728,000
Long Island Sound arm of the Atlantic, between N Long Island & S Conn.
lon·gi·tude (län′jə to͞od′, -tyo͞od′) *n.* [< L. *longitudo* < *longus,* LONG[1]] **1.** length **2.** distance east or west on the earth's surface, measured as an arc of the equator (in degrees up to 180° or by the difference in time) between the meridian passing through a particular place and a standard or prime meridian, usually the one passing through Greenwich, England
lon·gi·tu·di·nal (län′jə to͞od′'n əl, -tyo͞od′-) *adj.* **1.** of or in length **2.** running or placed lengthwise **3.** of longitude —**lon′gi·tu′di·nal·ly** *adv.*
long johns [Colloq.] long underwear: also **long′ies**
long jump a track and field event that is a jump for distance rather than height
long-lived (lôŋ′līvd′, -livd′) *adj.* having or tending to have a long life span or existence
long-play·ing (lôŋ′plā′iŋ) *adj.* designating or of a phonograph record with microgrooves, for playing at 33 1/3 revolutions per minute
long-range (-rānj′) *adj.* **1.** having a range of great distance **2.** taking the future into consideration [*long-range plans*]
long·shore·man (-shôr′mən) *n., pl.* **-men** [(*a*)*longshore* + *man*] a person who works on the waterfront loading and unloading ships
long shot [Colloq.] a betting choice that has little chance of winning and, hence, carries great odds —**not by a long shot** [Colloq.] not at all
long·sight·ed (-sīt′id) *adj. same as* FARSIGHTED
long·stand·ing (-stan′diŋ) *adj.* having continued for a long time
long-suf·fer·ing (-suf′ər iŋ) *adj.* bearing injuries, insults, trouble, etc. patiently for a long time —*n.* long and patient endurance of trials —**long′-suf′fer·ing·ly** *adv.*
long suit **1.** the suit in which a card player holds the most cards **2.** something at which one excels
long-term (-turm′) *adj.* **1.** for or extending over a long time **2.** designating or of a capital gain, loan, etc. that involves a relatively long period
long·time (-tīm′) *adj.* over a long period of time
long ton the British ton, equal to 2,240 pounds
‡**lon·gueur** (lōn gër′; *E.* lôŋ gur′) *n.* [Fr.] a long, boring section, as in a novel, musical work, etc.
long-waist·ed (lôŋ′wās′tid) *adj.* with a low waistline
long·ways (-wāz′) *adv. same as* LENGTHWISE: also **long′wise′** (-wīz′)
long-wind·ed (-win′did) *adj.* **1.** not easily winded by exertion **2.** *a)* speaking or writing at great length *b)* tiresomely long —**long′-wind′ed·ly** *adv.* —**long′-wind′ed·ness** *n.*
loo[1] (lo͞o) *n.* [< Fr. *lanturelu*] a card game played for a pool made up of stakes and forfeits
loo[2] (lo͞o) *n.* [< Fr. *lieux,* short for *les lieux d'aisances,* lit., places of conveniences] [Brit. Slang] a toilet

look (look) *vi.* [OE. *locian*] **1.** to see **2.** *a)* to direct one's eyes in order to see *b)* to direct one's attention mentally upon something **3.** to search **4.** to appear; seem **5.** to be facing in a specified direction **6.** to expect (followed by an infinitive) —*vt.* **1.** to direct one's eyes on [*look* him in the face] **2.** to express by one's looks [to *look* one's disgust] **3.** to appear as having attained (some age) [he *looks* his years] —*n.* **1.** the act of looking; glance **2.** outward aspect [the *look* of a beggar] **3.** [Colloq.] *a)* [*usually pl.*] appearance [from the *looks* of things] *b)* [*pl.*] personal appearance, esp. of a pleasing nature [to have *looks* and youth] —*interj.* **1.** see! **2.** pay attention! —**look after** to take care of —**look alive** (or **sharp**)! be alert! —**look down on** (or **upon**) to regard with contempt —**look for** **1.** to search for **2.** to expect —**look forward to** to anticipate, esp. eagerly —**look in (on)** to pay a brief visit (to) —**look on** **1.** to be an observer or spectator **2.** to consider; regard —**look (like) oneself** to seem in normal health, spirits, etc. —**look out** to be on the watch; be careful —**look out for** **1.** to be wary about **2.** to take care of —**look over** to examine; inspect —**look to** **1.** to take care of **2.** to rely upon; resort to **3.** to expect —**look up** **1.** to search for in a reference book, etc. **2.** [Colloq.] to pay a visit to **3.** [Colloq.] to improve —**look up to** to admire —**look′er** *n.*

look·er-on (look′ər än′) *n., pl.* **look′ers-on′** an observer or spectator; onlooker

looking glass a (glass) mirror

look·out (look′out′) *n.* **1.** a careful watching for someone or something **2.** a place for keeping watch, esp. a high place **3.** a person detailed to watch **4.** [Chiefly Brit.] outlook **5.** [Colloq.] concern; worry

loom¹ (lo͞om) *n.* [OE. (*ge*)*loma,* tool, utensil] a machine for weaving thread or yarn into cloth —*vt.* to weave on a loom

loom² (lo͞om) *vi.* [< ?] to appear, take shape, or come in sight indistinctly, esp. in a large or threatening form [the peak *loomed* up before us, disaster *loomed* ahead]

loon¹ (lo͞on) *n.* [earlier *loom* < ON. *lomr*] a fish-eating, diving bird with a sharp bill and webbed feet: noted for its weird cry

loon² (lo͞on) *n.* [Scot. *loun* < ?] **1.** a clumsy, stupid person **2.** a crazy person

loon·y (lo͞o′nē) *adj.* **loon′i·er, loon′i·est** [< LUNATIC] [Slang] crazy; demented —*n., pl.* **loon′ies** [Slang] a loony person Also **loon′ey**

loop (lo͞op) *n.* [< Anglo-N. forms corresponding to ON. *hlaup,* a leap, *hlaupa,* to run] **1.** the figure formed by a line, thread, wire, etc. that curves back to cross itself **2.** anything having or forming this figure, as a written *l* **3.** a sharp bend, as in a mountain road **4.** a ring-shaped fastening or ornament **5.** a plastic intrauterine contraceptive device (usually with *the*) **6.** *Aeron.* a maneuver in which an airplane describes a closed curve or circle in the vertical plane —*vt.* **1.** to make a loop or loops in or of **2.** to wrap around one or more times [*loop* the wire around the post] **3.** to fasten with a loop or loops —*vi.* **1.** to form a loop or loops **2.** *Aeron.* to perform a loop or loops —**knock** (or **throw**) **for a loop** [Slang] to throw into a state of confusion or shock —**loop the loop** to make a vertical loop in the air, as in an airplane —**loop′er** *n.*

loop·hole (-hōl′) *n.* [prob. < MDu. *lupen,* to peer + HOLE] **1.** a hole or narrow slit in the wall of a fort, etc. for looking or shooting through **2.** a means of evading an obligation, a law, etc.

loose (lo͞os) *adj.* [< ON. *lauss*] **1.** not confined or restrained; free **2.** not put up in a package [*loose* salt] **3.** readily available [*loose* cash] **4.** not firmly fastened down or in [a *loose* wheel] **5.** not taut; slack **6.** not tight [*loose* clothing] **7.** not compact or compactly constructed [*loose* soil, a *loose* frame] **8.** not restrained [*loose* talk] **9.** not precise; inexact [a *loose* translation] **10.** sexually immoral; lewd **11.** *a)* not strained [a *loose* cough] *b)* moving freely or excessively [*loose* bowels] **12.** [Colloq.] relaxed; easy —*adv.* loosely; in a loose manner —*vt.* **loosed, loos′ing** **1.** to make loose; specif., *a)* to set free; unbind *b)* to make less tight *c)* to make less compact *d)* to free from restraint; relax **2.** to let fly; release [he *loosed* the arrow] —*vi.* to loose something or become loose —**break loose** to free oneself; escape —**cast loose** to untie or unfasten —**let loose (with)** to release; let go —**on the loose** **1.** not confined or bound; free **2.** [Colloq.] having fun in a free, unrestrained manner —**set** (or **turn**) **loose** to make free; release —**loose′ly** *adv.* —**loose′ness** *n.*

loose ends minor bits of unfinished work, etc. —**at loose ends** unsettled, unoccupied, unemployed, etc.

loose-joint·ed (-join′tid) *adj.* **1.** having loose joints **2.** moving freely; limber —**loose′-joint′ed·ly** *adv.* —**loose′-joint′ed·ness** *n.*

loose-leaf (-lēf′) *adj.* having leaves, or sheets, that can easily be removed or replaced

loos·en (lo͞os′'n) *vt., vi.* to make or become loose or looser —**loosen up** [Colloq.] **1.** to talk freely **2.** to give money generously **3.** to relax —**loos′en·er** *n.*

loose·strife (-strīf′) *n.* [transl. of L. *lysimachia* < Gr. < *lyein,* to slacken + *machē,* battle] **1.** a plant with leafy stems and loose spikes of white, rose, or yellow flowers **2.** a plant (**purple loosestrife**) with spikes of purple flowers

loot (lo͞ot) *n.* [Hindi *lūt* < Sans. *lunt,* to rob] **1.** goods stolen or taken by force; plunder; spoils **2.** [Slang] money, gifts, etc. —*vt., vi.* to plunder —**loot′er** *n.*

lop¹ (läp) *vt.* **lopped, lop′ping** [OE. *loppian,* prob. < Scand.] **1.** to trim (a tree, etc.) by cutting off branches or twigs **2.** to remove by or as by cutting off —*n.* something lopped off —**lop′per** *n.*

lop² (läp) *vi.* **lopped, lop′ping** [prob. akin to LOB] **1.** to hang down loosely **2.** to move in a halting way —*adj.* hanging down loosely

lope (lōp) *vi.* **loped, lop′ing** [< ON. *hlaupa,* to leap] to move with a long, swinging stride or in an easy canter —*vt.* to cause to lope —*n.* a long, easy, swinging stride

lop-eared (läp′ird′) *adj.* having ears that droop or hang down

lop·sid·ed (-sīd′id) *adj.* **1.** noticeably heavier, bigger, or lower on one side **2.** not balanced; uneven —**lop′sid′ed·ly** *adv.* —**lop′sid′ed·ness** *n.*

lo·qua·cious (lō kwā′shəs) *adj.* [< L. *loquax* < *loqui,* to speak] very talkative; fond of talking —**lo·qua′cious·ly** *adv.* —**lo·qua′cious·ness** *n.*

lo·quac·i·ty (-kwas′ə tē) *n.* talkativeness, esp. when excessive

Lo·rain (lô rān′) [ult. after LORRAINE (France)] city in N Ohio, on Lake Erie: pop. 75,000

Lor·an (lôr′an) *n.* [< *Lo(ng) Ra(nge) N(avigation)*] [*also* **l-**] a system by which a ship or aircraft can determine its position by the difference in time between radio signals sent from two or more known stations

lord (lôrd) *n.* [OE. *hlaford* < *hlaf,* loaf + *weard,* keeper] **1.** a person having great power and authority; ruler; master **2.** the head of a feudal estate **3.** [**L-**] *a)* God *b)* Jesus Christ **4.** in Great Britain, *a)* a nobleman holding the rank of baron, viscount, earl, or marquess; member of the House of Lords *b)* a man who by courtesy or because of his office is given the title of Lord **5.** [**L-**] [*pl.*] the House of Lords in the British Parliament (usually with *the*) **6.** [**L-**] in Great Britain, the title of a lord, variously used —*interj.* [*often* **L-**] an exclamation of surprise or irritation —**lord it (over)** to domineer (over)

lord·ly (-lē) *adj.* **-li·er, -li·est** of, like, characteristic of, or suitable to a lord; specif., *a)* noble; grand *b)* haughty; overbearing —*adv.* in the manner of a lord —**lord′li·ness** *n.*

Lord of hosts Jehovah; God

Lord's day Sunday

lord·ship (lôrd′ship′) *n.* **1.** the rank or authority of a lord **2.** rule; dominion **3.** [*also* **L-**] a title used in speaking of or to a lord: with *his* or *your*

Lord's Prayer the prayer beginning *Our Father,* which Jesus taught his disciples: Matt. 6:9–13

lords spiritual the archbishops and bishops who are members of the British House of Lords

Lord's Supper **1.** *same as* LAST SUPPER **2.** Holy Communion; Eucharist

lords temporal those members of the British House of Lords who are not clergymen

lore (lôr) *n.* [OE. *lar*] knowledge or learning; specif., all the knowledge concerning a particular subject, esp. that of a traditional nature

Lor·e·lei (lôr′ə lī′) [G.] *German Legend* a siren whose singing on a rock in the Rhine lured sailors to shipwreck on the reefs

Lo·ret·ta (lô ret′ə, lə-) [dim. of LAURA] a feminine name

lor·gnette (lôr nyet′) *n.* [Fr. < *lorgner,* to spy, peep < OFr. *lorgne,* squinting] a pair of eyeglasses, or an opera glass, attached to a handle

LORGNETTE

lorn (lôrn) *adj.* [ME., pp. of *losen,* to lose] **1.** [Obs.] lost; ruined **2.** [Archaic] forsaken, forlorn, bereft, or desolate

Lor·raine (lô rān′; *Fr.* lô ren′) [Fr.] **1.** a feminine name **2.** former province of NE France: see ALSACE-LORRAINE

lor·ry (lôr′ē, lär′-) *n., pl.* **-ries** [prob. < dial. *lurry, lorry,* to tug] **1.** a low, flat wagon without sides **2.** [Brit.] a motor truck

lo·ry (lôr′ē) *n., pl.* **-ries** [Malay *lūrī*] a small, brightly colored parrot native to Australia and nearby islands

Los An·gel·es (lôs an′jə ləs, läs; aŋ′gə ləs; -lēz′) [Sp., lit., the angels] city & seaport on the SW coast of Calif.: pop. 2,967,000 (met. area 7,446,000)

lose (lo͞oz) *vt.* **lost, los′ing** [< OE. *losian,* to be lost + *leosan,* to lose] **1.** to bring to ruin or destruction **2.** to become unable to find; mislay [I *lost* my key] **3.** to have taken from one by accident, death, removal, etc.; suffer the loss of **4.** to get rid of [dieting to *lose* weight] **5.** to fail to keep or maintain [to *lose* one's temper, to *lose* one's job] **6.** *a)* to fail to see, hear, or understand *b)* to fail to keep in sight, mind, etc. **7.** to fail to have, get, take, etc.; miss **8.** to fail to win [to *lose* a game] **9.** to cause the loss of [it *lost* him his job] **10.** to wander from and not be able to find (one's way, etc.) **11.** to confuse, bewilder, or alienate **12.** to waste; squander [to *lose* time] **13.** to outdistance **14.** to engross or preoccupy [to be *lost* in reverie] **15.** to go slower by [my watch *lost* a minute] *—vi.* **1.** to suffer loss **2.** to be defeated in a contest, etc. **3.** to be slow: said of a timepiece **—lose oneself 1.** to go astray; become bewildered **2.** to become engrossed **—lose out** [Colloq.] to fail **—lose out on** [Colloq.] to fail to take advantage of or gain **—los′a·ble** *adj.*

los·er (lo͞o′zər) *n.* **1.** one that loses; esp., [Colloq.] one that seems doomed to lose **2.** a person who reacts to loss as specified [a poor *loser*]

los·ing (-ziŋ) *n.* [*pl.*] losses by gambling *—adj.* **1.** that loses [a *losing* team] **2.** resulting in loss [a *losing* game]

loss (lôs, läs) *n.* [< ? OE. *los,* ruin] **1.** a losing or being lost **2.** the damage, disadvantage, etc. caused by losing something **3.** the person, thing, or amount lost **4.** *Insurance a)* death, damage, etc. that is the basis for a valid claim *b)* the amount paid by the insurer **5.** *Mil. a)* the losing of military personnel in combat by death, injury, or capture *b)* [*pl.*] those lost in this way *c)* [*pl.*] ships, aircraft, etc. lost in battle **—at a loss (to)** puzzled or uncertain (how to)

loss leader any article that a store sells cheaply or below cost to attract customers

lost (lôst, läst) *pt. & pp. of* LOSE *—adj.* **1.** destroyed; ruined **2.** not to be found; missing **3.** no longer held, possessed, seen, heard, or known **4.** not gained or won **5.** having wandered from the way **6.** bewildered; ill at ease **7.** wasted; squandered **—lost in** engrossed in **—lost on** without effect on **—lost to 1.** no longer in the possession of **2.** no longer available to **3.** insensible to

lost tribes the ten tribes making up the kingdom of Israel that were carried off into Assyrian captivity about 722 B.C.: II Kings 17:6

lot (lät) *n.* [OE. *hlot*] **1.** any of a number of counters, etc. drawn from at random to decide a matter by chance **2.** the use of such a method [to choose men by *lot*] **3.** the decision arrived at by this means **4.** what one receives as the result of such a decision; share **5.** one's portion in life; fortune [her unhappy *lot*] **6.** a plot of ground **7.** *a)* a number of persons or things regarded as a group *b)* a quantity of material processed at the same time **8.** [*often pl.*] [Colloq.] a great number or amount **9.** [Colloq.] sort (of person) [he's a bad *lot*] **10.** a motion-picture studio *—adv.* very much [a *lot* richer] : also **lots** *—vt.* **lot′ted, lot′ting** to divide into lots *—vi.* to draw or cast lots **—cast** (or **throw**) **in one's lot with** to share the fortunes of **—draw** (or **cast**) **lots** to decide an issue by using lots **—the lot** [Colloq.] the entire amount or number

Lot (lät) *Bible* Abraham's nephew, who, warned by angels, fled from Sodom: his wife looked back to see it destroyed and was turned into a pillar of salt: Gen. 19:1–26

loth (lōth) *adj. alt. sp. of* LOATH

Lo·thar·i·o (lō ther′ē ō′) *n., pl.* **-i·os′** [after the young rake in a play by Nicholas Rowe (1674–1718)] [*often* **l-**] a lighthearted seducer of women

lo·tion (lō′shən) *n.* [< L. < pp. of *lavare,* to wash] a liquid preparation used, as on the skin, for washing, soothing, healing, etc.

lot·ter·y (lät′ər ē) *n., pl.* **-ter·ies** [< MFr. < MDu. < *lot,* lot] **1.** a game of chance in which people buy numbered chances on prizes, the winning numbers being drawn by lot **2.** any undertaking involving chance selection, as by the drawing of lots [military draft *lottery*]

lot·to (lät′ō) *n.* [It. < Fr. < MDu. *lot,* lot] a game of chance played with cards having squares numbered in rows: counters are placed on those numbers corresponding to numbered disks drawn by lot

lo·tus, lo·tos (lōt′əs) *n.* [L. < Gr. *lōtos* < Heb. *lōṭ*] **1.** *Gr. Legend* a plant whose fruit induced a dreamy languor and forgetfulness **2.** any of several tropical African and Asiatic waterlilies, as the **white lotus** of Egypt **3.** a plant of the legume family, with irregular leaves and yellow, purple, or white flowers

lo·tus-eat·er (-ēt′ər) *n.* in the *Odyssey,* one of a people who ate the fruit of the lotus and became indolent, dreamy, and forgetful of duty

lotus position in yoga, an erect sitting posture with the legs crossed, each foot resting on the opposite thigh

loud (loud) *adj.* [OE. *hlud*] **1.** strongly audible: said of sound **2.** sounding with great intensity [a *loud* bell] **3.** noisy **4.** clamorous; emphatic [*loud* denials] **5.** [Colloq.] too vivid; flashy [a *loud* pattern] **6.** [Colloq.] unrefined; vulgar *—adv.* in a loud manner **—loud′ish** *adj.* **—loud′ly** *adv.* **—loud′ness** *n.*

loud·mouthed (-mouтht′, -mouthd′) *adj.* talking in a loud, irritating voice **—loud′mouth′** *n.*

loud·speak·er (-spē′kər) *n.* a device for converting electric current into sound waves and for amplifying this sound

Lou·is (lo͞o′ē; *for 1, usually* lo͞o′is; *Fr.* lwē) [Fr., ult. < OHG. *Hluodowig* < Gmc. bases meaning "famous in war"] **1.** a masculine name: dim. *Lou, Louie* **2. Louis XIV** 1638–1715; king of France (1643–1715) **3. Louis XV** 1710–74; king of France (1715–74): great-grandson of *prec.* **4. Louis XVI** 1754–93; king of France (1774–92): guillotined: grandson of *prec.*

lou·is d'or (lo͞o′ē dôr′) [Fr., gold louis] **1.** an old French gold coin of varying value **2.** a later French gold coin worth 20 francs

Lou·ise (loo wēz′) [Fr., fem. of LOUIS] **1.** a feminine name: dim. *Lou;* var. *Louisa* **2. Lake,** small lake in SW Alberta, Canada

Lou·i·si·an·a (loo wē′zē an′ə, lo͞o′ə zē-) [< Fr., ult. after LOUIS XIV] Southern State of the U.S., on the Gulf of Mexico: 48,523 sq. mi.; pop. 4,204,000; cap. Baton Rouge: abbrev. **La., LA —Lou·i′si·an′i·an, Lou·i′si·an′an** *adj., n.*

Louis Napoleon (surname *Bonaparte*) 1808–73; president of France (1848–52) &, as Napoleon III, emperor (1852–70): deposed: nephew of NAPOLEON I

Lou·is·ville (lo͞o′ē vil; *locally* lo͞o′ə vəl) [after LOUIS XVI] city in N Ky.: pop. 298,000 (met. area 902,000)

lounge (lounj) *vi.* **lounged, loung′ing** [Scot. dial. < ? *lungis,* laggard] **1.** to stand, move, sit, etc. in a relaxed or lazy way **2.** to spend time in idleness *—vt.* to spend (time) by lounging *—n.* **1.** an act or time of lounging **2.** a room, as in a hotel or theater, with comfortable furniture and, often, an adjoining toilet or toilets **3.** a couch or sofa **—loung′er** *n.*

loupe (lo͞op) *n.* [Fr., ult. prob. < OHG. *luppa,* shapeless mass] a small, high-powered magnifying lens held close to the eye, used by jewelers, etc.

lour (lour) *vi., n. same as* LOWER[2]

Lourdes (loord, loordz; *Fr.* lo͞ord) town in SW France: site of a famous Catholic shrine

louse (lous; *also, for v.,* louz) *n., pl.* **lice** [OE. *lus* (pl. *lys*)] **1.** *a)* a small, wingless, parasitic insect that infests the hair or skin of man and some other mammals *b)* any of various arthropods that suck blood or juice from other animals or plants **2.** any similar insect, arachnid, etc., as the wood louse **3.** *pl.* **lous′es** [Slang] a person regarded as mean, contemptible, etc. *—vt.* **loused, lous′ing** [Rare] to delouse **—louse up** [Slang] to botch; spoil; ruin

lous·y (lou′zē) *adj.* **lous′i·er, lous′i·est 1.** infested with lice **2.** [Slang] dirty, disgusting, or contemptible **3.** [Slang] poor; inferior: a generalized epithet of disapproval **4.** [Slang] oversupplied (*with*) **—lous′i·ly** *adv.* **—lous′i·ness** *n.*

lout (lout) *n.* [prob. < ME. *lutien,* to lurk < OE. *lutian*] a clumsy, stupid fellow; boor **—lout′ish** *adj.* **—lout′ish·ly** *adv.* **—lout′ish·ness** *n.*

lou·ver (lo͞o′vər) *n.* [MFr. *lover* < MDu. *love,* theater gallery] **1.** an opening fitted with sloping slats so as to admit light and air but shed rain **2.** any of these slats: also **louver board 3.** any set of slats or fins used to control ventilation, etc. Also **lou′vre —lou′vered** *adj.*

Lou·vre (lo͞o′vrə, lo͞ov; *Fr.* lo͞o′vr′) ancient royal palace in Paris, now an art museum

lov·a·ble (luv′ə b′l) *adj.* inspiring love; easily loved; endearing: also sp. **love′a·ble —lov′a·bil′i·ty, lov′a·ble·ness** *n.* **—lov′a·bly** *adv.*

love (luv) *n.* [OE. *lufu*] **1.** a deep affection for or attachment or devotion to someone, or the expression of this **2.** good will toward others **3.** *a)* a strong liking for or interest in something [a *love* of music] *b)* the object of such liking **4.** *a)* a strong, usually passionate, affection of one person for another *b)* the object of this; sweetheart **5.** sexual passion or intercourse **6.** [**L-**] *a)* Cupid *b)* [Rare] Venus **7.** *Tennis* a score of zero *—vt.* **loved, lov′ing 1.** to feel love for **2.** to show love for by fondling, kissing, etc. **3.** to take great pleasure in [to *love* books] **4.** to benefit from [plants *love* light] *—vi.* to feel the emotion of love **—fall in love (with)** to begin to feel love (for) **—for the love of** for the sake of **—in love** feeling love **—make love 1.** to embrace, kiss, etc. **2.** to have sexual intercourse

love affair an amorous relationship between two people not married to each other

love apple [Archaic] the tomato

love·bird (-burd′) *n.* any of various small parrots, often kept as cage birds: the mates appear to be greatly attached to each other

love-hate (-hāt′) *adj.* characterized simultaneously by feelings of love and hate [a *love-hate* relationship]

Love·lace (luv′lās′), **Richard** 1618–58; Eng. poet
love·less (-lis) ***adj.*** without love; specif., *a)* feeling no love *b)* unloved —**love′less·ly *adv.*** —**love′less·ness *n.***
love-lies-bleed·ing (-līz′blēd′iŋ) ***n.*** a cultivated amaranth with spikes of small, red flowers
love·lorn (-lôrn′) ***adj.*** deserted by one's sweetheart; pining from love
love·ly (-lē) ***adj.*** **-li·er, -li·est** having qualities that inspire love, admiration, etc.; specif., *a)* beautiful *b)* morally or spiritually attractive *c)* [Colloq.] highly enjoyable *[a lovely party]* —***n.,*** *pl.* **-lies** [Colloq.] a beautiful young woman —**love′li·ly *adv.*** —**love′li·ness *n.***
love·mak·ing (-mā′kiŋ) ***n.*** the act of making love
love potion a magic drink supposed to arouse in the drinker love for a certain person
lov·er (-ər) ***n.*** a person who loves; specif., *a)* a sweetheart *b)* [*pl.*] a couple in love with each other *c)* a partner, esp. the male partner, in a love affair *d)* a person who greatly enjoys some (specified) thing *[a lover of good music]* —**lov′er·ly *adj., adv.***
love seat a small sofa seating two persons
love·sick (-sik′) ***adj.*** **1.** so much in love as to be unable to act normally **2.** expressive of such a condition —**love′sick′ness *n.***
lov·ing (-iŋ) ***adj.*** feeling or expressing love —**lov′ing·ly *adv.***
loving cup a large drinking cup with two handles, formerly passed among guests at banquets: now often given as a trophy in sports, etc.
lov·ing·kind·ness (-kīnd′nis) ***n.*** kindness resulting from or expressing love
low[1] (lō) ***adj.*** [ME. *lah* < ON. *lagr*] **1.** *a)* not high or tall *b)* not far above the ground **2.** depressed below the surrounding surface *[low land]* **3.** of little depth; shallow **4.** of little quantity, degree, value, etc. **5.** of less than normal height, depth, degree, etc. **6.** below others in order, position, etc. **7.** near the horizon *[the sun is low]* **8.** near the equator *[low latitudes]* **9.** exposing the neck and shoulders *[a dress with a low neckline]* **10.** in hiding *[stay low]* **11.** deep *[a low bow]* **12.** lacking energy; weak **13.** depressed; melancholy **14.** not of high rank; humble **15.** vulgar; coarse **16.** mean; contemptible *[a low trick]* **17.** unfavorable *[to have a low opinion of someone]* **18.** having less than a normal amount of some usual element *[low in calories]* **19.** not advanced in evolution, development, etc. *[a low form of plant life]* **20.** relatively recent *[a manuscript of low date]* **21.** designating or of the gear ratio of a motor vehicle transmission which produces the lowest speed and greatest power **22.** *a)* not well supplied with *[low on fuel]* *b)* [Colloq.] short of ready cash **23.** *a)* not loud *b)* deep in pitch **24.** very informal in matters of ceremony, doctrine, etc. **25.** *Phonet.* produced with the tongue held low in the mouth: said of some vowels, as (ä) —***adv.*** **1.** in, to, or toward a low position, level, etc. **2.** in a low manner **3.** quietly; softly **4.** with a deep pitch —***n.*** something low; specif., *a)* low gear (see *adj.* 21), or a similar arrangement in an automatic transmission *b)* a low level, point, degree, etc. *c)* *Meteorol.* an area of low barometric pressure —**lay low 1.** to cause to fall by hitting **2.** to overcome or kill —**lie low 1.** to keep oneself hidden **2.** to wait patiently —**low′ness *n.***
low[2] (lō) ***vi.*** [OE. *hlowan*] to make the characteristic sound of a cow; moo —***n.*** the characteristic sound of a cow
low·born (-bôrn′) ***adj.*** of humble birth
low·boy (-boi′) ***n.*** a chest of drawers mounted on short legs to about the height of a table
low·bred (-bred′) ***adj.*** ill-mannered; vulgar
low·brow (-brou′) ***n.*** [Colloq.] a person lacking intellectual tastes —***adj.*** [Colloq.] of or for a lowbrow
low-cal (-kal′) ***adj.*** having a low caloric value
Low Church that party of the Anglican Church which attaches little importance to the priesthood or to traditional rituals, doctrines, etc. —**Low′-Church′ *adj.***
low comedy comedy that gets its effect mainly from action and situation, as burlesque, farce, etc.
Low Countries the Netherlands, Belgium, & Luxembourg
low·down (lō′doun′; *for adj.* -doun′) ***n.*** [Slang] the pertinent facts (with *the*) —***adj.*** [Colloq.] mean; contemptible; despicable
Low·ell (lō′əl) [after F.C. *Lowell* (1775–1817), industrialist] city in NE Mass.: pop. 92,000
Low·ell (lō′əl) **1. Amy,** 1874–1925; U.S. poet **2. James Russell,** 1819–91; U.S. poet, essayist, & editor **3. Robert,** 1917–77; U.S. poet
low·er[1] (lō′ər) ***adj.*** *compar. of* LOW[1] **1.** below or farther down in place, rank, dignity, etc. **2.** less in quantity, value, intensity, etc. **3.** farther south, closer to the mouth of a river, etc. **4.** [L-] *Geol.* earlier: used of a division of a period —***vt.*** **1.** to let or put down *[lower the window]* **2.** to reduce in height, amount, value, etc. *[to lower prices]* **3.** to weaken or lessen *[to lower one's resistance]* **4.** to demean; degrade **5.** to reduce (a sound) in volume or in pitch —***vi.*** to become lower; sink; fall
low·er[2] (lou′ər) ***vi.*** [ME. *louren*] **1.** to scowl or frown **2.** to appear dark and threatening —***n.*** a lowering look
Lower California *same as* BAJA CALIFORNIA
lower case small-letter type used in printing, as distinguished from capital letters (*upper case*) —**low′er-case′ *adj.*** —**low′er-case′ *vt.* - cased′, -cas′ing**
lower class the social class below the middle class; working class, or proletariat
low·er·class·man (lō′ər klas′mən) ***n.,*** *pl.* **-men** a student who is a freshman or sophomore
Lower House [*often* **l- h-**] the larger and more representative branch of a legislature having two branches, as the U.S. House of Representatives
low·er·ing (lou′ər iŋ) ***adj.*** **1.** scowling; frowning darkly **2.** dark, as if about to rain or snow —**low′er·ing·ly *adv.***
lower world 1. *same as* NETHER WORLD **2.** the earth
low frequency any radio frequency between 30 and 300 kilohertz
Low German 1. *same as* PLATTDEUTSCH **2.** the West Germanic languages, other than High German, including Plattdeutsch, English, Dutch, Frisian, etc.
low-grade (lō′grād′) ***adj.*** **1.** of inferior quality **2.** of low degree *[a low-grade infection]*
low-key (-kē′) ***adj.*** of low intensity, tone, etc.; subdued or restrained: also **low′-keyed′**
low·land (lō′lənd; *also, for n.,* -land′) ***n.*** land that is below the level of the surrounding land —***adj.*** of, in, or from such a region —**the Lowlands** lowland region in SC Scotland —**low′land·er, Low′land·er *n.***
Low Latin nonclassical, esp. medieval, Latin
low·life (-līf′) ***n.*** [Slang] a disgusting person
low·ly (-lē) ***adj.*** **-li·er, -li·est 1.** of or suited to a low position or rank **2.** humble; meek **3.** ordinary —***adv.*** **1.** humbly; meekly **2.** in a low manner, position, etc. **3.** softly; gently —**low′li·ness *n.***
Low Mass a Mass said, not sung, less ceremonial than High Mass, and offered by one priest
low-mind·ed (-mīn′did) ***adj.*** having or showing a coarse, vulgar mind —**low′-mind′ed·ly *adv.*** —**low′-mind′ed·ness *n.***
low-pitched (-picht′) ***adj.*** **1.** low in pitch **2.** having little slope, as a roof **3.** of low intensity; restrained
low-pres·sure (-presh′ər) ***adj.*** **1.** *a)* having or using a relatively low pressure *b)* having a low barometric pressure **2.** not energetic or forceful
low profile an unobtrusive presence, or concealed activity
low-proof (-pro͞of′) ***adj.*** low in alcohol content
low-rise (-rīz′) ***adj.*** designating or of a building, esp. an apartment house, having only a few stories
low-spir·it·ed (-spir′i tid) ***adj.*** in low spirits; sad; depressed —**low′-spir′it·ed·ly *adv.***
low-test (-test′) ***adj.*** vaporizing at a relatively high temperature: said of gasoline
low tide 1. the lowest level reached by the ebbing tide **2.** the time when the tide is at this level **3.** the lowest point reached by anything
low water 1. *same as* LOW TIDE **2.** water at its lowest level, as in a stream
low-wa·ter mark (-wôt′ər, -wät′-) **1.** a mark showing low water **2.** the lowest point reached
lox[1] (läks) ***n.*** [via Yid. < G. *lachs,* salmon] a variety of salty smoked salmon
lox[2] (läks) ***n.*** [*l(iquid) ox(ygen)*] oxygen in a liquid state, used in a fuel mixture for rockets
loy·al (loi′əl) ***adj.*** [Fr. < OFr. < L. *legalis:* see LEGAL] **1.** faithful to one's country **2.** faithful to those persons, ideals, etc. that one is under obligation to defend or support **3.** relating to or indicating loyalty —**loy′al·ly *adv.***
loy·al·ist (-ist) ***n.*** **1.** a person who supports the established government of his country during times of revolt **2.** [*often* **L-**] in the American Revolution, a colonist who was loyal to the British government **3.** [**L-**] in the Spanish Civil War, one who remained loyal to the Republic, opposing Franco —**loy′al·ism *n.***
loy·al·ty (-tē) ***n.,*** *pl.* **-ties** quality, state, or instance of being loyal; faithful adherence, etc.
Loyola *see* IGNATIUS (OF) LOYOLA
loz·enge (läz′'nj) ***n.*** [OFr. *losenge,* prob. < Gaul.] **1.** a plane figure with four equal sides and two obtuse angles; diamond **2.** a cough drop, candy, etc., orig. in this shape
LP [*L(ong) P(laying)*] *a trademark for* a long-playing record —***n.*** a long-playing record
LPG liquefied petroleum gas: also **LP-gas**
LPN, L.P.N. Licensed Practical Nurse
Lr *Chem.* lawrencium
LSD [*l(y)s(ergic acid) d(iethylamide)*] a psychedelic drug that produces behavior and symptoms, as hallucinations, delusions, etc., like those of certain psychoses
L.S.D., £.s.d., l.s.d. [L. *librae, solidi, denarii*] pounds, shillings, pence
Lt. Lieutenant
Ltd., ltd. limited
Lu *Chem.* lutetium

Lu·an·da (lo͞o än′də, -an′-) capital of Angola, on the Atlantic: pop. 347,000
lu·au (lo͞o ou′, lo͞o′ou′) *n.* [Haw.] a Hawaiian feast, usually with entertainment
lub·ber (lub′ər) *n.* [< ME. < *lobbe-* (see LOB)] **1.** a big, slow, clumsy person **2.** a landlubber —**lub′ber·li·ness** *n.* —**lub′ber·ly** *adj., adv.*
Lub·bock (lub′ək) [after T.S. *Lubbock,* Confederate officer] city in NW Tex.: pop. 174,000
lube (lo͞ob) *n.* **1.** a lubricating oil: also **lube oil** **2.** [Colloq.] a lubrication
Lü·beck (lü′bek; *E.* lo͞o′-) city & port in N West Germany: pop. 243,000
lu·bri·cant (lo͞o′brə kənt) *adj.* reducing friction by providing a smooth film as a covering over parts that move against each other —*n.* a substance for reducing friction in this way, as oil or grease
lu·bri·cate (-kāt′) *vt.* **-cat′ed, -cat′ing** [< L. pp. of *lubricare* < *lubricus,* smooth] **1.** to make slippery or smooth **2.** to apply a lubricant to —*vi.* to serve as a lubricant —**lu′bri·ca′tion** *n.* —**lu′bri·ca′tive** *adj.* —**lu′bri·ca′tor** *n.*
lu·bric·i·ty (lo͞o bris′ə tē) *n., pl.* **-ties** [< Fr. < LL. *lubricitas*] **1.** slipperiness; smoothness **2.** trickiness **3.** lewdness —**lu·bri′cious** (-brish′əs), **lu′bri·cous** (-bri kəs) *adj.*
lu·cent (lo͞o′s′nt) *adj.* [< L. prp. of *lucere,* to shine] **1.** giving off light; shining **2.** translucent or clear —**lu′cen·cy** *n.* —**lu′cent·ly** *adv.*
Lu·cerne (lo͞o surn′; *Fr.* lü sern′), **Lake (of)** lake in C Switzerland
lu·cerne, lu·cern (lo͞o surn′) *n.* [< Fr. < ModPr., ult. < L. *lucerna,* a lamp < *lucere,* to shine] [Chiefly Brit.] *same as* ALFALFA
Lu·cia (lo͞o′shə) [It. < L., fem. of LUCIUS] a feminine name
Lu·cian (lo͞o′shən) [< L.: see LUCIUS] a masculine name
lu·cid (lo͞o′sid) *adj.* [< L. < *lucere,* to shine] **1.** [Poet.] bright; shining **2.** transparent **3.** designating an interval of sanity in a mental disorder **4.** clear to the mind; readily understood **5.** clearheaded; rational —**lu·cid′i·ty, lu′cid·ness** *n.* —**lu′cid·ly** *adv.*
Lu·ci·fer (lo͞o′sə fər) [OE. < L. < *lux* (gen. *lucis*), LIGHT[1] + *ferre,* to BEAR[1]] **1.** [Poet.] the planet Venus when it is the morning star **2.** *Theol.* Satan, esp. as leader of the revolt of the angels before his fall —*n.* [l-] an early type of friction match
Lu·cille, Lu·cile (lo͞o sēl′) [var. of LUCY] a feminine name
Lu·cite (lo͞o′sīt) [< L. *lux,* light + -ITE] *a trademark for* a transparent or translucent acrylic resin or plastic
Lu·cius (lo͞o′shəs) [L. < *lux,* LIGHT[1]] a masculine name
luck (luk) *n.* [prob. < MDu. *luk,* contr. < *gelucke*] **1.** the seemingly chance happening of events which affect one; fortune; fate **2.** good fortune, success, etc. —*vi.* [Colloq.] to be lucky enough to come (*into, on, through,* etc.) —**crowd** (or **push**) **one's luck** [Slang] to take superfluous risks —**down on one's luck** in misfortune; unlucky —**in luck** lucky —**luck out** [Colloq.] to have things turn out favorably for one —**out of luck** unlucky —**try one's luck** to try to do something without being sure of the outcome —**worse luck** unfortunately
luck·less (-lis) *adj.* having no good luck; unlucky —**luck′less·ly** *adv.* —**luck′less·ness** *n.*
Luck·now (luk′nou) city in NC India: pop. 595,000
luck·y (luk′ē) *adj.* **luck′i·er, luck′i·est** **1.** having good luck; fortunate **2.** resulting fortunately **3.** believed to bring good luck —**luck′i·ly** *adv.* —**luck′i·ness** *n.*
lu·cra·tive (lo͞o′krə tiv) *adj.* [< L. pp. of *lucrari,* to gain < *lucrum:* see ff.] producing wealth or profit; profitable remunerative *[a lucrative* investment*]* —**lu′cra·tive·ly** *adv.* —**lu′cra·tive·ness** *n.*
lu·cre (lo͞o′kər) *n.* [< L. *lucrum,* gain, riches] riches; money: chiefly derogatory, as in **filthy lucre**
Lu·cre·tius (lo͞o krē′shəs) (born *Titus Lucretius Carus*) 96?–55? B.C.; Rom. poet & philosopher
lu·cu·brate (lo͞o′kyo͞o brāt′) *vi.* **-brat′ed, -brat′ing** [< L. pp. of *lucubrare,* to work by candlelight < *lux,* light] **1.** to work, study, or write laboriously, esp. late at night **2.** to write in a scholarly manner —**lu′cu·bra′tor** *n.*
lu·cu·bra·tion (lo͞o′kyo͞o brā′shən) *n.* **1.** a lucubrating **2.** a learned or carefully elaborated work **3.** [*often pl.*] any literary composition: humorous usage suggesting pedantry
Lu·cul·lus (lo͞o kul′əs), **(Lucius Lucinius)** 110?–57? B.C.; Rom. general: proverbial for his wealth —**Lu·cul′lan** (-ən), **Lu·cul′li·an** (-ē ən) *adj.*
Lu·cy (lo͞o′sē) [prob. via Fr. < L. *Lucia,* fem. of LUCIUS] a feminine name
lu·di·crous (lo͞o′di krəs) *adj.* [L. *ludicrus* < *ludus,* a game] causing laughter because absurd or ridiculous —**lu′di·crous·ly** *adv.* —**lu′di·crous·ness** *n.*
luff (luf) *n.* [< ODu. *loef,* weather side (of a ship)] **1.** a sailing close to the wind **2.** the forward edge of a fore-and-aft sail —*vi.* to turn the bow of a ship toward the wind
lug[1] (lug) *vt.* **lugged, lug′ging** [ME. *luggen,* prob. < Scand.] to carry or drag with effort —*n.* **1.** an earlike projection by which a thing is held or supported **2.** a heavy nut used with a bolt to secure a wheel to an axle **3.** a shallow box in which fruit is shipped **4.** [Slang] a loutish fellow
lug[2] (lug) *n. clipped form of* LUGSAIL
lug[3] (lug) *n. clipped form of* LUGWORM
luge (lo͞ozh) *n.* [Fr.] a racing sled for one or two persons —*vi.* **luged, luge′ing** to race with luges
Lu·ger (lo͞o′gər) [G.] *a trademark for* a German semiautomatic pistol —*n.* [*often* l-] this pistol
lug·gage (lug′ij) *n.* [LUG[1] + -AGE] suitcases, valises, trunks, etc.; baggage
lug·ger (lug′ər) *n.* a small vessel equipped with a lugsail or lugsails
lug·sail (lug′s′l, -sāl′) *n.* [< ? LUG[1]] a four-sided sail attached to an upper yard that hangs obliquely on the mast
lu·gu·bri·ous (lo͝o go͞o′brē əs, -gyo͞o′-) *adj.* [L. *lugubris* < *lugere,* to mourn + -OUS] very sad or mournful, esp. in a way that seems exaggerated or ridiculous —**lu·gu′bri·ous·ly** *adv.* —**lu·gu′bri·ous·ness** *n.*
lug·worm (lug′wurm′) *n.* [< ? + WORM] a bristly, segmented worm that burrows in muddy sand along the shore and is used for bait

LUGSAIL

Luke (lo͝ok) [< LL. < Gr.] **1.** a masculine name **2.** *Bible a)* one of the four Evangelists, a physician and the reputed author of the third Gospel *b)* this book, the third in the New Testament
luke·warm (lo͞ok′wôrm′) *adj.* [ME. *luke,* tepid + *warm,* warm] **1.** barely or moderately warm: said of liquids **2.** not very eager or enthusiastic —**luke′warm′ly** *adv.* —**luke′warm′ness** *n.*
lull (lul) *vt.* [ME. *lullen,* origin echoic] **1.** to calm by gentle sound or motion: chiefly in **lull to sleep** **2.** to bring into a specified condition by soothing and reassuring **3.** to quiet; allay *[to lull* one's fears*]* —*vi.* to become calm —*n.* a short period of quiet or of comparative calm
lull·a·by (lul′ə bī′) *n., pl.* **-bies′** a song for lulling a baby to sleep —*vt.* **-bied′, -by′ing** to lull as with a lullaby
lum·ba·go (lum bā′gō) *n.* [< L. *lumbus,* loin] backache, esp. in the lower back
lum·bar (lum′bər, -bär) *adj.* [< L. *lumbus,* loin] of or near the loins; specif., designating or of the vertebrae, nerves, arteries, etc. in the part of the body just below the thoracic part
lum·ber[1] (lum′bər) *n.* [< ? LOMBARD: orig., pawnshop, hence pawned or stored articles] **1.** discarded household articles, furniture, etc. stored away or taking up room **2.** timber sawed into beams, boards, etc. of convenient sizes —*vt.* **1.** to clutter with useless articles or rubbish **2.** to remove (timber) from (an area) —*vi.* to cut down timber and saw it into lumber —**lum′ber·er** *n.* —**lum′ber·ing** *n.*
lum·ber[2] (lum′bər) *vi.* [ME. *lomeren* < ? Scand.] **1.** to move heavily, clumsily, and, often, noisily **2.** to rumble —**lum′ber·ing** *adj.* —**lum′ber·ing·ly** *adv.*
lum·ber·jack (lum′bər jak′) *n. same as* LOGGER
lum·ber·man (-mən) *n., pl.* **-men** **1.** *same as* LOGGER **2.** one who deals in lumber
lum·ber·yard (-yärd′) *n.* a place where lumber is kept for sale
lu·men (lo͞o′mən) *n., pl.* **-mi·na** (-mi nə), **-mens** [ModL. < L., light] **1.** a unit of measure for the flow of light, equal to the amount of flow from a uniform point source of one candle **2.** the bore of a hollow needle, catheter, etc. **3.** *Anat.* the passage within a tubular organ
lu·mi·nance (-mə nəns) *n.* [< L. *lumen* (see LUMEN) + -ANCE] **1.** a being luminous **2.** luminous intensity, expressed in candles per unit projected area
lu·mi·nar·y (-mə ner′ē) *n., pl.* **-nar′ies** [< OFr. < LL. < L. *luminare* < *lumen,* light] **1.** a body that gives off light, such as the sun or moon **2.** *a)* a famous intellectual *b)* any notable person
lu·mi·nesce (lo͞o′mə nes′) *vi.* **-nesced′, -nesc′ing** [back-formation < ff.] to be or become luminescent
lu·mi·nes·cence (-′ns) *n.* [< L. *lumen,* a light + -ESCENCE] any giving off of light caused by the absorption of radiant energy, etc. and not by incandescence; any cold light —**lu′mi·nes′cent** *adj.*
lu·mi·nif·er·ous (-nif′ər əs) *adj.* [< L. *lumen,* a light + -FEROUS] giving off or transmitting light

lu·mi·nous (lo͞o′mə nəs) ***adj.*** [L. *luminosus* < *lumen*, a light] **1.** giving off light; bright **2.** illuminated **3.** glowing in the dark, as paint with a phosphor in it **4.** enlightened or enlightening —**lu′mi·nos′i·ty** (-näs′ə tē), *pl.* **-ties, lu′mi·nous·ness** ***n.*** —**lu′mi·nous·ly** ***adv.***

lum·mox (lum′əks) ***n.*** [< ?] [Colloq.] a clumsy, stupid person

lump¹ (lump) ***n.*** [ME. *lumpe*] **1.** a solid mass of no special shape; hunk **2.** a small cube, or oblong piece, etc., specif. of sugar **3.** a swelling; bulge **4.** a large amount; mass **5.** a clodlike person **6.** [*pl.*] [Colloq.] hard blows, criticism, or the like: in **get** (or **take**) **one's lumps** or **give someone his lumps** —***adj.*** in lumps [*lump* sugar] —***vt.*** **1.** to put together in a lump or lumps **2.** to treat or deal with in a mass, or collectively **3.** to make lumps in —***vi.*** to become lumpy —**in the lump** all together —**lump in one's throat** a tight feeling in the throat, as from restrained emotion

lump² (lump) ***vt.*** [Early ModE., to look sour] [Colloq.] to put up with (something disagreeable) [if you don't like it, you can *lump* it]

lump·ish (lump′ish) ***adj.*** **1.** like a lump **2.** clumsy, dull, etc. —**lump′ish·ly** ***adv.*** —**lump′ish·ness** ***n.***

lump sum a gross, or total, sum paid at one time

lump·y (lum′pē) ***adj.*** **lump′i·er, lump′i·est** **1.** full of lumps [*lumpy* pudding] **2.** covered with lumps **3.** rough: said of water **4.** like a lump; heavy; clumsy —**lump′i·ly** ***adv.*** —**lump′i·ness** ***n.***

Lu·na (lo͞o′nə) [L., moon] **1.** *Rom. Myth.* the goddess of the moon **2.** the moon personified

lu·na·cy (lo͞o′nə sē) ***n.***, *pl.* **-cies** [LUNA(TIC) + -CY] **1.** [Now Rare] insanity **2.** utter foolishness

luna moth a large N. American moth with crescent-marked wings, the hind pair of which end in elongated tails

lu·nar (lo͞o′nər) ***adj.*** [< L. < *luna*, the moon] of, on, or like the moon

lunar eclipse *see* ECLIPSE (sense 1)

lunar month *see* MONTH (sense 3)

lunar year a period of twelve lunar months

lu·nate (lo͞o′nāt) ***adj.*** [< L. < *luna*, the moon] crescent-shaped: also **lu′nat·ed** —**lu′nate·ly** ***adv.***

lu·na·tic (lo͞o′nə tik) ***adj.*** [< OFr. < LL. *lunaticus*, moonstruck, crazy < L. *luna*, the moon] **1.** [Now Rare] *a)* insane *b)* of lunacy *c)* of or for insane persons **2.** utterly foolish —***n.*** an insane person

lunatic fringe the minority considered fanatical in any political, social, or other movement

lunch (lunch) ***n.*** [earlier, a piece: ? < Sp. *lonja*, slice of ham] any light meal; esp., the midday meal between breakfast and dinner —***vi.*** to eat lunch —***vt.*** to provide lunch for —**lunch′er** ***n.***

lunch·eon (lun′chən) ***n.*** [< prec., prob. after dial. *nuncheon*, a snack] a lunch; esp., a formal lunch with others

lunch·eon·ette (lun′chə net′) ***n.*** [see -ETTE] a small restaurant where light lunches can be had

lunch·room (lunch′ro͞om′) ***n.*** a restaurant where light, quick meals, as lunches, are served

lung (luŋ) ***n.*** [OE. *lungen*] either of the two spongelike respiratory organs in the thorax of vertebrates, that oxygenate the blood and remove carbon dioxide from it —**at the top of one's lungs** in one's loudest voice

LUNGS (A, trachea; B, bronchus; C, visceral pleura; D, parietal pleura; E, bronchiole; F, diaphragm; G, upper lobe; H, middle lobe; I, lower lobe)

lunge (lunj) ***n.*** [< Fr. < *allonger*, to lengthen < *a-* (< L. *ad*), to + *long* (< L. *longus*), long] **1.** a sudden thrust, as with a sword **2.** a sudden plunge forward —***vi., vt.*** **lunged, lung′ing** to move, or cause to move, with a lunge —**lung′er** ***n.***

lung·fish (luŋ′fish′) ***n.***, *pl.* **-fish′, -fish′es:** see FISH any of various fishes having lungs as well as gills

lung·wort (-wurt′) ***n.*** [OE. *lungenwyrt*] a plant with large, spotted leaves and clusters of blue or purple flowers

Lu·per·ca·li·a (lo͞o′pər kā′lē ə, -kāl′yə) ***n.pl.*** an ancient Roman fertility festival, held in February: also **Lu′per·cal′** (-kal′) ***n.sing.*** —**Lu′per·ca′li·an** ***adj.***

lu·pine¹ (lo͞o′pin) ***n.*** [< L. < *lupus*, a wolf] **1.** a plant of the legume family, with racemes of white, rose, yellow, or blue flowers and pods containing beanlike seeds **2.** the seed of this plant, used in some parts of Europe as food

lu·pine² (lo͞o′pīn) ***adj.*** [< L. < *lupus*, a wolf] **1.** of a wolf or wolves **2.** wolflike; fierce

lu·pus (lo͞o′pəs) ***n.*** [ModL. < L., a wolf] any of various diseases with skin lesions, esp. tuberculosis of the skin

lurch¹ (lurch) ***vi.*** [< ?] **1.** to roll, pitch, or sway suddenly forward or to one side **2.** to stagger —***n.*** a lurching movement

lurch² (lurch) ***vi.*** [var. of LURK] [Obs.] to lurk —***vt.*** [Archaic] to cheat; steal; rob

lurch³ (lurch) ***n.*** [Fr. *lourche*, name of a 16th-c. game, prob. < OFr. *lourche*, duped] a situation in certain card games, in which the loser has less than half the score of the winner —**leave in the lurch** to leave in a difficult situation

lure (loor) ***n.*** [< MFr. < OFr. *loirre*, prob. < Gmc.] **1.** a feathered device on the end of a long cord, used in falconry to recall the hawk **2.** *a)* the power of attracting or enticing *b)* anything having this power **3.** a bait used in fishing —***vt.*** **lured, lur′ing** to attract; entice —**lur′er** ***n.***

lu·rid (loor′id) ***adj.*** [L. *luridus*, pale yellow, ghastly] **1.** [Rare] deathly pale **2.** glowing through a haze, as flames enveloped by smoke **3.** *a)* startling; sensational *b)* characterized by violent passion or crime —**lu′rid·ly** ***adv.*** —**lu′rid·ness** ***n.***

lurk (lurk) ***vi.*** [ME. *lurken*, akin to *louren*, LOWER²] **1.** to stay hidden, ready to attack, etc. **2.** to exist unobserved, be present as a latent threat, etc. **3.** to move furtively —**lurk′er** ***n.***

lus·cious (lush′əs) ***adj.*** [ME. *lucius*, prob. var. of *licious*, DELICIOUS, infl. by ff.] **1.** very pleasing to taste or smell; delicious **2.** *a)* delighting any of the senses *b)* voluptuous —**lus′cious·ly** ***adv.*** —**lus′cious·ness** ***n.***

lush¹ (lush) ***adj.*** [< OFr. *lasche*, lax, loose, ult. < L. *laxus*] **1.** tender and full of juice **2.** of or characterized by rich growth [*lush* vegetation, *lush* fields] **3.** characterized by richness, abundance, or extravagance —**lush′ly** ***adv.*** —**lush′ness** ***n.***

lush² (lush) ***n.*** [< ? *Lushington*, former actors' club in London] [Slang] **1.** alcoholic liquor **2.** an alcoholic —***vi., vt.*** [Slang] to drink (liquor)

lust (lust) ***n.*** [OE., pleasure, appetite] **1.** a desire to satisfy one's sexual needs; esp., strong sexual desire **2.** *a)* excessive desire [a *lust* for power] *b)* great zest —***vi.*** to feel an intense desire, esp. sexual desire —**lust′ful** ***adj.*** —**lust′ful·ly** ***adv.*** —**lust′ful·ness** ***n.***

lus·ter (lus′tər) ***n.*** [< Fr. < It. < L. *lustrare*, to illumine] **1.** gloss; sheen **2.** brightness; radiance **3.** *a)* radiant beauty *b)* fame; glory **4.** a glossy fabric of cotton and wool **5.** the reflecting quality and brilliance of the surface of a mineral **6.** the metallic, sometimes iridescent appearance of glazed pottery —***vt.*** **1.** to give a lustrous finish to **2.** to add glory to —***vi.*** to be or become lustrous

lus·ter·ware (-wer′) ***n.*** highly glazed earthenware decorated by the application of metallic oxides to the glaze: also, chiefly Brit. sp., **lustreware**

lus·trate (lus′trāt) ***vt.*** **-trat·ed, -trat·ing** [< L. pp. of *lustrare:* see LUSTRUM] to purify by means of certain ceremonies —**lus·tra′tion** ***n.***

lus·tre (lus′tər) ***n., vt., vi.*** **-tred, -tring** *chiefly Brit. sp. of* LUSTER

lus·trous (-trəs) ***adj.*** having luster; shining; bright —**lus′trous·ly** ***adv.*** —**lus′trous·ness** ***n.***

lus·trum (lus′trəm) ***n.***, *pl.* **-trums, -tra** (-trə) [L., orig., prob. illumination] **1.** in ancient Rome, a purification of all the people by means of ceremonies held every five years **2.** a five-year period

lust·y (lus′tē) ***adj.*** **lust′i·er, lust′i·est** full of vigor; strong, robust, hearty, etc. —**lust′i·ly** ***adv.*** —**lust′i·ness** ***n.***

Lü·ta (lo͞o′dä′) urban complex in NE China, including two seaports on the Yellow Sea: pop. 3,600,000

lu·ta·nist, lu·te·nist (lo͞ot′'n ist) ***n.*** a lute player

lute¹ (lo͞ot) ***n.*** [< MFr. < OFr. < Ar. *al‘ūd*, lit., the wood] an early stringed instrument with a rounded back and a long, fretted neck often bent in a sharp angle

LUTE

lute² (lo͞ot) ***n.*** [< OFr. < L. *lutum*, mud, clay] a clayey cement used as a sealing agent for the joints of pipes, etc. —***vt.*** **lut′ed, lut′ing** to seal with lute

lu·te·in·iz·ing hormone (lo͞ot′ē in īz′iŋ) [ult. < (CORPUS) LUTEUM] a hormone of the pituitary that esp. stimulates ovulation and the development of the corpus luteum

lu·te·ti·um (lo͞o tē′shē əm) ***n.*** [ModL. < L. *Lutetia*, ancient Rom. name of Paris] a metallic chemical element of the rare-earth group: symbol, Lu; at. wt., 174.97; at. no., 71

Lu·ther (lo͞o′thər) [G. < OHG. *Chlothar* < Gmc. bases meaning "famous fighter"] **1.** a masculine name **2. Martin,** 1483–1546; Ger. theologian: leader of the Protestant Reformation in Germany

Lu·ther·an (-ən) ***adj.*** **1.** of Martin Luther **2.** of the Protestant denomination founded by Luther, or of its doctrines, etc. —***n.*** a member of a Lutheran church —**Lu′ther·an·ism** ***n.***

lut·ist (lo͞ot′ist) ***n.*** a lute player

Lux·em·bourg (luk′səm burg′; *Fr.* lük sän bo͞or′) **1.** grand duchy in W Europe, bounded by Belgium, West Germany, & France: 998 sq. mi.; pop. 337,000 **2.** its capital: pop. 79,000 Also sp. **Luxemburg**

Lux·or (luk′sôr, look′-) city in S Egypt, on the Nile, near the ruins of ancient Thebes

lux·u·ri·ant (lug zhoor′ē ənt, luk shoor′-) *adj.* [< L. prp. of *luxuriare:* see ff.] **1.** growing with vigor and in abundance; lush; teeming **2.** richly or extravagantly full, varied, elaborate, etc. **3.** *same as* LUXURIOUS —**lux·u′ri·ance, lux·u′ri·an·cy** *n.* —**lux·u′ri·ant·ly** *adv.*

lux·u·ri·ate (-āt′) *vi.* **-at′ed, -at′ing** [< L. pp. of *luxuriare,* to be too fruitful < *luxuria,* LUXURY] **1.** to grow with vigor and in great abundance **2.** to live in great luxury **3.** to revel (*in*) —**lux·u′ri·a′tion** *n.*

lux·u·ri·ous (-əs) *adj.* **1.** fond of or indulging in luxury **2.** filled with or providing luxury; splendid, rich, comfortable, etc. —**lux·u′ri·ous·ly** *adv.* —**lux·u′ri·ous·ness** *n.*

lux·u·ry (luk′shə rē, lug′zhə-) *n., pl.* **-ries** [< OFr. < L. *luxuria* < *luxus,* luxury] **1.** the enjoyment of the best and most costly things that offer the greatest comfort and satisfaction **2.** anything giving such enjoyment, usually something considered unnecessary to life and health **3.** any unusual pleasure or comfort —*adj.* characterized by luxury

Lu·zon (lo͞o zän′) main island of the Philippines: 40,420 sq. mi.; chief city, Manila

Lvov (lvôf) city in W Ukrainian S.S.R.: pop. 524,000

LXX Septuagint

-ly[1] (lē) [OE. *-lic*] *a suffix used to form adjectives and meaning:* **1.** like, characteristic of, suitable to *[manly]* **2.** happening (once) every (specified period of time) *[monthly]*

-ly[2] (lē) [OE. *-lice* < *-lic*] *a suffix used to form adverbs and meaning:* **1.** in a (specified) manner, to a (specified) extent or direction, in or at a (specified) time or place *[harshly, outwardly, hourly]* **2.** in the (specified) order of sequence *[secondly]*

‡**ly·cée** (lē sā′) *n.* [Fr. < L.: see ff.] in France, a public, college-preparatory secondary school

Ly·ce·um (lī sē′əm, lī′sē-) [L. < Gr. *Lykeion,* the Lyceum: from the temple of *Apollōn Lykeios* near it] the grove at Athens where Aristotle taught —*n.* **[l-] 1.** a lecture hall **2.** an organization presenting public lectures or discussions, concerts, etc.

Ly·cur·gus (lī kur′gəs) real or legendary Spartan lawgiver of about the 9th cent. B.C.

Lyd·i·a (lid′ē ə) [LL. < Gr. fem. of *Lydios,* Lydian] **1.** a feminine name **2.** ancient kingdom in W Asia Minor —**Lyd′i·an** *adj., n.*

lye (lī) *n.* [OE. *leag*] **1.** orig., a strong alkaline solution obtained by leaching wood ashes **2.** any strongly alkaline substance Lye is used in cleaning and in making soap

ly·ing[1] (lī′iŋ) *prp. of* LIE[1]

ly·ing[2] (lī′iŋ) *prp. of* LIE[2] —*adj.* false; not truthful —*n.* the telling of a lie or lies

ly·ing-in (-in′) *n.* confinement in childbirth —*adj.* of or for childbirth *[a lying-in hospital]*

Lyl·y (lil′ē), **John** 1554?–1606; Eng. writer

lymph (limf) *n.* [L. *lympha,* spring water (infl. by Gr. *nymphē,* NYMPH)] a clear, yellowish fluid resembling blood plasma, found in the lymphatic vessels of vertebrates

lym·phat·ic (lim fat′ik) *adj.* **1.** of, containing, or conveying lymph **2.** sluggish; without energy —*n.* a lymphatic vessel

lymph node any of many small, compact structures lying in groups along the course of the lymphatic vessels and producing lymphocytes: also, esp. formerly, **lymph gland**

lym·pho- *a combining form meaning* of lymph or the lymphatics: also, before a vowel, **lymph-**

lym·pho·cyte (lim′fə sīt′) *n.* [prec. + -CYTE] a variety of leukocyte formed in lymphatic tissue —**lym′pho·cyt′ic** (-sit′ik) *adj.*

lymph·oid (lim′foid) *adj.* of or like lymph or the tissue of the lymph nodes

lynch (linch) *vt.* [< LYNCH LAW] to murder (an accused person) by mob action and without lawful trial, as by hanging —**lynch′er** *n.* —**lynch′ing** *n.*

Lynch·burg (linch′burg) [after J. *Lynch,* reputed founder] city in C Va.: pop. 67,000

lynch law [after Capt. William *Lynch* (1742–1820), member of a vigilance committee in Pittsylvania, Virginia, in 1780] the practice of killing by lynching

Lynn (lin) [prob. < Brit. place name *Lynn* < Celt.] **1.** a masculine or feminine name **2.** city in NE Mass.: suburb of Boston: pop. 78,000

lynx (liŋks) *n., pl.* **lynx′es, lynx:** see PLURAL, II, D, 1 [L. < Gr. *lynx*] any of a group of wildcats found throughout the Northern Hemisphere and characterized by a short tail, long, tufted ears, and keen vision

lynx-eyed (-īd′) *adj.* having very keen sight

Lyon (lyōn) city in EC France, on the Rhone: pop. 528,000: Eng. name **Ly·ons** (lī′ənz)

ly·on·naise (lī′ə nāz′; *Fr.* lyô nez′) *adj.* [Fr., fem. of *Lyonnais,* of Lyon] prepared with finely sliced onions, as potatoes with fried onions

Ly·ra (lī′rə) a N constellation: it contains Vega

ly·rate (lī′rāt) *adj.* shaped like a lyre

lyre (līr) *n.* [< L. < Gr. *lyra*] a small stringed instrument of the harp family, played by the ancient Greeks

LYRE

lyre·bird (-burd′) *n.* an Australian songbird: the long tail feathers of the male resemble a lyre when spread

lyr·ic (lir′ik) *adj.* [< Fr. or L.: both < Gr. *lyrikos*] **1.** suitable for singing, as to the accompaniment of a lyre; songlike; specif., designating poetry expressing the poet's emotions and thoughts: sonnets, odes, etc. are lyric poems **2.** writing lyric poetry **3.** *same as* LYRICAL **4.** having a relatively high voice with a light, flexible quality *[a lyric tenor]* —*n.* **1.** a lyric poem **2.** [*usually pl.*] the words of a song, as distinguished from the music

lyr·i·cal (-i k′l) *adj.* **1.** *same as* LYRIC **2.** expressing rapture or great enthusiasm —**lyr′i·cal·ly** *adv.*

lyr·i·cism (lir′ə siz′m) *n.* lyric quality, style, expression, etc.

lyr·i·cist (-sist) *n.* a writer of lyrics, esp. lyrics for popular songs

Ly·san·der (lī san′dər) ?–395 B.C.; Spartan naval & military commander

ly·sin (lī′s′n) *n.* [< Gr. *lysis* (see ff.) + -IN[1]] any antibody capable of dissolving bacteria, blood corpuscles, etc.

ly·sis (lī′sis) *n.* [ModL. < Gr. *lysis,* a loosening < *lyein,* to loose] **1.** cell destruction by lysins **2.** the gradual ending of disease symptoms

-ly·sis (lə sis) [see prec.] *a combining form meaning* a loosing, dissolution, dissolving, destruction *[catalysis, paralysis]*

-lyte (līt) [< Gr. *lytos* < *lyein:* see LYSIS] *a combining form meaning* a substance subjected to a process of decomposition *[hydrolyte]*

-lyt·ic (lit′ik) **1.** *a combining form used to form adjectives corresponding to nouns ending in* -LYSIS *[catalytic]* **2.** *Biochem. a combining form meaning* hydrolysis by enzymes

-lyze (līz) *a combining form used to form verbs corresponding to nouns ending in* -LYSIS *[electrolyze]*

M

M, m (em) *n., pl.* **M's, m's 1.** the thirteenth letter of the English alphabet **2.** the sound of *M* or *m*

M (em) *n.* a Roman numeral for 1,000

M. 1. Manitoba **2.** Medieval **3.** *Music* mezzo **4.** Monday **5.** *pl.* **MM.** Monsieur

M., m. 1. majesty **2.** male **3.** married **4.** masculine **5.** *Physics* mass **6.** meridian **7.** mile(s) **8.** mill(s) **9.** minim **10.** minute(s) **11.** month **12.** [L. *meridies*] noon *[A.M., P.M.]*

m, m. meter; meters

ma (mä; *dial.* mô) *n.* [Colloq.] mamma; mother

MA Massachusetts

MA, M.A. *Psychol.* mental age

M.A. [L. *Magister Artium*] Master of Arts

ma'am (mam, mäm; *unstressed* məm, 'm) *n.* [Colloq.] madam: used in direct address

Ma·bel (mā'b'l) [< *Amabel* < L. *amabilis,* lovable] a feminine name

ma·ca·bre (mə käb'rə, mə käb', -kä'bər) *adj.* [Fr. < OFr. (*danse*) *Macabré,* (dance) of death] gruesome; grim and horrible: also **ma·ca'ber** (-kä'bər)

mac·ad·am (mə kad'əm) *n.* [after J. L. *McAdam* (1756–1836), Scot. engineer] **1.** small broken stones used in making roads, usually combined with tar or asphalt **2.** a macadamized road

mac·a·dam·i·a nut (mak'ə dā'mē ə) [after John *Macadam* (d. 1865), Scot. chemist in Australia] a spherical, hard-shelled, edible nut from an Australian tree cultivated in Hawaii, etc.

mac·ad·am·ize (mə kad'ə mīz') *vt.* **-ized', -iz'ing** to make, repair, or cover (a road) by rolling successive layers of macadam on it

Ma·cao (mə kou') Port. territory consisting of a peninsula on the SE coast of China & two small nearby islands: also, Port. sp., **Macau**

ma·caque (mə käk') *n.* [Fr. < Port. *macaco*] any of a group of monkeys of Asia, Africa, and the East Indies, with a nonprehensile tail

mac·a·ro·ni (mak'ə rō'nē) *n.* [It. *maccaroni,* pl. < LowGr. *makaria,* broth of barley, ult. < Gr. *makar,* blessed] **1.** pasta in the form of tubes, etc., often baked with cheese, ground meat, etc. **2.** *pl.* **-nies** an 18th-cent. English dandy

mac·a·roon (mak'ə ro͞on') *n.* [< Fr. < It. *maccaroni,* MACARONI] a small cookie made chiefly of egg white, crushed almonds or coconut, and sugar

Ma·cau·lay (mə kô'lē), **Thomas Bab·ing·ton** (bab'iŋ tən), 1st Baron Macaulay, 1800–59; Eng. historian, essayist, & statesman

ma·caw (mə kô') *n.* [Port. *macao,* prob. < Braz. (Tupi) native name] a large, bright-colored, harsh-voiced parrot of Central and South America

Mac·beth (mək beth', mak-) **1.** a tragedy (c. 1606) by Shakespeare **2.** its title character

Mac·ca·bae·us (mak'ə bē'əs), **Judas** *see* MACCABEES

Mac·ca·bees (mak'ə bēz') **1.** family of Jewish patriots who, under Judas Maccabaeus, headed a successful revolt against Syria (175–164 B.C.) **2.** *Bible* two books of the Old Testament Apocrypha that tell of this revolt —**Mac'ca·be'an** *adj.*

Mac·Dow·ell (mək dou'əl), **Edward Alexander** 1861–1908; U.S. composer & pianist

Mace (mās) [< ff.] *a trademark* (in full, **Chemical Mace**) *for* a chemical compound used as a tear gas and a nerve gas

mace[1] (mās) *n.* [< OFr. *masse*] **1.** a heavy, spiked, armor-breaking club, used in the Middle Ages **2.** *a*) a staff used as a symbol of authority by certain officials *b*) a person who carries a mace: also **mace'bear'er**

mace[2] (mās) *n.* [< OFr. *macis* < ML. < L. < Gr. *makir,* a fragrant resin] a spice, usually ground, made from the dried outer covering of the nutmeg

Mac·e·do·ni·a (mas'ə dō'nē ə, -dōn'yə) **1.** ancient kingdom in SE Europe, now divided among Greece, Yugoslavia, & Bulgaria **2.** republic of Yugoslavia, in the SE part: 9,928 sq. mi.; cap. Skopje —**Mac'e·do'ni·an** *adj., n.*

mac·er·ate (mas'ə rāt') *vt.* **-at'ed, -at'ing** [< L. pp. of *macerare,* to soften] **1.** to soften and break down the parts of by soaking in liquid for some time **2.** to steep (fruit or vegetables) as in wine or liquor **3.** loosely, to break, tear, chop, etc. into bits **4.** to cause to waste away or grow thin —*vi.* to waste away; grow thin —**mac'er·a'tion** *n.*

Mach (mäk) *n. clipped form of* MACH NUMBER

mach. **1.** machine **2.** machinery **3.** machinist

ma·che·te (mə shet'ē, -chet'ē) *n.* [Sp., dim. of *macho,* ult. < L. *marcus,* a hammer] a large, heavy-bladed knife used for cutting down sugar cane or underbrush in Central and South America

Mach·i·a·vel·li (mä'kyä vel'lē; *E.* mak'ē ə vel'ē), **Nic·co·lō (di Bernardo)** (nē'kô lô') 1469–1527; Florentine statesman & writer on government

Mach·i·a·vel·li·an (mak'ē ə vel'ē ən, -vel'yən) *adj.* of or like Machiavelli or the political principles and methods of craftiness and duplicity advocated by him —*n.* a follower of such principles and methods —**Mach'i·a·vel'li·an·ism** *n.*

MACHETE

ma·chic·o·late (mə chik'ə lāt') *vt.* **-lat'ed, -lat'ing** [< ML. pp. of *machicolare* < MFr., prob. < L. *masticare,* MASTICATE + *col,* the neck: from use of machicolations to drop stones, etc.] to put machicolations in (a parapet, etc.)

ma·chic·o·la·tion (mə chik'ə lā'shən) *n.* an opening, as in the floor of a parapet, through which hot liquids, rocks, etc. could be dropped by the defenders of a fortress

mach·i·nate (mak'ə nāt'; *sometimes* mash'-) *vi., vt.* **-nat'ed, -nat'ing** [< L. pp. of *machinari,* to plot < *machina,* a MACHINE] to devise, plan, or plot artfully, esp. to do evil —**mach'i·na'tor** *n.*

mach·i·na·tion (mak'ə nā'shən; *sometimes* mash'-) *n.* an artful plot or scheme, esp. an evil one: *usually used in pl.*

ma·chine (mə shēn') *n.* [Fr. < L. *machina* < Gr. < *mēchos,* contrivance] **1.** a vehicle, as an automobile: old-fashioned term **2.** a structure consisting of a framework and various fixed and moving parts, for doing some kind of work; mechanism *[a sewing machine]* **3.** a person or organization regarded as acting like a machine; esp., a smoothly functioning complex organization **4.** the members of a political party who control policy and confer patronage **5.** *Mech.* a device, as a lever or pulley, that transmits, or changes the application of, energy —*adj.* **1.** of a machine or machines **2.** made or done by machinery **3.** standardized; stereotyped —*vt.* **-chined', -chin'ing** to make, shape, etc. by machinery —**ma·chin'a·ble** *adj.*

machine gun an automatic gun, usually with a cooling apparatus, firing a rapid stream of bullets fed into it by a belt —**ma·chine'-gun'** (-gun') *vt.* **-gunned', -gun'ning**

ma·chin·er·y (mə shēn'ər ē, -shēn'rē) *n., pl.* **-er·ies** **1.** machines collectively **2.** the working parts of a machine **3.** any means by which something is kept in action or a desired result is obtained *[the machinery of government]*

machine shop a factory for making or repairing machines or machine parts

machine tool a power-driven tool, as an electric lathe or drill —**ma·chine'-tool'** *adj., vt.*

ma·chin·ist (-ist) *n.* **1.** a person who makes or repairs machinery **2.** a worker skilled in using machine tools or one who operates a machine

‡**ma·chis·mo** (mä chēz'mô) *n.* [< Sp. *macho* (see MACHO)] strong or aggressive masculinity; virility

Mach number (mäk) [after Ernst *Mach* (1838–1916), Austrian physicist] [*also* **m-**] a number representing the ratio of the speed of an object to the speed of sound through the same medium, as air

‡**ma·cho** (mä'chô) *adj.* [Sp. < Port., ult. < L. *masculus,* MASCULINE] masculine, virile, courageous, etc.

Mac·ken·zie (mə ken'zē) river in NW Canada, flowing from the Great Slave Lake into the Arctic Ocean

mack·er·el (mak'ər əl, mak'rəl) *n., pl.* **-el, -els:** see PLURAL, II, D, 2 [< OFr. *makerel* < ?] an edible fish of the North Atlantic, with a striped back and a silvery belly

mackerel sky a sky with rows of small, fleecy clouds, like the streaks on a mackerel's back

Mack·i·nac (mak'ə nô'), **Straits of** [see MACKINAW (COAT)] strait connecting Lake Huron & Lake Michigan

Mackinac Island small island in the Straits of Mackinac

Mack·i·naw (coat) (mak'ə nô') [CanadFr. *Mackinac* < AmInd. *mitchimakinak,* large turtle] a short, double-breasted coat made of heavy woolen cloth, usually plaid

mack·in·tosh, mac·in·tosh (mak'in täsh') *n.* [after C. *Macintosh* (1766–1843), the Scot. inventor] a waterproof raincoat, or the fabric for it

Ma·con (mā'kən) [after N. *Macon* (1758–1837), N.C. patriot] city in C Ga.: pop. 117,000

mac·ra·mé (mak'rə mā') *n.* [Fr. < It. < Turk. *makrama,* napkin < Ar. *miqramah,* a veil] a coarse fringe or lace of thread or cord knotted in designs

mac·ro- [< Gr. *makros,* long] *a combining form meaning* long (in extent or duration), large, enlarged, or elongated: also, before a vowel, **macr-**

mac·ro·bi·ot·ics (mak'rō bī ät'iks) *n.pl.* [*with sing. v.*] [< prec. + Gr. *biōtikos* < *bios,* life] the art of prolonging life, as by a special diet —**mac'ro·bi·ot'ic** *adj.*

mac·ro·ceph·a·ly (mak'rə sef'ə lē) *n.* [MACRO- + CEPHAL(O)- + -Y[3]] a condition in which the head or cranial capacity is abnormally large —**mac'ro·ceph'a·lous, mac'ro·ce·phal'ic** (-si fal'ik) *adj.*

mac·ro·cosm (mak'rə käz'm) *n.* [< Fr. < ML.: see MACRO- & COSMOS] **1.** the universe **2.** any large, complex entity —**mac'ro·cos'mic** *adj.*

mac·ro·e·co·nom·ics (mak'rō ē'kə näm'iks, -ek'ə-) *n.pl.* [*with sing. v.*] a branch of economics dealing with all the forces at work in an economy or with the interrelationship of large sectors, as in employment or income

mac·ro·mol·e·cule (mak'rə mäl'ə kyo͞ol') *n.* a very large molecule, as a polymer molecule, composed of hundreds or thousands of atoms: also **mac'ro·mole'** (-mōl')

ma·cron (mā'krən, -krän) *n.* [< Gr. neut. of *makros,* long] a short, straight mark (¯) placed horizontally over a vowel to indicate that it is long or is to be pronounced in a certain way

mac·u·la (mak'yoo lə) *n., pl.* **-lae'** (-lē'), **-las** [L.] a spot, blotch, etc.; esp., *a*) a discolored spot on the skin *b*) a sunspot —**mac'u·lar** *adj.*

macula lu·te·a (lo͞ot'ē ə) [ModL., lit., yellowish spot] a small yellowish area of especially keen vision on the retina

mad (mad) *adj.* **mad'der, mad'dest** [< OE. pp. of (*ge*)*mædan,* to drive mad] **1.** mentally ill; insane **2.** frenzied; frantic *[mad with fear]* **3.** foolish and rash; unwise

4. foolishly enthusiastic or fond *[mad about clothes]* 5. wildly amusing; hilarious 6. having rabies *[a mad dog]* 7. *a)* angry (often with *at*) *b)* showing anger —**have a mad on** [Colloq.] to be angry —**mad as a hatter** (or **March hare**) completely crazy

Mad·a·gas·car (mad′ə gas′kər) country that is an island off the SE coast of Africa: 228,000 sq. mi.; pop. 6,750,000

mad·am (mad′əm) *n., pl.* **mad′ams;** for 1, usually **mes·dames** (mā däm′) [< Fr., orig. *ma dame* < L. *mea domina,* my lady] 1. a woman; lady: a polite term of address 2. the mistress of a household 3. a woman in charge of a brothel

mad·ame (mad′əm; *Fr.* mȧ dȧm′) *n., pl.* **mes·dames** (mā däm′; *Fr.* mā dȧm′) [Fr.: see prec.] a married woman: French title equivalent to *Mrs.:* abbrev. **Mme., Mdme.**

mad·cap (mad′kap′) *n.* [MAD + CAP, fig. for head] a reckless, impulsive person, esp. a girl —*adj.* reckless and impulsive

mad·den (mad′′n) *vt., vi.* to make or become mad; make or become insane, angry, or wildly excited —**mad′den·ing** *adj.* —**mad′den·ing·ly** *adv.*

mad·der (mad′ər) *n.* [OE. *mædere*] 1. any of various plants of the madder family; esp., a perennial vine with small, yellow flowers 2. *a)* the red root of this vine *b)* a red dye made from this 3. crimson —*adj.* designating a family of chiefly tropical herbs, shrubs, and trees, including bedstraw, bluet, coffee, etc.

mad·ding (-iŋ) *adj.* [Rare] 1. raving; frenzied *[*"the *madding* crowd"*]* 2. making mad

made (mād) *pt. & pp. of* MAKE —*adj.* 1. constructed; formed 2. produced artificially *[made flowers]* 3. invented; contrived *[a made word]* 4. prepared from various ingredients *[a made dish]* 5. sure of success *[a made man]* —**have (got) it made** [Slang] to be assured of success

Ma·deir·a (mə dir′ə) 1. group of Port. islands in the Atlantic, off the W coast of Morocco 2. largest island of this group —*n.* [*also* **m-**] a strong white wine made on this island

mad·e·leine (mad′′l in) *n.* [Fr., after *Madeleine* Paulnier, 19th-c. Fr. cook] a small, rich cupcake

Mad·e·line (mad′′l in, -īn′) [< MAGDALENE] a feminine name

ma·de·moi·selle (mad′ə mə zel′, mam zel′; *Fr.* mȧd mwȧ zel′) *n.,* Fr. *pl.* **mesde·moi·selles** (mād mwȧ zel′) [Fr. < *ma,* my + *demoiselle,* young lady] an unmarried woman or girl: French title equivalent to *Miss:* abbrev. **Mlle., Mdlle.**

made-to-or·der (mād′tə ôr′dər) *adj.* made to conform to the customer's specifications; custom-made

made-up (-up′) *adj.* 1. put together; arranged *[a made-up page of type]* 2. invented; false *[a made-up story]* 3. with cosmetics applied

Madge (maj) [dim. of MARGARET] a feminine name

mad·house (mad′hous′) *n.* 1. [Archaic] a place of confinement for the mentally ill 2. any place of turmoil, noise, and confusion

Mad·i·son (mad′i s′n) [after ff.] capital of Wis., in the SC part: pop. 171,000

Mad·i·son (mad′i s′n), **James** 1751–1836; 4th president of the U.S. (1809–1817)

mad·ly (mad′lē) *adv.* 1. insanely 2. wildly; furiously 3. foolishly 4. extremely

mad·man (mad′man′, -mən) *n., pl.* **-men′** (-men′, -mən) an insane person; lunatic; maniac —**mad′wom′an** *n.fem., pl.* **-wom′en**

mad money [Colloq.] 1. a small amount of money carried by a woman for emergencies, as on a date to enable her to get home alone if she wishes 2. money saved for minor purchases, often for spending frivolously

mad·ness (-nis) *n.* 1. insanity 2. great anger 3. great folly 4. wild excitement 5. rabies

Ma·don·na (mə dän′ə) *n.* [It. < *ma,* my (< L. *mea*) + *donna,* lady (< L. *domina*)] 1. Mary, mother of Jesus 2. a picture or statue of Mary

Ma·dras (mə dras′, -dräs′) seaport on the SE coast of India: pop. 1,729,000

ma·dras (mad′rəs, mäd′-; mə dras′, -dräs′) *n.* [< prec.] a fine, firm cotton cloth, usually striped or plaid

‡**ma·dre** (mä′dre) *n.* [Sp.] mother

mad·re·pore (mad′rə pôr′) *n.* [< Fr. < It. < *madre,* mother + *poro,* a pore] any of various branching corals that form reefs and islands in tropical seas

Ma·drid (mə drid′; *Sp.* mä *th*rēth′) capital of Spain, in the C part: pop. 2,867,000

mad·ri·gal (mad′ri gəl) *n.* [< It. *madrigale* < ?] 1. a short poem, usually of love, that can be set to music 2. a contrapuntal part song, without accompaniment, popular in the 15th to 17th cent. 3. loosely, any song —**mad′ri·gal·ist** *n.*

Ma·du·ra (mä door′ä) island of Indonesia, northeast of Java: 1,770 sq. mi.

Ma·du·rai (mä də rī′) city in S India: pop. 425,000

Mae (mā) [dim. of MARY] a feminine name

Mae·ce·nas (mi sē′nəs), **(Gaius Cilnius)** 70?–8 B.C.; Rom. statesman & patron of Horace & Virgil —*n.* any wealthy, generous patron

Mael·strom (māl′strəm) [Early ModDu. < *malen,* to grind + *stroom,* a stream] a dangerous whirlpool off the W coast of Norway —*n.* [**m-**] 1. any large or violent whirlpool 2. a violently agitated state of mind, emotions, affairs, etc.

mae·nad (mē′nad) *n.* [< L. < Gr. < *mainesthai,* to rave] 1. [*often* **M-**] a female worshiper of Dionysus; bacchante 2. a frenzied woman —**mae·nad·ic** (mi nad′ik) *adj.*

ma·es·to·so (mīs tō′sō; *It.* mä′e stô′sô) *adj., adv.* [It.] *Music* with majesty or dignity

ma·es·tro (mīs′trō; mä es′-) *n., pl.* **-tros, -tri** (-trē) [It. < L. *magister,* a MASTER] a master in any art; esp., a great composer, conductor, or teacher of music

Mae·ter·linck (māt′ər liŋk′, met′-), Count **Maurice** 1862–1949; Belgian playwright & poet

Ma·fi·a, Maf·fi·a (mä′fē ə) *n.* [It. *maffia,* hostility to law] an alleged secret society of criminals in the U.S. and other countries

Ma·fi·o·si (mä′fē ō′sē) *n.pl., sing.* **-so′** (-sō′) [It.] members of the Mafia

mag. 1. magazine 2. magnetism 3. magnitude

mag·a·zine (mag′ə zēn′, mag′ə zēn′) *n.* [< Fr. < OFr. < It. < Ar. < *makhzan,* a granary < *khazana,* to store up] 1. a warehouse or military supply depot 2. a space in which explosives are stored, as in a fort or warship 3. a supply chamber, as the space in a rifle from which the cartridges are fed, the space in a camera from which the film is fed, etc. 4. things kept in a magazine, as munitions or supplies 5. a publication that appears at regular intervals and contains stories, articles, etc. and, usually, advertisements 6. a television program, appearing regularly, with brief documentary segments

Mag·da·lene (mag′də lēn, -lin) [LL. < Gr. < *Magdala,* town in Galilee] *same as* MARY MAGDALENE —*n.* [**m-**] a reformed and repentant prostitute

Mag·de·burg (mäg′də boorkh; *E.* mag′də burg′) city & port in W East Germany, on the Elbe: pop. 268,000

Ma·gel·lan (mə jel′ən), **Ferdinand** 1480?–1521; Port. navigator in the service of Spain

Magellan, Strait of channel between the S. American mainland & Tierra del Fuego

ma·gen·ta (mə jen′tə) *n.* [< *Magenta,* town in Italy] purplish red —*adj.* purplish-red

mag·got (mag′ət) *n.* [ME. *magotte*] 1. a wormlike insect larva, as the legless larva of the housefly 2. an odd notion; whim —**mag′got·y** *adj.*

Ma·gi (mā′jī) *n.pl., sing.* **Ma′gus** (-gəs) [L., pl. of *magus* < Gr. < OPer. *magus*] 1. the priestly caste in ancient Media and Persia 2. *Douay Bible* the wise men from the East who brought gifts to the infant Jesus: Matt. 2:1–13

mag·ic (maj′ik) *n.* [< OFr. < L. < Gr. < *magikos,* of the MAGI] 1. the use of charms, spells, etc. in seeking or pretending to control events or forces 2. any power or influence that seems mysterious or hard to explain *[the magic of love]* 3. the art of producing illusions by sleight of hand, etc. —*adj.* 1. of, produced by, or using magic 2. producing extraordinary results, as if by magic —**mag′i·cal** *adj.* —**mag′i·cal·ly** *adv.*

ma·gi·cian (mə jish′ən) *n.* [< OFr. *magicien*] an expert in magic; specif., *a)* a sorcerer; wizard *b)* a performer skilled in magic (sense 3)

magic lantern *old-fashioned term for* a slide projector

mag·is·te·ri·al (maj′is tir′ē əl) *adj.* [< ML. < LL. < L. *magister,* a MASTER] 1. of or suitable for a magistrate or master 2. authoritative 3. domineering; pompous —**mag′is·te′ri·al·ly** *adv.*

mag·is·tra·cy (maj′is trə sē) *n., pl.* **-cies** 1. the position, office, or jurisdiction of a magistrate 2. magistrates collectively

mag·is·trate (-trāt′, -trit) *n.* [< L. < *magister,* MASTER] 1. a civil officer empowered to administer the law: the President of the U.S. may be called the *chief magistrate* 2. a minor judicial official, as a justice of the peace

mag·ma (mag′mə) *n.* [L. < Gr. < *massein,* to knead] molten rock deep in the earth, from which igneous rock is formed

Mag·na Char·ta (or **Car·ta**) (mag′nə kär′tə) [ML., lit., great charter] 1. the charter that King John was forced by the English barons to grant at Runnymede, June 15, 1215, interpreted as guaranteeing certain civil and political liberties 2. any constitution guaranteeing certain liberties

‡**mag·na cum lau·de** (mäg′nä koom lou′de, mag′nə kum

lô'dē [L.] with great praise: phrase used to signify graduation with high honors from a university or college

mag·na·nim·i·ty (mag'nə nim'ə tē) ***n.*** **1.** a magnanimous quality or state **2.** *pl.* **-ties** a magnanimous act

mag·nan·i·mous (mag nan'ə məs) ***adj.*** [< L. < *magnus,* great + *animus,* soul] generous in overlooking injury or insult; rising above pettiness —**mag·nan'i·mous·ly** ***adv.***

mag·nate (mag'nāt) ***n.*** [< LL. < L. *magnus,* great] a very influential person, esp. in business

mag·ne·sia (mag nē'zhə, -shə) ***n.*** [ModL., ult. < Gr. *Magnēsia,* area in Thessaly] magnesium oxide, MgO, a white, tasteless powder used as a mild laxative and antacid, and as an insulating substance —**mag·ne'sian** ***adj.***

mag·ne·si·um (mag nē'zē əm, -zhē əm, -zhəm) ***n.*** [ModL. < prec.] a light, silver-white, malleable metallic chemical element: it burns with a hot, white light, and is used in photographic flashbulbs, etc.: symbol, Mg; at. wt., 24.312; at. no., 12

mag·net (mag'nit) ***n.*** [< OFr. < L. *magnes* < Gr. *Magnētis (lithos),* (stone) of Magnesia: see MAGNESIA] **1.** any piece of iron, steel, or lodestone that has the property of attracting iron, steel, etc. **2.** a person or thing that attracts

mag·net·ic (mag net'ik) ***adj.*** **1.** having the properties of a magnet **2.** of, producing, or caused by magnetism **3.** of the earth's magnetism **4.** that can be magnetized **5.** powerfully attractive *[a magnetic* personality*]* —**mag·net'i·cal·ly** ***adv.***

magnetic bottle *Physics* a geometrical configuration whose extent is outlined by magnetic lines of force that will confine a hot plasma

magnetic field a region of space in which there is an appreciable magnetic force

magnetic force the attracting or repelling force between a magnet and a ferromagnetic material, between a magnet and a current-carrying conductor, etc.

magnetic mine a naval mine exploded when the metal hull of a ship passing near it deflects a magnetic needle, thus detonating the charge

magnetic needle a slender bar of magnetized steel which, when swinging freely on a pivot, as in a compass, points toward the magnetic poles

magnetic north the direction toward which a magnetic needle points, usually not true north

magnetic pickup a phonograph pickup in which a part of the stylus assembly vibrates in a magnetic field between two coils so as to induce a current

magnetic pole **1.** either pole of a magnet **2.** either point on the earth's surface toward which a magnetic needle points: the north and south magnetic poles do not precisely coincide with the geographical poles

magnetic recording the recording of electrical signals by means of changes in areas of magnetization on a tape **(magnetic tape)** or disc

mag·net·ism (mag'nə tiz'm) ***n.*** **1.** the property or quality of being magnetic **2.** the force to which this is due **3.** the branch of physics dealing with magnetic phenomena **4.** personal charm

mag·net·ite (-tīt') ***n.*** a black iron oxide, Fe_3O_4, an important iron ore: called *lodestone* when magnetic

mag·net·ize (mag'nə tīz') ***vt.*** **-ized', -iz'ing** **1.** to give magnetic properties to (steel, iron, etc.) **2.** to attract or charm (a person) —***vi.*** to become magnetic —**mag'net·iz'a·ble** ***adj*** —**mag'net·i·za'tion** ***n.*** —**mag'net·iz'er** ***n.***

mag·ne·to (mag nēt'ō) ***n.,*** *pl.* **-tos** a dynamo in which one or more permanent magnets produce the magnetic field; esp., a small machine of this sort connected with an internal-combustion engine to generate the current providing a spark for the ignition

mag·ne·to- [see MAGNET] *a combining form meaning:* **1.** magnetism, magnetic force **2.** magnetoelectric

mag·ne·to·e·lec·tric (-i lek'trik) ***adj.*** designating or of electricity produced by changing magnetic fields in the vicinity of electric conductors —**mag·ne'to·e·lec'tric'i·ty** (-tris'ə tē) ***n.***

mag·ne·tom·e·ter (mag'nə täm'ə tər) ***n.*** an instrument for measuring magnetic forces

mag·ne·to·mo·tive (mag nēt'ō mōt'iv) ***adj.*** designating or of a force that causes magnetic flux

mag·ne·to·sphere (mag nēt'ə sfir') ***n.*** [MAGNETO- + -SPHERE] that region surrounding a planet in which the planetary magnetic field is stronger than the interplanetary field

mag·ne·tron (mag'nə trän') ***n.*** [MAGNE(T) + (ELEC)TRON] an electron tube in which the flow of electrons is acted upon by an externally applied magnetic field to produce microwave frequencies

magnet school a public school which offers innovative courses, specialized training, etc. in order to attract students from a broad urban area and thereby help to bring about desegregation

mag·ni- [< L. *magnus,* great] *a combining form meaning* great, big, large *[magnificent]*

Mag·nif·i·cat (mag nif'i kat', män yif'i kät') ***n.*** [L.] **1.** the hymn of the Virgin Mary in Luke 1:46–55 **2.** any musical setting for this

mag·ni·fi·ca·tion (mag'nə fi kā'shən) ***n.*** **1.** a magnifying or being magnified **2.** the power of magnifying **3.** a magnified image or model

mag·nif·i·cence (mag nif'ə s'ns) ***n.*** [OFr. < L. < *magnificus,* noble < *magnus,* great + *facere,* to do] richness and splendor, as of furnishings, color, dress, etc.; stately or imposing beauty; grandeur

mag·nif·i·cent (-s'nt) ***adj.*** [OFr. < LL. *magnificens:* see prec.] **1.** beautiful and grand or stately; rich or sumptuous, as in construction, decoration, etc. **2.** exalted: said of ideas, etc. **3.** [Colloq.] very good; excellent —**mag·nif'i·cent·ly** ***adv.***

mag·nif·i·co (-kō') ***n.,*** *pl.* **-coes', -cos'** [It. < L. *magnificus:* see MAGNIFICENCE] a person of high rank

mag·ni·fy (mag'nə fī') ***vt.*** **-fied', -fy'ing** [< OFr. < L. *magnificare:* see MAGNIFICENCE] **1.** [Rare] to make greater **2.** to exaggerate *[to magnify* one's sufferings*]* **3.** to increase the apparent size of, esp. by means of a lens **4.** [Archaic] to praise; extol —***vi.*** to have the power of increasing the apparent size of an object —**mag'ni·fi'er** ***n.***

magnifying glass a lens that increases the apparent size of an object seen through it

mag·nil·o·quent (mag nil'ə kwənt) ***adj.*** [< L. < *magnus,* great + prp. of *loqui,* to speak] **1.** pompous or grandiose in speech or style of expression **2.** boastful or bombastic —**mag·nil'o·quence** ***n.*** —**mag·nil'o·quent·ly** ***adv.***

mag·ni·tude (mag'nə to͞od', -tyo͞od') ***n.*** [< L. < *magnus,* great] **1.** greatness; specif., *a)* of size *b)* of extent *c)* of influence **2.** *a)* size *b)* loudness (of sound) *c)* importance **3.** *Astron.* the degree of brightness of a fixed star: the brightest stars are of the first magnitude **4.** *Math.* a number given to a quantity for purposes of comparison with other quantities of the same class —**of the first magnitude** of the greatest importance

mag·no·li·a (mag nō'lē ə, -nōl'yə) ***n.*** [ModL., after P. *Magnol* (1638–1715), Fr. botanist] **1.** any of a group of trees or shrubs with large, fragrant flowers of white, pink, or purple **2.** the flower

mag·num (mag'nəm) ***n.*** [L., neut. sing. of *magnus,* great] a wine bottle holding twice as much as the usual bottle, or about 2/5 of a gallon

‡**mag·num o·pus** (mag'nəm ō'pəs) [L.] **1.** a great work, esp. of art or literature; masterpiece **2.** a person's greatest work or undertaking

mag·pie (mag'pī') ***n.*** [< *Mag,* dim. of MARGARET + PIE[3]] **1.** a noisy bird related to the crows and jays, with black-and-white coloring and a long, tapering tail **2.** a person who chatters **3.** a person who collects odds and ends

mag·uey (mag'wā; *Sp.* mä ge'ē) ***n.*** [Sp.] **1.** a fleshy-leaved, fiber-yielding agave of the SW U.S., Mexico, and Central America; esp., the century plant **2.** its fiber

Mag·yar (mag'yär; *Hung.* mŏd'yär) ***n.*** [Hung.] **1.** a member of the people constituting the main ethnic group in Hungary **2.** their language; Hungarian —***adj.*** of the Magyars, their language, etc.

Ma·ha·bha·ra·ta (mə hä'bä'rə tə) [Sans.] one of the two great epics of India, written in Sanskrit about 200 B.C.

ma·ha·ra·jah, ma·ha·ra·ja (mä'hə rä'jə) ***n.*** [< Sans. < *mahā,* great + *rājā,* king] formerly in India, a prince; specif., the sovereign prince of a native state

ma·ha·ra·ni, ma·ha·ra·nee (-nē) ***n.*** [< Hindi < *mahā,* great + *rānī,* queen] in India, the wife of a maharajah

ma·hat·ma (mə hat'mə, -hät'-) ***n.*** [< Sans. < *mahā,* great + *ātman,* soul] *Theosophy & Buddhism* any of a class of wise and holy persons held in special regard or reverence

Ma·hi·can (mə hē'kən) ***n.*** [< Algonquian, lit., a wolf] **1.** a confederacy or tribe of Algonquian Indians who lived chiefly in the upper Hudson Valley **2.** an Indian of this confederacy **3.** *same as* MOHEGAN —***adj.*** of the Mahicans

mah-jongg, mah·jong (mä'jôŋ', -jäŋ', -zhôŋ', -zhäŋ') ***n.*** [< Chin. *ma-ch'iao,* lit., house sparrow (a figure on one of the tiles)] a game of Chinese origin, played with 136 or 144 small tiles

Mah·ler (mä'lər), **Gus·tav** (goos'täf) 1860–1911; Austrian composer & conductor, born in Bohemia

ma·hog·a·ny (mə häg'ə nē, -hôg'-) ***n.,*** *pl.* **-nies** [< ?] **1.** any of various tropical trees, esp. one of tropical America, with hard, reddish-brown wood valued for furniture **2.** the wood of any of these trees **3.** reddish brown —***adj.*** **1.** made of mahogany **2.** reddish-brown

Ma·hom·et (mə häm'it) *same as* MOHAMMED

ma·hout (mə hout') ***n.*** [< Hindi < Sans. *mahāmātra,* lit., great in measure] in India and the East Indies, an elephant driver or elephant keeper

maid (mād) *n.* [< ME. contr. < *maiden*] **1.** *a)* a girl or young unmarried woman *b)* a virgin **2.** a girl or woman servant
maid·en (mād'n) *n.* [OE. *mægden*] **1.** *a)* a girl or young unmarried woman *b)* a virgin **2.** a race horse that has never won a race —*adj.* **1.** of, characteristic of, for, or suitable for a maiden or maidens **2.** *a)* unmarried *b)* virgin **3.** untried; unused; new; fresh **4.** first or earliest [a *maiden* voyage]
maid·en·hair (-her') *n.* any of various ferns with delicate brown to black fronds: also **maidenhair fern**
maid·en·head (-hed') *n.* **1.** [Archaic] maidenhood; virginity **2.** the hymen
maid·en·hood (-hood') *n.* the state or time of being a maiden: also **maid'hood'**
maid·en·ly (-lē) *adj.* **1.** of a maiden **2.** like or suitable for a maiden; modest, gentle, etc. —*adv.* [Archaic] in a maidenly manner —**maid'en·li·ness** *n.*
maiden name the surname of a woman before her marriage
maid of honor **1.** an unmarried woman acting as chief attendant to the bride at a wedding **2.** an unmarried woman, usually of noble birth, attending a queen or princess
maid·ser·vant (-sur'vənt) *n.* a girl or woman servant
mail[1] (māl) *n.* [OFr. *male,* ult. < OHG. *malaha,* wallet] **1.** *a)* letters, papers, packages, etc. transported and delivered by the post office *b)* their collection or delivery at a certain time **2.** [*also pl.*] the postal system —*adj.* of mail —*vt.* to send by mail, as by putting into a mailbox —**mail'a·bil'i·ty** *n.* —**mail'a·ble** *adj.* —**mail'er** *n.*
mail[2] (māl) *n.* [OFr. *maille* < L. *macula,* a mesh of a net] **1.** a flexible body armor made of small metal rings, loops of chain, or scales **2.** the hard protective covering of some animals, as turtles —*vt.* to cover or protect as with mail —**mailed** *adj.*

MAIL

mail·bag (māl'bag') *n.* **1.** a bag, as of leather, in which a mailman carries the mail he delivers: also **mail pouch** **2.** a heavy canvas bag in which mail is transported: also **mail sack**
mail·box (-bäks') *n.* **1.** a box into which mail is put when delivered **2.** a box, as on a street, into which mail is put for collection Also **mail box**
mail carrier one whose work is carrying and delivering mail; mailman; postman
Mail·gram (māl'gram') *a trademark for* a telegram delivered with the regular mail —*n.* [*also* **m-**] such a telegram
mail·ing list (māl'iŋ) a special list of names and addresses used by an organization, business, etc. in mailing out its literature, advertising matter, etc.
mail·man (māl'man', -mən) *n., pl.* **-men'** (-men', -mən) *same as* MAIL CARRIER
mail order an order for goods to be sent through the mail —**mail'-or'der** *adj.*
mail-order house a business that takes mail orders
maim (mām) *vt.* [OFr. *mahaigner*] to deprive of the use of some necessary part of the body; cripple; mutilate; disable
Mai·mon·i·des (mī män'ə dēz') (born *Moses ben Maimon*) 1135–1204; Sp. rabbi, physician, & philosopher, in Egypt
Main (mīn; *E.* mān) river in S West Germany, flowing west into the Rhine
main[1] (mān) *n.* [OE. *mægen*] **1.** physical strength; force: now only in **with might and main,** with all one's strength **2.** the principal part or point: usually in **in the main,** mostly, chiefly **3.** a principal pipe or line in a distributing system for water, gas, etc. **4.** [Poet.] the ocean **5.** [Archaic] the mainland **6.** [Obs.] any broad expanse —*adj.* **1.** orig., strong; powerful **2.** chief in size, importance, etc.; principal —**by main force** (or **strength**) by sheer force (or strength)
main[2] (mān) *n.* [prob. < prec.] a series of matches in cockfighting
main clause in a complex sentence, a clause that can function syntactically as a complete sentence by itself
main drag [Slang] the main street of a city or town
Maine (mān) [prob. from its being the *main* part of New England] New England State of the U.S.: 33,215 sq. mi.; pop. 1,125,000; cap. Augusta: abbrev. **Me., ME**
main·frame (mān'frām') *n.* the central processing unit of a computer
main·land (mān'land', -lənd) *n.* the main land mass of a continent, as distinguished from nearby islands, etc. —**main'land'er** *n.*
main·line (-līn') *n.* the principal road, course, etc. —*vt.* **-lined', -lin'ing** [Slang] to inject (a narcotic drug) directly into a large vein —**main'lin'er** *n.*
main·ly (-lē) *adv.* chiefly; principally; in the main
main·mast (-məst, -mast') *n.* the principal mast of a vessel
main·sail (-s'l, -sāl') *n.* **1.** in a square-rigged vessel, the sail set from the main yard: also **main course** **2.** in a fore-and-aft-rigged vessel, the large sail set from the mainmast

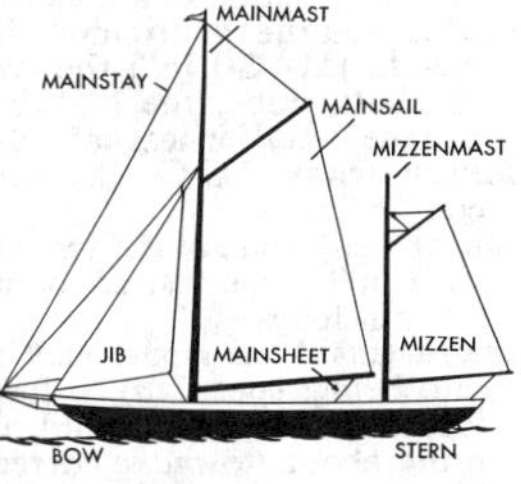

main·sheet (-shēt') *n.* the line controlling the angle at which a mainsail is set
main·spring (-spriŋ') *n.* **1.** the principal, or driving, spring in a clock, watch, etc. **2.** the chief motive, incentive, or impelling cause
main·stay (-stā') *n.* **1.** the supporting line run forward from the mainmast **2.** a chief support
main stem [Slang] *same as* MAIN DRAG
main·stream (-strēm') *n.* the main current or prevailing trend of thought, action, etc.
Main Street **1.** the principal street of any small town **2.** the typical inhabitants of a small town, regarded as provincial and conservative
main·tain (mān tān') *vt.* [< OFr. *maintenir,* ult. < L. *manu tenere,* to hold in the hand] **1.** to keep or keep up; carry on **2.** *a)* to keep in continuance [food *maintains* life] *b)* to keep in a certain condition, as of repair [to *maintain* roads] **3.** to hold (a place, etc.) against attack **4.** *a)* to uphold or defend, as by argument *b)* to declare positively; assert **5.** to support by aid, influence, etc. **6.** to provide the means of existence for [to *maintain* a family] —**main·tain'a·ble** *adj.* —**main·tain'er** *n.*
main·te·nance (mān't'n əns) *n.* **1.** a maintaining or being maintained; upkeep, continuance, support, defense, etc. **2.** means of support or sustenance; livelihood
main·top (mān'täp') *n.* a platform at the head of the lower section of the mainmast
main·top·mast (mān'täp'məst) *n.* the section of the mainmast above the maintop
main·top·sail (-s'l, -sāl) *n.* the sail above the mainsail on the mainmast
main yard the lower yard on the mainmast
mai·tre d' (māt'ər dē') [< ff.] [Colloq.] a headwaiter
‡**maî·tre d'hô·tel** (me'tr' dô tel') [Fr., lit., master of the house] **1.** a butler or steward **2.** a headwaiter
maize (māz) *n.* [Sp. *maīz* < WInd. *mahiz*] **1.** *chiefly Brit. name for* CORN[1] (sense 2) **2.** the color of ripe corn; yellow —*adj.* yellow
Maj. Major
ma·jes·tic (mə jes'tik) *adj.* having majesty; grand, stately, dignified, lofty, etc.: also **ma·jes'ti·cal** —**ma·jes'ti·cal·ly** *adv.*
maj·es·ty (maj'is tē) *n., pl.* **-ties** [< OFr. < L. *majestas* < base of *major,* compar. of *magnus,* great] **1.** sovereign power or dignity **2.** [**M-**] a title used in speaking to or of a sovereign, preceded by *His, Her,* or *Your* **3.** grandeur or stateliness
ma·jol·i·ca (mə jäl'i kə, -yäl'-) *n.* [It. *maiolica* < *Maiolica,* MAJORCA] a variety of Italian pottery, enameled, glazed, and richly decorated
ma·jor (mā'jər) *adj.* [L., compar. of *magnus,* great] **1.** *a)* greater in size, amount, or extent *b)* greater in importance or rank **2.** of full legal age **3.** constituting the majority **4.** *Educ.* designating a field of study in which a student specializes **5.** *Music a)* designating an interval greater than the corresponding minor by a semitone *b)* characterized by major intervals, scales, etc. [the *major* key] *c)* based on the scale pattern of the major mode: see MAJOR SCALE —*vi. Educ.* to pursue a major subject [to *major* in physics] —*n.* **1.** a superior in some class or group **2.** *U.S. Mil.* an officer ranking above a captain **3.** *Educ. a)* a major field of study *b)* a student specializing in a (specified) subject **4.** *Law* a person of full legal age **5.** *Music* a major interval, key, etc. —**the Majors** *Baseball* the Major Leagues
Ma·jor·ca (mə jôr'kə) largest of the Balearic Islands
ma·jor-do·mo (mā'jər dō'mō) *n., pl.* **-mos** [< Sp. or It. < LL. < L. *major,* greater, an elder + gen. of *domus,* house] **1.** a man in charge of a great or royal household; chief steward **2.** any steward or butler: humorous usage
ma·jor·ette (mā'jər et') *n. short for* DRUM MAJORETTE
major general *pl.* **major generals** *U.S. Mil.* an officer ranking above a brigadier general
ma·jor·i·ty (mə jôr'ə tē, -jär'-) *n., pl.* **-ties** [< Fr. < ML. < L. *major:* see MAJOR] **1.** the greater part or larger number; more than half **2.** the excess of the larger number of votes cast for one candidate, bill, etc. over all the rest of

the votes 3. the group or party with the majority of votes 4. the state or time of being legally an adult 5. *Mil.* the rank or position of a major

major league a principal league in a professional sport; specif., [M- L-] [*pl.*] the two main leagues of professional baseball clubs, the National League and the American League —**ma′jor-league′** *adj.* —**ma′jor-leagu′er** *n.*

major order *R.C.Ch.* the order of priest, deacon, or subdeacon

major scale one of the two standard diatonic musical scales, with half steps instead of whole steps after the third and seventh tones

make (māk) *vt.* **made, mak′ing** [OE. *macian*] 1. to bring into being; specif., *a)* to form by shaping or putting parts, ideas, etc. together; build, create, devise, etc. *b)* to cause; bring about [*to make corrections*] *c)* to cause to be available; provide [*to make room*] 2. to cause to be, become, or seem [*make him chairman*] : sometimes used reflexively [*make yourself comfortable*] 3. to prepare for use [*make the beds*] 4. to amount to [*two pints make a quart*] 5. to have, or prove to have, the qualities of or for [*to make a fine leader*] 6. to set up; establish [*to make rules*] 7. *a)* to acquire, as by one's behavior [*to make friends*] *b)* to get by earning, investing, etc. [*to make a fortune*] 8. to cause the success of [*that venture made him*] 9. to understand [*what do you make of that?*] 10. to estimate to be [*I make the distance about 500 miles*] 11. *a)* to do, execute, accomplish, etc. [*to make a quick turn*] *b)* to engage in [*to make war*] 12. to deliver (a speech) or utter (remarks, etc.) 13. to cause or force [*make him behave*] 14. to arrive at; reach [*the ship made port*] 15. to go or travel; traverse [*to make 500 miles the first day*] 16. [Colloq.] to succeed in getting a position on, etc. [*to make the team*] 17. [Slang] to seduce sexually 18. *Elec.* to close (a circuit); effect (a contact) —*vi.* 1. to start (to do something) [*she made to go*] 2. to tend, extend, or point (*to, toward,* etc.) 3. to behave in a specified manner [*make bold, make merry*] 4. to cause something to be in a specified condition [*make ready*] —*n.* 1. the act or process of making 2. the amount made; output 3. the way in which something is made; style; build 4. type, sort, or brand 5. character; nature [*a man of this make*] 6. *Elec.* the closing of a circuit —**make after** to chase or follow —**make away with** 1. to steal 2. to get rid of 3. to kill —**make believe** to pretend —**make for** 1. to head for 2. to attack 3. to help effect —**make it** [Colloq.] to do or achieve a certain thing —**make like** [Slang] to imitate —**make off with** to steal —**make or break** to cause the success or failure of —**make out** 1. to see with some difficulty 2. to understand 3. to write out 4. to fill out (a blank form, etc.) 5. to (try to) show or prove to be 6. to succeed; get along 7. [Slang] *a)* to kiss and caress as lovers *b)* to have sexual intercourse —**make over** 1. to change; renovate 2. to transfer the ownership of 3. [Colloq.] to be demonstrative toward or about —**make up** 1. to put together; compose 2. to form; constitute 3. to invent 4. to complete by providing what is lacking 5. to compensate (*for*) 6. to become friendly again after a quarrel 7. to put cosmetics on 8. to decide (one's mind) 9. to select and arrange type, illustrations, etc. for (a book, page, etc.) —**make up to** to try to ingratiate oneself with —**on the make** 1. [Colloq.] trying to succeed, esp. in an aggressive way 2. [Slang] seeking a lover

make-be·lieve (māk′bə lēv′) *n.* 1. pretense; feigning 2. a pretender —*adj.* pretended; feigned

mak·er (-ər) *n.* 1. a person or thing that makes 2. [M-] God —**meet one's Maker** to die

make·shift (-shift′) *n.* a thing that will do for a while as a substitute; temporary expedient —*adj.* that will do for a while as a substitute

make·up, make-up (-up′) *n.* 1. the way in which something is put together; composition 2. nature; disposition 3. the cosmetics, wigs, costumes, etc. put on for theatrical roles 4. cosmetics generally 5. the arrangement of type, illustrations, etc. in a book, newspaper, etc.

make-work (-wurk′) *adj.* designating a job, project, assignment, etc. that serves no useful purpose other than to give an otherwise idle or unemployed person something to do

Ma·key·ev·ka (mä kā′yif kä′) city in SE Ukrainian S.S.R., in the Donets river valley: pop. 415,000

mak·ing (mā′kiŋ) *n.* 1. the act of one that makes or the process of being made 2. the cause of success or advancement [*an experience that will be the making of him*] 3. *a)* something made *b)* the quantity made at a single time 4. [*often pl.*] the material or potential qualities needed [*to have the making(s) of a good doctor*]

mal- [Fr. < L. < *male,* badly < *malus,* bad] *a prefix meaning* bad or badly, wrong, ill [*maladjustment*]

Mal. 1. Malachi 2. Malay 3. Malayan

Ma·la·bo (mä lä′bō) capital of Equatorial Guinea; seaport on the island portion of the country: pop. 20,000

Ma·lac·ca (mə lak′ə) **Strait of,** strait between Sumatra & the Malay Peninsula

Mal·a·chi (mal′ə kī′) *Bible* 1. a Hebrew prophet of the 5th cent. B.C. 2. the book containing prophecies attributed to him

mal·a·chite (mal′ə kīt′) *n.* [< L. < Gr. *malachē,* mallow: from its color] native basic copper carbonate, $CuCO_3$-$Cu(OH)_2$, a green mineral used as a source of copper and for table tops, vases, etc.

mal·ad·just·ed (mal′ə jus′tid) *adj.* poorly adjusted, esp. to the circumstances of one's life —**mal′ad·just′ment** *n.*

mal·ad·min·is·ter (-əd min′ə stər) *vt.* to administer badly or corruptly —**mal′ad·min′is·tra′tion** *n.*

mal·a·droit (mal′ə droit′) *adj.* [Fr.: see MAL- & ADROIT] awkward; clumsy; bungling —**mal′a·droit′ly** *adv.* —**mal′a·droit′ness** *n.*

mal·a·dy (mal′ə dē) *n., pl.* **-dies** [< OFr. *malade,* sick < VL. *male habitus,* out of condition: see MAL- & HABIT] a disease; illness; sickness

Má·la·ga (mä′lä gä′; *E.* mal′ə gə) seaport in S Spain, on the Mediterranean: pop. 330,000

Mal·a·ga (mal′ə gə) *n.* 1. a large, white, oval grape 2. a white, sweet wine, orig. from Málaga

Mal·a·gas·y (mal′ə gas′ē) *n.* 1. *pl.* **-gas′y, -gas′ies** a native or inhabitant of Madagascar 2. the Indonesian language of the Malagasy

Malagasy Republic *former name of* MADAGASCAR

ma·laise (ma lāz′) *n.* [Fr. < *mal,* bad (see MAL-) + *aise,* EASE] a vague feeling of physical discomfort or uneasiness, as early in an illness

mal·a·mute (mal′ə myōōt′) *n.* [< *Malemute,* name of an Eskimo tribe] a strong dog with a thick coat of gray or black-and-white and a bushy tail: it was developed as a sled dog by the Alaskan Eskimo: in full, **Alaskan malamute:** also sp. **malemute, malemiut**

mal·a·prop (mal′ə präp′) *adj.* [< ff.] using or characterized by malapropisms: also **mal′a·prop′i·an** (-ē ən) —*n. same as* MALAPROPISM

mal·a·prop·ism (mal′ə präp iz′m) *n.* [after Mrs. *Malaprop,* a character in Sheridan's *The Rivals*] 1. ludicrous misuse of words, esp. of words that sound somewhat alike 2. an instance of this

mal·ap·ro·pos (mal′ap rə pō′, mal ap′-) *adj., adv.* [Fr.: see MAL- & APROPOS] inappropriate(ly); inopportune(ly)

ma·lar·i·a (mə ler′ē ə) *n.* [It., contr. of *mala aria,* bad air] an infectious disease, generally recurrent, caused by protozoans transmitted to man by the bite of an infected mosquito, esp. the anopheles: it is characterized by severe chills and fever —**ma·lar′i·al, ma·lar′i·an, ma·lar′i·ous** *adj.*

ma·lar·key, ma·lar·ky (mə lär′kē) *n.* [< ? Irish surname] [Slang] insincere talk; nonsense

mal·a·thi·on (mal′ə thī′än) *n.* an organic phosphate, $C_{10}H_{19}O_6S_2P$, used as an insecticide

Ma·la·wi (mä′lä wē) country in SE Africa: a member of the Commonwealth: 46,066 sq. mi.; pop. 4,530,000

Ma·lay (mā′lā, mə lā′) *n.* 1. a member of a large group of brown-skinned peoples living in the Malay Peninsula, the Malay Archipelago, and nearby islands 2. their Indonesian language —*adj.* of the Malays, their country, language, culture, etc.

Ma·lay·a (mə lā′ə) 1. *same as* MALAY PENINSULA 2. group of eleven states at the S end of the Malay Peninsula: it is a part of Malaysia and is called *West Malaysia*

Ma·lay·an (mə lā′ən) *adj. same as* INDONESIAN (sense 2) —*n.* 1. *same as* MALAY (sense 1) 2. *same as* INDONESIAN (sense 3)

Malay Archipelago large group of islands between the mainland of SE Asia & Australia

Ma·lay·o-Pol·y·ne·sian (mə lā′ō päl′ə nē′zhən, -shən) *adj.* designating or of a family of languages spoken over a large area in the C & W Pacific, including Polynesian, Indonesian, etc. —*n.* these languages

Malay Peninsula peninsula in SE Asia, including the S part of Thailand & the states of Malaya

Ma·lay·sia (mə lā′zhə, -shə) country in SE Asia, consisting of the states of Malaya and two states on N Borneo: a member of the Commonwealth: 128,654 sq. mi.; pop. 10,190,000; cap. Kuala Lumpur —**Ma·lay′sian** *adj., n.*

Mal·colm (mal′kəm) [Celt. *Maolcolm,* lit., servant of (St.) Columba] a masculine name

mal·con·tent (mal′kən tent′) *adj.* [OFr.: see MAL- & CONTENT[1]] dissatisfied or rebellious —*n.* a dissatisfied or rebellious person

‡**mal de mer** (mål də mer′) [Fr.] seasickness

Mal·den (môl′dən) [after *Maldon,* town in England] city in E Mass.: suburb of Boston: pop. 53,000

Mal·dive Islands (mal′dīv) country on a group of islands in the Indian Ocean, southwest of Ceylon: 115 sq. mi.; pop. 104,000: also **Mal′dives**

male (māl) *adj.* [< OFr. < L. *masculus,* dim. of *mas,* a male] 1. designating or of the sex that fertilizes the ovum of the female and begets offspring 2. of, like, or suitable for members of this sex; masculine 3. consisting of men or boys **4.** designating or having a part shaped to fit into a corresponding hollow part **5.** *Bot.* designating or of fertilizing bodies, organs, etc. —*n.* **1.** a male person; man or boy **2.** a male animal or plant —**male′ness** *n.*

mal·e·dic·tion (mal′ə dik′shən) *n.* [OFr. < LL. *maledictio* < L., abuse: see MAL- & DICTION] a calling down of evil on someone; curse

mal·e·fac·tion (-fak′shən) *n.* wrongdoing; crime

mal·e·fac·tor (mal′ə fak′tər) *n.* [L. < pp. of *malefacere* < *male,* evil + *facere,* to do] an evildoer or criminal

ma·lef·i·cent (mə lef′ə s'nt) *adj.* [see prec.] harmful; hurtful; evil —**ma·lef′i·cence** *n.*

ma·lev·o·lent (mə lev′ə lənt) *adj.* [< OFr. < L. < *male,* evil + prp. of *velle,* to wish] wishing evil or harm to others; spiteful; malicious —**ma·lev′o·lence** *n.* —**ma·lev′o·lent·ly** *adv.*

mal·fea·sance (mal fē′z'ns) *n.* [obs. Fr. *malfaisance* < *mal,* evil + prp. of *faire,* to do] wrongdoing or misconduct, esp. by a public official: distinguished from MISFEASANCE, NONFEASANCE —**mal·fea′sant** *adj.*

mal·for·ma·tion (mal′fôr mā′shən) *n.* faulty, irregular, or abnormal formation of a body or part —**mal·formed′** (-fôrmd′) *adj.*

mal·func·tion (mal fuŋk′shən) *vi.* to fail to function as it should —*n.* the act or an instance of malfunctioning

Ma·li (mä′lē) country in W Africa, south & east of Mauritania: 464,873 sq. mi.; pop. 4,929,000

mal·ic acid (mal′ik, mā′lik) [< Fr. < L. < Gr. *mēlon,* apple] a colorless acid, $C_4H_6O_5$, occurring in apples and other fruits

mal·ice (mal′is) *n.* [OFr. < L. < *malus,* bad] **1.** active ill will; desire to harm another; spite **2.** *Law* evil intent —**malice aforethought** a deliberate intention and plan to do something unlawful

ma·li·cious (mə lish′əs) *adj.* having, showing, or caused by malice; spiteful —**ma·li′cious·ly** *adv.* —**ma·li′cious·ness** *n.*

ma·lign (mə līn′) *vt.* [< OFr. < LL. < L. *malignus,* wicked < *male,* ill + base of *genus,* born] to speak evil of; slander —*adj.* **1.** showing ill will; malicious **2.** evil; sinister **3.** very harmful; malignant —**ma·lign′er** *n.*

ma·lig·nan·cy (mə lig′nən sē) *n.* **1.** a being malignant: also **ma·lig′nance** **2.** *pl.* **-cies** a malignant tumor

ma·lig·nant (-nənt) *adj.* [< LL. < L. *malignus:* see MALIGN] **1.** having an evil influence; malign **2.** wishing evil; malevolent **3.** very harmful **4.** very virulent; causing or likely to cause death [a cancer is a *malignant* growth] —**ma·lig′nant·ly** *adv.*

ma·lig·ni·ty (-nə tē) *n.* **1.** intense ill will or desire to harm others; great malice **2.** the quality of being very harmful or dangerous **3.** *pl.* **-ties** a malignant act, event, or feeling

ma·lines (mə lēn′; *Fr.* mȧ lēn′) *n.* [< *Malines,* Belgian city] a thin, somewhat stiff, silk net: also **ma·line′**

ma·lin·ger (mə liŋ′gər) *vi.* [< Fr. *malingre,* sickly] to pretend to be ill in order to escape duty or work; shirk —**ma·lin′ger·er** *n.*

mall (môl, mal) *n.* [var. of MAUL] **1.** a shaded walk or public promenade **2.** *a*) a street for pedestrians only, with shops on each of the sides *b*) a completely enclosed, air-conditioned shopping center like this

mal·lard (mal′ərd) *n., pl.* **-lards, -lard:** see PLURAL, II, D, 1 [OFr. *malart*] the common wild duck, from which the domestic duck is descended: the male has a green head and a band of white around the neck

Mal·lar·mé (mȧ lȧr mā′), **Sté·phane** (stā fȧn′) 1842–98; Fr. poet

mal·le·a·ble (mal′ē ə b'l) *adj.* [< ML. < L. *malleare,* to hammer < *malleus,* a hammer] **1.** that can be hammered, pounded, or pressed into various shapes without breaking **2.** pliable; adaptable —**mal′le·a·bil′i·ty, mal′le·a·bleness** *n.*

mal·let (mal′it) *n.* [< MFr. dim. of *mail* < OFr. *maile:* see MAUL] **1.** a kind of hammer, usually with a wooden head and a short handle, for driving a chisel, etc. **2.** *a*) a long-handled hammer used in playing croquet *b*) a similar instrument used in playing polo **3.** a small, light hammer used for playing a vibraphone, xylophone, etc.

mal·le·us (mal′ē əs) *n., pl.* **mal′le·i′** (-ī′) [L., a hammer] the outermost of the three small bones in the middle ear of mammals, shaped somewhat like a hammer

Mal·lor·ca (mäl yôr′kä, mä-) *Sp. name of* MAJORCA

mal·low (mal′ō) *n.* [OE. *mealuwe* < L. *malva*] **1.** any of a group of plants, with dissected or lobed leaves and large, showy flowers **2.** any of various other related plants, as the marsh mallow

Malm·ö (mälm′ö; *E.* mal′mō) seaport in S Sweden: pop. 254,000

malm·sey (mäm′zē) *n.* [< ML. < Gr. *Monembasia,* Greek town] **1.** a strong, full-flavored, sweet white wine **2.** the grape from which this is made

mal·nour·ished (mal nʉr′isht) *adj.* improperly nourished

mal·nu·tri·tion (mal′no͞o trish′ən) *n.* faulty or inadequate nutrition; poor nourishment

mal·o·dor·ous (mal ō′dər əs) *adj.* having a bad odor; stinking —**mal·o′dor** *n.* —**mal·o′dor·ous·ly** *adv.*

Mal·o·ry (mal′ər ē), Sir **Thomas** ?–1471?; Eng. compiler & translator of Arthurian tales taken mostly from Fr. sources

mal·prac·tice (mal prak′tis) *n.* **1.** injurious or unprofessional treatment of a patient by a physician or surgeon **2.** misconduct or improper practice in any professional or official position —**mal′prac·ti′tion·er** (-tish′ən ər) *n.*

malt (môlt) *n.* [OE. *mealt*] **1.** barley or other grain softened by soaking and then kiln-dried: used for brewing and distilling certain alcoholic liquors **2.** such liquor, esp. beer, ale, etc. **3.** [Colloq.] *same as* MALTED MILK —*adj.* made with malt —*vt.* **1.** to change (barley, etc.) into malt **2.** to prepare (milk, etc.) with malt or malt extract —*vi.* **1.** to be changed into malt **2.** to change barley, etc. into malt —**malt′y** *adj.* **malt′i·er, malt′i·est**

Mal·ta (môl′tə) **1.** country on a group of islands in the Mediterranean, south of Sicily: a member of the Commonwealth: 122 sq. mi.; pop. 328,000 **2.** main island of this group

malted milk a drink made by mixing a powdered preparation of dried milk and malted cereals with milk and, usually, ice cream and a flavoring

Mal·tese (môl tēz′) *adj.* of Malta, its inhabitants, etc. —*n.* **1.** *pl.* **-tese′** a native or inhabitant of Malta **2.** the Arabic language of Malta **3.** a variety of domestic cat with bluish-gray fur: in full, **Maltese cat**

Maltese cross a cross whose arms look like arrowheads pointing inward

malt extract a sticky, sugary substance obtained from malt soaked in water

Mal·thu·sian (mal tho͞o′zhən, -zē ən) *adj.* [after R. *Malthus* (1766–1834), Eng. economist] designating or of a theory that the increasing population of the world is naturally restricted by war, famine, and disease —*n.* a supporter of this theory

malt liquor beer, ale, etc. made from malt by fermentation

malt·ose (môl′tōs) *n.* a white, crystalline sugar, $C_{12}H_{22}O_{11} \cdot H_2O$, obtained by the action of the diastase of malt on starch: also called **malt sugar**

mal·treat (mal trēt′) *vt.* [< Fr.: see MAL- & TREAT] to treat roughly, unkindly, or brutally; abuse —**mal·treat′ment** *n.*

malt·ster (môlt′stər) *n.* one who makes malt

mam·bo (mäm′bō) *n.* [AmSp.] a rhythmic ballroom dance to music of Cuban Negro origin in 4/4 time with a heavy accent on the second and fourth beats —*vi.* to dance the mambo

mam·ma[1] (mä′mə; *occas.* mə mä′) *n.* [like L. *mamma,* mother, Sans. *mā,* Gr. *mammē* < baby talk] mother: a child's word: also **ma′ma**

mam·ma[2] (mam′ə) *n., pl.* **-mae** (-ē) [L., breast] a gland for secreting milk, present in the female of all mammals; mammary gland

mam·mal (-əl) *n.* [< ModL. < LL. < L. *mamma:* see prec.] any of a large class of warmblooded vertebrates whose offspring are fed with milk secreted by the female mammary glands —**mam·ma·li·an** (mə mā′lē ən, ma-) *adj., n.*

mam·ma·ry (mam′ər ē) *adj.* designating or of the milk-secreting glands; of the mammae

mam·mon (mam′ən) *n.* [< LL. < Gr. < Aram. *māmōnā,* riches] [*often* **M-**] riches regarded as an object of worship and greedy pursuit —**mam′mon·ism** *n.*

mam·moth (mam′əth) *n.* [Russ. *mamont*] an extinct elephant with a hairy skin and long tusks curving upward —*adj.* very big; huge; enormous

HAIRY MAMMOTH (to 13 ft. high at shoulder)

mam·my (mam′ē) *n., pl.* **-mies** [dial. var. of MAMMA[1]] **1.** mamma; mother: a child's word **2.** a Negro woman who takes care of white children, esp. in the southern States

man (man) *n., pl.* **men** (men) [OE. *mann*] **1.** a human being; person; specif., one of that species (see HOMO SAPIENS) of primates having the most highly developed brain and articulate speech **2.** the human race; mankind: used without *the* or *a* **3.** an adult male human being **4.** *a*) an adult male servant, follower, subordinate, etc. *b*) a male employee *c*) [Archaic] a vassal **5.** a husband or a lover **6.** a person with qualities conventionally regarded as manly **7.** any of the pieces used in chess, checkers, etc. **8.** [Slang] fellow; chap —*vt.* **manned, man′ning 1.** to furnish with men for work, defense, etc. *[*to *man* a ship*]* **2.** to take assigned places in, on, or at *[man* the guns!*]* **3.** to strengthen; brace *[*to *man* oneself for an ordeal*]* —*interj.* [Slang] an exclamation of emphasis: often used neutrally to preface or resume one's remarks —*adj.* male —**as a** (or **one**) **man** in unison; unanimously —**be one's own man 1.** to be free and independent **2.** to be in full control of oneself —**man and boy** first as a boy and then as a man —**the Man** [Slang] the person having authority over one, as a policeman —**to a man** with no one as an exception

-man (mən, man) *a combining form meaning* man or person of a specified kind, in a specified activity, etc. *[Frenchman, sportsman]*

Man. 1. Manila (paper) **2.** Manitoba

Man (man), **Isle of** one of the Brit. Isles, between Northern Ireland & England: 227 sq. mi.; pop. 48,000

ma·na (mä′nä) *n.* [< Polynesian] the supernatural force to which certain primitive peoples attribute good fortune, magical powers, etc.

man about town a worldly man who spends much time in fashionable restaurants, clubs, etc.

man·a·cle (man′ə k'l) *n.* [< OFr. < L. *manicula,* dim. of *manus,* hand] **1.** a handcuff; fetter or shackle for the hand **2.** any restraint *Usually used in pl.* —*vt.* **-cled, -cling 1.** to put handcuffs on; fetter **2.** to restrain; hamper

man·age (man′ij) *vt.* **-aged, -ag·ing** [It. *maneggiare* < *mano,* hand < L. *manus*] **1.** orig., to train (a horse) in his paces **2.** to control the movement or behavior of **3.** to have charge of; direct *[*to *manage* a household*]* **4.** [Rare] to handle or use carefully **5.** to get (a person) to do what one wishes, esp. by tact, flattery, etc. **6.** to succeed in accomplishing; contrive —*vi.* **1.** to conduct or direct affairs; carry on business **2.** to contrive to get along; succeed in handling matters

man·age·a·ble (man′ij ə b'l) *adj.* that can be managed; controllable —**man′age·a·bil′i·ty, man′age·a·ble·ness** *n.* —**man′age·a·bly** *adv.*

managed currency a currency regulated through procedures that alter the amount of money in circulation so as to control credit, prices, etc.

man·age·ment (man′ij mənt) *n.* **1.** the act, art, or manner of managing, controlling, etc. **2.** skillful managing **3.** executive ability **4.** the persons managing a business, institution, etc.

man·ag·er (-ij ər) *n.* a person who manages the affairs of a business, institution, client, team, etc. —**man′ag·er·ship′** *n.*

man·a·ge·ri·al (man′ə jir′ē əl) *adj.* of a manager or management —**man′a·ge′ri·al·ism** *n.* —**man′a·ge′ri·al·ly** *adv.*

Ma·na·gua (mä nä′gwä) **1.** lake in W Nicaragua **2.** capital of Nicaragua, on this lake: pop. 300,000 (1967): devastated by an earthquake, 1972

‡**ma·ña·na** (mä nyä′nä) *n.* [Sp.] tomorrow —*adv.* **1.** tomorrow **2.** at some indefinite future time

Ma·nas·seh (mə nas′ə) *Bible* **1.** the elder son of Joseph **2.** the tribe of Israel descended from him

man-at-arms (man′ət ärmz′) *n., pl.* **men′-at-arms′** (men′-) formerly, a soldier; esp., a heavily armed medieval soldier on horseback

man·a·tee (man′ə tē′, man′ə tē′) *n.* [Sp. *manatí* < native (Carib) name] a large, plant-eating aquatic mammal living in shallow tropical waters, having flippers and a broad, flat, rounded tail; sea cow

Man·ches·ter (man′ches′tər, -chi stər) **1.** city & port in NW England: pop. 603,000 **2.** [after prec.] city in S N.H.: pop. 91,000

Man·chu (man cho͞o′, man′cho͞o) *n.* **1.** *pl.* **-chus′, -chu′** a member of a Mongolian people of Manchuria: the Manchus conquered China in 1643–44 and ruled until 1912 **2.** the language of the Manchus —*adj.* of Manchuria, the Manchus, their language, etc.

Man·chu·ri·a (man choor′ē ə) region of NE China, north of Korea —**Man·chu′ri·an** *adj., n.*

-man·cy (man′sē) [< OFr. < LL. < Gr. *manteia,* divination] *a combining form meaning* divination *[chiromancy]*

man·da·la (mun′də lə) *n.* [Sans. *maṇḍala*] a circular design of concentric geometric forms symbolizing the universe or wholeness in Hinduism and Buddhism

Man·da·lay (man′də lā′, man′də lā′) city in C Burma, on the Irrawaddy River: pop. 322,000

man·da·mus (man dā′məs) *n.* [L., we command] *Law* a writ commanding that a specified thing be done, issued by a higher court to a lower one, or to a corporation, agency, official, etc.

man·da·rin (man′də rin) *n.* [< Port. < Hindi *mantrī,* minister of state < Sans. < *mantra,* counsel] **1.** a high official of China under the Empire **2.** a member of any elite group **3.** [M-] the official or main dialect of Chinese **4.** a small, sweet orange with a loose rind: in full, **mandarin orange** —*adj.* elegant or overrefined, as in literary style —**man′da·rin·ism** *n.*

man·date (man′dāt) *n.* [< L. neut. pp. of *mandare,* to command < *manus,* a hand + pp. of *dare,* to give] **1.** an authoritative order or command **2.** *a)* formerly, a commission from the League of Nations to a country to administer some region, colony, etc. *b)* the area that is so administered **3.** the wishes of constituents expressed to a representative, etc. and regarded as an order **4.** *Law* an order from a higher court or official to a lower one —*vt.* **-dat·ed, -dat·ing** to assign (a region, etc.) as a mandate —**man·da′tor** *n.*

man·da·to·ry (man′də tôr′ē) *adj.* **1.** of, like, or containing a mandate **2.** authoritatively commanded or required; obligatory **3.** holding a mandate (sense 2) —**man′da·to′ri·ly** *adv.*

man·di·ble (man′də b'l) *n.* [OFr. < LL. < *mandibulum* < L. *mandere,* to chew] the jaw; specif., *a)* the lower jaw of a vertebrate *b)* either of the most forward pair of biting jaws of an insect or other arthropod *c)* either jaw of a beaked animal —**man·dib′u·lar** (-dib′yo͞o lər) *adj.*

man·do·lin (man′d'l in′, man′də lin′) *n.* [< Fr. < It. dim. of *mandola* < LL. < LGr. *pandoura,* kind of lute] a musical instrument with four or five pairs of strings and a deep, rounded sound box: it is played with a plectrum —**man′do·lin′ist** *n.*

MANDOLIN

man·drake (man′drāk) *n.* [by folk etym. < OE. *mandragora* < LL. < L. < Gr. *mandragoras*] **1.** *a)* a poisonous plant of the nightshade family, with a short stem and a thick root *b)* the root, formerly used in medicine as a narcotic Also **man·drag·o·ra** (man drag′ər ə) **2.** *same as* MAY APPLE

man·drel, man·dril (man′drəl) *n.* [prob. < Fr. *mandrin*] **1.** a spindle or bar inserted into something to hold it while it is being machined **2.** a metal bar used as a core around which metal, glass, etc. is cast, molded, or shaped

man·drill (man′dril) *n.* [MAN + DRILL[4]] a large, fierce, strong baboon of W Africa

mane (mān) *n.* [OE. *manu*] the long hair growing from the top or sides of the neck of certain animals, as the horse, lion, etc. —**maned** *adj.* —**mane′less** *adj.*

ma·nège, ma·nege (ma nezh′, -nāzh′) *n.* [Fr. < It. *maneggio:* see MANAGE] **1.** the art of riding and training horses **2.** a school teaching this art **3.** the paces of a trained horse

ma·nes (mā′nēz) *n.pl.* [L.] [*often* **M-**] *Ancient Rom. Religion* the deified souls of the dead, esp. of dead ancestors

Ma·net (må nā′), **É·douard** (ā dwår′) 1832–83; Fr. impressionist painter

ma·neu·ver (mə no͞o′vər, -nyo͞o′-) *n.* [Fr. *manoeuvre* < VL. < L. *manu operare,* to work by hand] **1.** a planned and controlled movement of troops, warships, aircraft, etc. **2.** [*pl.*] large-scale practice movements of troops, warships, aircraft, etc. **3.** any skillful change of movement or direction in driving a vehicle, controlling an aircraft, etc. **4.** a stratagem; scheme —*vi., vt.* **1.** to perform or cause to perform maneuvers **2.** to manage or plan skillfully; scheme **3.** to move, get, put, make, etc. by some stratagem —**ma·neu′ver·a·bil′i·ty** *n.* —**ma·neu′ver·a·ble** *adj.*

man Friday *see* FRIDAY

man·ful (man′fəl) *adj.* manly; brave, resolute, strong, etc. —**man′ful·ly** *adv.* —**man′ful·ness** *n.*

man·ga·nese (maŋ′gə nēs′, -nēz′) *n.* [< Fr. < It., by metathesis < ML. *magnesia:* see MAGNESIA] a grayish-white, metallic chemical element, usually hard and brittle, which rusts like iron but is not magnetic: used in various alloys: symbol, Mn; at. wt., 54.9380; at. no., 25

mange (mānj) *n.* [< OFr. *mangeue,* an itch, ult. < L. *manducare:* see MANGER] a skin disease of mammals caused by parasitic mites and characterized by itching, loss of hair, etc.

man·gel-wur·zel (maŋ′g'l wur′z'l, -wurt′-) *n.* [G., ult. < *mangold,* beet + *wurzel,* a root] a variety of large beet, used as food for cattle, esp. in Europe: also **mangel**

man·ger (mān′jər) *n.* [OFr. *mangeure,* ult. < L. *manducare,* to eat < *mandere,* to chew] a box or trough to hold hay, etc. for horses or cattle to eat

man·gle[1] (maŋ′g'l) *vt.* **-gled, -gling** [Anglo-Fr. *mangler* < OFr. *mehaigner,* to maim] **1.** to mutilate by repeatedly and roughly cutting, hacking, etc. **2.** to spoil; botch; mar —**man′gler** *n.*

man·gle[2] (maŋ′g'l) *n.* [Du. *mangel* < G. < MHG. < L. < Gr. *manganon,* war machine] a machine for pressing and smoothing cloth, esp. sheets and other flat pieces, between heated rollers —*vt.* **-gled, -gling** to press in a mangle —**man′gler** *n.*

man·go (maŋ′gō) *n., pl.* **-goes, -gos** [Port. *manga* < Malay < Tamil *mān-kāy*] **1.** a yellow-red, somewhat acid tropical fruit with a thick rind and juicy pulp **2.** the tree on which it grows

man·grove (maŋ′grōv) *n.* [altered (after GROVE) < Port. *mangue* < Sp. *mangle* < the WInd. name] a tropical tree with branches that spread and send down roots, thus forming more trunks

man·gy (mān′jē) *adj.* **-gi·er, -gi·est 1.** having or caused by the mange **2.** shabby and filthy; squalid **3.** mean and low; despicable —**man′gi·ly** *adv.* —**man′gi·ness** *n.*

man·han·dle (man′han′d'l) *vt.* **-dled, -dling 1.** [Rare] to move or do by human strength only, without mechanical aids **2.** to handle roughly

Man·hat·tan (man hat′'n, mən-) [< Du.] **1.** island in SE N.Y., between the Hudson & East rivers: also **Manhattan Island 2.** borough of New York City, of which this island forms the major part: pop. 1,428,000 —*n.* [*often* **m-**] a cocktail made of whiskey and vermouth, usually with a dash of bitters

man·hole (man′hōl′) *n.* a hole through which a man can get into a sewer, conduit, ship's tank, etc. for repair work or inspection

man·hood (man′hood′) *n.* **1.** the state or time of being a man **2.** manly qualities; virility, courage, resolution, etc. **3.** men collectively

man-hour (-our′) *n.* an industrial time unit equal to one hour of work done by one person

man·hunt (-hunt′) *n.* a hunt for a man, esp. for a fugitive: also **man hunt**

ma·ni·a (mā′nē ə, mān′yə) *n.* [LL. < Gr. *mania* < *mainesthai,* to rage] **1.** wild or violent mental disorder; specif., the manic phase of manic-depressive psychosis, characterized generally by abnormal excitability, excessive activity, etc. **2.** an excessive, steady enthusiasm; obsession; craze

-ma·ni·a (mā′nē ə, mān′yə) [see prec.] *a combining form meaning:* **1.** a (specified) type of mental disorder *[kleptomania]* **2.** a continuing, intense enthusiasm or craving for *[bibliomania]*

ma·ni·ac (mā′nē ak′) *adj.* wildly insane; raving —*n.* a violently insane person; lunatic —**ma·ni·a·cal** (mə nī′ə k'l) *adj.* —**ma·ni′a·cal·ly** *adv.*

man·ic (man′ik; *chiefly Brit.* mā′nik) *adj.* having, characterized by, or like mania

man·ic-de·pres·sive (-di pres′iv) *adj.* designating, of, or having a psychosis characterized by alternating periods of mania and mental depression —*n.* a person who has this psychosis

Man·i·chae·ism, Man·i·che·ism (man′ə kē′iz'm) *n.* [after *Manichaeus,* 3d-cent. Persian prophet] a religious philosophy of the 3d to 7th cent. A.D. emphasizing a universal conflict between good and evil: also **Man′i·chae′an·ism** —**Man′i·chae′an** *n., adj.*

man·i·cot·ti (man′i kät′ē; *It.* mä′nē kôt′tē) *n.* [It., pl., lit., muffs] broad tubes of pasta, stuffed with cheese and baked with a tomato sauce

man·i·cure (man′ə kyoor′) *n.* [Fr. < L. *manus,* a hand + *cura,* care] the care of the hands; esp., a trimming, polishing, etc. of the fingernails —*vt.* **-cured′, -cur′ing 1.** *a)* to trim, polish, etc. (the fingernails) *b)* to give a manicure to **2.** [Colloq.] to trim, clip, etc. meticulously *[to manicure a lawn]* —**man′i·cur′ist** *n.*

man·i·fest (man′ə fest′) *adj.* [< OFr. < L. *manifestus,* lit., struck by the hand, palpable] apparent to the senses, esp. to sight, or to the mind; evident; obvious —*vt.* **1.** to make clear or evident; reveal **2.** to prove; be evidence of —*vi.* to appear to the senses —*n.* **1.** an itemized list of a ship's cargo, to be shown to customs officials **2.** a list of passengers and cargo on an aircraft —**man′i·fest′ly** *adv.*

man·i·fes·ta·tion (man′ə fes tā′shən, -fəs-) *n.* **1.** a manifesting or being manifested **2.** something that manifests *[his smile was a manifestation of joy]* **3.** any of the forms in which a being is thought to manifest itself **4.** a public demonstration

man·i·fes·to (man′ə fes′tō) *n., pl.* **-toes** [It. < *manifestare,* to MANIFEST] a public declaration of motives and intentions by a government or by an important person or group

man·i·fold (man′ə fōld′) *adj.* [OE. *manigfeald:* see MANY & -FOLD] **1.** having many and various forms, parts, etc. **2.** of many sorts *[manifold duties]* **3.** being such in many ways *[a manifold villain]* **4.** made up of or operating several units or parts of one kind —*n.* **1.** something that is manifold **2.** a pipe with one inlet and several outlets or with one outlet and several inlets, for connecting with other pipes, as the cylinder exhaust system in an automobile —*vt.* **1.** to make manifold **2.** to make a number of copies of *[to manifold a letter with carbon paper]* —**man′i·fold′er** *n.* —**man′i·fold′ly** *adv.*

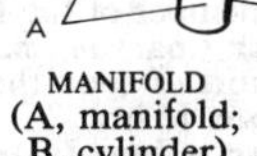

MANIFOLD (A, manifold; B, cylinder)

man·i·kin (man′ə k'n) *n.* [Du. *manneken* < *man,* man + dim. suffix *-ken*] **1.** a little man; dwarf **2.** *same as* MANNEQUIN

Ma·nil·a (mə nil′ə) capital & seaport of the Philippines, in SW Luzon: pop. 1,499,000 (met. area 3,100,000) —*n.* [*often* **m-**] *same as:* **1.** MANILA HEMP **2.** MANILA PAPER Also, for *n.,* **Ma·nil′la**

Manila hemp [*often* **m-**] a strong, tough fiber from the leafstalks of the abacá, used in making rope, paper, etc.

Manila paper [*often* **m-**] strong, buff or brownish paper orig. made of Manila hemp, now of various fibers

man in the street the average person

man·i·oc (man′ē äk′) *n.* [Fr. < Tupi *manioca*] *same as* CASSAVA

man·i·ple (man′ə p'l) *n.* [ult. < L. *manus,* a hand] a silk band worn over the left forearm by priests at Mass

ma·nip·u·late (mə nip′yə lāt′) *vt.* **-lat′ed, -lat′ing** [ult. < Fr. < L. *manipulus,* handful < *manus,* a hand + base of *plere,* to fill] **1.** to work, operate, or treat with or as with the hands, esp. with skill **2.** to manage or control artfully, often in an unfair or fraudulent way **3.** to change or falsify (figures, accounts, etc.) for one's own purposes —**ma·nip′u·la·ble, ma·nip′u·lat′a·ble** *adj.* —**ma·nip′u·la′tion** *n.* —**ma·nip′u·la′tive** *adj.*

ma·nip·u·la·tor (-lāt′ər) *n.* **1.** a person or thing that manipulates **2.** a mechanical device operated by remote control, as for handling radioactive materials

Man·i·to·ba (man′ə tō′bə) **1.** province of SC Canada: 251,000 sq. mi.; pop. 1,022,000; cap. Winnipeg: abbrev. **Man. 2. Lake,** lake in S Manitoba

man·i·tou (man′ə to͞o′) *n.* [< Algonquian name] any of various nature spirits believed in by Algonquian Indians: also **man′i·tu′, man′i·to′** (-tō′)

man·kind (man′kīnd′; *also, & for 2 always,* man′kīnd′) *n.* **1.** all human beings; the human race **2.** all human males

man·like (man′līk′) *adj.* **1.** like or characteristic of a man or men **2.** fit for a man; masculine

man·ly (-lē) *adj.* **-li·er, -li·est 1.** having qualities regarded as befitting a man; strong, brave, resolute, etc. **2.** fit for a man; masculine *[manly sports]* —*adv.* in a manly way —**man′li·ness** *n.*

man-made (-mād′) *adj.* made by man; synthetic

Mann (man; *for 2* män) **1. Horace,** 1796–1859; U.S. educator **2. Thom·as** (*G.* tō′mäs), 1875–1955; Ger. novelist in the U.S. & Switzerland

man·na (man′ə) *n.* [OE. < LL. < Gr. < Aram. *mannā* < Heb. *mān*] **1.** *Bible* food miraculously provided for the Israelites in the wilderness: Ex. 16:14–36 **2.** anything badly needed that comes unexpectedly

man·ne·quin (man′ə kin) *n.* [Fr. < Du.: see MANIKIN] **1.** a model of the human body, used by window dressers, artists, etc. **2.** a woman whose work is modeling clothes in stores, etc.

man·ner (man′ər) *n.* [< OFr., ult. < L. *manuarius,* of the hand < *manus,* a hand] **1.** a way or method in which something is done or happens **2.** a way of acting; personal, esp. customary, behavior or bearing **3.** [*pl.*] *a)* ways of social life *[a comedy of manners]* *b)* ways of social behavior; deportment *[good manners]* *c)* polite ways of social behavior *[the child lacks manners]* **4.** characteristic style or method in art, etc. **5.** *a)* kind; sort *[what manner of man is he?]* *b)* [*with pl. v.*] kinds; sorts *[all manner of things]* —**by all manner of means** of course; surely —**by any manner of means** in any way; at all —**by no manner of means** in no way; definitely not —**in a manner of speaking** in a certain sense or way —**to the manner born** accustomed from birth to the way or usage spoken of —**man′ner·less** *n.*

man·nered (-ərd) *adj.* **1.** having manners or a manner of a specified sort *[ill-mannered,* soberly *mannered]* **2.** artificial, stylized, or affected

man·ner·ism (man′ər iz'm) *n.* **1.** excessive use of some distinctive manner in art, literature, speech, or behavior **2.** a peculiarity of manner in behavior, speech, etc. that has become a habit —**man′ner·ist** *n.* —**man′ner·is′tic** *adj.*

man·ner·ly (-lē) *adj.* showing good manners; polite —*adv.* politely —**man′ner·li·ness** *n.*

Mann·heim (man′hīm; *G.* män′-) city in SW West Germany, on the Rhine: pop. 324,000

man·ni·kin (man′ə kin) *n. alt. sp. of* MANIKIN

man·nish (man′ish) *adj.* of, like, or fit for a man *[she walks with a mannish stride]* —**man′nish·ly** *adv.* —**man′nish·ness** *n.*

ma·noeu·vre (mə no͞o′vər, -nyo͞o′-) *n., vi., vt.* **-vred, -vring** *chiefly Brit. sp. of* MANEUVER

man of God 1. a holy man; saint, hermit, etc. **2.** a clergyman; minister, priest, rabbi, etc.

man of letters a writer, scholar, etc., esp. one whose work is in the field of literature

man of the world a man familiar with and tolerant of various sorts of people and their ways
man-of-war (man′əv wôr′, -ə wôr′) *n., pl.* **men′-of-war′** an armed naval vessel; warship
man-of-war bird *same as* FRIGATE BIRD
ma·nom·e·ter (mə näm′ə tər) *n.* [< Fr. < Gr. *manos,* rare (in sense "thin, sparse") + Fr. *-mètre,* -METER] an instrument for measuring the pressure of gases or liquids —**man·o·met·ric** (man′ə met′rik), **man′o·met′ri·cal** *adj.*
man·or (man′ər) *n.* [< OFr. < *manoir,* to dwell < L. *manere,* to remain] **1.** in England, a landed estate, orig. of a feudal lord and subject to the jurisdiction of his court **2.** in colonial America, a district granted as a manor and leased to tenants **3.** a mansion, as on an estate —**ma·no·ri·al** (mə nôr′ē əl) *adj.*
manor house the house of the lord of a manor
man·pow·er (man′pou′ər) *n.* **1.** power furnished by human physical strength **2.** the collective strength or availability for work of the people in a given area, nation, etc. Also **man power**
‡**man·qué** (mäŋ kā′) *adj.* [Fr. < It. < L. *mancus,* defective] **1.** that falls short of the goal; unsuccessful **2.** potential but unrealized; would-be Placed after the noun it modifies [a scholar *manqué*]
man·sard (roof) (man′särd) [after F. *Mansard,* 17th-c. Fr. architect] a roof with two slopes on each of the four sides, the lower steeper than the upper

MANSARD ROOF

manse (mans) *n.* [< ML. < pp. of L. *manere,* to dwell] **1.** a parsonage **2.** [Archaic] a mansion
man·ser·vant (man′sur′vənt) *n., pl.* **men·ser·vants** (men′sur′vənts) a male servant: also **man servant**
Mans·field (manz′fēld′, mans′-) [after J. *Mansfield* (1759–1830), surveyor] city in NC Ohio: pop. 54,000
man·sion (man′shən) *n.* [OFr. < L. *mansio,* a dwelling < pp. of *manere,* to dwell] a large, imposing house
man-sized (man′sīzd′) *adj.* [Colloq.] of a size fit for a man; large; big: also **man′-size′**
man·slaugh·ter (-slôt′ər) *n.* the killing of a human being by another, esp. when unlawful but without malice
man·ta (ray) (man′tə) [Sp. < LL. *mantum,* a cloak] *same as* DEVILFISH (sense 1)
man·tel (man′t'l) *n.* [see MANTLE] **1.** the facing of stone, marble, etc. about a fireplace, including a shelf or slab above it **2.** the shelf or slab
man·tel·et (man′t'l it, mant′lit) *n.* [OFr., dim. of prec.] **1.** a short mantle or cape **2.** a protective shelter or screen: also **mant′let**
man·tel·piece (man′t'l pēs′) *n.* a mantel shelf, or this shelf and the side elements framing the fireplace in front
man·til·la (man til′ə, -tē′ə) *n.* [Sp. < LL. < L. *mantellum,* a mantle] a woman's scarf, as of lace, worn over the hair and shoulders, as in Spain or Mexico
man·tis (man′tis) *n., pl.* **-tis·es, -tes** (-tēz) [ModL. < Gr. *mantis,* prophet, seer] a long, slender insect that feeds on other insects and grasps its prey with stout, spiny forelegs often held up together as if praying
man·tis·sa (man tis′ə) *n.* [L., (useless) addition] the decimal part of a logarithm
man·tle (man′t'l) *n.* [< OE. & OFr. < L. *mantellum*] **1.** a loose, sleeveless cloak or cape **2.** anything that cloaks or envelops **3.** a small, mesh hood which becomes white-hot over a flame and gives off light **4.** *same as* MANTEL **5.** *Geol. a)* the layer of the earth's interior between the crust and the core *b) same as* MANTLEROCK **6.** *Zool.* the glandular flap or folds of the body wall of a mollusk, etc., typically secreting a shell-forming fluid —*vt.* **-tled, -tling** to cover with or as with a mantle; cloak —*vi.* **1.** to be or become covered, as a surface with froth **2.** to blush or flush
man·tle·rock (-räk′) *n.* the loose, unconsolidated material on the solid rock of the earth's crust
man·tra (mun′trə, man′-) *n.* [Sans., akin to *mantar,* thinker] *Hinduism* a hymn or text, esp. from the Veda, chanted as an incantation or prayer
man·u·al (man′yoo wəl) *adj.* [< OFr. < L. < *manus,* a hand] **1.** of a hand or the hands **2.** made, done, worked, or used by the hands **3.** involving or doing hard physical work requiring use of the hands —*n.* **1.** a handy book of instructions, etc. for use as a guide **2.** a keyboard of an organ console or harpsichord **3.** prescribed drill in the handling of a rifle: also **manual of arms** —**man′u·al·ly** *adv.*
manual training training in practical arts and crafts, as metalworking, etc.
man·u·fac·ture (man′yə fak′chər) *n.* [Fr. < ML. < L. < *manus,* a hand + *factura,* a making < *facere,* to make] **1.** the making of goods by hand or, esp., by machinery, often on a large scale and with division of labor **2.** anything so made **3.** the making of something in a way regarded as mechanical —*vt.* **-tured, -tur·ing** **1.** to make by hand or, esp., by machinery, often on a large scale, etc. **2.** to work (wool, steel, etc.) into usable form **3.** to produce (something) in a way regarded as mechanical **4.** to make up (excuses, evidence, etc.)
man·u·fac·tur·er (-chər ər) *n.* a person or company in the business of manufacturing; esp., a factory owner
man·u·mis·sion (man′yə mish′ən) *n.* [see ff.] a freeing or being freed from slavery; emancipation
man·u·mit (-mit′) *vt.* **-mit′ted, -mit′ting** [< OFr. < L. < *manus,* a hand + *mittere,* to send] to free from slavery —**man′u·mit′ter** *n.*
ma·nure (mə noor′, -nyoor′) *vt.* **-nured′, -nur′ing** [< Anglo-Fr. < OFr. *manouvrer,* to work with the hands, cultivate] to put manure on or into (soil) —*n.* animal excrement or other substance used to fertilize soil
man·u·script (man′yə skript′) *adj.* [< L. < *manus,* a hand + pp. of *scribere,* to write] **1.** written by hand or with a typewriter **2.** designating writing that consists of unconnected letters resembling print; not cursive —*n.* **1.** a written or typewritten book, article, etc.; esp., an author's copy of his work, as submitted to a publisher or printer **2.** writing as distinguished from print
Manx (maŋks) *adj.* of the Isle of Man, its people, etc. —*n.* their Goidelic language, now nearly extinct —**the Manx** the people of the Isle of Man
Manx cat [*also* **m-**] any of a breed of domestic cat that has no tail
Manx·man (-mən) *n., pl.* **-men** a native or inhabitant of the Isle of Man —**Manx′wom′an** *n.fem., pl.* **-wom′en**
man·y (men′ē) *adj.* **more, most** [OE. *manig*] **1.** consisting of some large, indefinite number; numerous **2.** relatively numerous (preceded by *as, too,* etc.) —*n.* a large number (of persons or things) —*pron.* many persons or things **Many a** (or **an, another**) with a singular noun or pronoun is equivalent to *many* with the plural (e.g., *many a* man) —**a good many** [*with pl. v.*] a relatively large number —**a great many** [*with pl. v.*] an extremely large number —**the many** **1.** the majority of people **2.** the people; the masses
man·y-sid·ed (-sīd′id) *adj.* **1.** having many sides or aspects **2.** having many possibilities, qualities, interests, or accomplishments —**man′y-sid′ed·ness** *n.*
man·za·ni·ta (man′zə nēt′ə) *n.* [AmSp. < Sp., dim. of *manzana,* apple] any of several shrubs or small trees of the heath family, found in the W U.S.
Mao·ism (mou′iz'm) *n.* the communist theories and policies of Mao Tse-tung —**Mao′ist** *adj., n.*
Ma·o·ri (mou′rē, mä′ô rē; mä ôr′ē) *n.* **1.** *pl.* **-ris, -ri** any of a brown-skinned people native to New Zealand, of Polynesian origin **2.** their Polynesian language —*adj.* of the Maoris, their language, etc.
mao-tai (mou′tī′) *n.* [after *Mao-t'ai,* town in SW China] a strong, colorless, Chinese distilled liquor made from grain: also written **mao tai**
Mao Tse-tung (mou′ dzu′dooŋ′) 1893–1976; Chin. statesman; chairman of the People's Republic of China (1949–59) & of the Chin. Communist Party (1949–76)
map (map) *n.* [< ML. *mappa (mundi),* map (of the world) < L. *mappa,* napkin] **1.** a representation, usually flat, of all or part of the earth's surface, ordinarily showing countries, bodies of water, cities, etc. **2.** a similar representation of the sky, showing stars, planets, etc. **3.** any maplike representation **4.** [Slang] the face —*vt.* **mapped, map′ping** **1.** to make a map of; represent on a map **2.** to plan in detail [to *map* out a project] **3.** to survey for making a map —**put on the map** to make well known —**wipe off the map** to put out of existence —**map′per** *n.*
ma·ple (mā′p'l) *n.* [OE. *mapel(treo)*] **1.** any of a large group of trees with opposite leaves and two-winged fruits, grown for wood, sap, or shade **2.** the hard, fine-grained, light-colored wood **3.** the flavor of maple syrup or of maple sugar —*adj.* **1.** of maple **2.** flavored with maple
maple sugar sugar from boiled-down maple syrup
maple syrup syrup made by boiling down the sap of the sugar maple
Ma·pu·to (mə poot′ō) capital of Mozambique; seaport on the Indian Ocean: pop. 799,000
ma·quis (mä kē′; *Fr.* må kē′) *n.* [Fr. < It. *macchia,* a thicket] **1.** a zone of shrubby, evergreen plants in the Mediterranean area, used as a hiding place by guerrilla fighters, etc. **2.** [*often* **M-**] *pl.* **-quis′** (-kēz′; *Fr.* -kē′) a member of the French underground in World War II
mar (mär) *vt.* **marred, mar′ring** [OE. *mierran,* to hinder] to hurt or spoil the looks, value, perfection, etc. of; impair
Mar. March
mar·a·bou (mar′ə boo′) *n.* [Fr. < Port. < Ar. *murābit,* hermit] **1.** any of certain large storks; esp., *a)* a dark-green African species *b)* the Indian adjutant **2.** soft feathers from the wings and tail of the marabou
ma·ra·ca (mə rä′kə) *n.* [Port. *maracá* < the Braz. native name] a percussion instrument consisting of a dried gourd or a gourd-shaped rattle with loose pebbles in it, shaken to beat out a rhythm

Mar·a·cai·bo (mar′ə kī′bō; *Sp.* mä′rä kī′bô) seaport in NW Venezuela: pop. 625,000

mar·a·schi·no (mar′ə skē′nō, -shē′-) ***n.*** [It. < *marasca,* kind of cherry < *amaro,* bitter] a strong, sweet liqueur made from the fermented juice of a black wild cherry

maraschino cherries cherries in a syrup flavored with maraschino

Ma·rat (mȧ rȧ′), **Jean Paul** (zhän pôl) 1743–93; Fr. Revolutionary leader, born in Switzerland

Mar·a·thon (mar′ə thän′) ancient Greek village in E Attica, or a plain nearby, where the Athenians defeated the Persians (490 B.C.)

mar·a·thon (mar′ə thän′) ***n.*** **1.** a footrace of 26 miles, 385 yards: so called in allusion to the Greek runner who carried word of the victory at Marathon to Athens **2.** any long-distance or endurance contest

mar·a·thon·er (mar′ə thän′ər) ***n.*** a person who competes in a marathon

ma·raud (mə rôd′) ***vi.*** [< Fr. < *maraud,* vagabond, prob. < dial. *maraud,* tomcat, echoic of cry] to rove in search of plunder; make raids —***vt.*** to raid; plunder —**ma·raud′er** ***n.***

mar·ble (mär′b′l) ***n.*** [< OFr. < L. < Gr. *marmaros,* white glistening stone] **1.** a hard, metamorphic limestone, white or colored and sometimes streaked or mottled, which can take a high polish **2.** *a*) a piece or slab of this stone, used as a monument, etc. *b*) a sculpture in marble **3.** anything like marble in hardness, coldness, etc. **4.** *a*) a little ball of stone, glass, or clay, used in games *b*) [*pl., with sing. v.*] a children's game in which a marble is propelled with the thumb at other marbles in a marked circle **5.** [*pl.*] [Slang] brains; good sense [*to lose one's marbles*] —***adj.*** of or like marble —***vt.*** **-bled, -bling** **1.** to stain (book edges) to look mottled or streaked like marble **2.** to cause fat to be evenly distributed in narrow streaks through (meat) —**mar′bled, mar′bly** ***adj.***

mar·ble·ize (-īz′) ***vt.*** **-ized′, -iz′ing** to make, color, grain, or streak in imitation of marble

Marc Antony *see* ANTONY

mar·ca·site (mär′kə sīt′) ***n.*** [< Fr. < ML. < Ar. *marqashīṭā*] **1.** a pale, crystallized pyrite (**white iron pyrite**) **2.** this mineral or polished steel cut and used like brilliants

mar·cel (mär sel′) ***n.*** [after *Marcel* Grateau, early 20th-c. Fr. hairdresser] a series of even waves put in the hair with a curling iron: also **marcel wave** —***vt.*** **-celled′, -cel′ling** to put such waves in (hair)

March (märch) ***n.*** [< OFr. < L. *Martius* (*mensis*), (month) of Mars] the third month of the year, having 31 days: abbrev. **Mar.**

march[1] (märch) ***vi.*** [Fr. *marcher* < OFr., prob. < Frank.] **1.** to walk with regular, steady steps, as in a military formation **2.** to walk in a grave, stately way **3.** to advance or progress steadily —***vt.*** to make march or go —***n.*** **1.** a marching **2.** a steady advance; progress **3.** a regular, steady step or pace **4.** the distance covered in marching [*a day's march*] **5.** a long, tiring walk **6.** a piece of music for marching **7.** an organized walk by people demonstrating on a public issue [*a peace march*] —**on the march** marching —**steal a march on** to get an advantage over secretly —**march′er** ***n.***

march[2] (märch) ***n.*** [OFr. *marche* < Frank. hyp. *marka,* boundary] a boundary, border, or frontier

March hare a hare in breeding time, proverbially regarded as an example of madness

marching orders orders to march, go, or leave

mar·chion·ess (mär′shə nis, mär′shə nes′) ***n.*** [< ML. fem. of *marchio,* prefect of the marches, or borderlands] **1.** the wife or widow of a marquess **2.** a lady whose own rank equals that of a marquess

march·pane (märch′pān′) ***n.*** *same as* MARZIPAN

Mar·cia (mär′shə) [< L., ult. < *Mars,* MARS] a feminine name

Mar·co·ni (mär kō′nē; *It.* mär kô′nē), Marchese **Gu·gliel·mo** (gōō lyel′mô) 1874–1937; It. physicist: developed wireless telegraphy

Marco Polo *see* POLO

Mar·cus Aurelius (mär′kəs) *see* AURELIUS

Mar·di gras (mär′di grä′) [Fr., lit., fat Tuesday] Shrove Tuesday, the last day before Lent: a day of carnival, as in New Orleans

mare[1] (mer) ***n.*** [OE. *mere,* fem. of *mearh,* horse] a fully mature female horse, mule, donkey, etc.

ma·re[2] (mer′ē, mär′ē) ***n., pl.*** **-ri·a** (-ē ə) [L., sea] **1.** a sea **2.** a large, dark area on the surface of the moon or of Mars

mare's-nest (merz′nest′) ***n.*** **1.** a hoax; delusion **2.** a disorderly or confused condition; mess

mare's-tail (-tāl′) ***n.*** long, narrow formations of cirrus cloud, shaped somewhat like a horse's tail

Mar·ga·ret (mär′grit, -gər it) [< OFr. < L. *margarita,* a pearl] a feminine name: dim. *Marge;* var. *Margery, Margot, Marguerite*

mar·ga·rine (mär′jə rin) ***n.*** [Fr.] a spread or cooking fat made of refined vegetable oils processed to the consistency of butter, often churned with pasteurized skim milk, and generally fortified with vitamins A and D: also **mar′ga·rin**

marge (märj) ***n.*** [Fr. < L. *margo,* margin] [Archaic or Poet.] a border; edge; margin

mar·gin (mär′jən) ***n.*** [L. *margo* (gen. *marginis*)] **1.** a border, edge, or brink **2.** the blank border of a printed or written page **3.** a limit to what is desirable or possible **4.** *a*) an amount of money, supplies, etc. beyond what is needed *b*) provision for increase, addition, or advance **5.** the amount by which something is higher or lower **6.** *Business, Finance a*) the difference between the cost and selling price of goods *b*) money or collateral deposited with a broker, etc. either to meet legal requirements or to insure him against loss on contracts which he undertakes for a buyer or seller of stocks, etc. **7.** *Econ.* the minimum return of profit needed to continue activities —***vt.*** **1.** to provide with a margin **2.** *Business* to deposit a margin upon

mar·gin·al (-'l) ***adj.*** **1.** written or printed in the margin **2.** of a margin **3.** at, on, or close to the margin —**mar′gin·al′i·ty** (-al′ə tē) ***n.*** —**mar′gin·al·ly** ***adv.***

mar·gin·ate (mär′jə nāt′; *also for adj.* -nit) ***vt.*** **-at′ed, -at′ing** to provide with a margin —***adj.*** having a distinct margin: also **mar′gin·at′ed** —**mar′gin·a′tion** ***n.***

mar·grave (mär′grāv) ***n.*** [< MDu. < MHG. < OHG. < *marc,* a border + *graf,* a count] **1.** orig., a military governor of a border province in Germany **2.** the title of certain princes of Germany

mar·gra·vine (mär′grə vēn′) ***n.*** a margrave's wife

mar·gue·rite (mär′gə rēt′) ***n.*** [Fr., a pearl] **1.** *same as* DAISY (sense 1) **2.** a cultivated chrysanthemum with a single flower **3.** any of various daisylike plants of the composite family

Ma·ri·a (mə rī′ə, -rē′-) [see MARY] a feminine name

ma·ri·a (mer′ē ə, mär′-) ***n.*** *pl. of* MARE[2]

ma·ri·a·chi (mär′ē ä′chē) ***n.,*** *pl.* **-chis** [MexSp. < ?] **1.** one of a strolling band of musicians in Mexico **2.** such a band **3.** their music

Mar·i·an (mer′ē ən, mar′-) [var. of MARION] a feminine name: var. *Marianne* —***adj.*** of the Virgin Mary

Ma·ri·an·a Islands (mer′ē an′ə, mar′-) group of islands in the W Pacific: (except Guam); a commonwealth of the U.S. called **Northern Marianas**: pop. 15,000

Maria Theresa 1717–80; queen of Bohemia & Hungary & archduchess of Austria (1740–80): mother of MARIE ANTOINETTE

mar·i·cul·ture (mar′ə kul′chər) ***n.*** [< L. *mare,* sea + CULTURE] saltwater aquaculture

Ma·rie (mə rē′) [var. of MARY] a feminine name

Marie An·toi·nette (an′twə net′, -tə-), (**Josèphe Jeanne**) 1755–93; wife of Louis XVI; queen of France (1774–92): guillotined

Marie Louise 1791–1847; 2d wife of Napoleon I & empress of France (1810–15)

mar·i·gold (mar′ə gōld′) ***n.*** [< *Marie* (prob. the Virgin Mary) + *gold,* GOLD] **1.** a plant of the composite family, with red, yellow, or orange flowers **2.** its flower **3.** any of several unrelated plants

ma·ri·jua·na, ma·ri·hua·na (mar′ə wä′nə, mär′-; -hwä′-) ***n.*** [AmSp. < ? native word] **1.** *same as* HEMP (sense 1 *a*) **2.** its dried leaves and flowers, smoked for the psychological effects

Mar·i·lyn (mar′ə lin) [var. of MARY] a feminine name

ma·rim·ba (mə rim′bə) ***n.*** [< Afr. (Bantu), a kind of percussive instrument] a kind of xylophone, usually with resonators under the wooden bars

ma·ri·na (mə rē′nə) ***n.*** [It. & Sp., seacoast < L. *marinus:* see MARINE] a small harbor with dockage, supplies, and services for small pleasure craft

mar·i·nade (mar′ə nād′) ***n.*** [Fr. < Sp. < *marinar,* to pickle, ult. < L. *marinus:* see MARINE] **1.** a spiced pickling solution, esp. with oil and wine or vinegar, in which meat, fish, or salad is steeped **2.** meat, etc. so steeped —***vt.*** **-nad′ed, -nad′ing** *same as* MARINATE

mar·i·nate (mar′ə nāt′) ***vt.*** **-nat′ed, -nat′ing** [< It. < *marinare,* to pickle: see prec.] to steep (meat, etc.) in a marinade —**mar′i·na′tion** ***n.***

ma·rine (mə rēn′) ***adj.*** [< L. *marinus* < *mare,* the sea] **1.** of, found in, or formed by the sea or ocean **2.** *a*) of navigation on, or shipping by, the sea; nautical; maritime *b*) naval **3.** used, or to be used, at sea **4.** *a*) trained for service at sea, etc., as certain troops *b*) of such troops —***n.*** **1.** one of a marine military force; specif. [*often* **M-**], a member of the MARINE CORPS **2.** naval or merchant ships collectively; fleet [*the merchant marine*] **3.** in some countries, the governmental department of naval affairs **4.** a picture of a ship or sea scene

Marine Corps a branch of the U.S. armed forces trained for land, sea, and aerial combat

mar·i·ner (mar′ə nər) ***n.*** [< Anglo-Fr. < ML. < L. *marinus*, MARINE] a sailor; seaman

Mar·i·on (mar′ē ən, mer′-) [Fr., orig. dim. of *Marie*, MARY] a masculine or feminine name

mar·i·o·nette (mar′ē ə net′) ***n.*** [Fr., dim. of MARION] a puppet or little jointed doll moved by strings or wires from above, often on a little stage

Mar·i·po·sa lily (or **tulip**) (mar′ə pō′zə, -sə) [AmSp. < Sp. *mariposa*, butterfly] **1.** a plant of the lily family, of W N. America, with tuliplike flowers **2.** its flower

Ma·ri·tain (mȧ rē tan′), **Jacques** (zhȧk) 1882–1973; Fr. philosopher

mar·i·tal (mar′ə t'l) ***adj.*** [< L. < *maritus*, a husband] of marriage —**mar′i·tal·ly** ***adv.***

mar·i·time (mar′ə tīm′) ***adj.*** [L. *maritimus* < *mare*, the sea] **1.** on, near, or living near the sea **2.** of sea navigation, shipping, etc. **3.** nautical

Maritime Provinces Canad. provinces of Nova Scotia, New Brunswick, & Prince Edward Island

mar·jo·ram (mär′jər əm) ***n.*** [< OFr. < ML., prob. < L. *amaracus* < Gr. *amarakos*] any of various perennial plants of the mint family; esp., **sweet marjoram,** having aromatic leaves used in cooking

Mar·jo·rie, Mar·jo·ry (mär′jər ē) [var. of MARGARET] a feminine name

Mark (märk) **1.** [< L. *Marcus* < *Mars*, MARS] a masculine name **2.** *Bible* *a*) one of the four Evangelists, the reputed author of the second Gospel *b*) this book, the second in the New Testament

mark[1] (märk) ***n.*** [OE. *mearc*, orig., boundary] **1.** a line, spot, stain, scratch, mar, etc. on a surface **2.** a sign, symbol, or indication; specif., *a*) a printed or written sign or stroke [punctuation *marks*] *b*) a brand, label, etc. put on an article to show the owner, maker, etc. *c*) a sign of some quality, character, etc. [courtesy is the *mark* of a gentleman] *d*) a grade; rating [a *mark* of B in history] *e*) a cross, etc. made by a person unable to write his signature **3.** a standard of quality, etc. [up to the *mark*] **4.** importance; distinction [a man of *mark*] **5.** impression; influence [left his *mark* in history] **6.** a visible object of known position, serving as a guide **7.** a line, dot, etc. used to indicate position, as on a graduated scale **8.** an object aimed at; target; end; goal **9.** the butt of an attack, criticism, etc. **10.** a taking notice; heed **11.** *Sports* *a*) the starting line of a race *b*) a spare or strike in bowling —***vt.*** **1.** to put or make a mark or marks on **2.** to identify as by a mark **3.** to draw, write, record, etc. **4.** to show by a mark **5.** to show plainly; manifest [a smile *marking* joy] **6.** to distinguish; characterize **7.** to take notice of; heed **8.** to grade; rate **9.** to put price tags on **10.** to keep (score, etc.); record —***vi.*** **1.** to make a mark or marks **2.** to observe; take note **3.** *Games* to keep score —**hit the mark** **1.** to achieve one's aim **2.** to be right —**make one's mark** to achieve fame —**mark down** **1.** to write down; record **2.** to mark for sale at a reduced price —**mark off** (or **out**) to mark the limits of —**mark time** **1.** to keep time while at a halt by lifting the feet as if marching **2.** to suspend progress for a time —**mark up** **1.** to cover with marks **2.** to mark for sale at an increased price —**miss the mark** **1.** to fail in achieving one's aim **2.** to be inaccurate —**wide of** (or **beside**) **the mark** **1.** not striking the point aimed at **2.** irrelevant —**mark′er** ***n.***

mark[2] (märk) ***n.*** [< OE. < ON. *mǫrk*, a half pound of silver] a monetary unit of the old German Empire, superseded by the reichsmark, and of East Germany: see MONETARY UNITS, table

Mark Antony *see* ANTONY

mark·down (märk′doun′) ***n.*** **1.** a marking for sale at a reduced price **2.** the amount of reduction

marked (märkt) ***adj.*** **1.** having a mark or marks **2.** singled out as an object of hostility, etc. [a *marked* man] **3.** noticeable; distinct [a *marked* change] —**mark′ed·ly** (mär′kid lē) ***adv.*** —**mark′ed·ness** ***n.***

mar·ket (mär′kit) ***n.*** [< ONormFr. < L. *mercatus*, trade < pp. of *mercari*, to trade < *merx*, merchandise] **1.** *a*) a gathering of people for buying and selling things *b*) the people gathered **2.** an open space or a building with goods for sale from stalls, etc.: also **mar′ket·place′** **3.** a store selling provisions [a meat *market*] **4.** a region where goods can be bought and sold [the European *market*] **5.** *a*) trade in goods, stocks, etc. [an active *market*] *b*) trade in a specified commodity [the wheat *market*] *c*) the people associated in such trade **6.** *short for* STOCK MARKET **7.** demand (for goods or services) [a good *market* for new products] **8.** supply (of goods or services) [reduced labor *market*] —***vt.*** **1.** to send or take to market **2.** to offer for sale **3.** to sell —***vi.*** **1.** to buy or sell **2.** to buy provisions —**be in the market for** to be seeking to buy —**be on the market** to be offered for sale —**buyer's market** a state of trade favorable to the buyer (relatively heavy supply and low prices) —**put on the market** to offer for sale —**seller's market** a state of trade favorable to the seller (relatively heavy demand and high prices) —**mar′ket·a·bil′i·ty** ***n.*** —**mar′ket·a·ble** ***adj.*** —**mar′ket·er, mar′ket·eer′** (-kə tir′) ***n.*** —**mar′ket·ing** ***n.***

market price the prevailing price of a commodity

market value the price that a commodity can be expected to bring in a given market

mark·ing (mär′kiŋ) ***n.*** **1.** the act of making a mark or marks **2.** a mark or marks **3.** the characteristic arrangement of marks, as on fur or feathers

mark·ka (märk′kä) ***n.***, *pl.* **-kaa** (-kä) [Finn. < Sw. *mark*: see MARK[2]] see MONETARY UNITS, table (Finland)

marks·man (märks′mən) ***n.***, *pl.* **-men** a person who shoots, esp. with skill —**marks′man·ship′** ***n.***

mark·up (märk′up′) ***n.*** **1.** a marking for sale at an increased price **2.** the amount of increase

marl (märl) ***n.*** [< OFr. < ML. dim. of L. *marga*, marl < Gaul.] a crumbly mixture of clay, sand, and limestone, usually with shell fragments —***vt.*** to cover or fertilize with marl —**marl′y** ***adj.***

Marl·bor·ough (märl′bʉr′ō, -ə; *Brit.* môl′bər ə), 1st Duke of, (*John Churchill*) 1650–1722; Eng. general & statesman

mar·lin (mär′lin) ***n.***, *pl.* **-lin, -lins:** see PLURAL, II, D, 2 [< MARLINSPIKE] any of several large, slender deep-sea fishes related to the sailfish, esp. the **blue marlin** of the Atlantic

mar·line (mär′lin) ***n.*** [Du. *marlijn*, altered (after *lijn*, LINE[1])] a small cord of two loose strands for winding around the ends of ropes to prevent fraying: also **mar′lin, mar′ling** (-liŋ)

mar·line·spike, mar·lin·spike (-spīk′) ***n.*** a pointed iron instrument for separating rope strands, as in splicing: also **mar′ling·spike′** (-liŋ-)

Mar·lowe (mär′lō), **Christopher** 1564–93; Eng. dramatist & poet

mar·ma·lade (mär′mə lād′) ***n.*** [< OFr. < Port. < *marmelo*, quince < L. *melimelum* < Gr. < *meli*, honey + *mēlon*, apple] a jamlike preserve made of oranges or some other fruits and sugar

Mar·ma·ra (mär′mə rə), **Sea of** sea between European & Asiatic Turkey, connected with the Black Sea by the Bosporus & with the Aegean Sea by the Dardanelles: also sp. **Marmora**

mar·mo·re·al (mär môr′ē əl) ***adj.*** [< L. < *marmor*, marble + -AL] of or like marble: also **mar·mo′re·an** —**mar·mo′re·al·ly** ***adv.***

mar·mo·set (mär′mə zet′, -set′) ***n.*** [< OFr. *marmouset*, grotesque figure] a very small monkey of South and Central America, with thick, soft fur

MARMOSET (body to 15 in. long; tail to 17 in. long)

mar·mot (mär′mət) ***n.*** [< Fr. < earlier *marmottaine*, prob. < L. *mus montanus*, mountain mouse] any of a group of thick-bodied, gnawing and burrowing rodents with coarse fur and a short, bushy tail, as the woodchuck

Marne (märn) river in NE France, flowing northwest into the Seine at Paris

ma·roon[1] (mə ro͞on′) ***n.***, ***adj.*** [Fr. *marron*, chestnut < It. *marrone*] dark brownish red

ma·roon[2] (mə ro͞on′) ***n.*** [< Fr. < AmSp. *cimarrón*, wild < OSp. *cimarra*, thicket] in the West Indies and Surinam, **1.** orig., a fugitive Negro slave **2.** a descendant of such slaves —***vt.*** **1.** to put (a person) ashore in some desolate place and abandon him there **2.** to leave abandoned, helpless, etc.

mar·plot (mär′plät′) ***n.*** a person or, sometimes, a thing spoiling a plan by officious interference

Marq. **1.** Marquess **2.** Marquis

marque[1] (märk) ***n.*** [MFr. < Pr. *marca*] reprisal: obsolete except in LETTERS OF MARQUE

marque[2] (märk) ***n.*** [Fr., ult. < OIt. *marca*, a mark] an identifying nameplate or emblem on an automobile

mar·quee (mär kē′) ***n.*** [< Fr. *marquise* (misunderstood as pl.), orig. a canopy over an officer's tent] **1.** [Chiefly Brit.] a large tent, as for an outdoor entertainment **2.** a rooflike projection or awning over an entrance, as to a theater

mar·quess (mär′kwis) ***n.*** **1.** a British nobleman ranking above an earl and below a duke **2.** *same as* MARQUIS —**mar′quess·ate** (-kwə zit) ***n.***

mar·que·try, mar·que·terie (mär′kə trē) ***n.*** [< Fr. < *marque*, a mark] decorative inlaid work of wood, ivory, etc., as in furniture or flooring

Mar·quette (mär ket′), **Jacques** (zhȧk) 1637–75; Fr. Jesuit missionary & explorer, in N. America: called *Père Marquette*

mar·quis (mär′kwis; *Fr.* mȧr kē′) ***n.***, *pl.* **-quis·es;** *Fr.* **-quis′** (-kē′) [< OFr. < ML. *marchisus*, prefect of a frontier town < *marca*, borderland] in some European countries, a nobleman ranking above an earl or count and below a duke: cf. MARQUESS —**mar′quis·ate** (-kwə zit) ***n.***

mar·quise (mär kēz′; *Fr.* mȧr kēz′) ***n.*** **1.** the wife or widow of a marquis **2.** a lady whose rank in her own right equals that of a marquis **3.** a gem cut as a pointed oval

mar·qui·sette (mär′ki zet′, -kwi-) ***n.*** [dim. of Fr. *marquise*, awning: see MARQUEE] a thin, meshlike fabric used for curtains, dresses, etc.

Mar·ra·kech, Mar·ra·kesh (mə rä′kesh, mar′ə kesh′) city in C Morocco; traditional S capital: pop. 295,000

mar·riage (mar′ij) ***n.*** [OFr. < *marier:* see MARRY] **1.** the state of being married; relation between husband and wife; wedlock **2.** the act or rite of marrying; wedding **3.** any close union

mar·riage·a·ble (mar′i jə b'l) ***adj.*** old enough to get married —**mar′riage·a·bil′i·ty** ***n.***

marriage portion *same as* DOWRY

mar·ried (mar′ēd) ***adj.*** **1.** living together as husband and wife **2.** having a husband or wife **3.** of marriage or married people **4.** closely joined —***n.*** a married person: chiefly in **young marrieds**

mar·row (mar′ō) ***n.*** [OE. *mearg*] **1.** the soft, vascular, fatty tissue that fills the cavities of most bones **2.** the innermost, essential, or choicest part; pith —**mar′row·y** ***adj.***

mar·row·bone (-bōn′) ***n.*** a bone having marrow

mar·row·fat (-fat′) ***n.*** a variety of large, rich pea: also **marrowfat pea, marrow pea**

mar·ry[1] (mar′ē) ***vt.*** **-ried, -ry·ing** [< OFr. *marier* < L. < *maritus*, a husband] **1.** *a)* to join as husband and wife *b)* to join (a man) to a woman as her husband, or (a woman) to a man as his wife **2.** to take as husband or wife **3.** to join closely —***vi.*** **1.** to get married **2.** to enter into a close relationship —**marry off** to give in marriage: said of a parent or guardian —**mar′ri·er** ***n.***

mar·ry[2] (mar′ē) ***interj.*** [euphemistic respelling of (the Virgin) *Mary*] [Archaic or Dial.] an exclamation of surprise, anger, etc.

Mars (märz) **1.** *Rom. Myth.* the god of war: identified with the Greek god Ares **2.** *a personification of* war **3.** a planet of the solar system, fourth in distance from the sun: diameter, c.4,200 miles

Mar·sa·la (mär sä′lä) ***n.*** [< *Marsala*, seaport in W Sicily] a light, sweet white wine

Mar·seil·laise (mär′sə lāz′; *Fr.* mȧr se yez′) [Fr., lit., of Marseille] the French national anthem, composed (1792) during the French Revolution

Mar·seille (mȧr se′y′; *E.* mär sā′) seaport in SE France, on the Mediterranean: pop. 889,000

Mar·seilles (mär sā′; *chiefly Brit.* -sālz′; *for n.* -sālz′) *Eng. sp. of* MARSEILLE —***n.*** a thick, strong cotton cloth with a raised weave

marsh (märsh) ***n.*** [OE. *merisc*] a tract of low, wet, soft land; swamp; bog; morass

Mar·shal (mär′shəl) [< ff.] a masculine name

mar·shal (mär′shəl) ***n.*** [< OFr. *mareschal* < OHG. < *marah*, horse + *scalh*, servant] **1.** a high official of a medieval royal household **2.** a military commander; specif., *a) same as* FIELD MARSHAL *b)* in various foreign armies, a general officer of the highest rank **3.** an official in charge of ceremonies, processions, etc. **4.** a U.S. officer of various kinds; specif., *a)* a Federal officer appointed to a judicial district to perform functions like those of a sheriff *b)* the head of a police or fire department in some cities —***vt.*** **-shaled** or **-shalled, -shal·ing** or **-shal·ling 1.** to arrange (troops, things, ideas, etc.) in order; dispose **2.** *a)* to direct as a marshal; manage *b)* to lead or guide ceremoniously —**mar′shal·cy, mar′shal·ship′** ***n.***

Mar·shall (mär′shəl) **1. George C(atlett),** 1880–1959; U.S. general & statesman **2. John,** 1755–1835; U.S. jurist; chief justice of the U.S. (1801–35)

Mar·shall Islands (mär′shəl) group of islands in the W Pacific: see Trust Territory of the PACIFIC ISLANDS

marsh gas a gaseous product, chiefly methane, formed from decomposing vegetable matter

marsh·mal·low (marsh′mel′ō, -mal′ō) ***n.*** **1.** orig., a confection made from the root of the marsh mallow **2.** a soft, spongy confection of sugar, starch, corn syrup, and gelatin

marsh mallow a pink-flowered, perennial, European plant with a root sometimes used in medicine

marsh marigold a marsh plant of the buttercup family, with bright-yellow flowers

marsh·y (mär′shē) ***adj.*** **marsh′i·er, marsh′i·est 1.** of, like, or containing a marsh or marshes; swampy **2.** growing in marshes —**marsh′i·ness** ***n.***

mar·su·pi·al (mär sōō′pē əl) ***adj.*** **1.** of or like a marsupium **2.** of an order of mammals whose young are carried by the female for several months after birth in an external pouch of the abdomen —***n.*** an animal of this kind, as a kangaroo, opossum, etc.

mar·su·pi·um (-əm) ***n.***, *pl.* **-pi·a** (-ə) [ModL. < L. < Gr. dim. of *marsypos*, a pouch] the pouch on the abdomen of a female marsupial

mart (märt) ***n.*** [MDu., var. of *markt*] a market

Mar·tel (mär tel′), **Charles** 688?–741 A.D.; ruler of the Franks (714–741): grandfather of CHARLEMAGNE

mar·ten (mär′t'n) ***n.***, *pl.* **-tens, -ten:** see PLURAL, II, D, 1 [< OFr. < *martre*] **1.** a small, flesh-eating mammal like a weasel but larger, with soft, thick, valuable fur **2.** the fur

Mar·tha (mär′thə) [LL. < Gr. < Aram. *Mārthā*, lit., lady] **1.** a feminine name **2.** *Bible* a woman rebuked by Jesus for fussing over chores while he talked with her sister Mary: Luke 10:40

Mar·tial (mär′shəl) (*Marcus Valerius Martialis*) 40?–104? A.D.; Rom. epigrammatist & poet

mar·tial (mär′shəl) ***adj.*** [< L. *martialis*, of Mars] **1.** of or connected with war, soldiers, etc.; military *[martial* music*]* **2.** warlike; militaristic *[martial* spirit*]* —**mar′tial·ism** ***n.*** —**mar′tial·ist** ***n.*** —**mar′tial·ly** ***adv.***

martial law temporary rule by the military authorities over the civilians, as in time of war

Mar·tian (mär′shən) ***adj.*** of Mars (god or planet) —***n.*** an imagined inhabitant of the planet Mars

Mar·tin (mär′t'n) [Fr. < L. < *Mars* (gen. *Martis*), Mars: hence, lit., warlike] **1.** a masculine name **2.** Saint, 315?–397? A.D.; bishop of Tours: see MARTINMAS

mar·tin (mär′t'n) ***n.*** [Fr.] **1.** a stout-billed bird of the swallow family, as the purple martin **2.** any of various swallowlike birds

mar·ti·net (mär′t'n et′) ***n.*** [after Gen. J. *Martinet*, 17th-c. Fr. drillmaster] a very strict disciplinarian or stickler for rigid regulations

mar·tin·gale (mär′t'n gāl′) ***n.*** [Fr., prob. < Sp. *almártaga*, check, rein < Ar.] **1.** the strap of a horse's harness passing from the noseband to the girth between the forelegs, to keep the horse from rearing or throwing back its head **2.** a lower stay for the jib boom of a sailing vessel Also **mar′tingal′** (-gal′)

mar·ti·ni (mär tē′nē) ***n.***, *pl.* **-nis** [altered < earlier *Martinez:* reason for name unc.] [*also* **M-**] a cocktail of gin (or vodka) and dry vermouth

Mar·ti·nique (mär′tə nēk′) French island possession in the Windward group of the West Indies

Mar·tin·mas (mär′t'n məs) ***n.*** [see -MAS] Saint Martin's Day, a church festival held on November 11

mar·tyr (mär′tər) ***n.*** [OE. < LL. < Gr. *martyr*, a witness] **1.** a person tortured or killed because of his faith or beliefs **2.** a person suffering great pain or misery a long time —***vt.*** to make a martyr of —**mar′tyr·dom** ***n.***

mar·tyr·ize (mär′tə rīz′) ***vt.*** **-ized′, -iz′ing** to make a martyr of —***vi.*** to be or become a martyr —**mar′tyr·i·za′tion** ***n.***

mar·tyr·ol·o·gy (mär′tə räl′ə jē) ***n.***, *pl.* **-gies 1.** a list of martyrs **2.** a historical account of religious martyrs **3.** such accounts collectively —**mar′tyr·ol′o·gist** ***n.***

mar·vel (mär′v'l) ***n.*** [< OFr. *merveille* < VL. < L. neut. pl. of *mirabilis*, wonderful < *mirari*, to admire] a wonderful or astonishing thing; prodigy or miracle —***vi.*** **-veled** or **-velled, -vel·ing** or **-vel·ling** to be amazed; wonder —***vt.*** to wonder at or about (followed by a clause)

Mar·vell (mär′v'l), **Andrew** 1621–78; Eng. poet

mar·vel·ous (mär′v'l əs) ***adj.*** **1.** causing wonder; astonishing, extraordinary, incredible, etc. **2.** [Colloq.] fine; splendid Also, chiefly Brit. sp., **mar′vel·lous** —**mar′vel·ous·ly** ***adv.*** —**mar′vel·ous·ness** ***n.***

Mar·vin (mär′vin) [prob. ult. < Gmc. bases meaning "sea" & "friend"] a masculine name

Marx (märks), **Karl (Heinrich)** 1818–83; Ger. social philosopher & political economist whose doctrines are the basis of modern socialism

Marx·ism (märk′siz'm) ***n.*** the system of thought developed by Karl Marx, his co-worker Friedrich Engels, and their followers: also **Marx′i·an·ism** —**Marx′ist, Marx′i·an** ***adj., n.***

Mar·y (mer′ē, mar′ē, mā′rē) [< OE. < LL. *Maria* < Gr. < Heb. *Miryām* or Aram. *Maryam*, lit., rebellion] **1.** a feminine name **2. Mary I** (*Mary Tudor*) 1516–58; queen of England (1553–58): daughter of HENRY VIII & wife of PHILIP II of Spain **3. Mary II** 1662–94; queen of England, Scotland, & Ireland, ruling jointly with her husband, WILLIAM III **4.** *Bible a)* mother of Jesus: Matt. 1:18–25 *b)* sister of Martha: Luke 10:38–42 *c) same as* MARY MAGDALENE

Mary Janes *a trademark for* low-heeled, patent-leather slippers with a strap, for little girls

Mar·y·land (mer′ə lənd) [after Queen Henrietta *Maria,* wife of CHARLES I of England] E State of the U.S., on the Atlantic: 10,577 sq. mi.; pop. 4,216,000; cap. Annapolis: abbrev. **Md., MD**

Mary Magdalene *Bible* woman out of whom Jesus cast seven devils: Luke 8:2: identified with the repentant woman in Luke 7:37 ff.

Mary, Queen of Scots (*Mary Stuart*) 1542–87; queen of Scotland (1542–67): beheaded

mar·zi·pan (mär′zi pan′) *n.* [G. < It. *marzapane,* confection < ML. < Ar.] a confection of various shapes and colors made of a paste of ground almonds, sugar, and egg white

-mas (məs) *a combining form for* MASS *meaning* a (specified) church festival *[Martinmas]*

Ma·sai (mä sī′) *n.* **1.** *pl.* **-sai′, -sais′** any member of a pastoral people of Kenya and Tanzania **2.** their language

masc., mas. masculine

Mas·ca·gni (mäs kä′nyē), **Pie·tro** (pye′trô) 1863–1945; It. composer of operas

mas·ca·ra (mas kar′ə) *n.* [< Sp. < It. *maschera:* see MASK] a cosmetic for coloring the eyelashes —*vt.* **-ca′raed, -ca′ra·ing** to put mascara on

mas·con (mäs′kän′) *n.* [*mas(s) con(centration)*] a concentration of very dense material beneath the surface of the moon

mas·cot (mas′kät, -kət) *n.* [< Fr. < Pr. dim. of *masco,* sorcerer] any person, animal, or thing supposed to bring good luck by being present

mas·cu·line (mas′kyə lin) *adj.* [< OFr. < L. < *masculus,* male < *mas,* male] **1.** male; of men or boys **2.** having qualities regarded as characteristic of men and boys, as strength, vigor, etc. **3.** suitable for or typical of a man **4.** mannish **5.** *Gram.* designating or of the gender of words referring to males or things orig. regarded as male **6.** *Prosody* designating or of a rhyme of stressed final syllables (Ex.: enjoy, destroy) —*n. Gram.* **1.** the masculine gender **2.** a word or form in this gender —**mas′cu·line·ly** *adv.* —**mas′cu·lin′i·ty** *n.*

mas·cu·lin·ize (-li nīz′) *vt.* **-ized′, -iz′ing** to make masculine; esp., to produce male characteristics in (a female) —**mas′cu·lin′i·za′tion** *n.*

Mase·field (mās′fēld, māz′-), **John** 1878–1967; Eng. writer, esp. of poetry

ma·ser (mā′zər) *n.* [*m(icrowave) a(mplification by) s(timulated) e(mission of) r(adiation)*] a device, operating at microwave, infrared, etc. frequencies, in which atoms in a crystal or gas are concentrated, raised to a higher energy level, then emitted in a very narrow beam

mash (mash) *n.* [< OE. *masc-,* in *mascwyrt,* infused malt] **1.** crushed or ground malt or meal soaked in hot water for making wort, used in brewing beer **2.** a mixture of bran, meal, etc. in warm water for feeding horses, etc. **3.** any soft mixture or mass —*vt.* **1.** to mix (crushed malt, etc.) in hot water for making wort **2.** to change into a soft mass by beating, crushing, etc. **3.** to crush and injure or damage

mash·er (-ər) *n.* **1.** one that mashes; specif., a device for mashing vegetables, etc. **2.** [Slang] a man who makes unwanted advances to women not acquainted with him, esp. in public places

mask (mask) *n.* [Fr. *masque* < It. *maschera,* prob. < Ar. *maskhara,* buffoon] **1.** a covering to conceal or disguise all or part of the face **2.** anything that conceals or disguises **3.** a masque or masquerade **4.** a person wearing a mask **5.** *a)* a sculptured or molded likeness of the face *b)* a grotesque or comic representation of a face, worn to amuse or frighten **6.** a protective covering for the face or head *[a gas mask]* **7.** a covering for the mouth and nose, as for administering an anesthetic, preventing infection, etc. **8.** the face or head of a dog, fox, etc. —*vt.* to conceal, cover, disguise, etc. with or as with a mask —*vi.* **1.** to put on a mask **2.** to hide or disguise one's true motives, character, etc. —**masked** *adj.* —**mask′er** *n.*

MASKS

masked ball a ball at which masks and fancy costumes are worn

mask·ing tape (mas′kiŋ) an adhesive tape for covering borders, etc., as during painting

mas·och·ism (mas′ə kiz′m, maz′-) *n.* [after L. von Sacher-*Masoch* (1835–1895), Austrian writer] the getting of pleasure, specif. sexual pleasure, from being dominated or hurt physically or psychologically —**mas′och·ist** *n.* —**mas′och·is′tic** *adj.* —**mas′och·is′ti·cal·ly** *adv.*

ma·son (mā′s′n) *n.* [< OFr. < ML. *matio*] **1.** a person whose work is building with stone, brick, etc. **2.** [**M-**] *same as* FREEMASON

Ma·son-Dix·on line (mā′s′n dik′s′n) [after C. *Mason* & J. *Dixon,* who surveyed it, 1763–67] boundary line between Pa. & Md., regarded as separating the North from the South: also **Mason and Dixon's line**

Ma·son·ic (mə sän′ik) *adj.* [*also* **m-**] of Masons (Freemasons) or Masonry (Freemasonry)

Ma·son·ite (mā′s′n īt′) [after W. H. *Mason* (1877–1947?), U.S. engineer] *a trademark for* a kind of hardboard made from pressed wood fibers, used as building material, etc. —*n.* such hardboard

Mason jar [patented in 1858 by J. *Mason* of New York] [*also* **m-**] a wide-mouthed glass jar with a screw top, for preserving foods, esp. in home canning

ma·son·ry (mā′s′n rē) *n., pl.* **-ries** **1.** the trade or art of a mason **2.** something built by a mason or masons; brickwork or stonework **3.** [*usually* **M-**] *same as* FREEMASONRY

masque (mask) *n.* [see MASK] **1.** a masquerade; masked ball **2.** a former kind of dramatic entertainment with a mythical or allegorical theme and lavish costumes, music, etc. —**masqu′er** *n.*

mas·quer·ade (mas′kə rād′) *n.* [< Fr. < It. dial. var. of *mascherata* (< *maschera*): see MASK] **1.** a ball or party at which masks and fancy costumes are worn **2.** a costume for such a ball, etc. **3.** *a)* a disguise; pretense *b)* a living or acting under false pretenses —*vi.* **-ad′ed, -ad′ing** **1.** to take part in a masquerade **2.** to live or act under false pretenses —**mas′quer·ad′er** *n.*

Mass (mas) *n.* [OE. *mæsse* < LL. < *missa* in L. *ite, missa est* (*contio*), go, (the meeting) is dismissed] [*also* **m-**] **1.** the service of the Eucharist in the Roman Catholic Church and some other churches, consisting of a series of prayers and ceremonies **2.** a musical setting for certain parts of this service

mass (mas) *n.* [OFr. *masse* < L. < Gr. *maza,* barley cake] **1.** a piece or amount of indefinite shape or size *[a mass of* clay, a *mass* of cold air*]* **2.** a large quantity or number *[a mass* of bruises*]* **3.** bulk; size **4.** the main part; majority **5.** *Physics* the quantity of matter in a body as measured in its relation to inertia —*adj.* **1.** *a)* of a large number of things *[mass production] b)* of a large number of persons *[a mass* demonstration*]* **2.** of, like, or for the masses *[mass* education*]* —*vt., vi.* to gather or form into a mass —**in the mass** collectively —**the masses** the great mass of common people; specif., the working people

Mas·sa·chu·setts (mas′ə cho͞o′sits) [< Algonquian *Massaadchu-es-et,* lit., at the big hill] New England State of the U.S.: 8,257 sq. mi.; pop. 5,737,000; cap. Boston: abbrev. **Mass., MA**

mas·sa·cre (mas′ə kər) *n.* [Fr. < OFr. *maçacre,* shambles] **1.** the indiscriminate, merciless killing of human beings **2.** a large-scale slaughter of animals —*vt.* **-cred, -cring** to kill indiscriminately and mercilessly and in large numbers —**mas′sa·crer** (-krər) *n.*

mas·sage (mə säzh′) *n.* [Fr. < *masser,* to massage < Ar. *massa,* to touch] a rubbing, kneading, etc. of part of the body, as to stimulate circulation and make muscles or joints supple —*vt.* **-saged′, -sag′ing** to give a massage to —**mas·sag′er** *n.*

mass·cult (mas′kult′) *n.* [MASS + CULT(URE)] [Colloq.] an artificial, commercialized culture popularized for the masses through the mass media

Mas·se·net (mas′ə nā′; *Fr.* mȧs ne′), **Jules (Émile Frédéric)** (zhül) 1842–1912; Fr. composer

mas·sé (shot) (ma sā′) [Fr. < *masse,* billiard cue] a stroke in billiards made by hitting the cue ball off center with the cue held vertically so as to make the ball move in a curve

mas·seur (ma sʉr′, mə-; *Fr.* mȧ sër′) *n.* [Fr.] a man whose work is giving massages —**mas·seuse′** (-so͞oz′, -so͞oz′; *Fr.* -söz′) *n.fem.*

mas·sive (mas′iv) *adj.* **1.** *a)* forming or consisting of a large mass; big and solid; bulky *b)* larger or greater than normal *[a massive* dose of drugs*]* **2.** large and imposing or impressive **3.** large-scale; extensive —**mas′sive·ly** *adv.* —**mas′sive·ness** *n.*

mass media those means of communication that reach and influence large numbers of people, esp. newspapers, magazines, radio, and television

mass meeting a large public meeting to discuss public affairs, demonstrate public approval or disapproval, etc.

mass noun a noun used to denote an abstraction or something that is uncountable (Ex.: *love, girlhood, butter, news*)

mass number *Physics, Chem.* the number of neutrons and protons in the nucleus of an atom

mass production quantity production of goods, esp. by machinery and division of labor —**mass′-pro·duce′** *vt.* **-duced′, -duc′ing**

mast[1] (mast) *n.* [OE. *mæst*] **1.** a tall spar or hollow metal structure rising vertically from the keel or deck of a vessel and used to support the sails, yards, radar and radio equipment, etc. **2.** any vertical pole, as in a crane —*vt.* to put masts on —**before the mast** [Now Rare] as a common sailor

mast[2] (mast) *n.* [OE. *mæst*] beechnuts, acorns, chestnuts, etc., esp. as food for hogs

mas·ta·ba, mas·ta·bah (mas′tə bə) ***n.*** [< Ar.] an oblong structure with a flat roof and sloping sides, built over the opening of a mummy chamber or burial pit in ancient Egypt and used as a tomb

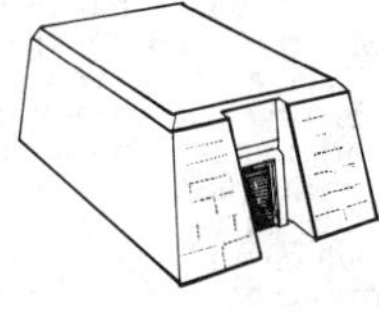
MASTABA

mas·ter (mas′tər) ***n.*** [< OE. *mægester* & OFr. *maistre;* both < L. *magister* < base of L. *magnus,* great] **1.** a man who rules others or has control, authority, or power over something; specif., *a)* a man who is head of a household or institution *b)* an employer *c)* an owner of an animal or slave *d)* the captain of a merchant ship *e)* a victor *f)* [Chiefly Brit.] a male schoolteacher *g)* a person whose teachings in religion, philosophy, etc. one follows *h)* [**M-**] Jesus Christ (with *our, the,* etc.) **2.** a person very skilled in some work, profession, etc.; expert; specif., *a)* a highly skilled workman qualified to follow his trade independently *b)* an artist regarded as great **3.** [**M-**] a title variously applied to *a)* any man or youth: now superseded by the variant *Mister,* usually written *Mr. b)* a boy regarded as too young to be addressed as *Mr. c)* a man who heads some institution, group, etc. *d)* in Scotland, the heir apparent of a viscount or baron *e)* a person who is a MASTER OF ARTS (or SCIENCE, etc.) **4.** *Law* any of several court officers appointed to assist the judge —***adj.*** **1.** being a master **2.** of a master **3.** chief; main; controlling; specif., designating a mechanism or contrivance that controls others, sets a standard or norm, etc. *[a master* switch*]* —***vt.*** **1.** to become master of; control, conquer, etc. **2.** to become an expert in (an art, science, etc.)

master builder **1.** a person skilled in building; esp., formerly, an architect **2.** a building contractor

mas·ter·ful (-fəl) ***adj.*** **1.** fond of acting the part of a master; imperious **2.** having or showing the ability of a master; expert; skillful —**mas′ter·ful·ly** ***adv.*** —**mas′ter·ful·ness** ***n.***

master key a key that will open every one of a set of locks

mas·ter·ly (-lē) ***adj.*** showing the ability or skill of a master; expert —***adv.*** in a masterly manner —**mas′ter·li·ness** ***n.***

master mechanic a skilled mechanic, esp. one serving as foreman

mas·ter·mind (-mīnd′) ***n.*** a very intelligent person, esp. one with the ability to plan or direct a group project —***vt.*** to be the mastermind of (a project)

Master of Arts (or **Science,** etc.) **1.** a degree given by a college or university to a person who has completed a prescribed course of graduate study in the humanities (or in science, etc.) **2.** a person who has this degree

master of ceremonies **1.** a person who supervises a ceremony **2.** a person who presides over an entertainment, introducing the participants, filling in the intervals with jokes, etc.

mas·ter·piece (-pēs′) ***n.*** **1.** a thing made or done with masterly skill **2.** the greatest work made or done by a person or group: also **mas′ter·work′**

Mas·ters (mas′tərz), **Edgar Lee** 1869–1950; U.S. poet

master sergeant *U.S. Mil.* a noncommissioned officer of high rank

mas·ter·ship (mas′tər ship′) ***n.*** **1.** the state of being a master; rule; control **2.** the position, duties, or term of office of a master **3.** masterly ability

mas·ter·stroke (-strōk′) ***n.*** a masterly action, move, or achievement

mas·ter·y (mas′tər ē, -trē) ***n.,*** *pl.* **-ter·ies** **1.** mastership **2.** ascendancy or victory; the upper hand **3.** expert skill or knowledge *[his mastery* of chess*]*

mast·head (mast′hed′) ***n.*** **1.** the top part of a ship's mast **2.** that part of a newspaper or magazine stating its address, publishers, editors, etc. —***vt.*** to display at the masthead

mas·tic (mas′tik) ***n.*** [OFr. < LL. < L. < Gr. *mastichē*] **1.** a yellowish resin obtained from a Mediterranean evergreen tree, used as an astringent and in making varnish, adhesives, etc. **2.** the tree: in full, **mastic tree**

mas·ti·cate (mas′tə kāt′) ***vt.*** **-cat′ed, -cat′ing** [< LL. pp. of *masticare* < Gr. *mastichan,* to gnash < *mastax,* a mouth] **1.** to chew up (food, etc.) **2.** to grind, cut, or knead (rubber, etc.) to a pulp —**mas′ti·ca′tion** ***n.*** —**mas′ti·ca′tor** ***n.***

mas·ti·ca·to·ry (-kə tôr′ē) ***adj.*** of or for mastication; specif., adapted for chewing —***n.,*** *pl.* **-ries** any substance chewed but not swallowed, to increase saliva flow

mas·tiff (mas′tif) ***n.*** [< OFr. *mastin,* ult. < L. *mansuetus,* tame] a large, powerful, smooth-coated dog with hanging lips and drooping ears

mas·to- [< Gr. *mastos,* the breast] *a combining form meaning* of or like a breast: also **mast-**

mas·to·don (mas′tə dän′) ***n.*** [ModL. < Fr. < Gr. *mastos,* a breast + *odous,* a tooth: from the nipplelike processes on its molars] a large, extinct animal resembling the elephant but larger

mas·toid (mas′toid) ***adj.*** [< Gr. < *mastos,* a breast + *eidos,* form] **1.** shaped like a breast or nipple **2.** designating, of, or near a projection of the temporal bone behind the ear —***n.*** **1.** the mastoid projection **2.** [Colloq.] *same as* MASTOIDITIS

mas·toid·i·tis (mas′toi dīt′is) ***n.*** inflammation of the mastoid

mas·tur·bate (mas′tər bāt′) ***vi., vt.*** **-bat′ed, -bat′ing** [< L. pp. of *masturbari,* ult. < *manus,* hand + *stuprum,* defilement] to manipulate one's own genitals, or the genitals of (another), for sexual gratification —**mas′tur·ba′tion** ***n.*** —**mas′tur·ba′tor** ***n.*** —**mas′tur·ba·to′ry** (-bə tôr′ē) ***adj.***

mat¹ (mat) ***n.*** [< OE. *meatt* < LL. *matta* < Phoen.] **1.** a flat, coarse fabric of woven or plaited hemp, straw, etc. **2.** a piece of this or of corrugated rubber, etc., used as a doormat, etc. **3.** a flat piece of cloth, woven straw, etc. put under a vase, dish, etc. **4.** a thickly padded floor covering, as in a gymnasium for wrestling, etc. **5.** anything growing or interwoven in a thick tangle *[a mat* of hair*]* —***vt.*** **mat′ted, mat′ting** **1.** to cover as with a mat **2.** to form into a thick tangle —***vi.*** to become felted or thickly tangled

mat² (mat) ***adj.*** [Fr. < OFr. *mat,* defeated, prob. < L. *mattus,* drunk < *madere,* to be drunk] *same as* MATTE —***n.*** **1.** *same as* MATTE **2.** a border, as of cardboard or cloth, put around a picture, usually between the picture and the frame —***vt.*** **mat′ted, mat′ting** **1.** to produce a dull surface or finish on **2.** to frame (a picture) with a mat

mat³ (mat) ***n.*** [Colloq.] a matrix; printing mold

mat·a·dor (mat′ə dôr′) ***n.*** [Sp. < *matar,* to kill < *mate,* checkmate] the bullfighter who kills the bull with a sword after performing a series of actions with a cape to anger and tire the animal

Ma·ta·mo·ros (mä′tä mô′rôs; *E.* mat′ə môr′əs) city in NE Mexico, on the Rio Grande, opposite Brownsville, Tex.: pop. 175,000

match¹ (mach) ***n.*** [< OFr. *mesche,* prob. < L. *myxa,* lamp wick < Gr.] **1.** orig., a wick or cord prepared to burn at a uniform rate, used for firing guns or explosives **2.** a slender piece of wood, cardboard, etc. tipped with a composition that catches fire by friction, sometimes only on a specially prepared surface

match² (mach) ***n.*** [OE. *(ge)mæcca,* a mate] **1.** any person or thing equal or similar to another in some way; specif., *a)* a person, group, or thing able to cope with another as an equal *b)* a counterpart or facsimile **2.** two or more persons or things that go together in appearance, size, etc. **3.** a contest or game; competition **4.** a marriage or mating **5.** a person regarded as a suitable mate —***vt.*** **1.** to join in marriage; mate **2.** to compete with successfully **3.** to put in opposition (*with*); pit (*against*) **4.** to be equal, similar, or suitable to **5.** to make, show, or get a competitor, counterpart, or equivalent to *[match* this cloth*]* **6.** to suit or fit (one thing) to another **7.** to fit (things) together **8.** to compare **9.** *a)* to flip or reveal (coins) to decide something contested, the winner being determined by the combination of faces thus exposed *b)* to match coins with (another person) —***vi.*** to be equal, similar, suitable, etc. in some way —**match′a·ble** ***adj.*** —**match′er** ***n.***

match·box (-bäks′) ***n.*** a small box for holding matches

match·less (mach′lis) ***adj.*** having no equal; peerless —**match′less·ly** ***adv.*** —**match′less·ness** ***n.***

match·lock (-läk′) ***n.*** **1.** an old type of gunlock in which the charge of powder was ignited by a slow-burning match (wick or cord) **2.** a musket with such a gunlock

match·mak·ing¹ (-mā′kiŋ) ***n.*** the work or business of making matches (for burning) —**match′mak′er** ***n.***

match·mak·ing² (-mā′kiŋ) ***n.*** **1.** the arranging of marriages for others **2.** the arranging of wrestling or boxing matches, etc. —**match′mak′er** ***n.***

match play *Golf* a form of play in which the score is calculated by counting holes won rather than strokes taken: cf. MEDAL PLAY

mate¹ (māt) ***n.*** [MDu. < *gemate* < Gmc.] **1.** a companion or fellow worker **2.** one of a matched pair **3.** *a)* a husband or wife *b)* the male or female of paired animals **4.** *Naut. a)* an officer of a merchant ship, ranking below the captain *b)* an assistant **5.** *U.S. Navy* any of various petty officers *[a carpenter's mate]* —***vt., vi.*** **mat′ed, mat′ing** **1.** to join as a pair **2.** to couple in marriage or sexual union

mate² (māt) ***n., interj., vt.*** **mat′ed, mat′ing** *same as* CHECKMATE

ma·té (mä′tā, mat′ā) ***n.*** [AmSp. < Quechua *mati,* calabash (used to steep the brew)] **1.** a beverage made from the dried leaves of a S. American tree 2. this tree or its leaves Also sp. **mate**

ma·ter (māt′ər, mät′-) ***n.*** [L.] [Chiefly Brit. Colloq.] mother: often preceded by *the*

ma·te·ri·al (mə tir′ē əl) ***adj.*** [< LL. < L. *materia*, matter] **1.** of matter; relating to or consisting of what occupies space; physical *[a material object]* **2.** *a)* of the body or bodily needs, etc. *[material pleasures]* *b)* of or fond of comfort, wealth, etc.; worldly *[material success]* **3.** important, essential, etc. (*to* the matter under discussion) **—*n.*** **1.** what a thing is, or may be, made of; elements or parts **2.** ideas, notes, etc. that may be worked up; data **3.** cloth or other fabric **4.** [*pl.*] tools, articles, etc. for a specified use *[writing materials]* **—ma·te′ri·al′i·ty** (-al′ə tē) ***n.***

ma·te·ri·al·ism (-iz′m) ***n.*** **1.** the philosophical doctrine that everything in the world, including thought, will, and feeling, can be explained only in terms of matter **2.** the tendency to be more concerned with material than with spiritual values **—ma·te′ri·al·ist** ***adj., n.*** **—ma·te′ri·al·is′tic** ***adj.*** **—ma·te′ri·al·is′ti·cal·ly** ***adv.***

ma·te·ri·al·ize (mə tir′ē ə līz′) ***vt.*** **-ized′, -iz′ing** **1.** to represent in material form **2.** to make (a spirit, etc.) appear in bodily form **—*vi.*** **1.** to become fact; be realized *[a plan that never materialized]* **2.** to take on, or appear in, bodily form: said of spirits, etc. **3.** to appear suddenly or unexpectedly **—ma·te′ri·al·i·za′tion** ***n.***

ma·te·ri·al·ly (-lē) ***adv.*** **1.** with regard to the matter, content, etc. and not the form **2.** physically **3.** to a great extent; considerably

ma·te·ri·a med·i·ca (mə tir′ē ə med′i kə) [ML. < L. *materia*, matter + fem. of *medicus*, medical] **1.** the drugs and other remedial substances used in medicine **2.** the branch of medical science that deals with such substances, their uses, etc.

ma·te·ri·el, ma·té·ri·el (mə tir′ē el′) ***n.*** [Fr.: see MATERIAL] the necessary materials and tools; specif., weapons, supplies, etc. of armed forces

ma·ter·nal (mə tur′n′l) ***adj.*** [< MFr. < L. < *mater*, a mother] **1.** of or like a mother; motherly **2.** derived or inherited from a mother **3.** related through the mother's side of the family *[maternal grandparents]* **—ma·ter′nal·ly** ***adv.***

ma·ter·ni·ty (mə tur′nə tē) ***n.*** **1.** the state of being a mother; motherhood **2.** the qualities of a mother; motherliness **—*adj.*** **1.** for pregnant women *[a maternity dress]* **2.** for the care of women giving birth and of newborn babies *[a maternity ward]*

math (math) ***n.*** *clipped form of* MATHEMATICS

math. **1.** mathematical **2.** mathematician **3.** mathematics

math·e·mat·i·cal (math′ə mat′i k′l) ***adj.*** [< ML. < L. < Gr. < *mathēma*, what is learned < *manthanein*, to learn] **1.** of, like, or concerned with mathematics **2.** rigorously precise, accurate, etc. **—math′e·mat′i·cal·ly** ***adv.***

math·e·ma·ti·cian (math′ə mə tish′ən, math′mə-) ***n.*** an expert or specialist in mathematics

math·e·mat·ics (math′ə mat′iks) ***n.pl.*** [*with sing. v.*] [see MATHEMATICAL & -ICS] the group of sciences (arithmetic, geometry, algebra, calculus, etc.) dealing with quantities, magnitudes, and forms, and their relationships, attributes, etc., by the use of numbers and symbols

Math·er (math′ər) **1. Cot·ton** (kät′'n), 1663–1728; Am. clergyman & writer: son of *ff.* **2. In·crease** (in′krēs), 1639–1723; Am. clergyman & writer

Ma·til·da, Ma·thil·da (mə til′də) [< ML. < OHG. < *maht*, power + *hiltia*, battle] a feminine name

mat·in (mat′'n) ***n.*** [OFr. < L. *matutinus*, of the morning < *Matuta*, goddess of dawn] **1.** [*pl.*] [*often* **M-**] *a) R.C.Ch.* the first of the seven canonical hours *b) Anglican Ch.* the service of public morning prayer **2.** [Poet.] a morning song **—*adj.*** **1.** of matins **2.** of morning **—mat′in·al** ***adj.***

mat·i·nee, mat·i·née (mat′'n ā′, mat′'n ā′) ***n.*** [< Fr.: see prec.] a daytime reception, etc.; esp., a performance, as of a play, in the afternoon

Ma·tisse (mà tēs′), **Hen·ri** (än rē′) 1869–1954; Fr. painter

ma·tri- [< L. *mater* (gen. *matris*), a mother] *a combining form meaning* mother *[matriarch]*

ma·tri·arch (mā′trē ärk′) ***n.*** [prec. + -ARCH] a mother who rules her family or tribe; specif., a woman who is head of a matriarchy **—ma′tri·ar′chal** (-är′k'l) ***adj.***

ma·tri·ar·chy (-trē är′kē) ***n.***, *pl.* **-chies** **1.** a form of social organization in which the mother is head of the family or tribe, descent being traced through the female line **2.** rule or domination by women **—ma′tri·ar′chic** ***adj.***

mat·ri·cide (mat′rə sīd′, mā′trə-) ***n.*** [< L. < *mater*, mother + *caedere*, to kill] **1.** the act of killing one's mother **2.** a person who kills his mother **—mat′ri·ci′dal** ***adj.***

ma·tric·u·late (mə trik′yoo lāt′; *also, for n.*, -lit) ***vt., vi.*** **-lat′ed, -lat′ing** [< ML. pp. of *matriculare*, to register < LL. dim. of *matrix*, MATRIX] to enroll, esp. as a student in a college or university **—*n.*** a person so enrolled **—ma·tric′u·lant** ***n.*** **—ma·tric′u·la′tion** ***n.***

mat·ri·mo·ny (mat′rə mō′nē) ***n.***, *pl.* **-nies** [< OFr. < L. *matrimonium* < *mater*, a mother] **1.** the act or rite of marriage **2.** the state of being husband and wife **3.** married life **—mat′ri·mo′ni·al** ***adj.*** **—mat′ri·mo′ni·al·ly** ***adv.***

ma·trix (mā′triks) ***n.***, *pl.* **-tri·ces′** (mā′trə sēz′, mat′rə-), **-trix·es** [LL., womb, ult. < L. *mater* (gen. *matris*), mother] **1.** orig., the womb; uterus **2.** that within which something originates, takes form, etc.; specif., a die or mold for casting or shaping **3.** *Printing* *a)* a metal mold for casting the face of type *b)* an impression, as of papier-mâché, from which a plate can be made

ma·tron (mā′trən) ***n.*** [< OFr. < L. *matrona* < *mater*, a mother] **1.** a wife or widow, esp. one with a mature manner **2.** a woman manager of the domestic arrangements of a hospital, prison, or other institution **3.** a woman guard, as in a jail **—ma′tron·al** ***adj.*** **—ma′tron·li·ness** ***n.*** **—ma′tron·ly** ***adj.***

matron of honor a married woman acting as principal attendant to the bride at a wedding

Matt. Matthew

matte (mat) ***n.*** [var. of MAT²] a dull surface or finish, often roughened **—*adj.*** not shiny or glossy; dull Also sp. **matt** **—mat′ted** ***adj.***

mat·ted (mat′id) ***adj.*** **1.** closely tangled together in a dense mass **2.** covered with matting or mats

mat·ter (mat′ər) ***n.*** [< OFr. < L. *materia*, material] **1.** what a thing is made of; constituent material **2.** whatever occupies space and is perceptible to the senses in some way: in modern physics, matter and energy are regarded as mutually convertible equivalents **3.** any specified sort of substance *[coloring matter]* **4.** material or content of thought or expression, as distinguished from style or form **5.** an amount or quantity *[a matter of a few days]* **6.** *a)* a thing or affair *[business matters]* *b)* cause or occasion *[no laughing matter]* **7.** importance; significance *[it's of no matter]* **8.** trouble; difficulty (with *the*) *[what's the matter?]* **9.** mail *[second-class matter]* **10.** pus **11.** *Printing* *a)* copy *b)* type set up **—*vi.*** **1.** to be of importance; have significance **2.** to form and discharge pus; suppurate **—as a matter of fact** in fact; really **—for that matter** as far as that is concerned: also **for the matter of that** **—no matter** **1.** it is of no importance **2.** regardless of *[no matter what you say]*

Mat·ter·horn (mat′ər hôrn′) mountain of the Pennine Alps, on the border between Switzerland & Italy

mat·ter-of-course (mat′ər əv kôrs′) ***adj.*** **1.** coming naturally in the course of events; routine **2.** reacting to events in a calm and natural way

matter of course a thing to be expected as a natural or logical occurrence

mat·ter-of-fact (-əv fakt′, -ə fakt′) ***adj.*** sticking strictly to facts; literal, unimaginative, etc. **—mat′ter-of-fact′ly** ***adv.*** **—mat′ter-of-fact′ness** ***n.***

Mat·thew (math′yoo) [< OFr. < LL. < Gr. < Heb. *mattithyāh*, lit., gift of God] **1.** a masculine name: dim. *Mat(t)*; var. *Matthias* **2.** *Bible* *a)* one of the four Evangelists and the reputed author of the first Gospel *b)* this book, the first of the New Testament

mat·ting¹ (mat′iŋ) ***n.*** **1.** a fabric of fiber, as straw or hemp, for mats, floor covering, wrapping, etc. **2.** mats collectively **3.** the making of mats

mat·ting² (mat′iŋ) ***n.*** [see MATTE] **1.** the production of a dull surface or finish **2.** such a surface or finish **3.** a mat, or border

mat·tins (mat′'nz) ***n.pl.*** *Brit. var. of* MATINS (see MATIN, *n.* 1)

mat·tock (mat′ək) ***n.*** [OE. *mattuc*] a tool like a pickax but with at least one flat blade, for loosening the soil, digging up roots, etc.

MATTOCK

mat·tress (mat′ris) ***n.*** [< OFr. < It. *materasso* < Ar. *maṭraḥ*, cushion] **1.** a casing of strong cloth filled with cotton, hair, foam rubber, etc., and usually coiled springs, and used on or as a bed **2.** an inflatable pad used in the same way: in full, **air mattress**

mat·u·rate (mach′oo rāt′, mat′yoo-) ***vi.*** **-rat′ed, -rat′ing** [< L. pp. of *maturare*, to MATURE] **1.** to suppurate; discharge pus **2.** to ripen; mature **—ma·tur·a·tive** (mə tyoor′ə tiv, mach′oo rāt′iv, mat′yoo-) ***adj.*** **—mat′u·ra′tion** ***n.***

ma·ture (mə toor′, -choor′, -tyoor′) ***adj.*** [< L. *maturus*, ripe] **1.** *a)* full-grown, as plants or animals *b)* ripe, as fruits *c)* fully developed, as a person **2.** fully developed, perfected, etc. *[a mature scheme]* **3.** of a state of full development *[of mature age]* **4.** due: said of a note, bond, etc. **—*vt.*** **-tured′, -tur′ing** **1.** to bring to full growth, or to ripeness **2.** to develop fully **—*vi.*** **1.** to become fully grown or ripe **2.** to become due: said of a note, etc. **—ma·ture′ly** ***adv.*** **—ma·ture′ness** ***n.***

ma·tu·ri·ty (-ə tē) ***n.*** **1.** *a)* a being full-grown, ripe, or fully developed *b)* a being perfect, complete, or ready

2. *a*) a becoming due *b*) the time at which a note, etc. becomes due

ma·tu·ti·nal (mə to͞ot′'n əl, -tyo͞ot′-; *chiefly Brit.* mach′o͞o ti′n'l) ***adj.*** [< L. < *matutinus:* see MATIN] of or in the morning; early —**ma·tu′ti·nal·ly** ***adv.***

mat·zo (mät′sə, -sô) ***n.,*** *pl.* **mat′zot, mat′zoth** (-sōt), **mat′zos** [< Heb. *matstsāh,* unleavened] flat, thin unleavened bread eaten by Jews during the Passover, or a piece of this

Maud, Maude (môd) [< MATILDA] a feminine name

maud·lin (môd′lin) ***adj.*** [< ME. *Maudeleyne,* (Mary) Magdalene (often represented as weeping)] **1.** foolishly and tearfully or weakly sentimental **2.** tearfully sentimental from too much liquor

Maugham (môm), **(William) Som·er·set** (sum′ər set′) 1874–1965; Eng. novelist & playwright

mau·gre, mau·ger (mô′gər) ***prep.*** [< OFr. *maugré,* lit., with displeasure] [Archaic] in spite of

Mau·i (mou′ē) [Haw.] island of Hawaii, southeast of Oahu

maul (môl) ***n.*** [< OFr. < L. *malleus,* a hammer] a very heavy hammer or mallet for driving stakes, etc. —***vt.*** **1.** to bruise or lacerate **2.** to handle roughly —**maul′er** ***n.***

Mau·na Lo·a (mou′nə lō′ə) [Haw., lit., long mountain] active volcano on the island of Hawaii

maun·der (môn′dər) ***vi.*** [prob. freq. of obs. *maund,* to beg] **1.** to move or act in a vague, aimless way **2.** to talk in an incoherent, rambling way —**maun′der·er** ***n.***

Maun·dy Thursday (môn′dē) [OFr. *mandé* < LL. *mandatum,* commandment of God < L.: from use in a prayer on that day] the Thursday before Easter

Mau·pas·sant (mō′pə sänt′; *Fr.* mō pá sän′) **(Henri René Albert) Guy de** (gē də) 1850–93; Fr. writer

Mau·re·ta·ni·a (môr′ə tā′nē ə, -tān′yə) ancient country & Roman province in NW Africa

Mau·rice (môr′is, mär′-; mô rēs′) [Fr. < LL. *Maurus,* a Moor] a masculine name

Mau·ri·ta·ni·a (môr′ə tā′nē ə, -tān′yə) country in W Africa, on the Atlantic: 419,230 sq. mi.; pop. 1,120,000 —**Mau′ri·ta′ni·an** ***adj., n.***

Mau·ri·ti·us (mô rish′ē əs, -rish′əs) island country in the Indian Ocean, east of Madagascar: a member of the Commonwealth: 809 sq. mi.; pop. 810,000

Mau·so·le·um (mô′sə lē′əm, -zə-) the tomb of Mausolus, king of an ancient land in Asia Minor —***n.*** **[m-]** *pl.* **-le′ums, -le′a** (-lē′ə) a large, imposing tomb

mauve (mōv, môv) ***n.*** [Fr., mallow < L. *malva,* mallow] any of several shades of delicate purple

ma·ven (mā′vən) ***n.*** [Yid. < LHeb. *mēvin*] an expert or connoisseur, often, specif., a self-proclaimed one

mav·er·ick (mav′ər ik, mav′rik) ***n.*** [after S. *Maverick,* 19th-c. Texas rancher who did not brand his cattle] **1.** an unbranded animal, esp. a strayed calf, formerly the property of the first one who branded it **2.** [Colloq.] a person who acts independently of his political party or group

ma·vis (mā′vis) ***n.*** [< OFr.] *same as* SONG THRUSH

maw (mô) ***n.*** [OE. *maga*] **1.** orig., the stomach **2.** the throat, gullet, jaws, etc. of a voracious animal **3.** anything thought of as devouring without end

mawk·ish (mô′kish) ***adj.*** [lit., maggoty < ON. *mathkr,* maggot] **1.** insipid or nauseating **2.** sentimental in a weak, insipid way, so as to be sickening —**mawk′ish·ly** ***adv.*** —**mawk′ish·ness** ***n.***

max. maximum

max·i- [< MAXI(MUM)] *a combining form meaning* maximum, very large, very long *[maxicoat]*

max·il·la (mak sil′ə) ***n.,*** *pl.* **-lae** (-ē) [L.] **1.** in vertebrates, the upper jaw, or a major bone or cartilage of it **2.** in insects, crabs, etc., one of the first or second pair of jaws or head appendages situated just behind the mandibles

max·il·lar·y (mak′sə ler′ē; *chiefly Brit.* mak sil′ə rē) ***adj.*** designating, of, or near the jaw or jawbone —***n.,*** *pl.* **-lar′ies** *same as* MAXILLA

max·im (mak′sim) ***n.*** [< MFr. < ML. < LL. *maxima* (*propositio*), the greatest (premise): see MAXIMUM] a concisely expressed rule of conduct; precept

max·i·ma (mak′sə mə) ***n.*** *alt. pl. of* MAXIMUM

max·i·mal (-m'l) ***adj.*** highest or greatest possible; of or constituting a maximum —**max′i·mal·ly** ***adv.***

Max·i·mil·ian (mak′sə mil′yən) [? a blend of the L. names *Maximus & Aemilianus*] **1.** a masculine name: dim. *Max* **2.** (*Ferdinand Maximilian Joseph*) 1832–67; archduke of Austria; emperor of Mexico (1864–67): executed

max·i·mize (mak′sə mīz′) ***vt.*** **-mized′, -miz′ing** to increase to the maximum —**max′i·mi·za′tion** ***n.*** —**max′i·miz′er** ***n.***

max·i·mum (-məm) ***n.,*** *pl.* **-mums, -ma** (-mə) [L., neut. of *maximus,* superl. of *magnus,* great] **1.** the greatest quantity, number, etc. possible or permissible **2.** the highest degree or point reached or recorded —***adj.*** **1.** greatest possible, permissible, or reached **2.** marking a maximum

Max·ine (mak sēn′) [fem. of *Max:* see MAXIMILIAN] a feminine name

May[1] (mā) ***n.*** [OFr. < L. < *Maia,* goddess of increase] **1.** the fifth month of the year, having 31 days **2.** the springtime of life; youth

May[2] (mā) [contr. of MARY, MARGARET] a feminine name

may (mā) ***v.aux.*** *pt.* **might** [OE. *mæg*] an auxiliary preceding an infinitive (without *to*) and expressing: **1.** orig., ability or power: now generally replaced by *can* **2.** possibility or likelihood *[it may rain]* **3.** permission *[you may go]* **4.** contingency, as in clauses of purpose, result, concession, or condition *[they died that we may be free]* **5.** wish, hope, or prayer *[may he rest in peace]*

Ma·ya (mä′yə) ***n.*** **1.** *pl.* **Ma′yas, Ma′ya** a member of a tribe of Indians in SE Mexico and Central America, who had a highly developed civilization **2.** their language —***adj.*** of the Mayas —**Ma′yan** ***adj., n.***

Ma·ya·güez (mä′yä gwes′) seaport in W Puerto Rico: pop. 69,000

May apple **1.** a woodland plant with shield-shaped leaves and a single large, white flower, found in the E U.S. **2.** its edible, yellow, oval fruit

may·be (mā′bē) ***adv.*** [ME. (for *it may be*)] perhaps

May·day (mā′dā′) ***n.*** [< Fr. (*venez*) *m'aider,* (come) help me] the international radiotelephone signal for help, used by ships and aircraft in distress

May Day May 1: as a traditional spring festival, often celebrated by dancing, crowning a May queen, etc.; as an international labor holiday, observed in many countries by parades, demonstrations, etc.

may·est (mā′ist) *archaic 2d pers. sing., pres. indic., of* MAY: *used with* thou

May·fair (mā′fer′) a fashionable residential district of the West End of London

may·flow·er (-flou′ər) ***n.*** a plant that flowers in early spring; esp., *a*) in the U.S., the trailing arbutus, etc. *b*) in England, the cowslip, marsh marigold, etc. —**[M-]** the ship on which the Pilgrims came to America (1620)

may·fly (-flī′) ***n.,*** *pl.* **-flies′** a slender insect with gauzy wings held vertically when at rest: the adult lives only a few hours or a few days

MAYFLY (body to 1 in.)

may·hap (mā′hap′, mā′hap′) ***adv.*** [< *it may hap*(*pen*)] [Archaic] perhaps; maybe: also **may′hap′pen**

may·hem (mā′hem, mā′əm) ***n.*** [see MAIM] **1.** *Law* the offense of maiming a person; specif., *a*) orig., injury inflicted on another so as to cause loss of a part or function necessary for self-defense *b*) any intentional mutilation of another's body **2.** loosely, any deliberate destruction or violence

May·ing (mā′iŋ) ***n.*** [*also* **m-**] the celebration of May Day, as by gathering flowers, dancing, etc.

May·nard (mā′nərd, -närd) [< Anglo-Fr. < OHG. < *magan,* power + *hart,* strong] a masculine name

may·n't (mā′'nt, mānt) may not

may·o (mā′ō) ***n.*** [Colloq.] *clipped form of* MAYONNAISE

may·on·naise (mā′ə nāz′) ***n.*** [Fr., prob. ult. < *Mahón,* Minorca] a creamy salad dressing made by beating together egg yolks, oil, lemon juice or vinegar, and seasoning

may·or (mā′ər, mer) ***n.*** [< OFr. *maire* < L. *major,* greater] the chief administrative official (or, under a city-manager plan, the formal head) of a city, town, or other municipality —**may′or·al** ***adj.***

may·or·al·ty (-əl tē) ***n.,*** *pl.* **-ties** the office or term of office of a mayor

May·pole (mā′pōl′) ***n.*** a high pole wreathed with streamers, around which merrymakers dance on May Day

May queen a girl chosen to be queen of the merrymakers on May Day

mayst (māst) *archaic 2d pers. sing., pres. indic., of* MAY: *used with* thou

May·time (mā′tīm′) ***n.*** the month of May: also **May′tide′**

Ma·za·rin (mà zà ran′; *E.* maz′ər in), **Jules** (zhül), Cardinal, (born *Giulio Mazarini*) 1602–61; Fr. statesman & prelate, born in Italy

maze (māz) ***n.*** [< OE. *amasian,* to amaze & pp. *amasod,* puzzled] **1.** a confusing, intricate network of winding pathways; labyrinth, specif. one used in psychological experiments and tests **2.** a state of confusion or bewilderment —**ma′zy** ***adj.*** **-zi·er, -zi·est —ma′zi·ly** ***adv.*** **—ma′zi·ness** ***n.***

‡**maz·el tov** (mä′z'l tōv′, tôf′) [Heb. (often via Yid.)] good luck: an expression of congratulation: also **maz′el·tov′, maz′zel tov**

ma·zur·ka, ma·zour·ka (mə zur′kə, -zoor′-) ***n.*** [Pol. *mazurka,* woman from Mazovia, region of C Poland] **1.** a lively Polish dance like the polka **2.** music for this, generally in 3/4 or 3/8 time

Maz·zi·ni (mät tsē′nē, mäd dzē′nē), **Giu·sep·pe** (joo zep′pe) 1805–72; It. patriot & revolutionist

M.B.A. Master of Business Administration

MBS Mutual Broadcasting System

M.C. 1. Master of Ceremonies **2.** Member of Congress

Mc·Car·thy·ism (mə kär′thē iz′m) ***n.*** [after J. *McCarthy,* U.S. senator (1946–57)] the use of indiscriminate, often unfounded, accusations, inquisitorial investigative methods, etc., ostensibly in the suppression of communism

Mc·Clel·lan (mə klel′ən), **George Brin·ton** (brin′t'n) 1826–85; Union general in the Civil War

Mc·Cor·mick (mə kôr′mik), **Cyrus Hall** (hôl) 1809–84, U.S. inventor of the reaping machine

Mc·Coy (mə koi′), **the (real)** [Slang] the real person or thing, not a substitute

Mc·In·tosh (mak′in täsh′) ***n.*** [after J. *McIntosh,* of Ontario, Can., who first cultivated it (1796)] a late-maturing variety of red apple: also **McIntosh Red**

Mc·Kin·ley (mə kin′lē), **Mount** [after ff.] mountain in SC Alas.: highest peak in N. America: 20,320 ft.

Mc·Kin·ley (mə kin′lē), **William** 1843–1901; 25th president of the U.S. (1897–1901): assassinated

Md *Chem.* mendelevium

Md., MD Maryland

M.D. [L. *Medicinae Doctor*] Doctor of Medicine

Mdlle. *pl.* **Mdlles.** Mademoiselle

Mdm. *pl.* **Mdms.** Madam

Mdme. *pl.* **Mdmes.** Madame

mdse. merchandise

MDu. Middle Dutch

me (mē) ***pron.*** [OE.] *objective case of* I: also used colloquially as a predicate complement with a linking verb (Ex.: that's *me*)

ME. Middle English

Me., ME Maine

M.E. 1. Master of Education **2.** Mechanical Engineer **3.** Methodist Episcopal **4.** Mining Engineer

‡**me·a cul·pa** (mē′ə kul′pə, mā′ä kool′pä) [L.] (by) my fault; I am to blame

mead[1] (mēd) ***n.*** [OE. *meodu*] an alcoholic drink made from fermented honey, often with spices, fruit, malt, etc. added

mead[2] (mēd) ***n.*** [OE. *mæd*] [Poet.] a meadow

Mead (mēd), **Lake** [after E. *Mead* (1858–1936), U.S. engineer] lake in SE Nev. & NW Ariz., formed by the Hoover Dam on the Colorado River

Mead (mēd), **Margaret** 1901–78; U.S. anthropologist

Meade (mēd), **George Gordon** 1815–72; Union general in the Civil War

mead·ow (med′ō) ***n.*** [< OE. *mædwe,* oblique case of *mæd*] **1.** a piece of grassland, esp. one whose grass is grown for use as hay **2.** low, level grassland near a stream, etc. —**mead′ow·y** ***adj.***

mead·ow·lark (-lärk′) ***n., pl.*** **-larks′, -lark′**: see PLURAL, II, D, 1 either of two N. American songbirds having brown-and-black upper parts and a yellow breast

mea·ger (mē′gər) ***adj.*** [< OFr. < L. *macer,* lean] **1.** thin; lean; emaciated **2.** of poor quality or small amount; inadequate Also, Brit., **mea′gre —mea′ger·ly** ***adv.*** **—mea′ger·ness** ***n.***

meal[1] (mēl) ***n.*** [OE. *mæl*] **1.** any of the times for eating; breakfast, lunch, dinner, etc. **2.** the food served or eaten at such a time

meal[2] (mēl) ***n.*** [OE. *melu*] **1.** any edible grain, coarsely ground and unbolted *[cornmeal]* **2.** any substance similarly ground or powdered

meal·ie (mēl′ē) ***n.*** [Afrik. *milje* < Port. *milho,* millet] in South Africa, **1.** [*pl.*] *same as* CORN[1] (sense 2) **2.** an ear of corn

meal ticket 1. a ticket entitling one to a specified value in meals at a particular restaurant **2.** [Slang] a person, job, skill, etc. depended on as one's means of support

meal·time (mēl′tīm′) ***n.*** the usual time for serving or eating a meal

meal·y (mēl′ē) ***adj.*** **meal′i·er, meal′i·est 1.** like meal; powdery, dry, soft, etc. **2.** of or containing meal **3.** covered with meal **4.** floury in color; pale **5.** mealy-mouthed —**meal′i·ness** ***n.***

meal·y-mouthed (-mouthd′, -moutht′) ***adj.*** evasive, euphemistic, insincere, etc. in what one says

mean[1] (mēn) ***vt.*** **meant** (ment), **mean′ing** [OE. *mænan*] **1.** to have in mind; intend; purpose *[he means to go]* **2.** *a)* to intend for a certain person or purpose *[a gift meant for you]* *b)* to destine *[he was meant to be a doctor]* **3.** to intend to express or imply *[to say what one means]* **4.** to signify; denote *[the German word "ja" means "yes"]* —***vi.*** **1.** to have a purpose in mind: chiefly in **mean well,** to have good intentions **2.** to have a (specified) degree of importance, effect, etc. *[she means little to him]* —**mean well by** to have good intentions toward

mean[2] (mēn) ***adj.*** [OE. (*ge*)*mæne*] **1.** low in quality, value, or importance; poor *[paid no mean sum]* **2.** poor in appearance; shabby *[a mean dwelling]* **3.** ignoble; base; petty **4.** stingy; miserly **5.** bad-tempered; unmanageable: said of a horse, etc. **6.** contemptibly bad-tempered, selfish, etc. **7.** humiliated **8.** [Colloq.] in poor health **9.** [Slang] hard to cope with; difficult —**mean′ly** ***adv.*** **—mean′ness** ***n.***

mean[3] (mēn) ***adj.*** [< OFr. < L. *medianus* < *medius,* middle] **1.** halfway between extremes; intermediate as to quantity, quality, etc. **2.** average; middling —***n.*** **1.** what is between extremes; intermediate state, quality, course, etc. **2.** moderation **3.** *Math. a)* a number between the smallest and largest values of a set of quantities, obtained by some prescribed method: unless otherwise qualified, *same as* ARITHMETIC MEAN *b)* the second or third term of a four-term proportion See also MEANS

me·an·der (mē an′dər) ***n.*** [< L. < Gr. *maiandros* < the name of a winding river in Asia Minor] **1.** [*pl.*] windings or convolutions, as of a stream **2.** an aimless wandering —***vi.*** **1.** to take a winding course: said of a stream **2.** to wander aimlessly or idly —**me·an′drous** (-drəs) ***adj.***

mean·ie, mean·y (mē′nē) ***n., pl.*** **mean′ies** [Colloq.] a person who is mean, selfish, cruel, etc.

mean·ing (mē′niŋ) ***n.*** **1.** what is meant; what is intended to be, or in fact is, signified, indicated, etc.; import, sense, or significance *[the meaning of a word]* **2.** [Archaic] intention —***adj.*** **1.** that has meaning; significant **2.** intending

mean·ing·ful (-fəl) ***adj.*** full of meaning; having significance or purpose —**mean′ing·ful·ly** ***adv.*** **—mean′ing·fulness** ***n.***

mean·ing·less (-lis) ***adj.*** having no meaning; without significance or purpose —**mean′ing·less·ly** ***adv.*** **—mean′ingless·ness** ***n.***

means (mēnz) ***n.pl.*** [< MEAN[3], *n.*] **1.** [*with sing. or pl. v.*] that by which something is done or obtained; agency *[a fast means of travel]* **2.** resources or wealth *[a person of means]* —**by all means 1.** without fail **2.** certainly —**by any means** in any way possible; somehow —**by means of** by using; with the aid of —**by no (manner of) means** not at all; certainly not —**means to an end** a method of getting what one wants

mean (solar) time time having exactly equal divisions

means test a financial investigation of a person's eligibility for welfare aid, public housing, etc.

meant (ment) *pt. & pp. of* MEAN[1]

mean·time (mēn′tīm′) ***adv.*** **1.** in or during the intervening time **2.** at the same time —***n.*** the intervening time Also, and for adv. now usually, **mean′while′** (-hwīl′)

mea·sles (mē′z'lz) ***n.pl.*** [*with sing. v.*] [ME. *maseles,* ? infl. by ME. *mesel,* leper < OFr. < L. *misellus,* wretch] **1.** an acute, infectious, communicable virus disease, characterized by small red spots on the skin, high fever, nasal discharge, etc., and occurring most frequently in childhood **2.** any of various similar but milder diseases; esp., rubella (called *German measles*)

mea·sly (mēz′lē) ***adj.*** **-sli·er, -sli·est 1.** infected with measles **2.** [Colloq.] contemptibly slight, worthless, or skimpy

meas·ur·a·ble (mezh′ər ə b'l) ***adj.*** that can be measured —**meas′ur·a·bil′i·ty** ***n.*** **—meas′ur·a·bly** ***adv.***

meas·ure (mezh′ər, mā′zhər) ***n.*** [< OFr. *mesure* < L. *mensura* < pp. of *metiri,* to measure] **1.** the extent, dimensions, capacity, etc. of anything, esp. as determined by a standard **2.** a determining of extent, dimensions, etc.; measurement **3.** *a)* unit of measurement, as an inch, yard, or bushel *b)* any standard of valuation; criterion **4.** a system of measurement *[dry measure]* **5.** an instrument or container for measuring *[a quart measure]* **6.** a definite quantity measured out **7.** an extent or degree not to be exceeded *[remain within measure]* **8.** proportion, quantity, or degree *[in large measure]* **9.** course of action; step *[reform measures]* **10.** a statute; law **11.** *a)* rhythm in verse; meter *b)* a metrical unit; foot of verse **12.** a dance or dance movement **13.** [*pl.*] *Geol.* strata: now chiefly in **coal measures** **14.** *Music a)* the notes or rests, or both, contained between two bars on the staff *b)* musical time —***vt.*** **-ured, -ur·ing 1.** to find out or estimate the extent, dimensions, etc. of, esp. by a standard **2.** to set apart or mark off by measuring (often with *off* or *out*) **3.** to make a judgment of

by comparing *[to measure one's foe]* **4.** to bring into comparison or rivalry (*against*) **5.** to be a device for measuring *[a clock measures time]* —*vi.* **1.** to get or take measurements **2.** to be of specified measurements **3.** to allow of measurement —**beyond** (or **above**) **measure** exceedingly; extremely —**for good measure** as a bonus or something extra —**in a measure** to some extent; somewhat —**made to measure** custom-made: said of clothes —**measure up** to prove to be qualified —**measure up to** to meet (expectations, a standard, etc.) —**take measures** to do things to accomplish a purpose —**take someone's measure** to estimate someone's ability, character, etc. —**meas′ur·er** *n.*

meas·ured (-ərd, -zhərd) *adj.* **1.** determined by a standard **2.** regular or uniform **3.** *a)* rhythmical *b)* metrical **4.** calculated, deliberate, etc., as speech —**meas′ured·ly** *adv.*

meas·ure·less (mezh′ər lis, mā′zhər-) *adj.* too large to be measurable; vast; immense —**meas′ure·less·ly** *adv.* —**meas′ure·less·ness** *n.*

meas·ure·ment (-mənt) *n.* **1.** a measuring or being measured **2.** extent or quantity determined by measuring **3.** a system of measuring

measuring worm the caterpillar larva of any geometrid moth

meat (mēt) *n.* [OE. *mete*] **1.** food: now dialectal except in **meat and drink** **2.** the flesh of animals used as food; esp., the flesh of mammals and, sometimes, of fowl **3.** the edible, inner part *[the meat of a nut]* **4.** the substance or essence *[the meat of a story]* **5.** [Archaic] a meal —**one's meat** [Slang] something that one especially enjoys or is skillful at *[golf's my meat]* —**meat′less** *adj.*

meat·ball (-bôl′) *n.* a small ball of ground meat, seasoned and cooked, often with sauce, etc.

meat·pack·ing (-pak′iŋ) *n.* the process or industry of slaughtering animals and preparing their meat for market —**meat′pack′er** *n.*

me·a·tus (mē āt′əs) *n., pl.* **-tus·es, -tus** [LL. < L., a passage, pp. of *meare,* to pass] a natural passage or duct in the body, or its opening

meat·y (mēt′ē) *adj.* **meat′i·er, meat′i·est** **1.** of, like, or having the flavor of, meat **2.** full of meat **3.** full of substance; thought-provoking; pithy —**meat′i·ness** *n.*

Mec·ca (mek′ə) religious capital of Saudi Arabia: birthplace of Mohammed, to which Muslims make pilgrimages: pop. c.250,000 —*n.* [*often* **m-**] any place that many people feel drawn to —**Mec′can** *adj., n.*

mech. **1.** mechanical **2.** mechanics

me·chan·ic (mə kan′ik) *adj.* [< L. < Gr. < *mēchanē,* a machine] *rare or archaic var. of* MECHANICAL —*n.* a worker skilled in using tools or in making, operating, and repairing machines

me·chan·i·cal (-i k'l) *adj.* **1.** having to do with, or having skill in the use of, machinery or tools **2.** produced or operated by machinery **3.** of, or in accordance with, the science of mechanics **4.** automatic, as if from force of habit; machinelike —**me·chan′i·cal·ly** *adv.*

mechanical advantage the rates of the output force of a mechanism to the input force

mechanical drawing drawing done, as by a draftsman, with T squares, scales, compasses, etc.

mech·a·ni·cian (mek′ə nish′ən) *n.* a person skilled in the design, operation, care, etc. of machinery

me·chan·ics (mə kan′iks) *n.pl.* [*with sing. v.*] **1.** the branch of physics that deals with the motion of material bodies and the action of forces on bodies: cf. STATICS, DYNAMICS, KINEMATICS **2.** knowledge of machinery **3.** the mechanical aspect; technical part *[the mechanics of writing]*

mech·a·nism (mek′ə niz'm) *n.* [< ModL. < Gr. *mēchanē,* a machine] **1.** the working parts of a machine; works *[the mechanism of a clock]* **2.** *a)* a system whose parts work together as in a machine *[the mechanism of the universe]* *b)* any physical or mental process by which some result is produced **3.** the mechanical aspect; technical part **4.** the theory that all phenomena can ultimately be explained in terms of physics and chemistry —**mech′a·nist** *n.* —**mech′a·nis′tic** *adj.* —**mech′a·nis′ti·cal·ly** *adv.*

mech·a·nize (mek′ə nīz′) *vt.* **-nized′, -niz′ing** **1.** to make mechanical **2.** to do or operate by machinery, not by hand **3.** to bring about the use of machinery in (an industry, etc.) **4.** to equip (an army, etc.) with motor vehicles, tanks, etc. —**mech′a·ni·za′tion** *n.* —**mech′a·niz′er** *n.*

mech·an·o·ther·a·py (mek′ə nō ther′ə pē) *n.* [< Gr. *mēchanē,* a machine + THERAPY] the treatment of disease by mechanical means, such as massage

med. **1.** medical **2.** medicine **3.** medieval **4.** medium

M.Ed. Master of Education

med·al (med′'l) *n.* [< Fr. < It. *medaglia,* ult. < LL. *medialis,* MEDIAL] **1.** a small, flat piece of metal with a design or inscription on it, made to commemorate some event, or awarded for some distinguished action, merit, etc. **2.** a disk bearing a religious symbol, blessed as by a priest and worn as a religious token

med·al·ist (-'l ist, -list) *n.* **1.** a person who designs or makes medals **2.** a person who has been awarded a medal **3.** *Golf* the low scorer in a qualifying round of medal play preliminary to a tournament Also, Brit. sp., **med′al·list**

me·dal·lion (mə dal′yən) *n.* [< Fr. < It.: see MEDAL] **1.** a large medal **2.** any of various designs, carvings, etc. like a medal in shape, used decoratively, as in architecture **3.** a small, thin, round or oval portion of meat, as beef or veal

medal play *Golf* a form of play in which the score is calculated by counting the total number of strokes taken to play the designated number of holes: cf. MATCH PLAY

med·dle (med′'l) *vi.* **-dled, -dling** [< OFr. *medler* < VL. < L. *miscere,* to mix] **1.** to concern oneself with other people's affairs without being asked or needed; interfere (*in* or *with*) **2.** to tamper (*with*) —**med′dler** *n.*

med·dle·some (-səm) *adj.* meddling or inclined to meddle —**med′dle·some·ness** *n.*

Mede (mēd) *n.* a native or inhabitant of Media

Me·de·a (mi dē′ə) *Gr. Myth.* a sorceress who helped Jason get the Golden Fleece

Me·del·lín (me′de yēn′) city in northwestern Colombia: pop. 968,000

Med·ford (med′fərd) [? for the meadlike marshes once there] city in E Mass.: suburb of Boston: pop. 58,000

Me·di·a (mē′dē ə) ancient kingdom in the part of SW Asia that is now NW Iran —**Me′di·an** *adj., n.*

me·di·a (mē′dē ə) *n. alt. pl. of* MEDIUM: see MEDIUM (*n.* 3)

me·di·ae·val (mē′dē ē′v'l, med′ē-, mid′ē-) *adj. same as* MEDIEVAL —**me′di·ae′val·ism** *n.*

me·di·al (mē′dē əl) *adj.* [< LL. < L. *medius,* middle] **1.** of or in the middle; median **2.** average; mean —**me′di·al·ly** *adv.*

me·di·an (-ən) *adj.* [< L. < *medius,* middle] **1.** middle; intermediate **2.** *a)* designating a line from a vertex of a triangle to the middle of the opposite side *b)* designating a line joining the midpoints of the nonparallel sides of a trapezoid **3.** *Statistics* designating the middle number in a series arranged in order of size, or, if there is no middle value, the average of the two middle numbers —*n.* **1.** a median number, point, or line **2.** a strip of land separating opposing traffic on a divided highway: in full, **median strip** —**me′di·an·ly** *adv.*

me·di·ate (mē′dē āt′; *for adj.* -it) *vi.* **-at′ed, -at′ing** [< LL. pp. of *mediare* < L. *medius,* middle] **1.** to be in an intermediate position **2.** to be an intermediary between persons or sides —*vt.* **1.** to settle by mediation **2.** to be the medium for bringing about (a result) —*adj.* dependent on, acting by, or connected through some intervening agency —**me′di·ate·ly** *adv.* —**me′di·a′tor** *n.*

me·di·a·tion (mē′dē ā′shən) *n.* a mediating; intervention for settling differences between persons, nations, etc. —**me′di·a′tive** *adj.* —**me′di·a·to′ry** (-ə tôr′ē) *adj.*

med·ic[1] (med′ik) *n.* [Colloq.] **1.** a physician or surgeon **2.** a medical student or intern **3.** a member of a military medical corps

med·ic[2] (med′ik) *n.* [< L. < Gr. *mēdikē* (*poa*), (grass) of Media] any of various leguminous plants, as alfalfa: also sp. **med′ick**

med·i·ca·ble (med′i kə b'l) *adj.* that can be cured, healed, or relieved by medical treatment

Med·i·caid (med′i kād′) *n.* [MEDIC(AL) + AID] [*also* **m-**] a State and Federal public health plan for persons with low income or no income

med·i·cal (med′i k'l) *adj.* [< Fr. < LL. < L. *medicus,* physician] of or connected with the practice or study of medicine —**med′i·cal·ly** *adv.*

medical jurisprudence the application of medical knowledge to questions of law, as in determining cause of death, proper medical practice, etc.

med·i·ca·ment (med′i kə mənt, mə dik′ə-) *n. same as* MEDICATION (sense 2)

Med·i·care (med′i ker′) *n.* [MEDI(CAL) + CARE] [*also* **m-**] a national health program for providing medical and hospital care for the aged from Federal, mostly social security, funds

med·i·cate (med′ə kāt′) *vt.* **-cat′ed, -cat′ing** [< L. pp. of *medicari,* to heal] **1.** to treat with medicine **2.** to add a medicinal substance to —**med′i·ca′tive** *adj.*

med·i·ca·tion (med′ə kā′shən) *n.* **1.** a medicating or being medicated **2.** a medicine; substance for curing or healing, or for relieving pain

Med·i·ci (med′ə chē′; *It.* me′dē chē′) family of rich, powerful bankers, merchants, & rulers of Florence & Tuscany in the 14th to 16th cent.; specif., *a)* **Catherine de'**, 1519–89; queen of Henry II of France (1547–59) *b)* **Lo·ren·zo de'** (lô *ren'*tsô de), 1449–92; ruler of Florence (1469–92) *c)* **Maria de'**, 1573–1642; queen of Henry IV of France (1600–10); queen regent (1610–17) —**Med'i·ce'an** (-sē'ən, -chē'ən) ***adj.***

me·dic·i·nal (mə dis''n 'l) ***adj.*** of, or having the properties of, medicine; curing, healing, or relieving —**me·dic'i·nal·ly** ***adv.***

med·i·cine (med'ə s'n; *Brit.* med'sin) ***n.*** [< OFr. < L. < *medicus,* physician] **1.** the science and art of diagnosing, treating, and preventing disease **2.** the branch of this science that makes use of drugs, diet, etc., as distinguished esp. from surgery **3.** any substance, as a drug, used in treating disease, healing, relieving pain, etc. **4.** among North American Indians, *a)* any object, rite, etc. supposed,tf to have supernatural powers as a remedy, preventive, etc. *b)* magical power —***vt.*** **-cined, -cin·ing** to give medicine to —**take one's medicine** to endure just punishment, etc.

medicine ball a large, heavy, leather-covered ball, tossed from one person to another for exercise

medicine man among North American Indians, etc., a man supposed to have supernatural powers of curing disease and controlling spirits; shaman

med·i·co (med'i kō') ***n., pl.*** **-cos'** [It.] [Colloq.] **1.** a doctor **2.** a medical student

me·di·e·val (mē'dē ē'v'l, med'ē-, mid'ē-) ***adj.*** [< L. *medius,* middle + *aevum,* age] of, like, characteristic of, or suggestive of the Middle Ages —**me'di·e'val·ly** ***adv.***

Medieval Greek the Greek language as it was used in the Middle Ages, from c.600–c.1500 A.D.

me·di·e·val·ism (-iz'm) ***n.*** **1.** medieval spirit, beliefs, customs, etc. **2.** devotion to these **3.** a belief, custom, etc. of the Middle Ages

me·di·e·val·ist (-ist) ***n.*** **1.** a specialist in medieval history, literature, art, etc. **2.** a person devoted to medieval customs, beliefs, etc.

Medieval Latin the Latin language used in Europe in the Middle Ages, from c.600–c.1500 A.D.

Me·di·na (mə dē'nə) city in NW Saudi Arabia: site of Mohammed's tomb: pop. c.60,000

me·di·o·cre (mē'dē ō'kər, mē'dē ō'kər) ***adj.*** [< Fr. < L. *mediocris* < *medius,* middle + *ocris,* a peak] **1.** neither very good nor very bad; ordinary; average **2.** not good enough; inferior

me·di·oc·ri·ty (mē'dē äk'rə tē) ***n., pl.*** **-ties** **1.** a being mediocre **2.** mediocre ability or attainment **3.** a person of mediocre abilities, etc.

med·i·tate (med'ə tāt') ***vt.*** **-tat'ed, -tat'ing** [< L. pp. of *meditari*] **1.** [Rare] to study; ponder **2.** to plan or intend —***vi.*** to think deeply and continuously; reflect —**med'i·ta'tive** ***adj.*** —**med'i·ta'tive·ly** ***adv.*** —**med'i·ta'tor** ***n.***

med·i·ta·tion (med'ə tā'shən) ***n.*** **1.** act of meditating; deep reflection, esp. on sacred matters **2.** [*often pl.*] oral or written material, as a sermon, based on meditation

Med·i·ter·ra·ne·an (med'i tə rā'nē ən) ***adj.*** [< L. < *medius,* middle + *terra,* land] **1.** of the Mediterranean Sea or nearby regions **2.** designating or of a style of furniture made to simulate the massive lines and ornate carving of a kind of Renaissance furniture —***n.*** a person who lives near the Mediterranean Sea

Mediterranean Sea large sea surrounded by Europe, Africa, & Asia: c.2,300 mi. long

me·di·um (mē'dē əm) ***n., pl.*** **-di·ums;** also (except sense 7), and for sense 3 usually, **-di·a** (-ə) [L., neut. of *medius,* middle] **1.** *a)* something intermediate *b)* a middle state or degree; mean **2.** an intervening thing through which a force acts **3.** any means, agency, etc.; specif., a means of communication that reaches the general public and carries advertising: in this sense, a singular form **media** (*pl.* **medias**) is now sometimes heard **4.** any surrounding substance in which bodies exist **5.** environment **6.** a nutritive substance, as agar, for cultivating bacteria, etc. **7.** a person through whom communications are supposedly sent from the spirits of the dead **8.** any material or technique as used in art **9.** a liquid mixed with pigments to give fluency —***adj.*** **1.** intermediate in quality, amount, degree, size, etc. **2.** neither rare nor well-done: said of meat

medium frequency any radio frequency between 300 kilohertz and 3 megahertz

med·lar (med'lər) ***n.*** [< OFr. < L. < Gr. *mespilon*] **1.** a small tree of the rose family, growing in Europe and Asia **2.** its applelike fruit, eaten when partly decayed

med·ley (med'lē) ***n., pl.*** **-leys** [< OFr. < pp. of *medler:* see MEDDLE] **1.** a mixture of things not usually placed together **2.** a musical piece made up of passages from other works

me·dul·la (mi dul'ə) ***n., pl.*** **-dul'las, -dul'lae** (-ē) [L., the marrow] **1.** *Anat. a) same as* MEDULLA OBLONGATA *b)* the inner substance of an organ *c)* bone marrow **2.** *Bot. same as* PITH (*n.* 1) —**med·ul·lar·y** (med'ə ler'ē, mej'-) ***adj.***

medulla ob·lon·ga·ta (äb'lôŋ gät'ə, -gāt'-) [ModL., oblong medulla] the widening continuation of the spinal cord forming the lowest part of the brain: it controls breathing, circulation, etc.

Me·du·sa (mə dōō'sə, -dyōō'-; -zə) *Gr. Myth.* one of the three Gorgons, slain by Perseus —***n.*** [**m-**] *pl.* **-sas, -sae** (-sē, -zē) *Zool. same as* JELLYFISH —**me·du'san** ***adj., n.***

meed (mēd) ***n.*** [OE. *med*] [Archaic] a merited reward

meek (mēk) ***adj.*** [< ON. *miukr,* gentle] **1.** patient and mild; not inclined to anger or resentment **2.** too submissive; spineless; spiritless —**meek'ly** ***adv.*** —**meek'ness** ***n.***

meer·schaum (mir'shəm, -shôm) ***n.*** [G. < *meer,* sea + *schaum,* foam] **1.** a soft, white, claylike mineral used for tobacco pipes, etc. because heat-resistant **2.** a pipe made of this

meet[1] (mēt) ***vt.*** **met, meet'ing** [OE. *metan*] **1.** to come upon; esp., to come face to face with **2.** to be present at the arrival of *[*to *meet* a bus*]* **3.** to come into contact, connection, etc. with *[*the ball *met* the bat*]* **4.** *a)* to come into the presence of *b)* to be introduced to; get acquainted with *c)* to keep an appointment with **5.** *a)* to contend with *b)* to face *[*to *meet* angry words with a laugh*]* *c)* to deal with effectively *[*to *meet* an objection*]* **6.** to experience *[*to *meet* disaster*]* **7.** to come within the perception of (the eye, ear, etc.) **8.** *a)* to comply with; satisfy (a demand, etc.) *b)* to pay (a bill, etc.) —***vi.*** **1.** to come together, as from different directions **2.** to come into contact, connection, etc. **3.** to become acquainted; be introduced **4.** to be opposed in or as in battle; fight **5.** to be united **6.** to assemble **7.** to come together for discussion, etc. (*with*) —***n.*** **1.** a meeting, gathering, etc. *[*a track *meet]* **2.** the people who meet or the place of meeting —**meet with** **1.** to experience **2.** to receive **3.** to encounter

meet[2] (mēt) ***adj.*** [< OE. (*ge*)*mæte,* fitting] [Now Rare] suitable; proper; fit —**meet'ly** ***adv.***

meet·ing (mēt'iŋ) ***n.*** **1.** a coming together of persons or things **2.** an assembly; gathering of people **3.** an assembly or place of assembly for worship **4.** a series of horse or dog races **5.** a point of contact; junction

meet·ing·house (-hous') ***n.*** a building used for public meetings, esp. for public worship

meg·a- [Gr. < *megas,* great] *a combining form meaning:* **1.** large, great, powerful *[megaphone]* **2.** a million (of) *[megaton]* Also, before a vowel, **meg-**

meg·a·death (meg'ə deth') ***n.*** [see MEGA-] one million dead persons, as from a hypothetical nuclear explosion

meg·a·hertz (-hurts') ***n., pl.*** **-hertz'** [see MEGA-] one million hertz: formerly **meg'a·cy'cle** (-sī'k'l)

meg·a·lo- [ModL. < Gr. < *megas,* large] *a combining form meaning:* **1.** large, great, powerful *[megalomania]* **2.** abnormal enlargement

meg·a·lo·ma·ni·a (meg'ə lō mā'nē ə, -mān'yə) ***n.*** [ModL.: see prec. & MANIA] a mental disorder characterized by delusions of grandeur, wealth, power, etc. —**meg'a·lo·ma'ni·ac'** (-ak') ***adj., n.*** —**meg'a·lo·ma·ni'a·cal** (-mə nī'ə k'l) ***adj.*** —**meg'a·lo·man'ic** (-man'ik) ***adj.***

meg·a·lop·o·lis (meg'ə läp'ə ləs) ***n.*** [Gr., great city] a vast, heavily populated urban area, including many cities —**meg'a·lo·pol'i·tan** (-lə päl'ə t'n) ***adj., n.***

meg·a·phone (meg'ə fōn') ***n.*** [see MEGA-] a large, funnel-shaped device for increasing the volume of the voice and directing it —***vt., vi.*** **-phoned', -phon'ing** to magnify or direct (the voice) with a megaphone —**meg'a·phon'ic** (-fän'ik) ***adj.***

meg·a·ton (-tun') ***n.*** [see MEGA-] the explosive force of a million tons of TNT —**meg'a·ton'nage** ***n.***

me·grim (mē'grəm) ***n.*** [< OFr.: see MIGRAINE] **1.** [Archaic] a whim; fancy **2.** [*pl.*] [Rare] low spirits

mei·o·sis (mī ō'sis) ***n.*** [ModL. < Gr. < *meioun,* to make smaller] the process of nuclear division in the formation of germ cells that halves the number of chromosomes present in the somatic cells of an animal or plant —**mei·ot'ic** (-ät'ik) ***adj.***

Meis·ter·sing·er (mīs'tər siŋ'ər, -ziŋ'ər) ***n., pl.*** **-sing'er** [G., lit., master singer] a member of one of the German guilds organized in the 14th-16th cent. for cultivating music and poetry

Mé·ji·co (me'hē kô') *Sp. name of* MEXICO

Me·kong (mā'käŋ', -kôŋ') river flowing from SW China through Indochina into the South China Sea

mel·a·mine (mel'ə mēn') ***n.*** [G. *melamin*] a white, crystalline compound, $C_3H_6N_6$, used in making synthetic resins

mel·an·cho·li·a (mel'ən kō'lē ə, -kōl'yə) ***n.*** [ModL. < LL.: see ff.] a mental disorder characterized by extreme depression, brooding, etc. —**mel'an·cho'li·ac'** (-kō'lē ak') ***adj., n.***

mel·an·chol·y (mel'ən käl'ē) ***n., pl.*** **-chol'ies** [< OFr. < LL. < Gr. *melancholia* < *melas,* black + *cholē,* bile: orig., referring to black bile as the humor causing this] **1.** *a)* sadness and depression of spirits *b)* a tendency to be sad or depressed **2.** pensiveness *—adj.* **1.** sad and depressed; gloomy **2.** causing sadness or depression **3.** pensive **—mel′an·chol′ic** *adj.* **—mel′an·chol′i·cal·ly** *adv.*

Mel·a·ne·sia (mel′ə nē′zhə, -shə) a major division of the Pacific islands, south of the equator, west of the international date line, & east of Australia & New Guinea

Mel·a·ne·sian (-zhən, -shən) *adj.* of Melanesia, its people, or their languages *—n.* **1.** a member of the dark-skinned native people of Melanesia **2.** the branch of Malayo-Polynesian languages of Melanesia

mé·lange (mā länzh′, -länj′) *n.* [Fr. < *mêler,* to mix] a mixture or medley; hodgepodge

mel·a·nin (mel′ə nin) *n.* [< Gr. *melas,* black + -IN[1]] a brownish-black pigment found in skin, hair, etc.

Mel·ba toast (mel′bə) [after Nellie *Melba* (1861–1931), Australian soprano] [*also* **m-**] slightly stale bread sliced thin and toasted until brown and crisp

Mel·bourne (mel′bərn) seaport in SE Australia: pop. 2,110,000

meld (meld) *vt., vi.* [G. *melden,* to announce] *Card Games* to declare (a combination of cards in one's hand), esp. by putting them face up on the table *—n.* **1.** a melding **2.** the cards melded

me·lee, mê·lée (mā′lā, mā lā′) *n.* [Fr. *mêlée* < OFr.: see MEDLEY] a noisy, confused, hand-to-hand fight among a number of people

mel·io·rate (mēl′yə rāt′) *vt., vi.* **-rat′ed, -rat′ing** [< LL. pp. of *meliorare* < L. *melior,* better] to make or become better; improve **—mel′io·ra·ble** (-yər ə b′l) *adj.* **—mel′io·ra′tion** *n.* **—mel′io·ra′tive** *adj.* **—mel′io·ra′tor** *n.*

mel·lif·lu·ous (mə lif′loo wəs) *adj.* [< L. < *mel,* honey + *fluere,* to flow] sounding sweet and smooth; honeyed [*mellifluous* tones] : also **mel·lif′lu·ent** (-wənt) **—mel·lif′lu·ous·ly** *adv.* **—mel·lif′lu·ous·ness** *n.*

mel·low (mel′ō) *adj.* [prob. < OE. *melu,* MEAL[2]] **1.** soft, sweet, and juicy because ripe: said of fruit **2.** full-flavored; matured: said of wine, etc. **3.** full, rich, soft, and pure: said of sound, light, etc. **4.** moist and rich: said of soil **5.** grown gentle and understanding *—vt., vi.* to make or become mellow **—mel′low·ly** *adv.* **—mel′low·ness** *n.*

me·lo·de·on (mə lō′dē ən) *n.* [G. *melodion* < *melodie,* melody] a small keyboard organ in which air is drawn through metal reeds by means of a bellows

me·lod·ic (mə läd′ik) *adj.* **1.** of or like melody **2.** *same as* MELODIOUS **—me·lod′i·cal·ly** *adv.*

me·lo·di·ous (mə lō′dē əs) *adj.* **1.** containing or producing melody **2.** pleasing to hear; tuneful **—me·lo′di·ous·ly** *adv.* **—me·lo′di·ous·ness** *n.*

mel·o·dist (mel′ə dist) *n.* a singer or composer of melodies

mel·o·dra·ma (mel′ə drä′mə, -dram′ə) *n.* [< Fr., ult. < Gr. *melos,* a song + *drama,* drama] **1.** orig., a sensational or romantic stage play with interspersed songs **2.** now, a drama with exaggerated conflicts and emotions, stereotyped characters, etc. **3.** any sensational, highly emotional action, utterance, etc. **—mel′o·dram′a·tist** (-dram′ə tist) *n.*

mel·o·dra·mat·ic (mel′ə drə mat′ik) *adj.* of or like melodrama; sensational and extravagantly emotional **—mel′o·dra·mat′i·cal·ly** *adv.* **—mel′o·dra·mat′ics** *n.pl.*

mel·o·dy (mel′ə dē) *n., pl.* **-dies** [< OFr. < LL. < Gr. *melōidia* < *melos,* song + *aeidein,* to sing] **1.** any pleasing series of sounds **2.** *Music a)* a sequence of single tones to produce a rhythmic whole; often, a tune, song, etc. *b)* the leading part in a harmonic composition

mel·on (mel′ən) *n.* [< OFr. < LL. *melo* for L. *melopepo* < Gr. < *mēlon,* apple + *pepōn,* melon] the large, juicy, many-seeded fruit of certain trailing plants of the gourd family, as the watermelon, cantaloupe, etc. **—cut a melon** [Slang] to distribute profits, etc., as among stockholders

Mel·pom·e·ne (mel päm′ə nē′) *Gr. Myth.* the Muse of tragedy

melt (melt) *vt., vi.* **melt′ed, melt′ing,** archaic pp. **molt′en** [OE. *meltan, vi., mieltan, vt.*] **1.** to change from a solid to a liquid state, generally by heat **2.** to dissolve; disintegrate **3.** to disappear or cause to disappear gradually (often with *away*) **4.** to merge gradually; blend [the sea *melts* into the sky] **5.** to soften [a tale to *melt* hearts] *—n.* a melting or being melted **—melt down** to melt (previously formed metal) so that it can be cast or molded again **—melt in one's mouth** **1.** to require little chewing **2.** to taste especially delicious **—melt′a·ble** *adj.* **—melt′er** *n.* **—melt′ing·ly** *adv.*

melt·down (-doun′) *n.* a situation in which dangerous radiation is released by a nuclear reactor if the fuel rods melt because of a defect in the cooling system

melting point the temperature at which a specified solid becomes liquid: abbrev. **melt. pt.**

melting pot a country, etc. in which people of various nationalities and races are assimilated

mel·ton (mel′t′n) *n.* [< *Melton* Mowbray, England] a heavy woolen cloth with a short nap

Mel·ville (mel′vil), **Herman** 1819–91; U.S. novelist

Mel·vin (mel′vin) [< ? OE. *mæl,* council + *wine,* friend] a masculine name

mem. **1.** member **2.** memorandum

mem·ber (mem′bər) *n.* [< OE. < L. *membrum*] **1.** a limb or other part or organ of a person, animal, or plant **2.** a distinct part of a whole, as of a series, an equation, a structure, etc. **3.** a person belonging to an organization or group

mem·ber·ship (-ship′) *n.* **1.** the state of being a member **2.** all the members of a group **3.** the number of members

mem·brane (mem′brān) *n.* [L. *membrana* < *membrum,* member] a thin, soft, pliable layer of animal or plant tissue that covers or lines an organ or part **—mem′braned** *adj.* **—mem′bra·nous** (-brə nəs) *adj.* **—mem′bra·nous·ly** *adv.*

me·men·to (mi men′tō, mə-) *n., pl.* **-tos, -toes** [L., imperative of *meminisse,* to remember] anything serving as a reminder; esp., a souvenir

‡**me·men·to mo·ri** (mi men′tō mō′rī, -rē) [L., remember you must die] any reminder of death

mem·o (mem′ō) *n., pl.* **-os** *clipped form of* MEMORANDUM

mem·oir (mem′wär) *n.* [< Fr. *mémoire* < L. *memoria,* MEMORY] **1.** a biography **2.** [*pl.*] an autobiography **3.** [*pl.*] a record of events based on the writer's personal observation or knowledge **4.** a report of a scientific study, etc.

mem·o·ra·bil·i·a (mem′ər ə bil′ē ə, -bil′yə; -bēl′-) *n.pl., sing.* **mem′o·rab′i·le** (-ə rab′ə lē) [L.] things worth remembering or recording and collecting

mem·o·ra·ble (mem′ər ə b′l, mem′rə-) *adj.* worth remembering; notable **—mem′o·ra·bil′i·ty** *n.* **—mem′o·ra·bly** *adv.*

mem·o·ran·dum (mem′ə ran′dəm) *n., pl.* **-dums, -da** (-də) [L.] **1.** *a)* a short note written to help one remember something *b)* a record, as of events, for future use **2.** an informal written communication, as in a business office **3.** a short written statement of the terms of an agreement, contract, or transaction

me·mo·ri·al (mə môr′ē əl) *adj.* [see MEMORY] serving to help people remember some person or event *—n.* **1.** anything meant to help people remember some person or event, as a statue, holiday, etc. **2.** a statement of facts, often with a petition for action, sent to a government, official, etc.

Memorial Day a U.S. holiday (the last Monday in May in most States) in memory of dead servicemen of all wars

me·mo·ri·al·ize (-īz′) *vt.* **-ized′, -iz′ing** **1.** to commemorate **2.** to present a petition to

mem·o·rize (mem′ə rīz′) *vt.* **-rized′, -riz′ing** to commit to memory **—mem′o·ri·za′tion** *n.*

mem·o·ry (mem′ər ē, mem′rē) *n., pl.* **-ries** [< OFr. < L. *memoria* < *memor,* mindful] **1.** the power, act, or process of recalling to mind facts or experiences **2.** the total of what one remembers **3.** a person, thing, etc. remembered **4.** the period over which remembering extends [within the *memory* of living men] **5.** commemoration or remembrance [in *memory* of his son] **6.** reputation after death **7.** the components of a computer, etc. that retain information

Mem·phis (mem′fis) **1.** capital of ancient Egypt, on the Nile just south of Cairo **2.** [after prec.] city in SW Tenn., on the Mississippi: pop. 646,000 (met. area 910,000)

mem·sa·hib (mem sä′ib, -säb′) *n.* [Anglo-Ind.: *mem* for MA'AM + Hindi *ṣāḥib,* SAHIB] in India formerly, a term of address for a European married woman as used by servants, etc.

men (men) *n. pl. of* MAN

men·ace (men′is) *n.* [< OFr. < L. *minacia* < *minax,* threatening < *minari,* to threaten] **1.** a threat or threatening **2.** anything threatening harm or evil **3.** [Colloq.] an annoying person *—vt., vi.* **-aced, -ac·ing** to threaten **—men′ac·ing·ly** *adv.*

me·nad (mē′nad) *n. alt. sp. of* MAENAD

mé·nage, me·nage (mā näzh′, mə-) *n.* [< Fr. < OFr. *manage* < *manoir* (see MANOR)] **1.** a household **2.** the management of a household

me·nag·er·ie (mə naj′ər ē, -nazh′-) *n.* [< Fr. < *ménage:* see prec.] **1.** a collection of wild animals kept in cages for exhibition **2.** a place where such animals are kept

Men·cken (meŋ′k′n), **H(enry) L(ouis)** 1880–1956; U.S. writer, editor, & critic

mend (mend) *vt.* [ME. *menden,* shortened from *amenden,* AMEND] **1.** to repair; restore to good condition **2.** to make better; improve; reform [*mend* your manners] **3.** to atone for: now only in **least said, soonest mended** *—vi.* **1.** to improve, esp. in health **2.** to grow together again or heal, as a fracture —*n.* **1.** a mending; improvement **2.** a mended place —**on the mend** improving, esp. in health —**mend′a·ble** *adj.* —**mend′er** *n.*

men·da·cious (men dā′shəs) *adj.* [< L. *mendax* (gen. *mendacis*)] not truthful; lying; false —**men·da′cious·ly** *adv.* —**men·da′cious·ness** *n.* —**men·dac·i·ty** (-das′ə tē) *n., pl.* **-ties**

Men·del (men′d'l), **Gre·gor Jo·hann** (grā′gôr yō′hän) 1822–84; Austrian monk & botanist: see MENDEL'S LAWS —**Men·de′li·an** (-dē′lē ən, -dēl′yən) *adj.* —**Men′del·ism** *n.* —**Men′del·ist** *adj., n.*

men·de·le·vi·um (men′də lē′vē əm) *n.* [ModL., after D.I. *Mendeleev* (1834–1907), Russ. chemist] a radioactive chemical element of the actinide series: symbol, Md; at. wt., 258(?); at. no., 101

Mendel's laws the principles of hereditary phenomena discovered and formulated by Mendel, holding that characters, as height, color, etc., are inherited in definite, predictable combinations

Men·dels·sohn (men′d'l sən; *G.* -dəls zōn′), **Fe·lix** (fā′liks) 1809–47; Ger. composer

men·di·cant (men′di kənt) *adj.* [< L. prp. of *mendicare*, to beg] asking for alms; begging *[mendicant* friars*]* —*n.* **1.** a beggar **2.** a mendicant friar —**men′di·can·cy, men·dic·i·ty** (mən dis′ə tē) *n.*

Men·e·la·us (men′ə lā′əs) *Gr. Myth.* a king of Sparta, brother of Agamemnon, and husband of Helen

men·folk (men′fōk′) *n.pl.* [Dial. or Colloq.] men: also **men′folks′**

men·ha·den (men hād′'n) *n., pl.* **-den, -dens:** see PLURAL, II, D, 2 [< Algonquian name] a sea fish related to the herring, common along the Atlantic coast: used for making oil and fertilizer

me·ni·al (mē′nē əl, mēn′yəl) *adj.* [< Anglo-Fr. < OFr. *meisniee*, household < L. *mansio:* see MANSION] **1.** of or fit for servants **2.** servile; low; mean —*n.* **1.** a domestic servant **2.** a servile, low person —**me′ni·al·ly** *adv.*

me·nin·ges (mə nin′jēz) *n.pl., sing.* **me·ninx** (mē′niŋks) [ModL., pl. of *meninx* < Gr. *mēninx*, a membrane] the three membranes that envelop the brain and spinal cord —**me·nin′ge·al** (-jē əl) *adj.*

men·in·gi·tis (men′in jīt′is) *n.* inflammation of the meninges, esp. as the result of infection —**men′in·git′ic** (-jit′ik) *adj.*

me·nis·cus (mi nis′kəs) *n., pl.* **-nis′cus·es, -nis′ci** (-nis′ī, -kī) [ModL. < Gr. *mēniskos*, dim. of *mēnē*, the moon] **1.** a crescent-shaped thing **2.** a lens convex on one side and concave on the other **3.** the curved upper surface of a column of liquid

MENISCUS (left, mercury; right, water)

Men·non·ite (men′ə nīt′) *n.* [after *Menno* Simons (1496?–1561?), a leader] a member of an evangelical Christian sect: Mennonites oppose the taking of oaths and military service, and favor plain dress

‡me·no (me′nô) *adv.* [It.] *Music* less

men·o·pause (men′ə pôz′) *n.* [< Gr. *mēn*, month + *pauein*, to make cease] the permanent cessation of menstruation; change of life —**men′o·paus′al** *adj.*

men·o·rah (mə nō′rə, -nôr′ə) *n.* [Heb., lamp stand] a candelabrum with seven branches, a symbol of Judaism, or with nine branches, used during Hanuka

Me·nor·ca (me nôr′kä) *Sp. name of* MINORCA

Me·not·ti (mə nät′ē), **Gian Car·lo** (jän kär′lō) 1911– ; It. operatic composer, in U.S. since 1928

men·ses (men′sēz) *n.pl.* [L., pl. of *mensis*, month] the periodic flow of blood from the uterus: normally every four weeks, from puberty to menopause

Men·she·vik (men′shə vik′) *n., pl.* **-viks′, -vik′i** (-vē′kē) [Russ. < *menshe*, the smaller] [*also* **m-**] a member of the minority faction of the Social Democratic Party of Russia, which opposed the Bolsheviks from 1903 on —**Men′she·vism** *n.* —**Men′she·vist** *n., adj.*

men·stru·ate (men′stroo wāt′, -strāt) *vi.* **-at′ed, -at′ing** [< L. pp. of *menstruare* < *mensis*, month] to have a discharge of the menses —**men′stru·al** *adj.* —**men′stru·a′tion** *n.*

men·sur·a·ble (men′shər ə b'l, -sər-) *adj.* that can be measured; measurable —**men′sur·a·bil′i·ty** *n.*

men·su·ra·tion (men′shə rā′shən, -sə-) *n.* [< LL. < pp. of *mensurare* < L. *mensura*, MEASURE] **1.** a measuring **2.** the branch of mathematics dealing with the determination of length, area, or volume —**men′su·ra′tive** (-rāt′iv) *adj.*

-ment (mənt, mint) [< OFr. < L. *-mentum*] *a suffix meaning:* **1.** a result or product *[improvement]* **2.** a means or instrument *[adornment]* **3.** the act, process, or art *[movement]* **4.** the state, fact, or degree *[disappointment]*

men·tal (men′t'l) *adj.* [< MFr. < LL. < L. *mens* (gen. *mentis*), the mind] **1.** of or for the mind *[mental* aids*]* **2.** done by or in the mind *[mental* arithmetic*]* **3.** mentally ill *[*a *mental* patient*]* **4.** for the mentally ill *[*a *mental* hospital*]* **5.** having to do with telepathy, etc. —**men′tal·ly** *adv.*

mental healing the treatment of diseases by mental concentration or hypnotic suggestion

men·tal·i·ty (men tal′ə tē) *n., pl.* **-ties** mental capacity, power, or activity; mind

mental reservation a qualification (of a statement) that one thinks but does not express

mental retardation congenital subnormality of intelligence: it ranges from *mild* (IQ of 70–85) to *moderate* (IQ of 50–70) and *severe* (IQ below 50): these terms have replaced *moron, imbecile,* and *idiot:* formerly called **mental deficiency**

men·thol (men′thōl, -thôl, -thäl) *n.* [G. < L. *mentha*, MINT[2] + *-ol*, -OL[1]] a white, waxy, crystalline alcohol, $C_{10}H_{19}OH$, obtained from oil of peppermint and used in medicine, cosmetics, etc.

men·tho·lat·ed (men′thə lāt′id) *adj.* containing or impregnated with menthol

men·tion (men′shən) *n.* [OFr. < L. *mentio* < stem of *mens*, the mind] **1.** a brief reference or statement **2.** a citing for honor —*vt.* **1.** to refer to or speak about briefly or incidentally **2.** to cite for honor —**make mention of** to mention —**not to mention** without even mentioning —**men′tion·a·ble** *adj.*

Men·tor (men′tər, -tôr) *Gr. Myth.* the loyal friend and adviser of Odysseus —*n.* [**m-**] **1.** a wise, loyal adviser **2.** a teacher or coach

men·u (men′yoo, mān′-) *n., pl.* **men′us** [Fr., small, detailed < L. *minutus:* see MINUTE[2]] **1.** a detailed list of the foods served at a meal or available at a restaurant **2.** the foods served

me·ow, me·ou (mē ou′, myou) *n.* [echoic] the characteristic vocal sound made by a cat —*vi.* to make such a sound

me·per·i·dine (mə per′ə dēn′) *n.* a synthetic narcotic, $C_{15}H_{21}O_2N$, used as a sedative and analgesic

Meph·i·stoph·e·les (mef′ə stäf′ə lēz′) a devil in medieval legend to whom Faust sells his soul for knowledge and power —*n.* a crafty, powerful, sardonic person Also **Me·phis·to** (mə fis′tō) —**Me·phis·to·phe·le·an, Me·phis·to·phe·li·an** (mef′is tə fē′lē ən, mə fis′-) *adj.*

me·phit·ic (mə fit′ik) *adj.* [< L. *mephitis*, a stench] **1.** bad-smelling **2.** poisonous; noxious

me·pro·ba·mate (mə prō′bə māt′) *n.* a bitter, white powder, $C_9H_{18}N_2O_4$, used as a tranquilizer

mer·can·tile (mur′kən til, -tīl′, -tēl′) *adj.* [Fr. < It. < *mercante*, a merchant < L. prp. of *mercari:* see MERCHANT] **1.** of or characteristic of merchants or trade; commercial **2.** of mercantilism

mer·can·til·ism (-iz'm) *n.* the earlier doctrine that the economic interests of a nation could be strengthened by the government through protective tariffs, by a balance of exports over imports, etc. —**mer′can·til·ist** *n., adj.*

Mer·ca·tor projection (mər kāt′ər) [after G. *Mercator* (1512–94), Fl. cartographer] a method of making maps on which the meridians are equally spaced parallel straight lines and the parallels of latitude are parallel straight lines spaced farther apart as they get farther from the equator: areas are increasingly distorted toward the poles

mer·ce·nar·y (mur′sə ner′ē) *adj.* [< L. < *merces*, wages] **1.** working or done for payment only; venal; greedy **2.** designating a soldier serving for pay in a foreign army —*n., pl.* **-nar′ies** **1.** a mercenary soldier **2.** a hireling —**mer′ce·nar′i·ly** *adv.* —**mer′ce·nar′i·ness** *n.*

mer·cer (mur′sər) *n.* [< OFr. < *merz*, goods < L. *merx*] [Brit.] a dealer in textiles

mer·cer·ize (mur′sə rīz′) *vt.* **-ized′, -iz′ing** [after J. *Mercer* (1791–1866), Eng. calico dealer] to treat (cotton thread or fabric) with a caustic soda solution in order to strengthen it, give it a silky luster, and make it more receptive to dyes

mer·chan·dise (mur′chən dīz′; *for n., also* -dīs′) *n.* [< OFr. < *marchant:* see ff.] things bought and sold; goods; wares —*vt., vi.* **-dised′, -dis′ing** **1.** to buy and sell; carry on trade in (some kind of goods) **2.** to promote and organize the sale of (a product) Also sp. **merchandize** —**mer′chan·dis′er** *n.*

mer·chant (mur′chənt) *n.* [OFr. *marchant*, ult. < L. *mercari*, to trade < *merx*, wares] **1.** a person whose business is buying and selling goods for profit **2.** a person who sells goods at retail; storekeeper —*adj.* **1.** of or used in trade **2.** of the merchant marine —*vt.* to deal in; trade

mer·chant·a·ble (-ə b'l) *adj.* that can be sold; marketable

mer·chant·man (-mən) *n., pl.* **-men** a ship used in commerce

merchant marine **1.** all the ships of a nation that are used in commerce **2.** their personnel

‡mer·ci (mer sē′) *interj.* [Fr.] thank you

Mer·cia (mur′shə) former Anglo-Saxon kingdom in central and southern England

Mer·cian (-shən) *adj.* of Mercia, its people, etc. —*n.* **1.** a native or inhabitant of Mercia **2.** the Old English dialect of the Mercians

mer·ci·ful (mur′si fəl) *adj.* full of mercy; having, feeling, or showing mercy; lenient; clement —**mer′ci·ful·ly** *adv.* —**mer′ci·ful·ness** *n.*

mer·ci·less (-lis) *adj.* without mercy; having, feeling, or showing no mercy; pitiless; cruel —**mer′ci·less·ly** *adv.* —**mer′ci·less·ness** *n.*

mer·cu·ri·al (mər kyoor′ē əl) *adj.* **1.** [M-] of Mercury (the god or planet) **2.** of or containing mercury **3.** caused by the use of mercury **4.** having qualities suggestive of mercury; quick, quick-witted, changeable, fickle, etc. —*n.* a drug or preparation containing mercury —**mer·cu′ri·al·ly** *adv.* —**mer·cu′ri·al·ness** *n.*

mer·cu·ric (mər kyoor′ik) *adj.* of or containing mercury, esp. with a valence of two

mercuric chloride a very poisonous, white, crystalline compound, $HgCl_2$, used as an antiseptic, etc.

Mer·cu·ro·chrome (mər kyoor′ə krōm′) [see MERCURY, *n.* & -CHROME] *a trademark for* a compound used as an antiseptic in the form of a red solution —*n.* [m-] this solution

mer·cu·rous (mər kyoor′əs, mur′kyoo rəs) *adj.* of or containing mercury, esp. with a valence of one

Mer·cu·ry (mur′kyoo rē) [L. *Mercurius*] **1.** *Rom. Myth.* the messenger of the gods, god of commerce, manual skill, eloquence, and cleverness: identified with the Greek god Hermes **2.** the smallest planet in the solar system and the one nearest to the sun: diameter, c.3,000 mi. —*n.* [< ML. < L., Mercury] [m-] **1.** a heavy, silver-white metallic chemical element, liquid at ordinary temperatures; quicksilver: it is used in thermometers, dentistry, etc.: symbol, Hg; at. wt., 200.59; at. no., 80 **2.** the mercury column in a thermometer or barometer

mer·cu·ry-va·por lamp (-vā′pər) a discharge tube containing mercury vapor

mer·cy (mur′sē) *n., pl.* **-cies** [< OFr. < L. *merces,* payment, reward] **1.** a refraining from harming or punishing offenders, enemies, etc.; kindness in excess of what may be expected **2.** imprisonment rather than death for those found guilty of capital crimes **3.** a disposition to forgive or be kind **4.** the power to forgive or be kind; clemency **5.** kind or compassionate treatment **6.** a fortunate thing; blessing —*interj.* a mild exclamation of surprise, annoyance, etc. —**at the mercy of** completely in the power of

mere[1] (mir) *adj. superl.* **mer′est** [< L. *merus,* unmixed, pure] nothing more or other than; only (as said to be) *[a mere* boy*]*

mere[2] (mir) *n.* [OE.] **1.** [Poet.] a lake or pond **2.** [Obs.] the sea or an arm of the sea

-mere (mir) [< Gr. *meros,* a part] *a combining form meaning* part

Mer·e·dith (mer′ə dith), **George** 1828–1909; Eng. novelist & poet

mere·ly (mir′lē) *adv.* **1.** no more than; and nothing else; only **2.** [Obs.] absolutely

mer·e·tri·cious (mer′ə trish′əs) *adj.* [< L. < *meretrix,* a prostitute < *mereri,* to serve for hire] **1.** alluring by false, showy charms; flashy; tawdry **2.** superficially plausible; specious —**mer′e·tri′cious·ly** *adv.* —**mer′e·tri′cious·ness** *n.*

mer·gan·ser (mər gan′sər) *n., pl.* **-sers, -ser:** see PLURAL, II, D, 1 [ModL. < L. *mergus,* diver + *anser,* goose] a large, fish-eating, diving duck with a long, slender beak and, usually, a crested head

merge (murj) *vi., vt.* **merged, merg′ing** [L. *mergere,* to dip] **1.** to lose or cause to lose identity by being absorbed, swallowed up, or combined **2.** to unite; combine

merg·er (mur′jər) *n.* a merging; specif., the combination of several companies, corporations, etc. in one

Mer·i·den (mer′i dən) [MERRY + DEN (in obs. sense of "valley")] city in C Conn.: pop. 57,000

me·rid·i·an (mə rid′ē ən) *adj.* [< OFr. < L. < *meridies,* noon, ult. < *medius,* middle + *dies,* day] **1.** of or at noon **2.** of or passing through the highest point in the daily course of any heavenly body **3.** of or at the highest point, as of power **4.** of or along a meridian —*n.* **1.** orig., the highest point reached by a heavenly body in its course **2.** the highest point of power, prosperity, etc.; zenith **3.** a great circle of the celestial sphere passing through the poles of the heavens and the zenith and nadir of any given point **4.** *a)* a great circle of the earth passing through the geographical poles and any given point on the earth's surface *b)* the half of such a circle between the poles *c)* any of the lines of longitude on a globe or map, representing such a half circle

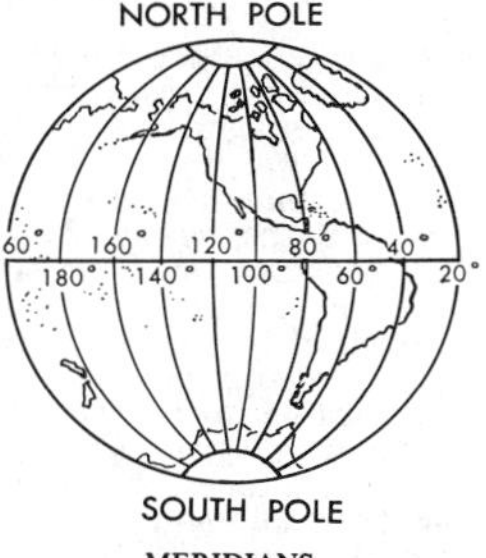

MERIDIANS

me·ringue (mə raŋ′) *n.* [Fr. < ?] **1.** egg whites beaten stiff and mixed with sugar, often browned in the oven and used as a covering for pies, cakes, etc. **2.** a baked shell made of this

me·ri·no (mə rē′nō) *n., pl.* **-nos** [Sp., prob. < (Beni) *Merin,* name of a nomadic Berber tribe] **1.** one of a hardy breed of sheep with long, fine wool **2.** the wool **3.** a fine, soft yarn made from this wool **4.** a soft, thin cloth made of this yarn —*adj.* designating or of this sheep, wool, etc.

mer·it (mer′it) *n.* [< OFr. < L. *meritum* < pp. of *mereri,* to earn] **1.** [*sometimes pl.*] the state, fact, or quality of deserving well or ill; desert **2.** worth; value; excellence **3.** something deserving reward, praise, etc. **4.** a mark, badge, etc. awarded for excellence **5.** [*pl.*] essential rightness or wrongness *[*to decide a case on its *merits]* —*vt.* to deserve —**mer′it·less** *adj.*

mer·i·toc·ra·cy (mer′ə täk′rə sē) *n.* an intellectual elite, based on academic achievement —**mer′it·o·crat′** *n.* —**mer′it·o·crat′ic** *adj.*

mer·i·to·ri·ous (mer′ə tôr′ē əs) *adj.* having merit; deserving reward, praise, etc. —**mer′i·to′ri·ous·ly** *adv.* —**mer′i·to′ri·ous·ness** *n.*

merit system a system of hiring and promoting people to civil service positions on the basis of merit as determined by competitive examinations

merl, merle (murl) *n.* [< OFr. < L. *merula*] [Archaic or Poet.] the European blackbird

Merle (murl) [Fr., prob. < *merle,* blackbird: see prec.] a masculine or feminine name

Mer·lin (mur′lin) *Arthurian Legend* a magician and seer, helper of King Arthur

mer·maid (mur′mād′) *n.* [see MERE[2] & MAID] **1.** an imaginary sea creature with the body of a beautiful woman and the tail of a fish **2.** a woman who swims well —**mer′man′** *n.masc., pl.* **-men′**

-mer·ous (mər əs) [< Gr. *meros,* a part] *a suffix meaning* having (a specified number of) parts

Mer·o·vin·gi·an (mer′ə vin′jē ən, -jən) *adj.* designating or of the Frankish line of kings who reigned in Gaul (ancient France) from c. 500 to 751 A.D. —*n.* a king of this line

mer·ri·ment (mer′i mənt) *n.* merrymaking; gaiety and fun; mirth; hilarity

mer·ry (mer′ē) *adj.* **-ri·er, -ri·est** [OE. *myrge*] **1.** full of fun and laughter; gay; mirthful **2.** festive *[*the *merry* month of May*]* —**make merry** to have fun —**mer′ri·ly** *adv.* —**mer′ri·ness** *n.*

mer·ry-an·drew (mer′ē an′droo) *n.* [MERRY + ANDREW: orig. unc.] a buffoon; clown

mer·ry-go-round (-gō round′) *n.* **1.** a circular, revolving platform with wooden animals and seats on it, used as an amusement ride; carrousel **2.** a whirl or busy round, as of pleasure

mer·ry·mak·ing (-mā′kiŋ) *n.* **1.** a making merry and having fun; conviviality; festivity **2.** a merry festival or entertainment —*adj.* taking part in merrymaking; gay and festive —**mer′ry·mak′er** *n.*

Mer·sey (mur′zē) river in NW England, flowing into the Irish Sea at Liverpool

Mer·thi·o·late (mər thī′ə lāt′) [*sodium ethyl-*) *mer*(*curi-*)*thio*(*salicy*)*late*] *a trademark for* a compound used chiefly in solutions as an antiseptic for surface wounds

Mer·vin (mur′vin) [prob. var. of MARVIN] a masculine name: var. *Mervyn, Merwin, Merwyn*

Me·sa (mā′sə) [see ff.] city in SC Ariz., near Phoenix: pop. 152,000

me·sa (mā′sə) *n.* [Sp. < L. *mensa,* a table] a small, high plateau or flat tableland with steep sides, esp. in the SW U.S.

mes·cal (mes kal′) *n.* [Sp. *mezcal* < Nahuatl *mexcalli*] **1.** a colorless, alcoholic, Mexican liquor made from the fermented juice of various agaves **2.** any plant from which this liquor is made **3.** a small cactus whose buttonlike tops (**mescal buttons**) when chewed cause hallucinations

mes·ca·line (mes′kə lēn′, -lin) *n.* [prec. + -INE[4]] a white, crystalline alkaloid, $C_{11}H_{17}O_3N$, a psychedelic drug obtained from mescal buttons

mes·dames (mā däm′; *Fr.* mā dȧm′) *n. pl. of* MADAME, MADAM (sense 1), or MRS.: abbrev. **Mmes.**

mes·de·moi·selles (mā′də mə zel′; *Fr.* mād mwȧ zel′) *n. pl. of* MADEMOISELLE: abbrev. **Mlles.**

me·seems (mē sēmz′) *v.impersonal pt.* **me·seemed′** [Archaic] (it) seems to me: also **me·seem′eth**

mes·en·ter·y (mez′'n ter′ē, mes′-) *n., pl.* **-ter′ies** [< ML. < Gr. < *mesos,* middle + *enteron,* intestine] a supporting membrane or membranes enfolding some internal organ and attaching it to the body wall or to another organ —**mes'en·ter'ic** *adj.*

mesh (mesh) *n.* [prob. < MDu. *maesche*] **1.** any of the open spaces of a net, screen, sieve, etc. **2.** [*pl.*] the threads, cords, etc. forming these openings **3.** a net or network **4.** a netlike, woven material, as that used for stockings **5.** a structure of interlocking metal links **6.** anything that entangles or snares —*vt., vi.* **1.** to entangle or become entangled **2.** to engage or become engaged: said of gears or gear teeth **3.** to interlock —**in mesh** in gear; interlocked —**mesh'y** *adj.*

‡**me·shu·ga** (mə shoog'ə) *adj.* [< Yid. < Heb.] crazy; insane: also **meshugga, meshugah, etc.**

mesh·work (mesh'wurk') *n.* meshes; network

mes·mer·ism (mez'mər iz'm, mes'-) *n.* [after F. A. *Mesmer* (1734–1815), G. physician] **1.** hypnotism **2.** irresistible attraction —**mes·mer'ic** (-mer'ik) *adj.* —**mes·mer'i·cal·ly** *adv.* —**mes'mer·ist** *n.*

mes·mer·ize (-īz') *vt.* **-ized', -iz'ing** to hypnotize; esp., to spellbind, or fascinate —**mes'mer·i·za'tion** *n.* —**mes'mer·iz'er** *n.*

mes·o- [< Gr. *mesos,* middle] *a combining form meaning* in the middle, intermediate: also **mes-**

mes·o·blast (mes'ə blast', mez'-) *n.* [MESO- + -BLAST] *same as* MESODERM —**mes'o·blas'tic** *adj.*

mes·o·carp (-kärp') *n.* [MESO- + -CARP] the middle layer of the wall of a ripened ovary or fruit, as the flesh of a plum —**mes'o·car'pic** *adj.*

mes·o·derm (-durm') *n.* [MESO- + -DERM] the middle layer of cells of an embryo, from which the skeleton, muscles, etc. develop —**mes'o·der'mal, mes'o·der'mic** *adj.*

mes·o·lith·ic (mes'ə lith'ik, mez'-) *adj.* [MESO- + -LITHIC] designating or of an old-world cultural period between the paleolithic and neolithic, during which certain animals and plants were domesticated

mes·o·mor·phic (-môr'fik) *adj.* [MESO- + -MORPHIC] designating or of the muscular type of human body, in which the structures developed from the mesoderm predominate —**mes'o·morph'** *n.*

mes·on (mes'än, mez'-; mē'sän, -zän) *n.* [MES(O)- + (ELECTR)ON] an unstable particle between the electron and proton in mass, first observed in cosmic rays —**me·son·ic** (me sän'ik, -zän'-; mē-) *adj.*

Mes·o·po·ta·mi·a (mes'ə pə tā'mē ə) ancient country in SW Asia, between the Tigris & Euphrates rivers: part of modern Iraq —**Mes'o·po·ta'mi·an** *adj., n.*

Mes·o·zo·ic (mes'ə zō'ik, mez'-) *adj.* [MESO- + ZO- + -IC] designating or of a geologic era after the Paleozoic and before the Cenozoic —**the Mesozoic** the Mesozoic Era or its rocks: see GEOLOGY, chart

Mes·quite (mes kēt') [after the *mesquite* trees found there] city in NE Tex.: suburb of Dallas: pop. 67,000

mes·quite, mes·quit (mes kēt', mes'kēt) *n.* [Sp. *mezquite* < Nahuatl *mizquitl*] a thorny tree or shrub common in the SW U.S. and in Mexico: its sugary, beanlike pods are used as fodder

mess (mes) *n.* [< OFr. < L. *missus,* a course (at a meal)] **1.** a quantity of food for a meal or dish **2.** a portion of soft food, as porridge **3.** unappetizing food **4.** *a*) a group of people who regularly have their meals together, as in the army *b*) the meal eaten by such a group **5.** a jumble; hodgepodge **6.** *a*) a state of trouble or difficulty *b*) a state of being untidy or dirty *c*) [Colloq.] a person in either of these states —*vt.* **1.** to supply meals to **2.** to make dirty or untidy; also, to bungle; botch: often with *up* —*vi.* **1.** to eat as one of a mess (sense 4 *a*) **2.** to make a mess **3.** to putter or meddle —**mess around** (or **about**) **1.** to putter around **2.** [Colloq.] to get involved (*with*)

mes·sage (mes'ij) *n.* [OFr. < ML. < pp. of L. *mittere,* to send] **1.** a report, request, etc. sent between persons **2.** a formal, official report [the President's *message* to Congress] **3.** the chief idea that an artist, writer, etc. seeks to communicate in a work —*vt., vi.* **-saged, -sag·ing** to send (as) a message —**get the message** [Colloq.] to get the implications of a hint, etc.

mes·sen·ger (mes''n jər) *n.* [< OFr. *messagier:* see MESSAGE] **1.** a person who carries a message or is sent on an errand **2.** [Archaic] a harbinger

mess hall a room or building where a group, as of soldiers, regularly have their meals

Mes·si·ah (mə sī'ə) [< LL. < Gr. *Messias* < Aram. < Heb. *māshīah,* lit., anointed] **1.** *Judaism* the promised and expected deliverer of the Jews **2.** *Christianity* Jesus Also **Mes·si'as** (-əs) —*n.* [**m-**] any expected savior —**Mes·si·an·ic** (mes'ē an'ik) *adj.*

mes·sieurs (mes'ərz; *Fr.* mā syö') *n. pl. of* MONSIEUR: abbrev. **MM.**: see also MESSRS.

Mes·si·na (mə sē'nə, me-) seaport in NE Sicily, on a strait (**Strait of Messina**) between Sicily & Italy: pop. 269,000

mess jacket a man's short, closefitting jacket, as that worn by waiters or busboys

mess kit the compactly arranged metal or plastic plates and eating utensils carried by a soldier or camper for use in the field: also **mess gear**

mess·mate (mes'māt') *n.* a person with whom one regularly has meals, as in the army

Messrs. (mes'ərz) Messieurs: now used chiefly as the pl. of MR.

mess·y (mes'ē) *adj.* **mess'i·er, mess'i·est** in or like a mess; untidy, disordered, dirty, etc. —**mess'i·ly** *adv.* —**mess'i·ness** *n.*

mes·ti·zo (mes tē'zō) *n., pl.* **-zos, -zoes** [Sp. < LL. *misticius,* of mixed race < L. pp. of *miscere,* to mix] a person of mixed parentage; esp., the offspring of a Spaniard and an American Indian —**mes·ti'za** (-zə) *n.fem.*

met (met) *pt. & pp. of* MEET[1]

met. metropolitan

met·a- [< Gr. *meta,* along with, after, between] *a prefix meaning:* **1.** changed, transposed [*metamorphosis, metathesis*] **2.** after, beyond, higher [*metaphysics*] Also, before a vowel, **met-**

me·tab·o·lism (mə tab'ə liz'm) *n.* [< Gr. *metabolē,* change < *meta,* beyond + *ballein,* to throw] the continuous processes in living organisms and cells, comprising those by which food is built up into protoplasm and those by which protoplasm is broken down into simpler substances or waste matter, with the release of energy for all vital functions —**met·a·bol·ic** (met'ə bäl'ik) *adj.*

me·tab·o·lize (-līz') *vt., vi.* **-lized', -liz'ing** to change by or subject to metabolism —**me·tab'o·liz'a·ble** *adj.*

me·tab·o·lous (-ləs) *adj.* [< Gr. *metabolos,* changeable + -OUS] of or undergoing metamorphosis

met·a·car·pus (met'ə kär'pəs) *n., pl.* **-pi** (-pī) [ModL. < Gr. < *meta,* beyond + *karpos,* the wrist] **1.** the part of the hand consisting of the five bones between the wrist and the fingers **2.** the part of a land vertebrate's forelimb between the carpus and the phalanges —**met'a·car'pal** *adj., n.*

met·al (met''l) *n.* [OFr. < L. *metallum* < Gr. *metallon,* mine] **1.** *a*) any of a class of chemical elements, as iron, gold, aluminum, etc., generally characterized by ductility, luster, conductivity of heat and electricity, and the ability to replace the hydrogen of an acid to form a salt *b*) an alloy of such elements, as brass, bronze, etc. **2.** any substance consisting of metal **3.** material; substance **4.** molten material for making glassware **5.** [Brit.] broken stones, cinders, etc. used as in making roads —*adj.* made of metal —*vt.* **-aled** or **-alled, -al·ing** or **-al·ling** to cover or supply with metal

metal., metall. **1.** metallurgical **2.** metallurgy

metal lath lath of expanded metal or metal mesh

me·tal·lic (mə tal'ik) *adj.* **1.** of, or having the nature of, metal **2.** containing, yielding, or producing metal **3.** like or suggestive of metal [a *metallic* sound] —**me·tal'li·cal·ly** *adv.*

met·al·lif·er·ous (met''l if'ər əs) *adj.* [< L. < *metallum,* metal + *ferre,* to BEAR[1] + -OUS] containing, yielding, or producing metal or ore

met·al·lur·gy (met''l ur'jē) *n.* [ModL. < Gr. < *metallon,* metal, mine + *ergon,* work] the science of separating metals from their ores and preparing them for use, by smelting, refining, etc. —**met'al·lur'gi·cal, met'al·lur'gic** *adj.* —**met'al·lur'gi·cal·ly** *adv.* —**met'al·lur'gist** *n.*

met·al·ware (-wer') *n.* kitchenware, etc. of metal

met·al·work (-wurk') *n.* **1.** things made of metal **2.** the making of such things: also **met'al·work'ing** —**met'al·work'er** *n.*

met·a·mor·phic (met'ə môr'fik) *adj.* of, characterized by, causing, or formed by metamorphism or metamorphosis

met·a·mor·phism (-môr'fiz'm) *n.* **1.** *same as* METAMORPHOSIS **2.** change in the structure of rocks under pressure, heat, etc. which turns limestone into marble, granite into gneiss, etc.

met·a·mor·phose (-fōz, -fōs) *vt., vi.* **-phosed, -phos·ing** to change in form or nature; transform

met·a·mor·pho·sis (-môr'fə sis, -môr fō'sis) *n., pl.* **-ses** (-sēz) [L. < Gr. < *metamorphoun,* to transform < *meta,* over + *morphē,* form] **1.** *a*) change of form or structure, as, in myths, by magic *b*) the form resulting from this **2.** a marked change of character, appearance, etc. **3.** *Biol.* a change in form or function as a result of development; specif., the transformation undergone by various animals after the embryonic state, as of the tadpole to the frog

met·a·phor (met'ə fôr', -fər) *n.* [< Fr. < L. < Gr., ult. < *meta,* over + *pherein,* to carry] a figure of speech that suggests a likeness by speaking of one thing as if it were another, different thing (Ex.: the curtain of night, "all the world's a stage"): cf. SIMILE —**mix metaphors** to use two or more inconsistent metaphors in a single expression (Ex.: the storm of protest was nipped in the bud) —**met'a·phor'i·cal, met'a·phor'ic** *adj.* —**met'a·phor'i·cal·ly** *adv.*

met·a·phys·i·cal (met'ə fiz'i k'l) *adj.* **1.** of, or having the nature of, metaphysics **2.** so subtle as to be hard to understand **3.** supernatural **4.** designating or of the school of early 17th-cent. English poets, whose verse is characterized by subtle and fanciful images —**met′a·phys′i·cal·ly** ***adv.***

met·a·phys·ics (met′ə fiz′iks) ***n.pl.*** [*with sing. v.*] [< ML. < Gr. (*ta*) *meta* (*ta*) *physika*, lit., (that) after (the) *Physics* (in Aristotle's works)] **1.** the branch of philosophy that deals with first principles and seeks to explain the nature of being and of the origin and structure of the world **2.** speculative philosophy in general —**met′a·phy·si′cian** (-fə zish′ən) ***n.***

me·tas·ta·sis (mə tas′tə sis) ***n., pl.*** **-ses′** (-sēz′) [ModL. < LL. < Gr. < *meta*, after + *histanai*, to place] the spread of disease from one part of the body to another unrelated to it, as of cancer cells by way of the bloodstream —**met·a·stat·ic** (met′ə stat′ik) ***adj.*** —**met′a·stat′i·cal·ly** ***adv.***

me·tas·ta·size (-sīz′) ***vi.*** **-sized′, -siz′ing** to spread to other parts of the body by metastasis

met·a·tar·sus (met′ə tär′səs) ***n., pl.*** **-tar′si** (-sī) [ModL. < Gr. *meta-*, after + *tarsus*, sole of the foot] **1.** the part of the human foot consisting of the five bones between the ankle and toes **2.** the part of a land vertebrate's hind limb, between the tarsus and phalanges —**met′a·tar′sal** ***adj., n.***

me·tath·e·sis (mə tath′ə sis) ***n., pl.*** **-ses′** (-sēz′) [LL. < Gr. < *meta*, over + *tithenai*, to place] transposition or interchange; specif., the transposition of letters or sounds in a word, as in *clasp* (from Middle English *clapse*) —**met·a·thet·ic** (met′ə thet′ik), **met′a·thet′i·cal** ***adj.***

met·a·zo·an (met′ə zō′ən) ***n.*** [ModL. *metazoa* (see META- & -ZOA) + -AN] any of the very large zoological division made up of all animals whose bodies are composed of many cells arranged into definite organs —***adj.*** of the metazoans

mete[1] (mēt) ***vt.*** **met′ed, met′ing** [OE. *metan*] **1.** to allot; apportion (usually with *out*) **2.** [Archaic] to measure

mete[2] (mēt) ***n.*** [OFr. < L. *meta*] a boundary

me·tem·psy·cho·sis (mi temp′si kō′sis, -tem′-; met′əm-sī-) ***n., pl.*** **-ses** (-sēz) [LL. < Gr. < *meta*, over + *empsychoun*, to put a soul into < *en*, in + *psychē*, soul] the supposed passing of the soul at death into another body; transmigration

me·te·or (mēt′ē ər) ***n.*** [< ML. < Gr. < *meteōra*, things in the air < *meta*, beyond + *eōra*, a hovering in the air] **1.** the flash and streak of light, the ionized trail, etc. occurring when a meteoroid is heated by its entry into the earth's atmosphere: popularly called *shooting* (or *falling*) *star* **2.** loosely, a meteoroid or meteorite

me·te·or·ic (mēt′ē ôr′ik, -är′-) ***adj.*** **1.** atmospheric or meteorological **2.** of a meteor or meteors **3.** like a meteor; momentarily brilliant, flashing, or swift —**me′te·or′i·cal·ly** ***adv.***

me·te·or·ite (mēt′ē ə rīt′) ***n.*** that part of a relatively large meteoroid that falls to earth as a mass of metal or stone —**me′te·or·it′ic** (-rit′ik) ***adj.***

me·te·or·oid (mēt′ē ə roid′) ***n.*** any of the many small, solid bodies traveling through outer space, which are seen as meteors when they enter the earth's atmosphere

me·te·or·o·log·i·cal (mēt′ē ər ə läj′i k'l) ***adj.*** **1.** of weather or climate **2.** of meteorology: also **me′te·or·o·log′ic** —**me′te·or·o·log′i·cal·ly** ***adv.***

me·te·or·ol·o·gy (mēt′ē ə räl′ə jē) ***n.*** [< Gr.: see METEOR & -LOGY] the science of the atmosphere and its phenomena; study of weather and climate —**me′te·or·ol′o·gist** ***n.***

me·ter[1] (mēt′ər) ***n.*** [< OFr. < L. < Gr. *metron*, measure] **1.** *a*) rhythm in verse; measured, patterned arrangement of syllables, primarily according to stress and length *b*) the specific rhythmic pattern of a stanza **2.** rhythm in music; esp., the division into measures, or bars, having a uniform number of beats **3.** the basic unit of length in the metric system, equal to 39.37 inches

me·ter[2] (mēt′ər) ***n.*** **1.** [< METE[1] + -ER] a person who measures **2.** [< ff.] *a*) an instrument or apparatus for measuring and recording the quantity or rate of flow of gas, electricity, water, etc. passing through it *b*) *same as* PARKING METER —***vt.*** to measure or record with a meter

-me·ter (mēt′ər, mi tər) [Fr. *-mètre* or ModL. *-metrum*, both < Gr. *metron*, a measure] *a suffix meaning:* **1.** a device for measuring *[barometer]* **2.** *a*) (a specified number of) meters *[kilometer]* *b*) (a specified fraction of) a meter *[centimeter]* **3.** having (a specified number of) metrical feet *[pentameter]*

me·ter·age (mēt′ər ij) ***n.*** measurement as by a meter, or the charge for this

me·ter-kil·o·gram-sec·ond (-kil′ə gram sek′ənd) ***adj.*** designating or of a system of measurement in which the meter, kilogram, and second are used as the units of length, mass, and time, respectively

Meth. Methodist

meth·a·done (meth′ə dōn′) ***n.*** [an acronym of the chemical name] a synthetic narcotic drug, $C_{21}H_{27}ON$, sometimes used in the treatment of hard-drug addicts

meth·ane (meth′ān) ***n.*** [METH(YL) + -ANE] a colorless, odorless, flammable gas, CH_4, present in marsh gas, firedamp, and natural gas: it is used as a fuel, etc.

methane series a series of saturated hydrocarbons having the general formula C_nH_{2n+2}: methane is the first member

meth·a·nol (meth′ə nôl′, -nōl′) ***n.*** [METHAN(E) + -OL[1]] a colorless, flammable, poisonous liquid, CH_3OH, obtained by the destructive distillation of wood and used as a fuel, solvent, and antifreeze, and in the making of paints, etc.

me·thinks (mi thiŋks′) ***v.impersonal pt.*** **me·thought′** [< OE. < *me*, to me + *thyncth*, it seems < *thyncan*, to seem] [Archaic] it seems to me

meth·od (meth′əd) ***n.*** [< Fr. < L. < Gr. *methodos*, pursuit < *meta*, after + *hodos*, a way] **1.** a way of doing anything; mode; process; esp., a regular, orderly procedure or way of teaching, investigating, etc. **2.** a system in doing things or handling ideas **3.** regular, orderly arrangement

me·thod·i·cal (mə thäd′i k'l) ***adj.*** characterized by method; orderly; systematic: also **me·thod′ic** —**me·thod′i·cal·ly** ***adv.*** —**me·thod′i·cal·ness** ***n.***

Meth·od·ism (meth′ə diz'm) ***n.*** **1.** the doctrines, organization, etc. of the Methodists **2.** [**m-**] excessive adherence to systematic procedure

Meth·od·ist (-dist) ***n.*** a member of a Protestant Christian denomination that developed from the evangelistic teachings of John and Charles Wesley —***adj.*** of or characteristic of the Methodists or Methodism: also **Meth′od·is′tic**

meth·od·ize (-dīz′) ***vt.*** **-ized′, -iz′ing** to make methodical; systematize —**meth′od·iz′er** ***n.***

meth·od·ol·o·gy (meth′ə däl′ə jē) ***n., pl.*** **-gies** [ModL.: see METHOD & -LOGY] **1.** the science of method, or orderly arrangement **2.** a system of methods, as in any particular science —**meth′od·o·log′i·cal** (-də läj′i k'l) ***adj.*** —**meth′od·o·log′i·cal·ly** ***adv.*** —**meth′od·ol′o·gist** ***n.***

me·thought (mi thôt′) *pt. of* METHINKS

Me·thu·se·lah (mə thōō′zə lə, -thyōō′-) *Bible* one of the patriarchs, who lived 969 years: Gen. 5:27

meth·yl (meth′əl) ***n.*** [< Fr., ult. < Gr. *methy*, wine + *hylē*, wood] the monovalent hydrocarbon radical CH_3, normally existing only in combination

methyl alcohol *same as* METHANOL

methyl chloride a gas, CH_3Cl, which when compressed becomes a sweet, transparent liquid: it is used as a refrigerant and local anesthetic

me·tic·u·lous (mə tik′yoo ləs) ***adj.*** [L. *meticulosus*, fearful < *metus*, fear] extremely or excessively careful about details; scrupulous or finicky —**me·tic′u·lous·ly** ***adv.*** —**me·tic′u·lous·ness, me·tic′u·los′i·ty** (-läs′ə tē) ***n.***

mé·tier (mā tyā′) ***n.*** [Fr. < OFr. *mestier* < L.: see MINISTRY] a trade, profession, or occupation

me·ton·y·my (mə tän′ə mē) ***n., pl.*** **-mies** [< LL. < Gr. < *meta*, change + *onyma*, name] use of the name of one thing for that of another associated with it (Ex.: "the press" for "journalists") —**met·o·nym·ic** (met′ə nim′ik) ***adj.***

me·tre (mē′tər) ***n.*** *chiefly Brit. sp. of* METER[1]

met·ric (met′rik) ***adj.*** **1.** *same as* METRICAL **2.** *a*) of the meter (unit of length) *b*) designating or of the system of measurement based on the meter: see METRIC SYSTEM

met·ri·cal (-ri k'l) ***adj.*** **1.** of or composed in meter or verse **2.** of, involving, or used in measurement; metric —**met′ri·cal·ly** ***adv.***

met·ri·ca·tion (met′rə kā′shən) ***n.*** the process of changing over to the metric system of weights and measures

met·ri·cize (met′rə sīz′) ***vt.*** **-cized′, -ciz′ing** to change into the metric system of weights and measures

metric system a decimal system of weights and measures in which the gram, the meter, and the liter are the basic units of weight, length, and capacity, respectively: see TABLES OF WEIGHTS AND MEASURES in Supplements

metric ton a measure of weight equal to 1,000 kilograms or 2,204.62 pounds

met·ro·nome (met′rə nōm′) ***n.*** [< Gr. *metron*, measure + *nomos*, law] a clockwork device with an inverted pendulum that beats time, as in setting a musical tempo, at a rate determined by the position of a sliding weight on the pendulum —**met′ro·nom′ic** (-näm′ik) ***adj.***

METRONOME

me·trop·o·lis (mə träp′'l is) ***n., pl.*** **-lis·es** [L. < Gr. < *mētēr*, a mother + *polis*, a city] **1.** the main city, often the capital, of a country, state, etc. **2.** any large city or center of population, culture, etc. **3.** the main diocese of an ecclesiastical province

met·ro·pol·i·tan (met′rə päl′ə t'n) ***adj.*** **1.** of or constituting a metropolis (senses 1

& 2) **2.** designating or of a metropolitan (sense 2) **3.** designating or of a population area consisting of a central city and smaller surrounding communities *—n.* **1.** a person who lives in and is wise in the ways of a metropolis (senses 1 & 2) **2.** *a)* an archbishop having authority over the bishops of a church province *b)* a bishop just below a Patriarch in the Orthodox Eastern Church

-me·try (mə trē) [< Gr. < *metron,* measure] *a terminal combining form meaning* the process, art, or science of measuring *[geometry]*

Met·ter·nich (met′ər nik; *G.* met′ər niH′), Prince **(Klemens Wenzel Nepomuk Lothar) von** 1773–1859; Austrian statesman & diplomat

met·tle (met′'l) *n.* [var. of METAL, used figuratively] quality of character; spirit; courage; ardor **—on one's mettle** prepared to do one's best

met·tle·some (met′'l səm) *adj.* full of mettle; spirited

Meuse (myo͞oz; *Fr.* möz) river flowing from NE France, through Belgium & the Netherlands into the North Sea

mev, Mev (mev) *n., pl.* **mev, Mev** [M(ILLION) E(LECTRON-) V(OLTS)] a unit of energy equal to one million electron-volts

mew[1] (myo͞o) *n.* [< OFr. < *muer* < L. *mutare,* to change] **1.** a cage, as for hawks while molting **2.** a secret place or den See also MEWS *—vt.* to confine in or as in a cage

mew[2] (myo͞o) *n.* [echoic] the characteristic vocal sound made by a cat *—vi.* to make this sound

mew[3] (myo͞o) *n.* [OE. *mæw*] a sea gull

mewl (myo͞ol) *vi.* [freq. of MEW[2]] to cry weakly, like a baby; whimper or whine **—mewl′er** *n.*

mews (myo͞oz) *n.pl.* [*usually with sing. v.*] [< MEW[1]] [Chiefly Brit.] **1.** stables or carriage houses, now often converted into dwellings, as along an alley **2.** such an alley

Mex. 1. Mexican **2.** Mexico

Mex·i·cal·i (mek′sə kal′ē) city in Baja California, NW Mexico, on the U.S. border: pop. 427,000

Mex·i·can (mek′si kən) *adj.* of Mexico, its people, their dialect of Spanish, or their culture *—n.* **1.** a native or inhabitant of Mexico **2.** Nahuatl

Mexican War a war between the U.S. and Mexico (1846–48)

Mex·i·co (mek′si kō′) **1.** country in N. America, south of the U.S.: 760,373 sq. mi.; pop. 48,313,000; cap. Mexico City **2. Gulf of,** arm of the Atlantic, east of Mexico & south of the U.S. Mexican name **Méx·i·co** (me′hē kô′), Spanish name, MÉJICO

Mexico City capital of Mexico, in a federal district, **México, D(istrito) F(ederal),** in the SC part of Mexico: pop. 3,484,000 (of district, 5,584,000)

me·zu·za (mə zo͝o′zə) *n., pl.* **-zot** (-zōt), **-zas** [Heb. *mĕzūzāh,* doorpost] *Judaism* a small scroll inscribed with Biblical verses (Deuteronomy 6:4–9 & 11:13–21) and attached in a case to the doorpost of the home: also sp. **me·zu′zah**

mez·za·nine (mez′ə nēn′, mez′ə nēn′) *n.* [Fr. < It. < *mezzano,* middle, ult. < L. *medius*] **1.** a low-ceilinged story between two main stories in a building, usually in the form of a balcony projecting partly over the main floor: also **mezzanine floor 2.** the first few rows of a theater balcony

mez·zo (met′sō, med′zō, mez′ō) *adj.* [It. < L. *medius,* middle] *Music* medium; moderate; half *—adv. Music* moderately; somewhat *—n., pl.* **-zos** *clipped form of:* **1.** MEZZO-SOPRANO **2.** MEZZOTINT

mez·zo-so·pra·no (-sə pran′ō, -prä′nō) *n., pl.* **-nos, -ni** (-ē, -nē) [It.] **1.** a woman's voice or part between soprano and contralto **2.** a singer with such a voice

mez·zo·tint (-tint′) *n.* [< It.: see MEZZO & TINT] **1.** a method of engraving on a copper or steel plate by scraping or polishing parts of a roughened surface to produce impressions of light and shade **2.** an engraving so produced *—vt.* to engrave by this method

MF, M.F., mf, m.f. medium frequency

mf *Music* mezzo forte

mfg. manufacturing

MFr. Middle French

mfr. *pl.* **mfrs.** manufacturer

Mg *Chem.* magnesium

mg, mg. milligram; milligrams

MGr. Medieval (or Middle) Greek

Mgr. 1. Manager **2.** Monseigneur **3.** Monsignor

MHG. Middle High German

MHz, Mhz megahertz

MI Michigan

mi (mē) *n.* [ML.: see GAMUT] *Music* a syllable representing the third tone of the diatonic scale

mi. 1. mile(s) **2.** mill(s)

Mi·am·i (mī am′ē, -ə) [< Fr.] city on the SE coast of Fla.: pop. 347,000 (met. area 1,574,000)

Miami Beach resort city in SE Fla., on an island opposite Miami: pop. 96,000

mi·aow, mi·aou (mē ou′, myou) *n., vi. same as* MEOW

mi·as·ma (mī az′mə, mē-) *n., pl.* **-mas, -ma·ta** (-mə tə) [ModL. < Gr. < *miainein,* to pollute] **1.** a vapor rising as from marshes or decomposing organic matter, formerly supposed to poison the air **2.** an unwholesome atmosphere, influence, etc. **—mi·as′mal, mi′as·mat′ic** (-mat′ik), **mi·as′mic** *adj.*

Mic. Micah

mi·ca (mī′kə) *n.* [ModL. < L., a crumb, infl. by *micare,* to shine] any of a group of minerals that crystallize in thin, somewhat flexible, easily separated layers, resistant to heat and electricity: a transparent form is often called ISINGLASS

Mi·cah (mī′kə) *Bible* **1.** a Hebrew prophet of the 8th cent. B.C. **2.** the book containing his prophecy

mice (mīs) *n. pl. of* MOUSE

Mich. 1. Michaelmas **2.** Michigan

Mi·chael (mī′k'l) [LL. < Gr. < Heb. *mīkhā'ēl,* lit., who is like God?] **1.** a masculine name: dim. *Mike, Mickey* **2.** *Bible* one of the archangels

Mich·ael·mas (-məs) *n.* [see -MAS] the feast of the archangel Michael, celebrated on September 29 **(Michaelmas Day)**

Mi·chel·an·ge·lo (Buonarroti) (mī′k'l an′jə lō′, mik′'l-) 1475–1564; It. sculptor, painter, architect, & poet

Mi·chel·son (mī′k'l s'n), **Albert Abraham** 1852–1931; U.S. physicist, born in Germany

Mich·i·gan (mish′ə gən) [< Fr. < Algonquian, lit., great water] **1.** Middle Western State of the U.S.: 58,216 sq. mi.; pop. 9,258,000; cap. Lansing: abbrev. **Mich., MI 2. Lake,** one of the Great Lakes, between Mich. & Wis.: 22,178 sq. mi. **—Mich′i·gan′der** (-gan′dər) *n.* **—Mich′i·ga′ni·an** (-gā′nē ən), **Mich′i·gan·ite′** (-īt′) *adj., n.*

Mick·ey Finn (mik′ē fin′) [*also* **m- f-**] [Slang] a drink of liquor to which a drug or purgative has been secretly added: often shortened to **Mick′ey, mick′ey** *n., pl.* **-eys**

Mickey Mouse [< a trademark for a cartoon character created by Walt Disney (1901–66), U.S. motion-picture producer] [Slang] **[m- m-]** childish, oversimplified, unrelated to reality, etc.

mick·le (mik′'l) *adj., adv., n.* [OE. *micel*] [Scot.] much

Mic·mac (mik′mak) *n., pl.* **-macs, -mac** [Algonquian, lit., allies] a member of a tribe of Indians in Newfoundland and the Maritime Provinces of Canada

mi·cra (mī′krə) *n. alt. pl. of* MICRON

mi·cro- [< Gr. < *mikros,* small] *a combining form meaning:* **1.** little; small; minute *[microfilm]* **2.** enlarging or amplifying *[microscope, microphone]* **3.** microscopic *[microchemistry]* **4.** one millionth part of (a specified unit) *[microgram]*

mi·crobe (mī′krōb) *n.* [Fr. < Gr. *mikros,* small + *bios,* life] a microscopic organism; esp., a disease germ **—mi·cro′bic, mi·cro′bi·al, mi·cro′bi·an** *adj.*

mi·cro·bi·ol·o·gy (mī′krō bī äl′ə jē) *n.* the branch of biology that deals with microorganisms **—mi′cro·bi′o·log′i·cal** (-ə läj′ə k'l) *adj.* **—mi′cro·bi·ol′o·gist** *n.*

mi·cro·ceph·a·ly (mī′krə sef′'l ē) *n.* [MICRO- + CEPHAL(O)- + -Y[3]] a condition in which the head or cranial capacity is abnormally small **—mi′cro·ceph′a·lous, mi′cro·ce·phal′ic** (-sə fal′ik) *adj.*

mi·cro·chem·is·try (-kem′is trē) *n.* the chemistry of microscopic or submicroscopic quantities or objects

mi·cro·com·put·er (mī′krō kəm pyo͞ot′ər) *n.* a very small computer controlled by a tiny silicon chip containing all the logical elements for handling data, performing calculations, etc.

mi·cro·cop·y (mī′krə käp′ē) *n., pl.* **-cop′ies** a copy of printed matter, etc. produced in very greatly reduced size, as by microfilming

mi·cro·cosm (mī′krə käz'm) *n.* a little world; miniature universe; specif., man, a community, etc. regarded as a miniature of the world **—mi′cro·cos′mic** *adj.*

mi·cro·fiche (mī′krə fēsh′) *n.* [Fr. < *micro-,* MICRO- + *fiche,* a small card] a small sheet of microfilm, containing a number of pages of microcopy

mi·cro·film (-film′) *n.* film on which documents, printed pages, etc. are photographed in a reduced size as for easier storage *—vt., vi.* to photograph on microfilm

mi·cro·form (-fôrm′) *n.* any form of photographically reduced document, print, etc., as microfilm

mi·cro·gram (-gram′) *n.* one millionth of a gram: also, chiefly Brit. sp., **mi′cro·gramme′**

mi·cro·groove (-gro͞ov′) *n.* a very narrow needle groove, as for a long-playing phonograph record

mi·crom·e·ter (mī kräm′ə tər) *n.* [< Fr.: see MICRO- & -METER] **1.** an instrument for measuring very small distances, angles, etc., used on a telescope or microscope **2.** *same as* MICROMETER CALIPER

MICROMETER

micrometer caliper (or **calipers**) calipers with a micrometer screw, for extremely accurate measurement

micrometer screw a finely threaded screw of definite pitch, with a head graduated to show how much the screw has been moved in or out

mi·crom·e·try (-trē) *n.* measurement with micrometers

mi·cron (mī′krän) ***n.,*** *pl.* **-crons, -cra** (-krə) [ModL. < Gr. *mikros,* small] one millionth of a meter, or one thousandth of a millimeter

Mi·cro·ne·sia (mī′krə nē′zhə, -shə) a major division of the Pacific islands, north of the equator, west of the international date line, & east of the Philippines

Mi·cro·ne·sian (-zhən, -shən) ***adj.*** of Micronesia, its people, their language, etc. —***n.*** **1.** a native of Micronesia **2.** any of the Malayo-Polynesian languages of Micronesia

mi·cro·or·gan·ism (mī′krō ôr′gə niz′m) ***n.*** any microscopic or ultramicroscopic animal or vegetable organism; esp., any of the bacteria, viruses, etc.

mi·cro·phone (mī′krə fōn′) ***n.*** [MICRO- + -PHONE] an instrument containing a device that converts the mechanical energy of sound waves into an electric signal, as for radio —**mi′cro·phon′ic** (-fän′ik) ***adj.***

mi·cro·print (-print′) ***n.*** a photographic copy so greatly reduced that it can be read only through a magnifying device

mi·cro·scope (mī′krə skōp′) ***n.*** [< ModL.: see MICRO- & -SCOPE] an instrument consisting essentially of a lens or combination of lenses, for making very small objects, as microorganisms, look larger

mi·cro·scop·ic (mī′krə skäp′ik) ***adj.*** **1.** so small as to be invisible or obscure except through a microscope; minute **2.** of or with a microscope **3.** like or suggestive of a microscope Also **mi′cro·scop′i·cal** —**mi′cro·scop′i·cal·ly** ***adv.***

mi·cros·co·py (mī kräs′kə pē; *occas.* mī′krə skō′pē) ***n.*** the use of a microscope; investigation by means of a microscope —**mi·cros′co·pist** ***n.***

mi·cro·wave (mī′krə wāv′) ***adj.*** **1.** designating or of the electromagnetic spectrum lying between the far infrared and some lower frequency limit, usually between 300,000 and 300 megahertz **2.** designating an oven that cooks quickly by causing microwaves to penetrate the food, generating internal heat —***n.*** any electromagnetic wave of microwave frequency —***vt.*** **-waved′, -wav′ing** to cook in a microwave oven

mic·tu·rate (mik′choo rāt′) ***vi.*** **-rat′ed, -rat′ing** [< L. pp. of *micturire* < *mingere,* to urinate] to urinate —**mic′tu·ri′tion** (-rish′ən) ***n.***

mid[1] (mid) ***adj.*** [OE. *midd*] **1.** *same as* MIDDLE **2.** *Phonet.* produced with the tongue in a position midway between high and low: said of some vowels, as (e)

mid[2] (mid) ***prep.*** [Poet.] amid: also **'mid**

mid- *a combining form meaning* middle or middle part of *[midbrain, midday]*

mid·air (-er′) ***n.*** any point in space, not in contact with the ground or other surface

Mi·das (mī′dəs) *Gr. Myth.* a king of Phrygia able to turn everything that he touched into gold

mid·brain (mid′brān′) ***n.*** the middle part of the brain

mid·day (mid′dā′) ***n.*** [OE. *middæg*] the middle part of the day; noon —***adj.*** of midday

mid·den (mid′'n) ***n.*** [prob. < Scand.] **1.** [Brit.] a dunghill or refuse heap **2.** *short for* KITCHEN MIDDEN

mid·dle (mid′'l) ***adj.*** [OE. *middel*] **1.** halfway between two given points, times, limits, etc.; also, equally distant from the ends, etc.; in the center **2.** in between; intermediate **3.** [M-] *Geol.* designating a division, as of a period, between *Upper* and *Lower* **4.** [M-] *Linguis.* designating a stage in language development intermediate between *Old* and *Modern [Middle* English*]* —***n.*** **1.** a point or part halfway between extremes; middle point, time, etc. **2.** something intermediate **3.** the middle part of the body; waist —***vt., vi.*** **-dled, -dling** to put in the middle

middle age the time of life between youth and old age: now usually the years from about 40 to about 65 —**mid′dle-aged′** ***adj.***

Middle Ages the period of European history between ancient and modern times, 476 A.D.–c.1450 A.D.

Middle America **1.** Mexico, Central America, and, sometimes, the West Indies **2.** the American middle class, esp. of the Middle West

Middle Atlantic States New Jersey, New York, & Pennsylvania

mid·dle·brow (mid′'l brou′) ***n.*** [Colloq.] a person regarded as having the conventional, anti-intellectual tastes or opinions of the middle class —***adj.*** [Colloq.] of or for a middlebrow

middle C the musical note of the first leger line below the treble staff and the first above the bass staff

middle class the social class between the aristocracy or very wealthy and the lower working class —**mid′dle-class′** ***adj.***

middle ear the eardrum and the adjacent cavity containing the hammer, the anvil, and the stirrup

Middle East **1.** area from Afghanistan to Egypt, including Arabia, Cyprus, & Asiatic Turkey **2.** sometimes, the Near East, excluding the Balkans —**Middle Eastern**

Middle English the English language as written and spoken between c.1100 and c.1500

Middle French the French language as written and spoken between the 14th and 16th centuries

Middle Greek *same as* MEDIEVAL GREEK

Middle High German the High German language as written and spoken between c.1100 and c.1500

Middle Irish the Irish language as written and spoken from the 11th to the 15th century

Middle Latin *same as* MEDIEVAL LATIN

Middle Low German the Low German language as written and spoken between c.1100 and c.1500

mid·dle·man (mid′'l man′) ***n.,*** *pl.* **-men′** (-men′) **1.** a trader who buys commodities from the producer and sells them to the retailer or, sometimes, directly to the consumer **2.** a go-between

mid·dle·most (-mōst′) ***adj.*** *same as* MIDMOST

mid·dle-of-the-road (-əv *th*ə rōd′) ***adj.*** avoiding extremes, esp. of the political left or right

middle school a school between elementary school and high school, variously between grades 5 and 9

mid·dle·weight (-wāt′) ***n.*** a boxer or wrestler between a welterweight and a light heavyweight (in boxing, 148–160 pounds)

Middle West region of the NC U.S. between the Rocky Mountains & the E border of Ohio, north of the Ohio River & the S borders of Kans. & Mo. —**Middle Western**

mid·dling (mid′liŋ) ***adj.*** of middle size, quality, grade, state, etc.; medium —***adv.*** [Colloq.] moderately; somewhat —***n.*** **1.** [*pl.*] products of medium quality, size, or price **2.** [*pl.*] particles of coarsely ground grain, often mixed with bran —**fair to middling** [Colloq.] moderately good or well

mid·dy (mid′ē) ***n.,*** *pl.* **-dies** **1.** [Colloq.] a midshipman **2.** a loose blouse with a sailor collar, worn by women and children: in full, **middy blouse**

Mid·gard (mid′gärd′) *Norse Myth.* the earth: also **Mid′garth′** (-gär*th*′)

midge (mij) ***n.*** [OE. *mycg*] **1.** a small, two-winged, gnatlike insect **2.** a very small person

midg·et (mij′it) ***n.*** **1.** a very small person **2.** anything very small of its kind —***adj.*** very small of its kind; miniature

Mi·di (mē dē′) [Fr.] southern France

mid·i·ron (mid′ī′ərn) ***n.*** a golf club with a metal head, used for fairway shots of medium distance: now usually called *number 2 iron*

Mid·land (mid′lənd) [from being about midway between Fort Worth & El Paso] city in WC Tex.: pop. 71,000

mid·land (mid′lənd) ***n.*** **1.** the middle region of a country; interior **2.** [M-] *a)* an English dialect of the Midlands *b)* a dialect of American English spoken chiefly in the area that extends westward to the Coast across the middle of the U.S. from the Middle Atlantic States —***adj.*** **1.** of or in the midland; inland **2.** [M-] of the Midlands —**the Midlands** region in WC England, around Birmingham

mid·most (mid′mōst′) ***adj.*** exactly in the middle, or nearest the middle —***adv.*** in the middle or midst —***prep.*** in the middle or midst of —***n.*** the middle part

mid·night (-nīt′) ***n.*** the middle of the night; twelve o'clock at night —***adj.*** **1.** of or at midnight **2.** like midnight; very dark —**burn the midnight oil** to study very late at night

midnight sun the sun visible at midnight in the arctic or antarctic regions during the summer

mid·point (-point′) ***n.*** a point at or close to the middle or center, or equally distant from the ends

mid·rib (-rib′) ***n.*** the central vein of a leaf

mid·riff (-rif) ***n.*** [< OE. < *midd,* MID[1] + *hrif,* belly] **1.** *same as* DIAPHRAGM (sense 1) **2.** the middle part of the torso, between the abdomen and the chest —***adj.*** designating or of a garment that bares this part

mid·ship (-ship′) ***adj.*** of the middle of a ship

mid·ship·man (-ship′mən) ***n.,*** *pl.* **-men** **1.** a student in training for the rank of ensign; specif., such a student at the U.S. Naval Academy at Annapolis **2.** formerly, a junior British naval officer ranking just above a naval cadet

mid·ships (-ships′) ***adv.*** *same as* AMIDSHIPS

midst[1] (midst, mitst) ***n.*** the middle; central part: now mainly in phrases as below —**in our** (or **your, their**) **midst** among us (or you, them) —**in the midst of** **1.** in the middle of **2.** during

midst[2] (midst, mitst) ***prep.*** [Poet.] in the midst of; amidst

mid·stream (mid′strēm′) ***n.*** the middle of a stream

mid·sum·mer (-sum′ər) ***n.*** **1.** the middle of summer **2.** popularly, the time of the summer solstice, about June 21 —***adj.*** of, in, or like midsummer

mid·term (-turm′) ***adj.*** occurring in the middle of the term —***n.*** [Colloq.] a midterm examination, as in a college course

mid-Vic·to·ri·an (mid′vik tôr′ē ən) ***adj.*** **1.** of or characteristic of the middle part of Queen Victoria's reign in

Great Britain (c.1850–1890) **2.** old-fashioned, prudish, morally strict, etc. —*n.* **1.** a person who lived during this period **2.** a person of mid-Victorian ideas, manners, etc.
mid·way (mid′wā′; *also, for adj. & adv.,* -wā′) *n.* **1.** orig., a middle way or course **2.** that part of a fair or exposition where sideshows and other amusements are located —*adj., adv.* in the middle
Midway Islands U.S. territory in the North Pacific, northwest of Hawaii, consisting of an atoll & two islets
mid·week (-wēk′) *n., adj.* (in) the middle of the week
Mid·west (mid′west′) *n. same as* MIDDLE WEST —*adj. same as* MIDWESTERN
Mid·west·ern (-ərn) *adj.* of, in, or characteristic of the Middle West —**Mid′west′ern·er** *n.*
mid·wife (mid′wīf′) *n., pl.* **-wives′** (-wīvz′) [OE. *mid,* with + *wif,* woman] a person whose work is helping women in childbirth —**mid′wife′ry** (-wī′fə rē, -wīf′rē) *n.*
mid·win·ter (-win′tər) *n.* **1.** the middle of the winter **2.** popularly, the time of the winter solstice, about December 22 —*adj.* of, in, or like midwinter
mid·year (-yir′) *adj.* occurring in the middle of the (calendar or academic) year —*n.* [Colloq.] a midyear examination, as in a college course
mien (mēn) *n.* [< DEMEAN², but altered after Fr. *mine,* look, air] **1.** a way of carrying and conducting oneself; manner **2.** a way of looking; appearance
miff (mif) *n.* [prob. echoic of a sound of disgust] [Colloq.] a trivial quarrel or fit of the sulks; tiff or huff —*vt., vi.* [Colloq.] to offend or take offense
MIG, MiG (mig) *n.* [after A. *Mi*koyan & M. *G*urevich, its Soviet designers] a small, fast jet military aircraft
might¹ (mīt) *v.* [OE. *mihte*] **1.** *pt. of* MAY **2.** an auxiliary with present or future sense, generally equivalent to *may [it might rain]*
might² (mīt) *n.* [OE. *miht*] **1.** great or superior strength, power, force, or vigor **2.** strength or power of any degree
might·y (-ē) *adj.* [OE. *mihtig*] **might′i·er, might′i·est 1.** having might; powerful; strong **2.** remarkably large, extensive, etc.; great —*adv.* [Colloq.] very; extremely —**might′i·ly** *adv.* —**might′i·ness** *n.*
mi·gnon (min′yän; *Fr.* mē nyōn′) *adj.* [Fr.] small and delicate —**mi·gnonne** (min′yən; *Fr.* mē nyôn′) *adj.fem.*
mi·gnon·ette (min′yə net′) *n.* [< Fr. dim. of *mignon:* see prec.] a plant bearing spikes of small greenish, whitish, or reddish flowers
mi·graine (mī′grān) *n.* [Fr. < OFr. < LL. *hemicrania* < Gr. < *hēmi-,* half + *kranion,* skull] a type of intense, periodically returning headache, usually limited to one side of the head —**mi·grain′ous** *adj.*
mi·grant (mī′grənt) *adj.* migrating; migratory —*n.* a person, bird, or animal that migrates; specif., a farm laborer who moves from place to place to harvest seasonal crops
mi·grate (mī′grāt) *vi.* **-grat·ed, -grat·ing** [< L. pp. of *migrare,* to migrate] **1.** to move from one place to another, esp. to another country **2.** to move from one region to another with the change in seasons, as many birds **3.** to move from place to place to harvest seasonal crops —**mi′gra·tor** *n.*
mi·gra·tion (mī grā′shən) *n.* **1.** a migrating **2.** a group of people or birds, fishes, etc. migrating together **3.** *Chem. a)* the shifting of position of one or more atoms within a molecule *b)* the movement of ions toward an electrode —**mi·gra′tion·al** *adj.*
mi·gra·to·ry (mī′grə tôr′ē) *adj.* **1.** migrating; characterized by migration **2.** of migration **3.** roving; wandering
mi·ka·do (mi kä′dō) *n., pl.* **-dos** [Jap. < *mi,* exalted + *kado,* gate] [*often* **M-**] the emperor of Japan: title no longer used
mike (mīk) *n.* [Colloq.] a microphone —*vt.* **miked, mik′ing** [Colloq.] to record, amplify, etc. by means of a microphone
mil (mil) *n.* [< L. *mille,* thousand] **1.** a unit of length, equal to 1/1000 inch, used in measuring the diameter of wire **2.** a unit of angle measurement for artillery fire, missile launching, etc., equal to 1/6400 of the circumference of a circle **3.** *see* MONETARY UNITS, table (Cyprus)
mil. 1. military **2.** militia
mi·la·dy, mi·la·di (mi lā′dē) *n.* [Fr. < E. *my lady*] **1.** an English noblewoman or gentlewoman **2.** a woman of fashion: advertisers' term
mil·age (mīl′ij) *n. alt. sp. of* MILEAGE
Mi·lan (mi lan′) city in NW Italy: pop. 1,684,000: It. name **Mi·la·no** (mē lä′nō) —**Mil·a·nese** (mil′ə nēz′) *adj., n., pl.* **-nese′**
milch (milch) *adj.* [OE. *-milce*] giving milk; kept for milking *[milch cows]*
mild (mīld) *adj.* [OE. *milde*] **1.** *a)* gentle or kind in disposition, action, or effect; not severe, harsh, etc. *b)* not extreme; moderate *[a mild winter]* **2.** having a soft, pleasant flavor; not strong, bitter, etc.: said of tobacco, cheese, etc. —**mild′ly** *adv.* —**mild′ness** *n.*
mil·dew (mil′do͞o′, -dyo͞o′) *n.* [OE. *meledeaw,* lit., honeydew] **1.** a fungus that attacks various plants or appears on damp cloth, paper, etc. as a furry, whitish coating **2.** any such coating or discoloration —*vt., vi.* to affect or become affected with mildew —**mil′dew′y** *adj.*
Mil·dred (mil′drid) [< OE. < *milde,* mild + *thryth,* power] a feminine name: dim. *Millie, Milly*
mile (mīl) *n., pl.* **miles,** dial. **mile** [< OE. < L. *milia (passuum),* thousand (paces)] a unit of linear measure, equal to 1,760 yards (5,280 feet or 1,609.35 meters): in full, **statute mile**: see NAUTICAL MILE
mile·age (-ij) *n.* **1.** an allowance per mile for traveling expenses **2.** total number of miles traveled, etc. **3.** rate per mile **4.** the amount of use one can get from something
mile·post (-pōst′) *n.* a signpost showing the distance in miles from a specified place
mil·er (mīl′ər) *n.* one who competes in mile races
Miles (mīlz) [OFr. < OHG. *Milo,* lit., mild, peaceful] a masculine name
mile·stone (mīl′stōn′) *n.* **1.** a stone or pillar set up to show the distance in miles from a specified place **2.** a significant event in history, in one's career, etc.
Mil·ford (mil′fərd) [? after *Milford,* town in England] city in SW Conn., near Bridgeport: pop. 49,000
Mil·haud (mē yō′), **Da·rius** (dá ryüs′) 1892–1974; Fr. composer
mi·lieu (mēl yoo′; *Fr.* mē lyö′) *n., pl.* **-lieus′**; Fr. **-lieux′** (-lyö′) [Fr. < OFr. *mi,* middle + *lieu,* a place] environment; esp., social setting
mil·i·tant (mil′i tənt) *adj.* [< L. prp. of *militare,* to serve as a soldier < *miles* (gen. *militis*), a soldier] **1.** fighting **2.** ready and willing to fight; esp., vigorous in support of a cause —*n.* a militant person —**mil′i·tan·cy** *n.* —**mil′i·tant·ly** *adv.*
mil·i·ta·rism (mil′ə tər iz′m) *n.* **1.** military spirit or its dominance in a nation **2.** the policy of maintaining a strong military organization in aggressive preparedness for war —**mil′i·ta·rist** *n.* —**mil′i·ta·ris′tic** *adj.* —**mil′i·ta·ris′ti·cal·ly** *adv.*
mil·i·ta·rize (mil′i tə rīz′) *vt.* **-rized′, -riz′ing 1.** to equip and prepare for war **2.** to fill with warlike spirit —**mil′i·ta·ri·za′tion** *n.*
mil·i·tar·y (mil′ə ter′ē) *adj.* [< Fr. < L. *militaris* < *miles:* see MILITANT] **1.** of, characteristic of, for, fit for, or done by soldiers or the armed forces **2.** of, for, or fit for war **3.** of the army —**the military** the army or the armed forces; esp., army officers as an influential force —**mil′i·tar′i·ly** (*also* mil′ə ter′ə lē) *adv.*
military attaché an army officer attached to his nation's embassy or legation in a foreign country
military police soldiers assigned to carry on police duties for the army
mil·i·tate (mil′ə tāt′) *vi.* **-tat′ed, -tat′ing** [< L. pp. of *militare:* see MILITANT] to be directed (*against*); operate or work (*against* or, rarely, *for*): said of facts, actions, etc.
mi·li·tia (mə lish′ə) *n.* [L., soldiery < *miles:* see MILITANT] any army composed of citizens rather than professional soldiers, called up in time of emergency —**mi·li′tia·man** (-mən) *n., pl.* **-men**
milk (milk) *n.* [OE. *meolc*] **1.** a white liquid secreted by the mammary glands of female mammals for suckling their young **2.** cow's milk, etc. drunk by humans as a food or used to make butter, cheese, etc. **3.** any liquid or juice like this *[coconut milk, milk of magnesia]* —*vt.* **1.** to draw milk from the mammary glands of (a cow, etc.) **2.** to extract (something) as if by milking *[to milk venom from a snake]* **3.** to extract something from as if by milking *[to milk a rich uncle for his money]* —*vi.* **1.** to give milk **2.** to draw milk —**cry over spilt milk** to mourn or regret something that cannot be undone —**milk′ing** *n.*
milk-and-wa·ter (-ən wôt′ər, -wät′-) *adj.* insipid; weak; wishy-washy; namby-pamby
milk·er (mil′kər) *n.* **1.** a person who milks **2.** a machine for milking **3.** a cow or other animal that gives milk
milk glass a nearly opaque whitish glass
milk leg *a former term for* a painful swelling of the leg, caused by clotting in the femoral veins, as in childbirth
milk·maid (milk′mād′) *n.* a girl or woman who milks cows or works in a dairy; dairymaid
milk·man (-man′) *n., pl.* **-men′** (-men′) a man who sells or delivers milk for a dairy
milk of magnesia a milky-white fluid, a suspension of magnesium hydroxide, $Mg(OH)_2$, in water, used as a laxative and antacid
milk·shake (-shāk′) *n.* a drink made of milk, flavoring, and, usually, ice cream, mixed until frothy
milk·shed (-shed′) *n.* [MILK + (WATER)SHED] all the dairy farms supplying milk for a given city
milk snake a harmless snake, gray or reddish with black-rimmed markings: it feeds on rodents, etc.
milk·sop (-säp′) *n.* an unmanly man or boy; sissy
milk sugar *same as* LACTOSE
milk tooth any of the temporary, first set of teeth in a child or the young of other mammals

milk·weed (-wēd′) ***n.*** any of a group of plants with a milky juice and pods which when ripe burst to release plumed seeds

MILKWEED PODS

milk·y (mil′kē) ***adj.* milk′i·er, milk′i·est 1.** like milk; esp., white as milk **2.** of or containing milk **3.** timid, meek, etc. **—milk′i·ness *n.***

Milky Way a broad, faint band of light seen as an arch across the sky at night, created by billions of distant stars and masses of gas

mill[1] (mil) ***n.*** [OE. *mylen,* ult. < LL. *molina* < L. *mola,* millstone] **1.** *a)* a building with machinery for grinding grain into flour or meal *b)* a machine for grinding grain **2.** a machine for grinding or crushing any solid material *[a coffee mill]* **3.** *a)* any of various machines for cutting, stamping, shaping, etc. *b)* [Colloq.] a place where things are done, produced, issued, etc. in a rapid, mechanical way *[a diploma mill]* **4.** a factory *[a textile mill]* **5.** a raised edge, ridged surface, etc. made by milling **—*vt.* 1.** to grind, work, form, etc. by, in, or as in a mill **2.** to raise and ridge the edge of (a coin) **—*vi.*** to move slowly in a circle, as cattle, or aimlessly, as a confused crowd (often with *around* or *about*) **—in the mill** in preparation **—through the mill** [Colloq.] through a hard, painful, instructive experience **—milled *adj.***

mill[2] (mil) ***n.*** [for L. *millesimus,* thousandth < *mille,* thousand] one tenth of a cent; $.001: a unit used in calculating but not as a coin

Mill (mil), **John Stuart** 1806–73; Eng. philosopher & political economist

mill·age (mil′ij) ***n.*** [MILL[2] + -AGE] taxation in mills per dollar of valuation

Mil·lais (mi lā′), Sir **John Everett** 1829–96; Eng. painter

Mil·lay (mi lā′), **Edna St. Vincent** 1892–1950; U.S. poet

mill·dam (mil′dam′) ***n.*** a dam built across a stream to raise its level enough to provide water power for turning a mill wheel

mil·len·ni·um (mi len′ē əm) ***n., pl.* -ni·ums, -ni·a** (-ə) [ModL. < L. *mille,* thousand + *annus,* year] **1.** a period of 1,000 years **2.** *Theol.* the period of a thousand years during which some believe Christ will reign on earth (with *the*): Rev. 20:1–5 **3.** a period of peace and happiness for everyone **—mil·len′ni·al *adj.* —mil·len′ni·al·ism *n.***

mil·le·pede (mil′ə pēd′) ***n.*** *same as* MILLIPEDE

mil·le·pore (mil′ə pôr′) ***n.*** [< Fr. < *mille,* thousand + *pore* < L. *porus,* PORE[2]] any of a genus of hydrozoans that form leaflike, porous masses of coral

mill·er (mil′ər) ***n.* 1.** a person who owns or operates a mill, esp. a flour mill **2.** a tool used for milling **3.** a moth with wings that look dusty, suggesting a miller's clothes

Mil·ler (mil′ər) **1. Arthur,** 1915– ; U.S. playwright **2. Joaquin** (wä kēn′), (pseud. of *Cincinnatus Heine Miller*) 1839?–1913; U.S. poet

mill·er's-thumb (mil′ərz thum′) ***n.*** any of several small freshwater fishes with spiny fins and a broad, flat head

mil·let (mil′it) ***n.*** see PLURAL, II, D, 3 [< MFr., dim. of *mil* < L. *milium,* millet] **1.** a cereal grass whose small grain is used for food in Europe and Asia **2.** the grain

Mil·let (mē le′; *E.* mi lā′), **Jean Fran·çois** (zhän frän′swȧ′) 1814–75; Fr. painter

mil·li- [< L. *mille,* thousand] *a combining form meaning* a 1000th part of *[millimeter]*

mil·li·am·pere (mil′ē am′pir) ***n.*** one thousandth of an ampere

mil·liard (mil′yərd, -yärd′) ***n.*** [Fr. < *million* (see MILLION) + *-ard* (see -ARD), orig. "large million"] [Brit.] 1,000 millions; billion

Mil·li·cent (mil′ə s′nt) [< OFr. < OHG. < *amal,* work + hyp. *swind,* strong] a feminine name

mil·lieme (mēl yem′, mē-) ***n.*** [< Fr. < MFr. < *mille,* a thousand < L.] *see* MONETARY UNITS, table (Libya)

mil·li·gram (mil′ə gram′) ***n.*** one thousandth of a gram: also, chiefly Brit. sp., **mil′li·gramme′**

mil·li·li·ter (-lēt′ər) ***n.*** one thousandth of a liter: also, chiefly Brit. sp., **mil′li·li′tre**

mil·lime (mil′ēm, -im) ***n.*** [Fr.: see MILLIEME] *see* MONETARY UNITS, table (Tunisia)

mil·li·me·ter (mil′ə mēt′ər) ***n.*** one thousandth of a meter: also, chiefly Brit. sp., **mil′li·me′tre**

mil·li·mi·cron (mil′ə mī′krän) ***n., pl.* -crons, -cra** (-krə) one thousandth of a micron, or ten angstroms: a unit of length for measuring waves of light, etc.

mil·li·ner (mil′ə nər) ***n.*** [< *Milaner,* importer of dress wares from Milan] a person who designs, makes, trims, or sells women's hats

mil·li·ner·y (mil′ə ner′ē; *chiefly Brit.* -nər i) ***n.* 1.** women's hats, headdresses, etc. **2.** the work or business of a milliner

mill·ing (mil′iŋ) *prp. of* MILL[1] **—*n.* 1.** the process or business of grinding grain into flour or meal **2.** the grinding, cutting, or processing of metal, cloth, etc. in a mill

milling machine a machine with a table on which material rests as it is fed against a rotating cutter (**milling cutter**) for cutting, grinding, shaping, etc.

mil·lion (mil′yən) ***n.*** [OFr. < It. *milione* < *mille,* thousand < L.] a thousand thousands; 1,000,000 **—*adj.* 1.** amounting to one million in number **2.** very many **—mil′lionth *adj., n.***

mil·lion·aire (mil′yə ner′) ***n.*** [< Fr.] a person worth at least a million dollars, pounds, etc.

mil·li·pede (mil′ə pēd′) ***n.*** [< L. < *mille,* thousand + *pes* (gen. *pedis*), a foot] a many-legged arthropod with two pairs of legs on most of its segments

mill·pond (mil′pänd′) ***n.*** a pond from which water flows for driving a mill wheel

mill·race (-rās′) ***n.* 1.** the current of water that drives a mill wheel **2.** the channel in which it runs

mill-run (-run′) ***adj.*** just as it comes out of the mill; ordinary; average

mill·stone (-stōn′) ***n.* 1.** either of a pair of large, flat, round stones between which grain or other substances are ground **2.** a heavy burden **3.** something that grinds, pulverizes, or crushes

mill·stream (-strēm′) ***n.*** water flowing in a millrace

mill wheel the wheel, usually a water wheel, that drives the machinery in a mill

mill·work (-wurk′) ***n.* 1.** doors, windows, etc. made in a planing mill **2.** work done in a mill **—mill′work′er *n.***

mill·wright (-rīt′) ***n.* 1.** one who designs, builds, or installs mills or their machinery **2.** a worker who installs or repairs the machinery in a plant

Milne (miln), **A(lan) A(lexander)** 1882–1956; Eng. playwright & writer of children's books

mi·lord (mi lôrd′) ***n.*** [Fr. < E. *my lord*] an English nobleman: used as a term of address

milque·toast (milk′tōst′) ***n.*** [< Caspar *Milquetoast,* comic-strip character by H. T. Webster (1885–1952), U.S. cartoonist] a timid, apologetic person

milt (milt) ***n.*** [prob. < Scand.] **1.** the reproductive glands of male fishes, esp. when filled with germ cells and the milky fluid containing them **2.** fish sperm **—*adj.*** breeding: said of male fishes **—*vt.*** to fertilize (fish roe) with milt **—milt′er *n.***

Mil·ti·a·des (mil tī′ə dēz′) ?–489? B.C.; Athenian general: defeated the Persians at Marathon

Mil·ton (mil′t′n) [< OE. *Middel-tun,* Middletown, or *Mylen-tun,* Mill town] **1.** a masculine name: dim. *Milt* **2. John,** 1608–74; Eng. poet **—Mil·ton′ic** (-tän′ik), **Mil·to′ni·an** (-tō′nē ən) ***adj.***

Mil·wau·kee (mil wô′kē) [< Fr. < Algonquian, lit., good land] city in SE Wis., on Lake Michigan: pop. 636,000 (met. area 1,393,000)

mime (mīm) ***n.*** [< L. < Gr. *mimos*] **1.** an ancient Greek or Roman farce, in which people and events were mimicked and burlesqued **2.** the representation of an action, character, mood, etc. by means of gestures rather than words **3.** an actor who performs in mimes **—*vt.* mimed, mim′ing** to mimic or act out as a mime **—*vi.*** to act as a mime, usually without speaking **—mim′er *n.***

mim·e·o·graph (mim′ē ə graf′, mim′yə-) ***n.*** [a former trademark < Gr. *mimeomai,* I imitate + -GRAPH] a machine for making copies of written, drawn, or typewritten matter by means of a stencil **—*vt.* 1.** to make copies of on such a machine **2.** to make (copies) on such a machine

mi·met·ic (mi met′ik, mī-) ***adj.*** [< Gr. < *mimeisthai,* to imitate] **1.** of or characterized by imitation; imitative **2.** of or characterized by mimicry **—mi·met′i·cal·ly *adv.***

mim·ic (mim′ik) ***adj.*** [< L. < Gr. < *mimos,* a mime] **1.** imitative **2.** of, or having the nature of, mimicry or imitation **3.** make-believe; mock **—*n.*** a person or thing that imitates; esp., an actor skilled in mimicry **—*vt.* mim′icked, mim′ick·ing 1.** to imitate in speech or action, as in ridicule **2.** to copy closely **3.** to take on the appearance of **—mim′ick·er *n.***

mim·ic·ry (-rē) ***n., pl.* -ries 1.** the practice, art, instance, or way of mimicking **2.** close resemblance, in color, form, or behavior, of one organism to another or to some object in its environment

mi·mo·sa (mi mō′sə) ***n.*** [ModL. < L. *mimus:* see MIME] a tree, shrub, or herb of the legume family, growing in warm regions, with heads or spikes of small white, yellow, or pink flowers

min. 1. mineralogy **2.** minim(s) **3.** minimum **4.** mining **5.** minor **6.** minute(s)

mi·na (mī′nə) ***n.*** *same as* MYNA: also sp. **mi′nah**

min·a·ret (min′ə ret′, min′ə ret′) ***n.*** **[**Fr. < Turk. < Ar. *manārah,* lighthouse**]** a high, slender tower attached to a Moslem mosque, with balconies from which a muezzin calls the people to prayer

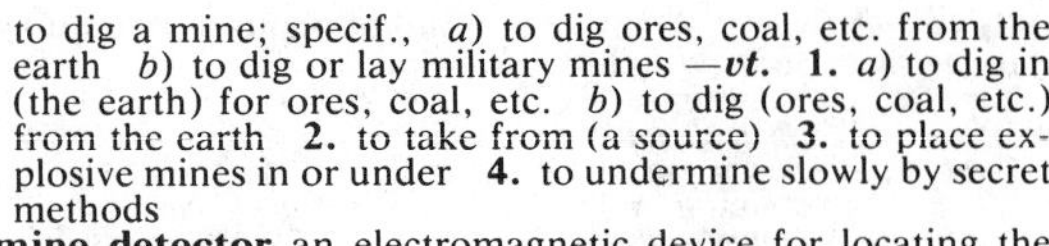

MINARET

min·a·to·ry (min′ə tôr′ē) ***adj.*** **[**< OFr. < LL. < pp. of L. *minari,* to threaten**]** menacing; threatening

mince (mins) ***vt.*** **minced, minc′ing** **[**OFr. *mincier,* ult. < L. *minutus,* small**]** **1.** to cut up (meat, etc.) into very small pieces **2.** to express or do with affected elegance or daintiness **3.** to lessen the force of; weaken *[*to *mince* no words*]* —***vi.*** **1.** to speak or act with affected elegance or daintiness **2.** to walk with short steps or in an affected, dainty manner —***n.*** *same as* MINCEMEAT —**not mince matters** to speak frankly —**minc′er** ***n.***

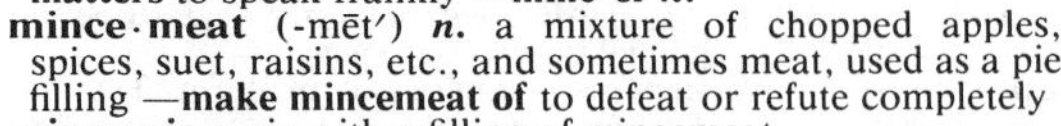

mince·meat (-mēt′) ***n.*** a mixture of chopped apples, spices, suet, raisins, etc., and sometimes meat, used as a pie filling —**make mincemeat of** to defeat or refute completely

mince pie a pie with a filling of mincemeat

minc·ing (min′siŋ) ***adj.*** **1.** affectedly elegant or dainty **2.** with short steps or affected daintiness *[*a *mincing* walk*]* —**minc′ing·ly** ***adv.***

mind (mīnd) ***n.*** **[**OE. *(ge)mynd***]** **1.** memory or remembrance *[*to bring to *mind* a story*]* **2.** what one thinks; opinion *[*speak your *mind]* **3.** *a)* that which thinks, perceives, feels, etc.; the seat of consciousness *b)* the intellect *c)* attention *d)* the psyche (sense 2) **4.** reason; sanity *[*to lose one's *mind]* **5.** a person having intelligence *[*the great *minds* of today*]* **6.** way, state, or direction of thinking and feeling *[*the reactionary *mind]* —***vt.*** **1.** to direct one's mind to; specif., *a)* [Now Dial.] to perceive; observe *b)* to pay attention to; heed *c)* to obey *d)* to take care of; look after *[mind* the baby*]* *e)* to be careful about *[mind* those rickety stairs*]* **2.** *a)* to care about; feel concern about *b)* to object to; dislike *[*to *mind* the cold*]* **3.** [Dial.] to remember **4.** [Dial. or Archaic] to remind —***vi.*** **1.** to pay attention; give heed **2.** to be obedient **3.** to be careful **4.** *a)* to care; feel concern *b)* to object —**bear** (or **keep**) **in mind** to remember —**be in one's right mind** to be sane —**blow one's mind** [Slang] **1.** to be hallucinated as by drugs **2.** to be amazed, confused, etc. —**call to mind** **1.** to remember **2.** to be a reminder of —**change one's mind** to change one's opinion or one's intention —**give (someone) a piece of one's mind** to criticize or rebuke sharply —**have a (good** or **great) mind to** to feel (strongly) inclined to —**have half a mind to** to be somewhat inclined to —**have in mind** **1.** to remember **2.** to think of **3.** to intend; purpose —**know one's own mind** to know one's own real thoughts, desires, etc. —**make up one's mind** to form a definite opinion or decision —**meeting of (the) minds** an agreement —**never mind** don't be concerned; it doesn't matter —**on one's mind** **1.** occupying one's thoughts **2.** worrying one —**out of one's mind** **1.** insane **2.** frantic (*with* worry, grief, etc.) —**put in mind** to remind —**set one's mind on** to be determinedly desirous of —**take one's mind off** to turn one's thoughts or attention from —**to one's mind** in one's opinion —**mind′er** ***n.***

Min·da·na·o (min′də nou′, -nä′ō) 2d largest island of the Philippines, at the S end of the group: 36,906 sq. mi.

mind·ed (mīn′did) ***adj.*** **1.** having a (specified kind of) mind *[*high-*minded]* **2.** inclined; disposed

mind·ful (mīnd′f'l) ***adj.*** having in mind; aware or careful (*of*) *[*to be *mindful* of the danger*]* —**mind′ful·ly** ***adv.*** —**mind′ful·ness** ***n.***

mind·less (-lis) ***adj.*** **1.** showing little or no intelligence; thoughtless **2.** taking no thought; heedless (*of*) —**mind′less·ly** ***adv.*** —**mind′less·ness** ***n.***

Min·do·ro (min dôr′ō) island of the Philippines, south of Luzon: 3,759 sq. mi.

mind reader one who professes to be able to perceive another's thoughts —**mind reading**

mind's eye the imagination

mine[1] (mīn) ***pron.*** **[**OE. *min***]** that or those belonging to me: used without a following noun *[*this is *mine, mine* are better*]*: also used after *of* to indicate possession *[*a friend of *mine]* —***possessive pronominal adj.*** [Mainly Archaic] my: formerly used before a vowel or *h [mine* eyes, *mine* honor*]*, now used after a noun in direct address *[*daughter *mine]*

mine[2] (mīn) ***n.*** **[**< MFr. < ? Celt.**]** **1.** *a)* a large excavation made in the earth, from which to extract metallic ores, coal, etc. *b)* a deposit of ore, coal, etc. **2.** any great source of supply *[*a *mine* of information*]* **3.** a firework that explodes in the air and scatters a number of smaller fireworks **4.** *Mil. a)* a tunnel dug under an enemy's trench, fort, etc., in which an explosive is placed to destroy the enemy fortifications *b)* an explosive charge in a container, buried in the ground for destroying enemy troops on land, or placed in the sea for destroying enemy ships —***vi.*** **mined, min′ing** to dig a mine; specif., *a)* to dig ores, coal, etc. from the earth *b)* to dig or lay military mines —***vt.*** **1.** *a)* to dig in (the earth) for ores, coal, etc. *b)* to dig (ores, coal, etc.) from the earth **2.** to take from (a source) **3.** to place explosive mines in or under **4.** to undermine slowly by secret methods

mine detector an electromagnetic device for locating the position of hidden explosive mines

mine field an area on land or in water where explosive mines have been set

mine·lay·er (mīn′lā′ər) ***n.*** a ship especially equipped to lay explosive mines in the water

min·er (-ər) ***n.*** a person whose work is digging coal, ore, etc. in a mine

min·er·al (min′ər əl, min′rəl) ***n.*** **[**OFr. < ML. neut. of *mineralis* < *minera,* a mine**]** **1.** an inorganic substance occurring naturally in the earth and having distinctive physical properties and a composition expressible by a chemical formula: sometimes applied to organic substances in the earth, such as coal **2.** an ore **3.** any substance that is neither vegetable nor animal **4.** any of certain elements, as iron, vital to animals and plants —***adj.*** of, like, or containing a mineral or minerals

mineral. **1.** mineralogical **2.** mineralogy

min·er·al·ize (min′ər ə līz′, min′rə-) ***vt.*** **-ized′, -iz′ing** **1.** to convert (organic matter) into a mineral **2.** to impregnate (water, etc.) with minerals **3.** to convert (a metal) into an ore —**min′er·al·i·za′tion** ***n.*** —**min′er·al·iz′er** ***n.***

min·er·al·o·gy (min′ə räl′ə jē, -ral′-) ***n.*** **1.** the scientific study of minerals **2.** *pl.* **-gies** a book about minerals —**min′er·a·log′i·cal** (-ər ə läj′i k'l) ***adj.*** —**min′er·a·log′i·cal·ly** ***adv.*** —**min′er·al′o·gist** ***n.***

mineral oil **1.** any oil found in the rock strata of the earth; specif., petroleum **2.** a colorless, tasteless oil derived from petroleum and used as a laxative

mineral water water naturally or artificially impregnated with mineral salts or gases

mineral wool a fibrous material made from rock and melted slag and used to insulate buildings

Mi·ner·va (mi nʉr′və) [L.] **1.** a feminine name **2.** the ancient Roman goddess of wisdom, technical skill, and invention: identified with the Greek goddess Athena

mi·ne·stro·ne (min′ə strō′nē; *occas.* -strōn′) ***n.*** **[**It., ult. < L. *ministrare,* to serve**]** a thick vegetable soup containing vermicelli, barley, etc. in a meat broth

mine sweeper a ship for destroying enemy mines

Ming (miŋ) Chin. dynasty (1368–1644): period noted for scholarly achievements & artistic works

min·gle (miŋ′g'l) ***vt.*** **-gled, -gling** **[**< OE. *mengan,* to mix**]** to mix together; combine; blend —***vi.*** **1.** to be or become mixed, blended, etc. **2.** to join or unite with others —**min′gler** ***n.***

min·i- **[**< MINI(ATURE)**]** *a combining form meaning:* **1.** miniature, very small, very short *[miniskirt]* **2.** of less scope, extent, etc. than usual *[mini-*crisis*]*

min·i·a·ture (min′ē ə chər, min′i chər) ***n.*** **[**< It. *miniatura* < ML. < L. *miniare,* to paint red < *minium,* red lead**]** **1.** *a)* a very small painting, esp. a portrait *b)* the art of making these **2.** a copy or model on a very small scale —***adj.*** on or done on a very small scale; minute —**in miniature** on a small scale; greatly reduced —**min′i·a·tur·ist** ***n.***

min·i·a·tur·ize (-īz′) ***vt.*** **-ized′, -iz′ing** to make in a small and compact form —**min′i·a·tur′i·za′tion** ***n.***

min·im (min′im) ***n.*** **[**< L. *minimus:* see MINIMUM**]** **1.** the smallest liquid measure, 1/60 fluid dram, or about a drop **2.** a tiny portion **3.** [Brit.] *same as* HALF NOTE —***adj.*** smallest; tiniest

min·i·mize (min′ə mīz′) ***vt.*** **-mized′, -miz′ing** to reduce to or estimate at a minimum, or the least possible amount, degree, etc. —**min′i·mi·za′tion** ***n.*** —**min′i·miz′er** ***n.***

min·i·mum (-məm) ***n.,*** *pl.* **-mums, -ma** (-mə) [L., neut. of *minimus,* least < *minor,* minor**]** **1.** the smallest quantity, number, or degree possible or permissible **2.** the lowest degree or point reached or recorded —***adj.*** **1.** smallest possible, permissible, or reached **2.** of, marking, or setting a minimum or minimums —**min′i·mal** ***adj.*** —**min′i·mal·ly** ***adv.***

minimum wage a wage established by contract or by law as the lowest that may be paid to employees doing a specified type of work

min·ing (mī′niŋ) ***n.*** the act, process, or work of removing ores, coal, etc. from a mine

min·ion (min′yən) ***n.*** [Fr. *mignon,* darling**]** **1.** a favorite, esp. one who is a servile follower: term of contempt **2.** a subordinate official **3.** *Printing* a size of type, 7 point —***adj.*** [Rare] dainty

minion of the law *same as* POLICEMAN

min·is·cule (min′ə skyōōl′) ***adj.*** *mistaken sp. of* MINUSCULE

min·i·skirt (min′ē skʉrt′) ***n.*** **[**MINI- + SKIRT**]** a very short skirt ending well above the knee

min·is·ter (min′is tər) ***n.*** **[**< OFr. < L. *minister,* a servant

< *minor,* lesser] **1.** a person appointed to take charge of some governmental department **2.** a diplomatic officer sent to a foreign nation to represent his government **3.** anyone authorized to carry out the spiritual functions of a church, conduct worship, preach, etc.; pastor **4.** any person or thing thought of as serving as the agent of some power, force, etc. *—vt.* [Archaic] to administer *—vi.* **1.** to serve as a minister in a church **2.** to give help (*to*)

min·is·te·ri·al (min′is tir′ē əl) *adj.* **1.** of a minister or (the) ministry **2.** subordinate or instrumental **3.** administrative; executive **—min′is·te′ri·al·ly** *adv.*

minister plenipotentiary *pl.* **ministers plenipotentiary** a diplomatic representative with full authority to negotiate

min·is·trant (min′is trənt) *adj.* serving as a minister; ministering *—n.* a person who ministers, or serves

min·is·tra·tion (min′is trā′shən) *n.* **1.** the act of serving as a minister or clergyman **2.** the act of giving help

min·is·try (min′is trē) *n., pl.* **-tries 1.** the act of ministering, or serving **2.** *a)* the office or function of a minister of religion *b)* such ministers collectively; clergy **3.** *a)* the department under a minister of government *b)* his term of office *c)* his headquarters *d)* such ministers collectively

min·i·ver (min′ə vər) *n.* [< OFr. < *menu,* small + *vair,* kind of fur < L. *varius,* variegated] a white fur used for trimming garments, esp. ceremonial robes, as of royalty

mink (miŋk) *n., pl.* **minks, mink:** see PLURAL, II, D, 1 [< Scand.] **1.** a slim, carnivorous mammal with partly webbed feet; esp., a dark-brown weasel living in water part of the time **2.** its valuable fur, soft, thick, and white to brown in color

MINK (17–28 in. long, including tail)

Minn. Minnesota

Min·ne·ap·o·lis (min′ē ap′′l is) [after a nearby waterfall (< Sioux *minne,* water, and *haha,* waterfall) + Gr. *polis,* city] city in E Minn., on the Mississippi: pop. 371,000 (met. area, with adjacent St. Paul, 2,109,000)

min·ne·sing·er (min′i siŋ′ər) *n.* [G. < MHG. *minne,* love + *senger,* singer] any of a number of German lyric poets and singers of the 12th to 14th cent.

Min·ne·so·ta (min′ə sōt′ə) [< Sioux, lit., milky blue water] Middle Western State of the U.S.: 84,068 sq. mi.; pop. 4,077,000; cap. St. Paul: abbrev. **Minn., MN —Min′ne·so′tan** *adj., n.*

min·now (min′ō) *n., pl.* **-nows, -now:** see PLURAL, II, D, 1 [< or akin to OE. *myne*] **1.** any of a large number of usually small freshwater fishes, used commonly as bait **2.** any very small fish Also [Dial. or Colloq.] **min′ny** (-ē), *pl.* **-nies**

Mi·no·an (mi nō′ən) *adj.* [< MINOS + -AN] designating or of an advanced prehistoric culture that flourished in Crete from c.2800–c.1100 B.C.

mi·nor (mī′nər) *adj.* [L.] **1.** *a)* lesser in size, amount, or extent *b)* lesser in importance or rank **2.** under full legal age **3.** constituting the minority **4.** sad; melancholy **5.** *Educ.* designating a field of study in which a student specializes, but to a lesser degree than in his major **6.** *Music a)* designating an interval smaller than the corresponding major by a semitone *b)* characterized by minor intervals, scales, etc. *c)* based on the scale pattern of the minor mode: see MINOR SCALE *—vi. Educ.* to pursue a minor subject *[*to *minor* in French*]* *—n.* **1.** a person under full legal age **2.** *Educ.* a minor field of study **3.** *Music* a minor interval, key, etc. **—the minors** the minor leagues, esp. in baseball

Mi·nor·ca (mi nôr′kə) 2d largest of the Balearic Islands

mi·nor·i·ty (mə nôr′ə tē, mī-; -när′-) *n., pl.* **-ties 1.** the lesser part or smaller number; less than half **2.** a racial, religious, or political group smaller than and differing from the larger, controlling group **3.** the period or condition of being under full legal age

minor league any league in a professional sport, as baseball, other than the major leagues **—mi′nor-league′** *adj.* **—mi′nor-leagu′er** *n.*

minor order *R.C.Ch.* any of the four lower orders below that of subdeacon, requisite for aspirants to major orders

minor scale one of the two standard diatonic scales, with half steps instead of whole steps, in ascending, after the second and seventh tones (**melodic minor scale**) or after the second, fifth, and seventh tones (**harmonic minor scale**)

minor suit *Bridge* diamonds or clubs

Mi·nos (mī′nəs, -näs) *Gr. Myth.* a king of Crete who after he died became a judge of the dead in the lower world

Min·o·taur (min′ə tôr′) *Gr. Myth.* a monster with the body of a man and the head of a bull, confined by Minos in a labyrinth and annually fed young Athenians, until killed by Theseus

Minsk (minsk; *Russ.* mēnsk) capital of the Byelorussian S.S.R.: pop. 818,000

min·ster (min′stər) *n.* [OE. *mynster* < LL. *monasterium,* MONASTERY] **1.** the church of a monastery **2.** any of various large churches or cathedrals

min·strel (min′strəl) *n.* [< OFr., servant, orig., official < LL. < L. *ministerium,* ministry] **1.** any of a class of lyric poets and singers of the Middle Ages, who traveled from place to place singing and reciting **2.** [Poet.] a poet, singer, or musician **3.** a performer in a minstrel show

minstrel show a comic variety show presented by a company of performers in blackface, who sing, tell jokes, etc.

min·strel·sy (-sē) *n., pl.* **-sies 1.** the art or occupation of a minstrel **2.** a group of minstrels **3.** a collection of minstrels' ballads or songs

mint[1] (mint) *n.* [OE. *mynet,* coin < L. < *Moneta,* epithet of Juno, in whose temple money was coined] **1.** a place where money is coined by the government **2.** a large amount *[*a *mint* of ideas*]* **3.** a source of manufacture or invention *—adj.* new, as if freshly minted *[*a postage stamp in *mint* condition*]* *—vt.* **1.** to coin (money) **2.** to invent or create; fabricate **—mint′er** *n.*

mint[2] (mint) *n.* [OE. *minte*] **1.** a plant of the mint family with leaves used for flavoring and in medicine **2.** a candy flavored with mint *—adj.* designating a family of plants, as the spearmint, peppermint, and basil, with aromatic leaves, volatile oil, and square stems

mint·age (min′tij) *n.* **1.** the act or process of minting money **2.** money so produced **3.** the cost of minting money **4.** the impression made on a coin

mint jelly (or **sauce**) a jelly (or sauce) flavored with mint leaves, served esp. with lamb

mint julep a frosted drink consisting of whiskey or brandy, sugar, and mint leaves

min·u·end (min′yoo wend′) *n.* [< L. gerundive of *minuere:* see MINUTE[2]] *Arith.* the number or quantity from which another is to be subtracted

min·u·et (min′yoo wet′) *n.* [Fr. *menuet* (see MENU), orig., very small: from the small steps taken] **1.** a slow, stately dance of the 17th and 18th cent., for groups of couples **2.** the music for this, in 3/4 time

mi·nus (mī′nəs) *prep.* [L., neut. sing. of *minor,* less] **1.** reduced by the subtraction of; less *[*four *minus* two*]* **2.** [Colloq.] without *[minus* a toe*]* *—adj.* **1.** indicating subtraction *[*a *minus* sign*]* **2.** negative *[*a *minus* quantity*]* **3.** somewhat less than *[*a grade of A *minus]* **4.** *Elec. same as* NEGATIVE *[*the *minus* terminal*]* *—n.* **1.** a minus sign **2.** a negative quantity

mi·nus·cule (mi nus′kyo͞ol, min′ə skyo͞ol′) *adj.* [Fr. < L. *minusculus,* rather small] very small

minus sign *Math.* a sign (–), indicating subtraction or negative quantity

min·ute[1] (min′it) *n.* [< OFr. < ML. *minuta* < L. (*pars*) *minuta* (*prima*), (first) small (part): see ff.] **1.** the sixtieth part of any of certain units; specif., *a)* 1/60 of an hour; sixty seconds *b)* 1/60 of a degree of an arc **2.** a moment; instant **3.** a specific point in time **4.** a measure of the distance usually covered in a minute *[*ten *minutes* from downtown*]* **5.** a note or memorandum; specif., [*pl.*] an official record of what was said and done at a meeting, etc. *—vt.* **-ut·ed, -ut·ing** to make minutes of; record **—the minute (that)** just as soon as **—up to the minute** in the latest style, fashion, etc.

mi·nute[2] (mī no͞ot′, mi-; -nyo͞ot′) *adj.* [< L. pp. of *minuere,* to lessen < *minor,* less] **1.** very small; tiny **2.** of little importance; trifling **3.** of or attentive to tiny details; exact; precise **—mi·nute′ness** *n.*

minute hand the longer hand of a clock or watch, which indicates the minutes and moves around the dial once every hour

mi·nute·ly (mī no͞ot′lē, mi-; -nyo͞ot′-) *adv.* **1.** in a minute manner or in minute detail **2.** into tiny pieces

min·ute·man (min′it man′) *n., pl.* **-men′** (-men′) [*also* **M-**] a member of the American citizen army during the American Revolution who volunteered to be ready for military service at a minute's notice

min·ute steak (min′it) a small, thin steak that can be cooked quickly

mi·nu·ti·ae (mi no͞o′shi ē′, -nyo͞o′-) *n.pl., sing.* **-ti·a** (-shē ə, -shə) [L. < *minutus,* MINUTE[2]] small or relatively unimportant details

minx (miŋks) *n.* [< ?] a pert, saucy young woman

Mi·o·cene (mī′ə sēn′) *adj.* [< Gr. *meiōn,* less + *kainos,* recent] designating or of the fourth epoch of the Tertiary Period in the Cenozoic Era **—the Miocene** the Miocene Epoch or its rocks: see GEOLOGY, chart

Mi·ra·beau (mir′ə bō′; *Fr.* mē rȧ bō′), comte (**Honoré Gabriel Riqueti) de** 1749–91; Fr. revolutionist & statesman

mir·a·cle (mir′ə k'l) ***n.*** [OFr. < L. *miraculum* < *mirari*, to wonder at < *mirus*, wonderful] **1.** an event or action that apparently contradicts known scientific laws [the *miracles* in the Bible] **2.** a remarkable thing; marvel **3.** a wonderful example [a *miracle* of tact] **4.** *same as* MIRACLE PLAY
miracle play any of a class of medieval religious dramas dealing with events in the lives of the saints: cf. MYSTERY PLAY
mi·rac·u·lous (mi rak′yoo ləs) ***adj.*** **1.** having the nature of a miracle; supernatural **2.** like a miracle; marvelous **3.** able to work miracles —**mi·rac′u·lous·ly** ***adv.*** —**mi·rac′u·lous·ness** ***n.***
mi·rage (mi räzh′) ***n.*** [Fr. < (*se*) *mirer*, to be reflected < VL. *mirare*, to look at, for L. *mirari*: see MIRACLE] **1.** an optical illusion in which the image of a distant object, as an oasis, is made to appear nearby: it is caused by the refraction of light rays from the object through layers of air of different temperatures and densities **2.** something that falsely appears to be real
mire (mīr) ***n.*** [< ON. *myrr*] **1.** an area of wet, soggy ground; bog **2.** deep mud or slush —***vt.*** **mired, mir′ing** **1.** to cause to get stuck in or as in mire **2.** to soil with mud or dirt —***vi.*** to sink or stick in mud
Mir·i·am (mir′ē əm) [< Heb.: see MARY] **1.** a feminine name **2.** *Bible* the sister of Moses and Aaron: Ex. 15:20
mirk (murk) ***n.*** *alt. sp. of* MURK —**mirk′y** ***adj.*** **mirk′i·er, mirk′i·est**
Mi·ró (mē rō′), **Joan** (hwän) 1893– ; Sp. painter
mir·ror (mir′ər) ***n.*** [< OFr. < VL. *mirare*: see MIRAGE] **1.** a smooth surface that reflects images; esp., a looking glass **2.** anything that truly pictures or describes [a play that is a *mirror* of life] —***vt.*** to reflect as in a mirror
mirth (murth) ***n.*** [OE. *myrgth* < base of *myrig*, pleasant] joyfulness, gaiety, or merriment, esp. when characterized by laughter
mirth·ful (-fəl) ***adj.*** full of, expressing, or causing mirth; merry —**mirth′ful·ly** ***adv.*** —**mirth′ful·ness** ***n.***
mirth·less (-lis) ***adj.*** without mirth or joy —**mirth′less·ly** ***adv.*** —**mirth′less·ness** ***n.***
mir·y (mīr′ē) ***adj.*** **mir′i·er, mir′i·est** **1.** boggy; swampy **2.** muddy; dirty —**mir′i·ness** ***n.***
mis- [OE. *mis-* or OFr. *mes-*] *a prefix meaning:* **1.** wrong or wrongly, bad or badly [*misplace, misrule*] **2.** no, not [*mistrust, misfire*]
mis·ad·ven·ture (mis′əd ven′chər) ***n.*** an unlucky accident; bad luck; mishap
mis·ad·vise (-əd vīz′) ***vt.*** **-vised′, -vis′ing** to advise badly —**mis′ad·vice′** (-vīs′) ***n.***
mis·al·li·ance (-ə lī′əns) ***n.*** an improper alliance; esp., an unsuitable marriage
mis·al·ly (-ə lī′) ***vt.*** **-lied′, -ly′ing** to ally unsuitably or inappropriately
mis·an·thrope (mis′ən thrōp′, miz′-) ***n.*** [< Gr. < *misein*, to hate + *anthrōpos*, a man] one who hates or distrusts all people: also **mis·an·thro·pist** (mis an′thrə pist) —**mis′an·throp′ic** (-thräp′ik), **mis′an·throp′i·cal** ***adj.*** —**mis′an·throp′i·cal·ly** ***adv.***
mis·an·thro·py (mis an′thrə pē) ***n.*** hatred or distrust of all people
mis·ap·ply (mis′ə plī′) ***vt.*** **-plied′, -ply′ing** to apply or use badly or improperly [to *misapply* one's energies, a trust fund, etc.] —**mis′ap·pli·ca′tion** ***n.***
mis·ap·pre·hend (-ap rə hend′) ***vt.*** to misunderstand —**mis′ap·pre·hen′sion** (-hen′shən) ***n.***
mis·ap·pro·pri·ate (mis′ə prō′prē āt′) ***vt.*** **-at′ed, -at′ing** to appropriate to a bad, incorrect, or dishonest use —**mis′ap·pro′pri·a′tion** ***n.***
mis·be·come (-bi kum′) ***vt.*** **-came′, -come′, -com′ing** to be unbecoming to; be unsuitable for
mis·be·got·ten (-bi gät′'n) ***adj.*** wrongly or unlawfully begotten; specif., born out of wedlock: also **mis′be·got′**
mis·be·have (-bi hāv′) ***vi.*** **-haved′, -hav′ing** to behave wrongly —***vt.*** to conduct (oneself) improperly —**mis′be·hav′er** ***n.*** —**mis′be·hav′ior** (-yər) ***n.***
mis·be·lief (-bə lēf′) ***n.*** wrong, false, or unorthodox belief
misc. **1.** miscellaneous **2.** miscellany
mis·cal·cu·late (mis kal′kyə lāt′) ***vt., vi.*** **-lat′ed, -lat′ing** to calculate incorrectly; miscount or misjudge —**mis′cal·cu·la′tion** ***n.***
mis·call (-kôl′) ***vt.*** to call by a wrong name
mis·car·riage (-kar′ij) ***n.*** **1.** failure to carry out what was intended [a *miscarriage* of justice] **2.** failure of mail, freight, etc. to reach its destination **3.** the expulsion of a fetus from the womb before it is sufficiently developed to survive: see ABORTION
mis·car·ry (-kar′ē) ***vi.*** **-ried, -ry·ing** **1.** *a*) to go wrong; fail: said of a plan, project, etc. *b*) to go astray; fail to arrive: said of mail, freight, etc. **2.** to suffer a miscarriage of a fetus
mis·cast (-kast′) ***vt.*** **-cast′, -cast′ing** to cast (an actor or a play) unsuitably
mis·ce·ge·na·tion (mis′i jə nā′shən, mi sej′ə-) ***n.*** [coined (c.1863) < L. *miscere*, to mix + *genus*, race + -ATION] marriage or sexual relations between a man and woman of different races, esp., in the U.S., between a white and a black
mis·cel·la·ne·ous (mis′ə lā′nē əs, -yəs) ***adj.*** [< L. < *miscellus*, mixed < *miscere*, to mix] **1.** consisting of various kinds; varied; mixed **2.** having various qualities, etc.; many-sided —**mis′cel·la′ne·ous·ly** ***adv.*** —**mis′cel·la′ne·ous·ness** ***n.***
mis·cel·la·ny (mis′ə lā′nē; *Brit.* mi sel′ə nē) ***n., pl.*** **-nies** [see prec.] **1.** a miscellaneous collection, esp. of literary works **2.** [*often pl.*] such a collection of writings, as in a book
mis·chance (mis chans′) ***n.*** bad luck; misadventure
mis·chief (mis′chif) ***n.*** [< OFr. < *meschever*, to come to grief < *mes-*, mis- + *chief*, end] **1.** harm or damage, esp. that done by a person **2.** *a*) action that causes harm or trouble *b*) a person causing damage or annoyance **3.** a tendency to annoy with playful tricks **4.** *a*) a prank; playful, annoying trick *b*) playful, harmless teasing
mis·chief-mak·er (-mā′kər) ***n.*** a person who causes mischief; esp., one who creates trouble by gossiping —**mis′chief-mak′ing** ***n., adj.***
mis·chie·vous (mis′chi vəs) ***adj.*** **1.** causing mischief; specif., *a*) injurious; harmful *b*) prankish; teasing **2.** inclined to annoy with playful tricks; naughty —**mis′chie·vous·ly** ***adv.*** —**mis′chie·vous·ness** ***n.***
mis·ci·ble (mis′ə b'l) ***adj.*** [< ML. < L. *miscere*, to mix] that can be mixed —**mis′ci·bil′i·ty** ***n.***
mis·con·ceive (mis′kən sēv′) ***vt., vi.*** **-ceived′, -ceiv′ing** to conceive or interpret wrongly; misunderstand —**mis′con·cep′tion** (-sep′shən) ***n.***
mis·con·duct (-kən dukt′; *for n.* mis kän′dukt) ***vt.*** **1.** to manage badly or dishonestly **2.** to conduct (oneself) improperly —***n.*** **1.** bad or dishonest management **2.** willfully improper behavior
mis·con·strue (-kən stroo′) ***vt.*** **-strued′, -stru′ing** to construe wrongly; misinterpret —**mis′con·struc′tion** (-struk′shən) ***n.***
mis·count (mis kount′; *for n. usually* mis′kount) ***vt., vi.*** to count incorrectly —***n.*** an incorrect count
mis·cre·ant (mis′krē ənt) ***adj.*** [OFr. *mescreant*, unbelieving < *mes-*, mis- + prp. of *croire*, to believe] **1.** villainous; evil **2.** [Archaic] unbelieving —***n.*** **1.** a criminal; villain **2.** [Archaic] an unbeliever —**mis′cre·an·cy** ***n.***
mis·cue (mis kyoo′) ***n.*** **1.** *Billiards* a shot spoiled by the cue's slipping off the ball **2.** [Colloq.] a mistake; error —***vi.*** **-cued′, -cu′ing** **1.** to make a miscue **2.** *Theater* to miss one's cue
mis·date (-dāt′) ***vt.*** **-dat′ed, -dat′ing** to date (a letter, etc.) incorrectly —***n.*** a wrong date
mis·deal (-dēl′) ***vt., vi.*** **-dealt′, -deal′ing** to deal (playing cards) wrongly —***n.*** a wrong deal —**mis′deal′er** ***n.***
mis·deed (mis dēd′) ***n.*** a wrong or wicked act; crime, sin, etc.
mis·de·mean (mis′di mēn′) ***vt., vi.*** [Rare] to conduct (oneself) badly; misbehave
mis·de·mean·or (-ər) ***n.*** **1.** [Rare] a misbehaving **2.** *Law* any minor offense, as the breaking of a municipal ordinance, for which statute provides a lesser punishment than for a felony, usually a fine or a short term in a local jail, workhouse, etc. Brit. sp. **mis′de·mean′our**
mis·di·rect (mis′də rekt′, -dī-) ***vt.*** to direct wrongly or badly —**mis′di·rec′tion** ***n.***
mis·do (mis doo′) ***vt.*** **-did′, -done′, -do′ing** to do wrongly —**mis·do′er** ***n.*** —**mis·do′ing** ***n.***
mis·doubt (-dout′) ***vt.*** [Archaic] **1.** to distrust **2.** to fear —***vi.*** [Archaic] to have doubts —***n.*** [Archaic] suspicion; doubt
‡**mise en scène** (mē zän sen′) [Fr.] **1.** the staging of a play, motion picture, etc. including the setting, arrangement of the actors, etc. **2.** surroundings; environment
mis·em·ploy (mis′em ploi′) ***vt.*** to employ wrongly or badly; misuse —**mis′em·ploy′ment** ***n.***
mi·ser (mī′zər) ***n.*** [L., wretched] a greedy, stingy person who hoards money for its own sake, even at the expense of his own comfort
mis·er·a·ble (miz′ər ə b'l, miz′rə-) ***adj.*** [< Fr. < L. *miserabilis* < *miser*, wretched] **1.** in a condition of misery; wretched **2.** causing misery, discomfort, etc. [*miserable* weather] **3.** bad; inferior; inadequate [a *miserable* performance] **4.** pitiable **5.** shameful —**mis′er·a·ble·ness** ***n.*** —**mis′er·a·bly** ***adv.***
Mis·e·re·re (miz′ə rer′ē, -rir′-) ***n.*** [LL., have mercy: first word of the psalm in the Vulgate] **1.** the 51st Psalm (50th in the Douay Version) **2.** a musical setting for this
mi·ser·ly (mī′zər lē) ***adj.*** like or characteristic of a miser; greedy and stingy —**mi′ser·li·ness** ***n.***
mis·er·y (miz′ər ē) ***n., pl.*** **-er·ies** [< OFr. < L. < *miser*, wretched] **1.** a condition of great wretchedness or suffering, because of pain, sorrow, poverty, etc.; distress **2.** a cause of such suffering; pain, sorrow, poverty, squalor, etc.

mis·fea·sance (mis fē'z'ns) *n.* [< OFr. < *mes-*, mis- + *faire* (< L. *facere*), to do] *Law* wrongdoing; specif., the doing of a lawful act in an unlawful or improper manner infringing on the rights of others: distinguished from MALFEASANCE, NONFEASANCE —**mis·fea'sor** (-zər) *n.*

mis·file (-fīl') *vt.* **-filed', -fil'ing** to file (papers, etc.) in the wrong place or order

mis·fire (-fīr') *vi.* **-fired', -fir'ing** **1.** to fail to ignite properly: said of an internal-combustion engine **2.** to fail to be discharged: said of a firearm, missile, etc. **3.** to fail to achieve the desired effect —*n.* an act or instance of misfiring

mis·fit (mis fit'; *for n. also, & for 3 always,* mis'fit') *vt., vi.* **-fit'ted, -fit'ting** to fit badly —*n.* **1.** a misfitting **2.** a garment, etc. that misfits **3.** a person not suited to his position, associates, etc.

mis·for·tune (mis fôr'chən) *n.* **1.** bad luck; ill fortune; trouble; adversity **2.** an instance of this; unlucky accident; mishap

mis·give (-giv') *vt.* **-gave', -giv'en, -giv'ing** to cause fear, doubt, or suspicion in [his heart *misgave* him] —*vi.* to feel fear, doubt, etc.

mis·giv·ing (-giv'iŋ) *n.* [*often pl.*] a disturbed feeling of fear, doubt, apprehension, etc.

mis·gov·ern (-guv'ərn) *vt.* to govern or administer badly —**mis·gov'ern·ment** *n.*

mis·guide (-gīd') *vt.* **-guid'ed, -guid'ing** to guide wrongly; lead into error or misconduct; mislead —**mis·guid'ance** *n.* —**mis·guid'ed·ly** *adv.* —**mis·guid'ed·ness** *n.*

mis·han·dle (mis han'd'l) *vt.* **-dled, -dling** to handle badly or roughly; abuse, mismanage, etc.

mis·hap (mis'hap') *n.* an unlucky accident

mish·mash (mish'mash') *n.* a hodgepodge; jumble: also **mish'mosh'** (-mäsh')

Mish·na, Mish·nah (mish nä', mish'nə) *n., pl.* **Mish·na·yot** (mish'nä yōt') [< ModHeb. < Heb. *shānāh*, to repeat, learn] the first part of the Talmud, containing interpretations of scriptural ordinances, compiled by the rabbis about 200 A.D.

mis·in·form (mis'in fôrm') *vt.* to supply with false or misleading information —**mis'in·form'ant, mis'in·form'er** *n.* —**mis'in·for·ma'tion** *n.*

mis·in·ter·pret (-in tur'prit) *vt.* to interpret wrongly; understand or explain incorrectly —**mis'in·ter'pre·ta'tion** *n.* —**mis'in·ter'pret·er** *n.*

mis·judge (mis juj') *vt., vi.* **-judged', -judg'ing** to judge wrongly or unfairly —**mis·judg'ment, mis·judge'ment** *n.*

mis·la·bel (-lā'b'l) *vt., vi.* **-beled** or **-belled, -bel·ing** or **-bel·ling** to label incorrectly

mis·lay (-lā') *vt.* **-laid', -lay'ing** **1.** to put in a place afterward forgotten **2.** to put down or install improperly [to *mislay* floor tiles]

mis·lead (-lēd') *vt.* **-led', -lead'ing** **1.** to lead in a wrong direction; lead astray **2.** to deceive or delude **3.** to lead into wrongdoing —**mis·lead'ing** *adj.* —**mis·lead'ing·ly** *adv.*

mis·man·age (-man'ij) *vt., vi.* **-aged, -ag·ing** to manage or administer badly —**mis·man'age·ment** *n.*

mis·match (-mach') *vt.* to match badly or unsuitably —*n.* a bad or unsuitable match

mis·mate (mis māt') *vt., vi.* **-mat'ed, -mat'ing** to mate badly or unsuitably

mis·name (-nām') *vt.* **-named', -nam'ing** to give or apply a wrong name to

mis·no·mer (mis nō'mər) *n.* [< OFr. < *mes-*, mis- + *nomer*, to name < L. *nominare:* see NOMINATE] **1.** the use of a wrong name or epithet for some person or thing **2.** a name or epithet wrongly used

mis·o- [< Gr. < *misein*, to hate] *a combining form meaning* hatred or hating [*misogyny*] : also **mis-**

mi·sog·a·my (mi säg'ə mē) *n.* [prec. + -GAMY] hatred of marriage —**mi·sog'a·mist** *n.*

mi·sog·y·ny (mi säj'ə nē) *n.* [< Gr.: see MISO- & -GYNY] hatred of women —**mi·sog'y·nist** *n.* —**mi·sog'y·nous, mi·sog'y·nic** *adj.*

mis·place (mis plās') *vt.* **-placed', -plac'ing** **1.** to put in a wrong place **2.** to bestow (one's trust, affection, etc.) unwisely **3.** *same as* MISLAY (sense 1) —**mis·place'ment** *n.*

mis·play (-plā') *vt., vi.* to play wrongly or badly, as in a game —*n.* a wrong or bad play

mis·print (mis print'; *for n. usually* mis'print') —*vt.* to print incorrectly —*n.* an error in printing

mis·pri·sion (mis prizh'ən) *n.* [< OFr. < pp. of *mesprendre*, to take wrongly < *mes-*, mis- + *prendre* < L. *prehendere*, to take] *Law* **1.** misconduct or neglect of duty, esp. by a public official **2.** act of contempt against a government or court

misprision of felony (or **treason**) *Law* the offense of concealing knowledge of another's felony (or treason)

mis·prize (mis prīz') *vt.* **-prized', -priz'ing** [< OFr. < *mes-*, mis- + LL. *pretiare*, to value < L. *pretium*, a price] to despise or undervalue

mis·pro·nounce (mis'prə nouns') *vt., vi.* **-nounced', -nounc'ing** to give (a word) a pronunciation different from any of the accepted standard pronunciations —**mis'pro·nun'ci·a'tion** (-nun'sē ā'shən) *n.*

mis·quote (mis kwōt') *vt., vi.* **-quot'ed, -quot'ing** to quote incorrectly —**mis'quo·ta'tion** *n.*

mis·read (-rēd') *vt., vi.* **-read'** (-red'), **-read'ing** (-rēd'iŋ) to read wrongly, esp. so as to misinterpret or misunderstand

mis·rep·re·sent (mis'rep ri zent') *vt.* **1.** to represent falsely; give an untrue idea of **2.** to be a bad representative of —**mis'rep·re·sen·ta'tion** *n.*

mis·rule (mis ro͞ol') *vt.* **-ruled', -rul'ing** to rule badly or unjustly; misgovern —*n.* **1.** misgovernment **2.** disorder or riot —**mis·rul'er** *n.*

miss[1] (mis) *vt.* [OE. *missan*] **1.** to fail to hit, meet, catch, do, see, hear, etc. **2.** to let (an opportunity, etc.) go by **3.** to escape; avoid [he *missed* being hit] **4.** to fail or forget to do, keep, attend, etc. [he *missed* a class] **5.** to notice, feel, or regret the absence or loss of —*vi.* **1.** to fail to hit something aimed at **2.** to fail to be successful **3.** to misfire, as an engine —*n.* a failure to hit, obtain, etc.

miss[2] (mis) *n., pl.* **miss'es** [contr. of MISTRESS] **1.** [**M-**] a title used in speaking to or of an unmarried woman or girl, placed before the name [*Miss* Smith, the *Misses* Smith] **2.** a young unmarried woman or girl **3.** [*pl.*] a series of sizes in clothing for women and girls of average proportions

Miss. Mississippi

miss. **1.** mission **2.** missionary

mis·sal (mis''l) *n.* [< ML. < LL. *missa*, MASS] *R.C.Ch.* a book containing all the prayers, rites, etc. for the Mass throughout the year

mis·shape (mis shāp') *vt.* **-shaped', -shaped'** or archaic **-shap'en, -shap'ing** to shape badly; deform

mis·shap·en (-'n) *adj.* badly shaped; deformed —**mis·shap'en·ly** *adv.* —**mis·shap'en·ness** *n.*

mis·sile (mis''l) *adj.* [L. *missilis* < pp. of *mittere*, to send] that can be, or is, thrown or shot —*n.* a weapon or other object, as a spear, bullet, rocket, etc., designed to be thrown or launched toward a target; often, specif., a guided missile

mis·sile·ry, mis·sil·ry (-rē) *n.* **1.** the science of building and launching guided missiles **2.** guided missiles collectively

miss·ing (mis'iŋ) *adj.* absent; lost; lacking; specif., absent after combat, but not definitely known to be dead or taken prisoner

mis·sion (mish'ən) *n.* [L. *missio* < pp. of *mittere*, to send] **1.** a sending out or being sent out with authority to perform a special duty, as by a church, government, etc. **2.** *a)* a group of persons sent by a church to spread its religion, esp. in a foreign land *b)* its headquarters *c)* [*pl.*] organized missionary work **3.** a diplomatic delegation; embassy **4.** a group of technicians, etc. sent to a foreign country **5.** the special duty or function for which someone is sent **6.** the special task for which a person is apparently destined in life; calling **7.** any charitable or religious organization for doing welfare work for the needy **8.** *Mil.* an assigned combat operation; esp., a single combat flight by an airplane or group of airplanes —*adj.* of a mission or missions —*vt.* to send on a mission

mis·sion·ar·y (-er'ē) *adj.* of or characteristic of religious missions or missionaries —*n., pl.* **-ar'ies** a person sent on a mission; specif., a person sent out by his church to preach, teach, and proselytize, as in a foreign country considered heathen: also **mis'sion·er**

mis·sis (mis'əz) *n.* [altered < MRS.] [Dial.] one's wife: also used with *the:* also **mis'sus**

Mis·sis·sip·pi (mis'ə sip'ē) [< Fr. < Algonquian, lit., big river] **1.** river in C U.S., flowing from N Minn. to the Gulf of Mexico: 2,348 mi. **2.** Southern State of the U.S.: 47,716 sq. mi.; pop. 2,521,000; cap. Jackson: abbrev. **Miss., MS**

Mis·sis·sip·pi·an (-ən) *adj.* **1.** of the Mississippi River **2.** of the State of Mississippi **3.** designating or of the first coal-forming period of the Paleozoic Era in N. America —*n.* a native or inhabitant of Mississippi —**the Mississippian** the Mississippian Period or its rocks: see GEOLOGY, chart

mis·sive (mis'iv) *n.* [Fr. < ML. < L. pp. of *mittere*, to send] a letter or written message

Mis·sour·i (mi zoor'ē) [< Algonquian, lit., people of the big canoes] **1.** river in WC U.S., flowing from NW Mont. to the Mississippi: 2,466 mi. **2.** Middle Western State of the C U.S.: 69,686 sq. mi.; pop. 4,917,000; cap. Jefferson City: abbrev. **Mo., MO** —**from Missouri** [Colloq.] not easily convinced —**Mis·sour'i·an** *adj., n.*

mis·speak (mis spēk′) ***vt., vi.*** **-spoke′, -spok′en, -speak′ing** to speak or say incorrectly
mis·spell (-spel′) ***vt., vi.*** **-spelled′** or **-spelt′, -spell′ing** to spell incorrectly
mis·spell·ing (-spel′iŋ) ***n.*** (an) incorrect spelling
mis·spend (-spend′) ***vt.*** **-spent′, -spend′ing** to spend improperly or wastefully
mis·state (-stāt′) ***vt.*** **-stat′ed, -stat′ing** to state incorrectly or falsely —**mis·state′ment** ***n.***
mis·step (mis step′) ***n.*** **1.** a wrong or awkward step **2.** a mistake in conduct; faux pas
mist (mist) ***n.*** **[**OE.**]** **1.** a large mass of water vapor like a light fog **2.** a cloud of dust, gas, etc. **3.** a fine spray, as of perfume **4.** a film before the eyes, blurring the vision *[*through a *mist* of tears*]* **5.** anything that obscures the understanding, memory, etc. —***vt., vi.*** to obscure with or as with a mist
mis·take (mi stāk′) ***vt.*** **-took′, -tak′en** or obs. **-took′, -tak′ing [**ON. *mistaka,* to take wrongly**]** **1.** to understand or perceive wrongly **2.** to take to be another *[*he *mistook* me for another*]* —***vi.*** to make a mistake —***n.*** **1.** a fault in understanding, interpretation, etc. **2.** a blunder; error —**and no mistake** [Colloq.] certainly —**mis·tak′a·ble** ***adj.***
mis·tak·en (-stāk′'n) ***adj.*** **1.** wrong; having an incorrect understanding, perception, etc.: said of persons **2.** incorrect; misunderstood: said of ideas, etc. —**mis·tak′en·ly** ***adv.***
mis·ter (mis′tər) ***n.*** **[**weakened form of MASTER**]** **1.** [M-] *a)* a title used in speaking to or of a man, placed before his name or office and usually written *Mr.* *b)* a title before the name of a place, occupation, etc. to designate an outstanding man in it **2.** [Colloq.] sir: in direct address, not followed by a name **3.** [Dial.] one's husband: also used with *the*
mis·time (mis tīm′) ***vt.*** **-timed′, -tim′ing** **1.** to do at an inappropriate time **2.** to judge incorrectly the time of
mis·tle·toe (mis′'l tō′) ***n.*** **[**< OE. < *mistel,* mistletoe + *tan,* a twig**]** **1.** an evergreen plant with yellowish-green leaves and waxy white, poisonous berries, parasitic on trees **2.** a sprig of this, hung as a Christmas decoration
mis·took (mi stook′) *pt. & obs. pp. of* MISTAKE
mis·tral (mis′trəl, mi sträl′) ***n.*** **[**Fr. < Pr., lit., master-wind < L. < *magister,* MASTER**]** a cold, dry, north wind that blows over the Mediterranean coast of France and nearby regions
mis·treat (mis trēt′) ***vt.*** to treat wrongly or badly —**mis·treat′ment** ***n.***
mis·tress (mis′tris) ***n.*** **[**< OFr. fem. of *maistre,* MASTER**]** **1.** a woman who rules others or controls something; specif., *a)* a woman head of a household or institution *b)* [Chiefly Brit.] a woman schoolteacher **2.** [*sometimes* **M-**] something regarded as feminine that has control, power, etc. *[*England was *Mistress* of the seas*]* **3.** a woman who has sexual relations with, and may be supported by, a man to whom she is not married **4.** [Archaic] a sweetheart **5.** [M-] formerly, a title prefixed to the name of a woman: now replaced by *Mrs.* or *Miss*
mis·tri·al (mis trī′əl) ***n.*** *Law* a trial made void because of an error in the proceedings, or because the jury cannot reach a verdict
mis·trust (-trust′) ***n.*** lack of trust or confidence; suspicion —***vt., vi.*** to have no trust or confidence in; doubt —**mis·trust′ful** ***adj.*** —**mis·trust′ful·ly** ***adv.*** —**mis·trust′ful·ness** ***n.***
mist·y (mis′tē) ***adj.*** **mist′i·er, mist′i·est** **1.** of or like mist **2.** characterized by or covered with mist **3.** *a)* blurred or dimmed, as by mist *b)* obscure or vague —**mist′i·ly** ***adv.*** —**mist′i·ness** ***n.***
mis·un·der·stand (mis′un dər stand′, mis un′-) ***vt.*** **-stood′, -stand′ing** to fail to understand correctly; miscomprehend or misinterpret
mis·un·der·stand·ing (-stan′diŋ) ***n.*** **1.** a failure to understand correctly **2.** a quarrel; disagreement
mis·un·der·stood (-stood′) ***adj.*** **1.** not properly understood **2.** not properly appreciated
mis·us·age (mis yōō′sij, -zij) ***n.*** **1.** incorrect usage, as of words **2.** bad or harsh treatment
mis·use (mis yōōz′; *for n.* -yōōs′) ***vt.*** **-used′, -us′ing** **1.** to use improperly; misapply **2.** to treat badly or harshly; abuse —***n.*** incorrect or improper use —**mis·us′er** ***n.***
mis·val·ue (-val′yōō) ***vt.*** **-ued, -u·ing** to fail to value properly or adequately
mis·word (-wurd′) ***vt.*** to word incorrectly
mis·write (-rīt′) ***vt.*** **-wrote′, -writ′ten, -writ′ing** to write incorrectly
Mitch·ell (mich′əl), **Maria** 1818–89; U.S. astronomer
mite[1] (mīt) ***n.*** **[**OE.**]** any of a large number of tiny arachnids, often parasitic upon animals, insects, or plants, or infesting prepared foods
mite[2] (mīt) ***n.*** **[**< MDu., ult. same as prec.**]** **1.** *a)* a very small sum of money *b)* formerly, a coin of very small value **2.** a bit; a little *[*a *mite* slow*]* **3.** a very small creature
mi·ter[1] (mīt′ər) ***n.*** **[**< OFr. < L. < Gr. *mitra,* a headband**]** **1.** a tall, ornamented cap with peaks in front and back, worn by bishops and abbots as a mark of office **2.** the office or rank of a bishop —***vt.*** to invest with the office of bishop

MITER

mi·ter[2] (mīt′ər) ***n.*** **[**prob. < prec.**]** *Carpentry* **1.** a kind of joint formed by fitting together two pieces, beveled to form a corner (usually a right angle): also **miter joint** **2.** either of the facing surfaces of such a joint —***vt.*** **1.** to fit together in a miter **2.** to bevel the edges of to form a miter

MITER JOINT

mit·i·gate (mit′ə gāt′) ***vt., vi.*** **-gat′ed, -gat′ing [**< L. pp. of *mitigare,* to make mild < *mitis,* mild + *agere,* to drive**]** to make or become milder, less severe, or less painful —**mit′i·ga·ble** (-i gə b'l) ***adj.*** —**mit′i·ga′tion** ***n.*** —**mit′i·ga′tive** ***adj.*** —**mit′i·ga′tor** ***n.*** —**mit′i·ga·to′ry** (-gə tôr′ē) ***adj.***
Mit·i·lí·ni (mit′'l ē′nē) *same as* LESBOS
mi·to·sis (mī tō′sis, mi-) ***n., pl.*** **-ses** (-sēz) **[**ModL. < Gr. *mitos,* thread + -OSIS**]** *Biol.* the indirect method of nuclear division of cells: the nuclear chromatin first appears as long threads which in turn break into chromosomes that are split lengthwise —**mi·tot′ic** (-tät′ik) ***adj.*** —**mi·tot′i·cal·ly** ***adv.***
mi·tral (mī′trəl) ***adj.*** of or like a miter
mitral valve the valve between the left atrium and left ventricle of the heart
mi·tre (mīt′ər) ***n., vt.*** **-tred, -tring** *Brit. sp. of* MITER
mitt (mit) ***n.*** **[**contr. < MITTEN**]** **1.** a woman's glove covering part of the arm, the hand, and sometimes part of the fingers **2.** *same as* MITTEN **3.** [Slang] a hand **4.** *a) Baseball* a padded glove worn for protection *[*catcher's *mitt]* *b)* a boxing glove
mit·ten (mit′'n) ***n.*** **[**< OFr. *mitaine***]** **1.** a glove with a thumb but no separately divided fingers **2.** *earlier var. of* MITT (sense 1)
mix (miks) ***vt.*** **mixed** or **mixt, mix′ing [**prob. < *mixt,* mixed < Fr. < L. pp. of *miscere,* to mix**]** **1.** to blend together in a single mass or compound **2.** to make by blending ingredients *[*to *mix* a cake*]* **3.** to join; combine *[*to *mix* work and play*]* **4.** to cause to associate *[*to *mix* boys with girls in a school*]* —***vi.*** **1.** to be mixed; be blended; mingle **2.** to associate or get along —***n.*** **1.** a mixing or being mixed **2.** a state of confusion **3.** a mixture, as of ingredients for making something **4.** soda, ginger ale, etc. for mixing with alcoholic liquor —**mix up** **1.** to mix thoroughly **2.** to confuse **3.** to involve (*in* some matter) —**mix′a·ble** ***adj.***
mixed (mikst) ***adj.*** **1.** joined or blended in a single mass or compound **2.** made up of different parts, elements, races, etc. **3.** consisting of or involving both sexes *[mixed* company*]* **4.** confused; muddled
mixed bag a random assortment or mixture, esp. of diverse elements, types of people, etc.
mixed marriage marriage between persons of different religions or races
mixed media **1.** the use of more than two media for an effect, as by combining acting, flashing lights, tape recordings, etc. **2.** *Painting* the use of different media, as oil and crayon, in the same composition
mixed number a number consisting of a whole number and a fraction, as 3 2/3
mix·er (mik′sər) ***n.*** **1.** one that mixes; specif., *a)* a person with reference to his sociability *b)* a machine or an electric appliance for mixing **2.** [Slang] a social gathering for getting people acquainted
mix·ture (miks′chər) ***n.*** **1.** a mixing or being mixed **2.** something mixed **3.** *Chem.* a substance containing two or more ingredients: distinguished from COMPOUND[1] in that the constituents are not in fixed proportions, retain their individual characteristics, and are physically separable
mix-up (miks′up′) ***n.*** **1.** a condition or instance of confusion **2.** [Colloq.] a fight
miz·zen, miz·en (miz′'n) ***adj.*** **[**< or akin to MFr. *misaine* < It. < L. *medianus:* see MEDIAN**]** of the mizzenmast —***n.*** **1.** a fore-and-aft sail set on the mizzenmast **2.** *clipped form of* MIZZENMAST
miz·zen·mast (-məst, -mast′) ***n.*** the mast nearest the stern in a ship with two or three masts
mk. *pl.* **mks.** **1.** mark (monetary unit) **2.** markka
mks, m.k.s., M.K.S. meter-kilogram-second
mkt. market
ML. Medieval (or Middle) Latin
ml. **1.** mail **2.** milliliter(s): also **ml**
Mlle. *pl.* **Mlles.** Mademoiselle
MLowG. Middle Low German

mm, mm. 1. millimeter(s) 2. [L. *millia*] thousands
MM. Messieurs
Mme. Madame
Mmes. Mesdames
MN Minnesota
Mn *Chem.* manganese
mne·mon·ic (nē män′ik) *adj.* [< Gr. < *mnēmōn,* mindful < *mnasthai,* to remember] 1. helping, or meant to help, the memory 2. of mnemonics or memory —**mne·mon′i·cal·ly** *adv.*
mne·mon·ics (-iks) *n.pl.* 1. [*with sing. v.*] a technique for improving memory by the use of certain formulas 2. such formulas
-mo (mō) [< L. abl. ending] *a suffix meaning* having (a specified number of) leaves as a result of folding a sheet of paper *[twelvemo]*
Mo *Chem.* molybdenum
Mo. 1. Missouri: also **MO** 2. Monday
mo. 1. money order 2. *pl.* **mos.** month
M.O., MO 1. Medical Officer 2. money order
m.o. money order
mo·a (mō′ə) *n.* [< native (Maori) name] any of an extinct group of very large, flightless birds of New Zealand, resembling the ostrich
Mo·ab (mō′ab) ancient kingdom east & south of the Dead Sea —**Mo′ab·ite′** (-ə bīt′) *adj., n.*
moan (mōn) *n.* [prob. < base of OE. *mænan,* to complain] 1. formerly, a lamentation 2. a low, mournful sound of sorrow or pain 3. any similar sound, as of the wind —*vi.* 1. to make a moan 2. to complain, lament, etc. —*vt.* 1. to say with a moan 2. to bewail *[to moan one's fate]*
moat (mōt) *n.* [OFr. *mote*] a deep, broad ditch dug around a fortress or castle, and often filled with water, for protection against invasion —*vt.* to surround with or as with a moat
mob (mäb) *n.* [< L. *mobile (vulgus),* movable (crowd)] 1. a disorderly and lawless crowd; rabble 2. any crowd 3. the common people: contemptuous term 4. [Slang] a gang of criminals —*vt.* **mobbed, mob′bing** 1. to crowd around and attack, jostle, annoy, etc. 2. to throng
mob·cap (mäb′kap′) *n.* [< MDu. *mop,* woman's cap + CAP] formerly, a woman's cap, worn indoors, with a high, puffy crown, often tied under the chin
Mo·bile (mō bēl′, mō′bēl) [< Fr. < AmInd.] seaport in SW Ala., on an arm **(Mobile Bay)** of the Gulf of Mexico: pop. 200,000
mo·bile (mō′b′l, -bīl; *also, & for n. usually,* -bēl) *adj.* [OFr. < L. *mobilis* < *movere,* to move] 1. *a)* moving, or able to move, from place to place *b)* movable by means of a motor vehicle *[a mobile home]* 2. that can change rapidly or easily, as to suit moods or needs; flexible, adaptable, fluid, etc. 3. designating or of a society in which one may move freely or advance from one class to another —*n.* an abstract sculpture with parts that can move, as a suspended arrangement of thin forms, rings, etc. —**mo·bil·i·ty** (mō bil′ə tē) *n.*
mobile home a movable dwelling with no permanent foundation, but connected to utility lines and set more or less permanently at a location
mo·bi·lize (mō′bə līz′) *vt.* **-lized′, -liz′ing** 1. *a)* to make movable *b)* to put into motion, circulation, or use 2. to make ready for immediate active service in war 3. to organize (people, resources, etc.) for any active service or use —*vi.* to become mobilized, as for war —**mo′bi·liz′a·ble** *adj.* —**mo′bi·li·za′tion** *n.* —**mo′bi·liz′er** *n.*
Mö·bi·us strip (mā′bē əs, mō′-) [after A. *Möbius* (1790–1868), G. mathematician] a surface with only one side, formed from a narrow strip of paper given a half twist and then pasted together
mob·oc·ra·cy (mäb äk′rə sē) *n., pl.* **-cies** [MOB + (DEM)OCRACY] 1. rule by a mob 2. the mob as ruler
mob·ster (mäb′stər) *n.* [Slang] a gangster
Mo·çam·bi·que (moo′səm bē′kə) *Port. name of* MOZAMBIQUE
moc·ca·sin (mäk′ə s′n) *n.* [< Algonquian] 1. a heelless slipper of soft, flexible leather, worn orig. by N. American Indians 2. a similar slipper, but with a hard sole and heel 3. *same as* WATER MOCCASIN
moccasin flower *same as* LADY-SLIPPER
mo·cha (mō′kə) *n.* [after *Mocha,* seaport in Yemen] 1. a choice grade of coffee grown orig. in Arabia 2. [Colloq.] any coffee 3. a flavoring made from coffee or coffee and chocolate 4. a type of soft, velvety leather —*adj.* 1. flavored with coffee or coffee and chocolate 2. reddish-brown

MOCCASINS

mock (mäk) *vt.* [OFr. *mocquer,* to mock] 1. to hold up to scorn or contempt; ridicule 2. to mimic, as in fun or derision 3. to lead on and disappoint; deceive 4. to defy and make futile —*vi.* to express scorn, ridicule, etc. —*n.* 1. a mocking 2. an object of ridicule 3. an imitation —*adj.* sham; imitation —**mock′er** *n.* —**mock′ing·ly** *adv.*
mock·er·y (-ər ē) *n., pl.* **-er·ies** 1. a mocking 2. an object of ridicule 3. a false, derisive, or impertinent imitation 4. vain effort; futility
mock-he·ro·ic (-hi rō′ik) *adj.* mocking, or burlesquing, heroic manner, action, or character —**mock′-he·ro′i·cal·ly** *adv.*
mock·ing·bird (mäk′iŋ burd′) *n.* an American songbird able to imitate many birdcalls
mock orange any of a genus of shrubs with fragrant white flowers like those of the orange
mock turtle soup a soup made from calf's head, veal, etc., spiced to taste like green turtle soup
mock-up (mäk′up′) *n.* a scale model or replica of a structure or apparatus, used for instructional or experimental purposes
mod (mäd) *adj.* [< MOD(ERN)] [*also* **M-**] designating a flamboyant style of clothing popular among young people, originating in England in the 1960's
mod. 1. moderate 2. modern
mod·al (mōd′'l) *adj.* of or indicating a mode or mood; specif., *Gram.* of or expressing mood —**mo·dal·i·ty** (mō dal′ə tē) *n., pl.* **-ties** —**mod′al·ly** *adv.*
modal auxiliary an auxiliary verb used with another to indicate its mood: *can, may, might, must, should,* and *would* are *modal auxiliaries*
mode (mōd) *n.* [L. *modus,* measure, manner] 1. a manner or way of acting, doing, or being 2. [Fr. < L. *modus*] customary usage, or current fashion or style 3. *Gram. same as* MOOD[2] 4. *Music* the arrangement, or any specific arrangement, of tones and semitones in a scale 5. *Statistics* the value, number, etc. that appears most frequently in a given series
mod·el (mäd′'l) *n.* [< Fr. < It. *modello,* dim. of *modo* < L. *modus,* MODE] 1. *a)* a small copy or representation of an existing or planned object, as a ship, building, etc. *b) same as* ARCHETYPE (sense 1) *c)* a representation of the supposed structure of something *d)* a piece of sculpture in wax or clay from which a finished work in bronze, marble, etc. is to be made 2. a person or thing considered as a standard of excellence to be imitated 3. a style or design *[a 1972 model]* 4. *a)* a person who poses for an artist or photographer *b)* any person or thing serving as a subject for an artist *c)* a person employed to display clothes by wearing them —*adj.* 1. serving as a model, or standard of excellence 2. representative; typical —*vt.* **-eled** or **-elled, -el·ing** or **-el·ling** 1. *a)* to make a model of *b)* to plan or form after a model *c)* to make conform to a standard of excellence 2. to shape or form in or as in clay, wax, etc. 3. to display (a dress, etc.) by wearing —*vi.* 1. to make a model or models 2. to serve as a model (sense 4) —**mod′el·er, mod′el·ler** *n.*
mod·er·ate (mäd′ər it; *for v.* -ə rāt′) *adj.* [< L. pp. of *moderare,* to restrain] 1. within reasonable limits; avoiding extremes; temperate 2. mild; not violent *[moderate weather]* 3. of average or medium quality, range, etc. *[moderate skills]* —*n.* a person holding moderate views, as in politics or religion —*vt., vi.* **-at′ed, -at′ing** 1. to make or become moderate 2. to preside over (a meeting, etc.) —**mod′er·ate·ly** *adv.* —**mod′er·ate·ness** *n.*
mod·er·a·tion (mäd′ə rā′shən) *n.* 1. a moderating, or bringing within bounds 2. avoidance of extremes 3. absence of violence; calmness —**in moderation** to a moderate degree; without excess
mod·e·ra·to (-rät′ō) *adj., adv.* [It.] *Music* with moderation in tempo
mod·er·a·tor (mäd′ə rāt′ər) *n.* a person or thing that moderates; specif., a person who presides at a meeting, debate, etc. —**mod′er·a′tor·ship′** *n.*
mod·ern (mäd′ərn) *adj.* [< Fr. < LL. *modernus* < L. *modo,* just now, orig. abl. of *modus,* measure] 1. of the present or recent times; specif., *a)* of the latest styles, methods, ideas, etc.; up-to-date *b)* designating or of certain contemporary trends in art, music, literature, dance, etc. 2. of the period of history from c.1450 A.D. to now 3. [*often* **M-**] designating the most recent stage of a language *[Modern English]* —*n.* 1. a person living in modern times 2. a person with modern ideas, standards, etc. —**mo·der′ni·ty** (mä dur′nə tē, mə-) *n., pl.* **-ties** —**mod′ern·ly** *adv.* —**mod′ern·ness** *n.*
Modern English the English language since about the mid-15th cent.: cf. EARLY MODERN ENGLISH
Modern Hebrew Hebrew in post-Biblical times, esp. as the language of modern Israel

mod·ern·ism (-iz'm) *n.* **1.** *a)* modern practices, ideas, etc., or sympathy with these *b)* a modern idiom, practice, or usage **2.** [M-] *Christianity* any movement redefining doctrine in the light of modern science, etc. —**mod'ern·ist** *n., adj.* —**mod'ern·is'tic** *adj.* —**mod'ern·is'ti·cal·ly** *adv.*
mod·ern·ize (mäd'ər nīz') *vt., vi.* **-ized', -iz'ing** to make or become modern in style, design, methods, etc. —**mod'ern·i·za'tion** *n.* —**mod'ern·iz'er** *n.*
Modern Latin the Latin used since c.1500, chiefly in scientific literature
mod·est (mäd'ist) *adj.* [< Fr. < L. *modestus* < *modus,* measure] **1.** having or showing a moderate opinion of one's own value, abilities, etc.; not vain **2.** not forward; shy or reserved *[modest* behavior*]* **3.** behaving, dressing, etc. decorously or decently **4.** moderate or reasonable; not extreme *[*a *modest* request*]* **5.** quiet and humble in appearance, style, etc. *[*a *modest* home*]* —**mod'est·ly** *adv.*
Mo·des·to (mə des'tō) [Sp., lit., modest] city in C Calif.: pop. 106,000
mod·es·ty (mäd'is tē) *n.* the quality or state of being modest; specif., *a)* unassuming or humble behavior *b)* moderation *c)* decency; decorum
ModGr. Modern Greek
ModHeb. Modern Hebrew
mod·i·cum (mäd'i kəm) *n.* [L., neut. of *modicus,* moderate] a small amount; bit
mod·i·fi·ca·tion (mäd'ə fi kā'shən) *n.* a modifying or being modified; specif., *a)* a partial or slight change in form *b)* a product of this *c)* a slight reduction *d)* a qualification or limitation of meaning
mod·i·fi·er (mäd'ə fī'ər) *n.* a person or thing that modifies; esp., a word, phrase, or clause that limits the meaning of another word or phrase *[*adjectives and adverbs are *modifiers]*
mod·i·fy (mäd'ə fī') *vt.* **-fied', -fy'ing** [< MFr. < L. *modificare,* to limit < *modus,* measure + *facere,* to make] **1.** to change or alter, esp. slightly or partially **2.** to limit or lessen slightly; moderate *[*to *modify* a penalty*]* **3.** *Gram.* to limit the meaning of; qualify *[*"old" *modifies* "man" in *old man]* **4.** *Linguis.* to change (a vowel) by umlaut —*vi.* to be modified —**mod'i·fi'a·ble** *adj.*
Mo·di·glia·ni (mô'dē lyä'nē), **A·me·de·o** (ä'me de'ô) 1884–1920; It. painter, in France
mod·ish (mōd'ish) *adj.* in the latest style; fashionable —**mod'ish·ly** *adv.* —**mod'ish·ness** *n.*
mo·diste (mō dēst') *n.* [Fr. < *mode:* see MODE] a woman who makes or deals in fashionable clothes, hats, etc. for women: somewhat old-fashioned term
ModL. Modern Latin
mod·u·lar (mäj'ə lər) *adj.* **1.** of a module or modulus **2.** designating or of units of standardized size, design, etc. that can be arranged or fitted together in various ways
mod·u·late (-lāt') *vt.* **-lat'ed, -lat'ing** [< L. pp. of *modulari* < dim. of *modus,* measure] **1.** to regulate, adjust, or adapt **2.** to vary the pitch, intensity, etc. of (the voice) **3.** *Radio* to vary the amplitude, frequency, or phase of (an oscillation, as a carrier wave) in accordance with some signal —*vi.* to shift from one key to another within a musical composition —**mod'u·la'tion** *n.* —**mod'u·la'tor** *n.* —**mod'u·la·to'ry** *adj.*
mod·ule (mäj'ōōl) *n.* [Fr. < L. dim. of *modus,* measure] **1.** a standard or unit of measurement, as in architecture **2.** *a)* any of a set of units, as cabinets, designed to be arranged or joined in various ways *b)* a detachable section, compartment, or unit with a specific function, as in a spacecraft *c)* *Electronics* a compact assembly functioning as a component of a larger unit
mod·u·lus (mäj'ə ləs) *n., pl.* **-u·li'** (-lī') [ModL. < L.: see prec.] *Physics* a constant expressing the measure of some property, as elasticity
‡**mo·dus o·pe·ran·di** (mō'dəs äp'ə ran'dī, -dē) [L.] mode of operation; procedure
‡**modus vi·ven·di** (vi ven'dī, -dē) [L.] **1.** mode of living **2.** a temporary compromise in a dispute
Mo·gul (mō'gul, -g'l; mō gul') *n.* [Per. *Mughul*] **1.** a Mongol, or Mongolian; esp., any of the Mongolian conquerors of India or their descendants **2.** [m-] a powerful or important person
mo·hair (mō'her) *n.* [< OIt. < Ar. *mukhayyar*] **1.** the hair of the Angora goat **2.** yarn or a fabric made from this hair —*adj.* of mohair
Mo·ham·med (mō ham'id) 570?–632 A.D.; Arabian prophet: founder of the Moslem religion
Mo·ham·med·an (mō ham'i d'n) *adj.* of Mohammed or the Moslem religion —*n. same as* MOSLEM: term used mainly by non-Moslems
Mo·ham·med·an·ism (-iz'm) *n. same as* ISLAM: term used mainly by non-Moslems
Mo·ha·ve (mō hä'vē) *n.* [< Mohave words for "three" & "mountain"] **1.** *pl.* **-ves, -ve** a member of an Indian tribe living along the Colorado River in Arizona **2.** their language —*adj.* of the Mohaves
Mo·hawk¹ (mō'hôk) *n.* [< Algonquian word meaning "man-eaters"] **1.** *pl.* **-hawks, -hawk** a member of an Iroquoian Indian tribe orig. of the Mohawk Valley, New York, now in Canada and New York **2.** their language —*adj.* of the Mohawks
Mo·hawk² (mō'hôk') [< prec.] river in C & E N.Y., flowing into the Hudson
Mo·he·gan (mō hē'gən) *n.* [< Algonquian, lit., a wolf] **1.** *pl.* **-gans, -gan** a member of a Mahican tribe of Algonquian Indians who lived in Connecticut **2.** *same as* MAHICAN —*adj.* of the Mohegans
Mo·hi·can (mō hē'kən) *n., adj. same as* MAHICAN
moi·e·ty (moi'ə tē) *n., pl.* **-ties** [< OFr. < L. < *medius,* middle] **1.** a half **2.** an indefinite part
moil (moil) *vi.* [< OFr. *moillier,* to moisten < L. *mollis,* soft] to toil —*vt.* [Archaic] to moisten or soil —*n.* **1.** toil **2.** turmoil —**moil'er** *n.*
moire (mwär, môr) *n.* [Fr., watered silk < E. MOHAIR] a fabric, as silk, rayon, or acetate, having a watered, or wavy, pattern
moi·ré (mwä rā', mô-; môr'ā) *adj.* [Fr.] having a watered, or wavy, pattern —*n.* **1.** a watered pattern pressed into cloth, etc. with engraved rollers **2.** *same as* MOIRE
moist (moist) *adj.* [OFr. *moiste* < L. *mucidus,* moldy < *mucus,* mucus] **1.** slightly wet; damp **2.** tearful —**moist'ly** *adv.* —**moist'ness** *n.*
mois·ten (mois''n) *vt., vi.* to make or become moist —**mois'·ten·er** *n.*
mois·ture (-chər) *n.* water, etc. causing a slight wetness or dampness —**mois'ture·less** *adj.*
mois·tur·ize (-īz') *vt., vi.* **-ized', -iz'ing** to add or restore moisture to (the skin, air, etc.) —**mois'tur·iz'er** *n.*
Mo·ja·ve (mō hä'vē) *n., adj. same as* MOHAVE
Mojave Desert desert in SE Calif.
mol (mōl) *n. same as* MOLE⁴
MOL manned orbiting laboratory
mol. **1.** molecular **2.** molecule
mo·lar (mō'lər) *adj.* [< L. < *mola,* millstone] **1.** used for or capable of grinding **2.** designating or of a tooth or teeth adapted for grinding —*n.* a molar tooth: in man there are twelve molars
mo·las·ses (mə las'iz) *n.* [< Port. *melaco* < LL. *mellaceum,* must < L. < *mel,* honey] a thick, usually dark brown syrup produced during the refining of sugar, or from sorghum, etc.
mold¹ (mōld) *n.* [OFr. *molle* < L. *modulus:* see MODULE] **1.** a hollow form for shaping something plastic or molten **2.** a frame, shaped core, etc. on or around which something is modeled **3.** a pattern or model for something **4.** something formed in or on, or as if in or on, a mold; often, specif., a gelatin dessert, aspic, etc. so formed **5.** form or shape, esp. that given by a mold **6.** distinctive character or nature —*vt.* **1.** to make or shape in or on, or as if in or on, a mold **2.** to influence (opinion, etc.) strongly **3.** to fit closely to the contours of **4.** to ornament by or with molding **5.** to make a mold of for a casting —**mold'a·ble** *adj.* —**mold'er** *n.*
mold² (mōld) *n.* [ME. *moul:* sp. prob. infl. by ff.] **1.** a downy or furry fungous growth on organic matter, esp. in the presence of dampness or decay **2.** any fungus producing such a growth —*vt., vi.* to make or become moldy
mold³ (mōld) *n.* [OE. *molde,* earth] loose, soft soil, esp. when rich with decayed organic matter
Mol·da·vi·a (mäl dā'vē ə, -dāv'yə) **1.** region in E Romania **2.** republic of the U.S.S.R., adjacent to this region: 13,000 sq. mi.; pop. 3,500,000; cap. Kishinev: in full, **Moldavian Soviet Socialist Republic** —**Mol·da'vi·an** *adj., n.*
mold·board (mōld'bôrd') *n.* **1.** a curved iron plate on a plowshare, for turning over the soil **2.** a large plate like this at the front of a bulldozer or snowplow, angled to push material aside **3.** one of the boards used to form a mold for concrete
mold·er (mōl'dər) *vi., vt.* [see MOLD³ & -ER] to crumble into dust; decay
mold·ing (mōl'diŋ) *n.* **1.** the act of one that molds **2.** something molded **3.** *a)* the ornamental contour of a cornice, jamb, etc. *b)* a cornice or similar projecting or sunk ornamentation *c)* a shaped strip of wood, etc., for finishing or decorating walls (esp. near the ceiling), furniture, etc.

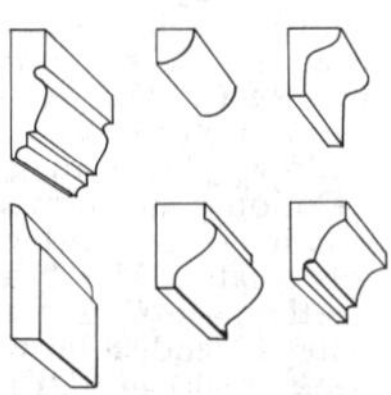
MOLDINGS

mold·y (mōl'dē) *adj.* **mold'i·er, mold'i·est** **1.** covered with a growth of mold **2.** musty or stale, as from age or decay —**mold'i·ness** *n.*
mole¹ (mōl) *n.* [OE. *mal*] a small, congenital spot on the human skin, usually dark-colored and slightly raised, often hairy

mole² (mōl) ***n.*** [< or akin to MDu. *mol*] a small, burrowing, insect-eating mammal with small eyes and ears, shovel-like forefeet, and soft fur: moles live mainly underground
mole³ (mōl) ***n.*** [< Fr. < LGr. < L. *moles*, a mass] **1.** a breakwater **2.** a harbor formed by a breakwater
mole⁴ (mōl) ***n.*** [< G. *mol*] *Chem.* the quantity of a substance having a weight in grams numerically equal to its molecular weight
Mo·lech (mō′lek) *Bible* an ancient god of the Phoenicians, etc., to whom children were sacrificed by burning —***n.*** anything demanding terrible sacrifice
mo·lec·u·lar (mə lek′yə lər) ***adj.*** of, produced by, or existing between molecules —**mo·lec′u·lar′i·ty** (-lar′ə tē) ***n.*** —**mo·lec′u·lar·ly** ***adv.***
molecular biology the branch of biology dealing with the chemical and physical structure and activities of the molecules in living matter
molecular weight the sum of the atomic weights of all atoms in a given molecule
mol·e·cule (mäl′ə kyo͞ol′) ***n.*** [< Fr. < ModL. *molecula*, dim. of L. *moles*, a mass] **1.** the smallest particle of an element or compound that can exist in the free state and still retain the characteristics of the element or compound **2.** a small particle
mole·hill (mōl′hil′) ***n.*** a small ridge or mound of earth, formed by a burrowing mole
mole·skin (-skin′) ***n.*** **1.** the soft, dark-gray skin of the mole, used as fur **2.** *a)* a strong cotton fabric with a soft nap, used for work clothes, etc. *b)* [*pl.*] trousers of this **3.** a soft fabric, often with an adhesive backing, used for foot pads
mo·lest (mə lest′, mō-) ***vt.*** [< OFr. < L. < *molestus*, troublesome < *moles*, a burden] **1.** to annoy or meddle with so as to trouble or harm **2.** to make improper sexual advances to (esp. a child) —**mo·les·ta·tion** (mō′les tā′shən, mäl′əs-) ***n.*** —**mo·lest′er** ***n.***
Mo·lière (mōl yer′; *Fr.* mô lyer′) (pseud. of *Jean Baptiste Poquelin*) 1622–73; Fr. dramatist
moll (mäl) ***n.*** [< var. of name MOLLY] [Slang] **1.** a gangster's mistress **2.** a prostitute
mol·lah (mäl′ə) ***n.*** *same as* MULLAH
mol·li·fy (mäl′ə fī′) ***vt.*** **-fied′, -fy′ing** [< MFr. < LL. < L. *mollis*, soft + *facere*, to make] **1.** to soothe, pacify, or appease **2.** to make less severe or violent —**mol′li·fi·ca′tion** ***n.*** —**mol′li·fi′er** ***n.***
mol·lusk, mol·lusc (mäl′əsk) ***n.*** [< Fr. < ModL. < L. *molluscus*, soft < *mollis*, soft] any of a large group of invertebrate animals, including clams, oysters, snails, squids, etc., having a soft, usually unsegmented body often enclosed in a hard shell and usually having gills and a foot —**mol·lus·kan, mol·lus·can** (mə lus′kən) ***adj., n.***
Mol·ly (mäl′ē) [dim. of MARY] a feminine name: also **Mol′lie**
mol·ly (mäl′ē) ***n., pl.*** **-lies** [< ModL. < F. N. *Mollien* (1758–1850), Fr. statesman] any of certain brightly colored tropical and subtropical American fishes often kept in aquariums: also **mol′lie**
mol·ly·cod·dle (mäl′ē käd′'l) ***n.*** [MOLLY + CODDLE] a man or boy used to being coddled, or protected, pampered, etc. —***vt.*** **-dled, -dling** to pamper; coddle —**mol′ly·cod′dler** ***n.***
Mo·loch (mō′läk, mäl′ək) *same as* MOLECH
Mo·lo·kai (mō′lō kī′) [Haw.] island of Hawaii: site of a leper colony
Mo·lo·tov cocktail (mô′lə täf) [after V. M. *Molotov* (1890–), Russ. statesman] [Slang] a bottle of gasoline, etc., plugged with a rag, ignited, and hurled as a grenade against vehicles, etc.
molt (mōlt) ***vi.*** [OE. (*be*)*mutian*, to exchange < L. *mutare*, to change] to shed skin, feathers, etc., prior to replacement by a new growth: said of reptiles, birds, etc. —***vt.*** to shed thus —***n.*** **1.** a molting **2.** the parts shed —**molt′er** ***n.***
mol·ten (mōl′t'n) *archaic pp. of* MELT —***adj.*** **1.** melted or liquefied by heat **2.** made by being melted and cast in a mold
mol·to (mōl′tō) ***adv.*** [It.] *Music* very; much
Mo·luc·cas (mō luk′əz) group of islands in Indonesia, between Celebes & New Guinea: also **Molucca Islands**
mol. wt. molecular weight
mo·lyb·de·nite (mə lib′də nīt′) ***n.*** a scaly or foliated, lead-gray ore of molybdenum, MoS_2
mo·lyb·de·num (-nəm) ***n.*** [ModL. < L. *molybdaena* < Gr. < *molybdos*, lead] a soft, lustrous, silver-white metallic chemical element, used in alloys, etc.: symbol, Mo; at. wt., 95.94; at. no., 42
mom (mäm) ***n.*** [Colloq.] mother
Mom·ba·sa (mäm bä′sə, -bas′ə) seaport on the SE coast of Kenya: pop. 180,000
mo·ment (mō′mənt) ***n.*** [< L. *momentum*, movement < *movere*, to move] **1.** an indefinitely brief period of time; instant **2.** a definite point in time **3.** a brief time of being important or outstanding **4.** importance; consequence [*news of great moment*] **5.** *Mech.* *a)* the tendency to cause rotation about a point or axis *b)* a measure of this —**the moment** the present time
mo·men·tar·i·ly (mō′mən ter′ə lē) ***adv.*** **1.** for a moment or short time **2.** in an instant **3.** from moment to moment; at any moment
mo·men·tar·y (mō′mən ter′ē) ***adj.*** **1.** lasting for only a moment; passing **2.** [Now Rare] recurring every moment **3.** likely to occur at any moment —**mo′men·tar′i·ness** ***n.***
mo·ment·ly (mō′mənt lē) ***adv.*** **1.** every moment **2.** at any moment **3.** for a single moment
mo·men·tous (mō men′təs) ***adj.*** of great moment; very important [*a momentous* decision] —**mo·men′tous·ly** ***adv.*** —**mo·men′tous·ness** ***n.***
mo·men·tum (mō men′təm) ***n.,*** *pl.* **-tums, -ta** (-tə) [ModL. < L.: see MOMENT] **1.** the impetus of or as of a moving object **2.** *Physics & Mech.* the quantity of motion of a moving body, equal to the product of its mass and its velocity
mom·my (mäm′ē) ***n.,*** *pl.* **-mies** *child's term for* MOTHER¹
mon- *same as* MONO-: used before a vowel
Mon. **1.** Monastery **2.** Monday **3.** Monsignor
mon. **1.** monastery **2.** monetary
Mon·a·co (män′ə kō, mə nä′kō) principality on the Mediterranean; enclave in SE France: 1/2 sq. mi.; pop. 23,000
mo·nad (mō′nad, män′ad) ***n.*** [LL. *monas* (gen. *monadis*) < Gr. < *monos*, alone] **1.** a unit; something simple and indivisible **2.** *Biol.* any simple, single-celled organism **3.** *Chem.* an atom, element, or radical with a valence of one —***adj.*** of a monad or monads —**mo·nad′ic, mo·nad′i·cal** ***adj.***
mon·arch (män′ərk, -ärk) ***n.*** [< LL. < Gr. < *monos*, alone + *archein*, to rule] **1.** the hereditary head of a state; king, queen, etc. **2.** a person or thing surpassing others of the same kind **3.** a large, migrating butterfly of N. America
mo·nar·chal (mə när′k'l) ***adj.*** of a monarch: also **mo·nar′chi·al** (-kē əl) —**mo·nar′chal·ly** ***adv.***
mo·nar·chi·cal (-ki k'l) ***adj.*** **1.** of or like a monarch or monarchy **2.** favoring a monarchy Also **mo·nar′chic** —**mo·nar′chi·cal·ly** ***adv.***
mon·ar·chism (män′ər kiz'm, -är-) ***n.*** monarchical principles or the advocacy of these —**mon′ar·chist** ***n., adj.*** —**mon′ar·chis′tic** ***adj.***
mon·ar·chy (-kē) ***n.,*** *pl.* **-ar·chies** a government or state headed by a monarch
mon·as·ter·y (män′ə ster′ē) ***n.,*** *pl.* **-ter′ies** [< LL. < LGr. *monastērion* < *monazein*, to be alone < *monos*, alone] the residence of a group of people, esp. monks, retired from the world under religious vows —**mon′as·te′ri·al** (-stir′ē əl) ***adj.***
mo·nas·tic (mə nas′tik) ***adj.*** **1.** of or characteristic of monasteries **2.** of or characteristic of monks or nuns; ascetic; self-denying Also **mo·nas′ti·cal** —***n.*** a monastic person —**mo·nas′ti·cal·ly** ***adv.***
mo·nas·ti·cism (-tə siz'm) ***n.*** the monastic system, state, or way of life
mon·au·ral (män ôr′'l) ***adj.*** [MON(O)- + AURAL] designating or of sound reproduction that uses only one source of sound, giving a monophonic effect —**mon·au′ral·ly** ***adv.***
mon·a·zite (män′ə zīt′) ***n.*** [G. *monazit* < Gr. *monazein*, to be alone] a native phosphate of the rare-earth metals, a major source of cerium, lanthanum, etc. and thorium
Mon·day (mun′dē, -dā) ***n.*** [OE. *monandæg*, moon's day] the second day of the week
Mon·days (-dēz, -dāz) ***adv.*** on or during every Monday
‡monde (mōnd) ***n.*** [Fr.] the world; society
‡mon Dieu (mōn dyö′) [Fr.] my God
Mon·dri·an (môn′drē än′), **Piet** (pēt) (born *Pieter Cornelis Mondriaan*) 1872–1944; Du. painter
mo·ne·cious (mə nē′shəs, mō-) ***adj.*** *same as* MONOECIOUS
Mo·nel metal (mō nel′) [after A. *Monell* (d. 1921), U.S. manufacturer] *a trademark for* an alloy mainly of nickel and copper, very resistant to corrosion
Mo·net (mō nā′, mə-; *Fr.* mô ne′), **Claude** 1840–1926; Fr. painter
mon·e·tar·y (män′ə ter′ē, mun′-) ***adj.*** [< LL. < L. *moneta*, a MINT¹] **1.** of the coinage or currency of a country: see table of MONETARY UNITS on next page **2.** of money; pecuniary —**mon′e·tar′i·ly** ***adv.***
mon·e·tize (-tīz′) ***vt.*** **-tized′, -tiz′ing** [< L. *moneta*, a MINT¹ + -IZE] **1.** to coin into money **2.** to legalize as money —**mon′e·ti·za′tion** ***n.***
mon·ey (mun′ē) ***n.,*** *pl.* **-eys, -ies** [< OFr. < L. *moneta*, a

Monetary Units of All Nations

(The exchange rates in this list are unofficial.)

Country	*Basic Unit*	*Equiv. in U.S. Currency*	*Chief Fractional Unit*
Afghanistan	afghani	.028	pul
Albania	lek	.215	qintar
Algeria	dinar	.268	centime
Andorra	franc	.22	centime
	peseta	.013	centimo
Angola	kwanza	.041	lwei
Argentina	peso	.0005	centavo
Australia	dollar	1.18	cent
Austria	schilling	.07	groschen
Bahamas	dollar	1.01	cent
Bahrain	dinar	2.66	fils
Bangladesh	taka	.07	paisa
Barbados	dollar	.52	cent
Belgium	franc	.032	centime
Benin	franc	.004	centime
Bhutan	ngultrum	.11	chhetrum
Bolivia	peso boliviano	.05	centavo
Botswana	pula	1.32	thebe
Brazil	cruzeiro	.017	centavo
Bulgaria	lev	1.17	stotinka
Burma	kyat	.158	pya
Burundi	franc	.012	centime
Cameroun	franc	.005	centime
Canada	dollar	.84	cent
Cape Verde	escudo	.03	centavo
Central African Republic	franc	.004	centime
Chad	franc	.004	centime
Chile	peso	.0275	centavo
China	yuan	.66	fen
China (Taiwan)	dollar	.029	cent
Colombia	peso	.023	centavo
Comoros	franc	.004	centime
Congo	franc	.004	centime
Costa Rica	colon	.12	centimo
Cuba	peso	1.49	centavo
Cyprus	pound	2.90	mil
Czechoslovakia	koruna	.19	haler
Denmark	krone	.167	ore
Djibouti	franc	.006	centime
Dominica	dollar	.40	cent
Dominican Republic	peso	1.00	centavo
Ecuador	sucre	.04	centavo
Egypt	pound	1.45	piaster
El Salvador	colon	.40	centavo
Equatorial Guinea	ekuele	.017	centimo
Ethiopia	birr	.49	santim
Fiji	dollar	1.26	cent
Finland	markka	.27	penni
France	franc	.22	centime
Gabon	franc	.004	centime
Gambia	dalasi	.60	butut
Germany, East	mark	.29	pfennig
Germany, West	deutsche mark	.51	pfennig
Ghana	cedi	.37	pesewa
Greece	drachma	.024	lepton
Grenada	dollar	.40	cent
Guatemala	quetzal	1.00	centavo
Guinea	syli	.06	kori
Guinea-Bissau	peso	.025	centavo
Guyana	dollar	.42	cent
Haiti	gourde	.20	centime
Honduras	lempira	.50	centavo
Hungary	forint	.05	fillér
Iceland	króna	.002	eyrir
India	rupee	.13	paisa
Indonesia	rupiah	.002	sen
Iran	rial	.014	dinar
Iraq	dinar	3.41	fils
Ireland	pound	1.90	penny
Israel	shekel	.195	agora
Italy	lira	.001	centesimo
Ivory Coast	franc	.004	centime
Jamaica	dollar	.57	cent
Japan	yen	.0049	sen
Jordan	dinar	3.39	fils
Kampuchea	(no currency)		
Kenya	shilling	.14	cent
Kiribati	dollar	1.18	cent
Korea, North	won	.52	chon
Korea, South	won	.002	
Kuwait	dinar	3.68	fils
Laos	kip	.003	at
Lebanon	pound	.28	piaster
Lesotho	loti	1.34	lisente
Liberia	dollar	1.00	cent
Libya	dinar	3.42	millieme
Liechtenstein	franc	.56	rappen
Luxembourg	franc	.032	centime
Madagascar	franc	.004	centime
Malawi	kwacha	1.25	tambala
Malaysia	ringgit	.45	cent
Maldive Is.	rupee	.12	cent
Mali	franc	.002	centime
Malta	pound	2.93	penny
Mauritania	ougiya	.023	khoms
Mauritius	rupee	.128	cent
Mexico	peso	.045	centavo
Monaco	franc	.235	centime
Mongolia	tugrik	.30	mongo
Morocco	dirham	.243	franc
Mozambique	metical	.035	centavo
Nauru	dollar	1.18	cent
Nepal	rupee	.087	pice
Netherlands	guilder	.47	cent
New Zealand	dollar	.96	cent
Nicaragua	cordoba	.143	centavo
Niger	franc	.004	centime
Nigeria	naira	1.91	kobo
Norway	krone	.194	ore
Oman	rial	2.90	paisa
Pakistan	rupee	.102	paisa
Panama	balboa	1.00	centesimo
Papua New Guinea	kina	1.54	toea
Paraguay	guarani	.008	centimo
Peru	sol	.004	centavo
Philippines	peso	.135	centavo
Poland	zloty	.035	grosz
Portugal	escudo	.02	centavo
Qatar	riyal	.28	dirham
Romania	leu	.23	ban
Rwanda	franc	.011	centime
San Marino	lira	.001	centesimo
São Tomé and Príncipe	dobra	.029	centavo
Saudi Arabia	riyal	.30	qursh
Senegal	franc	.004	centime
Seychelles	rupee	.19	cent
Sierra Leone	leone	.99	cent
Singapore	dollar	.478	cent
Solomon Is.	dollar	1.18	cent
Somalia	shilling	.16	cent
South Africa	rand	1.34	cent
Spain	peseta	.013	centimo
Sri Lanka	rupee	.057	cent
St. Lucia	dollar	.40	cent
St. Vincent	dollar	.40	cent
Sudan	pound	2.02	piaster
Surinam	guilder	.57	cent
Swaziland	lilangeni	1.34	cent
Sweden	krona	.23	ore
Switzerland	franc	.56	rappen
Syria	pound	.26	piaster
Tanzania	shilling	.12	cent
Thailand	baht	.051	satang
Togo	franc	.004	centime
Tonga	pa'anga	1.40	seniti
Trinidad & Tobago	dollar	.43	cent
Tunisia	dinar	2.50	millime
Turkey	lira	.012	piaster
Tuvalu	dollar	1.18	cent
Uganda	shilling	.13	cent
United Arab Emirates	dirham	.27	fils
United Kingdom	pound	2.40	penny
United States	dollar	1.00	cent
Upper Volta	franc	.004	centime
Uruguay	peso	.11	centesimo
U.S.S.R.	ruble	1.56	kopeck
Vanuatu	pound	2.40	penny
	franc	.004	centime
Vatican City	lira	.001	centesimo
Venezuela	bolívar	.233	centimo
Vietnam	dong	.456	sau
Western Samoa	tala	1.35	sene
Yemen, People's Democratic Republic of	dinar	2.95	fils
Yemen Arab Rep.	riyal	.22	bugshah
Yugoslavia	dinar	.04	para
Zaire	zaire	.34	likuta
Zambia	kwacha	1.32	ngwee
Zimbabwe	dollar	1.53	cent

MINT[1]] **1.** *a*) pieces of gold, silver, copper, etc., stamped by government authority and used as a medium of exchange; coin or coins: also called **hard money** *b*) any paper note authorized to be so used; bank notes; bills: see PAPER MONEY **2.** anything used as a medium of exchange **3.** any sum of money **4.** wealth **5.** *same as* MONEY OF ACCOUNT —**for one's money** [Colloq.] in one's opinion —**in the money** [Slang] wealthy —**make money** to gain profits —**one's money's worth** full value or benefit —**place** (or **put**) **money on** to bet on —**put money into** to invest money in —**mon′ey·less** *adj.*

mon·ey·bag (-bag′) *n.* **1.** a bag for money **2.** [*pl., with sing. v.*] [Colloq.] a rich person

mon·ey-chang·er (-chān′jər) *n.* **1.** a person whose business is money-changing **2.** a device holding stacked coins for making change quickly

mon·ey-chang·ing (-chān′jiŋ) *n.* the exchanging of currency, usually of different countries, esp. at an established or official rate

mon·eyed (mun′ēd) *adj.* **1.** wealthy; rich **2.** of, from, or representing money [*moneyed* interests]

mon·ey·lend·er (-len′dər) *n.* a person whose business is lending money at interest

mon·ey·mak·er (-mā′kər) *n.* a person or thing that makes money or a profit —**mon′ey·mak′ing** *adj., n.*

money of account a monetary denomination used in keeping accounts, etc., esp. one not issued in coin or in paper money (e.g., the U.S. mill)

money order an order for the payment of a specified sum of money, as one issued for a fee at one post office or bank and payable at another

Mong. **1.** Mongolia **2.** Mongolian

mon·ger (muŋ′gər, mäŋ′-) *n.* [OE. *mangere* < L. *mango*, dealer] a dealer or trader: usually in compounds [*fishmonger*]: sometimes used figuratively [*scandalmonger*]: chiefly Brit. in literal uses

mon·go (mäŋ′gō) *n., pl.* **-gos** *see* MONETARY UNITS, table (Mongolia)

Mon·gol (mäŋ′g'l, -gōl) *adj. same as* MONGOLIAN —*n.* **1.** a native of Mongolia (sense 1) or of an adjacent region in E Siberia **2.** *same as* MONGOLOID **3.** any Mongolic language, esp. that of the Mongolian People's Republic

Mongol. Mongolian

Mon·go·li·a (mäŋ gō′lē ə, män-; -gōl′yə) **1.** region in EC Asia, consisting of Inner Mongolia & Mongolia (sense 2) **2.** country in EC Asia, north of China: 592,600 sq. mi.; pop. 1,174,000: in full, **Mongolian People's Republic**

Mon·go·li·an (-ən, -yən) *adj.* **1.** of Mongolia, its people, or their culture **2.** *same as* MONGOLOID **3.** *same as* MONGOLIC (*adj.* 1) —*n.* **1.** a native of Mongolia **2.** *same as* MONGOLOID **3.** any Mongolic language

Mon·gol·ic (mäŋ gäl′ik, män-) *adj.* **1.** designating or of a subfamily of Altaic languages spoken by the Mongols and including Kalmuck **2.** *same as:* *a*) MONGOLIAN (*adj.* 1) *b*) MONGOLOID (*adj.* 1 & 2) —*n.* any Mongolic language

Mon·gol·ism (mäŋ′gə liz'm) *n.* [*often* **m-**] *earlier term for* DOWN'S SYNDROME

Mon·gol·oid (-loid′) *adj.* **1.** of or characteristic of the natives of Mongolia **2.** designating or of one of the major groups of mankind: it includes most of the peoples of Asia, the Eskimos, the N. American Indians, etc. **3.** [*often* **m-**] of or having Down's syndrome —*n.* **1.** a member of the Mongoloid group **2.** a person having Down's syndrome

mon·goose (mäŋ′go͞os) *n., pl.* **-goos·es** [< native name] an old-world, ferretlike, flesh-eating mammal, noted for its ability to kill rodents, snakes, etc.

MONGOOSE (body 9–25 in. long; tail 9–20 in. long)

mon·grel (muŋ′grəl, mäŋ′-) *n.* [< base of OE. *mengan*, to mix] **1.** an animal or plant produced by crossing breeds or varieties; esp., a dog of this kind **2.** anything produced by indiscriminate mixture —*adj.* of mixed breed, race, origin, or character Often a derogatory usage —**mon′grel·i·za′tion** *n.* —**mon′grel·ize′** *vt.* **-ized′, -iz′ing**

'mongst, mongst (muŋst) *prep. archaic var. of* AMONGST

mon·ied (mun′ēd) *adj. same as* MONEYED

mon·ies (mun′ēz) *n. alt. pl. of* MONEY

mon·i·ker, mon·ick·er (män′i kər) *n.* [< ?] [Slang] a person's name or nickname

mo·nism (mō′niz'm, män′iz'm) *n.* [ModL. *monismus* < Gr. *monos*, single] *Philos.* the doctrine that there is only one ultimate substance or principle, whether mind (*idealism*), matter (*materialism*), or something that is the basis of both —**mo′nist** *n.* —**mo·nis′tic, mo·nis′ti·cal** *adj.* —**mo·nis′ti·cal·ly** *adv.*

mo·ni·tion (mō nish′ən) *n.* [OFr. < L. < pp. of *monere*, to warn] **1.** admonition; warning; caution **2.** an official or legal notice

mon·i·tor (män′ə tər) *n.* [L. < pp. of *monere*, to warn] **1.** [Rare] one who advises or warns **2.** in some schools, a student chosen to help keep order, record attendance, etc. **3.** a reminder **4.** a large, flesh-eating lizard of Africa, S Asia, and Australia **5.** formerly, an armored warship with a low, flat deck and heavy guns in revolving turrets **6.** a person who monitors **7.** a device or instrument used for monitoring **8.** *Radio & TV* a receiver or speaker, as in a control room, for checking the quality of transmission —*vt., vi.* **1.** to watch or check on (a person or thing) for some reason **2.** to check on or regulate the performance of (a machine, airplane, etc.) **3.** to test for radioactive contamination with a monitor **4.** to listen in on (a broadcast, another's telephone conversation, etc.) to gather some specified type of information **5.** *Radio & TV* to check with a monitor —**mon′i·to′ri·al** (-tôr′ē əl) *adj.* —**mon′i·tor·ship′** *n.*

mon·i·to·ry (män′ə tôr′ē) *adj.* giving monition; admonishing —*n., pl.* **-ries** a monitory letter

monk (muŋk) *n.* [OE. *munuc* < LL. < LGr. < Gr. *monos*, alone] **1.** orig., a man living in solitary self-denial for religious reasons **2.** a member of certain male religious orders, generally under vows, as of poverty, obedience, and chastity —**monk′ish** *adj.* —**monk′ish·ly** *adv.*

mon·key (muŋ′kē) *n., pl.* **-keys** [prob. < or akin to MLowG. *Moneke*, the son of Martin the Ape in the medieval beast epic *Reynard the Fox*] **1.** any of the primates except man and the lemurs; specif., any of the smaller, long-tailed primates **2.** a person regarded as like a monkey, as a mischievous child —*vi.* [Colloq.] to play, trifle, or meddle

monkey business [Colloq.] foolish, mischievous, or deceitful tricks or behavior

mon·key·shine (-shīn′) *n.* [Colloq.] a mischievous trick or prank: *usually used in pl.*

monkey wrench a wrench with one movable jaw, adjusted by a screw to fit various sizes of nut, etc.

monk's cloth a heavy cloth, as of cotton, with a basket weave, used for drapes, etc.

monks·hood (muŋks′hood′) *n. same as* ACONITE (sense 1)

mon·o (män′ō) *adj. clipped form of* MONOPHONIC —*n. clipped form of* MONONUCLEOSIS

mon·o- [Gr. < *monos*, single] *a prefix meaning* one, alone, single [*monograph*]

mon·o·bas·ic (män′ə bā′sik) *adj. Chem.* designating an acid whose molecule contains one hydrogen atom replaceable by a metal or positive radical

mon·o·chro·mat·ic (-krō mat′ik) *adj.* [< L. < Gr.: see ff. & -IC] of or having one color: also **mon′o·chro′ic** (-krō′ik) —**mon′o·chro·mat′i·cal·ly** *adv.*

mon·o·chrome (män′ə krōm′) *n.* [< ML. < Gr. < *monos*, single + *chrōma*, color] a painting, drawing, or photograph in one color or shades of one color —**mon′o·chro′mic** *adj.* —**mon′o·chro′mist** *n.*

mon·o·cle (män′ə k'l) *n.* [Fr. < LL. *monoculus*, one-eyed < Gr. *monos*, single + L. *oculus*, eye] an eyeglass for one eye only —**mon′o·cled** *adj.*

mon·o·cli·nal (män′ə klī′n'l) *adj. Geol.* designating or of strata dipping in one direction —*n. same as* MONOCLINE

mon·o·cline (män′ə klīn′) *n.* [< MONO- + Gr. *klinein*, to incline] a monoclinal rock fold or structure

mon·o·clin·ic (män′ə klin′ik) *adj.* [see prec. & -IC] designating a crystalline form that has three unequal axes, two of which intersect at right angles while the third is oblique to one of the others

mon·o·cli·nous (män′ə klī′nəs) *adj.* [< ModL. < MONO- + Gr. *klinē*, a bed] *Bot.* having stamens and pistils in the same flower

mon·o·cot·y·le·don (män′ə kät′'l ē′d'n) *n.* a flowering plant with one seed leaf (cotyledon) —**mon′o·cot′y·le′don·ous** *adj.*

mon·o·dy (män′ə dē) *n., pl.* **-dies** [< LL. < Gr. *monōidia* < *monos*, alone + *aeidein*, to sing] **1.** a solo lament or dirge, as in ancient Greek tragedy **2.** a poem mourning someone's death **3.** *Music* *a*) a style of composition in which the melody is carried by one part, or voice *b*) a composition in this style —**mo·nod·ic** (mə näd′ik), **mo·nod′i·cal** *adj.* —**mo·nod′i·cal·ly** *adv.*

mo·noe·cious (mə nē′shəs, mō-) *adj.* [< MON(O)- + Gr. *oikos*, a house] *Bot.* having separate male flowers and female flowers on the same plant, as in maize —**mo·noe′cism** (-siz'm) *n.*

mo·nog·a·my (mə näg′ə mē) *n.* [< Fr. < LL. < Gr.: see MONO- & -GAMY] **1.** the practice or state of being married to only one person at a time **2.** *Zool.* the practice of having only one mate —**mo·nog′a·mist** *n.* —**mo·nog′a·mous, mon·o·gam·ic** (män′ə gam′ik) *adj.*

mon·o·gram (män′ə gram′) *n.* [< LL. < Gr. *mono-*, MONO- + *gramma,* letter] the initials of a name, combined in a single design —*vt.* **-grammed′, -gram′ming** to put a monogram on —**mon′o·gram·mat′ic** (-grə mat′ik) *adj.*

mon·o·graph (män′ə graf′) *n.* [MONO- + -GRAPH] a writing, esp. a scholarly one, on a single subject or aspect of a subject —**mon′o·graph′ic** *adj.*

mon·o·lith (män′ə lith′) *n.* [< Fr. < L. < Gr. < *monos,* single + *lithos,* stone] **1.** a single large block or piece of stone **2.** something made of this, as an obelisk **3.** something like a monolith in size, unity of structure or purpose, etc. —**mon′o·lith′ic** *adj.* —**mon′o·lith′ism** *n.*

mon·o·logue, mon·o·log (män′ə lôg′, -läg′) *n.* [Fr. < Gr. < *monos,* alone + *legein,* to speak] **1.** a long speech, esp. one monopolizing a conversation **2.** a poem, etc. in the form of a soliloquy **3.** a part of a play in which one character speaks alone; soliloquy **4.** a play, skit, or recitation for one actor only —**mon′o·logu′ist, mo·nol·o·gist** (mə näl′ə jist) *n.*

mon·o·ma·ni·a (män′ə mā′nē ə) *n.* **1.** an excessive interest in or enthusiasm for some one thing; craze **2.** a mental disorder characterized by irrational preoccupation with one subject —**mon′o·ma′ni·ac′** (-mā′nē ak′) *n.* —**mon′o-ma·ni′a·cal** (-mə nī′ə k′l) *adj.*

mon·o·mer (män′ə mər) *n.* [MONO- + Gr. *meros,* a part] a simple molecule that can form polymers by combining with identical or similar molecules —**mon′o·mer′ic** (-mer′ik) *adj.*

mon·o·met·al·lism (män′ə met′'l iz'm) *n.* the use of only one metal, usually gold or silver, as the monetary standard —**mon′o·me·tal′lic** (-mə tal′ik) *adj.* —**mon′o·met′al·list** *n.*

mo·no·mi·al (mō nō′mē əl, mä-) *adj.* [MO(NO)- + (BI)NOMIAL] consisting of only one term, esp. in algebra —*n.* a monomial expression, quantity, etc.

Mo·non·ga·he·la (mə näŋ′gə hē′lə) [< Algonquian] river in N W.Va. & SW Pa., joining the Allegheny to form the Ohio: 128 mi.

mon·o·nu·cle·o·sis (män′ə no͞o′klē ō′sis, -nyo͞o-) *n.* [MONO- + NUCLE(US) + -OSIS] **1.** *same as* INFECTIOUS MONONUCLEOSIS **2.** presence in the blood of too many cells with a single nucleus

mon·o·phon·ic (-fän′ik) *adj.* designating or of sound reproduction using a single channel

mon·o·plane (män′ə plān′) *n.* an airplane with only one pair of wings

mo·nop·o·list (mə näp′ə list) *n.* **1.** a person who has a monopoly **2.** a person who favors monopoly —**mo·nop′o-lis′tic** *adj.* —**mo·nop′o·lis′ti·cal·ly** *adv.*

mo·nop·o·lize (-līz′) *vt.* **-lized′, -liz′ing** **1.** to get, have, or exploit a monopoly of **2.** to get full possession or control of; dominate or occupy completely —**mo·nop′o·li·za′tion** *n.* —**mo·nop′o·liz′er** *n.*

mo·nop·o·ly (-lē) *n., pl.* **-lies** [< L. < Gr. < *monopōlia,* exclusive sale < *monos,* single + *pōlein,* to sell] **1.** exclusive control of a commodity or service in a given market, or control that makes possible the fixing of prices **2.** such control granted by a government **3.** any exclusive possession or control **4.** something held or controlled as a monopoly **5.** a company, etc. that has a monopoly

mon·o·rail (män′ə rāl′) *n.* **1.** a single rail serving as a track for cars suspended from it or balanced on it **2.** a railway with such a track

mon·o·so·di·um glu·ta·mate (män′ə sō′dē əm glo͞o′tə māt′) a white, crystalline powder, $C_5H_8O_4NaN$, used in foods as a flavor intensifier

mon·o·syl·lab·ic (män′ə si lab′ik) *adj.* **1.** having only one syllable **2.** consisting of, using, or speaking in monosyllables —**mon′o·syl·lab′i·cal·ly** *adv.*

mon·o·syl·la·ble (män′ə sil′ə b'l) *n.* a word of one syllable

mon·o·the·ism (män′ə thē iz'm) *n.* [MONO- + THEISM] the doctrine or belief that there is only one God —**mon′o·the-ist** *n.* —**mon′o·the·is′tic, mon′o·the·is′ti·cal** *adj.* —**mon′-o·the·is′ti·cal·ly** *adv.*

mon·o·tint (män′ə tint′) *n. same as* MONOCHROME

mon·o·tone (-tōn′) *n.* **1.** utterance of successive words without change of pitch or key **2.** monotony of tone, style, color, etc. **3.** a single, unchanging musical tone **4.** recitation, singing, etc. in such a tone **5.** a person who sings in such a tone —*adj. same as* MONOTONOUS —**mon′o·ton′ic** (-tän′ik) *adj.*

mo·not·o·nous (mə nät′'n əs) *adj.* [< LL. < Gr.: see MONO- & TONE] **1.** going on in the same tone without variation **2.** having little or no variation or variety **3.** tiresome because unvarying —**mo·not′o·nous·ly** *adv.* —**mo·not′o-nous·ness** *n.*

mo·not·o·ny (-ē) *n.* **1.** sameness of tone or pitch **2.** lack of variety **3.** tiresome sameness

mon·o·treme (män′ə trēm′) *n.* [< ModL. < Gr. *monos,* single + *trēma,* hole] any of the lowest order of mammals (platypuses and echidnas), which lay eggs and have a single opening for the excretory and genital organs —**mon′o-trem′a·tous** (-trem′ə təs, -trē′mə-) *adj.*

mon·o·type (-tīp′) *n.* [MONO- + -TYPE] **1.** *Biol.* the only type of its group **2.** *Printing* type produced by Monotype —[M-] *a trademark for* either of a pair of machines for casting and setting up type in separate characters: one, a casting machine, is controlled by a paper tape perforated on the other, a keyboard machine

mon·o·va·lent (män′ə vā′lənt) *adj. Chem. same as* UNIVALENT —**mon′o·va′lence, mon′o·va′len·cy** *n.*

mon·ox·ide (mə näk′sīd, män äk′-) *n.* an oxide with one atom of oxygen in each molecule

Mon·roe (mən rō′) [after ff.] city in N La.: pop. 58,000

Mon·roe (mən rō′), **James** 1758–1831; 5th president of the U.S. (1817–25)

Monroe Doctrine the doctrine, stated by President Monroe, that the U.S. would regard as an unfriendly act any attempt by a European nation to interfere in the affairs of, or increase its possessions in, the Americas

Mon·ro·vi·a (mən rō′vē ə) capital of Liberia; seaport on the Atlantic: pop. c.100,000

Mon·sei·gneur (män′sen yʉr′; *Fr.* mōn se nyër′) *n., pl.* **Mes·sei·gneurs** (mes′en yʉrz′; *Fr.* mā se nyër′) [Fr., lit., my lord] **1.** a French title of honor given to persons of high birth or rank, as princes, bishops, etc. **2.** [*often* **m-**] a person with this title

mon·sieur (mə syʉr′; *Fr.* mə syö′) *n., pl.* **mes·sieurs** (mes′ərz; *Fr.* mā syö′) [Fr., lit., my lord] a man; gentleman: French title [**M-**], equivalent to *Mr.* or *Sir:* abbrev. **M., Mons.**

Monsig. **1.** Monseigneur **2.** Monsignor

Mon·si·gnor (män sēn′yər; *It.* môn′sē nyôr′) *n., pl.* **-gnors** (-yərz); *It.* **-gno′ri** (-nyô′rē) [It., lit., my lord] **1.** a title of certain Roman Catholic prelates **2.** [*often* **m-**] a person with this title

mon·soon (män so͞on′) *n.* [< MDu. < Port. < Ar. *mausim,* a season] **1.** a seasonal wind of the Indian Ocean and S Asia, blowing from the southwest from April to October, and from the northeast the rest of the year **2.** the rainy season, when this wind blows from the southwest —**mon·soon′al** *adj.*

mon·ster (män′stər) *n.* [< OFr. < L. *monstrum,* divine portent < *monere,* to warn] **1.** any plant or animal greatly malformed, lacking parts, etc. **2.** any imaginary creature with striking incongruities in form, as a centaur or unicorn **3.** something monstrous **4.** any very cruel or wicked person **5.** any huge animal or thing —*adj.* huge; enormous; monstrous

mon·strance (män′strəns) *n.* [OFr. < ML. < L. *monstrare,* to show] *R.C.Ch.* a receptacle in which the consecrated Host is exposed for adoration

mon·stros·i·ty (män sträs′ə tē) *n.* **1.** the state or quality of being monstrous **2.** *pl.* **-ties** a monstrous thing or creature

mon·strous (män′strəs) *adj.* **1.** abnormally large; enormous **2.** very unnatural in shape, type, or character **3.** having the character or appearance of a monster **4.** horrible; hideous; shocking **5.** hideously wrong or evil; atrocious —*adv.* [Chiefly Dial.] very; extremely —**mon′strous·ly** *adv.* —**mon′strous·ness** *n.*

mon·tage (män täzh′, mōn-) *n.* [Fr. < *monter,* MOUNT[2]] **1.** *a)* the art or process of making a composite picture from a number of different pictures *b)* a picture so made **2.** *Motion Pictures a)* the art or process of producing a sequence of abruptly alternating or superimposed scenes or images *b)* such a sequence **3.** any technique, as in literature, with a similar sequence of elements —*vt.* **-taged′, -tag′ing** to incorporate in a montage

Mon·ta·gnard (män′tən yärd′) *n.* [Fr., lit., mountaineer] a member of a people living in the hills of central Vietnam

Mon·taigne (män tān′; *Fr.* mōn ten′y′), **Mi·chel Ey·quem de** (mē shel′ e kem′ də) 1533–92; Fr. essayist

Mon·tan·a (män tan′ə) [L. *montana,* mountainous region] Mountain State of the NW U.S.: 147,138 sq. mi.; pop. 787,000; cap. Helena: abbrev. **Mont., MT** —**Mon·tan′an** *adj., n.*

Mont·calm (mōn kålm′; *E.* mänt käm′), marquis **Louis Jo·seph de** (zhô zef′ də) 1712–59; Fr. general defeated & killed by Brit. forces at Quebec

mon·te (män′tē) *n.* [Sp., lit., mountain, hence heap of cards] a game in which players bet on the color of cards to be turned up

Mon·te Car·lo (män′ti kär′lō) town in Monaco: gambling resort: pop. 9,500

Mon·te·ne·gro (män′tə nē′grō) republic of S Yugoslavia: 5,333 sq. mi. —**Mon′te·ne′grin** (-grin) *adj., n.*

Mon·te·rey Park (män′tə rā′) city in SW Calif: suburb of Los Angeles: pop. 54,000

Mon·ter·rey (män′tə rā′; *Sp.* môn′ter rā′) city in NE Mexico: pop. 1,012,000

Mon·tes·quieu (mōn tes kyö′; *E.* män′təs kyo͞o′), (Baron **de la Brède et de**) 1689–1755; Fr. philosophical writer on history

Mon·tes·so·ri method (or **system**) (män′tə sôr′ē) [after Maria *Montessori* (1870–1952), It. educator who devised it] a system of teaching young children which emphasizes training of the senses and guidance intended to encourage self-education

Mon·te·ver·di (môn′te ver′dē), **Clau·dio (Giovanni Antonio)** (klou′dyô) 1567–1643; It. composer

Mon·te·vid·e·o (män′tə vi dā′ō; *Sp.* môn′te vē *the*′ô) capital of Uruguay, on the Río de la Plata: pop. 1,204,000

Mon·te·zu·ma II (män′tə zo͞o′mə) 1479?–1520; Aztec emperor of Mexico (1502–20)

Mont·gom·er·y (mənt gum′ər ē, mänt-, mən-; -gum′rē) [after Gen. R. *Montgomery* (1736?–75)] capital of Ala., in the SC part: pop. 178,000

month (munth) *n.* [OE. *monath*] **1.** any of the twelve parts into which the calendar year is divided: also **calendar month** **2.** *a)* the time from any day of one month to the corresponding day of the next *b)* a period of four weeks or 30 days **3.** the period of a complete revolution of the moon (in full, **lunar month**) **4.** one twelfth of the solar year (in full, **solar month**) **—month after month** every month **—month by month** each month **—month in, month out** every month

month·ly (munth′lē) *adj.* **1.** continuing or lasting for a month **2.** done, happening, payable, etc. every month **—*n.*,** *pl.* **-lies** **1.** a periodical published once a month **2.** [Colloq.] [*also pl.*] the menses **—*adv.*** once a month; every month

Mon·ti·cel·lo (män′tə sel′ō, -chel′ō) [It., little mountain] home of Thomas Jefferson, in C Va.

Mont·mar·tre (mōn mȧr′tr′) district in Paris, in N part: noted for its cafés and as an artists' quarter

Mont·pel·ier (mänt pēl′yər) [after ff.] capital of Vt., in the NC part: pop. 8,000

Mont·pel·lier (mōn pel yā′) city in S France: pop. 162,000

Mont·re·al (män′trē ôl′, mun′-) seaport in SW Quebec, Canada, on an island in the St. Lawrence River: pop. 1,081,000 (met. area 2,802,000): Fr. name **Mont·ré·al** (mōn rā ȧl′)

Montreal North suburb of Montreal: pop. 97,000: Fr. name **Montréal Nord** (nôr)

Mont-St-Mi·chel (mōn san mē shel′) islet off the NW coast of France: noted for its fortified abbey: also **Mont Saint Michel**

mon·u·ment (män′yə mənt) *n.* [OFr. < L. *monumentum* < *monere,* to remind] **1.** something set up to keep alive the memory of a person or event, as a tablet, statue, building, etc. **2.** a writing, etc. serving as a memorial **3.** *a)* a work of enduring significance [*monuments* of learning] *b)* an outstanding example [*a monument* of bigotry] **4.** a stone boundary marker **5.** [Obs.] a tomb

mon·u·men·tal (män′yə men′t′l) *adj.* **1.** of, suitable for, or serving as a monument **2.** like a monument; massive, enduring, etc. **3.** of lasting importance; historically notable **4.** very great; colossal [*monumental* pride] **—mon′u·men′tal·ly** *adv.*

mon·u·men·tal·ize (-īz′) *vt.* **-ized′, -iz′ing** to memorialize as by a monument; make monumental

-mo·ny (mō′nē) [L. *-monia, -monium*] *a suffix meaning* a resulting thing or state [*patrimony*]

moo (mo͞o) *n., pl.* **moos** [echoic] the vocal sound made by a cow; lowing sound **—*vi.*** **mooed, moo′ing** to make this sound; low

mooch (mo͞och) *vi., vt.* [ult. < OFr. *muchier,* to hide] [Slang] to get (food, money, etc.) by begging or sponging **—mooch′er** *n.*

mood[1] (mo͞od) *n.* [OE. *mod,* mind] **1.** a particular state of mind or feeling; humor, or temper **2.** a prevailing feeling, spirit, or tone **3.** [*pl.*] fits of morose, sullen, or uncertain temper

mood[2] (mo͞od) *n.* [< MODE, altered after prec.] *Gram.* that aspect of verbs which indicates whether the action or state expressed is regarded as a fact (*indicative mood*), as a matter of supposition, desire, etc. (*subjunctive mood*), or as a command (*imperative mood*)

mood·y (mo͞o′dē) *adj.* **mood′i·er, mood′i·est** **1.** subject to or characterized by gloomy, sullen, or changing moods **2.** resulting from or indicating such a mood **—mood′i·ly** *adv.* **—mood′i·ness** *n.*

moon (mo͞on) *n.* [OE. *mona*] **1.** the satellite of the earth, that revolves around it once in 29½ days and shines at night by reflecting the sun's light **2.** this body as it appears at a particular time of the month: see NEW MOON, HALF-MOON, FULL MOON, OLD MOON **3.** a month; esp., a lunar month **4.** *same as* MOONLIGHT **5.** anything shaped like the moon (i.e., an orb or crescent) **6.** any satellite of a planet **—*vi.*** to behave in an idle, dreamy, or abstracted way **—*vt.*** to pass (time) in mooning

PHASES OF THE MOON

moon·beam (-bēm′) *n.* a ray of moonlight

moon·calf (-kaf′) *n.* **1.** an idiot or fool **2.** a youth who spends time mooning about

moon-faced (-fāst′) *adj.* round-faced

moon·fish (-fish′) *n., pl.* **-fish′, -fish′es:** see FISH an oval-shaped sea fish found in the warmer coastal waters of North and South America

moon·let (-lit) *n.* a small moon or artificial satellite

moon·light (-līt′) *n.* the light of the moon **—*adj.*** **1.** of moonlight **2.** lighted by the moon **3.** done or occurring by moonlight, or at night

moon·light·ing (-līt′iŋ) *n.* [from the usual night hours of such jobs] the practice of holding a second regular job in addition to one's main job

moon·lit (-lit′) *adj.* lighted by the moon

moon·quake (-kwāk′) *n.* a trembling of the surface of the moon, thought to be caused by internal rock slippage or, possibly, meteorite impact

moon·scape (-skāp′) *n.* [MOON + (LAND)SCAPE] the surface of the moon or a representation of it

moon·shine (-shīn′) *n.* **1.** the light of the moon **2.** foolish or empty talk, notions, etc. **3.** [Colloq.] whiskey unlawfully made or smuggled

moon·shin·er (-shī′nər) *n.* [Colloq.] a person who makes and sells alcoholic liquor unlawfully

moon·shot (-shät′) *n.* the launching of a rocket to the moon

moon·stone (-stōn′) *n.* a translucent feldspar with a pearly luster, used as a gem

moon·struck (-struk′) *adj.* **1.** crazed; lunatic **2.** romantically dreamy **3.** dazed or distracted Also **moon′strick′en** (-strik′′n)

moon·walk (-wôk′) *n.* a walking about by an astronaut on the surface of the moon

moon·y (-ē) *adj.* **moon′i·er, moon′i·est** mooning; listless; dreamy

Moor (moor) *n.* [< OFr. < L. < Gr. *Mauros*] **1.** a member of a Moslem people of mixed Arab and Berber descent living in NW Africa **2.** a member of a group of this people that invaded and occupied Spain in the 8th cent. A.D. **—Moor′ish** *adj.*

moor[1] (moor) *n.* [OE. *mor*] [Brit.] a tract of open wasteland, usually covered with heather and often marshy; heath

moor[2] (moor) *vt.* [< or akin to MDu. *maren,* LowG. *moren,* to tie] **1.** to hold (a ship, etc.) in place by cables or chains as to a pier or buoy **2.** to cause to be held in place; secure **—*vi.*** **1.** to moor a ship, etc. **2.** to be secured as by cables **—moor′age** (-ij) *n.*

Moore (moor, môr) **1. George (Augustus),** 1852–1933; Ir. novelist & playwright **2. Henry,** 1898– ; Eng. sculptor **3. Thomas,** 1779–1852; Ir. poet

moor·hen (moor′hen′) *n.* a common gallinule of Europe and the E U.S.

moor·ing (-iŋ) *n.* **1.** [*often pl.*] the lines, cables, etc. by which a ship, etc. is moored **2.** [*pl.*] a place where a ship, etc. is moored **3.** [*often pl.*] beliefs, habits, ties, etc. that make one feel secure

moor·land (-land′) *n.* [Brit.] *same as* MOOR[1]

moose (mo͞os) *n., pl.* **moose** [< Algonquian] **1.** the largest animal of the deer family, native to the N U.S. and Canada: the male has huge antlers **2.** *same as* ELK (sense 1)

MOOSE (4½–6 ft. high at shoulder)

moot (mo͞ot) *n.* [OE. *mot, gemot,* a meeting] **1.** an early English assembly of freemen to administer justice, etc. **2.** a discussion or argument, esp. of a case in a moot court: see ff. **—*adj.*** **1.** debatable **2.** so hypothetical as to be meaningless **—*vt.*** **1.** to debate or discuss **2.** to propose for discussion or debate

moot court a mock court in which hypothetical cases are tried as an exercise for law students

mop (mäp) *n.* [ult. < ? L. *mappa,* napkin] **1.** a bundle of rags or yarn, or a sponge, etc., fastened to the end of a stick, as for washing floors **2.** anything suggestive of this, as a thick head of hair **—*vt.*** **mopped, mop′ping** to wash, wipe, or remove with or as with a mop **—mop up** [Colloq.] to finish **—mop′per** *n.*

mope (mōp) *vi.* **moped, mop′ing** [akin to MDu. *mopen*] to be gloomy and apathetic **—*n.*** **1.** a person who mopes **2.** [*pl.*] low spirits **—mop′er** *n.* **—mop′ey, mop′y, mop′ish** *adj.* **—mop′ish·ly** *adv.*

mo·per·y (mō′pər ē) ***n.*** [MOP(E) + -ERY] [Slang] a trivial or imaginary violation of law
mop·pet (mäp′it) ***n.*** [< ?] [Colloq.] a little child: a term of affection
Mor. Morocco
mo·raine (mə rān′, mô-) ***n.*** [Fr. < *morre*, a muzzle] a mass of rocks, gravel, sand, etc. deposited by a glacier, along its side (**lateral moraine**), at its lower end (**terminal moraine**), or beneath the ice (**ground moraine**) —**mo·rain′al, mo·rain′ic** ***adj.***
mor·al (môr′əl, mär′-) ***adj.*** [< L. < *mos*, pl. *mores*, manners, morals] **1.** relating to, dealing with, or capable of distinguishing between, right and wrong in conduct **2.** of, teaching, or in accordance with, the principles of right and wrong **3.** good or right in conduct or character; sometimes, specif., sexually virtuous **4.** designating support, etc. that involves sympathy without action **5.** being virtually such because of its effect on thoughts, attitudes, etc. [*a moral victory*] **6.** based on strong probability [*a moral certainty*] —***n.*** **1.** a moral lesson taught by a fable, event, etc. **2.** [*pl.*] principles, standards, or habits with respect to right or wrong in conduct; ethics; sometimes, specif., standards of sexual behavior —**mor′al·ly** ***adv.***
mo·rale (mə ral′, mô-) ***n.*** [Fr., fem. of *moral*: see prec.] moral or mental condition with respect to courage, discipline, confidence, enthusiasm, etc. [*the morale of the troops was low*]
mor·al·ist (môr′əl ist, mär′-) ***n.*** **1.** a person who moralizes **2.** a person who adheres to a system of moral teaching **3.** a person who seeks to impose his morals on others —**mor′al·is′tic** ***adj.*** —**mor′al·is′ti·cal·ly** ***adv.***
mo·ral·i·ty (mə ral′ə tē, mô-) ***n.***, *pl.* **-ties** **1.** moral quality or character; rightness or wrongness, as of an action **2.** a being in accord with the principles or standards of right conduct; virtue **3.** principles of right and wrong in conduct; ethics **4.** moral instruction or lesson **5.** a narrative with a moral lesson **6.** *same as* MORALITY PLAY
morality play any of a class of allegorical dramas of the 15th and 16th cent., whose characters were personifications, as Everyman, Vice, etc.
mor·al·ize (môr′ə līz′, mär′-) ***vi.*** **-ized′, -iz′ing** to consider or discuss matters of right and wrong, often in a self-righteous way —***vt.*** **1.** *a)* to explain in terms of right and wrong *b)* to draw a moral from **2.** to improve the morals of —**mor′al·i·za′tion** ***n.*** —**mor′al·iz′er** ***n.***
moral philosophy *same as* ETHICS
mo·rass (mə ras′, mô-) ***n.*** [< Du. < OFr. < Frank. *marisk*, a swamp] a tract of low, soft, watery ground; bog; swamp: often used figuratively of a difficult or troublesome state of affairs
mor·a·to·ri·um (môr′ə tôr′ē əm, mär′-) ***n.***, *pl.* **-ri·ums, -ri·a** (-ə) [ModL. < LL. < L. < *mora*, a delay] **1.** a legal authorization, usually by an emergency law, to delay payment of money due **2.** the effective period of such an authorization **3.** any authorized delay or stopping of some specified activity
Mo·ra·vi·a (mô rā′vē ə, mə-) region in C Czechoslovakia: chief city, Brno
Mo·ra·vi·an (mô rā′vē ən, mə-) ***adj.*** **1.** of Moravia, its people, etc. **2.** of the religious sect of Moravians —***n.*** **1.** a native or inhabitant of Moravia **2.** the Czech dialect of Moravia **3.** a member of a Protestant sect founded by people from Moravia (c.1722)
mo·ray (môr′ā; mô rā′, mə-) ***n.*** [< Port. < L. *muraena*, kind of fish < Gr. *myraina*] a voracious, brilliantly colored eel, found esp. among coral reefs: in full, **moray eel**
mor·bid (môr′bid) ***adj.*** [L. *morbidus*, sickly < *morbus*, disease] **1.** of, having, or caused by disease; diseased **2.** having or showing an interest in gruesome or gloomy matters **3.** gruesome; horrible [*morbid details of a crime*] —**mor·bid′i·ty, mor′bid·ness** ***n.*** —**mor′bid·ly** ***adv.***
mor·dant (môr′d′nt) ***adj.*** [< OFr. prp. of *mordre* < L. *mordere*, to bite] **1.** biting, caustic, or sarcastic [*mordant wit*] **2.** corrosive **3.** acting as a mordant —***n.*** **1.** a substance used in dyeing to fix the colors **2.** an acid, etc. used in etching to bite lines, areas, etc. into the surface —**mor′dan·cy** ***n.*** —**mor′dant·ly** ***adv.***
more (môr) ***adj.*** *superl.* MOST [OE. *mara*] **1.** greater in amount, quantity, or degree: used as the comparative of MUCH **2.** greater in number: used as the comparative of MANY **3.** additional; further [*take more tea*] —***n.*** **1.** a greater amount, quantity, or degree **2.** [*with pl. v.*] a greater number (*of*) [*more of us are going*] **3.** something additional or further [*more can be said*] —***adv.*** *superl.* MOST **1.** in or to a greater degree or extent: used with many adjectives and adverbs (regularly with those of three or more syllables) to form comparatives **2.** in addition; further —**more and more** **1.** increasingly **2.** a constantly increasing amount, quantity, etc. —**more or less** **1.** somewhat **2.** approximately
More (môr), Sir **Thomas** 1478–1535; Eng. statesman & writer: executed: canonized in 1935
mo·rel (mə rel′, mô-) ***n.*** [< Fr. < MDu. < OHG. *morhila*, dim. of *morha*, carrot] an edible mushroom that looks like a sponge on a stalk

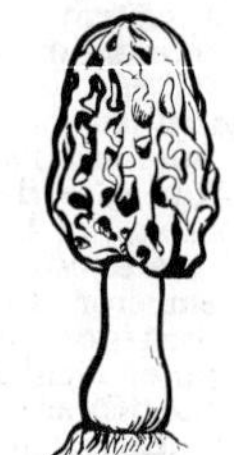
MOREL

more·o·ver (môr ō′vər) ***adv.*** in addition to what has been said; besides; further; also
mo·res (môr′ēz, -āz) ***n.pl.*** [L., pl. of *mos*, custom] folkways that, through general observance, develop the force of law
Mor·gan (môr′gən), **J(ohn) P(ierpont)** 1837–1913; U.S. financier
mor·ga·nat·ic (môr′gə nat′ik) ***adj.*** [< ML. < *morganaticum*, altered < OHG. *morgengeba*, morning gift given to one's bride (in lieu of a dower)] designating or of a form of marriage in which a man of royalty or nobility marries a woman of inferior social status with the provision that neither she nor their offspring may lay claim to his rank or property —**mor′ga·nat′i·cal·ly** ***adv.***
morgue (môrg) ***n.*** [Fr.] **1.** a place where the bodies of unknown dead persons or those dead of unknown causes are kept to be examined, identified, etc. **2.** a newspaper office's reference library of back numbers, clippings, etc.
mor·i·bund (môr′ə bund′) ***adj.*** [< L. *moribundus* < *mori*, to die] **1.** dying **2.** coming to an end **3.** having little or no vitality left —**mor′i·bund′i·ty** ***n.***
mo·ri·on (môr′ē än′) ***n.*** [Fr. < Sp. < *morra*, crown of the head] a crested, visorless helmet of the 16th and 17th cent., with a curved brim coming to a peak in front and in back
Mo·ris·co (mə ris′kō, mô-) ***adj.*** [Sp. < *Moro*, Moor] Moorish —***n.***, *pl.* **-cos, -coes** a Moor; esp., one of the Moors of Spain
Mor·mon (môr′mən) ***n.*** a member of the Church of Jesus Christ of Latter-day Saints (commonly called the *Mormon Church*), founded in the U.S. in 1830 by Joseph Smith —***adj.*** of the Mormons or their religion —**Mor′mon·ism** ***n.***
morn (môrn) ***n.*** [OE. *morne*] [Poet.] morning
morn·ing (môr′niŋ) ***n.*** [ME. *morweninge* (by analogy with EVENING) < OE. *morgen*] **1.** the first or early part of the day, from midnight, or esp. dawn, to noon **2.** the first or early part [*the morning of life*] **3.** dawn; daybreak —***adj.*** of, suited to, or occurring, appearing, etc. in the morning
morning dress formal daytime dress for men, including a cutaway (**morning coat**)
morning glory a twining annual vine with heart-shaped leaves and trumpet-shaped flowers of lavender, blue, pink, or white
morn·ings (-niŋz) ***adv.*** during every morning or most mornings
morning star a planet, esp. Venus, visible in the eastern sky before sunrise
Mo·ro (môr′ō) ***n.*** [Sp., a Moor] **1.** *pl.* **-ros, -ro** a member of a group of Moslem Malay tribes living in the S Philippines **2.** their language
Mo·roc·co (mə rä′kō) kingdom on the NW coast of Africa: c.171,300 sq. mi.; pop. 15,102,000; cap. Rabat —***n.*** [**m-**] a fine, soft leather made, orig. in Morocco, from goatskins: also **morocco leather** —**Mo·roc′can** ***adj., n.***
mo·ron (môr′än) ***n.*** [arbitrary use of Gr. neut. of *mōros*, foolish] **1.** a person having mild mental retardation: an obsolescent term: see MENTAL RETARDATION **2.** a very stupid person —**mo·ron′ic** ***adj.*** —**mo·ron′i·cal·ly** ***adv.*** —**mo·ron′i·ty, mo′ron·ism** ***n.***
mo·rose (mə rōs′, mô-) ***adj.*** [L. *morosus*, fretful < *mos* (gen. *moris*), manner] **1.** ill-tempered; gloomy, sullen, etc. **2.** characterized by gloom —**mo·rose′ly** ***adv.*** —**mo·rose′ness** ***n.***
-morph (môrf) [< Gr. *morphē*, form] *a combining form meaning* one having a (specified) form
mor·pheme (môr′fēm) ***n.*** [< Fr. < Gr. *morphē*, form] the smallest meaningful unit or form in a language: it may be an affix (*re-* in *refill*), a base (*do* in *undo*), or an inflectional form (*-s* in *girls*) —**mor·phe′mic** ***adj.*** —**mor·phe′mi·cal·ly** ***adv.***
Mor·pheus (môr′fē əs, -fyo͞os) *Gr. Myth.* the god of dreams
-mor·phic (môr′fik) [< Gr. *morphē*, form + -IC] *a combining form meaning* having a (specified) form or shape [*anthropomorphic*]
mor·phine (môr′fēn) ***n.*** [< G. or Fr. < ModL. *morphium* < L. *Morpheus*, MORPHEUS] a bitter, white or colorless, crystalline alkaloid derived from opium and used in medicine to relieve pain
mor·phol·o·gy (môr fäl′ə jē) ***n.*** [< G. < Gr. *morphē*, form + -LOGY] **1.** the branch of biology dealing with the form and structure of animals and plants **2.** the branch of linguistics dealing with the internal structure and forms of words —**mor′pho·log′i·cal** (-fə läj′i k′l), **mor′pho·log′ic** ***adj.*** —**mor′pho·log′i·cal·ly** ***adv.*** —**mor·phol′o·gist** ***n.***
-mor·phous (môr′fəs) [< Gr. < *morphē*, form] *same as* -MORPHIC

Mor·ris (môr′is, mär′-) **1.** [var. of MAURICE] a masculine name **2. William,** 1834–96; Eng. poet, artist, craftsman, & socialist

Morris chair [after Wm. MORRIS] an armchair with an adjustable back

mor·ro (mär′ō) ***n.,*** *pl.* **-ros** [Sp.] a rounded hill or point of land

mor·row (mär′ō, môr′ō) ***n.*** [< OE. *morgen,* morning] [Poet.] **1.** morning **2.** the next day **3.** the time just after some particular event

Morse (môrs) ***adj.*** [after ff.] [*often* **m-**] designating or of a code, or alphabet, consisting of a system of dots and dashes, or short and long sounds, used in telegraphy, etc. —***n.*** the Morse code

Morse (môrs), **Samuel F(inley) B(reese)** 1791–1872; U.S. inventor of the telegraph

mor·sel (môr′s'l) ***n.*** [< OFr. dim. of *mors* < L. *morsum,* a bite < pp. of *mordere,* to bite] **1.** a small bite or portion of food **2.** a small amount; bit

mor·tal (môr′t'l) ***adj.*** [< OFr. < L. *mortalis* < *mors* (gen. *mortis*), death] **1.** that must eventually die **2.** of man as a being who must eventually die **3.** of this world **4.** of death **5.** causing death; fatal **6.** to the death [*mortal* combat] **7.** not to be pacified [a *mortal* enemy] **8.** very intense; grievous [*mortal* terror] **9.** [Colloq.] *a*) extreme; very great *b*) very long and tedious *c*) possible [of no *mortal* good to anyone] **10.** *R.C.Ch.* causing spiritual death: said of sins regarded as serious —***n.*** a being who must eventually die; esp., a human being —***adv.*** [Dial.] extremely —**mor′tal·ly** ***adv.***

mor·tal·i·ty (môr tal′ə tē) ***n.*** **1.** the mortal nature of man **2.** death on a large scale, as from disease or war **3.** the proportion of deaths to the population of a region, nation, etc.; death rate **4.** the proportion that fail **5.** human beings collectively

mor·tar (môr′tər) ***n.*** [< OE. & OFr. < L. *mortarium*] **1.** a very hard bowl in which substances are ground or pounded to a powder with a pestle **2.** a short-barreled cannon with a low muzzle velocity, which hurls shells in a high trajectory **3.** a mixture of cement or lime with sand and water, used between bricks, etc., or as plaster —***vt.*** **1.** to plaster together with mortar **2.** to attack with mortar shells

mor·tar·board (-bôrd′) ***n.*** **1.** a square board with a handle beneath, on which mortar is carried **2.** an academic cap with a square, flat top, worn at commencements, etc.

mort·gage (môr′gij) ***n.*** [< OFr. < *mort,* dead + *gage,* GAGE[1]] *Law* **1.** the pledging of property to a creditor as security for the payment of a debt **2.** the deed by which this pledge is made —***vt.*** **-gaged, -gag·ing 1.** *Law* to pledge (property) by a mortgage **2.** to put an advance claim or liability on [he *mortgaged* his future]

mort·ga·gee (môr′gə jē′) ***n.*** a person to whom property is mortgaged

mort·ga·gor, mort·gag·er (môr′gi jər) ***n.*** a person who mortgages property

mor·tice (môr′tis) ***n., vt.*** *alt. sp. of* MORTISE

mor·ti·cian (môr tish′ən) ***n.*** [< L. *mors,* death + -ICIAN] *same as* FUNERAL DIRECTOR

mor·ti·fi·ca·tion (môr′tə fi kā′shən) ***n.*** **1.** a mortifying or being mortified; specif., *a*) the control of physical desires by self-denial, fasting, etc. *b*) shame, humiliation, etc. **2.** something causing shame, humiliation, etc. **3.** *old term for* GANGRENE

mor·ti·fy (môr′tə fī′) ***vt.*** **-fied′, -fy′ing** [< OFr. < LL. *mortificare,* to kill < L. *mors,* death (see MORTAL) + *facere,* to make] **1.** to punish (one's body) or control (one's physical desires) by self-denial, fasting, etc. **2.** to shame, humiliate, etc. **3.** [Now Rare] to make gangrenous —***vi.*** [Now Rare] to become gangrenous —**mor′ti·fi′er** ***n.***

mor·tise (môr′tis) ***n.*** [MFr. *mortaise* < Ar. *murtazza,* joined] a notch or hole cut, as in a piece of wood, to receive a projecting part (*tenon*) shaped to fit —***vt.*** **-tised, -tis·ing 1.** to join or fasten securely, esp. with a mortise and tenon **2.** to cut a mortise in

mort·main (môrt′mān′) ***n.*** [< OFr. < ML. < L. pp. of *mori,* to die + *manus,* hand] *Law* a transfer of lands or houses to a corporate body, as a church, for perpetual ownership

Mor·ton (môr′t'n) [< OE. < *mor,* a moor + *tun,* town] a masculine name

mor·tu·ar·y (môr′choo wer′ē) ***n.,*** *pl.* **-ar′ies** [< LL. < L. *mortuus,* dead] a place where dead bodies are kept before burial or cremation, as a morgue or funeral home —***adj.*** **1.** of or having to do with the burial of the dead **2.** of death

mos. months

Mo·sa·ic (mō zā′ik) ***adj.*** of Moses or the writings, principles, etc. attributed to him

mo·sa·ic (mō zā′ik) ***n.*** [< OFr. < ML. *musaicum* < LL. < L. *musa,* MUSE] **1.** the process of making pictures or designs by inlaying small bits of colored stone, glass, etc. in mortar **2.** a picture or design so made **3.** anything resembling this **4.** the photosensitive plate in a television camera tube —***adj.*** of or resembling mosaic or a mosaic —***vt.*** **-icked, -ick·ing** to make by or as by mosaic —**mo·sa′i·cal·ly** ***adv.*** —**mo·sa′i·cist** (-ə sist) ***n.***

Mosaic law the ancient Hebrew law, ascribed to Moses and contained mainly in the Pentateuch

Mos·cow (mäs′kou, -kō) capital of the U.S.S.R. & the R.S.F.S.R., in W R.S.F.S.R.: pop. 6,942,000 (met. area 7,061,000): Russ. name, **Mos·kva** (môs kvä′)

Mo·selle (mō zel′) river in NE France & N West Germany, flowing into the Rhine

Mo·ses (mō′ziz) [LL. < Gr. < Heb. *mōsheh,* prob. < Egypt. *mes,* child] **1.** a masculine name **2.** *Bible* the leader who brought the Israelites out of slavery in Egypt and led them to the Promised Land, and who received the Ten Commandments

mo·sey (mō′zē) ***vi.*** [< *vamose,* var. of VAMOOSE] [Slang] **1.** to amble along **2.** to go away

Mos·lem (mäz′ləm, muz′-, mäs′-) ***n.*** [Ar. *muslim,* true believer < *aslama,* to resign oneself (to God)] an adherent of Islam —***adj.*** of Islam or the Moslems: also **Mos·lem′ic** (-lem′ik) —**Mos′lem·ism** ***n.***

mosque (mäsk) ***n.*** [< MFr. < It. < Ar. *masjid* < *sajada,* to pray] a Moslem temple or place of worship

mos·qui·to (mə skēt′ō, -ə) ***n.,*** *pl.* **-toes, -tos** [Sp. & Port., dim. of *mosca* < L. *musca,* a fly] a two-winged insect, the female of which has skin-piercing, bloodsucking mouthparts: some varieties transmit diseases, as malaria and yellow fever —**mos·qui′to·ey** (-ē) ***adj.***

mosquito net (or **netting**) a fine mesh curtain for keeping out mosquitoes

moss (môs, mäs) ***n.*** [OE. *mos,* a swamp] **1.** a very small, green plant growing in velvety clusters on rocks, trees, moist ground, etc. **2.** any of various similar plants, as some lichens, algae, etc. —***vt.*** to cover with a growth of moss —**moss′like′** ***adj.***

moss agate agate with mosslike markings

moss·back (-bak′) ***n.*** [Colloq.] an old-fashioned or very conservative person

moss rose **1.** *same as* PORTULACA **2.** a variety of the cabbage rose with a roughened, mossy flower stalk and calyx

moss·y (-ē) ***adj.*** **moss′i·er, moss′i·est 1.** full of or covered with moss or a mosslike growth **2.** like moss —**moss′i·ness** ***n.***

most (mōst) ***adj.*** *compar.* MORE [OE *mast*] **1.** greatest in amount, quantity, or degree: used as the superlative of MUCH **2.** greatest in number: used as the superlative of MANY **3.** in the greatest number of instances [*most* fame is fleeting] —***n.*** **1.** the greatest amount, quantity, or degree **2.** [*with pl. v.*] the greatest number (*of*) —***adv.*** **1.** *compar.* MORE in or to the greatest degree or extent: used with many adjectives and adverbs (regularly with those of three or more syllables) to form superlatives **2.** very [a *most* beautiful morning] **3.** [Colloq.] almost; nearly —**at (the) most** at the very limit; not more than —**make the most of** to take the fullest advantage of

-most (mōst) [OE. *-mest*] *a suffix used in forming superlatives* [*foremost, hindmost*]

most·ly (mōst′lē) ***adv.*** **1.** for the most part **2.** chiefly; principally **3.** usually; generally

Mo·sul (mō sōōl′) city in N Iraq, on the Tigris River: pop. 243,000

mot (mō) ***n.*** [Fr., a word < L. *muttum,* a grunt] a witticism or pithy remark

mote (mōt) ***n.*** [OE. *mot*] a speck, as of dust

mo·tel (mō tel′) ***n.*** [MO(TORIST) + (HO)TEL] a hotel for those traveling by car, with accessible parking

mo·tet (mō tet′) ***n.*** [< OFr. dim. of *mot,* a word] a contrapuntal, polyphonic song of a sacred nature

moth (môth) ***n.,*** *pl.* **moths** (mô*th*z, môths) [OE. *moththe*] a four-winged, chiefly night-flying insect related to the butterfly but generally smaller and less brightly colored; specif., a small moth (**clothes moth**) whose larvae eat holes in woolens, furs, etc.

moth·ball (-bôl′) ***n.*** a small ball of naphthalene, the fumes of which repel moths, as from woolens, furs, etc. —***vt.*** to store with protective covering —***adj.*** in storage or reserve [a *mothball* fleet] —**in** (or **out of**) **mothballs** put into (or taken from) storage

moth-eat·en (-ēt′'n) ***adj.*** **1.** gnawed away in patches by moths, as cloth **2.** worn-out **3.** outdated

moth·er[1] (mu*th*′ər) ***n.*** [OE. *modor*] **1.** a woman who has borne a child; esp., a woman as she is related to her child **2.** *a)* a stepmother *b)* a mother-in-law **3.** the female parent of a plant or animal **4.** that which is the origin, source, or nurturer of something **5.** *a)* a woman having the responsibility and authority of a mother *b)* a woman who is the head (**mother superior**) of a religious establishment **6.** an elderly woman: used as a title of affectionate respect —***adj.*** **1.** of, like, or like that of a mother **2.** native [*mother* tongue] —***vt.*** **1.** to be the mother of **2.** to care for as a mother does —**moth′er·less** ***adj.***

moth·er[2] (mu*th*′ər) ***n.*** [altered (after prec.) < MDu. *moeder*] *same as* MOTHER OF VINEGAR

Mother Car·ey's chicken (ker′ēz) [< ?] any of various oceanic petrels; esp., *same as* STORMY PETREL (sense 1)

mother country *same as* MOTHERLAND

Mother Goose the imaginary creator of a collection of English nursery rhymes

moth·er·hood (mu*th*′ər hood′) ***n.*** **1.** the state of being a mother **2.** the qualities or character of a mother

Mother Hub·bard (hub′ərd) a full, loose gown for women

mother image (or **figure**) a person substituted in one's mind for one's mother

moth·er-in-law (-ən lô′) ***n.***, *pl.* **moth′ers-in-law′** the mother of one's husband or wife

moth·er·land (-land′) ***n.*** a person's native land or, sometimes, the land of his ancestors

mother lode the main vein of ore in a region

moth·er·ly (-lē) ***adj.*** of, like, or befitting a mother; maternal —**moth′er·li·ness** ***n.***

moth·er-of-pearl (-əv purl′) ***n.*** the hard, pearly internal layer of certain marine shells, as of the pearl oyster, used for making pearl buttons, etc.; nacre

mother of vinegar [see MOTHER[2]] a stringy, gummy, slimy substance formed by bacteria in vinegar or on the surface of fermenting liquids

Mother's Day the second Sunday in May, a day set aside (in the U.S.) in honor of mothers

mother tongue **1.** one's native language **2.** a language from which another derives

mother wit native intelligence; common sense

moth·proof (môth′pro͞of′) ***adj.*** treated chemically so as to repel moths —***vt.*** to make mothproof

moth·y (môth′ē) ***adj.*** **moth′i·er, moth′i·est** **1.** infested with moths **2.** moth-eaten

mo·tif (mō tēf′) ***n.*** [Fr.: see MOTIVE] **1.** a main element, idea, etc.; specif., a theme or subject that is repeated with various changes, as in a piece of music, a book, etc. **2.** a repeated figure in a design

mo·tile (mōt′'l) ***adj.*** [< L. pp. of *movere*, to move + -ILE] *Biol.* capable of or exhibiting spontaneous motion —**mo·til·i·ty** (mō til′ə tē) ***n.***

mo·tion (mō′shən) ***n.*** [< L. *motio* < pp. of *movere*, to move] **1.** a moving from one place to another; movement **2.** a moving of the body or any of its parts **3.** a meaningful movement of the hand, eyes, etc.; gesture **4.** a suggestion; esp., a proposal formally made in an assembly or meeting —***vi.*** to make a meaningful movement of the hand, head, etc. —***vt.*** to direct or command by a meaningful gesture —**go through the motions** to do something in a mechanical or merely formal way —**in motion** moving or in operation —**mo′tion·less** ***adj.*** —**mo′tion·less·ly** ***adv.***

motion picture **1.** a sequence of photographs or drawings projected on a screen in such rapid succession as to create the optical illusion of moving persons and objects **2.** a play, story, etc. photographed as a motion picture

motion sickness sickness characterized by nausea, dizziness, etc., and caused by the motion of an aircraft, boat, etc.

mo·ti·vate (mōt′ə vāt′) ***vt.*** **-vat′ed, -vat′ing** to provide with, or affect as, a motive or motives; incite —**mo′ti·va′tion** ***n.*** —**mo′ti·va′tion·al** ***adj.*** —**mo′ti·va′tive** ***adj.*** —**mo′ti·va′tor** ***n.***

mo·tive (mōt′iv) ***n.*** [< OFr. *motif* < ML. < L. pp. of *movere*, to move] **1.** some inner drive, impulse, etc. that causes one to act in a certain way; incentive; goal **2.** *same as* MOTIF —***adj.*** of, causing, or tending to cause motion —***vt.*** **-tived, -tiv·ing** *same as* MOTIVATE —**mo′tive·less** ***adj.***

-mo·tive (mōt′iv) [< prec. (*adj.*)] *a suffix meaning* moving, of motion [*automotive, locomotive*]

mot·ley (mät′lē) ***adj.*** [< ?] **1.** of many colors **2.** wearing many-colored garments [a *motley* fool] **3.** of many different elements [a *motley* group] —***n.*** **1.** cloth of mixed colors **2.** a garment of various colors, worn by a jester **3.** a combination of diverse elements

mo·to·cross (mō′tō krôs′) ***n.*** [Fr. < *motocyclette*, motorcycle + Eng. *cross-country*] a cross-country race for lightweight motorcycles

mo·tor (mōt′ər) ***n.*** [L., a mover < pp. of *movere*, to move] **1.** anything that produces or imparts motion **2.** an engine; esp., an internal-combustion engine for propelling a vehicle **3.** *Elec.* a machine for converting electrical energy into mechanical energy —***adj.*** **1.** producing motion **2.** of or powered by a motor [a *motor* bicycle] **3.** of, by, or for motor vehicles [a *motor* trip] **4.** for motorists [a *motor* inn] **5.** designating or of a nerve carrying impulses from the central nervous system to a muscle producing motion **6.** of, manifested by, or involving muscular movements [*motor* skills] —***vi.*** to travel by automobile

mo·tor·bike (-bīk′) ***n.*** [Colloq.] **1.** a bicycle propelled by a motor **2.** a light motorcycle

mo·tor·boat (-bōt′) ***n.*** a boat propelled by a motor

mo·tor·bus (-bus′) ***n.*** a passenger bus propelled by a motor: also **motor coach**

mo·tor·cade (-kād′) ***n.*** [MOTOR + (CAVAL)CADE] a procession of automobiles

mo·tor·car (-kär′) ***n.*** **1.** *same as* AUTOMOBILE **2.** a small, open car propelled by a motor and used on a railroad by workmen: also **motor car**

mo·tor·cy·cle (-sī′k'l) ***n.*** a two-wheeled vehicle, like a bicycle, propelled by an internal-combustion engine —***vi.*** **-cled, -cling** to ride a motorcycle —**mo′tor·cy′clist** ***n.***

motor hotel *same as* MOTEL: also **motor court, motor inn, motor lodge**

mo·tor·ist (mōt′ər ist) ***n.*** a person who drives an automobile or travels by automobile

mo·tor·ize (mōt′ə rīz′) ***vt.*** **-ized′, -iz′ing** **1.** to equip with motor-driven vehicles **2.** to make mobile by mounting on a motor vehicle **3.** to equip (a vehicle, etc.) with a motor —**mo′tor·i·za′tion** ***n.***

mo·tor·man (mōt′ər mən) ***n.***, *pl.* **-men** a person who drives an electric streetcar or electric locomotive

motor pool a group of motor vehicles kept for use as needed, as by military personnel

motor truck a motor-driven truck for hauling loads

motor vehicle a vehicle on wheels having its own motor and not running on rails, for use on streets or highways, as an automobile or bus

mot·tle (mät′'l) ***vt.*** **-tled, -tling** [back-formation < *mottled* < MOTLEY + -ED] to mark with blotches or streaks of different colors —**mot′tled** ***adj.***

mot·to (mät′ō) ***n.***, *pl.* **-toes, -tos** [It., a word: see MOT] **1.** a word, phrase, or sentence chosen as expressive of the goals or ideals of a nation, group, etc. and inscribed on something **2.** a maxim adopted as a principle of behavior

‡**moue** (mo͞o) ***n.***, *pl.* **moues** (mo͞o) [Fr. < OFr. *moue*, a grimace] a pouting grimace

mould (mōld) ***n., vt., vi.*** *chiefly Brit. sp. of* MOLD (all terms and senses) —**mould′y** ***adj.*** **mould′i·er, mould′i·est**

mould·board (-bôrd′) ***n.*** *chiefly Brit. sp. of* MOLDBOARD

mould·ing (mōl′diŋ) ***n.*** *chiefly Brit. sp. of* MOLDING

moult (mōlt) ***n., vt., vi.*** *chiefly Brit. sp. of* MOLT

mound (mound) ***n.*** [< ? MDu. *mond*, protection, infl. by MOUNT[1]] **1.** a heap or bank of earth, sand, etc., whether built or natural; small hill **2.** *Baseball* the slightly raised area on which the pitcher must stand when pitching —***vt.*** to heap up in a mound

Mound Builders the early Indian peoples who built the burial mounds and other earthworks found in the Middle West and the Southeast

mount[1] (mount) ***n.*** [< OE. *munt* & OFr. *mont*, both < L. *mons*] a mountain or hill: now poetic or [**M-**] before a proper name [*Mount* McKinley]

mount[2] (mount) ***vi.*** [< OFr. *munter*, ult. < L. *mons*: see prec.] **1.** to climb; ascend (often with *up*) **2.** to climb up on something; esp., to get on a horse or bicycle, etc. for riding **3.** to increase in amount [profits are *mounting*] —***vt.*** **1.** to go up; ascend; climb [to *mount* stairs] **2.** *a)* to get up on (a horse, bicycle, etc.) for riding *b)* to set on or provide with a horse *c)* to get up on (a platform, stool, etc.) **3.** to place on something raised (with *on*) [*mount* the statue on a pedestal] **4.** to place or fix on or in the proper support, backing, etc., as a gem in a setting, a specimen on a microscope slide, a picture on a mat, etc. **5.** to arrange (a skeleton, dead animal, etc.) for exhibition **6.** to furnish the costumes, settings, etc. for producing (a play) **7.** to prepare for and undertake (an expedition, campaign, etc.) **8.** *Mil.* *a)* to place (a gun) into position for use *b)* to be armed with (cannon) [this ship *mounts* six cannon] *c)* to post (a guard) on sentry duty *d)* to go on (guard) as a sentry —***n.*** **1.** the act or manner of mounting (a horse, etc.) **2.** a horse, bicycle, etc. for riding **3.** the support, setting, etc. on or in which something is mounted

moun·tain (moun′t'n) ***n.*** [< OFr. *montaigne*, ult. < L. *mons*, MOUNT[1]] **1.** a natural raised part of the earth's surface, larger than a hill **2.** [*pl.*] a chain or group of such elevations: also **mountain chain, mountain range** **3.** a large pile, heap, or mound **4.** a very large amount —***adj.***

1. of mountains 2. situated, living, or used in the mountains 3. like a mountain
mountain ash a small tree with clusters of white flowers and red berries
mountain dew [Colloq.] whiskey, esp. when illegally distilled, as by mountaineers
moun·tain·eer (moun′t'n ir′) *n.* 1. a person who lives in a mountainous region 2. a mountain climber —*vi.* to climb mountains, as for sport
mountain goat *same as* ROCKY MOUNTAIN GOAT
mountain laurel an evergreen shrub of E N. America, with pink and white flowers and shiny leaves
mountain lion *same as* COUGAR
moun·tain·ous (moun′t'n əs) *adj.* 1. full of mountains 2. like a mountain; esp., very large
mountain sheep any of various wild sheep found in mountain regions; esp., *same as* BIGHORN
moun·tain·side (-sīd′) *n.* the side of a mountain
Mountain Standard Time *see* STANDARD TIME
Mountain State any of the eight States of the W U.S. through which the Rocky Mountains pass
moun·tain·top (-täp′) *n.* the top of a mountain
Mountain View city in W Calif., near San Jose: pop. 59,000
moun·te·bank (moun′tə baŋk′) *n.* [< It. < *montare,* to mount + *in,* on + *banco,* a bench] 1. orig., a person who sold quack medicines in a public place, attracting an audience by tricks, stories, etc. 2. any charlatan, or quack —*vi.* to act as a mountebank —**moun′te·bank′er·y** *n.*
mount·ed (moun′tid) *adj.* provided with a mount, or horse, vehicle, support, etc. [*mounted* police]
Mount·ie, Mount·y (moun′tē) *n., pl.* **-ies** [Colloq.] a member of the Royal Canadian Mounted Police
mount·ing (moun′tiŋ) *n.* something serving as a backing, support, setting, etc.
Mount Vernon 1. [after E. *Vernon* (see GROG)] home of George Washington, in N Va., on the Potomac 2. [after prec.] city in SE N.Y.: suburb of New York City: pop. 67,000
mourn (môrn) *vi., vt.* [OE. *murnan*] 1. to feel or express sorrow for (something regrettable) 2. to grieve for (someone who has died) —**mourn′er** *n.*
mourn·ful (-fəl) *adj.* 1. of mourning; feeling or expressing grief or sorrow 2. causing sorrow; melancholy —**mourn′ful·ly** *adv.* —**mourn′ful·ness** *n.*
mourn·ing (môr′niŋ) *n.* 1. a sorrowing; specif., the expression of grief at someone's death, or the period of this 2. black clothes, drapery, etc., worn or displayed as a sign of grief —*adj.* of or expressing mourning —**mourn′ing·ly** *adv.*
mourning dove a gray, wild dove of the U.S.: so called because of its cooing, regarded as mournful
mouse (mous; *for v., usually* mouz) *n., pl.* **mice** [OE. *mus*] 1. any of numerous small rodents found throughout the world; esp., the **house mouse,** which infests human dwellings 2. a timid or spiritless person 3. [Slang] a dark, swollen bruise under the eye —*vi.* **moused, mous′ing** 1. to hunt for mice 2. to search for something busily and stealthily —*vt.* to hunt for
mous·er (mou′zər, -sər) *n.* a cat, dog, etc. with reference to its ability to catch mice
mous·ey (mou′sē, -zē) *adj. same as* MOUSY
mousse (mo͞os) *n.* [Fr., foam, prob. < L. *mulsa,* kind of mead] a light chilled or frozen food made with egg white, gelatin, whipped cream, etc., often served with fruit or flavoring for dessert
mous·tache (mə stash′, mus′tash) *n. var. of* MUSTACHE
mous·y (mou′sē, -zē) *adj.* **mous′i·er, mous′i·est** 1. of, characteristic of, or like a mouse; quiet, timid, etc. 2. infested with mice —**mous′i·ness** *n.*
mouth (mouth; *for v.* mou*th*) *n., pl.* **mouths** (mou*th*z) [OE. *muth*] 1. the opening through which an animal takes in food; specif., the cavity in the head which contains the teeth and tongue and through which sounds are uttered 2. the mouth regarded as the organ of eating and speaking 3. a grimace 4. any opening regarded as like the mouth [the *mouth* of a river, of a jar, of a cavern, etc.] —*vt.* 1. to say, esp. in an affected or pompous manner 2. to form (a word) with the mouth soundlessly 3. to rub with the mouth or lips —*vi.* to speak in a pompous manner; declaim —**down in** (or **at**) **the mouth** [Colloq.] depressed; unhappy —**mouth′er** (mou*th*′-) *n.* —**mouth′like′** *adj.*
-mouthed (mou*th*d) *a combining form meaning* having a (specified kind of) mouth, voice, etc. [*loudmouthed*]
mouth·ful (mouth′fool′) *n., pl.* **-fuls′** 1. as much as the mouth can hold 2. the usual amount taken into the mouth 3. a small amount 4. [Slang] a pertinent remark: chiefly in **say a mouthful**
mouth organ *same as* HARMONICA
mouth·part (-pärt′) *n.* any of various structures or organs around the mouth in arthropods, used for biting, grasping, etc.: *usually used in pl.*
mouth·piece (-pēs′) *n.* 1. a part placed at, or forming, a mouth 2. the part of a musical instrument held in or to the mouth 3. a person, periodical, etc. used by others to express their views, ideas, etc. 4. [Slang] a criminal's lawyer
mouth·wash (-wôsh′, -wäsh′) *n.* a flavored liquid used for rinsing the mouth or gargling
mouth·wa·ter·ing (-wôt′ər iŋ, -wät′ər-) *adj.* appetizing enough to make the mouth water; tasty
mouth·y (mou′*th*ē, -thē) *adj.* **mouth′i·er, mouth′i·est** overly talkative, esp. in a bombastic or rude way —**mouth′i·ly** *adv.* —**mouth′i·ness** *n.*
mou·ton (mo͞o′tän) *n.* [Fr., sheep: see MUTTON] lambskin, processed to resemble beaver, seal, etc.
mov·a·ble (mo͞o′və b'l) *adj.* 1. that can be moved from one place to another 2. changing in date from one year to the next [*movable* holidays] —*n.* 1. something movable 2. *Law* personal property, as furniture: *usually used in pl.* Also **move′a·ble** —**mov′a·bil′i·ty** *n.* —**mov′a·bly** *adv.*
move (mo͞ov) *vt.* **moved, mov′ing** [< Anglo-Fr. < OFr. < L. *movere*] 1. to change the place or position of 2. to set or keep in motion; impel, stir, etc. 3. to cause (*to act, do, say,* etc.); prompt 4. to arouse the emotions, passions, etc. of 5. to propose; esp., to propose formally, as in a meeting 6. to cause (the bowels) to evacuate 7. *Commerce* to dispose of (goods) by selling —*vi.* 1. to change place or position 2. to change one's residence 3. to be active [to *move* in artistic circles] 4. to make progress; advance 5. to take action 6. to be, or be set, in motion; turn, revolve, etc. 7. to make a formal application (*for*) [*move* for a new trial] 8. to evacuate: said of the bowels 9. [Colloq.] to depart [time to be *moving on*] 10. *Chess, Checkers,* etc. to change the position of a piece 11. *Commerce* to be disposed of by sale: said of goods —*n.* 1. act of moving; movement 2. one of a series of actions toward some goal 3. a change of residence 4. *Chess, Checkers,* etc. the act of moving or one's turn to move —**get a move on** [Slang] 1. to start moving 2. to hurry —**move in on** [Slang] to draw near to and try to gain control of —**move up** to promote or be promoted —**on the move** [Colloq.] moving about from place to place
move·ment (-mənt) *n.* 1. the act, process, or manner of moving; specif., *a)* an action of a person or group *b)* a shift in position *c)* an evacuation (of the bowels) *d) Mil.* a change in the location of troops, ships, etc., as part of a maneuver 2. *a)* organized action by people working together toward some goal *b)* those active in this way 3. a tendency; trend 4. the progress of events in a literary work; action 5. the effect of motion in painting, sculpture, etc. 6. *Mech.* the moving parts of a mechanism [the *movement* of a clock] 7. *Music a)* any of the principal divisions of a symphony or other long composition *b) same as* TEMPO or RHYTHM 8. *Prosody* rhythmic flow
mov·er (-ər) *n.* a person or thing that moves; specif., a person whose work or business is moving furniture, etc. for those changing residence
mov·ie (mo͞o′vē) *n.* [contr. < MOVING PICTURE] 1. a motion picture 2. a motion-picture theater —**the movies** 1. the motion-picture industry 2. a showing of a motion picture
mov·ie·go·er (-gō′ər) *n.* a person who goes to see motion pictures, esp. often or regularly
mov·ing (mo͞o′viŋ) *adj.* 1. that moves; specif., *a)* changing, or causing to change, place or position *b)* causing motion or action *c)* stirring the emotions 2. involving a moving motor vehicle [a *moving* violation (of a traffic law)] —**mov′ing·ly** *adv.*
moving picture *same as* MOTION PICTURE
moving staircase (or **stairway**) *same as* ESCALATOR
mow[1] (mō) *vt., vi.* **mowed, mowed** or **mown, mow′ing** [OE. *mawan*] 1. to cut down (standing grass or grain) with a sickle, lawn mower, etc. 2. to cut grass or grain from (a lawn, field, etc.) —**mow down** 1. to cause to fall like grass or grain being cut 2. to kill or destroy 3. to overwhelm (an opponent) —**mow′er** *n.*
mow[2] (mou) *n.* [OE. *muga*] 1. a stack or heap of hay, grain, etc., esp. in a barn 2. the part of a barn where hay or grain is stored
mown (mōn) *alt. pp. of* MOW[1]
Mo·zam·bique (mō′zəm bēk′) country on the SE coast of Africa: formerly a Port. territory: c. 302,300 sq. mi.; pop. 8,519,000; cap. Maputo
Mo·zart (mō′tsärt), **Wolf·gang A·ma·de·us** (vôlf′gäŋk′ ä′mä dā′oos) 1756–91; Austrian composer
moz·za·rel·la (mät′sə rel′ə) *n.* [It.] a soft, white, mild-flavored Italian cheese
MP, M.P. Military Police
mp [It. *mezzo piano*] *Music* moderately soft

M.P. 1. Member of Parliament 2. Mounted Police
M.P., m.p. melting point
mpg, m.p.g. miles per gallon
mph, m.p.h. miles per hour
Mr. (mis′tər) *pl.* **Messrs.** (mes′ərz) mister: used before the name or title of a man
Mrs. (mis′iz) *pl.* **Mmes.** (mā däm′) mistress: now used as a title before the name of a married woman
MS 1. Mississippi 2. multiple sclerosis
MS., ms., ms *pl.* **MSS., mss., mss** manuscript
Ms. (miz, mis) a title, free of reference to marital status, used before the name of a woman in place of either *Miss* or *Mrs.*
M.S., M.Sc. Master of Science
MScand. Middle Scandinavian
MSG monosodium glutamate
Msgr. Monsignor
MSgt, M/Sgt Master Sergeant
m'sieur (mə syʉr′; *Fr.* mə syö′) ***n.*** monsieur
MST, M.S.T. Mountain Standard Time
MT Montana
Mt., mt. *pl.* **mts.** 1. mount 2. mountain
M.T. metric ton
mtg. 1. meeting 2. mortgage: also **mtge.**
mtn. mountain
mu (myo͞o, mo͞o) ***n.*** [< Gr.] the twelfth letter of the Greek alphabet (M, μ)
much (much) ***adj.*** **more, most** [OE. *mycel*] great in quantity, amount, degree, etc. —***adv.*** 1. to a great degree or extent [*much* happier] 2. just about; nearly [*much* the same] 3. at frequent intervals; often [do you dine out *much?*] —***n.*** 1. a great amount or quantity [*much* to be done] 2. something great, outstanding, etc. [not *much* to look at] —**as much as** 1. to the degree that 2. practically; virtually —**make much of** to treat or consider as of great importance —**much as** 1. almost as 2. however —**much′ness** ***n.***
mu·ci·lage (myo͞o′s'l ij) ***n.*** [< MFr. < LL. *mucilago*, musty juice < L. *mucere*, to be moldy] 1. any of various thick, sticky substances produced in certain plants 2. any watery solution of gum, glue, etc. used as an adhesive
mu·ci·lag·i·nous (myo͞o′sə laj′ə nəs) ***adj.*** 1. of or like mucilage; sticky 2. producing mucilage
muck (muk) ***n.*** [< or akin to ON. *myki*, dung] 1. moist manure 2. black earth containing decaying matter, used as a fertilizer 3. anything unclean or degrading; dirt; filth —***vt.*** 1. to fertilize with muck 2. [Colloq.] to dirty as with muck —**muck′y** ***adj.*** **muck′i·er, muck′i·est**
muck·er (-ər) ***n.*** [prob. < G. < *mucken*, to grumble] [Slang] a coarse or vulgar person; cad
muck·rake (-rāk′) ***vi.*** **-raked′, -rak′ing** [coined c.1906: see MUCK & RAKE[1]] to search for and publicize corruption by public officials, businessmen, etc. —**muck′rak′er** ***n.***
mu·cous (myo͞o′kəs) ***adj.*** 1. of, containing, or secreting mucus 2. like mucus or covered with or as with mucus; slimy
mucous membrane a mucus-secreting membrane lining body cavities and canals, as the mouth, etc., connecting with the external air
mu·cus (myo͞o′kəs) ***n.*** [L.] the slimy secretion that moistens and protects the mucous membranes
mud (mud) ***n.*** [prob. < a LowG. source] wet, soft, sticky earth —***vt.*** **mud′ded, mud′ding** to cover or soil with or as with mud
mud·der (mud′ər) ***n.*** a race horse that performs especially well on a wet, muddy track
mud·dle (mud′'l) ***vt.*** **-dled, -dling** [< MUD] 1. to mix up; jumble; bungle 2. to confuse; befuddle, as with liquor —***vi.*** to act or think in a confused way —***n.*** mess, confusion, etc. —**muddle through** [Chiefly Brit.] to succeed in spite of confusion
mud·dler (-lər) ***n.*** a stick to stir mixed drinks
mud·dy (-ē) ***adj.*** **-di·er, -di·est** 1. full of or spattered with mud 2. not clear; cloudy [*muddy* coffee] 3. confused, obscure, etc. [*muddy* thinking] —***vt., vi.*** **-died, -dy·ing** to make or become muddy —**mud′di·ly** ***adv.*** —**mud′di·ness** ***n.***
mud·fish (-fish′) ***n., pl.*** **-fish′, -fish′es:** see FISH any of various fishes that live in mud or muddy water
mud·guard (-gärd′) ***n.*** *older name for* FENDER (sense *a*)
mud hen any of various birds that live in marshes, as the coot, gallinule, etc.
mud·pack (-pak′) ***n.*** a paste made up of fuller's earth, astringents, etc., used as a facial
mud puppy a N. American salamander that lives in mud under water
mud·sling·ing (-sliŋ′iŋ) ***n.*** unscrupulous attacks against an opponent, as in a political campaign —**mud′sling′er** ***n.***
mud snake a long, bluish-black snake with a spine at the tip of the tail, found in the SE U.S.
mud turtle a small turtle of North and Central America that lives in muddy ponds, streams, etc.

Muen·ster (mun′stər, mo͞on′-) ***n.*** [after *Munster*, in E France] a semisoft, mild cheese
mu·ez·zin (myo͞o ez′in) ***n.*** [< Ar. *mu'adhdhin* < *adhana*, to proclaim] a Moslem crier who calls the people to prayer at the proper hours
muff (muf) ***n.*** [Du. *mof* < Walloon < Fr. *moufle*, a mitten] 1. a cylindrical covering of fur, etc. into which the hands are placed from either end for warmth 2. *a) Baseball*, etc. a failure to hold the ball when catching it *b)* any bungling action —***vt., vi.*** to do (something) badly or awkwardly; specif., to bungle (a play), as in baseball
muf·fin (muf′'n) ***n.*** [? akin to OFr. *moufflet*, soft] a quick bread made with eggs, baked in a small, cup-shaped mold and usually eaten hot
muf·fle (muf′'l) ***vt.*** **-fled, -fling** [prob. akin to OFr. *enmouflé*, muffled < *moufle*, a mitten] 1. to wrap in a shawl, blanket, etc. so as to hide, keep warm, etc. 2. to wrap or cover in order to deaden or prevent sound 3. to deaden (a sound) 4. to stifle —***n.*** a covering, etc. used for muffling
muf·fler (-lər) ***n.*** 1. a scarf worn around the throat, as for warmth 2. a device for silencing noises, as a section in the exhaust pipe of an internal-combustion engine

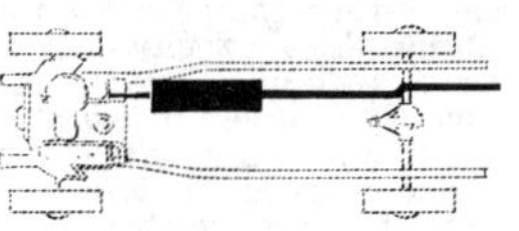

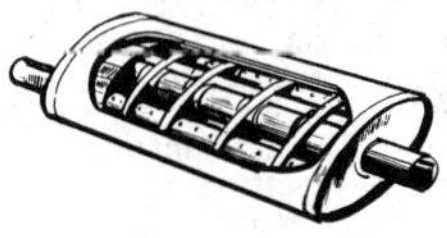

MUFFLER

muf·ti (muf′tē) ***n., pl.*** **-tis** [Ar. < *āftā*, to judge] 1. in Moslem countries, an interpreter of religious law 2. ordinary clothes, esp. when worn by one who usually wears a uniform
mug (mug) ***n.*** [prob. < Scand.] 1. a heavy drinking cup of earthenware or metal with a handle 2. as much as a mug will hold 3. [Slang] *a)* the face *b)* the mouth —***vt.*** **mugged, mug′ging** 1. to assault, esp. from behind and usually with intent to rob 2. [Slang] to photograph, as for police records —***vi.*** 1. to mug, or assault, someone 2. [Slang] to grimace, esp. in overacting —**mug′ger** ***n.***
mug·gy (mug′ē) ***adj.*** **-gi·er, -gi·est** [prob. < or akin to ON. *mugga*, a drizzle] hot, damp, and close [*muggy* weather] —**mug′gi·ness** ***n.***
mug·wump (mug′wump′) ***n.*** [< Algonquian *mugquomp*, chief] an independent, esp. in politics
Mu·ham·mad (mo͞o ham′əd) *same as* MOHAMMED —**Mu·ham′mad·an** ***adj., n.*** —**Mu·ham′mad·an·ism** ***n.***
‡**mu·jik** (mo͞o zhēk′, mo͞o′zhik) ***n.*** *same as* MUZHIK
Muk·den (mo͝ok′dən, mo͝ok den′) *former name of* SHENYANG
muk·luk (muk′luk′) ***n.*** [Esk. *muklok*, a large seal] 1. an Eskimo boot made of sealskin or reindeer skin 2. a canvas or rubber boot like this
mu·lat·to (mə lat′ō, myo͞o-) ***n., pl.*** **-toes** [Sp. & Port. *mulato*, of mixed breed < *mulo*, mule < L. *mulus*] 1. a person who has one Negro parent and one white parent 2. popularly, any person with mixed Negro and Caucasoid ancestry
mul·ber·ry (mul′ber′ē, -bər ē) ***n., pl.*** **-ries** [OE. *morberie* < L. *morum*, mulberry + OE. *berie*, a berry] 1. any of several trees that bear edible fruits resembling the raspberry 2. this fruit 3. purplish red —***adj.*** designating a family of plants including the mulberry, fig, and breadfruit
mulch (mulch) ***n.*** [ME. *molsh*, soft] leaves, straw, peat moss, etc., spread on the ground around plants to prevent evaporation of water from the soil, freezing of roots, etc. —***vt.*** to apply mulch to
mulct (mulkt) ***vt.*** [L. *mulctare* < *multa*, a fine] 1. to punish by a fine or by depriving of something 2. to extract (money) from (someone), as by fraud —***n.*** a fine or similar penalty
mule[1] (myo͞ol) ***n.*** [< OFr. < L. *mulus*] 1. the (usually sterile) offspring of a donkey and a horse, esp. of a jackass and a mare 2. a machine that draws and spins cotton fibers into yarn and winds the yarn 3. [Colloq.] a stubborn person
mule[2] (myo͞ol) ***n.*** [Fr., ult. < L. *mulleus*, red shoe] a lounging slipper that does not cover the heel
mule deer a long-eared deer of the western U.S.
mule skinner [Colloq.] a driver of mules
mu·le·ta (mo͞o lāt′ə, -let′ə) ***n.*** [Sp.] a red flannel cloth draped over a stick and manipulated by the matador in a bullfight
mu·le·teer (myo͞o′lə tir′) ***n.*** [< OFr.] a driver of mules
Mül·heim (mül′hīm′) city in W West Germany, on the Ruhr: pop. 189,000
mul·ish (myo͞ol′ish) ***adj.*** like a mule; stubborn; obstinate —**mul′ish·ly** ***adv.*** —**mul′ish·ness** ***n.***
mull[1] (mul) ***vt., vi.*** [OE. *myl*, dust] [Colloq.] to cogitate or ponder (usually with *over*)

mull[2] (mul) *vt.* [< ?] to heat, sweeten, and flavor with spices (ale, cider, wine, etc.)

mul·lah, mul·la (mul′ə, mool′-) *n.* [Turk., Per., & Hindi *mulla* < Ar. *mawlā*] a Moslem teacher or interpreter of the religious law: used as a title of respect for a learned man

mul·lein (mul′in) *n.* [OFr. *moleine,* ult. < L. *mollis,* soft] a tall plant of the figwort family, with spikes of yellow, lavender, or white flowers

mul·let (mul′it) *n., pl.* **-lets, -let:** see PLURAL, II, D, 1 [OFr. *mulet,* dim. < L. *mullus,* red mullet] any of a group of edible, spiny-rayed fishes found in fresh and salt waters; specif., the **striped** (or **gray**) **mullet**

mul·li·gan (mul′i g'n) *n.* [prob. < personal name] **1.** [Slang] a stew made of odd bits of meat and vegetables, esp. as made by hobos: also **mulligan stew** **2.** *Golf* a free drive, esp. off the first tee after a poor shot

mul·li·ga·taw·ny (mul′i gə tô′nē) *n.* [Tamil *milagutaṇṇir,* pepper water] an East Indian soup of meat, etc., flavored with curry

mul·lion (mul′yən) *n.* [prob. < OFr. *moienel* < L. *medianus,* middle] a slender, vertical dividing bar between the lights of windows, panels, etc. —*vt.* to furnish with mullions —**mul′lioned** *adj.*

MULLIONS

mul·tan·gu·lar (mul taŋ′gyoo lər) *adj.* having many angles: also **mul′ti·an′gu·lar** (mul′tē aŋ′-)

mul·ti- [L. < *multus,* much, many] *a combining form meaning:* **1.** having many *[multicolored]* **2.** more than two *[multilateral]* **3.** many times more than *[multimillionaire]* Also, before a vowel, **mult-** The meanings of the following words can be determined by combining the meanings of their component elements:

multicellular
multicolored
multidimensional
multidirectional
multifold
multifoliate
multilevel
multilinear
multilingual
multilobate
multinational
multinucleate
multiphase
multipinnate
multipolar
multipurpose
multiracial
multispeed
multispiral
multistoried
multivalve
multivitamin
multivoiced
multivolume

mul·ti·far·i·ous (mul′tə far′ē əs, -fer′-) *adj.* [L. *multifarius* < *multus,* many] having many kinds of parts or elements; of great variety —**mul′ti·far′i·ous·ly** *adv.* —**mul′ti·far′i·ous·ness** *n.*

mul·ti·flo·ra rose (-flôr′ə) a rose with thick clusters of small flowers, grown esp. for hedges

mul·ti·lat·er·al (mul′ti lat′ər əl) *adj.* **1.** many-sided **2.** involving more than two nations, etc. *[a multilateral treaty]* —**mul′ti·lat′er·al·ly** *adv.*

mul·ti·me·di·a (-mē′dē ə) *n. same as* MIXED MEDIA

mul·ti·mil·lion·aire (-mil′yə ner′) *n.* a person whose wealth amounts to many millions of dollars, francs, pounds, etc.

mul·ti·na·tion·al (-nash′ə n'l) *adj.* **1.** of or involving a number of nations **2.** designating or of a corporation with branches in a number of countries **3.** comprising persons of many nationalities —*n.* a multinational corporation

mul·tip·a·rous (mul tip′ər əs) *adj.* [< ModL.: see MULTI- & -PAROUS] *Zool.* normally bearing more than one offspring at a delivery

mul·ti·par·tite (mul′ti pär′tīt) *adj.* **1.** divided into many parts **2.** *same as* MULTILATERAL (sense 2)

mul·ti·ple (mul′tə p'l) *adj.* [Fr. < L. *multiplex* < *multus,* many + *-plex,* -fold: see DUPLEX] **1.** having or consisting of many parts, elements, etc.; manifold **2.** *Elec.* designating or of a circuit with two or more conductors in parallel —*n.* a number that is a product of some specified number and another number *[10 is a multiple of 5]*

multiple sclerosis a disease of the central nervous system, marked by speech defects, lack of coordination, etc.

mul·ti·plex (-pleks') *adj.* [L. *multiplex,* MULTIPLE] **1.** multiple **2.** designating or of a system for transmitting or receiving simultaneously two or more messages or signals over a common circuit, carrier wave, etc. —*vt.* to send (messages or signals) by a multiplex system

mul·ti·pli·cand (mul′tə pli kand′) *n.* [< L. *multiplicandus,* to be multiplied] *Math.* the number that is, or is to be, multiplied by another (the *multiplier*)

mul·ti·pli·ca·tion (-pli kā′shən) *n.* a multiplying or being multiplied; specif., *Math.* a method used to find the result of adding a specified quantity repeated a specified number of times

mul·ti·plic·i·ty (-plis′ə tē) *n.* [< LL. < L. *multiplex,* MULTIPLE] **1.** a being manifold or various **2.** a great number

mul·ti·pli·er (mul′tə plī′ər) *n.* **1.** a person or thing that multiplies or increases **2.** *Math.* the number by which another number (the *multiplicand*) is, or is to be, multiplied

mul·ti·ply[1] (mul′tə plī′) *vt.* **-plied′, -ply′ing** [< OFr. < L. *multiplicare* < *multiplex,* MULTIPLE] **1.** to cause to increase in number, amount, degree, etc. **2.** *Math.* to find the product of by multiplication —*vi.* **1.** to increase in number, amount, etc., esp. by procreation **2.** *Math.* to do multiplication

mul·ti·ply[2] (mul′tə plē) *adv.* in multiple ways

mul·ti·stage (mul′ti stāj′) *adj.* having several propulsion systems, used and discarded in sequence: said of a rocket or missile

mul·ti·tude (mul′tə tood′, -tyood′) *n.* [OFr. < L. *multitudo* < *multus,* many] **1.** a large number of persons or things; host, myriad, etc. **2.** the masses (preceded by *the*)

mul·ti·tu·di·nous (mul′tə tood′'n əs, -tyood′-) *adj.* **1.** many **2.** consisting of many parts, elements, etc.

mul·ti·va·lent (mul′ti vā′lənt, mul tiv′ə lənt) *adj. Chem. same as* POLYVALENT (sense 2) —**mul′ti·va′lence** *n.*

mul·ti·ver·si·ty (mul′tə vur′sə tē) *n., pl.* **-ties** the modern large and complex university with its many colleges, extensions, etc., regarded as being impersonal, bureaucratic, etc.

mum[1] (mum) *vi.* **mummed, mum′ming** [< OFr. *momer* < *momo,* echoic for grimace] to wear a mask or costume in fun; specif., to act as a mummer at Christmas time

mum[2] (mum) *n.* [Colloq.] a chrysanthemum

mum[3] (mum) *adj.* [ME. *momme,* echoic of sound made with closed lips] silent; not speaking —*interj.* do not speak! —**mum's the word** say nothing

mum·ble (mum′b'l) *vt., vi.* **-bled, -bling** [ME. *momelen*] **1.** to speak or say indistinctly, as with the mouth partly closed **2.** [Rare] to chew gently and ineffectively —*n.* a mumbled utterance —**mum′bler** *n.* —**mum′bling·ly** *adv.*

mum·ble·ty·peg (mum′b'l tē peg′) *n.* a game in which a jackknife is tossed in various ways to make it land with the blade in the ground

mum·bo jum·bo (mum′bō jum′bō) [of Afr. orig.: < ?] **1.** [**M- J-**] among certain West African tribes, an idol or god supposed to protect the people from evil **2.** any idol or fetish **3.** meaningless ritual, gibberish, etc.

mum·mer (mum′ər) *n.* [see MUM[1]] **1.** one who wears a mask or disguise for fun; specif., in England, any of the masked and costumed persons who act out pantomimes at Christmas time **2.** any actor

mum·mer·y (-ē) *n., pl.* **-mer·ies** **1.** performance by mummers **2.** any show or ceremony regarded as hypocritical

mum·mi·fy (mum′ə fī′) *vt.* **-fied′, -fy′ing** to make into or like a mummy —*vi.* to shrivel or dry up —**mum′mi·fi·ca′tion** *n.*

mum·my (mum′ē) *n., pl.* **-mies** [< Fr. < ML. < Ar. *mūmiyā* < Per. *mum,* wax] **1.** a dead body preserved by embalming, as by the ancient Egyptians **2.** any well-preserved dead body

mumps (mumps) *n.pl.* [*with sing. v.*] [pl. of obs. *mump,* a grimace] an acute communicable disease, caused by a virus and characterized by swelling of the salivary glands

mun. municipal

munch (munch) *vt., vi.* [ME. *monchen,* echoic] to chew steadily, often with a crunching sound

Mun·chau·sen (mun′chou′zən, moon′-; -chô′-), Baron 1720–97; Ger. soldier & adventurer known for his exaggerated tales of his exploits

Mun·cie (mun′sē) [after the *Munsee* (Delaware) Indians] city in EC Ind.: pop. 77,000

mun·dane (mun dān′, mun′dān) *adj.* [< OFr. < L. < *mundus,* world] **1.** of the world; esp., worldly, as distinguished from heavenly, spiritual, etc. **2.** commonplace; everyday; ordinary

Mu·nich (myoo′nik) city in SE West Germany; capital of Bavaria: pop. 1,244,000: Ger. name **Mün·chen** (mün′Hən)

mu·nic·i·pal (myoo nis′ə p'l) *adj.* [< L. < *municeps,* citizen of a free town < *munia,* official duties + *capere,* to take] **1.** of or having to do with a city, town, etc. or its local government **2.** having local self-government —**mu·nic′i·pal·ly** *adv.*

mu·nic·i·pal·i·ty (myoo nis′ə pal′ə tē) *n., pl.* **-ties** a city, town, etc. having its own incorporated government

mu·nic·i·pal·ize (myoo nis′ə pə līz′) *vt.* **-ized′, -iz′ing** **1.** to bring under the control or ownership of a municipality **2.** to make a municipality of —**mu·nic′i·pal·i·za′tion** *n.*

mu·nif·i·cent (myoo nif′ə s'nt) *adj.* [< L. < *munificus,* bountiful < *munus,* a gift + *facere,* to make] **1.** very generous in giving **2.** given with great generosity —**mu·nif′i·cence** *n.* —**mu·nif′i·cent·ly** *adv.*

mu·ni·tion (myoo nish′ən) *vt.* to provide with munitions
mu·ni·tions (-ənz) *n.pl.* [< MFr. < L. *munire*, to fortify] war supplies; esp., weapons and ammunition
Mün·ster (mün′stər) city in NW West Germany: pop. 203,000
mu·on (myōō′än) *n.* [MU + (MES)ON] a positively or negatively charged subatomic particle with a mass 207 times that of an electron
mu·ral (myoor′əl) *adj.* [Fr. < L. *muralis* < *murus*, a wall] **1.** of, on, in, or for a wall **2.** like a wall —*n.* a picture or photograph, esp. a large one, painted or applied directly on a wall —**mu′ral·ist** *n.*
Mur·ci·a (mur′shə, -shē ə; *Sp.* moor′thyä) city in SE Spain: pop. 262,000
mur·der (mur′dər) *n.* [OE. *morthor* & OFr. *mordre*] the unlawful and malicious or premeditated killing of one human being by another —*vt.* **1.** to kill unlawfully and with malice **2.** to spoil or botch, as in performance [*she murdered* that song] —*vi.* to commit murder —**get away with murder** [Slang] to escape detection or punishment for a blameworthy act —**mur′der·er** *n.* —**mur′der·ess** *n.fem.*
mur·der·ous (-əs) *adj.* **1.** of, having the nature of, or characteristic of murder; brutal **2.** capable or guilty of, or intending, murder **3.** [Colloq.] very dangerous, trying, etc.—**mur′der·ous·ly** *adv.* —**mur′der·ous·ness** *n.*
mu·ri·at·ic acid (myoor′ē at′ik) [< Fr. < L. < *muria*, brine] hydrochloric acid: a commercial term
Mu·ri·el (myoor′ē əl) [prob. < Celt. < *muir*, sea + *geal*, bright] a feminine name
Mu·ril·lo (moo rē′lyô; *E.* myoo ril′ō), **Bar·to·lo·mé Es·te·ban** (bär′tô lô me′ es te′bän) 1617–82; Sp. painter
murk (murk) *n.* [< ON. *myrkr*, dark] darkness; gloom —*adj.* [Archaic] dark or dim
murk·y (mur′kē) *adj.* **murk′i·er, murk′i·est** **1.** dark or gloomy **2.** heavy and obscure with smoke, mist, etc. —**murk′i·ly** *adv.* —**murk′i·ness** *n.*
Mur·mansk (moor mänsk′) seaport on the NW coast of the U.S.S.R., on the Arctic Ocean: pop. 296,000
mur·mur (mur′mər) *n.* [< OFr. < L.: echoic word] **1.** a low, indistinct, continuous sound, as of a stream, far-off voices, etc. **2.** a mumbled complaint **3.** *Med.* any abnormal sound heard by auscultation, esp. such a sound in the region of the heart —*vi.* **1.** to make a murmur **2.** to mumble a complaint —*vt.* to say in a murmur —**mur′mur·er** *n.* —**mur′mur·ing** *adj.* —**mur′mur·ous** *adj.*
Mur·phy bed (mur′fē) [after W. L. *Murphy*, its U.S. inventor (c.1900)] a bed that swings up or folds into a closet or cabinet when not in use
mur·rain (mur′in) *n.* [< OFr. *morine* < L. *mori*, to die] **1.** any of various infectious diseases of cattle **2.** [Archaic] a pestilence; plague
Mur·ray[1] (mur′ē) [< the surname *Murray*] a masculine name
Mur·ray[2] (mur′ē) river in SE Australia, flowing into the Indian Ocean
mur·ther (mur′*th*ər) *n., vt., vi. dial. var. of* MURDER
mus. **1.** museum **2.** music **3.** musical
mus·ca·dine (mus′kə din, -dīn′) *n.* [altered < MUSCATEL] a variety of grape grown in the SE U.S.
mus·cat (mus′kət, -kat) *n.* [Fr . < Pr. < It. *moscato*, musk, wine < LL. *muscus*, musk] **1.** a variety of sweet European grape from which muscatel and raisins are made **2.** *same as* MUSCATEL (sense 1)
mus·ca·tel (mus′kə tel′) *n.* [OFr. *muscadel*, ult. < It. *moscato*, MUSCAT] **1.** a rich, sweet wine made from the muscat **2.** *same as* MUSCAT (sense 1) Also **mus′ca·del′** (-del′)
mus·cle (mus′'l) *n.* [Fr. < L. *musculus*, dim. of *mus*, a mouse] **1.** any of the body organs consisting of bundles of fibers that can be contracted and expanded to produce bodily movements **2.** the tissue making up such an organ **3.** muscular strength; brawn **4.** [Colloq.] power based on force —*vi.* **-cled, -cling** [Colloq.] to make one's way by sheer force (usually with *in*)
mus·cle-bound (-bound′) *adj.* having some of the muscles enlarged and less elastic, as from too much exercise
Mus·co·vite (mus′kə vīt′) *n.* a Russian, esp. of Moscow —*adj.* of Russia or of Moscow
Mus·co·vy (mus′kə vē) **1.** former grand duchy surrounding & including Moscow **2.** *former name of* RUSSIA
Muscovy duck [altered < *musk duck*] a common domesticated duck with a large crest and red wattles
mus·cu·lar (mus′kyə lər) *adj.* **1.** of, consisting of, or accomplished by a muscle or muscles **2.** having well-developed muscles; strong; brawny —**mus′cu·lar′i·ty** (-lar′ə tē) *n.* —**mus′cu·lar·ly** *adv.*
muscular dystrophy a chronic disease characterized by a progressive wasting of the muscles
mus·cu·la·ture (mus′kyə lə chər) *n.* [Fr.] the arrangement of the muscles of a body or of some part of the body; muscular system
Muse (myōōz) *n.* [< OFr. < L. < Gr. *mousa*] **1.** *Gr. Myth.* any of the nine goddesses who presided over literature and the arts and sciences **2.** [m-] the spirit regarded as inspiring a poet or artist
muse (myōōz) *vi.* **mused, mus′ing** [< OFr. *muser*, to loiter] to think deeply; meditate —*vt.* to think or say meditatively —*n.* deep meditation
mu·se·um (myōō zē′əm) *n.* [L. < Gr. *mouseion*, place for the Muses < *mousa*, a Muse] a building, room, etc. for preserving and exhibiting artistic, historical, or scientific objects
mush[1] (mush) *n.* [prob. var. of MASH] **1.** a thick porridge of boiled cornmeal **2.** any thick, soft mass **3.** [Colloq.] maudlin sentimentality
mush[2] (mush) *interj.* [prob. < *mush on*, altered < Fr. *marchons*, let's go] in Canada and Alaska, a shout commanding sled dogs to start or to go faster —*vi.* to travel on foot over snow, usually with a dog sled —*n.* a journey by mushing
mush·room (mush′rōōm′, -room′) *n.* [OFr. *moisseron* < LL. *mussirio*] **1.** any of various rapid-growing, fleshy fungi having a stalk with an umbrellalike top; popularly, any edible variety, as distinguished from the poisonous ones (*toadstools*) **2.** anything like a mushroom in shape or rapid growth —*adj.* **1.** of or made with mushrooms **2.** like a mushroom in shape or rapid growth —*vi.* **1.** to grow or spread rapidly **2.** to flatten out at the end so as to resemble a mushroom
mush·y (mush′ē) *adj.* **mush′i·er, mush′i·est** **1.** like mush; thick and soft **2.** [Colloq.] maudlin and sentimental —**mush′i·ly** *adv.* —**mush′i·ness** *n.*
mu sic (myōō′zik) *n.* [< OFr. < L. < Gr. *mousikē* (*technē*), musical (art) < *mousa*, a Muse] **1.** the art and science of combining tones in varying melody, harmony, etc., esp. so as to form complete and expressive compositions **2.** the tones so arranged, or their arrangement **3.** any rhythmic sequence of pleasing sounds, as of birds, etc. **4.** a musical composition or compositions; esp., the written or printed score **5.** ability to respond to or take pleasure in music —**face the music** [Colloq.] to accept the consequences, however unpleasant —**set to music** to compose music for (a poem, etc.)
mu·si·cal (-zi k'l) *adj.* **1.** of or for the creation or performance of music **2.** melodious or harmonious **3.** fond of or skilled in music **4.** set to music —*n.* a theatrical or film production with dialogue and a musical score with popular songs and dances: in full, **musical comedy** (or **play**, or **drama**) —**mu′si·cal′i·ty** (-kal′ə tē) *n.* —**mu′si·cal·ly** *adv.*
musical chairs a game in which the players march to music around empty chairs (one fewer than the number of players) and rush to sit down each time the music stops: the player with no seat drops out
mu·si·cale (myōō′zə kal′) *n.* [Fr.] a party or social affair featuring a musical program
music box a mechanical musical instrument containing a bar with tuned steel teeth that are struck by pins so arranged on a revolving cylinder as to produce a certain tune or tunes
music hall **1.** an auditorium for musical productions **2.** [Brit.] a vaudeville theater
mu·si·cian (myōō zish′ən) *n.* a person skilled in music; esp., a professional performer of music —**mu·si′cian·ly** *adv.* —**mu·si′cian·ship′** *n.*
mu·si·col·o·gy (myōō′zi käl′ə jē) *n.* [< It.: see MUSIC & -LOGY] the systematized study of the science, history, and methods of music —**mu′si·co·log′i·cal** (-kə läj′i k'l) *adj.* —**mu′si·col′o·gist** *n.*
mus·ing (myōō′ziŋ) *adj.* that muses; meditative —*n.* meditation; reflection —**mus′ing·ly** *adv.*
musk (musk) *n.* [< OFr. < LL. < Gr. < Per. *mušk*, musk < Sans. *muṣka*, testicle] **1.** a substance with a strong, penetrating odor, obtained from a small sac (**musk bag**) under the skin of the abdomen in the male musk deer: used as the basis of numerous perfumes **2.** the odor of this substance, now often created synthetically —**musk′like′** *adj.*
musk deer a small, hornless deer of the uplands of C Asia: the male secretes musk
mus·kel·lunge (mus′kə lunj′) *n., pl.* **-lunge′** [< Ojibway *maskinoje*] a large pike of the Great Lakes and upper Mississippi: also called **mus′kie** (-kē)
mus·ket (mus′kit) *n.* [< MFr. < It. *moschetto*, orig. fledged arrow < L. *musca*, a fly] a smooth-bore, long-barreled firearm, used, as by infantry soldiers, before the invention of the rifle
mus·ket·eer (mus′kə tir′) *n.* a soldier armed with a musket
mus·ket·ry (mus′kə trē) *n.* **1.** the skill of firing muskets or other small arms **2.** muskets or musketeers, collectively
musk·mel·on (musk′mel′ən) *n.* [MUSK + MELON] any of several roundish fruits growing on a vine of the gourd family, as the cantaloupe: they have a thick rind and sweet, juicy flesh
Mus·ko·ge·an (mus kō′gē ən, -jē-) *adj.* designating or of a N. American Indian language family of the SE U.S.: also **Mus·kho′ge·an**

musk ox a hardy ox of arctic America and Greenland, with a long, coarse, hairy coat, large, curved horns, and a musklike odor

musk·rat (musk′rat′) ***n.,*** *pl.* **-rats′, -rat′**: see PLURAL, II, D, 1 **1.** a N. American rodent living in water and having glossy brown fur and a musklike odor **2.** its fur

MUSKRAT (body 9–13 in. long; tail 7–11 in. long)

musk·y (mus′kē) ***adj.*** **musk′i·er, musk′i·est** of, like, or smelling of musk —**musk′i·ness** ***n.***

Mus·lim (muz′ləm, mooz′-) ***n., adj.*** *same as* MOSLEM

mus·lin (muz′lin) ***n.*** [< Fr. < It. *mussolino* < *Mussolo,* Mosul, city in Iraq] a strong, often sheer cotton cloth of plain weave; esp., a heavy variety used for sheets, pillowcases, etc.

muss (mus) ***n.*** [prob. var. of MESS] **1.** [Now Rare] a mess **2.** [Old Slang or Dial.] a squabble —***vt.*** to make messy (often with *up*)

mus·sel (mus′'l) ***n.*** [< OE., ult. < L. *musculus,* mussel, MUSCLE] any of various bivalve mollusks; specif., *a)* an edible saltwater variety *b)* a large freshwater variety with a pearly shell formerly made into buttons

Mus·so·li·ni (moo̅s′sô lē′nē; *E.* moos′ə lē′nē, mus′-), **Be·ni·to** (be nē′tô) 1883–1945; It. dictator; Fascist prime minister of Italy (1922–43): executed

Mus·sorg·sky (moo sôrg′skē), **Mo·dest Pe·tro·vich** (mô-dyest′ pyi trô′vich) 1839–81; Russ. composer

Mus·sul·man (mus′'l mən) ***n.,*** *pl.* **-mans** [< Per. < Ar. *muslim*] [Now Rare] a Moslem

muss·y (mus′ē) ***adj.*** **muss′i·er, muss′i·est** [Colloq.] messy; disordered, rumpled, etc. —**muss′i·ness** ***n.***

must[1] (must; *unstressed* məst) ***v.aux.*** *pt.* **must** [< OE. *moste,* pt. of *motan,* may] an auxiliary used with the infinitive of various verbs (without *to*) to express: **1.** compulsion, obligation, or necessity *[I must pay her]* **2.** probability *[you must be my cousin]* **3.** certainty *[all men must die]* *Must* is sometimes used with the verb understood *[shoot if you must]* —***n.*** [Colloq.] something that must be done, had, read, seen, etc. *[this book is a must]* —***adj.*** [Colloq.] that must be done, etc.

must[2] (must) ***n.*** [OE. < L. *mustum,* new wine < *mustus,* fresh] the juice pressed from grapes or other fruit before it has fermented

must[3] (must) ***n.*** a musty quality or state

mus·tache (mə stash′, mus′tash) ***n.*** [< Fr. < It. *mostacchio* < MGr. < Gr. *mystax,* upper lip] **1.** the hair on the upper lip of men **2.** the hair or bristles growing about an animal's mouth

mus·ta·chio (məs tä′shō, -shē ō′) ***n.,*** *pl.* **-chios** [< Sp. or It.] a mustache, esp. a large, bushy one —**mus·ta′chioed** ***adj.***

Mustafa Kemal *same as* KEMAL ATATURK

mus·tang (mus′taŋ) ***n.*** [< AmSp. < Sp. *mesteño,* belonging to the graziers, wild] a small wild or half-wild horse of the SW plains of the U.S.

mus·tard (mus′tərd) ***n.*** [< OFr. *moustarde* < L. *mustum,* MUST[2] (orig. added to the condiment)] **1.** any of several plants with yellow flowers and slender pods **2.** the ground or powdered seeds from these pods, often prepared as a paste, used as a pungent seasoning **3.** a dark yellow —***adj.*** designating or of a family of plants with cross-shaped flowers, including cabbage, turnip, radish, alyssum, etc. —**cut the mustard** [Colloq.] to do the work required of one

mustard gas [from its mustardlike odor] a volatile liquid, $(CH_2ClCH_2)_2S$, used as a poison gas in war

mustard plaster a plaster made with powdered mustard, applied to the skin as a counterirritant

mus·ter (mus′tər) ***vt.*** [< OFr. < ML. < L. *monstrare,* to show < *monere,* to warn] **1.** to assemble (troops, etc.) **2.** to gather up; collect; summon (often with *up*) *[to muster up strength]* **3.** to total in number —***vi.*** to assemble as for inspection or roll call —***n.*** **1.** an assembling, as of troops for inspection **2.** *a)* the persons or things assembled *b)* the total of these **3.** the list of persons in a military or naval unit: also **muster roll** —**muster in** (or **out**) to enlist in (or discharge from) military service —**pass muster** to measure up to the required standards

must·n't (mus′'nt) must not

mus·ty (mus′tē) ***adj.*** **-ti·er, -ti·est** [ult. < ? MOIST] **1.** having a stale, moldy smell or taste **2.** stale, trite, or antiquated *[musty ideas]* —**mus′ti·ly** ***adv.*** —**mus′ti·ness** ***n.***

mu·ta·ble (myo̅o̅t′ə b'l) ***adj.*** [< L. < *mutare,* to change] **1.** that can be changed **2.** given to changing; inconstant **3.** subject to mutation —**mu′ta·bil′i·ty, mu′ta·ble·ness** ***n.*** —**mu′ta·bly** ***adv.***

mu·tant (myo̅o̅t′'nt) ***adj.*** [< L. prp. of *mutare,* to change] undergoing mutation —***n.*** an animal or plant with inheritable characters that differ from those of the parents

mu·tate (myo̅o̅′tāt) ***vi., vt.*** **-tat·ed, -tat·ing** [< L. pp. of *mutare,* to change] to change; specif., to undergo or cause to undergo mutation

mu·ta·tion (myo̅o̅ tā′shən) ***n.*** **1.** a changing or being changed **2.** a change, as in form, nature, etc. **3.** *Biol. a)* a sudden variation in some inheritable character of an animal or plant *b)* an individual resulting from such variation; mutant —**mu·ta′tion·al** ***adj.*** —**mu·ta′tion·al·ly** ***adv.***

mute (myo̅o̅t) ***adj.*** [< OFr. < L. *mutus*] **1.** not speaking; voluntarily silent **2.** unable to speak **3.** not spoken *[a mute appeal]* **4.** not pronounced; silent, as the *e* in *mouse* **5.** *Law* refusing to plead when arraigned —***n.*** **1.** a person who does not speak; specif., one who cannot speak because deaf; deaf-mute **2.** a letter that is not pronounced **3.** *Law* a defendant who refuses to plead when arraigned **4.** *Music* a device used to soften the tone of an instrument —***vt.*** **mut′ed, mut′ing** **1.** to soften the sound of, as with a mute **2.** to tone down (a color) —**mute′ly** ***adv.*** —**mute′ness** ***n.***

MUTES (A, violin mute; B, on violin bridge; C, trumpet mute; D, in bell of trumpet)

mu·ti·late (myo̅o̅t′'l āt′) ***vt.*** **-lat′ed, -lat′ing** [< L. pp. of *mutilare* < *mutilus,* maimed] **1.** to cut off or damage a limb, etc. of (a person or animal) **2.** to damage or otherwise make imperfect, esp. by removing an essential part or parts —**mu′ti·la′tion** ***n.*** —**mu′ti·la′tive** ***adj.*** —**mu′ti·la′tor** ***n.***

mu·ti·neer (myo̅o̅t′'n ir′) ***n.*** one guilty of mutiny

mu·ti·nous (myo̅o̅t′'n əs) ***adj.*** **1.** taking part or likely to take part in a mutiny **2.** of or having to do with mutiny —**mu′ti·nous·ly** ***adv.*** —**mu′ti·nous·ness** ***n.***

mu·ti·ny (myo̅o̅t′'n ē) ***n.,*** *pl.* **-nies** [< Fr. < OFr. *mutin,* riotous < *meute,* a revolt, ult. < L. *movere,* to move] forcible revolt against constituted authority; esp., rebellion of soldiers or sailors against their officers —***vi.*** **-nied, -ny·ing** to take part in a mutiny; revolt

mutt (mut) ***n.*** [prob. < *muttonhead,* a dolt] [Slang] **1.** a stupid person; blockhead **2.** a mongrel dog; cur

mut·ter (mut′ər) ***vi., vt.*** [ME. *moteren*] to speak or say in low tones with the lips almost closed, often in a complaining way; grumble —***n.*** **1.** a muttering **2.** something muttered —**mut′ter·er** ***n.***

mut·ton (mut′'n) ***n.*** [OFr. *moton,* a ram < ML. *multo,* sheep] the flesh of sheep, esp. a grown sheep, used as food —**mut′ton·y** ***adj.***

mutton chop **1.** a piece cut from the rib of a sheep for broiling or frying **2.** [*pl.*] side whiskers shaped like mutton chops

mu·tu·al (myo̅o̅′choo wəl) ***adj.*** [< MFr. < L. *mutuus,* reciprocal < *mutare,* to change] **1.** *a)* done, felt, etc. by each of two or more for or toward the other or others; reciprocal *[mutual admiration]* *b)* of each other *[mutual enemies]* **2.** shared in common; joint *[our mutual friend]* —**mu′tu·al′i·ty** (-wal′ə tē) ***n.,*** *pl.* **-ties** —**mu′tu·al·ly** ***adv.***

mutual fund a trust or corporation that invests funds from its shareholders in various securities

mu·tu·el (myo̅o̅′choo wəl) ***n.*** *same as* PARIMUTUEL

muu·muu (mo̅o̅′mo̅o̅) ***n.*** [< Haw., lit., cut off] a full, long, loose garment for women, usually in a bright print as orig. worn in Hawaii

Mu·zak (myo̅o̅′zak) *a trademark for* a system of transmitting recorded music to restaurants, factories, etc. —***n.*** the music transmitted

‡**mu·zhik, mu·zjik** (mo̅o̅ zhēk′, mo̅o̅′zhik) ***n.*** [Russ.] in czarist Russia, a peasant

muz·zle (muz′'l) ***n.*** [< OFr. *musel,* snout < ML. *musum* < ?] **1.** the part of the head of a dog, horse, etc. including the mouth, nose, and jaws **2.** a device, as of straps, fastened over the mouth of an animal to prevent its biting or eating **3.** anything that prevents free speech **4.** the front end of the barrel of a firearm —***vt.*** **-zled, -zling** **1.** to put a muzzle on (an animal) **2.** to prevent from talking or expressing an opinion —**muz′zler** ***n.***

muz·zle·load·er (-lōd′ər) ***n.*** any firearm loaded through the muzzle —**muz′zle·load′ing** ***n.***

my (mī; *unstressed, often* mə) ***possessive pronominal adj.*** [OE. *min*] of, belonging to, made, or done by me —***interj.*** an exclamation of surprise, dismay, etc.

my·ce·li·um (mī sē′lē əm) ***n.,*** *pl.* **-li·a** (-ə) [ModL. < Gr. *mykēs,* a mushroom] the thallus, or vegetative part, of a

fungus, made of a mass of threadlike tubes —**my·ce′li·al** *adj.*
My·ce·nae (mī sē′nē) ancient city in the NE Peloponnesus
My·ce·nae·an (mī′sə nē′ən) *adj.* **1.** of Mycenae **2.** designating or of a civilization that existed in Greece, Asia Minor, etc. from 1500 to 1100 B.C.
-my·cete (mī′sēt, mī sēt′) [< ModL. < Gr. < *mykēs*, a mushroom] *a combining form meaning* one of a specified class of fungi
my·co- [< Gr. *mykēs*, fungus] *a combining form meaning* fungus: also, before a vowel, **myc-**
my·col·o·gy (mī käl′ə jē) *n.* [< ModL.: see prec. & -LOGY] the branch of botany dealing with fungi —**my·co·log·ic** (mī′kə läj′ik), **my′co·log′i·cal** *adj.* —**my·col′o·gist** *n.*
my·co·sis (mī kō′sis) *n., pl.* **-ses** (-sēz) [ModL.: see MYC(O)- & -OSIS] **1.** the growth of parasitic fungi in any part of the body **2.** a disease caused by such fungi —**my·cot′ic** (-kät′ik) *adj.*
my·e·li·tis (mī′ə līt′is) *n.* [ModL. < Gr. *myelos*, marrow + -ITIS] inflammation of the spinal cord or the bone marrow
my·e·lo·gram (mī′ə lō gram′) *n.* [< Gr. *myelos*, marrow + -GRAM] an X-ray of the spinal cord, taken after the injection of a contrast substance —**my′e·log′ra·phy** (-läg′rə fē) *n.*
My·lar (mī′lär) *a trademark for* a polyester used for recording tapes, fabrics, etc. —*n.* [**m-**] this substance
my·na, my·nah (mī′nə) *n.* [Hindi *mainā*] any of a group of tropical birds of SE Asia related to the starling: some species can mimic speech
my·o- [< Gr. *mys* (gen. *myos*), a muscle] *a combining form meaning* muscle: also, before a vowel, **my-**
my·o·car·di·um (mī′ə kär′dē əm) *n.* [ModL.: see prec. + CARDIO-] the muscular substance of the heart —**my′o·car′di·al** *adj.*
my·o·pi·a (mī ō′pē ə) *n.* [ModL. < Gr. < *myein*, to close + *ōps*, an eye] abnormal vision in which light rays from distant objects focus in front of the retina instead of on it, so that the objects are not seen distinctly; nearsightedness —**my·op′ic** (-äp′ik) *adj.* —**my·op′i·cal·ly** *adv.*
My·ra (mī′rə) [< ? Ir. *Moira*] a feminine name
myr·i·ad (mir′ē əd) *n.* [< Gr. *myrias* (gen. *myriados*), ten thousand < *myrios*, countless] **1.** orig., ten thousand **2.** any indefinitely large number **3.** a great number of persons or things —*adj.* **1.** countless; innumerable **2.** of a highly varied nature
myr·i·a·pod (mir′ē ə päd′) *adj.* [see prec. & -POD] having many legs; specif., of a large group of arthropods having a long body of many segments, each with one or more pairs of jointed legs, as the centipedes —*n.* any animal of this group
Myr·mi·don (mʉr′mə dän′, -dən) *n., pl.* **-dons, Myr·mid·o·nes** (mər mid′ə nēz′) **1.** *Gr. Legend* any of a tribe of Thessalian warriors who fought under Achilles, their king, in the Trojan War **2.** [**m-**] an unquestioning follower or subordinate
myrrh (mʉr) *n.* [< OE. & OFr. < L. < Gr. *myrrha* < Ar. *murr*] **1.** a fragrant, bitter-tasting gum resin exuded from any of several plants of Arabia and E Africa, used in making incense, perfume, etc. **2.** any of these plants
Myr·tle (mʉr′t'l) [< ff.] a feminine name
myr·tle (mʉr′t'l) *n.* [< OFr. < ML. dim. of L. *myrtus* < Gr. *myrtos*] **1.** a shrub with evergreen leaves, white or pink flowers, and dark berries **2.** any of various other evergreen plants, as the periwinkle —*adj.* designating a family of evergreen trees and shrubs, including myrtle, eucalyptus, guava, clove, and blue gum
my·self (mī self′, mə-) *pron.* a form of the 1st pers. sing. pronoun, used: *a)* as an intensive *[I went myself]* *b)* as a reflexive *[I hurt myself]* *c)* as a quasi-noun meaning "my real or true self" *[I am not myself today]*
My·sore (mī sôr′) city in S India: pop. 254,000
mys·te·ri·ous (mis tir′ē əs) *adj.* of, containing, implying, or characterized by mystery —**mys·te′ri·ous·ly** *adv.* —**mys·te′ri·ous·ness** *n.*
mys·ter·y[1] (mis′tə rē, -trē) *n., pl.* **-ter·ies** [< L. < Gr. *mystērion*, ult. < *myein*, to initiate into the mysteries, orig., to close (eyes or mouth)] **1.** something unexplained, unknown, or kept secret **2.** *a)* anything that remains so secret or obscure as to excite curiosity *b)* a novel, play, etc. involving an event of this kind, esp. one about a crime and its solution **3.** obscurity or secrecy **4.** [*pl.*] secret rites or doctrines known only to the initiated *[the Eleusinian mysteries]* **5.** *same as* MYSTERY PLAY **6.** *Theol.* any religious truth divinely revealed and to be accepted on faith
mys·ter·y[2] (mis′tə rē) *n., pl.* **-ter·ies** [< ML. *misterium*, altered < L. *ministerium*, office, by confusion with *mysterium*, a secret rite] [Archaic] a craft or craft guild
mystery play any of a class of medieval dramatic representations of Biblical events
mys·tic (mis′tik) *adj.* [< L. < Gr. *mystikos* < *mystēs*, one initiated] **1.** *same as* MYSTICAL **2.** mysterious, secret, occult, awe-inspiring, etc. *[mystic rites, mystic powers]* —*n.* one who professes to undergo mystical experiences by which he learns truths beyond human understanding
mys·ti·cal (-ti k'l) *adj.* **1.** of mystics or mysticism; esp., based on intuition, meditation, etc. of a spiritual nature **2.** spiritually symbolic **3.** *same as* MYSTIC (sense 2) —**mys′ti·cal·ly** *adv.*
mys·ti·cism (-tə siz'm) *n.* **1.** the beliefs or practices of mystics **2.** the doctrine that knowledge of spiritual truths can be acquired by intuition and meditation **3.** vague or obscure thinking or belief
mys·ti·fy (mis′tə fī′) *vt.* **-fied′, -fy′ing** [< Fr. < *mystère*, mystery + *-fier*, -FY] **1.** *a)* to puzzle or perplex *b)* to bewilder deliberately **2.** to involve in mystery; make obscure —**mys′ti·fi·ca′tion** *n.*
mys·tique (mis tēk′) *n.* [Fr., mystic] the quasi-mystical attitudes and feelings surrounding some person, institution, activity, etc.
myth (mith) *n.* [< LL. < Gr. *mythos*, a word, legend] **1.** a traditional story of unknown authorship, serving usually to explain some phenomenon of nature, the origin of man, or the customs, religious rites, etc. of a people: cf. LEGEND **2.** such stories collectively; mythology **3.** any fictitious story **4.** any imaginary person or thing
myth. mythology
myth·i·cal (-i k'l) *adj.* **1.** of, or having the nature of, a myth or myths **2.** existing only in myth **3.** imaginary or fictitious; not based on fact Also **myth′ic** —**myth′i·cal·ly** *adv.*
my·thol·o·gize (mi thäl′ə jīz′) *vi.* **-gized′, -giz′ing** to relate, compile, or explain myths —*vt.* to make into a myth: also **myth·i·cize** (mith′ə sīz′) **-cized′, -ciz′ing** —**my·thol′o·giz′er** *n.*
my·thol·o·gy (mi thäl′ə jē) *n., pl.* **-gies** [< LL. < Gr. < *mythos*, myth + *-logia*, -LOGY] **1.** the study of myths **2.** myths collectively; esp., all the myths of a specific people or about a specific being —**myth·o·log·i·cal** (mith′ə läj′i k'l), **myth′o·log′ic** *adj.* —**myth′o·log′i·cal·ly** *adv.* —**my·thol′o·gist** *n.*
myth·os (mith′äs, mī′thäs) *n.* **1.** a myth or body of myths **2.** the attitudes, beliefs, etc. most characteristic of a particular group or society
Myt·i·le·ne (mit′'l ē′nē) *same as* LESBOS

N

N, n (en) *n., pl.* **N's, n's** **1.** the fourteenth letter of the English alphabet **2.** the sound of *N* or *n*
n (en) *n.* **1.** *Math. the symbol for* an indefinite number **2.** *Physics the symbol for* neutron
N *Chem.* nitrogen
N, N., n, n. **1.** north **2.** northern
n. **1.** net **2.** neuter **3.** noon **4.** noun **5.** number
Na [L. *natrium*] *Chem.* sodium
N.A. North America
NAACP, N.A.A.C.P. National Association for the Advancement of Colored People
nab (nab) *vt.* **nabbed, nab′bing** [prob. var. of dial. *nap*, to snatch < Scand.] [Colloq.] **1.** to seize suddenly; snatch **2.** to arrest or catch (a felon or wrongdoer) —**nab′ber** *n.*
na·bob (nā′bäb) *n.* [< Hindi < Ar. *nuwwāb*, pl. of *nā'ib*, deputy] **1.** a native provincial deputy or governor of the old Mogul Empire in India **2.** a very rich man
na·celle (nə sel′) *n.* [Fr. < LL. *navicella*, dim. of L. *navis*, a ship] a streamlined enclosure on an aircraft, esp. that which houses an engine
na·cre (nā′kər) *n.* [Fr. < It. < Ar. *naqqārah*, drum] *same as* MOTHER-OF-PEARL

na·cre·ous (-krē əs) ***adj.*** **1.** of or like nacre **2.** yielding nacre **3.** iridescent; lustrous
Na·dine (nə dēn′, nā-) [Fr. < Russ. *nadezhda*, hope] a feminine name
na·dir (nā′dər, -dir) ***n.*** [< MFr. < ML. < Ar. *naẓīr (as-samt)*, opposite (the zenith)] **1.** that point of the celestial sphere directly opposite to the zenith and directly below the observer **2.** the lowest point
nae (nā) ***adv.*** [Scot.] no; not —***adj.*** no
nag[1] (nag) ***vt.*** **nagged, nag′ging** [< Scand.] **1.** to annoy by continual scolding, faultfinding, urging, etc. **2.** to keep troubling, worrying, etc. —***vi.*** **1.** to urge, scold, etc. constantly **2.** to cause continual discomfort, pain, etc. —***n.*** a person, esp. a woman, who nags: also **nag′ger** —**nag′ging·ly** ***adv.*** —**nag′gy** ***adj.*** **-gi·er, -gi·est**
nag[2] (nag) ***n.*** [ME. *nagge* < ?] **1.** a horse that is worn-out, old, etc. **2.** [Slang] a racehorse, esp. an inferior one
Na·ga·sa·ki (nä′gə sä′kē) seaport on the W coast of Kyushu, Japan: partly destroyed (Aug. 9, 1945) by a U.S. atomic bomb: pop. 405,000
Na·go·ya (nä′gô yä′) seaport in S Honshu, Japan: pop. 1,935,000
Nag·pur (näg′poor) city in C India: pop. 690,000
Na·hua·tl (nä′wät ′l) ***n.*** [Nahuatl] **1.** *pl.* **Na′hua·tls, Na′hua·tl** a member of any of a number of Indian tribes of Mexico **2.** their Uto-Aztecan language **3.** a branch of the Uto-Aztecan language family, spoken in Mexico and C America
Na·hum (nā′əm, -həm) *Bible* **1.** a Hebrew prophet of the 7th cent. B.C. **2.** the book containing his prophecies: abbrev. **Nah.**
nai·ad (nā′ad, nī′-; -əd) ***n.***, *pl.* **-ads, -a·des′** (-ə dēz′) [< Fr. < L. < Gr. *Naïas* < *naein*, to flow] **1.** [*also* N-] *Gr. & Rom. Myth.* any of the nymphs living in and giving life to springs, fountains, rivers, etc. **2.** a girl or woman swimmer **3.** *Zool.* the aquatic nymph of certain insects
na·if, na·ïf (nä ēf′) ***adj.*** [Fr.] *same as* NAIVE
nail (nāl) ***n.*** [OE. *nægl*] **1.** *a)* the thin, horny substance growing out at the ends of the fingers and toes *b)* a claw **2.** a tapered piece of metal, commonly pointed and with a head, driven with a hammer to hold pieces of wood together, serve as a peg, etc. —***vt.*** **1.** to attach, fasten together, or fasten shut with nails **2.** to fix (the eyes, attention, etc.) steadily on an object **3.** to discover or expose (a lie, etc.) **4.** [Colloq.] to catch, capture, etc. **5.** [Colloq.] to hit squarely —**hit the nail on the head** to do or say whatever is exactly right —**nail down** to settle definitely; make sure —**nail′er** ***n.***

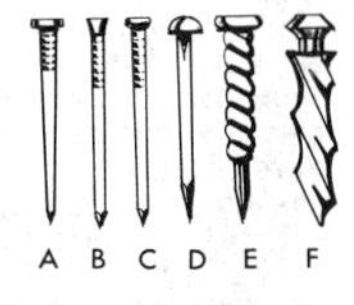

NAILS (A, common wire; B, flooring; C, finishing; D, boat; E, screw; F, masonry)

nail file a small, flat file for trimming the fingernails
nail polish a kind of lacquer, usually colored, applied to the fingernails or toenails as a cosmetic
nail set a tool for sinking a nail so that it is below the surface of the wood
nain·sook (nān′sook) ***n.*** [< Hindi < *nain*, the eye + *sukh*, pleasure] a thin, lightweight cotton fabric
nai·ra (nī′rə) ***n.***, *pl.* **nai′ra** [dim. of NIGERIA] the monetary unit of Nigeria: see MONETARY UNITS, table
Nai·ro·bi (nī rō′bē) capital of Kenya: pop. 479,000
na·ive, na·ïve (nä ēv′) ***adj.*** [Fr., fem. of *naïf* < L. *nativus*, natural] **1.** unaffectedly or foolishly simple; artless; unsophisticated **2.** not suspicious; credulous —**na·ive′ly, na·ïve′ly** ***adv.***
na·ive·té, na·ïve·té (nä ēv tā′, -ēv′tā) ***n.*** [Fr.] **1.** a being naive **2.** a naive action or remark Also **na·ive′ness, na·ïve′ness, na·ive′ty** (-tē), **na·ïve′ty**
na·ked (nā′kid) ***adj.*** [OE. *nacod*] **1.** *a)* completely unclothed; nude *b)* uncovered; exposed: said of parts of the body **2.** destitute **3.** without protection or defense **4.** without its usual covering; specif., *a)* out of its sheath [*a naked* sword] *b)* without decoration, etc. [*a naked* wall] **5.** without additions, etc.; plain [*the naked* truth] **6.** not aided by a microscope, telescope, etc. [*the naked* eye] —**na′ked·ly** ***adv.*** —**na′ked·ness** ***n.***
NAM, N.A.M. National Association of Manufacturers
nam·by-pam·by (nam′bē pam′bē) ***adj.*** [orig. satirical nickname of *Ambrose Philips*, 18th-c. Eng. poet] weakly sentimental; insipidly pretty or nice —***n.***, *pl.* **-bies** **1.** namby-pamby talk or writing **2.** a namby-pamby person
name (nām) ***n.*** [OE. *nama*] **1.** a word or phrase by which a person, thing, or class of things is known; title **2.** a word or phrase expressing some quality considered descriptive; epithet **3.** *a)* reputation *b)* good reputation **4.** a family or clan **5.** appearance only, not reality [*chief in name* only] **6.** a famous person —***adj.*** **1.** well-known [*a name* brand] **2.** carrying a name [*a name* tag] —***vt.*** **named, nam′ing** **1.** to give a name or title to **2.** to designate or refer to by name **3.** to identify by the right name [*name* the oceans] **4.** to nominate or appoint to a post or office **5.** to set or specify (a day, price, etc.) **6.** to speak about; mention —**call names** to swear at —**in the name of** **1.** in appeal to **2.** by the authority of **3.** as belonging to —**to one's name** belonging to one —**name′a·ble, nam′a·ble** ***adj.*** —**nam′er** ***n.***
name-call·ing (-kôl′iŋ) ***n.*** the use of abusive names in attacking another —**name′-call′er** ***n.***
name-drop·per (-dräp′ər) ***n.*** a person who tries to impress others by often mentioning famous persons in a familiar way —**name′-drop′ping** ***n.***
name·less (-lis) ***adj.*** **1.** without a name **2.** left unnamed **3.** not well known **4.** illegitimate **5.** indescribable **6.** too horrid to specify [*nameless* crimes] —**name′less·ly** ***adv.*** —**name′less·ness** ***n.***
name·ly (-lē) ***adv.*** that is to say; to wit
name·plate (-plāt′) ***n.*** a piece of metal, etc. on which a name is inscribed
name·sake (-sāk′) ***n.*** a person with the same name as another, esp. if named after the other
Na·mib·i·a (nä mib′ē ə) *official (UN) name for* SOUTH WEST AFRICA
Nan·cy (nan′sē) [prob. by faulty division of MINE[1] + *Ancy*, dim. of ME. *Annis*, Agnes] a feminine name
nan·keen, nan·kin (nan kēn′) ***n.*** [< ff.] **1.** a buff-colored, durable cotton cloth, orig. from China **2.** [*pl.*] trousers made of this
Nan·king (nan′kiŋ′, nän′-) city in E China, on the Yangtze River: pop. 2,700,000
Nan·nette, Na·nette (na net′) [dim. of ANNA] a feminine name
nan·ny (nan′ē) ***n.***, *pl.* **-nies** [< *Nan*, dim. of ANN(A)] [Brit.] a child's nurse
nanny goat [see prec.] [Colloq.] a female goat
na·no- [< Gr. *nanos*, dwarf] *a combining form meaning* one billionth part of
na·no·sec·ond (nan′ō sek′ənd) ***n.*** one billionth of a second
Nan·sen (nän′sən), **Fridt·jof** (frit′yäf) 1861–1930; Norw. arctic explorer, naturalist, & statesman
Nantes (nänt; *E.* nants) **1.** city in W France, on the Loire: pop. 259,000 **2. Edict of,** a decree issued (1598) in France, giving political equality to the Huguenots: it was revoked in 1685
Nan·tuck·et (nan tuk′it) [AmInd., lit., faraway land] island of Mass., south of Cape Cod
Na·o·mi (nā ō′mē, na-; nā′ə mī′) [Heb. *nā'omī*, lit., my delight] **1.** a feminine name **2.** *Bible* the mother-in-law of Ruth: Ruth 1
nap[1] (nap) ***vi.*** **napped, nap′ping** [OE. *hnappian*] **1.** to sleep lightly for a short time **2.** to be careless or unprepared —***n.*** a brief, light sleep
nap[2] (nap) ***n.*** [< or akin to MDu. & MLowG. *noppe*] **1.** the downy or hairy surface of cloth formed by short hairs or fibers, raised by brushing, etc. **2.** any similar surface, as of the flesh side of leather —***vt.*** **napped, nap′ping** to raise a nap on by brushing, etc. —**nap′less** ***adj.*** —**napped** ***adj.***
na·palm (nā′päm) ***n.*** [*na(phthene)* + *palm(itate)*, salt of palmitic acid] a jellylike substance with gasoline or oil in it, used in flame throwers and bombs —***vt.*** to attack or burn with napalm
nape (nāp, nap) ***n.*** [ME.] the back of the neck
na·per·y (nā′pər ē) ***n.*** [< MFr. < OFr. *nappe*: see NAPKIN] household linen; esp., table linen
naph·tha (naf′thə, nap′-) ***n.*** [L. < Gr. < Per. *neft*, pitch] **1.** a flammable, volatile liquid made by distilling petroleum, coal tar, wood, etc. and used as a fuel, solvent, etc. **2.** *same as* PETROLEUM
naph·tha·lene (-lēn′) ***n.*** [prec. + *-l-* + -ENE] a white, crystalline, aromatic hydrocarbon, $C_{10}H_8$, made by distilling coal tar and used in moth repellents and in certain dyes, etc.: also **naph′tha·lin′** —**naph′tha·len′ic** (-lē′nik, -len′ik) ***adj.***
naph·thol (naf′thōl, -thôl; nap′-) ***n.*** [NAPHTH(ALENE) + -OL[1]] either of two white, crystalline compounds, $C_{10}H_7OH$, derived from naphthalene and used as antiseptics and in dyes, etc.
nap·kin (nap′kin) ***n.*** [< OFr. *nappe* < L. *mappa*, cloth] **1.** a small cloth or paper used while eating for protecting the clothes and wiping the fingers or lips **2.** any small cloth, towel, etc.
Na·ples (nā′p'lz) **1.** seaport in S Italy, on the Bay of Naples: pop. 1,263,000 **2. Bay of,** inlet of the Tyrrhenian Sea, on the S coast of Italy

na·po·le·on (nə pō′lē ən, -pōl′yən) *n.* [after ff.] **1.** a former gold coin of France, equivalent to 20 francs **2.** a card game similar to euchre **3.** a layered puff pastry with a custardlike filling

Na·po·le·on I (nə pō′lē ən, -pōl′yən) (full Fr. name *Napoléon Bonaparte*) 1769–1821; Fr. military leader & emperor of France (1804–15) —**Na·po′le·on′ic** (-pō′lē än′ik) *adj.*

Napoleon III *see* LOUIS NAPOLEON

Na·po·li (nä′pô lē′) *It. name of* NAPLES

nap·py¹ (nap′ē) *n., pl.* **-pies** [< obs. *nap,* a bowl < OE. *hnæp*] a shallow bowl for serving food

nap·py² (nap′ē) *adj.* **-pi·er, -pi·est** covered with nap; downy, shaggy, etc. —**nap′pi·ness** *n.*

Nar·ba·da (nur′bud′ə) river in C India, flowing west into the Arabian Sea: c.800 mi.

nar·cis·sism (när′sə siz′m; *chiefly Brit.* när sis′iz′m) *n.* [< G.: see NARCISSUS & -ISM] **1.** self-love **2.** *Psychoanalysis* the first stage of libidinal development, in which the self is an erotic object Also **nar′cism** —**nar′cis·sist** *n., adj.* —**nar′cis·sis′tic** *adj.*

Nar·cis·sus (när sis′əs) *Gr. Myth.* a beautiful youth who pined away for love of his own reflection in a spring and was changed into the narcissus —*n.* [n-] *pl.* **-cis′sus, -cis′sus·es, -cis′si** (-ī) [ModL. < L. < Gr. *narkissos,* ? akin to *narkē* (see NARCOTIC): in reference to the narcotic properties] any of a genus of bulb plants with smooth leaves and white, yellow, or orange flowers, including the daffodils and jonquils

nar·co- [< Gr. *narkē,* stupor] *a combining form meaning* narcosis, sleep, stupor: also, before a vowel, **narc-**

nar·co·sis (när kō′sis) *n.* a condition of deep stupor which passes into unconsciousness, caused by a narcotic or certain chemicals

nar·co·syn·the·sis (när′kō sin′thə sis) *n.* [NARCO- + SYNTHESIS] a method of treating an acute traumatic neurosis by working with a patient while he is under the influence of a hypnotic drug

nar·cot·ic (när kät′ik) *n.* [< OFr. < ML. < Gr. *narkoun,* to benumb < *narkē,* numbness] **1.** a drug, as opium, used to relieve pain and induce sleep: narcotics are often addictive and in excessive doses can cause stupor, coma, or death **2.** anything with a soothing, lulling, or dulling effect —*adj.* **1.** of, like, or producing narcosis **2.** of, by, or for narcotic addicts

nar·co·tism (när′kə tiz′m) *n.* **1.** *same as* NARCOSIS **2.** addiction to narcotics

nar·co·tize (när′kə tīz′) *vt.* **-tized′, -tiz′ing** **1.** to subject to a narcotic; stupefy **2.** to lull or dull the senses of —**nar′co·ti·za′tion** *n.*

nard (närd) *n.* [< OFr. < L. < Gr. *nardos,* ult. < Sans.] *same as* SPIKENARD (sense 2)

nar·es (ner′ēz) *n.pl., sing.* **nar′is** (-is) [L.] the nasal passages; esp., the nostrils —**nar′i·al** (-ē əl), **nar′ine** (-in, -īn) *adj.*

nar·ghi·le (när′gə lē′, -lā′) *n.* [< Turk. & Per. < Per. *nargīl,* coconut tree: orig. made of coconut shell] *same as* HOOKAH: also sp. **nar′gi·le′, nar′gi·leh′**

Nar·ra·gan·sett Bay (nar′ə gan′sit) [after an extinct tribe of Algonquian Indians who lived around the bay] inlet of the Atlantic, extending into R.I.

nar·rate (nar′āt, na rāt′) *vt., vi.* **-rat·ed, -rat·ing** [< L. pp. of *narrare,* to relate] **1.** to tell (a story) **2.** to give an account of (events)

nar·ra·tion (na rā′shən) *n.* **1.** a narrating **2.** *same as* NARRATIVE **3.** writing or speaking that narrates, as fiction —**nar·ra′tion·al** *adj.*

nar·ra·tive (nar′ə tiv) *adj.* **1.** in story form **2.** concerned with narration —*n.* **1.** a story; account; tale **2.** the art or practice of relating stories or accounts —**nar′ra·tive·ly** *adv.*

nar·ra·tor (nar′āt ər, na rāt′ər) *n.* **1.** a person who relates a story, etc. **2.** a person who reads narrative passages, as between scenes of a play

nar·row (nar′ō, ner′ō) *adj.* [OE. *nearu*] **1.** small in width; not wide **2.** limited in meaning, size, amount, or extent *[a narrow* majority*]* **3.** limited in outlook; not liberal; prejudiced **4.** close; careful *[a narrow* inspection*]* **5.** with barely enough space, time, etc. *[a narrow* escape*]* **6.** limited in means *[narrow* circumstances*]* **7.** *Phonetics* tense: said of the tongue —*vi., vt.* to decrease or limit in width, extent, or scope —*n.* **1.** a narrow part or place, esp. in a valley, road, etc. **2.** [*usually pl.*] a narrow passage; strait —**nar′row·ly** *adv.* —**nar′row·ness** *n.*

narrow gauge **1.** a width (between railroad rails) less than standard (56½ in.) **2.** a narrow-gauge railroad or car —**nar′row-gauge′, nar′row-gauged′** *adj.*

nar·row-mind·ed (-mīn′did) *adj.* limited in outlook; not liberal; prejudiced —**nar′row-mind′ed·ly** *adv.* —**nar′row-mind′ed·ness** *n.*

nar·thex (när′theks) *n.* [LGr., exterior portico] **1.** in early Christian churches, a porch or portico **2.** a church vestibule leading to the nave

nar·whal (när′wəl, -hwəl) *n.* [< Scand., as in Norw. & Dan. *narhval*] an arctic cetacean valued for its oil and ivory: the male has a long, spiral tusk extending from the upper jaw: also **nar′wal** (-wəl), **nar′whale′** (-hwāl′)

NARWHAL (body 11–16 ft. long; tusk to 9 ft. long)

nar·y (ner′ē) *adj.* [< *ne'er a,* never a] [Dial.] not any; no (with *a* or *an*) *[nary* a doubt*]*

NASA (nas′ə) National Aeronautics and Space Administration

na·sal (nā′z′l) *adj.* [< ModL. < L. *nasus,* a nose] **1.** of the nose **2.** produced by making breath go through the nose, as the sounds of *m, n, ng* (ŋ) **3.** characterized by such sounds *[a nasal* voice*]* —*n.* a nasal sound —**na·sal·i·ty** (nā zal′ə tē) *n.* —**na′sal·ly** *adv.*

na·sal·ize (nā′zə līz′) *vt., vi.* **-ized′, -iz′ing** to pronounce or speak with a nasal sound or sounds —**na′sal·i·za′tion** *n.*

Nas·by (naz′bē), **Pe·tro·le·um V.** (pə trō′lē əm) (pseud. of *David Ross Locke*) 1833–88; U.S. humorist

nas·cent (nas′′nt, nā′s′nt) *adj.* [< L. prp. of *nasci,* to be born] **1.** coming into being; being born **2.** beginning to form, grow, or develop: said of ideas, cultures, etc. —**nas′cence, nas′cen·cy** *n.*

Nash·u·a (nash′oo wə) [< Algonquian, lit., ? the land between] city in S N.H.: pop. 68,000

Nash·ville (nash′vil) [after Gen. F. *Nash* (1720–77)] capital of Tenn., on the Cumberland River: coextensive with Davidson county with which it constitutes a metropolitan government (**Nashville-Davidson**): pop. 456,000 (met. area 829,000)

na·so- [< L. *nasus,* nose] *a combining form meaning:* **1.** nose, nasal **2.** nasal and

Nas·sau (nas′ô) capital of the Bahamas: pop., with the island on which it is located, 81,000

Nas·ser (nas′ər), **Ga·mal Ab·del** (gä mäl′ äb′dəl) 1918–70; Egypt. president of the United Arab Republic (1958–70)

na·stur·tium (nə stur′shəm, na-) *n.* [L. < *nasus,* nose + pp. of *torquere,* to twist: from its pungent odor] **1.** a plant with shield-shaped leaves and red, yellow, or orange flowers **2.** the flower

nas·ty (nas′tē) *adj.* **-ti·er, -ti·est** [< ? or akin to Du. *nestig,* dirty] **1.** very dirty; filthy **2.** nauseating **3.** morally offensive; indecent **4.** very unpleasant, mean, or harmful —**nas′ti·ly** *adv.* —**nas′ti·ness** *n.*

nat. **1.** national **2.** native **3.** natural

Na·tal (nə tal′, -täl′) province of E South Africa, on the Indian Ocean

na·tal (nāt′′l) *adj.* [< L. *natalis* < pp. of *nasci,* to be born] **1.** of or connected with one's birth **2.** dating from birth **3.** native: said of a place

Nat·a·lie (nat′′l ē) [Fr. < LL. < L. *natalis* (*dies*), natal (day), name given to children born on Christmas Day] a feminine name

na·tant (nāt′′nt) *adj.* [< L. prp. of *natare,* to swim] swimming or floating

na·ta·to·ri·al (nāt′ə tôr′ē əl) *adj.* [< LL. < L. *natator,* swimmer (see prec.) + -AL] of, characterized by, or adapted for swimming: also **na′ta·to′ry**

na·ta·to·ri·um (-əm) *n., pl.* **-ri·ums, -ri·a** (-ə) [LL.] a swimming pool

natch (nach) *adv.* [Slang] naturally; of course

na·tes (nā′tēz) *n.pl.* [L.] the buttocks

Na·than (nā′thən) [Heb. *nāthān,* lit., gift] a masculine name: dim. *Nat, Nate*

Na·than·a·el (nə than′yəl, -ē əl) [LL. < Gr. < Heb. *nĕthan'ēl,* lit., gift of God] a masculine name: dim. *Nat:* also sp. **Nathaniel**

nathe·less (nāth′lis, nath′-) *adv.* [< OE. < *na,* never + *the,* the + *læs,* less] [Archaic] nevertheless —*prep.* [Archaic] notwithstanding Also **nath′less** (nath′-)

na·tion (nā′shən) *n.* [< OFr. < L. *natio* < pp. of *nasci,* to be born] **1.** a community of people with a territory, history, economic life, culture, and language in common **2.** the people of a territory united under a single government; country **3.** a people or tribe —**na′tion·hood′** (-hood′) *n.*

na·tion·al (nash′ə n′l) *adj.* **1.** of a nation or the nation **2.** affecting a (or the) nation as a whole **3.** maintained by the Federal government —*n.* a citizen of a nation —**na′tion·al·ly** *adv.*

national bank **1.** a bank or system of banks owned and operated by a government **2.** in the U.S., a member bank of the Federal Reserve System

National Guard in the U.S., the organized militia forces of individual States, part of the U.S. Army when called into active Federal service

na·tion·al·ism (-iz′m) *n.* **1.** *a)* patriotism *b)* narrow, jingoist patriotism **2.** the putting of national interests and security above international considerations **3.** the desire for or advocacy of national independence —**na′tion·al·ist** (-ist) ***n., adj.*** —**na′tion·al·is′tic** ***adj.*** —**na′tion·al·is′ti·cal·ly** ***adv.***

na·tion·al·i·ty (nash′ə nal′ə tē) ***n.,*** *pl.* **-ties** **1.** national quality or character **2.** the status of belonging to a particular nation by birth or naturalization **3.** the condition or fact of being a nation **4.** a national group, esp. of immigrants from some other country: in full, **nationality group**

na·tion·al·ize (nash′ə nə līz′) ***vt.*** **-ized′, -iz′ing** **1.** to make national **2.** to transfer ownership or control of (land, industries, etc.) to the nation —**na′tion·al·i·za′tion** ***n.*** —**na′tion·al·iz′er** ***n.***

National Weather Service the division of the Department of Commerce that gathers data on weather conditions, on which weather forecasts are based

na·tion·wide (nā′shən wīd′) ***adj.*** by or throughout the whole nation; national

na·tive (nāt′iv) ***adj.*** **[**< MFr. < L. *nativus* < pp. of *nasci*, to be born**]** **1.** inborn; innate; natural **2.** belonging to a locality or country by birth, production, or growth; indigenous *[*a *native* Bostonian, *native* plants*]* **3.** *a)* being the place of one's birth *[*one's *native* land*]* *b)* belonging to one because of the place of one's birth *[*one's *native* language*]* **4.** as found in nature; unaltered by man **5.** occurring in a pure state in nature *[native* gold*]* **6.** of or characteristic of the people born in a certain place —***n.*** **1.** a person born in the region indicated, esp. one whose ancestors were also born there or as distinguished from an invader, colonist, etc. **2.** a plant or animal indigenous to a place and growing or living there naturally **3.** a permanent resident, not a mere visitor —**go native** to adopt a simple way of life —**na′tive·ly** ***adv.*** —**na′tive·ness** ***n.***

na·tive-born (-bôrn′) ***adj.*** born in a specified place or country

na·tiv·i·ty (nə tiv′ə tē, nā-) ***n.,*** *pl.* **-ties** **[**see NATIVE**]** **1.** birth **2.** *Astrol.* the horoscope for one's birth —**the Nativity** **1.** the birth of Jesus **2.** Christmas Day

natl. national

NATO (nā′tō) North Atlantic Treaty Organization

nat·ty (nat′ē) ***adj.*** **-ti·er, -ti·est** **[**< ? NEAT[1]**]** trim and smart in appearance or dress *[*a *natty* suit*]* —**nat′ti·ly** ***adv.*** —**nat′ti·ness** ***n.***

nat·u·ral (nach′ər əl, nach′rəl) ***adj.*** **[**< OFr. < L. *naturalis*, by birth**]** **1.** of or arising from nature **2.** produced or existing in nature; not artificial **3.** dealing with nature *[*a *natural* science*]* **4.** as found in nature; unaltered by man **5.** real or physical, rather than spiritual, intellectual, or imaginary **6.** *a)* innate; inborn *[natural* abilities*]* *b)* having certain qualities innately *[*a *natural* comedian*]* **7.** based on instinctive moral feeling *[natural* rights*]* **8.** true to nature; lifelike *[*a *natural* likeness*]* **9.** normal or usual *[*a *natural* outcome*]* **10.** customarily expected *[*a *natural* courtesy*]* **11.** free from affectation **12.** *a)* illegitimate *[*a *natural* child*]* *b)* not adoptive *[natural* parents*]* **13.** *Music* *a)* without flats or sharps *b)* neither sharped nor flatted —***n.*** **1.** an idiot **2.** [Colloq.] a person who is naturally expert **3.** [Colloq.] a sure success **4.** *Music* *a)* the sign (♮) canceling a preceding sharp or flat: in full, **natural sign** *b)* the note affected *c)* a white key on the piano —**nat′u·ral·ness** ***n.***

natural gas a mixture of gaseous hydrocarbons, chiefly methane, occurring naturally in the earth and conveyed through pipes to be used as a fuel

natural history the study of the animal, vegetable, and mineral world, esp. in a popular way

nat·u·ral·ism (-iz'm) ***n.*** **1.** action or thought based on natural desires or instincts **2.** *Literature, Art,* etc. faithful adherence to nature; realism: specif. applied to the realism of a group of 19th-cent. French writers **3.** *Philos.* the belief that the natural world is all that exists

nat·u·ral·ist (-ist) ***n.*** **1.** a person who studies animals and plants **2.** a person who believes in or practices naturalism —***adj.*** *same as* NATURALISTIC

nat·u·ral·is·tic (nach′ər ə lis′tik) ***adj.*** **1.** of natural history or naturalists **2.** of or characterized by naturalism **3.** in accordance with, or in imitation of, nature —**nat′u·ral·is′ti·cal·ly** ***adv.***

nat·u·ral·ize (nach′ər ə līz′, nach′rə-) ***vt.*** **-ized′, -iz′ing** **1.** to confer citizenship upon (an alien) **2.** to adopt and make common (a custom, word, etc.) from another place **3.** to adapt (a plant or animal) to a new environment —***vi.*** to become naturalized —**nat′u·ral·i·za′tion** ***n.***

nat·u·ral·ly (nach′ər əl ē, nach′rə lē) ***adv.*** **1.** in a natural manner **2.** by nature; innately **3.** as one might expect; of course

natural number any positive integer, as 1, 2, etc.

natural philosophy *earlier name for* NATURAL SCIENCE (specif., physics)

natural resources the forms of wealth supplied by nature, as coal, oil, water power, etc.

natural science the systematized knowledge of nature, including biology, chemistry, physics, etc.

natural selection the process in evolution by which those individuals (of a species) with characters that help them to become adapted to their specific environment tend to transmit their characters, while those less able to become adapted tend to die out

na·ture (nā′chər) ***n.*** **[**< OFr. < L. *natura* < pp. of *nasci*, to be born**]** **1.** the quality or qualities that make something what it is; essence **2.** inborn character, disposition, or tendencies **3.** kind; sort **4.** the basic biological functions, instincts, drives, etc. **5.** normal or acceptable behavior **6.** the sum total of all things in the physical universe **7.** [*sometimes* N-] the power, force, etc. that seems to regulate this **8.** the primitive state of man **9.** a simple way of life close to or in the outdoors **10.** natural scenery, and the plants and animals in it —**by nature** naturally; inherently —**of (or in) the nature of** having the essential character of; like

-na·tured (nā′chərd) *a combining form meaning* having or showing a (specified kind of) nature, disposition, or temperament *[*good-*natured]*

Naug·a·hyde (nôg′ə hīd′) [arbitrary coinage] *a trademark for* a kind of imitation leather, used for upholstery —***n.*** [n-] this material

naught (nôt) ***n.*** **[**< OE. < *na*, no + *wiht*, a person**]** **1.** nothing **2.** *Arith.* the figure zero (0) —***adj.*** [Archaic or Obs.] **1.** worthless **2.** evil —**set at naught** to defy; scorn

naugh·ty (nôt′ē) ***adj.*** **-ti·er, -ti·est** **[**< obs. *naught*, wicked**]** **1.** not behaving properly; disobedient: used esp. of children **2.** improper or obscene —**naugh′ti·ly** ***adv.*** —**naugh′ti·ness** ***n.***

Na·u·ru (nä o͞o′ro͞o) country on an island in the W Pacific, near the equator: 8 sq. mi.; pop. 7,000

nau·se·a (nô′shə, -sē ə, -zē ə, -zhə) ***n.*** **[**L. < Gr. *nausia*, seasickness < *naus*, a ship**]** **1.** a feeling of sickness at the stomach, with an urge to vomit **2.** disgust —**nau′se·ant** ***adj., n.***

nau·se·ate (-shē āt′, -sē-, -zē-, -zhē-) ***vt., vi.*** **-at′ed, -at′ing** to feel or cause to feel nausea —**nau′se·at′ing·ly** ***adv.*** —**nau′se·a′tion** ***n.***

nau·seous (nô′shəs, -zē əs, -sē-) ***adj.*** **1.** causing nausea; sickening **2.** [Colloq.] feeling nausea —**nau′seous·ly** ***adv.*** —**nau′seous·ness** ***n.***

naut. nautical

nautch (nôch) ***n.*** **[**< Hindi < Prakrit < Sans. *nṛtya*, dancing < *nṛt*, to dance**]** in India, a performance by professional dancing girls (**nautch girls**)

nau·ti·cal (nôt′i k'l) ***adj.*** **[**< Fr. < L. < Gr. < *nautēs*, sailor < *naus*, a ship**]** of or relating to sailors, ships, or navigation —**nau′ti·cal·ly** ***adv.***

nautical mile an international unit of distance for sea and air navigation, equal to 6,076.11549 ft. (1,852 meters)

nau·ti·lus (nôt′'l əs) ***n.,*** *pl.* **-lus·es, -li′** (-ī′) **[**ModL. < L. < Gr. *nautilos*, sailor < *naus*, a ship**]** **1.** any of a genus of tropical, cephalopod mollusks with a many-chambered, spiral shell having a pearly interior **2.** *same as* PAPER NAUTILUS

NAUTILUS
(shown in
cross section)

nav. **1.** naval **2.** navigation **3.** navigator

Nav·a·ho (nav′ə hō′) ***n.*** **[**< Sp. < AmInd. *Navahú*, lit., great fields**]** **1.** *pl.* **-hos′, -ho′, -hoes′** a member of an Indian tribe, the largest in the U.S., of Arizona, New Mexico, and Utah **2.** their Athapascan language Also sp. **Nav′a·jo′**

na·val (nā′v'l) ***adj.*** **[**< Fr. < L. *navalis* < *navis*, a ship**]** of, having, characteristic of, or for a navy, its ships, personnel, etc.

Na·varre (nə vär′) region in NE Spain & SW France: formerly a kingdom

nave[1] (nāv) ***n.*** **[**ML. *navis* < L., a ship**]** the main part of a church, extending between side aisles from the chancel to the principal entrance

nave[2] (nāv) ***n.*** **[**OE. *nafu***]** the hub of a wheel

na·vel (nā′v'l) ***n.*** **[**OE. *nafela***]** the small scar or depression in the middle of the abdomen, where the umbilical cord was attached to the fetus

navel orange a seedless orange having a navellike depression containing a small, secondary fruit

navig. **1.** navigation **2.** navigator

nav·i·ga·ble (nav′i gə b'l) ***adj.*** **[**see ff.**]** **1.** wide or deep enough, or free enough from obstructions, for ships, etc. to go through 2. that can be steered or directed *[a navigable balloon]* —**nav'i·ga·bil'i·ty** *n.* —**nav'i·ga·bly** *adv.*

nav·i·gate (nav'ə gāt') *vi.* **-gat'ed, -gat'ing** [< L. pp. of *navigare* < *navis,* a ship + *agere,* to lead] **1.** to steer, or direct, a ship or aircraft **2.** [Colloq.] to make one's way; walk —*vt.* **1.** to travel through or over (water, air, or land) in a ship or aircraft **2.** to steer, or direct the course of (a ship or aircraft) **3.** [Colloq.] to make one's way on or through

nav·i·ga·tion (nav'ə gā'shən) *n.* **1.** the act or practice of navigating; esp., the science of locating the position and plotting the course of ships and aircraft **2.** traffic by ship —**nav'i·ga'tion·al** *adj.* —**nav'i·ga'tion·al·ly** *adv.*

nav·i·ga·tor (nav'ə gāt'ər) *n.* **1.** a person who navigates; esp., one skilled in the navigation of a ship or aircraft **2.** an explorer by ship

nav·vy (nav'ē) *n., pl.* **-vies** [abbrev. of prec.] [Brit.] an unskilled laborer, as on canals, roads, etc.

na·vy (nā'vē) *n., pl.* **-vies** [< OFr. *navie,* ult. < L. *navis,* a ship] **1.** [Archaic] a fleet of ships **2.** all warships of a nation **3.** [*often* **N-**] *a)* the entire sea force of a nation, including vessels, personnel, stores, yards, etc. *b)* the governmental department in charge of this **4.** *same as* NAVY BLUE

navy bean [from common use in the U.S. Navy] a small, white variety of kidney bean

navy blue [from the color of the Brit. naval uniform] very dark, purplish blue

navy yard a dockyard for building and repairing naval ships, storing naval supplies, etc.

na·wab (nə wäb', -wôb') *n.* [Hindi *navāb*] *same as* NABOB

nay (nā) *adv.* [< ON. < *ne,* not + *ei,* ever] **1.** no: now seldom used except in a voice vote **2.** not that only, but also *[he is well-off, nay, rich]* —*n.* **1.** a refusal or denial **2.** a negative vote or a person voting in the negative **3.** a negative answer

Naz·a·rene (naz'ə rēn', naz'ə rēn') *adj.* of Nazareth or the Nazarenes —*n.* **1.** a native or inhabitant of Nazareth **2.** a member of an early sect of Jewish Christians —**the Nazarene** Jesus

Naz·a·reth (naz'ər əth) town in Galilee, N Israel, where Jesus lived as a child

Naz·a·rite, Naz·i·rite (naz'ə rīt') *n.* [< LL. < Gr. < Heb. *nāzar,* to consecrate] among the ancient Hebrews, a person adhering to certain strict religious vows

Na·zi (nät'sē, nat'-) *adj.* [G., contr. of *Nationalsozialistische* in party name] designating or of the German fascist political party (*National Socialist German Workers' Party*), that ruled Germany under Hitler (1933–45) —*n.* **1.** a member of this party **2.** [*often* **n-**] a supporter of this party or its ideology; fascist —**Na'zi·fi·ca'tion** *n.* —**Na'zi·fy', na'zi·fy'** *vt.* **-fied', -fy'ing** —**Na'zism** (-siz'm), **Na'zi·ism** (-sē iz'm) *n.*

Nb *Chem.* niobium

N.B. New Brunswick

N.B., n.b. [L. *nota bene*] note well

NBA, N.B.A. **1.** National Basketball Association **2.** National Boxing Association

NBC National Broadcasting Company

NBS, N.B.S. National Bureau of Standards

N.C., NC **1.** no charge **2.** North Carolina **3.** nurse corps

NCAA, N.C.A.A. National Collegiate Athletic Association

NCO, N.C.O. noncommissioned officer

Nd *Chem.* neodymium

N.D., n.d. no date

N.Dak., ND North Dakota

ne- *same as* NEO-: used before a vowel

Ne *Chem.* neon

NE Nebraska

NE, N.E., n.e. **1.** northeast **2.** northeastern

N.E. **1.** Naval Engineer **2.** New England

NEA, N.E.A. National Education Association

Neal (nēl) [prob. < Ir. *Niul* < *niadh,* a champion] a masculine name

Ne·an·der·thal (nē an'dər thôl', -täl') *adj.* [name of German valley where remains were found] **1.** designating or of a form of primitive man of the paleolithic period **2.** *a)* crude or primitive *b)* reactionary; regressive

neap (nēp) *adj.* [OE. *nep-* in *nepflod,* neap tide] designating either of the two lowest monthly tides, occurring just after the first and third quarters of the lunar month —*n.* neap tide

Ne·a·pol·i·tan (nē'ə päl'ə t'n) *adj.* of Naples —*n.* a native or inhabitant of Naples

near (nir) *adv.* [OE. *near,* nearer, compar. of *neah,* nigh] **1.** at a short distance in space or time **2.** relatively close in degree; almost *[near right]* : now usually *nearly* **3.** closely; intimately —*adj.* **1.** close in distance or time; not far **2.** close in relationship; akin **3.** close in friendship; intimate **4.** *a)* close in degree; narrow *[a near escape]* *b)* almost happening *[a near accident]* **5.** on the left side, facing forward: said of an animal in double harness, a wagon wheel, etc.: opposed to OFF **6.** short or direct *[the near way]* **7.** stingy **8.** somewhat resembling; approximating —*prep.* close to in space, time, degree, etc. —*vt., vi.* to draw near (to); approach —**near at hand** very close in time or space —**near'ness** *n.*

near·by (nir'bī') *adj., adv.* near; close at hand

Near East **1.** countries near the E end of the Mediterranean, including those of SW Asia, NE Africa, &, sometimes, the Balkans **2.** [Brit.] the Balkans

near·ly (-lē) *adv.* almost; not quite *[nearly finished]* —**not nearly** not at all; far from

near·sight·ed (-sīt'id) *adj.* having better vision for near things than for far ones; myopic —**near'sight'ed·ly** *adv.* —**near'sight'ed·ness** *n.*

neat[1] (nēt) *adj.* [< Fr. < L. *nitidus,* shining, trim < *nitere,* to shine] **1.** *a)* clean and orderly; trim; tidy *b)* tidy, skillful, and precise *[a neat worker]* *c)* free of superfluities; simple **2.** unmixed; straight *[to drink whiskey neat]* **3.** well-proportioned; shapely **4.** cleverly or smartly phrased or done; adroit **5.** [Slang] nice, pleasing, etc. —**neat'ly** *adv.* —**neat'ness** *n.*

neat[2] (nēt) *n., pl.* **neat** [OE. *neat*] [Now Rare] a bovine animal; ox, cow, etc.

neat·en (nēt''n) *vt.* to make neat

'neath, neath (nēth) *prep.* [Poet.] beneath

neat·herd (nēt'hurd') *n.* [Now Rare] a cowherd

neat's-foot oil (nēts'foot') a light-yellow oil obtained by boiling the feet and shinbones of cattle, used mainly as a dressing for leather

neb (neb) *n.* [OE. *nebb*] [Now Chiefly Brit. Dial.] **1.** a beak, nose, or snout **2.** a nib

Ne·bras·ka (nə bras'kə) [< Siouan name of Platte River, lit., flat water] Middle Western State of the U.S.: 77,227 sq. mi.; pop. 1,570,000; cap. Lincoln: abbrev. **Nebr., NE** —**Ne·bras'kan** *adj., n.*

Neb·u·chad·nez·zar (neb'yə kəd nez'ər, neb'ə-) ?–562 B.C.; king of Babylonia (605?–562), who conquered Jerusalem & deported many Jews into Babylonia: II Kings 24; Dan. 1–4 Also **Neb'u·chad·rez'zar** (-rez'ər)

neb·u·la (neb'yə lə) *n., pl.* **-lae'** (-lē'), **-las** [ModL. < L., fog] any of several vast cloudlike patches seen in the night sky, consisting of very distant groups of stars or of gaseous masses or of galaxies —**neb'u·lar** *adj.*

nebular hypothesis the theory that the solar system was formed by the condensation of a nebula

neb·u·los·i·ty (neb'yə läs'ə tē) *n.* **1.** a nebulous quality or condition **2.** *pl.* **-ties** a nebula

neb·u·lous (neb'yə ləs) *adj.* **1.** of or like a nebula **2.** unclear; vague; indefinite Also **neb'u·lose'** (-lōs') —**neb'u·lous·ly** *adv.* —**neb'u·lous·ness** *n.*

nec·es·sar·i·ly (nes'ə ser'ə lē, nes'ə ser'-) *adv.* **1.** because of necessity **2.** as a necessary result

nec·es·sar·y (nes'ə ser'ē) *adj.* [< L. < *necesse,* unavoidable < *ne-,* not + *cedere,* to give way] **1.** that cannot be done without; essential; indispensable **2.** that must happen; inevitable **3.** that must be done; required **4.** that follows logically; undeniable —*n., pl.* **-sar'ies** a thing necessary to life, to some purpose, etc.: *often used in pl.*

ne·ces·si·tate (nə ses'ə tāt') *vt.* **-tat'ed, -tat'ing** **1.** to make (something) necessary or unavoidable **2.** [Now Rare] to compel —**ne·ces'si·ta'tion** *n.*

ne·ces·si·tous (-təs) *adj.* **1.** needy **2.** necessary **3.** urgent —**ne·ces'si·tous·ly** *adv.*

ne·ces·si·ty (-tē) *n., pl.* **-ties** [< OFr. < L. < *necesse:* see NECESSARY] **1.** natural causation; fate **2.** anything inevitable, unavoidable, etc. **3.** *a)* the compulsion of circumstances, custom, law, etc. *b)* what is required by this **4.** great need **5.** something that cannot be done without; necessary thing: *often used in pl.* **6.** the state or quality of being necessary —**of necessity** necessarily

neck (nek) *n.* [OE. *hnecca*] **1.** that part of man or animal joining the head to the body **2.** a narrow part between the head, or end, and the body, or base, of any object, as of a violin **3.** that part of a garment which covers or is nearest the neck **4.** a narrow, necklike part; specif., *a)* a narrow strip of land *b)* the narrowest part of a bottle, vase, etc. or of an organ of the body *c)* a strait —*vt., vi.* [Slang] to hug, kiss, and caress in making love —**get it in the neck** [Slang] to be severely reprimanded or punished —**neck and neck** very close or even, as in a race —**neck of the woods** a region or locality —**risk one's neck** to put one's life, career, etc. in danger —**stick one's neck out** to expose oneself to possible failure, ridicule, etc. —**neck'er** *n.* —**neck'ing** *n.*

neck·band (-band') *n.* **1.** a band worn around the neck **2.** the part of a garment that encircles the neck; esp., the part fastened to the collar

neck·er·chief (nek'ər chif, -chēf') *n.* a kerchief worn around the neck

neck·lace (nek'lis) *n.* [NECK + LACE] a string of beads, jewels, etc. or a fine chain of gold, silver, etc. worn as an ornament around the neck

neck·line (-līn') *n.* the line formed by the edge of a garment around or nearest the neck

neck·piece (-pēs′) ***n.*** **1.** a decorative scarf, esp. of fur **2.** a piece of armor for the neck
neck·tie (-tī′) ***n.*** a decorative band for the neck, tied in front in a slipknot or bow
neck·wear (-wer′) ***n.*** articles worn about the neck, as neckties, scarfs, etc.
nec·ro- [< Gr. *nekros*, dead body] *a combining form meaning* death, corpse: also **necr-**
ne·crol·o·gy (ne kräl′ə jē) ***n., pl.*** **-gies** [see prec. & -LOGY] **1.** a list of people who have died **2.** an obituary —**nec·ro·log·i·cal** (nek′rə läj′i k'l) ***adj.*** —**nec′ro·log′i·cal·ly** ***adv.*** —**ne·crol′o·gist** ***n.***
nec·ro·man·cy (nek′rə man′sē) ***n.*** [< OFr. < ML. *nigromantia* < L. < Gr. *nekros*, corpse + *manteia*, divination] **1.** divination by alleged communication with the dead **2.** sorcery —**nec′ro·man′cer** ***n.*** —**nec′ro·man′tic** ***adj.***
ne·crop·o·lis (nə kräp′ə lis) ***n., pl.*** **-lis·es** [< Gr. < *nekros*, dead body + *polis*, city] a cemetery, esp. one belonging to an ancient city
ne·cro·sis (ne krō′sis) ***n., pl.*** **-ses** (-sēz) [ModL. < LL. < Gr. < *nekroun*, to make dead < *nekros*, dead body] the death or decay of tissue in a part of a living body or plant, as from disease —**ne·crose** (ne krōs′, nek′rōs) ***vt., vi.*** **-crosed′, -cros′ing** —**ne·crot′ic** (-krät′ik) ***adj.***
nec·tar (nek′tər) ***n.*** [L. < Gr. *nektar*, lit., that overcomes death] **1.** *Gr. Myth.* the drink of the gods **2.** any very delicious beverage **3.** *Bot.* the sweetish liquid in many flowers, made into honey by bees —**nec′tar·ous** ***adj.***
nec·tar·ine (nek′tə rēn′, nek′tə rēn′) ***n.*** [orig. adj. of *nectar*] a variety of peach having a smooth skin without down
nec·ta·ry (nek′tər ē) ***n., pl.*** **-ries** a nectar-secreting flower part —**nec·tar′i·al** (-ter′ē əl) ***adj.***
Ne·der·land (nā′dər länt′) *Du. name of* NETHERLANDS
nee, née (nā; *now often* nē) ***adj.*** [Fr., fem. pp. of *naître* < L. *nasci*, to be born] born: used to indicate the maiden name of a married woman [Mrs. Helen Jones, *nee* Smith]
need (nēd) ***n.*** [OE. *nied*] **1.** necessity or obligation **2.** lack of something required or desired **3.** something required or desired [one's daily *needs*] **4.** *a*) a condition of deficiency, or one requiring relief or supply [a friend in *need*] *b*) poverty; extreme want —***vt.*** to have need of; lack; require *Need* is often used as an auxiliary followed by an infinitive with or without *to*, meaning "to be obliged, must" [he *need* not come, he *needs* to be careful] —***vi.*** **1.** [Archaic] to be necessary [it *needs* not] **2.** to be in need See also NEEDS —**have need to** to be compelled to; must —**if need be** if it is required —**need′er** ***n.***
need·ful (-fəl) ***adj.*** **1.** necessary **2.** [Archaic] needy —**need′ful·ly** ***adv.*** —**need′ful·ness** ***n.***
nee·dle (nēd′'l) ***n.*** [OE. *nædl*] **1.** a small, slender, sharp-pointed piece of steel with a hole for thread, used for sewing **2.** *a*) a slender, hooked rod of steel, bone, etc., for crocheting *b*) a similar but hookless rod, for knitting **3.** a short, pointed piece of metal, etc. that moves in phonograph-record grooves to transmit vibrations **4.** a pointed instrument for etching or engraving **5.** the pointer of a compass, gauge, meter, etc. **6.** the thin, short, pointed leaf of the pine, spruce, etc. **7.** a thin rod that opens or closes a passage in a valve (**needle valve**) **8.** the sharp, very slender metal tube at the end of a hypodermic syringe **9.** *same as* ELECTRIC NEEDLE **10.** a needlelike structure or part —***vt.*** **-dled, -dling** **1.** to sew, puncture, etc. with a needle **2.** [Colloq.] *a*) to goad *b*) to tease or heckle —**nee′dle·like′** ***adj.*** —**nee′dler** ***n.***

A
B
C
NEEDLES
(A, sewing machine; B, straight; C, surgical)

nee·dle·point (-point′) ***n.*** **1.** an embroidery of woolen threads on canvas, as in tapestry **2.** lace made on a paper pattern, with a needle instead of a bobbin: in full, **needlepoint lace**
need·less (nēd′lis) ***adj.*** not needed; unnecessary —**need′less·ly** ***adv.*** —**need′less·ness** ***n.***
nee·dle·wom·an (nēd′'l woom′ən) ***n., pl.*** **-wom′en** a woman who does needlework; esp., a seamstress
nee·dle·work (-wurk′) ***n.*** work done with a needle; sewing or fancywork —**nee′dle·work′er** ***n.***
need·n't (nēd′'nt) need not
needs (nēdz) ***adv.*** [OE. *nedes*] of necessity; necessarily (with *must*) [he must *needs* obey]
need·y (nēd′ē) ***adj.*** **need′i·er, need′i·est** in need; very poor; destitute —**need′i·ness** ***n.***
ne'er (ner) ***adv.*** [Poet.] never
ne'er-do-well (-doo wel′) ***n.*** a shiftless, irresponsible person —***adj.*** lazy, worthless, etc.
ne·far·i·ous (ni fer′ē əs) ***adj.*** [< L. < *nefas*, crime < *ne-*, not + *fas*, lawful] very wicked; iniquitous —**ne·far′i·ous·ly** ***adv.*** —**ne·far′i·ous·ness** ***n.***
neg. **1.** negative **2.** negatively
ne·gate (ni gāt′) ***vt.*** **-gat′ed, -gat′ing** [see ff.] **1.** to deny the existence or truth of **2.** to make ineffective —**ne·ga′tor, ne·gat′er** ***n.***
ne·ga·tion (ni gā′shən) ***n.*** [< Fr. < L. < pp. of *negare*, to deny] **1.** a denying; denial **2.** the lack or opposite of something positive
neg·a·tive (neg′ə tiv) ***adj.*** [see prec.] **1.** expressing denial or refusal; saying "no" **2.** opposite to or lacking what is positive [a *negative* personality]; specif., *a*) *Biol.* directed away from the source of a stimulus [*negative* tropism] *b*) *Math.* less than zero; minus *c*) *Med.* not indicating the presence of symptoms, bacteria, etc. *d*) *Photog.* reversing the relation of light and shade of the original subject **3.** *Elec.* *a*) of, generating, or charged with NEGATIVE ELECTRICITY *b*) having an excess of electrons —***n.*** **1.** a word, phrase, statement, etc. expressing denial, rejection, or refusal **2.** the point of view opposing the positive or affirmative **3.** an impression of a sculpture, etc. that shows it in reverse **4.** the plate in a voltaic battery where the lower potential is **5.** *Math.* a negative quantity **6.** *Photog.* an exposed and developed negative film or plate, from which positive prints are made —***vt.*** **-tived, -tiv·ing** **1.** *a*) to refuse; reject *b*) to veto **2.** to deny; contradict **3.** to disprove **4.** to neutralize —**in the negative** **1.** in refusal or denial of a plan, etc. **2.** with a negative answer —**neg′a·tive·ly** ***adv.*** —**neg′a·tive·ness, neg′a·tiv′i·ty** ***n.***
negative electricity the kind of electricity in a body of resin rubbed with wool: it has an excess of electrons
neg·a·tiv·ism (neg′ə tiv iz'm) ***n.*** *Psychol.* an attitude characterized by ignoring or resisting suggestions or orders from others —**neg′a·tiv·ist** ***n., adj.*** —**neg′a·tiv·is′tic** ***adj.***
Ne·gev (neg′ev) region in S Israel of partially reclaimed desert: also **Ne′geb** (-eb)
neg·lect (ni glekt′) ***vt.*** [< L. pp. of *neglegere* < *neg-*, not + *legere*, to gather] **1.** to ignore or disregard **2.** to fail to attend to properly **3.** to leave undone —***n.*** **1.** a neglecting or being neglected **2.** lack of proper care —**neg·lect′er, neg·lec′tor** ***n.***
neg·lect·ful (-fəl) ***adj.*** negligent (often with *of*) —**neg·lect′ful·ly** ***adv.*** —**neg·lect′ful·ness** ***n.***
neg·li·gee (neg′lə zhā′, neg′lə zhā′) ***n.*** [< Fr., fem. pp. of *négliger*, to neglect] **1.** a woman's loosely fitting dressing gown **2.** any informal or careless attire —***adj.*** carelessly or incompletely dressed
neg·li·gence (neg′li jəns) ***n.*** **1.** the quality or condition of being negligent **2.** an instance of this
neg·li·gent (-jənt) ***adj.*** [< OFr. < L. prp. of *negligere*: see NEGLECT] **1.** habitually failing to do the required thing **2.** careless, lax, inattentive, etc. —**neg′li·gent·ly** ***adv.***
neg·li·gi·ble (neg′li jə b'l) ***adj.*** that can be neglected or disregarded because small, unimportant, etc. —**neg′li·gi·bil′i·ty** ***n.*** —**neg′li·gi·bly** ***adv.***
ne·go·ti·a·ble (ni gō′shē ə b'l, -shə b'l) ***adj.*** that can be negotiated; specif., *a*) legally transferable, as a promissory note *b*) that can be passed, crossed, etc. —**ne·go′ti·a·bil′i·ty** ***n.***
ne·go·ti·ate (-shē āt′) ***vi.*** **-at′ed, -at′ing** [< L. pp. of *negotiari* < *negotium*, business < *nec-*, not + *otium*, ease] to confer or discuss with a view to reaching agreement —***vt.*** **1.** to settle or conclude (a transaction, treaty, etc.) **2.** to transfer or sell (negotiable paper) **3.** to succeed in crossing, moving through, etc. —**ne·go′ti·a′tor** ***n.***
ne·go·ti·a·tion (ni gō′shē ā′shən) ***n.*** a negotiating; specif., [*often pl.*] a conferring or bargaining to reach agreement —**ne·go′ti·a·to′ry** (-ə tôr′ē) ***adj.***
Ne·gress (nē′gris) ***n.*** a Negro woman or girl: term regarded by some as patronizing or discriminatory
Ne·gri·to (nə grēt′ō) ***n., pl.*** **-tos, -toes** [Sp., dim. of *negro*, NEGRO] a member of any of various groups of dwarfish Negroid peoples of the East Indies, the Philippines, and Africa —**Ne·grit′ic** (-grit′ik) ***adj.***
ne·gri·tude (neg′rə tood′, nē′grə-; -tyood′) ***n.*** [Fr. *négritude*, coined < *nègre*, black + *-i-* + *-tude*, -TUDE] [*also* **N-**] the affirmation by Negroes of their distinctive cultural heritage, esp. in Africa
Ne·gro[1] (nē′grō) ***n., pl.*** **-groes** [Sp. & Port. *negro* < L. *niger*, black] **1.** a member of the Negroid peoples of Africa, living chiefly south of the Sahara **2.** *same as* NEGROID **3.** any person with Negro ancestors See BLACK (*n.* 3) —***adj.*** of Negroes
Ne·gro[2] (nā′grō; *Port.* -groo; *Sp.* -grô) river in N Brazil, flowing southeast into the Amazon: c.1,400 mi.
Ne·groid (nē′groid) ***adj.*** designating or of a major group of mankind that includes the dark-skinned peoples of Africa and of Melanesia, New Guinea, etc. —***n.*** a Negroid person

Ne·gros (nā′grōs) island of the C Philippines, between Cebu & Panay: 4,905 sq. mi.

ne·gus (nē′gəs) ***n.*** [after Col. Francis *Negus* (d. 1732), who first made it] a beverage of hot water, wine, and lemon juice, sweetened and spiced

Ne·he·mi·ah (nē′ə mī′ə) *Bible* **1.** a Hebrew leader of about the 5th cent. B.C. **2.** the book that tells about his work: abbrev. **Neh.** In the Douay Bible, **Ne′he·mi′as** (-əs)

Neh·ru (nā′ro͞o), **Ja·wa·har·lal** (jə wä′hər läl′) 1889–1964; prime minister of India (1947–64)

neigh (nā) ***vi.*** [OE. *hnægan*] to utter the characteristic cry of a horse; whinny —***n.*** this cry

neigh·bor (nā′bər) ***n.*** [< OE. < *neah* (see NIGH) + *gebur,* farmer] **1.** a person who lives near another **2.** a person or thing situated near another **3.** a fellow man —***adj.*** nearby; adjacent —***vt., vi.*** to live or be situated near or nearby Also, Brit. sp., **neighbour**

neigh·bor·hood (-ho͝od′) ***n.*** **1.** a being neighbors **2.** a district or area, esp. with regard to some characteristic **3.** people living near one another; community —**in the neighborhood of** [Colloq.] **1.** near (a place) **2.** approximately

neigh·bor·ly (nā′bər lē) ***adj.*** like or appropriate to neighbors; friendly —**neigh′bor·li·ness** ***n.***

Neil (nēl) [var. of NEAL] a masculine name

nei·ther (nē′*th*ər, nī′-) ***adj., pron.*** [OE. *na-hwæther,* lit., not whether] not either *[neither* boy went, *neither* of them sings*]* —***conj.*** **1.** not either: in the pair of correlatives *neither . . . nor [*can *neither* laugh *nor* cry*]* **2.** nor *[*he doesn't smoke, *neither* does he drink*]* —***adv.*** [Dial. or Colloq.] also (after negative expressions) *[*if she won't go, I won't *neither]*

Nejd (nezhd) district in C & E Saudi Arabia

Nell (nel) [dim. of HELEN] a feminine name

Nel·lie, Nel·ly (nel′ē) [dim. of HELEN] a feminine name

Nel·son (nel′s′n) [< the surname *Nelson,* Neal's son] **1.** a masculine name **2. Horatio,** Viscount Nelson, 1758–1805; Eng. admiral

nel·son (nel′s′n) ***n.*** [< personal name *Nelson*] a wrestling hold; specif., a hold **(half nelson)** in which one arm is placed under the opponent's arm from behind with the hand pressing the back of his neck, or a hold **(full nelson)** in which both arms are so placed under the opponent's arms

nem·a·tode (nem′ə tōd′) ***n.*** [< ModL. < Gr. *nēma* (gen. *nēmatos*), thread + -ODE] any of a phylum of long, cylindrical worms, as the hookworm

Nem·e·sis (nem′ə sis) [L. < Gr. < *nemein,* to deal out] *Gr. Myth.* the goddess of retribution or vengeance —***n.*** [*usually* **n-**] *pl.* **-ses′** (-sēz′) **1.** *a)* just punishment *b)* one who imposes it **2.** anyone or anything that it seems will surely defeat or thwart one

N.Eng. 1. New England **2.** North England

ne·o- [< Gr. *neos,* new] *a combining form meaning:* **1.** [*often* **N-**] new, recent *[neolithic]* **2.** in a new or different way *[neocolonialism]*

ne·o·clas·sic (nē′ō klas′ik) ***adj.*** designating or of a revival of classic style in art, literature, etc.: also **ne′o·clas′si·cal** —**ne′o·clas′si·cism** ***n.*** —**ne′o·clas′si·cist** ***n.***

ne·o·co·lo·ni·al·ism (-kə lō′nē əl iz′m) ***n.*** the survival or revival of colonialism, as by the exploitation of a supposedly independent region by a foreign power —**ne′o·co·lo′ni·al** ***adj.*** —**ne′o·co·lo′ni·al·ist** ***n., adj.***

ne·o·dym·i·um (nē′ə dim′ē əm) ***n.*** [< NEO- + (DI)DYMIUM] a metallic chemical element of the rare-earth group: symbol, Nd; at. wt., 144.24; at. no., 60

ne·o·lith·ic (nē′ə lith′ik) ***adj.*** [NEO- + -LITHIC] designating or of the later part of the Stone Age, during which polished stone tools and metal tools were first used

ne·ol·o·gism (nē äl′ə jiz′m) ***n.*** [< Fr.: see NEO-, -LOGY, & -ISM] **1.** a new word or a new meaning for an established word **2.** the use of these Also **ne·ol′o·gy,** *pl.* **-gies** —**ne·ol′o·gis′tic, ne·ol′o·gis′ti·cal** ***adj.***

ne·ol·o·gize (-jīz′) ***vi.*** **-gized′, -giz′ing** to invent or use neologisms —**ne·ol′o·gist** ***n.***

ne·o·my·cin (nē′ə mī′sin) ***n.*** [< NEO- + Gr. *mykēs,* fungus + -IN¹] a broad-spectrum antibiotic used esp. in treating infections of the skin and eye

ne·on (nē′än) ***n.*** [ModL. < Gr. *neon,* neut. of *neos,* new] a rare, colorless, and inert gaseous chemical element: symbol, Ne; at. wt., 20.183; at. no., 10

neon lamp a tube containing neon, which glows red when an electric current is sent through it

ne·o·phyte (nē′ə fīt′) ***n.*** [< LL. < Gr. < *neos,* new + *phytos* < *phyein,* to produce] **1.** a new convert **2.** any beginner; novice

ne·o·plasm (-plaz′m) ***n.*** [NEO- + -PLASM] an abnormal growth of tissue, as a tumor —**ne′o·plas′tic** ***adj.***

ne·o·prene (nē′ə prēn′) ***n.*** [NEO- + (*chloro*)*prene,* an acetylene derivative] a synthetic rubber highly resistant to oil, heat, light, and oxidation

Ne·pal (ni pôl′, ne-; -päl′) country in the Himalayas, between India & Tibet: 54,362 sq. mi.; pop. 10,845,000; cap. Katmandu —**Nep·a·lese** (nep′ə lēz′) ***adj., n.,*** *pl.* **-lese′**

ne·pen·the (ni pen′thē) ***n.*** [L. < Gr. < *nē-,* not + *penthos,* sorrow] **1.** a drug supposed by the ancient Greeks to cause forgetfulness of sorrow **2.** anything causing this Also **ne·pen′thes** (-thēz) —**ne·pen′the·an** (-thē ən) ***adj.***

neph·ew (nef′yo͞o; *chiefly Brit.* nev′-) ***n.*** [< OFr. < L. *nepos*] **1.** the son of one's brother or sister **2.** the son of one's brother-in-law or sister-in-law

ne·phrid·i·um (ne frid′ē əm) ***n.,*** *pl.* **-i·a** (-ə) [ModL. < Gr. dim. of *nephros,* kidney] **1.** an excretory tubule of many invertebrates, as worms, mollusks, etc. **2.** any of the excretory tubules of a vertebrate embryo

ne·phrit·ic (ne frit′ik) ***adj.*** [< LL. < Gr. < *nephros,* kidney] **1.** of a kidney or the kidneys; renal **2.** of or having nephritis

ne·phri·tis (ne frīt′əs) ***n.*** [see ff. & -ITIS] disease of the kidneys, characterized by inflammation, fibrosis, etc.

neph·ro- [< Gr. *nephros,* kidney] *a combining form meaning* kidney: also, before a vowel, **nephr-**

ne plus ul·tra (nē plus ul′trə) [L., no more beyond] the highest point of perfection

nep·o·tism (nep′ə tiz′m) ***n.*** [< Fr. < It. < L. *nepos* (gen. *nepotis*), nephew] favoritism shown to relatives, esp. in appointment to desirable positions —**nep′o·tist** ***n.*** —**nep′o·tis′tic** ***adj.***

Nep·tune (nep′to͞on, -tyo͞on) **1.** *Rom. Myth.* the god of the sea: identified with the Greek god Poseidon **2.** a planet of the solar system, eighth in distance from the sun: diameter, c.29,500 mi.

nep·tu·ni·um (nep to͞o′nē əm, -tyo͞o′-) ***n.*** [ModL.: named after the planet Neptune] a radioactive chemical element produced by irradiating uranium atoms with neutrons: symbol, Np; at. wt., 237.00; at. no., 93

nerd (nʉrd) ***n.*** [< ?] [Slang] a person regarded as contemptibly ineffective, dull, unsophisticated, etc.

Ne·re·id (nir′ē id) ***n.*** *Gr. Myth.* any of the sea nymphs, the fifty daughters of Nereus

Ne·re·us (nir′o͞os, -ē əs) *Gr. Myth.* a benevolent sea god, father of the fifty Nereids

Ne·ro (nir′ō) (*Nero Claudius Caesar Drusus Germanicus*) 37–68 A.D.; emperor of Rome (54–68)

ner·va·tion (nər vā′shən) ***n.*** *same as* VENATION

nerve (nʉrv) ***n.*** [< OFr. < L. *nervus*] **1.** a tendon: now chiefly in **strain every nerve,** to try as hard as possible **2.** any of the cordlike fibers carrying impulses between the body organs and the central nervous system **3.** emotional control; courage *[*a man of *nerve]* **4.** strength; vigor **5.** [*pl.*] the nervous system regarded as indicating health, emotional stability, etc. **6.** [*pl.*] nervousness **7.** [Colloq.] impudent boldness; audacity **8.** *Biol.* a vein in a leaf or insect's wing —***vt.*** **nerved, nerv′ing** to give strength or courage to —**get on one's nerves** [Colloq.] to make one irritable

nerve block a method of local anesthesia by stopping the impulses through a particular nerve

nerve cell 1. *same as* NEURON **2.** occasionally, a nerve cell body without its processes

nerve center 1. any group of nerve cells that function together in controlling some specific sense or bodily activity, as breathing **2.** a control center; headquarters

nerve gas any of several liquids whose vapors can paralyze the respiratory and central nervous systems when absorbed through the eyes, lungs, or skin

nerve impulse an electrical wave transmitted along a nerve that has been stimulated

nerve·less (nʉrv′lis) ***adj.*** **1.** without strength, force, courage, etc.; weak; unnerved **2.** not nervous; calm **3.** *Biol.* without nerves —**nerve′less·ly** ***adv.*** —**nerve′less·ness** ***n.***

nerve-rack·ing, nerve-wrack·ing (-rak′iŋ) ***adj.*** very trying to one's patience or equanimity

nerv·ous (nʉr′vəs) ***adj.*** **1.** orig., strong; sinewy **2.** vigorous in expression; animated **3.** of the nerves **4.** made up of or containing nerves **5.** characterized by or having a disordered state of the nerves **6.** emotionally tense, restless, agitated, etc. **7.** fearful; apprehensive —**nerv′ous·ly** ***adv.*** —**nerv′ous·ness, ner·vos′i·ty** (-väs′ə tē) ***n.***

nervous breakdown a psychotic or neurotic disorder that impairs the ability to function normally: a popular, nontechnical term

nervous system all the nerve cells and nervous tissues in an organism, including, in the vertebrates, the brain, spinal cord, nerves, etc.

ner·vure (nʉr′vyoor) ***n.*** [Fr.: see NERVE & -URE] *Zool. same as* VEIN (*n.* 2)

nerv·y (nʉr′vē) ***adj.*** **nerv′i·er, nerv′i·est** **1.** [Brit.] nervous; excitable **2.** full of courage; bold **3.** [Colloq.] brazen; impudent —**nerv′i·ly** ***adv.*** —**nerv′i·ness** ***n.***

nes·ci·ent (nesh′ənt, -ē ənt) ***adj.*** [< L. prp. of *nescire* < *ne-,* not + *scire,* to know] ignorant —**nes′ci·ence** ***n.***

-ness (nis, nəs) [OE. *-nes(s)*] *a suffix meaning* state, quality, or instance of being *[greatness, sadness, weakness]*

nest (nest) *n.* [OE.] **1.** the structure made or the place chosen by birds for laying their eggs and sheltering their young **2.** the place used by hornets, fish, etc. for spawning or breeding **3.** a cozy place to live; retreat **4.** a resort, haunt, or den or its frequenters *[a nest of thieves]* **5.** a swarm or colony of birds, insects, etc. **6.** a set of similar things, each fitting within the one next larger *—vi.* **1.** to build or live in a nest **2.** to fit one into another *—vt.* **1.** to make a nest for **2.** to place in or as in a nest **3.** to fit (an object) closely within another **—nest′a·ble** *adj.*

‡**n'est-ce pas?** (nes pä′) [Fr.] isn't that so?

nest egg 1. an artificial or real egg left in a nest to induce a hen to lay more eggs there **2.** money, etc. put aside as a reserve or to set up a fund

nes·tle (nes′'l) *vi.* **-tled, -tling** [OE. *nestlian*] **1.** to settle down comfortably and snugly **2.** to press close for comfort or in affection **3.** to lie sheltered or partly hidden, as a house among trees *—vt.* **1.** to rest or press in a snug, affectionate manner **2.** to shelter as in a nest **—nes′tler** *n.*

nest·ling (nest′liŋ, nes′-) *n.* **1.** a young bird not yet ready to leave the nest **2.** a young child

Nes·tor (nes′tər) *Gr. Myth.* a wise old counselor who fought with the Greeks at Troy

net[1] (net) *n.* [OE. *nett*] **1.** a fabric of string, cord, etc., loosely knotted in an openwork pattern and used to snare birds, fish, etc. **2.** a trap; snare **3.** a meshed fabric used to hold, protect, or mark off something *[a hairnet, tennis net]* **4.** a fine, meshed, lacelike cloth **5.** *same as* NETWORK (sense 2) *—vt.* **net′ted, net′ting 1.** to make into a net **2.** to snare as with a net **3.** to shelter or enclose as with a net *—vi.* to make nets or network **—net′like′** *adj.*

net[2] (net) *adj.* [Fr.: see NEAT[1]] **1.** remaining after certain deductions or allowances have been made, as for expenses, weight of containers, etc. **2.** final *[net result]* *—n.* a net amount, profit, weight, price, etc. *—vt.* **net′ted, net′ting** to gain as profit, etc.

neth·er (ne*th*′ər) *adj.* [OE. *neothera*] lower or under *[the nether world, nether garments]*

Neth·er·lands (ne*th*′ər ləndz) **1.** country in W Europe, on the North Sea: 12,978 sq. mi.; pop. 13,033,000; cap. Amsterdam; seat of govt. The Hague **2.** kingdom consisting of the independent states of the Netherlands & Netherlands Antilles Often with *the* Abbrev. **Neth. —Neth′er·land′er** (-lan′dər, -lən dər) *n.*

Netherlands Antilles three islands off the coast of Venezuela & two islands & part of another in the Leeward Islands, together constituting a state of the Netherlands

neth·er·most (ne*th*′ər mōst′) *adj.* lowest

nether world *Theol. & Myth.* the world of the dead or of punishment after death; hell

Net·tie, Net·ty (net′ē) [dim. of ANTOINETTE, etc.] a feminine name

net·ting (net′iŋ) *n.* **1.** the act or process of making nets or fishing with them **2.** netted material

net·tle (net′'l) *n.* [OE. *netele*] any of a number of related weeds with stinging hairs *—vt.* **-tled, -tling 1.** to sting with or as with nettles **2.** to irritate; annoy; vex

net ton *same as* SHORT TON

net·work (net′wʉrk′) *n.* **1.** any arrangement or fabric of parallel wires, threads, etc. crossed at regular intervals by others so as to leave open spaces **2.** a thing resembling this; specif., *a)* a system of connecting roads, canals, etc. *b) Radio & TV* a chain of transmitting stations controlled and operated as a unit *c)* a system, etc. of cooperating individuals *—adj.* broadcast over the stations of a network

Neuf·châ·tel (cheese) (nōō′shə tel′, nyōō′-) [after a town in N France] a soft, white cheese prepared from whole or skim milk

neu·ral (noor′əl, nyoor′-) *adj.* [NEUR(O)- + -AL] of a nerve, nerves, or the nervous system

neu·ral·gia (noo ral′jə, nyoo-) *n.* [ModL.: see NEURO- & -ALGIA] severe pain along the course of a nerve **—neu·ral′gic** (-jik) *adj.*

neu·ras·the·ni·a (noor′əs thē′nē ə, nyoor′-) *n.* [ModL. < NEUR(O)- + Gr. *astheneia,* weakness] a type of neurosis, usually the result of emotional conflicts, characterized by irritability, fatigue, anxiety, etc. **—neu′ras·then′ic** (-then′ik) *adj., n.*

neu·ri·tis (noo rīt′əs, nyoo-) *n.* [ModL.: see ff. & -ITIS] inflammation of a nerve or nerves, accompanied by pain **—neu·rit′ic** (-rit′ik) *adj.*

neu·ro- [< Gr. *neuron,* nerve] *a combining form meaning* of a nerve, nerves, or the nervous system *[neuropathy]* : also, before a vowel, **neur-**

neu·rol·o·gy (noo räl′ə jē, nyoo-) *n.* [ModL.: see prec. & -LOGY] the branch of medicine dealing with the nervous system and its diseases **—neu·ro·log·i·cal** (noor′ə läj′i k'l, nyoor′-) *adj.* **—neu·rol′o·gist** *n.*

neu·ron (noor′än, nyoor′-) *n.* [ModL. < Gr. *neuron,* nerve] the structural and functional unit of the nervous system, consisting of the nerve cell body and all its processes: also **neu′rone** (-ōn) **—neu′ro·nal** (-ə nəl), **neu·ron·ic** (noo rän′ik, nyoo-) *adj.*

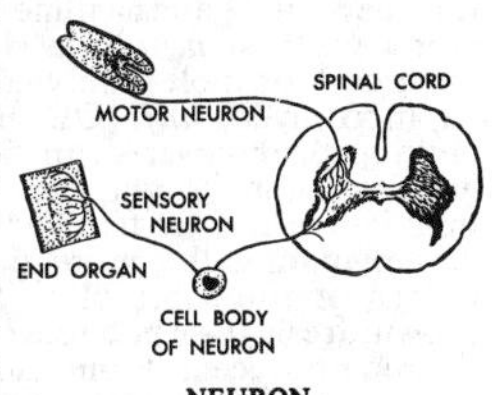

NEURON

neu·rop·a·thy (noo räp′ə thē, nyoo-) *n.* [NEURO- + -PATHY] any disease of the nerves or the nervous system **—neu·ro·path·ic** (noor′ə path′ik, nyoor′-) *adj.*

neu·ro·psy·chi·a·try (noor′ō sə kī′ə trē, nyoor′-) *n.* a branch of medicine combining neurology and psychiatry

neu·rop·ter·an (noo räp′tər ən, nyoo-) *n.* [< ModL. < NEURO- + Gr. *pteron,* wing + -AN] any of an order of insects with four membranous wings and biting mouthparts **—neu·rop′ter·ous** *adj.*

neu·ro·sis (noo rō′sis, nyoo-) *n., pl.* **-ses** (-sēz) [ModL.: see NEURO- & -OSIS] a functional mental disorder characterized by combinations of anxiety, compulsions and obsessions, phobias, depression, etc.

neu·ro·sur·ger·y (noor′ō sʉr′jər ē, nyoor′-) *n.* the branch of surgery involving some part of the nervous system, including the brain and spinal cord **—neu′ro·sur′geon** *n.*

neu·rot·ic (noo rät′ik, nyoo-) *adj.* of or having a neurosis *—n.* a neurotic person **—neu·rot′i·cal·ly** *adv.* **—neu·rot′i·cism** (-ə siz'm) *n.*

neut. neuter

neu·ter (nōōt′ər, nyōōt′-) *adj.* [< MFr. < L. < *ne-,* not + *uter,* either] **1.** [Archaic] neutral **2.** *Biol. a)* having no sexual organs; asexual *b)* having undeveloped or imperfect sexual organs in the adult, as the worker bee **3.** *Gram.* designating or of the gender that refers to things regarded as neither male nor female *—n.* **1.** a castrated or spayed animal **2.** *Biol.* a neuter plant or animal **3.** *Gram. a)* the neuter gender *b)* a neuter word *—vt.* to castrate or spay

neu·tral (nōō′trəl, nyōō′-) *adj.* [Fr. < ML. < L. < *neuter:* see prec.] **1.** not taking part in either side of a quarrel or war **2.** of or characteristic of a nation not taking part in a war or not taking sides in a power struggle **3.** not one thing or the other; indifferent **4.** having little or no decided color **5.** *Biol. same as* NEUTER **6.** *Chem.* neither acid nor alkaline **7.** *Elec.* neither negative nor positive **8.** *Phonet.* pronounced as the vowel is in most unstressed syllables, which tends to become (ə) *—n.* **1.** a nation not taking part in a war **2.** a neutral person **3.** a neutral color **4.** *Mech.* a disengaged position of gears, when they do not transmit power from the engine **—neu′tral·ly** *adv.*

neu·tral·ism (-iz'm) *n.* a policy, or the advocacy of a policy, of remaining neutral, esp. in international power conflicts **—neu′tral·ist** *adj., n.* **—neu′tral·is′tic** *adj.*

neu·tral·i·ty (nōō tral′ə tē, nyōō-) *n.* **1.** the quality, state, or character of being neutral **2.** the status or policy of a nation not participating directly or indirectly in a war between other nations

neu·tral·ize (nōō′trə līz′, nyōō′-) *vt.* **-ized′, -iz′ing 1.** to declare (a nation, etc.) neutral in war **2.** to destroy or counteract the effectiveness, force, etc. of **3.** *Chem.* to destroy the active properties of *[an alkali neutralizes an acid]* **4.** *Elec.* to make electrically neutral **—neu′tral·i·za′tion** *n.* **—neu′tral·iz′er** *n.*

neutral spirits ethyl alcohol of 190 proof or over, used in blended whiskeys, liqueurs, cordials, etc.

neu·tri·no (nōō trē′nō, nyōō-) *n., pl.* **-nos** [It., coined by E. FERMI < *neutrone* (< NEUTRON) + dim. suffix *-ino*] *Physics* a neutral particle having a mass approaching zero

neu·tron (nōō′trän, nyōō′-) *n.* [NEUTR(AL) + (ELECTR)ON] a fundamental particle in the nucleus of an atom: neutrons are uncharged and have about the same mass as protons

neutron bomb a small thermonuclear warhead for battlefield use, intended to disable or kill enemy soldiers without destroying buildings, vehicles, etc.

neutron star a heavenly object hypothesized to be a collapsed star consisting of immense numbers of densely packed neutrons

Ne·vad·a (nə vad′ə, -vä′də) [< (SIERRA) NEVADA] Mountain State of the U.S.: 110,540 sq. mi.; pop. 799,000; cap. Carson City: abbrev. **Nev., NV —Ne·vad′an** *adj., n.*

nev·er (nev′ər) *adv.* [OE. *næfre* < *ne,* not + *æfre,* ever] **1.** not ever; at no time **2.** not at all; in no case

nev·er·more (nev′ər môr′) *adv.* never again

never-never land [after the fairyland in J. M. Barrie's *Peter Pan*] an unreal or unrealistic place or situation

nev·er·the·less (nev′ər *thə* les′) ***adv.*** in spite of that; nonetheless; however

Nev·il, Nev·ille (nev″l) [< *Neuville,* town in Normandy (lit., new city)] a masculine name

ne·vus (nē′vəs) ***n., pl.* ne′vi** (-vī) [ModL. < L. *naevus*] a birthmark or mole —**ne′void** (-void) ***adj.***

new (no͞o, nyo͞o) ***adj.*** [OE. *niwe*] **1.** appearing, thought of, developed, discovered, made, etc. for the first time; never existing before **2.** *a)* different *[*a *new* hairdo*]* *b)* strange; unfamiliar **3.** not yet familiar or accustomed *[new* to the job*]* **4.** designating the more or most recent of two or more things of the same class *[*the *new* library*]* **5.** recently grown; fresh *[new* potatoes*]* **6.** not previously used or worn **7.** modern; recent; fashionable **8.** more; additional **9.** starting as a repetition of a cycle, series, etc. *[*the *new* year*]* **10.** having just reached a position, rank, place, etc. *[*a *new* arrival*]* **11.** refreshed in spirits, health, etc. *[*a *new* man*]* **12.** [N-] *same as* MODERN (sense 3) —***n.*** something new (with *the*) —***adv.*** **1.** again **2.** newly; recently —**new′ish** ***adj.*** —**new′ness** ***n.***

New Amsterdam Du. colonial town on Manhattan Island: renamed (1664) New York by the British

New·ark (no͞o′ərk, nyo͞o′-) [after *Newark,* England] city in NE N.J.: pop. 329,000 (met. area 1,964,000)

new ball game [Colloq.] a situation so drastically changed as to require new approaches, solutions, etc.

New Bed·ford (bed′fərd) [after W. Russell, Duke of *Bedford* (1639–83)] seaport in SE Mass.: pop. 98,000

new blood new people, regarded as a potential source of fresh ideas, renewed vigor, etc.

new·born (no͞o′bôrn′, nyo͞o′-) ***adj.*** **1.** recently born; just born **2.** reborn

New Britain city in C Conn.: pop. 74,000

New Brunswick province of SE Canada, on the Gulf of St. Lawrence: 28,354 sq. mi.; pop. 677,000; cap. Fredericton: abbrev. **N.B.**

New·burg (-bərg) ***adj.*** served in a rich, creamy sauce made with butter, egg yolks, and wine

New Caledonia Fr. island in the SW Pacific, west of Australia

new candle *see* CANDLE (*n.* 3)

New·cas·tle (no͞o′kas″l, nyo͞o′-; -käs′-) seaport in N England: pop. 254,000: in full, **New′cas′tle-up·on-Tyne′** (-tīn′) —**carry coals to Newcastle** **1.** to take things to a place where they are plentiful **2.** to do an unnecessary thing

new·com·er (no͞o′kum′ər, nyo͞o′-) ***n.*** a recent arrival

New Deal the economic and political principles and policies adopted by President Franklin D. Roosevelt in the 1930's to advance economic and social welfare —**New Dealer**

New Delhi capital of India, adjacent to the old city of Delhi: pop. 261,000

new·el (no͞o′əl, nyo͞o′-) ***n.*** [< OFr. < LL. *nucalis,* like a nut < L. *nux,* nut] **1.** the upright pillar around which the steps of a winding staircase turn **2.** the post at the top or bottom of a flight of stairs, supporting the handrail: also **newel post**

New England [so named (1616) by Capt. John SMITH] the six NE States of the U.S.: Me., Vt., N.H., Mass., R.I., and Conn. —**New Englander**

New English Bible a British translation of the Bible, published in 1970

new·fan·gled (no͞o′faŋ′g'ld, nyo͞o′-) ***adj.*** [< ME. < *newe,* new + *-fangel* < base of OE. *fon,* to take] new; novel: a humorously derogatory term

New·found·land (no͞o′fənd land′, -lənd; nyo͞o′-; nyo͞o found′land′) **1.** an island of Canada, off the E coast **2.** province of E Canada, including this island & Labrador: 156,185 sq. mi.; pop. 558,000; cap. St. John's: abbrev. **Nfld.** —**New′found·land′er** ***n.***

Newfoundland dog any of a North American breed of large, powerful, shaggy-haired dogs

New·gate (no͞o′gāt, nyo͞o′-) former prison in London: torn down in 1902

New Guinea large island in the East Indies, north of Australia: divided between West Irian (in Indonesia) & the country of Papua New Guinea

New Hamp·shire (hamp′shir, ham′-) [after *Hampshire,* county in England] New England State of the U.S.: 9,304 sq. mi.; pop. 921,000; cap. Concord: abbrev. **N.H., NH**

New Ha·ven (hā′vən) city in S Conn., on Long Island Sound: pop. 126,000

New Hebrides group of islands in the SW Pacific, which in 1980 became the independent nation of VANUATU

New High German *see* GERMAN, HIGH GERMAN

New Jersey [after the island of JERSEY] Eastern State of the U.S.: 7,836 sq. mi.; pop. 7,364,000; cap. Trenton: abbrev. **N.J., NJ** —**New Jer′sey·ite′** (-īt′)

New Jerusalem *Bible* heaven: Rev. 21:2

new·ly (no͞o′lē, nyo͞o′-) ***adv.*** **1.** recently; lately **2.** anew; afresh **3.** in a new way or style

new·ly·wed (-wed′) ***n.*** a recently married person

New·man (no͞o′mən, nyo͞o′-), **John Henry,** Cardinal Newman, 1801–90; Eng. theologian & writer

new math a system for teaching basic mathematics based on the use of sets

New Mexico [transl. of Sp. *Nuevo Méjico*] Mountain State of the U.S.: 121,666 sq. mi.; pop. 1,300,000; cap. Santa Fe: abbrev. **N.Mex., NM** —**New Mexican**

new moon the moon when it is between the earth and the sun, with its dark side toward the earth: it emerges as a crescent curving to the right

New Neth·er·land (ne*th*′ər lənd) Du. colony (1613–64) in E N. America: taken by England & divided into the colonies of New York & New Jersey

New Or·le·ans (ôr′lē ənz, ôr lēnz′; *chiefly Southern* ôr′lənz) [after ORLÉANS, France] city in SE La., on the Mississippi: pop. 557,000 (met. area 1,184,000)

New·port (no͞o′pôrt′, nyo͞o′-) seaport in SE Wales: pop. 112,000

Newport News [< ?] seaport in SE Va.: pop. 145,000

New Ro·chelle (rə shel′) [after *La Rochelle,* France] city in SE N.Y., on Long Island Sound: pop. 71,000

news (no͞oz, nyo͞oz) ***n.pl.*** [*with sing. v.*] [after OFr. *noveles* or ML. *nova,* pl. of *novum,* what is new] **1.** new information about anything; information previously unknown **2.** reports of recent happenings, esp. those broadcast, printed in a newspaper, etc. **3.** any person or thing featured in such reports —**make news** to do something reported as news

news·boy (-boi′) ***n.*** a boy who sells or delivers newspapers

news·cast (-kast′) ***n.*** [NEWS + (BROAD)CAST] a program of news broadcast over radio or TV —**news′cast′er** ***n.***

news·deal·er (-dēl′ər) ***n.*** a person who sells newspapers, magazines, etc., esp. as a retailer

news·let·ter (-let′ər) ***n.*** a news bulletin issued at regular intervals to a special group

news·man (-man′, -mən) ***n., pl.* -men** (-men′, -mən) a newsperson, esp. a male —**news′wom′an** ***n.fem., pl.* -wom′en**

New South Wales state of SE Australia, on the Pacific

news·pa·per (-pā′pər) ***n.*** a regular publication, usually a daily or weekly, containing news, opinions, advertisements, etc. —**news′pa′per·man′** ***n., pl.* -men′** —**news′pa′per·wom′an** ***n.fem., pl.* -wom′en**

new·speak (no͞o′spēk′, nyo͞o′-) ***n.*** [*sometimes* **N-**] the use of ambiguous and deceptive talk, as by government officials, in seeking to mold public opinion

news·per·son (no͞oz′pur′s'n, nyo͞oz′-) ***n.*** a person involved in the gathering, writing, editing, or reporting of news, often specif. for TV or radio

news·print (no͞oz′print′, nyo͞oz′-) ***n.*** a cheap paper, made mainly from wood pulp, for newspapers, etc.

news·reel (-rēl′) ***n.*** a short motion picture of news events

news·stand (-stand′) ***n.*** a stand at which newspapers, magazines, etc. are sold

New Style the method of reckoning time in accordance with the Gregorian calendar

news·wor·thy (no͞oz′wur′*thē,* nyo͞oz′-) ***adj.*** timely and important or interesting

news·y (-ē) ***adj.* news′i·er, news′i·est** [Colloq.] containing much news

newt (no͞ot, nyo͞ot) ***n.*** [by syllabic merging of ME. *an eute* < OE. *efeta,* eft] any of various small salamanders that can live on land or in water

NEWT (3–4 in. long)

New Testament the part of the Bible containing the life and teachings of Jesus and his followers

New·ton[1] (no͞ot″n, nyo͞ot″n) [< *New Towne,* orig. name of Cambridge, Mass.] city in E Mass.: suburb of Boston: pop. 84,000

New·ton[2] (no͞ot″n, nyo͞ot″n) [< surname *Newton* < Eng. place name < OE. *neowa tun,* new town] **1.** a masculine name **2.** Sir **Isaac,** 1642–1727; Eng. mathematician & natural philosopher —**New·to′ni·an** (-tō′nē ən) ***adj., n.***

new·ton (no͞ot″n, nyo͞ot″n) ***n.*** [after Sir Isaac NEWTON] the unit of force in the mks system: the force which imparts to a mass of 1 kilogram an acceleration of 1 meter per second per second

New Town **1.** any of a number of planned communities built in Great Britain since World War II **2.** [*often* **n- t-**] any housing development like this

New World the Western Hemisphere —**new′-world′** ***adj.***

new year [*also* **N- Y-**] **1.** the year just about to begin or just begun (usually with *the*) **2.** the first day or days of the new year

New Year's (Day) January 1, the first day of a calendar year, usually a legal holiday

New Year's Eve the evening before New Year's Day

New York [after the Duke of *York*] **1.** State of the NE U.S.: 49,576 sq. mi.; pop. 17,557,000; cap. Albany: abbrev. **N.Y., NY** **2.** city in SE N.Y., at the mouth of the Hudson:

often called **New York City:** pop. 7,071,000 (met. area 10,803,000) —**New York′er**

New York State Barge Canal system of waterways, including the Erie Canal, connecting Lake Erie & the Hudson River

New Zea·land (zē′lənd) country made up of two large islands & several small islands in the S Pacific, southeast of Australia: a member of the Commonwealth: 103,736 sq. mi.; pop. 2,809,000; cap. Wellington —**New Zea′land·er**

next (nekst) ***adj.*** *older superl. of* NIGH [OE. *neahst,* superl. of *neah,* nigh] nearest; immediately preceding or following —***adv.*** **1.** in the time, place, degree, or rank immediately preceding or following **2.** on the first subsequent occasion [when *next* we meet] —***prep.*** beside; nearest to [sit *next* the tree] —***n.*** the one immediately following —**get next to** [Slang] to become friendly or intimate with —**next door (to) 1.** in or at the house adjacent (to) **2.** almost

next-door (neks′dôr′) ***adj.*** in or at the next house, building, etc.

next of kin one's relative(s) most nearly related

nex·us (nek′səs) ***n.,*** *pl.* **-us·es, nex′us** [L. < pp. of *nectere,* to bind] **1.** a connection, tie, or link between individuals of a group, members of a series, etc. **2.** the group or series connected

Nez Per·cé (nez′ pər sā′, purs′) *pl.* **Nez Per·cés′, Nez Per·cé′** [Fr., lit., pierced nose: from the false notion that they pierced the nose] a member of a N. American Indian tribe of the Northwest

Nfld., Nfd. Newfoundland

N.G. 1. National Guard: also **NG 2.** New Guinea

N.G., n.g. [Slang] no good

ngul·trum (′n ool′troom) ***n.*** [Bhutanese] *see* MONETARY UNITS, table (Bhutan)

ngwee (′n gwē′) ***n.,*** *pl.* **ngwee** [native term, lit., bright] *see* MONETARY UNITS, table (Zambia)

N.H., NH New Hampshire

Ni *Chem.* nickel

N.I. Northern Ireland

ni·a·cin (nī′ə sin) ***n.*** [NI(COTINIC) AC(ID) + -IN[1]] a white, odorless substance, $C_6H_5O_2N$, found in protein foods: it is a member of the vitamin B complex, used in treating pellagra

Ni·ag·a·ra (nī ag′rə, -ər ə) [< Iroquoian town name] river between W N.Y. & SE Ontario, Canada, flowing from Lake Erie into Lake Ontario

Niagara Falls 1. waterfall on the Niagara River: divided by an island into two falls, Horseshoe, or Canadian, Falls & American Falls **2.** city in W N.Y., at Niagara Falls: pop. 71,000 **3.** city in SE Ontario, opposite Niagara Falls, N.Y.: pop. 69,000

nib (nib) ***n.*** [var. of NEB] **1.** the bill or beak of a bird **2.** the point of a pen **3.** the projecting end of anything; point

nib·ble (nib′'l) ***vt., vi.*** **-bled, -bling** [prob. akin to MLowG. *nibbelen*] **1.** to eat (food) with quick, small bites, as a mouse does **2.** to bite at with small, gentle bites —***n.*** **1.** a small bite or morsel **2.** a nibbling —**nib′bler *n.***

Ni·be·lung (nē′bə looŋ′) ***n.*** [G.] *Germanic Legend* any of a race of dwarfs who owned a magic ring and a hoard of gold, taken from them by Siegfried

Ni·be·lung·en·lied (nē′bə looŋ′ən lēt′) a Middle High German epic poem by an unknown author of the 13th cent.: see SIEGFRIED

nibs (nibz) ***n.*** [< ?] [Colloq.] an important, or esp. self-important, person (with *his*)

Nic·a·ra·gua (nik′ə rä′gwə) **1.** country in Central America, on the Caribbean & the Pacific: 54,342 sq. mi.; pop. 1,984,000; cap. Managua **2. Lake,** lake in S Nicaragua —**Nic′a·ra′guan** ***adj., n.***

Nice (nēs) seaport & resort in SE France: pop. 322,000

nice (nīs) ***adj.*** **nic′er, nic′est** [OFr., stupid < L. *nescius,* ignorant < *ne-,* not + *scire,* to know] **1.** difficult to please; fastidious **2.** delicate; precise; discriminative; subtle [a *nice* distinction] **3.** calling for accuracy, care, tact, etc. [a *nice* problem] **4.** *a)* finely discriminating *b)* minutely accurate **5.** morally scrupulous **6.** *a)* agreeable; pleasant *b)* attractive; pretty *c)* kind; considerate *d)* respectable *e)* good; excellent —***adv.*** pleasingly, attractively, etc.: regarded as substandard, dialectal, or colloquial —**nice and** [Colloq.] altogether; very [my tea is *nice and* hot] —**nice′ly *adv.*** —**nice′ness *n.***

Ni·cene Creed (nī′sēn, nī sēn′) [< *Nicaea,* ancient city in Asia Minor where it was formulated] a confession of faith for Christians adopted in 325 A.D.: now used in various forms by most denominations

ni·ce·ty (nī′sə tē) ***n.,*** *pl.* **-ties 1.** a being nice; specif., *a)* scrupulosity *b)* precision; accuracy, as of discrimination or perception *c)* fastidiousness; refinement **2.** the quality of calling for delicacy or precision in handling **3.** a subtle or minute detail, distinction, etc. **4.** something choice or dainty —**to a nicety** exactly

niche (nich) ***n.*** [Fr. < OFr., ult. < L. *nidus,* a nest] **1.** a recess in a wall for a statue, bust, or vase **2.** a place or position particularly suitable to the person or thing in it **3.** *Ecol.* the particular role of an organism in its total environment —***vt.*** **niched, nich′ing** to place in a niche

STATUE IN NICHE

Nich·o·las (nik′'l əs) [< OFr. < L. < Gr. < *nikē,* victory + *laos,* the people] **1.** a masculine name: dim. *Nick* **2. Nicholas I** 1796–1855; czar of Russia (1825–55) **3. Nicholas II** 1868–1918; last czar of Russia (1894–1917): forced to abdicate; executed **4.** Saint, 4th cent. A.D.: patron saint of Russia, of Greece, & of young people, sailors, etc.: cf. SANTA CLAUS

nick (nik) ***n.*** [prob. akin to *nocke,* notch] a small cut, chip, etc. made on the edge or surface of wood, metal, china, etc.; notch —***vt.*** **1.** to make a nick or nicks in **2.** *a)* to wound slightly *b)* to strike glancingly **3.** to hit or catch at the right time **4.** [Slang] *a)* to fine *b)* to overcharge or cheat —**in the nick of time** just before it is too late; exactly when needed

nick·el (nik′'l) ***n.*** [Sw. < G. *kupfernickel,* copper demon: so called because the copperlike ore contains no copper] **1.** a hard, silver-white, malleable metallic chemical element, used in alloys and for plating: symbol, Ni; at. wt., 58.71; at. no., 28 **2.** a U.S. or Canadian coin made of an alloy of nickel and copper and equal to five cents —***vt.*** **-eled** or **-elled, -el·ing** or **-el·ling** to plate with nickel

nick·el·o·de·on (nik′ə lō′dē ən) ***n.*** [< NICKEL + Fr. *odéon,* concert hall] **1.** formerly, a motion-picture theater, etc. where admission was five cents **2.** a player piano or early type of jukebox operated by the insertion of a nickel in a slot

nickel plate a thin layer of nickel deposited by electrolysis on metallic objects to prevent rust —**nick′el-plate′ *vt.*** **-plat′ed, -plat′ing**

nickel silver a hard, tough, ductile, malleable alloy composed essentially of nickel, copper, and zinc

nick·er (nik′ər) ***vi.*** [prob. < freq. of NEIGH] to utter a low, whinnying sound: said of a horse —***n.*** this sound

nick·nack (nik′nak′) ***n.*** *same as* KNICKKNACK

nick·name (nik′nām′) ***n.*** [by syllabic merging of ME. *an ekename,* a surname] **1.** a substitute, often descriptive name given to a person or thing, as in fun, affection, etc., as "Doc," "Shorty," etc. **2.** a familiar form of a name, as "Dick" for "Richard" —***vt.*** **-named′, -nam′ing** to give a nickname to

Nic·o·si·a (nik′ə sē′ə) capital of Cyprus: pop. 109,000

nic·o·tine (nik′ə tēn′, -tin) ***n.*** [Fr. < ModL., after J. *Nicot,* 16th-c. Fr. diplomat who introduced tobacco into France] a poisonous alkaloid, $C_{10}H_{14}N_2$, found in tobacco leaves and used as an insecticide —**nic′o·tin′ic** (-tin′ik, -tē′nik) ***adj.***

nicotinic acid *same as* NIACIN

nic·tate (nik′tāt) ***vi.*** **-tat·ed, -tat·ing** *same as* NICTITATE

nic·ti·tate (nik′tə tāt′) ***vi.*** **-tat′ed, -tat′ing** [< ML. pp. of *nictitare,* freq. < L. *nictare,* to wink] to wink or blink rapidly, as birds and animals with a nictitating membrane —**nic′ti·ta′tion *n.***

nictitating membrane a transparent third eyelid hinged at the inner side or lower lid of the eye of various animals

niece (nēs) ***n.*** [< OFr. < LL. < L. *neptis*] **1.** the daughter of one's brother or sister **2.** the daughter of one's brother-in-law or sister-in-law

Nie·tzsche (nē′chə), **Frie·drich Wil·helm** (frē′driH vil′helm) 1844–1900; Ger. philosopher —**Nie′tzsche·an** (-chē ən) ***adj., n.***

nif·ty (nif′tē) ***adj.*** **-ti·er, -ti·est** [prob. < MAGNIFICENT] [Slang] attractive, smart, stylish, enjoyable, etc. —***n.,*** *pl.* **-ties** a nifty thing; esp., a clever remark

Ni·ger (nī′jər) **1.** river in W Africa, flowing from Guinea through Mali, Niger, & Nigeria into the Atlantic **2.** country in WC Africa, north of Nigeria: c.458,500 sq. mi.; pop. 4,016,000

Ni·ger·i·a (nī jir′ē ə) country in WC Africa, on the Atlantic: a member of the Commonwealth: 327,186 sq. mi.; pop. 61,450,000; cap. Lagos —**Ni·ger′i·an** ***adj., n.***

nig·gard (nig′ərd) ***n.*** [prob. < Scand.] a stingy person; miser —***adj.*** stingy; miserly

nig·gard·ly (-lē) ***adj.*** **1.** stingy; miserly **2.** small, few, or scanty —***adv.*** stingily —**nig′gard·li·ness *n.***

nig·gle (nig′'l) ***vi.*** **-gled, -gling** [prob. akin to Norw. dial.

nigla] to work fussily; be finicky —**nig′gler** ***n.*** —**nig′gling** ***adj., n.***
nigh (nī) ***adv.*** [OE. *neah*] [Chiefly Archaic or Dial.] **1.** near in time, place, etc. **2.** almost —***adj.*** **nigh′er, nigh′est** or, older, **next** [Chiefly Archaic or Dial.] **1.** near; close **2.** direct or short **3.** on the left: said of animals, vehicles, etc. —***prep.*** [Chiefly Archaic or Dial.] near —***vi., vt.*** [Archaic] to approach
night (nīt) ***n.*** [OE. *niht*] **1.** the period of darkness between sunset and sunrise **2.** the evening at the end of a specified day *[Christmas night]* **3.** the darkness of night **4.** any period or condition of darkness or gloom; specif., *a)* a period of intellectual or moral degeneration *b)* a time of grief *c)* death —***adj.*** **1.** of, for, or at night **2.** active or working at night —**make a night of it** to celebrate all night —**night and day** continuously or continually
night blindness imperfect vision in the dark or in dim light: a symptom of vitamin A deficiency
night-bloom·ing cereus (-blōō′miŋ) any of various cactuses that bloom at night
night·cap (-kap′) ***n.*** **1.** a cap worn in bed, esp. formerly, to protect the head from cold **2.** [Colloq.] an alcoholic drink taken at bedtime
night clothes clothes to be worn in bed, as pajamas
night·club (-klub′) ***n.*** a place of entertainment open at night for eating, drinking, dancing, etc.
night crawler any large earthworm that comes to the surface at night, commonly used as fish bait
night·fall (-fôl′) ***n.*** the close of day; dusk
night gown (-goun′) ***n.*** a loose gown worn in bed by women or girls
night·hawk (-hôk′) ***n.*** **1.** any of a group of new-world night birds related to the goatsuckers and the whippoorwill **2.** *same as: a)* NIGHTJAR *b)* NIGHT OWL
night·ie (nīt′ē) ***n.*** *colloq. dim. of* NIGHTGOWN
night·in·gale (nīt′'n gāl′, -iŋ-) ***n.*** [< OE. < *niht*, night + base of *galan*, to sing] a small European thrush with a russet back and buff underparts, known for the melodious singing of the male, esp. at night
Night·in·gale (nīt′'n gāl′, -iŋ-), **Florence** 1820–1910; Eng. nurse: pioneer in modern nursing
night·jar (nīt′jär′) ***n.*** [NIGHT + JAR[1]] the European goatsucker
night latch a door latch with a bolt opened from the outside by a key and from the inside by a knob
night letter a long telegram sent at night at a cheaper rate than a regular telegram
night light a small, dim light kept on all night, as in a hallway, bathroom, sickroom, etc.
night·long (-lôŋ′) ***adj.*** lasting the entire night —***adv.*** during the entire night
night·ly (-lē) ***adj.*** **1.** of or like the night **2.** done or occurring every night —***adv.*** **1.** at night **2.** every night
night·mare (-mer′) ***n.*** [< ME. < *niht*, night + *mare*, demon] **1.** a frightening dream, often accompanied by a feeling of oppression and helplessness **2.** any frightening experience —**night′mar′ish** ***adj.***
night owl a person who works at night or otherwise stays up late
nights (nīts) ***adv.*** on every night or most nights
night school a school held in the evening, as for adults unable to attend by day
night·shade (nīt′shād′) ***n.*** [OE. *nihtscada*] **1.** any of a large genus of flowering plants of the nightshade family, including BLACK NIGHTSHADE **2.** *same as* BELLADONNA (sense 1) —***adj.*** designating a large family of poisonous and nonpoisonous plants, including the tobacco, tomato, potato, petunia, and eggplant
night·shirt (-shurt′) ***n.*** a long, loose, shirtlike garment, worn in bed, esp. formerly, by men or boys
night·spot (-spät′) ***n.*** *colloq. var. of* NIGHTCLUB
night stand a small table at the bedside
night stick a club carried by a policeman
night·time (-tīm′) ***n.*** the period of darkness from sunset to sunrise
night·wear (-wer′) ***n.*** *same as* NIGHT CLOTHES
night·y (-ē) ***n.***, *pl.* **night′ies** *alt. sp. of* NIGHTIE
NIH, N.I.H. National Institutes of Health
ni·hil·ism (nī′ə liz'm, nē′-, ni′hi-) ***n.*** [< L. *nihil*, nothing + -ISM] **1.** *Philos. a)* the denial of the existence of any basis for knowledge *b)* the general rejection of customary beliefs in morality, religion, etc. **2.** the belief that there is no meaning or purpose in existence **3.** *a)* [N-] a revolutionary movement in Russia (c.1860–1917) which advocated the destruction of existing social, political, and economic institutions *b)* loosely, any terroristic revolutionary movement —**ni′hil·ist** ***n.*** —**ni′hil·is′tic** ***adj.***
Ni·ke (nī′kē) *Gr. Myth.* the winged goddess of victory
nil (nil) ***n.*** [L., contr. of *nihil*] nothing
Nile (nīl) river in NE Africa, flowing through Egypt into the Mediterranean: with one of its principal headstreams, over 4,000 mi.
nil·gai (nil′gī) ***n.***, *pl.* **-gais, -gai:** see PLURAL, II, D, 1 [Per. *nīlgāw*, blue cow] a large, gray Indian antelope: also **nil′-gau** (-gô)
nim·ble (nim′b'l) ***adj.*** **-bler, -blest** [< OE. *numol* < *niman*, to take] **1.** quick-witted; alert *[a nimble mind]* **2.** showing mental quickness *[a nimble reply]* **3.** moving quickly and lightly —**nim′ble·ness** ***n.*** —**nim′bly** ***adv.***
nim·bo·stra·tus (nim′bō strāt′əs, -strat′əs) ***n.*** [ModL.: see ff. & STRATUS] an extensive, dark, low-level cloud, commonly bringing rain or snow
nim·bus (nim′bəs) ***n.***, *pl.* **-bi** (-bī), **-bus·es** [L., rain cloud] **1.** orig., any rain-producing cloud **2.** a bright cloud supposedly surrounding gods or goddesses appearing on earth **3.** an aura of splendor about any person or thing **4.** a halo surrounding the heads of saints, etc., as in pictures
Nim·rod (nim′räd) *Bible* a mighty hunter: Gen. 10:8–9 —***n.*** [*often* **n-**] a hunter
nin·com·poop (nin′kəm pōōp′, niŋ′-) ***n.*** [< ?] a stupid, silly person; fool; simpleton
nine (nīn) ***adj.*** [OE. *nigon*] totaling one more than eight —***n.*** **1.** the cardinal number between eight and ten; 9; IX **2.** anything having nine units or members, or numbered nine; specif., a baseball team —**the Nine** the nine Muses —**to the nines** **1.** to perfection **2.** in the most elaborate manner *[dressed to the nines]*
nine·fold (-fōld′) ***adj.*** [see -FOLD] **1.** having nine parts **2.** having nine times as much or as many —***adv.*** nine times as much or as many
nine·pins (-pinz′) ***n.pl.*** [*with sing. v.*] a British version of tenpins, in which nine pins are used
nine·teen (-tēn′) ***adj.*** [OE. *nigontyne*] nine more than ten —***n.*** the cardinal number between eighteen and twenty; 19; XIX
nine·teenth (-tēnth′) ***adj.*** **1.** preceded by eighteen others in a series; 19th **2.** designating any of the nineteen equal parts of something —***n.*** **1.** the one following the eighteenth **2.** any of the nineteen equal parts of something; 1/19
nine·ti·eth (nīn′tē ith) ***adj.*** **1.** preceded by eighty-nine others in a series; 90th **2.** designating any of the ninety equal parts of something —***n.*** **1.** the one following the eighty-ninth **2.** any of the ninety equal parts of something; 1/90
nine·ty (nīn′tē) ***adj.*** [OE. *nigontig*] nine times ten —***n.***, *pl.* **-ties** the cardinal number between eighty-nine and ninety-one; 90; XC (or LXXXX) —**the nineties** the numbers or years, as of a century, from ninety through ninety-nine
Nin·e·veh (nin′ə və) capital of ancient Assyria
nin·ny (nin′ē) ***n.***, *pl.* **-nies** [prob. by syllabic merging and contr. of *an innocent*] a fool; dolt
ninth (nīnth) ***adj.*** [OE. *nigonthe*] **1.** preceded by eight others in a series; 9th **2.** designating any of the nine equal parts of something —***n.*** **1.** the one following the eighth **2.** any of the nine equal parts of something; 1/9 —**ninth′ly** ***adv.***
Ni·o·be (nī′ə bē′) *Gr. Myth.* a queen of Thebes, daughter of Tantalus, who, weeping for her slain children, was turned into a stone from which tears continued to flow
ni·o·bi·um (nī ō′bē əm) ***n.*** [ModL. < L. *Niobe*, NIOBE: from association with tantalum: see TANTALUM] a gray or white metallic chemical element used in chromium steels, in jet engines and rockets, etc.: symbol, Nb; at. wt., 92.906; at. no., 41
nip[1] (nip) ***vt.*** **nipped, nip′ping** [prob. < MLowG. *nippen* or ON. *hnippa*] **1.** to pinch or squeeze, as between two surfaces; bite **2.** to sever (shoots, etc.) as by pinching or clipping **3.** to check the growth of **4.** to have a painful or injurious effect on because of cold *[frost nipped the plants]* —***vi.*** to give a nip or nips —***n.*** **1.** a nipping; pinch; bite **2.** a piece nipped off **3.** a stinging quality, as in cold air **4.** stinging cold; frost —**nip and tuck** so close or critical as to leave the outcome in doubt
nip[2] (nip) ***n.*** [prob. < Du. < base of *nippen*, to sip] a small drink of liquor; dram; sip —***vt., vi.*** to drink (liquor) in nips
nip·per (nip′ər) ***n.*** **1.** anything that nips, or pinches **2.** [*pl.*] any of various tools for grasping or severing, as pliers, pincers, or forceps **3.** the pincerlike claw of a crab, lobster, etc. **4.** [Brit. Colloq.] a small boy
nip·ple (nip′'l) ***n.*** [prob. < dim. of NEB] **1.** the part of a breast or udder through which a baby or young animal sucks milk from its mother; teat **2.** a teatlike part, as of rubber, for a baby's bottle **3.** any projection or thing resembling a nipple in shape or function
Nip·pon (nip′än, ni pän′) *a Jap. name for* JAPAN —**Nip′-pon·ese′** (-ə nēz′) ***adj., n.***, *pl.* **-ese′**
nip·py (nip′ē) ***adj.*** **-pi·er, -pi·est** **1.** tending to nip **2.** cold in a stinging way —**nip′pi·ness** ***n.***
nir·va·na (nir vä′nə, nər-; -van′ə) ***n.*** [< Sans.] [*also* **N-**] *Buddhism* the state of perfect blessedness achieved by the extinction of the self and by the absorption of the soul into the supreme spirit, or by the extinction of all desires or passions

Ni·san (nē sän′, nis′ən) *n.* [Heb.] the seventh month of the Jewish year: see JEWISH CALENDAR
ni·sei (nē′sā) *n., pl.* **ni′sei, ni′seis** [Jap., lit., second generation] [*also* **N-**] a native U.S. or Canadian citizen born of immigrant Japanese parents
nit (nit) *n.* [OE. *hnitu*] **1.** the egg of a louse or similar insect **2.** a young louse, etc.
ni·ter (nīt′ər) *n.* [< MFr. < L. < Gr. *nitron*] *same as:* **1.** POTASSIUM NITRATE **2.** SODIUM NITRATE Also, chiefly Brit., **ni′tre**
nit-pick·ing (nit′pik′iŋ) *adj., n.* paying too much attention to petty details —**nit′-pick′er** *n.*
ni·trate (nī′trāt) *n.* [Fr. < *nitre,* NITER] **1.** a salt or ester of nitric acid **2.** potassium nitrate or sodium nitrate, used as a fertilizer —*vt.* **-trat·ed, -trat·ing** to treat or combine with nitric acid or a nitrate —**ni·tra′tion** *n.*
ni·tric (nī′trik) *adj.* **1.** of or containing nitrogen **2.** designating or of compounds in which nitrogen has a higher valence than in the corresponding nitrous compounds
nitric acid a colorless, corrosive acid, HNO_3
ni·tride (nī′trīd) *n.* [NITR(O)- + -IDE] a compound of nitrogen with a more electropositive element
ni·tri·fy (nī′trə fī′) *vt.* **-fied′, -fy′ing** [< Fr.: see NITER & -FY] **1.** to impregnate (soil, etc.) with nitrates **2.** to cause the oxidation of (ammonium salts, atmospheric nitrogen, etc.) to nitrites and nitrates, as by the action of soil bacteria, etc. —**ni′tri·fi·ca′tion** *n.* —**ni′tri·fi′er** *n.*
ni·trite (nī′trīt) *n.* a salt or ester of nitrous acid
ni·tro- [see NITER] *a combining form used to indicate:* **1.** the presence of nitrogen compounds made as by the action of nitric or nitrous acid *[nitrocellulose]* **2.** the presence of the NO_2 radical *[nitrobenzene]* Also, before a vowel, **nitr-**
ni·tro·ben·zene (nī′trō ben′zēn) *n.* a poisonous yellow liquid, $C_6H_5NO_2$, prepared by treating benzene with nitric acid, used in dyes, etc.
ni·tro·cel·lu·lose (-sel′yoo lōs′) *n.* a substance produced by the action of nitric acid upon wood, cotton, etc.: used in making explosives, plastics, etc. —**ni′tro·cel′lu·los′ic** *adj.*
ni·tro·gen (nī′trə jən) *n.* [< Fr.: see NITRO- & -GEN] a colorless, tasteless, odorless gaseous chemical element forming nearly four fifths of the atmosphere: it is a component of all living things: symbol N; at. wt., 14.0067; at. no., 7 —**ni·trog·e·nous** (nī träj′ə nəs) *adj.*
nitrogen dioxide a poisonous, reddish-brown gas, NO_2, used in making nitric acid, as a rocket-fuel oxidizer, etc.
nitrogen fixation 1. the conversion of atmospheric nitrogen into nitrates by soil bacteria (**nitrogen fixers**) in the nodules of legumes **2.** the conversion of free nitrogen into useful nitrogenous compounds by various industrial processes —**ni′tro·gen-fix′ing** *adj.*
ni·trog·e·nize (nī träj′ə nīz′, nī′trə jə-) *vt.* **-nized′, -niz′ing** to combine with nitrogen or its compounds
nitrogen mustard any of a class of compounds similar to mustard gas, used in cancer research and treatment
ni·tro·glyc·er·in, ni·tro·glyc·er·ine (nī′trə glis′ər in, -trō-) *n.* a thick, explosive oil, $C_3H_5(ONO_2)_3$, prepared by treating glycerin with a mixture of nitric and sulfuric acids: used in medicine and in making dynamites and propellants
ni·trous (nī′trəs) *adj.* **1.** of, like, or containing niter **2.** designating or of compounds in which nitrogen has a lower valence than in the corresponding nitric compounds
nitrous acid an acid, HNO_2, known only in solution or in the form of its salts (*nitrites*)
nitrous oxide a colorless, nonflammable gas, N_2O, used as an anesthetic and in aerosols
nit·ty (nit′ē) *adj.* **-ti·er, -ti·est** full of nits
nit·ty-grit·ty (-grit′ē) *n.* [rhyming extension of GRITTY] [Slang] the actual, basic facts, elements, issues, etc.
nit·wit (nit′wit′) *n.* [*nit* (< G. dial. for G. *nicht,* not) or ? NIT + WIT[1]] a stupid person
nix[1] (niks) *n., pl.* **nix′es,** G. **nix′e** (nik′sə) [G.] *Germanic Myth.* a water sprite —**nix·ie** (nik′sē) *n.fem.*
nix[2] (niks) *adv.* [G. *nichts*] [Slang] **1.** no; not so **2.** not at all —*interj.* [Slang] an exclamation meaning: **1.** stop! **2.** I forbid, refuse, disagree, etc. —*n.* [Slang] **1.** nothing **2.** rejection —*vt.* [Slang] to disapprove of or put a stop to
Nix·on (nik′s′n), **Richard M(ilhous)** 1913– ; 37th president of the U.S. (1969–74)
N.J., NJ New Jersey
NLRB, N.L.R.B. National Labor Relations Board
N.Mex. New Mexico: also **NM, N.M.**
NNE, N.N.E., n.n.e. north-northeast
NNW, N.N.W., n.n.w. north-northwest
no[1] (nō) *adv.* [OE. *na* < *ne a,* lit., not ever] **1.** [Scot. or Rare] not *[*whether or *no]* **2.** not in any degree *[no* worse*]* **3.** nay; not so: the opposite of YES, used to deny, refuse, or disagree —*adj.* not any; not a *[no* errors*]* —*n., pl.* **noes, nos 1.** refusal or denial **2.** a negative vote or voter

no[2] (nō) *n., pl.* **no** [Jap. *nō*] [*often* **N-**] a classic form of Japanese drama with music and dancing
No *Chem.* nobelium
No. 1. north **2.** northern **3.** number: also **no.**
NOAA National Oceanic and Atmospheric Administration
no-ac·count (nō′ə kount′) *adj.* [Colloq.] worthless; good-for-nothing —*n.* a shiftless person
No·ah (nō′ə) [Heb. *nōah,* lit., rest, comfort] **1.** a masculine name **2.** *Bible* the patriarch commanded by God to build the ark on which he, his family, and two of every kind of creature survived the Flood: Gen. 5:28–10:32
nob·by (näb′ē) *adj.* **-bi·er, -bi·est** [< ? slang *nob,* the head] [Chiefly Brit. Slang] stylish
No·bel (nō bel′), **Al·fred Bern·hard** (äl′fred ber′närd) 1833–96; Swed. industrialist & inventor of dynamite: established the Nobel prizes
No·bel·ist (nō bel′ist) *n.* a person who has been awarded a Nobel prize
no·bel·i·um (nō bel′ē əm) *n.* [after *Nobel* Institute in Stockholm, where discovered] a radioactive chemical element produced by the nuclear bombardment of curium: symbol, No; at. wt., 255(?); at. no., 102
Nobel prizes annual international prizes given by the Nobel Foundation for distinction in physics, chemistry, medicine, economics, and literature, and for promoting peace
no·bil·i·ty (nō bil′ə tē) *n., pl.* **-ties 1.** a being noble **2.** high station or rank in society **3.** the class of people of noble rank: in Great Britain, the peerage (with *the*)
no·ble (nō′b′l) *adj.* **-bler, -blest** [OFr. < L. *nobilis,* lit., well-known] **1.** famous or renowned **2.** having or showing high moral qualities **3.** having excellent qualities **4.** grand; stately *[a noble* view*]* **5.** of high rank or title; aristocratic —*n.* a person having hereditary rank or title; nobleman; peer —**no′ble·ness** *n.* —**no′bly** *adv.*
no·ble·man (-mən) *n., pl.* **-men** a member of the nobility; peer —**no′ble·wom′an** *n.fem., pl.* **-wom′en**
no·blesse o·blige (nō bles′ ō blēzh′) [Fr., lit., nobility obliges] the obligation of people of high rank or social position to be kind and generous
no·bod·y (nō′bud′ē, -bäd′ē, -bəd ē) *pron.* not anybody; no one —*n., pl.* **-bod′ies** a person of no importance
nock (näk) *n.* [< Scand.] **1.** a notch for holding the string at either end of a bow **2.** the notch in the end of an arrow, for the bowstring
noc·tu·id (näk′choo wid) *n.* [< ModL. < L. *noctua,* night owl < *nox,* night] any of a large family of moths which fly at night, including many of those flying into lighted houses
noc·tur·nal (näk tur′n′l) *adj.* [LL. *nocturnalis* < L. < *nox,* night] **1.** of, done, or happening in the night **2.** active during the night —**noc·tur′nal·ly** *adv.*
noc·turne (näk′tərn) *n.* [Fr.] **1.** a painting of a night scene **2.** a romantic, dreamy musical composition, appropriate to night
nod (näd) *vi.* **nod′ded, nod′ding** [ME. *nodden*] **1.** to bend the head forward quickly, as in agreement, greeting, command, etc. **2.** to let the head fall forward involuntarily because of drowsiness **3.** to be careless; make a slip **4.** to sway to and fro, as plumes —*vt.* **1.** to bend (the head) forward quickly **2.** to signify (assent, approval, etc.) by doing this —*n.* **1.** a nodding **2.** [**N-**] the imaginary realm of sleep and dreams: usually **land of Nod**
nodding acquaintance a slight, not intimate, acquaintance with a person or thing
nod·dy (näd′ē) *n., pl.* **-dies** [< ? NOD] **1.** a fool; simpleton **2.** a tropical sea bird with dark feathers and a short tail
node (nōd) *n.* [L. *nodus,* knot] **1.** a knot; knob; swelling **2.** a central point **3.** *Astron.* either of the two diametrically opposite points at which the orbit of a heavenly body intersects a fundamental plane **4.** *Bot.* that part of a stem from which a leaf starts to grow **5.** *Physics* the point, line, or surface of a vibrating object where there is comparatively no vibration —**nod′al** *adj.*

VIBRATING STRING
N N
L L L

NODES
(N, nodes formed when vibrating string is stopped at intervals along its length; L, loops between nodes)

nod·ule (näj′ool) *n.* [L. *nodulus,* dim of *nodus,* a knot] **1.** a small knot or rounded lump **2.** *Bot.* a knot on a root, containing nitrogen-fixing bacteria —**nod′u·lar, nod′u·lose, nod′u·lous** *adj.*
no·el, no·ël (nō el′) *n.* [Fr. *noël* < OFr. < L. *natalis,* NATAL] **1.** a Christmas carol **2.** [**N-**] *same as* CHRISTMAS
no-fault (nō′fôlt′) *adj.* **1.** designating or of insurance in which the victim of an accident collects damages although blame for the accident is not established **2.** designating a divorce granted without blame being indicated

nog, nogg (näg) ***n.*** [< East Anglian dial.] **1.** [Brit.] a strong ale **2.** *same as* EGGNOG

nog·gin (näg′in) ***n.*** [prob. < prec.] **1.** a small cup or mug **2.** one fourth of a pint: a measure for ale or liquor **3.** [Colloq.] the head

no-good (nō′good′) ***adj.*** [Slang] contemptible

No·gu·chi (nō go͞o′chē), **Hi·de·yo** (hē′de yō′) 1876–1928; Jap. bacteriologist in the U.S.

no-hit·ter (nō′hit′ər) ***n.*** a baseball game in which the pitcher allows the opposing team no base hits

no·how (nō′hou′) ***adv.*** [Dial.] in no manner

noise (noiz) ***n.*** [OFr. < L. *nausea:* see NAUSEA] **1.** *a)* loud shouting; clamor *b)* any loud, disagreeable sound **2.** sound *[*the *noise* of rain*]* **3.** any unwanted electrical signal within a communication system —***vt.*** **noised, nois′ing** to spread (a report, rumor, etc.)

noise·less (-lis) ***adj.*** with little or no noise; silent —**noise′less·ly** ***adv.*** —**noise′less·ness** ***n.***

noi·some (noi′səm) ***adj.*** [see ANNOY & -SOME[1]] **1.** injurious to health; harmful **2.** foul-smelling; offensive —**noi′some·ly** ***adv.*** —**noi′some·ness** ***n.***

nois·y (noi′zē) ***adj.*** **nois′i·er, nois′i·est** **1.** making noise **2.** making more sound than is expected or customary **3.** full of noise; clamorous —**nois′i·ly** ***adv.*** —**nois′i·ness** ***n.***

‡**no·lens vo·lens** (nō′lenz vō′lenz) [L.] unwilling (or) willing; whether or not one wishes it

nol·le pros·e·qui (näl′ē präs′ə kwī′) [L., to be unwilling to prosecute] *Law* formal notice that prosecution in a criminal case or civil suit will be partly or entirely ended

no·lo con·ten·de·re (nō′lō kən ten′də rē) [L., I do not wish to contest (it)] *Law* a plea by the defendant in a criminal case declaring that he will not make a defense, but not admitting guilt

nol-pros (näl′präs′) ***vt.*** **-prossed′, -pros′sing** [< abbrev. of NOLLE PROSEQUI] to abandon (all or part of a suit) by entering a nolle prosequi on the court records

nom. nominative

no·mad (nō′mad) ***n.*** [< L. < Gr. < *nemein,* to pasture] **1.** a member of a tribe or people having no permanent home, but moving about constantly in search of food, pasture, etc. **2.** a wanderer —***adj.*** wandering: also **no·mad′ic** —**no·mad′i·cal·ly** ***adv.*** —**no′mad·ism** ***n.***

no man's land **1.** a piece of land to which no one has a recognized title **2.** the area on a battlefield separating the combatants **3.** an indefinite area of operation, involvement, etc.

nom de guerre (näm′ də ger′) *pl.* **noms′ de guerre′** [Fr., lit., a war name] a pseudonym

nom de plume (näm′ də plo͞om′) *pl.* **noms′ de plume′** [Fr.] a pen name; pseudonym

Nome (nōm) [< nearby Cape *Nome,* prob. < *? name,* query on an early map, misread as *C. Nome*] city in W Alas., on the Bering Sea: pop. 2,500

no·men·cla·ture (nō′mən klā′chər) ***n.*** [< L. < *nomen,* name + pp. of *calare,* to call] **1.** the system of names used in a branch of learning, or for the parts of a mechanism **2.** a system of naming

nom·i·nal (näm′i n′l) ***adj.*** [< L. < *nomen,* a name] **1.** of, or having the nature of, a name **2.** of or having to do with a noun **3.** in name only, not in fact *[*the *nominal* leader*]* **4.** relatively very small *[*a *nominal* fee*]* —***n.*** a noun; also, any word or phrase, as an adjective, used like a noun —**nom′i·nal·ly** ***adv.***

nom·i·nate (näm′ə nāt′) ***vt.*** **-nat′ed, -nat′ing** [< L. < pp. of *nominare* < *nomen,* a name] **1.** to name or appoint to an office or position **2.** *a)* to name as a candidate for election or appointment *b)* to propose as a candidate for an award or honor —**nom′i·na′tion** ***n.*** —**nom′i·na′tor** ***n.***

nom·i·na·tive (näm′ə nə tiv; *for adj. 1, also* -nāt′iv) ***adj.*** **1.** named or appointed to a position or office **2.** *Gram.* designating or of the case of the subject of a finite verb and the words (appositives, predicate adjectives, etc.) that agree with it; active case —***n.*** **1.** the nominative case **2.** a word in this case

nom·i·nee (näm′ə nē′) ***n.*** [NOMIN(ATE) + -EE] a person who is nominated, esp. a candidate for election

-no·my [< Gr. < *nomos,* law] *a combining form meaning* the systematized knowledge of *[astronomy]*

non- [< L. *non,* not] *a prefix meaning* not: used to give a negative force, esp. to nouns, adjectives, and adverbs: *non-* is less emphatic than *in-* and *un-*, which often give a word an opposite meaning (Ex.: *nonhuman, inhuman*) The list below includes the more common compounds formed with *non-* that do not have special meanings; they will be understood if *not* is used before the meaning of the base word

non·age (nän′ij, nō′nij) ***n.*** [< Anglo-Fr. < OFr.: see NON- & AGE] **1.** *Law* the state of being under full legal age, usually twenty-one **2.** the period of immaturity

non·a·ge·nar·i·an (nän′ə ji ner′ē ən, nō′nə-) ***adj.*** [< L. < *nonaginta,* ninety] ninety years old, or between the ages of ninety and one hundred —***n.*** a person of this age

non·ag·gres·sion pact (nän′ə gresh′ən) an agreement between two nations not to attack each other, usually for a specified period of years

non·a·gon (nän′ə gän′) ***n.*** [< L. *nonus,* ninth + -GON] a polygon with nine angles and nine sides

non·a·ligned (nän′ə līnd′) ***adj.*** not aligned with either side in a conflict —**non′a·lign′ment** ***n.***

nonce (näns) ***n.*** [ME. (*for the*) *nones,* formed by syllabic merging < (*for then*) *ones,* lit., for the once] the present use, occasion, or time; time being: chiefly in **for the nonce**

nonce word a word coined and used for a single or particular occasion

non·cha·lant (nän′shə länt′, nän′shə lənt) ***adj.*** [Fr. < *non,* not + *chaloir,* to care for < L. *calere,* to be warm] **1.** without warmth or enthusiasm **2.** showing cool lack of concern; casually indifferent —**non′cha·lance′** ***n.*** —**non′cha·lant′ly** ***adv.***

non·com (nän′käm′) ***n.*** *colloq. clipped form of* NONCOMMISSIONED OFFICER

non·com·bat·ant (nän käm′bə tənt, nän′kəm bat′ənt) ***n.*** **1.** a member of the armed forces whose activities do not include actual combat, as a chaplain **2.** any civilian in wartime —***adj.*** of noncombatants

non·com·mis·sioned officer (nän′kə mish′ənd) an enlisted person of any of various grades in the armed forces, as, in the U.S. Army, from corporal to sergeant major: see also PETTY OFFICER

non·com·mit·tal (-kə mit′'l) ***adj.*** not committing one to any point of view or course of action —**non′com·mit′tal·ly** ***adv.***

non·com·pli·ance (-kəm plī′əns) ***n.*** failure or refusal to comply —**non′com·pli′ant** ***adj.***

non com·pos men·tis (nän′ käm′pəs men′tis) [L.] *Law* not of sound mind; mentally incapable of handling one's own affairs: often **non compos**

---

nonabrasive
nonabsorbent
nonacademic
nonacceptance
nonacid
nonactinic
nonactive
nonaddictive
nonadjacent
nonadjectival
nonadjustable
nonadministrative
nonadvantageous
nonadverbial
nonaesthetic
nonaffiliated
non-African
nonaggressive
nonagreement
nonagricultural
nonalcoholic
nonalgebraic
nonallergenic
nonallergic
nonalphabetic
nonamendable
non-American
nonanalytic
non-Anglican
nonantagonistic
nonapologetic
nonapostolic
nonappearance
nonappearing
nonapplicable
nonaquatic
non-Arab
non-Arabic
nonaristocratic
nonarithmetical
nonartistic
non-Aryan
non-Asiatic
nonassertive
nonassessable
nonassignable
nonassimilable
nonassimilation
nonathletic
nonatmospheric
nonattendance
nonattributive
nonautomatic
nonbacterial
nonbasic
nonbeliever
nonbelieving
nonbelligerent
non-Biblical
nonblooming
nonbreakable
non-British
non-Buddhist
nonbudding
nonbureaucratic
nonburnable
nonbusiness
noncaloric
noncancerous
noncanonical
noncapitalistic
noncarbonated
noncarnivorous
noncategorical
non-Catholic
non-Caucasoid
noncellular
noncereal
noncertified
nonchargeable
nonchemical
non-Christian
noncitizen
noncivilized
nonclassical
nonclassifiable
nonclerical
nonclinical
noncoagulating
noncoalescing
noncoercive
noncohesive
noncollapsible
noncollectable
noncollectible
noncollegiate
noncombat
noncombining
noncombustible
noncommercial
noncommunicable
noncommunicant
noncommunicating
non-Communist
noncompensating
noncompetency
noncompetent
noncompeting
noncompetitive
noncomplacent
noncompletion
noncomplying

non·con·duc·tor (nän′kən duk′tər) ***n.*** a substance that does not readily transmit certain forms of energy, as electricity, sound, heat, etc.

non·con·form·ist (-kən fôr′mist) ***adj.*** not following established customs, beliefs, etc. —***n.*** a person who is nonconformist; esp. [**N-**], a Protestant in England who is not a member of the Anglican Church —**non′con·form′ism, non′con·form′i·ty** ***n.***

non·co·op·er·a·tion (-kō äp′ə rā′shən) ***n.*** **1.** failure to work together or act jointly **2.** refusal to cooperate with a government, as by nonpayment of taxes: used as a form of protest —**non′co·op′er·a′tion·ist** ***n.*** —**non′co·op′er·a·tive** ***adj.*** —**non′co·op′er·a′tor** ***n.***

non·de·script (nän′di skript′, nän′di skript′) ***adj.*** [< L. *non*, not + pp. of *describere*, DESCRIBE] belonging to no definite class or type; hard to classify or describe —***n.*** a nondescript person or thing

non·du·ra·ble goods (-door′ə b'l, -dyoor′-) goods usable for a relatively short time, as food, apparel, or fabrics: also **nondurables** ***n.pl.***

none[1] (nun) ***pron.*** [OE. *nan* < *ne*, not + *an*, one] **1.** no one; not anyone *[none* but Jack can do it*]* **2.** [*usually with pl. v.*] no persons or things; not any *[*there are *none* on the table*]* —***n.*** no part; nothing *[*I want *none* of it*]* —***adv.*** in no way; not at all *[none* the worse for wear*]*

none[2] (nōn) ***n.*** [OE. *non:* see NOON] *Eccles.* [*often* **N-**] the fifth of the canonical hours

non·en·ti·ty (nän en′tə tē) ***n.***, *pl.* **-ties** **1.** the state of not existing **2.** something that exists only in the mind **3.** a person of no importance

nones (nōnz) ***n.pl.*** [< L. < *nonus*, ninth < *novem*, nine] **1.** in the ancient Roman calendar, the ninth day before the ides of a month **2.** *same as* NONE[2]

non·es·sen·tial (nän′i sen′shəl) ***adj.*** not essential; of relatively no importance; unnecessary —***n.*** a nonessential person or thing

none·such (nun′such′) ***n.*** a person or thing unrivaled or unequaled; nonpareil

none·the·less (nun′*th*ə les′) ***adv.*** in spite of that; nevertheless: also **none the less**

non-Eu·clid·e·an (nän′yoo klid′ē ən) ***adj.*** designating or of a geometry that rejects any of Euclid's postulates

non·fea·sance (nän fē′z'ns) ***n.*** *Law* failure to do what duty requires to be done

non·fer·rous (-fer′əs) ***adj.*** **1.** not made of or containing iron **2.** designating or of metals other than iron

non·he·ro (nän′hir′ō) ***n.*** *same as* ANTIHERO

no·nil·lion (nō nil′yən) ***n.*** [Fr. < L. *nonus*, ninth + Fr. *million*] **1.** in the U.S. and France, the number represented by 1 followed by 30 zeros **2.** in Great Britain and Germany, the number represented by 1 followed by 54 zeros —***adj.*** amounting to one nonillion in number

non·in·ter·ven·tion (nän′in tər ven′shən) ***n.*** the state or fact of not intervening; esp., a refraining by one nation from interference in the affairs of another —**non′in·ter·ven′tion·ist** ***adj.***, ***n.***

---

noncompressible
noncompression
noncompulsory
nonconciliating
nonconclusive
nonconcurrence
noncondensing
nonconducive
nonconducting
nonconferrable
nonconfidential
nonconflicting
nonconformance
nonconforming
noncongealing
noncongenital
non-Congressional
nonconnective
nonconscious
nonconsecutive
nonconsent
nonconservative
nonconstitutional
nonconstructive
nonconsultative
noncontagious
noncontemporary
noncontentious
noncontiguous
noncontinental
noncontinuance
noncontinuous
noncontraband
noncontradictory
noncontributory
noncontrolled
noncontroversial
nonconventional
nonconvergent
nonconvertible
nonconviction
noncoordinating
noncorrective
noncorresponding
noncorrodible
noncorroding
noncorrosive
noncreative
noncriminal
noncritical
noncrucial
noncrystalline
nonculpable
noncumulative
noncurrent
nondamageable
nondecaying
nondeceptive
nondeciduous
nondeductible
nondefamatory
nondefensive
nondefilement
nondefining
nondehiscent
nondelivery
nondemand
nondemocratic
nondenominational
nondepartmental
nondeparture
nondependence
nondepositor
nondepreciating
nonderivative
nonderogatory
nondestructive
nondetachable
nondetonating
nondevelopment
nondevotional
nondialectal
nondictatorial
nondidactic
nondifferentiation
nondiffractive
nondiffusible
nondiffusing
nondiplomatic
nondirectional
nondisappearing
nondischarging
nondisciplinary
nondiscrimination
nondiscriminatory
nondisparaging
nondisposal
nondistinctive
nondivergent
nondivisible
nondoctrinal
nondocumentary
nondogmatic
nondramatic
nondrinker
nondriver
nondrying
nondutiable
nondynastic
nonearning
nonecclesiastical
noneconomic
nonedible
noneditorial
noneducable
noneducational
noneffective
nonefficient
nonelastic
nonelective
nonelectric
nonelectrolyte
nonemotional
nonendemic
nonenforceable
non-English
nonentailed
nonepiscopal
nonequal
nonequivalent
nonerotic
noneternal
nonethical
noneugenic
non-European
nonevangelical
nonevolutionary
nonexchangeable
nonexclusive
nonexcusable
nonexecutive
nonexempt
nonexistence
nonexistent
nonexpansive
nonexpendable
nonexperienced
nonexperimental
nonexpert
nonexplosive
nonexportable
nonextension
nonextraditable
nonfactual
nonfading
nonfat
nonfatal
nonfatalistic
nonfattening
nonfederal
nonfederated
nonfertile
nonfestive
nonfiction
nonfictional
nonfigurative
nonfilterable
nonfinancial
nonfireproof
nonfiscal
nonfissionable
nonflammable
nonflowering
nonflowing
nonfluctuating
nonflying
nonfocal
nonforfeiture
nonformal
nonfreezing
non-French
nonfulfillment
nonfunctional
nonfundamental
nongaseous
nongenetic
non-Germanic
nongovernmental
nongranular
non-Greek
nongregarious
nonhabitable
nonhabitual
nonhabituating
nonhazardous
non-Hellenic
nonhereditary
nonheritable
nonhistoric
nonhuman
nonhumorous
nonidentical
nonidiomatic
nonimaginary
nonimitative
nonimmune
nonimmunized
nonimportation
nonimpregnated
noninclusive
nonindependent
non-Indian
nonindictable
nonindividualistic
nonindustrial
noninfected
noninfectious
noninflammable
noninflammatory
noninflationary
noninflectional
noninformative
noninheritable
noninjurious
noninstructional
noninstrumental
nonintegrated
nonintellectual
nonintelligent
nonintercourse
noninterference
noninternational
nonintersecting
nonintoxicant
nonintoxicating
nonintuitive

---

non·ju·ror (nän joor′ər) ***n.*** a person who refuses to take an oath of allegiance, as to his ruler or government —**non·ju′ring** ***adj.***

non·met·al (-met′'l) ***n.*** an element lacking the characteristics of a metal; specif., any of the elements (e.g., oxygen, carbon, nitrogen, fluorine) whose oxides form acids —**non′me·tal′lic** ***adj.***

non·mor·al (-môr′əl, -mär′-) ***adj.*** not connected in any way with morality; not moral and not immoral

non·nu·cle·ar (-no͞o′klē ər) ***adj.*** not nuclear; specif., not operated by or using nuclear energy

non·ob·jec·tive (nän′əb jek′tiv) ***adj.*** *same as* NONREPRESENTATIONAL —**non′ob·jec′tiv·ism** ***n.***

non·pa·reil (nän′pə rel′) ***adj.*** [Fr. < *non,* not + *pareil,* equal, ult. < L. *par,* equal] unequaled; peerless —***n.*** **1.** someone or something unequaled or unrivaled **2.** a small wafer of chocolate covered with tiny sugar pellets **3.** *Printing* a size of type between agate and minion; 6 point

non·par·ti·san (nän pär′tə z'n) ***adj.*** not partisan; esp., not controlled by, or supporting, any single political party: also **non·par′ti·zan** —**non·par′ti·san·ship′** ***n.***

non·per·son (nän′pur′s'n) ***n.*** a person who is officially ignored by the government of his country

non·plus (nän plus′, nän′plus′) ***n.*** [L. *non,* not + *plus,* more] a condition of perplexity in which one is unable to go, speak, or act further —***vt.*** **-plused′** or **-plussed′, -plus′ing** or **-plus′sing** to put in a nonplus; bewilder

non·pro·duc·tive (nän′prə duk′tiv) ***adj.*** **1.** not productive **2.** not directly related to the production of goods, as clerks, salesmen, etc. —**non′pro·duc′tive·ly** ***adv.***

non·prof·it (nän präf′it) ***adj.*** not intending or intended to earn a profit

non·pro·lif·er·a·tion (nän′prō lif′ə rā′shən) ***n.*** a not proliferating; specif., the limitation of production of nuclear weapons

non-pros (-präs′) ***vt.*** **-prossed′, -pros′sing** to enter a judgment of non prosequitur against (a plaintiff or his suit)

non pro·se·qui·tur (nän′ prō sek′wi tər) [L., he does not prosecute] *Law* a judgment entered against a plaintiff who fails to appear at the court proceedings of his suit

non·rat·ed (nän rāt′id) ***adj.*** *U.S. Navy* designating an enlisted man who is not a petty officer

non·rep·re·sen·ta·tion·al (nän′rep ri zən tā′shən 'l) ***adj.*** designating or of art that does not attempt to represent in recognizable form any object in nature; abstract —**non′rep·re·sen·ta′tion·al·ism** ***n.***

non·res·i·dent (nän rez′ə dənt) ***adj.*** not residing in a specified place; esp., not residing in the locality where one works, attends school, etc. —***n.*** a nonresident person —**non·res′i·dence, non·res′i·den·cy** ***n.*** —**non′res·i·den′tial** ***adj.***

non·re·sist·ant (nän′ri zis′tənt) ***adj.*** not resistant; submitting to force or arbitrary authority —***n.*** a person who believes that force should not be used to oppose arbitrary authority, however unjust —**non′re·sist′ance** ***n.***

non·re·stric·tive (-ri strik′tiv) ***adj.*** *Gram.* designating a clause, phrase, or word felt as not essential to the sense, or purely descriptive, and hence usually set off by commas (Ex.: John, *who is six feet tall,* is younger than Bill)

non·sched·uled (nän skej′oold) ***adj.*** designating or of an airline, plane, etc. making commercial flights on demand, not on a regular schedule

non·sec·tar·i·an (nän′sek ter′ē ən) ***adj.*** not sectarian; not confined to any specific religion

non·sense (nän′sens, -səns) ***n.*** [NON- + SENSE] **1.** words or actions that convey an absurd meaning or no meaning at all **2.** things of relatively no importance or value **3.** impudent or foolish behavior —***adj.*** designating or of syllables or words constructed so as to have no meaning —***interj.*** how foolish! how absurd!

non·sen·si·cal (nän sen′si k'l) ***adj.*** unintelligible, foolish, absurd, etc. —**non·sen′si·cal·ly** ***adv.***

non se·qui·tur (nän′ sek′wi tər) [L., lit., it does not follow] **1.** a conclusion or inference that does not follow

---

noninvolvement
noniodized
nonionized
nonirradiated
nonirritant
nonirritating
non-Islamic
non-Jewish
nonjudicial
non-Latin
nonlegal
nonlethal
nonlicensed
nonlinear
nonliquefying
nonliquid
nonliquidating
nonliterary
nonliterate
nonliving
nonlocal
nonmagnetic
nonmailable
nonmaintenance
nonmalignant
nonmalleable
nonmarital
nonmaritime
nonmarrying
nonmartial
nonmaterial
nonmaterialistic
nonmaternal
nonmathematical
nonmechanical
nonmedicinal
nonmelodious
nonmember
nonmercantile
nonmetaphysical
nonmetropolitan
nonmigratory
nonmilitant
nonmilitary
nonmineral
nonmortal
non-Moslem
nonmotile
nonmunicipal
nonmuscular
nonmystical
nonmythical
nonnarcotic
nonnational
nonnative
nonnatural
nonnavigable
nonnegotiable
non-Negro
nonneutral
nonnucleated
nonnutritious
nonnutritive
nonobedience
nonobligatory
nonobservance
nonobservant
nonobstructive
nonoccupational
nonoccurrence
nonodorous
nonofficial
nonoperating
nonoperational
nonoperative
non-Oriental
nonorthodox
nonoxidizing
nonoxygenated
nonpalatal
nonpapal
nonparallel
nonparasitic
nonparental
nonparishioner
nonparliamentary
nonparochial
nonparticipant
nonpaying
nonpayment
nonperceptual
nonperforated
nonperformance
nonperiodical
nonperishable
nonpermanent
nonpermeable
nonpermissible
nonperpendicular
nonpersecution
nonpersistent
nonphilosophical
nonphysical
nonphysiological
nonplastic
nonpoetic
nonpoisonous
nonpolitical
nonporous
nonpossession
nonpredatory
nonpredictable
nonpreferential
nonprejudicial
nonprescriptive
nonproducer
nonprofessional
nonprofessorial
nonprofitable
nonprogressive
nonprohibitive
nonprolific
nonprophetic
nonproportional
nonproprietary
nonproscriptive
nonprotective
nonprotein
non-Protestant
nonpsychic
nonpublic
nonpuncturable
nonpunishable
nonpurulent
nonracial
nonradiating
nonradical
nonradioactive
nonratable
nonrational
nonreactive
nonreader
nonrealistic
nonreality
nonreciprocal
nonreciprocating
nonrecognition
nonrecoverable
nonrecurrent
nonrecurring
nonredeemable
nonrefillable
nonregenerating
nonregimented
nonregistered
nonregistrable
nonregulation
nonreigning
nonrelative
nonreligious
nonremovable
nonrenewable
nonrepayable
nonrepentance
nonrepresentative
nonreproductive
nonresidual
nonresonant
nonrestricted
nonretentive
nonretiring
nonretractile
nonreturnable
nonreversible
nonrevertible
nonrevolving
nonrhetorical
nonrhyming
nonrhythmic
nonrigid
nonritualistic
nonrival
non-Roman
nonromantic
nonrotating
nonroyal
nonrural
nonsacred
nonsacrificial
nonsalable
nonsalaried
nonsalutary
nonsaturated
non-Scandinavian
nonscholastic
nonscientific
nonscoring
nonseasonal
nonsecret
nonsecretory
nonsectional
nonsecular
nonsedentary
nonseditious
nonsegregated
nonsegregation
nonselective
non-Semitic
nonsensitive
nonsensitized
nonsensory
nonsensuous

from the premises 2. a remark having no bearing on what has just been said
non·skid (nän′skid′) ***adj.*** so constructed as to reduce skidding: said of a tire tread, etc.
non·stand·ard (nän stan′dərd) ***adj.*** not standard; specif., designating or of locutions, pronunciations, etc. not considered to be standard speech, as slang usages, obscenities, etc.
non·stop (-stäp′) ***adj., adv.*** without a stop
non·such (nun′such′) ***n.*** *same as* NONESUCH
non·suit (nän′so͞ot′) ***n.*** [< Anglo-Fr.: see NON- & SUIT] *Law* a judgment against a plaintiff due to his failure to proceed to trial or to establish a valid case or adequate evidence —***vt.*** to bring a nonsuit against (a plaintiff or his case)
non·sup·port (nän′sə pôrt′) ***n.*** failure to provide for a legal dependent
non trop·po (nän trō′pō) [It.] *Music* not too much; moderately
non·un·ion (nän yo͞on′yən) ***n.*** failure to mend or unite: said of a broken bone —***adj.*** **1.** not belonging to a labor union **2.** not made or serviced under conditions required by a labor union **3.** refusing to recognize a labor union —**non·un′ion·ism** ***n.*** —**non·un′ion·ist** ***n.***
non·vi·o·lence (-vī′ə ləns) ***n.*** an abstaining from violence or physical force, as in opposing government policy —**non·vi′o·lent** ***adj.***
non·vot·er (nän vōt′ər) ***n.*** a person who does not vote or is not permitted to vote —**non·vot′ing** ***adj.***
noo·dle[1] (no͞o′d'l) ***n.*** [prob. < earlier *noddle,* the head] **1.** a simpleton; fool **2.** [Slang] the head
noo·dle[2] (no͞o′d'l) ***n.*** [G. *nudel*] a flat, narrow strip of dry dough, usually made with egg and served in soup, etc.
noo·dle[3] (no͞o′d'l) ***vi.*** **-dled, -dling** [prob. var. of DOODLE] [Colloq.] **1.** to play idly or improvise on a musical instrument **2.** to explore an idea
nook (no͝ok) ***n.*** [ME. *nok*] **1.** a corner, esp. of a room **2.** a small recess or secluded spot
noon (no͞on) ***n.*** [OE. *non* < L. *nona* (*hora*), ninth (hour): cf. NONES, now recited at midday] **1.** twelve o'clock in the daytime; midday **2.** the highest point or culmination —***adj.*** of or occurring at noon (midday)
noon·day (-dā′) ***n., adj.*** noon (midday)
no one no person; not anybody; nobody
noon·time (-tīm′) ***n., adj.*** noon (midday): also **noon′tide′**
noose (no͞os) ***n.*** [prob. via Pr. < L. *nodus*] **1.** a loop formed in a rope, cord, etc. by means of a slipknot so that the loop tightens as the rope is pulled **2.** anything that restricts one's freedom; tie, bond, etc. —***vt.*** **noosed, noos′ing** **1.** to catch or hold as in a noose **2.** to form a noose in (a rope, etc.) —**the noose** death by hanging
no-par (nō′pär′) ***adj.*** having no stated par value [*a no-par certificate of stock*]
nope (nōp) ***adv.*** [Slang] no: a negative reply
nor (nôr; *unstressed* nər) ***conj.*** [ME., contr. of *nother,* neither] and not; and not either: used as the second of the correlatives *neither. . . nor* or after some other negative [*I can neither go nor stay; not for sale, nor for rent*]
nor′, nor (nôr) north: used especially in compounds [*nor'western*]
Nor. **1.** North **2.** Norway **3.** Norwegian
No·ra (nôr′ə) [Ir., dim. of ELEANOR] a feminine name
Nor·dic (nôr′dik) ***adj.*** [< ModL. < Fr. < *nord,* north < OE. *north*] designating or of a physical type of the Caucasoid peoples exemplified by the long-headed, tall, blond people of Scandinavia
nor·ep·i·neph·rine (nôr′ep′ə nef′rin, -rēn) ***n.*** [< NOR(MAL) + EPINEPHRINE] a hormone, $C_8H_{11}NO_3$, of the adrenal medulla, that constricts blood vessels, helps transmit nerve impulses, etc.
Nor·folk (nôr′fək) [after *Norfolk,* county in England] seaport in SE Va., on Hampton Roads & Chesapeake Bay: pop. 267,000
Norfolk jacket (or **coat**) a loose-fitting, single-breasted, belted jacket with box pleats
Nor·ge (nôr′gə) *Norw. name of* NORWAY
no·ri·a (nôr′ē ə) ***n.*** [Sp. < Ar. *nā'ūrah*] in Spain and the Orient, a water wheel with buckets at its circumference to raise and discharge water

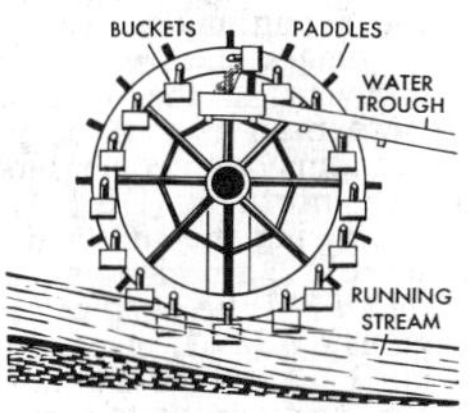

NORIA

norm (nôrm) ***n.*** [< L. *norma,* carpenter's square] a standard, model, or pattern; esp., *a*) a standard of achievement as represented by the average achievement of a large group *b*) an ideal standard of conduct or one typical of a certain group
Norm. Norman
Nor·ma (nôr′mə) [< ? L. *norma:* see NORM] a feminine name
nor·mal (nôr′m'l) ***adj.*** [< L. < *norma,* a rule] **1.** conforming with or constituting an accepted standard or norm; esp., corresponding to the average of a large group; natural; usual; regular **2.** naturally occurring [*normal immunity*] **3.** *Chem. a*) designating or of a salt formed by replacing all the replaceable hydrogen of an acid *b*) designating a solution of an acid or base containing 1.00797 grams of hydrogen ions per liter **4.** *Math.* perpendicular; at right angles **5.** *Med., Psychol. a*) free from disease, disorder, etc.; esp., average in intelligence or development *b*) mentally sound —***n.*** **1.** anything normal **2.** the usual state, amount, degree, etc. **3.** *Math.* a perpendicular —**nor′mal·cy, nor·mal′i·ty** (-mal′ə tē) ***n.***
nor·mal·ize (nôr′mə līz′) ***vt., vi.*** **-ized′, -iz′ing** **1.** to bring or come to the normal, or usual, state **2.** to bring or come into conformity with a standard —**nor′mal·i·za′tion** ***n.*** —**nor′mal·iz′er** ***n.***
nor·mal·ly (-lē) ***adv.*** **1.** in a normal manner **2.** under normal circumstances; ordinarily
normal school esp. formerly, a school for training high-school graduates to become teachers
Nor·man[1] (nôr′mən) **1.** [< OE. < OHG. *Nordemann,* lit., Northman] a masculine name: dim. *Norm* **2.** [ult. after A. *Norman,* railroad surveyor] city in C Okla., near Oklahoma City: pop. 68,000
Nor·man[2] (nôr′mən) ***n.*** [< OFr. *Normant* or ML. *Normannus,* both < Frank.] **1.** any of the Scandinavians who oc-

nonserious
nonservile
nonsexual
non-Shakespearean
nonsharing
nonshattering
nonshrinkable
nonsinkable
nonslaveholding
non-Slavic
nonsmoker
nonsocial
nonsocialist
nonsolid
nonsolvent
non-Spanish
nonsparing
nonspeaking
nonspecialist
nonspecialized
nonspecializing
nonspecific
nonspeculative
nonspherical
nonspiritual
nonspirituous
nonspottable
nonstaining
nonstandardized
nonstarting
nonstatic
nonstationary
nonstatistical
nonstatutory
nonstrategic
nonstretchable
nonstriated
nonstriker
nonstriking
nonstructural
nonsubmissive
nonsubscriber
nonsuccessful
nonsuccessive
nonsupporting
nonsuppurative
nonsustaining
nonsymbolic
nonsymmetrical
nonsympathizer
nonsymphonic
nonsymptomatic
nonsynchronous
nonsyntactic
nonsynthesized
nonsystematic
nontarnishable
nontaxable
nonteachable
nontechnical
nonterrestrial
nonterritorial
nontestamentary
nontheatrical
nontheological
nontherapeutic
nonthinking
nontoxic
nontraditional
nontragic
nontransferable
nontransitional
nontransparent
nontreasonable
nontributary
nontropical
nontuberculous
nontypical
nontyrannical
nonulcerous
nonunderstandable
nonuniform
nonuniversal
nonusable
nonuse
nonuser
nonuterine
nonutilitarian
nonutilized
nonvascular
nonvegetative
nonvenereal
nonvenomous
nonvenous
nonverbal
nonvernacular
nonvertical
nonviable
nonviolation
nonvirulent
nonviscous
nonvisual
nonvitreous
nonvocal
nonvocational
nonvolatile
nonvolcanic
nonvoluntary
nonwhite
nonworker
nonwoven
nonyielding

cupied Normandy in the 10th cent. A.D. **2.** a descendant of the Normans and French who conquered England in 1066 **3.** *same as* NORMAN FRENCH **4.** a native or inhabitant of Normandy —*adj.* of Normandy, the Normans, their language, or culture —**Nor′man·esque′** (-esk′) *adj.*

Norman Conquest the conquest of England by the Normans under William the Conqueror in 1066

Nor·man·dy (nôr′mən dē) region & former province in NW France, on the English Channel

Norman French the French spoken in England by the Norman conquerors; Anglo-French —**Nor′man-French′** *adj.*

norm·a·tive (nôr′mə tiv) *adj.* of or establishing a norm, or standard —**norm′a·tive·ly** *adv.*

Nor·ris (nôr′is, när′-) **Frank,** (born *Benjamin Franklin Norris, Jr.*) 1870–1902; U.S. novelist

Norse (nôrs) *adj.* [prob. < Du. *Noorsch,* a Norwegian < *noord,* north] Scandinavian, esp. West Scandinavian —*n.* **1.** the Scandinavian, esp. the West Scandinavian, group of languages **2.** *same as* NORWEGIAN —**the Norse 1.** the Scandinavians **2.** the West Scandinavians

Norse·man (-mən) *n., pl.* **-men** a member of the ancient Scandinavian people; Northman

north (nôrth) *n.* [OE.] **1.** the direction to the right of a person facing the sunset (0° or 360° on the compass, opposite south) **2.** a region or district in or toward this direction **3.** [*often* **N-**] the northern part of the earth, esp. the arctic regions —*adj.* **1.** in, of, to, or toward the north **2.** from the north **3.** [**N-**] designating the northern part of a country, etc. —*adv.* in or toward the north —**the North** that part of the U.S. bounded on the south by Maryland, the Ohio River, and S Missouri

North, Frederick, 2d Earl of Guilford; 1732–92; Eng. statesman; prime minister of Great Britain (1770–82): called *Lord North*

North America N continent in the Western Hemisphere: including adjacent islands, c.9,330,000 sq. mi.; pop. 376,000,000 —**North American**

north·bound (-bound′) *adj.* going northward

North Carolina [see CAROLINA[1]] Southern State of the U.S.: 52,712 sq. mi.; pop. 5,874,000; cap. Raleigh: abbrev. **N.C., NC** —**North Carolinian**

North Charleston city in SE S.C., near Charleston: pop. 66,000

North Dakota [see DAKOTA[1]] Middle Western State of the U.S.: 70,665 sq. mi.; pop. 653,000; cap. Bismarck: abbrev. **N.Dak., ND** —**North Dakotan**

north·east (nôrth′ēst′; *nautical,* nôr-) *n.* **1.** the direction halfway between north and east; 45° east of due north **2.** a region or district in or toward this direction —*adj.* **1.** in, of, to, or toward the northeast **2.** from the northeast, as a wind —*adv.* in, toward, or from the northeast —**the Northeast** the northeastern part of the U.S., esp. New England

north·east·er (nôrth′ēs′tər; *nautical,* nôr-) *n.* a storm or strong wind from the northeast

north·east·er·ly (-tər lē) *adj., adv.* **1.** in or toward the northeast **2.** from the northeast

north·east·ern (-tərn) *adj.* **1.** in, of, or toward the northeast **2.** from the northeast **3.** [**N-**] of or characteristic of the Northeast or New England —**North′east′ern·er** *n.*

north·east·ward (nôrth′ēst′wərd; *nautical,* nôr-) *adv., adj.* toward the northeast: also **north′east′wards** *adv.* —*n.* a northeastward direction, point, or region

north·east·ward·ly (-lē) *adj., adv.* **1.** toward the northeast **2.** from the northeast, as a wind

north·er (nôr′*th*ər) *n.* a storm or strong wind from the north

north·er·ly (-lē) *adj., adv.* **1.** toward the north **2.** from the north

north·ern (nôr′*th*ərn) *adj.* **1.** in, of, or toward the north **2.** from the north **3.** [**N-**] of or characteristic of the North —**north′ern·most′** *adj.*

north·ern·er (nôr′*th*ər nər, -*th*ə nər) *n.* a native or inhabitant of the north, specif. [**N-**] of the northern part of the U.S.

Northern Hemisphere that half of the earth north of the equator

Northern Ireland division of the United Kingdom, in the NE part of the island of Ireland: 5,462 sq. mi.; pop. 1,512,000; cap. Belfast

northern lights *same as* AURORA BOREALIS

Northern Rhodesia *former name of* ZAMBIA

Northern Spy a yellowish-red winter apple

Northern Territory territory of N Australia, on the Pacific

North Island N island of the two main islands of New Zealand

north·land (nôrth′land′, -lənd) *n.* [*also* **N-**] the northern region of a country —**north′land′er** *n.*

North Little Rock city in C Ark., on the Arkansas River opposite Little Rock: pop. 64,000

North·man (-mən) *n., pl.* **-men** *same as* NORSEMAN

north-north·east (nôrth′nôrth′ēst′; *nautical,* nôr′nôr-) *n.* the direction halfway between due north and northeast; 22°30′ east of due north —*adj., adv.* **1.** in or toward this direction **2.** from this direction

north-north·west (-west′) *n.* the direction halfway between due north and northwest; 22°30′ west of due north —*adj., adv.* **1.** in or toward this direction **2.** from this direction

North Pole the northern end of the earth's axis

North Sea arm of the Atlantic, between Great Britain & the European mainland, esp. Norway & Denmark

North Star Polaris, the bright star almost directly above the North Pole; polestar

North·um·bri·a (nôr thum′brē ə) former Anglo-Saxon kingdom in Great Britain, south of the Firth of Forth

North·um·bri·an (-ən) *adj.* of Northumbria, its people, or their dialect —*n.* **1.** a native or inhabitant of Northumbria **2.** the Old English dialect of Northumbria

north·ward (nôrth′wərd; *nautical,* nôr′*th*ərd) *adv., adj.* toward the north: also **north′wards** *adv.* —*n.* a northward direction, point, etc.

north·ward·ly (-lē) *adj., adv.* **1.** toward the north **2.** from the north

north·west (nôrth′west′; *nautical,* nôr-) *n.* **1.** the direction halfway between north and west; 45° west of due north **2.** a district or region in or toward this direction —*adj.* **1.** in, of, or toward the northwest **2.** from the northwest —*adv.* in, toward, or from the northwest —**the Northwest** the northwestern part of the U.S., esp. Wash., Oreg., and Ida.

north·west·er (nôrth′wes′tər; *nautical,* nôr-) *n.* a storm or strong wind from the northwest

north·west·er·ly (-tər lē) *adj., adv.* **1.** in or toward the northwest **2.** from the northwest

north·west·ern (-tərn) *adj.* **1.** in, of, or toward the northwest **2.** from the northwest **3.** [**N-**] of or characteristic of the Northwest —**North′west′ern·er** *n.*

Northwest Territories division of Canada, on the Arctic Ocean: 1,304,903 sq. mi.; pop. 43,000; cap. Yellowknife: abbrev. **N.W.T.**

Northwest Territory region north of the Ohio River, between Pa. & the Mississippi (established 1787): it now forms Ohio, Ind., Ill., Mich., Wis., & part of Minn.

north·west·ward (nôrth′west′wərd; *nautical,* nôr-) *adv., adj.* toward the northwest: also **north′west′wards** *adv.* —*n.* a northwestward direction, point, or region

north·west·ward·ly (-lē) *adj., adv.* **1.** toward the northwest **2.** from the northwest, as a wind

Norw. 1. Norway **2.** Norwegian

Nor·walk (nôr′wôk′) [< AmInd.] **1.** city in SW Calif.: suburb of Los Angeles: pop. 85,000 **2.** city in SW Conn., on Long Island Sound: pop. 78,000

Nor·way (nôr′wā′) country in N Europe, occupying the W & N parts of the Scandinavian Peninsula: 125,064 sq. mi.; pop. 3,851,000; cap. Oslo

Nor·we·gian (nôr wē′jən) *adj.* of Norway, its people, their language, etc. —*n.* **1.** a native or inhabitant of Norway **2.** the North Germanic language of the Norwegians

Nor·wich (nôr′ij, -ich; när′-) city in E England: pop. 119,000

Nos., nos. numbers

nose (nōz) *n.* [OE. *nosu*] **1.** the part of the human face between the mouth and the eyes, having two openings for breathing and smelling **2.** the corresponding part in animals; snout, muzzle, etc. **3.** the sense of smell **4.** power to track or perceive as by scent *[a nose* for news*]* **5.** anything noselike in shape or position; projecting part, as a prow, front of an airplane, etc. —*vt.* **nosed, nos′ing 1.** to discover or perceive as by smell **2.** to rub with the nose **3.** to push with the nose (with *aside,* etc.) **4.** to push (a way, etc.) with the front forward —*vi.* **1.** to smell; sniff **2.** to pry inquisitively **3.** to advance; move forward —**by a nose 1.** by the length of the animal's nose in horse racing, etc. **2.** by a very small margin —**lead by the nose** to dominate completely —**look down one's nose at** [Colloq.] to be disdainful of —**nose out 1.** to defeat by a very small margin **2.** to discover, as by smelling —**nose over** to turn over on its nose: said of an airplane moving on the ground —**on the nose** [Slang] **1.** that (a specified horse, etc.) will finish first in a race **2.** precisely; exactly —**pay through the nose** to pay an unreasonable price —**turn up one's nose at** to sneer at; scorn —**under one's (very) nose** in plain view

nose bag *same as* FEED BAG

nose·band (nōz′band′) *n.* that part of a bridle or halter which passes over the animal's nose

nose·bleed (-blēd′) *n.* a bleeding from the nose

nose cone the cone-shaped foremost part of a rocket or missile, resistant to intense heat

nose dive 1. a swift, downward plunge of an airplane, nose first **2.** any sudden, sharp drop —**nose′-dive′** *vi.* **-dived′, -div′ing**

nose drops medication administered through the nose with a dropper

no-see-um (nō sē′əm) *n.* [alt. after *no see (th)em*: in reference to its very small size] *same as* BITING MIDGE

nose·gay (nōz′gā′) ***n.*** [NOSE + GAY (in obs. sense of "gay object")] a small bouquet
nose·piece (-pēs′) ***n.*** **1.** that part of a helmet which protects the nose **2.** *same as* NOSEBAND **3.** anything nose-like in form or position **4.** the bridge of a pair of eyeglasses
nos·ey (nō′zē) ***adj.*** **nos′i·er, nos′i·est** *same as* NOSY
nosh (näsh) ***vt., vi.*** [< Yid. < G. *naschen,* to nibble] [Slang] to eat (a snack) —***n.*** [Slang] a snack —**nosh′er** ***n.***
no-show (nō′shō′) ***n.*** [Colloq.] a person who fails to claim or cancel a reservation, as for a flight
nos·tal·gia (näs tal′jə, nəs-, nôs-; -jē ə) ***n.*** [ModL. < Gr. *nostos,* a return + -ALGIA] **1.** a longing for home; homesickness **2.** a longing for something far away or of former times —**nos·tal′gic** (-jik) ***adj.*** —**nos·tal′gi·cal·ly** ***adv.***
nos·tril (näs′trəl) ***n.*** [OE. *nosthyrl* < *nosu,* nose + *thyrel,* hole] either of the openings into the nose
nos·trum (näs′trəm) ***n.*** [L., ours] **1.** *a)* a medicine made by the person selling it *b)* a quack medicine **2.** a pet scheme for solving some problem
nos·y (nō′zē) ***adj.*** **nos′i·er, nos′i·est** [Colloq.] prying; inquisitive —**nos′i·ly** ***adv.*** —**nos′i·ness** ***n.***
Nosy Par·ker (pär′kər) [NOSY + proper name *Parker*] [*also* **n- p-, n- P-**] [Colloq.] a nosy person
not (nät) ***adv.*** [ME., unstressed form of *nought*] in no manner; to no degree: a term of negation
‡**no·ta be·ne** (nō′tə bē′nē, nō′tä be′nā) [L.] note well; take particular notice
no·ta·bil·i·ty (nōt′ə bil′ə tē) ***n.*** **1.** *pl.* **-ties** a notable person **2.** the quality of being notable
no·ta·ble (nōt′ə b'l) ***adj.*** [OFr. < L. *notabilis* < *notare,* to note] worthy of notice; remarkable —***n.*** a famous or well-known person —**no′ta·bly** ***adv.***
no·tar·i·al (nō ter′ē əl) ***adj.*** of or done by a notary public —**no·tar′i·al·ly** ***adv.***
no·ta·rize (nōt′ə rīz′) ***vt.*** **-rized′, -riz′ing** to certify or attest (a document) as a notary public —**no′ta·ri·za′tion** ***n.***
no·ta·ry (nōt′ər ē) ***n.,*** *pl.* **-ries** [< OFr. < L. < *notare,* to note] *clipped form of* NOTARY PUBLIC
notary public *pl.* **notaries public, notary publics** an official authorized to certify or attest documents, take depositions and affidavits, etc.
no·ta·tion (nō tā′shən) ***n.*** [< L. < *notare,* to NOTE] **1.** the use of a system of signs or symbols for words, quantities, etc. **2.** any such system used in algebra, music, etc. **3.** a brief note jotted down **4.** the noting of something in writing —**no·ta′tion·al** ***adj.***
notch (näch) ***n.*** [by syllabic merging of ME. *an oche* < OFr. *oche,* a notch] **1.** a V-shaped cut in an edge or surface **2.** a narrow, deep pass; gap **3.** [Colloq.] a step; degree *[a notch* below average*]* —***vt.*** **1.** to cut a notch or notches in **2.** to record or tally, as by notches —**notched** ***adj.*** —**notch′er** ***n.***
note (nōt) ***n.*** [OFr. < L. *nota,* a mark, sign < pp. of *noscere,* to know] **1.** a distinguishing feature *[a note* of joy*]* **2.** importance or distinction *[a man of note]* **3.** *a)* a brief, written statement of a fact, etc., as to aid memory *b)* [*pl.*] a record of experiences, etc. **4.** a comment or explanation, as at the foot of a page **5.** notice; heed *[worthy of note]* **6.** *a)* a short, informal letter *b)* a formal diplomatic or other official communication **7.** *a)* any of certain commercial papers relating to debts or payment of money *[a promissory note]* *b)* a piece of paper currency **8.** a cry or call, as of a bird **9.** a signal or intimation *[a note* of warning*]* **10.** [Archaic] a tune or song **11.** *Music a)* a tone of definite pitch *b)* a symbol for a tone, indicating pitch and duration *c)* a key of a piano, etc. —***vt.*** **not′ed, not′ing** **1.** to heed; observe **2.** to put in writing; make a note of **3.** to mention specially **4.** to signify or indicate —**compare notes** to exchange views —**take notes** to write down notes, as during a lecture —**note′less** ***adj.***

NOTES
(A, whole; B, half; C, quarter; D, eighth; E, sixteenth; F, thirty-second; G, sixty-fourth)

note·book (-book′) ***n.*** a book for memorandums
not·ed (nōt′id) ***adj.*** distinguished; renowned; eminent —**not′ed·ly** ***adv.*** —**not′ed·ness** ***n.***
note paper paper for writing notes, or letters
note·wor·thy (-wur′thē) ***adj.*** worthy of note; outstanding; remarkable —**note′wor′thi·ly** ***adv.*** —**note′wor′thi·ness** ***n.***
noth·ing (nuth′iŋ) ***n.*** [OE. *na thing*] **1.** *a)* no thing; not anything *b)* no part, trace, etc. **2.** nothingness **3.** a thing that does not exist **4.** *a)* something of little or no value, importance, etc. *b)* a person considered of no value or importance **5.** a nought; zero —***adv.*** not at all —**for nothing** **1.** at no cost; free **2.** in vain **3.** without reason —**in nothing flat** [Colloq.] in almost no time at all —**make nothing of** **1.** to treat as of little importance **2.** to fail to understand —**nothing but** nothing other than —**nothing doing** [Colloq.] **1.** no: used in refusal **2.** no result, accomplishment, etc. —**nothing less than** no less than: also **nothing short of** —**think nothing of** **1.** to attach no importance to **2.** to regard as easy to do
noth·ing·ness (-nis) ***n.*** **1.** nonexistence **2.** lack of value, meaning, etc. **3.** unconsciousness or death **4.** anything nonexistent, useless, etc.
no·tice (nōt′is) ***n.*** [MFr. < L. *notitia* < *notus:* see NOTE] **1.** announcement or warning **2.** a brief mention or review of a book, play, etc. **3.** a written or printed sign giving some public information, warning, or rule **4.** *a)* attention; regard; heed *b)* courteous attention **5.** a formal warning of intention to end an agreement or contract at a certain time *[to give a tenant notice]* —***vt.*** **-ticed, -tic·ing** **1.** *a)* to refer to or comment on *b)* to review briefly **2.** *a)* to observe; pay attention to *b)* to be courteous or responsive to —**serve notice** to give formal warning, as of intentions; announce —**take notice** to pay attention; observe
no·tice·a·ble (-ə b'l) ***adj.*** **1.** readily noticed; conspicuous **2.** significant —**no′tice·a·bly** ***adv.***
no·ti·fi·ca·tion (nōt′ə fi kā′shən) ***n.*** **1.** a notifying or being notified **2.** the notice given or received **3.** the letter, form, etc. notifying
no·ti·fy (nōt′ə fī′) ***vt.*** **-fied′, -fy′ing** [< MFr. < L. < *notus* (see NOTE) + *facere,* to make] **1.** to give notice to; inform **2.** [Chiefly Brit.] to give notice of; announce —**no′ti·fi′er** ***n.***
no·tion (nō′shən) ***n.*** [Fr. < L. < *notus:* see NOTE] **1.** *a)* a mental image *b)* a vague thought **2.** a belief; opinion; view **3.** an inclination; whim **4.** an intention **5.** [*pl.*] small, useful articles, as needles, thread, etc., sold in a store
no·tion·al (-'l) ***adj.*** **1.** of or expressing notions, or concepts **2.** imaginary; not actual **3.** having visionary ideas; fanciful
no·to·ri·e·ty (nōt′ə rī′ə tē) ***n.*** the quality or state of being notorious
no·to·ri·ous (nō tôr′ē əs) ***adj.*** [ML. *notorius* < LL. < L. *notus:* see NOTE] **1.** well-known **2.** widely but unfavorably known or talked about —**no·to′ri·ous·ly** ***adv.*** —**no·to′ri·ous·ness** ***n.***
no-trump (nō′trump′) ***adj.*** *Bridge* with no suit being trumps —***n.*** *Bridge* a no-trump bid or hand
Not·ting·ham (nät′iŋ əm) city in C England: pop. 305,000
not·with·stand·ing (nät′with stan′diŋ, -with-) ***prep.*** in spite of *[he flew on, notwithstanding the storm]* —***adv.*** all the same; nevertheless *[he will go, notwithstanding]* —***conj.*** although
nou·gat (nōō′gət) ***n.*** [Fr. < Pr. < *noga* < L. *nux,* nut] a confection of sugar paste with nuts
nought (nôt) ***n.*** [OE. *nowiht* < *ne,* not + *awiht,* aught] **1.** nothing **2.** *Arith.* the figure zero (0) —***adj.*** [Archaic or Obs.] **1.** worthless **2.** evil —***adv.*** [Archaic] in no way; not at all —**set at nought** to defy; scorn
noun (noun) ***n.*** [< OFr. < L. *nomen,* a name] *Gram.* **1.** any of a class of words naming or denoting a person, thing, action, quality, etc. *[Ex.: boy, water,* and *truth* are *nouns]* **2.** any word, phrase, or clause so used —**noun′al** ***adj.***
nour·ish (nur′ish) ***vt.*** [< OFr. *norrir* < L. *nutrire*] **1.** to feed or sustain with substances necessary to life and growth **2.** to foster; develop; promote (a feeling, attitude, habit, etc.) —**nour′ish·er** ***n.*** —**nour′ish·ing** ***adj.*** —**nour′ish·ing·ly** ***adv.***
nour·ish·ment (-mənt) ***n.*** **1.** a nourishing or being nourished **2.** something that nourishes
nou·veau riche (nōō′vō rēsh′) *pl.* **nou·veaux riches** (nōō′vō rēsh′) [Fr., newly rich] a newly rich person: often connoting lack of culture
Nov. November
no·va (nō′və) ***n.,*** *pl.* **-vae** (-vē), **-vas** [ModL. < L. *nova* (*stella*), new (star)] *Astron.* a star that suddenly becomes vastly brighter and then loses brightness through months or years
No·va Sco·tia (nō′və skō′shə) province of SE Canada, consisting of a peninsula & an island at the mouth of the Gulf of St. Lawrence: 21,425 sq. mi.; pop. 829,000; cap. Halifax: abbrev. **N.S.** —**No′va Sco′tian**
nov·el (näv′'l) ***adj.*** [< OFr. < L. *novellus,* dim. of *novus,* new] new and unusual —***n.*** [< It. < L. *novella,* new things < *novellus*] **1.** a relatively long fictional prose narrative with a more or less complex plot **2.** the literary form including all such narratives (with *the*) —**nov′el·is′tic** ***adj.***
nov·el·ette (näv′ə let′) ***n.*** a short novel
nov·el·ist (näv′'l ist) ***n.*** a person who writes novels
nov·el·ize (näv′ə līz′) ***vt.*** **-ized′, -iz′ing** to make into or like a novel —**nov′el·i·za′tion** ***n.***

no·vel·la (nō vel′ə; *It.* nô vel′lä) ***n.,*** *pl.* **-las, -le** (-ē; *It.* -le) [It.] **1.** a short prose narrative, often satiric, as a tale by Boccaccio **2.** a short novel; novelette

nov·el·ty (näv′'l tē) ***n.,*** *pl.* **-ties 1.** the quality of being novel **2.** something novel; innovation **3.** a small, often cheap, cleverly made article, as for play: *usually used in pl.*

No·vem·ber (nō vem′bər) ***n.*** [< OFr. < L. < *novem,* nine: the ancient Roman year began with March] the eleventh month of the year, having 30 days: abbrev. **Nov., N.**

no·ve·na (nō vē′nə) ***n.*** [ML. < L. < *novem,* nine] *R.C.Ch.* a nine-day period of devotions

nov·ice (näv′is) ***n.*** [OFr. < L. *novicius* < *novus,* new] **1.** a person on probation in a religious group before taking vows **2.** a person new to an activity, etc.; beginner

no·vi·ti·ate (nō vish′ē it, -āt′; -vish′it) ***n.*** **1.** the period or state of being a novice **2.** a novice **3.** the quarters of religious novices

No·vo·cain (nō′və kān′) [L. *nov(us),* new + (C)OCAIN(E)] *a trademark for* PROCAINE: also sp. **Novocaine**

No·vo·kuz·netsk (nô′vô ko͞oz nyetsk′) city in SC R.S.F.S.R.: pop. 495,000

No·vo·si·birsk (-si birsk′) city in the SC R.S.F.S.R., on the Ob River: pop. 1,079,000

now (nou) ***adv.*** [OE. *nu*] **1.** *a)* at the present time *b)* at once **2.** at the time referred to; then; next *[now* the war began*]* **3.** *a)* very recently *[*he left just *now] b)* very soon *[*he's leaving just *now]* **4.** with things as they are *[now* I'll never know*]* *Now* is often used for emphasis or in making transitions *[now* look here*]* ***—conj.*** since; seeing that *[now* that you know*]* ***—n.*** the present time *[*that's all for *now]* ***—adj.*** of the present time *[*the *now* generation*]* ***—interj.*** an exclamation of warning, reproach, etc. **—now and then** sometimes: also **now and again**

now·a·days (nou′ə dāz′) ***adv.*** in these days; at the present time ***—n.*** the present time

no·way (nō′wā′) ***adv.*** in no manner; by no means; not at all; nowise: also **no′ways′** (-wāz′)

no·where (nō′hwer′, -wer′) ***adv.*** not in, at, or to any place; not anywhere: also [Dial. or Colloq.] **no′wheres′** ***—n.*** **1.** a place that is nonexistent, remote, etc. **2.** a place or state of obscurity **—nowhere near** not nearly

no-win (-win′) ***adj.*** designating or of a situation, policy, etc. that will be unsuccessful no matter what is done

no·wise (-wīz′) ***adv.*** in no manner; noway

nox·ious (näk′shəs) ***adj.*** [< L. < *noxa,* injury < *nocere, to hurt*] harmful to health or morals; injurious; unwholesome **—nox′ious·ly** ***adv.*** **—nox′ious·ness** ***n.***

noz·zle (näz′'l) ***n.*** [dim. of NOSE] **1.** a spout at the end of a hose, etc., for controlling a stream of liquid or gas **2.** [Slang] the nose

Np *Chem.* neptunium

N.P., n.p. Notary Public

NRC, N.R.C. Nuclear Regulatory Commission

N/S, n/s *Banking* not sufficient funds: also **N.S.F.**

N.S. 1. New Style **2.** Nova Scotia

N.S.W. New South Wales

-n't a contracted form of *not [aren't]*

NT., NT, N.T. New Testament

nth (enth) ***adj.*** **1.** expressing the ordinal equivalent to *n* **2.** of the indefinitely large or small quantity represented by *n* **—to the nth degree** (or **power**) **1.** to an indefinite degree or power **2.** to an extreme

nt. wt. net weight

nu (no͞o, nyo͞o) ***n.*** [Gr.] the thirteenth letter of the Greek alphabet (Ν, ν)

nu·ance (no͞o′äns, nyo͞o′-; no͞o äns′) ***n.*** [Fr. < *nuer,* to shade, ult. < L. *nubes,* a cloud] a slight or delicate variation in tone, color, meaning, etc. **—nu′anced** ***adj.***

nub (nub) ***n.*** [var. of *knub,* for KNOB] **1.** *a)* a knob or lump *b)* small piece **2.** [Colloq.] the point of a story or gist of a matter

nub·bin (nub′in) ***n.*** [dim. of NUB] **1.** a small or imperfect ear of Indian corn **2.** anything small or undeveloped *[nubbins* of coal*]*

nub·ble (nub′'l) ***n.*** [dim. of NUB] a small knob or lump **—nub′bly** ***adj.*** **-bli·er, -bli·est**

nub·by (-ē) ***adj.*** **-bi·er, -bi·est** covered with small nubs, or lumps; having a rough, knotted surface *[*a *nubby* fabric*]* **—nub′bi·ness** ***n.***

Nu·bi·a (no͞o′bē ə, nyo͞o′-) region & former kingdom in NE Africa, between the Red Sea & the Sahara, in Egypt & Sudan **—Nu′bi·an** ***adj., n.***

nu·bile (no͞o′b'l, nyo͞o′-; -bīl) ***adj.*** [Fr. < L. < *nubere,* to marry] marriageable: said of a young woman with reference to her age or physical development **—nu·bil′i·ty** ***n.***

nu·cle·ar (no͞o′klē ər, nyo͞o′-) ***adj.*** **1.** of, like, or forming a nucleus **2.** of or relating to atomic nuclei *[nuclear* energy*]* **3.** of or operated by atomic energy *[nuclear weapons]* **4.** of, having, or involving nuclear weapons *[nuclear* war*]*

nuclear fission the splitting of the nuclei of atoms, with conversion of some mass into energy, as in an atomic bomb

nuclear fusion the fusion of atomic nuclei into a nucleus of heavier mass, with a resultant loss in the combined mass, which is converted into energy, as in a hydrogen bomb

nuclear reactor a device for initiating and maintaining a controlled nuclear chain reaction in a fissionable fuel for the production of energy or additional fissionable material

nu·cle·ase (no͞o′klē ās′, nyo͞o′-) ***n.*** [NUCLE(O)- + -ASE] any of various enzymes that speed up the hydrolysis of nucleic acids

nu·cle·ate (-it; *also, & for v. always,* -āt′) ***adj.*** having a nucleus ***—vt.*** **-at′ed, -at′ing** to form into or around a nucleus ***—vi.*** to form a nucleus **—nu′cle·a′tion** ***n.*** **—nu′cle·a′tor** ***n.***

nu·cle·i (no͞o′klē ī′, nyo͞o′-) ***n.*** *pl. of* NUCLEUS

nu·cle·ic acid (no͞o klē′ik, nyo͞o-) any of a group of complex organic acids found esp. in the nucleus of all living cells and essential to life

nu·cle·o- *a combining form meaning:* **1.** nucleus **2.** nuclear **3.** nucleic acid Also **nu·cle-**

nu·cle·o·lus (no͞o klē′ə ləs, nyo͞o-) ***n.,*** *pl.* **-li′** (-lī′) [ModL. < LL., dim. of L. *nucleus*] a conspicuous, usually spherical body in the nucleus of most cells: also **nu′cle·ole′** **—nu·cle′o·lar** ***adj.***

nu·cle·on (no͞o′klē än′, nyo͞o′-) ***n.*** [NUCLE(US) + (PROT)ON] a neutron or proton, either of the fundamental particles of the atomic nucleus **—nu′cle·on′ic** ***adj.***

nu·cle·on·ics (no͞o′klē än′iks, nyo͞o′-) ***n.pl.*** [*with sing. v.*] the branch of physics dealing with nucleons or with nuclear phenomena

nu·cle·us (no͞o′klē əs, nyo͞o′-) ***n.,*** *pl.* **-cle·i′** (-ī′), **-cle·us·es** [ModL. < L., a kernel] **1.** a central thing or part around which other things or parts are grouped **2.** any center of growth or development **3.** *Astron.* the bright central part of a comet head **4.** *Biol.* the central, usually rounded mass of protoplasm in most plant and animal cells, necessary to growth, reproduction, etc. **5.** *Chem., Physics* the central part of an atom, the fundamental particles of which are the proton and neutron: it carries a positive charge **6.** *Organic Chem.* a stable arrangement of atoms that may occur in many compounds

nu·clide (-klīd) ***n.*** [NUCL(EUS) + *-ide* < Gr. *eidos,* form] a specific type of atom that exists for a measurable time and is characterized by a distinct nuclear structure **—nu·clid′ic** (-klid′ik) ***adj.***

nude (no͞od, nyo͞od) ***adj.*** [L. *nudus*] completely unclothed or uncovered; naked; bare ***—n.*** **1.** a nude person **2.** a nude figure in painting, sculpture, etc. **3.** the condition of being nude *[*in the *nude]* **—nude′ly** ***adv.*** **—nude′ness** ***n.***

nudge (nuj) ***vt.*** **nudged, nudg′ing** [prob. akin to Norw. dial. *nyggja,* to push] to push gently, esp. with the elbow, so as to get attention, etc. ***—n.*** a gentle push with the elbow, etc. **—nudg′er** ***n.***

nud·ism (no͞o′diz'm) ***n.*** the practice or cult of going nude for hygienic reasons **—nud′ist** ***n., adj.***

nu·di·ty (-də tē) ***n.*** **1.** a being nude; nakedness **2.** *pl.* **-ties** a nude figure, as in art

nud·nik (no͝od′nik) ***n.*** [< Yid. < Russ.] [Slang] a dull, tiresome person

nu·ga·to·ry (no͞o′gə tôr′ē, nyo͞o′-) ***adj.*** [< L. < pp. of *nugari,* to trifle] **1.** trifling; worthless **2.** not operative; invalid

nug·get (nug′it) ***n.*** [prob. dim. of E. dial. *nug,* lump] a lump, esp. of native gold

nui·sance (no͞o′s'ns, nyo͞o′-) ***n.*** [< OFr. < *nuisir* < L. *nocere,* to annoy] an act, thing, person, etc. causing trouble, annoyance, or inconvenience

nuisance tax a tax considered a nuisance because paid in very small amounts by the consumer

null (nul) ***adj.*** [< MFr. < L. *nullus,* none < *ne-,* not + *ullus,* any] **1.** without legal force; invalid: usually in **null and void** **2.** amounting to nought; nil **3.** of no value, effect, etc.; insignificant **4.** *Math.* designating, of, or being zero

nul·li·fy (nul′ə fī′) ***vt.*** **-fied′, -fy′ing** [< LL. < L. *nullus,* none + *facere,* to make] **1.** to make legally null; make void **2.** to make valueless or useless **3.** to cancel out **—nul′li·fi·ca′tion** ***n.*** **—nul′li·fi′er** ***n.***

nul·li·ty (nul′ə tē) ***n.*** **1.** a being null **2.** *pl.* **-ties** anything that is null

Num. (the book of) Numbers

num. 1. number **2.** numeral(s)

numb (num) ***adj.*** [< ME. *nomen,* pp. of *nimen,* to take] weakened in or deprived of the power of feeling or moving; deadened; insensible ***—vt.*** to make numb **—numb′ly** ***adv.*** **—numb′ness** ***n.***

num·ber (num′bər) ***n.*** [< OE. < L. *numerus*] **1.** a symbol or word, or a group of either of these, showing how many or which one in a series: see CARDINAL NUMBER, ORDINAL NUMBER **2.** [*pl.*] *same as* ARITHMETIC **3.** the sum or total of persons or units **4.** a collection of persons or things; assemblage **5.** *a)* [*often pl.*] a large group *b)* [*pl.*] numerical superiority **6.** quantity, as consisting of units **7.** *a)* a single issue of a periodical *[*the May *number] b)* a single song, skit, etc. in a program **8.** [Colloq.] a person or thing singled out [this hat is a smart *number*] **9.** *Gram. a*) the differentiation in form to show whether one or more than one is meant *b*) the form itself See SINGULAR, PLURAL **10.** [*pl.*] *a*) metrical form; meter *b*) metrical lines; verses —*vt.* **1.** to count; enumerate **2.** to give a number to; designate by number **3.** to include as one of a group (*among*) **4.** to limit the number of [his days are *numbered*] **5.** to comprise; total —*vi.* **1.** to total; count **2.** to be numbered —**a number of** several or many —**beyond** (or **without**) **number** too many to be counted —**do a number on** [Slang] to abuse in some way, as by injuring, cheating, etc. —**get** (or **have**) **one's number** [Slang] to discover (or know) one's true character or motives —**one's number is up** [Slang] one's time to die, suffer punishment, etc. has arrived —**the numbers** an illegal lottery involving small bets on the order of numbers in a tabulation, as of published financial reports: also called **numbers pool** (or **racket**, etc.) —**without number** too numerous to be counted —**num′ber·er** *n.*

num·ber·less (-lis) *adj.* **1.** innumerable; countless **2.** without a number or numbers

number one [Colloq.] **1.** oneself **2.** the first, usually the very best, quality or grade

Num·bers (num′bərz) [so named from containing the census of the Hebrews after the Exodus] the fourth book of the Pentateuch in the Bible

numb·skull (num′skul′) *n. same as* NUMSKULL

nu·mer·a·ble (no͞o′mər ə b'l, nyo͞o′-) *adj.* that can be numbered or counted

nu·mer·al (-mər əl) *adj.* [< LL. < L. *numerus,* number] of, expressing, or denoting a number or numbers —*n.* a figure, letter, or word, or a group of any of these, expressing a number: see ARABIC NUMERALS, ROMAN NUMERALS

nu·mer·ate (-mə rāt′) *vt.* **-at′ed, -at′ing 1.** *same as* ENUMERATE **2.** to read as words (numbers expressed in figures)

nu·mer·a·tion (no͞o′mə rā′shən, nyo͞o′-) *n.* **1.** a numbering or counting **2.** a system of numbering **3.** a numerating (sense 2)

nu·mer·a·tor (no͞o′mə rāt′ər, nyo͞o′-) *n.* **1.** a person or thing that numbers **2.** *Math.* the term above the line in a fraction, indicating how many of the specified parts of a unit are taken

nu·mer·i·cal (noo mer′i k'l, nyoo-) *adj.* **1.** of, or having the nature of, number **2.** in or by numbers **3.** denoting (a) number **4.** expressed by numbers, not letters —**nu·mer′i·cal·ly** *adv.*

nu·mer·ol·o·gy (no͞o′mə räl′ə jē, nyo͞o′-) *n.* [< L. *numerus,* a number + -LOGY] divination based on assigning meanings to numbers, as those of birth dates

nu·mer·ous (no͞o′mər əs, nyo͞o′-) *adj.* [< L. < *numerus,* a number] **1.** consisting of many **2.** very many —**nu′merous·ly** *adv.* —**nu′mer·ous·ness** *n.*

Nu·mid·i·a (no͞o mid′ē ə, nyo͞o-) ancient country in N Africa, mainly in what is now E Algeria —**Nu·mid′i·an** *adj., n.*

nu·mis·mat·ic (no͞o′miz mat′ik, nyo͞o′-; -mis-) *adj.* [< Fr. < L. *numisma,* a coin < Gr. < *nomizein,* to sanction < *nomos,* law] **1.** of coins or medals **2.** of or having to do with currency **3.** of numismatics

nu·mis·mat·ics (-iks) *n.pl.* [*with sing. v.*] the study or collection of coins, medals, etc. —**nu·mis·ma·tist** (no͞o miz′mə tist, nyo͞o-; -mis′-) *n.*

num·skull (num′skul′) *n.* [NUM(B) + SKULL] a stupid person; dolt; dunce

nun (nun) *n.* [< OE. < LL. *nonna*] a woman devoted to a religious life, esp. in a convent under vows of poverty, chastity, and obedience

Nunc Di·mit·tis (nuŋk′ di mit′is, nooŋk′) [L., now thou lettest depart] **1.** a hymn based on the words in Luke 2: 29–32 **2.** [**n- d-**] *a*) departure or farewell *b*) dismissal

nun·ci·o (nun′shē ō′, -sē-) *n., pl.* **-ci·os′** [It. < L. *nuntius,* messenger] an ambassador of the Pope to a foreign state

nun·ner·y (nun′ər ē) *n., pl.* **-ner·ies** *a former name for* CONVENT

nup·tial (nup′shəl) *adj.* [< L. < *nuptiae,* marriage < pp. of *nubere,* to marry] **1.** of marriage **2.** of mating —*n.* [*pl.*] a wedding

Nu·rem·berg (noor′əm burg′, nyoor′-) city in NC Bavaria, West Germany: pop. 472,000: Ger. name **Nürn·berg** (nürn′berkh′)

nurse (nurs) *n.* [< OFr. < LL. < L. < *nutrix* < *nutrire,* to nourish] **1.** a woman hired to take full care of another's young child or children **2.** a person trained to take care of the sick or aged, assist surgeons, etc. **3.** a person or thing that fosters, protects, etc. —*vt.* **nursed, nurs′ing 1.** to give milk from the breast to (an infant) **2.** to suck milk from the breast of **3.** to take care of (a child or children) **4.** to bring up; rear **5.** to tend (the sick or aged) **6.** to nourish or foster [to *nurse* a grudge] **7.** to treat, or try to cure [to *nurse* a cold] **8.** *a*) to use, handle, etc. carefully, so as to avoid pain, etc. [to *nurse* an injured leg] *b*) to consume, spend, etc. slowly or carefully so as to conserve [to *nurse* a drink] **9.** to hold carefully —*vi.* **1.** to feed at the breast **2.** to suckle a child **3.** to tend the sick, etc. as a nurse

nurse·maid (-mād′) *n.* a woman hired to take care of a child or children: also **nurs′er·y·maid′**

nurs·er·y (nur′sə rē, nurs′rē) *n., pl.* **-er·ies 1.** a room in a home, set aside for the children **2.** *same as: a*) NURSERY SCHOOL *b*) DAY NURSERY **3.** a place where young trees or plants are raised for sale, etc.

nurs·er·y·man (-mən) *n., pl.* **-men** (-mən) one who owns, operates, or works for a nursery (sense 3)

nursery rhyme a short poem for children

nursery school a prekindergarten school for young children aged usually 3 to 5

nursing home a residence providing care for the infirm, chronically ill, disabled, etc.

nurs·ling (nurs′liŋ) *n.* **1.** a young baby still being nursed **2.** anything that is being carefully tended Also **nurse′ling**

nur·ture (nur′chər) *n.* [< OFr. < LL. pp. of L. *nutrire,* to nourish] **1.** anything that nourishes; food **2.** training, upbringing, fostering, etc.: also **nur′tur·ance 3.** the environmental influences as distinguished from genetic nature —*vt.* **-tured, -tur·ing 1.** to nourish **2.** to train, rear, foster, etc. —**nur′tur·ant, nur′tur·al** *adj.* —**nur′tur·er** *n.*

nut (nut) *n.* [OE. *hnutu*] **1.** a dry, one-seeded fruit, consisting of a kernel, often edible, in a woody or leathery shell, as the walnut, chestnut, pecan, acorn, etc. **2.** the kernel itself **3.** loosely, any hard-shelled fruit keeping more or less indefinitely, as a peanut **4.** a small, usually metal block with a center threaded hole for screwing onto a bolt, etc. **5.** [Colloq.] the cost of an undertaking that must be recovered before a profit can be made **6.** [Slang] *a*) a foolish, crazy, or eccentric person *b*) a devotee; fan See also NUTS —*vi.* **nut′ted, nut′ting** to hunt for or gather nuts —**hard** (or **tough**) **nut to crack** a person or thing hard to understand or deal with —**off one's nut** [Slang] foolish, silly, or crazy

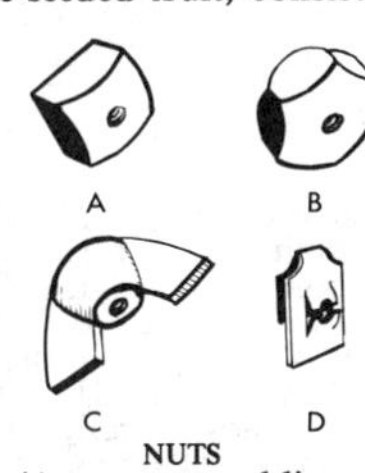

NUTS
(A, square neckline; B, hexagon machine; C, wing; D, snap-on)

nut·crack·er (-krak′ər) *n.* a device, usually hinged, for cracking the shells of nuts

nut·gall (-gôl′) *n.* a small, nut-shaped gall on the oak and other trees

nut·hatch (-hach′) *n.* a small, nut-eating bird with a sharp beak and short tail

nut·meat (-mēt′) *n.* the kernel of a nut

nut·meg (nut′meg′) *n.* [ME. *notemygge,* partial transl. of OFr. *noiz muscade,* lit., musky nut] **1.** the hard, aromatic seed of an East Indian tree: it is grated and used as a spice **2.** the tree

nut·pick (nut′pik′) *n.* a small, sharp instrument for digging out the kernels of cracked nuts

nu·tri·a (no͞o′trē ə, nyo͞o′-) *n.* [Sp. < L. *lutra,* otter] **1.** a S. American water-dwelling rodent with webbed feet and a long, almost hairless tail **2.** its short-haired, soft, brown fur

nu·tri·ent (no͞o′trē ənt, nyo͞o′-) *adj.* [< L. prp. of *nutrire,* to nourish] nutritious; nourishing —*n.* anything nutritious

nu·tri·ment (-trə mənt) *n.* [< L. < *nutrire,* to nourish] anything that nourishes; food

nu·tri·tion (no͞o trish′ən, nyo͞o-) *n.* [< L. *nutrire,* to nourish] **1.** a nourishing or being nourished; esp., the series of processes by which an organism takes in and assimilates food for promoting growth and repairing tissues **2.** nourishment **3.** the science or study of proper diet —**nu·tri′tion·al** *adj.* —**nu·tri′tion·al·ly** *adv.* —**nu·tri′tion·ist** *n.*

nu·tri·tious (-əs) *adj.* nourishing; of value as food —**nu·tri′tious·ly** *adv.* —**nu·tri′tious·ness** *n.*

nu·tri·tive (no͞o′trə tiv, nyo͞o′-) *adj.* **1.** having to do with nutrition **2.** nutritious —**nu′tri·tive·ly** *adv.*

nuts (nuts) *adj.* [see NUT, 6] [Slang] crazy; foolish —*interj.* [Slang] an exclamation of disgust, scorn, refusal, etc.: often in the phrase **nuts to (someone or something)** —**be nuts about** [Slang] to love or like very much

nuts and bolts [Colloq.] the basic elements or practical aspects of something —**nuts′-and-bolts′** *adj.*

nut·shell (nut′shel′) *n.* the shell enclosing the kernel of a nut —**in a nutshell** concisely

nut·ty (nut′ē) *adj.* **-ti·er, -ti·est 1.** containing or producing nuts **2.** nutlike in flavor **3.** [Slang] *a*) very enthusiastic *b*) crazy —**nut′ti·ly** *adv.* —**nut′ti·ness** *n.*

nux vom·i·ca (nuks′väm′i kə) [ML. < L. *nux,* nut + *vomere,* to vomit] **1.** the poisonous seed of an Asiatic tree, containing strychnine **2.** the tree
nuz·zle (nuz′'l) *vt.* **-zled, -zling** [< NOSE] to push against or rub with the nose, snout, etc. —*vi.* **1.** to push or rub with the nose, etc. against or into something **2.** to nestle; snuggle —**nuz′zler** *n.*
NV Nevada
NW, N.W., n.w. 1. northwest **2.** northwestern
N.W.T. Northwest Territories
N.Y., NY New York
Nya·sa (nyä′sä, nī as′ə), **Lake** lake in SE Africa, between Malawi & Mozambique
Nya·sa·land (-land′) *former name of* MALAWI
N.Y.C. New York City
nyc·ta·lo·pi·a (nik′tə lō′pē ə) *n.* [LL. < Gr. < *nyx* (gen. *nyktos*), night + *alaos,* blind + *ōps,* eye] *same as* NIGHT BLINDNESS —**nyc′ta·lop′ic** (-läp′ik) *adj.*
nyl·ghai (nil′gī) *n. same as* NILGAI
ny·lon (nī′län) *n.* [arbitrary coinage] **1.** a synthetic polymeric amide made into fiber, bristles, etc. of great strength and elasticity **2.** any of the materials made from nylon; specif., [*pl.*] stockings of nylon yarn
nymph (nimf) *n.* [< OFr. < L. < Gr. *nymphē*] **1.** *Gr. & Rom. Myth.* any of a group of minor nature goddesses, represented as beautiful maidens living in rivers, trees, etc. **2.** a lovely young woman **3.** *Entomology* the young of an insect with incomplete metamorphosis —**nymph′al, nymph′e·an** *adj.*
nymph·et (nim′fət, nim fet′) *n.* [< Fr. dim. of *nymphe:* see prec.] a pubescent girl, esp. one who is sexually precocious —**nym·phet′ic** *adj.*
nym·pho·ma·ni·a (nim′fə mā′nē ə, -mān′yə) *n.* [ModL. < Gr. *nymphē,* bride, nymph + -MANIA] abnormal and uncontrollable desire by a woman for sexual intercourse —**nym′pho·ma′ni·ac′** (-ak′) *adj., n.*
Nyx (niks) [Gr.] *Gr. Myth.* the goddess of night
N.Z., N.Zeal. New Zealand

O

O, o (ō) *n., pl.* **O's, o's 1.** the fifteenth letter of the English alphabet **2.** a sound of *O* or *o* **3.** the numeral zero **4.** an object shaped like O or o **5.** *Physics the symbol for* ohm —*adj.* circular or oval in shape
O (ō) *interj.* an exclamation variously used: **1.** in direct address [*O Lord!*] **2.** to express surprise, fear, wonder, pain, etc.: now usually *oh* **3.** at the end of a line in some ballads —*n., pl.* **O's** a use of this exclamation
o' (ə, ō) *prep. an abbreviated form of:* **1.** of [*o'clock*] **2.** [Archaic or Dial.] on
O 1. *Linguis.* Old [*OFr.*] **2.** *Chem.* oxygen
O. 1. Ocean **2.** October **3.** Ohio **4.** Ontario
O., o. 1. octavo **2.** old **3.** [L. *octarius*] *Pharmacy* pint
oaf (ōf) *n.* [< ON. *alfr,* elf] a stupid, clumsy fellow; lout —**oaf′ish** *adj.* —**oaf′ish·ly** *adv.* —**oaf′ish·ness** *n.*
O·a·hu (ō ä′hōō) [Haw. < ?] chief island of Hawaii, on which Honolulu is located
oak (ōk) *n.* see PLURAL, II, D, 3 [OE. *ac*] **1.** a large hardwood tree or bush bearing nuts called *acorns* **2.** its wood **3.** any of various plants resembling an oak —*adj.* of oak: also **oak′en**
oak apple an applelike gall on oak trees
Oak·land (ōk′lənd) [after *oak* groves orig. there] seaport in W Calif., on San Francisco Bay, opposite San Francisco: pop. 339,000: see SAN FRANCISCO
Oak Ridge [after the many *oak* trees there] city in E Tenn.: center for atomic research: pop. 28,000
oak tag a kind of sturdy cardboard originally made from oak fibers, used for posters, folders, etc.
oa·kum (ō′kəm) *n.* [OE. *acumba* < *a-,* out + *camb,* a comb] loose, stringy, hemp fiber got by taking apart old ropes: used in caulking
oar (ôr) *n.* [OE. *ar*] **1.** a long pole with a broad blade at one end, used in rowing **2.** a person who uses an oar; rower —*vt., vi.* to row —**put one's oar in** to meddle —**rest on one's oars** to stop to rest or relax —**oared** *adj.*
oar·fish (ôr′fish′) *n., pl.* **-fish′, -fish′es:** see FISH a narrow, serpentlike, deep-sea fish, up to 30 ft. long, with a fin the length of the back
oar·lock (-läk′) *n.* a device, often U-shaped, for holding the oar in place in rowing
oars·man (ôrz′mən) *n., pl.* **-men** a man who rows; esp., an expert at rowing —**oars′man·ship′** *n.*
OAS, O.A.S. Organization of American States
o·a·sis (ō ā′sis; *occas.* ō′ə sis) *n., pl.* **-ses** (-sēz) [L. < Gr. *ōasis:* orig. Coptic] **1.** a fertile place in a desert, due to the presence of water **2.** any place or thing offering welcome relief in the midst of difficulty, dullness, etc.
oat (ōt) *n.* [OE. *ate*] **1.** [*usually pl.*] *a*) a hardy cereal grass *b*) its edible grain **2.** any related grass; esp., the wild oat **3.** [Obs. or Poet.] a musical pipe made of an oat stalk —**feel one's oats** [Slang] **1.** to be frisky **2.** to feel and act important —**oat′en** *adj.*
oat·cake (-kāk′) *n.* a thin, flat cake of oatmeal
oath (ōth) *n., pl.* **oaths** (ōthz, ōths) [OE. *ath*] **1.** *a*) a ritualistic declaration, as by appeal to God, that one will speak the truth, keep a promise, etc. *b*) the thing declared **2.** the profane use of the name of God or of a sacred thing in anger or emphasis **3.** a swearword —**take oath** to promise or declare with an oath
oat·meal (ōt′mēl′) *n.* **1.** oats ground or rolled into meal or flakes **2.** a porridge made from this
Ob (ōb; *Russ.* ôb′y′) river in W Siberia, flowing northwest & north into the Arctic Ocean: 2,495 mi.
ob- [< L. *ob*] *a prefix meaning:* **1.** to, toward, before [*object*] **2.** opposed to, against [*obnoxious*] **3.** upon, over [*obfuscate*] **4.** completely, totally [*obsolete*] **5.** inversely, oppositely [*objurgate*] In words of Latin origin, *ob-* assimilates to *o-* before *m, oc-* before *c, of-* before *f,* and *op-* before *p*
OB, O.B. 1. obstetrician **2.** obstetrics
ob. [L. *obiit*] he (or she) died
O·ba·di·ah (ō′bə dī′ə) *Bible* **1.** a minor Hebrew prophet **2.** the book containing his prophecies: abbrev. **Ob., Obad.**
ob·bli·ga·to (äb′lə gät′ō) *adj.* [It., lit., obliged < L.] *Music* indispensable: said earlier of a required accompaniment but now usually of an optional one —*n., pl.* **-tos, -ti** (-ē) such an accompaniment
ob·du·rate (äb′door ət, -dyoor-) *adj.* [< L. pp. of *obdurare* < *ob-,* intens. + *durare,* to harden] **1.** hardhearted **2.** hardened and unrepenting **3.** stubborn —**ob′du·ra·cy** (-ə sē) *n.* —**ob′du·rate·ly** *adv.*
o·be·di·ence (ō bē′dē əns, ə-) *n.* the state, fact, or an instance of obeying; a being obedient
o·be·di·ent (-ənt) *adj.* [< OFr. < L. prp. of *obedire,* OBEY] obeying or willing to obey; submissive —**o·be′di·ent·ly** *adv.*
o·bei·sance (ō bā′s'ns, -bē′-) *n.* [< OFr. < prp. of *obeir,* OBEY] **1.** a gesture of respect or reverence, as a bow **2.** homage; deference —**o·bei′sant** *adj.*
ob·e·lisk (äb′ə lisk, ō′bə-) *n.* [< L. < Gr. *obeliskos,* dim. of *obelos,* a spit] a tall, four-sided stone pillar tapering toward its pyramidal top

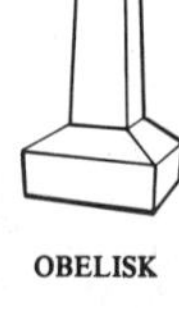
OBELISK

O·ber·am·mer·gau (ō′bər äm′ər gou′) village in Bavaria, S West Germany: site of a Passion play performed usually every ten years
O·ber·hau·sen (ō′bər hou′z'n) city in W West Germany: pop. 260,000
O·ber·on (ō′bə rän′, -bər ən) in early folklore, the king of fairyland and husband of Titania
o·bese (ō bēs′) *adj.* [< L. pp. of *obedere* < *ob-* (see OB-) + *edere,* to eat] very fat —**o·be′si·ty** *n.*
o·bey (ō bā′, ə-) *vt.* [< OFr. < L. *obedire* < *ob-* (see OB-) + *audire,* to hear] **1.** to carry out the orders of **2.** to carry out (an order) **3.** to be guided by [*to obey one's conscience*] —*vi.* to be obedient —**o·bey′er** *n.* —**o·bey′ing·ly** *adv.*
ob·fus·cate (äb′fəs kāt′, äb fus′kāt) *vt.* **-cat′ed, -cat′ing** [< L. pp. of *obfuscare* < *ob-* (see OB-) + *fuscare,* to obscure < *fuscus,* dark] **1.** to darken; obscure **2.** to muddle; confuse —**ob′fus·ca′tion** *n.*
o·bi (ō′bē) *n.* [Jap.] a broad sash with a bow in back, worn with a Japanese kimono
o·bit (ō′bit, äb′it) *n. same as* OBITUARY
ob·i·ter dic·tum (äb′i tər dik′təm, ō′bi-) *pl.* **ob′i·ter dic′ta** (-tə) [L.] **1.** an incidental opinion expressed by a judge **2.** any incidental remark
o·bit·u·ar·y (ō bich′oo wer′ē, ə-) *n., pl.* **-ar′ies** [ult. < L. *obitus,* death < pp. of *obire,* to die < *ob-* (see OB-) + *ire,*

to go] a notice of someone's death, usually with a brief biography —*adj.* of or recording a death or deaths

obj. 1. object 2. objection 3. objective

ob·ject (äb′jikt; *for v.* əb jekt′, äb-) *n.* [< ML. *objectum*, something thrown in the way < L. pp. of *objicere* < *ob-* (see OB-) + *jacere*, to throw] **1.** a thing that can be seen or touched; material thing **2.** a person or thing to which action, thought, or feeling is directed **3.** aim; purpose; goal **4.** *Gram.* a noun or substantive receiving the action of a verb (see DIRECT OBJECT, INDIRECT OBJECT), or one governed by a preposition **5.** *Philos.* anything that can be perceived by the mind —*vt.* to state in opposition or disapproval —*vi.* **1.** to put forward an objection; be opposed **2.** to feel or express disapproval —**ob′ject·less** *adj.* —**ob·jec′tor** *n.*

object glass *same as* OBJECTIVE (*n.* 4)

ob·jec·ti·fy (əb jek′tə fī′, äb-) *vt.* **-fied′, -fy′ing** to make objective —**ob·jec′ti·fi·ca′tion** *n.*

ob·jec·tion (əb jek′shən, äb-) *n.* **1.** an objecting **2.** a feeling or expression of opposition, disapproval, or dislike **3.** a reason for opposing, disapproving, or disliking

ob·jec·tion·a·ble (-ə b'l) *adj.* causing objection; disagreeable; offensive —**ob·jec′tion·a·bly** *adv.*

ob·jec·tive (əb jek′tiv, äb-) *adj.* **1.** of or having to do with a known or perceived object that is not merely in the mind **2.** having existence independent of the mind; real **3.** concerned with the actual features of the thing dealt with rather than the thoughts, feelings, etc. of the artist, writer, or speaker [an *objective* description] **4.** without bias or prejudice **5.** being the aim or goal **6.** minimizing subjective factors in answering and grading, as a multiple-choice or true-false test **7.** *Gram.* designating or of the case of an object (sense 4) —*n.* **1.** anything external to or independent of the mind; reality **2.** aim; goal **3.** *Gram.* *a)* the objective case *b)* a word in this case **4.** *Optics* the lens or lenses nearest the object observed, as in a microscope or telescope —**ob·jec′tive·ly** *adv.* —**ob·jec′tive·ness** *n.*

ob·jec·tiv·i·ty (äb′jek tiv′ə tē) *n.* **1.** the state or quality of being objective **2.** objective reality

ob·jec·tiv·ize (əb jek′tə vīz′, äb-) *vt.* **-ized′, -iz′ing** to make objective —**ob·jec′ti·vi·za′tion** *n.*

object lesson an actual or practical demonstration or exemplification of some principle

ob·jet d'art (äb′zhā där′, ub′-) *pl.* **ob·jets d'art** (äb′zhā-, ub′-) [Fr.] a relatively small object of artistic value, as a figurine, vase, etc.

ob·jur·gate (äb′jər gāt′, əb jur′gāt) *vt.* **-gat′ed, -gat′ing** [< L. pp. of *objurgare* < *ob-* (see OB-) + *jurgare*, to chide] to chide vehemently; upbraid sharply; berate —**ob′jur·ga′tion** *n.* —**ob·jur′ga·to′ry** (-gə tôr′ē) *adj.*

obl. 1. oblique 2. oblong

ob·late[1] (äb′lāt, äb lāt′) *adj.* [ModL. *oblatus* < OB- + *-latus* as in *prolatus:* see PROLATE] *Geom.* flattened at the poles [an *oblate* spheroid]

ob·late[2] (äb′lāt) *n.* [< ML. *oblatus* < L. pp. of *offerre*, to OFFER] *R.C.Ch.* a person living in or associated with a religious community but not bound by vows

ob·la·tion (ä blā′shən) *n.* [OFr. < L. < *oblatus*, pp. of *offerre:* see OFFER] an offering made to God or a god —**ob·la′tion·al** *adj.*

ob·li·gate (äb′lə gāt′) *vt.* **-gat′ed, -gat′ing** [< L. pp. of *obligare:* see OBLIGE] to bind by a contract, promise, sense of duty, etc.

ob·li·ga·tion (äb′lə gā′shən) *n.* **1.** an obligating or being obligated **2.** *a)* a legal or moral responsibility *b)* the thing that such a responsibility binds one to do **3.** binding power of a contract, promise, etc. **4.** indebtedness for a favor, service, etc. —**ob′li·ga′tion·al** *adj.*

ob·li·ga·to (äb′lə gät′ō) *adj., n., pl.* **-tos, -ti** (-ē) *same as* OBBLIGATO

ob·lig·a·to·ry (ə blig′ə tôr′ē, äb′lig ə-) *adj.* legally or morally binding; required —**ob·lig′a·to′ri·ly** *adv.* —**ob·lig′a·to′ri·ness** *n.*

o·blige (ə blīj′, ō-) *vt.* **o·bliged′, o·blig′ing** [< OFr. < L. *obligare* < *ob-* (see OB-) + *ligare*, to bind] **1.** to compel by moral, legal, or physical force; constrain **2.** to make indebted for a kindness; do a favor for —*vi.* to do a favor —**o·blig′er** *n.*

o·blig·ing (ə blī′jiŋ) *adj.* ready to do favors; helpful; accommodating —**o·blig′ing·ly** *adv.*

ob·lique (ə blēk′, ō-; *also, esp. in mil. use*, -blīk′) *adj.* [< L. *obliquus* < *ob-* (see OB-) + *liquis*, awry] **1.** neither perpendicular nor horizontal; slanting **2.** not straight to the point; indirect **3.** evasive, underhanded, etc. **4.** indirectly aimed at or attained **5.** *Gram.* designating or of any case but the nominative and vocative —*n.* an oblique angle, muscle, etc. —*vi.* **-liqued′, -liqu′ing** to veer from the perpendicular; slant —**ob·lique′ly** *adv.* —**ob·liq·ui·ty** (ə blik′wə tē, ō-), **ob·lique′ness** *n.*

oblique angle any angle other than a right angle; acute or obtuse angle

ob·lit·er·ate (ə blit′ə rāt′, ō-) *vt.* **-at′ed, -at′ing** [< L. pp. of *obliterare*, to blot out < *ob-* (see OB-) + *litera*, a letter] **1.** to blot out or wear away, leaving no traces; efface **2.** to do away with; destroy —**ob·lit′er·a′tion** *n.* —**ob·lit′er·a′tive** *adj.* —**ob·lit′er·a′tor** *n.*

ob·liv·i·on (ə bliv′ē ən, ō-) *n.* [< OFr. < L. < *oblivisci*, to forget] **1.** a forgetting or having forgotten; forgetfulness **2.** a being forgotten

ob·liv·i·ous (-əs) *adj.* **1.** forgetful or unmindful (usually with *of* or *to*) **2.** causing forgetfulness —**ob·liv′i·ous·ly** *adv.* —**ob·liv′i·ous·ness** *n.*

ob·long (äb′lôŋ) *adj.* [< L. < *ob-* (see OB-) + *longus*, long] longer than broad; elongated; specif., rectangular and longer in one direction than in the other —*n.* an oblong figure

ob·lo·quy (äb′lə kwē) *n., pl.* **-quies** [< LL. < *obloqui*, to speak against < *ob-* (see OB-) + *loqui*, to speak] **1.** verbal abuse of a person or thing; esp., widespread censure **2.** disgrace or infamy resulting from this

ob·nox·ious (əb näk′shəs, äb-) *adj.* [< L. < *obnoxius*, in danger < *ob-* (see OB-) + *noxa*, a harm] very unpleasant; objectionable; offensive —**ob·nox′ious·ly** *adv.* —**ob·nox′ious·ness** *n.*

o·boe (ō′bō) *n.* [It. < Fr. *hautbois:* see HAUTBOY] a double-reed woodwind instrument having a high, penetrating, melancholy tone —**o′bo·ist** *n.*

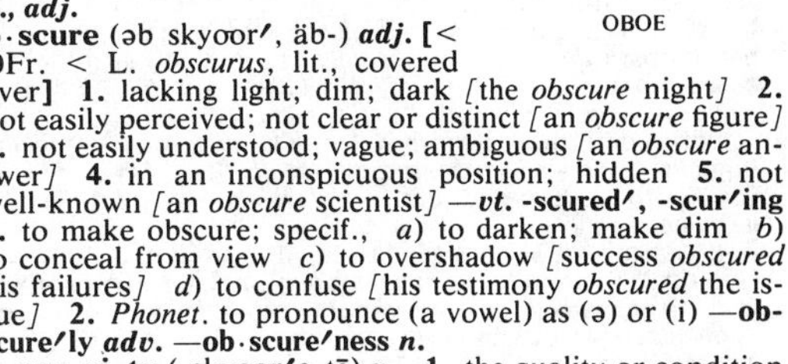

OBOE

Obs., obs. obsolete

ob·scene (äb sēn′, əb-) *adj.* [< Fr. < L. *obscenus*, filthy, repulsive] **1.** offensive to one's feelings, or to prevailing notions, of modesty or decency; lewd **2.** disgusting; repulsive —**ob·scene′ly** *adv.* —**ob·scen′i·ty** (-sen′ə tē) *n., pl.* **-ties**

ob·scu·rant·ism (äb skyoor′ənt iz'm, əb-) *n.* [< L. *obscurans*, obscuring] **1.** opposition to human progress or enlightenment **2.** the practice of being deliberately obscure or vague —**ob·scu′rant·ist** *n., adj.*

ob·scure (əb skyoor′, äb-) *adj.* [< OFr. < L. *obscurus*, lit., covered over] **1.** lacking light; dim; dark [the *obscure* night] **2.** not easily perceived; not clear or distinct [an *obscure* figure] **3.** not easily understood; vague; ambiguous [an *obscure* answer] **4.** in an inconspicuous position; hidden **5.** not well-known [an *obscure* scientist] —*vt.* **-scured′, -scur′ing** **1.** to make obscure; specif., *a)* to darken; make dim *b)* to conceal from view *c)* to overshadow [success *obscured* his failures] *d)* to confuse [his testimony *obscured* the issue] **2.** *Phonet.* to pronounce (a vowel) as (ə) or (i) —**ob·scure′ly** *adv.* —**ob·scure′ness** *n.*

ob·scu·ri·ty (-skyoor′ə tē) *n.* **1.** the quality or condition of being obscure **2.** *pl.* **-ties** an obscure person or thing

ob·se·quies (äb′sə kwēz) *n.pl.* [< OFr. < ML. *obsequiae* (pl.) (< L. *obsequium:* see ff.), substituted for L. *exsequiae*, funeral] funeral rites

ob·se·qui·ous (əb sē′kwē əs, äb-) *adj.* [< L. < *obsequium*, compliance < *obsequi*, to comply with] showing too great a willingness to serve or obey; fawning —**ob·se′qui·ous·ly** *adv.* —**ob·se′qui·ous·ness** *n.*

ob·serv·a·ble (əb zur′və b'l, äb-) *adj.* **1.** that can be observed; visible; noticeable **2.** deserving of attention **3.** that can or must be kept or celebrated [an *observable* holiday] —**ob·serv′a·bly** *adv.*

ob·serv·ance (-vəns) *n.* **1.** the act or practice of observing a law, duty, custom, etc. **2.** a customary act, rite, etc. **3.** observation **4.** *R.C.Ch.* the rule to be observed by a religious order

ob·serv·ant (-vənt) *adj.* **1.** strict in observing a rule, custom, etc. (often with *of*) **2.** paying careful attention **3.** perceptive or alert —**ob·serv′ant·ly** *adv.*

ob·ser·va·tion (äb′zər vā′shən) *n.* **1.** *a)* the act, practice, or power of noticing *b)* something noticed **2.** a being seen or noticed **3.** *a)* a noting and recording of facts and events, as for some scientific study *b)* the data so noted and recorded **4.** a comment based on something observed **5.** the act of determining the altitude of the sun, a star, etc., in order to find a ship's position at sea —*adj.* for observing —**ob′ser·va′tion·al** *adj.*

ob·serv·a·to·ry (əb zur′və tôr′ē, äb-) *n., pl.* **-ries** **1.** a building or institution equipped for scientific observation, esp. one with a large telescope for astronomical research **2.** any building or place providing an extensive view of the surrounding land

ob·serve (əb zʉrv′, äb-) ***vt.*** **-served′, -serv′ing** [< OFr. < L. *observare*, to watch < *ob-* (see OB-) + *servare*, to keep] **1.** to adhere to or keep (a law, custom, duty, etc.) **2.** to celebrate (a holiday, etc.) according to custom **3.** *a*) to notice or perceive (something) *b*) to pay special attention to **4.** to conclude after study **5.** to say casually; remark **6.** to examine scientifically —***vi.*** **1.** to take notice or make observations **2.** to comment (*on* or *upon*) —**ob·serv′er** ***n.*** —**ob·serv′ing·ly** ***adv.***

ob·sess (əb ses′, äb-) ***vt.*** [< L. *obsessus*, pp. of *obsidere*, to besiege < *ob-* (see OB-) + *sedere*, to sit] to haunt or trouble in mind, esp. to an abnormal degree; preoccupy greatly —**ob·ses′sive** ***adj.*** —**ob·ses′sive·ly** ***adv.*** —**ob·ses′sive·ness** ***n.***

ob·ses·sion (-sesh′ən) ***n.*** **1.** the fact or state of being obsessed with an idea, desire, emotion, etc. **2.** such a persistent idea, desire, etc. —**ob·ses′sion·al** ***adj.***

ob·sid·i·an (əb sid′ē ən, äb-) ***n.*** [< ModL. < L. *Obsidianus*, a faulty reading for *Obsianus*, after Obsius, who, according to Pliny, discovered it] a hard, dark volcanic glass, used as a gemstone

ob·so·lesce (äb′sə les′) ***vi.*** **-lesced′, -lesc′ing** to be or become obsolescent

ob·so·les·cent (-les′'nt) ***adj.*** in the process of becoming obsolete —**ob′so·les′cence** ***n.*** —**ob′so·les′cent·ly** ***adv.***

ob·so·lete (äb′sə lēt′, äb′sə lēt′) ***adj.*** [< L. pp. of *obsolescere* < *ob-* (see OB-) + *solere*, to become accustomed] **1.** no longer in use or practice; discarded **2.** out-of-date; passé —***vt.*** **-let′ed, -let′ing** to make obsolete, as by replacing with something newer —**ob′so·lete′ly** ***adv.*** —**ob′so·lete′ness** ***n.***

ob·sta·cle (äb′sti k'l) ***n.*** [OFr. < L. *obstaculum* < *ob-* (see OB-) + *stare*, to stand] anything that gets in the way or hinders; obstruction

ob·stet·ric (əb stet′rik, äb-) ***adj.*** [< ModL. < L. < *obstetrix*, midwife, lit., she who stands before] of childbirth or obstetrics: also **ob·stet′ri·cal** —**ob·stet′ri·cal·ly** ***adv.***

ob·ste·tri·cian (äb′stə trish′ən) ***n.*** a medical doctor who specializes in obstetrics

ob·stet·rics (əb stet′riks, äb-) ***n.pl.*** [*with sing. v.*] the branch of medicine concerned with the care and treatment of women in pregnancy, childbirth, and the period immediately following

ob·sti·na·cy (äb′stə nə sē) ***n.*** **1.** the state or quality of being obstinate **2.** *pl.* **-cies** an obstinate act, attitude, etc.

ob·sti·nate (äb′stə nit) ***adj.*** [< L. pp. of *obstinare*, to resolve on, ult. < *ob-* (see OB-) + *stare*, to stand] **1.** unreasonably determined to have one's own way; stubborn; dogged **2.** resisting treatment [an *obstinate* fever] **3.** not easily subdued, ended, etc. —**ob′sti·nate·ly** ***adv.*** —**ob′sti·nate·ness** ***n.***

ob·strep·er·ous (əb strep′ər əs, äb-) ***adj.*** [< L., ult. < *ob-* (see OB-) + *strepere*, to roar] noisy, boisterous, or unruly, esp. in resisting or opposing —**ob·strep′er·ous·ly** ***adv.*** —**ob·strep′er·ous·ness** ***n.***

ob·struct (əb strukt′, äb-) ***vt.*** [< L. pp. of *obstruere* < *ob-* (see OB-) + *struere*, to pile up] **1.** to block (a passage) with obstacles; clog **2.** to hinder (progress, an activity, etc.); impede **3.** to block (the view) —**ob·struct′er, ob·struc′tor** ***n.*** —**ob·struc′tive** ***adj.*** —**ob·struc′tive·ly** ***adv.*** —**ob·struc′tive·ness** ***n.***

ob·struc·tion (əb struk′shən, äb-) ***n.*** **1.** an obstructing or being obstructed **2.** anything that obstructs; hindrance

ob·struc·tion·ist (-ist) ***n.*** anyone who obstructs progress; esp., a member of a legislature who hinders legislation by technical maneuvers —***adj.*** of obstructionists: also **ob·struc′tion·is′tic** —**ob·struc′tion·ism** ***n.***

ob·tain (əb tān′, äb-) ***vt.*** [< OFr. < L. *obtinere* < *ob-* (see OB-) + *tenere*, to hold] to get possession of by effort; procure —***vi.*** to be in force or in effect; prevail [peace will *obtain*] —**ob·tain′a·ble** ***adj.*** —**ob·tain′er** ***n.*** —**ob·tain′ment** ***n.***

ob·trude (əb trōōd′, äb-) ***vt.*** **-trud′ed, -trud′ing** [< L. *obtrudere* < *ob-* (see OB-) + *trudere*, to thrust] **1.** to thrust forward; push out; eject **2.** to force (oneself, one's opinions, etc.) upon others unasked or unwanted —***vi.*** to obtrude oneself (*on* or *upon*) —**ob·trud′er** ***n.*** —**ob·tru′sion** (-trōō′zhən) ***n.***

ob·tru·sive (-trōō′siv) ***adj.*** **1.** inclined to obtrude **2.** obtruding itself —**ob·tru′sive·ly** ***adv.*** —**ob·tru′sive·ness** ***n.***

ob·tuse (äb tōōs′, əb-; -tyōōs′) ***adj.*** [< L. pp. of *obtundere*, to blunt < *ob-* (see OB-) + *tundere*, to strike] **1.** not sharp or pointed; blunt **2.** greater than 90 degrees and less than 180 degrees [an *obtuse* angle] **3.** slow to understand or perceive; dull or insensitive **4.** not acute [an *obtuse* pain] —**ob·tuse′ly** ***adv.*** —**ob·tuse′ness, ob·tu′si·ty** ***n.***

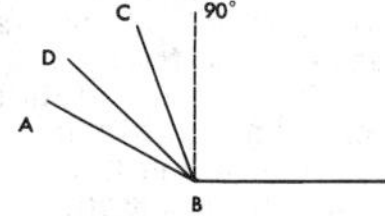

OBTUSE ANGLES (ABE, DBE, CBE)

ob·verse (äb vʉrs′, əb-; *also, & for n. always*, äb′vərs) ***adj.*** [< L. pp. of *obvertere* < *ob-* (see OB-) + *vertere*, to turn] **1.** turned toward the observer **2.** narrower at the base than at the top [an *obverse* leaf] **3.** forming a counterpart —***n.*** **1.** the side, as of a coin or medal, bearing the main design **2.** the front or main surface of anything **3.** a counterpart —**ob·verse′ly** ***adv.***

ob·vi·ate (äb′vē āt′) ***vt.*** **-at′ed, -at′ing** [< L. pp. of *obviare* < *obvius*: see OBVIOUS] to do away with or prevent by effective measures; make unnecessary —**ob′vi·a′tion** ***n.***

ob·vi·ous (äb′vē əs) ***adj.*** [L. *obvius*, in the way: see OB- & VIA] easy to see or understand; evident —**ob′vi·ous·ly** ***adv.*** —**ob′vi·ous·ness** ***n.***

oc- *see* OB-

o/c overcharge

Oc., oc. ocean

oc·a·ri·na (äk′ə rē′nə) ***n.*** [It., dim. of *oca* < LL. *auca*, a goose: from its shape] a small, simple wind instrument with finger holes and a mouthpiece: it produces soft, hollow tones

OCARINA

O'Ca·sey (ō kā′sē), **Sean** (shôn) 1880–1964; Ir. playwright

occas. 1. occasion **2.** occasional **3.** occasionally

oc·ca·sion (ə kā′zhən) ***n.*** [< OFr. < L. < pp. of *occidere* < *ob-* (see OB-) + *cadere*, to fall] **1.** a favorable time; opportunity **2.** a fact or event that makes something else possible **3.** *a*) a happening; occurrence *b*) a particular time [on the *occasion* of his birth] **4.** a special time or event, suitable for celebration **5.** need arising from circumstances —***vt.*** to give occasion to; cause —**on occasion** once in a while; sometimes —**rise to the occasion** to meet an emergency —**take (the) occasion** to use the opportunity (to do something)

oc·ca·sion·al (-'l) ***adj.*** **1.** occurring on a particular occasion **2.** of or for a special occasion **3.** acting only on special occasions **4.** happening now and then; infrequent —**oc·ca′sion·al·ly** ***adv.***

oc·ci·dent (äk′sə dənt) ***n.*** [< OFr. < L. *occidens*, direction of the setting sun < *occidere*: see OCCASION] the west: now rare, except [**O-**] the part of the world west of Asia, esp. Europe and the Americas —**oc′ci·den′tal, Oc′ci·den′tal** ***adj.***, ***n.***

oc·cip·i·tal (äk sip′ə t'l) ***adj.*** of the occiput or the occipital bone —***n.*** *same as* OCCIPITAL BONE —**oc·cip′i·tal·ly** ***adv.***

occipital bone the bone that forms the back part of the skull

oc·ci·put (äk′si put′) ***n.***, *pl.* **oc·cip′i·ta** (-sip′ə tə), **-puts′** [< MFr. < L. < *ob-* (see OB-) + *caput*, head] the back part of the skull or head

oc·clude (ə klōōd′, ä-) ***vt.*** **-clud′ed, -clud′ing** [< L. *occludere* < *ob-* (see OB-) + *claudere*, to shut] **1.** to close or block (a passage) **2.** to shut in or out **3.** *Chem.* to retain or absorb (a gas, liquid, or solid) —***vi.*** *Dentistry* to meet with the cusps fitting closely —**oc·clud′ent** ***adj.*** —**oc·clu′sion** (-klōō′zhən) ***n.*** —**oc·clu′sive** ***adj.***

oc·cult (ə kult′, ä′kult) ***adj.*** [< L. pp. of *occulere*, to conceal < *ob-* (see OB-) + *celare*, hide] **1.** hidden **2.** secret; esoteric **3.** beyond human understanding; mysterious **4.** designating or of such alleged mystic arts as alchemy, astrology, etc. —***vt., vi.*** to hide or become hidden —**the occult** the occult arts —**oc·cult′ism** ***n.*** —**oc·cult′ist** ***n.*** —**oc·cult′ly** ***adv.*** —**oc·cult′ness** ***n.***

oc·cul·ta·tion (äk′ul tā′shən) ***n.*** **1.** the state of becoming hidden or disappearing from view **2.** *Astron.* an eclipse in which the eclipsed body seems much smaller than the eclipsing body

oc·cu·pan·cy (äk′yə pən sē) ***n.***, *pl.* **-cies** **1.** an occupying; a taking or keeping in possession **2.** *Law* the taking possession of a previously unowned object

oc·cu·pant (-pənt) ***n.*** **1.** one who occupies a house, post, etc. **2.** one who acquires possession by occupancy

oc·cu·pa·tion (äk′yə pā′shən) ***n.*** **1.** an occupying or being occupied; specif., the seizure and control of a country or area by military forces **2.** (one's) trade, profession, or business —**oc′cu·pa′tion·al** ***adj.*** —**oc′cu·pa′tion·al·ly** ***adv.***

occupational disease a disease commonly acquired by people in a particular occupation [silicosis is an *occupational disease* of miners]

occupational therapy therapy by means of work, as arts and crafts, designed to divert the mind or to correct a physical defect

oc·cu·py (äk′yə pī′) ***vt.*** **-pied′, -py′ing** [< OFr. < L. *occupare*, to possess < *ob-* (see OB-) + *capere*, to seize] **1.** to take possession of by settlement or seizure **2.** to hold possession of by tenure; specif., *a*) to dwell in *b*) to hold (a position or office) **3.** to take up or fill up (space, time, etc.) **4.** to employ or busy (oneself, one's mind, etc.) —**oc′cu·pi′er** ***n.***

oc·cur (ə kʉr′) ***vi.*** **-curred′, -cur′ring** [< L. *occurrere* <

ob- (see OB-) + *currere,* to run] **1.** to be found; exist *[fish occur* in most waters*]* **2.** to present itself; come to mind *[an idea occurred* to him*]* **3.** to take place; happen

oc·cur·rence (-əns) *n.* **1.** the act or fact of occurring **2.** an event; incident —**oc·cur′rent** *adj.*

o·cean (ō′shən) *n.* [< OFr. < L. *oceanus* < Gr. *Ōkeanos*] **1.** the great body of salt water that covers about 71% of the earth's surface **2.** any of its five principal divisions: the Atlantic, Pacific, Indian, Arctic, or Antarctic Ocean **3.** any great expanse or quantity —**o·ce·an·ic** (ō′shē an′ik) *adj.*

o·cean·aut (-ôt′) *n.* [< OCEAN + Gr. *nautēs,* sailor] *same as* AQUANAUT

o·cean·go·ing (-gō′iŋ) *adj.* of, having to do with, or made for, travel on the ocean

O·ce·an·i·a (ō′shē an′ē ə) islands in the Pacific, including Melanesia, Micronesia, & Polynesia &, sometimes, Australia, New Zealand, & the Malay Archipelago: also **O′ce-an′i·ca** (-i kə) —**O′ce·an′i·an** *adj., n.*

o·ce·an·og·ra·phy (ō′shə näg′rə fē, ō′shē ə-) *n.* the study of the environment in the oceans —**o′ce·an·og′ra·pher** *n.* —**o′ce·an·o·graph′ic** (-nə graf′ik), **o′ce·an·o·graph′i·cal** *adj.*

o·ce·an·ol·o·gy (-näl′ə jē) *n.* **1.** the study of the sea in all its aspects, including oceanography **2.** *same as* OCEANOGRAPHY —**o′ce·an·ol′o·gist** *n.*

ocean sunfish a large, sluggish ocean fish, with a globelike body and stumpy tail

o·cel·lus (ō sel′əs) *n., pl.* **-li** (-ī) [L., dim. of *oculus,* an eye] **1.** the simple eyespot of certain invertebrates **2.** an eyelike spot —**o·cel′lar** *adj.*

o·ce·lot (äs′ə lät′, ō′sə-) *n., pl.* **-lots, -lot:** see PLURAL, II, D, 1 [Fr. < Nahuatl *ocelotl,* jaguar] a large cat of N. and S. America, with a yellow or gray coat marked with black spots

OCelt. Old Celtic

o·cher (ō′kər) *n.* [< L. < Gr. < *ōchros,* pale-yellow] **1.** a yellow or reddish-brown clay colored by iron oxide, used as a pigment **2.** the color of ocher; esp., dark yellow —*vt.* to color with ocher —**o′cher·ous** *adj.*

o·chre (ō′kər) *n., vt.* **o′chred, o′chring** *alt. sp. of* OCHER —**o′chre·ous** (-kər əs, -krē əs) *adj.*

-ock (ək) [OE. *-oc, -uc,* dim.] *a suffix used orig. to form the diminutive [hillock]*

o'clock (ə kläk′, ō-) *adv.* **1.** of or according to the clock **2.** as if on a clock dial

oct- *same as:* **1.** OCTA- **2.** OCTO- Used before a vowel

Oct. October

oct. octavo

oc·ta- [Gr. *okta-* < *oktō,* eight] *a combining form meaning* eight *[octagon]*

oc·ta·gon (äk′tə gän′) *n.* [< L. < Gr.: see OCTA- & -GON] a plane figure with eight angles and eight sides —**oc·tag′o·nal** (-tag′ə n'l) *adj.* —**oc·tag′o·nal·ly** *adv.*

oc·ta·he·dron (äk′tə hē′drən) *n., pl.* **-drons, -dra** (-drə) [< Gr.: see OCTA- & -HEDRON] a solid figure with eight plane surfaces —**oc′ta·he′dral** *adj.*

oc·tane (äk′tān) *n.* [< OCT(O)- + -ANE] an oily paraffin hydrocarbon, C_8H_{18}, found in petroleum

octane number (or **rating**) a number representing the antiknock quality of a gasoline, etc.: the higher the number, the greater this quality

oc·tave (äk′tiv, -tāv) *n.* [< OFr. < L. *octavus,* eighth < *octo,* eight] **1.** *a)* the eighth day inclusive following a church festival *b)* the period between the festival and this day **2.** the first eight lines of a sonnet **3.** any group of eight **4.** *Music a)* the eighth full tone above or below a given tone *b)* the interval of eight diatonic degrees between a tone and either of its octaves *c)* the series of tones (a full scale) within this interval, or the keys of an instrument producing such a series *d)* a tone and either of its octaves sounded together —*adj.* consisting of eight, or an octave —**oc·ta·val** (äk tā′v'l, äk′tə v'l) *adj.*

Oc·ta·vi·an (äk tā′vē ən) *see* AUGUSTUS (sense 2)

oc·ta·vo (äk tā′vō, -tä′-) *n., pl.* **-vos** [< L. (*in*) *octavo,* (in) eight] **1.** the page size (about 6 by 9 inches) of a book made up of printer's sheets folded into eight leaves **2.** a book with pages of this size Also written **8vo** or **8°** —*adj.* with pages of this size

oc·tet, oc·tette (äk tet′) *n.* [< OCT(O)- + (DU)ET] **1.** any group of eight; esp., an octave (sense 2) **2.** *Music a)* a composition for eight voices or eight instruments *b)* the eight performers of this

oc·to- [Gr. *oktō-* < *oktō,* eight] *a combining form meaning* eight

Oc·to·ber (äk tō′bər) *n.* [OE. < L. < *octo,* eight: it was the eighth month of the ancient Roman year] the tenth month of the year, having 31 days: abbrev. **Oct., O.**

oc·to·ge·nar·i·an (äk′tə ji ner′ē ən) *adj.* [< L. < *octoginta,* eighty] eighty years old, or between the ages of eighty and ninety —*n.* a person of this age

oc·to·pus (äk′tə pəs) *n., pl.* **-pus·es, -pi′** (-pī′), **oc·top·o·des** (äk täp′ə dēz′) [ModL. < Gr. < *oktō,* eight + *pous,* a foot] **1.** a mollusk with a soft body and eight arms covered with suckers **2.** anything suggesting an octopus; esp., a powerful organization with many branches

OCTOPUS (diameter with outspread arms, from 1 in. to 25 ft.)

oc·to·roon (äk′tə ro͞on′) *n.* [OCTO- + (QUAD)ROON] a person with one eighth Negro ancestry

oc·tu·ple (äk′too p'l, -tyoo-; äk to͞o′-, -tyo͞o′-) *adj.* [< L. < *octo,* eight + *-plus,* -fold] eightfold —*n.* something that is eight times as great as something else —*vt.* **-pled, -pling** to multiply by eight

oc·u·lar (äk′yə lər) *adj.* [< LL. < L. *oculus,* the eye] **1.** of, for, or like the eye **2.** by eyesight *[an ocular* demonstration*]* —*n.* the eyepiece of an optical instrument

oc·u·list (-list) *n.* [< Fr. < L. *oculus,* the eye] *earlier term for* OPHTHALMOLOGIST

OD (ō′dē′) *n., pl.* **ODs, OD's** [Slang] an overdose, esp. of a narcotic —*vi.* **OD'd** or **ODed, OD'ing** or **ODing** [Slang] to take an overdose, esp. a fatal overdose of a narcotic

OD, O.D. 1. Officer of the Day **2.** olive drab

o·da·lisque, o·da·lisk (ōd′'l isk) *n.* [Fr. < Turk. *ōdalik,* chambermaid] a female slave or concubine in a harem

odd (äd) *adj.* [< ON. *oddi,* triangle, hence (from the third angle) odd number] **1.** *a)* remaining or separated from a pair, a set, etc. *[an odd* glove, a few *odd* volumes of Dickens*]* *b)* remaining after the others are paired, grouped, taken, etc. **2.** having a remainder of one when divided by two; not even: said of numbers **3.** numbered with an odd number *[the odd* months*]* **4.** *a)* in addition to that mentioned in a round number *[ten* dollars and some *odd* change*]* *b)* with a relatively small number over that specified *[thirty odd* years ago*]* **5.** occasional; incidental *[odd* jobs*]* **6.** *a)* singular; peculiar *b)* queer; eccentric **7.** out-of-the-way *[in odd* corners*]* —**odd′ly** *adv.* —**odd′ness** *n.*

odd·ball (-bôl) *n.* [ODD + BALL[1]] [Slang] an eccentric or nonconforming person —*adj.* strange or unconventional

odd·i·ty (äd′ə tē) *n.* **1.** queerness; peculiarity **2.** *pl.* **-ties** an odd person or thing

odd·ment (-mənt) *n.* something odd or left over

odds (ädz) *n.pl.* **1.** [Now Rare] difference **2.** difference in favor of one side over the other; advantage **3.** an equalizing advantage given by a bettor or competitor in proportion to the assumed chances in his favor —**at odds** in disagreement; quarreling —**by (all) odds** by far —**the odds are** the likelihood is

odds and ends scraps; remnants; oddments

odds-on (-än′, -ôn′) *adj.* having better than an even chance of winning *[an odds-on* favorite*]*

ode (ōd) *n.* [Fr. < LL. < Gr. *ōidē,* song < *aeidein,* to sing] a lyric poem typically addressed to some person or thing and characterized by lofty feeling and dignified style —**od′ic** (ō′dik) *adj.*

-ode (ōd) [< Gr. *hodos*] *a suffix meaning* way, path

O·der (ō′dər) river in C Europe, flowing northeast through Czechoslovakia & Poland into the Baltic

O·des·sa (ō des′ə; *Russ.* ô de′sä) **1.** seaport in S Ukrainian S.S.R., on the Black Sea: pop. 797,000 **2.** city in WC Tex.: pop. 90,000

O·din (ō′din) *Norse Myth.* the chief god: identified with the Teutonic god Woden

o·di·ous (ō′dē əs) *adj.* [< OFr. < L. < *odium:* see ff.] arousing or deserving hatred or loathing; disgusting —**o′di·ous·ly** *adv.* —**o′di·ous·ness** *n.*

o·di·um (-əm) *n.* [L. *odium,* hatred < *odi,* I hate] **1.** *a)* hatred *b)* a being hated **2.** the disgrace brought on by hateful action; opprobrium

O·do·a·cer (ō′dō ā′sər) 435?–493 A.D.; 1st barbarian ruler of Italy (476–493)

o·dom·e·ter (ō däm′ə tər) *n.* [< Fr. < Gr. < *hodos,* way + *metron,* a measure] an instrument for measuring the distance traveled by a vehicle

-o·dont (ə dänt′) [< Gr. *odōn* (gen. *odontos*)] *a combining form meaning* tooth

o·dont·o- [see prec.] *a combining form meaning* tooth or teeth: also, before a vowel, **odont-**

o·don·tol·o·gy (ō′dän täl′ə jē) *n.* [< Fr.: see prec. & -LOGY] the science dealing with the structure, growth, and diseases of the teeth —**o·don′to·log′i·cal** (-tə läj′i k'l) ***adj.*** —**o·don′to·log′i·cal·ly** ***adv.*** —**o′don·tol′o·gist** ***n.***

o·dor (ō′dər) ***n.*** [< OFr. < L.] **1.** *a)* that characteristic of a substance which makes it perceptible to the sense of smell *b)* a smell, whether pleasant or unpleasant; fragrance, stench, etc. **2.** [Archaic] a perfume —**be in bad** (or **ill**) **odor** to be in ill repute —**o′dor·less** ***adj.***

o·dor·if·er·ous (ō′də rif′ər əs) ***adj.*** giving off an odor, often, specif., a fragrant one —**o′dor·if′er·ous·ly** ***adv.*** —**o′dor·if′er·ous·ness** ***n.***

o·dor·ous (ō′dər əs) ***adj.*** having an odor; esp., fragrant —**o′dor·ous·ly** ***adv.*** —**o′dor·ous·ness** ***n.***

o·dour (ō′dər) ***n.*** *Brit. sp. of* ODOR

-o·dus (ə dəs) [ModL. < Gr. *-odous* < *odōn*, tooth] *a combining form meaning* having teeth, toothed

-o·dyn·i·a (ə din′ē ə, -dīn′-) [ModL. < Gr. < *odynē*, pain] *a combining form meaning* pain in (a specified organ or part)

O·dys·se·us (ō dis′yōōs, -dis′ē əs) the hero of the *Odyssey*, a king of Ithaca and one of the Greek leaders in the Trojan War: Latin name, *Ulysses*

Od·ys·sey (äd′ə sē) an ancient Greek epic poem, ascribed to Homer, about the wanderings of Odysseus during the ten years after the fall of Troy —***n.*** [*sometimes* **o-**] *pl.* **-seys** any extended wandering

oe- an earlier variant spelling for many words of Gr. and L. origin now usually written with *e-*

OE., OE, O.E. Old English

OED, O.E.D. Oxford English Dictionary

Oed·i·pal (ed′ə pəl, e′də-) ***adj.*** [*also* **o-**] of or relating to the Oedipus complex

Oed·i·pus (-pəs) *Gr. Myth.* a king of Thebes who unwittingly killed his father and married his mother

Oedipus complex *Psychoanalysis* the unconscious tendency of a child, sometimes unresolved in adulthood, to be attached to the parent of the opposite sex and hostile toward the other parent

o'er (ôr) ***prep., adv.*** *chiefly poet. contr. of* OVER

oe·soph·a·gus (i säf′ə gəs) ***n.*** *chiefly Brit. sp. of* ESOPHAGUS

oes·trus (es′trəs, ēs′-) ***adj.*** *Brit. sp. of* ESTRUS

of (uv, äv; *unstressed* əv, ə) ***prep.*** [OE., unstressed var. of *af, æf*, away (from)] **1.** from; specif., *a)* derived or coming from [men *of* Ohio] *b)* as relates to [how wise *of* her] *c)* resulting from; through [to die *of* fever] *d)* at a distance from [east *of* the city] *e)* proceeding as a product from; by [the poems *of* Poe] *f)* separated from [robbed *of* his money] *g)* from the whole constituting [part *of* the time] *h)* made from [a sheet *of* paper] **2.** belonging to [pages *of* a book] **3.** *a)* possessing [a man *of* property] *b)* containing [a bag *of* nuts] **4.** specified as [a height *of* six feet] **5.** with (something specified) as object, goal, etc. [a reader *of* books] **6.** characterized by [a man *of* honor] **7.** concerning; about [think well *of* me] **8.** set aside for [a day *of* rest] **9.** during [*of* late years] **10.** before: used in telling time [ten *of* nine] **11.** [Archaic] by [rejected *of* men] *Of* is also used in various idiomatic expressions, many of which are entered in this dictionary under the key words

of- *see* OB-

off (ôf) ***adv.*** [LME. variant of *of*, OF] **1.** so as to be or keep away or at a distance [to move *off*, to ward *off*] **2.** so as to be measured, divided, etc. [to mark *off*] **3.** so as to be no longer on, attached, etc. [take *off* your hat] **4.** (a specified distance) away in space or time [200 yards *off*, two weeks *off*] **5.** so as to be no longer in operation, function, etc. [turn the motor *off*] **6.** so as to be less, smaller, etc. [5% *off* for cash] **7.** so as to lose consciousness [to doze *off*] **8.** away from one's work [take a day *off*] —***prep.*** **1.** no longer (or not) on, attached, etc. [the car is *off* the road] **2.** away from [to live *off* the campus] **3.** *a)* from the substance of; on [to live *off* the land] *b)* at the expense of **4.** branching out from [an alley *off* Main Street] **5.** free or relieved from [*off* duty] **6.** not up to the usual level, standard, etc. of [*off* one's game] **7.** [Colloq.] no longer using, supporting, etc. [to be *off* liquor] **8.** [Colloq.] from [to buy it *off* him] —***adj.*** **1.** not on, attached, etc. [his hat is *off*] **2.** not in operation, function, etc. [the motor is *off*] **3.** on the way [be *off* to bed] **4.** less, smaller, etc. [sales are *off*] **5.** away from work, etc. [the maid is *off* today] **6.** not up to what is usual, standard, etc. [an *off* day] **7.** more remote; further [on the *off* chance] **8.** designating the horse on the right in double harness, etc. **9.** in (specified) circumstances [to be well *off*] **10.** not correct; in error [his figures are *off*] **11.** *Cricket* designating the side of the field facing the batsman **12.** *Naut.* toward the sea —***n.*** the fact or condition of being off —***interj.*** go away! stay away! —**off and on** now and then —**off with!** take off! remove! —**off with you!** go away! depart!

off. **1.** office **2.** officer **3.** official

of·fal (ôf′'l, äf′-) ***n.*** [ME. *ofall*, lit., off-fall] **1.** [*with sing. or pl. v.*] the entrails, etc. of a butchered animal **2.** refuse; garbage

off·beat (ôf′bēt′) ***adj.*** [< a rhythm in jazz music] [Colloq.] not conforming to the usual pattern or trend; unconventional, unusual, etc.

off-Broad·way (-brôd′wā′) ***adj., adv.*** outside the main commercial theatrical district in New York City —***n.*** off-Broadway theaters and their productions Also written **Off Broadway**

off-col·or (-kul′ər) ***adj.*** **1.** varying from the usual, standard, or required color **2.** not quite proper; risqué [an *off-color* joke]

Of·fen·bach (ôf′'n bäk′), **Jacques** (zhäk) (born *Jakob Eberscht*) 1819?–80; Fr. composer, born in Germany

of·fence (ə fens′) ***n.*** *Brit. sp. of* OFFENSE

of·fend (ə fend′) ***vi.*** [< OFr. < L. *offendere* < *ob-* (see OB-) + *fendere*, to hit] **1.** to commit a sin or crime; do wrong **2.** to create resentment, anger, etc. —***vt.*** **1.** to hurt the feelings of; make resentful, angry, etc. **2.** to be displeasing to (the taste, sense, etc.) —**of·fend′er** ***n.***

of·fense (ə fens′; ôf′fens, äf′-) ***n.*** **1.** an offending; specif., *a)* a breaking of the law; sin or crime *b)* a creating of resentment, anger, etc. **2.** a being offended; esp., a feeling hurt, resentful, or angry **3.** [Rare] something that causes wrongdoing **4.** something that causes resentment, anger, etc. **5.** *a)* the act of attacking *b)* the action of seeking to score in any contest **6.** *a)* the person, army, etc. that is attacking *b)* the side that is seeking to score in any contest —**give offense** to anger, insult, etc.; offend —**take offense** to become offended; feel hurt, angry, etc. —**of·fense′less** ***adj.***

of·fen·sive (ə fen′siv) ***adj.*** **1.** attacking; aggressive **2.** of or for attack **3.** designating or of the side that is seeking to score in any contest **4.** unpleasant; disgusting; repugnant [an *offensive* odor] **5.** causing resentment, anger, etc.; insulting —***n.*** **1.** attitude or position of attack **2.** an attack or hostile action, esp. by armed forces —**of·fen′sive·ly** ***adv.*** —**of·fen′sive·ness** ***n.***

of·fer (ôf′ər, äf′-) ***vt.*** [OE. *offrian* < LL. *offerre*, to sacrifice < *ob-* (see OB-) + *ferre*, to bring] **1.** to present in an act of worship [to *offer* prayers] **2.** to present for acceptance or consideration [to *offer* one's services, a suggestion, etc.] **3.** to express willingness or intention (to do something) [to *offer* to go] **4.** to show or give signs of [to *offer* resistance] **5.** *a)* to present for sale *b)* to bid (a price, etc.) —***vi.*** **1.** to make a presentation in worship **2.** to occur; present itself [when the opportunity *offers*] —***n.*** the act of offering or thing offered —**of′fer·er, of′fer·or** ***n.***

of·fer·ing (-iŋ) ***n.*** **1.** the act of making an offer **2.** something offered; specif., *a)* a contribution *b)* a presentation made in an act of worship *c)* something offered for sale *d)* a theatrical presentation

of·fer·to·ry (ôf′ər tôr′ē, äf′-) ***n.***, *pl.* **-ries** [< ML. < LL. *offertorium*, place for offerings < *offerre*, OFFER] [*often* **O-**] **1.** that part of Holy Communion during which the Eucharistic bread and wine are offered to God **2.** any collection of money at a church service, or the part of the service for this **3.** the prayers or music accompanying the offertory

off·hand (ôf′hand′) ***adv.*** without prior preparation; extemporaneously —***adj.*** **1.** said or done offhand; extemporaneous **2.** casual, curt, etc. Also **off′hand′ed** —**off′hand′ed·ly** ***adv.*** —**off′hand′ed·ness** ***n.***

of·fice (ôf′is, äf′-) ***n.*** [< OFr. < L. *officium* < *opus*, a work + *facere*, to do] **1.** something done for another; (specified kind of) service [done through his good (or ill) *offices*] **2.** an assigned duty, esp. one that is an essential part of one's work; function; task **3.** a position of authority or trust, esp. in a government, business, etc. **4.** *a)* any of the branches of the U.S. Government ranking next below the departments [the Printing *Office*] *b)* [Chiefly Brit.] a governmental department [the Foreign *Office*] **5.** a place where work or business that is clerical, administrative, professional, etc. is carried on **6.** a religious ceremony or rite; specif., *a)* [**O-**] *shortened form of* DIVINE OFFICE *b)* [*often pl.*] any special rites

office boy a boy who works in an office, doing odd jobs and errands

of·fice·hold·er (-hōl′dər) ***n.*** a government official

of·fi·cer (ôf′ə sər, äf′-) ***n.*** **1.** anyone holding an office or position of authority in a government, business, society, etc. **2.** a policeman **3.** a person holding a position of authority in the armed forces; specif., *same as* COMMISSIONED OFFICER **4.** the captain or any of the mates of a nonnaval ship —***vt.*** **1.** to provide with officers **2.** to command; direct

officer of the day the military officer in overall charge of the interior guard and security of his garrison for any given day

of·fi·cial (ə fish′əl) ***adj.*** **1.** of or holding an office, or position of authority **2.** by, from, or with the proper authority; authorized or authoritative [an *official* request] **3.** formal or ceremonious and often involving persons of authority **4.** formally set or prescribed [the *official* date of publication] —***n.*** **1.** a person holding office **2.** *Sports* one who supervises an athletic contest —**of·fi′cial·ly** ***adv.***

of·fi·cial·dom (-dəm) *n.* **1.** officials collectively **2.** the domain or position of officials
of·fi·cial·ese (ə fish′ə lēz′) *n.* the pompous, wordy, and involved language typical of official communications and reports
of·fi·cial·ism (ə fish′əl iz'm) *n.* **1.** the characteristic practices of officials **2.** officials collectively
of·fi·ci·ate (ə fish′ē āt′) *vi.* **-at′ed, -at′ing** **1.** to perform the duties of an office **2.** to perform the functions of a priest, minister, rabbi, etc. at a religious ceremony **3.** *Sports* to act as referee, umpire, etc. —**of·fi′ci·a′tion** *n.*
of·fi·cious (ə fish′əs) *adj.* [< L. < *officium,* OFFICE] offering unwanted advice or services; meddlesome —**of·fi′cious·ly** *adv.* —**of·fi′cious·ness** *n.*
off·ing (ôf′iŋ) *n.* [< OFF] **1.** the distant part of the sea visible from the shore **2.** distance, or position at a distance, from the shore —**in the offing** **1.** at some distance but in sight **2.** at some indefinite time in the future
off·ish (ôf′ish) *adj.* [Colloq.] aloof; standoffish —**off′ish·ly** *adv.* —**off′ish·ness** *n.*
off-key (ôf′kē′) *adj.* **1.** not on the right note; flat or sharp **2.** not quite in accord with what is normal, fitting, etc.
off-lim·its (-lim′its) *adj.* ruled to be a place that cannot be entered, visited, patronized, etc. by a specific group
off·scour·ing (-skour′iŋ) *n.* [*usually pl.*] something scoured off; refuse, dregs, etc.
off·set (ôf′set′; *for v. usually* ôf set′) *n.* **1.** an offshoot; extension; branch; spur **2.** anything that balances or compensates for something else **3.** a ledge formed in a wall by a reduction in its thickness above **4.** *Mech.* a bend in a pipe, etc. to permit it to pass an obstruction **5.** *a)* *same as* OFFSET PRINTING *b)* an impression made by this process —*adj.* **1.** of, relating to, or being an offset **2.** that is offset —*vt.* **-set′, -set′ting** **1.** to balance, compensate for, etc. **2.** to make an offset in **3.** to make (an impression) by offset printing —*vi.* to project or develop as an offset
offset printing a lithographic printing process in which the inked impression is first made on a rubber-covered roller, then transferred to paper
off·shoot (ôf′shōōt′) *n.* **1.** a shoot growing from the main stem of a plant **2.** anything that branches off, or derives from, a main source
off·shore (-shôr′) *adj.* **1.** moving away from the shore **2.** at some distance from shore **3.** engaged in outside the U.S., as by U.S. banks or manufacturers [*offshore* investments, *offshore* production] —*adv.* **1.** away from the shore **2.** outside the U.S. [to borrow money *offshore*]
off·side (-sīd′) *adj. Sports* not in the proper position for play, as, in football, ahead of the ball before the play has begun —*n.* an offside play
off·spring (-spriŋ′) *n., pl.* **-spring′, -springs′** **1.** a child or animal as related to its parent **2.** progeny **3.** a result
off·stage (-stāj′) *n.* that part of a stage, as the wings, not seen by the audience —*adj.* in or from the offstage —*adv.* **1.** to the offstage **2.** when not actually appearing before the public
off-white (-hwīt′, -wīt′) *adj.* of any of various shades of grayish-white or yellowish-white
off year **1.** a year in which a major election does not take place **2.** a year of little production, poor crops, etc.
OFr. Old French
oft (ôft) *adv.* [OE.] *chiefly poet. var. of* OFTEN
of·ten (ôf′'n, ôf′t'n) *adv.* [ME. var. of prec.] many times; frequently —*adj.* [Archaic] frequent
of·ten·times (-tīmz′) *adv. same as* OFTEN: also [Chiefly Poet.] **oft′times′**
Og·den (äg′dən, ôg′-) [after P. *Ogden,* local fur trader] city in N Utah: pop. 64,000
o·gee (ō′jē, ō jē′) *n.* [< OFr. *ogive*] **1.** an S-shaped curve, line, molding, etc. **2.** a pointed arch formed with the curve of an ogee on each side: also **ogee arch**

OGEE ARCH

o·gle (ō′g'l, ä′-) *vi., vt.* **o′gled, o′gling** [prob. < LowG. *oegeln* < *oog,* the eye] to keep looking (at) boldly and with obvious desire; make eyes (at) —*n.* an ogling look —**o′gler** *n.*
o·gre (ō′gər) *n.* [Fr. < ? L. *Orcus,* Pluto, Hades] **1.** in fairy tales and folklore, a man-eating monster or giant **2.** a hideous or cruel man —**o′gre·ish, o′grish** *adj.* —**o′gress** *n.fem.*
oh (ō) *interj.* **1.** an exclamation of surprise, fear, wonder, pain, etc. **2.** a word used in direct address [*oh,* waiter!] —*n., pl.* **oh's, ohs** any instance of this exclamation
OH Ohio
O. Henry *see* HENRY
OHG, OHG., O.H.G. Old High German
O·hi·o (ō hī′ō) **1.** [after the river] Middle Western State of the U.S.: 41,222 sq. mi.; pop. 10,797,000; cap. Columbus: abbrev. **O., OH** **2.** [ult. < Iroquoian, lit., large river] river flowing from SW Pa. southwestward into the Mississippi —**O·hi′o·an** *adj., n.*
ohm (ōm) *n.* [after G. S. *Ohm* (1789–1854), G. physicist] the mks unit of electrical resistance, equal to the resistance of a circuit in which an electromotive force of one volt maintains a current of one ampere —**ohm′ic** *adj.*
ohm·me·ter (-mēt′ər) *n.* an instrument for measuring directly electrical resistance in ohms
-oid (oid) [< Gr. < *eidos,* a form, shape] *a suffix meaning* like, resembling [*crystalloid*]
oil (oil) *n.* [< OFr. < L. *oleum* < Gr. *elaion,* (olive) oil] **1.** any of various greasy, combustible substances obtained from animal, vegetable, and mineral sources: oils are liquid at ordinary temperatures and soluble in certain organic solvents, as ether, but not in water **2.** *same as* PETROLEUM **3.** any of various substances with the consistency of oil **4.** *same as: a)* OIL COLOR *b)* OIL PAINTING —*vt.* to lubricate or supply with oil —*adj.* of, from, like, or yielding oil, or having to do with the production or use of oil —**oiled** *adj.* —**oil′er** *n.*
oil cake a mass of crushed linseed, cottonseed, etc. from which the oil has been extracted, used as livestock feed and as a fertilizer
oil·cloth (-klôth′, -kläth′) *n.* cloth made waterproof with oil or with heavy coats of paint
oil color paint made by grinding a pigment in oil
oil of vitriol *same as* SULFURIC ACID
oil painting **1.** a picture painted in oil colors **2.** the art of painting in oil colors
oil·pa·per (-pā′pər) *n.* paper made transparent and waterproof by treatment with oil
oil·skin (-skin′) *n.* **1.** cloth made waterproof by treatment with oil **2.** [*often pl.*] a garment or outfit made of this
oil slick a film of oil on water, forming a smooth area
oil·stone (-stōn′) *n.* a whetstone treated with oil
oil well a well bored through layers of rock, etc. to a supply of petroleum
oil·y (-ē) *adj.* **oil′i·er, oil′i·est** **1.** of, like, or containing oil **2.** covered with oil; greasy **3.** too smooth; unctuous —**oil′i·ly** *adv.* —**oil′i·ness** *n.*
oink (oiŋk) *n.* the grunt of a pig, or a sound imitating it —*vi.* to grunt as or like a pig
oint·ment (oint′mənt) *n.* [< OFr., ult. < L. *unguentum:* see UNGUENT] a fatty substance applied to the skin as a salve or cosmetic; unguent
O·jib·wa (ō jib′wā, -wä, -wə) *n.* [Algonquian *ojibway,* to pucker: from the puckered seam on their moccasins] **1.** *pl.* **-was, -wa** a member of a group of N. American tribes living from Michigan to North Dakota **2.** their Algonquian language —*adj.* of these tribes Also **O·jib′way** (-wā)
OK, O.K. (ō′kā′; *also, & for v. & n. usually,* ō′kā′) *adj., adv., interj.* [abbrev. for "oll korrect," jocular misspelling of *all correct*] all right; correct —*n., pl.* **OK's, O.K.'s** approval —*vt.* **OK'd, O.K.'d, OK'ing, O.K.'ing** to put an OK on; approve
OK Oklahoma
o·ka·pi (ō kä′pē) *n., pl.* **-pis, -pi:** see PLURAL, II, D, 1 [native Afr. name] an African animal related to the giraffe, but having a much shorter neck

OKAPI (to 5 ft. high at shoulder)

o·kay (ō′kā′) *adj., adv., interj., n., vt. colloq. var. of* OK
O·kee·cho·bee (ō′kē chō′bē), **Lake** [< AmInd.] lake in SE Fla., at the N edge of the Everglades
O·ke·fe·no·kee Swamp (ō′kə fə nō′kē) [< AmInd., lit., trembling earth] swamp in SE Ga. & NE Fla.
O·khotsk (ō kätsk′; *Russ.* ô khôtsk′), **Sea of** arm of the Pacific, off the E coast of Siberia
O·kie (ō′kē) *n.* [OK(LAHOMA) + -IE] a migratory farm worker, esp. one forced from Oklahoma by drought, farm foreclosure, etc., in the late 1930's
O·ki·na·wa (ō′kə nä′wə) largest island of the Ryukyus, northeast of Taiwan
O·kla·ho·ma (ō′klə hō′mə) [< Choctaw *okla,* people + *homma,* red] State of the SC U.S.: 69,919 sq. mi.; pop. 3,025,000; cap. Oklahoma City: abbrev. **Okla., OK** —**O′kla·ho′man** *adj., n.*
Oklahoma City capital of Okla., in the central part: pop. 403,000 (met. area 830,000)
o·kra (ō′krə) *n.* [< WAfr. name] **1.** a tall plant with slen-

der, ribbed, sticky green pods **2.** the pods, used as a cooked vegetable, in soups, etc.

-ol[1] (ōl, ôl) [< (ALCOH)OL] *a suffix used in chemistry to mean* an alcohol or phenol *[menthol]*

-ol[2] (ōl, ôl) *var. of* -OLE

OL., O.L. Old Latin

old (ōld) ***adj.*** **old′er** or **eld′er, old′est** or **eld′est** [OE. *ald*] **1.** having lived or existed for a long time; aged **2.** of or characteristic of aged people **3.** of a certain age *[a* boy ten years *old]* **4.** made some time ago; not new **5.** known from the past *[*up to his *old* tricks*]* **6.** *[often* **O-**] designating the earliest stage of a language *[Old* English*]* **7.** worn out by age or use; shabby **8.** former **9.** having had long experience *[an old* hand at this work*]* **10.** having existed long ago; ancient *[an old* civilization*]* **11.** of long standing *[an old* joke*]* **12.** designating the earlier or earliest of two or more *[*the *Old* World*]* **13.** [Colloq.] dear: a term of affection *[old* boy*]* Also used as a colloquial intensive *[a* fine *old* time*]* —*n.* **1.** time long past; yore *[*days of *old]* **2.** a person of a specified age: used in hyphenated compounds *[a* six-year-*old]* **3.** something old (with *the*) —**old′ish** *adj.* —**old′ness** *n.*

old age the advanced years of life, when strength and vigor decline: cf. MIDDLE AGE

old country the country from which an immigrant came, esp. a country in Europe

old·en (ōl′d'n) *adj.* [Poet.] (of) old; ancient

Old English the West Germanic, Low German language of the Anglo-Saxons, spoken in England from c. 400 to c. 1100 A.D.

old-fash·ioned (ōld′fash′ənd) *adj.* suited to or favoring the styles, ideas, etc. of past times; out-of-date —*n.* [*also* **O- F-**] a cocktail made with whiskey, soda water, bitters, sugar, and fruit

old fogy, old fogey *see* FOGY

Old French the French language from c. 800 to c. 1550 A.D., esp. from the 9th to the 14th century

Old Glory the flag of the United States

old gold a soft, yellowish, metallic color

Old Guard [after Napoleon's imperial guard (1804)] **1.** any group that has long defended a cause **2.** the conservative element of a group, party, etc.

old hand a person with much skill or experience

old hat [Slang] **1.** old-fashioned **2.** well-known to the point of being trite or commonplace

Old High German the High German language from the 8th to the 12th century

old·ie, old·y (ōl′dē) *n., pl.* **old′ies** [Colloq.] an old joke, song, movie, etc.

Old Irish Irish Gaelic before the 11th century

old lady [Slang] **1.** one's mother **2.** one's wife

Old Latin the Latin language before c. 75 B.C.

old-line (ōld′līn′) *adj.* **1.** old and well-established **2.** following tradition; conservative

Old Low German the Low German language from its earliest period to the 12th century A.D.

old maid **1.** a woman, esp. an older woman, who has never married; spinster **2.** a prim, prudish, fussy person —**old′-maid′ish** *adj.*

old man [Slang] **1.** one's father **2.** one's husband **3.** [*usually* **O- M-**] any man in authority, as the head of a company, captain of a vessel, etc.

old master **1.** any great European painter before the 18th cent. **2.** a painting by any of these

old moon the moon in its last quarter, when it appears as a crescent curving to the left

Old Nick [prob. contr. < NICHOLAS] the Devil; Satan: also **Old Harry**

Old Norman French *same as* NORMAN FRENCH

Old Norse the North Germanic language of the Scandinavian peoples before the 14th century

Old Prussian a Baltic language which became extinct in the 17th century

old rose grayish or purplish red —**old′-rose′** *adj.*

Old Saxon a West Germanic language known chiefly from manuscripts of the 9th and 10th centuries A.D.

old school a group of people who cling to traditional or conservative ideas, methods, etc.

Old South the South before the Civil War

old·ster (ōld′stər) *n.* [Colloq.] a person who is no longer a youngster; old or elderly person

old style **1.** an old style of type with narrow, light letters **2.** [**O- S-**] the old method of reckoning time according to the Julian calendar, which was off one day every 128 years —**old′-style′** *adj.*

Old Testament *Christian designation for* the Holy Scriptures of Judaism, the first of the two general divisions of the Christian Bible

old-time (ōld′tīm′) *adj.* **1.** of or like past times **2.** of long standing or experience

old-tim·er (-tī′mər) *n.* [Colloq.] **1.** a longtime resident, employee, etc. **2.** an old-fashioned person

old wives' tale a silly story or superstition such as gossipy old women might pass around

old-wom·an·ish (-woom′ən ish) ***adj.*** like, typical of, or suitable for an old woman; fussy

Old World the Eastern Hemisphere, often esp. Europe —**old′-world′** *adj.*

-ole (ōl) [< L. *oleum,* oil] *a suffix used in chemistry indicating:* **1.** a five-member, closed-chain compound **2.** a compound without hydroxyl

o·le·ag·i·nous (ō′lē aj′i nəs) *adj.* [< Fr. < L. < *olea,* olive tree] oily; unctuous —**o′le·ag′i·nous·ness** *n.*

o·le·an·der (ō′lē an′dər, ō′lē an′dər) *n.* [ML.] a poisonous evergreen shrub with fragrant white, pink, or red flowers

o·le·ate (ō′lē āt′) *n.* a salt or ester of oleic acid

o·le·ic (ō lē′ik, ō′lē-) *adj.* [< L. *oleum,* oil + -IC] **1.** of or from oil **2.** of oleic acid

oleic acid an oily acid, $C_{17}H_{33}COOH$, present in most fats and oils as an ester, used in soaps, etc.

o·le·in (ō′lē in) *n.* [< Fr. < L. *oleum,* an oil] **1.** a liquid glyceride, present in olive oil, etc. **2.** the liquid part of a fat

o·le·o (ō′lē ō′) *n. clipped form of* OLEOMARGARINE

o·le·o- [< L. *oleum,* an oil] *a combining form meaning* oil, olein, or oleic *[oleomargarine]*

o·le·o·mar·ga·rine, o·le·o·mar·ga·rin (ō′lē ō mär′jə rin) *n.* [< Fr.: see prec. & MARGARINE] *full name of* MARGARINE

o·le·o·res·in (ō′lē ō rez′'n) *n.* **1.** a mixture of a resin and an essential oil, as turpentine, occurring naturally in various plants **2.** a prepared solution of resin in an essential oil

ol·fac·tion (äl fak′shən, ōl-) *n.* [see ff.] **1.** the sense of smell **2.** the act of smelling

ol·fac·to·ry (-tər ē, -trē) *adj.* [< L. pp. of *olfacere,* to smell < *olere,* to have a smell + *facere,* to make] of the sense of smell: also **ol·fac′tive** —*n., pl.* **-ries** [*usually pl.*] an organ of smell

OLG, OLG., O.L.G. Old Low German

ol·i·garch (äl′ə gärk′) *n.* any of the rulers of an oligarchy

ol·i·gar·chy (-gär′kē) *n., pl.* **-chies** [Gr. *oligarchia:* see OLIGO- & -ARCHY] **1.** a form of government with the ruling power belonging to a few **2.** a state so governed **3.** those ruling such a state —**ol′i·gar′chic, ol′i·gar′chi·cal, ol′i·gar′chal** (-k'l) *adj.*

ol·i·go- [Gr. < *oligos,* small] *a combining form meaning* few, small, a deficiency of: also **olig-**

Ol·i·go·cene (äl′ə gō sēn′) *adj.* [< prec. + Gr. *kainos,* new] designating or of the third epoch of the Tertiary Period in the Cenozoic Era —**the Oligocene** the Oligocene Epoch or its rocks: see GEOLOGY, chart

ol·i·gop·o·ly (äl′ə gäp′ə lē) *n., pl.* **-lies** [OLIG(O)- + (MON)OPOLY] control of a commodity or service by a few companies or suppliers —**ol′i·gop′o·list** *n.* —**ol′i·gop′o·lis′tic** *adj.*

o·li·o (ō′lē ō′) *n., pl.* **o′li·os′** [< Sp. *olla:* see OLLA] **1.** a spicy stew **2.** a medley or miscellany

ol·ive (äl′iv) *n.* [OFr. < L. *oliva* < Gr. *elaia*] **1.** *a)* an evergreen tree of the olive family, native to S Europe and the Near East, with an edible fruit *b)* the small, oval fruit, eaten green or ripe, or pressed to extract its oil *c)* the wood of this tree **2.** an olive branch or wreath **3.** the dull, yellowish-green color of the unripe fruit —*adj.* **1.** of the olive **2.** olive-colored **3.** designating a family of trees and shrubs with loose clusters of four-parted flowers, including the olives, ashes, lilacs, etc.

olive branch **1.** the branch of the olive tree, a symbol of peace **2.** any peace offering

olive drab **1.** a shade of greenish brown **2.** woolen cloth dyed this color and used for U.S. Army uniforms **3.** [*pl.*] such a uniform —**ol′ive-drab′** *adj.*

olive oil a light-yellow oil pressed from ripe olives, used in cooking, soap, etc.

Ol·i·ver (äl′ə vər) [Fr. *Olivier,* prob. < MLowG. < *alf,* elf + *hari,* an army] a masculine name

ol·i·vine (äl′ə vēn′) *n.* [OLIV(E) + -INE[4]] a green silicate of magnesium and iron

ol·la (äl′ə; *Sp.* ôl′yä) *n.* [Sp. < L.] **1.** a large-mouthed pot or jar **2.** a spicy stew

Ol·mec (äl′mek) *n., pl.* **-mecs, -mec** a member of an ancient Indian people in Mexico —*adj.* of the Olmecs

ol·o·gy (äl′ə jē) *n., pl.* **-gies** [< -LOGY] a branch of learning; science: humorous usage

O·lym·pi·a (ō lim′pē ə, ə-) **1.** plain in the W Peloponnesus: site of the ancient Olympic games **2.** [ult. < Mount OLYMPUS] capital of Wash., on Puget Sound: pop. 27,000

O·lym·pi·ad (-ad′) *n.* [*often* **o-**] **1.** in ancient Greece, a four-year period between Olympic games **2.** a celebration of the modern Olympic games

O·lym·pi·an (-ən) *n.* **1.** *Gr. Myth.* any of the gods on Mount Olympus **2.** a native of Olympia **3.** a participant in the Olympic games —*adj.* **1.** of Olympia or Mount Olympus **2.** exalted; majestic; celestial **3.** of the ancient Olympic games

O·lym·pic (ō lim′pik, ə-) *adj. same as* OLYMPIAN —*n.* [*pl.*] the Olympic games (preceded by *the*)
Olympic games **1.** an ancient Greek festival with contests in athletics, poetry, and music, held every four years at Olympia to honor Zeus **2.** a modern international athletic competition held every four years in a selected city
O·lym·pus (ō lim′pəs, ə-), **Mount** mountain in N Greece, between Thessaly & Macedonia: in Greek mythology, the home of the gods
-o·ma (ō′mə) [ModL. < Gr. *-ōma*] *a suffix meaning* tumor *[sarcoma]*
O·ma·ha (ō′mə hô, -hä) [ult. < Siouan tribal name, lit., ? upstream people] city in E Nebr., on the Missouri River: pop. 312,000 (met. area 566,000)
O·man (ō män′) country in SE Arabia, on the Arabian Sea: 82,000 sq. mi.; pop. c.750,000
O·mar Khay·yám (ō′mär kī yäm′, ō′mər kī yam′) ?–1123?; Persian poet & mathematician
o·ma·sum (ō mā′səm) *n., pl.* **-sa** (-sə) [ModL. < L., bullock's tripe < Gaul.] the third division in the stomach of a cud-chewing animal, as the cow
O.M.B. Office of Management and Budget
om·buds·man (äm′bədz mən) *n., pl.* **-men** [Sw.] a public official appointed to investigate citizens' complaints that government agencies may be violating their rights
o·me·ga (ō mā′gə, -meg′ə, -mē′gə) *n.* [Gr. *o mega,* lit., great (i.e., long) *o*] **1.** the twenty-fourth and final letter of the Greek alphabet (Ω, ω) **2.** the last (of any series); end
om·e·let, om·e·lette (äm′lit, äm′ə let) *n.* [< Fr., ult. < L. *lamella,* small plate] eggs beaten up, often with milk or water, cooked as a pancake in a frying pan and served usually folded over and often with a filling, as of jelly
o·men (ō′mən) *n.* [L.] a thing or happening supposed to foretell a future event; augury —*vt.* to be an omen of
om·i·cron, om·i·kron (äm′ə krän′, ō′mə-; *Brit.* ō mī′-krən) *n.* [Gr. *o mikron,* lit., small *o*] the fifteenth letter of the Greek alphabet (Ο, ο)
om·i·nous (äm′ə nəs) *adj.* [L. *ominosus*] of or serving as an evil omen; threatening; sinister —**om′i·nous·ly** *adv.* —**om′i·nous·ness** *n.*
o·mis·si·ble (ō mis′ə b'l) *adj.* that can be omitted
o·mis·sion (ō mish′ən) *n.* [< LL. *omissio*] **1.** an omitting or being omitted **2.** anything omitted
o·mit (ō mit′) *vt.* **o·mit′ted, o·mit′ting** [< L. *omittere* < *ob-* (see OB-) + *mittere,* to send] **1.** to fail to include; leave out **2.** to fail to do; neglect —**o·mit′ter** *n.*
om·ni- [L. < *omnis,* all] *a combining form meaning* all, everywhere *[omniscient]*
om·ni·bus (äm′nə bəs, -ni bus′) *n., pl.* **-bus·es** [Fr. < L., lit., for all] **1.** *same as* BUS (sense 1) **2.** a one-volume collection of previously published works —*adj.* providing for many things at once
omnibus bill a legislative bill containing many miscellaneous provisions, appropriations, etc.
om·ni·far·i·ous (äm′nə fer′ē əs) *adj.* [< L. *omnifarius* < *omnis,* all + *fari,* to speak] of all kinds, varieties, or forms
om·nip·o·tence (äm nip′ə təns) *n.* **1.** the state or quality of being omnipotent **2.** [O-] God
om·nip·o·tent (-tənt) *adj.* [OFr. < L. < *omnis,* all + *potens,* able] having unlimited power or authority; all-powerful —**the Omnipotent** God —**om·nip′o·tent·ly** *adv.*
om·ni·pres·ent (äm′ni prez′'nt) *adj.* [< ML. < L. *omnis,* all + *praesens,* present] present in all places at the same time —**om′ni·pres′ence** *n.*
om·nis·cient (äm nish′ənt) *adj.* [< ML. < L. *omnis,* all + prp. of *scire,* to know] knowing all things —**the Omniscient** God —**om·nis′cience** *n.* —**om·nis′cient·ly** *adv.*
om·ni·um-gath·er·um (äm′nē əm gath′ər əm) *n.* [L. *omnium,* all + Latinized form of GATHER] a miscellaneous collection of persons or things
om·niv·o·rous (äm niv′ər əs) *adj.* [< L.: see OMNI- & -VOROUS] **1.** eating any sort of food **2.** taking in everything indiscriminately *[an omnivorous* reader*]* —**om·niv′o·rous·ly** *adv.* —**om·niv′o·rous·ness** *n.*
Omsk (ômsk) city in W Siberia, on the Irtysh River: pop. 800,000
on (än, ôn) *prep.* [OE. *on, an*] **1.** above, but in contact with and supported by; upon **2.** in contact with; covering or attached to **3.** so as to be supported by *[*to lean *on* one's elbow*]* **4.** in the surface of **5.** near to *[*a cottage *on* the lake*]* **6.** at the time of *[on* entering*]* **7.** with (something specified) as the basis *[on* purpose*]*. **8.** connected with, as a part *[on* the faculty*]* **9.** engaged in *[on* a trip*]* **10.** in a state of *[on* parole*]* **11.** as a result of *[*a profit *on* the sale*]* **12.** in the direction of *[*a light shone *on* us*]* **13.** so as to affect *[*to put a curse *on* someone*]* **14.** through the use or medium of *[*to live *on* bread*]* **15.** concerning *[*an essay *on* war*]* **16.** coming after *[*insult *on* insult*]* **17.** [Colloq.] chargeable to *[*a drink *on* the house*]* **18.** [Slang] using; addicted to *[*to be *on* drugs*]* —*adv.* **1.** in a situation of contacting, being supported by, or covering *[*put your shoes *on]* **2.** in a direction toward *[*looked *on]* **3.** forward; ahead *[*move *on]* **4.** continuously *[*she sang *on]* **5.** into operation or action *[*turn the light *on]* **6.** *Baseball* on base **7.** *Theater* on stage —*adj.* **1.** in action or operation *[*the TV is *on]* **2.** planned for *[*tomorrow's game is still *on]* —**and so on** and more like the preceding —**on and off** intermittently —**on and on** continuously —**on to** [Slang] aware of, esp. aware of the real nature of
-on (än) *a suffix designating:* **1.** [< *-on* in *argon*] an inert gas *[radon]* **2.** [< *-on* in *ion*] a subatomic particle *[electron]*
ON., ON, O.N. Old Norse
o·nan·ism (ō′nə niz'm) *n.* [< *Onan* (Gen. 38:9)] **1.** withdrawal in coition before ejaculation **2.** masturbation —**o′nan·ist** *n.* —**o′nan·is′tic** *adj.*
once (wuns) *adv.* [ME. *ones,* gen. of *on,* ONE] **1.** one time; one time only **2.** at any time; ever **3.** formerly **4.** by one degree *[*a cousin *once* removed*]* —*conj.* as soon as; if ever —*adj.* former —*n.* one time *[*go this *once]* —**all at once** **1.** all at the same time **2.** suddenly —**at once** **1.** immediately **2.** at the same time —**for once** for at least one time —**once (and) for all** conclusively —**once in a while** occasionally —**once or twice** a few times —**once upon a time** long ago
once-o·ver (wuns′ō′vər) *n.* [Colloq.] **1.** a swiftly appraising glance **2.** a quick cleaning or going-over
on·com·ing (än′kum′iŋ) *adj.* approaching *[oncoming* traffic*]* —*n.* approach
one (wun) *adj.* [OE. *an*] **1.** being a single thing **2.** forming a whole; united **3.** designating a person or thing as contrasted with another *[*from *one* day to another*]* **4.** being uniquely the person or thing specified *[*the *one* solution to the problem*]* **5.** single in kind; the same *[*all of *one* mind*]* **6.** a certain but unspecified *[one* day last week*]* : also used as an intensive substitute for the indefinite article *[*she's *one* beautiful girl*]* —*n.* **1.** the number expressing unity or designating a single unit; the first and lowest cardinal number; 1; I **2.** a single person or thing **3.** anything consisting of a single unit or numbered one; specif., [Colloq.] a one-dollar bill —*pron.* **1.** some, or a certain, person or thing **2.** any person or thing **3.** the person or thing previously mentioned —**all one** making no difference —**at one** in accord —**one and all** everybody —**one another** each one the other; each other: see EACH OTHER, under EACH —**one of those things** something inevitable
-one (ōn) [arbitrary use of Gr. *-ōnē*] *a suffix used in chemistry, meaning* a ketone *[acetone]*
one-horse (wun′hôrs′) *adj.* **1.** drawn by or using one horse **2.** [Colloq.] small, unimportant, etc.
O·nei·da (ō nī′də) *n.* [Iroquois *Oneiute,* lit., standing rock] **1.** *pl.* **-das, -da** a member of a tribe of Indians orig. of New York State but now also of Wisconsin and Ontario **2.** their Iroquoian language
O'Neill (ō nēl′), **Eugene** 1888–1953; U.S. playwright
one·ness (wun′nis) *n.* **1.** singleness; unity **2.** unity of mind, feeling, etc. **3.** sameness; identity
one-night stand (wun′nīt′) a single appearance in a town by a traveling show, lecturer, etc.
one-on-one (wun′än wun′, -ôn-) *adj., adv.* **1.** contending individually against a single opposing player, as in basketball **2.** in direct, personal confrontation
on·er·ous (än′ər əs, ō′nər-) *adj.* [< MFr. < L. *onerosus* < *onus,* a load] burdensome; oppressive —**on′er·ous·ly** *adv.*
one·self (wun′self′, wunz′-) *pron.* a person's own self: also **one's self** —**be oneself** **1.** to function normally **2.** to be natural —**by oneself** alone; unaccompanied —**come to oneself** to recover one's senses or capacity for judgment
one-sid·ed (wun′sīd′id) *adj.* **1.** on, having, or involving only one side **2.** larger, heavier, etc. on one side; lopsided **3.** favoring one side; unfair **4.** uneven or unequal *[*a *one-sided* race*]* —**one′-sid′ed·ly** *adv.* —**one′-sid′ed·ness** *n.*
one-step (-step′) *n.* an old ballroom dance with quick walking steps in 2/4 time
one-time (-tīm′) *adj.* at a past time; former
one-to-one (wun′tə wun′) *adj.* **1.** permitting the pairing of an element of one group uniquely with a corresponding element of another group **2.** *Math.* with each member of one set having a partner in the other set
one-track (wun′trak′) *adj.* **1.** having a single track **2.** [Colloq.] able or willing to deal with only one thing at a time *[*a *one-track* mind*]*
one-up (-up′) *adj.* [Colloq.] having an advantage (over another): often in **be one-up on** —*vt.* **-upped′, -up′ping** [Colloq.] to have or seize an advantage over (another) —**one′-up′man·ship′** *n.*

one-way (-wā′) *adj.* **1.** moving, or allowing movement, in one direction only [*a one-way* street] **2.** without reciprocal action or obligation

on·go·ing (än′gō′iŋ) *adj.* going on; in process

on·ion (un′yən) *n.* [< OFr. < L. *unio,* a kind of single onion] **1.** a plant of the lily family, with an edible bulb having a strong, sharp smell and taste **2.** the bulb

on·ion·skin (-skin′) *n.* a tough, thin, translucent paper, often used for carbon copies

on-line (än′līn′, ôn′-) *adj.* designating or of instruments, equipment, or devices directly connected to and controlled by the unit of a computer that interprets and executes instructions

on·look·er (än′look′ər) *n.* one who watches without taking part; spectator —**on′look′ing** *adj., n.*

on·ly (ōn′lē) *adj.* [OE. *anlic* < *an,* one + *-lic,* -LY[1]] **1.** alone of its or their kind; sole **2.** alone in superiority; best —*adv.* **1.** and no other; and no (or nothing) more; solely [drink water *only*] **2.** (but) in what follows or in the end [to meet one crisis, *only* to face another] **3.** as recently as [*only* last fall] —*conj.* [Colloq.] except that; but [I'd go, *only* it's late] —**if . . . only** would that; I wish that —**only too** very

on·o·mat·o·poe·ia (än′ə mat′ə pē′ə, -mät′-) *n.* [LL. < Gr. < *onoma,* a name + *poiein,* to make] **1.** formation of a word by imitating the sound associated with an object or action (Ex.: *buzz*) **2.** the use of such words, as in poetry —**on′o·mat′o·poe′ic, on′o·mat′o·po·et′ic** (-pō et′ik) *adj.*

On·on·da·ga (än′ən dô′gə, ōn′-; -dä′-) *n.* [Iroquois *Onontaʼge′,* lit., on top of the hill] **1.** *pl.* **-gas, -ga** a member of a tribe of Indians orig. of New York State but now also of Ontario **2.** their Iroquoian language —**On′on·da′gan** *adj.*

ONormFr. Old Norman French

on·rush (än′rush′, ôn′-) *n.* a headlong dash forward; strong onward rush —**on′rush′ing** *adj.*

on·set (-set′) *n.* **1.** an attack **2.** a beginning

on·shore (-shôr′) *adj.* **1.** moving onto or toward the shore **2.** on land [an *onshore* patrol] —*adv.* toward the shore

on·slaught (-slôt′) *n.* [< Du. *annslag* < *slagen,* to strike] a violent, intense attack

On·tar·i·o (än ter′ē ō) **1.** [after the lake, below] province of SC Canada, between the Great Lakes & Hudson Bay: 412,582 sq. mi.; pop. 8,264,000; cap. Toronto: abbrev. **Ont. 2.** [after prec.] city in S Calif.: pop. 89,000 **3. Lake,** [ult. < Iroquoian, lit., fine lake] smallest & easternmost of the Great Lakes, between N.Y. & Ontario, Canada: 7,313 sq. mi. —**On·tar′i·an** *adj., n.*

on·to (än′to͞o, ôn′-; -tə) *prep.* **1.** to a position on **2.** [Slang] aware of the real nature, etc. of [he's *onto* our schemes] Also **on to**

on·to- [< Gr. prp. of *einai,* to be] *a combining form meaning:* **1.** being; existence **2.** organism

on·tog·e·ny (än täj′ə nē) *n.* [prec. + -GENY] the development of an individual organism: distinguished from PHYLOGENY: also **on·to·gen·e·sis** (än′tə jen′ə sis) —**on′to·ge·net′ic** (-jə net′ik), **on′to·gen′ic** *adj.*

on·tol·o·gy (än täl′ə jē) *n.* the study of the nature of being or reality —**on·to·log·i·cal** (än′tə läj′i k'l) *adj.*

o·nus (ō′nəs) *n.* [L.] **1.** a hard or unpleasant task, duty, etc.; burden **2.** responsibility for a wrong; blame **3.** *same as* BURDEN OF PROOF

on·ward (än′wərd) *adv.* toward or at a position ahead; forward: also **on′wards** —*adj.* moving or directed ahead; advancing

on·yx (än′iks; *occas.* ō′niks) *n.* [< OFr. < L. < Gr. *onyx,* nail, claw: its color resembles that of the fingernail] **1.** a variety of agate with alternate colored layers **2.** a translucent, often banded, stalagmitic calcite: also **onyx marble**

o·o- [< Gr. *ōion*] *a combining form meaning* egg or ovum: also written **oö-**

oo·dles (o͞o′d'lz) *n.pl.* [< ? HUDDLE] [Colloq.] a great amount; very many

o·o·lite (ō′ə līt′) *n.* [< Fr.: see OO- & -LITE] **1.** a tiny calcium carbonate particle with concentric layers, formed in the sea: also **o′o·lith** (-lith) **2.** a rock of these —**o′o·lit′ic** (-lit′ik) *adj.*

o·ol·o·gy (ō äl′ə jē) *n.* [OO- + -LOGY] the study of birds' eggs —**o·o·log·i·cal** (ō′ə läj′i k'l) *adj.* —**o·ol′o·gist** *n.*

oo·long (o͞o′lôŋ) *n.* [< Chin. *wulung,* lit., black dragon] a dark Chinese tea, partly fermented before being dried

oo·mi·ac, oo·mi·ak (o͞o′mē ak′) *n. same as* UMIAK

o·o·pho·ro- (ō′ə fə rō′) [< Gr. *ōion,* an egg + *-phoros,* bearing] *a combining form meaning* ovary or ovaries: also, before a vowel, **oophor-**

oops (o͞ops, oops) *interj. same as* WHOOPS

ooze[1] (o͞oz) *n.* [OE. *wos,* sap] an oozing or something that oozes —*vi.* **oozed, ooz′ing 1.** to flow or leak out slowly, as through tiny holes; seep **2.** to give forth moisture, as through pores —*vt.* to exude

ooze[2] (o͞oz) *n.* [OE. *wase*] **1.** soft mud or slime; esp., the sediment at the bottom of a lake, ocean, etc. **2.** a bog

oo·zy[1] (o͞o′zē) *adj.* **-zi·er, -zi·est** oozing moisture —**oo′zi·ly** *adv.* —**oo′zi·ness** *n.*

oo·zy[2] (o͞o′zē) *adj.* **-zi·er, -zi·est** full of or like ooze; slimy —**oo′zi·ly** *adv.* —**oo′zi·ness** *n.*

op- *see* OB-

op. 1. opera **2.** operation **3.** opposite **4.** opus

O.P. Order of Preachers (Dominicans)

O.P., OP, o.p., op out of print

o·pac·i·ty (ō pas′ə tē) *n.* **1.** opaque state, quality, or degree **2.** *pl.* **-ties** an opaque thing

o·pal (ō′p'l) *n.* [< L. < Gr. *opallios* < Sans. *upala,* precious stone] an amorphous silica, of various colors, typically iridescent: some varieties are semiprecious stones

o·pal·es·cent (ō′pə les′'nt) *adj.* iridescent like opal —**o′pal·esce′** *vi.* **-esced′, -esc′ing** —**o′pal·es′cence** *n.*

o·pal·ine (ō′p'l in, -ēn′, -īn′) *adj.* of or like opal —*n.* a translucent, milky glass

o·paque (ō pāk′) *adj.* [L. *opacus,* shady] **1.** not letting light through **2.** not reflecting light or not shining **3.** hard to understand; obscure **4.** slow in understanding; obtuse —*n.* anything opaque —*vt.* **o·paqued′, o·paqu′ing** to make opaque —**o·paque′ly** *adv.* —**o·paque′ness** *n.*

op (art) (äp) [< OP(TICAL)] abstract painting using geometrical patterns to create various optical effects, such as the illusion of movement

op. cit. [L. *opere citato*] in the work cited

ope (ōp) *adj., vt., vi.* **oped, op′ing** [Poet.] open

OPEC (ō′pek) Organization of Petroleum Exporting Countries

o·pen (ō′p'n) *adj.* [OE.] **1.** allowing access, entrance, or exit; not closed or shut **2.** allowing freedom of view or passage; unenclosed or unobstructed **3.** unsealed; unwrapped **4.** *a)* not covered *b)* unprotected or undefended **5.** spread out; unfolded **6.** having spaces, gaps, etc. [*open* ranks] **7.** free from ice **8.** *a)* not excluding anyone [an *open* meeting] *b)* ready to admit customers, clients, etc. **9.** free to be argued; not settled [an *open* question] **10.** *a)* not prejudiced or narrow-minded *b)* liberal; generous **11.** *a)* free from legal or discriminatory restrictions [*open* housing] *b)* free from effective regulation [the city is wide *open*] *c)* not regulated, organized, or conducted along traditional lines [*open* marriage, *open* education] **12.** socially mobile, politically free, etc. [an *open* society] **13.** in force or operation [an *open* account] **14.** *a)* not already taken or engaged [the job is *open*] *b)* free to be accepted or rejected **15.** accessible; available **16.** not secret; public **17.** frank; candid **18.** *Music a)* not stopped by the finger: said of a string *b)* not closed at the top: said of an organ pipe *c)* produced by an open string or pipe or without a slide or key: said of a tone *d)* not muted **19.** *Phonetics a)* low *b)* fricative *c)* ending in a vowel or diphthong: said of a syllable —*vt.* **1.** to make open, or no longer closed, shut, obstructed, etc. **2.** *a)* to make an opening in *b)* to produce (a hole, way, etc.) **3.** to spread out; expand **4.** to expose (to an influence or action) **5.** to make available without restriction, fee, etc. **6.** *a)* to free from prejudice *b)* to make liberal and generous **7.** to reveal; disclose **8.** to begin (bidding, a session, etc.) **9.** to start operating, going, etc. [to *open* a new shop] —*vi.* **1.** to become open **2.** to spread out; expand; unfold **3.** to become revealed, disclosed, etc. **4.** to give access (with *to, into, on,* etc.) **5.** to begin; start **6.** to start operating, going, etc.; specif., in the stock exchange, to show an indicated initial price level [steel *opened* high] **7.** to begin a series of performances, games, etc. —*n.* [*usually* **O-**] any of various golf tournaments for both professionals and amateurs —**open out 1.** to expand **2.** to develop **3.** to reveal —**open to 1.** willing to receive, discuss, etc. **2.** liable to **3.** available or accessible to or for —**open up 1.** to make or become open **2.** to unfold **3.** to start; begin **4.** [Colloq.] to begin firing a gun or guns **5.** [Colloq.] to speak freely **6.** [Colloq.] to go or make go faster —**the open 1.** any open, unobstructed area **2.** the outdoors **3.** public knowledge —**o′pened** *adj.* —**o′pen·er** *n.* —**o′pen·ly** *adv.* —**o′pen·ness** *n.*

open air the outdoors —**o′pen-air′** *adj.*

o·pen-and-shut (ō′p'n 'n shut′) *adj.* easily decided; obvious [an *open-and-shut* case]

open chain the structural form of certain molecules in which the chain of atoms does not form a ring

open city a city left open to enemy occupation to gain immunity from attack

open door 1. unrestricted admission **2.** equal, unrestricted opportunity for all nations to trade with a given nation —**o′pen-door′** *adj.*

o·pen-end (-end′) *adj.* **1.** of an investment company not limiting the shares issued **2.** allowing additional borrowing on the original security [an *open-end* mortgage] **3.** *same as* OPEN-ENDED

o·pen-end·ed (-en′did) *adj.* **1.** unrestricted in duration, scope, etc., as a discussion **2.** open to change **3.** allowing for a freely formulated answer rather than one chosen from among predetermined answers: said of a question

o·pen-eyed (-īd′) ***adj.*** with the eyes open or wide open, as in awareness or amazement

o·pen-faced (-fāst′) ***adj.*** **1.** having a frank, honest face **2.** designating a sandwich without a top slice of bread: also **o′pen-face′**

o·pen·hand·ed (-han′did) ***adj.*** generous —**o′pen-hand′ed·ly** ***adv.*** —**o′pen·hand′ed·ness** ***n.***

o·pen·heart·ed (-här′tid) ***adj.*** **1.** not reserved; frank **2.** kindly; generous —**o′pen·heart′ed·ly** ***adv.*** —**o′pen-heart′ed·ness** ***n.***

o·pen-hearth (-härth′) ***adj.*** designating or using a furnace with a wide, saucer-shaped hearth and a low roof, for making steel

OPEN-HEARTH FURNACE (A, lining; B, metal; C, heater ports; D, gas; E, air: fired alternately from either end)

o·pen-heart surgery (-härt′) heart surgery with the chest opened and the blood recirculated and oxygenated by mechanical means

open house informal reception of visitors freely coming and going, at one's home, a school, etc.

o·pen·ing (-iŋ) ***n.*** **1.** a becoming or making open **2.** an open place; hole; gap **3.** a clearing in a wooded area **4.** *a*) a beginning *b*) a first performance **5.** an opportunity **6.** a job available **7.** *Chess, Checkers,* etc. the series of first moves

open letter a letter written as to a specific person but published in a newspaper, etc. for all to read

open market *same as* FREE MARKET

o·pen-mind·ed (-mīn′did) ***adj.*** open to new ideas; not biased —**o′pen-mind′ed·ly** ***adv.*** —**o′pen-mind′ed·ness** ***n.***

o·pen-mouthed (-mouthd′, -moutht′) ***adj.*** **1.** having the mouth open **2.** gaping, as in astonishment

open primary a primary election in which the voter need not declare party affiliation

open punctuation punctuation characterized by relatively few commas or other marks

open sea **1.** the expanse of sea away from coastlines, bays, inlets, etc. **2.** *same as* HIGH SEAS

open secret something supposed to be secret but known to almost everyone

open sesame **1.** magic words spoken to open the door of the thieves' den in the story of Ali Baba **2.** any sure means of achieving an end

open shop a factory, business, etc. employing workers regardless of union membership

open stock merchandise, as dishes, available in sets, with individual pieces kept in stock

o·pen·work (-wurk′) ***n.*** ornamental work, as in cloth, with openings in the material

op·er·a[1] (äp′ər ə, äp′rə) ***n.*** **[**It. < L., a work**]** **1.** a play with most or all the text sung to orchestral accompaniment and usually with elaborate costuming, sets, and choreography **2.** the art of such plays **3.** the score, libretto, or performance of an opera **4.** a theater for operas

o·pe·ra[2] (ō′pə rə, äp′ər ə) ***n. pl. of*** OPUS

op·er·a·ble (äp′ər ə b'l) ***adj.*** **[**< ML.: see OPERATE & -ABLE**]** **1.** practicable **2.** treatable surgically —**op′er·a·bil′i·ty** ***n.*** —**op′er·a·bly** ***adv.***

‡**o·pé·ra bouffe** (ô pā rȧ bōōf′; *E.* äp′ər ə bōōf′) **[**Fr.**]** comic, esp. farcical, opera

opera glasses a small binocular telescope used at the opera, in theaters, etc.

opera hat a man's tall, collapsible silk hat

opera house a theater chiefly for operas

op·er·ant (äp′ər ənt) ***adj.*** operating, or producing an effect or effects —***n.*** one that operates

op·er·ate (äp′ə rāt′) ***vi.*** **-at′ed, -at′ing** **[**< L. pp. of *operari,* to work < *opus* (gen. *operis*), a work**]** **1.** to be in action; work **2.** to produce a certain effect **3.** to carry on military movements **4.** to perform a surgical operation —***vt.*** **1.** [Now Rare] to effect **2.** *a*) to put or keep in action; work (a machine, etc.) *b*) to conduct or manage (a business, etc.) **3.** [Colloq.] to do a surgical operation on

op·er·at·ic (äp′ə rat′ik) ***adj.*** of or like the opera —**op′er·at′i·cal·ly** ***adv.***

op·er·a·tion (äp′ə rā′shən) ***n.*** **1.** the act, process, or method of operating **2.** the condition of being in action or at work **3.** a procedure that is part of a series in some work **4.** any strategic military movement; also, [*pl.*] a center where this is monitored or supervised **5.** any specific plan, project, etc. *[Operation* Cleanup*]* **6.** any surgical procedure to remedy a physical ailment or defect **7.** *Math.* any process, as addition, involving a change in quantity —**in operation** **1.** in action; working **2.** in force

op·er·a·tion·al (-'l) ***adj.*** **1.** of the operation of a device, system, process, etc. **2.** *a*) that can be used or operated *b*) in use; operating **3.** of or ready for use in a military operation —**op′er·a′tion·al·ly** ***adv.***

op·er·a·tion·al·ize (-'l īz′) ***vt.*** **-ized′, -iz′ing** to make operational; put into operation —**op′er·a′tion·al·i·za′tion** ***n.***

operations research systematic, scientific analysis of problems, as in government, military, or business operations: also **operations analysis**

op·er·a·tive (äp′ə rā′tiv, äp′ər ə-) ***adj.*** **1.** capable of or in operation **2.** effective **3.** connected with physical work or mechanical action **4.** of or resulting from a surgical operation —***n.*** **1.** a worker, esp. a skilled industrial worker **2.** a detective or spy —**op′er·a′tive·ly** ***adv.***

op·er·a·tor (äp′ə rāt′ər) ***n.*** **1.** one who operates; specif., *a*) a person who effects something; agent *b*) a person who works a machine *c*) a person engaged in commercial or industrial operations or enterprises **2.** [Slang] a clever person who generally manages to achieve his ends

o·per·cu·lum (ō pur′kyoo ləm) ***n., pl.*** **-la** (-lə), **-lums** **[**ModL. < L., lid, dim. < *operire,* to close**]** any of various covering flaps or lidlike structures in plants and animals, as the bony covering protecting the gills of fishes —**o·per′cu·lar** ***adj.*** —**o·per′cu·late** (-lit, -lāt′), **o·per′cu·lat′ed** ***adj.***

op·er·et·ta (äp′ə ret′ə) ***n.*** **[**It., dim. of *opera,* OPERA[1]**]** a light, amusing opera with spoken dialogue

oph·thal·mi·a (äf thal′mē ə) ***n.*** **[**< LL. < Gr. < *ophthalmos,* the eye**]** severe inflammation of the eyeball or conjunctiva

oph·thal·mic (-mik) ***adj.*** of the eye; ocular

oph·thal·mo- **[**< Gr. *ophthalmos,* the eye**]** *a combining form meaning* the eye: also **oph·thalm-**

oph·thal·mol·o·gy (äf′thal mäl′ə jē, äp′-; -thə-) ***n.*** the branch of medicine dealing with the structure, functions, and diseases of the eye —**oph′thal·mo·log′i·cal** (-mə läj′i-k'l) ***adj.*** —**oph′thal·mol′o·gist** ***n.***

oph·thal·mo·scope (äf thal′mə skōp′, äp-) ***n.*** **[**OPHTHALMO- & -SCOPE**]** an instrument for examining the interior of the eye —**oph·thal′mo·scop′ic** (-skäp′ik) ***adj.*** —**oph′thal-mos′co·py** (-thəl mäs′kə pē) ***n.***

-o·pi·a (ō′pē ə) **[**< Gr. < *ōps,* an eye**]** *a combining form meaning* a (specified kind of) eye defect

o·pi·ate (ō′pē it, -āt′) ***n.*** **1.** any medicine containing opium or any of its derivatives, and acting as a sedative and narcotic **2.** anything quieting, soothing, etc. —***adj.*** **1.** containing opium **2.** bringing sleep, quiet, etc.; narcotic

o·pine (ō pīn′) ***vt., vi.*** **o·pined′, o·pin′ing** **[**< MFr. < L. *opinari,* to think**]** to hold or express (some opinion): now usually humorous

o·pin·ion (ə pin′yən) ***n.*** **[**< OFr. < L. < *opinari,* to think**]** **1.** a belief not based on certainty or knowledge but on what seems true, valid, or probable **2.** an evaluation, estimation, etc. **3.** an expert's formal judgment **4.** *Law* the formal statement by a judge, court referee, etc. of the law bearing on a case

o·pin·ion·at·ed (-āt′id) ***adj.*** holding unreasonably or obstinately to one's own opinions —**o·pin′ion·at′ed·ly** ***adv.*** —**o·pin′ion·at′ed·ness** ***n.***

o·pin·ion·a·tive (-āt′iv, -ə tiv) ***adj.*** **1.** of, or of the nature of, opinion **2.** opinionated —**o·pin′ion·a′tive·ly** ***adv.*** —**o·pin′ion·a′tive·ness** ***n.***

o·pi·um (ō′pē əm) ***n.*** **[**L. < Gr. < *opos,* vegetable juice**]** a narcotic drug made from the juice of the seed capsules of the opium poppy, used as an intoxicant and medicinally to relieve pain and produce sleep

opium poppy an annual poppy with large, white or purple flowers, the source of opium

O·por·to (ō pôr′tō) seaport in N Portugal: pop. 305,000

o·pos·sum (ə päs′əm) ***n., pl.*** **-sums, -sum:** see PLURAL, II, D, 1 **[**< Algonquian, lit., white beast**]** any of several American marsupials; esp., the **American** (or **Virginian**) **opossum,** a small, tree-dwelling mammal: it is active at night and pretends to be dead when trapped

OPOSSUM (body 12–20 in. long; tail 10–21 in. long)

opp. **1.** opposed **2.** opposite

op·po·nent (ə pō′nənt) ***n.*** **[**< L. prp. of *opponere* < *ob-* (see OB-) + *ponere,* to set**]** one who opposes, as in a fight, game, etc.; adversary —***adj.*** opposing; antagonistic

op·por·tune (äp′ər tōōn′, äp′ər-tyōōn′) ***adj.*** **[**< MFr. < L. *opportunus,* lit., before the port < *ob-* (see OB-) + *portus,* a port**]** **1.** right for the purpose: said of time **2.** happening or done at the right time; timely **—op′por·tune′ly** *adv.*

op·por·tun·ism (-iz'm) *n.* the adapting of one's actions, judgments, etc. to circumstances, as in politics, for one's own benefit without regard for principles **—op′por·tun′ist** *n.* **—op′por·tun·is′tic** *adj.* **—op′por·tun·is′ti·cal·ly** *adv.*

op·por·tu·ni·ty (äp′ər to͞o′nə tē, -tyo͞o′-) *n., pl.* **-ties 1.** a combination of circumstances favorable for the purpose **2.** a good chance or occasion

op·pos·a·ble (ə pō′zə b'l) *adj.* **1.** that can be resisted **2.** that can be placed opposite something else **—op·pos′a·bil′i·ty** *n.*

op·pose (ə pōz′) *vt.* **-posed′, -pos′ing** [< OFr. < L. *opponere:* see OB- & POSITION] **1.** to set against; place opposite, in balance or contrast **2.** to contend with in speech or action; resist *—vi.* to act in opposition **—op·pos′er** *n.*

op·po·site (äp′ə zit) *adj.* [OFr. < L. pp. of *opponere:* see prec.] **1.** set against, facing, or back to back; at the other end or side (often with *to*) **2.** hostile; resistant **3.** entirely different; exactly contrary **4.** *Bot.* growing in pairs, but separated by a stem *—n.* anything opposed or opposite *—adv.* on opposing sides or in an opposite position *—prep.* across from **—op′po·site·ly** *adv.* **—op′po·site·ness** *n.*

op·po·si·tion (äp′ə zish′ən) *n.* **1.** an opposing **2.** an opposed condition; resistance, contrast, etc. **3.** anything that opposes; specif., [*often* **O-**] a political party opposing the party in power **4.** *Astrol., Astron.* the position of two heavenly bodies 180° apart in longitude **—op′po·si′tion·al** *adj.* **—op′po·si′tion·ist** *n., adj.*

op·press (ə pres′) *vt.* [< OFr. < ML. < L. pp. of *opprimere* < *ob-* (see OB-) + *premere,* PRESS[1]] **1.** to weigh heavily on the mind, spirits, or senses of **2.** to keep down by the cruel or unjust use of power; tyrannize over **—op·pres′sor** *n.*

op·pres·sion (ə presh′ən) *n.* **1.** an oppressing or being oppressed **2.** a thing that oppresses **3.** physical or mental distress

op·pres·sive (ə pres′iv) *adj.* **1.** hard to put up with **2.** cruelly overbearing; tyrannical **3.** weighing heavily on the mind, etc.; distressing **—op·pres′sive·ly** *adv.* **—op·pres′sive·ness** *n.*

op·pro·bri·ous (ə prō′brē əs) *adj.* **1.** expressing opprobrium; abusive **2.** [Now Rare] disgraceful **—op·pro′bri·ous·ly** *adv.* **—op·pro′bri·ous·ness** *n.*

op·pro·bri·um (-əm) *n.* [L. < *opprobare,* to reproach < *ob-* (see OB-) + *probrum,* a disgrace] **1.** the disgrace or infamy attached to conduct viewed as grossly shameful **2.** anything bringing shame or disgrace **3.** reproachful contempt

-op·sis (äp′sis) [< Gr. < *opsis,* a sight] *a combining form meaning* sight or view

opt (äpt) *vi.* [< Fr. < L. *optare*] to make a choice (often with *for*) **—opt out (of)** to choose not to be or continue in (an activity, group, etc.)

opt. 1. optical **2.** optician **3.** optional

op·ta·tive (äp′tə tiv) *adj.* [< Fr. < LL. < L. *optare,* to desire] expressing wish or desire, as a mood in Greek grammar *—n.* the optative mood, or a verb in this mood

op·tic (äp′tik) *adj.* [< Fr. < ML. < Gr. *optikos*] of the eye or sense of sight

op·ti·cal (-'l) *adj.* **1.** of the sense of sight; visual **2.** of optics **3.** for aiding vision *[optical* instruments*]* **—op′ti·cal·ly** *adv.*

op·ti·cian (äp tish′ən) *n.* a person who makes or deals in optical instruments, esp. one who prepares and dispenses eyeglasses

optic nerve either of a pair of nerves which connect the retina of the eye with the brain

op·tics (äp′tiks) *n.pl. [with sing. v.]* [< OPTIC] the branch of physics dealing with the nature and properties of light and vision

op·ti·mal (äp′tə məl) *adj.* most favorable or desirable; best; optimum **—op′ti·mal·ly** *adv.*

op·ti·mism (-miz'm) *n.* [< Fr. < L. *optimus,* best] **1.** *Philos. a)* the doctrine that the existing world is the best possible *b)* the belief that good ultimately prevails over evil **2.** the tendency to take the most hopeful or cheerful view of matters **—op′ti·mist** (-mist) *n.* **—op′ti·mis′tic** (-mis′tik), **op′ti·mis′ti·cal** *adj.* **—op′ti·mis′ti·cal·ly** *adv.*

op·ti·mum (-məm) *n., pl.* **-mums, -ma** (-mə) [L., neut. of *optimus,* best < *ops,* riches] the best or most favorable degree, condition, amount, etc. *—adj.* most favorable or desirable; best

op·tion (äp′shən) *n.* [Fr. < L. *optio* < *optare,* to wish] **1.** a choosing; choice **2.** the right or liberty of choosing **3.** something that is or can be chosen **4.** the right to buy, sell, or lease at a fixed price, sign a contract, etc. within a specified time

op·tion·al (-'l) *adj.* left to one's option, or choice; elective **—op′tion·al·ly** *adv.*

op·tom·e·try (äp täm′ə trē) *n.* [see OPTIC & -METRY] **1.** measurement of the range and power of vision **2.** the profession of examining the eyes for errors in refraction and of prescribing glasses to correct such defects **—op·to·met·ric** (äp′tə met′rik), **op′to·met′ri·cal** *adj.* **—op·tom′e·trist** *n.*

op·u·lent (äp′yə lənt) *adj.* [< L. < *ops,* wealth] **1.** wealthy; rich **2.** abundant; profuse **—op′u·lence, op′u·len·cy** *n.* **—op′u·lent·ly** *adv.*

o·pus (ō′pəs) *n., pl.* **o·pe·ra** (ō′pə rə, äp′ər ə), **o′pus·es** [L., a work] a work; composition; esp., any of the musical works of a composer numbered in order of composition or publication

-o·py (ō′pē) *same as* -OPIA

or[1] (ôr; *unstressed* ər) *conj.* [ME., in form a contr. of *other,* either, but actually < OE. *oththe*] a coordinating conjunction introducing: *a)* an alternative possibility *[*beer *or* wine, either go *or* stay*] b)* a synonymous term *[*ill, *or* sick*]*

or[2] (ôr) *n.* [Fr. < L. *aurum,* gold] *Heraldry* gold

-or (ər; *occas.* ôr) [< OFr. < L. *-or*] *a suffix meaning:* **1.** a person or thing that *[inventor]* **2.** quality or condition *[error]* : in Brit. usage, often **-our**

OR Oregon

or·a·cle (ôr′ə k'l, är′-) *n.* [OFr. < L. *oraculum* < *orare,* to pray < *os* (gen. *oris*), the mouth] **1.** in ancient Greece and Rome, *a)* the place where, or medium by which, deities were consulted *b)* the revelation of a medium or priest **2.** *a)* any person or agency believed to be in communication with a deity *b)* any person of great wisdom *c)* opinion or statements of any such oracle

o·rac·u·lar (ô rak′yoo lər) *adj.* of or like an oracle; wise, mysterious, etc. **—o·rac′u·lar·ly** *adv.*

o·ral (ôr′əl) *adj.* [< L. *os* (gen. *oris*), the mouth] **1.** uttered; spoken **2.** of or using speech **3.** of, at, or near the mouth **4.** *Psychoanalysis* of an early stage of psychosexual development focusing on mouth functions *—n.* a spoken examination, as in a college **—o′ral·ly** *adv.*

oral history 1. the gathering of historical data consisting of personal recollections, usually in the form of tape-recorded interviews **2.** such an interview or interviews

O·ran (ō ran′) seaport in N Algeria, on the Mediterranean: pop. 430,000

Or·ange (ôr′inj, är′-; *also, for 3, Fr.* ô ränzh′) **1.** [prob. after the *orange* groves there] city in SW Calif.: suburb of Los Angeles: pop. 92,000 **2.** river in South Africa, flowing from NE Lesotho into the Atlantic **3.** former principality in W Europe, in what is now SE France

or·ange (ôr′inj, är′-) *n.* [< OFr. < Pr. *auranja* < Sp. < Ar. < Per. < Sans. *naranga*] **1.** a reddish-yellow, round, edible citrus fruit with a sweet, juicy pulp **2.** the evergreen tree it grows on **3.** reddish yellow *—adj.* **1.** reddish-yellow **2.** of oranges **—or′ang·y** (-in jē) *adj.*

or·ange·ade (-ād′) *n.* a drink made of orange juice and water, usually sweetened

Orange Free State province of South Africa, west of Lesotho

Or·ange·man (ôr′inj mən, är′-) *n., pl.* **-men** [after the Prince of *Orange,* later WILLIAM III] a member of a secret society organized in northern Ireland in 1795 to support Protestantism

orange pekoe a black tea of Ceylon and India

orange stick an orangewood stick, for manicuring

or·ange·wood (ôr′inj wood′, är′-) *n.* the wood of the orange tree *—adj.* of orangewood

o·rang·u·tan (ô raŋ′oo tan′, ə-; -taŋ′) *n.* [< Malay < *oran,* man + *utan,* forest] an ape of Borneo and Sumatra, with shaggy, reddish-brown hair, very long arms, small ears, and a hairless face: also sp. **o·rang′ou·tang′** (-taŋ′)

ORANGUTAN (standing height to 60 in.)

o·rate (ô rāt′, ôr′āt) *vi.* **o·rat′ed, o·rat′ing** [< ff.] to make an oration; speak pompously or bombastically: a humorously derogatory term

o·ra·tion (ô rā′shən) *n.* [< L. *oratio* < *orare,* to speak] a formal speech, as at a ceremony

or·a·tor (ôr′ət ər, är′-) *n.* **1.** a person who delivers an oration **2.** an eloquent public speaker

or·a·tor·i·cal (ôr′ə tôr′i k'l, är′-) *adj.* **1.** of or characteristic of orators or oratory **2.** given to oratory **—or′a·tor′i·cal·ly** *adv.*

or·a·to·ri·o (ôr′ə tôr′ē ō′, är′-) *n., pl.* **-os′** [It., small chapel: from performances at a chapel in Rome] a long, dramatic musical work, usually on a religious theme, consisting of arias, recitatives, choruses, etc. with orchestral accompaniment but without stage action, scenery, etc.

or·a·to·ry (ôr′ə tôr′ē, är′-) *n., pl.* **-ries** [L. *oratoria*] **1.** the art of an orator; skill in public speaking **2.** [< LL. < L. *oratorius* < *orator*] a small chapel, esp. for private prayer

orb (ôrb) *n.* [L. *orbis,* a circle] **1.** a globe; sphere **2.** any heavenly sphere, as the sun or moon **3.** a small globe with a cross, as a symbol of royal power **4.** [Poet.] the eye *—vt.*

1. to form into a sphere or circle 2. [Poet.] to enclose or encircle —**orbed** *adj.* —**orb′y** *adj.*

or·bic·u·lar (ôr bik′yoo lər) *adj.* [< LL. < L. dim. of *orbis,* a circle] 1. in the form of an orb; spherical or circular 2. *Bot.* round and flat, as some leaves Also **or·bic′u·late** (-lit, -lāt′), **or·bic′u·lat′ed** (-lāt′id) —**or·bic′u·lar′i·ty** (-lar′ə tē) *n.* —**or·bic′u·lar·ly** *adv.*

or·bit (ôr′bit) *n.* [< MFr. < ML. < L. *orbita,* path < *orbis,* a circle] 1. the bony cavity containing the eye; eye socket 2. *a)* the path of a heavenly body in its revolution around another *b)* the path of an artificial satellite or spacecraft around a heavenly body 3. the range of one's experience or activity —*vi.* to move in an orbit or circle —*vt.* 1. to put into an orbit in space 2. to move in an orbit around —**or′bit·al** *adj.*

or·bit·er (-ər) *n.* one that moves in an orbit; specif., an artificial satellite designed to orbit a planet, etc.

or·chard (ôr′chərd) *n.* [< OE. *ortgeard,* ult. < L. *hortus,* a garden + OE. *geard,* enclosure] 1. an area of land where fruit trees or nut trees are grown 2. such trees

or·ches·tra (ôr′kis trə, -kes′-) *n.* [L. < Gr. *orchēstra,* space for the chorus in front of the stage < *orcheisthai,* to dance] 1. the space in front of and below the stage, where the musicians sit: in full, **orchestra pit** 2. *a)* the main-floor seats of a theater, esp. the front section *b)* the main floor itself 3. *a)* a group of musicians playing together; esp., *same as* SYMPHONY ORCHESTRA *b)* their instruments —**or·ches′tral** (-kes′trəl) *adj.* —**or·ches′tral·ly** *adv.*

or·ches·trate (ôr′kis trāt′) *vt., vi.* **-trat′ed, -trat′ing** 1. to compose or arrange (music) for an orchestra 2. to furnish (a ballet, etc.) with an orchestral score 3. to combine harmoniously —**or′ches·tra′tion** *n.* —**or′ches·tra′tor, or′ches·trat′er** *n.*

or·chid (ôr′kid) *n.* [< L.: see ff.] 1. any of a family of plants having bulbous roots and flowers with three petals, one lip-shaped 2. the flower 3. a light bluish red —*adj.* of this color

or·chis (ôr′kis) *n.* [L. < Gr. *orchis,* lit., testicle: from the shape of the roots] an orchid; specif., one with small flowers growing in spikes

ord. 1. order 2. ordinal 3. ordinance

or·dain (ôr dān′) *vt.* [< OFr. < L. *ordinare* < *ordo,* an order] 1. to decree; order; establish; enact 2. to invest with the functions or office of a minister, priest, or rabbi —*vi.* to command; decree —**or·dain′er** *n.* —**or·dain′ment** *n.*

or·deal (ôr dēl′, -dē′əl; ôr′dēl) *n.* [OE. *ordal*] 1. an old method of trial exposing the accused to physical dangers from which he was supposedly protected if innocent 2. a painful or severe test

or·der (ôr′dər) *n.* [< OFr. < L. *ordo,* straight row] 1. social position 2. a state of peace; orderly conduct 3. arrangement of things or events; series 4. a fixed or definite plan; system 5. a group set off from others by some quality 6. a group of persons organized for military, monastic, or social purposes [the Masonic *Order*] 7. *a)* a group of persons distinguished by having received a certain award or citation *b)* the group's insignia 8. a condition in which everything is in its right place and functioning properly 9. condition in general [in working *order*] 10. a command, direction, etc., usually backed by authority 11. class; kind; sort [sentiments of a high *order*] 12. an established method, as of conduct in meetings, court, etc. 13. *a)* a request or commission to supply something *b)* the goods supplied *c)* a single portion of some food, as in a restaurant 14. *Archit. a)* any of several classical styles of structure, as Doric, determined chiefly by the type of column and entablature *b)* a style of building 15. *Biol.* a classification ranking above a family and below a class 16. *Finance* written instructions to pay money or surrender property 17. *Theol. a)* any of the nine grades of angels *b)* any rank in the Christian clergy *c)* [*pl.*] the position of ordained minister —*vt.* 1. to put or keep in order; arrange 2. *a)* to command *b)* to command to go (*to, out of,* etc.) 3. to request or direct (something to be supplied) —*vi.* 1. to give a command 2. to request that something be supplied —**by order of** according to the command of —**call to order** to request to be quiet, as to start (a meeting) —**in** (or **out of**) **order** 1. in (or not in) proper sequence or position 2. in (or not in) good condition 3. in (or not in) accordance with the rules 4. being (or not being) suitable to the occasion —**in order that** so that; to the end that —**in order to** as a means to —**in short order** without delay —**on order** ordered but not yet supplied —**on the order of** 1. similar to 2. approximately —**to order** as specified by the buyer —**or′der·er** *n.*

or·der·ly (ôr′dər lē) *adj.* 1. *a)* neatly arranged *b)* conforming to some regular order; systematic 2. well-behaved; law-abiding —*adv.* in proper order; methodically —*n., pl.* **-lies** 1. *Mil.* an enlisted man assigned as a personal attendant or given a specific task 2. a male hospital attendant —**or′der·li·ness** *n.*

or·di·nal (ôr′d'n əl) *adj.* [< LL. *ordinalis* < L. *ordo,* an order] 1. expressing order, specif. of a number in a series: see ORDINAL NUMBER 2. of an order of animals or plants —*n.* 1. *same as* ORDINAL NUMBER 2. [*often* **O-**] a book of religious rituals

ordinal number a number used to indicate order (e.g., ninth, 25th, etc.) in a series: distinguished from CARDINAL NUMBER

or·di·nance (ôr′d'n əns) *n.* [< OFr. < *ordener:* see ORDAIN] 1. an authoritative command 2. an established practice, rite, etc. 3. a governmental, now esp. municipal, statute or regulation

or·di·nar·i·ly (ôr′d'n er′ə lē) *adv.* 1. usually; as a rule 2. in an ordinary way

or·di·nar·y (ôr′d'n er′ē) *n., pl.* **-nar′ies** [< OFr. < ML. < L. *ordinarius,* an overseer < *ordo,* an order] 1. an official of church or court whose power is original, not delegated 2. [Brit.] *a)* a set meal at a fixed price *b)* an inn, etc. serving such meals 3. *Eccles.* [*often* **O-**] the unvarying part of the Mass —*adj.* 1. customary; usual 2. *a)* unexceptional; common *b)* relatively inferior —**in ordinary** in regular service —**out of the ordinary** unusual —**or′di·nar′i·ness** *n.*

or·di·nate (ôr′d'n it, -āt′) *n.* [< ModL. (*linea*) *ordinate* (*applicata*), line applied in an ordered manner] *Math.* in a system of coordinates, the distance of a point from the horizontal axis as measured along a line parallel to the vertical axis: cf. ABSCISSA

or·di·na·tion (ôr′d'n ā′shən) *n.* an ordaining or being ordained

ord·nance (ôrd′nəns) *n.* [contr. < ORDINANCE] 1. cannon or artillery 2. all military weapons together with ammunition, vehicles, equipment, etc. 3. a military unit supplying and storing ordnance

Or·do·vi·cian (ôr′də vish′ən) *adj.* [< L. *Ordovices,* a tribe in Wales] designating or of the second period of the Paleozoic Era —**the Ordovician** the Ordovician Period or its rocks: see GEOLOGY, chart

or·dure (ôr′jər, -dyoor) *n.* [OFr. < *ord,* filthy < L. *horridus,* horrid] dung; excrement

ore (ôr) *n.* [OE. *ar,* brass, copper] 1. any natural combination of minerals, esp. one from which a metal or metals can be profitably extracted 2. a natural substance from which a nonmetallic material, as sulfur, can be extracted

ö·re (ö′rə) *n., pl.* **ö′re** [Sw., ult. < L. *aurum,* gold] *see* MONETARY UNITS, table (Sweden)

ø·re (ö′rə) *n., pl.* **ø′re** [Dan. & Norw.: see prec.] *see* MONETARY UNITS, table (Denmark, Norway)

o·reg·a·no (ô reg′ə nō, ə-) *n.* [Sp. *orégano,* ult. < Gr. *origanon*] any of several plants of the mint family, with fragrant leaves used for seasoning

Or·e·gon (ôr′i gən, är′-; *also, but not locally,* -gän′) [prob. < AmInd. name of the Columbia River] NW State of the U.S.: 96,981 sq. mi.; pop. 2,633,000; cap. Salem: abbrev. **Oreg., OR** —**Or′e·go′ni·an** (-gō′nē ən) *adj., n.*

O·res·tes (ô res′tēz, ə-) *Gr. Myth.* brother of Electra: see ELECTRA

Ö·re·sund (*Swed.* ö′rə sund′) strait between Sweden & the Danish island of Zealand

or·gan (ôr′gən) *n.* [< OFr. & OE. < L. *organum* < Gr. *organon,* an instrument < *ergon,* work] 1. *a)* a large wind instrument consisting of various sets of pipes which, opened by keys on one or more keyboards, allow passage to a column of compressed air causing sound by vibration: also called **pipe organ** *b)* any of several musical instruments producing similar sounds, as a reed organ 2. in animals and plants, a part composed of specialized tissues and adapted to perform a specific function or functions 3. a means for performing some action 4. a means of communicating ideas, as a periodical

or·gan·dy, or·gan·die (ôr′gən dē) *n., pl.* **-dies** [Fr. *organdi* < ?] a very sheer, crisp cotton fabric, used for dresses, curtains, etc.

or·gan·elle (ôr′gə nel′) *n.* [ult. < L. *organum,* a tool + *-ella,* dim. suffix] a specialized structure within a cell, as a chloroplast or cilium

organ grinder a person who makes a living by playing a barrel organ in the streets

or·gan·ic (ôr gan′ik) *adj.* 1. of or having to do with an organ 2. inherent; constitutional 3. made up of systematically interrelated parts; organized 4. *a)* designating or of any chemical compound containing carbon *b)* designating or of the branch of chemistry dealing with carbon compounds 5. of, like, or derived from living organisms 6. grown with only animal or vegetable fertilizers 7. *Law* designating or of fundamental, or constitutional, law 8.

Med. producing or involving alteration in the structure of an organ: cf. FUNCTIONAL **—or·gan′i·cal·ly** *adv.*

or·gan·ism (ôr′gə niz'm) *n.* **1.** any animal or plant with organs and parts that function together to maintain life **2.** anything like a living thing in its complexity of structure or functions **—or′gan·is′mic** *adj.* **—or′gan·is′mi·cal·ly** *adv.*

or·gan·ist (ôr′gə nist) *n.* one who plays the organ

or·gan·i·za·tion (ôr′gə ni zā′shən, -nī-) *n.* **1.** an organizing or being organized **2.** the way in which the parts of a thing are organized **3.** any unified group or systematized whole; esp., *a*) a body of persons organized for some purpose, as a club, union, etc. *b*) the administrative or executive structure of a business or political party **—or′gan·i·za′tion·al** *adj.* **—or′gan·i·za′tion·al·ly** *adv.*

or·gan·ize (ôr′gə nīz′) *vt.* **-ized′, -iz′ing 1.** to provide with an organic structure; esp., *a*) to arrange in an orderly way *b*) to bring into a unified, coherent form *c*) to make plans and arrange for **2.** to bring into being; establish **3.** to enlist in, or cause to form, a labor union **4.** [Colloq.] to set (oneself) into an orderly state of mind *—vi.* **1.** to become organized **2.** to form an organization, esp. a labor union **—or′gan·iz′a·ble** *adj.* **—or′gan·iz′er** *n.*

or·gan·za (ôr gan′zə) *n.* [< ?] a stiff, sheer fabric of rayon, silk, etc.

or·gasm (ôr′gaz'm) *n.* [< Fr. < Gr. *orgasmos* < *organ,* to swell with moisture] a frenzy; esp., the climax of a sexual act **—or·gas′mic, or·gas′tic** *adj.*

or·gy (ôr′jē) *n., pl.* **-gies** [< Fr. < L. < Gr. *orgia,* pl., secret rites] **1.** [*usually pl.*] in ancient Greece and Rome, wild celebration in worship of certain gods **2.** any wild, licentious merrymaking **3.** unrestrained indulgence in any activity **—or′gi·as′tic** (-as′tik) *adj.* **—or′gi·as′ti·cal·ly** *adv.*

o·ri·el (ôr′ē əl) *n.* [< OFr. < ? ML. *oriolum,* porch] a large window built out from a wall and resting on a bracket or corbel

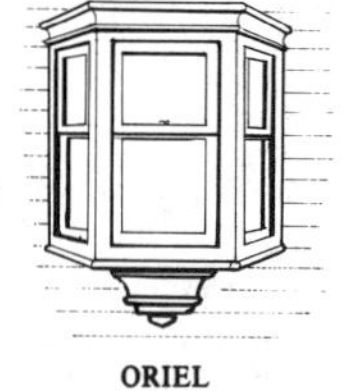
ORIEL

o·ri·ent (ôr′ē ənt; *also, and for v. usually,* -ent′) *n.* [OFr. < L. *oriens,* direction of the rising sun, prp. of *oriri,* to arise] the east: now rare, except [**O-**] the East, or Asia; esp., the Far East *—adj.* **1.** shining, as pearls **2.** [Poet.] *a*) eastern; oriental *b*) rising, as the sun *—vt.* **1.** to arrange with reference to the east **2.** to set (a map or chart) in agreement with the points of the compass **3.** to adjust or adapt to a particular situation (often used reflexively)

o·ri·en·tal (ôr′ē en′t'l) *adj.* **1.** [Poet.] eastern **2.** [**O-**] of the Orient, its people, or their culture; Eastern *—n.* [*usually* **O-**] a native of the Orient or a member of a people native to that region

O·ri·en·tal·ism (-iz'm) *n.* **1.** any trait, quality, etc. associated with people of the East **2.** study of Eastern culture **—O′ri·en′tal·ist** *n.*

Oriental poppy a perennial poppy often grown for its red, pink, or white flowers

Oriental rug (or **carpet**) a carpet hand-woven in the Orient, usually with intricate, colorful designs

o·ri·en·tate (ôr′ē ən tāt′, -en-) *vt.* **-tat′ed, -tat′ing** *same as* ORIENT *—vi.* **1.** to face east, or in any specified direction **2.** to adjust to a situation

o·ri·en·ta·tion (ôr′ē ən tā′shən, -en-) *n.* **1.** an orienting or being oriented **2.** *a*) awareness of one's environment as to time, space, objects, and persons *b*) a period of introduction and adjustment

or·i·en·teer·ing (ôr′ē en tir′iŋ) *n.* [< Swed. *orientering,* lit., orientation] a timed cross-country competition in which runners follow a course, using compass and map

or·i·fice (ôr′ə fis, är′-) *n.* [Fr. < LL. *orificium* < L. *os* (gen. *oris*), mouth + *facere,* to make] an opening or mouth, as of a tube or cavity

or·i·flamme (ôr′ə flam′, är′-) *n.* [Fr. < OFr. < L. < *aurum,* gold + *flamma,* flame] **1.** the ancient royal standard of France, a red silk banner with flame-shaped streamers **2.** any battle standard

orig. 1. origin **2.** original **3.** originally

o·ri·ga·mi (ôr′ə gä′mē) *n.* [Jap.] **1.** a traditional Japanese art of folding paper to form flowers, animal figures, etc. **2.** an object so made

or·i·gin (ôr′ə jin, är′-) *n.* [< MFr. < L. *origo* (gen. *originis*) < *oriri,* to rise] **1.** a coming into existence or use; beginning **2.** parentage; birth; lineage **3.** source; root **4.** *Math.* the point at which coordinate axes intersect

o·rig·i·nal (ə rij′ə n'l) *adj.* **1.** having to do with an origin; first; earliest **2.** never having been before; new; novel **3.** capable of creating something new, or thinking or acting in an independent, fresh way; inventive **4.** coming from someone as the originator, maker, author, etc. **5.** being that from which copies, reproductions, translations, etc. have been made *—n.* **1.** a primary type that has given rise to varieties **2.** an original work of art, writing, etc., as distinguished from a copy, etc. **3.** the person or thing depicted in a painting, etc. **4.** a person of original mind and unusual creativity **—o·rig′i·nal·ly** *adv.*

o·rig·i·nal·i·ty (ə rij′ə nal′ə tē) *n.* **1.** a being original **2.** the ability to be original, inventive, or creative

original sin *Christian Theology* sinfulness and depravity regarded as innate in man as a direct result of Adam's sin

o·rig·i·nate (ə rij′ə nāt′) *vt.* **-nat′ed, -nat′ing** to bring into being; esp., to create (something original); invent *—vi.* to come into being; begin; start **—o·rig′i·na′tion** *n.* **—o·rig′i·na′tive** *adj.* **—o·rig′i·na′tor** *n.*

O·ri·no·co (ôr′ə nō′kō) river in Venezuela, flowing from N Brazil into the Atlantic: c. 1,700 mi.

o·ri·ole (ôr′ē ōl′) *n.* [< OFr. < ML. < L. *aureolus,* golden < *aurum,* gold] **1.** any of a family of yellow and black birds found from Europe to Australia **2.** any of a group of American birds, including the Baltimore oriole, that have orange and black plumage and build hanging nests

O·ri·on (ō rī′ən, ô-) an equatorial constellation near Taurus, containing the bright star Rigel

or·i·son (ôr′i z'n, är′-; -s'n) *n.* [< OFr. < LL. *oratio,* a prayer < L.: see ORATION] a prayer

Ork·ney Islands (ôrk′nē) group of islands north of Scotland, constituting a region (**Orkney**) of Scotland

Or·lan·do (ôr lan′dō) [after *Orlando* Reeves, an Indian runner] city in C Fla.: pop. 128,000 (met. area 695,000)

Or·lé·ans (ôr′*lā än′*; *E.* ôr′lē ənz) city in NC France, on the Loire: pop. 96,000

Or·lon (ôr′län) [arbitrary coinage, after (NYL)ON] *a trademark for* a synthetic fiber somewhat like nylon, or a fabric made from this fiber *—n.* [**o-**] this fiber or fabric

Or·mazd (ôr′məzd) [Per.] *Zoroastrianism* the supreme deity and creator of the world: also sp. **Or′muzd**

or·mo·lu (ôr′mə lo͞o′) *n.* [< Fr. *or moulu,* ground gold] an imitation gold consisting of an alloy of copper and tin, used as decoration, etc.

or·na·ment (ôr′nə mənt; *for v.* -ment′) *n.* [< OFr. < L. *ornamentum* < *ornare,* to adorn] **1.** anything that adorns; decoration; embellishment **2.** a person whose character or talent adds luster to his surroundings, society, etc. **3.** an adorning or being adorned **4.** mere external display **5.** *Music* an embellishing trill, arpeggio, etc. *—vt.* to furnish with ornaments or be an ornament to; decorate

or·na·men·tal (ôr′nə men′t'l) *adj.* serving as an ornament; decorative *—n.* something ornamental; specif., a decorative plant **—or′na·men′tal·ly** *adv.*

or·na·men·ta·tion (-men tā′shən) *n.* **1.** an ornamenting or being ornamented **2.** ornaments collectively

or·nate (ôr nāt′) *adj.* [< L. pp. of *ornare,* to adorn] **1.** heavily ornamented; overadorned **2.** showy or flowery, as some literary styles **—or·nate′ly** *adv.* **—or·nate′ness** *n.*

or·ner·y (ôr′nər ē) *adj.* [altered < ORDINARY] [Chiefly Dial.] **1.** having an ugly or mean disposition **2.** obstinate **3.** base; low **—or′ner·i·ness** *n.*

or·ni·thol·o·gy (ôr′nə thäl′ə jē) *n.* [< ModL. < Gr. *ornis* (gen. *ornithos*), bird + -LOGY] the branch of zoology dealing with birds **—or·ni·tho·log·i·cal** (ôr′ni thə läj′i k'l) *adj.* **—or′ni·tho·log′i·cal·ly** *adv.* **—or′ni·thol′o·gist** *n.*

o·ro·tund (ôr′ə tund′) *adj.* [< L. *ore rotundo,* lit., with round mouth] **1.** clear, strong, and deep: said of the voice **2.** bombastic or pompous, as speech **—o′ro·tun′di·ty** *n.*

O·roz·co (ô *rôs′*kô), **Jo·sé Cle·men·te** (hô se′ kle men′te) 1883–1949; Mex. painter

or·phan (ôr′fən) *n.* [< LL. < Gr. *orphanos*] a child whose parents are dead *—adj.* **1.** being an orphan **2.** of or for orphans *—vt.* to cause to become an orphan

or·phan·age (-ij) *n.* **1.** the state of being an orphan **2.** an institution housing orphans

Or·phe·us (ôr′fē əs, -fyo͞os) *Gr. Myth.* a poet-musician with magic musical powers who lost his chance to lead his wife, Eurydice, out from the world of the dead when he looked back at her

Or·phic (-fik) *adj.* **1.** of or characteristic of Orpheus **2.** [*also* **o-**] *a*) like the music attributed to Orpheus; entrancing *b*) mystic; occult

or·pine (ôr′pin) *n.* [< MFr. < OFr. < L. *auripigmentum,* pigment of gold] a plant with fleshy leaves and white, yellow, or purple flowers

or·ris (ôr′is, är′-) *n.* [prob. < MIt. < L. *iris,* iris] any of several European irises, esp. a species whose rootstocks yield orrisroot

or·ris·root (-ro͞ot′) *n.* the rootstock of the orris, ground and used in perfumery, tooth powders, etc.

or·tho- [< Gr. *orthos,* straight] *a combining form meaning:* **1.** straight *[orthodontics]* **2.** right angle *[orthoclase]* **3.** correct or standard *[orthography]* **4.** *Med.* correction of deformities *[orthopedics]* Also, before a vowel, **orth-**

or·tho·clase (ôr′thə klās′, -klāz′) *n.* [< G. < Gr. *orthos* (see ORTHO-) + *klasis,* fracture, because of 90° cleavage] potassium feldspar, common in granitic rocks

or·tho·don·tics (ôr′thə dän′tiks) *n.pl.* [*with sing. v.*] [<

ModL.: see ORTH(O)-, -ODONT, & -ICS] the branch of dentistry concerned with correcting irregularities of the teeth and poor occlusion: also **or′tho·don′ti·a** (-dän′shə, -shē ə) —**or′tho·don′tic** *adj.* —**or′tho·don′tist** *n.*

or·tho·dox (ôr′thə däks′) *adj.* [< Fr. < LL. < LGr. < Gr. *orthos,* correct + *doxa,* opinion < *dokein,* to think] **1.** conforming to the usual beliefs or established doctrines, esp. in religion; conventional; specif., *a)* conforming to the Christian faith as formulated in the early creeds *b)* **[O-]** strictly observing the ceremonial rites and traditions of Judaism, such as kashrut, the Sabbath, etc. **2.** **[O-]** designating or of any church in the Orthodox Eastern Church —**or′tho·dox′y** *n., pl.* **-dox′ies**

Orthodox Eastern Church the Christian church dominant in E Europe, W Asia, and N Africa, orig. made up of four patriarchates (Constantinople, Alexandria, Antioch, Jerusalem), now also including the autonomous churches of the Soviet Union, Greece, Romania, Bulgaria, etc.

or·tho·e·py (ôr thō′ə pē, ôr′thō-) *n.* [< ModL. < Gr. < *orthos,* right + *epos,* a word] **1.** the study of pronunciation; phonology **2.** the standard pronunciation of a language —**or·tho·ep·ic** (ôr′thō ep′ik), **or′tho·ep′i·cal** *adj.* —**or′tho·ep′i·cal·ly** *adv.* —**or·tho′e·pist** *n.*

or·thog·ra·phy (ôr thäg′rə fē) *n., pl.* **-phies** [< MFr. < L. < Gr.: see ORTHO- & -GRAPHY] **1.** spelling in accord with accepted usage **2.** any method of spelling **3.** spelling as a subject for study —**or·thog′ra·pher** *n.* —**or·tho·graph·ic** (ôr′thə graf′ik), **or′tho·graph′i·cal** *adj.* —**or′tho·graph′i·cal·ly** *adv.*

or·tho·pe·dics, or·tho·pae·dics (ôr′thə pē′diks) *n.pl.* [*with sing. v.*] [< Fr. < Gr. *orthos,* straight + *paideia,* training of children < *pais,* child] the branch of surgery dealing with the treatment of deformities, diseases, and injuries of the bones, joints, etc. —**or′tho·pe′dic, or′tho·pae′dic** *adj.* —**or′tho·pe′dist, or′tho·pae′dist** *n.*

or·thop·ter·an (ôr thäp′tər ən) *n.* [< ORTHO- + Gr. *pteron,* wing] any of an order of insects, including crickets, grasshoppers, etc., having chewing mouthparts and hard forewings covering membranous hind wings —**or·thop′ter·ous** *adj.*

or·to·lan (ôr′t′l ən) *n.* [Fr. < Pr. < It. < L. *hortulanus,* dim. of *hortus,* a garden] an old-world bunting, prized as choice food

Or·well (ôr′wel, -wəl), **George** (pseud. of *Eric Arthur Blair*) 1903–50; Eng. writer —**Or·well′i·an** *adj.*

-o·ry (ôr′ē, ər ē) [< OFr. < L. *-orius, -oria, -orium*] *a suffix meaning:* **1.** of, having the nature of *[contradictory]* **2.** a place or thing for *[laboratory]*

o·ryx (ôr′iks, är′-) *n., pl.* **o′ryx·es, o′ryx:** see PLURAL, II, D, 1 [ModL. < L., wild goat < Gr., lit., pickax] any of a group of large African and Asian antelopes with long horns

‡**os**[1] (äs) *n., pl.* **os′sa** (-ə) [L.] a bone

‡**os**[2] (äs) *n., pl.* **o·ra** (ôr′ə) [L.] a mouth; opening

Os *Chem.* osmium

OS, O.S. Old Style

OS., OS, O.S. Old Saxon

O·sage orange (ō sāj′, ō′sāj) [< *Osage,* AmInd. tribe] **1.** a thorny tree with hard, yellow wood, used for hedges, etc. **2.** its orangelike, inedible fruit

O·sa·ka (ô′sä kä′; *E.* ō sä′kə) seaport in S Honshu, Japan: pop. 3,156,000

Os·car (äs′kər) [< OE. < *os,* a god + *gar,* a spear] a masculine name —*n.* [< ?] [Slang] any of the statuettes awarded annually in the U.S. for achievements in motion pictures

os·cil·late (äs′ə lāt′) *vi.* **-lat′ed, -lat′ing** [< L. pp. of *oscillare,* to swing] **1.** to swing back and forth **2.** to be indecisive; vacillate **3.** *Physics* to vary between maximum and minimum values, as electric current —*vt.* to cause to oscillate —**os′cil·la′tor** *n.* —**os′cil·la·to′ry** *adj.*

os·cil·la·tion (äs′ə lā′shən) *n.* **1.** an oscillating **2.** fluctuation; instability **3.** *Physics a)* variation between maximum and minimum values, as of current *b)* a single swing of an oscillating object

os·cil·lo·graph (ä sil′ə graf′, ə-) *n.* [< L. *oscillare,* to swing + -GRAPH] an instrument for displaying or recording electrical oscillations in a wavy line (**oscillogram**) —**os·cil′lo·graph′ic** *adj.*

os·cil·lo·scope (-skōp′) *n.* [< L. *oscillare,* to swing + -SCOPE] a type of oscillograph that visually displays an electrical wave on a fluorescent screen, as of a cathode-ray tube —**os·cil′lo·scop′ic** (-skäp′ik) *adj.*

os·cine (äs′in, -īn) *adj.* [< ModL. < L. *oscen,* bird whose notes were used in divining] designating or of a group of perching birds, as the finches, larks, etc., typically with highly developed vocal organs —*n.* an oscine bird

os·cu·late (äs′kyə lāt′) *vt., vi.* **-lat′ed, -lat′ing** [< L. pp. of *osculari* < *osculum,* kiss, dim. of *os,* a mouth] **1.** to kiss: a jocular usage **2.** to touch closely —**os′cu·lant** *adj.* —**os′cu·la′tion** *n.* —**os′cu·la·to′ry** *adj.*

-ose[1] (ōs) [Fr. < (*gluc*)*ose:* see GLUCOSE] *a suffix designating:* **1.** a carbohydrate *[sucrose]* **2.** the product of a protein hydrolysis *[proteose]*

-ose[2] (ōs) [L. *-osus*] *a suffix meaning* full of, having the qualities of, like *[verbose]*

Osh·a·wa (äsh′ə wə, -wô) city in SE Ontario, Canada, on Lake Ontario: pop. 107,000

Osh·kosh (äsh′käsh) [after *Oshkosh* (1795–1850), Am. Indian chief] city in E Wis.: pop. 50,000

o·sier (ō′zhər) *n.* [< OFr. < ML. *ausaria,* bed of willows] **1.** any of several willows whose branches or stems are used for baskets and furniture **2.** a willow branch used for wickerwork

O·si·ris (ō sī′ris) the ancient Egyptian god of the lower world, brother and husband of Isis

-o·sis (ō′sis) [L. < Gr. *-ōsis*] *a suffix meaning:* **1.** state, condition, action *[osmosis]* **2.** an abnormal or diseased condition *[neurosis]*

-os·i·ty (äs′ət ē) [< Fr. < L. *-ositas*] *a suffix used to form nouns from adjectives ending in* -OSE[2] *or* -OUS

Os·lo (äs′lō, äz′-; *Norw.* o͝os′lo͞o) capital of Norway; seaport in the SE part: pop. 487,000

Os·man·li (äz man′lē, äs-) *n.* [Turk. < *Osman* (1259–1326), leader & founder of the Ottoman Empire] **1.** *pl.* **-lis** an Ottoman Turk **2.** *same as* TURKISH (*n.* 1) —*adj. same as* TURKISH

os·mics (äz′miks) *n.pl.* [*with sing. v.*] [< Gr. *osmē,* odor + -ICS] the science of smell

os·mi·um (äz′mē əm) *n.* [ModL. < Gr. *osmē,* odor: after the odor of one of its oxides] a very hard, bluish-white, metallic chemical element that occurs in the form of an alloy with platinum and iridium: symbol, Os; at. wt., 190.2; at. no., 76

os·mose (äs′mōs, äz′-) *vt., vi.* **-mosed, -mos·ing** to undergo osmosis

os·mo·sis (äs mō′sis, äz-) *n.* [ModL., ult. < Gr. *ōsmos,* impulse < *ōthein,* to push] **1.** the tendency of a solvent to pass through a semipermeable membrane, as the wall of a living cell, so as to equalize concentrations on both sides of the membrane **2.** the diffusion of fluids through a porous partition —**os·mot′ic** (-mät′ik) *adj.* —**os·mot′i·cal·ly** *adv.*

os·prey (äs′prē) *n., pl.* **-preys** [< L. *ossifraga,* lit., the bonebreaker < *os,* a bone + *frangere,* to break] a large diving bird of prey of the hawk family with a blackish back and white breast, that feeds solely on fish

OSPREY (20–24 in. long)

Os·sa (äs′ə) mountain in Thessaly, NE Greece: see PELION

‡**os·sa** (äs′ə) *n. pl. of* OS[1]

os·se·ous (äs′ē əs) *adj.* [< L. < *os,* a bone] composed of, containing, or like bone; bony

Os·sian (äsh′ən, äs′ē ən) *Gaelic Folklore* a bard and hero of the 3d cent. —**Os′si·an′ic** *adj.*

os·si·fy (äs′ə fī′) *vt., vi.* **-fied′, -fy′ing** [< L. *os* (gen. *ossis*), a bone + -FY] **1.** to change or develop into bone **2.** to settle or fix rigidly in a practice, custom, etc. —**os′si·fi·ca′tion** *n.*

Os·si·ning (äs′ə niŋ) [< Delaware *ossingsing,* lit., at the standing stone] village in SE N.Y., on the Hudson: site of Sing Sing, a State prison

os·te·al (äs′tē əl) *adj.* osseous; bony

os·te·i·tis (äs′tē īt′əs) *n.* [OSTE(O)- + -ITIS] inflammation of the bone or bony tissue

Ost·end (äs tend′, äs′tend) seaport & summer resort in NW Belgium, on the North Sea: pop. 58,000

os·ten·si·ble (äs ten′sə b′l, əs-) *adj.* [Fr. < ML. < L. *ostendere,* to show < *ob(s)*-, against + *tendere,* to stretch] apparent; seeming; professed —**os·ten′si·bly** *adv.*

os·ten·sive (äs ten′siv) *adj.* **1.** directly pointing out; clearly demonstrative **2.** *same as* OSTENSIBLE —**os·ten′sive·ly** *adv.*

os·ten·ta·tion (äs′tən tā′shən) *n.* [< L., ult. < *ostendere:* see OSTENSIBLE] showy display, as of wealth, knowledge, etc.; pretentiousness —**os′ten·ta′tious** *adj.* —**os′ten·ta′tious·ly** *adv.* —**os′ten·ta′tious·ness** *n.*

os·te·o- [ModL. < Gr. *osteon*] *a combining form meaning* a bone or bones *[osteopath]* : also, before a vowel, **oste-**

os·te·ol·o·gy (äs′tē äl′ə jē) *n.* [ModL.: see prec. & -LOGY] the study of the structure and function of bones —**os′te·o·log′i·cal** (-ə läj′i k′l) *adj.* —**os′te·ol′o·gist** *n.*

os·te·o·ma (äs′tē ō′mə) *n., pl.* **-mas, -ma·ta** (-mə tə) [ModL.: see OSTEO- & -OMA] a tumor composed of bony tissue

os·te·o·ma·la·cia (-ō mə lā′shə) *n.* [ModL. < OSTEO- + *malacia,* a softness of tissue] a bone disease characterized by a softening of the bones from a deficiency in calcium salts

os·te·o·my·e·li·tis (-ō mī′ə lit′is) ***n.*** [ModL.: see OSTEO- & MYELITIS] infection of bone marrow or structures

os·te·op·a·thy (äs′tē äp′ə thē) ***n.*** [ModL.: see OSTEO- & -PATHY] a school of medicine and surgery emphasizing the interrelationship of the musculoskeletal system to all other body parts —**os′te·o·path′** (-ə path′) ***n.*** —**os′te·o·path′ic** ***adj.*** —**os′te·o·path′i·cal·ly** ***adv.***

os·te·o·po·ro·sis (-ō pô rō′sis) ***n.*** [ModL. < OSTEO- + *porosis,* a porous condition] a bone disease in which the bones become brittle because of a loss of calcium

Ös·ter·reich (ös′tər riH′) *Ger. name of* AUSTRIA

ost·ler (äs′lər) ***n.*** *same as* HOSTLER

os·tra·cism (äs′trə siz′m) ***n.*** [see ff.] **1.** in ancient Greece, the temporary banishment of a citizen by popular vote **2.** an exclusion by general consent, as from society

os·tra·cize (-sīz′) ***vt.*** **-cized′, -ciz′ing** [Gr. *ostrakizein,* to exile by votes written on potsherds < *ostrakon,* a potsherd] to banish, exclude, etc. by ostracism

os·trich (ôs′trich, äs′-) ***n.,*** *pl.* **-trich·es, -trich:** see PLURAL, II, D, 1 [< OFr. < VL. < L. *avis,* bird + *struthio,* ostrich] **1.** a swift-running, non-flying bird of Africa and the Near East, the largest living bird, with a long neck and legs and small wings **2.** *same as* RHEA (*see* RHEA *n.*)

Os·tro·goth (äs′trə gäth′) ***n.*** an East Goth; esp., a member of the tribe which conquered Italy in the 5th cent. A.D. —**Os′tro·goth′ic** ***adj.***

Oś·wie·çim (ôsh vyan′tsim) *Pol. name of* AUSCHWITZ

OT., OT, O.T. Old Testament

O·thel·lo (ə thel′ō, ô-) a tragedy by Shakespeare in which the title character, made madly jealous by the villainous Iago, kills his faithful wife, Desdemona

OSTRICH (to 8 ft. high)

oth·er (uth′ər) ***adj.*** [OE.] **1.** being the remaining one or ones of two or more *[*Bill and the *other* boy(s)*]* **2.** different or distinct from that or those implied *[*some *other* girl*]* **3.** different *[*it is *other* than you think*]* **4.** additional *[*to have no *other* coat*]* **5.** former *[*in *other* times*]* —***pron.*** **1.** the other one *[*each loved the *other]* **2.** some other person or thing *[*to do as *others* do*]* —***adv.*** otherwise; differently *[*he can't do *other* than go*]* —**of all others** above all others —**the other day** (or **night, etc.**) not long ago —**oth′er·ness** ***n.***

oth·er·wise (-wīz′) ***adv.*** **1.** in another manner; differently *[*to believe *otherwise]* **2.** in all other respects *[*an *otherwise* intelligent man*]* **3.** in other circumstances —***adj.*** different *[*his answer could not be *otherwise]*

other world a supposed world after death

oth·er·world·ly (-wurld′lē) ***adj.*** being apart from earthly interests —**oth′er·world′li·ness** ***n.***

-ot·ic (ät′ik) [Gr. *-ōtikos*] *a suffix meaning:* **1.** of or affected with *[sclerotic]* **2.** producing *[narcotic]*

o·ti·ose (ō′shē ōs′, ōt′ē-) ***adj.*** [< L. < *otium,* leisure] **1.** idle; indolent **2.** ineffective; futile **3.** useless; superfluous —**o′ti·ose′ly** ***adv.*** —**o′ti·os′i·ty** (-äs′ə tē) ***n.***

O·tis (ōt′əs) **1.** [orig. family name] a masculine name **2. James,** 1725–83; Am. Revolutionary statesman

o·ti·tis (ō tīt′əs) ***n.*** [ModL.: see OTO- & -ITIS] inflammation of the ear

o·to- [< Gr. *ous* (gen. *ōtos*), the ear] *a combining form meaning* the ear *[otology]* : also, before a vowel, **ot-**

o·tol·o·gy (ō täl′ə jē) ***n.*** [OTO- + -LOGY] the branch of medicine dealing with the ear and its disorders —**o·to·log·i·cal** (ōt′ə läj′i k′l) ***adj.*** —**o·tol′o·gist** ***n.***

o·to·scle·ro·sis (ōt′ō skli rō′sis) ***n.*** [OTO- + SCLEROSIS] a growth of spongy bone in the inner ear causing deafness

O·tran·to (ō trän′tō), **Strait of** strait between Italy & Albania, connecting the Adriatic & Ionian seas

Ot·ta·wa[1] (ät′ə wə, -wä′) ***n.*** **1.** *pl.* **-was, -wa** a member of a tribe of Indians who lived in SE Canada and in Michigan **2.** their Algonquian language —***adj.*** of the Ottawas

Ot·ta·wa[2] (ät′ə wə, -wä′) capital of Canada, in SE Ontario: pop. 304,000

ot·ter (ät′ər) ***n.,*** *pl.* **-ters, -ter:** see PLURAL, II, D, 1 [OE. *oter*] **1.** a furry, flesh-eating mammal related to the weasel and mink, with webbed feet and a long tail **2.** its fur **3.** *same as* SEA OTTER

Ot·to (ät′ō) [< OHG. < *auda,* rich] **1.** a masculine name **2. Otto I** 912–973 A.D.; king of Germany (936–973) & emperor of the Holy Roman Empire (962–973): called *the Great*

Ot·to·man (ät′ə mən) ***adj.*** [ult. < Ar. *'Uthmāni,* of Osman: see OSMANLI] *same as* TURKISH —***n.,*** *pl.* **-mans** **1.** a Turk **2.** [**o-**] *a*) a low, cushioned seat or couch without a back or arms *b*) a cushioned footstool

Ottoman Empire empire (c.1300–1918) of the Turks, including at its peak much of SE Europe, SW Asia, & NE Africa

ouch (ouch) ***interj.*** an exclamation of pain

ought[1] (ôt) ***v.aux.*** [orig., pt. of *owe* < OE. pp. of *agan,* to owe] an auxiliary used with infinitives to express obligation or duty *[*he *ought* to pay his debts*]* or desirability *[*you *ought* to eat more*]* or probability *[*it *ought* to be over soon*]*

ought[2] (ôt) ***n.*** [var. of AUGHT] anything whatever; aught —***adv.*** [Archaic] to any degree; aught

ought[3] (ôt) ***n.*** [by faulty division of *a nought*] a nought; the figure zero (0)

ought·n't (-'nt) ought not

‡**oui** (wē) ***adv.*** [Fr.] yes

Oui·ja (wē′jə, -jē) [Fr. *oui,* yes + G. *ja,* yes] *a trademark for* a device consisting of a planchette and a board bearing the alphabet and other symbols, used in spiritualistic séances, etc.

ounce[1] (ouns) ***n.*** [< OFr. < L. *uncia,* a twelfth] **1.** a unit of weight equal to 1/16 pound avoirdupois, or 1/12 pound troy **2.** *same as* FLUID OUNCE **3.** any small amount Abbrev. **oz.** (*sing. & pl.*)

ounce[2] (ouns) ***n.*** [< OFr. *l'once* < VL. < L. *lynx,* lynx] *same as* SNOW LEOPARD

our (our, är) ***possessive pronominal adj.*** [OE. *ure*] of, belonging to, made, or done by us

Our Father *same as* LORD'S PRAYER

ours (ourz, ärz) ***pron.*** that or those belonging to us: used without a following noun *[ours* are better*]* : also used after *of* to indicate possession *[*a friend of *ours]*

our·self (our self′, är-) ***pron.*** a form corresponding to OURSELVES, used, as in royal proclamations, by one person

our·selves (-selvz′) ***pron.*** a form of the 1st pers. pl. pronoun, used: *a*) as an intensive *[*we went *ourselves] b*) as a reflexive *[*we hurt *ourselves] c*) as a quasi-noun meaning "our real or true selves" *[*we are not *ourselves* today*]*

-ous (əs) [< OFr. < L. *-osus*] *a suffix meaning:* **1.** having, full of, characterized by *[dangerous]* **2.** *Chem.* having a lower valence than is indicated by the suffix *-ic [nitrous]*

ou·sel (ōō′z'l) ***n.*** *same as* OUZEL

oust (oust) ***vt.*** [< Anglo-Fr. < OFr. *ouster* < L. *ostare* < *ob-,* against + *stare,* to stand] to force or drive out; expel, dispossess, eject, etc.

oust·er (ous′tər) ***n.*** **1.** a person or thing that ousts **2.** *Law* an ousting or being ousted, esp. from real property; legal eviction or unlawful dispossession

out (out) ***adv.*** [OE. *ut*] **1.** *a*) away or forth from a place, position, etc. *[*they live ten miles *out] b*) away from home *c*) away from shore *d*) on strike **2.** into the open air *[*come *out* and play*]* **3.** into existence or activity *[*disease broke *out]* **4.** *a*) to a conclusion *[*argue it *out] b*) completely *[*tired *out] c*) in full bloom, or in leaf **5.** into sight or notice *[*the moon came *out]* **6.** *a*) into or in circulation *[*to put *out* a new style*] b*) into or in society *[*debutantes who come *out]* **7.** from existence or activity *[*fade *out]* **8.** so as to remove from power or office *[*vote them *out]* **9.** aloud *[*sing *out]* **10.** beyond a regular surface, condition, etc. *[*stand *out,* eke *out]* **11.** away from the interior or midst *[*spread *out]* **12.** from one state, as of composure, to another, as of annoyance *[*friends may fall *out]* **13.** into disuse, discard, etc. *[*long skirts went *out]* **14.** from a number or stock *[*pick *out]* **15.** [Slang] into unconsciousness *[*to pass *out]* **16.** *Baseball,* etc. in a manner that results in an out *[*to fly *out]* —***adj.*** **1.** external: usually in combination *[outpost]* **2.** beyond regular limits **3.** outlying **4.** directed outward *[*an *out* flight*]* **5.** away from work, etc. **6.** deviating from what is accurate **7.** *a*) not in operation, use, etc. *b*) turned off; extinguished **8.** not to be considered; not possible **9.** not in power **10.** [Colloq.] having suffered a loss *[out* five dollars*]* **11.** [Colloq.] outmoded **12.** *Baseball* having failed to get on base —***prep.*** **1.** out of; through to the outside **2.** along the way of *[*to drive *out* a driveway*]* **3.** [Poet.] forth from: usually after *from* —***n.*** **1.** something that is out **2.** a person, group, etc. that is not in power, etc.: *usually used in pl.* **3.** [Slang] a way out; means of avoiding **4.** *Baseball* the failure of a batter or runner to reach base safely **5.** *Tennis, Squash,* etc. a service or return that lands out of bounds —***vi.*** to come out; esp., to become known —***vt.*** to put out —***interj.*** get out! —**on the outs** [Colloq.] on unfriendly terms —**out and away** by far; without comparison —**out and out** completely; thoroughly —**out for** making a determined effort to get or do —**out of** **1.** from inside of **2.** from the number of **3.** beyond **4.** from (material, etc.) *[*made *out of* stone*]* **5.** because of *[out of* spite*]* **6.** having no *[out of* gas*]* **7.** not in a condition of *[out of* order*]* **8.** so as to deprive *[*cheat *out of* money*]* —**out one's way** [Colloq.] to or near one's neighborhood —**out to** making a determined effort to

out- [< OUT] *a combining form meaning:* **1.** at or from a point away, outside *[outbuilding]* **2.** going away or forth, outward *[outbound]* **3.** better, greater, or more than *[outdo]* :a frequent usage as in the following self-explanatory terms:

outact	**outhit**	**outscore**
outbox	**outperform**	**outshout**
outfight	**outproduce**	**outspend**

out·age (out′ij) ***n.*** [OUT- + -AGE] an accidental suspension of operation, as of electric power

out-and-out (out′'n out′) ***adj.*** complete; thorough

out·back (out′bak′) ***n.*** [*also* **O**-] the sparsely settled, flat, arid inland region of Australia

out·bal·ance (out′bal′əns) ***vt.*** **-anced, -anc·ing** to be greater than in weight, value, etc.

out·bid (-bid′) ***vt.*** **-bid′, -bid′ding** to bid or offer more than (someone else)

out·board (out′bôrd′) ***adj., adv.*** **1.** outside the hull or bulwarks of a ship or boat **2.** away from the fuselage or hull of an aircraft **3.** outside the main body of a spacecraft —***n.*** **1.** *same as* OUTBOARD MOTOR **2.** a boat with an outboard motor

outboard motor a portable gasoline engine mounted outboard on a boat to propel it

out·bound (-bound′) ***adj.*** outward bound

out·break (-brāk′) ***n.*** a breaking out; sudden occurrence, as of disease, war, rioting, etc.

out·build·ing (-bil′diŋ) ***n.*** a structure, as a garage, separate from the main building

out·burst (-burst′) ***n.*** a sudden release, as of feeling

out·cast (-kast′) ***adj.*** driven out; rejected —***n.*** a person or thing cast out or rejected

out·class (out′klas′) ***vt.*** to surpass; excel

out·come (out′kum′) ***n.*** result; consequence

out·crop (out′kräp′; *for v.* -kräp′) ***n.*** **1.** the emergence of a mineral from the earth so as to be exposed on the surface **2.** the mineral —***vi.*** **-cropped′, -crop′ping 1.** to emerge in this way **2.** to break forth

out·cry (-krī′) ***n., pl.*** **-cries′ 1.** a crying out **2.** a strong protest or objection

out·dat·ed (out′dāt′id) ***adj.*** no longer popular

out·dis·tance (-dis′təns) ***vt.*** **-tanced, -tanc·ing** to leave behind, as in a race

out·do (-dōō′) ***vt.*** **-did′, -done′, -do′ing** to exceed or surpass —**outdo oneself** to do better than one expected to

out·door (out′dôr′) ***adj.*** **1.** being or taking place outdoors **2.** of, or fond of, the outdoors

out·doors (-dôrz′) ***adv.*** in or into the open; outside —***n.*** **1.** any area outside a building **2.** countryside, etc. where there are few houses

out·er (out′ər) ***adj.*** **1.** located farther out; exterior **2.** relatively far removed *[the outer regions]*

out·er·coat (-kōt′) ***n.*** a topcoat, overcoat, etc.

Outer Mongolia *former name of* MONGOLIAN PEOPLE'S REPUBLIC

out·er·most (-mōst′) ***adj.*** located farthest without

outer space 1. space beyond the atmosphere of the earth **2.** space outside the solar system

out·er·wear (-wer′) ***n.*** outer garments, as topcoats

out·face (out′fās′) ***vt.*** **-faced′, -fac′ing 1.** to subdue with a look or stare **2.** to defy or resist

out·field (out′fēld′) ***n.*** *Baseball* **1.** the playing area beyond the infield **2.** the outfielders

out·field·er (-ər) ***n.*** *Baseball* a player whose position is in the outfield

out·fit (-fit′) ***n.*** **1.** *a*) a set of articles for equipping *b*) the equipment used in any craft or activity **2.** articles of clothing worn together **3.** a group of people associated in some activity, as a military unit —***vt.*** **-fit′ted, -fit′ting** to equip —***vi.*** to obtain an outfit —**out′fit′ter *n.***

out·flank (out′flaŋk′) ***vt.*** **1.** to go around and beyond the flank of (enemy troops) **2.** to thwart; outwit

out·flow (out′flō′) ***n.*** **1.** the act of flowing out **2.** *a*) that which flows out *b*) amount flowing out

out·fox (out′fäks′) ***vt.*** to outwit; outsmart

out·gen·er·al (-jen′ər əl) ***vt.*** **-aled** or **-alled, -al·ing** or **-al·ling** to surpass, as in leadership

out·go (out′gō′; *for n.* out′gō′) ***vt.*** **-went′, -gone′, -go′ing** to surpass; go beyond —***n., pl.*** **-goes′ 1.** a going out **2.** that which goes or is paid out; outflow or expenditure

out·go·ing (out′gō′iŋ) ***adj.*** **1.** going out; leaving **2.** sociable, friendly, etc. —***n.*** the act of going out

out·grow (out′grō′) ***vt.*** **-grew′, -grown′, -grow′ing 1.** to grow faster or larger than **2.** to lose or get rid of by becoming mature **3.** to grow too large for

out·growth (out′grōth′) ***n.*** **1.** a growing out **2.** a result; consequence; development **3.** an offshoot

out·guess (out′ges′) ***vt.*** to outwit; anticipate

out·house (out′hous′) ***n.*** an outbuilding; specif., a small outbuilding with a toilet over a pit

out·ing (-iŋ) ***n.*** **1.** a pleasure trip or holiday away from home **2.** an outdoor walk, ride, etc.

out·land·er (-lan′dər) ***n.*** a foreigner; stranger

out·land·ish (out lan′dish) ***adj.*** **1.** very odd; fantastic **2.** remote; out-of-the-way —**out·land′ish·ly *adv.***

out·last (-last′) ***vt.*** **1.** to endure longer than **2.** to outlive

out·law (out′lô′) ***n.*** [OE. *utlaga* < ON. *utlagr*] **1.** orig., a person deprived of legal rights and protection **2.** a notorious criminal who is a fugitive from the law —***vt.*** **1.** orig., to declare to be an outlaw **2.** to remove the legal force of (contracts, etc.) **3.** to declare illegal **4.** to bar, or ban —**out′law′ry *n., pl.*** **-ries**

out·lay (out′lā′; *for v., usually* out′lā′) ***n.*** **1.** a spending (of money, energy, etc.) **2.** money, etc. spent —***vt.*** **-laid′, -lay′ing** to spend (money)

out·let (out′let′) ***n.*** **1.** a passage for letting something out **2.** a means of expression *[an outlet for rage]* **3.** a stream, river, etc. that flows out from a lake **4.** *a*) a market for goods *b*) a store, etc. that sells the goods of a specific manufacturer or wholesaler **5.** a point in a wiring system at which electric current may be taken by inserting a plug

out·line (-līn′) ***n.*** **1.** a line bounding the limits of an object **2.** a sketch showing the contours of an object **3.** [*also pl.*] an undetailed general plan **4.** a systematic listing of the important points of a subject —***vt.*** **-lined′, -lin′ing 1.** to draw in outline **2.** to list the main points of

out·live (out′liv′) ***vt.*** **-lived′, -liv′ing 1.** to live or endure longer than **2.** to live through; outlast

out·look (out′look′) ***n.*** **1.** *a*) a place for looking out *b*) the view from such a place **2.** a looking out **3.** viewpoint **4.** prospect; probable result

out·ly·ing (-lī′iŋ) ***adj.*** relatively far out from a certain point or center; remote

out·man (out′man′) ***vt.*** **-manned′, -man′ning** to surpass in number of men

out·ma·neu·ver, out·ma·noeu·vre (-mə nōō′vər) ***vt.*** **-vered** or **-vred, -ver·ing** or **-vring** to maneuver with better effect than; outwit

out·match (-mach′) ***vt.*** to surpass; outdo

out-mi·grant (out′mī′grənt) ***adj.*** leaving one region, etc. to go to another —***n.*** an out-migrant person

out·mod·ed (out′mōd′id) ***adj.*** no longer in fashion or accepted; obsolete

out·most (out′mōst′) ***adj.*** most remote; outermost

out·num·ber (out′num′bər) ***vt.*** to exceed in number

out-of-date (out′əv dāt′) ***adj.*** no longer in style or use; outmoded; old-fashioned

out-of-door (-dôr′) ***adj.*** *same as* OUTDOOR

out-of-doors (-dôrz′) ***adv., n.*** *same as* OUTDOORS

out-of-the-way (-*th*ə wā′) ***adj.*** **1.** secluded **2.** unusual **3.** not conventional

out·pa·tient (out′pā′shənt) ***n.*** a patient, not an inmate, receiving treatment at a hospital

out·play (out′plā′) ***vt.*** to play better than

out·point (-point′) ***vt.*** to score more points than

out·post (out′pōst′) ***n.*** **1.** *Mil. a*) a small group stationed at a distance from the main force, to prevent a surprise attack *b*) the station so occupied *c*) any military base in a foreign country **2.** a frontier settlement

out·pour (out′pôr′; *for v.* out′pôr′) ***n.*** **1.** a pouring out **2.** outflow Also **out′pour′ing** —***vt., vi.*** to pour out

out·put (out′poot′) ***n.*** **1.** the work done or amount produced, esp. over a given period **2.** in computers, *a*) information transferred or delivered *b*) the act or process of transferring or delivering this information *c*) any of various devices involved in this process **3.** *Elec. a*) the useful current delivered by amplifiers, generators, etc. or by a circuit *b*) the terminal where such energy is delivered

out·rage (out′rāj′) ***n.*** [< OFr. < *outre*, beyond < L. *ultra*] **1.** an extremely vicious or violent act **2.** a deep insult or offense **3.** great anger, indignation, etc. aroused by such an act or offense —***vt.*** **-raged′, -rag′ing 1.** to commit an outrage upon; specif., *a*) to offend, insult, or wrong *b*) to rape **2.** to cause great anger, etc. in

out·ra·geous (out rā′jəs) ***adj.*** **1.** involving or doing great injury or wrong **2.** very offensive or shocking —**out·ra′geous·ly *adv.*** —**out·ra′geous·ness *n.***

out·rank (out′raŋk′) ***vt.*** to exceed in rank

‡**ou·tré** (ōō trā′; *E.* -trā′) ***adj.*** [Fr.] **1.** exaggerated **2.** eccentric; bizarre

out·reach (out′rēch′; *for n.* out′rēch′) ***vt., vi.*** **1.** to reach farther (than); surpass **2.** to reach out; extend —***n.*** **1.** a reaching out **2.** the extent of reach

out·ride (out′rīd′) *vt.* **-rode′, -rid′den, -rid′ing 1.** to surpass in riding **2.** to endure successfully
out·rid·er (out′rīd′ər) *n.* **1.** an attendant on horseback who rides ahead of or beside a carriage **2.** a cowboy who rides over a range to prevent cattle from straying **3.** a trailblazer; forerunner
out·rig·ger (-rig′ər) *n.* **1.** any framework extended beyond the rail of a ship, as a projecting brace for an oarlock **2.** a timber rigged out from the side of a native canoe to prevent tipping; also, a canoe of this type

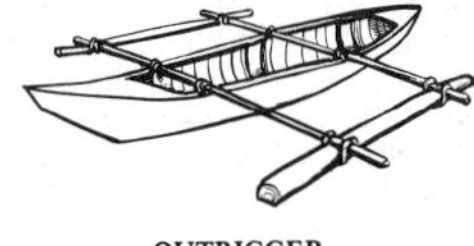
OUTRIGGER

out·right (out′rīt′; *for adv.* out′rīt′) *adj.* **1.** without reservation; downright **2.** straightforward **3.** complete; whole —*adv.* **1.** entirely **2.** openly **3.** at once —**out′right′-ness** *n.*
out·run (out′run′) *vt.* **-ran′, -run′, -run′ning 1.** to run faster or farther than **2.** to exceed **3.** to escape (a pursuer) as by running
out·sell (-sel′) *vt.* **-sold′, -sell′ing 1.** to sell in greater amounts than **2.** to excel in salesmanship
out·set (out′set′) *n.* a setting out; beginning
out·shine (out′shīn′) *vt.* **-shone′** or **-shined′, -shin′ing 1.** to shine brighter or longer than (another) **2.** to surpass; excel —*vi.* to shine forth
out·shoot (out′sho͞ot′; *for n.* out′sho͞ot′) *vt., vi.* **-shot′, -shoot′ing** to shoot better than (another) —*n.* that which shoots out or protrudes
out·side (out′sīd′, out′-; -sīd′) *n.* **1.** the outer side, part, or surface; exterior **2.** *a*) outward aspect or appearance *b*) that which is obvious or superficial **3.** any place or area not inside —*adj.* **1.** of or on the outside; outer **2.** coming from or situated beyond given limits; from some other place, person, group, etc. *[*to accept no *outside* help*]* **3.** extreme *[*an *outside* estimate*]* **4.** mere; slight *[*an *outside* chance*]* —*adv.* **1.** on or to the outside **2.** beyond certain limits **3.** outdoors —*prep.* **1.** on or to the outer side of **2.** beyond the limits of —**at the outside** at the very most —**outside of 1.** outside **2.** [Colloq.] other than
out·sid·er (out′sīd′ər) *n.* one who is outside or not included; esp., one not a member of a given group
out·sit (-sit′) *vt.* **-sat′, -sit′ting** to sit longer than or beyond the time of
out·size (out′sīz′) *n.* **1.** an odd size; esp., an unusually large size **2.** a garment, etc. of such a size —*adj.* of nonstandard size; esp., unusually large: also **out′sized′**
out·skirts (-skurts′) *n.pl.* the outer areas, as of a city
out·smart (out′smärt′) *vt.* [Colloq.] to overcome by cunning or cleverness; outwit
out·spo·ken (out′spō′kən) *adj.* **1.** unrestrained in speech; frank **2.** spoken boldly or candidly —**out′spo′ken·ly** *adv.* —**out′spo′ken·ness** *n.*
out·spread (out′spred′; *for adj. & n.* out′spred′) *vt., vi.* **-spread′, -spread′ing** to spread out; extend; expand —*n.* a spreading out —*adj.* spread out; extended; expanded
out·stand·ing (out′stand′iŋ) *adj.* **1.** projecting **2.** prominent; distinguished **3.** unsettled **4.** unpaid **5.** that have been issued and sold: said of stocks and bonds —**out′-stand′ing·ly** *adv.*
out·stare (-ster′) *vt.* **-stared′, -star′ing** to outdo in staring; stare down; outface
out·stay (-stā′) *vt.* **1.** to stay longer than **2.** to stay beyond the time of; overstay
out·stretch (-strech′) *vt.* **1.** to extend **2.** to stretch beyond —**out′stretched′** *adj.*
out·strip (-strip′) *vt.* **-stripped′, -strip′ping 1.** to go at a faster pace than; get ahead of **2.** to surpass; excel
out·talk (-tôk′) *vt.* to talk more skillfully, loudly, or forcibly than; surpass in talking
out·think (-thiŋk′) *vt.* **-thought′, -think′ing 1.** to think deeper, faster, or more cunningly than **2.** to outwit by such thinking
out·vote (-vōt′) *vt.* **-vot′ed, -vot′ing** to defeat or surpass in voting
out·ward (out′wərd) *adj.* **1.** having to do with the outside; outer **2.** readily seen; visible **3.** to or toward the outside **4.** having to do with the physical as opposed to the mind or spirit **5.** superficial or external —*adv.* **1.** toward the outside; away **2.** visibly; publicly Also **out′wards** *adv.* —*n.* that which is outward —**out′ward·ness** *n.*
out·ward·ly (-lē) *adv.* **1.** toward or on the outside **2.** in regard to outward appearance or action
out·wear (out′wer′) *vt.* **-wore′, -worn′, -wear′ing 1.** to wear out **2.** to be more lasting than
out·weigh (-wā′) *vt.* **1.** to weigh more than **2.** to be more important, valuable, etc. than
out·wit (-wit′) *vt.* **-wit′ted, -wit′ting** to get the better of by cunning or cleverness
out·work (out′wurk′; *for v.* out′wurk′) *n.* a lesser fortification built out beyond the main defenses —*vt.* **-worked′** or **-wrought′, -work′ing** to work better or harder than
ou·zel (o͞o′z′l) *n.* [OE. *osle*] any of several perching birds including the dippers, of Europe, Asia, and the New World; esp., *same as* WATER OUZEL
o·va (ō′və) *n. pl. of* OVUM
o·val (ō′v′l) *adj.* [< Fr. < L. *ovum,* an egg] **1.** shaped like the cross section of an egg lengthwise; elliptical **2.** having the form of an egg —*n.* anything oval —**o′val·ly** *adv.*
Oval Office the oval-shaped office of the President in the White House; also, his position, authority, or power
o·var·i·ec·to·my (ō ver′ē ek′tə mē) *n., pl.* **-mies** [see -ECTOMY] the surgical removal of one or both ovaries
o·va·ry (ō′vər ē) *n., pl.* **-ries** [< ModL. < L. *ovum,* an egg] **1.** *Anat., Zool.* either of the pair of female reproductive glands producing eggs and, in vertebrates, sex hormones **2.** *Bot.* the enlarged hollow part of the pistil, containing ovules —**o·var·i·an** (ō ver′ē ən) *adj.*
o·vate (ō′vāt) *adj.* [< L. < *ovum,* an egg] **1.** egg-shaped **2.** *Bot.* shaped like the longitudinal section of an egg, esp. with the broader end at the base, as some leaves —**o′vate·ly** *adv.*
o·va·tion (ō vā′shən) *n.* [L. *ovatio* < *ovare,* to celebrate a triumph] an enthusiastic outburst of applause or an enthusiastic public welcome
ov·en (uv′ən) *n.* [OE. *ofen*] a compartment or receptacle for baking or roasting food or for heating or drying things
ov·en·bird (-burd′) *n.* a N. American warbler that builds a domelike nest on the ground
o·ver (ō′vər) *prep.* [OE. *ofer*] **1.** *a*) in, at, or to a position up from; above *b*) across and down from *[*to fall *over* a cliff*]* **2.** while engaged in *[*discuss it *over* dinner*]* **3.** upon the surface of *[*spread icing *over* the cake*]* **4.** so as to cover *[*shutters *over* the windows*]* **5.** upon, as an effect or influence *[*he cast a spell *over* us*]* **6.** with care, concern, etc. for *[*watch *over* the flock*]* **7.** above in authority, power, etc. **8.** along or across, or above and to the other side of *[*fly *over* the lake*]* **9.** on the other side of *[*a city *over* the border*]* **10.** through all or many parts of *[over* the whole State*]* **11.** during *[over* a decade*]* **12.** more than *[over* ten dollars*]* **13.** up to and including *[*stay *over* Easter*]* **14.** rather than **15.** concerning; about **16.** through the medium of *[over* the radio*]* —*adv.* **1.** *a*) above, across, or to the other side *b*) across the brim or edge **2.** more; beyond *[*three hours or *over]* **3.** longer or till a time later *[*please stay *over]* **4.** covering the entire area *[*the wound healed *over]* **5.** from start to finish *[*count the money *over]* **6.** *a*) from an upright position *[*he fell *over] b*) upside down *[*turn the cup *over]* **7.** again *[*do it *over]* **8.** at or on the other side, as of an intervening space *[over* in Spain*]* **9.** from one side, viewpoint, person, etc. to another *[*they won him *over]* —*adj.* **1.** upper, outer, superior, excessive, or extra: often in combination *[overcoat, overseer, oversupply]* **2.** finished; past *[*his life is *over]* **3.** having reached the other side **4.** [Colloq.] as a surplus; extra *[*an hour *over* for the week*]* —*n.* something in addition; surplus —*interj.* turn the page, etc. over —**over again** another time; anew —**over all** from end to end —**over and above** more than —**over and over (again)** repeatedly
o·ver- *a combining form meaning:* **1.** above in position, outer, upper, superior *[overhead, overlord]* **2.** passing across or beyond *[overrun]* **3.** involving a movement downward from above *[overflow]* **4.** excessive(ly), too much *[overload, oversell]* : the list below includes some common compounds formed with *over-* that can be understood if *too* or *too much* is added to the meaning of the base word

overabundance
overabundant
overactive
overambitious
overanxious
overattentive
overbold
overbuild
overburden
overbusy
overbuy
overcapitalize
overcareful
overcareless
overcautious
overcompensate
overconfident
overconscientious
overconservative
overcook
overcritical
overcrowd
overdecorate
overdependent
overdye
overeager
overeat
overemotional
overemphasize
overenthusiastic
overexercise
overexert
overexpand
overexpose
overexpand
overfed
overfond
overgenerous
overgreedy
overhasty
overheat
overindulge
overindulgence
overinflate
overinvert
overladen
overlong
overnice
overorganize
overpay
overpayment
overpeopled
overpopulate
overpraise
overprecise
overrefined
overreligious
overripe
oversensitive
oversentimental
oversolicitous
overspecialize
overstimulate
overstretch
overstrict
overstudy
oversubtle
oversufficient
oversuspicious
overtire
overuse
overvalue
overwind
overvalue
overzealous

o·ver·act (ō′vər akt′) *vt., vi.* to act with exaggeration

o·ver·age[1] (ō′vər āj′) *adj.* **1.** over the age fixed as a standard **2.** so old as to be of no use

o·ver·age[2] (ō′vər ij) *n.* [OVER- + -AGE] a surplus or excess, as of goods

o·ver·all (ō′vər ôl′; *for adv.* -ôl′) *adj.* **1.** from end to end **2.** including everything; total —*adv.* **1.** from end to end **2.** in general

o·ver·alls (-ôlz′) *n.pl.* loose-fitting trousers, often with an attached bib, worn over other clothing to protect against dirt and wear

o·ver·arm (-ärm′) *adj.* performed by raising the arm above the shoulder, as in swimming

o·ver·awe (ō′vər ô′) *vt.* **-awed′, -aw′ing** to overcome or subdue by inspiring awe

o·ver·bal·ance (ō′vər bal′əns; *for n.* ō′vər bal′əns) *vt.* **-anced, -anc·ing 1.** *same as* OUTWEIGH **2.** to throw off balance —*n.* something that overbalances

o·ver·bear (ō′vər ber′) *vt.* **-bore′, -borne′, -bear′ing 1.** to press down by weight or physical power **2.** to dominate or subdue —*vi.* to be too fruitful

o·ver·bear·ing (-iŋ) *adj.* **1.** arrogant or domineering **2.** dominant or overriding —**o′ver·bear′ing·ly** *adv.* —**o′ver·bear′ing·ness** *n.*

o·ver·bid (ō′vər bid′; *for n.* ō′vər bid′) *vt., vi.* **-bid′, -bid′ding 1.** to outbid (another person) **2.** to bid more than the worth of (a thing, as one's hand in bridge) —*n.* a higher or excessive bid

o·ver·blown[1] (ō′vər blōn′) *adj.* past the stage of full bloom

o·ver·blown[2] (ō′vər blōn′) *adj.* **1.** stout; obese **2.** *a)* overdone; excessive *b)* pompous; bombastic

o·ver·board (ō′vər bôrd′) *adv.* **1.** over a ship's side **2.** from a ship into the water —**go overboard** [Colloq.] to go to extremes

o·ver·cast (ō′vər kast′; *for v. 1, usually* ō′vər kast′) *n.* a covering, esp. of clouds —*adj.* **1.** cloudy: said of the sky or weather **2.** *Sewing* made with overcasting —*vt., vi.* **-cast′, -cast′ing 1.** to overcloud **2.** *Sewing* to sew over (an edge) with long, loose stitches to prevent raveling

o·ver·charge (ō′vər chärj′; *for n.* ō′vər chärj′) *vt., vi.* **-charged′, -charg′ing 1.** to charge too high a price **2.** to overload **3.** to exaggerate —*n.* **1.** an excessive charge **2.** too full or heavy a load

o·ver·cloud (-kloud′) *vt., vi.* **1.** to darken or cover over with clouds; dim **2.** to make or become gloomy, angry, etc. in appearance

o·ver·coat (ō′vər kōt′) *n.* a coat, esp. a heavy coat, worn over the usual clothing for warmth

o·ver·come (ō′vər kum′) *vt.* **-came′, -come′, -com′ing 1.** to get the better of; defeat; conquer **2.** to master, prevail over, or surmount *[to overcome obstacles]* **3.** to overpower or overwhelm *[overcome by laughter]* —*vi.* to win

o·ver·de·vel·op (-di vel′əp) *vt.* **1.** to develop too much **2.** *Photog.* to develop (a film, plate, etc.) too long or in too strong a developer —**o′ver·de·vel′op·ment** *n.*

o·ver·do (-do͞o′) *vt.* **-did′, -done′, -do′ing 1.** to do too much, or to excess **2.** to spoil the effect of by exaggeration **3.** to cook too long **4.** to exhaust; tire —*vi.* to do too much

o·ver·dose (ō′vər dōs′; *for v.* ō′vər dōs′) *n.* too large a dose —*vt.* **-dosed′, -dos′ing** to dose to excess

o·ver·draft (ō′vər draft′) *n.* **1.** an overdrawing of money from a bank **2.** the amount overdrawn

o·ver·draw (ō′vər drô′) *vt.* **-drew′, -drawn′, -draw′ing 1.** to spoil the effect of by exaggeration **2.** to draw on in excess of the amount credited to the drawer

o·ver·dress (-dres′) *vt., vi.* to dress too warmly, too showily, or too formally for the occasion

o·ver·drive (ō′vər drīv′) *n.* a gear that automatically reduces an engine's power output without reducing its driving speed

o·ver·due (ō′vər do͞o′, -dyo͞o′) *adj.* **1.** past or delayed beyond the time set for payment, arrival, etc. **2.** that should have come about sooner

o·ver·es·ti·mate (-es′tə māt′; *for n.* -mit) *vt.* **-mat′ed, -mat′ing** to set too high an estimate on or for —*n.* an estimate that is too high —**o′ver·es′ti·ma′tion** *n.*

o·ver·ex·tend (-ik stend′) *vt.* to extend beyond reasonable limits or beyond one's capacity to meet obligations —**o′ver·ex·ten′sion** (-ik sten′shən) *n.*

o·ver·flow (ō′vər flō′; *for n.* ō′vər flō′) *vt.* **1.** to flow or spread across; flood **2.** to flow over the brim or edge of **3.** to cause to overflow by filling beyond capacity —*vi.* **1.** to run over **2.** to be superabundant —*n.* **1.** an overflowing or being overflowed **2.** the amount that overflows; surplus **3.** an outlet for overflowing liquids

o·ver·fly (ō′vər flī′) *vt.* **-flew′, -flown′, -fly′ing** to fly an aircraft over (a specified area) or beyond (a specified place), as for reconnaissance —**o′ver·flight′** *n.*

o·ver·grow (-grō′) *vt.* **-grew′, -grown′, -grow′ing 1.** to overspread with growth or foliage so as to cover up **2.** to outgrow —*vi.* **1.** to grow too large or too fast **2.** to grow beyond normal size —**o′ver·grown′** *adj.* —**o′ver·growth′** *n.*

o·ver·hand (ō′vər hand′) *adj.* **1.** with the hand over the object it grasps **2.** done with the hand raised above the shoulder **3.** designating or of sewing in which the stitches are passed over two edges to sew them together —*adv.* in an overhand manner —*vt.* to sew overhand —*n. Sports* an overhand stroke

o·ver·hang (ō′vər haŋ′; *for n.* ō′vər haŋ′) *vt.* **-hung′, -hang′ing 1.** to hang or project over or beyond **2.** to impend; threaten —*vi.* to project or jut out over something —*n.* **1.** the projection of one thing over or beyond another **2.** an overhanging or projecting part

o·ver·haul (ō′vər hôl′; *for n.* ō′vər hôl′) *vt.* **1.** to haul over, as for examination **2.** *a)* to check thoroughly for needed repairs, adjustments, etc. *b)* to make such repairs, etc., as on a motor **3.** to catch up with —*n.* an overhauling

o·ver·head (ō′vər hed′; *for adv.* ō′vər hed′) *adj.* **1.** located or operating above the level of the head **2.** in the sky **3.** on a higher level, with reference to related objects —*n.* the regular costs of running a business, as of rent, maintenance, taxes, etc. —*adv.* above the head; aloft

o·ver·hear (ō′vər hir′) *vt.* **-heard′, -hear′ing** to hear (something spoken or a speaker) without the speaker's knowledge or intention

o·ver·joy (-joi′) *vt.* to give great joy to; delight

o·ver·kill (ō′vər kil′) *n.* **1.** the capacity of a nation's nuclear weapon stockpile to kill many times the total population of any given nation **2.** much more of something than is necessary, appropriate, etc.; esp., an excess of effort in trying to achieve some end

o·ver·land (-land′, -lənd) *adv., adj.* by, on, or across land

O·ver·land Park (ō′vər lənd) [after the *Overland,* or Santa Fe, Trail which passed through the area] city in NE Kans.: suburb of Kansas City: pop. 82,000

o·ver·lap (ō′vər lap′; *for n.* ō′vər lap′) *vt., vi.* **-lapped′, -lap′ping** to lap over; to extend over (something or each other) so as to coincide in part —*n.* **1.** an overlapping **2.** a part that overlaps **3.** the extent or place of overlapping

o·ver·lay (ō′vər lā′; *for n.* ō′vər lā′) *vt.* **-laid′, -lay′ing 1.** to lay or spread over **2.** to cover, as with a decorative layer —*n.* **1.** a covering **2.** a decorative layer or the like **3.** a transparent flap showing additional details, areas of color, etc. placed over a map, art work, etc.

o·ver·leaf (ō′vər lēf′) *adj., adv.* on the other side of the page or sheet

o·ver·leap (ō′vər lēp′) *vt.* **1.** to leap over or across **2.** to omit; pass over **3.** to overreach (oneself) by leaping too far

o·ver·lie (-lī′) *vt.* **-lay′, -lain′, -ly′ing** to lie on or over

o·ver·load (ō′vər lōd′; *for n.* ō′vər lōd′) *vt.* to put too great a load in or on —*n.* too great a load

o·ver·look (ō′vər look′; *for n.* ō′vər look′) *vt.* **1.** to look at from above **2.** to give a view of from above **3.** to rise above **4.** *a)* to look beyond and not see *b)* to ignore; neglect **5.** to pass over indulgently; excuse **6.** to oversee; supervise —*n.* a height or the view from it

o·ver·lord (ō′vər lôrd′) *n.* a lord ranking above other lords, esp. in the feudal system

o·ver·ly (-lē) *adv.* too or too much; excessively

o·ver·man (ō′vər man′) *vt.* **-manned′, -man′ning** to supply with more men than necessary

o·ver·mas·ter (-mas′tər) *vt.* to overcome; conquer

o·ver·match (-mach′) *vt.* **1.** to be more than a match for **2.** to match against a superior opponent

o·ver·much (ō′vər much′) *adj., adv.* too much —*n.* too great a quantity; excessive amount

o·ver·night (ō′vər nīt′; *for adj.* ō′vər nīt′) *adv.* **1.** during the night **2.** on or during the previous evening **3.** very suddenly —*adj.* **1.** done or going on during the night **2.** of the previous evening **3.** for one night *[an overnight guest]* **4.** of or for a brief trip *[an overnight bag]*

o·ver·pass (ō′vər pas′) *n.* a bridge or other passageway over a road, railway, etc.

o·ver·play (ō′vər plā′) *vt.* **1.** to overact, overdo, or overemphasize **2.** *Card Games* to overestimate the strength of (one's hand)

o·ver·pop·u·late (-päp′yə lāt′) *vt.* **-lat′ed, -lat′ing** to populate (an area) too heavily for the available resources —**o′ver·pop′u·la′tion** *n.*

o·ver·pow·er (-pou′ər) *vt.* **1.** to get the better of; make helpless; subdue; overwhelm **2.** to supply with more power than is needed —**o′ver·pow′er·ing** *adj.* —**o′ver·pow′er·ing·ly** *adv.*

o·ver·print (ō′vər print′; *for n.* ō′vər print′) *vt.* to print over (a previously printed surface) —*n.* anything overprinted, as (on) a stamp

o·ver·pro·duce (ō′vər prə do͞os′, -dyo͞os′) *vt., vi.* **-duced′, -duc′ing** to produce in a quantity that exceeds the need or demand —**o′ver·pro·duc′tion** *n.*
o·ver·pro·tect (-prə tekt′) *vt.* to protect more than is necessary; specif., to seek to shield (one's child, etc.) from normal hurts or conflicts —**o′ver·pro·tec′tive** *adj.*
o·ver·rate (-rāt′) *vt.* **-rat′ed, -rat′ing** to rate or estimate too highly
o·ver·reach (-rēch′) *vt.* **1.** to reach beyond or above **2.** to reach too far for and miss **3.** to outwit or cheat —*vi.* to reach too far —**overreach oneself 1.** to fail because of trying more than one can do **2.** to fail because of being too crafty or eager —**o′ver·reach′er** *n.*
o·ver·re·act (-rē akt′) *vi.* to react in an extreme, highly emotional way, as by undue use of force
o·ver·ride (-rīd′) *vt.* **-rode′, -rid′den, -rid′ing 1.** to ride over **2.** to trample down **3.** to suppress or prevail over **4.** to disregard, overrule, or nullify **5.** to fatigue (a horse, etc.) by riding too long
o·ver·rule (-ro͞ol′) *vt.* **-ruled′, -rul′ing 1.** to set aside or decide against, as by higher authority; rule against or rule out **2.** to prevail over
o·ver·run (-run′; *for n.* ō′vər run′) *vt.* **-ran′, -run′, -run′ning 1.** to spread out over so as to cover **2.** to swarm over, as vermin, or ravage, as an army **3.** to invade or conquer by a rapid advance **4.** to spread swiftly throughout, as ideas **5.** to run beyond (certain limits) *[to overrun second base]* —*vi.* **1.** to overflow **2.** to run over or beyond certain limits —*n.* **1.** an act or instance of overrunning **2.** the amount that overruns
o·ver·seas (ō′vər sēz′) *adv.* over or beyond the sea —*adj.* **1.** foreign **2.** over or across the sea Also, chiefly Brit., **o′ver·sea′**
o·ver·see (ō′vər sē′) *vt.* **-saw′, -seen′, -see′ing 1.** to supervise; superintend **2.** to catch sight of secretly or accidentally **3.** to survey; watch
o·ver·se·er (ō′vər sē′ər) *n.* a person who directs the work of others; supervisor
o·ver·sell (ō′vər sel′) *vt.* **-sold′, -sell′ing 1.** to sell more than can be supplied **2.** to promote to an extreme degree that defeats one's purposes
o·ver·set (ō′vər set′; *for n.* ō′vər set′) *vt.* **-set′, -set′ting 1.** to upset **2.** to overturn or overthrow —*vi.* to tip over —*n.* an overturning
o·ver·shad·ow (ō′vər shad′ō) *vt.* **1.** *a)* to cast a shadow over *b)* to darken **2.** to be more significant or important than by comparison
o·ver·shoe (ō′vər sho͞o′) *n.* a kind of boot of rubber or fabric worn over the regular shoe to protect against cold or dampness; galosh
o·ver·shoot (ō′vər sho͞ot′) *vt.* **-shot′, -shoot′ing 1.** to shoot or pass over or beyond (a target, mark, etc.) **2.** to go farther than (an intended or normal limit); exceed —*vi.* to shoot or go too far
o·ver·shot (ō′vər shät′) *adj.* **1.** with the upper part or half extending past the lower *[an overshot jaw]* **2.** driven by water flowing onto the upper part *[an overshot water wheel]*
o·ver·sight (-sīt′) *n.* a careless mistake or omission
o·ver·sim·pli·fy (ō′vər sim′plə fī′) *vt., vi.* **-fied′, -fy′ing** to simplify to an extent that distorts, as by ignoring essential details —**o′ver·sim′pli·fi·ca′tion** *n.*
o·ver·size (-sīz′) *adj.* **1.** too large **2.** larger than the normal or usual Also **o′ver·sized′** —*n.* a size larger than regular sizes
o·ver·skirt (-skurt′) *n.* an outer skirt
o·ver·sleep (ō′vər slēp′) *vi.* **-slept′, -sleep′ing** to sleep past the intended time for getting up
o·ver·spread (-spred′) *vt.* **-spread′, -spread′ing** to spread over; cover the surface of
o·ver·state (-stāt′) *vt.* **-stat′ed, -stat′ing** to give a magnified account of (facts, truth, etc.); exaggerate —**o′ver·state′ment** *n.*
o·ver·stay (-stā′) *vt.* to stay beyond the time, duration, or limits of
o·ver·step (-step′) *vt.* **-stepped′, -step′ping** to go beyond the limits of; exceed
o·ver·stock (ō′vər stäk′; *for n.* ō′vər stäk′) *vt.* to stock more of than is needed —*n.* too large a stock
o·ver·strung (ō′vər struŋ′) *adj.* too highly strung; tense
o·ver·stuff (-stuf′) *vt.* **1.** to stuff with too much of something **2.** to upholster (furniture) with deep stuffing —**o′ver·stuffed′** *adj.*
o·ver·sub·scribe (-səb skrīb′) *vt., vi.* **-scribed′, -scrib′ing** to subscribe for more (of) than is available or asked —**o′ver·sub·scrip′tion** (-skrip′shən) *n.*
o·ver·sup·ply (-sə plī′) *vt.* **-plied′, -ply′ing** to supply in excess —*n., pl.* **-plies** too great a supply
o·vert (ō vurt′, ō′vurt) *adj.* [< MFr. pp. of *ovrir* < L. *aperire,* to open] **1.** not hidden; open **2.** *Law* done publicly, without attempt at concealment —**o·vert′ly** *adv.* —**o·vert′ness** *n.*
o·ver·take (ō′vər tāk′) *vt.* **-took′, -tak′en, -tak′ing 1.** to catch up with and, often, go beyond **2.** to come upon unexpectedly or suddenly
o·ver·tax (-taks′) *vt.* **1.** to tax too heavily **2.** to make excessive demands on
o·ver·throw (ō′vər thrō′; *for n.* ō′vər thrō′) *vt.* **-threw′, -thrown′, -throw′ing 1.** to throw or turn over; upset **2.** to conquer; end **3.** to throw a ball, etc. beyond (the intended receiver or target) —*n.* **1.** an overthrowing or being overthrown **2.** destruction; end
o·ver·time (ō′vər tīm′; *for v.* -tīm′) *n.* **1.** time beyond the established limit, as of working hours **2.** pay for work done in such time **3.** *Sports* an extra period added to the game to decide a tie —*adj., adv.* of, for, or during (an) overtime —*vt.* **-timed′, -tim′ing** to allow too much time for (a photographic exposure, etc.)
o·ver·tone (ō′vər tōn′) *n.* **1.** any of the attendant higher tones heard with a fundamental musical tone **2.** an implication; nuance: *usually used in pl. [a reply full of overtones]*
o·ver·top (ō′vər täp′) *vt.* **-topped′, -top′ping 1.** to rise above **2.** to excel; surpass
o·ver·ture (ō′vər chər, ō′və-) *n.* [< OFr. < L. *apertura,* APERTURE] **1.** an introductory proposal or offer **2.** a musical introduction to an opera, oratorio, etc.
o·ver·turn (ō′vər turn′; *for n.* ō′vər turn′) *vt.* **1.** to turn over; upset **2.** to conquer —*vi.* to tip over; capsize —*n.* an overturning or being overturned
o·ver·view (ō′vər vyo͞o′) *n.* a general survey
o·ver·ween·ing (ō′vər wē′niŋ) *adj.* [< OE. *oferwenan:* see OVER- & WEEN] **1.** arrogant; excessively proud **2.** exaggerated; excessive —**o′ver·ween′ing·ly** *adv.*
o·ver·weigh (-wā′) *vt.* **1.** *same as* OUTWEIGH **2.** to burden; oppress
o·ver·weight (ō′vər wāt′; *for adj. & v.,* ō′vər wāt′) *n.* extra or surplus weight —*adj.* above the normal, desirable, or allowed weight —*vt. same as* OVERWEIGH
o·ver·whelm (ō′vər hwelm′, -welm′) *vt.* [see OVER- & WHELM] **1.** to pour down on and bury beneath **2.** to crush; overpower —**o′ver·whelm′ing** *adj.* —**o′ver·whelm′ing·ly** *adv.*
o·ver·work (ō′vər wurk′; *for n.* ō′vər wurk′) *vt.* to work or use to excess —*vi.* to work too hard or too long —*n.* work that is severe or burdensome
o·ver·write (ō′vər rīt′) *vt., vi.* **-wrote′, -writ′ten, -writ′ing 1.** to write over (other writing) **2.** to write too much, or in a labored style, about (some subject) **3.** to receive a commission on the sales of (a subagent)
o·ver·wrought (ō′vər rôt′) *adj.* **1.** very nervous or excited **2.** with the surface adorned **3.** too elaborate
o·vi- [< L. *ovum,* an egg] *a combining form meaning* egg or ovum *[oviduct, oviform]*
Ov·id (äv′id) (L. name, *Publius Ovidius Naso*) 43 B.C.–17? A.D.; Rom. poet
o·vi·duct (ō′vi dukt′) *n.* [< ModL.: see OVI- & DUCT] a duct or tube through which the ovum passes from an ovary to the uterus or to the outside
o·vi·form (-fôrm′) *adj.* [OVI- & -FORM] egg-shaped
o·vip·a·rous (ō vip′ər əs) *adj.* [< L.: see OVI- & -PAROUS] producing eggs which hatch after leaving the body —**o·vip′a·rous·ly** *adv.*
o·vi·pos·i·tor (ō′vi päz′i tər) *n.* [ModL. < OVI- + L. *positor,* one who places < *ponere,* to place] a special organ of many female insects, usually at the end of the abdomen, for depositing eggs
o·void (ō′void) *adj.* [OV(I)- + -OID] egg-shaped: also **o·void′al** —*n.* anything of ovoid form
o·vu·late (ō′vyə lāt′, äv′yə-) *vi.* **-lat′ed, -lat′ing** [OVUL(E) + -ATE[1]] to produce and discharge ova from the ovary —**o′vu·la′tion** *n.* —**o′vu·la·to′ry** (-lə tôr′ē) *adj.*
o·vule (ō′vyo͞ol, äv′yo͞ol) *n.* [Fr. < ModL. dim. of L. *ovum,* egg] a small egg or seed, esp. one in an early stage of development; specif., *a) Bot.* the part of a plant which develops into a seed after fertilization *b) Zool.* the immature ovum —**o′vu·lar** *adj.*
o·vum (ō′vəm) *n., pl.* **o·va** (ō′və) [L., an egg] *Biol.* a mature female germ cell
ow (ou) *interj.* a cry of pain
owe (ō) *vt.* **owed, ow′ing** [OE. *agan,* to own] **1.** to be indebted to (someone) for (a specified amount or thing) **2.** to feel the need to do, give, etc. **3.** to cherish (a feeling) toward another: only in **owe a grudge** —*vi.* to be in debt
O·wens·bor·o (ō′ənz bur′ō) [after a Col. *Owens* (1769–1811)] city in NW Ky., on the Ohio: pop. 54,000
ow·ing (ō′iŋ) *adj.* **1.** that owes **2.** due; unpaid *[ten dollars owing on a bill]* —**owing to** because of; as a result of
owl (oul) *n.* [OE. *ule*] a night bird of prey found throughout the world, having a large face, large eyes, a short, hooked beak, and feathered legs with sharp talons: applied figuratively to a person who is active at night, looks solemn, etc. —**owl′ish** *adj.* —**owl′ish·ly** *adv.* —**owl′like′** *adj.*
owl·et (-it) *n.* a young or small owl

own (ōn) *adj.* [OE. *agen,* pp. of *agan,* to possess] belonging or relating to oneself or itself: used to strengthen a preceding possessive *[his own book]* —*n.* that which belongs to oneself *[the car is his own]* —*vt.* **1.** to possess; have **2.** to admit; acknowledge —*vi.* to confess (*to*) —**come into one's own** to receive what properly belongs to one, esp. recognition —**of one's own** belonging strictly to oneself —**on one's own** [Colloq.] by one's own efforts; independent —**own up (to)** to confess (to) —**own′er** *n.* —**own′er·less** *adj.* —**own′er·ship′** *n.*

ox (äks) *n., pl.* **ox′en,** rarely **ox:** see PLURAL, II, D, 1 [OE. *oxa*] **1.** any of several bovine mammals, as the buffalo, bison, yak, etc. **2.** a castrated bull, used as a draft animal —**ox′like′** *adj.*

ox·al·ic acid (äk sal′ik) [< Fr. < L. < Gr. *oxalis,* sorrel < *oxys,* acid] a colorless, poisonous, crystalline acid, $(COOH)_2$, found in many plants and used in dyeing, bleaching, etc.

ox·blood (äks′blud′) *n.* a deep red color

ox·bow (-bō′) *n.* **1.** the U-shaped part of an ox yoke which passes under and around the animal's neck **2.** something shaped like this, as a bend in a river

ox·en (äk′s′n) *n. pl. of* ox

ox·eye (äks′ī′) *n.* **1.** any of several composite plants, as a sunflowerlike perennial of E N. America **2.** any of various birds, as the dunlin

ox-eyed (-īd′) *adj.* having large, full eyes

oxeye daisy *same as* DAISY (sense 1)

Ox·ford (äks′fərd) city in SC England: site of Oxford University: pop. 109,000

ox·ford (äks′fərd) *n.* [after prec.] [*sometimes* **O-**] **1.** a low shoe laced over the instep: also **oxford shoe** **2.** a cotton or rayon fabric with a basketlike weave, used for shirts, etc.: also **oxford cloth**

Oxford gray a very dark gray, nearly black

ox·heart (äks′härt′) *n.* a large, heart-shaped cherry

ox·i·dant (äk′sə dənt) *n.* an oxidizing agent

ox·i·da·tion (äk′sə dā′shən) *n.* an oxidizing or being oxidized —**ox′i·da′tive** *adj.*

ox·ide (äk′sīd) *n.* [Fr. < Gr. *oxys,* sour + Fr. (*ac*)*ide,* acid] a binary compound of oxygen with another element or a radical

ox·i·dize (äk′sə dīz′) *vt.* **-dized′, -diz′ing** [< prec. + -IZE] **1.** to unite with oxygen, as in burning or rusting **2.** to increase the positive valence or decrease the negative valence of (an element or ion) —*vi.* to become oxidized —**ox′i·diz′a·ble** *adj.* —**ox′i·diz′er** *n.*

ox·lip (äks′lip′) *n.* [< OE. < *oxa,* ox + *slyppe,* dropping] a perennial plant related to the primrose, having yellow flowers in early spring

Ox·nard (äks′närd) [after H. *Oxnard,* local businessman] city in SW Calif.: pop. 108,000

Ox·o·ni·an (äk sō′nē ən) *adj.* of Oxford (England) or Oxford University —*n.* **1.** a student or alumnus of Oxford University **2.** a native or inhabitant of Oxford, England

ox·tail (äks′tāl′) *n.* the tail of an ox or steer, esp. when skinned and used in soup or stew

ox·y-¹ [< OXY(GEN)] *a combining form meaning* containing oxygen

ox·y-² [< Gr. *oxys,* sharp] *a combining form meaning* sharp, pointed, or acid *[oxymoron, oxygen]*

ox·y·a·cet·y·lene (äk′sē ə set′'l ēn′) *adj.* of or using a mixture of oxygen and acetylene, as for producing an extremely hot flame used in welding or cutting metals *[oxyacetylene torch]*

ox·y·gen (äk′si jən) *n.* [< Fr.: see OXY-² & -GEN] a colorless, odorless, tasteless, gaseous chemical element, the most abundant of all elements: it occurs free in the atmosphere, forming one fifth of its volume, and is able to combine with nearly all other elements; it is essential to life processes and to combustion: symbol, O; at. wt., 15.9994; at. no., 8 —**ox′y·gen′ic** (-jen′ik) *adj.*

ox·y·gen·ate (äk′si jə nāt′) *vt.* **-at′ed, -at′ing** to mix, treat, or combine with oxygen: also **ox′y·gen·ize′, -ized′, -iz′ing** —**ox′y·gen·a′tion** *n.* —**ox′y·gen·a′tor** *n.*

oxygen tent a transparent enclosure into which oxygen is released, fitted around a bed patient to help him breathe

ox·y·hy·dro·gen (äk′si hī′drə jən) *adj.* of or using a mixture of oxygen and hydrogen, as for producing a hot flame used in welding *[oxyhydrogen torch]*

ox·y·mo·ron (äk′si môr′än) *n., pl.* **-mo′ra** (-ə) [LGr. < *oxys,* sharp + *moros,* dull] a figure of speech in which contradictory ideas or terms are combined (Ex.: sweet sorrow)

o·yez, o·yes (ō′yez′, -yes′, -yā′) *interj.* [Anglo-Fr., hear ye, ult. < L. *audire,* to hear] hear ye! attention!: usually cried out three times by an official to command silence before a proclamation is made —*n.* a cry of "oyez"

oys·ter (oi′stər) *n.* [< OFr. < L. *ostrea* < Gr. *ostreon*] **1.** a marine mollusk with an irregular, bivalve shell, found esp. on the ocean floor and widely used as food **2.** any of several similar bivalve mollusks

oyster bed a natural or artificially prepared place on the ocean floor for breeding oysters

oyster crab any of various small crabs that live in the gill cavities of oysters, clams, etc.

oyster cracker a small, round, salted soda cracker

oyster plant *same as* SALSIFY

oz. *pl.* **oz., ozs.** ounce

O·zark Mountains (ō′zärk) [< Fr. *aux Arcs,* to the (region of the) Arc (Arkansa) Indians, a Siouan-speaking tribe] highland region in NW Ark., SW Mo., & NE Okla.: also **Ozarks**

o·zone (ō′zōn) *n.* [Fr. < Gr. *ozein,* to smell] **1.** a pale-blue gas, O_3, with a strong odor: it is an allotropic form of oxygen, formed by a silent electrical discharge in air and used as a bleaching agent, water purifier, etc. **2.** [Slang] pure, fresh air —**o·zon′ic** (-zän′ik, -zō′nik) *adj.*

o·zon·ize (ō′zō nīz′) *vt.* **-ized′, -iz′ing** **1.** to change (oxygen) into ozone **2.** to treat with ozone —**o′zon·i·za′tion** *n.* —**o′zon·iz′er** *n.*

P

P, p (pē) *n., pl.* **P's, p's** **1.** the sixteenth letter of the English alphabet **2.** the sound of *P* or *p* —**mind one's p's and q's** to be careful what one does

P **1.** *Chess* pawn **2.** *Chem.* phosphorus **3.** police **4.** *Physics* power or pressure

p [Brit.] penny; pennies

P., p. **1.** pitcher **2.** power **3.** pressure

p. **1.** *pl.* **pp.** page **2.** participle **3.** past **4.** penny **5.** per **6.** piano **7.** pint

pa (pä; *dial. often* pô) *n.* [Colloq.] father; papa

Pa *Chem.* protactinium

Pa., PA Pennsylvania

P.A. public address (system)

pa·'an·ga (pä äŋ′ä) *n., pl.* **pa·'an′ga** [Polynesian (Tongan), a kind of seedpod] *see* MONETARY UNITS, table (Tonga)

Pab·lum (pab′ləm) [< ff.] *a trademark for* a soft, bland cereal food for infants —*n.* [**p-**] any oversimplified or tasteless writing, ideas, etc.

pab·u·lum (pab′yoo ləm) *n.* [L.] **1.** food **2.** nourishment for the mind **3.** *same as* PABLUM

pac (pak) *n.* [< AmInd. *pacu,* moccasin] a high, insulated, waterproof, laced boot

pace (pās) *n.* [< OFr. *pas* < L. *passus,* a step] **1.** a step in walking, running, etc. **2.** the length of a step or stride (30 in. to 40 in.) **3.** the rate of speed in walking, etc. **4.** rate of movement, progress, development, etc. **5.** a particular way of walking, etc.; gait **6.** the gait of a horse in which both legs on the same side are raised together —*vt.* **paced, pac′ing** **1.** to walk back and forth across **2.** to measure by paces (often with *off*) **3.** to train or guide the pace of (a horse) **4.** to set the pace for (a runner, etc.) **5.** to go before and lead **6.** to cover (a certain distance) —*vi.* **1.** to walk with regular steps **2.** to raise both legs on the same side at the same time in moving: said of a horse —**change of pace** variation in tempo or mood or in speed of delivery —**keep pace (with)** to maintain the same speed or rate of progress (as) —**put through one's paces** to test one's abilities, etc. —**set the pace** **1.** to go at a speed that others try to equal, as in a race **2.** to do or be something for others to emulate —**pac′er** *n.*

pace·mak·er (-mā′kər) *n.* **1.** *a)* a runner, horse, etc. that sets the pace for others, as in a race *b)* a person, group, or thing that serves as a model Also **pace′set′ter** **2.** *Med.* an electronic device surgically implanted in the body to stimulate or regulate the heartbeat —**pace′mak′ing** *n.*

pa·chi·si (pə chē′zē) *n.* [< Hindi < *pacīs,* twenty-five (the highest throw)] **1.** in India, a game in which the moves of pieces around a board are determined by the throwing of cowrie shells **2.** *same as* PARCHEESI

pach·y·derm (pak′ə durm′) *n.* [< Fr. < Gr. < *pachys,* thick + *derma,* a skin] **1.** a large, thick-skinned, hoofed animal, as the elephant, rhinoceros, or hippopotamus **2.** an insensitive, stolid person —**pach′y·der′mal, pach′y·der′mic** *adj.* —**pach′y·der′ma·tous, pach′y·der′mous** *adj.*

pach·y·san·dra (pak′ə san′drə) *n.* [ModL. < Gr. *pachys,* thick + ModL. *-andrus,* -ANDROUS] a low, dense-growing, hardy evergreen plant, often used for a ground cover

Pa·cif·ic (pə sif′ik) [< ff., after its tranquil appearance] largest of the earth's oceans, between Asia and the American continents —*adj.* of, in, on, or near this ocean

pa·cif·ic (pə sif′ik) *adj.* [< Fr. < L. < *pacificare,* PACIFY] **1.** making or tending to make peace **2.** peaceful; calm; tranquil —**pa·cif′i·cal·ly** *adv.*

pa·cif·i·cate (-ə kāt′) *vt.* **-cat′ed, -cat′ing** *same as* PACIFY —**pac·i·fi·ca·tion** (pas′ə fi kā′shən) *n.* —**pa·cif′i·ca′tor** *n.* —**pa·cif′i·ca·to′ry** (-kə tôr′ē) *adj.*

Pacific Islands, Trust Territory of the U.S. trust territory in the W Pacific, consisting of the Caroline & Marshall islands: 420 sq. mi.; pop. 110,000

Pacific Standard Time *see* STANDARD TIME

pac·i·fi·er (pas′ə fī′ər) *n.* **1.** a person or thing that pacifies **2.** a nipple or teething ring for babies

pac·i·fism (-fiz′m) *n.* [< Fr.: see PACIFIC & -ISM] opposition to the use of force under any circumstances; specif., refusal for reasons of conscience to participate in war —**pac′i·fist** *n., adj.* —**pac′i·fis′tic** *adj.* —**pac′i·fis′ti·cal·ly** *adv.*

pac·i·fy (pas′ə fī′) *vt.* **-fied′, -fy′ing** [< Fr. < L. *pacificare* < *pax,* peace + *facere,* to make] **1.** to make peaceful or calm; appease; tranquilize **2.** *a)* to secure peace in (a nation, etc.) *b)* to seek to neutralize or win over (people in occupied areas) —**pac′i·fi′a·ble** *adj.*

pack[1] (pak) *n.* [MDu. *pak* < MFl. *pac*] **1.** a bundle of things tied up for carrying, as on the back; load; burden **2.** a container in which something may be stored compactly [parachute *pack*] **3.** a group or set [a *pack* of lies or liars]; specif., *a)* a package of a standard number [a *pack* of cigarettes] *b)* a set of playing cards; deck *c)* a set of hunting hounds *d)* a group of wild animals living and hunting together **4.** *same as* ICE PACK **5.** *a)* treatment by wrapping a patient in sheets, etc. that are wet or dry and hot or cold *b)* the sheets so used **6.** a cosmetic paste applied to the skin and left to dry [*mudpack*] **7.** *a)* the amount of food put in cans, etc. in a season or year *b)* a method of packing or canning —*vt.* **1.** to make a pack of **2.** *a)* to put together in a box, trunk, etc. *b)* to fill (a box, trunk, etc.) **3.** to put (food) in (cans, etc.) for preservation **4.** *a)* to crowd; cram [the hall was *packed*] *b)* to crowd (people) together **5.** to fill in tightly, as for prevention of leaks [to *pack* valves] **6.** to press together firmly [*packed* earth] **7.** to load (an animal) with a pack **8.** to carry (goods, etc.) in a pack: said of an animal **9.** to send (*off*) **10.** [Slang] to wear or carry (a gun, etc.) as part of one's equipment **11.** [Slang] *a)* to deliver (a blow, punch, etc.) with force *b)* to provide or contain [a play that *packs* a message] —*vi.* **1.** to make up packs **2.** to put one's clothes, etc. into luggage for a trip **3.** to crowd together in a small space **4.** to admit of being folded compactly, put in a container, etc. [this suit *packs* well] **5.** to settle into a compact mass —*adj.* **1.** used in or suitable for packing **2.** formed into packs **3.** used for carrying packs, loads, etc. [a *pack* animal] —**send packing** to dismiss (a person) abruptly —**pack′a·bil′i·ty** *n.* —**pack′a·ble** *adj.*

pack[2] (pak) *vt.* [orig. unc., but infl. by prec.] to choose (a jury, court, etc.) in such a way as to get desired results

-pack (pak) *a combining form meaning* a carton of (a specified number of) bottles or cans, as of beer

pack·age (pak′ij) *n.* **1.** orig., the act or process of packing **2.** a wrapped or boxed thing; parcel **3.** a container, wrapping, etc., esp. one in which a commodity is packed for sale **4.** a number of items, plans, etc. offered as an inseparable unit —*vt.* **-aged, -ag·ing** to put into a package

package store a store where alcoholic liquor is sold by the bottle to be drunk off the premises

pack·er (pak′ər) *n.* a person or thing that packs; specif., *a)* one who packs goods for shipping, sale, etc. *b)* one who owns or manages a packing house

pack·et (-it) *n.* **1.** a small package **2.** *same as* PACKET BOAT —*vt.* to make up into a packet

packet boat a boat that travels a regular route carrying passengers, freight, and mail

pack·ing (pak′iŋ) *n.* **1.** the act or process of a person or thing that packs; specif., the large-scale processing and packaging of meats, fruits, etc. **2.** material used to pack

pack·ing·house (-hous′) *n.* a plant where meats are processed and packed for sale; also, a similar plant for packing fruits and vegetables

pack rat a N. American rat that often hides small articles in its nest

pack·sad·dle (-sad′′l) *n.* a saddle with fastenings to secure the load carried by a pack animal

pack·thread (-thred′) *n.* strong, thick thread or twine for tying bundles, packages, etc.

pack train a procession of pack animals

pact (pakt) *n.* [< OFr. < L. < pp. of *paciscere,* to agree < *pax,* peace] an agreement between persons or nations

pad[1] (pad) *n.* [echoic, but infl. by PAD[3]] the dull sound made by a footstep or staff on the ground

pad[2] (pad) *n.* [? var. of POD] **1.** a soft, stuffed saddle **2.** anything made of or stuffed with soft material to fill out a shape, protect from friction, jarring, blows, etc. [a shoulder *pad*] **3.** a piece of folded gauze, etc. used as a dressing on a wound, etc. **4.** *a)* the foot of certain animals, as the wolf, fox, etc. *b)* any of the cushionlike parts on the underside of such a foot **5.** the floating leaf of a water plant, as the waterlily **6.** a tablet of paper for writing on **7.** a small cushion soaked with ink for inking a rubber stamp: in full, **stamp pad** or **ink pad** **8.** *same as* LAUNCH PAD **9.** [Slang] *a)* a bed *b)* the room, apartment, etc. where one lives —*vt.* **pad′ded, pad′ding** **1.** to stuff, cover, or line with a pad or padding **2.** to lengthen (a speech or writing) with unnecessary material **3.** to fill (an expense account, etc.) with invented or inflated entries

pad[3] (pad) *vi.* **pad′ded, pad′ding** [< Du. *pad,* path] **1.** to travel on foot; walk **2.** to walk or run with a soft step

pad·ding (pad′iŋ) *n.* **1.** the action of one who pads **2.** any soft material used to pad, as cotton, felt, etc. **3.** unnecessary material used to lengthen a speech or writing

pad·dle[1] (pad′′l) *n.* [< ?] **1.** a short oar with a wide blade, used without an oarlock **2.** any of various implements shaped like this and used as in washing clothes, working butter, flogging, hitting a ball in some games, etc. **3.** any of the propelling boards in a water wheel or paddle wheel —*vt., vi.* **-dled, -dling** **1.** to propel (a canoe, etc.) with a paddle **2.** to punish by beating as with a paddle; spank **3.** to stir, work, etc. with a paddle —**paddle one's own canoe** to depend entirely on oneself —**pad′dler** *n.*

pad·dle[2] (pad′′l) *vi.* **-dled, -dling** [prob. freq. of PAD[3]] **1.** to move the hands or feet about in the water; dabble **2.** to walk like a small child; toddle —**pad′dler** *n.*

paddle ball a game similar to handball, but played with a short-handled, perforated paddle

pad·dle·fish (-fish′) *n., pl.* **-fish′, -fish′es:** see FISH a large fish of the Mississippi and Yangtze river systems, with a paddle-shaped snout

paddle wheel a wheel with paddles around it for propelling a steamboat

pad·dock (pad′ək) *n.* [< OE. *pearruc,* enclosure] **1.** a small enclosure near a stable, in which horses are exercised **2.** an enclosure at a race track, where horses are saddled and walked before a race

pad·dy (pad′ē) *n., pl.* **-dies** [Malay *padī*] **1.** rice in the husk, growing or gathered **2.** rice in general **3.** a rice field: often **rice paddy**

PADDLE WHEEL

paddy wagon *slang name for* PATROL WAGON

Pa·de·rew·ski (pä′de ref′skē; *E.* pad′ə ref′skē), **I·gnace (Jan)** (ē′nyȧs′) 1860–1941; Pol. pianist & composer

pad·lock (pad′läk′) *n.* [< ME. < *pad* (< ?) + *lokke,* LOCK[1]] a removable lock with a hinged link to be passed through a staple, chain, or eye —*vt.* to fasten or keep shut as with a padlock

pa·dre (pä′drā, -drē; *It.* -dre; *Sp.* -thre) *n., pl.* **-dres** (-drāz, -drēz; *Sp.* -thres); It. **pa′dri** (-drē) [Sp., It., Port. < L. *pater,* a father] **1.** father: the title of a priest in Italy, Spain, Portugal, and Latin America **2.** [Slang] a priest or chaplain

Pad·u·a (paj′o͞o ə, pad′yo͞o ə) city in N Italy: pop. 226,000: It. name **Pa·do·va** (pä′dô vä)

pae·an (pē′ən) *n.* [L. < Gr. < *Paian,* epithet of Apollo] a song of joy, triumph, praise, etc.

pae·do- *same as* PEDO-: also **paed-**

pa·el·la (pä yel′ə; *Sp.* pä e′lyä) *n.* [Catalan, ult. < L. *patella,* a small pan] a dish of rice cooked with chicken, seafood, etc., seasoned with saffron

pa·gan (pā′gən) *n.* [LL. *paganus,* a heathen < L., a peasant < *pagus,* country] **1.** anyone not a Christian, Moslem, or Jew; heathen **2.** a person who has no religion —*adj.* **1.** of pagans **2.** not religious —**pa′gan·dom** *n.* —**pa′gan·ish** *adj.* —**pa′gan·ism** *n.*

Pa·ga·ni·ni (pä′gä nē′nē; *E.* pag′ə nē′nē), **Ni·co·lò** (nē′kô lô′) 1782–1840; It. violinist & composer

pa·gan·ize (pā′gə nīz′) ***vt., vi.*** **-ized′, -iz′ing** to make or become pagan —**pa′gan·iz′er** ***n.***

page[1] (pāj) ***n.*** [Fr. < L. *pagina* < base of *pangere*, to fasten] **1.** *a)* one side of a leaf of a book, newspaper, etc. *b)* the printing or writing on it *[*the sports *pages]* *c)* an entire leaf in a book, etc. **2.** *[often pl.]* a record of events *[*the *pages* of history*]* **3.** an event or series of events that might fill a page *[*a colorful *page* in his life*]* —***vt.*** **paged, pag′ing** to number the pages of —***vi.*** to turn pages in scanning (*through* a book, etc.)

page[2] (pāj) ***n.*** [OFr. < It. *paggio*] **1.** formerly, a boy training for knighthood **2.** a boy attendant, esp. one serving a person of high rank, as in court **3.** a boy, or sometimes a girl, who runs errands, carries messages, etc., as in a hotel, legislature, etc. —***vt.*** **paged, pag′ing** to try to find (a person) by calling his name, as a hotel page does

pag·eant (paj′ənt) ***n.*** [Anglo-L. *pagina*, scene displayed on a stage, stage < L., PAGE[1]] **1.** a spectacular exhibition, elaborate parade, etc., as a procession with floats **2.** a drama, often staged outdoors, celebrating a historical event or events **3.** empty pomp or display

pag·eant·ry (-ən trē) ***n.,*** *pl.* **-ries** **1.** grand spectacle; gorgeous display **2.** empty show or display

pag·i·nate (paj′ə nāt′) ***vt.*** **-nat′ed, -nat′ing** to number the pages of (a book, etc.)

pag·i·na·tion (paj′ə nā′shən) ***n.*** **1.** the numbering of the pages of a book, etc. **2.** the figures with which pages are numbered in sequence

pa·go·da (pə gō′də) ***n.*** [< Port., prob. < Per. < *but*, idol + *kadah*, house, prob. infl. by Prakrit *bhagodī*, divine] in the Orient, a temple that is a tapering tower with rooflike, upward curving projections between its several stories

Pa·go Pa·go (päŋ′ō päŋ′ō, pä′gō pä′gō) seaport on the S coast of Tutuila Island, American Samoa: pop. 2,500

paid (pād) *pt. & pp. of* PAY[1]

pail (pāl) ***n.*** [OE. *pægel*, small measure < LL. *pagella*, in VL. a measure of area or volume] **1.** a cylindrical container, usually with a hoop-shaped handle, for carrying liquids, etc.; bucket **2.** the amount held by a pail: also **pail′ful′**, *pl.* **-fuls′**

pain (pān) ***n.*** [< OFr. < L. *poena*, punishment < Gr. *poinē*, penalty] **1.** orig., penalty or punishment **2.** a sensation of hurting caused by injury, disease, etc., transmitted by the nervous system **3.** the distress or suffering caused by anxiety, grief, disappointment, etc. **4.** [*pl.*] the labor of childbirth **5.** [*pl.*] great care *[*to take *pains* with one's work*]* **6.** [Slang] an annoyance —***vt.*** to cause pain to; hurt —***vi.*** to have or cause pain —**on** (or **upon** or **under**) **pain of** at the risk of bringing upon oneself (punishment, death, etc.) —**pain′less** ***adj.*** —**pain′less·ly** ***adv.*** —**pain′less·ness** ***n.***

Paine (pān), **Thomas** 1737–1809; Am. Revolutionary patriot, writer, & political theorist, born in England

pained (pānd) ***adj.*** **1.** hurt or distressed; offended **2.** showing hurt feelings or resentment

pain·ful (pān′fəl) ***adj.*** **1.** causing pain; hurting; distressing **2.** having pain; aching **3.** exacting and difficult **4.** annoying —**pain′ful·ly** ***adv.*** —**pain′ful·ness** ***n.***

pains·tak·ing (pānz′tā′kiŋ) ***n.*** great care or diligence —***adj.*** **1.** very careful; diligent **2.** characterized by great care —**pains′tak′ing·ly** ***adv.***

paint (pānt) ***vt.*** [< OFr. pp. of *peindre* < L. *pingere*] **1.** *a)* to make (a picture, etc.) in colors applied to a surface *b)* to depict with paints *[*to *paint* a landscape*]* **2.** to describe colorfully; depict in words **3.** to cover or decorate with paint *[*to *paint* a wall*]* **4.** to apply such cosmetics as lipstick, rouge, etc. to **5.** to apply (a medicine, etc.) with a brush or swab —***vi.*** **1.** to practice the art of painting pictures **2.** to use cosmetics —***n.*** **1.** a mixture of pigment with oil, water, etc. used as a covering or coloring or for making pictures on canvas, etc. **2.** a dried coat of paint **3.** *a)* coloring matter, as lipstick, rouge, etc., used as a cosmetic *b) same as* GREASEPAINT **4.** [Dial.] a piebald horse; pinto —**paint out** to cover up as with a coat of paint —**paint the town (red)** [Slang] to go on a boisterous spree —**paint′a·ble** ***adj.*** —**paint′y** ***adj.*** **paint′i·er, paint′i·est**

paint·brush (-brush′) ***n.*** a brush used for applying paint

paint·er[1] (pānt′ər) ***n.*** **1.** an artist who paints pictures **2.** a person whose work is covering surfaces, as walls, with paint

paint·er[2] (pānt′ər) ***n.*** [< OFr., ult. < L. *pendere*, to hang] a rope attached to the bow of a boat for tying it to a dock, etc.

paint·er[3] (pānt′ər) ***n.*** [altered < PANTHER] *dial. var. of* COUGAR

paint·ing (pānt′iŋ) ***n.*** **1.** the work or art of one who paints **2.** a picture made with paints

pair (per) ***n.,*** *pl.* **pairs;** sometimes, after a number, **pair** [< OFr. < L. neut. pl. of *par*, equal] **1.** two similar or corresponding things associated or used together *[*a *pair* of shoes*]* **2.** a single thing with two joined corresponding parts *[*a *pair* of pants*]* **3.** two persons or animals; specif., *a)* a married, engaged, or courting couple *b)* two mated animals *c)* two people with something in common *[*a *pair* of thieves*]* *d)* a brace; span *[*a *pair* of oxen*]* *e)* two legislators on opposing sides of a question who agree to withhold their vote so as to offset each other; also, such an agreement **4.** two playing cards of the same denomination —***vt.*** **1.** to make a pair of (two persons or things) or of (one *with* another) by matching, joining, etc. **2.** to arrange in pairs —***vi.*** **1.** to form a pair; match **2.** to mate —**pair off** **1.** to join (two people or things) in a pair **2.** to separate into pairs

pai·sa (pī′sä) ***n.,*** *pl.* **-se** (-se) [Hindi *paisā*] *see* MONETARY UNITS, table (Bangladesh, India, Pakistan)

pais·ley (pāz′lē) ***adj.*** [after *Paisley*, city in Scotland where orig. made] [*also* **P-**] **1.** of or having an elaborate, colorful pattern of intricate, curved figures **2.** made of cloth having such a pattern —***n.*** [*also* **P-**] a paisley cloth, shawl, necktie, etc.

PAISLEY PATTERN

Pai·ute (pī′yo͞ot, pī yo͞ot′) ***n.*** [< Shoshonean *pah-ute*, lit., water Ute] **1.** *pl.* **-utes, -ute** a member of any of various groups of N. American Indians living in Nevada, California, Utah, and Arizona **2.** any of their Shoshonean dialects

pa·ja·mas (pə jam′əz, -jä′məz) ***n.pl.*** [< Hindi < Per. *pāi*, a leg + *jāma*, garment] a loosely fitting sleeping or lounging suit consisting of jacket and trousers —**pa·ja′ma** ***adj.***

Pa·ki·stan (pä′ki stän′, pak′i stan′) country in S Asia, on the Arabian Sea: 310,403 sq. mi.; pop. 42,900,000; cap. Islamabad

Pa·ki·stan·i (pä′ki stä′nē, pak′i stan′ē) ***adj.*** of Pakistan or its people —***n.*** a native or inhabitant of Pakistan

pal (pal) ***n.*** [Eng. Romany < Sans. *bhrātr*, brother] [Colloq.] an intimate friend; comrade; chum —***vi.*** **palled, pal′ling** [Colloq.] **1.** to associate as pals **2.** to be a pal (*with* another)

pal·ace (pal′is) ***n.*** [< OFr. < L. < *Palatium*, one of the seven hills of Rome, where Augustus lived] **1.** the official residence of a king, emperor, etc. **2.** any large, magnificent house or building

pal·a·din (pal′ə din) ***n.*** [< Fr. < It. < L. *palatinus*, a palace officer: see prec.] **1.** any of the twelve legendary peers of Charlemagne's court **2.** a knight or heroic champion

pa·lae·o- *same as* PALEO-: also **pa·lae-**

pal·an·quin, pal·an·keen (pal′ən kēn′) ***n.*** [< Port. < Jav. < Sans. *palyaṅka*] formerly in eastern Asia, a covered litter for one person, carried by poles on men's shoulders

pal·at·a·ble (pal′it ə b'l) ***adj.*** [PALAT(E) + -ABLE] **1.** pleasant or acceptable to the taste **2.** acceptable to the mind —**pal′at·a·bil′i·ty, pal′at·a·ble·ness** ***n.*** —**pal′at·a·bly** ***adv.***

pal·a·tal (pal′it 'l) ***adj.*** **1.** of the palate **2.** pronounced with the tongue raised against or near the hard palate, as *y* in *yes* —***n.*** a palatal sound —**pal′a·tal·ly** ***adv.***

pal·a·tal·ize (-īz′) ***vt.*** **-ized′, -iz′ing** to pronounce as a palatal *[*the *t* in *nature* is *palatalized* to *ch]* —**pal′a·tal·i·za′tion** ***n.***

pal·ate (pal′it) ***n.*** [L. *palatum*] **1.** the roof of the mouth, consisting of a hard, bony forward part (the *hard palate*) and a soft, fleshy back part (the *soft palate*) **2.** taste

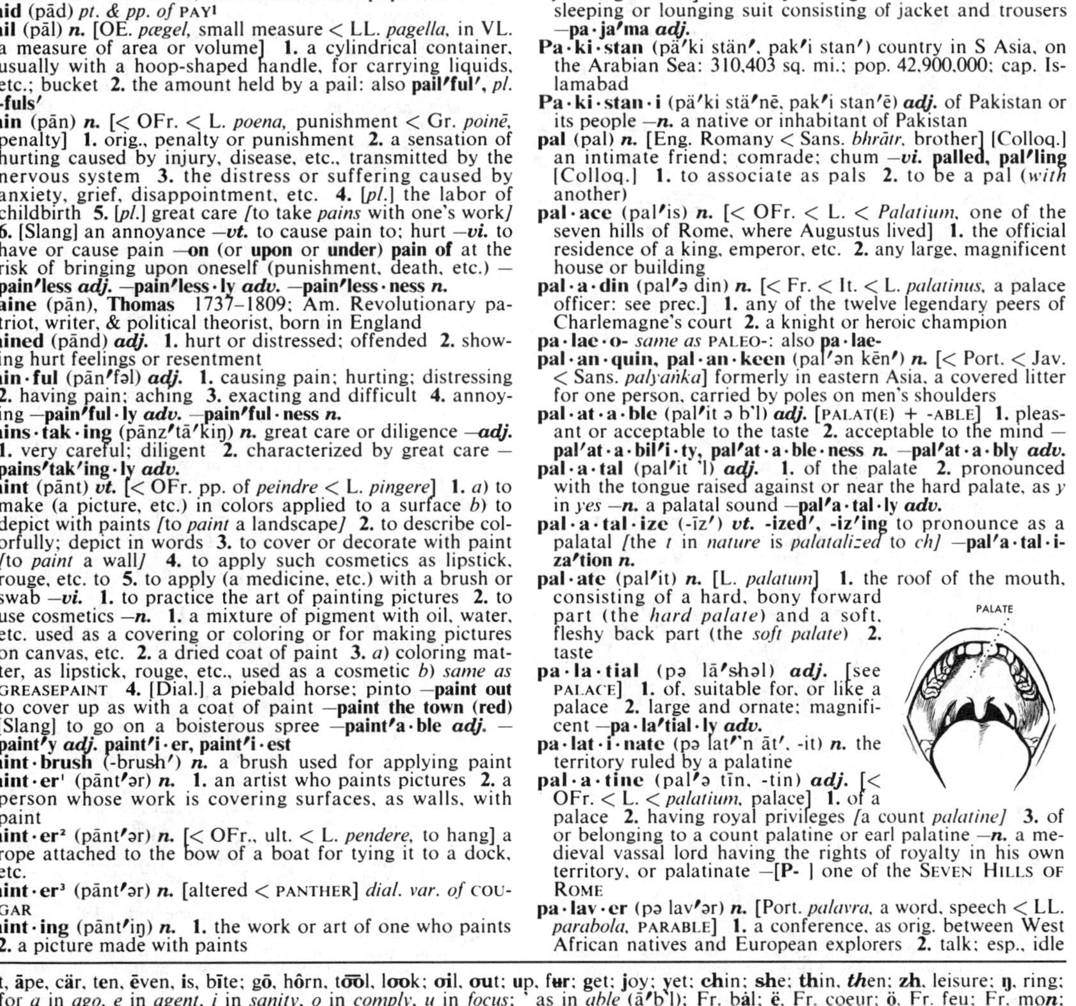

pa·la·tial (pə lā′shəl) ***adj.*** [see PALACE] **1.** of, suitable for, or like a palace **2.** large and ornate; magnificent —**pa·la′tial·ly** ***adv.***

pa·lat·i·nate (pə lat′'n āt′, -it) ***n.*** the territory ruled by a palatine

pal·a·tine (pal′ə tīn, -tin) ***adj.*** [< OFr. < L. < *palatium*, palace] **1.** of a palace **2.** having royal privileges *[*a count *palatine]* **3.** of or belonging to a count palatine or earl palatine —***n.*** a medieval vassal lord having the rights of royalty in his own territory, or palatinate —[**P-**] one of the SEVEN HILLS OF ROME

pa·lav·er (pə lav′ər) ***n.*** [Port. *palavra*, a word, speech < LL. *parabola*, PARABLE] **1.** a conference, as orig. between West African natives and European explorers **2.** talk; esp., idle

chatter 3. flattery; cajolery —*vi.* 1. to talk, esp. idly or flatteringly 2. to confer —*vt.* to flatter or wheedle
Pa·la·wan (pä lä′wän) island in the W Philippines, southwest of Mindoro: 4,550 sq. mi.
pale[1] (pāl) *adj.* [OFr. < L. < *pallere,* to be pale] 1. of a whitish or colorless complexion; pallid; wan 2. lacking intensity; faint: said of color, light, etc. 3. feeble; weak [*a pale imitation*] —*vi., vt.* **paled, pal′ing** to make or become pale —**pale′ly** *adv.* —**pale′ness** *n.* —**pal′ish** *adj.*
pale[2] (pāl) *n.* [< MFr. < L. *palus,* a stake] 1. a narrow, pointed stake used in fences; picket 2. a fence; enclosure; boundary: now chiefly figurative 3. a district enclosed within bounds
pale·face (pāl′fās′) *n.* a white person: a term allegedly first used by N. American Indians
pa·le·o- [< Gr. *palaios,* ancient] *a combining form meaning* ancient, prehistoric, primitive, etc. [*Paleozoic, paleolithic*] : also **pa·le-**
Pa·le·o·cene (pā′lē ə sēn′, pal′ē-) *adj.* [< prec. + Gr. *kainos,* recent] designating or of the first epoch of the Tertiary Period in the Cenozoic Era —**the Paleocene** the Paleocene Epoch or its rocks: see GEOLOGY, chart
pa·le·og·ra·phy (pā′lē äg′rə fē, pal′ē-) *n.* 1. ancient writing or forms of writing 2. the study of describing or deciphering ancient writings —**pa′le·og′ra·pher** *n.* —**pa′le·o·graph′ic** (-ə graf′ik), **pa′le·o·graph′i·cal** *adj.*
pa·le·o·lith·ic (pā′lē ə lith′ik, pal′ē-) *adj.* [PALEO- + -LITHIC] designating or of the middle part of the early Stone Age, during which stone and bone tools were used
pa·le·on·tol·o·gy (-än täl′ə jē) *n.* [< Fr.: see PALE(O)- & ONTO- & -LOGY] the branch of geology that deals with prehistoric life through the study of fossils —**pa′le·on′to·log′i·cal** (-tə läj′i k′l), **pa′le·on′to·log′ic** *adj.* —**pa′le·on·tol′o·gist** *n.*
Pa·le·o·zo·ic (-ə zō′ik) *adj.* [PALEO- + ZO- + -IC] designating or of the era between the Precambrian and the Mesozoic —**the Paleozoic** the Paleozoic era or its rocks: see GEOLOGY, chart
Pa·ler·mo (pə lur′mō; *It.* pä ler′mô) seaport on the N coast of Sicily: pop. 659,000
Pal·es·tine (pal′əs tīn′) 1. region on the E coast of the Mediterranean, the country of the Jews in Biblical times 2. Brit. mandated territory (1923–48) in this region, west of the Jordan River, before the establishment of the state of Israel —**Pal′es·tin′i·an** (-tin′ē ən) *adj., n.*
Pal·es·tri·na (pä′les trē′nä; *E.* pal′ə strē′nə), **Gio·van·ni (Pierluigi) da** (jô vän′nē dä) 1525?–94; It. composer
pal·ette (pal′it) *n.* [Fr. < L. *pala,* a shovel] 1. a thin board with a hole for the thumb at one end, on which an artist arranges and mixes his paints 2. the colors used, as by a particular artist
pal·frey (pôl′frē) *n., pl.* **-freys** [< OFr. < ML., ult. < Gr. *para,* beside + L. *veredus,* post horse] [Archaic] a saddle horse, esp. one for a woman
Pa·li (pä′lē) *n.* the Old Indic dialect which has become the religious language of Buddhism
pal·imp·sest (pal′imp sest′) *n.* [< L. < Gr. < *palin,* again + *psēn,* to rub smooth] a parchment, tablet, etc. that has been written upon several times, with previous, erased texts still partly visible

PALETTE

pal·in·drome (pal′in drōm′) *n.* [< Gr. < *palin,* again + *dramein,* to run] a word, phrase, or sentence that reads the same backward or forward (Ex.: madam)
pal·ing (pāl′iŋ) *n.* 1. a fence made of pales 2. the action of making such a fence 3. a pale, or pales collectively
pal·i·sade (pal′ə sād′, pal′ə sād′) *n.* [< Fr. < Pr. < L. *palus,* a stake] 1. any of a row of large pointed stakes set in the ground to form a fence as for fortification 2. such a fence 3. [*pl.*] a line of steep cliffs —*vt.* **-sad′ed, -sad′ing** to fortify or defend with a palisade
pall[1] (pôl) *vi.* **palled, pall′ing** [ME. *pallen,* short for *appallen,* APPALL] 1. to become cloying, insipid, etc. 2. to become satiated or bored —*vt.* to satiate, bore, or disgust
pall[2] (pôl) *n.* [< OE. < L. *pallium,* a cover] 1. a piece of velvet, etc. used to cover a coffin, hearse, or tomb 2. a dark or gloomy covering [*a pall of smoke*] 3. a cloth, or cardboard covered with cloth, used to cover the chalice in some Christian churches —*vt.* **palled, pall′ing** to cover as with a pall
Pal·la·dio (päl lä′dyô), **An·dre·a** (än dre′ä) (born *Andrea di Pietro*) 1518–80; It. architect —**Pal·la·di·an** (pə lā′dē ən, -lä′-) *adj.*
Pal·la·di·um (pə lā′dē əm) *n., pl.* **-di·a** (-ə) 1. the legendary statue of Pallas Athena in Troy believed to guard the city 2. [**p-**] any safeguard
pal·la·di·um (pə lā′dē əm) *n.* [ModL., ult. < Gr. *Pallas,* the goddess] a rare, silvery-white, metallic chemical element: it is used as a catalyst, or in alloys with gold, silver, etc.: symbol, Pd; at. wt., 106.4; at. no., 46
Pal·las (pal′əs) *Gr. Myth.* Athena, goddess of wisdom: also **Pallas Athena** —**Pal·la·di·an** (pə lā′dē ən) *adj.*
pall·bear·er (pôl′ber′ər) *n.* [PALL[2] + BEARER] one of the persons who bear the coffin at a funeral
pal·let[1] (pal′it) *n.* [< MFr.: see PALETTE] 1. a wooden tool consisting of a flat blade with a handle; esp., such a tool for smoothing pottery 2. *same as* PALETTE (sense 1) 3. a low, portable platform for storing goods in warehouses, etc. 4. any of the clicks or pawls in the escapement of a clock, etc. which engage the ratchet wheel to regulate the speed
pal·let[2] (pal′it) *n.* [< MFr. < OFr. *paille,* straw < L. *palea,* chaff] a small, inferior bed or a mattress filled as with straw and used on the floor
pal·li·ate (pal′ē āt′) *vt.* **-at′ed, -at′ing** [< LL. pp. of *palliare,* to conceal < *pallium,* a cloak] 1. to lessen the pain or severity of without curing; alleviate 2. to make appear less serious or offensive; excuse —**pal′li·a′tion** *n.* —**pal′li·a′tive** (-āt′iv, -ə tiv) *adj., n.* —**pal′li·a′tor** *n.*
pal·lid (pal′id) *adj.* [L. *pallidus,* PALE[1]] faint in color; pale —**pal′lid·ly** *adv.* —**pal′lid·ness** *n.*
Pall Mall (pel′mel′, pal′mal′, pôl′môl′) a London street, noted for its clubs for men
pal·lor (pal′ər) *n.* [L. < *pallere:* see PALE[1]] lack of color; unnatural paleness, as of the face
palm[1] (päm; *occas.* pälm) *n.* [OE. < L. *palma:* from its handlike fronds] 1. any of a family of tropical or subtropical trees with a tall, branchless trunk and a bunch of large leaves at the top 2. a leaf of this tree carried as a symbol of victory, triumph, etc. 3. victory; triumph —*adj.* designating or of a family of plants including the coconut palm, date palm, etc. —**bear** (or **carry off**) **the palm** to be the winner —**pal·ma·ceous** (pal mā′shəs, pä-) *adj.*
palm[2] (päm; *occas.* pälm) *n.* [< OFr. < L. *palma*] 1. the inner surface of the hand between the fingers and wrist 2. the part of a glove, etc. that covers the palm 3. the broad, flat part of an antler, as of a moose 4. a unit of measure based either on the width of the hand (3 to 4 inches) or its length (7 to 9 inches) 5. any broad, flat part at the end of an arm, handle, etc. —*vt.* to hide (something) in the palm or between the fingers, as in a sleight-of-hand trick —**have an itching palm** [Colloq.] to desire money greedily —**palm off** to pass off by fraud or deceit —**pal·mar** (pal′mər, pä′-) *adj.*
Pal·ma (päl′mä) seaport on Majorca: chief city of the Balearic Islands: pop. 208,000: in full, **Palma de Mallorca**
pal·mate (pal′māt, pä′-) *adj.* [< L. < *palma,* PALM[2]] shaped like a hand with the fingers spread; specif., *a*) *Bot.* having veins or lobes radiating from a common center, as some leaves *b*) *Zool.* web-footed Also **pal′mat·ed** —**pal′mate·ly** *adv.* —**pal·ma′tion** *n.*
Palm Beach resort town on the SE coast of Fla.
palm·er (päm′ər, päl′mər) *n.* 1. a pilgrim who carried a palm leaf as a sign that he had been to the Holy Land 2. any pilgrim
Palm·er·ston (päm′ər stən), 3d Viscount, (*Henry John Temple*) 1784–1865; Brit. statesman; prime minister (1855–58; 1859–65)
pal·met·to (pal met′ō) *n., pl.* **-tos, -toes** [Sp. *palmito,* dim. < *palma* < L., PALM[1]] any of several new-world palms with fan-shaped leaves, as the cabbage palm
palm·is·try (päm′is trē, päl′mis-) *n.* [< ME., prob. contr. < *paume,* PALM[2] + *maistrie,* mastery] the pretended art of telling a person's fortune by the lines, etc. on the palm of his hand —**palm′ist** *n.*
pal·mit·ic acid (pal mit′ik, pä-) [< Fr.] a fatty acid found in many natural fats and oils
palm leaf the leaf of a palm tree, esp. of a palmetto, used to make fans, hats, etc.
palm oil an oil obtained from the fruit of certain palms, used in making soap, candles, etc.
Palm Springs resort city in S Calif.
Palm Sunday the Sunday before Easter, commemorating Jesus' triumphal entry into Jerusalem
palm·y (päm′ē, päl′mē) *adj.* **palm′i·er, palm′i·est** 1. abounding in or shaded by palm trees 2. of or like a palm 3. prosperous [*palmy days*]
pal·my·ra (pal mī′rə) *n.* [< Port. < *palma* < L., PALM[1]] a palm tree grown in India, Ceylon, and Africa for its durable wood, its leaves used for thatching, etc.
Pal·o Al·to (pal′ō al′tō) [Sp., lit., tall tree (the redwood)] city in W Calif., near San Francisco: pop. 55,000
pal·o·mi·no (pal′ə mē′nō) *n., pl.* **-nos** [AmSp. < Sp., dove-colored, ult. < L. *palumbes,* pigeon] a cream, golden, or light-chestnut horse with white mane and tail
palp (palp) *n. same as* PALPUS —**pal′pal** *adj.*
pal·pa·ble (pal′pə b′l) *adj.* [< LL. < L. *palpare,* to touch] 1. that can be touched, felt, etc.; tangible 2. easily perceived by the senses; recognizable, perceptible, etc. 3. obvious; plain —**pal′pa·bil′i·ty** *n.* —**pal′pa·bly** *adv.*
pal·pate (pal′pāt) *vt.* **-pat·ed, -pat·ing** [< L. pp. of *pal-*

pare, to touch] to examine by touching, as for medical diagnosis —**pal·pa′tion** ***n.***

pal·pi·tate (pal′pə tāt′) ***vi.*** **-tat′ed, -tat′ing** [< L. pp. of *palpitare,* freq. of *palpare,* to feel] **1.** to beat rapidly or flutter: said of the heart **2.** to throb; quiver —**pal′pi·tant** ***adj.*** —**pal′pi·ta′tion** ***n.***

pal·pus (pal′pəs) ***n.,*** *pl.* **pal′pi** (-pī) [ModL. < L. *palpus,* the soft palm of the hand] a jointed organ or feeler for touching or tasting, attached to one of the head appendages of insects, lobsters, etc.

pal·sy (pôl′zē) ***n.,*** *pl.* **-sies** [< OFr. < L. *paralysis,* PARALYSIS] paralysis of any voluntary muscle, sometimes accompanied by uncontrollable tremors —***vt.*** **-sied, -sy·ing** to afflict with or as with palsy; paralyze

pal·ter (pôl′tər) ***vi.*** [freq. < dial. *palt,* a rag] **1.** to talk or act insincerely; prevaricate **2.** to trifle **3.** to quibble

pal·try (pôl′trē) ***adj.*** **-tri·er, -tri·est** [prob. < LowG. *paltrig* < *palte,* a rag] worthless; trifling; petty —**pal′tri·ness** ***n.***

pam·pas (pam′pəz; *for adj., usually* -pəs) ***n.pl.*** [AmSp., pl. of *pampa* < Quechua, plain] the extensive treeless plains of S. America, esp. of Argentina —***adj.*** of the pampas —**pam·pe·an** (pam′pē ən, pam pē′-) ***adj., n.***

pam·per (pam′pər) ***vt.*** [< LowG. source] **1.** orig., to feed too much; glut **2.** to be overindulgent with; coddle *[to pamper* a child*]* —**pam′per·er** ***n.***

pam·phlet (pam′flit) ***n.*** [< OFr. *Pamphilet,* popular name of a ML. poem] **1.** a small, unbound booklet, usually with a paper cover **2.** a treatise in this form, as on some topic of current interest

pam·phlet·eer (pam′flə tir′) ***n.*** a writer of pamphlets, esp. those dealing with political or social issues —***vi.*** to write or publish pamphlets

Pan (pan) *Gr. Myth.* a god of fields, forests, wild animals, flocks, and shepherds, represented with the legs of a goat

pan[1] (pan) ***n.*** [OE. *panne*] **1.** any broad, shallow container, usually of metal and without a cover, used in cooking, etc.: often in combination *[saucepan]* **2.** a pan-shaped part or object; specif., *a)* a container for washing out gold, etc. from gravel *b)* either receptacle in a pair of scales **3.** *same as* HARDPAN (sense 1) **4.** the part holding the powder in a flintlock **5.** [Slang] a face —***vt.*** **panned, pan′ning** **1.** to cook in a pan **2.** [Colloq.] to criticize unfavorably, as in reviewing **3.** *Mining a)* to wash (gravel) in a pan *b)* to separate (gold, etc.) from gravel in this way —***vi.*** *Mining* **1.** to wash gravel in a pan **2.** to yield gold in this process —**pan out** **1.** *Mining* to yield gold, as gravel, a mine, etc. **2.** [Colloq.] to turn out; esp., to turn out well

pan[2] (pan) ***vt., vi.*** **panned, pan′ning** [< PAN(ORAMA)] to move (a motion-picture or television camera) so as to get a panoramic effect or follow a moving object —***n.*** the act of panning

pan- [< Gr. *pan,* neut. of *pas,* all, every] *a combining form meaning:* **1.** all *[pantheism]* **2.** [**P-**] *a)* of, comprising, or common to every *[Pan-*American*]* *b)* (belief in) the union or cooperation of all members of (a specified group) *[Pan-*Americanism*]* In sense 2, usually with a hyphen, as in the following words:

Pan-African	**Pan-European**
Pan-Arabic	**Pan-Islamic**
Pan-Asiatic	**Pan-Slavic**

pan·a·ce·a (pan′ə sē′ə) ***n.*** [L. < Gr. < *pan,* all + *akeisthai,* to cure] a supposed remedy or cure for all diseases or ills; cure-all —**pan′a·ce′an** ***adj.***

pa·nache (pə nash′) ***n.*** [Fr., ult. < LL. *pinnaculum,* plume] **1.** a plume on a helmet **2.** carefree self-confidence or style; flamboyance

Pan·a·ma (pan′ə mä′, -mô′) **1.** country in Central America, on the Isthmus of Panama: 29,201 sq. mi.; pop. 1,425,000 **2.** its capital, on the Pacific: pop. 412,000: also **Panama City** **3. Isthmus of,** strip of land connecting South America & Central America —**Pan′a·ma′ni·an** (-mā′nē ən) ***adj., n.***

Panama Canal ship canal across the Isthmus of Panama, connecting the Caribbean Sea & the Pacific Ocean: 50.7 mi. long

Panama (hat) [< *Panama* (city)] a fine, hand-plaited hat made from select leaves of a Central and South American plant

Pan-A·mer·i·can (pan′ə mer′ə kən) ***adj.*** of North, Central, and South America, collectively

Pan-A·mer·i·can·ism (-iz′m) ***n.*** a policy of political and economic cooperation, mutual cultural understanding, etc. among the Pan-American nations

pan·a·tel·a, pan·a·tel·la (pan′ə tel′ə) ***n.*** [AmSp., orig. a long biscuit < It., dim. of *pane,* bread] a long, slender cigar

Pa·nay (pä nī′; *E.* pə nī′) island of the C Philippines, between Mindoro & Negros: 4,446 sq. mi.

pan·broil (pan′broil′) ***vt.*** to fry in a pan with little or no fat

pan·cake (pan′kāk′) ***n.*** **1.** a thin, flat cake of batter fried on a griddle or in a pan; griddlecake; flapjack **2.** a landing in which the plane levels off, stalls, then drops almost vertically: in full, **pancake landing** —***vi., vt.*** **-caked′, -cak′ing** to make, or cause to make, a pancake landing

pancake makeup a thin cake of compressed powder used as cosmetic or theatrical makeup

pan·chro·mat·ic (pan′krō mat′ik) ***adj.*** sensitive to light of all colors *[panchromatic* film*]* —**pan·chro·ma·tism** (pan-krō′mə tiz′m) ***n.***

pan·cre·as (pan′krē əs, paŋ′-) ***n.*** [ModL. < Gr. < *pan,* all + *kreas,* flesh] a large, elongated gland that secretes an alkaline digestive juice (**pancreatic juice**) into the small intestine: the pancreas of animals, used as food, is called *sweetbread* —**pan′cre·at′ic** (-at′ik) ***adj.***

pan·da (pan′də) ***n.*** [Fr. < native name in Nepal] *clipped form of:* **1.** GIANT PANDA **2.** LESSER PANDA

pan·dem·ic (pan dem′ik) ***adj.*** [< LL. < Gr. < *pan,* all + *dēmos,* the people] epidemic over a large region —***n.*** a pandemic disease

Pan·de·mo·ni·um (pan′də mō′nē əm) [ModL. < Gr. *pan-* + *daimōn,* demon] the capital of Hell in Milton's *Paradise Lost* —***n.*** [**p-**] wild disorder, noise, or confusion, or a place where this exists

pan·der (pan′dər) ***n.*** [< L. *Pandarus,* who, in the story of Troilus and Cressida, acts as their go-between] **1.** a go-between in a sexual intrigue; pimp **2.** one who provides the means of helping to satisfy the ambitions, vices, etc. of another Also **pan′der·er** —***vi.*** to act as a pander (*to*)

pan·dit (pun′dit, pan′-) ***n.*** [var. of PUNDIT] in India, a learned man: used [**P-**] as a title of respect

P. and L., P. & L. profit and loss

Pan·do·ra (pan dôr′ə) [L. < Gr. < *pan,* all + *dōron,* a gift] *Gr. Myth.* the first mortal woman, who in curiosity opened a box, letting out all human ills into the world

pan·dow·dy (pan dou′dē) ***n.,*** *pl.* **-dies** [prob. < obs. E. dial. *pandoulde,* custard] deep-dish apple pie, having a top crust only

pane (pān) ***n.*** [< OFr. < L. *pannus,* piece of cloth] **1.** a flat piece, side, or face **2.** *a)* a single division of a window, etc., consisting of a sheet of glass in a frame *b)* such a sheet of glass **3.** a panel, as of a door

pan·e·gyr·ic (pan′ə jir′ik) ***n.*** [< Fr. < L. < Gr. *panēgyris,* public meeting < *pan,* all + *ageirein,* to bring together] **1.** a formal speech or writing praising a person or event **2.** high or exaggerated praise —**pan′e·gyr′i·cal** ***adj.*** —**pan′e·gyr′i·cal·ly** ***adv.*** —**pan′e·gyr′ist** ***n.*** —**pan′e·gy·rize′** (-jə rīz′) ***vt., vi.*** **-rized′, -riz′ing**

pan·el (pan′'l) ***n.*** [< OFr., ult. < L. *pannus,* piece of cloth] **1.** a section or division of a surface; specif., *a)* a flat piece, usually rectangular, forming a part of the surface of a wall, door, etc., usually raised, recessed, framed, etc. *b)* a similar piece used as a cover, a light diffuser, a built-in heating element, etc. *c)* a pane of a window *d)* a board, or flat surface, for instruments or controls **2.** *a)* a thin board for an oil painting *b)* a painting on such a board *c)* a picture much longer than it is wide **3.** *a)* a list of persons summoned for jury duty *b)* the jury itself **4.** a group of persons selected for a specific purpose, as for judging a contest, discussing an issue, etc. **5.** a lengthwise strip, as of contrasting material, in a skirt or dress —***vt.*** **-eled** or **-elled, -el·ing** or **-el·ling** to provide, decorate, etc. with panels

panel discussion a discussion carried on by a selected group of speakers before an audience

pan·el·ing, pan·el·ling (-iŋ) ***n.*** **1.** panels collectively; series of panels in a wall, etc. **2.** sections of plastic, wood, etc. from which to cut panels

pan·el·ist (-ist) ***n.*** a member of a panel (*n.* 4)

panel truck a small, enclosed pickup truck

pan·e·tel·a, pan·e·tel·la (pan′ə tel′ə) ***n.*** *same as* PANATELA

pan fish a fish that can be fried whole in a pan

pan-fry (pan′frī′) ***vt.*** **-fried′, -fry′ing** to fry in a shallow skillet or frying pan

pang (paŋ) ***n.*** [< ?] a sudden, sharp, brief pain, physical or emotional; spasm of distress

pan·go·lin (paŋ gō′lin) ***n.*** [Malay *pĕngulin,* roller < *gulin,* to roll] any of various toothless, scaly mammals of Asia and Africa, able to roll into a ball when attacked

pan·han·dle[1] (pan′han′d'l) ***n.*** **1.** the handle of a pan **2.** [*often* **P-**] a strip of land like the handle of a pan, as the northern extension of Texas

pan·han·dle[2] (pan′han′d'l) ***vt., vi.*** **-dled, -dling** [ult. < PAN[1] + HANDLE, *vt.*] [Colloq.] to beg (from), esp. on the streets —**pan′han′dler** ***n.***

Pan·hel·len·ic (pan′hə len′ik) ***adj.*** **1.** of all the Greek peoples **2.** of all Greek-letter fraternities and sororities

pan·ic[1] (pan′ik) ***n.*** [L. *panicum*, kind of millet < *panus*, a swelling] any of several related grasses, as millet, used as fodder: also **panic grass**

pan·ic[2] (pan′ik) ***adj.*** [< Fr. < Gr. *panikos*, of Pan] **1.** literally, of Pan or of sudden fear supposedly inspired by him **2.** like, showing, or resulting from, panic —***n.*** **1.** a sudden, unreasoning, hysterical fear, often spreading quickly **2.** a widespread fear of financial collapse, resulting in stock-market decline, withdrawals of bank deposits, etc. **3.** [Slang] a very comical person or thing —***vt.*** **-icked, -icking** **1.** to affect with panic **2.** [Slang] to convulse (an audience, etc.) with laughter, etc. —***vi.*** to give way to or show panic —**push** (or **press, hit,** etc.) **the panic button** [Slang] to react to a crisis by some frantic action —**pan′i·cal·ly** ***adv.*** —**pan′ick·y** ***adj.***

pan·i·cle (pan′i k'l) ***n.*** [< L. dim. of *panus*, a swelling, ear of millet] a loose, irregularly branched flower cluster; compound raceme —**pan·i·cled, pa·nic·u·late** (pa nik′yə lit, -lāt′) ***adj.***

PANICLE OF OATS

pan·ic-strick·en (pan′ik strik′'n) ***adj.*** stricken with panic; badly frightened: also **panic-struck**

pan·jan·drum (pan jan′drəm) ***n.*** [arbitrary coinage] a self-important, pompous official

pan·nier, pan·ier (pan′yər, -ē ər) ***n.*** [< MFr. < L. *panarium*, breadbasket < *panis*, bread] **1.** *a)* a large basket for carrying loads on the back *b)* either of a pair of baskets hung across the back of a donkey, horse, etc. **2.** *a)* a framework, as of wire, used formerly to puff out a skirt at the hips *b)* a skirt so puffed

pan·ni·kin (pan′ə kin) ***n.*** [Chiefly Brit.] a small pan or cup

pa·no·cha (pə nō′chə) ***n.*** [AmSp. < Sp. *pan*, bread < L. *panis*] **1.** a coarse Mexican sugar **2.** *var. of* PENUCHE: also **pa·no′che** (-chē)

pan·o·ply (pan′ə plē) ***n.***, *pl.* **-plies** [< Gr. < *pan*, all + *hopla*, arms] **1.** a complete suit of armor **2.** any complete or magnificent covering or array —**pan′o·plied *adj.***

pan·o·ra·ma (pan′ə ram′ə) ***n.*** [< PAN- + Gr. *horama*, a view] **1.** *a)* a picture unrolled in such a way as to give the impression of a continuous view *b) same as* CYCLORAMA (sense 1) **2.** an open view in all directions **3.** a full review of a subject **4.** a constantly changing scene *[*the *panorama* of the waterfront*]* —**pan′o·ram′ic *adj.*** —**pan′o·ram′i·cal·ly *adv.***

pan·pipe (pan′pīp′) ***n.*** [*also* **P-**] a primitive musical instrument made of a row of reeds or tubes of graduated lengths, played by blowing across the open ends: also **panpipes, Pan's pipes**

pan·sy (pan′zē) ***n.***, *pl.* **-sies** [Fr. *pensée*, a thought < *penser*, to think] **1.** a small, flowering plant with flat, broad, velvety petals in many colors **2.** [Slang] a male homosexual

pant[1] (pant) ***vi.*** [prob. < OFr. *pantaisier*, ult. < L. *phantasia*, nightmare] **1.** to breathe rapidly and heavily, as from running fast **2.** to beat rapidly; throb **3.** to yearn eagerly (with *for* or *after*) —***vt.*** to gasp out —***n.*** **1.** any of a series of rapid, heavy breaths; gasp **2.** a throb, as of the heart **3.** a puff of an engine

pant[2] (pant) ***n., adj.*** *see* PANTS

pan·ta·lets, pan·ta·lettes (pan′t'l ets′) ***n.pl.*** [dim. of ff.] **1.** long, loose drawers showing below the skirt, worn by women in the 19th cent. **2.** detachable ruffles for the legs of drawers

pan·ta·loon (pan′t'l o͞on′) [< Fr. < It., ult. after the Venetian patron saint *Pantalone*] [**P-**] **1.** a foolish old man in early Italian comedy, typically slender and in tightfitting trousers **2.** a similar buffoon in modern pantomime —***n.*** [*pl.*] trousers

pant·dress (pant′dres′) ***n.*** a woman's garment with the lower part like pants instead of a skirt

pan·the·ism (pan′thē iz'm) ***n.*** **1.** the belief that God is not a personality but the sum of all beings, things, forces, etc. in the universe **2.** the worship of all gods —**pan′the·ist *n.*** —**pan′the·is′tic, pan′the·is′ti·cal *adj.*** —**pan′the·is′ti·cal·ly *adv.***

pan·the·on (pan′thē än′, -ən) ***n.*** [< L. < Gr. < *pan*, all + *theos*, a god] **1.** a temple for all the gods; esp., [**P-**] a temple built in Rome in 27 B.C.: used since 609 A.D. as a Christian church **2.** all the gods of a people **3.** [*often* **P-**] a building in which the famous dead of a nation are entombed or commemorated

pan·ther (pan′thər) ***n.***, *pl.* **-thers, -ther:** see PLURAL, II, D, 1 [< OFr. < L. < Gr. *panthēr*] **1.** a leopard; specif., *a)* a black leopard *b)* a leopard that is very large or fierce **2.** *same as: a)* COUGAR *b)* JAGUAR —**pan′ther·ess *n.fem.***

pant·ies (pan′tēz) ***n.pl.*** women's or children's short underpants: also **pan′tie** (-tē)

pan·to- [< Gr. *pantos*, gen. of *pan*, all, every] *a combining form meaning* all or every: also **pant-**

pan·to·graph (pan′tə graf′) ***n.*** [< Fr.: see prec. & -GRAPH] a mechanical device for reproducing a drawing on the same or a different scale

pan·to·mime (pan′tə mīm′) ***n.*** [< L. < Gr. < *pantos* (see PANTO-) + *mimos*, a mimic] **1.** *a)* a play, skit, etc. performed without words, using actions and gestures only *b)* the art of acting in this way **2.** actions and gestures without words —***vt., vi.*** **-mimed′, -mim′ing** to express or act in pantomime —**pan′to·mim′ic** (-mim′ik) ***adj.*** —**pan′to·mim′ist** (-mī′mist, -mim′ist) ***n.***

pan·to·then·ic acid (pan′tə then′ik) [< Gr. *pantothen*, from every side] a yellow, viscous oil, $C_9H_{17}O_5N$, a member of the vitamin B complex, found in all living tissues

pan·try (pan′trē) ***n.***, *pl.* **-tries** [< OFr. < ML. *panetaria* < L. *panis*, bread] **1.** a small room off the kitchen where cooking ingredients and utensils, china, etc. are kept **2.** *same as* BUTLER'S PANTRY

pants (pants) ***n.pl.*** [abbrev. of PANTALOON(S)] **1.** trousers **2.** drawers or panties As an adjective or in compounds, usually **pant** *[pant* legs, *pantdress]*

pant·suit (pant′so͞ot′) ***n.*** a woman's outfit of a matched jacket and pants: also **pants suit**

pan·ty (pan′tē) ***n.***, *pl.* **-ties** *same as* PANTIES

panty girdle a girdle with a crotch like panties

panty hose a woman's undergarment combining panties with hose: also **pan′ty·hose′** (-hōz′) ***n.***

pan·ty·waist (-wāst′) ***n.*** **1.** orig., a child's two-piece undergarment **2.** [Slang] a sissy

pan·zer (pan′zər; *G.* pän′tsər) ***adj.*** [G., armor] armored *[*a *panzer* division*]*

Pao·tou (bou′dō′) city in Inner Mongolia, NE China: pop. 1,500,000: also sp. **Paotow**

pap[1] (pap) ***n.*** [prob. orig. < baby talk] [Archaic] a nipple or teat

pap[2] (pap) ***n.*** [orig. < baby talk] **1.** any soft food for babies or invalids **2.** any oversimplified or tasteless writing, ideas, etc.

pa·pa (pä′pə; *now less freq.* pə pä′) ***n.*** [< baby talk, as also in Fr. & L. *papa*] father: a child's word

pa·pa·cy (pā′pə sē) ***n.***, *pl.* **-cies** [< ML. < LL. *papa*, pope] **1.** the position or authority of the Pope **2.** the period during which a pope rules **3.** the succession of popes **4.** [*also* **P-**] the government of the Roman Catholic Church, headed by the Pope

pa·pal (pā′pəl) ***adj.*** [< MFr. < ML.: see POPE & -AL] **1.** of the Pope or the papacy **2.** of the Roman Catholic Church —**pa′pal·ly *adv.***

pa·paw (pô′pô, pə pô′) ***n.*** [prob. < ff.] **1.** *same as* PAPAYA **2.** *a)* a tree of central and southern U.S. having a yellowish, edible fruit with many seeds *b)* its fruit

pa·pa·ya (pə pä′yə) ***n.*** [Sp. < Carib name] **1.** a palmlike tropical American tree bearing a large, yellowish-orange fruit like a melon **2.** its fruit

pa·per (pā′pər) ***n.*** [< OFr. < L. *papyrus*, PAPYRUS] **1.** a thin, flexible material usually in sheets, made from wood pulp, rags, etc., and used for writing or printing on, for packaging, etc. **2.** a single piece or sheet of this **3.** a printed or written paper; specif., *a)* an official document *b)* an essay, dissertation, etc. *c)* a written examination, report, etc. **4.** *same as: a)* COMMERCIAL PAPER *b)* PAPER MONEY **5.** *clipped form of: a)* NEWSPAPER *b)* WALLPAPER **6.** a small wrapper of paper, usually including its contents *[*a *paper* of pins*]* **7.** any material like paper, as papyrus **8.** [*pl.*] *a)* documents identifying a person; credentials *b)* a collection of letters, writings, etc. —***adj.*** **1.** of paper; made of paper **2.** like paper; thin **3.** existing only in written form; theoretical *[paper* profits*]* —***vt.*** **1.** to cover with paper, esp. wallpaper **2.** to wrap in paper —***vi.*** to hang wallpaper —**on paper** **1.** in written or printed form **2.** in theory —**pa′per·er *n.*** —**pa′per·like′, pa′per·y *adj.***

pa·per·back (-bak′) ***n.*** a book bound in paper —**pa′per-backed′, pa′per·bound′** (-bound′) ***adj.***

paper birch the N. American birch having white or ash-colored paperlike bark

pa·per·boy (-boi′) ***n.*** a boy or man who sells or delivers newspapers

paper clip a flexible clasp of metal wire for holding loose sheets of paper together

paper cutter **1.** *same as* PAPER KNIFE **2.** a device for cutting and trimming several sheets of paper at a time

pa·per·hang·er (-haŋ′ər) ***n.*** a person whose work is covering walls with wallpaper —**pa′per·hang′ing *n.***

paper knife a knifelike blade, as of metal, used to slit sealed envelopes and uncut book pages

paper money noninterest-bearing notes, as dollar bills, issued by a government or its banks, circulating as legal tender

paper nautilus an eight-armed mollusk related to the octopus: the female has a paperlike shell in which the young develop

paper tiger a person, nation, etc. that seems to pose a threat but is actually powerless

pa·per·weight (-wāt′) ***n.*** any small, heavy object set on papers to keep them from being scattered

paper work the keeping of records, filing of reports, etc. incidental to some work or task

pa·pier-mâ·ché (pā′pər mə shā′) ***n.*** [Fr. *papier,* paper + pp. of *mâcher,* to chew] a material made of paper pulp mixed with size, glue, etc., that is easily molded when moist and dries strong and hard —***adj.*** made of papier-mâché

pa·pil·la (pə pil′ə) ***n., pl.*** **-lae** (-ē) [L., dim. of *papula,* pimple] **1.** a small bulge of flesh, as at the root of a hair, a developing tooth, etc., or on the surface of the tongue **2.** *Bot.* a tiny, protruding cell —**pap·il·lar·y** (pap′ə ler′ē, pə pil′ər ē) ***adj.*** —**pap·il·late** (pap′ə lāt′, pə pil′it) ***adj.***

pap·il·lo·ma (pap′ə lō′mə) ***n., pl.*** **-ma·ta** (-mə tə), **-mas** [ModL.: see PAPILLA & -OMA] a benign tumor of the skin or mucous membrane, consisting of a thickened and enlarged papilla or group of papillae, as a corn or wart

pa·pist (pā′pist) ***n.*** [< ModL. < LL. *papa,* POPE] **1.** one who believes in papal supremacy **2.** a Roman Catholic —***adj.*** Roman Catholic A hostile term

pa·poose (pa po͞os′, pə-) ***n.*** [< Algonquian *papoos*] a North American Indian baby

pap·pus (pap′əs) ***n., pl.*** **pap′pi** (-ī) [ModL. < L. < Gr. *pappos,* old man] *Bot.* a tuft of bristles, hairs, etc.

pap·py (pap′ē) ***n., pl.*** **-pies** [Dial. or Colloq.] father

pa·pri·ka (pa prē′kə, pə-; pap′ri kə) ***n.*** [Hung. < Serb. < Gr. *peperi,* pepper] a mild, red condiment ground from the fruit of certain peppers

Pap test (pap) [after G. *Papanicolaou* (1883–1962), U.S. anatomist] the microscopic examination of a smear (**Pap smear**) taken from the cervix of a woman: a test for cancer

Pap·u·a New Guinea (pap′yo͞o wə, pä′po͞o wə) country occupying the E half of the island of New Guinea, and nearby islands: c. 180,000 sq. mi.; pop. 2,756,000

pap·ule (pap′yo͞ol) ***n.*** [L. *papula*] a pimple —**pap′u·lar** (-lər) ***adj.*** —**pap′u·lose′** (-lōs′) ***adj.***

pa·py·rus (pə pī′rəs) ***n., pl.*** **-ri** (-rī), **-rus·es** [L. < Gr. *papyros,* prob. < Egypt.] **1.** a tall water plant abundant in the Nile region in Egypt **2.** a writing material made from this plant by the ancient Egyptians, Greeks, and Romans **3.** any ancient document or manuscript on papyrus

par (pär) ***n.*** [L., an equal] **1.** the established value of the money of one country in terms of the money of another **2.** an equal status, footing, level, etc.: usually in **on a par (with) 3.** the average state, condition, etc. *[*work that is above *par]* **4.** *Commerce* the face value of stocks, bonds, etc. **5.** *Golf* the number of strokes established as a skillful score for a hole or course —***adj.*** **1.** of or at par **2.** average; normal —***vt.*** **parred, par′ring** *Golf* to score par on (a given hole or course)

par. 1. paragraph **2.** parallel **3.** parenthesis **4.** parish

Pa·rá (pä rä′) river in NE Brazil, forming the S estuary of the Amazon

pa·ra (pä rä′, pär′ə) ***n.*** [Turk. < Per. *pārah,* a piece] *see* MONETARY UNITS, table (Yugoslavia)

par·a- [< Gr. < *para,* at the side of] *a prefix meaning:* **1.** by or at the side of, beyond, aside from *[paramilitary]* **2.** *Med. a)* in a secondary capacity *b)* functionally disordered, abnormal *c)* like or resembling *[paratyphoid]*

par·a-a·mi·no·ben·zo·ic acid (par′ə ə mē′nō ben zō′ik, -am′ə nō′-) a crystalline compound, $C_7H_7NO_2$, considered a member of the vitamin B complex

par·a·ble (par′ə b′l) ***n.*** [< MFr. < LL. < L. < Gr. *parabolē,* a comparing: ult. < *para-,* beside + *ballein,* to throw] a short, simple story teaching a moral or religious lesson

pa·rab·o·la (pə rab′ə lə) ***n.*** [ModL. < Gr. *parabolē:* see prec.] *Geom.* a plane curve formed by the intersection of a cone with a plane parallel to its side

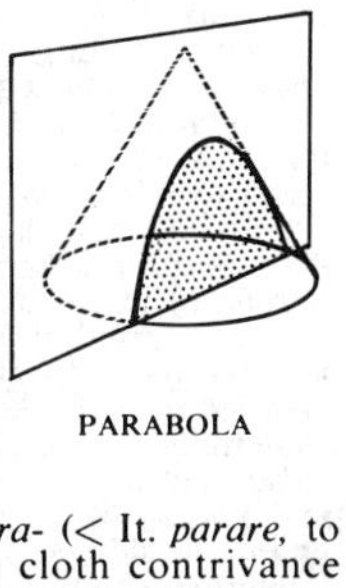

PARABOLA

par·a·bol·ic[1] (par′ə bäl′ik) ***adj.*** of, like, or expressed by a parable: also **par′a·bol′i·cal** —**par′a·bol′i·cal·ly** ***adv.***

par·a·bol·ic[2] (par′ə bäl′ik) ***adj.*** **1.** of or like a parabola **2.** concave with the regular outline of a parabola, as a reflector —**par′a·bol′i·cal·ly** ***adv.***

Par·a·cel·sus (par′ə sel′səs), **Phi·lip·pus Au·re·o·lus** (fi lip′əs ô rē′ə ləs) (born *Theophrastus Bombastus von Hohenheim*) 1493–1541; Swiss physician & alchemist

par·a·chute (par′ə sho͞ot′) ***n.*** [Fr. < *para-* (< It. *parare,* to ward off) + *chute,* a fall] **1.** a large cloth contrivance shaped like an umbrella when it opens up, used to retard the speed of a person or thing dropping from an airplane, etc. **2.** something shaped like or having the effect of a parachute —***vt., vi.*** **-chut′ed, -chut′ing** to drop or descend by parachute —**par′a·chut′ist** ***n.***

pa·rade (pə rād′) ***n.*** [Fr. < Sp. *parada,* ult. < L. *parare,* to prepare] **1.** ostentatious display **2.** *a)* a military assembly; esp., a review of marching troops *b)* a place where troops assemble regularly for parade **3.** any organized procession or march, as for display **4.** *a)* a public walk or promenade *b)* persons promenading —***vt.*** **-rad′ed, -rad′ing 1.** to bring together (troops, etc.) for inspection or display **2.** to march or walk through (the streets, etc.), as for display **3.** to show off *[*he *parades* his knowledge*]* —***vi.*** **1.** to march in a parade **2.** to walk about ostentatiously **3.** to assemble in military formation for review or display —**on parade** on display —**pa·rad′er** ***n.***

par·a·digm (par′ə dim, -dīm′) ***n.*** [< Fr. < LL. < Gr. < *para,* beside + *deigma,* example < *deiknynai,* to show] **1.** a pattern, example, or model **2.** *Gram.* an example of a declension or conjugation, giving all the inflectional forms of a word —**par′a·dig·mat′ic** (-dig mat′ik) ***adj.***

par·a·dise (par′ə dīs′) ***n.*** [< OFr. < LL. < L. < Gr. *paradeisos,* a garden] **1.** [P-] the garden of Eden **2.** *same as* HEAVEN **3.** any place or state of perfection, happiness, etc. —**par′a·di·si′a·cal** (-di sī′ə k′l), **par′a·dis′i·ac′** (-dis′ē ak′) ***adj.***

par·a·dox (par′ə däks′) ***n.*** [< L. < Gr. < *para-,* beyond + *doxa,* opinion < *dokein,* to think] **1.** a statement that seems contradictory, absurd, etc. but may be true in fact **2.** a statement that contradicts itself and is false **3.** a person, situation, etc. that seems inconsistent or full of contradictions —**par′a·dox′i·cal** ***adj.*** —**par′a·dox′i·cal·ly** ***adv.***

par·af·fin (par′ə fin) ***n.*** [G. < L. *parum,* too little + *affinis,* akin: from its chemical inertness] **1.** a white, waxy substance consisting of a mixture of hydrocarbons, distilled from petroleum and used for making candles, sealing jars, etc. **2.** *Chem.* any hydrocarbon of the methane series —***vt.*** to coat or impregnate with paraffin

paraffin series *same as* METHANE SERIES

par·a·gon (par′ə gän′, -gən) ***n.*** [MFr. < It. *paragone,* touchstone < Gr. < *para-,* against + *akonē,* whetstone] a model of perfection or excellence

par·a·graph (par′ə graf′) ***n.*** [< OFr. < ML. < Gr. *paragraphos* < *para-,* beside + *graphein,* to write] **1.** a distinct section of a chapter, letter, etc. dealing with a particular point: it is begun on a new line, often indented **2.** a mark (¶) used as by proofreaders to indicate the beginning of a paragraph **3.** a brief item in a newspaper or magazine —***vt.*** **1.** to write about in paragraphs **2.** to arrange in paragraphs —**par′a·graph′ic** ***adj.***

Par·a·guay (par′ə gwā′, -gwī′; *Sp.* pä rä gwī′) **1.** inland country in SC S. America: 157,042 sq. mi.; pop. 2,303,000; cap. Asunción **2.** river flowing from S Brazil through Paraguay into the Paraná —**Par′a·guay′an** ***adj., n.***

Paraguay tea *same as* MATÉ

par·a·keet (par′ə kēt′) ***n.*** [MFr. *paroquet,* prob. < *perrot,* parrot] any of various small, slender parrots with a long, tapering tail

par·a·le·gal (par′ə lē′gəl) ***adj.*** [PARA- + LEGAL] designating or of persons trained to aid lawyers but not licensed to practice law —***n.*** a person doing paralegal work

par·al·lax (par′ə laks′) ***n.*** [< Fr. < Gr. < *para-,* beyond + *allassein,* to change] **1.** the apparent change in the position of an object resulting from a change in the viewer's position **2.** the amount of such change; specif., *Astron.* the apparent difference in the position of a heavenly body with reference to some point on the surface of the earth and some other point, as the center of the earth —**par′al·lac′tic** ***adj.***

par·al·lel (par′ə lel′, -ləl) ***adj.*** [< Fr. < L. < Gr. < *para-,* side by side + *allēlos,* one another] **1.** extending in the same direction and at a constant distance apart, so as never to meet, as lines, planes, etc. **2.** having parallel parts or movements, as some machines **3.** *a)* similar or corresponding, as in purpose, time, or essential parts *b)* having a balanced arrangement, esp. of phrases or clauses *[parallel* structure*]* **4.** *Elec.* designating a circuit in parallel —***adv.*** in a parallel manner —***n.*** **1.** a parallel line, surface, etc. **2.** any person or thing similar or corresponding to another; counterpart **3.** a being parallel **4.** any comparison showing likeness **5.** *a)* any of the imaginary lines parallel to the equator and representing degrees of latitude *b)* such a line drawn on a map or globe: in full, **parallel of latitude 6.** [*pl.*] a sign (∥) used as a reference mark **7.** *Elec.* a circuit connection in which the negative terminals are joined to

fat, āpe, cär, ten, ēven, is, bīte; gō, hôrn, to͞ol, look; oil, out; up, fur; get; joy; yet; chin; she; thin, *th*en; zh, leisure; ŋ, ring; ə for *a* in *ago, e* in *agent, i* in *sanity, o* in *comply, u* in *focus;* ′ as in *able* (ā′b′l); Fr. bål; ë, Fr. coeur; ö, Fr. feu; Fr. mon; ô, Fr. coq; ü, Fr. duc; r, Fr. cri; H, G. ich; kh, G. doch; ‡foreign; *hypothetical; < derived from. See inside front cover.

one conductor and the positive to another: usually in phrase, **in parallel** —*vt.* **-al·leled′** or **-al·lelled′, -al·lel′ing** or **-al·lel′ling** **1.** *a)* to make (one thing) parallel to another *b)* to make parallel to each other **2.** to be parallel with [the road *parallels* the river] **3.** to compare (things) in order to show similarity **4.** to be or find a counterpart for; match

parallel bars two parallel, horizontal bars set on adjustable upright posts: used in gymnastics

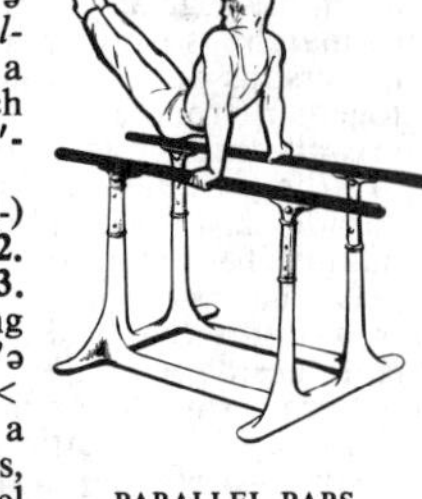

PARALLEL BARS

par·al·lel·e·pi·ped (par′ə lel′ə pī′pid, -pip′id) *n.* [< Gr. *parallēlos,* parallel + *epipedos,* plane] a solid with six faces, each of which is a parallelogram: also **par′al·lel′e·pip′e·don′** (-pip′ə dän′)

par·al·lel·ism (par′ə lel iz′m, -ləl-) *n.* **1.** the state of being parallel **2.** close resemblance; similarity **3.** use of parallel structure in writing

par·al·lel·o·gram (par′ə lel′ə gram′) *n.* [< Fr. < L. < Gr. < *parallēlos,* PARALLEL + *grammē,* a line] a plane figure with four sides, having the opposite sides parallel and equal

pa·ral·y·sis (pə ral′ə sis) *n., pl.* **-ses′** (-sēz′) [L. < Gr. < *paralyein,* to loosen at the side < *para-,* beside + *lyein,* to loose] **1.** partial or complete loss of the power of motion or sensation, esp. voluntary motion, in some part or all of the body **2.** any condition of helpless inactivity or inability to act —**par·a·lyt·ic** (par′ə lit′ik) *adj., n.*

par·a·lyze (par′ə līz′) *vt.* **-lyzed′, -lyz′ing** **1.** to cause paralysis in **2.** to make inactive, ineffective, or powerless —**par′a·ly·za′tion** *n.* —**par′a·lyz′er** *n.*

Par·a·mar·i·bo (par′ə mar′i bō′) seaport & capital of Suriname: pop. c.150,000

par·a·me·ci·um (par′ə mē′shē əm, -sē əm) *n., pl.* **-ci·a** (-ə) [ModL. < Gr. *paramēkēs,* oval] a one-celled, elongated protozoan that moves by means of cilia

par·a·med·ic[1] (par′ə med′ik) *n.* [< PARA(CHUTE) + MEDIC[1]] a medic, esp. a medical corpsman, who parachutes to combat or rescue areas

par·a·med·ic[2] (par′ə med′ik) *n.* [back-formation < ff.] a person in paramedical work

par·a·med·i·cal (par′ə med′i k'l) *adj.* [PARA- + MEDICAL] designating or of auxiliary medical personnel, as midwives, corpsmen, nurses' aides, etc.

pa·ram·e·ter (pə ram′ə tər) *n.* [< ModL. < Gr. *para,* alongside + *metron,* measure] **1.** *Math.* a quantity whose value varies with the circumstances of its application **2.** any constant, with variable values, used as a reference for other variables —**par·a·met·ric** (par′ə met′rik) *adj.*

par·a·mil·i·tar·y (par′ə mil′ə ter′ē) *adj.* [PARA- + MILITARY] designating or of forces working along with, or in place of, a regular military organization, often as a semiofficial or secret auxiliary

par·a·mount (par′ə mount′) *adj.* [< Anglo-Fr. < OFr. *par* (L. *per*), by + *amont* (< L. *ad montem*), uphill] ranking higher than any other; chief; supreme —*n.* a supreme ruler; overlord —**par′a·mount′cy** (-sē) *n.* —**par′a·mount′ly** *adv.*

par·a·mour (par′ə moor′) *n.* [< OFr. *par amour,* with love] **1.** a lover; esp., the illicit sexual partner of a married person **2.** [Archaic] a sweetheart

Pa·ra·ná (pä′rä nä′) river flowing from S Brazil through NE Argentina into the Río de la Plata

par·a·noi·a (par′ə noi′ə) *n.* [ModL. < Gr. < *para-,* beside + *nous,* the mind] a mental disorder characterized by systematized delusions, as of grandeur or, esp., persecution —**par′a·noid′, par′a·noi′ac** (-ak) *adj., n.* —**par′a·noi′dal** *adj.*

par·a·pet (par′ə pit, -pet′) *n.* [Fr. < It. < *parare,* to guard + *petto,* breast < L. *pectus*] **1.** a wall or bank for screening troops from enemy fire **2.** a low wall or railing, as on a balcony or bridge

par·a·pher·na·li·a (par′ə fər nāl′yə, -fə nāl′-; -nā′lē ə) *n.pl.* [*often with sing. v.*] [ML. < LL. *parapherna* < Gr. < *para-,* beyond + *phernē,* a dowry] **1.** personal belongings **2.** equipment; apparatus; gear

par·a·phrase (par′ə frāz′) *n.* [Fr. < L. < Gr. *paraphrasis,* ult. < *para-,* beyond + *phrazein,* to tell] a rewording of the meaning of something spoken or written —*vt., vi.* **-phrased′, -phras′ing** to express in a paraphrase —**par′a·phras′er, par′a·phrast′** (-frast′) *n.* —**par′a·phras′tic** *adj.*

par·a·ple·gi·a (par′ə plē′jē ə, -jə) *n.* [ModL. < Gr. *paraplēgia,* a stroke at one side: see PARA- & -PLEGIA] paralysis of the entire lower half of the body —**par′a·ple′gic** (-plē′jik, -plej′ik) *adj., n.*

par·a·pro·fes·sion·al (-prə fesh′ən 'l) *n.* a worker trained to perform certain functions, as in medicine, but not licensed to practice as a professional

par·a·psy·chol·o·gy (-sī käl′ə jē) *n.* [PARA- + PSYCHOLOGY] the study of such psychic phenomena as telepathy, ESP, etc.

Pará rubber crude rubber obtained from several tropical S. American trees

par·a·site (par′ə sīt′) *n.* [< L. < Gr. *parasitos,* one who eats at the table of another < *para-,* beside + *sitos,* food] **1.** a person who lives at others' expense without making any useful return **2.** a plant or animal that lives on or within another from which it derives sustenance —**par′a·sit′ic** (-sit′ik), **par′a·sit′i·cal** *adj.* —**par′a·sit′i·cal·ly** *adv.* —**par′a·sit′ism** (-sīt′iz′m) *n.*

par·a·sit·ize (-si tīz′, -sī-) *vt.* **-ized′, -iz′ing** **1.** to live on, in, or with as a parasite **2.** to infest with parasites

par·a·si·tol·o·gy (par′ə sī täl′ə jē, -si-) *n.* the science dealing with parasites —**par′a·si·tol′o·gist** *n.*

par·a·sol (par′ə sôl′, -säl′) *n.* [Fr. < It. < *parare,* to ward off + *sole,* the sun] a light umbrella carried as a sunshade

par·a·sym·pa·thet·ic (par′ə sim′pə thet′ik) *adj.* [PARA- + SYMPATHETIC] designating or of that part of the autonomic nervous system whose functions include the slowing of the heartbeat and stimulation of certain digestive glands: cf. SYMPATHETIC

par·a·thi·on (par′ə thī′än) *n.* [< Gr. *para-,* alongside + *theion,* sulfur] a poisonous insecticide, $C_{10}H_{14}O_5NPS$

par·a·thy·roid (-thī′roid) *adj.* [PARA- + THYROID] designating or of any of four small glands on or near the thyroid gland: their hormonal secretions help control the body's calcium-phosphorus balance —*n.* a parathyroid gland

par·a·troops (par′ə tro͞ops′) *n.pl.* [< PARA(CHUTE) + TROOP] troops trained and equipped to parachute into a combat area —**par′a·troop′** *adj.* —**par′a·troop′er** *n.*

par·a·ty·phoid (par′ə tī′foid) *adj.* [PARA- + TYPHOID] designating, of, or causing a disease similar to typhoid fever but milder and caused by various bacteria

‡**par a·vion** (pȧr ȧ vyōn′) [Fr.] by air mail

par·boil (pär′boil′) *vt.* [< OFr. < *par* (< L. *per*), through + *boullir* (< L. *bullire*), to boil: meaning infl. by Eng. *part*] **1.** to boil until partly cooked, as before roasting **2.** to make uncomfortably hot

par·buck·le (pär′buk′'l) *n.* [altered (after BUCKLE[1]) < Early ModE. *parbunkel*] a sling for a log, barrel, etc. made by passing a doubled rope around the object and pulling the ends through the loop —*vt.* **-led, -ling** to raise or lower by using a parbuckle

Par·cae (pär′sē) *n.pl. Rom. Myth.* the three Fates

par·cel (pär′s'l) *n.* [< MFr., ult. < L. *particula:* see PARTICLE] **1.** a small, wrapped bundle; package **2.** a quantity of items put up for sale **3.** a group; pack [a *parcel* of fools] **4.** a piece, as of land —*vt.* **-celed** or **-celled, -cel·ing** or **-cel·ling** **1.** to separate into parts and distribute (with *out*) **2.** to make up in or as a parcel

parcel post a postal service for carrying and delivering parcels (fourth-class mail)

parch (pärch) *vt.* [< ?] **1.** to expose (corn, etc.) to great heat, so as to dry or roast **2.** to make hot and dry **3.** to make very thirsty **4.** to dry up and shrivel with cold —*vi.* to become very hot, dry, thirsty, etc.

Par·chee·si (pär chē′zē) *a trademark for* a game like pachisi, in which dice are thrown —*n.* **[p-]** this game or the game of pachisi: also sp. **par·che′si, par·chi′si**

parch·ment (pärch′mənt) *n.* [< OFr., ult. < L. (*charta*) *Pergamena,* (paper) of Pergamum, city in Asia Minor] **1.** an animal skin, as of a sheep or goat, prepared as a surface for writing or painting **2.** paper treated to resemble this **3.** a manuscript, diploma, etc. on parchment

pard (pärd) *n.* [< OFr. < L. < Gr. *pardos*] [Archaic or Poet.] a leopard, or panther

pard·ner (pärd′nər) *n.* [altered < PARTNER] [Chiefly Dial.] a partner: often clipped to **pard**

par·don (pär′d'n) *vt.* [< OFr. < LL. < L. *per-,* through + *donare,* to give] **1.** to release (a person) from punishment **2.** to cancel penalty for (an offense); forgive **3.** to excuse (a person) for (a minor fault, discourtesy, etc.) —*n.* **1.** a pardoning or being pardoned; forgiveness **2.** an official document granting a pardon **3.** *R.C.Ch. same as* INDULGENCE —**par′don·a·ble** *adj.* —**par′don·a·bly** *adv.*

par·don·er (-ər) *n.* **1.** in the Middle Ages, a person authorized to sell ecclesiastical pardons, or indulgences **2.** a person who pardons

pare (per) *vt.* **pared, par′ing** [< MFr. < L. *parare,* to prepare] **1.** to cut or trim away (the rind, skin, covering, etc.) of (anything); peel **2.** to reduce gradually —**par′er** *n.*

par·e·gor·ic (par′ə gôr′ik, -gär′-) *n.* [< LL. < Gr. < *parēgoros,* speaking, consoling < *para-,* beside + *agora,* assembly] **1.** orig., a medicine that lessens pain **2.** a camphorated tincture of opium, used to relieve diarrhea

pa·ren·chy·ma (pə reŋ′ki mə) *n.* [ModL. < Gr., ult. < *para-,* beside + *en-,* in + *cheein,* to pour] **1.** *Anat.* the functional tissue of an organ, as distinguished from its connective tissue, etc. **2.** *Bot.* a soft tissue of thin-walled cells in plant leaves and stems, fruit pulp, etc. —**pa·ren′chy·mal, par·en·chym·a·tous** (par′eŋ kim′ə təs) *adj.*

par·ent (per′ənt, par′-) ***n.*** [OFr. < L. *parens,* parent, orig. prp. of *parere,* to beget] **1.** a father or mother **2.** a progenitor or ancestor **3.** any organism in relation to its offspring **4.** a source; origin —**pa·ren·tal** (pə ren′t'l) ***adj.*** —**pa·ren′tal·ly** ***adv.*** —**par′ent·hood′** ***n.***

par·ent·age (-ij) ***n.*** **1.** descent from parents or ancestors; lineage **2.** the position or relation of a parent; parenthood

pa·ren·the·sis (pə ren′thə sis) ***n., pl.*** **-ses′** (-sēz′) [LL. < Gr., ult. < *para-,* beside + *entithenai,* to insert] **1.** a word, clause, remark, etc. added as an explanation or comment within a complete sentence and usually marked off by curved lines, commas, etc. **2.** either or both of the curved lines ( ) so used **3.** an episode or interlude —**par·en·thet·i·cal** (par′ən thet′i k'l), **par′en·thet′ic** ***adj.*** —**par′en·thet′·i·cal·ly** ***adv.***

pa·ren·the·size (-sīz′) ***vt.*** **-sized′, -siz′ing** **1.** to insert (a word, etc.) as a parenthesis **2.** to put into parentheses (sense 2)

par·ent·ing (per′ənt iŋ, par′-) ***n.*** the work or skill of a parent in raising a child or children

pa·re·sis (pə rē′sis, par′ə sis) ***n., pl.*** **-ses** (-sēz) [ModL. < Gr. < *parienai,* to relax] **1.** partial or slight paralysis **2.** a syphilitic brain disease marked by dementia, paralytic attacks, etc.: in full, **general paresis** —**pa·ret′ic** (-ret′ik, -rē′-tik) ***n., adj.***

par ex·cel·lence (pär ek′sə läns′) [Fr.] in the greatest degree of excellence; beyond comparison

par·fait (pär fā′) ***n.*** [Fr., lit., perfect] **1.** a frozen dessert of cream, eggs, syrup, etc. in a tall, slender, short-stemmed glass **2.** a dessert of layers of ice cream, crushed fruit, etc. in such a glass

par·he·li·on (pär hē′lē ən, -hēl′yən) ***n., pl.*** **-li·a** (-ə, -yə) [< L. < Gr. < *para-,* beside + *hēlios,* the sun] a bright, colored spot of light on a solar halo —**par·he′lic** ***adj.***

pa·ri·ah (pə rī′ə; *chiefly Brit.* par′ē ə) ***n.*** [< Tamil *paṛaiyan,* a drummer: the pariah was a hereditary drumbeater] **1.** a member of a low caste in India **2.** any outcast

pa·ri·e·tal (pə rī′ə t'l) ***adj.*** [< Fr. < LL. < L. *paries,* a wall] *Anat.* of the walls of a cavity, etc.; esp., designating either of two bones forming part of the top and sides of the skull

par·i·mu·tu·el (par′ə myōō′choo wəl) ***n.*** [Fr., lit., a mutual bet] **1.** a system of betting on races in which the winning bettors share the total amount bet, minus a percentage for the track operators, taxes, etc. **2.** a machine for recording such bets and computing payoffs

par·ing (per′iŋ) ***n.*** a thin piece or strip pared off

‡**pa·ri pas·su** (per′ē pas′ōō, par′ē) [L.] **1.** with equal speed **2.** in equal proportion

Par·is[1] (par′is) *Gr. Legend* a son of Priam: he kidnapped Helen, thus causing the Trojan War

Par·is[2] (par′is; *Fr.* pȧ′rē′) capital of France, on the Seine: pop. 2,591,000 (urbanized area, 8,197,000) —**Pa·ri·sian** (pə rizh′ən, -rē′zhən) ***adj., n.***

Paris green a poisonous, bright-green chemical powder used chiefly as an insecticide

par·ish (par′ish) ***n.*** [< OFr. < LL. < LGr. *paroikia,* diocese, ult. < Gr. *para-,* beside + *oikos,* dwelling] **1.** a district of British local government **2.** an administrative district of various churches, esp. a part of a diocese, under the charge of a priest or minister **3.** *a)* the members of a church congregation *b)* the territory they live in **4.** a civil division in Louisiana, corresponding to a county

pa·rish·ion·er (pə rish′ə nər) ***n.*** a member of a parish

par·i·ty (par′ə tē) ***n., pl.*** **-ties** [< Fr. < L. < *par,* equal] **1.** a being the same in power, value, etc.; equality **2.** resemblance; similarity **3.** equivalence in value of a currency in terms of another country's currency **4.** equality of value at a given ratio between different kinds of money, commodities, etc. **5.** a controlled price for farm products, to keep the farmers' purchasing power at a specified level

park (pärk) ***n.*** [< OFr. < ML. *parricus*] **1.** land with woods, lakes, etc., held as part of a private estate or as a hunting preserve **2.** an area of public land; specif., *a)* an area for public recreation, usually with walks, playgrounds, etc. *b)* an open square in a city, with benches, trees, etc. *c) same as* AMUSEMENT PARK *d)* a large area with natural scenery, preserved by a government **3.** *same as* BALLPARK **4.** that arrangement in an automatic transmission of a motor vehicle that holds the vehicle in place when it is parked **5.** an area for parking motor vehicles **6.** *Mil.* an area for storing and servicing vehicles and other equipment —***vt.*** **1.** to enclose as in a park **2.** to assemble (military equipment) in a park **3.** to leave (a vehicle) in a certain place temporarily **4.** to maneuver (a vehicle) into a space for parking **5.** [Colloq.] to put, leave, or deposit in a certain place —***vi.*** to park a vehicle

par·ka (pär′kə) ***n.*** [Aleutian < Russ.] **1.** a hip-length pullover fur garment with a hood, worn in arctic regions **2.** a similar hooded jacket

parking lot an area for parking motor vehicles

parking meter a coin-operated timing device at a parking space to show the length of time that a parked vehicle may occupy that space

Par·kin·son's disease (pär′kin sənz) [after J. *Parkinson* (1755–1824), Eng. physician] a brain disease characterized by a tremor and muscular rigidity

park·land (pärk′land′) ***n.*** wooded land set aside as, or suitable for, a public park

Park·man (pärk′mən), **Francis** 1823–93; U.S. historian

park·way (park′wā′) ***n.*** **1.** a broad roadway edged or divided with plantings of trees, bushes, and grass **2.** the landscaped center strip or border

Parl. **1.** Parliament **2.** Parliamentary

parl·ance (pär′ləns) ***n.*** [< Anglo-Fr. < OFr. < *parler,* to speak] a style or manner of speaking or writing; language; idiom *[military parlance]*

par·lan·do (pär län′dō) ***adj., adv.*** [It.] *Music* to be sung in a style suggesting or approximating speech

par·lay (pär′lā, -lē; *for v., also* pär lā′) ***vt., vi.*** [< Fr. < It. < *paro,* an equal < L. *par*] **1.** to bet (an original wager plus its winnings) on another race, etc. **2.** to exploit (an asset) successfully *[to parlay one's voice into fame]* —***n.*** a bet or series of bets made by parlaying

par·ley (pär′lē) ***vi.*** [< Fr. *parler,* to speak < LL. < *parabola,* PARABLE] to confer, esp. with an enemy —***n., pl.*** **-leys** a conference; specif., a military conference with an enemy to discuss terms

par·lia·ment (pär′lə mənt) ***n.*** [< OFr. *parlement* < *parler:* see prec.] **1.** an official conference or council concerned with government **2.** [**P-**] the national legislative body of Great Britain, composed of the House of Commons and the House of Lords **3.** [**P-**] a similar body in other countries

par·lia·men·tar·i·an (pär′lə men ter′ē ən, -mən-) ***n.*** a person skilled in parliamentary rules or debate

par·lia·men·ta·ry (pär′lə men′tər ē, -trē) ***adj.*** **1.** of, like, or established by a parliament **2.** conforming to the rules of a parliament or other public assembly **3.** having or governed by a parliament; specif., of a government in which the prime minister holds office only so long as he commands a majority in the parliament

par·lor (pär′lər) ***n.*** [< OFr. < *parler:* see PARLEY] **1.** *a)* orig., a room set aside for the entertainment of guests *b)* any living room: old-fashioned term **2.** a small, semiprivate room in a hotel, etc., used as for conferences **3.** a business establishment, esp. one with specialized services *[a beauty parlor]* Brit. sp. **parlour**

par·lous (pär′ləs) ***adj.*** [ME., contr. of *perilous*] [Chiefly Archaic] **1.** perilous **2.** cunning, shrewd, etc. —***adv.*** [Chiefly Archaic] extremely

Par·ma (pär′mə; *for 1, also It.* pär′mä) **1.** city in N Italy: pop. 172,000 **2.** [ult. after prec.] city in NE Ohio: suburb of Cleveland: pop. 93,000

Par·men·i·des (pär men′ə dēz′) 5th cent. B.C.; Gr. philosopher

Par·me·san (cheese) (pär′mə zän′, -zən, -zan′) [Fr. < It. < *Parma,* city in Italy] a very hard, dry Italian cheese made from skim milk and usually grated for sprinkling on spaghetti, soup, etc.

Par·nas·sus (pär nas′əs) mountain in C Greece: sacred to Apollo and the Muses in ancient times —***n.*** **1.** poetry or poets collectively **2.** any center of poetic or artistic activity —**Par·nas′si·an** (-ē ən) ***adj.***

Par·nell (pär′n'l, pär nel′), **Charles Stewart** 1846–91; Ir. nationalist leader

pa·ro·chi·al (pə rō′kē əl) ***adj.*** [OFr. < ML. < LL. *parochia:* see PARISH] **1.** of or in a parish or parishes **2.** narrow; provincial; limited —**pa·ro′chi·al·ism** ***n.*** —**pa·ro′chi·al·ist** ***n.*** —**pa·ro′chi·al·ly** ***adv.***

parochial school a school supported and controlled by a church

par·o·dy (par′ə dē) ***n., pl.*** **-dies** [< Fr. < L. < Gr. *parōidia* < *para-,* beside + *ōidē,* song] **1.** a literary or musical composition imitating the style of a writer or composer in a nonsensical way, as in ridicule **2.** a weak imitation —***vt.*** **-died, -dy·ing** to make a parody of —**pa·rod·ic** (pə räd′ik), **pa·rod′i·cal** ***adj.*** —**par′o·dist** ***n.*** —**par′o·dis′tic** ***adj.***

pa·role (pə rōl′) ***n.*** [Fr. < LL. *parabola,* PARABLE] **1.** word of honor; esp., the promise of a prisoner of war not to fight further if released **2.** the condition of being on parole **3.** *a)* the release of a prisoner before his sentence has expired, on condition of future good behavior *b)* the freedom thus granted, or its duration —***vt.*** **-roled′, -rol′ing** to release on parole —**on parole** at liberty under conditions of parole

pa·rol·ee (pə rō′lē′) ***n.*** a person on parole from prison
pa·rot·id (pə rät′id) ***adj.*** [< ML. < L. < Gr. *parōtis* < *para-*, beside + *ous* (gen. *ōtos*), ear] designating or of either of the salivary glands below and in front of each ear —***n.*** a parotid gland
-par·ous (pər əs) [< L. < *parere*, to bear] *a combining form meaning* bringing forth, producing, bearing [*viviparous*]
par·ox·ysm (par′ək siz′m) ***n.*** [< Fr. < ML. < Gr. < *para-*, beyond + *oxynein*, to sharpen < *oxys*, sharp] **1.** a sudden attack, or intensification of the symptoms, of a disease, usually recurring periodically **2.** a sudden outburst of laughter, rage, etc.; fit; spasm —**par′ox·ys′mal** (-siz′m′l) ***adj.***
par·quet (pär kā′) ***n.*** [Fr. < MFr. dim. of *parc*, a park] **1.** the main floor of a theater, esp. from the orchestra pit to the parquet circle: usually called *orchestra* **2.** a flooring of parquetry —***vt.*** **-queted′** (-kād′), **-quet′ing** (-kā′iŋ) **1.** to use parquetry to make (a floor, etc.) **2.** to decorate the floor of (a room) with parquetry
parquet circle the part of a theater beneath the balcony and behind the parquet
par·quet·ry (pär′kə trē) ***n.*** inlaid woodwork in geometric forms: used esp. in flooring
parr (pär) ***n.***, *pl.* **parrs, parr:** see PLURAL, II, D, 1 [< ?] a young salmon before it enters salt water
par·ra·keet (par′ə kēt′) ***n.*** *alt. sp. of* PARAKEET
par·ri·cide (par′ə sīd′) ***n.*** [Fr. < L. *parricida*, a relative + *-cida*, -CIDE] **1.** a person who murders his parent or another near relative **2.** the act of a parricide —**par′ri·ci′dal** ***adj.***

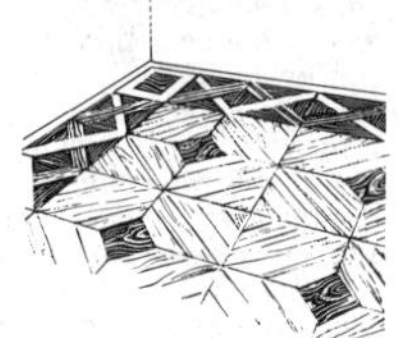
PARQUETRY

par·rot (par′ət) ***n.*** [Fr. dial. *perrot*] **1.** any of several related tropical or subtropical birds with a hooked bill, brightly colored feathers, and feet having two toes pointing forward and two backward: some parrots can learn to imitate human speech **2.** a person who mechanically repeats the words or acts of others —***vt.*** to repeat or imitate, esp. without understanding
parrot fever *same as* PSITTACOSIS
parrot fish any of various related, brightly colored, tropical ocean fishes with parrotlike jaws
par·ry (par′ē) ***vt.*** **-ried, -ry·ing** [prob. < imper. of Fr. *parer* < It. *parare*, to ward off < L. *parare*, to prepare] **1.** to ward off or deflect (a blow, sword thrust, etc.) **2.** to turn aside (a question, etc.) as by a clever or evasive reply —***vi.*** to make a parry —***n.***, *pl.* **-ries 1.** a warding off of a blow, etc. **2.** an evasive reply
parse (pärs) ***vt., vi.*** **parsed, pars′ing** [< L. *pars* (*orationis*), part (of speech)] [Now Rare] **1.** to separate (a sentence) into its parts, explaining the grammatical form, function, etc. of each part **2.** to describe the form, part of speech, etc. of (a word in a sentence)
Par·see, Par·si (pär′sē, pär sē′) ***n.*** [Per. *Pārsī*, a Persian] a member of a Zoroastrian religious sect in India descended from Persian refugees from the Moslem persecutions of the 7th and 8th cent. —**Par′see·ism, Par′si·ism** ***n.***
Par·si·fal (pär′si fäl′, -fəl) the title character in Wagner's opera (1882) about the knights of the Holy Grail
par·si·mo·ny (pär′sə mō′nē) ***n.*** [< L. *parcimonia* < *parcere*, to spare] a tendency to be very careful in spending; stinginess —**par′si·mo′ni·ous** ***adj.*** —**par′si·mo′ni·ous·ly** ***adv.*** —**par′si·mo′ni·ous·ness** ***n.***
pars·ley (pärs′lē) ***n.*** [< OE. & OFr. < L. *petroselinum* < Gr. < *petros*, a rock + *selinon*, celery] a plant of the parsley family, with aromatic, often curled leaves used to flavor or garnish some foods —***adj.*** designating a family of hollow-stemmed, herbaceous plants having umbels, including the parsnip, carrot, etc.
pars·nip (pär′snip) ***n.*** [altered (after ME. *nepe*, turnip) < OFr. < L. *pastinaca* < *pastinare*, to dig up] **1.** a plant of the parsley family, with a long, thick, sweet, white root used as a vegetable **2.** its root
par·son (pär′s′n) ***n.*** [< OFr. < ML. *persona*, orig., person < L.: see PERSON] **1.** a clergyman in charge of a parish **2.** any clergyman
par·son·age (-ij) ***n.*** the dwelling provided by a church for the use of its parson
part (pärt) ***n.*** [OE. & OFr., both < L. *pars* (gen. *partis*)] **1.** a division or portion of a whole; specif., *a*) any of several equal quantities, numbers, pieces, etc. into which something can be divided *b*) an essential, separable element [*radio parts*] *c*) a certain amount but not all *d*) a segment or organ as of the body **2.** a share assigned or given; specif., *a*) duty [*to do one's part*] *b*) interest; concern [*to have some part in a matter*] *c*) [*usually pl.*] talent; ability [*a man of parts*] *d*) a role in a play *e*) *Music* any voice or instrument in an ensemble, or the score for it **3.** a region; esp., [*usually pl.*] a portion of a country; district **4.** one of the sides in a transaction, dispute, etc. **5.** the dividing line made by combing the hair in different directions —***vt.*** [< OFr. < L. *partire* < the *n.*] **1.** to break or divide into parts **2.** to comb (the hair) so as to leave a part **3.** to break up or separate; break or hold apart **4.** [Archaic] to apportion —***vi.*** **1.** to break or divide into parts **2.** to separate and go different ways **3.** to cease associating **4.** *a*) to go away *b*) to die —***adj.*** not total; partial —***adv.*** not fully; partly —**for one's part** as far as one is concerned —**for the most part** mostly; generally —**in good part** good-naturedly —**in part** to some extent or degree; partly —**on the part of one 1.** as far as one is concerned **2.** by or coming from one Also **on one's part** —**part with** to give up; relinquish —**play a part 1.** to behave unnaturally in trying to deceive **2.** to participate: also **take part** —**take some-one's part** to side with someone
part. 1. participial **2.** participle
par·take (pär tāk′) ***vi.*** **-took′, -tak′en, -tak′ing** [< *partaker*, contr. of *part taker*] **1.** to take part (*in* an activity); participate **2.** to take a portion; specif., to eat or drink, esp. with others (usually with *of*) **3.** to have or show a trace (*of*); have some of the qualities (*of*) —**par·tak′er** ***n.***
par·terre (pär ter′) ***n.*** [Fr. < *par*, on + *terre*, earth] **1.** an ornamental garden area **2.** *same as* PARQUET CIRCLE
par·the·no·gen·e·sis (pär′thə nō jen′ə sis) ***n.*** [ModL. < Gr. *parthenos*, virgin + *genesis*, origin] reproduction by the development of an unfertilized ovum, seed, or spore, as in certain insects, algae, etc. —**par′the·no·ge·net′ic** (-jə-net′ik) ***adj.*** —**par′the·no·ge·net′i·cal·ly** ***adv.***
Par·the·non (pär′thə nän′, -nən) [L. < Gr. < *parthenos*, a virgin (i.e., Athena)] the Doric temple of Athena built (5th cent. B.C.) on the Acropolis
Par·thi·a (pär′thē ə) ancient country southeast of the Caspian Sea —**Par′thi·an** ***adj., n.***
Parthian shot any hostile gesture or remark made in leaving: Parthian cavalrymen shot at the enemy while retreating or pretending to retreat
par·tial (pär′shəl) ***adj.*** [MFr. < ML. < L. *pars*, PART] **1.** favoring one person, faction, etc. more than another; biased **2.** not complete or total —**partial to** fond of —**par′tial·ly** ***adv.***
par·ti·al·i·ty (pär′shē al′ə tē, pär shal′-) ***n.*** **1.** the state or quality of being partial; bias **2.** particular fondness or liking
par·tic·i·pant (pär tis′ə pənt, pər-) ***adj.*** participating —***n.*** a person who participates
par·tic·i·pate (-pāt′) ***vi.*** **-pat′ed, -pat′ing** [< L. pp. of *participare* < *pars*, PART + *capere*, to take] to have or take a share with others (*in* an activity, etc.) —**par·tic′i·pa′tion, par·tic′i·pance** ***n.*** —**par·tic′i·pa′tive** ***adj.*** —**par·tic′i·pa′tor** ***n.*** —**par·tic′i·pa·to′ry** (-pə tôr′ē) ***adj.***
par·ti·cip·i·al (pär′tə sip′ē əl) ***adj.*** of, based on, or having the nature and use of a participle —**par′ti·cip′i·al·ly** ***adv.***
par·ti·ci·ple (pär′tə sip′'l) ***n.*** [OFr. < L. < *particeps*, partaking < *pars*, PART + *capere*, to take] a verbal form having the qualities of both verb and adjective Participles are used: *a*) in verb phrases (are *asking*) *b*) as verbs (*seeing* her, he stopped) *c*) as adjectives (the *beaten* path) *d*) as nouns (*seeing* is *believing*) *e*) as adverbs (*raving* mad) *f*) as connectives (*saving* those present)
par·ti·cle (pär′ti k'l) ***n.*** [< MFr. < L. *particula*, dim. of *pars*, PART] **1.** *a*) a tiny fragment *b*) the slightest trace; speck **2.** *Gram.* *a*) a short, usually uninflected part of speech used to show syntactical relationships, as an article, preposition, conjunction, or interjection *b*) an uninflected stem **3.** *Physics* a piece of matter so small as to be considered without magnitude
par·ti-col·ored (pär′tē kul′ərd) ***adj.*** [< Fr. pp. of *partir*: see PARTY] **1.** having different colors in different parts **2.** diversified
par·tic·u·lar (pər tik′yə lər, pär-) ***adj.*** [< MFr. < LL. < L. *particula*, PARTICLE] **1.** of or belonging to a single, definite person, group, or thing **2.** regarded separately; specific **3.** unusual; special **4.** itemized; detailed **5.** hard to please; exacting —***n.*** **1.** a distinct fact, item, or instance **2.** a detail; item —**in particular** particularly; especially
par·tic·u·lar·i·ty (pər tik′yə lar′ə tē, pär-) ***n.***, *pl.* **-ties 1.** the state, quality, or fact of being particular; specif., *a*) individuality *b*) attention to detail **2.** something particular; specif., *a*) a peculiarity *b*) a minute detail
par·tic·u·lar·ize (-tik′yə lə rīz′) ***vt.*** **-ized′, -iz′ing** to specify; itemize —***vi.*** to give particulars or details —**par-tic′u·lar·i·za′tion** ***n.***
par·tic·u·lar·ly (-tik′yə lər lē) ***adv.*** **1.** in detail **2.** especially; unusually **3.** specifically
par·tic·u·late (pär tik′yə lit, -lāt′) ***adj.*** [< L. *particula*, particle + -ATE[1]] of or pertaining to tiny, separate particles —***n.*** a tiny particle
part·ing (pärt′iŋ) ***adj.*** **1.** dividing; separating **2.** departing **3.** given, spoken, done, etc. at parting —***n.*** **1.** a

breaking or separating 2. a dividing point or line 3. something that separates or divides 4. a leave-taking or departure 5. death

par·ti·san (pärt′ə z'n, -s'n) *n.* [MFr. < It. *partigiano* < L. *pars,* PART] 1. a strong supporter of a side, party, or person; often, specif., an unreasoning, emotional adherent 2. any of a group of guerrilla fighters, esp. in a civilian force —*adj.* of or like a partisan Also sp. **par′ti·zan** —**par′ti·san·ship′** *n.*

par·ti·ta (pär tēt′ə) *n.* [It. < fem. pp. of *partire,* to divide < L. *pars,* part] *Music* 1. a kind of suite, esp. of the 18th cent. 2. an air with variations

par·tite (pär′tīt) *adj.* [< L. pp. of *partire,* to part] in parts: often in compounds *[tripartite]*

par·ti·tion (pär tish′ən, pər-) *n.* [< L. *partitio*] 1. division into parts 2. something that divides, as a wall separating rooms 3. a part or section —*vt.* 1. to divide into parts 2. to divide by a partition —**par·ti′tion·er** *n.*

par·ti·tive (pärt′ə tiv) *adj.* [< ML.: see PARTITE & -IVE] 1. making a division 2. *Gram.* restricting to or involving only a part of a whole —*n.* a partitive word or form —**par′ti·tive·ly** *adv.*

part·ly (pärt′lē) *adv.* in part; not fully

part·ner (pärt′nər) *n.* [altered (after *part*) < *parcener,* joint inheritor] one who takes part in an activity with another or others; specif., *a*) one of two or more persons heading the same business enterprise *b*) a husband or wife *c*) either of two persons dancing together *d*) either of two players on the same side or team playing against two others —*vt.* 1. to join (others) together as partners 2. to be or provide a partner for

part·ner·ship (-ship′) *n.* 1. the state of being a partner 2. the relationship of partners; joint interest 3. *a*) an association of partners in a business enterprise *b*) the contract for this

part of speech any of the classes of words of a given language, variously based on form, function, meaning, etc.: in traditional English grammar, the parts of speech are noun, verb, adjective, adverb, pronoun, preposition, conjunction, and interjection

par·took (pär took′) *pt. of* PARTAKE

par·tridge (pär′trij) *n., pl.* **-tridg·es, -tridge:** see PLURAL, II, D, 1 [< OFr. < L. < Gr. *perdix*] 1. a quaillike game bird, orig. of Europe and now also of N. America, with an orange-brown head, grayish neck, and rust-colored tail 2. any of various game birds like the partridge, as the pheasant

PARTRIDGE (to 14 in. long; wingspread to 13 in.)

part song a song for several voices singing in harmony, usually unaccompanied: also **part′-song′** *n.*

part-time (pärt′tīm′) *adj.* designating, of, or engaged in work, study, etc. for periods regarded as taking less time than a full schedule

part time as a part-time employee, student, etc. *[to work part time]*

par·tu·ri·ent (pär tyoor′ē ənt, -toor′-) *adj.* [< L. prp. of *parturire,* to be in labor < *parere,* to produce] 1. giving birth or about to give birth to young 2. of childbirth —**par·tu′ri·en·cy** *n.*

par·tu·ri·tion (pär′choo rish′ən, -tyoo-, -too-) *n.* [< L.: see prec.] a giving birth; childbirth

part·way (pärt′wā′) *adv.* to some point, degree, etc.

par·ty (pär′tē) *n., pl.* **-ties** [< OFr. < *partir,* to divide < L. < *pars,* PART] 1. a group working to establish or promote certain principles of government; esp., a political group which tries to elect its candidates to office 2. any group acting together to accomplish or do something *[a surveying party]* 3. a gathering for social entertainment, or the entertainment itself *[a cocktail party]* 4. a participant in an action, plan, etc. (often with *to*) *[he is a party to the plan]* 5. either of the persons or sides concerned in a legal matter 6. [Colloq.] a person —*adj.* 1. of a political party 2. for a social gathering *[party clothes]* —*vi.* **-tied, -ty·ing** to attend or hold social parties —*vt.* to be host to at a party

party line 1. a single circuit connecting two or more telephone users with the exchange 2. the line of policy followed by a political party —**par′ty-lin′er** *n.*

par value the value of a stock, bond, etc. fixed at the time of its issue; face value

par·ve·nu (pär′və noo′, -nyoo′) *n.* [Fr., pp. of *parvenir* < L. *parvenire,* to arrive] a person who has suddenly acquired wealth or power and is considered an upstart —*adj.* like or characteristic of a parvenu

pas (pä) *n., pl.* **pas** (päz; *Fr.* pä) [Fr. < L. *passus,* a step] a step or series of steps in dancing: in ballet, a **pas de deux** (pä′də doo′) is a dance for two, a **pas de trois** (pät trwä′) is for three, a **pas de qua·tre** (pät kå′tr′) is for four

Pas·a·de·na (pas′ə dē′nə) 1. [< Ojibwa, lit., valley town] city in SW Calif., near Los Angeles: pop. 119,000 2. [after prec.] city in SE Tex., near Houston: pop. 113,000

Pas·cal (pås kål′; *E.* pas kal′), **Blaise** (blez) 1623–62; Fr. mathematician, physicist, & philosopher

Pas·cal celery (pas′k'l) [< ?] a large, dark-green variety of celery with firm stalks

Pasch (pask) *n.* [< OFr. < LL. < Gr. *pascha* < Heb. *pesah,* the Passover] *same as:* 1. PASSOVER 2. EASTER —**pas′chal** (pas′k'l) *adj.*

pasch flower (pask) *same as* PASQUEFLOWER

pa·sha (pə shä′, pä′shə, pash′ə) *n.* [Turk. *pasha*] formerly, in Turkey, 1. a title of honor placed after the name 2. a high official

Pash·to (push′tō, päsh′-) *n.* an Iranian language of Afghanistan and West Pakistan

pasque·flow·er (pask′flou′ər) *n.* [< MFr. < *passer,* PASS[2] + *fleur,* a flower, altered after Fr. *pasque,* PASCH] any of several plants of the buttercup family; esp., a N. American wildflower with hairy leaves and cup-shaped, bluish flowers

pass[1] (pas) *n.* [see PACE] a narrow passage or opening, esp. between mountains; gap; defile

pass[2] (pas) *vi.* [< OFr. *passer,* ult. < L. *passus,* a step] 1. to go forward, through, or out 2. to extend; lead *[a road passing around the hill]* 3. to be handed on from person to person 4. to go or be conveyed from one place, condition, possession, etc. to another 5. to be exchanged between persons, as greetings 6. *a*) to cease *[the fever passed]* *b*) to go away; depart 7. to die (usually with *away, on*) 8. to go by or past 9. to slip by or elapse *[an hour passed]* 10. to make a way (with *through* or *by*) 11. to take place or be accepted without question 12. to be sanctioned or approved, as by a legislative body 13. *a*) to go through a test, course, etc. successfully; satisfy requirements *b*) to be barely acceptable as a substitute 14. to take place; happen 15. to give a judgment, sentence, etc.; decide (*on* or *upon*) 16. to be rendered or pronounced *[the judgment passed against us]* 17. *Card Games* to decline a chance to bid, play, etc. 18. *Sports* to make a pass of the ball, etc. —*vt.* 1. to go by, beyond, past, over, or through; specif., *a*) to leave behind *b*) to undergo (usually with *through*) *c*) to go by without noticing *d*) to omit paying (a regular dividend) *e*) to go through (a test, course, etc.) successfully *f*) to surpass; excel 2. to cause or allow to go or move; specif., *a*) to send; dispatch *b*) to guide into position *[to pass a rope around a stake]* *c*) to cause to go through *d*) to make move past *e*) to cause or allow to get by an obstacle, etc. *f*) to ratify, enact, or approve *g*) to cause or allow to go through a test, course, etc. successfully *h*) to spend (time) *i*) to excrete; void *j*) *Baseball* to walk (a batter) 3. to make move from place to place or person to person; specif., *a*) to hand to another *b*) to put into circulation *[to pass a bad check]* *c*) to throw or hit (a ball, etc.) from one player to another 4. *a*) to give (an opinion or judgment) *b*) to utter (a remark) —*n.* 1. an act of passing; passage 2. *a*) the successful completion of a course or test in school, esp. without honors *b*) a mark indicating this 3. condition or situation *[a strange pass]* 4. *a*) a ticket, etc. giving one free entry or exit *b*) a ticket that permits unlimited rides on a bus, etc. for a specified period *c*) *Mil.* a written leave of absence for a brief period 5. a motion of the hands meant to deceive, as in card tricks 6. a motion of the hand, as in hypnotism 7. *a*) a motion of the hand as if to strike *b*) a tentative attempt 8. [Slang] an attempt to embrace or kiss, often an overly familiar one 9. *Aeron.* a flight over a specified point or at a target 10. *Card Games* a declining of a chance to bid, play, etc. 11. *Sports* *a*) an intentional transfer of the ball, etc. to another player during play *b*) a lunge or thrust in fencing *c*) a walk in baseball —**bring to pass** to make happen —**come to pass** to happen —**pass for** to be accepted or looked upon as *[it is a sham but passes for the real thing]* —**pass off** 1. to cease 2. to take place, as a transaction 3. to be or cause to be accepted as genuine, etc., esp. through deceit —**pass out** 1. to distribute 2. to faint —**pass over** 1. to disregard; ignore; omit 2. to not consider (someone) for a promotion, etc. —**pass up** [Colloq.] to reject, refuse, or let go by, as an opportunity —**pass′er** *n.*

pass. 1. passenger 2. passim 3. passive

pass·a·ble (-ə b'l) *adj.* 1. that can be passed, traveled over, or crossed 2. that can be circulated, as coin 3. barely satisfactory; fair 4. that can be enacted, as a proposed law —**pass′a·ble·ness** *n.* —**pass′a·bly** *adv.*

pas·sage (pas′ij) *n.* [OFr. < *passer:* see PASS[2] & -AGE] 1. the act of passing; specif., *a*) migration *b*) transition *c*) the enactment of a law by a legislature 2. permission, right, or a chance to pass **3.** a journey, esp. by water; voyage **4.** *a)* passenger accommodations, esp. on a ship *b)* the charge for this **5.** a way or means of passing; specif., *a)* a road or path *b)* a channel, duct, etc. *c)* a passageway **6.** an interchange, as of blows or words **7.** a short section of something written or spoken or of a musical composition

pas·sage·way (-wā′) *n.* a narrow way for passage, as a hall, corridor, or alley

Pas·sa·ic (pə sā′ik) [after *Passaic* River (on which the city is located) < Delaware *passajeck,* valley] city in NE N.J.: pop. 52,000

pass·book (pas′bo͝ok′) *n. same as* BANKBOOK

pas·sé (pa sā′, pas′ā) *adj.* [Fr., lit., past] **1.** out-of-date; old-fashioned **2.** rather old

passed ball *Baseball* a pitch that the catcher should have caught but that gets by him, allowing a base runner to advance

pas·sen·ger (pas′'n jər) *n.* [< MFr. < OFr. *passage,* PASSAGE] a person traveling in a vehicle, esp. when not operating it

passenger pigeon a N. American pigeon formerly abundant but now extinct

pass·er-by (pas′ər bī′) *n., pl.* **pass′ers-by′** a person who passes by

pas·ser·ine (pas′ər in, -ə rīn′) *adj.* [< L. < *passer,* a sparrow] of the order of perching songbirds to which most birds belong —*n.* a bird of this order

‡**pas·sim** (pas′im) *adv.* [L.] here and there; in various parts (of a book, etc.)

pass·ing (pas′iŋ) *adj.* **1.** going by, beyond, past, over, or through **2.** only brief; momentary **3.** casual; incidental *[a passing* remark*]* **4.** satisfying requirements *[a passing* grade*]* —*adv.* [Chiefly Archaic] very —*n.* **1.** the act of one that passes; specif., death **2.** a means or place of passing —**in passing 1.** casually **2.** incidentally

passing shot *Tennis* a sharp shot sent past an opposing player who is at the net or moving toward it

pas·sion (pash′ən) *n.* [OFr. < LL. < L. pp. of *pati,* to suffer] **1.** orig., suffering, as of a martyr **2.** [P-] the suffering of Jesus during the Crucifixion or after the Last Supper **3.** *a)* any emotion, as hate, grief, love, etc. *b)* [*pl.*] all of these emotions **4.** extreme emotion; specif., *a)* rage; fury *b)* enthusiasm *[a passion* for music*] c)* strong love or affection *d)* sexual desire; lust **5.** the object of strong desire or fondness —**pas′sion·al** *adj.* —**pas′sion·less** *adj.*

pas·sion·ate (-it) *adj.* **1.** having or showing strong emotions **2.** hot-tempered **3.** intense; ardent **4.** readily aroused sexually —**pas′sion·ate·ly** *adv.*

pas·sion·flow·er (-flou′ər) *n.* [from the supposed resemblance of parts of the flowers to Jesus' wounds, crown of thorns, etc.] any of a number of tropical plants with variously colored flowers and yellow or purple, egglike fruit **(passion fruit)**

Passion play a religious play representing the Passion of Jesus

pas·sive (pas′iv) *adj.* [< L. *passivus* < pp. of *pati,* to suffer] **1.** acted upon without acting in return **2.** not resisting; submissive **3.** taking no active part; inactive **4.** *Gram.* denoting the voice or form of a verb whose subject is the receiver (object) of the action of the verb —*n. Gram.* the passive voice —**pas′sive·ly** *adv.* —**pas′sive·ness, pas·siv·i·ty** (pa siv′ə tē) *n.*

passive resistance opposition, as to a government, by refusal to comply with orders, or by such nonviolent acts as fasting, public demonstrations, etc.

pass·key (pas′kē′) *n.* **1.** *same as: a)* MASTER KEY *b)* SKELETON KEY **2.** any private key

Pass·o·ver (pas′ō′vər) *n.* [PASS[2] & OVER] a Jewish holiday (*Pesach*) of eight (or seven) days beginning on the 14th of Nisan and commemorating the ancient Hebrews' deliverance from slavery in Egypt: Ex. 12

pass·port (-pôrt′) *n.* [< Fr. < *passer,* PASS[2] & *port,* PORT[1]] **1.** a government document issued to a citizen for travel abroad, subject to visa requirements, certifying his identity and citizenship and entitling him to protection **2.** anything making a person accepted or admitted

pass-through (-thro͞o′) *n.* an opening in a wall, as for passing food, etc. from a kitchen to another room

pass·word (-wurd′) *n.* **1.** a secret word or phrase that must be uttered by someone wishing to pass a guard **2.** any means of gaining entrance, etc.

past (past) *rare pp. of* PASS[2] —*adj.* **1.** gone by; ended **2.** of a former time **3.** just gone by *[the past* week*]* **4.** having served formerly *[a past* chairman*]* **5.** *Gram.* indicating a time or condition gone by or an action completed or in progress at a former time —*n.* **1.** time gone by **2.** the history or former life of a person, group, etc.: often used to indicate a hidden or questionable past *[a* woman with a *past]* **3.** *Gram. a)* the past tense *b)* a verb form in this tense —*prep.* **1.** later than **2.** farther on than **3.** beyond in amount or degree **4.** beyond the extent, power, etc. of *[past* belief*]* —*adv.* to and beyond a point in time or space —**not put it past someone** to believe someone is not unlikely (to do a certain thing) *[I* would *not put it past* him to lie*]*

pas·ta (päs′tə) *n.* [It. < LL.: see ff.] **1.** dough made as of semolina and shaped and dried in the form of spaghetti, macaroni, etc. **2.** spaghetti, macaroni, etc. cooked in some way

paste (pāst) *n.* [OFr. < LL. *pasta* < Gr. *pastē,* barley porridge] **1.** *a)* dough for making rich pastry *b) same as* PASTA **2.** any soft, moist, smooth-textured substance *[toothpaste]* **3.** a foodstuff, pounded or ground until creamy *[almond paste]* **4.** a mixture of flour or starch, water, resin, etc., used as an adhesive for paper, etc. **5.** the moistened clay used to make pottery or porcelain **6.** *a)* a hard, brilliant glass for making artificial gems *b)* such a gem or gems **7.** [Slang] a blow or punch —*vt.* **past′ed, past′ing 1.** to make adhere, as with paste **2.** to cover with pasted material **3.** [Slang] to punch —**past′er** *n.*

paste·board (-bôrd′) *n.* a stiff material made of layers of paper pasted together or of pressed and dried paper pulp —*adj.* **1.** of pasteboard **2.** flimsy

pas·tel (pas tel′) *n.* [Fr. < It. *pastello* < LL. *pasta,* PASTE] **1.** *a)* ground coloring matter formed into a crayon *b)* the crayon **2.** a picture drawn with such crayons **3.** drawing with pastels as an art form **4.** a soft, pale shade of any color —*adj.* **1.** soft and pale: said of colors **2.** of pastel **3.** drawn with pastels —**pas·tel′ist, pas·tel′list** *n.*

pas·tern (pas′tərn) *n.* [< MFr. < *pasture,* a tether, ult. < L. *pastor:* see PASTOR] the part of a horse's foot between the fetlock and the hoof

PASTERN

Pas·teur (pas tur′; *Fr.* pȧs tėr′), **Louis** 1822–95; Fr. chemist & bacteriologist

pas·teur·i·za·tion (pas′chər i zā′shən, pas′tər-) *n.* a method of destroying and checking bacteria in milk, beer, etc. by heating the liquid to a specified temperature for a specified period of time

pas·teur·ize (pas′chə rīz′, pas′tə-) *vt.* **-ized′, -iz′ing** [after L. PASTEUR] to subject (milk, beer, etc.) to pasteurization —**pas′teur·iz′er** *n.*

pas·tiche (pas tēsh′) *n.* [Fr. < It. *pasticcio*] **1.** *a)* a literary, artistic, or musical composition made up of bits from various sources; potpourri *b)* such a composition intended to imitate or ridicule another artist's style **2.** a jumbled mixture; hodgepodge

pas·tie (pas′tē) *n. same as* PASTY[2]

pas·tille (pas tēl′) *n.* [Fr. < L. *pastillus,* lozenge < *pascere,* to feed] **1.** a small tablet or lozenge containing medicine, flavoring, etc. **2.** a pellet of aromatic paste, burned for fumigating or deodorizing Also **pas·til** (pas′til)

pas·time (pas′tīm′) *n.* [transl. of Fr. *passe-temps*] a way of spending spare time pleasantly

past master 1. a former master, as in a lodge **2.** an expert —**past mistress** *fem.*

pas·tor (pas′tər) *n.* [< OFr. < L., a shepherd < *pascere,* to feed] a clergyman in charge of a church or congregation —**pas′tor·ship′** *n.*

pas·to·ral (-tər əl) *adj.* [< L. < *pastor,* a shepherd] **1.** of shepherds or their work, etc. **2.** of or characteristic of rural life idealized as peaceful, simple, and natural **3.** of a pastor or his duties —*n.* **1.** a poem, play, etc. having an idealized pastoral setting with shepherds, etc. **2.** a pastoral picture or scene **3.** a letter from a pastor or bishop to those in his charge **4.** *same as* PASTORALE —**pas′to·ral·ly** *adv.*

pas·to·rale (pas′tə ral′, -rä′lē) *n.* [It., lit., pastoral] *Music* a composition suggesting rural scenes or life

pas·tor·ate (pas′tər it) *n.* **1.** the position, rank, or term of office of a pastor **2.** a group of pastors

past participle a participle used: *a)* with auxiliaries and typically expressing completed action or a time or state gone by (as *started* in "he has started") *b)* as an adjective (as *grown* in "a grown man")

past perfect 1. a tense indicating an action or state as completed before a specified or implied time in the past **2.** a verb form in this tense (Ex.: had gone)

pas·tra·mi (pə strä′mē) *n.* [Yid. < Romanian < *pastra,* to preserve] highly spiced, smoked beef

pas·try (pās′trē) *n., pl.* **-tries** [see PASTE & -ERY] **1.** *a)* flour dough made with shortening, as for pie crust, tarts, etc. *b)* foods made with this **2.** all fancy baked goods **3.** a single pie, cake, etc.

pas·tur·age (pas′chər ij) *n. same as* PASTURE

pas·ture (pas′chər) *n.* [OFr. < LL. *pastura* < L. *pascere,* to feed] **1.** grass or other growing plants used as food by grazing animals **2.** ground suitable, or a field set aside, for grazing —*vt.* **-tured, -tur·ing 1.** to put (cattle, etc.) out to graze in a pasture **2.** to graze on (grass, etc.) **3.** to provide with pasture: said of land —*vi.* to graze —**put out to pasture 1.** to pasture (cattle) **2.** to cause to retire from work —**pas′tur·a·ble** *adj.* —**pas′tur·er** *n.*

past·y¹ (pās′tē) *adj.* **past′i·er, past′i·est** of or like paste in color or texture —**past′i·ness** *n.*

pas·ty² (pas′tē, päs′-, pās′-) *n., pl.* **pas′ties** [< OFr. < *paste,* PASTE] [Chiefly Brit.] a meat pie

pat¹ (pat) *adj.* [prob. < ff.] **1.** apt; timely; opportune **2.** exactly suitable *[a pat* hand in poker*]* **3.** so glibly plausible as to seem contrived —*adv.* in a pat manner —**have (down) pat** [Colloq.] to know or have memorized thoroughly —**stand pat** to stick to an opinion, course of action, etc. —**pat′ly** *adv.* —**pat′ness** *n.*

pat² (pat) *n.* [prob. echoic] **1.** a gentle tap or stroke with the hand or other flat surface **2.** the sound made by this **3.** a small lump, as of butter —*vt.* **pat′ted, pat′ting 1.** *a)* to tap or stroke gently, esp. with the hand, as in affection, sympathy, etc. *b)* to tap lightly with a flat surface **2.** to shape, apply, etc. by patting —*vi.* **1.** to pat a surface **2.** to move with a patting sound

pat. 1. patent **2.** patented

Pat·a·go·ni·a (pat′ə gō′nē ə, -gōn′yə) dry, grassy region in the S parts of Argentina & Chile, east of the Andes —**Pat′a·go′ni·an** *adj., n.*

patch (pach) *n.* [prob. < OFr. *pieche,* PIECE] **1.** a piece of material to cover or mend a hole or tear or to strengthen a weak spot **2.** a dressing for a wound **3.** a shield worn over an injured eye **4.** a differing part of a surface area *[patches* of blue sky*]* **5.** a small plot of ground *[a* potato *patch]* **6.** *a)* a scrap of material; remnant *b) same as* BEAUTY SPOT (sense 1) **7.** *Mil.* a cloth insignia of unit identification worn high on the sleeve —*vt.* **1.** to put a patch on **2.** to be a patch for **3.** to make (a quilt, etc.) out of patches **4.** to make or put together crudely or hurriedly (often with *up* or *together)* —**patch up** to end or settle (differences, a quarrel, etc.) —**patch′er** *n.*

patch·ou·li, patch·ou·ly (pach′oo lē, pə chōō′lē) *n.* [Fr., altered < E. *patch leaf* < Tamil < *paccu,* green + *ilai,* leaf] **1.** an East Indian plant that yields a heavy, dark-brown, fragrant oil **2.** a perfume made from this oil

patch pocket a pocket made by sewing a patch of shaped material to the outside of a garment

patch test a test for determining allergy to a specific substance, made by attaching a sample of it to the skin and observing the reaction

patch·work (pach′wurk′) *n.* **1.** anything made of odd, miscellaneous parts; jumble **2.** needlework, as a quilt, made of odd patches of cloth sewn together at the edges **3.** any design or surface like this

patch·y (pach′ē) *adj.* **patch′i·er, patch′i·est 1.** of or like patches **2.** not consistent or uniform; irregular —**patch′i·ly** *adv.* —**patch′i·ness** *n.*

pate (pāt) *n.* [< ?] **1.** the head, esp. the top of the head **2.** the brain or intellect A humorous term

pâ·té (pä tā′) *n.* [Fr.] **1.** a pie **2.** a meat paste

pâ·té de foie gras (pä tā′ də fwä′ grä′, pät′ā) [Fr.] a paste made of the livers of fattened geese

pa·tel·la (pə tel′ə) *n., pl.* **-las, -lae** (-ē) [L., dim. of *patina,* a pan < Gr. *patanē*] *same as* KNEECAP —**pa·tel′lar** *adj.*

pat·en (pat′'n) *n.* [< OFr. < L. *patina:* see prec.] a metal plate, esp. for the Eucharistic bread

pa·ten·cy (pāt′'n sē, pat′-) *n.* the state or quality of being patent, or obvious

pat·ent (pat′'nt; *Brit., & for adj. 2, 3, & 4, usually* pāt′-) *adj.* [MFr. < L. prp. of *patere,* to be open] **1.** *a)* open to public inspection: said of a document granting a right, esp. to an invention *[letters patent] b)* granted or appointed by letters patent **2.** generally accessible or available **3.** obvious; evident *[a patent* lie*]* **4.** open or unobstructed **5.** *a)* protected by a patent *b)* of or having to do with patents *c)* made or sold under a patent —*n.* **1.** an official document granting a right or privilege; letters patent; esp., a document granting the exclusive right to produce, sell, or get a profit from an invention, process, etc. for a specific period **2.** *a)* the right so granted *b)* the thing so protected **3.** any exclusive right or license —*vt.* **1.** to grant a patent to or for **2.** to get a patent for —**pat′ent·a·ble** *adj.* —**pat·ent·ee** (pat′'n tē′) *n.* —**pat·en·tor** (pat′'n tər) *n.*

patent leather leather with a hard, glossy, usually black finish: formerly patented

pa·tent·ly (pāt′'nt lē, pat′-) *adv.* in a patent manner; clearly; obviously; openly

patent medicine a trademarked medical preparation obtainable without a prescription

pa·ter (pāt′ər) *n.* [L.] [Chiefly Brit. Colloq.] father

Pa·ter (pāt′ər), **Walter (Horatio)** 1839–94; Eng. essayist & critic

pa·ter·fa·mil·i·as (pāt′ər fə mil′ē əs, pät′-) *n.* [L.] the father of a family

pa·ter·nal (pə tur′n'l) *adj.* [< ML. < L. < *pater,* father] **1.** of or like a father; fatherly **2.** derived or inherited from a father **3.** related through the father's side of the family *[paternal* grandparents*]* —**pa·ter′nal·ly** *adv.*

pa·ter·nal·ism (-iz'm) *n.* the system of controlling a country, employees, etc. as a father might his children —**pa·ter′nal·ist** *n., adj.* —**pa·ter′nal·is′tic** *adj.* —**pa·ter′nal·is′ti·cal·ly** *adv.*

pa·ter·ni·ty (pə tur′nə tē) *n.* **1.** the state of being a father **2.** male parentage **3.** origin in general

pa·ter·nos·ter (pät′ər nôs′tər; pat′ər näs′tər, pāt′-) *n.* [L., our father] **1.** the Lord's Prayer, esp. in Latin: often **Pater Noster 2.** each large bead on a rosary on which this is said

Pat·er·son (pat′ər s'n) [after W. *Paterson* (1745–1806), State governor] city in NE N.J.: pop. 138,000

path (path) *n.* [OE. *pæth*] **1.** a way worn by footsteps **2.** a walk for use by people on foot, as in a park **3.** a course along which something moves **4.** a course of conduct or procedure —**path′less** *adj.*

pa·thet·ic (pə thet′ik) *adj.* [< LL. < Gr. *pathētikos,* akin to *pathos,* suffering] **1.** expressing or arousing pity, sympathy, etc.; pitiful **2.** pitifully unsuccessful, ineffective, etc. **3.** of the emotions: now only in PATHETIC FALLACY Also **pa·thet′i·cal** —**pa·thet′i·cal·ly** *adv.*

pathetic fallacy the ascribing of human feelings, etc. to nonhuman things (Ex.: the angry sea)

path·find·er (path′fīn′dər) *n.* one who makes a way where none had existed, as in a wilderness

-path·i·a (path′ē ə) [ModL.] *same as* -PATHY

-path·ic (path′ik) *a combining form used to form adjectives from nouns ending in* -PATHY

path·o- [< Gr. *pathos,* suffering] *a combining form meaning* suffering, disease, feeling: also, before a vowel, **path-**

path·o·gen (path′ə jən) *n.* [prec. + -GEN] any microorganism or virus that can cause disease —**path′o·gen′ic** (-jen′ik) *adj.* —**path′o·gen′i·cal·ly** *adv.*

path·o·gen·e·sis (path′ə jen′ə sis) *n.* [ModL.: see PATHO- & GENESIS] the development of a disease: also **pa·thog·e·ny** (pə thäj′ə nē) —**path′o·ge·net′ic** (-jə net′ik) *adj.*

pa·thol·o·gy (pə thäl′ə jē, pa-) *n., pl.* **-gies** [< Fr. or ModL. < Gr.: see ff. & -LOGY] **1.** the branch of medicine dealing with the nature of disease, esp. with the structural and functional changes caused by disease **2.** all the conditions, processes, or results of a particular disease —**path·o·log·i·cal** (path′ə läj′i k'l), **path′o·log′ic** *adj.* —**path′o·log′i·cal·ly** *adv.* —**pa·thol′o·gist** *n.*

pa·thos (pā′thäs, -thôs) *n.* [Gr., suffering] **1.** the quality in something experienced or observed which arouses feelings of pity, sorrow, sympathy, or compassion **2.** the feeling aroused

path·way (path′wā′) *n. same as* PATH

-pa·thy (pə thē) [< ModL. < Gr. < *pathos,* suffering] *a combining form meaning:* **1.** feeling, suffering *[antipathy]* **2.** disease, treatment of disease *[osteopathy]*

pa·tience (pā′shəns) *n.* [< OFr. < L. *patientia* < *pati,* to suffer] **1.** the state, quality, or fact of being patient **2.** [Chiefly Brit.] any game of solitaire

pa·tient (pā′shənt) *adj.* [< OFr. < L. prp. of *pati,* to suffer] **1.** enduring pain, trouble, etc. with composure and without complaint **2.** calmly tolerating insult, delay, confusion, etc. **3.** showing calm endurance *[a patient* face*]* **4.** diligent; persevering *[a patient* worker*]* —*n.* a person receiving medical care —**pa′tient·ly** *adv.*

pat·i·na (pat′'n ə, pə tē′nə) *n.* [Fr. < It.] **1.** a fine greenish crust formed by oxidation on bronze or copper, often valued as ornamental **2.** any surface change due to age, as on old wood

pa·ti·o (pat′ē ō′, pät′-) *n., pl.* **-ti·os′** [Sp.] **1.** a courtyard or inner area open to the sky, as in Spanish and Spanish-American architecture **2.** a paved area, as one next to a house, with chairs, tables, etc. for outdoor lounging, dining, etc.

pat·ois (pat′wä; *Fr.* pȧ twȧ′) *n., pl.* **-ois** (-wäz; *Fr.* -twȧ′) [Fr.] **1.** a form of a language differing from the accepted standard, as a provincial or local dialect **2.** *same as* JARGON (sense 4)

pat. pend. patent pending

pat·ri- [L. < Gr. < *patēr,* father] *a combining form meaning* father

pa·tri·arch (pā′trē ärk′) *n.* [< OFr. < LL. < Gr., ult. < *patēr,* father + *archein,* to rule] **1.** the father and ruler of a family or tribe: in the Bible, Abraham, Isaac, Jacob, and Jacob's twelve sons were patriarchs **2.** a person regarded as the founder of a religion, business, etc. **3.** a man of great age and dignity **4.** [*often* **P-**] *a)* any of certain bishops in the early Christian Church *b) R.C.Ch.* the Pope **(Patriarch of the West)**, or any of certain Eastern bishops *c) Orthodox Eastern Ch.* the highest-ranking bishop at Constantinople, Alexandria, Antioch, Jerusalem, Moscow, etc. —**pa′tri·ar′chal** *adj.*

pa·tri·ar·chate (-är′kit, -kāt) *n.* the position, rank, jurisdiction, etc. of a patriarch
pa·tri·ar·chy (-är′kē) *n., pl.* **-chies** **1.** a form of social organization in which the father is the head of the family or tribe, descent being traced through the male line **2.** rule or domination by men —**pa′tri·ar′chic** *adj.*
Pa·tri·cia (pə trish′ə, -trē′shə) [L., fem. of *patricius:* see PATRICK] a feminine name: dim. *Pat, Patty*
pa·tri·cian (pə trish′ən) *n.* [< MFr. < L. *patricius* < *patres,* pl. of *pater,* father] **1.** in ancient Rome, *a)* orig., a member of any of the Roman citizen families *b)* later, a member of the nobility **2.** an aristocrat —*adj.* **1.** of or characteristic of patricians **2.** noble; aristocratic
pat·ri·cide (pat′rə sīd′) *n.* [< ML.: see PATRI- & -CIDE] **1.** the act of killing one's father **2.** a person who kills his father —**pat′ri·ci′dal** *adj.*
Pat·rick (pat′rik) [L. *patricius,* patrician] **1.** a masculine name **2.** Saint, 385?–461? A.D.; Brit. missionary in, and patron saint of, Ireland
pat·ri·mo·ny (pat′rə mō′nē) *n., pl.* **-nies** [< OFr. < L. *patrimonium* < *pater,* father] **1.** property inherited from one's father or ancestors **2.** property endowed to a church, etc. **3.** anything inherited; heritage —**pat′ri·mo′ni·al** *adj.*
pa·tri·ot (pā′trē ət, -ät′; *chiefly Brit.* pat′rē-) *n.* [< Fr. < LL. < Gr. < *patris,* fatherland] a person who loves and loyally or zealously supports his own country —**pa′tri·ot′ic** *adj.* —**pa′tri·ot′i·cal·ly** *adv.*
pa·tri·ot·ism (-ə tiz′m) *n.* love and loyal or zealous support of one's own country
pa·tris·tic (pə tris′tik) *adj.* [< G. < L. *patres,* pl. of *pater,* father] of the early leaders, or fathers, of the Christian Church or their writings, etc.: also **pa·tris′ti·cal** —**pa·tris′ti·cal·ly** *adv.*
pa·trol (pə trōl′) *vt., vi.* **-trolled′, -trol′ling** [Fr. *patrouiller* < OFr. *patouiller,* to paddle] to make a regular, repeated circuit of (an area, camp, etc.), as in guarding —*n.* **1.** a patrolling **2.** a person or group patrolling **3.** a group of ships, airplanes, etc. used in patrolling **4.** a subdivision of a troop of Boy Scouts or Girl Scouts —**pa·trol′ler** *n.*
pa·trol·man (-mən) *n., pl.* **-men** a policeman assigned to patrol a specific beat
patrol wagon a small, enclosed truck used by the police in transporting prisoners
pa·tron (pā′trən) *n.* [< OFr. < ML., ult. < L. *pater,* father] **1.** a person who is like a father in some respects; protector; benefactor **2.** a wealthy or influential person who sponsors and supports some person, activity, etc. **3.** a regular customer —**pa′tron·ess** *n.fem.*
pa·tron·age (pā′trən ij, pat′rən-) *n.* **1.** *a)* the function or status of a patron *b)* support, sponsorship, etc. given by a patron **2.** favor, courtesy, etc. shown to people considered inferior; condescension **3.** *a)* clientele; customers *b)* business; trade **4.** *a)* the power to appoint to office or grant other political favors *b)* the distribution of such offices or favors *c)* the offices, etc. thus distributed
pa·tron·ize (pā′trə nīz′, pat′rə-) *vt.* **-ized′, -iz′ing** **1.** to act as a patron toward; sponsor; support **2.** to treat kindly but as an inferior **3.** to be a regular customer of (a store, etc.)
patron saint a saint looked upon as the special guardian of a person, place, institution, etc.
pat·ro·nym·ic (pat′rə nim′ik) *n.* [< LL. < Gr. < *patēr,* father + *onyma,* a name] a name showing descent from a given person as by the addition of a prefix or suffix (e.g., *Stevenson,* son of Steven, *O'Brien,* descendant of Brien)
pa·troon (pə tro͞on′) *n.* [Du., protector < Fr. *patron,* PATRON] a person who held an estate with manorial rights under the old Dutch governments of New York and New Jersey
pat·sy (pat′sē) *n., pl.* **-sies** [prob. < It. *pazzo,* an insane person] [Slang] a person easily imposed upon or victimized
pat·ten (pat′'n) *n.* [MFr. *patin,* a clog < *pate,* a paw] a thick wooden sandal or clog
pat·ter[1] (pat′ər) *vi.* [freq. of PAT[2]] to make, or move so as to make, a patter —*n.* a series of quick, light taps
pat·ter[2] (pat′ər) *vt., vi.* [< *pater,* in PATERNOSTER] to speak rapidly or glibly; recite mechanically —*n.* **1.** language peculiar to a group, class, etc.; jargon **2.** glib, rapid speech, as of salesmen, comedians, etc. **3.** idle, meaningless chatter
pat·ter[3] (pat′ər) *n.* a person or thing that pats
pat·tern (pat′ərn) *n.* [< OFr. *patron,* patron, hence model, pattern] **1.** a person or thing considered worthy of imitation or copying **2.** a model, plan, or set of forms used as a guide in making things *[a dress pattern]* **3.** something representing a class or type; sample **4.** an arrangement of form; design *[wallpaper patterns]* **5.** a regular, mainly unvarying way of acting *[behavior patterns]* **6.** a predictable or prescribed route, movement, etc. *[traffic pattern]* —*vt.* to make, do, shape, or plan in imitation of a model or pattern (with *on, upon,* or *after*)
pat·tern·mak·er (-māk′ər) *n.* a person who makes patterns, as for molds or for various articles to be mass-produced: also **pattern maker**
pat·ty (pat′ē) *n., pl.* **-ties** [Fr. *pâté,* a pie] **1.** a small pie **2.** a small, flat cake of ground meat, fish, etc., usually fried **3.** any disk-shaped piece, as of candy
patty shell a pastry case in which individual portions of creamed foods, etc. are served
pau·ci·ty (pô′sə tē) *n.* [< MFr. < L. < *paucus,* few] **1.** fewness; small number **2.** scarcity; insufficiency
Paul (pôl) [L. *Paulus,* Rom. surname, prob. < *paulus,* small] **1.** a masculine name **2.** *Bible* the apostle of Christianity to the Gentiles, author of many Epistles: also *Saint Paul* **3. Paul VI** 1897–1978; Pope (1963–78)
Paul·a (-ə) [L., fem. of prec.] a feminine name
Paul Bun·yan (bun′yən) *American Folklore* a giant lumberjack, who, with the help of his blue ox, Babe, performed various superhuman feats
Paul·ine[1] (pô lēn′) [L. *Paulina,* fem. of *Paulinus:* see ff.] a feminine name
Paul·ine[2] (pôl′īn, -ēn) *adj.* [ModL. *Paulinus*] of the Apostle Paul, his writings, or doctrines
Paul·ing (pôl′iŋ), **Li·nus (Carl)** (lī′nəs) 1901– ; U.S. chemist
paunch (pônch) *n.* [< MFr. < L. *pantex,* belly] the abdomen, or belly; esp., a potbelly —**paunch′i·ness** *n.* —**paunch′y** *adj.*
pau·per (pô′pər) *n.* [L., poor person] **1.** a person who lives on charity, esp. public charity **2.** an extremely poor person
pau·per·ism (-iz′m) *n.* **1.** the condition of being a pauper **2.** paupers collectively Also **pau′per·dom** (-dəm)
pau·per·ize (pô′pə rīz′) *vt.* **-ized′, -iz′ing** to make a pauper of —**pau′per·i·za′tion** *n.*
pause (pôz) *n.* [MFr. < L. < Gr. *pausis,* a stopping < *pauein,* to stop] **1.** a temporary stop or rest, as in working or speaking **2.** hesitation; delay *[pursuit without pause]* **3.** *Music same as* FERMATA **4.** *Prosody* a rhythm break or caesura —*vi.* **paused, paus′ing** **1.** to make a pause; stop; hesitate **2.** to dwell or linger (*on* or *upon*) —**give one pause** to make one hesitant or uncertain —**paus′er** *n.*
pave (pāv) *vt.* **paved, pav′ing** [< OFr. *paver,* ult. < L. *pavire,* to beat] **1.** to cover the surface of (a road, etc.), as with concrete, asphalt, etc. **2.** to be the top surface of —**pave the way (for)** to prepare the way (for) —**pav′er** *n.*
pave·ment (pāv′mənt) *n.* **1.** a paved surface, as of concrete, brick, etc.; specif., a paved street or road **2.** the material used in paving
pa·vil·ion (pə vil′yən) *n.* [< OFr. < L. *papilio,* butterfly, also tent] **1.** a large tent, usually with a peaked top **2.** a building, often partly open, for exhibits, etc., as at a fair or park **3.** part of a building jutting out **4.** any of the separate or connected parts of a group of related buildings, as of a hospital —*vt.* to furnish with or shelter in a pavilion
pav·ing (pā′viŋ) *n.* **1.** a pavement **2.** material for a pavement
Pav·lov (päv′lôf; *E.* pav′lôv), **I·van Pe·tro·vich** (i vän′ pye trô′vich) 1849–1936; Russ. physiologist —**Pav·lov·i·an** (pav lô′vē ən) *adj.*
Pav·lo·va (päv′lô vä; *E.* päv lō′və), **An·na (Matveyevna)** (än′ä) 1885?–1931; Russ. ballet dancer
paw (pô) *n.* [< OFr. *poue* < Frank.] **1.** the foot of a four-footed animal having claws **2.** [Colloq.] a hand —*vt., vi.* **1.** to touch, dig, strike, etc. with the paws or feet **2.** to handle clumsily, roughly, or overintimately —**paw′er** *n.*
pawl (pôl) *n.* [akin ? to Du. *pal,* pole] a mechanical device allowing rotation in only one direction, as a hinged tongue which engages the notches of a ratchet wheel, preventing backward motion

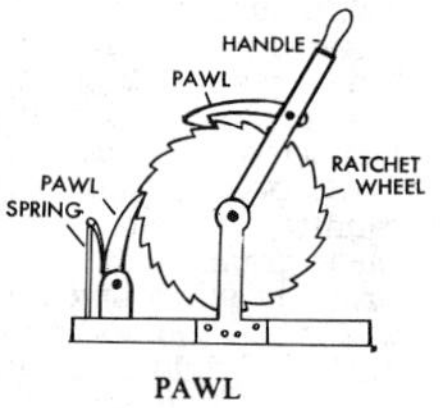

PAWL

pawn[1] (pôn) *n.* [< MFr. *pan*] **1.** anything given as security, as for a debt; pledge **2.** the state of being pledged *[his ring was in pawn]* **3.** the act of pawning —*vt.* **1.** to put in pawn **2.** to stake or risk —**pawn′age** *n.* —**pawn′er, paw′nor** *n.*
pawn[2] (pôn) *n.* [< OFr. < ML. *pedo,* foot soldier, ult. < L. *pes,* foot] **1.** a chessman of the lowest value **2.** a person used to advance another's purposes
pawn·bro·ker (-brō′kər) *n.* a person licensed to lend money at interest on personal belongings left with him as security —**pawn′bro′king** *n.*
Paw·nee (pô nē′) *n.* [< ? Algonquian *pani,* slave] **1.** *pl.* **-nees′, -nee′** a member of an Indian tribe formerly living in Nebraska and now in N Oklahoma **2.** their language —*adj.* of this tribe or their language
pawn·shop (pôn′shäp′) *n.* a pawnbroker's shop
pawn ticket a receipt for goods in pawn
paw·paw (pô′pô′) *n. same as* PAPAW
Paw·tuck·et (pô tuk′it) [< Algonquian, little falls] city in NE R.I., adjacent to Providence: pop. 71,000
‡**pax vo·bis·cum** (paks vō bis′kəm, päks-) [L.] peace (be) with you

pay[1] (pā) ***vt.*** **paid** or obs. (except in phrase *pay out*, sense 2) **payed, pay′ing** [< OFr. < L. *pacare*, to pacify < *pax*, peace] **1.** to give to (a person) what is due, as for goods or services; remunerate **2.** to give (what is due) in return, as for goods or services **3.** to make a deposit or transfer of (money) [to *pay* $10 into savings] **4.** to settle (a debt, etc.) **5.** *a)* to give (a compliment, respects, etc.) *b)* to make (a visit, etc.) **6.** to yield as a recompense [this job *pays* $90] **7.** to be profitable to [it will *pay* him to listen] —***vi.*** **1.** to give due compensation; make payment **2.** to be profitable **3.** to yield return as specified [that stock *pays* poorly] —***n.*** **1.** a paying or being paid; payment **2.** money paid; esp., wages or salary —***adj.*** **1.** operated or made available by depositing a coin [a *pay* telephone] **2.** designating a service, facility, etc. paid for by subscription, fees, etc. [*pay* TV] —**in the pay of** employed and paid by —**pay as you go** to pay expenses as they arise —**pay back 1.** to repay **2.** to get even with —**pay for 1.** to undergo punishment because of **2.** to atone for —**pay off 1.** to pay all that is owed **2.** to take revenge on (a wrongdoer) or for (a wrong done) —**pay out 1.** to give out (money, etc.) **2.** to let out a rope, cable, etc. gradually —**pay up** to pay in full or on time —**pay′er** ***n.***

pay[2] (pā) ***vt.*** **payed, pay′ing** [ONormFr. *peier* < L. < *pix*, pitch] to coat (the seams of a vessel, etc.) as with tar, in order to make waterproof

pay·a·ble (pā′ə b′l) ***adj.*** **1.** that can be paid **2.** that is to be paid (*on* a specified date); due

pay·check (-chek′) ***n.*** a check in payment of wages, etc.

pay·day (-dā′) ***n.*** the day on which wages, etc. are paid

pay dirt soil, gravel, ore, etc. rich enough in minerals to make mining profitable —**hit** (or **strike**) **pay dirt** [Colloq.] to discover a source of wealth, success, etc.

pay·ee (pā ē′) ***n.*** the person to whom a check, note, money, etc. is payable

pay·load (pā′lōd′) ***n.*** **1.** a cargo, or the part of a cargo, producing income: also **pay load 2.** *a)* the warhead of a ballistic missile, the spacecraft launched by a rocket, etc. *b)* the weight of this

pay·mas·ter (-mas′tər) ***n.*** the official in charge of paying employees —**pay′mis′tress** ***n.fem.***

pay·ment (-mənt) ***n.*** **1.** a paying or being paid **2.** something paid **3.** penalty or reward

pay·nim (pā′nim) ***n.*** [< OFr. < LL. *paganismus*, paganism] [Archaic] **1.** a pagan or the pagan world **2.** a non-Christian; esp., a Moslem

pay·off (pā′ôf′) ***n.*** **1.** the act or time of payment **2.** settlement or reckoning **3.** that which is paid off; recompense **4.** [Colloq.] a bribe **5.** [Colloq.] an unexpected or improbable climax or outcome

pay·o·la (pā ō′lə) ***n.*** [PAY[1] + *-ola*, as in *Pianola* (trademark for a player piano)] [Slang] **1.** the paying of bribes or graft for commercial advantage or special favors, as to a disc jockey for promoting a song unfairly **2.** such a bribe or graft

pay·roll (pā′rōl′) ***n.*** **1.** a list of employees to be paid, with the amount due to each **2.** the total amount needed for this for a given period

payt., pay′t payment

pa·zazz (pə zaz′) ***n.*** *same as* PIZAZZ

Pb [L. *plumbum*] *Chem.* lead

PBS Public Broadcasting Service

PBX, P.B.X. [< *p*(*rivate*) *b*(*ranch*) *ex*(*change*)] the telephone connections on the switchboard of an office, company, etc.

pc. 1. piece **2.** price(s)

p.c. 1. percent: also **pct. 2.** postal card **3.** post card

Pd *Chem.* palladium

pd. paid

P.D. 1. per diem: also **p.d. 2.** Police Department **3.** postal district

pea (pē) ***n.***, *pl.* **peas,** archaic or Brit. dial. **pease** [< ME. *pese*, a pea, taken as pl. < OE. *pise* < L. < Gr. *pison*] **1.** a climbing plant with white or pinkish flowers and green seedpods **2.** its small, round seed, eaten as a vegetable **3.** any similar plant —**as like as two peas (in a pod)** exactly alike

peace (pēs) ***n.*** [< OFr. *pais* < L. *pax*] **1.** freedom from or a stopping of war **2.** a treaty or agreement to end war **3.** freedom from public disturbance; law and order **4.** harmony in a group; concord **5.** an undisturbed state of mind; serenity: in full, **peace of mind 6.** calm; quiet —***vi.*** [Obs. except in imperative] to be or become silent or quiet —**at peace** free from war, conflict, etc. —**hold** (or **keep**) **one's peace** to be silent —**keep the peace** to maintain law and order —**make peace** to end hostilities

peace·a·ble (-ə b′l) ***adj.*** **1.** fond of or promoting peace; not quarrelsome **2.** at peace; peaceful —**peace′a·bly** ***adv.***

peace conference a conference for ending a war or for seeking ways to establish lasting peace

Peace Corps an agency of the U.S., established to provide volunteers skilled in teaching, construction, etc. to assist underdeveloped areas abroad

peace·ful (-fəl) ***adj.*** **1.** not quarrelsome; peaceable **2.** free from disturbance; calm **3.** of or characteristic of a time of peace —**peace′ful·ly** ***adv.*** —**peace′ful·ness** ***n.***

peace·mak·er (-mā′kər) ***n.*** a person who makes peace, as by settling the quarrels of others —**peace′mak′ing** ***n., adj.***

peace pipe *same as* CALUMET

peace·time (-tīm′) ***n.*** a time of peace —***adj.*** of or characteristic of such a time

peach[1] (pēch) ***n.*** [< OFr. < VL., ult. < L. *Persicum* (*malum*), Persian (apple)] **1.** a small tree with pink blossoms and round, juicy, orange-yellow fruit with a fuzzy skin and a rough pit **2.** its fruit **3.** the color of this fruit **4.** [Slang] any person or thing well liked —**peach′like′** ***adj.***

peach[2] (pēch) ***vi.*** [ult. < OFr. *empechier*, IMPEACH] [Old Slang] to inform against another

peach·y (pē′chē) ***adj.*** **peach′i·er, peach′i·est 1.** peachlike, as in color or texture **2.** [Old Slang] fine; excellent —**peach′i·ness** ***n.***

pea·cock (pē′käk′) ***n.***, *pl.* **-cocks′, -cock′**: see PLURAL, II, D, 1 [< OE. *pea* < L. *pavo*, peacock + *cok*, COCK[1]] **1.** the male of a species of peafowls, with a crest and long tail coverts having rainbow-colored, eyelike spots: these coverts can be erected and fanned out **2.** any male peafowl **3.** a vain, strutting person —***vi.*** to display vanity in behavior, dress, etc. —**pea′cock′ish, pea′cock′y** ***adj.***

pea·fowl (-foul′) ***n.***, *pl.* **-fowls′, -fowl′**: see PLURAL, II, D, 1 any of a genus of pheasantlike birds of S Asia and the East Indies, including the peacock that is widely domesticated

pea green a light yellowish green

pea·hen (-hen′) ***n.*** a female peafowl

pea jacket [< Du. < *pij*, coarse cloth + *jekker*, jacket] a hip-length, heavy woolen coat worn as by seamen: also **pea′coat′** ***n.***

peak (pēk) ***n.*** [var. of *pike* (summit)] **1.** a pointed end or top, as of a cap, roof, etc. **2.** *a)* the summit of a mountain ending in a point *b)* a mountain with such a summit **3.** the highest point or degree; maximum [the *peak* of production] **4.** *Naut.* *a)* the top rear corner of a fore-and-aft sail *b)* the upper end of the gaff *c)* the narrowed part of the hull, front or rear —***adj.*** maximum [*peak* production] —***vt., vi.*** **1.** to bring or come to a vertical position, as a sail yard **2.** to come or cause to come to a peak

peaked[1] (pēkt; *occas.* pē′kid) ***adj.*** having a peak

peak·ed[2] (pē′kid) ***adj.*** [< ?] thin and drawn, or weak and wan, as from illness —**peak′ed·ness** ***n.***

peal (pēl) ***n.*** [ME. *pele* < *apele*, appeal] **1.** the loud ringing of a bell or bells **2.** a set of bells; chimes **3.** any loud, prolonged sound, as of gunfire, laughter, etc. —***vt., vi.*** to sound in a peal; resound; ring

pe·an (pē′ən) ***n.*** *alt. sp. of* PAEAN

pea·nut (pē′nut′) ***n.*** **1.** an annual vine of the legume family, with brittle pods ripening underground and containing edible seeds **2.** the pod or its seed **3.** [*pl.*] [Slang] a trifling sum

PEANUT PLANT

peanut butter a food paste or spread made by grinding roasted peanuts

pear (per) ***n.*** [< OE. < VL. *pira* < L. pl. of *pirum*] **1.** a tree with soft, juicy fruit, round at the base and narrowing toward the stem **2.** this fruit

Pearl (purl) [< ff.] a feminine name

pearl (purl) ***n.*** [< MFr., ult. < L. *perna*, a sea mussel] **1.** a smooth, hard, usually white or bluish-gray, roundish growth formed around a foreign body within the shell of some oysters and other mollusks: it is used as a gem **2.** *same as* MOTHER-OF-PEARL **3.** anything pearllike in size, color, beauty, value, etc. **4.** the color of some pearls, a bluish gray —***vi.*** to fish for pearl-bearing mollusks —***adj.*** **1.** of or having pearls **2.** like a pearl in shape or color **3.** made of mother-of-pearl [*pearl* buttons] —**pearl′er** ***n.*** —**pearl′i·ness** ***n.*** —**pearl′y** ***adj.*** **-i·er, -i·est**

pearl ash a refined potash

pearl diver (or **fisher**) a person who dives for pearl-bearing mollusks

pearl gray a pale bluish gray

Pearl Harbor [after the *pearl* oysters once there] inlet on the S coast of Oahu, Hawaii, near Honolulu: site of a U.S. naval base bombed by Japan, Dec. 7, 1941

Pearly Gates [Colloq.] the gates of heaven: cf. Rev. 21:21

pear-shaped (per′shāpt′) ***adj.*** **1.** shaped like a pear **2.** full, clear, and resonant: said of sung tones

peart (pirt) ***adj.*** [var. of PERT] [Dial.] lively, chipper, sprightly, smart, etc. —**peart′ly** ***adv.*** —**peart′ness** ***n.***

Pear·y (pir′ē), **Robert Edwin** 1856–1920; U.S. arctic explorer, the first to reach the North Pole

peas·ant (pez′'nt) ***n.*** [< Anglo-Fr. < MFr. < OFr. < *païs*, country < LL. < *pagus*, district] **1.** any person of the class of small farmers or of farm laborers, as in Europe or Asia **2.** a person regarded as coarse, boorish, ignorant, etc.

peas·ant·ry (-'n trē) ***n.*** peasants collectively

pease (pēz) ***n.*** **1.** *pl.* **peas′es, peas′en** (-'n) [Obs.] a pea **2.** *archaic or Brit. dial. pl. of* PEA

pease·cod, peas·cod (pēz′käd′) ***n.*** [Archaic] the pod of the pea plant

peat (pēt) ***n.*** [ML. *peta*, piece of turf < Celt.] **1.** partly decayed plant matter found in ancient bogs and swamps **2.** a dried block of this used as fuel —**peat′y** ***adj.*** **peat′i·er, peat′i·est**

peat moss **1.** *same as* SPHAGNUM **2.** peat composed of residues of mosses, used as a mulch

pea·vey (pē′vē) ***n.***, *pl.* **-veys** [prob. after J. *Peavey*, said to be its inventor, c. 1872] a heavy wooden lever with a pointed tip and hinged hook near the end: used by lumbermen in handling logs: also sp. **pea′vy**, *pl.* **-vies**

peb·ble (peb′'l) ***n.*** [< OE. *papol(stan)*, pebble (stone)] **1.** a small stone worn smooth and round, as by the action of water **2.** clear, transparent quartz or a lens made from it **3.** a surface treated to make it irregular or indented, as on leather (**pebble leather**), paper, etc. —***vt.*** **-bled, -bling** **1.** to cover as with pebbles **2.** to stamp (leather) so as to give it a pebble surface

peb·bly (-lē) ***adj.*** **-bli·er, -bli·est** **1.** having many pebbles **2.** having a pebble surface

pe·can (pi kan′, -kän′; pē′kan, -kän) ***n.*** [< Algonquian *pakan*] **1.** an olive-shaped, edible nut with a thin shell **2.** the N. American tree on which it grows

pec·ca·dil·lo (pek′ə dil′ō) ***n.***, *pl.* **-loes, -los** [< Sp. dim. of *pecado* < L. < *peccare*, to sin] a minor or petty sin; slight fault

pec·cant (pek′ənt) ***adj.*** [< L. prp. of *peccare*, to sin] sinful; sinning —**pec′can·cy** ***n.***, *pl.* **-cies** —**pec′cant·ly** ***adv.***

pec·ca·ry (pek′ər ē) ***n.***, *pl.* **-ries, -ry:** see PLURAL, II, D, 1 [AmSp. *pecari* < native Carib name] a grayish, piglike animal of N. and S. America, with sharp tusks and porklike flesh

peck[1] (pek) ***vt.*** [< ME. var. of *picken*, PICK[2]] **1.** to strike with a pointed object, as a beak **2.** to make by doing this [*to peck a hole*] **3.** to pick up or get by pecking —***vi.*** to make strokes as with a pointed object —***n.*** **1.** a stroke so made, as with the beak **2.** a mark made as by pecking **3.** [Colloq.] a quick, casual kiss —**peck at** **1.** to make a pecking motion at **2.** [Colloq.] to eat very little of **3.** [Colloq.] to criticize constantly —**peck′er** ***n.***

peck[2] (pek) ***n.*** [< OFr. *pek*] **1.** a unit of dry measure equal to 1/4 bushel or eight quarts **2.** any container that will hold a peck **3.** [Colloq.] a large amount, as of trouble

pec·tin (pek′tin) ***n.*** [< Gr. *pēktos*, congealed + -IN[1]] a water-soluble carbohydrate obtained from certain ripe fruits, which yields a gel that is the basis of jellies and jams —**pec′tic, pec′tin·ous** ***adj.***

pec·to·ral (pek′tər əl) ***adj.*** [< L. < *pectus* (gen. *pectoris*), breast] **1.** of or located in or on the breast or chest **2.** worn on the chest or breast [*a pectoral cross*] —***n.*** a pectoral fin or muscle

pectoral fin either of a pair of fins just behind the head of a fish

pec·u·late (pek′yə lāt′) ***vt., vi.*** **-lat′ed, -lat′ing** [< L. pp. of *peculari*, to embezzle] to steal or misuse (money or property in one's care); embezzle —**pec′u·la′tion** ***n.*** —**pec′u·la′tor** ***n.***

pe·cul·iar (pi ky͞ool′yər) ***adj.*** [< L. < *peculium*, private property] **1.** of only one person, thing, group, etc.; exclusive **2.** particular; special [*a matter of peculiar interest*] **3.** queer; odd; strange —**pe·cul′iar·ly** ***adv.***

pe·cu·li·ar·i·ty (pi ky͞oo′lē ar′ə tē, -ky͞ool′yar′-) ***n.*** **1.** a being peculiar **2.** *pl.* **-ties** something that is peculiar, as a trait

pe·cu·ni·ar·y (pi ky͞oo′nē er′ē) ***adj.*** [< L. < *pecunia*, money] **1.** of or involving money **2.** involving a money penalty, or fine —**pe·cu′ni·ar′i·ly** ***adv.***

ped- *same as:* **1.** PEDO- **2.** PEDI- Used before a vowel

ped·a·gog·ic (ped′ə gäj′ik, -gō′jik) ***adj.*** [see ff.] of or characteristic of teachers or of teaching: also **ped′a·gog′i·cal** —**ped′a·gog′i·cal·ly** ***adv.***

ped·a·gogue, ped·a·gog (ped′ə gäg′, -gôg′) ***n.*** [< OFr. < L. < Gr. < *pais*, a child + *agein*, to lead] a teacher; often specif., a pedantic, dogmatic teacher

ped·a·go·gy (-gō′jē, -gäj′ē) ***n.*** [see prec.] **1.** the profession of teaching **2.** the art or science of teaching; esp., instruction in teaching methods

ped·al (ped′'l; *also, for adj. 1*, pēd′-) ***adj.*** [< L. < *pes* (gen. *pedis*), a foot] **1.** of the foot or feet **2.** of or operated by a pedal —***n.*** a lever operated by the foot to transmit motion, as in a bicycle, or to change the tone or volume of an organ, harp, etc. —***vt., vi.*** **-aled** or **-alled, -al·ing** or **-al·ling** to operate by a pedal or pedals; use the pedals (of)

pedal pushers calf-length pants for women or girls, used originally for bicycle riding

ped·ant (ped′'nt) ***n.*** [< Fr. < It. *pedante*, ult. < Gr. *paidagōgos:* see PEDAGOGUE] **1.** a person who emphasizes trivial points of learning, showing a scholarship lacking in judgment **2.** a narrow-minded teacher who insists on exact adherence to rules —**pe·dan·tic** (pi dan′tik) ***adj.*** —**pe·dan′ti·cal·ly** ***adv.***

ped·ant·ry (ped′'n trē) ***n.***, *pl.* **-ries** **1.** the qualities, practices, etc. of a pedant; showy display of knowledge, or an instance of this **2.** adherence to rules

ped·ate (ped′āt) ***adj.*** [< L. < *pes*, foot] **1.** *Bot.* palmately divided into three main divisions **2.** *Zool.* *a*) having a foot or feet *b*) footlike

ped·dle (ped′'l) ***vi.*** **-dled, -dling** [back-formation < *peddler* < ? ME. *ped*, a basket] to go from place to place selling small articles —***vt.*** **1.** to carry from place to place and offer for sale **2.** to deal out or circulate (gossip, etc.) —**ped′dler** ***n.***

-pede (pēd) [< L. *pes*, a foot] *a combining form meaning* foot or feet [*centipede*]: also **-ped**

ped·er·as·ty (ped′ə ras′tē, pē′də-) ***n.*** [< ModL. < Gr. < *pais* (gen. *paidos*), boy + *eran*, to love] sodomy between males, esp. by a man with a boy —**ped′er·ast′** ***n.*** —**ped′er·as′tic** ***adj.*** —**ped′er·as′ti·cal·ly** ***adv.***

ped·es·tal (ped′is t'l) ***n.*** [< Fr. < It. < *piè* (< L. *pes*), a foot + *di*, of + *stal* (< Gmc. hyp. *stal*), a rest] **1.** the bottom support of a column, statue, etc. **2.** any foundation, base, etc. —***vt.*** **-taled** or **-talled, -tal·ing** or **-tal·ling** to furnish with a pedestal —**put** (or **set**) **on a pedestal** to idolize

pe·des·tri·an (pə des′trē ən) ***adj.*** [< L. *pedester* < *pes* (gen. *pedis*), a foot + -IAN] **1.** going or done on foot **2.** of or for pedestrians [*a pedestrian crossing*] **3.** lacking interest or imagination; prosaic; dull —***n.*** one who goes on foot; a walker —**pe·des′tri·an·ism** ***n.***

ped·i- [< L. *pes* (gen. *pedis*), a foot] *a combining form meaning* foot or feet [*pedicure*]

pe·di·a·tri·cian (pē′dē ə trish′ən) ***n.*** a specialist in pediatrics: also **pe′di·at′rist** (-at′rist)

pe·di·at·rics (-at′riks) ***n.pl.*** [*with sing. v.*] [< PED(O)- + -IATRICS] the branch of medicine dealing with the care of infants and children and the treatment of their diseases —**pe′di·at′ric** ***adj.***

ped·i·cab (ped′i kab′) ***n.*** [PEDI- + CAB] a three-wheeled passenger vehicle, esp. in SE Asia, which the driver propels by pedaling like a bicycle

ped·i·cel (ped′i s'l) ***n.*** [< ModL. dim. of L. *pediculus*, dim. of *pes*, a foot] **1.** *Bot.* the stalk of a single flower, fruit, grass spikelet, etc. **2.** *Zool.* *a*) a small, stalklike structure *b*) a small, footlike part Also **ped′i·cle** (-k'l) —**ped′i·cel′·late** (-sel′it, -āt) ***adj.***

pe·dic·u·lo·sis (pi dik′yə lō′sis) ***n.*** [< L. dim. of *pedis*, a louse + -OSIS] infestation with lice —**pe·dic′u·lous** (-ləs) ***adj.***

ped·i·cure (ped′i kyoor′) ***n.*** [< Fr. < L. *pes*, a foot + *cura*, care] **1.** *early term for* PODIATRIST **2.** care of the feet; esp., a trimming, polishing, etc. of the toenails —**ped′i·cur′ist** ***n.***

ped·i·gree (ped′ə grē′) ***n.*** [< MFr. *piè de grue*, lit., crane's foot: from the lines in the genealogical tree] **1.** a list of ancestors; family tree **2.** descent; lineage **3.** a recorded line of descent, esp. of a purebred animal —**ped′i·greed′** ***adj.***

ped·i·ment (ped′ə mənt) ***n.*** [altered (after L. *pes*, gen. *pedis*, a foot) < earlier *periment*, prob. < PYRAMID] **1.** a low-pitched gable on the front of some buildings of Grecian architecture **2.** any similar triangular piece, as over a doorway, etc. —**ped′i·men′·tal** ***adj.*** —**ped′i·men′ted** ***adj.***

PEDIMENT

ped·i·palp (ped′i palp′) ***n.*** [< ModL.: see PEDI- & PALPUS] either of the second pair of appendages of arachnids, developed for grasping, sensing, etc.

ped·lar, ped·ler (ped′lər) ***n.*** one who peddles; peddler

pe·do- [< Gr. *pais* (gen. *paidos*), a child] *a combining form meaning* child, children

pe·dom·e·ter (pi däm′ə tər) ***n.*** [< Fr. < L. *pes* (gen. *pedis*), a foot + Gr. *metron*, a measure] an instrument which measures the distance covered in walking by recording the number of steps

pe·dun·cle (pi duŋ′k'l, pē′duŋ k'l) ***n.*** [< ModL. dim. of L. *pes*, foot] **1.** *Anat., Med., Zool.* a stalklike part **2.** *Bot.* a stalk of a flower cluster or solitary flower —**pe·dun′cu·lar** (-kyə lər) ***adj.*** —**pe·dun′cu·late** (-kyə lit, -lāt′) ***adj.***

peek (pēk) ***vi.*** [< ?] to glance or look quickly and furtively, as through an opening —***n.*** such a glance

peek·a·boo (pēk′ə bo͞o′) ***n.*** a child's game in which someone hides his face, as behind his hands, and then suddenly reveals it, calling "peekaboo!" —***adj.*** made of openwork or sheer fabric, as a blouse

peel[1] (pēl) ***vt.*** [< OFr. < L. *pilare,* to make bald < *pilus,* a hair] to cut away or strip off (the rind, skin, surface, etc.) of (anything); pare —***vi.*** **1.** to shed skin, bark, etc. **2.** to come off in layers or flakes, as old paint **3.** [Slang] to undress —***n.*** the rind or skin of fruit —**peel off** *Aeron.* to veer away from a flight formation abruptly —**peel rubber** (or **tires**) [Slang] to accelerate an automobile quickly —**peel′er** ***n.***

peel[2] (pēl) ***n.*** [< OFr. < L. *pala,* a spade] a long shovellike tool used by bakers for moving bread into and out of ovens

Peel (pēl), Sir **Robert** 1788–1850; Brit. statesman; prime minister (1834–35; 1841–46)

peel·ing (pēl′iŋ) ***n.*** a peeled-off strip, as of apple skin

peen (pēn) ***n.*** [prob. < Scand.] the part of certain hammer heads opposite to the flat striking surface: often ball-shaped (**ball peen**) or wedge-shaped —***vt.*** to hammer, bend, etc. with a peen

peep[1] (pēp) ***vi.*** [orig. echoic] **1.** to make the short, high-pitched cry of a young bird **2.** to speak in a weak voice, as from fear —***n.*** **1.** a short, high-pitched sound **2.** a slight vocal sound —**peep′er** ***n.***

peep[2] (pēp) ***vi.*** [? akin to ME. *piken,* peek] **1.** to look through a small opening or from a place of hiding **2.** to peer slyly or secretly **3.** to show or appear gradually or partially [stars *peeped* through the clouds] —***vt.*** to cause to appear or protrude —***n.*** **1.** a brief look; secret or furtive glimpse **2.** the first appearance, as of dawn

peep·er (-ər) ***n.*** **1.** a person who peeps or pries **2.** [Slang] *a)* [*pl.*] the eyes *b)* a private detective

peep·hole (-hōl′) ***n.*** a hole to peep through

Peeping Tom **1.** *Eng. Legend* the tailor who was struck blind after peeping at Lady Godiva **2.** [**p- T-**] a person who gets pleasure, esp. sexual pleasure, from furtively watching others

peer[1] (pir) ***n.*** [< OFr. *per* < L. *par,* an equal] **1.** one that has the same rank, value, etc. as another; specif., an equal before the law **2.** a noble; esp., a British duke, marquess, earl, viscount, or baron

peer[2] (pir) ***vi.*** [? short for APPEAR] **1.** to look closely, as in trying to see more clearly **2.** to come partly into sight **3.** [Poet.] to appear

peer·age (pir′ij) ***n.*** **1.** all the peers of a particular country **2.** the rank or dignity of a peer **3.** a book or list of peers with their lineage

peer·ess (-is) ***n.*** **1.** the wife of a peer **2.** a woman having the rank of peer in her own right

peer group a group of people of about the same age and status and having the same set of values

peer·less (-lis) ***adj.*** without equal; unrivaled —**peer′less·ly** ***adv.*** —**peer′less·ness** ***n.***

peeve (pēv) ***vt.*** **peeved, peev′ing** [< ff.] [Colloq.] to make peevish —***n.*** [Colloq.] **1.** an object of dislike; annoyance **2.** a peevish state

pee·vish (pē′vish) ***adj.*** [< ?] **1.** irritable; fretful **2.** showing ill humor or impatience, as a remark —**pee′vish·ly** ***adv.*** —**pee′vish·ness** ***n.***

pee·wee (pē′wē′) ***n.*** [prob. echoic redupl. of WEE] [Colloq.] an unusually small person or thing

peg (peg) ***n.*** [prob. < LowG. source] **1.** a short pin or bolt used to hold parts together, close an opening, hang things on, fasten ropes to, mark the score in a game, etc. **2.** *a)* the distance between pegs *b)* a step or degree *c)* a fixed level, as for a price **3.** any of the pins that regulate the tension of the strings of a violin, etc. **4.** a point or prong for tearing, hooking, etc. **5.** a point of reference, esp. an excuse or reason **6.** [Colloq.] the foot or leg **7.** [Colloq.] an act of throwing —***vt.*** **pegged, peg′ging** **1.** to put a peg or pegs into so as to fasten, mark, etc. **2.** to maintain (prices, etc.) at a fixed level **3.** to score (points) in cribbage **4.** [Colloq.] to identify or categorize [*pegged* him as a scholar] **5.** [Colloq.] to throw (a ball) —***vi.*** **1.** to keep score with pegs, as in cribbage **2.** to move energetically (with *along,* etc.) —**peg away (at)** to work steadily and persistently (at) —**round peg in a square hole** one in a position, etc. for which he is unfitted: also **square peg in a round hole** —**take down a peg** to lower the pride or conceit of

Peg·a·sus (peg′ə səs) **1.** *Gr. Myth.* a winged horse, symbol of poetic inspiration **2.** a large northern constellation

peg·board (peg′bôrd′) ***n.*** **1.** a small board with holes in it for inserting scoring pegs for cribbage **2.** a piece of boardlike material with rows of holes for hooks to hold displays, tools, etc.: as a trademark, **Peg-Board**

Peg·gy (peg′ē) [dim. of MARGARET] a feminine name

peg leg [Colloq.] **1.** a wooden leg **2.** a person with a wooden leg

peg-top (peg′täp′) ***adj.*** designating trousers that are full at the hips and narrow at the cuffs

peg top **1.** a child's spinning top, pear-shaped with a metal tip **2.** [*pl.*] peg-top trousers

P.E.I. Prince Edward Island

peign·oir (pān wär′, pen-; pān′wär, pen′-) ***n.*** [Fr. < *peigner,* to comb, ult. < L. *pecten,* a comb] a negligee

Pei·ping (bā′piŋ′) *former name of* PEKING

Peirce (purs), **Charles San·ders** (san′dərz) 1839–1914; U.S. philosopher & mathematician

pe·jo·ra·tion (pē′jə rā′shən, pej′ə-) ***n.*** [see ff.] **1.** a worsening **2.** a change for the worse in the meaning of a word

pe·jo·ra·tive (pi jôr′ə tiv, pej′ə rāt′iv) ***adj.*** [< L. pp. of *pejorare,* to make worse < *pejor,* worse] **1.** declining; making or becoming worse: said of a word whose basic meaning has changed for the worse (Ex.: *cretin*) **2.** disparaging or derogatory —***n.*** a pejorative word or form

Pe·king (pē′kiŋ′; *Chin.* bā′jiŋ′) capital of China, in the NE part: pop. c. 7,000,000

Pe·king·ese (pē′kiŋ ēz′; *for n. 3, usually* -kə nēz′) ***adj.*** of Peking, China, or its people —***n.,*** *pl.* **Pekingese** **1.** a native or inhabitant of Peking **2.** the Chinese dialect of Peking **3.** a small dog with long, silky hair, short legs, and a pug nose Also **Pe′kin·ese′** (-kə nēz′)

Peking man a type of early man of the Pleistocene age, known from fossil remains found near Peking

pe·koe (pē′kō; *Brit. often* pek′ō) ***n.*** [< Chin. *pek-ho,* lit., white down (on the young leaves used)] a black, small-leaved tea of Ceylon and India

pe·lag·ic (pi laj′ik) ***adj.*** [< L. < Gr. < *pelagos,* the sea] of the open sea or ocean

pel·ar·go·ni·um (pel′är gō′nē əm) ***n.*** [ModL. < Gr. *pelargos,* stork] any of a group of plants with lobed leaves and showy flowers; geranium

pelf (pelf) ***n.*** [akin to MFr. *pelfre,* booty] **1.** orig., booty **2.** wealth regarded with contempt

pel·i·can (pel′i kən) ***n.*** [< OE. < LL. < Gr. *pelekan*] a large water bird with webbed feet and an expandable pouch in the lower bill for scooping up fish

Pe·li·on (pē′lē ən) mountain in NE Greece: in Greek mythology, the Titans piled Pelion on Ossa and both on Olympus in a futile attempt to attack the gods

pe·lisse (pə lēs′) ***n.*** [Fr., ult. < L. *pellicius,* made of skins < *pellis,* a skin] a long cloak or outer coat, esp. one of fur

pel·la·gra (pə lag′rə, -lā′grə) ***n.*** [It. < *pelle* (< L. *pellis*), the skin + *-agra* < Gr. *agra,* seizure] a chronic disease caused by a deficiency of niacin in the diet and causing skin eruptions and mental disorders —**pel·la′grous** ***adj.***

pel·let (pel′ət) ***n.*** [< OFr. *pelote* < VL. dim. of L. *pila,* a ball] **1.** a little ball, as of clay, paper, medicine, compressed food, etc. **2.** *a)* a crude projectile, as used in a catapult *b)* a bullet, or imitation bullet *c)* a small lead shot —***vt.*** **1.** to make pellets of **2.** to shoot or hit with pellets

pel·let·ize (-īz′) ***vt.*** **-ized′, -iz′ing** to make pellets of the iron-containing particles recovered from low-grade iron (ore) —**pel′let·i·za′tion** ***n.***

pell-mell, pell·mell (pel′mel′) ***adv., adj.*** [< Fr. < OFr. *pesle mesle,* redupl. < *mesler,* to mix] **1.** in a jumbled, confused mass or manner **2.** in reckless haste; headlong —***n.*** confusion; disorder

pel·lu·cid (pə lo͞o′sid) ***adj.*** [< L. < *pellucere* < *per,* through + *lucere,* to shine] **1.** transparent or translucent; clear **2.** clear and simple in style —**pel′lu·cid′i·ty, pel·lu′cid·ness** ***n.*** —**pel·lu′cid·ly** ***adv.***

Pel·o·pon·ne·sus, Pel·o·pon·ne·sos (pel′ə pə nē′səs) peninsula forming the S part of the mainland of Greece —**Pel′o·pon·ne′sian** (-shən, -zhən) ***adj., n.***

pelt[1] (pelt) ***vt.*** [? ult. < L. *pillare,* to drive] **1.** to throw things at **2.** to beat heavily and repeatedly **3.** to throw (missiles) —***vi.*** **1.** to strike heavily or steadily, as hard rain **2.** to hurry —***n.*** a blow —**(at) full pelt** at full speed

pelt[2] (pelt) ***n.*** [prob. < PELTRY] **1.** the skin of a fur-bearing animal, esp. after it is stripped from the carcass **2.** the human skin: a humorous usage

pel·tate (pel′tāt) ***adj.*** [< L. *pelta,* light shield + -ATE[1]] *Bot.* shield-shaped: having the stalk attached to the lower surface within the margin: said of a leaf —**pel′tate·ly** ***adv.***

pelt·ry (pel′trē) ***n.***, *pl.* **-ries** [< OFr. < *peletier,* furrier < *pel,* a skin] pelts, or fur-bearing skins, collectively

pel·vis (pel′vis) ***n.***, *pl.* **-vis·es, -ves** (-vēz) [ModL. < L., a basin] *Anat., Zool.* any basinlike structure; specif., *a*) the basinlike cavity in the posterior part of the trunk of man and many other vertebrates *b*) the ring of bones forming this cavity: also **pelvic girdle** —**pel′vic *adj.***

pem·mi·can (pem′i kən) ***n.*** [< Cree *pemikkân,* fat meat < *pimiy,* fat] **1.** dried lean meat, pounded into a paste with fat and preserved as pressed cakes **2.** a concentrated food of dried beef, suet, dried fruit, etc., used for emergency rations, as by explorers

pen¹ (pen) ***n.*** [OE. *penn*] **1.** a small yard or enclosure for domestic animals **2.** the animals inside it **3.** any small enclosure —***vt.*** **penned** or **pent, pen′ning** to confine or enclose as in a pen

pen² (pen) ***n.*** [< OFr. < L. *penna,* a feather] **1.** orig., a heavy quill trimmed to a split point, for writing with ink **2.** any of various devices used in writing or drawing with ink, often with a metal point split into two nibs: see also BALL POINT PEN, FOUNTAIN PEN **3.** the metal point for this device **4.** *a*) writing as a profession *b*) literary style —***vt.*** **penned, pen′ning** to write as with a pen

pen³ (pen) ***n.*** [Slang] a penitentiary

pen⁴ (pen) ***n.*** [< ?] a female swan

Pen., pen. peninsula

pe·nal (pē′n'l) ***adj.*** [< L. < *poena,* punishment] **1.** of, for, or involving punishment, esp. legal punishment **2.** making one liable to punishment, as an offense —**pe′nal·ly *adv.***

penal code a body of law dealing with various crimes or offenses and their legal penalties

pe·nal·ize (pē′n'l īz′, pen′'l-) ***vt.*** **-ized′, -iz′ing** **1.** to set a penalty for **2.** to impose a penalty on, as for breaking some rule **3.** to put at a disadvantage —**pe′nal·i·za′tion *n.***

pen·al·ty (pen′'l tē) ***n.***, *pl.* **-ties** **1.** a punishment fixed by law, as for a crime **2.** the handicap, fine, forfeit, etc. imposed upon an offender or one who does not fulfill a contract or obligation **3.** any unfortunate consequence **4.** *Sports* a loss of yardage, the removal of a player, etc. imposed for breaking a rule

pen·ance (pen′əns) ***n.*** [< OFr. < L. < *paenitens:* see PENITENT] **1.** *R.C.Ch. & Orthodox Eastern Ch.* a sacrament involving the confession of sin, repentance, and submission to penalties imposed, followed by absolution **2.** any voluntary suffering to show repentance for wrongdoing —***vt.*** **-anced, -anc·ing** to impose a penance on —**do penance** to perform an act of penance

Pe·nang (pi naŋ′) seaport in Malaysia, on an island (**Penang**) off the NW coast of the Malay Peninsula: pop. 325,000

pe·na·tes (pi nāt′ēz) ***n.pl.*** [L.] the household gods of the ancient Romans: see LARES AND PENATES

pence (pens; *in compounds,* pəns) ***n.*** [Brit.] *pl. of* PENNY: used also in compounds *[twopence]*

pen·chant (pen′chənt; *Fr.* pän shän′) ***n.*** [Fr. < *pencher,* to incline, ult. < L. *pendere,* to hang] a strong liking or fondness; inclination

pen·cil (pen′s'l) ***n.*** [< MFr. < L. *penicillus* < dim. of *penis,* a tail] **1.** orig., an artist's brush **2.** the style of a given artist **3.** a pointed, rod-shaped instrument with a core of graphite or crayon, used for writing, drawing, etc. **4.** something shaped or used as a pencil *[a styptic pencil]* **5.** a series of lines coming to or spreading out from a point —***vt.*** **-ciled** or **-cilled, -cil·ing** or **-cil·ling** **1.** to write, draw, etc. as with a pencil **2.** to use a pencil on —**pen′cil·er, pen′cil·ler *n.***

pend (pend) ***vi.*** [< OFr. < L. *pendere,* to hang] to await judgment or decision

pend·ant (pen′dənt) ***n.*** [< OFr. prp. of *pendre* < L. *pendere,* to hang] **1.** an ornamental hanging object, as from an earring **2.** anything hanging, as the pull chain on a lamp **3.** a decorative piece suspended from a ceiling or roof —***adj.*** *same as* PENDENT —**pend′ant·ly *adv.***

pend·ent (-dənt) ***adj.*** [see prec.] **1.** suspended **2.** overhanging **3.** undecided; pending —***n.*** *same as* PENDANT —**pend′en·cy *n.*** —**pend′ent·ly *adv.***

pend·ing (pen′diŋ) ***adj.*** **1.** not decided or established *[patent pending]* **2.** impending —***prep.*** **1.** throughout the course of; during **2.** while awaiting; until *[pending his arrival]*

pen·drag·on (pen drag′ən) ***n.*** [W. *pen,* head + *dragon,* leader < L. *draco,* cohort's standard] supreme chief or leader: a title used in ancient Britain

pen·du·lous (pen′joo ləs, -dyoo-) ***adj.*** [L. *pendulus* < *pendere,* to hang] **1.** hanging freely or loosely; suspended so as to swing **2.** drooping —**pen′du·lous·ly *adv.*** —**pen′du·lous·ness *n.***

pen·du·lum (pen′joo ləm, -dyoo-, -d'l əm) ***n.*** [ModL. < L.: see prec.] a body hung from a fixed point so as to swing freely to and fro under the combined forces of gravity and momentum: often used to regulate clock movements —**pen′du·lar *adj.***

Pe·nel·o·pe (pə nel′ə pē) [L. < Gr. *Pēnelopē*] **1.** a feminine name: dim. *Penny* **2.** Ulysses' wife, who waited faithfully for his return

pen·e·tra·ble (pen′i trə b'l) ***adj.*** that can be penetrated —**pen′e·tra·bil′i·ty, pen′e·tra·ble·ness *n.*** —**pen′e·tra·bly *adv.***

pen·e·trate (pen′ə trāt′) ***vt.*** **-trat′ed, -trat′ing** [< L. pp. of *penetrare* < base of *penitus,* inward] **1.** to find or force a way into or through; enter as by piercing **2.** to see into the interior of **3.** to have an effect throughout; permeate **4.** to affect or move deeply **5.** to understand —***vi.*** **1.** to make a way into or through something **2.** to have a marked effect on the mind or emotions

pen·e·trat·ing (-trāt′iŋ) ***adj.*** **1.** that can penetrate *[a penetrating oil]* **2.** sharp; piercing *[a penetrating smell]* **3.** that has entered deeply *[a penetrating wound]* **4.** discerning *[a penetrating mind]* Also **pen′e·tra′tive** —**pen′e·trat′ing·ly, pen′e·tra′tive·ly *adv.***

pen·e·tra·tion (pen′ə trā′shən) ***n.*** **1.** a penetrating **2.** the depth to which something penetrates **3.** sharp discernment; insight

pen·guin (peŋ′gwin, pen′-) ***n.*** [prob. < W. *pen gwyn,* lit., white head] any of a group of flightless birds of the Southern Hemisphere, having webbed feet and paddlelike flippers for swimming

PENGUIN (to 4 ft. high)

pen·hold·er (pen′hōl′dər) ***n.*** **1.** the holder into which a pen point fits **2.** a container for a pen

pen·i·cil·lin (pen′ə sil′in) ***n.*** [< ff. + -IN¹] any of several antibiotic compounds obtained from certain molds or produced synthetically

pen·i·cil·li·um (-ē əm) ***n.***, *pl.* **-li·ums, -li·a** (-ə) [ModL. < L. *penicillus,* a brush: from the tuftlike ends] any of a group of fungi growing as green mold on stale bread, decaying fruit, etc.

pen·in·su·la (pə nin′sə lə, -syoo-) ***n.*** [< L. < *paene,* almost + *insula,* an isle] **1.** a land area almost entirely surrounded by water, connected with the mainland by an isthmus **2.** any land area projecting into the water —**pen·in′su·lar *adj.***

pe·nis (pē′nis) ***n.***, *pl.* **-nis·es, -nes** (-nēz) [L., a tail, penis] the male organ of sexual intercourse: in mammals it is also the organ through which urine is ejected —**pe′nile** (-nīl, -nil) ***adj.***

pen·i·tent (pen′ə tənt) ***adj.*** [< OFr. < L. prp. of *paenitere,* to repent] sorry for having done wrong and willing to atone; repentant —***n.*** **1.** a penitent person **2.** *R.C.Ch.* a person undergoing penance —**pen′i·tence *n.*** —**pen′i·tent·ly *adv.***

pen·i·ten·tial (pen′ə ten′shəl) ***adj.*** of, constituting, or expressing penitence or penance —***n.*** **1.** a penitent **2.** a list or book of rules governing religious penance —**pen′i·ten′tial·ly *adv.***

pen·i·ten·tia·ry (pen′ə ten′shə rē) ***adj.*** [< ML. < L.: see PENITENT] **1.** of or for penance **2.** used in punishing and reforming **3.** making one liable to imprisonment in a penitentiary —***n.***, *pl.* **-ries** a prison; specif., a State or Federal prison for persons convicted of serious crimes

pen·knife (pen′nīf′) ***n.***, *pl.* **-knives′** (-nīvz′) a small pocketknife; orig., one used in making quill pens

pen·light, pen·lite (pen′līt′) ***n.*** a flashlight that is as small and slender as a fountain pen

pen·man (pen′mən) ***n.***, *pl.* **-men** **1.** a person employed to write or copy; scribe **2.** a person skilled in penmanship **3.** an author

pen·man·ship (-ship′) ***n.*** **1.** handwriting as an art or skill **2.** a style of handwriting

Penn (pen), **William** 1644–1718; Eng. Quaker leader: founder of Pennsylvania

Penn., Penna. Pennsylvania

pen name a name used by an author in place of his true name; nom de plume

pen·nant (pen′ənt) ***n.*** [< PENNON, altered after PENDANT] **1.** any long, narrow flag **2.** any such flag symbolizing a championship, esp. in baseball

pen·ni (pen′ē) ***n.***, *pl.* **-ni·a** (-ə), **-nis, -ni** [Finn., akin to PENNY] *see* MONETARY UNITS, table (Finland)

pen·ni·less (pen′i lis) ***adj.*** without even a penny; extremely poor —**pen′ni·less·ness *n.***

Pen·nine Alps (pen′īn, -in) division of the W Alps, along the Swiss-Italian border

pen·non (pen′ən) ***n.*** [< OFr. < *penne:* see PEN²] **1.** a long, narrow, triangular or swallow-tailed flag used as an ensign by knights or lancers **2.** any flag or pennant **3.** a pinion; wing

Penn·syl·va·ni·a (pen′s'l vān′yə, -vā′nē ə) [after Wm. PENN + L. *sylvania,* wooded (land), ult. < *sylva,* forest] State of the NE U.S.: 45,333 sq. mi.; pop. 11,867,000; cap. Harrisburg: abbrev. **Pa., PA**

Pennsylvania Dutch **1.** the descendants of early German immigrants, who settled mainly in E Pennsylvania **2.** their High German dialect: also called **Pennsylvania German** **3.** their folk art, featuring stylized decorations of flowers, birds, etc. —**Penn′syl·va′ni·a-Dutch′** *adj.*

Penn·syl·va·ni·an (pen′s'l vān′yən, -vā′nē ən) *adj.* **1.** of Pennsylvania **2.** designating or of the sixth period of the Paleozoic Era in N. America —*n.* a native or inhabitant of Pennsylvania —**the Pennsylvanian** the Pennsylvanian Period or its rocks: see GEOLOGY, chart

pen·ny (pen′ē) *n., pl.* **-nies;** for 1 (esp. collectively), **pence** [OE. *pening,* ult. < L. *pannus,* cloth (a medium of exchange)] **1.** in the United Kingdom and certain Commonwealth countries, *a)* formerly, a unit of currency equal to one twelfth of a shilling *b)* a unit of currency equal to one 100th part of a pound: in full, **new penny** **2.** a U.S. or Canadian cent **3.** a sum of money —**a pretty penny** [Colloq.] a large sum of money

-pen·ny (pen′ē) *a combining form meaning* costing (a specified number of) pennies *[sixpenny]* : as applied to nails, now a measure of their length

penny arcade a public amusement hall with various coin-operated game and vending machines

penny pincher a person who is extremely frugal or stingy —**pen′ny-pinch′ing** *n., adj.*

pen·ny·roy·al (pen′ē roi′əl) *n.* [< Anglo-Fr. < OFr. *poliol* (< L. *pulegium,* fleabane) + *real,* royal] **1.** a European mint with lavender flowers **2.** a similar N. American mint that yields an aromatic oil

pen·ny·weight (pen′ē wāt′) *n.* a unit of weight, equal to 24 grains or 1/20 ounce troy weight

pen·ny-wise (pen′ē wīz′) *adj.* careful or thrifty in small matters —**penny-wise and pound-foolish** thrifty in small matters but wasteful in major ones

pen·ny·worth (-wurth′) *n.* **1.** the amount that can be bought for one penny **2.** the value in money of something paid for **3.** a small amount

pe·nol·o·gy (pē näl′ə jē) *n.* [Gr. *poinē,* penalty + -LOGY] the study of the reformation and rehabilitation of criminals and of prison management —**pe·no·log·i·cal** (pē′nə läj′i k'l) *adj.* —**pe·nol′o·gist** *n.*

pen pal a person, esp. a stranger in another country, with whom one arranges to exchange letters

Pen·sa·co·la (pen′sə kō′lə) [< Choctaw, hair people < *pansha,* hair + *okla,* people] seaport in NW Fla., on the Gulf of Mexico: pop. 58,000

pen·sion (pen′shən; *for n. 3,* pän′sē än′, *Fr.* pän syōn′) *n.* [< MFr. < L. *pensio* < pp. of *pendere,* to pay] **1.** a regular payment, not wages, to one who has fulfilled certain requirements, as of service, age, disability, etc. **2.** a regular payment, not a fee, given to an artist, etc. by his patron; subsidy **3.** in France, etc., *a)* a boardinghouse *b)* room and board —*vt.* to grant a pension to —**pension off** to dismiss from service with a pension —**pen′sion·a·ble** *adj.* —**pen′sion·ar′y** *adj., n.* —**pen′sion·er** *n.*

pen·sive (pen′siv) *adj.* [< OFr. < *penser* < L. *pensare,* to consider, freq. of *pendere,* to weigh] **1.** thinking deeply, often of sad or melancholy things **2.** expressing deep thoughtfulness, often with some sadness —**pen′sive·ly** *adv.* —**pen′sive·ness** *n.*

pen·stock (pen′stäk′) *n.* [PEN[1] + STOCK] **1.** a sluice for controlling the flow of water **2.** a tube or trough for carrying water to a water wheel

pent (pent) *alt. pt. & pp. of* PEN[1] —*adj.* held or kept in; penned (often with *up*)

pen·ta- [Gr. *penta-* < *pente,* five] *a combining form meaning* five: also, before a vowel, **pent-**

pen·ta·gon (pen′tə gän′) *n.* [< L. < Gr.: see prec. & -GON] a plane figure with five angles and five sides —**the Pentagon** a five-sided building in Arlington, Va., housing the Department of Defense; hence, the U.S. military establishment —**pen·tag′o·nal** (-tag′ə n'l) *adj.*

pen·ta·he·dron (pen′tə hē′drən) *n., pl.* **-drons, -dra** (-drə) [ModL.: see PENTA- & -HEDRON] a solid figure with five plane surfaces —**pen′ta·he′dral** *adj.*

pen·tam·er·ous (pen tam′ər əs) *adj.* [PENTA- + -MEROUS] *Biol.* made up of five parts: also written **5-merous**

pen·tam·e·ter (-ə tər) *n.* [L. < Gr.: see PENTA- & METER[1]] **1.** a line of verse containing five metrical feet **2.** verse consisting of pentameters —*adj.* having five metrical feet

Pen·ta·teuch (pen′tə to͞ok′, -tyo͞ok′) *n.* [< LL. < Gr. < *penta-,* five + *teuchos,* a book] the first five books of the Bible

pen·tath·lon (pen tath′län, -lən) *n.* [< Gr. < *penta-,* five + *athlon,* a contest] an athletic contest in which each contestant takes part in five track and field events

pen·ta·va·lent (pen′tə vā′lənt) *adj.* **1.** having a valence of five **2.** *same as* QUINQUEVALENT (sense 1)

Pen·te·cost (pen′tə kôst′, -käst′) *n.* [< LL. < Gr. *pentēkostē* (*hēmera*), the fiftieth (day) after Passover] **1.** *same as* SHAVUOT **2.** a Christian festival on the seventh Sunday after Easter, celebrating the descent of the Holy Spirit upon the Apostles; Whitsunday —**Pen′te·cos′tal** *adj.*

pent·house (pent′hous′) *n.* [< MFr. *apentis,* ult. < L. *appendere,* APPEND] **1.** a small structure with a sloping roof, or such a roof, attached to the side of a building **2.** an apartment or houselike structure built on the roof of a building

pen·tode (pen′tōd) *n.* [PENT(A)- + -ODE] an electron tube containing five electrodes, usually a cathode, anode, and three grids

Pen·to·thal Sodium (pen′tə thôl′) *a trademark for* THIOPENTAL SODIUM: often clipped to **Pentothal**

pent-up (pent′up′) *adj.* held in check; curbed; confined *[pent-up* emotion*]*

pe·nu·che, pe·nu·chi (pə no͞o′chē) *n.* [var. of PANOCHA] a fudgelike candy made of brown sugar, milk, butter, and, sometimes, nuts

pe·nult (pē′nult, pi nult′) *n.* [< L. < *paene,* almost + *ultimus,* last] the one next to the last; specif., the second last syllable in a word

pe·nul·ti·mate (pi nul′tə mit) *adj.* **1.** next to the last **2.** of the penult —*n. same as* PENULT —**pe·nul′ti·mate·ly** *adv.*

pe·num·bra (pi num′brə) *n., pl.* **-brae** (-brē), **-bras** [ModL. < L. *paene,* almost + *umbra,* shade] **1.** the partly lighted area surrounding the complete shadow of a body, as the moon, in full eclipse **2.** the less dark region around the central area of a sunspot **3.** a vague, indefinite, or borderline area —**pe·num′bral** *adj.*

pe·nu·ri·ous (pə nyoor′ē əs, -noor′-) *adj.* **1.** unwilling to part with money or possessions; miserly; stingy **2.** characterized by penury; destitute —**pe·nu′ri·ous·ly** *adv.* —**pe·nu′ri·ous·ness** *n.*

pen·u·ry (pen′yə rē) *n.* [< L. *penuria,* want] lack of money, property, or necessities; destitution

pe·on (pē′än, -ən) *n.* [< Sp. < ML. *pedo,* foot soldier] **1.** in Latin America, a person of the laboring class **2.** in the SW U.S., formerly, a person forced into servitude to work off a debt **3.** an exploited laborer

pe·on·age (pē′ə nij) *n.* **1.** the condition of a peon **2.** the system by which debtors or legal prisoners are forced to labor for their creditors or for persons who lease their services from the state

pe·o·ny (pē′ə nē) *n., pl.* **-nies** [< OE. & OFr. < L. < Gr. *Paiōn,* epithet for Apollo, god of medicine: from its former medicinal use] **1.** any of a group of plants with large pink, white, red, or yellow, showy flowers **2.** the flower

peo·ple (pē′p'l) *n., pl.* **-ple;** for 1 & 10, **-ples** [< Anglo-Fr. < OFr. < L. *populus,* nation] **1.** all the persons of a racial, national, religious, linguistic, or cultural group; nation, race, ethnic group, etc. **2.** the persons belonging to a certain place, community, or class *[*the *people* of Ohio, *people* of wealth*]* **3.** the persons under the leadership or control of a particular person or body **4.** the members of (someone's) class, occupation, set, race, etc. *[*the miner spoke for his *people]* **5.** one's relatives or ancestors; family **6.** persons without wealth, privilege, etc.; populace **7.** the electorate of a state **8.** persons considered indefinitely *[*what will *people* say?*]* **9.** human beings **10.** a group of creatures *[*the ant *people]* —*vt.* **-pled, -pling** to fill with or as with people; populate

people's front *same as* POPULAR FRONT

Pe·or·i·a (pē ôr′ē ə) [< Fr. < Algonquian *piwarea,* ? he carries a pack] city in C Ill.: pop. 124,000

pep (pep) *n.* [< PEPPER] [Colloq.] energy; vigor; liveliness —*vt.* **pepped, pep′ping** [Colloq.] to fill with pep; invigorate; stimulate (with *up*)

pep·lum (pep′ləm) *n., pl.* **-lums, -la** (-lə) [L. < Gr. *peplos,* a shawl] **1.** a large scarf worn draped about the body by women in ancient Greece **2.** a flounce attached at the waist of a dress, coat, etc. and extending around the hips

pep·per (pep′ər) *n.* see PLURAL, II, D, 3 [< OE. < L. *piper* < Gr. *peperi*] **1.** *a)* a pungent condiment obtained from the small, dried fruits of an East Indian plant: see BLACK PEPPER, WHITE PEPPER *b)* the plant itself **2.** any of various plants possessing aromatic and pungent properties, used as flavoring **3.** *a) same as* CAPSICUM *b)* the fruit of the capsicum: see RED PEPPER, GREEN PEPPER, SWEET PEPPER **4.** any of various pungent spices, as cayenne pepper —*vt.* **1.** to season with ground pepper **2.** to sprinkle thickly **3.** to shower with many small objects *[*a roof *peppered* with hailstones*]* **4.** to beat or hit with quick jabs

pep·per-and-salt (-'n sôlt′) *adj.* speckled with contrasting colors, esp. black and white

pep·per·corn (-kôrn′) *n.* [OE. *piporcorn*] the dried berry of the black PEPPER (*n.* 1)

pep·per·grass (-gras′) ***n.*** a plant of the mustard family, with small, whitish flowers and flattened pods
pepper mill a hand mill used to grind peppercorns
pep·per·mint (-mint′, -mənt) ***n.*** **1.** a plant of the mint family, with lance-shaped leaves and whitish or purplish flowers **2.** the pungent oil it yields, used for flavoring **3.** a candy flavored with this oil
pep·per·o·ni (pep′ə rō′nē) ***n., pl.*** **-nis, -ni** [< It. *peperoni*] a highly spiced Italian sausage
pepper pot any of various stews or soups of vegetables, meat, etc. flavored with hot spices
pepper shaker a container with a perforated top, for sprinkling ground pepper: also **pep′per·box′** (-bäks′) ***n.***
pepper tree a S. American ornamental tree with loose clusters of yellowish flowers and pinkish-red berries
pep·per·y (-ē) ***adj.*** **1.** of, like, or highly seasoned with pepper **2.** sharp or fiery, as speech or writing **3.** hot-tempered; irritable —**pep′per·i·ness** ***n.***
pep pill [Slang] any of various pills containing a stimulant, esp. amphetamine
pep·py (pep′ē) ***adj.*** **-pi·er, -pi·est** [Colloq.] full of pep, or energy; brisk; vigorous; spirited —**pep′pi·ly** ***adv.*** —**pep′pi·ness** ***n.***
pep·sin (pep′s'n) ***n.*** [G. < Gr. < *peptein,* to digest] **1.** an enzyme secreted in the stomach, aiding in the digestion of proteins **2.** an extract of pepsin from the stomachs of calves, etc., formerly used to help in digesting food
pep talk a talk, as to an athletic team by its coach, to instill enthusiasm, etc.
pep·tic (pep′tik) ***adj.*** [< L. < Gr. < *peptein,* to digest] **1.** of or aiding digestion **2.** of or relating to pepsin **3.** related to, or caused to some extent by, digestive secretions *[a peptic ulcer]*
pep·tone (-tōn) ***n.*** [< G. < Gr. *peptos,* digested] any of a group of soluble and diffusible derived proteins formed by the action of enzymes on proteins, as in digestion —**pep·ton′ic** (-tän′ik) ***adj.***
Pepys (pēps; *occas.* peps, pep′is, pē′pis), **Samuel** 1633–1703; Eng. government official, known for his diary
Pe·quot (pē′kwät) ***n.*** [< Algonquian *paquatanog,* destroyers] **1.** *pl.* **-quots, -quot** any member of a tribe of Indians in Connecticut until dispersed in 1637 **2.** their Algonquian language —***adj.*** of this tribe
per (pʉr; *unstressed* pər) ***prep.*** [L.] **1.** through; by; by means of **2.** for each *[fifty cents per yard]* **3.** [Colloq.] according to *[per his instructions]*
per- [< L. *per,* through] *a prefix meaning:* **1.** through; throughout *[perceive, percolate]* **2.** thoroughly; very *[persuade]* **3.** *Chem.* containing a specified element or radical in its maximum, or a relatively high, valence *[peroxide]*
Per. **1.** Persia **2.** Persian
per. **1.** period **2.** person
per·ad·ven·ture (pʉr′əd ven′chər) ***adv.*** [< OFr. < *par,* by + *aventure,* chance] [Archaic] **1.** possibly **2.** by chance —***n.*** chance; doubt
per·am·bu·late (pər am′byoo lāt′) ***vt.*** **-lat′ed, -lat′ing** [< L. pp. of *perambulare* < *per,* through + *ambulare,* to walk] to walk through, over, around, etc., as in inspecting —***vi.*** to stroll —**per·am′bu·la′tion** ***n.*** —**per·am′bu·la·to′ry** (-lə tôr′ē) ***adj.***
per·am·bu·la·tor (-lāt′ər) ***n.*** **1.** a person who perambulates **2.** [Chiefly Brit.] a baby carriage
per an·num (pər an′əm) [L.] by the year; yearly
per·cale (pər kāl′, -kal′) ***n.*** [Fr. < Per. *pargāla*] closely woven cotton cloth, used for sheets, etc.
per cap·i·ta (pər kap′ə tə) [ML., lit., by heads] for each person
per·ceive (pər sēv′) ***vt., vi.*** **-ceived′, -ceiv′ing** [< OFr. < L. *percipere* < *per,* through + *capere,* to take] **1.** to grasp or take in mentally **2.** to become aware (of) through the senses —**per·ceiv′a·ble** ***adj.*** —**per·ceiv′a·bly** ***adv.*** —**per·ceiv′er** ***n.***
per·cent (pər sent′) ***adv., adj.*** [< It. < L. *per centum*] in or for every hundred *[a 20 percent rate means 20 in every hundred]*: symbol, %: also **per cent** or, now rare, **per cent.,** **per cen·tum** (sen′təm) —***n.*** **1.** a hundredth part **2.** [Colloq.] percentage **3.** [*pl.*] bonds, etc. bearing regular interest of a (stated) percentage *[the four percents]*
per·cent·age (-ij) ***n.*** **1.** a given part or amount in every hundred **2.** any amount, as of interest, stated in percent **3.** part; portion *[a percentage of the audience]* **4.** [Colloq.] *a)* use; advantage *b)* [*usually pl.*] a risk based on favorable odds
per·cen·tile (pər sen′tīl, -sent′'l) ***n.*** *Statistics* **1.** any value in a series dividing the distribution of its members into 100 groups of equal frequency **2.** any of these groups —***adj.*** of a percentile
per·cept (pʉr′sept) ***n.*** [< PERCEPTION] a recognizable sensation or impression received by the mind through the senses
per·cep·ti·ble (pər sep′tə b'l) ***adj.*** that can be perceived —**per·cep′ti·bil′i·ty** ***n.*** —**per·cep′ti·bly** ***adv.***
per·cep·tion (-shən) ***n.*** [< L. < pp. of *percipere:* see PERCEIVE] **1.** *a)* the act of perceiving or the ability to perceive; awareness *b)* insight or intuition **2.** the understanding, knowledge, etc. or a specific idea, concept, etc. got by perceiving —**per·cep′tion·al** ***adj.*** —**per·cep′tu·al** (-choo əl) ***adj.***
per·cep·tive (-tiv) ***adj.*** **1.** of or capable of perception **2.** able to perceive quickly and easily —**per·cep′tive·ly** ***adv.*** —**per·cep′tive·ness, per′cep·tiv′i·ty** ***n.***
perch[1] (pʉrch) ***n., pl.*** **perch, perch′es:** see PLURAL, II, D, 2 [< OFr. < L. < Gr. *perkē*] **1.** a small, spiny-finned, freshwater food fish **2.** any of various bony, spiny-rayed, usually saltwater fishes
perch[2] (pʉrch) ***n.*** [< OFr. < L. *pertica,* a pole] **1.** a horizontal pole, branch, etc. serving as a roost for birds **2.** any resting place, esp. a high or insecure one **3.** *a)* a measure of length, equal to 5½ yards *b)* a measure of area, equal to 30¼ square yards —***vi., vt.*** to alight and rest, or place, on or as on a perch —**perch′er** ***n.***
per·chance (pər chans′) ***adv.*** [< OFr. *par,* by + *chance,* chance] [Archaic] **1.** by chance **2.** perhaps; possibly
Per·che·ron (pʉr′chə rän′, -shə-) ***n.*** [Fr. < *Perche,* region in France] a breed of large, fast-trotting draft horses: also **Percheron Norman**
per·cip·i·ent (pər sip′ē ənt) ***adj.*** perceiving, esp. keenly or readily —***n.*** a person who perceives —**per·cip′i·ence, per·cip′i·en·cy** ***n.*** —**per·cip′i·ent·ly** ***adv.***
Per·ci·val (pʉr′sə v'l) [< OFr., prob. < *perce val,* pierce valley] **1.** a masculine name **2.** a knight in Arthurian legend, who saw the Holy Grail: usually **Per′ci·vale** (-v'l)
per·co·late (pʉr′kə lāt′) ***vt.*** **-lat′ed, -lat′ing** [< L. pp. of *percolare* < *per,* through + *colare,* to strain] **1.** to pass (a liquid) gradually through a porous substance; filter **2.** to drain or ooze through (a porous substance); permeate **3.** to brew (coffee) in a percolator —***vi.*** **1.** to ooze through a porous substance **2.** to permeate **3.** to start bubbling up, as percolated coffee —**per′co·la′tion** ***n.***
per·co·la·tor (-lāt′ər) ***n.*** a coffeepot in which boiling water bubbles up through a tube and filters back down through the ground coffee
per·cus·sion (pər kush′ən) ***n.*** [< L. < pp. of *percutere,* to strike] **1.** the hitting of one body against another, as the hammer of a firearm against a powder cap **2.** the impact of sound waves on the ear **3.** percussion instruments collectively **4.** *Med.* the tapping of the chest, back, etc. with the fingers to determine from the sound produced the condition of internal organs —**per·cus′sive** ***adj.*** —**per·cus′sive·ly** ***adv.*** —**per·cus′sive·ness** ***n.***
percussion cap a small paper or metal container holding a charge that explodes when struck
percussion instrument a musical instrument in which the tone is produced when some part is struck, as the drums, cymbals, xylophone, etc.
per·cus·sion·ist (-ist) ***n.*** a musician who plays percussion instruments
Per·cy (pʉr′sē) **1.** a masculine name: see PERCIVAL **2.** **Sir Henry,** 1364–1403; Eng. soldier & rebel against Henry IV
per di·em (dē′əm, dī′əm) [L.] **1.** by the day; daily **2.** a daily allowance, as for expenses
per·di·tion (pər dish′ən) ***n.*** [< OFr. < LL. < L. pp. of *perdere,* to lose] **1.** [Archaic] complete and irreparable loss; ruin **2.** *Theol.* *a)* the loss of the soul; damnation *b)* *same as* HELL
‡père (per) ***n.*** [Fr.] father: often used after the surname, like English *Senior [Dumas père]*
per·e·gri·nate (per′ə gri nāt′) ***vt., vi.*** **-nat′ed, -nat′ing** [< L. pp. of *peregrinari* < *peregrinus:* see PILGRIM] to travel, esp. walk (along or through) —**per′e·gri·na′tion** ***n.*** —**per′e·gri·na′tor** ***n.***
per·e·grine (falcon) (per′ə grin, -grēn′) [see prec.] a very swift European falcon with a spotted breast: used in falconry
per·emp·to·ry (pə remp′tər ē) ***adj.*** [< LL. < L. < pp. of *perimere,* to destroy < *per-,* intens. + *emere,* to take] **1.** *Law* *a)* barring further action, debate, etc.; final; decisive *b)* not requiring that any cause be shown *[a peremptory challenge of a juror]* **2.** that cannot be denied, delayed, etc., as a command **3.** intolerantly positive; dogmatic *[a peremptory manner]* —**per·emp′to·ri·ly** ***adv.*** —**per·emp′to·ri·ness** ***n.***
per·en·ni·al (pə ren′ē əl) ***adj.*** [< L. < *per,* through + *annus,* a year] **1.** lasting or active throughout the whole year **2.** continuing for a long time *[a perennial youth]* **3.** becoming active again and again; perpetual **4.** having a life cycle of more than two years: said of plants —***n.*** a perennial plant —**per·en′ni·al·ly** ***adv.***
perf. **1.** perfect **2.** perforated
per·fect (pʉr′fikt; *for v., usually* pər fekt′) ***adj.*** [< OFr. < L. pp. of *perficere* < *per,* through + *facere,* to do] **1.** complete in all respects; flawless **2.** in a condition of excellence, as in skill or quality **3.** completely accurate; exact

[a perfect copy] **4.** utter; absolute *[a perfect fool]* **5.** *Gram.* expressing a state or action completed at the time of speaking or at the time indicated: verbs have three perfect tenses: present perfect, past perfect, and future perfect **6.** *Music* designating an interval, as an octave, whose character is not altered by inversion and which has no alternative major and minor forms —*vt.* **1.** to bring to completion **2.** to make perfect or more nearly perfect according to a given standard, as by training, etc. —*n.* **1.** the perfect tense **2.** a verb form in this tense —**per·fect′er** *n.* —**per′fect·ness** *n.*

per·fect·i·ble (pər fek′tə b'l) *adj.* that can become, or be made, perfect or more nearly perfect —**per·fect′i·bil′i·ty** *n.*

per·fec·tion (pər fek′shən) *n.* **1.** the act or process of perfecting **2.** a being perfect **3.** a person or thing that is the perfect embodiment of some quality —**to perfection** completely; perfectly

per·fec·tion·ism (-iz'm) *n.* extreme or obsessive striving for perfection, as in one's work —**per·fec′tion·ist** *n., adj.* —**per·fec′tion·is′tic** *adj.*

per·fect·ly (pur′fikt lē) *adv.* **1.** to a perfect degree **2.** completely; fully

per·fec·to (pər fek′tō) *n., pl.* **-tos** [Sp., perfect] a cigar of a standard shape, thick in the center and tapering to a point at each end

perfect participle *same as* PAST PARTICIPLE

perfect pitch *a popular term for* ABSOLUTE PITCH

per·fer·vid (pər fur′vid) *adj.* extremely fervid

per·fi·dy (pur′fə dē) *n., pl.* **-dies** [< Fr. < L. *perfidia* < *per fidem* (*decipi*), (to deceive) through faith] betrayal of trust; treachery —**per·fid·i·ous** (pər fid′ē əs) *adj.* —**per·fid′i·ous·ly** *adv.*

per·fo·li·ate (pər fō′lē it, -āt′) *adj.* [< ModL. < L. *per*, through + *folium*, a leaf] having a stem that seems to pass through it: said of a leaf —**per·fo′li·a′tion** *n.*

PERFOLIATE LEAVES

per·fo·rate (pur′fə rāt′; *for adj., usually* -rit) *vt., vi.* **-rat′ed, -rat′ing** [< L. pp. of *perforare* < *per*, through + *forare*, to bore] **1.** to make a hole or holes through, as by punching or boring **2.** to pierce with holes in a row, as a pattern, computer tape, etc. —*adj.* pierced with holes, esp. in a row, for easy tearing: also **per′fo·rat′ed** —**per′fo·ra·ble** *adj.* —**per′fo·ra′tor** *n.*

per·fo·ra·tion (pur′fə rā′shən) *n.* **1.** a perforating or being perforated **2.** a hole made by piercing, ulceration, etc. **3.** any of a series of punched holes, as those between postage stamps on a sheet

per·force (pər fôrs′) *adv.* [< OFr.: see PER & FORCE] by or through necessity; necessarily

per·form (pər fôrm′) *vt.* [< Anglo-Fr. < OFr. *parfournir*, to consummate < *par* (< L. *per-*, intens.) + *fornir*, to accomplish] **1.** to act on so as to complete; do (a task, process, etc.) **2.** to fulfill (a promise, etc.) **3.** to render or enact (a piece of music, a dramatic role, etc.) —*vi.* to execute an action or process; esp., to act in a play, dance, etc. before an audience —**per·form′a·ble** *adj.* —**per·form′er** *n.*

per·form·ance (-fôr′məns) *n.* **1.** the act of performing; execution, accomplishment, etc. **2.** functioning, usually with regard to effectiveness, as of a machine **3.** a deed or feat **4.** *a*) a formal exhibition or presentation before an audience, as a play; show *b*) one's part in this

per·fume (pər fyōōm′; *for n., usually* pur′fyōōm) *vt.* **-fumed′, -fum′ing** [< MFr. < It. < L. *per-*, intens. + *fumare*, to smoke] **1.** to fill with a pleasing odor **2.** to put perfume on —*n.* **1.** a sweet scent; fragrance **2.** a substance producing a pleasing odor; esp., a volatile oil, as that extracted from flowers

per·fum·er (pər fyōō′mər) *n.* **1.** one who makes or sells perfumes **2.** one who or that which perfumes

per·fum·er·y (-ē) *n., pl.* **-er·ies** **1.** the trade or art of a perfumer **2.** perfumes collectively **3.** a place where perfume is made or sold

per·func·to·ry (pər fuŋk′tər ē) *adj.* [< LL. < L. pp. of *perfungi* < *per-*, intens. + *fungi*, to perform] **1.** done merely as a routine; superficial *[a perfunctory examination]* **2.** without concern; indifferent *[a perfunctory teacher]* —**per·func′to·ri·ly** *adv.* —**per·func′to·ri·ness** *n.*

per·go·la (pur′gə lə) *n.* [It., arbor < L. *pergula*, projecting cover] an arbor, esp. one with an open roof of cross rafters supported on columns, usually with climbing vines

per·haps (pər haps′, -aps′) *adv.* [PER + *haps*, pl. of HAP] possibly; maybe

pe·ri (pir′ē) *n.* [Per. *parī*] *Persian Myth.* **1.** a fairy or elf **2.** any fairylike being

per·i- [< Gr. < *peri*] *a prefix meaning:* **1.** around, about *[periscope]* **2.** near *[perigee]*

per·i·anth (per′ē anth′) *n.* [< ModL. < Gr. *peri-*, around + *anthos*, a flower] the outer envelope of a flower, including the calyx and corolla

per·i·car·di·tis (per′ə kär dīt′is) *n.* inflammation of the pericardium

per·i·car·di·um (-kär′dē əm) *n., pl.* **-di·a** (-ə) [ModL. < Gr. < *peri-*, around + *kardia*, heart] in vertebrates, the thin, membranous sac around the heart —**per′i·car′di·al, per′i·car′di·ac′** *adj.*

per·i·carp (per′ə kärp′) *n.* [< ModL. < Gr.: see PERI- & -CARP] *Bot.* the wall of a ripened ovary —**per′i·car′pi·al** *adj.*

Per·i·cles (per′ə klēz′) 495?–429 B.C.; Athenian statesman & general —**Per′i·cle′an** (-klē′ən) *adj.*

per·i·cra·ni·um (per′ə krā′nē əm) *n., pl.* **-ni·a** (-ə) [ModL. < Gr. < *peri-*, around + *kranion*, skull] the tough membrane covering the skull

per·i·gee (per′ə jē′) *n.* [< Fr. < ModL. < Gr. < *peri-*, near + *gē*, earth] **1.** the point nearest to the earth, the moon, or another planet, in the orbit of a satellite or spacecraft around it **2.** the lowest or nearest point —**per′i·ge′an, per′i·ge′al** *adj.*

per·i·he·li·on (per′ə hē′lē ən, -hēl′yən) *n., pl.* **-li·ons, -li·a** (-ə) [ModL. < Gr. *peri-*, around + *hēlios*, the sun] the point nearest the sun in the orbit around it of a planet, comet, or man-made satellite: cf. APHELION

per·il (per′əl) *n.* [OFr. < L. *periculum*, danger] **1.** exposure to harm or injury; danger **2.** something that may cause harm or injury —*vt.* **-iled** or **-illed, -il·ing** or **-il·ling** to expose to danger

per·il·ous (-əs) *adj.* involving peril or risk; dangerous —**per′il·ous·ly** *adv.* —**per′il·ous·ness** *n.*

pe·rim·e·ter (pə rim′ə tər) *n.* [< L. < Gr. < *peri-*, around + *metron*, a measure] **1.** the outer boundary of a figure or area **2.** the total length of this —**per·i·met·ric** (per′ə met′rik), **per′i·met′ri·cal** *adj.* —**per′i·met′ri·cal·ly** *adv.*

per·i·ne·um (per′ə nē′əm) *n., pl.* **-ne′a** (-ə) [ModL. < LL. < Gr. < *peri-*, around + *inein*, to discharge] the region between the thighs; specif., the small area between the anus and the vulva or the scrotum —**per′i·ne′al** *adj.*

pe·ri·od (pir′ē əd) *n.* [< MFr. < L. < Gr. *periodos*, a cycle < *peri-*, around + *hodos*, way] **1.** the interval between the successive occurrences of an astronomical event, as between two full moons **2.** a portion of time distinguished by certain processes, conditions, etc.; stage *[a period of change]* **3.** any of the portions of time into which a game, school day, etc. is divided **4.** the full course, or one of the stages, of a disease **5.** the menses **6.** an end or conclusion *[death put a period to his plans]* **7.** a subdivision of a geologic era **8.** *Gram.* *a*) a sentence, esp. a well-balanced sentence *b*) the pause in speaking or a mark of punctuation (.) used at the end of a declarative sentence *c*) the dot (.) following many abbreviations **9.** *Physics* the interval of time necessary for a complete cycle of a regularly recurring motion —*adj.* of or like that of an earlier period or age *[period furniture]*

pe·ri·od·ic (pir′ē äd′ik) *adj.* **1.** appearing or recurring at regular intervals *[a periodic fever]* **2.** occurring from time to time; intermittent **3.** of or characterized by periods **4.** of a sentence (**periodic sentence**) in which the essential elements are withheld until the end

pe·ri·od·i·cal (-i k'l) *adj.* **1.** *same as* PERIODIC **2.** published at regular intervals, as weekly, monthly, etc. **3.** of a periodical —*n.* a periodical publication —**pe′ri·od′i·cal·ly** *adv.*

pe·ri·o·dic·i·ty (pir′ē ə dis′ə tē) *n., pl.* **-ties** the tendency or fact of recurring at regular intervals

periodic law the law that properties of chemical elements recur periodically when the elements are arranged in order of their atomic numbers

periodic table an arrangement of the chemical elements according to their atomic numbers, to exhibit the periodic law

per·i·o·don·tal (per′ē ə dän′t'l) *adj.* [PERI- + -ODONT + -AL] occurring around a tooth or affecting the gums

per·i·os·te·um (per′i äs′tē əm) *n., pl.* **-te·a** (-ə) [ModL. < L. < Gr. < *peri-*, around + *osteon*, a bone] the membrane of connective tissue covering all bones except at the joints —**per′i·os′te·al** *adj.*

per·i·pa·tet·ic (per′i pə tet′ik) *adj.* [< Fr. < L. < Gr., ult. < *peri-*, around + *patein*, to walk] **1.** [**P-**] of the philosophy or followers of Aristotle, who walked about while he was teaching **2.** walking or moving about; itinerant —*n.* **1.** [**P-**] a follower of Aristotle **2.** a person who walks from place to place —**per′i·pa·tet′i·cal·ly** *adv.*

pe·riph·er·al (pə rif′ər əl) *adj.* **1.** of, belonging to, or forming a periphery **2.** *Anat.* of, at, or near the surface of the body **3.** merely incidental; tangential *[of peripheral interest]* —*n.* a piece of equipment that can be used with a computer to increase its functional range or efficiency, as a printer or disc —**pe·riph'er·al·ly** *adv.*

pe·riph·er·y (-ē) *n., pl.* **-er·ies** [< MFr. < LL. < Gr. < *peri-*, around + *pherein,* to bear] **1.** a boundary line or outside surface, esp. of a rounded figure **2.** surrounding space or area

pe·riph·ra·sis (pə rif'rə sis) *n., pl.* **-ses'** (-sēz') [L. < Gr. < *peri-*, around + *phrazein,* to speak] the use of many words where a few would do; roundabout way of speaking: also **per·i·phrase** (per'ə frāz')

per·i·phras·tic (per'ə fras'tik) *adj.* **1.** of, like, or expressed in periphrasis **2.** *Gram.* formed with a particle or auxiliary verb instead of by inflection, as the phrase *did sing* used for *sang* —**per'i·phras'ti·cal·ly** *adv.*

pe·rique (pə rēk') *n.* [AmFr.] a strong, rich black tobacco grown in Louisiana, used in blending

per·i·sarc (per'ə särk') *n.* [< PERI- + Gr. *sarx,* flesh] the tough, nonliving, outer skeleton layer of many hydroid colonies

per·i·scope (per'ə skōp') *n.* [PERI- + -SCOPE] an optical instrument consisting of a tube equipped with lenses and mirrors or prisms, so arranged that a person looking through one end can see objects reflected at the other end: used on submerged submarines, etc. —**per'i·scop'ic** (-skäp'ik) *adj.*

PERISCOPE

per·ish (per'ish) *vi.* [< OFr. < L. *perire,* to perish < *per-*, intens. + *ire,* to go] **1.** to be destroyed, ruined, or wiped out **2.** to die; esp., to die a violent or untimely death —**perish the thought!** do not even consider such a possibility!

per·ish·a·ble (-ə b'l) *adj.* that may perish; esp., liable to spoil, as some foods —*n.* something, esp. a food, liable to spoil or deteriorate —**per'ish·a·bil'i·ty, per'ish·a·ble·ness** *n.*

per·i·stal·sis (per'ə stôl'sis, -stal'-) *n., pl.* **-ses** (-sēz) [ModL. < Gr. < *peri-*, around + *stellein,* to place] the wavelike muscular contractions and dilations of the walls of the alimentary canal and certain other hollow organs, that move the contents onward —**per'i·stal'tic** *adj.*

per·i·style (per'ə stīl') *n.* [< Fr. < L. < Gr. < *peri-*, around + *stylos,* a column] **1.** a row of columns forming an enclosure or supporting a roof **2.** any area so formed, as a court —**per'i·sty'lar** (-stī'lər) *adj.*

per·i·to·ne·um (per'it 'n ē'əm) *n., pl.* **-ne'a** (-ə), **-ne'ums** [LL. < Gr. < *peri-*, around + *teinein,* to stretch] the serous membrane lining the abdominal cavity and covering the visceral organs —**per'i·to·ne'al** *adj.*

per·i·to·ni·tis (-īt'əs) *n.* inflammation of the peritoneum

per·i·wig (per'ə wig') *n.* [earlier *perwyke* < Fr. *perruque,* PERUKE] a wig, formerly worn by men

per·i·win·kle[1] (per'ə wiŋ'k'l) *n.* [< OE. < L. *pervinca*] a European creeper with blue, white, or pink flowers, grown as a ground cover

per·i·win·kle[2] (per'ə wiŋ'k'l) *n.* [OE. *pinewincle*] **1.** any of various small saltwater snails having a thick, cone-shaped shell **2.** such a shell

per·jure (pur'jər) *vt.* **-jured, -jur·ing** [< OFr. < L. < *per,* through + *jurare,* to swear] to make (oneself) guilty of perjury —**per'jur·er** *n.*

per·jured (-jərd) *adj.* guilty of, or characterized by, perjury: also **per·ju·ri·ous** (pər joor'ē əs)

per·ju·ry (-jər ē) *n., pl.* **-ries** [< OFr. < L. < *perjurus,* false] **1.** the willful telling of a lie while under oath **2.** the breaking of any oath

perk[1] (purk) *vt.* [< ? ONormFr. *perquer,* to perch] **1.** to raise (the head, ears, etc.) briskly (often with *up*) **2.** to make smart in appearance (often with *up* or *out*) **3.** to give or restore freshness, vivacity, etc. to (usually with *up*) —*vi.* **1.** to straighten one's posture jauntily **2.** to become lively or recover one's spirits (with *up*)

perk[2] (purk) *vt., vi. colloq. clip of* PERCOLATE

perk[3] (purk) *n.* [Chiefly Brit. Colloq.] *clipped form of* PERQUISITE

perk·y (pur'kē) *adj.* **perk'i·er, perk'i·est** **1.** self-confident **2.** sprightly; jaunty —**perk'i·ly** *adv.* —**perk'i·ness** *n.*

Perm (perm) city in E European R.S.F.S.R.: pop. 850,000

per·ma·frost (pur'mə frôst', -fräst') *n.* [PERMA(NENT) + FROST] permanently frozen subsoil

per·ma·nence (pur'mə nəns) *n.* the state or quality of being permanent

per·ma·nen·cy (-nən sē) *n.* **1.** *same as* PERMANENCE **2.** *pl.* **-cies** something permanent

per·ma·nent (-nənt) *adj.* [MFr. < L. prp. of *permanere* < *per,* through + *manere,* to remain] lasting or intended to last indefinitely or for a relatively long time —*n. colloq. clip of* PERMANENT WAVE —**per'ma·nent·ly** *adv.*

permanent wave a hair wave, produced by applying heat or chemicals, that is relatively long lasting

per·man·ga·nate (pər maŋ'gə nāt') *n.* a salt of permanganic acid, generally dark purple

per·man·gan·ic acid (pur'man gan'ik) an unstable acid, $HMnO_4$, that is an oxidizing agent

per·me·a·bil·i·ty (pur'mē ə bil'ə tē) *n.* **1.** a being permeable **2.** *Physics a)* the measure of ease with which magnetic lines of force are carried *b)* the rate of diffusion of a fluid through a porous body

per·me·a·ble (pur'mē ə b'l) *adj.* that can be permeated, as by liquids —**per'me·a·bly** *adv.*

per·me·ate (-āt') *vt.* **-at'ed, -at'ing** [< L. pp. of *permeare* < *per,* through + *meare,* to glide] to pass into or through and affect every part of; spread through *[ink permeates blotting paper]* —*vi.* to spread or diffuse (with *through* or *among*) —**per'me·a'tion, per'me·ance** *n.* —**per'me·a'tive** (-āt'iv) *adj.*

Per·mi·an (pur'mē ən) *adj.* [after *Perm,* former province of Russia] designating or of the seventh and last period of the Paleozoic Era —**the Permian** the Permian Period or its rocks: see GEOLOGY, chart

per·mis·si·ble (pər mis'ə b'l) *adj.* that can be permitted; allowable —**per·mis'si·bil'i·ty** *n.* —**per·mis'si·bly** *adv.*

per·mis·sion (pər mish'ən) *n.* the act of permitting; esp., formal consent; leave

per·mis·sive (-mis'iv) *adj.* **1.** giving permission **2.** allowing freedom; indulgent —**per·mis'sive·ly** *adv.* —**per·mis'sive·ness** *n.*

per·mit (pər mit'; *for n., usually* pur'mit) *vt.* **-mit'ted, -mit'ting** [< L. < *per,* through + *mittere,* to send] **1.** to allow; consent to *[smoking is not permitted]* **2.** to give permission to; authorize *[to permit women to vote]* **3.** to give opportunity for *[to permit light to enter]* —*vi.* to give opportunity *[if time permits]* —*n.* **1.** *same as* PERMISSION **2.** a document granting permission; license —**per·mit'ter** *n.*

per·mu·ta·tion (pur'myoo tā'shən) *n.* **1.** any radical alteration **2.** *Math.* any one of the total number of groupings, or subsets, into which a group, or set, of elements can be arranged: the permutations of 1, 2, and 3 taken two at a time are 12, 21, 13, 31, 23, 32 —**per'mu·ta'tion·al** *adj.*

per·mute (pər myoot') *vt.* **-mut'ed, -mut'ing** [< L. *permutare* < *per-*, intens. + *mutare,* to change] to rearrange the order or sequence of —**per·mut'a·ble** *adj.*

Per·nam·bu·co (pur'nəm boo'kō; *Port.* per'nänm boo'koo) *same as* RECIFE

per·ni·cious (pər nish'əs) *adj.* [< Fr. < L. < *pernecare* < *per,* thoroughly + *necare,* to kill < *nex* (gen. *necis*), death] **1.** causing great injury, destruction, or ruin **2.** [Rare] wicked; evil —**per·ni'cious·ly** *adv.* —**per·ni'cious·ness** *n.*

pernicious anemia a form of anemia characterized by a reduction of the red blood cells and by gastrointestinal and nervous disturbances, etc.

per·nick·et·y (pər nik'ə tē) *adj. same as* PERSNICKETY

per·o·rate (per'ə rāt') *vi.* **-rat'ed, -rat'ing** **1.** to make a lengthy oration **2.** to sum up or conclude a speech

per·o·ra·tion (per'ə rā'shən) *n.* [< L. < pp. of *perorare* < *per,* through + *orare,* to speak] **1.** the concluding part of a speech, including a summing up **2.** a bombastic speech

per·ox·ide (pə räk'sīd) *n.* [PER- + OXIDE] any oxide containing the oxygen (O_2) group linked by a single bond; specif., hydrogen peroxide —*vt.* **-id·ed, -id·ing** to bleach (hair, etc.) with hydrogen peroxide —*adj.* bleached with hydrogen peroxide

per·pen·dic·u·lar (pur'pən dik'yə lər) *adj.* [< OFr. < L. < *perpendiculum,* plumb line < *per-*, intens. + *pendere,* to hang] **1.** at right angles to a given plane or line **2.** exactly upright; vertical **3.** very steep —*n.* **1.** a line at right angles to another line or plane **2.** a perpendicular position —**per'pen·dic'u·lar'i·ty** (-lar'ə tē) *n.* —**per'pen·dic'u·lar·ly** *adv.*

PERPENDICULAR

per·pe·trate (pur'pə trāt') *vt.* **-trat'ed, -trat'ing** [< L. pp. of *perpetrare* < *per,* thoroughly + *patrare,* to effect] **1.** to do (something evil, criminal, or offensive) **2.** to commit (a blunder), impose (a hoax), etc. —**per'pe·tra'tion** *n.* —**per'pe·tra'tor** *n.*

per·pet·u·al (pər pech'oo wəl) *adj.* [< OFr. < L. < *perpetuus,* constant] **1.** lasting forever or for an indefinitely long time **2.** continuing indefinitely without interruption; constant *[a perpetual nuisance]* —**per·pet'u·al·ly** *adv.*

perpetual motion the motion of a hypothetical device which, once set in motion, would operate indefinitely by creating its own energy

per·pet·u·ate (pər pech'oo wāt') *vt.* **-at'ed, -at'ing** to make perpetual; cause to continue or be remembered —**per·pet'u·a'tion** *n.* —**per·pet'u·a'tor** *n.*

per·pe·tu·i·ty (pʉr′pə to͞o′ə tē, -tyo͞o′-) ***n.,*** *pl.* **-ties** **1.** a being perpetual **2.** something perpetual, as a pension to be paid indefinitely **3.** unlimited time; eternity —**in perpetuity** forever

per·plex (pər pleks′) ***vt.*** **[**< MFr. < L. *perplexus*, confused < *per*, through + pp. of *plectere*, to twist**]** **1.** to make (a person) uncertain, hesitant, etc.; confuse **2.** to make intricate or complicated —**per·plexed′** ***adj.*** —**per·plex′ing** ***adj.*** —**per·plex′ing·ly** ***adv.***

per·plex·i·ty (-plek′sə tē) ***n.*** **1.** the state of being perplexed; bewilderment **2.** *pl.* **-ties** something that perplexes

per·qui·site (pʉr′kwə zit) ***n.*** **[**< ML. < pp. of *perquirere*, to obtain < L. < *per-*, intens. + *quaerere*, to seek**]** **1.** something additional to regular profit or pay, resulting from one's employment **2.** a tip or gratuity **3.** a prerogative or right, by virtue of one's status, position, etc.

Per·ry (per′ē) **1.** **[**? < Fr. < L. *Petrus*, Peter**]** a masculine name **2. Matthew Cal·braith** (kal′breth), 1794–1858; U.S. naval officer **3. Oliver Haz·ard** (haz′ərd), 1785–1819; U.S. naval officer: brother of *prec.*

Pers. **1.** Persia **2.** Persian

pers. **1.** person **2.** personal

per se (pʉr′ sē′, sā′) **[**L.**]** by (or in) itself; intrinsically

per second per second for each second every second: used of a rate of acceleration

per·se·cute (pʉr′sə kyo͞ot′) ***vt.*** **-cut′ed, -cut′ing** **[**< MFr. < L. < *persequi*, to pursue < *per*, through + *sequi*, to follow**]** **1.** to afflict constantly so as to injure or distress, esp. for reasons of religion, politics, or race **2.** to annoy constantly *[persecuted* by mosquitoes*]* —**per′se·cu′tion** ***n.*** —**per′se·cu′tive** ***adj.*** —**per′se·cu′tor** ***n.***

Per·seph·o·ne (pər sef′ə nē) *Gr. Myth.* the daughter of Zeus and Demeter, abducted by Hades (Pluto) to be his wife: identified with the Roman goddess Proserpina

Per·seus (pʉr′syo͞os, -sē əs) **1.** *Gr. Myth.* a son of Zeus and slayer of Medusa: he married Andromeda after rescuing her from a sea monster **2.** a N constellation

per·se·ver·ance (pʉr′sə vir′əns) ***n.*** **1.** the act of persevering **2.** persistence; steadfastness

per·sev·er·ate (pər sev′ə rāt′) ***vi.*** **-at′ed, -at′ing** to experience or display perseveration

per·sev·er·a·tion (pər sev′ə rā′shən) ***n.*** the tendency of an idea, experience, or response to persist in an individual

per·se·vere (pʉr′sə vir′) ***vi.*** **-vered′, -ver′ing** **[**< OFr. < L. < *perseverus* < *per-*, intens. + *severus*, severe**]** to continue in some effort, course of action, etc. in spite of difficulty, opposition, etc.; persist —**per′se·ver′ing·ly** ***adv.***

Per·shing (pʉr′shiŋ), **John Joseph** 1860–1948; U.S. general: commander of U.S. forces in World War I

Per·sia (pʉr′zhə, -shə) **1.** *former official name of* IRAN **2.** *same as* PERSIAN EMPIRE

Per·sian (-zhən, -shən) ***adj.*** of Persia, its people, their language, etc.; Iranian —***n.*** **1.** a native or inhabitant of Persia **2.** the Iranian language of Iran

Persian Empire ancient empire in SW Asia, including at its peak the area from the Indus River to the W borders of Asia Minor & Egypt: founded by Cyrus the Great & conquered by Alexander the Great

Persian Gulf arm of the Arabian Sea, between SW Iran & Arabia

Persian lamb **1.** the lamb of the karakul sheep **2.** the black or gray pelt of newborn karakul lambs, having small, tight curls

Persian rug (or **carpet**) an Oriental rug made in Persia, with a richly colored, intricate pattern

per·si·flage (pʉr′sə fläzh′) ***n.*** **[**Fr. < *persifler*, to banter < *per-* (see PER-) + *siffler*, to whistle**]** **1.** a light, frivolous style of writing or speaking **2.** talk or writing of this kind

per·sim·mon (pər sim′ən) ***n.*** **[**< AmInd.**]** **1.** any of various trees with white flowers, hard wood, and plumlike fruit **2.** the fruit, sour and astringent when green, but sweet and edible when ripe

per·sist (pər sist′, -zist′) ***vi.*** **[**< MFr. < L. < *per*, through + *sistere*, to cause to stand**]** **1.** to refuse to give up, esp. when faced with opposition **2.** to continue insistently, as in repeating a question **3.** to endure; remain; last

per·sist·ence (-sis′təns, -zis′-) ***n.*** **1.** a persisting; stubborn continuance **2.** a persistent or lasting quality; tenacity: also **per·sist′en·cy**

per·sist·ent (-tənt) ***adj.*** **1.** continuing, esp. in the face of opposition, etc.; stubborn **2.** continuing to exist or endure **3.** constantly repeated; continued —**per·sist′ent·ly** ***adv.***

per·snick·e·ty (pər snik′ə tē) ***adj.*** **[**< Scot. dial.**]** [Colloq.] **1.** too particular or precise; fussy **2.** showing or requiring careful treatment

per·son (pʉr′s′n) ***n.*** **[**< OFr. < L. *persona*, lit., actor's mask, hence a person**]** **1.** a human being; individual man, woman, or child **2.** *a)* a living human body *b)* bodily appearance *[*to be neat about one's *person]* **3.** personality; self **4.** *Gram.* *a)* division into three sets of pronouns (**personal pronouns**), and, usually, corresponding verb forms, to identify the subject: see FIRST PERSON, SECOND PERSON, THIRD PERSON *b)* any of these sets **5.** *Law* any individual or incorporated group having certain legal rights and responsibilities —**in person** actually present

-per·son (pʉr′s′n) *a combining form meaning* person (of either sex) in a specified activity: used in coinages to avoid the masculine implication of *-man [*"chairperson"*]*

per·so·na (pər sō′nə) ***n.,*** *pl.* **-nae** (-nē); for sense 2, **-nas** [L.: see prec.] **1.** [*pl.*] the characters of a drama, novel, etc. **2.** *Psychol.* the outer personality presented to others by an individual

per·son·a·ble (pʉr′s′n ə b′l) ***adj.*** having a pleasing appearance and personality; attractive —**per′son·a·ble·ness** ***n.*** —**per′son·a·bly** ***adv.***

per·son·age (-ij) ***n.*** **1.** an important person **2.** any person **3.** a character in history, a play, novel, etc.

‡**per·so·na gra·ta** (pər sō′nə grät′ə, grāt′ə) **[**L.**]** a person who is acceptable or welcome

per·son·al (pʉr′s′n əl) ***adj.*** **1.** private; individual **2.** done in person or by oneself *[*a *personal* interview*]* **3.** involving human beings *[personal* relationships*]* **4.** of the body or physical appearance **5.** *a)* having to do with the character, conduct, etc. of a certain person *[*a *personal* remark*]* *b)* tending to make personal remarks *[*to get *personal* in an argument*]* **6.** of or like a person or rational being **7.** *Gram.* indicating grammatical person, as the inflectional endings of verbs in Latin and Greek **8.** *Law* of property (**personal property**) that is movable or not attached to the land —***n.*** **1.** a local news item about a person or persons **2.** a classified advertisement about a personal matter

per·son·al·i·ty (pʉr′sə nal′ə tē) ***n.,*** *pl.* **-ties** **1.** the quality or fact of being a person **2.** the quality or fact of being a particular person; individuality **3.** *a)* distinctive individual qualities of a person, considered collectively *b)* such qualities applied to a group, nation, etc. **4.** *a)* the sum of such qualities as impressing others *b)* personal attractiveness **5.** a person; esp., a notable person **6.** [*pl.*] any offensive remarks aimed at a person

per·son·al·ize (pʉr′s′n ə līz′) ***vt.*** **-ized′, -iz′ing** **1.** to apply to a particular person, esp. to oneself **2.** *same as* PERSONIFY **3.** to have marked with one's name or initials *[personalized* checks*]*

per·son·al·ly (-ə lē) ***adv.*** **1.** without the help of others; in person **2.** as a person *[*I dislike him *personally*, but admire his art*]* **3.** in one's own opinion **4.** as though directed at oneself *[*to take a remark *personally]*

per·son·al·ty (-əl tē) ***n.,*** *pl.* **-ties** *same as* PERSONAL PROPERTY: see PERSONAL (sense 8)

‡**per·so·na non gra·ta** (pər sō′nə nän grät′ə, grāt′ə) **[**L.**]** a person who is not acceptable

per·son·ate (pʉr′sə nāt′) ***vt.*** **-at′ed, -at′ing** **1.** to act the part of, as in a drama **2.** *Law* to assume the identity of with intent to defraud —**per′son·a′tion** ***n.*** —**per′son·a′tive** ***adj.*** —**per′son·a′tor** ***n.***

per·son·i·fi·ca·tion (pər sän′ə fi kā′shən) ***n.*** **1.** a personifying or being personified **2.** a person or thing thought of as representing some quality, idea, etc.; perfect example *[*Cupid is the *personification* of love*]* **3.** a figure of speech in which a thing or idea is represented as a person

per·son·i·fy (pər sän′ə fī′) ***vt.*** **-fied′, -fy′ing** **1.** to think or speak of (a thing) as a person *[*to *personify* a ship by referring to it as "she"*]* **2.** to symbolize (an abstract idea) by a human figure, as in art **3.** to be a symbol or perfect example of (something); typify —**per·son′i·fi′er** ***n.***

per·son·nel (pʉr′sə nel′) ***n.*** **[**Fr.**]** **1.** persons employed in any work, enterprise, service, etc. **2.** a personnel department or office for hiring employees, etc. —***adj.*** of or in charge of personnel

per·spec·tive (pər spek′tiv) ***adj.*** **[**< LL. < L. *perspicere* < *per*, through + *specere*, to look**]** **1.** of perspective **2.** drawn in perspective —***n.*** **1.** the art of picturing objects or a scene, e.g., by converging lines, so as to show them as they appear to the eye with reference to relative distance or depth **2.** *a)* the appearance of objects as determined by their relative distance and positions *b)* the effect of relative distance and position **3.** the relationship of the parts of a whole, regarded from a particular standpoint or point in time **4.** *a)* a specific point of view in judging things or events *b)* the ability to see things in a true relationship —**per·spec′tive·ly** ***adv.***

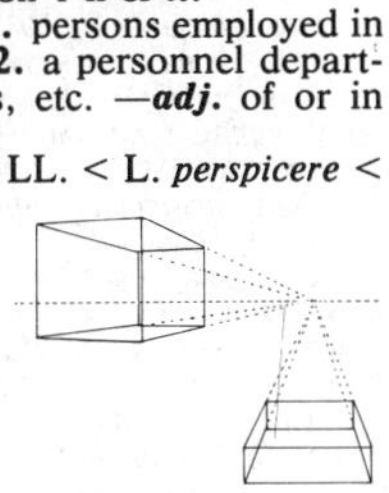

PERSPECTIVE

per·spi·ca·cious (pur'spə kā'shəs) *adj.* [L. *perspicax* < *perspicere:* see prec.] having keen judgment or understanding; discerning —**per'spi·ca'cious·ly** *adv.* —**per'spi·cac'i·ty** (-kas'ə tē), **per'spi·ca'cious·ness** *n.*

per·spic·u·ous (pər spik'yoo wəs) *adj.* [L. *perspicuus,* transparent < *perspicere:* see PERSPECTIVE] clear in statement or expression; easily understood —**per·spi·cu·i·ty** (pur'spə kyoo'ə tē), **per·spic'u·ous·ness** *n.* —**per·spic'u·ous·ly** *adv.*

per·spi·ra·tion (pur'spə rā'shən) *n.* [Fr.] **1.** a perspiring; sweating **2.** sweat —**per·spir·a·to·ry** (pər spīr'ə tôr'ē) *adj.*

per·spire (pər spīr') *vt., vi.* **-spired', -spir'ing** [< Fr. < L. *perspirare* < *per,* through + *spirare,* to breathe] to give forth (a characteristic salty moisture) through the pores of the skin; sweat

per·suade (pər swād') *vt.* **-suad'ed, -suad'ing** [< MFr. < L. *persuadere* < *per-,* intens. + *suadere,* to urge] to cause to do something, esp. by reasoning, urging, etc.; induce; convince —**per·suad'a·ble, per·sua'si·ble** (-swā'sə b'l) *adj.* —**per·suad'er** *n.* —**per·sua'si·bil'i·ty** *n.*

per·sua·sion (pər swā'zhən) *n.* **1.** a persuading or being persuaded **2.** power of persuading **3.** a strong belief; conviction **4.** *a)* a particular religious belief *b)* a particular sect, party, group, etc. **5.** [Colloq.] kind, sort, sex, etc.: used jocularly

per·sua·sive (-siv) *adj.* having the power, or tending, to persuade —**per·sua'sive·ly** *adv.* —**per·sua'sive·ness** *n.*

pert (purt) *adj.* [aphetic for *apert* < OFr. < L. *apertus,* open] **1.** bold or impudent in speech or behavior; saucy **2.** chic and jaunty **3.** [Dial.] lively; brisk —**pert'ly** *adv.* —**pert'ness** *n.*

per·tain (pər tān') *vi.* [< OFr. < L. *pertinere,* to reach < *per-,* intens. + *tenere,* to hold] **1.** to belong; be connected or associated; be a part, etc. **2.** to be appropriate *[*conduct that *pertains* to a lady*]* **3.** to have reference; be related *[*laws *pertaining* to the case*]*

Perth (purth) capital of Western Australia: pop. 626,000

per·ti·na·cious (pur'tə nā'shəs) *adj.* [< L. *pertinax* (gen. *pertinacis*), firm < *per-,* intens. + *tenax* < *tenere,* to hold] **1.** holding firmly or stubbornly to some purpose, belief, or action **2.** hard to get rid of; persistent —**per'ti·na'cious·ly** *adv.* —**per'ti·nac'i·ty** (-nas'ə tē) *n.*

per·ti·nent (pur't'n ənt) *adj.* [< MFr. < L. prp. of *pertinere:* see PERTAIN] of or connected with the matter at hand; relevant —**per'ti·nence, per'ti·nen·cy** *n.* —**per'ti·nent·ly** *adv.*

per·turb (pər turb') *vt.* [< MFr. < L. < *per-,* intens. + *turbare,* to disturb] **1.** to cause to be alarmed, agitated, or upset; disturb or trouble greatly **2.** to cause confusion in —**per·turb'a·ble** *adj.* —**per·turb'ed·ly** *adv.* —**per·turb'er** *n.*

per·tur·ba·tion (pur'tər bā'shən) *n.* **1.** a perturbing or being perturbed **2.** a disturbance **3.** *Astron.* an irregularity in the orbit of a heavenly body, caused by the attraction of a body other than the one around which it orbits —**per'tur·ba'tion·al** *adj.*

per·tus·sis (pər tus'is) *n.* [ModL. < L. *per-,* intens. + *tussis,* a cough] *same as* WHOOPING COUGH

Pe·ru (pə roo') country in W S.America, on the Pacific: 496,222 sq. mi.; pop. 13,586,000; cap. Lima —**Pe·ru·vi·an** (pə roo'vē ən) *adj., n.*

pe·ruke (pə rook') *n.* [< Fr. *perruque*] *same as* PERIWIG

pe·rus·al (pə roo'z'l) *n.* a perusing

pe·ruse (pə rooz') *vt.* **-rused', -rus'ing** [prob. < L. *per-,* intens. + ME. *usen,* to use] **1.** to read carefully; study **2.** to read —**pe·rus'er** *n.*

per·vade (pər vād') *vt.* **-vad'ed, -vad'ing** [< L. *pervadere* < *per,* through + *vadere,* to go] **1.** to pass through; spread throughout **2.** to be prevalent throughout —**per·va'sion** (-vā'zhən) *n.* —**per·va'sive** *adj.* —**per·va'sive·ly** *adv.* —**per·va'sive·ness** *n.*

per·verse (pər vurs') *adj.* [< OFr. < L. pp. of *pervertere:* see PERVERT] **1.** deviating from what is considered right or good; improper, wicked, etc. **2.** persisting in error; stubbornly contrary **3.** obstinately disobedient **4.** obstinate; stubborn —**per·verse'ly** *adv.* —**per·verse'ness, per·ver'si·ty** *n., pl.* **-ties**

per·ver·sion (-vur'zhən, -shən) *n.* **1.** a perverting or being perverted **2.** something perverted **3.** any sexual act or practice considered abnormal

per·vert (pər vurt'; *for n.* pur'vərt) *vt.* [< OFr. < L. < *per-,* intens. + *vertere,* to turn] **1.** to lead astray from what is right or good; misdirect; corrupt **2.** to misuse **3.** to misinterpret; distort **4.** to debase —*n.* a perverted person; esp., one who practices sexual perversion —**per·ver'sive** (-vur'siv) *adj.* —**per·vert'ed** *adj.* —**per·vert'er** *n.*

per·vi·ous (pur'vē əs) *adj.* [< L. < *per,* through + *via,* way] **1.** allowing passage through; permeable **2.** having a mind open to influence, argument etc. —**per'vi·ous·ly** *adv.* —**per'vi·ous·ness** *n.*

Pe·sach (pā'säkh) *n.* [Heb. *pesaḥ,* a passing over] *same as* PASSOVER

pe·se·ta (pə sāt'ə; *Sp.* pe se'tä) *n.* [Sp., dim. of *peso,* PESO] the monetary unit and a coin of Spain: see MONETARY UNITS, table

pes·e·wa (pes'ə wä) *n., pl.* **-e·was, -e·wa** [< native word *kpesaba,* a seed] *see* MONETARY UNITS, table (Ghana)

pes·ky (pes'kē) *adj.* **-ki·er, -ki·est** [prob. var. of *pesty* < PEST + -Y²] [Colloq.] annoying; troublesome —**pes'ki·ly** *adv.* —**pes'ki·ness** *n.*

pe·so (pā'sō; *Sp.* pe'sô) *n., pl.* **- sos** [Sp. < L. pp. of *pendere,* to weigh] the monetary unit of Argentina, Colombia, Cuba, Mexico, etc.: see MONETARY UNITS, table

peso bo·liv·i·a·no (bô lē'vyä'nô) *pl.* **pesos bolivianos** *see* MONETARY UNITS, table (Bolivia)

pes·sa·ry (pes'ər ē) *n., pl.* **-ries** [< LL. < L. < Gr. *pessos,* pebble] a device worn in the vagina to support the uterus or prevent conception

pes·si·mism (pes'ə miz'm) *n.* [< Fr. < L. *pessimus,* worst, superl. of *pejor,* worse] **1.** *a)* the belief that the existing world is the worst possible *b)* the belief that the evil in life outweighs the good **2.** the tendency to expect the worst outcome in any circumstance; a looking on the dark side of things —**pes'si·mist** *n.* —**pes'si·mis'tic** *adj.* —**pes'si·mis'ti·cal·ly** *adv.*

pest (pest) *n.* [< Fr. < L. *pestis,* a plague] **1.** a person or thing that causes trouble, annoyance, etc.; nuisance; specif., any destructive insect, small animal, weed, etc. **2.** [Rare] bubonic plague

pes·ter (pes'tər) *vt.* [< OFr. *empestrer,* orig., to hobble a horse: infl. by prec.] to annoy repeatedly with petty irritations; bother —**pes'ter·er** *n.*

pest·hole (pest'hōl') *n.* a place infested or likely to be infested with an epidemic disease

pes·ti·cide (pes'tə sīd') *n.* any chemical used for killing insects, weeds, etc. —**pes'ti·ci'dal** *adj.*

pes·tif·er·ous (pes tif'ər əs) *adj.* [< L. < *pestis,* a plague + *ferre,* to bear] **1.** orig., *a)* bringing or carrying disease *b)* infected with an epidemic disease **2.** dangerous to the welfare of society; evil **3.** [Colloq.] annoying; bothersome —**pes·tif'er·ous·ly** *adv.* —**pes·tif'er·ous·ness** *n.*

pes·ti·lence (pes't'l əns) *n.* [see ff.] **1.** any contagious or infectious disease that is fatal or very harmful, esp. an epidemic of such disease, as bubonic plague **2.** anything, as a doctrine, regarded as harmful —**pes'ti·len'tial** (-tə len'shəl) *adj.* —**pes'ti·len'tial·ly** *adv.*

pes·ti·lent (-ənt) *adj.* [< L. < *pestis,* plague] **1.** likely to cause death; deadly **2.** dangerous to the security and welfare of society; pernicious **3.** annoying; troublesome —**pes'ti·lent·ly** *adv.*

pes·tle (pes''l) *n.* [< OFr. < L. *pistillum* < *pinsere,* to pound] **1.** a tool used to pound or grind substances, as in a mortar **2.** a heavy bar used in pounding or stamping —*vt., vi.* **-tled, -tling** to pound, grind, crush, etc. with or as with a pestle

pes·to (pes'tō) *n.* [It., ult. < L. *pinsere*: see PESTLE] a sauce of ground fresh basil and garlic mixed with olive oil, used esp. over pasta

pet¹ (pet) *n.* [orig. Scot. dial.] **1.** an animal that is domesticated and kept as a companion or treated with fondness **2.** a person who is liked or treated better than others; favorite —*adj.* **1.** kept or treated as a pet **2.** especially liked; favorite **3.** greatest; particular *[*one's *pet* peeve*]* **4.** showing fondness *[*a *pet* name*]* —*vt.* **pet'ted, pet'ting** **1.** to stroke or pat gently; fondle; caress **2.** to pamper —*vi.* [Colloq.] to kiss, fondle intimately, etc. in making love —**pet'ter** *n.*

pet² (pet) *n.* [< obs. phr. *to take the pet* < ?] a state of sulky peevishness or ill humor

Pet. Peter

pet·al (pet''l) *n.* [< ModL. < Gr. < *petalos,* outspread] any of the component parts, or leaves, of a corolla —**pet'aled, pet'alled** *adj.* —**pet'al·like'** *adj.* —**pet'al·ous** *adj.*

pe·tard (pi tärd') *n.* [< Fr. < *péter,* ult. < L. *pedere,* to break wind] a metal cone filled with explosives: formerly used to break an opening in a wall or gate

pet·cock (pet'käk') *n.* [< obs. *pet,* breaking wind + COCK¹] a small valve for draining excess water or air from pipes, radiators, boilers, etc.

Pe·ter (pē'tər) [< LL. < Gr. < *petros,* a rock] **1.** a masculine name: dim. *Pete* **2.** *Bible a)* ?–64? A.D.; one of the Twelve Apostles, a fisherman and the reputed author of the Epistles of Peter: also called *Simon Peter b)* either of these books **3. Peter I** 1672–1725; czar of Russia (1682–1725): called *Peter the Great*

pe·ter (pē'tər) *vi.* [< ?] [Colloq.] to become gradually smaller, weaker, etc. and cease (with *out*)

Pe·ter·bor·ough (pē'tər bur'ō) city in SE Ontario, Canada, near Toronto: pop. 56,000

pet·i·ole (pet'ē ōl') *n.* [< ModL. < L. *petiolus,* dim. of *pes,* a foot] **1.** *Bot. same as* LEAFSTALK **2.** *Zool.* a stalklike part; peduncle —**pet'i·o·lar** (-ə lər) *adj.* —**pet'i·o·late'** (-ə lāt', -lit) *adj.*

pet·it (pet'ē; *Fr.* pə tē') *adj.* [< OFr.: see PETTY] small; petty: now used chiefly in law

pe·tite (pə tēt′) ***adj.*** [Fr., fem. of *petit*] small and trim of figure: said of a woman —**pe·tite′ness** ***n.***

pe·tit four (pet′ē fôr′; *Fr.* pə tē fo͞or′) *pl.* **pe·tits fours** (pet′ē fôrz′; *Fr.* pə tē fo͞or′), **pe·tit fours** (pet′ē fôrz′) [Fr. < *petit,* small + *four,* lit., oven] a small cake cut from spongecake, etc. and decorated with icing

pe·ti·tion (pə tish′ən) ***n.*** [< OFr. < L. *petitio* < *petere,* to ask] **1.** a solemn, earnest request to a superior or to those in authority; entreaty **2.** a formal document making such a request, often signed by a number of persons **3.** something that is asked or entreated **4.** *Law* a written plea asking for specific court action —***vt.*** **1.** to address a petition to **2.** to ask for; solicit —***vi.*** to make a petition —**pe·ti′tion·ar′y** ***adj.*** —**pe·ti′tion·er** ***n.***

petit jury a group of twelve citizens picked to weigh the evidence in and decide the issues of a trial in court: cf. GRAND JURY

petit larceny *see* LARCENY

Pe·trarch (pē′trärk) (It. name *Francesco Petrarca*) 1304–74; It. lyric poet & scholar

pet·rel (pet′rəl) ***n.*** [? a dim. of PETER, in allusion to St. Peter's walking on the sea] any of various small, dark sea birds with long wings; esp., *same as* STORMY PETREL

pe·tri dish (pē′trē) [after J. *Petri* (1852–1921), G. bacteriologist] [*also* **P- d-**] a shallow, cylindrical, transparent dish with a cover, used for the culture of microorganisms

pet·ri·fy (pet′rə fī′) ***vt.*** **-fied′, -fy′ing** [< Fr. < L. *petra,* a rock + *facere,* to make] **1.** to replace the normal cells of (organic matter) with silica, etc.; re-form as a stony substance **2.** to make rigid; harden or deaden **3.** to paralyze, as with fear; stun —***vi.*** to become petrified —**pet′ri·fac′tion** (-fak′shən), **pet′ri·fi·ca′tion** ***n.***

pet·ro- [< Gr. *petra* or *petros*] *a combining form meaning* rock or stone: also, before a vowel, **petr-**

pet·ro·chem·i·cal (pet′rō kem′i k′l) ***n.*** [PETRO(LEUM) + CHEMICAL] a chemical derived ultimately from petroleum, as ethylene glycol, etc.

pet·ro·dol·lars (pet′rō däl′ərz) ***n.pl.*** [PETRO(LEUM) + DOLLARS] the revenue obtained by the major oil-exporting countries from the sale of petroleum

Pet·ro·grad (pet′rə grad; *Russ.* pyet′rô grät′) *former name (1914–24) of* LENINGRAD

pe·trog·ra·phy (pi träg′rə fē) ***n.*** [< ModL.: see PETRO- & -GRAPHY] the science of the description or classification of rocks —**pe·trog′ra·pher** ***n.*** —**pet·ro·graph·ic** (pet′rə graf′ik), **pet′ro·graph′i·cal** ***adj.***

pet·rol (pet′rəl) ***n.*** [< Fr. < ML. *petroleum:* see PETROLEUM] *Brit. term for* GASOLINE

pet·ro·la·tum (pet′rə lāt′əm, -lät′-) ***n.*** [ModL. < ff. + L. *-atus:* see -ATE[1]] a greasy, jellylike substance consisting of a mixture of hydrocarbons obtained from petroleum

pe·tro·le·um (pə trō′lē əm) ***n.*** [ML. < L. *petra,* a rock + *oleum,* oil] an oily, liquid solution of hydrocarbons, yellowish-green to black in color, occurring naturally in certain rock strata: it yields paraffin, fuel oil, kerosine, gasoline, benzine, etc.

petroleum jelly *same as* PETROLATUM

pe·trol·o·gy (pi träl′ə jē) ***n.*** [PETRO- + -LOGY] the study of the composition, structure, and origin of rocks —**pet·ro·log·ic** (pet′rə läj′ik), **pet′ro·log′i·cal** ***adj.*** —**pet′ro·log′i·cal·ly** ***adv.*** —**pe·trol′o·gist** ***n.***

pet·ti·coat (pet′i kōt′) ***n.*** [< PETTY + COAT] **1.** a skirt, now esp. an underskirt, worn by women and girls **2.** [Colloq.] a woman or girl —***adj.*** of or by women

pet·ti·fog·ger (pet′ē fäg′ər, -fôg′-) ***n.*** [PETTY + obs. *fogger* < ?] **1.** a lawyer who handles petty cases, esp. by using unethical methods **2.** a trickster **3.** a quibbler —**pet′ti·fog′** ***vi.*** **-fogged′, -fog′ging** —**pet′ti·fog′ger·y** ***n.***

pet·tish (pet′ish) ***adj.*** [< PET[2] + -ISH] peevish; petulant; cross —**pet′tish·ly** ***adv.*** —**pet′tish·ness** ***n.***

pet·ty (pet′ē) ***adj.*** **-ti·er, -ti·est** [OFr. *petit*] **1.** relatively unimportant; trivial **2.** narrow-minded, mean, etc. **3.** relatively low in rank; subordinate —**pet′ti·ness** ***n.***

petty cash a cash fund for incidental expenses

petty jury *same as* PETIT JURY

petty larceny *see* LARCENY

petty officer any of certain naval enlisted men whose ratings correspond to those of army noncommissioned officers

pet·u·lant (pech′oo lənt) ***adj.*** [< L. *petulans* < *petere,* to attack] impatient or irritable, esp. over a petty annoyance —**pet′u·lance, pet′u·lan·cy** ***n.*** —**pet′u·lant·ly** ***adv.***

pe·tu·ni·a (pə to͞on′yə, -tyo͞on′-; -ē ə) ***n.*** [ModL. < Fr. < Tupi *petun,* tobacco] a plant of the nightshade family, with variously colored, funnel-shaped flowers

pew (pyo͞o) ***n.*** [< OFr. *puie* < L. pl. of *podium,* balcony < Gr. *podion* < *pous,* a foot] **1.** any of the benches with a back fixed in rows in a church **2.** any of the boxlike enclosures with seats, in some churches, for one family, etc.

pe·wee (pē′wē) ***n.*** [echoic of its call] any of several small flycatchers

pe·wit (pē′wit, pyo͞o′it) ***n.*** [echoic of its call] *same as:* **1.** LAPWING **2.** PEWEE

pew·ter (pyo͞ot′ər) ***n.*** [< OFr. *peautre*] **1.** a dull, silvery-gray alloy of tin with brass, copper, or, esp., lead **2.** articles made of pewter —***adj.*** made of pewter

pe·yo·te (pā ōt′ē; *Sp.* pe yô′te) ***n.*** [AmSp. < Nahuatl *peyotl,* caterpillar, in reference to the downy center] *same as* MESCAL (sense 3): also **pe·yo′tl** (-′l; *Sp.* -t′l)

pf. **1.** perfect **2.** pianoforte **3.** preferred: also **pfd.**

Pfc, Pfc., PFC Private First Class

pfen·nig (fen′ig; *G.* pfen′iH) ***n.,*** *pl.* **-nigs,** G. **-ni·ge** (-i gə) [G., akin to PENNY] *see* MONETARY UNITS, table (Germany)

PG parental guidance suggested: a motion-picture rating cautioning parents that they may find the film unsuitable for children

pg. page

pH (pē′āch′) [< Fr. *p(ouvoir) h(ydrogène),* hydrogen power] *a symbol for* the degree of acidity (values from 0 to 7) or alkalinity (values from 7 to 14)

Phae·dra (fē′drə) *Gr. Myth.* wife of Theseus: she loved her stepson, Hippolytus, who rejected her

Pha·ë·thon (fā′ə thən) *Gr. & Rom. Myth.* son of Helios: he tried to drive his father's sun chariot and would have set the world on fire had not Zeus prevented him

pha·e·ton, pha·ë·ton (fā′ət ′n) ***n.*** [< Fr. < L.: see prec.] **1.** a light, four-wheeled carriage with front and back seats and, usually, a folding top **2.** *same as* TOURING CAR

-phage (fāj) [< Gr. *phagein,* to eat] *a combining form meaning* eating or destroying

phag·o- [< Gr. *phagein,* to eat] *a combining form meaning:* **1.** eating or destroying *[phagocyte]* **2.** phagocyte Also, before a vowel, **phag-**

phag·o·cyte (fag′ə sīt′) ***n.*** [prec. + -CYTE] any leukocyte that ingests and destroys other cells, microorganisms, etc. in the blood and tissues —**phag′o·cyt′ic** (-sit′ik) ***adj.***

-pha·gous (fə gəs) [< Gr. < *phagein,* to eat] *a combining form meaning* that eats (a thing specified)

-pha·gy (fə jē) [< ModL. < Gr. *phagein,* to eat] *a combining form meaning* the practice of eating (a thing specified): also **-pha·gi·a** (fā′jē ə, -jə)

pha·lan·ger (fə lan′jər) ***n.*** [ModL. < Gr. *phalanx,* bone between two joints: with reference to the structure of the hind feet] any of various small Australian marsupials with a long, bushy tail

pha·lanx (fā′laŋks, fal′aŋks) ***n.,*** *pl.* **-lanx·es;** also, & for 4 always, **pha·lan·ges** (fə lan′jēz) [L. < Gr., line of battle] **1.** an ancient military formation of infantry in close ranks with shields together **2.** a massed group of individuals **3.** a group of individuals united for a common purpose **4.** any of the bones of the fingers or toes: also **phal·ange** (fal′ənj, fāl′-; fə lanj′) —**pha·lan·ge·al** (fə lan′jē əl) ***adj.***

phal·lic (fal′ik) ***adj.*** **1.** of or like the phallus **2.** of or relating to phallicism **3.** *same as* GENITAL

phal·li·cism (fal′ə siz′m) ***n.*** worship of the phallus as a symbol of the male generative power: also **phal′lism**

phal·lus (fal′əs) ***n.,*** *pl.* **-li** (-ī), **-lus·es** [L. < Gr. *phallos*] an image of the penis as a symbol of generative power

phan·tasm (fan′taz′m) ***n.*** [< OFr. < L. < Gr. *phantasma* < *phantazein,* to show] **1.** a figment of the mind; esp., a specter, or ghost **2.** a deceptive likeness —**phan·tas′mal, phan·tas′mic** ***adj.***

phan·tas·ma·go·ri·a (fan taz′mə gôr′ē ə) ***n.*** [< Fr. < Gr. *phantasma,* phantasm + *ageirein,* to assemble] a rapidly changing series of things seen or imagined, as in a dream: also **phan·tas′ma·go′ry,** *pl.* **-ries** —**phan·tas′ma·go′ri·al, phan·tas′ma·go′ric, phan·tas′ma·go′ri·cal** ***adj.***

phan·ta·sy (fan′tə sē) ***n.,*** *pl.* **-sies** *same as* FANTASY

phan·tom (fan′təm) ***n.*** [< OFr. *fantosme:* see PHANTASM] **1.** something not real that one seems to see; apparition; specter **2.** something feared **3.** an illusion **4.** a person or thing that is something in appearance but not in fact *[a phantom of a leader]* **5.** any mental image or representation —***adj.*** of, like, or constituting a phantom; illusory

Phar·aoh (fer′ō) ***n.*** [ult. < Egypt. *pr-'o,* great house] the title of the rulers of ancient Egypt —**Phar′a·on′ic** (-ā än′ik), **Phar′a·on′i·cal** ***adj.***

Phar·i·sa·ic (far′ə sā′ik) ***adj.*** **1.** of the Pharisees **2.** [**p-**] *a)* observing the letter but not the spirit of religious law *b)* hypocritical: also **phar′i·sa′i·cal** —**phar′i·sa′i·cal·ly** ***adv.***

Phar·i·sa·ism (far′ə sā′iz′m) ***n.*** **1.** the beliefs and practices of the Pharisees **2.** **[p-]** pharisaic behavior, character, principles, etc.

Phar·i·see (far′ə sē′) ***n.*** **1.** a member of an ancient Jewish party that carefully observed the written and the oral, or traditional, law **2.** **[p-]** a pharisaic person —**Phar′i·see′ism** ***n.***

Pharm., pharm. **1.** pharmaceutical **2.** pharmacist **3.** pharmacopeia **4.** pharmacy

phar·ma·ceu·ti·cal (fär′mə so͞ot′i k'l, -syo͞ot′-) ***adj.*** [< LL. < Gr., ult. < *pharmakon,* a medicine] **1.** of pharmacy or pharmacists **2.** of or by drugs Also **phar′ma·ceu′tic** —***n.*** a pharmaceutical product; drug —**phar′ma·ceu′ti·cal·ly** ***adv.***

phar·ma·ceu·tics (-iks) ***n.pl.*** [*with sing. v.*] *same as* PHARMACY (sense 1)

phar·ma·cist (fär′mə sist) ***n.*** a person licensed to practice pharmacy; druggist

phar·ma·cog·no·sy (fär′mə käg′nə sē) ***n.*** [< Gr. *pharmakon,* a drug + *-gnōsia* < *gnōsis,* knowledge] the science dealing with properties of drugs in their crude state

phar·ma·col·o·gy (-käl′ə jē) ***n.*** [< ModL. < Gr. *pharmakon,* a drug] **1.** orig., the study of the preparation, qualities, and uses of drugs **2.** the science dealing with the effects of drugs —**phar′ma·co·log′i·cal** (-kə läj′i k'l), **phar′ma·co·log′ic** ***adj.*** —**phar′ma·co·log′i·cal·ly** ***adv.*** —**phar′ma·col′o·gist** ***n.***

phar·ma·co·pe·ia, phar·ma·co·poe·ia (fär′mə kə pē′ə) ***n.*** [ModL. < Gr. < *pharmakon,* a drug + *poiein,* to make] an authoritative book containing a list of drugs and medicines and the lawful standards for their production, dispensation, etc. —**phar′ma·co·pe′ial, phar′ma·co·poe′ial** ***adj.***

phar·ma·cy (fär′mə sē) ***n.,*** *pl.* **-cies** [< MFr. < LL. < Gr. < *pharmakon,* a drug] **1.** the art or profession of preparing and dispensing drugs and medicines **2.** a place where this is done; drugstore

phar·yn·gi·tis (far′in jīt′əs) ***n.*** inflammation of the mucous membrane of the pharynx; sore throat

phar·ynx (far′iŋks) ***n.,*** *pl.* **phar′ynx·es, pha·ryn·ges** (fə rin′jēz) [ModL. < Gr. *pharynx*] the cavity leading from the mouth and nasal passages to the larynx and esophagus: see EPIGLOTTIS, illus. —**pha·ryn·ge·al** (fə rin′jē əl, far′ən jē′əl), **pha·ryn′gal** (-riŋ′gəl) ***adj.***

phase (fāz) ***n.*** [< ModL. < Gr. *phasis* < *phainesthai,* to appear] **1.** any stage in the illumination or appearance of the moon or a planet **2.** any stage or form in a series of changes, as in development **3.** aspect; side; part *[a problem with many phases]* **4.** a solid, liquid, or gaseous homogeneous form *[ice is a phase of* H_2O*]* **5.** the fractional part of a cycle through which a periodic wave, as of light, sound, etc., has advanced at any instant, with reference to a standard position **6.** a characteristic variation in the color of an animal's fur or plumage, according to season, age, etc. —***vt.*** **phased, phas′ing** **1.** to plan, introduce, carry out, etc. in phases (often with *in, into,* etc.) **2.** to put in phase —***vi.*** to move by phases —**in** (or **out of**) **phase** in (or not in) synchronization —**phase out** to terminate (an activity) by stages —**pha·sic** (fā′zik) ***adj.***

phase modulation *Radio* variation in the phase of a carrier wave in accordance with some signal, as speech

phase-out (fāz′out′) ***n.*** a phasing out; gradual termination, withdrawal, etc.

Ph.D. [L. *Philosophiae Doctor*] Doctor of Philosophy

pheas·ant (fez′'nt) ***n.,*** *pl.* **-ants, -ant:** see PLURAL, II, D, 1 [< Anglo-Fr. < OFr. < L. < Gr. *phasianos,* lit., (bird) of *Phasis,* river in Asia] **1.** a chickenlike game bird with a long tail and brilliant feathers **2.** any of various birds resembling the pheasant, as the ruffed grouse

RING-NECKED PHEASANT (to 35 in. long, including beak and tail)

phel·lem (fel′em) ***n.*** [< Gr. *phellos*] *same as* CORK (*n.* 4)

phen- [< Fr. < Gr. *phainein,* to show] *a combining form meaning* of or derived from benzene: also **phe·no-**

phe·nac·e·tin (fi nas′ə tin) ***n.*** [PHEN- + ACET(O)- + -IN¹] *same as* ACETOPHENETIDIN

Phe·ni·cia (fə nish′ə, -nē′shə) *same as* PHOENICIA

phe·no·bar·bi·tal (fē′nə bär′bə tôl′, -tal′) ***n.*** [PHENO- + BARBITAL] an odorless, white powder, $C_{12}O_3N_2H_{12}$, used as a sedative and antispasmodic

phe·no·cryst (fē′nə krist, fen′ə-) ***n.*** [< Fr. < Gr. *phainein,* to show + *krystallos,* crystal] a conspicuous crystal found in porphyritic rock

phe·nol (fē′nōl, -nôl, -näl) ***n.*** [PHEN- + -OL¹] a white crystalline compound, C_6H_5OH, produced from coal tar and used in making explosives, etc.: its dilute aqueous solution is commonly called carbolic acid —**phe·no′lic** ***adj.***

phe·nol·phthal·ein (fē′nōl thal′ēn, -nôl-; -fthal′-; -ē ən) ***n.*** [< PHENOL + NAPHTHALENE] a white to pale-yellow, crystalline powder, $C_{20}H_{14}O_4$, used as a laxative, in making dyes, and as an acid-base indicator in chemical analysis

phe·nom·e·na (fi näm′ə nə) ***n.*** *pl. of* PHENOMENON

phe·nom·e·nal (fi näm′ə n'l) ***adj.*** **1.** of or constituting a phenomenon or phenomena **2.** very unusual; extraordinary —**phe·nom′e·nal·ly** ***adv.***

phe·nom·e·non (fi näm′ə nän′, -nən) ***n.,*** *pl.* **-na** (-nə); also, esp. for 3 and 4, **-nons′** [< LL. < Gr. *phainomenon,* neut. prp. of *phainesthai,* to appear] **1.** any fact or experience that is apparent to the senses and can be scientifically described, as an eclipse **2.** the appearance of something experienced as distinguished from the thing in itself **3.** anything extremely unusual **4.** [Colloq.] a person who is extraordinary in some way

phe·no·type (fē′nə tīp′) ***n.*** [G. *phänotypus*] *Biol.* the manifest characters of an organism collectively, resulting from both its heredity and its environment —**phe′no·typ′ic** (-tip′ik), **phe′no·typ′i·cal** ***adj.*** —**phe′no·typ′i·cal·ly** ***adv.***

phen·yl (fen′il, fē′nil) ***n.*** [PHEN- + -YL] the monovalent radical, C_6H_5, forming the basis of phenol, benzene, aniline, and some other compounds

phen·yl·al·a·nine (fen′il al′ə nēn′, fē′nil-) ***n.*** an essential amino acid, $C_9H_{11}O_2N$, occurring in proteins

phen·yl·ke·to·nu·ri·a (-kēt′ə nyoor′ē ə) ***n.*** [PHENYL + KETON(E) + -URIA] a genetic disorder of phenylalanine metabolism, which, if untreated, causes severe mental retardation in infants

pher·o·mone (fer′ə mōn′) ***n.*** [< Gr. *pherein,* BEAR¹ + E. *-o-* + (HOR)MONE] a chemical substance secreted by certain animals, as ants, that produces responses in other individuals in the same species

phew (fyo͞o, fyoo: *conventionalized pronun.*) ***interj.*** a breathy sound expressing disgust, surprise, etc.

phi (fī, fē) ***n.*** [MGr.] the 21st letter of the Greek alphabet (Φ, φ)

phi·al (fī′əl) ***n.*** [< OFr. < Pr. < ML. < L. < Gr. *phialē,* shallow bowl] a small glass bottle; vial

Phi Be·ta Kap·pa (fī′ bāt′ə kap′ə, bēt′ə) **1.** an honorary society of U.S. college students of high scholastic rank **2.** a member of this society

Phid·i·as (fid′ē əs) 5th cent. B.C.; Gr. sculptor —**Phid′i·an** ***adj.***

Phil. **1.** Philippians **2.** Philippine

Phil·a·del·phi·a (fil′ə del′fē ə, -fyə) [Gr. *philadelphia,* brotherly love < *philos,* loving + *adelphos,* brother] city & port in SE Pa.: pop. 1,688,000 (met. area 4,701,000) —**Phil′a·del′phi·an** ***adj., n.***

phi·lan·der (fi lan′dər) ***vi.*** [< Gr. < *philos,* loving + *anēr* (gen. *andros*), a man] to make love insincerely: said of a man —**phi·lan′der·er** ***n.***

phil·an·throp·ic (fil′ən thräp′ik) ***adj.*** of, showing, or constituting philanthropy; charitable; benevolent; humane: also **phil′an·throp′i·cal** —**phil′an·throp′i·cal·ly** ***adv.***

phi·lan·thro·py (fi lan′thrə pē) ***n.*** [< LL. < Gr. < *philein,* to love + *anthrōpos,* man] **1.** a desire to help mankind, as by gifts to charitable or humanitarian institutions **2.** *pl.* **-pies** a philanthropic act, gift, institution, etc. —**phi·lan′thro·pist** ***n.***

phi·lat·e·ly (fi lat′'l ē) ***n.*** [< Fr. < Gr. *philos,* loving + *ateleia,* exemption from (further) tax taken as equivalent of "postage prepaid"] the collection and study of postage stamps, postmarks, etc. —**phil·a·tel·ic** (fil′ə tel′ik) ***adj.*** —**phil′a·tel′i·cal·ly** ***adv.*** —**phi·lat′e·list** ***n.***

-phile (fīl, fil) [< Gr. *philos,* loving] *a combining form meaning* loving, liking, favorably disposed to *[Anglophile]* : also **-phil** (fil)

Phi·le·mon (fi lē′mən, fī-) a book of the New Testament, an epistle from the Apostle Paul to his friend Philemon: abbrev. **Philem.**

phil·har·mon·ic (fil′här män′ik, fil′ər-) ***adj.*** [< Fr. < Gr. *philos,* loving + *harmonia,* harmony] loving or devoted to music: used in the title of some symphony orchestras —***n.*** **1.** a society formed to sponsor a symphony orchestra **2.** [Colloq.] such an orchestra or one of its concerts

Phil·ip (fil′əp) [< L. < Gr. < *philos,* loving + *hippos,* a horse] **1.** a masculine name: dim. *Phil:* also sp. **Phil·lip** **2.** *Bible* one of the twelve apostles **3. Philip II** *a)* 382–336 B.C.; king of Macedonia (359–336): father of ALEXANDER THE GREAT *b)* 1165–1223; king of France (1180–1223) *c)* 1527–98; king of Spain (1556–98): sent the Armada against England (1588)

Phi·lip·pi (fi lip′ī) ancient city in Macedonia —**Phi·lip′pi·an** (-ē ən) ***adj., n.***

Phi·lip·pi·ans (-ē ənz) a book of the New Testament, an epistle from the Apostle Paul to the Christians of Philippi

Phi·lip·pic (fi lip′ik) ***n.*** **1.** any of the orations of Demosthenes against Philip, king of Macedon **2.** **[p-]** any bitter verbal attack

Phil·ip·pine (fil′ə pēn′) ***adj.*** of the Philippine Islands or their people

Philippine mahogany the reddish wood of various trees of the Philippines and SE Asia

Phil·ip·pines (fil′ə pēnz′) country occupying a group of c. 7,100 islands (**Philippine Islands**) in the SW Pacific off the SE coast of Asia: 114,830 sq. mi.; pop. 43,751,000; cap. Manila

Phi·lis·ti·a (fə lis′tē ə) country of the Philistines, in ancient SW Palestine

Phil·is·tine (fil′is tēn′; fi lis′tin, -tēn) ***n.*** **1.** a member of a non-Semitic people who lived in Philistia and repeatedly warred with the Israelites **2.** [*often* **p-**] a person regarded as smugly conventional, indifferent to cultural values, etc. —***adj.*** **1.** of the ancient Philistines **2.** [*often* **p-**] smugly conventional, lacking in culture, etc. —**Phil′is·tin·ism** ***n.***

Phil·lips (fil′əps) [after H. *Phillips* (?–1958), its U.S. developer] *a trademark for* a screwdriver (**Phillips screwdriver**) with a tip that can be used on a screw (**Phillips screw**) that has two slots crossing at the center of the head

phil·o- [< Gr. *philos,* loving] *a combining form meaning* loving, liking, having a predilection for *[philology]* : also, before a vowel, **phil-**

phil·o·den·dron (fil′ə den′drən) ***n.*** [ModL. < Gr. *philos,* loving + *dendron,* a tree] a tropical American vine of the arum family, often with heart-shaped leaves

phi·log·y·ny (fi läj′ə nē) ***n.*** [< Gr. < *philein,* to love + *gynē,* woman] love of or fondness for women —**phi·log′y·nist** ***n.*** —**phi·log′y·nous** ***adj.***

phi·lol·o·gy (fi läl′ə jē) ***n.*** [< Fr. < L. < Gr. *philologia,* love of literature < *philein,* to love + *logos,* a word] **1.** the study of literary texts, etc. in order to determine their authenticity, meaning, etc. **2.** *earlier term for* LINGUISTICS —**phil·o·log·i·cal** (fil′ə läj′i k′l), **phil′o·log′ic** ***adj.*** —**phil′o·log′i·cal·ly** ***adv.*** —**phi·lol′o·gist** ***n.***

philos. philosophy

phi·los·o·pher (fi läs′ə fər) ***n.*** [< OFr. < L. < Gr. < *philos,* loving + *sophos,* wise] **1.** a person who studies or is learned in philosophy **2.** a person who lives by a system of philosophy **3.** *a)* a person who meets difficulties with calmness and composure *b)* a person who philosophizes

philosophers' (or **philosopher's**) **stone** an imaginary substance that alchemists believed would change base metals into gold or silver

phil·o·soph·ic (fil′ə säf′ik) ***adj.*** **1.** of a philosophy or philosopher **2.** devoted to or learned in philosophy **3.** calm, as in a difficult situation; rational Also **phil′o·soph′i·cal** —**phil′o·soph′i·cal·ly** ***adv.***

phi·los·o·phize (fi läs′ə fīz′) ***vi.*** **-phized′, -phiz′ing** **1.** to deal philosophically with abstract matter; reason like a philosopher **2.** to express superficial philosophic ideas, truisms, etc.; esp., to moralize —**phi·los′o·phiz′er** ***n.***

phi·los·o·phy (-fē) ***n., pl.*** **-phies** [< OFr. < L. < Gr.: see PHILOSOPHER] **1.** theory or logical analysis of the principles underlying conduct, thought, knowledge, and the nature of the universe **2.** the general principles of a field of knowledge *[*the *philosophy* of economics*]* **3.** a particular system of principles for the conduct of life **4.** *a)* a study of human morals, character, and behavior *b)* mental composure; calmness

-phi·lous (fi ləs) [< Gr. *philos,* loving] *a combining form meaning* loving, liking

phil·ter (fil′tər) ***n.*** [< MFr. < L. < Gr. *philtron* < *philein,* to love] **1.** a potion or charm thought to arouse sexual love, esp. toward a specific person **2.** any magic potion —***vt.*** to charm or arouse with a philter

phle·bi·tis (fli bīt′is) ***n.*** [see ff. & -ITIS] inflammation of a vein —**phle·bit′ic** (-bit′ik) ***adj.***

phleb·o- [< Gr. *phleps* (gen. *phlebos*), a vein] *a combining form meaning* vein: also, before a vowel, **phleb-**

phle·bot·o·my (fli bät′ə mē) ***n.*** [< OFr. < LL. < Gr.: see prec. & -TOMY] the act of bloodletting as a therapeutic measure —**phle·bot′o·mist** ***n.***

phlegm (flem) ***n.*** [< MFr. < LL. < Gr. *phlegma,* inflammation < *phlegein,* to burn] **1.** the thick secretion of the mucous glands of the respiratory tract, discharged from the throat, as during a cold **2.** [Obs.] that one of the four humors believed to cause sluggishness **3.** *a)* sluggishness *b)* calmness; composure —**phlegm′y** ***adj.***

phleg·mat·ic (fleg mat′ik) ***adj.*** [ult. < Gr. *phlegma:* see prec.] hard to rouse to action; specif., *a)* sluggish; dull; apathetic *b)* calm; cool; stolid Also **phleg·mat′i·cal** —**phleg·mat′i·cal·ly** ***adv.***

phlo·em (flō′em) ***n.*** [G. < Gr. *phloos,* bark] the cell tissue serving as a path for the distribution of food material in a plant

phlo·gis·ton (flō jis′tän, -tən) ***n.*** [ModL., ult. < Gr. *phlegein,* to burn] an imaginary element formerly believed to cause combustion; principle of fire —**phlo·gis′tic** ***adj.***

phlox (fläks) ***n.*** [ModL. < L. < Gr. *phlox,* a flame < *phlegein,* to burn] any of a group of chiefly N. American plants, with opposite leaves and white, pink, red, or bluish flowers

PHLOX

Phnom Penh (p′nôm′ pen′) capital of Kampuchea (see CAMBODIA): pop. c. 300,000 (in 1979): also **Pnom-Penh**

-phobe (fōb) [Fr. < L. < Gr. < *phobos,* a fear] a suffix meaning one who fears or hates *[Francophobe]*

pho·bi·a (fō′bē ə) ***n.*** [< Gr. *phobos,* a fear] an irrational, persistent fear of some particular thing or situation —**pho′bic** ***adj.***

-pho·bi·a (fō′bē ə) [see prec.] *a combining form meaning* fear, dread, hatred *[claustrophobia]*

Phoe·be (fē′bē) [L. < Gr. < *phoibos,* bright] **1.** a feminine name **2.** *Gr. Myth. same as* ARTEMIS

phoe·be (fē′bē) ***n.*** [echoic, with sp. after prec.] any of several American flycatchers with a gray or brown back and a short crest

Phoe·bus (fē′bəs) *Gr. Myth. same as* APOLLO

Phoe·ni·cia (fə nish′ə, -nē′shə) ancient region of city-states at the E end of the Mediterranean, in the region of present-day Syria & Lebanon

Phoe·ni·cian (-nish′ən, -nē′shən) ***adj.*** of Phoenicia, its people, their language, etc. —***n.*** **1.** a native of Phoenicia **2.** the extinct Semitic language of the Phoenicians

Phoe·nix (fē′niks) [in allusion to the ff.] capital of Ariz., in the SC part: pop. 765,000 (met. area 1,512,000)

phoe·nix (fē′niks) ***n.*** [< OE. & OFr. *fenix* < L. *phoenix* < Gr. *phoinix*] *Egyptian Myth.* a beautiful bird which lived for 500 or 600 years and then consumed itself in fire, rising renewed from the ashes: a symbol of immortality

phon (fän) ***n.*** [< Gr. *phōnē,* a sound] a measure of the apparent loudness of a sound

pho·nate (fō′nāt) ***vi.*** **-nat·ed, -nat·ing** [< Gr. *phōnē,* a voice + -ATE[1]] to utter a voiced sound —**pho·na′tion** ***n.***

phone[1] (fōn) ***n.*** [Gr. *phōnē,* a sound] any single speech sound: a phoneme is composed of phones

phone[2] (fōn) ***n., vt., vi.*** **phoned, phon′ing** *colloq. shortened form of* TELEPHONE

-phone (fōn) [< Gr. *phōnē,* a sound] *a combining form meaning:* **1.** a device producing or transmitting sound *[saxophone]* **2.** a telephone *[radiophone]*

pho·neme (fō′nēm) ***n.*** [< Fr. < Gr. *phōnēma,* a sound < *phōnē,* a voice] *Linguis.* a set of similar sounds in a language that are heard as the same sound and represented in phonemic transcription by the same symbol, as the sounds of *p* in *pin, spin,* and *tip*

pho·ne·mic (fə nē′mik, fō-) ***adj.*** **1.** of, characterized by, or based on, phonemes **2.** of phonemics

pho·ne·mics (fə nē′miks, fō-) ***n.pl.*** [*with sing. v.*] **1.** the branch of language study dealing with the phonemic systems of languages **2.** the description and classification of the phonemes of a language —**pho·ne′mi·cist** (-mə sist) ***n.***

pho·net·ic (fə net′ik, fō-) ***adj.*** [< ModL. < Gr. < *phōnētos,* to be spoken, ult. < *phōnē,* a sound] **1.** of speech sounds **2.** of phonetics **3.** conforming to pronunciation *[phonetic* spelling*]* —**pho·net′i·cal·ly** ***adv.***

pho·net·ics (-iks) ***n.pl.*** [*with sing. v.*] **1.** the branch of language study dealing with speech sounds, their production and combination, and their representation by written symbols **2.** the phonetic system of a particular language —**pho·ne·ti·cian** (fō′nə tish′ən), **pho·ne·tist** (fō′nə tist) ***n.***

pho·ney (fō′nē) ***adj., n.*** [Colloq.] *same as* PHONY

phon·ic (fän′ik, fō′nik) ***adj.*** [< Gr. *phōnē,* a sound] **1.** of, or having the nature of, sound; esp., of speech sounds **2.** of phonics —**phon′i·cal·ly** ***adv.***

phon·ics (fän′iks, fō′niks) ***n.pl.*** [*with sing. v.*] [< prec.] a method of teaching beginners to read by learning the usual sounds of certain letters or groups of letters

pho·no- [< Gr. *phōnē,* a sound] *a combining form meaning* sound, speech: also, before a vowel, **phon-**

pho·no·gram (fō′nə gram′) ***n.*** [prec. + -GRAM] a symbol representing a word, syllable, or sound, as in shorthand —**pho′no·gram′ic, pho′no·gram′mic** ***adj.***

pho·no·graph (fō′nə graf′) ***n.*** [PHONO- + -GRAPH] an instrument for reproducing sound that has been transcribed in a spiral groove on a disk or cylinder: a needle or stylus follows this groove —**pho′no·graph′ic** ***adj.*** —**pho′no·graph′i·cal·ly** ***adv.***

pho·nog·ra·phy (fō näg′rə fē) ***n.*** [PHONO- + -GRAPHY] **1.** a written representation of the sounds of speech **2.** any system of shorthand based on a phonetic transcription of speech

pho·nol·o·gy (fō näl′ə jē, fə-) ***n.*** [PHONO- + -LOGY] **1.** phonetics or phonemics or, esp., both considered as a system of speech sounds **2.** the study of the changes in speech sounds in a language or dialect —**pho·no·log·i·cal** (fō′nə läj′i k'l), **pho′no·log′ic** ***adj.*** —**pho′no·log′i·cal·ly** ***adv.*** —**pho·nol′o·gist** ***n.***

pho·non (fō′nän) ***n.*** [PHON(O)- + *-on,* as in PHOTON] a quantum of sound energy that is a carrier of heat

pho·ny (fō′nē) ***adj.*** **-ni·er, -ni·est** [< Brit. thieves' argot *fawney,* a gilt ring (passed off as gold) < Ir. *fáinne*] [Colloq.] not genuine; false, counterfeit, pretentious, etc. —***n.,*** *pl.* **-nies** [Colloq.] **1.** something not genuine; fake **2.** a person who deceives, dissembles, is insincere, etc.; fraud —**pho′ni·ness** ***n.***

-pho·ny (fə nē, fō′nē) [< Gr. *phōnē,* a sound] *a combining form meaning* a (specified kind of) sound: also **-pho·ni·a** (fō′nē ə)

-phore (fôr) [< ModL. < Gr. *-phoros* < *pherein,* to bear] *a combining form meaning* bearer, producer

-phor·ous (fər əs) [see prec.] *a combining form meaning* bearing, producing

phos·gene (fäs′jēn) ***n.*** [< Gr. *phōs,* light + *-gene* (for -GEN)] a colorless, volatile liquid, $COCl_2$, used as a poison gas, in making dyes, etc.

phos·phate (fäs′fāt) ***n.*** [Fr.] **1.** a salt or ester of phosphoric acid **2.** a fertilizer containing phosphates **3.** a soft drink made with soda water, syrup, and, orig., a few drops of phosphoric acid —**phos·phat′ic** (-fat′ik) ***adj.***

phos·pha·tide (fäs′fə tīd′) ***n.*** [PHOSPHAT(E) + -IDE] any of a group of fatty compounds, as lecithin, found in animal and plant cells

phos·phide (-fīd) ***n.*** a compound consisting of trivalent phosphorus with another element or a radical

phos·phite (-fīt) ***n.*** [Fr.] a salt or ester of phosphorous acid

phos·pho- [< PHOSPHORUS] *a combining form meaning* phosphorous or phosphoric acid: also **phosph-**

Phos·phor (fäs′fər) [see PHOSPHORUS] [Poet.] the morning star, esp. Venus —***n.*** [**p-**] **1.** *same as* PHOSPHORUS: now esp. in **phosphor bronze,** a bronze with a little phosphorus in it **2.** a phosphorescent or fluorescent substance

phos·pho·rate (-fə rāt′) ***vt.*** **-rat′ed, -rat′ing** to combine or impregnate with phosphorus

phos·pho·resce (fäs′fə res′) ***vi.*** **-resced′, -resc′ing** to show or undergo phosphorescence

phos·pho·res·cence (-res′'ns) ***n.*** [Fr.: see PHOSPHORUS & -ESCENCE] **1.** *a)* the condition or property of giving off light after exposure to radiant energy, as light, X-rays, etc. *b)* such light **2.** a giving off of light without noticeable heat, as from phosphorus —**phos′pho·res′cent** ***adj.***

phos·pho·ret·ed, phos·pho·ret·ted (fäs′fə ret′id) ***adj.*** combined or impregnated with phosphorus: also **phos′phu·ret′ed** (-fyoo-), **phos′phu·ret′ted**

phos·phor·ic (fäs fôr′ik, -fär′-) ***adj.*** of, like, or containing phosphorus, esp. with a valence of five

phosphoric acid any of several oxygen acids of phosphorus

phos·pho·ro- *a combining form meaning* phosphorus or phosphorescence: also **phosphor-**

phos·pho·rous (fäs′fər əs, fäs fôr′əs) ***adj.*** of, like, or containing phosphorus, esp. with a valence of three

phosphorous acid a white or yellowish, crystalline acid, H_3PO_3, that absorbs oxygen readily

phos·pho·rus (fäs′fər əs) ***n.*** [ModL. < L. *Phosphorus,* morning star < Gr. < *phōs,* a light + *pherein,* to bear] **1.** orig., any phosphorescent substance or object **2.** a nonmetallic chemical element, normally a white, phosphorescent, waxy solid, becoming yellow when exposed to light: it is poisonous and ignites spontaneously at room temperature: when heated in sealed tubes it becomes red, nonpoisonous, and less flammable: symbol, P; at. wt., 30.9738; at. no., 15: a radioactive isotope (**phosphorus 32**) is used in medical treatment, as a tracer in research, etc.

pho·tic (fōt′ik) ***adj.*** [< Gr. *phōs* (gen. *phōtos*), a light + -IC] **1.** of light, esp. in its effect on organisms **2.** designating or of the upper layer (**photic zone**) in a body of water into which daylight penetrates and influences living organisms

pho·to (fōt′ō) ***n.,*** *pl.* **-tos** *clipped form of* PHOTOGRAPH

pho·to- [< Gr. *phos* (gen. *phōtos*), a light] *a combining form meaning:* **1.** of or produced by light *[photograph]* **2.** of a photograph or photography

pho·to·chem·is·try (fōt′ō kem′is trē) ***n.*** the branch of chemistry having to do with the effect of light, etc. in producing chemical action, as in photography —**pho′to·chem′i·cal** (-i k'l) ***adj.***

pho·to·com·po·si·tion (-käm′pə zish′ən) ***n.*** any of various methods of preparing matter for printing by projecting light images of the letters on a photosensitive surface to produce a negative from which plates can be made —**pho′to·com·pose′** (-kəm pōz′) ***vt.*** **-posed′, -pos′ing**

pho·to·con·duc·tive (-kən duk′tiv) ***adj.*** designating or of a substance, as selenium, whose conductivity varies with the illumination striking it —**pho′to·con·duc′tor** ***n.***

pho·to·cop·y (fōt′ə käp′ē) ***n.,*** *pl.* **-cop′ies** a photographic copy of printed or other graphic material —***vt.*** **-cop′ied, -cop′y·ing** to make a photocopy of

pho·to·de·tec·tor (fōt′ō di tek′tər) ***n.*** a demodulator that is sensitive to light

pho·to·e·lec·tric (-i lek′trik) ***adj.*** of or having to do with the electric effects produced by light or other radiation, esp. as in the emission of electrons by certain substances when subjected to radiation of suitable wavelength

photoelectric cell any device in which light controls the electron emission from a cathode, the electrical resistance of an element, etc.: usually used in an electric circuit for mechanical devices, as for opening doors, etc.; electric eye

pho·to·e·lec·tron (-i lek′trän) ***n.*** an electron emitted by a photoelectric effect

pho·to·en·grav·ing (-in grā′viŋ) ***n.*** **1.** a photomechanical process by which photographs are reproduced in relief on printing plates **2.** a plate so made **3.** a print from such a plate —**pho′to·en·grave′** ***vt.*** **-graved′, -grav′ing** —**pho′to·en·grav′er** ***n.***

photo finish **1.** a race so close that the winner can be determined only from a photograph at the finish line **2.** any close finish of a game, contest, etc.

pho·to·fin·ish·ing (-fin′ish iŋ) ***n.*** the developing and printing of photographs —**pho′to·fin′ish·er** ***n.***

pho·to·flash (fōt′ə flash′) ***adj.*** *Photog.* designating or of a light, esp. a flashbulb, electrically synchronized with the shutter —***n.*** a photoflash bulb, lamp, photograph, etc.

pho·to·flood (-flud′) ***adj.*** *Photog.* designating or of a high-intensity electric lamp used for sustained illumination —***n.*** a photoflood bulb, lamp, photograph, etc.

photog. **1.** photographic **2.** photography

pho·to·gen·ic (fōt′ə jen′ik) ***adj.*** [PHOTO- + -GENIC] **1.** giving off light **2.** that looks or is likely to look attractive in photographs: said esp. of a person —**pho′to·gen′i·cal·ly** ***adv.***

pho·to·graph (fōt′ə graf′) ***n.*** a picture made by photography —***vt.*** to take a photograph of —***vi.*** **1.** to take photographs **2.** to appear (as specified) in photographs *[to photograph well]* —**pho·tog·ra·pher** (fə täg′rə fər) ***n.***

pho·to·graph·ic (fōt′ə graf′ik) ***adj.*** **1.** of or like a photograph or photography **2.** used in or made by photography **3.** retaining or recalling in precise detail *[a photographic memory]* —**pho′to·graph′i·cal·ly** ***adv.***

pho·tog·ra·phy (fə täg′rə fē) ***n.*** [PHOTO- + -GRAPHY] the art or process of producing images of objects upon a photosensitive surface by the chemical action of light or other radiant energy

pho·to·gra·vure (fōt′ə grə vyoor′) ***n.*** [Fr.] **1.** a photomechanical process by which photographs are reproduced on intaglio printing plates **2.** a plate so made **3.** a print from such a plate, usually with a satinlike finish

pho·to·li·thog·ra·phy (-li thäg′rə fē) ***n.*** a printing process combining photography and lithography

pho·tol·y·sis (fō täl′ə sis) ***n.*** [see PHOTO- & -LYSIS] chemical decomposition due to the action of light —**pho·to·lyt·ic** (fōt′ə lit′ik) ***adj.***

pho·to·me·chan·i·cal (fōt′ō mə kan′i k'l) ***adj.*** designating or of any process by which printing plates are made by a photographic method —**pho′to·me·chan′i·cal·ly** ***adv.***

pho·tom·e·ter (fō täm′ə tər) ***n.*** [PHOTO- + -METER] a device used to measure the intensity of light

pho·tom·e·try (-trē) ***n.*** the measurement of the intensity of light, esp. as a branch of optics —**pho·to·met·ric** (fōt′ə-met′rik) ***adj.*** —**pho′to·met′ri·cal·ly** ***adv.***

pho·to·mon·tage (fōt′ə män täzh′, -mōn-) ***n.*** montage done in or with photographs

pho·to·mu·ral (-myoor′əl) ***n.*** a very large photograph used as a mural

pho·ton (fō′tän) ***n.*** [PHOT(O)- + (ELECTR)ON] a quantum of electromagnetic energy, as of light, X-rays, etc., having both particle and wave behavior

pho·to-off·set (fōt′ō ôf′set′) ***n.*** a method of offset printing in which the pictures or text are photographically transferred to a metal plate from which inked impressions are made on the rubber roller

pho·to·re·cep·tor (-ri sep′tər) ***n.*** *Biol.* a sense organ, as an eye, specialized to detect light —**pho′to·re·cep′tive** ***adj.***

pho·to·sen·si·tive (-sen′sə tiv) ***adj.*** reacting or sensitive to radiant energy, esp. to light —**pho′to·sen′si·tiv′i·ty** ***n.*** —**pho′to·sen′si·tize′** (-tīz′) ***vt.*** **-tized′, -tiz′ing**

pho·to·sphere (fōt′ə sfir′) ***n.*** [PHOTO- + SPHERE] the visible surface of the sun —**pho′to·spher′ic** (-sfer′ik) ***adj.***

Pho·to·stat (-stat′) [PHOTO- + -STAT] *a trademark for* a device for making photographic copies of printed matter, drawings, etc. directly as positives upon special paper —***n.*** [**p-**] a copy so made —***vt.*** [**p-**] **-stat′ed** or **-stat′ted, -stat′ing** or **-stat′ting** to make a photostat of —**pho′to·stat′ic** ***adj.***

pho·to·syn·the·sis (fōt′ə sin′thə sis) ***n.*** the formation in green plants of organic substances, chiefly sugars, from carbon dioxide and water in the presence of light and chlorophyll —**pho′to·syn′the·size′** (-sīz′) ***vt., vi.*** **-sized′, -siz′ing**

—**pho′to·syn·thet′ic** (-sin thet′ik) ***adj.*** —**pho′to·syn·thet′i·cal·ly** ***adv.***

pho·tot·ro·pism (fō tät′rə piz′m) ***n.*** *Bot.* movement of a part of a plant toward or away from light sources: see HELIOTROPISM —**pho·to·trop·ic** (fōt′ə träp′ik) ***adj.***

phrase (frāz) ***n.*** [< L. *phrasis,* diction < Gr. < *phrazein,* to speak] **1.** a manner or style of speech or expression **2.** a short, colorful or forceful expression **3.** *Gram.* a sequence of two or more words conveying a single thought or forming a distinct part of a sentence but not containing a subject and predicate: cf. CLAUSE **4.** *Music* a short, distinct passage, usually of two, four, or eight measures —***vt.*** **phrased, phras′ing 1.** to express in words or in a phrase **2.** *Music* to mark off (notes) into phrases —**phras′al** ***adj.***

phra·se·ol·o·gy (frā′zē äl′ə jē) ***n.,*** *pl.* **-gies** [< ModL.: see PHRASE & -LOGY] choice and pattern of words; way of speaking or writing —**phra′se·ol′o·gist** ***n.***

phre·net·ic (fri net′ik) ***adj.*** [< OFr. < L. < Gr. *phrenētikos,* mad] *earlier sp. of* FRENETIC

phre·nol·o·gy (fri näl′ə jē) ***n.*** [< Gr. *phrēn,* mind + -LOGY] a system, now rejected, by which character and mental faculties are analyzed by studying the shape and protuberances of the skull —**phren·o·log·i·cal** (fren′ə läj′i k′l) ***adj.*** —**phre·nol′o·gist** ***n.***

Phryg·i·a (frij′ē ə) ancient country in WC Asia Minor —**Phryg′i·an** ***adj., n.***

PHS, P.H.S. Public Health Service

phthi·sis (thī′sis, tī′-, fthī′-) ***n.*** [L. < Gr. < *phthiein,* to waste away] *old term for* any wasting disease, esp. tuberculosis of the lungs —**phthis·ic** (tiz′ik) ***adj., n.*** —**phthis′i·cal, phthis′ick·y** ***adj.***

phy·co·my·cete (fī′kō mī′sēt, -mī sēt′) ***n.*** [< Gr. *phykos,* seaweed + -MYCETE] any of a class of fungi resembling the algae —**phy′co·my·ce′tous** (-mī sēt′əs) ***adj.***

Phyfe (fīf), **Duncan** (born *Duncan Fife*) 1768–1854; U.S. cabinetmaker & furniture designer, born in Scotland

phy·la (fī′lə) ***n.*** *pl. of* PHYLUM

phy·lac·ter·y (fi lak′tər ē, -trē) ***n.,*** *pl.* **-ter·ies** [< ML. < LL. < Gr. *phylaktērion,* a safeguard < *phylassein,* to guard] a small leather case holding slips inscribed with Scripture passages: one is worn on the forehead and one on the left arm by Orthodox or Conservative Jewish men during morning prayer

PHYLACTERIES

-phyll (fil) [ModL. < Gr. *phyllon,* a leaf] *a combining form meaning* leaf *[chlorophyll]*

Phyl·lis (fil′is) [L. < Gr. *Phyllis,* lit., a leaf] a feminine name

phyl·lo- [< Gr. *phyllon,* a leaf] *a combining form meaning* leaf: also, before a vowel, **phyll-**

phyl·lo·tax·is (fil′ə tak′sis) ***n.*** [ModL. < prec. + Gr. *taxis,* arrangement] *Bot.* **1.** the arrangement of leaves on a stem **2.** the study or principles of such arrangement Also **phyl′lo·tax′y** (-sē) —**phyl′lo·tac′tic** (-tik) ***adj.***

-phyl·lous (fil′əs) [see PHYLLO- & -OUS] *a combining form meaning* having (a specified number or kind of) leaves, leaflets, etc.

phyl·lox·e·ra (fil′ək sir′ə, fi läk′sər ə) ***n.,*** *pl.* **-rae** (-ē), **-ras** [ModL. < Gr. *phyllon,* a leaf + *xēros,* dry] any of various plant lice that attack the leaves and roots of certain plants, as grapevines

phy·lo- [< Gr. *phylon,* tribe] *a combining form meaning* tribe, race, phylum, etc.: also **phyl-**

phy·log·e·ny (fī läj′ə nē) ***n.,*** *pl.* **-nies** [< G.: see PHYLO- & -GENY] descent, development, or evolution, as of a species or race: distinguished from ONTOGENY Also **phy·lo·gen·e·sis** (fī′lə jen′ə sis) —**phy′lo·ge·net′ic** (-jə net′ik), **phy′lo·gen′ic** (-jen′ik) ***adj.*** —**phy′lo·ge·net′i·cal·ly** ***adv.***

phy·lum (fī′ləm) ***n.,*** *pl.* **-la** (-lə) [< Gr. *phylon,* tribe] **1.** any principal division of the animal kingdom: sometimes, unofficially, a main subdivision of the plant kingdom **2.** *a)* a language stock *b)* loosely, a language family

phys. 1. physical **2.** physician **3.** physics

phys. ed. physical education

phys·ic (fiz′ik) ***n.*** [< OFr. < L. *physica,* natural science < Gr. < *physis,* nature < *phyein,* to produce] **1.** [Archaic] medical science **2.** a medicine, esp. a cathartic —***vt.*** **-icked, -ick·ing 1.** to dose with medicine, esp. with a cathartic **2.** to cure; heal

phys·i·cal (fiz′i k′l) ***adj.*** [< ML. < L.: see prec.] **1.** of nature and all matter; natural; material **2.** of natural science **3.** of or according to the laws of nature **4.** of, or produced by the forces of, physics **5.** of the body as opposed to the mind —***n.*** a general medical examination: in full, **physical examination** —**phys′i·cal·ly** ***adv.***

physical chemistry chemistry dealing with physical properties in relation to chemical properties

physical education instruction in the exercise, hygiene, etc. of the human body; esp., a course in gymnastics, athletics, etc., as in a school or college

physical geography the study of the features and nature of the earth's surface, atmosphere, climate, etc.

physical science any science dealing with inanimate matter or energy, as physics, chemistry, etc.

physical therapy therapy using exercise, massage, heat, etc. instead of drugs —**physical therapist**

phy·si·cian (fə zish′ən) ***n.*** [< OFr. < L.: see PHYSIC] **1.** a person licensed to practice medicine **2.** a medical doctor other than a surgeon **3.** any person or thing that heals or relieves

phys·i·cist (fiz′ə sist) ***n.*** a specialist in physics

phys·ics (fiz′iks) ***n.pl.*** [*with sing. v. in senses 1 & 2*] [transl. of L. *physica,* physics] **1.** orig., natural science **2.** *a)* the science dealing with the properties, changes, etc. of matter and energy, with energy considered either as continuous (**classical physics**) or as discrete (**quantum physics**) *b)* a specific system of physics **3.** physical properties or processes

phys·i·o- [< Gr. *physis,* nature] *a combining form meaning:* **1.** nature; natural *[physiography]* **2.** physical *[physiotherapy]* Also, before a vowel, **physi-**

phys·i·og·no·my (fiz′ē äg′nə mē; *chiefly Brit.* -än′ə-) ***n.*** [< MFr. < ML. < Gr. < *physis,* nature + *gnōmōn,* one who knows] **1.** the practice of trying to judge character and mental qualities by observation of bodily, esp. facial, features **2.** facial features, esp. as supposedly indicative of character **3.** outward features —**phys′i·og·nom′ic** (-äg näm′ik, -ə näm′-), **phys′i·og·nom′i·cal** ***adj.*** —**phys′i·og·nom′i·cal·ly** ***adv.*** —**phys′i·og′no·mist** ***n.***

phys·i·og·ra·phy (fiz′ē äg′rə fē) ***n.*** [PHYSIO- + -GRAPHY] **1.** a description of the features and phenomena of nature **2.** *same as* PHYSICAL GEOGRAPHY —**phys′i·og′ra·pher** ***n.*** —**phys′i·o·graph′ic** (-ə graf′ik), **phys′i·o·graph′i·cal** ***adj.***

physiol. 1. physiological **2.** physiology

phys·i·ol·o·gy (fiz′ē äl′ə jē) ***n.*** [< Fr. < L. < Gr.: see PHYSIO- & -LOGY] **1.** the study of the functions and vital processes of living organisms or their parts and organs **2.** the functions and vital processes (*of* an organism, etc.) —**phys′i·o·log′i·cal** (-ə läj′i k′l), **phys′i·o·log′ic** ***adj.*** —**phys′i·o·log′i·cal·ly** ***adv.*** —**phys′i·ol′o·gist** ***n.***

phys·i·o·ther·a·py (fiz′ē ō ther′ə pē) ***n.*** *same as* PHYSICAL THERAPY —**phys′i·o·ther′a·pist** ***n.***

phy·sique (fi zēk′) ***n.*** [Fr.] the structure, constitution, strength, or appearance of the body

-phyte (fīt) [< Gr. *phyton,* a plant] *a combining form meaning:* **1.** a plant growing in a (specified) way or place *[sporophyte]* **2.** plantlike *[zoophyte]*

phy·to- [< Gr. *phyton,* a plant] *a combining form meaning* a plant, vegetation: also, before a vowel, **phyt-**

pi[1] (pī) ***n.,*** *pl.* **pies** [see PIE[2]] **1.** a mixed, disordered collection of printing type **2.** any jumble or mixture —***vt.*** **pied, pie′ing** or **pi′ing** to make jumbled; mix up (type)

pi[2] (pī) ***n.*** [Gr.] **1.** the sixteenth letter of the Greek alphabet (Π, π) **2.** *a)* the symbol (π) designating the ratio of the circumference of a circle to its diameter *b)* this ratio, equal to 3.14159265+

pi·a ma·ter (pī′ə māt′ər, pē′ə mät′ər) [ML., lit., gentle mother < L.] the vascular membrane that is the innermost of the three membranes around the brain and spinal cord

pi·an·ism (pē an′iz'm, pē′ən-) ***n.*** a pianist's technique

pi·a·nis·si·mo (pē′ə nis′ə mō′) ***adj., adv.*** [It., superl. of *piano,* soft] *Music* very soft: a direction to the performer —***n.,*** *pl.* **-mos′, -mi′** (-mē′) a pianissimo note or passage

pi·an·ist (pē an′ist, pyan′-, pē′ən-) ***n.*** a person who plays the piano, esp. skillfully

pi·an·o[1] (pē an′ō, pyan′ō) ***n.,*** *pl.* **-os** [It., contr. < *pianoforte*] a large, stringed percussion instrument played from a keyboard: each key operates a felt-covered hammer that strikes and vibrates a rigid steel wire or set of wires

pi·a·no[2] (pē ä′nō, pyä′-) ***adj., adv.*** [It., soft, smooth < L. *planus,* smooth] *Music* soft: a direction to the performer —***n.,*** *pl.* **-nos** a note or passage played softly

pi·an·o·for·te (pē an′ə fôrt′, pē an′ə fôr′tē) ***n.*** [It. < *piano,* soft + *forte,* strong] *same as* PIANO[1]

pi·as·ter (pē as′tər) ***n.*** [< Fr. < It., ult. < L. *emplastrum,* plaster] a unit of currency in Egypt, Lebanon, Sudan, Syria, and Turkey: see MONETARY UNITS, table Also, Brit. sp., **pi·as′tre**

pi·az·za (pē az′ə, -at′sə; *It.* pyät′tsä) ***n.*** [It. < L. *platea:* see

PLACE] **1.** in Italy, an open public square, esp. with buildings around it **2.** a covered gallery or arcade **3.** a large, covered porch

pi·broch (pē′bräk) ***n.*** [< Gael. *piobaireachd,* ult. < *piob,* bagpipe] a piece of music for the bagpipe, usually martial but sometimes dirgelike

pi·ca (pī′kə) ***n.*** [< ? ML., directory: perhaps in reference to the type used in printing it] **1.** a size of type, 12 point **2.** the height of this type, about 1/6 inch: used as a unit of measure

pic·a·dor (pik′ə dôr′) ***n.*** [Sp. < *picar,* to prick] in bullfighting, any of the horsemen who prick the bull's neck with a lance to weaken him

Pic·ar·dy (pik′ər dē) region & former province of N France: Fr. **Pi·car·die** (pē kȧr dē′)

pic·a·resque (pik′ə resk′) ***adj.*** [< Sp. < *pícaro,* a rascal] of or dealing with sharp-witted vagabonds and their adventures *[a picaresque* novel*]*

Pi·cas·so (pi kä′sō, -kas′ō), **Pa·blo** (pä′blō) 1881–1973 ; Sp. painter & sculptor in France

pic·a·yune (pik′ē ōōn′, -ə yōōn′) ***n.*** [Fr. *picaillon,* small coin < Pr.] **1.** a coin of small value **2.** anything trivial or worthless **—*adj.*** trivial; petty; small or small-minded: also **pic′a·yun′ish**

Pic·ca·dil·ly (pik′ə dil′ē) street in London, a traditional center of fashionable shops, clubs, & hotels

pic·ca·lil·li (pik′ə lil′ē) ***n.*** [prob. < PICKLE] a relish of chopped vegetables, mustard, spices, etc.

pic·co·lo (pik′ə lō′) ***n., pl.*** **-los′** [It., small] a small flute, pitched an octave above the ordinary flute

pice (pīs) ***n., pl.*** **pice** [Hindi *paisā*] *see* MONETARY UNITS, table (Nepal)

pick[1] (pik) ***n.*** [var. of PIKE[4]] **1.** a heavy tool with a long, pointed metal head set at a right angle to the handle, used for breaking up soil, rock, etc. **2.** a pointed instrument for picking *[toothpick]* **3.** *same as* PLECTRUM **4.** a pin used to hold hair rollers in place

pick[2] (pik) ***vt.*** [ME. *picken,* akin to ON. *pikka,* to pierce] **1.** to break up, pierce, or dig up (soil, rock, etc.) with something pointed **2.** to make (a hole) with something pointed **3.** *a*) to dig, probe, or scratch at in trying to remove *b*) to clear something from (the teeth, etc.) in this way **4.** to remove by pulling; specif., to gather (flowers, berries, etc.) **5.** to clear thus, as a fowl of its feathers or a tree of its fruit **6.** to eat sparingly or daintily **7.** to pull (fibers, rags, etc.) apart **8.** to choose **9.** to find occasion for (a quarrel or fight) **10.** to search out *[to pick* flaws*]* **11.** *a*) to pluck (the strings on a guitar, etc.) *b*) to play (a guitar, etc.) thus **12.** to open (a lock) with a wire, etc. instead of a key **13.** to steal from (another's pocket, etc.) **—*vi.*** **1.** to eat sparingly or fussily **2.** to thieve **3.** to use a pick **4.** to gather growing berries, flowers, etc. **5.** to select, esp. in a fussy way **—*n.*** **1.** a stroke or blow with something pointed **2.** the act of choosing or a thing chosen **3.** the best or most desirable one(s) **4.** the amount of a crop gathered at one time **—pick and choose** to choose or select carefully **—pick at 1.** to eat small portions of, esp. in a fussy way **2.** [Colloq.] to find fault with **3.** to toy with; finger **—pick off 1.** to pluck **2.** to hit with a carefully aimed shot **—pick on 1.** to choose **2.** [Colloq.] to single out for abuse, criticism, etc. **—pick one's way** to move slowly and cautiously **—pick out 1.** to choose **2.** to single out from among a group; distinguish **3.** to make out (meaning) **4.** to play (a tune) note by note **—pick over** to sort out, item by item **—pick up 1.** to grasp and lift **2.** to get or learn, esp. by chance or casually **3.** to stop for and take along **4.** to take into custody; arrest **5.** to gain (speed) **6.** to regain (health, power, etc.); improve **7.** to resume (an activity, etc.) after a pause **8.** to bring into range of sight, hearing, radio or TV reception, etc. **9.** to make (a room, etc.) tidy **10.** [Colloq.] to get to know casually, esp. for lovemaking **—pick′er *n.***

pick·a·back (pik′ə bak′, pik′ē-) ***adv., adj.*** [var. of *pickapack,* redupl. of PACK[1]] *same as* PIGGYBACK

pick·ax, pick·axe (pik′aks′) ***n.*** [altered (after *ax*) < OFr. *picquois*] a pick with a point at one end of the head and a chiselike edge at the other **—*vt., vi.*** **-axed′, -ax′ing** to use a pickax (on)

picked (pikt) ***adj.*** [< PICK[2]] **1.** selected with care **2.** gathered directly from plants, as berries

pick·er·el (pik′ər əl, pik′rəl) ***n., pl.*** **-el, -els:** see PLURAL, II, D, 2 [dim. of PIKE[3]] **1.** any of various small N. American freshwater fishes related to the pike **2.** *a local name for* WALLEYED PIKE

pick·er·el·weed (-wēd′) ***n.*** any of certain N. American aquatic plants, esp. a shallow-water plant with arrow-shaped leaves and bluish flowers

PICKAX

pick·et (pik′it) ***n.*** [< Fr. dim. of *pic,* PIKE[2]] **1.** a stake, usually pointed, used in a fence, as a hitching post, etc. **2.** a soldier or soldiers stationed to guard troops from surprise attack **3.** a ship or airplane patrol **4.** a person stationed, as by a labor union, outside a factory, store, public building, etc. to demonstrate protest, keep strikebreakers out, etc. **—*vt.*** **1.** to enclose with a picket fence **2.** to hitch (an animal) to a picket **3.** *a*) to post as a military picket *b*) to guard (troops) with a picket **4.** to place pickets, or serve as a picket, at (a factory, etc.) **—*vi.*** to serve as a picket (sense 4) **—pick′et·er *n.* —pick′et·ing *n.***

picket fence a fence made of upright stakes

picket line a line of people serving as pickets

pick·ing (pik′iŋ) ***n.*** **1.** the act of one that picks **2.** [*usually pl.*] something picked, or the amount of this; specif., *a*) small scraps that may be gleaned *b*) something got by effort; returns or spoils

pick·le (pik′'l) ***n.*** [< MDu. *pekel*] **1.** any brine, vinegar, or spicy solution used to preserve or marinate food **2.** a vegetable, specif. a cucumber, so preserved **3.** a chemical bath to clear metal of scale, preserve wood, etc. **4.** [Colloq.] an awkward or difficult situation **—*vt.*** **-led, -ling** to treat or preserve in a pickle solution **—pick′ler *n.***

pick·led (-'ld) ***adj.*** [Slang] intoxicated; drunk

pick-me-up (pik′mē up′) ***n.*** [Colloq.] an alcoholic drink taken to raise one's spirits

pick·pock·et (-päk′it) ***n.*** a thief who steals from the pockets of persons, as in crowds

pick·up (pik′up′) ***n.*** **1.** a picking up **2.** an increasing in speed; acceleration **3.** a small, open truck for light loads **4.** [Colloq.] a casual acquaintance, as for lovemaking **5.** [Colloq.] improvement, as in business **6.** [Colloq.] *a*) a stimulant *b*) stimulation **7.** *a*) in an electric phonograph, a device producing audio-frequency currents from the vibrations of a needle in a record groove *b*) the pivoted arm holding this **8.** *Radio & TV a*) reception of sound or light for conversion into electrical energy in the transmitter*b*) the apparatus used *c*) any place outside a studio where a broadcast originates *d*) the electrical system connecting this place to the broadcasting station **—*adj.*** [Colloq.] assembled, organized, etc. informally or hastily

pick·y (pik′ē) ***adj.*** **pick′i·er, pick′i·est** [Colloq.] overly fastidious or exacting; fussy

pic·nic (pik′nik) ***n.*** [< Fr., prob. < *piquer,* to pick + *nique,* a trifle] **1.** a pleasure outing, with an outdoor meal **2.** a shoulder cut of pork, cured like ham: also **picnic ham, picnic shoulder** **3.** [Slang] *a*) a pleasant experience *b*) an easy task **—*vi.*** **-nicked, -nick·ing** to hold or attend a picnic **—pic′nick·er *n.***

pi·co- [prob. < It. *piccolo,* small] *a combining form meaning* one trillionth

Pi·co Ri·ver·a (pē′kō rə ver′ə) [after P. *Pico,* gov. of Mexican Calif. + *Rivera,* from its being between two rivers] city in SW Calif.: suburb of Los Angeles: pop. 53,000

pi·cot (pē′kō) ***n., pl.*** **-cots** (-kōz) [Fr., dim. of *pic,* a point] any of the small loops in an ornamental edging on lace, ribbon, etc. **—*vt., vi.*** **-coted** (-kōd), **-cot·ing** (-kō iŋ) to edge with these

pic·ric acid (pik′rik) [< Fr. < Gr. *pikros,* bitter] a poisonous, yellow, crystalline, bitter acid, $C_6H_3O_7N_3$, used in dyes, explosives, etc.

Pict (pikt) ***n.*** any of an ancient people of Great Britain, driven into Scotland by the Britons and Romans **—Pict′ish *adj., n.***

pic·to·graph (pik′tə graf′) ***n.*** [< L. *pictus* (see PICTURE) + -GRAPH] **1.** a picture or picturelike symbol representing an idea, as in ancient writing **2.** a diagram using pictured objects to convey ideas **—pic′to·graph′ic *adj.* —pic′to·graph′i·cal·ly *adv.* —pic·tog′ra·phy** (-täg′rə fē) ***n.***

pic·to·ri·al (pik tôr′ē əl) ***adj.*** **1.** of, containing, or expressed in pictures **2.** suggesting a mental image; graphic **—*n.*** a periodical featuring many pictures **—pic·to′ri·al·i·za′tion *n.* —pic·to′ri·al·ize′ *vt.* -ized′, -iz′ing —pic·to′ri·al·ly *adv.***

pic·ture (pik′chər) ***n.*** [< L. *pictura* < *pictus,* pp. of *pingere,* to paint] **1.** *a*) a likeness of an object, person, or scene produced on a flat surface, as by painting or photography *b*) a printed reproduction of this **2.** anything resembling or typifying something else *[*he's the *picture* of health*]* **3.** anything regarded as like a painting, etc. **4.** a mental image; idea **5.** a vivid description **6.** all the facts of an event **7.** *same as: a*) TABLEAU *b*) MOTION PICTURE **8.** the image on a TV screen **—*vt.*** **-tured, -tur·ing** **1.** to make a picture of by painting, drawing, etc. **2.** to make visible; show clearly **3.** to describe or explain **4.** to imagine **—in** (or **out of) the picture** considered as involved (or not involved) in a situation

pic·tur·esque (pik′chə resk′) ***adj.*** **1.** like a picture; specif., *a*) having a wild beauty, as mountain scenery *b*) pleasantly unfamiliar; quaint **2.** suggesting a mental picture; vivid **—pic′tur·esque′ly *adv.* —pic′tur·esque′ness *n.***

picture tube *same as* KINESCOPE (sense 1)

picture window a large window, esp. in a living room, that seems to frame the outside view
picture writing writing that uses pictographs
pid·dle (pid′'l) *vi., vt.* **-dled, -dling** [child's word for URINATE] to dawdle —**pid′dler** *n.*
pid·dling (pid′liŋ) *adj.* trifling; petty
pidg·in (pij′in) *n.* [a supposed Chin. pronun. of BUSINESS] a jargon, as pidgin English, incorporating the vocabulary of one or more languages
pidgin English **1.** a simplified form of English with a Chinese or Melanesian syntax, used by Orientals, etc. as a trade language **2.** any jargon similarly intermixed with English
pie[1] (pī) *n.* [akin ? to PIE[3]] **1.** a baked dish consisting of fruit, meat, etc. with an under or upper crust, or both **2.** a layer cake with a filling of custard, jelly, etc. **3.** [Slang] something extremely good or easy —**(as) easy as pie** [Colloq.] extremely easy
pie[2] (pī) *n., vt.* [< ? prec.] *chiefly Brit. sp. of* PI[1]
pie[3] (pī) *n.* [OFr. < L. *pica*] *same as* MAGPIE
pie·bald (pī′bôld′) *adj.* [PIE[3] + BALD] covered with patches or spots of two colors, esp. white and black —*n.* a piebald horse or other animal
piece (pēs) *n.* [OFr. *pece,* prob. < Gaul.] **1.** a part broken or separated from the whole **2.** a section or quantity of a whole, regarded as complete in itself **3.** a single thing, specimen, etc.; specif., *a)* an artistic work, as of music *b)* an action or its result *[a piece of business] c)* a firearm *d)* a coin or token *e)* one of a set, as of china *f)* a counter as used in games **4.** the quantity or size, as of cloth, manufactured as a unit **5.** an amount of work constituting a single job **6.** [Archaic or Dial.] an amount of time or space —*vt.* **pieced, piec′ing** **1.** to add pieces to, as in repairing or enlarging **2.** to join (*together*) the pieces of, as in mending —**go to pieces** **1.** to fall apart **2.** to lose all self-control —**of a (or one) piece** of the same sort; alike —**speak one's piece** to vent one's views or opinions —**piec′er** *n.*
‡**pièce de ré·sis·tance** (pyes′ də rā zēs täns′) [Fr., piece of resistance] **1.** the principal dish of a meal **2.** the main item or event in a series
piece goods *same as* YARD GOODS
piece·meal (pēs′mēl′) *adv.* [< ME. < *pece,* PIECE + *-mele,* a measure] piece by piece; in small amounts or degrees —*adj.* made or done in pieces or one piece at a time
piece of eight the obsolete Spanish dollar
piece·work (-wurk′) *n.* work paid for at a fixed rate **(piece rate)** per piece —**piece′work′er** *n.*
pied (pīd) *adj.* covered with spots or patches of two or more colors; piebald; variegated
Pied·mont (pēd′mänt) **1.** hilly, upland region of the E U.S., between the Atlantic coastal plain & the Appalachians **2.** region of NW Italy, on the border of Switzerland & France: chief city, Turin
pied·mont (pēd′mänt) *adj.* [< PIEDMONT, Italy] at the base of a mountain —*n.* a piedmont area, etc.
pie·plant (pī′plant′) *n.* [PIE[1] + PLANT] the rhubarb: so called from its use in pies
pier (pir) *n.* [ML. *pera,* ult. < ? or akin to L. *petra,* stone] **1.** a heavy structure supporting the spans of a bridge **2.** a structure built out over water and supported by pillars: used as a landing place, pavilion, etc. **3.** *Archit. a)* a heavy supporting column *b)* the part of a wall between windows or other openings *c)* a buttress
pierce (pirs) *vt.* **pierced, pierc′ing** [OFr. *percer,* ult. < L. *per,* through + *tundere,* to strike] **1.** to pass into or through as a pointed instrument does; stab **2.** to affect sharply the senses or feelings of **3.** to make a hole in; perforate; bore **4.** to make (a hole), as by boring **5.** to break into or through **6.** to sound sharply through **7.** to penetrate with the sight or mind —*vi.* to penetrate —**pierc′er** *n.* —**pierc′ing·ly** *adv.*
Pierce (pirs), **Franklin** 1804–69; 14th president of the U.S. (1853–57)
pier glass a tall mirror set in the pier, or wall section, between windows
Pi·er·i·an (pī ir′ē ən) *adj.* **1.** of a region **(Pieria)** in northern Greece, where the Muses were worshiped **2.** of the Muses or the arts
Pi·erre[1] (pē er′; *Fr.* pyer) [Fr., var. of PETER] a masculine name
Pierre[2] (pir) [after *Pierre* Chonteau, early fur trader] capital of S.Dak., on the Missouri River: pop. 12,000
Pi·er·rot (pē′ə rō′; *Fr.* pye rō′) [Fr., dim. of *Pierre,* PETER] a stock comic character in old French pantomime, having a whitened face and loose white pantaloons and jacket
pi·e·tism (pī′ə tiz'm) *n.* religious piety, esp. when exaggerated —**pi′e·tis′tic, pi′e·tis′ti·cal** *adj.*
pi·e·ty (pī′ə tē) *n., pl.* **-ties** [< OFr. < LL. *pietas* < L. < *pius,* pious] **1.** devotion to religious duties and practices **2.** loyalty and devotion to parents, family, etc. **3.** a pious act, statement, etc.
piezoelectric effect the property exhibited by certain crystals of generating voltage when subjected to pressure, and, conversely, undergoing mechanical stress when subjected to voltage: a piezoelectric crystal when ground and cut to a particular size oscillates or resonates at a precise frequency
pi·e·zo·e·lec·tric·i·ty (pē ā′zō i lek′tris′ə tē) *n.* [< Gr. *piezein,* to press + ELECTRICITY] electricity resulting from the piezoelectric effect —**pi·e′zo·e·lec′tric, pi·e′zo·e·lec′tri·cal** *adj.* —**pi·e′zo·e·lec′tri·cal·ly** *adv.*
pif·fle (pif′'l) *n.* [< Brit. dial.] [Colloq.] talk, action, etc. regarded as insignificant or nonsensical —*interj.* nonsense! —**pif′fling** *adj.*
pig (pig) *n., pl.* **pigs, pig:** see PLURAL, II, D, 1 [ME. *pigge,* orig., young pig] **1.** a domesticated animal with a long, broad snout and a thick, fat body covered with coarse bristles; swine; hog **2.** a young hog of less than c. 100 lbs. **3.** pork **4.** a person regarded as piggish or like a pig **5.** [Slang] a slattern or slut **6.** *a)* an oblong casting of iron, etc. poured from the smelting furnace *b)* the mold used *c) clipped form of* PIG IRON —*vi.* **pigged, pig′ging** **1.** to bear pigs **2.** to live like a pig, esp. in the phrase **pig it** —**buy a pig in a poke** to buy, get, or agree to something without sight or knowledge of it in advance
pi·geon[1] (pij′ən) *n., pl.* **-geons, -geon:** see PLURAL, II, D, 1 [< MFr. < LL. *pipio,* chirping bird < *pipire,* to peep] **1.** any of various related birds with a small head, plump body, and short legs, larger than doves **2.** *same as* CLAY PIGEON **3.** a young woman **4.** [Slang] a dupe
pi·geon[2] (pij′ən) *n. same as* PIDGIN
pigeon breast a deformity of the human chest, as from rickets, in which the sternum projects sharply like that of a pigeon —**pi′geon-breast′ed** *adj.*
pigeon hawk a small N. American falcon
pi·geon·hole (-hōl′) *n.* **1.** a small recess for pigeons to nest in **2.** a small, open compartment, as in a desk, for filing papers —*vt.* **-holed′, -hol′ing** **1.** to put in the pigeonhole of a desk, etc. **2.** to put aside indefinitely **3.** to classify
pi·geon-toed (-tōd′) *adj.* having the toes or feet turned in
pig·ger·y (pig′ər ē) *n., pl.* **-ger·ies** *chiefly Brit. var. of* PIGPEN
pig·gish (pig′ish) *adj.* like a pig; gluttonous or filthy —**pig′gish·ly** *adv.* —**pig′gish·ness** *n.*
pig·gy (pig′ē) *n., pl.* **-gies** a little pig: also sp. **pig′gie** —*adj.* **-gi·er, -gi·est** *same as* PIGGISH
pig·gy·back (pig′ē bak′) *adv., adj.* [alt. of PICKABACK] **1.** on the shoulders or back **2.** of or by a system in which loaded truck trailers are carried on railroad flatcars —*vt.* to carry piggyback
piggy bank any small savings bank, often in the form of a pig, with a slot for coins
pig·head·ed (-hed′id) *adj.* stubborn; obstinate —**pig′head′ed·ly** *adv.* —**pig′head′ed·ness** *n.*
pig iron [see PIG, *n.* 6] crude iron, as it comes from the blast furnace
pig·let (pig′lit) *n.* a little pig, esp. a suckling
pig·ment (pig′mənt) *n.* [< L. *pigmentum* < base of *pingere,* to paint] **1.** coloring matter, usually as an insoluble powder mixed with oil, water, etc. to make paints **2.** coloring matter in the cells and tissues of plants or animals —*vi., vt.* to take on or make take on pigment: also **pig′ment·ize′** **-ized′, -iz′ing** —**pig′men·tar′y** (-mən ter′ē) *adj.*
pig·men·ta·tion (pig′mən tā′shən) *n.* coloration in plants or animals due to pigment in the tissue
Pig·my (pig′mē) *adj., n., pl.* **-mies** *same as* PYGMY
pig·nut (pig′nut′) *n.* **1.** any of several bitter-tasting hickory nuts **2.** any tree they grow on
pig·pen (-pen′) *n.* a pen where pigs are confined
pig·skin (-skin′) *n.* **1.** the skin of a pig **2.** leather made from this **3.** [Colloq.] a football
pig·stick·ing (-stik′iŋ) *n.* the hunting of wild boars, esp. on horseback with spears —**pig′stick′er** *n.*
pig·sty (-stī′) *n., pl.* **-sties′** *same as* PIGPEN
pig·tail (-tāl′) *n.* **1.** tobacco in a twisted roll **2.** a braid of hair hanging at the back of the head
pi·ka (pī′kə) *n.* [< E. Siberian name] any of various small, rabbitlike mammals of rocky, usually high areas in western N. America and in Asia
pike[1] (pīk) *n. clipped form of* TURNPIKE
pike[2] (pīk) *n.* [< Fr. < *piquer,* to pierce < ? L. *picus,* woodpecker] a weapon, formerly used by foot soldiers, with a metal spearhead on a long, wooden shaft —*vt.* **piked, pik′ing** to pierce with a pike —**pike′man** (-mən) *n., pl.* **-men**
pike[3] (pīk) *n., pl.* **pike, pikes:** see PLURAL, II, D, 2 [prob. < *pike* (see PIKE[4]), from the pointed head] **1.** a slender, voracious, freshwater game fish of northern waters, having a narrow, pointed head and sharp teeth: also **northern pike**

2. any of several related fishes, as the pickerel 3. a fish resembling the true pike, as the walleyed pike
pike[4] (pīk) *n.* [OE. *pic*, a pickax] a spike or point, as the pointed tip of a spear
pik·er (pī′kər) *n.* [orig., prob. one from *Pike* County, Mo.] [Slang] a person who does things in a petty or very cautious way
Pikes Peak (pīks) [after Z. *Pike* (1779–1813), Am. explorer] mountain in C Colo.: 14,110 ft.
pike·staff (pīk′staf′) *n., pl.* **-staves** (-stāvz′) 1. the shaft of a pike 2. a traveler's staff with a sharp point
pi·laf, pi·laff (pi läf′, pē′läf) *n.* [Pers. & Turk. *pilāw*] a dish of rice boiled in a seasoned liquid, and usually containing meat or fish
pi·las·ter (pi las′tər) *n.* [< Fr. < It. *pilastro* < L. *pila*, a pile] a rectangular support projecting partially from a wall and treated architecturally as a column, with a base, shaft, and capital

PILASTER

Pi·late (pī′lət), **Pon·tius** (pän′shəs, -chəs, -tē əs) 1st cent. A.D.; Rom. governor of Judaea & Samaria (26?–36?) who condemned Jesus to be crucified
pi·lau, pi·law (pi lô′) *n. same as* PILAF
pil·chard (pil′chərd) *n.* [earlier *pilcher* < ?] 1. a small saltwater fish of the herring family, the commercial sardine of western Europe 2. any of several related fishes; esp., the **Pacific sardine,** found off the western coast of the U.S.
Pil·co·ma·yo (pēl′kô mä′yô) river flowing from Bolivia along the Argentine-Paraguay border into the Paraguay River
pile[1] (pīl) *n.* [< MFr. < L. *pila*, a pillar] 1. a mass of things heaped together 2. a heap of wood, etc. on which a corpse or sacrifice is burned 3. a large building or group of buildings 4. [Colloq.] *a*) a large amount or number *b*) a lot of money 5. *Elec.* *a*) orig., a series of alternate plates of unlike metals with acid-saturated cloth or paper between them, for making an electric current *b*) any similar arrangement that produces an electric current; battery 6. *an earlier name for* NUCLEAR REACTOR —*vt.* **piled, pil′ing** 1. to put in a pile; heap up 2. to cover with a pile; load 3. to accumulate Often with *up* —*vi.* 1. to form a pile or heap 2. to move confusedly in a mass (with *in, out, on,* etc.)
pile[2] (pīl) *n.* [< L. *pilus*, a hair] 1. a soft, velvety, raised surface on a rug, fabric, etc., consisting of yarn loops that are often sheared 2. soft, fine hair, as on wool, fur, etc. —**piled** *adj.*
pile[3] (pīl) *n.* [OE. *pil*] 1. a long, heavy beam driven into the ground, sometimes under water, to support a bridge, dock, etc. 2. any similar support —*vt.* **piled, pil′ing** 1. to drive piles into 2. to support with piles
pi·le·ate (pī′lē it, pil′ē-; -āt′) *adj.* [< L. < *pileus*, cap] having a crest extending from the bill to the nape, as some birds Also **pi′le·at′ed** (-āt′id)
pileated woodpecker a N. American woodpecker with a black and white body and a red crest
pile driver (or **engine**) a machine with a drop hammer for driving piles
pi·le·ous (pī′lē əs, pil′ē-) *adj.* [< L. *pilus*, a hair + -EOUS] hairy or furry
piles (pīlz) *n.pl.* [< L. *piloe*, pl. of *pila*, a ball] *same as* HEMORRHOIDS (see HEMORRHOID)
pi·le·um (pī′lē əm, pil′ē-) *n., pl.* **-le·a** (-ə) [ModL. < L. *pilleum*, felt cap] the top of a bird's head from the bill to the nape
pile·up (pīl′up′) *n.* 1. a piling up 2. [Colloq.] a collision involving several vehicles
pi·le·us (pī′lē əs, pil′ē-) *n., pl.* **-le·i′** (-ī′) [< L. *pilleus* (or *pilleum*), felt cap] *Bot.* the cap of a mushroom, or a similar part of other fungi
pil·fer (pil′fər) *vt., vi.* [MFr. *pelfrer* < *pelfre*, booty] to steal (esp. small sums, petty objects, etc.) —**pil′fer·age** *n.* —**pil′fer·er** *n.*
pil·grim (pil′grəm) *n.* [< OFr. < LL. < L. *peregrinus*, foreigner, ult. < *per*, through + *ager*, country] 1. a wanderer 2. a traveler to a shrine or holy place 3. [P-] any member of the band of English Puritans who founded Plymouth Colony in 1620
pil·grim·age (-ij) *n.* 1. a pilgrim's journey, esp. to a shrine, etc. 2. any similar long journey
Pilgrim Fathers the Pilgrims
Pilgrim's Progress a religious allegory by John Bunyan (1678)
pil·ing (pī′liŋ) *n.* 1. piles collectively 2. a structure of piles
Pil·i·pi·no (pil′ə pē′nō) *n.* [Tag. < obs. Sp. *Philippino*, FILIPINO] *same as* TAGALOG (sense 2): official national language of the Philippines
pill (pil) *n.* [contr. < L. *pilula*, dim. of *pila*, a ball] 1. a small ball, tablet, or capsule of medicine to be swallowed whole 2. a thing that is unpleasant but unavoidable 3. [Slang] a baseball, golf ball, etc. 4. [Slang] an unpleasant person —*vt.* to dose with pills —*vi.* to form into small balls of fuzz on a fabric —**the pill** [Colloq.] a contraceptive taken as a pill by women
pil·lage (pil′ij) *n.* [< MFr. < *piller*, to rob] 1. a plundering 2. booty; loot —*vt.* **-laged, -lag·ing** 1. to deprive of money or property by violence; loot 2. to take as booty or loot —*vi.* to take loot —**pil′lag·er** *n.*
pil·lar (pil′ər) *n.* [< OFr., ult. < L. *pila*, a column] 1. a slender, vertical structure used as a support; column 2. a column standing alone as a monument 3. a person who is a main support of an institution, movement, etc. —*vt.* to support as with pillars —**from pillar to post** from one predicament, place of appeal, etc. to another
Pillars of Hercules two headlands on either side of the Strait of Gibraltar
pill·box (pil′bäks′) *n.* 1. a small, shallow box, often cylindrical, for pills 2. a low, enclosed gun emplacement of concrete and steel
pil·lion (pil′yən) *n.* [< Gael. < *peall*, a hide, ult. < L. *pellis*, a skin] 1. a cushion behind a saddle for an extra rider, esp. a woman 2. an extra saddle behind the driver's on a motorcycle
pil·lo·ry (pil′ər ē) *n., pl.* **-ries** [OFr. *pilori*] 1. a wooden board with holes for the head and hands, in which petty offenders were formerly locked and exposed to public scorn 2. any exposure to public scorn —*vt.* **-ried, -ry·ing** 1. to punish by placing in a pillory 2. to lay open to public ridicule, scorn, or abuse

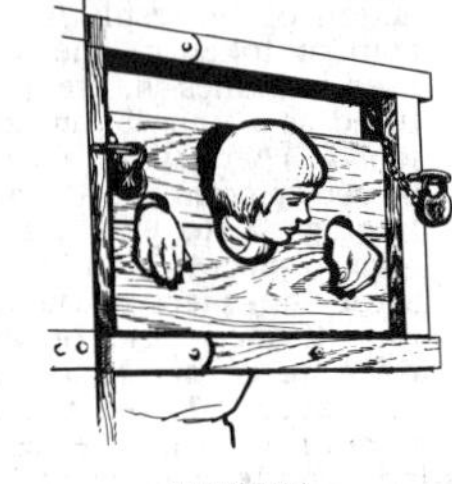

PILLORY

pil·low (pil′ō) *n.* [OE. *pyle*] 1. a cloth case filled with feathers, foam rubber, etc., used as a support, as for the head in sleeping 2. anything like a pillow in form or function —*vt.* 1. to rest as on a pillow 2. to be a pillow for —*vi.* to rest the head as on a pillow —**pil′low·y** *adj.*
pil·low·case (-kās′) *n.* a removable cloth case to cover a pillow: also **pil′low·slip′** (-slip′)
pillow sham a decorative cover for a bed pillow
pi·lose (pī′lōs) *adj.* [< L. < *pilus*, a hair] covered with hair, esp. fine, soft hair: also **pi′lous** (-ləs) —**pi·los·i·ty** (pī läs′ə tē) *n.*
pi·lot (pī′lət) *n.* [< MFr. < It. *pilota*, ult. < Gr. *pēdon*, oar blade] 1. a steersman; specif., a person licensed to direct or steer ships into or out of a harbor or through difficult waters 2. a qualified operator of an aircraft 3. a guide; leader 4. a device guiding the action of a machine or machine part 5. *same as:* *a*) COWCATCHER *b*) PILOT LIGHT *c*) PILOT FILM (or TAPE) —*vt.* 1. to act as a pilot of, on, in, or over 2. to guide; lead —*adj.* 1. that guides or activates 2. that serves as a testing unit —**pi′lot·less** *adj.*
pi·lot·age (-ij) *n.* a piloting, or the fee for it
pilot balloon a small balloon sent up to determine the direction and velocity of the wind
pilot biscuit (or **bread**) *same as* HARDTACK
pilot film (or **tape**) a film (or videotape) of a single segment of a projected television series, for showing to prospective commercial sponsors
pilot fish any of various fishes seemingly acting as pilots, as the remora
pi·lot·house (-hous′) *n.* an enclosed place on the upper deck of a ship, for the helmsman
pilot lamp an electric lamp placed in an electric circuit to indicate when the current is on
pilot light 1. a small gas burner kept lighted to rekindle a principal burner when needed: also **pilot burner** 2. *same as* PILOT LAMP
Pil·sener, Pil·sner (pilz′nər, pils′-) *adj.* [after Pilsen (*Plzeň*), city in Bohemia, where first made] [*often* **p-**] designating a light, Bohemian lager beer often served in a tall, conical glass (**Pilsener glass**)
Pilt·down man (pilt′doun′) a supposed species of prehistoric man presumed on the basis of bone fragments found in Piltdown (Sussex, England) in 1911 and exposed as a hoax in 1953
Pi·ma (pē′mə) *n.* [< Sp. < Pima] 1. *pl.* **-mas, -ma** any member of a N. American Indian tribe in Arizona 2. their language —**Pi′man** *adj.*
Pima cotton [< *Pima* County, Ariz.] a strong, smooth cotton grown in the SW U.S.
pi·men·to (pi men′tō) *n., pl.* **-tos** [< Sp. < L. *pigmentum*, lit., PIGMENT (in VL. & ML., spice)] 1. a sweet variety of the capsicum pepper, or its red fruit, used as a relish, etc. 2. *same as* ALLSPICE
pimento cheese a cheese containing pimentos

pi·mien·to (pi myen′tō, -men′-) ***n.*** *same as* PIMENTO

pimp (pimp) ***n.*** [prob. < or akin to MFr. *pimper*, to allure] a man who is an agent for prostitutes —***vi.*** to act as a pimp

pim·per·nel (pim′pər nel′, -nəl) ***n.*** [< OFr. < LL., ult. < L. *piper*, PEPPER: its fruit resembles peppercorns] any of certain related plants with clustered flowers and leafless stems; esp., the **scarlet pimpernel,** with red, white, or blue, starlike flowers which close in bad weather

pim·ple (pim′p'l) ***n.*** [prob. < or akin to OE. *piplian*, to break out in pimples] any small, rounded, usually inflamed swelling of the skin

pim·ply (pim′plē) ***adj.*** **-pli·er, -pli·est** having pimples: also **pim′pled** (-p'ld)

pin (pin) ***n.*** [OE. *pinn*] **1.** a peg of wood, metal, etc., used for fastening things together, as a support to hang things, etc. **2.** a little piece of stiff wire with a pointed end and flattened or rounded head, for fastening things together **3.** something worthless or insignificant; trifle **4.** *clipped form of* CLOTHESPIN, SAFETY PIN, COTTER PIN, etc. **5.** anything like a pin in form, use, etc. **6.** an ornament, badge, or emblem with a pin or clasp for fastening to clothes **7.** a peg for regulating the tension of a string in a piano, harp, etc. **8.** [Colloq.] the leg: *usually used in pl.* **9.** *Bowling* any of the wooden clubs at which the ball is rolled **10.** *Golf* a pole with a flag attached, in and marking the hole of a green **11.** *Naut.* *a)* *same as* THOLE *b)* a peg or bolt to fasten rigging —***vt.*** **pinned, pin′ning** **1.** to fasten as with a pin **2.** to pierce with a pin **3.** to hold firmly in one position **4.** [Slang] to give one's fraternity pin to, as an informal token of betrothal —**pin down** **1.** to get (someone) to commit himself as to his opinion, plans, etc. **2.** to determine or confirm (a fact, details, etc.) —**pin someone's ears back** [Colloq.] to beat, defeat, or scold someone soundly —**pin (something) on someone** [Colloq.] to lay the blame for (something) on someone

pin·a·fore (pin′ə fôr′) ***n.*** [PIN + AFORE] **1.** a sleeveless, apronlike garment worn by little girls over the dress **2.** a sleeveless housedress

pin·ball machine (pin′bôl′) a game machine with an inclined board having pins, holes, etc. marked with scores for a spring-driven ball to contact

pince-nez (pans′nā′, pins′-; *Fr.* pans nā′) ***n.***, *pl.* **pince′-nez′** (-nāz′; *Fr.* -nā′) [Fr., nose-pincher] eyeglasses without sidepieces, kept in place by a spring gripping the bridge of the nose

pin·cers (pin′sərz) ***n.pl.*** [*occas. with sing. v.*] [< OFr. *pincier*, to pinch] **1.** a tool with two pivoted parts for gripping or nipping things **2.** a grasping claw, as of a crab —**pin′cer·like′** ***adj.***

PINCERS

pinch (pinch) ***vt.*** [ult. < OFr. *pincier*] **1.** to squeeze as between finger and thumb or between two edges **2.** to nip off the end of (a plant shoot) **3.** to press painfully upon (a part of the body) **4.** to cause distress or discomfort to **5.** to make thin, cramped, etc., as by hunger or cold **6.** to restrict closely; straiten: usually in the passive **7.** [Slang] *a)* to steal *b)* to arrest —***vi.*** **1.** to squeeze painfully **2.** to be stingy or frugal —***n.*** **1.** a pinching; squeeze **2.** a quantity graspable between finger and thumb; small amount **3.** distress; hardship **4.** an emergency **5.** [Slang] *a)* a theft *b)* an arrest —**pinch pennies** to be very frugal —**pinch′er** ***n.***

pinch·beck (pinch′bek′) ***n.*** [after C. *Pinchbeck*, 18th-cent. Eng. jeweler] **1.** an alloy of copper and zinc used to imitate gold in jewelry **2.** anything cheap or imitation —***adj.*** of or like pinchbeck

pinch·ers (pin′chərz) ***n.pl.*** *same as* PINCERS

pinch-hit (pinch′hit′) ***vi.*** **-hit′, -hit′ting** **1.** *Baseball* to bat in place of the batter whose turn it is, esp. when a hit is needed **2.** to act as a substitute (*for*) in an emergency —**pinch hitter**

pin·cush·ion (pin′kooosh′ən) ***n.*** a small cushion to stick pins and needles in, to keep them handy

Pin·dar (pin′dər) 522?–438? B.C.; Gr. lyric poet —**Pin·dar·ic** (pin dar′ik) ***adj.***

pine[1] (pīn) ***n.*** see PLURAL, II, D, 3 [OE. *pin* < L. *pinus*, pine tree] **1.** any of various evergreen trees of the pine family: many pines are valuable for wood and for resin, from which turpentine, tar, etc. are obtained **2.** the wood —***adj.*** designating a family of trees with needlelike leaves and, usually, woody cones and valuable wood, including the pines, firs, hemlocks, etc.

pine[2] (pīn) ***vi.*** **pined, pin′ing** [OE. *pinian*, to torment < *pin* < L. *poena*, a pain] **1.** to waste (*away*) with grief, longing, etc. **2.** to have an intense desire; yearn (*for* or *after*)

pin·e·al body (pin′ē əl) [< Fr. < L. *pinea*, a pine cone] a small, cone-shaped body on the dorsal portion of the brain of all vertebrates: its function is obscure

pine·ap·ple (pīn′ap′'l) ***n.*** [ME. *pinappel*, pine cone (see PINE[1] & APPLE)] **1.** a juicy, edible tropical fruit somewhat resembling a pine cone **2.** the plant it grows on, with spiny-edged leaves

Pine Bluff city in central Ark., on the Arkansas River: pop. 57,000

pine tar a thick, dark liquid obtained from pine wood, used in disinfectants, tar paints, etc.

pin·ey (pī′nē) ***adj.*** **pin′i·er, pin′i·est** **1.** abounding in pines **2.** of or like pines

pin·feath·er (pin′feth′ər) ***n.*** an undeveloped feather that is just emerging through the skin

ping (piŋ) ***n.*** [echoic] a sharp sound, as of a bullet striking, an engine knocking, etc. —***vi., vt.*** to make or cause to make such a sound

Ping-Pong (piŋ′pôŋ′, -päŋ′) [echoic] *a trademark for* table tennis equipment —***n.*** [**p- p-**] *same as* TABLE TENNIS

pin·head (pin′hed′) ***n.*** **1.** the head of a pin **2.** anything tiny or trifling **3.** a stupid or silly person —**pin′head′ed** ***adj.*** —**pin′head′ed·ness** ***n.***

pin·hole (-hōl′) ***n.*** **1.** a tiny hole made as by a pin **2.** a hole into which a pin or peg goes

pin·ion[1] (pin′yən) ***n.*** [< Fr., ult. < L. *pinna*, bucket of a paddle wheel, lit., feather] a small cogwheel with teeth that fit into a gearwheel or rack

pin·ion[2] (pin′yən) ***n.*** [< OFr. < L. *pinna*, a feather] **1.** the end joint of a bird's wing **2.** a wing **3.** any wing feather —***vt.*** **1.** to cut off or bind the pinions of (a bird) to keep it from flying **2.** to bind (the wings) **3.** to disable or impede by binding the arms of **4.** to confine

pink[1] (piŋk) ***n.*** [< ?] **1.** any of certain annual and perennial plants of the pink family **2.** the flower **3.** pale red **4.** the finest example, degree, etc. **5.** [Colloq.] a person of somewhat radical political views: a derogatory term —***adj.*** **1.** designating a family of plants with bright-colored flowers, including the carnation, sweet william, etc. **2.** pale-red **3.** [Colloq.] somewhat radical —**in the pink** [Colloq.] in good physical condition; healthy —**pink′ish** ***adj.*** —**pink′ness** ***n.***

pink[2] (piŋk) ***vt.*** [akin ? to OE. *pyngan*, to prick] **1.** to ornament (cloth, paper, etc.) by making perforations in a pattern **2.** to cut a saw-toothed edge on (cloth, etc.) to prevent unraveling or for decoration **3.** to prick or stab **4.** to adorn or embellish —**pink′er** ***n.***

pink·eye (piŋk′ī′) ***n.*** an acute, contagious form of conjunctivitis, in which the eyeball also is inflamed

pink·ie, pink·y (piŋ′kē) ***n.***, *pl.* **pink′ies** [prob. < Du. dim. of *pink*, little finger] the fifth, or smallest, finger

pink·ing shears (piŋ′kiŋ) shears with notched blades, for pinking the edges of cloth, etc.

pink salmon a widespread species of salmon, often canned

pink tea [Colloq.] a frivolous social gathering

pin money **1.** orig., an allowance given to a wife for small personal expenses **2.** any small sum of money, as for incidental minor expenses

pin·na (pin′ə) ***n.***, *pl.* **-nae** (-ē), **-nas** [L., a feather] **1.** *Anat.* the external ear **2.** *Bot.* a leaflet of a pinnately compound leaf **3.** *Zool.* a feather, wing, fin, etc. —**pin′nal** ***adj.***

pin·nace (pin′is) ***n.*** [< Fr. < Sp., ult. < L. *pinus*, PINE[1]] **1.** a small sailing ship **2.** a ship's boat

pin·na·cle (pin′ə k'l) ***n.*** [< MFr. < LL. dim. of L. *pinna*, wing] **1.** a small turret or spire on a buttress, etc. **2.** a slender, pointed formation, as a mountain peak **3.** the highest point; acme —***vt.*** **-cled, -cling** **1.** to set on a pinnacle **2.** to furnish with pinnacles **3.** to form the pinnacle of

pin·nate (pin′āt, -it) ***adj.*** [ModL. < L. < *pinna*, a feather] **1.** resembling a feather **2.** *Bot.* with featherlike leaflets on each side of a common axis —**pin′nate·ly** ***adv.*** —**pin·na′tion** ***n.***

pi·noch·le, pi·noc·le (pē′nuk′'l, -näk′'l) ***n.*** [earlier *binochle* < G. dial. < Fr. *binocle*, eyeglasses] a card game using a 48-card deck made up of two of every card above the eight

pi·ñon (pin′yən, -yōn; *Sp.* pē nyôn′) ***n.***, *pl.* **-ñons**; Sp. **-ño′nes** (-nyô′nes) [< AmSp. < Sp., ult. < L. *pinus*, PINE[1]] **1.** any of several small pines with large, edible seeds, found in western N. America **2.** the seed

pin·point (pin′point′) ***vt.*** **1.** to show the location of (a place on a map, etc.) by sticking in a pin **2.** to locate, define, or focus on precisely —***n.*** **1.** the point of a pin **2.** something trifling

pin·prick (-prik′) ***n.*** **1.** a tiny hole made as by a pin **2.** a minor irritation or annoyance

pins and needles a prickling feeling as in a numb limb —**on pins and needles** in anxious suspense

pin·set·ter (-set′ər) ***n.*** **1.** a person that sets up bowling pins on the alley **2.** a device that does this automatically Also **pin′spot′ter** (-spät′ər)

pin stripe **1.** a very thin stripe, as in some suits **2.** a pattern of such stripes in parallel

pint (pīnt) ***n.*** **[**< MFr. < ML. *pinta:* orig. prob. a painted spot marking the level in a measure**]** **1.** a measure of capacity (liquid or dry) equal to 1/2 quart **2.** a pint container Abbrev. **pt., p.**

pin·tail (pin′tāl′) ***n.,*** *pl.* **-tails′**, **-tail′**: see PLURAL, II, D, 1 **1.** any of several ducks, esp. one with long, pointed middle tail feathers **2.** a grouse with a long, pointed tail —**pin′tailed′** ***adj.***

pin·tle (pin′t'l) ***n.*** **[**OE. *pintel,* penis**]** a pin or bolt upon which some other part pivots or turns

pin·to (pin′tō) ***adj.*** **[**AmSp. < Sp., ult. < L. pp. of *pingere,* to paint**]** marked with patches of white and another color —***n.,*** *pl.* **-tos** **1.** a pinto horse **2.** *same as* PINTO BEAN

pinto bean a mottled kidney bean grown in the southwestern U.S. for food and fodder

pint-size (pīnt′sīz′) ***adj.*** tiny: also **pint′-sized′**

pin·up (pin′up′) ***adj.*** **1.** that is or can be pinned up on or fastened to a wall *[*a *pinup* lamp*]* **2.** [Colloq.] designating or of a girl whose sexual attractiveness makes her a suitable subject for the kind of pictures often pinned up on walls, as of a barracks —***n.*** [Colloq.] a pinup girl, picture, etc.

pin·wheel (-hwēl′, -wēl′) ***n.*** **1.** a small wheel with colored vanes of paper, etc., pinned to a stick so as to revolve in the wind **2.** a firework that revolves when set off

pin·worm (-wurm′) ***n.*** a small, unsegmented worm sometimes parasitic in the human large intestine

pin·y (pī′nē) ***adj.*** **pin′i·er, pin′i·est** *same as* PINEY

pi·on (pī′än′) ***n.*** **[**PI[2] + (MES)ON**]** any of three mesons, positive, negative, or neutral, with a mass approximately 270 times that of an electron

pi·o·neer (pī′ə nir′) ***n.*** **[**< Fr. < OFr. *peonier,* foot soldier < *peon:* see PEON**]** one who goes before, preparing the way for others, as an early settler or a scientist in research —***adj.*** of a pioneer —***vi.*** to be a pioneer —***vt.*** **1.** to prepare or open (a way, etc.) **2.** to be a pioneer in or of

pi·ous (pī′əs) ***adj.*** **[**L. *pius***]** **1.** having or showing religious devotion **2.** springing from actual or pretended religious devotion **3.** virtuous in a hypocritical way **4.** sacred —**pi′ous·ly** ***adv.*** —**pi′ous·ness** ***n.***

pip[1] (pip) ***n.*** **[**contr. < PIPPIN**]** a small seed, as of an apple, pear, orange, etc.

pip[2] (pip) ***n.*** **[**earlier *peep* < ?**]** **1.** any of the spots on playing cards, dice, etc. **2.** *same as* BLIP (sense 1)

pip[3] (pip) ***vi.*** **pipped, pip′ping** **[**prob. var. of PEEP[1]**]** to peep or chirp, as a young bird —***vt.*** to break through (the shell): said of a hatching bird

pip[4] (pip) ***n.*** **[**< MDu., ult. < L. *pituita,* phlegm**]** **1.** a contagious disease of fowl, characterized by the secretion of mucus in the throat **2.** [Colloq.] any unspecified human ailment: a jocular usage

pipe (pīp) ***n.*** **[**OE., ult. < L. *pipare,* to chirp**]** **1.** a cylindrical tube, as of wood or metal, into which air is blown to make musical sounds; specif., [*pl.*] *same as:* *a)* PANPIPE *b)* BAGPIPE **2.** any of the tubes in an organ that produce the tones **3.** a boatswain's whistle **4.** a high, shrill sound, as of a birdcall **5.** [*often pl.*] the vocal organs, esp. as used in singing **6.** a long tube of concrete, metal, etc., for conveying water, oil, etc. **7.** a tubular organ of the body; esp., [*pl.*] the respiratory organs **8.** anything tubular in form **9.** *a)* a tube with a small bowl at one end, in which tobacco, etc. is smoked *b)* enough tobacco, etc. to fill such a bowl **10.** *a)* a cask holding about 126 gallons *b)* this volume as a unit of measure —***vi.*** **piped, pip′ing** **1.** to play on a pipe **2.** to utter shrill sounds —***vt.*** **1.** to play (a tune, etc.) on a pipe **2.** to utter in a shrill voice **3.** to bring, call, etc. by piping **4.** to convey (water, oil, etc.) by pipes **5.** to provide with pipes **6.** to trim (a dress, etc.) with piping **7.** [Slang] to look at —**pipe down** [Slang] to become quiet, stop shouting, etc. —**pipe up** **1.** to begin to play or sing (music) **2.** to speak up or say, esp. in a piping voice

pipe clay a white, plastic clay used for making tobacco pipes, whitening leather, etc.

pipe cleaner a short length of wires twisted to hold tiny tufts of yarn, for cleaning pipestems

pipe cutter a tool that is rotated around a metal pipe and cuts it by sharp disks in a curved jaw

pipe dream [Colloq.] a fantastic idea or vain hope, such as an opium smoker might have

pipe fitter a mechanic who installs and maintains plumbing pipes, etc. —**pipe fitting**

pipe·ful (pīp′fool′) ***n.,*** *pl.* **-fuls′** the amount (of tobacco, etc.) put in a pipe at one time

pipe·line (-līn′) ***n.*** **1.** a line of pipes for conveying water, gas, oil, etc. **2.** any means whereby something is conveyed *[*a *pipeline* of information*]* —***vt.*** **-lined′, -lin′ing** to convey by, or supply with, a pipeline

pipe of peace *same as* CALUMET

pipe organ *same as* ORGAN (sense 1 *a*)

pip·er (-ər) ***n.*** a person who plays on a pipe; esp., a bagpiper —**pay the piper** to suffer the consequences of doing as one pleases

pipe·stem (-stem′) ***n.*** **1.** the slender stem of a tobacco pipe **2.** anything like this in form

pi·pette, pi·pet (pī pet′, pi-) ***n.*** **[**Fr., dim. of *pipe,* a pipe**]** a slender tube for measuring or transferring small amounts of liquids

pip·ing (pīp′iŋ) ***n.*** **1.** the act of one who pipes **2.** music made by pipes **3.** a shrill sound **4.** a system of pipes **5.** material used for pipes **6.** a narrow, rounded fold of material with which edges or seams are trimmed —***adj.*** **1.** playing on a pipe **2.** shrill —**piping hot** so hot as to sizzle; very hot

pip·it (pip′it) ***n.*** **[**echoic of its cry**]** a small songbird with a slender bill and streaked breast

pip·kin (pip′kin) ***n.*** **[**? dim. of PIPE, *n.* 10**]** a small earthenware pot

pip·pin (pip′in) ***n.*** **[**OFr. *pepin,* seed, pip**]** any of a number of varieties of apple

pip·sis·se·wa (pip sis′ə wə) ***n.*** **[**< Algonquian**]** a N. American evergreen plant with jagged, leathery leaves formerly used in medicine

pip·squeak (pip′skwēk′) ***n.*** **[**PIP[3] + SQUEAK**]** [Colloq.] a person, etc. regarded as small or insignificant

pi·quant (pē′kənt, -känt; *now occas.* -kwənt) ***adj.*** **[**Fr. prp. of *piquer,* to prick**]** **1.** pleasantly sharp or spicy to the taste **2.** exciting interest; stimulating; provocative —**pi′quan·cy** (-kən sē), **pi′quant·ness** ***n.*** —**pi′quant·ly** ***adv.***

pique (pēk) ***n.*** **[**Fr. < *piquer,* to prick**]** **1.** resentment at being slighted; ruffled pride **2.** a fit of displeasure —***vt.*** **piqued, piqu′ing** **1.** to arouse resentment in, as by slighting **2.** to arouse (one's curiosity, etc.)

pi·qué (pē kā′) ***n.*** **[**Fr., pp. of *piquer,* to prick**]** a firmly woven cotton fabric with ribbed wales

pi·quet (pi ket′, -kā′) ***n.*** **[**Fr. < *pic,* orig., a sting**]** a game of cards for two, played with 32 cards

pi·ra·cy (pī′rə sē) ***n.,*** *pl.* **-cies** **[**< ML.: see PIRATE**]** **1.** robbery of ships on the high seas **2.** the unauthorized publication or use of a copyrighted or patented work

Pi·rae·us (pī rē′əs) seaport in SE Greece: part of Athens metropolitan area: pop. 184,000

Pi·ran·del·lo (pir′ən del′ō; *It.* pē′rän del′lô), **Lu·i·gi** (lōō ē′jē) 1867–1936; It. playwright & novelist

pi·ra·nha (pi rän′yə, -ran′-) ***n.*** **[**Braz. Port. < Tupi, toothed fish**]** a small, fiercely voracious freshwater fish of South America

pi·rate (pī′rət) ***n.*** **[**< L. < Gr. *peiratēs* < *peiran,* to attack**]** **1.** a person who practices piracy; esp., a robber of ships on the high seas **2.** a pirates' ship —***vt., vi.*** **-rat·ed, -rat·ing** **1.** to practice piracy (upon) **2.** to take (something) by piracy **3.** to publish or reproduce without authorization (a literary work, musical recording, etc.), esp. in violation of a copyright —**pi·rat·i·cal** (pī rat′i k'l), **pi·rat′ic** ***adj.*** —**pi·rat′i·cal·ly** ***adv.***

pi·rogue (pi rōg′) ***n.*** **[**< Fr. < Sp. *piragua* < Carib**]** a canoe made by hollowing out a log

pir·ou·ette (pir′oo wet′) ***n.*** **[**Fr., spinning top; prob. < dial. *piroue,* a top**]** a whirling around on one foot or the point of the toe, esp. in ballet —***vi.*** **-et′ted, -et′ting** to do a pirouette

Pi·sa (pē′zə; *It.* pē′sä) city in W Italy: famous for its Leaning Tower, a bell tower which leans more than 17 ft. from the perpendicular: pop. 103,000

pis·ca·to·ri·al (pis′kə tôr′ē əl) ***adj.*** **[**< L. < *piscator,* fisherman**]** of fishermen or fishing: also **pis′ca·to′ry** —**pis′ca·to′ri·al·ly** ***adv.***

Pis·ces (pī′sēz, pis′ēz) **[**L., pl. of *piscis,* a fish**]** **1.** a constellation south of Andromeda **2.** the twelfth sign of the zodiac: see ZODIAC, illus.

pis·ci- **[**< L. *piscis,* a fish**]** *a combining form meaning* fish *[pisciculture]*

pis·ci·cul·ture (pis′i kul′chər) ***n.*** **[**prec. + CULTURE**]** the breeding of fish as a science or industry

pis·cine (pis′īn, -ēn; pī′sēn) ***adj.*** **[**< L. *piscis,* a fish**]** of or resembling fish

Pi·sis·tra·tus (pī sis′trə təs, pi-) 600?–527 B.C.; tyrant of Athens (560–527, with two interruptions)

pis·mire (pis′mīr′, piz′-) ***n.*** **[**< ME. < *pisse,* urine + *mire,* ant: from the odor of ants' formic acid**]** an ant

pis·mo clam (piz′mō) **[**after *Pismo* Beach, Calif.**]** a heavy-shelled, edible clam found on sandy beaches of California and Mexico

Pis·sar·ro (pē sȧ rō′; *E.* pi sär′ō), **Ca·mille** (kȧ mē′y') 1830–1903; Fr. painter

pis·ta·chi·o (pi stä′shē ō′, -stash′ē ō′, -stash′ō) ***n.,*** *pl.*

-chi·os′ [< It. < L. < Gr. *pistakē* < OPer. *pistah*] **1.** a small tree related to the cashew **2.** its edible, greenish seed **(pistachio nut) 3.** the flavor of this nut **4.** a light yellow-green color

pis·til (pis′t′l) ***n.*** [Fr. < L. *pistillum,* PESTLE] the seedbearing organ of a flowering plant, consisting of one carpel or of several united carpels

PISTIL

pis·til·late (pis′tə lit, -lāt′) ***adj.*** having a pistil or pistils; specif., having pistils but no stamens

pis·tol (pis′t′l) ***n.*** [< Fr. < G. < Czech *pišt′al,* prob. < *pisk,* a whistling sound] **1.** a small firearm held and fired with one hand **2.** such a firearm in which the chamber is part of the barrel: cf. REVOLVER —***vt.* -toled** or **-tolled, -tol·ing** or **-tol·ling** to shoot with a pistol

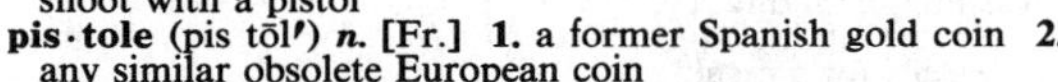

pis·tole (pis tōl′) ***n.*** [Fr.] **1.** a former Spanish gold coin **2.** any similar obsolete European coin

pis·tol-whip (pis′t′l hwip′, -wip′) ***vt.* -whipped′, -whip′ping** to beat with a pistol, esp. about the head

pis·ton (pis′t′n) ***n.*** [Fr. < It. < *pistare,* to beat, ult. < L. *pinsere,* to pound] **1.** a disk or short cylinder closely fitted in a hollow cylinder and moved back and forth by the pressure of a fluid so as to transmit reciprocating motion to a rod **(piston rod),** or moved by the rod so as to exert pressure on the fluid **2.** *Music* a sliding valve moved in the cylinder of a brass-wind instrument to change the pitch

piston ring a split metal ring placed around a piston to make it fit the cylinder closely

pit[1] (pit) ***n.*** [Du. < MDu. *pitte*] the hard stone, as of the plum, peach, etc., which contains the seed —***vt.* pit′ted, pit′ting** to remove the pit from

pit[2] (pit) ***n.*** [OE. *pytt,* ult. < L. *puteus,* a well] **1.** a hole in the ground **2.** an abyss **3.** hell: used with *the* **4.** a covered hole used to trap wild animals; pitfall **5.** any concealed danger; trap **6.** an enclosed area in which animals are kept or made to fight [a bear *pit*] **7.** *a)* the shaft of a coal mine *b)* the mine itself **8.** a hollow on a part of the human body [an *armpit*] **9.** a small hollow in a surface; specif., a smallpox scar on the skin **10.** [Brit.] *a)* the rear part of the ground floor of a theater *b)* the spectators in that section **11.** the sunken section in front of the stage, where the orchestra sits **12.** the part of the floor of an exchange where a special branch of business is transacted [the corn *pit*] **13.** an area off the side of a racing speedway for servicing cars —***vt.* pit′ted, pit′ting 1.** to put or store in a pit **2.** to make pits in **3.** to mark with small scars **4.** to set (cocks, etc.) in a pit to fight **5.** to set in competition (*against*) —***vi.*** to become marked with pits —**the pits** [Slang] the worst possible place, condition, etc.

PISTON

pi·ta (pē′tä, -tə) ***n.*** [Heb. < *pāt,* loaf] a round, flat bread of the Middle East that can be split open to form a pocket for a filling

pit·a·pat (pit′ə pat′) ***adv.*** [echoic] with rapid beating; palpitatingly —***n.*** a rapid succession of beats —***vi.* -pat′ted, -pat′ting** to go pitapat

Pit·cairn Island (pit′kern) Brit. island in Polynesia, South Pacific: settled by Brit. mutineers in 1790

pitch[1] (pich) ***n.*** [OE. *pic* < L. *pix*] **1.** a black, sticky substance formed in the distillation of coal tar, petroleum, etc. and used for waterproofing, pavements, etc. **2.** natural asphalt **3.** a resin from certain evergreen trees —***vt.*** to cover or smear as with pitch

pitch[2] (pich) ***vt.*** [ME. *picchen*] **1.** to set up [to *pitch* a tent] **2.** to throw; fling; toss **3.** to fix or set at a particular point, level, degree, etc. **4.** *Baseball a)* to throw (the ball) to the batter *b)* to serve as pitcher for (a game) **5.** *Golf* to loft (a ball), esp. in making an approach **6.** *Music* to set the key of (a tune, an instrument, or the voice) —***vi.* 1.** to encamp **2.** to take up one's position; settle **3.** to hurl or toss anything, as hay, a baseball, etc. **4.** to fall or plunge forward or headlong **5.** to incline downward; dip **6.** to toss with the bow and stern rising and falling: said of a ship **7.** to move in a like manner in the air: said of an aircraft **8.** to act as pitcher in a ball game —***n.* 1.** act or manner of pitching **2.** a throw; toss **3.** the pitching of a ship or aircraft in rough sea or air **4.** anything pitched **5.** the amount pitched **6.** a point or degree [emotion was at a high *pitch*] **7.** the degree of slope or inclination **8.** a card game in which the suit of the first card led becomes trump **9.** [Slang] a line of talk, such as a salesman or hawker uses **10.** *Machinery* the distance between corresponding points, as on two adjacent gear teeth or on two adjacent threads of a screw **11.** *Music,* etc. *a)* that quality of a tone or sound determined by the frequency of vibration of the sound waves: the greater the frequency, the higher the pitch *b)* a standard of pitch for tuning instruments —**make a pitch for** [Slang] to speak in favor of —**pitch in** [Colloq.] **1.** to set to work energetically **2.** to make a contribution —**pitch into** [Colloq.] to attack

pitch-black (pich′blak′) ***adj.*** very black

pitch·blende (-blend′) ***n.*** [< G. < *pech,* PITCH[1] + *blende,* BLENDE] a brown to black lustrous mineral, the chief ore of uranium

pitch-dark (-därk′) ***adj.*** very dark

pitched battle (picht) **1.** a battle in which placement of troops and the line of combat are fixed before the action **2.** a hard-fought battle

pitch·er[1] (pich′ər) ***n.*** [< OFr. < VL. *bicarium,* a jug, cup: see BEAKER] a container, usually with a handle and lip, for holding and pouring liquids —**pitch′er·ful′** ***n., pl.*** **-fuls′**

pitch·er[2] (pich′ər) ***n.*** [PITCH[2] + -ER] *Baseball* the player who pitches the ball to opposing batters

pitcher plant a plant with pitcherlike leaves which attract and trap insects

pitch·fork (pich′fôrk′) ***n.*** a large, long-handled fork used for lifting and tossing hay, etc. —***vt.*** to lift and toss as with a pitchfork

pitch·man (-mən) ***n., pl.*** **-men 1.** a person who hawks novelties, etc. from a stand, as at a carnival **2.** [Slang] any high-pressure salesman or advertiser

pitch·out (-out′) ***n.*** *Baseball* a ball pitched deliberately away from the plate so that the catcher can try to throw out a runner who is off base

pitch pine a resinous pine from which pitch or turpentine is obtained

pitch pipe a small pipe which produces a fixed tone as a standard for tuning instruments, etc.

pitch·y (pich′ē) ***adj.* pitch′i·er, pitch′i·est 1.** full of or smeared with pitch **2.** thick and sticky like pitch **3.** black

pit·e·ous (pit′ē əs) ***adj.*** arousing or deserving pity —**pit′e·ous·ly** ***adv.*** —**pit′e·ous·ness** ***n.***

pit·fall (pit′fôl′) ***n.*** [< ME. < *pit,* PIT[2] + *falle,* a trap < OE. *fealle*] **1.** a lightly covered pit used as a trap for animals **2.** any hidden danger or difficulty

pith (pith) ***n.*** [OE. *pitha*] **1.** the soft, spongy tissue in the center of certain plant stems **2.** any soft core, as of a bone **3.** the essential part; gist **4.** importance: now usually in the phrase **of great pith and moment** —***vt.* 1.** to remove the pith from (a plant stem) **2.** to pierce or sever the spinal cord of (an animal)

Pith·e·can·thro·pus e·rec·tus (pith′ə kan′thrə pəs i rek′təs, -kan thrō′pəs) [ModL. < Gr. *pithēkos,* an ape + *anthrōpos,* man] *an earlier name for* JAVA MAN

pith·y (pith′ē) ***adj.* pith′i·er, pith′i·est 1.** of, like, or full of pith **2.** terse and full of substance or meaning —**pith′i·ly** ***adv.*** —**pith′i·ness** ***n.***

pit·i·a·ble (pit′ē ə b′l) ***adj.*** arousing or deserving pity, sometimes mixed with scorn or contempt —**pit′i·a·ble·ness** ***n.*** —**pit′i·a·bly** ***adv.***

pit·i·ful (pit′i fəl) ***adj.* 1.** exciting or deserving pity **2.** deserving contempt; despicable —**pit′i·ful·ly** ***adv.*** —**pit′i·ful·ness** ***n.***

pit·i·less (-lis) ***adj.*** without pity; merciless —**pit′i·less·ly** ***adv.*** —**pit′i·less·ness** ***n.***

pit·man (pit′mən) ***n., pl.*** **-men** a person who works in a pit; esp., a coal miner

pi·ton (pē′tän; *Fr.* pē tōn′) ***n., pl.*** **-tons** (-tänz; *Fr.* -tōn′) [Fr. < MFr., a spike] a metal spike that is driven into rock or ice for support in mountain climbing: it has an eye to which a rope can be secured

Pitt (pit), **William 1.** 1st Earl of Chatham, 1708–78; Eng. statesman; prime minister (1766–68) **2.** 1759–1806; Eng. statesman; prime minister (1783–1801; 1804–06): son of *prec.*

pit·tance (pit′′ns) ***n.*** [< OFr. *pitance,* food allowed a monk, ult. < L. *pietas,* PIETY] **1.** a meager allowance of money **2.** a small amount or share

pit·ter-pat·ter (pit′ər pat′ər) ***n.*** [echoic] a rapid succession of light beating or tapping sounds, as of raindrops —***adv.*** with a pitter-patter —***vi.*** to fall, etc. with a pitter-patter

Pitts·burgh (pits′bərg) [after Wm. PITT (the father)] city in SW Pa.: pop. 424,000 (met. area 2,261,000)

Pitts·field (pits′fēld′) [after Wm. PITT (the father)] city in W Mass.: pop. 52,000

pi·tu·i·tar·y (pi to͞o′ə ter′ē, -tyo͞o′-) ***adj.*** [< L. < *pituita,* phlegm] of the pituitary gland —***n., pl.*** **-tar′ies** *same as* PITUITARY GLAND

pituitary gland (or **body**) a small, oval endocrine gland attached to the base of the brain: it secretes hormones influencing body growth, the activity of other endocrine glands, etc.

pit viper any of a family of poisonous snakes, as the rattlesnake, copperhead, etc., with a pit on each side of the head

pit·y (pit′ē) ***n.,*** *pl.* **pit′ies** [< OFr. < L. *pietas,* PIETY] **1.** sorrow for another's suffering or misfortune; compassion **2.** a cause for sorrow or regret —***vt., vi.*** **pit′ied, pit′y·ing** to feel pity (for) —**have** (or **take**) **pity on** to show pity for —**pit′i·er *n.*** —**pit′y·ing·ly *adv.***

‡**più** (pyōō) ***adv.*** [It.] more: a direction in music, as in *più allegro,* more quickly

Pi·us (pī′əs) name of twelve popes; esp., **Pius XII** 1876–1958; Pope (1939–58)

piv·ot (piv′ət) ***n.*** [Fr.] **1.** a point, shaft, etc. on which something turns **2.** a person or thing on which something turns or depends **3.** a pivoting movement —***adj.*** *same as* PIVOTAL —***vt.*** to provide with or mount on a pivot —***vi.*** to turn as on a pivot

piv·ot·al (-'l) ***adj.*** **1.** of or acting as a pivot **2.** on which something turns or depends; crucial

pix·ie, pix·y (pik′sē) ***n.,*** *pl.* **pix′ies** [< Brit. dial.] a fairy or sprite, esp. one that is puckish —**pix′ie·ish, pix′y·ish *adj.***

pix·i·lat·ed (pik′sə lāt′id) ***adj.*** [altered < *pixy-led,* lost] eccentric, daft, puckish, etc.

Pi·zar·ro (pē thär′rô; *E.* pi zä′rō), **Fran·cis·co** (frän thēs′kô) 1470?–1541; Sp. conqueror of Peru

pi·zazz, piz·zazz (pə zaz′) ***n.*** [prob. echoic of exuberant cry] [Slang] **1.** energy, vitality, spirit, etc. **2.** smartness, style, flair, etc. —**pi·zaz′zy, piz·zaz′zy *adj.***

piz·za (pēt′sə) ***n.*** [It.] an Italian dish made by baking a thin layer of dough covered with a spiced preparation of tomatoes, cheese, etc.

piz·ze·ri·a (pēt′sə rē′ə) ***n.*** [It.] a place where pizzas are prepared and sold

piz·zi·ca·to (pit′sə kät′ō; *It.* pēt′tsē kä′tô) ***adj.*** [It.] *Music* plucked: a direction to pluck the strings of a violin, viola, etc. —***adv.*** in a pizzicato manner —***n.,*** *pl.* **-ca′ti** (-ē; *It.* -tē) a note or passage played in this way

pk. *pl.* **pks. 1.** pack **2.** park **3.** peak **4.** peck

pkg. package; packages

pkwy. parkway

pl. 1. place **2.** plate **3.** plural

plac·a·ble (plak′ə b'l, plā′kə-) ***adj.*** [< OFr. < L. < *placare,* to soothe] capable of being placated; forgiving —**plac′a·bil′i·ty *n.*** —**plac′a·bly *adv.***

plac·ard (plak′ärd, -ərd) ***n.*** [< MFr. < MDu. *placke,* a piece] **1.** a notice for display in a public place; poster **2.** a small card or plaque —***vt.*** **1.** to place placards on or in **2.** to advertise by means of placards **3.** to display as a placard —***vi.*** to set up placards

pla·cate (plā′kāt, plak′āt) ***vt.*** **-cat·ed, -cat·ing** [< L. pp. of *placare,* to appease] to stop from being angry; appease; pacify —**pla′cat·er *n.*** —**pla·ca′tion *n.*** —**pla′ca′tive *adj.*** —**pla′ca·to′ry *adj.***

place (plās) ***n.*** [OFr. < L. *platea* < Gr. *plateia,* a street < *platys,* broad] **1.** a square or court in a city **2.** a short street **3.** space; room **4.** a region or locality **5.** *a)* the part of space occupied by a person or thing *b)* situation or state **6.** a city, town, or village **7.** a residence; dwelling **8.** a building or space devoted to a special purpose [*a place* of amusement] **9.** a particular spot on or part of something [*a sore place* on the leg] **10.** a particular passage or page in a book, etc. **11.** position or standing, esp. one of importance [*one's place* in history] **12.** a step or point in a sequence [*in the first place*] **13.** the customary or proper position, time, or character **14.** a space reserved or occupied by a person, as a seat in a theater, etc. **15.** a job or position; employment **16.** official position **17.** the duties of any position **18.** one's duty or business **19.** *Arith.* the position of an integer, as in noting decimals [*the third decimal place*] **20.** *Racing* the first, second, or third position at the finish, specif. the second position —***vt.*** **placed, plac′ing 1.** *a)* to put in a particular place, condition, or relation *b)* to identify by associating with the correct place or circumstances **2.** to find employment or a position for **3.** to assign (a value) **4.** to offer for consideration, etc. **5.** to repose (trust, etc.) *in* a person or thing **6.** to finish in (a specified position) in a competition —***vi.*** to finish among the first three in a contest; specif., to finish second in a horse or dog race —**give place 1.** to make room **2.** to yield —**go places** [Slang] to achieve success —**in** (or **out of**) **place 1.** in (or out of) the customary or proper place **2.** being (or not being) fitting or timely —**in place of** instead of —**put someone in his place** to humble someone who is overstepping bounds —**take place** to occur —**take the place of** to be a substitute for

pla·ce·bo (plə sē′bō) ***n.,*** *pl.* **-bos, -boes** [L., I shall please] *Med.* a sugar pill or the like given merely to humor a patient

place card a small card with the name of a guest, set at the place that he is to occupy at a table

place kick *Football* a kick made while the ball is held in place on the ground, as in attempting a field goal —**place′-kick′ *vi.***

place mat a small mat serving as an individual table cover for a person at a meal

place·ment (plās′mənt) ***n.*** **1.** a placing or being placed **2.** the finding of employment for a person **3.** location or arrangement

pla·cen·ta (plə sen′tə) ***n.,*** *pl.* **-tas, -tae** (-tē) [ModL. < L., lit., a cake, ult. < Gr. *plax,* a flat object] a vascular organ developed within the uterus, connected by the umbilical cord to the fetus and supplying it with nourishment —**pla·cen′tal, pla·cen′tate *adj.***

plac·er[1] (plās′ər) ***n.*** a person who places

plac·er[2] (plas′ər) ***n.*** [AmSp. < Catal. < *plassa,* a place] a waterborne or glacial deposit of gravel or sand containing particles of gold, platinum, etc. that can be washed out

plac·er mining (plas′ər) mining in placer deposits by washing, dredging, etc.

place setting the china, silverware, etc. for setting one place at a table for a meal

plac·id (plas′id) ***adj.*** [L. *placidus*] undisturbed; tranquil; calm —**pla·cid·i·ty** (plə sid′ə tē), **plac′id·ness *n.*** —**plac′id·ly *adv.***

plack·et (plak′it) ***n.*** [prob. < PLACARD, in related obs. sense] a slit at the waist of a skirt or dress to make it easy to put on and take off

pla·gia·rism (plā′jə riz′m, -jē ə riz′m) ***n.*** [< L. *plagiarius,* kidnapper] **1.** the act of plagiarizing **2.** an idea, plot, etc. that has been plagiarized Also **pla′gia·ry,** *pl.* **-ries** —**pla′gia·rist *n.*** —**pla′gia·ris′tic *adj.***

pla·gia·rize (-rīz′) ***vt., vi.*** **-rized′, -riz′ing** to take (ideas, writings, etc.) from (another) and pass them off as one's own —**pla′gia·riz′er *n.***

pla·gi·o·clase (plā′jē ə klās′) ***n.*** [< G. < Gr. *plagios,* oblique + *klasis,* a cleaving] any of a series of common rock-forming feldspars

plague (plāg) ***n.*** [< MFr. < L. *plaga* < Gr. *plēgē,* misfortune] **1.** anything that afflicts or troubles; calamity **2.** any deadly epidemic disease; specif., *same as* BUBONIC PLAGUE **3.** [Colloq.] a nuisance —***vt.*** **plagued, plagu′ing 1.** to afflict with a plague **2.** to vex; torment —**plagu′er *n.***

plaice (plās) ***n.,*** *pl.* **plaice, plaic′es:** see PLURAL, II, D, 2 [< OFr. < LL. *platessa,* flatfish < Gr. *platys,* broad] a kind of American or European flatfish

plaid (plad) ***n.*** [Gael. *plaide,* a blanket] **1.** a long woolen cloth with a crossbarred pattern, worn over the shoulder by Scottish Highlanders **2.** a fabric with such a pattern **3.** any pattern of this kind —***adj.*** having such a pattern: also **plaid′ed**

plain (plān) ***adj.*** [OFr. < L. *planus,* flat] **1.** orig., flat; level **2.** not obstructed; open [*in plain view*] **3.** clearly understood; obvious [*his meaning was plain*] **4.** *a)* outspoken; frank [*plain talk*] *b)* downright [*plain nonsense*] **5.** not luxurious [*a plain coat*] **6.** not complicated; simple [*plain sewing*] **7.** homely [*a plain face*] **8.** unfigured, undyed, etc. [*plain cloth*] **9.** unmixed [*plain soda*] **10.** not of high rank; ordinary [*a plain man*] —***n.*** an extent of level country —***adv.*** clearly or simply —**plain′ly *adv.*** —**plain′ness *n.***

plain·clothes man (plān′klōz′, -klōthz′) a police detective who wears civilian clothes on duty: also **plain′clothes′man** (-mən) ***n.,*** *pl.* **-men**

plains·man (plānz′mən) ***n.,*** *pl.* **-men** an inhabitant of the plains; esp., a frontiersman on the Great Plains

plain·song (plān′sôŋ′) ***n.*** early Christian church music, still used in some churches, in free rhythm and sung in unison: also **plain′chant′** (-chant′)

plain-spo·ken (plān′spō′k'n) ***adj.*** speaking or spoken plainly or frankly —**plain′-spo′ken·ness *n.***

plaint (plānt) ***n.*** [< OFr. < L. < pp. of *plangere,* to lament] **1.** [Poet.] lament **2.** a complaint

plain·tiff (plān′tif) ***n.*** [< OFr. < *plaindre,* to complain: see prec.] a person who brings a suit into a court of law; complainant

plain·tive (-tiv) ***adj.*** [< OFr.: see prec.] expressing sorrow or melancholy; sad —**plain′tive·ly *adv.*** —**plain′tive·ness *n.***

plait (plāt; *chiefly Brit.* plat) ***n.*** [< OFr. < L. pp. of *plicare,* to fold] **1.** *same as* PLEAT **2.** a braid of hair, ribbon, etc. —***vt.*** **1.** *same as* PLEAT **2.** to braid or make by braiding —**plait′er *n.***

plan (plan) ***n.*** [Fr., plan: merging of *plan* (< L. *planus,* flat) with MFr. *plant* < It. *pianta* < L. *planta,* sole of the foot] **1.** a diagram showing the arrangement in horizontal section of a structure, piece of ground, etc. **2.** *a)* a scheme for making, doing, or arranging something; project, schedule, etc. *b)* a method of proceeding **3.** any outline or sketch —***vt.*** **planned, plan′ning 1.** to make a plan of (a structure, etc.) **2.** to devise a scheme for doing, making, etc. **3.** to have in mind as a project or purpose —***vi.*** to make plans —**plan′ner *n.***

plan·chette (plan chet′, -shet′) ***n.*** [Fr., dim. of *planche*, PLANK] a small, three-cornered device used on a Ouija board: it is believed to move without guidance to letters or words as the fingers rest on it

Planck (pläŋk), **Max** (mäks) 1858–1947; Ger. physicist

plane[1] (plān) ***n.*** [< MFr. < L. < Gr. < *platys*, broad: from its broad leaves] any of several trees with maplelike leaves and bark that comes off in large patches: also **plane tree**

plane[2] (plān) ***adj.*** [L. *planus*] **1.** flat; level **2.** *Math.* *a)* on a surface that is a plane *b)* of such surfaces —***n.*** **1.** a surface that wholly contains a straight line joining any two points lying in it **2.** a flat or level surface **3.** a level of achievement, existence, etc. **4.** *clipped form of* AIRPLANE **5.** any airfoil; esp., a wing of an airplane

plane[3] (plān) ***n.*** [< OFr. < LL. < *planare*, to make level < L. *planus*, level] a carpenter's tool for shaving a wood surface to make it smooth, level, etc. —***vt.*** **planed, plan′ing 1.** to make smooth or level with a plane **2.** to remove with a plane (with *off* or *away*) —***vi.*** **1.** to work with a plane **2.** to do the work of a plane —**plan′er** ***n.***

PLANE

plane[4] (plān) ***vi.*** **planed, plan′ing** [Fr. *planer* < OFr. (term used in falconry)] **1.** to soar or glide **2.** to rise from the water, as a hydroplane does **3.** to travel by airplane

plane geometry the branch of geometry dealing with plane figures

plan·et (plan′it) ***n.*** [< OFr. < LL. < Gr. *planētēs*, wanderer < *planan*, to wander] **1.** orig., any heavenly body with apparent motion, including the sun, moon, Venus, Mars, etc. **2.** now, any heavenly body shining by reflected sunlight and revolving about the sun: the major planets, in their order from the sun, are Mercury, Venus, Earth, Mars, Jupiter, Saturn, Uranus, Neptune, and Pluto **3.** *Astrol.* any heavenly body regarded as influencing human lives

plan·e·tar·i·um (plan′ə ter′ē əm) ***n.***, *pl.* **-i·ums, -i·a** (-ə) [ModL. < LL. *planeta*, PLANET + L. (*sol*)*arium*, SOLARIUM] **1.** an arrangement for projecting the images of the sun, moon, planets, and stars inside a large dome by means of a complex optical instrument that is revolved to show the celestial motions **2.** the room or building containing this

plan·e·tar·y (plan′ə ter′ē) ***adj.*** **1.** of a planet or the planets **2.** terrestrial; global **3.** wandering; erratic **4.** moving in an orbit, like a planet **5.** designating or of an epicyclic train of gears, as in an automobile transmission **6.** *Astrol.* under the influence of a planet

plan·e·tes·i·mal (plan′ə tes′i m′l) ***adj.*** [PLANET + (INFINIT)ESIMAL] of very small bodies in space that move in planetary orbits: according to the **planetesimal hypothesis** the planets were formed by the uniting of planetesimals —***n.*** any of these bodies

plan·et·oid (plan′ə toid′) ***n.*** [PLANET + -OID] *same as* ASTEROID (*n.* 1)

plank (plaŋk) ***n.*** [< ONormFr. < OFr. < LL. *planca*, ult. < Gr. *phalanx*, PHALANX] **1.** a long, broad, thick board **2.** timber cut into planks **3.** something that supports **4.** any of the principles in a platform, as of a political party —***vt.*** **1.** to cover, lay, etc. with planks **2.** to broil and serve (steak, etc.) on a board **3.** [Colloq.] *a)* to lay or set (*down*) with force *b)* to pay (usually with *down* or *out*) —**walk the plank** to walk off a plank projecting out from a ship's side, as pirates' victims were forced to do

plank·ing (-iŋ) ***n.*** **1.** the act of laying planks **2.** planks collectively

plank·ton (plaŋk′tən) ***n.*** [G. < Gr. *planktos*, wandering < *plazesthai*, to wander] the microscopic animal and plant life floating in bodies of water, used as food by fish —**plank·ton′ic** (-tän′ik) ***adj.***

planned parenthood the planning of the number and spacing of the births of one's children

pla·no- [< L. *planus*, flat] *a combining form meaning:* **1.** plane, flat **2.** having one side plane and (the other as specified)

pla·no-con·cave (plā′nō kän kāv′, -kän′kāv) ***adj.*** having one side plane and the other concave

pla·no-con·vex (-kän veks′, -kän′veks) ***adj.*** having one side plane and the other convex

plan position indicator a circular radarscope on which the center represents the location of the transmitter and echoes represent the location of objects

plant (plant) ***n.*** [OE. *plante* < L. *planta*, a sprout] **1.** a living organism that, unlike an animal, cannot move voluntarily, synthesizes food from carbon dioxide, and has no sense organs **2.** a young tree, shrub, or herb, ready to put into other soil to mature **3.** a soft-stemmed organism of this kind, as distinguished from a tree or shrub **4.** the machinery, buildings, etc. of a factory **5.** the equipment, buildings, etc. of an institution, as a school **6.** the apparatus for a certain mechanical operation [*a ship's power plant*] **7.** [Slang] a person placed, or thing used, to trick or trap —***vt.*** **1.** *a)* to put into the ground to grow *b)* to set plants in (a piece of ground) **2.** to set firmly in position **3.** to fix in the mind; implant **4.** to settle; found; establish **5.** to stock with animals **6.** to put a stock of (fish, etc.) in a body of water **7.** [Slang] to deliver (a punch, etc.) with force **8.** [Slang] *a)* to place (a person or thing) in such a way as to trick, trap, etc. *b)* to place (an ostensible news item) in a newspaper, etc. **9.** [Slang] to hide or conceal —**plant′like′** ***adj.***

Plan·tag·e·net (plan taj′ə nit) the ruling family of England (1154–1399), or any member of it

plan·tain[1] (plan′tin) ***n.*** [OFr. < L. *plantago*] any of various related plants with leaves at the base of the stem and spikes of tiny, greenish flowers

plan·tain[2] (plan′tin) ***n.*** [< Sp. *plá(n)tano*, lit., plane tree < L. *platanus:* see PLANE[1]] **1.** a tropical banana plant with a coarse fruit eaten as a cooked vegetable **2.** this fruit

plantain lily a plant of the lily family, with broad leaves and white or bluish flowers

plan·tar (plan′tər) ***adj.*** [< L. < *planta*, sole of the foot] of or on the sole of the foot

plan·ta·tion (plan tā′shən) ***n.*** [< L. < *plantare*, to plant] **1.** formerly, a colony **2.** an area growing cultivated crops **3.** an estate, as in the South, cultivated by workers living on it **4.** a large, cultivated planting of trees

plant·er (plan′tər) ***n.*** **1.** the owner of a plantation **2.** a person or machine that plants **3.** a decorative container for house plants

plan·ti·grade (plan′tə grād′) ***adj.*** [Fr. < L. *planta*, sole + Fr. *-grade*, -GRADE] walking on the whole sole of the foot, as a bear, man, etc. —***n.*** a plantigrade animal

plant louse *same as* APHID

plaque (plak) ***n.*** [Fr. < MDu. *placke*, a disk] **1.** *a)* any thin, flat piece of metal, wood, etc. with a design, etc. used as a wall ornamentation *b)* a wall tablet commemorating or identifying something **2.** a platelike brooch **3.** *a)* an abnormal patch on the skin, mucous membrane, etc. *b)* a thin, transparent film on a tooth surface

plash[1] (plash) ***n.*** [OE. *plæsc*, prob. echoic] a pool or puddle —**plash′y** ***adj.*** **plash′i·er, plash′i·est**

plash[2] (plash) ***vt., vi., n.*** [echoic] *same as* SPLASH

-pla·si·a (plā′zhə, -zhē ə) [ModL. < Gr. < *plassein*, to mold] *a combining form meaning* change, development

-plasm (plaz′m) [see ff.] *a combining form meaning:* **1.** the fluid substances of an animal or vegetable cell **2.** protoplasm [*ectoplasm*]

plas·ma (plaz′mə) ***n.*** [G. < Gr., something molded < *plassein*, to form] **1.** the fluid part of blood, without the corpuscles **2.** the fluid part of lymph, milk, or intramuscular liquid **3.** *same as* PROTOPLASM **4.** a high-temperature, ionized gas composed of nearly equal numbers of electrons and positive ions —**plas·mat′ic** (-mat′ik) ***adj.***

plasma membrane a very thin living membrane surrounding the cytoplasm of a plant or animal cell

plas·ter (plas′tər) ***n.*** [< OE. & OFr. < LL. *plastrum* < L. *emplastrum* < Gr. < *emplassein*, to daub over] **1.** a pasty mixture of lime, sand, and water, hard when dry, for coating walls, ceilings, etc. **2.** *same as* PLASTER OF PARIS **3.** a pasty preparation spread on cloth and applied to the body as a medicine —***vt.*** **1.** to cover, smear, etc. as with plaster **2.** to apply or affix like a plaster [*to plaster posters on walls*] **3.** to make lie smooth and flat **4.** [Colloq.] to affect or strike with force —**plas′ter·er** ***n.*** —**plas′ter·y** ***adj.***

plas·ter·board (-bôrd′) ***n.*** a thin board formed of layers of plaster and paper, used in wide sheets

plas·tered (plas′tərd) ***adj.*** [Slang] intoxicated; drunk

plaster of Paris [from use of gypsum from Paris, France] a heavy white powder, calcined gypsum, which, when mixed with water, forms a thick paste that sets quickly: used for casts, statuary, etc.

plas·tic (plas′tik) ***adj.*** [< L. < Gr. *plastikos* < *plassein*, to form] **1.** molding or shaping matter; formative **2.** *a)* that can be molded or shaped *b)* made of a plastic **3.** in a flexible state; impressionable **4.** dealing with molding or modeling **5.** *Physics* capable of change of shape without breaking apart —***n.*** any of various nonmetallic compounds, synthetically produced, which can be molded and hardened, or formed into pliable sheets, etc. —**plas′ti·cal·ly** ***adv.*** —**plas·tic′i·ty** (-tis′ə tē) ***n.***

-plas·tic (plas′tik) [< Gr.: see prec.] *a combining form meaning* forming, developing

Plas·ti·cine (plas′tə sēn′) [PLASTIC + -INE[4]] *a trademark*

for an oil-base modeling paste, used like clay or wax —*n.* [p-] this paste: also **plas′ti·cene′** (-sēn)

plas·ti·cize (-sīz′) *vt., vi.* **-cized′, -ciz′ing** to make or become plastic

plas·ti·ciz·er (-sī′zər) *n.* any substance added to a plastic material to keep it soft and viscous

plastic surgery surgery dealing with the repair of injured, deformed, or destroyed parts of the body, esp. by transferring skin, bone, etc. from other parts —**plastic surgeon**

plas·tid (plas′tid) *n.* [< G. < Gr. < *plastēs,* molder < *plassein,* to form] a specialized protoplasmic structure in the cytoplasm of some plant cells

plas·tron (plas′trən) *n.* [Fr. < It. < *piastra,* thin plate of metal] **1.** a metal breastplate **2.** a chest protector for a fencer **3.** the under shell of a turtle

-plas·ty (plas′tē) [< Gr. < *plastos,* formed < *plassein,* to mold] *a combining form meaning* plastic surgery

plat¹ (plat) *vt.* **plat′ted, plat′ting** [see PLAIT] [Dial.] to plait or braid —*n.* [Dial.] a plait or braid

plat² (plat) *n.* [var. of PLOT] **1.** a small piece of ground **2.** a map or plan, esp. of a piece of land divided into building lots —*vt.* **plat′ted, plat′ting** to make a map or plan of

Pla·ta (plä′tä), **Ri·o de la** (rē′ô de lä) estuary of the Paraná & Uruguay rivers, between Argentina & Uruguay

plate (plāt) *n.* [OFr., flat object, ult. < Gr. *platys,* flat] **1.** a smooth, flat, thin piece of metal, etc. **2.** *same as* SHEET METAL **3.** *a*) any of the thin sheets of metal used in one kind of armor (**plate armor**) *b*) such armor **4.** *a*) a thin, flat piece of metal on which an engraving is cut *b*) an impression taken from this **5.** a print of a woodcut, lithograph, etc. **6.** a full-page book illustration printed on special paper **7.** dishes, utensils, etc. of, or plated with, gold or silver **8.** a shallow dish from which food is eaten **9.** *same as* PLATEFUL **10.** the food in a dish; course *[a fruit plate]* **11.** food and service for an individual at a meal *[a dollar a plate]* **12.** a container passed in churches, etc. for donations of money **13.** a thin cut of beef from the forequarter, just below the short ribs **14.** *Anat., Zool.* a thin layer or scale, as of horny tissue, etc. **15.** *Archit.* a horizontal wooden girder that supports the trusses of a roof **16.** *Baseball short for* HOME PLATE **17.** *Dentistry a*) that part of a denture which fits to the mouth and holds the teeth *b*) [*often pl.*] loosely, a full set of false teeth **18.** *Elec. same as* ANODE (sense 1) **19.** *Philately* the impression surface from which a sheet of stamps is printed **20.** *Photog.* a sheet of glass, metal, etc. coated with a film sensitive to light, upon which the image is formed **21.** *Printing* a cast, to be printed from, made from a mold of set type by the electrotype or stereotype process —*vt.* **plat′ed, plat′ing 1.** to coat with gold, tin, etc. **2.** to cover with metal plates for protection **3.** *Printing* to make a plate of

pla·teau (pla tō′) *n., pl.* **-teaus′, -teaux′** (-tōz′) [Fr. < OFr. < *plat:* see PLATE] **1.** an elevated tract of more or less level land **2.** a period of little change or progress, as represented by a flat extent on a graph, etc.

plat·ed (plāt′id) *adj.* **1.** protected with plates, as of armor **2.** coated with a metal *[silver-plated]*

plate·ful (-fool′) *n., pl.* **-fuls′** as much as a plate will hold

plate glass polished, clear glass in thick sheets, used for shop windows, mirrors, etc.

plate·let (plāt′lit) *n.* [PLATE + -LET] any of certain roundish disks, smaller than a red blood cell, found in the blood of mammals and associated with blood clotting

plat·en (plat′′n) *n.* [< OFr. *platine,* flat plate < *plat:* see PLATE] **1.** a flat metal plate, as that in a printing press which presses the paper against the inked type **2.** in a typewriter, the roller against which the keys strike

plat·er (plāt′ər) *n.* a person or thing that plates

plate tec·ton·ics (tek tän′iks) [see TECTONIC] the theory that the earth's surface consists of plates, or large crustal slabs, whose constant motion accounts for continental drift, mountain building, etc.

plat·form (plat′fôrm′) *n.* [Fr. *plate-forme,* lit., flat form: see PLATE & FORM] **1.** a raised horizontal surface; specif., *a*) a raised flooring beside railroad tracks, etc. *b*) a vestibule at the end of a railroad car *c*) a raised stage for performers, speakers, etc. **2.** a statement of principles, as of a political party —*adj.* **1.** *a*) designating a woman's shoe with a thick sole of cork, leather, etc. *b*) designating such a sole **2.** designating a rocking chair (**platform rocker**) that rocks atop an attached, stationary base

plat·ing (plāt′iŋ) *n.* **1.** the act or process of one that plates **2.** an external layer of metal plates **3.** a thin coating of gold, silver, tin, etc.

plat·i·num (plat′′n əm) *n.* [ModL. < Sp. *platina* < *plata,* silver] a steel-gray, ductile metallic chemical element, resistant to corrosion and electrochemical attack: used as a chemical catalyst, for dental alloys, jewelry, etc.: symbol, Pt; at. wt., 195.09; at. no., 78

platinum blonde 1. a girl or woman with very light, silvery blonde hair **2.** such a color

plat·i·tude (plat′ə to͞od′, -tyo͞od′) *n.* [Fr. < *plat,* flat (see PLATE), after *latitude,* etc.] **1.** dullness or triteness of ideas, etc. **2.** a trite remark, esp. one uttered as though it were fresh —**plat′i·tu′di·nous** *adj.* —**plat′i·tu′di·nous·ly** *adv.*

plat·i·tu·di·nize (plat′ə to͞o′d′n īz′, -tyo͞o′-) *vi.* **-nized′, -niz′ing** to write or speak platitudes

Pla·to (plā′tō) 427?–347? B.C.; Gr. philosopher

Pla·ton·ic (plə tän′ik, plā-) *adj.* **1.** of or characteristic of Plato or his philosophy **2.** idealistic or impractical **3.** [*usually* p-] not amorous or sexual, but purely spiritual or intellectual *[platonic love]* —**pla·ton′i·cal·ly** *adv.*

Pla·to·nism (plāt′′n iz′m) *n.* the idealistic philosophy of Plato or his school —**Pla′to·nist** *n.* —**Pla′to·nis′tic** *adj.*

pla·toon (plə to͞on′) *n.* [Fr. *peloton,* a ball, group < *pelote,* a ball] **1.** a military unit composed of two or more squads **2.** a group like this *[a platoon of police]* **3.** any of the specialized squads on a team, as an offensive or defensive squad in football —*vt.* to divide into, or use as or on, a platoon

Platt·deutsch (plät′doich′, plat′-) *n.* [G. < Du. *plat,* clear, lit., flat + *duitsch,* German, Dutch] any Low German vernacular dialect of N Germany

Platte (plat) [< Fr. *Rivière Platte,* lit., flat river] river formed in C Nebr. & flowing east into the Missouri

plat·ter (plat′ər) *n.* [< Anglo-Fr. < OFr. *plat:* see PLATE] **1.** a large, shallow dish, usually oval, from which food, esp. meat or fish, is served **2.** [Slang] a phonograph record

plat·y- [< Gr. *platys,* flat] *a combining form meaning* broad or flat *[platypus]* : also, before a vowel, **plat-**

plat·y·hel·minth (plat′ē hel′minth) *n.* [prec. + HELMINTH] any of a large group of flattened worms, as the tapeworms, flukes, etc.: many are parasitic —**plat′y·hel·min′thic** *adj.*

plat·y·pus (plat′ə pəs) *n., pl.* **-pus·es, -pi′** (-pī′) [ModL. < Gr. < *platys,* flat + *pous,* a foot] a small, aquatic, egg-laying mammal of Australia and Tasmania, with webbed feet, a tail like a beaver's, and a bill like a duck's: in full, **duckbill platypus**

PLATYPUS (16–24 in. long, including tail)

plau·dit (plô′dit) *n.* [< L. pl. imper. of *plaudere,* to applaud] [*usually pl.*] **1.** a round of applause **2.** any strong expression of approval or praise

plau·si·ble (plô′zə b′l) *adj.* [< L. *plausibilis* < *plaudere,* to applaud] **1.** seemingly true, acceptable, etc.: often implying disbelief **2.** seemingly honest, trustworthy, etc.: often implying distrust —**plau′si·bil′i·ty** *n.* —**plau′si·bly** *adv.*

Plau·tus (plô′təs), (**Titus Maccius**) 254?–184 B.C.; Rom. writer of comic dramas

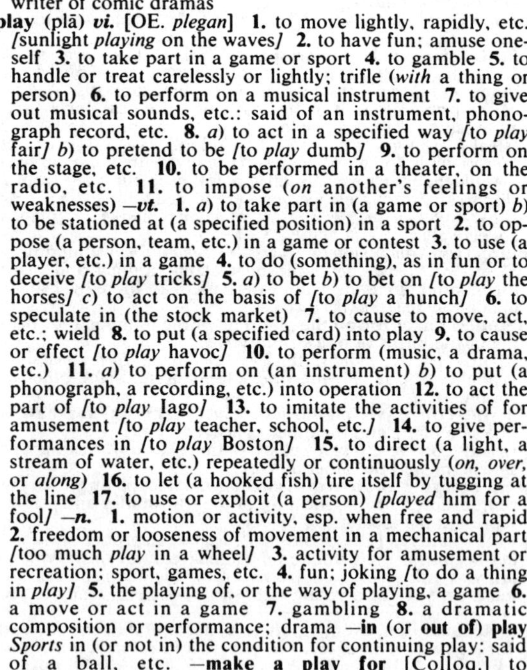

play (plā) *vi.* [OE. *plegan*] **1.** to move lightly, rapidly, etc. *[sunlight playing on the waves]* **2.** to have fun; amuse oneself **3.** to take part in a game or sport **4.** to gamble **5.** to handle or treat carelessly or lightly; trifle (*with* a thing or person) **6.** to perform on a musical instrument **7.** to give out musical sounds, etc.: said of an instrument, phonograph record, etc. **8.** *a*) to act in a specified way *[to play fair] b*) to pretend to be *[to play dumb]* **9.** to perform on the stage, etc. **10.** to be performed in a theater, on the radio, etc. **11.** to impose (*on* another's feelings or weaknesses) —*vt.* **1.** *a*) to take part in (a game or sport) *b*) to be stationed at (a specified position) in a sport **2.** to oppose (a person, team, etc.) in a game or contest **3.** to use (a player, etc.) in a game **4.** to do (something), as in fun or to deceive *[to play tricks]* **5.** *a*) to bet *b*) to bet on *[to play the horses] c*) to act on the basis of *[to play a hunch]* **6.** to speculate in (the stock market) **7.** to cause to move, act, etc.; wield **8.** to put (a specified card) into play **9.** to cause or effect *[to play havoc]* **10.** to perform (music, a drama, etc.) **11.** *a*) to perform on (an instrument) *b*) to put (a phonograph, a recording, etc.) into operation **12.** to act the part of *[to play Iago]* **13.** to imitate the activities of for amusement *[to play teacher, school, etc.]* **14.** to give performances in *[to play Boston]* **15.** to direct (a light, a stream of water, etc.) repeatedly or continuously (*on, over,* or *along*) **16.** to let (a hooked fish) tire itself by tugging at the line **17.** to use or exploit (a person) *[played him for a fool]* —*n.* **1.** motion or activity, esp. when free and rapid **2.** freedom or looseness of movement in a mechanical part *[too much play in a wheel]* **3.** activity for amusement or recreation; sport, games, etc. **4.** fun; joking *[to do a thing in play]* **5.** the playing of, or the way of playing, a game **6.** a move or act in a game **7.** gambling **8.** a dramatic composition or performance; drama —**in** (or **out of**) **play** *Sports* in (or not in) the condition for continuing play: said of a ball, etc. —**make a play for** [Colloq.] to employ one's arts or skills to obtain, win, etc.; court —**play along (with)** to cooperate (with), often just for expediency —**play around** **1.** to behave in a frivolous way **2.** to be sexually unfaithful or promiscuous —**play at** **1.** to pretend to be engaged in **2.** to work at halfheartedly —**play down** to make seem not too important —**played out** **1.** finished **2.** exhausted —**play into (someone's) hands** to act in a way that gives the advantage to (someone) —**play it** to act in a (specified) manner *[to play it smart]* —**play off** **1.** to pit (one) against another **2.** to break (a tie) by playing once more —**play out** **1.** to play to the finish; end **2.** to pay out (a rope, etc.) —**play up** to give prominence to —**play up to** [Colloq.] to try to please by flattery —**play′a·ble** ***adj.***

play·act (plā′akt′) ***vi.*** **1.** to act in a play **2.** to pretend **3.** to behave in an affected or dramatic manner

play·back (-bak′) ***n.*** the playing of a phonograph record or tape to listen to or check the sound recorded on it

play·bill (-bil′) ***n.*** **1.** a poster or circular advertising a play **2.** a program of a play

play·boy (-boi′) ***n.*** a man of means who is given to pleasure-seeking, sexual promiscuity, etc.

play·er (-ər) ***n.*** **1.** a person who plays a game **2.** an actor **3.** a person who plays a musical instrument **4.** a gambler **5.** a thing that plays; specif., a RECORD PLAYER

player piano a piano that can play mechanically

play·ful (-fəl) ***adj.*** **1.** fond of play or fun; frisky; frolicsome **2.** said or done in fun; jocular —**play′ful·ly** ***adv.*** —**play′ful·ness** ***n.***

play·go·er (-gō′ər) ***n.*** a person who goes to the theater frequently —**play′go′ing** ***n., adj.***

play·ground (-ground′) ***n.*** a place, often part of a schoolyard, for outdoor games and play

play hook·y (hook′ē) [*hooky* prob. < *hook it,* to run away] to stay away from school without permission

play·house (plā′hous′) ***n.*** **1.** a theater **2.** a small house for children to play in **3.** a doll house

playing cards cards used in playing various games, arranged in four suits (spades, hearts, diamonds, and clubs): a standard deck has 52 cards

play·let (-lit) ***n.*** a short drama

play·mate (-māt′) ***n.*** a companion in games and recreation: also **play′fel′low** (-fel′ō)

play-off (-ôf′) ***n.*** a game or any of a series of games played to break a tie or to decide a championship

play on words a pun or punning

play·pen (-pen′) ***n.*** a small, portable enclosure in which an infant can play, crawl, etc.

play·thing (-thiŋ′) ***n.*** a thing to play with; toy

play·time (-tīm′) ***n.*** time for play or recreation

play·wright (-rīt′) ***n.*** a writer of plays; dramatist

pla·za (plä′zə, plaz′ə) ***n.*** [Sp. < L. *platea:* see PLACE] **1.** a public square in a city or town **2.** *same as* SHOPPING CENTER **3.** an area along a superhighway, with a restaurant, service station, etc.

plea (plē) ***n.*** [< OFr. < L. *placitum,* an opinion < pp. of *placere,* to please] **1.** a statement in defense **2.** an appeal; entreaty **3.** *Law* a defendant's statement, answering the charges against him or showing why he should not answer

plea bargaining pretrial negotiations in which the defendant agrees to plead guilty to a lesser charge in exchange for having more serious charges dropped

plead (plēd) ***vi.*** **plead′ed** or **pled** or **plead** (pled), **plead′ing** [< OFr.: see PLEA] **1.** to present a case or a plea in a law court **2.** to make an appeal; beg *[to plead for mercy]* —***vt.*** **1.** to argue (a law case) **2.** to declare oneself to be (guilty or not guilty) of a charge **3.** to offer as an excuse *[to plead ignorance]* —**plead′a·ble** ***adj.*** —**plead′er** ***n.***

plead·ings (-iŋz) ***n.pl.*** the statements setting forth to the court the claims of the plaintiff and the answer of the defendant

pleas·ance (plez′′ns) ***n.*** [< MFr. < *plaisant:* see ff.] a pleasant area or garden, as on an estate

pleas·ant (-′nt) ***adj.*** [< MFr. prp. of *plaisir,* to please] **1.** agreeable to the mind or senses; pleasing **2.** having an agreeable manner, appearance, etc. —**pleas′ant·ly** ***adv.*** —**pleas′ant·ness** ***n.***

pleas·ant·ry (plez′′n trē) ***n.,*** *pl.* **-ries** **1.** pleasant jocularity in conversation **2.** *a)* a humorous remark or action *b)* a polite social remark

please (plēz) ***vt.*** **pleased, pleas′ing** [MFr. *plaisir* < L. *placere*] **1.** to be agreeable to; give pleasure to; satisfy **2.** to be the will or wish of *[it pleased him to remain]* —***vi.*** **1.** to be agreeable; satisfy *[to aim to please]* **2.** to have the will or wish; like *[to do as one pleases]* *Please* is also used for politeness in requests to mean "be obliging enough (to)" *[please sit down]* —**if you please** if you wish or like

pleas·ing (plē′ziŋ) ***adj.*** giving pleasure; agreeable —**pleas′ing·ly** ***adv.*** —**pleas′ing·ness** ***n.***

pleas·ur·a·ble (plezh′ər ə b′l) ***adj.*** pleasant; enjoyable —**pleas′ur·a·ble·ness** ***n.*** —**pleas′ur·a·bly** ***adv.***

pleas·ure (plezh′ər, plā′zhər) ***n.*** **1.** a pleased feeling; delight **2.** one's wish, will, or choice *[what is your pleasure?]* **3.** a thing that gives delight or satisfaction **4.** sensual satisfaction **5.** amusement; fun —**pleas′ure·ful** ***adj.***

pleat (plēt) ***n.*** [ME. *pleten:* cf. PLAIT] a flat double fold in cloth or other material, pressed or stitched in place —***vt.*** to lay and press (cloth) in a pleat or pleats —**pleat′er** ***n.***

plebe (plēb) ***n.*** [short for PLEBIAN] a member of the freshman class at the U.S. Military Academy or Naval Academy

ple·be·ian (pli bē′ən) ***n.*** [< L. < *plebs,* common people] **1.** a member of the ancient Roman lower class **2.** one of the common people **3.** a vulgar, coarse person —***adj.*** **1.** of or characteristic of the lower class in ancient Rome or of the common people anywhere **2.** vulgar or common

pleb·i·scite (pleb′ə sīt′, -sit) ***n.*** [< Fr. < L. < *plebs,* common people + *scitum,* decree] a direct vote of the people on a political issue, as on a choice between independence for their region or union with another nation

plec·trum (plek′trəm) ***n.,*** *pl.* **-trums, -tra** (-trə) [L. < Gr. *plēktron* < *plēssein,* to strike] a thin piece of metal, bone, plastic, etc., used for plucking the strings of a guitar, mandolin, etc.

pled (pled) *alt. pt. & pp. of* PLEAD

pledge (plej) ***n.*** [< OFr. or ML., prob. < OS. *plegan,* to guarantee] **1.** the condition of being given or held as security for a contract, payment, etc. **2.** a person or thing given or held as such security; something pawned; hostage **3.** a token **4.** the drinking of a toast to someone **5.** a promise or agreement **6.** something promised, esp. money to be donated **7.** a person undergoing a trial period before initiation into a fraternity —***vt.*** **pledged, pledg′ing** **1.** to present as security, esp. for the repayment of a loan; pawn **2.** to drink a toast to **3.** to bind by a promise **4.** to promise to give (loyalty, a donation, etc.) **5.** *a)* to accept tentative membership in (a fraternity) *b)* to accept as a pledge (*n.* 7) —**take the pledge** to vow not to drink alcoholic liquor —**pledg′er** ***n.***

pledg·ee (plej ē′) ***n.*** a person to whom a pledge is delivered: distinguished from PLEDGOR

pledg·or (plej′ər, plej′ôr′) ***n.*** *Law* a person who delivers something as security

-ple·gia (plē′jē ə, -jə) [ModL. < Gr. < *plēgē,* a stroke] *a combining form meaning* paralysis *[paraplegia]*

Ple·ia·des (plē′ə dēz′, plī′-) ***n.pl.,*** *sing.* **Ple′iad** (-ad) **1.** *Gr. Myth.* the seven daughters of Atlas, placed by Zeus among the stars **2.** *Astron.* a cluster of stars in the constellation Taurus

Plei·o·cene (plī′ə sēn′) ***adj.*** *same as* PLIOCENE

Pleis·to·cene (plīs′tə sēn′) ***adj.*** [< Gr. *pleistos,* most + *kainos,* recent] designating or of the first epoch of the Quaternary Period in the Cenozoic Era —**the Pleistocene** the Pleistocene Epoch or its rocks: see GEOLOGY, chart

ple·na·ry (plē′nə rē, plen′ə-) ***adj.*** [< LL. < L. *plenus,* full] **1.** full; complete *[plenary power]* **2.** for attendance by all members *[a plenary session]* —**ple′na·ri·ly** (-rə lē) ***adv.***

plenary indulgence *R.C.Ch.* an indulgence remitting in full the temporal punishment due a sinner

plen·i·po·ten·ti·ar·y (plen′i pə ten′shē er′ē, -shə rē) ***adj.*** [< ML. < LL. < L. *plenus,* full + *potens,* powerful] having or giving full authority —***n.,*** *pl.* **-ar′ies** a person given full authority to act as diplomatic representative of a government

plen·i·tude (plen′ə to͞od′, -tyo͞od′) ***n.*** [OFr. < L. < *plenus,* full] **1.** fullness; completeness **2.** abundance; plenty —**plen′i·tu′di·nous** ***adj.***

plen·te·ous (plen′tē əs) ***adj.*** plentiful; abundant —**plen′te·ous·ly** ***adv.*** —**plen′te·ous·ness** ***n.***

plen·ti·ful (plen′ti fəl) ***adj.*** **1.** having or yielding plenty **2.** ample or abundant —**plen′ti·ful·ly** ***adv.*** —**plen′ti·ful·ness** ***n.***

plen·ty (plen′tē) ***n.,*** *pl.* **-ties** [< MFr. < L. *plenitas* < *plenus,* full] **1.** prosperity; opulence **2.** an ample supply; enough **3.** a large number *[plenty of errors]* —***adj.*** [Colloq.] ample; enough —***adv.*** [Colloq.] quite *[plenty good]*

ple·o·nasm (plē′ə naz′m) ***n.*** [< LL. < Gr. < *pleonazein,* to be in excess < *pleōn,* more, compar. of *polys,* much] **1.** the use of more words than are necessary for the meaning **2.** a redundant word or expression —**ple′o·nas′tic** ***adj.***

pleth·o·ra (pleth′ə rə) ***n.*** [ML. < Gr. < *plēthos,* fullness] the state of being too full; overabundance; excess —**ple·thor·ic** (plə thôr′ik, pleth′ə rik) ***adj.***

pleu·ra (ploor′ə) ***n.,*** *pl.* **-rae** (-ē) [ML. < Gr. *pleura,* a rib] the thin serous membrane lining each half of the chest cavity and covering a lung —**pleu′ral** ***adj.***

pleu·ri·sy (ploor′ə sē) ***n.*** [< MFr. < LL. < L. < Gr. < *pleura,* a rib] inflammation of the pleura, characterized by painful breathing —**pleu·rit·ic** (ploo rit′ik) ***adj.***

pleu·ro- [< Gr. *pleura,* a rib] *a combining form meaning:* **1.** on or near the side **2.** of, involving, or near the pleura Also, before a vowel, **pleur-**

Plex·i·glas (plek′sə glas′) [< L. *plexus,* a twining + GLASS] *a trademark for* a lightweight, transparent, thermoplastic resin, used for aircraft canopies, lenses, etc. —*n.* this material: also **plex′i·glass′**

plex·us (plek′səs) ***n.,*** *pl.* **-us·es, -us** [ModL. < L. < pp. of *plectere,* to twine] a network; specif., *Anat.* a network of blood vessels, nerves, etc.

pli·a·ble (plī′ə b′l) ***adj.*** [< MFr. < *plier,* to bend < L. *plicare,* to fold] **1.** easily bent; flexible **2.** easily influenced or persuaded **3.** adjusting readily; adaptable —**pli′a·bil′i·ty, pli′a·ble·ness** ***n.*** —**pli′a·bly** ***adv.***

pli·ant (plī′ənt) ***adj.*** [see prec.] **1.** easily bent; pliable **2.** adaptable or compliant —**pli′an·cy, pli′ant·ness** ***n.***

pli·cate (plī′kāt) ***adj.*** [< L. pp. of *plicare,* to fold] having lengthwise folds —**pli·ca′tion** ***n.***

pli·er (plī′ər) ***n.*** a person or thing that plies

pli·ers (plī′ərz) ***n.pl.*** [< PLY[1]] small pincers for gripping small objects, bending wire, etc.

plight[1] (plīt) ***n.*** [< Anglo-Fr. *plit,* for OFr. *pleit,* a fold] a condition or state of affairs; esp., an awkward, sad, or dangerous situation

plight[2] (plīt) ***vt.*** [OE. *plihtan,* to pledge < *pliht,* danger] to pledge or promise, or bind by a pledge —**plight one's troth** to make a promise of marriage

A B C
PLIERS
(A, slip joint; B, needle nose; C, arc joint)

Plim·soll mark (or **line**) (plim′səl, -säl, -sôl) [after S. *Plimsoll* (1824–98), Eng. statesman] a line or set of lines on the outside of merchant ships, showing the water level to which they may legally be loaded

plink (pliŋk) ***n.*** [echoic] a light, sharp, ringing or clinking sound —***vt., vi.*** **1.** to make such sounds on (a piano, banjo, etc.) **2.** to shoot at (tin cans, etc.) —**plink′er** ***n.***

plinth (plinth) ***n.*** [< L. < Gr. *plinthos,* a brick, tile] **1.** the square block at the base of a column, pedestal, etc. **2.** the base on which a statue rests

Plin·y (plin′ē) **1.** (L. name *Gaius Plinius Secundus*) 23–79 A.D.; Rom. naturalist & writer: called *the Elder* **2.** (L. name *Gaius Plinius Caecilius Secundus*) 62?–113? A.D.; Rom. writer & statesman: called *the Younger:* nephew of *prec.*

Pli·o·cene (plī′ə sēn′) ***adj.*** [< Gr. *pleōn,* more + *kainos,* new] designating or of the last epoch of the Tertiary Period in the Cenozoic Era —**the Pliocene** the Pliocene Epoch or its rocks: see GEOLOGY, chart

plis·sé, plis·se (pli sā′) ***n.*** [< Fr. < pp. of *plisser,* to pleat] **1.** a crinkled finish given to cotton, nylon, etc. with a caustic soda solution **2.** a fabric with this finish

PLO, P.L.O. Palestine Liberation Organization

plod (pläd) ***vi.*** **plod′ded, plod′ding** [prob. echoic] **1.** to walk or move heavily and laboriously; trudge **2.** to work steadily and monotonously; drudge —*n.* **1.** the act of plodding **2.** the sound of a heavy step —**plod′der** ***n.*** —**plod′ding·ly** ***adv.***

plonk (pläŋk, pluŋk) ***vt., vi., n.*** *same as* PLUNK

plop (pläp) ***vt., vi.*** **plopped, plop′ping** [echoic] **1.** to drop with a sound like that of something flat falling into water **2.** to drop heavily —*n.* the act of plopping or the sound made by this —*adv.* with a plop

plo·sive (plō′siv) ***adj.*** [< (EX)PLOSIVE] *Phonet.* produced by the stoppage and sudden release of the breath, as the sounds of *k, p,* and *t* when used initially —*n.* a plosive sound

plot (plät) ***n.*** [OE., a piece of land] **1.** a small area of ground *[a garden plot]* **2.** a chart or diagram, as of a building or estate **3.** a secret, usually evil, scheme **4.** the plan of action of a play, novel, etc. —*vt.* **plot′ted, plot′ting 1.** *a)* to draw a plan of (a ship's course, etc.) *b)* to mark the position or course of on a map **2.** to make secret plans for **3.** to plan the action of (a story, etc.) **4.** *a)* to determine the location of (a point) on a graph by means of coordinates *b)* to represent (an equation) by joining points on a graph to form a curve —*vi.* to scheme or conspire —**plot′less** ***adj.*** —**plot′less·ness** ***n.*** —**plot′ter** ***n.***

plough (plou) ***n., vt., vi.*** *chiefly Brit. sp. of* PLOW

plov·er (pluv′ər, plō′vər) ***n.,*** *pl.* **plov′ers, plov′er:** see PLURAL, II, D, 1 [< OFr., ult. < L. *pluvia,* rain] a shore bird with a short tail, long, pointed wings, and a short beak

plow (plou) ***n.*** [ME. *ploh* < Late OE.] **1.** a farm implement used to cut and turn up the soil **2.** anything like this; specif., a SNOWPLOW —*vt.* **1.** to cut and turn up (soil) with a plow **2.** to make furrows in with or as with a plow **3.** to make as if by plowing *[he plowed his way in]* **4.** to cut a way through (water) —*vi.* **1.** to use a plow in tilling the soil **2.** to cut a way (*through* water, etc.) **3.** to plod **4.** to begin work vigorously (with *into*) **5.** to collide forcefully (with *into*) —**plow back** to reinvest (profits) in the same business enterprise —**plow under 1.** to bury (crops or vegetation) by plowing, so as to enrich the soil or in seeking to prevent overproduction **2.** [Colloq.] to destroy; obliterate —**plow up 1.** to remove with a plow **2.** to till (soil) thoroughly —**plow′a·ble** ***adj.*** —**plow′er** ***n.***

plow·man (-mən) ***n.,*** *pl.* **-men 1.** a man who guides a plow **2.** a farm worker

plow·share (-sher′) ***n.*** the share, or cutting blade, of a moldboard plow

ploy (ploi) ***n.*** [? < (EM)PLOY] an action or maneuver intended to outwit or disconcert another person

pluck (pluk) ***vt.*** [OE. *pluccian*] **1.** to pull off or out; pick **2.** to drag or snatch **3.** to pull feathers or hair from *[to pluck a chicken, pluck eyebrows]* **4.** to pull at (the strings of a musical instrument) and release quickly to sound tones **5.** [Slang] to rob or swindle —*vi.* **1.** to pull; tug; snatch (often with *at*) **2.** to pluck a musical instrument —*n.* **1.** a pulling; tug **2.** courage to meet danger or difficulty; fortitude —**pluck′er** ***n.***

pluck·y (-ē) ***adj.*** **pluck′i·er, pluck′i·est** brave; spirited; resolute —**pluck′i·ly** ***adv.*** —**pluck′i·ness** ***n.***

plug (plug) ***n.*** [MDu. *plugge*] **1.** an object used to stop up a hole, drain, etc. **2.** *a)* a cake of pressed tobacco *b)* a piece of chewing tobacco **3.** a device, as with projecting prongs, for fitting into an electric outlet, appliance, etc. to make electrical contact **4.** *same as: a)* SPARK PLUG *b)* FIREPLUG **5.** [Colloq.] a defective or shopworn article **6.** [Slang] an old, worn-out horse **7.** [Colloq.] a boost, advertisement, etc., esp. one slipped into the entertainment part of a radio or TV program, a magazine article, etc. —*vt.* **plugged, plug′ging 1.** to stop up (a hole, etc.) with a plug (often with *up*) **2.** to insert (something) as a plug **3.** [Colloq.] *a)* to promote (a song) by frequent performance *b)* to promote with a plug (*n.* 7) **4.** [Slang] to shoot a bullet into —*vi.* [Colloq.] to work or study hard and steadily; plod —**plug in** to connect (an electrical device) with an outlet, etc. by inserting a plug in a socket or jack —**pull the plug** [Colloq.] **1.** to disconnect a device being used to maintain a terminal patient's life **2.** to put an end to something

plum (plum) ***n.*** [OE. *plume*] **1.** *a)* any of various small trees bearing a smooth-skinned, edible fruit with a flattened stone *b)* the fruit **2.** a raisin, when used in pudding or cake **3.** the dark bluish-red or reddish-purple color of some plums **4.** something choice or desirable

plum·age (plo͞o′mij) ***n.*** [MFr. < L. *pluma,* a feather] a bird's feathers

plumb (plum) ***n.*** [< MFr. < L. *plumbum,* LEAD[2]] a lead weight (**plumb bob**) hung at the end of a line (**plumb line**), used to determine how deep water is or whether a wall, etc. is vertical —*adj.* perfectly vertical —*adv.* **1.** straight down; directly **2.** [Colloq.] entirely; absolutely *[plumb crazy]* —*vt.* **1.** to test or sound with a plumb **2.** to discover the facts of; solve **3.** to make vertical —**out of** (or **off**) **plumb** not vertical

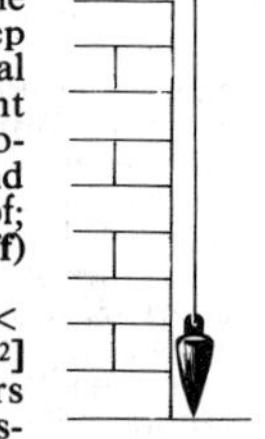

PLUMB

plumb·er (plum′ər) ***n.*** [< MFr. < L. < *plumbarius,* lead-worker < *plumbum,* LEAD[2]] a skilled worker who installs and repairs pipes, fixtures, etc., as of water or gas systems

plumb·ing (plum′iŋ) ***n.*** **1.** the using of a plumb **2.** the work of a plumber **3.** the pipes and fixtures with which a plumber works

plume (plo͞om) ***n.*** [OFr. < L. *pluma*] **1.** *a)* a feather, esp. a large, showy one *b)* a cluster of these **2.** an ornament made of such a feather or feathers, or a feathery tuft of hair, esp. when worn on a hat, helmet, etc. **3.** a token of worth or achievement; prize **4.** something like a plume in shape or lightness *[a plume of smoke]* —*vt.* **plumed, plum′ing 1.** to provide, cover, or adorn with plumes **2.** to preen (its feathers): said of a bird **3.** to pride (oneself)

plum·met (plum′it) ***n.*** [< MFr. dim. of *plombe:* see PLUMB] **1.** a plumb **2.** a thing that weighs heavily —*vi.* to fall or drop straight downward

plu·mose (plo͞o′mōs) ***adj.*** [< L. < *pluma,* a feather] **1.** feathered **2.** like a feather —**plu·mos′i·ty** (-mäs′ə tē) ***n.***

plump[1] (plump) ***adj.*** [< MDu. *plomp,* bulky] full and rounded in form; chubby —***vt., vi.*** to make plump; fill out (sometimes with *up* or *out*) —**plump′ish** ***adj.*** —**plump′ly** ***adv.*** —**plump′ness** ***n.***

plump[2] (plump) ***vi.*** [< MDu. *plompen:* orig. echoic] **1.** to fall or bump (*against*) suddenly or heavily **2.** to offer strong support (*for* someone or something) —*vt.* to drop, throw, or put down heavily or all at once —*n.* a sudden or heavy fall or the sound of this —*adv.* **1.** suddenly or heavily **2.** straight down **3.** in plain words; bluntly —*adj.* blunt; direct

plum pudding [orig. made with plums] a rich pudding made of raisins, currants, flour, suet, etc., boiled or steamed, as in a linen bag

plu·mule (plo͞om′yo͞ol) *n.* [< L. dim. of *pluma*, a feather] **1.** the growing stem tip of the embryo of a plant seed **2.** a down feather

plum·y (plo͞o′mē) *adj.* **plum′i·er, plum′i·est 1.** covered or adorned with plumes **2.** like a plume; feathery

plun·der (plun′dər) *vt.* [< G. *plunder*, baggage] **1.** to rob (a person or place) by force, esp. in warfare **2.** to take (property) by force or fraud —*vi.* to engage in plundering —*n.* **1.** the act of plundering; pillage **2.** goods taken by force or fraud; loot; booty —**plun′der·er** *n.* —**plun′der·ous** *adj.*

plunge (plunj) *vt.* **plunged, plung′ing** [< OFr. *plongier*, ult. < L. *plumbum*, LEAD²] to thrust or throw suddenly (*into* a liquid, hole, condition, etc.) —*vi.* **1.** to dive or rush, as into water, a fight, etc. **2.** to move violently and rapidly downward or forward **3.** to pitch, as a ship **4.** to extend far down in a revealing way [*a plunging* neckline] **5.** [Colloq.] to spend, gamble, or speculate heavily —*n.* **1.** *a*) a dive or downward leap *b*) a swim **2.** any sudden, violent plunging motion **3.** [Colloq.] a heavy, rash investment —**take the plunge** to start on some new and uncertain enterprise, esp. after some hesitation

plung·er (plun′jər) *n.* **1.** a person who plunges **2.** a large, rubber suction cup with a long handle, used to free clogged drains **3.** any cylindrical device that operates with a plunging motion, as a piston

plunk (pluŋk) *vt.* [echoic] **1.** to pluck or strum (a banjo, guitar, etc.) **2.** to throw or put down heavily; plump —*vi.* **1.** to give out a twanging sound, as a banjo **2.** to fall heavily **3.** [Colloq.] *same as* PLUMP² (*vi.* 2) —*n.* the act or sound of plunking —*adv.* with a twang or thud —**plunk down** [Colloq.] to pay —**plunk′er** *n.*

plu·per·fect (plo͞o pur′fikt) *adj.* [abbrev. of L. *plus quam perfectum*, more than perfect] designating a tense in any of certain languages corresponding to the past perfect in English —*n.* a pluperfect tense or a form in this tense

plu·ral (ploor′əl) *adj.* [L. *pluralis* < *plus* (gen. *pluris*), more] **1.** of or including more than one **2.** of or involving a plurality of persons or things [*plural* marriage] **3.** *Gram.* designating or of that category of number referring to more than one, or in languages having dual number, more than two —*n. Gram.* **1.** the plural number **2.** a plural form of a word **3.** a word in plural form The plurals of nouns are formed in English according to the principles listed below. Words with alternative plurals in the regular -(*e*)*s* form are marked (*).

I. REGULAR ENGLISH PLURALS
- A. Add *-s* in all cases except as noted below
- B. Add *-es* after final *-ss, -sh, -ch, -s, -x, -z*, and *-zz: glass-es, ash-es, witch-es, gas-es, box-es, adz-es, buzz-es*
- C. Add *-es* after *-y* preceded by a consonant or by *-qu-*, and change the *-y* to *-i: fly, fli-es; soliloquy, soliloqui-es;* etc. (Add *-s* after *-y* preceded by a vowel: *day, day-s; monkey, monkey-s;* etc.)
- D. Add *-s* to most words ending in *-o* preceded by a consonant, and to all words ending in *-o* preceded by a vowel: *piano-s, radio-s, studio-s*, etc. (Add *-es* to some words ending in *-o* preceded by a consonant: **buffalo-es*, **domino-es, echo-es, hero-es, potato-es,* etc.)

II. OTHER ENGLISH PLURALS
- A. Change *-f* to *-v* in many words, and add *-es: half, self, life, leaf,* **scarf*¹, **wharf*, etc.
- B. Plural formed by:
  1. *-en: ox-en*
  2. *-ren: child-ren*
  3. Vowel change: *man, men; foot, feet; mouse, mice;* etc.
- C. Plural the same as the singular: *alms, barracks, Chinese, deer* (occas. *deers*), *forceps, gross, means, moose, sheep*, etc.
- D. Plural either different from or the same as the singular:
  1. Plural usually different, but sometimes the same, esp. in the usage of hunters and fishermen: *antelope, badger, brant, buffalo, cougar, giraffe, mullet, shrimp, sturgeon, tarpon*, etc.
  2. Plural usually the same, but different if referring to different kinds, species, varieties, etc. [the *fishes* of the South Pacific]: *cod, elk, gar, mackerel, shad, springbok, trout*, etc.
  3. Plural usually lacking, but given in -(*e*)*s* form when different kinds are referred to [the many *steels* produced]: *brass, coffee, fruit, iron, linen, wool*, etc.
  4. Plural and collective singular interchangeable: *seeds, seed;* etc.

III. FORMS SINGULAR OR PLURAL ONLY
- A. Singular only (or when a generalized abstraction): *clearness, fishing, information, knowledge, luck, music, nonsense, truth*, etc.
- B. Plural only (even when singular in meaning), including certain senses of nouns otherwise singular: *Balkans, blues* (depression), *glasses, overalls, pliers, remains* (corpse), *scissors, tongs, trousers*, etc.
- C. Plural in form but used with singular verbs: *checkers* (game), *measles, mumps, news*, etc.
- D. Nouns ending in *-ics* are singular when they denote scientific subjects, as *mathematics, physics*, etc., and plural when they denote activities or qualities, as *acrobatics, acoustics*, etc.

IV. LATIN AND GREEK PLURALS
- A. With Latin suffix *-i* replacing singular ending *-us: alumnus, alumn-i;* **focus, foc-i;* **nucleus, nucle-i;* **radius, radi-i;* etc.
- B. With Latin suffix *-ae* replacing singular ending *-a: alumna, alumn-ae;* **formula, formul-ae;* etc.
- C. With suffix *-a* replacing singular ending:
  1. Latin nouns in *-um:* **agendum, agend-a; datum, dat-a;* **medium, medi-a;* etc.
  2. Greek nouns in *-on:* **criterion, criteri-a;* **phenomenon, phenomen-a;* etc.
- D. With suffix *-es:*
  1. Latin suffix *-ex* or *-ix* replaced by *-ices:* **appendix, append-ices;* **index, ind-ices;* etc.
  2. Latin or Greek suffix *-is* replaced by *-es: analysis, analys-es; axis, ax-es;* etc.
- E. Miscellaneous Latin and Greek plurals: **phalanx, phalang-es;* **stigma, stigma-ta; corpus, corp-ora;* **genus, gen-era;* etc.

V. OTHER FOREIGN PLURALS
- A. Hebrew: **cherub, cherub-im; kibbutz, kibbutz-im;* **matzo, matzo-t(h)*
- B. Italian: **bandit, bandit-ti;* **dilettante, dilettant-i;* **virtuoso, virtuos-i;* etc.
- C. French: *bijou, bijou-x;* **château, château-x;* **portmanteau, portmanteau-x;* etc.

VI. PLURALS OF NUMBERS, LETTERS, SIGNS, WORDS (when thought of as things), etc. add *-'s* (or now often *-s*): *8's* (or *8s*), *B's* (or *Bs*), *&'s* (or *&s*), *but's* (or *buts*)

plu·ral·ism (ploor′əl iz′m) *n.* **1.** a being plural, or existing in more than one part or form **2.** the existence within a society of groups that differ ethnically, culturally, etc. **3.** *Philos.* the theory that reality is composed of a number of ultimate beings, principles, or substances —**plu′ral·ist** *n., adj.* —**plu′ral·is′tic** *adj.* —**plu′ral·is′ti·cal·ly** *adv.*

plu·ral·i·ty (ploo ral′ə tē) *n., pl.* **-ties 1.** a being plural or numerous **2.** a great number; multitude **3.** *a*) the total number of votes received by the leading candidate in an election *b*) the number of votes that the leading candidate of more than two obtains over the next highest candidate **4.** *same as* MAJORITY

plu·ral·ize (ploor′ə līz′) *vt., vi.* **-ized′, -iz′ing** to make or become plural —**plu′ral·i·za′tion** *n.* —**plu′ral·iz′er** *n.*

plu·ral·ly (-əl ē) *adv.* in the plural number

plu·ri- [L. < *plus* (gen. *pluris*), several] *a combining form meaning* several or many

plus (plus) *prep.* [L., more] **1.** added to [2 *plus* 2 equals 4] **2.** in addition to [salary *plus* bonus] —*adj.* **1.** designating a sign (**plus sign**) indicating addition [+ is a *plus* sign] **2.** positive [a *plus* quantity] **3.** somewhat higher than [a grade of B *plus*] **4.** involving extra gain or advantage [a *plus* factor] **5.** [Colloq.] and more [she has personality *plus*] **6.** *Elec. same as* POSITIVE [the *plus* terminal] —*adv.* [Colloq.] moreover [he has the time *plus* he has the money] —*n., pl.* **plus′es, plus′ses 1.** a plus sign **2.** an added or favorable quantity or thing **3.** a positive quantity

plus fours [orig. indicating added length of material for overlap below the knee] loose knickerbockers worn, esp. formerly, for active sports

plush (plush) *n.* [< Fr. < *peluche*, ult. < L. *pilus*, hair] a fabric with a soft, thick, deep pile —*adj.* **1.** of plush **2.** [Slang] luxurious, as in furnishings —**plush′i·ly** *adv.* —**plush′i·ness** *n.* —**plush′y** *adj.* **plush′i·er, plush′i·est**

Plu·tarch (plo͞o′tärk) 46?–120? A.D.; Gr. biographer & historian

Plu·to (plo͞ot′ō) **1.** *Gr. & Rom. Myth.* the god ruling the lower world **2.** the outermost planet of the solar system: diameter, c. 3,700 mi. —**Plu·to′ni·an** *adj.*

plu·toc·ra·cy (ploo täk′rə sē) ***n.**, pl.* **-cies** [< Gr. < *ploutos,* wealth + *kratein,* to rule] **1.** government by the wealthy **2.** a group of wealthy people who control a government

plu·to·crat (ploot′ə krat′) ***n.*** **1.** a member of a wealthy ruling class **2.** a person whose wealth gives him control or great influence —**plu′to·crat′ic** ***adj.*** —**plu′to·crat′i·cal·ly** ***adv.***

plu·ton·ic (ploo tän′ik) ***adj.*** [after PLUTO] *Geol.* formed far below the surface of the earth by intense heat and slow cooling, as some rocks

plu·to·ni·um (ploo tō′nē əm) ***n.*** [ModL. after *Pluto* (planet)] a radioactive, metallic chemical element: symbol, Pu; at. wt., 239.05; at. no., 94

plu·vi·al (ploo′vē əl) ***adj.*** [< L. < *pluvia,* rain] **1.** *a)* of or having to do with rain *b)* having much rain **2.** *Geol.* formed by the action of rain

ply[1] (plī) ***vt.*** **plied, ply′ing** [< OFr. < L. *plicare,* to fold] [Now Rare] to bend, twist, fold, or mold —***n.**, pl.* **plies** **1.** a single thickness or layer, as of plywood, doubled cloth, etc. **2.** one of the twisted strands in rope, yarn, etc. **3.** bias or inclination —***adj.*** having (a specified number of) layers, strands, etc. *[three-ply]*

ply[2] (plī) ***vt.*** **plied, ply′ing** [ME. *plien,* short for *applien,* APPLY] **1.** to work with; wield or use (a tool, faculty, etc.) **2.** to work at (a trade) **3.** to address (someone) urgently (*with* questions, etc.) **4.** to keep supplying (*with* gifts, food, etc.) **5.** to sail back and forth across *[boats ply the channel]* —***vi.*** **1.** to keep busy or work (*at* something or *with* a tool, etc.) **2.** to travel regularly (*between* places): said of ships, buses, etc.

Ply·mouth (plim′əth) **1.** seaport in SW England, on the English Channel: pop. 257,000 **2.** village on the SE coast of Mass.: settled by the Pilgrims (1620) as **Plymouth Colony**

Plymouth Rock **1.** boulder at Plymouth, Mass., where the Pilgrims are said to have landed **2.** any of a breed of American chickens

ply·wood (plī′wood′) ***n.*** [PLY[1] + WOOD] a material made of thin layers of wood glued and pressed together, usually with the grains at right angles

Pm *Chem.* promethium

pm. **1.** phase modulation **2.** premium

P.M. **1.** Paymaster **2.** Postmaster **3.** Prime Minister

P.M., p.m., PM [L. *post meridiem*] after noon: used to designate the time from noon to midnight

p.m. post-mortem

pmk. postmark

pneu·mat·ic (noo mat′ik, nyoo-) ***adj.*** [< L. < Gr. < *pneuma,* breath] **1.** of or containing wind, air, or gases **2.** *a)* filled with compressed air *[pneumatic tire]* *b)* worked by compressed air *[pneumatic drill]* —**pneu·mat′i·cal·ly** ***adv.***

pneu·mat·ics (-iks) ***n.pl.*** [*with sing. v.*] the branch of physics dealing with such properties of air and other gases as pressure, density, etc.

pneu·mo·coc·cus (noo′mə käk′əs, nyoo′-) ***n.**, pl.* **-coc′ci** (-käk′sī) [ModL. < Gr. *pneumōn,* a lung + COCCUS] a bacterium that is a causative agent of pneumonia —**pneu′mo·coc′cal** (-käk′'l), **pneu′mo·coc′cic** (-käk′sik) ***adj.***

pneu·mo·en·ceph·a·lo·gram (-en sef′ə lō gram′) ***n.*** [< Gr. *pneumōn,* a lung + *en-,* in + *kephalē,* the head + -GRAM] an X-ray photograph of the brain made after cerebrospinal fluid has been replaced with air or oxygen

pneu·mo·ni·a (noo mōn′yə, nyoo-; -mō′nē ə) ***n.*** [ModL. < Gr. < *pneumōn,* a lung < *pnein,* to breathe] inflammation or infection of the alveoli of the lungs, caused by any of various agents, such as bacteria or viruses —**pneu·mon′ic** (-män′ik) ***adj.***

Pnom-Penh (p′nôm′pen′) *same as* PHNOM PENH

Po (pō) river in N Italy, flowing from the Alps east into the Adriatic

Po *Chem.* polonium

P.O., p.o. **1.** petty officer: also **PO** **2.** post office **3.** post office box

poach[1] (pōch) ***vt.*** [< MFr. < *poche,* a pocket: the yolk is "pocketed" in the white] to cook (fish, an egg without its shell, etc.) in water or other liquid near the boiling point, or in a small receptacle put over boiling water —**poach′er** ***n.***

poach[2] (pōch) ***vt.*** [< Fr. < OFr. *pochier,* to tread upon < MHG. *puchen,* to plunder] **1.** to trample **2.** *a)* to trespass on (private property), esp. for hunting or fishing *b)* to hunt or catch (game or fish) illegally, esp. by trespassing **3.** to steal —***vi.*** to hunt or fish illegally, esp. as a trespasser —**poach′er** ***n.***

Po·ca·hon·tas (pō′kə hän′təs) 1595?–1617; Am. Indian princess: reputed to have saved Captain John Smith from execution

pock (päk) ***n.*** [OE. *pocc*] **1.** a pustule, esp. one caused by smallpox **2.** *same as* POCKMARK —**pocked** ***adj.*** —**pock′y** ***adj.*** **pock′i·er, pock′i·est**

pock·et (päk′it) ***n.*** [< Anglo-Fr. < ONormFr. dim. of *poque,* a bag] **1.** *a)* a little bag or pouch, now usually sewn into or on clothing, for carrying money and small articles *b)* any usually small container, compartment, pouch, etc. **2.** a cavity for holding something **3.** a small area or group *[a pocket of poverty]* **4.** a confining or frustrating situation **5.** funds *[a drain on one's pocket]* **6.** *Aeron. same as* AIR POCKET **7.** any of the pouches at the sides and corners of a billiard or pool table **8.** *Geol.* *a)* a cavity filled with ore, oil, gas, or water *b)* a small deposit of ore, etc. —***adj.*** **1.** *a)* that is or can be carried in a pocket *b)* smaller than standard **2.** not widespread; isolated *[pocket resistance]* —***vt.*** **1.** to put into a pocket **2.** to provide with pockets **3.** to envelop; enclose **4.** to take dishonestly; appropriate (money, etc.) for one's own use **5.** to put up with (an insult, etc.) without answering or showing anger **6.** to hide, suppress, or set aside *[pocket one's pride]* —**out of pocket** from money at hand

pocket battleship a small battleship within certain treaty limits as to tonnage and guns

pocket billiards *same as* POOL[2] (*n.* 2)

pock·et·book (-book′) ***n.*** **1.** a case, as of leather, for carrying money and papers in one's pocket; billfold **2.** a woman's purse **3.** monetary resources

pocket book a book small enough to be carried in one's pocket

pock·et·ful (-fool′) ***n.**, pl.* **-fuls′** as much as a pocket will hold

pock·et·knife (-nīf′) ***n.**, pl.* **-knives′** (-nīvz′) a knife with blades that fold into the handle

pocket money cash for small expenses

pock·et-size (-sīz′) ***adj.*** of a small size; esp., of a size to fit in a pocket: also **pock′et-sized′**

pocket veto the indirect veto by the President of the U.S. of a bill presented to him by Congress within ten days of its adjournment, by his failing to sign and return the bill before Congress adjourns

pock·mark (päk′märk′) ***n.*** a scar or pit left by a pustule, as of smallpox, or any mark like this —***vt.*** to cover with pockmarks —**pock′marked′** ***adj.***

po·co (pō′kō) ***adv.*** [It.] *Music* somewhat

pod (päd) ***n.*** [< ?] **1.** a dry fruit or seed vessel enclosing one or more seeds, as a legume **2.** a contoured enclosure, as the housing of a jet engine —***vi.*** **pod′ded, pod′ding** **1.** to bear pods **2.** to swell out into a pod —**pod′like′** ***adj.***

-pod (päd) [< Gr. *pous* (gen. *podos*), a foot] *a combining form meaning:* **1.** foot **2.** (one) having (a specified number or kind of) feet *[tripod]* Also **-pode** (pōd)

podg·y (päj′ē) ***adj.*** **podg′i·er, podg′i·est** *var. of* PUDGY

po·di·a·try (pō dī′ə trē, pə-) ***n.*** [< Gr. *pous* (see -POD) + -IATRY] the profession dealing with the care of the feet and with the treatment of foot disorders —**po·di′a·trist** ***n.*** —**po′di·at′ric** ***adj.***

po·di·um (pō′dē əm) ***n.**, pl.* **-di·a** (-ə); for 1 usually, **-di·ums** [L. < Gr. *podion,* dim. of *pous* (see -POD)] **1.** a low platform, esp. for the conductor of an orchestra **2.** *Zool.* a foot or footlike structure

Po·dunk (pō′duŋk′) [after a village in Mass. or Conn.] [Colloq.] any typically dull small town in the U.S.

Poe (pō), **Edgar Allan** 1809–49; U.S. poet, short-story writer, & critic

po·em (pō′əm) ***n.*** [< MFr. < L. < Gr. *poiēma* < *poiein,* to make] **1.** an arrangement of words written or spoken, traditionally a rhythmical or metrical composition, sometimes rhymed **2.** anything suggesting a poem in its effect

po·e·sy (pō′ə sē′, -zē′) ***n.**, pl.* **-sies** [< OFr. < L. < Gr. *poiēsis* < *poiein,* to make] **1.** *old-fashioned var. of* POETRY **2.** [Obs.] a poem

po·et (pō′ət) ***n.*** [< OFr. < L. < Gr. *poiētēs* < *poiein,* to make] **1.** a person who writes poems **2.** a person who expresses himself with beauty of thought and language —**po′et·ess** [Now Rare] ***n.fem.***

poet. **1.** poetic **2.** poetry

po·et·as·ter (pō′ə tas′tər) ***n.*** [see POET & -ASTER] a writer of mediocre verse; rhymester

po·et·ic (pō et′ik) ***adj.*** **1.** of, like, or fit for a poet or poetry **2.** written in verse **3.** having the beauty, imagination, etc. of poetry **4.** imaginative or creative Also **po·et′i·cal** —**po·et′i·cal·ly** ***adv.***

po·et·i·cize (-ə sīz′) ***vt.*** **-cized′, -ciz′ing** **1.** to make poetic **2.** to express, or deal with, in poetry —***vi.*** to write poetry

poetic justice justice, as in some plays, etc., in which good is rewarded and evil punished

poetic license **1.** disregard of strict fact or of rigid form, as by a poet, for artistic effect **2.** freedom to do this

po·et·ics (pō et′iks) ***n.pl.*** [*with sing. v.*] **1.** *a)* the theory or structure of poetry *b)* a treatise on this **2.** the poetic theory or practice of a specific poet

po·et·ize (pō′ə tīz′) ***vt., vi.*** **-ized′, -iz′ing** *same as* POETICIZE

poet laureate *pl.* **poets laureate, poet laureates** **1.** the court poet of England, appointed for life by the monarch to write poems celebrating official occasions, national events, etc. **2.** any official poet of any nation, region, etc.

po·et·ry (pō′ə trē) ***n.*** [< OFr. < ML. < L. *poeta*, a poet] **1.** the art, theory, or structure of poems **2.** poems **3.** *a)* poetic qualities *b)* the expression or embodiment of such qualities

po·go stick (pō′gō) [arbitrary coinage] a stilt with pedals and a spring at one end, used as a toy on which one can move along in a series of bounds

po·grom (pō gräm′, -grum′; pō′grəm) ***n.*** [Russ., devastation] an organized persecution and massacre of a minority group, esp. of Jews (as in Czarist Russia)

poi (poi, pō′ē) ***n.*** [Haw.] Hawaiian food made of mashed, fermented taro root

poign·ant (poin′yənt; *chiefly Brit.* -ənt) ***adj.*** [MFr. prp. of *poindre* < L. *pungere*, to prick] **1.** *a)* sharp or pungent to the smell or, formerly, the taste *b)* keenly affecting the other senses *[poignant* beauty*]* **2.** *a)* sharply painful to the feelings *b)* evoking pity, compassion, etc. **3.** sharp, biting, etc. *[poignant* wit*]* —**poign′an·cy** ***n.*** —**poign′ant·ly** ***adv.***

poi·kil·o·ther·mal (poi kil′ō thur′m′l) ***adj.*** [< Gr. *poikilos*, variegated + THERMAL] *Zool. same as* COLD-BLOODED (sense 1)

poin·ci·a·na (poin′sē an′ə, -ā′nə) ***n.*** [ModL., after M. de *Poinci*, a governor of the Fr. West Indies] any of various small tropical trees with showy red, orange, or yellow flowers

poin·set·ti·a (poin set′ē ə, -set′ə) ***n.*** [ModL., after J. R. *Poinsett* (d. 1851), U.S. ambassador to Mexico] a Mexican and Central American plant with yellow flowers surrounded by petallike red leaves

point (point) ***n.*** [OFr., a dot, prick < L. < *punctus*, pp. of *pungere*, to prick] **1.** a minute mark or dot **2.** a dot in print or writing, as a period, decimal point, etc. **3.** *a)* an element in geometry having definite position, but no size, shape, or extension *b)* a particular position, location, spot, etc. *[points* on an itinerary*]* **4.** *a)* the position of a player, as in cricket *b)* the player **5.** the exact moment *[*at the *point* of death*]* **6.** a stage, condition, level, or degree reached *[*a boiling *point]* **7.** an item *[*explain it *point* by *point]* **8.** *a)* a distinguishing characteristic *b)* a physical characteristic of an animal, used as a standard in judging breeding **9.** a unit, as of measurement, value, game scores, etc. **10.** *a)* a sharp end; tip *b)* something with a sharp end **11.** needlepoint lace **12.** a projecting piece of land; cape **13.** a branch of a deer's antler *[*a ten-*point* buck*]* **14.** *a)* the essential fact or idea under consideration *b)* the main idea or feature of a story, etc. **15.** aim; purpose; object *[*there's no *point* in going*]* **16.** *a)* an impressive argument or fact *[*he has a *point* there!*]* *b)* a helpful hint **17.** the number that the thrower must make to win in craps **18.** *Ballet* the position of being on the tips of the toes **19.** *Elec.* either of the two tungsten or platinum contacts that make or break the circuit in a distributor **20.** *Finance a)* a standard unit of value, equal to $1, used in quoting prices, as of stocks *b)* a percentage of a mortgage required to be paid in advance by the borrower **21.** *Navigation a)* any of the 32 marks showing direction on a compass card *b)* the angle between two successive compass points **22.** *Printing* a measuring unit for type bodies and printed matter, equal to about 1/72 of an inch —***vt.*** **1.** *a)* to put punctuation marks in *b)* to mark (*off* a sum, etc.) with (decimal) points **2.** to sharpen (a pencil, etc.) to a point **3.** to give (a story, remark, etc.) emphasis (usually with *up*) **4.** to show or call attention to (usually with *out*) *[point* the way*]* **5.** to aim or direct (a gun, finger, etc.) **6.** to extend the foot so as to bring (the toe) more nearly in line with the leg **7.** to show the location of (game) by standing still and facing toward it: said of hunting dogs **8.** *Masonry* to rake out mortar from the joints of (brickwork) and finish with fresh mortar —***vi.*** **1.** to direct one's finger or the like (*at* or *to*) **2.** to call attention (*to*); hint (*at*) **3.** to aim or be directed (*to* or *toward*) **4.** to point game: said of a hunting dog —**at the point of** very close to —**beside the point** not pertinent —**in point of** in the matter of —**make a point of** **1.** to make (something) one's strict rule, practice, etc. **2.** to call special attention to —**on** (or **upon**) **the point of** on the verge of —**stretch** (or **strain**) **a point** to make an exception or concession —**to the point** pertinent; apt: also **in point** —**point′a·ble** ***adj.***

point-blank (-blaŋk′) ***adj.*** [POINT + BLANK (white center of the target)] **1.** aimed horizontally, straight at a mark **2.** straightforward; plain *[*a *point-blank* answer*]* —***adv.*** **1.** in a direct line; straight **2.** without quibbling; bluntly *[*to refuse *point-blank]*

point·ed (poin′tid) ***adj.*** **1.** *a)* having a point, or sharp end *b)* tapering **2.** sharp; incisive, as an epigram **3.** aimed at someone *[*a *pointed* remark*]* **4.** very evident; emphasized —**point′ed·ly** ***adv.*** —**point′ed·ness** ***n.***

point·er (-tər) ***n.*** **1.** a person or thing that points **2.** a long, tapered rod for pointing to things, as on a map **3.** an indicator on a clock, meter, etc. **4.** a large, lean hunting dog with a smooth coat: it smells out game and then points **5.** [Colloq.] a helpful hint —**the Pointers** *Astron.* the two stars in the Big Dipper that are almost in a line with the North Star

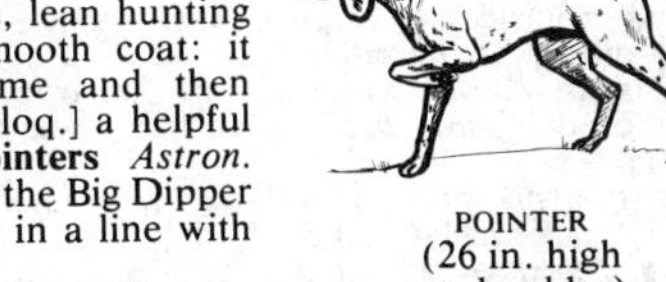

POINTER
(26 in. high at shoulder)

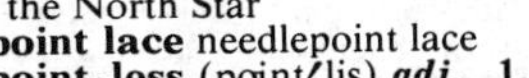

point lace needlepoint lace

point·less (point′lis) ***adj.*** **1.** without a point **2.** without meaning, relevance, or force; senseless —**point′less·ly** ***adv.*** —**point′less·ness** ***n.***

point of honor a matter affecting one's honor

point of order a question as to whether the rules of parliamentary procedure are being observed

point of view **1.** the place from which, or way in which, something is viewed; standpoint **2.** a mental attitude

point·y (poin′tē) ***adj.*** **point′i·er, point′i·est** **1.** that comes to a sharp point **2.** having many points

poise (poiz) ***n.*** [< OFr. < VL. < L. *pensum*, something weighed < *pendere*, to weigh] **1.** balance; stability **2.** ease and dignity of manner; composure **3.** the condition of being calm or serene **4.** carriage; bearing, as of the body —***vt.*** **poised, pois′ing** **1.** to balance; keep steady **2.** to suspend (usually passive or reflexive) —***vi.*** **1.** to be suspended or balanced **2.** to hover

poi·son (poi′z′n) ***n.*** [< OFr. < L. *potio*, potion] **1.** a substance causing illness or death when eaten, drunk, or absorbed in small quantities **2.** anything harmful to happiness or welfare —***vt.*** **1.** to harm or destroy by means of poison **2.** to put poison on or into **3.** to influence wrongfully *[*to *poison* one's mind*]* —***adj.*** poisonous or poisoned —**poi′son·er** ***n.***

poison dogwood *same as* POISON SUMAC

poison ivy **1.** any of several plants having leaves of three leaflets and ivory-colored berries: it can cause a severe rash on contact **2.** such a rash

poison oak *name variously used for:* **1.** POISON IVY **2.** POISON SUMAC

poi·son·ous (poi′z′n əs) ***adj.*** capable of injuring or killing by or as by poison; full of poison; venomous —**poi′son·ous·ly** ***adv.*** —**poi′son·ous·ness** ***n.***

poison sumac a swamp plant with clusters of grayish fruit and leaves made up of 7 to 13 leaflets: it can cause a severe rash on contact

POISON IVY

poke[1] (pōk) ***vt.*** **poked, pok′ing** [MDu. or LowG. *poken*] **1.** *a)* to push or jab with a stick, finger, etc. *b)* [Slang] to hit with the fist **2.** to make (a hole, etc.) by poking **3.** to stir up (a fire) **4.** to thrust (something) forward; intrude *[*to *poke* one's head out a window*]* —***vi.*** **1.** to jab with a stick, poker, etc. (*at*) **2.** to intrude; meddle **3.** to search (sometimes with *about* or *around*) **4.** to stick out; protrude **5.** to move slowly or lazily; loiter (often with *along*) —***n.*** **1.** *a)* a poking; jab; thrust *b)* [Slang] a blow with the fist **2.** *same as* SLOWPOKE **3.** a poke bonnet —**poke fun (at)** to ridicule or deride

poke[2] (pōk) ***n.*** [OFr. *poke, poque* < Frank.] **1.** [Dial.] a sack or bag **2.** [Slang] *a)* a wallet or purse *b)* all of one's money

poke[3] (pōk) ***n.*** [< AmInd. *puccoon*] *same as* POKEWEED: also **poke′ber′ry** (-ber′ē), *pl.* **-ries**

poke bonnet a bonnet with a wide front brim

pok·er[1] (pō′kər) ***n.*** [< ?] a card game in which the players bet on the value of their hands, forming a pool to be taken by the winner: see DRAW POKER, STUD POKER

pok·er[2] (pō′kər) ***n.*** **1.** a person or thing that pokes **2.** a bar, as of iron, for stirring a fire

poker face [Colloq.] an expressionless face, as of a poker player hiding the nature of his hand

poke·weed (pōk′wēd′) ***n.*** [see POKE[3]] a N. American plant with purplish-white flowers, reddish-purple berries, and poisonous roots

pok·ey (pō′kē) ***n.***, *pl.* **pok′eys, pok′ies** [< ?] [Slang] a jail: also **pok′y**

pok·y (pō′kē) ***adj.*** **pok′i·er, pok′i·est** [POKE[1] + -Y[2]] **1.** slow; dull **2.** small; stuffy *[*a *poky* room*]* **3.** shabbily dressed Also **pok′ey** —**pok′i·ly** ***adv.*** —**pok′i·ness** ***n.***

pol (päl) ***n.*** [Slang] an experienced politician

Pol. **1.** Poland **2.** Polish

Po·land (pō′lənd) country in C Europe, on the Baltic Sea: 120,625 sq. mi.; pop. 32,807,000; cap. Warsaw

Poland China an American breed of large hog, usually black and white
po·lar (pō′lər) ***adj.*** [< ML. < L. *polus:* see POLE²] **1.** of or near the North or South Pole **2.** of a pole or poles **3.** having polarity **4.** opposite in character, direction, etc. **5.** guiding, like the polestar
polar bear a large, white bear of the Arctic regions
polar circle *same as:* **1.** ARCTIC CIRCLE **2.** ANTARCTIC CIRCLE
Po·la·ris (pō lar′is) [ModL. < ML. (*stella*) *polaris,* polar (star)] *same as* NORTH STAR
po·lar·i·scope (pō lar′ə skōp′) ***n.*** [POLARI(ZE) + -SCOPE] an instrument for demonstrating or detecting the polarization of light —**po·lar′i·scop′ic** (-skäp′ik) ***adj.***
po·lar·i·ty (pō lar′ə tē) ***n.,*** *pl.* **-ties 1.** the tendency of bodies having opposite magnetic poles to become aligned so that their two extremities point to the two magnetic poles of the earth **2.** any tendency to turn, feel, etc. in a certain way, as if magnetized **3.** the having of two contrary qualities, powers, etc. **4.** the condition of being positive or negative with respect to some reference point or object
po·lar·i·za·tion (pō′lər i zā′shən) ***n.*** **1.** the producing or acquiring of polarity **2.** the accumulation of gases around the electrodes of an electric cell during electrolysis, causing a reduction in the flow of current **3.** *Optics* a condition, or the production of a condition, of light in which the transverse vibrations of the waves are in one plane or direction only
po·lar·ize (pō′lə rīz′) ***vt.*** **-ized′, -iz′ing** [< Fr. < *polaire,* POLAR] to give polarity to; produce polarization in —***vi.*** to acquire polarity; specif., to separate into diametrically opposed groups, etc. —**po′lar·iz′a·ble *adj.*** —**po′lar·iz′er *n.***
Po·lar·oid (pō′lə roid′) [POLAR + -OID] *a trademark for:* **1.** a transparent material capable of polarizing light **2.** a camera that develops and prints snapshots: in full, **Polaroid (Land) camera**
Pole (pōl) ***n.*** a native or inhabitant of Poland
pole¹ (pōl) ***n.*** [OE. *pal* < L. *palus,* a stake] **1.** a long, slender piece of wood, metal, etc. *[a tent pole]* **2.** a unit of measure, equal to one rod or one square rod **3.** the innermost position on a race track —***vt., vi.*** **poled, pol′ing 1.** to propel (a boat or raft) with a pole **2.** to impel, support, etc. (something) as with a pole
pole² (pōl) ***n.*** [L. *polus* < Gr. *polos*] **1.** either end of any axis, as of the earth, of the celestial sphere, etc. **2.** the region around the North Pole or South Pole **3.** either of two opposed forces, parts, etc., such as the ends of a magnet, the terminals of a battery, etc. —**poles apart** widely separated
pole·ax, pole·axe (pōl′aks′) ***n.,*** *pl.* **-ax′es** (-ak′siz) [< *pol,* POLL + *ax,* AX] **1.** a long-handled battle-ax **2.** any ax with a spike, hook, etc. opposite the blade —***vt.*** **-axed′, -ax′ing** to attack with a poleax
pole·cat (pōl′kat′) ***n.,*** *pl.* **-cats′, -cat′:** see PLURAL, II, D, 1 [prob. < OFr. *poule:* see PULLET & CAT] **1.** a small, weasel-like carnivore of Europe **2.** *same as* SKUNK
po·lem·ic (pə lem′ik, pō-) ***adj.*** [< Fr. < Gr. *polemikos* < *polemos,* a war] **1.** of or involving dispute; controversial **2.** argumentative Also, esp. for 2, **po·lem′i·cal** —***n.*** **1.** an argument or controversial discussion **2.** a person inclined to argument —**po·lem′i·cal·ly *adv.***
po·lem·ics (-iks) ***n.pl.*** [*with sing. v.*] the art or practice of disputation —**po·lem′i·cist** (-ə sist) ***n.***
pole·star (pōl′stär′) ***n.*** **1.** Polaris, the North Star **2.** a guiding principle **3.** a center of attraction
pole vault *Track and Field* **1.** an event in which the contestants leap for height, vaulting over a bar with the aid of a long, flexible pole **2.** such a leap —**pole′-vault′ *vi.*** —**pole′-vault′er *n.***
po·lice (pə lēs′) ***n.*** [Fr. < LL. < Gr. *politeia,* the state < *politēs,* citizen < *polis,* city] **1.** the regulation of morals, safety, etc.; law enforcement **2.** the governmental department (of a city, state, etc.) for keeping order, enforcing the law, and preventing and detecting crimes **3.** [*with pl. v.*] the members of such a department, or of a private organization like this *[security police]* **4.** *U.S. Army* *a)* the duty of keeping a camp, etc. clean and orderly *b)* [*with pl. v.*] the soldiers charged with this —***vt.*** **-liced′, -lic′ing 1.** to control, protect, etc. with police or the like *[to police the streets]* **2.** to keep (a camp, etc.) clean and orderly
police dog a dog specially trained to assist police; esp., in popular usage, a German shepherd dog
po·lice·man (-mən) ***n.,*** *pl.* **-men** a member of a police force —**po·lice′wom′an *n.fem.,*** *pl.* **-wom′en**
police state a government that uses a secret police force to suppress political opposition
pol·i·clin·ic (päl′i klin′ik) ***n.*** [< G. < Gr. *polis,* city + G. *klinik,* clinic] the department of a hospital where outpatients are treated
pol·i·cy¹ (päl′ə sē) ***n.,*** *pl.* **-cies** [< OFr. < L. < Gr. *politeia:* see POLICE] **1.** wise or prudent management **2.** any governing principle, plan, etc.
pol·i·cy² (päl′ə sē) ***n.,*** *pl.* **-cies** [< MFr. < It. *polizza* < ML., ult. < Gr. *apodeixis,* proof < *apodeiknynai,* to display] a written contract (**insurance policy**) in which one party guarantees to insure another against a specified loss, injury, etc.
policy (racket) *same as* THE NUMBERS (see NUMBER)
po·li·o (pō′lē ō′) ***n.*** *clipped form of* POLIOMYELITIS
po·li·o·my·e·li·tis (pō′lē ō mī′ə līt′əs) ***n.*** [ModL. < Gr. *polios,* gray + MYELITIS] an acute infectious disease, esp. of children, caused by a virus inflammation of the gray matter of the spinal cord, often resulting in muscular paralysis
Pol·ish (pō′lish) ***adj.*** of Poland, its people, their language, or culture —***n.*** the West Slavic language of the Poles
pol·ish (päl′ish) ***vt.*** [< OFr. < L. *polire*] **1.** *a)* to smooth and brighten, as by rubbing *b)* to coat with wax, etc. and make glossy **2.** to improve or refine (manners, etc.) by removing crudeness **3.** to complete or embellish —***vi.*** to take a polish; become glossy, refined, etc. —***n.*** **1.** a surface gloss **2.** elegance; refinement **3.** a substance used for polishing **4.** a polishing or being polished —**polish off** [Colloq.] to finish or get rid of —**polish up** [Colloq.] to improve —**pol′ished *adj.*** —**pol′ish·er *n.***
Po·lit·bu·ro (päl′it byoor′ō, pō′lit-) ***n.*** [< Russ. < *Polit(icheskoe) Byuro,* political bureau] the executive committee of the Communist Party of the Soviet Union and of certain other countries
po·lite (pə līt′) ***adj.*** [< L. pp. of *polire,* to polish] **1.** polished; cultured; refined *[polite society]* **2.** having good manners; courteous —**po·lite′ly *adv.*** —**po·lite′ness *n.***
pol·i·tesse (päl′ə tes′) ***n.*** [Fr.] politeness
pol·i·tic (päl′ə tik) ***adj.*** [< MFr. < L. < Gr. < *politēs:* see POLICE] **1.** having practical wisdom; prudent **2.** crafty; unscrupulous **3.** artful; expedient *[a politic plan]* **4.** [Rare] political: see BODY POLITIC —***vi.*** **-ticked, -tick·ing** to engage in political campaigning —**pol′i·tic·ly *adv.***
po·lit·i·cal (pə lit′i k′l) ***adj.*** **1.** of or concerned with government, politics, etc. **2.** having a definite governmental organization **3.** engaged in politics *[political parties]* **4.** of or characteristic of political parties or politicians —**po·lit′i·cal·ly *adv.***
political economy *earlier name for* ECONOMICS
political science the science of the principles, organization, and methods of government —**political scientist**
pol·i·ti·cian (päl′ə tish′ən) ***n.*** a person actively engaged in politics, often one holding or seeking political office: often used derogatorily of one who seeks only to advance himself or his party, as by scheming: cf. STATESMAN
po·lit·i·co (pə lit′i kō′) ***n.,*** *pl.* **-cos′** [Sp. or It.] *same as* POLITICIAN
pol·i·tics (päl′ə tiks) ***n.pl.*** [*with sing. or pl. v.*] **1.** the science of government; political science **2.** political affairs **3.** participation in political affairs **4.** political methods, tactics, etc. **5.** political opinions, principles, etc. **6.** factional scheming for power within a group
pol·i·ty (päl′ə tē) ***n.,*** *pl.* **-ties** [< MFr. < L. *politia:* see POLICY¹] **1.** the government organization of a state, church, etc. **2.** a society or institution with a government; state
Polk (pōk), **James Knox** 1795–1849; 11th president of the U.S. (1845–49)
pol·ka (pōl′kə) ***n.*** [Czech < Pol. fem. of *Polak,* a Pole] **1.** a fast dance for couples **2.** music for this dance, in duple time —***vi.*** to dance the polka
pol·ka dot (pō′kə) **1.** one of the small round dots regularly spaced to form a pattern on cloth **2.** a pattern or cloth with such dots —**pol′ka-dot′ *adj.***
poll (pōl) ***n.*** [< or akin to MDu. *pol,* head] **1.** the head; esp., the crown, back, or hair of the head **2.** a counting, listing, etc. of persons, esp. of voters **3.** the number of votes recorded **4.** [*pl.*] a place where votes are cast and recorded **5.** *a)* a canvassing of a selected or random group to collect information, or to attempt to discover public opinion *b)* a report on this —***vt.*** **1.** to cut off or cut short **2.** to trim the wool, branches, etc. of **3.** *a)* to register the votes of *b)* to require each member of (a jury, etc.) to declare his vote individually **4.** to receive (a certain number of votes) **5.** to cast (a vote) **6.** to canvass in a poll (sense 5 *a*) —***vi.*** to vote in an election —**poll′er *n.***
pol·len (päl′ən) ***n.*** [ModL. < L., dust] the yellow, powderlike male sex cells on the stamens of a flower
pol·li·nate (päl′ə nāt′) ***vt.*** **-nat′ed, -nat′ing** to transfer pollen from a stamen to a pistil of (a flower) —**pol′li·na′tion *n.*** —**pol′li·na′tor *n.***
pol·li·wog (päl′ē wäg′, -wôg′) ***n.*** [prob. < *pol,* POLL + *wigelen,* to WIGGLE] *same as* TADPOLE: also sp. **pol′ly·wog′**
poll·ster (pōl′stər) ***n.*** a person whose work is taking public opinion polls
poll tax a tax per head: in some States payment of a poll tax is a prerequisite for voting
pol·lu·tant (pə lo͞ot′'nt) ***n.*** something that pollutes, as a harmful chemical discharged into the air
pol·lute (pə lo͞ot′) ***vt.*** **-lut′ed, -lut′ing** [< L. pp. of *pol-*

luere] to make unclean, impure, or corrupt; defile —**pol·lut′er** ***n.*** —**pol·lu′tion** ***n.***

Pol·lux (päl′əks) **1.** *Gr. & Rom. Myth.* the immortal twin of Castor **2.** the brightest star in the constellation Gemini

Pol·ly·an·na (päl′ē an′ə) ***n.*** [the heroine of novels by Eleanor H. Porter (1868–1920), U.S. writer] a persistently optimistic person

po·lo (pō′lō) ***n.*** [prob. < Tibet. *pulu*, the ball] **1.** a game played on horseback by two teams who try to drive a small wooden ball through the opponents' goal with long-handled mallets **2.** *same as* WATER POLO —**po′lo·ist** ***n.***

Po·lo (pō′lō), **Mar·co** (mär′kō) 1254?–1324?; Venetian traveler in E Asia

po·lo·naise (päl′ə nāz′, pō′lə-) ***n.*** [Fr. < fem. of *polonais*, Polish] **1.** a stately Polish dance in triple time **2.** music for this dance

po·lo·ni·um (pə lō′nē əm) ***n.*** [ModL. < ML. *Polonia*, Poland: coinage of Marie Curie, its co-discoverer] a radioactive chemical element formed by the disintegration of radium: symbol, Po; at. wt., 210.05; at. no., 84

polo shirt a knitted pullover sport shirt

Pol·ska (pôl′skä) *Pol. name of* POLAND

pol·troon (päl tro͞on′) ***n.*** [< Fr. < It. *poltrone*, coward < *poltro*, colt] a thorough coward —***adj.*** cowardly —**pol·troon′er·y** ***n.***

pol·y- [ModL. < Gr. *poly-* < *polys*, much, many] *a combining form meaning* much, many, more than one

pol·y·an·dry (päl′ē an′drē, päl′ē an′-) ***n.*** [< Gr. < *poly-*, many + *anēr*, a man] the state or practice of having two or more husbands at the same time —**pol′y·an′dric** ***adj.*** —**pol′y·an′drist** ***n.*** —**pol′y·an′drous** ***adj.***

pol·y·an·thus (päl′ē an′thəs) ***n.*** [ModL. < Gr. < *poly-*, many + *anthos*, a flower] **1.** any of various primroses with many flowers **2.** a sweet-scented narcissus with clusters of star-shaped flowers

pol·y·cen·tric (päl′i sen′trik) ***adj.*** [POLY- + CENT(E)R + -IC] of or relating to independent centers of power within a political system —**pol′y·cen′trism** ***n.*** —**pol′y·cen′trist** ***adj., n.***

pol·y·clin·ic (-klin′ik) ***n.*** [POLY- + CLINIC] a clinic or hospital treating various kinds of diseases

pol·y·es·ter (päl′ē es′tər) ***n.*** [POLY(MER) + ESTER] any of several polymeric synthetic resins used in making plastics, fibers, etc.

pol·y·eth·yl·ene (päl′ē eth′ə lēn′) ***n.*** [POLY(MER) + ETHYLENE] any of several thermoplastic resins, $(C_2H_4)_n$, used in making plastics, films, etc.

po·lyg·a·my (pə lig′ə mē) ***n.*** [< Fr. < Gr.: see POLY- & -GAMY] the practice of having two or more wives or husbands at the same time —**po·lyg′a·mist** ***n.*** —**po·lyg′a·mous** ***adj.*** —**po·lyg′a·mous·ly** ***adv.***

pol·y·glot (päl′i glät′) ***adj.*** [< Gr. < *poly-*, many + *glōtta*, the tongue] **1.** speaking or writing several languages **2.** containing or written in several languages —***n.*** **1.** a polyglot person **2.** a polyglot book

pol·y·gon (päl′i gän′) ***n.*** [< LL. < Gr.: see POLY- & -GON] a closed plane figure, esp. one with more than four sides and angles —**po·lyg·o·nal** (pə lig′ə n′l) ***adj.***

pol·y·graph (-graf′) ***n.*** **1.** an early device for reproducing writings or drawings **2.** an instrument for recording changes in blood pressure, pulse rate, etc.: see LIE DETECTOR —**pol′y·graph′ic** ***adj.***

po·lyg·y·ny (pə lij′ə nē) ***n.*** [ModL. < POLY- + Gr. *gynē*, a woman] the practice of having two or more wives or concubines at the same time —**po·lyg′y·nous** (-nəs) ***adj.***

pol·y·he·dron (päl′i hē′drən) ***n.***, *pl.* **-drons, -dra** (-drə) [ModL. < Gr.: see POLY- & -HEDRON] a solid figure, esp. one with more than six plane surfaces —**pol′y·he′dral** ***adj.***

Pol·y·hym·ni·a (-him′nē ə) *Gr. Myth.* the Muse of sacred poetry: also **Po·lym′ni·a** (pə lim′-)

pol·y·math (päl′i math′) ***n.*** [< Gr. < *poly-* (see POLY-) + *manthanein*, to learn] a person of great and diversified learning —**pol′y·math′ic** ***adj.***

pol·y·mer (päl′i mər) ***n.*** [G. < Gr.: see POLY- & -MEROUS] a naturally occurring or synthetic substance made up of giant molecules formed by polymerization

pol·y·mer·ic (päl′i mer′ik) ***adj.*** composed of the same chemical elements in the same proportions by weight, but differing in molecular weight —**pol′y·mer′i·cal·ly** ***adv.***

po·lym·er·i·za·tion (pə lim′ər i zā′shən, päl′i mər-) ***n.*** the process of joining two or more like molecules to form a more complex molecule whose molecular weight is a multiple of the original and whose physical properties are different —**po·lym′er·ize′** (-īz′) ***vt., vi.*** **-ized′, -iz′ing**

pol·y·mor·phous (päl′i môr′fəs) ***adj.*** [< Gr.: see POLY- & -MORPH] having, occurring in, or passing through several or various forms: also **pol′y·mor′phic** —**pol′y·mor′phism** ***n.*** —**pol′y·mor′phous·ly** ***adv.***

Pol·y·ne·sia (päl′ə nē′zhə, -shə) a major division of the Pacific islands east of the international date line, including Hawaii, Samoa, Tonga, Society Islands, etc.

Pol·y·ne·sian (-zhən, -shən) ***adj.*** of Polynesia, its people, their language, etc. —***n.*** **1.** a member of the brown people of Polynesia, including the Hawaiians, Tahitians, Samoans, and Maoris **2.** the group of Malayo-Polynesian languages of Polynesia

pol·y·no·mi·al (päl′i nō′mē əl) ***n.*** [POLY- + (BI)NOMIAL] **1.** *Algebra* an expression consisting of two or more terms (Ex.: $x^3 + 3x + 2$) **2.** *Biol.* a species or subspecies name having two or more terms —***adj.*** consisting of polynomials

pol·yp (päl′ip) ***n.*** [< Fr. < L. < Gr. < *poly-*, many + *pous*, a foot] **1.** any of various coelenterates having a mouth fringed with tentacles at the top of a tubelike body, as the sea anemone, hydra, etc. **2.** a projecting growth of mucous membrane inside the nose, bladder, etc. —**pol′yp·ous** ***adj.***

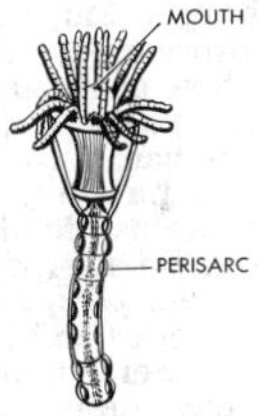

MOUTH

PERISARC

POLYP (sense 1)

pol·y·pet·al·ous (-pet′'l əs) ***adj.*** [POLY- + PETAL + -OUS] *Bot.* having separate petals

pol·y·phon·ic (päl′i fän′ik) ***adj.*** [< Gr.: see POLY- & -PHONE] **1.** having or making many sounds **2.** *Music* of or characterized by polyphony; contrapuntal Also **po·lyph·o·nous** (pə lif′ə nəs) —**pol′y·phon′i·cal·ly** ***adv.***

po·lyph·o·ny (pə lif′ə nē) ***n.*** **1.** multiplicity of sounds, as in an echo **2.** *Music* a combining of a number of individual but harmonious melodies; counterpoint

pol·y·pro·pyl·ene (päl′i prō′pə lēn′) ***n.*** [POLY(MER) + PROPYLENE] polymerized propylene, a very light thermoplastic resin used in packaging, tubing, etc.

pol·y·some (päl′i sōm′) ***n.*** [POLY- + -SOME[3]] a group of ribosomes in which protein synthesis occurs

pol·y·so·mic (päl′i sō′mik) ***adj.*** [< prec. + -IC] *Genetics* having extra chromosomes, not in a set

pol·y·sty·rene (-stī′rēn) ***n.*** a tough plastic, a polymer of styrene, used to make containers, etc.

pol·y·syl·lab·ic (-si lab′ik) ***adj.*** **1.** having several, esp. four or more, syllables **2.** characterized by polysyllables Also **pol′y·syl·lab′i·cal** —**pol′y·syl·lab′i·cal·ly** ***adv.***

pol·y·syl·la·ble (päl′i sil′ə b'l) ***n.*** a polysyllabic word

pol·y·tech·nic (päl′i tek′nik) ***adj.*** [< Fr. < Gr. < *poly-*, many + *technē*, an art] of or providing instruction in many scientific and technical subjects —***n.*** a polytechnic school

pol·y·the·ism (päl′i thē iz′m) ***n.*** [< Fr. < Gr. < *poly-*, many + *theos*, god] belief in more than one god —**pol′y·the·ist** ***adj., n.*** —**pol′y·the·is′tic, pol′y·the·is′ti·cal** ***adj.*** —**pol′y·the·is′ti·cal·ly** ***adv.***

pol·y·un·sat·u·rat·ed (päl′i un sach′ə rāt′id) ***adj.*** [POLY- + UNSATURATED] containing more than one double or triple bond in the molecule, as certain vegetable and animal fats and oils

pol·y·u·re·thane (-yoor′ə thān′) ***n.*** [POLY- + *urethane*, a chemical compound with the basic structure of polyurethane] any of certain synthetic rubber polymers used in cushions, molded products, etc.

pol·y·va·lent (-vā′lənt) ***adj.*** **1.** designating a vaccine for two or more strains of the same microorganism **2.** *Chem.* *a)* having a valence of more than two *b)* having more than one valence —**pol′y·va′lence** ***n.***

pol·y·wa·ter (-wôt′ər, -wät′-) ***n.*** [POLY(MERIC) + WATER] a viscous substance variously identified as a new form of water, highly contaminated water, etc.

pom·ace (pum′is) ***n.*** [ML. *pomacium*, cider < L. *pomum*, a fruit] **1.** the crushed pulp of apples or other fruit pressed for juice **2.** the crushed matter of anything pressed, as seeds for oil

po·ma·ceous (pō mā′shəs) ***adj.*** [< L. *pomum*, a fruit] of or like apples or other pomes

po·made (pä mād′, pō-, pə-; -mäd′) ***n.*** [< Fr. < It. *pomata*, ult. < L. *pomum*, fruit: orig. perfumed with apple pulp] a perfumed preparation, as for grooming the hair: also **po·ma·tum** (pō māt′əm) —***vt.*** **-mad′ed, -mad′ing** to apply pomade to

pome (pōm) ***n.*** [OFr., ult. < L. *pomum*, fruit] any fleshy fruit with a core and seeds, as the apple, pear, etc.

pome·gran·ate (päm′gran′it, päm′ə-; pum′-) ***n.*** [< OFr. < *pome*, apple + *granade* < L. *granatum*, lit., having seeds] **1.** a round fruit with a thick, red rind and many seeds covered with red, juicy, edible flesh **2.** the bush or small tree that bears it

Pom·er·a·ni·a (päm′ə rā′nē ə) region in C Europe, on the Baltic, now divided between Poland & East Germany

Pom·er·a·ni·an (-ən) ***adj.*** of Pomerania or its people —***n.***

1. a native or inhabitant of Pomerania 2. any of a breed of small dog with long, silky hair, pointed ears, and a bushy tail

pom·mel (pum′'l; *also, for n.*, päm′'l) ***n.*** [< OFr. dim. of *pome:* see POME] **1.** a round knob on the end of some sword hilts **2.** the rounded, upward-projecting front part of a saddle —***vt.*** **-meled** or **-melled, -mel·ing** or **-mel·ling** *same as* PUMMEL

po·mol·o·gy (pō mäl′ə jē) ***n.*** [< ModL.: see POME & -LOGY] the science of fruit cultivation —**po′mo·log′i·cal** (-mə läj′i k'l) ***adj.*** —**po·mol′o·gist** ***n.***

Po·mo·na (pə mō′nə) [after *Pomona,* Rom. goddess of fruits & fruit trees] city in S Calif., east of Los Angeles: pop. 93,000

pomp (pämp) ***n.*** [< MFr. < L. < Gr. *pompē,* solemn procession] **1.** stately display; splendor **2.** ostentatious show or display

pom·pa·dour (päm′pə dôr′) ***n.*** [after ff.] a hairdo in which the hair is swept or brushed up high from the forehead

Pom·pa·dour (päm′pə dôr′, -door′; *Fr.* pōn pȧ do͞or′), marquise **de** (də) 1721–64; mistress of Louis XV

pom·pa·no (päm′pə nō′) ***n.***, *pl.* **-no′, -nos′:** see PLURAL, II, D, 2 [Sp. *pámpano*] a spiny-finned, saltwater food fish of N. America and the West Indies

Pom·pei·i (päm pā′ē, -pā′) ancient city on the S coast of Italy: destroyed by the eruption of Mount Vesuvius (79 A.D.) —**Pom·pei′an** (-pā′ən) ***adj., n.***

Pom·pey (päm′pē) (L. name *Gnaeus Pompeius*) 106–48 B.C.; Rom. general & statesman: called *the Great* (L. *Magnus*)

pom-pom (päm′päm′) ***n.*** [echoic] **1.** any of several rapid-firing automatic weapons **2.** *same as* POMPON (sense 1): also **pom′pom′**

pom·pon (päm′pän′, -päm′) ***n.*** [Fr.] **1.** an ornamental ball or tuft as of silk or wool, worn as on hats or waved by cheerleaders **2.** *a)* a kind of chrysanthemum, dahlia, etc. with small, round flowers *b)* the flower

pom·pous (päm′pəs) ***adj.*** **1.** full of pomp; magnificent **2.** pretentious, as in speech or manner; self-important —**pom·pos′i·ty** (-päs′ə tē), *pl.* **-ties, pom′pous·ness** ***n.*** —**pom′pous·ly** ***adv.***

Pon·ce (pôn′se) seaport on the S coast of Puerto Rico: pop. 126,000

Pon·ce de Le·ón (pôn′the *the* le ôn′; *E.* päns′ də lē′ən), **Juan** (hwän) 1460?–1521; Sp. explorer: discovered Florida

pon·cho (pän′chō) ***n.***, *pl.* **-chos** [< SAmInd.] **1.** a cloak like a blanket with a hole in the middle for the head **2.** a garment, esp. a raincoat, like this

pond (pänd) ***n.*** [< ME. var. of POUND³] a body of standing water smaller than a lake, often man-made

pon·der (pän′dər) ***vt., vi.*** [< MFr. < L. *ponderare,* to weigh < *pondus,* a weight] to think deeply (about); deliberate —**pon′der·a·bil′i·ty** ***n.*** —**pon′der·a·ble** ***adj.*** —**pon′der·er** ***n.***

pon·der·o·sa (pine) (pän′də rō′sə) [< ModL. (*Pinus*) *ponderosa,* lit., heavy (pine)] **1.** a yellow pine of western N. America **2.** its wood

pon·der·ous (pän′dər əs) ***adj.*** [< L. < *pondus* (gen. *ponderis*), a weight] **1.** very heavy **2.** unwieldy because of weight **3.** bulky; massive **4.** labored; dull *[a ponderous* style*]* —**pon′der·ous·ly** ***adv.*** —**pon′der·ous·ness, pon′der·os′i·ty** (-äs′ə tē) ***n.***

pond lily *same as* WATERLILY

pond scum a mass of filamentous algae forming a green scum on the surface of ponds, etc.

pond·weed (pänd′wēd′) ***n.*** any of various related water plants, with submerged or floating leaves

pone (pōn) ***n.*** [< Algonquian] [Chiefly Southern] **1.** corn bread in small, oval loaves **2.** such a loaf

pon·gee (pän jē′) ***n.*** [< Chin. dial. *pen-chi,* domestic loom] **1.** a soft, thin silk cloth, usually left in its natural light-brown color **2.** a cloth like this

pon·iard (pän′yərd) ***n.*** [< Fr., ult. < L. *pugnus,* fist] a dagger —***vt.*** to stab with a poniard

pons (pänz) ***n.***, *pl.* **pon·tes** (pän′tēz) [L., a bridge] *Anat., Zool.* a piece of connecting tissue

Pon·ti·ac¹ (pän′tē ak′) 1720?–69; Ottawa Indian chief

Pon·ti·ac² (pän′tē ak′) [after prec.] city in SE Mich., just north of Detroit: pop. 77,000

pon·ti·fex (pän′tə feks′) ***n.***, *pl.* **pon·tif·i·ces** (pän tif′ə sēz′) [L.: see ff.] in ancient Rome, a member of the supreme college of priests

pon·tiff (pän′tif) ***n.*** [< Fr. < LL. *pontifex,* bishop < L., high priest] **1.** a bishop; specif., [**P-**] the Pope (in full, **Supreme Pontiff**) **2.** a high priest

pon·tif·i·cal (pän tif′i k'l) ***adj.*** **1.** having to do with a high priest **2.** celebrated by a bishop or other highranking prelate *[a pontifical* Mass*]* **3.** papal **4.** having the pomp, dogmatism, and dignity of a pontiff; sometimes, specif., arrogant or haughty —***n.*** **1.** [*pl.*] a pontiff's vestments and insignia **2.** a book of rites as performed by a bishop —**pon·tif′i·cal·ly** ***adv.***

pon·tif·i·cate (-kit; *also, and for v. always,* -kāt′) ***n.*** the office or tenure of a pontiff —***vi.*** **-cat′ed, -cat′ing** **1.** to officiate as a pontiff **2.** to speak in a pompous or dogmatic way —**pon·tif′i·ca′tor** ***n.***

Pon·tine Marshes (pän′tēn, -tīn) region in C Italy, southeast of Rome: formerly swampy, now reclaimed

pon·toon (pän to͞on′) ***n.*** [Fr. < L. *ponto* < *pons,* a bridge] **1.** a flat-bottomed boat **2.** any of a number of these, or of hollow, floating cylinders, etc., used to support a temporary bridge (**pontoon bridge**) **3.** a float on an aircraft Also **pon′ton** (-t'n)

po·ny (pō′nē) ***n.***, *pl.* **-nies** [< Scot., prob. < OFr. dim of *poulain,* a colt, ult. < L. *pullus,* foal] **1.** a small horse of any of several breeds, usually not over 58 in. high at the withers **2.** something small of its kind; specif., a small liqueur glass or its contents **3.** [Colloq.] a literal translation of a foreign work, used in doing schoolwork, often dishonestly **4.** [Slang] a racehorse —***vt., vi.*** **-nied, -ny·ing** [Slang] to pay (money), as to settle an account (with *up*)

po·ny·tail (pō′nē tāl′) ***n.*** a hairdo in which long hair, tied tight high at the back of the head, hangs free

pooch (po͞och) ***n.*** [Slang] a dog

poo·dle (po͞o′d'l) ***n.*** [G. *pudel* < LowG. < *pudeln,* to splash] any of a breed of dog with a solid-colored, curly coat

pooh¹ (po͞o) ***interj.*** [prob. echoic] an exclamation of disdain, disbelief, or impatience

pooh² (po͞o) ***vt.*** [Slang] *same as* POOP²

pooh-pooh (po͞o′po͞o′) ***vt.*** [redupl. of POOH¹] to minimize; make light of; belittle

pool¹ (po͞ol) ***n.*** [OE. *pol*] **1.** a small pond, as in a garden **2.** a puddle **3.** *same as* SWIMMING POOL **4.** a deep, still spot in a river **5.** a natural underground accumulation of oil or gas —***vi.*** to form, or accumulate in, a pool

pool² (po͞ol) ***n.*** [Fr. *poule* < LL. *pulla,* hen: associated in E. with prec.] **1.** the total stakes played for, as in a single deal of a card game **2.** a game of billiards played with object balls numbered 1 to 15 and a cue ball, on a table with six pockets **3.** *a)* a combination of resources, funds, etc. for some common purpose *b)* the persons or parties forming it **4.** a combination of business firms for creating a monopoly **5.** a supply of equipment, personnel, etc. shared by a group —***vt., vi.*** to contribute to a common fund; form a pool (of)

Poo·na (po͞o′nə) city in W India: pop. 737,000

poop¹ (po͞op) ***n.*** [< MFr., ult. < L. *puppis*] **1.** orig., the stern of a ship **2.** on sailing ships, a raised deck at the stern, sometimes forming the roof of a cabin: also **poop deck** —***vt.*** to break over the poop or stern of: said of waves

poop² (po͞op) ***vt.*** [echoic] [Slang] to tire: usually in the passive voice —**poop out** [Slang] **1.** to become exhausted **2.** to cease functioning

poop³ (po͞op) ***n.*** [prob. < *poop,* feces] [Slang] **1.** a contemptible person **2.** the pertinent facts

poor (poor) ***adj.*** [< OFr. < L. *pauper,* poor] **1.** *a)* having little or no means to support oneself; needy *b)* indicating or characterized by poverty **2.** lacking in some quality or thing; specif., *a)* scanty; inadequate *[poor* crops*]* *b)* barren; sterile *[poor* soil*]* *c)* lacking nourishment; feeble *d)* lacking excellence; inferior *e)* mean-spirited; contemptible *f)* lacking pleasure or comfort *[*to have a *poor* time*]* *g)* lacking skill *[a poor* cook*]* **3.** worthy of pity; unfortunate —**the poor** poor, or needy, people —**poor′ly** ***adv.*** —**poor′ness** ***n.***

poor-boy sandwich (poor′boi′) *same as* HERO SANDWICH

poor·house (-hous′) ***n.*** formerly, an institution for paupers, supported from public funds

poor-mouth (-mouth′) ***vi.*** [Colloq.] to complain about one's lack of money: also **talk** (or **cry**) **poor-mouth**

poor white a white person, esp. in the South, who lives in great poverty: often an offensive term

pop¹ (päp) ***n.*** [echoic] **1.** a sudden, short, light explosive sound **2.** a shot with a revolver, rifle, etc. **3.** any carbonated, nonalcoholic beverage **4.** *Baseball* a ball popped into the infield: also **pop′-up′** —***vi.*** **popped, pop′ping** **1.** to make, or burst with, a pop **2.** to move, go, come, etc. suddenly and quickly **3.** to open wide suddenly, or protrude: said of the eyes **4.** to shoot a pistol, etc. **5.** *Baseball* to hit the ball high in the air into the infield —***vt.*** **1.** to cause (corn) to pop, as by roasting, etc. **2.** *a)* to fire (a pistol, etc.) *b)* to shoot **3.** to put suddenly or quickly *[*to *pop* one's head in the door*]* **4.** [Slang] to swallow (a pill, capsule, etc.) **5.** *Baseball* to hit (the ball) high in the air into the infield —***adv.*** with or like a pop —**pop off** [Slang] **1.** to die suddenly **2.** to speak or write emotionally, etc. **3.** [Chiefly Brit.] to leave hastily —**pop the question** [Colloq.] to propose marriage

pop² (päp) ***n.*** [< PAPA] [Slang] father: also a familiar term of address for any elderly man

pop³ (päp) ***adj.*** *clipped form of* POPULAR *[pop* music*]*

pop. **1.** popular **2.** popularly **3.** population

pop (art) (päp) a realistic style of painting and sculpture, using techniques and popular subjects from commercial art and mass media, such as comic strips

pop concert a popular concert, chiefly of semiclassical and light classical music

pop·corn (-kôrn′) ***n.*** **1.** a variety of Indian corn with small ears and hard grains which pop open in a white, puffy mass when heated **2.** the popped grains, often salted for eating

pope (pōp) ***n.*** [OE. *papa* < LL., ult. < Gr. *pappas,* father] [*usually* **P-**] *R.C.Ch.* the bishop of Rome and head of the Church —**pope′dom** (-dəm) ***n.***

Pope (pōp), **Alexander** 1688–1744; Eng. poet

pop·er·y (pōp′ər ē) ***n.*** the doctrines and rituals of the Roman Catholic Church: a hostile term

pop·eyed (päp′īd′) ***adj.*** having protruding eyes

pop·gun (-gun′) ***n.*** a toy gun that shoots pellets by air compression, with a pop

pop·in·jay (päp′in jā′) ***n.*** [< MFr. *papagai* < Ar. *babaghā,* parrot] a talkative, conceited person

pop·ish (pōp′ish) ***adj.*** having to do with popery: a hostile term —**pop′ish·ly** ***adv.*** —**pop′ish·ness** ***n.***

pop·lar (päp′lər) ***n.*** [< OFr. *poplier,* ult. < L. *populus*] **1.** any of various tall, fast-growing trees with alternate leaves and catkins **2.** the wood of any of these **3.** *same as: a*) TULIP TREE *b*) TULIPWOOD (sense 1)

pop·lin (päp′lən) ***n.*** [Fr. *papeline,* prob. < (*draps de*) *Poperinghes,* (cloths from) Poperinge, city in Flanders] a sturdy fabric of cotton, rayon, etc. with fine ribbing

Po·po·ca·té·petl (pô pô′kä te′pet′l; *E.* pō′pə kat′ə-pet′'l) volcano in SC Mexico

pop·o·ver (päp′ō′vər) ***n.*** a puffy, hollow muffin

pop·per (-ər) ***n.*** **1.** a person or thing that pops **2.** a covered wire basket or pan for popping corn

pop·pet (päp′it) ***n.*** [var. of PUPPET] a valve that moves into and from its seat, as in a gasoline engine: in full, **poppet valve**

pop·py (päp′ē) ***n., pl.*** **-pies** [OE. *popæg* < L. *papaver*] **1.** any of various related plants with a milky juice and showy, variously colored flowers **2.** the flower of any of these **3.** an extract, as opium, made from poppy juice **4.** yellowish red, the color of some poppies: also **poppy red**

pop·py·cock (-käk′) ***n.*** [Du. *pappekak,* dung] [Colloq.] nonsense

poppy seed the small, dark seed of the poppy, used in baking, etc. as a flavoring or topping

Pop·si·cle (päp′si k'l) [blend < POP[1] + (I)CICLE] *a trademark for* a flavored ice frozen around a stick —***n.*** [**p-**] such a confection

pop·u·lace (päp′yə lis) ***n.*** [Fr. < It. < L. *populus,* PEOPLE] **1.** the common people; the masses **2.** *same as* POPULATION (sense 1 *a*)

pop·u·lar (päp′yə lər) ***adj.*** [< L. < *populus,* PEOPLE] **1.** of or carried on by people generally **2.** suitable or intended for the general public [*popular* music] **3.** within the means of the ordinary person [*popular* prices] **4.** common; prevalent [a *popular* notion] **5.** liked by very many people [a *popular* actor] **6.** having many friends —**pop′u·lar′i·ty** (-lar′ə tē) ***n.*** —**pop′u·lar·ly** ***adv.***

popular front a political coalition of leftist and liberal groups, as in France (1936–39) to combat fascism

pop·u·lar·ize (päp′yə lə rīz′) ***vt.*** **-ized′, -iz′ing** **1.** to make popular **2.** to make understandable to the general public —**pop′u·lar·i·za′tion** ***n.*** —**pop′u·lar·iz′er** ***n.***

pop·u·late (päp′yə lāt′) ***vt.*** **-lat′ed, -lat′ing** [< ML. pp. of *populare* < L. *populus,* PEOPLE] **1.** to inhabit **2.** to supply with inhabitants

pop·u·la·tion (päp′yə lā′shən) ***n.*** **1.** *a*) all the people in a country, region, etc. *b*) the number of these *c*) a (specified) part of the people in a given area [the Japanese *population* of Hawaii] **2.** a populating or being populated **3.** *Biol.* all the organisms living in a given area **4.** *Statistics* a group of persons or things

population explosion the very great and continuing increase in human population in modern times

Pop·u·list (päp′yə list) ***n.*** [< L. *populus,* PEOPLE] a member of a U.S. political party (**Populist party** or **People's party,** 1891–1904) advocating free coinage of gold and silver, public ownership of utilities, an income tax, etc. —***adj.*** of this party: also **Pop′u·lis′tic** —**Pop′u·lism** ***n.***

pop·u·lous (päp′yə ləs) ***adj.*** full of people; thickly populated —**pop′u·lous·ly** ***adv.*** —**pop′u·lous·ness** ***n.***

por·ce·lain (pôr′s'l in, pôrs′lin) ***n.*** [< Fr. < It. *porcellana,* a kind of shell, shaped like a pig, ult. < L. *porcus,* pig] **1.** a hard, white, nonporous, translucent ceramic ware, made of kaolin, feldspar, and quartz or flint **2.** porcelain dishes or ornaments, collectively —***adj.*** made of porcelain —**por′ce·la′ne·ous, por′cel·la′ne·ous** (-sə lā′nē əs) ***adj.***

por·ce·lain·ize (-īz′) ***vt.*** **-ized′, -iz′ing** to coat with porcelain or a substance like it

porch (pôrch) ***n.*** [< OFr. < L. *porticus* < *porta,* a gate] **1.** a covered entrance to a building, usually with a roof that is held up by posts **2.** an open or enclosed room on the outside of a building **3.** [Obs.] a portico

por·cine (pôr′sīn, -sin) ***adj.*** [< Fr. < L. < *porcus,* a hog] of or like pigs or hogs

por·cu·pine (pôr′kyə pīn′) ***n., pl.*** **-pines′, -pine′**: see PLURAL, II, D, 1 [< MFr. < OIt. < L. *porcus,* a pig + *spina,* a spine] any of various large, related rodents having coarse hair mixed with long, stiff, sharp spines

pore[1] (pôr) ***vi.*** **pored, por′ing** [< ?] **1.** to read or study carefully [to *pore* over a book] **2.** to ponder (with *over*)

pore[2] (pôr) ***n.*** [< L. < Gr. *poros,* a passage] **1.** a tiny opening, as in plant leaves, skin, etc., through which fluids may be absorbed or discharged **2.** a similar tiny opening in rocks or other substances

por·gy (pôr′gē) ***n., pl.*** **-gies, -gy**: see PLURAL, II, D, 1 [prob. < Sp. or Port. *pargo* < L. *pagrus* < Gr. *phagros,* sea bream] **1.** a saltwater food fish having spiny fins and a wide body, as the scup **2.** any of various other fishes, as the menhaden

pork (pôrk) ***n.*** [< OFr. < L. *porcus,* a pig] the flesh of a pig or hog used, fresh or cured, as food

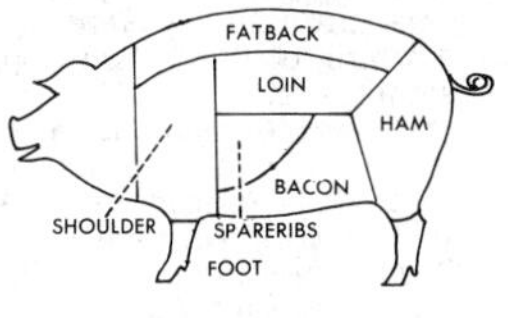

pork barrel [Colloq.] government money spent for political patronage, as for local improvements to please the voters in a district —**pork′-bar′rel·ing** ***n.***

pork·er (pôr′kər) ***n.*** a hog, esp. a young one, fattened for use as food

CUTS OF PORK

pork pie **1.** a meat pie made with chopped pork **2.** a man's soft hat with a round, flat crown: now often **pork′pie′** ***n.,*** **porkpie hat**

pork·y (pôr′kē) ***adj.*** **pork′i·er, pork′i·est** **1.** of or like pork **2.** fat, as though overfed **3.** [Slang] saucy, cocky, etc.

por·nog·ra·phy (pôr näg′rə fē) ***n.*** [< Gr. < *porne,* a prostitute + *graphein,* to write] writings, pictures, etc. intended primarily to arouse sexual desire —**por·nog′ra·pher** ***n.*** —**por′no·graph′ic** (-nə graf′ik) ***adj.*** —**por′no·graph′i·cal·ly** ***adv.***

po·rous (pôr′əs) ***adj.*** full of pores, through which fluids, air, or light may pass —**po·ros·i·ty** (pô räs′ə tē, pə-), **po′rous·ness** ***n.*** —**po′rous·ly** ***adv.***

por·phy·ry (pôr′fər ē) ***n., pl.*** **-ries** [< OFr. < ML., ult. < Gr. *porphyros,* purple] **1.** orig., an Egyptian rock with large feldspar crystals in a purplish rock mass **2.** any igneous rock resembling this —**por′phy·rit′ic** (-fə rit′ik) ***adj.***

por·poise (pôr′pəs) ***n., pl.*** **-pois·es, -poise**: see PLURAL, II, D, 1 [< OFr. *porpeis* < L. *porcus,* a pig + *piscis,* a fish] **1.** any of a number of small, toothed whales with a blunt snout, found in most seas, esp. the **harbor porpoise** **2.** a dolphin or any of several other small cetaceans

por·ridge (pôr′ij, pär′-) ***n.*** [altered < POTTAGE by confusion with ME. *porrey* < OFr. < VL. *porrata,* leek broth < L. *porrum,* leek] [Chiefly Brit.] a soft food made of cereal or meal boiled in water or milk

por·rin·ger (-in jər) ***n.*** [< Fr. *potager,* soup dish: altered after prec.] a bowl for porridge, cereal, etc., esp. one of metal used by children

port[1] (pôrt) ***n.*** [OFr. & OE. < L. *portus,* a haven] **1.** a harbor **2.** a city with a harbor where ships can load and unload cargo **3.** *same as* PORT OF ENTRY

port[2] (pôrt) ***n.*** [< *Oporto,* city in Portugal] a sweet, fortified, usually dark-red wine

port[3] (pôrt) ***vt.*** [< MFr. < L. *portare,* to carry] to hold or place (a rifle or sword) diagonally in front of one, as for inspection —***n.*** way of carrying the head and body

port[4] (pôrt) ***n.*** [prob. < PORT[1]] the left-hand side of a ship or airplane as one faces forward, toward the bow —***adj.*** of or on the port —***vt., vi.*** to move or turn (the helm) to the port side

port[5] (pôrt) ***n.*** [< OFr. < L. *porta,* a door] **1.** *a*) *same as* PORTHOLE *b*) a porthole covering **2.** an opening, as in a valve face, for the passage of steam, gas, etc.

Port. **1.** Portugal **2.** Portuguese

port·a·ble (pôr′tə b'l) ***adj.*** [< MFr. < LL. < L. *portare,* to carry] **1.** that can be carried **2.** *a*) easily carried or moved, esp. by hand [a *portable* TV] *b*) that can be used anywhere because battery-operated [a *portable* radio] —***n.*** something portable —**port′a·bil′i·ty** ***n.***

por·tage (pôr′tij; *for n. 2 & v., also Canad.* pôr täzh′) ***n.*** [MFr. < ML. *portaticum* < L. *portare,* to carry] **1.** the act of carrying **2.** *a*) a carrying of boats and supplies overland between navigable rivers, lakes, etc. *b*) any route over which this is done —***vt., vi.*** **-taged, -tag·ing** to carry (boats, etc.) over a portage

por·tal (pôr′t'l) *n.* [MFr. < ML. < L. *porta,* a gate] a doorway, gate, or entrance, esp. a large or imposing one

Port Arthur [after *Arthur* Stilwell, local philanthropist] seaport in SE Tex.: pop. 61,000

Port-au-Prince (pôrt′ō prins′; *Fr.* pôr tō prans′) capital of Haiti; seaport on the Caribbean: pop. 250,000

port authority a government commission in charge of the traffic, regulations, etc. of a port

port·cul·lis (pôrt kul′is) *n.* [< MFr. < *porte,* a gate + *coleïce,* sliding < L. *colare,* to filter] a heavy iron grating suspended by chains and lowered between grooves to bar the gateway of a castle or fortified town

Port du Sa·lut (pôr′ doo sa lo͞o′) [Fr.] a semihard, whole-milk, yellowish cheese

porte-co·chere, porte-co·chère (pôrt′kō sher′) *n.* [Fr., coach gate] **1.** a large gateway into a courtyard **2.** a kind of porch roof projecting over a driveway at an entrance to a house, etc.

Port Elizabeth seaport in S Cape Province, South Africa: pop. 381,000

por·tend (pôr tend′) *vt.* [< L. *portendere* < *por-,* akin to *per-,* through + *tendere,* to stretch] **1.** to be an omen or warning of; foreshadow; presage **2.** to be an indication of; signify

por·tent (pôr′tent) *n.* **1.** something that portends an event about to occur, esp. an unfortunate event; omen **2.** a portending; significance **3.** a marvel

por·ten·tous (pôr ten′təs) *adj.* **1.** being a portent; ominous **2.** marvelous; amazing **3.** pompous —**por·ten′tous·ly** *adv.* —**por·ten′tous·ness** *n.*

por·ter[1] (pôr′tər) *n.* [< OFr. < LL. *portarius* < L. *porta,* a gate] a doorman or gatekeeper

por·ter[2] (pôr′tər) *n.* [< OFr. < LL. < L. *portare,* to carry] **1.** a man whose work is to carry luggage, as at a railroad station **2.** a man who sweeps, cleans, does errands, etc. in a bank, store, etc. **3.** a railroad employee who waits on passengers in a sleeper or parlor car **4.** [abbrev. of *porter's ale*] a dark-brown beer resembling light stout, made from charred or browned malt

Por·ter (pôr′tər) **1. Katherine Anne,** 1890–1980; U.S. short-story writer & novelist **2. William Sydney,** *see* O. HENRY

por·ter·house (-hous′) *n.* **1.** formerly, a place serving beer, porter, etc. (and sometimes steaks and chops) **2.** a choice cut of beef from the loin just before the sirloin: in full, **porterhouse steak**

port·fo·li·o (pôrt fō′lē ō′) *n., pl.* **-li·os′** [< It. *portafoglio* < L. *portare,* to carry + *folium,* a leaf] **1.** a flat, portable case for carrying loose papers, drawings, etc. **2.** such a case for state documents **3.** the office of a minister of state **4.** a list of an investor's stocks, bonds, etc. **5.** a selection of representative works, as of an artist

port·hole (pôrt′hōl′) *n.* **1.** an opening in a ship's side, as for admitting light and air **2.** an opening to shoot through; embrasure **3.** any similar opening

por·ti·co (pôr′tə kō′) *n., pl.* **-coes′, -cos′** [It. < L. *porticus:* see PORCH] a porch or covered walk, consisting of a roof supported by columns

PORTICO

por·tiere, por·tière (pôr tyer′, -tē er′) *n.* [Fr. < *porte,* a door] a curtain hung in a doorway

por·tion (pôr′shən) *n.* [< OFr. < L. *portio* (gen. *portionis*)] **1.** a part, esp. as allotted to a person, set aside for some purpose, etc.; share **2.** the part of an estate received by an heir **3.** a dowry **4.** one's lot; destiny **5.** a helping of food —*vt.* **1.** to divide into portions **2.** to give as a portion to **3.** to give a portion to —**por′tion·less** *adj.*

Port·land (pôrt′lənd) **1.** [after ff.] city & port in NW Oreg., on the Columbia River: pop. 366,000 (met. area 1,236,000) **2.** [after *Portland,* town in England] seaport on the coast of SE Maine: pop. 62,000

portland cement [concrete made from it resembles stone from the Isle of *Portland,* England] [*sometimes* **P-**] a kind of cement that hardens under water, made by burning limestone and clay

port·ly (pôrt′lē) *adj.* **-li·er, -li·est** [PORT[3] + -LY[1]] **1.** large and heavy in a dignified or stately way **2.** stout; corpulent —**port′li·ness** *n.*

port·man·teau (pôrt man′tō, pôrt′man tō′) *n., pl.* **-teaus, -teaux** (-tōz) [< Fr. < *porter,* to carry + *manteau,* a cloak] a stiff leather suitcase that opens like a book into two compartments

portmanteau word a word that is a combination of two others (Ex.: *smog,* from *smoke* and *fog*)

Pôr·to (pôr′too) *Port. name of* OPORTO

Pôr·to A·le·gre (ä le′grə) seaport in S Brazil, on the Atlantic: pop. 641,000

port of call a regular stopover port for ships

port of entry any place where customs officials check people and foreign goods entering a country

Port-of-Spain (pôrt′əv spān′) seaport on NW Trinidad; capital of Trinidad and Tobago: pop. 98,000

Por·to No·vo (pôr′tō nō′vō) capital of Benin; seaport on the Atlantic: pop. 100,000

Por·to Ri·co (pôr′tə rē′kō) *former name of* PUERTO RICO

por·trait (pôr′trit, -trāt) *n.* [MFr., pp. of *portraire:* see PORTRAY] **1.** a painting, photograph, etc. of a person, esp. of his face **2.** a description, portrayal, etc. of a person —**por′trait·ist** *n.*

por·trai·ture (pôr′tri chər) *n.* **1.** the making of portraits **2.** a portrait

por·tray (pôr trā′) *vt.* [MFr. *portraire* < L. < *pro-,* forth + *trahere,* to draw] **1.** to make a picture or portrait of **2.** to make a word picture of; describe **3.** to play the part of in a play, movie, etc. —**por·tray′a·ble** *adj.* —**por·tray′al** *n.*

Port Sa·id (sä ēd′, sä′id) seaport in NE Egypt, at the Mediterranean end of the Suez Canal: pop. 244,000

Ports·mouth (pôrts′məth) **1.** seaport in S England, on the English Channel: pop. 212,000 **2.** [after prec.] seaport in SE Va., on Hampton Roads: pop. 105,000

Por·tu·gal (pôr′chə gəl; *Port.* pôr′too gäl′) country in SW Europe, on the Atlantic, including the Azores & Madeira: 35,509 sq. mi.; pop. 9,526,000; cap. Lisbon

Por·tu·guese (pôr′chə gēz′) *adj.* of Portugal, its people, their language, etc. —*n.* **1.** *pl.* **-guese′** a native or inhabitant of Portugal **2.** the Romance language spoken in Portugal and Brazil

Portuguese man-of-war a large, warm-sea animal having long, dangling tentacles that sting, and a large, bladderlike sac that enables it to float on water

por·tu·lac·a (pôr′chə lak′ə) *n.* [ModL. < L., purslane] a fleshy annual plant with yellow, pink, or purple flowers

pose[1] (pōz) *vt.* **posed, pos′ing** [< OFr. *poser* < VL. < LL. *pausare,* to pause: infl. by L. *positus,* pp. of *ponere,* to place] **1.** to put forth; assert *[to pose a claim]* **2.** to propose (a question, problem, etc.) **3.** to put (a model, photographic subject, etc.) in a certain attitude —*vi.* **1.** to assume a certain attitude, as in modeling for an artist **2.** to strike attitudes for effect *[look at her posing]* **3.** to pretend to be what one is not *[to pose as an officer]* —*n.* **1.** a bodily attitude, esp. one held for an artist, photographer, etc. **2.** behavior or speech assumed for effect; pretense

pose[2] (pōz) *vt.* **posed, pos′ing** [< APPOSE, OPPOSE] to baffle, as by a difficult question

Po·sei·don (pō sī′d'n, pə-) *Gr. Myth.* god of the sea: identified with the Roman god Neptune

pos·er[1] (pō′zər) *n.* **1.** a person who poses **2.** a person who behaves in an affected way

pos·er[2] (pō′zər) *n.* a baffling question or problem

po·seur (pō zur′) *n.* [Fr.] a person who assumes attitudes or manners merely for their effect upon others

posh (päsh) *adj.* [prob. < obs. Brit. slang *posh,* a dandy] [Colloq.] luxurious and fashionable; elegant —**posh′ly** *adv.* —**posh′ness** *n.*

pos·it (päz′it) *vt.* [< L. *positus,* pp. of *ponere,* to place] **1.** to set in place or position; situate **2.** to set down or assume as fact; postulate

po·si·tion (pə zish′ən) *n.* [MFr. < L. *positio* < pp. of *ponere,* to place] **1.** the manner in which a person or thing is placed or arranged; attitude **2.** one's attitude toward or opinion on a subject; stand **3.** the place where a person or thing is, esp. in relation to others; location or situation **4.** the usual or proper place; station *[the players are in position]* **5.** a location or condition of advantage *[to jockey for position]* **6.** a person's relative place, as in society; rank; status **7.** a place high in society, business, etc. *[a man of position]* **8.** a post of employment; job; office —*vt.* to put in a particular position; place —**po·si′tion·al** *adj.* —**po·si′tion·er** *n.*

pos·i·tive (päz′ə tiv) *adj.* [< OFr. < L. *positivus* < pp. of *ponere,* to place] **1.** *a)* definitely set; explicit; specific *[positive instructions]* *b)* allowing no doubt; certain; sure **2.** *a)* sure in mind; confident; assured *[a positive person]* *b)* overconfident or dogmatic **3.** showing resolution or agreement; affirmative *[a positive answer]* **4.** tending in the direction regarded as that of increase, progress, etc. **5.** making a definite contribution; constructive *[positive criticism]* **6.** unrelated to anything else; absolute; unqualified **7.** having real existence in itself *[a positive good]* **8.** based on reality or facts *[positive proof]* **9.** concerned only with real things and experience; empirical; practical **10.** [Colloq.] complete; downright *[a positive fool]* **11.** *Biol.* directed toward the source of a stimulus *[positive tropism]* **12.** *Elec. a)* of, generating, or charged with POSITIVE ELECTRICITY *b)* having a deficiency of electrons **13.** *Gram.* of an adjective or adverb in its uninflected or unmodified form or degree: neither comparative nor superlative **14.** *Math.* greater than zero; plus **15.** *Med.* indicating the presence or existence of a condition, symptoms, bacteria, etc. **16.** *Photog.* with the relation of light and shade the same as in the thing photographed —*n.* something positive, as a degree, quality, etc.; specif., *a*) the plate in a voltaic battery where the higher potential is *b*) *Gram.* the positive degree, or a word in it *c*) *Math.* a positive quantity *d*) *Photog.* a positive print —**pos′i·tive·ly** *adv.* —**pos′i·tive·ness** *n.*

positive electricity the kind of electricity in a glass body rubbed with silk; it is deficient in electrons

pos·i·tiv·ism (päz′ə tiv iz'm) *n.* **1.** a being positive; certainty; assurance **2.** overconfidence or dogmatism **3.** a system of philosophy based solely on observable scientific facts and rejecting speculation about ultimate origins —**pos′i·tiv·ist** *n., adj.* —**pos′i·tiv·is′tic** *adj.*

pos·i·tron (päz′ə trän′) *n.* [POSI(TIVE) + (ELEC)TRON] the positive antiparticle of an electron, with about the same mass and magnitude of charge

poss. **1.** possession **2.** possessive **3.** possibly

pos·se (päs′ē) *n.* [ML., short for *posse comitatus*, power of the county] a body of men summoned by a sheriff, to assist him in keeping the peace

pos·sess (pə zes′) *vt.* [< MFr. < L. pp. of *possidere*] **1.** to have as something that belongs to one; own **2.** to have as an attribute, quality, etc. *[*to *possess* wisdom*]* **3.** to gain or keep influence or control over; dominate *[possessed* by an idea*]* **4.** to cause (someone) to have property, facts, etc. (usually with *of*) **5.** [Archaic] to seize; gain —**pos·ses′sor** *n.*

pos·sessed (pə zest′) *adj.* **1.** owned **2.** controlled as by an evil spirit; crazed —**possessed of** having

pos·ses·sion (pə zesh′ən) *n.* **1.** a possessing or being possessed; ownership, hold, etc. **2.** anything possessed **3.** [*pl.*] property; wealth **4.** territory ruled by an outside country **5.** *Sports* actual control of the ball or puck in play

pos·ses·sive (pə zes′iv) *adj.* **1.** of possession, or ownership **2.** showing or desiring possession *[*a *possessive* person*]* **3.** *Gram.* designating or of a case, form, or construction expressing possession (Ex.: *men's, of men, her, whose*) —*n. Gram.* **1.** the possessive case **2.** a possessive form —**pos·ses′sive·ly** *adv.* —**pos·ses′sive·ness** *n.*

pos·set (päs′it) *n.* [< ?] a hot drink made of milk and ale, wine, etc., usually spiced

pos·si·bil·i·ty (päs′ə bil′ə tē) *n.* **1.** a being possible **2.** *pl.* **-ties** something that is possible

pos·si·ble (päs′ə b'l) *adj.* [OFr. < L. < *posse*, to be able] **1.** that can be **2.** that may or may not happen **3.** that can be done, known, chosen, etc., depending on circumstances **4.** permissible

pos·si·bly (-blē) *adv.* **1.** by any possible means *[*it can't *possibly* work*]* **2.** perhaps; maybe

pos·sum (päs′əm) *n.* [Colloq.] *same as* OPOSSUM —**play possum** to feign death, unawareness, etc.

post[1] (pōst) *n.* [OE. < L. *postis*] **1.** a piece of wood, metal, etc., usually long and square or cylindrical, set upright to support a building, sign, fence, etc. **2.** the starting point of a horse race —*vt.* **1.** to put up (a notice, etc.) on (a wall, post, etc.) **2.** to announce or publicize thus *[post* a reward*]* **3.** to warn persons against trespassing on (grounds, etc.) by posted notices **4.** to put (a name) on a posted or published list

post[2] (pōst) *n.* [< Fr. < It., ult. < L. *positum*, neut. pp. of *ponere*, to place] **1.** the place where a soldier, guard, etc. is stationed **2.** *a*) a place where troops are stationed *b*) the troops there; garrison **3.** a local unit of a veterans' organization **4.** a place where a person or group is stationed, as at a machine **5.** an assigned or appointed position, job, or duty **6.** *clipped form of* TRADING POST —*vt.* **1.** to station at or assign to a post **2.** to put up or deposit (a bond, etc.)

post[3] (pōst) *n.* [< Fr. < It. < L. fem. pp. of *ponere:* see prec.] **1.** formerly, any of a number of riders or runners posted at intervals to carry mail, etc. in relays along a route *b*) a stage of a post route *c*) a post horse *d*) a packet boat **2.** [Chiefly Brit.] *a*) (the) mail *b*) a post office *c*) a mailbox —*vi.* **1.** formerly, to travel in posts or stages **2.** to travel fast **3.** to rise and sink back in the saddle in rhythm with the horse's trot —*vt.* **1.** formerly, to send by post **2.** [Chiefly Brit.] to mail **3.** to inform, as of events: usually passive *[*keep me *posted]* **4.** *Bookkeeping* *a*) to transfer (an item) to the ledger *b*) to enter all necessary items in (a ledger, etc.) —*adv.* **1.** by post or postal courier **2.** speedily

post- [L. < *post*, after] *a prefix meaning:* **1.** after in time, following *[postglacial]* **2.** after in space, behind

post·age (pōs′tij) *n.* [< POST[3] + -AGE] the amount charged for mailing a letter or package, esp. as represented by stamps or indicia

postage meter a machine that prints indicia on mail, indicating that postage has been paid

postage stamp a government stamp for a letter or package, showing postage paid

post·al (pōs′t'l) *adj.* having to do with mail or post offices —*n.* [Colloq.] a postal card

postal card **1.** a card with a printed postage stamp, issued by a government at a rate lower than that for letters **2.** *same as* POST CARD

post-bel·lum (pōst bel′əm) *adj.* [L.] after the war; specif., after the American Civil War

post·box (pōst′bäks′) *n. chiefly Brit. var. of* MAILBOX

post card **1.** an unofficial card, often a picture card, for mailing when a postage stamp is affixed **2.** *same as* POSTAL CARD

post chaise a closed, four-wheeled coach drawn by fast horses, formerly used to carry mail and passengers

post·date (pōst′dāt′) *vt.* **-dat′ed, -dat′ing** **1.** to assign a later date to than the actual or current date **2.** to put such a date on **3.** to follow in time

post·er (pōs′tər) *n.* **1.** a person who posts notices, bills, etc. **2.** a large advertisement or notice, often illustrated, posted publicly

pos·te·ri·or (päs tir′ē ər, pōs-) *adj.* [L., compar. of *posterus*, following < *post*, after] **1.** later; following after **2.** coming after in order; succeeding **3.** at or toward the rear; hinder; back: opposed to ANTERIOR —*n.* *[formerly also pl.]* the buttocks —**pos·te′ri·or′i·ty** (-ôr′ə tē) *n.* —**pos·te′ri·or·ly** *adv.*

pos·ter·i·ty (päs ter′ə tē) *n.* [< MFr. < L. < *posterus:* see prec.] **1.** all of a person's descendants **2.** all future generations

pos·tern (pōs′tərn, päs′-) *n.* [< OFr. < LL. *posterula* < *posterus:* see POSTERIOR] a back door or gate; private entrance at the side or rear —*adj.* of a postern; rear, etc.

post exchange a nonprofit general store at an army post, selling merchandise, as to servicemen

post·gla·cial (pōst′glā′shəl) *adj.* existing or happening after the disappearance of glaciers from a specific area

post·grad·u·ate (-graj′oo wit, -wāt′) *adj.* of or taking a course of study after graduation —*n.* a postgraduate student

post·haste (pōst′hāst′) *adv.* with great haste

post horse formerly, a horse kept at an inn (**post house**) for couriers or for hire to travelers

post·hu·mous (päs′choo məs, -tyoo-) *adj.* [< LL. < L. *postumus*, last, superl. of *posterus* (see POSTERIOR): altered after *humare*, to bury] **1.** born after the father's death **2.** published after the author's death **3.** arising or continuing after one's death —**post′hu·mous·ly** *adv.*

post·hyp·not·ic (pōst′hip nät′ik) *adj.* of, or carried out in, the period following a hypnotic trance *[posthypnotic* suggestion*]*

pos·til·ion, pos·til·lion (pōs til′yən, päs-) *n.* [Fr. < It. < *posta*, POST[3]] a person riding the left-hand leading horse of a four-horse carriage or the left-hand horse of a two-horse carriage

post·im·pres·sion·ism (pōst′im presh′ən iz'm) *n.* the theory or practice of some late 19th-cent. painters reacting against impressionism and emphasizing what is subjective or formal —**post′im·pres′sion·ist** *adj., n.* —**post′im·pres′sion·is′tic** *adj.*

post·lude (pōst′lood′) *n.* [POST- + (PRE)LUDE] **1.** a solo on the organ at the end of a church service **2.** a concluding musical section

post·man (-mən) *n., pl.* **-men** *same as* MAIL CARRIER

post·mark (-märk′) *n.* a post-office mark stamped on a piece of mail, canceling the postage stamp and recording the date and place —*vt.* to stamp with a postmark

post·mas·ter (-mas′tər) *n.* a person in charge of a post office —**post′mas′ter·ship′** *n.* —**post′mis′tress** *n.fem.*

postmaster general *pl.* **postmasters general, postmaster generals** the head of a government's postal system

post·me·rid·i·an (pōst′mə rid′ē ən) *adj.* [< L.: see POST- & MERIDIAN] of or in the afternoon

post me·ri·di·em (-ē əm) [L.] after noon: abbrev. **P.M., p.m., PM**

post-mor·tem (pōst′môr′təm) *adj.* [L., after death] **1.** happening or done after death **2.** designating or of an examination of a human body after death —*n.* **1.** a post-mortem examination: see AUTOPSY **2.** a detailed evaluation of some event just ended

post·na·sal drip (pōst′nā′z'l) a dripping of mucus from behind the nose onto the pharynx

post·na·tal (pōst′nāt′'l) *adj.* after birth

post office **1.** the governmental department in charge of the mails **2.** an office or building where mail is sorted, postage stamps are sold, etc.

post·op·er·a·tive (pōst′äp′ər ə tiv, -äp′rə-; -ə rāt′iv) *adj.* of or in the period after surgery —**post′op′er·a·tive·ly** *adv.*

post·paid (pōst′pād′) *adj.* with the postage prepaid

post·pone (pōst pōn′, pōs-) *vt.* **-poned′, -pon′ing** [< L.

post, after + *ponere*, to put] to put off until later; defer; delay —**post·pon′a·ble** *adj.* —**post·pone′ment** *n.* —**post·pon′er** *n.*
post·pran·di·al (pōst′pran′dē əl) *adj.* [< POST- + L. *prandium*, noonday meal] after a meal —**post′pran′di·al·ly** *adv.*
post road a road over which the post, or mail, is or formerly was carried
post·script (pōst′skript′, pōs′-) *n.* [< ModL. < L. pp. of *postscribere* < *post-*, after + *scribere*, to write] a note, paragraph, etc. added below the signature of a letter, or to a book, speech, etc. to give more facts, ideas, etc.
post time the scheduled starting time of a horse race
pos·tu·lant (päs′chə lənt) *n.* [Fr. < L. prp. of *postulare*: see ff.] a petitioner, esp. for admission into a religious order
pos·tu·late (päs′chə lāt′; *for n., usually* -lit) *vt.* **-lat′ed, -lat′ing** [< L. pp. of *postulare*, to demand] **1.** to claim; demand; require **2.** to assume without proof to be true, real, or necessary, esp. as a basis for argument **3.** to take for granted; assume —*n.* **1.** something postulated; assumption or axiom **2.** a prerequisite **3.** a basic principle —**pos′tu·la′tion** *n.* —**pos′tu·la′tor** (-ər) *n.*
pos·ture (päs′chər) *n.* [MFr. < It. < L. *positura* < *ponere*, to place] **1.** the position or carriage of the body; bearing **2.** a position assumed as in posing for an artist **3.** the way things stand; condition [the *posture* of foreign affairs **4.** *a)* frame of mind *b)* an attitude assumed merely for effect **5.** an official stand on an issue —*vt.* **-tured, -tur·ing** to place in a posture; pose —*vi.* to assume a bodily or mental posture, esp. for effect; pose —**pos′tur·al** *adj.* —**pos′tur·er** *n.*
pos·tur·ize (-chə rīz′) *vt., vi.* **-ized′, -iz′ing** *same as* POSTURE
post·war (pōst′wôr′) *adj.* after the (or a) war
po·sy (pō′zē) *n., pl.* **-sies** [contr. < POESY] **1.** orig., a verse or motto inscribed inside a ring, etc. **2.** a flower or bouquet: an old-fashioned usage
pot (pät) *n.* [OE. *pott*] **1.** a round vessel of metal, etc., for holding liquids, cooking food, etc. **2.** a pot with its contents **3.** *same as* POTFUL **4.** a pot of liquor **5.** *shortened form for* FLOWERPOT, CHIMNEY POT, etc. **6.** a toilet: a vulgar usage **7.** [Colloq.] *a)* all the money bet at a single time *b)* a large amount of money **8.** [Colloq.] a potshot **9.** [Slang] *same as: a)* MARIJUANA *b)* POTBELLY —*vt.* **pot′ted, pot′ting** **1.** to put into a pot **2.** to cook or preserve in a pot **3.** to shoot (game) for food, not for sport **4.** to hit or get as by a potshot —**go to pot** to go to ruin
po·ta·ble (pōt′ə b'l) *adj.* [Fr. < LL. < L. *potare*, to drink] fit to drink; drinkable —*n.* something drinkable; beverage —**po′ta·bil′i·ty, po′ta·ble·ness** *n.*
‡**po·tage** (pô tȧzh′) *n.* [Fr.] soup or broth
pot·ash (pät′ash′) *n.* [< Du. < *pot*, pot + *asch*, ash] **1.** *same as: a)* POTASSIUM CARBONATE *b)* POTASSIUM HYDROXIDE **2.** any substance containing potassium; esp., any potassium compound used in fertilizers
po·tas·si·um (pə tas′ē əm) *n.* [ModL. < Du.: see prec.] a soft, silver-white, waxlike metallic chemical element: its native salts are used in fertilizers, glass, etc.: symbol, K; at. wt., 39.102; at. no., 19 —**po·tas′sic** *adj.*
potassium bromide a white, crystalline compound, KBr, used in photography, medicine, etc.
potassium carbonate an alkaline, crystalline compound, K_2CO_3, used in making soap, glass, etc.
potassium chlorate a crystalline salt, $KClO_3$, a strong oxidizing agent used in medicine and in making matches, etc.
potassium chloride a crystalline salt, KCl, used in fertilizers, as a source of potassium salts, etc.
potassium cyanide an extremely poisonous crystalline compound, KCN, used in metallurgy, in electroplating, etc.
potassium hydroxide a strongly alkaline, crystalline compound, KOH, used in making soap, glass, etc.
potassium nitrate a crystalline compound, KNO_3, used in fertilizers, gunpowder, etc. and as an oxidizing agent
potassium permanganate a dark-purple, crystalline compound, $KMnO_4$, used as an oxidizing agent, disinfectant, etc.
po·ta·tion (pō tā′shən) *n.* [< MFr. < L. < *potare*, to drink] **1.** the act of drinking **2.** a drink or draft, esp. of liquor
po·ta·to (pə tāt′ō, -ə) *n., pl.* **-toes** [Sp. *patata* < WInd. name] **1.** orig., *same as* SWEET POTATO **2.** *a)* the starchy tuber of a widely cultivated plant of the nightshade family, cooked as a vegetable *b)* the plant
potato beetle (or **bug**) *same as* COLORADO BEETLE
potato chip a very thin slice of potato fried crisp and then salted: also, Brit., **potato crisp**
pot·bel·ly (pät′bel′ē) *n., pl.* **-lies** a protruding belly —**pot′bel′lied** *adj.*
pot·boil·er (-boil′ər) *n.* a piece of writing, etc., usually inferior, done quickly for money
Po·tem·kin (pä tyôm′kin; *E.* pō tem′kin), **Gri·go·ri A·le·ksan·dro·vich** (grē gô′rē ä′lyek sän′drô vich) 1739–91; Russian field marshal & statesman; favorite of Catherine II
po·tent (pōt′'nt) *adj.* [L. *potens* (gen. *potentis*), prp. of *posse*, to be able] **1.** having authority or power; mighty **2.** convincing; cogent **3.** effective or powerful in action, as a drug **4.** able to have an erection and hence to engage in sexual intercourse —**po′ten·cy,** *pl.* **-cies, po′tence** *n.* —**po′tent·ly** *adv.*
po·ten·tate (pōt′'n tāt′) *n.* a ruler; monarch
po·ten·tial (pə ten′shəl) *adj.* [< ML. < L.: see POTENT] **1.** that can, but has not yet, come into being; possible; latent **2.** *Gram.* expressing possibility, capability, etc. ["I can go" is in the *potential* mood] —*n.* **1.** something potential **2.** *Elec.* the relative voltage at a point in an electric circuit or field with respect to some reference point in the same circuit or field —**po·ten′tial·ly** *adv.*
potential energy inactive energy resulting from position or structure instead of motion, as in a coiled spring
po·ten·ti·al·i·ty (pə ten′shē al′ə tē) *n.* **1.** possibility or capability of becoming, developing, etc.; latency **2.** *pl.* **-ties** something potential
po·ten·ti·ate (pə ten′shē āt′) *vt.* **-at′ed, -at′ing** [< L. *potentia*, potency + -ATE[1]] to increase (the effect of a drug or toxin) by previous or simultaneous use of another drug or toxin —**po·ten′ti·a′tion** *n.* —**po·ten′ti·a′tor** *n.*
po·ten·ti·om·e·ter (pə ten′shē äm′ə tər) *n.* [< POTENTIAL + -METER] an instrument for measuring, comparing, or controlling electric potentials
pot·ful (pät′fool′) *n., pl.* **-fuls′** as much as a pot will hold
pot·head (-hed′) *n.* [Slang] a habitual user of marijuana
poth·er (päth′ər) *n.* [< ?] **1.** a cloud of smoke, dust, etc. **2.** a commotion or fuss —*vt., vi.* to fuss or bother
pot·herb (pät′urb′, -hurb′) *n.* any herb whose leaves and stems are boiled for food or used as a flavoring
pot·hold·er (-hōl′dər) *n.* a small pad, or piece of thick cloth, for handling hot pots, etc.
pot·hole (-hōl′) *n.* **1.** a deep hole or pit **2.** *chiefly Brit. var. of* CHUCKHOLE
pot·hook (-hook′) *n.* **1.** an S-shaped hook for hanging a pot or kettle over a fire **2.** a hooked rod for lifting hot pots, etc. **3.** a curved mark in writing
pot·house (-hous′) *n.* [Brit.] a small tavern
po·tion (pō′shən) *n.* [< OFr. < L. < *potare*, to drink] a drink or liquid dose, as of medicine or poison
pot·luck (pät′luk′) *n.* whatever the family meal happens to be [invited in to take *potluck*]
Po·to·mac (pə tō′mək) [< Algonquian town name, lit., ? where tribute is brought] river forming a boundary of W.Va., Md., & Va., and flowing into Chesapeake Bay
pot·pie (pät′pī′) *n.* **1.** a meat pie made in a pot or deep dish, usually with only a top crust **2.** a stew with dumplings
pot·pour·ri (pō′poo rē′, pät poor′ē) *n.* [Fr. < *pot*, a pot + pp. of *pourrir*, to rot] **1.** a mixture of dried flower petals with spices, kept in a jar for its fragrance **2.** a medley, miscellany, or anthology
pot roast meat, usually a large cut of beef, cooked in one piece by braising
Pots·dam (päts′dam′; *G.* pôts däm′) city in East Germany, near Berlin: pop. 111,000
pot·sherd (pät′shurd′) *n.* [see POT & SHARD] a piece of broken pottery
pot·shot (-shät′) *n.* **1.** an easy shot **2.** a random shot **3.** a haphazard try **4.** a random criticism
pot·tage (pät′ij) *n.* [< MFr. < *pot*, a pot < Du.] a thick soup or stew of vegetables, or meat and vegetables
pot·ted (pät′id) *adj.* **1.** put into a pot **2.** cooked or preserved in a pot or can **3.** [Slang] drunk
pot·ter[1] (-ər) *n.* a maker of earthenware pots, dishes, etc.
pot·ter[2] (pät′ər) *vi., vt.* [< OE. *potian*, to push] *chiefly Brit. var. of* PUTTER[3]
potter's field [cf. Matt. 27:7] a burial ground for paupers or unknown persons
potter's wheel a rotating horizontal disk upon which clay is molded into bowls, etc.
pot·ter·y (pät′ər ē) *n., pl.* **-ter·ies** [< MFr. < *potier*, a potter < *pot*, a pot] **1.** a potter's workshop or factory **2.** the art of a potter **3.** pots, bowls, etc. made of clay hardened by heat; earthenware

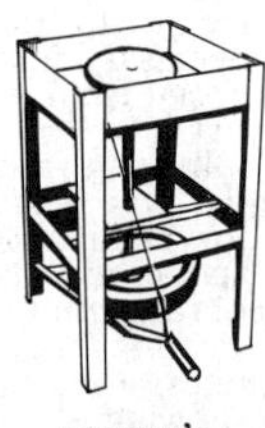
POTTER'S WHEEL

pot·tle (pät′'l) *n.* [< MFr. dim. of *pot*, a pot] **1.** formerly, a half-gallon liquid measure **2.** *a)* a pot holding a half gallon *b)* its contents; esp., alcoholic liquor
pot·ty[1] (pät′ē) *n., pl.* **-ties** **1.** a child's small chamber pot **2.** a child's chair for toilet training, having an open seat with a pot beneath: in full, **potty chair** **3.** a toilet: a child's word
pot·ty[2] (pät′ē) *adj.* **-ti·er, -ti·est** [Brit. Colloq.] **1.** trivial **2.** slightly crazy —**pot′ti·ness** *n.*

pouch (pouch) ***n.*** [MFr. *poche*, var. of *poque*, a poke] **1.** a small bag or sack, as for pipe tobacco **2.** a mailbag **3.** any pouchlike cavity, part, etc. **4.** *a)* a saclike structure on the abdomen of some animals; marsupium *b)* a baglike part, as of a gopher's cheeks, for carrying food —***vt.*** **1.** to put into a pouch **2.** to make into a pouch —***vi.*** to form a pouch —**pouched** ***adj.***

poul·ter·er (pōl′tər ər) ***n.*** [Brit.] a dealer in poultry and game: also [Archaic] **poul′ter**

poul·tice (pōl′tis) ***n.*** [ML. *pultes*, orig. pl. of L. *puls*, pap] a hot, soft, moist mass, as of flour, mustard, etc., applied, sometimes on a cloth, to a sore part of the body —***vt.*** **-ticed, -tic·ing** to apply a poultice to

poul·try (pōl′trē) ***n.*** [< MFr. < OFr. *poulet:* see PULLET] domestic fowls, as chickens, raised for meat or eggs

poul·try·man (-mən) ***n.,*** *pl.* **-men** a person who raises or deals in poultry

pounce[1] (pouns) ***n.*** [< ? MFr. *poinçon:* see PUNCHEON[1]] **1.** a claw or talon of a bird of prey **2.** the act of pouncing; swoop, leap, etc. —***vi.*** **pounced, pounc′ing** to swoop down, spring, or leap (*on, upon,* or *at*) as in attacking —**pounc′er** ***n.***

pounce[2] (pouns) ***n.*** [< Fr. < L. *pumex*, pumice] **1.** a fine powder, as of cuttlefish bone, formerly used to keep ink from blotting **2.** a fine powder sprinkled over a stencil to make a design, as on cloth —***vt.*** **pounced, pounc′ing** to use pounce on

pound[1] (pound) ***n.,*** *pl.* **pounds,** collectively **pound** [OE. *pund* < L. *pondo*, abl. of *pondus*, weight] **1.** a unit of weight, equal to 16 oz. (7,000 grains) avoirdupois or 12 oz. (5,760 grains) troy: abbrev. **lb. 2.** the monetary unit of the United Kingdom, equal to 20 shillings or 100 (new) pennies, symbol £, and of various other countries, as of Ireland, Israel, etc.: see MONETARY UNITS, table

pound[2] (pound) ***vt.*** [OE. *punian*] **1.** to beat to a pulp, powder, etc. **2.** to strike or drive with repeated heavy blows **3.** to make by pounding —***vi.*** **1.** to deliver repeated, heavy blows (*at* or *on* a door, etc.) **2.** to move with heavy steps, thumps, etc. **3.** to beat heavily; throb —***n.*** a pounding, or the sound of it —**pound one's ear** [Slang] to sleep —**pound out 1.** to flatten, smooth, etc. by pounding **2.** to produce (musical notes, typed copy, etc.) with a very heavy touch —**pound the pavement** [Slang] to walk the streets, as in looking for work —**pound′er** ***n.***

pound[3] (pound) ***n.*** [< OE. *pund-*] **1.** a municipal enclosure for confining stray animals **2.** an enclosure for keeping animals **3.** an enclosure for trapping animals **4.** a place of confinement, as for arrested persons **5.** an enclosed area for catching or keeping fish

pound·age (poun′dij) ***n.*** **1.** a tax, etc. per pound (sterling or weight) **2.** weight in pounds

pound·al (poun′d'l) ***n.*** [< POUND[1]] a unit of force producing an acceleration of one foot per second every second on a one-pound mass

pound·cake (pound′kāk′) ***n.*** a rich cake made with a pound each of flour, butter, sugar, etc.

-pound·er (poun′dər) *a combining form meaning* something weighing or worth (a specified number of pounds)

pound-fool·ish (pound′fo͞ol′ish) ***adj.*** not handling large sums of money wisely: see PENNY-WISE

pour (pôr) ***vt.*** [< ?] **1.** to make flow in a continuous stream **2.** to emit, utter, etc. profusely or steadily —***vi.*** **1.** to flow freely, continuously, or copiously **2.** to rain heavily **3.** to swarm **4.** to act as a hostess by pouring tea, coffee, etc. for guests at a reception —***n.*** **1.** a pouring **2.** a heavy rain —**pour it on** [Slang] **1.** to flatter **2.** to try or work very hard —**pour′er** ***n.***

‡**pour·boire** (po͞or bwår′) ***n.*** [Fr. < *pour*, for + *boire*, to drink] a tip, or gratuity

pout[1] (pout) ***vi.*** [ME. *pouten*] **1.** to thrust out the lips, as in sullenness **2.** to sulk **3.** to protrude: said of the lips —***vt.*** **1.** to thrust out (the lips) **2.** to utter with a pout —***n.*** **1.** a pouting **2.** a fit of sulking: also **the pouts**

pout[2] (pout) ***n.,*** *pl.* **pout, pouts:** see PLURAL, II, D, 2 [OE. *-pute*] any of several stout-bodied fishes, as the horned pout, eelpout, etc.

pout·er (-ər) ***n.*** **1.** a person who pouts **2.** any of a breed of pigeon that can distend its crop: also **pouter pigeon**

pov·er·ty (päv′ər tē) ***n.*** [< OFr. < L. < *pauper*, poor] **1.** the condition or quality of being poor; need **2.** inferiority; inadequacy **3.** scarcity

pov·er·ty-strick·en (-strik′'n) ***adj.*** very poor

pow (pou) ***interj.*** an exclamation suggesting the sound of a shot, explosion, etc.

POW, P.O.W. prisoner of war

pow·der (pou′dər) ***n.*** [< OFr. *poudre* < L. *pulvis*] **1.** any dry substance in the form of fine, dustlike particles, produced by crushing, grinding, etc. **2.** a specific kind of powder [face *powder*] **3.** *same as* GUNPOWDER —***vt.*** **1.** to put powder on **2.** to make into powder —***vi.*** **1.** to be made into powder **2.** to use powder as a cosmetic —**take a powder** [Slang] to run away; leave —**pow′der·er** ***n.***

powder blue pale blue —**pow′der-blue′** ***adj.***

powder burn a skin burn caused by gunpowder exploding at close range

pow·dered sugar (pou′dərd) granulated sugar ground to a powder

powder horn a container made of an animal's horn, for carrying gunpowder

powder puff a soft pad for applying cosmetic powder

powder room a lavatory for women

pow·der·y (pou′dər ē) ***adj.*** **1.** of, like, or in the form of, powder **2.** easily made into powder **3.** covered with or as if with powder

POWDER HORN

pow·er (pou′ər) ***n.*** [< OFr. *poeir*, earlier *poter*, ult. < L. *posse*, to be able] **1.** ability to do, act, or produce **2.** a specific ability or faculty [the *power* of sight] **3.** great ability to do, act, or affect; vigor; force **4.** *a)* the ability to control others; influence *b)* [*pl.*] special authority of a person or group in office *c)* legal authority **5.** *a)* physical force or energy [water *power*] *b)* the capacity to exert such force [200 *horsepower*] **6.** a person or thing of great influence, force, or authority **7.** a nation, esp. one dominating others **8.** a spirit or divinity **9.** military strength **10.** *Math.* *a)* the result of multiplying a quantity by itself [4 is the second *power* of 2 (2^2)] *b)* *same as* EXPONENT (sense 3) **11.** *Optics* the degree of magnification of a lens, telescope, etc. —***vt.*** to supply with power —***adj.*** **1.** operated by electricity, etc. [*power* tools] **2.** using an auxiliary, engine-powered system [*power* steering] **3.** carrying electricity [*power* lines] —**in power 1.** in authority **2.** in office —**the powers that be** the persons in control —**pow′ered** ***adj.***

pow·er·boat (-bōt′) ***n.*** *same as* MOTORBOAT

power dive *Aeron.* a dive speeded by engine power —**pow′er-dive′** ***vi., vt.*** **-dived′, -div′ing**

pow·er·ful (-fəl) ***adj.*** having much power; strong —***adv.*** [Dial.] very —**pow′er·ful·ly** ***adv.*** —**pow′er·ful·ness** ***n.***

pow·er·house (-hous′) ***n.*** **1.** a building where electric power is generated **2.** [Colloq.] a powerful person, team, etc.

pow·er·less (-lis) ***adj.*** without power; weak, impotent, etc. —**pow′er·less·ly** ***adv.*** —**pow′er·less·ness** ***n.***

power of attorney a written statement legally authorizing a person to act for one

power pack *Radio* a unit in an amplifier that converts power-line or battery voltage to required voltages

power structure those persons or groups who hold the ruling power in a nation, organization, etc. because of their social, economic, and institutional position

pow·wow (pou′wou′) ***n.*** [< Algonquian *powwaw*, priest] **1.** a N. American Indian ceremony to effect a cure, success in war, etc. as by magic, attended by feasting, dancing, etc. **2.** a conference of or with N. American Indians **3.** [Colloq.] any conference or gathering —***vi.*** **1.** to hold a powwow **2.** [Colloq.] to confer

pox (päks) ***n.*** [for *pocks:* see POCK] **1.** a disease characterized by skin eruptions, as smallpox **2.** syphilis

Poz·nań (pôz′nän′y′) city in W Poland: pop. 462,000

pp, pp. *Music* pianissimo

pp. **1.** pages **2.** past participle

P.P., p.p. **1.** parcel post **2.** past participle **3.** postpaid **4.** prepaid

ppd. **1.** postpaid **2.** prepaid

PPI plan position indicator

ppm, p.p.m., PPM parts per million

ppr., p.pr. present participle

P.P.S., p.p.s. [L. *post postscriptum*] an additional postscript

P.Q. Province of Quebec

Pr *Chem.* praseodymium

Pr. **1.** Prince **2.** Provençal

pr. **1.** pair(s) **2.** present **3.** price **4.** pronoun

P.R., PR **1.** Puerto Rico **2.** public relations

prac·ti·ca·ble (prak′ti kə b'l) ***adj.*** [< Fr. < *pratiquer:* see PRACTICE] **1.** that can be done or put into practice; feasible [a *practicable* plan] **2.** that can be used; usable [a *practicable* tool] —**prac′ti·ca·bil′i·ty, prac′ti·ca·ble·ness** ***n.*** —**prac′ti·ca·bly** ***adv.***

prac·ti·cal (prak′ti k'l) ***adj.*** [obs. *practic* < LL. *practicus:* see PRACTICE] **1.** of or from practice or action [*practical* knowledge] **2.** *a)* usable; workable; useful and sensible [*practical* proposals] *b)* designed for use; utilitarian **3.**

concerned with application to useful ends, rather than theory, speculation, etc. *[practical science]* **4.** given to actual practice *[a practical farmer]* **5.** of, concerned with, or realistic and sensible about everyday activities, work, etc. **6.** that is so in practice; virtual **7.** matter-of-fact —**prac′ti·cal′i·ty** (-kal′ə tē), *pl.* **-ties, prac′ti·cal·ness** *n.*

practical joke a trick played on someone but meant in fun —**practical joker**

prac·ti·cal·ly (prak′tik lē, -tik ′l ē) *adv.* **1.** in a practical way **2.** from a practical viewpoint **3.** in effect; virtually **4.** [Colloq.] nearly

practical nurse a nurse, often licensed, with less training than a registered nurse

prac·tice (prak′tis) *vt.* **-ticed, -tic·ing** [< MFr. < *pratiquer* < ML. < LL. < Gr. *praktikos*, practical < *prassein*, to do] **1.** to do or engage in regularly; make a habit of *[to practice thrift]* **2.** to do repeatedly so as to gain skill **3.** *a)* to work at, esp. as a profession *[to practice law]* *b)* to observe, or adhere to (beliefs, ideals, etc.) *[to practice one's religion]* —*vi.* **1.** to do something repeatedly so as to gain skill **2.** to work at a profession —*n.* **1.** the act, result, etc. of practicing; specif., *a)* a usual action; habit *b)* a usual method or custom; convention **2.** *a)* repeated action for gaining skill *b)* the resulting condition of being skilled *[out of practice]* **3.** knowledge put into action **4.** *a)* exercise of a profession *b)* a business based on this *[to buy another's law practice]* —**prac′tic·er** *n.*

prac·ticed (-tist) *adj.* **1.** skilled through practice **2.** learned or perfected by practice

practice teacher *same as* STUDENT TEACHER —**practice teaching**

prac·tise (-tis) *vt., vi.* **-tised, -tis·ing** *chiefly Brit. sp. of* PRACTICE

prac·ti·tion·er (prak tish′ə nər) *n.* **1.** a person who practices a profession, art, etc. **2.** a Christian Science healer

prae- [L.: see PRE-] *same as* PRE-

prae·no·men (prē nō′mən) *n., pl.* **-no′mens, -nom′i·na** (-näm′i nə) [L. < *prae-*, before + *nomen*, a name] the first name of an ancient Roman

prae·tor (prēt′ər) *n.* [L., ult. < *prae-*, before + *ire*, to go] an ancient Roman magistrate, next below a consul in rank —**prae·to·ri·al** (pri tôr′ē əl) *adj.*

prae·to·ri·an (pri tôr′ē ən) *adj.* **1.** of a praetor **2.** [*often* **P-**] designating or of the bodyguard (**Praetorian Guard**) of a Roman emperor

prag·mat·ic (prag mat′ik) *adj.* [< L. < Gr. *pragmatikos* < *pragma*, business < *prassein*, to do] **1.** concerned with actual practice, not with theory; practical **2.** dealing with historical facts as causally related **3.** of pragmatism Also, for senses 1 & 3, **prag·mat′i·cal** —**prag·mat′i·cal·ly** *adv.*

pragmatic sanction any of various royal decrees that had the force of fundamental law

prag·ma·tism (prag′mə tiz'm) *n.* **1.** the quality or condition of being pragmatic **2.** a philosophy that tests all concepts by practical results —**prag′ma·tist** *n., adj.*

Prague (präg) capital of Czechoslovakia, in the W part: pop. 1,034,000: Czech name **Pra·ha** (prä′hä)

prai·rie (prer′ē) *n.* [Fr. < OFr. *praerie* < *pré* < L. *pratum*, meadow + *-erie*, -ERY] a large area of level or slightly rolling grassland

prairie chicken either of two brown-and-white henlike grouse, with a short, rounded tail, of N. American prairies and the coast of the Gulf of Mexico: also **prairie hen**

prairie dog a small, squirrellike, burrowing rodent of N. America, with a barking cry

Prairie Provinces Canad. provinces of Manitoba, Saskatchewan, & Alberta

prairie schooner a large covered wagon used by pioneers to cross the American prairies

prairie wolf *same as* COYOTE

praise (prāz) *vt.* **praised, prais′ing** [< OFr. < LL. < L. *pretium*, worth] **1.** to commend the worth of; express admiration of **2.** to laud the glory of (God, etc.), as in song; glorify —*n.* a praising or being praised; commendation; glorification —**sing someone's praise** (or **praises**) to praise someone highly —**prais′er** *n.*

PRAIRIE DOG (to 15 in. long, including tail)

praise·wor·thy (-wur′thē) *adj.* worthy of praise; laudable —**praise′wor′thi·ly** *adv.* —**praise′wor′thi·ness** *n.*

Pra·krit (prä′krit) *n.* [Sans. *prākṛta*, natural < *pra-*, before + *kṛ*, to do] any of several Old Indic languages not of Sanskrit origin, spoken in ancient India

pra·line (prā′lēn; *chiefly South* prä′-) *n.* [Fr., after Marshal Duplessis-*Praslin* (1598–1675), whose cook created it] **1.** a crisp candy made of a pecan, almond, etc. browned in boiling sugar **2.** a similar patty of pecans, brown sugar, etc.

pram (pram) *n.* [Brit. Colloq.] a perambulator

prance (prans) *vi.* **pranced, pranc′ing** [< ?] **1.** to rise up on the hind legs in a lively way, esp. while moving along: said of a horse **2.** to ride on a prancing horse **3.** to caper like a prancing horse **4.** to swagger; strut —*vt.* to make (a horse) prance —*n.* a prancing —**pranc′er** *n.* —**pranc′ing·ly** *adv.*

prank[1] (praŋk) *n.* [< ? or akin ? to ff.] a playful trick, often one causing some mischief —**prank′ish** *adj.* —**prank′ish·ly** *adv.* —**prank′ish·ness** *n.* —**prank′ster** *n.*

prank[2] (praŋk) *vt., vi.* [prob. < LowG. source] to dress up or adorn showily

pra·se·o·dym·i·um (prā′zē ō dim′ē əm, -sē-) *n.* [ModL. < Gr. *prasios*, green + (DI)DYMIUM] a metallic chemical element of the rare-earth group, whose salts are generally green: symbol, Pr; at. wt., 140.907; at. no., 59

prat (prat) *n.* [< ?] [Slang] the buttocks

prate (prāt) *vi.* **prat′ed, prat′ing** [< MDu. *praten*; prob. echoic] to talk on and on, foolishly; chatter —*vt.* to tell idly; blab —*n.* chatter —**prat′er** *n.* —**prat′ing·ly** *adv.*

prat·fall (prat′fôl′) *n.* [Slang] a fall on the buttocks, esp. for comic effect, as in burlesque

prat·tle (prat′'l) *vi., vt.* **-tled, -tling** [MLowG. *pratelen*] **1.** *same as* PRATE **2.** to speak childishly; babble —*n.* **1.** idle chatter **2.** childish babble —**prat′tler** *n.*

prau (prou, prä′o͞o) *n. same as* PROA

prawn (prôn) *n.* [< ?] any of various related edible, shrimplike crustaceans or larger shrimp

Prax·it·e·les (prak sit′ə lēz′) 4th cent. B.C.; Athenian sculptor

pray (prā) *vt.* [< OFr. < LL. < L. *precari* < *prex* (gen. *precis*), prayer] **1.** to implore: no longer used except in a shortened form of direct request *[(I) pray (you) tell me]* **2.** to ask for by prayer; beg for imploringly **3.** to recite (a prayer) **4.** to effect, get, etc. by praying —*vi.* to make supplication or offer prayers

prayer[1] (prer) *n.* [< OFr. < ML. < L. *precarius*, got by begging < *precari*, to entreat] **1.** the act of praying **2.** an earnest request; entreaty **3.** *a)* an earnest request to God, etc. *b)* an utterance of praise, etc. to God *c)* a set of words used in praying *[evening prayer]* **4.** [*often pl.*] a religious prayer service **5.** something prayed for —**prayer′ful** *adj.* —**prayer′ful·ly** *adv.* —**prayer′ful·ness** *n.*

PRAWN (from 1 in. to 2 ft. long)

pray·er[2] (prā′ər) *n.* a person who prays

prayer book a book of formal religious prayers

praying mantis *same as* MANTIS

pre- [< Fr. *pré-* or L. *prae-* < L. *prae*, before] *a prefix meaning:* **1.** before in time, place, or rank *[prewar]* **2.** preliminary to *[preschool]*

preach (prēch) *vi.* [< OFr. < LL. < L. < *prae-*, before + *dicare*, to proclaim] **1.** to give a sermon **2.** to give moral or religious advice, esp. tediously —*vt.* **1.** to teach, advocate, or urge as by preaching **2.** to deliver (a sermon)

preach·er (prē′chər) *n.* a person who preaches; esp., a clergyman

preach·i·fy (-chə fī′) *vi.* **-fied′, -fy′ing** [Colloq.] to preach or moralize tiresomely

preach·ment (prēch′mənt) *n.* a preaching or sermon, esp. a long, tiresome one

preach·y (prē′chē) *adj.* **preach′i·er, preach′i·est** [Colloq.] given to or marked by preaching

pre·am·ble (prē′am′b'l, prē am′-) *n.* [< MFr., ult. < L. < *prae-*, before + *ambulare*, to go] **1.** an introduction, esp. to a constitution, statute, etc., stating its reason and purpose **2.** an introductory fact, event, etc.; preliminary

pre·am·pli·fi·er (prē am′plə fī′ər) *n.* in a radio, phonograph, etc., an amplifier to boost the voltage of a weak signal before it reaches the main amplifier

pre·ar·range (prē′ə rānj′) *vt.* **-ranged′, -rang′ing** to arrange beforehand —**pre′ar·range′ment** *n.*

preb·end (preb′ənd) *n.* [< MFr. < ML. *praebenda*, things to be supplied < L. *praebere*, to give] **1.** the amount paid a clergyman by his cathedral or collegiate church **2.** the church property yielding this amount **3.** *same as* PREBENDARY

preb·en·dar·y (preb′ən der′ē) *n., pl.* **-dar′ies** a person receiving a prebend

prec. preceding

Pre·cam·bri·an (prē kam′brē ən) *adj.* designating or of the geologic era covering all the time before the Cambrian Period —**the Precambrian** the Precambrian Era or its rocks: see GEOLOGY, chart

pre·can·cel (prē kan′s'l) *vt.* **-celed** or **-celled, -cel·ing** or **-cel·ling** to cancel (a postage stamp) before use in mailing —*n.* a precanceled stamp

pre·can·cer·ous (-kan′sər əs) *adj.* that may or is likely to become cancerous

pre·car·i·ous (pri ker′ē əs) ***adj.*** [L. *precarius:* see PRAYER[1]] **1.** dependent upon circumstances; insecure *[a precarious* living*]* **2.** dependent upon chance; risky *[a precarious* foothold*]* —**pre·car′i·ous·ly** ***adv.*** —**pre·car′i·ous·ness** ***n.***

pre·cast concrete (prē′kast) blocks, slabs, etc. of concrete cast into form before being put into position

pre·cau·tion (pri kô′shən) ***n.*** [< Fr. < LL. < L. pp. of *praecavere* < *prae-,* before + *cavere,* to take care] **1.** care taken beforehand **2.** a measure taken beforehand against possible danger, failure, etc. —**pre·cau′tion·ar′y** ***adj.***

pre·cede (pri sēd′) ***vt., vi.*** **-ced′ed, -ced′ing** [< MFr. < L. < *prae-,* before + *cedere,* to go] to be, come, or go before in time, order, rank, importance, etc.

prec·e·dence (pres′ə dəns, pri sēd′'ns) ***n.*** **1.** the act, right, or fact of preceding; priority in time, order, rank, etc. **2.** a ranking of dignitaries in order of importance Also **prec′e·den·cy**

pre·ced·ent (pri sēd′'nt; *for n.* pres′ə dənt) ***adj.*** that precedes —***n.*** **1.** an act, decision, etc. that may serve as an example, reason, or justification for a later one **2.** a practice resulting from such precedents

prec·e·den·tial (pres′ə den′shəl) ***adj.*** **1.** of, like, or serving as a precedent **2.** having precedence

pre·cen·tor (pri sen′tər) ***n.*** [< LL. < L. < *prae,* before + *canere,* to sing] a person who directs church singing —**pre·cen·to·ri·al** (prē′sen tôr′ē əl) ***adj.***

pre·cept (prē′sept) ***n.*** [< L. < *praecipere,* to teach < *prae-,* before + *capere,* to take] **1.** a direction meant as a rule of action or conduct (Ex.: Look before you leap) **2.** a rule of moral conduct **3.** a rule or direction, as in technical matters —**pre·cep′tive** ***adj.***

pre·cep·tor (pri sep′tər) ***n.*** [see prec.] a teacher —**pre·cep·to·ri·al** (prē′sep tôr′ē əl) ***adj.*** —**pre·cep′tor·ship′** ***n.*** —**pre·cep′tress** ***n.fem.***

pre·ces·sion (pri sesh′ən) ***n.*** **1.** a preceding; precedence **2.** *Mech.* a change in direction of the rotational axis of a spinning body, in which the axis describes a cone —**pre·ces′sion·al** ***adj.***

pre·cinct (prē′siŋkt) ***n.*** [< ML. < L. pp. of *praecingere,* to encompass < *prae-,* before + *cingere,* to surround] **1.** [*usually pl.*] an enclosure between buildings, walls, etc. **2.** [*pl.*] environs; neighborhood **3.** *a)* a division of a city, as for police administration *b)* a subdivision of a ward, as for voting **4.** any limited area **5.** a boundary

pre·ci·os·i·ty (presh′ē äs′ə tē) ***n., pl.*** **-ties** [see PRECIOUS] great fastidiousness or affectation, esp. in language

pre·cious (presh′əs) ***adj.*** [< OFr. < L. *pretiosus* < *pretium,* a price] **1.** of great price or value; costly **2.** much loved or cherished; dear **3.** overrefined or affected **4.** very great *[a precious* liar*]* —***adv.*** [Colloq.] very —**pre′cious·ly** ***adv.*** —**pre′cious·ness** ***n.***

precious stone a rare and costly gem

prec·i·pice (pres′ə pis) ***n.*** [< Fr. < L. < *praeceps,* headlong < *prae-,* before + *caput,* a head] **1.** a vertical, almost vertical, or overhanging rock face; steep cliff **2.** the brink of disaster, defeat, etc.

pre·cip·i·tant (pri sip′ə tənt) ***adj.*** [< L. prp. of *praecipitare:* see ff.] *same as* PRECIPITATE —***n.*** a substance causing formation of a precipitate —**pre·cip′i·tan·cy,** *pl.* **-cies, pre·cip′i·tance** ***n.*** —**pre·cip′i·tant·ly** ***adv.***

pre·cip·i·tate (pri sip′ə tāt′; *also, for adj. & n.,* -tit) ***vt.*** **-tat′ed, -tat′ing** [< L. pp. of *praecipitare* < *praeceps:* see PRECIPICE] **1.** to throw headlong; hurl downward **2.** to make happen before expected, needed, etc.; hasten **3.** *Chem.* to cause (a dissolved substance) to become insoluble and separate out from a solution, as by a reagent **4.** *Meteorol.* to condense (vapor) and make fall as rain, snow, etc. —***vi.*** **1.** *Chem.* to be precipitated **2.** *Meteorol.* to condense and fall as rain, snow, etc. —***adj.*** **1.** falling steeply, rushing headlong, etc. **2.** acting, happening, or done very hastily or rashly; impetuous **3.** very sudden; abrupt —***n.*** a substance precipitated out from a solution —**pre·cip′i·tate·ly** ***adv.*** —**pre·cip′i·tate·ness** ***n.*** —**pre·cip′i·ta′tive** ***adj.*** —**pre·cip′i·ta′tor** ***n.***

pre·cip·i·ta·tion (pri sip′ə tā′shən) ***n.*** **1.** a precipitating or being precipitated **2.** sudden or rash haste **3.** *Chem.* a precipitating or precipitate **4.** *Meteorol.* *a)* rain, snow, etc. *b)* the amount of this

pre·cip·i·tous (pri sip′ə təs) ***adj.*** **1.** steep like a precipice **2.** having precipices **3.** *same as* PRECIPITATE —**pre·cip′i·tous·ly** ***adv.*** —**pre·cip′i·tous·ness** ***n.***

pré·cis (prā sē′, prā′sē) ***n., pl.*** **pré·cis′** (-sēz′, -sēz) [Fr.: see ff.] a summary or abstract —***vt.*** to make a précis of

pre·cise (pri sīs′) ***adj.*** [MFr. *precis* < L. pp. of *praecidere,* to cut off < *prae-,* before + *caedere,* to cut] **1.** strictly defined; accurately stated; definite **2.** speaking definitely or distinctly **3.** minutely exact **4.** *a)* very careful or strict in following a procedure, rules, etc. *b)* finicky —**pre·cise′ly** ***adv.*** —**pre·cise′ness** ***n.***

pre·ci·sion (pri sizh′ən) ***n.*** **1.** the quality of being precise; exactness, accuracy, etc. **2.** the degree of this —***adj.*** characterized by precision, as in measurement, operation, etc. —**pre·ci′sion·ist** ***n.***

pre·clude (pri klo͞od′) ***vt.*** **-clud′ed, -clud′ing** [< L. *praecludere* < *prae-,* before + *claudere,* to shut] to make impossible, esp. in advance; shut out —**pre·clu′sion** (-klo͞o′zhən) ***n.*** —**pre·clu′sive** (-siv) ***adj.*** —**pre·clu′sive·ly** ***adv.***

pre·co·cious (pri kō′shəs) ***adj.*** [L. *praecox,* ult. < *prae-,* before + *coquere,* to cook] **1.** matured beyond normal for one's age, esp. in mental capacity, talent, etc. **2.** of or showing premature development —**pre·co′cious·ly** ***adv.*** —**pre·co′cious·ness, pre·coc′i·ty** (-käs′ə tē) ***n.***

pre·cog·ni·tion (prē′käg nish′ən) ***n.*** supposed perception, esp. extrasensory, of something before it occurs —**pre·cog′ni·tive** (-nə tiv) ***adj.***

pre·con·ceive (prē′kən sēv′) ***vt.*** **-ceived′, -ceiv′ing** to form a conception or opinion of beforehand —**pre′con·cep′tion** ***n.***

pre·con·cert (-kən sʉrt′) ***vt.*** to arrange or settle beforehand —**pre′con·cert′ed** ***adj.*** —**pre′con·cert′ed·ly** ***adv.***

pre·con·di·tion (-kən dish′ən) ***vt.*** to prepare (someone or something) to react, etc. in a certain way under certain conditions —***n.*** a condition required in advance for something to occur, be done, etc.

pre·cook (prē ko͝ok′) ***vt.*** to cook partially or completely, for final preparation later

pre·cur·sor (pri kʉr′sər) ***n.*** [< L. < *praecurrere,* to run ahead] **1.** a person or thing that comes before and indicates, or prepares the way for, what will follow; forerunner **2.** a predecessor, as in office

pre·cur·so·ry (-sə rē) ***adj.*** **1.** serving as a precursor **2.** introductory; preliminary

pred. predicate

pre·da·cious, pre·da·ceous (pri dā′shəs) ***adj.*** [< L. *praedari,* to prey upon < *praeda,* a prey + -ACEOUS] preying on other animals —**pre·dac′i·ty** (-das′ə tē), **pre·da′cious·ness, pre·da′ceous·ness** ***n.***

pre·date (prē dāt′) ***vt.*** **-dat′ed, -dat′ing** **1.** to date before the actual date **2.** to come before in date

pre·da·tion (pri dā′shən) ***n.*** [< L. < pp. of *praedari:* see PREDACIOUS] **1.** a plundering or preying **2.** the method of existence of predatory animals

pred·a·tor (pred′ə tər) ***n.*** a predatory person or animal

pred·a·to·ry (-tôr′ē) ***adj.*** [< L. < *praeda,* a prey] **1.** plundering, robbing, or exploiting **2.** capturing and feeding upon other animals —**pred′a·to′ri·ly** ***adv.*** —**pred′a·to′ri·ness** ***n.***

pre·de·cease (prē′di sēs′) ***vt., vi.*** **-ceased′, -ceas′ing** to die before (someone else)

pred·e·ces·sor (pred′ə ses′ər, pred′ə ses′ər; *chiefly Brit.* prē′di-) ***n.*** [< MFr. < LL. < L. *prae-,* before + *decessor,* retiring officer < *decessus:* see DECEASE] **1.** a person preceding another, as in office **2.** a thing replaced by another thing, as in use

pre·des·ig·nate (prē dez′ig nāt′) ***vt.*** **-nat′ed, -nat′ing** to designate beforehand —**pre·des′ig·na′tion** ***n.***

pre·des·ti·nate (prē des′tə nit; *for v.* -nāt′) ***adj.*** predestined or foreordained —***vt.*** **-nat′ed, -nat′ing** to foreordain, specif., *Theol.,* by divine decree —**pre·des′ti·na′tor** ***n.***

pre·des·ti·na·tion (prē des′tə nā′shən) ***n.*** **1.** *Theol.* divine foreordaining of everything, specif. of certain souls to salvation and, esp. in Calvinism, of others to damnation **2.** destiny; fate

pre·des·tine (prē des′tin) ***vt.*** **-tined, -tin·ing** to destine or decree beforehand; foreordain

pre·de·ter·mine (prē′di tʉr′mən) ***vt.*** **-mined, -min·ing** **1.** to determine or decide beforehand **2.** to bias or prejudice beforehand —**pre′de·ter′mi·nate** (-mə nit) ***adj.*** —**pre′de·ter′mi·na′tion** ***n.***

pred·i·ca·ble (pred′i kə b'l) ***adj.*** that can be predicated —***n.*** something predicable —**pred′i·ca·bil′i·ty, pred′i·ca·ble·ness** ***n.*** —**pred′i·ca·bly** ***adv.***

pre·dic·a·ment (pri dik′ə mənt) ***n.*** [< LL. *praedicamentum* < L. *praedicare:* see PREACH] a condition or situation, esp. one that is difficult, embarrassing, or comical

pred·i·cate (pred′ə kāt′; *for n. and adj.,* -kit) ***vt.*** **-cat′ed, -cat′ing** [< L. pp. of *praedicare:* see PREACH] **1.** orig., to proclaim; affirm **2.** to affirm as a quality, attribute, etc. *[*to *predicate* the honesty of one's motives*]* **3.** to base (something) *on* or *upon* facts, conditions, etc. **4.** to imply or connote —***vi.*** to make an affirmation —***n.*** **1.** *Gram.* the verb or verbal phrase, including any complements, objects, and modifiers, that is one of the two constituents of a sentence or clause, the other being the subject **2.** *Logic* something that is affirmed or denied about the subject of a proposition

(Ex.: *green* in "grass is green") —***adj.*** *Gram.* of, or having the nature of, a predicate —**pred′i·ca′tion** ***n.*** —**pred′i·ca′tive** ***adj.*** —**pred′i·ca′tive·ly** ***adv.***

pre·dict (pri dikt′) ***vt., vi.*** [< L. pp. of *praedicere* < *prae-*, before + *dicere*, to tell] to state (what one believes will happen); foretell —**pre·dict′a·bil′i·ty** ***n.*** —**pre·dict′a·ble** ***adj.*** —**pre·dict′a·bly** ***adv.*** —**pre·dic′tive** ***adj.*** —**pre·dic′tive·ly** ***adv.*** —**pre·dic′tor** ***n.***

pre·dic·tion (pri dik′shən) ***n.*** **1.** a predicting or being predicted **2.** something predicted

pre·di·gest (prē′di jest′, -dī-) ***vt.*** to digest beforehand; specif., to treat (food) as with enzymes for easier digestion —**pre′di·ges′tion** ***n.***

pre·di·lec·tion (pred′'l ek′shən, prēd′-) ***n.*** [< Fr. < ML. < L. *prae-*, before + *diligere*, to prefer] a preconceived liking; partiality (*for*)

pre·dis·pose (prē′dis pōz′) ***vt.*** **-posed′, -pos′ing** to make receptive beforehand —**pre′dis·po·si′tion** (-pə zish′ən) ***n.***

pre·dom·i·nant (pri däm′ə nənt) ***adj.*** **1.** having authority or influence over others; superior **2.** most frequent; prevailing —**pre·dom′i·nance, pre·dom′i·nan·cy** ***n., pl.*** **-cies, pre·dom′i·nant·ly** ***adv.***

pre·dom·i·nate (-nāt′; *for adj.* -nit) ***vi.*** **-nat′ed, -nat′ing** **1.** to have influence or authority (*over* others); hold sway **2.** to prevail; preponderate —***adj.*** *same as* PREDOMINANT —**pre·dom′i·nate·ly** ***adv.*** —**pre·dom′i·na′tion** ***n.***

pre·em·i·nent, pre-em·i·nent (prē em′ə nənt) ***adj.*** eminent above others; surpassing: also **pre·ëm′i·nent** —**pre·em′i·nence, pre-em′i·nence** ***n.*** —**pre·em′i·nent·ly, pre-em′i·nent·ly** ***adv.***

pre·empt, pre-empt (-empt′) ***vt.*** [< ff.] **1.** to acquire (public land) by preemption **2.** to seize before anyone else can; appropriate **3.** *Radio & TV* to replace (a regularly scheduled program) —***vi.*** *Bridge* to make a preemptive bid Also **pre·ëmpt′** —**pre·emp′tor, pre-emp′tor** ***n.***

pre·emp·tion, pre-emp·tion (-emp′shən) ***n.*** [< ML. pp. of *preemere* < L. *prae-*, before + *emere*, to buy] **1.** the act or right of buying land, etc. before, or in preference to, others **2.** action taken to check other action beforehand Also **pre·ëmp′tion**

pre·emp·tive, pre-emp·tive (-emp′tiv) ***adj.*** **1.** having to do with preemption **2.** *Bridge* designating a high bid intended to shut out opposing bids Also **pre·ëmp′tive** —**pre·emp′tive·ly, pre-emp′tive·ly** ***adv.***

preen (prēn) ***vt.*** [< OE. < *proinen*] **1.** to clean and trim (the feathers) with the beak: said of birds **2.** to dress up or adorn (oneself) **3.** to show satisfaction with or vanity in (oneself) —***vi.*** to primp —**preen′er** ***n.***

pre·ex·ist, pre-ex·ist (prē′ig zist′) ***vt., vi.*** to exist previously or before (another person or thing): also **pre′ëx·ist′** —**pre′ex·ist′ence, pre′-ex·ist′ence** ***n.*** —**pre′ex·ist′ent, pre′-ex·ist′ent** ***adj.***

pref. **1.** preface **2.** preferred **3.** prefix

pre·fab (prē′fab′) ***n.*** [Colloq.] a prefabricated building

pre·fab·ri·cate (prē fab′rə kāt′) ***vt.*** **-cat′ed, -cat′ing** **1.** to fabricate beforehand **2.** to make (houses, etc.) in standardized sections for shipment and quick assembly —**pre′fab·ri·ca′tion** ***n.***

pref·ace (pref′is) ***n.*** [< MFr. < ML. < L. *prae-*, before + pp. of *fari*, to speak] **1.** an introductory statement to an article, book, or speech, telling its subject, purpose, etc. **2.** something introductory —***vt.*** **-aced, -ac·ing** **1.** to furnish or introduce with a preface **2.** to be or serve as a preface to

pref·a·to·ry (pref′ə tôr′ē) ***adj.*** of, like, or serving as a preface: also **pref′a·to′ri·al** —**pref′a·to′ri·ly** ***adv.***

pre·fect (prē′fekt) ***n.*** [< OFr. < L. pp. of *praeficere*, to set over < *prae-*, before + *facere*, to make] **1.** in ancient Rome, any of various officials in charge of governmental or military departments **2.** any of various administrators; specif., the head of a department of France

pre·fec·ture (prē′fek chər) ***n.*** the office, authority, territory, or residence of a prefect —**pre·fec′tur·al** ***adj.***

pre·fer (pri fur′) ***vt.*** **-ferred′, -fer′ring** [< MFr. < L. < *prae-*, before + *ferre*, BEAR[1]] **1.** to promote; advance **2.** to put before a magistrate, court, etc. to be considered **3.** to choose before another; like better —**pre·fer′rer** ***n.***

pref·er·a·ble (pref′ər ə b'l, pref′rə-) ***adj.*** to be preferred; more desirable —**pref′er·a·bil′i·ty, pref′er·a·ble·ness** ***n.*** —**pref′er·a·bly** ***adv.***

pref·er·ence (pref′ər əns, pref′rəns) ***n.*** **1.** a preferring or being preferred **2.** the right, power, etc. of prior choice or claim **3.** something preferred **4.** a giving of advantage to one person, country, etc. over others, as in granting credit or setting tariff rates

pref·er·en·tial (pref′ə ren′shəl) ***adj.*** **1.** of, giving, or receiving preference **2.** offering a preference **3.** designating a union shop which gives preference to union members in hiring, layoffs, etc. —**pref′er·en′tial·ly** ***adv.***

pre·fer·ment (pri fur′mənt) ***n.*** **1.** a preferring **2.** an advancement in rank or office; promotion **3.** an office, rank, or honor to which a person is advanced

preferred stock stock on which dividends must be paid before those of common stock

pre·fig·ure (prē fig′yər) ***vt.*** **-ured, -ur·ing** [< LL. < L. *prae-*, before + *figurare*, to fashion] **1.** to be a type of or foreshadow (something that will appear later) **2.** to imagine beforehand —**pre′fig·u·ra′tion** (-yə rā′shən) ***n.*** —**pre·fig′ur·a·tive** ***adj.*** —**pre·fig′ur·a·tive·ly** ***adv.*** —**pre·fig′ur·a·tive·ness** ***n.*** —**pre·fig′ure·ment** ***n.***

pre·fix (prē′fiks; *also, for v.*, prē fiks′) ***vt.*** [< MFr. < L. pp. of *praefigere* < *prae-*, before + *figere*, to fix] to fix to the beginning of a word, etc.; esp., to add as a prefix —***n.*** **1.** a syllable or group of syllables joined to the beginning of a word to alter its meaning or create a new word [*pre-* is a prefix added to *cool* to form *precool*] **2.** a title before a person's name, as *Dr.* —**pre′fix·al** ***adj.*** —**pre·fix′ion** ***n.***

pre·fron·tal (prē frunt′'l) ***adj.*** of or situated near the front of the brain or of the head of a vertebrate

preg·na·ble (preg′nə b'l) ***adj.*** [< MFr. < *prendre*, to take] that can be captured or attacked —**preg′na·bil′i·ty** ***n.***

preg·nant (preg′nənt) ***adj.*** [< L. *pregnans* (gen. *pregnantis*) < *prae-*, before + base of OL. *gnasci*, to be born] **1.** having (an) offspring developing in the uterus; with young or with child **2.** mentally fertile; inventive **3.** productive of results; fruitful **4.** full of meaning, significance, etc. **5.** filled (*with*) or rich (*in*); abounding —**preg′nan·cy** ***n., pl.*** **-cies** —**preg′nant·ly** ***adv.***

pre·hen·sile (pri hen′s'l) ***adj.*** [< Fr. < L. pp. of *prehendere*, to take] adapted for seizing or grasping, esp. by wrapping itself around something as a monkey's tail does —**pre·hen·sil·i·ty** (prē′hen sil′ə tē) ***n.***

pre·his·tor·ic (prē′his tôr′ik, -tär′-) ***adj.*** of the period before recorded history: also **pre′his·tor′i·cal** —**pre′his·tor′i·cal·ly** ***adv.***

pre·judge (prē juj′) ***vt.*** **-judged′, -judg′ing** [< Fr. < L.: see PRE- & JUDGE] to judge beforehand, or without all the evidence —**pre·judg′ment, pre·judge′ment** ***n.***

prej·u·dice (prej′ə dis) ***n.*** [< MFr. < L. < *prae-*, before + *judicium*, judgment] **1.** an opinion formed before the facts are known; preconceived idea, usually one that is unfavorable **2.** *a*) an opinion held in disregard of facts that contradict it; unreasonable bias *b*) the holding of such opinions **3.** intolerance or hatred of other races, creeds, etc. **4.** harm resulting as from some judgment or action of another —***vt.*** **-diced, -dic·ing** **1.** to harm or damage, as by some judgment or action **2.** to cause to have prejudice; bias

prej·u·di·cial (prej′ə dish′əl) ***adj.*** causing prejudice, or harm; injurious; detrimental —**prej′u·di′cial·ly** ***adv.***

prel·a·cy (prel′ə sē) ***n., pl.*** **-cies** **1.** *a*) the office or rank of a prelate *b*) prelates collectively Also **prel′a·ture** (-chər) **2.** church government by prelates: often a hostile term: also **prel′a·tism** (-it iz'm)

prel·ate (-it) ***n.*** [< OFr. < LL. < L. pp. of *praeferre*, to PREFER] a high-ranking ecclesiastic, as a bishop —**prel′ate·ship′** ***n.*** —**pre·lat·ic** (pri lat′ik) ***adj.***

pre·lim (prē′lim) ***n.*** [Slang] *clipped form of* PRELIMINARY

prelim. preliminary

pre·lim·i·nar·y (pri lim′ə ner′ē) ***adj.*** [< Fr. or ModL. < L. *prae-*, before + *liminaris* < *limen*, threshold] leading up to the main action, business, etc.; introductory; preparatory —***n., pl.*** **-nar′ies** [*often pl.*] **1.** a preliminary step, procedure, etc. **2.** a preliminary examination **3.** a contest before the main one —**pre·lim′i·nar′i·ly** ***adv.***

prel·ude (prel′yo͞od; prā′lo͞od, prē′-) ***n.*** [< Fr. < ML. < L. < *prae-*, before + *ludere*, to play] **1.** a preliminary part; preface; opening **2.** *Music* *a*) an introductory section of a suite, fugue, etc. *b*) since the 19th cent., any short, romantic composition —***vt., vi.*** **-ud·ed, -ud·ing** **1.** to serve as or be a prelude (to) **2.** to play (as) a prelude —**pre·lu·di·al** (pra lo͞o′dē əl, prē-) ***adj.***

pre·mar·i·tal (prē mar′ə t'l) ***adj.*** before marriage

pre·ma·ture (prē′mə to͞or′, -cho͞or′, -tyo͞or′) ***adj.*** [< L.: see PRE- & MATURE] happening, done, arriving, or existing before the proper or usual time; specif., born before the full period of gestation —**pre′ma·ture′ly** ***adv.*** —**pre′ma·tu′ri·ty, pre′ma·ture′ness** ***n.***

pre·med (prē′med′) ***adj.*** *clipped form of* PREMEDICAL —***n.*** a premedical student

pre·med·i·cal (prē med′i k'l) ***adj.*** designating or of the studies preparatory to the study of medicine

pre·med·i·tate (pri med′ə tāt′) ***vt.*** **-tat′ed, -tat′ing** to think out or plan beforehand —***vi.*** to meditate beforehand —**pre·med′i·tat′ed** ***adj.*** —**pre·med′i·tat′ed·ly** ***adv.*** —**pre·med′i·ta′tive** ***adj.*** —**pre·med′i·ta′tor** ***n.***

pre·med·i·ta·tion (pri med′ə tā′shən, prē′med-) ***n.*** **1.** a premeditating **2.** *Law* a degree of forethought sufficient to show intent to commit an act

pre·mier (pri mir′, -myir′; prē′mē ər) ***adj.*** [MFr. < L. *primarius* < *primus*, first] **1.** first in importance; chief **2.** first in time —***n.*** a chief official; specif., *the title of* *a*) the prime minister in certain countries *b*) the governor of a Canadian province —**pre·mier′ship** ***n.***

pre·mière, pre·miere (pri myer′, -mir′, -mē er′) ***n.*** [Fr., fem. of *premier:* see prec.] a first performance of a play, movie, etc. —***adj.*** **1.** being the leading woman performer, as in ballet **2.** *same as* PREMIER —***vt., vi.*** **-mièred′** or **-miered′, -mièr′ing** or **-mier′ing** to exhibit (a play, movie, etc.) for the first time

prem·ise (prem′is; *for v., also* pri mīz′) ***n.*** [< ML. < L. pp. of *praemittere* < *prae-*, before + *mittere*, to send] **1.** a previous statement serving as a basis for an argument; specif., either of the two propositions of a syllogism from which the conclusion is drawn: also sp. **prem′iss** **2.** [*pl.*] *a*) the part of a deed or lease that states the parties and property involved, etc. *b*) the property so mentioned **3.** [*pl.*] a piece of real estate [keep off the *premises*] —***vt.*** **-ised, -is·ing** **1.** to state as a premise **2.** to preface (a discourse, etc.) —***vi.*** to make a premise

pre·mi·um (prē′mē əm, prēm′yəm) ***n.***, *pl.* **-ums** [< L. < *prae-*, before + *emere*, to take] **1.** a reward or prize, esp. as an added inducement to buy or do something **2.** an amount paid in addition to the regular charge, interest, etc. **3.** a payment, as for an insurance policy **4.** very high value [to put a *premium* on honesty] **5.** the amount by which one form of money exceeds another (of the same nominal value), as in exchange value —***adj.*** rated as superior and higher in price —**at a premium** **1.** at a value or price higher than normal **2.** very valuable, as because of scarcity

pre·mo·lar (prē mō′lər) ***adj.*** designating or of any bicuspid tooth in front of the molars —***n.*** a premolar tooth

pre·mo·ni·tion (prē′mə nish′ən, prem′ə-) ***n.*** [< MFr. < LL. < L. < *prae-*, before + *monere*, to warn] **1.** a forewarning **2.** a foreboding —**pre·mon·i·to·ry** (pri män′ə tôr′ē) ***adj.***

pre·na·tal (prē nāt′'l) ***adj.*** [PRE- + NATAL] existing or taking place before birth —**pre·na′tal·ly** ***adv.***

pre·nup·tial (prē nup′shəl, -chəl) ***adj.*** **1.** before a marriage or wedding **2.** before mating

pre·oc·cu·pa·tion (prē äk′yə pā′shən) ***n.*** a preoccupying or being preoccupied: also **pre·oc′cu·pan·cy**, *pl.* **-cies**

pre·oc·cu·py (-äk′yə pī′) ***vt.*** **-pied′, -py′ing** [< MFr. < L.: see PRE- & OCCUPY] **1.** to occupy completely the thoughts of; engross; absorb **2.** to occupy or take possession of before someone else or beforehand

pre·or·dain (prē′ôr dān′) ***vt.*** to ordain or decree beforehand —**pre′or·di·na′tion** (-d'n ā′shən) ***n.***

prep (prep) ***adj.*** [Colloq.] *clipped form of* PREPARATORY —***vi.*** **prepped, prep′ping** [Colloq.] to prepare oneself by study, etc. —***vt.*** to prepare (one) for something; specif., to prepare (a patient) as for surgery

prep. **1.** preparation **2.** preparatory **3.** preposition

pre·pack·age (prē pak′ij) ***vt.*** **-aged, -ag·ing** to package (goods, esp. foods) in certain amounts or weights before selling

pre·paid (prē pād′) *pt. & pp. of* PREPAY

prep·a·ra·tion (prep′ə rā′shən) ***n.*** **1.** a preparing or being prepared **2.** a preparatory measure **3.** something prepared for a special purpose, as a medicine, cosmetic, etc.

pre·par·a·tive (pri par′ə tiv) ***adj.*** *same as* PREPARATORY —***n.*** *same as* PREPARATION (sense 2, 3)

pre·par·a·to·ry (-tôr′ē) ***adj.*** **1.** that prepares or serves to prepare; introductory **2.** undergoing preparation, esp. for college entrance —**pre·par′a·to′ri·ly** ***adv.***

preparatory school a private secondary school for preparing students to enter college

pre·pare (pri par′, -per′) ***vt.*** **-pared′, -par′ing** [< MFr. < L. < *prae-*, before + *parare*, to get ready] **1.** to make ready or suitable **2.** to make receptive; dispose **3.** to equip or furnish; fit out **4.** to put together; construct; compound [to *prepare* a dinner or a medicine] —***vi.*** **1.** to make things ready **2.** to make oneself ready —**pre·par′ed·ly** (-id lē) ***adv.***

pre·par·ed·ness (-id nis) ***n.*** the state of being prepared, esp. for waging war, as by stockpiling weapons

pre·pay (prē pā′) ***vt.*** **-paid′, -pay′ing** to pay or pay for in advance —**pre·pay′ment** ***n.***

pre·pense (pri pens′) ***adj.*** [< OFr. < *pur-*, pro- + *penser*, to think] planned beforehand

pre·pon·der·ant (pri pän′dər ənt) ***adj.*** greater in amount, power, influence, etc.; predominant —**pre·pon′der·ance, pre·pon′der·an·cy** ***n.*** —**pre·pon′der·ant·ly** ***adv.***

pre·pon·der·ate (-də rāt′) ***vi.*** **-at′ed, -at′ing** [< L. pp. of *praeponderare* < *prae-*, before + *ponderare*, to weigh < *pondus*, a weight] to be greater in amount, power, influence, etc.; predominate —**pre·pon′der·a′tion** ***n.***

prep·o·si·tion (prep′ə zish′ən) ***n.*** [< L. < pp. of *praeponere* < *prae-*, before + *ponere*, to place] **1.** a relation word, as *in, by, for, with, to*, etc., that connects a noun or pronoun, or a noun phrase, to another element, as to another noun (Ex.: the sound *of* rain), to a verb (Ex.: he went *to* the store), or to an adjective (Ex.: late *for* the tea party) **2.** any construction having a similar function (Ex.: *in back of*, equivalent to *behind*) —**prep′o·si′tion·al** ***adj.*** —**prep′o·si′tion·al·ly** ***adv.***

prepositional phrase a preposition and its object

pre·pos·sess (prē′pə zes′) ***vt.*** **1.** orig., to occupy beforehand or before another **2.** to preoccupy to the exclusion of later thoughts, feelings, etc. **3.** to prejudice or bias **4.** to impress favorably at once —**pre′pos·ses′sion** ***n.***

pre·pos·sess·ing (-iŋ) ***adj.*** that prepossesses, or impresses favorably; pleasing —**pre′pos·sess′ing·ly** ***adv.*** —**pre′pos·sess′ing·ness** ***n.***

pre·pos·ter·ous (pri päs′tər əs) ***adj.*** [< L. < *prae-*, before + *posterus*, coming after < *post*, after] so contrary to nature, common sense, etc. as to be laughable; absurd —**pre·pos′ter·ous·ly** ***adv.*** —**pre·pos′ter·ous·ness** ***n.***

pre·puce (prē′pyo͞os) ***n.*** [< MFr. < L. *praeputium*] the fold of skin covering the end of the penis —**pre·pu′tial** (-pyo͞o′shəl) ***adj.***

Pre-Raph·a·el·ite (prē raf′ē ə līt′, -rā′fē-) ***n.*** **1.** a member of a society of artists (**Pre-Raphaelite Brotherhood**) formed in England in 1848 to revive the qualities of Italian art before Raphael **2.** any artist with similar aims —***adj.*** of or like Pre-Raphaelites —**Pre-Raph′a·el·it′ism** ***n.***

pre·re·cord (prē′ri kôrd′) ***vt.*** *Radio & TV* to record (an announcement, program, etc.) in advance, for later broadcasting

pre·req·ui·site (pri rek′wə zit) ***adj.*** required beforehand, esp. as a necessary condition for something following —***n.*** something prerequisite

pre·rog·a·tive (pri räg′ə tiv) ***n.*** [< MFr. < L. *praerogativa*, called upon to vote first, ult. < *prae-*, before + *rogare*, to ask] **1.** a prior or exclusive privilege, esp. one peculiar to a rank, class, etc. **2.** a superior advantage —***adj.*** of or having a prerogative

Pres. **1.** Presbyterian: also **Presb.** **2.** President

pres. **1.** present **2.** presidency

pres·age (pres′ij; *for v., usually* pri sāj′) ***n.*** [< MFr. < L. < *prae-*, before + *sagire*, to perceive] **1.** a sign or warning of a future event; portent **2.** a foreboding **3.** foreshadowing quality [of ominous *presage*] —***vt.*** **-aged′, -ag′ing** **1.** to give a warning of; portend **2.** to have a foreboding of **3.** to predict —***vi.*** to make a prediction —**pres·ag′er** ***n.***

pres·by·ter (prez′bi tər, pres′-) ***n.*** [LL.: see PRIEST] **1.** in the early Christian church and in the Presbyterian Church, an elder **2.** in the Episcopal Church, a priest or minister —**pres′by·te′ri·al** (-bə tir′ē əl), **pres·byt′er·al** (-bit′ər əl) ***adj.***

pres·by·te·ri·an (prez′bə tir′ē ən, pres′-) ***adj.*** **1.** having to do with church government by presbyters **2.** [**P-**] designating or of a church of a Calvinistic Protestant denomination governed by presbyters, or elders —***n.*** [**P-**] a member of a Presbyterian church —**Pres′by·te′ri·an·ism** ***n.***

pres·by·ter·y (prez′bə ter′ē, pres′-) ***n.***, *pl.* **-ter′ies** **1.** *a*) in Presbyterian churches, a governing body made up of all the ministers and an equal number of elders from all the churches in a district *b*) such a district **2.** the part of a church reserved for the officiating clergy

pre·school (prē′sko͞ol′) ***adj.*** designating, of, or for a child between infancy and school age, usually between the ages of two and five (or six) —**pre·school′er** ***n.***

pre·sci·ence (prē′shē əns, presh′əns) ***n.*** [< OFr. < LL., ult. < L. *prae-*, before + *scire*, to know] apparent knowledge of things before they happen; foreknowledge —**pre′sci·ent** ***adj.*** —**pre′sci·ent·ly** ***adv.***

pre·scribe (pri skrīb′) ***vt.*** **-scribed′, -scrib′ing** [< L. < *prae-*, before + *scribere*, to write] **1.** to set down as a rule or direction; order **2.** to order or advise as a medicine or treatment: said of physicians, etc. —***vi.*** **1.** to set down or impose rules **2.** to give medical advice or prescriptions —**pre·scrib′er** ***n.***

pre·script (pri skript′; *also, and for n. always*, prē′skript) ***adj.*** prescribed —***n.*** something prescribed; direction; rule

pre·scrip·tion (pri skrip′shən) ***n.*** **1.** a prescribing **2.** something prescribed; order **3.** *a*) a doctor's written direction for the preparation and use of a medicine, the grinding of eyeglass lenses, etc. *b*) a medicine so prescribed —***adj.*** made according to, or purchasable only with, a doctor's prescription —**pre·scrip′tive** ***adj.*** —**pre·scrip′tive·ly** ***adv.***

pres·ence (prez′'ns) ***n.*** **1.** the fact or condition of being present **2.** immediate surroundings [admitted to his *presence*] **3.** one that is present, esp. a person of high station or imposing appearance **4.** *a*) a person's bearing, appearance, etc. *b*) poised and confident bearing, as that of a performer before an audience (**stage presence**) **5.** a spirit or ghost felt to be present

presence of mind ability to think clearly and act quickly and intelligently in an emergency

pres·ent (prez′'nt; *for v.* pri zent′) ***adj.*** [OFr. < L. *praesens*, prp. of *praeesse* < *prae-*, before + *esse*, to be] **1.** *a)* being at the specified place; in attendance *b)* existing (*in* a particular thing) [nitrogen is *present* in the air] **2.** existing or happening now **3.** now being discussed, considered, etc. [the *present* writer] **4.** *Gram.* indicating action as now taking place (Ex.: he *goes*) or state as now existing (Ex.: the plums *are* ripe), action that is habitual (Ex.: he *speaks* softly), or action that is always true (Ex.: two and two *is* four) —***n.*** **1.** the present time **2.** the present occasion **3.** *Gram.* the present tense or a verb in it **4.** [*pl.*] *Law* this very document [know by these *presents*] **5.** something presented, or given; gift —***vt.*** [< OFr. < L. *praesentare*, to place in the presence of < *praesens*: see the *adj.*] **1.** to introduce (a person *to* someone) **2.** to offer for viewing or notice; exhibit; show **3.** to offer for consideration **4.** to give (a gift, award, etc.) to (someone) **5.** to hand over, send, etc. (a bill, credentials, etc.) to **6.** to point or aim (a weapon, etc.) —**present arms** *Mil.* **1.** to hold a rifle vertically in front of the body: a position of salute **2.** *a)* this position *b)* the command to assume it —**pre·sent′er** ***n.***

pre·sent·a·ble (pri zen′tə b'l) ***adj.*** **1.** that can be presented; fit to be shown, given, etc. to others **2.** properly dressed for meeting people —**pre·sent′a·bil′i·ty, pre·sent′a·ble·ness** ***n.*** —**pre·sent′a·bly** ***adv.***

pre·sen·ta·tion (prē′zen tā′shən, prez′'n-) ***n.*** **1.** a presenting or being presented **2.** something presented, as a theatrical performance, a gift, etc. —**pre′sen·ta′tion·al** ***adj.***

pres·ent-day (prez′'nt dā′) ***adj.*** of the present time

pre·sen·ti·ment (pri zen′tə mənt) ***n.*** [MFr. < L.: see PRE- & SENTIMENT] a feeling that something, esp. of an unfortunate nature, is about to take place; foreboding

pres·ent·ly (prez′'nt lē) ***adv.*** **1.** in a little while; soon **2.** at present; now **3.** [Archaic] instantly

pre·sent·ment (pri zent′mənt) ***n.*** **1.** *same as* PRESENTATION **2.** a grand-jury report of an offense initiated by the jury without their having received a bill of indictment

present participle a participle used *a)* with auxiliaries to express present or continuing action or state of being [as *going* in "I am going"] *b)* as an adjective [as *going* in "a going concern"]

present perfect **1.** a tense indicating an action or state as completed at the time of speaking but not at any definite time in the past **2.** a verb form in this tense (Ex.: has gone)

pre·ser·va·tive (pri zʉr′və tiv) ***adj.*** preserving —***n.*** anything that preserves; esp., a substance added to food to keep it from spoiling

pre·serve (pri zʉrv′) ***vt.*** **-served′, -serv′ing** [< MFr., ult. < L. *prae-*, before + *servare*, to keep] **1.** to keep from harm, damage, etc.; protect; save **2.** to keep from spoiling or rotting **3.** to prepare (food), as by canning, salting, etc., for future use **4.** to keep up; maintain [to *preserve* liberty] —***vi.*** to preserve fruit, etc. —***n.*** **1.** [*usually pl.*] fruit preserved whole or in large pieces by cooking with sugar **2.** a place where game, fish, etc. are maintained and protected, esp. for regulated hunting and fishing **3.** the special domain or sphere of some person or group —**pre·serv′a·ble** ***adj.*** —**pres·er·va·tion** (prez′ər vā′shən) ***n.*** —**pre·serv′er** ***n.***

pre·set (prē set′) ***vt.*** **-set′, -set′ting** to set (the controls of an automatic apparatus) beforehand

pre-shrunk (prē′shruŋk′) ***adj.*** shrunk by a special process in manufacture so as to minimize shrinkage in laundering or dry cleaning

pre·side (pri zīd′) ***vi.*** **-sid′ed, -sid′ing** [< Fr. < L. *praesidere* < *prae-*, before + *sedere*, to sit] **1.** to be in charge of an assembly; act as chairman **2.** to have authority, control, etc. (usually with *over*) —**pre·sid′er** ***n.***

pres·i·den·cy (prez′i dən sē) ***n.***, *pl.* **-cies** **1.** the office, function, or term of president **2.** [*often* **P-**] the office of President of the U.S.

pres·i·dent (prez′i dənt) ***n.*** [< MFr. < L. prp. of *praesidere*: see PRESIDE] **1.** the highest executive officer of a company, society, university, club, etc. **2.** [*often* **P-**] the chief executive, or sometimes the formal head, of a republic **3.** any presiding officer —**pres′i·den′tial** (-den′shəl) ***adj.*** —**pres′i·den′tial·ly** ***adv.***

pres·i·dent-e·lect (-i lekt′) ***n.*** an elected president who has not yet taken office

pre·sid·i·o (pri sid′ē ō′) ***n.***, *pl.* **-i·os** [Sp. < L. *praesidium*] a military post, esp. in the SW U.S.

pre·sid·i·um (pri sid′ē əm) ***n.***, *pl.* **-i·a** (-ə), **-i·ums** [< Russ. < L. *praesidium*, a presiding over] **1.** in the Soviet Union, *a)* any of a number of permanent administrative committees *b)* [**P-**] the permanent administrative committee of the Supreme Soviet **2.** [**P-**] a chief administrative committee as in Albania, Romania, etc.

pre·sig·ni·fy (prē sig′nə fī′) ***vt.*** **-fied′, -fy′ing** to indicate beforehand; foreshadow

press[1] (pres) ***vt.*** [< MFr. < L. *pressare*, freq. of *premere*, to press] **1.** to act on with steady force or weight; push steadily against; squeeze **2.** to squeeze (juice, etc.) from (grapes, etc.) **3.** *a)* to squeeze so as to make smooth, compact, etc.; compress *b)* to iron (clothes, etc.) with a heavy iron or a steam machine **4.** to embrace closely **5.** to force; compel; constrain **6.** to urge persistently; entreat **7.** to try to force acceptance of [she *pressed* the gift on us] **8.** to lay stress on; emphasize **9.** to distress or trouble [to be *pressed* for time] **10.** to urge on **11.** to shape (a phonograph record, plastic item, etc.), using a form **12.** [Archaic] to crowd; throng **13.** [Obs.] *same as* OPPRESS —***vi.*** **1.** to exert pressure; specif., *a)* to weigh down; bear heavily *b)* to go forward with determined effort *c)* to force one's way *d)* to crowd; throng *e)* to be urgent or insistent *f)* to try too hard **2.** to iron clothes, etc. **3.** to undergo pressing in a specified way —***n.*** **1.** a pressing or being pressed; pressure, urgency, etc. **2.** a crowd; throng **3.** an instrument or machine by which something is crushed, stamped, smoothed, etc. by pressure **4.** the condition of clothes as to smoothness, creases, etc. after pressing **5.** *a) clipped form of* PRINTING PRESS *b)* a printing or publishing establishment *c)* the art or business of printing *d)* newspapers, magazines, etc. or the persons who write for them *e)* publicity, criticism, etc., as in newspapers **6.** an upright closet for clothes, etc. —**go to press** to start to be printed —**press′er** ***n.***

press[2] (pres) ***vt.*** [altered (after prec.) < obs. *prest*, to enlist for military service by advance pay < OFr., ult. < L. *praes*, surety + *stare*, to stand] **1.** to force into service, esp. military or naval service **2.** to use in a way different from the ordinary, esp. in an emergency

press agent a person whose work is to get publicity for an individual, organization, etc. —**press′-a′gent·ry** ***n.***

press box a place reserved for reporters at sports events, etc.

press conference a collective interview granted to newsmen as by a celebrity or personage

press gang [for *prest gang*: see PRESS[2]] a group who round up others and force them into military or naval service

press·ing (pres′iŋ) ***adj.*** calling for immediate attention; urgent —***n.*** something stamped, squeezed, etc. with a press [a *pressing* of phonograph records] —**press′ing·ly** ***adv.***

press·man (-mən) ***n.***, *pl.* **-men** **1.** an operator of a printing press **2.** [Brit.] a newspaperman

press of sail (or canvas) the maximum amount of sail that a ship can safely carry under given conditions

pres·sure (presh′ər) ***n.*** [OFr. < L. *pressura* < pp. of *premere*, to PRESS[1]] **1.** a pressing or being pressed; compression; squeezing **2.** a state of distress or strain **3.** a feeling as though a part of the body is being compressed **4.** a compelling influence [social *pressure*] **5.** pressing demands; urgency **6.** *clipped form of: a)* AIR PRESSURE *b)* BLOOD PRESSURE **7.** *Physics* the force pressing against a surface, expressed in units of force per unit of area —***vt.*** **-sured, -sur·ing** to exert pressure on

pressure cooker an airtight container for quick cooking by steam under pressure —**pres′sure-cook′** ***vt.***

pressure group any group exerting pressure on legislators and the public through lobbies, propaganda, etc. to affect legislation, etc.

pressure suit a type of G-suit designed to maintain normal respiration and circulation, esp. in spaceflights

pres·sur·ize (presh′ər īz′) ***vt.*** **-ized′, -iz′ing** **1.** to keep nearly normal air pressure inside of (an airplane, spacesuit, etc.), as at high altitudes **2.** to subject to high pressure —**pres′sur·i·za′tion** ***n.*** —**pres′sur·iz′er** ***n.***

press·work (pres′wʉrk′) ***n.*** **1.** the operation of a printing press **2.** work done by a printing press

pres·ti·dig·i·ta·tion (pres′tə dij′i tā′shən) ***n.*** [Fr. < *preste* < It. *presto*, quick + L. *digitus*, a finger] the doing of tricks by quick, skillful use of the hands; sleight of hand —**pres′ti·dig′i·ta′tor** ***n.***

pres·tige (pres tēzh′, -tēj′) ***n.*** [Fr. < LL. *praestigium*, illusion, ult. < L. *praestringere*, to blind] **1.** the power to impress or influence, as because of success, wealth, etc. **2.** reputation based on high achievement, character, etc. —**pres·tige′ful, pres·ti′gious** (-tij′əs, -tē′jəs) ***adj.***

pres·tis·si·mo (pres tis′ə mō′) ***adv., adj.*** [It., superl. of *presto*: see ff.] *Music* very fast —***n.***, *pl.* **-mos′** a prestissimo passage or movement

pres·to (pres′tō) ***adv., adj.*** [It., quick < L. *praestus*, ready] **1.** fast **2.** *Music* in fast tempo —***n.***, *pl.* **-tos** *Music* a presto passage or movement

pre·stressed concrete (prē′strest′) concrete containing steel cables, wires, etc. under tension to produce compressive stress and lend greater strength

pre·sume (pri zo͞om′, -zyo͞om′) ***vt.*** **-sumed′, -sum′ing** [< OFr. < L. < *prae-*, before + *sumere*, to take] **1.** to take upon oneself without permission or authority; dare (to say or do something); venture **2.** to take for granted, lacking proof; suppose **3.** to constitute reasonable evidence for supposing [a signed invoice *presumes* receipt of goods]

—*vi.* **1.** to act presumptuously; take liberties **2.** to rely too much (*on* or *upon*), as in taking liberties —**pre·sum′a·ble** *adj.* —**pre·sum′a·bly** *adv.* —**pre·sum′ed·ly** *adv.*

pre·sump·tion (pri zump′shən) *n.* **1.** a presuming; specif., *a*) an overstepping of proper bounds; effrontery *b*) a taking of something for granted **2.** the thing presumed; supposition **3.** a ground or reason for presuming **4.** *Law* the inference that a fact exists, based on other known facts

pre·sump·tive (-tiv) *adj.* **1.** giving reasonable ground for belief [*presumptive* evidence] **2.** based on probability; presumed [an heir *presumptive*] —**pre·sump′tive·ly** *adv.*

pre·sump·tu·ous (-cho͞o wəs) *adj.* too bold or forward; overstepping proper bounds; showing presumption —**pre·sump′tu·ous·ly** *adv.* —**pre·sump′tu·ous·ness** *n.*

pre·sup·pose (prē′sə pōz′) *vt.* **-posed′, -pos′ing** **1.** to suppose or assume beforehand; take for granted **2.** to require or imply as a preceding condition —**pre′sup·po·si′tion** (-sup ə zish′ən) *n.*

pret. preterit

pre·tend (pri tend′) *vt.* [< MFr. < L. < *prae-*, before + *tendere*, to stretch] **1.** to claim; profess [to *pretend* ignorance of the law] **2.** to claim or profess falsely; feign [to *pretend* illness] **3.** to make believe, as in play [to *pretend* to be astronauts] —*vi.* **1.** to lay claim (with *to*) **2.** to make believe in play or deception —**pre·tend′ed** *adj.*

pre·tend·er (-ten′dər) *n.* **1.** a person who pretends **2.** a person who lays claim to something, esp. to a throne

pre·tense (pri tens′, prē′tens) *n.* [< Anglo-Fr., ult. < L. pp. of *praetendere:* see PRETEND] **1.** a claim; pretension [making no *pretense* to being rich] **2.** a false claim or profession [a *pretense* of friendship] **3.** a false show of something **4.** a pretending, as at play; make-believe **5.** a pretext **6.** pretentiousness Also, Brit. sp., **pretence**

pre·ten·sion (pri ten′shən) *n.* [< ML. < L.: see prec.] **1.** a pretext or allegation **2.** a claim, as to a right, title, etc. **3.** assertion of a claim **4.** pretentiousness

pre·ten·tious (-shəs) *adj.* [< Fr.] claiming or pretending to be more important, elegant, etc. than is really so; affectedly grand; ostentatious —**pre·ten′tious·ly** *adv.* —**pre·ten′tious·ness** *n.*

pret·er·it, pret·er·ite (pret′ər it) *adj.* [< MFr. < L. pp. of *praeterire* < *praeter-*, beyond + *ire*, to go] *Gram.* expressing past action or state —*n.* **1.** the past tense **2.** a verb in this tense

pre·ter·mit (prēt′ər mit′) *vt.* **-mit′ted, -mit′ting** [< L. < *praeter-*, beyond + *mittere*, to send] to neglect, omit, or overlook —**pre′ter·mis′sion** *n.*

pre·ter·nat·u·ral (-nach′ər əl) *adj.* [< ML. < L. *praeter-*, beyond + *naturalis*, natural] **1.** differing from or beyond what is natural; abnormal **2.** *same as* SUPERNATURAL —**pre′ter·nat′u·ral·ism** *n.* —**pre′ter·nat′u·ral·ly** *adv.*

pre·test (prē′test′; *for v.* prē′test′) *n.* a preliminary test, as of a product —*vt., vi.* to test in advance

pre·text (prē′tekst) *n.* [< L. pp. of *praetexere*, to pretend: see PRE- & TEXTURE] **1.** a false reason or motive put forth to hide the real one; excuse **2.** a cover-up; front

pre·tor (prēt′ər) *n. same as* PRAETOR —**pre·to·ri·al** (pri tôr′ē əl) *adj.* —**pre·to′ri·an** *adj., n.*

Pre·to·ri·a (pri tôr′ē ə) capital of the Transvaal & the seat of the government of South Africa: pop. 493,000

pre·tri·al (prē′trī′əl) *adj.* occurring, presented, etc. before a court trial begins [a *pretrial* motion]

pret·ti·fy (prit′ə fī′) *vt.* **-fied′, -fy′ing** to make pretty

pret·ty (prit′ē, pur′tē) *adj.* **-ti·er, -ti·est** [< OE. *prætig*, crafty < *prætt*, a trick] **1.** pleasing or attractive, esp. in a light, dainty, or graceful way **2.** *a*) fine; nice: often used ironically [a *pretty* fix] *b*) skillful [a *pretty* move] **3.** [Colloq.] considerable; quite large [a *pretty* price] —*adv.* **1.** fairly; somewhat; quite [*pretty* sure] **2.** [Colloq.] prettily [to talk *pretty*] —*n., pl.* **-ties** a pretty person or thing —*vt.* **-tied, -ty·ing** to make pretty (usually with *up*) —**sitting pretty** [Slang] in a favorable position —**pret′ti·ly** *adv.* —**pret′ti·ness** *n.* —**pret′ty·ish** *adj.*

pret·zel (pret′s′l) *n.* [G. *brezel* < OHG., ult. < L. *brachium*, an arm] a hard, brittle biscuit usually in the form of a loose knot or stick, sprinkled with salt

PRETZEL

pre·vail (pri vāl′) *vi.* [< L. < *prae-*, before + *valere*, to be strong] **1.** to gain the advantage or mastery; be victorious (*over* or *against*) **2.** to be effective; succeed **3.** to be or become stronger or more widespread; predominate **4.** to exist widely; be prevalent —**prevail on** (or **upon, with**) to persuade; induce

pre·vail·ing (-iŋ) *adj.* **1.** superior in strength, influence, or effect **2.** most frequent; predominant **3.** widely existing; prevalent —**pre·vail′ing·ly** *adv.*

prev·a·lent (prev′ə lənt) *adj.* [see PREVAIL] **1.** [Rare] dominant **2.** widely existing, practiced, or accepted; common —**prev′a·lence** *n.* —**prev′a·lent·ly** *adv.*

pre·var·i·cate (pri var′ə kāt′) *vi.* **-cat′ed, -cat′ing** [< L. pp. of *praevaricari*, lit., to walk crookedly < *prae-*, before + *varicare*, to straddle, ult. < *varus*, bent] **1.** to turn aside from, or evade, the truth; equivocate **2.** to tell an untruth; lie —**pre·var′i·ca′tion** *n.* —**pre·var′i·ca′tor** *n.*

pre·vent (pri vent′) *vt.* [< L. pp. of *praevenire* < *prae-*, before + *venire*, to come] **1.** to stop or keep (*from* doing something) **2.** to keep from happening; make impossible by prior action; hinder —**pre·vent′a·ble, pre·vent′i·ble** *adj.* —**pre·vent′er** *n.*

pre·ven·tion (pri ven′shən) *n.* **1.** a preventing **2.** [Now Rare] a means of preventing; preventive

pre·ven·tive (-tiv) *adj.* preventing or serving to prevent; esp., preventing disease —*n.* anything that prevents; esp., anything that prevents disease; prophylactic Also **pre·vent′a·tive** —**pre·ven′tive·ly** *adv.* —**pre·ven′tive·ness** *n.*

pre·view (prē′vyo͞o) *vt.* to view or show beforehand —*n.* **1.** a previous or preliminary view or survey **2.** *a*) a restricted showing, as of a movie, before exhibition to the public generally *b*) a showing of scenes from a movie, TV show, etc. to advertise it

pre·vi·ous (prē′vē əs) *adj.* [< L. < *prae-*, before + *via*, a way] **1.** occurring before in time or order; prior **2.** [Colloq.] too soon; premature —**previous to** before —**pre′vi·ous·ly** *adv.*

previous question the question, put as a motion, whether a matter under consideration by a parliamentary body should be voted on immediately

pre·vi·sion (prē vizh′ən) *n.* [< Fr. < ML. < L. pp. of *praevidere* < *prae-*, before + *videre*, to see] **1.** foresight or foreknowledge **2.** a prediction or prophecy —*vt.* to foresee —**pre·vi′sion·al, pre·vi′sion·ar′y** *adj.*

pre·vue (prē′vyo͞o) *n. same as* PREVIEW (esp. sense 2)

pre·war (prē′wôr′) *adj.* before a (or the) war

prex·y (prek′sē) *n., pl.* **prex′ies** [Slang] the president, esp. of a college, etc.

prey (prā) *n.* [OFr. *preie* < L. *praeda*] **1.** orig., plunder; booty **2.** an animal hunted for food by another animal **3.** a person or thing that falls victim to someone or something **4.** the mode of living by preying on other animals [a bird of *prey*] —*vi.* **1.** to plunder; rob **2.** to hunt other animals for food **3.** to profit by swindling **4.** to have a wearing or destructive influence Generally used with *on* or *upon* —**prey′er** *n.*

Pri·am (prī′əm) *Gr. Legend* the last king of Troy, who reigned during the Trojan War: father of Hector and Paris

pri·ap·ic (prī ap′ik) *adj.* [< PRIAPUS + -IC] **1.** *same as* PHALLIC **2.** overly concerned with one's virility

Pri·a·pus (prī ā′pəs) [L. < Gr.] *Gr. & Rom. Myth.* the god personifying the male procreative power

price (prīs) *n.* [< OFr. < L. *pretium*] **1.** the amount of money, etc. asked or paid for something; cost **2.** value or worth **3.** a reward for the capture or death of a person **4.** the cost, as in life, labor, etc., of obtaining some benefit —*vt.* **priced, pric′ing** **1.** to fix the price of **2.** [Colloq.] to ask or find out the price of —**at any price** no matter what the cost —**beyond** (or **without**) **price** priceless; invaluable —**pric′er** *n.*

price control the setting of ceiling prices on basic commodities by a government, as to fight inflation

price index *see* INDEX (sense 5 *b*)

price·less (prīs′lis) *adj.* **1.** too valuable to be measured by price **2.** [Colloq.] very amusing or absurd

prick (prik) *n.* [OE. *prica*, a dot] **1.** a very small puncture or dot made by a sharp point **2.** [Archaic] a pointed object, as a thorn **3.** a pricking **4.** a sharp pain caused as by being pricked —*vt.* **1.** to make (a tiny hole) in (something) with a sharp point **2.** to pain sharply [*pricked* by remorse] **3.** to mark by dots, points, or punctures **4.** to cause to point or stick up (with *up*) **5.** [Archaic] to goad —*vi.* **1.** to cause or feel a slight, sharp pain **2.** to point or stick up: said esp. of ears —**prick up one's ears** to listen closely —**prick′er** *n.*

prick·le (prik′'l) *n.* [OE. *pricel* < base of *prica*, prick] **1.** any sharp point; specif., a thornlike process on a plant **2.** a prickly sensation; tingling —*vt.* **-led, -ling** **1.** to prick as with a thorn **2.** to cause to feel a tingling sensation —*vi.* to tingle

prick·ly (-lē) *adj.* **-li·er, -li·est** **1.** full of prickles **2.** stinging; tingling —**prick′li·ness** *n.*

prickly heat an itching skin disease with small eruptions caused by inflammation of the sweat glands

prickly pear **1.** any of various cactus plants, some of

which have barbed spines **2.** its pear-shaped, edible fruit
pride (prīd) ***n.*** [OE. *pryte* < *prut,* proud] **1.** *a)* an overhigh opinion of oneself; exaggerated self-esteem *b)* haughtiness; arrogance **2.** a sense of one's own dignity; self-respect **3.** delight or satisfaction in one's achievements, one's children, etc. **4.** a person or thing that one is proud of **5.** the best of a class, group, etc.; pick **6.** the best part; prime *[in the pride of manhood]* **7.** *a)* a group or family (of lions) *b)* [Colloq.] any impressive group —***vt.*** **prid'ed, prid'ing** [Rare] to make proud —**pride oneself on** to be proud of —**pride'ful** ***adj.*** —**pride'ful·ly** ***adv.*** —**pride'ful·ness** ***n.***
prie-dieu (prē'dyōō') ***n.*** [Fr. < *prier,* to pray + *dieu,* God] a narrow, upright frame with a ledge for kneeling on at prayer and an upper ledge, as for a book
pri·er (prī'ər) ***n.*** a person who pries
priest (prēst) ***n.*** [OE. *preost* < LL. *presbyter,* an elder < Gr. < *presbys,* old] **1.** a person whose function is to make sacrificial offerings and perform other religious rites **2.** in some Christian churches, a clergyman authorized to administer the sacraments **3.** any clergyman —**priest'hood'** ***n.*** —**priest'li·ness** ***n.*** —**priest'ly** ***adj.*** **-li·er, -li·est**
priest·ess (prēs'tis) ***n.*** a girl or woman priest, esp. of a pagan religion
Priest·ley (prēst'lē), **Joseph** 1733–1804; Eng. scientist & theologian: discoverer of oxygen
prig (prig) ***n.*** [< 16th-c. slang] an annoying person who is excessively proper and smug in his moral behavior and attitudes —**prig'ger·y, prig'gism** ***n.*** —**prig'gish** ***adj.*** —**prig'gish·ly** ***adv.*** —**prig'gish·ness** ***n.***
prim (prim) ***adj.*** **prim'mer, prim'mest** [< ? MFr. *prim,* prime, sharp, neat < L. *primus,* first] stiffly formal, precise, moral, etc.; proper; demure —***vt., vi.*** **primmed, prim'ming** to get a prim look on (one's face or mouth) —**prim'ly** ***adv.*** —**prim'ness** ***n.***
prim. **1.** primary **2.** primitive
pri·ma ballerina (prē'mə) [It., lit., first ballerina] the principal woman dancer in a ballet company
pri·ma·cy (prī'mə sē) ***n.,*** *pl.* **-cies** [< MFr. < ML. < LL. *primas:* see PRIMATE] **1.** the state of being first in time, order, rank, etc. **2.** the rank or authority of a primate
pri·ma don·na (prē'mə dän'ə, prim'ə) *pl.* **pri'ma don'nas** [It., lit., first lady] **1.** the principal woman singer, as in an opera **2.** [Colloq.] a temperamental or arrogant person
pri·ma fa·ci·e (prī'mə fā'shi ē', fā'shē) [L.] at first sight: used to designate legal evidence (**prima facie evidence**) that is enough to establish a fact unless refuted
pri·mal (prī'm'l) ***adj.*** [< ML. < L. *primus,* first] **1.** first in time; original **2.** first in importance; chief
primal therapy a treatment of mental disorder in which the patient, often in group sessions, is induced to reenact his infancy and to express his emotions violently in screams, shouts, etc.: also **primal scream (therapy)**
pri·ma·quine (prī'mə kwēn') ***n.*** a synthetic chemical compound, $C_{15}H_{21}N_3O$, used as a cure for malaria
pri·ma·ri·ly (prī mer'ə lē, prī'mer'-) ***adv.*** **1.** at first; originally **2.** mainly; principally
pri·ma·ry (prī'mer'ē, -mər ē) ***adj.*** [< L. *primarius* < *primus,* first] **1.** first in time or order of development; primitive; original **2.** *a)* from which others are derived; fundamental *b)* designating colors regarded as basic, from which all others may be derived: see COLOR (*n.* 2 & 3) **3.** first in importance; chief; principal *[a primary concern]* **4.** firsthand; direct *[a primary source of information]* **5.** *Elec.* designating or of an inducing current, input circuit, or input coil in a transformer, etc. **6.** *Zool.* of the large feathers on the end joint of a bird's wing —***n.,*** *pl.* **-ries** **1.** something first in order, quality, etc. **2.** in the U.S., *a)* a local meeting of voters of a given political party to nominate candidates for public office, etc. *b) same as* DIRECT PRIMARY ELECTION **3.** any of the primary colors **4.** *Elec.* a primary coil **5.** *Zool.* a primary feather
primary accent (or **stress**) **1.** the heavier stress or force given to one syllable in a spoken word or to one word in an utterance **2.** the mark to show this (')
primary cell a battery cell whose energy is derived from an essentially irreversible electrochemical reaction
primary school *same as* ELEMENTARY SCHOOL
pri·mate (prī'māt; *also, for 1,* -mit) ***n.*** [< OFr. < LL. *primas* (gen. *primatis*), chief < L. *primus,* first] **1.** an archbishop, or the highest-ranking bishop in a province, etc. **2.** any of an order of mammals, including man, the apes, monkeys, etc. —**pri'mate·ship'** ***n.*** —**pri·ma·tial** (prī mā'shəl) ***adj.***
prime (prīm) ***adj.*** [MFr. < L. *primus,* first < OL. *pri,* before] **1.** first in time; original; primitive **2.** first in rank; chief *[prime minister]* **3.** first in importance; principal *[a prime advantage]* **4.** first in quality; first-rate *[prime beef]* **5.** from which others are derived; fundamental **6.** *Finance* designating the most favorable interest rate on bank loans **7.** *Math. a)* of or being a prime number *b)* having no factor in common except 1 *[9 and 16 are prime to each other]* —***n.*** [OE. *prim* < L. *prima (hora),* first (hour): see the *adj.*] **1.** [*often* **P-**] the first daylight canonical hour **2.** the first or earliest part; dawn, springtime, youth, etc. **3.** *a)* the best or most vigorous period or stage of a person or thing *b)* the best part; pick **4.** *a)* any of a number of equal parts, usually sixty, into which a unit, as a degree, is divided *b)* the mark (') indicating this: it is also used to distinguish a letter, etc. from another of the same kind, as A' **5.** *Math. same as* PRIME NUMBER **6.** *Music same as* UNISON —***vt.*** **primed, prim'ing** **1.** to make ready; prepare **2.** to prepare (a gun) for firing or (a charge) for exploding by providing with priming or a primer **3.** *a)* to get (a pump) into operation by pouring in water *b)* to get (an empty carburetor) into operation by pouring in gasoline **4.** to undercoat, size, etc. (a surface) for painting **5.** to provide (a person) beforehand with information, answers, etc. —***vi.*** to prime a person or thing —**prime'ness** ***n.***
prime meridian the meridian from which longitude is measured east and west; 0° longitude: see GREENWICH TIME
prime minister in parliamentary governments, the chief executive and, usually, head of the cabinet —**prime ministry**
prime number an integer that can be evenly divided by no other whole number than itself and 1, as 2, 3, 5, or 7
prim·er[1] (prim'ər; *Brit.* prī'mər) ***n.*** [< ML. < L. *primus,* first] **1.** a simple book for first teaching children to read **2.** a textbook giving the first principles of any subject
prim·er[2] (prī'mər) ***n.*** a person or thing that primes; specif., *a)* a small cap, tube, etc. containing an explosive, used to set off the main charge *b)* a preliminary coat of paint, etc.
prime time *Radio & TV* the hours, esp. the evening hours, when the largest audience is readily available
pri·me·val (prī mē'v'l) ***adj.*** [< L. *primaevus* (< primus, first + *aevum,* an age) + -AL] of the earliest times or ages; primordial —**pri·me'val·ly** ***adv.***
prim·ing (prī'miŋ) ***n.*** **1.** the explosive used to set off the charge in a gun, etc. **2.** paint, sizing, etc. used as a primer
prim·i·tive (prim'ə tiv) ***adj.*** [< MFr. < L. *primitivus* < *primus,* first] **1.** of or existing in the earliest times or ages; original **2.** *a)* characteristic of the earliest ages *b)* crude, simple, etc. **3.** not derivative; primary —***n.*** **1.** a primitive person or thing **2.** *a)* an artist or a work of art of an early culture *b)* an artist or a work of art characterized by lack of formal training —**prim'i·tive·ly** ***adv.*** —**prim'i·tive·ness** ***n.***
prim·i·tiv·ism (-iz'm) ***n.*** **1.** belief in or practice of primitive ways, living, etc. **2.** the qualities, etc. of primitive art or artists —**prim'i·tiv·ist** ***n., adj.***
pri·mo·gen·i·tor (prī'mə jen'i tər) ***n.*** [LL. < L. *primus,* first + *genitor,* a father] **1.** an ancestor; forefather **2.** the earliest ancestor of a family, race, etc.
pri·mo·gen·i·ture (-chər) ***n.*** [< ML. < L. *primus,* first + *genitura,* a begetting] **1.** the condition or fact of being the firstborn of the same parents **2.** *Law* the exclusive right of the eldest son to inherit his father's estate
pri·mor·di·al (prī môr'dē əl) ***adj.*** [< LL. < L. *primordium,* the beginning < *primus,* first + *ordiri,* to begin] **1.** existing at or from the beginning; primitive **2.** fundamental; original —**pri·mor'di·al·ly** ***adv.***
primp (primp) ***vt., vi.*** [prob. extension of PRIM] to groom or dress up in a fussy way
prim·rose (prim'rōz') ***n.*** [< MFr. altered (after *rose,* ROSE[1]) < OFr. *primerole* < ML. *primula* < L. *primus,* first] **1.** any of a number of related plants having variously colored, tubelike flowers: also **prim'u·la** (-yoo lə) **2.** the flower of any of these plants **3.** the light yellow of some primroses —***adj.*** **1.** of the primrose **2.** light-yellow
primrose path [cf. *Hamlet* I, iii] the path of pleasure, self-indulgence, etc.
prin. **1.** principal **2.** principle
prince (prins) ***n.*** [OFr. < L. *princeps,* chief < *primus,* first + *capere,* to take] **1.** orig., any male monarch; esp., a king **2.** a ruler whose rank is below that of a king; head of a principality **3.** a nonreigning male member of a royal family **4.** in Great Britain, a son or grandson of the sovereign **5.** *a)* a preeminent person in any class or group *[a merchant prince]* *b)* [Colloq.] a fine, generous, helpful fellow —**prince'dom** ***n.***
Prince Albert a long, double-breasted frock coat
prince consort the husband of a queen or empress reigning in her own right
Prince Edward Island island province of SE Canada, in the Gulf of St. Lawrence: 2,184 sq. mi.; pop. 118,000; cap. Charlottetown: abbrev. **P.E.I.**
prince·ling (prins'liŋ) ***n.*** a young, small, or subordinate prince: also **prince'kin, prince'let**
prince·ly (-lē) ***adj.*** **-li·er, -li·est** **1.** of a prince; royal **2.** characteristic or worthy of a prince; magnificent; generous
Prince of Darkness *a name sometimes given to* SATAN
Prince of Peace *a name sometimes given to* JESUS
Prince of Wales *title conferred on* the oldest son and heir apparent of a British king or queen

prin·cess[1] (prin′sis, -ses) ***n.*** **1.** orig., any female monarch **2.** a nonreigning female member of a royal family **3.** in Great Britain, a daughter of the sovereign or of a son of the sovereign **4.** the wife of a prince

prin·cess[2] (prin′sis, prin ses′) ***adj.*** [< Fr. *princesse*, a princess] of or designating a woman's one-piece, closefitting, gored dress, etc.: also **prin·cesse′** (-ses′)

Prince·ton (prins′tən) [after the *Prince* of Orange, later WILLIAM III] borough in C N.J., near Trenton: scene of a battle of the Revolutionary War: pop. 12,000

prin·ci·pal (prin′sə pəl) ***adj.*** [OFr. < L. *principalis* < *princeps:* see PRINCE] **1.** first in rank, authority, importance, etc. **2.** that is or has to do with principal (*n.* 3) —***n.*** **1.** a principal person or thing; specif., *a)* a chief; head *b)* a governing officer, as of a school *c)* a main actor or other kind of performer **2.** any of the main end rafters of a roof **3.** *Finance a)* the amount of a debt, investment, etc. minus the interest *b)* the face value of a stock or bond *c)* the main portion of an estate, etc., as distinguished from income **4.** *Law a)* one who employs another to act as his agent *b)* the one primarily responsible for an obligation *c)* one who commits a crime: cf. ACCESSORY —**prin′ci·pal·ly** ***adv.*** —**prin′ci·pal·ship′** ***n.***

prin·ci·pal·i·ty (prin′sə pal′ə tē) ***n.,*** *pl.* **-ties** **1.** the rank, dignity, or jurisdiction of a prince **2.** the territory ruled by a prince

principal parts the principal inflected forms of a verb, from which the other forms may be derived: in English, they are the present infinitive, the past tense, the past participle, and, sometimes, the present participle (Ex.: *drink, drank, drunk, drinking; go, went, gone, going*)

Prín·ci·pe (prin′sə pē′; *Port.* prēn′sə pə) see SÃO TOMÉ

prin·ci·ple (prin′sə pəl) ***n.*** [< MFr. < L. *principium* < *princeps:* see PRINCE] **1.** the ultimate source or cause **2.** a natural or original tendency, faculty, etc. **3.** a fundamental truth, law, etc., upon which others are based [moral *principles*] **4.** *a)* a rule of conduct *b)* such rules collectively *c)* adherence to them; integrity [a man of *principle*] **5.** an essential element or quality [the active *principle* of a medicine] **6.** *a)* the scientific law that explains a natural action [the *principle* of cell division] *b)* the method of a thing's operation —**in principle** theoretically or in essence

prin·ci·pled (-pəld) ***adj.*** having or based on principles, as of conduct

prink (priŋk) ***vt., vi.*** [prob. < PRANK[2]] *same as* PRIMP

print (print) ***n.*** [< OFr. < pp. of *preindre* < L. *premere*, to PRESS[1]] **1.** a mark made on a surface by pressing or hitting with an object; imprint [the *print* of a heel] **2.** an object for making such a mark, as a stamp, die, etc. **3.** a cloth printed with a design, or a dress, blouse, etc. made of this **4.** the condition of being printed **5.** printed lettering **6.** the impression made by inked type **7.** a picture or design printed from a plate, block, etc., as an etching or lithograph **8.** printed material [*newsprint*] **9.** a photograph, esp. one made from a negative —***vt.*** **1.** to make a print on or in **2.** to stamp or draw, trace, etc. (a mark, letter, etc.) on or in a surface **3.** to produce on (paper, etc.) the impression of inked type, plates, etc. by means of a printing press **4.** to produce (a book, etc.) by typesetting, presswork, etc. **5.** to publish in print [to *print* a story] **6.** to write in letters resembling printed ones **7.** to produce (a photograph) from (a negative) **8.** in computers, to deliver (information) by means of a printer: often with *out* **9.** to impress upon the mind, memory, etc. —***vi.*** **1.** to practice the trade of a printer **2.** to produce an impression, photograph, etc. **3.** to write in letters resembling printed ones **4.** to produce newspapers, books, etc. by means of a printing press —**in** (or **out of**) **print** still (or no longer) for sale by the publisher: said of books, etc. —**print′a·ble** ***adj.***

printed circuit an electrical circuit formed by applying conductive material in fine lines or other shapes to an insulating surface

print·er (-ər) ***n.*** **1.** one whose work or business is printing **2.** a device that prints; esp., in computers, a device that produces information in printed form

printer's devil an apprentice in a printing shop

print·ing (-iŋ) ***n.*** **1.** the act of a person or thing that prints **2.** the production of printed matter **3.** the art of a printer **4.** something printed **5.** *same as* IMPRESSION (sense 5 *b*) **6.** written letters made like printed ones

printing press a machine for printing from inked type, plates, or rolls

print·out (-out′) ***n.*** the output of a computer presented in printed or typewritten form

print shop **1.** a shop where printing is done: also **printing office** **2.** a shop where prints, etchings, etc. are sold

pri·or (prī′ər) ***adj.*** [L., former, superior] **1.** preceding in time; earlier **2.** preceding in order or importance [a *prior* choice] —***n.*** [OE. & OFr., both < ML. < L.] **1.** the head of a priory **2.** in an abbey, the person in charge next below the abbot —**prior to** before in time —**pri′or·ate** (-it), **pri′or·ship′** ***n.*** —**pri′or·ess** ***n.fem.***

pri·or·i·tize (prī ôr′ə tīz′, -är′-) ***vt.*** **-tized′, -tiz′ing** **1.** to arrange (items) in order of priority **2.** to assign (an item) to a particular level of priority

pri·or·i·ty (prī ôr′ə tē, -är′-) ***n.,*** *pl.* **-ties** **1.** a being prior; precedence **2.** *a)* a right to precedence over others in obtaining, buying, or doing something *b)* an order granting this **3.** something given or to be given prior attention

pri·o·ry (prī′ər ē) ***n.,*** *pl.* **-ries** a monastery governed by a prior, or a convent governed by a prioress

Pris·cil·la (pri sil′ə) [L., ult. < *priscus*, ancient] a feminine name

prise (prīz) ***vt.*** **prised, pris′ing** [Chiefly Brit.] to prize, or pry, as with a lever

prism (priz′'m) ***n.*** [< LL. < Gr. *prisma*, lit., something sawed < *prizein*, to saw] **1.** a solid figure whose ends are equal and parallel polygons and whose sides are parallelograms **2.** anything that refracts light, as a drop of water **3.** *Optics a)* a transparent body, as of glass, whose ends are equal and parallel triangles, and whose three sides are parallelograms: used for refracting or dispersing light, as into the spectrum *b)* any similar body of three or more sides

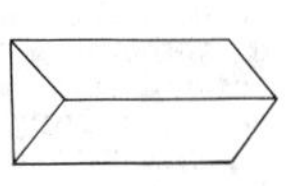
TRIANGULAR PRISM

pris·mat·ic (priz mat′ik) ***adj.*** **1.** of or like a prism **2.** that refracts light as a prism **3.** that forms prismatic colors **4.** many-colored; brilliant —**pris·mat′i·cal·ly** ***adv.***

prismatic colors the colors of the visible spectrum; red, orange, yellow, green, blue, indigo, and violet

pris·on (priz′'n) ***n.*** [OFr. < L. *prensio*, for *prehensio* < *prehendere*, to take] **1.** a place where persons are confined **2.** a building, usually with cells, where persons convicted by trial or awaiting trial are confined; specif., such a building maintained by a State or the Federal government **3.** imprisonment

pris·on·er (priz′nər, -'n ər) ***n.*** **1.** a person confined in prison, as for some crime **2.** a person held in custody **3.** a person captured or held captive [a *prisoner* of love]

prisoner of war a member of the regular or irregular armed forces of a nation at war held captive by the enemy

pris·sy (pris′ē) ***adj.*** **-si·er, -si·est** [prob. PR(IM) + (S)ISSY] [Colloq.] very prim or precise; fussy, prudish, etc. —**pris′si·ly** ***adv.*** —**pris′si·ness** ***n.***

pris·tine (pris′tēn, -tin; pris tēn′) ***adj.*** [L. *pristinus*, former] **1.** characteristic of the earliest period or condition; original **2.** still pure; uncorrupted; unspoiled [*pristine* beauty] —**pris′tine·ly** ***adv.***

prith·ee (prith′ē) ***interj.*** [< *pray thee*] [Archaic] I pray thee; please

pri·va·cy (prī′və sē; *Brit. also* priv′ə-) ***n.,*** *pl.* **-cies** **1.** the quality or condition of being private; withdrawal from public view **2.** secrecy [told in strict *privacy*] **3.** one's private life or personal affairs [an invasion of one's *privacy*]

pri·vate (prī′vit) ***adj.*** [< L. *privatus*, belonging to oneself, ult. < *privus*, separate] **1.** of or concerning only one particular person or group; not general [*private* property, his *private* affairs] **2.** not open to or controlled by the public [a *private* school] **3.** for an individual person [a *private* room] **4.** not holding public office [a *private* citizen] **5.** away from public view; secluded [a *private dining room*] **6.** secret; confidential [a *private* matter] **7.** not connected with an institution or organization; independent [*private* medical practice; a *private* detective] —***n.*** an enlisted man of either of the two lowest ranks in the U.S. Army or of the lowest rank in the U.S. Marine Corps —**in private** not publicly —**pri′vate·ly** ***adv.***

private enterprise *same as* FREE ENTERPRISE

pri·va·teer (prī′və tir′) ***n.*** [< PRIVAT(E) + -EER] **1.** a privately owned and manned armed ship commissioned in a war to attack and capture enemy ships, esp. merchant ships **2.** a commander or crew member of a privateer: also **pri′va·teers′man,** *pl.* **-men** —***vi.*** to sail as a privateer

private eye [Slang] a private detective

private first class an enlisted man ranking just below a corporal in the U.S. Army and just below a lance corporal in the U.S. Marine Corps

pri·va·tion (prī vā′shən) ***n.*** [< L. *privatio:* see PRIVATE] **1.** deprivation; the loss or absence of some quality or condition **2.** lack of the ordinary necessities of life

priv·a·tive (priv′ə tiv) ***adj.*** **1.** depriving or tending to deprive **2.** *Gram.* indicating negation, absence, or loss —*n.* *Gram.* a privative term or affix, as *a-*, *un-*, *non-*, or *-less* —**priv′a·tive·ly** *adv.*

priv·et (priv′it) *n.* [< ?] any of various shrubs of the olive family, with bluish-black berries and white flowers

priv·i·lege (priv′'l ij, priv′lij) *n.* [< OFr. < L. *privilegium*, a law for or against an individual < *privus*, separate + *lex* (gen. *legis*), a law] **1.** a right, advantage, favor, etc. specially granted to a certain person, group, or class **2.** a basic civil right, guaranteed by a government [the *privilege* of trial by jury] —*vt.* **-leged, -leg·ing** to grant a privilege to

priv·y (priv′ē) *adj.* [< OFr. < L. *privatus*, PRIVATE] **1.** orig., private; personal **2.** [Archaic] hidden, secret, etc. —*n.*, *pl.* **priv′ies** a toilet; esp., an outhouse —**privy to** privately informed about —**priv′i·ly** *adv.*

privy council a body of advisers or confidential counselors appointed by or serving a ruler —**privy councilor**

privy seal in Great Britain, the seal placed on documents which later receive the great seal or which are not important enough to receive it

prize[1] (prīz) *vt.* **prized, priz′ing** [see PRICE] **1.** formerly, to price or appraise **2.** to value highly; esteem —*n.* **1.** something offered or given to the winner of a contest, lottery, etc. **2.** a reward, premium, etc. **3.** anything worth striving for; any highly valued possession —*adj.* **1.** that has received a prize **2.** worthy of a prize **3.** given as a prize

prize[2] (prīz) *n.* [< OFr. *prise*, fem. pp. of *prendre* < L. *prehendere*, to take] something taken by force, as in war; esp., a captured enemy warship —*vt.* **prized, priz′ing 1.** to seize as a prize of war **2.** to pry, as with a lever

prize court a court that decides how captured property, esp. that taken at sea in wartime, is to be distributed

prize·fight (prīz′fīt′) *n.* a professional boxing match —**prize′fight′er** *n.* —**prize′fight′ing** *n.*

prize ring 1. a square platform, enclosed by ropes, for prizefights **2.** prizefighting

pro[1] (prō) *adv.* [L., for] on the affirmative side; favorably —*adj.* favorable —*prep.* in favor of; for —*n.*, *pl.* **pros** a reason, vote, position, etc. in favor of something

pro[2] (prō) *adj.*, *n.*, *pl.* **pros** *short form of* PROFESSIONAL

pro-[1] [Gr. < *pro*, before] *a prefix meaning* before in place or time [*proboscis*]

pro-[2] [L. < *pro*, forward] *a prefix meaning:* **1.** forward or ahead [*progress*] **2.** forth [*produce*] **3.** substituting for, acting for [*pronoun*] **4.** supporting, favoring [*prolabor*]

pro·a (prō′ə) *n.* [Malay *prau*] a Malayan boat having a triangular sail and one outrigger

PROA

prob. 1. probable **2.** probably **3.** problem

prob·a·bil·i·ty (präb′ə-bil′ə tē) *n.*, *pl.* **-ties 1.** the quality or state of being probable; likelihood **2.** a probable thing or event **3.** *Math.* the ratio of the number of times a particular event can occur to the total number of likely events involved —**in all probability** very likely

prob·a·ble (präb′ə b'l) *adj.* [MFr. < L. < *probare*, to prove] **1.** likely to occur or be; that can reasonably but not certainly be expected [the *probable* winner] **2.** reasonably so, as on the basis of evidence, but not proved [the *probable* cause of a disease] —**prob′a·bly** *adv.*

pro·bate (prō′bāt) *n.* [< L. pp. of *probare:* see PROBE] **1.** the act or process of proving or establishing that a document submitted for official certification and registration, as a will, is genuine **2.** all matters coming under the jurisdiction of probate courts —*adj.* having to do with probate or a probate court —*vt.* **-bat·ed, -bat·ing 1.** to establish officially the genuineness or validity of (a will) **2.** popularly, to certify in a probate court as mentally unsound —**pro′ba·tive** (-bə tiv, präb′ə-), **pro′ba·to′ry** (-tôr′ē) *adj.*

probate court a court having jurisdiction over the probating of wills, the administration of estates, and, usually, the guardianship of minors and incompetents

pro·ba·tion (prō bā′shən) *n.* [< OFr. < L. < *probare:* see PROBE] **1.** a testing or trial, as of a person's character, fitness for a position, etc. **2.** the suspension of sentence of a person convicted but not imprisoned, on condition of continued good behavior and regular reporting to a probation officer **3.** *a)* the status of a person being tested or on trial *b)* the period of testing or trial —**pro·ba′tion·ar′y, pro·ba′tion·al** *adj.*

pro·ba·tion·er (-ər) *n.* a person on probation

probation officer an officer appointed by a court to supervise persons placed on probation

probe (prōb) *n.* [LL. *proba*, proof < L. *probare*, to test < *probus*, proper] **1.** a slender, blunt surgical instrument for exploring a wound or the like **2.** the act of probing **3.** a searching examination; specif., *a)* an investigation, as by a legislative committee, into corruption, etc. *b)* an exploratory survey **4.** an instrumented spacecraft for exploring the upper atmosphere, outer space, another planet, etc. —*vt.* **probed, prob′ing 1.** to explore (a wound, etc.) with a probe **2.** to examine or investigate thoroughly —*vi.* to search; investigate —**prob′er** *n.*

prob·i·ty (prō′bə tē, präb′ə-) *n.* [< L. < *probus*, good] uprightness; honesty; integrity

prob·lem (präb′ləm) *n.* [< MFr. < L. < Gr. *problēma* < *pro-*, forward + *ballein*, to throw] **1.** a question or matter to be thought about or worked out [a math *problem*] **2.** a matter, person, etc. that is perplexing or difficult —*adj.* **1.** depicting a social problem [a *problem* play] **2.** very difficult to deal with, esp. to train or discipline [a *problem* child]

prob·lem·at·ic (präb′lə mat′ik) *adj.* **1.** having the nature of a problem; hard to solve or deal with **2.** uncertain Also **prob′lem·at′i·cal** —**prob′lem·at′i·cal·ly** *adv.*

‡**pro bo·no pu·bli·co** (prō bō′nō pub′li kō′) [ML.] for the public good or welfare

pro·bos·cis (prō bäs′is) *n.*, *pl.* **-cis·es, -ci·des′** (-ə dēz′) [L. < Gr. < *pro-*, before + *boskein*, to feed] **1.** an elephant's trunk, or a long, flexible snout, as of a tapir **2.** any tubular organ for sucking, food-gathering, sensing, etc., as of some insects, worms, and mollusks **3.** a person's nose, esp. if large: a jocular usage

pro·caine (prō′kān) *n.* [PRO-[2] + (CO)CAINE] a synthetic crystalline compound used as a local anesthetic

pro·ce·dure (prə sē′jər, prō-) *n.* **1.** the act, method, or manner of proceeding in some action; esp., the order of steps to be followed **2.** a particular course or method of action **3.** the established way of carrying on the business of a legislature, law court, etc. —**pro·ce′dur·al** *adj.* —**pro·ce′dur·al·ly** *adv.*

pro·ceed (prə sēd′, prō-) *vi.* [< MFr. < L. < *procedere* < *pro-*, forward + *cedere*, to go] **1.** to advance or go on, esp. after stopping **2.** to go on speaking, esp. after an interruption **3.** to undertake and carry on some action [to *proceed* to build a fire] **4.** to move along or be carried on [things *proceeded* smoothly] **5.** to take legal action (often with *against*) **6.** to come forth, issue, or arise (*from*)

pro·ceed·ing (-iŋ) *n.* **1.** an advancing or going on with what one has been doing **2.** the carrying on of an action or course of action **3.** a particular action or course of action **4.** [*pl.*] a record of the business transacted by a learned society, etc. **5.** [*pl.*] legal action

pro·ceeds (prō′sēdz) *n.pl.* the sum or profit derived from a sale, venture, etc.

proc·ess (präs′es; *chiefly Brit. & Canad.*, prō′ses) *n.* [< OFr. < L. pp. of *procedere:* see PROCEED] **1.** a series of changes by which something develops or is brought about [the *process* of digestion, growth, etc.] **2.** a particular method of making or doing something, in which there are a number of steps **3.** *Biol.* a projecting part of a structure or organism **4.** *Law* *a)* an action or suit *b)* a written order, as a summons to appear in court —*vt.* to prepare by or subject to a special process —*adj.* prepared by a special process —**in process** in the course of being done —**in (the) process of** in or during the course of —**proc′es·sor, proc′ess·er** *n.*

process cheese a cheese made by heating and blending together several natural cheeses with an emulsifying agent: also **proc′essed cheese**

pro·ces·sion (prə sesh′ən, prō-) *n.* [OFr. < L. < *procedere:* see PROCEED] **1.** the act of proceeding, esp. in an orderly manner **2.** a number of persons or things moving forward, as in a parade, in an orderly, formal way

pro·ces·sion·al (-'l) *adj.* of or relating to a procession —*n.* **1.** a hymn sung at the beginning of a church service during the entrance of the clergy **2.** any musical composition to accompany a procession

pro·claim (prō klām′, prə-) *vt.* [< MFr. < L. < *pro-*, before + *clamare*, to cry out] **1.** to announce to the public officially; announce to be **2.** to show to be [acts that *proclaimed* him a friend] **3.** to praise or extol

proc·la·ma·tion (präk′lə mā′shən) *n.* **1.** a proclaiming or being proclaimed **2.** something that is proclaimed

pro·cliv·i·ty (prō kliv′ə tē) *n.*, *pl.* **-ties** [L. *proclivitas* < *pro-*, before + *clivus*, a slope] a natural or habitual tendency or inclination

pro·con·sul (prō kän′s'l) *n.* [L. < *pro consule*, (acting) for the consul] a Roman official with consular authority who commanded an army in the provinces, often acting as provincial governor —**pro·con′sul·ar** (-ər) *adj.* —**pro·con′sul·ate** (-it), **pro·con′sul·ship′** *n.*

pro·cras·ti·nate (prō kras′tə nāt′, prə-) *vi.*, *vt.* **-nat′ed, -nat′ing** [< L. pp. of *procrastinare*, ult. < *pro-*, forward + *cras*, tomorrow] to put off doing (something) until later; delay —**pro·cras′ti·na′tion** *n.* —**pro·cras′ti·na′tor** *n.*

pro·cre·ate (prō′krē āt′) *vt., vi.* **-at′ed, -at′ing** [< L. pp. of *procreare* < *pro-*, before + *creare*, to create] **1.** to produce (young); beget **2.** to produce or bring into existence —**pro′cre·ant** *adj.* —**pro′cre·a′tion** *n.* —**pro′cre·a′tive** *adj.* —**pro′cre·a′tor** *n.*

Pro·crus·te·an (prō krus′tē ən) *adj.* **1.** of or like Procrustes or his actions **2.** securing conformity at any cost

Pro·crus·tes (-tēz) *Gr. Myth.* a giant who seized travelers, tied them to a bedstead, and either stretched them or cut off their legs to make them fit it

proc·tol·o·gy (präk täl′ə jē) *n.* [< Gr. *prōktos*, anus + -LOGY] the branch of medicine dealing with the rectum and anus and their diseases —**proc′to·log′ic** (-tə läj′ik), **proc′to·log′i·cal** *adj.* —**proc·tol′o·gist** *n.*

proc·tor (präk′tər) *n.* [< ME., contr.: see PROCURATOR] **1.** a person employed to manage another's affairs **2.** a college or university official who maintains order, supervises examinations, etc. —*vt.* to supervise (an examination) —**proc·to·ri·al** (präk tôr′ē əl) *adj.* —**proc′tor·ship′** *n.*

pro·cum·bent (prō kum′bənt) *adj.* [< L. prp. of *pro cumbere*, ult. < *pro-*, forward + *cubare*, to lie down] **1.** lying face down **2.** *Bot.* trailing along the ground: said of a stem

proc·u·ra·tor (präk′yə rāt′ər) *n.* [< OFr. < L. < *procurare:* see ff.] **1.** in the Roman Empire, an administrator of a province **2.** a person employed to manage another's affairs; agent —**proc′u·ra·to′ri·al** (-yər ə tôr′ē əl) *adj.*

pro·cure (prō kyoor′, prə-) *vt.* **-cured′, -cur′ing** [< MFr. < L. < *pro*, for + *curare*, to attend to < *cura*, a care] **1.** to get or bring about by some effort; obtain; secure **2.** to obtain (women) for the purpose of prostitution —**pro·cur′a·ble** *adj.* —**pro·cure′ment, pro·cur′ance, pro·cur′al** *n.*

pro·cur·er (-ər) *n.* a person who procures; specif., a man who obtains women for the purpose of prostitution; pimp —**pro·cur′ess** *n.fem.*

Pro·cy·on (prō′sē än′) [L. < Gr. < *pro-*, before + *kyōn*, dog: it rises before the Dog Star] a star of the first magnitude in Canis Minor

prod (präd) *vt.* **prod′ded, prod′ding** [< ?] **1.** to jab or poke as with a pointed stick **2.** to urge or stir into action —*n.* **1.** a prodding; jab, poke, thrust, etc. **2.** something that prods; specif., a rod or pointed stick used in driving cattle —**prod′der** *n.*

prod·i·gal (präd′i gəl) *adj.* [MFr. < L. < *prodigere*, to waste < *pro-*, forth + *agere*, to drive] **1.** wasteful in a reckless way **2.** extremely generous; lavish **3.** extremely abundant; profuse —*n.* a person who recklessly wastes his wealth, resources, etc. —**prod′i·gal′i·ty** (-gal′ə tē) *n., pl.* **-ties** —**prod′i·gal·ly** *adv.*

prodigal son *Bible* a wastrel son who repented and was welcomed home: Luke 15:11–32

pro·di·gious (prə dij′əs) *adj.* [< L.: see ff.] **1.** wonderful; amazing **2.** enormous; huge —**pro·di′gious·ly** *adv.* —**pro·di′gious·ness** *n.*

prod·i·gy (präd′ə jē) *n., pl.* **-gies** [L. *prodigium*, omen] a person or thing so extraordinary as to inspire wonder; specif., a child who is extremely talented or intelligent

pro·duce (prə do͞os′, -dyo͞os′; *for n.* präd′o͞os, -yo͞os; prō′do͞os, -dyo͞os) *vt.* **-duced′, -duc′ing** [L. *producere* < *pro-*, forward + *ducere*, to lead] **1.** to bring to view; offer for inspection *[*to *produce* identification*]* **2.** to bring forth; bear; yield *[*a well that *produces* oil*]* **3.** *a)* to make or manufacture *b)* to create **4.** to cause; give rise to *[*war *produces* devastation*]* **5.** to get ready and present (a play, movie, etc.); be the producer (sense 2) of **6.** *Econ.* to create (anything having exchange value) **7.** *Geom.* to extend (a line or plane) —*vi.* to bear, yield, create, manufacture, etc. something —*n.* something produced; yield; esp., fresh fruits and vegetables —**pro·duc′i·bil′i·ty** *n.* —**pro·duc′i·ble** *adj.*

pro·duc·er (prə do͞os′ər, -dyo͞os′-) *n.* **1.** a person or thing that produces; specif., one who produces goods and services: opposed to CONSUMER **2.** a person in charge of the financing and coordination of all activities in connection with the production of a play, movie, etc.

prod·uct (präd′əkt) *n.* [< ML. < L. pp. of *producere:* see PRODUCE] **1.** something produced by nature or by man **2.** result; outgrowth **3.** *Chem.* any substance resulting from a chemical change **4.** *Math.* the quantity obtained by multiplying two or more quantities together

pro·duc·tion (prə duk′shən) *n.* **1.** the act or process of producing **2.** the rate of producing or the amount produced **3.** *a)* something produced; product *b)* a work of art, literature, etc. *c)* a show, movie, etc. **4.** the creation of economic value; producing of goods and services —**make a production (out) of** [Colloq.] to dwell on or fuss over needlessly

pro·duc·tive (-tiv) *adj.* **1.** fertile **2.** marked by abundant production or effective results **3.** bringing as a result (with *of*) *[*war is *productive* of much misery*]* **4.** of or engaged in the creating of economic value —**pro·duc′tive·ly** *adv.* —**pro·duc·tiv·i·ty** (prō′dək tiv′ə tē, präd′ək-, prə duk′-), **pro·duc′tive·ness** *n.*

pro·em (prō′em) *n.* [< MFr. < L. < Gr. < *pro-*, before + *oimē*, song] a brief introduction; preface

prof (präf) *n.* [Colloq.] *shortened form of* PROFESSOR

Prof. Professor

prof·a·na·tion (präf′ə nā′shən) *n.* a profaning or being profaned; desecration —**pro·fan·a·to·ry** (prə fan′ə tôr′ē, prō-) *adj.*

pro·fane (prə fān′, prō-) *adj.* [< MFr. < L. < *pro-*, before (i.e., outside of) + *fanum*, a temple] **1.** not connected with religion; secular *[profane* art*]* **2.** not hallowed **3.** showing disrespect or contempt for sacred things; irreverent —*vt.* **-faned′, -fan′ing** **1.** to treat (sacred things) with disrespect or contempt **2.** to put to a base or improper use —**pro·fane′ly** *adv.* —**pro·fane′ness** *n.* —**pro·fan′er** *n.*

pro·fan·i·ty (-fan′ə tē) *n.* **1.** the state or quality of being profane **2.** *pl.* **-ties** something profane; esp., profane language or the use of profane language

pro·fess (prə fes′, prō-) *vt.* [< L. pp. of *profiteri* < *pro-*, before + *fateri*, to avow] **1.** to make an open declaration of; affirm *[*to *profess* one's love*]* **2.** to claim to have (some feeling, knowledge, etc.): often connoting insincerity or pretense **3.** to practice as one's profession **4.** to declare one's belief in *[*to *profess* Christianity*]*

pro·fessed (-fest′) *adj.* **1.** openly declared; avowed **2.** insincerely avowed; pretended **3.** having made one's profession (sense 4) **4.** professing to be duly qualified *[*a *professed* economist*]* —**pro·fess′ed·ly** (-fes′id lē) *adv.*

pro·fes·sion (prə fesh′ən) *n.* **1.** a professing, or declaring; avowal, as of love, religious belief, etc. **2.** a faith or religion professed **3.** *a)* an occupation requiring advanced education and involving intellectual skills, as medicine, law, theology, engineering, teaching, etc. *b)* the body of persons in any such occupation *c)* loosely, any occupation **4.** the act or ceremony of taking vows on entering a religious order —**the oldest profession** prostitution: a jocular usage

pro·fes·sion·al (-'l) *adj.* **1.** of, engaged in, or worthy of the standards of, a profession **2.** designating or of a school offering instruction in a profession **3.** earning one's living from an activity, such as a sport, not normally thought of as an occupation **4.** engaged in by professional players *[professional* hockey*]* **5.** engaged in a specific occupation for pay *[*a *professional* writer*]* **6.** being such in the manner of one practicing a profession *[*a *professional* hatemonger*]* —*n.* **1.** a person who is professional (esp. in sense 3) **2.** a person who does something with great skill —**pro·fes′sion·al·ism** *n.* —**pro·fes′sion·al·ly** *adv.*

pro·fes·sion·al·ize (-'l īz′) *vt.* **-ized′, -iz′ing** to cause to have professional qualities, status, etc. —**pro·fes′sion·al·i·za′tion** *n.*

pro·fes·sor (prə fes′ər) *n.* **1.** a person who professes something **2.** a teacher; specif., a college teacher of the highest rank —**pro·fes·so·ri·al** (prō′fə sôr′ē əl) *adj.* —**pro′fes·so′ri·al·ly** *adv.* —**pro·fes′sor·ship′, pro·fes′sor·ate** (-it) *n.*

prof·fer (präf′ər) *vt.* [< Anglo-Fr. & OFr. < *por-*, PRO-[2] + *offrir*, ult. < L. *offerre*, to offer] to offer (advice, friendship, etc.) —*n.* an offer or proposal

pro·fi·cient (prə fish′ənt) *adj.* [< L. prp. of *proficere*, to advance < *pro-*, forward + *facere*, to make] highly competent; skilled —*n.* an expert —**pro·fi′cien·cy** (-ən sē) *n., pl.* **-cies** —**pro·fi′cient·ly** *adv.*

pro·file (prō′fīl; *chiefly Brit.* -fēl) *n.* [< It. < *profilare*, to outline < *pro-* (< L. *pro-*), before + *filo* (< L. *filum*), a thread] **1.** *a)* a side view of the face *b)* a drawing of this **2.** outline *[*the *profile* of a hill*]* **3.** a short, vivid biographical and character sketch **4.** a graph, writing, etc. presenting data about a particular subject **5.** *Archit.* a side or sectional elevation of a building, etc. —*vt.* **-filed, -fil·ing** to sketch, write, or make a profile of

prof·it (präf′it) *n.* [OFr. < L. pp. of *proficere*, to profit: see PROFICIENT] **1.** advantage; gain; benefit **2.** [*often pl.*] income from money invested in stocks, bonds, etc. **3.** [*often pl.*] the sum remaining after all costs are deducted from the income of a business —*vi.* **1.** to make a profit **2.** to benefit; gain —*vt.* to be of profit or advantage to —**prof′it·er** *n.* —**prof′it·less** *adj.*

prof·it·a·ble (-ə b'l) *adj.* yielding profit, gain, or benefit —**prof′it·a·bil′i·ty, prof′it·a·ble·ness** *n.* —**prof′it·a·bly** *adv.*

prof·i·teer (präf′ə tir′) *n.* [PROFIT + -EER] a person who makes an unfair profit by charging very high prices when there is a short supply of something that people need —*vi.* to be a profiteer

profit sharing the practice of dividing a share of the profits of a business among employees, in addition to paying them their wages —**prof′it-shar′ing** ***adj.***

prof·li·gate (präf′lə git) ***adj.*** [< L. pp. of *profligare,* to rout, ruin < *pro-,* forward + *fligere,* to drive] **1.** immoral and shameless; dissolute **2.** recklessly extravagant —***n.*** a profligate person —**prof′li·ga·cy** (-gə sē), **prof′li·gate·ness** ***n.*** —**prof′li·gate·ly** ***adv.***

pro·found (prə found′) ***adj.*** [< OFr. < L. *profundus* < *pro-,* forward + *fundus,* bottom] **1.** very deep or low [a *profound* abyss, sigh, etc.] **2.** marked by intellectual depth [*profound* talk] **3.** deeply or intensely felt [*profound* grief] **4.** thoroughgoing [*profound* changes] **5.** unbroken [a *profound* silence] —**pro·found′ly** ***adv.*** —**pro·found′ness** ***n.***

pro·fun·di·ty (-fun′də tē) ***n.,*** *pl.* **-ties** **1.** depth **2.** intellectual depth **3.** a profound idea, matter, etc.

pro·fuse (prə fyo͞os′) ***adj.*** [< L. pp. of *profundere* < *pro-,* forth + *fundere,* to pour] **1.** giving freely; generous [*profuse* in her apologies] **2.** given or poured forth freely and abundantly —**pro·fuse′ly** ***adv.*** —**pro·fuse′ness** ***n.***

pro·fu·sion (-fyo͞o′zhən) ***n.*** **1.** a pouring forth with great liberality or wastefulness **2.** great liberality or wastefulness **3.** rich or lavish supply; abundance

pro·gen·i·tor (prō jen′ə tər, prə-) ***n.*** [< MFr. < L., ult. < *pro-,* forth + *gignere,* to beget] **1.** a forefather; ancestor in direct line **2.** an originator or precursor

prog·e·ny (präj′ə nē) ***n.,*** *pl.* **-nies** [< MFr. < L. < *progignere:* see prec.] children, descendants, or offspring

pro·ges·ter·one (prō jes′tə rōn′) ***n.*** [PRO-[1] + GE(STATION) + STER(OL) + -ONE] a steroid hormone, $C_{21}H_{30}O_2$, that prepares the uterus for the fertilized ovum and the mammary glands for milk secretion

prog·na·thous (präg′nə thəs, präg nā′-) ***adj.*** [PRO-[1] + Gr. *gnathos,* a jaw] having the jaws projecting beyond the upper face: also **prog·nath′ic** (-nath′ik) —**prog′na·thism** ***n.***

prog·no·sis (präg nō′sis) ***n.,*** *pl.* **-no′ses** (-sēz) [< LL. < Gr. < *pro-,* before + *gignōskein,* to know] a forecast or forecasting; esp., a prediction of the probable course of a disease in an individual and the chances of recovery

prog·nos·tic (-näs′tik) ***n.*** [see prec.] **1.** a sign; omen **2.** a forecast —***adj.*** **1.** foretelling **2.** *Med.* of, or serving as a basis for, prognosis

prog·nos·ti·cate (-näs′tə kāt′) ***vt.*** **-cat′ed, -cat′ing** **1.** to foretell or predict **2.** to indicate beforehand —**prog·nos′ti·ca′tion** ***n.*** —**prog·nos′ti·ca′tive** (-kāt′iv) ***adj.*** —**prog·nos′ti·ca′tor** ***n.***

pro·gram (prō′gram, -grəm) ***n.*** [< Fr. < LL. < Gr. *programma,* an edict < *pro-,* before + *graphein,* to write] **1.** *a*) the acts, speeches, musical pieces, etc. that make up an entertainment, ceremony, etc. *b*) a printed list of these **2.** a scheduled broadcast on radio or television **3.** a plan or procedure **4.** all the activities offered at a camp, resort, etc. **5.** *a*) a sequence of operations to be performed by a digital computer, as in solving a problem *b*) the coded instructions and data for this —***vt.*** **-grammed** or **-gramed, -gram·ming** or **-gram·ing** **1.** to schedule in a program **2.** to prepare (a textbook) for use in programmed learning **3.** *a*) to furnish (a computer) with a program *b*) to incorporate in a computer program —***vi.*** to prepare a program Also, Brit. sp., **pro′gramme** —**pro·gram·mat·ic** (prō′grə-mat′ik) ***adj.*** —**pro′gram·mer, pro′gram·er** ***n.***

programmed learning learning that a pupil acquires on his own, step by step, from a textbook that has a series of questions with the answers given elsewhere in the book

program music instrumental music that is meant to suggest a particular scene, story, etc.

prog·ress (präg′res, -rəs; *chiefly Brit.* prō′gres; *for v.* prə-gres′) ***n.*** [< L. pp. of *progredi* < *pro-,* before + *gradi,* to step] **1.** a moving forward or onward **2.** forward course; development **3.** advance toward perfection; improvement —***vi.*** **1.** to move forward or onward **2.** to move forward toward completion, a goal, etc. **3.** to advance toward perfection; improve —**in progress** going on

pro·gres·sion (prə gresh′ən) ***n.*** **1.** a moving forward or onward **2.** a succession, as of acts, happenings, etc. **3.** *Math.* a series of numbers increasing or decreasing by a constant difference between terms: see ARITHMETIC PROGRESSION, GEOMETRIC PROGRESSION —**pro·gres′sion·al** ***adj.***

pro·gres·sive (-gres′iv) ***adj.*** **1.** moving forward or onward **2.** continuing by successive steps **3.** of, or concerned with, progression **4.** designating a tax whose rate increases as the base increases **5.** favoring or working for progress, as through political or social reform **6.** of education that stresses self-expression, etc. **7.** *Gram.* indicating continuing action: said of certain verb forms, as *am working* **8.** *Med.* becoming more severe: said of a disease —***n.*** **1.** a person who is progressive, esp. one who favors political progress or reform **2.** [P-] a member of a Progressive Party —**pro·gres′sive·ly** ***adv.*** —**pro·gres′sive·ness** ***n.***

Progressive Party any of several U.S. political parties; specif., *a*) one formed in 1912 by followers of Theodore Roosevelt *b*) one formed in 1924 and led by Robert LaFollette *c*) one formed in 1948, orig. led by Henry Wallace (1888–1965)

pro·hib·it (prō hib′it, prə-) ***vt.*** [< L. pp. of *prohibere* < *pro-,* before + *habere,* to have] **1.** to refuse to permit; forbid by law or by an order **2.** to prevent; hinder —**pro·hib′it·er, pro·hib′i·tor** ***n.***

pro·hi·bi·tion (prō′ə bish′ən) ***n.*** **1.** a prohibiting or being prohibited **2.** an order or law that forbids **3.** the forbidding by law of the manufacture or sale of alcoholic liquors; specif., [P-] in the U.S., the period (1920–1933) of prohibition by Federal law —**pro′hi·bi′tion·ist** ***n.***

pro·hib·i·tive (prō hib′ə tiv, prə-) ***adj.*** **1.** prohibiting or tending to prohibit something **2.** such as to prevent purchase, use, etc. [*prohibitive* prices] Also **pro·hib′i·to′ry** (-tôr′ē) —**pro·hib′i·tive·ly** ***adv.***

proj·ect (präj′ekt, -ikt; *for v.* prə jekt′) ***n.*** [< L. pp. of *projicere* < *pro-,* before + *jacere,* to throw] **1.** a proposal; plan **2.** an organized undertaking, as a special unit of work, research, etc. in school **3.** a complex of inexpensive apartments or houses, usually owned publicly —***vt.*** **1.** to propose (a plan of action) **2.** to throw forward **3.** *a*) to cause (one's voice) to be heard clearly and at a distance *b*) to get (ideas, feelings, etc.) across to others effectively **4.** to send forth in one's imagination [to *project* oneself into the future] **5.** to cause to jut out **6.** to cause (a shadow, image, etc.) to fall upon a surface **7.** *same as* EXTRAPOLATE **8.** *Geom.* to transform the points of (a geometric figure) into the points of another figure, usually by lines of correspondence —***vi.*** **1.** to jut out **2.** to project one's voice, ideas, etc.

pro·jec·tile (prə jek′t'l, -tīl) ***n.*** **1.** an object designed to be shot forward, as a cannon shell, bullet, or rocket **2.** anything thrown forward —***adj.*** **1.** designed to be hurled forward, as a javelin **2.** hurling forward [*projectile* energy]

pro·jec·tion (-shən) ***n.*** **1.** a projecting or being projected **2.** something that projects, or juts out **3.** something that is projected; specif., in map making, the representation on a plane of all or part of the earth's surface or of the celestial sphere **4.** an extrapolation **5.** *Psychiatry* the unconscious act of ascribing to others one's own ideas, impulses, or emotions **6.** *Photog.* the process of projecting an image, as from a transparent slide, upon a screen, etc. —**pro·jec′tion·al** ***adj.*** —**pro·jec′tive** ***adj.***

pro·jec·tion·ist (-ist) ***n.*** the operator of a motion-picture or slide projector

pro·jec·tor (prə jek′tər) ***n.*** a person or thing that projects; specif., a machine for throwing an image on a screen, as from a motion-picture film

Pro·kof·iev (prô kôf′yef; *E.* prə kō′fē ef′), **Ser·gei (Sergeevich)** (syer gyā′) 1891–1953; Russ. composer

pro·lapse (prō′laps; *also, and for v. usually,* prō laps′) ***n.*** [< ModL. < LL. < pp. of *prolabi* < *pro-,* forward + *labi,* to fall] *Med.* the slipping out of place of an internal organ, as the uterus: also **pro·lap′sus** (-lap′səs) —***vi.*** **-lapsed′, -laps′ing** *Med.* to slip out of place

pro·late (prō′lāt) ***adj.*** [< L. pp. of *proferre,* to bring forward] extended or elongated at the poles [a *prolate* spheroid]

pro·le·tar·i·at (prō′lə ter′ē ət) ***n.*** [< Fr. < L. *proletarius,* a citizen of the poorest class, who served the state only by having children < *proles,* offspring] **1.** [Rare] the class of lowest status in any society **2.** the working class; esp., the industrial working class —**pro′le·tar′i·an** ***adj., n.***

pro·lif·er·ate (prō lif′ə rāt′, prə-) ***vt., vi.*** **-at′ed, -at′ing** [ult. < ML. < L. *proles,* offspring + *ferre,* to bear] **1.** to reproduce (new parts) in quick succession **2.** to create in profusion; multiply rapidly —**pro·lif′er·a′tion** ***n.*** —**pro·lif′er·ous** (-rəs) ***adj.***

pro·lif·ic (prə lif′ik, prō-) ***adj.*** [< Fr. < ML. < L. *proles,* offspring + *facere,* to make] **1.** producing many young or much fruit **2.** creating many products of the mind [a *prolific* poet] **3.** fruitful; abounding (often with *in* or *of*) —**pro·lif′i·ca·cy** (-i kə sē) ***n.*** —**pro·lif′i·cal·ly** ***adv.***

pro·lix (prō liks′, prō′liks) ***adj.*** [< L. *prolixus,* extended] **1.** so wordy as to be tiresome; verbose **2.** long-winded —**pro·lix′i·ty** ***n.*** —**pro·lix′ly** ***adv.***

pro·logue (prō′lôg, -läg) ***n.*** [< MFr. < L. < Gr. < *pro-,* before + *logos,* a discourse] **1.** an introduction to a poem, play, etc.; esp., introductory lines spoken before a dramatic performance **2.** the actor speaking such lines **3.** any preliminary act, event, etc.

pro·long (prə lôŋ′) ***vt.*** [< MFr. < LL. < L. *pro-,* forth + *longus,* long] to lengthen in time or space: also **pro·lon′gate** (-gāt) **-gat·ed, -gat·ing** —**pro·lon·ga·tion** (prō′lôŋ-gā′shən) ***n.*** —**pro·long′er** ***n.***

prom (präm) ***n.*** [contr. < ff.] [Colloq.] a ball or dance, as of a particular class at a school or college

prom·e·nade (präm′ə nād′, -näd′) ***n.*** [Fr. < *promener,* to take for a walk < LL. < L. *pro-,* forth + *minare,* to herd] **1.** a leisurely walk taken for pleasure, to display one's finery, etc. **2.** a public place for such a walk, as an avenue

3. *a*) a ball, or formal dance *b*) a march of all the guests, beginning a formal ball —*vi., vt.* **-nad′ed, -nad′ing** to take a promenade (along or through); parade —**prom′e·nad′er** *n.*

Pro·me·theus (prə mē′thyo͞os, -thē əs) *Gr. Myth.* a Titan who stole fire from heaven to benefit mankind: in punishment, Zeus chained him to a rock where a vulture ate away at his liver —**Pro·me′the·an** (-thē ən) *adj., n.*

pro·me·thi·um (-thē əm) *n.* [ModL. < prec.] a metallic chemical element of the rare-earth group: symbol, Pm; at. wt., 145(?); at. no., 61

prom·i·nence (präm′ə nəns) *n.* **1.** a being prominent **2.** something prominent

prom·i·nent (-nənt) *adj.* [< L. prp. of *prominere*, to project] **1.** sticking out; projecting [a *prominent* chin] **2.** noticeable at once; conspicuous **3.** widely and favorably known [a *prominent* artist] —**prom′i·nent·ly** *adv.*

pro·mis·cu·ous (prə mis′kyoo wəs) *adj.* [< L. < *pro-*, forth + *miscere*, to mix] **1.** consisting of different elements mixed together without sorting **2.** showing little or no taste or care in choosing; specif., engaging in sexual intercourse with many persons casually **3.** without plan or purpose; casual —**prom·is·cu·i·ty** (präm′is kyo͞o′ə tē, prō′mis-), *pl.* **-ties, pro·mis′cu·ous·ness** *n.* —**pro·mis′cu·ous·ly** *adv.*

prom·ise (präm′is) *n.* [< L. *promissum*, ult. < *pro-*, forth + *mittere*, to send] **1.** an agreement to do or not to do something; vow **2.** a sign that gives reason for expecting success **3.** something promised —*vi.* **-ised, -is·ing 1.** to make a promise **2.** to give a basis for expectation—*vt.* **1.** to make a promise of (something) *to* somebody **2.** to engage or pledge (with an infinitive or clause) [to *promise* to go] **3.** to give a basis for expecting **4.** [Colloq.] to assure —**prom′is·er,** *Law* **prom′i·sor′** (-i sôr′) *n.*

Promised Land 1. *Bible* Canaan, promised by God to Abraham and his descendants: Gen. 17:8 **2.** [p- l-] a place where one expects to have a better life

prom·is·ing (präm′i siŋ) *adj.* showing promise of success, excellence, etc. —**prom′is·ing·ly** *adv.*

prom·is·so·ry (präm′i sôr′ē) *adj.* **1.** containing a promise **2.** stipulating conditions that must be complied with to keep an insurance contract valid

promissory note a written promise to pay a certain sum of money to a certain person or bearer on demand or on a specified date

prom·on·to·ry (präm′ən tôr′ē) *n., pl.* **-ries** [< LL. < L. *promunturium*, prob. < *prominere*, to project] a peak of high land that juts out into a body of water; headland

pro·mote (prə mōt′) *vt.* **-mot′ed, -mot′ing** [< L. pp. of *promovere* < *pro-*, forward + *movere*, to move] **1.** to raise or advance to a higher position or rank [she was *promoted* to manager] **2.** to help bring about or further the growth or establishment of [to *promote* the general welfare] **3.** to further the popularity, sales, etc. of by publicizing and advertising [to *promote* a product] **4.** to move forward a grade in school —**pro·mot′a·ble** *adj.*

pro·mot·er (-mōt′ər) *n.* a person or thing that promotes; specif., a person who begins, secures financing for, and helps to organize an undertaking, as a business

pro·mo·tion (-mō′shən) *n.* a promoting; specif., *a*) advancement in rank, grade, or position *b*) furtherance of an enterprise, cause, etc. —**pro·mo′tion·al** *adj.*

prompt (prämpt) *adj.* [< MFr. < L. < pp. of *promere* < *pro-*, forth + *emere*, to take] **1.** quick to act or to do what is required; ready, punctual, etc. **2.** done, spoken, etc. at once or without delay —*n.* a notice of payment due —*vt.* **1.** to urge into action **2.** to remind (a person) of something he has forgotten; specif., to help (an actor, etc.) with a cue **3.** to move or inspire by suggestion —**prompt′ly** *adv.* —**prompt′ness** *n.*

prompt·er (prämp′tər) *n.* a person who prompts; specif., one who cues performers when they forget their lines

promp·ti·tude (-tə to͞od′, -tyo͞od′) *n.* the quality of being prompt; promptness

prom·ul·gate (präm′əl gāt′, prō mul′gāt) *vt.* **-gat′ed, -gat′ing** [< L. pp. of *promulgare*, to publish, altered < ? *pro-*, before + *vulgus*, the people] **1.** to publish or make known officially (a decree, law, dogma, etc.) **2.** to make widespread [to *promulgate* culture] —**prom′ul·ga′tion** *n.* —**prom′ul·ga′tor** *n.*

pron. 1. pronominal **2.** pronoun **3.** pronounced **4.** pronunciation

prone (prōn) *adj.* [< L. *pronus* < *pro*, before] **1.** lying or leaning face downward **2.** lying flat or prostrate **3.** having a natural bent; disposed or inclined (*to*) [*prone* to error] **4.** groveling —**prone′ly** *adv.* —**prone′ness** *n.*

prong (prôŋ) *n.* [akin to MLowG. *prangen*, to pinch] **1.** any of the pointed ends of a fork; tine **2.** any pointed projecting part, as the tip of an antler —*vt.* to pierce or break up with a prong —**pronged** *adj.*

prong·horn (prôŋ′hôrn′) *n., pl.* **-horns′, -horn′**: see PLURAL, II, D, 1 an antelopelike deer of Mexico and the western U.S., having curved horns

pro·nom·i·nal (prō näm′i n′l) *adj. Gram.* of, or having the function of, a pronoun —**pro·nom′i·nal·ly** *adv.*

pro·noun (prō′noun) *n.* [< MFr. < L. *pronomen* < *pro*, for + *nomen*, noun] *Gram.* a word that can assume the functions of a noun and be used in place of a noun: *I, you, them, it, ours, who, which, myself, anybody*, etc. are *pronouns*

pro·nounce (prə nouns′) *vt.* **-nounced′, -nounc′ing** [< OFr. < L. < *pro-*, before + *nuntiare*, to announce < *nuntius*, messenger] **1.** to say officially, solemnly, etc. [the judge *pronounced* sentence] **2.** to declare to be as specified [to *pronounce* a man guilty] **3.** *a*) to utter or articulate (a sound or word) *b*) to utter in the required or standard manner [he couldn't *pronounce* my name] —*vi.* **1.** to make a pronouncement (*on*) **2.** to pronounce words, syllables, etc. —**pro·nounce′a·ble** *adj.* —**pro·nounc′er** *n.*

pro·nounced (-nounst′) *adj.* **1.** spoken or uttered **2.** clearly marked; unmistakable; decided [a *pronounced* change] —**pro·nounc′ed·ly** (-noun′sid lē) *adv.*

pro·nounce·ment (-nouns′mənt) *n.* **1.** a pronouncing **2.** a formal statement of a fact, opinion, or judgment

pron·to (prän′tō) *adv.* [Sp. < L. *promptus*: see PROMPT] [Slang] at once; quickly; immediately

pro·nun·ci·a·men·to (prə nun′sē ə men′tō, prō-) *n., pl.* **-tos** [Sp. < L.: see PRONOUNCE] **1.** a public declaration; proclamation **2.** *same as* MANIFESTO

pro·nun·ci·a·tion (-ā′shən) *n.* **1.** the act or manner of pronouncing words **2.** *a*) any of the accepted or standard pronunciations of a word *b*) the representation in phonetic symbols of such a pronunciation —**pro·nun′ci·a′tion·al** *adj.*

proof (pro͞of) *n.* [< OFr. *prueve* < LL. *proba*: see PROBE] **1.** a proving, testing, or trying of something **2.** anything serving to establish the truth of something; conclusive evidence **3.** the establishment of the truth of something [to work on the *proof* of a theory] **4.** a test or trial of the truth, worth, quality, etc. of something **5.** the state of having been tested or proved **6.** tested or proved strength, as of armor **7.** the relative strength of an alcoholic liquor with reference to the standard for proof spirit: see PROOF SPIRIT **8.** *Law* all the facts, admissions, and conclusions which together operate to determine a verdict **9.** *Photog.* a trial print of a negative **10.** *Printing* an impression of composed type taken for checking errors and making changes —*adj.* **1.** of tested and proved strength **2.** able to resist, withstand, etc. (with *against*) [*proof* against criticism] **3.** used in proving or testing **4.** of standard strength: said of alcoholic liquors —*vt.* **1.** to make a proof of **2.** *clipped form of* PROOFREAD

-proof (pro͞of) *a combining form meaning:* **1.** impervious to [*waterproof*] **2.** protected from [*rustproof*] **3.** resistant to [*fireproof*]

proof·read (pro͞of′rēd′) *vt., vi.* to read and mark corrections on (printers' proofs, etc.) —**proof′read′er** *n.*

proof spirit an alcoholic liquor that is 100 proof and contains 50% of its volume of alcohol having a specific gravity of 0.7939 at 60° F

prop[1] (präp) *n.* [MDu. *proppe*, a prop] **1.** a support, as a stake or pole, placed under or against a structure or part **2.** a person or thing that gives support to a person, institution, etc. —*vt.* **propped, prop′ping 1.** to support or hold up, as with a prop (often with *up*) **2.** to place or lean (something) *against* a support **3.** to sustain or bolster

prop[2] (präp) *n. same as* PROPERTY (sense 5)

prop[3] (präp) *n. clipped form of* PROPELLER

prop. 1. proper(ly) **2.** property **3.** proposition

prop·a·gan·da (präp′ə gan′də, prō′pə-) *n.* [ModL., short for *congregatio de propaganda fide*, congregation for propagating the faith] **1.** [P-] *R.C.Ch.* a committee of cardinals in charge of the foreign missions **2.** the systematic, widespread promotion of a certain set of ideas, doctrines, etc., esp. to further one's own cause: also **prop′a·gan′dism 3.** ideas, doctrines, or allegations so spread, esp. if regarded as spread by deception —**prop′a·gan′dist** *n., adj.* —**prop′a·gan·dis′tic** *adj.* —**prop′a·gan·dis′ti·cal·ly** *adv.*

prop·a·gan·dize (-dīz) *vt., vi.* **-dized, -diz·ing 1.** to spread (certain ideas or propaganda) **2.** to subject (people) to propaganda

prop·a·gate (präp′ə gāt′) *vt.* **-gat′ed, -gat′ing** [< L. pp. of *propagare*, to peg down < *propago*, slip (of a plant)] **1.** to cause (a plant or animal) to reproduce itself; raise or breed **2.** to reproduce (itself): said of a plant or animal **3.** to spread (ideas, customs, etc.) **4.** to extend or transmit (sound waves, etc.) through air or water —*vi.* to reproduce, as plants or animals —**prop′a·ga′tion** *n.* —**prop′a·ga′tive** *adj.* —**prop′a·ga′tor** *n.*

pro·pane (prō′pān) *n.* [PROP(YL) + (METH)ANE] a heavy, gaseous hydrocarbon, C_3H_8, of the methane series, used as a fuel, in refrigerants, etc.

‡**pro pa·tri·a** (prō pä′trē ə) [L.] for (one's) country

pro·pel (prə pel′) *vt.* **-pelled′, -pel′ling** [< L. < *pro-*, forward + *pellere,* to drive] to push, drive, or impel onward, forward, or ahead —**pro·pel′lant** *n.* —**pro·pel′lent** *adj., n.*

pro·pel·ler (-ər) *n.* a person or thing that propels; specif., a device (**screw propeller**) consisting of blades twisted to move in a spiral as they rotate with the hub, and serving to propel a ship or aircraft forward

pro·pen·si·ty (prə pen′sə tē) *n., pl.* **-ties** [< L. pp. of *propendere,* to hang forward + -ITY] a natural inclination or tendency; bent

prop·er (präp′ər) *adj.* [< OFr. < L. *proprius,* one's own] **1.** specially adapted or suitable; appropriate *[*the *proper* tool for a job*]* **2.** naturally belonging or peculiar (*to*) *[*weather *proper* to May*]* **3.** conforming to an accepted standard or to good usage; correct **4.** fitting; seemly; right **5.** decent or decorous or exceedingly respectable **6.** in its most restricted sense; strictly so called *[*Chicago *proper* (i.e., apart from its suburbs)*]* **7.** [Chiefly Brit. Colloq.] complete; thorough *[*a *proper* scoundrel*]* **8.** [Archaic or Dial.] *a)* fine; excellent *b)* handsome **9.** *Gram.* designating a noun that names a specific individual, place, etc., is not used with an article, and is normally capitalized, as *Donald, Boston,* etc. —*adv.* [Dial.] completely; thoroughly —**prop′er·ly** *adv.* —**prop′er·ness** *n.*

proper fraction *Math.* a fraction in which the numerator is less than the denominator (Ex.: 2/5)

prop·er·tied (präp′ər tēd) *adj.* owning property

prop·er·ty (präp′ər tē) *n., pl.* **-ties** [< OFr. < L. *proprietas* < *proprius,* one's own] **1.** *a)* the right to possess, use, and dispose of something; ownership *b)* something, as a piece of writing, in which copyright or other rights are held **2.** a thing or things owned; possessions; esp., land or real estate owned **3.** a specific piece of land or real estate **4.** any trait or attribute proper to a thing; characteristic or essential quality *[*the *properties* of a chemical compound*]* **5.** any of the movable articles used as part of a stage setting, except the costumes, backdrops, etc.

proph·e·cy (präf′ə sē) *n., pl.* **-cies** [< OFr. < LL. < Gr. < *prophētēs:* see PROPHET] **1.** prediction of the future by a prophet, as supposedly influenced by the guidance of God or a god **2.** any prediction **3.** something prophesied

proph·e·sy (-sī′) *vt., vi.* **-sied′, -sy′ing** **1.** to declare or predict (something) by or as by the influence of divine guidance; utter (prophecies) **2.** to predict (a future event) in any way —**proph′e·si′er** *n.*

proph·et (präf′it) *n.* [< OFr. < LL. < Gr. *prophētēs,* interpreter of a god's will < *pro-*, before + *phanai,* to speak] **1.** a person who claims to speak for God, or a religious leader who claims to be, or is thought to be, divinely inspired **2.** a spokesman for some cause, group, etc. **3.** a person who predicts the future —**the Prophet** *a name used for* MOHAMMED (by Moslems) *or for* Joseph SMITH (by Mormons) —**the Prophets** **1.** the prophetic books of the Bible that include Isaiah, Jeremiah, etc. **2.** the authors or subjects of these books —**proph′et·ess** *n.fem.*

pro·phet·ic (prə fet′ik) *adj.* **1.** of, or having the powers of, a prophet **2.** of or containing a prophecy **3.** that predicts Also **pro·phet′i·cal** —**pro·phet′i·cal·ly** *adv.*

pro·phy·lac·tic (prō′fə lak′tik) *adj.* [< Gr., ult. < *pro-*, before + *phylassein,* to guard] preventive or protective; esp., preventing disease —*n.* a prophylactic medicine, device, etc.; esp., a condom

pro·phy·lax·is (-sis) *n., pl.* **-lax′es** (-sēz) the prevention of or protection from disease; specif., a cleaning of the teeth by a dentist, to remove plaque and tartar

pro·pin·qui·ty (prō piŋ′kwə tē) *n.* [< MFr. < L. < *propinquus,* near] **1.** nearness in time or place **2.** nearness of relationship; kinship

pro·pi·ti·ate (prə pish′ē āt′, prō-) *vt.* **-at′ed, -at′ing** [< L. pp. of *propitiare* < *propitius:* see ff.] to win or regain the good will of; appease or conciliate —**pro·pi′ti·a·ble** *adj.* —**pro·pi′ti·a′tion** *n.* —**pro·pi′ti·a′tor** *n.* —**pro·pi′ti·a·to′ry** (-ə tôr′ē), **pro·pi′ti·a′tive** (-āt′iv) *adj.*

pro·pi·tious (prə pish′əs, prō-) *adj.* [< OFr. < L. *propitius* < *pro-*, before + *petere,* to seek] **1.** favorably inclined; gracious *[*the *propitious* gods*]* **2.** favorable; auspicious *[*a *propitious* omen*]* **3.** that favors *[propitious* winds*]* —**pro·pi′tious·ly** *adv.* —**pro·pi′tious·ness** *n.*

prop·jet (präp′jet′) *n. same as* TURBOPROP

pro·po·nent (prə pō′nənt) *n.* [< L. prp. of *proponere* < *pro-*, forth + *ponere,* to place] **1.** a person who makes a proposal or proposition **2.** a person who espouses or supports a cause, etc.

pro·por·tion (prə pôr′shən) *n.* [< MFr. < L. < *pro-*, for + *portio,* a part] **1.** the comparative relation between things with respect to size, amount, etc.; ratio **2.** a part, share, etc., esp. in its relation to the whole; quota **3.** balance or symmetry **4.** size, degree, etc. relative to a standard **5.** [*pl.*] dimensions **6.** *Math. a)* an equality between ratios (Ex.: 2 is to 6 as 3 is to 9): also called **geometrical proportion** *b) same as* RULE OF THREE —*vt.* **1.** to cause to be in proper relation, balance, etc. *[proportion* the penalty to the crime*]* **2.** to arrange the parts of (a whole) so as to be harmonious —**pro·por′tioned** *adj.* —**pro·por′tion·ment** *n.*

pro·por·tion·al (-′l) *adj.* **1.** of or determined by proportion; relative **2.** in proportion *[*pay *proportional* to work done*]* **3.** *Math.* having the same ratio —*n.* a quantity in a mathematical proportion —**pro·por′tion·al′i·ty** (-al′ə tē) *n.* —**pro·por′tion·al·ly** *adv.*

proportional representation a system of voting that allows each political party to be represented in a legislature in proportion to its share of the popular vote

pro·por·tion·ate (prə pôr′shə nit; *for v.* -nāt′) *adj.* in proper proportion; proportional —*vt.* **-at′ed, -at′ing** to make proportionate —**pro·por′tion·ate·ly** *adv.*

pro·pos·al (prə pō′z′l) *n.* **1.** a proposing **2.** a plan or action proposed **3.** an offer of marriage

pro·pose (prə pōz′) *vt.* **-posed′, -pos′ing** [< OFr. < L. pp. of *proponere:* see PROPONENT] **1.** to put forth for consideration or acceptance **2.** to plan or intend **3.** to present as a toast in drinking **4.** to nominate for membership, office, etc. —*vi.* **1.** to make a proposal; form a purpose, etc. **2.** to offer marriage —**pro·pos′er** *n.*

prop·o·si·tion (präp′ə zish′ən) *n.* **1.** a proposing **2.** *a)* something proposed; plan *b)* [Colloq.] an immoral proposal, esp. in sexual relations **3.** [Colloq.] a proposed deal, as in business **4.** [Colloq.] a person, problem, etc. to be dealt with **5.** a subject to be discussed **6.** *Logic* an expression in which the predicate affirms or denies something about the subject **7.** *Math.* a theorem to be demonstrated or a problem to be solved —*vt.* to make a proposition, esp. an improper one, to —**prop′o·si′tion·al** *adj.*

pro·pound (prə pound′) *vt.* [< L. *proponere:* see PROPONENT] to put forth for consideration; propose —**pro·pound′er** *n.*

pro·pri·e·tar·y (prə prī′ə ter′ē) *n., pl.* **-tar′ies** [< LL. < L. *proprietas:* see PROPERTY] **1.** a proprietor **2.** a group of proprietors **3.** proprietorship —*adj.* **1.** belonging to a proprietor **2.** holding property **3.** of property or proprietorship **4.** held under patent, trademark, or copyright *[*a *proprietary* medicine*]*

pro·pri·e·tor (prə prī′ə tər) *n.* [< PROPRIET(ARY) + -OR] **1.** a person who has exclusive right to some property; owner **2.** one who owns and operates a business establishment —**pro·pri′e·tor·ship′** *n.* —**pro·pri′e·tress** (-tris) *n.fem.*

pro·pri·e·ty (-ə tē) *n., pl.* **-ties** [< OFr.: see PROPERTY] **1.** the quality of being proper, fitting, etc.; fitness **2.** conformity with what is proper or fitting or with accepted standards of behavior —**the proprieties** accepted standards of behavior in polite society

pro·pul·sion (prə pul′shən) *n.* [< L. pp. of *propellere* (see PROPEL) + -ION] **1.** a propelling or being propelled **2.** something that propels; propelling or driving force —**pro·pul′sive, pro·pul′so·ry** *adj.*

pro·pyl (prō′pil) *n.* [< PRO(TO)- + Gr. *piōn,* fat + -YL] the monovalent radical C_3H_7, occurring in two isomeric forms —**pro·pyl′ic** *adj.*

pro·pyl·ene (prō′pə lēn′) *n.* [prec. + -ENE] a flammable, colorless gas, used in making polypropylene, synthetic glycerol, etc.

propylene glycol a colorless, viscous liquid used as antifreeze, in making polyester resins, etc.

pro ra·ta (prō rāt′ə, rät′ə) [L. *pro rata* (*parte*), according to the calculated (share)] in proportion; proportionate or proportionately

pro rate (prō rāt′, prō′rāt′) *vt., vi.* **-rat′ed, -rat′ing** [< prec.] to divide, assess, or distribute proportionately —**pro·rat′a·ble** *adj.* —**pro·ra′tion** *n.*

pro·rogue (prō rōg′) *vt., vi.* **-rogued′, -rogu′ing** [< MFr. < L. *prorogare,* to defer < *pro-*, for + *rogare,* to ask] to discontinue or end a session of (a legislative assembly) —**pro′ro·ga′tion** (-rō gā′shən) *n.*

pro·sa·ic (prō zā′ik) *adj.* [< ML. < L. *prosa,* PROSE] **1.** of or like prose; unpoetic **2.** commonplace; dull —**pro·sa′i·cal·ly** *adv.* —**pro·sa′ic·ness** *n.*

pro·sce·ni·um (prō sē′nē əm) *n., pl.* **-ni·ums, -ni·a** (-ə) [L. < Gr. < *pro-*, before + *skēnē,* a tent] **1.** the apron of a stage **2.** the plane separating the stage proper from the audience and including the arch (**proscenium arch**) and its curtain

pro·sciut·to (prə sho͞ot′ō) *n.* [It. < *prosciugare,* to dry out] a spicy Italian ham, cured by drying and served in very thin slices

pro·scribe (prō skrīb′) *vt.* **-scribed′, -scrib′ing** [< L. < *pro-*, before + *scribere,* to write] **1.** in ancient Rome, to publish the name of (a person) condemned to death, banishment, etc. **2.** to deprive of the protection of the law; outlaw **3.** to banish; exile **4.** to denounce or forbid the

practice of —**pro·scrib′er** *n.* —**pro·scrip′tion** (-skrip′shən) *n.* —**pro·scrip′tive** *adj.* —**pro·scrip′tive·ly** *adv.*
prose (prōz) *n.* [MFr. < L. *prosa,* for *prorsa* (*oratio*), direct (speech), ult. < pp. of *provertere,* to turn forward] **1.** the ordinary form of language, without rhyme or meter: cf. VERSE, POETRY **2.** dull, commonplace talk —*adj.* **1.** of or in prose **2.** dull; prosaic —*vt., vi.* **prosed, pros′ing** to speak or write in prose —**pros′er** *n.*
pros·e·cute (präs′ə kyōōt′) *vt.* **-cut′ed, -cut′ing** [< L. pp. of *prosequi* < *pro-,* before + *sequi,* to follow] **1.** to pursue (something) to a conclusion [*to prosecute* a war] **2.** to carry on; engage in **3.** *a*) to conduct legal proceedings against, esp. in court for a crime *b*) to try to get, enforce, etc. by legal process —*vi.* to institute and carry on a legal suit —**pros′e·cut′a·ble** *adj.* —**pros′e·cu′tor** *n.*
prosecuting attorney a public official who conducts criminal proceedings on behalf of the State; prosecutor
pros·e·cu·tion (präs′ə kyōō′shən) *n.* **1.** a prosecuting, or following up **2.** the conducting of a lawsuit **3.** the State as the party that institutes and carries on criminal proceedings in court
pros·e·lyte (präs′ə līt′) *n.* [< LL. < Gr. *prosēlytos*] a person who has been converted from one religion, belief, etc. to another —*vt., vi.* **-lyt′ed, -lyt′ing** **1.** to try to convert (a person), esp. to one's religion **2.** to persuade to do or join something —**pros′e·lyt′er** *n.* —**pros′e·lyt·ism** (-li tiz'm, -līt iz'm) *n.*
pros·e·lyt·ize (-li tīz′) *vi., vt.* **-ized′, -iz′ing** *same as* PROSELYTE —**pros′e·lyt·iz′er** *n.*
Pro·ser·pi·na (prō sʉr′pi nə) *Rom. Myth.* the daughter of Ceres and wife of Pluto: identified with the Greek goddess Persephone: also **Pro·ser′pi·ne′** (-nē′, präs′ər pīn′)
‡**pro·sit** (prō′zit; *E.* prō′sit) *interj.* [G. < L. *prodesse,* to do good] to your health: a toast, esp. among Germans
pros·o·dy (präs′ə dē) *n., pl.* **-dies** [< L. < Gr. *prosōidia,* tone, accent < *pros,* to + *ōidē,* song] **1.** the science or art of versification, including the study of metrical structure, rhyme, etc. **2.** a system of versification [Poe's *prosody*] —**pro·sod·ic** (prə säd′ik), **pro·sod′i·cal** *adj.* —**pro·sod′i·cal·ly** *adv.* —**pros′o·dist** *n.*
pros·pect (präs′pekt) *n.* [L. *prospectus,* lookout, ult. < *pro-,* forward + *specere,* to look] **1.** *a*) a broad view; scene *b*) a place from which one can see such a view **2.** a mental view; survey **3.** the view from any particular point; outlook **4.** a looking forward; anticipation **5.** *a*) something hoped for *b*) [*usually pl.*] apparent chance for success **6.** a likely customer, candidate, etc. —*vt., vi.* to explore or search (*for*) [*to prospect* for gold] —**in prospect** expected
pro·spec·tive (prə spek′tiv, prä-) *adj.* **1.** looking toward the future **2.** expected; likely —**pro·spec′tive·ly** *adv.*
pros·pec·tor (präs′pek tər) *n.* a person who prospects for valuable ores, oil, etc.
pro·spec·tus (prə spek′təs, prä-) *n.* [L.: see PROSPECT] a statement outlining the main features of a new work, business enterprise, etc. or of an established institution
pros·per (präs′pər) *vi.* [< MFr. < L. < *prosperus,* favorable] to succeed, thrive, grow, etc. vigorously —*vt.* [Archaic] to cause to prosper
pros·per·i·ty (prä sper′ə tē) *n.* prosperous condition; good fortune, wealth, success, etc.
pros·per·ous (präs′pər əs) *adj.* **1.** prospering; flourishing **2.** well-to-do; well-off **3.** conducive to success; favorable —**pros′per·ous·ly** *adv.*
pros·tate (präs′tāt) *adj.* [< ML. < Gr. *prostatēs,* one standing before, ult. < *pro-,* before + *histanai,* to stand] of or relating to the prostate gland: also **pros·tat′ic** (-tat′ik) —*n. same as* PROSTATE GLAND
prostate gland a partly muscular gland surrounding the urethra at the base of the bladder in most male mammals
pros·the·sis (präs′thə sis; *for 2, often* präs thē′-) *n., pl.* **-the·ses′** (-sēz′) [< LL. < Gr. < *pros,* to + *tithenai,* to place] *Med.* **1.** the replacement of a missing limb, eye, etc. by an artificial substitute **2.** such a substitute —**prosthet′ic** (-thet′ik) *adj.*
pros·ti·tute (präs′tə tōōt′, -tyōōt′) *vt.* **-tut′ed, -tut′ing** [< L. pp. of *prostituere* < *pro-,* before + *statuere,* to make stand] **1.** to sell the services of (oneself or another) for purposes of sexual intercourse **2.** to sell (oneself, one's integrity, etc.) for unworthy purposes —*n.* **1.** a woman who engages in promiscuous sexual intercourse for pay **2.** a writer, artist, etc. who sells his services for unworthy purposes —**pros′ti·tu′tion** *n.* —**pros′ti·tu′tor** *n.*
pros·trate (präs′trāt) *adj.* [< L. pp. of *prosternere* < *pro-,* before + *sternere,* to stretch out] **1.** lying with the face downward in humility or submission **2.** lying flat, prone, or supine **3.** thrown or fallen to the ground **4.** *a*) laid low; overcome *b*) physically weak or exhausted **5.** *Bot.* trailing on the ground —*vt.* **-trat·ed, -trat·ing** **1.** to lay flat on the ground **2.** to lay low; overcome or exhaust —**pros·tra′tion** *n.*
pro·style (prō′stīl) *adj.* [< L. < Gr. < *pro,* before + *stylos,* pillar] having a portico with columns, usually four, across the front only —*n.* such a portico
pros·y (prō′zē) *adj.* **pros′i·er, pros′i·est** **1.** like, or having the nature of, prose **2.** prosaic, dull, etc. —**pros′i·ly** *adv.* —**pros′i·ness** *n.*
Prot. Protestant
pro·tac·tin·i·um (prō′tak tin′ē əm) *n.* [ModL.: see PROTO- & ACTINIUM] a rare, radioactive, metallic chemical element: symbol, Pa; at. wt., 231.10; at. no., 91
pro·tag·o·nist (prō tag′ə nist) *n.* [< Gr. *prōtos,* first + *agōnistēs,* actor] **1.** the main character in a drama, novel, or story **2.** a person playing a leading or active part
Pro·tag·o·ras (prō tag′ər əs) 481?–411? B.C.; Gr. philosopher
prot·a·sis (prät′ə sis) *n.* [LL. < Gr. < *pro-,* before + *teinein,* to stretch] *Gram.* the clause that expresses the condition in a conditional sentence: cf. APODOSIS
pro·te·an (prōt′ē ən, prō tē′ən) *adj.* **1.** [P-] of or like Proteus **2.** readily taking on different shapes or forms
pro·te·ase (prōt′ē ās′) *n.* [PROTE(IN) + (DIAST)ASE] an enzyme that digests proteins
pro·tect (prə tekt′) *vt.* [< L. pp. of *protegere* < *pro-,* before + *tegere,* to cover] **1.** to shield from injury, danger, or loss; defend **2.** to set aside funds for paying (a note, draft, etc.) at maturity **3.** *Econ.* to guard (domestic goods) by tariffs on imports —**pro·tect′a·ble** *adj.*
pro·tec·tion (prə tek′shən) *n.* **1.** a protecting or being protected **2.** a person or thing that protects **3.** a passport **4.** [Colloq.] *a*) money extorted by racketeers threatening violence *b*) bribes paid by racketeers to avoid prosecution **5.** *Econ.* the system of protecting domestic goods by taxing imports
pro·tec·tion·ism (-iz'm) *n.* *Econ.* the system, theory, or policy of protection —**pro·tec′tion·ist** *n., adj.*
pro·tec·tive (prə tek′tiv) *adj.* **1.** protecting or intended to protect **2.** *Econ.* intended to protect domestic products, industries, etc. in competition with foreign ones [*a protective* tariff] —**pro·tec′tive·ly** *adv.* —**pro·tec′tive·ness** *n.*
pro·tec·tor (prə tek′tər) *n.* **1.** one that protects; guardian **2.** *a*) a person ruling a kingdom during the minority, incapacity, etc. of the sovereign *b*) [P-] the title (in full **Lord Protector**) held by Oliver Cromwell (1653–1658) and his son Richard (1658–1659), during the Protectorate —**pro·tec′tor·ship′** *n.* —**pro·tec′tress** (-tris) *n.fem.*
pro·tec·tor·ate (-it) *n.* **1.** government by a protector **2.** the office or term of a protector **3.** [P-] the government of England under the Protectors (1653–1659) **4.** *a*) the relation of a strong state to a weaker state under its control and protection *b*) a state so controlled
pro·té·gé (prōt′ə zhā′, prōt′ə zhā′) *n.* [Fr., pp. of *protéger* < L.: see PROTECT] a person receiving guidance and help, esp. in furthering his career, from an influential person —**pro′té·gée′** (-zhā′, -zhā′) *n.fem.*
pro·tein (prō′tēn, prōt′ē in) *n.* [G. < Fr. < Gr. *prōteios,* prime < *prōtos,* first] any of a class of complex nitrogenous substances occurring in all animal and vegetable matter and essential to the diet of animals
pro tem·po·re (prō tem′pə rē′) [L.] for the time (being); temporary or temporarily: shortened to **pro tem**
pro·te·ol·y·sis (prōt′ē äl′ə sis) *n.* [ModL.: see PROTEIN & -LYSIS] *Biochem.* the breaking down of proteins, as by gastric juices, into simpler substances —**pro′te·o·lyt′ic** (-ə lit′ik) *adj.*
pro·te·ose (prōt′ē ōs′) *n.* [PROTE(IN) + -OSE[1]] any of a class of water-soluble products, formed in the hydrolysis of proteins, that can be broken down into peptones
pro·test (prə test′; *for n.* prō′test) *vt.* [< MFr. < L. < *pro-,* forth + *testari,* to affirm < *testis,* a witness] **1.** to state positively; declare or affirm strongly **2.** to speak strongly against **3.** to make a written declaration of the nonpayment of (a promissory note, check, etc.) —*vi.* **1.** to make solemn affirmation **2.** to express disapproval; object —*n.* **1.** the act or an instance of protesting; objection **2.** a document formally objecting to something **3.** *Law* a formal declaration that a bill or note has not been honored by the drawer —**under protest** while expressing one's objections; unwillingly —**pro·test′er, pro·tes′tor** *n.*
Prot·es·tant (prät′is tənt; *for n. 2 & adj. 2, also* prə tes′tənt) *n.* [Fr. < G. < L. prp. of *protestari:* see prec.] **1.** a member of any of the Christian churches resulting or deriving from the Reformation under the leadership of Luther, Calvin, Wesley, etc. **2.** [p-] a person who protests —*adj.* **1.** of Protestants or Protestant beliefs, practices, etc. **2.** [p-] protesting —**Prot′es·tant·ism** *n.*
Protestant Episcopal Church the Protestant church in the

U.S. that conforms to the practices and principles of the Church of England

prot·es·ta·tion (prät'is tā'shən, prō'tes-) *n.* **1.** a strong declaration or affirmation **2.** the act of protesting **3.** a protest; objection

Pro·teus (prōt'ē əs, prō'tyōōs) *Gr. Myth.* a sea god who could change his own form at will

pro·thal·li·um (prō thal'ē əm) *n., pl.* **-li·a** (-ə) [ModL. < Gr. *pro-,* before + *thallos,* a shoot] the part of a fern that bears the sex organs, a small, flat, greenish disc usually attached to the ground by hairlike roots: also **pro·thal'lus** (-əs), *pl.* **-li** (-ī), **-lus·es**

pro·throm·bin (prō thräm'bin) *n.* [PRO-1 + THROMBIN] a factor in the blood plasma that is converted into thrombin during blood clotting

pro·to- [< Gr. < *prōtos,* first] *a combining form meaning:* **1.** first in time, original, primitive *[prototype]* **2.** first in importance, chief *[protagonist]* Also **prot-**

pro·to·col (prōt'ə kôl', -käl') *n.* [< MFr. < ML. < LGr. *prōtokollon,* first leaf glued to a manuscript (noting the contents) < Gr. *prōtos,* first + *kolla,* glue] **1.** an original draft or record of a document, negotiation, etc. **2.** the code of ceremonial forms and courtesies used in official dealings, as between heads of state or diplomats *—vt., vi.* **-colled'** or **-coled', -col'ling** or **-col'ing** to draw up, or state in, a protocol

pro·ton (prō'tän) *n.* [ModL. < Gr. neut. of *prōtos,* first] a fundamental particle in the nucleus of all atoms: it carries a unit positive charge of electricity and has a mass approximately 1836 times that of an electron: cf. NEUTRON

proton synchrotron a synchrotron for accelerating protons and other heavy particles to very high energies

pro·to·plasm (prōt'ə plaz'm) *n.* [< G.: see PROTO- & PLASMA] a semifluid, colloidal substance that is the essential living matter of all animal and plant cells **—pro'to·plas'mic** *adj.*

pro·to·type (prōt'ə tīp') *n.* [see PROTO- & TYPE] **1.** the first thing or being of its kind; original **2.** a model for another of its kind **3.** a perfect example of a particular type **—pro'·to·typ'al** (-tī'p'l), **pro'to·typ'ic** (-tip'ik), **pro'to·typ'i·cal** *adj.*

pro·to·zo·an (prōt'ə zō'ən) *n.* [ModL. *Protozoa* (see PROTO- & -ZOA) + -AN] any of a large group of mostly microscopic, one-celled animals living chiefly in water but sometimes parasitic: also **pro'to·zo'on** (-än), *pl.* **-zo'a** (-ə) *—adj.* of the protozoans: also **pro'to·zo'ic** (-ik)

pro·tract (prō trakt') *vt.* [< L. pp. of *protrahere* < *pro-,* forward + *trahere,* to draw] **1.** to draw out in time; prolong **2.** to draw to scale, using a protractor and scale **3.** *Zool.* to thrust out; extend **—pro·tract'ed·ly** *adv.* **—pro·tract'ed·ness** *n.* **—pro·tract'i·ble** *adj.* **—pro·trac'tion** *n.* **—pro·trac'tive** *adj.*

pro·trac·tile (prō trak't'l) *adj.* capable of being protracted or thrust out; extensible

pro·trac·tor (-tər) *n.* [ML.] **1.** a person or thing that protracts **2.** a graduated, semicircular instrument for plotting and measuring angles

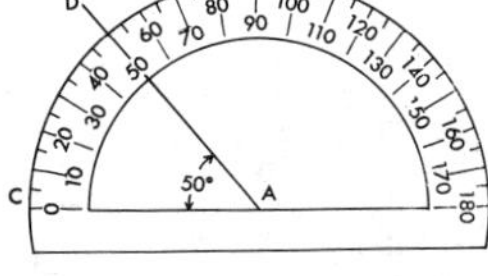

PROTRACTOR
(DAC, angle measured)

pro·trude (prō trōōd') *vt., vi.* **-trud'ed, -trud'ing** [< L. < *pro-,* forth + *trudere,* to thrust] to thrust or jut out; project **—pro·tru'sion** (-trōō'zhən) *n.*

pro·tru·sile (-trōō's'l) *adj.* that can be protruded, or thrust out, as a tentacle, etc.: also **pro·tru'si·ble**

pro·tru·sive (-trōō'siv) *adj.* **1.** protruding; jutting or bulging out **2.** *same as* OBTRUSIVE **—pro·tru'sive·ly** *adv.* **—pro·tru'sive·ness** *n.*

pro·tu·ber·ance (prō tōō'bər əns, -tyōō'-) *n.* **1.** a being protuberant **2.** a part or thing that protrudes; projection; bulge; swelling Also **pro·tu'ber·an·cy** (-ən sē), *pl.* **-cies**

pro·tu·ber·ant (-ənt) *adj.* [< LL. prp. of *protuberare,* to bulge out < L. *pro-,* forth + *tuber,* a bump] bulging or swelling out; protruding; prominent **—pro·tu'ber·ant·ly** *adv.*

proud (proud) *adj.* [OE. *prud* < OFr. < LL. *prode,* beneficial < L. *prodesse,* to be useful] **1.** having or showing a proper pride in oneself, one's position, etc. **2.** having or showing an overweening opinion of oneself; haughty; arrogant **3.** feeling or causing great pride or joy *[his proud* parents, a *proud* moment*]* **4.** caused by pride; presumptuous **5.** stately; splendid *[a proud* fleet*]* **6.** spirited *[a proud* stallion*]* **—do oneself proud** [Colloq.] to do extremely well **—proud of** highly pleased with **—proud'ly** *adv.*

proud flesh [< the notion of swelling up] an abnormal growth of flesh around a healing wound

Proust (prōōst), **Mar·cel** (mär sel') 1871–1922; Fr. novelist **—Proust'i·an** *adj.*

Prov. 1. Provençal **2.** Proverbs **3.** Province

prov. 1. province **2.** provincial **3.** provisional **4.** provost

prove (prōōv) *vt.* **proved, proved** or **prov'en, prov'ing** [< OFr. *prover* < L.: see PROBE] **1.** to test by experiment, a standard, etc.; try out **2.** to establish as true; demonstrate to be a fact **3.** to establish the validity of (a will, etc.) **4.** to show (oneself) to be capable, dependable, etc. **5.** *Math.* to test the correctness of (a calculation, etc.) *—vi.* to be found by experience or trial; turn out to be **—prov'a·bil'·i·ty, prov'a·ble·ness** *n.* **—prov'a·ble** *adj.* **—prov'a·bly** *adv.* **—prov'er** *n.*

prov·e·nance (präv'ə nəns) *n.* [Fr. < L. < *pro-,* forth + *venire,* to come] origin; derivation; source

Pro·ven·çal (prō'vən säl', präv'ən-) *adj.* of Provence, its people, their language, etc. *—n.* **1.** the vernacular of S France, a Romance language which, in its medieval form, was an important literary language **2.** a native or inhabitant of Provence

Pro·vence (prô väns') region & former province of SE France, on the Mediterranean

prov·en·der (präv'ən dər) *n.* [< MFr. < ML. *praebenda:* see PREBEND] **1.** dry food for livestock, as hay, corn, etc. **2.** [Colloq.] provisions; food

prov·erb (präv'ərb) *n.* [< OFr. < L. < *pro-,* before + *verbum,* a word] **1.** a short, popular saying that expresses some obvious truth; adage; maxim **2.** a person or thing that has become commonly recognized as a type; byword

pro·ver·bi·al (prə vur'bē əl) *adj.* **1.** of, or having the nature of, a proverb **2.** expressed in a proverb **3.** well-known because commonly referred to **—pro·ver'bi·al·ly** *adv.*

Prov·erbs (präv'ərbz) a book of the Bible containing maxims ascribed to Solomon and others

pro·vide (prə vīd') *vt.* **-vid'ed, -vid'ing** [< L. < *pro-,* before + *videre,* to see] **1.** to make available; supply **2.** to supply (someone *with* something) **3.** to state as a condition; stipulate *—vi.* **1.** to prepare (*for* or *against*) a possible situation, event, etc. **2.** to furnish the means of support (*for*) **—pro·vid'er** *n.*

pro·vid·ed (-vīd'id) *conj.* on the condition or understanding; if (often with *that*)

Prov·i·dence (präv'ə dəns) [named by Roger WILLIAMS] capital of Rhode Island, on Narragansett Bay: pop. 157,000 (met. area 918,000)

prov·i·dence (präv'ə dəns) *n.* [< MFr. < L. < prp. of *providere:* see PROVIDE] **1.** a looking to, or preparation for, the future; provision **2.** skill in management; prudence **3.** *a)* the benevolent guidance of God or nature *b)* an instance of this **4.** [P-] God

prov·i·dent (-dənt) *adj.* [< L. *providens,* prp. of *providere:* see PROVIDE] **1.** providing for future needs or events **2.** prudent or economical **—prov'i·dent·ly** *adv.*

prov·i·den·tial (präv'ə den'shəl) *adj.* of, by, or as if decreed by divine providence **—prov'i·den'tial·ly** *adv.*

pro·vid·ing (prə vīd'iŋ) *conj.* on the condition or understanding; provided (often with *that*)

prov·ince (präv'ins) *n.* [< OFr. < L. *provincia*] **1.** an outside territory governed by ancient Rome **2.** an administrative division of a country; specif., any of the ten main divisions of Canada **3.** *a)* a territorial district; territory *b)* [*pl.*] the parts of a country removed from the capital and major cities **4.** range of duties or functions **5.** a field of knowledge, activity, etc. **6.** a division of a country under the jurisdiction of an archbishop or metropolitan

pro·vin·cial (prə vin'shəl) *adj.* **1.** of or belonging to a province **2.** having the ways, speech, attitudes, etc. of a certain province **3.** rural; countrified; rustic **4.** narrow or limited in outlook; unsophisticated *—n.* **1.** a native of a province **2.** a provincial, esp. unsophisticated, person **—pro·vin'cial·ly** *adv.*

pro·vin·cial·ism (-iz'm) *n.* **1.** a being provincial **2.** narrowness of outlook **3.** a provincial custom, characteristic, etc. **4.** a word, phrase, etc. peculiar to a province Also **pro·vin'ci·al'i·ty** (-shē al'ə tē), *pl.* **-ties —pro·vin'cial·ist** *n.*

proving ground a place for testing new equipment, new theories, etc.

pro·vi·sion (prə vizh'ən) *n.* [MFr. < L. < pp. of *providere:* see PROVIDE] **1.** a providing or supplying **2.** something provided for the future; specif., [*pl.*] a stock of food **3.** a preparatory arrangement or measure taken in advance **4.** a clause, as in a legal document, stipulating some specific thing *—vt.* to supply with provisions, esp. with a stock of food **—pro·vi'sion·er** *n.*

pro·vi·sion·al (-'l) *adj.* conditional or temporary, pending a permanent arrangement **—pro·vi'sion·al·ly** *adv.*

pro·vi·so (prə vī'zō) *n., pl.* **-sos, -soes** [ML. *proviso* (*quod*), provided that] **1.** a clause, as in a document, making some condition **2.** a condition or stipulation

pro·vi·so·ry (-zər ē) *adj.* **1.** containing a proviso; conditional **2.** *same as* PROVISIONAL **—pro·vi'so·ri·ly** *adv.*

Pro·vo (prō'vō) [after Étienne *Provot,* early fur trader] city in NC Utah: pop. 74,000

prov·o·ca·tion (präv′ə kā′shən) ***n.*** **1.** a provoking **2.** something that provokes; esp., a cause of anger or irritation

pro·voc·a·tive (prə väk′ə tiv) ***adj.*** provoking or tending to provoke; stimulating, erotic, irritating, etc. —***n.*** something that provokes —**pro·voc′a·tive·ly** ***adv.*** —**pro·voc′a·tive·ness** ***n.***

pro·voke (prə vōk′) ***vt.*** **-voked′, -vok′ing** [< MFr. < L. < *pro-*, forth + *vocare*, to call] **1.** to excite to some action or feeling **2.** to anger or irritate **3.** to stir up (action or feeling) **4.** to evoke —**pro·vok′er** ***n.*** —**pro·vok′ing·ly** ***adv.***

pro·vo·lo·ne (prō′və lō′nē, präv′ə-) ***n.*** [It.] a hard, light-colored Italian cheese, usually smoked

pro·vost (prō′vōst; präv′əst; *esp. military* prō′vō) ***n.*** [< OE. & OFr., both < ML. *propositus*, for L. *praepositus*, chief, ult. < *prae-*, before + *ponere*, to place] **1.** a superintendent; official in charge **2.** the chief magistrate of a Scottish burgh **3.** the head of a cathedral chapter or principal church **4.** the head of, or an administrator in, some colleges and universities —**pro′vost·ship′** ***n.***

pro·vost guard (prō′vō) a detail of military police under the command of an officer (**provost marshal**)

prow (prou) ***n.*** [< Fr., ult. < L. < Gr. *prōira*] **1.** the forward part of a ship **2.** anything like this

prow·ess (prou′is, prō′-) ***n.*** [< OFr. *prouesse* < *prou*, brave, var. of *prud*: see PROUD] **1.** bravery; valor **2.** superior ability, skill, etc.

prowl (proul) ***vi., vt.*** [ME. *prollen* < ?] to roam about furtively as in search of prey —***n.*** a prowling —**on the prowl** prowling about —**prowl′er** ***n.***

prowl car *same as* SQUAD CAR

prox. proximo

prox·i·mal (präk′sə m′l) ***adj.*** **1.** proximate; next or nearest **2.** situated near the point of attachment of a limb, etc. —**prox′i·mal·ly** ***adv.***

prox·i·mate (präk′sə mit) ***adj.*** [< LL. pp. of *proximare*, to come near < L. *proximus*, nearest, superl. of *prope*, near] **1.** next or nearest in space, order, time, etc. **2.** approximate —**prox′i·mate·ly** ***adv.***

prox·im·i·ty (präk sim′ə tē) ***n.*** [< MFr. < L. < *proximus*: see prec.] nearness in space, time, etc.

prox·i·mo (präk′sə mō′) ***adv.*** [L. *proximo* (*mense*), in the next (month)] in or of the next month [*on the 9th proximo*]

prox·y (präk′sē) ***n.***, *pl.* **prox′ies** [ME. *prokecie* < *procuracie*, office of a procurator] **1.** the function of a deputy **2.** *a*) the authority to act for another, or a person given this authority *b*) a document giving this authority, as in voting at a stockholders' meeting

prs. pairs

prude (pro͞od) ***n.*** [Fr. < *prudefemme*, excellent woman] a person who is overly modest or proper in behavior, dress, speech, etc., esp. in a way that annoys others —**prud′ish** ***adj.*** —**prud′ish·ly** ***adv.*** —**prud′ish·ness** ***n.***

pru·dence (pro͞od′'ns) ***n.*** **1.** the quality or fact of being prudent **2.** careful management; economy

pru·dent (pro͞od′'nt) ***adj.*** [OFr. < L. *prudens*, for *providens*, PROVIDENT] **1.** exercising sound judgment in practical matters, esp. as concerns one's own interests **2.** cautious in conduct; sensible; not rash **3.** managing carefully and with economy —**pru′dent·ly** ***adv.***

pru·den·tial (proo den′shəl) ***adj.*** **1.** characterized by or exercising prudence **2.** having an advisory function —**pru·den′tial·ly** ***adv.***

prud·er·y (pro͞od′ər ē) ***n.*** a being prudish

prune¹ (pro͞on) ***n.*** [< MFr. < VL. < L. *prunum* < Gr. *proumnon*, plum] **1.** a plum dried for eating **2.** [Slang] a dull or otherwise unpleasant person

prune² (pro͞on) ***vt.*** **pruned, prun′ing** [< MFr., prob. ult. < *provain* (< L. *propago*), a slip] **1.** to remove dead or living parts from (a plant), as to increase fruit or flower production **2.** to cut out as being unnecessary **3.** to shorten by removing unnecessary parts [*to prune a novel*] —***vi.*** to remove unnecessary parts —**prun′er** ***n.***

pruning hook a long tool or shears with a hooked blade, for pruning plants

pru·ri·ent (proor′ē ənt) ***adj.*** [L. *pruriens* < *prurire*, to itch, long for] **1.** having lustful ideas or desires **2.** full of or causing lust; lascivious; lewd —**pru′ri·ence, pru′ri·en·cy** ***n.*** —**pru′ri·ent·ly** ***adv.***

pru·ri·tus (proo rīt′əs) ***n.*** [< L. pp. of *prurire*, to itch] intense itching without a rash —**pru·rit′ic** (-rit′ik) ***adj.***

Prus·sia (prush′ə) former kingdom in N Europe (1701–1871) & the dominant state of the German Empire (1871–1919) —**Prus′sian** ***adj., n.***

Prussian blue any of a group of dark-blue iron pigments used in paints, printing inks, etc.

prus·sic acid (prus′ik) *same as* HYDROCYANIC ACID

pry¹ (prī) ***n.***, *pl.* **pries** [back-formation < PRIZE²] **1.** a lever or crowbar **2.** leverage —***vt.*** **pried, pry′ing** **1.** to raise or move with a lever or crowbar **2.** to draw forth with difficulty

pry² (prī) ***vi.*** **pried, pry′ing** [ME. *prien* < ?] to look (*into*) closely or inquisitively; peer or snoop —***n.***, *pl.* **pries** **1.** a prying **2.** a person who is too inquisitive

pry·er (prī′ər) ***n.*** *same as* PRIER

pry·ing (-iŋ) ***adj.*** improperly curious or inquisitive —**pry′ing·ly** ***adv.***

Ps., Psa. Psalm; Psalms

ps. pieces

P.S. **1.** Privy Seal **2.** Public School

P.S., p.s., PS postscript

psalm (säm) ***n.*** [OE. *sealm* < LL. < Gr. *psalmos* < *psallein*, to pluck (a harp)] **1.** a sacred song or poem **2.** [*usually* **P-**] any of the sacred songs in praise of God that make up the Book of Psalms in the Bible

psalm·book (-book′) ***n.*** a collection of psalms for use in religious worship

psalm·ist (-ist) ***n.*** a composer of psalms —**the Psalmist** King David, to whom some or all of the Psalms are attributed

psal·mo·dy (säm′ə dē, sal′mə-) ***n.*** [< LL. < Gr. < *psalmos* (see PSALM) + *ōidē*, a song] **1.** the singing of psalms **2.** psalms collectively **3.** the arrangement of psalms for singing —**psal′mo·dist** ***n.***

Psalms (sämz) a book of the Bible, consisting of 150 psalms: also **Book of Psalms**

Psal·ter (sôl′tər) ***n.*** [< OE. & OFr., both < L. < Gr. *psaltērion*, psaltery < *psallein*, to pluck] the Book of Psalms —***n.*** [*also* **p-**] a version of the Psalms for use in religious services

psal·ter·y (sôl′tər ē, sôl′trē) ***n.***, *pl.* **-ter·ies** [< OFr. < L.: see PSALTER] an ancient stringed instrument with a shallow sound box, played by plucking the strings

PSALTERY

pseud. pseudonym

pseu·do (so͞o′dō, syo͞o′-) ***adj.*** [see ff.] sham; false; spurious; pretended; counterfeit

pseu·do- [< LL. < Gr. < *pseudēs*, false < *pseudein*, to deceive] *a combining form meaning:* **1.** fictitious, sham [*pseudonym*] **2.** counterfeit, spurious **3.** closely or deceptively similar to (a specified thing): also **pseud-**

pseu·do·nym (so͞o′də nim′, syo͞o′-) ***n.*** [< Fr. < Gr. < *pseudēs*, false + *onyma*, a name] a fictitious name, esp. one assumed by an author; pen name —**pseu′do·nym′i·ty** ***n.*** —**pseu·don′y·mous** (-dän′ə məs) ***adj.*** —**pseu·don′y·mous·ly** ***adv.***

pseu·do·po·di·um (so͞o′də pō′dē əm, syo͞o′də-) ***n.***, *pl.* **-di·a** (-ə) [ModL.: see PSEUDO- & PODIUM] a temporary jutting out of a part of a single cell, as in an amoeba, by means of which it can move about or take in food: also **pseu′do·pod′** (-päd′) —**pseu·dop′o·dal** (-däp′ə dəl) ***adj.***

pseu·do·sci·ence (-dō sī′əns) ***n.*** any system of theories that claims to be a science but has no scientific basis —**pseu′do·sci′en·tif′ic** ***adj.***

psf, p.s.f. pounds per square foot

pshaw (shô) ***interj., n.*** an exclamation of impatience, disgust, contempt, etc.

psi (sī, psē) ***n.*** [LGr. < Gr.] the twenty-third letter of the Greek alphabet (Ψ, ψ)

psi, p.s.i. pounds per square inch

psi·lo·cy·bin (sī′lə sī′bin, sil′ə-) ***n.*** [< ModL. *Psilocybe*, genus of mushrooms] a hallucinogenic drug obtained from certain mushrooms

psit·ta·co·sis (sit′ə kō′sis) ***n.*** [ModL. < L. < Gr. *psittakos*, a parrot + -OSIS] an acute, infectious virus disease of birds of the parrot family, often transmitted to man

pso·ri·a·sis (sə rī′ə sis) ***n.*** [ModL. < Gr. < *psōra*, an itch] a chronic skin disease in which scaly, reddish patches are formed —**pso·ri·at·ic** (sôr′ē at′ik) ***adj.***

psst (pst) ***interj.*** a sound made to get someone's attention quickly and quietly

PST, P.S.T. Pacific Standard Time

psych (sīk) ***vt.*** **psyched, psych′ing** [clipped < PSYCHOANALYZE] [Slang] to figure out the motives of, esp. in order to outwit, control, etc. (often with *out*)

Psy·che (sī′kē) [L. < Gr. < *psychē*, the soul] *Rom. Myth.* a maiden who becomes the wife of Cupid and is made immortal

psy·che (sī′kē) ***n.*** [L. < Gr. < *psychē*, the soul] **1.** the human soul **2.** the human mind

psy·che·del·ic (sī′kə del′ik) ***adj.*** [< PSYCHE + Gr. *delein,* to make manifest] **1.** of or causing extreme changes in the conscious mind, with hallucinations, delusions, etc. **2.** of or like the intense, distorted sights, sounds, colors, etc. produced by such changes in the mind —***n.*** a psychedelic drug —**psy′che·del′i·cal·ly** ***adv.***

psy·chi·a·trist (sə kī′ə trist, sī-) ***n.*** a doctor of medicine specializing in psychiatry

psy·chi·a·try (-trē) ***n.*** [ModL.: see PSYCHO- & -IATRY] the branch of medicine dealing with disorders of the mind, including psychoses and neuroses —**psy·chi·at·ric** (sī′kē-at′rik), **psy′chi·at′ri·cal** ***adj.*** —**psy′chi·at′ri·cal·ly** ***adv.***

psy·chic (sī′kik) ***adj.*** [< Gr. < *psychē,* the soul] **1.** of the psyche, or mind **2.** beyond natural or known physical processes **3.** apparently sensitive to supernatural forces Also **psy′chi·cal** —***n.*** a person who is supposedly sensitive to supernatural forces —**psy′chi·cal·ly** ***adv.***

psy·cho (sī′kō) ***adj., n.*** *colloq. clipped form of* PSYCHOTIC, PSYCHOPATHIC, PSYCHOPATH

psy·cho- [< Gr. *psychē,* soul] *a combining form meaning* the mind or mental processes *[psychology]*: also, before a vowel, **psych-**

psy·cho·ac·tive (sī′kō ak′tiv) ***adj.*** [PSYCHO- + ACTIVE] designating or of a drug, chemical, etc. that has a strong or specific effect on the mind

psy·cho·a·nal·y·sis (sī′kō ə nal′ə sis) ***n.*** [ModL.: see PSYCHO- & ANALYSIS] a method or practice, originated by Freud, of treating neuroses and some other mental disorders through analysis of emotional conflicts, repressions, etc. by getting the patient to talk freely, analyzing his dreams, etc. —**psy′cho·an′a·lyt′ic** (-an′ə lit′ik), **psy′cho-an′a·lyt′i·cal** ***adj.*** —**psy′cho·an′a·lyt′i·cal·ly** ***adv.***

psy·cho·an·a·lyst (-an′əl ist) ***n.*** a specialist in psychoanalysis

psy·cho·an·a·lyze (-an′ə līz′) ***vt.*** **-lyzed′, -lyz′ing** to treat by means of psychoanalysis

psy·cho·dra·ma (sī′kə drä′mə) ***n.*** a form of psychotherapy in which each patient in a group acts out situations related to his problem —**psy′cho·dra·mat′ic** (-drə mat′ik) ***adj.***

psy·cho·dy·nam·ics (sī′kō dī nam′iks) ***n.pl.*** [*with sing. v.*] the study of the mental and emotional motives underlying human behavior —**psy′cho·dy·nam′ic** ***adj.*** —**psy′cho-dy·nam′i·cal·ly** ***adv.***

psy·cho·gen·ic (sī′kə jen′ik) ***adj.*** [PSYCHO- + -GENIC] caused by mental conflicts; psychic —**psy′cho·gen′i·cal-ly** ***adv.***

psy·cho·ki·ne·sis (sī′kō ki nē′sis) ***n.*** [PSYCHO- + Gr. *kinēsis,* motion] the supposed ability to influence physical objects or events by thought processes —**psy′cho·ki·net′ic** (-net′ik) ***adj.***

psy·cho·log·i·cal (sī′kə läj′i k′l) ***adj.*** **1.** of psychology **2.** of the mind; mental **3.** affecting or intended to affect the mind Also **psy′cho·log′ic** —**psy′cho·log′i·cal·ly** ***adv.***

psychological moment **1.** the moment when one is mentally ready for something **2.** the critical moment

psychological warfare the use of psychological means, as propaganda, to influence the thinking of or undermine the morale of an enemy

psy·chol·o·gist (sī käl′ə jist) ***n.*** a specialist in psychology

psy·chol·o·gize (-ə jīz′) ***vi.*** **-gized′, -giz′ing** **1.** to study psychology **2.** to reason psychologically —***vt.*** to analyze psychologically

psy·chol·o·gy (-jē) ***n.,*** *pl.* **-gies** [< ModL.: see PSYCHO- & -LOGY] **1.** *a)* the science dealing with the mind and with mental and emotional processes *b)* the science of human and animal behavior **2.** the sum of a person's actions, traits, thoughts, etc. **3.** a system of psychology

psy·cho·neu·ro·sis (sī′kō noo rō′sis, -nyoo-) ***n.,*** *pl.* **-ro′ses** (-sēz) [ModL.: see PSYCHO- & NEUROSIS] *same as* NEUROSIS —**psy′cho·neu·rot′ic** (-rät′ik) ***adj., n.***

psy·cho·path (sī′kə path′) ***n.*** *same as* PSYCHOPATHIC PERSONALITY (sense 1)

psy·cho·path·ic (sī′kə path′ik) ***adj.*** characterized by psychopathy; mentally ill —**psy′cho·path′i·cal·ly** ***adv.***

psychopathic personality **1.** a person with serious personality defects, whose behavior is amoral and asocial (often criminal), generally without psychotic symptoms **2.** the personality of such a person

psy·cho·pa·thol·o·gy (sī′kō pa thäl′ə jē) ***n.*** **1.** the science dealing with mental disorders **2.** the behavior of the mentally ill —**psy′cho·path′o·log′i·cal** (-path′ə läj′i k′l) ***adj.*** —psy′cho·pa·thol′o·gist *n.*

psy·chop·a·thy (sī käp′ə thē) ***n.*** [PSYCHO- + -PATHY] mental disorder

psy·cho·phar·ma·col·o·gy (sī′kō fär′mə käl′ə jē) ***n.*** the study of the effects of drugs on the mind —**psy′cho-phar′ma·co·log′i·cal** (-kə läj′i k′l), **psy′cho·phar′ma·co-log′ic** ***adj.***

psy·cho·sex·u·al (-sek′shoo wəl) ***adj.*** having to do with the psychological aspects of sexuality in contrast to the physical aspects —**psy′cho·sex′u·al′i·ty** (-wal′ə tē) ***n.***

psy·cho·sis (sī kō′sis) ***n.,*** *pl.* **-cho′ses** (-sēz) [ModL.: see PSYCHO- & -OSIS] a major mental disorder in which the personality is very seriously disorganized and one's sense of reality is usually altered

psy·cho·so·cial (sī′kō sō′shəl) ***adj.*** of the psychological development of an individual in relation to his social environment

psy·cho·so·mat·ic (-sō mat′ik) ***adj.*** [PSYCHO- + SOMATIC] **1.** designating or of a physical disorder originating in or aggravated by one's psychic or emotional processes **2.** designating a system of medicine using a coordinated psychological and physiological approach toward such disorders —**psy′cho·so·mat′i·cal·ly** ***adv.***

psy·cho·ther·a·py (-ther′ə pē) ***n.*** [PSYCHO- + THERAPY] treatment of mental disorder by counseling, psychoanalysis, etc. —**psy′cho·ther′a·peu′tic** ***adj.*** —**psy′cho·ther′a·pist** ***n.***

psy·chot·ic (sī kät′ik) ***adj.*** of or having a psychosis —***n.*** a person having a psychosis —**psy·chot′i·cal·ly** ***adv.***

psy·chot·o·mi·met·ic (sī kät′ō mi met′ik) ***adj.*** [< PSYCHOT(IC) + *-o-* + MIMETIC] designating or of certain drugs, as LSD and mescaline, that produce hallucinations, psychotic symptoms, etc. —***n.*** a psychotomimetic drug

psy·cho·tox·ic (sī′kō täk′sik) ***adj.*** [PSYCHO- + TOXIC] of or pertaining to substances capable of damaging the brain

Pt *Chem.* platinum

pt. *pl.* **pts.** **1.** part **2.** pint **3.** point

p.t. **1.** past tense **2.** pro tempore

P.T.A. Parent-Teacher Association

ptar·mi·gan (tär′mə gən) ***n.,*** *pl.* **-gans, -gan:** see PLURAL, II, D, 1 [altered (after PTERO-) < Scot. *tarmachan*] any of several varieties of northern or alpine grouse, having feathered legs and undergoing seasonal color changes

PT boat [*p*(*atrol*) *t*(*orpedo*) *boat*] a high-speed motorboat equipped with torpedoes and machine guns

pter·i·do·phyte (ter′ə dō fīt′, tə rid′ə-) ***n.*** [< Gr. *pteris,* a fern + -PHYTE] a group of plants reproducing by means of spores and including the ferns —**pter′id·o·phyt′ic** (-fit′ik), **pter′i·doph′y·tous** (-däf′i təs) ***adj.***

pter·o- [ModL. < Gr. *pteron*] *a combining form meaning* feather, wing *[pterodactyl]*

pter·o·dac·tyl (ter′ə dak′t′l) ***n.*** [< ModL.: see prec. & DACTYL] an extinct flying reptile, having wings of skin stretched between the hind limb and a long digit of the forelimb —**pter′o-dac′tyl·oid′, pter′o·dac′tyl·ous** ***adj.***

PTERODACTYL (wingspread to 20 ft.)

-pter·ous (tər əs) [see PTERO- & -OUS] *a combining form meaning* having (a specified number or kind of) wings *[homopterous]*

Ptol·e·ma·ic (täl′ə mā′ik) ***adj.*** **1.** of Ptolemy, the astronomer, or his theory that the earth is the center of the universe and that the heavenly bodies move around it **2.** of the Ptolemies who ruled Egypt

Ptol·e·my (täl′ə mē) **1.** (L. name *Claudius Ptolemaeus*) 2d cent. A.D.; Gr. astronomer, mathematician, & geographer of Alexandria **2.** *pl.* **-mies** Macedonian family whose members formed the ruling dynasty of Egypt (305?–30 B.C.); esp., *a)* **Ptolemy I** 367?–283; 1st king of this dynasty (305?–285) *b)* **Ptolemy II** 309?– 247?; king of Egypt (285–247?)

pto·maine (tō′mān) ***n.*** [< It. < Gr. *ptōma,* a corpse < *piptein,* to fall] any of a class of alkaloid substances, some of which are poisonous, formed in decaying animal or vegetable matter by bacteria

ptomaine poisoning *earlier term for* FOOD POISONING (erroneously thought to be from ptomaines)

pty·a·lin (tī′ə lin) ***n.*** [< Gr. < *ptyein,* to spit + -IN[1]] an enzyme in the saliva of man (and some animals) that converts starch to dextrin and maltose

Pu *Chem.* plutonium

pub (pub) ***n.*** *chiefly Brit. colloq. clipped form of* PUBLIC HOUSE (sense 2)

pub. **1.** public **2.** published **3.** publisher **4.** publishing

pu·ber·ty (pyōō′bər tē) ***n.*** [< L. < *puber,* adult] the state of physical development when sexual reproduction first becomes possible: the age is generally fixed in common law at 14 for boys and 12 for girls —**pu′ber·tal** ***adj.***

pu·bes[1] (pyōō′bēz) ***n.*** [L., pubic hair] **1.** the body hair appearing at puberty; esp., the hair surrounding the genitals **2.** the region of the abdomen covered by such hair

pu·bes[2] (pyōō′bēz) ***n.*** *pl. of* PUBIS

pu·bes·cent (pyōō bes′'nt) ***adj.*** [Fr. < L. prp. of *pubescere,* to reach puberty < *pubes,* adult] **1.** reaching or having reached puberty **2.** covered with a soft down, as many plants and insects —**pu·bes′cence** ***n.***

pu·bic (pyōō′bik) ***adj.*** of or in the region of the pubes

pu·bis (-bis) *n., pl.* **pu′bes** (-bēz) [ModL. < L.: see PUBES[1]] that part of either hipbone forming, with the other, the front arch of the pelvis

pub·lic (pub′lik) *adj.* [L. *publicus,* ult. < *populus,* the people] **1.** of, belonging to, or concerning the people as a whole; of the community at large *[*the *public* welfare*]* **2.** for the use or benefit of all; esp., government-supported *[*a *public* park*]* **3.** acting in an official capacity on behalf of the people as a whole *[*the *public* prosecutor*]* **4.** known by all or most people *[*a *public* figure*]* —*n.* **1.** the people as a whole; community at large **2.** a specific part of the people *[*the reading *public]* —**go public** *Finance* to offer corporation stock for sale to the public —**in public** openly; not in privacy or secret —**pub′lic·ly** *adv.*

pub·li·can (pub′li kən) *n.* **1.** in ancient Rome, a tax collector **2.** [Brit.] a saloonkeeper; innkeeper

pub·li·ca·tion (pub′lə kā′shən) *n.* [< L. < *publicare:* see PUBLISH] **1.** a publishing or being published; public notification **2.** the printing and distribution, usually for sale, of books, magazines, newspapers, etc. **3.** something published, esp. a periodical

public domain **1.** public lands, for the use of everyone **2.** the condition of being free from copyright or patent, and available to anyone

public enemy a hardened criminal or other person who is a menace to society

public house **1.** an inn **2.** [Brit.] an establishment where alcoholic drinks are served; bar

pub·li·cist (pub′lə sist) *n.* **1.** a specialist in international law **2.** a journalist who writes about public affairs **3.** a specialist in public relations

pub·lic·i·ty (pə blis′ə tē) *n.* **1.** a being public, or commonly known **2.** *a)* any information that makes a person, place, etc. known or well-known to the public *b)* the work of handling such information **3.** a being noticed by the public **4.** any procedure or act intended to gain public notice

pub·li·cize (pub′lə sīz′) *vt.* **-cized′, -ciz′ing** to give publicity to; draw public attention to

public opinion the opinion held by people generally

public relations relations of an organization with the public through publicity seeking to form public opinion

public school **1.** in the U.S., an elementary or secondary school that is part of a system of free schools maintained by public taxes and supervised by local authorities **2.** in England, any of several private, expensive, endowed boarding schools for boys, preparing them for the universities or the public service

public servant an elected or appointed government official or a civil-service employee

pub·lic-spir·it·ed (pub′lik spir′i tid) *adj.* having or showing zeal for the public welfare

public utility an organization that supplies water, electricity, transportation, etc. to the public: it may be operated either by a private corporation **(public-service corporation)** under governmental regulation or by the government itself

public works works constructed by the government for public use or service, as highways or dams

pub·lish (pub′lish) *vt.* [< OFr. < L. *publicare* < *publicus,* PUBLIC] **1.** to make publicly known; announce; proclaim **2.** *a)* to issue (a printed work, etc.) to the public, as for sale *b)* to issue the written work of (an author) —*vi.* **1.** to issue books, newspapers, etc. to the public **2.** to write books, etc. that are published —**pub′lish·a·ble** *adj.*

pub·lish·er (-ər) *n.* a person or firm that publishes books, newspapers, magazines, etc.

Puc·ci·ni (po͞ot chē′nē), **Gia·co·mo** (jä′kô mô′) 1858–1924; It. operatic composer

puce (pyo͞os) *n.* [Fr., lit., a flea] brownish purple

puck[1] (puk) *n.* [akin to POKE[1]] *Ice Hockey* a hard rubber disk which the players try to drive into the opponents' goal

puck[2] (puk) *n.* [OE. *puca*] a mischievous sprite or elf, as **[P-]** the one in Shakespeare's *A Midsummer Night's Dream* —**puck′ish** *adj.* —**puck′ish·ly** *adv.* —**puck′ish·ness** *n.*

puck·a (puk′ə) *adj.* same as PUKKA

puck·er (puk′ər) *vt., vi.* [freq. form of POKE[2]] to draw up into wrinkles or small folds —*n.* such a wrinkle or fold —**pucker up** to contract the lips as in preparing to kiss —**puck′er·y** *adj.*

pud·ding (po͝od′iŋ) *n.* [akin ? to OE. *puduc,* a swelling] **1.** [Scot.] a kind of boiled sausage **2.** a soft, mushy food, usually made with a base of flour, cereal, etc. and boiled or baked **3.** a sweetened dessert of this kind, variously containing eggs, milk, fruit, etc.

pud·dle (pud′'l) *n.* [dim. < OE. *pudd,* a ditch] **1.** a small pool of water, esp. stagnant or muddy water **2.** a thick mixture of clay, and sometimes sand, with water —*vt.* **-dled, -dling** **1.** to make muddy **2.** to make a thick mixture of (wet clay and sand) **3.** to keep water from penetrating by using this mixture **4.** to treat (iron) by the puddling process —*vi.* to dabble or wallow in muddy water —**pud′dler** *n.* —**pud′dly** *adj.* **-dli·er, -dli·est**

pud·dling (-liŋ) *n.* the process of making wrought iron from pig iron by heating and stirring it in the presence of oxidizing agents

pu·den·dum (pyo͞o den′dəm) *n., pl.* **-den′da** (-də) [ModL., ult. < L. *pudere,* to be ashamed] [*usually pl.*] the external human sex organs, esp. of the female —**pu·den′dal** (-d'l) *adj.*

pudg·y (puj′ē) *adj.* **pudg′i·er, pudg′i·est** [prob. < Scot. *pud,* belly] short and fat —**pudg′i·ness** *n.*

Pueb·lo (pweb′lō) [see ff.] city in SC Colo., on the Arkansas River: pop. 102,000

pueb·lo (pweb′lō) *n., pl.* **-los;** also, for 2, **-lo** [Sp. < L. *populus,* people] **1.** an Indian village of the SW U.S.; specif., one in which the Indians live together in one or more terraced, flat-roofed structures of stone or adobe **2.** **[P-]** an Indian, as a Hopi, living in a pueblo

pu·er·ile (pyo͞o′ər əl, pyoor′əl; -īl) *adj.* [< Fr. < L. < *puer,* boy] childish; silly; immature —**pu′er·ile·ly** *adv.* —**pu′er·il′i·ty** (-ə ril′ə tē) *n., pl.* **-ties**

pu·er·per·al (pyo͞o ʉr′pər əl) *adj.* [< L. < *puer,* boy + *parere,* to bear] of or connected with childbirth

puerperal fever septic poisoning occurring during childbirth: a term no longer used

Puer·to Ri·co (pwer′tə rē′kō, pôr′-) island in the West Indies, constituting a commonwealth associated with the U.S.: 3,421 sq. mi.; pop. 2,712,000; cap. San Juan: abbrev. **P.R., PR** —**Puer′to Ri′can**

puff (puf) *n.* [OE. *pyff* < the *v.*] **1.** *a)* a short, sudden gust, as of wind, or an expulsion, as of breath *b)* a small quantity of vapor, smoke, etc. expelled at one time **2.** a drawing into the mouth of smoke from a cigarette, etc. **3.** a swelling or protuberance **4.** a shell of light pastry filled with whipped cream, etc. **5.** a soft, bulging mass of material, gathered in at the edges **6.** a soft roll of hair on the head **7.** a soft pad for dabbing powder on the skin or hair **8.** a quilted bed covering with a filling of down, etc. **9.** undue or exaggerated praise, as in a book review —*vi.* [OE. *pyffan*] **1.** to blow in puffs, as the wind **2.** *a)* to give forth puffs of smoke, steam, etc. *b)* to breathe rapidly and hard **3.** to move (*away, out, in,* etc.), giving forth puffs **4.** to fill, become inflated, or swell (*out* or *up*), as with air or pride **5.** to take a puff or puffs on a cigarette, etc. —*vt.* **1.** to blow, drive, etc. in or with a puff or puffs **2.** to inflate; swell **3.** to praise unduly, as in a book review **4.** to smoke (a cigarette, etc.) **5.** to set (the hair) in puffs —**puff′i·ly** *adv.* —**puff′i·ness** *n.* —**puff′y** *adj.* **puff′i·er, puff′i·est**

puff adder **1.** a large, poisonous African snake which hisses or puffs loudly when irritated **2.** *same as* HOGNOSE SNAKE

puff·ball (-bôl′) *n.* any of various round, white-fleshed fungi that burst at the touch when mature, and discharge a brown powder

puff·er (-ər) *n.* **1.** one that puffs **2.** any of various fishes that can expand the body by swallowing air or water

puf·fin (puf′in) *n.* [ME. *poffin* < ?] a northern sea bird with a short neck, ducklike body, and brightly colored triangular beak

PUFFIN (to 13½ in. long)

pug[1] (pug) *n.* [< ? PUCK[2]] **1.** a small, short-haired dog with a wrinkled face, snub nose, and curled tail **2.** *same as* PUG NOSE

pug[2] (pug) *vt.* **pugged, pug′ging** [< dial.: prob. echoic of pounding] **1.** to mix (wet, plastic clay) for making bricks, earthenware, etc. **2.** to fill in with clay, mortar, etc. for soundproofing —*n.* wet, plastic clay

pug[3] (pug) *n.* [Slang] a pugilist

Pu·get Sound (pyo͞o′jit) [after P. *Puget,* Eng. explorer] inlet of the Pacific, extending southward into NW Wash.

pug·ging (pug′iŋ) *n.* **1.** the mixing of pug (wet clay) **2.** clay, mortar, etc. used for soundproofing

pu·gil·ism (pyo͞o′jə liz'm) *n.* [< L. *pugil,* boxer, akin to *pugnare,* to fight + -ISM] *same as* BOXING —**pu′gil·ist** *n.* —**pu′gil·is′tic** *adj.*

pug·na·cious (pug nā′shəs) *adj.* [< L. < *pugnare,* to fight + -OUS] eager and ready to fight; quarrelsome —**pug·na′cious·ly** *adv.* —**pug·nac′i·ty** (-nas′ə tē), **pug·na′cious·ness** *n.*

pug nose a short, thick, turned-up nose —**pug′-nosed′** (-nōzd′) *adj.*

pu·is·sant (pyo͞o′i sənt, pyo͞o is′'nt, pwis′'nt) *adj.* [OFr.

fat, āpe, cär, ten, ēven, is, bīte; gō, hôrn, to͞ol, look; oil, out; up, fʉr; get; joy; yet; chin; she; thin, *th*en; zh, leisure; ŋ, ring; ə for *a* in *ago, e* in *agent, i* in *sanity, o* in *comply, u* in *focus;* ′ as in *able* (ā′b'l); Fr. bál; ë, Fr. coeur; ö, Fr. feu; Fr. mo*n*; ô, Fr. coq; ü, Fr. duc; *r,* Fr. cri; H, G. ich; kh, G. doch; ‡foreign; *hypothetical; < derived from. See inside front cover.

< *poeir:* see POWER] [Archaic] powerful; strong —**pu′is·sance** ***n.*** —**pu′is·sant·ly** ***adv.***

puke (pyo͞ok) ***n., vi., vt.*** **puked, puk′ing** [akin ? to G. *spucken*, to spit] *same as* VOMIT: avoided by some as vulgar

puk·ka (puk′ə) ***adj.*** [Hindi *pakkā*, ripe] [Anglo-Indian] **1.** good or first-rate of its kind **2.** genuine; real

pul (po͝ol) ***n.,*** *pl.* **puls, pul** [< Per., ult. < L., orig., bellows, hence bag, moneybag] *see* MONETARY UNITS, table (Afghanistan)

Pu·las·ki (po͝o las′kē; *Pol.* po͞o lä′skē), **Cas·i·mir** (kaz′i-mir) 1748–79; Pol. general in the Am. Revolutionary army

pul·chri·tude (pul′krə to͞od′, -tyo͞od′) ***n.*** [< L. < *pulcher*, beautiful] physical beauty —**pul′chri·tu′di·nous** (-'n əs) ***adj.***

pule (pyo͞ol) ***vi.*** **puled, pul′ing** [echoic] to whine or whimper, as a sick or fretful child

Pul·it·zer (po͝ol′it sər; *now often* pyo͞o′lit-), **Joseph** 1847–1911; U.S. newspaper owner & philanthropist, born in Hungary

Pulitzer Prize any of various yearly prizes established by Joseph Pulitzer, for work in journalism, literature, and music

pull (po͝ol) ***vt.*** [OE. *pullian*, to pluck] **1.** to exert force or influence on so as to make move toward or after the source of the force; drag, tug, draw, etc. **2.** *a)* to draw or pluck out; extract (a tooth, etc.) *b)* to pick or uproot (weeds, etc.) **3.** to draw apart; tear **4.** to stretch (taffy, etc.) back and forth repeatedly **5.** to strain and injure *[to pull a muscle]* **6.** [Colloq.] to carry out; perform *[to pull a raid]* **7.** [Colloq.] to restrain *[to pull one's punches]* **8.** [Colloq.] *a)* to take out (a gun, etc.) so as to threaten *b)* to force (a wheel, etc.) off or out **9.** *Baseball, Golf* to hit (the ball) so it goes to the left or, if left-handed, to the right **10.** *Printing* to take (a proof) on a hand press **11.** *Rowing a)* to work (an oar) by drawing it toward one *b)* to be rowed normally by *[this boat pulls four oars]* —***vi.*** **1.** to exert force in or for dragging, tugging, or attracting something **2.** to take a deep draft of a drink, a puff on a cigarette, etc. **3.** to be capable of being pulled **4.** to move or drive a vehicle (*away, ahead, out,* etc.) —***n.*** **1.** the act or force of pulling; specif., *a)* a dragging, tugging, attracting, etc. *b)* a drink, a puff on a cigarette, etc. *c)* a hard, steady effort *d)* the force to move something **2.** something to be pulled, as a drawer handle **3.** [Colloq.] *a)* influence or special advantage *b)* drawing power; appeal —**pull apart** to find fault with —**pull down 1.** to tear down **2.** to degrade; humble **3.** to reduce **4.** [Colloq.] to get (a specified wage, grade, etc.) —**pull for** [Colloq.] to cheer on, or hope for the success of —**pull in 1.** to arrive **2.** to draw in **3.** [Slang] to arrest and take to police headquarters —**pull off** [Colloq.] to accomplish or do —**pull oneself together** to regain one's poise, courage, etc. —**pull out 1.** to depart **2.** to withdraw or retreat **3.** to escape from a responsibility, etc. —**pull over** to drive (a vehicle) to or toward the curb —**pull through** to get over (an illness, difficulty, etc.) —**pull up 1.** to uproot **2.** to bring or come to a stop **3.** to drive (a vehicle) to a specified place **4.** to check or rebuke —**pull′er** ***n.***

pul·let (po͝ol′it) ***n.*** [< OFr. dim. of *poule*, hen < L. *pullus*, chicken] a young hen, usually not more than a year old

pul·ley (po͝ol′ē) ***n.,*** *pl.* **-leys** [< OFr. < ML. *poleia*, ult. < Gr. dim. of *polos*, axis] **1.** a small wheel with a grooved rim in which a rope or chain runs, as to raise a weight attached at one end by pulling on the other end **2.** a combination of such wheels, used to increase the applied power **3.** a wheel that turns or is turned by a belt, rope, chain, etc., so as to transmit power

PULLEYS (A, anchor; E, energy; W, weight)

Pull·man (po͝ol′mən) ***n.*** **1.** [after G.M. *Pullman* (1831–1897), U.S. inventor] a railroad car with private compartments or seats that can be made up into berths for sleeping: also **Pullman car** **2.** [*often* **p-**] a suitcase that opens flat and has a hinged divider inside: also **pullman case**

Pullman kitchen [*also* **p-**] a small, compact kitchen, typically built into an alcove, as in some apartments

pull·out (po͝ol′out′) ***n.*** **1.** a pulling out; esp., a removal, withdrawal, etc. **2.** something to be pulled out, as a magazine insert

pull·o·ver (-ō′vər) ***adj.*** that is put on by being pulled over the head —***n.*** a pullover sweater, shirt, etc.

pull·up (po͝ol′up′) ***n.*** *Gym.* the act of chinning oneself

pul·mo·nar·y (pul′mə ner′ē, po͝ol′-) ***adj.*** [< L. < *pulmo* (gen. *pulmonis*), a lung] **1.** of, like, or affecting the lungs **2.** having lungs **3.** designating the artery conveying blood from the heart to the lungs or any of the veins conveying blood from the lungs to the heart Also **pul·mon′ic** (-män′ik)

Pul·mo·tor (po͝ol′mōt′ər, pul′-) [< L. *pulmo*, a lung + MOTOR] *a trademark for* an apparatus that gives artificial respiration by forcing oxygen into the lungs —***n.*** [**p-**] such an apparatus

pulp (pulp) ***n.*** [< Fr. < L. *pulpa*, flesh] **1.** a soft, moist, formless mass **2.** the soft, juicy part of a fruit **3.** the soft pith of a plant stem **4.** the soft, sensitive substance under the dentin of a tooth **5.** ground-up, moistened fibers of wood, rags, etc., from which paper is made **6.** a magazine printed on rough, inferior paper, often featuring shocking stories about sex, crime, etc. —***vt.*** **1.** to reduce to pulp **2.** to remove the pulp from —***vi.*** to become pulp —**pulp′i·ly** ***adv.*** —**pulp′i·ness** ***n.*** —**pulp′y** ***adj.*** **pulp′i·er, pulp′i·est**

pul·pit (po͝ol′pit, pul′-) ***n.*** [L. *pulpitum*, a stage] **1.** a raised platform from which a clergyman preaches in a church **2.** preachers as a group

pulp·wood (pulp′wo͝od′) ***n.*** **1.** soft wood for making paper **2.** wood ground to pulp for paper

pul·que (po͝ol′kē; *Sp.* po͞ol′ke) ***n.*** [AmSp., prob. of Mex. Ind. origin] a fermented drink, popular in Mexico, made from the juice of an agave

pul·sar (pul′sär, -sər) ***n.*** [PULS(E)[1] + -AR] any of several small heavenly objects in the Milky Way that emit radio pulses at regular intervals

pul·sate (pul′sāt) ***vi.*** **-sat·ed, -sat·ing** [< L. pp. of *pulsare*, to beat] **1.** to beat or throb rhythmically, as the heart **2.** to vibrate; quiver —**pul·sa′tion** ***n.*** —**pul′sa·tive** (-sə tiv) ***adj.*** —**pul′sa′tor** ***n.*** —**pul′sa·to′ry** ***adj.***

pulse[1] (puls) ***n.*** [< OFr., ult. < L. pp. of *pellere*, to beat] **1.** the regular beating in the arteries, caused by the contractions of the heart **2.** any regular or rhythmical beat, signal, etc. **3.** the underlying feelings of a group, the public, etc. **4.** a brief surge of electric current **5.** a very short burst of radio waves —***vi.*** **pulsed, puls′ing** to pulsate —***vt.*** to make pulsate —**puls′er** ***n.***

pulse[2] (puls) ***n.*** [< OFr. < L. *puls*, a pottage] **1.** the edible seeds of peas, beans, lentils, and similar plants having pods **2.** any such plant

pulse·jet (engine) (-jet′) a jet engine in which the air-intake valves of the combustion chamber open and close in a pulselike manner

pul·ver·ize (pul′və rīz′) ***vt.*** **-ized′, -iz′ing** [< MFr. < LL. < L. *pulvis*, dust] **1.** to crush, grind, etc. into a powder or dust **2.** to demolish —***vi.*** to be pulverized into a powder or dust —**pul′ver·iz′a·ble, pul′ver·a·ble** (-vər ə b'l) ***adj.*** —**pul′ver·i·za′tion** ***n.*** —**pul′ver·iz′er** ***n.***

pu·ma (pyo͞o′mə, po͞o′-) ***n.,*** *pl.* **-mas, -ma:** see PLURAL, II, D, 1 [AmSp. < Quechua] *same as* COUGAR

pum·ice (pum′is) ***n.*** [< OFr. < L. *pumex*] a light, porous, volcanic rock used in solid or powdered form to scour, smooth, and polish: also **pumice stone** —***vt.*** **-iced, -ic·ing** to scour, etc. with pumice —**pu·mi·ceous** (pyo͞o mish′əs) ***adj.***

pum·mel (pum′'l) ***vt.*** **-meled** or **-melled, -mel·ing** or **-mel·ling** [< POMMEL] to beat or hit with repeated blows, esp. with the fist

pump[1] (pump) ***n.*** [< MDu. *pompe* < Sp. *bomba*, prob. of echoic origin] any of various machines that force a liquid or gas into or through, or draw it out of, something, as by suction or pressure —***vt.*** **1.** to move (fluids) with a pump **2.** to remove water, etc. from, as with a pump **3.** to drive air into, as with a pump **4.** to force in, draw out, move up and down, etc. in the manner of a pump **5.** to apply force to with a pumping motion **6.** [Colloq.] *a)* to question closely and persistently *b)* to get (information) in this way —***vi.*** **1.** to work a pump **2.** to move water, etc. with a pump **3.** to move or go up and down like a pump handle **4.** to flow in, out, or through by, or as if by, being pumped —**pump′er** ***n.***

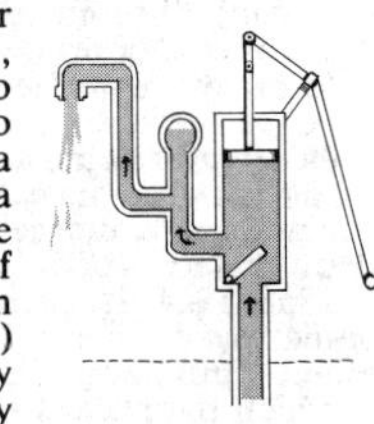

PUMP

pump[2] (pump) ***n.*** [< ? Fr. *pompe*, an ornament] a low-cut shoe without straps or ties

pump·er·nick·el (pum′pər nik′'l) ***n.*** [G.] a coarse, dark, sour bread made of unsifted rye

pump·kin (pum′kin, pump′-, puŋ′-) ***n.*** [< MFr. < L. < Gr. *pepōn*, lit., ripe] **1.** a large, round, orange-yellow fruit with many seeds, cooked and eaten in pies, etc. **2.** the vine on which it grows **3.** [Brit.] any of several squashes

pun (pun) ***n.*** [< ? It. *puntiglio*, fine point] the humorous use of words that have the same sound or spelling, but have different meanings; a play on words —***vi.*** **punned, pun′ning** to make a pun or puns —**pun′ner** ***n.***

Punch (punch) [< PUNCHINELLO] the hero of the puppet show **Punch and Judy**, a humpbacked figure with a hooked nose, constantly fighting with his wife, Judy —**pleased as Punch** greatly pleased

punch[1] (punch) ***n.*** [see PUNCHEON[1]] **1.** *a)* a tool driven or pressed against a surface that is to be shaped or stamped *b)* a tool driven against a nail, bolt, etc. that is to be worked in or out **2.** a device or machine for making holes, cuts, etc. **3.** the hole, cut, etc. so made —***vt.*** **1.** to pierce, stamp, etc. with a punch **2.** to make (a hole, etc.) with a punch —**punch′er** ***n.***

punch[2] (punch) ***vt.*** [ME. *punchen*] **1.** to prod or poke with a stick **2.** to herd (cattle) as by prodding **3.** to strike with the fist —***n.*** **1.** a thrusting blow with the fist **2.** [Colloq.] effective force; vigor —**pull one's punches** [Colloq.] to deliver blows, criticisms, etc. intended to have little or no effect —**punch a (time) clock** to insert a timecard into a time clock when arriving at or leaving work —**punch in** (or **out**) to record one's arrival (or departure) by punching a time clock —**punch′er** ***n.***

punch[3] (punch) ***n.*** [Hindi *pā̃c*, five: it orig. had five ingredients] a sweet drink of fruit juices, carbonated beverages, sherbet, etc., often mixed with wine or liquor, and served in cups from a large bowl (**punch bowl**)

punch·board (-bôrd′) ***n.*** a board or card with covered holes to be punched out, used as a game of chance: the holes contain slips or disks with hidden numbers, etc. usually designating prizes

punch card a card with holes or notches positioned in it, esp. by a key punch for data processing

punch-drunk (-druŋk′) ***adj.*** dazed, unsteady in gait, confused in speech, etc., as because of many blows to the head in boxing

pun·cheon[1] (pun′chən) ***n.*** [< MFr., ult. < L. pp. of *pungere*, to prick] **1.** a short, upright wooden post used in framework **2.** a heavy piece of timber roughly dressed with one side flat **3.** a device for punching, stamping, etc.

pun·cheon[2] (pun′chən) ***n.*** [OFr. *poinçon*] a large cask of varying capacity (72–120 gal.), for beer, wine, etc.; also, as much as it will hold

pun·chi·nel·lo (pun′chə nel′ō) ***n.***, *pl.* **-los** [< a character's name in a Neapolitan puppet play] a buffoon; clown

punching bag a stuffed or inflated leather bag hung up in order to be punched for exercise or practice

punch line the line carrying the point of a joke

punch press a press in which dies are fitted for cutting, shaping, or stamping metal

punch·y (pun′chē) ***adj.*** **punch′i·er, punch′i·est** [Colloq.] **1.** forceful; vigorous **2.** *same as* PUNCH-DRUNK

punc·til·i·o (puŋk til′ē ō′) ***n.***, *pl.* **-os′** [< Sp. or It., ult. < L. *punctum*, a point] **1.** a nice point of conduct, ceremony, etc. **2.** punctiliousness

punc·til·i·ous (-ē əs) ***adj.*** **1.** very careful about every detail of behavior, ceremony, etc. **2.** very exact; scrupulous —**punc·til′i·ous·ly** ***adv.*** —**punc·til′i·ous·ness** ***n.***

punc·tu·al (puŋk′cho͞o wəl) ***adj.*** [< ML. *punctualis* < L. *punctus*, a point] on time; prompt —**punc′tu·al′i·ty** (-wal′ə tē) ***n.*** —**punc′tu·al·ly** ***adv.*** —**punc′tu·al·ness** ***n.***

punc·tu·ate (puŋk′cho͞o wāt′) ***vt.*** **-at′ed, -at′ing** [< ML. pp. of *punctuare* < L. *punctus*, a point] **1.** *a)* to insert punctuation marks in *b)* to function as a punctuation mark in **2.** to break in on here and there [a speech *punctuated* with applause] **3.** to emphasize; accentuate —***vi.*** to use punctuation marks —**punc′tu·a′tor** ***n.***

punc·tu·a·tion (puŋk′cho͞o wā′shən) ***n.*** **1.** a punctuating; specif., the use of standardized marks in writing and printing to separate sentences or sentence elements or to make meaning clearer **2.** a punctuation mark or marks

punctuation mark any of the marks used in punctuation, as a period or comma

punc·ture (puŋk′chər) ***n.*** [< L. < *pungere*, to pierce] **1.** a perforating or piercing **2.** a hole made by a sharp point —***vt.*** **-tured, -tur·ing** **1.** to perforate or pierce with a sharp point **2.** to reduce or put an end to [to *puncture* one's pride] —***vi.*** to be punctured —**punc′tur·a·ble** ***adj.***

pun·dit (pun′dit) ***n.*** [< Hindi < Sans. *paṇḍita*] **1.** in India, a Brahman learned in Sanskrit, Hindu philosophy, etc. **2.** a person who has great learning

pun·gent (pun′jənt) ***adj.*** [< L. prp. of *pungere*, to prick] **1.** producing a sharp sensation of taste or smell; acrid **2.** sharp to the mind; poignant **3.** sharply penetrating; biting [*pungent* language] **4.** keenly clever —**pun′gen·cy** ***n.*** —**pun′gent·ly** ***adv.***

Pu·nic (pyo͞o′nik) ***adj.*** [L. *Punicus* < *Poeni*, the Carthaginians] **1.** of ancient Carthage or its people **2.** like the Carthaginians, regarded by the Romans as faithless and treacherous

pun·ish (pun′ish) ***vt.*** [< OFr. < L. *punire*, to punish < *poena*, punishment] **1.** to cause to undergo pain, loss, or suffering for a crime or wrongdoing **2.** to impose a penalty for (an offense) **3.** to treat harshly **4.** [Colloq.] to consume or use up —***vi.*** to deal out punishment —**pun′ish·a·bil′i·ty** ***n.*** —**pun′ish·a·ble** ***adj.*** —**pun′ish·er** ***n.***

pun·ish·ment (-mənt) ***n.*** **1.** a punishing or being punished **2.** a penalty imposed on an offender for wrongdoing **3.** harsh treatment

pu·ni·tive (pyo͞o′nə tiv) ***adj.*** inflicting or concerned with punishment: also **pu′ni·to′ry** (-tôr′ē) —**pu′ni·tive·ly** ***adv.*** —**pu′ni·tive·ness** ***n.***

punitive damages *same as* EXEMPLARY DAMAGES

Pun·jab (pun jäb′, pun′jäb, -jab) **1.** region in NW India & NE Pakistan, between the Indus & Jumna rivers **2.** state of India, in this region: 19,403 sq. mi.; pop. 11,147,000

punk[1] (puŋk) ***n.*** [var. of SPUNK] any substance, as decayed wood, that smolders when ignited, used as tinder; esp., a fungous substance shaped into slender, fragile sticks and used to light fireworks, etc.

punk[2] (puŋk) ***n.*** [< ?] [Slang] **1.** a young hoodlum **2.** anyone, esp. a youngster, regarded as inexperienced, insignificant, etc. —***adj.*** [Slang] poor or bad in quality

pun·kah, pun·ka (puŋ′kə) ***n.*** [Hindi *pankhā*] in India, a large fan made from the palmyra leaf, or a large, swinging fan hung from the ceiling

pun·ster (pun′stər) ***n.*** a person who is fond of making puns

punt[1] (punt) ***n.*** [< slang of Rugby School, England] *Football* a kick in which the ball is dropped from the hands and then kicked before it strikes the ground —***vt., vi.*** to kick (a football) in this way —**punt′er** ***n.***

punt[2] (punt) ***n.*** [OE. < L. *ponto*: see PONTOON] a flat-bottomed boat with square ends, usually propelled by a long pole —***vt.*** **1.** to propel (a boat) by pushing with a pole against the bottom of a shallow river or lake **2.** to carry in a punt —***vi.*** to go in a punt —**punt′er** ***n.***

punt[3] (punt) ***vi.*** [< Fr. < Sp. *punto* < L. *punctum*, a point] **1.** in certain card games, to bet against the banker **2.** [Brit.] to gamble; bet —**punt′er** ***n.***

pu·ny (pyo͞o′nē) ***adj.*** **-ni·er, -ni·est** [< Fr. < OFr. *puis*, after + *né*, born] of inferior size, strength, or importance; weak —**pu′ni·ness** ***n.***

pup (pup) ***n.*** **1.** *a)* a young dog; puppy *b)* a young fox, wolf, etc. **2.** a young seal, whale, etc. —***vi.*** **pupped, pup′ping** to give birth to pups

pu·pa (pyo͞o′pə) ***n.***, *pl.* **-pae** (-pē), **-pas** [ModL. < L., a girl, doll] an insect in the stage between the larval and adult forms: some pupae are enclosed in cocoons —**pu′pal** ***adj.***

PUPA

pu·pate (-pāt) ***vi.*** **-pat·ed, -pat·ing** to go through the pupal stage —**pu·pa′tion** ***n.***

pu·pil[1] (pyo͞o′p'l) ***n.*** [< MFr. < L. *pupillus* (dim. of *pupus*, boy), *pupilla* (dim. of *pupa*, girl), ward] a person being taught by a teacher or tutor, as in a school —**pu′pil·age, pu′pil·lage** ***n.***

pu·pil[2] (pyo͞o′p'l) ***n.*** [< Fr. < L. *pupilla*, one's figure reflected in another's eye; special use of *pupilla*: see prec.] the contractile circular opening in the center of the iris of the eye

pup·pet (pup′it) ***n.*** [< OFr., ult. < L. *pupa*, a girl, doll] **1.** orig., a doll **2.** a small, usually jointed figure, as of a human being, moved with the hands or by strings, wires, or rods, usually in a puppet show **3.** a person whose actions, ideas, etc. are controlled by another

pup·pet·eer (pup′i tir′) ***n.*** a person who operates or designs puppets or produces puppet shows

pup·pet·ry (pup′i trē) ***n.*** the art or work of a puppeteer

puppet show a play or performance with puppets

pup·py (pup′ē) ***n.***, *pl.* **-pies** [< MFr. *popee*, doll < OFr.: see PUPPET] **1.** a young dog **2.** an insolent, conceited, or silly young man —**pup′py·ish** ***adj.***

puppy love immature love between a boy and a girl

pup tent *same as* SHELTER TENT

pur·blind (pur′blīnd′) ***adj.*** [ME. *pur blind*, quite blind] **1.** orig., completely blind **2.** partly blind **3.** slow in perceiving or understanding —**pur′blind′ness** ***n.***

Pur·cell (pur′s'l), **Henry** 1659?–95; Eng. composer

pur·chase (pur′chəs) ***vt.*** **-chased, -chas·ing** [< OFr. < *pour*, for + *chacier*, to chase] **1.** to get for money; buy **2.** to get at a cost, as of suffering **3.** *a)* to move or raise by applying mechanical power *b)* to get a fast hold on so as to do this —***n.*** **1.** anything obtained by buying **2.** a buying **3.** *a)* a fast hold applied to move something mechanically or to keep from slipping *b)* an apparatus for applying such a hold —**pur′chas·a·ble** ***adj.*** —**pur′chas·er** ***n.***

pur·dah (pur′də) ***n.*** [Hindi & Per. *pardah*, a veil] a curtain or veil used by some Hindus and Moslems to hide their women from strangers; also, this practice of hiding women

pure (pyoor) ***adj.*** [< OFr. < L. *purus*] **1.** *a)* free from any adulterant [*pure* maple syrup] *b)* free from anything harmful [*pure* water] **2.** simple; mere [*pure* luck] **3.** utter; absolute **4.** free from defects **5.** free from sin or guilt **6.** virgin or chaste **7.** of unmixed stock; purebred **8.** abstract or theoretical *[pure* physics*]* **—pure′ly** *adv.* **— pure′ness** *n.*

pure·bred (-bred′) *adj.* belonging to a recognized breed through generations of unmixed descent **—*n.*** such a plant or animal

pu·rée (pyoo rā′; pyoor′ā, -ē) *n.* [Fr. < OFr. < L. < *purus,* pure] **1.** food prepared by putting cooked vegetables, fruits, etc. through a sieve or blender **2.** a thick, smooth soup made with this **—*vt.* -réed′, -rée′ing** to make a purée of Also sp. **puree**

pur·ga·tion (pər gā′shən) *n.* the act of purging

pur·ga·tive (pər′gə tiv) *adj.* **1.** that purges **2.** causing bowel movement **—*n.*** a substance that purges; specif., a cathartic **—pur′ga·tive·ly** *adv.*

pur·ga·to·ry (pər′gə tôr′ē) *n., pl.* **-ries** [< OFr. < ML. < LL. < L. *purgare:* see ff.] **1.** [*often* **P-**] in R.C. and other Christian doctrine, a state or place in which those who have died in the grace of God expiate their sins **2.** any state or place of temporary punishment or remorse **—pur′ga·to′ri·al** *adj.*

purge (pərj) *vt.* **purged, purg′ing** [< OFr. < L. *purgare* < *purus,* clean + *agere,* to do] **1.** to cleanse of impurities, foreign matter, etc. **2.** to cleanse of guilt, sin, etc. **3.** to remove by cleansing **4.** *a)* to rid (a nation, political party, etc.) of individuals regarded as disloyal or undesirable *b)* to kill or otherwise get rid of (such individuals) **5.** *Med. a)* to empty (the bowels) *b)* to make the bowels of (a person) become empty **—*vi.* 1.** to become clean, clear, or pure **2.** to have or cause a thorough bowel movement **—*n.* 1.** a purging **2.** that which purges; esp., a cathartic **—purg′er** *n.*

pu·ri·fy (pyoor′ə fī′) *vt.* **-fied′, -fy′ing** [< OFr. < L. *purificare* < *purus,* pure + *facere,* to make] **1.** to rid of impurities or pollution **2.** to free from guilt, sin, corruption, etc. **—*vi.*** to become purified **—pu′ri·fi·ca′tion** *n.* **—pu·rif·i·ca·to·ry** (pyoo rif′ə kə tôr′ē) *adj.* **—pu′ri·fi′er** *n.*

Pu·rim (poor′im, pōō rēm′) *n.* [Heb. *pūrīm,* pl., lit., lots] a Jewish holiday celebrated on the 14th day of Adar, commemorating the deliverance of the Jews by Esther from a massacre: also called **Feast of Lots**

pur·ism (pyoor′iz′m) *n.* **1.** strict observance of or insistence on precise usage or style, as in applying formal rules of grammar, art, etc. **2.** an instance of this **—pur′ist** *n.* **—pu·ris′tic, pu·ris′ti·cal** *adj.* **—pu·ris′ti·cal·ly** *adv.*

Pu·ri·tan (pyoor′ə t′n) *n.* [see PURITY & -AN] **1.** a member of a Protestant group in England and America who, in the 16th and 17th centuries, wanted to make the Church of England simpler in its services and stricter about morals **2.** [**p-**] a person regarded as excessively strict in morals and religion **—*adj.* 1.** of the Puritans **2.** [**p-**] puritanical **—Pu′ri·tan·ism, pu′ri·tan·ism** *n.*

pu·ri·tan·i·cal (pyoor′ə tan′i k′l) *adj.* **1.** [**P-**] of the Puritans **2.** excessively strict in morals and religion Also **pu′ri·tan′ic —pu′ri·tan′i·cal·ly** *adv.*

pu·ri·ty (pyoor′ə tē) *n.* [< MFr. < LL. < L. *purus,* pure] the quality or condition of being pure; specif., *a)* freedom from adulterating matter *b)* cleanness; clearness *c)* innocence or chastity *d)* freedom from elements regarded as corrupting

purl[1] (pərl) *vi.* [< ? Scand.] **1.** to move in ripples or with a murmuring sound **2.** to eddy; swirl **—*n.*** a stream or rill that purls, or its murmuring sound

purl[2] (pərl) *vt., vi.* [prob. < a Romance source] **1.** to edge (lace) with small loops **2.** to invert (stitches) in knitting **—*n.* 1.** metal thread, for embroidery **2.** a small loop or chain of loops on the edge of lace **3.** an inversion of knitting stitches

pur·lieu (pər′lōō, pərl′yōō) *n.* [< Anglo-Fr. < OFr. < *pur-,* through + *aler,* to go] **1.** orig., an outlying part of a royal forest, returned to private owners **2.** a place one visits often **3.** [*pl.*] *a)* bounds; limits *b)* environs **4.** an outlying part

pur·lin, pur·line (pər′lin) *n.* [< ?] a horizontal timber supporting rafters of a roof

pur·loin (pər loin′, pər′loin) *vt., vi.* [< OFr. < *pur-,* for + *loin,* far] to steal; filch **—pur·loin′er** *n.*

pur·ple (pər′p′l) *n.* [OE. < L. *purpura* < Gr. *porphyra,* shellfish yielding purple dye] **1.** a dark color that is a blend of red and blue **2.** esp. formerly, *a)* deep crimson *b)* cloth or clothing of such color: an emblem of royalty or high rank **—*adj.* 1.** of the color purple **2.** imperial; royal **3.** *a)* flowery *[purple* prose*]* *b)* strong and often offensive *[purple* language*]* **—*vt., vi.* -pled, -pling** to make or become purple **—born to** (or **in**) **the purple** of royal or high birth **—pur′plish, pur′ply** *adj.*

Purple Heart a decoration awarded to members of the U.S. armed forces wounded in action

purple martin a large N. American swallow with bluish-black plumage

pur·port (pər pôrt′; *also, & for n. always,* pər′pôrt) *vt.* [< Anglo-Fr. < OFr. < *por-,* forth + *porter,* to bear] **1.** to profess or claim as its meaning or intent **2.** to give the appearance, often falsely, of being, intending, etc. **—*n.*** meaning; main idea **—pur·port′ed** *adj.* **—pur·port′ed·ly** *adv.*

pur·pose (pər′pəs) *vt., vi.* **-posed, -pos·ing** [< OFr. var. of *proposer,* to PROPOSE] to plan, intend, or resolve **—*n.* 1.** what one plans to get or do; intention; aim **2.** resolution; determination **3.** the reason or use for something *[*a room with no *purpose]* **—on purpose** not by accident; intentionally **—to good purpose** advantageously **—to little** (or **no**) **purpose** with little or no effect **—to the purpose** apt; relevant **—pur′pose·less** *adj.* **—pur′pose·less·ly** *adv.* **—pur′pose·less·ness** *n.*

pur·pose·ful (-fəl) *adj.* **1.** resolutely aiming at a specific goal **2.** directed toward a specific end; not meaningless **— pur′pose·ful·ly** *adv.* **—pur′pose·ful·ness** *n.*

pur·pose·ly (-lē) *adv.* with a definite purpose; intentionally; deliberately

pur·pos·ive (pər′pə siv) *adj.* **1.** serving a purpose **2.** having purpose **—pur′pos·ive·ly** *adv.*

purr (pər) *n.* [echoic] **1.** a low, vibratory sound made by a cat when it seems to be pleased **2.** any sound like this **— *vi., vt.*** to make, or express by, such a sound

purse (pərs) *n.* [OE. *purs* < ML. *bursa,* a bag < LL., a hide < Gr. *byrsa*] **1.** a small bag or pouch for carrying money **2.** finances; money **3.** a sum of money given as a present or prize **4.** a woman's handbag **—*vt.* pursed, purs′ing** to pucker (one's lips, brows, etc.)

purs·er (pər′sər) *n.* [ME., a purse bearer] a ship's officer in charge of accounts, freight, tickets, etc., esp. on a passenger vessel

purse strings a drawstring for certain purses **—hold the purse strings** to be in control of the money **—tighten** (or **loosen**) **the purse strings** to make funds less (or more) readily available

purs·lane (pərs′lin, -lān) *n.* [< MFr. < LL. *porcilaca* < L. *portulaca*] any of a number of trailing weeds with pink, fleshy stems and small, yellow flowers; esp., an annual used as a potherb and in salads

pur·su·ance (pər sōō′əns, -syōō′-) *n.* a pursuing, or carrying out, as of a project, plan, etc.

pur·su·ant (-ənt) *adj.* [Now Rare] pursuing **—pursuant to 1.** following upon **2.** in accordance with

pur·sue (pər sōō′, -syōō′) *vt.* **-sued′, -su′ing** [< OFr. < VL. < L. < *pro-,* forth + *sequi,* to follow] **1.** to follow in order to overtake, capture, etc.; chase **2.** to follow or go on with (a specified course, action, etc.) **3.** to strive for; seek after *[*to *pursue* success*]* **4.** to have as one's occupation, profession, or study; devote oneself to **5.** to keep on harassing; hound **—*vi.* 1.** to chase **2.** to go on; continue **—pur·su′a·ble** *adj.* **—pur·su′er** *n.*

pur·suit (-sōōt′, -syōōt′) *n.* **1.** a pursuing **2.** a career, interest, etc. to which one devotes oneself

pursuit plane a fighter plane: see FIGHTER (sense 3)

pur·sui·vant (pər′si vənt, -swi-) *n.* [< OFr. < *poursuir:* see PURSUE] **1.** in England, an officer ranking below a herald **2.** a follower; attendant

pur·sy[1] (pər′sē) *adj.* **-si·er, -si·est** [< Anglo-Fr. *pursif,* for OFr. *polsif* < *polser,* to push, pant < L. *pulsare,* to beat] **1.** short-winded, esp. from being fat **2.** fat **—pur′si·ness** *n.*

pur·sy[2] (pər′sē) *adj.* **-si·er, -si·est** pursed; puckered

pu·ru·lent (pyoor′ə lənt, -yoo lənt) *adj.* [Fr. < L. < *pus* (gen. *puris*), pus] of, like, containing, or discharging pus **—pu′ru·lence, pu′ru·len·cy** *n.* **—pu′ru·lent·ly** *adv.*

pur·vey (pər vā′) *vt.* [< Anglo-Fr. < OFr. < L. *providere:* see PROVIDE] to supply (esp. food or provisions) **—pur·vey′ance** *n.* **—pur·vey′or** *n.*

pur·view (pər′vyōō) *n.* [< Anglo-Fr. *purvere (est),* (it is) provided, ult. < L. *providere:* see PROVIDE] **1.** the body and scope of an act or bill **2.** extent or range of control, activity, concern, etc.; province

pus (pus) *n.* [L.] the usually yellowish-white liquid matter produced in certain infections, consisting of bacteria, white corpuscles, serum, etc.

Pu·san (pōō′sän′) seaport on the SE coast of South Korea: pop. 1,879,000

push (poosh) *vt.* [< MFr. < OFr. < L. *pulsare,* to beat < pp. of *pellere,* to drive] **1.** *a)* to exert pressure or force against, esp. so as to move *b)* to move in this way *c)* to thrust, shove, or drive (*up, down, in, out,* etc.) **2.** *a)* to urge on; impel *b)* to follow up vigorously; promote (a campaign, claim, etc.) *c)* to extend or expand (business activities, etc.) **3.** to bring into a critical state; press *[*be *pushed* for time*]* **4.** to urge or promote the use, sale, etc. of **5.** [Colloq.] to be near or close to *[pushing* sixty years*]* **—*vi.* 1.** to press against a thing so as to move it **2.** to try hard to advance, succeed, etc. **3.** to move forward against opposition **4.** to move by being pushed **—*n.* 1.** a pushing **2.** a vigorous effort, campaign, etc. **3.** pressure of circumstances **4.** [Colloq.] enterprise; drive **—push off** [Colloq.] to set out; depart **—push on** to go forward; proceed

push button a small knob or button that is pushed to cause

something to operate, as by closing an electric circuit —**push′-but′ton** ***adj.***
push·cart (poosh′kärt′) ***n.*** a cart pushed by hand, esp. one used by street vendors
push·er (-ər) ***n.*** **1.** a person or thing that pushes **2.** [Slang] a person peddling drugs, esp. narcotics, illegally
push·ing (-iŋ) ***adj.*** **1.** aggressive; enterprising **2.** forward; officious —**push′ing·ly** ***adv.***
Push·kin (pōōsh′kin; *E.* poosh′-), **A·lek·san·dr (Sergeyevich)** (ä′lyik sän′dr′) 1799–1837; Russ. poet
push·o·ver (poosh′ō′vər) ***n.*** [Slang] **1.** anything very easy to do **2.** a person, group, etc. easily persuaded, defeated, seduced, etc.
Push·tu (push′tōō) ***n.*** *same as* PASHTO
push-up, push·up (poosh′up′) ***n.*** an exercise in which a person lying face down, with hands palm down under the shoulders, pushes the body up by straightening the arms and lowers it by bending the arms
push·y (poosh′ē) ***adj.*** **push′i·er, push′i·est** [Colloq.] annoyingly aggressive and persistent —**push′i·ness** ***n.***
pu·sil·lan·i·mous (pyōō′s'l an′ə məs) ***adj.*** [< LL. < L. *pusillus*, tiny + *animus*, the mind] **1.** timid or cowardly **2.** proceeding from or showing a lack of courage —**pu′sil·la·nim′i·ty** (-ə nim′ə tē) ***n.*** —**pu′sil·lan′i·mous·ly** ***adv.***
puss[1] (poos) ***n.*** [orig. ? echoic of the spitting of a cat] **1.** a cat: pet name **2.** a girl: term of affection
puss[2] (poos) ***n.*** [prob. < IrGael. *pus*, mouth] [Slang] **1.** the face **2.** the mouth
pus·sy[1] (pus′ē) ***adj.*** **-si·er, -si·est** containing or like pus
puss·y[2] (poos′ē) ***n.,*** *pl.* **puss′ies** [dim. of PUSS[1]] a cat, esp. a kitten: also **puss′y·cat′** (-kat′)
puss·y·foot (-foot′) ***vi.*** [Colloq.] **1.** to move with stealth, like a cat **2.** to shy away from giving a definite opinion, taking a firm stand, etc. —**puss′y·foot′er** ***n.***
pussy willow any of several willows bearing silvery, velvetlike catkins before the leaves appear
pus·tu·lant (pus′chə lənt) ***adj.*** making pustules form
pus·tu·lar (-lər) ***adj.*** of, like, or covered with pustules: also **pus′tu·lous** (-ləs)
pus·tu·late (-lāt′; *for adj.* -lit) ***vt., vi.*** **-lat′ed, -lat′ing** [< LL. pp. of *pustulare* < *pustula*, a pustule] to form into pustules —***adj.*** covered with pustules —**pus′tu·la′tion** ***n.***
pus·tule (pus′chōōl) ***n.*** [L. *pustula*] **1.** a small swelling in the skin, containing pus **2.** any small swelling like a blister or pimple
put (poot) ***vt.*** **put, put′ting** [< or akin to OE. *potian*, to push] **1.** *a)* to drive or send by a blow, shot, or thrust *b)* to throw with an overhand thrust from the shoulder *[put* the shot*]* **2.** to make do something; impel; force **3.** to make be in a specified place, condition, relation, etc.; place; set *[put* her at ease*]* **4.** to make undergo; subject **5.** to impose (a burden, tax, etc.) **6.** *a)* to bring to bear (*on*); apply (*to*) *b)* to bring in; add; inject *c)* to bring about; effect **7.** to attribute; assign; ascribe *[put* the blame on him*]* **8.** to express; state *[put* it plainly*]* **9.** to translate **10.** to present for consideration, decision, etc. *[put* the question*]* **11.** *a)* to estimate as being (with *at*) *[*to *put* the cost at $50*]* *b)* to fix or set (a price, value, etc.) *on* **12.** to fit (words) to music **13.** *a)* to bet (money) *on* *b)* to invest (money) *in* or *into* —***vi.*** to go (*in, out, back*, etc.) —***n.*** a cast or thrust —***adj.*** [Colloq.] fixed *[*stay *put]* —**put about** to turn from one tack or direction to another —**put across** [Colloq.] **1.** to make understood or accepted **2.** to carry out with success **3.** to carry out by trickery —**put aside** (or **by**) **1.** to keep for later **2.** to discard —**put away** **1.** *same as* PUT ASIDE **2.** [Colloq.] *a)* to put in a jail, etc. *b)* to consume (food or drink) *c)* to kill (a pet) to prevent suffering —**put down** **1.** *a)* to crush; repress *b)* to strip of power, rank, etc.; degrade **2.** to write down; record **3.** to attribute (to) **4.** to consider as; classify **5.** to land (an aircraft) **6.** [Slang] to belittle, reject, criticize, or humiliate —**put forth** **1.** to grow (leaves, etc.) **2.** to exert (effort, etc.) **3.** to propose; offer **4.** to leave port —**put in** **1.** to enter a port or haven **2.** to enter (a claim, etc.) **3.** [Colloq.] to spend (time) —**put in for** to apply for —**put it** (or **something**) **over on** [Colloq.] to deceive; trick —**put off** **1.** to postpone; delay **2.** to evade or divert **3.** to perturb; upset —**put on** **1.** to clothe, adorn, or cover oneself with **2.** to take on; add **3.** to assume or pretend **4.** to apply (a brake, etc.) **5.** to stage (a play) **6.** [Slang] to fool (someone) by taking advantage of his readiness to believe; hoax —**put on to** to inform (someone) about (something) —**put out** **1.** to expel; dismiss **2.** to stop from burning; extinguish (a fire or light) **3.** to spend (money) **4.** to disconcert or vex **5.** to inconvenience **6.** to publish, produce, or supply **7.** *Baseball* to cause (a batter or runner) to be out by a fielding play —**put over** [Colloq.] *same as* PUT ACROSS —**put through** **1.** to carry out successfully **2.** to cause to do or undergo **3.** to connect (someone) by telephone with someone else —**put to it** to place in a difficult situation; press hard —**put up** **1.** to offer, as for consideration, decision, sale, etc. **2.** to offer as a candidate **3.** to preserve or can (fruits, etc.) **4.** to erect; build **5.** to lodge, or provide lodgings for **6.** *a)* to advance or provide (money) *b)* [Slang] to do or produce what is needed or wanted **7.** to arrange (the hair) with curlers, bobby pins, etc. **8.** to carry on *[*to *put up* a struggle*]* **9.** [Colloq.] to incite (a person) *to* some action —**put upon** to impose on; victimize —**put up with** to tolerate; bear
pu·ta·tive (pyōōt′ə tiv) ***adj.*** [< L. < *putare*, to suppose] reputed; supposed —**pu′ta·tive·ly** ***adv.***
put-down (poot′doun′) ***n.*** [Slang] a belittling remark or crushing retort
put-on (poot′än′) ***adj.*** feigned —***n.*** [Slang] a fooling of someone by taking advantage of his readiness to believe
put·out (-out′) ***n.*** *Baseball* a play in which the batter or runner is retired, or put out
put-put (put′put′) ***n., vi.*** **put′-put′ted, put′-put′ting** *same as* PUTT-PUTT
pu·tre·fac·tion (pyōō′trə fak′shən) ***n.*** [see ff.] the rotting of organic matter by bacteria, fungi, and oxidation, with resulting foul-smelling products —**pu′tre·fac′tive** ***adj.***
pu·tre·fy (pyōō′trə fī′) ***vt., vi.*** **-fied′, -fy′ing** [< L. *putrefacere* < *putris*, putrid + *facere*, to make] to make or become putrid or rotten —**pu′tre·fi′er** ***n.***
pu·tres·cent (pyōō tres′'nt) ***adj.*** [L. prp. of *putrescere*, to become rotten < *putris*, rotten] **1.** rotting **2.** of or relating to putrefaction —**pu·tres′cence** ***n.***
pu·trid (pyōō′trid) ***adj.*** [< Fr. < L. *putridus* < *putrere*, to be rotten] **1.** rotten and smelling bad **2.** of or from decay **3.** corrupt or depraved **4.** [Colloq.] very unpleasant —**pu·trid′i·ty, pu′trid·ness** ***n.*** —**pu′trid·ly** ***adv.***
‡**Putsch** (pooch) ***n.*** [G.] an uprising or rebellion, esp. an unsuccessful one
putt (put) ***n.*** [< PUT, *v.*] *Golf* a light stroke made on the putting green in trying to put the ball into the hole —***vt., vi.*** to hit (the ball) thus
put·tee (pu tē′, put′ē) ***n.*** [< Hindi *paṭṭī*, a bandage < Sans. *paṭṭa*, a strip of cloth] a cloth or leather legging or a cloth strip wound spirally to cover the leg from ankle to knee
put·ter[1] (poot′ər) ***n.*** a person or thing that puts
putt·er[2] (put′ər) ***n.*** *Golf* **1.** a short, straight-faced club used in putting **2.** a person who putts
put·ter[3] (put′ər) ***vi.*** [var. of POTTER[2]] to busy oneself in an ineffective or aimless way; dawdle (often with *around*, etc.) —***vt.*** to fritter (*away*)
putt·ing green (put′iŋ) *Golf* the area of smooth, closely mowed turf in which the hole is sunk
putt-putt (put′put′) ***n.*** [echoic] **1.** the chugging or popping sounds of a motorboat engine, etc. **2.** [Colloq.] a boat, etc. making such sounds —***vi.*** **putt′-putt′ed, putt′-putt′ing** to make, move along, or operate with such sounds

PUTTEES

put·ty (put′ē) ***n.*** [< Fr. *potée*, lit., potful < *pot*, a pot] **1.** a soft, plastic mixture of powdered chalk and linseed oil, used to hold glass panes in place, to fill small cracks, etc. **2.** any similar substance —***vt.*** **-tied, -ty·ing** to cement, fill, etc. with putty —**put′ti·er** ***n.***
Pu·tu·ma·yo (pōō′tōō mä′yô) river flowing from SW Colombia into the Amazon in NW Brazil
put-up (poot′up′) ***adj.*** [Colloq.] planned secretly beforehand *[*a *put-up* job*]*
puz·zle (puz′'l) ***vt.*** **-zled, -zling** [< ?] to perplex; bewilder —***vi.*** **1.** to be perplexed, etc. **2.** to exercise one's mind, as on a problem —***n.*** **1.** a puzzled state **2.** a puzzling problem, etc. **3.** a toy or problem to test skill or ingenuity —**puzzle out** to solve by deep thought —**puzzle over** to give deep thought to —**puz′zle·ment** ***n.*** —**puz′zler** ***n.***
Pvt. *Mil.* Private
PW Prisoner of War
PWA, P.W.A. Public Works Administration
pwt. pennyweight(s)
PX post exchange
pya (pyä) ***n.,*** *pl.* **pyas** [Burmese] *see* MONETARY UNITS, table (Burma)
py·e·mi·a (pī ē′mē ə) ***n.*** [ModL.: see PYO- & -EMIA] blood poisoning caused by pus-producing organisms —**py·e′mic** ***adj.***
Pyg·ma·li·on (pig māl′yən, -mā′lē ən) *Gr. Legend* a sculptor who fell in love with his statue of a maiden, later brought to life as Galatea by Aphrodite

Pyg·my (pig′mē) ***n., pl.*** **-mies** [< L. < Gr. *pygmaios*, of the length of the *pygmē*, forearm and fist] **1.** a member of any of several African and Asian peoples of small stature **2.** [**p-**] any abnormally undersized or insignificant person or thing —***adj.*** **1.** of Pygmies **2.** [**p-**] very small

py·ja·mas (pə jam′əz, -jä′məz) ***n.pl.*** *Brit. sp. of* PAJAMAS

py·lon (pī′län) ***n.*** [Gr. *pylōn*, gateway] **1.** a gateway, as of an Egyptian temple **2.** a towerlike structure, as for supporting electric lines, marking an aircraft course, etc.

py·lo·rus (pī lôr′əs, pə-) ***n., pl.*** **-ri** (-ī) [LL. < Gr. *pylōros*, gatekeeper < *pylē*, a gate + *ouros*, watchman] the opening from the stomach into the duodenum —**py·lor′ic** ***adj.***

py·o- [< Gr. *pyon*, pus] *a combining form meaning:* **1.** pus **2.** pus-forming Also **py-**

Pyong·yang (pyuŋ′yäŋ′) capital of North Korea, in the W part: pop. 1,500,000

py·or·rhe·a, py·or·rhoe·a (pī′ə rē′ə) ***n.*** [ModL.: see PYO- & -RRHEA] a discharge of pus; specif., *short for* PYORRHEA ALVEOLARIS —**py′or·rhe′al, py′or·rhoe′al** ***adj.***

pyorrhea al·ve·o·la·ris (al vē′ə ler′is) an infection of the gums and tooth sockets, in which pus forms and the teeth become loose

pyr·a·mid (pir′ə mid) ***n.*** [L. *pyramis* (gen. *pyramidis*) < Gr.] **1.** any huge structure with a square base and four sloping, triangular sides meeting at the top, as those built for royal tombs in ancient Egypt **2.** anything shaped like this **3.** *Geom.* a solid figure the base of which is a polygon whose sides are the bases of triangular surfaces meeting at a common vertex —***vi., vt.*** to build up or grow as in the form of a pyramid —**py·ram·i·dal** (pi ram′ə d'l) ***adj.*** —**py·ram′i·dal·ly** ***adv.*** —**pyr′a·mid′ic, pyr′a·mid′i·cal** ***adj.***

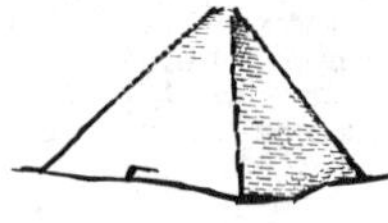

EGYPTIAN PYRAMID

pyre (pīr) ***n.*** [< L. < Gr. < *pyr*, a fire] a pile, esp. of wood, for burning a corpse in a funeral rite

Pyr·e·nees (pir′ə nēz′) mountain range along the border between France & Spain —**Pyr′e·ne′an** (-nē′ən) ***adj.***

py·re·thrum (pī rē′thrəm) ***n.*** [ModL. < L. < Gr. *pyrethron*, feverfew] **1.** any of several chrysanthemums, with white, pink, red, or purple flower heads **2.** an insecticide made from the dried flower heads of certain chrysanthemums

py·ret·ic (pī ret′ik) ***adj.*** [< ModL. < Gr. *pyretos*, fever < *pyr*, a fire] of or causing fever

Py·rex (pī′reks) [arbitrary coinage < PIE[1] + *-r-* + *-ex*] *a trademark for* a heat-resistant glassware for cooking, etc.

pyr·i·dine (pir′ə dēn′, -din) ***n.*** [PYR(O)- + -ID + -INE[4]] a flammable, liquid base, C_5H_5N, with a sharp odor, produced by distilling coal tar, etc. and used in the synthesis of vitamins and drugs, etc.

pyr·i·dox·ine (pir′ə däk′sēn′, -sin) ***n.*** [PYRID(INE) + OX(Y)-[1] + -INE[4]] a pyridine derivative, $C_8H_{11}O_3N$, a vitamin of the B complex, found in cereal grains, liver, yeast, etc.

py·rite (pī′rīt) ***n., pl.*** **py·ri·tes** (pə rīt′ēz, pi-; pī′rīts) [< L. < Gr. *pyritēs*, flint < *pyr*, a fire] iron sulfide, FeS_2, a lustrous, yellow mineral that is an important ore of sulfur

py·ri·tes (pə rīt′ēz, pī-; pī′rīts) ***n.*** any of various native metallic sulfides, as pyrite —**py·rit′ic** (-rit′ik), **py·rit′i·cal** ***adj.***

py·ro- [< Gr. *pyr*, a fire] *a combining form meaning* fire, heat *[pyromania]*: also **pyr-**

Py·ro·ce·ram (pī′rō sə ram′) [prec. + CERAM(IC)] *a trademark for* a heavy, glasslike, ceramic material highly resistant to heat and breakage

py·rog·ra·phy (pī räg′rə fē) ***n.*** [PYRO- + -GRAPHY] **1.** the art of burning designs on wood or leather with heated tools **2.** a design so made —**py·rog′ra·pher** ***n.*** —**py′ro·graph′ic** (-rə graf′ik) ***adj.***

py·ro·ma·ni·a (pī′rə mā′nē ə, -mān′yə) ***n.*** [ModL.: see PYRO- & -MANIA] an uncontrollable desire to start destructive fires —**py′ro·ma′ni·ac′** (-nē ak′) ***n., adj.*** —**py′ro·ma·ni′a·cal** (-mə nī′ə k'l) ***adj.***

py·rom·e·ter (pī räm′ə tər) ***n.*** [PYRO- + -METER] an instrument for measuring unusually high temperatures —**py′ro·met′ric** (-rə met′rik) ***adj.*** —**py′ro·met′ri·cal·ly** ***adv.*** —**py·rom′e·try** (-trē) ***n.***

py·ro·tech·nic (pī′rə tek′nik) ***adj.*** [< Fr. < Gr. *pyr*, fire + *technē*, art] **1.** of fireworks **2.** designating or of spacecraft devices or materials that ignite or explode to activate propellants, etc. **3.** dazzling *[pyrotechnic* wit*]* Also **py′ro·tech′ni·cal** —**py′ro·tech′ni·cal·ly** ***adv.***

py·ro·tech·nics (-niks) ***n.pl.*** **1.** [*with sing. v.*] the art of making and using fireworks: also **py′ro·tech′ny** (-nē) **2.** *a)* a display of fireworks *b)* fireworks; esp., rockets, flares, etc., as for signaling *c)* pyrotechnic devices in spacecraft **3.** a dazzling display, as of eloquence —**py′ro·tech′nist** ***n.***

py·rox·y·lin, py·rox·y·line (pī räk′sə lin) ***n.*** [< Fr. < Gr. *pyr*, fire + *xylon*, wood] nitrocellulose, esp. in less explosive forms than guncotton, used in making paints, lacquers, etc.

Pyr·rhic victory (pir′ik) [after *Pyrrhus*, king of Epirus, who defeated the Romans in 280 and 279 B.C., suffering extremely heavy losses] a victory that is too costly

Py·thag·o·ras (pi thag′ər əs) 6th cent. B.C.; Gr. philosopher & mathematician —**Py·thag′o·re′an** (-ə rē′ən) ***adj., n.***

Pyth·i·an (pith′ē ən) ***adj.*** [< L. < Gr. *Pythios*, of *Pythō*, older name for DELPHI] **1.** of Apollo as patron of Delphi and the Delphic oracle **2.** designating or of the games held at Delphi every four years in ancient Greece in honor of Apollo

Pythias *see* DAMON AND PYTHIAS

py·thon (pī′thän, -thən) ***n.*** [< L. < Gr. *Pythōn*, a serpent slain by Apollo] **1.** any of a group of large, nonpoisonous snakes of Asia, Africa, and Australia, that crush their prey to death **2.** popularly, any large snake that crushes its prey

py·tho·ness (pī′thə nis) ***n.*** [< MFr. < ML. < LL. < Gr. *Pythō*: see PYTHIAN] **1.** a priestess of Apollo at Delphi **2.** any woman soothsayer; prophetess

pyx (piks) ***n.*** [< L. < Gr. *pyxis*, a box < *pyxos*, the box tree] the container in which the consecrated wafer of the Eucharist is kept or carried

pyx·is (pik′sis) ***n., pl.*** **pyx′i·des′** (-sə dēz′) [L.: see prec.] *Bot.* a dry fruit whose upper portion splits off as a lid

Q

Q, q (kyōō) ***n., pl.*** **Q's, q's** **1.** the seventeenth letter of the English alphabet **2.** the sound of *Q* or *q*

Q *Chess* queen

Q. **1.** Quebec **2.** Queen **3.** Question

q. **1.** quart **2.** quarter **3.** quarto **4.** queen **5.** question **6.** quetzal **7.** quintal: also **ql.** **8.** quire

Qa·tar (kä′tär) independent Arab sheikdom occupying a peninsula in E Arabia on the Persian gulf: 8,500 sq. mi.; pop. 130,000

Q.C. Queen's Counsel

Q.E.D. [L. *quod erat demonstrandum*] which was to be proved

qin·tar (kin tär′) ***n.*** [Alb., ult. < L. *centum*, cent] *see* MONETARY UNITS, table (Albania)

QM, Q.M. Quartermaster

qr. *pl.* **qrs.** **1.** quarter **2.** quire

qt. **1.** quantity **2.** quart(s)

Q.T., q.t. [Slang] quiet: usually in **on the Q.T.** (or **q.t.**), in secret

qto. quarto

qua (kwā, kwä) ***adv.*** [L. < *qui*, who] in the function or capacity of *[*the President *qua* Commander in Chief*]*

quack[1] (kwak) ***vi.*** [echoic] to utter the sound or cry of a duck, or a sound like it —***n.*** the sound made by a duck, or any sound like it

quack[2] (kwak) ***n.*** [short for QUACKSALVER] **1.** a person who practices medicine without having been trained, licensed, etc. **2.** any person who pretends to have knowledge or skill that he does not have; charlatan —***adj.*** **1.** characterized by grand claims that have little or no foundation **2.** dishonestly claiming to bring about a cure —***vi.*** to engage in quackery —**quack′ish** ***adj.*** —**quack′ish·ly** ***adv.***

quack·er·y (-ər ē) ***n.*** the claims or methods of a quack

quack·sal·ver (-sal′vər) ***n.*** [< MDu. < *quacken*, to brag + *zalf*, salve] [Now Rare] a quack; charlatan

quad[1] (kwäd) ***n.*** *same as:* **1.** QUADRANGLE (of a college) **2.** QUADRUPLET

quad[2] (kwäd) ***n.*** [< QUAD(RAT)] *Printing* a piece of type metal lower than the face of the type, used for spacing, etc. —***vt.*** **quad′ded, quad′ding** to fill out (a line) with quads

Quad·ra·ges·i·ma (kwäd′rə jes′i mə) ***n.*** [LL. < fem. of L. *quadragesimus*, fortieth] the first Sunday in Lent: also **Quadragesima Sunday**
quad·ran·gle (kwäd′raŋ′g'l) ***n.*** [< MFr. < LL. < L.: see QUADRI- & ANGLE[1]] **1.** a plane figure with four angles and four sides **2.** *a)* an area surrounded on four sides by buildings *b)* the buildings themselves —**quad·ran′gu·lar** (-gyə lər) ***adj.***
quad·rant (kwäd′rənt) ***n.*** [< L. *quadrans*, fourth part] **1.** a fourth part of the circumference of a circle; an arc of 90° **2.** a quarter section of a circle **3.** an instrument for measuring altitudes or angular elevations in astronomy and navigation —**quad·ran′tal** (-ran′t'l) ***adj.***
quad·ra·phon·ic (kwäd′rə fän′ik) ***adj.*** [< L. *quadra*, a square + PHONIC] designating or of sound reproduction, as on records or tapes or in broadcasting, using four channels to carry and reproduce through separate speakers a blend of sounds from separate sources
quad·rat (kwäd′rat) ***n.*** [var. of ff.] **1.** *same as* QUAD[2] **2.** *Ecol.* a plot of ground used to study plant and animal life
quad·rate (-rāt; *also, for adj. & n.,* -rit) ***adj.*** [< L. pp. of *quadrare*, to make square, ult. < *quattuor*, four] square or nearly square —***n.*** **1.** a square or rectangle **2.** a square or rectangular space, thing, etc. —***vi.*** **-rat·ed, -rat·ing** to square; agree (*with*) —***vt.*** to make square
quad·rat·ic (kwäd rat′ik) ***adj.*** [< prec. + -IC] *Algebra* involving a quantity or quantities that are squared but none that are raised to a higher power —***n.*** *Algebra* a quadratic term, expression, or equation —**quad·rat′i·cal·ly** ***adv.***
quadratic equation *Algebra* an equation in which the second power, or square, is the highest to which the unknown quantity is raised
quad·ra·ture (kwäd′rə chər) ***n.*** [< LL. < L. pp. of *quadrare:* see QUADRATE] **1.** the act of squaring **2.** the determining of the dimensions of a square equal in area to a given surface **3.** *Astron.* the relative position of two heavenly bodies when 90° distant from each other
quad·ren·ni·al (kwäd ren′ē əl) ***adj.*** [< L. < *quadri-* (see ff.) + *annus*, a year] **1.** lasting four years **2.** occurring once every four years —***n.*** a quadrennial event —**quad·ren′ni·al·ly** ***adv.***
quad·ri- [L. < base of *quattuor*, four] *a combining form meaning* four times, fourfold: also, before a vowel, **quadr-**
quad·ri·lat·er·al (kwäd′rə lat′ər əl) ***adj.*** [< L.: see QUADRI- & LATERAL] four-sided —***n.*** **1.** *Geom.* a plane figure having four sides and four angles **2.** a four-sided area —**quad′ri·lat′er·al·ly** ***adv.***

QUADRILATERALS

qua·drille (kwə dril′, kwä-) ***n.*** [Fr. < Sp. *cuadrilla*, dim. < *cuadro*, a square] **1.** a square dance performed by four couples **2.** music for this dance
quad·ril·lion (kwäd ril′yən) ***n.*** [Fr. < *quadri-* (see QUADRI-) + (MI)LLION] **1.** in the U.S. and France, the number represented by 1 followed by 15 zeros **2.** in Great Britain and Germany, the number represented by 1 followed by 24 zeros —***adj.*** amounting to one quadrillion in number —**quad·ril′lionth** ***adj., n.***
quad·ri·ple·gi·a (kwäd′rə plē′jē ə, -jə) ***n.*** [ModL.: see QUADRI- & -PLEGIA] total paralysis of the body from the neck down —**quad′ri·ple′gic** (-plē′jik, -plej′ik) ***adj., n.***
quad·ri·va·lent (kwäd′rə vā′lənt, kwä driv′ə-) ***adj.*** **1.** having four valences **2.** *same as* TETRAVALENT (sense 1) —**quad′ri·va′lence, quad′ri·va′len·cy** ***n.***
quad·roon (kwä dro͞on′) ***n.*** [< Sp. < *cuarto*, a fourth < L. *quartus:* see QUART] a person who has one Negro grandparent
quad·ru·ped (kwäd′roo ped′) ***n.*** [< L. < *quadru-* (for *quadri-*), four + *pes*, a foot] an animal, esp. a mammal, with four feet —***adj.*** having four feet —**quad·ru·pe·dal** (kwä dro͞o′pi d'l, kwäd′rə ped′'l) ***adj.***
quad·ru·ple (kwä dro͞o′p'l, -drup′'l; kwäd′roo-) ***adj.*** [MFr. < L. < *quadru-* (see prec.) + *-plus*, -fold] **1.** consisting of four **2.** four times as much or as many; fourfold **3.** *Music* having four beats to the measure —***n.*** an amount four times as much or as many —***vt., vi.*** **-pled, -pling** to make or become four times as much or as many
quad·ru·plet (kwä drup′lit, -dro͞o′plit; kwäd′roo plit) ***n.*** [dim. of prec.] **1.** any of four offspring born at a single birth **2.** a group of four, usually of one kind
quad·ru·pli·cate (kwä dro͞o′plə kāt′; *for adj. & n., usually* -kit) ***vt.*** **-cat′ed, -cat′ing** [< L. pp. of *quadruplicare* < *quadru-* (see QUADRUPED) + *plicare*, to fold] to make four identical copies of —***adj.*** **1.** fourfold **2.** designating the fourth of identical copies —***n.*** any of four identical copies —**in quadruplicate** in four identical copies —**quad·ru′pli·ca′tion** ***n.***
quaes·tor (kwes′tər, kwēs′-) ***n.*** [L. < pp. of *quaerere*, to inquire] in ancient Rome, **1.** orig., a judge in certain criminal cases **2.** later, any of certain state treasurers —**quaes·to′ri·al** (-tôr′ē əl) ***adj.*** —**quaes′tor·ship′** ***n.***
quaff (kwäf, kwaf) ***vt., vi.*** [prob. (by misreading of *-ss-* as *-ff-*) < LowG. *quassen*, to overindulge] to drink deeply in a hearty or thirsty way —***n.*** **1.** a quaffing **2.** a drink that is quaffed —**quaff′er** ***n.***
quag·ga (kwag′ə) ***n.,*** *pl.* **-ga, -gas** see PLURAL, II, D, 2 [Afrik. < native name] a striped wild ass of Africa, now extinct
quag·gy (kwag′ē) ***adj.*** **-gi·er, -gi·est** **1.** like a quagmire; boggy; miry **2.** soft; flabby
quag·mire (kwag′mīr′) ***n.*** [< earlier *quag*, a bog + MIRE] **1.** wet, boggy ground, yielding under the feet **2.** a difficult or dangerous situation from which it is hard to escape *[a quagmire* of debts*]*
qua·hog, qua·haug (kwô′hôg, kō′-; -häg) ***n.*** [< AmInd. name] an edible clam of the eastern coast of N. America, having a very hard, solid shell
quail[1] (kwāl) ***vi.*** [prob. < OFr. *coaillier* < L. *coagulare*, to coagulate] to draw back in fear; lose courage; cower
quail[2] (kwāl) ***n.,*** *pl.* **quails, quail:** see PLURAL, II, D, 1 [< OFr. < ML. *cuacula*, prob. < Gmc. echoic name] **1.** any of various small game birds, resembling partridges **2.** *same as* BOBWHITE
quaint (kwānt) ***adj.*** [< OFr. *cointe* < L. *cognitus*, known: see COGNITION] **1.** unusual or old-fashioned in a pleasing way **2.** unusual; curious **3.** fanciful; whimsical —**quaint′ly** ***adv.*** —**quaint′ness** ***n.***
quake (kwāk) ***vi.*** **quaked, quak′ing** [OE. *cwacian*] **1.** to tremble or shake, as the ground does in an earthquake **2.** to shudder or shiver, as from fear or cold —***n.*** **1.** a shaking or tremor **2.** an earthquake
Quak·er (kwāk′ər) ***n.*** [orig. mocking: said to be from founder's admonition to "quake" at the word of the Lord] *a popular name for* a member of the Society of Friends: see SOCIETY OF FRIENDS —**Quak′er·ess** [Now Rare] ***n.fem.*** —**Quak′er·ish** ***adj.*** —**Quak′er·ism** ***n.*** —**Quak′er·ly** ***adj., adv.***
quaking aspen a poplar with small, flat-stemmed leaves that tremble in the slightest breeze
quak·y (kwā′kē) ***adj.*** **quak′i·er, quak′i·est** inclined to quake; shaky —**quak′i·ly** ***adv.*** —**quak′i·ness** ***n.***
qual·i·fi·ca·tion (kwäl′ə fi kā′shən) ***n.*** **1.** a qualifying or being qualified **2.** a thing or condition that qualifies or limits; modification or restriction **3.** any skill, knowledge, experience, etc. that fits a person for a position, office, etc. **4.** a condition that must be met, as to be eligible
qual·i·fied (kwäl′ə fīd′) ***adj.*** **1.** having met conditions or requirements set **2.** having the necessary or desirable qualities; competent **3.** limited; modified *[qualified* approval*]* —**qual′i·fied′ly** ***adv.*** —**qual′i·fied′ness** ***n.***
qual·i·fy (-fī′) ***vt.*** **-fied′, -fy′ing** [< Fr. < ML. < L. *qualis*, of what kind + *facere*, to make] **1.** to describe by giving the qualities or characteristics of **2.** to make fit for an office, position, etc. **3.** to make legally capable; license **4.** to modify; restrict; limit **5.** to moderate; soften **6.** to change the strength of (a liquor, etc.) **7.** *Gram.* to modify the meaning of (a word) —***vi.*** to be or become qualified —**qual′i·fi′a·ble** ***adj.*** —**qual′i·fi′er** ***n.*** —**qual′i·fy′ing·ly** ***adv.***
qual·i·ta·tive (-tāt′iv) ***adj.*** having to do with quality or qualities —**qual′i·ta′tive·ly** ***adv.***
qualitative analysis the branch of chemistry dealing with the determination of the elements or ingredients of which a compound or mixture is composed
qual·i·ty (kwäl′ə tē) ***n.,*** *pl.* **-ties** [< OFr. < L. < *qualis*, of what kind] **1.** any of the features that make something what it is; characteristic; attribute **2.** basic nature; character; kind **3.** the degree of excellence which a thing possesses **4.** excellence; superiority **5.** [Archaic] *a)* high social position *b)* people of such position **6.** the property of a tone determined by its overtones; timbre
quality control a system for maintaining desired standards in a product, esp. by inspecting samples
qualm (kwäm) ***n.*** [OE. *cwealm*, disaster] **1.** a sudden feeling of sickness, faintness, or nausea **2.** a sudden feeling of uneasiness or doubt; misgiving **3.** a twinge of conscience; scruple —**qualm′ish** ***adj.*** —**qualm′ish·ly** ***adv.*** —**qualm′ishness** ***n.***
quan·da·ry (kwän′drē, -dər ē) ***n.,*** *pl.* **-ries** [< ? L. *quande*, how much] a state of perplexity; dilemma
quan·ta (kwän′tə) ***n.*** *pl. of* QUANTUM
quan·ti·fy (kwän′tə fī′) ***vt.*** **-fied′, -fy′ing** [ML. < L. *quantus*, how much + *facere*, to make] to determine or express the quantity of; measure —**quan′ti·fi′a·ble** ***adj.*** —**quan′ti·fi·ca′tion** ***n.*** —**quan′ti·fi′er** ***n.***
quan·ti·ta·tive (kwän′tə tāt′iv) ***adj.*** **1.** having to do

with quantity **2.** capable of being measured —**quan′ti·ta′tive·ly** *adv.* —**quan′ti·ta′tive·ness** *n.*

quantitative analysis the branch of chemistry dealing with the measurement of the amounts or percentages of the various components of a compound or mixture

quan·ti·ty (kwän′tə tē) *n., pl.* **-ties** [< OFr. < L. *quantus*, how much] **1.** an amount; portion **2.** any bulk, weight, or number not definitely specified **3.** the exact amount of something **4.** [*also pl.*] a great amount **5.** that property of anything which can be determined by measurement **6.** the relative length of a vowel, syllable, musical tone, etc. **7.** *Math.* *a*) a thing that has the property of being measurable in dimensions, amounts, etc. *b*) a number or symbol expressing a quantity

quan·tum (-təm) *n., pl.* **-ta** (-tə) [L., neut. sing. of *quantus*, how much] *Physics* an (or the) elemental unit, as of energy: the **quantum theory** states that energy is not absorbed or radiated continuously, but discontinuously, in quanta

quar·an·tine (kwôr′ən tēn′, kwär′-) *n.* [It. *quarantina*, lit., forty days, ult. < L. *quadraginta*, forty] **1.** *a*) the period, orig. 40 days, during which a vessel suspected of carrying contagious disease is detained in a port in isolation *b*) the place where such a vessel is stationed **2.** any isolation or restriction on travel to keep contagious diseases, insect pests, etc. from spreading **3.** a place where persons, animals, or plants having such diseases, etc. are isolated **4.** the state of being quarantined —*vt.* **-tined′, -tin′ing 1.** to place under quarantine **2.** to isolate politically, commercially, socially, etc. —**quar′an·tin′a·ble** *adj.*

quark (kwôrk) *n.* [orig. a word coined by James Joyce in *Finnegan's Wake*] any of three proposed particles thought of as the building blocks of baryons and mesons

quar·rel[1] (kwôr′əl, kwär′-) *n.* [< OFr., ult. < dim. of L. *quadrus*, a square] **1.** a square-headed arrow shot from a crossbow **2.** a small, diamond-shaped or square pane of glass

quar·rel[2] (kwôr′əl, kwär′-) *n.* [< OFr. < L. *querela*, complaint < *queri*, to complain] **1.** a cause for dispute **2.** a dispute, esp. one marked by anger and resentment **3.** a breaking up of friendly relations —*vi.* **-reled** or **-relled, -rel·ing** or **-rel·ling 1.** to find fault; complain **2.** to dispute heatedly **3.** to have a breach in friendship —**quar′rel·er, quar′rel·ler** *n.*

quar·rel·some (-səm) *adj.* inclined to quarrel —**quar′rel·some·ly** *adv.* —**quar′rel·some·ness** *n.*

quar·ry[1] (kwôr′ē, kwär′ē) *n., pl.* **-ries** [< OFr. *cuiree*, altered (after *cuir*, a hide) < pp. of *curer*, to eviscerate] **1.** an animal that is being hunted down **2.** anything pursued

quar·ry[2] (kwôr′ē, kwär′ē) *n., pl.* **-ries** [< ML., ult. < L. *quadrare*, to square] a place where building stone, marble, or slate is excavated —*vt.* **-ried, -ry·ing 1.** to excavate from a quarry **2.** to make a quarry in (land)

quar·ry·man (-mən) *n., pl.* **-men** a person who works in a stone quarry: also **quar·ri·er** (kwôr′ē ər, kwär′-)

quart (kwôrt) *n.* [< MFr. < OFr. < L. *quartus*, fourth < base of *quattuor*, four] **1.** a liquid measure, equal to 1/4 gallon (57.75 cu. in.) **2.** a dry measure, equal to 1/8 peck **3.** any container that can hold one quart

quar·ter (kwôr′tər) *n.* [< OFr. < L. *quartarius*, a fourth < *quartus*, fourth] **1.** any of the four equal parts of something; fourth **2.** *a*) one fourth of a year; three months *b*) a school or college term, usually one fourth of a school year **3.** *a*) one fourth of an hour; 15 minutes *b*) the moment marking the end of each fourth of an hour **4.** *a*) one fourth of a dollar; 25 cents *b*) a coin of the U.S. and Canada equal to 25 cents: in the U.S., made of cupronickel **5.** any leg of a four-legged animal, with the adjoining parts **6.** *a*) any of the four main points of the compass *b*) any of the regions of the earth thought of as under these **7.** a particular district in a city [the Latin *quarter*] **8.** [*pl.*] lodgings; place of abode **9.** mercy granted to a surrendering foe **10.** a particular person, group, place, etc., esp. one serving as a source [news from the highest *quarters*] **11.** *a*) the period of time in which the moon makes one fourth of its revolution around the earth *b*) a phase of the moon when it is half lighted **12.** *Football, Basketball*, etc. any of the four periods into which a game is divided **13.** *Heraldry* *a*) any of the four equal divisions of a shield *b*) the charge occupying such a division **14.** *Naut.* *a*) the after part of a ship's side *b*) an assigned station or post —*vt.* **1.** to divide into four equal parts **2.** loosely, to separate into any number of parts **3.** to dismember (the body of a person put to death) into four parts **4.** to provide lodgings for; specif., to assign (soldiers) to lodgings **5.** to pass over (an area) in many directions, as hounds do in searching for game **6.** *Heraldry* to place (different coats of arms) on the quarters of a shield, or to add (a coat of arms) to a shield thus —*vi.* **1.** to be lodged or stationed (*at* or *with*) **2.** to range over a field, etc., as hounds in hunting **3.** *Naut.* to blow on the quarter of a ship: said of the wind —*adj.* constituting or equal to a quarter —**at close quarters** at close range —**cry quarter** to beg for mercy —**quar′ter·ing** *adj., n.*

quar·ter·back (-bak′) *n.* *Football* the offensive back who calls the signals and directs the plays —*vt., vi.* **1.** to act as quarterback for (a team) **2.** to direct or lead; manage

quarter day any of the four days regarded as beginning a new quarter of the year, when quarterly payments on rents, etc. are due

quar·ter-deck, quar·ter·deck (-dek′) *n.* **1.** the after part of a ship's upper deck, usually reserved for officers **2.** *U.S. Navy* the part of a ship's upper deck reserved for official ceremonies

quar·tered (kwôr′tərd) *adj.* **1.** divided into quarters **2.** provided with quarters or lodgings **3.** quartersawed

quar·ter·fi·nal (kwôr′tər fī′n′l; *for n. usually* kwôr′tər-fī′n′l) *adj.* coming just before the semifinals, as of a tournament —*n.* **1.** a quarterfinal match **2.** [*pl.*] a quarterfinal round —**quar′ter·fi′nal·ist** *n.*

quarter horse an American breed of horse with a low, compact, muscular body and great sprinting speed for distances up to a quarter of a mile

quar·ter·ly (kwôr′tər lē) *adj.* **1.** occurring or appearing at regular intervals four times a year **2.** consisting of a quarter —*adv.* once every quarter of the year —*n., pl.* **-lies** a publication issued every three months

quar·ter·mas·ter (-mas′tər) *n.* **1.** *Mil.* an officer whose duty it is to provide troops with quarters, clothing, equipment, etc. **2.** a ship's petty officer who attends to navigation, signals, etc.

quar·tern (kwôr′tərn) *n.* [< OFr.: see QUART] **1.** orig., a fourth part **2.** [Brit.] one fourth of a pint, a peck, etc.

quarter note *Music* a note having one fourth the duration of a whole note; crotchet: see NOTE, illus.

quar·ter·saw (kwôr′tər sô′) *vt.* **-sawed′, -sawed′** or **-sawn′, -saw′ing** to saw (a log) into quarters lengthwise and then into boards, in order to show off the grain of the wood

quarter section a division of public lands that is one fourth of a section (160 acres) and is half a mile square

quarter sessions 1. in England, a court that sits quarterly in civil proceedings, with limited criminal jurisdiction **2.** in the U.S., any of various courts that sit quarterly

quar·ter·staff (-staf′) *n., pl.* **-staves′** (-stāvz′) a stout, iron-tipped wooden staff, six to eight feet long, formerly used in England as a weapon

quarter tone *Music* an interval of one half of a semitone

quar·tet, quar·tette (kwôr tet′) *n.* [< Fr. < It. dim. of *quarto* < L. *quartus*, a fourth] **1.** any group of four **2.** *Music* *a*) a composition for four voices or four instruments *b*) the four performers of such a composition

quar·to (kwôr′tō) *n., pl.* **-tos** [< L. (*in*) *quarto*, (in) a fourth] **1.** the page size (about 9 by 12 in.) of a book made up of printer's sheets folded into four leaves **2.** a book with pages of this size —*adj.* with pages of this size

quartz (kwôrts) *n.* [G. *quarz* < ?] a brilliant, crystalline mineral, silicon dioxide, SiO_2, occurring most often in a colorless, transparent form, but also as variously colored semiprecious stones —**quartz·ose** (kwôrt′sōs) *adj.*

quartz crystal *Electronics* a thin plate or rod cut from quartz and ground so as to vibrate at a particular frequency

quartz lamp a mercury-vapor lamp with a quartz tube for transmitting ultraviolet rays

qua·sar (kwā′sär, -zär, -sər) *n.* [< *quas*(*i-stell*)*ar* (*radio source*)] any of a number of extremely distant starlike objects that emit powerful radio waves

quash[1] (kwäsh) *vt.* [< MFr. < LL. *cassare*, to destroy < L. *cassus*, empty] *Law* to annul or set aside (an indictment)

quash[2] (kwäsh) *vt.* [< MFr. < L. *quassare*, to shatter < pp. of *quatere*, to break] to put down or overcome as by force; suppress; quell [to *quash* an uprising]

qua·si (kwā′sī, -zī; kwä′sē, -zē) *adv.* [L. < *quam*, as + *si*, if] as if; seemingly; in part —*adj.* seeming Often hyphenated as a prefix [*quasi*-judicial]

qua·si-stel·lar radio source (-stel′ər) *same as* QUASAR

quas·si·a (kwäsh′ē ə, kwäsh′ə) *n.* [ModL. < Graman *Quassi*, Surinam Negro who prescribed it for fever, c. 1730] **1.** any of a group of tropical trees related to the ailanthus **2.** the wood of certain of these or a drug extracted from it

qua·ter·na·ry (kwät′ər ner′ē, kwə tur′nər ē) *adj.* [< L. < *quaterni*, four each] **1.** consisting of four **2.** [Q-] designating or of the geologic period following the Tertiary in the Cenozoic Era —**the Quaternary** the Quaternary Period or its rocks: see GEOLOGY, chart

quat·rain (kwä′trān) *n.* [Fr. < *quatre* < L. *quattuor*, four] a stanza or poem of four lines

quat·re·foil (kat′ər foil′, kat′rə-) *n.* [< MFr. < *quatre* (< L. *quattuor*), four + *feuille* (< L. *folium*), a leaf] **1.** a flower with four petals or a leaf with four leaflets **2.** *Archit.* a circular design of four converging arcs

qua·ver (kwā′vər) *vi.* [ME. *cwafien*] **1.** to shake or tremble **2.** to be tremulous: said of the voice **3.** to make a trill in singing or playing —*vt.* **1.** to utter in a tremulous voice **2.** to sing or play with a trill —*n.* **1.** a tremulous quality in a voice or tone **2.** [Brit.] *same as* EIGHTH NOTE —**qua′ver·er** *n.* —**qua′ver·ing·ly** *adv.* —**qua′ver·y** *adj.*

quay (kē) ***n.*** [MFr. *cai* < Celt.] a wharf for loading and unloading ships, usually one of stone or concrete

Que. Quebec

quean (kwēn) ***n.*** [OE. *cwene*] **1.** a hussy **2.** a prostitute

quea·sy (kwē′zē) ***adj.*** **-si·er, -si·est** [ME. *qwesye* < Scand.] **1.** causing or feeling nausea **2.** squeamish; easily nauseated **3.** uncomfortable; uneasy **—quea′si·ly** ***adv.*** **—quea′si·ness** ***n.***

Que·bec (kwi bek′) **1.** province of E Canada: 594,860 sq. mi.; pop. 6,234,000; abbrev. **Que., P.Q. 2.** its capital, on the St. Lawrence River: pop. 177,000 (met. area 413,000) Fr. **Qué·bec** (kā bek′)

Que·bec·ois (ke′be kwä′) ***n.,*** *pl.* **-ois′** [CanadFr. *Québecois*] a French-speaking native or inhabitant of the province of Quebec

Quech·ua (kech′wä, -wə) ***n.*** [Sp. < Quechua name] **1.** *pl.* **-uas, -ua** a member of any of a group of S. American Indian tribes dominant in the former Inca Empire **2.** their language, still widely spoken **—Quech′uan** ***adj., n.***

queen (kwēn) ***n.*** [OE. *cwen*] **1.** the wife of a king **2.** a woman who rules over a monarchy in her own right **3.** a woman who is foremost among others, as in beauty or accomplishments **4.** a place or thing regarded as the finest of its kind **5.** the fully developed, reproductive female in a colony of bees, ants, etc. **6.** a playing card with a picture of a queen on it **7.** [Slang] a male homosexual, esp. one with feminine characteristics **8.** *Chess* the most powerful piece: it can move in any straight or diagonal direction **—queen it** to act like a queen; domineer **—queen′dom** ***n.*** **—queen′hood′** ***n.*** **—queen′like′** ***adj.***

Queen Anne's lace *same as* WILD CARROT

queen consort the wife of a reigning king

queen dowager the widow of a king

queen·ly (-lē) ***adj.*** **-li·er, -li·est** of, like, or fit for a queen; royal; regal **—queen′li·ness** ***n.***

queen mother a queen dowager who is mother of a reigning sovereign

queen post *Carpentry* either of two vertical posts set between the rafters and the base of a truss, at equal distances from the apex

QUEEN POSTS

Queens (kwēnz) [after *Queen* Catherine, wife of CHARLES II of England] borough of New York City, on W Long Island: pop. 1,891,000

queen's English *see* KING'S ENGLISH

queen-size (kwēn′sīz′) ***adj.*** [Colloq.] larger than usual, but less than king-size

Queens·land (kwēnz′land′, -lənd) state of NE Australia

queer (kwir) ***adj.*** [< ? G. *quer,* crosswise] **1.** differing from what is usual or ordinary: odd; strange **2.** slightly ill; giddy, queasy, etc. **3.** [Colloq.] doubtful; suspicious **4.** [Colloq.] having mental quirks; eccentric **5.** [Slang] counterfeit; not genuine **6.** [Slang] homosexual *—vt.* [Slang] **1.** to spoil the success of **2.** to put (oneself) into an unfavorable position *—n.* [Slang] **1.** counterfeit money **2.** an eccentric person **3.** a homosexual **—queer′ish** ***adj.*** **—queer′ly** ***adv.*** **—queer′ness** ***n.***

quell (kwel) ***vt.*** [OE. *cwellan,* to kill] **1.** to crush; subdue [to *quell* a mutiny] **2.** to quiet; allay [to *quell* fears]

quench (kwench) ***vt.*** [OE. *cwencan,* caus. of *cwincan,* to go out] **1.** to extinguish; put out [water *quenched* the fire] **2.** to overcome; subdue **3.** to satisfy; slake [he *quenched* his thirst] **4.** to cool (hot steel, etc.) suddenly by plunging into water, oil, etc. **—quench′a·ble** ***adj.*** **—quench′er** ***n.*** **—quench′less** ***adj.***

quern (kwʉrn) ***n.*** [OE. *cweorn*] a primitive hand mill, esp. for grinding grain

quer·u·lous (kwer′ə ləs, -yə-) ***adj.*** [< L. < *queri,* to complain] **1.** inclined to find fault; complaining **2.** full of complaint; peevish **—quer′u·lous·ly** ***adv.*** **—quer′u·lous·ness** ***n.***

que·ry (kwir′ē) ***n.,*** *pl.* **-ries** [< L. *quaere,* 2d pers. sing., imper., of *quaerere,* to ask] **1.** a question; inquiry **2.** a doubt **3.** a question mark (?) *—vt.* **-ried, -ry·ing 1.** to call in question; ask about **2.** to question (a person) **3.** to question the accuracy of (written or printed matter) by marking with a question mark *—vi.* to ask questions or express doubt **—que′rist** ***n.***

ques. question

quest (kwest) ***n.*** [< OFr. < ML., ult. < L. *quaesitus,* pp. of *quaerere,* to seek] **1.** a seeking; hunt; search **2.** a journey in search of adventure, etc., as those undertaken by knights-errant in medieval times **3.** the persons participating in a quest *—vi.* to go in search or pursuit *—vt.* to seek **—quest′er** ***n.***

ques·tion (kwes′chən) ***n.*** [< Anglo-Fr. < OFr. < L. *quaestio* < pp. of *quaerere,* to ask] **1.** an asking; inquiry **2.** something asked; interrogative sentence **3.** doubt; uncertainty **4.** something in controversy before a court **5.** a problem; matter open to discussion or inquiry **6.** a matter or case of difficulty [not a *question* of money] **7.** *a)* a point being debated or a resolution brought up before an assembly *b)* the putting of such a matter to a vote *—vt.* **1.** to ask questions of; interrogate **2.** to express uncertainty about; doubt **3.** to dispute; challenge *—vi.* to ask a question or questions **—beside the question** not relevant **—beyond (all) question** without any doubt **—in question** being considered, debated, etc. **—out of the question** impossible; not to be considered **—ques′tion·er** ***n.*** **—ques′tion·ing** ***adj.***

ques·tion·a·ble (-ə b′l) ***adj.*** **1.** that can or should be questioned; open to doubt **2.** suspected with good reason of being immoral, dishonest, etc. **3.** uncertain [of *questionable* excellence] **—ques′tion·a·bly** ***adv.***

question mark **1.** a mark of punctuation (?) put after a sentence, word, etc. to indicate a direct question, or to express doubt, uncertainty, etc. **2.** an unknown factor

ques·tion·naire (kwes′chə ner′) ***n.*** [Fr.] a written or printed list of questions used in gathering information from one or more persons

quet·zal (ket säl′) ***n.*** [AmSp. < Nahuatl < *quetzalli,* tail feather] **1.** a Central American bird, usually brilliant green above and red below, with long, streaming tail feathers in the male **2.** *pl.* **-zal′es** (-sä′les) *see* MONETARY UNITS, table (Guatemala)

QUETZAL
(length, including plumes, to 42 in.)

queue (kyo͞o) ***n.*** [Fr. < OFr. *coue* < L. *cauda,* tail] **1.** a pigtail **2.** [Chiefly Brit.] a line, as of persons waiting to be served *—vi.* **queued, queu′ing** [Chiefly Brit.] to form in a line (often with *up*)

Que·zon (ke′sôn; *E.* kā′zän), **Man·uel Lu·is** (mä nwel′ lo͞o ēs′) 1878–1944; Philippine statesman

quib·ble (kwib′′l) ***n.*** [< L. *quibus* (formerly common in legal documents), abl. pl. of *qui,* who, which] **1.** a petty evasion; cavil **2.** a petty objection or criticism *—vi.* **-bled, -bling** to evade the truth of a point under discussion by caviling **—quib′bler** ***n.***

‡**quiche Lor·raine** (kēsh lô ren′) *pl.* **quiches Lor·raine** (kēsh) [Fr., lit., Lorraine pastry: *quiche* < G. dial. *küche,* dim of *kuchen,* cake] a kind of custard pie made with cheese, bacon, etc. and served hot

quick (kwik) ***adj.*** [OE. *cwicu,* living] **1.** [Archaic] living **2.** *a)* rapid in action; swift [a *quick* walk, a *quick* worker] *b)* prompt [a *quick* reply] **3.** lasting a short time [a *quick* look] **4.** prompt to understand or learn **5.** sensitive [a *quick* sense of smell] **6.** easily stirred; fiery [a *quick* temper] *—adv.* quickly; rapidly *—n.* **1.** the living, esp. in **the quick and the dead** **2.** the sensitive flesh under a fingernail or toenail **3.** the deepest feelings [cut to the *quick*] **—quick′ly** ***adv.*** **—quick′ness** ***n.***

quick bread any bread, as muffins, corn bread, etc., leavened with baking powder, soda, etc., and baked as soon as the batter or dough is mixed

quick·en (kwik′ən) ***vt.*** **1.** to animate; enliven **2.** to stir; arouse; stimulate **3.** to make move more rapidly; hasten *—vi.* **1.** to become enlivened; revive **2.** *a)* to begin to show signs of life *b)* to enter the stage of pregnancy in which the movement of the fetus can be felt **3.** to become more rapid; speed up [the pulse *quickens* with fear] **—quick′en·er** ***n.***

quick-freeze (-frēz′) ***vt.*** **-froze′, -froz′en, -freez′ing** to subject (food) to sudden freezing so that flavor and natural juices are retained and the food can be stored at low temperatures for a long time

quick·ie (-ē) ***n.*** [Slang] anything done or made quickly *—adj.* [Slang] done or made quickly

quick·lime (-līm′) ***n.*** lime, or calcium oxide, which gives off much heat in combining with water; unslaked lime

quick·sand (-sand′) ***n.*** [see QUICK & SAND] a deep deposit of loose, wet sand in which a person or heavy object may be easily engulfed

quick·set (-set′) ***n.*** [Chiefly Brit.] **1.** a live slip or cutting, as of hawthorn, planted, as for a hedge **2.** a hedge

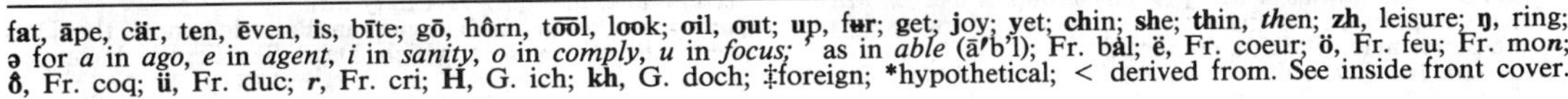

quick·sil·ver (-sil′vər) ***n.*** the metal mercury *—vt.* to cover with mercury *—adj.* of or like mercury

quick·step (-step′) ***n.*** **1.** the step used for marching in quick time **2.** a march in the rhythm of quick time **3.** a spirited dance step

quick-tem·pered (-tem′pərd) ***adj.*** easily angered

quick time the normal rate of marching: in the U.S. Army, 120 (30-inch) paces a minute

quick-wit·ted (-wit′id) *adj.* nimble of mind; alert —**quick′-wit′ted·ly** *adv.* —**quick′-wit′ted·ness** *n.*

quid[1] (kwid) *n.* [var. of *cud*] a piece, as of tobacco, to be chewed

quid[2] (kwid) *n., pl.* **quid** [Brit. Slang] a sovereign, or one pound sterling

quid·di·ty (kwid′ə tē) *n., pl.* **-ties** [< ML. < L. *quid,* what] **1.** essential quality **2.** a quibble

quid·nunc (kwid′nuŋk′) *n.* [L., lit., what now?] an inquisitive, gossipy person; busybody

quid pro quo (kwid′ prō kwō′) [L.] **1.** one thing in return for another **2.** something equivalent; substitute

qui·es·cent (kwī es′'nt) *adj.* [< L. prp. of *quiescere,* to become quiet] quiet; still; inactive —**qui·es′cence** *n.* —**qui·es′cent·ly** *adv.*

qui·et (kwī′ət) *adj.* [< OFr. < L. *quietus,* pp. of *quiescere,* to keep quiet < *quies* (gen. *quietis*), rest] **1.** still; calm; motionless **2.** *a)* not noisy; hushed *b)* not speaking; silent **3.** not agitated; gentle *[a quiet sea]* **4.** not easily excited *[a quiet disposition]* **5.** not bright or showy *[quiet furnishings]* **6.** not forward; unobtrusive *[a quiet manner]* **7.** secluded *[a quiet den]* **8.** peaceful; relaxing *[a quiet evening]* **9.** *Commerce* not busy *[a quiet market]* —*n.* **1.** a quiet state; calmness, stillness, etc. **2.** a quiet or peaceful quality —*vt., vi.* to make or become quiet —*adv.* in a quiet manner —**qui′et·er** *n.* —**qui′et·ly** *adv.* —**qui′et·ness** *n.*

qui·et·en (-'n) *vt., vi.* [Brit. or Dial.] to make or become quiet

qui·e·tude (kwī′ə to͞od′, -tyo͞od′) *n.* a state of being quiet; rest; calmness

qui·e·tus (kwī ēt′əs) *n.* [< ME. *quietus (est)* < ML., (he is) quit < L., QUIET] **1.** discharge or release from debt, obligation, etc. **2.** discharge or release from life; death **3.** anything that kills

quill (kwil) *n.* [prob. < MLowG. or MDu.] **1.** any of the large, stiff wing or tail feathers of a bird **2.** *a)* the hollow, horny stem of a feather *b)* anything made from this, as a pen or plectrum **3.** any of the spines of a porcupine or hedgehog

quilt (kwilt) *n.* [< OFr. < L. *culcita,* a bed] **1.** a bedcover made of two layers of cloth filled with down, wool, etc. and stitched together in lines or patterns **2.** anything like or used as a quilt —*vt.* **1.** to stitch as or like a quilt *[to quilt a potholder]* **2.** to fasten between two pieces of material **3.** to line or pad with quilting —*vi.* to make a quilt or quilts —**quilt′er** *n.*

quilt·ing (-iŋ) *n.* **1.** the act of making quilts **2.** material for quilts **3.** *same as* QUILTING BEE

quilting bee (or **party**) a social gathering of women at which they work together sewing quilts

quince (kwins) *n.* [orig. pl. of ME. *quyn* < OFr. < L. < Gr. *kydōnion*] **1.** a golden or greenish-yellow, hard, apple-shaped fruit used in preserves **2.** the tree that bears this fruit

Quin·cy (kwin′zē) [after J. *Quincy* (1689–1767), a local official] city in E Mass.: suburb of Boston: pop. 85,000

qui·nine (kwī′nīn; *chiefly Brit.* kwi nēn′) *n.* [< *quina,* cinchona bark (< Sp. < Quechua name) + -INE[4]] **1.** a bitter, crystalline substance, $C_{20}H_{24}N_2O_2$, extracted from cinchona bark **2.** any compound of this used in medicine, esp. for treating malaria

quinine water *same as* TONIC (*n.* 2)

Quin·qua·ges·i·ma (kwiŋ′kwə jes′i mə) *n.* [LL. *quinquagesima (dies),* fiftieth (day)] the Sunday before Lent: also **Quinquagesima Sunday**

quin·quen·ni·al (kwiŋ kwen′ē əl) *adj.* [< L. < *quinque,* five + *annus,* year] **1.** lasting five years **2.** taking place every five years —*n.* a quinquennial event —**quin·quen′ni·al·ly** *adv.*

quin·que·va·lent (kwiŋ′kwə vā′lənt) *adj.* [L. *quinque,* five + -VALENT] **1.** having five valences **2.** *same as* PENTAVALENT (sense 1) —**quin′que·va′lence, quin′que·va′len·cy** *n.*

quin·sy (kwin′zē) *n.* [< ML. *quinancia* < LL. *cynanche* < Gr. *kynanchē,* lit., dog-choking < *kyōn,* dog + *anchein,* to choke] *an earlier term for* TONSILLITIS

quint (kwint) *n. shortened form of* QUINTUPLET

quin·tal (kwin′t'l) *n.* [< MFr. < ML. < Ar. *qintār,* ult. < L. *centenarius:* see CENTENARY] **1.** a hundredweight (100 lbs. in the U.S., 112 lbs. in Great Britain) **2.** a metric unit of weight, equal to 100 kilograms (220.46 lbs.)

quin·tes·sence (kwin tes′'ns) *n.* [< MFr. < ML. *quinta essentia,* fifth essence, or ultimate substance] **1.** the essence of something in its purest form **2.** the perfect type or example of something —**quin′tes·sen′tial** (-tə sen′shəl) *adj.*

quin·tet, quin·tette (kwin tet′) *n.* [< Fr. < It. dim. of *quinto* < L. *quintus,* a fifth] **1.** any group of five **2.** *Music a)* a composition for five voices or five instruments *b)* the five performers of such a composition

Quin·til·ian (kwin til′yən, -ē ən) (L. name *Marcus Fabius Quintilianus*) 30?–96? A.D.; Rom. rhetorician, born in Spain

quin·til·lion (kwin til′yən) *n.* [< L. *quintus,* a fifth + (M)ILLION] **1.** in the U.S. and France, the number represented by 1 followed by 18 zeros **2.** in Great Britain and Germany, the number represented by 1 followed by 30 zeros —*adj.* amounting to one quintillion in number —**quin·til′lionth** *adj., n.*

quin·tu·ple (kwin to͞o′p'l, -tyo͞o′-, -tup′'l; kwin′too p'l) *adj.* [MFr. < LL. < L. *quintus,* a fifth + *-plex,* -fold] **1.** consisting of five **2.** five times as much or as many; fivefold —*n.* an amount five times as much or as many —*vt., vi.* **-pled, -pling** to make or become five times as much or as many

quin·tu·plet (kwin tup′lit, -to͞o′plit, -tyo͞o′-; kwin′too plit) *n.* [dim. of prec.] **1.** any of five offspring born at a single birth **2.** a group of five, usually of one kind

quip (kwip) *n.* [< L. *quippe,* indeed] **1.** a witty, or, esp. formerly, sarcastic remark; jest **2.** a quibble **3.** something curious or odd —*vi.* **quipped, quip′ping** to utter quips —**quip′ster** *n.*

quire[1] (kwīr) *n. archaic var. of* CHOIR

quire[2] (kwīr) *n.* [< OFr. < VL. *quaternum,* paper in sets of four < L. *quaterni,* four each] a set of 24 or 25 sheets of paper of the same size and stock

quirk (kwurk) *n.* [< ? ON. *kverk,* a bird's crop] **1.** *a)* a sudden twist, turn, etc. *[a quirk of fate] b)* a flourish in writing **2.** a quibble **3.** a peculiar trait or mannerism —**quirk′i·ly** *adv.* —**quirk′i·ness** *n.* —**quirk′y** *adj.* **quirk′i·er, quirk′i·est**

quirt (kwurt) *n.* [AmSp. *cuarta*] a riding whip with a braided leather lash and a short handle —*vt.* to strike with a quirt

quis·ling (kwiz′liŋ) *n.* [after Vidkun *Quisling* (1887–1945), Norw. collaborationist with the Nazis] a traitor

quit (kwit) *vt.* **quit** or **quit′ted, quit′ting** [< OFr. < ML. *quietus,* free: see QUIET] **1.** to free (oneself) *of* **2.** to discharge (a debt); repay **3.** to give up **4.** to leave; depart from **5.** to stop, discontinue, or resign from —*vi.* **1.** *a)* to stop doing something *b)* to give up, as in discouragement **2.** to give up one's job; resign —*adj.* clear, free, or rid, as of an obligation

quitch (kwich) *n.* [< OE. < *cwicu,* alive] *same as* COUCH GRASS

quit·claim (kwit′klām′) *n.* [< Anglo-Fr. & OFr.: see QUIT & CLAIM] **1.** the relinquishment of a claim, right, title, etc. **2.** a legal paper in which a person relinquishes to another a claim or title to some property or right: in full, **quitclaim deed** —*vt.* to give up a claim or title to

quite (kwīt) *adv.* [ME. form of QUIT, *adj.*] **1.** completely; entirely **2.** really; truly **3.** to a considerable degree or extent —**quite a few** (or **bit,** etc.) [Colloq.] more than a few (or bit, etc.) —**quite (so)!** certainly!

Qui·to (kē′tō) capital of Ecuador: pop. 463,000

quit·rent (kwit′rent′) *n.* a rent paid in lieu of feudal services: also **quit rent**

quits (kwits) *adj.* [prob. contr. < ML. *quittus,* var. of *quietus:* see QUIETUS] on even terms, as by paying a debt, retaliating, etc. —**call it quits** [Colloq.] **1.** to stop working, playing, etc. **2.** to end an association or friendship; stop being intimate

quit·tance (kwit′'ns) *n.* [see QUIT] **1.** *a)* payment of a debt or obligation *b)* a document certifying this; receipt **2.** recompense; repayment

quit·ter (kwit′ər) *n.* [Colloq.] a person who quits or gives up easily, without trying hard

quiv·er[1] (kwiv′ər) *vi.* to shake with a tremulous motion; tremble —*n.* the act or condition of quivering; tremor —**quiv′er·y** *adj.*

quiv·er[2] (kwiv′ər) *n.* [OFr. *coivre* < Gmc.] **1.** a case for holding arrows **2.** the arrows in it

‡**qui vive?** (kē vēv′) [Fr., (long) live who? (i.e., whose side are you on?)] who goes there?: a sentry's challenge —**on the qui vive** on the lookout; on the alert

Quixote, Don *see* DON QUIXOTE

quix·ot·ic (kwik sät′ik) *adj.* **1.** [*often* **Q-**] of or like Don Quixote **2.** extravagantly chivalrous or romantically idealistic; visionary; impractical Also **quix·ot′i·cal** —**quix·ot′i·cal·ly** *adv.* —**quix′ot·ism** (-sə tiz'm) *n.*

quiz (kwiz) *n., pl.* **quiz′zes** [prob. arbitrary use of L. *quis,* what?] **1.** formerly, a practical joke; hoax **2.** a questioning; esp., a short examination to test one's knowledge —*vt.* **quizzed, quiz′zing** **1.** [Obs.] to make fun of **2.** to ask questions of, as in interrogating —**quiz′zer** *n.*

quiz program (or **show**) a radio or TV program in which a group of people compete in answering questions posed by a master of ceremonies (**quizmaster**)

quiz·zi·cal (kwiz′i k'l) *adj.* **1.** odd; comical **2.** teasing; bantering **3.** perplexed —**quiz′zi·cal′i·ty** (-kal′ə tē), **quiz′zi·cal·ness** *n.* —**quiz′zi·cal·ly** *adv.*

Qum·ran (koom rän′) region in Palestine, near the Dead Sea: site of caves in which Dead Sea Scrolls have been found

quoin (koin, kwoin) ***n.*** [var. of COIN] **1.** the external corner of a building; esp., any of the stones forming the corner of a building **2.** a wedgelike piece of stone, etc., such as the keystone of an arch **3.** a wedge-shaped wooden or metal block used to lock something in place

QUOINS

quoit (kwoit; *chiefly Brit.* koit) ***n.*** [< Anglo-Fr., prob. < OFr. *coite,* a cushion] **1.** a ring of rope or metal thrown at an upright peg: the object of the game is to encircle the peg with the ring **2.** [*pl., with sing. v.*] this game

quon·dam (kwän′dəm) ***adj.*** [L.] that was at one time; former *[a quondam* pacifist*]*

Quon·set hut (kwän′sit) [< *Quonset* Point, R.I., where first manufactured] *a trademark for* a prefabricated metal shelter shaped like the longitudinal half of a cylinder resting on its flat surface

quo·rum (kwôr′əm) ***n.*** [L., gen. pl. of *qui,* who] the minimum number of members required to be present at an assembly or meeting before it can validly transact business

quo·ta (kwōt′ə) ***n.*** [ML., short for L. *quota pars,* how large a part] **1.** a share which each of a number is to contribute or receive; proportional share **2.** the number or proportion that is allowed or admitted *[*nationality *quotas* for immigrants to the U.S.*]*

quot·a·ble (kwōt′ə b'l) ***adj.*** worthwhile quoting or suitable for quotation —**quot′a·bil′i·ty *n.*** —**quot′a·bly *adv.***

quo·ta·tion (kwō tā′shən) ***n.*** **1.** a quoting **2.** the words or passage quoted **3.** *Commerce* the current quoted price of a stock, bond, commodity, etc.

quotation mark either of a pair of punctuation marks (". . .") used to enclose a direct quotation, or of single marks ('. . .') for enclosing a quotation within a quotation

quote (kwōt) ***vt.* quot′ed, quot′ing** [< ML. *quotare,* to number (chapters, etc.) < L. *quotus,* of what number] **1.** to repeat a passage from or statement of **2.** to repeat (a passage, statement, etc.) **3.** to cite as an example or authority **4.** to state (the price of something) —***vi.*** to make a quotation, as from a book —***n.*** [Colloq.] *same as:* **1.** QUOTATION **2.** QUOTATION MARK —***interj.*** I shall quote: used in speech before a quotation —**quot′er *n.***

quoth (kwōth) ***vt.*** [< OE. < *cwethan,* to speak] [Archaic] said: followed by a subject in the first or third person

quoth·a (-ə) ***interj.*** [< *quoth he*] [Archaic] indeed!

quo·tid·i·an (kwō tid′ē ən) ***adj.*** [< OFr. < L. < *quotidie,* daily < *quot,* as many as + *dies,* day] **1.** daily; recurring every day **2.** everyday; ordinary —***n.*** anything, esp. a fever, that recurs daily

quo·tient (kwō′shənt) ***n.*** [< L. *quoties,* how often < *quot,* how many] *Arith.* the result obtained when one number is divided by another

quo war·ran·to (kwō wô ran′tō) *pl.* **quo war·ran′tos** [ML., by what warrant] a legal proceeding undertaken to recover an office, franchise, etc. from the one in possession

qursh (koorsh) ***n., pl.* qu·rush** (koo′rəsh) [< Ar. *taqrush,* to earn < *qrsh,* to collect] *see* MONETARY UNITS, table (Saudi Arabia)

q.v. [L. *quod vide*] which see

R

R, r (är) ***n., pl.* R's, r's** **1.** the eighteenth letter of the English alphabet **2.** a sound of *R* or *r*

R **1.** *Chem.* radical **2.** *Math.* ratio **3.** *Elec.* resistance **4.** *Chess* rook —**the three R's** reading, writing, and arithmetic, regarded as the basic studies

R restricted: a motion-picture rating meaning that no one under the age of seventeen will be admitted unless accompanied by a parent or guardian

r **1.** *Math.* radius **2.** roentgen(s) **3.** ruble

R. **1.** Radical **2.** Republic(an)

R., r. **1.** [L. *Rex*] king **2.** [L. *Regina*] queen **3.** rabbi **4.** radius **5.** railroad **6.** right **7.** river **8.** road **9.** ruble **10.** *Baseball* runs **11.** *pl.* **Rs., Rs, rs.** rupee

r. **1.** rare **2.** retired **3.** rod(s)

Ra[1] (rä) the sun god and chief god of the ancient Egyptians, usually depicted as having the head of a hawk

Ra[2] *Chem.* radium

Ra·bat (rä bät′, rə-) capital of Morocco: pop. 435,000

ra·bat (rab′ē, rə bat′) ***n.*** [MFr.] a plain, black dickey worn with a clerical collar by some clergymen

rab·bet (rab′it) ***n.*** [< OFr. < *rabattre:* see REBATE] a groove or cut made in the edge of a board, etc. so that another piece may be fitted into it to form a joint (**rabbet joint**) —***vt.*** **1.** to cut a rabbet in **2.** to join by means of a rabbet —***vi.*** to be joined by a rabbet

rab·bi (rab′ī) ***n., pl.* -bis, -bies** [< LL. < Gr. < Heb. *rabbī,* my master] a teacher of the Jewish law, now usually one that is ordained and the spiritual head of a congregation

rab·bin·ate (rab′i nit, -nāt′) ***n.*** **1.** the position or office of rabbi **2.** rabbis as a group

Rab·bin·ic (rə bin′ik) ***adj.*** **1.** designating the Hebrew language as used in the writings of rabbis of the Middle Ages **2.** [**r-**] *same as* RABBINICAL

rab·bin·i·cal (-i k'l) ***adj.*** of the rabbis, their doctrines, learning, language, etc., esp. in the early Middle Ages —**rab·bin′i·cal·ly *adv.***

rab·bit (rab′it) ***n., pl.* -bits, -bit:** see PLURAL, II, D, 1 [ME. *rabette*] **1.** a burrowing mammal that is usually smaller than the hare, produces unfurred young, and has soft fur, long ears, and a stubby tail **2.** its fur —***vi.*** to hunt rabbits

rabbit ears [Colloq.] an indoor TV antenna with two adjustable rods that swivel apart at a V-shaped angle

rabbit fever *same as* TULAREMIA

rabbit punch *Boxing* a sharp blow to the back of the neck

rab·ble (rab′'l) ***n.*** [< ? or akin to ML. *rabulus,* noisy < L. *rabula,* a pettifogger] a noisy, disorderly crowd; mob —***vt.*** **-bled, -bling** to attack by a rabble; mob —**the rabble** the common people; the masses: a term of contempt

rab·ble-rous·er (-rouz′ər) ***n.*** a person who tries to arouse people to violent action by appeals to emotions, prejudices, etc.; demagogue —**rab′ble-rous′ing *adj., n.***

Rab·e·lais (rà ble′; *E.* rab′ə lā′), **Fran·çois** (frän swà′) 1495?–1553; Fr. satirist & humorist —**Rab·e·lai·si·an** (rab′ə lā′zhən, -zē ən) ***adj., n.***

rab·id (rab′id; *for 3 occas.* rā′bid) ***adj.*** [< L. < *rabere,* to rage] **1.** violent; raging **2.** fanatical or unreasonably zealous **3.** of or having rabies —**ra·bid′i·ty** (rə bid′ə tē), **rab′id·ness *n.*** —**rab′id·ly *adv.***

ra·bies (rā′bēz) ***n.*** [L., madness] an infectious virus disease of mammals, passed on to man by the bite of an infected animal: it causes choking, convulsions, etc.

rac·coon (ra ko͞on′) ***n., pl.* -coons′, -coon′:** see PLURAL, II, D, 1 [< Algonquian *äräkun,* lit., scratcher] **1.** a small, tree-climbing, chiefly flesh-eating mammal of N. America, active largely at night and having long, yellowish-gray fur and a long, black-ringed tail **2.** its fur

race[1] (rās) ***n.*** [< ON. *rās,* a running] **1.** a competition of speed in running, riding, etc. **2.** [*pl.*] a series of such competitions for horses, cars, etc., on a regular course **3.** any contest likened to a race *[*the *race* for mayor*]* **4.** a steady onward movement **5.** *a*) a swift current of water *b*) a channel for this, esp. one built to use the water in industry *[*a *millrace]* —***vi.* raced, rac′ing** **1.** to take part in a race **2.** to go or move very fast or too fast —***vt.*** **1.** to compete with in a race **2.** to enter or run (a horse, etc.) in a race **3.** to make go very fast or too fast **4.** to run (an engine) at high speed with the transmission system not engaged

race[2] (rās) ***n.*** [Fr. < It. *razza*] **1.** any of the different varieties of mankind, mainly the Caucasoid, Mongoloid, or Negroid groups, distinguished by kind of hair, color of skin, stature, etc.: now often replaced in scientific use by *ethnic stock* or *group* **2.** any geographical, national, or tribal ethnic grouping **3.** any group of people having the same ancestry **4.** any group of people having the same habits, ideas, etc. **5.** *Biol.* *a*) a subspecies, or variety *b*) *same as* BREED (*n.* 1) —**the (human) race** mankind

race·course (-kôrs′) ***n.*** *same as* RACE TRACK

race·horse (-hôrs′) ***n.*** a horse bred and trained for racing

ra·ceme (rā sēm′, rə-) *n.* [L. *racemus,* cluster of grapes] a flower cluster with individual flowers growing on small stems at intervals along one central stem, as in the lupine —**rac·e·mose** (ras′ə mōs′) *adj.*

RA-CEME

rac·er (rās′ər) *n.* **1.** any person, animal, vehicle, etc. that takes part in races **2.** any of several slim, swift, harmless snakes

race riot violence and fighting in a community, brought on by racial hostility

race track a course prepared for racing

race·way (rās′wā′) *n.* **1.** a narrow channel for water **2.** a race track for harness racing **3.** a race track for drag races, racing stock cars, etc.

Ra·chel (rā′chəl) [LL. < Gr. < Heb. *rāḥēl,* lit., ewe] **1.** a feminine name **2.** *Bible* the younger of the two wives of Jacob: Gen. 29–35

ra·chi·tis (rə kīt′əs, ra-) *n.* [ModL. < Gr. *rhachitis,* inflammation of the spine < *rhachis,* spine] *same as* RICKETS —**ra·chit′ic** (-kit′ik) *adj.*

Rach·ma·ni·noff (räkh mä′nü nôf; *E.* räk mä′ni nôf′), **Ser·gei V(assilievich)** (syer gā′) 1873–1943; Russ. composer, conductor, & pianist: also sp. **Rachmaninov**

ra·cial (rā′shəl) *adj.* **1.** of a race, or ethnic group **2.** of or between races —**ra′cial·ly** *adv.*

ra·cial·ism (-iz′m) *n.* **1.** a doctrine or teaching, without scientific support, that claims to find racial differences in character, intelligence, etc. and that seeks to maintain the supposed superiority and purity of some one race **2.** *same as* RACISM (sense 2) —**ra′cial·ist** *n., adj.*

Ra·cine (rə sēn′) [Fr., root, after the nearby Root River] city in SE Wis., on Lake Michigan: pop. 86,000

Ra·cine (rȧ sēn′; *E.* rə sēn′), **Jean Bap·tiste** (zhän bȧ tēst′) 1639–99; Fr. poet & dramatist

rac·ism (rā′siz′m) *n.* **1.** *same as* RACIALISM (sense 1) **2.** the practice of racial discrimination, segregation, etc., based on racialism —**rac′ist** *n., adj.*

rack[1] (rak) *n.* [prob. < MDu. *rek* < *recken,* to stretch] **1.** a framework, stand, etc. for holding things *[clothes rack]* **2.** the triangular device in which the balls are set up at the start of a pool game **3.** a device for lifting an automobile for repairs from below **4.** a toothed bar that meshes with a cogwheel, etc. **5.** a frame on which a victim is tortured by stretching his limbs out of place **6.** any great torment **7.** a wrenching or upheaval, as by a storm —*vt.* **1.** to put in or on a rack **2.** to torture on a rack **3.** to torment or afflict **4.** to oppress, as by demanding excessive rent —**off the rack** ready-made: said of clothing —**on the rack** in a very painful situation —**rack one's brains** (or **memory,** etc.) to try very hard to think of something —**rack up** [Slang] **1.** to gain or score **2.** to beat decisively

rack[2] (rak) *n., vi.* [< ?] *same as* SINGLE-FOOT

rack[3] (rak) *n.* [var. of WRACK] destruction: now only in **go to rack and ruin,** to become ruined

rack[4] (rak) *n.* [prob. < Scand.] a broken mass of clouds blown by the wind

rack·et[1] (rak′it) *n.* [prob. echoic] **1.** a noisy confusion; uproar **2.** *a)* an obtaining of money illegally, as by fraud *b)* [Colloq.] any dishonest scheme **3.** [Slang] *a)* an easy, profitable source of income *b)* any business, profession, etc. —*vi.* to make a racket, or uproar —**rack′et·y** *adj.*

rack·et[2] (rak′it) *n.* [MFr. *raquette* < ML. *rasceta* < Ar. *rāḥah,* palm of the hand] **1.** a light bat for tennis, etc., with a network of catgut, nylon, etc. in an oval or round frame attached to a handle **2.** loosely, a table-tennis paddle **3.** [*pl., with sing. v.*] the game of racquets

A B C D

RACKETS
(A, squash; B, tennis; C, badminton; D, racquetball)

rack·et·eer (rak′ə tir′) *n.* [see RACKET[1] & -EER] one who gets money illegally, as by fraud, blackmail, or, esp., extortion —*vi.* to get money thus —**rack′et·eer′ing** *n.*

ra·clette (ra klet′) *n.* [Fr. < *racler,* to scrape] a Swiss dish consisting of cheese that is melted, as over a fire, and scraped onto boiled potatoes or crusty bread

rac·on·teur (rak′än tur′) *n.* [Fr. < *raconter,* to recount] a person skilled at telling stories or anecdotes

ra·coon (ra ko͞on′) *n., pl.* **-coons′, -coon′:** see PLURAL, II, D, 1 *same as* RACCOON

rac·quet (rak′it) *n.* **1.** *same as* RACKET[2] **2.** [*pl., with sing. v.*] a game similar to court tennis: see TENNIS

rac·quet·ball (-bôl′) *n.* a game similar to handball, but played with a short-handed racket

rac·y (rā′sē) *adj.* **rac′i·er, rac′i·est** [RACE[2] + -Y[2]] **1.** having the taste or quality required to be genuine *[racy fruit]* **2.** lively; spirited **3.** piquant; pungent **4.** indecent; risqué —**rac′i·ly** *adv.* —**rac′i·ness** *n.*

rad (rad) *n.* [< *rad(iation)*] the unit of absorbed dose of ionizing radiation, equal to 100 ergs of energy per gram of matter

rad. 1. radical **2.** radius

ra·dar (rā′där) *n.* [*ra(dio) d(etecting) a(nd) r(anging)*] a system or device for sending out radio waves in order to detect an object by the waves reflected back from the object and thus find out its direction, distance, height, or speed: used also in mapping, navigation, etc. —**ra′dar·man** (-mən) *n., pl.* **-men**

ra·dar·scope (rā′där skōp′) *n.* an instrument that displays on a screen the reflected radio waves picked up by radar

ra·di·al (rā′dē əl) *adj.* [< ML.: see RADIUS] **1.** of or like a ray or rays; branching out in all directions from a common center **2.** of or like a radius **3.** *Anat.* of or near the radius —*n.* a radial part —**ra′di·al·ly** *adv.*

radial (ply) tire an automobile tire with the ply cords almost at right angles to the center line of the tread

ra·di·ant (rā′dē ənt) *adj.* [< L. prp. of *radiare:* see RADIATE] **1.** shining brightly **2.** filled with light **3.** showing joy, love, well-being, etc. **4.** issuing (from a source) in or as in rays —*n.* a source of heat or light rays —**ra′di·ance, ra′di·an·cy** *n.* —**ra′di·ant·ly** *adv.*

radiant energy energy traveling in waves; esp., electromagnetic radiation, as heat, light, X-rays, etc.

radiant heating a method of heating by radiation, as from electric coils or steam pipes in the floor or walls

ra·di·ate (rā′dē āt′) *vi.* **-at′ed, -at′ing** [< L. pp. of *radiare* < *radius:* see RADIUS] **1.** to send out rays of heat, light, etc. **2.** to spread out in rays **3.** to branch out in lines from a center —*vt.* **1.** to send out (heat, light, etc.) in rays **2.** to give forth (happiness, love, etc.) —*adj.* having rays or raylike parts; radial —**ra′di·ate·ly** *adv.*

ra·di·a·tion (rā′dē ā′shən) *n.* **1.** a radiating; specif., the process in which radiant energy is sent out from atoms and molecules as they undergo internal change **2.** such radiant energy **3.** energetic nuclear particles, as alpha and beta particles, etc. —**ra′di·a′tion·al** *adj.* —**ra′di·a′tive** *adj.*

radiation sickness sickness produced by overexposure to radiation from X-rays, nuclear explosions, etc. and resulting in nausea, diarrhea, bleeding, etc.

ra·di·a·tor (rā′dē āt′ər) *n.* anything that radiates; specif., *a)* a series of pipes with hot water or steam circulating in them so as to radiate heat into a room, etc. *b)* a device of tubes and fins, as in a motor vehicle, through which circulating water passes so as to take away the extra heat and thus cool the engine

rad·i·cal (rad′i k′l) *adj.* [< LL. < L. *radix* (gen. *radicis*), a root] **1.** *a)* of or from the root or source; fundamental; basic *b)* extreme; thorough **2.** *a)* favoring basic or extreme change, as in the social or economic structure *b)* [**R-**] designating or of any of various modern political parties, as in Europe, ranging from moderate to conservative —*n.* **1.** *a)* a basic part of something *b)* a fundamental **2.** *a)* a person having radical views *b)* [**R-**] a member of a Radical party **3.** *Chem.* a group of two or more atoms that acts as a single atom and goes through a reaction unchanged, or is replaced by a single atom **4.** *Math. a)* an expression showing that a root is to be extracted *b)* *same as* RADICAL SIGN —**rad′i·cal·ly** *adv.* —**rad′i·cal·ness** *n.*

rad·i·cal·ism (-iz′m) *n.* **1.** the quality or state of being radical **2.** radical principles, methods, or practices

rad·i·cal·ize (-īz′) *vt., vi.* **-ized′, -iz′ing** to make or become politically radical —**rad′i·cal·i·za′tion** *n.*

radical sign *Math.* the sign used before a quantity to show that its root is to be extracted

rad·i·cand (rad′i kand′) *n.* *Math.* a quantity from which a root is to be extracted, shown with a radical sign

rad·i·cle (rad′i k′l) *n.* [< L. dim. of *radix,* a root] *Bot.* the lower part of the axis of an embryo seedling

ra·di·i (rā′dē ī′) *n. alt. pl. of* RADIUS

ra·di·o (rā′dē ō′) *n., pl.* **-os′** [contr. < RADIOTELEGRAPH] **1.** a way of communicating over a distance by changing sounds or signals into electromagnetic waves that are sent through space, without wires, to a receiving set, which changes them back into sounds or signals **2.** such a receiving set **3.** broadcasting by radio as an industry, entertainment, etc. —*adj.* **1.** of, using, used in, or sent by radio **2.** of electromagnetic wave frequencies from c.10 kilohertz to c.300,000 megahertz —*vt., vi.* **-oed′, -o′ing** to send (a message, etc.) or communicate with (a person, etc.) by radio

ra·di·o- [Fr. < L. *radius,* ray: see RADIUS] *a combining form meaning:* **1.** ray, raylike **2.** by radio **3.** using radiant energy *[radiotherapy]* **4.** radioactive *[radioisotope]*

ra·di·o·ac·tive (rā′dē ō ak′tiv) *adj.* giving off radiant energy in particles or rays by the disintegration of the atomic nuclei: said of such elements as radium and uranium —**ra′di·o·ac′tive·ly** *adv.* —**ra′di·o·ac·tiv′i·ty** (-ak tiv′ə tē) *n.*

radio astronomy astronomy dealing with radio waves in space in order to get data about the universe

radio beacon a radio transmitter that gives off special signals to help ships or aircraft determine their positions or come in safely, as in a fog

ra·di·o·broad·cast (-brôd′kast′) ***n.*** a broadcast by radio —***vt., vi.*** **-cast′** or **-cast′ed, -cast′ing** to broadcast by radio —**ra′di·o·broad′cast′er** ***n.***

ra·di·o·car·bon (-kär′bən) ***n.*** *same as* CARBON 14: see CARBON

radio frequency any frequency between normally audible sound waves and infrared light, from c.10 kilohertz to c.300,000 megahertz

ra·di·o·gram (rā′dē ō gram′) ***n.*** **1.** a message sent by radio: also **ra′di·o·tel′e·gram′** **2.** *same as* RADIOGRAPH

ra·di·o·graph (-graf′) ***n.*** a picture made on a sensitized film or plate by X-rays —**ra′di·og′ra·pher** (-äg′rə fər) ***n.*** —**ra′di·o·graph′ic** ***adj.*** —**ra′di·og′ra·phy** ***n.***

ra·di·o·i·so·tope (rā′dē ō ī′sə tōp′) ***n.*** a natural or artificial radioactive isotope of a chemical element

ra·di·ol·o·gy (rā′dē äl′ə jē) ***n.*** [RADIO- + -LOGY] the science dealing with X-rays and other radiant energy, esp. as used in medicine and radiotherapy —**ra′di·o·log′i·cal** (-ə läj′i k′l) ***adj.*** —**ra′di·o·log′i·cal·ly** ***adv.*** —**ra′di·ol′o·gist** ***n.***

ra·di·om·e·ter (-äm′ə tər) ***n.*** an instrument for measuring radiant energy —**ra′di·om′e·try** ***n.***

ra·di·o·pho·to (rā′dē ō fōt′ō) ***n., pl.*** **-tos** a photograph or picture transmitted by radio: also **ra′di·o·pho′to·graph′**

ra·di·os·co·py (-äs′kə pē) ***n.*** [RADIO- + -SCOPY] the direct examination of the inside structure of opaque objects by radiation, as by X-rays —**ra′di·o·scop′ic** (-ə skäp′ik) ***adj.***

ra·di·o·sonde (rā′dē ō sänd′) ***n.*** [Fr. < *radio* (cf. RADIO) + *sonde,* a sounding line] a compact package made up of a radio transmitter and meteorological instruments sent into the upper atmosphere, as by balloon, to record and radio back temperature, pressure, and humidity data

radio spectrum the complete range of frequencies of electromagnetic radiation useful in radio, from c.10 kilohertz to c.300,000 megahertz

ra·di·o·tel·e·graph (rā′dē ō tel′ə graf′) ***n.*** *same as* WIRELESS TELEGRAPHY: also **ra′di·o·te·leg′ra·phy** (-tə leg′rə fē) —***vt., vi.*** to send (a message, etc.) by radiotelegraph

ra·di·o·tel·e·phone (-tel′ə fōn′) ***n.*** the equipment needed at one station for two-way voice communication by radio: also **ra′di·o·phone′** —**ra′di·o·tel′e·phon′ic** (-fän′ik) ***adj.*** —**ra′di·o·te·leph′o·ny** (-tə lef′ə nē) ***n.***

radio telescope a radio antenna or array of antennas for use in radio astronomy

ra·di·o·ther·a·py (-ther′ə pē) ***n.*** the treatment of disease by X-rays or by rays from a radioactive substance

rad·ish (rad′ish) ***n.*** [OE. *rædic* < L. *radix,* a root] **1.** an annual plant of the mustard family, with an edible root **2.** the pungent root, eaten raw as a relish or in a salad

ra·di·um (rā′dē əm) ***n.*** [ModL. < L. *radius,* a ray] a radioactive metallic chemical element, found in uranium minerals: symbol, Ra; at. wt., 226.00; at. no., 88

radium therapy the treatment of cancer or other diseases by the use of radium

ra·di·us (rā′dē əs) ***n., pl.*** **-di·i′** (-ī′), **-us·es** [L., a spoke (of a wheel), hence ray (of light)] **1.** a raylike part, as a spoke of a wheel **2.** *a)* a straight line from the center to the periphery of a circle or sphere *b)* its length **3.** *a)* the circular area or distance within the sweep of such a line [*no house within a radius of five miles*] *b)* the distance a ship or airplane can go and still get back without refueling **4.** any limited extent, scope, etc. [*within the radius of one's experience*] **5.** the shorter and thicker of the two bones of the forearm on the same side as the thumb

RAdm Rear Admiral

ra·dome (rā′dōm′) ***n.*** [RA(DAR) + DOME] a domed housing for a radar antenna, esp. on aircraft

ra·don (rā′dän) ***n.*** [RAD(IUM) + -ON] a radioactive gaseous chemical element formed in the atomic disintegration of radium: symbol, Rn; at. wt., 222.00; at. no., 86

RAF, R.A.F. Royal Air Force

raf·fi·a (raf′ē ə) ***n.*** [< Malagasy native name] **1.** a palm tree of Madagascar, with large, pinnate leaves **2.** fiber from its leaves, woven into baskets, hats, etc.

raff·ish (raf′ish) ***adj.*** [(RIFF)RAFF + -ISH] **1.** disreputable, rakish, etc. **2.** tawdry; vulgar; low —**raff′ish·ly** ***adv.*** —**raff′ish·ness** ***n.***

raf·fle (raf′′l) ***n.*** [MFr. *rafle,* dice game < OHG. *raffel,* a rake] a lottery in which a chance or chances to win a prize are bought —***vt.*** **-fled, -fling** to offer as a prize in a raffle (often with *off*) —**raf′fler** ***n.***

raft[1] (raft) ***n.*** [< ON. *raptr,* a log] **1.** a flat structure of logs, boards, etc. fastened together and floated on water **2.** an inflatable boat or pad, as of rubber, for floating on water —***vt.*** to carry on a raft —***vi.*** to travel, work, etc. on a raft —**rafts′man** (-mən) ***n., pl.*** **-men**

raft[2] (raft) ***n.*** [< Brit. Dial. *raff,* rubbish] [Colloq.] a large number, collection, or quantity; lot

raft·er (raf′tər) ***n.*** [OE. *ræfter*] any of the beams that slope from the ridge of a roof to the eaves and serve to support the roof

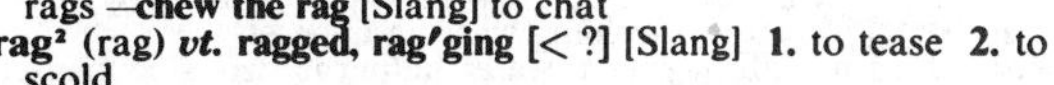

RAFTERS

rag[1] (rag) ***n.*** [ult. < ON. *rögg,* tuft of hair] **1.** a waste piece of cloth, esp. an old or torn one **2.** a small cloth for dusting, washing, etc. **3.** anything regarded as having as little value as a rag **4.** [*pl.*] *a)* old, worn clothes *b)* any clothes: humorous term **5.** [Slang] any newspaper regarded with contempt —***adj.*** made of rags —**chew the rag** [Slang] to chat

rag[2] (rag) ***vt.*** **ragged, rag′ging** [< ?] [Slang] **1.** to tease **2.** to scold

rag[3] (rag) ***n.*** **1.** *clipped form of* RAGTIME **2.** a composition in ragtime —***vt.*** **ragged, rag′ging** to play in ragtime

ra·ga (rä′gə) ***n.*** [Sans. *rāga,* lit., color] any of various traditional melodies used in improvising by Hindu musicians

rag·a·muf·fin (rag′ə muf′in) ***n.*** [ME. *Ragamoffyn,* name of a demon in *Piers Plowman,* a poem attributed to William Langland] a dirty, ragged person; esp., a poor, ragged child

rag·bag (rag′bag′) ***n.*** **1.** a bag for rags **2.** a collection of odds and ends

rage (rāj) ***n.*** [< OFr. < LL. < L. *rabies,* madness] **1.** furious, uncontrolled anger; esp., a brief spell of raving fury **2.** violence or intensity, as of the wind **3.** strong emotion, enthusiasm, or desire —***vi.*** **raged, rag′ing** **1.** to show violent anger in action or speech **2.** to be violent, uncontrolled, etc. [*a raging sea*] **3.** to spread unchecked, as a disease —**(all) the rage** anything thought of as a fad or craze

rag·ged (rag′id) ***adj.*** **1.** shabby or torn from wear **2.** wearing shabby or torn clothes **3.** uneven; rough **4.** shaggy; unkempt [*ragged hair*] **5.** not finished; imperfect **6.** harsh; strident —**run ragged** to make (someone) exhausted —**rag′ged·ly** ***adv.*** —**rag′ged·ness** ***n.***

rag·ged·y (rag′i dē) ***adj.*** somewhat ragged, or tattered

rag·lan (rag′lən) ***n.*** [after Lord *Raglan* (1788–1855), Brit. general] a loose overcoat or topcoat without shoulder seams, each sleeve **(raglan sleeve)** continuing in one piece to the collar

rag·man (rag′man′) ***n., pl.*** **-men′** (-men′) a man who collects, buys, and sells rags, old paper, etc.

ra·gout (ra go͞o′) ***n.*** [< Fr. < *ragoûter,* to revive the appetite of] a highly seasoned stew of meat and vegetables —***vt.*** **-gouted′** (-go͞od′), **-gout′ing** (-go͞o′iŋ) to make into a ragout

rag·pick·er (rag′pik′ər) ***n.*** a person who makes his living by picking up and selling rags and junk

rag rug a rug of rag strips woven or sewn together

rag·tag (and bobtail) (rag′tag′) [RAG[1] + TAG] the lowest classes; the rabble: term of contempt

rag·time (rag′tīm′) ***n.*** [prob. < *ragged time*] **1.** a type of strongly syncopated American music in fast, even time, popular 1890–1915 **2.** its rhythm

rag·weed (rag′wēd′) ***n.*** [from the tattered appearance of the leaves] any of a genus of chiefly N. American plants of the composite family, having tassellike, greenish flowers with a pollen that is a major cause of hay fever

rag·wort (-wurt′) ***n.*** [see prec.] *same as* GROUNDSEL

rah (rä) ***interj.*** hurrah: used as a cheer

raid (rād) ***n.*** [< ROAD, in obs. sense "a riding"] **1.** a sudden, hostile attack, as by troops, aircraft, bandits, etc. **2.** any sudden invasion of some place by police, to discover violations of the law **3.** an attempt to lure employees from a competitor **4.** an attempt by speculators to make stock market prices fall —***vt., vi.*** to make a raid (on) —**raid′er** ***n.***

rail[1] (rāl) ***n.*** [< OFr. < L. *regula,* a rule] **1.** a bar of wood, metal, etc. placed horizontally between posts as a barrier or support **2.** a fence or railing **3.** any of a series of parallel metal bars laid on crossties, etc. to make a track for trains, etc. **4.** a railroad as a means of transportation [*travel by rail*] **5.** the rim of a billiard table **6.** a narrow wooden piece at the top of a ship's bulwarks —***vt.*** to supply with rails or a railing; fence

rail[2] (rāl) ***vi.*** [< MFr. *railler* < Pr., ult. < LL. *ragere,* to bellow] to complain violently (with *against* or *at*)

rail[3] (rāl) ***n., pl.*** **rails, rail:** see PLURAL, II, D, 1 [< MFr. < *raaler,* to screech] any of a number of small, cranelike

fat, āpe, cär, ten, ēven, is, bīte; gō, hôrn, to͞ol, look; oil, out; up, fur; get; joy; yet; chin; she; thin, *th*en; zh, leisure; ŋ, ring; ə for *a* in *ago*, *e* in *agent*, *i* in *sanity*, *o* in *comply*, *u* in *focus*; ′ as in *able* (ā′b′l); Fr. bål; ë, Fr. coeur; ö, Fr. feu; Fr. mo*n*; ô, Fr. coq; ü, Fr. duc; r, Fr. cri; H, G. ich; kh, G. doch; ‡foreign; *hypothetical; < derived from. See inside front cover.

wading birds living in marshes and having short wings and tail, long toes, and a harsh cry

rail·ing (rāl′iŋ) *n.* **1.** material for rails **2.** rails collectively **3.** a fence or balustrade made of rails and posts

rail·ler·y (rāl′ər ē) *n., pl.* **-ler·ies** [Fr. *raillerie:* see RAIL[2] & -ERY] **1.** light ridicule; banter **2.** a teasing act or remark

rail·road (rāl′rōd′) *n.* **1.** a road laid with parallel steel rails along which locomotives draw cars in a train **2.** a complete system of such roads, including land, rolling stock, etc. **3.** the corporation owning such a system *—vt.* **1.** to transport by railroad **2.** [Colloq.] to rush through quickly, so as to prevent careful consideration **3.** [Slang] to cause to go to prison on a trumped-up charge or after a hasty trial *—vi.* to work on a railroad **—rail′road′er** *n.*

rail-split·ter (-split′ər) *n.* a person who splits logs into rails **—the Rail-Splitter** *nickname of* Abraham LINCOLN

rail·way (-wā′) *n.* **1.** *a)* a railroad for light vehicles *[a street railway]* *b)* [Brit.] any railroad **2.** any track with rails for guiding wheels

rai·ment (rā′mənt) *n.* [ME. *rayment* < *arayment:* see ARRAY & -MENT] [Archaic] clothing; wearing apparel

rain (rān) *n.* [OE. *regn*] **1.** water falling in drops condensed from the moisture in the atmosphere **2.** the falling of such drops; shower **3.** *a)* rainy weather *b)* [*pl.*] the rainy season (preceded by *the*) **4.** a rapid falling or propulsion of many small objects *[a rain of ashes]* *—vi.* **1.** to fall: said of rain *[it is raining]* **2.** to fall like rain **3.** to cause rain to fall *—vt.* **1.** to pour down (rain or something likened to rain) **2.** to give in large quantities **—rain cats and dogs** [Colloq.] to rain heavily **—rain out** to cause (an event) to be postponed or canceled because of rain **—rain′less** *adj.*

rain·bow (-bō′) *n.* an arc containing the colors of the spectrum in bands, formed in the sky by the refraction, reflection, and dispersion of the sun's rays in falling rain or in mist *—adj.* of many colors

rainbow trout a game fish native to the mountain streams and rivers of the Pacific Coast of N. America

rain check **1.** the stub of a ticket to a ball game, etc., entitling the holder to be admitted at a future date if the original event is rained out **2.** a bid for, or an offer of, a future invitation in place of one turned down

rain·coat (rān′kōt′) *n.* a waterproof or water-repellent coat for giving protection from rain

rain·drop (-dräp′) *n.* a single drop of rain

rain·fall (-fôl′) *n.* **1.** a falling of rain; shower **2.** the amount of water falling as rain, snow, etc. over a given area in a given period of time: measured in inches of depth of water that has fallen into a rain gauge

rain forest a dense, evergreen forest in a tropical region having abundant rainfall throughout the year

rain gauge an instrument for measuring rainfall

Rai·nier (rā nir′, rā′nir), **Mount** [after an 18th-cent. Brit. Adm. *Rainier*] mountain of the Cascade Range, in WC Wash.: 14,410 ft.

rain·proof (rān′proo͞f′) *adj.* not letting rain through *—vt.* to make rainproof

rain·storm (-stôrm′) *n.* a storm with a heavy rain

rain·wa·ter (-wôt′ər, -wät′ər) *n.* water that falls or has fallen as rain and is soft and fairly free of mineral matter

rain·wear (-wer′) *n.* rainproof clothing

rain·y (rā′nē) *adj.* **rain′i·er, rain′i·est** **1.** that has rain or much rain *[the rainy season]* **2.** wet with rain **3.** bringing rain **—rain′i·ness** *n.*

rainy day a possible future time of difficulty or need

raise (rāz) *vt.* **raised, rais′ing** [< ON. *reisa*] **1.** *a)* to make rise; lift *b)* to put upright **2.** to construct (a building, etc.) **3.** to stir up; arouse; incite *[to raise a revolt]* **4.** to increase in size, value, amount, etc. *[to raise prices]* **5.** to increase in degree, intensity, etc. *[to raise one's voice]* **6.** to improve the position or rank of *[to raise oneself from poverty]* **7.** to cause to arise, appear, or come; esp., to bring back as from death *[to raise the dead]* **8.** to produce; provoke *[the joke raised a laugh]* **9.** to bring forward for consideration *[to raise a question]* **10.** to collect or procure (an army, money, etc.) **11.** to utter (a cry, shout, etc.) **12.** to bring to an end *[to raise a siege]* **13.** to leaven (bread, etc.) **14.** *a)* to make (corn, etc.) grow *b)* to breed (cattle, etc.) *c)* to rear (children) **15.** to contact by radio **16.** to make (a blister) form **17.** to make (a nap on cloth) with teasels, etc. **18.** *Bridge* to increase (one's partner's bid in a suit) **19.** *Naut.* to come within sight of (land, etc.) **20.** *Poker* to bet more than (the highest preceding bet or bettor) *—vi.* **1.** [Dial.] to rise or arise **2.** *Poker* to increase the bet *—n.* **1.** a raising **2.** an increase in amount; specif., an increase in salary or wages **—raise Cain** (or **the devil, hell, a rumpus, the roof,** etc.) [Slang] to create a disturbance; cause trouble

raised (rāzd) *adj.* **1.** made in low relief; embossed **2.** having a napped surface **3.** leavened with yeast

rai·sin (rā′z'n) *n.* [< OFr. < L. *racemus,* cluster of grapes] a sweet, dried grape, usually seedless

rai·son d'être (rā′zōn det′, det′rə; *Fr.* re zōn de′tr′) [Fr.] reason for being; justification for existence

raj (räj) *n.* [see ff.] in India, rule; sovereignty; dominion

ra·jah, ra·ja (rä′jə) *n.* [< Hindi < Sans. *rājan* < *rāj,* to rule] **1.** formerly, a prince or chief in India **2.** esp. formerly, a Malay chief

rake[1] (rāk) *n.* [OE. *raca*] a long-handled tool with teeth or prongs at one end, used for gathering loose grass, leaves, etc. *—vt.* **raked, rak′ing** **1.** *a)* to gather with or as with a rake *b)* to make (a lawn, etc.) tidy with a rake **2.** to gather with great care **3.** to scratch or smooth as with a rake **4.** to search through carefully **5.** to direct gunfire along (a line of troops, etc.): often used figuratively *—vi.* **1.** to use a rake **2.** to search as if with a rake **3.** to scrape or sweep (with *over, across,* etc.) **—rake in** to gather an abundant amount of rapidly **—rake up** to uncover facts or gossip about (the past, a scandal, etc.)

rake[2] (rāk) *n.* [contr. of *rakehell,* prob. < ME. *rakel,* rash] a man who leads a wild, dissolute life: also **rake′hell′** (-hel′)

rake[3] (rāk) *vi., vt.* **raked, rak′ing** [? akin to Sw. *raka,* to project] to be or make slightly inclined, as a ship's masts; slant *—n.* a slanting or inclining

rake-off (rāk′ôf′) *n.* [Slang] a commission, rebate, or share, esp. one gained in a shady deal

rak·ish[1] (rā′kish) *adj.* [< RAKE[3] + -ISH] **1.** having a trim, neat appearance suggesting speed: said of a ship **2.** dashing and gay; jaunty **—rak′ish·ly** *adv.* **—rak′ish·ness** *n.*

rak·ish[2] (rā′kish) *adj.* like a rake; wild and carefree **—rak′ish·ly** *adv.* **—rak′ish·ness** *n.*

Ra·leigh (rô′lē, rä′-) [after ff.] capital of N.C., in the C part: pop. 150,000

Ra·leigh (rô′lē, rä′-), Sir **Walter** 1552?–1618; Eng. statesman, explorer, & poet: also sp. **Ralegh**

ral·len·tan·do (räl′ən tän′dō) *adj., adv.* [It., prp. of *rallentare,* to slow down] *Music* gradually slower: abbrev. **rall.**

ral·ly[1] (ral′ē) *vt.* **-lied, -ly·ing** [< Fr. < OFr. < *re-,* again + *alier,* to join: see ALLY] **1.** to gather together (retreating troops) and restore to a state of order **2.** to bring (persons) together for a common purpose **3.** to revive (one's spirits, etc.) *—vi.* **1.** to return to a state of order: said esp. of retreating troops **2.** to come together for a common purpose **3.** to come in order to help *[to rally to a friend]* **4.** to revive; recover *[to rally from a fever]* **5.** *Commerce* to rise in price after having fallen: said of stocks, etc. **6.** *Sports* to come from behind in scoring **7.** *Tennis,* etc. to take part in a rally *—n., pl.* **-lies** **1.** a rallying or being rallied; specif., a mass meeting **2.** an organized run, esp. of sports cars, over a course, designed to test driving skills: also sp. **ral′lye** **3.** *Tennis,* etc. an exchange of several strokes before the point is won **—ral′li·er** *n.*

ral·ly[2] (ral′ē) *vt., vi.* **-lied, -ly·ing** [Fr. *rallier,* to RAIL[2]] to tease or mock playfully; banter

Ralph (ralf; *Brit. usually* rāf) [< ON. < *rath,* counsel + *ulfr,* a wolf] a masculine name

ram (ram) *n.* [OE. *ramm*] **1.** a male sheep **2.** *same as* BATTERING RAM **3.** *a)* formerly, a sharp projection at a prow, for piercing enemy vessels *b)* a ship with this **4.** *same as* HYDRAULIC RAM **5.** the striking part of a pile driver **6.** the plunger of a force pump **—[R-]** Aries *—vt.* **rammed, ram′ming** **1.** to strike against with great force **2.** to force into place **3.** to force acceptance of (an idea, legislative bill, etc.) **4.** to stuff or cram (*with* something) *—vi.* **1.** to strike with force; crash **2.** to move rapidly **—ram′mer** *n.*

Ram·a·dan (ram′ə dän′) *n.* [Ar. *ramaḍān,* lit., the hot month < *ramaḍa,* to be hot] the ninth month of the Moslem year, a period of daily fasting from sunrise to sunset

Ra·ma·ya·na (rä mä′yə nə) one of the two great epics of India, written in Sanskrit after the Mahabharata

ram·ble (ram′b'l) *vi.* **-bled, -bling** [< ME. *romblen,* freq. of *romen,* to roam] **1.** to roam about; esp., to stroll about idly **2.** to talk or write aimlessly, without sticking to any point **3.** to spread in all directions, as a vine *—vt.* to roam through *—n.* a rambling, esp. a stroll

ram·bler (ram′blər) *n.* **1.** a person or thing that rambles **2.** any of certain climbing roses

ram·bunc·tious (ram buŋk′shəs) *adj.* [altered < *robustious* < *robust*] wild, boisterous, unruly, etc. **—ram·bunc′tious·ly** *adv.* **—ram·bunc′tious·ness** *n.*

ram·e·kin, ram·e·quin (ram′ə kin) *n.* [Fr. *ramequin* < MDu. *rammeken,* cheese dish] **1.** a food mixture, specif. of bread crumbs, cheese, and eggs, baked in individual baking dishes **2.** a baking dish of this kind

Ram·e·ses (ram′ə sēz) *var. of* RAMSES

ram·i·fi·ca·tion (ram′ə fi kā′shən) *n.* **1.** a ramifying or being ramified **2.** *a)* a branch or offshoot *b)* a derived effect, consequence, or result

ram·i·fy (ram′ə fī′) *vt., vi.* **-fied′, -fy′ing** [< Fr. < ML. < L. *ramus,* a branch + *facere,* to make] to divide or spread out into branches or branchlike divisions

ram·jet (engine) (ram′jet′) a jet engine in which the air for burning the fuel is compressed by being rammed into the inlet by the aircraft's velocity

ra·mose (rā′mōs, rə mōs′) *adj.* [L. *ramosus* < *ramus,* a

branch] **1.** bearing many branches or branchlike projections **2.** branching —**ra'mose·ly** *adv.*
ra·mous (rā'məs) *adj.* **1.** *same as* RAMOSE **2.** branchlike
ramp[1] (ramp) *n.* [Fr. *rampe* < OFr.: see ff.] **1.** a sloping walk, road, plank, etc. joining different levels **2.** a wheeled staircase rolled up to an airplane for use in getting on or off **3.** a sloping runway for launching boats, as from trailers
ramp[2] (ramp) *vi.* [OFr. *ramper,* to climb] **1.** to rear up on the hind legs; specif., *Heraldry* to be shown rampant **2.** to rampage or rage —*n.* a ramping
ram·page (ram pāj'; *also, and for n. always,* ram'pāj) *vi.* **-paged', -pag'ing** [prob. < RAMP[2]] to rush violently or wildly about; rage —*n.* a rampaging: chiefly in **on the** (or **a**) **rampage** —**ram·pa'geous** *adj.* —**ram·pag'er** *n.*
ramp·ant (ram'pənt) *adj.* [< OFr.: see RAMP[2]] **1.** growing or spreading unchecked; rife **2.** violent and uncontrollable **3.** standing up on the hind legs; specif., *Heraldry* shown so in profile, one forepaw above the other *[a lion rampant]* —**ramp'an·cy** *n.* —**ramp'ant·ly** *adv.*
ram·part (ram'pärt, -pərt) *n.* [Fr. < *re-,* again + *emparer* < Pr. *amparer,* to fortify < L. *ante,* before + *parare,* to prepare] **1.** a defensive embankment around a castle, fort, etc., with a parapet at the top **2.** any defense or bulwark
ram·rod (ram'räd') *n.* a rod for ramming down the charge in a gun loaded through the muzzle
Ram·ses (ram'sēz) any of a number of Egyptian kings who ruled from c. 1315 to c. 1090 B.C.
ram·shack·le (ram'shak''l) *adj.* [< freq. of RANSACK] loose and rickety; likely to fall to pieces
ran (ran) *pt. of* RUN
ranch (ranch) *n.* [< RANCHO] **1.** a large farm, esp. in western States, for raising many cattle, horses, or sheep **2.** any large farm for raising a particular crop or livestock *[a fruit ranch]* **3.** *same as* RANCH HOUSE —*vi.* to work on or manage a ranch —**ranch'er** *n.* —**ranch'man** (-mən) *n., pl.* **-men**
ranch house **1.** the owner's residence on a ranch **2.** a house with all the rooms on one floor, usually with a garage attached
ran·cho (ran'chō, rän'-) *n., pl.* **-chos** [AmSp.] in Spanish America, *same as* RANCH
ran·cid (ran'sid) *adj.* [< L. < *rancere,* to be rank] having the bad smell or taste of spoiled fats or oils —**ran·cid'i·ty** (-sid'ə tē), **ran'cid·ness** *n.* —**ran'cid·ly** *adv.*
ran·cor (raŋ'kər) *n.* [OFr. < LL. < L. *rancere,* to be rank] a continuing and bitter hate or ill will; deep spite: also, Brit. sp., **ran'cour** —**ran'cor·ous** *adj.* —**ran'cor·ous·ly** *adv.*
rand (rand, ränd) *n., pl.* **rand** [Afrik., orig., shield] *see* MONETARY UNITS, table (South Africa)
R & B, r & b rhythm and blues
R & D, R. and D. research and development
Ran·dolph (ran'dälf, -dôlf) [< ML. < OE. *randwulf,* lit., shield wolf] a masculine name
ran·dom (ran'dəm) *n.* [< OFr. *randon,* violence, speed < *randir,* to run violently] haphazard movement: now only in **at random,** without careful choice, aim, plan, etc.; haphazardly —*adj.* **1.** made, done, etc. in an aimless or haphazard way **2.** not uniform **3.** *Statistics* with each in a set or group having an equal opportunity of occurring or of occurring with a particular frequency —**ran'dom·ly** *adv.* —**ran'dom·ness** *n.*
ran·dom·ize (-īz') *vt.* **-ized', -iz'ing** to pick at random so as to get an unbiased result, often using a table of random numbers —**ran'dom·i·za'tion** *n.*
R & R, R and R *Mil.* rest and recuperation (leave)
ran·dy (ran'dē) *adj.* **-di·er, -di·est** [prob. < *rand,* dial. var. of RANT + -Y[2]] sexually aroused; lustful
ra·nee (rä'nē) *n. alt. sp. of* RANI
rang (raŋ) *pt. of* RING[1]
range (rānj) *vt.* **ranged, rang'ing** [< OFr. var. of *rengier* < *renc,* a row] **1.** to put in a certain order, esp. in a row or rows **2.** to classify **3.** to place with others in a cause, party, etc. *[to range oneself with the rebels]* **4.** to aim (a gun, telescope, etc.) properly **5.** to roam over or through **6.** to move along parallel to *[ranging the coastline]* **7.** to put out (cattle, etc.) to graze on a range —*vi.* **1.** to extend in a given direction *[hills ranging south]* **2.** to wander about; roam **3.** to vary between stated limits *[ages ranging from 1 to 7]* **4.** *Biol., Zool.* to be native to a specified region —*n.* **1.** a row, line, or series; rank **2.** a class, kind, or order **3.** a chain or single system of mountains **4.** *a)* the firing distance, either maximum or to a target, of a weapon *b)* the flight path of a missile or rocket **5.** the farthest distance a plane, etc. can go without refueling **6.** *a)* a place for shooting practice *b)* a place for testing rockets in flight **7.** the full extent over which something moves or is heard, seen, effective, etc.; scope **8.** the full extent of pitch, from highest to lowest tones, of a voice, instrument, etc. **9.** a large, open area of land for grazing livestock **10.** the limits within which there are changes or differences in amount, degree, etc. *[a wide range in price]* **11.** a cooking unit typically with an oven and surface heating units **12.** *Biol., Zool.* the region to which a plant or animal is native —*adj.* of a range (sense 9)
range finder any of various instruments to determine the distance of a target or object from a gun, camera, etc.
rang·er (rān'jər) *n.* **1.** one who ranges; roamer **2.** *a)* a member of a special military or police force that patrols a region *b)* [*often* **R-**] a soldier of a group trained for raiding **3.** *a)* in England, the chief official of a royal park or forest *b)* in the U.S., a warden patrolling government forests
Ran·goon (raŋ go͞on') capital of Burma, a seaport in the S part, on the Irrawaddy: pop. 1,759,000
rang·y (rān'jē) *adj.* **rang'i·er, rang'i·est** **1.** ranging about **2.** long-limbed and slender **3.** having range —**rang'i·ness** *n.*
ra·ni (rä'nē) *n.* [< Hindi < Sans. fem. of *rājan:* see RAJAH] the wife of a rajah
rank[1] (raŋk) *n.* [< MFr. < OFr. *renc*] **1.** a row, line, or series; specif., a set of organ pipes of the same kind **2.** an orderly arrangement **3.** a social class *[people from all ranks of life]* **4.** a high position in society *[a man of rank]* **5.** an official grade *[the rank of captain]* **6.** a relative position as measured by quality, etc. *[a poet of the first rank]* **7.** a row of soldiers, etc., side by side **8.** [*pl.*] all those in an organization, as the army, who are not officers or leaders *[to rise from the ranks]*: also **rank and file** —*vt.* **1.** to place in a rank or ranks **2.** to assign a relative position to **3.** to outrank —*vi.* to hold a certain position *[to rank third]* —**pull (one's) rank** [Slang] to use one's higher rank to get others to obey, etc.
rank[2] (raŋk) *adj.* [OE. *ranc,* strong] **1.** growing vigorously and coarsely; too luxuriant *[rank grass]* **2.** producing a luxuriant crop, often to excess **3.** very bad in smell or taste **4.** coarse; indecent **5.** utter; extreme *[rank injustice]* —**rank'ly** *adv.* —**rank'ness** *n.*
rank·ing (raŋ'kiŋ) *adj.* **1.** of the highest rank *[the ranking officer]* **2.** prominent or outstanding
ran·kle (raŋ'k'l) *vi., vt.* **-kled, -kling** [< OFr. < *draoncle* < ML. *dracunculus,* a fester < L. dim. of *draco,* dragon] **1.** orig., to fester **2.** to cause or fill with long-lasting rancor, resentment, etc.
ran·sack (ran'sak) *vt.* [< ON. < *rann,* a house + *sækja,* to search] **1.** to search through every part of **2.** to search through for plunder; pillage —**ran'sack·er** *n.*
ran·som (ran'səm) *n.* [< OFr. *raençon* < L. *redemptio,* REDEMPTION] **1.** the securing of the release of a captive or of seized property by paying money or meeting other demands **2.** the price so paid or demanded —*vt.* to get (a captive, etc.) released by paying the demanded price —**ran'som·er** *n.*
rant (rant) *vi., vt.* [< obs. Du. *ranten,* to rave] to talk or say in a loud, wild, extravagant way; declaim violently; rave —*n.* ranting talk —**rant'er** *n.* —**rant'ing·ly** *adv.*
rap[1] (rap) *vt.* **rapped, rap'ping** [prob. echoic] **1.** to strike quickly and sharply; tap **2.** [Slang] to criticize sharply —*vi.* **1.** to knock quickly and sharply **2.** [Slang] to talk; chat —*n.* **1.** a quick, sharp knock; tap **2.** [Slang] a talking; chat **3.** [Slang] blame or punishment; specif., a judicial sentence, as to prison: usually in **beat** (escape) or **take** (receive) **the rap,** or **bum** (unfair) **rap** —**rap out** to utter sharply —**rap'per** *n.*
rap[2] (rap) *n.* [< ?] [Colloq.] the least bit: in **not care** (or **give**) **a rap,** not care anything at all
ra·pa·cious (rə pā'shəs) *adj.* [< L. *rapax* (gen. *rapacis*) < *rapere,* to seize] **1.** taking by force; plundering **2.** greedy; voracious **3.** living on captured prey; predatory —**ra·pa'cious·ly** *adv.* —**ra·pac·i·ty** (rə pas'ə tē), **ra·pa'cious·ness** *n.*
rape[1] (rāp) *n.* [ME. < L. *rapere,* to seize] **1.** *a)* the crime of having sexual intercourse with a woman or girl forcibly and without her consent, or **(statutory rape)** with a girl below the age of consent *b)* any sexual assault upon a person **2.** [Now Rare] a seizing and carrying away by force **3.** any violent or outrageous assault —*vt., vi.* **raped, rap'ing** to commit rape (on) —**rap'ist** *n.*
rape[2] (rāp) *n.* [L. *rapa, rapum,* turnip] an annual old-world plant of the mustard family, with seed **(rape'seed')** yielding an oil **(rape oil, rapeseed oil)** and with leaves used for fodder
Raph·a·el (rā'fē əl; *also, and for 2 usually,* raf'ē-) [LL. < Gr. < Heb. *rephā'ēl,* lit., God hath healed] **1.** an archangel mentioned in the Apocrypha **2.** (born *Raffaello Santi* or *Sanzio*) 1483–1520; It. painter & architect
rap·id (rap'id) *adj.* [L. *rapidus* < *rapere,* to rush] moving,

occurring, or acting with speed; swift; fast; quick —*n.* **1.** [*usually pl.*] a part of a river where the current is swift, as because of a narrowing of the river bed **2.** a rapid transit car, train, or system —**ra·pid·i·ty** (rə pid′ə tē), **rap′id·ness** *n.* —**rap′id·ly** *adv.*

rap·id-fire (-fīr′) *adj.* **1.** firing shots in rapid succession: said of guns **2.** done, carried on, etc. in a swift, sharp way

rapid transit a system of rapid public transportation in an urban area, using electric trains running along an unimpeded right of way

ra·pi·er (rā′pē ər, rāp′yər) *n.* [Fr. *rapière*] **1.** orig., a slender, two-edged sword with a large cup hilt **2.** later, a light, sharp-pointed sword used only for thrusting

rap·ine (rap′in) *n.* [OFr. < L. *rapina* < *rapere,* to seize] the act of seizing property by force; plunder; pillage

rap·pel (ra pel′, rə-) *n.* [Fr., lit., a recall] a descent down a steep cliff by a climber using a double rope secured above —*vi.* **-pelled′, -pel′ling** to make such a descent

rap·pen (räp′ən) *n., pl.* **-pen** [G. < *rappe,* raven: after the eagle on an earlier Alsatian coin] *see* MONETARY UNITS, table (Liechtenstein, Switzerland)

rap·port (ra pôr′, -pôrt′) *n.* [Fr. < OFr. < *re-,* again + *aporter* < L. < *ad-,* to + *portare,* to carry] relationship, esp. of a sympathetic kind; agreement; harmony

rap·proche·ment (ra prōsh′män; *Fr.* rȧ prôsh män′) *n.* [Fr.] an establishing or restoring of friendly relations

rap·scal·lion (rap skal′yən) *n.* [< earlier *rascallion,* extension of RASCAL] a rascal; rogue

rapt (rapt) *adj.* [< L. pp. of *rapere,* to seize] **1.** carried away with joy, love, etc.; full of or showing rapture **2.** absorbed (*in* meditation, study, etc.)

rap·to·ri·al (rap tôr′ē əl) *adj.* [< L. < pp. of *rapere,* to seize] **1.** predatory; specif., of or belonging to a group of birds of prey with a strong notched beak and sharp talons, as the eagle **2.** adapted for seizing prey *[raptorial* claws*]*

rap·ture (rap′chər) *n.* [RAPT + -URE] **1.** the state of being carried away with joy, love, etc.; ecstasy **2.** an expression of great joy, pleasure, etc. —**rap′tur·ous** *adj.*

rare[1] (rer) *adj.* **rar′er, rar′est** [MFr. < L. *rarus*] **1.** not often seen, done, found, etc.; uncommon **2.** unusually good; excellent *[a rare* teacher*]* **3.** not dense; thin *[rare* atmosphere*]* —**rare′ness** *n.*

rare[2] (rer) *adj.* **rar′er, rar′est** [OE. *hrere*] not fully cooked; partly raw: said esp. of meat —**rare′ness** *n.*

rare[3] (rer) *vi.* **rared, rar′ing 1.** *dial. var. of* REAR[2] *vi.* **2.** [Colloq.] to be eager: used in prp. *[raring* to go*]*

rare·bit (rer′bit) *n. same as* WELSH RABBIT

rare earth 1. any of certain similar basic oxides; specif., any of the oxides of the rare-earth metals **2.** any of the rare-earth metals

rare-earth metals (or **elements**) (rer′urth′) a group of rare metallic chemical elements with consecutive atomic numbers of 57 to 71 inclusive

rar·e·fy (rer′ə fī′) *vt., vi.* **-fied′, -fy′ing** [< MFr. < L. < *rarus,* rare + *facere,* to make] **1.** to make or become thin, or less dense **2.** to make or become more refined, subtle, or lofty —**rar′e·fac′tion** (-fak′shən) *n.*

rare·ly (rer′lē) *adv.* **1.** not often; seldom **2.** beautifully, excellently, etc. **3.** uncommonly; unusually

rar·i·ty (rer′ə tē) *n.* **1.** a being rare; specif., *a)* uncommonness; scarcity *b)* excellence *c)* lack of density **2.** *pl.* **-ties** a rare or uncommon thing

ras·cal (ras′k'l) *n.* [OFr. *rascaille,* scrapings, ult. < L. pp. of *radere,* to scrape] a scoundrel; rogue; scamp: often used playfully, as of a mischievous child

ras·cal·i·ty (ras kal′ə tē) *n.* **1.** the character or behavior of a rascal **2.** *pl.* **-ties** a low, mean, or dishonest act

ras·cal·ly (ras′k'l ē) *adj.* of or like a rascal; base; dishonest; mean —*adv.* in a rascally way

rase (rāz) *vt.* **rased, ras′ing** *alt. Brit. sp. of* RAZE

rash[1] (rash) *adj.* [ME. *rasch*] too hasty and careless; reckless —**rash′ly** *adv.* —**rash′ness** *n.*

rash[2] (rash) *n.* [MFr. *rasche*] **1.** a breaking out of red spots on the skin **2.** a sudden appearance of a large number *[a rash* of complaints*]*

rash·er (rash′ər) *n.* [< ? obs. *rash,* to cut] **1.** a thin slice of bacon or, rarely, ham, for frying or broiling **2.** a serving of several such slices

rasp (rasp) *vt.* [< OFr. < OHG. *raspon,* to scrape together] **1.** to scrape or rub as with a file **2.** to utter in a rough, grating tone **3.** to grate upon; irritate —*vi.* **1.** to scrape; grate **2.** to make a rough, grating sound —*n.* **1.** a type of rough file with sharp, projecting points **2.** a rough, grating sound —**rasp′er** *n.* —**rasp′ing·ly** *adv.*

rasp·ber·ry (raz′ber′ē, -bər ē) *n., pl.* **-ries** [earlier *raspis berry* < *raspis,* raspberry] **1.** the small, juicy, edible fruit of various brambles of the rose family: it is a cluster of red, purple, or black drupelets **2.** the bramble bearing this **3.** [Slang] a jeering sound made by blowing out so as to vibrate the tongue between the lips

Ras·pu·tin (räs po͞o′tin; *E.* ras pyo͞ot′'n), **Gri·go·ri E·fi·mo·vich** (gri gô′ri ye fē′mə vich) 1871?–1916; Russ. religious mystic & faith healer: assassinated

rasp·y (ras′pē) *adj.* **rasp′i·er, rasp′i·est 1.** rasping; grating **2.** easily irritated —**rasp′i·ness** *n.*

ras·sle (ras′'l) *n., vi., vt.* **-sled, -sling** *dial. or colloq. var. of* WRESTLE

rat (rat) *n.* [OE. *ræt*] **1.** *a)* any of numerous long-tailed rodents resembling, but larger than, the mouse, very destructive, and carriers of disease *b)* any of various ratlike rodents **2.** [Slang] a sneaky, contemptible person; informer, traitor, etc. —*vi.* **rat′ted, rat′ting 1.** to hunt rats **2.** [Slang] *a)* to desert or betray a cause, movement, etc. *b)* to act as an informer —*vt.* to tease (the hair) —**rats!** [Slang] an exclamation of disgust, disappointment, etc. —**smell a rat** to suspect a trick, plot, etc.

rat·a·ble (rāt′ə b'l) *adj.* **1.** that can be rated, or estimated, etc. **2.** figured at a certain rate; proportional **3.** [Brit.] taxable Also sp. **rate′a·ble** —**rat′a·bly, rate′a·bly** *adv.*

rat-a-tat (rat′ə tat′) *n.* [echoic] a series of sharp, quick rapping sounds: also **rat′-a-tat′-tat′**

ra·ta·touille (rä′tä twē′) *n.* [Fr. < *ra-,* intensifier + *ta-,* reduplicated syllable + *touiller,* to stir, mix < L. *tudiculare,* to stir about] a vegetable stew of eggplant, zucchini, tomatoes, etc. flavored with garlic and served hot or cold

ratch·et (rach′it) *n.* [< Fr. < It. *rocchetto,* dim. of *rocca,* distaff] **1.** a toothed wheel (in full, **ratchet wheel**) or bar whose teeth slope in one direction so as to catch and hold a pawl, which thus prevents backward movement **2.** such a pawl **3.** such a wheel (or bar) and pawl as a unit

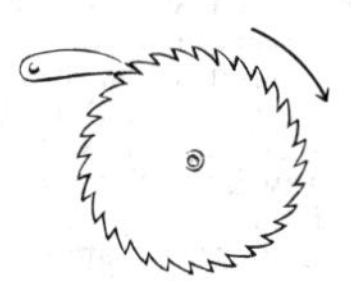
RATCHET WHEEL

rate[1] (rāt) *n.* [OFr. < L. *rata* (*pars*), reckoned (part) < pp. of *reri,* to reckon] **1.** the amount, degree, etc. of anything in relation to units of something else *[*the *rate* of pay per month*]* **2.** a fixed ratio; proportion *[*the *rate* of exchange*]* **3.** a price or value; specif., the cost per unit of some commodity, service, etc. **4.** speed of movement or action **5.** a class or rank *[*of the first *rate]* **6.** [Brit.] a local property tax **7.** *U.S. Navy* any of the grades of an enlisted man with a rating —*vt.* **rat′ed, rat′ing 1.** to estimate the value, capacity, skill, etc. of; appraise **2.** *a)* to put into a particular class or rank *b) U.S. Navy* to assign a rate to **3.** to consider; esteem **4.** to fix or determine the rates for **5.** [Colloq.] to deserve —*vi.* **1.** to be classed or ranked **2.** to have value, status, or rating —**at any rate 1.** in any event **2.** anyway

rate[2] (rāt) *vt., vi.* **rat′ed, rat′ing** [ME. *raten*] to scold severely; chide

rate·pay·er (rāt′pā′ər) *n.* [Brit. & Canad.] one who pays rates, or local taxes

-rat·er (rāt′ər) *a combining form meaning* one of a (specified) rate, or class *[*first-*rater]*

rath·er (rath′ər; *for interj.* ra′thur′) *adv.* [OE. *hrathor,* compar. of *hrathe,* quickly] **1.** more willingly; preferably **2.** with more justice, reason, etc. **3.** more accurately; more precisely **4.** on the contrary **5.** to some degree; somewhat —*interj.* [Chiefly Brit.] certainly —**had** (or **would**) **rather 1.** would choose to **2.** would prefer that —**rather than** instead of

raths·kel·ler (rät′skel′ər, rath′-) *n.* [G. < *rat,* council + *keller,* cellar] a restaurant of the German type, usually below street level, where beer is served

rat·i·fy (rat′ə fī′) *vt.* **-fied′, -fy′ing** [< MFr. < ML. < L. *ratus* (see RATE[1]) + *facere,* to make] to approve or confirm; esp., to give official sanction to —**rat′i·fi·ca′tion** *n.*

ra·ti·né (rat′'n ā′) *n.* [Fr., frizzed: of the nap] a loosely woven fabric of cotton, wool, rayon, etc., with a nubby surface: also **ra·tine** (ra tēn′)

rat·ing (rāt′iŋ) *n.* **1.** a rank or grade; specif., a classification of armed-forces personnel according to specialties **2.** a placement in a certain rank or class **3.** an evaluation of the credit or financial standing of a businessman, firm, etc. **4.** an amount determined as a grade **5.** *Radio & TV* the relative popularity of a program, as shown by polls

ra·tio (rā′shō, -shē ō′) *n., pl.* **-tios** [L.: see REASON] **1.** a fixed relation in degree, number, etc. between two similar things; proportion *[a ratio* of two boys to three girls*]* **2.** *Math.* the quotient of one quantity divided by another of the same kind, usually expressed as a fraction

ra·ti·o·ci·nate (rash′ē ō′sə nāt′, rat′ē-; -äs′ə nāt′) *vi.* **-nat′ed, -nat′ing** [< L. pp. of *ratiocinari* < *ratio:* see REASON] to reason, esp. using formal logic —**ra′ti·o′ci·na′tion** *n.* —**ra′ti·o′ci·na′tive** *adj.* —**ra′ti·o′ci·na′tor** *n.*

ra·tion (rash′ən, rā′shən) *n.* [MFr. < ML. < L. *ratio:* see REASON] **1.** a fixed portion; share; allowance **2.** a fixed allowance of food or provisions, as a daily allowance for one soldier, etc. 3. [*pl.*] food or food supply —*vt.* 1. to give rations to 2. to distribute (food, clothing, etc.) in rations, as in times of scarcity —**ra′tion·ing** *n.*

ra·tion·al (rash′ən ′l) *adj.* [L. *rationalis* < *ratio:* see REASON] 1. of or based on reasoning 2. able to reason; reasoning 3. showing reason; sensible [a *rational* plan] 4. *Math.* designating or of a number that can be expressed as the quotient of two integers or as an integer —**ra′tion·al′i·ty** (-ə nal′ə tē) *n., pl.* **-ties** —**ra′tion·al·ly** *adv.*

ra·tion·a·le (rash′ə nal′, -nā′lē) *n.* [L.: see prec.] 1. the rational basis for something 2. an explanation of reasons or principles

ra·tion·al·ism (rash′ən ′l iz′m) *n.* the principle or practice of accepting reason as the only source of knowledge and as the only basis for forming one's opinions, beliefs, or course of action —**ra′tion·al·ist** *n., adj.* —**ra′tion·al·is′tic** *adj.* —**ra′tion·al·is′ti·cal·ly** *adv.*

ra·tion·al·ize (rash′ən ə līz′) *vt.* **-ized′, -iz′ing** 1. to make rational; make conform to reason 2. to explain on the basis of reason or logic 3. *Psychol.* to think of explanations for (one's acts, beliefs, etc.) that seem to make sense but do not truly reveal one's motives —*vi.* 1. to think in a rational or rationalistic manner 2. to rationalize one's acts, beliefs, etc. —**ra′tion·al·i·za′tion** *n.* —**ra′tion·al·iz′er** *n.*

rat·ite (rat′īt) *adj.* [< L. < *ratis,* a raft] of a group of large, flightless birds having a flat breastbone without the keellike ridge of flying birds —*n.* any bird of this group, as the ostrich

rat·line (rat′lin) *n.* [altered by folk etym. < LME. *ratling* < ?] any of the small, thin pieces of tarred rope that join the shrouds of a ship and serve as a ladder: also sp. **rat′lin**

rat race [Slang] a mad scramble or intense competitive struggle, as in the business world

rats·bane (rats′bān′) *n.* [see BANE] rat poison

rat·tail (rat′tāl′) *adj.* shaped like a rat's tail; slim and tapering: also **rat′tailed′**

rat·tan (ra tan′) *n.* [Malay *rotan* < *raut,* to strip] 1. a climbing palm with long, slender, tough stems 2. these stems, used in making wickerwork, etc. 3. a cane or switch made from such a stem

RATLINES

rat·ter (rat′ər) *n.* 1. a dog or cat skilled at catching rats 2. [Slang] a betrayer or informer

rat·tle (rat′′l) *vi.* **-tled, -tling** [ME. *ratelen:* prob. echoic] 1. to make a rapid series of sharp, short sounds 2. to move with such sounds [a cart *rattled* over the stones] 3. to chatter (often with *on*) —*vt.* 1. to cause to rattle [he *rattled* the handle] 2. to utter or perform rapidly (usually with *off*) 3. to confuse or upset [catcalls *rattled* the speaker] —*n.* 1. a quick succession of short, sharp sounds 2. a rattling noise in the throat, as of a dying person 3. a noisy uproar 4. the series of horny rings at the end of a rattlesnake's tail 5. a device, as a baby's toy, intended to rattle when shaken —**rattle around in** to occupy (a place too big for one's needs) —**rat′tly** *adj.*

rat·tle·brain (-brān′) *n.* a frivolous, talkative person: also **rat′tle·pate′** (-pāt′) —**rat′tle·brained′** *adj.*

rat·tler (rat′lər) *n.* 1. a person or thing that rattles 2. a rattlesnake 3. [Colloq.] a freight train

rat·tle·snake (rat′′l snāk′) *n.* any of various poisonous American pit vipers having a series of horny rings at the end of the tail that rattle when shaken

rat·tle·trap (-trap′) *n.* anything worn out, rickety, or rattling; esp., an old, worn-out automobile

rat·tling (rat′liŋ) *adj.* 1. that rattles 2. [Colloq.] very fast, good, etc. —*adv.* [Colloq.] very [a *rattling* good time]

rat·ty (rat′ē) *adj.* **-ti·er, -ti·est** 1. of, like, or full of rats 2. [Slang] shabby or run-down

rau·cous (rô′kəs) *adj.* [L. *raucus*] 1. hoarse; rough-sounding [a *raucous* shout] 2. loud and rowdy [a *raucous* party] —**rau′cous·ly** *adv.* —**rau′cous·ness** *n.*

raun·chy (rôn′chē, rän′-) *adj.* **-chi·er, -chi·est** [< ?] [Slang] 1. dirty, cheap, sloppy, etc. 2. earthy, risqué, lustful, etc. —**raun′chi·ly** *adv.* —**raun′chi·ness** *n.*

rau·wol·fi·a (rô wool′fē ə, rou-) *n.* [ModL., after L. *Rauwolf,* 16th-c. G. botanist] 1. any of a group of tropical trees and shrubs, some of which yield medicinal substances 2. the root of one of these trees, a source of reserpine

rav·age (rav′ij) *n.* [Fr. < *ravir:* see RAVISH] 1. the act or practice of violently destroying 2. ruin; devastating damage —*vt.* **-aged, -ag·ing** to destroy violently; devastate; ruin —*vi.* to commit ravages —**rav′ag·er** *n.*

rave (rāv) *vi.* **raved, rav′ing** [prob. < OFr. *raver*] 1. to talk incoherently or wildly, as when delirious or demented 2. to talk with excessive enthusiasm (*about*) 3. to rage, as a storm —*vt.* to utter incoherently —*n.* 1. a raving 2. [Colloq.] an excessively enthusiastic commendation: often used before a noun [a *rave* review] —**rav′er** *n.*

rav·el (rav′′l) *vt.* **-eled** or **-elled, -el·ing** or **-el·ling** [MDu. *ravelen*] 1. orig., to make complicated or tangled 2. to separate the parts, esp. threads, of; untwist 3. to make clear; disentangle —*vi.* to become separated into its parts, esp. threads; fray (*out*) —*n.* a raveling, or a raveled thread —**rav′el·er, rav′el·ler** *n.*

Ra·vel (rȧ vel′; E. ra vel′), **Mau·rice (Joseph)** (mô rēs′) 1875–1937; Fr. composer

rav·el·ing, rav·el·ling (rav′′l iŋ, rav′liŋ) *n.* anything raveled, as a thread raveled from knitted or woven fabric

ra·ven (rā′vən) *n.* [OE. *hræfn*] a large bird of the crow family, with shiny black feathers and a sharp beak —*adj.* black and shiny

rav·en·ing (rav′′n iŋ) *adj.* [see RAVENOUS] greedily searching for prey

rav·e·nous (rav′ə nəs) *adj.* [< OFr. < *ravine* < L. *rapina,* RAPINE] 1. greedily hungry 2. greedy [*ravenous* for praise] 3. rapacious —**rav′e·nous·ly** *adv.* —**rav′e·nous·ness** *n.*

ra·vine (rə vēn′) *n.* [Fr., flood < OFr.: see prec.] a long, deep hollow in the earth's surface, worn by a stream; gorge

rav·ing (rā′viŋ) *adj.* 1. raging; delirious 2. [Colloq.] exciting raving admiration [a *raving* beauty] —*adv.* so as to cause raving [*raving* mad] —*n.* delirious, incoherent speech

ra·vi·o·li (rav′ē ō′lē) *n.pl.* [*with sing. v.*] [It.] small casings of dough containing seasoned ground meat, cheese, etc., boiled and served usually in a savory tomato sauce

rav·ish (rav′ish) *vt.* [< stem of OFr. *ravir,* ult. < L. *rapere,* to seize] 1. to seize and carry away forcibly 2. to rape 3. to enrapture —**rav′ish·er** *n.* —**rav′ish·ment** *n.*

rav·ish·ing (-iŋ) *adj.* causing great joy or delight; entrancing —**rav′ish·ing·ly** *adv.*

raw (rô) *adj.* [OE. *hreaw*] 1. not cooked 2. in its natural condition; not changed by art, manufacture, etc. [*raw* silk] 3. not processed, edited, etc. [*raw* data] 4. inexperienced [a *raw* recruit] 5. with the skin rubbed off; sore and inflamed [a *raw* cut] 6. uncomfortably cold and damp [a *raw* wind] 7. *a*) brutal or coarse in frankness *b*) indecent; bawdy 8. [Colloq.] harsh or unfair [a *raw* deal] —**in the raw** 1. in the natural state 2. naked —**raw′ly** *adv.* —**raw′ness** *n.*

Ra·wal·pin·di (rä′wəl pin′dē) city in NE Pakistan: pop. 340,000

raw·boned (rô′bōnd′) *adj.* having little fat; lean; gaunt

raw·hide (-hīd′) *n.* 1. an untanned or partially tanned cattle hide 2. a whip made of this —*vt.* **-hid′ed, -hid′ing** to beat with such a whip

Ray (rā) [dim. of RAYMOND] a masculine name

ray[1] (rā) *n.* [< OFr. < L. *radius:* see RADIUS] 1. any of the thin lines, or beams, of light that appear to come from a bright source 2. any of several lines coming out from a center 3. a tiny amount [a *ray* of hope] 4. *Bot., Zool.* any part of a structure with parts coming like rays from a center, as the petals of certain flowers, the limbs of a starfish, etc. 5. *Physics* *a*) a stream of particles given off by a radioactive substance, or any of the particles *b*) a straight line along which any part of a wave of radiant energy is regarded as traveling —*vi.* 1. to shine forth in rays 2. to radiate —*vt.* 1. to send out in rays 2. to supply with rays or radiating lines —**ray′less** *adj.* —**ray′like′** *adj.*

ray[2] (rā) *n.* [< MFr. < L. *raia*] any of several fishes, as the stingray, electric ray, skate, etc., having a horizontally flat body with both eyes on top, wide fins at each side, and a slender or whiplike tail

ray flower any of the flowers around the margin of the head of certain composite plants, as the daisy: also **ray floret**

Ray·mond (rā′mənd) [< ONormFr. < Frank. *Raginmund,* lit., wise protection] a masculine name

ray·on (rā′än) *n.* [arbitrary coinage < RAY[1]] 1. any of various synthetic textile fibers produced by pressing a cellulose solution through very small holes and solidifying it in the form of filaments 2. any fabric woven or knitted from such fibers

raze (rāz) *vt.* **razed, raz′ing** [< OFr. *raser,* ult. < L. pp. of *radere,* to scrape] to tear down completely; level to the ground: demolish

ra·zor (rā′zər) *n.* [< OFr. < *raser:* see prec.] 1. a sharp-edged cutting instrument for shaving off or cutting hair 2. *same as* SHAVER (sense 2)

ra·zor·back (-bak′) *n.* 1. a wild or semiwild hog of the S U.S., with a ridged back and long legs 2. a sharp ridge

razz (raz) *vt., vi.* [contr. < RASPBERRY] [Slang] to tease, ridicule, heckle, etc. —*n.* [Slang] *same as* RASPBERRY (sense 3)

raz·zle-daz·zle (raz′'l daz′'l) *n.* [Slang] a flashy display intended to confuse, bewilder, or deceive

razz·ma·tazz (raz′mə taz′) *n.* [Slang] **1.** lively spirit; excitement **2.** flashy display; showiness

Rb *Chem.* rubidium

rbi, RBI, r.b.i. *Baseball* run(s) batted in

R.C. **1.** Red Cross **2.** Roman Catholic

R.C.Ch. Roman Catholic Church

Rd., rd. **1.** road **2.** rod **3.** round

R.D. Rural Delivery

re[1] (rā) *n.* [It. < L. *re(sonare)*: see GAMUT] *Music* a syllable representing the second tone of the diatonic scale

re[2] (rē, rā) *prep.* [L., abl. of *res*, thing] in the case or matter of; as regards: short for *in re*

re- [< Fr. *re-, ré-* < L. *re-, red-*, back] *a prefix meaning:* **1.** back *[repay]* **2.** again, anew *[reappear]* It is used with a hyphen: 1) to distinguish between a word in which the prefix means *again* or *anew* and a word having a special meaning (Ex.: *re-sound, resound*) 2) to avoid ambiguity in forming nonce words *[re-urge]* 3) esp. formerly, before words beginning with an *e [re-edit]*: now usually solid *[reedit]* The following list contains some of the more common words in which *re-* means *again* or *anew*

reabsorb
reabsorption
reaccuse
reaccustom
reacquaint
reacquire
readapt
readdress
readjust
readmission
readmit
readmittance
readopt
reaffiliate
reaffirm
reaffirmation
realliance
reallocation
reallot
reappearance
reapplication
reapply
reappoint
reappointment
rearrest
reascend
reassemble
reassembly
reassert
reassertion
reassess
reassign
reassociate
reassume
reassumption
reattach
reattack
reattain
reattempt
reawaken
rebaptism
rebaptize
rebeautify
rebid
rebill
rebind
reborn
rebuild
rebury
recalculate
recapitalize
recarry
recertify
rechannel
recharge
recharter
recheck
rechew
recirculate
reclassification
reclassify
reclothe
recode
recolor
recombine
recommence
recommission
recompose
recompress
recompute
recondense
reconduct
reconfine
reconfirm
reconquer
reconquest
reconsecrate
reconsign
reconsolidate
reconstitute
recontaminate
reconvene
reconvey
recook
recopy
recross
recrystallize
recultivate
redecorate
rededicate
redefine
redefinition
redeliver
redemand
redeposit
redescribe
redesign
redetermine
redevelop
rediscover
rediscovery
redistribute
redistribution
redraft
redraw
redry
redye
reedit
reelect
reelection
reembark
reembody
reembrace
reemerge
reemergence
reemphasize
reenact
reengage
reenlist
reenlistment
reenter
reentrance
reequip
reestablish
reevaluate
reexamination
reexamine
reexchange
reexperience
reexplain
reexport
reface
refashion
refasten
refigure
refile
refilter
refocus
refold
reformulate
refortify
reframe
refreeze
refuel
refurnish
regather
regild
reglaze
reglorify
reglue
regrade
regrind
regrow
rehandle
rehang
rehire
rehospitalize
rehouse
reignite
reimpose
reimprisonment
reincorporate
reincur
reinduce
reinfect
reinflate
reinform
reinfuse
reinoculate
reinsert
reinspect
reinspire
reinstall
reinstitute
reinstruct
reinsure
reinterment
reinterpret
reinterrogate
reintroduce
reintroduction
reinvest
reinvestigate
reinvigorate
reinvite
reinvolve
reissue
rekindle
reknit
relabel
relace
relaunder
relearn
relet
relight
reload
reman
remarriage
remarry
rematch
remeasure
remelt
remerge
remilitarize
remix
remodify
remold
rename
renegotiate
renominate
renotify
renumber
reobtain
reoccupy
reoccur
reoccurrence
reopen
reoppose
reorient
repack
repaint
repanel
repaper
repark
repartition
repave
rephotograph
replan
replant
replaster
replate
replay
repolish
repopularize
repopulate
repot
repour
re-present
reprice
reprocess
reprosecute
re-prove
republication
republish
repurchase
repurify
requalify
reread
rerecord
reroll
resaddle
reschedule
rescore
rescreen
reseal
reseed
reseize
resell
resend
resentence
re-serve
resettle
resew
reshape
resharpen
reshine
reshow
reshuffle
re-sign
resilver
resituate
resmooth
resolder
resolidify
re-solve
re-sound
respace
respread
restabilize
restaff
restage
restamp
restart
restimulate
restitch
restock
restraighten
re-strain
restrengthen
restretch
restrike
restring
restudy
restyle
resubmit
resubscribe
resummon
resupply
resurvey
reswallow
resynthesize
retabulate
retack
retape
reteach
retelevise
retell
retest
retestify
rethread
retie
retitle
retold
retrain
retransfer
retranslate
re-treat
retrial
retrim
retry
retune
retwist
retype
reupholster
reusable
reuse
revaccinate
revaluation
revalue
revarnish
reverify
revibrate
revisit
revisualize
revitalize
revote
rewaken
rewarm
rewash
reweave
reweigh
reweld
rewin
rework
rezone

Re *Chem.* rhenium

reach (rēch) *vt.* [OE. *ræcan*] **1.** to thrust out or extend (the hand, etc.) **2.** to extend to, or touch, by thrusting out, etc. **3.** to obtain and hand over *[reach* me the salt*]* **4.** to go as far as; attain **5.** to carry as far as *[*the news *reached* him late*]* **6.** to add up to *[*to *reach* hundreds of dollars*]* **7.** to influence; affect **8.** to get in touch with, as by telephone —*vi.* **1.** to thrust out the hand, foot, etc. **2.** to stretch, or be extended, in amount, influence, space, time, etc. **3.** to carry, as sight, sound, etc. **4.** to try to obtain something **5.** to try too hard to make a point, joke, etc. **6.** *Naut.* to sail on a reach —*n.* **1.** a stretching or thrusting out **2.** the power of stretching, obtaining, etc. **3.** the distance or extent covered in stretching, obtaining, etc. **4.** a continuous extent or stretch, esp. of water **5.** *Naut.* a tack sailed with the wind coming from abeam —**reach′a·ble** *adj.* —**reach′er** *n.*

re·act (rē akt′) *vi.* **1.** to act in return or reciprocally **2.** to act in opposition **3.** to go back to a former condition, stage, etc. **4.** to respond to a stimulus, influence, etc. **5.** *Chem.* to act with another substance in producing a chemical change —*vt.* to produce a chemical change in

re-act (rē′akt′) *vt.* to act or do again

re·act·ance (rē ak′təns) *n. Elec.* opposition to the flow of alternating current, caused by inductance or capacitance

re·act·ant (-tənt) *n.* any of the substances taking part in a chemical reaction

re·ac·tion (rē ak′shən) *n.* **1.** a returning or opposing action, influence, etc. **2.** a response, as to a stimulus **3.** a movement back to a former or less advanced condition, stage, etc.; esp., such a movement in politics **4.** *Chem.* *a)* the mutual action of substances undergoing chemical change *b)* a process that produces changes in an atomic nucleus **5.** *Med.* *a)* an action induced by resistance to another action *b)* the effect produced by an allergen *c)* depression or exhaustion following nervous tension, overstimulation, etc. *d)* increased activity following depression —**re·ac′tion·al** *adj.* —**re·ac′tive** *adj.* —**re·ac′tive·ly** *adv.* —**re′ac·tiv′i·ty** *n.*

re·ac·tion·ar·y (-shə ner′ē) *adj.* of, showing, or favoring reaction, esp. in politics —*n., pl.* **-ar′ies** a reactionary person

reaction engine an engine, as a rocket, that develops thrust by the reaction to the jet of gases ejected from it
reaction time *Psychol.* the time between stimulation and the beginning of the response
re·ac·ti·vate (rē ak′tə vāt′) *vt.* **-vat′ed, -vat′ing** to make active again; specif., to restore to active military status —*vi.* to be reactivated —**re·ac′ti·va′tion** *n.*
re·ac·tor (-tər) *n.* **1.** a person or thing that reacts **2.** *same as* NUCLEAR REACTOR
read[1] (rēd) *vt.* **read** (red), **read′ing** (rēd′iŋ) [OE. *rædan,* to counsel] **1.** to get the meaning of (something written or printed) by interpreting its characters or signs *[*to *read* books, music, Braille, etc.*]* **2.** to utter aloud (something written or printed) **3.** to interpret movements of (the lips of a person speaking) **4.** to know (a language) well enough to interpret its written form **5.** to understand the nature, significance, or thinking of **6.** to interpret (dreams, omens, etc.) or foretell (the future) **7.** to interpret (a printed passage, a signal, etc.) as having a particular meaning **8.** to give as a reading in a certain passage *[*for "shew" *read* "show"*]* **9.** to study *[*to *read* law*]* **10.** to register *[*the thermometer *reads* 80°*]* **11.** to put into a specified state by reading **12.** to obtain (information) from (punch cards, tape, etc.): said of a computer **13.** [Slang] to hear and understand *[*I *read* you loud and clear*]* —*vi.* **1.** to read something written or printed **2.** to learn by reading (with *about* or *of*) **3.** to study **4.** to give a particular meaning when read **5.** to be drawn up in certain words *[*the sentence *reads* as follows*]* **6.** to admit of being read *[*it *reads* well*]* —**read into** (or **in**) to interpret in a certain way —**read out** to display or record with a readout device —**read out of** to expel from (a political party, society, etc.) —**read up (on)** to become well informed (about) by reading
read[2] (red) *pt. & pp. of* READ[1] —*adj.* having knowledge got from reading; informed *[*well-*read]*
read·a·ble (rēd′ə b′l) *adj.* **1.** interesting or easy to read **2.** capable of being read; legible —**read′a·bil′i·ty, read′a·ble·ness** *n.* —**read′a·bly** *adv.*
Reade (rēd), **Charles** 1814–84; Eng. novelist
read·er (rēd′ər) *n.* **1.** a person who reads **2.** a person who reads lessons, prayers, etc. aloud in church **3.** *a)* a schoolbook containing stories, poems, etc. for use in teaching how to read *b)* an anthology of stories, essays, etc.
read·er·ship (-ship′) *n.* all the people who read a particular publication, author, etc.
Read·ing (red′iŋ) **1.** city in SC England: pop. 127,000 **2.** [after prec.] city in SE Pa.: pop. 79,000
read·ing (rēd′iŋ) *adj.* **1.** that reads **2.** of or for reading —*n.* **1.** the act or practice of one who reads **2.** the reciting of a literary work in public **3.** material read or to be read **4.** the extent to which a person has read **5.** the amount measured by a barometer, thermometer, etc. **6.** the way something is written, read, performed, understood, etc. *[*a superb *reading* of Hamlet*]*
read·out (rēd′out′) *n.* **1.** a retrieving of information from storage in a digital computer **2.** this information, displayed visually or recorded, as by typewriter or on tape, for immediate use **3.** information immediately displayed or recorded from various electronic instruments
read·y (red′ē) *adj.* **read′i·er, read′i·est** [OE. *ræde*] **1.** prepared to act or be used immediately *[ready* to go, *ready* for occupancy*]* **2.** unhesitant; willing *[*a *ready* worker*]* **3.** *a)* likely or liable immediately *[ready* to cry*]* *b)* apt; inclined *[*always *ready* to blame others*]* **4.** done without delay; prompt *[*a *ready* reply*]* **5.** available immediately *[ready* cash*]* —*vt.* **read′ied, read′y·ing** to make ready (often used reflexively) —**at the ready** being prepared for immediate use *[*to hold a gun *at the ready]* —**make ready** to prepare —**read′i·ly** *adv.* —**read′i·ness** *n.*
read·y-made (-mād′) *adj.* made so as to be ready for immediate use or sale; not made-to-order: also, as applied to clothing, **read′y-to-wear′** (-tə wer′)
Rea·gan (rā′gən), **Ronald (Wilson)** 1911– ; 40th president of the U.S. (1981–)
re·a·gent (rē ā′jənt) *n.* [RE- + AGENT] *Chem.* a substance used to detect or measure another substance or to convert one substance into another
re·al[1] (rē′əl, rēl) *adj.* [OFr. < ML. *realis* < L. *res,* thing] **1.** existing or happening as or in fact; actual, true, etc. **2.** *a)* authentic; genuine *b)* not pretended; sincere **3.** designating wages or income as measured by purchasing power **4.** *Law* of or relating to permanent, immovable things *[real* property*]* **5.** *Philos.* existing objectively —*adv.* [Colloq.] very —**for real** [Slang] real or really
re·al[2] (rē′əl; *Sp.* re äl′) *n., pl.* **re′als;** Sp. **re·al′es** (-ä′les) [Sp. & Port., lit., royal < L. *regalis:* see REGAL] a former silver coin of Spain
re·al[3] (re äl′) *n. sing. of* REIS

real estate **1.** land, including the buildings or improvements on it and its natural assets, as minerals, water, timber, etc. **2.** ownership of or property in land, etc.
re·a·lign (rē′ə līn′) *vt., vi.* to align again; specif., to readjust alliances (between) —**re′a·lign′ment** *n.*
re·al·ism (rē′ə liz′m) *n.* **1.** a tendency to face facts and be practical **2.** the picturing in art and literature of people and things as they really appear to be, without idealizing **3.** *Philos. a)* the doctrine that universals are objectively actual *b)* the doctrine that material objects exist in themselves apart from the mind's consciousness of them —**re′al·ist** *n.*
re·al·is·tic (rē′ə lis′tik) *adj.* **1.** of, having to do with, or in the style of, realism or realists **2.** tending to face facts; practical rather than visionary —**re′al·is′ti·cal·ly** *adv.*
re·al·i·ty (rē al′ə tē) *n., pl.* **-ties** **1.** the quality or fact of being real **2.** a person or thing that is real; fact **3.** the quality of being true to life **4.** *Philos.* that which is real —**in reality** in fact; actually
re·al·ize (rē′ə līz′) *vt.* **-ized′, -iz′ing** **1.** to make real; bring into being; achieve **2.** to make appear real **3.** to understand fully *[*to *realize* one's danger*]* **4.** to convert (assets, rights, etc.) into money **5.** to gain; obtain *[*to *realize* a profit*]* **6.** to be sold for, or bring as profit (a specified sum) —**re′al·iz′a·ble** *adj.* —**re′al·i·za′tion** *n.*
re·al-life (rē′əl līf′) *adj.* actual; not imaginary
re·al·ly (rē′ə lē, rēl′ē) *adv.* **1.** in reality; in fact; actually **2.** truly or genuinely *[really* hot*]* —*interj.* indeed
realm (relm) *n.* [< OFr. *reaume* < L. *regimen,* rule, infl. by L. *regalis,* REGAL] **1.** a kingdom **2.** a region; sphere; area *[*the *realm* of imagination*]*
real number *Math.* any rational or irrational number
real time **1.** time in which the occurrence and recording of an event are almost simultaneous **2.** the actual time used by a computer to solve a problem the answer to which is immediately available to control a process that is going on at the same time
Re·al·tor (rē′əl tər) *n.* [< ff. + -OR] a real estate broker who is a member of the National Association of Real Estate Boards
re·al·ty (rē′əl tē) *n.* [REAL[1] + -TY[1]] *same as* REAL ESTATE
ream[1] (rēm) *n.* [< MFr. < Ar. *rizma,* a bale] **1.** a quantity of paper varying from 480 sheets (20 quires) to 516 sheets **2.** *[pl.]* [Colloq.] a great amount
ream[2] (rēm) *vt.* [OE. *reman,* akin to *ryman,* lit., to make roomy < base of *rum,* room] **1.** *a)* to enlarge or taper (a hole) *b)* to enlarge the bore of (a gun) **2.** to remove (a defect) by reaming **3.** to squeeze the juice from in a reamer **4.** [Slang] to cheat or deceive
ream·er (-ər) *n.* a person or thing that reams; specif., *a)* a sharp-edged tool for enlarging or tapering holes *b)* a utensil in which oranges, etc. are squeezed for juice

REAMER

re·an·i·mate (rē an′ə māt′) *vt.* **-mat′ed, -mat′ing** to give new life, power, vigor, courage, etc. to —**re·an′i·ma′tion** *n.*
reap (rēp) *vt.* [OE. *ripan*] **1.** to cut (grain) with a scythe, machine, etc. **2.** to gather (a crop, harvest, etc.) **3.** to harvest grain from (a field) **4.** to get as the result of action, work, etc. —*vi.* to reap a harvest, reward, etc.
reap·er (rē′pər) *n.* **1.** a person who reaps **2.** a machine for reaping grain —**the (Grim) Reaper** death
re·ap·por·tion (rē′ə pôr′shən) *vt.* to apportion again, as with the intent of having all legislative districts contain about the same number of people —**re′ap·por′tion·ment** *n.*
re·ap·praise (-prāz′) *vt.* **-praised′, -prais′ing** to make a fresh appraisal of; reconsider —**re′ap·prais′al** *n.*
rear[1] (rir) *n.* [< ARREAR(S)] **1.** the back part **2.** the position behind or at the back **3.** the part of an army, etc. farthest from the battle front **4.** [Slang] the buttocks: also **rear end** —*adj.* of, at, or in the rear —**bring up the rear** to come at the end, as of a procession
rear[2] (rir) *vt.* [OE. *ræran,* caus. of *risan,* to rise] **1.** to put upright; elevate **2.** to build; erect **3.** to grow or breed (animals or plants) **4.** to bring to maturity by educating, nourishing, etc. *[*to *rear* children*]* —*vi.* **1.** to rise on the hind legs, as a horse **2.** to rise (*up*) in anger, etc.
rear admiral a naval officer next in rank above a captain and below a vice admiral
rear guard a military detachment to protect the rear of a main force or body
re·arm (rē ärm′) *vt., vi.* **1.** to arm again **2.** to arm with new or more effective weapons —**re·ar′ma·ment** *n.*
rear·most (rir′mōst′) *adj.* farthest in the rear
re·ar·range (rē′ə rānj′) *vt.* **-ranged′, -rang′ing** **1.** to ar-

range again **2.** to arrange in a different manner —**re'ar·range'ment** ***n.***
rear·ward (rir'wərd) ***adj.*** at, in, or toward the rear —***adv.*** toward the rear: also **rear'wards**
rea·son (rē'z'n) ***n.*** [< OFr. < L. *ratio*, a reckoning < pp. of *reri*, to think] **1.** an explanation or justification of an act, idea, etc. **2.** a cause or motive **3.** the ability to think, draw conclusions, etc. **4.** sound thought or judgment; good sense **5.** normal mental powers; sanity —***vi.*** **1.** to think logically; draw conclusions from facts known or assumed **2.** to argue or talk in a logical way —***vt.*** **1.** to think logically about; analyze **2.** to argue, conclude, or infer [he *reasoned* that the method was too costly] **3.** to justify with reason **4.** to persuade by reasoning (*into* or *out of* something) —**by reason of** because of —**in** (or **within**) **reason** in accord with what is reasonable —**out of all reason** unreasonable —**stand to reason** to be logical or reasonable —**with reason** justifiably; rightly —**rea'son·er** ***n.***
rea·son·a·ble (-ə b'l) ***adj.*** **1.** capable of reasoning or being reasoned with **2.** using or showing reason, or sound judgment; sensible **3.** *a*) not extreme or excessive *b*) not expensive —**rea'son·a·ble·ness** ***n.*** —**rea'son·a·bly** ***adv.***
rea·son·ing (-iŋ) ***n.*** **1.** the drawing of inferences or conclusions from known or assumed facts **2.** the reasons, proofs, etc. used in this process
re·as·sure (rē'ə shoor') ***vt.*** **-sured', -sur'ing** **1.** to assure again or anew **2.** to restore to confidence **3.** [Brit.] to insure anew —**re'as·sur'ance** ***n.*** —**re'as·sur'ing·ly** ***adv.***
re·bate (rē'bāt; *also for v.* ri bāt') ***vt.*** **-bat·ed, -bat·ing** [< OFr. < *re-*, re- + *abattre*: see ABATE] **1.** to give back (part of an amount paid) **2.** to make a deduction from (a bill) —***n.*** a return of part of the amount paid, as for goods
re·bec, re·beck (rē'bek) ***n.*** [Fr. < OFr. *rebebe* < Ar. *rabāb*] a medieval pear-shaped instrument played with a bow like a violin
Re·bec·ca (ri bek'ə) [LL. < Gr. < Heb. *ribbqāh*, lit., noose] **1.** a feminine name **2.** *Bible* the wife of Isaac and mother of Jacob and Esau: usually sp. **Rebekah**
reb·el (reb''l; *for v.* ri bel') ***n.*** [< OFr. < L. < *re-*, again + *bellare*, to war < *bellum*, war] **1.** a person who takes up arms against the government of his own country **2.** a person who resists any authority or control **3.** [*often* **R-**] *an epithet for* a Confederate soldier —***adj.*** **1.** rebellious **2.** of rebels —***vi.*** **-elled', -el'ling** **1.** to be a rebel against the government of one's country **2.** to resist any authority or control **3.** to feel or show strong aversion
re·bel·lion (ri bel'yən) ***n.*** [< MFr. < L.: see prec.] **1.** an act or state of armed, open resistance to one's government **2.** defiance of any authority or control
re·bel·lious (-yəs) ***adj.*** **1.** resisting authority; engaged in rebellion **2.** of or like rebels or rebellion **3.** opposing any control; defiant **4.** difficult to treat or handle —**re·bel'lious·ly** ***adv.*** —**re·bel'lious·ness** ***n.***
re·birth (rē burth', rē'burth') ***n.*** **1.** a new or second birth **2.** a reawakening; revival
re·bound (ri bound'; *also, & for n. usually,* rē'bound') ***vi.*** **1.** to bound or spring back, as upon impact or in recovery **2.** to reecho —***vt.*** to make bound or spring back —***n.*** **1.** a rebounding; recoil **2.** a basketball that bounds back after an attempted basket, or the play made in getting this ball —**on the rebound** **1.** after bouncing off the ground, a wall, etc. **2.** just after and while reacting to rejection, as in love
re·bo·zo (ri bō'zō; *Sp.* re bô'thô, -sô) ***n.,*** *pl.* **-zos** (-zōz; *Sp.* -thôs, -sôs) [Sp., a shawl] a long scarf worn by women around the head and shoulders, as in Mexico
re·broad·cast (rē brôd'kast') ***vt., vi.*** **-cast'** or **-cast'ed, -cast'ing** **1.** to broadcast again **2.** to broadcast (a program, etc. received in a relay system from another station) —***n.*** **1.** a rebroadcasting **2.** a program that is being or has been rebroadcast
re·buff (ri buf') ***n.*** [< MFr. < It. *rabbuffo*, ult. < Gmc.] **1.** a blunt refusal of offered help, advice, etc. **2.** any check or repulse —***vt.*** **1.** to refuse bluntly; snub **2.** to check
re·buke (ri byōōk') ***vt.*** **-buked', -buk'ing** [< Anglo-Fr. < OFr. < *re-*, back + *buchier*, to beat] to blame or scold in a sharp way; reprimand —***n.*** a sharp scolding or reprimand —**re·buk'er** ***n.*** —**re·buk'ing·ly** ***adv.***
re·bus (rē'bəs) ***n.*** [L., lit., by things] a kind of puzzle consisting of pictures of things combined so as to suggest words or phrases [a picture of a bee plus the figure 4 is a *rebus* for "before"]
re·but (ri but') ***vt.*** **-but'ted, -but'ting** [< Anglo-Fr. < OFr. < *re-*, back + *buter*, to push] to contradict or oppose, esp. in a formal manner by argument, proof, etc. —***vi.*** to provide opposing arguments —**re·but'ta·ble** ***adj.*** —**re·but'ter** ***n.***
re·but·tal (-'l) ***n.*** a rebutting, as in law
rec (rek) ***n.*** *shortened form of* RECREATION in such compounds as **rec room, rec hall**
rec. **1.** receipt **2.** recipe **3.** record(ed)
re·cal·ci·trant (ri kal'si trənt) ***adj.*** [< L. prp. of *recalcitrare* < *re-*, back + *calcitrare*, to kick < *calx*, a heel] **1.** refusing to obey authority, regulation, etc.; stubbornly defiant **2.** hard to handle or deal with —***n.*** a recalcitrant person —**re·cal'ci·trance, re·cal'ci·tran·cy** ***n.*** —**re·cal'ci·trant·ly** ***adv.***
re·call (ri kôl'; *for n. also* rē'kôl') ***vt.*** **1.** to call back; order to return **2.** to bring back to mind; remember **3.** to take back; revoke **4.** to bring back in awareness, attention, etc. —***n.*** **1.** a recalling **2.** the ability to remember; memory **3.** the process of removing, or the right to remove, a public official from office by popular vote —**re·call'a·ble** ***adj.***
re·cant (ri kant') ***vt., vi.*** [< L. < *re-*, back + *cantare*, freq. of *canere*, to sing] to take back or confess being wrong about (former beliefs, statements, etc.), esp. formally or publicly —**re·can·ta·tion** (rē'kan tā'shən) ***n.***
re·cap[1] (rē kap'; *also, & for n. always,* rē'kap') ***vt.*** **-capped', -cap'ping** [RE- + CAP] to cement, mold, and vulcanize a strip of rubber on the outer surface of (a worn pneumatic tire); retread —***n.*** a recapped tire
re·cap[2] (rē'kap') ***n.*** a recapitulation, or summary —***vi., vt.*** **-capped', -cap'ping** to recapitulate
re·ca·pit·u·late (rē'kə pich'ə lāt') ***vi., vt.*** **-lat'ed, -lat'ing** [see RE- & CAPITULATE] to tell again briefly; summarize
re·ca·pit·u·la·tion (-pich'ə lā'shən) ***n.*** **1.** a recapitulating **2.** a summary, or brief restatement —**re'ca·pit'u·la'tive, re'ca·pit'u·la·to'ry** (-lə tôr'ē) ***adj.***
re·cap·ture (rē kap'chər) ***vt.*** **-tured, -tur·ing** **1.** to capture again; retake; reacquire **2.** to bring back by remembering —***n.*** a recapturing or being recaptured
re·cast (rē kast'; *for n.* rē'kast') ***vt.*** **-cast', -cast'ing** **1.** to cast again or anew **2.** to improve the form of by redoing; reconstruct [to *recast* a sentence] —***n.*** a recasting
recd., rec'd. received
re·cede[1] (ri sēd') ***vi.*** **-ced'ed, -ced'ing** [< L.: see RE- & CEDE] **1.** to go or move back [the flood *receded*] **2.** to withdraw [to *recede* from a promise] **3.** to slope backward [her chin *recedes*] **4.** to lessen, dim, etc.
re·cede[2] (rē'sēd') ***vt.*** **-ced'ed, -ced'ing** to cede back
re·ceipt (ri sēt') ***n.*** [< Anglo-Fr. < ML. < L. < pp. of *recipere*: see RECEIVE] **1.** *old-fashioned var. of* RECIPE **2.** a receiving or being received **3.** a written acknowledgment that something, as goods, money, etc., has been received **4.** [*pl.*] the thing or amount received, as of money taken in by a business —***vt.*** **1.** to mark (a bill) paid **2.** to write a receipt for (goods, etc.)
re·ceiv·a·ble (ri sē'və b'l) ***adj.*** **1.** that can be received **2.** suitable for acceptance **3.** due in payment from one's customers —***n.*** [*pl.*] accounts or bills receivable
re·ceive (ri sēv') ***vt.*** **-ceived', -ceiv'ing** [< Anglo-Fr. < OFr. < L. *recipere* < *re-*, back + *capere*, to take] **1.** to take or get (something given, offered, sent, etc.) **2.** to meet with; experience [to *receive* acclaim] **3.** to undergo; suffer [to *receive* a blow] **4.** to take the force of; bear [each wheel *receives* equal weight] **5.** to react to as specified [the song was well *received*] **6.** to get knowledge of; learn [to *receive* news] **7.** to accept as authentic, valid, etc. **8.** *a*) to let enter; admit *b*) to have room for; contain **9.** to greet (visitors, etc.) —***vi.*** **1.** to be a recipient **2.** to greet guests or visitors **3.** *Radio & TV* to convert incoming electromagnetic waves into sound or light, thus reproducing the sounds or images being transmitted **4.** *Sports* to catch a ball or be prepared to return a thrown, kicked, etc. ball
re·ceiv·er (ri sē'vər) ***n.*** **1.** a person who receives (in various senses); specif., *Law* a person appointed by the court to administer or hold in trust property in bankruptcy or in a lawsuit **2.** a thing that receives; specif., *a*) a receptacle *b*) an apparatus that converts electrical signals, etc. into sound or light, as a radio or television receiving set, or that part of a telephone held to the ear
re·ceiv·er·ship (-ship') ***n.*** *Law* **1.** the duties or office of a receiver **2.** the state of being administered or held by a receiver
receiving set an apparatus for receiving radio or television signals; receiver
re·cent (rē's'nt) ***adj.*** [MFr. < L. *recens* < *re-*, again + base akin to Gr. *kainos*, new] **1.** done, made, etc. just before the present time; modern; new **2.** of a time just before the present **3.** [**R-**] designating or of the present epoch, extending from the close of the Pleistocene —**the Recent** the Recent Epoch or its rocks: see GEOLOGY, chart —**re'cent·ly** ***adv.*** —**re'cent·ness** ***n.***
re·cep·ta·cle (ri sep'tə k'l) ***n.*** [L. *receptaculum* < freq. of *recipere*: see RECEIVE] **1.** anything used to contain or hold something else; container **2.** *Bot.* *a*) the part of the stalk from which the flower grows *b*) a cuplike or disklike part supporting spores, seeds, etc.
re·cep·tion (ri sep'shən) ***n.*** [OFr. < L. < pp. of *recipere*: see RECEIVE] **1.** *a*) a receiving or being received *b*) the manner of this [a friendly *reception*] **2.** a social function, often formal, for the receiving of guests **3.** *Radio & TV* the manner of receiving, with reference to quality [poor *reception*]

re·cep·tion·ist (-ist) ***n.*** an office employee who receives callers, gives information, etc.

re·cep·tive (ri sep′tiv) ***adj.*** **1.** receiving or tending to receive, admit, or contain **2.** able or ready to receive requests, suggestions, new ideas, etc. **3.** of reception or receptors —**re·cep′tive·ly** ***adv.*** —**re·cep′tiv′i·ty, re·cep′tive·ness** ***n.***

re·cep·tor (-tər) ***n.*** *Physiol.* a nerve ending specialized for the reception of stimuli; sense organ

re·cess (rē′ses; *also, and for v. usually,* ri ses′) ***n.*** [< L. pp. of *recedere,* to recede] **1.** a receding or hollow place, as in a wall; niche **2.** a secluded or withdrawn place [the *recesses* of the subconscious] **3.** a temporary halting of work, study, etc. —***vt.*** **1.** to place in a recess **2.** to form a recess in —***vi.*** to take a recess

re·ces·sion[1] (ri sesh′ən) ***n.*** [L. *recessio* < pp. of *recedere,* to recede] **1.** a going backward; withdrawal **2.** a departing procession, as of clergy and choir after a church service **3.** a receding part, as of a wall **4.** a temporary falling off of business activity during a prosperous period

re·ces·sion[2] (rē sesh′ən) ***n.*** [RE- + CESSION] a ceding back, as to a former owner

re·ces·sion·al (-′l) ***adj.*** of a recession —***n.*** a hymn or other music sung or played during a church recession

re·ces·sive (ri ses′iv) ***adj.*** **1.** receding or tending to recede **2.** *Genetics* designating or of that one of any pair of allelic characters which, when both are present in the germ plasm, remains latent: opposed to DOMINANT —**re·ces′sive·ly** ***adv.*** —**re·ces′sive·ness** ***n.***

re·cher·ché (rə sher′shā, -sher′shā′) ***adj.*** [Fr., pp. of *rechercher:* see RESEARCH] **1.** sought out with care; choice **2.** having refinement or contrived elegance **3.** too refined; too studied

re·cid·i·vism (ri sid′ə viz′m) ***n.*** [< L. < *recidere* < *re-,* back + *cadere,* to fall + -ISM] relapse, or tendency to relapse, esp. into crime or antisocial behavior —**re·cid′i·vist** ***n., adj.*** —**re·cid′i·vis′tic, re·cid′i·vous** ***adj.***

Re·ci·fe (re sē′fə) seaport in NE Brazil, on the Atlantic: pop. 1,079,000

rec·i·pe (res′ə pē) ***n.*** [L., imperative of *recipere:* see RECEIVE] **1.** formerly, a medicinal prescription **2.** a list of ingredients and directions for preparing a dish or drink **3.** any procedure for bringing about a desired result

re·cip·i·ent (ri sip′ē ənt) ***n.*** [< L. prp. of *recipere:* see RECEIVE] a person or thing that receives —***adj.*** receiving, or ready or able to receive —**re·cip′i·ence, re·cip′i·en·cy** ***n.***

re·cip·ro·cal (ri sip′rə k′l) ***adj.*** [< L. *reciprocus,* returning] **1.** done, felt, given, etc. in return **2.** on both sides; mutual **3.** corresponding but reversed **4.** equivalent or interchangeable; complementary **5.** *Gram.* expressing mutual action or relation [*each other* is a *reciprocal* pronoun] **6.** *Math.* of reciprocals —***n.*** **1.** anything that has a reciprocal relation to another; counterpart **2.** *Math.* the quantity resulting from the division of 1 by the given quantity [the *reciprocal* of 7 is 1/7] —**re·cip′ro·cal′i·ty** (-kal′ə tē) ***n.*** —**re·cip′ro·cal·ly** ***adv.***

re·cip·ro·cate (-kāt′) ***vt., vi.*** **-cat′ed, -cat′ing** [< L. pp. of *reciprocare* < *reciprocus:* see prec.] **1.** *a)* to give and get reciprocally *b)* to give, do, feel, etc. (something similar) in return **2.** to move alternately back and forth —**re·cip′ro·ca′tion** ***n.*** —**re·cip′ro·ca′tive, re·cip′ro·ca·to′ry** (-kə tôr′ē) ***adj.*** —**re·cip′ro·ca′tor** ***n.***

rec·i·proc·i·ty (res′ə präs′ə tē) ***n., pl.*** **-ties** [< Fr.] **1.** reciprocal state or relationship **2.** mutual exchange; esp., exchange of special privileges between two countries, as mutual reduction of tariffs

re·cit·al (ri sīt′′l) ***n.*** **1.** *a)* a reciting; specif., a telling in detail *b)* the account, story, etc. told **2.** a detailed statement **3.** a musical or dance program given by a soloist, soloists, or a small ensemble —**re·cit′al·ist** ***n.***

rec·i·ta·tion (res′ə tā′shən) ***n.*** **1.** a recital (sense 1) **2.** *a)* the speaking aloud in public of something memorized *b)* the piece so presented **3.** a reciting by pupils of answers to questions on a prepared lesson, etc.

rec·i·ta·tive (res′ə tə tēv′) ***n.*** [It. *recitativo* < L. *recitare,* to RECITE] *Music* **1.** a type of declamatory singing, free in rhythm and tempo, as in the dialogue of operas **2.** a work or passage in this style **3.** music for such passages —***adj.*** in the style of recitative

re·cite (ri sīt′) ***vt., vi.*** **-cit′ed, -cit′ing** [< OFr. < L. *recitare:* see RE- & CITE] **1.** to speak aloud, as from memory, (a lesson) in class or (a poem, etc.) before an audience **2.** to tell in detail or narrate (something) —**re·cit′er** ***n.***

reck (rek) ***vi., vt.*** [OE. *reccan*] [Archaic] **1.** to have care or concern (*for*) or take heed (*of*) **2.** to concern or be of concern; matter (to)

reck·less (rek′lis) ***adj.*** [see prec. & -LESS] **1.** careless; heedless **2.** not regarding consequences; rash —**reck′less·ly** ***adv.*** —**reck′less·ness** ***n.***

reck·on (rek′ən) ***vt.*** [OE. *-recenian*] **1.** to count; figure up; compute **2.** *a)* to consider as; regard as being [*reckon* them friends] *b)* to judge; estimate **3.** [Colloq. or Dial.] to suppose —***vi.*** **1.** to count up; figure **2.** [Colloq.] to rely (with *on*) **3.** [Colloq.] to suppose —**reckon with** **1.** to settle accounts with **2.** to take into consideration

reck·on·ing (-iŋ) ***n.*** **1.** the act of one who reckons; count or computation **2.** a calculated guess **3.** *a)* a bill; account *b)* settlement of an account **4.** the giving of rewards or punishments [day of *reckoning*] **5.** *Naut.* the determination of the position of a ship; esp., *short for* DEAD RECKONING

re·claim (ri klām′) ***vt.*** [< OFr. < L. *reclamare:* see RE- & CLAIM] **1.** to rescue or bring back (someone) from error, vice, etc. **2.** to make (wasteland, etc.) capable of being cultivated or lived on, as by irrigating, etc. **3.** to recover (useful materials) from waste products —***n.*** reclamation [beyond *reclaim*] —**re·claim′a·ble** ***adj.*** —**re·claim′ant, re·claim′er** ***n.***

re-claim (rē′klām′) ***vt.*** to claim back; demand the return of; try to get back

rec·la·ma·tion (rek′lə mā′shən) ***n.*** a reclaiming or being reclaimed, as of wasteland or of useful materials from waste products

re·cline (ri klīn′) ***vt., vi.*** **-clined′, -clin′ing** [< L. < *re-,* back + *clinare,* to lean] to lie or cause to lie back or down; lean back —**rec·li·na·tion** (rek′lə nā′shən) ***n.***

re·clin·er (-klī′nər) ***n.*** **1.** one that reclines **2.** an upholstered armchair that can be adjusted for reclining: also **reclining chair**

rec·luse (rek′lōōs, ri klōōs′) ***adj.*** [< OFr. < LL. < L. pp. of *recludere* < *re-,* back + *claudere,* to shut] secluded; solitary —***n.*** a person who leads a secluded, solitary life —**re·clu·sion** (ri klōō′zhən) ***n.*** —**re·clu′sive** ***adj.***

rec·og·ni·tion (rek′əg nish′ən) ***n.*** [< L. < pp. of *recognoscere:* see ff.] **1.** *a)* a recognizing or being recognized; acknowledgment *b)* approval, gratitude, etc. [in *recognition* of his services] **2.** formal acceptance by a government of the sovereignty of a newly established state or government **3.** identification of a person or thing as being known to one **4.** notice, as in passing; greeting —**re·cog·ni·to·ry** (ri käg′nə tôr′ē), **re·cog′ni·tive** ***adj.***

re·cog·ni·zance (ri käg′ni zəns, -kän′i-) ***n.*** [< OFr. < L. < *re-,* again + *cognoscere,* to know: see COGNITION] *Law* **1.** a bond or obligation of record binding a person to some act, as to appear in court **2.** a sum of money that one must forfeit if this obligation is not fulfilled

rec·og·nize (rek′əg nīz′) ***vt.*** **-nized′, -niz′ing** [altered (after prec.) < OFr.: see prec.] **1.** to identify as known before **2.** to know by some detail, as of appearance **3.** to be aware of the significance of **4.** to acknowledge the existence, validity, etc. of [to *recognize* a claim] **5.** to accept as a fact; admit [to *recognize* defeat] **6.** to acknowledge as worthy of appreciation or approval **7.** to formally acknowledge the legal standing of (a government or state) **8.** to show acquaintance with (a person) by greeting **9.** to grant (a person) the right to speak, as in a meeting —**rec′og·niz′a·bil′i·ty** ***n.*** —**rec′og·niz′a·ble** ***adj.*** —**rec′og·niz′a·bly** ***adv.*** —**rec′og·niz′er** ***n.***

re·coil (ri koil′; *also for n., esp. of weapons,* rē′koil′) ***vi.*** [< OFr. < *re-,* back + *cul* < L. *culus,* the buttocks] **1.** to draw, start, or shrink back, as in fear, surprise, disgust, etc. **2.** to fly back when released, as a spring, or kick back when fired, as a gun **3.** to return as to the starting point or source; react (*on* or *upon*) —***n.*** **1.** a recoiling **2.** the state of having recoiled —**re·coil′er** ***n.*** —**re·coil′less** ***adj.***

re-coil (rē′koil′) ***vt., vi.*** to coil anew or again

rec·ol·lect (rek′ə lekt′) ***vt.*** [< L.: see RE- & COLLECT[1]] **1.** to call back to mind; remember, esp. with some effort **2.** to recall to (oneself) something temporarily forgotten —***vi.*** to remember —**rec′ol·lec′tion** ***n.*** —**rec′ol·lec′tive** ***adj.***

re-col·lect (rē′kə lekt′) ***vt.*** **1.** to collect again (what has been scattered) **2.** to rally (one's courage, etc.) **3.** to compose (oneself): in this sense sometimes written **recollect**

rec·om·mend (rek′ə mend′) ***vt.*** [< ML.: see RE- & COMMEND] **1.** to give in charge; entrust [*recommended* to his care] **2.** to suggest favorably as suited for some function, position, etc. **3.** to make acceptable or pleasing [his charm *recommends* him] **4.** to advise; counsel —**rec′om·mend′a·ble** ***adj.*** —**rec′om·mend′a·to′ry** ***adj.*** —**rec′om·mend′er** ***n.***

rec·om·men·da·tion (-mən dā′shən) ***n.*** **1.** a recommending **2.** anything that recommends or makes a favorable or pleasing impression; specif., a letter recommending a person or thing **3.** advice; counsel

re·com·mit (rē′kə mit′) *vt.* **-mit′ted, -mit′ting 1.** to commit again **2.** to refer (a question, bill, etc.) back to a committee —**re′com·mit′ment, re′com·mit′tal** *n.*

rec·om·pense (rek′əm pens′) *vt.* **-pensed′, -pens′ing** [< MFr. < LL.: see RE- & COMPENSATE] **1.** to repay (a person, etc.); reward **2.** to compensate (a loss, injury, etc.) —*n.* **1.** something given or done in return for something else; requital, reward, etc. **2.** something given or done to make up for a loss, injury, etc.; compensation

rec·on·cile (rek′ən sīl′) *vt.* **-ciled′, -cil′ing** [< OFr. < L.: see RE- & CONCILIATE] **1.** to make friendly again **2.** to settle (a quarrel, etc.) **3.** to make (facts, ideas, texts, etc.) consistent or compatible **4.** to make content or acquiescent (*to*) —**rec′on·cil′a·bil′i·ty** *n.* —**rec′on·cil′a·ble** *adj.* —**rec′on·cil′a·bly** *adv.* —**rec′on·cil′i·a′tion** (-sil′ē ā′shən), **rec′on·cile′ment** *n.* —**rec′on·cil′i·a·to′ry** (-sil′ē ə tôr′ē) *adj.*

rec·on·dite (rek′ən dīt′, ri kän′dīt) *adj.* [< L. pp. of *recondere* < *re-*, back + *condere*, to store up, hide] **1.** beyond the grasp of ordinary understanding; profound **2.** dealing with abstruse or difficult subjects **3.** obscure or concealed —**rec′on·dite′ly** *adv.* —**rec′on·dite′ness** *n.*

re·con·di·tion (rē′kən dish′ən) *vt.* to put back in good condition by cleaning, repairing, etc.

re·con·nais·sance (ri kän′ə səns, -zəns) *n.* [Fr.: see RECOGNIZANCE] an exploratory survey or examination, as in seeking out information about enemy positions

re·con·noi·ter (rē′kə noit′ər, rek′ə-) *vt., vi.* [< Fr. < OFr.: see RECOGNIZANCE] to make a reconnaissance (of): also, chiefly Brit. sp., **rec′on·noi′tre -tred, -tring** —**rec′on-noi′ter·er, rec′on·noi′trer** (-noi′trər) *n.*

re·con·sid·er (rē′kən sid′ər) *vt., vi.* to consider again; think over, as with a view to changing a decision —**re′con-sid′er·a′tion** *n.*

re·con·sti·tute (rē kän′stə to͞ot′, -tyo͞ot′) *vt.* **-tut′ed, -tut′ing** to constitute again or anew; specif., to restore (a dehydrated or condensed substance) to its full liquid form by adding water —**re·con′sti·tu′tion** *n.*

re·con·struct (rē′kən strukt′) *vt.* **1.** to construct again; make over **2.** to build up again (something in its original form), as from remaining parts —**re′con·struc′tive** *adj.*

re·con·struc·tion (-struk′shən) *n.* **1.** *a)* a reconstructing *b)* something reconstructed **2.** [R-] the period (1867–77) or the process, after the Civil War, of reestablishing the Southern States in the Union

re·con·vert (rē′kən vurt′) *vt., vi.* to change back, as to a former status, religion, etc. —**re′con·ver′sion** *n.*

re·cord (ri kôrd′; *for n. & adj.*, rek′ərd) *vt.* [< OFr. < L. *recordari*, to remember < *re-*, again + *cor* (gen. *cordis*), heart, mind] **1.** *a)* to put in writing, print, etc. for future use *b)* to make an official note of [to *record* a vote] **2.** *a)* to indicate automatically and permanently, as on a graph [a seismograph *records* earthquakes] *b)* to show, as on a dial **3.** to remain as evidence of **4.** *a)* to register (sound or visual images) in some permanent form, as on a phonograph disc, magnetic tape, etc. for reproduction on a playback device *b)* to register the performance of in this way —*vi.* **1.** to record something **2.** to admit of being recorded —*n.* **1.** the condition of being recorded **2.** *a)* an account of events *b)* anything that serves as evidence of an event, etc. *c)* an official report of public proceedings, as in a court **3.** anything that written evidence is put on or in, as a register, monument, etc. **4.** *a)* the known facts about anyone or anything, as about one's career *b)* the recorded offenses of a person who has been arrested one or more times **5.** a thin, flat, grooved disc for playing on a phonograph **6.** the best performance, highest speed, greatest amount, etc. achieved, esp. when officially recorded —*adj.* establishing a record as the best, largest, etc. [a *record* crop] —**go on record** to state one's opinions publicly or officially —**off the record** confidential(ly) —**on (the) record** publicly declared

record changer a phonograph device that automatically sets in place each record from a stack placed on a spindle

re·cord·er (ri kôr′dər) *n.* **1.** a public officer who keeps records of deeds or other official papers **2.** a machine or device that records; esp., *same as* TAPE RECORDER **3.** an early form of flute

RECORDER

re·cord·ing (ri kôr′diŋ) *adj.* that records —*n.* **1.** the act of one that records **2.** *a)* what is recorded, as on a disc or tape *b)* the record itself

record player a phonograph having the pickup, turntable, amplifier, speaker, etc. operate electrically or electronically

re·count (ri kount′) *vt.* [< Anglo-Fr.: see RE- & COUNT[1]] to tell in detail; narrate; enumerate —**re·count′al** *n.*

re-count (rē′kount′; *for n.* rē′kount′) *vt.* to count again —*n.* a second or additional count, as of votes: also written **recount**

re·coup (ri ko͞op′) *vt.* [< Fr. < *re-*, again + *couper*, to cut] **1.** *a)* to make up for [to *recoup* a loss] *b)* to regain [to *recoup* one's health] **2.** to pay back —*n.* a recouping —**re·coup′a·ble** *adj.* —**re·coup′ment** *n.*

re·course (rē′kôrs, ri kôrs′) *n.* [< OFr. < L. *recursus*, a running back: see RE- & COURSE] **1.** a turning for aid, safety, etc. [he had *recourse* to the law] **2.** that to which one turns seeking aid, safety, etc. [one's last *recourse*]

re·cov·er (ri kuv′ər) *vt.* [< OFr. < L. *recuperare*: see RECUPERATE] **1.** *a)* to get back (something lost, stolen, etc.) *b)* to regain (health, etc.) **2.** to compensate for [to *recover* losses] **3.** *a)* to get (oneself) back to a state of control, balance, etc. *b)* to save (oneself) from a slip, betrayal of feeling, etc. **4.** to reclaim (land from the sea, useful substances from waste, etc.) **5.** *Law* to get or get back by final judgment in a court —*vi.* **1.** to regain health, balance, control, etc. **2.** to save oneself from a slip, self-betrayal, etc. **3.** *Law* to receive judgment in one's favor —**re·cov′er·a·ble** *adj.*

re-cov·er (rē′kuv′ər) *vt.* to cover again or anew

re·cov·er·y (ri kuv′ər ē) *n., pl.* **-er·ies** the act or an instance of recovering; specif., *a)* a regaining of something lost or stolen *b)* a return to health, consciousness, etc. *c)* a regaining of balance, composure, etc. *d)* a retrieval of a capsule, nose cone, etc. after a spaceflight *e)* the removal of valuable substances from waste material, byproducts, etc.

rec·re·ant (rek′rē ənt) *adj.* [OFr. prp. of *recreire*, to surrender allegiance < ML. < L. *re-*, back + *credere*, to believe] **1.** *a)* orig., crying for mercy *b)* cowardly **2.** disloyal; traitorous —*n.* **1.** a coward **2.** a disloyal person; traitor —**rec′re·an·cy** *n.* —**rec′re·ant·ly** *adv.*

rec·re·ate (rek′rē āt′) *vt.* **-at′ed, -at′ing** [< L. pp. of *recreare*: see RE- & CREATE] to refresh in body or mind —*vi.* to take recreation —**rec′re·a′tive** *adj.*

re-cre·ate (rē′krē āt′) *vt.* **-at′ed, -at′ing** to create anew —**re′-cre·a′tion** *n.* —**re′-cre·a′tive** *adj.*

rec·re·a·tion (rek′rē ā′shən) *n.* [see RECREATE] **1.** refreshment in body or mind, as after work, by some form of play, amusement, or relaxation **2.** any form of play, amusement, etc. used for this purpose, as games, sports, etc. —**rec′re·a′tion·al** *adj.*

re·crim·i·nate (ri krim′ə nāt′) *vi.* **-nat′ed, -nat′ing** [< ML.: see RE- & CRIMINATE] to answer an accuser by accusing him in return —**re·crim′i·na′tion** *n.* —**re·crim′i·na·to′ry** (-nə tôr′ē), **re·crim′i·na′tive** *adj.*

re·cru·desce (rē′kro͞o des′) *vi.* **-desced′, -desc′ing** [< L. < *re-*, again + *crudescere*, to become harsh < *crudus*, raw] to break out again after being relatively inactive —**re′cru·des′cence** *n.* —**re′cru·des′cent** *adj.*

re·cruit (ri kro͞ot′) *vt.* [< Fr. < pp. of *recroître*, to grow again < L. *re-*, again + *crescere*, to grow] **1.** to raise or strengthen (an army, navy, etc.) by enlisting personnel **2.** to enlist (personnel) into an army or navy **3.** *a)* to enlist (new members) for a party, organization, etc. *b)* to hire or engage the services of —*vi.* to enlist new personnel, esp. for a military force —*n.* **1.** a recently enlisted or drafted soldier, sailor, etc. **2.** a new member of any group, etc. —**re·cruit′er** *n.* —**re·cruit′ment** *n.*

rec. sec. recording secretary

rec·tal (rek′t'l) *adj.* of, for, or near the rectum —**rec′tal·ly** *adv.*

rec·tan·gle (rek′taŋ′g'l) *n.* [Fr. < ML.: see RECTI- & ANGLE[1]] any four-sided plane figure with four right angles

RECTANGLES

rec·tan·gu·lar (rek taŋ′gyə lər) *adj.* **1.** shaped like a rectangle **2.** having right-angled corners, as a building **3.** right-angled —**rec·tan′gu·lar′i·ty** (-lar′ə tē) *n.* —**rec·tan′gu·lar·ly** *adv.*

rec·ti- [LL. < L. *rectus*] *a combining form meaning* straight, right [*rectilinear*]: also, before a vowel, **rect-**

rec·ti·fi·er (rek′tə fī′ər) *n.* **1.** a person or thing that rectifies **2.** *Elec.* a device that converts alternating current into direct current

rec·ti·fy (rek′tə fī′) *vt.* **-fied′, -fy′ing** [< MFr. < LL.: see RECTI- & -FY] **1.** to put right; correct **2.** *Chem.* to refine or purify (a liquid) by distillation **3.** *Elec.* to convert (alternating current) to direct current —**rec′ti·fi′a·ble** *adj.* —**rec′ti·fi·ca′tion** *n.*

rec·ti·lin·e·ar (rek′tə lin′ē ər) *adj.* [< LL. < *rectus*, straight + *linea*, LINE[1]] **1.** in or forming a straight line **2.** bounded, formed, or characterized by straight lines Also **rec′ti·lin′e·al** —**rec′ti·lin′e·ar·ly** *adv.*

rec·ti·tude (rek′tə to͞od′, -tyo͞od′) *n.* [MFr. < LL. < L. *rectus*, straight] **1.** strict honesty; uprightness of character **2.** correctness of judgment or method

rec·to (rek′tō) *n., pl.* **-tos** [< ModL. (*folio*) *recto*, on (the page) to the right] *Printing* any right-hand page of a book; front side of a leaf: opposed to VERSO

rec·tor (rek′tər) *n.* [L. < pp. of *regere,* to rule] **1.** a clergyman or minister in charge of a parish, esp. in the Protestant Episcopal Church or an Anglican Church **2.** *R.C.Ch.* *a*) a priest in charge of a seminary, college, etc. *b*) [Brit.] the head priest of a parish **3.** in certain schools, colleges, etc., the head or headmaster —**rec′tor·ate** (-it) *n.* —**rec·to′ri·al** (-tôr′ē əl) *adj.*

rec·to·ry (rek′tər ē) *n., pl.* **-ries** the residence of a clergyman who is a rector

rec·tum (rek′təm) *n., pl.* **-tums, -ta** (-tə) [ModL. < L. *rectum* (*intestinum*), straight (intestine)] the lowest, or last, segment of the large intestine, ending at the anus

re·cum·bent (ri kum′bənt) *adj.* [< L. < *re-,* back + *cumbere,* to lie down] **1.** lying down; reclining **2.** resting; idle —**re·cum′ben·cy** *n.* —**re·cum′bent·ly** *adv.*

re·cu·per·ate (ri ko͞o′pə rāt′, -kyo͞o′-) *vt.* **-at′ed, -at′ing** [< L. pp. of *recuperare,* to recover] to get back, or recover (losses, health, etc.) —*vi.* **1.** to get well again **2.** to recover losses, etc. —**re·cu′per·a′tion** *n.* —**re·cu′per·a′tive** (-pə rāt′iv, -pər ə tiv) *adj.* —**re·cu′per·a′tor** *n.*

re·cur (ri kʉr′) *vi.* **-curred′, -cur′ring** [< L. *re-,* back + *currere,* to run] **1.** to have recourse (*to*) **2.** to return in thought, talk, etc. [*to recur* to a topic] **3.** to occur again, as in memory **4.** to happen or appear again or at intervals

re·cur·rent (ri kʉr′ənt) *adj.* **1.** appearing again or periodically **2.** turning back in the opposite direction, as some nerves —**re·cur′rence** *n.* —**re·cur′rent·ly** *adv.*

re·curve (ri kʉrv′) *vt., vi.* **-curved′, -curv′ing** to curve or bend back or backward —**re·cur·vate** (ri kʉr′vit, -vāt) *adj.*

re·cy·cle (rē sī′k′l) *vt., vi.* **-cled, -cling** **1.** to pass through a cycle again, as for treating **2.** to use again and again, as a single supply of water

red[1] (red) *n.* [OE. *read*] **1.** a primary color varying in hue from that of blood to pink **2.** a pigment producing this color **3.** [*often* **R-**] a political radical; esp., a communist **4.** anything colored red, as a red checker piece —*adj.* **red′der, red′dest** **1.** of the color red **2.** having red hair **3.** *a*) having a reddish skin *b*) florid, flushed, or blushing *c*) bloodshot *d*) sore **4.** [**R-**] *a*) politically radical; esp., communist *b*) of the Soviet Union —**in the red** in debt or losing money —**see red** [Colloq.] to be or become angry —**red′dish** *adj.* —**red′ly** *adv.* —**red′ness** *n.*

red[2] (red) *vt., vi.* **red, red′ding** *var. of* REDD

re·dact (ri dakt′) *vt.* [< L. pp. of *redigere,* to reduce to order] to arrange in proper form for publication; edit —**re·dac′tion** *n.* —**re·dac′tor** *n.*

red algae a group of red, brownish-red, pink, or purple algae that form shrublike masses in the depths of the oceans

red·bait (red′bāt′) *vi., vt.* to denounce (a person or group) as being communist, esp. with little or no valid evidence —**red′bait′er** *n.*

red blood cell *same as* ERYTHROCYTE: also called **red blood corpuscle**

red-blood·ed (red′blud′id) *adj.* high-spirited and strong-willed; vigorous, lusty, etc.

red·breast (-brest′) *n.* any of several birds with a reddish breast; esp., the American robin and the European robin

red·bud (-bud′) *n. same as* JUDAS TREE

red·cap (-kap′) *n.* a porter in a railway station, air terminal, etc.

red carpet **1.** a long red carpet laid out for important guests to walk on, as at a reception **2.** a very grand welcome and entertainment (with *the*) —**roll out the red carpet (for)** to welcome and entertain in a very grand style —**red′-car′pet** *adj.*

red·coat (red′kōt′) *n.* a British soldier in a uniform with a red coat, as during the American Revolution

Red Cross **1.** a red cross on a white ground, emblem of neutrality in war, used since 1864 to mark hospitals, ambulances, etc. **2.** *a*) an international society (in full, **International Red Cross**) for the relief of suffering in time of war or disaster *b*) any national branch of this

redd (red) *vt., vi.* **redd** or **redd′ed, redd′ing** [< ? OE. *hreddan,* to free] [Colloq.] to make (a place) tidy (usually with *up*)

red deer **1.** a deer native to Europe and Asia **2.** the white-tailed deer in its reddish summer coat

red·den (red′'n) *vt.* to make red —*vi.* to become red; esp., to blush or flush

re·deem (ri dēm′) *vt.* [< MFr. < L. *redimere* < *re*(*d*)-, back + *emere,* to get] **1.** to get or buy back; recover **2.** to pay off (a mortgage, etc.) **3.** *a*) to convert (paper money) into coin or bullion *b*) to convert (stocks, bonds, etc.) into cash *c*) to turn in (trading stamps or coupons) for a prize, premium, etc. **4.** *a*) to set free by paying a ransom *b*) to deliver from sin and its penalties **5.** to fulfill (a promise or pledge) **6.** *a*) to make amends or atone for *b*) to restore (oneself) to favor by making amends *c*) to make worthwhile —**re·deem′a·ble, re·demp′ti·ble** (-demp′tə b'l) *adj.* —**re·deem′er** *n.*

re·demp·tion (ri demp′shən) *n.* [OFr. < L. < pp. of *redimere:* see prec.] **1.** a redeeming or being redeemed **2.** something that redeems —**re·demp′tion·al** *adj.* —**re·demp′tive, re·demp′to·ry** *adj.*

re·de·ploy (rē′di ploi′) *vt., vi.* to move (troops, etc.) from one front or area to another —**re′de·ploy′ment** *n.*

red-eye (red′ī′) *adj.* [from the bloodshot eyes of one who has not slept] [Slang] designating a late-night or all-night commercial airline flight —*n.* [Slang] such a flight

red fox **1.** the common European fox with reddish fur **2.** the similar related fox of N. America

red-hand·ed (red′han′did) *adv., adj.* **1.** with hands covered with a victim's blood **2.** in the very act of committing a crime **3.** in a situation that makes one seem guilty

red·head (red′hed′) *n.* **1.** a person with red hair **2.** a N. American duck related to the canvasback: the male has a red head —**red′head′ed** *adj.*

redheaded woodpecker a N. American woodpecker with a bright-red head and neck

red herring **1.** a smoked herring **2.** something used to turn attention away from the basic issue: from drawing a herring across the trace in hunting, to confuse the hounds

red-hot (red′hät′) *adj.* **1.** hot enough to glow; very hot **2.** very excited, angry, etc. **3.** very new; up-to-the-minute [*red-hot* news] —*n.* [Colloq.] a frankfurter

red·in·gote (red′iŋ gōt′) *n.* [Fr., altered < E. *riding coat*] **1.** formerly, a man's long, full-skirted overcoat **2.** a long, lightweight coat, open down the front, worn by women

red·in·te·grate (red in′tə grāt′, ri din′-) *vt.* **-grat′ed, -grat′ing** [< L. pp. of *redintegrare:* see RE- & INTEGRATE] to make whole again; reunite —**red·in′te·gra′tion** *n.*

re·di·rect (rē′di rekt′, -dī-) *vt.* to direct again or direct to a different place —*adj. Law* designating the examination of one's own witness again, after his cross-examination by the opposing lawyer —**re′di·rec′tion** *n.*

re·dis·count (rē dis′kount) *vt.* to discount (esp. commercial paper) for a second time —*n.* **1.** a rediscounting **2.** rediscounted commercial paper —**re′dis·count′a·ble** *adj.*

re·dis·trict (rē dis′trikt) *vt.* to divide anew into districts, esp. so as to reapportion representatives

red lead red oxide of lead, Pb_3O_4, used in making paint, in glassmaking, etc.

red-let·ter (red′let′ər) *adj.* designating a memorable or joyous day or event: from the custom of marking holidays on the calendar in red ink

red light **1.** any warning signal **2.** a red stoplight

red·lin·ing (red′lī′niŋ) *n.* [from the practice of outlining such areas in red on a map] the systematic refusal by lending institutions or insurance companies to issue mortgage loans or insurance on property in certain neighborhoods regarded by them as deteriorating

red man a North American Indian

red meat meat that is red before cooking; esp., beef or mutton as distinguished from pork, veal, poultry, etc.

re·do (rē do͞o′) *vt.* **-did′, -done′, -do′ing** **1.** to do again or do over **2.** to redecorate (a room, etc.)

red·o·lent (red′'l ənt) *adj.* [OFr. < L. prp. of *redolere* < *re*(*d*)-, intens. + *olere,* to smell] **1.** sweet-smelling; fragrant **2.** smelling (*of*) [*redolent* of tar] **3.** suggestive (*of*) —**red′o·lence, red′o·len·cy** *n.* —**red′o·lent·ly** *adv.*

Re·don·do Beach (rə dän′dō) [< Sp. *redondo,* circular] city in SW Calif.: suburb of Los Angeles: pop. 57,000

re·dou·ble (rē dub′'l) *vt.* **-bled, -bling** [MFr. *redoubler:* see RE- & DOUBLE] **1.** *a*) to increase fourfold *b*) to make twice as much or twice as great *c*) to make much greater **2.** to refold —*vi.* **1.** *a*) to become twice as great or twice as much *b*) to increase fourfold **2.** [Archaic] to reecho **3.** to turn sharply backward, as on one's tracks **4.** *Bridge* to double a bid that an opponent has already doubled —*n. Bridge* a redoubling

re·doubt (ri dout′) *n.* [< Fr. < It. *ridotto* < ML. *reductus,* orig. pp. of L. *reducere:* see REDUCE] **1.** a breastwork outside or within a fortification **2.** any stronghold

re·doubt·a·ble (-ə b'l) *adj.* [< MFr. < *redouter,* to fear < L. *re-,* intens. + *dubitare,* to doubt] **1.** inspiring fear **2.** commanding respect —**re·doubt′a·bly** *adv.*

re·dound (ri dound′) *vi.* [< MFr. < L. *redundare,* to overflow < *re*(*d*)-, intens. + *undare,* to surge] **1.** to have a result (*to* the credit or discredit of someone or something) **2.** to come back; recoil (*upon*): said of honor or disgrace

red pepper **1.** a plant with a red, many-seeded fruit, as the cayenne **2.** the fruit **3.** the ground fruit or seeds, used for seasoning

red·poll (red′pōl′) *n.* any of a number of finches the males of which usually have a red crown

re·dress (ri dres′; *for n., usually* rē′dres) *vt.* [< OFr.: see RE- & DRESS] **1.** to set right; rectify, as by making compensation for (a wrong, etc.) **2.** [Now Rare] to make amends to —*n.* **1.** compensation, as for a wrong **2.** a redressing —**re·dress′a·ble** *adj.* —**re·dress′er** *n.*

re-dress (rē′dres′) *vt.* to dress again

Red River **1.** river flowing along the Tex.-Okla. border, through Ark. & La. into the Mississippi **2.** river flowing along the N.Dak.-Minn. border into Lake Winnipeg in Manitoba: in full, **Red River of the North**

red salmon *same as* SOCKEYE

Red Sea sea between NE Africa & W Arabia, connected with the Mediterranean Sea by the Suez Canal

red·shirt (red′shurt′) *vt.* [from red shirts worn by a scrimmage team] [Slang] to withdraw (a player) from the varsity team so that he will be eligible to play an extra year later —*n.* such a player

red snapper a reddish, deep-water food fish, found in the Gulf of Mexico and in adjacent Atlantic waters

red spider a small, red, vegetarian mite

red squirrel a N. American tree squirrel, with reddish fur

red·start (red′stärt′) *n.* [RED[1] + obs. *start,* tail] **1.** an American fly-catching warbler **2.** a small European warbler with a reddish tail

red tape [from the tape used to tie official papers] **1.** official forms and routines **2.** rigid adherence to routine and regulations, causing delay in getting business done

red tide a reddish discoloration of sea waters, caused by large numbers of certain red protozoans that release poisons that kill fishes and other organisms

red·top (-täp′) *n.* a grass grown in the cooler parts of N. America for hay, pasturage, and lawns

re·duce (ri do͞os′, -dyo͞os′) *vt.* **-duced′, -duc′ing** [< L. < *re-,* back + *ducere,* to lead] **1.** *a)* to lessen in any way, as in size, amount, value, price, etc. *b)* to put into a simpler or more concentrated form **2.** to bring into a certain order; systematize **3.** to change to a different form, as by melting, grinding, etc. **4.** to lower, as in rank; demote **5.** *a)* to bring to order, obedience, etc., as by persuasion or force *b)* to subdue or conquer **6.** *a)* to bring into difficult circumstances *[reduced* to poverty*]* *b)* to compel by need *[reduced* to stealing*]* **7.** to make thin **8.** *Arith.* to change in denomination or form without changing in value *[*to *reduce* 4/8 to 1/2*]* **9.** *Chem. a)* to decrease the positive valence of (an atom or ion) *b)* to increase the number of electrons of (an atom or ion) *c)* to remove the oxygen from *d)* to combine with hydrogen *e)* to bring into the metallic state by removing nonmetallic elements **10.** *Photog.* to weaken the density of (a negative) **11.** *Surgery* to restore to normal position *[*to *reduce* a fracture*]* —*vi.* **1.** to become reduced **2.** to lose weight, as by being on a diet —**re·duc′er** *n.* —**re·duc′i·bil′i·ty** *n.* —**re·duc′i·ble** *adj.* —**re·duc′i·bly** *adv.*

reducing agent *Chem.* any substance that reduces another substance and is itself oxidized in the process

‡**re·duc·ti·o ad ab·sur·dum** (ri duk′tē ō′ ad ab sur′dəm, -shē ō′) [L., lit., reduction to absurdity] *Logic* the disproof of a proposition by showing the logical conclusions drawn from it to be absurd

re·duc·tion (ri duk′shən) *n.* **1.** *a)* a reducing or being reduced *b)* the amount of this **2.** anything made or brought about by reducing, as a smaller copy —**re·duc′tion·al** *adj.* —**re·duc′tive** *adj.* —**re·duc′tive·ly** *adv.*

re·dun·dan·cy (ri dun′dən sē) *n., pl.* **-cies** **1.** a being redundant **2.** an overabundance **3.** the use of redundant words **4.** the part of a statement that is redundant or unnecessary Also **re·dun′dance**

re·dun·dant (-dənt) *adj.* [< L. prp. of *redundare:* see REDOUND] **1.** more than enough; excess; superfluous **2.** wordy **3.** unnecessary to the meaning: said of words and affixes —**re·dun′dant·ly** *adv.*

re·du·pli·cate (ri do͞o′plə kāt′, -dyo͞o′-; *for adj. & n., usually* -kit) *vt.* **-cat′ed, -cat′ing** [< ML.: see RE- & DUPLICATE] **1.** to redouble, double, or repeat **2.** to double (a syllable or word) to form a new word (as *tom-tom*), sometimes with changes (as *chitchat*) —*vi.* to become reduplicated —*adj.* reduplicated; doubled —*n.* something reduplicated —**re·du′pli·ca′tion** *n.* —**re·du′pli·ca′tive** *adj.*

red·wing (red′wiŋ′) *n.* **1.** a small European thrush with an orange-red patch on the underside of the wings **2.** *same as* RED-WINGED BLACKBIRD

red-winged blackbird a N. American blackbird with a bright-red patch on the top surface of the wings in the male: also **redwing blackbird**

red·wood (-wood′) *n.* **1.** a giant evergreen having enduring, soft wood, found on the coast of California and S Oregon **2.** *same as* BIG TREE **3.** the wood of these trees

Redwood City [after prec.] city in W Calif., on San Francisco Bay: suburb of San Francisco: pop. 55,000

re·ech·o, re-ech·o (rē ek′ō) *vt., vi.* **-ech′oed, -ech′o·ing** to echo back or again; resound —*n., pl.* **-ech′oes** the echo of an echo Also **re·ëch′o**

reed (rēd) *n.* [OE. *hreod*] **1.** *a)* any of various tall, slender grasses growing in wet or marshy land *b)* the stem of any of these *c)* such plants collectively **2.** a rustic musical pipe made from a hollow stem **3.** *Music a)* a thin strip of some flexible substance placed within the opening of the mouthpiece of certain wind instruments, as the clarinet: when vibrated by the breath, it produces a musical tone *b)* an instrument with a reed *c)* in some organs, a similar device that vibrates in a current of air

OBOE REED SIDE VIEW
OBOE REED TOP VIEW
CLARINET REED SIDE VIEW
REEDS

Reed (rēd), **Walter** 1851–1902; U.S. army surgeon & bacteriologist

reed organ an organ with a set of free metal reeds instead of pipes to produce the tones

re·ed·u·cate, re-ed·u·cate (rē ej′ə kāt′) *vt.* **-cat′ed, -cat′ing** to educate anew, esp. so as to rehabilitate or adapt to new situations: also **re·ëd′u·cate′** —**re·ed′u·ca′tion, re-ed′u·ca′tion** *n.* —**re·ed′u·ca′tive, re-ed′u·ca′tive** *adj.*

reed·y (rēd′ē) *adj.* **reed′i·er, reed′i·est** **1.** full of reeds **2.** made of reed or reeds **3.** like a reed; slender, fragile, etc. **4.** sounding like a reed instrument; thin; piping —**reed′i·ly** *adv.* —**reed′i·ness** *n.*

reef[1] (rēf) *n.* [prob. < ON. *rif,* a rib] a ridge of rock, coral, or sand at or near the surface of the water

reef[2] (rēf) *n.* [< or akin to prec.] **1.** a part of a sail which can be folded and tied down to reduce the area exposed to the wind **2.** the act of reefing —*vt.* **1.** to reduce (a sail) by taking in part of it **2.** to lower (a spar or mast) or reduce the projection of (a bowsprit)

reef·er (rē′fər) *n.* **1.** a person who reefs **2.** a short, thick, double-breasted coat like a seaman's jacket **3.** [from the rolled appearance of a *reef* (of a sail)] [Slang] a marijuana cigarette

reef knot a square knot used for reefing

reek (rēk) *n.* [OE. *rec*] **1.** vapor; fume **2.** a strong, unpleasant smell; stench —*vi.* **1.** to fume **2.** to have a strong, offensive smell **3.** to be permeated with anything very unpleasant —*vt.* to emit or exude (vapor, fumes, etc.) —**reek′y** *adj.*

reel[1] (rēl) *vi.* [< the *n.*] **1.** to give way or fall back; sway or stagger as from being struck **2.** to lurch or stagger about, as from drunkenness **3.** to go around and around; whirl **4.** to feel dizzy —*vt.* to cause to reel —*n.* [OE. *hreol*] a reeling motion; whirl, stagger, etc.

reel[2] (rēl) *n.* [prob. < REEL[1], *n.*] **1.** *a)* a lively Scottish dance *b) same as* VIRGINIA REEL **2.** music for either of these

reel[3] (rēl) *n.* [OE. *hreol*] **1.** a frame or spool on which thread, wire, film, etc. is wound **2.** such a frame on a fishing rod for winding line **3.** the quantity of wire, thread, film, etc. usually wound on one reel **4.** in a lawn mower, a set of spiral steel blades rotating on a horizontal bar —*vt., vi.* to wind on a reel —**reel in** **1.** to wind on a reel **2.** to pull in (a fish) by winding a line on a reel —**reel off** to tell, write, etc. easily and quickly —**reel out** to unwind from a reel —**(right) off the reel** without hesitation

re·en·force, re-en·force (rē′in fôrs′) *vt.* **-forced′, -forc′ing** *same as* REINFORCE: also **re′ën·force′**

re·en·try, re-en·try (rē en′trē) *n., pl.* **-tries** **1.** a reentering; specif., a coming back, as of a space vehicle, into the earth's atmosphere **2.** a second or repeated entry **3.** *Bridge, Whist* a card that will win a trick and regain the lead Also **re·ën′try**

reeve[1] (rēv) *n.* [OE. *gerefa*] **1.** in English history, *a)* the chief officer of a town or district *b)* the overseer of a manor; steward **2.** the elected head of a town council in certain Canadian provinces

reeve[2] (rēv) *vt.* **reeved** or **rove, rove** or **rov′en, reev′ing** [prob. < Du. *reven*] *Naut.* **1.** to slip (a rope, etc.) through a block, ring, etc. **2.** *a)* to pass in, through, or around something *b)* to fasten by so doing **3.** to pass a rope through (a block or pulley)

ref (ref) *n., vt., vi. same as* REFEREE

ref. **1.** referee **2.** reference **3.** reformed

re·fec·tion (ri fek′shən) *n.* [OFr. < L. < pp. of *reficere* < *re-,* again + *facere,* to make] **1.** food or drink taken to refresh oneself **2.** a light meal

re·fec·to·ry (-tər ē) *n., pl.* **-ries** a dining hall in a monastery, convent, college, etc.

re·fer (ri fur′) *vt.* **-ferred′, -fer′ring** [< MFr. < L. *referre* < *re-,* back + *ferre,* to bear] **1.** to assign or attribute (*to*) as cause or origin **2.** to assign or regard as belonging (*to* a kind, class, etc.) **3.** to submit (a quarrel, etc.) for settlement **4.** to direct (*to* someone or something) for aid, information, etc. —*vi.* **1.** to relate or apply (*to*) **2.** to direct attention, or make reference (*to*) *[*to *refer* to an earlier event*]* **3.** to turn for information, aid, etc. (*to*) *[*to *refer* to a map*]* —**ref·er·a·ble** (ref′ər ə b′l), **re·fer′ra·ble, re·fer′ri·ble** (ri fur′-) *adj.* —**re·fer′rer** *n.*

ref·er·ee (ref′ə rē′) *n.* **1.** a person to whom something is referred for decision **2.** an official who enforces the rules in certain sports contests **3.** *Law* a person appointed by a court to study, and report on, a matter —*vt., vi.* **-eed′, -ee′ing** to act as referee (in)

ref·er·ence (ref′ər əns, ref′rəns) *n.* **1.** a referring or being referred **2.** relation; regard *[*in *reference* to his letter*]* **3.** *a)* the direction of attention to a person or thing *b)* a mention or allusion **4.** *a)* an indication, as in a book, of some other work to be consulted *b)* the work so indicated *c)* a number or symbol (in full, **reference mark**) directing the reader to a footnote, etc. **5.** *a)* the giving of the name of a person who can offer information or recommendation *b)* the person so indicated *c)* a written statement giving the qualifications, abilities, etc. of someone seeking a position, etc. **6.** *a)* a source of information: often attributive *[reference* books*]* *b)* a book, etc. used for reference —*vt.* **-enced, -enc·ing** to provide with references —**make reference to** refer to; mention —**ref′er·en′tial** (-ə ren′shəl) *adj.* —**ref′er·en′tial·ly** *adv.*

ref·er·en·dum (ref′ə ren′dəm) *n., pl.* **-dums** or **-da** (-də) [ModL. < L., gerund of *referre:* see REFER] **1.** the submission of a law, proposed or already in effect, to a direct vote of the people **2.** the right of the people to vote on such laws, overruling the legislature **3.** the vote itself

ref·er·ent (ref′ər ənt) *n.* something referred to; specif., *Linguis.* the thing referred to by a term or expression

re·fer·ral (ri fur′əl) *n.* **1.** a referring or being referred, as for professional service **2.** a person who is referred or directed to another person, an agency, etc.

re·fill (rē fil′; *for n.* rē′fil) *vt., vi.* to fill again —*n.* a new filling; esp., *a)* a unit to replace the used-up contents of a container *b)* any additional filling of a prescription for medicine —**re·fill′a·ble** *adj.*

re·fi·nance (rē′fə nans′, rē fī′nans) *vt.* **-nanced′, -nanc′-ing** to finance again; specif., to provide or obtain a new loan or more capital for

re·fine (ri fīn′) *vt., vi.* **-fined′, -fin′ing** [RE- + FINE[1], *v.*] **1.** to free or become free from impurities, dross, etc.; purify **2.** to free or become free from imperfection, coarseness, etc.; make or become more polished **3.** to make or become more subtle, as in thinking or speaking —**refine on** (or **upon**) to improve, as by adding refinements —**re·fin′er** *n.*

re·fined (ri fīnd′) *adj.* **1.** made free from impurities; purified **2.** free from coarseness; cultivated; elegant **3.** characterized by great subtlety, precision, etc.

re·fine·ment (ri fīn′mənt) *n.* **1.** *a)* a refining or being refined *b)* the result of this **2.** delicacy or elegance of language, speech, manners, etc.; polish **3.** a development; improvement; elaboration **4.** a fine distinction; subtlety

re·fin·er·y (ri fīn′ər ē) *n., pl.* **-er·ies** an establishment or plant for refining, or purifying, such raw materials as oil, metal, sugar, etc.

re·fin·ish (rē fin′ish) *vt.* to give a new surface to (wood, etc.) —**re·fin′ish·er** *n.*

re·fit (rē fit′; *also for n.* rē′fit′) *vt., vi.* **-fit′ted, -fit′ting** to make or be made ready or fit for use again, as by repairing, reequipping, etc. —*n.* an act or instance of refitting

refl. **1.** reflection **2.** reflex **3.** reflexive

re·flect (ri flekt′) *vt.* [< MFr. < L. < *re-*, back + *flectere*, to bend] **1.** to bend or throw back (light, heat, or sound) **2.** to give back an image of; mirror or reproduce **3.** to bring back as a consequence (with *on*) *[*deeds that *reflect* honor on him*]* **4.** to express or show *[*skills that *reflect* years of training*]* **5.** to recollect or realize after thought (*that*) **6.** to fold or turn back: *usually used in pp.* —*vi.* **1.** to be thrown back *[*light *reflecting* from the water*]* **2.** to throw back light, heat, etc. *[*a *reflecting* surface*]* **3.** *a)* to give back an image *b)* to be mirrored **4.** to think seriously; contemplate (*on* or *upon*) **5.** to cast blame or discredit (*on* or *upon*)

re·flec·tance (-flek′t′ns) *n.* *Physics* the ratio of the total electromagnetic radiation, usually light, reflected by a surface to the total striking the surface

re·flec·tion (ri flek′shən) *n.* **1.** a reflecting or being reflected **2.** the throwing back by a surface of sound, light, etc. **3.** anything reflected; specif., an image; likeness **4.** *a)* serious thought; contemplation *b)* an idea, remark, etc. that comes from such thought **5.** *a)* blame; discredit *b)* a statement casting, or an action bringing, blame or discredit **6.** *Anat.* a bending back on itself —**re·flec′tion·al** *adj.*

re·flec·tive (-tiv) *adj.* **1.** reflecting **2.** of or produced by reflection **3.** meditative; thoughtful —**re·flec′tive·ly** *adv.* —**re·flec′tive·ness, re′flec·tiv′i·ty** *n.*

re·flec·tor (-tər) *n.* **1.** a person or thing that reflects; esp., a surface, object, or device that reflects radiant energy, as light, sound, etc. **2.** a reflecting telescope: see TELESCOPE

re·flex (rē′fleks; *for v.* ri fleks′) *n.* [< L. pp. of *reflectere:* see REFLECT] **1.** reflection, as of light **2.** a reflected image or reproduction **3.** *a)* *Physiol.* a reflex action *b)* any quick, automatic or habitual response *c)* [*pl.*] ability to react quickly and effectively *[*a boxer with good *reflexes]* —*adj.* **1.** turned or bent back **2.** coming in reaction; esp., *Physiol.* designating or of an involuntary action, as a sneeze, resulting when a stimulus carried to a nerve center is directly transmitted to the muscle or gland that responds **3.** *Geom.* designating an angle greater than a straight angle (180°) —*vt.* to bend, turn, or fold back —**re′flex·ly** *adv.*

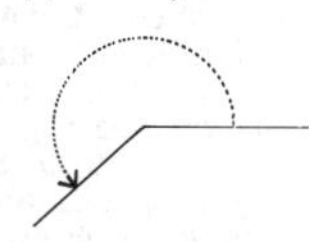
REFLEX ANGLE

re·flex·ion (ri flek′shən) *n.* *Brit. var. of* REFLECTION

re·flex·ive (-siv) *adj.* **1.** reflex **2.** *Gram.* *a)* designating a verb whose subject and direct object refer to the same person or thing (e.g., *wash* in "I wash myself") *b)* designating a pronoun used as the direct object of such a verb, as *myself* in the above example —*n.* a reflexive verb or pronoun —**re·flex′ive·ly** *adv.* —**re·flex′ive·ness, re·flex·iv·i·ty** (rē′flek siv′ə tē) *n.*

re·for·est (rē fôr′ist, -fär′-) *vt., vi.* to plant new trees on (land once forested) —**re′for·est·a′tion** *n.*

re·form (ri fôrm′) *vt.* [< OFr. < L. *reformare:* see RE- & FORM] **1.** to make better by removing faults; correct *[*to *reform* a calendar*]* **2.** *a)* to make better by stopping abuses, introducing better procedures, etc. *b)* to put a stop to (abuses, etc.) **3.** to cause (a person) to give up misconduct and behave better —*vi.* to become better; give up one's bad ways —*n.* **1.** a correction of faults or evils, as in government or society **2.** an improvement in character and conduct —*adj.* [**R-**] designating or of a movement in Judaism that emphasizes its ethical aspects rather than traditional ritual —**re·form′a·ble** *adj.* —**re·form′a·tive** *adj.* —**re·formed′** *adj.*

re-form (rē′fôrm′) *vt., vi.* to form again

ref·or·ma·tion (ref′ər mā′shən) *n.* **1.** a reforming or being reformed **2.** [**R-**] the 16th-cent. religious movement that aimed at reforming the Roman Catholic Church and resulted in establishing the Protestant churches —**ref′or·ma′tion·al** *adj.*

re·form·a·to·ry (ri fôr′mə tôr′ē) *adj.* reforming or aiming at reform —*n., pl.* **-ries** **1.** an institution to which young law offenders are sent for training and discipline intended to reform them: also **reform school** **2.** a penitentiary for women

re·form·er (ri fôr′mər) *n.* a person who seeks to bring about reform, esp. political or social reform

re·form·ism (-miz'm) *n.* the practice or advocacy of reform, esp. political or social reform —**re·form′ist** *n., adj.*

re·fract (ri frakt′) *vt.* [< L. *refractus*, pp. of *refringere* < *re-*, back + *frangere*, to break] **1.** to cause (a ray or wave of light, heat, or sound) to undergo refraction **2.** *Optics* to measure the degree of refraction of (an eye or lens) —**re·frac′tive** *adj.* —**re·frac′tive·ly** *adv.* —**re·frac·tiv·i·ty** (rē′frak tiv′ə tē), **re·frac′tive·ness** *n.*

re·frac·tion (ri frak′shən) *n.* **1.** the bending of a ray or wave of light, heat, or sound, as it passes obliquely from one medium to another of different density **2.** *Optics* the ability of the eye to refract light entering it, so as to form an image on the retina

re·frac·tor (ri frak′tər) *n.* **1.** something that refracts **2.** a refracting telescope: see TELESCOPE

re·frac·to·ry (ri frak′tər ē) *adj.* [< L. < *refractus:* see REFRACT] **1.** hard to manage; stubborn; obstinate **2.** resistant to heat; hard to melt or work: said of ores or metals **3.** not yielding to treatment, as a disease —**re·frac′to·rily** *adv.* —**re·frac′to·ri·ness** *n.*

re·frain[1] (ri frān′) *vi.* [< OFr. < L. < *re-*, back + *frenare*, to curb < *frenum*, a rein] to hold back; keep oneself (*from* doing something); forbear

re·frain[2] (ri frān′) *n.* [MFr., ult. < L. *refringere:* see REFRACT] **1.** a phrase or verse repeated at intervals in a song or poem, as after each stanza **2.** music for this

re·fran·gi·ble (ri fran′jə b'l) *adj.* [< RE- + L. *frangere*, to break + -IBLE] that can be refracted, as light rays —**re·fran′gi·bil′i·ty, re·fran′gi·ble·ness** *n.*

re·fresh (ri fresh′) *vt.* [< OFr.: see RE- & FRESH[1]] **1.** to make fresh by cooling, wetting, etc. *[*rains *refreshing* parched plants*]* **2.** to make (another or oneself) feel cooler, stronger, etc., as by food, drink, or sleep **3.** to replenish, as by new supplies, etc. **4.** to revive (the memory, etc.) —*vi.* **1.** to become fresh again; revive **2.** to take refreshment, as food or drink —**re·fresh′er** *n.* —**re·fresh′ing** *adj.* —**re·fresh′ing·ly** *adv.*

refresher course a course of study reviewing material previously studied

re·fresh·ment (ri fresh′mənt) ***n.*** **1.** a refreshing or being refreshed **2.** something that refreshes, as food, drink, etc. **3.** [*pl.*] food or drink or both, esp. when not a full meal

re·frig·er·ant (ri frij′ər ənt) ***adj.*** **1.** that refrigerates; cooling or freezing **2.** reducing heat or fever —***n.*** **1.** a substance used to reduce fever **2.** a substance used in refrigeration; specif., any of various liquids that vaporize at a low temperature, used in mechanical refrigeration

re·frig·er·ate (-ə rāt′) ***vt.*** **-at′ed, -at′ing** [< L. pp. of *refrigerare* < *re-*, intens. + *frigerare*, to cool < *frigus*, cold] **1.** to make or keep cool or cold; chill **2.** to preserve (food, etc.) by keeping cold or freezing —**re·frig′er·a′tion** ***n.*** —**re·frig′er·a′tive, re·frig′er·a·to′ry** ***adj.***

re·frig·er·a·tor (-rāt′ər) ***n.*** something that refrigerates; esp., a box, cabinet, or room in which food, etc. is kept cool, as by ice or mechanical refrigeration

reft (reft) ***adj.*** robbed or deprived (*of* something); bereft

ref·uge (ref′yo͞oj) ***n.*** [< OFr. < L., ult. < *re-*, back + *fugere*, to flee] **1.** shelter or protection from danger, difficulty, etc. **2.** a place of safety; shelter; safe retreat

ref·u·gee (ref′yoo jē′, ref′yoo jē′) ***n.*** a person who flees from his home or country to seek refuge elsewhere, as in a time of war, persecution, etc.

re·ful·gent (ri ful′jənt) ***adj.*** [< L. prp. of *refulgere*: see RE- & FULGENT] shining; radiant; resplendent —**re·ful′gence, re·ful′gen·cy** ***n.*** —**re·ful′gent·ly** ***adv.***

re·fund[1] (ri fund′; *for n.* rē′fund′) ***vt., vi.*** [< MFr. < L. < *re-*, back + *fundere*, to pour] to give back (money, etc.); repay —***n.*** the act of refunding or the amount refunded; repayment —**re·fund′a·ble** ***adj.***

re·fund[2] (rē′fund′) ***vt.*** to fund again or anew; specif., *Finance* to use borrowed money, as from the sale of a bond issue, to pay back (a loan)

re·fur·bish (ri fur′bish) ***vt.*** [RE- + FURBISH] to brighten, freshen, or polish up again; renovate —**re·fur′bish·ment** ***n.***

re·fus·al (ri fyo͞o′z′l) ***n.*** **1.** the act of refusing **2.** the right or chance to accept or refuse something before it is offered to another; option

re·fuse[1] (ri fyo͞oz′) ***vt.*** **-fused′, -fus′ing** [< OFr. *refuser*, ult. < L. pp. of *refundere*: see REFUND[1]] **1.** to decline to accept; reject **2.** to decline to do, give, grant, obey, etc.; deny [*to refuse a request, to refuse to go*] **3.** to stop short at (a fence, etc.) without jumping it: said of a horse —***vi.*** to decline to accept, agree to, or do something —**re·fus′er** ***n.***

ref·use[2] (ref′yo͞os, -yo͞oz) ***n.*** [< OFr. pp. of *refuser*: see prec.] anything thrown away or rejected as worthless or useless; waste; rubbish —***adj.*** thrown away or rejected as worthless or useless

re·fute (ri fyo͞ot′) ***vt.*** **-fut′ed, -fut′ing** [L. *refutare*, to repel: see RE- & CONFUTE] **1.** to prove (a person) to be wrong; confute **2.** to prove (an argument or statement) to be false or wrong, by argument or evidence —**re·fut′a·ble** (-fyo͞ot′ə b'l, ref′yoo tə-) ***adj.*** —**re·fut′a·bly** ***adv.*** —**ref·u·ta·tion** (ref′yə tā′shən), **re·fut′al** ***n.*** —**re·fut′er** ***n.***

reg. **1.** regiment **2.** region **3.** register **4.** registered **5.** registrar **6.** regular **7.** regulation

re·gain (ri gān′) ***vt.*** **1.** to get back again; recover **2.** to succeed in reaching again; get back to

re·gal (rē′gəl) ***adj.*** [MFr. < L. *regalis* < *rex* (gen. *regis*), a king] **1.** of a king; royal **2.** characteristic of, like, or fit for a king; splendid, stately, etc. —**re·gal·i·ty** (rē gal′ə tē) ***n.*** —**re′gal·ly** ***adv.***

re·gale (ri gāl′) ***vt.*** **-galed′, -gal′ing** [< Fr. < *ré-* (see RE-) + OFr. *gale*, joy] **1.** to entertain by providing a splendid feast **2.** to delight with something pleasing or amusing —***vi.*** to feast —**re·gale′ment** ***n.*** —**re·gal′er** ***n.***

re·ga·li·a (ri gāl′yə, -gā′lē ə) ***n.pl.*** [L., neut. pl. of *regalis*: see REGAL] **1.** the emblems and insignia of kingship, as a crown, scepter, etc. **2.** the insignia or decorations of any rank, society, etc. **3.** splendid clothes; finery

re·gard (ri gärd′) ***n.*** [< OFr. < *regarder*: see RE- & GUARD] **1.** a firm, fixed look; gaze **2.** consideration; concern [*have regard for your health*] **3.** respect and affection; esteem [*to have high regard for one's teachers*] **4.** reference; relation [*in regard to your plan*] **5.** [*pl.*] good wishes; respects [*give my regards to Bill*] —***vt.*** **1.** to look at with a firm, steady gaze **2.** to take into account; consider **3.** [Archaic] to give attentive heed to **4.** to hold in affection and respect **5.** to think of in a certain light [*to regard taxes as a burden*] **6.** to have relation to; concern [*this regards your welfare*] —***vi.*** to look or pay heed —**as regards** concerning —**without regard to** without considering

re·gard·ful (-fəl) ***adj.*** **1.** mindful (*of*) **2.** respectful

re·gard·ing (-iŋ) ***prep.*** with regard to; concerning; about

re·gard·less (-lis) ***adj.*** heedless; careless —***adv.*** [Colloq.] without regard for objections, difficulties, etc.; anyway —**regardless of** in spite of —**re·gard′less·ly** ***adv.***

re·gat·ta (ri gät′ə, -gat′-) ***n.*** [It.] **1.** a boat race **2.** a series of such races

re·gen·cy (rē′jən sē) ***n.***, *pl.* **-cies** **1.** the position, function, or authority of a regent or group of regents **2.** a group of men serving as regents **3.** a country governed by a regent or a group of regents **4.** the time during which a regent or regency governs; specif., [**R-**] in England, the period between 1811 and 1820

re·gen·er·ate (ri jen′ər it; *for v.* -ə rāt′) ***adj.*** [< L. pp. of *regenerare*: see RE- & GENERATE] **1.** spiritually reborn **2.** renewed or restored —***vt.*** **-at′ed, -at′ing** **1.** to cause to be spiritually reborn **2.** to cause to be completely reformed or improved **3.** to bring into existence again; reestablish **4.** *Biol.* to grow anew (a part to replace one hurt or lost) **5.** *Electronics* to increase the amplification of (a signal) by feeding energy back from an amplifier output to its input **6.** *Physics* to restore (a battery, etc.) to its original state or properties —***vi.*** **1.** to form again, or be made anew **2.** to be regenerated, or spiritually reborn —**re·gen′er·a·cy** (-ə sē) ***n.*** —**re·gen′er·a′tion** ***n.*** —**re·gen′er·a′tive** ***adj.***

re·gent (rē′jənt) ***adj.*** [MFr. < ML. < L. prp. of *regere*, to rule] acting in place of a king or ruler [*a prince regent*] —***n.*** **1.** a person appointed to rule a monarchy when the sovereign is absent, too young, or incapacitated **2.** a member of a governing board, as of a State university or a State system of schools —**re′gent·ship′** ***n.***

reg·i·cide (rej′ə sīd′) ***n.*** [< ML. < L. *rex* (see REGAL) + *-cida*: see -CIDE] **1.** a person who kills a king **2.** the killing of a king —**reg′i·ci′dal** ***adj.***

re·gime, ré·gime (rə zhēm′, rā-) ***n.*** [< Fr. < L. *regimen*: see ff.] **1.** *a)* a political system *b)* a form of government or rule **2.** a social system or order **3.** the period that a person or system is in power **4.** *same as* REGIMEN

reg·i·men (rej′ə mən) ***n.*** [L., rule < *regere*, to rule] a regulated system of diet, exercise, rest, etc. for promoting the health

reg·i·ment (rej′ə mənt; *for v.* -ment′) ***n.*** [< MFr. < LL. *regimentum*, government < L. *regere*, to rule] **1.** a military unit consisting of two or more battalions **2.** a large number (of persons, etc.) —***vt.*** **1.** to form into regiments **2.** to assign to a regiment **3.** to organize systematically, as into uniform groups **4.** to organize in a rigid system under strict discipline and control —**reg′i·men′tal** ***adj.*** —**reg′i·men′tal·ly** ***adv.*** —**reg′i·men·ta′tion** ***n.***

reg·i·men·tals (rej′ə men′t'lz) ***n.pl.*** **1.** a regiment's uniform and insignia **2.** military uniform

Re·gi·na (ri jī′nə) [L., a queen] capital of Saskatchewan, Canada, in the S part: pop. 150,000 —***n.*** [*also* **r-**] queen

Reg·i·nald (rej′i nəld) [ult. < Gmc. bases meaning "wise ruler"] a masculine name: dim. *Reggie*

re·gion (rē′jən) ***n.*** [< Anglo-Fr. < OFr. < L. *regio* < *regere*, to rule] **1.** a part of the earth's surface, esp. a part having a specified position or feature [*a coastal region, tropical regions*] **2.** any area, place, space, etc. or sphere, realm, etc. [*the upper regions of the air, a region of research*] **3.** an administrative division of a country, as in Italy or the U.S.S.R. **4.** a division or part of the body

re·gion·al (-'l) ***adj.*** **1.** of a whole region, not just a locality **2.** of some particular region, district, etc. —**re′gion·al·ism** ***n.*** —**re′gion·al·ly** ***adv.***

reg·is·ter (rej′is tər) ***n.*** [< MFr. < ML. *registrum* < LL. < L. pp. of *regerere*, to record] **1.** *a)* a record or list of names, events, items, etc. *b)* a book in which this is kept *c)* an entry in such a record **2.** registration; enrollment **3.** a device, as a meter or counter, for recording fares paid, money deposited, etc. [*a cash register*] **4.** an opening into a room by which the amount of air passing, as from a furnace, can be controlled **5.** *Music a)* a part of a range of tones of the human voice or of an instrument having a specified quality *b)* an organ stop, or the tone quality it produces **6.** *Printing* exact placing of lines, pages, colors, etc. —***vt.*** **1.** to enter in or as in a record or list; enroll **2.** to indicate as on a scale [*a thermometer registers temperature*] **3.** to show, as by facial expression [*to register surprise*] **4.** to safeguard (mail) by having its committal to the postal system recorded, for a fee **5.** *Printing* to cause to be in register —***vi.*** **1.** to enter one's name, as in a hotel register, a list of eligible voters, etc. **2.** to enroll in a school, college, etc. **3.** to make an impression —**reg′is·trant** (-trənt) ***n.***

reg·is·tered (-tərd) ***adj.*** officially or legally recorded, enrolled, or certified

registered nurse a nurse who has completed extensive training and has passed a State examination so as to qualify for performing complete nursing services

reg·is·trar (rej′i strär′, rej′i strär′) ***n.*** **1.** an official who keeps records, as of the students in a college **2.** a trust company that keeps the records of stock transfers, etc.

reg·is·tra·tion (rej′i strā′shən) ***n.*** **1.** a registering or being registered **2.** an entry in a register **3.** the number of persons registered

reg·is·try (rej′is trē) ***n.***, *pl.* **-tries** **1.** *same as* REGISTRATION **2.** an office where registers are kept **3.** an official record or list; register **4.** a certificate on which is shown the nation-

ality of a merchant ship as recorded in an official register
reg·nant (reg′nənt) ***adj.*** [< L. prp. of *regnare*, to reign] **1.** reigning; ruling **2.** predominant **3.** prevalent; widespread —**reg′nan·cy** ***n.***
re·gorge (ri gôrj′) ***vt.*** **-gorged′, -gorg′ing** [< Fr.: see RE- & GORGE] to throw up or back; disgorge
re·gress (rē′gres; *for v.* ri gres′) ***n.*** [< L. pp. of *regredi* < *re-*, back + *gradi*, to go] **1.** a going or coming back **2.** backward movement; retrogression —***vi.*** **1.** to go back; move backward **2.** to revert to an earlier form or to earlier or more infantile behavior patterns —**re·gres′sion** ***n.*** —**re·gres′sive** ***adj.*** —**re·gres′sive·ly** ***adv.*** —**re·gres′sor** ***n.***
re·gret (ri gret′) ***vt.*** **-gret′ted, -gret′ting** [< OFr. *regreter*, to mourn < a Gmc. base] **1.** to be sorry about or mourn for (a person or thing gone, lost, etc.) **2.** to feel troubled or remorseful over (an occurrence, one's acts, etc.) —***n.*** **1.** a troubled feeling or remorse, esp. over one's acts or omissions **2.** sorrow over a person or thing gone, lost, etc. —**(one's) regrets** a polite expression of regret, as at declining an invitation —**re·gret′ful** ***adj.*** —**re·gret′ful·ly** ***adv.*** —**re·gret′ful·ness** ***n.*** —**re·gret′ta·ble** ***adj.*** —**re·gret′ta·bly** ***adv.*** —**re·gret′ter** ***n.***
re·group (rē grōōp′) ***vt., vi.*** to group again; specif., *Mil.* to reorganize (one's forces), as after a battle
reg·u·lar (reg′yə lər) ***adj.*** [< MFr. < L. < *regula:* see RULE] **1.** conforming in form or arrangement to a rule, principle, type, etc.; orderly; symmetrical **2.** characterized by conformity to a fixed principle or procedure **3.** *a)* usual; customary *b)* not a substitute; established [the *regular* quarterback] **4.** consistent, habitual, steady, etc. [a *regular* customer] **5.** recurring at set times or functioning in a normal way **6.** conforming to a generally accepted rule of conduct; proper **7.** properly qualified [a *regular* doctor] **8.** [Colloq.] thorough; absolute [a *regular* nuisance] **9.** [Colloq.] pleasant, friendly, etc. [a *regular* fellow] **10.** *Bot.* having all similar parts of the same shape and size: said of flowers **11.** *Eccles.* belonging to a religious order, etc. and adhering to its rule **12.** *Gram.* conforming to the usual type as in inflection **13.** *Math.* having all angles and sides equal, as a polygon, or all faces equal, as a polyhedron **14.** *Mil.* *a)* designating or of the standing army of a country *b)* designating soldiers recognized in international law as legitimate combatants in warfare **15.** *Politics* designating, of, or loyal to the party leadership, candidates, etc. —***n.*** **1.** a member of a religious order **2.** a member of a regular army **3.** a regular member of an athletic team **4.** a clothing size for men of average height **5.** *Politics* one who is loyal to the party leadership, candidates, etc. —**reg′u·lar′i·ty** (-lar′ə tē) ***n.,*** *pl.* **-ties** —**reg′u·lar·ly** ***adv.***
reg·u·late (reg′yə lāt′) ***vt.*** **-lat′ed, -lat′ing** [< LL. pp. of *regulare* < L. *regula:* see RULE] **1.** to control or direct according to a rule, principle, etc. **2.** to adjust to a standard, rate, degree, etc. [*regulate* the heat] **3.** to adjust (a clock, etc.) so as to make operate accurately **4.** to make uniform, methodical, etc. —**reg′u·la′tive, reg′u·la·to′ry** (-lə tôr′ē) ***adj.***
reg·u·la·tion (reg′yə lā′shən) ***n.*** **1.** a regulating or being regulated **2.** a rule or law by which conduct, etc. is regulated —***adj.*** **1.** required by regulation [a *regulation* uniform] **2.** usual; normal
reg·u·la·tor (reg′yə lāt′ər) ***n.*** a person or thing that regulates; specif., *a)* a mechanism for controlling the movement of machinery, fluids, etc.; governor *b)* the device in a watch or clock by which its speed is adjusted
re·gur·gi·tate (ri gʉr′jə tāt′) ***vi., vt.*** **-tat′ed, -tat′ing** [< ML. pp. of *regurgitare* < *re-*, back + LL. *gurgitare*, to surge] to surge or flow back, or cause to do this; specif., to bring (partly digested food) from the stomach back to the mouth —**re·gur′gi·tant** ***adj.*** —**re·gur′gi·ta′tion** ***n.***
re·ha·bil·i·tate (rē′hə bil′ə tāt′, rē′ə-) ***vt.*** **-tat′ed, -tat′ing** [< ML.: see RE- & HABILITATE] **1.** to restore to rank, privileges, reputation, etc. which one has lost **2.** to put back in good condition **3.** *a)* to restore to a normal state of health, etc. as by medical treatment *b)* to make (the handicapped or disadvantaged) able to be employed by giving them special training —**re′ha·bil′i·ta′tion** ***n.*** —**re′ha·bil′i·ta′tive** ***adj.***
re·hash (rē hash′; *for n.* rē′hash) ***vt.*** [RE- + HASH[1]] to work up again or go over again [to *rehash* the same old arguments] —***n.*** the act or result of rehashing
re·hear (rē hir′) ***vt.*** **-heard′** (-hʉrd′), **-hear′ing** *Law* to hear (a case) a second time —**re·hear′ing** ***n.***
re·hears·al (ri hʉr′s′l) ***n.*** a rehearsing; specif., a practice performance of a play, concert, etc.
re·hearse (ri hʉrs′) ***vt.*** **-hearsed′, -hears′ing** [< OFr. < *re-*, again + *herser*, to harrow < *herse*, a harrow] **1.** to repeat aloud as heard or read; recite **2.** to tell in detail **3.** to perform (a play, concert, etc.) for practice in preparation for a public performance **4.** to drill (a person) in what he is to do —***vi.*** to rehearse a play, etc.
re·heat (rē hēt′) ***vt.*** to heat again; specif., to add heat to (a fluid), as in an afterburner —**re·heat′er** ***n.***
Reich (rīk; *G.* rīH) ***n.*** [G.] Germany or the German government; specif., the German fascist state under the Nazis from 1933 to 1945 **(Third Reich)**
reichs·mark (rīks′märk′; *G.* rīHs′märk′) ***n.,*** *pl.* **-marks′, -mark′** [G.] the monetary unit of Germany from 1924 to 1948
Reichs·tag (rīks′täg′; *G.* rīHs′täkh′) ***n.*** [G.] formerly, the legislative assembly of Germany
reign (rān) ***n.*** [< OFr. < L. *regnum* < *regere*, to rule] **1.** royal power or rule **2.** dominance; prevalence [the *reign* of fashion] **3.** the period of rule, dominance, etc. —***vi.*** **1.** to rule as a sovereign **2.** to be widespread; prevail [peace *reigns*]
Reign of Terror the period of the French Revolution from 1793 to 1794, during which many persons were executed
re·im·burse (rē′im bʉrs′) ***vt.*** **-bursed′, -burs′ing** [RE- + archaic *imburse*, after Fr. *rembourser*] **1.** to pay back (money spent) **2.** to compensate (a person) for expenses, damages, losses, etc. —**re′im·burs′a·ble** ***adj.*** —**re′im·burse′ment** ***n.***
Reims (rēmz; *Fr.* raɴs) city in NE France: pop. 153,000
rein (rān) ***n.*** [< OFr. *resne*, ult. < L. *retinere:* see RETAIN] **1.** a narrow strip of leather attached to each end of a horse's bit and held by the rider or driver to control the animal: *usually used in pl.* **2.** [*pl.*] a means of guiding, controlling, etc. [the *reins* of government] —***vt.*** to guide, control, etc. as with reins —***vi.*** to stop or slow down as with reins (with *in* or *up*) —**draw rein** to slow down or stop: also **draw in the reins** —**give (free) rein to** to allow to act without restraint

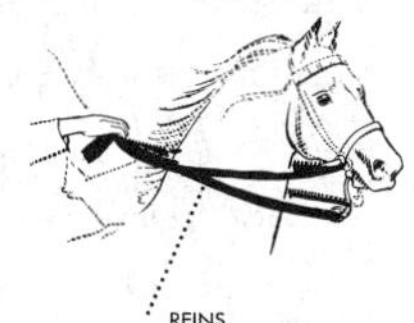
REINS

re·in·car·nate (rē′in kär′nāt) ***vt.*** **-nat·ed, -nat·ing** to cause to undergo reincarnation
re·in·car·na·tion (-kär nā′shən) ***n.*** **1.** a rebirth of the soul in another body, as in Hindu religious belief **2.** a new incarnation **3.** the doctrine that the soul reappears after death in another and different bodily form
rein·deer (rān′dir′) ***n.,*** *pl.* **-deer′**, occas. **-deers′** [< ON. < *hreinn*, reindeer + *dȳr*, deer] a large deer with branching antlers, found in northern regions: domesticated there as a beast of burden and for its milk, meat, and leather
reindeer moss an arctic lichen eaten by grazing animals
re·in·force (rē′in fôrs′) ***vt.*** **-forced′, -forc′ing** [RE- + var. of ENFORCE] **1.** to strengthen (a military or naval force) with more troops, ships, planes, etc. **2.** to strengthen, as by propping, adding new material, etc. **3.** to make more compelling [to *reinforce* an argument] —**re′in·forc′er** ***n.***
reinforced concrete concrete masonry containing steel bars or mesh to increase its tensile strength
re·in·force·ment (-mənt) ***n.*** **1.** a reinforcing or being reinforced **2.** anything that reinforces; specif., [*pl.*] additional troops, ships, etc.
reins (rānz) ***n.pl.*** [< OFr. < L. pl. of *ren*, kidney] [Archaic] **1.** the kidneys **2.** the loins, thought of as the seat of the emotions and affections
re·in·state (rē′in stāt′) ***vt.*** **-stat′ed, -stat′ing** to instate again; restore to a former condition, position, etc. —**re′in·state′ment** ***n.***
reis (rās) ***n.pl.,*** *sing.* **re·al** (re äl′) [Port.] a former Portuguese and Brazilian money of account
re·it·er·ate (rē it′ə rāt′) ***vt.*** **-at′ed, -at′ing** [< L. pp. of *reiterare:* see RE- & ITERATE] to say or do again or repeatedly —**re·it′er·a′tion** ***n.*** —**re·it′er·a′tive** (-ə rāt′iv, -ər ə-tiv) ***adj.*** —**re·it′er·a′tive·ly** ***adv.***
re·ject (ri jekt′; *for n.* rē′jekt) ***vt.*** [< L. pp. of *rejicere* < *re-*, back + *jacere*, to throw] **1.** to refuse to take, agree to, use, believe, etc. **2.** to discard or throw out as worthless **3.** to pass over (a phonograph record set by a record changer) **4.** to vomit **5.** to deny love or acceptance to (someone) **6.** *Physiol.* to be incompatible with (a part or organ transplanted into the body) —***n.*** a rejected thing or person —**re·ject′ee′** ***n.*** —**re·ject′er, re·jec′tor** ***n.*** —**re·jec′tion** ***n.*** —**re·jec′tive** ***adj.***
re·joice (ri jois′) ***vi.*** **-joiced′, -joic′ing** [< OFr. *rejoir* < *re-*, again + *joir* < L. *gaudere*, to rejoice] to be glad or happy (often with *at* or *in*) —***vt.*** to make glad; delight —**re·joic′ing·ly** ***adv.***
re·join[1] (rē join′) ***vt.*** [< MFr.: see ff.] **1.** to come into the company of again **2.** to join together again; reunite **3.** to renew membership in (an organization) after a lapse —***vi.*** to become joined together again

re·join² (ri join′) ***vt.*** [< Anglo-Fr. < MFr. *rejoindre:* see RE- & JOIN] to say in answer —***vi.*** to answer

re·join·der (-dər) ***n.*** [< Anglo-Fr. substantive use of *rejoindre:* see prec.] **1.** *a)* an answer to a reply *b)* any answer **2.** *Law* the defendant's answer to the plaintiff's replication

re·ju·ve·nate (ri jo͞o′və nāt′) ***vt.*** **-nat′ed, -nat′ing** [< RE- + L. *juvenis,* young + -ATE¹] **1.** to make young again; bring back to youthful strength, appearance, etc. **2.** to make seem new or fresh again —**re·ju′ve·na′tion** ***n.*** —**re·ju′ve·na′tor** ***n.***

re·lapse (ri laps′; *for n., also* rē′laps) ***vi.*** **-lapsed′, -laps′ing** [< L. pp. of *relabi,* to slip back: see RE- & LAPSE] to slip back into a former condition, esp. after improvement or seeming improvement —***n.*** **1.** a relapsing **2.** the recurrence of a disease after apparent improvement —**re·laps′er** ***n.***

re·late (ri lāt′) ***vt.*** **-lat′ed, -lat′ing** [< L. pp. of *referre,* to bring back: see REFER] **1.** to tell the story of; narrate **2.** to connect, as in thought or meaning; show a relation between *[*to *relate* theory and practice*]* —***vi.*** **1.** *a)* to have some connection (*to*) *b)* to show sympathy and understanding **2.** to have reference (*to*) —**re·lat′a·ble** ***adj.*** —**re·lat′er, re·la′tor** ***n.***

re·lat·ed (-lāt′id) ***adj.*** **1.** narrated; told **2.** connected or associated, as by origin, kinship, marriage, etc.; of the same family —**re·lat′ed·ness** ***n.***

re·la·tion (ri lā′shən) ***n.*** **1.** a narrating, telling, etc. **2.** what is narrated; recital **3.** connection, as in thought, meaning, etc. **4.** connection of persons by blood or marriage; kinship **5.** a person related to others by kinship; relative **6.** [*pl.*] *a)* the connections between or among persons, groups, nations, etc. *b)* sexual intercourse —**in** (or **with**) **relation to** concerning; regarding —**re·la′tion·al** ***adj.***

re·la·tion·ship (-ship′) ***n.*** **1.** the state or an instance of being related **2.** connection by blood or marriage; kinship

rel·a·tive (rel′ə tiv) ***adj.*** **1.** related each to the other; referring to each other **2.** having to do with; relevant **3.** regarded in relation to something else; comparative **4.** meaningful only in relationship *[*"cold" is a *relative* term*]* **5.** *Gram.* *a)* designating a word that introduces a subordinate clause and refers to an antecedent *[*"which" is a *relative* pronoun in "the hat which you bought"*]* *b)* introduced by such a word *[*a *relative* clause*]* —***n.*** **1.** a relative word or thing **2.** a person related to others by kinship; member of the same family —**relative to 1.** concerning; about **2.** corresponding to; in proportion to —**rel′a·tive·ness** ***n.***

relative humidity *see* HUMIDITY

rel·a·tive·ly (-lē) ***adv.*** in a relative manner; in relation to or compared to something else; not absolutely *[*a *relatively* unimportant matter*]*

rel·a·tiv·ism (-iz'm) ***n.*** any theory of ethics or knowledge based on the idea that all values or judgments are relative, differing according to circumstances, persons, etc. —**rel′a·tiv·ist** ***n.*** —**rel′a·tiv·is′tic** ***adj.***

rel·a·tiv·i·ty (rel′ə tiv′ə tē) ***n.*** **1.** a being relative **2.** *Physics* the fact, principle, or theory of the relative, rather than absolute, character of motion, velocity, mass, time, etc.: as developed esp. by Albert Einstein, the theory includes the statements that: 1) the velocity of light is constant; 2) the mass of a body in motion varies with its velocity; 3) matter and energy are equivalent; 4) space and time are interdependent and form a four-dimensional continuum

re·lax (ri laks′) ***vt., vi.*** [< L. < *re-,* back + *laxare,* to loosen < *laxus,* loose] **1.** to make or become looser, or less firm, stiff, or tense **2.** to make or become less strict, severe, or intense, as discipline, effort, etc. **3.** to rest or give rest to, from work, worry, etc. —**re·laxed′** ***adj.*** —**re·lax′ed·ly** (-lak′sid lē) ***adv.*** —**re·lax′er** ***n.***

re·lax·ant (-ənt) ***adj.*** of or causing relaxation, esp. of muscular tension —***n.*** a relaxant drug or agent

re·lax·a·tion (rē′lak sā′shən) ***n.*** **1.** a relaxing or being relaxed; loosening, lessening of severity, etc. **2.** *a)* a lessening of or rest from work, worry, etc. *b)* recreation or other activity for bringing this about

re·lay (rē′lā; *for v., also* ri lā′) ***n.*** [MFr. *relais* (pl.), orig. relays of hunting hounds < *re-,* back + *laier,* to leave] **1.** a fresh supply of horses, etc. ready to relieve others, as for a stage of a journey **2.** a crew of workers relieving others; shift **3.** *a)* *same as* RELAY RACE *b)* any of the laps of a relay race **4.** a conveying or transmitting as by relays **5.** *same as* SERVOMOTOR **6.** *Elec.* a device activated by variations in conditions in one electric circuit and controlling a larger current or activating other devices in the same or another circuit: used in telegraphy, etc. —***vt.*** **-layed, -lay·ing** **1.** to convey by or as by relays *[*to *relay* news*]* **2.** *Elec.* to control, operate, or send on by a relay

re-lay (rē′lā′) ***vt.*** **-laid′, -lay′ing** to lay again or anew: also written **re′lay′**

relay race a race between teams, each runner going in turn only part of the total distance

re·lease (ri lēs′) ***vt.*** **-leased′, -leas′ing** [< OFr. < L. *relaxare:* see RELAX] **1.** to set free, as from confinement, duty, work, etc. **2.** to let (a missile, etc.) go **3.** to permit to be issued, published, broadcast, etc. **4.** *Law* to give up to someone else (a claim, right, etc.) —***n.*** **1.** a freeing or being freed, as from prison, pain, an obligation, etc. **2.** relief from tension as by expressing emotion freely **3.** a document authorizing release, as from prison, etc. **4.** a letting loose of something caught, held, etc. **5.** a device for releasing a catch, etc., as on a machine **6.** *a)* a releasing to the public, as of a book, film, news, etc. *b)* the book, film, news, etc. released **7.** *Law* *a)* a giving up of a claim or right *b)* the document by which this is done

re-lease (rē′lēs′) ***vt.*** **-leased′, -leas′ing** to lease again

released time periods during school time when pupils in a public school may leave the school in order to receive religious instruction elsewhere

rel·e·gate (rel′ə gāt′) ***vt.*** **-gat′ed, -gat′ing** [< L. pp. of *relegare* < *re-,* away + *legare,* to send] **1.** to exile or banish (*to*) **2.** to consign or assign to an inferior position **3.** to assign to a class, sphere, etc. **4.** to refer, commit, or hand over for decision or action —**rel′e·ga′tion** ***n.***

re·lent (ri lent′) ***vi.*** [ult. < L. < *re-,* again + *lentus,* pliant] to soften in temper, resolution, etc.; become less severe, stern, or stubborn —**re·lent′ing·ly** ***adv.***

re·lent·less (-lis) ***adj.*** **1.** not relenting; harsh; pitiless **2.** persistent; unremitting —**re·lent′less·ly** ***adv.*** —**re·lent′less·ness** ***n.***

rel·e·vant (rel′ə vənt) ***adj.*** [< ML. prp. of *relevare:* see RELIEVE] bearing upon or relating to the matter in hand; pertinent; to the point —**rel′e·vance, rel′e·van·cy** ***n.*** —**rel′e·vant·ly** ***adv.***

re·li·a·ble (ri lī′ə b'l) ***adj.*** that can be relied on; dependable —**re·li′a·bil′i·ty, re·li′a·ble·ness** ***n.*** —**re·li′a·bly** ***adv.***

re·li·ance (-əns) ***n.*** **1.** the act of relying **2.** trust, dependence, or confidence **3.** a thing relied on

re·li·ant (-ənt) ***adj.*** having or showing trust, dependence, or confidence; dependent (*on*) —**re·li′ant·ly** ***adv.***

rel·ic (rel′ik) ***n.*** [< OFr. < L. *reliquiae* (pl.), remains < *relinquere:* see RELINQUISH] **1.** *a)* an object, custom, etc. that has survived from the past *b)* a keepsake or souvenir **2.** [*pl.*] remaining fragments; ruins **3.** *R.C.Ch. & Orthodox Eastern Ch.* the bodily remains of a saint, martyr, etc., or an object associated with him, reverenced as a memorial

rel·ict (rel′ikt) ***n.*** [< L. pp. of *relinquere:* see RELINQUISH] [Archaic] a widow

re·lief (ri lēf′) ***n.*** [< OFr. *relever:* see ff.] **1.** an easing, as of pain, anxiety, a burden, etc. **2.** anything that lessens tension, or offers a pleasing change **3.** aid in the form of goods or money given, as by a government agency, to those unable to support themselves **4.** any aid given in times of need, danger, or disaster, as supplies sent into a flooded area **5.** *a)* release from work or duty *b)* the person or persons bringing such release by taking over a post **6.** *a)* the projection of sculptured figures and forms from a flat surface, so that they stand wholly or partly free *b)* a work of art so made **7.** *a)* the differences in height, collectively, of land forms in any particular area *b)* these differences as shown by lines, colors, or raised areas on a map (**relief map**) **8.** *Law* the assistance sought by a complainant as in a court of equity **9.** *a)* *Painting* the apparent solidity or projection of objects *b)* distinctness of outline; contrast —***adj.*** *Baseball* designating a pitcher regularly used to replace another during a game —**in relief** carved or molded so as to project from a surface —**on relief** receiving relief from a government agency

re·lieve (ri lēv′) ***vt.*** **-lieved′, -liev′ing** [< OFr. < L. < *re-,* again + *levare,* to raise < *levis,* light] **1.** *a)* to ease, lighten, or reduce (pain, anxiety, etc.) *b)* to free from pain, distress, etc. **2.** to lighten (pressure, stress, etc.) on (something) **3.** to give or bring aid or assistance to *[*to *relieve* a besieged city*]* **4.** *a)* to set free from a burden, obligation, etc. *b)* to remove (a burden, etc.) **5.** to set free from duty or work by replacing with oneself or another *[*to *relieve* a nurse*]*; specif., *Baseball* to serve as a relief pitcher for **6.** to make less tedious, etc. by providing a pleasing change **7.** to set off by contrast; make distinct or prominent **8.** to ease (oneself) by urinating or defecating —**re·liev′a·ble** ***adj.*** —**re·liev′er** ***n.***

re·lie·vo (ri lē′vō, ril yev′ō) ***n.,*** *pl.* **-vos** *same as* RELIEF (SENSE 6)

re·li·gion (ri lij′ən) ***n.*** [< OFr. < L. *religio* < ? < *re-,* back + *ligare,* to bind] **1.** *a)* belief in a superhuman power or powers to be obeyed and worshiped as the creator(s) and ruler(s) of the universe *b)* expression of this belief in conduct and ritual **2.** any specific system of belief, worship, etc., often involving a code of ethics *[*the Christian *religion]* **3.** the state or way of life of a person in a monastic order, etc. **4.** any object that is seriously or zealously pursued

re·li·gi·os·i·ty (ri lij′ē äs′ə tē) ***n.*** the quality of being excessively or mawkishly religious —**re·li′gi·ose′** (-ōs′) ***adj.***

re·li·gious (ri lij′əs) ***adj.*** **1.** that believes in or supports a religion; devout; pious **2.** of or concerned with religion *[religious* books*]* **3.** belonging to a community of monks, nuns, etc. **4.** conscientiously exact; scrupulous —***n.,*** *pl.* **-gious** a member of a community of monks, nuns, etc. —**re·li′gious·ly** ***adv.*** —**re·li′gious·ness** ***n.***

re·line (rē līn′) ***vt.*** **-lined′, -lin′ing** **1.** to mark with new lines **2.** to provide with a new lining

re·lin·quish (ri liŋ′kwish) ***vt.*** [< OFr. < L. < *re-*, from + *linquere,* to leave] **1.** to give up (a plan, policy, etc.) **2.** to surrender (something owned, a right, etc.) **3.** to let go (a grasp, etc.) —**re·lin′quish·ment** ***n.***

rel·i·quar·y (rel′ə kwer′ē) ***n.,*** *pl.* **-quar′ies** [< Fr. < L.: see RELIC] a small box, casket, or shrine in which relics are kept and shown

rel·ique (rel′ik, re lēk′) ***n.*** *archaic var. of* RELIC

rel·ish (rel′ish) ***n.*** [< OFr. *relais,* something remaining < *relaisser:* see RELEASE] **1.** the distinctive flavor something has **2.** a trace (of some quality) **3.** an appetizing flavor; pleasing taste **4.** *a)* pleasure; enjoyment *b)* liking or craving **5.** anything that gives pleasure, zest, etc. **6.** pickles, olives, etc. served with a meal to add flavor or as an appetizer —***vt.*** to enjoy; like —***vi.*** **1.** to have the flavor (*of* something) **2.** to have a pleasing taste

re·live (rē liv′) ***vt.*** **-lived′, -liv′ing** to experience again (a past event) as in the imagination

re·lo·cate (rē lō′kāt) ***vt., vi.*** **-cat·ed, -cat·ing** **1.** to locate again **2.** to move to a new location —**re′lo·ca′tion** ***n.***

re·luc·tance (ri luk′təns) ***n.*** **1.** a being reluctant; unwillingness **2.** *Elec.* a measure of the opposition presented to the lines of force in a magnetic circuit

re·luc·tant (-tənt) ***adj.*** [< L. prp. of *reluctari* < *re-*, against + *luctari,* to struggle] **1.** unwilling or disinclined (*to* do something) **2.** marked by unwillingness *[*a *reluctant* answer*]* —**re·luc′tant·ly** ***adv.***

re·ly (ri lī′) ***vi.*** **-lied′, -ly′ing** [< OFr. < L. *religare:* see RELIGION] to have confidence; depend (with *on* or *upon*)

REM (rem) ***n.,*** *pl.* **REMs** [*r(apid) e(ye) m(ovement)*] the periodic, rapid, jerky movement of the eyeballs under closed lids while asleep and dreaming

re·main (ri mān′) ***vi.*** [< OFr. < L. < *re-*, back + *manere,* to stay] **1.** to be left over when the rest has been taken away, destroyed, etc. **2.** to stay on as while others go *[*to *remain* at home*]* **3.** to go on being *[*to *remain* a cynic*]* **4.** to continue to exist; persist *[*hope *remains]* **5.** to be left to be dealt with, done, etc.

re·main·der (-dər) ***n.*** **1.** those remaining **2.** what is left when a part is taken away **3.** a copy or copies of a book still held by the publisher when the sale has fallen off, usually disposed of at a very low price **4.** *Arith. a)* what is left when a smaller number is subtracted from a larger *b)* what is left undivided when one number is not evenly divisible by another —***vt.*** to sell (books, etc.) as remainders

re·mains (ri mānz′) ***n.pl.*** **1.** what is left after part has been used, destroyed, etc. **2.** a dead body; corpse **3.** writings left unpublished by an author at his death

re·make (rē māk′; *for n.* rē′māk′) ***vt.*** **-made′, -mak′ing** to make again or anew —***n.*** **1.** a remaking **2.** something remade, as a motion picture

re·mand (ri mand′) ***vt.*** [< OFr., ult. < L. *re-*, back + *mandare,* to order] **1.** to send back **2.** *Law a)* to send (a prisoner or accused person) back into custody, as to await trial, etc. *b)* to send (a case) back to a lower court for further proceedings —***n.*** a remanding or being remanded

re·mark (ri märk′) ***vt.*** [Fr. *remarquer* < *re-*, again + *marquer,* to mark] **1.** to notice; observe; perceive **2.** to say or write as an observation or comment —***vi.*** to make an observation or comment (with *on* or *upon*) —***n.*** **1.** a noticing or observing **2.** something said briefly; comment

re·mark·a·ble (-ə b'l) ***adj.*** **1.** worthy of remark or notice **2.** unusual; extraordinary —**re·mark′a·ble·ness** ***n.*** —**re·mark′a·bly** ***adv.***

Rem·brandt (Harmensz) van Rijn (rem′brant van rīn′; *Du.* rem′bränt vän rīn′) 1606–69; Du. painter & etcher

re·me·di·a·ble (ri mē′dē ə b'l) ***adj.*** that can be remedied —**re·me′di·a·ble·ness** ***n.*** —**re·me′di·a·bly** ***adv.***

re·me·di·al (-əl) ***adj.*** **1.** providing, or intended to provide, a remedy **2.** *Educ.* of or being a course for helping students having difficulty in the subject *[remedial* reading*]* —**re·me′di·al·ly** ***adv.***

rem·e·dy (rem′ə dē) ***n.,*** *pl.* **-dies** [< Anglo-Fr. < OFr. < L. *remedium* < *re-*, again + *mederi,* to heal] **1.** any medicine or treatment that cures, heals, or relieves a disease or tends to restore health **2.** something that corrects or counteracts an evil or wrong; relief **3.** a legal means by which a violation of a right is prevented or compensated for —***vt.*** **-died, -dy·ing** to act as a remedy for; cure, counteract, correct, etc. —**rem′e·di·less** ***adj.***

re·mem·ber (ri mem′bər) ***vt.*** [< OFr. < LL. < L. *re-*, again + *memorare,* to bring to mind < *memor,* mindful] **1.** to have (an event, thing, person, etc.) come to mind again; think of again **2.** to bring back to mind by an effort; recall **3.** to bear in mind; be careful not to forget **4.** to keep (a person) in mind for a present, legacy, etc. **5.** to mention as sending greetings *[remember* me to your sister*]* —***vi.*** **1.** to bear in mind or call back to mind **2.** to have memory

re·mem·brance (-brəns) ***n.*** **1.** a remembering or being remembered **2.** the power to remember **3.** a memory **4.** the extent of time over which one can remember **5.** a souvenir or keepsake **6.** commemoration **7.** [*pl.*] greetings

Remembrance Day a British and Canadian holiday in November, equivalent to VETERANS DAY

re·mind (ri mīnd′) ***vt., vi.*** [RE- + MIND, *v.*] to put (a person) in mind (*of* something); cause to remember —**re·mind′er** ***n.***

re·mind·ful (-fəl) ***adj.*** reviving memory; reminding

Rem·ing·ton (rem′iŋ tən), **Frederic** 1861–1909; U.S. painter, sculptor, & illustrator

rem·i·nisce (rem′ə nis′) ***vi.*** **-nisced′, -nis′cing** [< ff.] to think, talk, or write about one's past experiences

rem·i·nis·cence (-'ns) ***n.*** [Fr. < LL. < L. prp. of *reminisci* < *re-*, again + *memini,* to remember] **1.** a remembering of past experiences **2.** a memory or recollection **3.** [*pl.*] an account, written or spoken, of remembered experiences

rem·i·nis·cent (-'nt) ***adj.*** **1.** characterized by or given to reminiscence **2.** bringing to mind something else; suggestive (*of*) —**rem′i·nis′cent·ly** ***adv.***

re·miss (ri mis′) ***adj.*** [see REMIT] **1.** careless in, or negligent about, carrying out a task **2.** showing carelessness or negligence —**re·miss′ness** ***n.***

re·mis·si·ble (-ə b'l) ***adj.*** that can be remitted

re·mis·sion (ri mish′ən) ***n.*** the act or an instance of remitting; forgiveness of sins or debts, lessening or leaving of pain or symptoms, etc. —**re·mis′sive** ***adj.***

re·mit (ri mit′) ***vt.*** **-mit′ted, -mit′ting** [< L. *remittere* (pp. *remissus*) < *re-*, back + *mittere,* to send] **1.** to forgive or pardon (sins, etc.) **2.** to free someone from (a debt, tax, penalty, etc.) **3.** to let slacken; lessen *[*without *remitting* one's efforts*]* **4.** to refer (a matter) for consideration, judgment, etc.; specif., *Law same as* REMAND **5.** to send (money) in payment —***vi.*** **1.** *a)* to moderate; slacken *b)* to have its symptoms lessen or disappear: said of an illness **2.** to send money in payment —**re·mit′ment** ***n.*** —**re·mit′ta·ble** ***adj.*** —**re·mit′ter** ***n.***

re·mit·tal (-'l) ***n.*** *same as* REMISSION

re·mit·tance (-'ns) ***n.*** **1.** the sending of money, as by mail **2.** the money sent

re·mit·tent (-'nt) ***adj.*** remitting; abating for a while or at intervals, as a fever —**re·mit′tent·ly** ***adv.***

rem·nant (rem′nənt) ***n.*** [< OFr. prp. of *remaindre:* see REMAIN] **1.** what is left over **2.** [*often pl.*] a small remaining part, amount, or number **3.** a trace; vestige **4.** a piece of cloth, ribbon, etc. left over, as at the end of the bolt —***adj.*** remaining

re·mod·el (rē mäd′'l) ***vt.*** **-eled** or **-elled, -el·ing** or **-el·ling** **1.** to model again **2.** to make over; rebuild

re·mon·strance (ri män′strəns) ***n.*** a remonstrating; protest, complaint, etc., or a statement of this

re·mon·strant (-strənt) ***adj.*** remonstrating —***n.*** a person who remonstrates —**re·mon′strant·ly** ***adv.***

re·mon·strate (-strāt) ***vt.*** **-strat·ed, -strat·ing** [< ML. pp. of *remonstrare* < L. *re-*, again + *monstrare,* to show] to say or plead in protest, objection, etc. —***vi.*** to present and urge reasons in opposition or complaint; protest —**re·mon·stra·tion** (rē′män strā′shən, rem′ən-) ***n.*** —**re·mon′stra·tive** (-strə tiv) ***adj.*** —**re·mon′stra·tive·ly** ***adv.*** —**re·mon′strator** (-strāt ər) ***n.***

rem·o·ra (rem′ər ə) ***n.*** [L., lit., hindrance] an ocean fish with a sucking disc on the head, by which it clings to sharks, ships, etc.

REMORA
(7 in. to 3 ft. long)

re·morse (ri môrs′) ***n.*** [< OFr. < LL. < L. pp. of *remordere* < *re-*, again + *mordere,* to bite] **1.** a deep, torturing sense of guilt over a wrong one has done; self-reproach **2.** pity: now only in **without remorse,** pitilessly —**re·morse′ful** ***adj.*** —**re·morse′ful·ly** ***adv.*** —**re·morse′ful·ness** ***n.*** —**re·morse′less** ***adj.*** —**re·morse′less·ly** ***adv.*** —**re·morse′less·ness** ***n.***

re·mote (ri mōt′) ***adj.*** **-mot′er, -mot′est** [< L. pp. of *removere,* to remove] **1.** distant in space or time; far off **2.** far off and hidden; secluded **3.** distant in connection, relation, etc. [a question *remote* from the subject] **4.** distantly related [a *remote* cousin] **5.** distant in manner; aloof **6.** slight; faint [a *remote* chance] —**re·mote′ly** *adv.* —**re·mote′ness** *n.*

remote control control of aircraft, missiles, or other apparatus from a distance, as by radio waves

re·mount (rē mount′; *for n. usually* rē′mount′) *vt., vi.* to mount again —*n.* a fresh horse to replace another

re·mov·a·ble (ri mo͞o′və b'l) *adj.* that can be removed —**re·mov′a·bil′i·ty** *n.* —**re·mov′a·bly** *adv.*

re·mov·al (ri mo͞o′v'l) *n.* a removing or being removed; esp., *a)* a taking away *b)* dismissal, as from an office *c)* a moving to somewhere else, as of a store

re·move (ri mo͞ov′) *vt.* **-moved′, -mov′ing** [< OFr. < L. *removere:* see RE- & MOVE] **1.** to move (something) from where it is; take away **2.** to take off [*remove* your hat] **3.** *a)* to kill *b)* to dismiss, as from an office *c)* to get rid of [to *remove* the causes of war] **4.** to extract or separate (*from*) —*vi.* **1.** [Poet.] to go away **2.** to move away, as to another place of residence **3.** to be removable [paint that *removes* easily] —*n.* **1.** a removing **2.** the space or time in which a move is made **3.** any step, interval, or degree [but one *remove* from war] —**re·mov′er** *n.*

re·moved (ri mo͞ovd′) *adj.* **1.** distant by (a specified number of degrees of relationship) [one's first cousin once *removed* is the child of one's first cousin] **2.** remote; distant; unconnected (*from*)

re·mu·ner·ate (ri myo͞o′nə rāt′) *vt.* **-at′ed, -at′ing** [< L. pp. of *remunerari,* to reward < *re-,* again + *munus,* a gift] to pay (a person) for (a service, loss, etc.); reward; recompense —**re·mu′ner·a·ble** *adj.* —**re·mu′ner·a′tion** *n.* —**re·mu′ner·a′tive** (-nə rāt′iv, -nər ə tiv) *adj.* —**re·mu′ner·a′tive·ly** *adv.* —**re·mu′ner·a′tive·ness** *n.* —**re·mu′ner·a′tor** *n.*

Re·mus (rē′məs) [L.] *see* ROMULUS

ren·ais·sance (ren′ə säns′, -zäns′; *chiefly Brit.* ri nā′s'ns) *n.* [Fr. < *re-,* again + *naître* (ult. < L. *nasci*), to be born] **1.** a rebirth; revival **2.** [**R-**] *a)* the great revival of art, literature, and learning in Europe in the 14th, 15th, and 16th centuries *b)* the period of this *c)* the style of art, literature, architecture, etc. of this period *d)* any similar revival —*adj.* [**R-**] of, or in the style of, the Renaissance

re·nal (rē′n'l) *adj.* [< Fr. < L. *renalis* < *renes,* kidneys] of or near the kidneys

re·nas·cence (ri nas′'ns, -nās′-) *n.* [*also* **R-**] *same as* RENAISSANCE

re·nas·cent (-'nt) *adj.* [< L.: see RE- & NASCENT] having or showing new life, strength, or vigor

rend (rend) *vt.* **rent, rend′ing** [OE. *rendan*] **1.** to tear or pull with violence (with *from, off,* etc.) **2.** to tear apart or split with violence: often figurative [a roar *rends* the air] —*vi.* to tear; split apart

ren·der (ren′dər) *vt.* [< OFr., ult. < L. < *re-,* back + *dare,* to give] **1.** to hand over, or submit, as for approval, consideration, payment, etc. [*render* an account of your actions] **2.** to give (*up*); surrender **3.** to give in return [*render* good for evil] **4.** to give or pay as due [to *render* thanks] **5.** to cause to be; make [to *render* one helpless] **6.** *a)* to give (aid, etc.) *b)* to do (a service, etc.) **7.** to represent; depict **8.** to recite (a poem, etc.), play (music), act (a role), etc. **9.** to translate **10.** to deliver (a judgment, verdict, etc.) **11.** to melt down (fat) —**ren′der·a·ble** *adj.* —**ren′der·er** *n.* —**ren′der·ing** *n.*

ren·dez·vous (rän′dā vo͞o′, -dē-, -də-) *n., pl.* **-vous′** (-vo͞oz′) [< Fr. *rendez vous,* betake yourself] **1.** a place set for a meeting, as of troops, ships, spacecraft, etc. **2.** a place where people gather; meeting place **3.** *a)* an agreement to meet at a certain time or place *b)* the meeting itself —*vi., vt.* **-voused′** (-vo͞od′), **-vous′ing** (-vo͞o′iŋ) to bring or come together at a rendezvous

ren·di·tion (ren dish′ən) *n.* a rendering or result of rendering; specif., *a)* a performance (*of* a piece of music, a role, etc.) *b)* a translation

ren·e·gade (ren′ə gād′) *n.* [< Sp. pp. of *renegar,* to deny, ult. < L. *re-,* again + *negare,* to deny] a person who abandons his religion, party, principles, etc. to join the other side; apostate; traitor —*adj.* disloyal; traitorous

re·nege (ri nig′, -neg′, -nēg′) *vi.* **-neged′, -neg′ing** [ML. *renegare:* see prec.] **1.** to go back on a promise **2.** *Card Games* to play a card of another suit, against the rules, when holding any of the suit called for —*n. Card Games* an act of reneging —**re·neg′er** *n.*

re·new (ri no͞o′, -nyo͞o′) *vt.* **1.** to make new or as if new again; make fresh or strong again **2.** to cause to exist again; reestablish **3.** to begin again; resume **4.** to go over again; repeat [*renew* a promise] **5.** to replace as by a fresh supply of **6.** to give or get an extension of [to *renew* a lease] —**re·new′a·bil′i·ty** *n.* —**re·new′a·ble** *adj.* —**re·new′al** *n.* —**re·new′ed·ly** *adv.* —**re·new′er** *n.*

ren·i- [< L. *renes,* kidneys] *a combining form meaning* kidney, kidneys

Rennes (ren) city in NW France: pop. 181,000

ren·net (ren′it) *n.* [< OE. *gerennan,* to coagulate] **1.** *a)* the membrane lining the stomach of an unweaned animal, esp. the fourth stomach of a calf *b)* the contents of such a stomach **2.** *a)* an extract of this membrane or of the stomach contents, used to curdle milk, as in making cheese or junket *b)* any substance used to curdle milk

ren·nin (ren′in) *n.* [RENN(ET) + -IN[1]] a coagulating enzyme that can curdle milk, found in rennet

Re·no (rē′nō) [after U.S. Gen. J. L. *Reno* (1823–62)] city in W Nev.: pop. 101,000

Re·noir (rə nwȧr′; *E.* ren′wär), **Pierre Au·guste** (ô güst′) 1841–1919; Fr. painter

re·nounce (ri nouns′) *vt.* **-nounced′, -nounc′ing** [OFr. < L. < *re-,* back + *nuntiare,* to tell < *nuntius,* messenger] **1.** to give up formally (a claim, right, etc.) **2.** to give up (a pursuit, practice, belief, etc.) **3.** to cast off or disown [to *renounce* a son] —**re·nounce′ment** *n.*

ren·o·vate (ren′ə vāt′) *vt.* **-vat′ed, -vat′ing** [< L. pp. of *renovare* < *re-,* again + *novare,* to make new < *novus,* new] to make fresh or sound again, as though new; clean up, replace worn parts in, repair, rebuild, etc. —**ren′o·va′tion** *n.* —**ren′o·va′tive** *adj.* —**ren′o·va′tor** *n.*

re·nown (ri noun′) *n.* [< Anglo-Fr. < OFr. < *re-,* again + *nom(m)er,* to name < L. < *nomen,* a name] great fame or reputation —**re·nowned′** *adj.*

rent[1] (rent) *n.* [< OFr. < LL. hyp. form for L. *reddita* (*pecunia*), paid (money)] **1.** a stated payment at fixed intervals for the use of a house, land, etc. **2.** *Econ.* income from the use of land —*vt.* **1.** to get or give temporary possession of (a house, land, etc.) in return for rent **2.** to get or give temporary use of (a car, tool, etc.) in return for a fee —*vi.* to be leased or let for rent or a fee —**for rent** available to be rented —**rent′a·ble** *adj.* —**rent′er** *n.*

rent[2] (rent) *pt. & pp. of* REND

rent[3] (rent) *n.* [n. use of obs. var. of REND] **1.** a hole or gap made by tearing or splitting **2.** a split in an organization; schism

rent·al (ren′t'l) *n.* **1.** an amount paid or received as rent **2.** a house, apartment, car, etc. offered for rent —*adj.* of, in, or for rent

re·nun·ci·a·tion (ri nun′sē ā′shən) *n.* [< L.: see RENOUNCE] a renouncing, as of a right, claim, pursuit, etc. —**re·nun′ci·a·tive, re·nun′ci·a·to′ry** (-ə tôr′ē) *adj.*

re·or·der (rē ôr′dər) *n.* a repeated order for the same goods —*vt.* **1.** to order again **2.** to put in order again —*vi.* to order goods again

re·or·gan·i·za·tion (rē ôr′gə ni zā′shən, rē′ôr-) *n.* **1.** a reorganizing or being reorganized **2.** a thorough reconstruction of a business corporation as effected after, or in anticipation of, a failure

re·or·gan·ize (rē ôr′gə nīz′) *vt., vi.* **-ized′, -iz′ing** to organize again or anew; effect a reorganization (of) —**re·or′gan·iz′er** *n.*

rep (rep) *n.* [Fr. *reps* < Eng. *ribs*] a ribbed fabric of silk, wool, cotton, rayon, etc.

Rep. 1. Representative **2.** Republic **3.** Republican

rep. 1. repeat **2.** report(ed) **3.** reporter

re·pack·age (rē pak′ij) *vt.* **-aged, -ag·ing** to package again or anew, as in a more secure or attractive package

re·paid (rē pād′) *pt. & pp. of* REPAY

re·pair[1] (ri per′) *vt.* [< OFr. < L. < *re-,* again + *parare,* to prepare] **1.** to put back in good condition after damage, decay, etc.; fix **2.** to renew; restore (one's health, etc.) **3.** to set right; remedy (a mistake, etc.) **4.** to make amends for (a wrong, etc.) —*n.* **1.** a repairing **2.** [*usually pl.*] an instance of, or work done in, repairing **3.** the state of being repaired [a car kept in *repair*] **4.** state with respect to being repaired [in bad *repair*] —**re·pair′a·ble** *adj.* —**re·pair′er** *n.*

re·pair[2] (ri per′) *vi.* [< OFr. < LL. *repatriare* < L. *re-,* back + *patria,* one's native country] to go (*to* a place)

re·pair·man (-mən, -man′) *n., pl.* **-men** (-mən, -men′) a man whose work is repairing things

rep·a·ra·ble (rep′ər ə b'l) *adj.* that can be repaired, remedied, etc. —**rep′a·ra·bly** *adv.*

rep·a·ra·tion (rep′ə rā′shən) *n.* [< MFr. < LL. < pp. of L. *reparare:* see REPAIR[1]] **1.** a repairing or being repaired **2.** a making up for a wrong or injury **3.** compensation; specif., [*usually pl.*] compensation by a defeated nation for damage done by it in a war, payable in money, goods, etc.

rep·ar·tee (rep′ər tē′; -är-; -tā′) *n.* [< Fr. pp. of *repartir,* to reply < *re-,* back + *partir,* to part] **1.** a quick, witty reply; retort **2.** a series of such retorts; banter **3.** skill in making witty replies

re·past (ri past′) *n.* [< OFr. < *re-,* RE- + *past,* food < L. < pp. of *pascere,* to feed] food and drink; a meal

re·pa·tri·ate (rē pā′trē āt′; *for n. usually* -it) *vt., vi.* **-at′ed, -at′ing** [< LL. pp. of *repatriare:* see REPAIR[2]] to send back or return to the country of birth, citizenship, or allegiance [to *repatriate* prisoners of war] —*n.* a person who has been repatriated —**re·pa′tri·a′tion** *n.*

re·pay (ri pā′) *vt.* **-paid′, -pay′ing** [OFr. *repaier*] **1.** *a)* to pay back (money); refund *b)* to pay back (a person) **2.**

to make some return for [*repay* a kindness] **3.** to make some return to (a person), as for some service —***vi.*** to make a repayment or return —**re·pay′a·ble** ***adj.*** —**re·pay′-ment** ***n.***

re·peal (ri pēl′) ***vt.*** [< OFr. *rapeler:* see RE- & APPEAL] to revoke; cancel; annul [to *repeal* a law] —***n.*** the act of repealing —**re·peal′a·ble** ***adj.*** —**re·peal′er** ***n.***

re·peat (ri pēt′) ***vt.*** [< OFr. < L. < *re-*, again + *petere,* to seek] **1.** to say or utter again **2.** to say over; recite, as a poem **3.** to say (something) as said by someone else **4.** to tell to others [to *repeat* a secret] **5.** to do or make again [*repeat* an operation] **6.** to say again what has been said before by (oneself) —***vi.*** **1.** to say or do again what has been said or done before **2.** to occur again; recur **3.** to vote (illegally) more than once in an election —***n.*** **1.** a repeating **2.** *a*) anything said or done again *b*) a rebroadcast of a radio or TV program **3.** *Music* *a*) a passage repeated in playing *b*) a symbol for this —**re·peat′a·bil′i·ty** ***n.*** —**re·peat′a·ble** ***adj.***

re·peat·ed (-id) ***adj.*** said, made, or done again, or again and again —**re·peat′ed·ly** ***adv.***

re·peat·er (-ər) ***n.*** **1.** a person or thing that repeats **2.** *same as* REPEATING FIREARM **3.** a person who fraudulently votes more than once in the same election **4.** a student who repeats a course or grade in school

repeating decimal a decimal in which some digit or group of digits is repeated continuously (Ex.: .3333, .037037)

repeating firearm a firearm that can fire a number of shots (from a magazine or clip) without reloading

re·pel (ri pel′) ***vt.*** **-pelled′, -pel′ling** [< L. < *re-*, back + *pellere,* to drive] **1.** to drive back or force back [to *repel* an attack] **2.** to refuse, reject, or spurn [she *repelled* his attentions] **3.** to cause dislike in; disgust [the odor *repels* me] **4.** *a*) to be resistant to, or present an opposing force to [plastic *repels* water] *b*) to fail to mix with [water *repels* oil] —***vi.*** to cause distaste, dislike, aversion, etc. —**re·pel′-ler** ***n.***

re·pel·lent (-ənt) ***adj.*** **1.** that repels; pushing away or driving back **2.** causing distaste, dislike, etc. **3.** able to resist the absorption of liquid, esp. water, to a limited extent —***n.*** something that repels; specif., *a*) a solution applied to fabric to make it water-repellent *b*) any substance used to repel insects Also **re·pel′lant** —**re·pel′lence, re·pel′-len·cy** ***n.*** —**re·pel′lent·ly** ***adv.***

re·pent (ri pent′) ***vi., vt.*** [< OFr. < VL. < L. *re-*, again + *paenitere,* to repent] **1.** to feel sorry for (a past error, sin, omission, etc.) **2.** to feel such regret over (some past act, intention, etc.) as to change one's mind —**re·pent′er** ***n.***

re·pent·ance (-'ns) ***n.*** a repenting or being penitent; feeling of sorrow, etc., esp. for wrongdoing; remorse —**re·pent′ant** ***adj.*** —**re·pent′ant·ly** ***adv.***

re·peo·ple (rē pē′p'l) ***vt.*** **-pled, -pling** to people anew; provide with new inhabitants

re·per·cus·sion (rē′pər kush′ən, rep′ər-) ***n.*** [< L. pp. of *repercutere:* see RE- & PERCUSSION] **1.** formerly, a recoil **2.** reflection, as of sound **3.** a reaction to some event or action: *usually used in pl.* —**re′per·cus′sive** ***adj.***

rep·er·toire (rep′ər twär′, rep′ə-) ***n.*** [< Fr. < LL. *repertorium:* see ff.] **1.** the stock of plays, operas, roles, songs, etc. that a company, actor, singer, etc. knows and is ready to perform **2.** the stock of special skills of a certain person or group

rep·er·to·ry (rep′ər tôr′ē, rep′ə-) ***n., pl.*** **-ries** [LL. *repertorium* < L. pp. of *reperire,* to discover] **1.** a storehouse, or the things in it **2.** *same as* REPERTOIRE **3.** the system of play production used by a repertory theater

repertory theater a theater whose actors perform several plays a season, alternating them at regular intervals

rep·e·ti·tion (rep′ə tish′ən) ***n.*** [< MFr. < L. *repetitio*] **1.** a repeating; a doing or saying again **2.** something repeated **3.** a copy or imitation —**re·pet′i·tive** (ri pet′ə tiv) ***adj.*** —**re·pet′i·tive·ly** ***adv.***

rep·e·ti·tious (-əs) ***adj.*** full of or using repetition, esp. tiresome or boring repetition —**rep′e·ti′tious·ly** ***adv.*** —**rep′e-ti′tious·ness** ***n.***

re·phrase (rē frāz′) ***vt.*** **-phrased′, -phras′ing** to phrase again, esp. in a different way

re·pine (ri pīn′) ***vi.*** **-pined′, -pin′ing** [RE- + PINE²] to feel or express discontent; complain; fret —**re·pin′er** ***n.*** —**re-pin′ing·ly** ***adv.***

re·place (ri plās′) ***vt.*** **-placed′, -plac′ing** **1.** to put back in a former or the proper place or position **2.** to take the place of **3.** to provide an equivalent for [*replace* a worn tire] **4.** to put back or pay back; restore [*replace* stolen goods] —**re·place′a·ble** ***adj.*** —**re·plac′er** ***n.***

re·place·ment (-mənt) ***n.*** **1.** a replacing or being replaced **2.** a person or thing that takes the place of another that is lost, worn out, dismissed, etc.

re·plen·ish (ri plen′ish) ***vt.*** [< OFr. < L. *re-*, again + *plenus,* full] **1.** to make full or complete again, as with a new supply **2.** to supply again with fuel, etc. —**re-plen′ish·er** ***n.*** —**re·plen′ish·ment** ***n.***

re·plete (ri plēt′) ***adj.*** [< OFr. < L. pp. of *replere* < *re-*, again + *plere,* to fill] **1.** well-filled; plentifully supplied **2.** stuffed with food and drink —**re·ple′tion** ***n.***

re·plev·in (ri plev′in) ***n.*** [< OFr. *re-*, again + *plevir,* to pledge] *Law* **1.** the recovery by a person of goods claimed to be his, on his promise to test the matter in court and give up the goods if defeated **2.** the writ by which this is done —***vt.*** to take back (goods) under such a writ: usually **re·plev′y** **-plev′ied, -plev′y·ing**

rep·li·ca (rep′li kə) ***n.*** [It. < ML. < L. *replicare:* see REPLY] a reproduction or close copy, esp. of a work of art

rep·li·ca·tion (rep′lə kā′shən) ***n.*** [< MFr. < L. < pp. of *replicare:* see ff.] *Law* the plaintiff's answer to the plea of the defendant

re·ply (ri plī′) ***vi.*** **-plied′, -ply′ing** [< OFr. < L. < *re-*, back + *plicare,* to fold] **1.** to answer in speech or writing **2.** to respond by some action [to *reply* to enemy fire] **3.** *Law* to answer a defendant's plea —***vt.*** to say in answer [she *replied* that she agreed] —***n., pl.*** **-plies′** **1.** an answer in speech or writing **2.** a response by some action —**re-pli′er** ***n.***

re·port (ri pôrt′) ***vt.*** [< OFr. < L. < *re-*, back + *portare,* to carry] **1.** to give an account of; give information about; recount **2.** to carry and repeat (a message, etc.) **3.** to write an account of for publication, as in a newspaper **4.** to make known the presence, approach, etc. of **5.** to give an official account of **6.** to present (something referred for study, etc.) with conclusions, recommendations, etc. [the committee *reported* the bill out] **7.** to make a charge about (an offense or offender) to a person in authority —***vi.*** **1.** to make a report **2.** to work as a reporter **3.** to present oneself or make one's presence known [to *report* for duty] **4.** to be responsible (*to* a superior) —***n.*** **1.** rumor; gossip [*report* has it that he will resign] **2.** reputation [a man of good *report*] **3.** a statement or account brought in and presented, often for publication **4.** a formal or official presentation of facts or of the record of an investigation, court case, etc. **5.** a loud noise, esp. one made by an explosion —**re·port′a·ble** ***adj.*** —**re·port′ed-ly** ***adv.*** —**re·port′ing** ***n.***

re·port·age (-ij) ***n.*** the reporting of news events

report card a written report of a pupil's progress and behavior, sent to his parents or guardian at regular intervals

re·port·er (-ər) ***n.*** a person who reports; specif., *a*) a person who reports legal or legislative proceedings *b*) a person who gathers information and writes reports for a newspaper, magazine, etc. *c*) a person who reports news on radio or TV —**rep·or·to·ri·al** (rep′ər tôr′ē əl) ***adj.*** —**rep′or·to′ri·al·ly** ***adv.***

re·pose¹ (ri pōz′) ***vt.*** **-posed′, -pos′ing** [< OFr. < LL. < L. *re-*, again + LL. *pausare,* to rest] to lay or place for rest [to *repose* oneself on a bed] —***vi.*** **1.** to lie at rest **2.** to rest from work, travel, etc. **3.** to rest in death or a grave **4.** to rest or be supported [the shale *reposes* on limestone] —***n.*** **1.** a reposing, or resting **2.** *a*) rest *b*) sleep **3.** ease of manner; composure **4.** calm; peace —**re·pose′ful** ***adj.*** —**re·pose′ful·ly** ***adv.***

re·pose² (ri pōz′) ***vt.*** **-posed′, -pos′ing** [< L. *repositus:* see ff.] **1.** to place (trust, etc.) in someone **2.** to place (power, etc.) in the control of someone

re·pos·i·to·ry (ri päz′ə tôr′ē) ***n., pl.*** **-ries** [< L. < pp. of *reponere* < *re-*, back + *ponere,* to place] **1.** a box, chest, closet, or room in which things may be placed for safekeeping **2.** a center for storing [a *repository* of information] **3.** a person to whom something is confided

re·pos·sess (rē′pə zes′) ***vt.*** to get possession of again; specif., to take back from a buyer who has failed to keep up payments —**re′pos·ses′sion** (-zesh′ən) ***n.***

rep·re·hend (rep′ri hend′) ***vt.*** [< L. < *re-*, back + *prehendere,* to take] **1.** to reprimand or rebuke (a person) **2.** to find fault with (something done) —**rep·re·hen·sion** (-hen′shən) ***n.*** —**rep′re·hen′sive** ***adj.*** —**rep′re·hen′sive-ly** ***adv.***

rep·re·hen·si·ble (-hen′sə b'l) ***adj.*** deserving to be reprehended —**rep′re·hen′si·bil′i·ty** ***n.*** —**rep′re·hen′si·bly** ***adv.***

rep·re·sent (rep′ri zent′) ***vt.*** [< OFr. < L.: see RE- & PRESENT, *v.*] **1.** to present or picture to the mind **2.** to present or be a likeness of **3.** to describe or set forth, often in order to influence, persuade, etc. **4.** *a*) to be a sign or symbol for [*x represents* the unknown] *b*) to express by symbols, characters, etc. **5.** to be the equivalent of [a cave *represents* home to them] **6.** to act the part of (a character), as in a play **7.** to act in place of; be a substitute for

8. to speak and act for by conferred authority, as a legislator for his constituents **9.** to serve as a specimen, example, type, etc. of —**rep′re·sent′a·ble** ***adj.***

rep·re·sen·ta·tion (rep′ri zen tā′shən) ***n.*** **1.** a representing or being represented **2.** legislative representatives, collectively **3.** a likeness, image, etc. **4.** *[often pl.]* an account of facts, arguments, etc. intended to influence action, etc. **5.** the production or performance of a play, etc.

rep·re·sen·ta·tion·al (-'l) ***adj.*** **1.** of representation **2.** designating or of art that represents in recognizable form objects in nature —**rep′re·sen·ta′tion·al·ism** ***n.*** —**rep′re·sen·ta′tion·al·ist** ***n.*** —**rep′re·sen·ta′tion·al·ly** ***adv.***

rep·re·sen·ta·tive (rep′rə zen′tə tiv) ***adj.*** **1.** representing; specif., *a)* picturing; portraying *b)* acting in the place of or on behalf of another or others; esp., serving as an elected delegate **2.** of or based on representation of the people by elected delegates *[representative* government*]* **3.** typical —***n.*** **1.** an example or type **2.** a person authorized to act or speak for others, as an elected legislator or a salesman, agent, etc. **3.** [**R-**] a member of the lower house of Congress or of a State legislature —**rep′re·sent′a·tive·ly** ***adv.*** —**rep′re·sent′a·tive·ness** ***n.***

re·press (ri pres′) ***vt.*** [< L. pp. of *reprimere:* see RE- & PRESS[1]] **1.** to hold back; restrain *[*to *repress* a sigh*]* **2.** to put down; subdue **3.** to control so strictly as to stifle free, natural behavior *[*to *repress* a child*]* **4.** *Psychiatry a)* to force (painful ideas, impulses, etc.) into the unconscious *b)* to prevent (unconscious ideas, etc.) from becoming conscious —**re·press′er, re·pres′sor** ***n.*** —**re·press′i·ble** ***adj.*** —**re·pres′sive** ***adj.*** —**re·pres′sive·ly** ***adv.*** —**re·pres′sive·ness** ***n.***

re-press (rē′pres′) ***vt.*** to press again; esp., to make new copies of (a recording) from the original master

re·pres·sion (ri presh′ən) ***n.*** **1.** a repressing or being repressed **2.** *Psychiatry* what is repressed

re·prieve (ri prēv′) ***vt.*** **-prieved′, -priev′ing** [ult. < Fr. pp. of *reprendere,* to take back] **1.** to postpone the punishment of; esp., to postpone the execution of (a condemned person) **2.** to give temporary relief to, as from pain —***n.*** a reprieving or being reprieved; specif., *a)* a postponement of a penalty, esp. of execution *b)* a temporary relief, as from trouble or pain

rep·ri·mand (rep′rə mand′; *also for v.,* rep′rə mand′) ***n.*** [< Fr. < L. *reprimendus,* that is to be repressed < *reprimere,* REPRESS] a severe or formal rebuke —***vt.*** to rebuke severely or formally

re·print (rē print′; *for n. usually* rē′print′) ***vt.*** to print again; print an additional impression of —***n.*** something reprinted; specif., an additional impression or edition, as of an earlier book, pamphlet, etc.

re·pris·al (ri prī′z'l) ***n.*** [< MFr. < It. < *riprendere,* to take back < L. *reprehendere:* see REPREHEND] **1.** the use of force, short of war, against another nation to obtain redress of grievances **2.** injury done in return for injury received, esp. in war, as the killing of prisoners

re·prise (ri prēz′) ***n.*** [< OFr. pp. of *reprendre,* to take back] in a musical play, the repetition of all or part of a song performed earlier —***vt.*** **-prised′, -pris′ing** to present a reprise of (a song)

re·pro (rē′prō) ***n., pl.*** **-pros** *shortened form of* REPRODUCTION PROOF: also **repro proof**

re·proach (ri prōch′) ***vt.*** [OFr. *reprochier:* ult. < L. *re-,* back + *prope,* near] to accuse of and blame for a fault; rebuke; reprove —***n.*** **1.** shame, disgrace, or blame, or a source or cause of this **2.** a blaming, or an expression of blame; rebuke —**re·proach′a·ble** ***adj.*** —**re·proach′er** ***n.*** —**re·proach′ing·ly** ***adv.***

re·proach·ful (-fəl) ***adj.*** full of or expressing reproach —**re·proach′ful·ly** ***adv.*** —**re·proach′ful·ness** ***n.***

rep·ro·bate (rep′rə bat′) ***vt.*** **-bat′ed, -bat′ing** [< LL. pp. of *reprobare:* see REPROVE] **1.** to disapprove of strongly; condemn **2.** to reject or abandon —***adj.*** **1.** depraved; corrupt **2.** *Theol.* lost in sin; rejected by God —***n.*** a reprobate person —**rep′ro·ba′tion** ***n.*** —**rep′ro·ba′tive** ***adj.***

re·pro·duce (rē′prə do͞os′, -dyo͞os′) ***vt.*** **-duced′, -duc′ing** to produce again; specif., *a)* to bring forth others of (its kind), esp. by sexual intercourse *b)* to make (a lost part or organ) grow again *c)* to make a copy, imitation, etc. of (a picture, sound, etc.) *d)* to repeat —***vi.*** **1.** to produce offspring, esp. by sexual intercourse **2.** to undergo copying, duplication, etc. —**re′pro·duc′er** ***n.*** —**re′pro·duc′i·ble** ***adj.***

re·pro·duc·tion (rē′prə duk′shən) ***n.*** **1.** a reproducing or being reproduced **2.** something made by reproducing; copy **3.** the process by which animals and plants produce new individuals

reproduction proof an especially fine proof of type, etc. to be photographed for making a printing plate

re·pro·duc·tive (-tiv) ***adj.*** **1.** reproducing **2.** of or for reproduction —**re′pro·duc′tive·ly** ***adv.*** —**re′pro·duc′tive·ness** ***n.***

re·proof (ri pro͞of′) ***n.*** a reproving or something said in reproving; rebuke: also **re·prov′al** (-pro͞o′v'l)

re·prove (ri pro͞ov′) ***vt.*** **-proved′, -prov′ing** [< OFr. < LL. *reprobare:* see RE- & PROVE] **1.** to speak to in disapproval; rebuke **2.** to express disapproval of (something done or said) —**re·prov′a·ble** ***adj.*** —**re·prov′er** ***n.*** —**re·prov′ingly** ***adv.***

rep·tile (rep′t'l, -tīl) ***n.*** [LL. < neut. of L. *reptilis,* crawling < pp. of *repere,* to creep] **1.** any of a group of coldblooded vertebrates having a body covered with scales or horny plates and including snakes, lizards, turtles, crocodiles, etc. and dinosaurs **2.** a mean, sneaky person —***adj.*** of or like a reptile —**rep·til·i·an** (rep til′ē ən) ***adj., n.***

re·pub·lic (ri pub′lik) ***n.*** [< MFr. < L. < *res,* thing + *publica,* public] **1.** a nation in which the supreme power rests in all the citizens entitled to vote and is exercised by representatives elected by them **2.** the government of such a state **3.** a nation with a president as its head **4.** any of certain divisions of the U.S.S.R. or Yugoslavia

re·pub·li·can (ri pub′li kən) ***adj.*** **1.** of or like a republic **2.** favoring a republic **3.** [**R-**] of the Republican Party —***n.*** **1.** a person who favors a republican form of government **2.** [**R-**] a member of the Republican Party

re·pub·li·can·ism (-iz'm) ***n.*** **1.** republican government **2.** republican principles, or adherence to them **3.** [**R-**] the policies, etc. of the Republican Party

Republican Party one of the two major political parties in the U.S., organized in 1854

re·pu·di·ate (ri pyo͞o′dē āt′) ***vt.*** **-at′ed, -at′ing** [< L. pp. of *repudiare,* to divorce < *repudium,* separation] **1.** to disown or cast off publicly **2.** *a)* to refuse to accept or support (a belief, treaty, etc.) *b)* to deny the truth of (a charge, etc.) **3.** to refuse to acknowledge or pay (a debt, etc.) —**re·pu′di·a′tion** ***n.*** —**re·pu′di·a′tor** ***n.***

re·pug·nance (ri pug′nəns) ***n.*** [< MFr. < L. < prp. of *repugnare* < *re-,* back + *pugnare,* to fight] **1.** inconsistency **2.** extreme dislike or distaste Also **re·pug′nan·cy**

re·pug·nant (-nənt) ***adj.*** **1.** contradictory or opposed **2.** causing repugnance; offensive —**re·pug′nant·ly** ***adv.***

re·pulse (ri puls′) ***vt.*** **-pulsed′, -puls′ing** [< L. pp. of *repellere,* REPEL] **1.** to drive back; repel (an attack, etc.) **2.** to repel with discourtesy, coldness, etc.; rebuff **3.** to be repulsive to —***n.*** **1.** a repelling or being repelled **2.** a refusal, rejection, or rebuff

re·pul·sion (ri pul′shən) ***n.*** **1.** a repelling or being repelled **2.** strong dislike, distaste, or aversion **3.** *Physics* the mutual action by which bodies or particles of matter tend to repel each other: opposed to ATTRACTION

re·pul·sive (-siv) ***adj.*** **1.** tending to repel **2.** causing strong dislike or aversion **3.** of repulsion —**re·pul′sively** ***adv.*** —**re·pul′sive·ness** ***n.***

rep·u·ta·ble (rep′yoo tə b'l) ***adj.*** **1.** having a good reputation; respectable **2.** in proper or good usage *[*a *reputable* word*]* —**rep′u·ta·bil′i·ty** ***n.*** —**rep′u·ta·bly** ***adv.***

rep·u·ta·tion (rep′yoo tā′shən) ***n.*** [< L. < pp. of *reputare:* see ff.] **1.** the regard, favorable or not, shown for a person or thing by the public, community, etc.; repute **2.** such regard when favorable *[*to lose one's *reputation]* **3.** fame; distinction

re·pute (ri pyo͞ot′) ***vt.*** **-put′ed, -put′ing** [< MFr. < L. < *re-,* again + *putare,* to think] to consider to be as specified *[*he is *reputed* to be rich*]* —***n.*** *same as* REPUTATION (senses 1, 3)

re·put·ed (-id) ***adj.*** generally regarded as being such *[*the *reputed* owner*]* —**re·put′ed·ly** ***adv.***

re·quest (ri kwest′) ***n.*** [< OFr. < ML., ult. < L. *requirere:* see REQUIRE] **1.** an asking for something; petition **2.** something asked for **3.** state of being asked for; demand *[*a song much in *request]* —***vt.*** **1.** to ask for, esp. in a polite or formal way **2.** to ask (a person) to do something —**by request** in response to a request

Re·qui·em (rek′wē əm, rāk′-, rēk′-) ***n.*** [L., acc. of *requies,* rest: first word of the Mass] *[also* **r-**] **1.** *R.C.Ch. a)* a Mass for the repose of the dead *b)* a musical setting for this **2.** a dirge

‡**re·qui·es·cat in pa·ce** (rāk′wē es′kät in pä′chā, rek′-) [L.] may he (or she) rest in peace

re·quire (ri kwīr′) ***vt.*** **-quired′, -quir′ing** [< OFr. < L. *requirere* < *re-,* again + *quaerere,* to ask] **1.** to ask or insist upon, as by right or authority; demand **2.** to order; command *[*to *require* him to go*]* **3.** to need *[*to *require* help*]* **4.** to call for as needed *[*the work *requires* skill*]* —***vi.*** to make a demand

re·quire·ment (-mənt) ***n.*** **1.** a requiring **2.** something required or demanded **3.** something needed; necessity

req·ui·site (rek′wə zit) ***adj.*** [< L. pp. of *requirere:* see REQUIRE] required; necessary; indispensable —***n.*** something requisite

req·ui·si·tion (rek′wə zish′ən) ***n.*** **1.** a requiring, as by authority **2.** a formal written request, as for equipment **3.** the state of being demanded for use —***vt.*** **1.** to demand or take, as by authority *[*to *requisition* food for troops*]* **2.** to demand from *[*to *requisition* a town for food*]* **3.** to submit a written request for (equipment, etc.)

re·quite (ri kwīt′) ***vt.*** **-quit′ed, -quit′ing [**RE- + *quite,* obs. var. of QUIT**]** to repay or make return to (a person, group, etc.) for (a benefit, service, etc. or an injury, wrong, etc.) —**re·quit′al** ***n.*** —**re·quit′er** ***n.***

rere·dos (rir′däs, rer′ə-) ***n.*** **[**< Anglo-Fr. < OFr. *arere* (see ARREARS) + *dos,* back**]** an ornamental screen or partition wall behind an altar in a church

re·route (rē ro͞ot′, -rout′) ***vt.*** **-rout′ed, -rout′ing** to send by a new or different route

re·run (rē run′; *for n.* rē′run′) ***vt.*** **-ran′, -run′ning** to run again —***n.*** **1.** a rerunning; esp., a repeat showing of a movie, taped TV program, etc. **2.** the movie, etc. so shown

res (rās, rēz) ***n., pl.*** **res [**L., a thing**]** *Law* **1.** a thing; object **2.** matter; case; point; action

res. 1. reserve **2.** residence **3.** resides **4.** resolution

re·sal·a·ble (rē sāl′ə b'l) ***adj.*** that can be sold again

re·sale (rē′sāl′) ***n.*** the act of selling again

re·scind (ri sind′) ***vt.*** **[**L. *rescindere* < *re-,* back + *scindere,* to cut**]** to revoke, repeal, or cancel (a law, order, etc.) —**re·scind′a·ble** ***adj.*** —**re·scind′er** ***n.***

re·scis·sion (ri sizh′ən) ***n.*** a rescinding

re·script (rē′skript) ***n.*** **[**< L. < pp. of *rescribere* < *re-,* back + *scribere,* to write**]** an official decree or order; specif., one issued by a court to its clerk

res·cue (res′kyo͞o) ***vt.*** **-cued, -cu·ing [**< OFr. < *re-,* again + *escorre,* to shake < L. < *ex-,* off + *quatere,* to shake**]** **1.** to free or save from danger, evil, etc. **2.** *Law* to take out of legal custody by force —***n.*** a rescuing —**res′cu·a·ble** ***adj.*** —**res′cu·er** ***n.***

re·search (ri surch′; *for n. equally* rē′surch) ***n.*** **[**< MFr.: see RE- & SEARCH**]** [*sometimes pl.*] systematic investigation in a field of knowledge, to discover or establish facts or principles —***vi., vt.*** to do research (on or in) —**re·search′a·ble** ***adj.*** —**re·search′er, re·search′ist** ***n.***

re·seat (rē sēt′) ***vt.*** **1.** to seat again or in another seat **2.** to supply with a new seat or seats

re·sect (ri sekt′) ***vt.*** **[**< L. pp. of *resecare* < *re-,* back + *secare,* to cut**]** *Surgery* to remove part of (an organ, bone, etc.) —**re·sec′tion** ***n.***

re·sem·blance (ri zem′bləns) ***n.*** **1.** a resembling; likeness **2.** a point, degree, or sort of likeness

re·sem·ble (ri zem′b'l) ***vt.*** **-bled, -bling [**< OFr. < *re-,* again + *sembler* < L. *simulare:* see SIMULATE**]** to be like or similar to in appearance or nature

re·sent (ri zent′) ***vt.*** **[**< Fr. < OFr. < *re-,* again + *sentir* < L. *sentire,* to feel**]** to feel or show hurt or indignation at (some act, etc.) or toward (a person), from a sense of being offended —**re·sent′ful** ***adj.*** —**re·sent′ful·ly** ***adv.*** —**re·sent′ful·ness** ***n.*** —**re·sent′ment** ***n.***

re·ser·pine (ri sur′pin, -pēn; res′ər pēn′) ***n.*** **[**G. *reserpin***]** a crystalline alkaloid, $C_{33}H_{40}N_2O_9$, obtained from the root of a rauwolfia: used in the treatment of hypertension and as a sedative

res·er·va·tion (rez′ər vā′shən) ***n.*** **1.** a reserving or the thing reserved; specif., *a*) public land set aside for some special use *[*an Indian *reservation]* *b*) an arrangement by which a hotel room, theater ticket, etc. is set aside for use at a certain time or until called for *c*) anything so reserved **2.** a limiting condition or qualification, expressed or implied: see also MENTAL RESERVATION

re·serve (ri zurv′) ***vt.*** **-served′, -serv′ing [**< OFr. < L. < *re-,* back + *servare,* to hold**]** **1.** to keep back, store up, or set apart for later use or a special purpose **2.** to hold over to a later time **3.** to set aside or have set aside (a theater seat, etc.) for someone **4.** to retain for oneself *[*to *reserve* the right to refuse*]* —***n.*** **1.** something reserved **2.** a limitation: now rare except in **without reserve** (see below) **3.** the practice of keeping one's thoughts, feelings, etc. to oneself; aloofness **4.** reticence; silence **5.** restraint in artistic expression; freedom from exaggeration **6.** [*pl.*] *a*) manpower kept out of action and ready for emergency use or for replacing others *b*) military forces not on active duty but subject to call; militia (with *the*) **7.** cash, or any liquid assets, kept aside by a bank, business, etc. to meet expected or unexpected demands **8.** land set apart for special use —***adj.*** being, or having the nature of, a reserve —**in reserve** reserved for later use —**without reserve** subject to no limitation

re·served (ri zurvd′) ***adj.*** **1.** set apart for some purpose, person, etc. **2.** showing reserve; aloof or reticent —**re·serv′ed·ly** (-zur′vid lē) ***adv.*** —**re·serv′ed·ness** ***n.***

re·serv·ist (ri zur′vist) ***n.*** a member of a country's military reserves

res·er·voir (rez′ər vwär′, rez′ə-; -vwôr′, -vôr′) ***n.*** **[**< Fr. < *réserver:* see RESERVE**]** **1.** a place where anything is collected and stored; esp., a natural or artificial lake in which water is stored for use **2.** a receptacle (in an apparatus) for a fluid, as oil or ink **3.** a reserve supply

re·set (rē set′; *for n.* rē′set′) ***vt.*** **-set′, -set′ting** to set again —***n.*** **1.** a resetting **2.** something reset **3.** a device for resetting something

re·ship (rē ship′) ***vt.*** **-shipped′, -ship′ping 1.** to ship again **2.** to transfer to another ship —**re·ship′ment** ***n.***

re·side (ri zīd′) ***vi.*** **-sid′ed, -sid′ing [**< MFr. < L. *residere* < *re-,* back + *sedere,* to sit**]** **1.** to dwell for a long time; live (*in* or *at*) **2.** to be present or exist (*in*): said of qualities, etc. **3.** to be vested (*in*): said of rights, powers, etc.

res·i·dence (rez′i dəns) ***n.*** **1.** a residing **2.** the fact or status of living or staying in a place while working or in training, school, etc. **3.** the place where one resides; one's abode; esp., a house or mansion **4.** the time during which a person resides in a place

res·i·den·cy (-dən sē) ***n., pl.*** **-cies 1.** *same as* RESIDENCE **2.** a period of advanced, specialized medical or surgical training at a hospital

res·i·dent (-dənt) ***adj.*** **1.** having a residence (*in* or *at*); residing **2.** being in residence (sense 2) *[*a *resident* physician of a hospital*]* **3.** present or existing (*in*) **4.** not migratory: said of birds, etc. —***n.*** **1.** a person who lives in a place and is not a visitor or transient **2.** a doctor who is serving a residency **3.** a nonmigratory bird, etc.

res·i·den·tial (rez′ə den′shəl) ***adj.*** **1.** of or connected with residence **2.** of or suitable for residences, or homes *[*a *residential* area*]* **3.** chiefly for residents rather than transients *[*a *residential* hotel*]* —**res′i·den′tial·ly** ***adv.***

re·sid·u·al (ri zij′oo wəl) ***adj.*** of or like a residue; leftover; remaining —***n.*** **1.** something remaining, as at the end of a process **2.** [*pl.*] extra fees paid to performers for reruns, as on TV **3.** *Math.* the difference between an actual and an estimated value —**re·sid′u·al·ly** ***adv.***

re·sid·u·ar·y (-oo wer′ē) ***adj.*** **1.** residual; leftover **2.** *Law* *a*) relating to the residue of an estate *b*) receiving such a residue *[*a *residuary* legatee*]*

res·i·due (rez′ə do͞o′, -dyo͞o′) ***n.*** **[**< MFr. < L. neut. of *residuus,* remaining < *residere:* see RESIDE**]** **1.** what is left after part is removed; remainder **2.** *Chem.* matter remaining after evaporation, combustion, etc. **3.** *Law* that part of a testator's estate left after all claims and bequests have been satisfied

re·sid·u·um (ri zij′oo wəm) ***n., pl.*** **-u·a** (-wə) **[**L.**]** *same as* RESIDUE

re·sign (ri zīn′) ***vt., vi.*** **[**< MFr. < L. < *re-,* back + *signare,* to sign**]** to give up or relinquish (a claim, office, position, etc.), esp. by formal notice (often with *from*) —**resign oneself (to)** to submit or become reconciled (to)

res·ig·na·tion (rez′ig nā′shən) ***n.*** **1.** *a*) a resigning *b*) formal notice of this, esp. in writing **2.** patient submission; acquiescence

re·signed (ri zīnd′) ***adj.*** feeling or showing resignation —**re·sign′ed·ly** (-zīn′id lē) ***adv.*** —**re·sign′ed·ness** ***n.***

re·sil·ience (ri zil′yəns, -ē əns) ***n.*** the quality of being resilient: also **re·sil′ien·cy**

re·sil·ient (-yənt, -ē ənt) ***adj.*** **[**< L. prp. of *resilire* < *re-,* back + *salire,* to jump**]** **1.** springing back into shape, position, etc. after being stretched, bent, or compressed **2.** recovering strength, spirits, etc. quickly —**re·sil′ient·ly** ***adv.***

res·in (rez′'n) ***n.*** **[**< MFr. < L. *resina***]** **1.** a solid or semisolid, viscous, organic substance exuded from various plants and trees: natural resins are used in varnishes and lacquers **2.** *same as:* *a*) SYNTHETIC RESIN *b*) ROSIN —***vt.*** to treat or rub with resin: also **res′in·ate′** (-ə nāt′) **-at′ed, -at′ing** —**res′in·ous, res′in·y** ***adj.***

re·sist (ri zist′) ***vt.*** **[**< MFr. < L. < *re-,* back + *sistere,* to set**]** **1.** to withstand; fend off; stand firm against **2.** *a*) to oppose actively; fight or work against *b*) to refuse to cooperate with, submit to, etc. **3.** to keep from yielding to or enjoying —***vi.*** to oppose or withstand something; offer resistance —***n.*** a resistant substance, as a protective coating —**re·sist′er** ***n.*** —**re·sist′i·bil′i·ty** ***n.*** —**re·sist′i·ble** ***adj.*** —**re·sis′tive** ***adj.*** —**re·sis·tiv·i·ty** (rē′zis tiv′ə tē, ri-zis′-) ***n.***

re·sist·ance (ri zis′təns) ***n.*** **1.** a resisting; opposition **2.** power or capacity to resist; specif., the ability of an organism to ward off disease **3.** opposition of some force, thing, etc. to another **4.** a force that retards or opposes motion **5.** [*often* **R-**] an underground movement in a country fighting against a foreign occupying power, etc. **6.** *Elec.* *a*) the property by which a conductor opposes current flow and thus generates heat *b*) *same as* RESISTOR —**re·sist′ant** ***adj., n.***

re·sist·less (ri zist′lis) ***adj.*** **1.** that cannot be resisted; irresistible **2.** without power to resist —**re·sist′less·ly** ***adv.*** —**re·sist′less·ness** ***n.***

re·sis·tor (ri zis′tər) ***n.*** *Elec.* a device, as a wire coil, used to produce resistance in a circuit

fat, āpe, cär; ten, ēven; is, bīte; gō, hôrn, to͞ol, look; oil, out; up, fur; get; joy; yet; chin; she; thin, *th*en; zh, leisure; ŋ, ring; ə for *a* in *ago, e* in *agent, i* in *sanity, o* in *comply, u* in *focus;* ′ as in *able* (ā′b'l); Fr. bål; ë, Fr. coeur; ö, Fr. feu; Fr. mo*n*; ô, Fr. coq; ü, Fr. duc; *r,* Fr. cri; H, G. ich; kh, G. doch; ‡foreign; *hypothetical; < derived from. See inside front cover.

re·sole (rē′sōl′) ***vt.*** **-soled′, -sol′ing** to put a new sole on (a shoe, etc.) —***n.*** a new sole for a shoe, etc.

re·sol·u·ble (ri zäl′yoo b'l, rez′əl-) ***adj.*** that can be resolved —**re·sol′u·bil′i·ty, re·sol′u·ble·ness** ***n.***

res·o·lute (rez′ə lo͞ot′) ***adj.*** [< L. pp. of *resolvere:* see RE- & SOLVE] having or showing a fixed, firm purpose; determined; resolved —**res′o·lute′ly** ***adv.*** —**res′o·lute′ness** ***n.***

res·o·lu·tion (rez′ə lo͞o′shən) ***n.*** **1.** *a)* a resolving of something or breaking it up into its separate parts *b)* the result of this **2.** *a)* a determining or deciding *b)* a decision as to future action **3.** a resolute quality of mind **4.** a formal statement of opinion adopted by a group **5.** a solving or answering; solution **6.** the unraveling of the plot in a drama or narrative

re·solve (ri zälv′, -zôlv′) ***vt.*** **-solved′, -solv′ing** [< L.: see RE- & SOLVE] **1.** to break up into separate parts; analyze **2.** to change or transform [the talk *resolved* itself into a dispute] **3.** to cause to decide [this *resolved* him to go] **4.** to reach as a decision; determine [to *resolve* to go] **5.** *a)* to find an answer to; solve *b)* to make a decision about, esp. by vote or formally *c)* to explain or make clear (a problem, a fictional plot, etc.) *d)* to remove (doubt, etc.) **6.** *Music* to make (a dissonant chord or tone) become consonant —***vi.*** **1.** to be resolved, as by analysis **2.** to come to a decision —***n.*** **1.** a fixed purpose or intention **2.** a formal resolution, as by a group —**re·solv′a·bil′i·ty** ***n.*** —**re·solv′a·ble** ***adj.*** —**re·solv′er** ***n.***

re·solved (-zälvd′, -zôlvd′) ***adj.*** firm and fixed in purpose; resolute —**re·solv′ed·ly** (-zäl′vid lē, -zôl′-) ***adv.***

res·o·nance (rez′ə nəns) ***n.*** **1.** a being resonant **2.** the reinforcing and prolonging of a sound or musical tone by reflection or by sympathetic vibration of other bodies **3.** *Elec.* the condition arising in a circuit when an incoming current is at the same, or nearly the same, frequency as the circuit, thus producing much greater currents **4.** *Physics* the effect produced when the natural vibration frequency of a body is greatly amplified by vibrations at this same frequency from another body

res·o·nant (-nənt) ***adj.*** [< L. prp. of *resonare,* to resound] **1.** resounding or reechoing **2.** producing resonance [*resonant* walls] **3.** of, full of, or intensified by resonance [a *resonant* voice] —**res′o·nant·ly** ***adv.***

res·o·nate (-nāt′) ***vi., vt.*** **-nat′ed, -nat′ing** to be or make resonant

res·o·na·tor (-nāt′ər) ***n.*** **1.** a device for producing resonance or increasing sound by resonance **2.** *Electronics* an apparatus or system that can be put into oscillation by oscillations in another system

re·sorb (ri sôrb′) ***vt.*** [< L. < *re-,* again + *sorbere,* to suck up] to absorb again —**re·sorp′tion** (-sôrp′shən) ***n.***

res·or·cin·ol (ri zôr′si nōl′, -nôl′) ***n.*** [< RES(IN) + It. *orcello,* a kind of lichen] a colorless crystalline compound, $C_6H_4(OH)_2$, used in making dyes, celluloid, pharmaceuticals, etc.: also **res·or′cin** (-sin)

re·sort (ri zôrt′) ***vi.*** [< OFr. < *re-,* again + *sortir,* to go out] **1.** to go; esp., to go often **2.** to have recourse; turn (*to*) for help, support, etc. —***n.*** **1.** a place people often go to for rest or recreation, as on a vacation **2.** a frequent getting together or visiting [a place of general *resort*] **3.** a person or thing one turns to for help, support, etc. **4.** a turning for help, support, etc.; recourse —**as a** (or **the**) **last resort** as the last available means

re·sound (ri zound′) ***vi.*** [< OFr. < L. < *re-,* again + *sonare,* to sound] **1.** to echo or be filled with sound; reverberate **2.** to make a loud, echoing or prolonged sound **3.** to be echoed **4.** to be praised —***vt.*** **1.** to give back (sound); echo **2.** to give forth or utter loudly

re·sound·ing (-iŋ) ***adj.*** **1.** reverberating **2.** thoroughgoing; complete [a *resounding* victory] **3.** high-sounding —**re·sound′ing·ly** ***adv.***

re·source (rē′sôrs, -zôrs; ri sôrs′, -zôrs′) ***n.*** [< Fr. < OFr. < *re-,* again + *sourdre,* to spring up < L. *surgere,* to rise] **1.** something ready for use or available as needed **2.** [*pl.*] wealth; assets **3.** [*pl.*] something useful, as coal or oil, that a country, state, etc. has **4.** a means to an end; expedient **5.** [*pl.*] a source of strength or ability within oneself: in full, **inner resources** **6.** a being resourceful

re·source·ful (ri sôrs′fəl, -zôrs′-) ***adj.*** full of resource; able to deal promptly and effectively with difficulties, etc. —**re·source′ful·ly** ***adv.*** —**re·source′ful·ness** ***n.***

re·spect (ri spekt′) ***vt.*** [< L. pp. of *respicere* < *re-,* back + *specere,* to look at] **1.** to hold in high regard; show honor or courtesy to **2.** to show consideration for; avoid intruding upon, etc. [*respect* others' privacy] **3.** to concern; relate to —***n.*** **1.** a feeling of high regard; esteem **2.** a being held in honor **3.** deference or dutiful regard [*respect* for law] **4.** courteous consideration **5.** [*pl.*] courteous expressions of regard: now chiefly in **pay one's respects,** to show polite regard as by visiting **6.** a particular point or detail [right in every *respect*] **7.** reference; relation [with *respect* to this] —**in respect of** with reference to —**re·spect′er** ***n.***

re·spect·a·ble (ri spek′tə b'l) ***adj.*** **1.** worthy of respect or esteem **2.** socially acceptable; proper **3.** fairly good in quality **4.** fairly large **5.** good enough to be seen, worn, etc. —**re·spect′a·bil′i·ty** ***n.*** —**re·spect′a·bly** ***adv.***

re·spect·ful (ri spekt′fəl) ***adj.*** full of or showing respect; polite —**re·spect′ful·ly** ***adv.*** —**re·spect′ful·ness** ***n.***

re·spect·ing (ri spek′tiŋ) ***prep.*** concerning; about

re·spec·tive (-tiv) ***adj.*** as relates individually to each of two or more [their *respective* merits]

re·spec·tive·ly (-tiv lē) ***adv.*** in regard to each in the order named [the first and second prizes went to Mary and George, *respectively*]

re·spell (rē spel′) ***vt.*** to spell again; specif., to spell differently in an attempt to show the pronunciation [to respell the word "calf" as (kaf)]

res·pi·ra·tion (res′pə rā′shən) ***n.*** **1.** act or process of respiring; breathing **2.** the processes by which a living organism or cell takes in oxygen, distributes and utilizes it in oxidation, and gives off products, esp. carbon dioxide **3.** a similar process in anaerobic organisms —**res′pi·ra′tion·al** ***adj.***

res·pi·ra·tor (res′pə rāt′ər) ***n.*** **1.** a device, as of gauze, worn over the mouth and nose, as to prevent the inhaling of harmful substances **2.** an apparatus for giving artificial respiration

res·pi·ra·to·ry (res′pər ə tôr′ē, ri spīr′ə-) ***adj.*** of, for, or involving respiration

re·spire (ri spīr′) ***vi., vt.*** **-spired′, -spir′ing** [< OFr. < L. < *re-,* back + *spirare,* to breathe] to breathe; inhale and exhale (air)

res·pite (res′pit) ***n.*** [< OFr. < L. pp. of *respicere:* see RESPECT] **1.** a delay or postponement, esp. in carrying out a death sentence; reprieve **2.** a period of temporary relief, as from pain, work, etc. —***vt.*** **-pit·ed, -pit·ing** to give a respite to

re·splend·ent (ri splen′dənt) ***adj.*** [< L. prp. of *resplendere* < *re-,* again + *splendere,* to shine] shining brightly; dazzling —**re·splend′ence, re·splend′en·cy** ***n.*** —**re·splend′ent·ly** ***adv.***

re·spond (ri spänd′) ***vi.*** [< OFr. < L. < *re-,* back + *spondere,* to pledge] **1.** to answer; reply **2.** to act in return, as if in answer **3.** to react favorably, as to medical treatment **4.** *Law* to be answerable or liable —***vt.*** to say in answer

re·spond·ent (-spän′dənt) ***adj.*** responding; answering —***n.*** **1.** a person who responds **2.** *Law* a defendant —**re·spond′ence, re·spond′en·cy** ***n.***

re·spond·er (-dər) ***n.*** **1.** a person or thing that responds **2.** *Electronics* a device, as a transponder, that indicates reception of a signal

re·sponse (ri späns′) ***n.*** [< ML. < L. pp. of *respondere:* see RESPOND] **1.** something said or done in answer; reply or reaction **2.** *Eccles.* a word, phrase, etc. sung or spoken in answer, as by a congregation or choir in answer to an officiating clergyman **3.** *Electronics* the ratio of output to input of a device or system **4.** *Physiol., Psychol.* a reaction to a stimulus

re·spon·si·bil·i·ty (ri spän′sə bil′ə tē) ***n., pl.*** **-ties** **1.** a being responsible; obligation, accountability, etc. **2.** a person or thing that one is responsible for

re·spon·si·ble (ri spän′sə b'l) ***adj.*** [< MFr. < L.: see RESPONSE] **1.** expected or obliged to account (*for* something, *to* someone); answerable **2.** involving obligation or duties [a *responsible* job] **3.** that can be charged with being the cause, agent, etc. of something **4.** able to think and act rationally, and hence accountable for one's behavior **5.** dependable or reliable, as in meeting obligations —**re·spon′si·ble·ness** ***n.*** —**re·spon′si·bly** ***adv.***

re·spon·sive (-siv) ***adj.*** **1.** answering **2.** reacting readily, as to suggestion [a *responsive* audience] **3.** containing responses [*responsive* reading in church] —**re·spon′sive·ly** ***adv.*** —**re·spon′sive·ness** ***n.***

rest[1] (rest) ***n.*** [OE.] **1.** *a)* peace, ease, and refreshment, as produced by sleep *b)* sleep or repose **2.** refreshing inactivity after work or exertion, or a period of this **3.** *a)* relief from anything distressing, tiring, etc. *b)* peace of mind **4.** the repose of death **5.** absence of motion **6.** a place for resting; lodging place, as for travelers **7.** a thing that supports [a foot *rest*] **8.** *Music* *a)* a measured interval of silence between tones *b)* a symbol for this —***vi.*** **1.** *a)* to get refreshed by sleeping, lying down, ceasing work, etc. *b)* to sleep **2.** to be at ease or at peace **3.** to be dead **4.** to be quiet or still for a while **5.** to remain unchanged [let the matter *rest*] **6.** *a)* to lie, sit, or lean *b)* to be placed or based (*in, on,* etc.) **7.** to be or lie (where specified) [the fault *rests* with him] **8.** to be fixed [his eyes *rested* on her] **9.** to rely; depend **10.** *Law* to end voluntarily the introduction of evidence in a case —***vt.***

MUSICAL RESTS (A, whole; B, half; C, quarter; D, eighth; E, sixteenth)

1. to give rest to; refresh by rest **2.** to put or lay for ease, support, etc. *[rest* your head on the pillow*]* **3.** to base; ground *[*to *rest* an argument on facts*]* **4.** to fix (the eyes, etc.) **5.** to bring to rest; stop **6.** *Law* to cause (a case) to rest —**at rest 1.** asleep **2.** immobile **3.** free from distress, care, etc. **4.** dead —**lay to rest** to bury —**rest′er** *n.*

rest² (rest) *n.* [< OFr. < L. *restare,* to remain < *re-,* back + *stare,* to stand] **1.** what is left; remainder **2.** [*with pl. v.*] the others Used with *the* —*vi.* to go on being *[rest* assured*]*

re·state (rē stāt′) *vt.* **-stat′ed, -stat′ing** to state again, esp. in a different way —**re·state′ment** *n.*

res·tau·rant (res′tə rənt, -ränt′) *n.* [Fr. < prp. of *restaurer:* see RESTORE] a place where meals can be bought and eaten

res·tau·ra·teur (res′tər ə tʉr′) *n.* [Fr.] a person who owns or operates a restaurant

rest·ful (rest′fəl) *adj.* **1.** full of or giving rest **2.** quiet; peaceful **3.** having a soothing effect —**rest′ful·ly** *adv.* —**rest′ful·ness** *n.*

res·ti·tu·tion (res′tə to͞o′shən, -tyo͞o′-) *n.* [< MFr. < L. < pp. of *restituere,* to restore < *re-,* again + *statuere,* to set up] **1.** restoration to the rightful owner of something lost or taken away **2.** a making good for loss or damage **3.** a return to a former condition

res·tive (res′tiv) *adj.* [< OFr. < *rester:* see REST²] **1.** hard to control; unruly, balky, etc. **2.** nervous or impatient under restraint; restless —**res′tive·ly** *adv.* —**res′tive·ness** *n.*

rest·less (rest′lis) *adj.* **1.** unable to rest or relax **2.** giving no rest or relaxation; disturbed *[restless* sleep*]* **3.** never or seldom still; always moving **4.** seeking change; discontented —**rest′less·ly** *adv.* —**rest′less·ness** *n.*

res·to·ra·tion (res′tə rā′shən) *n.* **1.** a restoring or being restored, as of a person or thing to a former condition or position, or of something taken away or lost to its rightful owner **2.** a reconstruction of the original form of a building, fossil animal, etc. **3.** a restored thing —**the Restoration 1.** reestablishment of the monarchy in England in 1660 under Charles II **2.** the period of his reign (1660–85)

re·stor·a·tive (ri stôr′ə tiv) *adj.* **1.** of restoration **2.** restoring or able to restore health, consciousness, etc. —*n.* a thing that restores

re·store (ri stôr′) *vt.* **-stored′, -stor′ing** [< OFr. < L. < *re-,* again + *-staurare,* to place] **1.** to give back (something taken away, lost, etc.) **2.** to bring back to a former or normal condition, as by repairing, rebuilding, etc. **3.** to put (a person) back into a position, rank, etc. **4.** to bring back to health, strength, etc. **5.** to bring back into being, use, etc. —**re·stor′a·ble** *adj.* —**re·stor′er** *n.*

restr. restaurant

re·strain (ri strān′) *vt.* [< OFr. < L. < *re-,* back + *stringere,* to draw tight] **1.** to hold back from action; check; curb **2.** to keep under control **3.** to deprive of physical liberty, as by shackling **4.** to limit; restrict —**re·strain′a·ble** *adj.* —**re·strain′ed·ly** *adv.* —**re·strain′er** *n.*

re·straint (ri strānt′) *n.* **1.** a restraining or being restrained **2.** a restraining influence or action **3.** a means of restraining **4.** loss or limitation of liberty **5.** control of emotions, impulses, etc.; reserve

restraint of trade restriction or prevention of business competition, as by monopoly, price fixing, etc.

re·strict (ri strikt′) *vt.* [< L. pp. of *restringere:* see RESTRAIN] to keep within certain limits; limit; confine

re·strict·ed (ri strik′tid) *adj.* limited; confined; specif., *a)* that may be seen only by authorized personnel *[*a *restricted* document*]* *b)* excluding certain groups, esp. minorities

re·stric·tion (-shən) *n.* **1.** restricting or being restricted **2.** something that restricts; limitation

re·stric·tion·ism (-shən iz′m) *n.* the policy of favoring restriction, as of trade, immigration, etc. —**re·stric′tion·ist** *n., adj.*

re·stric·tive (ri strik′tiv) *adj.* **1.** restricting or tending to restrict **2.** *Gram.* designating a clause, phrase, or word felt as limiting what it modifies and so not set off with commas (Ex.: the man *who spoke to us* is my uncle) —**re·stric′tive·ly** *adj.* —**re·stric′tive·ness** *n.*

rest·room (rest′ro͞om′) *n.* a room or rooms in a public building, with toilets, washbowls, and, sometimes, couches, etc.: also **rest room**

re·struc·ture (rē struk′chər) *vt.* **-tured, -tur·ing** to plan or provide a new structure or organization for

re·sult (ri zult′) *vi.* [< ML. < L. *resultare,* to rebound, freq. of *resilire:* see RESILIENT] **1.** to happen because of something else; follow as an effect (often with *from*) **2.** to end (*in* something) as an effect or development —*n.* **1.** *a)* what comes about from an action, process, etc.; consequence; outcome *b)* [*pl.*] desired effects **2.** the number, quantity, etc. obtained by mathematical calculation

re·sult·ant (-'nt) *adj.* that results —*n.* **1.** a result **2.** *Physics* a force, velocity, etc. with an effect equal to that of two or more such forces, etc. acting together

re·sume (ri zo͞om′, -zyo͞om′) *vt.* **-sumed′, -sum′ing** [< MFr. < L. < *re-,* again + *sumere,* to take] **1.** to take or occupy again **2.** to begin again or go on with again after interruption —*vi.* to begin again or go on again

ré·su·mé (rez′oo mā′, rā′zoo-; rā′zoo mā′) *n.* [Fr., pp. of *résumer:* see prec.] a summary; specif., a statement of a job applicant's previous employment experience, education, etc.: also written **resume, resumé**

re·sump·tion (ri zump′shən) *n.* [< L. < pp. of *resumere*] the act of resuming

re·sur·face (rē sʉr′fis) *vt.* **-faced, -fac·ing** to put a new surface on —*vi.* to come to the surface again

re·surge (ri sʉrj′) *vi.* **-surged′, -surg′ing 1.** to rise again; revive **2.** to surge back again

re·sur·gent (-sʉr′jənt) *adj.* rising or tending to rise again; resurging —**re·sur′gence** *n.*

res·ur·rect (rez′ə rekt′) *vt.* [< ff.] **1.** *Theol.* to bring back to life **2.** to bring back into notice, use, etc. —*vi. Theol.* to rise from the dead

res·ur·rec·tion (rez′ə rek′shən) *n.* [< OFr. < LL. < L. *resurrectus,* pp. of *resurgere,* to rise again] **1.** *Theol. a)* a rising from the dead, or coming back to life *b)* the state of having so risen **2.** a return to notice, use, etc.; revival —**the Resurrection** *Theol.* **1.** the rising of Jesus from the dead **2.** the rising of all the dead at the Last Judgment —**res′ur·rec′tion·al** *adj.*

resurrection plant any of various small plants that curl up when dry and spread their branches or become green again when watered

re·sus·ci·tate (ri sus′ə tāt′) *vt., vi.* **-tat′ed, -tat′ing** [< L. pp. of *resuscitare* < *re-,* again + *suscitare,* to revive] to revive (someone who is unconscious, apparently dead, etc.) —**re·sus′ci·ta′tion** *n.* —**re·sus′ci·ta′tive** *adj.* —**re·sus′ci·ta′tor** *n.*

ret (ret) *vt.* **ret′ted, ret′ting** [MDu. *reten*] to dampen or soak (flax, hemp, etc.) in water to separate the fibers from woody tissue

ret. 1. retain **2.** retired **3.** return(ed)

re·tail (rē′tāl; *for vt. 2, usually* ri tāl′) *n.* [< OFr. *retailler,* to cut up < *re-,* again + *tailler,* to cut] the sale of goods in small quantities directly to the consumer: cf. WHOLESALE —*adj.* having to do with the selling of goods in this way —*adv.* in small amounts or at a retail price —*vt.* **1.** to sell as retail goods **2.** to repeat or pass on (gossip, etc.) —*vi.* to be sold as retail goods —**re′tail·er** *n.*

re·tain (ri tān′) *vt.* [< OFr. < L. < *re-,* back + *tenere,* to hold] **1.** to keep in possession **2.** to keep in a fixed state **3.** to continue to hold (heat, etc.) **4.** to continue to use, etc. **5.** to keep in mind; remember **6.** to engage (a lawyer, etc.) by an advance fee called a retainer —**re·tain′ment** *n.*

re·tain·er (ri tā′nər) *n.* **1.** a person or thing that retains **2.** a servant, attendant, etc., as of a person or family of rank or wealth **3.** *Law a)* the retaining of the services of a lawyer, consultant, etc. *b)* a fee paid in advance to make such services available when needed

retaining wall a wall built to keep a bank of earth from sliding or water from flooding

re·take (rē tāk′; *for n.* rē′tāk′) *vt.* **-took′, -tak′en, -tak′ing 1.** to take again, take back, or recapture **2.** to photograph again —*n.* **1.** a retaking **2.** a movie scene, etc. rephotographed or to be rephotographed

re·tal·i·ate (ri tal′ē āt′) *vi.* **-at′ed, -at′ing** [< L. pp. of *retaliare* < *re-,* back + *talio,* punishment in kind] to return like for like; esp., to pay back injury for injury —*vt.* to return in kind (an injury, wrong, etc. suffered) —**re·tal′i·a′tion** *n.* —**re·tal′i·a′tive, re·tal′i·a·to′ry** *adj.*

re·tard (ri tärd′) *vt.* [< OFr. < L. < *re-,* back + *tardare,* to make slow < *tardus,* slow] to hinder, delay, or slow the advance or progess of —*n.* a retarding; delay

re·tard·ant (-'nt) *n.* something that retards; esp., a substance that delays a chemical reaction: also **re·tard′er** —*adj.* tending to retard

re·tard·ate (ri tär′dāt) *n.* a mentally retarded person

re·tar·da·tion (rē′tär dā′shən) *n.* **1.** a retarding or being retarded **2.** something that retards **3.** *same as* MENTAL RETARDATION —**re·tard·a·tive** (ri tär′də tiv), **re·tard′a·to′ry** (-tôr′ē) *adj.*

re·tard·ed (ri tär′did) *adj.* delayed in development or progress, esp. because of mental retardation

retch (rech) *vi.* [OE. *hræcan,* to hawk, spit] to strain to vomit, esp. without bringing anything up

retd. 1. retained **2.** retired **3.** returned

re·ten·tion (ri ten′shən) *n.* [L.] **1.** a retaining or being retained 2. power of or capacity for retaining 3. *a*) memory *b*) ability to remember

re·ten·tive (-tiv) ***adj.*** 1. retaining or able to retain 2. having good recall or a good memory —**re·ten′tive·ly** ***adv.*** —**re·ten′tive·ness, re·ten·tiv·i·ty** (rē′ten tiv′ə tē) ***n.***

re·think (rē thiŋk′) ***vt.*** **-thought′, -think′ing** to think over again, with a view to changing; reconsider

ret·i·cence (ret′ə s'ns) ***n.*** quality, state, or instance of being reticent; reserve: also **ret′i·cen·cy**

ret·i·cent (-s'nt) ***adj.*** [< L. prp. of *reticere* < *re-*, again + *tacere*, to be silent] 1. not willing to say much; tending to keep one's thoughts, etc. to oneself; reserved 2. having a restrained, quiet, or understated quality —**ret′i·cent·ly** ***adv.***

re·tic·u·lar (ri tik′yə lər) ***adj.*** [see RETICULE] 1. netlike 2. intricate —**re·tic′u·lar·ly** ***adv.***

re·tic·u·late (-lit; *also, and for v. always,* -lāt′) ***adj.*** [< L. < *reticulum:* see ff.] like a net or network, as the veins of some leaves: also **re·tic′u·lat′ed** —***vt., vi.*** **-lat′ed, -lat′ing** to divide, mark, or be marked so as to look like network —**re·tic′u·late·ly** ***adv.*** —**re·tic′u·la′tion** ***n.***

ret·i·cule (ret′ə kyo͞ol′) ***n.*** [< Fr. < L. *reticulum*, dim. of *rete*, a net] a woman's drawstring handbag, orig. of net

re·tic·u·lum (ri tik′yə ləm) ***n.,*** *pl.* **-la** (-lə) [L.: see RETICULE] 1. network 2. the second division of the stomach of cud-chewing animals, as cows

ret·i·na (ret′'n ə) ***n.,*** *pl.* **-nas, -nae′** (-ē′) [ML., prob. < L. *rete*, a net] the innermost coat of the back part of the eyeball, on which the image is formed by the lens —**ret′i·nal** ***adj.***

ret·i·nue (ret′'n o͞o′, -yo͞o′) ***n.*** [< OFr. < pp. of *retenir:* see RETAIN] a body of assistants, servants, etc. attending a person of rank or importance; train of attendants

re·tire (ri tīr′) ***vi.*** **-tired′, -tir′ing** [< Fr. < *re-*, back + *tirer*, to draw] 1. to withdraw to a private or secluded place 2. to go to bed 3. to retreat, as in battle 4. to give up one's work, career, etc., esp. because of advanced age 5. to move back or away —***vt.*** 1. to withdraw or move (troops) in retreat 2. to take (money, paid-off bonds, etc.) out of circulation 3. to cause to retire from a job, etc. 4. to withdraw (an outdated or worn-out thing) from use 5. *Baseball*, etc. to end the batting turn of (a batter, side, etc.)

re·tired (ri tīrd′) ***adj.*** 1. secluded or private 2. *a*) that has given up one's work, etc., esp. because of advanced age *b*) of or for such retired persons

re·tir·ee (ri tīr′ē′) ***n.*** one who has retired from work, etc.: also **re·tir′ant** (-ənt)

re·tire·ment (ri tīr′mənt) ***n.*** 1. a retiring or being retired, specif. from work, etc. 2. *a*) privacy; seclusion *b*) a place of privacy or seclusion

re·tir·ing (-iŋ) ***adj.*** 1. that retires 2. reserved; modest; shy

re·took (rē to͝ok′) *pt. of* RETAKE

re·tool (rē to͞ol′) ***vt., vi.*** to adapt the machinery of (a factory) for making a different product by changing the tools and dies

re·tort[1] (ri tôrt′) ***vt., vi.*** [< L. *retortus*, pp. of *retorquere* < *re-*, back + *torquere*, to twist] 1. to return in kind (an insult, etc. received) 2. to answer back, esp. in a sharp, quick, or clever way —***n.*** a retorting or the response so made

re·tort[2] (ri tôrt′) ***n.*** [< Fr. < ML. *retorta* < L. fem. pp.: see prec.] 1. a container for distilling, usually of glass and with a long tube 2. a vessel for heating ore to extract metal, coal to produce gas, etc.

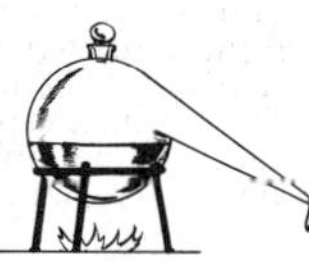
RETORT

re·touch (rē tuch′; *for n., also* rē′tuch′) ***vt.*** to touch up or change details in (a painting, the negative or print of a photograph, etc.) —***n.*** a retouching or thing retouched —**re·touch′er** ***n.***

re·trace (ri trās′) ***vt.*** **-traced′, -trac′ing** [Fr. *retracer:* see RE- & TRACE[1]] 1. to go back over again, esp. in the reverse direction [to *retrace* one's steps] 2. to trace again the story of, from the beginning

re-trace (rē′trās′) ***vt.*** **-traced′, -trac′ing** to trace the lines of (a drawing, engraving, etc.) over again

re·tract (ri trakt′) ***vt., vi.*** [< L.: ult. < *re-*, back + *trahere*, to draw] 1. to draw back or in [to *retract* claws] 2. to withdraw or take back (a statement, offer, charge, etc.); recant —**re·tract′a·bil′i·ty** ***n.*** —**re·tract′a·ble** ***adj.*** —**re·trac′tion** ***n.*** —**re·trac′tive** ***adj.***

re·trac·tile (ri trak′t'l, -tīl) ***adj.*** [Fr.] that can be retracted, or drawn back or in, as the claws of a cat

re·trac·tor (-tər) ***n.*** one that retracts; esp., *a*) a muscle that retracts an organ, protruded part, etc. *b*) a surgical device for retracting a part or organ

re·tread (rē tred′; *for n.* rē′tred′) ***vt., n.*** *same as* RECAP[1]

re-tread (rē′tred′) ***vt.*** **-trod′, -trod′den** or **-trod′, -tread′ing** to tread again

re·treat (ri trēt′) ***n.*** [< OFr., ult. < L. *re-*, back + *trahere*, to draw] 1. a going back or backward; withdrawal in the face of opposition, etc. 2. withdrawal to a safe or private place 3. a safe, quiet, or secluded place 4. a period of seclusion, esp. for religious contemplation, often as part of a group 5. *Mil.* *a*) the forced withdrawal of troops under attack, or a signal for this *b*) a signal by bugle or drum at sunset for lowering the national flag, or this ceremony —***vi.*** 1. to withdraw; go back 2. to slope backward —**beat a retreat** to retreat or withdraw in a hurry

re·trench (rē trench′) ***vt., vi.*** [< MFr.: see RE- & TRENCH] to cut down or reduce (esp. expenses); curtail, economize, etc. —**re·trench′ment** ***n.***

ret·ri·bu·tion (ret′rə byo͞o′shən) ***n.*** [< OFr. < LL., ult. < L. < *re-*, back + *tribuere*, to pay] deserved punishment for evil done, or, sometimes, reward for good done —**re·trib·u·tive** (ri trib′yoo tiv), **re·trib′u·to′ry** (-tôr′ē) ***adj.*** —**re·trib′u·tive·ly** ***adv.***

re·triev·al (ri trē′v'l) ***n.*** 1. a retrieving 2. possibility of recovery or restoration

re·trieve (ri trēv′) ***vt.*** **-trieved′, -triev′ing** [< OFr. < *re-*, again + *trouver*, to find] 1. to get back; recover 2. to restore; revive [to *retrieve* one's spirits] 3. to rescue or save 4. to set right or repair (a loss, error, etc.) 5. to recall to mind 6. to recover (information) from data stored in a computer 7. *Hunting* to find and bring back (killed or wounded game): said of dogs 8. *Tennis*, etc. to return (a ball hard to reach) —***vi.*** *Hunting* to retrieve game —***n.*** a retrieving —**re·triev′a·ble** ***adj.***

re·triev·er (-ər) ***n.*** 1. a person or thing that retrieves 2. a dog trained to retrieve game; specif., any of several breeds of dog developed for this purpose

ret·ro (ret′rō) ***n.,*** *pl.* **-ros** *clipped form of* RETROROCKET

ret·ro- [< L. *retro*, backward] *a combining form meaning* backward, back, behind [*retroactive*]

ret·ro·ac·tive (ret′rō ak′tiv) ***adj.*** applying to, or going into effect as of, the preceding period [a *retroactive* pay increase] —**ret′ro·ac′tive·ly** ***adv.*** —**ret′ro·ac·tiv′i·ty** ***n.***

ret·ro·cede (ret′rə sēd′) ***vi.*** **-ced′ed, -ced′ing** [< L. < *retro-*, back + *cedere*, to yield, go] to go back; recede —***vt.*** to cede (territory) back —**ret′ro·ces′sion** (-sesh′ən) ***n.***

ret·ro·fire (ret′rə fīr′) ***vi., vt.*** **-fired′, -fir′ing** to ignite: said of a retrorocket —***n.*** a retrofiring

ret·ro·fit (-fit′) ***n.*** [RETRO- + FIT[1]] a change in design, construction, etc., as of an aircraft, to incorporate later improvements —***vt., vi.*** **-fit′ted, -fit′ting** to modify with a retrofit

ret·ro·flex (-fleks′) ***adj.*** [< L.: see RETRO- & FLEX] 1. bent or turned backward 2. *Phonet.* pronounced with the tip of the tongue raised and bent slightly backward Also **ret′ro·flexed′** —***n.*** *Phonet.* a retroflex sound

ret·ro·grade (ret′rə grād′) ***adj.*** [< L. *retrogradi:* see RETRO- & GRADE] 1. moving or directed backward 2. going back to an earlier, esp. worse, condition —***vi.*** **-grad′ed, -grad′ing** 1. to go or move backward 2. to deteriorate

ret·ro·gress (ret′rə gres′, ret′rə gres′) ***vi.*** [< L. pp. of *retrogradi:* see prec.] to move backward, esp. into an earlier or worse condition —**ret′ro·gres′sion** (-gresh′ən) ***n.*** —**ret′ro·gres′sive** ***adj.*** —**ret′ro·gres′sive·ly** ***adv.***

ret·ro·rock·et, ret·ro-rock·et (ret′rō räk′it) ***n.*** a small rocket on a larger rocket or spacecraft, used to produce thrust against flight direction so as to reduce speed

ret·ro·spect (ret′rə spekt′) ***n.*** [< L. pp. of *retrospicere* < *retro-*, back + *specere*, to look] a looking back on or thinking about things past —**in retrospect** in reviewing the past —**ret′ro·spec′tion** ***n.***

ret·ro·spec·tive (ret′rə spek′tiv) ***adj.*** 1. looking or directed back, to the past, etc. 2. retroactive —***n.*** an art show of typical works of an artist over all or part of his lifetime —**ret′ro·spec′tive·ly** ***adv.***

ret·rous·sé (ret′ro͞o sā′) ***adj.*** [Fr., turned up] turned up at the tip [a *retroussé* nose]

ret·si·na (ret′si nə) ***n.*** [ModGr.] a wine of Greece, flavored with pine resin

re·turn (ri turn′) ***vi.*** [< OFr. *retourner:* see RE- & TURN] 1. to go or come back 2. to answer; retort —***vt.*** 1. to bring, send, carry, or put back 2. to pay back by doing or giving the same; reciprocate [to *return* a visit, a compliment, etc.] 3. to produce (a profit, revenue, etc.); yield 4. to report officially or formally 5. to elect or reelect, as to a legislature 6. to render (a verdict, etc.) 7. *Sports* to hit back or throw back (a ball) —***n.*** 1. a coming or going back 2. a bringing, sending, carrying, or putting back 3. something returned 4. repayment; requital; reciprocation 5. *a*) profit made on an exchange of goods *b*) [*often pl.*] yield or profit, as from investments 6. an answer; retort 7. *a*) an official or formal report *b*) [*usually pl.*] a report on a vote count [*election returns*] *c*) a form for reporting income tax due: in full, **(income) tax return**—***adj.*** 1. of or for returning [a *return* ticket] 2. given, sent, done, etc. again or in return [a *return* visit] 3. returning

or returned —**in return** as a return; as an equivalent, etc.
re·turn·a·ble (ri tur′nə b'l) *adj.* that can or may be returned —*n.* a container, as a glass beer bottle, that can be returned for reuse and for a refund of a deposit on it
re·turn·ee (ri tur′nē′) *n.* a person who returns, as home from military service
Reu·ben (ro͞o′bin) [via LL. < Gr. < Heb. *rĕ'ūbēn,* lit., behold, a son] **1.** a masculine name **2.** *Bible a)* the eldest son of Jacob *b)* the tribe of Israel descended from him
Reuben (sandwich) [? after *Reuben* Kay, Omaha grocer c. 1930] a sandwich made with rye bread, corned beef, sauerkraut, Swiss cheese, and a dressing and served hot
re·u·ni·fy (rē yo͞o′nə fī′) *vt., vi.* **-fied′, -fy′ing** to unify again after being divided —**re′u·ni·fi·ca′tion** *n.*
Ré·un·ion (rā ü nyōn′; *E.* rē yo͞on′yən) French island possession in the Indian Ocean, east of Madagascar
re·un·ion (rē yo͞on′yən) *n.* **1.** a reuniting **2.** a gathering of persons after separation *[a family reunion]*
re·u·nite (rē′yoo nīt′) *vt., vi.* **-nit′ed, -nit′ing** to unite again; bring or come together again
rev (rev) *n.* [Colloq.] a revolution, as of an engine —*vt., vi.* **revved, rev′ving** [Colloq.] to speed up (an engine, motor, etc.): usually with *up*
Rev. 1. *Bible* Revelation **2.** *pl.* **Revs.** Reverend
rev. 1. revenue **2.** reverse **3.** review(ed) **4.** revise(d) **5.** revision **6.** revolution **7.** revolving
re·val·u·ate (rē val′yoo wāt′) *vt.* **-at′ed, -at′ing** to make a new valuation or appraisal of —**re·val′u·a′tion** *n.*
re·vamp (rē vamp′) *vt.* **1.** to put a new vamp on (a shoe or boot) **2.** to make over; revise —*n.* a revamping
re·vanch·ism (rə vänsh′iz'm, -vänch′-) *n.* [< Fr. *revanche,* revenge + -ISM] the revengeful spirit moving a defeated nation to aggressively seek restoration of territories, etc. —**re·vanch′ist** *adj., n.*
re·veal (ri vēl′) *vt.* [< OFr. < L. *revelare,* lit., to draw back the veil < *re-,* back + *velum,* a veil] **1.** to make known (something hidden or secret); disclose **2.** to expose to view; show; display —**re·veal′a·ble** *adj.* —**re·veal′er** *n.*
re·veil·le (rev′ə lē; *Brit.* ri val′ē, -vel′-) *n.* [< Fr. imper. of *(se) réveiller,* to wake up, ult. < L. *re-,* again + *vigilare,* to watch] *Mil.* **1.** a signal on a bugle, drum, etc. early in the morning to wake soldiers or sailors or call them to first assembly **2.** the first assembly of the day
rev·el (rev′'l) *vi.* **-eled** or **-elled, -el·ing** or **-el·ling** [< MFr. < L. *rebellare:* see REBEL] **1.** to make merry; be noisily festive **2.** to take much pleasure *(in) [to revel in sports]* —*n.* **1.** merrymaking; revelry **2.** [*often pl.*] an occasion of merrymaking —**rev′el·er, rev′el·ler** *n.*
rev·e·la·tion (rev′ə lā′shən) *n.* **1.** a revealing, or disclosing **2.** something disclosed, especially when it comes as a great surprise **3.** *Theol.* God's revealing of himself and his will to man —[**R-**] the last book of the New Testament (in full, **The Revelation of Saint John the Divine**): also **Revelations** —**rev′e·la′tor** *n.* —**rev′e·la·to′ry** (-lə tôr′ē) *adj.*
rev·el·ry (rev′'l rē) *n., pl.* **-ries** reveling; noisy merrymaking; boisterous festivity
re·venge (ri venj′) *vt.* **-venged′, -veng′ing** [< OFr. *re-,* again + *vengier,* to take vengeance < L. *vindicare:* see VINDICATE] **1.** to inflict injury or punishment in return for (an injury, insult, etc.) **2.** to avenge (a person, oneself, etc.) —*n.* **1.** a revenging; vengeance **2.** what is done in revenging **3.** desire to take vengeance **4.** a chance to retaliate, as by a return match after a defeat —**be revenged** to get revenge —**re·veng′er** *n.* —**re·veng′ing·ly** *adv.*
re·venge·ful (-fəl) *adj.* full of or desiring revenge —**re·venge′ful·ly** *adv.* —**re·venge′ful·ness** *n.*
rev·e·nue (rev′ə no͞o′, -nyo͞o′) *n.* [< MFr. < *re-,* back + *venir* < L. *venire,* to come] **1.** the income or return from property or investment **2.** a source of income **3.** the income of a government from taxes, licenses, etc.
rev·e·nu·er (-ər) *n.* [Colloq.] a Treasury Department revenue agent, esp. one concerned with halting the illegal distilling of alcohol and bootlegging
re·ver·ber·ant (ri vur′bər ənt) *adj.* reverberating
re·ver·ber·ate (-bə rāt′) *vt.* **-at′ed, -at′ing** [< L. < *re-,* again + *verberare,* to beat < *verber,* a lash] **1.** to cause (a sound) to reecho **2.** to reflect (light, heat, etc.) —*vi.* **1.** to reecho or resound **2.** to be reflected, as light or sound waves **3.** to recoil; rebound
re·ver·ber·a·tion (ri vur′bə rā′shən) *n.* **1.** a reverberating or being reverberated; reflection of light or sound waves, etc. **2.** something reverberated, as reechoed sound —**re·ver′ber·a′tive** (-bə rāt′iv, -bər ə tiv) *adj.* —**re·ver′ber·a′tive·ly** *adv.* —**re·ver′ber·a·to′ry** (-bər ə tôr′ē) *adj.*
Re·vere (ri vir′), **Paul** 1735–1818; Am. patriot
re·vere (ri vir′) *vt.* **-vered′, -ver′ing** [< Fr. < L. < *re-,* again + *vereri,* to fear] to regard with deep respect, love, and awe; venerate
rev·er·ence (rev′ər əns, rev′rəns) *n.* **1.** a feeling or attitude of deep respect, love, and awe; veneration **2.** a manifestation of this; specif., a bow or curtsy **3.** [**R-**] a title used in speaking to or of a clergyman: preceded by *your* or *his* —*vt.* **-enced, -enc·ing** to treat with reverence
rev·er·end (-ər ənd, -rənd) *adj.* [< MFr. < L. *reverendus,* gerundive of *revereri:* see REVERE] worthy of reverence: used [*usually* **the R-**] as a title of respect for a clergyman, often before the name —*n. colloq. term for* CLERGYMAN
rev·er·ent (-ər ənt, -rənt) *adj.* feeling or showing reverence —**rev′er·ent·ly** *adv.*
rev·er·en·tial (rev′ə ren′shəl) *adj.* showing or caused by reverence —**rev′er·en′tial·ly** *adv.*
rev·er·ie (rev′ər ē) *n.* [< Fr. < MFr. < *rever,* to wander] **1.** dreamy thinking, esp. of agreeable things; daydreaming **2.** a fanciful notion or daydream
re·vers (ri vir′, -ver′) *n., pl.* **-vers′** (-virz′, -verz′) [Fr. < L. *reversus:* see REVERSE] a part (of a garment) turned back to show the reverse side or facing, as a lapel: also **re·vere′**
re·ver·sal (ri vur′s'l) *n.* a reversing or being reversed
re·verse (ri vurs′) *adj.* [< OFr. < L. pp. of *revertere:* see REVERT] **1.** *a)* turned backward; opposite or contrary, as in position, direction, etc. *b)* with the back showing **2.** reversing the usual effect, as to show white letters on a black background **3.** acting or moving in a way opposite or contrary to the usual **4.** causing movement backward or in the opposite direction —*n.* **1.** the opposite or contrary **2.** the back, as the side of a coin or medal that does not show the main design **3.** a reversing; esp., a change from good fortune to bad; defeat; check **4.** a mechanism, etc. for reversing, as a gear or an arrangement in an automatic transmission that causes a machine or motor vehicle to run backward —*vt.* **-versed′, -vers′ing 1.** to turn in an opposite position or direction, upside down, or inside out **2.** to change to the opposite **3.** to cause to go in an opposite direction **4.** to transfer (the charges for a telephone call) to the party being called **5.** *Law* to revoke or annul (a decision, etc.) —*vi.* **1.** to go or turn in the opposite direction **2.** to put a motor, engine, etc. in reverse —**re·verse′ly** *adv.* —**re·vers′er** *n.*
re·vers·i·ble (ri vur′sə b'l) *adj.* **1.** that can be reversed, as cloth, coats, etc. finished so that either side can be used as the outer side **2.** that can reverse, as a chemical reaction —*n.* a reversible coat, jacket, etc. —**re·vers′i·bil′i·ty** *n.*
re·ver·sion (ri vur′zhən, -shən) *n.* **1.** a return, as to a former state, custom, etc. **2.** *Biol.* a return to a former or primitive type; atavism **3.** *Law a)* the right of succession, future possession, etc. *b)* the return of an estate to the grantor and his heirs after a grant terminates —**re·ver′sion·ar′y, re·ver′sion·al** *adj.*
re·vert (ri vurt′) *vi.* [< OFr. < L. < *re-,* back + *vertere,* to turn] **1.** to go back; return, as to a former practice, subject, etc. **2.** *Biol.* to return to an earlier type **3.** *Law* to go back to a former owner or his heirs —**re·vert′i·ble** *adj.*
rev·er·y (rev′ər ē) *n., pl.* **-er·ies** *same as* REVERIE
re·vet·ment (ri vet′mənt) *n.* [< Fr. < OFr., ult. < L. *re-,* again + *vestire,* to clothe] **1.** a facing, as of stone, to protect an embankment, etc. **2.** *same as* RETAINING WALL
re·view (ri vyo͞o′) *n.* [< MFr. < L. < *re-,* again + *videre,* to see] **1.** a looking at or looking over again **2.** a general survey or report **3.** a looking back, as on past events **4.** reexamination, as by a higher court of the decision of a lower court **5.** a critical report and evaluation, as in a newspaper, of a book, play, concert, etc. **6.** a magazine containing articles of criticism and evaluation *[a law review]* **7.** the act of going over a lesson again, as in recitation **8.** *same as* REVUE **9.** a formal inspection, as of troops on parade —*vt.* **1.** to look back on (past events, etc.) **2.** to survey in thought, speech, or writing **3.** to inspect (troops, etc.) formally **4.** to give or write a critical report of (a book, play, etc.) **5.** to reexamine (a lower court's decision) **6.** to go over (lessons, etc.) again —*vi.* to review books, plays, etc.
re·view·er (-ər) *n.* a person who reviews; esp., one who reviews books, plays, etc. as for a newspaper
re·vile (ri vīl′) *vt.* **-viled′, -vil′ing** [< OFr. *reviler,* to treat as vile: see RE- & VILE] to call bad names in talking to or about —**re·vile′ment** *n.* —**re·vil′er** *n.*
re·vise (ri vīz′) *vt.* **-vised′, -vis′ing** [< Fr. < L. < *re-,* back + *visere,* to survey, freq. of *videre,* to see] **1.** to read (a manuscript, etc.) over carefully and correct and improve it **2.** to change or amend —*n.* a revising or a revision —**re·vis′al** *n.* —**re·vis′er, re·vi′sor** *n.*
Revised Standard Version a mid-20th-cent. revision of an earlier version of the Bible, made by certain U.S. scholars
re·vi·sion (ri vizh′ən) *n.* **1.** act, process, or work of revising **2.** a revised form, as of a book, etc. —**re·vi′sion·ar′y, re·vi′sion·al** *adj.*

re·vi·sion·ist (-ist) ***n.*** a person who favors the revision of some accepted theory, etc. —***adj.*** of revisionists —**re·vi′sion·ism** ***n.***

re·vi·so·ry (ri vī′zər ē) ***adj.*** of, or having the nature or power of, revision

re·viv·al (ri vī′v'l) ***n.*** a reviving or being revived; specif., *a*) a bringing or coming back into use, being, etc. *b*) a new presentation of an earlier play, movie, etc. *c*) restoration to vigor and activity *d*) a bringing or coming back to life or consciousness *e*) a stirring up of religious feelings, usually by the excited preaching of evangelists at public meetings *f*) a series of such meetings

re·viv·al·ist (-ist) ***n.*** a person who promotes or conducts religious revivals —**re·viv′a·lism** ***n.*** —**re·viv′a·lis′tic** ***adj.***

re·vive (ri vīv′) ***vi., vt.*** **-vived′, -viv′ing** [< OFr. < L. < *re-*, again + *vivere*, to live] **1.** to come or bring back to life or consciousness **2.** to come or bring back to health and vigor **3.** to come or bring back into use, operation, or attention **4.** to come or bring to mind again **5.** to present (a play or movie) in a revival —**re·viv′a·bil′i·ty** ***n.*** —**re·viv′a·ble** ***adj.*** —**re·viv′er** ***n.***

re·viv·i·fy (ri viv′ə fī′) ***vt., vi.*** **-fied′, -fy′ing** to give or acquire new life or vigor; revive —**re·viv′i·fi·ca′tion** ***n.*** —**re·viv′i·fi′er** ***n.***

rev·o·ca·ble (rev′ə kə b'l) ***adj.*** that can be revoked: also **re·vok·a·ble** (ri vō′kə b'l) —**rev′o·ca·bil′i·ty** ***n.*** —**rev′o·ca·bly** ***adv.***

rev·o·ca·tion (rev′ə kā′shən) ***n.*** a revoking or being revoked; repeal; annulment

rev·o·ca·to·ry (rev′ə kə tôr′ē) ***adj.*** revoking or tending to revoke

re·voke (ri vōk′) ***vt.*** **-voked′, -vok′ing** [< MFr. < L. < *re-*, back + *vocare*, to call] to withdraw, repeal, or cancel (a law, permit, etc.) —***vi.*** *same as* RENEGE (sense 2) —***n.*** *same as* RENEGE —**re·vok′er** ***n.***

re·volt (ri vōlt′) ***n.*** [< Fr. < It., ult. < L. *revolvere:* see REVOLVE] **1.** a rising up against the government; rebellion **2.** any refusal to submit to authority **3.** the state of a person or persons revolting —***vi.*** **1.** to rise up against the government **2.** to refuse to submit to authority; rebel **3.** to be disgusted or shocked (with *at* or *against*) —***vt.*** to disgust —**re·volt′er** ***n.***

re·volt·ing (-vōl′tiŋ) ***adj.*** **1.** rebellious **2.** causing revulsion; disgusting —**re·volt′ing·ly** ***adv.***

rev·o·lu·tion (rev′ə lo͞o′shən) ***n.*** [< OFr. < LL. < L. pp. of *revolvere:* see REVOLVE] **1.** *a*) movement of a body in an orbit or circle *b*) the time taken for a body to go around an orbit **2.** a turning motion of a body around its center or axis; rotation **3.** a complete cycle of events **4.** a complete or radical change of any kind **5.** overthrow of a government or social system, with another taking its place

rev·o·lu·tion·ar·y (-er′ē) ***adj.*** **1.** of, like, favoring, or causing a revolution in a government or social system **2.** bringing about a very great change **3.** [**R-**] having to do with the American Revolution **4.** revolving or rotating —***n., pl.*** **-ar′ies** a revolutionist

Revolutionary War *see* AMERICAN REVOLUTION

rev·o·lu·tion·ist (-ist) ***n.*** a person who favors or takes part in a revolution

rev·o·lu·tion·ize (-īz′) ***vt.*** **-ized′, -iz′ing** **1.** to make a complete and basic change in **2.** [Rare] to bring about a political revolution in

re·volve (ri välv′) ***vt.*** **-volved′, -volv′ing** [< L. < *re-*, back + *volvere*, to roll] **1.** to turn over in the mind; reflect on **2.** to cause to travel in a circle or orbit **3.** to cause to rotate —***vi.*** **1.** to move in a circle or orbit **2.** to rotate **3.** to seem to move (*around* or *about* something) **4.** to recur at intervals **5.** to be pondered on —**re·volv′a·ble** ***adj.***

re·volv·er (ri väl′vər) ***n.*** a handgun with a revolving cylinder holding several bullets which can be fired without reloading

re·volv·ing (-viŋ) ***adj.*** **1.** that revolves **2.** designating a fund that is regularly replenished, for making loans, etc. **3.** designating credit, as for a charge account, renewed by regular payments to maintain a specified amount

revolving door a door consisting of four vanes hung on a central axle, and turned around by pushing on a vane

re·vue (ri vyo͞o′) ***n.*** [Fr.: see REVIEW] a musical show consisting of skits, songs, and dances, often poking fun at personages, fashions, etc.

re·vul·sion (ri vul′shən) ***n.*** [< Fr. < L. < pp. of *revellere* < *re-*, back + *vellere*, to pull] **1.** a sudden, complete, and violent change of feeling **2.** extreme disgust —**re·vul′sive** ***adj.***

re·ward (ri wôrd′) ***n.*** [< ONormFr. (for OFr. *regarde*) < *regarder:* see REGARD] **1.** something given in return for good or, sometimes, evil, or for service or merit **2.** money offered, as for the capture of a criminal, etc. **3.** compensation; profit —***vt.*** **1.** to give a reward to **2.** to give a reward for (service, etc.) —**re·ward′a·ble** ***adj.*** —**re·ward′er** ***n.***

re·ward·ing (-iŋ) ***adj.*** giving a sense of reward, or return —**re·ward′ing·ly** ***adv.***

re·wind (rē wīnd′) ***vt.*** **-wound′, -wind′ing** to wind again; specif., to wind (film, tape, etc.) back on the reel —***n.*** **1.** something rewound **2.** a rewinding

re·wire (-wīr′) ***vt., vi.*** **-wired′, -wir′ing** to wire again; specif., *a*) to put new wires in or on (a house, motor, etc.) *b*) to telegraph again

re·word (rē wurd′) ***vt.*** to state again in other words; change the wording of

re·work (-wurk′) ***vt.*** to work again; specif., *a*) to rewrite or revise *b*) to process (something used) for use again

re·write (rē rīt′; *for n.* rē′rīt′) ***vt., vi.*** **-wrote′, -writ′ten, -writ′ing** **1.** to write again **2.** to revise **3.** to write (news turned in by a reporter) in a different form for publication —***n.*** an article so written —**re·writ′er** ***n.***

Rex (reks) [L., a king] a masculine name —***n.*** [*also* **r-**] king

Rey·kja·vík (rā′kyə vēk′) capital of Iceland: seaport on the SW coast: pop. 81,000

Reyn·ard (ren′ərd, rā′nərd, rā′närd) [OFr. *Renard* < OHG.] the fox in the medieval beast epic *Reynard the Fox;* hence, a name for any fox

Reyn·olds (ren′əldz), Sir **Joshua** 1723–92; Eng. portrait painter

RF, R.F., r.f. **1.** radio frequency **2.** rapid-fire

rf., rf *Baseball* right field (or fielder)

RFD, R.F.D. Rural Free Delivery

Rh **1.** *see* RH FACTOR **2.** *Chem.* rhodium

r.h. relative humidity

r.h., R.H., RH right hand

Rhad·a·man·thus (rad′ə man′thəs) *Gr. Myth.* a son of Zeus who after he died became a judge of the dead in the lower world —**Rhad′a·man′thine** (-thin) ***adj.***

rhap·sod·ic (rap säd′ik) ***adj.*** of, or having the nature of, rhapsody; extravagantly enthusiastic: also **rhap·sod′i·cal** —**rhap·sod′i·cal·ly** ***adv.***

rhap·so·dize (rap′sə dīz′) ***vi., vt.*** **-dized′, -diz′ing** to speak, write, or recite in a rhapsodic manner or form —**rhap′so·dist** ***n.***

rhap·so·dy (-dē) ***n., pl.*** **-dies** [< Fr. < L. < Gr. *rhapsōidia*, ult. < *rhaptein*, to stitch together + *ōidē*, song] **1.** any ecstatic or extravagantly enthusiastic speech or writing **2.** great delight **3.** *Music* an instrumental composition of free, irregular form, suggesting improvisation

Rhe·a (rē′ə) *Gr. Myth.* the daughter of Uranus and Gaea, wife of Cronus, and mother of Zeus, Hera, etc. —***n.*** [**r-**] a large S. American nonflying bird, resembling the African ostrich but smaller and having a feathered neck and head

Rheims (rēmz; *Fr.* rans) *former sp. of* REIMS

Rhein (rīn) *Ger. name of the* RHINE

Rhein·gold (rīn′gōld′; *G.* rīn′gôlt′) [G., Rhine gold] *Germanic Legend* the hoard of gold guarded by the Rhine maidens and later owned by the Nibelungs and Siegfried

Rhen·ish (ren′ish) ***adj.*** of the Rhine or the regions around it —***n.*** [Now Rare] *same as* RHINE WINE

rhe·ni·um (rē′nē əm) ***n.*** [ModL. < L. *Rhenus*, Rhine] a rare metallic chemical element resembling manganese: symbol, Re; at. wt., 186.2; at no., 75

rhe·o- [< Gr. *rheos*, current < *rhein*, to flow] *a combining form meaning* a flow, current [*rheostat*]

rhe·o·stat (rē′ə stat′) ***n.*** [RHEO- + -STAT] a device for varying the resistance of an electric circuit without interrupting the circuit, used as to dim or brighten electric lights —**rhe′o·stat′ic** ***adj.***

rhe·sus (rē′səs) ***n.*** [ModL. < L. < Gr. proper name] a brownish-yellow macaque of India, often kept in zoos and used in medical research: in full, **rhesus monkey**

RHESUS MONKEY (head & body to 18 in.; tail to 8 in.)

rhet·o·ric (ret′ər ik) ***n.*** [< OFr. < L. < Gr. *rhētorikē* (*technē*), oratorical (art) < *rhētōr*, orator] **1.** the art of using words effectively in speaking or writing; esp., now, the art of prose composition **2.** a book on this **3.** artificial eloquence; showiness in literary style

rhe·tor·i·cal (ri tôr′i k'l, -tär′-) ***adj.*** **1.** of, having the nature of, or according to rhetoric **2.** artificially eloquent; showy and elaborate in literary style —**rhe·tor′i·cal·ly** ***adv.***

rhetorical question a question asked only to produce an effect, no spoken answer being expected

rhet·o·ri·cian (ret′ə rish′ən) ***n.*** **1.** a person skilled in using or teaching the art of rhetoric **2.** a person who speaks or writes in a showy, elaborate way

rheum (ro͞om) ***n.*** [< OFr. < L. < Gr. *rheuma*, a flow] **1.** any watery discharge from the mucous membranes, as of the mouth, eyes, or nose **2.** a cold; rhinitis —**rheum′y** ***adj.*** **rheum′i·er, rheum′i·est**

rheu·mat·ic (roo mat′ik) ***adj.*** of, caused by, or having rheumatism *—n.* a person who has rheumatism **—rheu·mat′i·cal·ly** *adv.*

rheumatic disease any of a group of diseases of connective tissue, as rheumatoid arthritis, gout, etc.

rheumatic fever a disease in which there is fever, the joints ache and swell, and the heart becomes inflamed

rheu·ma·tism (ro͞o′mə tiz'm) *n.* [< L. < Gr. *rheumatismos:* see RHEUM] *a popular term for* any of various painful conditions in which the joints and muscles become inflamed and stiff, as rheumatoid arthritis, bursitis, etc.

rheu·ma·toid (-toid′) *adj.* of or like rheumatism

rheumatoid arthritis a chronic disease in which the joints become inflamed, painful, and swollen often to the extent that fingers, toes, etc. become deformed

Rh factor (är′āch′) [RH(ESUS): first discovered in rhesus monkeys] a group of antigens, usually present in human red blood cells, which may cause hemolytic reactions during pregnancy or after tranfusion of blood containing this factor into someone lacking it: people who have this factor are **Rh positive;** those who lack it are **Rh negative**

Rhin (ran) *Fr. name of the* RHINE

rhi·nal (rī′n'l) *adj.* [RHIN(O)- + -AL] of the nose; nasal

Rhine (rīn) river in W Europe, flowing from E Switzerland through Germany & the Netherlands into the North Sea

Rhine·land (rīn′land′, -lənd) that part of Germany west of the Rhine

rhine·stone (rīn′stōn′) *n.* [transl. of Fr. *caillou du Rhin:* so called because orig. made at Strasbourg (on the Rhine)] a bright, artificial gem made of hard, colorless glass, often cut to imitate a diamond

Rhine wine **1.** any of various wines produced in the Rhine Valley, esp. any such light, dry white wine **2.** a wine like this produced elsewhere

rhi·ni·tis (rī nīt′əs) *n.* [ModL.: see RHINO- & -ITIS] inflammation of the mucous membrane of the nose

rhi·no (rī′nō) *n., pl.* **-nos, -no** *shortened form of* RHINOCEROS

rhi·no- [< Gr. *rhis* (gen. *rhinos*), the nose] *a combining form meaning* nose: also, before a vowel, **rhin-**

rhi·noc·er·os (rī näs′ər əs) *n., pl.* **-os·es, -os:** see PLURAL, II, D, 1 [< L. < Gr. < *rhis* (see prec.) + *keras,* horn] any of various large, thick-skinned, plant-eating mammals of Africa and Asia, with one or two upright horns on the snout

INDIAN RHINOCEROS (3–6½ ft. high at shoulder)

rhi·zo- [< Gr. *rhiza,* a root] *a combining form meaning* root: also, before a vowel, **rhiz-**

rhi·zoid (rī′zoid) *adj.* [prec. + -OID] rootlike *—n.* any of the rootlike filaments in a moss, fern, etc. that attach the plant to the substratum **—rhi·zoi′dal** *adj.*

rhi·zome (rī′zōm) *n.* [ModL. < Gr., ult. < *rhiza,* a root] a creeping stem lying, usually horizontally, at or under the surface of the soil: it has scale leaves, bears leaves or aerial shoots near its tips, and produces roots from its undersurface **—rhi·zom′a·tous** (-zäm′ə təs, -zō′mə-) *adj.*

rhi·zo·pod (rī′zə päd′) *n.* [RHIZO- + -POD] any of a class of one-celled animals with pseudopodia, including the amoebas, foraminifers, etc. **—rhi·zop′o·dous** (-zäp′ə dəs) *adj.*

RHIZOME OF GRASS

rho (rō) *n.* [Gr.] the seventeenth letter of the Greek alphabet (Ρ, ρ)

Rhode Island (rōd) [< ? Du. *Roodt Eylandt,* red island or < ? RHODES] New England State of the U.S.: 1,214 sq. mi.; pop. 947,000; cap. Providence: abbrev. **R.I., RI —Rhode Islander**

Rhode Island Red any of a breed of American chickens with reddish-brown feathers and a black tail

Rhode Island White any of a breed of chickens similar to Rhode Island Reds, but with white feathers

Rhodes (rōdz) largest island of the Dodecanese, in the Aegean: 545 sq. mi. **—Rho·di·an** (rō′dē ən) *adj., n.*

Rho·de·sia (rō dē′zhə, -zhē ə) *former name of* ZIMBABWE **—Rho·de′sian** *adj., n.*

Rhodesian man [skeletal remains found in Northern *Rhodesia*] a form of primitive man of the later Pleistocene, with massive brow ridges

rho·di·um (rō′dē əm) *n.* [ModL. < Gr. *rhodon,* a rose: from the color of its salts in solution] a hard, gray-white metallic chemical element, used in alloys with platinum and gold: symbol, Rh; at. wt., 102.905; at. no., 45

rho·do- [< Gr. *rhodon,* a rose] *a combining form meaning* rose, rose-red: also, before a vowel, **rhod-**

rho·do·den·dron (rō′də den′drən) *n.* [L. < Gr. < *rhodon,* a rose + *dendron,* a tree] any of a genus of trees and shrubs, mainly evergreen, with showy flowers of pink, white, or purple

rhom·boid (räm′boid) *n.* [< Fr. < L. < Gr.: see RHOMBUS & -OID] a parallelogram with oblique angles and only the opposite sides equal *—adj.* shaped like a rhomboid or rhombus: also **rhom·boi′dal**

RHOMBOID

rhom·bus (räm′bəs) *n., pl.* **-bus·es, -bi** (-bī) [L. < Gr. *rhombos,* turnable object] an equilateral parallelogram, esp. one with oblique angles: also **rhomb —rhom′bic** *adj.*

RHOMBUS

Rhone, Rhône (rōn) river flowing from SW Switzerland south through France into the Mediterranean

rhu·barb (ro͞o′bärb) *n.* [< OFr. < ML. < LL. < Gr. *rhēon,* rhubarb + *barbaron,* foreign] **1.** a perennial plant having large leaves whose long, thick, sour stalks are cooked into a sauce or baked in pies **2.** the roots or rhizomes of certain Asiatic varieties, used as a cathartic **3.** [Slang] a heated argument

rhumb (rum, rumb) *n.* [< Port. & Sp. *rumbo,* prob. < L. *rhombus,* RHOMBUS] any of the points of a mariner's compass

rhum·ba (rum′bə) *n. alt. sp. of* RUMBA

rhumb line a course keeping a constant compass direction, charted as a line cutting all meridians at the same angle

rhyme (rīm) *n.* [< OFr. < *rimer,* to rhyme, prob. < Frank. hyp. *rim,* a row: form infl. by L. *rhythmus,* rhythm] **1.** likeness of sounds at the ends of words or lines of verse **2.** a word that has the same end sound as another *[*"lazy" is a *rhyme* for "daisy"*]* **3.** a poem, or verse in general, using such end sounds *—vi.* **rhymed, rhym′ing** **1.** to make verse, esp. rhyming verse **2.** to form a rhyme *[*"more" *rhymes* with "door"*]* **3.** to be composed in metrical form with rhymes: said of verse *—vt.* **1.** to put into rhyme **2.** to compose in metrical form with rhymes **3.** to use as a rhyme *[*to *rhyme* "new" with "true"*]* **—rhyme or reason** order or sense: preceded by *without, no,* etc. **—rhym′er** *n.*

rhyme·ster (rīm′stər) *n.* a maker of simple or inferior verse or rhymes; poetaster

rhyming slang **1.** a word or phrase that rhymes with, and is a slang term for, a particular word (Ex.: *bees and honey* for *money*) **2.** such words or phrases collectively

rhythm (rith′'m, rith′əm) *n.* [< Fr. < L. < Gr. *rhythmos,* measure < *rhein,* to flow] **1.** *a)* flow or movement having a regularly repeated pattern of accents, beats, etc. *[*the *rhythm* of the waves, of dancing, of the heartbeat, etc.*]* *b)* the pattern of this **2.** *Biol.* a periodic occurrence in living organisms of specific physiological changes **3.** *Music a)* regular, repeated grouping of strong and weak beats, or heavily and lightly accented tones *b)* the form or pattern of this *[*waltz *rhythm]* **4.** *Prosody* the form or pattern of the regularly repeated stressed and unstressed or long and short syllables *[*iambic *rhythm]* **—rhyth′mic** (rith′mik), **rhyth′mi·cal** *adj.* **—rhyth′mi·cal·ly** *adv.*

rhythm and blues a form of popular U.S. Negro music, influenced by the blues and having a strong beat

rhythm method a method of seeking birth control by abstaining from sexual intercourse during the woman's probable monthly ovulation period

R.I., RI Rhode Island

ri·al (rī′əl) *n.* [Per. < Ar. < Sp. *real,* REAL²] *see* MONETARY UNITS, table (Iran and Oman)

ri·al·to (rē al′tō) *n., pl.* **-tos** [< *Rialto,* a bridge in Venice, Italy] a trading area or marketplace

rib (rib) *n.* [OE. *rib*] **1.** any of the curved bones attached to the backbone and enclosing the chest cavity: in man there are twelve pairs of such bones: see TRUE RIBS, FALSE RIBS, FLOATING RIBS **2.** a cut of meat having one or more ribs, as spareribs **3.** a raised ridge in woven or knitted material **4.** any riblike piece used to form a framework, or to shape or strengthen something *[*an umbrella *rib]* **5.** any of the main veins of a leaf **6.** [Slang] a playfully teasing remark or action *—vt.* **ribbed, rib′bing** **1.** to provide, form, or strengthen with ribs **2.** [Slang] to tease playfully **—ribbed** *adj.* **—rib′ber** *n.* **—rib′less** *adj.*

rib·ald (rib′əld) *adj.* [OFr. *ribaud,* debauchee, ult. < OHG. *riban,* to copulate] characterized by coarse joking; esp., dealing with sex in a humorously earthy or direct way *—n.* a ribald person

rib·ald·ry (-əl drē) *n.* ribald language or humor

rib·and (rib′ənd, -ən) *n. archaic var. of* RIBBON

rib·bing (rib′iŋ) *n.* an arrangement or series of ribs, as in knitted fabric, a ship's framework, etc.

rib·bon (rib′ən) *n.* [MFr. *riban*] **1.** a narrow strip as of silk or rayon, used for decorating or tying, for badges, etc. **2.** anything suggesting such a strip *[a ribbon of blue sky]* **3.** [*pl.*] torn strips or shreds; tatters *[a sleeve torn to ribbons]* **4.** a narrow strip of cloth inked for use in a typewriter, etc. —*vt.* **1.** to decorate, trim, or mark with ribbons **2.** to tear into ribbonlike shreds —*vi.* to extend in a ribbonlike strip —**rib′bon·like′** *adj.*

ri·bo·fla·vin (rī′bə flā′vin) *n.* [< *ribose,* a sugar + FLAVIN] a factor of the vitamin B complex, found in milk, eggs, liver, fruits, leafy vegetables, etc.: lack of riboflavin in the diet causes stunted growth, loss of hair, etc.

ri·bo·nu·cle·ase (rī′bō no͞o′klē ās′, -nyo͞o′-) *n.* [RIBO(SE) + NUCLEASE] any of various enzymes that split ribonucleic acid

ri·bo·nu·cle·ic acid (-no͞o klē′ik, -nyo͞o-) [RIBO(SE) + NUCLEIC ACID] an essential component in the cytoplasm of all living cells, composed of long chains of phosphate and ribose along with several bases bonded to the ribose: one form carries the genetic information needed for protein synthesis in the cell

ri·bose (rī′bōs) *n.* [< G. *rib(onsäure),* an acid containing four OH radicals + -OSE[1]] a sugar, $C_5H_{10}O_5$, derived from nucleic acids

ri·bo·some (rī′bə sōm′) *n.* [RIBO(SE) + -SOME[3]] any of the minute particles composed of RNA and proteins, found in cell cytoplasm and functioning in the production of proteins —**ri′bo·so′mal** *adj.*

-ric (rik) [OE. *rice,* reign] *a combining form meaning* jurisdiction, realm *[bishopric]*

rice (rīs) *n.* [OFr. *ris* < It. < L. < Gr. *oryza:* of Oriental origin] **1.** a cereal grass of warm climates, planted in ground under water **2.** its starchy seeds or grain, used as food —*vt.* **riced, ric′ing** to form (cooked potatoes, etc.) into ricelike granules

rice paper **1.** a thin paper made from the straw of rice **2.** a fine, delicate paper made by cutting and pressing the pith of an Asian plant (the **rice-paper plant**)

ric·er (rī′sər) *n.* a utensil for ricing cooked potatoes, etc. by forcing them through small holes

rich (rich) *adj.* [OE. *rice,* noble, powerful < OFr. < Gmc.] **1.** having much money or property; wealthy **2.** having abundant natural resources *[a rich region]* **3.** well supplied (*with*); abounding (*in*) **4.** valuable *[a rich prize]* **5.** costly and elegant; sumptuous *[rich gifts]* **6.** *a)* containing much butter (or other fat), cream, sugar, flavoring, etc. *[rich foods]* *b)* strong and flavorful *[rich wine]* **7.** *a)* full and mellow: said of sounds, the voice, etc. *b)* deep; vivid: said of colors *c)* very fragrant: said of odors **8.** abundant; ample *[a rich fund of stories]* **9.** yielding in abundance, as soil, etc. **10.** [Colloq.] *a)* very amusing *b)* absurd; preposterous —**the rich** wealthy people collectively —**rich′ly** *adv.* —**rich′ness** *n.*

Rich·ard (rich′ərd) [< OFr. < OHG. *Richart* < Gmc. bases meaning "strong king"] **1.** a masculine name **2.** **Richard I,** 1157–99; king of England (1189–99): called **Richard the Lion-Hearted** (Fr. *Richard Coeur de Lion*) **3.** **Richard II,** 1367–1400; king of England (1377–99) **4.** **Richard III,** 1452–85; king of England (1483–85)

Rich·ard·son (rich′ərd sən), **Samuel** 1689–1761; Eng. novelist

Ri·che·lieu (rish′ə lo͞o′; *Fr.* rēsh lyö′), duc **de** (*Armand Jean du Plessis*) 1585–1642; Fr. cardinal & statesman

rich·en (rich′′n) *vt.* to make rich or richer

rich·es (-iz) *n.pl.* [ME. *richess, n. sing.* < OFr. *richesse*] valuable possessions; much money, property, etc.; wealth

Rich·mond (rich′mənd) **1.** [after Duke of *Richmond,* son of CHARLES II] borough of New York City, including Staten Island: pop. 352,000 **2.** [after *Richmond,* city in SE England] *a)* capital of Va.; port on the James River: pop. 219,000 (met. area 631,000) *b)* seaport in W Calif., on San Francisco Bay: pop. 75,000

Rich·ter scale (rik′tər) [devised by C. *Richter* (1900–), U.S. seismologist] a scale for measuring the magnitude of earthquakes, with each of its 10 steps about 60 times greater than the preceding step

rick (rik) *n.* [OE. *hreac*] a stack of hay, straw, etc. in a field, esp. one covered for protection from rain —*vt.* to pile (hay, etc.) into ricks

rick·ets (rik′its) *n.* [altered < ? RACHITIS] a disease, chiefly of children, characterized by a softening and, often, bending of the bones: it is caused by lack of vitamin D

rick·ett·si·a (ri ket′sē ə) *n., pl.* **-si·ae′** (-ē′), **-si·as** [ModL., after H. T. *Ricketts* (1871–1910), U.S. pathologist] any of a genus of microorganisms that cause certain diseases, as typhus, and are transmitted by the bite of certain lice and ticks —**rick·ett′si·al** *adj.*

rick·et·y (rik′it ē) *adj.* **1.** of or having rickets **2.** weak in the joints; tottering **3.** liable to fall apart or break down; shaky —**rick′et·i·ness** *n.*

rick·rack (rik′rak′) *n.* [redupl. of RACK[1]] flat, zigzag braid for trimming dresses, etc.

rick·shaw, rick·sha (rik′shô) *n. same as* JINRIKISHA

ric·o·chet (rik′ə shā′, rik′ə shā′; *also, chiefly Brit.,* -shet′) *n.* [Fr.] **1.** the rebound or skipping of a bullet, stone, etc. after striking a surface at an angle **2.** a bullet, etc. that ricochets —*vi.* **-cheted′** (-shād′) or **-chet′ted** (-shet′id), **-chet′ing** (-shā′iŋ) or **-chet′ting** (-shet′iŋ) to move with such a motion

ri·cot·ta (ri kät′ə; *It.* rē kôt′tä) *n.* [It. < L. pp. of *recoquere,* to boil again] a soft, dry or moist Italian cheese made from whey left from making other cheeses

rid (rid) *vt.* **rid** or **rid′ded, rid′ding** [ON. *rythja,* to clear (land)] to free, clear, or relieve, as of something undesirable *[to rid a garden of weeds]* —**be rid of** to be freed from —**get rid of** **1.** to get free from **2.** to do away with; dispose of

rid·dance (rid′′ns) *n.* a ridding or being rid; clearance or removal, as of something undesirable —**good riddance!** welcome relief or deliverance!

rid·den (rid′′n) *pp. of* RIDE —*adj.* controlled or obsessed (by the thing specified) *[fear-ridden]*

rid·dle[1] (rid′′l) *n.* [OE. *rædels,* akin to *rædan,* to guess] **1.** a puzzle in the form of a question or statement with a tricky meaning or answer that is hard to guess; conundrum **2.** any puzzling or perplexing person or thing; enigma —*vt.* **-dled, -dling** to solve or explain (a riddle) —*vi.* to utter riddles —**rid′dler** *n.*

rid·dle[2] (rid′′l) *n.* [OE. *hriddel*] a coarse sieve —*vt.* **-dled, -dling** **1.** to sift through a riddle **2.** *a)* to make many holes in, as with buckshot *b)* to affect every part of *[riddled with errors]*

ride (rīd) *vi.* **rode** or archaic **rid** (rid), **rid′den** or archaic **rid** or **rode, rid′ing** [OE. *ridan*] **1.** *a)* to sit on and control a horse or other animal in motion *b)* to be carried along (*in* a vehicle, *on* a bicycle, etc.) *c)* to move along as if so carried *d)* to be carried or supported in motion (*on* or *upon*) *[tanks ride on treads]* **2.** to admit of being ridden *[the car rides smoothly]* **3.** to move, lie, or float on the water **4.** to be dependent (*on*) *[the change rides on his approval]* **5.** to be placed as a bet (*on*) **6.** [Colloq.] to continue undisturbed, with no action taken —*vt.* **1.** to sit on or in and control so as to move along *[to ride a horse]* **2.** to move along on or be carried or supported on *[to ride the waves]* **3.** to move over, along, or through (a road, area, etc.) by horse, car, etc. **4.** to cover (a specified distance) by riding **5.** to engage in by riding *[to ride a race]* **6.** to cause to ride **7.** to control, dominate, or oppress *[ridden by fear]* **8.** [Colloq.] to torment or tease, as with ridicule, criticism, etc. —*n.* **1.** *a)* a riding; esp., a journey by horse, car, bicycle, etc. *b)* a way or chance to ride *c)* the way a car, etc. rides **2.** a road, etc. for riding **3.** a roller coaster, Ferris wheel, or other thing to ride, as at a carnival —**ride down** **1.** to knock down by riding against **2.** to overtake by riding **3.** to overcome **4.** to exhaust (a horse, etc.) by riding —**ride herd (on)** to keep under close control —**ride out** to withstand or endure (a storm, crisis, etc.) successfully —**ride up** to move upward out of place, as an article of clothing —**take for a ride** [Slang] **1.** to take somewhere, as in a car, and kill **2.** to cheat or swindle —**rid′a·ble, ride′a·ble** *adj.*

rid·er (-ər) *n.* **1.** a person who rides **2.** *a)* an addition or amendment to a contract, etc. *b)* a clause, usually dealing with an unrelated matter, added to a legislative bill when it is up for passage **3.** any of various pieces moving or resting on something else —**rid′er·less** *adj.*

rid·er·ship (-ship′) *n.* the passengers using a particular system of public transportation over a given period of time, or the estimated number of these

ridge (rij) *n.* [OE. *hrycg*] **1.** the long, narrow top or crest of something, as of an animal's back, a wave, etc. **2.** a long, narrow elevation of land or similar range of hills or mountains **3.** any narrow, raised strip, as on fabric **4.** the horizontal line formed by the meeting of two sloping surfaces *[the ridge of a roof]* —*vt., vi.* **ridged, ridg′ing** to form into or mark with a ridge or ridges —**ridge′like′** *adj.*

ridge·pole (-pōl′) *n.* the horizontal timber or beam at the ridge of a roof: also **ridge′piece′**

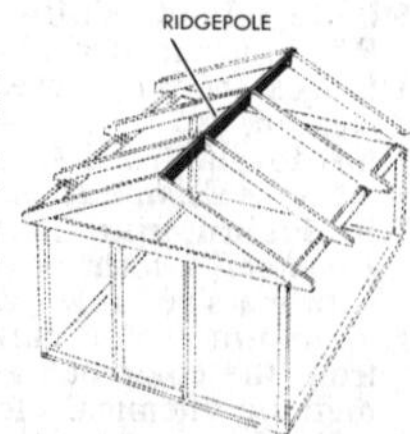

rid·i·cule (rid′i kyo͞ol′) *n.* [Fr. < L. *ridiculum,* a jest, ult. < *ridere,* to laugh] **1.** the act of making someone or something the object of scornful laughter by joking, mocking, etc.; derision **2.** words or actions used in doing this —*vt.* **-culed′, -cul′ing** to make fun of or make others laugh at; deride; mock

ri·dic·u·lous (ri dik′yə ləs) *adj.* deserving ridicule; absurd —**ri·dic′u·lous·ly** *adv.* —**ri·dic′u·lous·ness** *n.*

rid·ing[1] (rīd′iŋ) *adj.* **1.** that rides or is ridden **2.** of or for riders on horseback —*n.* the act of one that rides

rid·ing[2] (rīd′iŋ) *n.* [OE. *-thrithing,* a third part] formerly, any of the three administrative divisions of Yorkshire, England

Rif (rif) mountain range along the Mediterranean coast of Morocco: also **Er Rif** (er)

rife (rīf) ***adj.*** [OE. *ryfe*] **1.** frequently or commonly occurring; widespread [gossip was *rife*] **2.** *a*) abundant *b*) abounding; filled [*rife* with error] —**rife′ness** ***n.***

Riff (rif) *same as* RIF —***n.***, *pl.* **Riffs, Riff′i** (-ē) a member of a Berber people living in or near the Rif

rif·fle (rif′'l) ***n.*** [< ? or akin to G. *riffel*, a groove] **1.** *a*) a shoal, reef, etc. in a stream, producing a stretch of ruffled or choppy water *b*) a stretch of such water, or a ripple on it **2.** the act or a method of riffling cards —***vt., vi.* -fled, -fling** **1.** to ruffle or ripple **2.** to leaf rapidly (through) by releasing pages, etc. along their edge with the thumb **3.** to shuffle (playing cards) by holding part of the deck in each hand and mixing the cards together with riffling motions

riff·raff (rif′raf′) ***n.*** [< OFr. *rif et raf* < *rifler*, to scrape + *rafle*, a raking in] **1.** those people regarded as worthless, insignificant, etc.; rabble **2.** [Dial.] trash

ri·fle¹ (rī′f'l) ***vt.* -fled, -fling** [Fr. *rifler*, to scrape < OFr. < MHG. *riffeln*, to scratch] **1.** to cut spiral grooves on the inside of (a gun barrel, etc.) **2.** to hurl or throw with great speed —***n.*** **1.** a shoulder gun with spiral grooves cut into the inner surface of the barrel: see RIFLING **2.** [*pl.*] troops armed with rifles

ri·fle² (rī′f'l) ***vt.* -fled, -fling** [< OFr. *rifler*, to plunder, orig. to scratch: see prec.] **1.** to ransack and rob; pillage; plunder **2.** to take as plunder; steal —**ri′fler** ***n.***

ri·fle·man (-mən) ***n.***, *pl.* **-men** **1.** a soldier armed with a rifle **2.** a man who uses a rifle

rifle range a place for target practice with a rifle

ri·fle·ry (-rē) ***n.*** the skill or practice of shooting at targets with rifles

ri·fling (rī′fliŋ) ***n.*** **1.** the cutting of spiral grooves within a gun barrel, to make the projectile spin when fired **2.** a system of such grooves

rift (rift) ***n.*** [Dan., a fissure < *rive*, to tear] **1.** an opening caused by splitting; fissure; cleft **2.** an open break in friendly relations —***vt., vi.*** to burst open; split

rig (rig) ***vt.* rigged, rig′ging** [< Scand.] **1.** *a*) to fit (a ship, mast, etc.) with sails, shrouds, etc. *b*) to fit (a ship's sails, shrouds, etc.) to the masts, yards, etc. **2.** to fit (*out*); equip **3.** to prepare for use, esp. in a hurry (often with *up*) **4.** to arrange in a dishonest way [to *rig* a contest] **5.** [Colloq.] to dress; clothe (usually with *out*) —***n.*** **1.** the arrangement of sails, masts, etc. on a vessel **2.** equipment; gear **3.** *a*) a carriage, etc. with its horse or horses *b*) a tractor-trailer **4.** [Colloq.] dress; costume —**rig′ger** ***n.***

Ri·ga (rē′gə) capital of the Latvian S.S.R.; seaport on the Baltic Sea: pop. 733,000

rig·a·ma·role (rig′ə mə rōl′) ***n.*** *var. of* RIGMAROLE

ri·ga·to·ni (rig′ə tō′nē; *It.* rē′gä tô′nē) ***n.*** [It., pl. < pp. of *rigare*, to mark with lines] short, ridged casings of pasta, often stuffed with ground meat, cheese, etc.

Ri·gel (rī′j'l, -g'l) [Ar. *rijl*, foot: in the left foot of Orion] a bright, bluish star, brightest in the constellation Orion

rig·ging (rig′iŋ) ***n.*** **1.** the chains, ropes, etc. used for supporting and working the masts, sails, etc. of a vessel **2.** equipment; gear

right (rīt) ***adj.*** [OE. *riht*] **1.** orig., straight [a *right* line] **2.** *a*) formed by a straight line perpendicular to a base [a *right* angle] *b*) having the axis perpendicular to the base [a *right* cylinder] **3.** in accordance with justice, law, morality, etc.; virtuous [*right* conduct] **4.** in accordance with fact, reason, etc.; correct; true [the *right* answer] **5.** *a*) fitting; suitable *b*) most convenient or favorable **6.** designating the side meant to be seen [the *right* side of cloth] **7.** having sound physical or mental health **8.** *a*) designating or of that side of one's body which is toward the east when one faces north *b*) designating or of the corresponding side of anything *c*) closer to the right side of a person facing the thing mentioned [the top *right* drawer] **9.** of the bank of a river on the right of a person facing downstream **10.** of the political right; conservative or reactionary —***n.*** **1.** what is right, or just, lawful, proper, etc. **2.** *a*) a power, privilege, etc. that a person has or gets by law, nature, tradition, etc. [the *right* of free speech] *b*) [*often pl.*] an interest in property, real or intangible **3.** the true report, as of a happening (with *the*) **4.** *a*) the right side *b*) a turn toward the right side **5.** *Boxing a*) the right hand *b*) a blow delivered with the right hand **6.** [*often* **R-**] *Politics* a conservative or reactionary position, party, etc. (often with *the*): from the location of their seats in some European legislatures —***adv.*** **1.** in a straight line; directly [go *right* home] **2.** in a way that is correct, proper, just, favorable, etc.; well **3.** completely [soaked *right* through his coat] **4.** exactly [*right* here] **5.** immediately [come *right* down] **6.** on or toward the right hand **7.** very [he knows *right* well]: colloquial except in certain titles [the *right* reverend] —***interj.*** agreed! I understand! —***vt.*** **1.** to put in or restore to an upright position [we *righted* the boat] **2.** to correct **3.** to put in order [she *righted* the room] **4.** to make amends for —***vi.*** to regain an upright position —**by right** (or **rights**) in justice; properly —**in one's own right** through one's own status, ability, etc. —**in the right** on the side supported by truth, justice, etc. —**right away** (or **off**) without delay; at once —**right on!** [Slang] precisely! exactly! that's right!: an exclamation of approval or encouragement —**to rights** [Colloq.] in or into proper condition or order —**right′a·ble** ***adj.*** —**right′er** ***n.*** —**right′ness** ***n.***

right·a·bout (rīt′ə bout′) ***n.*** **1.** *same as* RIGHTABOUT-FACE **2.** the direction faced after turning completely about —***adv., adj.*** with, in, or by a rightabout-face

right·a·bout-face (-fās′) ***n.*** **1.** a turning directly about so as to face the opposite direction **2.** a complete reversal of belief, conduct, etc. —***interj.*** a military command to perform a rightabout-face

right angle an angle of 90 degrees, made by the meeting of two straight lines perpendicular to each other

right-an·gled (rīt′aŋ′g'ld) ***adj.*** having or forming one or more right angles; rectangular: also **right′-an′gle**

RIGHT ANGLE

right·eous (rī′chəs) ***adj.*** [altered < OE. *rihtwis*: see RIGHT & -WISE] **1.** acting justly; doing what is right; upright; virtuous [a *righteous* man] **2.** morally right or having a sound moral basis [*righteous* anger] —**right′eous·ly** ***adv.*** —**right′eous·ness** ***n.***

right·ful (rīt′fəl) ***adj.*** **1.** fair; just; right **2.** having a just, lawful claim [the *rightful* owner] **3.** belonging or owned by just or lawful claim [a *rightful* rank] **4.** proper; fitting —**right′ful·ly** ***adv.*** —**right′ful·ness** ***n.***

right-hand (rīt′hand′) ***adj.*** **1.** on or directed toward the right **2.** of, for, or with the right hand **3.** most helpful or reliable [the president's *right-hand* man]

right-hand·ed (-han′did) ***adj.*** **1.** using the right hand more skillfully than the left **2.** done with the right hand **3.** made for use with the right hand **4.** turning from left to right; clockwise —***adv.*** with the right hand [to throw *right-handed*] —**right′-hand′ed·ly** ***adv.*** —**right′-hand′ed·ness** ***n.*** —**right′-hand′er** ***n.***

right·ist (rīt′ist) ***n.*** a person whose political position is conservative or reactionary; member of the right —***adj.*** conservative or reactionary —**right′ism** ***n.***

right·ly (rīt′lē) ***adv.*** **1.** with justice; fairly **2.** properly; suitably **3.** correctly

right-mind·ed (rīt′mīn′did) ***adj.*** thinking or believing what is right; having correct views or sound principles —**right′-mind′ed·ly** ***adv.*** —**right′-mind′ed·ness** ***n.***

right·o (rīt′ō, rī′tō′) ***interj.*** [Chiefly Brit.] yes; certainly

right of asylum the right of a nation to extend protection to refugees, esp. political refugees, from another nation

right of way **1.** the legal right to move in front of others, as at a traffic intersection **2.** the right to use a certain route, as over another's property **3.** *a*) a strip of land used by a railroad for its tracks *b*) land over which a public road, a power line, etc. passes Also **right′-of-way′**

right-on (rit′än′, -ôn′) ***adj.*** [Slang] sophisticated, informed, current, etc.

right-to-work (rīt′tə wurk′) ***adj.*** designating or of laws prohibiting the union shop

right triangle a triangle with one right angle

right·ward (-wərd) ***adv., adj.*** on or toward the right: also **right′wards** ***adv.***

right whale a large-headed whalebone whale without teeth or dorsal fin

right wing [see RIGHT, *n.* 6] the more conservative or reactionary section of a political party, group, etc. —**right′-wing′** ***adj.*** —**right′-wing′er** ***n.***

rig·id (rij′id) ***adj.*** [< L. < *rigere*, to be stiff] **1.** not bending or flexible; stiff [a *rigid* metal girder] **2.** not moving; set **3.** severe, strict, or rigorous [a *rigid* taskmaster, a *rigid* rule] **4.** *Aeron.* having a rigid framework that encloses containers for the gas, as a dirigible —**ri·gid·i·ty** (ri jid′ə tē), **rig′id·ness** ***n.*** —**rig′id·ly** ***adv.***

ri·gid·i·fy (ri jid′ə fī′) ***vt., vi.* -fied′, -fy′ing** to make or become rigid —**ri·gid′i·fi·ca′tion** ***n.***

rig·ma·role (rig′mə rōl′) ***n.*** [< *ragman roll* < ME. *rageman rolle*, a document] **1.** rambling talk; nonsense **2.** a fussy or time-wasting procedure

rig·or (rig′ər; *for 4, also* rī′gôr) ***n.*** [< MFr. < L. < *rigere*, to be rigid] **1.** harshness or severity; specif., *a*) strictness [the *rigor* of martial law] *b*) extreme hardship [the *rigors* of life] **2.** exact precision or accuracy **3.** a severe, harsh, or oppressive act, etc. **4.** stiffness or rigidity, esp. in body tissues Also, Brit. sp., **rig′our**

rig·or mor·tis (rig′ər môr′tis, rī′gôr) [ModL., stiffness of death] the stiffening of the muscles after death

rig·or·ous (rig′ər əs) ***adj.*** **1.** very strict or harsh *[rigorous* rules*]* **2.** very severe or sharp *[*a *rigorous* climate*]* **3.** exactly precise or accurate *[rigorous* scholarship*]* **—rig′or·ous·ly** ***adv.*** **—rig′or·ous·ness** ***n.***

Ri·je·ka (rē ye′kä) seaport in NW Yugoslavia, on the Adriatic: pop. 101,000

Rijn (rīn) *Du. name of the* RHINE

rile (rīl) ***vt.*** **riled, ril′ing** [var. of ROIL] [Colloq. or Dial.] **1.** *same as* ROIL **2.** to anger; irritate

Ri·ley (rī′lē), **James Whit·comb** (hwit′kəm, wit′-) 1849–1916; U.S. poet

rill (ril) ***n.*** [< Du. *ril* or LowG. *rille*] a little brook

rim (rim) ***n.*** [OE. *rima,* an edge] **1.** an edge, border, or margin, esp. of something circular **2.** *a)* the outer part of a wheel *b)* the metal flange of an automobile wheel, on which the tire is mounted **3.** *Basketball* the metal hoop to which the net is attached ***—vt.*** **rimmed, rim′ming 1.** to put a rim on or around **2.** to roll around the rim of *[*the golf ball *rimmed* the hole*]* **—rim′less** ***adj.***

Rim·baud (ran bō′), **(Jean Nicolas) Ar·thur** (år tür′) 1854–91; Fr. poet

rime[1] (rīm) ***n., vt., vi.*** **rimed, rim′ing** *same as* RHYME **—rim′er** ***n.***

rime[2] (rīm) ***n.*** [OE. *hrim*] a white frost on grass, leaves, etc.; hoarfrost ***—vt.*** **rimed, rim′ing** to coat with rime

Rim·sky-Kor·sa·kov (rēm′skē kôr′sä kôf′; *E.* rim′skē kôr′sə kôf′), **Ni·ko·lai (Andreyevich)** (nē kô lī′) 1844–1908; Russ. composer: also sp. **Rimski-Korsakoff**

rind (rīnd) ***n.*** [OE.] a thick, hard, or tough outer layer or coating, as on fruit, cheese, bacon, etc.

rin·der·pest (rin′dər pest′) ***n.*** [G. *rinder,* cattle + *pest,* a plague] an acute infectious disease of cattle and, often, sheep and goats

ring[1] (riŋ) ***vi.*** **rang** or now chiefly dial. **rung, rung, ring′ing** [OE. *hringan*] **1.** to give forth the clear, resonant sound of a bell **2.** to produce, as by sounding, a specified impression *[*promises that *ring* false*]* **3.** to cause a bell to sound, esp. as a summons *[*to *ring* for a maid*]* **4.** to sound loudly; resound *[*the room *rang* with laughter*]* **5.** to have a sensation as of ringing, etc.: said of the ears or head ***—vt.*** **1.** to cause (a bell, etc.) to ring **2.** to sound (a peal, knell, etc.) as by ringing a bell **3.** to signal, announce, etc. as by ringing **4.** to call by telephone (often with *up*) **5.** [Slang] to substitute fraudulently (often with *in*) ***—n.*** **1.** the sound of a bell **2.** any similar sound, esp. when loud and continued **3.** a characteristic sound or impression *[*the *ring* of sincerity*]* **4.** the act of ringing a bell, etc. **5.** a telephone call: chiefly in **give (someone) a ring,** to telephone (someone) **—ring a bell** to stir up a memory **—ring down** (or **up**) **the curtain 1.** to signal for a theater curtain to be lowered (or raised) **2.** to end (or begin) something **—ring up** to record (a specified amount) on a cash register

ring[2] (riŋ) ***n.*** [OE. *hring*] **1.** a small, circular band, esp. of precious metal, to be worn on the finger **2.** any similar band used for some special purpose *[*a key *ring]* **3.** a circular line, mark, or figure **4.** the outer edge, or rim, as of a wheel **5.** any of the circular marks seen in the cross section of a tree trunk: each ring represents a year's growth: in full, **annual ring 6.** a number of people or things grouped in a circle **7.** a group of people working together to advance their own selfish interests, as in politics, etc. **8.** an enclosed area, often circular, for contests, exhibitions, etc. *[*a circus *ring]* **9.** *a)* an enclosure, now a square, in which boxing and wrestling matches are held *b)* prizefighting (with *the*) **10.** a contest: often used in **throw one's hat into the ring,** to enter a contest, esp. one for political office **11.** *Chem.* a number of atoms united in such a way that they can be represented as a ring ***—vt.*** **ringed, ring′ing 1.** to encircle as with a ring **2.** to form into, or furnish with, a ring or rings **3.** in some games, to toss a ring, horseshoe, etc. so that it encircles (a peg) **4.** to cut a circle of bark from (a tree) ***—vi.*** to form in a ring or rings **—run rings around** [Colloq.] **1.** to run much faster than **2.** to excel greatly **—ringed** ***adj.***

ring·bolt (-bōlt′) ***n.*** a bolt with a ring at the head

ring·dove (-duv′) ***n.*** **1.** the European wood pigeon **2.** a small dove of Europe and Asia, with a dark ring around the neck

ring·er[1] (riŋ′ər) ***n.*** **1.** a horseshoe, quoit, etc. thrown so that it encircles the peg **2.** such a throw

ring·er[2] (riŋ′ər) ***n.*** **1.** a person or thing that rings a bell, chime, etc. **2.** [Slang] *a)* a horse, player, etc. fraudulently entered, or substituted for another, in a competition *b)* a person or thing very closely resembling another

ring·git (riŋ′git) ***n., pl.*** **ring′git** [native term] *see* MONETARY UNITS, table (Malaysia)

ring·lead·er (riŋ′lēd′ər) ***n.*** a person who leads others, esp. in unlawful acts, etc.

ring·let (-lit) ***n.*** **1.** a little ring **2.** a curl of hair, esp. a long one **—ring′let·ed** ***adj.***

ring·mas·ter (riŋ′mas′tər) ***n.*** a man who directs the performances in a circus ring

ring-necked pheasant (-nekt′) an Asian game fowl with a whitish collar around the neck in the male, now widespread in N. America

ring·side (-sīd′) ***n.*** **1.** the place just outside the ring, as at a boxing match or circus **2.** any place that provides a close view of something

ring·worm (-wurm′) ***n.*** any contagious skin disease caused by a fungus that produces ring-shaped patches

rink (riŋk) ***n.*** [< Scot. < OFr. *renc,* RANK[1]] **1.** a smooth expanse of ice, often enclosed, for ice-skating or for playing hockey **2.** a smooth floor, usually of wood and enclosed, for roller-skating **3.** the building enclosing a rink

rinse (rins) ***vt.*** **rinsed, rins′ing** [< OFr. *rincer,* ult. < L. *recens,* fresh] **1.** to wash lightly, as by dipping into clear water **2.** *a)* to remove soap, dirt, etc. from by such washing *b)* to remove (soap, dirt, etc.) by such washing **3.** to flush (the mouth or teeth), as with clear water **4.** *a)* to dip (fabrics, etc.) into a dye solution *b)* to use a rinse on (the hair) ***—vi.*** to undergo rinsing ***—n.*** **1.** a rinsing **2.** the water or solution used in rinsing **3.** a substance mixed with water and used to tint hair **—rins′er** ***n.***

Ri·o de Ja·nei·ro (rē′ō dā′ zhə ner′ō, dē′, də; jə nir′ō) seaport in SE Brazil, on the Atlantic: pop. 4,297,000

Ri·o Grande (rē′ō grand′, gran′dē, grän′dā) river flowing from S Colo. through N.Mex., then southeast as the boundary of Texas & Mexico into the Gulf of Mexico: 1,885 mi.

ri·ot (rī′ət) ***n.*** [OFr. *riote* < *rihoter,* to make a disturbance] **1.** wild or violent disorder, confusion, etc.; tumult **2.** a violent, public disturbance of the peace by a number of persons (in law, usually three or more) assembled together **3.** a brilliant display *[*a *riot* of color*]* **4.** [Now Rare] *a)* debauchery *b)* unrestrained revelry or a wild revel **5.** [Colloq.] an extremely amusing person, thing, or event ***—vi.*** **1.** to take part in a riot or public disturbance **2.** [Now Rare] to revel **—read the riot act to** to command to stop doing something, under threat of punishment **—run riot 1.** to act in a wild, unrestrained manner **2.** to grow in profusion **—ri′ot·er** ***n.***

ri·ot·ous (rī′ət əs) ***adj.*** **1.** *a)* having the nature of a disturbance of the peace *b)* engaging in rioting **2.** disorderly or boisterous **3.** debauched; immoral *[riotous* living*]* **4.** luxuriant or profuse **—ri′ot·ous·ly** ***adv.*** **—ri′ot·ous·ness** ***n.***

rip[1] (rip) ***vt.*** **ripped, rip′ping** [prob. < or akin to Fl. *rippen,* to tear] **1.** *a)* to cut or tear apart roughly *b)* to remove as by cutting or tearing (with *off, out,* etc.) *c)* to make (a hole) in this way *d)* to slash with a sharp instrument *e)* to cut or tear (stitches) so as to open (a seam, hem, etc.) **2.** to saw or split (wood) along the grain ***—vi.*** **1.** to become torn or split apart **2.** [Colloq.] to move with speed or violence ***—n.*** a torn place or burst seam; split **—rip into** [Colloq.] to attack violently, often with words **—rip off** [Slang] **1.** to steal or rob **2.** to cheat, exploit, etc. **—rip out** [Colloq.] to utter sharply, as in anger **—rip′per** ***n.***

rip[2] (rip) ***n.*** [< ? prec.] an extent of rough water caused by cross currents or tides meeting

rip[3] (rip) ***n.*** [var. of *rep,* prob. abbrev. of REPROBATE] [Colloq.] a debauched, dissipated person

R.I.P. *abbrev. of* REQUIESCAT IN PACE

ri·par·i·an (ri per′ē ən, rī-) ***adj.*** [< L. < *ripa,* a bank] of, adjacent to, or living on the bank of a river or, sometimes, of a lake, pond, etc.

rip cord a cord, etc. pulled to open a parachute during descent

ripe (rīp) ***adj.*** [OE.] **1.** fully grown or developed; specif., ready to be harvested for food, as grain or fruit **2.** like ripe fruit, as in being ruddy and full *[ripe* lips*]* **3.** sufficiently processed to be ready for use *[ripe* cheese*]* **4.** fully or highly developed; mature *[ripe* wisdom*]* **5.** advanced in years *[*the *ripe* age of ninety*]* **6.** fully prepared *[ripe* for marriage*]* **7.** ready for some treatment or process *[*a boil *ripe* for lancing*]* **8.** far enough along (*for* some purpose): said of time **—ripe′ly** ***adv.*** **—ripe′ness** ***n.***

rip·en (rī′pən) ***vi., vt.*** to become or make ripe; mature, age, cure, etc. **—rip′en·er** ***n.***

rip-off (rip′ôf′) ***n.*** [Slang] a stealing, robbing, cheating, exploiting, etc.

ri·poste, ri·post (ri pōst′) ***n.*** [< Fr. < It. *risposta* < L. *respondere:* see RESPOND] **1.** *Fencing* a sharp, swift thrust made after parrying an opponent's lunge **2.** a sharp, swift retort ***—vi.*** **-post′ed, -post′ing** to make a riposte

rip·ping (rip′iŋ) ***adj.*** **1.** that rips or tears **2.** [Chiefly Brit. Slang] excellent; fine **—rip′ping·ly** ***adv.***

rip·ple (rip′'l) ***vi.*** **-pled, -pling** [prob. < RIP[1] + *-le,* freq. suffix] **1.** *a)* to form or have little waves on the surface, as water stirred by a breeze *b)* to flow with such waves on the surface **2.** to give the effect of rippling water, as by alternately rising and falling *[*laughter *rippling* through the hall*]* ***—vt.*** to cause to ripple ***—n.*** **1.** a small wave or undulation, as on the surface of water **2.** a movement, appearance, etc. like this 3. a sound like that of rippling water —**rip′pler** *n.* —**rip′ply** (-lē) *adj.* **-pli·er, -pli·est**

ripple effect the spreading effects experienced as the result of a single event

rip-roar·ing (-rôr′iŋ) *adj.* [Slang] boisterous; uproarious

rip·saw (-sô′) *n.* [RIP[1] + SAW[1]] a saw with coarse teeth, for cutting wood along the grain

rip·tide (-tīd′) *n.* [RIP[2] + TIDE] a tide opposing another tide, producing rough waters

rise (rīz) *vi.* **rose, ris·en** (riz′'n), **ris′ing** [OE. *risan*] **1.** to stand or assume an erect or nearly erect position after sitting, lying etc. **2.** to get up after sleeping or resting **3.** to rebel; revolt **4.** to end an official assembly or meeting **5.** to return to life after dying **6.** to go to a higher place or position; ascend **7.** to appear above the horizon *[the moon rose]* **8.** to attain a higher level *[the river is rising]* **9.** to advance in status, rank, etc.; become rich, famous, etc. **10.** to become erect or rigid **11.** to extend or incline upward *[hills rising steeply]* **12.** to increase in amount, degree, etc. **13.** to become louder, shriller, etc. **14.** to become stronger, more vivid, etc. **15.** to become larger and puffier, as dough with yeast **16.** to originate; begin **17.** to have its source: said of a stream **18.** to happen; occur **19.** to become apparent to the senses or the mind *[land rising ahead of the ship]* **20.** to become aroused *[to make one's temper rise]* **21.** to be built *[the house rose quickly]* —*vt.* to cause to rise, as birds from cover —*n.* **1.** the appearance of the sun, moon, etc. above the horizon **2.** upward motion; ascent **3.** an advance in status, rank, etc. **4.** the appearance of a fish at the water's surface **5.** a piece of rising ground; hill **6.** a slope upward **7.** the vertical height of something, as a staircase **8.** *a)* an increase in height, as of water level *b)* an increase in pitch of a sound *c)* an increase in degree, amount, etc. **9.** a beginning, origin, etc. **10.** [Brit.] a raise (in wages) —**get a rise out of** [Slang] to draw a desired response from, as by teasing —**give rise to** to bring about; begin —**rise to** to prove oneself capable of coping with *[to rise to the occasion]*

ris·er (rīz′ər) *n.* **1.** a person or thing that rises **2.** a vertical piece between the steps in a stairway

ris·i·bil·i·ty (riz′ə bil′ə tē) *n., pl.* **-ties 1.** the quality or state of being risible **2.** [*usually pl.*] a sense of the ridiculous or amusing

ris·i·ble (riz′ə b'l) *adj.* [Fr. < LL. < L. pp. of *ridere,* to laugh] **1.** able or inclined to laugh **2.** of or connected with laughter **3.** causing laughter; laughable; funny

ris·ing (rī′ziŋ) *adj.* **1.** that rises; ascending, advancing, etc. **2.** growing; maturing *[the rising generation]* **3.** [Colloq. or Dial.] somewhat more than; also, approaching *[a man rising fifty]* : in these senses sometimes regarded as a preposition —*n.* **1.** the act of one that rises; esp., an uprising; revolt **2.** something that rises; projection

risk (risk) *n.* [Fr. *risque* < It. *risco*] **1.** the chance of injury, damage, or loss; dangerous chance; hazard **2.** *a)* the chance or likelihood that a person or thing insured may suffer injury, damage, or loss *b)* the person or thing insured, in relation to such chance or likelihood —*vt.* **1.** to expose to risk; hazard *[to risk one's life]* **2.** to take the chance of *[to risk a fight]* —**run** (or **take**) **a risk** to expose oneself to a risk; take a chance —**risk′er** *n.*

risk·y (ris′kē) *adj.* **risk′i·er, risk′i·est** involving risk; hazardous; dangerous —**risk′i·ly** *adv.* —**risk′i·ness** *n.*

ris·qué (ris kā′) *adj.* [Fr., pp. of *risquer,* to risk] very close to being improper or indecent; daring; suggestive

Ri·ta (rēt′ə) [It.] a feminine name

ri·tar·dan·do (rē′tär dän′dō) *adj., adv.* [It., gerund of *ritardare:* see RETARD] *Music* becoming gradually slower

rite (rīt) *n.* [L. *ritus*] **1.** a solemn or ceremonial act or observance in accordance with prescribed rule, as in religious use *[marriage rites]* **2.** any formal, customary observance, practice, or procedure *[the rites of courtship]* **3.** *a)* a particular system or form of ceremonial procedure; ritual *b)* [*often* **R-**] liturgy; esp., any of the forms of the Eucharistic service **4.** [*often* **R-**] either of the two major divisions (**Eastern Rite** and **Western Rite**) of the Christian (Catholic) Church, according to the liturgy used

rit·u·al (rich′oo wəl) *adj.* [L. *ritualis*] of, having the nature of, or done as a rite —*n.* **1.** a system of rites, religious or otherwise **2.** the observance of set forms or rites, as in worship **3.** a book containing rites **4.** a practice, service, or procedure done as a rite —**rit′u·al·ly** *adv.*

rit·u·al·ism (-iz'm) *n.* **1.** the observance of ritual **2.** an excessive devotion to ritual **3.** the study of religious ritual —**rit′u·al·ist** *n., adj.* —**rit′u·al·is′tic** *adj.* —**rit′u·al·is′ti·cal·ly** *adv.*

ritz·y (rit′sē) *adj.* **ritz′i·er, ritz′i·est** [< the *Ritz* hotels] [Old Slang] luxurious, fashionable, elegant, etc. —**ritz′i·ness** *n.*

ri·val (rī′v'l) *n.* [Fr. < L. *rivalis,* orig., one using the same stream as another < *rivus,* a brook] **1.** a person who tries to get the same thing as another, or to equal or surpass another; competitor **2.** an equal or a satisfactory substitute *[plastics are rivals of many metals]* —*adj.* acting as a rival; competing —*vt.* **-valed** or **-valled, -val·ing** or **-val·ling 1.** to try to equal or surpass **2.** to equal —*vi.* [Archaic] to be a rival

ri·val·ry (-rē) *n., pl.* **-ries** the act of rivaling or the fact or state of being a rival or rivals; competition

rive (rīv) *vt., vi.* **rived, rived** or **riv·en** (riv′'n), **riv′ing** [ON. *rifa*] **1.** to tear apart; rend **2.** to split; cleave

riv·er (riv′ər) *n.* [< OFr. < VL. < L. *riparius:* see RIPARIAN] **1.** a natural stream of water larger than a creek and emptying into an ocean, a lake, or another river **2.** any plentiful stream or flow —**sell down the river** to betray, deceive, etc. —**up the river** [Slang] to or confined in a penitentiary

Ri·ve·ra (rē ve′rä; *E.* ri ver′ə), **Die·go** (dye′gô) 1886–1957; Mex. painter, esp. of murals

river basin the area drained by a river and its tributaries

riv·er·bed (riv′ər bed′) *n.* the channel in which a river flows or has flowed

Riv·er·side (riv′ər sīd′) [< Santa Ana *River,* near which it is located] city in S Calif.: pop. 171,000

riv·er·side (riv′ər sīd′) *n.* the bank of a river —*adj.* on or near the bank of a river

riv·et (riv′it) *n.* [< MFr. < *river,* to clinch] **1.** a metal bolt with a head on one end, used to fasten beams together by being inserted through holes: the plain end is then hammered into a head **2.** a similar device used to strengthen seams, as on work clothes —*vt.* **1.** to fasten with rivets **2.** to hammer the end of (a bolt, etc.) into a head **3.** to fasten firmly **4.** to hold (the eyes, attention, etc.) firmly —**riv′et·er** *n.*

A B C D

RIVETS (A, rivet holding steel beams together; B, C, D, rivets)

Riv·i·er·a (riv′ē er′ə; *It.* rē vye′rä) coastal strip of the Mediterranean in SE France & NW Italy: a famous resort area

riv·u·let (riv′yoo lit) *n.* [< It. *rivoletto,* ult. < L. *rivus,* a brook] a little stream

Ri·yadh (rē yäd′) political capital of Saudi Arabia: pop. c. 300,000: cf. MECCA

ri·yal (rē yäl′, -yôl′) *n., pl.* **-yals′** [Ar. *riyāl* < Sp. *real:* see REAL[2]] *see* MONETARY UNITS, table (Qatar, Saudi Arabia, Yemen)

rm. *pl.* **rms. 1.** ream **2.** room

Rn *Chem.* radon

R.N. 1. Registered Nurse: also **RN 2.** Royal Navy

RNA ribonucleic acid

roach[1] (rōch) *n.* **1.** *same as* COCKROACH **2.** [Slang] the butt of a marijuana cigarette

roach[2] (rōch) *n., pl.* **roach, roach′es:** see PLURAL, II, D, 2 [OFr. *roche,* prob. < Gmc.] **1.** a freshwater fish of the carp family, found in N Europe **2.** any of various similar American fishes

roach[3] (rōch) *vt.* [< ?] **1.** to brush (a person's hair) so that it arches in a roll **2.** to cut (a horse's mane) so that it stands up

road (rōd) *n.* [OE. *rad,* a ride < *ridan,* to ride] **1.** *a)* a way made for traveling between places by automobile, horseback, etc.; highway *b) same as* ROADBED (sense 2) **2.** a way; path; course *[the road to fortune]* **3.** *same as* RAILROAD **4.** [*often pl.*] a protected place near shore where ships can ride at anchor —**one for the road** [Slang] a last alcoholic drink before leaving —**on the road 1.** traveling, as a salesman **2.** on tour, as actors —**take to the road** to start traveling —**the road** the cities visited by touring theatrical companies

road·a·bil·i·ty (rōd′ə bil′ə tē) *n.* the degree of operating ease and riding comfort of a vehicle on the road

road·bed (rōd′bed′) *n.* **1.** a layer of crushed rock, cinders, etc. on which the ties and rails of a railroad are laid **2.** the foundation and surface of a road, or highway

road·block (-bläk′) *n.* **1.** a blockade set up in a road to prevent movement of vehicles **2.** any hindrance

road·house (-hous′) *n.* a tavern, inn, or, esp., nightclub along a country road, as in the 1920's

road runner a long-tailed, crested desert bird of the southwestern U.S. and northern Mexico, that can run swiftly

road·side (-sīd′) *n.* the side of a road —*adj.* on or at the side of a road *[a roadside park]*

road·stead (-sted′) *n. same as* ROAD (sense 4)

road·ster (-stər) *n.* an earlier type of open automobile with a single seat for two or three persons and, sometimes, a rumble seat

road test a test of a vehicle, tires, etc. under actual operating conditions —**road′-test′** *vt.*

road·way (-wā′) *n.* **1.** a road **2.** that part of a road intended for cars, trucks, and other vehicles to travel on
roam (rōm) *vi.* [ME. *romen*] to travel from place to place, esp. with no special plan or purpose; wander —*vt.* to wander over or through *[*to *roam* the streets*]* —*n.* the act of roaming; ramble —**roam′er** *n.*
roan (rōn) *adj.* [OFr. < OSp. *roano,* ult. < *ravus*] of a solid color, as reddish-brown, black, etc., with a thick sprinkling of white hairs: said chiefly of horses —*n.* **1.** a roan color **2.** a roan horse or other animal
Ro·a·noke (rō′ə nōk′) [< Algonquian *Roanok,* northern people] **1.** city in SW Va.: pop. 100,000 **2.** island off the NE coast of N.C.: site of an abortive Eng. colony (1585–87)
roar (rôr) *vi.* [OE. *rarian*] **1.** to utter a loud, deep, rumbling sound, as a lion **2.** to talk or laugh loudly and boisterously **3.** to operate with a loud noise, as a motor or gun **4.** to resound with a noisy din —*vt.* **1.** to utter with a roar **2.** to make, put, etc. by roaring *[*to *roar* oneself hoarse*]* —*n.* **1.** a loud, deep, rumbling sound, as of a lion, bull, crowd shouting, etc. **2.** a loud noise, as of waves, a motor, etc.; din —**roar′er** *n.*
roast (rōst) *vt.* [OFr. *rostir* < Frank.] **1.** to cook (something) with little or no moisture, as in an oven or over an open fire **2.** to dry, parch, or brown (coffee, etc.) by exposure to heat **3.** to expose to great heat **4.** to heat (ore, etc.) in a furnace in order to remove impurities or cause oxidation **5.** [Colloq.] to criticize or ridicule severely —*vi.* **1.** to be cooked by being roasted **2.** to be or become very hot —*n.* **1.** roasted meat **2.** a cut of meat for roasting **3.** a roasting or being roasted **4.** a picnic at which food is roasted *[*a steer *roast]* —*adj.* roasted *[roast* pork*]* —**roast′ing** *adj.*
roast·er (rōs′tər) *n.* **1.** a person or thing that roasts **2.** a pan, oven, etc. for roasting meat **3.** a young pig, chicken, etc. suitable for roasting
rob (räb) *vt.* **robbed, rob′bing** [OFr. *rober* < Gmc.] **1.** *a) Law* to take personal property, money, etc. from unlawfully by using or threatening force *b)* popularly, to steal something from in any way **2.** to deprive (someone) *of* something belonging to or due him *[*the accident *robbed* him of health*]* —*vi.* to commit robbery —**rob′ber** *n.*
rob·ber·y (räb′ər ē) *n., pl.* **-ber·ies** a robbing; specif., the committing of a felony by taking another's property while he is present, by violence or threat of violence
robe (rōb) *n.* [OFr., a robe, orig., booty < Gmc.] **1.** a long, loose outer garment; specif., *a)* such a garment worn on formal occasions, to show rank or office, as by a judge *b)* a bathrobe or dressing gown **2.** [*pl.*] [Archaic] clothes; costume **3.** *short for* LAP ROBE —*vt., vi.* **robed, rob′ing** to dress in or cover with a robe
Rob·ert (räb′ərt) [< OFr. < OHG. < *hruod-,* fame + *perht,* bright] **1.** a masculine name: dim. *Bob, Rob, Robin* **2. Robert I** *see* BRUCE (sense 2)
Ro·ber·ta (rə bur′tə, rō-) [fem. of ROBERT] a feminine name
Ro·bes·pierre (rô bes pyer′; *E.* rōbs′pyer, -pir), **Max·i·mi·lien (François Marie Isidore de)** (mák sē mē lyan′) 1758–94; Fr. revolutionist & Jacobin leader: guillotined
rob·in (räb′in) *n.* [< OFr. dim. of *Robert*] **1.** a large N. American thrush with a dull-red breast and belly **2.** a small European warbler with a yellowish-red breast Also **robin redbreast**
Robin Good·fel·low (good′fel′ō) *Eng. Folklore* a mischievous elf or fairy: identified with Puck
Robin Hood *Eng. Legend* an outlaw of the 12th cent. who lived with his followers in Sherwood Forest and robbed the rich to help the poor
rob·in's-egg blue (räb′inz eg′) a light greenish blue
Rob·in·son (räb′in s'n), **Edwin Ar·ling·ton** (är′liŋ tən) 1869–1935; U.S. poet
Robinson Cru·soe (krōō′sō) the hero of Defoe's novel (1719) of the same name, a sailor who is shipwrecked on a tropical island
ro·bot (rō′bət, -bät) *n.* [< Czech *robota,* forced labor < OBulg. < *rabu,* servant] **1.** *a)* any manlike mechanical being, as those in Karel Čapek's play *R.U.R.* *b)* any mechanical device operated automatically, esp. by remote control, to perform in a seemingly human way **2.** an automaton; esp., a person who acts or works mechanically —**ro′bot·ism** *n.*
robot bomb a small, jet-propelled bomb with wings, steered by an automatic pilot and carrying high explosives
ro·bust (rō bust′, rō′bust) *adj.* [L. *robustus* < *robur,* hard variety of oak] **1.** *a)* strong and healthy; hardy *b)* strongly built; muscular or sturdy **2.** suited to or requiring physical strength *[robust* work*]* **3.** rough; coarse; boisterous **4.** full and rich, as in flavor *[*a *robust* port wine*]* —**ro·bust′ly** *adv.* —**ro·bust′ness** *n.*
roc (räk) *n.* [< Ar. < Per. *rukh*] *Arabian & Persian Legend* a fabulous bird, so huge and strong that it could carry off large animals
Rochelle salt [after La *Rochelle,* France] a colorless, crystalline compound, $KNaC_4H_4O_6.4H_2O$, used as a piezoelectric material, etc.
Roch·es·ter (rä′ches′tər, räch′is-) **1.** [after N. *Rochester,* Revolutionary officer] city in W N.Y., on Lake Ontario: pop. 242,000 (met. area 970,000) **2.** [after prec.] city in SE Minn.: pop. 58,000
roch·et (räch′it) *n.* [< OFr. < *roc,* a cloak < MHG. < OHG. *roch*] a vestment of lawn or linen, like a surplice, worn by bishops
rock[1] (räk) *n.* [< OFr. *roche*] **1.** a large mass of stone **2.** *a)* a large stone detached from the mass; boulder *b)* broken pieces of any size of such stone **3.** *a)* mineral matter formed in masses in the earth's crust *b)* a particular kind or mass of this **4.** anything like a rock, as in strength; esp., a firm support, basis, etc. **5.** [Colloq. or Dial.] any stone **6.** [Slang] a diamond or other gem —**on the rocks** [Colloq.] **1.** in a condition of ruin or catastrophe **2.** without money; bankrupt **3.** served undiluted over ice cubes: said of liquor, wine, etc.
rock[2] (räk) *vt.* [OE. *roccian*] **1.** to move back and forth or from side to side (a cradle, a child in the arms, etc.) **2.** to make or put by moving this way *[*to *rock* a baby to sleep*]* **3.** *a)* to sway strongly; shake *[*the explosion *rocked* the house*]* *b)* to upset emotionally —*vi.* **1.** to move back and forth or from side to side **2.** to sway strongly; shake —*n.* **1.** a rocking **2.** a rocking motion **3.** *a) same as* ROCK-AND-ROLL *b)* popular music evolved from rock-and-roll, variously containing elements of folk music, country music, etc.
rock-and-roll (räk′'n rōl′) *n.* a form of popular music, having a strong and regular rhythm, which evolved from jazz and the blues: also sp. **rock 'n' roll**
rock bottom the lowest level, point, or position; very bottom —**rock′-bot′tom** *adj.*
rock-bound (-bound′) *adj.* surrounded or covered by rocks *[*a *rock-bound* coast*]*
rock candy large, hard, clear crystals of sugar formed on a string dipped in a solution of boiled sugar
Rock Cornish (hen) *same as* CORNISH (sense 2 *b*)
rock crystal a transparent, esp. colorless, quartz
Rock·e·fel·ler (räk′ə fel′ər) **1. John D(avison),** 1839–1937; U.S. industrialist & philanthropist **2. John D(avison), Jr.,** 1874–1960; U.S. industrialist & philanthropist: son of *prec.*
rock·er (räk′ər) *n.* **1.** either of the curved pieces on the bottom of a cradle, rocking chair, etc. **2.** *same as* ROCKING CHAIR **3.** any of various devices that work with a rocking motion —**off one's rocker** [Slang] crazy; insane
rock·et (räk′it) *n.* [It. *rocchetta,* a spool, orig. dim. of *rocca,* a distaff < OHG.] **1.** any of various devices, typically cylindrical, containing a combustible substance which when ignited produces gases that escape through a rear vent and drive the container forward by the principle of reaction: rockets are used as fireworks and projectile weapons and to propel spacecraft **2.** a spacecraft, missile, etc. propelled by a rocket —*vi.* **1.** to dart ahead swiftly like a rocket **2.** to travel in a rocket **3.** to soar *[*prices *rocketed]* —*vt.* to convey in a rocket —**rock·e·teer** (räk′ə tir′) *n.*
rock·et·ry (räk′ə trē) *n.* **1.** the science of designing, building, and launching rockets **2.** rockets collectively
Rock·ford (räk′fərd) [after the *rocky*-bottomed *ford* there] city in N Ill.: pop. 140,000
rock garden a garden with flowers and plants growing among rocks variously arranged
Rock·ies (räk′ēz) *same as* ROCKY MOUNTAINS
rocking chair a chair mounted on rockers or springs, so as to allow a rocking movement
rocking horse a toy horse mounted on rockers or springs and big enough for a child to ride
Rock Island [< the name of the *rocky island* in the river] city in NW Ill., on the Mississippi: pop. 47,000
rock-ribbed (räk′ribd′) *adj.* **1.** having rocky ridges *[rock-ribbed* coasts*]* **2.** firm; unyielding
rock salt common salt in solid masses
rock wool a fibrous material that looks like spun glass, made from molten rock or slag through which steam is forced: it is used for insulation, esp. in buildings
rock·y[1] (räk′ē) *adj.* **rock′i·er, rock′i·est 1.** full of rocks **2.** consisting of rock **3.** like a rock; firm, hard, unfeeling, etc. **4.** full of obstacles *[*the *rocky* road to success*]* —**rock′i·ness** *n.*
rock·y[2] (räk′ē) *adj.* **rock′i·er, rock′i·est 1.** *a)* inclined to rock, or sway *b)* uncertain; shaky **2.** [Slang] weak or dizzy, as from illness; unwell —**rock′i·ness** *n.*
Rocky Mountain goat a white, goatlike antelope of the mountains of northwest N. America
Rocky Mountains mountain system in W N.America, extending from C N.Mex. to N Alas.
Rocky Mountain sheep *same as* BIGHORN
Rocky Mountain spotted fever an acute infectious disease caused by a rickettsia
ro·co·co (rə kō′kō; *occas.* rō′kə kō′) *n.* [Fr. < *rocaille,*

shell work] a style of architecture and decoration using elaborate ornamentation imitating foliage, shell work, scrolls, etc.: popular in the 18th cent. —*adj.* **1.** of or in rococo **2.** too elaborate; florid and tasteless

rod (räd) ***n.*** [OE. *rodd*] **1.** *Bible* a branch of a family or tribe **2.** any straight stick, bar, etc., as of wood, metal, etc. *[*curtain *rods]* **3.** *a)* a stick for beating as punishment *b)* punishment **4.** *a)* a staff, scepter, etc., carried as a symbol of office or rank *b)* power; authority **5.** *same as* FISHING ROD **6.** a stick used to measure something **7.** *a)* a measure of length equal to 5½ yards *b)* a square rod, equal to 30¼ square yards **8.** [Slang] a pistol or revolver **9.** [Slang] *same as* HOT ROD **10.** *Biol.* a rod-shaped cell, microorganism, etc. —**rod′like′** ***adj.***

rode (rōd) *pt. & archaic pp. of* RIDE

ro·dent (rōd′'nt) ***adj.*** [< L. prp. of *rodere,* to gnaw] **1.** gnawing **2.** of or like rodents —***n.*** any of various gnawing mammals, including rats, mice, beavers, etc., that have constantly growing incisors; esp., a rat or mouse

ro·de·o (rō′dē ō′; *also, esp. for 1,* rō dā′ō) ***n.,*** *pl.* **-de·os′** [Sp. < *rodear,* surround < L. *rotare:* see ROTATE] **1.** [Now Rare] a roundup of cattle **2.** a public exhibition of the skills of cowboys, as broncobusting, lassoing, etc.

Ro·din (*rô* dan′; *E.* rō dan′), **(François) Au·guste (René)** (ô güst′) 1840–1917; Fr. sculptor

rod·o·mon·tade (räd′ə män tād′, rō′də-; -täd′) ***n.*** [Fr. < It. *Rodomonte,* boastful Saracen leader in *Orlando Furioso,* 16th-c. epic] arrogant boasting or blustering talk —***adj.*** arrogantly boastful —***vi.*** **-tad′ed, -tad′ing** to boast

roe[1] (rō) ***n.*** [akin to or < ? ON. *hrogn*] fish eggs, esp. when still massed in the ovarian membrane

roe[2] (rō) ***n.,*** *pl.* **roe, roes:** see PLURAL, II, D, 2 [OE. *ra*] a small, agile, graceful European and Asian deer

roe·buck (rō′buk′) ***n.,*** *pl.* **-bucks′, -buck′:** see PLURAL, II, D, 1 the male of the roe deer

roent·gen (rent′gən, ren′chən) ***n.*** [after W. K. *Roentgen* (1845–1923), Ger. physicist] the international unit used in measuring ionizing radiation, as X-rays or gamma rays

Roentgen ray [*also* **r-**] *same as* X-RAY

ro·ga·tion (rō gā′shən) ***n.*** [< L. < *rogare,* to ask] a supplication or prayer, esp. as chanted during the three days **(Rogation Days)** before Ascension Day

Rog·er (räj′ər) [OFr. < OHG. < *hruod-,* fame + base meaning "spear"] a masculine name —***interj.*** [< conventional name of international signal flag for *R*] [*also* **r-**] **1.** received: term used in radiotelephony to indicate reception of a message **2.** [Colloq.] right! OK!

Ro·get (rō zhā′), **Peter Mark** 1779–1869; Eng. writer: compiler of a thesaurus

rogue (rōg) ***n.*** [< ? L. *rogare,* to ask] **1.** formerly, a vagabond **2.** a scoundrel **3.** a fun-loving, mischievous person **4.** an animal that wanders alone and is fierce and wild —***vt.*** **rogued, rogu′ing** to cheat —***vi.*** to live or act like a rogue

ro·guer·y (rō′gər ē) ***n.,*** *pl.* **-guer·ies** the behavior of a rogue; specif., *a)* trickery; cheating *b)* playful mischief

rogues' gallery a collection of photographs of criminals, as used by police in identification

ro·guish (rō′gish) ***adj.*** of or like a rogue; specif., *a)* dishonest; unscrupulous *b)* playfully mischievous —**ro′guish·ly** ***adv.*** —**ro′guish·ness** ***n.***

roil (roil) ***vt.*** [< Fr. < OFr. *rouil,* rust, ult. < L. *robigo,* rust] **1.** to make (a liquid) cloudy, muddy, etc. by stirring up the sediment **2.** to stir up; agitate **3.** to make angry or irritable —***vi.*** to be agitated —**roil′y** ***adj.*** **roil′i·er, roil′i·est**

roist·er (rois′tər) ***vi.*** [< OFr. < L. *rusticus:* see RUSTIC] **1.** to boast or swagger **2.** to be lively and noisy; revel boisterously —**roist′er·er** ***n.*** —**roist′er·ous** ***adj.***

Ro·land (rō′lənd) [Fr. < OHG. < *hruod-,* fame + *land,* land] **1.** a masculine name **2.** a hero famous for his courage who appears in legends about Charlemagne

role, rôle (rōl) ***n.*** [Fr. *rôle,* a roll: from roll containing actor's part] **1.** a part, or character, that an actor plays **2.** a function assumed by someone *[*an advisory *role]*

roll (rōl) ***vi.*** [OFr. *roller,* ult. < L. *rotula* (or *rotulus*), dim. of *rota,* wheel] **1.** to move by turning over and over **2.** *a)* to move on wheels *b)* to travel in a wheeled vehicle **3.** to pass *[*the years *rolled* by*]* **4.** to move in a periodical revolution: said of stars, planets, etc. **5.** *a)* to flow, as water, in a full, sweeping motion *b)* to be carried in a flow **6.** to extend in gentle swells or undulations **7.** to make a loud, rising and falling sound *[*thunder *rolls]* **8.** to rise and fall in a full, mellow cadence, as speech **9.** to trill **10.** to be wound into a ball or cylinder, as yarn **11.** to turn in a circular motion *[*with eyes *rolling]* **12.** to rock from side to side, as a ship **13.** to walk by swaying **14.** to become spread under a roller **15.** to make progress; advance **16.** to start operating *[*the presses *rolled]* **17.** [Colloq.] to abound (*in*) *[rolling* in wealth*]* **18.** *Football* to move laterally: said of the passer: in full, **roll out** —***vt.*** **1.** to move by turning over and over **2.** to move on wheels or rollers **3.** to cause to start operating **4.** to beat (a drum) with light, rapid blows **5.** to utter with a full, flowing sound **6.** to say with a trill *[*to *roll* one's r's*]* **7.** to give a swaying motion to **8.** to move around or from side to side *[*to *roll* one's eyes*]* **9.** to wind into a ball or cylinder *[*to *roll* a cigarette*]* **10.** to wrap or enfold **11.** to make flat or spread out, by using a roller, etc. **12.** to iron (sleeves, etc.) without forming a crease **13.** [Slang] to rob (a drunken or sleeping person) **14.** *Printing* to spread ink on (type, a form, etc.) with a roller —***n.*** **1.** the act or an instance of rolling **2.** *a)* a scroll *b)* something that is, or looks as if, rolled up **3.** a register; catalog **4.** a list of names for checking attendance **5.** a measure of something rolled into a cylinder *[*a *roll* of wallpaper*]* **6.** a cylindrical mass of something **7.** any of various small cakes of bread, etc. **8.** a roller (in various senses) **9.** a swaying motion **10.** a rapid succession of light blows on a drum **11.** a loud, reverberating sound, as of thunder **12.** a trill **13.** a slight swell on the surface, as of land **14.** [Slang] money; esp., a wad of paper money —**roll back** **1.** to move back **2.** to reduce (prices) to a previous level by government action —**roll in** to arrive or appear, usually in large numbers or amounts —**roll out** to spread out by unrolling —**roll over** **1.** to refinance (a maturing note, etc.) **2.** to reinvest (funds) so as to defer paying taxes —**roll up** **1.** to increase by accumulation **2.** [Colloq.] to arrive in a vehicle —**strike off** (or **from**) **the rolls** to expel from membership

roll·a·way (rōl′ə wā′) ***adj.*** having rollers for easy moving and storing when not in use *[*a *rollaway* bed*]*

roll bar a heavy metal bar reinforcing the roof of an automobile to reduce injury if the car should roll over

roll call the reading aloud of a roll, as in military formations, to find out who is absent

roll·er (rō′lər) ***n.*** **1.** a person or thing that rolls **2.** *a)* a cylinder on which something is rolled up *b)* a heavy rolling cylinder used to crush, smooth, or spread something **3.** a long bandage in a roll **4.** a long, heavy wave that breaks on the shoreline **5.** a canary that trills its notes

roller bearing a bearing in which the shaft turns on rollers in a ringlike track

roller coaster an amusement ride in which small, open cars move on tracks that dip and curve sharply

roller skate a skate with wheels: see SKATE[1] (sense 2) —**roll′-er-skate′** ***vi.*** **-skat′ed, -skat′ing** —**roller skater**

rol·lick (räl′ik) ***vi.*** [< ? FROLIC] to play or behave in a gay, carefree way —**rol′lick·ing, rol′lick·some** (-səm) ***adj.***

roll·ing (rōl′iŋ) ***adj.*** that rolls; specif., rotating or revolving, recurring, swaying, surging, resounding, trilling, etc. —***n.*** the action, motion, or sound of something that rolls

rolling mill **1.** a factory in which metal bars, sheets, etc. are rolled out **2.** a machine used for such rolling

rolling pin a heavy, smooth cylinder of wood, glass, etc., usually with a handle at each end, used to roll out dough

rolling stock all the locomotives, cars, etc. of a railroad, or the trucks, trailers, etc. of a trucking company

roll·o·ver (-ō′vər) ***n.*** the act or an instance of rolling over a maturing note, etc. or invested funds

roll-top (rōl′täp′) ***adj.*** made with a flexible top of parallel slats that slides back *[*a *roll-top* desk*]*

ro·ly-po·ly (rō′lē pō′lē) ***adj.*** [redupl. of ROLL] short and plump; pudgy —***n.,*** *pl.* **-lies** **1.** a roly-poly person or thing **2.** [Chiefly Brit.] a pudding made of rich dough and jam

rom, rom. roman (type)

Rom. **1.** Roman **2.** Romance **3.** Romania **4.** Romanian **5.** Romanic **6.** Romans (Epistle to the Romans)

Ro·ma (*rô′*mä) *It. name of* ROME

Ro·ma·ic (rō mā′ik) ***n.*** the everyday language of modern Greece —***adj.*** of this language

ro·maine (rō mān′, rō′mān) ***n.*** [Fr. < fem. of *romain,* Roman] a kind of lettuce with long leaves that form a cylindrical or conical head: also **romaine lettuce**

Ro·man (rō′mən) ***adj.*** **1.** of or characteristic of ancient or modern Rome, its people, etc. **2.** of the Roman Catholic Church **3.** [*usually* **r-**] designating or of the usual upright style of printing types; not italic —***n.*** **1.** a native, citizen, or inhabitant of ancient or modern Rome **2.** [*usually* **r-**] roman type or characters

Roman alphabet the alphabet of the ancient Romans, used with little change in most modern European languages

Roman arch a semicircular arch

Roman candle a firework consisting of a long tube that sends out balls of fire, sparks, etc.

Roman Catholic **1.** of the Roman Catholic Church **2.** a member of this church —**Roman Catholicism**

Roman Catholic Church the Christian church headed by the Pope

Ro·mance (rō mans′, rō′mans) ***adj.*** [see ff.] designating or of any of the languages derived from Vulgar Latin, as Italian, Spanish, French, etc. —***n.*** these languages

ro·mance (rō mans′; *also, for n.,* rō′mans) ***n.*** [OFr. *romanz,* Roman (i.e., the vernacular, not Latin), ult. < L. *Romanicus,* Roman] **1.** a long verse or prose narrative, orig. written in one of the Romance languages, about knights and chivalric deeds, adventure, and love **2.** a novel of love, adventure, etc. **3.** excitement, love, and adventure of the kind found in such literature **4.** the tendency to enjoy romantic adventures **5.** an exaggeration or fabrication **6.** a love affair —***vi.*** **-manced′, -manc′ing 1.** to write or tell romances **2.** to think or talk about romantic things —***vt.*** [Colloq.] to woo; court —**ro·manc′er *n.***

Roman Curia *R.C.Ch. see* CURIA (sense 2)

Roman Empire empire established by Augustus, including, at its peak, W & S Europe, Britain, Asia Minor, N Africa, & the lands at the E end of the Mediterranean: it existed from 27 B.C. until 395 A.D.

Ro·man·esque (rō′mə nesk′) ***adj.*** designating or of a style of European architecture of the 11th and 12th cent., based on the Roman and using round arches and vaults, massive walls, etc. —***n.*** this style of architecture

Roman holiday [after the ancient Roman gladiatorial contests] entertainment at the expense of others' suffering, or a spectacle yielding such entertainment

Ro·ma·nia, Ro·mâ·nia (rō mān′yə, -mā′nē ə; *Romanian* rô mu′nyä) country in SE Europe, on the Black Sea: 91,700 sq. mi.; pop. 20,470,000; cap. Bucharest

Ro·ma·nian (-mān′yən, -mā′nē ən) ***adj.*** of Romania, its people, language, etc. —***n.*** **1.** a native or inhabitant of Romania **2.** the Romance language of the Romanians

Ro·man·ic (-man′ik) ***adj., n.*** *same as* ROMANCE

Ro·man·ism (rō′mən iz'm) ***n.*** Roman Catholicism: hostile usage

Ro·man·ize (-īz′) ***vt.*** **-ized′, -iz′ing 1.** to make or become Roman in character, spirit, etc. **2.** to make or become Roman Catholic —**Ro′man·i·za′tion *n.***

Roman nose a nose with a prominent bridge

Roman numerals the Roman letters used as numerals until the 10th cent. A.D.: in Roman numerals I = 1, V = 5, X = 10, L = 50, C = 100, D = 500, and M = 1,000 The value of a symbol following another of the same or greater value is added (e.g., III = 3, XV = 15); the value of a symbol preceding one of greater value is subtracted (e.g., IX = 9)

Ro·ma·no (rō mä′nō) ***n.*** [It., ROMAN] a dry, sharp, very hard Italian cheese, usually grated

Ro·ma·nov (rô mä′nôf; *E.* rō′mə nôf′) ruling family of Russia from 1613 to 1917: also sp. **Romanoff**

Ro·mans (rō′mənz) a book of the New Testament, an epistle from the Apostle Paul to the Christians of Rome

ro·man·tic (rō man′tik) ***adj.*** **1.** of, like, or characterized by romance **2.** without a basis in fact; fanciful or fictitious **3.** not practical; visionary *[a romantic scheme]* **4.** full of thoughts, feelings, etc. of romance **5.** *a)* of or concerned with idealized lovemaking *b)* suited for romance, or lovemaking *[a romantic night]* **6.** [*often* **R-**] of or associated with the ROMANTIC MOVEMENT —***n.*** a romantic person —**ro·man′ti·cal·ly *adv.***

ro·man·ti·cism (rō man′tə siz'm) ***n.*** **1.** romantic spirit, outlook, etc. **2.** *a) same as* ROMANTIC MOVEMENT *b)* the spirit, style, etc. of, or adherence to, the Romantic Movement: contrasted with CLASSICISM, etc. —**ro·man′ti·cist *n.***

ro·man·ti·cize (-sīz′) ***vt.*** **-cized′, -ciz′ing** to treat or regard romantically —***vi.*** to have romantic ideas, attitudes, etc. —**ro·man′ti·ci·za′tion *n.***

Romantic Movement the revolt in the 18th and 19th cent. against neoclassicism in literature, music, art, etc.: it emphasized freedom of form, full expression of feeling, etc.

Rom·a·ny (räm′ə nē, rō′mə-) ***n.*** [Romany *romani,* Gypsy < *rom,* a man < Sans.] **1.** *pl.* **-ny, -nies** a Gypsy **2.** the Indic language of the Gypsies —***adj.*** of the Gypsies, their language, etc. Also sp. **Rom′ma·ny**

Rom. Cath. Roman Catholic

Rome (rōm) **1.** capital of Italy, on the Tiber River: formerly, the capital of the Roman Empire: pop. 2,731,000 **2.** [after prec.] city in C N.Y., near Utica: pop. 44,000 **3.** *same as* ROMAN CATHOLIC CHURCH

Ro·me·o (rō′mē ō′) the hero of Shakespeare's tragedy *Romeo and Juliet* (c. 1595), lover of Juliet —***n.,*** *pl.* **-os′** a man who is an ardent lover

Rom·ney (räm′nē, rum′-), **George** 1734–1802; Eng. painter

romp (rämp) ***n.*** [< earlier *ramp,* hussy, prob. < OFr. *ramper:* see RAMP²] **1.** a person who romps, esp. a girl **2.** boisterous, lively play **3.** *a)* an easy, winning gait in a race *[to win in a romp] b)* an easy victory —***vi.*** **1.** to play in a boisterous, lively way **2.** to win with ease

romp·er (räm′pər) ***n.*** **1.** one who romps **2.** [*pl.*] a young child's loose-fitting, one-piece outer garment with bloomer-like pants

Rom·u·lus (räm′yoo ləs) *Rom. Myth.* the founder and first king of Rome: he and his twin brother Remus, left as infants to die, were suckled by a she-wolf

Ron·ald (rän′'ld) [Scot. < ON. *Rögnvaldr:* see REGINALD] a masculine name

ron·deau (rän′dō) ***n.,*** *pl.* **-deaux** (-dōz) [Fr. < *rondel* < *rond,* round] a short lyrical poem of thirteen (or ten) lines and an unrhymed refrain that consists of the opening words and is used in two places

ron·del (-d'l, -del) ***n.*** [OFr.: see prec.] a kind of rondeau, usually with fourteen lines, two rhymes, and the first two lines used as a refrain in the middle and at the end

ron·do (rän′dō) ***n.,*** *pl.* **-dos** [It. < Fr.: see RONDEAU] *Music* a composition or movement having its principal theme stated three or more times in the same key, separated by subordinate themes

rood (ro͞od) ***n.*** [OE. *rod*] **1.** a crucifix **2.** in England, a measure of area usually equal to 1/4 acre (40 square rods)

roof (ro͞of, ro͝of) ***n.,*** *pl.* **roofs** [OE. *hrof*] **1.** the outside top covering of a building **2.** figuratively, a house or home **3.** anything like a roof *[the roof of the mouth]* —***vt.*** to cover as with a roof —**raise the roof** [Slang] to be very noisy, as in anger or joy —**roof′less *adj.***

roof·er (-ər) ***n.*** a person who builds or repairs roofs

roof garden 1. a garden on the flat roof of a building **2.** the roof or top floor of a building, decorated as a garden and used as a restaurant, etc.

roof·ing (-iŋ) ***n.*** **1.** the act of covering with a roof **2.** material for roofs **3.** a roof

roof·top (-täp′) ***n.*** the roof of a building

roof·tree (-trē′) ***n.*** **1.** the ridgepole of a roof **2.** a roof

rook¹ (ro͝ok) ***n.*** [OE. *hroc*] **1.** a crowlike European bird **2.** a swindler; cheat —***vt., vi.*** to swindle; cheat

rook² (ro͝ok) ***n.*** [< OFr. *roc* < Ar. < Per. *rukh*] *Chess* either of the two corner pieces shaped like a castle tower, movable only in a vertical or horizontal line; castle

rook·er·y (ro͝ok′ər ē) ***n.,*** *pl.* **-er·ies** a breeding place or colony of rooks, or of seals, penguins, etc.

rook·ie (ro͝ok′ē) ***n.*** [altered < ? RECRUIT] [Slang] **1.** an inexperienced recruit in the army **2.** any novice, as on a police force or in a professional sport

room (ro͞om, ro͝om) ***n.*** [OE. *rum*] **1.** space to contain something or in which to do something *[room for one more]* **2.** opportunity *[room for doubt]* **3.** a space within a building enclosed or set apart by walls **4.** [*pl.*] living quarters; lodgings **5.** the people in a room *[the whole room was silent]* —***vi., vt.*** to have, or provide with, lodgings

room and board lodging and meals

room clerk a clerk at a hotel or motel who registers guests, assigns them rooms, etc.

room·er (ro͞o′mər, ro͝o′-) ***n.*** a person who rents lodgings

room·ette (ro͞o met′, ro͝o-) ***n.*** a small compartment for one person in a railroad sleeping car

room·ful (ro͞om′fo͝ol′, ro͝om′-) ***n.,*** *pl.* **-fuls′ 1.** as much or as many as will fill a room **2.** the people or objects in a room, collectively

rooming house a house with furnished rooms for rent

room·mate (-māt′) ***n.*** a person with whom one shares a room or rooms

room·y (-ē) ***adj.*** **room′i·er, room′i·est** having plenty of room; spacious —**room′i·ly *adv.*** —**room′i·ness *n.***

roor·back, roor·bach (ro͝or′bak) ***n.*** [after a nonexistent book, *Roorback's Tour,* containing spurious charges against presidential candidate James K. POLK] a slanderous story spread to damage the reputation of a political candidate

Roo·se·velt (rō′zə velt′, -vəlt; rōz′velt) **1. Franklin Delano** (del′ə nō′), 1882–1945; 32d president of the U.S. (1933–45) **2. Theodore,** 1858–1919; 26th president of the U.S. (1901–09)

roost (ro͞ost) ***n.*** [OE. *hrost*] **1.** a perch on which birds, esp. domestic fowls, can rest or sleep **2.** a place with perches for birds **3.** a place for resting, sleeping, etc. —***vi.*** **1.** to sit, sleep, etc. on a perch **2.** to settle down, as for the night —**come home to roost** to come back in an unfavorable way to the doer; boomerang —**rule the roost** to be master

roost·er (ro͞os′tər) ***n.*** the male of the chicken

root¹ (ro͞ot, ro͝ot) ***n.*** [Late OE. *rote* < ON. *rot*] **1.** the part of a plant, usually below the ground, that lacks nodes, shoots, and leaves, holds the plant in place, and draws water and food from the soil **2.** loosely, any underground part of a plant **3.** the embedded part of a bodily structure, as of the teeth, hair, etc. **4.** the source or cause of an action, quality, condition, etc. **5.** an ancestor **6.** [*pl.*] the close ties one has with some place or people as through birth, upbringing, long association, etc. **7.** a supporting part; base **8.** an essential or basic part *[the root of the matter]* **9.** *Math. a)*

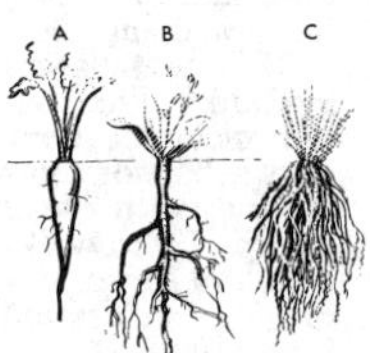

ROOTS
(A, B, taproot;
C, fibrous)

a quantity that, multiplied by itself a specified number of times, produces a given quantity *[4 is the square root (4 x 4) of 16 and the cube root (4 x 4 x 4) of 64]* *b)* a number that, when substituted for the unknown quantity in an equation, will satisfy the equation **10.** *Music* the basic tone of a chord **11.** *Linguis.* *same as* BASE[1] (*n.* 10) —*vi.* **1.** to begin to grow by putting out roots **2.** to become fixed, settled, etc. —*vt.* **1.** to fix the roots of in the ground **2.** to establish; settle —**root up** (or **out, away**) to pull out by the roots; remove completely —**take root 1.** to begin growing by putting out roots **2.** to become settled —**root′i·ness** *n.* —**root′y** *adj.*

root[2] (ro͞ot, root) *vt.* [OE. *wrotan* < *wrot,* snout] to dig (*up* or *out*) with or as with the snout —*vi.* **1.** to dig in the ground, as with the snout **2.** to search about; rummage **3.** [Colloq.] *a)* to encourage a contestant or team by applauding and cheering *b)* to lend moral support to one seeking success, recovery, etc. Usually with *for* —**root′er** *n.*

Root (ro͞ot, root), **E·li·hu** (el′ə hyo͞o′) 1845–1937; U.S. statesman; secretary of state (1905–09)

root beer a carbonated drink made of extracts from the roots and bark of certain plants, etc.

root canal a small, tubular channel, normally filled with pulp, in the root of a tooth

root crop a crop, as turnips, beets, etc., grown for the edible roots

root hair *Bot.* any of the hairlike tubular outgrowths from a growing root, which absorb water and minerals from the soil

root·less (-lis) *adj.* having no roots or ties —**root′less·ly** *adv.* —**root′less·ness** *n.*

root·let (-lit) *n.* a little root

root·stock (-stäk′) *n.* *Bot.* **1.** *same as* RHIZOME **2.** a plant onto which another is grafted as a new top

rope (rōp) *n.* [OE. *rap*] **1.** a thick, strong cord made of intertwisted strands of fiber, wires, etc. **2.** *a)* a noose for hanging a person *b)* death by hanging: with *the* **3.** *same as* LASSO **4.** a ropelike string of things *[a rope of pearls]* **5.** a ropelike, sticky formation, as in a liquid —*vt.* **roped, rop′ing 1.** to fasten or tie with a rope **2.** to connect by a rope **3.** to mark off or enclose with a rope (usually with *in, off,* or *out*) **4.** to catch with a lasso —*vi.* to become ropelike and sticky, as candy —**know the ropes** [Colloq.] to know the details or procedures, as of a job —**rope in** [Slang] to trick into doing something —**the end of one's rope** the end of one's endurance, resources, etc. —**rop′er** *n.*

rope·walk (-wôk′) *n.* a long, low, narrow shed, etc. in which ropes are made

rope·walk·er (-ər) *n.* a performer who walks or does tricks on a tightrope: also **rope′danc′er** (-dan′sər) —**rope′walk′ing** *n.*

rop·y (rō′pē) *adj.* **rop′i·er, rop′i·est 1.** forming sticky threads, as some liquids **2.** like rope —**rop′i·ness** *n.*

Roque·fort (cheese) (rōk′fərt) [< *Roquefort,* France, where orig. made] a strong cheese with a bluish mold, made from goats' and ewes' milk

ror·qual (rôr′kwəl) *n.* [Fr. < Norw. *röyrkval* < ON. *reytharhvalr,* lit., red whale] any of the whalebone whales with a well-developed dorsal fin, esp. a finback whale with lengthwise furrows on its belly and throat

Ror·schach test (rôr′shäk) [after H. *Rorschach* (1884–1922), Swiss psychiatrist] *Psychol.* a test for personality analysis, in which the person being tested tells what is suggested to him by a standard series of inkblot designs: his responses are then interpreted

ro·sa·ceous (rō zā′shəs) *adj.* **1.** of the rose family of plants, as the strawberry, plum, etc. **2.** like a rose **3.** rose-colored

Ros·a·lie (rō′zə lē′, räz′ə-) [Fr., prob. ult. < L. *rosa,* rose] a feminine name

Ros·a·lind (räz′ə lind) [Sp. *Rosalinda,* as if from *rosa linda,* pretty rose] a feminine name

Ro·sa·rio (rô sä′ryô) city & port in EC Argentina, on the Paraná River: pop. 672,000

ro·sa·ry (rō′zər ē) *n., pl.* **-ries** [L. *rosarium,* ult. < *rosa,* a rose] *R.C.Ch.* **1.** a string of beads used to keep count in saying certain prayers **2.** [*also* **R-**] the prayers said with these beads

Rose (rōz) [see ff.] a feminine name

rose[1] (rōz) *n.* [OE. < L. *rosa*] **1.** any of a genus of shrubs with prickly stems and five-parted, usually fragrant flowers of red, pink, white, yellow, etc. **2.** the flower of any of these **3.** any of several related plants **4.** pinkish red or purplish red **5.** anything like a rose in form, as a rosette, the perforated nozzle of a sprinkling can, a round cut of gem with many facets and a flat base, etc. —*adj.* **1.** of or having to do with roses **2.** rose-colored **3.** rose-scented **4.** designating a large family of wild and cultivated flowers, shrubs, and trees, including the hawthorns, roses, strawberries, apples, peaches, almonds, etc. —*vt.* **rosed, ros′ing** to make rose-colored —**under the rose** *same as* SUB ROSA

rose[2] (rōz) *pt. of* RISE

ro·sé (rō zā′) *n.* [Fr., lit., pink] a light, pink wine made by removing the grape husks after partial fermentation

ro·se·ate (rō′zē it, -āt′) *adj.* **1.** rose-colored; rosy **2.** cheerful or optimistic —**ro′se·ate·ly** *adv.*

rose·bud (rōz′bud′) *n.* the bud of a rose

rose·bush (-boosh′) *n.* a shrub that bears roses

rose chafer a small N. American beetle that feeds on the leaves and flowers of roses and other plants: also called **rose bug**

rose-col·ored (-kul′ərd) *adj.* **1.** pinkish-red or purplish-red **2.** cheerful or optimistic —**through rose-colored glasses** with optimism

rose fever a kind of hay fever believed to be caused by the pollen of roses: also **rose cold**

Rose·mar·y (rōz′mer′ē; *chiefly Brit.* -mə ri) [see ff.] a feminine name

rose·mar·y (-mer′ē; *chiefly Brit.* -mə ri) *n.* [altered (after ROSE[1] & MARY), ult. < L. *ros marinus,* lit., dew of the sea] an evergreen plant of the mint family, with small, light-blue flowers and fragrant leaves used in perfumery, cooking, etc.

rose of Sharon 1. a plant with white, red, pink, or purplish, bell-shaped flowers **2.** [Chiefly Brit.] a Saint Johnswort shrub with large, yellow flowers

ro·se·o·la (rō zē′ə lə, rō′zē ō′lə) *n.* [ModL., dim. < L. *roseus,* rosy] *same as* RUBELLA: also called **rose rash**

Ro·set·ta stone (rō zet′ə) a stone tablet, found in 1799 at Rosetta, Egypt, bearing inscriptions that provided a key for deciphering Egyptian hieroglyphics

ro·sette (rō zet′) *n.* [Fr. < OFr., dim. of *rose,* ROSE[1]] an ornament, arrangement, etc. resembling or suggesting a rose *[a rosette of ribbon]*

Rose·ville (rōz′vil) [after W. *Rose,* 1st local postmaster (1836)] city in SE Mich.: suburb of Detroit: pop. 54,000

rose water a preparation consisting of water and attar of roses, used as a perfume

rose window a circular window with roselike tracery or mullions arranged like the spokes of a wheel

rose·wood (rōz′wood′) *n.* [from its odor] **1.** any of a number of valuable hard, reddish, black-streaked woods, used in making furniture, etc. **2.** a tropical tree yielding such wood

Rosh Ha·sha·na (rōsh′ hə shô′nə, -shä′-; *Heb.* rōsh′ hä shä nä′) the Jewish New Year, celebrated on the 1st and 2d days of Tishri: also sp. **Rosh Hashona, Rosh Hashanah,** etc.

ros·in (räz′'n) *n.* [altered < MFr. *resine,* RESIN] the hard, brittle resin, light-yellow to almost black, left after the distillation of crude turpentine: it is rubbed on violin bows, used in making varnish, etc. —*vt.* to rub with rosin; put rosin on —**ros′in·ous, ros′in·y** *adj.*

ROSE WINDOW

Ross (rôs) **1. Bet·sy** (bet′sē), (*Mrs. Elizabeth Griscom Ross*) 1752–1836; Am. woman reputed to have made the first Am. flag **2.** Sir **James Clark,** 1800–62; Brit. polar explorer **3.** Sir **John,** 1777–1856; Brit. arctic explorer, born in Scotland: uncle of *prec.*

Ros·set·ti (rō zet′ē, -set′ē) **1. Chris·ti·na (Georgina)** (kris tē′nə), 1830–94; Eng. poet **2. Dante Gabriel,** 1828–82; Eng. painter & poet: brother of *prec.*

Ross Ice Shelf frozen S section of the Ross Sea: also called **Ross Shelf Ice**

Ros·si·ni (rôs sē′nē; *E.* rô sē′nē), **Gio·ac·chi·no (Antonio)** (jô′ä kē′nô) 1792–1868; It. composer

Ross Sea arm of the Pacific, along the coast of Antarctica

Ros·tand (rôs tän′; *E.* räs′tand), **Ed·mond** (ed mōn′) 1868–1918; Fr. dramatist & poet

ros·ter (räs′tər) *n.* [Du. *rooster,* orig., gridiron, hence a list (from ruled paper used for lists)] **1.** a list of military or naval personnel, with their assignments, duties, etc. **2.** any list; roll

Ros·tock (rôs′tôk; *E.* räs′täk) seaport in N East Germany, on the Baltic: pop. 195,000

Ros·tov (rô stôf′; *E.* räs′täv) seaport in SW R.S.F.S.R., at the mouth of the Don: pop. 789,000: also called **Ros′tov-on-Don′**

ros·trum (räs′trəm) *n., pl.* **-trums, -tra** (-trə) [L., (ship's) beak, hence the speakers' platform in the Forum, decorated with ramming beaks taken from captured ships] **1.** any platform for public speaking **2.** public speaking, or public speakers collectively —**ros′tral** *adj.*

ros·y (rō′zē) ***adj.*** **ros′i·er, ros′i·est** 1. like a rose, esp. in color; rose-red or pink *[rosy* cheeks*]* 2. [Archaic] made with roses 3. bright, promising, cheerful, etc. *[a rosy* future*]* —**ros′i·ly** ***adv.*** —**ros′i·ness** ***n.***

rot (rät) ***vi.*** **rot′ted, rot′ting** [OE. *rotian*] 1. to decompose gradually by the action of bacteria, etc.; decay 2. to become unhealthy, etc. *[to rot* in prison*]* 3. to become morally corrupt —***vt.*** 1. to cause to rot, or decompose 2. *same as* RET —***n.*** 1. a rotting or being rotten; decay 2. something rotting or rotten 3. any of various plant and animal diseases, esp. of sheep, causing decay 4. [Slang] nonsense —***interj.*** an exclamation of disgust, anger, etc.

ro·ta·ry (rōt′ər ē) ***adj.*** [< ML. < L. *rota*, a wheel] 1. turning around a central point or axis, as a wheel; rotating 2. *a)* having a rotating part or parts *b)* having blades that rotate on a hub *[a rotary* lawn mower*]* —***n.***, *pl.* **-ries** a rotary machine or engine

Rotary Club any local organization of an international club (**Rotary International**) of business and professional men, founded in 1905 to promote community welfare —**Ro·tar·i·an** (rō ter′ē ən) ***n., adj.*** —**Ro·tar′i·an·ism** ***n.***

rotary press a printing press with curved plates mounted on rotating cylinders, for printing on paper fed from a roll

ro·ta·ry-wing aircraft (-wiŋ′) an aircraft, as the helicopter, sustained in the air by rotors

ro·tate (rō′tāt) ***vi., vt.*** **-tat·ed, -tat·ing** [< L. pp. of *rotare* < *rota*, a wheel] 1. to move or turn around, as a wheel 2. to go or cause to go in a regular and recurring succession of changes *[to rotate* crops*]* —**ro′tat·a·ble** ***adj.*** —**ro·ta·tive** (rō′tāt iv, rōt′ə tiv) ***adj.*** —**ro′ta·tor** ***n.***

ro·ta·tion (rō tā′shən) ***n.*** 1. a rotating or being rotated 2. regular and recurring succession of changes —**ro·ta′tion·al** ***adj.***

rotation of crops a system of rotating in a fixed order the kinds of crops grown in the same field, to maintain soil fertility

ro·ta·to·ry (rō′tə tôr′ē) ***adj.*** 1. of, or having the nature of, rotation 2. rotating; rotary 3. going or following in rotation 4. causing rotation

ROTC, R.O.T.C. Reserve Officers' Training Corps

rote (rōt) ***n.*** [< ?] a fixed, mechanical way of doing something; routine —**by rote** by memory alone, without thought

ro·te·none (rōt′'n ōn′) ***n.*** [Jap. *roten*, an East Indian plant + -ONE] a white, odorless, crystalline substance, $C_{23}H_{22}O_6$, used in insecticides

rot·gut (rät′gut′) ***n.*** [ROT + GUT] [Slang] raw, low-grade whiskey or other liquor

Roth·schild (rôth′chīld′, räths′-; *G.* rōt′shilt) family of European bankers of the 18th & 19th cent., originally of Germany

ro·ti·fer (rōt′ə fər) ***n.*** [ModL. < L. *rota*, wheel + -FER] any of various microscopic, invertebrate freshwater animals, having a ring or rings of cilia at the front end of the body —**ro·tif·er·al** (rō tif′ər əl), **ro·tif′er·ous, ro·tif′er·an** ***adj.***

ro·tis·ser·ie (rō tis′ər ē) ***n.*** [Fr. < MFr., ult. < *rostir*, to ROAST] 1. a shop where roasted meats are sold 2. a grill with an electrically turned spit

ro·to (rōt′ō) ***n.***, *pl.* **-tos** *shortened form of* ROTOGRAVURE

ro·to·gra·vure (rōt′ə grə vyoor′) ***n.*** [< L. *rota*, a wheel + GRAVURE] 1. a printing process using photogravure cylinders on a rotary press 2. a print or newspaper pictorial section printed by this process

ro·tor (rōt′ər) ***n.*** [< ROTATE] 1. the rotating part of a motor, dynamo, etc. 2. a device, as on a helicopter, consisting of generally horizontal airfoils with their hub

Ro·to·till·er (rōt′ə til′ər) *a trademark for* a motorized cultivator with rotary blades —***n.*** [*also* **r-**] such a cultivator —**ro′to·till′** ***vt.***

rot·ten (rät′'n) ***adj.*** [ON. *rotinn*] 1. decayed; decomposed; spoiled 2. smelling of decay; putrid 3. morally corrupt or offensive; dishonest, etc. 4. unsound or weak, as if decayed within 5. [Slang] very bad, disagreeable, etc. *[a rotten* show*]* —**rot′ten·ly** ***adv.*** —**rot′ten·ness** ***n.***

rot·ter (rät′ər) ***n.*** [< ROT] [Chiefly Brit. Slang] a despicable fellow; cad; bounder

Rot·ter·dam (rät′ər dam′; *Du.* rôt′ər däm′) seaport in SW Netherlands, in the Rhine delta: pop. 687,000

ro·tund (rō tund′) ***adj.*** [L. *rotundus*, akin to *rota*, a wheel] 1. round or rounded out; plump or stout 2. full-toned; sonorous *[a rotund* voice*]* —**ro·tun′di·ty, ro·tund′ness** ***n.*** —**ro·tund′ly** ***adv.***

ro·tun·da (rō tun′də) ***n.*** [< It. < L. fem. of *rotundus*, rotund] a round building, hall, or room, esp. one with a dome

Rou·ault (ro͞o ō′), **Georges** (zhôrzh) 1871–1958; Fr. painter

rou·ble (ro͞o′b'l) ***n.*** *same as* RUBLE

rou·é (ro͞o ā′) ***n.*** [Fr., pp. of *rouer*, to break on the wheel < L. *rota*, a wheel] a dissipated man; debauchee; rake

Rou·en (ro͞o än′; *Fr.* rwän) city & port in NW France, on the Seine: pop. 120,000

rouge (ro͞ozh) ***n.*** [Fr., red < L. *rubeus*] 1. any of various reddish cosmetic powders, pastes, etc. for coloring the cheeks and lips 2. a reddish powder, mainly ferric oxide, for polishing jewelry, metal, etc. —***vi., vt.*** **rouged, roug′ing** to use cosmetic rouge (on)

rough (ruf) ***adj.*** [OE. *ruh*] 1. *a)* not smooth or level; uneven *[a rough* surface*]* *b)* not easily traveled; overgrown, wild, etc. *[rough* country*]* 2. shaggy *[a rough* coat*]* 3. moving violently; agitated; specif., *a)* stormy; tempestuous *[rough* weather*]* *b)* boisterous or disorderly *[rough* play*]* 4. harsh, rude, brutal, etc. *[a rough* temper*]* 5. sounding, feeling, or tasting harsh 6. lacking comforts and conveniences *[the rough* life of pioneers*]* 7. not refined or polished *[a rough* diamond*]* 8. not finished, perfected, etc. *[a rough* sketch, a *rough* estimate*]* 9. needing strength rather than skill or intelligence *[rough* labor*]* 10. [Colloq.] difficult, severe, etc. *[a rough* time*]* 11. *Phonet.* pronounced with an aspirate; having the sound of *h* —***n.*** 1. rough ground 2. rough material or condition 3. a rough sketch or draft 4. [Chiefly Brit.] a rough person; rowdy 5. *Golf* any part of the course where grass, weeds, etc. grow uncut —***adv.*** in a rough manner —***vt.*** 1. to make rough; roughen 2. to treat roughly (often with *up*) 3. to make or shape roughly (usually with *in* or *out*) *[rough* out a scheme*]* —***vi.*** to behave roughly —**in the rough** in a rough or crude state —**rough it** to live without comforts and conveniences —**rough′ish** ***adj.*** —**rough′ly** ***adv.*** —**rough′ness** ***n.***

rough·age (ruf′ij) ***n.*** rough or coarse substance; specif., coarse food or fodder, as bran, straw, etc., serving as a stimulus to peristalsis

rough-and-read·y (ruf′'n red′ē) ***adj.*** 1. rough, or crude, rude, etc., but effective *[rough-and-ready* methods*]* 2. characterized by rough vigor rather than refinement, formality, etc.

rough-and-tum·ble (-tum′b'l) ***adj.*** violent and disorderly, with no concern for rules —***n.*** a fight or struggle of this kind

rough·cast (ruf′kast′) ***n.*** 1. a coarse plaster for covering outside surfaces, as walls 2. a rough pattern or crude model —***vt.*** **-cast′, -cast′ing** 1. to cover (walls, etc.) with roughcast 2. to make or shape in a rough form

rough-dry (-drī′) ***vt.*** **-dried′, -dry′ing** to dry (washed laundry) without ironing: also **rough′dry′** —***adj.*** washed and dried but not ironed

rough·en (ruf′'n) ***vt., vi.*** to make or become rough

rough-hew (ruf′hyo͞o′) ***vt.*** **-hewed′, -hewed′** or **-hewn′, -hew′ing** 1. to hew (timber, stone, etc.) roughly, or without finishing or smoothing 2. to form roughly Also **rough′hew′**

rough·house (ruf′hous′) ***n.*** [Slang] rough or boisterous play, fighting, etc. —***vt.*** **-housed′, -hous′ing** [Slang] to treat roughly or boisterously —***vi.*** [Slang] to take part in roughhouse

rough·neck (-nek′) ***n.*** [Slang] a rough person; rowdy

rough·rid·er (-rīd′ər) ***n.*** 1. a person who breaks horses for riding 2. a person who does much hard, rough riding 3. [**R-**] a member of Theodore Roosevelt's volunteer cavalry regiment in the Spanish-American War: also **Rough Rider**

rough·shod (-shäd′) ***adj.*** shod with horseshoes that have metal points to prevent slipping —**ride roughshod over** to treat in a harsh, arrogant, inconsiderate manner

rou·lade (ro͞o läd′) ***n.*** [Fr. < *rouler*, to ROLL] 1. a rapid series of tones sung to one syllable 2. a slice of meat rolled and cooked

rou·lette (ro͞o let′) ***n.*** [Fr. < OFr. dim. of *roele*, a small wheel, ult. < L. *rota*, a wheel] 1. a gambling game played by rolling a small ball around a shallow bowl with a revolving inner disk (**roulette wheel**) with red and black numbered compartments 2. a small toothed wheel for making rows of marks or dots, as between postage stamps —***vt.*** **-let′ted, -let′ting** to make marks, dots, etc. in with a roulette

Rou·ma·nia (ro͞o mān′yə, -mā′nē ə) *same as* ROMANIA —**Rou·ma′nian** ***adj., n.***

round (round) ***adj.*** [< OFr. < L. *rotundus*, rotund] 1. shaped like a ball; spherical 2. *a)* shaped like a circle, ring, etc.; circular or curved *b)* shaped like a cylinder; cylindrical 3. plump or stout 4. with or involving a circular motion *[a round* dance*]* 5. full; complete *[a round* dozen*]* 6. expressed by a whole number, or in tens, hundreds, etc. 7. large in amount, size, etc. *[a round* sum*]* 8. mellow and full in tone; sonorous 9. brisk; vigorous *[a round* pace*]* 10. outspoken; plain and blunt 11. *Phonet.* pronounced with the lips forming an oval *[a round* vowel*]* —***n.*** 1. something round; thing that is spherical, circular, curved, etc. 2. a rung of a ladder or a chair 3. the part of a beef animal between the rump and the leg: in full, **round of beef** 4. movement in a circular course 5. *same as* ROUND DANCE 6. a series or succession of actions, events, etc. *[a round* of parties*]* 7. the complete extent *[the round* of human beliefs*]* 8. [*often pl.*] a regular, customary circuit, as by a watchman of his station 9. a single serving, as of drinks, for each in a group **10.** *a)* a single shot from a rifle, etc. or from a number of rifles fired together *b)* ammunition for such a shot **11.** a single outburst, as of applause **12.** *Games & Sports* a single period or division of action; specif., *a) Boxing* any of the timed periods of a fight *b) Golf* a number of holes as a unit of competition **13.** *Music* a short song for two or more persons or groups, in which the second starts when the first reaches the second phrase, etc. —***vt.*** **1.** to make round **2.** to pronounce with rounded lips **3.** to make plump **4.** to express as a round number (usually with *off*) **5.** to complete; finish **6.** to make a circuit of *[*we *rounded* the island*]* **7.** to make a turn about *[*to *round* a corner*]* —***vi.*** **1.** to make a complete or partial circuit **2.** to turn; reverse direction **3.** to become round or plump —***adv.*** **1.** in a circle; along a circular course **2.** through a recurring period of time *[*to work the year *round]* **3.** from one person or place to another *[*the peddler came *round]* **4.** for each of several *[*not enough to go *round]* **5.** in circumference **6.** on all sides; in every direction **7.** about; near **8.** in a roundabout way **9.** here and there **10.** with a rotating movement **11.** in or to the opposite direction **12.** in or to an opposite viewpoint —***prep.*** **1.** so as to encircle or surround **2.** on the circumference or border of **3.** on all sides of **4.** in the vicinity of **5.** in a circuit or course through **6.** here and there in **7.** so as to make a curve or circuit about In the U.S., *round* (*adv. & prep.*) is generally superseded by *around;* in Great Britain, *round* is preferred for most senses —**go the round** (or **rounds**) **1.** to be circulated widely, as a story, rumor, etc. **2.** to walk one's regular circuit: also **make one's rounds** —**in the round 1.** with the audience, etc. seated all around a central stage, etc. **2.** in full and completely rounded form, not in relief: said of sculpture **3.** in full detail —**out of round** not having perfect roundness —**round about 1.** in or to the opposite direction **2.** in every direction around —**round up 1.** to drive together in a herd, group, etc. **2.** [Colloq.] to gather or assemble —**round′ish** ***adj.*** —**round′ness** ***n.***

round·a·bout (round′ə bout′) ***adj.*** **1.** not straight or straightforward; indirect *[roundabout* methods*]* **2.** encircling; enclosing —***n.*** **1.** something that is indirect or circuitous **2.** a short, tight jacket formerly worn by men or boys **3.** *Brit. var. of* MERRY-GO-ROUND

round dance 1. a dance with the dancers moving in a circle **2.** any of several dances, as the waltz, polka, etc., in which the couples make circular movements

round·ed (roun′did) ***adj.*** **1.** made round **2.** having variety in tastes, abilities, etc. *[*a well-*rounded* person*]*

roun·de·lay (roun′də lā′) ***n.*** **[**< MFr. dim. of *rondel,* a rondel**]** a simple song in which some phrase, line, etc. is continually repeated

round·er (roun′dər) ***n.*** **1.** a person or thing that rounds, as a tool for rounding edges **2.** [Colloq.] a dissolute person or drunkard

Round·head (round′hed′) ***n.*** a member of the Parliamentary, or Puritan, party in England during the English civil war (1642–52)

round·house (-hous′) ***n.*** **1.** a building, generally circular, with a turntable in the center, for storing and repairing locomotives **2.** a cabin on the after part of a ship's quarter-deck **3.** *a) Baseball* a pitch with a wide curve *b) Boxing* a wide swing or hook, as to the head

round·ly (-lē) ***adv.*** **1.** in a round form **2.** in a round manner; specif., *a)* vigorously, severely, etc. *b)* fully

round robin 1. a petition, protest, etc. with the signatures written in a circle to conceal the order of signing **2.** a tournament in which every entrant is matched with every other one **3.** a letter circulated among the members of a group, forwarded by each in turn, often with added comments

round-shoul·dered (-shōl′dərd) ***adj.*** stooped because the shoulders are bent forward

round steak a cut from a round of beef: see ROUND (*n.* 3)

Round Table 1. the table around which King Arthur and his knights sat **2.** King Arthur and his knights, collectively **3.** [**r- t-**] *a)* an informal discussion group *b)* the informal discussion —**round′-ta′ble** ***adj.***

round-the-clock (-*th*ə kläk′) ***adj., adv.*** continuously

round trip a trip to a place and back again —**round′-trip′** ***adj.***

round·up (-up′) ***n.*** **1.** *a)* the act of driving cattle, etc. together on the range and collecting them in a herd, as for branding *b)* the cowboys, horses, etc. that do this work **2.** any similar driving together or collecting **3.** a summary, as of news

round·worm (-wurm′) ***n.*** **1.** *same as* NEMATODE **2.** a species of nematode worms, living as parasites, esp. in the intestines of man and other mammals

rouse (rouz) ***vt.*** **roused, rous′ing [**prob. < Anglo-Fr. or OFr.**]** **1.** to stir up (game) from cover to flight or attack **2.** to stir up, as to anger or action; excite **3.** to wake —***vi.*** **1.** to leave cover: said of game **2.** to wake **3.** to become active —***n.*** a rousing —**rous′er** ***n.*** —**rous′ing·ly** ***adv.***

Rous·seau (ro͞o sō′) **1. Hen·ri** (än rē′), 1844–1910; Fr. painter **2. Jean Jacques** (zhän zhäk), 1712–78; Fr. political philosopher & writer, born in Switzerland

roust·a·bout (roust′ə bout′) ***n.*** **[***roust,* dial. var. of ROUSE + ABOUT**]** **1.** a deckhand or waterfront laborer **2.** an unskilled or transient laborer, as in a circus or on a ranch

rout[1] (rout) ***n.*** **[**< OFr. < L. *rupta:* see ROUTE**]** **1.** a disorderly crowd; rabble **2.** a disorderly flight, as of defeated troops **3.** an overwhelming defeat **4.** [Archaic] a group of people; company —***vt.*** **1.** to put to disorderly flight **2.** to defeat overwhelmingly

rout[2] (rout) ***vi.*** **[**var. of ROOT[2]**]** **1.** to dig for food with the snout, as a pig **2.** to poke or rummage about —***vt.*** **1.** to dig up with the snout **2.** to force out —**rout out 1.** to expose to view **2.** to scoop, gouge, or hollow out **3.** to make (a person) get out —**rout up 1.** to get by poking about **2.** to make (a person) get up —**rout′er** ***n.***

route (ro͞ot; *also, and for n. 2 usually,* rout) ***n.*** **[**OFr. < L. *rupta (via),* broken (path) < pp. of *rumpere,* to break**]** **1.** a road, etc. for traveling; esp., a highway **2.** *a)* a regular course traveled as in delivering mail, milk, etc. *b)* a set of customers to whom one regularly makes deliveries —***vt.*** **rout′ed, rout′ing 1.** to send by a specified route *[*to *route* goods through Omaha*]* **2.** to fix the order of procedure of

rou·tine (ro͞o tēn′) ***n.*** **[**Fr. < *route:* see prec.**]** **1.** a regular, unvarying procedure, customary, prescribed, or habitual, as of work **2.** a theatrical skit **3.** a series of dance steps **4.** a set of coded instructions for a computer —***adj.*** having the nature of or using routine —**rou·tine′ly** ***adv.*** —**rou·tin′ism** ***n.*** —**rou·tin′ize** ***vt.*** **-ized, -iz·ing**

roux (ro͞o) ***n.*** **[**Fr. *roux (beurre),* reddish-brown (butter)**]** a cooked mixture of butter (or other fat) and flour, used for thickening sauces, soups, gravies, etc.

rove[1] (rōv) ***vi.*** **roved, rov′ing [**< ?**]** **1.** to wander about; roam **2.** to look around: said of the eyes —***vt.*** to wander over; roam through *[*he *roved* the woods*]* —***n.*** a roving; ramble —**rov′er** ***n.***

rove[2] (rōv) ***vt.*** **[**< ?**]** to twist (fibers) together and draw out into a strand (**roving**) before spinning

rove[3] (rōv) *alt. pt. & pp. of* REEVE[2]

rov·en (rōv′′n) *alt. pp. of* REEVE[2]

row[1] (rō) ***n.*** **[**OE. *rǣw***]** **1.** a number of people or things arranged in a line **2.** any of the lines of seats side by side in a theater, etc. **3.** a street with a line of buildings, as of a specified nature, on either side *[*fraternity *row]* —***vt.*** to arrange or put in rows —**hard** (or **long**) **row to hoe** anything hard or tiring to do —**in a row** one after the other

row[2] (rō) ***vt.*** **[**OE. *rowan***]** **1.** to move (a boat, etc.) on water by using oars **2.** to carry in a rowboat *[row* us across the lake*]* **3.** to use (oarsmen, a stroke, etc. as specified) in rowing **4.** to take part in (a race) by rowing —***vi.*** **1.** to use oars in moving a boat **2.** to be moved by oars: said of a boat —***n.*** **1.** a rowing **2.** a trip made by rowboat —**row′er** ***n.***

row[3] (rou) ***n.*** **[**< ? ROUSE**]** a noisy quarrel, dispute, or disturbance; squabble or brawl —***vi.*** to take part in a row

row·an (rō′ən, rou′-) ***n.*** **[**< Scand.**]** **1.** the mountain ash, a tree with white flowers and reddish berries **2.** its fruit: also **row′an·ber′ry,** *pl.* **-ries**

row·boat (rō′bōt′) ***n.*** a boat made to be rowed

row·dy (rou′dē) ***n.,*** *pl.* **-dies [**< ? ROW[3]**]** a person whose behavior is rough, quarrelsome, and disorderly; hoodlum —***adj.*** **-di·er, -di·est** of or like a rowdy —**row′di·ly** ***adv.*** —**row′di·ness** ***n.*** —**row′dy·ish** ***adj.*** —**row′dy·ism** ***n.***

row·el (rou′əl) ***n.*** **[**< OFr. *roele:* see ROULETTE**]** a small wheel with sharp projecting points, forming the end of a spur —***vt.*** **-eled** or **-elled, -el·ing** or **-el·ling** to spur or prick (a horse) with a rowel

ROWEL

row·lock (rul′ək, räl′-; rō′läk′) ***n.*** **[**altered (after ROW[2]) < OARLOCK**]** *chiefly Brit. term for* OARLOCK

Roy (roi) **[**as if < OFr. *roy* (Fr. *roi*), a king, but prob. < Gael. *rhu,* red**]** a masculine name

roy·al (roi′əl) ***adj.*** **[**< OFr. < L. *regalis:* see REGAL**]** **1.** of a king, queen, or other sovereign *[*a *royal* edict, the *royal* family*]* **2.** having the rank of a king or queen **3.** of a kingdom, its government, etc. *[*the *royal* fleet*]* **4.** *a)* founded or supported by a king or queen *b)* in the service of the Crown **5.** suitable for a king or queen; magnificent, stately, regal, etc. **6.** unusually large, fine, etc. —***n.*** a small sail set on the royal mast —**roy′al·ly** ***adv.***

royal blue a deep, vivid reddish or purplish blue

royal flush the highest poker hand, consisting of the ace, king, queen, jack, and ten of the same suit
roy·al·ist (-ist) *n.* a person who supports a king or a monarchy, esp. in times of revolution —**roy'al·ism** *n.*
royal jelly a highly nutritious food fed by worker bees to all very young larvae and continued to be fed to larvae chosen to be queens
royal mast a small mast above the topgallant mast
Royal Oak [after an oak in which CHARLES II is said to have hidden] city in SE Mich.: suburb of Detroit: pop. 71,000
royal palm any of a genus of tall, ornamental palm trees
roy·al·ty (roi'əl tē) *n., pl.* **-ties** **1.** the rank, status, or power of a king or queen **2.** a royal person or, collectively, royal persons **3.** a kingdom **4.** royal quality or character; regalness, nobility, etc. **5.** [*usually pl.*] a right, privilege, etc. of a monarch **6.** *a*) a share of the proceeds paid to the owner of a right, as a patent, for its use *b*) such a share paid to one who leases out lands rich in oil or minerals *c*) a share of the proceeds from his work paid to an author, composer, etc.

ROYAL PALM

rpm, r.p.m. revolutions per minute
R.R. **1.** railroad: also **RR** **2.** Right Reverend
-rrha·gi·a (rā'jē ə) [ModL. < Gr. < *rhēgnynai,* to burst] *a combining form meaning* abnormal discharge or flow: also **-rrhage** (rij), **-rrhag'y** (rā'jē)
-rrhe·a, -rrhoe·a (rē'ə) [ModL. < Gr. < *rhein,* to flow] *a combining form meaning* a flow, discharge
Rs, rs. rupees
R.S.F.S.R., RSFSR Russian Soviet Federated Socialist Republic
RSV, R.S.V. Revised Standard Version (of the Bible)
R.S.V.P., r.s.v.p. [Fr. *répondez s'il vous plâit*] please reply
rt. right
rte. route
Ru *Chem.* ruthenium
rub (rub) *vt.* **rubbed, rub'bing** [ME. *rubben,* akin to Dan. *rubbe*] **1.** to move (one's hand, a cloth, etc.) back and forth over (something) firmly **2.** to spread or apply (polish, salve, etc.) on a surface **3.** to move (a thing) against something else, or move (things) over each other with pressure and friction **4.** to put into a specified condition by applying pressure and friction [*rub* it dry] **5.** to make sore by rubbing **6.** to remove by rubbing (*out, off,* etc.) —*vi.* **1.** to move with pressure and friction (*on, against,* etc.) **2.** to rub something **3.** to admit of being rubbed or removed by rubbing (often with *off, out,* etc.) —*n.* **1.** a rubbing; specif., a massage **2.** an obstacle or difficulty **3.** something that irritates, annoys, etc. —**rub down** **1.** to massage **2.** to smooth, polish, etc. by rubbing —**rub it in** [Slang] to keep reminding someone of his failure or mistake —**rub off on** to be left on as a mark, as by rubbing or, figuratively, by close contact —**rub the wrong way** to annoy or irritate
ru·ba·to (rōō bät'ō) *adj., adv.* [It. < (*tempo*) *rubato,* stolen (time)] *Music* with some notes lengthened and others shortened in dropping strict tempo in a passage for effect —*n., pl.* **-toes** **1.** the use of rubato **2.** a rubato passage, phrase, etc.
rub·ber[1] (rub'ər) *n.* **1.** a person or thing that rubs **2.** [from use as an eraser] an elastic substance produced from the milky sap of various tropical plants, or synthetically **3.** something made of this substance; specif., *a*) an eraser *b*) a low-cut overshoe *c*) [Slang] a condom **4.** *Baseball* an oblong piece of rubber, etc. set into the pitcher's mound —*adj.* made of rubber —**rub'ber·like'** *adj.*
rub·ber[2] (rub'ər) *n.* [< ?] **1.** *Bridge* a series limited to three games, two of which must be won to win the series **2.** any game played to break a tie in games won: usually **rubber game**
rubber band a narrow, continuous band of rubber as for holding small objects together
rubber cement an adhesive made of unvulcanized rubber in a quickly evaporating solvent
rub·ber·ize (-īz') *vt.* **-ized', -iz'ing** to coat or impregnate with rubber
rub·ber·neck (-nek') *n.* [Old Slang] a person who gazes about in curiosity, as a sightseer —*vi.* [Old Slang] to gaze about in this way
rubber plant **1.** any plant yielding latex from which crude rubber is formed **2.** a house plant with large, glossy, leathery leaves
rubber stamp **1.** a stamp made of rubber, inked on a pad and used for printing signatures, dates, etc. **2.** [Colloq.] *a*) a person, bureau, etc. that approves something in a routine way, without thought *b*) any routine approval —**rub'ber-stamp'** *vt., adj.*
rub·ber·y (rub'ər ē) *adj.* like rubber in appearance, elasticity, toughness, etc. —**rub'ber·i·ness** *n.*
rub·bing (rub'iŋ) *n.* an impression of a raised or incised design, etc. taken by placing a paper over it and rubbing with graphite, wax, etc.
rub·bish (rub'ish) *n.* [ult. < base of RUB] **1.** any material thrown away as worthless; trash **2.** worthless, foolish ideas, statements, etc.; nonsense —**rub'bish·y** *adj.*
rub·ble (rub''l) *n.* [akin to RUBBISH, RUB] **1.** rough, broken pieces of stone, brick, etc. **2.** masonry made of such pieces: also **rub'ble·work'** **3.** debris from buildings, etc., resulting from earthquake, bombing, etc. —**rub'bly** *adj.*
rub·down (rub'doun') *n.* a massage
rube (rōōb) *n.* [< REUBEN] [Slang] a country person regarded as simple, unsophisticated, etc.
Rube Gold·berg (rōōb gōld'bərg) [< *Rube Goldberg* (1883–1970), U.S. cartoonist] designating a complicated device used to perform a simple operation
ru·bel·la (rōō bel'ə) *n.* [ModL. < L. *rubellus* < *ruber,* red] a contagious virus disease, characterized by swollen glands of the neck and small red spots on the skin; German measles
Ru·bens (rōō'bənz; *Fl.* rü'bəns), **Peter Paul** 1577–1640; Fl. painter
ru·be·o·la (rōō bē'ə lə, rōō'bē ō'lə) *n.* [ModL., neut. pl. dim. of L. *rubeus,* red] *same as* MEASLES (sense 1)
Ru·bi·con (rōō'bi kän') small river in N Italy crossed by Caesar to march on Rome with his army (49 B.C.), starting a civil war —**cross the Rubicon** to make a decisive move that cannot be undone
ru·bi·cund (rōō'bi kund') *adj.* [< Fr. < L. < *ruber,* red] reddish; ruddy —**ru'bi·cun'di·ty** *n.*
ru·bid·i·um (rōō bid'ē əm) *n.* [ModL. < L. *rubidus,* red (from red lines in its spectrum)] a soft, silvery-white metallic chemical element, resembling potassium: symbol, Rb; at. wt., 85.47; at. no., 37
ru·ble (rōō'b'l) *n.* [Russ. *rubl'*] the monetary unit of the U.S.S.R.: see MONETARY UNITS, table
ru·bric (rōō'brik) *n.* [< MFr. < L. *rubrica,* rubric < *ruber,* red] **1.** in early books and manuscripts, a chapter heading, initial letter, etc. printed or written in red, decorative lettering, etc. **2.** a heading, title, etc., as of a chapter, a law, etc. **3.** a direction in a prayer book **4.** a note of comment; gloss **5.** an established rule of procedure —**ru'bri·cal** *adj.* —**ru'bri·cal·ly** *adv.*
ru·by (rōō'bē) *n., pl.* **-bies** [< OFr. *rubi,* ult. < L. *rubeus,* red] **1.** a clear, deep-red variety of corundum, valued as a precious stone **2.** deep red —*adj.* deep-red
ruche (rōōsh) *n.* [Fr., lit., beehive < OFr. < Celt.] a fluting or pleating of lace, ribbon, net, etc. for trimming garments, esp. at the neck or wrist
ruch·ing (rōō'shiŋ) *n.* **1.** ruches collectively **2.** material used to make ruches
ruck·sack (ruk'sak', rook'-) *n.* [G. < *rücken,* the back + *sack,* a sack] a kind of knapsack
ruck·us (ruk'əs) *n.* [prob. a merging of earlier *ruction,* an uproar & RUMPUS] [Colloq.] noisy confusion; uproar; row; disturbance
rud·der (rud'ər) *n.* [OE. *rother,* steering oar] **1.** a broad, flat, movable piece of wood or metal hinged vertically at the stern of a boat or ship, used for steering **2.** a piece like this on an aircraft, etc. —**rud'der·less** *adj.*
rud·der·post (-pōst') *n.* the sternpost or the vertical shaft to which the rudder is fastened

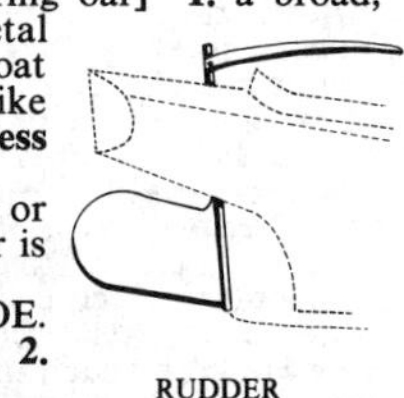
RUDDER

rud·dy (rud'ē) *adj.* **-di·er, -di·est** [OE. *rudig*] **1.** having a healthy red color **2.** red or reddish —**rud'di·ness** *n.*
ruddy duck a small, N. American duck, the adult male of which has a brownish-red upper body
rude (rōōd) *adj.* **rud'er, rud'est** [OFr. < L. *rudis*] **1.** crude or rough in form [*a rude* hut] **2.** barbarous or ignorant [*rude* savages] **3.** lacking refinement; coarse, uncouth, etc. **4.** discourteous; impolite [a *rude* reply] **5.** rough; harsh [a *rude* awakening] **6.** harsh in sound; discordant **7.** simple or primitive **8.** not carefully worked out —**rude'ly** *adv.* —**rude'ness** *n.*

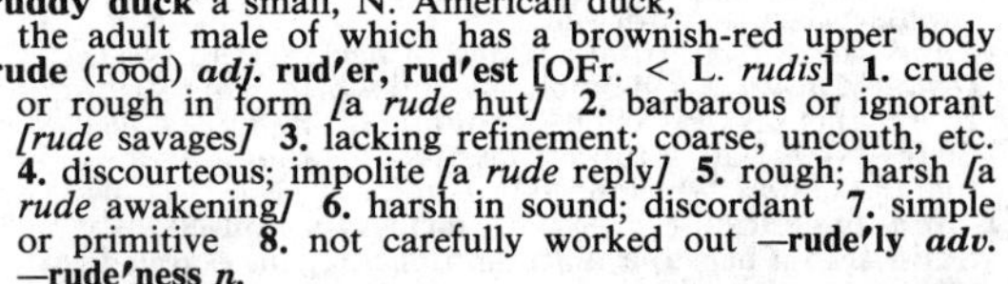

ru·di·ment (rōō'də mənt) *n.* [L. *rudimentum* < *rudis,* rude] **1.** a first principle or element, as of a subject to be learned [the *rudiments* of physics] **2.** a first slight beginning of something **3.** *Biol.* an incompletely developed or vestigial organ or part
ru·di·men·ta·ry (rōō'də men'tər ē, -men'trē) *adj.* **1.** of rudiments or first principles; elementary **2.** incompletely developed **3.** vestigial Also **ru'di·men'tal** —**ru'di·men'ta·ri·ly** *adv.* —**ru'di·men'ta·ri·ness** *n.*
Ru·dolf I (rōō'dälf, -dôlf) 1218–91; Ger. king & emperor of the Holy Roman Empire (1273–91)
Ru·dolph (rōō'dälf, -dôlf) [< G. < OHG. < *hruod-,* fame + *wolf,* a wolf] a masculine name: dim. *Rudy*

rue[1] (rōō) ***vt., vi.*** **rued, ru′ing** [OE. *hreowan*] to feel sorrow or remorse (for); regret; repent —***n.*** [Archaic] sorrow or regret

rue[2] (rōō) ***n.*** [< OFr. < L. *ruta* < Gr. *rhytē*] a strong-scented herb with yellow flowers and bitter-tasting leaves formerly used in medicine

rue·ful (rōō′fəl) ***adj.*** **1.** causing sorrow or pity **2.** feeling or showing sorrow or regret, esp. in a wry way —**rue′ful·ly** ***adv.*** —**rue′ful·ness** ***n.***

ruff[1] (ruf) ***n.*** [contr. of RUFFLE[1], *n.*] **1.** a high, frilled, stiff collar worn by men and women in the 16th and 17th cents. **2.** a ring of feathers or fur standing out about the neck of a bird or animal **3.** a Eurasian sandpiper the male of which grows a ruff in the breeding season —**ruffed** ***adj.***

RUFF

ruff[2] (ruf) ***n.*** [< OFr. *roffle*] *Card Games* the act of trumping —***vt., vi.*** *Card Games* to trump

ruffed grouse a N. American game bird with neck feathers that can be spread into a ruff: also called *partridge* in the northern U.S. and *pheasant* in the southern U.S.

ruf·fi·an (ruf′ē ən, ruf′yən) ***n.*** [< Fr. < It. *ruffiano,* a pander] a brutal, lawless person; hoodlum —***adj.*** brutal and lawless: also **ruf′fi·an·ly** —**ruf′fi·an·ism** ***n.***

ruf·fle[1] (ruf′'l) ***vt.*** **-fled, -fling** [< ON. or MLowG.] **1.** to disturb the smoothness of; ripple [wind *ruffling* the water] **2.** to gather into ruffles **3.** to put ruffles on **4.** to make (feathers, etc.) stand up as in a ruff **5.** to disturb or annoy **6.** *a)* to turn (pages) rapidly *b)* to shuffle (cards) —***vi.*** **1.** to become uneven **2.** to become disturbed, annoyed, etc. —***n.*** **1.** a strip of cloth, lace, etc. gathered in pleats or puckers and used for trimming **2.** a bird's ruff **3.** a disturbance; annoyance **4.** a ripple —**ruf′fly** ***adj.***

ruf·fle[2] (ruf′'l) ***n.*** [prob. echoic] a low, continuous beating of a drum —***vi., vt.*** **-fled, -fling** to beat (a drum, etc.) with a ruffle

ru·fous (rōō′fəs) ***adj.*** [L. *rufus,* red] brownish-red

rug (rug) ***n.*** [< Scand.] **1.** a piece of thick, often napped fabric, woven strips of rag, an animal skin, etc. used as a floor covering **2.** *chiefly Brit. term for* LAP ROBE

Rug·by (rug′bē) ***n.*** [first played at *Rugby,* a boys' school in C England] a kind of football in which there are 15 players on each side, action is continuous, and the oval ball may be kicked, thrown laterally, or run with

rug·ged (rug′id) ***adj.*** [< Scand.] **1.** having a surface that is uneven, rough, craggy, etc. [*rugged* ground] **2.** strong, irregular, and lined [a *rugged* face] **3.** stormy [*rugged* weather] **4.** sounding harsh **5.** severe; hard [a *rugged* life] **6.** not polished or refined; rude **7.** strong; robust; vigorous; hardy **8.** [Colloq.] requiring skill, endurance, etc. —**rug′ged·ly** ***adv.*** —**rug′ged·ness** ***n.***

Ruhr (roor; *G.* rōōr) **1.** river in C West Germany, flowing west into the Rhine **2.** major coal-mining & industrial region in the valley of this river: also called **Ruhr Basin**

ru·in (rōō′in) ***n.*** [< OFr. < L. *ruina* < *ruere,* to fall] **1.** [*pl.*] the remains of a fallen building, city, etc., or of something destroyed, devastated, decayed, etc. **2.** anything that has been destroyed, etc. **3.** the state of being destroyed, dilapidated, etc. **4.** downfall, destruction, decay, etc., as of a thing or person, or the cause of this [gambling was his *ruin*] —***vt.*** to bring to ruin; specif., *a)* to destroy, or damage greatly *b)* to make bankrupt *c)* to seduce (a chaste woman) —***vi.*** to go or come to ruin

ru·in·a·tion (rōō′ə nā′shən) ***n.*** **1.** a ruining or being ruined **2.** anything that ruins

ru·in·ous (rōō′ə nəs) ***adj.*** **1.** falling or fallen into ruin **2.** bringing ruin; disastrous —**ru′in·ous·ly** ***adv.***

rule (rōōl) ***n.*** [< OFr. < L. *regula,* straightedge < *regere,* to lead straight] **1.** *a)* an authoritative regulation for conduct, method, procedure, etc. *b)* an established practice that serves as a guide [*rules* of grammar] **2.** a set of regulations in a religious order **3.** a habit; custom **4.** customary course of events [famine is the *rule* following war] **5.** *a)* government; reign *b)* the period of a particular reign **6.** a ruler or straightedge **7.** *Law a)* a court regulation *b)* a decision, order, etc. made by a judge or court in regard to a specific question or point *c)* a legal principle **8.** *Printing* a thin strip of metal as high as type, used to print lines —***vt.*** **ruled, rul′ing** **1.** to have an influence over; guide **2.** to keep under control **3.** to have authority over; govern **4.** to settle by decree; determine **5.** to mark (lines) on (paper, etc.) as with a ruler —***vi.*** **1.** to govern **2.** to prevail **3.** to issue a formal decision —**as a rule** usually —**rule out** to decide to exclude from consideration

rule of three *Math.* the method of finding the fourth term of a proportion when three terms are given: the product of the first and last is equal to the product of the second and third

rule of thumb **1.** a rule based on experience or practice rather than on scientific knowledge **2.** any practical, though crude, method of estimating

rul·er (rōō′lər) ***n.*** **1.** a person or thing that rules or governs **2.** a thin strip of wood, metal, etc. with a straight edge, used in drawing lines, measuring, etc.

rul·ing (-liŋ) ***adj.*** that rules; governing, predominating, etc. —***n.*** **1.** a governing **2.** a decision made by a court **3.** *a)* the making of ruled lines b) the lines so made

rum[1] (rum) ***n.*** [short for *rumbullion,* orig. a dial. term, tumult < ?] **1.** an alcoholic liquor distilled from fermented sugar cane, molasses, etc. **2.** alcoholic liquor in general

rum[2] (rum) ***adj.*** [< obs. *rum,* good] [Chiefly Brit. Colloq.] **1.** odd; strange **2.** bad, poor, etc. [a *rum* joke]

rum[3] (rum) ***n.*** *same as* RUMMY[1]

Ru·ma·nia (rōō mān′yə, -mā′nē ə) *same as* ROMANIA —**Ru·ma′nian** ***adj., n.***

rum·ba (rum′bə, rōōm′-; *Sp.* rōōm′bä) ***n.*** [AmSp., prob. of Afr. origin] **1.** a dance of Cuban Negro origin **2.** a ballroom adaptation of this, characterized by rhythmic movements of the lower part of the body **3.** music for this dance —***vi.*** to dance the rumba

rum·ble (rum′b'l) ***vi.*** **-bled, -bling** [prob. < MDu. *rommelen*] **1.** to make a deep, heavy rolling sound, as thunder **2.** to move with such a sound —***vt.*** **1.** to cause to make, or move with, such a sound **2.** to utter with such a sound —***n.*** **1.** a deep, heavy rolling sound **2.** a widespread expression of discontent **3.** [Slang] a gang fight —**rum′bler** ***n.***

rumble seat in some earlier automobiles, an open rear seat that could be folded shut when not in use

ru·men (rōō′min) ***n.,*** *pl.* **-mi·na** (-mi nə) [ModL. < L., gullet] the first stomach of a ruminant

Rum·ford (rum′fərd), Count *see* Benjamin THOMPSON

ru·mi·nant (rōō′mə nənt) ***adj.*** [< L. prp. of *ruminare,* to ruminate < *rumen,* RUMEN] **1.** chewing the cud **2.** of the cud-chewing animals **3.** meditative —***n.*** any of a large group of four-footed, hoofed, even-toed, cud-chewing mammals, as the cattle, sheep, goat, deer, camel, etc. —**ru′mi·nant·ly** ***adv.***

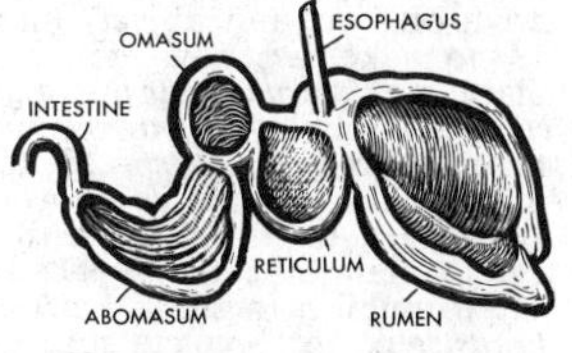

STOMACH OF A RUMINANT

ru·mi·nate (-nāt′) ***vt., vi.*** **-nat′ed, -nat′ing** [< L. pp. of *ruminare:* see prec.] **1.** to chew (the cud), as a cow does **2.** to meditate (on); muse —**ru′mi·na′tion** ***n.*** —**ru′mi·na′tive** ***adj.***

rum·mage (rum′ij) ***n.*** [< MFr. < *arrumer,* to stow cargo < *run,* ship's hold < Frank.] **1.** odds and ends **2.** a rummaging search —***vt.*** **-maged, -mag·ing** **1.** to search through (a place, etc.) thoroughly by moving the contents about **2.** to get or turn up by searching thoroughly (with *up* or *out*) —***vi.*** to make a thorough search —**rum′mag·er** ***n.***

rummage sale a sale of miscellaneous articles, used or new, to raise money for a charity

rum·my[1] (rum′ē) ***adj.*** **-mi·er, -mi·est** [RUM[2] + -Y[2]] [Chiefly Brit. Colloq.] odd; strange; queer —***n.*** any of certain card games in which the object is to match cards into sets of the same denomination or sequences of the same suit

rum·my[2] (rum′ē) ***n.,*** *pl.* **-mies** [RUM[1] + -Y[2]] [Slang] a drunkard —***adj.*** **-mi·er, -mi·est** of or like rum

ru·mor (rōō′mər) ***n.*** [< OFr. < L., noise] **1.** general talk not based on definite knowledge; hearsay **2.** an unconfirmed report, story, etc. in general circulation —***vt.*** to tell or spread by rumor Also, Brit. sp., **ru′mour**

ru·mor·mon·ger (-muŋ′gər, -mäŋ′-) ***n.*** a person who spreads rumors

rump (rump) ***n.*** [ON. *rumpr*] **1.** the hind part of an animal, where the legs and back join **2.** a cut of beef from this part, behind the loin and above the round **3.** the buttocks **4.** the last and unimportant part; remnant

rum·ple (rum′p'l) ***n.*** [< MDu. < *rompe,* a wrinkle] an uneven fold or crease; wrinkle —***vt., vi.*** **-pled, -pling** **1.** to make rumples (in); crumple **2.** to make or become disheveled —**rum′ply** ***adj.***

rum·pus (rum′pəs) ***n.*** [< ?] [Colloq.] noisy disturbance

rum·run·ner (rum′run′ər) ***n.*** a person, ship, etc. engaged in smuggling alcoholic liquor —**rum′run′ning** ***n.***

run (run) ***vi.*** **ran** or dial. **run, run, run′ning** [ON. *rinna* & OE. *rinnan*] **1.** to go by moving the legs faster than in walking **2.** *a)* to move swiftly [we *ran* to her aid] *b)* to go (*to*) for help [*run* to the doctor] **3.** to associate (*with*) **4.** to go, move, etc. easily and freely, without hindrance **5.** to flee **6.** to make a quick trip (*up to, down to,* etc.) for a brief stay **7.** *a)* to take part in a contest or race *b)* to be a candidate in an election **8.** to swim in migration: said of fish **9.** to go, as on a schedule [a bus *runs* between Chicago and Detroit] **10.** to pass lightly and rapidly [his eyes *ran* over the page] **11.** to be told repeatedly [a rumor *ran* through the town] **12.** to climb or creep, as a vine **13.** to ravel [her stocking *ran*] **14.** to operate with parts that revolve or slide [the machine is *running*] **15.** to flow [rivers *run* to the sea] **16.** to melt and flow, as wax **17.** *a)* to spread over cloth, etc. when moistened, as colors *b)* to be subject to this spreading, as fabric **18.** to be wet with a flow [her eyes *ran* with tears] **19.** *a)* to discharge pus, mucus, etc. *b)* to leak, as a faucet **20.** *a)* to appear in print, as in a newspaper *b)* to appear continuously [the play *ran* for a year] **21.** *a)* to continue in effect [the law *runs* for ten years] *b)* to continue to occur [talent *runs* in the family] **22.** to show a preference for (with *to*) [his taste *runs* to sweets] **23.** *a)* to extend in a continuous line [a fence *runs* through the woods] *b)* to extend in scope (*from* one thing *to* another) **24.** to pass into a specified condition, etc. [to *run* into trouble] **25.** to be written, expressed, etc. in a specified way [the adage *runs* like this] **26.** to be or continue at a specified size, price, etc. [apples *running* four to the pound] —***vt.*** **1.** to follow (a specified course) **2.** to travel over [horses *ran* the range] **3.** to perform as by running [to *run* a race] **4.** to incur (a risk) **5.** *a)* to get past [to *run* a blockade] *b)* to go through without making a required stop [to *run* a red light] **6.** to hunt (game, etc.) **7.** to compete with as in a race **8.** *a)* to enter (a horse, etc.) in a race *b)* to put up as a candidate for election **9.** *a)* to make run, move, etc. *b)* to cause to go between points, as on a schedule *c)* to cause (an engine, etc.) to idle for a while **10.** to bring or force into a specified condition by running [to *run* oneself into debt] **11.** *a)* to convey, as in a vehicle *b)* to smuggle **12.** to drive or force (an object) into, against, etc. (something) **13.** to make pass, flow, etc., esp. rapidly, in a specified way, place, etc. [to *run* water into a glass] **14.** *a)* to manage [to *run* a household] *b)* to conduct (a test, etc.) *c)* to cause to undergo a test, etc. **15.** to cost (an amount) **16.** to mark or draw (lines, as on a map) **17.** to trace [to *run* a story back to its source] **18.** to undergo (a fever, etc.) **19.** to melt or smelt (ore) **20.** to cast or mold; found **21.** to publish (a story, etc.) as in a newspaper **22.** *Billiards,* etc. to complete successfully (a sequence of shots, etc.) **23.** *Bridge* to lead (a suit) taking a series of tricks —***n.*** **1.** *a)* an act or period of running *b)* a running pace **2.** the distance covered or time spent in running **3.** a trip; journey; esp., *a)* a regular trip, as of a plane *b)* a route for making deliveries **4.** *a)* movement onward; progression *b)* a continuous course or period [a *run* of good luck] **5.** a continuous course of performances, etc., as of a play **6.** a continued series of demands, as for specified goods **7.** a continuous series or extent **8.** a flow or rush of water, etc., as of the tide **9.** a small, swift stream **10.** *a)* a period during which some fluid flows readily *b)* the amount of flow **11.** *a)* a period of operation of a machine *b)* the output during this period **12.** *a)* a kind or class, as of goods *b)* the usual or average kind **13.** *a)* an inclined pathway or course [a ski *run*] *b)* an enclosed area for domestic animals [a dog *run*] **14.** freedom to move about at will [to have the *run* of the house] **15.** *a)* a large number of fish migrating together *b)* such migration **16.** a ravel, as in a stocking **17.** *Baseball* a scoring point, made by a successful circuit of the bases **18.** *Billiards,* etc. a sequence of successful shots, etc. **19.** *Mil.* the approach to the target made by an airplane in bombing, etc. **20.** *Music* a rapid succession of tones —***adj.*** **1.** melted **2.** poured while in a melted state [*run* metal] —**a run for one's money** **1.** powerful competition **2.** satisfaction for what one has expended —**in the long run** in the final outcome; ultimately —**on the run** **1.** running **2.** running away —**run across** to encounter by chance —**run along** to depart —**run away** **1.** to flee **2.** to desert one's home or family **3.** to escape and run loose —**run away with** **1.** to steal **2.** to carry out of control [his anger *ran away with* him] **3.** *a)* to outdo all others in (a contest, etc.) *b)* to get (a prize, etc.) in this way —**run down** **1.** to stop operating **2.** to run or drive against so as to knock down **3.** to pursue and capture or kill **4.** to search out the source of **5.** to speak of with disapproval **6.** to make or become run-down **7.** to read through rapidly —**run for it** to run to escape something —**run in** **1.** to include (something additional) **2.** [Colloq.] to make a quick visit **3.** [Slang] to arrest —**run into** **1.** to encounter by chance **2.** to collide with **3.** to add up to (a large sum of money): also **run to** —**run off** **1.** to print, make copies of, etc. **2.** to cause to be run, played, etc. **3.** to drive (trespassers) away **4.** to drain **5.** *same as* RUN AWAY —**run on** **1.** to continue or be continued **2.** to add (something) at the end **3.** to talk continuously —**run out** **1.** to come to an end; expire **2.** to drive out —**run out of** to use up —**run out on** [Colloq.] to abandon or desert —**run over** **1.** to ride or drive over **2.** to overflow **3.** to go beyond a limit **4.** to examine, rehearse, etc. rapidly —**run scared** [Slang] to behave as if expecting to fail —**run through** **1.** to use up or spend quickly or recklessly **2.** to pierce **3.** to examine, rehearse, etc. rapidly —**run up** **1.** to raise, rise, or make rapidly **2.** to let (bills, etc.) go without paying them **3.** to sew with a rapid succession of stitches

run·a·bout (run′ə bout′) ***n.*** **1.** a person who runs about from place to place **2.** a light, one-seated, open carriage or automobile **3.** a light motorboat

run·a·round (-ə round′) ***n.*** [Colloq.] a series of evasive excuses, delays, etc.: usually in **get** (or **give**) **the runaround**

run·a·way (-ə wā′) ***n.*** **1.** a fugitive **2.** a horse, etc. that runs away **3.** a running away —***adj.*** **1.** running away or having run away **2.** of or done by runaways **3.** easily won, as a race **4.** *a)* rising rapidly, as prices *b)* having an uncontrolled rise of prices [*runaway* inflation]

run-down (-doun′) ***adj.*** **1.** not wound and therefore not running, as a clock **2.** in poor physical condition, as from overwork **3.** fallen into disrepair

run·down (-doun′) ***n.*** a concise summary

rune (ro͞on) ***n.*** [OE. *run*] **1.** any of the characters of an ancient Germanic alphabet **2.** something inscribed in such characters **3.** *a)* a Finnish or Old Norse poem or canto *b)* [Poet.] any poem, song, etc. that is mystical or obscure

rung[1] (ruŋ) ***n.*** [OE. *hrung,* a staff] **1.** any sturdy stick, bar, or rod used as a crossbar, support, etc.; specif., *a)* any of the steps of a ladder *b)* a crosspiece between the legs of a chair, or across the back, etc. **2.** a degree, as of social status, success, etc.

rung[2] (ruŋ) *pp. & chiefly dial. pt. of* RING[1]

ru·nic (ro͞o′nik) ***adj.*** **1.** consisting of or set down in runes **2.** like runes in decorative effect **3.** mystical; obscure

run-in (run′in′) ***adj.*** *Printing* made continuous without a break or paragraph —***n.*** **1.** *Printing* run-in matter **2.** [Colloq.] a quarrel, fight, etc.

run·nel (run′'l) ***n.*** [OE. *rynel* < *rinnan,* to run] a small stream; little brook: also **run′let** (-lit)

run·ner (run′ər) ***n.*** **1.** one that runs; specif., *a)* a racer *b)* *same as* BASE RUNNER **2.** a messenger, as for a bank or broker **3.** a smuggler **4.** a person who operates a machine, etc. **5.** a long, narrow cloth or rug **6.** a long ravel, as in hose; run **7.** a long, trailing stem, as of a strawberry, that puts out roots along the ground, thus producing new plants **8.** something on or in which something else moves **9.** either of the long, narrow pieces on which a sled or sleigh slides **10.** the blade of a skate

run·ner-up (-up′) ***n.,*** *pl.* **-ners-up′** a person or team that finishes second in a race, contest, etc.

run·ning (run′iŋ) ***n.*** **1.** the act of one that runs; racing, managing, etc. **2.** that which runs, or flows —***adj.*** **1.** moving or advancing rapidly **2.** flowing [*running* water] **3.** cursive: said of handwriting **4.** melting; becoming liquid **5.** discharging pus [a *running* sore] **6.** creeping or climbing: said of plants **7.** in operation, as machinery **8.** in a straight line [a *running* foot] **9.** without interruption; continuous [a *running* commentary] **10.** prevalent **11.** current [a *running* account] **12.** simultaneous [a *running* translation] **13.** moving easily or smoothly **14.** slipping or sliding easily, as a knot **15.** moving when pulled, as a rope **16.** done in or by a run [a *running* jump] **17.** of the normal run (of a train, bus, etc.) [*running* time] —***adv.*** in succession [for ten days *running*] —**in** (or **out of**) **the running** in (or out of) the competition

running board esp. formerly, a footboard along the lower part of the side of some automobiles

running fire a rapid succession of shots fired, remarks made, questions asked, etc.

running head (or **title**) a heading or title printed at the top of every, or every other, page

running knot *same as* SLIPKNOT

running lights the lights that a ship or aircraft traveling at night is required to display

running mate a candidate for a lesser office, as for the vice-presidency, in his relationship to the candidate for the greater office

run·ny (run′ē) ***adj.*** **-ni·er, -ni·est** **1.** that flows, esp. too freely **2.** that keeps on discharging mucus [a *runny* nose]

Run·ny·mede (run′ē mēd′) meadow on the south bank of the Thames, southwest of London: see MAGNA CHARTA

run-off (run′ôf′) ***n.*** **1.** something that runs off, as rain in excess of the amount absorbed by the ground **2.** a deciding, final race, election, etc., as in case of a tie

run-of-the-mill (run′əv *thə* mil′) ***adj.*** [see RUN, *n.*, 12 *b*] not selected or special; ordinary

run-on (run′än′) ***adj.*** *Printing* continuous without a break or new paragraph —***n.*** run-on matter

runt (runt) ***n.*** [< ?] **1.** a stunted or undersized animal, plant, thing, or (usually in a contemptuous sense) person **2.** the smallest animal of a litter —**runt′i·ness** ***n.*** —**runt′y** ***adj.*** **runt′i·er, runt′i·est**

run-through (run′thro͞o′) ***n.*** a full rehearsal without stopping

run·way (-wā′) ***n.*** a channel, track, chute, etc. in, on, or along which something moves; specif., *a*) a strip of leveled, usually paved ground for use by airplanes in taking off and landing *b*) a narrow extension of a stage out into the audience

ru·pee (ro͞o pē′, ro͞o′pē) ***n.*** [< Hindi < Sans. *rūpya*, wrought silver] the monetary unit of India, Pakistan, Ceylon, etc.: see MONETARY UNITS, table

ru·pi·ah (ro͞o pē′ə) ***n.*** [< Hindi] *see* MONETARY UNITS, table (Indonesia)

rup·ture (rup′chər) ***n.*** [< MFr. < L. < pp. of *rumpere*, to break] **1.** a breaking apart or being broken apart **2.** a breaking off of friendly or peaceful relations **3.** a hernia —***vt., vi.*** **-tured, -tur·ing 1.** to break apart or burst **2.** to affect with or undergo a rupture

ru·ral (roor′əl) ***adj.*** [< MFr. < LL. *ruralis* < L. *rus* (gen. *ruris*), the country] **1.** of or like the country, country folk, etc.; rustic **2.** living in the country **3.** having to do with farming —**ru′ral·ly** ***adv.***

rural delivery delivery of mail by carriers on routes in rural areas: formerly **rural free delivery**

ru·ral·ism (-iz'm) ***n.*** **1.** rural quality **2.** rural life **3.** a rural idiom, feature, etc. Also **ru·ral·i·ty** (roo ral′ə tē), *pl.* **-ties** —**ru′ral·ist** (-ist) ***n.***

ru·ral·ize (roor′ə līz′) ***vt.*** **-ized′, -iz′ing** to make rural —***vi.*** to live for a time in the country —**ru′ral·i·za′tion** ***n.***

Ru·ri·ta·ni·an (roor′ə tā′nē ən) ***adj.*** [after *Ruritania*, imaginary kingdom in novels by A. Hope (1863–1933)] of or characteristic of some quaint, romantic, unreal place

ruse (ro͞oz) ***n.*** [< MFr. < OFr. *reuser*, to deceive < L. *recusare*, to refuse] a stratagem or trick

rush[1] (rush) ***vi.*** [< Anglo-Fr. < MFr. < OFr. *reuser:* see prec.] **1.** *a*) to move swiftly or impetuously *b*) to dash recklessly **2.** to make a sudden attack (*on* or *upon*) **3.** to pass, come, go, etc. swiftly or suddenly **4.** *Football* to advance the ball by a running play —***vt.*** **1.** to move, send, push, etc. swiftly or violently **2.** to do, make, move, etc. with unusual speed or haste **3.** *a*) to attack suddenly *b*) to overcome or capture thus **4.** [Colloq.] *a*) to lavish attentions on, as in courting *b*) to entertain with parties, etc. prior to inviting to join a fraternity or sorority —***n.*** **1.** a rushing **2.** an eager movement of many people to get to a place **3.** intense activity; haste; hurry **4.** a sudden attack **5.** a scrimmage contest between groups of college students **6.** great pressure, as of much business requiring quick or hasty attention **7.** [*usually pl.*] *Motion Pictures* a first print of a scene or scenes, shown for the director, etc. to inspect —***adj.*** necessitating haste [*rush* orders] —**with a rush** suddenly and forcefully —**rush′er** ***n.***

rush[2] (rush) ***n.*** [OE. *risc*] **1.** any of a genus of grasslike plants usually growing in wet places and having, in some species, round stems and pliant leaves used in making baskets, mats, etc. **2.** any of various similar plants, as bulrushes —**rush′y** ***adj.*** **rush′i·er, rush′i·est**

rush candle a candle made with the pith of a rush as the wick: also **rush′light′** ***n.***, **rush light**

rush·ee (rush ē′) ***n.*** a college student who is being rushed by a fraternity or sorority

rush hour a time of the day when business, traffic, etc. are especially heavy —**rush′-hour′** ***adj.***

rusk (rusk) ***n.*** [Sp. *rosca*, twisted bread roll] **1.** sweet, raised bread or cake toasted in an oven until crisp, usually after being sliced **2.** a piece of this

Rus·kin (rus′kin), **John** 1819–1900; Eng. writer, art critic, & social reformer

Russ. **1.** Russia **2.** Russian

Rus·sell (rus′'l) **1.** [< surname *Russell*, orig. dim. of Fr. *roux*, red] a masculine name: dim. *Russ* **2. Bertrand** (**Arthur William**), 3d Earl Russell, 1872–1970; Brit. philosopher, mathematician, & writer, born in Wales

rus·set (rus′it) ***n.*** [< OFr. < L. *russus*, reddish] **1.** yellowish (or reddish) brown **2.** a coarse, brownish cloth, formerly used for clothing by country folk **3.** a winter apple with a rough, mottled skin —***adj.*** yellowish-brown or reddish-brown

Rus·sia (rush′ə) **1.** former empire (**Russian Empire**) in E. Europe & N Asia, 1547–1917, ruled by the czars **2.** *popular name for the* UNION OF SOVIET SOCIALIST REPUBLICS

Russia leather a fine, smooth leather, usually dyed dark red, orig. made in Russia: used in bookbinding, etc.

Rus·sian (rush′ən) ***adj.*** of Russia, its people, their language, etc. —***n.*** **1.** *a*) a native or inhabitant of Russia, specif. of the R.S.F.S.R. *b*) popularly, any citizen of the U.S.S.R. **2.** a member of the chief Slavic people of Russia **3.** the East Slavic language of the Russians; esp., its principal dialect (**Great Russian**), the official language of the U.S.S.R.

Russian dressing mayonnaise mixed with chili sauce, chopped pickles, pimentos, etc.: used on salads, etc.

Rus·sian·ize (-īz′) ***vt.*** **-ized′, -iz′ing** to make Russian in character —**Rus′sian·i·za′tion** ***n.***

Russian Revolution the revolution of 1917 in Russia in which the Czar's government was overthrown

Russian roulette a deadly game of chance in which a person spins the cylinder of a revolver holding only one bullet, aims at his head, and pulls the trigger

Russian Soviet Federated Socialist Republic largest republic of the U.S.S.R., from the Baltic Sea to the Pacific: 6,592,000 sq. mi.; pop. 130,100,000; cap. Moscow

Russian wolfhound *same as* BORZOI

Rus·si·fy (rus′ə fī′) ***vt.*** **-fied′, -fy′ing** *same as* RUSSIANIZE

Rus·so- *a combining form meaning:* **1.** Russia or Russian **2.** Russian and [*Russo*-Japanese]

rust (rust) ***n.*** [OE.] **1.** the reddish-brown coating (mainly ferric oxide) formed on iron or steel by oxidation, as during exposure to air and moisture **2.** any similar coating on other metals **3.** any stain or formation resembling iron rust **4.** any habit, influence, etc. injurious to usefulness, to the mind, etc. **5.** inactivity; idleness **6.** a reddish brown **7.** *a*) any of various plant diseases caused by parasitic fungi that produce reddish spots on stems and leaves *b*) such a fungus: in full, **rust fungus** —***vi., vt.*** **1.** to affect or be affected by a rust fungus **2.** to become or cause to be coated with rust **3.** to spoil, as from lack of use **4.** to become or make rust-colored —**rust′-col′ored** ***adj.*** —**rust′less** ***adj.***

rus·tic (rus′tik) ***adj.*** [< MFr. < L. *rusticus* < *rus:* see RURAL] **1.** of or living in the country, as distinguished from cities or towns; rural **2.** not refined or sophisticated; specif., *a*) simple, plain, or artless *b*) awkward, uncouth, or boorish **3.** made of bark-covered branches or roots [*rustic* furniture] —***n.*** a country person, esp. one regarded as simple, awkward, uncouth, etc. —**rus′ti·cal·ly** ***adv.*** —**rus·tic′i·ty** (-tis′ə tē) ***n.***

rus·ti·cate (rus′ti kāt′) ***vi.*** **-cat′ed, -cat′ing** **1.** to go to the country **2.** to live in the country —***vt.*** **1.** to send to live in the country **2.** [Brit.] to suspend (a student) temporarily from a university **3.** to make rustic —**rus′ti·ca′tion** ***n.*** —**rus′ti·ca′tor** ***n.***

rus·tle[1] (rus′'l) ***vi., vt.*** **-tled, -tling** [ult. < WGmc. echoic base] to make or cause to make soft sounds, as of leaves moved by a breeze —***n.*** a series of such sounds

rus·tle[2] (rus′'l) ***vi., vt.*** **-tled, -tling** [< ? RUSH[1] + HUSTLE] [Colloq.] **1.** to work with, or move or get by, energetic action **2.** to steal (cattle, etc.) —**rustle up** [Colloq.] to collect or get together, as by foraging around —**rus′tler** ***n.***

rust·proof (rust′pro͞of′) ***adj.*** resistant to rust —***vt.*** to make rustproof

rust·y (rus′tē) ***adj.*** **rust′i·er, rust′i·est** **1.** coated with rust, as a metal, or affected by rust, as a plant **2.** of or caused by rust **3.** not working freely because of or as if because of rust **4.** *a*) impaired by disuse, neglect, etc. *b*) having lost one's skill through lack of practice **5.** rust-colored **6.** faded, old-looking, or shabby —**rust′i·ly** ***adv.*** —**rust′i·ness** ***n.***

rut[1] (rut) ***n.*** [< ? MFr. *route*, ROUTE] **1.** a track or furrow, esp. one made by wheeled vehicles **2.** a fixed, routine procedure, way of acting, thinking, etc. —***vt.*** **rut′ted, rut′ting** to make a rut or ruts in

rut[2] (rut) ***n.*** [< OFr. < L. < *rugire*, to roar] **1.** the periodic sexual excitement of certain mammals, esp. males **2.** the period of this —***vi.*** **rut′ted, rut′ting** to be in rut

ru·ta·ba·ga (ro͞ot′ə bā′gə, ro͞ot′ə bä′gə) ***n.*** [Sw. dial. *rotabagge*] a turnip with a large, yellow root

Ruth (ro͞oth) [LL. < Heb. *rūth*, prob. contr. < *rēʿuth*, companion] **1.** a feminine name **2.** *Bible* *a*) a Moabite widow deeply devoted to her mother-in-law, Naomi *b*) the book of the Bible that tells her story **3. George Herman,** (nicknamed "*Babe*") 1895–1948; U.S. baseball player

ruth (ro͞oth) ***n.*** [ult. < OE. *hreowian*, to rue] [Now Rare] **1.** pity; compassion **2.** sorrow; grief; remorse

Ru·the·ni·a (ro͞o thē′nē ə) region in W Ukrainian S.S.R. —**Ru·the′ni·an** ***adj., n.***

ru·the·ni·um (ro͞o thē′nē əm) ***n.*** [ModL. < ML. *Ruthenia*, Russia, where first found] a rare, very hard, silvery-gray metallic chemical element, used in alloys and as a catalyst: symbol, Ru; at. wt., 101.07; at. no., 44

Ruth·er·ford (ru*th*′ər fərd), **Ernest,** 1st Baron Rutherford of Nelson, 1871–1937; Brit. physicist, born in New Zealand
ruth·ful (rōōth′fəl) ***adj.*** [Now Rare] full of ruth, or pity, sorrow, etc. —**ruth′ful·ly** ***adv.*** —**ruth′ful·ness** ***n.***
ruth·less (-lis) ***adj.*** without ruth; pitiless and relentless, as in seeking some goal —**ruth′less·ly** ***adv.*** —**ruth′less·ness** ***n.***
rut·ty (rut′ē) ***adj.*** **-ti·er, -ti·est** having or full of ruts *[a rutty road]* —**rut′ti·ness** ***n.***
Rwan·da (ʉr wän′dä, rōō wän′də) country in EC Africa, east of Zaire: 10,169 sq. mi.; pop. 3,724,000 —**Rwan′dan** ***adj., n.***
Rwy., Ry. Railway
Rx [< ℞, symbol for L. *recipe:* see RECIPE] *symbol for* PRESCRIPTION (sense 3) —***n.*** a prescription for any disorder
-ry (rē) *shortened form of* -ERY *[dentistry, jewelry]*
rye (rī) ***n.*** see PLURAL, II, D, 3 [OE. *ryge*] **1.** a hardy cereal grass widely grown for its grain and straw **2.** the grain or seeds of this plant, used for making flour and whiskey, and as feed for livestock **3.** *a)* whiskey distilled from this grain *b)* in the eastern U.S., a blended whiskey
rye bread bread made altogether or partly of rye flour
rye·grass (-gras′) ***n.*** any of various grasses that are annuals or that live for only a few years
Ryu·kyu Islands (ryōō′kyōō′) chain of Jap. islands in the W Pacific, between Kyushu & Taiwan

S

S, s (es) ***n., pl.*** **S's, s's** **1.** the nineteenth letter of the English alphabet **2.** a sound of *S* or *s*
S (es) ***n.*** **1.** something shaped like an *S* **2.** *Chem.* sulfur —***adj.*** shaped like *S*
-s [alt. form of -ES] **1.** the plural ending of most nouns *[hips, shoes]* **2.** the ending of the third person singular, present indicative, of verbs *[gives, runs]* **3.** a suffix used to form some adverbs *[betimes, days]*
-'s[1] [OE. *-es*] the ending of the possessive singular of nouns (and some pronouns) and of the possessive plural of nouns not ending in *s [*boy'*s*, one'*s*, women'*s]*
-'s[2] *the unstressed and assimilated form of:* **1.** is *[*he'*s* here*]* **2.** has *[*she'*s* eaten*]* **3.** does *[*what'*s* it matter?*]* **4.** us *[*let'*s* go*]*
S, S., s, s. **1.** south **2.** southern
S. **1.** Saturday **2.** September **3.** Sunday
S., s. **1.** *pl.* **SS., ss.** saint **2.** school
s. **1.** second(s) **2.** shilling(s) **3.** singular
SA Seaman Apprentice
S.A. **1.** Salvation Army **2.** South America
Saar (sär, zär) **1.** river flowing from NE France north into the Moselle River, SW West Germany **2.** rich coal-mining region in the valley of this river: also called **Saar Basin**
Saar·land (sär′land, zär′-; *G.* zär′länt′) state of SW West Germany, in the Saar River Basin
Sa·ba (sā′bə) ancient kingdom in S Arabia in the region of modern Yemen: Biblical name, *Sheba*
Sab·ba·tar·i·an (sab′ə ter′ē ən) ***adj.*** of the Sabbath and its observance —***n.*** **1.** a person, esp. a Christian, who observes the Sabbath (sense 1) **2.** a Christian favoring rigid observance of Sunday as the Sabbath —**Sab′ba·tar′i·an·ism** ***n.***
Sab·bath (sab′əth) ***n.*** [< OFr. & OE. *sabat,* both < L. < Gr. < Heb. < *shābath,* to rest] **1.** the seventh day of the week (Saturday), observed as a day of rest and worship by Jews and some Christian sects **2.** Sunday as the usual Christian day of rest and worship —***adj.*** of the Sabbath
Sab·bat·i·cal (sə bat′i k'l) ***adj.*** [< Fr. < LL. < Gr. *sabbatikos:* see prec.] **1.** of or suited to the Sabbath **2.** [**s-**] designating a year or shorter period of absence for study, rest, or travel, given at intervals, orig. every seven years, as to some college teachers —***n.*** [**s-**] a sabbatical year or leave Also **Sab·bat′ic**
sa·ber (sā′bər) ***n.*** [< Fr. < G. *sabel* < MHG. < Pol. & Hung.] a heavy cavalry sword with a slightly curved blade —***vt.*** to cut, wound, or kill with a saber
Sa·bin (sā′bin), **Albert B(ruce)** 1906– ; U.S. bacteriologist: developed an oral vaccine to prevent poliomyelitis
Sa·bine (sā′bīn) ***n.*** a member of an ancient tribe living in central Italy, conquered by the Romans, 3d century B.C.
sa·ble (sā′b'l) ***n., pl.*** **-bles, -ble:** see PLURAL, II, D, 1 [OFr. < ML. *sabelum,* ult. < Russian *sobol'*] **1.** *same as* MARTEN; esp., *a)* the **European marten,** with light-colored underfur *b)* the **American marten,** with a darker pelt **2.** *a)* the costly fur of the sable *b)* [*pl.*] a coat, etc. of this **3.** *Heraldry* the color black —***adj.*** **1.** made of or with the fur of the sable **2.** black or dark brown; dark
sa·bot (sab′ō, sa bō′) ***n.*** [Fr., ult. < Ar. *sabbât,* sandal] **1.** a shoe shaped from a single piece of wood **2.** a heavy leather shoe with a wooden sole

SABOT

sab·o·tage (sab′ə täzh′) ***n.*** [Fr. < *saboter,* to damage < *sabot:* see prec. & -AGE: from damage done to machinery by wooden shoes] **1.** intentional destruction of machines, waste of materials, etc., as during labor disputes **2.** destruction of railroads, bridges, etc. as by enemy agents or an underground resistance **3.** deliberate obstruction of or damage to any cause, effort, etc. —***vt.*** **-taged′, -tag′ing** to injure or destroy by sabotage —***vi.*** to engage in sabotage
sab·o·teur (sab′ə tʉr′) ***n.*** [Fr.] a person who sabotages
sa·bra (sä′brə) ***n.*** [ModHeb. *sābrāh,* lit., prickly fruit of a native cactus] a native-born Israeli
sa·bre (sā′bər) ***n., vt.*** **-bred, -bring** *same as* SABER
sac (sak) ***n.*** [Fr. < L. *saccus:* see SACK[1]] a pouchlike part in a plant or animal, esp. one filled with fluid —**sac′like′** ***adj.***
SAC, S.A.C. Strategic Air Command
sac·cha·ride (sak′ə rīd′) ***n.*** [see ff.] any of the carbohydrates; esp., any of the sugars, as glucose
sac·cha·rin (sak′ə rin) ***n.*** [< L. *saccharum,* sugar < Gr. *sakcharon,* ult. < Sans.] a white, crystalline coal-tar compound, $C_7H_5O_3NS$, about 500 times sweeter than cane sugar, used as a sugar substitute in diabetic diets, etc.
sac·cha·rine (-rin, -rīn′) ***adj.*** [see prec.] **1.** of, like, or producing sugar **2.** too sweet or syrupy *[*a *saccharine* voice*]* —***n.*** *same as* SACCHARIN —**sac′cha·rine·ly** ***adv.*** —**sac′cha·rin′i·ty** (-rin′ə tē) ***n.***
sac·er·do·tal (sas′ər dōt′'l, sak′-) ***adj.*** [< MFr. < L. < *sacerdos,* priest] of priests or the office of priest; priestly —**sac′er·do′tal·ly** ***adv.***
sa·chem (sā′chəm) ***n.*** [< Algonquian *sâchimau*] among some N. American Indian tribes, the chief
sa·chet (sa shā′; *chiefly Brit.* sash′ā) ***n.*** [Fr. < OFr., dim. of *sac:* see SAC] **1.** a small bag, pad, etc. filled with perfumed powder and put in dresser drawers, etc. to scent clothing **2.** such powder: also **sachet powder**
sack[1] (sak) ***n.*** [OE. *sacc* < L. *saccus* < Gr. < Heb. *śaq*] **1.** *a)* a bag, esp. a large bag of coarse cloth, for holding grain, foodstuffs, etc. *b)* the contents or capacity of a sack **2.** a loose-fitting jacket or dress **3.** [Slang] dismissal from a job (with *the*) **4.** [Slang] a bed, bunk, etc. **5.** *Baseball* a base —***vt.*** **1.** to put into sacks **2.** [Slang] to dismiss from a job; fire —**hit the sack** [Slang] to go to bed
sack[2] (sak) ***n.*** [< MFr. < It. *sacco,* plunder, lit., bag < L. *saccus:* see prec.] the plundering of a captured city, etc. —***vt.*** to plunder (a city, etc.)
sack[3] (sak) ***n.*** [< Fr. (*vin*) *sec,* dry (wine) < L. *siccus,* dry] any of various dry white wines from Spain or the Canary Islands
sack·but (sak′but′) ***n.*** [Fr. *saquebute* < OFr. *saquer,* to pull + *bouter,* to push] a medieval wind instrument, forerunner of the trombone: the word is also incorrectly used in the King James Version of the Bible to translate an Aramaic word for a kind of lyre
sack·cloth (-klôth′, -kläth′) ***n.*** **1.** *same as* SACKING **2.** a rough cloth worn as a symbol of mourning or penitence —**in sackcloth and ashes** in a state of great mourning or penitence
sack coat a man's loose-fitting, straight-backed coat, usually part of a business suit
sack·ful (sak′fool′) ***n., pl.*** **-fuls′** **1.** the amount a sack holds **2.** a large quantity
sack·ing (-iŋ) ***n.*** a cheap, coarse cloth of flax, hemp, jute, etc., used esp. for sacks
sa·cral[1] (sā′krəl) ***adj.*** [< L. neut. of *sacer,* sacred] of or for religious rites or observances
sa·cral[2] (sā′krəl) ***adj.*** [< ModL.: see SACRUM & -AL] of, or in the region of, the sacrum
sac·ra·ment (sak′rə mənt) ***n.*** [< OFr. < LL. *sacramentum,* ult. < L. *sacer,* sacred] **1.** any of certain rites variously observed by Christians as ordained by Jesus, as baptism,

Holy Communion, etc. **2.** [*sometimes* **S-**] the Eucharist, or Holy Communion; also, the consecrated bread and wine, or sometimes the bread alone **3.** something regarded as sacred

sac·ra·men·tal (sak′rə men′t'l) ***adj.*** of, like, or used in a sacrament —***n.*** *R.C.Ch.* something like a sacrament but instituted by the Church, as holy water —**sac′ra·men′tal·ly** ***adv.***

Sac·ra·men·to (sak′rə men′tō) [Sp., sacrament] **1.** river in C Calif., flowing south into San Francisco Bay **2.** capital of Calif., on this river: pop. 276,000 (met. area 1,011,000)

sa·cred (sā′krid) ***adj.*** [< OFr. < L. < *sacer,* holy] **1.** consecrated to a god or deity; holy **2.** having to do with religion or religious rites **3.** given the respect accorded holy things; venerated **4.** dedicated to a person, place, purpose, etc. *[sacred* to his memory*]* **5.** that must not be broken, ignored, etc.; inviolate *[a sacred* promise*]* —**sa′cred·ly** ***adv.*** —**sa′cred·ness** ***n.***

sacred cow any person or thing regarded as above criticism

sac·ri·fice (sak′rə fīs′) ***n.*** [< OFr. < L. *sacrificium* < *sacer,* sacred + *facere,* to make] **1.** *a)* an offering of the life of a person or animal, or of an object, in homage to a deity *b)* the thing offered **2.** *a)* a giving up, destroying, etc. of one thing for the sake of another *b)* the thing given up, etc. **3.** *a)* a selling or giving up of a thing at less than its value *b)* the loss incurred **4.** *Baseball same as* SACRIFICE BUNT —***vt.*** **-ficed′, -fic′ing** **1.** to offer as a sacrifice to a deity **2.** to give up, destroy, etc. for the sake of another thing **3.** to sell at less than value **4.** *Baseball* to advance (a base runner) by a sacrifice —***vi.*** to make a sacrifice

sacrifice bunt *Baseball* a bunt by the batter hit so that while he is being put out a base runner advances to another base: also **sacrifice hit**

sacrifice fly *Baseball* a play in which the batter flies out and a runner scores from third base after the catch

sac·ri·fi·cial (sak′rə fish′əl) ***adj.*** of, like, used in, or offering a sacrifice —**sac′ri·fi′cial·ly** ***adv.***

sac·ri·lege (sak′rə lij) ***n.*** [< MFr. < L. < *sacrilegus,* temple robber < *sacer,* sacred + *legere,* to take away] **1.** misuse or violation of what is consecrated to God or religion **2.** a desecrating of anything held sacred

sac·ri·le·gious (sak′rə lij′əs, -lē′jəs) ***adj.*** **1.** that is or involves sacrilege **2.** guilty of sacrilege —**sac′ri·le′gious·ly** ***adv.*** —**sac′ri·le′gious·ness** ***n.***

sac·ris·tan (sak′ris tən) ***n.*** a person in charge of a sacristy

sac·ris·ty (-tē) ***n., pl.*** **-ties** [< Fr. < ML. < L. < *sacrista,* sacristan] a room in a church where the sacred vessels, vestments, etc. are kept

sa·cro·il·i·ac (sā′krō il′ē ak′, sak′rō-) ***adj.*** [< SACRUM + ILIAC] of the sacrum and the ilium; esp., designating the joint between them —***n.*** the sacroiliac joint

sac·ro·sanct (sak′rō saŋkt′) ***adj.*** [< L. < *sacer,* sacred + *sanctus,* holy] very sacred, holy, or inviolable

sa·crum (sā′krəm, sak′rəm) ***n., pl.*** **-cra** (-krə, -rə) or **-crums** [ModL. < LL. (*os*) *sacrum,* sacred (bone): ? anciently used in sacrifices] a thick, triangular bone joining the ilia (see ILIUM) at the lower end of the spinal column

sad (sad) ***adj.*** **sad′der, sad′dest** [OE. *sæd,* sated] **1.** having or expressing low spirits or sorrow; unhappy; sorrowful **2.** causing or characterized by sorrow, dejection, etc. **3.** dark or dull in color; drab **4.** [Colloq.] very bad; deplorable **5.** [Dial.] heavy or soggy *[a sad* cake*]* —**sad′ly** ***adv.*** —**sad′ness** ***n.***

sad·den (sad′'n) ***vt., vi.*** to make or become sad

sad·dle (sad′'l) ***n.*** [OE. *sadol*] **1.** a seat, usually of padded leather, for a rider on a horse, bicycle, etc. **2.** a padded part of a harness worn over a horse's back **3.** the part of an animal's back where a saddle is put **4.** anything like a saddle in form, position, etc. **5.** a ridge between two peaks **6.** a cut of lamb, etc. including part of the backbone and the two loins —***vt.*** **-dled, -dling** **1.** to put a saddle upon **2.** to burden (a person) with (a debt, responsibility, obligation, etc.) —***vi.*** to put a saddle on a horse and mount it (often with *up*) —**in the saddle** **1.** seated on a saddle **2.** having control

sad·dle·bag (-bag′) ***n.*** **1.** a large bag, usually one of a pair, carried on either side of the back of a horse, etc., just behind the saddle **2.** a similar bag carried over the back wheel of a motorcycle, etc.

sad·dle·bow (-bō′) ***n.*** the arched front part of a saddle, the top of which is the pommel

sad·dle·cloth (-klôth′, -kläth′) ***n.*** a thick cloth placed under a saddle on an animal's back

saddle horse a horse trained for riding

sad·dler (sad′lər) ***n.*** a person whose work is making, repairing, or selling saddles, harnesses, etc.

saddle roof a roof with two gables and a ridge

sad·dler·y (sad′lə rē) ***n., pl.*** **-dler·ies** **1.** the work of a saddler **2.** articles made by a saddler **3.** a shop where these are sold

saddle shoes white oxford shoes with a band of contrasting leather across the instep

saddle soap a mild soap with neat's-foot oil in it, for cleaning and softening leather

Sad·du·cee (saj′oo sē′, sad′yoo-) ***n.*** a member of an ancient Jewish party accepting only the written law and rejecting the oral, or traditional, law —**Sad′du·ce′an** ***adj.***

Sade (säd), marquis **de** (full name, comte *Donatien Alphonse François de Sade*) 1740–1814; Fr. soldier & novelist

sa·dhu (sä′dōō) ***n.*** [Sans. < *sādhu,* straight] a Hindu holy man

sad·i·ron (sad′ī′ərn) ***n.*** [SAD (sense 5) + IRON] a heavy flatiron, pointed at both ends

sad·ism (sad′iz'm, sā′diz'm) ***n.*** [Fr., after marquis de SADE] the getting of pleasure, specif. sexual pleasure, from hurting or mistreating another or others —**sad′ist** ***n.*** —**sa·dis·tic** (sə dis′tik, sā-) ***adj.*** —**sa·dis′ti·cal·ly** ***adv.***

sad·o·mas·o·chism (sā′dō mas′ə kiz'm, sad′ō-; -maz′-) ***n.*** sadism and masochism in the same individual —**sad′o·mas′o·chist** ***n.*** —**sad′o·mas′o·chis′tic** ***adj.***

sad sack [Slang] a person who means well but is always blundering and in trouble

sa·fa·ri (sə fär′ē) ***n., pl.*** **-ris** [Swahili < Ar. < *safara,* to travel] a journey or hunting expedition, esp. in E Africa

safe (sāf) ***adj.*** **saf′er, saf′est** [OFr. *sauf* < L. *salvus*] **1.** *a)* free from danger, damage, etc.; secure *b)* having escaped injury; unharmed **2.** *a)* giving protection *b)* trustworthy **3.** unable to cause trouble or damage *[safe* in jail*]* **4.** taking or involving no risks **5.** *Baseball* having reached base without being put out —***n.*** **1.** a strong, locking metal container for valuables **2.** any compartment, box, etc. to store food, etc. —**safe′ly** ***adv.*** —**safe′ness** ***n.***

safe-con·duct (-kän′dukt) ***n.*** **1.** permission to travel through a dangerous area, as in time of war, with protection against arrest or harm **2.** a written pass giving this

safe-de·pos·it (-di päz′it) ***adj.*** designating or of a box or vault, esp. in a bank, for storing valuables: also **safe′ty-de·pos′it**

safe·guard (-gärd′) ***n.*** any person or thing that protects or guards against loss or injury; a precaution or protection —***vt.*** to protect or guard

safe·keep·ing (-kēp′iŋ) ***n.*** a keeping or being kept in safety; protection or custody

safe·ty (sāf′tē) ***n., pl.*** **-ties** **1.** a being safe; security **2.** a device to prevent accident, as a locking device (also **safety catch, safety lock**) on a firearm **3.** *Football a)* a play in which a player grounds the ball behind his own goal line when the ball was caused to pass the goal line by his own team: it scores two points for the opponents *b)* a player of a defensive backfield whose position is deep, behind the cornerbacks: in full, **safety man** —***adj.*** giving safety

safety belt **1.** *same as* LIFE BELT **2.** a belt attaching a person working at heights to something to prevent falling **3.** *same as* SEAT BELT

safety glass glass made to be shatterproof by fastening together two sheets of glass with a transparent, plastic substance between them

safety lamp a miner's lamp designed to avoid fire, etc.

safety match a match that will light only when it is struck on a prepared surface

safety pin a pin bent back on itself so as to form a spring, the point being held with a guard

safety razor a razor with guards for the blade to protect the skin from cuts

safety valve **1.** an automatic valve for a steam boiler, etc., to release steam if the pressure is too great **2.** any outlet for emotion, energy, etc.

saf·fi·an leather (saf′ē ən) [G. *saffian,* ult. < Per. *sāht,* hard] leather of sheepskin or goatskin tanned with sumac

saf·flow·er (saf′lou′ər) ***n.*** [< Du. or MFr., ult. < Ar. *aṣfar,* a yellow plant] a thistlelike annual plant of the composite family, with orange flower heads yielding a dyestuff and with seeds yielding oil used in paints, foods, etc.

saf·fron (saf′rən) ***n.*** [< OFr. *safran,* ult. < Ar. *za'farān*] **1.** a perennial old-world plant with funnel-shaped, purplish flowers having orange stigmas **2.** the dried, aromatic stigmas, used in flavoring and coloring foods **3.** orange yellow: also **saffron yellow** —***adj.*** orange-yellow

S. Afr. **1.** South Africa **2.** South African

sag (sag) ***vi.*** **sagged, sag′ging** [prob. < Scand.] **1.** to sink or bend; esp. in the middle, from weight or pressure **2.** to hang down unevenly **3.** to lose firmness, strength, etc.; weaken **4.** to decline in price, sales, etc. —***vt.*** to cause to sag —***n.*** **1.** a sagging **2.** a sunken place

sa·ga (sä′gə) ***n.*** [ON., a tale] **1.** a medieval Scandinavian story of battles, etc., generally telling the legendary history

of a Norse family **2.** any long story relating heroic deeds
sa·ga·cious (sə gā′shəs) ***adj.*** [< L. *sagax* (gen. *sagacis*), wise] keenly perceptive or discerning, farsighted, etc. **—sa·ga′cious·ly *adv.* —sa·ga′cious·ness *n.***
sa·gac·i·ty (sə gas′ə tē) ***n.,*** *pl.* **-ties** the quality or an instance of being sagacious
sag·a·more (sag′ə môr′) ***n.*** [< AmInd. *sāgimau*] a chief of second rank among certain tribes of N. American Indians
sage[1] (sāj) ***adj.*** **sag′er, sag′est** [< OFr., ult. < L. *sapiens,* orig. prp. of *sapere,* to know] having or showing wisdom or good judgment ***—n.*** a very wise man, esp. an old man respected for his wisdom, experience, etc. **—sage′ly *adv.***
sage[2] (sāj) ***n.*** [< OFr. < L. < *salvus,* safe: it reputedly had healing powers] **1.** any of various plants of the mint family, as the **scarlet sage,** with bright red flowers, or the **garden sage,** with leaves dried for seasoning meats, etc. **2.** *same as* SAGEBRUSH
sage·brush (-brush′) ***n.*** any of certain plants of the composite family, common in dry, alkaline areas of the western U.S.; esp., the **big sagebrush,** with small, aromatic leaves and minute flower heads
sage grouse a large grouse of sagebrush plains of western N. America: also, esp. for the female, **sage hen**
Sag·i·naw (sag′ə nô′) [< Ojibway village name, lit., at the mouth of a river] city in EC Mich.: pop. 78,000
Sag·it·ta·ri·us (saj′i ter′ē əs) [L., archer] **1.** a large S constellation in the Milky Way **2.** the ninth sign of the zodiac: see ZODIAC, illus.
sag·it·tate (saj′ə tāt′) ***adj.*** [< ModL. < L. *sagitta,* arrow] in the shape of an arrowhead, as some leaves
sa·go (sā′gō) ***n.,*** *pl.* **-gos** [Malay *sāgū*] **1.** an edible starch prepared from certain palm trees and other plants **2.** a palm tree yielding sago: also **sago palm**
sa·gua·ro (sə gwä′rō, -wä′-) ***n.,*** *pl.* **-ros** [MexSp. < native name] a giant cactus with a thick, spiny stem and white flowers, native to the southwestern U.S. and northern Mexico: also **sa·hua′ro** (-wä′-)
Sa·ha·ra (sə har′ə, -her′ə, -här′ə) [Ar. *ṣaḥrā,* a desert] vast desert region in N Africa **—Sa·ha′ran *adj.***
Sa·hel (sä hel′) region in NC Africa, south of the Sahara, characterized by periodic drought
sa·hib (sä′ib, -hib, -ēb, -hēb) ***n.*** [< Hindi < Ar. *ṣāḥib,* master] sir; master: title formerly used by natives in colonial India when speaking to or of a European
said (sed) *pt. & pp. of* SAY ***—adj.*** aforesaid; named before
Sai·gon (sī gän′) seaport in S Vietnam; capital of the former South Vietnam: now called **Ho Chi Minh City**
sail (sāl) ***n.*** [OE. *segl*] **1.** any of the shaped sheets of canvas, etc. spread to catch the wind and so drive certain vessels forward **2.** sails collectively **3.** a sailing vessel or vessels **4.** a trip in a ship or boat **5.** anything like a sail, as an arm of a windmill ***—vi.*** **1.** to be moved forward by means of sails or a propeller, etc. **2.** to travel on water **3.** to begin a trip by water **4.** to manage a sailboat, as in racing **5.** to glide through the air **6.** to move smoothly, like a ship sailing **7.** [Colloq.] to move quickly **8.** [Colloq.] to throw oneself (*into*) with energy **9.** [Colloq.] to attack or criticize someone severely (with *into*) ***—vt.*** **1.** to move through or upon (a body of water) in a boat or ship **2.** to manage or navigate (a boat or ship) **—in sail** with sails set **—make sail 1.** to spread out a ship's sail **2.** to begin a trip by water **—set sail 1.** to hoist the sails for departure **2.** to begin a trip by water **—take in sail** to lower sails **—under sail** sailing; with sails set **—sail′ing *n., adj.***
sail·boat (-bōt′) ***n.*** a boat having a sail or sails
sail·cloth (-klôth′, -kläth′) ***n.*** canvas or other cloth used in making sails, tents, etc.
sail·er (-ər) ***n.*** a ship or boat, esp. one with sails
sail·fish (-fish′) ***n.,*** *pl.* **-fish′, -fish′es:** see FISH a large, tropical marine fish with a large, saillike dorsal fin and a sword-shaped upper jaw
sail·or (-ər) ***n.*** **1.** a person who makes his living by sailing; seaman **2.** *a)* an enlisted man in the navy *b)* anyone in the navy **3.** a voyager on water, as affected by seasickness *[a bad sailor]* **4.** a straw hat with a low, flat crown and flat brim **—sail′or·ing *n.* —sail′or·ly *adj.***
sail·plane (sāl′plān′) ***n.*** a light glider designed for soaring ***—vi.*** **-planed′, -plan′ing** to fly a sailplane

SAILFISH
(to 11 ft. long)

saint (sānt) ***n.*** [< OFr. < LL. < L. *sanctus,* holy] **1.** a holy person **2.** a person who is unusually charitable, patient, etc. **3.** [*pl.*] those, esp. holy persons, who have died and are believed to be with God **4.** *a)* in the New Testament, any Christian *b)* **[S-]** a member of any religious group calling themselves *Saints* **5.** in certain Christian churches, a deceased person officially recognized as having lived an exceptionally holy life ***—vt.*** to make a saint of For names of

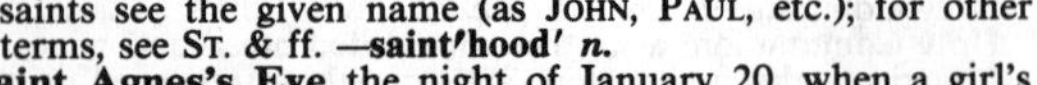

saints see the given name (as JOHN, PAUL, etc.); for other terms, see ST. & ff. **—saint′hood′ *n.***
Saint Agnes's Eve the night of January 20, when a girl's future husband was supposed to be revealed to her if she performed certain rites
Saint Ber·nard (bər närd′) a large, reddish-brown and white dog of a breed formerly trained by monks at the St. Bernard hospice, in the Swiss Alps, to rescue travelers
saint·ed (sān′tid) ***adj.*** **1.** of or fit for a saint; saintly **2.** regarded as a saint **3.** holy; sacred
Saint El·mo's fire (or **light**) (el′mōz) [after *St. Elmo,* patron saint of sailors] a visible electric discharge from tips of masts, spires, trees, etc. as during electrical storms
Saint-Ex·u·pé·ry (san teg zü pā rē′), **An·toine de** (än twån′ də) 1900–44; Fr. aviator & writer
Saint-Gau·dens (sānt gô′d′nz), **Augustus** 1848–1907; U.S. sculptor, born in Ireland
Saint Johns·wort (jänz′wurt′) [< ?] any of various plants with usually yellow flowers and spotted leaves
saint·ly (sānt′lē) ***adj.*** **-li·er, -li·est** like or suitable for a saint **—saint′li·ness *n.***
Saint Patrick's Day March 17, observed by the Irish in honor of Saint Patrick, the patron saint of Ireland
Saint-Saëns (san säns′), **Charles Ca·mille** (shårl kå mē′y′) 1835–1921; Fr. composer
Saint Valentine's Day February 14, observed in honor of a martyr of the 3d cent. and, coincidentally, as a day for sending valentines to sweethearts, etc.
Saint Vi·tus' dance (vī′təs) [after *St. Vitus,* patron saint of persons having chorea] *same as* CHOREA
saith (seth; *now also* sā′ith) *archaic 3d pers. sing., pres. indic., of* SAY
sake[1] (sāk) ***n.*** [OE. *sacu,* suit at law] **1.** purpose or reason; motive *[for the sake of peace]* **2.** advantage; behalf; benefit *[for my sake]* **—for heaven's** (or **gosh** or **Pete's**) **sake!** a mild exclamation of surprise, annoyance, etc.
sa·ke[2] (sä′kē) ***n.*** [Jap.] a Japanese alcoholic beverage made from fermented rice: also sp. **sa′ki**
Sa·kha·lin (sä khä lēn′; *E.* sak′ə lēn′) island of the U.S.S.R., off the E coast of Siberia
sal (sal) ***n.*** [L.] *Pharmacy* salt
sa·laam (sə läm′) ***n.*** [Ar. *salām,* peace] **1.** a Moslem greeting ("peace") **2.** an Oriental greeting made by bowing low with the palm of the right hand placed on the forehead **3.** a greeting showing respect ***—vt., vi.*** to make a salaam
sal·a·ble (sāl′ə b′l) ***adj.*** that can be sold; marketable
sa·la·cious (sə lā′shəs) ***adj.*** [< L. < *salire,* to leap] **1.** lecherous; lustful **2.** erotically stimulating; pornographic **—sa·la′cious·ly *adv.* —sa·la′cious·ness, sa·lac′i·ty** (-las′ə tē) ***n.***
sal·ad (sal′əd) ***n.*** [< MFr. < Pr. < L. pp. of *salare,* to salt < *sal,* salt] **1.** a dish, usually cold, of vegetables, usually raw, or fruits, served with a dressing, or molded in gelatin **2.** any green plant or herb used for such a dish
salad bar a bar or counter in a restaurant at which one may pick out vegetables to make a salad
salad days time of youth and inexperience
salad dressing a preparation of olive oil or other vegetable oil, vinegar, spices, etc. served with a salad
sal·a·man·der (sal′ə man′dər) ***n.*** [< OFr. < L. *salamandra* < Gr.] **1.** a mythological reptile that was said to live in fire **2.** any of a group of tailed amphibians related to frogs and toads, with a soft, moist skin
sa·la·mi (sə lä′mē) ***n.*** [It., pl., preserved meat, ult. < L. *sal,* salt] a highly spiced, salted sausage, orig. Italian, of pork and beef, or of beef alone
sal ammoniac *same as* AMMONIUM CHLORIDE
sal·a·ried (sal′ə rēd) ***adj.*** **1.** receiving a salary **2.** yielding a salary *[a salaried position]*
sal·a·ry (sal′ə rē) ***n.,*** *pl.* **-ries** [< L. *salarium,* orig., part of a Roman soldier's pay for buying salt < *sal,* salt] a fixed payment at regular intervals for services, esp. when clerical or professional
sale (sāl) ***n.*** [< OE. < ON. *sala*] **1.** a selling; the exchange of property or a service for an agreed sum of money or its equivalent **2.** opportunity to sell; market **3.** an auction **4.** a selling at prices lower than usual **5.** [*pl.*] receipts in business **6.** [*pl.*] the work, department, etc. of selling *[a job in sales]* **—for** (or **on**) **sale** to be sold
sale·a·ble (sāl′ə b′l) ***adj.*** *same as* SALABLE
Sa·lem (sā′ləm) [< Biblical place name] **1.** capital of Oreg., in the NW part: pop. 89,000 **2.** city on the NE coast of Mass.: suburb of Boston: pop. 38,000
sal·e·ra·tus (sal′ə rāt′əs) ***n.*** [ModL. *sal aeratus,* aerated salt] sodium bicarbonate; baking soda
Sa·ler·no (sä ler′nô; *E.* sə lur′nō) seaport in S Italy, on the Tyrrhenian Sea: pop. 151,000
sales·clerk (sālz′klurk′) ***n.*** a person employed to sell goods in a store
sales·man (sālz′mən) ***n.,*** *pl.* **-men** **1.** a man who is a salesclerk **2.** a traveling agent who sells goods or services
sales·man·ship (-ship′) ***n.*** the skill or technique of selling

sales·per·son (sālz′pʉr′s'n) *n.* a person employed to sell goods; esp., a salesclerk —**sales′peo′ple** (-pē′p'l) *n.pl.*
sales resistance resistance of potential customers to efforts aimed at getting them to buy
sales·room (-ro͞om′) *n.* a room in which goods are shown and offered for sale
sales talk any persuasion or argument used in trying to sell something or to persuade one to do something
sales tax a tax on sales and, sometimes, services
sales·wom·an (-woom′ən) *n., pl.* **-wom′en** (-wim′in) a woman salesclerk: also **sales′la′dy** (-lā′dē), *pl.* **-dies**
Sal·ic law (sal′ik, sā′lik) [< ML. < LL. *Salii,* a tribe of Franks] **1.** a code of laws of Germanic tribes, or any of these laws **2.** a law excluding women from succession to the throne in the French and Spanish monarchies
sa·lic·y·late (sə lis′ə lāt′; sal′ə sil′āt, -it) *n.* any salt or ester of salicylic acid
sal·i·cyl·ic acid (sal′ə sil′ik) [< Fr. *salicyle* (radical of the acid) < L. *salix,* willow + -IC] a white, crystalline compound, $C_7H_6O_3$, used in making aspirin, as a food preservative, etc.
sa·lient (sāl′yənt, sā′lē ənt) *adj.* [< L. prp. of *salire,* to leap] **1.** leaping **2.** pointing outward; projecting **3.** standing out; noticeable; prominent —*n.* **1.** the part of a battle line, fort, etc. projecting farthest toward the enemy **2.** a projecting angle, part, etc. —**sa′lience** *n.* —**sa′lien·cy** *n., pl.* **-cies** —**sa′lient·ly** *adv.*
Sa·li·nas (sə lē′nəs) [ult. < L. *salina,* salty < *sal,* salt] city in WC Calif., near San Jose: pop. 80,000
sa·line (sā′līn, -lēn; *for n. 1 also* sə lēn′) *adj.* [< L. < *sal,* salt] of, like, or containing salt; salty —*n.* **1.** a salt lick, salt marsh, etc. **2.** a salt of an alkali metal or of magnesium, used as a cathartic **3.** a saline solution —**sa·lin·i·ty** (sə lin′ə tē) *n.*
Salis·bur·y (sôlz′ber′ē, -bə rē) **1.** city in SC England: noted for its 13th-cent. cathedral: pop. 36,000 **2.** capital of Zimbabwe, in the NE part: pop. 385,000
Salisbury, 3d Marquess of, (*Robert Arthur Talbot Gascoyne-Cecil*) 1830–1903; Eng. statesman
Salisbury steak *same as* HAMBURGER (sense 2)
sa·li·va (sə lī′və) *n.* [L.] the thin, watery, slightly viscid fluid secreted by the salivary glands: it aids digestion by moistening and softening food, and contains an enzyme that converts starch to dextrin and maltose
sal·i·var·y (sal′ə ver′ē) *adj.* of or secreting saliva
sal·i·vate (-vāt′) *vt.* **-vat′ed, -vat′ing** [< L. pp. of *salivare*] to produce an excessive flow of saliva in —*vi.* to secrete saliva —**sal′i·va′tion** *n.*
Salk (sôlk), **Jonas E(dward)** 1914– ; U.S. bacteriologist: developed a vaccine for injection to prevent poliomyelitis
sal·low (sal′ō) *adj.* [OE. *salu*] of a sickly, pale-yellowish complexion —*vt.* to make sallow —**sal′low·ness** *n.*
Sal·ly (sal′ē) [dim. of SARAH] a feminine name
sal·ly (sal′ē) *n., pl.* **-lies** [MFr. *saillie,* ult. < L. *salire,* to leap] **1.** a sudden rushing forth, as of troops to attack besiegers **2.** any sudden start into activity **3.** a quick witticism; quip **4.** an excursion; jaunt —*vi.* **-lied, -ly·ing 1.** to make a sally **2.** *a)* to go outdoors *b)* to set out on a trip Used with *forth* or *out*
sal·ma·gun·di (sal′mə gun′dē) *n.* [Fr. *salmigondis* < ? It. *salame conditi,* pickled meat] **1.** a dish of chopped meat, eggs, onions, etc. **2.** any mixture
salm·on (sam′ən) *n., pl.* **-on, -ons:** see PLURAL, II, D, 2 [< MFr. < OFr. *saumon* < L. *salmo*] **1.** any of various bony fishes; specif., any of several varieties of game and food fishes of the N Hemisphere, with silver scales and flesh that is pink when cooked: salmon spawn in fresh water but usually live in salt water **2.** yellowish pink: also **salmon pink**
sal·mo·nel·la (sal′mə nel′ə) *n., pl.* **-nel′lae** (-ē), **-nel′la, -nel′las** [ModL.: after D. *Salmon* (d. 1914), U.S. veterinarian] any of certain rod-shaped bacteria that cause various diseases, as typhoid fever, food poisoning, etc.
Sa·lo·me (sə lō′mē; *occas.* sal′ə mā′) *traditional name of* the stepdaughter of Herod Antipas: her dancing pleased Herod so much that he granted her request for the head of John the Baptist: Matt. 14:8
sa·lon (sə län′, sal′än; *Fr.* så lōn′) *n.* [Fr.: see SALOON] **1.** a large reception hall **2.** a drawing room of a French private home **3.** a regular gathering of distinguished persons, writers, artists, etc. in a celebrity's home **4.** *a)* an art gallery *b)* an art exhibition **5.** a shop or business place for performing some personal service [*beauty salon*]
Sa·lo·ni·ka (sal′ə nē′kə, -nī′-; sə län′i kə) **1.** seaport in N Greece, on the Gulf of Salonika: pop. 251,000 **2. Gulf of,** N arm of the Aegean Sea Also sp. **Salonica**
sa·loon (sə lo͞on′) *n.* [Fr. *salon* < It. < *sala,* a hall] **1.** any large room or hall for receptions, exhibitions, etc.; specif., the main social cabin of a passenger ship **2.** a place where alcoholic drinks are sold to be drunk on the premises: an old-fashioned term
sa·loon·keep·er (-kēp′ər) *n.* a person who operates a saloon (sense 2)
sal·sa (säl′sə) *n.* [AmSp. < Sp., sauce] a kind of Latin American dance music of Afro-Cuban and Puerto Rican origin, influenced by jazz and rock
sal·si·fy (sal′sə fē′, -fī′) *n.* [< Fr. < It. *sassefrica*] a plant of the composite family, with white, edible, fleshy roots
sal soda crystallized sodium carbonate
salt (sôlt, sält) *n.* [OE. *sealt*] **1.** sodium chloride, NaCl, a white, crystalline substance found in natural beds, in sea water, etc., and used for seasoning and preserving food, etc. **2.** a chemical compound derived from an acid by replacing hydrogen, wholly or partly, with a metal or an electropositive radical **3.** that which lends tang or piquancy, as pungent wit **4.** *same as* SALTCELLAR **5.** [*pl.*] mineral salts used as a cathartic (as **Epsom salts**), to soften bath water (**bath salts**), as a restorative (**smelling salts**), etc. **6.** [Colloq.] a sailor —*adj.* **1.** containing salt **2.** preserved with salt **3.** tasting or smelling of salt **4.** *a)* flooded with salt water *b)* growing in salt water —*vt.* **1.** to sprinkle, season, or preserve with salt **2.** to treat or provide with salt **3.** to give tang to **4.** to put minerals in (a mine), oil in (a well), etc. so as to deceive prospective buyers —**salt away** (or **down**) **1.** to pack and preserve with salt **2.** [Colloq.] to store or save (money, etc.) —**with a grain** (or **pinch**) **of salt** with allowance or reserve; skeptically —**worth one's salt** worth one's wages, etc. —**salt′er** *n.* —**salt′ish** *adj.* —**salt′-like′** *adj.* —**salt′ness** *n.*
SALT (sôlt, sält) Strategic Arms Limitation Talks
salt-and-pep·per (-'n pep′ər) *adj. same as* PEPPER-AND-SALT
salt·box (sôlt′bäks′) *n.* **1.** a box for salt, with a sloping lid **2.** a house shaped like this, with two stories in front and one at the rear and a gable roof Also **salt box**
salt·cel·lar (-sel′ər) *n.* [< ME. < *salt,* salt + MFr. *salière,* saltcellar] a small dish or shaker for salt at the table
salt·ine (sôl tēn′) *n.* [SALT + -INE[4]] a flat, crisp cracker sprinkled with salt
Salt Lake City capital of Utah, near the SE end of the Great Salt Lake: pop. 163,000 (met. area 935,000)
salt lick **1.** an exposed natural deposit of rock salt which animals come to lick **2.** a block of rock salt placed in a pasture for cattle, etc. to lick
salt marsh grassland over which salt water flows at intervals
salt pork pork cured in salt
salt·shak·er (sôlt′shā′kər) *n.* a container for salt, with a perforated top for shaking out the salt
salt·wa·ter (-wôt′ər, -wät′ər) *adj.* of, having to do with, or living in salt water or the sea
salt·works (-wʉrks′) *n., pl.* **-works′** a place where salt is made, as by evaporation of natural brines
salt·wort (-wʉrt′) *n.* any of a genus of plants of the goosefoot family, growing on seashores or saline soils
salt·y (sôl′tē) *adj.* **salt′i·er, salt′i·est 1.** of, tasting of, or containing salt **2.** smelling of or suggesting the sea **3.** *a)* sharp; piquant *b)* coarse or earthy *c)* cross or caustic —**salt′i·ly** *adv.* —**salt′i·ness** *n.*
sa·lu·bri·ous (sə lo͞o′brē əs) *adj.* [L. *salubris* < *salus,* health] promoting health or welfare; healthful, wholesome, salutary, etc. —**sa·lu′bri·ous·ly** *adv.* —**sa·lu′bri·ty** (-brə tē), **sa·lu′bri·ous·ness** *n.*
sal·u·tar·y (sal′yoo ter′ē) *adj.* [< Fr. < L. < *salus* (gen. *salutis*), health] **1.** promoting health; healthful **2.** promoting some good purpose; beneficial —**sal′u·tar′i·ly** *adv.*
sal·u·ta·tion (sal′yoo tā′shən) *n.* [< MFr. < L. < pp. of *salutare:* see SALUTE] **1.** the act of greeting, addressing, etc. by gestures or words **2.** certain words serving as a greeting or as the opening of a letter, as "Dear Sir"
sa·lu·ta·to·ri·an (sə lo͞ot′ə tôr′ē ən) *n.* in some schools and colleges, the student, usually second highest in scholastic rank, who gives the salutatory
sa·lu·ta·to·ry (sə lo͞ot′ə tôr′ē) *adj.* of or expressing a salutation —*n., pl.* **-ries** an opening address, esp. at a school or college commencement exercise
sa·lute (sə lo͞ot′) *vt.* **-lut′ed, -lut′ing** [< L. *salutare* < *salus:* see SALUTARY] **1.** to greet in a friendly way, as by bowing, tipping the hat, etc. **2.** to honor ceremonially and officially by firing cannon, raising the right hand to the forehead, etc. **3.** to present itself to, as if in greeting **4.** to acknowledge with praise; commend —*vi.* to make a salute —*n.* **1.** an act, remark, or gesture made in saluting **2.** *Mil.* the position of the hand, etc. assumed in saluting
sal·va·ble (sal′və b'l) *adj.* that can be saved or salvaged
Sal·va·dor (sal′və dôr′; *Port.* säl′və dôr′) seaport in E Brazil, on the Atlantic: pop. 1,001,000

Sal·va·do·ran (sal′və dôr′ən) *adj.* of El Salvador, its people, or culture —*n.* a native or inhabitant of El Salvador Also **Sal′va·do′ri·an** (-dôr′ē ən)

sal·vage (sal′vij) *n.* [Fr. < MFr. < *salver,* to SAVE[1]] **1.** *a)* the rescue of a ship and cargo at sea from fire, shipwreck, etc. *b)* compensation paid for such rescue *c)* the ship or cargo so rescued *d)* the bringing up of a sunken ship or its cargo by divers, caissons, etc. **2.** *a)* the saving of any goods, etc. from destruction or waste *b)* goods, etc. so saved *c)* the proceeds from sale of such goods, etc. as in settling insurance claims —*vt.* **-vaged, -vag·ing** to save or rescue from shipwreck, fire, flood, etc.; engage or succeed in the salvage of (ships, goods, etc.) —**sal′vage·a·bil′i·ty** *n.* —**sal′vage·a·ble** *adj.* —**sal′vag·er** *n.*

sal·va·tion (sal vā′shən) *n.* [< OFr. < LL. < L. pp. of *salvare,* to SAVE[1]] **1.** a saving or being saved **2.** a person or thing that saves or rescues **3.** *Theol.* spiritual rescue from the consequences of sin —**sal·va′tion·al** *adj.*

Salvation Army a Christian organization that works to bring religion and help to the very poor

salve[1] (sav) *n.* [OE. *sealf*] **1.** any soothing or healing ointment applied to wounds, burns, sores, etc. **2.** anything that soothes or heals; balm —*vt.* **salved, salv′ing** to soothe

salve[2] (salv) *vt.* **salved, salv′ing** *same as* SALVAGE

sal·ver (sal′vər) *n.* [< Fr. < Sp. *salva* < *salvar,* to taste (so as to prove food wholesome) < L. *salvare,* to SAVE[1]] a tray on which something is served or presented

sal·vi·a (sal′vē ə) *n.* [ModL., genus name < L.] *same as* SAGE[2] (sense 1)

sal·vo (sal′vō) *n., pl.* **-vos, -voes** [< It. < L. *salve,* hail!] **1.** a discharge of a number of guns in succession or at the same time, either in salute or at a target **2.** the release of a load of bombs or the launching of several rockets at the same time **3.** a burst of cheers or applause

sal vo·la·ti·le (vō lat′′l ē′) [ModL., volatile salt] ammonium carbonate, used in smelling salts

Sal·ween (sal wēn′) river in SE Asia, flowing from Tibet through Burma into the Indian Ocean

Salz·burg (zälts′boorkh; *E.* sôlz′bərg) city in C Austria: pop. 108,000

SAM (sam) surface-to-air missile

Sam. Samuel

Sa·mar (sä′mär) island of the E Philippines, southeast of Luzon: 5,181 sq. mi.

sam·a·ra (sam′ər ə, sə mer′ə) *n.* [ModL. < L., elm seed] a dry, winged, seeded fruit, as of the maple

SAMARAS (A, maple; B, elm; C, ash; D, basswood)

Sa·mar·i·a (sə mer′ē ə, -mar′-) in ancient times, **1.** N kingdom of the Hebrews; Israel **2.** its capital **3.** district of Palestine between Galilee & Judea

Sa·mar·i·tan (-ə t'n) *n.* **1.** a native or inhabitant of Samaria **2.** *see* GOOD SAMARITAN —*adj.* of Samaria or its people

sa·mar·i·um (sə mer′ē əm, -mar′-) *n.* [ModL. < *samarskite,* a mineral, ult. < Col. *Samarski,* Russ. mining official] a metallic chemical element of the rare-earth group: symbol, Sm; at. wt., 150.35; at. no., 62

Sam·ar·kand (sam′ər kand′; *Russ.* sä mär känt′) city in E Uzbek S.S.R.: pop. 267,000

sam·ba (sam′bə, säm′-) *n.* [Port., prob. of Afr. origin] **1.** a Brazilian dance of African origin **2.** music for this dance —*vi.* to dance the samba

Sam Browne belt (sam′ broun′) [after 19th-c. Brit. Gen. *Samuel J. Browne*] a military officer's belt with a diagonal strap across the right shoulder

same (sām) *adj.* [ON. *samr*] **1.** being the very one; identical **2.** alike in kind, quality, amount, etc.; corresponding **3.** unchanged; not different *[he looks the same]* **4.** before-mentioned; just spoken of —*pron.* the same person or thing —*adv.* **1.** in the same way **2.** nevertheless The *adj.* & *pron.* are usually used with *the, this,* or *that;* the *adv.*, with *the* —**same′ness** *n.*

sam·i·sen (sam′ə sen′) *n.* [Jap. < Chin. *san hsien,* three strings] a three-stringed Japanese musical instrument, somewhat like a banjo

sam·ite (sam′īt, sā′mīt) *n.* [< MFr. < ML. < MGr. < *hexamitos,* woven with six threads] a heavy silk fabric interwoven with gold or silver threads, worn in the Middle Ages

Sa·mo·a (sə mō′ə) group of islands in the South Pacific, north of Tonga: seven of these islands constitute a possession (**American Samoa**) of the U.S., 76 sq. mi., pop. 28,000: see also WESTERN SAMOA —**Sa·mo′an** *adj., n.*

Sa·mos (sā′mäs; *Gr.* sä′môs) Gr. island in the Aegean, off the W coast of Turkey —**Sa·mi·an** (sā′mē ən) *adj., n.*

Sam·o·thrace (sam′ə thrās′) Gr. island in the NE Aegean

sam·o·var (sam′ə vär′, säm′ə vär′) *n.* [Russ., lit., self-boiler] a Russian metal urn with an internal tube for heating water for tea

SAMOVAR

Sam·o·yed, Sam·o·yede (sam′ə yed′) *n.* [Russ.] **1.** any of a Uralic people of Siberia **2.** their language **3.** any of a strong breed of Siberian dog, with a thick, white coat —*adj.* of the Samoyeds or their language: also **Sam′o·yed′ic**

samp (samp) *n.* [< Algonquian *nasaump,* softened by water] coarse cornmeal or a porridge of this

sam·pan (sam′pan) *n.* [Chin. *san-pan* < ? *san,* three + *pan,* a plank] any of various small boats used in China and Japan, rowed with a scull from the stern, and often having a sail and a small cabin formed of mats

sam·ple (sam′p'l) *n.* [< OFr.: see EXAMPLE] **1.** a part, piece, or item that shows what the whole thing or group is like; specimen or example *[samples* of wallpaper, a *sample* of his humor*]* **2.** *Statistics* a selected part of the population studied to gain knowledge of the whole —*vt.* **-pled, -pling** to take or test a sample of

sam·pler (-plər) *n.* **1.** a person who prepares or tests samples **2.** a cloth embroidered with designs, mottoes, etc. in different stitches

Sam·son (sam′s'n) [LL. < Gr. < Heb. *shimshōn* < ? *shemesh,* sun] *Bible* an Israelite noted for his great strength: betrayed by Delilah: Judges 13–16

Sam·u·el (sam′yoo wəl, sam′yool) [LL. < Gr. < Heb. *shĕmū′ēl,* lit., name of God] **1.** a masculine name: dim. *Sam, Sammy* **2.** *Bible a)* a Hebrew judge and prophet *b)* either of two books (I Samuel, II Samuel) telling of Samuel, Saul, and David

sam·u·rai (sam′ə rī′) *n., pl.* **-rai′** [Jap.] **1.** a member of a military class in feudal Japan **2.** a Japanese army officer or member of the military caste

‡**-san** (sän) [Jap.] a Japanese honorific suffix added to names, titles, etc.

San An·ge·lo (san an′jə lō′) [after *Santa Angela,* a Mex. nun] city in WC Tex.: pop. 73,000

San An·to·ni·o (san′ ən tō′nē ō′, an-) [Sp., St. Anthony, 13th-c. Franciscan friar of Padua] city in SC Tex.: site of the Alamo: pop. 785,000 (met. area 1,070,000)

san·a·to·ri·um (san′ə tôr′ē əm) *n., pl.* **-ri·ums, -ri·a** (-ə) [ModL. < LL. *sanatorius,* giving health < L. *sanare,* to heal] *chiefly Brit. var. of* SANITARIUM

San Ber·nar·di·no (san′ bur′nər dē′nō, -nə-) [Sp., St. Bernardine (of Siena)] city in S Calif., near Los Angeles: pop. 118,000

sanc·ti·fied (saŋk′tə fīd′) *adj.* **1.** made holy; consecrated **2.** sanctimonious

sanc·ti·fy (saŋk′tə fī′) *vt.* **-fied′, -fy′ing** [< OFr. < LL. *sanctificare:* see SAINT & -FY] **1.** to make holy; specif., *a)* to set apart as holy; consecrate *b)* to make free from sin; purify **2.** to make binding or inviolable by sanction —**sanc′ti·fi·ca′tion** *n.* —**sanc′ti·fi′er** *n.*

sanc·ti·mo·ni·ous (saŋk′tə mō′nē əs) *adj.* pretending to be very pious; affecting sanctity or righteousness —**sanc′ti·mo′ni·ous·ly** *adv.* —**sanc′ti·mo′ni·ous·ness** *n.*

sanc·ti·mo·ny (saŋk′tə mō′nē) *n.* [< OFr. < L. *sanctimonia* < *sanctus,* holy] affected piety or righteousness

sanc·tion (saŋk′shən) *n.* [< Fr. < L. < *sanctus,* holy] **1.** the confirming or ratifying of an action by authority; authorization **2.** support; approval **3.** something that gives binding force to a law, as the penalty for breaking it or a reward for carrying it out **4.** something, as a moral principle or influence, that makes a rule of conduct, etc. binding **5.** [*usually pl.*] a boycott, blockade, or similar coercive measure, as against one nation by others to enforce international law —*vt.* to give sanction to; specif., *a)* to ratify or confirm *b)* to authorize or permit —**sanc′tion·a·ble** *adj.*

sanc·ti·ty (saŋk′tə tē) *n., pl.* **-ties** [< L. < *sanctus,* holy] **1.** saintliness or holiness **2.** a being sacred or inviolable **3.** anything held sacred

sanc·tu·ar·y (saŋk′choo wer′ē) *n., pl.* **-ar′ies** [< MFr. < LL. < L. *sanctus,* sacred] **1.** a holy place, as a building set aside for worship; specif., *a)* the ancient Temple at Jerusalem *b)* any church, temple, etc. *c)* a holy place within a church, temple, etc., as the part around the altar, the holy of holies, etc. **2.** a place of refuge or protection **3.** refuge; immunity from punishment **4.** a reservation where animals or birds may not be hunted or trapped

sanc·tum (saŋk′təm) *n., pl.* **-tums, -ta** (-tə) [L., neut. of *sanctus,* holy] **1.** a sacred place **2.** a study or private room where one is not to be disturbed

sanctum sanc·to·rum (saŋk tôr′əm) [LL.] **1.** *same as* HOLY OF HOLIES **2.** a place of utmost privacy

sand (sand) *n.* [OE.] **1.** loose, gritty grains of disintegrated rock, as on beaches, in deserts, etc. **2.** [*usually pl.*] an area of sand; beach **3.** the sand in an hourglass **4.** [*pl.*] moments of time **5.** [Slang] grit; courage —*vt.* **1.** to sprinkle, fill, or mix with sand **2.** to smooth or polish with sand or sandpaper —**sand′ed** *adj.* —**sand′er** *n.*

Sand (sand; *Fr.* sänd), **George** (pseud. of *Amandine Aurore Lucie Dupin,* Baronne *Dudevant*) 1804–76; Fr. novelist

san·dal¹ (san′d'l) *n.* [< L. < Gr. dim. of *sandalon*] **1.** a kind of footwear consisting of a sole fastened in various ways to the foot by straps over the instep or toes, or around the ankles **2.** any of various low slippers —**san′daled, san′dalled** *adj.*

san·dal² (san′d'l) *n. same as* SANDALWOOD

san·dal·wood (-wood′) *n.* [< MFr. < ML., ult. < Sans. *candana*] **1.** the hard, sweet-smelling heartwood of any of certain Asiatic trees, used for carving and cabinetmaking or burned as incense **2.** any tree yielding such wood

sand·bag (sand′bag′) *n.* **1.** a bag filled with sand and used for ballast, in fortifications, for levees against floods, etc. **2.** a small, sand-filled bag used as a bludgeon —*vt.* **-bagged′, -bag′ging** **1.** to place sandbags in or around **2.** to hit with a sandbag **3.** [Colloq.] to force into doing something —**sand′bag′ger** *n.*

sand bar a ridge or narrow shoal of sand formed in a river or along a shore by the action of currents or tides

sand·blast (-blast′) *n.* **1.** a current of air or steam carrying sand at a high velocity, used in etching glass and in cleaning surfaces as of metals, stone, etc. **2.** the machine used to apply this blast —*vt.* to engrave, clean, etc. with a sandblast —**sand′blast′er** *n.*

sand·box (-bäks′) *n.* a box containing sand for children to play in

Sand·burg (sand′bərg, san′-), **Carl** 1878–1967; U.S. poet, writer, & ballad collector

sand flea **1.** any of various crustaceans found on sandy sea beaches, that jump like fleas **2.** *same as* CHIGGER

sand·hog (sand′hôg′, -häg′) *n.* a laborer in underground or underwater construction projects, working under compressed air, as in a caisson or tunnel

San Di·e·go (san′ dē ā′gō) [after *San Diego* (St. Didacus), 15th-cent. Sp. friar] seaport in S Calif., on the Pacific: pop. 876,000 (met. area 1,860,000)

sand·lot (sand′lät′) *adj.* having to do with games, esp. baseball, played by amateurs, orig. on a sandy lot or field —**sand′lot′ter** *n.*

S & M, s & m sexual sadism and masochism

sand·man (-man′) *n.* in fairy tales, etc. a person supposed to make children sleepy by dusting sand in their eyes

sand·pa·per (-pā′pər) *n.* a strong paper with sand glued on one side, used for smoothing and polishing —*vt.* to smooth or polish with sandpaper

sand·pip·er (-pī′pər) *n., pl.* **-pip′ers, -pip′er:** see PLURAL, II, D, 1 a small shore bird with a long, soft-tipped bill

San·dra (san′drə, sän′-) [< *Alexandra,* fem. of ALEXANDER] a feminine name

sand·stone (sand′stōn′) *n.* a common sedimentary rock much used for building, composed largely of sand grains, mainly quartz, cemented together by silica, etc.

sand·storm (-stôrm′) *n.* a windstorm in which large quantities of sand are blown about

sand trap a hollow filled with sand, serving as a hazard on a golf course

sand·wich (sand′wich, san′-) *n.* [< 4th Earl of *Sandwich* (1718–1792)] two or more slices of bread with a filling of meat, cheese, etc. between them: now sometimes used of a single slice of bread covered with meat, gravy, etc. —*vt.* to place between other persons, things, materials, etc.

sandwich man a man who walks the streets with two signboards hung from his shoulders, front and back

sand·y (san′dē) *adj.* **sand′i·er, sand′i·est** **1.** composed of, full of, or covered with sand **2.** like sand; gritty, shifting, etc. **3.** pale brown or dark yellow *[sandy* hair*]* —**sand′i·ness** *n.*

sane (sān) *adj.* **san′er, san′est** [L. *sanus,* healthy] **1.** having a normal, healthy mind; able to make sound, rational judgments **2.** showing good sense; sensible *[a sane* policy*]* —**sane′ly** *adv.* —**sane′ness** *n.*

San·for·ize (san′fə rīz′) *vt.* **-ized′, -iz′ing** [from the trademark *Sanforized:* after *Sanford* L. Cluett (1874–1968), the inventor] to preshrink (cloth) permanently by a patented process before making garments

San Fran·cis·co (san′ frən sis′kō) [prob. after St. FRANCIS OF ASSISI] seaport on the coast of C Calif., on an inlet (**San Francisco Bay**) of the Pacific: pop. 679,000 (met. area, incl. Oakland, 3,227,000)

sang (saŋ) *pt. of* SING

Sang·er (saŋ′ər), **Margaret** (born *Margaret Higgins*) 1883–1966; U.S. nurse: leader in birth-control education

sang-froid (saŋ′frwä′; *Fr.* sän frwå′) *n.* [Fr., lit., cold blood] cool self-possession or composure

san·gui·nar·y (saŋ′gwi ner′ē) *adj.* [< L. < *sanguis:* see ff.] **1.** with much bloodshed or killing **2.** of or stained with blood **3.** bloodthirsty —**san′gui·nar′i·ly** *adv.* —**san′gui·nar′i·ness** *n.*

san·guine (saŋ′gwin) *adj.* [< OFr. < L. < *sanguis* (gen. *sanguinis*), blood] **1.** of the color of blood; ruddy **2.** [from medieval notion about those in whom blood is the main humor] cheerful; confident; optimistic —**san′guine·ly** *adv.* —**san′guine·ness** *n.*

san·guin·e·ous (saŋ gwin′ē əs) *adj.* [see prec.] *same as:* **1.** SANGUINARY **2.** SANGUINE

San·he·drin (san hed′rin, -hē′drin) *n.* [< Heb. < Gr. < *syn-,* together + *hedra,* seat] the highest court and council of the ancient Jewish nation, having religious and civic functions

san·i·tar·i·um (san′ə ter′ē əm) *n., pl.* **-i·ums, -i·a** (-ə) [ModL. < L. *sanitas,* health] a nursing home, hospital, etc. for the care of invalids or convalescents, esp. one for treating a specific disease or disorder

san·i·tar·y (san′ə ter′ē) *adj.* [< Fr. < L. *sanitas,* health] **1.** of health or the rules and conditions of health; esp., promoting health by getting rid of dirt and of things that bring disease **2.** free from dirt, etc. that could bring disease; clean; hygienic —**san′i·tar′i·ly** *adv.* —**san′i·tar′i·ness** *n.*

sanitary napkin an absorbent pad of cotton, etc. worn by women during menstruation

san·i·ta·tion (san′ə tā′shən) *n.* **1.** the science and work of bringing about healthful and hygienic conditions **2.** drainage and disposal of sewage

san·i·tize (san′ə tīz′) *vt.* **-tized′, -tiz′ing** to make sanitary, as by sterilizing —**san′i·tiz′er** *n.*

san·i·ty (san′ə tē) *n.* [< OFr. < L. *sanitas,* health] **1.** the condition of being sane; soundness of mind; mental health **2.** soundness of judgment

San Joa·quin (san′ wô kēn′, wä-) [Sp., St. Joachim, reputed father of the Virgin Mary] river in C Calif., flowing south into the Sacramento River

San Jo·se (san′ hō zā′, ə zā′) [Sp. *San José,* St. Joseph] city in WC Calif.: pop. 637,000 (met. area 1,290,000)

San Jo·sé (sän′ hô se′) capital of Costa Rica, in the C part: pop. 203,000

San Juan (san′ hwän′, wôn′; *Sp.* sän′ hwän′) [Sp., St. John] capital of Puerto Rico; seaport on the Atlantic: pop. 445,000 (met. area 851,000)

sank (saŋk) *alt. pt. of* SINK

San Le·an·dro (san′ lē an′drō) [Sp., St. Leander, archbishop of Seville] city in W Calif., on San Francisco Bay: suburb of Oakland: pop. 64,000

San Ma·ri·no (sän′ mä rē′nô; *E.* san′ mə rē′nō) independent country within E Italy: 23 sq. mi.; pop. 19,000

San Mar·tín (sän′ mär tēn′), **Jo·sé de** (hô se′ de) 1778–1850; S. American revolutionary leader, born in Argentina

San Ma·te·o (san′ mə tā′ō) [Sp., St. Matthew] city in W Calif.: suburb of San Francisco: pop. 78,000

sans (sanz; *Fr.* sän) *prep.* [< OFr. *sanz* (Fr. *sans*) < L. *sine,* without] without; lacking

Sans. Sanskrit

San Sal·va·dor (san sal′və dôr′; *Sp.* sän säl′vä *th*ôr′) **1.** capital of El Salvador: pop. 256,000 **2.** island of the E Bahamas: prob. the place of Columbus' first landing (1492)

sans-cu·lotte (sanz′koo lät′, -kyoo-) *n.* [Fr., without breeches] a revolutionary: term of contempt applied by the aristocrats to the republicans in the French Revolution, who wore pantaloons instead of knee breeches

san·se·vi·e·ri·a (san′sə vir′ē ə, -vi ē′rē ə) *n.* [ModL., after the Prince of *Sanseviero* (1710–71)] any of a genus of succulent plants with thick, lance-shaped leaves

San·skrit (san′skrit) *n.* [< Sans. *saṃskṛta,* lit., made together, well arranged] the classical Old Indic literary language: important in the study of comparative Indo-European linguistics —*adj.* of or written in Sanskrit Also sp. **San′scrit** —**San·skrit′ic** *adj.* —**San′skrit·ist** *n.*

sans-ser·if (san ser′if) *n.* [see SANS & SERIF] a style of printing type with no serifs

San·ta (san′tə, -ti; *for adj., also* sän′tä) *short for* SANTA CLAUS —*adj.* [Sp. & It., saint, fem.] holy or saint: used in combinations *[Santa* Maria*]*

San·ta An·a (san′tə an′ə) [Sp., St. Anne] city in SW Calif.: suburb of Los Angeles: pop. 204,000

San·ta An·na (sän′tä ä′nä), **An·to·nio Ló·pez de** (än tô′nyô lô′pes de) 1795?–1876; Mex. revolutionist & general

San·ta Bar·ba·ra (san′tə bär′bə rə) [Sp., St. Barbara] city on the coast of SW Calif.: pop. 75,000

Santa Cat·a·li·na (kat′'l ē′nə) island off the SW coast of Calif.: a tourist resort

San·ta Cla·ra (kler′ə) [Sp., St. Clare (of Assisi)] city in W Calif., near San Jose: pop. 88,000

San·ta Claus, San·ta Klaus (san′tə klôz′, -ti) [< Du.

dial. < *Sant Nikolass,* St. NICHOLAS] *Folklore* a fat, white-bearded, jolly old man in a red suit, who distributes gifts at Christmas time: also called **Saint Nicholas, Saint Nick**

San·ta Fe (san′tə fā′) [Sp., holy faith] capital of N.Mex., in the NC part: pop. 49,000

Santa Fe Trail trade route between Santa Fe, N.Mex., & Independence, Mo.: important from 1821 to 1880

San·ta Mon·i·ca (san′tə män′i kə) [Sp., St. Monica, mother of St. AUGUSTINE (of North Africa)] city in SW Calif., on the Pacific: suburb of Los Angeles: pop. 88,000

San·ta Ro·sa (san′tə rō′zə) [Sp., holy rose] city in W Calif., north of San Francisco: pop. 83,000

San·ta·ya·na (san′tē an′ə, -ä′nə; *Sp.* sän′tä yä′nä), **George** (born *Jorge Augustín Nicolás de Santayana*) 1863–1952; Sp. philosopher & writer in English

San·ti·a·go (sän′tē ä′gô; *E.* san′tē ā′gō) capital of Chile, in the C part: pop. 2,566,000 (met. area 3,120,000)

san·tim (sun tēm′) *n., pl.* **san′ti·motch′** (-tē mäch′) [Amharic] *see* MONETARY UNITS, table (Ethiopia)

San·to Do·min·go (sän′tô dô miŋ′gô; *E.* san′tō dō miŋ′gō) capital of the Dominican Republic; seaport on the S coast: pop., of the district, 823,000

Saône (sōn) river in E France, flowing south into the Rhone

São Pau·lo (soun pou′lo͞o) city in SE Brazil: pop. 5,902,000

São To·mé and Prín·ci·pe (tō mā′ ənd prin′sə pē′) country off the W coast of Africa, comprising two islands (*São Tomé* and *Príncipe*): 372 sq. mi.; pop. 75,000

sap[1] (sap) *n.* [OE. *sæp*] **1.** the juice that circulates through a plant, esp. a woody plant, bearing water, food, etc. **2.** any fluid considered vital to life or health **3.** vigor; energy **4.** [Slang] a stupid person: in full, **sap′head′** (-hed′) —*vt.* **sapped, sap′ping** to drain of sap

sap[2] (sap) *n.* [MFr. *sappe,* a hoe < It. *zappe*] a trench for approaching or undermining an enemy position —*vt.* **sapped, sap′ping 1.** to undermine by digging away foundations **2.** to undermine in any way; weaken; exhaust —*vi.* **1.** to dig saps **2.** to approach a position by saps

sap[3] (sap) *n.* [prob. orig. contr. < SAPLING] [Slang] a blackjack, short club, etc. —*vt.* **sapped, sap′ping** [Slang] to hit on the head, or knock out, with a sap

sa·pi·ent (sā′pē ənt) *adj.* [< L. prp. of *sapere,* to taste, know] full of knowledge; wise; discerning —**sa′pi·ence** *n.*

sa·pi·en·tial (sā′pē en′shəl) *adj.* [see prec.] having, providing, or expounding wisdom

sap·ling (sap′liŋ) *n.* **1.** a young tree **2.** a youth

sap·o·dil·la (sap′ə dil′ə) *n.* [< Sp. < Nahuatl *tzapotl*] **1.** a tropical American evergreen tree, yielding chicle and having a brown fruit with a yellowish pulp **2.** the fruit

sap·o·na·ceous (sap′ə nā′shəs) *adj.* [< ModL. < L. *sapo,* soap] soapy or soaplike

sa·pon·i·fy (sə pän′ə fī′) *vt.* **-fied′, -fy′ing** [< Fr. < L. *sapo* (gen. *saponis*), soap + *facere,* to make] to convert (a fat) into soap by reaction with an alkali —*vi.* to be made into soap —**sa·pon′i·fi′a·ble** *adj.* —**sa·pon′i·fi·ca′tion** *n.*

sap·per (sap′ər) *n.* **1.** a soldier employed in digging saps, laying mines, etc. **2.** a person or thing that saps

sap·phire (saf′īr) *n.* [< OFr. < L. < Gr. *sappheiros*] **1.** a hard, transparent precious stone of a clear, deep-blue corundum **2.** its color **3.** a hard variety of corundum, varying in color **4.** a gem made of this —*adj.* deep-blue

Sap·pho (saf′ō) 7th cent. B.C.; Gr. lyric poetess of Lesbos —**Sap′phic** (-ik) *adj.*

Sap·po·ro (sä′pô rô′) chief city on the island of Hokkaido, Japan: pop. 821,000

sap·py (sap′ē) *adj.* **-pi·er, -pi·est 1.** full of sap; juicy **2.** [Slang] foolish; silly; fatuous —**sap′pi·ness** *n.*

sap·ro·phyte (sap′rə fīt′) *n.* [< Gr. *sapros,* rotten + -PHYTE] any organism that lives on dead or decaying organic matter, as some fungi —**sap′ro·phyt′ic** (-fit′ik) *adj.*

sap·suck·er (sap′suk′ər) *n.* any of several small American woodpeckers that often drill holes in trees for the sap

sap·wood (sap′wood′) *n.* the soft wood between the inner bark of a tree and the heartwood, serving to conduct water

sar·a·band (sar′ə band′) *n.* [< Fr. < Sp., ult. < Per. *sarband,* kind of dance] **1.** a graceful, stately, slow Spanish dance in triple time **2.** music for this dance

Sar·a·cen (sar′ə s′n) *n.* any Arab or any Moslem, esp. at the time of the Crusades —*adj.* of the Saracens

Sar·ah (ser′ə, sar′ə) [Heb. *śārāh,* lit., princess] **1.** a feminine name: dim. *Sadie, Sally;* var. *Sara* **2.** *Bible* the wife of Abraham and mother of Isaac: also **Sa·rai** (ser′ī)

Sa·ra·je·vo (sä′rä′ye vô; *E.* sar′ə yā′vō) capital of Bosnia and Hercegovina, in C Yugoslavia: scene of the assassination of an Austrian archduke (June 28, 1914), which precipitated World War I: pop. 175,000

sa·ran (sə ran′) *n.* [arbitrary coinage] any of various thermoplastic resins obtained, as by polymerization, from certain vinyl compounds: used in making fabrics, a transparent wrapping material, etc.

Sa·ra·tov (sä rä′tôf) city & port in SC European R.S.F.S.R., on the Volga: pop. 758,000

sar·casm (sär′kaz′m) *n.* [< LL. < Gr. < *sarkazein,* to tear flesh like dogs < *sarx,* flesh] **1.** a taunting or sneering remark; gibe or jeer, generally ironical **2.** the making of such remarks **3.** sarcastic quality

sar·cas·tic (sär kas′tik) *adj.* **1.** of, like, or full of sarcasm; sneering, caustic, etc. **2.** using, or fond of using, sarcasm —**sar·cas′ti·cal·ly** *adv.*

sar·co·carp (sär′kə kärp′) *n.* [< Gr. *sarx,* flesh + -CARP] the fleshy part of a stone fruit, as in the plum

sar·co·ma (sär kō′mə) *n., pl.* **-mas, -ma·ta** (-mə tə) [ModL. < Gr. < *sarx,* flesh] any of various malignant tumors that begin in connective tissue —**sar·co′ma·to′sis** (-tō′sis) *n.*

sar·coph·a·gus (sär käf′ə gəs) *n., pl.* **-gi′** (-jī′), **-gus·es** [L. < Gr. < *sarx,* flesh + *phagein,* to eat: because the limestone orig. used hastened disintegration] a stone coffin, esp. one on display, as in a monumental tomb

sard (särd) *n.* [L. *sarda*] a very hard, deep orange-red variety of chalcedony, used in jewelry, etc.

sar·dine (sär dēn′) *n., pl.* **-dines′, -dine′:** see PLURAL, II, D, 1 [< MFr. < L. *sarda,* kind of fish] any of various small ocean fishes preserved in tightly packed cans for eating; specif., *same as* PILCHARD

Sar·din·i·a (sär din′ē ə, -din′yə) It. island in the Mediterranean, south of Corsica: c.9,196 sq. mi.: It. name **Sar·degna** (sär dā′nyä) —**Sar·din′i·an** *adj., n.*

sar·don·ic (sär dän′ik) *adj.* [< Fr. < L. < Gr. < *sardanios,* bitter, scornful] disdainfully or bitterly sneering or sarcastic [*a sardonic smile*] —**sar·don′i·cal·ly** *adv.*

sar·do·nyx (sär′də niks) *n.* [L. < Gr. < *sardios,* sard + *onyx,* onyx] a variety of onyx made up of layers of white chalcedony and sard, used as a gem

sar·gas·sum (sär gas′əm) *n.* [ModL. < Port. < *sarga,* kind of grape] any of various floating, brown seaweeds having special branches with berrylike air sacs: also **sar·gas′so** (-ō), *pl.* **-sos, sargasso weed**

Sar·gent (sär′jənt), **John Sing·er** (siŋ′ər) 1856–1925; U.S. painter in Europe

sa·ri (sä′rē) *n.* [< Hindi < Sans.] an outer garment of Hindu women, a long cloth wrapped around the body with one end over the shoulder: also sp. **sa′ree**

SARI

Sar·ni·a (sär′nē ə) city & port in SE Ontario, Canada, at the S end of Lake Huron: pop. 55,000

sa·rod, sa·rode (sə rōd′) *n.* [Hindi *sarod* < Per.] a lutelike musical instrument of India, with many strings

sa·rong (sə rôŋ′, -räŋ′) *n.* [Malay *sārung*] a garment of men and women in the Malay Archipelago, the East Indies, etc., consisting of a long cloth, often brightly colored and printed, worn like a skirt

sar·sa·pa·ril·la (sas′pə ril′ə, särs′-, sär′sə-) *n.* [< Sp. < *zarza,* bramble + dim. of *parra,* vine] **1.** a tropical American plant with fragrant roots **2.** its dried root, or an extract **3.** a carbonated drink flavored with sarsaparilla

Sar·to (sär′tô), **An·dre·a del** (än dre′ä del) 1486–1531; Florentine painter

sar·to·ri·al (sär tôr′ē əl) *adj.* [< LL. *sartor,* a tailor] **1.** of tailors or their work **2.** of men's clothing or dress

Sar·tre (sår′tr′), **Jean-Paul** (zhän pôl) 1905–80; Fr. philosopher, playwright, & novelist

SASE self-addressed stamped envelope

sash[1] (sash) *n.* [Ar. *shāsh,* muslin] an ornamental ribbon or scarf worn over the shoulder or around the waist

sash[2] (sash) *n.* [taken as sing. of earlier *shashes* < Fr. *châssis,* a frame] **1.** a frame for holding the glass pane of a window or door, esp. a sliding frame **2.** such frames collectively

sa·shay (sa shā′) *vi.* [altered < *chassé* (dance)] [Colloq.] to move, walk, or go, esp. casually

sash cord a cord attached to either side of a sliding sash, having balancing weights **(sash weights)** for raising or lowering the window easily

Sas·katch·e·wan (sas kach′ə wän′, -wən) province of SC Canada: 251,700 sq. mi.; pop. 921,000; cap. Regina: abbrev. **Sask.**

Sas·ka·toon (sas′kə to͞on′) city in C Saskatchewan, Canada: pop. 134,000

sas·quatch (sas′kwach′) *n.* [< AmInd.] [*also* **S-**] a huge, hairy, manlike creature reputed to live in the mountains of NW North America

sass (sas) *n.* [var. of SAUCE] [Colloq.] impudent talk —*vt.* [Colloq.] to talk impudently to

sas·sa·fras (sas′ə fras′) *n.* [Sp. *sasafras*] **1.** a small eastern N. American tree bearing small, bluish fruits **2.** the dried root bark of this tree, used as a flavoring

sass·y (sas′ē) *adj.* **sass′i·er, sass′i·est** [dial. var. of SAUCY] [Colloq.] impudent; saucy —**sass′i·ly** *adv.* —**sass′i·ness** *n.*

sat (sat) *pt. & pp. of* SIT

SAT, S.A.T. Scholastic Aptitude Test

Sat. 1. Saturday **2.** Saturn

Sa·tan (sāt′'n) [OE., ult. < Heb. *sāṭan*, to plot against] *Christian Theol.* the chief evil spirit; the Devil

sa·tang (sä taŋ′) *n., pl.* **-tang′** [Siamese *satāŋ*] *see* MONETARY UNITS, table (Thailand)

sa·tan·ic (sā tan′ik, sə-) *adj.* of or like Satan; devilish; wicked: also **sa·tan′i·cal** —**sa·tan′i·cal·ly** *adv.*

satch·el (sach′əl) *n.* [< OFr. < L. dim. of *saccus*, a sack] a small bag for carrying clothes, books, etc.

sate[1] (sāt) *vt.* **sat′ed, sat′ing** [prob. < L. *satiare*, to fill full] **1.** to satisfy (an appetite, desire, etc.) to the full **2.** to satiate; surfeit; glut

sate[2] (sat, sāt) *archaic pt. & pp. of* SIT

sa·teen (sa tēn′, sə-) *n.* [< SATIN] a smooth, glossy cotton cloth, made to imitate satin

sat·el·lite (sat′'l īt′) *n.* [Fr. < L. *satelles*, an attendant] **1.** *a)* an attendant of some important person *b)* an obsequious follower **2.** *a)* a small planet revolving around a larger one *b)* a man-made object put into orbit around the earth, the moon, or some other heavenly body **3.** a small state that is economically dependent on a larger state

sa·tia·ble (sā′shə b'l, sā′shē ə-) *adj.* that can be sated or satiated —**sa′tia·bil′i·ty** *n.* —**sa′tia·bly** *adv.*

sa·ti·ate (sā′shē āt′; *for adj., usually* -it) *adj.* [< L. pp. of *satiare*, to satisfy < *satis*, enough] having had enough or more than enough —*vt.* **-at′ed, -at′ing** **1.** [Rare] to sate; satisfy fully **2.** to provide with more than enough, so as to weary or disgust; glut; surfeit —**sa′ti·a′tion** *n.*

sa·ti·e·ty (sə tī′ə tē) *n.* a being satiated; surfeit

sat·in (sat′'n) *n.* [< MFr. < Sp. < Ar. *zaitūnī*, of *Zaitūn*, former name of a Chinese seaport] a fabric of silk, nylon, rayon, etc. with a smooth, glossy finish on one side —*adj.* of or like satin; smooth and glossy —**sat′in·y** *adj.*

sat·in·wood (sat′'n wood′) *n.* **1.** any of several smooth, hard woods used in fine furniture, etc. **2.** a tree yielding such wood, esp. one in the East or one in the West Indies

sat·ire (sa′tīr) *n.* [Fr. < L. *satira*, orig. a dish of fruits, prob. < Etruscan] **1.** a literary work in which vices, follies, etc. are held up to ridicule and contempt **2.** such works collectively **3.** the use of ridicule, sarcasm, irony, etc. to attack or deride vices, follies, etc.

sa·tir·i·cal (sə tir′i k'l) *adj.* **1.** of, like, or containing satire **2.** using satire Also **sa·tir′ic** —**sa·tir′i·cal·ly** *adv.*

sat·i·rist (sat′ə rist) *n.* a writer of satires

sat·i·rize (-rīz′) *vt.* **-rized′, -riz′ing** to attack, ridicule, or criticize with satire —**sat′i·riz′er** *n.*

sat·is·fac·tion (sat′is fak′shən) *n.* **1.** a satisfying or being satisfied **2.** something that satisfies; specif., *a)* anything that brings pleasure or contentment *b)* settlement of debt *c)* reparation for injury or insult —**give satisfaction** **1.** to satisfy **2.** to accept a challenge to duel or fight

sat·is·fac·to·ry (-fak′tə rē, -trē) *adj.* satisfying; fulfilling a need, wish, requirement, etc. adequately —**sat′is·fac′to·ri·ly** *adv.* —**sat′is·fac′to·ri·ness** *n.*

sat·is·fy (sat′is fī′) *vt.* **-fied′, -fy′ing** [< OFr. < L. < *satis*, enough + *facere*, to make] **1.** to fulfill the needs or desires of; gratify **2.** to fulfill the requirements of **3.** to comply with (rules or obligations) **4.** *a)* to free from doubt; convince *b)* to answer (a doubt, etc.) adequately **5.** *a)* to give what is due to *b)* to discharge (a debt, etc.) **6.** to make reparation to or for —*vi.* to be adequate, sufficient, etc. —**sat′is·fi′a·ble** *adj.* —**sat′is·fi′er** *n.*

sa·to·ri (sä tôr′ē) *n.* [Jap.] *Zen Buddhism* spiritual enlightenment or illumination

sa·trap (sā′trap, sat′rap) *n.* [< L. < Gr. *satrapēs* < OPer.] **1.** the governor of a province in ancient Persia **2.** a ruler of a dependency, esp. a petty tyrant

sa·trap·y (sā′trə pē, sat′rə-) *n., pl.* **-trap·ies** the government, authority, or province of a satrap

sat·u·ra·ble (sach′ər ə b'l) *adj.* that can be saturated

sat·u·rate (sach′ə rāt′) *vt.* **-rat′ed, -rat′ing** [< L. pp. of *saturare*, to fill up < *satur*, full] **1.** to cause to be thoroughly soaked **2.** to cause to be so completely filled or supplied that no more can be taken up **3.** *Chem. a)* to cause (a substance) to combine to its full capacity with another *b)* to dissolve the maximum amount of (a gas, liquid, or solid) in a solution —**sat′u·ra′tor** *n.*

sat·u·ra·tion (sach′ə rā′shən) *n.* **1.** a saturating or being saturated **2.** the degree to which a color is free from mixture with white; intensity of hue

saturation point **1.** the point at which the maximum amount has been absorbed **2.** the limit beyond which something cannot be continued, endured, etc.

Sat·ur·day (sat′ər dē, -dā′) *n.* [OE. *Sæterdæg*, Saturn's day] the seventh and last day of the week

Saturday night special [from their use in weekend crimes] [Slang] any small, cheap, short-barreled handgun

Sat·ur·days (-dēz, -dāz′) *adv.* on or during every Saturday

Sat·urn (sat′ərn) **1.** *Rom. Myth.* the god of agriculture: identified with the Greek god Cronus **2.** a planet in the solar system, sixth in distance from the sun: diameter, c.72,000 mi. —**Sa·tur·ni·an** (sə tʉr′nē ən) *adj.*

Sat·ur·na·li·a (sat′ər nā′lē ə, -nāl′yə) *n.pl.* **1.** the ancient Roman festival of Saturn, held about December 17, with general feasting and revelry **2.** [**s-**] [*often with sing. v. & with a pl.* **-li·as**] a period of unrestrained revelry

sat·ur·nine (sat′ər nīn′) *adj.* **1.** *Astrol.* born under the supposed influence of the planet Saturn **2.** sluggish, grave, taciturn, etc. —**sat′ur·nine′ly** *adv.*

sat·yr (sāt′ər, sat′-) *n.* [< L. < Gr. *satyros*] **1.** *Gr. Myth.* a lecherous woodland deity, attendant on Bacchus, represented as having pointed ears, short horns, the head and body of a man, and the legs of a goat **2.** a lecherous man

sat·y·ri·a·sis (sat′ə rī′ə sis) *n.* [see prec.] abnormal and uncontrollable desire by a man for sexual intercourse: cf. NYMPHOMANIA

sau (sou) *n.* [Vietnamese] *see* MONETARY UNITS, table (Vietnam)

sauce (sôs) *n.* [< OFr. < L. *salsa*, salted food, ult. < *sal*, salt] **1.** *a)* a liquid or soft dressing served with food as a relish *b)* a flavored syrup put on ice cream **2.** stewed or preserved fruit **3.** something that adds interest or zest **4.** [Dial.] garden vegetables eaten as a side dish **5.** [Colloq.] impudence **6.** [Slang] alcoholic liquor: usually with *the* —*vt.* **sauced, sauc′ing** **1.** to flavor with a sauce **2.** to give flavor to **3.** [Colloq.] to be impudent or saucy to

sauce·pan (-pan′) *n.* a small pot with a projecting handle, used for cooking

sau·cer (sô′sər) *n.* [MFr. *saussier* < *sause*, SAUCE] **1.** a small, round, shallow dish, esp. one with an indentation to hold a cup **2.** anything round and shallow like a saucer

sau·cy (sô′sē) *adj.* **-ci·er, -ci·est** [SAUC(E) + -Y[2]] **1.** rude; impudent **2.** pert; sprightly [*a saucy smile*] **3.** stylish or smart —**sau′ci·ly** *adv.* —**sau′ci·ness** *n.*

Sa·u·di (sä ōō′dē, sou′dē) *adj.* of Saudi Arabia, its people, etc. —*n., pl.* **-dis** a native or inhabitant of Saudi Arabia

Saudi Arabia kingdom occupying most of Arabia: c. 617,000 sq. mi.; pop. 6,036,000; cap. Riyadh (Mecca is the religious capital)

sau·er·bra·ten (sour′brät′'n, zou′ər-) *n.* [G. < *sauer*, sour + *braten*, a roast] a dish made of beef marinated in vinegar with onion, spices, etc. before cooking

sau·er·kraut (sour′krout′) *n.* [G. *sauer*, sour + *kraut*, cabbage] chopped cabbage fermented in a brine of its own juice with salt

sau·ger (sô′gər) *n.* [< ?] a small American pikeperch

Saul (sôl) [< LL. < Gr. < Heb. *shā'ūl*, lit., asked (i.e., of God)] **1.** a masculine name **2.** *Bible a)* the first king of Israel *b) orig. name of the Apostle* PAUL

Sault Ste. Ma·rie (sōō′ sānt′ mə rē′) [< Fr. *Sault de Sainte Marie*, lit., falls of St. Mary] **1.** city in N Mich., on a river (*St. Marys River*) flowing from Lake Superior into Lake Huron: pop. 14,000 **2.** city opposite it, in Ontario, Canada: pop. 75,000 Also **Sault Sainte Marie** See also Soo

sau·na (sou′nə, sô′-) *n.* [Finn.] **1.** a Finnish bath, consisting of exposure to very hot, relatively dry air, with light beating of the skin with birch or cedar boughs **2.** the enclosure for such a bath

saun·ter (sôn′tər) *vi.* [< ?] to walk about idly; stroll —*n.* **1.** a leisurely and aimless walk **2.** a slow, leisurely gait

sau·ri·an (sôr′ē ən) *n.* [< Gr. *sauros*, a lizard] any of those reptiles that are lizards —*adj.* of or like lizards

-sau·rus (sôr′əs) [see prec.] *a combining form meaning* lizard

sau·sage (sô′sij) *n.* [< ONormFr. < VL. < L. *salsus*: see SAUCE] pork or other meat, chopped fine, highly seasoned, and either stuffed into membranous casings or made into patties for cooking

sau·té (sō tā′, sô-) *adj.* [Fr., pp. of *sauter*, to leap] fried quickly in a little fat —*vt.* **-téed′, -té′ing** to fry quickly in a pan with a little fat —*n.* a sautéed dish

sau·terne (sō tʉrn′, sô-) *n.* [< *Sauternes*, town in France] a white, usually sweet table wine

sav·age (sav′ij) *adj.* [< OFr. < VL. < L. *silvaticus*, wild < *silva*, a wood] **1.** wild; uncultivated [*a savage jungle*] **2.** fierce; untamed [*a savage tiger*] **3.** without civilization; barbarous [*a savage tribe*] **4.** crude; rude **5.** cruel; pitiless —*n.* **1.** a member of a primitive society or savage tribe **2.** a fierce, brutal person —*vt.* **-aged, -ag·ing** to attack violently, either physically or verbally —**sav′age·ly** *adv.*

sav·age·ry (-rē) *n., pl.* **-ries** **1.** the condition of being savage, wild, primitive, etc. **2.** savage act or behavior

sa·van·na, sa·van·nah (sə van′ə) *n.* [< Sp. < *zavana* < native name] a treeless plain or a grassland with scattered trees, esp. in or near the tropics

Sa·van·nah (sə van′ə) [< the native name of the Shawnees] seaport in SE Ga.: pop. 142,000

sa·vant (sə vänt′, sav′ənt) ***n.*** **[**Fr., orig. prp. of *savoir* < L. *sapere*, to know**]** a learned person

save[1] (sāv) ***vt.*** **saved, sav′ing [**< OFr. *salver* < L. < *salvus*, safe**]** **1.** to rescue or preserve from harm or danger **2.** to preserve for future use (often with *up*) **3.** to prevent loss or waste of *[*to *save* time*]* **4.** to avoid or lessen *[*to *save* wear and tear*]* **5.** to treat carefully in order to preserve, lessen wear, etc. **6.** *Theol.* to deliver from sin and punishment —***vi.*** **1.** to avoid expense, loss, waste, etc. **2.** to keep something or someone from danger, harm, etc. **3.** to hoard money or goods **4.** to keep; last **5.** *Theol.* to exercise power to redeem from sin —***n.*** *Sports* an action that keeps an opponent from scoring or winning —**sav′a·ble, save′a·ble** ***adj.*** —**sav′er** ***n.***

save[2] (sāv) ***prep.*** **[**< OFr. *sauf*, lit., SAFE**]** except; but —***conj.*** **1.** except; but **2.** [Archaic] unless

sav·ing[1] (sā′viŋ) ***adj.*** that saves; specif., *a)* rescuing *b)* economical *c)* containing an exception *[*a *saving* clause*]* *d)* compensating; redeeming *[*a *saving* grace*]* —***n.*** **1.** the act of one that saves **2.** [*often pl. with sing. v.*] any reduction in expense, time, etc. *[*a *saving(s)* of 10%*]* **3.** *a)* anything saved *b)* [*pl.*] sums of money saved

sav·ing[2] (sā′viŋ) ***prep.*** [Now Rare] **1.** with due respect for **2.** except; save —***conj.*** [Now Rare] save

savings account an account in a bank or savings association which receives and invests depositors' savings, on which it pays interest

savings and loan association a depositor-owned establishment in which depositors' savings draw interest and are used for making real-estate loans

sav·ior, sav·iour (sāv′yər) ***n.*** **[**< OFr. < LL. *salvator* < *salvare*, to SAVE[1]**]** a person who saves —**the Saviour** (or **Savior**) Jesus Christ

sa·voir-faire (sav′wär fer′) ***n.*** [Fr., to know (how) to do] ready knowledge of what to do or say, and of when and how to do or say it; social poise and tact

sa·vor (sā′vər) ***n.*** **[**< OFr. < L. *sapor***]** **1.** the taste or smell of something; flavor **2.** characteristic quality **3.** noticeable trace **4.** power to excite interest, zest, etc. —***vi.*** **1.** to have the particular taste, smell, or quality; smack (*of*) **2.** to show traces or signs (*of*) —***vt.*** **1.** to season or flavor **2.** to taste or smell, esp. with relish **3.** to dwell on with delight; relish Also, Brit. sp., **savour** —**sa′vor·er** ***n.*** —**sa′vor·less** ***adj.*** —**sa′vor·ous** ***adj.***

sa·vor·y[1] (sā′vər ē) ***adj.*** **-vor·i·er, -vor·i·est [**< OFr. pp. of *savourer*, to taste < *savour*, SAVOR**]** **1.** pleasing to the taste or smell **2.** pleasant, agreeable, etc. **3.** morally acceptable; respectable **4.** salty or piquant *[*a *savory* relish*]* —***n.***, *pl.* **-vor·ies** in England, a small, highly seasoned portion of food served at the end of a meal or as an appetizer Also, Brit. sp., **savoury** —**sa′vor·i·ness** ***n.***

sa·vor·y[2] (sā′vər ē) ***n.*** **[**< OFr. *savoreie*, altered (prob. after *savour*, SAVOR) < L. *satureia*, savory**]** a fragrant herb of the mint family, used in cooking

Sa·voy[1] (sə voi′) ruling family of Piedmont, the duchy of Savoy, the kingdom of Sardinia, & (1861–1946) Italy

Sa·voy[2] (sə voi′) region in SE France, on the borders of Italy & Switzerland: formerly, a duchy

Sa·voy·ard (sə voi′ərd) ***n.*** **[**< the *Savoy*, London theater**]** an actor, producer, or admirer of Gilbert and Sullivan operas

sav·vy (sav′ē) ***vi.*** **-vied, -vy·ing [**altered < Sp. *sabe* (*usted*), do (you) know? < *saber*, to know**]** [Slang] to understand; get the idea —***n.*** [Slang] **1.** shrewd understanding **2.** skill or know-how —***adj.*** [Slang] shrewd or discerning

saw[1] (sô) ***n.*** **[**OE. *sagu***]** **1.** a cutting tool having a thin, metal blade or disk with sharp teeth along the edge **2.** a machine that operates a saw —***vt.*** **sawed, sawed** or chiefly Brit. **sawn, saw′ing** **1.** to cut or shape with a saw **2.** to make sawlike cutting motions through or with (something) or produce with such motions —***vi.*** **1.** to cut with a saw or as a saw does **2.** to be cut with a saw *[*wood that *saws* easily*]* **3.** to make sawlike cutting motions —**saw′er** ***n.***

SAWS
(A, keyhole; B, hacksaw; C, handsaw; D, crosscut)

saw[2] (sô) ***n.*** **[**OE. *sagu***]** an old saying; maxim

saw[3] (sô) *pt. of* SEE[1]

saw·bones (sô′bōnz′) ***n.*** [Slang] a surgeon

saw·buck (-buk′) ***n.*** **1. [**Du. *zaagbok***]** a sawhorse with the legs projecting above the crossbar **2. [**from resemblance of the crossed legs of a sawbuck to an X (Roman numeral for 10)**]** [Slang] a ten-dollar bill

saw·dust (-dust′) ***n.*** tiny bits of wood formed in sawing

sawed-off (sôd′ôf′) ***adj.*** **1.** designating a shotgun with the barrel cut off short **2.** [Colloq.] short in stature

saw·fish (sô′fish′) ***n.***, *pl.* **-fish′, -fish′es:** see FISH any of a genus of tropical giant rays having a long, flat, sawlike snout edged with teeth on both sides

saw·fly (-flī′) ***n.***, *pl.* **-flies′** any of a group of four-winged insects the female of which has a pair of sawlike organs that cut into plants, the eggs being then deposited in the cuts

saw·horse (-hôrs′) ***n.*** a rack on which wood is placed while being sawed

saw·mill (-mil′) ***n.*** **1.** a place where logs are sawed into boards **2.** a large sawing machine

sawn (sôn) *chiefly Brit. pp. of* SAW[1]

saw-toothed (sô′to͞otht′) ***adj.*** having notches like the teeth of a saw; serrate: also **saw′tooth′**

saw·yer (sô′yər) ***n.*** a person whose work is sawing wood, as into planks and boards

sax (saks) ***n.*** [Colloq.] a saxophone

sax·horn (saks′hôrn′) ***n.*** **[**after A. J. *Sax* (1814–1894), Belgian inventor**]** any of a group of valved brass-wind instruments with a full, even tone

sax·i·frage (sak′sə frij) ***n.*** **[**MFr. < L. < *saxum*, a rock + base of *frangere*, to break: the plant grows in rock crevices**]** any of a group of plants with white, yellow, purple, or pinkish small flowers, and leaves often at the base of the plant

Sax·on (sak′s'n) ***n.*** **1.** a member of an ancient Germanic people of northern Germany: some Saxons conquered parts of England in the 5th and 6th cent. A.D. **2.** *same as* ANGLO-SAXON (*n.* 1 & 4) **3.** a native or inhabitant of modern Saxony **4.** any of the Low German dialects of the Saxon peoples —***adj.*** **1.** of the Saxons, their language, etc. **2.** of Saxony

Sax·on·y (sak′sə nē) **1.** region in S East Germany: formerly, a kingdom **2.** medieval duchy at the base of Jutland: now part of a West German state called *Lower Saxony*

sax·o·phone (sak′sə fōn′) ***n.*** **[**Fr., after A. J. *Sax* (see SAXHORN) & -PHONE**]** a single-reed, keyed wind instrument having a curved metal body —**sax′o·phon′ist** ***n.***

SAXOPHONE

say (sā) ***vt.*** **said, say′ing;** 3d pers. sing., pres. indic., **says** (sez), archaic **saith [**OE. *secgan***]** **1.** to utter; speak **2.** to express in words; state; declare **3.** to state positively or as an opinion *[*who can *say* what will be?*]* **4.** to indicate or show *[*the clock *says* ten*]* **5.** to recite; repeat *[*to *say* one's prayers*]* **6.** to estimate *[*he is, I'd *say*, forty*]* **7.** to allege; report *[*they *say* he's guilty*]* **8.** to communicate (an idea, feeling, etc.) *[*the painting *says* nothing*]* —***vi.*** to make a statement; speak; express an opinion —***n.*** **1.** a chance to speak *[*to have one's *say]* **2.** authority, as to make a final decision: often with *the* —***adv.*** **1.** for example *[*any fish, *say* perch*]* **2.** about; nearly *[*costing, *say*, $5*]* —***interj.*** an exclamation expressing surprise, admiration, etc. —**go without saying** to be too obvious to need explanation —**that is to say** in other words; that means —**to say the least** to understate —**say′er** ***n.***

say·ing (sā′iŋ) ***n.*** something said; esp., an adage, proverb, or maxim

‡**sa·yo·na·ra** (sä′yô nä′rä) ***n., interj.*** **[**< Jap.**]** farewell

say-so (sā′sō′) ***n.*** [Colloq.] **1.** (one's) word, opinion, assurance, etc. **2.** right of decision; authority

Sb [L. *stibium***]** *Chem.* antimony

Sc *Chem.* scandium

SC, S.C. South Carolina

Sc. **1.** Scotch **2.** Scots **3.** Scottish

sc. **1.** scene **2.** science **3.** scilicet

s.c. *Printing* small capitals

scab (skab) ***n.*** **[**ON. *skabb***]** **1.** a crust that forms over a sore or wound as it is healing **2.** a mangy skin disease, esp. of sheep **3.** a plant disease characterized by roughened, scablike spots **4.** *a)* [Old Slang] a scoundrel *b)* a worker who refuses to join a union *c)* a worker who refuses to strike, or who takes the place of a striking worker —***vi.*** **scabbed, scab′bing** **1.** to become covered with a scab **2.** to work or act as a scab

scab·bard (skab′ərd) ***n.*** **[**< Anglo-Fr. *escaubers* (pl.) < ? OHG. *scar*, sword + *bergan*, to hide**]** a sheath or case to hold the blade of a sword, dagger, etc. —***vt.*** to sheathe

scab·by (skab′ē) ***adj.*** **-bi·er, -bi·est** **1.** covered with or consisting of scabs **2.** low; base; mean —**scab′bi·ly** ***adv.*** —**scab′bi·ness** ***n.***

sca·bies (skā′bēz, -bē ēz) ***n.*** **[**L., itch < *scabere*, to scratch**]** a contagious skin disease caused by mites that burrow under the skin to deposit eggs, causing intense itching

sca·bi·o·sa (skā′bē ō′sə) ***n.*** **[**ModL., genus name < ML. < L.: see prec.: once considered a remedy for scabies**]** any of various related plants having showy flowers in flattened or dome-shaped heads: also **sca′bi·ous** (-əs)

scab·rous (skab′rəs, skā′brəs) ***adj.*** **[**< LL. < L. *scabere*, to scratch**]** **1.** rough, like a file; scaly, scabby, etc. **2.** full of difficulties **3.** indecent, scandalous, etc. —**scab′rous·ly** ***adv.*** —**scab′rous·ness** ***n.***

scad (skad) ***n.*** **[**< ?**]** [*usually pl.*] [Colloq.] a very large number or amount *[scads* of money*]*

scaf·fold (skaf′'ld, -ōld) ***n.*** **[**OFr. *escafalt:* prob. akin to CATAFALQUE**]** **1.** a temporary framework for supporting workmen during the erecting, repairing, or painting of a building, etc. **2.** a raised platform on which criminals are executed, as by hanging **3.** any raised framework —***vt.*** to furnish or support with a scaffold

scaf·fold·ing (-'l diŋ) ***n.*** **1.** the materials that form a scaffold **2.** a scaffold or scaffolds

sca·lar (skā′lər) ***adj.*** **1.** in, on, or of a scale **2.** *Math.* designating or of a quantity that has magnitude but no direction in space, as volume or temperature —***n.*** a scalar quantity: distinguished from VECTOR (sense 2 *a*)

scal·a·wag (skal′ə wag′) ***n.*** **[**< ?**]** **1.** a scamp; rascal **2.** a white Southern Republican during the Reconstruction: an opprobrious term Also sp. **scallawag**

scald[1] (skôld) ***vt.*** **[**< ONormFr. < OFr. < LL. *excaldare* < L. *ex-*, intens. + *calidus,* hot**]** **1.** to burn with hot liquid or steam **2.** to heat almost to the boiling point **3.** to use boiling liquid on, as in sterilizing, etc. —***vi.*** to be or become scalded —***n.*** **1.** a burn caused by scalding **2.** the act or an instance of scalding **3.** any of various plant diseases characterized by a whitening or browning of tissues

scald[2] (skôld, skäld) ***n.*** *var. of* SKALD —**scald′ic** ***adj.***

scale[1] (skāl) ***n.*** **[**< LL. *scala* < L., a ladder**]** **1.** orig., a ladder or flight of stairs **2.** *a*) a series of marks along a line, as at regular intervals, used in measuring or registering something *[*the *scale* of a thermometer*]* *b*) any instrument or ruler so marked **3.** *a*) the proportion that a map, model, etc. bears to the thing that it represents *[*a *scale* of one inch to a mile*]* *b*) a line marked off on a map to show this ratio **4.** *a*) a system of classifying in a series of degrees according to relative size, amount, rank, etc. *[*a wage *scale]* *b*) any point, level, or degree in such a series **5.** *Math.* a number system having a specified base *[*the binary *scale]* **6.** *Music* a sequence of tones, rising or falling in pitch, in accordance with any of various systems of intervals —***vt.*** **scaled, scal′ing** **1.** to climb up or over **2.** to make according to a scale —***vi.*** **1.** to climb; go up **2.** to go up in a graduated series —**on a large** (or **small**) **scale** to a relatively large (or small) degree or extent —**scale down** (or **up**) to reduce (or increase) according to a ratio —**scal′er** ***n.***

scale[2] (skāl) ***n.*** **[**< OFr. *escale,* husk & *escaille,* shell: both < Gmc.**]** **1.** any of the thin, flat, overlapping, horny plates forming the outer covering of many fishes and reptiles **2.** any thin, flaky or platelike layer or piece that forms part of, or peels off from, a surface **3.** a coating that forms on metals when heated or rusted *[scale* on the inside of a boiler*]* **4.** any small scalelike leaf or bract; esp., such a modified leaf covering the bud of a seed plant —***vt.*** **scaled, scal′ing** **1.** to strip or scrape scales from **2.** to remove in thin layers; pare down **3.** to cause scales to form on —***vi.*** **1.** to flake or peel off in scales **2.** to become covered with scale or scales —**scale′less** ***adj.***

scale[3] (skāl) ***n.*** **[** ON. *skāl,* bowl**]** **1.** either of the shallow dishes or pans of a balance **2.** [*often pl.*] a balance or other weighing device —***vt.*** **scaled, scal′ing** **1.** to weigh in scales **2.** to have a weight of —***vi.*** to be weighed —**the Scales** *same as* LIBRA —**turn the scales** to determine; decide

scale insect any of a large group of small, homopterous insects destructive to plants: the females secrete a round, wax scale under which they live and lay their eggs

sca·lene (skā lēn′, skā′lēn) ***adj.*** **[**< LL. < Gr. *skalēnos,* uneven**]** *Geom.* **1.** having unequal sides and angles: said of a triangle **2.** having the axis not perpendicular to the base: said of a cone, etc.

scaling ladder a ladder used for climbing high walls

scal·lion (skal′yən) ***n.*** **[**< ONormFr. *escalogne,* ult. < L. (*caepa*) *Ascalonia,* (onion of) Ascalon (in Philistia)**]** any of three varieties of onion; specif., *a*) the shallot *b*) the leek *c*) a green onion with an almost bulbless root

scal·lop (skäl′əp, skal′-) ***n.*** **[**OFr. *escalope* < *escale:* see SCALE[2]**]** **1.** a kind of mollusk with two deeply grooved, curved shells, that swims by means of a large muscle that rapidly snaps its shells together **2.** this muscle, used as food **3.** a single shell of such a mollusk; specif., one used as a baking dish **4.** any of a series of curves, projections, etc. forming an ornamental edge on cloth, lace, etc. —***vt.*** **1.** to cut the edge or border of in scallops **2.** to bake with a milk sauce and bread crumbs; escallop —***vi.*** to gather scallops —**scal′lop·er** ***n.***

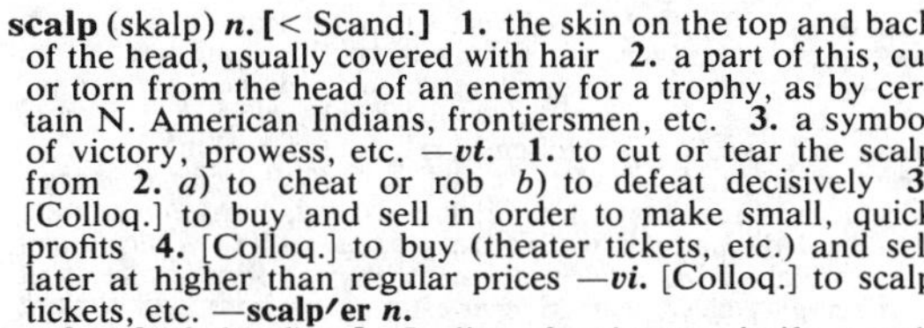

SCALLOP (sense 1)

scal·ly·wag (skal′ē wag′) ***n.*** *same as* SCALAWAG

scalp (skalp) ***n.*** **[**< Scand.**]** **1.** the skin on the top and back of the head, usually covered with hair **2.** a part of this, cut or torn from the head of an enemy for a trophy, as by certain N. American Indians, frontiersmen, etc. **3.** a symbol of victory, prowess, etc. —***vt.*** **1.** to cut or tear the scalp from **2.** *a*) to cheat or rob *b*) to defeat decisively **3.** [Colloq.] to buy and sell in order to make small, quick profits **4.** [Colloq.] to buy (theater tickets, etc.) and sell later at higher than regular prices —***vi.*** [Colloq.] to scalp tickets, etc. —**scalp′er** ***n.***

scal·pel (skal′pəl) ***n.*** **[**< L. dim. of *scalprum,* a knife < *scalpere,* to cut**]** a small, light, straight knife with a very sharp blade, used by surgeons and in anatomical dissections

scal·y (skā′lē) ***adj.*** **scal′i·er, scal′i·est** having, covered with, or resembling scales —**scal′i·ness** ***n.***

scamp[1] (skamp) ***n.*** **[**< obs. *scamp,* to roam < MFr. *escamper,* to flee, ult. < L. *ex-*, out + *campus,* battlefield**]** a mischievous or roguish fellow; rascal —**scamp′ish** ***adj.***

scamp[2] (skamp) ***vt.*** **[**akin to or < ON. *skammr,* short**]** to do in a careless, inadequate way —**scamp′er** ***n.***

scam·per (skam′pər) ***vi.*** **[**prob. freq. of obs. *scamp:* see SCAMP[1]**]** to run or go hurriedly or quickly —***n.*** the act of scampering —**scam′per·er** ***n.***

scam·pi (skam′pē) ***n.***, *pl.* **-pi, -pies** **[**It., pl. of *scampo***]** a kind of large prawn, valued as food

scan (skan) ***vt.*** **scanned, scan′ning** **[**< L. *scandere,* to climb**]** **1.** to analyze (verse), as by marking off the metrical feet and showing the rhythmic structure **2.** to look at closely or in a broad, searching way; scrutinize **3.** to glance at quickly **4.** in computers, to examine in sequence (data), esp. with an electronic device **5.** *Radar* to traverse (a region) with a succession of transmitted radar beams **6.** *TV* to traverse (a surface) rapidly and point by point with a beam of light or electrons in transmitting or reproducing an image —***vi.*** **1.** to scan verse **2.** to be in a certain poetic meter —***n.*** a scanning —**scan′na·ble** ***adj.*** —**scan′ner** ***n.***

Scan., Scand. **1.** Scandinavia **2.** Scandinavian

scan·dal (skan′d'l) ***n.*** **[**< OFr. < LL. *scandalum,* cause for stumbling < Gr. *skandalon,* a snare**]** **1.** any act, person, or thing that offends or shocks the moral feelings of people and leads to disgrace **2.** a reaction of shame, outrage, etc. caused by such an act, person, etc. **3.** disgrace or ignominy **4.** talk that harms a reputation; wicked gossip

scan·dal·ize (skan′də līz′) ***vt.*** **-ized′, -iz′ing** to outrage the moral feelings of by improper conduct —**scan′dal·iz′er** ***n.***

scan·dal·mon·ger (skan′d'l muŋ′gər, -mäŋ′-) ***n.*** a person who gossips maliciously and spreads scandal

scan·dal·ous (-əs) ***adj.*** **1.** causing scandal; shocking to people's moral feelings; shameful **2.** consisting of or spreading slander; libelous —**scan′dal·ous·ly** ***adv.*** —**scan′dal·ous·ness** ***n.***

Scan·di·na·vi·a (skan′də nā′vē ə) **1.** region in N Europe, including Norway, Sweden, & Denmark and, sometimes, Iceland **2.** peninsula in N Europe, consisting of Norway & Sweden: in full, **Scandinavian Peninsula**

Scan·di·na·vi·an (-ən) ***adj.*** of Scandinavia, its people, their languages, etc. —***n.*** **1.** any of the people of Scandinavia **2.** the subbranch of the Germanic languages spoken by them; North Germanic

scan·di·um (skan′dē əm) ***n.*** **[**ModL. < ML. < L. *Scandia,* N European lands**]** a rare metallic chemical element: symbol, Sc; at. wt., 44.956; at. no., 21

scan·sion (skan′shən) ***n.*** the act of scanning verse

scant (skant) ***adj.*** **[**< ON. < *skammr,* short**]** **1.** inadequate in size or amount; not enough; meager **2.** not quite up to full measure —***vt.*** **1.** to limit in size or amount; stint **2.** to fail to give full measure of **3.** to treat in an inadequate manner —***adv.*** [Dial.] scarcely; barely —**scant′ly** ***adv.*** —**scant′ness** ***n.***

scant·ling (skant′liŋ) ***n.*** **[**< ONormFr. < OFr. *eschandillon,* a measure**]** a small beam or timber; esp., a small upright timber, as in the frame of a structure

scant·y (skan′tē) ***adj.*** **scant′i·er, scant′i·est** **[**SCANT + -Y[2]**]** **1.** barely sufficient; not ample; meager **2.** insufficient; not enough —**scant′i·ly** ***adv.*** —**scant′i·ness** ***n.***

scape (skāp) ***n., vt., vi.*** **scaped, scap′ing** [Archaic] *same as* ESCAPE: also **'scape**

-scape (skāp) **[**< (LAND)SCAPE**]** *a combining form meaning* (a drawing, etc. of) a specified view or scene *[cityscape]*

scape·goat (skāp′gōt′) ***n.*** **[**SCAPE + GOAT**]** **1.** a goat over which the high priest of the ancient Jews confessed the sins of the people, after which it was allowed to escape: Lev. 16:7–26 **2.** a person, group, or thing upon whom the blame for the mistakes or crimes of others is thrust

scape·grace (-grās′) ***n.*** **[**SCAPE + GRACE**]** a graceless, unprincipled fellow; scamp; rogue

scap·u·la (skap′yoo lə) ***n.***, *pl.* **-lae′** (-lē′), **-las** **[**ModL. < L.**]** *same as* SHOULDER BLADE

scap·u·lar (-lər) *adj.* of the shoulder or scapula —*n.* **1.** a sleeveless outer garment falling from the shoulders, worn by monks **2.** two small pieces of cloth joined by strings, worn on the chest and back, under the clothes, by some Roman Catholics as a token of religious devotion

scar (skär) *n.* [< MFr. < LL. < Gr. *eschara,* orig., fireplace] **1.** a mark left after a wound, burn, ulcer, etc. has healed **2.** any mark like this, as on a plant where a leaf was attached **3.** the lasting mental or emotional effects of suffering —*vt., vi.* **scarred, scar′ring** to mark with or form a scar

scar·ab (skar′əb) *n.* [< Fr. < L. *scarabaeus*] **1.** any of various beetles, mostly stout-bodied and often brilliantly colored **2.** *a)* the black, winged dung beetle, held sacred by the ancient Egyptians *b)* an image of this beetle, cut from a stone or gem and formerly worn as a charm

scar·a·bae·id (skar′ə bē′id) *n.* [< ModL. family name] *same as* SCARAB (sense 1) —*adj.* of the scarab beetles

Scar·a·mouch (skar′ə mo͞osh′, -mo͞och′, -mouch′) [< Fr. < It. *Scaramuccia,* lit., a skirmish] a stock character in old Italian comedy, depicted as a braggart and a coward

scarce (skers) *adj.* [ONormFr. *escars,* ult. < L. *excerpere,* to select] **1.** not common; rarely seen **2.** not plentiful; hard to get —*adv. literary var. of* SCARCELY —**make oneself scarce** [Colloq.] to go or stay away —**scarce′ness** *n.*

scarce·ly (-lē) *adv.* **1.** hardly; not quite **2.** probably not or certainly not *[scarcely* true*]*

scar·ci·ty (sker′sə tē) *n., pl.* **-ties 1.** the condition of being scarce; inadequate supply **2.** rarity; uncommonness

scare (sker) *vt.* **scared, scar′ing** [ON. *skirra,* to scare < *skjarr,* timid] to fill with fear or terror; esp., to frighten suddenly —*vi.* to become frightened, esp. suddenly —*n.* **1.** a sudden fear **2.** a state of widespread fear *[*a war *scare]* —**scare up** [Colloq.] to produce or gather quickly

scare·crow (-krō′) *n.* **1.** a figure of a man, etc. made with sticks, old clothes, etc., put in a field to scare birds away from crops **2.** anything that frightens one but is harmless **3.** a person who is dressed like a scarecrow

scarf[1] (skärf) *n., pl.* **scarfs, scarves** [ONormFr. *escarpe,* a purse hung from the neck < ML. < L. < *scirpus,* a bulrush] **1.** a long or broad piece of cloth worn about the neck, head, etc. for warmth or decoration **2.** a long, narrow covering for a table, etc. **3.** a sash worn by soldiers or officials —*vt.* to cover as with a scarf

scarf[2] (skärf) *n., pl.* **scarfs** [prob. < Scand.] **1.** a joint made by notching, grooving, or cutting the ends of two pieces and fastening them so that they join into one continuous piece: also **scarf joint 2.** the ends so cut —*vt.* **1.** to join by a scarf **2.** to make a scarf in the end of

scar·i·fy (skar′ə fī′) *vt.* **-fied′, -fy′ing** [< MFr., ult. < Gr. *skariphasthai,* to scratch < *skariphos,* a stylus] **1.** to make a series of small cuts or punctures in (the skin), as in surgery **2.** to criticize sharply **3.** *Agric.* to loosen or stir (the topsoil) —**scar′i·fi·ca′tion** *n.*

scar·la·ti·na (skär′lə tē′nə) *n.* [ModL. < ML. (*febris*) *scarlatina*] *popular term for a mild form of* SCARLET FEVER

Scar·lat·ti (skär lät′tē) **1. A·les·san·dro** (ä′les sän′drô), 1660?–1725; It. composer **2. (Giuseppe) Do·me·ni·co** (dô me′nē kô′), 1685–1757; It. composer: son of *prec.*

scar·let (skär′lit) *n.* [< OFr. < ML. *scarlatum,* scarlet cloth < Per. < Ar., ult. < Gr. *kyklas,* encircling] **1.** very bright red with a slightly orange tinge **2.** cloth or clothing of this color —*adj.* **1.** of this color **2.** sinful

scarlet fever an acute contagious disease in which one has a sore throat, fever, and a scarlet rash

scarlet letter a scarlet letter A worn in earlier times by a person convicted of adultery

scarlet runner (bean) a climbing bean plant of tropical America, having scarlet flowers, and pods with red-and-black seeds

scarlet tanager a songbird native to the U.S., the male of which has a scarlet body and black wings and tail

scarp (skärp) *n.* [< It. *scarpa*] **1.** a steep slope; specif., an escarpment or cliff along the edge of a plateau **2.** the outer slope of a rampart, or a rear slope of a ditch below the rampart —*vt.* to make into a steep slope

scar tissue the fibrous, contracted tissue of a scar

scarves (skärvz) *n. alt. pl. of* SCARF[1]

scar·y (sker′ē) *adj.* **scar′i·er, scar′i·est** [Colloq.] **1.** causing fear **2.** easily frightened —**scar′i·ness** *n.*

scat[1] (skat) *vi.* **scat′ted, scat′ting** [? a hiss + CAT] [Colloq.] to go away: usually in the imperative

scat[2] (skat) *adj.* [< ?] *Jazz* designating or of singing in which meaningless syllables are used, often to imitate the sounds of a musical instrument —*n.* such singing —*vi.* **scat′ted, scat′ting** to engage in scat singing

scat[3] (skat) *n.* [< Gr. *skōr,* excrement] excrement left by an animal, esp. a wild animal

scathe (skā*th*) *vt.* **scathed, scath′ing** [< ON. < *skathi,* harm] **1.** [Archaic or Dial.] *a)* to injure *b)* to wither or sear **2.** to denounce fiercely —*n.* [Archaic or Dial.] injury or harm —**scathe′less** *adj.*

scath·ing (skā′*th*iŋ) *adj.* searing; harsh or caustic *[scathing* remarks*]* —**scath′ing·ly** *adv.*

sca·tol·o·gy (skə täl′ə jē) *n.* [< Gr. *skōr* (gen. *skatos*), excrement + -LOGY] obsession with the obscene, esp. with excrement or excretion, in literature —**scat·o·log·i·cal** (skat′ə läj′i k′l), **scat′o·log′ic** *adj.*

scat·ter (skat′ər) *vt.* [ME. *skateren*] **1.** to throw here and there or strew loosely; sprinkle **2.** to separate and drive in many directions; disperse —*vi.* to separate and go off in several directions *[*the crowd *scattered]* —*n.* **1.** a scattering **2.** what is scattered about —**scat′ter·er** *n.*

scat·ter·brain (-brān′) *n.* a person who is flighty and not able to think in a serious way —**scat′ter·brained′** *adj.*

scatter rug a small rug for covering only a limited area

scaup (skôp) *n., pl.* **scaups, scaup:** see PLURAL, II, D, 1 [obs. var. of *scalp,* mussel bed] any of several wild ducks related to the canvasback and redhead: also **scaup duck**

scav·enge (skav′inj) *vt.* **-enged, -eng·ing** [< ff.] **1.** to clean up (streets, etc.) **2.** to salvage (usable goods) by rummaging through refuse —*vi.* **1.** to act as a scavenger **2.** to look for food

scav·eng·er (-in jər) *n.* [< Anglo-Fr., ult. < Fl. *scawen* or OFrank. *scouwon,* to peer at] **1.** a person who gathers things that have been discarded by others **2.** any animal that eats refuse and decaying organic matter

sce·nar·i·o (si ner′ē ō′, -när′-) *n., pl.* **-i·os′** [It. < L. < *scaena,* stage, SCENE] **1.** a synopsis of a play, opera, or the like **2.** the working script of a movie, television play, etc. **3.** an outline for a planned series of events, real or imagined —**sce·nar′ist** *n.*

scene (sēn) *n.* [< MFr. < L. < Gr. *skēnē,* tent, stage] **1.** the place in which any event occurs *[*the *scene* of the crime*]* **2.** the setting of the action of a play, story, etc. *[*the *scene* of *Hamlet* is Denmark*]* **3.** a division of a play, usually part of an act **4.** a part of a play, story, etc. that constitutes a unit of action *[*a deathbed *scene]* **5.** *same as* SCENERY (sense 1) **6.** a view of people or places **7.** a display of strong feeling before others *[*she made a *scene* in court*]* **8.** an episode or event, real or imaginary, esp. as described **9.** [Colloq.] the locale or environment for a specified activity *[*the poetry *scene]* —**behind the scenes 1.** backstage **2.** in private or in secrecy; not for public knowledge —**make the scene** [Slang] **1.** to be present **2.** to participate actively or successfully

sce·ner·y (sē′nər ē) *n., pl.* **-ner·ies 1.** painted screens, backdrops, hangings, etc., used on the stage to represent places **2.** the features of a landscape

sce·nic (sē′nik, sen′ik) *adj.* **1.** *a)* of the stage; theatrical *b)* relating to stage effects or stage scenery **2.** *a)* having to do with natural scenery *b)* having beautiful scenery **3.** representing an action, event, etc. —**sce′ni·cal·ly** *adv.*

scent (sent) *vt.* [< OFr. < L. *sentire,* to feel] **1.** to smell **2.** to get a hint of; suspect **3.** to fill with an odor; perfume —*vi.* to hunt by the sense of smell —*n.* **1.** a smell; odor **2.** the sense of smell **3.** a perfume **4.** an odor left by an animal, by which it is tracked **5.** a track followed in hunting **6.** any clue by which something is followed —**scent′ed** *adj.* —**scent′less** *adj.*

scep·ter (sep′tər) *n.* [< OFr. < L. < Gr. *skēptron,* staff] **1.** a staff held by rulers on ceremonial occasions as a symbol of sovereignty **2.** royal authority; sovereignty —*vt.* to furnish with a scepter; invest with royal authority

scep·tic (skep′tik) *n., adj. chiefly Brit. sp. of* SKEPTIC —**scep′ti·cal** *adj.* —**scep′ti·cal·ly** *adv.* —**scep′ti·cism** *n.*

scep·tre (sep′tər) *n., vt.* **-tred, -tring** *chiefly Brit. sp. of* SCEPTER

sched·ule (skej′o͞ol, -əl; *Brit. & often Canad.* shed′yo͞ol, shej′o͞ol) *n.* [< OFr. < LL. dim. of L. *scheda,* a leaf of paper < Gr. *schidē,* splinter of wood] **1.** a list or catalog of details, as of a bill of sale **2.** a list of times of recurring events, arriving and departing trains, etc.; timetable **3.** a timed plan for a project —*vt.* **-uled, -ul·ing 1.** to place in a schedule **2.** to make a schedule of **3.** to plan for a certain time

Scheduled Castes the groups of people in India formerly belonging to the class of untouchables

Scheldt (skelt) river flowing from N France through Belgium & the Netherlands into the North Sea: Du. name **Schel·de** (skhel′də)

sche·ma (skē′mə) *n., pl.* **-ma·ta** (-mə tə) [Gr.: see SCHEME] an outline, diagram, scheme, plan, etc.

sche·mat·ic (skē mat′ik, skə-) *adj.* of, or having the nature of, a scheme, schema, plan, diagram, etc. —*n.* a diagram, as of the wiring of an electric circuit —**sche·mat′i·cal·ly** *adv.*

scheme (skēm) *n.* [< L. < Gr. *schēma,* a form] **1.** *a)* a systematic program for attaining some object *b)* a secret or underhanded plan; plot *c)* a visionary plan **2.** an orderly combination of things on a definite plan *[*a color *scheme]* **3.** an outline showing different parts of an object or system —*vt.* **schemed, schem′ing** to plan as a scheme; devise; contrive; plot —*vi.* **1.** to make schemes **2.** to plot; intrigue —**schem′er** *n.*

schem·ing (skē′miŋ) ***adj.*** given to forming schemes or plots; crafty, tricky, etc. —**schem′ing·ly *adv.***

Sche·nec·ta·dy (skə nek′tə dē) [< Du. < Iroquoian name (? lit., place of the pines) + Du. *stede,* place] city in E N.Y., on the Mohawk River: pop. 68,000

scher·zan·do (sker tsän′dō, -tsan′-) ***adj.*** [It. < *scherzo:* see ff.] *Music* playful —***adv.*** *Music* playfully

scher·zo (sker′tsō) ***n.,*** *pl.* **-zos, -zi** (-tsē) [It., a jest] a lively, playful movement, as of a sonata, in 3/4 time

Schick test (shik) [after B. *Schick* (1877–1967), U.S. pediatrician] a test for immunity to diphtheria, made by injecting dilute diphtheria toxin into the skin

Schil·ler (shil′ər), **(Johann Christoph) Fried·rich von** (frē′driH fôn) 1759–1805; Ger. dramatist & poet

schil·ling (shil′iŋ) ***n.*** [G.] *see* MONETARY UNITS, table (Austria)

schism (siz′'m; *now occas.* skiz′'m) ***n.*** [< OFr. < LL. < Gr. *schisma* < *schizein,* to cleave] **1.** a split in an organized group, esp. a church, caused by a difference of opinion **2.** the offense of trying to cause a split in a church

schis·mat·ic (siz mat′ik; *now occas.* skiz-) ***adj.*** **1.** of or having the nature of schism **2.** tending to or causing schism Also **schis·mat′i·cal** —***n.*** a person who causes or participates in schism —**schis·mat′i·cal·ly *adv.***

schist (shist) ***n.*** [< Fr. < L. < Gr. *schistos,* easily cleft < *schizein,* to cleave] any metamorphic rock of a type that splits easily into thin leaves —**schist′ose** (-ōs) ***adj.***

schis·to·so·mi·a·sis (shis′tə sō mī′ə sis) ***n.*** [ModL. < Gr. *schistos,* cleft + *sōma,* body + -IASIS] a chronic disease, caused by parasitic flukes in the bloodstream, that produces disorders of the liver, bladder, lungs, etc.

schiz·o (skit′sō, skiz′ō) ***adj., n.,*** *pl.* **schiz′os** *clipped form of* SCHIZOPHRENIC

schiz·o- [Modl. < Gr. *schizein,* to cleave] *a combining form meaning* split, division: also, before a vowel, **schiz-**

schiz·o·carp (skiz′ə kärp′, skit′sə-) ***n.*** [prec. + -CARP] *Bot.* a dry fruit, as of the maple, that splits into one-seeded carpels —**schiz′o·car′pous, schiz′o·car′pic *adj.***

schiz·oid (skit′soid, skiz′oid) ***adj.*** **1.** of, like, or having schizophrenia **2.** designating or of a type of person who is withdrawn, introverted, etc. —***n.*** a schizoid person

schiz·o·phre·ni·a (skit′sə frē′nē ə, skiz′ə-) ***n.*** [ModL. < SCHIZO- + Gr. *phrēn,* the mind] a major mental disorder of unknown cause in which, typically, a person's emotions are displayed in bizarre behavior, his sense of reality is distorted by delusions and hallucinations, etc. —**schiz′o·phren′ic** (-fren′ik, -frē′nik) ***adj., n.***

schle·miel (shlə mēl′) ***n.*** [Yid. < Heb. proper name *Shelumiēl*] [Slang] a bungling person who habitually fails or is easily victimized: also sp. **schle·mihl′**

Schles·wig-Hol·stein (shles′wig hōl′stīn; *G.* shlās′viH hōl′shtīn) state of N West Germany, at the base of Jutland

schmaltz (shmälts, shmôlts) ***n.*** [via Yid. < G. *schmalz,* lit., melted fat] [Slang] **1.** highly sentimental and banal music, literature, etc. **2.** banal sentimentalism Also **schmalz** —**schmaltz′y *adj.* schmaltz′i·er, schmaltz′i·est**

schnapps (shnäps, shnaps) ***n.,*** *pl.* **schnapps** [G., a dram] any strong alcoholic liquor: also sp. **schnaps**

schnau·zer (shnou′zər) ***n.*** [G. < *schnauzen,* to snarl] any of three breeds of sturdy, active dog with a close, wiry coat

SCHNAUZER (17–20 in. high at shoulder)

Schnitz·ler (shnits′lər), **Ar·thur** (är′toor) 1862–1931; Austrian playwright & novelist

schnoz·zle (shnäz′'l) ***n.*** [via Yid. < G. *schnauze*] [Slang] the nose: also **schnoz**

schol·ar (skäl′ər) ***n.*** [< OE. or OFr., both ult. < L. *schola,* a SCHOOL[1]] **1.** *a)* a learned person *b)* a specialist in a particular branch of learning, esp. in the humanities **2.** a student given scholarship aid **3.** any student or pupil

schol·ar·ly (-lē) ***adj.*** **1.** of or relating to scholars **2.** showing much knowledge and critical ability **3.** devoted to learning; studious —***adv.*** [Rare] like a scholar

schol·ar·ship (-ship′) ***n.*** **1.** the quality of knowledge and learning shown by a student **2.** the systematized knowledge of a learned man, or of scholars collectively **3.** a gift of money or other aid to help a student

scho·las·tic (skə las′tik) ***adj.*** [< L. < Gr. < *scholazein,* to be at leisure < *scholē,* a SCHOOL[1]] **1.** of schools, colleges, students, teachers, etc.; academic **2.** [*also* **S-**] of or relating to scholasticism Also **scho·las′ti·cal** —***n.*** [*also* **S-**] **1.** *same as* SCHOOLMAN (sense 1) **2.** a person who favors Scholasticism —**scho·las′ti·cal·ly *adv.***

scho·las·ti·cism (-tə siz'm) ***n.*** **1.** [*often* **S-**] a medieval system of Christian thought based on Aristotelian logic **2.** an insistence upon traditional doctrines and methods

scho·li·ast (skō′lē əst) ***n.*** [< ModL. < MGr. < Gr. *scholion,* a comment < *scholē,* a SCHOOL[1]] an ancient interpreter and annotator of the classics —**scho′li·as′tic *adj.***

Schön·berg (shän′bərg, shōn′-; *G.* shön′berkh), **Arnold** 1874–1951; U.S. composer, born in Austria

school[1] (skōōl) ***n.*** [OE. *scol* < L. *schola* < Gr. *scholē,* leisure, school] **1.** a place or institution for teaching and learning, as a public school, dancing school, college or university, etc. **2.** *a)* the building or buildings, classrooms, etc. of a school *b)* all of its students and teachers *c)* a regular session of teaching at a school **3.** *a)* attendance at a school [to miss *school* for a week] *b)* the process of being educated at a school [he finished *school*] **4.** any situation or experience through which one gains knowledge, training, etc. [the *school* of hard knocks] **5.** a particular division of an institution of learning, esp. of a university [the *school* of law] **6.** a group following the same teachings, beliefs, methods, etc. [the Impressionist *school*] **7.** a way of life [a gentleman of the old *school*] —***vt.*** **1.** to teach; instruct; educate **2.** to discipline or control —***adj.*** of a school or schools

school[2] (skōōl) ***n.*** [Du., a crowd] a large number of fish or water animals of the same kind swimming or feeding together —***vi.*** to move together in such a school

school board a group of people, elected or appointed, who are in charge of local public schools

school·book (skōōl′book′) ***n.*** a book used for study in schools; textbook

school·boy (-boi′) ***n.*** a boy attending school

school bus a vehicle for transporting students to and from school and on school-related trips

school·child (-chīld′) ***n.,*** *pl.* **-chil′dren** (-chil′drən) a child attending school

school·fel·low (-fel′ō) ***n.*** *same as* SCHOOLMATE

school·girl (-gurl′) ***n.*** a girl attending school

school guard a person whose duty it is to escort children across streets near schools

school·house (-hous′) ***n.*** a building used as a school

school·ing (-iŋ) ***n.*** **1.** training or education; esp., formal instruction at school **2.** cost of attending school

school·man (-mən; *for 2, often* -man′) ***n.,*** *pl.* **-men** (-mən; *for 2, often* -men′) **1.** [*often* **S-**] any of the medieval teachers of scholasticism **2.** a teacher or educator

school·marm (-märm′, -mäm′) ***n.*** [Colloq.] a woman schoolteacher, hence any person, who tends to be oldfashioned and prudish: also **school′ma'am′** (-mäm′, -mam′)

school·mas·ter (-mas′tər) ***n.*** **1.** a man who teaches in a school: an old-fashioned term **2.** [Brit.] a headmaster or master in a school —**school′mis′tress** (-mis′tris) ***n.fem.***

school·mate (-māt′) ***n.*** a person going to the same school at the same time as another

school·room (-rōōm′) ***n.*** a classroom

school·teach·er (-tē′chər) ***n.*** a person whose work is teaching in a school

school·work (-wurk′) ***n.*** lessons worked on in classes at school or done as homework

school year the part of a year when school is in session, usually from September to June

schoon·er (skōō′nər) ***n.*** [< ? Scot. dial. *scun,* to skip a flat stone across water] **1.** a ship with two or more masts, rigged fore and aft **2.** *short for* PRAIRIE SCHOONER **3.** a large beer glass

Scho·pen·hau·er (shō′pən hou′ər), **Arthur** 1788–1860; Ger. pessimist philosopher —**Scho′pen·hau′er·ism *n.***

schot·tische (shät′ish) ***n.*** [< G. (*der*) *schottische* (*tanz*), (the) Scottish (dance)] **1.** a form of round dance in 2/4 time, similar to the polka **2.** music for this —***vi.*** **-tisched, -tisch·ing** to dance a schottische

Schu·bert (shōō′bərt; *G.* shōō′bert), **Franz (Peter)** (fränts) 1797–1828; Austrian composer

Schu·mann (shōō′män), **Robert (Alexander)** 1810–56; Ger. composer

schuss (shoos) ***n.*** [G., lit., shot, rush] a straight run down a hill in skiing —***vi.*** to make such a run

schwa (shwä) ***n.*** [G. < Heb. *sh'wā*] **1.** the neutral vowel sound of most unstressed syllables in English; sound of *a* in *ago, e* in *agent,* etc. **2.** the symbol (ə) for this sound

Schweit·zer (shvīt′sər; *E.* shwīt′sər), **Al·bert** (äl′bert) 1875–1965; Alsatian medical missionary, theologian, & musician in Africa

sci. **1.** science **2.** scientific

sci·at·ic (sī at′ik) ***adj.*** [< MFr. < ML. < L. < Gr. *ischiadikos* < *ischion,* the hip] of, near, or affecting the hip or its nerves

sci·at·i·ca (sī at′i kə) ***n.*** any painful condition in the region of the hip and thighs; esp., neuritis of the long nerve (**sciatic nerve**) passing down the back of the thigh

sci·ence (sī′əns) ***n.*** **[**< OFr. < L. < prp. of *scire,* to know**]** **1.** orig., knowledge **2.** systematized knowledge derived from observation, study, and experimentation **3.** a branch of knowledge, esp. one concerned with establishing and systematizing facts, principles, and methods *[*the *science* of mathematics*]* **4.** *a)* the systematized knowledge of nature *b)* any branch of this See NATURAL SCIENCE **5.** skill based upon systematized training *[*the *science* of cooking*]* **6.** [S-] *shortened form of* CHRISTIAN SCIENCE

science fiction highly imaginative or fantastic fiction typically involving real or imagined scientific phenomena

sci·en·tif·ic (sī′ən tif′ik) ***adj.*** **1.** of, dealing with, or used in science *[scientific* study, *scientific* apparatus*]* **2.** *a)* based on, or using, the principles and methods of science; systematic and exact *b)* designating a method in which theories are based on data collected systematically and tested objectively **3.** *a)* done according to methods gained by systematic training *[scientific* boxing*]* *b)* having or showing such training —**sci′en·tif′i·cal·ly** ***adv.***

sci·en·tist (sī′ən tist) ***n.*** **1.** a specialist in science, as in biology, chemistry, etc. **2.** [S-] a Christian Scientist

sci-fi (sī′fī′) ***adj., n.*** *same as* SCIENCE FICTION

scil·i·cet (sil′i set′) ***adv.*** **[**L., contr. of *scire licet,* it is permitted to know**]** namely; that is to say

scim·i·tar, scim·i·ter (sim′ə tər) ***n.*** **[**It. *scimitarra* < ?**]** a short, curved sword with an edge on the convex side, used chiefly by Turks, Arabs, etc.

scin·til·la (sin til′ə) ***n.*** **[**L.**]** **1.** a spark **2.** the least trace

scin·til·late (sin′t'l āt′) ***vi.*** **-lat′ed, -lat′ing** **[**< L. pp. of *scintillare* < *scintilla,* a spark**]** **1.** to give off sparks; flash; sparkle **2.** to sparkle with wit **3.** to twinkle, as a star —**scin′til·lant** ***adj.*** —**scin′til·la′tor** ***n.***

scin·til·la·tion (sin′t'l ā′shən) ***n.*** **1.** a scintillating, or flashing, twinkling, sparkling, etc. **2.** a spark or flash **3.** the flash of light made by ionizing radiation upon striking a crystal detector or a phosphor

sci·o·lism (sī′ə liz'm) ***n.*** **[**< L. dim. of *scius,* knowing < *scire,* to know**]** superficial knowledge or learning —**sci′o·list** ***n.*** —**sci′o·lis′tic** ***adj.***

sci·on (sī′ən) ***n.*** **[**OFr. *cion* < ?**]** **1.** a shoot or bud of a plant, esp. one for grafting **2.** a descendant; offspring

Scip·i·o (sip′ē ō) **1.** (*Publius Cornelius Scipio Africanus*) 237?–183? B.C.; Rom. general: defeated Hannibal (202): called *Major* or *the Elder* **2.** (*Publius Cornelius Scipio Aemilianus Africanus Numantinus*) 184?–129? B.C.; Rom. general & statesman: destroyed Carthage (146): grandson of *prec.*: called *Minor* or *the Younger*

scis·sion (sizh′ən, sish′-) ***n.*** **[**Fr. < LL. < L. pp. of *scindere,* to cut**]** a cutting or splitting, or the state of being cut

scis·sor (siz′ər) ***vt.*** to cut with scissors —***n.*** *same as* SCISSORS

scis·sors (siz′ərz) ***n.pl.*** **[**< OFr. < LL. pl. of *cisorium,* cutting tool < L. *caedere,* to cut**]** **1.** a cutting instrument, smaller than shears, with two opposing blades which are pivoted together so that they work against each other: also **pair of scissors** **2.** [*with sing. v.*] *a)* a gymnastic feat in which the legs are moved in a way suggestive of scissors *b)* *same as* SCISSORS HOLD

scissors hold a wrestling hold in which one contestant clasps the other with his legs

scissors kick a swimming kick in which one leg is bent at the knee and the other thrust backward, then both brought together with a snap

scis·sor·tail (siz′ər tāl′) ***n.*** a pale gray and pink variety of flycatcher of the S U.S. and Mexico, having a forked tail

SCLC, S.C.L.C. Southern Christian Leadership Conference

scle·ra (sklir′ə) ***n.*** **[**< Gr. *sklēros,* hard**]** the tough, white, fibrous membrane covering all of the eyeball except the area covered by the cornea

scle·ren·chy·ma (skli reŋ′kə mə) ***n.*** **[**ModL. < Gr. *sklēros,* hard + *enchyma,* infusion**]** *Bot.* plant tissue of uniformly thick-walled, dead cells, as in nut shells

scle·ro- **[**< Gr. *sklēros,* hard**]** *a combining form meaning:* **1.** hard **2.** of the sclera Also, before a vowel, **scler-**

scle·ro·sis (skli rō′sis) ***n.,*** *pl.* **-ses** (-sēz) **[**< ML. < Gr. < *sklēros,* hard**]** **1.** an abnormal hardening of body tissues, esp. of the nervous system or the walls of arteries **2.** a disease characterized by such hardening

scle·rot·ic (-rät′ik) ***adj.*** **1.** hard **2.** of, characterized by, or having sclerosis **3.** of the sclera

scoff (skôf, skäf) ***n.*** **[**prob. < Scand.**]** **1.** an expression of scorn or derision; jeer **2.** an object of mocking contempt, scorn, etc. —***vt.*** to mock at or deride —***vi.*** to show scorn or derision; jeer (*at*) —**scoff′er** ***n.*** —**scoff′ing·ly** ***adv.***

scoff·law (-lô) ***n.*** **[**prec. + LAW**]** [Colloq.] a habitual or flagrant violator of laws, esp. traffic or liquor laws

scold (skōld) ***n.*** **[**< ON. *skald,* poet (prob. because of satirical verses)**]** a person, esp. a woman, who habitually uses abusive language —***vt.*** to find fault with angrily; rebuke —***vi.*** **1.** to find fault angrily **2.** to use abusive language habitually —**scold′er** ***n.*** —**scold′ing** ***adj., n.***

scol·lop (skäl′əp) ***n., vt.*** *var. of* SCALLOP

sconce[1] (skäns) ***n.*** **[**< OFr., ult. < L. *abscondere,* to hide**]** a bracket attached to a wall for holding a candle, etc.

sconce[2] (skäns) ***n.*** **[**Du. *schans,* a fortress, orig. wickerwork**]** a small fort, bulwark, etc. —***vt.*** **sconced, sconc′ing** [Archaic] **1.** to provide with a sconce **2.** to shelter or protect

scone (skōn) ***n.*** **[**Scot., contr. < ? MDu. *schoonbrot,* fine bread**]** a tea cake resembling a baking powder biscuit, usually baked on a griddle

scoop (sko͞op) ***n.*** **[**< MDu. *schope,* bailing vessel & *schoppe,* a shovel**]** **1.** any of various small, shovellike utensils; specif., *a)* a kitchen utensil used to take up sugar, flour, etc. *b)* a small utensil with a round bowl, for dishing up ice cream, mashed potatoes, etc. **2.** the deep shovel of a dredge or steam shovel, which takes up sand, etc. **3.** the act or motion of taking up with or as with a scoop **4.** the amount taken up at one time by a scoop **5.** a hollowed-out place **6.** [Colloq.] a large profit made by speculation **7.** [Colloq.] *a)* advantage gained over a competitor by being first, specif. as in the publication of a news item *b)* such a news item —***adj.*** designating a rounded, somewhat low neckline in a dress, etc. —***vt.*** **1.** to take up or out as with a scoop **2.** to dig (*out*); hollow (*out*) **3.** to make by digging out **4.** to gather (*in* or *up*) as if with a scoop **5.** [Colloq.] to effect a scoop (*n.* 7) in competition with —**scoop′er** ***n.***

scoop·ful (-fo͝ol′) ***n.,*** *pl.* **-fuls′** as much as a scoop will hold

scoot (sko͞ot) ***vi., vt.*** **[**prob. < ON. *skjōta,* to shoot**]** [Colloq.] to go or move quickly; hurry (off); dart —***n.*** [Colloq.] the act of scooting

scoot·er (-ər) ***n.*** **[**< prec.**]** **1.** a child's toy for riding on, consisting of a low footboard with a wheel or wheels at each end, and a raised handlebar for steering: it is moved by pushing one foot against the ground **2.** a similar vehicle with a seat, propelled by a motor: in full, **motor scooter** **3.** a sailboat with runners, for use on water or ice

scope (skōp) ***n.*** **[**< It. < L. < Gr. *skopos,* distant object viewed, watcher**]** **1.** the extent of the mind's grasp; range of understanding **2.** the range or extent of action, content, etc., or of an activity, concept, etc. *[*the *scope* of a book*]* **3.** room or opportunity for action or thought **4.** *short for* TELESCOPE, MICROSCOPE, RADARSCOPE, etc.

-scope (skōp) **[**< Gr. < *skopein,* to see**]** *a combining form meaning* an instrument, etc. for seeing or observing *[telescope]*

sco·pol·a·mine (skō päl′ə mēn′, -min) ***n.*** **[**< G. < ModL. *Scopolia,* a genus of plants, after G. A. *Scopoli* (1723–1788), It. naturalist + G. *amin,* amine**]** an alkaloid, $C_{17}H_{21}O_4N$, used in medicine as a sedative, hypnotic, etc.

-sco·py (skə pē) **[**< Gr. < *skopein,* to see**]** *a combining form meaning* a seeing, observing *[bioscopy]*

scor·bu·tic (skôr byo͞ot′ik) ***adj.*** **[**< ModL. < ML. *scorbutus,* scurvy < Russ. *skórbnut,* to wither**]** of, like, or having scurvy: also **scor·bu′ti·cal**

scorch (skôrch) ***vt.*** **[**< ? Scand.**]** **1.** *a)* to char or discolor the surface of by superficial burning *b)* to parch or shrivel by heat **2.** to criticize very sharply **3.** to burn and destroy everything in (an area) before yielding it to the enemy *[*a *scorched*-earth policy*]* —***vi.*** to become scorched —***n.*** a superficial burning or burn

scorch·er (-ər) ***n.*** anything that scorches; esp., [Colloq.] *a)* a very hot day *b)* a withering remark

score (skôr) ***n.*** **[**OE. *scoru* < ON. *skor***]** **1.** *a)* a scratch, mark, incision, etc. *b)* a drawn line, as one to mark a starting point *c)* notches, marks, etc. made to keep tally or account **2.** an amount due; debt **3.** a grievance one seeks to settle or get even for **4.** a reason or ground **5.** the number of points made in a game or contest **6.** a grade or rating, as on a test **7.** *a)* twenty people or things *b)* [*pl.*] very many **8.** [Colloq.] a successful action, remark, etc. **9.** [Colloq.] the way things really are: chiefly in **know the score** **10.** [Slang] the victim of a swindle; mark **11.** *Music* *a)* a written or printed copy of a composition, showing all parts for the instruments or voices *b)* the music for a stage production, motion picture, etc. —***vt.*** **scored, scor′ing** **1.** to mark or mark out with notches, lines, gashes, etc. **2.** to crease or partly cut (paper, etc.) for accurate folding or tearing **3.** to keep account of by lines or notches **4.** *a)* to make (runs, hits, goals, etc.) in a game *b)* to record the score of *c)* to add (points) to one's score *d)* *Baseball* to bring (a runner) home on one's hit, etc. **5.** to gain *[*to *score* a success*]* **6.** to grade, as in testing **7.** *a)* to raise welts on by lashing *b)* to upbraid **8.** *Music* to arrange in a score —***vi.*** **1.** to make points, as in a game **2.** to run up a score **3.** to keep score in a game **4.** to succeed in getting what one wants —**scor′er** ***n.***

score·board (-bôrd′) ***n.*** a large board for posting the score and other details of a game, as in a baseball stadium

score card **1.** a card for recording the score of a game, match, etc. **2.** a card printed with the names, positions, etc. of the players of competing teams Also **score′card′** ***n.***

score·keep·er (-kēp′ər) ***n.*** a person keeping score, esp. officially, at a game, competition, etc.

score·less (-lis) ***adj.*** with no points scored

sco·ri·a (skôr′ē ə) ***n.,*** *pl.* **-ri·ae′** (-ē′) [L. < Gr. < *skōr,* dung] **1.** the refuse left after metal has been smelted from ore **2.** cinderlike lava —**sco′ri·a′ceous** (-ā′shəs) ***adj.***

scorn (skôrn) ***n.*** [< OFr. < *escharnir,* to scorn] **1.** great contempt for someone or something, often with some indignation **2.** expression of this feeling **3.** the object of such contempt —***vt.*** **1.** to regard with scorn; treat with contempt **2.** to refuse or reject as wrong or disgraceful —***vi.*** [Obs.] to scoff; mock —**laugh to scorn** to ridicule

scorn·ful (-fəl) ***adj.*** filled with or showing scorn or contempt —**scorn′ful·ly** ***adv.*** —**scorn′ful·ness** ***n.***

Scor·pi·o (skôr′pē ō′) [L.] **1.** a S constellation: also **Scor′pi·us** (-əs) **2.** *Astrol.* the eighth sign of the zodiac: see ZODIAC, illus.

scor·pi·on (-ən) ***n.*** [OFr. < L. < Gr. *skorpios*] **1.** any of various arachnids found in warm regions, with a long tail ending in a curved, poisonous sting **2.** *Bible* a whip or scourge —[**S-**] *same as* SCORPIO

SCORPION (to 10 in. long)

Scot (skät) ***n.*** **1.** any member of a Gaelic tribe of northern Ireland that migrated to Scotland in the 5th cent. A.D. **2.** a native or inhabitant of Scotland

scot (skät) ***n.*** [ON. *skot,* tribute] money assessed or paid; tax; levy

Scot. 1. Scotch **2.** Scotland **3.** Scottish

Scotch (skäch) ***adj.*** of Scotland, its people, their language, etc.: cf. SCOTTISH —***n.*** *same as:* **1.** SCOTTISH **2.** SCOTCH WHISKY

scotch (skäch) ***vt.*** [prob. < Anglo-Fr. < OFr. *coche,* a notch] **1.** to cut; scratch; notch **2.** to wound without killing; maim **3.** to put an end to; stifle *[*to *scotch* a rumor*]* —***n.*** a cut or scratch

Scotch-Irish (-ī′rish) ***adj.*** designating or of those people of northern Ireland descended from Scottish settlers, esp. those who emigrated to America

Scotch·man (-mən) ***n.,*** *pl.* **-men** *var. of* SCOTSMAN

Scotch pine a hardy Eurasian pine, with yellow wood

Scotch tape [< *Scotch,* a trademark] a thin, transparent, cellulose adhesive tape

Scotch terrier *same as* SCOTTISH TERRIER

Scotch whisky whiskey, often having a smoky flavor, distilled in Scotland from malted barley

sco·ter (skōt′ər) ***n.,*** *pl.* **-ters, -ter:** see PLURAL, II, D, 1 [< ?] any of several large, dark-colored sea ducks found chiefly along the N coasts of Europe and N. America

scot-free (skät′frē′) ***adj.*** **1.** free from payment of scot, or tax **2.** unharmed or unpunished; free from penalty

Sco·tia (skō′shə) ***n.*** *poet. term for* SCOTLAND

Scot·land (skät′lənd) division of the United Kingdom, occupying the N half of Great Britain & nearby islands: 30,405 sq. mi.; pop. 5,217,000; cap. Edinburgh

Scotland Yard 1. headquarters of the metropolitan London police: officially, **New Scotland Yard 2.** the London police, esp. the detective bureau

Scots (skäts) ***adj., n.*** *same as* SCOTTISH

Scots·man (skäts′mən) ***n.,*** *pl.* **-men** a native or inhabitant of Scotland, esp. a man: *Scotsman* or *Scot* is preferred to *Scotchman* in Scotland —**Scots′wom′an** ***n.fem.,*** *pl.* **-wom′en**

Scott (skät) **1. Robert Fal·con** (fôl′kən), 1868–1912; Eng. antarctic explorer **2.** Sir **Walter,** 1771–1832; Scot. poet & novelist

Scot·ti·cism (skät′ə siz′m) ***n.*** a Scottish idiom, expression, word, pronunciation, etc.

Scot·tie, Scot·ty (skät′ē) ***n.,*** *pl.* **-ties** *colloq. name for* SCOTTISH TERRIER

Scot·tish (skät′ish) ***adj.*** of Scotland, its people, their English dialect, etc. *Scottish* is preferred in formal usage, but with some words, *Scotch* is almost invariably used (e.g., tweed, whisky), with others, *Scots* (e.g., law) —***n.*** the dialect of English spoken in Scotland —**the Scottish** the Scottish people

Scottish Gaelic the Celtic language of the Scottish Highlands: see GAELIC

Scottish terrier any of a breed of terriers with short legs, a squarish muzzle, rough, wiry hair, and pointed, erect ears

Scotts·dale (skäts′dāl′) [after Rev. W. *Scott,* chaplain in the Civil War] city in SC Ariz.: suburb of Phoenix: pop. 88,000

Scotus *see* DUNS SCOTUS

scoun·drel (skoun′drəl) ***n.*** [prob. < Anglo-Fr. *escoundre,* ult. < L. *abscondere,* ABSCOND] a mean, immoral, or wicked person; villain; rascal —***adj.*** characteristic of a scoundrel; mean: also **scoun′drel·ly**

scour[1] (skour) ***vt.*** [MDu. *scuren* < ? OFr. *escurer* < VL. < L. *ex-,* intens. + *curare,* to take care of] **1.** to clean or polish by vigorous rubbing, as with abrasives **2.** to remove dirt and grease from (wool, etc.) **3.** *a)* to wash or clear as by a swift current of water; flush *b)* to wash away **4.** to clear of (something undesirable) —***vi.*** **1.** to clean things by rubbing and polishing **2.** to become clean and bright by being scoured —***n.*** **1.** the act of scouring **2.** a cleansing agent used in scouring **3.** [*usually pl., with sing. v.*] dysentery in cattle, etc. —**scour′er** ***n.***

scour[2] (skour) ***vt.*** [< ? OFr. *escourre,* to run forth < VL. < L. *ex-,* out + *currere,* to run] to pass over quickly, or range over or through, as in search or pursuit *[*to *scour* a town for an escaped convict*]* —***vi.*** to run or range about, as in search or pursuit —**scour′er** ***n.***

scourge (skurj) ***n.*** [< OFr. < L. *ex,* off + *corrigia,* a whip] **1.** a whip or other instrument for flogging **2.** any means of severe punishment or any cause of great suffering *[*the *scourge* of war*]* —***vt.*** **scourged, scourg′ing 1.** to whip or flog **2.** to punish or make suffer severely —**scourg′er** ***n.***

scour·ings (skour′iŋz) ***n.pl.*** dirt, refuse, or remains removed by or as if by scouring

scout[1] (skout) ***n.*** [< OFr. < *escouter,* to hear < L. *auscultare,* to listen] **1.** a soldier, plane, etc. sent to spy out the strength, movements, etc. of the enemy **2.** a person sent out to learn the tactics of an opponent, to search out new talent, etc. *[*a baseball *scout]* **3.** a member of the Boy Scouts or Girl Scouts **4.** the act of reconnoitering **5.** [Slang] fellow; guy —***vt.*** **1.** to follow closely so as to spy upon **2.** to look for; watch **3.** to find by looking around (often with *out, up*) —***vi.*** **1.** to go out in search of information about the enemy; reconnoiter **2.** to go in search of something *[scout* around for some firewood*]* **3.** to work as a scout (*n.* 2) **4.** to be active in the Boy Scouts or Girl Scouts —**scout′er** ***n.*** —**scout′ing** ***n.***

scout[2] (skout) ***vt.*** [prob. < ON. *skuti,* a taunt] to reject as absurd; scoff at —***vi.*** to scoff (*at*)

scout·mas·ter (-mas′tər) ***n.*** the adult leader of a troop of Boy Scouts

scow (skou) ***n.*** [Du. *schouw*] a large, flat-bottomed boat with square ends, used for carrying coal, sand, etc. and often towed by a tug

scowl (skoul) ***vi.*** [prob. < Scand.] **1.** to contract the eyebrows and lower the corners of the mouth in showing displeasure; look angry, sullen, etc. **2.** to have a threatening look; lower —***vt.*** to affect or express with a scowl —***n.*** the act or expression of scowling; angry frown —**scowl′er** ***n.***

scrab·ble (skrab′'l) ***vi.*** **-bled, -bling** [Du. *schrabbelen* < *schrabben,* to scrape] **1.** to scratch, scrape, or paw as though looking for something **2.** to struggle **3.** to scribble —***vt.*** **1.** to scrape together quickly **2.** *a)* to scribble *b)* to scribble on —***n.*** a scrabbling; a scramble, scribble, scrawl, etc. —[**S-**] *a trademark for* a word game played with lettered tiles placed as in a crossword puzzle —**scrab′bler** ***n.***

scrag (skrag) ***n.*** [prob. < ON.] **1.** a thin, scrawny person, animal, or plant **2.** [Slang] the neck —***vt.*** **scragged, scrag′ging** [Slang] to choke or wring the neck of

scrag·gly (skrag′lē) ***adj.*** **-gli·er, -gli·est** [see ff. & -LY[1]] sparse, scrubby, irregular, uneven, ragged, or the like *[*a *scraggly* beard*]* —**scrag′gli·ness** ***n.***

scrag·gy (skrag′ē) ***adj.*** **-gi·er, -gi·est** [< SCRAG] **1.** rough or jagged **2.** lean; bony; skinny —**scrag′gi·ly** ***adv.***

scram (skram) ***vi.*** **scrammed, scram′ming** [contr. of ff.] [Slang] to leave or get out, esp. in a hurry

scram·ble (skram′b'l) ***vi.*** **-bled, -bling** [< ? SCAMPER + SCRABBLE] **1.** to climb, crawl, or clamber hurriedly **2.** to scuffle or struggle for something **3.** to rush pell-mell, as to get something highly prized *[*to *scramble* for political office*]* —***vt.*** **1.** *a)* to throw together haphazardly; jumble *b)* *Electronics* to modify (transmitted auditory or visual signals) so as to make unintelligible without special receiving equipment **2.** to cook (eggs) while stirring the mixed whites and yolks —***n.*** **1.** a hard, hurried climb or advance as over rough, difficult ground **2.** a disorderly struggle or rush, as for something prized **3.** a jumble —**scram′bler** ***n.***

Scran·ton (skrant′'n) [family name of the founders of a local ironworks] city in NE Pa.: pop. 88,000

scrap[1] (skrap) ***n.*** [< ON. *skrap*] **1.** a small piece; fragment; bit **2.** a bit of something written **3.** *a)* discarded metal suitable only for reprocessing *b)* discarded articles of rubber, leather, paper, etc. **4.** [*pl.*] bits of leftover food —***adj.*** **1.** in the form of pieces, leftovers, etc. **2.** used and discarded —***vt.*** **scrapped, scrap′ping 1.** to make into scrap **2.** to discard; junk —**scrap′per** ***n.***

scrap[2] (skrap) ***n.*** [prob. < *scrape,* orig., nefarious scheme] [Colloq.] a fight or quarrel —***vi.*** **scrapped, scrap′ping** [Colloq.] to fight or quarrel —**scrap′per** ***n.***

scrap·book (-book′) ***n.*** a book of blank pages for mounting clippings, pictures, etc.

scrape (skrāp) ***vt.* scraped, scrap′ing** [< ON. *skrapa*] **1.** to rub over the surface of with something rough or sharp **2.** to make smooth or clean by rubbing with a tool or abrasive **3.** to remove by rubbing with something sharp or rough (with *off, out,* etc.) **4.** to scratch or abrade by a rough, rubbing contact **5.** to rub with a harsh, grating sound *[*chalk *scraping* a blackboard*]* **6.** to gather slowly and with difficulty *[*to *scrape* up some money*]* —***vi.*** **1.** to rub against something harshly; grate **2.** to give out a harsh, grating noise **3.** to gather goods or money slowly and with difficulty **4.** to manage to get by (with *through, along, by*) **5.** to draw the foot back along the ground in bowing —***n.*** **1.** a scraping **2.** a scraped place; abrasion **3.** a harsh, grating sound **4.** a disagreeable situation; predicament **5.** a fight or conflict —**scrap′er *n.***

scrap·ing (skrā′piŋ) ***n.*** **1.** the act of a person or thing that scrapes **2.** the sound of this **3.** [*usually pl.*] something scraped off, together, or up

scrap iron discarded or waste pieces of iron, to be recast

scrap·ple (skrap′'l) ***n.*** [dim. of SCRAP[1]] cornmeal boiled with scraps of pork, allowed to set, sliced, and fried

scrap·py[1] (skrap′ē) ***adj.* -pi·er, -pi·est** [SCRAP[1] + -Y[2]] **1.** made of scraps **2.** disconnected *[scrappy* memories*]* —**scrap′pi·ly *adv.*** —**scrap′pi·ness *n.***

scrap·py[2] (skrap′ē) ***adj.* -pi·er, -pi·est** [SCRAP[2] + -Y[2]] [Colloq.] fond of fighting —**scrap′pi·ly *adv.*** —**scrap′pi·ness *n.***

Scratch (skrach) [altered (after ff.) < ON. *skratti,* devil] [*sometimes* **s-**] the Devil: usually **Old Scratch**

scratch (skrach) ***vt.*** [prob. altered < ME. *scratten,* to scratch, after *cracchen*] **1.** to mark or cut the surface of slightly with something pointed or sharp **2.** to tear or dig with the nails or claws **3.** *a*) to scrape lightly to relieve itching, etc. *b*) to chafe **4.** to rub or scrape with a grating noise **5.** to write or draw hurriedly or carelessly **6.** to strike out (writing, etc.) **7.** to gather with difficulty; scrape (*together* or *up*) **8.** *Politics* to strike out the name of (a candidate) on (a party ticket or ballot) **9.** *Sports* to withdraw (an entry) from a contest, specif. from a horse race —***vi.*** **1.** to use nails or claws in digging or wounding **2.** to scrape the skin lightly to relieve itching, etc. **3.** to manage to get by **4.** to make a harsh, scraping noise **5.** to withdraw from a race or contest **6.** *Billiards, Pool* to commit a scratch —***n.*** **1.** the act of scratching **2.** a mark, tear, or slight wound made by scratching **3.** a grating or scraping sound **4.** a scribble **5.** the starting line of a race **6.** [Slang] money **7.** *Billiards, Pool a*) a shot that results in a penalty *b*) a miss **8.** *Sports a*) the starting point or time of a contestant who receives no handicap *b*) such a contestant *c*) an entry withdrawn from a contest —***adj.*** **1.** used for hasty notes, preliminary figuring, etc. *[scratch* paper*]* **2.** having no handicap in a contest **3.** put together hastily, without selection **4.** *Baseball* designating a chance hit credited to the batter for a ball not hit sharply —**from scratch 1.** from the starting line, as in a race **2.** from nothing; without advantage —**scratch the surface** to do, consider, or affect something superficially —**up to scratch** [Colloq.] up to a standard —**scratch′er *n.***

scratch·y (-ē) ***adj.* scratch′i·er, scratch′i·est 1.** made with scratches **2.** making a scratching noise **3.** scratched together; haphazard **4.** that chafes, itches, etc. *[scratchy* cloth*]* —**scratch′i·ly *adv.*** —**scratch′i·ness *n.***

scrawl (skrôl) ***vt., vi.*** [< ?] to write, draw, or mark hastily, carelessly, or awkwardly —***n.*** **1.** sprawling handwriting, often hard to read **2.** something scrawled —**scrawl′er *n.*** —**scrawl′y *adj.* scrawl′i·er, scrawl′i·est**

scraw·ny (skrô′nē) ***adj.* -ni·er, -ni·est** [prob. < Scand.] **1.** very thin; skinny and bony **2.** stunted or scrubby —**scraw′ni·ness *n.***

scream (skrēm) ***vi.*** [akin to WFl. *schreemen,* to scream, G. *schrei,* a cry] **1.** to utter or make a shrill, piercing cry or sound **2.** to laugh loudly or hysterically **3.** to have a startling effect **4.** to shout or yell in anger, hysteria, etc. —***vt.*** **1.** to utter with or as with a scream **2.** to bring into a specified state by screaming *[*to *scream* oneself hoarse*]* —***n.*** **1.** a sharp, piercing cry or sound **2.** [Colloq.] a hilariously funny person or thing

scream·er (-ər) ***n.*** **1.** a person who screams **2.** [Slang] a sensational headline **3.** any of various long-toed S. American wading birds

scream·ing (-iŋ) ***adj.*** **1.** that screams **2.** startling in effect **3.** causing screams of laughter —**scream′ing·ly *adv.***

screech (skrēch) ***vi.*** [ON. *skraekja*] to utter or make a shrill, high-pitched, harsh shriek or sound —***vt.*** to utter with a screech —***n.*** a shrill, high-pitched, harsh shriek or sound —**screech′er *n.*** —**screech′y *adj.* screech′i·er, screech′i·est**

screech owl 1. a small owl with feathered ear tufts and an eerie, wailing cry **2.** [Brit.] *same as* BARN OWL

screed (skrēd) ***n.*** [ME. *screde,* var. of *schrede,* shred] a long, tiresome speech or piece of writing

screen (skrēn) ***n.*** [< OFr. *escren* < Gmc.] **1.** a curtain or movable partition, as a covered frame, used to separate, conceal, protect, etc. **2.** anything that functions to shield, conceal, etc. *[*a smoke *screen]* **3.** a coarse mesh of wire, etc. used as a sieve, as for grading coal **4.** a system for screening or testing persons **5.** a frame covered with a mesh, as of wire, used, as on a window, to keep insects out **6.** *a*) a white surface upon which movies, slides, etc. are projected *b*) the movie industry or art **7.** the surface area of a television or radar receiver on which the light pattern is traced —***vt.*** **1.** to separate, conceal, or protect, as with a screen **2.** to enclose or provide with a screen **3.** to sift through a screen **4.** *a*) to interview or test in order to separate according to skills, personality, etc. *b*) to separate in this way (usually with *out*) **5.** *a*) to project (movies, etc.) upon a screen *b*) to photograph with a movie camera *c*) to adapt (a story, play, etc.) as for a movie —***vi.*** to be screened or suitable for screening, as in movies —**screen′a·ble *adj.*** —**screen′er *n.*** —**screen′less *adj.***

screen·ing (-iŋ) ***n.*** **1.** the act of one that screens **2.** *a*) a screen or set of screens *b*) mesh used in a screen **3.** [*pl.*] material separated out by a sifting screen

screen·play (-plā′) ***n.*** a story written, or adapted from a novel, etc., for production as a movie

screw (skrōō) ***n.*** [MFr. *escroue,* hole in which a screw turns < L. *scrofa,* sow, infl. by *scrobis,* vulva] **1.** *a*) a cylindrical or conical piece of metal for fastening things by being turned: it is threaded evenly with an advancing spiral ridge and usually has a slotted head: also called **male** (or **external**) **screw** *b*) the internal thread, as of a nut, into which a male screw can be turned: also called **female** (or **internal**) **screw** *c*) a turning of such a screw **2.** any of various devices operating or threaded like a screw, as a screw propeller **3.** [Slang] a prison guard **4.** [Chiefly Brit. Colloq.] a stingy person **5.** [Brit. Colloq.] a salary —***vt.*** **1.** to twist; turn; tighten **2.** to fasten, tighten, insert, etc. as with a screw or screws **3.** to twist out of shape; contort **4.** to make stronger (often with *up*) **5.** to force or compel, as if by using screws **6.** [Slang] to cheat; swindle —***vi.*** **1.** to go together or come apart by being turned like a screw *[*a lid *screws* on*]* **2.** to be fitted for screws **3.** to twist; turn; wind **4.** to cheat; swindle —**have a screw loose** [Slang] to be eccentric, odd, etc. —**put the screws on** (or **to**) to subject to force or great pressure —**screw up** [Slang] to make a mess of; bungle

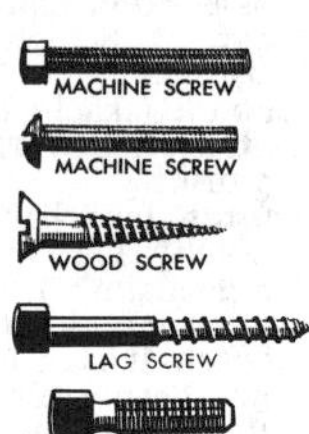

screw·ball (-bôl′) ***n.*** **1.** *Baseball* a ball thrown by a right-handed pitcher that curves to the right, or by a left-handed pitcher that curves to the left **2.** [Slang] a person who seems irrational, unconventional, unbalanced, etc. —***adj.*** [Slang] peculiar; irrational

screw·driv·er (-drī′vər) ***n.*** **1.** a tool used for turning screws, having an end that fits into the slot in the head of a screw **2.** a cocktail of orange juice and vodka

screw eye a screw with a loop for a head

screw hook a screw with a hook for a head

screw propeller *see* PROPELLER

screw thread the spiral ridge of a screw

screw·y (skrōō′ē) ***adj.* screw′i·er, screw′i·est** [Slang] **1.** mentally unbalanced; crazy **2.** peculiar, odd, etc. in a confusing way —**screw′i·ness *n.***

scrib·ble (skrib′'l) ***vt., vi.* -bled, -bling** [< ML. < L. *scribere,* to write] **1.** to write carelessly, hastily, or illegibly **2.** to cover with or make marks that are meaningless or hard to read —***n.*** scribbled writing, marks, etc.; scrawl —**scrib′bler *n.***

scribe (skrīb) ***n.*** [L. *scriba,* public writer < *scribere,* to write] **1.** a penman who copied manuscripts before the invention of printing **2.** a writer; author **3.** a person learned in the Jewish law who makes handwritten copies of the Torah **4.** a person employed by the public to write letters, etc. —***vi.* scribed, scrib′ing** to work as a scribe —**scrib′al *adj.***

scrim (skrim) ***n.*** [< ?] a light, sheer, loosely woven cotton or linen cloth, often used in the theater as a backdrop or as a semitransparent curtain

scrim·mage (skrim′ij) ***n.*** [altered < SKIRMISH] **1.** a tussle; confused struggle **2.** *Football a*) the play that follows the pass from center *b*) football practice in the form of actual play —***vi.* -maged, -mag·ing** to take part in a scrimmage

scrimp (skrimp) ***vt.*** [prob. < Scand.] **1.** to make too small, short, etc.; skimp **2.** to treat stingily; stint —***vi.*** to be sparing and frugal —**scrimp′er *n.*** —**scrimp′ing·ly *adv.***

scrimp·y (skrim′pē) ***adj.* scrimp′i·er, scrimp′i·est 1.** skimpy; scanty; meager **2.** frugal or economical —**scrimp′i·ly *adv.*** —**scrimp′i·ness *n.***

scrim·shaw (skrim′shô′) ***n.*** [< ?] **1.** carving done on shells, bone, ivory, etc., esp. by sailors **2.** an article or articles so made

scrip (skrip) ***n.*** [contr. < SCRIPT] **1.** a note, list, receipt, etc. **2.** a certificate of a right to receive something; specif., a certificate of indebtedness, issued as currency, as by a local government without funds

script (skript) ***n.*** [< MFr. < L. *scriptum*, neut. pp. of *scribere*, to write] **1.** handwriting, or a style of this **2.** *Printing* a typeface that looks like handwriting **3.** an original manuscript **4.** a copy of the text of a play or movie, or of a radio or television show —***vt.*** [Colloq.] to write the script for (a movie, etc.)

scrip·ture (skrip′chər) ***n.*** [< L. < *scriptus:* see SCRIPT] **1.** [S-] [*often pl.*] *a*) the sacred writings of the Jews, identical with the Old Testament of the Christians *b*) the Christian Bible; Old and New Testaments **2.** any sacred writing —**scrip′tur·al** ***adj.*** —**scrip′tur·al·ly** ***adv.***

script·writ·er (skript′rīt′ər) ***n.*** a person who writes scripts for movies, television shows, etc.

scrive·ner (skriv′nər, -′n ər) ***n.*** [< OFr., ult. < L. *scriba*, a SCRIBE] [Archaic] **1.** a scribe or clerk **2.** a notary

scrod (skräd) ***n.*** [prob. < MDu. *schrode*, strip] a young codfish or haddock, split and prepared for cooking

scrof·u·la (skräf′yə lə) ***n.*** [ML. < L. < dim. of *scrofa*, a sow] tuberculosis of the lymphatic glands, esp. of the neck, in which the glands become enlarged —**scrof′u·lous** ***adj.*** —**scrof′u·lous·ly** ***adv.*** —**scrof′u·lous·ness** ***n.***

scroll (skrōl) ***n.*** [altered (? after *roll*) < ME. *scrowe* < OFr. *escroue*, roll of writings] **1.** a roll of parchment, paper, etc., usually with writing on it **2.** anything having the form of a loosely rolled sheet of paper, as an ornamental design in coiled or spiral form —**scrolled** ***adj.***

SCROLL

scroll saw a thin, ribbonlike saw for cutting thin wood into spiral or ornamental designs (**scroll′work′**)

Scrooge (skrōōj) ***n.*** [after *Scrooge*, a character in Dickens' *A Christmas Carol*] [*also* **s-**] a hard, miserly old man

scro·tum (skrōt′əm) ***n.***, *pl.* **-ta** (-ə), **-tums** [L.] in most male mammals, the pouch of skin containing the testicles —**scro′tal** ***adj.***

scrounge (skrounj) ***vt.*** **scrounged, scroung′ing** [< ?] [Colloq.] **1.** to get or find by hunting around **2.** to get by begging or sponging **3.** to pilfer —***vi.*** [Colloq.] to search (*around*) for something —**scroung′er** ***n.***

scrub[1] (skrub) ***n.*** [dial. var. of *shrub*, infl. ? by ON. *skroppa*, a lean creature] **1.** *a*) short, stunted trees or bushes growing thickly together *b*) land covered with such growth **2.** any person, animal, or thing smaller than the usual, or considered inferior **3.** *Sports a*) a player not on the regular team *b*) [*pl.*] a secondary team made up of such players —***adj.*** **1.** mean; poor; inferior **2.** undersized; stunted **3.** *Sports* of or for the scrubs

scrub[2] (skrub) ***vt.*** **scrubbed, scrub′bing** [prob. < Scand.] **1.** to clean or wash by rubbing hard **2.** to rub hard **3.** to cleanse (a gas) of impurities **4.** [Colloq.] *a*) to cancel or call off *b*) to get rid of —***vi.*** to clean something by rubbing, as with a brush —***n.*** **1.** the act of scrubbing **2.** a person who scrubs —**scrub′ber** ***n.***

scrub·by (skrub′ē) ***adj.*** **-bi·er, -bi·est** **1.** undersized or inferior; stunted **2.** covered with brushwood **3.** paltry, shabby, etc. —**scrub′bi·ly** ***adv.*** —**scrub′bi·ness** ***n.***

scruff (skruf) ***n.*** [< ON. *skrufr*, tuft of hair] the back of the neck; nape

scruff·y (skruf′ē) ***adj.*** **scruff′i·er, scruff′i·est** [< dial. *scruff*, var. of SCURF + -Y[2]] shabby, unkempt, or untidy; grubby —**scruff′i·ly** ***adv.*** —**scruff′i·ness** ***n.***

scrum·mage (skrum′ij) ***n.*** [dial. var. of SCRIMMAGE] *Rugby* a play in which the two sets of forwards, lined up facing each other, try to kick the ball back to their teammates —***vi.*** **-maged, -mag·ing** to take part in a scrummage

scrump·tious (skrump′shəs) ***adj.*** [< SUMPTUOUS] [Colloq.] very pleasing, attractive, etc. —**scrump′tious·ly** ***adv.***

scru·ple (skrōō′p′l) ***n.*** [< MFr. < L. *scrupulus*, small sharp stone] **1.** a very small quantity **2.** an apothecaries' weight equal to 1/3 dram (20 grains) **3.** a doubt arising from difficulty in deciding what is right, proper, etc.; qualm —***vt., vi.*** **-pled, -pling** to hesitate (at) from doubt; have scruples (about)

scru·pu·lous (skrōō′pyə ləs) ***adj.*** **1.** having or showing scruples; conscientiously honest **2.** demanding or using precision, care, and exactness —**scru′pu·los′i·ty** (-läs′ə tē), *pl.* **-ties, scru′pu·lous·ness** ***n.*** —**scru′pu·lous·ly** ***adv.***

scru·ti·nize (skrōōt′′n īz′) ***vt.*** **-nized′, -niz′ing** to look at carefully or examine closely —**scru′ti·niz′er** ***n.***

scru·ti·ny (-′n ē) ***n.***, *pl.* **-nies** [< LL. < L. *scrutari*, to search into carefully] **1.** a close examination **2.** a careful, continuous watch **3.** a lengthy, searching look

scu·ba (skōō′bə) ***n.*** [*s*(elf-)*c*(ontained) *u*(nderwater) *b*(reathing) *a*(pparatus)] a diver's apparatus with compressed-air tanks connected to a mouthpiece for breathing under water

scud (skud) ***vi.*** **scud′ded, scud′ding** [prob. < ON.] **1.** to move swiftly **2.** to be driven before the wind —***n.*** **1.** a scudding **2.** spray, rain, or snow driven by the wind **3.** very low, dark, swiftly moving clouds

scuff (skuf) ***vt.*** [prob. < or akin to ON. *skufa*, to shove] **1.** to scrape (the ground, etc.) with the feet **2.** to wear a rough place on the surface of **3.** to scrape (one's feet) on the ground, etc. —***vi.*** **1.** to walk without lifting the feet; shuffle **2.** to become scraped or worn in patches —***n.*** **1.** a noise or act of scuffing **2.** a worn or rough spot **3.** a loose-fitting house slipper, esp. one without a counter

scuf·fle (skuf′′l) ***vi.*** **-fled, -fling** [freq. of prec.] **1.** to struggle or fight in rough confusion **2.** to move in a confused hurry **3.** to drag one's feet —***n.*** **1.** a rough, confused fight **2.** the act or sound of feet shuffling

scull (skul) ***n.*** [prob. < Scand.] **1.** an oar mounted at the stern and worked from side to side to move a boat forward **2.** either of a pair of light oars used by a single rower **3.** a light racing boat for one, two, or four rowers —***vt., vi.*** to propel with a scull or sculls —**scull′er** ***n.***

scul·ler·y (skul′ər ē) ***n.***, *pl.* **-ler·ies** [< OFr., ult. < *escuelle*, a dish < L. *scutella*, a tray] a room adjoining the kitchen, where pots and pans are cleaned, etc.

scul·lion (skul′yən) ***n.*** [< OFr. < L. *scopa*, a broom] [Archaic] a servant doing the rough, dirty work in a kitchen

scul·pin (skul′pin) ***n.***, *pl.* **-pin, -pins:** see PLURAL, II, D, 2 [prob. < Fr. *scorpene* < L. *scorpaena:* see SCORPION] any of certain spiny sea fishes with a big head and wide mouth

sculpt (skulpt) ***vt., vi.*** [Fr. *sculpter*, ult. < L. *sculpere:* see SCULPTURE] **1.** to carve or model as a sculptor **2.** to give sculpturelike form to (hair, fabric, etc.) Also **sculp**

sculp·tor (skulp′tər) ***n.*** [L. < *sculpere*, to carve] an artist who models, carves, or fashions figures or forms of clay, stone, metal, wood, etc. —**sculp′tress** [Now Rare] ***n.fem.***

sculp·ture (-chər) ***n.*** [< L. < pp. of *sculpere*, to carve] **1.** the art of carving wood, chiseling stone, casting or welding metal, modeling clay, etc. into statues, figures, or the like **2.** any work or works of sculpture —***vt.*** **-tured, -tur·ing** **1.** to carve, chisel, etc. into statues, figures, etc. **2.** to portray in sculpture **3.** to form like sculpture **4.** to decorate with sculpture —***vi.*** to work as a sculptor —**sculp′tu·ral** ***adj.*** —**sculp′tu·ral·ly** ***adv.***

sculp·tur·esque (skulp′chə resk′) ***adj.*** like sculpture

scum (skum) ***n.*** [< MDu. *schum*] **1.** a thin layer of impurities which forms on the top of liquids **2.** worthless parts or things; refuse **3.** a mean, despicable person, or such people collectively —***vi.*** **scummed, scum′ming** to form scum

scum·my (skum′ē) ***adj.*** **-mi·er, -mi·est** **1.** of, like, or covered with scum **2.** [Colloq.] despicable; low; mean

scup (scup) ***n.***, *pl.* **scup, scups:** see PLURAL, II, D, 2 [< AmInd.] a brown-and-white porgy of the N Atlantic

scup·per (skup′ər) ***n.*** [< ?] **1.** an opening in a ship's side to allow water to run off the deck **2.** an opening in a wall to allow water to run off a floor or roof

scup·per·nong (skup′ər nôŋ′, -näŋ′) ***n.*** [< the *Scuppernong* River, N. Carolina] **1.** a golden-green grape of the southern U.S. **2.** sweet wine made from this grape

scurf (skʉrf) ***n.*** [< ON. hyp. *skurfr*] **1.** little, dry scales shed by the skin, as dandruff **2.** any scaly coating —**scurf′y** ***adj.*** **scurf′i·er, scurf′i·est**

scur·ril·ous (skʉr′ə ləs) ***adj.*** [< L. < *scurra*, buffoon] using or containing coarse, vulgar, or abusive language —**scur·ril·i·ty** (skə ril′ə tē) ***n.***, *pl.* **-ties** —**scur′ril·ous·ly** ***adv.*** —**scur′ril·ous·ness** ***n.***

scur·ry (skʉr′ē) ***vi.*** **-ried, -ry·ing** [< HURRY-SCURRY] to run hastily —***vt.*** to cause to scurry —***n.*** a scurrying

scur·vy (skʉr′vē) ***adj.*** **-vi·er, -vi·est** [< SCURF] low; mean; contemptible —***n.*** a disease resulting from a deficiency of vitamin C in the body and causing weakness, anemia, spongy gums, bleeding from the mucous membranes, etc. —**scur′vi·ly** ***adv.*** —**scur′vi·ness** ***n.***

scut (skut) ***n.*** [< ?] **1.** a short, stumpy tail, esp. of a rabbit or deer **2.** a contemptible person

scu·tate (skyōō′tāt) ***adj.*** [ModL. < L. < *scutum*, a shield] **1.** *Bot. same as* PELTATE **2.** *Zool.* covered by bony or horny plates or scales

scutch·eon (skuch′ən) ***n.*** *same as* ESCUTCHEON

scu·tel·lum (skyōō tel′əm) ***n.***, *pl.* **-tel′la** (-ə) **1.** [ModL., mistaken for L. dim. of *scutum*, a shield] *Bot.* any shield-shaped part **2.** [ModL. < L. *scutella:* see ff.] *Zool.* a small, horny scale or plate

scut·tle[1] (skut′′l) ***n.*** [OE. *scutel*, a dish < L. *scutella*] a kind of bucket used for pouring coal on a fire: in full, **coal scuttle**

scut·tle[2] (skut′'l) ***vi.* -tled, -tling** [prob. akin to SCUD] to scurry, esp. away from trouble, etc. —***n.*** a scurry
scut·tle[3] (skut′'l) ***n.*** [< MFr. < Sp. *escotilla*, dim. of *escote*, a notch] **1.** an opening in a wall or roof, fitted with a cover **2.** a small, covered opening in the hull or deck of a ship —***vt.* -tled, -tling** **1.** to make or open holes in the hull of (a ship) below the waterline; esp., to sink in this way **2.** to abandon (a plan, undertaking, etc.)
scut·tle·butt (-but′) ***n.*** [orig. < *scuttled butt*, lidded cask] **1.** *Naut.* a drinking fountain on shipboard **2.** [Colloq.] rumor or gossip
scu·tum (skyo͞ot′əm) ***n.**, pl.* **scu′ta** (-ə) [L.] **1.** the long, leather-covered, wooden shield of Roman infantrymen **2.** *Zool.* a heavy, horny scale, as on certain reptiles or insects: also **scute** (skyo͞ot)
Scyl·la (sil′ə) a dangerous rock on the southern Italian coast, opposite the whirlpool Charybdis —**between Scylla and Charybdis** facing danger or evil on either hand
scythe (sī*th*) ***n.*** [altered (after L. *scindere*, to cut) < OE. *sithe*] a tool with a long, single-edged blade on a bent wooden shaft, used in cutting tall grass, grain, etc. by hand —***vt.* scythed, scyth′ing** to cut with a scythe
Scyth·i·a (sith′ē ə) ancient region in SE Europe, on the N coast of the Black Sea —**Scyth′i·an** ***adj., n.***
S.Dak., SD South Dakota
Se *Chem.* selenium
SE, S.E., s.e. **1.** southeast **2.** southeastern

SCYTHE

sea (sē) ***n.*** [OE. *sæ*] **1.** the ocean **2.** a large body of salt water wholly or partly enclosed by land [the Red *Sea*] **3.** a large body of fresh water [the *Sea* of Galilee] **4.** the condition of the ocean's surface [a calm *sea*] **5.** a heavy swell or wave **6.** a very great amount or expanse **7.** *Astron. same as* MARE[2] (sense 2) —***adj.*** of, connected with, or for use at sea —**at sea** **1.** on the open sea **2.** uncertain; bewildered —**follow the sea** to be a sailor —**go to sea** to become a sailor —**put (out) to sea** to sail away from land
sea anchor a large, canvas-covered frame, usually conical, let out from a ship as a drag to reduce drifting or to keep the ship heading into the wind
sea anemone a sea polyp having a firm, gelatinous body topped with colored, petallike tentacles
sea bag a large, cylindrical bag in which a sailor carries his clothes and personal belongings
sea bass **1.** any of numerous sea fishes; esp., *a)* the **black sea bass,** a food fish with large scales and a wide mouth, found along the Atlantic coast of the U.S. *b)* the **giant sea bass,** found along the California coast **2.** any of various similar fishes, as the **white sea bass,** a drum found along the California coast
Sea·bee (sē′bē′) ***n.*** [< *CB*, short for *Construction Battalion*] a member of any of the construction and engineering battalions of the U.S. Navy
sea bird a bird living on or near the sea: also **sea fowl**
sea·board (-bôrd′) ***n.*** land or coastal region bordering on the sea —***adj.*** bordering on the sea
sea·borne (-bôrn′) ***adj.*** **1.** carried on or by the sea **2.** afloat: said of ships
sea breeze a breeze blowing inland from the sea
sea·coast (-kōst′) ***n.*** land bordering on the sea
sea cow **1.** any of several sea mammals, as the dugong or manatee **2.** *earlier name for* WALRUS
sea cucumber an echinoderm with a cucumber-shaped, flexible body and long tentacles around the mouth
sea dog **1.** an experienced sailor **2.** any of various seals
sea elephant a large seal that is hunted for oil: the male has a long proboscis
sea·far·er (-fer′ər) ***n.*** a traveler by sea; esp., a sailor
sea·far·ing (-fer′iŋ) ***adj.*** of or engaged in life at sea —***n.*** **1.** the occupation of a sailor **2.** travel by sea
sea·food (-fo͞od′) ***n.*** food prepared from or consisting of saltwater fish or shellfish
sea·girt (-gʉrt′) ***adj.*** surrounded by the sea
sea·go·ing (-gō′iŋ) ***adj.*** **1.** made for use on the open sea [a *seagoing* schooner] **2.** *same as* SEAFARING
sea green a pale bluish green —**sea′-green′** ***adj.***
sea gull *same as* GULL[1]; esp., any gull living along a seacoast
sea horse **1.** a small, semitropical marine fish with a slender tail, plated body, and a head somewhat like that of a horse **2.** a mythical sea creature, half fish and half horse
Sea Islands chain of islands off the coasts of S.C., Ga., & N Fla.
seal[1] (sēl) ***n.*** [< OFr. < L. *sigillum*, a seal, dim. of *signum*, a sign] **1.** a design, initials, etc. placed on a letter, document, etc. to prove it is authentic: letters were once commonly sealed with a molten wax wafer impressed with such a design **2.** a stamp or signet ring for making such an impression **3.** a wax wafer, piece of paper, etc. bearing an impressed design recognized as official **4.** *a)* something that closes or fastens tightly or securely *b)* a tight closure, as against the passage of air or water **5.** anything that guarantees; pledge **6.** a sign; token [a handshake as a *seal* of friendship] **7.** an ornamental paper stamp [a Christmas *seal*] —***vt.*** **1.** to mark with a seal **2.** to secure the contents of (a letter, etc.) by closing with a wax seal, a gummed flap, etc. **3.** to confirm the truth of (a promise, etc.) by some action **4.** to certify as being official, accurate, exact, etc. by or as by fixing a seal to **5.** to settle or determine finally [to *seal* one's fate] **6.** *a)* to close, etc. as with a seal [to *seal* one's lips] *b)* to close completely as to make airtight or watertight *c)* to apply a nonpermeable coating to (a porous surface, as a wood) —**seal off** **1.** to close completely **2.** to surround with barriers, a cordon, etc. —**set one's seal to** **1.** to mark with one's seal **2.** to endorse —**seal′a·ble** ***adj.*** —**seal′er** ***n.***
seal[2] (sēl) ***n.**, pl.* **seals, seal:** see PLURAL, II, D, 1 [OE. *seolh*] **1.** a sea mammal with a sleek coat and four flippers: it lives in cold waters and eats fish **2.** the fur of a fur seal **3.** leather made from sealskin —***vi.*** to hunt seals
Sea·lab (sē′lab′) ***n.*** [SEA + LAB(ORATORY)] any of a series of underwater laboratories of the U.S. Navy for undersea exploration and research
sea lamprey a parasitic lamprey of the N Atlantic that spawns in streams and is now landlocked in the Great Lakes
sea lane a commonly used route for travel by sea

FUR SEAL
(5–7 ft. long)

seal·ant (sēl′ənt) ***n.*** [SEAL[1] + -ANT] a substance, as a wax, plastic, silicone, etc., used for sealing
sea legs the ability to walk without loss of balance on board ship, esp. in a rough sea
seal·er·y (sēl′ər ē) ***n.**, pl.* **-er·ies** **1.** a place where seals are hunted **2.** the work of hunting seals Also **seal fishery**
sea level the level of the surface of the sea, esp. the mean level between high and low tide: used as a standard in measuring heights and depths
sea lily a stalked and attached crinoid
sealing wax a hard mixture of resin and turpentine used for sealing letters, dry cells, etc.: it softens when heated
sea lion a large, eared seal of the N Pacific
seal ring *same as* SIGNET RING
seal·skin (sēl′skin′) ***n.*** **1.** the skin of the seal; esp., the soft undercoat dyed dark-brown or black **2.** a garment made of this —***adj.*** made of sealskin
Sea·ly·ham terrier (sē′lē ham′, -əm) [< *Sealyham*, an estate in Wales] any of a breed of small, white terrier with short legs and square jaws
seam (sēm) ***n.*** [OE. *seam*] **1.** the line formed by sewing together two pieces of material **2.** any line marking joining edges, as of boards **3.** a mark, line, etc. like this, as a scar, wrinkle, etc. **4.** a layer or stratum of ore, coal, etc. —***vt.*** **1.** to join together so as to form a seam **2.** to mark with a seamlike line, crack, etc. —**seam′less** ***adj.***
sea·man (sē′mən) ***n.**, pl.* **-men** **1.** a sailor **2.** *U.S. Navy* a nonrated enlisted man whose duties are concerned with deck maintenance, equipment, etc. —**sea′man·like′** ***adj.***
sea·man·ship (-ship′) ***n.*** skill in sailing, navigating, or working a ship
seam·stress (sēm′stris) ***n.*** a woman who sews expertly or who makes her living by sewing
seam·y (sē′mē) ***adj.*** **seam′i·er, seam′i·est** **1.** having or showing seams **2.** unpleasant, squalid, or sordid [the *seamy* side of life] —**seam′i·ness** ***n.***
sé·ance (sā′äns) ***n.*** [Fr. < OFr. *seoir* < L. *sedere*, to sit] a meeting at which spiritualists seek or profess to communicate with the dead
sea otter a web-footed sea mammal, found along the N Pacific coast: its dark-brown fur is valuable
sea·plane (sē′plān′) ***n.*** any airplane designed to land on and take off from water
sea·port (-pôrt′) ***n.*** **1.** a port or harbor used by ocean ships **2.** a town or city having such a port
sear (sir) ***adj.*** [OE.] withered; sere —***vt.*** **1.** to dry up; wither **2.** to scorch or burn the surface of **3.** to brand with a hot iron **4.** to make callous or unfeeling —***n.*** a mark produced by searing —**sear′ing·ly** ***adv.***
search (sʉrch) ***vt.*** [< OFr. *cercher* < LL. *circare*, to go about < *circus*, ring] **1.** to go over and look through in order to find something [*search* the records] **2.** to examine (a person) for something concealed **3.** to examine carefully; probe [to *search* one's soul] —***vi.*** to make a search —***n.*** the act of searching; examination —**in search of** trying to find —**search me** [Slang] I do not know —**search out** to seek and find by searching —**search′a·ble** ***adj.*** —**search′er** ***n.***
search·ing (-iŋ) ***adj.*** **1.** examining thoroughly **2.** keen; piercing —**search′ing·ly** ***adv.***

search·light (-līt′) *n.* **1.** an apparatus on a swivel, that projects a strong, far-reaching beam of light **2.** such a beam

search warrant a legal document authorizing a police search, as for stolen articles, etc.

sea·scape (sē′skāp′) *n.* [SEA + (LAND)SCAPE] **1.** a view of the sea **2.** a drawing, painting, etc. of this

sea·shell (-shel′) *n.* the shell of any saltwater mollusk

sea·shore (-shôr′) *n.* land along the sea; seacoast

sea·sick·ness (-sik′nis) *n.* nausea, dizziness, etc. caused by the rolling or pitching of a ship at sea —**sea′sick′** *adj.*

sea·side (-sīd′) *n.* land along the sea; seashore —*adj.* at or of the seaside

sea·son (sē′z′n) *n.* [< OFr. < VL. *satio,* sowing time < L. < base of *serere,* to sow] **1.** any of the four divisions into which the year is divided; spring, summer, fall (or autumn), or winter **2.** the time of the year when something specified takes place, is popular, permitted, at its best, etc. *[*the harvest *season,* the hunting *season]* **3.** a period of time *[*the busy *season* in a factory*]* **4.** the fitting or convenient time **5.** the time of a specified festival or holiday *[*the Easter *season]* —*vt.* **1.** to make (food) more tasty by adding salt, spices, etc. **2.** to add zest or interest to **3.** to make more fit for use, as by aging, curing, etc. **4.** to make used to; accustom *[*a *seasoned* traveler*]* **5.** to temper; soften —*vi.* to become seasoned, as wood by drying —**for a season** for a while —**in season 1.** available fresh for use as food **2.** at the legally established time for being hunted or caught: said of game, etc. **3.** in or at the proper time **4.** early enough: also **in good season 5.** in heat: said of animals —**out of season** not in season —**sea′son·er** *n.*

sea·son·a·ble (-ə b'l) *adj.* **1.** suitable to or usual for the time of year **2.** timely; opportune —**sea′son·a·bly** *adv.*

sea·son·al (-əl) *adj.* of or depending on a season or the seasons *[seasonal* rains, *seasonal* work*]* —**sea′son·al·ly** *adv.*

sea·son·ing (-iŋ) *n.* anything that adds zest; esp., salt, spices, etc. added to food to make it more tasty

season ticket a ticket or set of tickets as for a series of concerts, sports events, etc. or for transportation, etc. for a given period of time

seat (sēt) *n.* [ON. *sæti*] **1.** the manner of sitting, as on horseback **2.** *a)* a place to sit, or the right to such a place, esp. as shown by a ticket *b)* a thing to sit on; chair, bench, etc. **3.** *a)* the buttocks *b)* the part of a garment covering the buttocks *c)* the part of a chair, etc. that supports the buttocks **4.** the right to sit as a member; membership *[*a *seat* on the stock exchange*]* **5.** a part or surface on which another part rests or fits **6.** the chief location, or center *[*the *seat* of government*]* —*vt.* **1.** to put or set in or on a seat **2.** to lead to a seat **3.** to have seats for *[*the car *seats* six*]* **4.** to put a seat in or on; reseat **5.** to put in a certain place, position, etc. —**be seated 1.** to get in a seat; sit down: also **take a seat 2.** to be sitting **3.** to be located, settled, etc. —**seat′less** *adj.*

seat belt anchored straps buckled across the hips, to protect a seated passenger, as in an automobile or airplane

-seat·er (sēt′ər) *a combining form meaning* a vehicle, etc. having (a specified number of) seats *[*a two-*seater]*

seat·ing (-iŋ) *n.* **1.** a providing with a seat or seats **2.** material for covering chair seats, etc. **3.** the arrangement of seats

SEATO (sē′tō) Southeast Asia Treaty Organization

Se·at·tle (sē at′'l) [after *Seathl,* an Indian chief] seaport in WC Wash., on Puget Sound: pop. 494,000 (met. area 1,601,000)

sea urchin a small sea animal with a round body in a shell covered with long, movable spines

sea wall a wall made to break the force of the waves and to protect the shore from erosion

sea·ward (sē′wərd) *adj., adv.* toward the sea: also, for *adv.,* **sea′wards** —*n.* a seaward direction or position

sea·way (-wā′) *n.* **1.** a way or route by sea **2.** a ship's headway **3.** a rough sea **4.** an inland waterway to the sea for ocean ships

sea·weed (-wēd′) *n.* **1.** any sea plant or plants; esp., any marine alga: in full, **marine seaweed 2.** any similar freshwater plant: in full, **freshwater seaweed**

sea·wor·thy (-wur′*th*ē) *adj.* fit to travel in on the open sea; sturdy: said of a ship —**sea′wor′thi·ness** *n.*

se·ba·ceous (si bā′shəs) *adj.* [< L. < *sebum,* tallow] of or like fat, tallow, or sebum; esp., designating certain skin glands that secrete sebum

Se·bas·tian (si bas′chən) [L. < Gr. < *Sebastia,* ancient city in Asia Minor] **1.** a masculine name **2.** Saint, ?–288? A.D.; Christian martyr of Rome

se·bum (sē′bəm) *n.* [L., tallow] the semiliquid, greasy secretion of the sebaceous glands

‡**sec** (sek) *adj.* [Fr.] dry; not sweet: said of wine

SEC, S.E.C. Securities and Exchange Commission

sec secant

sec. 1. second(s) **2.** secondary **3.** secretary **4.** section(s) **5.** sector **6.** security

se·cant (sē′kənt, -kant) *adj.* [< L. prp. of *secare,* to cut] cutting; intersecting —*n.* **1.** *Geom.* any straight line intersecting a curve at two or more points **2.** *Trigonometry* the ratio of the hypotenuse of a right triangle to either of the other two sides with reference to the enclosed angle

se·cede (si sēd′) *vi.* **-ced′ed, -ced′ing** [< L. < *se-,* apart + *cedere,* to go] to withdraw formally from a larger body, as from a political union —**se·ced′er** *n.*

se·ces·sion (si sesh′ən) *n.* **1.** a seceding **2.** *[often* **S-***]* the withdrawal of the Southern States from the Federal Union at the start of the Civil War —**se·ces′sion·al** *adj.* —**se·ces′sion·ism** *n.* —**se·ces′sion·ist** *n.*

Seck·el (pear) (sek′'l) [after the Pa. fruitgrower who originated it] a small, sweet, juicy, reddish-brown pear

se·clude (si klōōd′) *vt.* **-clud′ed, -clud′ing** [< L. *secludere* < *se-,* apart + *claudere,* to shut] **1.** to keep away or shut off from others; isolate **2.** to make private or hidden

se·clud·ed (-klōōd′id) *adj.* shut off or kept apart from others; isolated; withdrawn —**se·clud′ed·ly** *adv.*

se·clu·sion (si klōō′zhən) *n.* **1.** a secluding or being secluded; retirement; isolation **2.** a secluded spot —**se·clu′sive** *adj.* —**se·clu′sive·ly** *adv.* —**se·clu′sive·ness** *n.*

sec·ond[1] (sek′ənd) *adj.* [OFr. < L. *secundus* < *sequi,* to follow] **1.** coming next after the first in order; 2d or 2nd **2.** another; other; additional *[*a *second* helping*]* **3.** being of the same kind as another *[*a *second* Caesar*]* **4.** alternate *[*every *second* day*]* **5.** next below the first in rank, value, merit, etc. **6.** *Music a)* lower in pitch *b)* performing a part lower in pitch —*n.* **1.** the second person, thing, class, place, etc. **2.** the next after the first **3.** an article of merchandise that is not of the first quality **4.** an aid or assistant, as to a duelist or boxer **5.** the second forward gear ratio of a motor vehicle **6.** [Slang] *[pl.]* a second helping of food —*vt.* **1.** to act as an aid to; assist **2.** to give support or encouragement to; reinforce **3.** to indicate formal support of (a motion, etc.) so that it may be discussed or voted on —*adv.* in the second place, group, etc. —**sec′ond·er** *n.*

sec·ond[2] (sek′ənd) *n.* [ML. (*pars minuta*) *secunda,* second (small part): from being a further division (i.e., beyond the minute)] **1.** 1/60 of a minute of time **2.** 1/60 of a minute of angular measurement **3.** a very short time; instant **4.** a specific point in time

Second Advent *same as* SECOND COMING

sec·ond·ar·y (sek′ən der′ē) *adj.* **1.** second, or below the first, in rank, importance, place, etc.; subordinate; minor **2.** *a)* coming from something considered primary or original; derivative *b)* second-hand; not original *[*a *secondary* source of information*]* *c)* designating colors derived by mixing two primary colors: see COLOR (*n.* 3) **3.** coming after the first in a series of processes, events, stages, etc. **4.** *Elec.* designating or of an induced current or its circuit **5.** *Zool.* designating or of the long flight feathers on the second joint of a bird's wing —*n., pl.* **-ar′ies 1.** a person or thing that is secondary, subordinate, etc. **2.** any of the secondary colors **3.** *Elec.* an output winding of a transformer from which the power is taken **4.** *Football* the defensive backfield —**sec′ond·ar′i·ly** *adv.*

secondary accent (or **stress**) **1.** any accent, or stress, that is weaker than the full, or primary, accent **2.** a mark (in this dictionary, ′) to show this

secondary school a school, as a high school, coming after elementary school

second banana [Slang] **1.** a subordinate performer in a show, esp. burlesque, as one who plays straight man to the top banana, or star comedian **2.** any person in a subordinate position

second base *Baseball* the base between first base and third base, located behind the pitcher

second childhood feeble and childish state due to old age

sec·ond-class (sek′ənd klas′) *adj.* **1.** of the class, rank, quality, etc. next below the highest **2.** designating or of travel accommodations next below the best **3.** designating or of a class of mail consisting of newspapers, periodicals, etc. **4.** inferior, inadequate, etc. —*adv.* **1.** with second-class accommodations **2.** as or by second-class mail

Second Coming in the theology of some Christian sects, the expected return of Christ, at the Last Judgment

second cousin the child of one's parent's first cousin

second growth tree growth on land stripped of virgin forest

sec·ond-guess (sek′ənd ges′) *vt., vi.* [Colloq.] to use hindsight in criticizing (someone or something), remaking (a decision), etc. —**sec′ond-guess′er** *n.*

sec·ond·hand (-hand′) *adj.* **1.** not direct from the original source; not original **2.** used or worn previously by

another; not new 3. of or dealing in merchandise that is not new —*adv.* not firsthand; not directly
second hand the hand (of a clock or watch) that indicates the seconds and moves around the dial once every minute
second lieutenant a commissioned officer of the lowest rank in the U.S. Army, Air Force, or Marine Corps
sec·ond·ly (sek′ənd lē) *adv.* in the second place; second
second nature acquired habits, etc. fixed so deeply as to seem part of a person's nature
second person that form of a pronoun (as *you*) or verb (as *are*) which refers to the person(s) spoken to
sec·ond-rate (-rāt′) *adj.* 1. second in quality, rank, etc,; second-class 2. inferior; mediocre —**sec′ond-rat′er** *n.*
second sight the supposed ability to see things not physically present, to foresee the future, etc.
sec·ond-string (-striŋ′) *adj.* [Colloq.] 1. *Sports* that is the second or a substitute choice for play at a specified position 2. second-rate; inferior —**sec′ond-string′er** *n.*
second wind 1. the return of normal ease in breathing after the feeling one has at first of being exhausted from hard exercise 2. recovered capacity for continuing any effort
se·cre·cy (sē′krə sē) *n., pl.* **-cies** 1. a being secret 2. the practice or habit of being secretive
se·cret (sē′krit) *adj.* [< OFr. < L. pp. of *secernere* < *se-*, apart + *cernere*, to sift, discern] 1. kept from the knowledge of others 2. remote; secluded 3. keeping one's affairs to oneself; secretive 4. beyond general understanding; mysterious 5. concealed from sight or notice; hidden [a *secret* drawer] 6. acting in secret [a *secret* society] —*n.* 1. something known only to some and kept from the knowledge of others 2. something not understood or explained; mystery 3. the true explanation, regarded as not obvious [the *secret* of success] —**in secret** without the knowledge of others; secretly —**se′cret·ly** *adv.*
secret agent a person who carries on espionage or similar work of a secret nature, as for a government
sec·re·tar·i·at (sek′rə ter′ē ət) *n.* 1. the office, position, or quarters of a secretary of high position in a government, etc. 2. a staff headed by a secretary-general
sec·re·tar·y (sek′rə ter′ē) *n., pl.* **-tar′ies** [ML. *secretarius*, one entrusted with secrets < L. *secretum*: see SECRET] 1. *a*) a person whose work is keeping records, handling correspondence, etc. as for an executive in a business office *b*) an officer of a company, club, etc. having somewhat similar duties 2. an official in charge of a department of government 3. a writing desk, esp. one topped with a small bookcase —**sec′re·tar′i·al** *adj.* —**sec′re·tar′y·ship′** *n.*
secretary bird [from the penlike feathers of its crest] a large, grayish-blue and black African bird of prey with a long neck and long legs
sec·re·tar·y-gen·er·al (-jen′ər əl) *n., pl.* **-tar′ies-gen′er·al** the chief administrative officer of an organization, in charge of a secretariat
se·crete (si krēt′) *vt.* **-cret′ed, -cret′ing** [< L. pp. of *secernere*: see SECRET] 1. to hide; conceal 2. to form and release (a specified secretion) as a gland, etc. does
se·cre·tion (si krē′shən) *n.* 1. a hiding or concealing of something 2. *a*) the process by which a substance is formed from the blood or sap and then released into the organism or as a waste product *b*) such a substance
se·cre·tive (sē′krə tiv; *also, & for 2 always,* si krēt′iv) *adj.* [SECRET + -IVE] 1. keeping one's affairs to oneself; not frank; reticent 2. *same as* SECRETORY —**se′cre·tive·ly** *adv.* —**se′cre·tive·ness** *n.*
se·cre·to·ry (si krēt′ər ē) *adj.* of, or having the function of, secretion —*n.* a secretory gland, etc.
secret police a police force that operates secretly, esp. in order to suppress opposition to the government
secret service a government service that carries on secret investigation; specif., [S- S-] a division of the U.S. Treasury Department for uncovering counterfeiters, protecting the President, etc.
sect (sekt) *n.* [< MFr. < L. < *sequi*, to follow] 1. a religious denomination, esp. one that has broken away from an established church 2. a group of people or a faction having a common leadership, philosophy, etc.
sec·tar·i·an (sek ter′ē ən) *adj.* 1. of or relating to a sect 2. devoted to some sect 3. narrow-minded —*n.* 1. a member of any religious sect 2. a person who is blindly devoted to a sect —**sec·tar′i·an·ism** *n.*
sec·ta·ry (sek′tər ē) *n., pl.* **-ries** a member of a sect
sec·tion (sek′shən) *n.* [< L. < pp. of *secare*, to cut] 1. a cutting or separating by cutting; specif., an incision in surgery 2. a part separated by cutting; slice; division 3. *a*) a division of a book, newspaper, etc. *b*) a numbered paragraph of a law, etc. 4. any distinct or separate part [a bookcase in *sections*] 5. a segment of an orange, etc. 6. a division of public lands that is a mile square (640 acres) 7. a drawing, etc. of a thing as it would appear if cut straight through in a given plane 8. any one of two or more buses, trains, or airplanes for a particular run or flight 9. *Railroading* *a*) a part of a sleeping car containing an upper and lower berth *b*) a division of the right of way maintained by a single crew —*vt.* 1. to divide into sections 2. to represent in sections
sec·tion·al (sek′shən ′l) *adj.* 1. of or devoted to a given section or district 2. made up of or divided into sections —*n.* a sectional sofa, bookcase, etc. —**sec′tion·al·ly** *adv.*
sec·tion·al·ism (-iz'm) *n.* narrow-minded concern shown for one section of a country —**sec′tion·al·ist** *adj., n.*
sec·tor (sek′tər) *n.* [LL. < L., cutter < *secare*, to cut] 1. part of a circle bounded by any two radii and the included arc 2. a mathematical instrument, as for measuring angles, consisting of two scaled rulers jointed together at one end 3. any of the districts into which an area is divided for military operations 4. a distinct part of a society or of an economy, group, etc. —*vt.* to divide into sectors —**sec′tor·al, sec·to′ri·al** (-tôr′ē əl) *adj.*
sec·u·lar (sek′yə lər) *adj.* [< OFr. < LL. < L. < *saeculum*, an age, generation] 1. *a*) not related to church or religion; not sacred or religious; temporal; worldly [*secular* schools] *b*) of secularism 2. living in the outside world and not bound by a monastic vow [the *secular* clergy] —*n.* a member of the secular clergy —**sec′u·lar·ly** *adv.*
sec·u·lar·ism (-iz'm) *n.* 1. worldly spirit, views, etc.; esp., a system of beliefs and practices that rejects any form of religious faith 2. the belief that religion should be strictly separated from the state or government, esp. from public education —**sec′u·lar·ist** *n., adj.* —**sec′u·lar·is′tic** *adj.*
sec·u·lar·ize (sek′yə lə rīz′) *vt.* **-ized′, -iz′ing** 1. to change from religious to civil ownership or use 2. to deprive of religious character, influence, etc. 3. to convert to secularism —**sec′u·lar·i·za′tion** *n.*
se·cure (si kyoor′) *adj.* [< L. < *se-*, free from + *cura*, care] 1. free from fear, care, doubt, etc.; not worried, troubled, etc. 2. free from danger; safe 3. in safekeeping 4. firm; stable [make the knot *secure*] 5. reliable; dependable —*vt.* **-cured′, -cur′ing** 1. to make secure, or safe; protect 2. to make sure or certain; guarantee, as with a pledge [to *secure* a loan with collateral] 3. to make firm, fast, etc. [*secure* the bolt] 4. to obtain; acquire; get [to *secure* aid] 5. to capture —*vi.* to give security —**se·cur′a·ble** *adj.* —**se·cur′ance** *n.* —**se·cure′ly** *adv.* —**se·cur′er** *n.*
se·cu·ri·ty (si kyoor′ə tē) *n., pl.* **-ties** 1. the state of being or feeling free from fear, anxiety, danger, doubt, etc. 2. protection or defense, as against attack, espionage, etc. [funds for national *security*] 3. *a*) something given as a pledge of repayment, etc. *b*) a person who promises to pay another's debt if he fails to pay it 4. a stock certificate or bond: *usually used in pl.*
Security Council the United Nations council responsible for maintaining international peace and security
secy., sec'y. secretary
se·dan (si dan′) *n.* [< ? L. *sedere*, to sit] 1. *same as* SEDAN CHAIR 2. an enclosed automobile with two or four doors, and two wide seats, front and rear
sedan chair an enclosed chair for one person, carried on poles by two men

SEDAN CHAIR

se·date[1] (si dāt′) *adj.* [< L. pp. of *sedare*, to settle] calm or composed; esp., serious and unemotional; decorous —**se·date′ly** *adv.* —**se·date′ness** *n.*
se·date[2] (si dāt′) *vt.* **-dat′ed, -dat′ing** [< SEDATIVE] to dose with a sedative
se·da·tion (si dā′shən) *n.* *Med.* 1. the reducing of excitement, nervousness, or irritation by means of sedatives 2. the calm state produced by sedatives
sed·a·tive (sed′ə tiv) *adj.* [see SEDATE[1]] tending to soothe or quiet; specif., *Med.* producing sedation —*n.* a sedative medicine
sed·en·tar·y (sed′'n ter′ē) *adj.* [< Fr. < L. < prp. of *sedere*, to sit] 1. *a*) tending to sit much of the time *b*) keeping one seated much of the time [a *sedentary* job] 2. *a*) not migratory, as some birds *b*) fixed to one spot, as a barnacle —**sed′en·tar′i·ly** *adv.* —**sed′en·tar′i·ness** *n.*
Se·der (sā′dər) *n., pl.* **Se·dar·im** (sə där′im), **Se′ders** [Heb. *sēdher*, arrangement] *Judaism* the Passover feast commemorating the exodus of the Jews from Egypt
sedge (sej) *n.* [OE. *secg*] any of several coarse, grasslike plants often found on wet ground or in water —**sedg′y** *adj.*
sed·i·ment (sed′ə mənt) *n.* [< Fr. < L. < *sedere*, to sit] 1. matter that settles to the bottom of a liquid 2. *Geol.* matter deposited by water or wind —**sed′i·men′tal** (-men′t'l) *adj.* —**sed′i·men·ta′tion** (-men tā′shən) *n.*
sed·i·men·ta·ry (sed′ə men′tər ē) *adj.* 1. of, like, or containing sediment 2. formed by the deposit of sediment, as certain rocks —**sed′i·men′ta·ri·ly** *adv.*
se·di·tion (si dish′ən) *n.* [OFr. < L. < *sed-*, apart + *itio*, a going < *ire*, to go] a stirring up of rebellion against the government —**se·di′tion·ist** *n.*

se·di·tious (si dish′əs) ***adj.*** **1.** of, like, or constituting sedition **2.** stirring up rebellion —**se·di′tious·ly** ***adv.*** —**se·di′tious·ness** ***n.***

se·duce (si do͞os′, -dyo͞os′) ***vt.*** **-duced′, -duc′ing** [< LL. < L. < *se-*, apart + *ducere*, to lead] **1.** *a)* to persuade to do something disloyal, disobedient, etc. *b)* to tempt to evil or wrongdoing; lead astray *c)* to persuade to engage in unlawful sexual intercourse, esp. for the first time **2.** to entice —**se·duce′ment** ***n.*** —**se·duc′er** ***n.*** —**se·duc′i·ble** ***adj.***

se·duc·tion (si duk′shən) ***n.*** **1.** a seducing or being seduced **2.** something that seduces

se·duc·tive (-tiv) ***adj.*** tending to seduce, or lead astray; enticing —**se·duc′tive·ly** ***adv.*** —**se·duc′tive·ness** ***n.***

se·duc·tress (-tris) ***n.*** a woman who seduces

sed·u·lous (sej′oo ləs) ***adj.*** [L. *sedulus*, ult. < *se-*, apart + *dolus*, trickery] working hard and steadily; diligent and persistent —**se·du·li·ty** (si dyo͞ol′ə tē, -do͞ol′-), **sed′u·lous·ness** ***n.*** —**sed′u·lous·ly** ***adv.***

se·dum (sē′dəm) ***n.*** [ModL., genus name < L.] any of a genus of plants found on rocks and walls, with fleshy stalks and leaves and white, yellow, or pink flowers

see[1] (sē) ***vt.*** **saw, seen, see′ing** [OE. *seon*] **1.** *a)* to get knowledge of through the eyes; look at *b)* to picture mentally **2.** *a)* to grasp mentally; understand *b)* to accept as proper [I can't *see* him as president] *c)* to consider; judge [*saw* it as his duty] **3.** to find out; learn [*see* who's there] **4.** to know by experience [has *seen* better days] **5.** to look over; inspect **6.** to make sure [*see* that he goes] **7.** *a)* to escort [to *see* someone home] *b)* to keep company with **8.** to encounter; meet **9.** to call on; visit or consult [*see* a lawyer] **10.** to admit to one's presence; receive [too ill to *see* anyone] **11.** to be a spectator at; view or attend [*see* a show] **12.** *Card Games* to meet (a bet) of (another) by staking an equal sum —***vi.*** **1.** to have the power of sight **2.** to discern objects, colors, etc. by using the eyes [able to *see* far] **3.** *a)* to take a look *b)* to investigate or inquire **4.** to understand **5.** to think something over; reflect [let's *see*, where is it?] —***interj.*** behold! look! —**see about** **1.** to inquire into **2.** to attend to —**see after** to take care of —**see fit (to)** to think it is proper (to do something) —**see into** **1.** to look into **2.** to perceive the true meaning or nature of —**see off** to go with and watch (another) leave by plane, boat, bus, etc. —**see out** **1.** to go through with; finish **2.** to wait till the end of —**see through** **1.** to perceive the true meaning or character of **2.** to carry out to the end; finish **3.** to help through a time of difficulty —**see to** to attend to —**see′a·ble** ***adj.***

see[2] (sē) ***n.*** [< OFr. *sie* < L. *sedes*, a seat] **1.** the official seat, or center of authority, of a bishop **2.** the position, authority, or jurisdiction of a bishop

seed (sēd) ***n., pl.*** **seeds, seed:** see PLURAL, II, D, 4 [OE. *sæd*] **1.** the part of a flowering plant that contains the embryo and will develop into a new plant if sown **2.** loosely, *a)* any part, as a bulb, from which a new plant will grow *b)* a small, seedlike fruit **3.** seeds used for sowing **4.** source; origin [the *seeds* of revolt] **5.** family stock; ancestry **6.** descendants; posterity **7.** *same as* SPAT[4] **8.** seed-bearing condition [in *seed*] **9.** *same as* SPORE (*n.* 2) **10.** sperm or semen **11.** something tiny, like a seed; esp., *a)* a tiny crystal or particle *b)* a tiny bubble, as in glassware **12.** *Sports* a seeded player —***vt.*** **1.** to plant with seeds **2.** to sow (seeds) **3.** to remove the seeds from **4.** to sprinkle particles of dry ice, silver iodide, etc. into (clouds), as in trying to produce rainfall **5.** to provide with the means or stimulus for growing or developing **6.** *Sports* *a)* to distribute the names of contestants in (the draw for position in a tournament) so as to avoid matching the most skilled too early *b)* to treat (any of the most skilled players) thus —***vi.*** **1.** to become ripe and produce seeds **2.** to shed seeds **3.** to sow seeds —**go** (or **run**) **to seed** **1.** to shed seeds after flowering **2.** to become weak, useless, etc. —**seed′ed** ***adj.*** —**seed′er** ***n.*** —**seed′less** ***adj.***

seed·bed (-bed′) ***n.*** a bed of soil, usually covered with glass, in which seedlings are grown for transplanting

seed·case (-kās′) ***n.*** *same as* SEED VESSEL

seed coral fragments of coral used in ornaments

seed leaf *same as* COTYLEDON

seed·ling (-liŋ) ***n.*** **1.** a plant grown from a seed, rather than from a cutting, etc. **2.** any young plant; esp., a young tree less than three feet high

seed money money made available to begin the financing of, or to attract additional funds for, a long-term project

seed oysters oyster spat; very young oysters, esp. at the stage suitable for relocation

seed pearl a very small pearl, often imperfect

seed plant *same as* SPERMATOPHYTE

seed·pod (-päd′) ***n.*** a carpel or pistil, enclosing ovules or seeds in angiosperms

seeds·man (sēdz′mən) ***n., pl.*** **-men** **1.** a sower of seeds **2.** a dealer in seeds Also **seed′man**

seed·time (sēd′tīm′) ***n.*** the season for sowing seeds

seed vessel any dry, hollow fruit, as a pod, containing seed

seed·y (sēd′ē) ***adj.*** **seed′i·er, seed′i·est** **1.** containing many seeds **2.** gone to seed **3.** shabby, run-down, or looking bad, ill, etc. —**seed′i·ly** ***adv.*** —**seed′i·ness** ***n.***

see·ing (sē′iŋ) ***n.*** **1.** the sense or power of sight **2.** the use of the eyes to see —***adj.*** having the sense of sight —***conj.*** considering; inasmuch as

Seeing Eye dog [*also* **s- e-**] a guide dog, specif. one trained by Seeing Eye, Inc., near Morristown, N.J.

seek (sēk) ***vt.*** **sought, seek′ing** [OE. *secan*] **1.** to try to find; look for **2.** to go to; resort to [to *seek* the woods for peace] **3.** *a)* to try to get or find out by asking or searching [to *seek* an answer] *b)* to request; ask for **4.** to try for; aim at [*seeking* perfection] **5.** to try: used with an infinitive [to *seek* to please] —***vi.*** to look for someone or something —**seek′er** ***n.***

seem (sēm) ***vi.*** [prob. < ON. *sæma*, to conform to] **1.** *a)* to appear to be [to *seem* glad] *b)* to appear: usually used with an infinitive [he *seems* to know] *c)* to have the impression; think: used with an infinitive [I *seem* to recall] **2.** to appear to exist [there *seems* no end] **3.** to be apparently true [it *seems* he was here]

seem·ing (-iŋ) ***adj.*** that seems real, true, etc. without necessarily being so; apparent [her *seeming* anger] —***n.*** outward appearance; semblance —**seem′ing·ly** ***adv.***

seem·ly (sēm′lē) ***adj.*** **-li·er, -li·est** [< ON. < *sæmr*, fitting] **1.** pleasing in appearance **2.** suitable, proper, decorous, etc. —***adv.*** in a seemly way —**seem′li·ness** ***n.***

seen (sēn) *pp. of* SEE[1]

seep (sēp) ***vi.*** [OE. *sipian*, to soak] to leak, drip, or flow out slowly through small openings; ooze —***n.*** **1.** a seeping **2.** liquid that seeps —**seep′age** (-ij) ***n.*** —**seep′y** ***adj.***

seer (sē′ər *for 1;* sir *for 2*) ***n.*** **1.** a person who sees **2.** a person with the supposed power to foretell the future

seer·suck·er (sir′suk′ər) ***n.*** [< Hindi < Per. *shir u shakar*, lit., milk and sugar] a light fabric of cotton, etc. woven with alternating crinkled stripes in various patterns

see·saw (sē′sô′) ***n.*** [redupl. of SAW[1]] **1.** a plank balanced at the middle, used by children at play, who ride the ends so that when one goes up, the other comes down **2.** such a riding **3.** any up-and-down or back-and-forth movement or change —***adj.*** moving up and down or back and forth —***vt., vi.*** to move on a seesaw or like a seesaw

seethe (sē*th*) ***vt.*** **seethed, seeth′ing** [OE. *sēothan*] **1.** to cook by boiling **2.** to soak or saturate in liquid —***vi.*** **1.** to boil or to surge, foam, etc. as if boiling **2.** to be violently agitated —***n.*** a seething

seg·ment (seg′mənt; *for v.* -ment) ***n.*** [L. *segmentum* < *secare*, to cut] **1.** any of the parts into which something is separated or separable; section **2.** *Geom.* any part, esp. of a circle or sphere, cut off by a line or plane —***vt., vi.*** to divide into segments —**seg·men′tal** (-men′t'l), **seg′men·tar′y** ***adj.*** —**seg·men′tal·ly** ***adv.***

seg·men·ta·tion (seg′mən tā′shən, -men-) ***n.*** **1.** a dividing or being divided into segments **2.** *Biol.* the progressive growth and cleavage of a single cell into others to form a new organism

se·go (sē′gō) ***n., pl.*** **-gos** [< AmInd.] **1.** a perennial bulb plant with trumpet-shaped flowers, found in western N. America: in full, **sego lily** **2.** its edible bulb

seg·re·gate (seg′rə gāt′; *for adj. usually* -git) ***adj.*** [< L. pp. of *segregare* < *se-*, apart + *grex* (gen. *gregis*), a flock] separate; set apart —***vt.*** **-gat′ed, -gat′ing** to set apart from others; isolate; specif., to impose a system of segregation on (racial groups, social facilities, etc.) —***vi.*** to become segregated —**seg′re·gat′ive** ***adj.***

seg·re·gat·ed (seg′rə gāt′id) ***adj.*** conforming to a system that segregates racial groups

seg·re·ga·tion (seg′rə gā′shən) ***n.*** a segregating or being segregated; specif., the policy or practice of compelling racial groups to live apart from each other, go to separate schools, etc. —**seg′re·ga′tion·ist** ***n., adj.***

se·gue (seg′wā, sā′gwā) ***vi.*** **-gued, -gue·ing** [< It., ult. < L. *sequi*, to follow] to continue without break (*to* or *into*) the next part or what follows —***n.*** a segueing

sei·del (zī′d'l, sī′-) ***n., pl.*** **-dels, -del** [G. < MHG. < L. *situla*, a bucket] a large beer mug, often with a hinged lid

sei·gneur (sen yʉr′, sān-, sēn-) ***n.*** [Fr. < MFr.: see SEIGNIOR] **1.** *same as* SEIGNIOR **2.** the owner of a seigneury (sense 2) —**sei·gneur′i·al** (-ē əl) ***adj.***

sei·gneur·y (sen′yər ē, sān′-, sēn′-) ***n., pl.*** **-gneur·ies** **1.** *same as* SEIGNIORY (sense 1) **2.** in French Canada, an estate granted by royal decree to 17th-cent. French settlers

sei·gnior (sēn′yər) ***n.*** [< Anglo-Fr. < OFr. < L. *senior:* see SENIOR] a lord or noble; specif., the lord of a fief

sei·gnio·ri·al, sei·gno·ri·al (sēn yôr′ē əl) ***adj.*** of or relating to a seignior: also **sei·gnior·al, sei·gnor·al** (sēn′-yər əl)

sei·gnior·y (sēn′yər ē) ***n.,*** *pl.* **-gnior·ies** **1.** the estate of a seignior **2.** the rights or authority of a feudal lord

Seine (sān; *Fr.* sen) river in N France, flowing through Paris into the English Channel

seine (sān) ***n.*** [OE. *segne,* ult. < L. < Gr. *sagēnē*] a large fishing net with floats along the top edge and weights along the bottom —***vt., vi.*** **seined, sein′ing** to fish with a seine

seis·mic (sīz′mik, sīs′-) ***adj.*** [< Gr. *seismos,* an earthquake < *seiein,* to shake] of, relating to, or caused by an earthquake or earthquakes or similar, but man-made, tremors —**seis′mi·cal·ly** ***adv.***

seis·mo- [< Gr. *seismos:* see prec.] *a combining form meaning* earthquake *[seismogram]*

seis·mo·gram (sīz′mə gram′, sīs′-) ***n.*** the chart of an earthquake as recorded by a seismograph

seis·mo·graph (-graf′) ***n.*** an instrument that records the intensity and duration of earthquakes and similar tremors —**seis·mog·ra·pher** (sīz mäg′rə fər, sīs-) ***n.*** —**seis′mo-graph′ic** ***adj.*** —**seis·mog′ra·phy** ***n.***

seis·mol·o·gy (sīz mäl′ə jē, sīs-) ***n.*** [SEISMO- + -LOGY] a geophysical science dealing with earthquakes and related phenomena —**seis′mo·log′ic** (-mə läj′ik), **seis′mo·log′i-cal** ***adj.*** —**seis′mo·log′i·cal·ly** ***adv.*** —**seis·mol′o·gist** ***n.***

seize (sēz) ***vt.*** **seized, seiz′ing** [< OFr. *saisir* < ML. *sacire,* prob. < Frank.] **1.** *a)* orig., to give a feudal holding to *b)* to give ownership to: in the passive voice *[seized* of the lands*]* **2.** *a)* to take possession of by legal power; confiscate *[*to *seize* contraband*]* *b)* to capture and put into custody; arrest; apprehend **3.** to take forcibly or quickly; grasp *[*to *seize* a weapon, to *seize* power*]* **4.** *a)* to suddenly fill the mind of *[*an idea *seized* him*]* *b)* to grasp with the mind, esp. suddenly **5.** to afflict suddenly *[seized* with tremors*]* **6.** *Naut.* to bind with cord, etc. —**seize on** (or **upon**) to grasp or take eagerly —**seiz′a·ble** ***adj.*** —**seiz′er** ***n.***

sei·zin (sē′zin) ***n.*** [< OFr.: see prec.] legal possession, esp. of a freehold estate —**sei′zor** ***n.***

sei·zure (sē′zhər) ***n.*** **1.** a seizing or being seized **2.** a sudden attack, as of disease

sel. **1.** selected **2.** selection(s)

sel·dom (sel′dəm) ***adv.*** [OE. *seldan*] not often; rarely —***adj.*** rare; infrequent —**sel′dom·ness** ***n.***

se·lect (sə lekt′) ***adj.*** [L. *selectus,* pp. of *seligere* < *se-,* apart + *legere,* to choose] **1.** chosen in preference to others; specially picked **2.** choice; excellent **3.** careful in choosing; discriminating **4.** limited to certain people or groups; exclusive —***vt., vi.*** to choose, as for excellence —**se·lect′ness** ***n.*** —**se·lec′tor** ***n.***

se·lect·ee (sə lek′tē′) ***n.*** a person inducted into the armed forces under selective service

se·lec·tion (sə lek′shən) ***n.*** **1.** a selecting or being selected **2.** *a)* a thing, person, or group chosen *b)* a variety to choose from **3.** *Biol.* any process by which certain organisms or genetic characters naturally survive over others or are bred to do so: see NATURAL SELECTION

se·lec·tive (-tiv) ***adj.*** **1.** of or characterized by selection **2.** having the power of selecting, or tending to select **3.** *Radio* excluding undesired frequencies when tuned to a specific station —**se·lec′tive·ly** ***adv.*** —**se·lec′tive·ness** ***n.***

selective service compulsory military training and service according to age, physical fitness, etc.

se·lec·tiv·i·ty (sə lek′tiv′ə tē) ***n.*** **1.** the state or quality of being selective **2.** the degree to which a radio receiver is selective

se·lect·man (sə lekt′mən; *locally, also* sē′lekt man′) ***n.,*** *pl.* **-men** (-mən, -men′) any of a board of officers elected in New England towns to manage municipal affairs

Se·le·ne (si lē′nē) the Greek goddess of the moon

sel·e·nite (sel′ə nīt′) ***n.*** [< L. < Gr. *selēnitēs* (*lithos*), lit., moon (stone)] a kind of gypsum in crystalline form

se·le·ni·um (sə lē′nē əm) ***n.*** [ModL. < Gr. *selēnē,* the moon] a nonmetallic chemical element whose electrical conductivity varies with the intensity of light: used in photoelectric devices, etc.: symbol, Se; at. wt., 78.96; at. no., 34

self (self) ***n.,*** *pl.* **selves** [OE.] **1.** the identity, character, or essential qualities of a person or thing **2.** one's own person or being as apart from all others **3.** one's own well-being or advantage —***pron.*** [Colloq.] myself, himself, herself, or yourself *[*tickets for *self* and wife*]* —***adj.*** **1.** uniform throughout **2.** of the same kind, color, material, etc. as the rest *[*a *self* lining*]*

self- *a prefix used in hyphenated compounds, meaning:* **1.** of oneself or itself *[self-*restraint*]* **2.** by oneself or itself *[self-*starting*]* **3.** in oneself or itself *[self-*centered*]* **4.** to, with, or for oneself or itself *[self-*addressed, *self-*pity*]*

self-a·base·ment (self′ə bās′mənt) ***n.*** abasement or humiliation of oneself

self-ab·ne·ga·tion (-ab′nə gā′shən) ***n.*** lack of consideration for oneself; self-denial

self-ab·sorp·tion (-əb zôrp′shən, -sôrp′-) ***n.*** absorption in one's own interests, affairs, etc. —**self′-ab·sorbed′** ***adj.***

self-a·buse (-ə byōōs′) ***n.*** *a euphemism for* MASTURBATION

self-act·ing (-ak′tiŋ) ***adj.*** working by itself; automatic

self-ad·dressed (-ə drest′) ***adj.*** addressed to oneself *[*a *self-addressed* envelope*]*

self-ad·vance·ment (-əd vans′mənt) ***n.*** the advancing or promoting of one's own interests

self-ap·point·ed (-ə point′tid) ***adj.*** acting as such on one's own, but not recognized as such by others *[*a *self-appointed* censor*]*

self-as·ser·tion (-ə sur′shən) ***n.*** the act of demanding recognition for oneself or of insisting upon one's rights, claims, etc. —**self′-as·ser′tive, self′-as·sert′ing** ***adj.***

self-as·sur·ance (-ə shoor′əns) ***n.*** confidence in oneself, one's own ability, talent, etc. —**self′-as·sured′** ***adj.***

self-cen·tered (-sen′tərd) ***adj.*** occupied or concerned only with one's own affairs; egocentric; selfish

self-col·ored (-kul′ərd) ***adj.*** **1.** of only one color **2.** of the natural or original color, as a fabric

self-com·mand (-kə mand′) ***n.*** *same as* SELF-CONTROL

self-com·pla·cent (-kəm plā′s′nt) ***adj.*** self-satisfied, esp. in a smug way —**self′-com·pla′cen·cy** ***n.***

self-con·ceit (-kən sēt′) ***n.*** too high an opinion of oneself; conceit —**self′-con·ceit′ed** ***adj.***

self-con·fessed (-kən fest′) ***adj.*** being such by one's own admission *[*a *self-confessed* thief*]*

self-con·fi·dence (-kän′fə dəns) ***n.*** confidence in oneself, one's own abilities, etc. —**self′-con′fi·dent** ***adj.*** —**self′-con′fi·dent·ly** ***adv.***

self-con·scious (-kän′shəs) ***adj.*** **1.** unduly conscious of oneself as an object of notice; embarrassed or ill at ease **2.** showing embarrassment *[*a *self-conscious* cough*]* —**self′-con′scious·ly** ***adv.*** —**self′-con′scious·ness** ***n.***

self-con·tained (-kən tānd′) ***adj.*** **1.** keeping one's affairs to oneself; reserved **2.** showing self-control **3.** having all working parts, complete with motive power, in an enclosed unit: said of machinery **4.** having within oneself or itself all that is necessary; self-sufficient, as a community —**self′-con·tain′ment** ***n.***

self-con·tent·ed (-kən ten′tid) ***adj.*** contented with what one is or has —**self′-con·tent′, self′-con·tent′ment** ***n.***

self-con·tra·dic·tion (-kän′trə dik′shən) ***n.*** **1.** contradiction of oneself or itself **2.** any statement or idea containing elements that contradict each other —**self′-con′tra·dic′to·ry** ***adj.***

self-con·trol (-kən trōl′) ***n.*** control of oneself, or of one's own emotions, desires, actions, etc.

self-de·cep·tion (-di sep′shən) ***n.*** the deceiving of oneself as to one's true feelings, motives, circumstances, etc.: also **self′-de·ceit′, self′-de·lu′sion** (-di lōō′zhən) —**self′-de·ceiv′ing** ***adj.***

self-de·feat·ing (-di fēt′iŋ) ***adj.*** that unwittingly defeats its own purpose or interests

self-de·fense (-di fens′) ***n.*** **1.** defense of oneself, one's rights, etc. **2.** boxing: usually in **manly art of self-defense** —**self′-de·fen′sive** ***adj.***

self-de·ni·al (-di nī′əl) ***n.*** denial or sacrifice of one's own desires or pleasures —**self′-de·ny′ing** ***adj.***

self-de·struct (-di strukt′) ***vi.*** *same as* DESTRUCT

self-de·struc·tion (-di struk′shən) ***n.*** destruction of oneself or itself; specif., suicide —**self′-de·struc′tive** ***adj.***

self-de·ter·mi·na·tion (-di tur′mə nā′shən) ***n.*** **1.** determination or decision according to one's own mind or will, without outside influence **2.** the right of a people to decide upon its own political status or form of government —**self′-de·ter′mined** ***adj.*** —**self′-de·ter′min·ing** ***adj.***

self-dis·ci·pline (-dis′ə plin) ***n.*** the disciplining or controlling of oneself, one's actions, etc. —**self′-dis′ci·plined** ***adj.***

self-doubt (-dout′) ***n.*** lack of self-confidence

self-ed·u·cat·ed (-ej′ə kāt′id) ***adj.*** educated by oneself, with little or no formal schooling

self-ef·face·ment (-i fās′mənt) ***n.*** modest, retiring behavior —**self′-ef·fac′ing** ***adj.***

self-em·ployed (-im ploid′) ***adj.*** working for oneself, with direct control over work, services, fees, etc. —**self′-em·ploy′ment** ***n.***

self-es·teem (-ə stēm′) ***n.*** **1.** belief in oneself; self-respect **2.** undue pride in oneself; conceit

self-ev·i·dent (-ev′ə dənt) ***adj.*** evident without need of proof or explanation —**self′-ev′i·dent·ly** ***adv.***

self-ex·am·i·na·tion (-ig zam′ə nā′shən) ***n.*** examination or analysis of oneself and one's conduct, motives, etc.

self-ex·ist·ent (-ig zis′tənt) ***adj.*** existing of or by itself without external cause —**self′-ex·ist′ence** ***n.***

self-ex·plan·a·to·ry (-ik splan′ə tôr′ē) ***adj.*** explaining itself: also **self′-ex·plain′ing**

self-ex·pres·sion (-ik spresh′ən) ***n.*** expression of one's own personality or emotions, as in the arts

self-ful·fill·ment (-fəl fil′mənt) ***n.*** fulfillment of one's aspirations, hopes, etc. through one's own efforts

self-gov·ern·ment (-guv′ər mənt, -ərn-) ***n.*** government of a group by its own members, as in electing representatives —**self′-gov′ern·ing** ***adj.***
self-hate (-hāt′) ***n.*** hate directed against oneself or one's own people, often in despair: also **self′-ha′tred**
self·heal (-hēl′) ***n.*** any of various plants supposed to have healing properties; esp., a common old-world weed of the mint family
self-help (-help′) ***n.*** care or betterment of oneself by one's own efforts, as through study
self-hyp·no·sis (-hip nō′sis) ***n.*** *same as* AUTOHYPNOSIS
self-im·age (-im′ij) ***n.*** one's concept of oneself and one's identity, abilities, worth, etc.
self-im·por·tant (-im pôr′t'nt) ***adj.*** having or showing an exaggerated opinion of one's own importance; pompous or officious —**self′-im·por′tance** ***n.***
self-im·posed (-im pōzd′) ***adj.*** imposed on oneself by oneself, as a duty
self-im·prove·ment (-im pro͞ov′mənt) ***n.*** improvement of one's status, mind, etc. by one's own efforts
self-in·crim·i·na·tion (-in krim′ə nā′shən) ***n.*** incrimination of oneself by one's own statements or answers —**self′-in·crim′i·nat′ing** ***adj.***
self-in·duced (-in do͞ost′) ***adj.*** **1.** induced by oneself or itself **2.** produced by self-induction
self-in·duc·tion (-in duk′shən) ***n.*** induction of a voltage in a circuit by the variation of current in that circuit
self-in·dul·gence (-in dul′jəns) ***n.*** indulgence of one's own desires, impulses, etc. —**self′-in·dul′gent** ***adj.***
self-in·flict·ed (-in flik′tid) ***adj.*** inflicted on oneself by oneself, as an injury
self-in·ter·est (-in′trist, -in′tər ist) ***n.*** **1.** one's own interest or advantage **2.** an exaggerated regard for this, esp. at the expense of others
self·ish (sel′fish) ***adj.*** **1.** too much concerned with one's own welfare or interests, with little or no thought or care for others **2.** showing or prompted by self-interest —**self′ish·ly** ***adv.*** —**self′ish·ness** ***n.***
self-jus·ti·fi·ca·tion (self′jus′tə fi kā′shən) ***n.*** the justifying or explaining away of one's actions or motives
self·less (self′lis) ***adj.*** devoted to others' welfare or interests and not one's own; unselfish —**self′less·ly** ***adv.*** —**self′less·ness** ***n.***
self-load·ing (self′lōd′iŋ) ***adj.*** loading again by its own action *[a self-loading gun]*
self-love (-luv′) ***n.*** love of self or regard for oneself and one's own interests
self-made (-mād′) ***adj.*** **1.** made by oneself or itself **2.** successful, rich, etc. through one's own efforts
self-o·pin·ion·at·ed (-ə pin′yə nāt′id) ***adj.*** stubborn or conceited with regard to one's own opinions
self-pit·y (-pit′ē) ***n.*** pity for oneself
self-pol·li·na·tion (-päl′ə nā′shən) ***n.*** pollination of a flower by itself or by another flower on the same plant —**self′-pol′li·nat′ed** ***adj.***
self-por·trait (-pôr′trit, -trāt) ***n.*** a painting, drawing, etc. of oneself, done by oneself
self-pos·ses·sion (-pə zesh′ən) ***n.*** full control of one's feelings, actions, etc.; self-control; composure —**self′-pos·sessed′** ***adj.***
self-pres·er·va·tion (-prez′ər vā′shən) ***n.*** **1.** preservation of oneself from danger, injury, or death **2.** the urge to preserve oneself, regarded as instinctive
self-pro·nounc·ing (-prə noun′siŋ) ***adj.*** showing pronunciation by marks added to the original spelling, not by phonetic respelling
self-pro·pelled (-prə peld′) ***adj.*** propelled by its own motor or power: also **self′-pro·pel′ling**
self-re·al·i·za·tion (-rē′ə li zā′shən) ***n.*** fulfillment of oneself, one's capabilities, etc.
self-re·cord·ing (-ri kôr′diŋ) ***adj.*** recording its own operations automatically, as a seismograph
self-re·gard (-ri gärd′) ***n.*** **1.** concern for oneself and one's own interests **2.** *same as* SELF-RESPECT
self-reg·u·lat·ing (-reg′yə lāt′iŋ) ***adj.*** regulating oneself or itself automatically or without outside control —**self′-reg′u·la′tion** ***n.***
self-re·li·ance (-ri lī′əns) ***n.*** reliance on oneself, one's abilities, etc. —**self′-re·li′ant** ***adj.***
self-re·proach (-ri prōch′) ***n.*** blame of oneself; guilt feeling —**self′-re·proach′ful** ***adj.***
self-re·spect (-ri spekt′) ***n.*** proper respect for oneself and one's worth as a person —**self′-re·spect′ing** ***adj.***
self-re·straint (-ri strānt′) ***n.*** restraint of oneself; self-control —**self′-re·strained′** ***adj.***
self-re·veal·ing (-ri vēl′iŋ) ***adj.*** revealing one's innermost thoughts, feelings, etc.: also **self′-rev′e·la·to′ry** (-rev′ə lə tôr′ē) —**self′-rev′e·la′tion** ***n.***
self-right·eous (-rī′chəs) ***adj.*** thinking oneself more righteous or moral than others —**self′-right′eous·ly** ***adv.*** —**self′-right′eous·ness** ***n.***
self-ris·ing (-rīz′iŋ) ***adj.*** rising by itself: said specif. of flour sold with a leavening agent blended in for quick breads or cakes
self-rule (-ro͞ol′) ***n.*** *same as* SELF-GOVERNMENT
self-sac·ri·fice (-sak′rə fīs′) ***n.*** sacrifice of oneself or one's interests to benefit others —**self′-sac′ri·fic′ing** ***adj.***
self·same (-sām′) ***adj.*** exactly the same; identical; (the) very same —**self′same′ness** ***n.***
self-sat·is·fied (-sat′is fīd′) ***adj.*** pleased with oneself or with what one has done —**self′-sat′is·fac′tion** ***n.***
self-sat·is·fy·ing (-sat′is fī′iŋ) ***adj.*** satisfying to oneself
self-seal·ing (-sēl′iŋ) ***adj.*** **1.** automatically sealing punctures, etc., as some tires **2.** sealable by pressure alone, as some envelopes
self-seek·er (-sē′kər) ***n.*** a person seeking only or mainly to further his own interests —**self′-seek′ing** ***n., adj.***
self-serv·ice (-sur′vis) ***n.*** the practice of serving oneself in a store, cafeteria, etc. and then paying a cashier —***adj.*** operating thus
self-serv·ing (-sur′viŋ) ***adj.*** serving one's own selfish interests, esp. at the expense of others
self-sown (-sōn′) ***adj.*** sown by wind, water, or other natural means, as some weeds
self-styled (-stīld′) ***adj.*** so named by oneself *[he is a self-styled expert]*
self-suf·fi·cient (-sə fish′ənt) ***adj.*** able to get along without help; independent —**self′-suf·fi′cien·cy** ***n.***
self-sup·port (-sə pôrt′) ***n.*** support of oneself or itself without aid or reinforcement —**self′-sup·port′ing** ***adj.***
self-sus·tain·ing (-sə stān′iŋ) ***adj.*** **1.** supporting or able to support oneself or itself **2.** able to continue once begun
self-taught (-tôt′) ***adj.*** **1.** having taught oneself **2.** learned by oneself without instruction
self·ward (-wərd) ***adv.*** toward oneself: also **self′wards** —***adj.*** directed toward oneself
self-willed (-wild′) ***adj.*** stubborn about getting one's own way; willful —**self′-will′** ***n.***
self-wind·ing (-wīn′diŋ) ***adj.*** winding automatically, as certain wristwatches
sell (sel) ***vt.*** **sold, sell′ing** [OE. *sellan,* to give] **1.** to exchange (property, goods, services, etc.) for money or its equivalent **2.** *a)* to offer for sale; deal in *b)* to make or try to make sales in or to *[to sell chain stores]* **3.** *a)* to deliver (a person) to his enemies, into slavery, etc. *b)* to betray (a country, cause, etc.) **4.** to give up (one's honor, etc.) for profit, etc. **5.** to promote the sale of *[television sells many products]* **6.** [Colloq.] *a)* to establish confidence or belief in *[to sell oneself to the public]* *b)* to persuade (someone) of the value of something (with *on*) *[sell him on the idea]* **7.** [Slang] to cheat or dupe —***vi.*** **1.** to sell something **2.** to work or act as a salesman or salesperson **3.** to be a popular item on the market **4.** to be sold (*for* or *at*) *[belts selling for two dollars]* **5.** [Colloq.] to be accepted, approved, etc. *[a scheme that won't sell]* —***n.*** [Slang] **1.** a trick or hoax **2.** selling or salesmanship —**sell out** **1.** to dispose of completely by selling **2.** [Colloq.] to betray (someone, a cause, etc.) —**sell short** **1.** to sell securities, etc. not yet owned, expecting to cover later at a lower price **2.** to undervalue —**sell′er** ***n.***
sell-off (-ôf′) ***n.*** a price decline for all or certain stocks and bonds, due to pressure to sell
sell·out (-out′) ***n.*** [Colloq.] **1.** a selling out, or betrayal **2.** a show, etc. for which all seats have been sold
Sel·ma (sel′mə) [< ? Gr. *selma,* a ship] a feminine name
Selt·zer (selt′sər) ***n.*** [< *Niederselters,* village near Wiesbaden, Germany] **1.** natural mineral water that is effervescent **2.** [*often* **s-**] any carbonated water Also **Seltzer water**
sel·vage, sel·vedge (sel′vij) ***n.*** [< SELF + EDGE, after MDu. *selfegge*] **1.** a specially woven edge to keep cloth from raveling **2.** an edge of fabric or paper that is to be trimmed off or covered
selves (selvz) ***n.*** *pl. of* SELF
Sem. **1.** Seminary **2.** Semitic
sem. **1.** semester **2.** semicolon
se·man·tic (sə man′tik) ***adj.*** [Gr. *sēmantikos,* significant < *sēmainein,* to show < *sēma,* a sign] **1.** of meaning, esp. in language **2.** of semantics —**se·man′ti·cal·ly** ***adv.***
se·man·tics (-tiks) ***n.pl.*** [*with sing. v.*] [see prec.] **1.** the branch of linguistics dealing with the meanings given to words and the changes that occur to these meanings as time goes on **2.** the relationships between symbols and the ideas given to them by their users **3.** loosely, the twisting of meaning to mislead or confuse, as in some advertising and propaganda —**se·man′ti·cist** (-tə sist) ***n.***

sem·a·phore (sem′ə fôr′) ***n.*** [< Fr. < Gr. *sēma,* a sign + *-phoros:* see -PHOROUS] any device or system for signaling, as by lights, flags, mechanical arms, etc. —***vt., vi.*** **-phored′, -phor′ing** to signal by semaphore —**sem′a·phor′ic** ***adj.*** —**sem′a·phor′ist** ***n.***

SEMAPHORE (signals for letters A, B, C, D)

Se·ma·rang (sə mä′räŋ) seaport in N Java, Indonesia: pop. 503,000

sem·blance (sem′bləns) ***n.*** [< OFr. < *sembler,* to seem, ult. < L. *similis,* like] **1.** outward look or show; seeming likeness **2.** a likeness, image, or representation **3.** a false, assumed, or deceiving form or appearance

se·men (sē′mən) ***n.*** [ModL. < L., a seed] the fluid secreted by the male reproductive organs, containing the spermatozoa

se·mes·ter (sə mes′tər) ***n.*** [G. < L. *semestris,* half-yearly < *sex,* six + *mensis,* month] either of the two terms which usually make up a school or college year —**se·mes′tral** ***adj.***

sem·i (sem′ī, -ē) ***n., pl.*** **sem′is** *clipped form of* SEMITRAILER (sense 2)

sem·i- (sem′i; *also variously* -ē, -ī, -ə) [L.] *a prefix meaning:* **1.** half *[semicircle]* **2.** partly *[semiskilled]* **3.** twice in a (specified period) *[semiannually]*

sem·i·an·nu·al (sem′ē an′yoo wəl) ***adj.*** **1.** happening, presented, etc. every half year **2.** lasting only half a year, as some plants —**sem′i·an′nu·al·ly** ***adv.***

sem·i·a·quat·ic (-ə kwät′ik, -kwat′-) ***adj.*** *Biol.* **1.** growing in or near water **2.** spending some time in water, as muskrats

sem·i·au·to·mat·ic (-ôt′ə mat′ik) ***adj.*** **1.** partly automatic and partly hand-controlled: said of machinery **2.** operating like an automatic firearm but requiring a trigger pull for each shot fired —***n.*** a semiautomatic firearm

sem·i·breve (sem′i brēv′) ***n.*** [Brit.] *same as* WHOLE NOTE

sem·i·cir·cle (sem′i sʉr′k′l) ***n.*** a half circle —**sem′i·cir′cu·lar** (-kyə lər) ***adj.***

semicircular canal any of the three loop-shaped, tubular structures of the inner ear that serve to maintain balance in the organism

sem·i·co·lon (sem′i kō′lən) ***n.*** a mark of punctuation (;) showing more separation than that marked by the comma and less than that marked by the period, etc.: used chiefly between units containing elements separated by commas and between some coordinate clauses

sem·i·con·duc·tor (sem′i kən duk′tər) ***n.*** a substance, as silicon, whose conductivity is improved by minute additions of certain substances or by application of heat, light, or voltage: used in transistors, etc.

sem·i·con·scious (-kän′shəs) ***adj.*** not fully conscious or awake —**sem′i·con′scious·ness** ***n.***

sem·i·de·tached (-di tacht′) ***adj.*** partly separate, as two houses joined by a common wall

sem·i·fi·nal (sem′i fī′n′l; *for n., usually* sem′i fī′n′l) ***adj.*** coming just before the final match, as of a tournament —***n.*** **1.** a semifinal match **2.** [*pl.*] a semifinal round —**sem′i·fi′nal·ist** ***n.***

sem·i·flu·id (sem′i flōō′id) ***adj.*** heavy or thick but able to flow —***n.*** a semifluid substance

sem·i·for·mal (-fôr′m′l) ***adj.*** designating or requiring attire that is less than strictly formal but not informal

sem·i·hard (-härd′) ***adj.*** somewhat hard, but easily cut

sem·i·lit·er·ate (-lit′ər it) ***adj.*** knowing how to read and write a little, or knowing only how to read

sem·i·month·ly (-munth′lē) ***adj.*** coming, happening, done, etc. twice a month —***n., pl.*** **-lies** something coming, appearing, issued, etc. twice a month —***adv.*** twice a month

sem·i·nal (sem′ə n′l) ***adj.*** [< MFr. < L. < *semen,* a seed] **1.** of or containing seed or semen **2.** of reproduction **3.** like seed in being a source or a first stage in development; germinal *[a seminal book]* **4.** being an early and influential example *[a seminal jazz band]*

sem·i·nar (sem′ə när′) ***n.*** [G. < L.: see ff.] **1.** a group of supervised students doing advanced study **2.** a course for such a group **3.** any similar group discussion

sem·i·nar·y (sem′ə ner′ē) ***n., pl.*** **-nar′ies** [< L. neut. of *seminarius,* of seed < *semen,* a seed] **1.** a school, esp. a private school for young women: an old-fashioned term **2.** a school or college where priests, ministers, or rabbis are trained —**sem′i·nar′i·an** (-ē ən) ***n.***

sem·i·nif·er·ous (sem′ə nif′ər əs) ***adj.*** [< L. *semen,* a seed + -FEROUS] **1.** seed-bearing **2.** containing semen

Sem·i·nole (sem′ə nōl′) ***n.*** [Creek *Simanóle,* lit., runaway] **1.** *pl.* **-noles′, -nole′** any of an American Indian people of S Florida and Oklahoma **2.** their Muskogean language

sem·i·of·fi·cial (sem′ē ə fish′′l) ***adj.*** having some, but not full, official authority —**sem′i·of·fi′cial·ly** ***adv.***

se·mi·ot·ics (sē′mē ät′iks) ***n.pl.*** [< Gr. < *sēmeion,* a sign] [*with sing. v.*] *Philos.* a general theory of signs and symbols; esp., the analysis of signs used in language

sem·i·per·me·a·ble (sem′i pʉr′mē ə b′l) ***adj.*** allowing some substances to pass; permeable to smaller molecules but not to larger ones

sem·i·pre·cious (-presh′əs) ***adj.*** designating gems, as garnets and opals, of lower value than precious gems

sem·i·pri·vate (-prī′vit) ***adj.*** partly but not completely private; specif., designating or of a hospital room with two, three, or, sometimes, four beds

sem·i·pro (sem′i prō′) ***adj., n.*** *shortened form of* SEMIPROFESSIONAL

sem·i·pro·fes·sion·al (sem′i prə fesh′ən ′l) ***adj.*** not fully professional; specif., *a)* engaging in a sport, etc. for pay but not as a regular occupation *b)* engaged in by semiprofessional players, etc. —***n.*** a semiprofessional player, etc. —**sem′i·pro·fes′sion·al·ly** ***adv.***

sem·i·qua·ver (sem′i kwā′vər) ***n.*** [Chiefly Brit.] a musical sixteenth note

sem·i·rig·id (sem′i rij′id) ***adj.*** somewhat or partly rigid; specif., designating an airship with a rigid internal keel

sem·i·skilled (-skild′) ***adj.*** **1.** partly skilled **2.** of or doing manual work that requires only limited training

sem·i·soft (-sôft′) ***adj.*** soft but firm and easily cut

sem·i·sol·id (-säl′id) ***adj.*** viscous and slowly flowing, as asphalt —***n.*** a semisolid substance

Sem·ite (sem′īt; *chiefly Brit.* sē′mīt) ***n.*** [prob. < Fr. < ModL. < *Semiticus:* see ff.] a member of any people speaking a Semitic language, as a Hebrew, Arab, etc.

Se·mit·ic (sə mit′ik) ***adj.*** [< G. < ModL. *Semiticus,* ult. < Gr. *Sem* < Heb. *Shēm,* SHEM] **1.** of or like the Semites **2.** designating or of a major division of a family of languages of SW Asia and N Africa, including Hebrew, Arabic, etc. —***n.*** this division, or any member of it

Sem·i·tism (sem′ə tiz′m) ***n.*** **1.** a Semitic word or idiom **2.** traits, customs, etc. of the Semites

sem·i·tone (sem′i tōn′) ***n.*** *Music* the difference in pitch between any two immediately adjacent keys on the piano

sem·i·trail·er (-trā′lər) ***n.*** **1.** a detachable trailer designed to be attached by a coupling to the rear part of a tractor (sense 2), on which it is partly supported **2.** a truck made up of such a trailer and tractor

sem·i·trop·i·cal (sem′i träp′i k′l) ***adj.*** somewhat like the tropics; nearly tropical: also **sem′i·trop′ic**

sem·i·vow·el (sem′i vou′əl) ***n.*** *Phonet.* a glide at the beginning of a syllable, as the sound of *w* in *wall*

sem·i·week·ly (sem′i wēk′lē) ***adj.*** appearing, happening, done, etc. twice a week —***n., pl.*** **-lies** a semiweekly publication —***adv.*** twice a week

sem·i·year·ly (-yir′lē) ***adj.*** coming, happening, done, etc. twice a year —***adv.*** twice a year

sem·o·li·na (sem′ə lē′nə) ***n.*** [< It. dim. of *semola,* bran] coarsely ground durum, a byproduct in the milling of flour, used in making macaroni, puddings, etc.

‡**sem·per fi·de·lis** (sem′pər fi dā′lis) [L.] always faithful: motto of the U.S. Marine Corps

‡**semper pa·ra·tus** (pə rät′əs, -rāt′əs) [L.] always prepared: motto of the U.S. Coast Guard

sem·pi·ter·nal (sem′pi tʉr′n′l) ***adj.*** [< ML. < L. < *semper,* always + *aeternus,* ETERNAL] everlasting; eternal

sen (sen) ***n., pl.*** **sen** [Jap.] the 100th part of a yen: a former monetary unit of Japan, now used only as a money of account See also MONETARY UNITS, table (Indonesia)

Sen., sen. **1.** senate **2.** senator **3.** senior

sen·ate (sen′it) ***n.*** [< OFr. < L. *senatus* < *senex,* old] **1.** the supreme council of the ancient Roman state **2.** a lawmaking assembly **3.** [S-] *a)* the upper branch of the legislature of the U.S., or of most of the States of the U.S. *b)* a similar body in other countries **4.** a governing body, as in some schools

sen·a·tor (sen′ə tər) ***n.*** a member of a senate —**sen′a·to′ri·al** (-tôr′ē əl) ***adj.***

send (send) ***vt.*** **sent, send′ing** [OE. *sendan*] **1.** *a)* to cause to go or be carried; convey *b)* to dispatch or transmit (a message) by mail, radio, etc. **2.** to direct or command to go *[send him home]* **3.** to enable to go or attend *[to send one's son to college]* **4.** to cause to move by hitting, throwing, etc. *[he sent the ball over the fence]* **5.** to drive into some condition *[sent him to his ruin]* **6.** to cause to happen, come, etc. *[joy sent by the gods]* **7.** [Slang] to excite; thrill —***vi.*** **1.** to send a message, messenger, etc. *[to send for help]* **2.** to transmit, as by radio —**send away** to dispatch or banish —**send down** [Brit.] to suspend or expel from a university —**send flying** **1.** to dismiss hurriedly **2.** to stagger, as with a blow **3.** to put to flight **4.** to scatter abruptly in all directions —**send for** **1.** to order to come; summon **2.** to request or order delivery of —**send forth** to give out or forth; produce, emit, etc. —**send in** **1.** to dispatch or send to one receiving **2.** to put (a player) in a game —**send off** **1.** to dispatch (a letter, gift, etc.) **2.** to dismiss **3.** to give a send-off to —**send up** **1.** to cause to rise **2.** [Colloq.] to sentence to prison —**send′er** ***n.***

send-off (send′ôf′) ***n.*** [Colloq.] **1.** a demonstration of friendly feeling toward someone starting out on a trip, career, etc. **2.** a start given to someone or something

Sen·e·ca¹ (sen′i kə) ***n.*** [< Oneida Indian name meaning "people of the standing rock"] **1.** *pl.* **-cas, -ca** any of a N. American Indian people of New York and Ontario **2.** their Iroquoian language —**Sen′e·can *adj.***

Sen·e·ca² (sen′i kə) (*Lucius Annaeus Seneca*) 4? B.C.–65 A.D.; Rom. philosopher, dramatist, & statesman

Sen·e·gal (sen′i gôl′) **1.** country in W Africa, on the Atlantic: 76,124 sq. mi.; pop. 3,780,000; cap. Dakar **2.** river flowing from W Mali, along the Senegal border into the Atlantic —**Sen′e·ga·lese′** (-gə lēz′) ***adj., n.,*** *pl.* **-lese′**

se·nes·cent (sə nes′'nt) ***adj.*** [< L. prp. of *senescere,* to grow old] growing old; aging —**se·nes′cence** (-'ns) ***n.***

sen·es·chal (sen′ə shəl) ***n.*** [< OFr. < Frank. *siniskalk,* oldest servant] a steward in a medieval household

se·nile (sē′nīl, sen′īl) ***adj.*** [L. *senilis* < *senex,* old] **1.** of or typical of old age **2.** showing the deterioration, esp. the mental confusion, memory loss, etc., often accompanying old age —**se′nile·ly *adv.*** —**se·nil·i·ty** (si nil′ə tē) ***n.***

sen·ior (sēn′yər) ***adj.*** [L., compar. of *senex,* old] **1.** the older: written *Sr.* after the name of a father whose son bears the same name **2.** of higher rank or longer service **3.** of or for seniors in a high school or college —***n.*** **1.** an older person **2.** a person of greater rank or longer service **3.** a student in the last year of a high school or college —**one's senior** a person older than oneself

senior citizen an elderly person, esp. one who is retired

senior high school high school, following junior high school: it usually includes the 10th, 11th, and 12th grades

sen·ior·i·ty (sēn yôr′ə tē, -yär′-) ***n.,*** *pl.* **-ties** **1.** a being senior, as in age or rank **2.** certain rights, esp. the right to continue to hold a certain job, based on length of service

sen·i·ti (sen′ə tē) ***n.,*** *pl.* **sen′i·ti** [Polynesian (Tongan), cent] *see* MONETARY UNITS, table (Tonga)

sen·na (sen′ə) ***n.*** [< Ar. *sanā*] **1.** any of a genus of plants of the legume family, with yellow flowers **2.** the dried leaflets of various sennas, used, esp. formerly, as a laxative

‡**se·ñor** (se nyôr′) ***n.,*** *pl.* **se·ño′res** (-nyô′res) [Sp. < L. *senior:* see SENIOR] a man; gentleman: Spanish title equivalent to *Mr.* or *Sir*

‡**se·ño·ra** (se nyô′rä) ***n.,*** *pl.* **se·ño′ras** (-räs) [Sp.] a married woman: Spanish title equivalent to *Mrs.* or *Madam*

‡**se·ño·ri·ta** (se′nyô rē′tä) ***n.,*** *pl.* **-ri′tas** (-täs) [Sp.] an unmarried woman or girl: Spanish title equivalent to *Miss*

sen·sa·tion (sen sā′shən) ***n.*** [< LL. < *sensatus,* intelligent < L. *sensus,* sense] **1.** the power or process of receiving conscious sense impressions through direct stimulation of the bodily organism [the *sensations* of hearing, seeing, etc.] **2.** a conscious feeling or sense impression [a *sensation* of cold] **3.** a generalized feeling [a *sensation* of joy] **4.** *a)* a state or feeling of general excitement [the play caused a *sensation*] *b)* the action, event, person, etc. causing this

sen·sa·tion·al (-'l) ***adj.*** **1.** of the senses or sensation **2.** *a)* intensely interesting or exciting *b)* intended to startle, shock, thrill, etc. **3.** [Colloq.] unusually good, fine, etc. —**sen·sa′tion·al·ize′** (-'l īz′) ***vt.*** **-ized′, -iz′ing** —**sen·sa′tion·al·ly *adv.***

sen·sa·tion·al·ism (-'l iz'm) ***n.*** **1.** the use of subject matter, style, etc. intended to shock, thrill, etc. **2.** *Philos.* the belief that all knowledge is acquired through the senses —**sen·sa′tion·al·ist *n.*** —**sen·sa′tion·al·is′tic *adj.***

sense (sens) ***n.*** [< Fr. < L. *sensus* < *sentire,* to feel] **1.** ability to receive and react to stimuli, as light, sound, etc.; specif., any of five faculties of receiving impressions through certain body organs (sight, touch, taste, smell, and hearing) **2.** these faculties collectively **3.** *a)* feeling, impression, or perception through the senses [a *sense* of warmth] *b)* a generalized feeling [a *sense* of longing] **4.** an ability to judge external conditions, sounds, etc. [a *sense* of direction, pitch, etc.] **5.** an ability to feel, appreciate, or understand some quality [a *sense* of humor, honor, etc.] **6.** *a)* sound thinking; normal intelligence and judgment *b)* something wise or reasonable [to talk *sense*] **7.** [*pl.*] normal ability to think or reason soundly [to come to one's *senses*] **8.** *a)* meaning; esp., any of several meanings of the same word or phrase *b)* essential meaning; gist **9.** the general opinion or attitude of a group —***vt.*** **sensed, sens′ing** **1.** to be aware of; perceive **2.** to understand **3.** to detect automatically, as by sensors —**in a sense** from one aspect; to a limited degree —**make sense** to be intelligible or logical

sense·less (-lis) ***adj.*** **1.** unconscious **2.** not showing good sense; stupid **3.** having no real point; meaningless —**sense′less·ly *adv.*** —**sense′less·ness *n.***

sense organ any organ or structure, as an eye or a taste bud, that receives specific stimuli and transmits them as sensations to the brain

sen·si·bil·i·ty (sen′sə bil′ə tē) ***n.,*** *pl.* **-ties** [< MFr. < LL. < L.: see ff.] **1.** the capacity for physical sensation; ability to feel **2.** [*often pl.*] *a)* the capacity for being affected emotionally or intellectually *b)* sensitive responsiveness to intellectual, moral, or aesthetic values

sen·si·ble (sen′sə b'l) ***adj.*** [< MFr. < L. *sensibilis* < pp. of *sentire,* to feel] **1.** that can cause physical sensation **2.** perceptible to the intellect **3.** easily perceived or noticed; striking **4.** capable of receiving sensation **5.** having appreciation or understanding; aware **6.** showing good sense or sound judgment; wise —**sen′si·bly *adv.***

sen·si·tive (sen′sə tiv) ***adj.*** [< MFr. < ML. *sensitivus* < L. *sensus:* see SENSE] **1.** of the senses or sensation; sensory **2.** receiving and responding to stimuli **3.** keenly susceptible to stimuli [a *sensitive* ear] **4.** easily hurt; tender **5.** highly responsive to whatever is stimulating intellectually, artistically, etc. **6.** easily offended, shocked, irritated, etc. **7.** highly responsive as to light, radio signals, etc. [*sensitive* equipment] **8.** indicating or measuring small changes or differences **9.** of or dealing with secret or delicate government matters —**sen′si·tive·ly *adv.*** —**sen′si·tiv′i·ty** (-ə tē), **sen′si·tive·ness *n.***

sensitive plant a tropical American plant with purplish flowers, whose leaflets fold and leafstalks droop when touched

sensitivity training a kind of psychotherapy in which a group of patients, under the guidance of a leader, seek a better understanding of themselves and others, as by the exchange of intimate feelings and experiences

sen·si·tize (sen′sə tīz′) ***vt.*** **-tized′, -tiz′ing** to make sensitive —**sen′si·ti·za′tion *n.*** —**sen′si·tiz′er *n.***

sen·sor (sen′sər, -sôr) ***n.*** [< L. pp. of *sentire,* to feel + -OR] a device designed to detect, measure, or record physical phenomena, as radiation, and to respond, as by transmitting information or operating controls

sen·so·ri·mo·tor (sen′sə rē mōt′ər) ***adj.*** [< SENSORY + MOTOR] *Physiol., Psychol.* of or involving both sensory and motor functions

sen·so·ry (sen′sər ē) ***adj.*** **1.** of the senses or sensation **2.** connected with the reception and transmission of sense impressions Also **sen·so′ri·al** (-sôr′ē əl)

sen·su·al (sen′shoo wəl) ***adj.*** [L. *sensualis* < *sensus,* SENSE] **1.** of the body and the senses as distinguished from the intellect or spirit **2.** *a)* connected or preoccupied with bodily or sexual pleasures *b)* lustful; lewd —**sen′su·al·ly *adv.***

sen·su·al·ism (-iz'm) ***n.*** **1.** frequent or excessive indulgence in sensual pleasures **2.** *a)* the belief that sensual pleasures are the greatest good for mankind *b)* expression of this belief, esp. in art —**sen′su·al·ist *n.***

sen·su·al·i·ty (sen′shoo wal′ə tē) ***n.*** **1.** a being sensual; fondness for or indulgence in sensual pleasures **2.** lasciviousness; lewdness

sen·su·al·ize (sen′shoo wə līz′) ***vt.*** **-ized′, -iz′ing** to make sensual —**sen′su·al·i·za′tion *n.***

sen·su·ous (sen′shoo wəs) ***adj.*** **1.** of, based on, or appealing to the senses **2.** enjoying or readily affected by sense impressions —**sen′su·ous·ly *adv.*** —**sen′su·ous·ness *n.***

sent (sent) *pt. & pp. of* SEND

sen·tence (sen′t'ns) ***n.*** [< OFr. < L. *sententia,* opinion, ult. < prp. of *sentire,* to feel] **1.** *a)* a decision or judgment, as of a court; esp., the determination by a court of a convicted person's punishment *b)* the punishment **2.** *Gram.* a word or group of words stating, asking, commanding, or exclaiming something, usually having a subject and predicate: in writing, it begins with a capital letter and ends with a period, question mark, etc. —***vt.*** **-tenced, -tenc·ing** to pronounce judgment upon (a convicted person); condemn (*to* a specified punishment) —**sen·ten′tial** (-ten′shəl) ***adj.***

sen·ten·tious (sen ten′shəs) ***adj.*** [< L. < *sententia:* see prec.] **1.** expressing much in few words; short and pithy **2.** full of, or fond of using, maxims, proverbs, etc., esp. in a pompously trite or moralizing way —**sen·ten′tious·ly *adv.***

sen·tient (sen′shənt, -shē ənt) ***adj.*** [< L. prp. of *sentire,* to feel] of, having, or capable of feeling or perception; conscious —**sen′tience, sen′tien·cy *n.*** —**sen′tient·ly *adv.***

sen·ti·ment (sen′tə mənt) ***n.*** [< OFr. < ML. < L. *sentire,* to feel] **1.** a complex combination of feelings and opinions **2.** an opinion, attitude, etc.: *often used in the pl.* **3.** susceptibility to emotional appeal; sensibility **4.** appeal to the emotions in literature or art **5.** sentimentality; maudlin emotion **6.** a short sentence expressing some thought or wish **7.** the real thought or meaning behind something

sen·ti·men·tal (sen′tə men′t'l) ***adj.*** **1.** having or showing tender or delicate feelings, as in literature or art, often in an excessive or maudlin way **2.** influenced more by emotion than reason **3.** of or resulting from sentiment —**sen′ti·men′tal·ism *n.*** —**sen′ti·men′tal·ist *n.*** —**sen′ti·men′tal·ly *adv.***

sen·ti·men·tal·i·ty (sen′tə men tal′ə tē) ***n.*** **1.** the quality or condition of being sentimental, esp. in a maudlin way **2.** *pl.* **-ties** any expression of this

sen·ti·men·tal·ize (-men′tə līz′) ***vi.*** **-ized′, -iz′ing** to be sentimental —***vt.*** to regard or treat sentimentally —**sen′ti·men′tal·i·za′tion** ***n.***

sen·ti·nel (sen′ti n'l) ***n.*** [< Fr. < It. *sentinella*, ult. < L *sentire*, to feel] a person or animal set to guard a group; specif., a sentry —***vt.*** **-neled** or **-nelled, -nel·ing** or **-nel·ling** **1.** to guard as a sentinel **2.** to furnish with a sentinel **3.** to post as a sentinel

sen·try (sen′trē) ***n.,*** *pl.* **-tries** [< ? obs. *centery*, guardhouse] a sentinel; esp., any member of a military guard posted to guard against, and warn of, danger

Se·oul (sōl; *Korean* syö′ool′) capital of South Korea, in the NW part: pop. 5,510,000

se·pal (sē′p'l; *chiefly Brit.* sep′'l) ***n.*** [< Fr. < ModL. *sepalum*, arbitrary blend < Gr. *skepē*, a covering + L. *petalum*, petal] *Bot.* any of the usually green, leaflike parts of the calyx —**se′paled, se′palled** ***adj.***

SEPALS

-sep·al·ous (sep′'l əs) *a combining form meaning* having (a specified number or kind of) sepals

sep·a·ra·ble (sep′ər ə b'l, sep′rə-) ***adj.*** that can be separated —**sep′a·ra·bil′i·ty** ***n.*** —**sep′a·ra·bly** ***adv.***

sep·a·rate (sep′ə rāt′; *for adj. & n.* sep′ər it, sep′rit) ***vt.*** **-rat′ed, -rat′ing** [< L. pp. of *separare* < *se-*, apart + *parare*, to arrange] **1.** to set apart into groups, sets, units, etc.; divide **2.** to tell apart; distinguish between **3.** to keep apart by being between *[*a wall *separates* the yards*]* **4.** to bring about a separation between (a man and wife) **5.** to set apart from others; segregate **6.** to take away (a part or ingredient) from a combination or mixture **7.** to discharge from military service or from a job —***vi.*** **1.** to withdraw or secede **2.** to part, become disconnected, etc. **3.** to part company; go in different directions **4.** to stop living together as man and wife but without getting a divorce **5.** to become distinct or disengaged, as from a mixture —***adj.*** **1.** set apart or divided from the rest or others **2.** not associated with others; distinct; individual **3.** having individual form or function **4.** not shared or held in common —***n.*** [*pl.*] articles of dress designed to be worn as a set or separately —**sep′a·rate·ly** ***adv.*** —**sep′a·rate·ness** ***n.*** —**sep·a·ra·tive** (sep′ə rā′tiv, -ər ə tiv), **sep′a·ra·to′ry** (-ər ə tôr′ē) ***adj.*** —**sep′a·ra′tor** ***n.***

sep·a·ra·tion (sep′ə rā′shən) ***n.*** **1.** a separating or being separated **2.** the place where this occurs; break; division **3.** something that separates **4.** an arrangement by which a man and wife live apart by agreement or court decree

sep·a·ra·tism (sep′ər ə tiz′m) ***n.*** a policy of or movement for political, religious, or racial separation —**sep·a·ra·tist** (sep′ər ə tist, -ə rāt′ist) ***n., adj.***

Se·phar·dim (sə fär′dim, -fär dēm′) ***n.pl.,*** *sing.* **Se·phard** (sə färd′), **Se·phar·di** (-fär′dē, -fär dē′) [< Heb.: cf. Obad. 20] the Jews of Spain and Portugal before the Inquisition, or their descendants —**Se·phar′dic** ***adj.***

se·pi·a (sē′pē ə) ***n.*** [L., cuttlefish < Gr. *sēpia* < *sēpein*, to cause to rot (from the inky fluid)] **1.** a dark-brown pigment prepared from the inky secretion of cuttlefish **2.** a dark reddish-brown color **3.** a photographic print in this color —***adj.*** **1.** of sepia **2.** dark reddish-brown

se·poy (sē′poi) ***n.*** [Port. *sipae* < Hindi & Per. *sipāhī* < *sipāh*, army] formerly, a native of India serving in the British army

sep·pu·ku (se pōō′kōō) ***n.*** [Jap.] *same as* HARA-KIRI

sep·sis (sep′sis) ***n.*** [ModL. < Gr. < *sēpein*, to make putrid] poisoning caused by the absorption into the blood of certain microorganisms and their products

Sept. **1.** September **2.** Septuagint

sep·ta (sep′tə) ***n.*** *alt. pl. of* SEPTUM

Sep·tem·ber (sep tem′bər, səp-) ***n.*** [< L. < *septem*, seven: the early Romans reckoned from March] the ninth month of the year, having 30 days

sep·ten·ni·al (sep ten′ē əl) ***adj.*** [< L. < *septum*, seven + *annus*, year] **1.** lasting seven years **2.** coming, happening, etc. every seven years —**sep·ten′ni·al·ly** ***adv.***

sep·tet, sep·tette (sep tet′) ***n.*** [G. < L. *septem*, seven + G. (*du*)*ett*] **1.** a group of seven persons or things **2.** *Music a*) a composition for seven voices or instruments *b*) the performers of this

sep·tic (sep′tik) ***adj.*** [< L. < Gr. *sēptikos* < *sēpein*, to make putrid] caused by or involving microorganisms that are infecting or putrefying —**sep′ti·cal·ly** ***adv.***

sep·ti·ce·mi·a (sep′tə sē′mē ə) ***n.*** [< Gr. *sēptikos*, putrefactive + *haima*, blood] a systemic disease caused by certain microorganisms and their toxic products in the blood —**sep′ti·ce′mic** ***adj.***

septic tank an underground tank in which waste matter is putrefied and decomposed through bacterial action

sep·til·lion (sep til′yən) ***n.*** [Fr. < L. *septem*, seven + Fr. (*m*)*illion*] **1.** in the U.S. and France, the number represented by 1 followed by 24 zeros **2.** in Great Britain and Germany, the number represented by 1 followed by 42 zeros —***adj.*** amounting to one septillion in number

sep·tu·a·ge·nar·i·an (sep′too wə ji ner′ē ən) ***adj.*** [< LL. < L. *septuageni*, seventy each < *septuaginta*, seventy] seventy years old, or between the ages of seventy and eighty —***n.*** a person of this age

Sep·tu·a·gint (sep′too wə jint, -tyoo-, -choo-) [< L. *septuaginta*, seventy: in tradition, done by 70 or 72 translators] a Greek translation of the Hebrew Scriptures made in the 3d cent. B.C.

sep·tum (sep′təm) ***n.,*** *pl.* **-tums, -ta** (-tə) [ModL. < L. < *sepire*, to enclose < *saepes*, a hedge] *Biol.* a part that separates two cavities or masses of tissue, as in the nose, a fruit, etc.; partition —**sep′tal** ***adj.***

sep·tu·ple (sep tōō′p'l, -tyōō′-, -tup′'l; sep′too p'l) ***adj.*** [LL. *septuplus* < L. *septem*, seven] **1.** consisting of seven **2.** seven times as much or as many —***vt., vi.*** **-pled, -pling** to multiply by seven

sep·ul·cher (sep′'l kər) ***n.*** [< OFr. < L. *sepulcrum* < *sepelire*, to bury] a vault for burial; grave; tomb —***vt.*** to bury in a sepulcher

se·pul·chral (sə pul′krəl) ***adj.*** **1.** of sepulchers, burial, etc. **2.** suggestive of the grave, etc.; dismal; gloomy **3.** deep and melancholy: said of sound —**se·pul′chral·ly** ***adv.***

sep·ul·chre (sep′'l kər) ***n., vt.*** **-chred, -chring** *Brit. sp. of* SEPULCHER

sep·ul·ture (sep′'l chər) ***n.*** burial; interment

seq. [L. *sequentes* or *sequentia*] the following: also **seqq.**

se·quel (sē′kwəl) ***n.*** [< MFr. < L. *sequela* < *sequi*, to follow] **1.** something that follows; continuation **2.** a result or consequence **3.** any literary work complete in itself but continuing a story begun in an earlier work

se·quence (sē′kwəns) ***n.*** [< MFr. < LL. < L. *sequens*: see ff.] **1.** *a*) the following of one thing after another; succession or continuity *b*) the order in which this occurs **2.** a continuous or related series **3.** a resulting event; consequence **4.** *Math.* an ordered set of quantities or elements **5.** *Motion Pictures* the series of shots forming a single, uninterrupted episode —***vt.*** **-quenced, -quenc·ing** to arrange in a sequence

se·quent (-kwənt) ***adj.*** [L. *sequens*, prp. of *sequi*, to follow] **1.** following in time or order; subsequent **2.** following as a result; consequent —***n.*** something sequent; consequence

se·quen·tial (si kwen′shəl) ***adj.*** **1.** *same as* SEQUENT **2.** characterized by or forming a regular sequence of parts

se·ques·ter (si kwes′tər) ***vt.*** [< MFr. < LL. *sequestrare*, to remove < L. *sequester*, trustee] **1.** to set apart; separate **2.** to take possession of (property) as security for a debt, claim, etc. **3.** to confiscate; seize, esp. by authority **4.** to withdraw; seclude —**se·ques′tered** ***adj.***

se·ques·trate (-trāt) ***vt.*** **-trat·ed, -trat·ing** *same as* SEQUESTER —**se′ques·tra′tor** ***n.***

se·ques·tra·tion (sē′kwes trā′shən, si kwes′-) ***n.*** **1.** a sequestering or being sequestered; seclusion; separation **2.** *a*) the legal seizure of property for security *b*) confiscation of property, as by court action

se·quin (sē′kwin) ***n.*** [Fr. < It. *zecchino* < *zecca*, a mint < Ar. *sikkah*, a stamp] **1.** an obsolete Italian gold coin **2.** a small, shiny spangle, as a metal disk, esp. one of many sewn on fabric for decoration —***vt.*** **-quined** or **-quinned, -quin·ing** or **-quin·ning** to adorn with sequins

se·quoi·a (si kwoi′ə) ***n.*** [ModL., genus name: after *Sequoya*, Am. Indian (c. 1760–1843) who devised the Cherokee syllabary] either of two giant evergreen trees; specif., *a*) BIG TREE *b*) REDWOOD

se·rag·lio (si ral′yō, -räl′-) ***n.,*** *pl.* **-lios** [It. *serraglio*, enclosure (infl. by Turk. *serai*, palace), ult. < LL. *serare*, to lock < *sera*, a lock] **1.** the part of a Moslem's household where his wives or concubines live; harem **2.** the palace of a Turkish sultan Also **se·rail** (sə ri′, -rīl′, -rāl′)

se·ra·pe (sə rä′pē) ***n.*** [MexSp.] a woolen blanket, often brightly colored, worn as an outer garment by men in Spanish-American countries

SERAPE

ser·aph (ser′əf) ***n.,*** *pl.* **-aphs, -a·phim′** (-ə fim′) [< LL. < Heb. *sĕrāphīm, pl.*] *Bible* one of the heavenly beings mentioned in Isaiah as surrounding the throne of God —**se·raph·ic** (sə raf′ik) ***adj.*** —**se·raph′i·cal·ly** ***adv.***

Serb (surb) ***n.*** **1.** a native or inhabitant of Serbia **2.** *same as* SERBIAN (*n.* 1) —***adj.*** *same as* SERBIAN

Ser·bi·a (sur′bē ə) republic of Yugoslavia, in the E part: 21,580 sq. mi.; cap. Belgrade

Ser·bi·an (-ən) ***adj.*** of Serbia, the Serbs, or their language —***n.*** **1.** Serbo-Croatian as spoken in Serbia **2.** *same as* SERB (*n.* 1)

Ser·bo-Cro·a·tian (sur′bō krō ā′shən) ***n.*** the major South Slavic language of Yugoslavia: it is generally written in the Roman alphabet in Croatia and in the

Cyrillic alphabet in Serbia *—adj.* of this language or the people who speak it

sere[1] (sir) ***n.*** [< SERIES] *Ecol.* the complete series of communities occurring in succession in an area

sere[2] (sir) ***adj.*** [var. of SEAR] [Poet.] withered

ser·e·nade (ser'ə nād') ***n.*** [< Fr. < It. *serenata,* ult. < L. *serenus,* clear] **1.** the act of playing or singing music outdoors at night, esp. by a lover under the window of his sweetheart **2.** a piece of music suitable for this ***—vt., vi.* -nad'ed, -nad'ing** to play or sing a serenade (*to*) **—ser'e·nad'er *n.***

ser·en·dip·i·ty (ser'ən dip'ə tē) ***n.*** [after the princes in a Per. fairy tale, *The Three Princes of Serendip,* who make such discoveries] a seeming gift for making fortunate discoveries accidentally **—ser'en·dip'i·tous *adj.***

se·rene (sə rēn') ***adj.*** [L. *serenus*] **1.** clear; unclouded [a *serene* sky] **2.** untroubled; calm, peaceful, etc. **3.** [S-] exalted: in titles [His *Serene* Highness] **—se·rene'ly *adv.* —se·ren'i·ty** (-ren'ə tē), **se·rene'ness *n.***

serf (surf) ***n.*** [OFr. < L. *servus,* a slave] **1.** a person in a slavelike condition under the feudal system, bound to his master's land and transferred with it **2.** a person treated like a slave **—serf'dom, serf'hood' *n.***

Serg., serg. sergeant

serge (surj) ***n.*** [< OFr. < L. < *sericus,* silken, lit., of the *Seres,* prob. the Chinese, prob. ult. < Chin. *se,* silk] a strong, twilled fabric made of wool, silk, rayon, etc. and used for suits, coats, linings, etc. ***—vt.* serged, serg'ing** to finish off (a cut or raveling edge) with overcast stitches

ser·geant (sär'jənt) ***n.*** [< OFr. < L. *serviens,* serving < *servire,* to serve] **1.** *same as* SERGEANT-AT-ARMS **2.** *a)* a noncommissioned officer of the fifth grade, ranking just above a corporal in the U.S. Army and Marine Corps *b)* generally, any of the noncommissioned officers in the U.S. armed forces with *sergeant* as part of the title of their rank **3.** a police officer ranking next below a captain or a lieutenant **—ser'gean·cy,** *pl.* **-cies, ser'geant·ship' *n.***

ser·geant-at-arms (-ət ärmz') ***n.,*** *pl.* **ser'geants-at-arms'** an officer appointed to keep order, as in a legislature

sergeant first class *U.S. Army* the seventh grade of enlisted man, ranking just below master sergeant

sergeant major *pl.* **sergeants major** **1.** the chief administrative noncommissioned officer of a military headquarters: an occupational title, not a rank **2.** *U.S. Army & Marine Corps* the highest ranking noncommissioned officer

se·ri·al (sir'ē əl) ***adj.*** [< ModL. < L. *series,* a row, SERIES] **1.** of, arranged in, or forming a series [*serial* numbers] **2.** appearing or published in a series of continuing parts at regular intervals **3.** of a serial or serials **4.** *same as* TWELVE-TONE ***—n.*** a story presented in serial form, as in periodicals, movies, radio, TV, etc. **—se'ri·al·ly *adv.***

se·ri·al·ize (-īz') ***vt.* -ized', -iz'ing** to put or publish (a story, etc.) in serial form **—se'ri·al·i·za'tion *n.***

serial number any of a series of numbers given to a person (as a soldier) or thing (as an engine) for identification

se·ri·a·tim (sir'ē āt'im) ***adv., adj.*** [ML. < L. *series*] one after another in order; serial(ly)

se·ries (sir'ēz) ***n.,*** *pl.* **-ries** [L. < *serere,* to join together] **1.** a number of similar things arranged in a row [a *series* of arches] **2.** a number of similar persons, things, or events coming one after another; sequence **3.** a number of things produced as a related group; set **4.** *Elec.* a circuit connection in which the components are joined end to end, forming a single path for the current: usually in the phrase **in series** **5.** *Geol.* a subdivision of a geologic system **6.** *Math.* a sequence, often infinite, of terms to be added or subtracted ***—adj.*** *Elec.* designating or of a circuit in series

ser·if (ser'if) ***n.*** [Du. *schreef,* a stroke < *schrijven,* to write < L. *scribere*] *Printing* a fine line projecting from a main stroke of a letter

ser·i·graph (ser'ə graf') ***n.*** [< L. *sericum,* silk + -GRAPH] a color print made by the silk-screen process and printed by the artist himself **—se·rig'ra·phy** (sə rig'rə fē) ***n.***

se·ri·o·com·ic (sir'ē ō käm'ik) ***adj.*** partly serious and partly comic **—se'ri·o·com'i·cal·ly *adv.***

se·ri·ous (sir'ē əs) ***adj.*** [< ML. *seriosus* < L. *serius*] **1.** earnest, grave, sober, or solemn [a *serious* man] **2.** *a)* meaning what one says; not joking or trifling *b)* meant in earnest **3.** concerned with grave, important matters; weighty [a *serious* novel] **4.** requiring careful consideration [a *serious* problem] **5.** giving cause for concern [a *serious* wound] **—se'ri·ous·ly *adv.* —se'ri·ous·ness *n.***

se·ri·ous-mind·ed (-mīn'did) ***adj.*** having or showing earnestness of purpose, etc.; not frivolous, jocular, etc. **—se'ri·ous-mind'ed·ly *adv.* —se'ri·ous-mind'ed·ness *n.***

ser·jeant (sär'jənt) ***n.*** *Brit. var. of* SERGEANT

ser·mon (sur'mən) ***n.*** [OFr. < LL. < L. *sermo,* a discourse] **1.** a speech, esp. by a clergyman during services, on some religious topic or on morals **2.** any serious or boring talk on one's behavior, responsibilities, etc. **—ser·mon'ic** (-män'ik) ***adj.***

ser·mon·ize (-mə nīz') ***vi., vt.* -ized', -iz'ing** to preach (to); lecture **—ser'mon·iz'er *n.***

Sermon on the Mount the sermon given by Jesus to his disciples: Matt. 5–7, Luke 6:20–49

se·rol·o·gy (si räl'ə jē) ***n.*** [< SERUM + -LOGY] the science dealing with the properties and actions of serums **—se·ro·log·ic** (sir'ə läj'ik), **se'ro·log'i·cal *adj.* —se·rol'o·gist *n.***

se·rous (sir'əs) ***adj.*** **1.** of or containing serum **2.** like serum; thin and watery

ser·pent (sur'pənt) ***n.*** [OFr. < L. < prp. of *serpere,* to creep] **1.** a snake, esp. a large or poisonous one **2.** a sly, treacherous person

ser·pen·tine (sur'pən tēn', -tīn') ***adj.*** of or like a serpent; esp., *a)* evilly cunning; treacherous *b)* coiled, twisted, or winding ***—n.*** **1.** a coil of thin paper thrown out to unwind as a streamer **2.** a green or brownish-red mineral, magnesium silicate

ser·rate (ser'āt, -it; *for v. usually* sə rāt') ***adj.*** [L. *serratus* < *serra,* a saw] having sawlike notches along the edge, as some leaves: also **ser·rat'ed** ***—vt.* -rat'ed, -rat'ing** to make serrate

ser·ra·tion (sə rā'shən) ***n.*** **1.** the condition of being serrate **2.** a single tooth or notch in a serrate edge **3.** a formation of these Also **ser·ra·ture** (ser'ə chər)

ser·ried (ser'ēd) ***adj.*** [pp. of obs. *serry* < Fr. *serrer,* to crowd < LL. *serare:* see SERAGLIO] placed close together; compact, as soldiers in ranks

se·rum (sir'əm) ***n.,*** *pl.* **-rums, -ra** (-ə) [L., whey] **1.** any watery animal fluid, esp. the yellowish fluid that is left after blood clots: in full, **blood serum** **2.** blood serum used as an antitoxin, taken from an animal made immune to a specific disease by inoculation **3.** whey **4.** watery plant fluid

serum albumin the most abundant protein of blood serum, serving to regulate osmotic pressure and used in the emergency treatment of shock

serv·ant (sur'vənt) ***n.*** [OFr. < prp. of *servir* < L. *servire,* to serve] **1.** a person hired to work in another's home as a maid, cook, chauffeur, etc. **2.** a person employed by a government: cf. PUBLIC SERVANT, CIVIL SERVANT **3.** a person who works earnestly for a cause, etc.

serve (surv) ***vt.* served, serv'ing** [< OFr. < L. *servire,* to serve < *servus,* a slave] **1.** to work for as a servant **2.** *a)* to do services for; aid; help *b)* to give reverence to, as God **3.** to do military or naval service for **4.** to pass or spend (a term of imprisonment, military service, etc.) **5.** to carry out the duties of (a position, office, etc.) **6.** to provide (customers) with (goods or services) **7.** to prepare and offer (food, etc.) to (a person or persons) **8.** *a)* to meet the needs of [a tool to *serve* many purposes] *b)* to promote or further [to *serve* the national interest] **9.** to be used by [one hospital *serves* the town] **10.** to function for [my memory *serves* me well] **11.** to treat [she was cruelly *served*] **12.** to deliver (a summons, subpoena, etc.) to (someone) **13.** to hit (a tennis ball, etc.) to one's opponent in order to start play **14.** to operate (a large gun) **15.** to copulate with (a female): said of an animal **16.** *Naut.* to put a binding around in order to strengthen (rope) ***—vi.*** **1.** to work as a servant **2.** to be in service [to *serve* in the navy] **3.** to carry out the duties of an office or position **4.** to be of service; function **5.** to meet needs or satisfy requirements **6.** to wait on table **7.** to be suitable: said of weather, wind, etc. **8.** to start play by hitting the ball, etc. ***—n.*** the act or manner of serving the ball in tennis, etc., or one's turn to serve **—serve (someone) right** to be what (someone) deserves, as for doing something wrong

serv·er (sur'vər) ***n.*** **1.** a person who serves, as a waiter, etc. **2.** a thing used in serving, as a tray, cart, etc.

serv·ice (sur'vis) ***n.*** [< OFr. < L. *servitium* < *servus,* a slave] **1.** the occupation or condition of a servant **2.** *a)* employment, esp. public employment *b)* a branch of this, including the people in it; specif., the armed forces **3.** work done or duty performed for others [repair *service*] **4.** a religious ceremony, esp. a meeting for prayer **5.** *a)* an act of assistance *b)* the result of this; benefit *c)* [*pl.*] friendly help; also, professional aid [a fee for *services*] **6.** the act or manner of serving food **7.** a set of utensils used in serving [a tea *service*] **8.** a system or method of providing people with electric power, water, transportation, etc. **9.** installation, maintenance, repairs, etc. provided to customers by a dealer, etc. **10.** the act or manner of serving the ball in tennis, etc., or one's turn to serve **11.** *Law* notification of legal action, esp. through the serving of a writ, etc. **12.** *Naut.* any strong material, as wire or twine, used in serving (ropes) ***—adj.*** **1.** of, for, or in service **2.** of, for, or used by servants, tradespeople, etc. [a rear *service* entrance]

—*vt.* **-iced, -ic·ing** 1. to furnish with a service 2. to copulate with (a female): said of an animal 3. to make or keep fit for service, as by adjusting, repairing, etc. —**at one's service** 1. ready to serve one 2. ready for one's use —**in service** 1. in use; functioning 2. in the armed forces 3. working as a servant —**of service** helpful; useful

serv·ice·a·ble (sʉr′vis ə b'l) ***adj.*** 1. that can be of service; useful 2. that will give good service; durable —**serv′ice·a·bil′i·ty, serv′ice·a·ble·ness** ***n.*** —**serv′ice·a·bly** ***adv.***

serv·ice·man (sʉr′vis man′, -mən) ***n., pl.*** **-men′** (-men′, -mən) 1. a member of the armed forces 2. a person whose work is servicing or repairing something: also **service man**

service mark a symbol, word, etc. used by a supplier of services, as transportation, laundry, etc., to distinguish the services from those of competitors: usually registered and protected by law: cf. TRADEMARK

service station 1. a place providing maintenance, parts, etc. as for electrical equipment 2. a place providing these, and selling gas and oil, for motor vehicles

service stripe a stripe, or any of the parallel diagonal stripes, worn on the left sleeve of a uniform to indicate years spent in the service

ser·vi·ette (sʉr′vē et′) ***n.*** [Fr. < MFr. < *servir*, to serve] a table napkin

ser·vile (sʉr′v'l, -vīl) ***adj.*** [< L. < *servus*, a slave] 1. of a slave or slaves 2. like that of slaves or servants [*servile* employment] 3. humbly yielding or submissive; cringing —**ser′vile·ly** ***adv.*** —**ser·vil·i·ty** (sər vil′ə tē), *pl.* **-ties, ser′vile·ness** ***n.***

serv·ing (-viŋ) ***n.*** a helping of food —***adj.*** used for serving food [a *serving* spoon]

ser·vi·tor (sʉr′və tər) ***n.*** a servant, attendant, etc.

ser·vi·tude (sʉr′və to͞od′, -tyo͞od′) ***n.*** [MFr. < L. < *servus*, a slave] 1. slavery or bondage 2. work imposed as punishment for crime

ser·vo·mech·a·nism (sʉr′vō mek′ə niz'm) ***n.*** [SERVO(MOTOR) + MECHANISM] an automatic control system in which the output is compared with the input through feedback so that any error in control is corrected

ser·vo·mo·tor (sʉr′vō mōt′ər) ***n.*** [< Fr. *servo-moteur* < L. *servus*, slave + Fr. *moteur*, MOTOR] a device, as an electric motor, that is controlled by an amplified signal as from a servomechanism

ses·a·me (ses′ə mē′) ***n.*** [< L. < Gr. *sēsamon*, of Sem. orig.] 1. an East Indian plant whose flat seeds yield an edible oil 2. its seeds, used for flavoring bread, rolls, etc. See also OPEN SESAME

ses·qui- [< L. < *semis*, half + *que*, and] *a combining form meaning* one and a half [*sesquicentennial*]

ses·qui·cen·ten·ni·al (ses′kwi sen ten′ē əl) ***adj.*** of or ending a period of 150 years —***n.*** a 150th anniversary or its celebration

ses·sile (ses′il, -īl) ***adj.*** [< L. pp. of *sedere*, to sit] 1. *Anat., Zool.* attached directly by its base 2. *Bot.* attached directly to the main stem

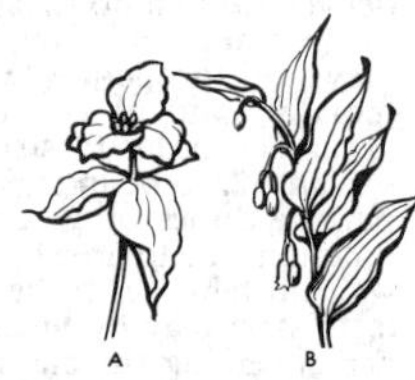

SESSILE LEAVES (A, trillium; B, Solomon's seal)

ses·sion (sesh′ən) ***n.*** [< L. *sessio* < *sedere*, to sit] 1. *a)* the sitting together or meeting of a court, legislature, council, etc. *b)* a continuous series of such meetings *c)* the period a session lasts 2. a school term or period of study, classes, etc. 3. the governing body of a Presbyterian church 4. any period of activity [a *session* of golf] —**in session** meeting —**ses′sion·al** ***adj.***

ses·tet (ses tet′, ses′tet) ***n.*** [< It. dim. of *sesto*, sixth < L. < *sex*, six] 1. *Music same as* SEXTET 2. *a)* the final six lines of a sonnet *b)* a poem of six lines

set (set) ***vt.*** **set, set′ting** [OE. *settan*] 1. to cause to sit; seat 2. *a)* to cause (a fowl) to sit on eggs to hatch them *b)* to put (eggs) under a fowl to hatch them 3. to put in a certain or designated place or position [*set* the book on the table, *set* the wheel on the axle] 4. to bring (something) into contact with something else [to *set* a match to paper] 5. to affix (one's signature, etc.) to a document 6. to cause to be in some condition or relation 7. to cause to be in working or proper condition; arrange; fix; specif., *a)* to fix (a net, trap, etc.) to catch animals *b)* to fix (a sail) to catch the wind *c)* to adjust; regulate [to *set* a clock] *d)* to place (oneself) in readiness for action *e)* to arrange (a table) with tableware for a meal *f)* to put (a dislocated or fractured bone) into normal position 8. *a)* to put into a fixed position [he *set* his jaw] *b)* to cause (one's mind, etc.) to be fixed, determined, etc. *c)* to cause to become firm [pectin *sets* jelly] *d)* to make (a color) fast in dyeing *e)* to mount (gems) in jewelry *f)* to decorate (jewelry) with gems *g)* to arrange (hair) in a certain style with lotion, hairpins, etc. 9. to cause to take a specified direction; direct [he *set* his face toward home] 10. to appoint; establish; specif., *a)* to station (a person) for certain duties *b)* to fix (limits or boundaries) *c)* to fix (a time) for (an event) *d)* to establish (a rule, record, etc.) *e)* to furnish (an example) for others *f)* to introduce (a fashion, etc.) *g)* to fix (a quota) for a given period *h)* to begin to apply (oneself) to a task 11. *a)* to fix (the amount of a price, fine, etc.) *b)* to fix or put as an estimate [to *set* little store by someone] 12. to point toward (game): said of dogs 13. *Baking* to put aside (leavened dough) to rise 14. *Bridge* to prevent (one's opponents) from making their bid 15. *Music* to write or fit (words *to* music or music *to* words) 16. *Printing a)* to arrange (type) for printing *b)* to put (manuscript) into type 17. *Theater a)* to place (a scene) in a given locale *b)* to arrange the scenery and properties on (the stage) —*vi.* 1. to sit on eggs: said of a fowl 2. to become firm or hard [the cement *set*] 3. to become fast, as a dye 4. *a)* to begin to move, travel, etc. (with *out, forth, on, off*, etc.) *b)* to get started [to *set* to work] 5. to have a certain direction; tend 6. *a)* to sink below the horizon *b)* to wane; decline 7. to hang or fit in a certain way [the jacket *sets* well] 8. to grow together: said of a broken bone 9. [Now Dial.] to sit 10. *Bot.* to begin to develop into a fruit —***adj.*** 1. fixed in advance [a *set* time] 2. established, as by authority 3. deliberate; intentional 4. conventional [a *set* speech] 5. fixed; rigid 6. *a)* resolute *b)* obstinate 7. firm in consistency 8. ready [get *set*] 9. formed; built —*n.* 1. a setting or being set; specif., the act of a dog in setting game 2. the way or position in which a thing is set; specif., *a)* direction, as of a current *b)* tendency; inclination *c)* warp; bend *d)* the way in which an article of clothing fits *e)* the position of a part of the body [the *set* of her head] 3. something which is set; specif., *a)* a twig, slip, young bulb, etc. for planting or grafting *b)* the constructed scenery for a play, movie, etc. 4. *a)* the act or a style of arranging hair *b)* the lotion, etc. used for this: in full, **hair set** 5. a group of persons or things classed or belonging together [the social *set*, a *set* of tools, books, china, etc.] 6. assembled equipment for radio or television reception 7. *Math.* a collection of elements or objects that satisfy a given condition 8. *Tennis* a group of games of which the winner must win a specified number, usually (and at least) six —**all set** [Colloq.] prepared; ready —**set about** to begin; start doing —**set against** 1. to balance 2. to compare 3. to make hostile toward —**set aside** 1. to reserve for a purpose: also **set apart** 2. to discard; reject 3. to annul —**set back** 1. to reverse or hinder the progress of 2. [Slang] to cost (a person) a specified sum of money —**set down** 1. to put down 2. to land (an airplane) 3. to put in writing or print 4. to establish (rules, etc.) 5. to ascribe —**set forth** 1. to publish 2. to express in words —**set in** 1. to begin 2. to insert —**set off** 1. to start (a person) doing something 2. to make begin 3. to make prominent by contrast 4. to enhance 5. to cause to explode —**set on** 1. to incite to attack 2. to attack: also **set upon** —**set out** 1. to display, as for sale 2. to plant 3. to undertake —**set to** 1. to get to work; begin 2. to begin fighting —**set up** 1. to place in an upright position 2. to raise to power, a high position, etc. 3. to present as specified 4. to put together or erect (a tent, machine, etc.) 5. to establish; found 6. to make detailed plans for 7. to begin 8. to make successful, etc.

se·ta (sēt′ə) ***n., pl.*** **-tae** (-ē) [ModL. < L., a stiff hair] *Bot., Zool.* a bristle or bristlelike part or organ

set·back (set′bak′) ***n.*** 1. a reversal or check in progress; relapse 2. a steplike recessed section, as in the upper part of a wall

Seth (seth) [LL. < Gr. < Heb. *shēth*, lit., appointed] 1. a masculine name 2. *Bible* the third son of Adam

set·off (set′ôf′) ***n.*** 1. a thing that makes up for something else; counterbalance 2. *a)* a debt claimed by a debtor against his creditor *b)* a claim for this

set piece 1. an artistic composition intended to impress others 2. a scenic display of fireworks 3. any situation carefully planned beforehand

set·screw (set′skro͞o′) ***n.*** a machine screw passing through one part and against or into another to prevent movement, as of a ring around a shaft

set·tee (se tē′) ***n.*** [prob. altered < SETTLE[1]] 1. a seat or bench with a back 2. a small or medium-sized sofa

set·ter (set′ər) ***n.*** 1. a person who sets or a thing used in setting 2. any of several breeds of long-haired bird dog trained to find game and point it out by standing rigid: see ENGLISH SETTER, IRISH SETTER

set·ting (set′iŋ) ***n.*** 1. the act of one that sets 2. the position of something, as a dial, that has been set 3. a thing in or on which something, as a gem, has been set 4. time and place, environment, etc. of an event, story, play, etc. 5. actual physical surroundings, real or artificial 6. the music for a set of words 7. the eggs in the nest of a setting hen 8. *same as* PLACE SETTING

set·tle[1] (set′'l) ***n.*** [OE. *setl*] a long wooden bench with a back and armrests

set·tle[2] (set′'l) ***vt.* -tled, -tling** [OE. < *setl,* a seat] **1.** to put in order; arrange as desired [to *settle* one's affairs] **2.** to set in place firmly or comfortably **3.** to establish as a resident or residents [he *settled* his family in London] **4.** to migrate to; colonize [New York was *settled* by the Dutch] **5.** to cause to sink and become more compact [the rain *settled* the dust] **6.** to clarify (a liquid) by causing the sediment to sink to the bottom **7.** to free (the mind, nerves, stomach, etc.) from disturbance **8.** to establish in business, marriage, etc. **9.** to fix definitely; decide (something in doubt) **10.** to end (a dispute) **11.** to pay (a bill, debt, etc.) **12.** to make over (property, etc.) to someone by legal action (with *on* or *upon*) **13.** to decide (a legal dispute) without court action —***vi.*** **1.** to stop moving and stay in one place **2.** to cast itself, as fog over a landscape or gloom over a person **3.** to become localized in a part of the body: said of pain or disease **4.** to take up permanent residence **5.** to move downward; sink [the car *settled* in the mud] **6.** to become more dense by sinking, as sediment **7.** to become clearer by the settling of dregs **8.** to become more stable or composed **9.** *a)* to reach a decision (with *with, on,* or *upon*) *b)* to accept something less than what is hoped for [he'll *settle* for any kind of work] **10.** to pay a bill or debt —**settle down** **1.** to take up permanent residence, a regular job, etc. **2.** to become less nervous, erratic, etc. **3.** to apply oneself steadily

set·tle·ment (-mənt) ***n.*** **1.** a settling or being settled **2.** a new colony **3.** a village **4.** a community established by a religious or social group **5.** an agreement, adjustment, etc. **6.** *a)* the disposition of property for the benefit of a person *b)* this property **7.** an institution, usually in a depressed neighborhood, offering social services and recreational and educational activities: also **settlement house**

set·tler (set′lər) ***n.*** **1.** a person or thing that settles **2.** one who settles in a new country

set·tlings (-liŋz) ***n.pl.*** sediment; dregs

set-to (set′to͞o′) ***n., pl.* -tos′** (-to͞oz′) [Colloq.] **1.** a fight or struggle **2.** any brisk or vigorous contest

set·up (set′up′) ***n.*** **1.** the way in which something is set up; specif., *a)* plan, makeup, etc., as of equipment, an organization, etc. *b)* details of a plan of action, etc. **2.** bodily posture; carriage **3.** the glass, ice, soda water, etc. for preparing an alcoholic drink **4.** [Colloq.] *a)* a contest deliberately arranged to result in an easy victory *b)* the contestant marked for defeat *c)* any undertaking that is, or is made, very easy *d)* a person easily tricked

Seu·rat (sö rȧ′), **Georges (Pierre)** (zhôrzh) 1859–91; Fr. painter

Se·vas·to·pol (sə vas′tə pōl; *Russ.* se′väs tô′pəl y') seaport in SW Crimea, on the Black Sea: pop. 229,000

sev·en (sev′'n) ***adj.*** [OE. *seofon*] totaling one more than six —***n.*** **1.** the cardinal number between six and eight; 7; VII **2.** anything having seven units or members, or numbered seven

sev·en·fold (-fōld′) ***adj.*** [see -FOLD] **1.** having seven parts **2.** having seven times as much or as many —***adv.*** seven times as much or as many

Seven Hills of Rome seven low hills on the E bank of the Tiber, on & about which Rome was originally built

seven seas all the oceans of the world

sev·en·teen (sev′'n tēn′) ***adj.*** [OE. *seofentyne*] seven more than ten —***n.*** the cardinal number between sixteen and eighteen; 17; XVII

sev·en·teenth (-tēnth′) ***adj.*** **1.** preceded by sixteen others in a series; 17th **2.** designating any of the seventeen equal parts of something —***n.*** **1.** the one following the sixteenth **2.** any of the seventeen equal parts of something; 1/17

sev·en·teen-year locust (sev′'n tēn′yir′) a cicada which lives underground as a larva for from thirteen to seventeen years before emerging as an adult

sev·enth (sev′'nth) ***adj.*** [< ME. < *seoven* + -TH[2]] **1.** preceded by six others in a series; 7th **2.** designating any of the seven equal parts of something —***n.*** **1.** the one following the sixth **2.** any of the seven equal parts of something; 1/7 **3.** *Music* *a)* the seventh tone of an ascending diatonic scale, or a tone six degrees above or below a given tone *b)* the interval between two such tones, or a combination of them —**sev′enth·ly** ***adv.***

seventh heaven **1.** in certain ancient cosmologies, the outermost of the spheres enclosing the earth, in which God and his angels are **2.** a state of perfect happiness

sev·en·ti·eth (sev′'n tē ith) ***adj.*** **1.** preceded by sixty-nine others in a series; 70th **2.** designating any of the seventy equal parts of something —***n.*** **1.** the one following the sixty-ninth **2.** any of the seventy equal parts of something; 1/70

sev·en·ty (-tē) ***adj.*** seven times ten —***n., pl.* -ties** the cardinal number between sixty-nine and seventy-one; 70; LXX —**the seventies** the numbers or years, as of a century, from seventy through seventy-nine

sev·er (sev′ər) ***vt., vi.*** [< OFr., ult. < L. *separare*] **1.** to separate; divide **2.** to part or break off; cut in two [to *sever* a cable, to *sever* a relationship] —**sev′er·a·ble** ***adj.***

sev·er·al (sev′ər əl, sev′rəl) ***adj.*** [< Anglo-Fr. < ML. < L. *separ,* separate] **1.** separate; distinct **2.** different; respective [parted and went their *several* ways] **3.** more than two but not many; few —***n.*** [*with pl. v.*] an indefinite but small number (*of* persons or things) —***pron.*** [*with pl. v.*] several persons or things; a few

sev·er·al·ly (-ē) ***adv.*** **1.** separately; distinctly **2.** respectively; individually

sev·er·ance (sev′ər əns, sev′rəns) ***n.*** a severing or being severed

severance pay extra pay given to an employee dismissed through no fault of his own

se·vere (sə vir′) ***adj.* -ver′er, -ver′est** [< MFr. < OFr. < L. *severus*] **1.** harsh or strict, as in treatment; stern **2.** serious; grave [a *severe* glance, a *severe* wound] **3.** rigidly accurate or demanding **4.** extremely plain or simple [a *severe* style] **5.** keen; intense [*severe* pain] **6.** difficult; rigorous [a *severe* test] —**se·vere′ly** ***adv.*** —**se·vere′ness** ***n.***

se·ver·i·ty (sə ver′ə tē) ***n.*** **1.** a being severe; specif., *a)* strictness; harshness *b)* seriousness; gravity *c)* rigid accuracy *d)* extreme plainness, as in style *e)* keenness, as of pain *f)* rigorousness **2.** *pl.* **-ties** something severe

Sev·ern (sev′ərn) river flowing from C Wales through England & into the Bristol Channel

Se·ville (sə vil′) city in SW Spain: pop. 622,000: Sp. name **Se·vil·la** (sā vē′lyä)

Sè·vres (sev′rə) ***n.*** [< *Sèvres,* suburb of Paris] a type of fine French porcelain

sew (sō) ***vt.* sewed, sewn** or **sewed, sew′ing** [OE. *siwian*] **1.** to join or fasten with stitches made with needle and thread **2.** to make, mend, etc. by such means —***vi.*** to work with needle and thread or at a sewing machine —**sew up** **1.** to close together the edges of with stitches **2.** [Colloq.] *a)* to get or have absolute control of *b)* to bring to a successful conclusion *c)* to make certain of success in

sew·age (so͞o′ij, syo͞o′-) ***n.*** the waste matter carried off by sewers or drains

Sew·ard (so͞o′ərd), **William Henry** 1801–72; U.S. statesman; secretary of state (1861–69)

sew·er[1] (so͞o′ər, syo͞o′-) ***n.*** [MFr. *esseweur,* ult. < L. *ex,* out + *aqua,* water] a pipe or drain, usually underground, for carrying off water and waste matter

sew·er[2] (sō′ər) ***n.*** a person or thing that sews

sew·er·age (so͞o′ər ij, syo͞o′-) ***n.*** **1.** removal of surface water and waste matter by sewers **2.** a system of sewers **3.** *same as* SEWAGE

sew·ing (sō′iŋ) ***n.*** **1.** the act or occupation of a person who sews **2.** material for sewing; needlework

sewing circle a group of women who meet regularly to sew, as for some charitable purpose

sewing machine a machine with a mechanically driven needle used for sewing and stitching

sewn (sōn) *alt. pp. of* SEW

sex (seks) ***n.*** [L. *sexus* < ? *secare,* to divide] **1.** either of the two divisions, male or female, of persons, animals, or plants, with reference to their reproductive functions **2.** the character of being male or female **3.** anything connected with sexual gratification or reproduction; esp., the attraction of one sex for the other **4.** sexual intercourse —***adj.*** [Colloq.] *same as* SEXUAL

sex- [< L. *sex,* six] *a combining form meaning* six

sex·a·ge·nar·i·an (sek′sə ji ner′ē ən) ***adj.*** [< L. < *sexageni,* sixty each] sixty years old, or between the ages of sixty and seventy —***n.*** a person of this age

sex appeal the physical attractiveness and erotic charm that attracts members of the opposite sex

sex chromosome a sex-determining chromosome in the germ cells of most animals and a few plants: in most animals, all the eggs carry an X chromosome and the spermatozoa either an X or Y chromosome, and an egg receiving an X chromosome at fertilization will develop into a female (XX) while one receiving a Y will develop into a male (XY)

sexed (sekst) ***adj.*** **1.** of or having sex **2.** having (a specified degree of) sexuality

sex hormone any hormone, as testosterone, estrogen, etc., having an effect upon the reproductive organs, sexual characteristics, etc.

sex·ism (sek′siz'm) ***n.*** [SEX + (RAC)ISM] the economic exploitation and social domination of members of one sex by the other, specif. of women by men —**sex′ist** ***adj., n.***

sex·less (seks′lis) ***adj.*** **1.** lacking the characteristics of sex: asexual **2.** lacking in normal sexual appetite or appeal —**sex′less·ly** ***adv.*** —**sex′less·ness** ***n.***

sex linkage *Genetics* the phenomenon by which inherited characters are determined by genes carried on one of the sex chromosomes —**sex′-linked′** (-liŋkt′) ***adj.***

sex·ol·o·gy (sek säl′ə jē) ***n.*** the science dealing with human sexual behavior —**sex·ol′o·gist** ***n.***

sex·ploi·ta·tion (seks′ploi tā′shən) ***n.*** [SEX + (EX)PLOITATION] the use of explicit sexual material, esp. in motion pictures, for promotional reasons

sext (sekst) ***n.*** [< ML. < L. *sexta (hora)*, sixth (hour)] [*often* **S-**] the fourth of the canonical hours, orig. set for the sixth hour of the day (counting from 6 A.M.), or noon

sex·tant (seks′tənt) ***n.*** [ModL. *sextans*, arc of a sixth part of a circle < L. < *sextus*, sixth] an instrument used by navigators for measuring the angular distance of the sun, a star, etc. from the horizon, as in finding the position of a ship

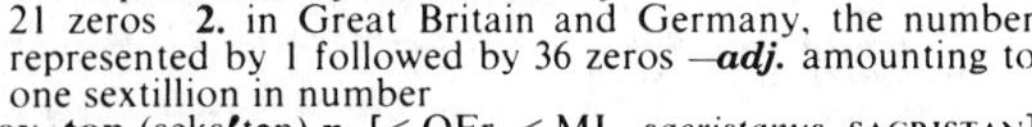
SEXTANT

sex·tet, sex·tette (seks tet′) ***n.*** [altered < SESTET] **1.** any group of six **2.** *Music a)* a composition for six voices or instruments *b)* the six performers of this

sex·til·lion (seks til′yən) ***n.*** [Fr. < L. *sextus*, sixth + Fr. *(m)illion*] **1.** in the U.S. and France, the number represented by 1 followed by 21 zeros **2.** in Great Britain and Germany, the number represented by 1 followed by 36 zeros —***adj.*** amounting to one sextillion in number

sex·ton (seks′tən) ***n.*** [< OFr. < ML. *sacristanus*, SACRISTAN] **1.** a church official in charge of the maintenance of church property **2.** an official in a synagogue who manages its day-to-day affairs

sex·tu·ple (seks tōō′p'l, -tyōō′-, -tup′'l; seks′too p'l) ***adj.*** [< L. *sextus*, sixth, after QUADRUPLE] **1.** consisting of six **2.** six times as much or as many **3.** *Music* having six beats to the measure —***n.*** an amount six times as much or as many —***vt., vi.*** **-pled, -pling** to multiply by six

sex·tu·plet (seks tup′lit, -tōō′plit, -tyōō′-; seks′too plit) ***n.*** [dim. of prec.] **1.** any of six offspring born at a single birth **2.** a group of six, usually of one kind

sex·u·al (sek′shoo wəl) ***adj.*** **1.** of or involving sex, the sexes, the organs of sex and their functions, etc. **2.** *Biol. a)* having sex *b)* designating or of reproduction by the union of male and female germ cells —**sex′u·al′i·ty** (-wal′ə-tē) ***n.*** —**sex′u·al·ly** ***adv.***

sex·y (sek′sē) ***adj.*** **sex′i·er, sex′i·est** [Colloq.] exciting or intended to excite sexual desire; erotic —**sex′i·ly** ***adv.*** —**sex′i·ness** ***n.***

Sey·chelles (sā shel′, -shelz′) country on a group of islands in the Indian Ocean, northeast of Madagascar: a member of the Commonwealth: 107 sq. mi.; pop. 58,000

sfor·zan·do (sfôr tsän′dō) ***adj., adv.*** [It. < *sforzare*, to force] *Music* with emphasis: abbrev. **sf., sfz.** —***n.***, *pl.* **-dos** a sforzando note or chord Also **sfor·za′to** (-tsä′tō)

sgraf·fi·to (skra fē′tō) ***n.***, *pl.* **-fi′ti** (-tē) [It. < *sgraffiare*, to scratch] **1.** the producing of a design on ceramics, stuccoed façades, etc. by incising the outer coating to reveal a ground of a different color **2.** such a design or the object bearing it

Sgt, Sgt. Sergeant

sh (sh: *a lengthened sound*) ***interj.*** hush!

shab·by (shab′ē) ***adj.*** **-bi·er, -bi·est** [< dial. *shab*, scab < OE. *sceabb*] **1.** run down; dilapidated **2.** *a)* showing much wear; threadbare: said of clothing *b)* wearing such clothing **3.** unworthy [*a shabby* offering] **4.** shameful [*shabby* treatment] —**shab′bi·ly** ***adv.*** —**shab′bi·ness** ***n.***

Sha·bu·oth (shä vōō′ōt, shə vōō′ōs) ***n.*** *var. of* SHAVUOT

shack (shak) ***n.*** [prob. < Scot. dial. *shachle*, a shanty] a small, crudely built cabin; shanty —**shack up with** [Slang] to share living quarters with (one's lover)

shack·le (shak′'l) ***n.*** [OE. *sceacul*] **1.** a metal fastening, usually one of a linked pair, for the wrist or ankle of a prisoner; fetter; manacle **2.** [*usually pl.*] anything that keeps one from acting, thinking, or developing freely **3.** any of several devices for fastening or coupling —***vt.*** **-led, -ling** to bind, fasten, or hinder with or as with shackles —**shack′ler** ***n.***

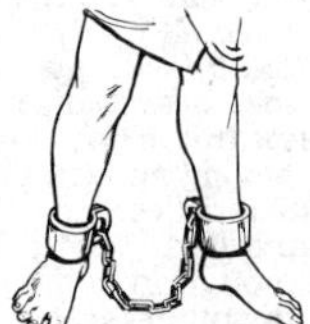
SHACKLES

shad (shad) ***n.***, *pl.* **shad, shads:** see PLURAL, II, D, 2 [OE. *sceadd*] **1.** any of several herringlike saltwater food fishes that spawn in rivers **2.** any of various similar fishes, esp. the **gizzard shad,** often stocked in fresh waters as food for other fish

shad·ber·ry (-ber′ē, -bər ē) ***n.***, *pl.* **-ries** *same as* JUNEBERRY: also called **shad·bush** (-boosh′)

shade (shād) ***n.*** [OE. *sceadu*] **1.** slight darkness caused by a more or less opaque object cutting off rays of light, as from the sun **2.** an area less brightly lighted than its surroundings, as an open place sheltered from sunlight **3.** [Archaic] *a)* a shadow *b)* [*often pl.*] a secluded place **4.** a representation of darkness in a painting, etc. **5.** degree of darkness of a color **6.** *a)* a small difference [*shades* of opinion] *b)* a slight amount or degree; trace [*a shade* of humor in his voice] **7.** [Chiefly Literary] *a)* a ghost *b)* anything lacking reality **8.** *a)* any device used to protect or screen from light [*a* window *shade*] *b)* a partial cover for an electric lamp, etc., for diffusing or directing light: in full, **lamp shade** **9.** [*pl.*] [Slang] sunglasses —***vt.*** **shad′ed, shad′ing** **1.** to protect or screen from light or heat **2.** to provide with a shade **3.** to hide or screen as with a shadow **4.** to darken; dim **5.** *a)* to represent the effects of shade in (a painting, etc.) *b)* to mark with gradations of light or color **6.** to change by very slight degrees or gradations **7.** to lessen (a price) slightly —***vi.*** to change or vary slightly or by degrees —**in** (or **into**) **the shade** **1.** in or into darkness or shadow **2.** in or into comparative obscurity —**shades of (something)**! how suggestive of (something past)! [*shades of* Prohibition!] —**the shades** **1.** the increasing darkness, as of evening **2.** Hades —**shade′less** ***adj.***

shad·ing (-iŋ) ***n.*** **1.** a shielding against light **2.** the representation of light or shade in a picture **3.** any small variation, as in quality

shad·ow (shad′ō) ***n.*** [< dat. & gen. of OE. *sceadu*, shade] **1.** the darkness or the dark shape cast upon a surface by something cutting off light from it **2.** [*pl.*] the growing darkness after sunset **3.** *a)* gloom, sadness, etc. *b)* anything causing gloom, doubt, etc. **4.** a dark or shaded area, as in a picture **5.** *a)* something imagined, not real *b)* a ghost; apparition **6.** a vague indication or omen **7.** *a)* a faint suggestion or appearance; trace [*a shadow* of hope] *b)* remnant; vestige **8.** a constant companion **9.** a person who trails another closely, as a spy —***vt.*** **1.** to throw a shadow upon **2.** to make dark or gloomy **3.** to foreshadow (often with *forth*) **4.** to follow closely, esp. in secret —**in** (or **under**) **the shadow of** **1.** very close to **2.** under the influence of —**under the shadow of** **1.** *see prec. phrase* **2.** in danger of —**shad′ow·er** ***n.*** —**shad′ow·less** ***adj.***

shad·ow·box (-bäks′) ***vi.*** to spar with an imaginary opponent, esp. in training as a boxer —**shad′ow·box′ing** ***n.***

shad·ow·y (shad′ə wē) ***adj.*** **1.** that is or is like a shadow; specif., *a)* without reality; illusory *b)* dim; indistinct **2.** shaded or full of shadow —**shad′ow·i·ness** ***n.***

shad·y (shād′ē) ***adj.*** **shad′i·er, shad′i·est** **1.** giving shade **2.** shaded, as from the sun; full of shade **3.** [Colloq.] of questionable character or honesty —**on the shady side of** beyond (a given age) —**shad′i·ly** ***adv.*** —**shad′i·ness** ***n.***

shaft (shaft) ***n.*** [OE. *sceaft*] **1.** *a)* the long stem or handle of an arrow or spear *b)* an arrow or spear **2.** a missile or something like a missile [*shafts* of light, wit, etc.] **3.** a long, slender part or object; specif., *a)* the stem of a feather *b)* a column or obelisk; also, the main, usually cylindrical, part between the ends of a column *c)* a flagpole *d)* a handle, as on some tools or implements *e)* either of the two poles between which an animal is harnessed to a vehicle *f)* a bar supporting, or transmitting motion to, a mechanical part [the drive *shaft* of an engine] **4.** a long, narrow opening sunk into the earth [*a* mine *shaft*] **5.** a vertical opening through the floors of a building **6.** a conduit for air, as in heating —***vt.*** [Slang] to cheat, trick, exploit, etc. —**get the shaft** [Slang] to be cheated, tricked, etc. —**give (someone) the shaft** [Slang] to cheat or trick (someone)

shag[1] (shag) ***n.*** [OE. *sceacga*] **1.** *a)* a long, heavy, coarse nap, as on some rugs *b)* fabric with such a nap **2.** any disordered, tangled mass **3.** coarse, shredded tobacco —***vt.*** **shagged, shag′ging** to make shaggy or rough

shag[2] (shag) ***vt.*** **shagged, shag′ging** [< ?] to chase after and retrieve (baseballs hit in batting practice)

shag·bark (shag′bärk′) ***n.*** **1.** a hickory tree with gray, shredding bark **2.** its wood **3.** its edible nut

shag·gy (shag′ē) ***adj.*** **-gi·er, -gi·est** **1.** covered with long, coarse hair or wool **2.** carelessly groomed; unkempt **3.** of tangled, coarse growth; straggly **4.** having a rough nap or surface —**shag′gi·ly** ***adv.*** —**shag′gi·ness** ***n.***

sha·green (shə grēn′) ***n.*** [Fr. *chagrin* < Turk. *saghri*, hide] **1.** rawhide with a rough, granular surface, made from the skin of a horse, seal, etc. **2.** the hard, rough skin of the shark or dogfish

shah (shä) ***n.*** [Per. *shāh*] a title of the ruler of Iran

Shak. Shakespeare

shake (shāk) ***vt.*** **shook, shak′en, shak′ing** [OE. *sceacan*] **1.** to cause to move up and down, back and forth, or from side to side with short, quick movements **2.** to bring, force, mix, scatter, etc. by abrupt, brisk movements [*shake* the medicine before taking it, *shake* salt on the steak] **3.** to cause to tremble **4.** *a)* to cause to totter or become unsteady *b)* to unnerve; upset [he was *shaken* by the news] **5.** to brandish; wave **6.** to clasp (another's hand), as in greeting **7.** [Colloq.] to get away from or rid of [to *shake* one's pursuers] **8.** *Music same as* TRILL —*vi.* **1.** to move quickly up and down, back and forth, etc.; vibrate **2.** to tremble, quiver, etc., as from cold or fear **3.** to become unsteady; totter **4.** to clasp each other's hand, as in greeting **5.** *Music same as* TRILL —*n.* **1.** an act of shaking **2.** an unsteady movement; tremor **3.** a natural fissure in rock or timber **4.** a long shingle split from a log **5.** [Colloq.] an earthquake **6.** *short for* MILKSHAKE **7.** [*pl.*] [Colloq.] a convulsive trembling (usually with *the*) **8.** [Colloq.] a moment [be back in a *shake*] **9.** [Colloq.] a kind of treatment [a fair *shake*] **10.** *Music same as* TRILL —**no great shakes** [Colloq.] not outstanding or unusual —**shake down** **1.** to bring down or cause to fall by shaking **2.** to cause to settle by shaking **3.** to test or condition (new equipment, etc.) **4.** [Slang] to extort money from —**shake off** to get away from or rid of —**shake out** to make fall out, empty, straighten out, etc. by shaking —**shake up** **1.** to shake, esp. so as to mix or loosen **2.** to disturb or rouse by or as by shaking **3.** to jar or shock **4.** to reorganize as by shaking —**shak′a·ble, shake′a·ble** *adj.*

shake·down (shāk′doun′) *n.* [Colloq.] **1.** an extortion of money, as by blackmail **2.** a thorough search of a person or place —*adj.* for testing the performance, acclimating the personnel, etc. [the *shakedown* cruise for a ship]

shak·en (-′n) *pp. of* SHAKE

shake·out (-out′) *n.* **1.** any movement in the prices of securities that forces speculators to sell **2.** any drop in economic activity that eliminates marginal or unprofitable businesses, products, etc.

shak·er (shā′kər) *n.* **1.** a person or thing that shakes **2.** a device used in shaking [a cocktail *shaker*] **3.** [S-] [short for earlier *Shaking Quaker*: from trembling under emotional stress of devotions] a member of a former religious sect practicing celibacy, communal living, etc.

Shake·speare (shāk′spir), **William** 1564–1616; Eng. poet & dramatist: also sp. **Shakespere, Shakspere,** etc. —**Shake·spear′e·an, Shake·spear′i·an** *adj., n.*

Shakespearean sonnet a sonnet composed of three quatrains and a final couplet

shake-up (shāk′up′) *n.* a shaking up; specif., an extensive reorganization, as in policy or personnel

shak·o (shak′ō) *n., pl.* **shak′os** [< Fr. < Hung. *csákó* < ? G. *zacke,* a peak] a stiff, cylindrical military dress hat, usually with a flat top and a plume

SHAKO

shak·y (shā′kē) *adj.* **shak′i·er, shak′i·est** **1.** not firm, substantial, etc.; weak, unsound, etc., as a structure, belief, etc. **2.** *a)* trembling *b)* nervous or jittery **3.** not dependable or reliable; questionable [*shaky* evidence] —**shak′i·ly** *adv.* —**shak′i·ness** *n.*

shale (shāl) *n.* [OE. *scealu,* a shell] a fine-grained rock formed largely by the hardening of clay: it splits easily into thin layers —**shal′y** *adj.* **shal′i·er, shal′i·est**

shall (shal; *unstressed* shəl) *v., pt.* **should** [OE. *sceal,* inf. *sceolan*] **1.** an auxiliary sometimes used to express the simple future in the first person [I *shall* tell him] and determination, obligation, etc. in the second and third persons [you *shall* obey]: see also WILL[2] **2.** an auxiliary regularly used: *a)* in questions in the first person asking for agreement [*shall* we dance?] *b)* in laws and resolutions [the fine *shall* not exceed $100]

shal·lop (shal′əp) *n.* [< Fr., prob. orig. fig. use of *chaloupe,* nutshell, ult. < OFr. *escalope,* SCALLOP] any of various earlier small open boats fitted with oars or sails or both

shal·lot (shə lät′) *n.* [obs. Fr. *eschalotte,* altered < OFr. *eschaloigne,* scallion] **1.** a small onion whose clustered bulbs, like garlic but milder, are used for flavoring **2.** *same as* GREEN ONION

shal·low (shal′ō) *adj.* [ME. *shalow* < OE. hyp. *scealw*] **1.** not deep [a *shallow* lake] **2.** lacking depth of character or intellect; superficial —*n.* [*usually pl., often with sing. v.*] a shallow place in water; shoal —*vt., vi.* to make or become shallow —**shal′low·ly** *adv.* —**shal′low·ness** *n.*

sha·lom (shä lōm′) *n., interj.* [Heb. *shālōm,* lit., peace] a word used as the traditional Jewish greeting or farewell

shalt (shalt; *unstressed* shəlt) *archaic 2d pers. sing., pres. indic., of* SHALL

sham (sham) *n.* [prob. < a dial. var. of SHAME] **1.** *a)* an imitation that is meant to deceive *b)* a hypocritical action, false appearance, etc. **2.** one who falsely affects a certain character **3.** *short for* PILLOW SHAM —*adj.* not genuine or real; false; fake —*vt., vi.* to fake; pretend —**sham′mer** *n.*

sha·man (shä′mən, shā′-; sham′ən) *n., pl.* **-mans** [Russ., ult. < Prakrit *śamana,* Buddhist monk] a priest or medicine man of shamanism —**sha·man·ic** (shə man′ik) *adj.*

sha·man·ism (-iz′m) *n.* **1.** a religion of northeast Asia, based on a belief in spirits who are influenced only by shamans **2.** a similar religion of some American Indians —**sha′man·ist** *n.* —**sha′man·is′tic** *adj.*

sham·ble (sham′b'l) *vi.* **-bled, -bling** [orig. *adj.,* in *shamble legs,* prob. < ff., in obs. sense of stool] to walk in a clumsy manner, barely lifting the feet —*n.* a shambling walk

sham·bles (-b'lz) *n.pl.* [*with sing. v.*] [OE. *scamol,* a bench, ult. < L. *scamellum,* dim. < *scamnum,* a bench] **1.** a slaughterhouse **2.** a scene of great slaughter or bloodshed **3.** any scene or condition of great destruction or disorder [the children left the room a *shambles*]

shame (shām) *n.* [OE. *scamu*] **1.** a painful feeling of having lost the respect of others because of the improper behavior, incompetence, etc. of oneself or another **2.** a capacity for such feeling **3.** dishonor or disgrace **4.** a person or thing that brings dishonor or disgrace **5.** something unfortunate or outrageous —*vt.* **shamed, sham′ing** **1.** to cause to feel shame **2.** to dishonor or disgrace **3.** to force by a sense of shame [*shamed* into apologizing] —**for shame!** you ought to be ashamed! —**put to shame** **1.** to cause to feel shame **2.** to do much better than; surpass

shame·faced (-fāst′) *adj.* [altered < OE. < *scamu,* shame + *fæst,* fast] **1.** shy or bashful **2.** showing a feeling of shame; ashamed —**shame·fac·ed·ly** (shām′fās′id lē, shām′fāst′lē) *adv.* —**shame′fac′ed·ness** *n.*

shame·ful (-fəl) *adj.* **1.** bringing or causing shame or disgrace; disgraceful **2.** not just, moral, or decent; offensive —**shame′ful·ly** *adv.* —**shame′ful·ness** *n.*

shame·less (-lis) *adj.* having or showing no shame, modesty, or decency; brazen —**shame′less·ly** *adv.* —**shame′less·ness** *n.*

sham·my (sham′ē) *n., pl.* **-mies;** *adj., vt.* **-mied, -my·ing** *same as* CHAMOIS (*n.* 2, *adj.* 1, *vt.*)

sham·poo (sham po͞o′) *vt.* **-pooed′, -poo′ing** [Hindi *chāmpo,* imper. of *chāmpnā,* to press] **1.** formerly, to massage **2.** to wash (the hair and scalp), esp. with shampoo **3.** to wash the hair and scalp of **4.** to wash (a rug, upholstery, etc.) with a shampoo —*n.* **1.** the act of washing hair, a rug, etc. **2.** a special soap, or soaplike preparation, that produces suds —**sham·poo′er** *n.*

sham·rock (sham′räk′) *n.* [< Ir. dim. of *seamar,* clover] any of certain clovers or cloverlike plants with leaflets in groups of three: the emblem of Ireland

Shang·hai (shaŋ′hī′, shäŋ′-) seaport in E China, near the mouth of the Yangtze: pop. c. 10,000,000

shang·hai (shaŋ′hī, shaŋ hī′) *vt.* **-haied, -hai·ing** [< prec., in allusion to such kidnapping for crews on the China run] **1.** to kidnap, usually by drugging, for service aboard ship **2.** [Slang] to induce (another) to do something through force or underhanded methods —**shang′hai·er** *n.*

Shan·gri-La (shaŋ′grə lä′) *n.* [< the scene of J. Hilton's novel, *Lost Horizon*] any imaginary, idyllic utopia or hidden paradise

shank (shaŋk) *n.* [OE. *scanca*] **1.** the part of the leg between the knee and the ankle in man or a corresponding part in animals **2.** the whole leg **3.** a cut of meat from the leg of an animal **4.** a straight, narrow part between other parts, as *a)* the part of a tool between the handle and the working part *b)* the narrow part of a shoe sole **5.** a projection on some buttons by which they are sewn to fabric **6.** the body of a piece of type —**ride** (or **go**) **on shank's mare** to walk —**shank of the evening** a relatively early part of the evening

Shan·non (shan′ən) river in WC Ireland, flowing southwestward into the Atlantic

shan't (shant) shall not

shan·tey (shan′tē) *n., pl.* **-teys** *var. of* CHANTEY

Shan·tung (shan′tuŋ′, shän′dooŋ′) province of NE China, on the Yellow Sea —*n.* [*sometimes* **s-**] a fabric of silk, rayon, etc. with an uneven surface

shan·ty[1] (shan′tē) *n., pl.* **-ties** [< CanadFr. *chantier,* workshop] a small, shabby dwelling; hut

shan·ty[2] (shan′tē) *n., pl.* **-ties** *var. of* CHANTEY

shan·ty·town (-toun′) *n.* the section of a city where there are many ramshackle houses

shape (shāp) *n.* [< OE. (*ge*)*sceap,* form, akin to *sceppan,* to create] **1.** the way a thing looks because of its outline; outer form **2.** the form of a particular person or thing, or class of things **3.** the contour of the body; figure **4.** assumed appearance; guise [a foe in the *shape* of a friend] **5.** a phantom **6.** a mold used for shaping **7.** definite or regular form [to begin to take *shape*] **8.** [Colloq.] *a*) condition; state [a patient in poor *shape*] *b*) good physical condition [exercises that keep one in *shape*] —*vt.* **shaped, shap′ing** **1.** to give definite shape to; make **2.** to arrange, express, or devise (a plan, answer, etc.) in definite form **3.** to adapt [*shape* your plans to your abilities] **4.** to direct or conduct (one's life, the course of events, etc.) —*vi.* [Colloq.] to take shape —**shape up** [Colloq.] **1.** to develop to a definite form, condition, etc. **2.** to develop satisfactorily **3.** to behave as required —**take shape** to begin to have definite form —**shap′er** *n.*

shape·less (-lis) ***adj.*** **1.** without distinct or regular form **2.** without a pleasing shape; unshapely —**shape′less·ly** ***adv.*** —**shape′less·ness** ***n.***

shape·ly (-lē) ***adj.*** **-li·er, -li·est** having a pleasing shape; well-proportioned: used esp. of a woman —**shape′li·ness** ***n.***

shard (shärd) ***n.*** [OE. *sceard*] a fragment or broken piece, esp. of pottery; potsherd

share[1] (sher) ***n.*** [OE. *scearu*] **1.** a part or portion that belongs to an individual, or the part contributed by one **2.** a just or full part [to do one's *share* of work] **3.** any of the parts into which the ownership of a property is divided; esp., any of the equal parts of the capital stock of a corporation —*vt.* **shared, shar′ing** **1.** to distribute in shares **2.** to receive, use, experience, etc. in common with another or others —*vi.* **1.** to have a share; participate (often with *in*) **2.** to share or divide something equally (often with *out* or *with*) —**go shares** to take part jointly, as in an enterprise —**share and share alike** with each having an equal share —**shar′er** *n.*

share[2] (sher) ***n.*** [OE. *scear*] the part of a plow or other agricultural tool that cuts the soil

share·crop (sher′kräp′) ***vi., vt.*** **-cropped′, -crop′ping** to work (land) for a share of the crop, esp. as a tenant farmer —**share′crop′per** ***n.***

share·hold·er (sher′hōl′dər) ***n.*** a person who holds or owns a share or shares, esp. in a corporation

shark[1] (shärk) ***n.*** [prob. < G. *schurke*, scoundrel] **1.** a person who victimizes others, as by swindling **2.** [Slang] a person with great ability in a given activity; expert

shark[2] (shärk) ***n.*** [? akin to prec.] any of numerous, usually large, mostly marine fishes with a tough, slate-gray skin: most sharks are fish-eaters and some will attack man

SHARK
(45 ft. maximum length)

shark·skin (-skin′) ***n.*** **1.** leather made from the skin of a shark **2.** a cloth of cotton, wool, rayon, etc. with a smooth, silky surface **3.** a fabric woven with a pebbly pattern

Shar·on (sher′ən) [? < ROSE OF SHARON] a feminine name

sharp (shärp) ***adj.*** [OE. *scearp*] **1.** having a very thin edge or fine point, suitable for cutting or piercing; keen **2.** having a point or edge; not rounded [a *sharp* ridge] **3.** not gradual; abrupt [a *sharp* turn] **4.** clearly defined; distinct [a *sharp* contrast] **5.** quick or acute in perception or intellect; specif., *a*) acutely sensitive in seeing, hearing, etc. *b*) clever **6.** attentive; vigilant [a *sharp* lookout] **7.** crafty; underhanded **8.** harsh, biting, or severe [*sharp* criticism] **9.** violent [a *sharp* attack] **10.** brisk; active [a *sharp* run] **11.** severe; intense [a *sharp* pain] **12.** strong; pungent, as in taste **13.** high-pitched; shrill [a *sharp* sound] **14.** cold and cutting [a *sharp* wind] **15.** [Slang] attractively dressed or groomed **16.** *Music a*) higher in pitch by a half step [C *sharp* (C♯)] *b*) above true pitch —*n.* **1.** [Colloq.] an expert **2.** [Colloq.] *same as* SHARK[1], SHARPER **3.** *Music a*) a tone one half step above another *b*) the symbol (♯) indicating this —*vt. Music* to make sharp —*vi. Music* to sing or play above true pitch —*adv.* **1.** in a sharp manner; specif., *a*) abruptly or briskly *b*) attentively or alertly *c*) so as to have a sharp point or edge *d*) keenly; piercingly *e*) *Music* above true pitch **2.** precisely [one o'clock *sharp*] —**sharp′ly** ***adv.*** —**sharp′ness** ***n.***

sharp·en (shär′p'n) ***vt., vi.*** to make or become sharp or sharper —**sharp′en·er** ***n.***

sharp·er (-pər) ***n.*** a person, esp. a gambler, who is dishonest in dealing with others; swindler

sharp·ie (shär′pē) ***n.*** [< SHARP] **1.** a long, narrow, flat-bottomed fishing boat with one or two masts, each with a triangular sail **2.** [Colloq.] a shrewd, cunning person

sharp·shoot·er (shärp′shōōt′ər) ***n.*** a person who shoots with great accuracy; good marksman —**sharp′shoot′ing** ***n.***

sharp-tongued (-tuŋd′) ***adj.*** using or characterized by sharp or harshly critical language

sharp-wit·ted (-wit′id) ***adj.*** having or showing keen intelligence; thinking quickly and effectively —**sharp′-wit′ted·ly** ***adv.*** —**sharp′-wit′ted·ness** ***n.***

Shas·ta (shas′tə), **Mount** [< a tribal name] volcanic mountain in the Cascade Range, N Calif.

Shasta daisy [after prec.] a daisylike chrysanthemum having large flowers

Shatt-al-A·rab (shat′əl ä′räb) river in SE Iraq, formed by the confluence of the Tigris & Euphrates rivers, & flowing into the Persian Gulf

shat·ter (shat′ər) ***vt.*** [ME. *schateren*, to scatter] **1.** to break into pieces suddenly, as with a blow **2.** to damage severely [to *shatter* one's health] —*vi.* to burst into pieces —*n.* [*pl.*] broken pieces: chiefly in **in** (or **into**) **shatters**

shave (shāv) ***vt.*** **shaved, shaved** or **shav′en, shav′ing** [OE. *sceafan*] **1.** to cut away thin slices from [to *shave* the edge of a door] **2.** to scrape into thin sections or slices [*shaved* ham] **3.** *a*) to cut off (hair, esp. the beard) at the surface of the skin (often with *off* or *away*) *b*) to cut the hair to the surface of [to *shave* the chin, the legs, etc.] *c*) to cut the beard of (a person) **4.** to barely touch or almost touch in passing; graze **5.** to trim (grass, etc.) closely —*vi.* to cut off hair with a razor or shaver; shave oneself —*n.* **1.** a tool used for cutting off thin slices **2.** something shaved off; shaving **3.** the act or an instance of shaving the beard

shav·en (shā′v'n) *alt. pp. of* SHAVE —***adj.*** **1.** shaved or tonsured **2.** closely trimmed

shav·er (-vər) ***n.*** **1.** a person who shaves **2.** an instrument used in shaving; esp., a device with a small electric motor that operates a set of cutters **3.** [Colloq.] a boy; lad

shave·tail (shāv′tāl′) ***n.*** [orig., an unbroken mule] [Slang] a second lieutenant, esp. one recently appointed

Sha·vi·an (shā′vē ən) ***adj.*** [< ModL. *Shavius*, Latinized < SHAW] of or characteristic of George Bernard Shaw or his work —*n.* an admirer of Shaw or his work

shav·ing (shā′viŋ) ***n.*** **1.** the act of one that shaves **2.** a thin piece of wood, metal, etc. shaved off

Sha·vu·ot (shä vōō′ōt, shə vōō′ōs) ***n.*** [Heb. *shābhūʿoth*, lit., weeks] a Jewish holiday, orig. celebrating the spring harvest, now chiefly commemorating the revelation of the Law at Mount Sinai

Shaw (shô), **George Bernard** 1856–1950; Brit. dramatist & critic, born in Ireland

shawl (shôl) ***n.*** [prob. via Urdu < Per. *shāl*] an oblong or square cloth worn, esp. by women, as a covering for the head or shoulders

shawm (shôm) ***n.*** [< MFr., ult. from L. *calamus*, a reed] an early double-reed wind instrument resembling the oboe

Shaw·nee (shô nē′, shô′nē) ***n.*** [< Algonquian < *shawun*, south + *ogi*, people] **1.** *pl.* **-nees′, -nee′** any member of a tribe of N. American Indians living at various times in the East and Midwest, and now chiefly in Oklahoma **2.** their Algonquian language

shay (shā) ***n.*** [back-formation < CHAISE, assumed as pl.] [Dial.] a light carriage; chaise

she (shē; *unstressed* shi) ***pron.*** *for pl. see* THEY [prob. after OE. *seo*, fem. def. article, replacing OE. *heo*, she] the woman, girl, or female animal (or the object regarded as female) previously mentioned: *she* is the nominative case form of the feminine third personal pronoun —*n., pl.* **shes** a woman, girl, or female animal

sheaf (shēf) ***n.***, *pl.* **sheaves** [OE. *sceaf*] **1.** a bunch of cut stalks of grain, etc. bound together **2.** a collection, as of papers, bound in a bundle —*vt. same as* SHEAVE[2]

shear (shir) ***vt.*** **sheared, sheared** or **shorn, shear′ing** [OE. *scieran*] **1.** to cut as with shears **2.** *a*) to remove (the hair, wool, etc.) by cutting *b*) to cut the hair, wool, etc. from **3.** to tear (*off*) by shearing stress **4.** to move through as if cutting **5.** to strip (*of* a power, right, etc.) —*vi.* **1.** to use shears, etc. in cutting wool, metal, etc. **2.** to break under a shearing stress **3.** to move as if by cutting —*n.* **1.** *a*) *rare var. of* SHEARS *b*) a single blade of a pair of shears **2.** a machine used in cutting metal **3.** the act or result of shearing; specif., the shearing of wool from an animal [a sheep of three *shears*] **4.** *same as* SHEARING STRESS —**shear′er** *n.*

sheared (shird) ***adj.*** subjected to shearing: said esp. of fur trimmed to give it an even surface [*sheared* beaver]

shearing stress the force causing two contacting parts to slide upon each other in opposite directions parallel to their plane of contact

shears (shirz) ***n.pl.*** [*also with sing. v.*] **1.** large scissors: also called **pair of shears** **2.** any of several large tools or machines with two opposed blades, used to cut metal, etc.

shear·wa·ter (shir′wôt′ər, -wät′-) ***n.*** any of various black-and-white sea birds, related to the albatrosses, that skim the water in flight

sheath (shēth) ***n.***, *pl.* **sheaths** (shē*th*z, shēths) [OE. *sceath*] **1.** a case for the blade of a knife, sword, etc. **2.** a covering resembling this, as the membrane around a muscle, etc. **3.** a woman's closefitting dress —*vt. same as* SHEATHE

sheathe (shē*th*) ***vt.*** **sheathed, sheath′ing** **1.** to put into a sheath or scabbard **2.** to enclose in a case or covering

sheath·ing (shē′*th*iŋ) ***n.*** something that sheathes, as the inner covering of boards or waterproof material on the roof or outside wall of a frame house

sheath knife a knife carried in a sheath

sheave[1] (shēv, shiv) *n.* [ME. *scheve*] a wheel with a grooved rim, as in a pulley block

sheave[2] (shēv) *vt.* **sheaved, sheav′ing** [< SHEAF] to gather and fix (grain, papers, etc.) in a sheaf or sheaves

sheaves[1] (shēvz) *n. pl. of* SHEAF

sheaves[2] (shēvz, shivz) *n. pl. of* SHEAVE[1]

She·ba (shē′bə) *Biblical name of* SABA

Sheba, Queen of *Bible* the queen who visited King Solomon to investigate his reputed wisdom: I Kings 10:1–13

she·bang (shə baŋ′) *n.* [Colloq.] an affair, business, contrivance, thing, etc.: chiefly in **the whole shebang**

She·bat (shə vät′) *n.* [Heb.] the fifth month of the Jewish year: see JEWISH CALENDAR

shed[1] (shed) *n.* [OE. *scead*] **1.** a small, rough building or lean-to, used for shelter or storage **2.** a large, barnlike or hangarlike structure for storage

shed[2] (shed) *vt.* **shed, shed′ding** [OE. *sceadan*, to separate] **1.** to pour out; emit **2.** to cause to flow; let fall in drops *[to shed tears]* **3.** to send forth or spread about; radiate *[to shed confidence]* **4.** to cause to flow off without going through; repel *[oilskin sheds water]* **5.** to cast off (a natural growth or covering, as leaves, hair, etc.) *—vi.* to shed leaves, hair, etc. *—n. same as* WATERSHED **—shed blood** to kill in a violent way **—shed′der** *n.*

she'd (shēd) **1.** she had **2.** she would

sheen (shēn) *n.* [< the adj.] **1.** brightness; luster **2.** bright attire *—adj.* [OE. *sciene*, beautiful] [Archaic] of shining beauty; bright *—vi.* [Dial.] to shine; gleam

sheep (shēp) *n., pl.* **sheep** [OE. *sceap*] **1.** a cud-chewing mammal related to the goats, with heavy wool and edible flesh called mutton **2.** leather made from sheepskin **3.** a person who is meek, stupid, timid, etc. **—make** (or **cast**) **sheep's eyes at** to look shyly but amorously at

sheep·cote (-kōt′) *n.* [cf. COTE] *chiefly Brit. var. of* SHEEPFOLD: also **sheep′cot′** (-kät′)

sheep-dip (-dip′) *n.* any chemical preparation used as a bath, as to free sheep from vermin or to clean the fleece

sheep dog any dog trained to herd and protect sheep

sheep·fold (-fōld′) *n.* a pen or enclosure for sheep

sheep·herd·er (-hur′dər) *n.* a person who herds or takes care of a large flock of grazing sheep **—sheep′herd′ing** *n.*

sheep·ish (-ish) *adj.* **1.** *a)* embarrassed by being caught in a mistake, lie, etc. *b)* awkwardly shy or bashful **2.** meek, timid, etc. like sheep **—sheep′ish·ly** *adv.* **—sheep′ish·ness** *n.*

sheep·man (-man′, -mən) *n., pl.* **-men′** (-men′, -mən) a person who raises sheep for the market

sheep·shank (-shaŋk′) *n.* a knot used for shortening a rope

sheeps·head (shēps′hed′) *n., pl.* **-head′, -heads′**: see PLURAL, II, D, 2 any of several fishes; esp., *a)* an ocean food fish of the eastern coast of the U.S. *b)* the freshwater drum of central N. America

sheep·skin (shēp′skin′) *n.* **1.** the skin of a sheep, esp. with the fleece left on **2.** parchment or leather made from the skin of a sheep **3.** [Colloq.] *same as* DIPLOMA

sheer[1] (shir) *vi.* [var. of SHEAR] to turn aside from a course; swerve; deviate *—vt.* to cause to sheer *—n.* **1.** deviation from a course **2.** the oblique heading of a ship riding at a single bow anchor **3.** the upward curve of a ship's deck lines as seen from the side

sheer[2] (shir) *adj.* [ON. *skærr*] **1.** very thin; transparent: said of textiles **2.** not mixed with anything else; pure **3.** absolute; downright *[sheer persistence]* **4.** extremely steep, as the face of a cliff *—adv.* **1.** completely; utterly **2.** very steeply *—n.* thin, fine material, or a garment made of it **—sheer′ly** *adv.* **—sheer′ness** *n.*

sheet[1] (shēt) *n.* [OE. *sceat*] **1.** a large piece of cotton, linen, etc., used on a bed **2.** *a)* a single piece of paper *b)* a large piece of paper with a number of pages printed on it, to be folded into a signature for binding into a book: *usually used in pl. c)* [Colloq.] a newspaper *[a scandal sheet]* **3.** a broad, continuous surface or layer, as of flame, water, etc. **4.** a broad, thin piece, as of glass, metal, etc. **5.** a flat baking pan *[a cookie sheet]* **6.** [Chiefly Poet.] a sail *—vt.* to cover or provide with, or form into, a sheet or sheets *—adj.* in the form of a sheet *[sheet iron]* **—sheet′like′** *adj.*

sheet[2] (shēt) *n.* [short for OE. *sceatline*] **1.** a rope for controlling the set of a sail, attached to a lower corner **2.** [*pl.*] the spaces not occupied by thwarts, at the bow and stern of an open boat

sheet anchor a large anchor used only in emergencies

sheet bend *Naut.* a knot used in fastening a rope to the bight of another rope or to an eye

sheet·ing (shēt′iŋ) *n.* **1.** cotton or linen material used for making sheets **2.** material used in covering or lining a surface *[copper sheeting]*

sheet metal metal rolled thin in the form of a sheet

sheet music music printed on unbound sheets of paper

Shef·field (shef′ēld) city in Yorkshire, NC England: pop. 525,000

sheik, sheikh (shēk) *n.* [Ar. *shaikh*, old man] **1.** the chief of an Arab family, tribe, or village **2.** an official in the Moslem religious organization **—sheik′dom, sheikh′dom** *n.*

Shei·la (shē′lə) [Ir.] a feminine name

shek·el (shek′'l) *n.* [< Heb. < *shāqal*, to weigh] **1.** among the ancient Hebrews, Babylonians, etc., a unit of weight (about half an ounce), or a gold or silver coin of this weight **2.** the monetary unit of Israel: see MONETARY UNITS, table **3.** [*pl.*] [Slang] money

shel·drake (shel′drāk′) *n., pl.* **-drakes′, -drake′**: see PLURAL, II, D, 1 [prob. < a ME. cognate of MDu. *schillede*, variegated + *drake*, drake] **1.** a large, old-world wild duck that feeds on fish, etc. and nests in burrows: the plumage is variegated **2.** *same as* MERGANSER

shelf (shelf) *n., pl.* **shelves** [prob. < MLowG. *schelf*] **1.** a thin, flat length of wood, metal, etc. fixed horizontally to a wall, or in a cupboard, etc., used for holding things **2.** the contents or capacity of a shelf **3.** something like a shelf; specif., *a)* a flat ledge of rock *b)* a sand bar or reef **—on the shelf** out of use, circulation, etc. **—shelf′like′** *adj.*

shell (shel) *n.* [OE. *sciel*] **1.** a hard outer covering, as of a turtle, egg, nut, etc. **2.** something like a shell in being hollow, empty, a covering, etc., as the hull of a boat, an unfilled pie crust, etc. **3.** a shy or uncommunicative manner *[to come out of one's shell]* **4.** a woman's pullover, sleeveless knit blouse **5.** a light, long, narrow racing boat rowed by a team of oarsmen **6.** an explosive artillery projectile containing high explosives and sometimes shrapnel, chemicals, etc. **7.** a small-arms cartridge *—vt.* **1.** to remove the shell or covering from *[to shell peas]* **2.** to separate (kernels of corn, etc.) from the ear **3.** to fire shells at from large guns; bombard *—vi.* to separate from the shell or covering **—shell out** [Colloq.] to pay out (money) **—shell′-like′** *adj.* **—shell′y** *adj.*

she'll (shēl; *unstressed* shil) **1.** she shall **2.** she will

shel·lac, shel·lack (shə lak′) *n.* [SHEL(L) + LAC, used as transl. of Fr. *laque en écailles*, lac in fine sheets] **1.** refined lac, a resin usually produced in thin, flaky layers, used in making varnish, phonograph records, etc. **2.** a thin varnish containing this resin and alcohol *—vt.* **-lacked′, -lack′ing 1.** to apply shellac to; cover with shellac **2.** [Slang] *a)* to beat *b)* to defeat decisively

shell·back (shel′bak′) *n.* [prob. referring to the shell of the sea turtle] **1.** an old, experienced sailor **2.** anyone who has crossed the equator by ship

shell·bark (-bärk′) *n. same as* SHAGBARK

-shelled (sheld) *a combining form meaning* having a (specified kind of) shell *[soft-shelled crab]*

Shel·ley (shel′ē), **Percy Bysshe** (bish) 1792–1822; Eng. poet

shell·fire (shel′fīr′) *n.* the firing of large shells

shell·fish (-fish′) *n., pl.* **-fish′, -fish′es**: see FISH any aquatic animal with a shell, esp. such an animal that is edible, as the clam, lobster, etc.

shell game 1. a swindling game in which the victim bets that a pea is under one of three shells manipulated by sleight of hand **2.** any scheme for victimizing people

shell·proof (-proof′) *adj.* proof against damage from shells or bombs

shell shock *an earlier term for* COMBAT FATIGUE **—shell′-shocked′** *adj.*

shel·ter (shel′tər) *n.* [< ? OE. *sceldtruma*, troop protected by interlocked shields < *scield*, shield + *truma*, a troop] **1.** something that covers or protects; place of protection against the elements, danger, etc. **2.** a being covered, protected, etc.; refuge *—vt.* to provide shelter or refuge for *—vi.* to find shelter or refuge **—shel′ter·less** *adj.*

sheltered workshop a workshop and training center for the handicapped, where they can earn wages but are free from the competitive stress of most jobs

shelter tent a small, portable tent that shelters two men: it is made from two sections (**shelter halves**), each of which is carried by a soldier in his field equipment

shelve (shelv) *vi.* **shelved, shelv′ing** [< SHELF] to slope gradually *—vt.* **1.** to furnish with shelves **2.** to put on a shelf or shelves **3.** *a)* to lay aside *[to shelve a discussion]* *b)* to dismiss from active service

shelves (shelvz) *n. pl. of* SHELF

shelv·ing (shel′viŋ) *n.* **1.** material for shelves **2.** shelves collectively **3.** the condition or degree of sloping

Shem (shem) *Bible* the eldest of Noah's sons: Gen. 5:32

Shem·ite (shem′īt) *n. rare var. of* SEMITE

Shen·an·do·ah (shen′ən dō′ə) [< AmInd., lit., ? spruce stream] river in N Va., flowing between the Blue Ridge & Allegheny mountains into the Potomac

she·nan·i·gan (shi nan′i g'n) *n.* [altered < ? Ir. *sionna-*

chuighim, I play the fox] [*usually pl.*] [Colloq.] nonsense; trickery; mischief
Shen·yang (shun′yäŋ′) city in NE China: pop. c. 4,000,000
She·ol (shē′ōl, shē ōl′) [< Heb. < *shā'al,* to dig] *Bible* a place in the earth conceived of as the dwelling of the dead
shep·herd (shep′ərd) ***n.*** [OE. *sceaphyrde:* see SHEEP & HERD²] **1.** a person who herds sheep **2.** a leader of a group; esp., a clergyman —***vt.*** to herd, guard, lead, etc. as a shepherd —**shep′herd·ess *n.fem.***
shepherd dog *same as* SHEEP DOG
shepherd's pie a meat pie with mashed potatoes on top
shepherd's purse a small weed of the mustard family, with triangular, pouchlike pods
Sher·a·ton (sher′ə tən) ***adj.*** [after T. *Sheraton* (1751–1806), Eng. cabinetmaker] designating or of a style of furniture having simplicity of form, straight lines, etc.
sher·bet (shur′bət) ***n.*** [< Turk. < Ar. *sharbah,* a drink] **1.** [Brit.] a beverage made of watered fruit juice and sugar **2.** a frozen dessert like an ice but with gelatin added
Sher·brooke (shur′brook) city in S Quebec, Canada: pop. 76,000
Sher·i·dan (sher′i d'n) **1. Philip Henry,** 1831–88; Union general in the Civil War **2. Richard Brins·ley** (brinz′lē), 1751–1816; Brit. dramatist & politician, born in Ireland
she·rif (shə rēf′) ***n.*** [Ar. *sharīf,* noble] **1.** a descendant of Mohammed through his daughter Fatima **2.** an Arab prince or chief
sher·iff (sher′if) ***n.*** [< OE. < *scir,* shire + *gerefa,* reeve] **1.** in England, esp. formerly, any of various officers of a shire, or county **2.** in the U.S., the chief law-enforcement officer of a county, charged with the keeping of the peace and the execution of court orders —**sher′iff·dom *n.***
Sher·man (shur′mən), **William Tecumseh** 1820–91; Union general in the Civil War
sher·ry (sher′ē) ***n.,*** *pl.* **-ries** [< earlier *sherris* < *Xeres* (now Jerez), Spain] **1.** a strong, yellow or brownish Spanish wine **2.** any similar wine made elsewhere
Sher·wood Forest (shur′wood) forest in C England, near Nottingham, made famous in the Robin Hood legends
she's (shēz) **1.** she is **2.** she has
Shet·land Islands (shet′lənd) group of islands northeast of the Orkney Islands, constituting a region (**Shetland**) of Scotland
Shetland pony any of a breed of sturdy ponies with a rough coat and long tail and mane, orig. from the Shetland Islands
She·vu·oth (shə vo͞o′ōt) ***n.*** [Heb.] *same as* SHAVUOT
shew (shō) ***n., vt., vi.*** **shewed, shewn** or **shewed, shew′ing** *archaic sp. of* SHOW
shew·bread (-bred′) ***n.*** [prec. + BREAD, transl. of Heb. *leḥem pānīm,* presence bread] the unleavened bread placed at the altar in the ancient Temple as an offering every Sabbath by the priests
SHF, S.H.F., shf, s.h.f. superhigh frequency
shib·bo·leth (shib′ə ləth) ***n.*** [< LL. < Heb. *shibbōleth,* a stream] **1.** *Bible* the test word used by the men of Gilead to distinguish the escaping Ephraimites, who pronounced the initial (sh) as (s): Judg. 12:4–6 **2.** something said or done that is a sign or test of belonging to a certain group
shied (shīd) *pt. & pp. of* SHY
shield (shēld) ***n.*** [OE. *scield*] **1.** a broad piece of armor carried in the hand or worn on the forearm to ward off blows or missiles **2.** any person or thing that guards or protects **3.** anything shaped like a triangular shield, broad at the top and with curved sides, as an escutcheon, badge, etc. **4.** a safety screen or guard, as over the moving parts of machinery **5.** a pad worn at the armpit to protect a garment from perspiration: also **dress shield** —***vt., vi.*** to be a shield (for); defend; protect —**shield′er *n.***
shift (shift) ***vt.*** [OE. *sciftan,* to divide] **1.** to move or transfer as from one person, place, direction, etc. to another **2.** to replace by another or others; change or exchange **3.** to change the arrangement of (gears) in driving a motor vehicle —***vi.*** **1.** to change position, direction, form, etc. **2.** to get along; manage [to *shift* for oneself] **3.** to use tricky or expedient methods **4.** to change from one gear arrangement to another **5.** in typing, to change from small letters, etc. to capitals, etc. by depressing a key (**shift key**) —***n.*** **1.** the act of shifting; change [a *shift* in public opinion, a *shift* in the wind] **2.** a plan of conduct, esp. for an emergency; expedient; stratagem **3.** a deceitful scheme; trick **4.** *short for* GEARSHIFT **5.** a group of people working in relay with other groups, or the work period involved [the night *shift*] **6.** *a*) [Now Rare] a woman's slip *b*) a loose dress that hangs straight with no waistline **7.** *Football* a regrouping of the offensive backfield shortly before the ball is put in play —**make shift** to do the best one can (*with* the means at hand) —**shift′a·ble *adj.*** —**shift′er *n.***
shift·less (-lis) ***adj.*** lazy or careless —**shift′less·ly *adv.*** —**shift′less·ness *n.***
shift·y (shif′tē) ***adj.*** **shift′i·er, shift′i·est** having or showing a nature that is not to be trusted; full of shifts; tricky —**shift′i·ly *adv.*** —**shift′i·ness *n.***
Shih·chia·chuang (shu′jyä′jwäŋ′) city in NE China, southwest of Peking: pop. 1,118,000
Shih Tzu (shē′ dzo͞o′) *pl.* **Shih Tzus, Shih Tzu** [< Chin. *shih,* lion + *tzu,* son] any of a Chinese breed of small dog with long, silky hair and short legs
Shi·ko·ku (shē′kô ko͞o′) smallest of the four major islands of Japan, south of Honshu: c. 6,860 sq. mi.
shill (shil) ***n.*** [< ?] [Slang] the confederate of a gambler, pitchman, auctioneer, etc. who pretends to buy, bet, or bid so as to lure others
shil·le·lagh, shil·la·lah (shi lā′lē, -lə) ***n.*** [< *Shillelagh,* Irish village] a club or cudgel: also sp. **shil·le′lah**
shil·ling (shil′iŋ) ***n.*** [OE. *scylling*] **1.** *a*) a British money of account and silver coin, equal to 1/20 of a pound: symbol, /: coinage discontinued in 1971 *b*) any of several monetary units used in other countries: see MONETARY UNITS, table **2.** a coin of colonial America
shil·ly-shal·ly (shil′ē shal′ē) ***vi.*** **-lied, -ly·ing** [a redupl. of *shall I?*] to be unable to make up one's mind; show indecision; vacillate —***n.*** the act of shilly-shallying
Shi·loh (shī′lō) [after an ancient town in Israel] region in SW Tenn.: scene of a Civil War battle (1862)
shim (shim) ***n.*** [< ?] a thin piece of wood, metal, etc. used for filling space, leveling, etc. —***vt.*** **shimmed, shim′ming** to fit with a shim or shims
shim·mer (shim′ər) ***vi.*** [OE. *scymrian*] **1.** to shine with an unsteady light; glimmer **2.** to form a wavering image, as by reflection from waves of heat —***n.*** a shimmering light
shim·my (shim′ē) ***n.*** [< CHEMISE] **1.** a jazz dance of the 1920's, with much shaking of the body **2.** a shaking or wobbling, as in the front wheels of an automobile —***vi.*** **-mied, -my·ing** to shake or wobble
shin (shin) ***n.*** [OE. *scinu*] **1.** the front part of the leg between the knee and the ankle **2.** the lower foreleg in beef —***vt., vi.*** **shinned, shin′ning** to climb (a rope, pole, etc.) by gripping with both hands and legs: often with *up*
shin·bone (shin′bōn′) ***n.*** *same as* TIBIA
shin·dig (shin′dig′) ***n.*** [folk-etym. form of colloq. *shindy,* commotion] [Colloq.] a dance, party, or other social affair
shine (shīn) ***vi.*** **shone** or, esp. for vt. 2, **shined, shin′ing** [OE. *scinan*] **1.** to give off or reflect light; gleam; glow **2.** to excel; be eminent **3.** to show itself clearly [love *shone* from her face] —***vt.*** **1.** to direct the light of [to *shine* a flashlight] **2.** to make shiny by polishing —***n.*** **1.** brightness; radiance **2.** luster; polish; gloss **3.** *short for* SHOESHINE **4.** splendor; brilliance **5.** sunshine; fair weather —**shine up to** [Slang] to curry favor with —**take a shine to** [Slang] to take a liking to (someone)
shin·er (-ər) ***n.*** **1.** a person or thing that shines **2.** *pl.* **-ers, -er:** see PLURAL, II, D, 1 any of a number of freshwater minnows with silvery scales **3.** [Slang] *same as* BLACK EYE
shin·gle¹ (shiŋ′g'l) ***n.*** [prob. < Scand.] [Chiefly Brit.] **1.** coarse, waterworn gravel, as on a beach **2.** an area covered with this —**shin′gly *adj.*** **-gli·er, -gli·est**
shin·gle² (shiŋ′g'l) ***n.*** [prob. altered < OE. *scindel,* ult. < L. *scindula,* a shingle] **1.** a thin, wedge-shaped piece of wood, slate, etc. laid with others in a series of overlapping rows as a covering for roofs, etc. **2.** a woman's short haircut with the hair over the nape shaped close to the head **3.** [Colloq.] a small signboard, as that of a doctor or lawyer —***vt.*** **-gled, -gling** to cover (a roof, etc.) with shingles
shin·gles (shiŋ′g'lz) ***n.*** [< ML. < L. *cingulum,* a girdle < *cingere,* to gird] *same as* HERPES ZOSTER
shin·ing (shīn′iŋ) ***adj.*** **1.** giving off or reflecting light; bright **2.** brilliant; splendid [a *shining* example]
shin·ny¹ (shin′ē) ***n.,*** *pl.* **-nies** [prob. < SHIN] **1.** a simple form of hockey played by children **2.** the curved stick used in this game Also sp. **shin′ney**
shin·ny² (shin′ē) ***vi.*** **-nied, -ny·ing** *same as* SHIN
shin·plas·ter (shin′plas′tər) ***n.*** **1.** a plaster or poultice for use on sore shins **2.** formerly, a piece of paper money having a face value of less than a dollar
shin·splints (-splints′) ***n.pl.*** [*with sing. v.*] [? < SHIN + *splint,* bony growth] painful strain of extensor muscles in the lower leg, caused by running on a hard surface
Shin·to (shin′tō) ***n.*** [Jap. < Chin. *shin,* god + *tao,* way] a religion of Japan, emphasizing worship of nature and of ancestors —**Shin′to·ism *n.*** —**Shin′to·ist *n., adj.***
shin·y (shīn′ē) ***adj.*** **shin′i·er, shin′i·est** **1.** bright; shining **2.** highly polished; glossy —**shin′i·ness *n.***
ship (ship) ***n.*** [OE. *scip*] **1.** any large vessel navigating deep water **2.** a sailing vessel with a bowsprit and at least three square-rigged masts **3.** a ship's officers and crew **4.** an aircraft —***vt.*** **shipped, ship′ping** **1.** to put or take on board a ship **2.** to send or transport by any carrier [to *ship* coal by rail] **3.** to take in (water) over the side, as in a heavy sea **4.** to put or fix in its proper place on a ship or boat

[*ship* the oars] 5. to hire for work on a ship 6. [Colloq.] to send (*away, out,* etc.); get rid of —*vi.* 1. to go aboard ship; embark 2. to be hired to serve on a ship 3. to travel by ship —**ship over** to enlist or reenlist in the U.S. Navy —**when** (or **if,** etc.) **one's ship comes in** (or **home**) when (or if, etc.) one's fortune is made —**ship′pa·ble** *adj.*

-ship (ship) [OE. *-scipe*] *a suffix meaning:* 1. the quality or state of [*friendship*] 2. *a*) the rank or office of [*governorship*] *b*) one having the rank of [*lordship*] 3. ability as [*leadership*] 4. all individuals (of the specified class) collectively [*readership*]

ship biscuit *same as* HARDTACK

ship·board (ship′bôrd′) *n.* a ship: chiefly in **on shipboard,** aboard a ship —*adj.* done, happening, used etc. on a ship [a *shipboard* romance]

ship·build·er (-bil′dər) *n.* one whose business is building ships —**ship′build′ing** *n.*

ship canal a canal large enough for seagoing ships

ship·load (-lōd′) *n.* the load of a ship

ship·mas·ter (-mas′tər) *n.* the officer in command of a merchant ship; captain

ship·mate (-māt′) *n.* a fellow sailor on the same ship

ship·ment (-mənt) *n.* 1. the shipping or transporting of goods 2. goods shipped

ship of the line formerly, a warship of the largest class, having a position in the line of battle

ship·own·er (-ō′nər) *n.* an owner of a ship or ships

ship·per (-ər) *n.* a person who ships goods

ship·ping (-iŋ) *n.* 1. the act or business of transporting goods 2. ships collectively, as of a nation or port, esp. with reference to tonnage

ship·shape (-shāp′) *adj.* having everything neatly in place, as on board ship; trim —*adv.* in a neat and orderly manner

ship·side (-sīd′) *n.* the area on a pier alongside a ship

ship·worm (-wurm′) *n.* any of various small mollusks with wormlike bodies: they burrow into submerged wood

ship·wreck (-rek′) *n.* 1. the remains of a wrecked ship 2. the loss or destruction of a ship through storm, collision, etc. 3. any ruin or destruction —*vt.* 1. to cause to undergo shipwreck 2. to destroy, ruin, or wreck

ship·wright (-rīt′) *n.* a man, esp. a carpenter, whose work is the construction and repair of ships

ship·yard (-yärd′) *n.* a place where ships are built and repaired

shire (shīr) *n.* [OE. *scir,* office] 1. any of the former districts in Great Britain coinciding generally with the modern county 2. any of the counties of Great Britain with a name ending in *-shire*

shirk (shurk) *vt., vi.* [? akin to G. *schurke,* rascal] to neglect or evade doing (something that should be done) —**shirk′er** *n.*

Shir·ley (shur′lē) [ult. < OE. *scire,* shire + *leah,* lea] a feminine name

shirr (shur) *n.* [< ?] *same as* SHIRRING —*vt.* 1. to make shirring in (cloth or a garment) 2. to bake (eggs) with crumbs in small buttered dishes

shirr·ing (-iŋ) *n.* 1. a gathering made in cloth by drawing the material up on parallel rows of short, running stitches 2. any trim made by shirring

shirt (shurt) *n.* [OE. *scyrte*] 1. *a*) the usual sleeved garment worn by men on the upper part of the body, often under a suit coat, typically having a collar and a buttoned opening down the front *b*) a similar garment for women 2. *same as* UNDERSHIRT —**keep one's shirt on** [Slang] to remain patient or calm —**lose one's shirt** [Slang] to lose everything

shirt·ing (-iŋ) *n.* material for making shirts

shirt-sleeve (-slēv′) *adj.* 1. in, or suitable for being in, one's shirt sleeves 2. plain; informal 3. homespun; homely [*shirt-sleeve* philosophy]

shirt·tail (shurt′tāl′) *n.* the part of a shirt extending below the waist

shirt·waist (-wāst′) *n.* 1. a woman's blouse tailored more or less like a shirt 2. a dress with a bodice like a shirtwaist: also **shirtwaist dress, shirt′dress′** *n.*

shish ke·bab (shish′ kə bäb′) [< Arm., ult. < Ar. *shīsh,* skewer + *kabāb,* kebab] a broiled dish consisting of small chunks of meat, esp. lamb, placed on skewers alternately with tomatoes, onions, etc.: also **shish′ ka·bob′**

shiv (shiv) *n.* [prob. < Romany *chiv,* a blade] [Slang] a knife, esp. one with a narrow blade used as a weapon

Shi·va (shē′və) *var. of* SIVA

shiv·a·ree (shiv′ə rē′, shiv′ə rē′) *n.* [< CHARIVARI] a mock serenade, as to newlyweds, with kettles, horns, etc. —*vt.* **-reed′, -ree′ing** to serenade with a shivaree

shiv·er[1] (shiv′ər) *n.* [ME. *schivere*] a fragment or splinter of something broken, as glass —*vt., vi.* to break into many fragments or splinters; shatter —**shiv′er·y** *adj.*

shiv·er[2] (shiv′ər) *vi.* [ME. *cheveren* < ? OE. *ceafl,* a jaw] to shake, tremble, etc., as from fear or cold —*n.* a shaking, trembling, etc., as from fear or cold —**the shivers** a fit of shivering —**shiv′er·y** *adj.*

shmaltz (shmälts) *n.* [Slang] *var. sp. of* SCHMALTZ —**shmaltz′y** *adj.* **shmaltz′i·er, shmaltz′i·est**

shoal[1] (shōl) *n.* [OE. *scolu*] 1. a large group; mass; crowd 2. a large school of fish —*vi.* to come together in or move about as a shoal

shoal[2] (shōl) *n.* [OE. *sceald,* shallow] 1. a shallow place in a river, sea, etc. 2. a sand bar, etc. forming a shallow place that is a danger to navigation, esp. one visible at low water —*vt., vi.* to make or become shallow —**shoal′y** *adj.* **shoal′i·er, shoal′i·est**

shoat (shōt) *n.* [< ?] a young hog of between about 100 and 180 lbs.

shock[1] (shäk) *n.* [< Fr. < MFr. *choquer,* prob. < MDu. *schokken,* to collide] 1. *a*) a sudden, powerful blow, shake, disturbance, etc. *b*) the effect of this 2. *a*) a sudden and strong upsetting of the mind or feelings *b*) something causing this [her accident was a *shock* to us] 3. the violent effect on the body of an electric current passed through it 4. [Colloq.] *short for* SHOCK ABSORBER: *used in pl.* 5. *Med.* a disorder caused by severe injury or damage to the body, loss of blood, etc., and marked by a sharp drop in blood pressure, a rapid pulse, etc. —*vt.* 1. to disturb emotionally; astonish, horrify, etc. 2. to affect with physical shock 3. to produce electric shock in —*vi.* to be shocked, distressed, etc. [one who does not *shock* easily] —**shock′er** *n.*

shock[2] (shäk) *n.* [prob. via MDu. or MLowG. *schok*] a number of grain sheaves, as of corn or wheat, stacked together on end to cure and dry —*vt., vi.* to gather in shocks

SHOCKS OF CORN

shock[3] (shäk) *n.* [< ? prec.] a thick, bushy or tangled mass, as of hair

shock absorber a device, as on the springs of a car, that lessens or absorbs the force of shocks

shock·ing (shäk′iŋ) *adj.* causing great surprise, horror, disgust, etc. —**shock′ing·ly** *adv.*

shock·proof (-prōōf′) *adj.* able to absorb shock without being damaged [a *shockproof* watch]

shock therapy a method of treating certain psychotic conditions by injecting certain drugs or by applying electric current to the brain, which results in convulsion or coma: also **shock treatment**

shock troops troops especially chosen, trained, and equipped to lead an attack

shod (shäd) *alt. pt. & pp. of* SHOE

shod·den (shäd′'n) *alt. pp. of* SHOE

shod·dy (shäd′ē) *n., pl.* **shod′dies** [< ?] 1. an inferior woolen yarn or cloth made from fibers of used fabrics 2. anything of less worth than it seems to have; esp., an inferior imitation —*adj.* **shod′di·er, shod′di·est** 1. *a*) made of shoddy *b*) made of any inferior material *c*) poorly done or made 2. sham 3. contemptible; low [a *shoddy* trick] —**shod′di·ly** *adv.* —**shod′di·ness** *n.*

shoe (shōō) *n.* [OE. *sceoh*] 1. an outer covering for the foot, made of leather, canvas, etc. and usually having a stiff sole and a heel 2. something like a shoe in shape or use; specif., *a*) *short for* HORSESHOE, BRAKE SHOE *b*) the metal strip along the bottom of a sled runner *c*) the casing of a pneumatic tire —*vt.* **shod** or **shoed, shod** or **shoed** or **shod′den, shoe′ing** to furnish with shoes —**fill one's shoes** to take one's place —**in another's shoes** in another's position

shoe·black (-blak′) *n. same as* BOOTBLACK

shoe·horn (-hôrn′) *n.* an implement of metal, horn, plastic, etc. with a troughlike blade, inserted at the back of a shoe to help in slipping the heel in —*vt.* to force or squeeze into a narrow space

shoe·lace (-lās′) *n.* a length of cord, leather, etc. used for lacing and fastening a shoe

shoe·mak·er (-māk′ər) *n.* a person whose business is making or repairing shoes —**shoe′mak′ing** *n.*

shoe·pac (-pak′) *n.* [altered (after SHOE & PAC) < AmInd. *shipak* < *paku,* shoe] *same as* PAC

sho·er (shōō′ər) *n.* a person who shoes horses

shoe·shine (-shīn′) *n.* the cleaning and polishing of a pair of shoes

shoe·string (-striŋ′) *n.* 1. *same as* SHOELACE 2. a small amount of money as capital [the business was started on a *shoestring*]

shoestring potatoes potatoes cut into long, very narrow strips and fried crisp in deep fat

shoe tree a form, as of wood or metal, put into a shoe to stretch it or preserve its shape

sho·gun (shō′gun′, -gōōn′) ***n.*** [Jap. < Chin. *chiang-chun,* leader of an army] any of the military governors who ruled Japan until 1868 —**sho′gun·ate** (-it, -gə nāt′) ***n.***

Sho·lo·khov (shô′lô khôf), **Mi·kha·il (Aleksandrovich)** (mi khä ēl′) 1905– ; Russ. novelist

Sho·lom A·leich·em (shô′ləm ä läkh′əm) (pseud. of *Solomon Rabinowitz*) 1859–1916; Russ. writer in Yiddish

shone (shōn) *pt. & pp. of* SHINE

shoo (shōō) ***interj.*** [echoic] **1.** an exclamation used in driving away chickens and other animals **2.** go away! get out! —***vi.*** **shooed, shoo′ing** to cry "shoo" —***vt.*** to drive away abruptly, by or as by crying "shoo"

shoo-in (shōō′in′) ***n.*** [SHOO + IN] [Colloq.] someone or something expected to win easily in an election, a race, etc.

shook (shook) *pt. and dial. pp. of* SHAKE —**shook up** [Slang] upset; disturbed

shoot (shōōt) ***vt.*** **shot, shoot′ing** [OE. *sceotan*] **1.** *a)* to move swiftly over, by, etc. *[to shoot the rapids in a canoe]* *b)* to make move with great force *[to shoot an elevator upward]* **2.** to pour, empty out, or dump, as down a chute **3.** *a)* to hurl or thrust out *[volcanoes shooting molten rock]* *b)* to cast (an anchor, net, etc.) *c)* to throw away or spoil (an opportunity, etc.) *d)* [Colloq.] to use up or waste (time, money, etc.) **4.** to slide (a door bolt) into or out of its fastening **5.** *a)* to streak or fleck (*with* another color or substance) *[blue shot with orange]* *b)* to vary (*with* something different) *[a story shot with humor]* **6.** to put forth (a branch, leaves, etc.) **7.** *a)* to launch (a rocket), discharge (a bullet, arrow, etc.), or fire (a gun, bow, etc.) *b)* to discharge (rays) with force **8.** to send forth (a question, fist, etc.) swiftly or with force **9.** to hit, wound, kill, or destroy with a bullet, arrow, etc. **10.** to take the altitude of (a star), as with a sextant **11.** to photograph or film **12.** to inject, as with drugs **13.** *Games, Sports a)* to throw or drive (a ball, etc.) toward the objective *b)* to score (a goal, points, etc.) *c)* to play (golf, pool, craps, etc.) *d)* to make (a specified bet), as in craps —***vi.*** **1.** *a)* to move swiftly, as an arrow from a bow *b)* to spurt or gush **2.** to be felt suddenly and keenly, as pain, etc. **3.** to grow or sprout rapidly **4.** to jut out; project **5.** to fire a missile, gun, etc. **6.** to use guns, bows and arrows, etc., as in hunting **7.** *a)* to photograph a scene *b)* to start movie cameras working **8.** *Sports a)* to propel a ball, etc. toward the objective *b)* to roll dice —***n.*** **1.** *a)* the act of shooting *b)* a shooting trip, party, or contest **2.** the act of sprouting **3.** a new growth; sprout or twig **4.** the launching of a rocket, guided missile, etc. **5.** a sloping trough; chute **6.** a spasm of pain —***interj.*** **1.** an exclamation of disgust, disappointment, etc. **2.** begin talking! —**shoot at** (or **for**) [Colloq.] to strive for —**shoot from the hip** to act or talk impetuously —**shoot off one's** (or **at the**) **mouth** [Slang] **1.** to speak without caution; blab **2.** to boast —**shoot′er** ***n.***

shooting star *same as* METEOR

shoot-out, shoot·out (shōōt′out′) ***n.*** [Slang] a battle with handguns, etc., as between police and criminals

shop (shäp) ***n.*** [OE. *sceoppa,* booth] **1.** *a)* a place where certain goods or services are offered for sale *b)* a specialized department in a large store *[the gourmet shop]* **2.** a place where a particular kind of work is done *[a printing shop]* **3.** in some schools, a manual-training course, class, or department —***vi.*** **shopped, shop′ping** to visit shops so as to examine or buy merchandise —**set up shop** to start a business —**shop around** **1.** to go from shop to shop, looking for bargains or special items **2.** to search for a good or better job, idea, etc. —**talk shop** to discuss one's work

shop·girl (-gurl′) ***n.*** [Chiefly Brit.] *same as* SALESWOMAN

shop·keep·er (shäp′kē′pər) ***n.*** a person who owns or operates a shop, or small store —**shop′keep′ing** ***n.***

shop·lift·er (-lif′tər) ***n.*** a person who steals articles from a store during shopping hours —**shop′lift′** ***vt., vi.***

shoppe (shäp) ***n.*** *var. of* SHOP (sense 1)

shop·per (shäp′ər) ***n.*** **1.** a person who shops; esp., one hired by a store to shop for others **2.** a person hired by a store to compare competitors' merchandise and prices

shopping center a complex of stores, restaurants, etc. with an adjoining parking lot

shop steward a person elected by his fellow workers in a union shop to represent them in dealing with the employer

shop·talk (shäp′tôk′) ***n.*** **1.** the specialized vocabulary of a particular occupation, etc. **2.** conversation about one's work, esp. after hours

shop·worn (-wôrn′) ***adj.*** **1.** soiled, faded, etc. from having been displayed in a shop **2.** drab, dull, trite, etc.

Shor·an (shôr′an) ***n.*** [*Sho(rt) Ra(nge) N(avigation)*] [*also* **s-**] a radar system for locating the position of a plane, etc. by signals from a pair of transponders on the ground

shore[1] (shôr) ***n.*** [< OE. hyp. *score* < or akin to *scorian,* to jut out] **1.** land at the edge of a body of water **2.** land as opposed to water

shore[2] (shôr) ***n.*** [akin to MDu. *schore,* OIce. *skortha,* a prop] a beam, etc. placed under or against something as a prop —***vt.*** **shored, shor′ing** to support or make stable as with shores (usually with *up*)

shore dinner a meal with a variety of seafood dishes

shore leave leave granted to a ship's crew for going ashore

shore·line (-līn′) ***n.*** the edge of a body of water

shore patrol a detail of the U.S. Navy, Coast Guard, or Marine Corps serving as military police on shore

shore·ward (-wərd) ***adv.*** toward the shore: also **shore′wards** —***adj.*** moving toward the shore

shor·ing (shôr′iŋ) ***n.*** **1.** the act of supporting with shores **2.** a system of shores used for support

shorn (shôrn) *alt. pp. of* SHEAR

short (shôrt) ***adj.*** [OE. *scort*] **1.** not extending far from end to end; not long **2.** not great in range or scope *[a short journey, view, etc.]* **3.** low in height; not tall **4.** lasting but a little time; brief **5.** not retentive *[a short memory]* **6.** condensed or concise **7.** brief to the point of rudeness; curt **8.** less than a sufficient or correct amount *[short on money]* **9.** not far enough to reach the objective *[the shot fell short]* **10.** having a tendency to crumble, as pastry **11.** *a)* not possessing at the time of sale the commodity or security one is selling *b)* designating or of a sale of commodities or securities which the seller does not have but expects to buy later at a lower price **12.** *Phonet. & Prosody* comparatively brief in duration, as sounds, syllables, etc. —***n.*** **1.** something short; specif., *a)* a short sound or syllable *b)* *same as* SHORT SUBJECT **2.** a variation of clothing size shorter than the average **3.** [*pl.*] *a)* formerly, knee breeches *b)* short trousers reaching partway to the knee *c)* a man's undergarment of similar form **4.** [*pl.*] items needed to make up a shortage or deficiency **5.** [*pl.*] a byproduct of wheat milling that consists of bran, germ, and coarse meal **6.** *clipped form of: a)* SHORTSTOP *b)* SHORT CIRCUIT —***adv.*** **1.** abruptly; suddenly **2.** rudely; curtly **3.** briefly; concisely **4.** so as to be short **5.** by surprise; unawares *[caught short]* **6.** by a short sale —***vt., vi.*** **1.** to give less than what is needed, usual, etc. **2.** *clipped form of: a)* SHORTCHANGE *b)* SHORT-CIRCUIT —**fall** (or **come**) **short** **1.** to be insufficient **2.** to fail to reach —**in short** **1.** in summing up **2.** briefly —**run short** to have less than enough —**short for** being an abbreviation of —**short of** **1.** less than **2.** lacking **3.** without actually resorting to —**the short end of the stick** the worst of a deal —**short′ish** ***adj.*** —**short′ness** ***n.***

short·age (-ij) ***n.*** a deficiency in amount; deficit

short·bread (-bred′) ***n.*** a rich, crumbly cake or cookie made with much shortening

short·cake (-kāk′) ***n.*** a light biscuit or a sweet cake served with fruit, etc. as a dessert

short·change (-chānj′) ***vt., vi.*** **-changed′, -chang′ing** [Colloq.] **1.** to give less money than is due in change **2.** to cheat —**short′chang′er** ***n.***

short-cir·cuit (-sur′kit) ***vt.*** **1.** *Elec.* to make a short circuit in **2.** to bypass (an obstruction, custom, etc.) **3.** to thwart —***vi.*** to develop a short circuit

short circuit **1.** a usually accidental low-resistance connection between two points in an electric circuit that deflects the current or causes excessive current flow **2.** popularly, a disrupted electric circuit resulting from this

short·com·ing (-kum′iŋ) ***n.*** a falling short of what is expected or required; defect or deficiency

short·cut (-kut′) ***n.*** **1.** a shorter way to get to the same place **2.** any way of saving time, effort, expense, etc.

short·en (shôrt′'n) ***vt., vi.*** to make or become short or shorter —**short′en·er** ***n.***

short·en·ing (shôrt′'n iŋ, shôrt′niŋ) ***n.*** **1.** a making or becoming short or shorter **2.** fat used to make pastry, etc. crisp or flaky

short·hand (-hand′) ***n.*** any system of special symbols for letters, words, and phrases for taking notes, dictation, etc. rapidly —***adj.*** written in or using shorthand

"THIS IS A SAMPLE OF SHORTHAND WRITING"

short-hand·ed (-han′did) ***adj.*** short of workers or helpers

short·head·ed (shôrt′hed′id) ***adj.*** having a short or broad head —**short′head′ed·ness** ***n.***

short·horn (-hôrn′) ***n.*** any of a breed of cattle with short, curved horns: they are raised for both beef and milk

short-lived (-līvd′, -livd′) ***adj.*** having or tending to have a short life span or existence

short·ly (-lē) ***adv.*** **1.** in a few words; briefly **2.** in a short time; soon **3.** abruptly and rudely; curtly

short order any food that can be cooked or served quickly when ordered, as at a lunch counter —**short′-or′der** ***adj.***

short-range (shôrt′rānj′) ***adj.*** **1.** having a range of short distance **2.** not looking far into the future [*short-range* plans]

short shrift very little care or attention, as from lack of patience or sympathy —**make short shrift of** to dispose of quickly and impatiently: also **give short shrift**

short·sight·ed (shôrt′sīt′id) ***adj.*** **1.** *same as* NEARSIGHTED **2.** having or showing a lack of foresight —**short′sight′ed·ly** ***adv.*** —**short′sight′ed·ness** ***n.***

short·stop (-stäp′) ***n.*** *Baseball* the infielder stationed between second and third base

short story a kind of story shorter than the novel or novelette and more limited in scope and number of characters

short subject any short film presentation shown along with the feature in a motion-picture program

short-tem·pered (-tem′pərd) ***adj.*** having a tendency to lose one's temper; easily or quickly angered

short-term (-turm′) ***adj.*** **1.** for a short time **2.** designating or of a capital gain, loan, etc. that involves a relatively short period

short ton a ton that is 2,000 pounds avoirdupois

short-waist·ed (-wās′tid) ***adj.*** with a high waistline

short·wave (-wāv′) ***n.*** **1.** a radio wave sixty meters or less in length **2.** a radio or radio band for broadcasting or receiving shortwaves: in full, **shortwave radio**

short-wind·ed (-win′did) ***adj.*** **1.** easily put out of breath by exertion **2.** breathing with quick, labored breaths

short·y, short·ie (-ē) ***n.***, *pl.* **short′ies** [Colloq.] a person or thing of less than average height or size

Sho·sho·ne (shō shō′nē) ***n.*** [< ? Shoshonean *tsosoni*, curly head] **1.** *pl.* **-sho′nes, -sho′ne** any member of a group of N. American Indians scattered over Idaho, Nevada, Utah, Wyoming, and California **2.** their Shoshonean language Also sp. **Sho·sho′ni**

Sho·sho·ne·an (shō shō′nē ən, shō′shə nē′ən) ***n.*** a branch of the Uto-Aztecan languages —***adj.*** **1.** of Shoshonean **2.** of the Shoshones

Sho·sta·ko·vich (shô′stä kô′vich; *E.* shäs′tə kō′vich), **Dmi·tri** (d′mē′trē) 1906–75; Russ. composer

shot[1] (shät) ***n.*** [OE. *sceot*] **1.** the act of shooting; discharge of a missile, esp. from a gun **2.** *a)* the distance a missile travels *b)* range; scope **3.** an attempt to hit with a missile **4.** *a)* any attempt or try *b)* a guess **5.** a pointed, critical remark **6.** the flight or path of an object thrown, driven, etc. in any of several games **7.** *a)* a projectile to be discharged from a firearm, esp. a solid ball or bullet *b)* such projectiles collectively **8.** a small pellet or pellets of lead, used for a charge of a shotgun **9.** the ball used in the shot put: see SHOT PUT **10.** a blast **11.** a marksman [a fair *shot*] **12.** *a)* a single photograph *b)* a sequence or view taken by a single continuous run of a movie or TV camera **13.** a hypodermic injection, as of vaccine **14.** a drink of liquor **15.** [Colloq.] a bet, with reference to the odds given [a ten-to-one *shot*] —***vt.*** **shot′ted, shot′ting** to load or weight with shot —**a shot in the arm** something that bolsters up, encourages, etc. —**call the shots** **1.** to give orders **2.** to control what happens —**have** (or **take**) **a shot at** [Colloq.] to make a try at —**like a shot** quickly or suddenly

shot[2] (shät) *pt. & pp. of* SHOOT —***adj.*** **1.** variegated, streaked, etc. with another color or substance **2.** varied with something different **3.** [Colloq.] ruined or worn out

shote (shōt) ***n.*** *var. of* SHOAT

shot·gun (shät′gun′) ***n.*** a smoothbore gun for firing a charge of small shot at short range —***vt., vi.*** to shoot, force, etc. with a shotgun

shot put (poot′) **1.** a contest in which a heavy metal ball is propelled by an overhand thrust from the shoulder **2.** a single put of the shot —**shot′-put′ter** ***n.*** —**shot′-put′ting** ***n.***

should (shood; *unstressed, often* shəd) ***v.*** [OE. *sceolde*, pt. of *sceal*, I am obliged] **1.** *pt. of* SHALL **2.** an auxiliary used to express: *a)* obligation, duty, etc. [he *should* help her] *b)* expectation or probability [he *should* be here soon] : equivalent to *ought to* *c)* futurity from the standpoint of the past in indirect quotations: replaceable by *would* [I said I *should* (or *would*) be home late] *d)* futurity in polite requests or in statements implying doubt: replaceable by *would* [I *should* (or *would*) think he'd like it] *e)* a future condition [if I *should* die tomorrow] *f)* a past condition: replaceable by *would* [I *should* (or *would*) have gone had you asked me] In the usage of some grammarians, the distinctions between *should* and *would* are the same as those between *shall* and *will*: *see* WILL[2]

shoul·der (shōl′dər) ***n.*** [OE. *sculdor*] **1.** *a)* the joint connecting the arm or forelimb with the body *b)* the part of the body including this joint, extending to the base of the neck **2.** [*pl.*] the two shoulders and the part of the back between them **3.** a cut of meat consisting of the upper foreleg and attached parts **4.** the part of a garment that covers the shoulder **5.** a shoulderlike projection **6.** the strip along the edge of a paved road; berm —***vt.*** **1.** to push along or through, as with the shoulder **2.** to carry upon the shoulder **3.** to assume the burden of —***vi.*** to push with the shoulder —**cry on someone's shoulder** to tell one's troubles to someone in seeking sympathy —**put one's shoulder to the wheel** to set to work vigorously —**shoulder arms** to rest a rifle against the shoulder, supporting the butt with the hand —**shoulder to shoulder** **1.** side by side and close together **2.** working together —**straight from the shoulder** **1.** moving straight forward from the shoulder: said of a blow **2.** without reserve; frankly —**turn** (or **give**) **a cold shoulder to** to treat with disdain; avoid

shoulder blade either of two flat bones in the upper back

shoulder harness a restraining strap passing over the shoulder and body to the hip, used for safety in a car

shoulder strap **1.** a strap, usually one of a pair, worn over the shoulder to support a garment **2.** a strap worn over the shoulder for carrying an attached purse, camera, etc. **3.** a flap of cloth on the shoulder of a uniform, coat, etc.

should·n't (shood′′nt) should not

shouldst (shoodst) *archaic 2d pers. sing. pt. of* SHALL: *used with* thou: also **should·est** (shood′ist)

shout (shout) ***n.*** [ME. *schoute*] a loud, sudden cry, call, or outburst —***vt., vi.*** to utter in a shout or cry out loudly —**shout down** to silence by loud shouting —**shout′er** ***n.***

shove (shuv) ***vt., vi.*** **shoved, shov′ing** [OE. *scufan*] **1.** to push, as along a surface **2.** to push roughly —***n.*** a push or thrust —**shove off** **1.** to push (a boat) away from shore **2.** [Colloq.] to start off; leave —**shov′er** ***n.***

shov·el (shuv′′l) ***n.*** [OE. *scofl*] **1.** *a)* a tool with a broad scoop or blade and a long handle: used in lifting and moving loose material *b)* any machine with a shovellike device **2.** *same as* SHOVELFUL —***vt.*** **-eled** or **-elled, -el·ing** or **-el·ling** **1.** to lift and move with a shovel **2.** to dig out (a path, etc.) with a shovel **3.** to put in large quantities [to *shovel* food in one's mouth] —***vi.*** to use a shovel

shov·el·er, shov·el·ler (shuv′′l ər, shuv′lər) ***n.*** **1.** a person or thing that shovels **2.** a freshwater duck with a long, broad, flattened bill: also **shov′el·bill′**

shov·el·ful (shuv′′l fool′) ***n.***, *pl.* **-fuls′** as much as a shovel will hold

show (shō) ***vt.*** **showed, shown** or **showed, show′ing** [OE. *sceawian*, to look] **1.** to bring or put in sight; make visible; exhibit; display **2.** to guide; conduct [*show* him to his room] **3.** to direct attention to; point out [we *showed* him the sights] **4.** to reveal, manifest, etc. [to *show* anger] **5.** to explain, prove, or demonstrate [to *show* how it works] **6.** to register [a clock *shows* the time] **7.** to grant or bestow (favor, mercy, etc.) —***vi.*** **1.** to be or become seen; appear **2.** to be noticeable [the scratch won't *show*] **3.** to finish third or no worse than third in a horse or dog race **4.** [Colloq.] to come or arrive as expected —***n.*** **1.** a showing or demonstration [a *show* of passion] **2.** a display or exhibition, esp. in public or for the public **3.** a spectacular, pompous display **4.** a trace as of metal, coal, etc. in the earth **5.** something false; pretense [her sorrow was mere *show*] **6.** a ridiculous spectacle **7.** a presentation of entertainment, as a TV program or a movie **8.** third position at the finish of a horse or dog race —**for show** in order to attract attention —**put** (or **get**) **the show on the road** [Slang] to start an activity, venture, etc. —**show off** **1.** to make a display of **2.** to do something meant to attract attention —**show up** **1.** to expose or be exposed **2.** to come; arrive **3.** [Colloq.] to surpass

show·boat (-bōt′) ***n.*** a boat with a theater in which plays are presented for people who live in river towns

show·bread (-bred′) ***n.*** *same as* SHEWBREAD

show business the theater, motion pictures, television, etc. as a business or industry: also [Colloq.] **show biz**

show·case (-kās′) ***n.*** **1.** a glass-enclosed case for protecting things on display **2.** a means of displaying to good advantage [the revue was a *showcase* for new talent] —***vt.*** **-cased′, -cas′ing** to display to good advantage

show·down (-doun′) ***n.*** [Colloq.] **1.** *Poker* the laying down of the cards face up to see who wins **2.** any action that brings matters to a climax or settles them

show·er[1] (shō′ər) ***n.*** a person who shows something

show·er[2] (shou′ər) ***n.*** [OE. *scur*] **1.** a brief fall of rain, hail, sleet, or snow **2.** a sudden, abundant fall or flow, as of tears, rays, sparks, etc. **3.** a party at which gifts are presented to the guest of honor **4.** *a)* a bath in which the body is sprayed with fine streams of water from a perforated nozzle: in full, **shower bath** *b)* an apparatus, or a room or enclosure, for this —*vt.* **1.** to make wet as with a spray of water **2.** to pour forth as in a shower [*showered* with praise] —*vi.* **1.** to fall or come as a shower **2.** to bathe under a shower —**show′er·y** *adj.*

show·girl (shō′gurl′) *n.* same as CHORUS GIRL

show·ing (shō′iŋ) *n.* an exhibition, display, or performance

show·man (shō′mən) *n., pl.* **-men** **1.** a person whose business is producing or presenting shows **2.** a person skilled at this or at presenting anything in a striking manner —**show′man·ship′** *n.*

shown (shōn) *alt. pp. of* SHOW

show·off (shō′ôf′) *n.* **1.** a showing off to attract attention **2.** a person who shows off

show·piece (-pēs′) *n.* **1.** something exhibited **2.** something that is a fine example of its kind

show·place (-plās′) *n.* **1.** a place that is exhibited to the public for its beauty, etc. **2.** any place that is beautiful, lavishly furnished, etc.

show·room (-ro͞om′) *n.* a room where merchandise is displayed, as for advertising or sale

show window a store window for displaying goods

show·y (-ē) *adj.* **show′i·er, show′i·est** **1.** of striking appearance **2.** attracting attention in a gaudy or flashy way —**show′i·ly** *adv.* —**show′i·ness** *n.*

shrank (shraŋk) *alt. pt. of* SHRINK

shrap·nel (shrap′n'l) *n.* [after H. *Shrapnel* (1761–1842), Brit. general who invented it] **1.** an artillery shell filled with an explosive charge and many small metal balls, set to explode in the air **2.** these metal balls or the shell fragments scattered by any exploding shell

shred (shred) *n.* [OE. *screade*] **1.** a long, narrow strip or piece cut or torn off **2.** a very small piece or amount; fragment [not a *shred* of truth] —*vt.* **shred′ded** or **shred, shred′ding** to cut or tear into shreds —**shred′der** *n.*

Shreve·port (shrēv′pôrt) [after H. M. *Shreve* (1785–1854), U.S. inventor] city in NW La.: pop. 206,000

shrew (shro͞o) *n.* [OE. *screawa*] **1.** a small, mouselike mammal with soft, brown fur and a long snout: also **shrew′mouse′**, *pl.* **-mice′** **2.** a nagging, bad-tempered woman —**shrew′ish** *adj.* —**shrew′ish·ness** *n.*

shrewd (shro͞od) *adj.* [< ME. pp. of *schrewen,* to curse < *schrewe,* shrew] keen-witted, clever, or sharp in practical affairs; astute —**shrewd′ly** *adv.* —**shrewd′ness** *n.*

shriek (shrēk) *vi.* [prob. < ON.] to make a loud, sharp, piercing cry or sound; screech; scream —*vt.* to utter with a shriek —*n.* a loud, piercing cry or sound —**shriek′er** *n.*

shrift (shrift) *n.* [OE. *scrift* < *scrifan,* to shrive] [Archaic] **1.** confession to and absolution by a priest **2.** the act of shriving See also SHORT SHRIFT

shrike (shrīk) *n.* [OE. *scric*] any of several shrill-voiced birds with hooked beaks: most types feed on insects, some on small birds, frogs, etc., which are sometimes impaled on thorns

shrill (shril) *adj.* [ME. *schrille:* echoic] **1.** having or producing a high, thin, piercing tone; high-pitched **2.** characterized or accompanied by shrill sounds **3.** irritatingly insistent —*vt., vi.* to utter with or make a shrill sound —**shrill′ness** *n.* —**shril′ly** *adv.*

shrimp (shrimp) *n., pl.* **shrimps, shrimp:** see PLURAL, II, D, 1 [< base of OE. *scrimman,* to shrink] **1.** a small, long-tailed crustacean, valued as food **2.** [Colloq.] a small, slight person —*vi.* to fish for shrimp —**shrimp′er** *n.*

SHRIMP (to 9 in. long)

shrine (shrīn) *n.* [OE. *scrin* < L. *scrinium,* box] **1.** a container holding sacred relics **2.** the tomb of a saint or revered person **3.** a place of worship, usually one whose center is a sacred scene or object **4.** a place or thing hallowed or honored because of its history or associations

shrink (shriŋk) *vi.* **shrank** or **shrunk, shrunk** or **shrunk′en, shrink′ing** [OE. *scrincan*] **1.** to contract, as from heat, cold, wetness, etc. **2.** to lessen, as in amount, worth, etc. **3.** to draw back in fear, dislike, etc.; cower or flinch —*vt.* to cause to shrink or contract —*n.* **1.** a shrinking **2.** [< (*head*)*shrink*(*er*)] [Slang] a psychiatrist: also **shrink′er**

shrink·age (shriŋ′kij) *n.* **1.** the act or process of shrinking, as of a fabric in washing **2.** decrease in value; depreciation **3.** the amount of shrink, decrease, etc.

shrinking violet a very shy or modest person

shrink-wrap (shriŋk′rap′) *vt.* **-wrapped′, -wrap′ping** to wrap (a commodity) in a tough, transparent plastic material which is then shrunk by heating to form a sealed, tightfitting package —*n.* a wrapping of such material

shrive (shrīv) *vt., vi.* **shrived** or **shrove, shriv′en** (shriv′'n) or **shrived, shriv′ing** [OE. *scrifan,* ult. < L. *scribere,* to write] [Archaic] **1.** to hear the confession of (a person) and, usually after penance, give absolution **2.** to get absolution for (oneself) by confessing and doing penance

shriv·el (shriv′'l) *vt., vi.* **-eled** or **-elled, -el·ing** or **-el·ling** [prob. < Scand.] **1.** to shrink and make or become wrinkled or withered **2.** to make or become helpless, useless, etc.

shroud (shroud) *n.* [OE. *scrud*] **1.** a cloth used to wrap a corpse for burial **2.** something that covers, protects, or screens; veil **3.** any of the ropes stretched from a ship's side to a masthead to offset lateral strain on the mast **4.** any of the lines from a parachute's canopy to the harness: in full, **shroud line** —*vt.* **1.** to wrap (a corpse) in a shroud **2.** to hide; cover; screen

shrove (shrōv) *alt. pt. of* SHRIVE

Shrove·tide (shrōv′tīd′) *n.* the three days before Ash Wednesday (**Shrove Sunday, Monday,** and **Tuesday**), formerly set aside as a period of confession and of festivity just before Lent

shrub[1] (shrub) *n.* [OE. *scrybb,* brushwood] a low, woody plant with several permanent stems instead of a single trunk; bush —**shrub′like′** *adj.*

shrub[2] (shrub) *n.* [< Ar. *sharāb,* drink] a drink made of fruit juice, sugar, and, usually, rum or brandy

shrub·ber·y (shrub′ər ē) *n., pl.* **-ber·ies** a group or heavy growth of shrubs, as around a house

shrub·by (-ē) *adj.* **-bi·er, -bi·est** **1.** covered with shrubs **2.** like a shrub —**shrub′bi·ness** *n.*

shrug (shrug) *vt., vi.* **shrugged, shrug′ging** [ME. *schruggen,* orig., to shiver] to draw up (the shoulders), as in expressing indifference, doubt, disdain, etc. —*n.* the gesture so made —**shrug off** to dismiss in a carefree way

shrunk (shruŋk) *alt. pt. & pp. of* SHRINK

shrunk·en (-'n) *alt. pp. of* SHRINK —*adj.* contracted in size

‡**shtet·l** (shtet′'l) *n., pl.* **shtet′lach** (-läkh); E. **shtet′ls** (-'lz) [Yid., dim. of *shtat,* city < G. *stadt*] any of the former Jewish village communities of E Europe, esp. in Russia

shtick (shtik) *n.* [Yid., pranks, caprice] [Slang] **1.** a comic piece of business, as in a vaudeville act **2.** a characteristic talent, trait, bit of behavior, etc.

shuck (shuk) *n.* [< ?] **1.** a shell, pod, or husk **2.** the shell of an oyster or clam **3.** [Slang] *a*) a hoax or fraud *b*) a phony —*vt.* **1.** to remove shucks from (corn, clams, etc.) **2.** to remove like a shuck [to *shuck* one's clothes] —*vi.* [Slang] to fool or deceive —**shuck′er** *n.*

shucks (shuks) *interj.* an exclamation of mild disappointment, embarrassment, etc.

shud·der (shud′ər) *vi.* [ME. *schoderen*] to shake or tremble suddenly and violently, as in horror —*n.* a shuddering; sudden, strong tremor —**the shudders** a feeling of horror, disgust, etc. —**shud′der·ing·ly** *adv.* —**shud′der·y** *adj.*

shuf·fle (shuf′'l) *vt.* **-fled, -fling** [prob. < or akin to LowG. *schuffeln* < base of SHOVE] **1.** to move (the feet) with a dragging gait **2.** to mix (playing cards) so as to change their order **3.** to mix together in a jumbled mass **4.** to shift (things) about from one place to another **5.** to bring, put, or thrust (*into* or *out of*) clumsily or trickily —*vi.* **1.** to move by dragging or scraping the feet, as in walking or dancing **2.** to act in a shifty, tricky, or dishonest manner **3.** to shift repeatedly from one position or place to another **4.** to shuffle playing cards —*n.* **1.** the act of shuffling **2.** a deceptive action; evasion; trick **3.** *a*) a shuffling of the feet *b*) a gait, dance, etc. characterized by this **4.** *a*) a shuffling of playing cards *b*) one's turn at this —**lose in the shuffle** to leave out in the confusion of things —**shuffle off** to get rid of —**shuf′fler** *n.*

shuf·fle·board (-bôrd′) *n.* [< earlier *shovel board,* after the shape of the cues] **1.** a game in which large disks are pushed with a cue along a smooth lane toward numbered squares **2.** the surface on which it is played

shun (shun) *vt.* **shunned, shun′ning** [OE. *scunian*] to keep away from; avoid strictly —**shun′ner** *n.*

shunt (shunt) *vt., vi.* [< ? or akin to prec.] **1.** to move or turn to one side; turn aside **2.** to switch (a train, etc.) from one track to another **3.** *Elec.* to divert or be diverted by a shunt —*n.* **1.** a shunting **2.** a railroad switch **3.** *Elec.* a conductor connecting two points in a circuit and diverting part of the current from the main circuit —**shunt′er** *n.*

shush (shush) *interj.* [echoic] hush! be quiet! —*vt.* to say "shush" to; tell (another) to be quiet

shut (shut) *vt.* **shut, shut′ting** [OE. *scyttan* < base of *sceotan,* to shoot] **1.** *a*) to move (a door, window, lid, etc.) into a position that covers the opening to which it is fitted *b*) to fasten (a door, etc.) securely, as with a bolt or catch **2.** to close (an opening, container, etc.) **3.** *a*) to prevent entrance to or exit from; bar *b*) to confine or enclose (*in* a room, cage, etc.) **4.** to fold up or close the parts of (an umbrella, a book, the eyes, etc.) **5.** to stop or suspend the operation of (a school, business, etc.) —*vi.* to be or become shut —*adj.* closed, fastened, etc. —*n.* the act or time of shutting —**shut down** **1.** to close by lowering **2.** to settle over (a place) so as to conceal, as fog or night **3.** to close (a factory, etc.), usually temporarily —**shut in** to surround or enclose —**shut off** **1.** to prevent the passage of (water, electricity, etc.) **2.** to prevent passage through (a road, faucet, etc.) **3.** to separate; isolate —**shut out** **1.** to deny entrance to; exclude (sound, a view, etc.) **2.** to prevent (the opposition) from scoring in a game —**shut up** **1.** to enclose, confine, or imprison **2.** to close all the entrances to **3.** [Colloq.] *a*) to stop or cause to stop talking *b*) to prevent from speaking or writing freely; censor

shut·down (-doun′) ***n.*** a stoppage or suspension of work or activity, as in a factory

shut-eye (-ī′) ***n.*** [Slang] sleep

shut-in (-in′) ***n.*** a person who is too ill, weak, etc. to go out —***adj.*** not able to go out

shut-off (-ôf′) ***n.*** **1.** something that shuts off a flow, as a valve **2.** a stoppage or interruption

shut·out (-out′) ***n.*** **1.** a preventing of the opposing team from scoring **2.** a game in which this occurs

shut·ter (shut′ər) ***n.*** **1.** a person or thing that shuts **2.** a movable, usually hinged cover for a window **3.** anything used to cover an opening; specif., a device for opening and closing the aperture of a camera lens to expose the film or plate —***vt.*** to close or furnish with shutters

shut·tle (shut′'l) ***n.*** [OE. *scytel,* missile: from being cast back and forth] **1.** *a*) a device used to pass the woof thread back and forth between the warp threads in weaving *b*) any of several devices having a similar use or motion, as the device that carries the lower thread back and forth on a sewing machine **2.** a bus, train, helicopter, etc. making frequent trips back and forth over a short route —***vt., vi.*** **-tled, -tling** **1.** to move rapidly to and fro **2.** to go by means of a shuttle

shut·tle·cock (-käk′) ***n.*** **1.** a rounded piece of cork having a flat end stuck with feathers: it is struck back and forth across a net by players in badminton or in battledore and shuttlecock **2.** the game of battledore and shuttlecock —***vt., vi.*** to go, send, or bandy back and forth

shy[1] (shī) ***adj.*** **shy′er** or **shi′er, shy′est** or **shi′est** [OE. *sceoh*] **1.** easily frightened or startled; timid **2.** not at ease with other people; bashful **3.** distrustful; wary **4.** [Slang] lacking in amount; short (*on* or *of*) —***vi.*** **shied, shy′ing** **1.** to move or pull back suddenly when startled; start **2.** to be or become cautious or unwilling; draw back (often with *at* or *from*) —***n.,*** *pl.* **shies** an act of shying; start, as of a horse —**fight shy of** to avoid or evade —**shy′er *n.*** —**shy′ly *adv.*** —**shy′ness *n.***

shy[2] (shī) ***vt., vi.*** **shied, shy′ing** [< ? or akin to prec.] to fling, esp. sidewise with a jerk *[shying* stones at a target*]* —***n.,*** *pl.* **shies** a shying; fling

Shy·lock (shī′läk′) the moneylender in Shakespeare's *Merchant of Venice* —***n.*** an exacting creditor

shy·ster (shī′stər) ***n.*** [prob. altered < G. *scheisser,* defecator] [Slang] a person, esp. a lawyer, who uses unethical or tricky methods

si (sē) ***n.*** *Music same as* TI

‡**sí** (sē) ***adv.*** [Sp.] yes: also [It.] **sì**

Si *Chem.* silicon

Si·am (sī am′) *former name of* THAILAND

Si·a·mese (sī′ə mēz′, -mēs′) ***n.,*** *pl.* **Si′a·mese′** *same as* THAI —***adj.*** *same as* THAI

Siamese cat a breed of short-haired cat characterized by blue eyes and a fawn-colored coat shading to a darker color at the face, ears, paws, and tail

Siamese twins [after such a pair born in Siam] any pair of twins born joined to each other

Si·an (shē′än′) city in NC China: pop. c. 1,500,000

sib (sib) ***n.*** [OE. *sibb*] **1.** blood relatives; kin **2.** a blood relative **3.** a brother or sister —***adj.*** related by blood

Si·be·li·us (si bā′lē oos; *E.* sə bāl′yəs), **Jean (Julius Christian)** (zhän) 1865–1957; Finn. composer

Si·ber·i·a (sī bir′ē ə) region in N Asia, between the Urals & the Pacific; Asiatic section of the R.S.F.S.R. —**Si·ber′i·an *adj., n.***

sib·i·lant (sib′'l ənt) ***adj.*** [< L. < *sibilare,* to hiss] having or making a hissing sound —***n.*** *Phonet.* a consonant characterized by a hissing sound, as (s), (z), (sh), (zh), (ch), and (j) —**sib′i·lance, sib′i·lan·cy *n.,*** *pl.* **-cies** —**sib′i·lant·ly *adv.***

sib·ling (sib′liŋ) ***n.*** [20th-c. readoption of OE. *sibling,* a relative] one of two or more persons born of the same parents, or, sometimes, having one parent in common; brother or sister

Sib·yl (sib′'l) [L. *Sibylla:* see ff.] a feminine name

sib·yl (sib′'l) ***n.*** [< L. < Gr. *sibylla*] **1.** any of certain women consulted as prophetesses or oracles by the ancient Greeks and Romans **2.** a prophetess; fortuneteller — **sib′yl·line′** (-'l īn′, -ēn′, -in) ***adj.***

‡**sic**[1] (sik) ***adv.*** [L.] thus; so: used within brackets, [*sic*], to show that a quoted passage, esp. one containing some error, is shown exactly as in the original

sic[2] (sik) ***vt.*** [var. of SEEK] **sicked, sick′ing** **1.** to pursue and attack: said esp. of or to a dog **2.** to urge to attack *[*to *sic* a dog on someone*]*

Sic·i·ly (sis′'l ē) island of Italy, off its S tip: with small nearby islands, 9,926 sq. mi.: It. name **Si·ci·lia** (sē-chēl′yä) —**Si·cil·ian** (si sil′yən, -ē ən) ***adj., n.***

sick[1] (sik) ***adj.*** [OE. *seoc*] **1.** suffering from disease; physically or mentally ill **2.** having nausea; vomiting or about to vomit **3.** characteristic of sickness *[*a *sick* expression*]* **4.** of or for sick people *[sick* leave*]* **5.** deeply disturbed, as by grief, failure, etc. **6.** disgusted by reason of excess *[sick* of his excuses*]*: often **sick and tired** **7.** unsound **8.** having a great longing (*for*) *[sick* for the hills*]* **9.** of sickly color; pale **10.** menstruating **11.** [Colloq.] sadistic, morbid, etc. *[*a *sick* joke*]* —**the sick** sick people collectively

sick[2] (sik) ***vt.*** *same as* SIC[2]

sick bay a ship's hospital or dispensary

sick·bed (sik′bed′) ***n.*** the bed of a sick person

sick call *Mil.* **1.** a daily formation for those who wish to receive medical attention **2.** the time for this

sick·en (sik′'n) ***vt., vi.*** to make or become sick, disgusted, etc. —**sick′en·er *n.***

sick·en·ing (-iŋ) ***adj.*** **1.** causing sickness or nausea **2.** disgusting —**sick′en·ing·ly *adv.***

sick headache **1.** any headache accompanied by nausea **2.** *same as* MIGRAINE

sick·ish (sik′ish) ***adj.*** **1.** somewhat sick or nauseated **2.** somewhat sickening or nauseating —**sick′ish·ly *adv.***

sick·le (sik′'l) ***n.*** [OE. *sicol,* ult. < L. *secula* < *secare,* to cut] a tool consisting of a crescent-shaped blade with a short handle, for cutting tall grass, etc.

sick leave leave from work granted for illness, often with pay (**sick pay**) for a limited number of days

sickle cell anemia an inherited chronic anemia found chiefly among Negroes, characterized by an abnormal red blood cell (**sickle cell**) containing a defective form of hemoglobin that causes the cell to become sickle-shaped when deprived of oxygen: also **sickle cell disease**

SICKLE

sick·ly (sik′lē) ***adj.*** **-li·er, -li·est** **1.** in poor health; sick much of the time **2.** of or produced by sickness *[*a *sickly* pallor*]* **3.** producing illness; unhealthful **4.** sickening, as an odor **5.** faint; feeble *[*a *sickly* light*]* **6.** weak; insipid *[*a *sickly* smile*]* —***adv.*** in a sick manner: also **sick′li·ly** —***vt.*** **-lied, -ly·ing** to make sickly, as in color, vigor, etc. —**sick′li·ness *n.***

sick·ness (-nis) ***n.*** **1.** a being sick or diseased; illness **2.** a particular disease or illness **3.** nausea

sick·room (-ro͞om′) ***n.*** the room to which a sick person is confined

Sid·dhar·tha Gau·ta·ma (sid där′tə gout′ə mə, gôt′-) *see* BUDDHA

side (sīd) ***n.*** [OE.] **1.** the right or left half of a human or animal body **2.** a position beside one **3.** *a*) any of the lines or surfaces that bound something *[*a square has four *sides]* *b*) either of the two bounding surfaces of an object that are not the front, back, top, or bottom **4.** either of the two surfaces of paper, cloth, etc. **5.** a particular or specified surface *[*the inner *side* of a vase, the visible *side* of the moon*]* **6.** a particular part or quality of a person or thing *[*his cruel *side,* the bright *side* of life*]* **7.** the slope of a hill, bank, etc. **8.** any location, area, space, etc. with reference to a central point or line, or to the speaker **9.** the ideas, opinions, or position of one person or faction opposing another *[*his *side* of the argument*]* **10.** one of the parties in a contest, conflict, etc. **11.** line of descent through either parent **12.** any of the pages containing an actor's part in a play **13.** [Brit. Slang] superior or patronizing manner **14.** [Brit.] *Billiards same as* ENGLISH (*n.* 3) —***adj.*** **1.** of, at, or on a side *[*a *side* door*]* **2.** to or from one side *[*a *side* glance*]* **3.** done, happening, etc. on the side *[*a *side* effect*]* **4.** not main; secondary *[*a *side* issue*]* —***vt.*** **sid′ed, sid′ing** to furnish with sides or siding —**on the side** in addition to the main thing, part, course, etc. —**side by side** beside each other; together —**side with** to support (one of opposing factions, etc.) —**take sides** to support one of the parties in a dispute, etc.

side arms weapons of the kind that may be worn at the side or at the waist, as a sword, pistol, etc.

side·board (sīd′bôrd′) ***n.*** a piece of dining-room furniture for holding table linen, silver, china, etc.

side·burns (-burnz′) ***n.pl.*** [reversed < BURNSIDES] **1.** *same as* BURNSIDES **2.** the hair growing on a man's face just in front of the ears, esp. when the rest of the beard is cut off

side·car (-kär′) ***n.*** a small car attached to the side of a motorcycle, for carrying a passenger, parcels, etc.

sid·ed (sīd′id) ***adj.*** having (a specified number or kind of) sides *[six-sided]*

side dish any food served along with the main course, usually in a separate dish

side·kick (-kik′) ***n.*** [Slang] **1.** a companion; close friend **2.** a partner; confederate

side·light (-līt′) ***n.*** **1.** a light coming from the side **2.** a bit of incidental information on a subject

side·line (-līn′) ***n.*** a line along the side; specif., *a)* either of the two lines marking the side limits of a playing area, as in football or basketball *b)* [*pl.*] the areas just outside these lines *c)* a line, as of merchandise or work, in addition to one's main line —***vt.*** **-lined′, -lin′ing** to remove from active participation, as because of injury —**side′lin′er** ***n.***

side·long (-lôŋ′) ***adv.*** toward the side; obliquely —***adj.*** **1.** inclined; slanting **2.** directed to the side, as a glance

side·man (-man′) ***n.***, *pl.* **-men′** (-men′) [as distinguished from the *front man,* or leader] a member of a jazz or dance band other than the leader

side·piece (-pēs′) ***n.*** a piece forming, or attached to, the side of something

si·de·re·al (sī dir′ē əl) ***adj.*** [< L. < *sidus* (gen. *sideris*), a star] **1.** of the stars or constellations; astral **2.** with reference to the stars —**si·de′re·al·ly** ***adv.***

sidereal day the time between two successive passages of the vernal equinox over the upper meridian: it measures one rotation of the earth and is equal to 23 hours, 56 minutes, 4.091 seconds of mean solar time

sidereal year *see* YEAR (sense 3)

sid·er·ite (sid′ə rīt′) ***n.*** [< G. < L. < Gr. < *sidēros,* iron] a yellowish to light-brown iron ore, $FeCO_3$ —**sid′er·it′ic** (-rit′ik) ***adj.***

side·sad·dle (sīd′sad′'l) ***n.*** a saddle for women wearing skirts, upon which the rider sits with both legs on the same side of the animal —***adv.*** on or as if on a sidesaddle

side·show (-shō′) ***n.*** **1.** a small show apart from the main show, as of a circus **2.** activity of minor importance

side·slip (-slip′) ***vi.*** **-slipped′, -slip′ping 1.** to slip sideways, as on skis **2.** *Aeron.* to move in a sideslip —***vt.*** to cause to sideslip —***n.*** **1.** a slip or skid to the side **2.** *Aeron.* a sideways and downward movement toward the inside of a turn by an airplane in a sharp bank

side·split·ting (-split′iŋ) ***adj.*** **1.** very hearty: said of laughter **2.** causing hearty laughter

side·step (-step′) ***vt.*** **-stepped′, -step′ping** to avoid by or as by stepping aside; dodge —***vi.*** to step to one side

side step a step to one side, as to avoid something, or a step taken sidewise

side·swipe (-swīp′) ***vt., vi.*** **-swiped′, -swip′ing** to hit along the side in passing —***n.*** a glancing blow of this kind

side·track (-trak′) ***vt., vi.*** **1.** to switch (a train, etc.) to a siding **2.** to turn away from the main issue —***n.*** a railroad siding

side·walk (-wôk′) ***n.*** a path for pedestrians, usually paved, along the side of a street

side·wall (-wôl′) ***n.*** the side of an automobile tire between the tread and the rim of a wheel

side·ward (-wərd) ***adv., adj.*** directed or moving toward one side: also **side′wards** ***adv.***

side·ways (-wāz′) ***adv.*** **1.** from the side **2.** with one side forward **3.** toward one side; obliquely —***adj.*** turned or moving toward or from one side Also **side′way, side′wise′** (-wīz′)

side-wheel (sīd′hwēl′, -wēl′) ***adj.*** designating a steamboat having a paddle wheel on each side —**side′-wheel′er** ***n.***

side whiskers whiskers at the side of the face

side·wind·er (sīd′wīn′dər) ***n.*** **1.** a small desert rattlesnake of the SW U.S. that moves by looping its body sideways **2.** [S-] an air-to-air missile

sid·ing (sīd′iŋ) ***n.*** **1.** shingles, boards, aluminum panels, etc. forming the outside covering of a frame building **2.** a short railroad track connected with a main track by a switch and used for unloading, bypassing, etc.

si·dle (sī′d'l) ***vi.*** **-dled, -dling** [< *sideling,* sideways] to move sideways, esp. in a shy or stealthy manner —***vt.*** to make go sideways —***n.*** a sidling movement

Sid·ney (sid′nē) **1.** [< the surname *Sidney,* prob. reduced from *St. Denis*] a masculine or feminine name: dim. *Sid* **2.** Sir **Philip,** 1554–86; Eng. poet, soldier, & statesman

Si·don (sī′d'n) chief city of ancient Phoenicia, on the Mediterranean in what is now SW Lebanon

siege (sēj) ***n.*** [OFr., ult. < L. *obsidere,* to besiege < *ob-,* against + *sedere,* to sit] **1.** the surrounding of a city, fort, etc. by an enemy army trying to capture it by continued blockade and attack **2.** any stubborn and continued effort to win or control something **3.** a long, distressing period *[a siege* of illness*]* **4.** [Obs.] a seat; throne —***vt.*** **sieged, sieg′ing** *same as* BESIEGE —**lay siege to** to subject to a siege

Sieg·fried (sēg′frēd, sig′-) a hero of Germanic legend who wins the treasure of the Nibelungs

si·en·na (sē en′ə) ***n.*** [It. *terra di Siena,* lit., earth of Siena, city in Italy] **1.** a yellowish-brown earth pigment containing iron and manganese **2.** a reddish-brown pigment made by burning this; burnt sienna **3.** either of these colors

si·er·ra (sē er′ə) ***n.*** [Sp. < L. *serra,* a saw] a range of mountains with a saw-toothed appearance

Si·er·ra Le·one (sē er′ə lē ōn′) country in W Africa, on the Atlantic, between Guinea & Liberia: a member of the Commonwealth: 27,925 sq. mi.; pop. 2,600,000

Si·er·ra Ma·dre (sē er′ə mä′drā; *Sp.* sye′rä mä′dre) mountain system of Mexico, consisting of three ranges bordering the central plateau

Sierra Nevada [Sp., lit., snowy range] mountain range in E Calif.: also called **the Si·er·ras** (sē er′əz)

si·es·ta (sē es′tə) ***n.*** [Sp. < L. *sexta* (*hora*), sixth (hour), noon] a brief nap or rest taken after the noon meal, esp. in Spain and some Latin American countries

‡**sieur** (syër) ***n.*** [OFr., inflected form of *sire,* SIRE] *archaic French title of respect meaning* SIR

sieve (siv) ***n.*** [OE. *sife*] a utensil having many small openings, used to strain solids from liquids or to separate fine particles from coarser ones; strainer; sifter —***vt., vi.*** **sieved, siev′ing** to pass through a sieve

sift (sift) ***vt.*** [OE. *siftan*] **1.** to pass through a sieve so as to separate the coarse from the fine particles, or to break up lumps, as of flour **2.** to scatter by or as by the use of a sieve **3.** to examine with care; weigh (evidence, etc.) **4.** to separate; screen *[to sift* fact from fable*]* —***vi.*** **1.** to sift something **2.** to pass as through a sieve —**sift′er** ***n.***

sift·ings (-iŋz) ***n.pl.*** sifted matter

sigh (sī) ***vi.*** [OE. *sican*] **1.** to take in and let out a long, deep, sounded breath, as in sorrow, relief, fatigue, etc. **2.** to make a sound like a sigh *[trees sighing* in the wind*]* **3.** to long or lament (*for*) —***vt.*** to express with a sigh —***n.*** the act or sound of sighing —**sigh′er** ***n.***

sight (sīt) ***n.*** [OE. (*ge*)*siht* < base of *seon,* to see] **1.** *a)* something seen; view *b)* a remarkable view; spectacle *c)* a thing worth seeing: *usually used in pl. [*the *sights* of the city*]* **2.** the act of seeing **3.** a look; glimpse **4.** any device used to aid the eyes in lining up a gun, optical instrument, etc. on its objective **5.** aim or an observation taken as with a sextant, gun, etc. **6.** the ability to see; vision; eyesight **7.** range of vision **8.** one's thinking or opinion *[a* hero in her *sight]* **9.** a person or thing not pleasant to look at **10.** [Dial.] a large amount; lot *[a sight* better than fighting*]* —***vt.*** **1.** to observe or examine by taking a sight **2.** to catch sight of; see **3.** *a)* to furnish with a sighting device *b)* to adjust the sights of **4.** to aim (a gun, etc.) at (a target), using the sights —***vi.*** **1.** to take aim or an observation with a sight **2.** to look carefully *[sight* along the line*]* —***adj.*** **1.** read, done, understood, etc. as soon as seen **2.** payable when presented *[a sight* draft*]* —**a sight for sore eyes** [Colloq.] a welcome sight —**at** (or **on**) **sight** when or as soon as seen —**by sight** by recognizing but not through being acquainted —**catch sight of** to see, esp. briefly; glimpse —**lose sight of 1.** to see no longer **2.** to forget —**not by a long sight 1.** not nearly **2.** not at all —**out of sight 1.** not in sight **2.** [Colloq.] extremely high, as in price, standards, etc. **3.** [Slang] excellent; wonderful —**sight unseen** without seeing (the thing) beforehand

sight·ed (-id) ***adj.*** **1.** having sight; not blind **2.** having (a specified kind of) sight: used in combination *[farsighted]*

sight·less (-lis) ***adj.*** **1.** blind **2.** unseen —**sight′less·ly** ***adv.*** —**sight′less·ness** ***n.***

sight·ly (-lē) ***adj.*** **-li·er, -li·est** pleasant to the sight

sight·see·ing (-sē′iŋ) ***n.*** the act of visiting places and things of interest —***adj.*** for or engaged in seeing sights —**sight′-se′er** ***n.***

sig·ma (sig′mə) ***n.*** [Gr.] the eighteenth letter of the Greek alphabet (Σ, σ)

sig·moid (-moid) ***adj.*** having a double curve like the letter S: also **sig·moi′dal** —**sig·moi′dal·ly** ***adv.***

sigmoid flexure 1. *Anat.* the last curving part of the colon, ending in the rectum **2.** *Zool.* an S-shaped curve

Sig·mund (sig′mənd) [< G. & ON.] a masculine name

sign (sīn) ***n.*** [< OFr. < L. *signum*] **1.** something that indicates a fact, quality, etc. *[black is a sign* of mourning*]* **2.** *a)* a gesture that tells something specified *[a nod is a sign* of approval*]* *b)* any of the gestures used in sign language **3.** a mark or symbol having a specific meaning *[the sign* ¢ for cent(s)*]* **4.** a publicly displayed board, placard, etc. bearing information, advertising, etc. **5.** any visible trace or indication *[the signs* of spring*]* **6.** an omen **7.** *same as* SIGN OF THE ZODIAC —***vt.*** **1.** to mark with a sign, esp. of the cross as in blessing **2.** to write one's name on, as in agreement, authorization, etc. **3.** to write (one's name) as a signature **4.** to hire by written contract —***vi.*** **1.** to write one's signature, as in attesting or confirming something **2.** to make a sign; signal —**sign away** (or **over**) to transfer title to (something) by signing a document —**sign in** (or **out**) to sign a register on arrival (or departure) —**sign off** to stop broadcasting, as for the day —**sign on** to hire or be hired —**sign up 1.** *same as* SIGN ON **2.** to enlist in military service —**sign′er** *n.*

sig·nal (sig′n'l) ***n.*** [< OFr. < VL. *signale,* ult. < L. *signum,* a sign] **1.** any sign, event, etc. that is a call to some kind of action *[*a bugle *signal* to attack*]* **2.** *a)* a sign given by gesture, a device, etc. to convey a command, direction, warning, etc. *b)* an object or device providing such a sign **3.** *Card Games* a bid or play designed to guide one's partner **4.** *Telegraphy, Radio & TV,* etc. the electrical impulses, sound or picture elements, etc. transmitted or received —***adj.*** **1.** not ordinary; notable **2.** used as a signal —***vt., vi.*** **-naled** or **-nalled, -nal·ing** or **-nal·ling 1.** to make a signal or signals (to) **2.** to communicate by signals —**sig′nal·er, sig′nal·ler** ***n.***

signal corps the part of an army in charge of communications, as by radio

sig·nal·ize (-īz′) ***vt.*** **-ized′, -iz′ing 1.** to make notable **2.** to draw attention to —**sig′nal·i·za′tion** ***n.***

sig·nal·ly (-ē) ***adj.*** notably; remarkably

sig·nal·man (-mən, -man′) ***n.,*** *pl.* **-men** (-mən, -men′) a person responsible for signaling or receiving signals

sig·na·to·ry (sig′nə tôr′ē) ***adj.*** that has or have joined in the signing of something —***n.,*** *pl.* **-ries** any of the persons, states, etc. that have signed a document

sig·na·ture (sig′nə chər) ***n.*** [< LL. < L. *signare,* to sign] **1.** a person's name written by himself **2.** the act of signing one's name **3.** an identifying characteristic or mark **4.** *Music* a sign or signs placed at the beginning of a staff to show key or time **5.** *Printing a)* a large sheet on which pages are printed in some multiple of four, and which, when folded to page size, forms one section of a book *b)* a letter or number on the first page of each sheet showing in what order that section is to be bound **6.** *Radio & TV* a theme song, picture, etc. used to identify a program

sign·board (sīn′bôrd′) ***n.*** a board bearing a sign, esp. one advertising a business, product, etc.

sig·net (sig′nit) ***n.*** [MFr. dim. of *signe,* a sign] **1.** a small seal used in marking documents as official, etc. **2.** a mark made by a signet

signet ring a finger ring containing a signet, often in the form of an initial or a monogram

sig·nif·i·cance (sig nif′ə kəns) ***n.*** **1.** that which is signified; meaning **2.** the quality of being significant; suggestiveness; expressiveness **3.** importance; consequence

sig·nif·i·cant (-kənt) ***adj.*** [< L. prp. of *significare,* to signify] **1.** *a)* having or expressing a meaning *b)* full of meaning **2.** important; momentous **3.** having or expressing a special or hidden meaning **4.** of a difference too large to be due to chance, as in statistics Also **sig·nif′i·ca′tive** (-kāt′iv) —**sig·nif′i·cant·ly** ***adv.***

sig·ni·fi·ca·tion (sig′nə fi kā′shən) ***n.*** **1.** significance; meaning **2.** a signifying; indication

sig·ni·fy (sig′nə fī′) ***vt.*** **-fied′, -fy′ing** [< OFr. < L. *significare* < *signum,* a sign + *facere,* to make] **1.** to be a sign or indication of; mean **2.** to show or make known by a sign, words, etc. —***vi.*** **1.** to be significant; matter **2.** [Chiefly Black Slang] to engage in verbal play involving boastful taunts, witty insults, indirect threats, etc. —**sig′ni·fi′a·ble** ***adj.*** —**sig′ni·fi′er** ***n.***

sign language communication of thoughts or ideas by means of signs and gestures of the hands and arms

sign of the zodiac any of the twelve divisions of the zodiac, each represented by a symbol: see ZODIAC

‡**si·gnor** (sē nyôr′; *E.* sēn′yôr) ***n.,*** *pl.* **si·gno′ri** (-nyô′rē); E. **si′gnors** [It.] **1.** [S-] Mr.: Italian title of respect, used before the name **2.** a gentleman; man

‡**si·gno·ra** (sē nyô′rä; *E.* sēn yôr′ə) ***n.,*** *pl.* **si·gno′re** (-re); E. **si·gno′ras** [It.] **1.** [S-] Mrs.; Madam: Italian title of respect **2.** a married woman

‡**si·gno·re** (sē nyô′re) ***n.,*** *pl.* **si·gno′ri** (-rē) [It.] **1.** [S-] sir: Italian title of respect, used in direct address without the name **2.** a gentleman; man

‡**si·gno·ri·na** (sē′nyô rē′nä; *E.* sēn′yə rē′nə) ***n.,*** *pl.* **-ri′ne** (-ne); E. **-ri′nas** [It.] **1.** [S-] Miss: Italian title of respect **2.** an unmarried woman or girl

sign·post (sīn′pōst′) ***n.*** **1.** a post with a sign on it, as for showing a route or direction **2.** a clear indication

Si·gurd (sig′ərd) a hero of Norse legend identified with the German SIEGFRIED

Sikh (sēk) ***n.*** [Hindi, a disciple] a member of a monotheistic Hindu religious sect that rejects the caste system —***adj.*** of Sikhs —**Sikh′ism** ***n.***

si·lage (sī′lij) ***n.*** [contr. (after SILO) < ENSILAGE] green fodder stored in a silo

Si·las (sī′ləs) [LL. < Gr. < Aram. *sh'ilâ,* lit., asked for] a masculine name: dim. *Si*

sild (sild) ***n.,*** *pl.* **sild, silds:** see PLURAL, II, D, 2 [Norw., herring] any of several small or young herrings canned as Norwegian sardines

si·lence (sī′ləns) ***n.*** **1.** the state or fact of keeping silent or still **2.** absence of any sound or noise; stillness **3.** a withholding of knowledge or omission of mention **4.** failure to communicate, write, etc. —***vt.*** **-lenced, -lenc·ing 1.** to make silent **2.** to put down; repress **3.** to put (enemy guns) out of action —***interj.*** be silent!

si·lenc·er (sī′lən sər) ***n.*** **1.** one that silences **2.** a device for muffling the report of a firearm **3.** [Chiefly Brit.] a muffler for an internal-combustion engine

si·lent (sī′lənt) ***adj.*** [< L. < prp. of *silere,* to be silent] **1.** making no vocal sound; mute **2.** seldom speaking; not talkative **3.** free from sound or noise; quiet; still **4.** not spoken, expressed, etc. *[silent* grief, the *silent* "b" in "debt"*]* **5.** making no mention, explanation, etc. **6.** not active *[*factories now *silent]* **7.** designating or of films without synchronized sound —**si′lent·ly** ***adv.***

silent butler a dish with a hinged cover and handle, in which to empty ashtrays, brush crumbs, etc.

silent partner a partner who shares in financing but not in managing a business, firm, etc.

Si·le·sia (sī lē′shə, si-; -zhə) region in E Europe, mainly in SW Poland —**Si·le′sian** ***adj., n.***

si·lex (sī′leks) ***n.*** [L.] **1.** silica, esp. in the form of flint or quartz **2.** heat-resistant glass of fused quartz

sil·hou·ette (sil′oo wet′) ***n.*** [Fr., after E. de *Silhouette,* 18th-c. Fr. minister of finance] **1.** *a)* a profile portrait in black or in some solid color, often a cutout mounted on a light background *b)* any dark shape seen against a light background **2.** the outline of a figure, garment, etc.; contour —***vt.*** **-et′ted, -et′ting** to show or project in silhouette

SILHOUETTE

sil·i·ca (sil′i kə) ***n.*** [ModL. < L. *silex,* flint] the dioxide of silicon, SiO_2, a hard, glassy mineral found in various forms, as in quartz, sand, opal, etc.

sil·i·cate (sil′i kit, -kāt′) ***n.*** a salt or ester derived from silica or a silicic acid

si·li·ceous (sə lish′əs) ***adj.*** **1.** of, containing, or like silica **2.** growing in soil that has much silica in it

si·lic·ic (sə lis′ik) ***adj.*** of, like, or derived from silicon

silicic acid any of several jellylike precipitates formed by acidifying sodium silicate solution

sil·i·con (sil′i kən, -kän′) ***n.*** [ModL., ult. < L. *silex,* flint] a nonmetallic chemical element second only to oxygen in its abundance in nature and found always in combination, as in silica: symbol, Si; at. wt., 28.086; at. no., 14

sil·i·cone (-kōn′) ***n.*** [SILIC(ON) + -ONE] any of a group of polymerized, organic silicon compounds highly resistant to heat, water, etc. and used in lubricants, polishes, etc.

silicone rubber a rubberlike polymer made from certain silicones: it keeps its elasticity over a wide temperature range and is used in gaskets, insulation, etc.

sil·i·co·sis (sil′ə kō′sis) ***n.*** [ModL.: see SILICON & -OSIS] a chronic lung disease caused in miners, stonecutters, etc. by inhaling silica dust over a long period of time

silk (silk) ***n.*** see PLURAL, II, D, 3 [OE. *seoluc,* ult. < ? L. *sericus:* see SERGE] **1.** the fine, soft, shiny fiber produced by silkworms **2.** thread or fabric made from this **3.** a garment or other article of such fabric **4.** any silklike filament or substance *[*corn *silk]* —***adj.*** of or like silk —**hit the silk** [Slang] to parachute from an aircraft

silk cotton *same as* KAPOK

silk·en (sil′k'n) ***adj.*** **1.** made of silk **2.** dressed in silk **3.** like silk, as in being soft, smooth, glossy, or luxurious

silk hat a tall, cylindrical hat covered with silk or satin, worn by men in formal dress

silk-screen (silk′skrēn′) ***adj.*** **1.** designating or of a stencil process of printing a design through a screen of silk or other fine cloth, parts of the screen being blocked as with an impermeable film **2.** designating a print made by this process —***vt.*** to print by this process

silk-stock·ing (-stäk′iŋ) ***adj.*** **1.** fashionably or richly dressed **2.** wealthy or aristocratic —***n.*** a member of the wealthy or aristocratic class

silk·worm (-wurm′) ***n.*** any of certain moth caterpillars that produce cocoons of silk fiber

silk·y (sil′kē) ***adj.*** **silk′i·er, silk′i·est** **1.** of or like silk; soft, smooth, lustrous, etc. **2.** having fine, soft hairs, as some leaves —**silk′i·ly** ***adv.*** —**silk′i·ness** ***n.***

sill (sil) ***n.*** [OE. *syll*] **1.** a heavy, horizontal timber or line of masonry supporting a house wall, etc. **2.** a horizontal piece forming the bottom frame of the opening into which a window or door is set

sil·la·bub (sil′ə bub′) ***n.*** *var. of* SYLLABUB

sil·ly (sil′ē) ***adj.*** **-li·er, -li·est** [OE. *sælig,* happy, blessed < *sæl,* happiness (sense development: happy → blissful → unaware of reality → foolish)] **1.** having or showing little sense or judgment; foolish, absurd, etc. **2.** frivolous or trivial **3.** [Colloq.] dazed or senseless, as from a blow —***n.,*** *pl.* **-lies** a silly person —**sil′li·ly** (or **sil′ly**) ***adv.*** —**sil′li·ness** ***n.***

si·lo (sī′lō) ***n.,*** *pl.* **-los** [Fr. < Sp. < L. < Gr. *siros*] **1.** an airtight pit or tower in which green fodder is stored **2.** a large, underground structure for storing and launching a long-range ballistic missile —***vt.*** **-loed, -lo·ing** to store in a silo

silt (silt) ***n.*** [prob. < Scand.] earthy sediment made up of fine particles carried or laid down by moving water —***vt., vi.*** to fill or choke up with silt —**sil·ta·tion** (sil tā′shən) ***n.*** —**silt′y** ***adj.*** **silt′i·er, silt′i·est**

Si·lu·ri·an (si loor′ē ən, sī-) ***adj.*** [< L. *Silures,* ancient tribe in Wales] designating or of the geological period after the Ordovician in the Paleozoic Era —**the Silurian** the Silurian Period or its rocks: see GEOLOGY, chart

sil·va (sil′və) ***n.*** [ModL. < L., a forest] **1.** the forest trees of an area **2.** *pl.* **-vas, -vae** (-vē) a book or treatise describing these

sil·van (sil′vən) ***adj., n.*** *same as* SYLVAN

sil·ver (sil′vər) ***n.*** [OE. *seolfer*] **1.** a white, metallic chemical element that is extremely ductile and malleable and takes a high polish: it is a precious metal and is used in coins, jewelry, etc.: symbol, Ag; at. wt., 107.868; at. no., 47 **2.** *a)* silver coin *b)* money; riches **3.** articles, esp. tableware, made of or plated with silver **4.** the lustrous, grayish-white color of silver **5.** something having this color, as the coating for a mirror —***adj.*** **1.** of or containing silver; silvery **2.** of or advocating silver as a currency standard **3.** having a silvery color, tone, etc. **4.** eloquent *[a silver tongue]* **5.** marking the 25th anniversary *[a silver wedding anniversary]* —***vt.*** **1.** to cover with silver **2.** to make silvery in color —***vi.*** to become silvery

silver birch *same as* PAPER BIRCH

silver certificate formerly, a type of U.S. paper currency redeemable in silver

sil·ver·fish (-fish′) ***n.*** **1.** *pl.* **-fish′, -fish′es:** see FISH any of various unrelated fishes of silvery color **2.** *pl.* **-fish′** a wingless insect with silvery scales and long feelers, found in damp, dark places

silver fox **1.** a N. American fox with white-tipped black fur **2.** this fur

silver iodide a yellow powder, AgI, that darkens in light: used in photography, to seed clouds, etc.

silver lining anything seen as hopeful or comforting in the midst of despair, misfortune, etc.

silver nitrate a colorless, crystalline salt, $AgNO_3$, used in silver-plating, photography, medicine, etc.

sil·ver-plate (-plāt′) ***vt.*** **-plat′ed, -plat′ing** to coat with silver, esp. by electroplating

silver plate tableware made of, or plated with, silver

silver salmon *same as* COHO

sil·ver·side (-sīd′) ***n.*** any of certain small, mostly saltwater fishes with silver stripes along the sides: also **sil′ver·sides′**

sil·ver·smith (-smith′) ***n.*** a skilled worker who makes articles of silver

silver standard a monetary standard in which the basic currency unit is made equal to and redeemable by a specified quantity of silver

sil·ver·ware (-wer′) ***n.*** **1.** articles, esp. tableware, made of or plated with silver **2.** any metal tableware

sil·ver·y (sil′vər ē) ***adj.*** **1.** like silver, as in color or luster **2.** covered with or containing silver **3.** soft and clear, like the sound of a silver bell —**sil′ver·i·ness** ***n.***

Sim·e·on (sim′ē ən) *Bible* the second son of Jacob and Leah, or the tribe of Israel descended from him

Simeon Sty·li·tes (stī lī′tēz), Saint 390?–459? A.D.; Syrian monk who lived & preached on top of a pillar near Antioch, for over 30 years

Sim·hat To·rah (sim khät′ tō rä′, sim′khäs tō′rə) [< Heb., lit., rejoicing in the Torah] a Jewish festival in early fall marking the end of the annual cycle of Torah readings and the beginning of the next cycle: also sp. **Simchath Torah**

sim·i·an (sim′ē ən) ***adj.*** [< L. *simia,* an ape, prob. < *simus,* flat-nosed < Gr.] of or like an ape or monkey —***n.*** an ape or monkey

sim·i·lar (sim′ə lər) ***adj.*** [< Fr. < L. *similis*] **1.** nearly but not exactly the same or alike **2.** *Geom.* having the same shape, but not the same size or position —**sim′i·lar·ly** ***adv.***

sim·i·lar·i·ty (sim′ə lar′ə tē) ***n.*** **1.** a being similar; likeness **2.** *pl.* **-ties** a point, feature, or instance in which things are similar

sim·i·le (sim′ə lē) ***n.*** [L., a likeness < *similis,* like] a figure of speech in which one thing is likened to another, dissimilar thing by using *like, as,* etc. (Ex.: a voice like thunder): cf. METAPHOR

si·mil·i·tude (sə mil′ə to͞od′, -tyo͞od′) ***n.*** [MFr. < L. *similitudo*] **1.** a person or thing resembling another; counterpart **2.** the form or likeness (*of* some person or thing) **3.** [Rare] a simile **4.** similarity; likeness

Si·mi Valley (sə mē′; *popularly,* sē′mē) [prob. < AmInd. *shimiji,* little white clouds] city in SW Calif., northwest of Los Angeles: pop. 78,000

sim·mer (sim′ər) ***vi.*** [of echoic origin] **1.** to remain at or just below the boiling point **2.** to be about to break out, as in anger, revolt, etc. —***vt.*** **1.** to make (a liquid) simmer **2.** to cook in such a liquid —***n.*** a simmering —**simmer down** **1.** to simmer, as a liquid, until the volume is reduced **2.** to become calm; cool off

Si·mon (sī′mən) [LL. < Gr. < Heb. *shim'ōn,* lit., heard] **1.** a masculine name **2.** *Bible* one of the twelve apostles, called *Peter* or *Simon Peter*

Simon Le·gree (lə grē′) **1.** the villainous slave overseer in H. B. STOWE's novel *Uncle Tom's Cabin* **2.** any cruel taskmaster

Simon Ma·gus (mā′gəs) *Bible* a Samaritan magician who offered money for instruction in the rite of imparting the Holy Ghost: Acts 8:9–24

si·mon-pure (sī′mən pyoor′) ***adj.*** [after *Simon Pure,* a Quaker in S. Centlivre's play *A Bold Stroke for a Wife* (1718)] genuine; authentic

si·mo·ny (sī′mə nē, sim′ə-) ***n.*** [< OFr. < ML. *simonia* < SIMON MAGUS] the buying or selling of sacred or spiritual things, as church offices

si·moom (si mo͞om′) ***n.*** [< Ar. < *samma,* to poison] a hot, violent, sand-laden wind of the African and Asiatic deserts: also **si·moon′** (-mo͞on′)

simp (simp) ***n.*** *slang clipped form of* SIMPLETON

sim·pa·ti·co (sim pät′i kō, -pat′-) ***adj.*** [< It. *simpatico* or Sp. *simpático*] compatible or congenial

sim·per (sim′pər) ***vi.*** [akin to MDu. *simperlijc,* dainty, affected] to smile in a silly or affected way —***vt.*** to say with a simper —***n.*** a silly or affected smile —**sim′per·er** ***n.*** —**sim′per·ing·ly** ***adv.***

sim·ple (sim′p'l) ***adj.*** **-pler, -plest** [OFr. < L. *simplex*] **1.** having only one part, feature, etc.; not compound or complex **2.** having few parts, etc.; not complicated or involved **3.** easy to do, solve, or understand, as a task, question, etc. **4.** without additions or qualifications *[the simple facts]* **5.** *a)* not ornate; unadorned *[simple clothes]* *b)* not luxurious; plain *[simple tastes]* **6.** pure; unadulterated **7.** without guile or deceit **8.** *a)* not showy or affected; natural *b)* not sophisticated; naive **9.** of low rank or position; lowly or ordinary **10.** insignificant; unimportant **11.** *a)* stupid or foolish *b)* uneducated or ignorant **12.** *Chem.* elementary or unmixed **13.** *Law* unconditional *[in fee simple]* **14.** *Zool.* not divided into parts; not compounded —***n.*** **1.** an ignorant or foolish person **2.** something having only one part, substance, etc. **3.** [Archaic] a medicinal plant or herb, or a medicine made from it —**sim′ple·ness** ***n.***

simple fraction a fraction in which both numerator and denominator are whole numbers, as 1/2

simple fracture a bone fracture in which the broken ends of bone do not pierce the skin

sim·ple-heart·ed (-här′tid) ***adj.*** artless or unsophisticated

simple interest interest computed on principal alone, not on principal plus interest

simple machine any of the basic mechanical devices, including the lever, wheel and axle, pulley, wedge, screw, and inclined plane, essential to any complex machine

sim·ple-mind·ed (-mīn′did) ***adj.*** **1.** artless; unsophisticated **2.** foolish; stupid; silly **3.** mentally retarded —**sim′ple-mind′ed·ly** ***adv.*** —**sim′ple-mind′ed·ness** ***n.***

simple sentence a sentence having one main clause and no subordinate clauses (Ex.: The boy ran home.)

sim·ple·ton (sim′p'l tən) ***n.*** [< SIMPLE] a person who is stupid or easily deceived; fool

sim·plic·i·ty (sim plis′ə tē) ***n.,*** *pl.* **-ties** **1.** a being simple; freedom from complexity or intricacy **2.** absence of luxury, elegance, etc.; plainness **3.** freedom from affectation **4.** lack of sense; foolishness

sim·pli·fy (sim′plə fī′) ***vt.*** **-fied′, -fy′ing** to make simpler, easier, less complex, etc. —**sim′pli·fi·ca′tion** ***n.*** —**sim′pli·fi′er** ***n.***

sim·plist (sim′plist) ***n.*** a person given to simplistic explanations, theories, etc. —***adj.*** *same as* SIMPLISTIC —**sim′plism** ***n.***

sim·plis·tic (sim plis′tik) ***adj.*** making complex problems seem to be simple; oversimplifying or oversimplified —**sim·plis′ti·cal·ly** ***adv.***

sim·ply (sim′plē) ***adv.*** **1.** in a simple way **2.** merely; only *[simply trying to help]* **3.** absolutely; completely

sim·u·la·crum (sim′yoo lā′krəm) ***n.**, pl.* **-cra** (-krə) [L. < *simulare:* see ff.] **1.** an image; likeness **2.** false appearance; semblance **3.** a mere pretense; sham

sim·u·late (sim′yoo lāt′) ***vt.*** **-lat′ed, -lat′ing** [< L. pp. of *simulare,* to feign < *simul,* likewise] **1.** to give a false appearance of; feign [to *simulate* an interest] **2.** to look or act like [an insect *simulating* a twig] —**sim′u·la′tion** ***n.*** —**sim′u·la′tive** ***adj.***

sim·u·la·tor (-lāt′ər) ***n.*** one that simulates; specif., a training device that duplicates artificially the conditions likely to be encountered in some operation, as in a spacecraft [a flight *simulator*]

si·mul·cast (sī′m'l kast′) ***vt.*** **-cast′** or **-cast′ed, -cast′ing** [SIMUL(TANEOUS) + (BROAD)CAST] to broadcast (a program, event, etc.) simultaneously by radio and television —***n.*** a program, etc. so broadcast

si·mul·ta·ne·ous (sī′m'l tā′nē əs, -tān′yəs) ***adj.*** [< ML., ult. < L. *simul,* at the same time] occurring, done, existing, etc. together or at the same time —**si′mul·ta·ne′i·ty** (-tə nē′ə tē), **si′mul·ta′ne·ous·ness** ***n.*** —**si′mul·ta′ne·ous·ly** ***adv.***

sin (sin) ***n.*** [OE. *synne*] **1.** *a)* the breaking of religious or moral law, esp. through a willful act *b)* the state of committing sins **2.** any offense or fault —***vi.*** **sinned, sin′ning** to commit a sin

sin sine

Si·nai (sī′nī; *occas.* sī′ni ī′), **Mount** *Bible* the mountain where Moses received the Law from God: Ex. 19

Sinai Peninsula broad peninsula in NE Egypt, between the Gulf of Suez & an E arm of the Red Sea

since (sins) ***adv.*** [< OE. *siththan,* ult. < *sith,* after + *thon,* instrumental form of *thæt,* that] **1.** from then until now [he came Monday and has been here ever *since*] **2.** at some or any time between then and now [he was ill last week but has *since* recovered] **3.** before now; ago [gone long *since*] —***prep.*** **1.** continuously from (the time given) until now [out walking *since* noon] **2.** during the period following [he's written twice *since* May] —***conj.*** **1.** after the time that [two years *since* he died] **2.** continuously from the time when [lonely ever *since* he left] **3.** inasmuch as; because [*since* you're tired, let's go home]

sin·cere (sin sir′) ***adj.*** **-cer′er, -cer′est** [< MFr. < L. *sincerus,* clean] **1.** without deceit or pretense; truthful; honest **2.** genuine; real [*sincere* grief] —**sin·cere′ly** ***adv.***

sin·cer·i·ty (sin ser′ə tē) ***n.**, pl.* **-ties** a being sincere; honesty, genuineness, etc.

Sin·clair (sin kler′), **Up·ton (Beall, Jr.)** (up′t'n) 1878–1968; U.S. novelist & socialist

Sind (sind) region in S Pakistan, in the Indus valley

sine (sīn) ***n.*** [ML. *sinus* (< L., a curve), used as transl. of Ar. *jaib,* bosom of a garment] *Trigonometry* the ratio between the side opposite a given acute angle in a right triangle and the hypotenuse

‡**si·ne** (sī′nē, sē′nā) ***prep.*** [L.] without

si·ne·cure (sī′nə kyoor, sin′ə-) ***n.*** [< ML. < L. *sine,* without + *cura,* care] **1.** a church benefice not involving spiritual care of members **2.** any position that brings profit without involving much work, responsibility, etc.

si·ne di·e (sī′nē dī′ē, sin′ā dē′ā) [LL.] without (a) day (being set for meeting again); for an indefinite period

si·ne qua non (sī′nē kwā nän′, sin′ā kwä nōn′) [L., without which not] something essential or indispensable

sin·ew (sin′yoo) ***n.*** [OE. *seonwe,* oblique form < nom. *seonu*] **1.** a tendon **2.** muscular power; strength **3.** [*often pl.*] any source of power —***vt.*** to strengthen as with sinews

sin·ew·y (-yoo wē) ***adj.*** **1.** of or like sinew; tough **2.** having many sinews, as a cut of meat **3.** having good muscular development **4.** vigorous; powerful

sin·ful (sin′fəl) ***adj.*** full of or characterized by sin; wicked —**sin′ful·ly** ***adv.*** —**sin′ful·ness** ***n.***

sing (siŋ) ***vi.*** **sang** or now rarely **sung, sung, sing′ing** [OE. *singan*] **1.** *a)* to produce musical sounds with the voice *b)* to perform musical selections vocally **2.** to use song in description, praise, etc. [of thee I *sing*] **3.** *a)* to make musical sounds like those of the human voice, as a songbird *b)* to whistle, buzz, hum, etc., as a teakettle, bee, etc. **4.** to admit of being sung **5.** to rejoice [his heart *sang*] —***vt.*** **1.** to render or utter by singing **2.** to chant **3.** to describe, proclaim, etc. in song **4.** to bring or put, as to sleep, by singing —***n.*** **1.** a sound of whistling, humming, etc. **2.** [Colloq.] *a)* a singing by a group gathered for the purpose *b)* the group —**sing out** [Colloq.] to speak or call out loudly —**sing′a·ble** ***adj.*** —**sing′er** ***n.***

sing. singular

sing-a·long (siŋ′ə lôŋ′) ***n.*** [Colloq.] an informal gathering of people to join in the singing of songs

Sin·ga·pore (siŋ′gə pôr′, siŋ′ə-) **1.** island country off the S tip of the Malay Peninsula: a member of the Commonwealth: 225 sq. mi.; pop. 2,110,000 **2.** its capital, a seaport: pop. c.1,000,000

singe (sinj) ***vt.*** **singed, singe′ing** [OE. *sengan*] **1.** to burn superficially or slightly **2.** to expose (a carcass) to flame in removing bristles or feathers —***n.*** a slight burn

Sin·gha·lese (siŋ′gə lēz′, -lēs′) ***adj., n.**, pl.* **-lese′** *same as* SINHALESE

sin·gle (siŋ′g'l) ***adj.*** [< OFr. < L. *singulus*] **1.** *a)* one only; one and no more *b)* distinct from others of the same kind [every *single* time] **2.** without another; alone **3.** of or for one person or family, as a house **4.** between two persons only [*single* combat] **5.** unmarried **6.** having only one part; not double, compound, etc. **7.** uniform **8.** unbroken **9.** having only one set of petals **10.** sincere —***vt.*** **-gled, -gling** to select from others (usually with *out*) —***vi.*** *Baseball* to hit a single —***n.*** **1.** a single person or thing; specif., *a)* a hotel room, a ticket, etc. for one person *b)* [Colloq.] a one-dollar bill **2.** *Baseball* a hit by which the batter reaches first base **3.** *Cricket* a hit by which one run is scored **4.** [*pl.*] *Tennis,* etc. a match with only one player on each side —**sin′gle·ness** ***n.***

sin·gle-breast·ed (-bres′tid) ***adj.*** overlapping over the breast just enough to be fastened with one button or one row of buttons, as a coat

single entry a system of bookkeeping in which a single account is kept, usually of cash and of debts owed to and by the concern in question

single file **1.** a single column of persons or things, one directly behind another **2.** in such a column

sin·gle-foot (-foot′) ***n.*** the gait of a horse in which the legs move in lateral pairs, each foot falling separately

sin·gle-hand·ed (-han′did) ***adj.*** **1.** having only one hand **2.** using or requiring the use of only one hand **3.** done or working alone —***adv.*** **1.** by means of only one hand **2.** without help —**sin′gle-hand′ed·ly** ***adv.***

sin·gle-heart·ed (-här′tid) ***adj.*** honest; sincere —**sin′gle-heart′ed·ly** ***adv.*** —**sin′gle-heart′ed·ness** ***n.***

sin·gle-mind·ed (-mīn′did) ***adj.*** **1.** *same as* SINGLE-HEARTED **2.** with only one aim or purpose —**sin′gle-mind′ed·ly** ***adv.*** —**sin′gle-mind′ed·ness** ***n.***

sin·gle-space (-spās′) ***vt., vi.*** **-spaced′, -spac′ing** to type (copy) so as to leave no line space between lines

single standard a moral code with the same standard for men and women alike, esp. in matters of sex

sin·gle·stick (-stik′) ***n.*** **1.** a swordlike stick formerly used for fencing **2.** the sport of fencing with such sticks

sin·glet (siŋ′glit) ***n.*** [Brit.] a man's undershirt or jersey

single tax **1.** a system of taxation with only one tax, as on the value of land **2.** such a tax —**sin′gle-tax′** ***adj.***

sin·gle·ton (siŋ′g'l tən) ***n.*** **1.** the only playing card held by a player in a given suit **2.** a single thing, all by itself

sin·gle·tree (-trē′) ***n.*** [< earlier *swingletree* < ME. *swingle,* a rod + *tre,* a tree] a pivoted crossbar at the front of a wagon, etc., to which the traces of a horse's harness are hooked

sin·gly (siŋ′glē) ***adv.*** **1.** as a single, separate person or thing; alone **2.** one by one **3.** without help; unaided

Sing Sing (siŋ′siŋ′) a N.Y. State penitentiary at Ossining

sing·song (siŋ′sôŋ′, -säŋ′) ***n.*** **1.** *a)* an unvarying rise and fall of tone *b)* speech, tones, etc. marked by this **2.** *a)* monotonous rhyme or rhythm in verse *b)* verse with this —***adj.*** monotonous because done in singsong

sin·gu·lar (siŋ′gyə lər) ***adj.*** [< OFr. < L. < *singulus,* single] **1.** being the only one of its kind; unique **2.** extraordinary; remarkable [*singular* beauty] **3.** strange; odd [a *singular* remark] **4.** [Archaic] separate; individual **5.** *Gram.* designating or of that category of number referring to only one —***n.*** *Gram.* **1.** the singular number **2.** the singular form of a word **3.** a word in singular form —**sin′gu·lar′i·ty** (-lar′ə tē) ***n.**, pl.* **-ties** —**sin′gu·lar·ly** ***adv.***

sin·gu·lar·ize (siŋ′gyə lə rīz′) ***vt.*** **-ized′, -iz′ing** to make singular

Sin·ha·lese (sin′hə lēz′, sin′ə-; -lēs′) ***adj.*** of Ceylon, its principal people, their language, etc. —***n.*** **1.** *pl.* **-lese′** any member of the Sinhalese people **2.** their language

sin·is·ter (sin′is tər) ***adj.*** [< L. *sinister,* left-hand or unlucky (side)] **1.** of or on the left-hand side (on a coat of arms, the right of the viewer) **2.** threatening harm, evil, etc.; ominous **3.** evil or dishonest, esp. in a dark, mysterious way [a *sinister* plot] **4.** unfortunate or disastrous [a *sinister* fate] —**sin′is·ter·ly** ***adv.*** —**sin′is·ter·ness** ***n.***

sin·is·tral (sin′is trəl) ***adj.*** [OFr. < L.: see prec.] **1.** on the left-hand side; left **2.** left-handed

sin·is·trorse (sin′is trôrs′) *adj.* [< ModL. < L. < *sinister,* left + pp. of *vertere,* to turn] *Bot.* twining upward to the left, as the stems of some vines

Si·nit·ic (si nit′ik) *n.* [see SINO-, -ITE, & -IC] a branch of Sino-Tibetan, including Chinese languages —*adj.* of China, the Chinese, their languages, etc.

sink (siŋk) *vi.* **sank** or **sunk, sunk** or obs. **sunk′en, sink′ing** [OE. *sincan*] **1.** to go beneath the surface of water, snow, etc. and be partly or completely covered **2.** *a)* to go down slowly *b)* to seem to descend, as the sun **3.** to become lower in level, as a lake **4.** to decrease in degree, volume, or strength, as wind, flames, a sound, etc. **5.** to become less in value or amount, as prices **6.** to become hollow; recede, as the cheeks **7.** to pass gradually (*into* sleep, despair, etc.) **8.** to become increasingly and dangerously ill; fail **9.** *a)* to lose social position, wealth, etc. *b)* to lose or abandon one's moral values and stoop (*to* an unworthy action) **10.** to become absorbed; penetrate —*vt.* **1.** to cause to sink; make go beneath a surface, make go down, make lower, etc. **2.** to make (a well, engraved design, etc.) by digging, drilling, or cutting **3.** *a)* to invest (money, capital, etc.) *b)* to lose by investing **4.** to hold back, suppress, or conceal (evidence, identity, etc.) **5.** to pay up (a debt) **6.** to defeat; undo; ruin **7.** *Sports* to put (a basketball) through the basket or (a golf ball) into the hole, and so score —*n.* **1.** a cesspool or sewer **2.** any place or thing considered morally filthy or corrupted **3.** a basin, as in a kitchen, with a drainpipe and, usually, a water supply **4.** *Geol. a)* an area of slightly sunken land, esp. one in which water collects *b) same as* SINKHOLE (sense 2) —**sink in** [Colloq.] to be grasped by the mind, esp. with difficulty —**sink′a·ble** *adj.*

sink·er (siŋ′kər) *n.* **1.** a person or thing that sinks **2.** a lead weight for fishing **3.** [Colloq.] a doughnut

sink·hole (siŋk′hōl′) *n.* **1.** *same as* CESSPOOL **2.** *Geol.* a hollow into which surface water flows and sinks

Sin·kiang (sin′kyaŋ′; *Chin.* shin′jyäŋ′) autonomous region of NW China, between Tibet & U.S.S.R.: 635,830 sq. mi.

sinking fund a fund made up of sums of money set aside at intervals, usually invested at interest, to pay a debt, meet expenses, etc.

sin·less (sin′lis) *adj.* without sin; innocent —**sin′less·ly** *adv.* —**sin′less·ness** *n.*

sin·ner (-ər) *n.* a person who sins; wrongdoer

Sinn Fein (shin′ fān′) [Ir., we ourselves] an early 20th-cent. Irish revolutionary movement working for independence and to revive Irish culture —**Sinn′ Fein′er**

Si·no- [< Fr. < LL. < Gr. *Sinai,* an Oriental people] *a combining form meaning:* **1.** of the Chinese people or language **2.** Chinese and

Si·nol·o·gy (sī näl′ə jē, si-) *n.* [SINO- + -LOGY] the study of Chinese languages, customs, etc. —**Si·no·log·i·cal** (sī′nə läj′i k'l, sin′ə-) *adj.* —**Si·nol′o·gist** *n.*

Si·no-Ti·bet·an (sī′nō ti bet′'n, sin′ō-) *adj.* designating or of a family of languages of C and SE Asia, including Sinitic, Tibetan, and Burmese —*n.* this family

sin·u·ate (sin′yoo wit; *also, and for v. always,* -wāt′) *adj.* [< L. pp. of *sinuare,* to bend < *sinus,* a bend] **1.** *same as* SINUOUS **2.** *Bot.* having an indented, wavy margin, as some leaves —*vi.* **-at′ed, -at′ing** to wind in and out —**sin′u·ate·ly** *adv.* —**sin′u·a′tion** *n.*

sin·u·ous (sin′yoo wəs) *adj.* [< L. < *sinus,* a bend] **1.** bending or winding in and out **2.** not straightforward; devious —**sin′u·os′i·ty** (-wäs′ə tē) *n., pl.* **-ties** —**sin′u·ous·ly** *adv.*

si·nus (sī′nəs) *n.* [L., a bent surface] **1.** a bend or curve **2.** a cavity, hollow, or passage; specif., *Anat., Zool. a)* any air cavity in the skull opening into a nasal cavity *b)* a channel for venous blood **3.** a channel leading from a pus-filled cavity

si·nus·i·tis (sī′nə sīt′əs) *n.* [ModL.: see prec. & -ITIS] inflammation of a sinus or sinuses, esp. of the skull

si·nu·soi·dal projection (sī′nə soi′d'l) [< ML. *sinus* < L.: see SINUS] a map projection showing the entire surface of the earth, with straight lines of latitude and curved lines of longitude

Si·on (sī′ən) *var. of* ZION

-sion (shən; *sometimes* zhən) [< L. *-sio*] *a suffix meaning* act, quality, condition, or result of *[discussion, confusion]*

Siou·an (so͞o′ən) *adj.* designating or of a language family of N. American Indians of the west central U.S., central Canada, etc.: it includes Dakota, Crow, etc. —*n.* this family of languages

Sioux (so͞o) *n., pl.* **Sioux** (so͞o, so͞oz) [Fr. < Ojibway dim. of *nadowe,* an adder, hence, an enemy] *same as* DAKOTA[1] (*n.* 1 & 2) —*adj. same as* DAKOTA[1] (*adj.* 1)

Sioux City city in W Iowa, on the Missouri River: pop. 82,000

Sioux Falls city in SE S.Dak.: pop. 81,000

sip (sip) *vt., vi.* **sipped, sip′ping** [akin to LowG. *sippen*] to drink a little at a time —*n.* **1.** a sipping **2.** a small quantity sipped —**sip′per** *n.*

si·phon (sī′fən) *n.* [Fr. < L. < Gr. *siphōn,* a tube] **1.** a bent tube for carrying liquid out over the edge of a container to a lower level through the atmospheric pressure on the surface of the liquid **2.** *same as* SIPHON BOTTLE **3.** a tubelike organ, as in a cuttlefish, for drawing in or ejecting liquids —*vt., vi.* to draw off, or pass, through a siphon —**si′phon·al** (-'l), **si·phon′ic** (-fän′ik) *adj.*

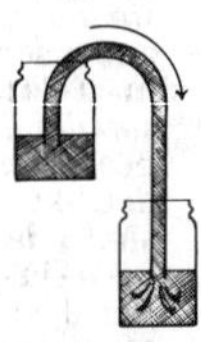
SIPHON

siphon bottle a heavy, sealed bottle with a tube inside connected at the top with a valve and nozzle used to release the pressurized, carbonated water within

sir (sur) *n.* [< *sire:* see ff.] **1.** [*sometimes* **S-**] a respectful term of address used to a man: not followed by the name: often used in the salutation of a letter **2.** [**S-**] the title used before the name of a knight or baronet **3.** [Archaic] a term of address used with the title of a man's office, etc. *[sir judge]*

sire (sīr) *n.* [< OFr., a master < L. *senior:* see SENIOR] **1.** a title of respect used in addressing a king **2.** [Poet.] a father or forefather **3.** the male parent of an animal —*vt.* **sired, sir′ing** to beget: said esp. of animals

si·ren (sī′rən) *n.* [< OFr., ult. < Gr. *Seirēn*] **1.** *Gr. & Rom. Myth.* any of several sea nymphs who lured sailors to their death on rocky coasts by seductive singing **2.** a seductive woman **3.** a device using steam or air driven against a rotating, perforated disk to make a loud, wailing sound, esp. as a warning signal —*adj.* of or like a siren; dangerously seductive

Sir·i·us (sir′ē əs) [L. < Gr. *Seirios,* lit., the scorcher] *same as* DOG STAR (sense 1)

sir·loin (sur′loin) *n.* [< MFr. < OFr. *sur,* over < *loigne,* loin] a choice cut, esp. of beef, from the loin end just in front of the rump

si·roc·co (sə räk′ō) *n., pl.* **-cos** [It. < Ar. *sharq,* the east] **1.** a hot, steady wind blowing from the Libyan deserts into S Europe **2.** any wind like this

sir·rah, sir·ra (sir′ə) *n.* [< SIR] [Archaic] a contemptuous term of address used to a man

sir·ree, sir·ee (sə rē′) *interj.* [< SIR] an interjection used for emphasis after *yes* or *no*

sir·up (sir′əp, sur′-) *n. same as* SYRUP —**sir′up·y** *adj.*

sis (sis) *n. colloq. shortened form of* SISTER

si·sal (sī′s'l) *n.* [< *Sisal,* Yucatán, a former seaport] **1.** a strong fiber obtained from a widely cultivated agave native to S Mexico, used for making rope, insulation, etc. **2.** the agave itself Also **sisal hemp**

sis·sy (sis′ē) *n., pl.* **-sies** [dim. of SIS] **1.** [Colloq.] *a)* an effeminate man or boy *b)* a coward **2.** [Slang] a homosexual —*adj.* [Colloq.] of or like a sissy: also **sis′si·fied′** (-ə fīd′) —**sis′sy·ish** *adj.*

sis·ter (sis′tər) *n.* [ON. *systir*] **1.** a female as she is related to other children of her parents **2.** a close friend who is like a sister **3.** a female fellow member of the same race, creed, profession, organization, etc. **4.** a member of a female religious order; nun **5.** one of the same kind, model, etc. **6.** [Brit.] a nurse, esp. a head nurse —*adj.* related as sisters

sis·ter·hood (-hood′) *n.* **1.** the state of being a sister or sisters **2.** an association of women united in a common interest, work, creed, etc.

sis·ter-in-law (-in lô′) *n., pl.* **sis′ters-in-law′** **1.** the sister of one's husband or wife **2.** the wife of one's brother **3.** the wife of the brother of one's husband or wife

sis·ter·ly (-lē) *adj.* **1.** of or like a sister **2.** friendly, kind, affectionate, etc. —**sis′ter·li·ness** *n.*

Sis·tine Chapel (sis′tēn) [< It. (after Pope *Sixtus* IV)] the principal chapel in the Vatican, with frescoes by Michelangelo

Sis·y·phus (sis′ə fəs) *Gr. Myth.* a greedy king doomed forever in Hades to roll uphill a heavy stone which always rolled down again

sit (sit) *vi.* **sat, sit′ting** [OE. *sittan*] **1.** *a)* to rest the body on the buttocks, as on a chair *b)* to rest on the haunches with forelegs braced, as a dog *c)* to perch, as a bird **2.** to cover eggs for hatching **3.** *a)* to occupy a seat as a judge, legislator, etc. *b)* to be in session, as a court **4.** to pose, as for a portrait **5.** to be inactive **6.** to be located *[a house sitting on a hill]* **7.** to hang on the wearer *[a coat sitting loosely]* **8.** to rest or lie as specified *[cares sit lightly on him]* **9.** *same as* BABY-SIT —*vt.* **1.** to cause to sit **2.** to stay seated on (a horse, etc.) **3.** to have seating space for —*n.* [Colloq.] the time spent seated —**sit back** **1.** to relax **2.** to be passive —**sit down** to take a seat —**sit in** to take part; attend (often with *on*) —**sit on** (or **upon**) **1.** to be on (a jury, committee, etc.) **2.** to confer on **3.** [Colloq.] to suppress, squelch, etc. —**sit out** **1.** to stay until the end of **2.** to stay seated during or take no part in (a dance, game, etc.) —**sit up** **1.** to rise to a sitting position **2.** to sit erect **3.** to put off going to bed **4.** [Colloq.] to become suddenly alert —**sit well with** to be agreeable to

si·tar (si tär′) ***n.*** [Hindi *sitār*] a lutelike instrument of India with a long, fretted neck, a resonating gourd or gourds, and strings that vibrate along with those being played —**si·tar′ist *n.***

SITAR

sit·com (sit′käm′) ***n.*** [Colloq.] *short for* SITUATION COMEDY

sit-down (sit′doun′) ***n.*** **1.** a strike in which strikers stay inside a factory, etc. refusing to work until agreement is reached: in full, **sit-down strike** **2.** a form of civil disobedience in which demonstrators sit down in streets, etc. and resist being moved —**sit′-down′er *n.***

site (sīt) ***n.*** [< L. *situs*, position < pp. of *sinere*, to put down] **1.** a piece of land considered for a certain purpose *[a good site for a town]* **2.** the place or scene of anything —***vt.*** **sit′ed, sit′ing** to locate on a site

sith (sith) ***adv., conj., prep.*** [OE. *siththa*] *archaic form of* SINCE

sit-in (sit′in′) ***n.*** a sit-down inside a public place by a group demonstrating for civil rights, against war, etc.

sit·ter (sit′ər) ***n.*** one that sits; specif., *a*) *short for* BABY SITTER *b*) a brooding hen

sit·ting (sit′iŋ) ***n.*** **1.** the act or position of one that sits **2.** a session or meeting, as of a court **3.** a period of being seated at some activity **4.** *a*) a brooding upon eggs *b*) a clutch of eggs being hatched —***adj.*** that sits; seated

Sitting Bull 1834?–90; Sioux Indian chief whose tribe annihilated the attacking troops of General Custer (1876)

sitting room *same as* LIVING ROOM

sit·u·ate (sich′oo wāt′) ***vt.*** **-at′ed, -at′ing** [< ML. pp. of *situare*, to place < L. *situs*, SITE] to put in a certain place or position; place; locate

sit·u·at·ed (-id) ***adj.*** **1.** placed as to site or position; located **2.** placed as to circumstances

sit·u·a·tion (sich′oo wā′shən) ***n.*** **1.** location; position **2.** a place; locality **3.** condition with regard to circumstances **4.** *a*) a combination of circumstances at a given time in real life or in the plot of a play, novel, etc. *b*) a difficult state of affairs **5.** a position of employment

sit·u·a·tion·al (-'l) ***adj.*** of, resulting from, or adjusted to fit a specific situation —**sit′u·a′tion·al·ly *adv.***

situation comedy a comedy, esp. a comic television series, made up of contrived episodes involving stock characters

sit-up, sit·up (sit′up′) ***n.*** an exercise in which a person lying flat on the back rises to a sitting position without using the hands and keeping the legs straight

sitz bath (sits, zits) [< G. *sitzbad*, a sitting bath] **1.** a bath in which only the hips and buttocks are covered **2.** the tub or basin for this

Si·va (sē′və, shē′-) Hindu god of destruction and reproduction, a member of the supreme Hindu trinity: see BRAHMA, VISHNU —**Si′va·ism *n.*** —**Si′va·is′tic *adj.***

Si·van (sē vän′, siv′ən) ***n.*** [Heb.] the ninth month of the Jewish year: see JEWISH CALENDAR

six (siks) ***adj.*** [OE. *sex*] totaling one more than five —***n.*** **1.** the cardinal number between five and seven; 6; VI **2.** a group of six; half a dozen **3.** anything having six units or members, or numbered six —**at sixes and sevens** [Colloq.] **1.** in confusion or disorder **2.** disagreeing

six·fold (-fōld′) ***adj.*** [see -FOLD] **1.** having six parts **2.** having six times as much or as many —***adv.*** six times as much or as many

six·pence (-pəns) ***n.*** **1.** the sum of six British (old) pennies **2.** a British coin of this value, discontinued (1971)

six·pen·ny (-pen′ē, -pə nē) ***adj.*** **1.** worth or costing sixpence **2.** designating a size of nails, two inches long

six-shoot·er (-shoōt′ər) ***n.*** [Colloq.] a revolver that fires six shots without reloading: also **six′-gun′**

six·teen (siks′tēn′) ***adj.*** [OE. *syxtene*] six more than ten —***n.*** the cardinal number between fifteen and seventeen; 16; XVI

six·teenth (siks′tēnth′) ***adj.*** **1.** preceded by fifteen others in a series; 16th **2.** designating any of the sixteen equal parts of something —***n.*** **1.** the one following the fifteenth **2.** any of the sixteen equal parts of something; 1/16

sixteenth note *Music* a note having one sixteenth the duration of a whole note: see NOTE, illus.

sixth (siksth) ***adj.*** [OE. *sixta*] **1.** preceded by five others in a series; 6th **2.** designating any of the six equal parts of something —***n.*** **1.** the one following the fifth **2.** any of the six equal parts of something; 1/6 **3.** *Music a*) the sixth tone of an ascending diatonic scale, or a tone five degrees above or below any given tone *b*) the interval between two such tones, or a combination of them —**sixth′ly *adv.***

sixth sense a power to perceive by intuition, thought of as a sense in addition to the commonly accepted five senses

six·ti·eth (siks′tē ith) ***adj.*** **1.** preceded by fifty-nine others in a series; 60th **2.** designating any of the sixty equal parts of something —***n.*** **1.** the one following the fifty-ninth **2.** any of the sixty equal parts of something; 1/60

six·ty (siks′tē) ***adj.*** [OE. *sixtig*] six times ten —***n.***, *pl.* **-ties** the cardinal number between fifty-nine and sixty-one; 60; LX —**the sixties** the numbers or years, as of a century, from sixty through sixty-nine

six·ty-fourth note (-fôrth′) *Music* a note having one sixty-fourth the duration of a whole note: see NOTE, illus.

siz·a·ble (sī′zə b'l) ***adj.*** quite large or bulky: also **size′a·ble** —**siz′a·ble·ness *n.*** —**siz′a·bly *adv.***

size[1] (sīz) ***n.*** [< OFr. *sise*, short for *assise*: see ASSIZE] **1.** that quality of a thing which determines how much space it occupies; dimensions **2.** any of a series of graded classifications for goods *[size ten shoes]* **3.** *a*) extent, amount, etc. *b*) sizable amount, dimensions, etc. **4.** ability to meet needs **5.** [Colloq.] true state of affairs —***vt.*** **sized, siz′ing** to make or arrange according to size —**of a size** of one or the same size —**size up** [Colloq.] to estimate; judge

size[2] (sīz) ***n.*** [ME. *syse*] any thin, pasty or gluey substance used as a glaze or filler on porous materials, as on paper or cloth —***vt.*** **sized, siz′ing** to apply size to

-sized (sīzd) *a combining form meaning* having (a specified) size *[small-sized]* : also **-size** *[life-size]*

siz·ing (sī′ziŋ) ***n.*** **1.** *same as* SIZE[2] **2.** the act or process of applying such size

siz·zle (siz′'l) ***vi.*** **-zled, -zling** [echoic] **1.** to make a hissing sound when in contact with heat **2.** to be extremely hot **3.** to simmer with suppressed rage —***n.*** a sizzling sound

S.J. Society of Jesus

Skag·er·rak (skag′ə rak′) arm of the North Sea, between Norway & Denmark

skald (skôld, skäld) ***n.*** [ON. *skāld*] any ancient Scandinavian poet, specif. of the Viking period —**skald′ic *adj.***

skate[1] (skāt) ***n.*** [assumed sing. < Du. *schaats*, a skate < ONormFr. < OFr. *eschace*, stilt < Frank.] **1.** *a*) a bladelike metal runner in a frame to be fastened to a shoe, used for gliding on ice *b*) a shoe with this attached Also **ice skate** **2.** a frame or shoe with two pairs of small wheels, for gliding on a sidewalk, etc.: also **roller skate** **3.** a skating —***vi.*** **skat′ed, skat′ing** to move along on skates —**skat′er *n.***

skate[2] (skāt) ***n.***, *pl.* **skates, skate:** see PLURAL, II, D, 1 [ON. *skata*] any of various rays with a broad, flat body and short, spineless tail

skate·board (skāt′bôrd′) ***n.*** a short, oblong board with two wheels at each end, which one rides on, usually while standing —***vi.*** **-board′ed, -board′ing** to ride on a skateboard

ske·dad·dle (ski dad′'l) ***vi.*** **-dled, -dling** [coinage of Civil War period] [Colloq.] to run off; leave fast

skeet (skēt) ***n.*** [ult. < ON. *skeyti*, a projectile] trapshooting done from different angles, usually eight

skein (skān) ***n.*** [< MFr. *escaigne*] **1.** a quantity of thread or yarn wound in a coil **2.** a coil of hair, etc.

skel·e·ton (skel′ə t'n) ***n.*** [ModL. < Gr. *skeleton* (*sōma*), dried (body) < *skeletos*, dried up] **1.** the hard framework of an animal, supporting the tissues and protecting the organs; specif., all the bones or bony framework of a human being or other vertebrate **2.** anything like a skeleton; specif., *a*) a very lean or thin person or animal *b*) a supporting framework, as of a ship *c*) an outline, as of a novel —***adj.*** of or like a skeleton; greatly reduced *[a skeleton force]* —**skeleton in the closet** some fact, as about a relative, kept secret because of shame —**skel′e·tal** (-t'l) ***adj.***

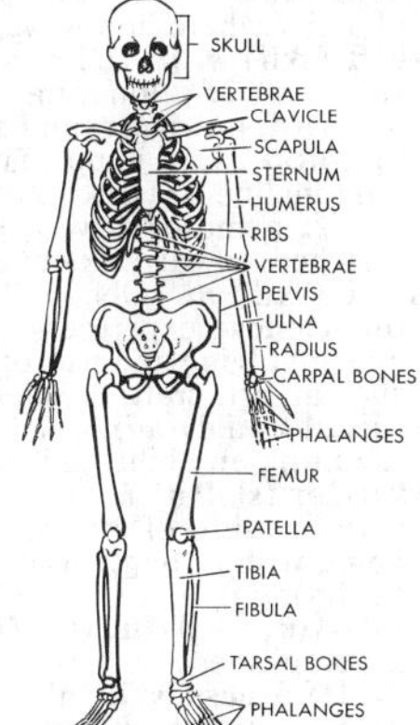

HUMAN SKELETON

skel·e·ton·ize (-īz′) ***vt.*** **-ized′, -iz′ing** **1.** to reduce to a skeleton **2.** to outline **3.** to reduce greatly in number or size

skeleton key a key with much of the bit filed away so that it can open any of various simple locks

skep·tic (skep′tik) ***adj.*** [< L. < Gr. *skeptikos*, inquiring] *var. of*

SKEPTICAL —*n.* **1.** [S-] a member of any of the ancient Greek philosophical schools that denied the possibility of real knowledge **2.** a believer in philosophical skepticism **3.** one who habitually doubts or questions matters generally accepted **4.** one who doubts religious doctrines

skep·ti·cal (skep′ti k'l) ***adj.*** **1.** of or characteristic of skeptics or skepticism **2.** not easily convinced; doubting; questioning **3.** doubting the fundamental doctrines of religion —**skep′ti·cal·ly** ***adv.***

skep·ti·cism (-siz'm) ***n.*** **1.** [S-] the doctrines of the ancient Greek Skeptics **2.** the philosophical doctrine that the truth of all knowledge must always be in question **3.** skeptical attitude; doubt, esp. about religious doctrines

sketch (skech) ***n.*** **[**Du. *schets* < It. *schizzo* < L. < Gr. *schedios,* extempore**]** **1.** a simple, rough drawing or design, done rapidly **2.** a brief plan; outline **3.** a short, light, informal story, description, skit, etc. —***vt., vi.*** to make a sketch (of) —**sketch′a·ble** ***adj.*** —**sketch′er** ***n.***

sketch·book (-book′) ***n.*** **1.** a book of drawing paper for making sketches **2.** a book of literary sketches Also **sketch book**

sketch·y (-ē) ***adj.*** **sketch′i·er, sketch′i·est** **1.** having the form of a sketch; not detailed **2.** not complete; inadequate —**sketch′i·ly** ***adv.*** —**sketch′i·ness** ***n.***

skew (skyōō) ***vi.*** **[**< ONormFr. *eskiuer,* altered < OFr. < OHG.: see ESCHEW**]** **1.** to take a slanting course; swerve or twist **2.** to glance sideways (*at*) —***vt.*** **1.** to make slanting or oblique **2.** to bias or distort —***adj.*** **1.** slanting; oblique **2.** not symmetrical —***n.*** **1.** a slant or twist **2.** a slanting part or movement —**skew′ness** ***n.***

skew·er (skyōō′ər) ***n.*** **[**< ON. *skifa,* a slice**]** **1.** a long pin used to hold meat together while cooking or as a brochette **2.** any similar pin or rod —***vt.*** to fasten or pierce as with skewers

SKEWERS

ski (skē; *Brit. also* shē) ***n., pl.*** **skis, ski** **[**Norw. < ON. *skith,* snowshoe, strip of wood**]** **1.** either of a pair of long, thin runners of wood, metal, etc., fastened to the shoes for gliding over snow **2.** a water ski: see WATER-SKI —***vi.*** **skied** (skēd), **ski′ing** **1.** to glide on skis, as down snow-covered hills **2.** *short for* WATER-SKI —**ski′er** ***n.***

skid (skid) ***n.*** [prob. < ON. *skith:* see SKI] **1.** a plank, log, etc. used as a support or as a track to slide or roll a heavy object on **2.** a low, movable platform for holding loads or stacks **3.** [*pl.*] a protective wooden fender put against the side of a ship **4.** a runner in place of a wheel on some aircraft landing gear **5.** a sliding wedge or drag used to check a vehicle's motion by pressure against a wheel **6.** a skidding —***vt.*** **skid′ded, skid′ding** **1.** to brake or lock (a wheel) with a skid **2.** to support or move on skids **3.** to cause (a wheel, vehicle, etc.) to skid —***vi.*** **1.** to slide without turning, as a wheel when brakes are applied on a slippery surface **2.** to slide, as a vehicle not gripping an icy road **3.** to decline sharply, as prices —**be on** (or **hit**) **the skids** [Slang] to be on the downgrade —**put the skids on** (or **under**) [Slang] to thwart or cause to fail —**skid′der** ***n.***

skid·dy (-ē) ***adj.*** **-di·er, -di·est** having a slippery surface on which vehicles are liable to skid

skid row **[**altered < *skid road,* a trail for dragging logs, hence a section of town where loggers gathered**]** a section of a city where hobos, vagrants, derelicts, etc. gather

skiff (skif) ***n.*** **[**< MFr. < It. *schifo* < Gmc.**]** **1.** any light rowboat **2.** a long, narrow rowboat, esp. one with a centerboard, outrigger, and a small sail

ski jump **1.** a jump made by a skier after skiing down a long incline or track **2.** such an incline or track

ski lift a motor-driven, endless cable, typically with seats attached, to carry skiers up a slope

skill (skil) ***n.*** **[**ON. *skil,* distinction**]** **1.** great ability or proficiency; expertness **2.** an art, craft, or science, esp. one involving the use of the hands or body **3.** ability in such an art, craft, or science

skilled (skild) ***adj.*** **1.** having skill; skillful **2.** having or requiring an ability gained by special experience or training

skil·let (skil′it) ***n.*** **[**< ? OFr. dim. of *escuelle,* basin < L. *scutella,* dim. of *scutra,* a dish**]** **1.** [Chiefly Brit.] a pot or kettle with a long handle **2.** a shallow pan with a handle, for frying food

skill·ful, skil·ful (skil′fəl) ***adj.*** having or showing skill; accomplished; expert —**skill′ful·ly, skil′ful·ly** ***adv.*** —**skill′ful·ness, skil′ful·ness** ***n.***

skim (skim) ***vt.*** **skimmed, skim′ming** **[**prob. akin to SCUM**]** **1.** *a)* to clear (a liquid) of floating matter *b)* to remove (floating matter) from a liquid **2.** to coat with a thin layer [a pond *skimmed* with ice] **3.** to look through (a book, etc.) hastily **4.** *a)* to glide swiftly over *b)* to throw so as to make ricochet lightly [*skim* a flat stone across water] —***vi.*** **1.** to move along swiftly and lightly; glide **2.** to read hastily (*through* or *over* a book, etc.) **3.** to become thinly coated, as with scum —***n.*** **1.** something skimmed **2.** a skimming **3.** a thin coating

skim·mer (-ər) ***n.*** **1.** one that skims **2.** a utensil for skimming liquids **3.** a hat, usually of straw, with a flat crown and a wide, straight brim

skim milk milk from which cream has been removed: also **skimmed milk**

skimp (skimp) ***adj.*** **[**prob. altered < SCRIMP**]** [Colloq.] *same as* SCANTY —***vi.*** [Colloq.] **1.** to give or allow too little; be stingy **2.** to keep expenses very low —***vt.*** [Colloq.] **1.** to do poorly or carelessly **2.** to be stingy in or toward; specif., to make too small, too short, etc.

skimp·y (skim′pē) ***adj.*** **skimp′i·er, skimp′i·est** [Colloq.] barely or not quite enough; scanty —**skimp′i·ness** ***n.***

skin (skin) ***n.*** **[**ON. *skinn***]** **1.** the outer covering of the animal body **2.** this covering removed and prepared for use; pelt **3.** a skinlike outer layer, as fruit rind, a film or scum, etc. **4.** a container made of animal skin, for holding liquids **5.** [Slang] [*pl.*] a set of drums —***vt.*** **skinned, skin′ning** **1.** to cover as with skin **2.** to remove skin from **3.** to injure by scraping (one's knee, etc.) **4.** [Colloq.] *a)* to defraud; swindle *b)* to criticize severely **5.** [Colloq.] to urge on (a mule, ox, etc.), esp. by whipping —***vi.*** [Colloq.] **1.** to climb (*up* or *down*) **2.** to move (*through*), pass (*by*), succeed, etc. by a tiny margin —**by the skin of one's teeth** by the tiniest margin; barely —**get under one's skin** [Colloq.] to anger or irritate one —**have a thick** (or **thin**) **skin** to be insensitive (or very sensitive) to criticism, etc. —**save one's skin** [Colloq.] to avoid death or injury —**skin′ner** ***n.***

skin-deep (-dēp′) ***adj.*** **1.** penetrating no deeper than the skin **2.** without real significance; superficial —***adv.*** so as to be skin-deep

skin diving underwater swimming in which the swimmer, without lines to the surface, is variously equipped with a face mask, flipperlike footgear, a snorkel or scuba equipment, etc. —**skin′-dive′** (-dīv′) ***vi.*** **-dived′, -div′ing** —**skin diver**

skin·flint (-flint′) ***n.*** **[**lit., one who would skin a flint for economy**]** a niggardly person; miser

skin grafting the surgical transplanting of skin (**skin graft**) to replace skin destroyed, as by burning

skink (skiŋk) ***n.*** **[**< L. < Gr. *skinkos***]** a lizard with a very long, shiny body and short legs

skin·less (skin′lis) ***adj.*** without a skin, casing, etc.

skinned (skind) ***adj.*** having skin (of a specified kind) [*dark-skinned*]

skin·ny (skin′ē) ***adj.*** **-ni·er, -ni·est** **1.** of or like skin **2.** without much flesh; emaciated; thin **3.** inferior; inadequate —**skin′ni·ness** ***n.***

skin·ny-dip (-dip′) ***vi.*** **-dipped′, -dip′ping** [Colloq.] to swim in the nude —***n.*** [Colloq.] a swim in the nude

skin test any test for detecting the presence of a disease or allergy from the reaction of the skin to a test substance

skin·tight (skin′tīt′) ***adj.*** clinging closely to the skin; tightfitting [a *skintight* dress]

skip (skip) ***vi.*** **skipped, skip′ping** [prob. < Scand.] **1.** to leap, jump, etc. lightly; specif., to move along by hopping lightly on one foot and then the other **2.** to be deflected from a surface; ricochet **3.** to pass from one point to another, omitting what lies between **4.** to be promoted in school beyond the next regular grade **5.** [Colloq.] to leave hurriedly; abscond —***vt.*** **1.** to leap lightly over **2.** to pass over or omit **3.** to fail to attend a session of (school, church, etc.) **4.** to cause to skip or ricochet **5.** to promote to the school grade beyond the next regular one **6.** [Colloq.] to leave (a town, etc.) hurriedly —***n.*** **1.** *a)* an act of skipping; leap *b)* a skipping gait alternating light hops on each foot **2.** a passing over or omitting —**skip it!** it doesn't matter!

ski pants pants that fit snugly at the ankles, worn for skiing and other winter sports

skip·jack (-jak′) ***n., pl.*** **-jacks′, -jack′:** see PLURAL, II, D, 1 any of several kinds of fish that play at the surface of the water

ski·plane (skē′plān′) ***n.*** an airplane with skis for landing gear, for use on snow

ski pole either of a pair of light poles with a sharp tip, used by skiers as a help in climbing, keeping balance, etc.

skip·per[1] (skip′ər) ***n.*** **1.** a person or thing that skips **2.** any of various skipping insects

skip·per[2] (skip′ər) ***n.*** **[**MDu. *schipper* < *schip,* a ship**]** **1.** the captain of a ship **2.** any leader, director, or captain —***vt.*** to act as skipper of

skirl (skurl) ***vt., vi.*** [prob. < Scand.] [Scot. & Dial.] to sound out in shrill, piercing tones, as a bagpipe —***n.*** a shrill sound, as of a bagpipe

skir·mish (skur′mish) ***n.*** **[**< MFr. < It. < *schermire,* to fight < Gmc.**]** **1.** a brief fight between small groups, usually an incident of a battle **2.** any slight, unimportant conflict —***vi.*** to take part in a skirmish —**skir′mish·er** ***n.***

skirt (skurt) ***n.*** **[**ON. *skyrt,* shirt**]** **1.** that part of a dress, coat, robe, etc. that hangs below the waist **2.** a woman's garment that hangs down from the waist 3. something like a skirt, as a flap hanging from a saddle 4. [*pl.*] the outer parts; outskirts, as of a city 5. [Old Slang] a girl or woman —*vt.* 1. to lie along or form the edge of 2. *a*) to move along the edge of or pass around *b*) to miss narrowly 3. to avoid (a difficult issue, problem, etc.) 4. to border or edge with something —*vi.* to be on, or move along, the edge — **skirt'ed** *adj.* —**skirt'er** *n.*

skit (skit) *n.* [prob. < Scand. var. of ON. *skjota*, to shoot] 1. a short piece of satirical or humorous writing 2. a short, comic theatrical sketch

ski tow a kind of ski lift enabling skiers to glide up the slope on their skis, towed by the endless cable

skit·ter (skit'ər) *vi.* [freq. of dial. *skite*, to dart about < Scand.] to skip or move along quickly or lightly, esp. over water —*vt.* to cause to skitter

skit·tish (skit'ish) *adj.* [see SKIT & -ISH] 1. lively or playful, esp. in a coy way 2. easily frightened; jumpy 3. fickle; undependable —**skit'tish·ly** *adv.* —**skit'tish·ness** *n.*

skit·tle (skit''l) *n.* [prob. < Scand. cognate of SHUTTLE] 1. [*pl. with sing. v.*] a British form of ninepins in which a wooden disk or ball is used to knock down the pins 2. any of these pins —(**not**) **all beer and skittles** (not) pure pleasure

skiv·vy (skiv'ē) *n.*, *pl.* **-vies** [< ?] [Slang] 1. a man's, esp. a sailor's, short-sleeved undershirt: usually **skivvy shirt** 2. [*pl.*] men's underwear

skoal (skōl) *interj.* [Dan. & Norw. *skaal*, a cup < ON. *skāl*, a bowl] to your health!: a toast

Sko·pje (skô'pye) city in SE Yugoslavia; capital of Macedonia: pop. 172,000

Skr., Skrt., Skt. Sanskrit

sku·a (skyōō'ə) *n.* [ModL., ult. < ON. *skūfr*, a tuft] any of several large, brown and white sea gulls, found in cold seas

skul·dug·ger·y, skull·dug·ger·y (skul dug'ər ē) *n.* [< ?] [Colloq.] sneaky, dishonest behavior; trickery

skulk (skulk) *vi.* [prob. < LowG. *schulken* or Dan. *skulke*] 1. to move about in a stealthy or sinister manner; slink 2. [Chiefly Brit.] to avoid work or responsibility; shirk —*n.* a person who skulks —**skulk'er** *n.* —**skulk'ing·ly** *adv.*

skull (skul) *n.* [< Scand.] 1. the bony framework of the head, enclosing the brain 2. the human head or mind

skull and crossbones a representation of two crossed thighbones under a human skull, used as a symbol of death or extreme danger

skull·cap (-kap') *n.* a light, closefitting, brimless cap

skunk (skuŋk) *n.* [< AmInd. *segonku*] 1. *a*) *pl.* **skunks, skunk**: see PLURAL, II, D, 1 a bushy-tailed mammal about the size of a cat: it has black fur with white stripes down its back, and ejects a foul-smelling liquid when molested *b*) its fur 2. [Colloq.] a despicable, offensive person —*vt.* [Slang] to defeat overwhelmingly in a game or contest

skunk cabbage a plant having large, cabbagelike leaves and a disagreeable smell

sky (skī) *n.*, *pl.* **skies** [ON., a cloud] 1. [*often pl.*] the upper atmosphere, esp. with reference to its appearance [blue *skies*, a cloudy *sky*] 2. the heavens, apparently arching over the earth 3. heaven —*vt.* **skied** or **skyed, sky'ing** [Colloq.] to hit, throw, etc. high in the air —**out of a clear (blue) sky** without warning —**to the skies** without reserve

sky blue a blue color like that of the sky on a clear day — **sky'-blue'** *adj.*

sky·cap (-kap') *n.* a porter at an air terminal

sky diving the sport of jumping from an airplane and executing free-fall maneuvers before opening the parachute — **sky'-dive'** (-dīv') *vi.* **-dived', -div'ing** —**sky diver**

sky-high (skī'hī') *adj., adv.* 1. very high 2. so as to be completely blasted; to pieces

sky·jack (-jak') *vt.* [Colloq.] to hijack (an aircraft) —**sky'-jack'er** *n.* —**sky'jack'ing** *n.*

sky·lark (-lärk') *n.* a Eurasian lark, famous for the song it utters as it soars toward the sky —*vi.* [SKY + LARK²] to play about boisterously; frolic

sky·light (-līt') *n.* a window in a roof or ceiling

sky·line (-līn') *n.* 1. the line along which sky and earth seem to meet 2. the outline, as of a city, seen against the sky

sky pilot [Slang] a clergyman; esp., a military chaplain

sky·rock·et (-räk'it) *n.* a firework rocket that explodes in midair, with colored flame, sparks, etc. —*vi., vt.* to rise or cause to rise rapidly to a great height, success, etc.

sky·sail (skī'sāl', -s'l) *n.* the small sail set above the royal at the top of a square-rigged mast

sky·scrap·er (-skrā'pər) *n.* a very tall building

sky·ward (-wərd) *adv., adj.* toward the sky: also **sky'wards** *adv.*

sky·ways (-wāz') *n.pl.* routes of air travel

sky·writ·ing (-rīt'iŋ) *n.* the tracing of words, etc. in the sky by trailing smoke from an airplane in flight —**sky'write'** *vi., vt.* **-wrote', -writ'ten, -writ'ing** —**sky'writ'er** *n.*

slab (slab) *n.* [ME. *sclabbe*] 1. a piece that is flat, broad, and fairly thick [a *slab* of concrete] 2. a rough piece cut from the outside of a log

slack¹ (slak) *adj.* [OE. *slæc*] 1. slow; sluggish 2. barely moving, as a current of air 3. not busy or active; dull [a *slack* period] 4. loose; not tight or taut 5. weak; lax 6. careless or negligent [a *slack* workman] —*vt.* 1. to make slack 2. to slake —*vi.* 1. to be or become slack; slacken 2. to be idle, careless, or negligent —*adv.* in a slack manner — *n.* 1. a part that is slack or hangs loose 2. a lack of tension 3. a stoppage of movement in a current 4. a dull period; lull —**slack off** to slacken —**slack up** to go more slowly — **slack'ly** *adv.* —**slack'ness** *n.*

slack² (slak) *n.* [akin to Fl. *slecke*, dross, Du. *slak*] a mixture of small pieces of coal, coal dust, and dirt left from the screening of coal

slack·en (slak''n) *vt., vi.* 1. to make or become less active, intense, etc. 2. to relax or loosen —**slack'en·er** *n.*

slack·er (-ər) *n.* 1. a person who shirks his work or duty 2. a person who evades military service in wartime

slacks (slaks) *n.pl.* trousers for men or women; esp., trousers that are not part of a suit

slag (slag) *n.* [MLowG. *slagge*] 1. the fused refuse separated from a metal in smelting 2. lava resembling this —*vt., vi.* **slagged, slag'ging** to form into slag

slain (slān) *pp. of* SLAY

slake (slāk) *vt.* **slaked, slak'ing** [OE. *slacian* < *slæc*, slack] 1. to make (thirst, desire, etc.) less intense by satisfying 2. to put out (a fire) 3. to produce a chemical change in (lime) by combination with water —*vi.* to become slaked

slaked lime *same as* CALCIUM HYDROXIDE

sla·lom (slä'ləm) *n.* [Norw., sloping trail] a downhill skiing race over a zigzag course —*vi.* to ski in a slalom

slam¹ (slam) *vt.* **slammed, slam'ming** [prob. < Scand.] 1. to shut with force and noise [to *slam* a door] 2. to hit, put, etc. with force and noise [to *slam* a baseball over the fence] 3. [Colloq.] to criticize severely —*vi.* to shut, go into place, etc. with force and noise —*n.* 1. the act or noise of slamming 2. [Colloq.] a severe criticism

slam² (slam) *n.* [< ?] *Bridge shortened form of* GRAND SLAM or LITTLE SLAM

slam·mer (slam'ər) *n.* [Slang] a prison or jail

slan·der (slan'dər) *n.* [< Anglo-Fr. < LL. *scandalum*: see SCANDAL] 1. the utterance of a falsehood damaging to a person's character or reputation: cf. LIBEL 2. such a spoken falsehood —*vt.* to utter a slanderous statement about — **slan'der·er** *n.*

slan·der·ous (-əs) *adj.* 1. containing slander 2. uttering slander —**slan'der·ous·ly** *adv.*

slang (slaŋ) *n.* [18th-c. cant < ?] 1. orig., the specialized vocabulary of criminals, tramps, etc.: now usually called CANT¹ 2. the specialized vocabulary of those in the same work, way of life, etc.: now usually called SHOPTALK, ARGOT, JARGON 3. highly informal language, usually short-lived and of a vigorous or colorful nature, that is usually avoided in formal speech and writing: it consists of both coined words and those with new meanings —*vi.* to use slang or abusive talk

slang·y (-ē) *adj.* **slang'i·er, slang'i·est** 1. of, like, or containing slang 2. given to using slang —**slang'i·ly** *adv.* — **slang'i·ness** *n.*

slant (slant) *vt., vi.* [< Scand.] 1. to turn or lie in a direction that is not straight up and down or straight across; slope 2. to write or tell so as to appeal to a particular interest or to express a particular bias —*n.* 1. *a*) a slanting surface, line, etc.; slope *b*) *same as* VIRGULE 2. a point of view or attitude, or one that shows bias —*adj.* oblique; sloping — **slant'ing** *adj.* —**slant'ing·ly** *adv.*

slant rhyme rhyme in which there is close but not exact correspondence of sounds (Ex.: *lid, lad; wait, made*)

slant·wise (-wīz') *adv.* so as to slant or slope; obliquely: also **slant'ways'** —*adj.* slanting; oblique

slap (slap) *n.* [LowG. *sklapp*: echoic] 1. *a*) a blow with something flat, as the palm of the hand *b*) the sound of this, or a sound like it 2. an insult; rebuff —*vt.* **slapped, slap'ping** 1. to strike with something flat 2. to put, hit, etc. carelessly or with force —*vi.* to make a dull, sharp noise, as upon impact —*adv.* 1. [Colloq.] straight; directly 2. [Brit. Colloq.] abruptly —**slap down** [Colloq.] to rebuke or rebuff sharply —**slap'per** *n.*

slap·dash (-dash′) ***n.*** something done carelessly and hastily —***adv.*** in a hasty, careless manner —***adj.*** hasty, careless, impetuous, etc.

slap-hap·py (-hap′ē) ***adj.*** [Slang] **1.** dazed, as by blows to the head **2.** silly or giddy

slap·jack (-jak′) ***n.*** *same as* FLAPJACK

slap·stick (-stik′) ***n.*** **1.** a device, formerly used by stage comedians, made of two wooden slats that slap together loudly when hit against something **2.** crude comedy full of horseplay —***adj.*** characterized by such comedy

slash (slash) ***vt.*** [< ? OFr. *esclachier,* to break] **1.** to cut or wound with sweeping strokes, as of a knife **2.** to whip viciously; lash **3.** to cut slits in (a fabric, dress, etc.), esp. so as to expose underlying material **4.** to reduce drastically *[to slash prices]* **5.** to criticize severely —***vi.*** to make a sweeping motion with or as with something sharp —***n.*** **1.** a sweeping stroke made as with a knife **2.** a cut made by such a stroke; gash **3.** *same as* VIRGULE **4.** a slit in a fabric, dress, etc. **5.** *a)* an open place in a forest, cluttered with branches, chips, etc. as from the cutting of timber *b)* such debris —**slash′er** ***n.***

slash·ing (-iŋ) ***adj.*** **1.** severe; violent **2.** dashing; spirited —***n.*** *same as* SLASH (*n.* 4 & 5) —**slash′ing·ly** ***adv.***

slat (slat) ***n.*** [OFr. *esclat,* fragment] **1.** a thin, narrow strip of wood, metal, etc. *[slats of a Venetian blind]* **2.** [*pl.*] [Slang] *a)* the ribs *b)* the buttocks —***vt.*** **slat′ted, slat′ting** to provide or make with slats

slate (slāt) ***n.*** [< OFr. fem. of *esclat:* see prec.] **1.** a hard, fine-grained rock that separates easily into thin, smooth layers **2.** its bluish-gray color: also **slate blue** **3.** a thin piece of slate, esp. one used as a roofing tile or as a tablet for writing on with chalk **4.** a list of candidates proposed for nomination or election —***vt.*** **slat′ed, slat′ing** **1.** to cover with slate **2.** to choose or schedule, as for a list of candidates, appointments, etc. —**a clean slate** a clean record without blemish —**slat′er** ***n.*** —**slat′y** ***adj.***

slat·tern (slat′ərn) ***n.*** [< dial. *slatter,* to slop] **1.** a woman who is careless and sloppy in her habits, appearance, etc. **2.** a slut —**slat′tern·li·ness** ***n.*** —**slat′tern·ly** ***adj., adv.***

slaugh·ter (slôt′ər) ***n.*** [ON. *slātr,* lit., slain flesh] **1.** the killing of animals for food; butchering **2.** the brutal killing of a human being **3.** the killing of people in large numbers, as in battle —***vt.*** **1.** to kill (animals) for food; butcher **2.** to kill (people) brutally or in large numbers —**slaugh′ter·er** ***n.*** —**slaugh′ter·ous** ***adj.***

slaugh·ter·house (-hous′) ***n.*** a place where animals are butchered for food; abattoir

Slav (släv, slav) ***n.*** a member of any of a group of Slavic-speaking peoples of E, SE, and C Europe, including the Russians, Ukrainians, Serbs, Croats, Bulgars, Czechs, Poles, Slovaks, etc. —***adj.*** *same as* SLAVIC

Slav. Slavic

slave (slāv) ***n.*** [< OFr. < ML. *sclavus,* slave, orig. Slav < LGr. *Sklabos:* first applied to captive Slavs] **1.** a human being who is owned as property by another and is under his absolute control **2.** a person who is dominated by some influence, habit, person, etc. *[slaves to fashion]* **3.** a person who slaves; drudge **4.** any ant enslaved by ants of other species: also **slave ant** **5.** a device actuated or controlled by another, similar device —***vi.*** **slaved, slav′ing** **1.** to work like a slave; drudge **2.** to deal in slaves

slave driver **1.** a person who oversees the work of slaves **2.** any merciless taskmaster

slave·hold·er (-hōl′dər) ***n.*** a person who owns slaves —**slave′hold′ing** ***adj., n.***

slav·er[1] (slav′ər) ***vi.*** [< Scand.] to let saliva run from the mouth; drool —***n.*** saliva drooling from the mouth

slav·er[2] (slā′vər) ***n.*** **1.** a ship used in the slave trade: also **slave ship** **2.** a person who deals in slaves

slav·er·y (slā′və rē, slāv′rē) ***n.*** **1.** the owning of slaves as a practice or institution **2.** the condition of being a slave; bondage **3.** a condition of domination by some influence, habit, etc. **4.** hard work or toil; drudgery

slave trade traffic in slaves; specif., the transportation of African Negroes to America for sale as slaves

slav·ey (slā′vē, slav′ē) ***n.,*** *pl.* **-eys** [Brit. Colloq.] a female domestic servant who does menial work

Slav·ic (släv′ik, slav′-) ***adj.*** of the Slavs, their languages, etc. —***n.*** a principal branch of the Indo-European family of languages, including Russian, Ukrainian, Byelorussian (**East Slavic**); Old Church Slavic, Bulgarian, Serbo-Croatian, Slovenian (**South Slavic**); and Polish, Sorbian, Czech, Slovak (**West Slavic**) Also **Sla·von·ic** (slə vän′ik)

slav·ish (slā′vish) ***adj.*** **1.** of or like slaves; specif., *a)* servile *b)* laborious **2.** blindly dependent *[slavish imitation]* —**slav′ish·ly** ***adv.*** —**slav′ish·ness** ***n.***

Sla·vo·ni·a (slə vō′nē ə) region in Croatia, N Yugoslavia —**Sla·vo′ni·an** ***adj., n.***

slaw (slô) ***n.*** *short for* COLESLAW

slay (slā) ***vt.*** **slew** or for 2 **slayed, slain, slay′ing** [OE. *slean*] **1.** to kill by violent means **2.** [Slang] to impress, delight, amuse, etc. greatly —**slay′er** ***n.***

sleaze (slēz) ***n.*** [< SLEAZY] [Slang] **1.** the quality or condition of being sleazy; sleaziness **2.** anything cheap, vulgar, shoddy, etc.

slea·zy (slē′zē) ***adj.*** **-zi·er, -zi·est** [< *Slesia,* var. of SILESIA] **1.** flimsy or thin in substance *[a sleazy fabric]* **2.** shoddy, cheap, etc. —**slea′zi·ly** ***adv.*** —**slea′zi·ness** ***n.***

sled (sled) ***n.*** [MLowG. or MDu. *sledde*] a vehicle mounted on runners for coasting or for carrying loads on snow, ice, etc. —***vt., vi.*** **sled′ded, sled′ding** to carry or ride on a sled

sledge[1] (slej) ***n., vt., vi.*** **sledged, sledg′ing** [OE. *slecge* < base of *slean,* to strike] *same as* SLEDGEHAMMER

sledge[2] (slej) ***n.*** [MDu. *sleedse*] a large, heavy sled for carrying loads over ice, snow, etc. —***vt.*** **sledged, sledg′ing** to carry by sledge

sledge·ham·mer (-ham′ər) ***n.*** [see SLEDGE[1]] a long, heavy hammer, usually held with both hands —***vt., vi.*** to strike as with a sledgehammer —***adj.*** crushingly powerful

sleek (slēk) ***adj.*** [var. of SLICK] **1.** smooth and shiny; glossy *[sleek fur]* **2.** having a healthy, glowing, well-groomed appearance **3.** speaking or acting in a smooth but insincere way **4.** luxurious, elegant, etc. —***vt.*** to make sleek: also **sleek′en** —**sleek′ly** ***adv.*** —**sleek′ness** ***n.***

sleep (slēp) ***n.*** [OE. *slæp*] **1.** *a)* a condition of rest for the body and mind at regular times, during which the eyes stay closed and there is dreaming *b)* a period of sleeping **2.** any state like sleep, as a coma —***vi.*** **slept, sleep′ing** **1.** to be in the state of sleep; slumber **2.** to be in a state like sleep, as hibernation **3.** [Colloq.] to have sexual intercourse (*with*) **4.** [Colloq.] to postpone a decision (*on*) —***vt.*** **1.** to have (a specified kind of sleep) *[to sleep the sleep of the just]* **2.** to provide sleeping accommodations for —**last sleep** death —**sleep away** to spend in sleep —**sleep in** **1.** to sleep at the place where one is in domestic service **2.** to sleep later than usual in the morning —**sleep off** to rid oneself of by sleeping —**sleep over** [Colloq.] to spend the night at another's home

sleep·er (slē′pər) ***n.*** **1.** one who sleeps, esp. as specified *[a light sleeper]* **2.** a beam laid flat for supporting something **3.** [Chiefly Brit.] a railroad tie **4.** *same as* SLEEPING CAR **5.** something that achieves an unexpected success, importance, etc. **6.** [*usually pl.*] pajamas that enclose the feet

sleeping bag a large bag with a warm lining, for sleeping in, esp. outdoors

sleeping car a railroad car with berths, compartments, etc. for passengers to sleep in

sleeping pill a pill or capsule containing a drug, esp. a barbiturate, that helps put one to sleep

sleeping sickness **1.** an infectious disease, esp. of tropical Africa, transmitted by the bite of the tsetse fly: it is characterized by fever, lethargy, and coma, usually ending in death **2.** inflammation of the brain, caused by a virus and inducing drowsiness, etc.

sleep·less (slēp′lis) ***adj.*** **1.** with little or no sleep *[a sleepless night]* **2.** always alert or active —**sleep′less·ly** ***adv.*** —**sleep′less·ness** ***n.***

sleep·walk·ing (slēp′wôk′iŋ) ***n.*** the act or practice of walking while asleep; somnambulism —**sleep′walk′** ***vi.*** —**sleep′walk′er** ***n.***

sleep·wear (-wer′) ***n.*** clothes to be worn in bed, as pajamas

sleep·y (slē′pē) ***adj.*** **sleep′i·er, sleep′i·est** **1.** ready or likely to fall asleep; drowsy **2.** not very active; dull; quiet *[a sleepy little town]* **3.** causing or showing drowsiness —**sleep′i·ly** ***adv.*** —**sleep′i·ness** ***n.***

sleet (slēt) ***n.*** [< OE. hyp. *sliete*] **1.** rain that freezes as it falls **2.** a mixture of rain and snow **3.** the icy coating formed when rain freezes on trees, streets, etc. —***vi.*** to shower in the form of sleet —**sleet′y** ***adj.***

sleeve (slēv) ***n.*** [OE. *sliefe*] **1.** that part of a garment that covers an arm or part of an arm **2.** a tube or tubelike part fitting around another part **3.** an envelope for a phonograph record —***vt.*** **sleeved, sleev′ing** to provide with sleeves —**up one's sleeve** hidden but ready at hand —**sleeved** ***adj.*** —**sleeve′less** ***adj.***

sleigh (slā) ***n.*** [Du. *slee,* contr. of *slede,* sled] a carriage with runners instead of wheels, for travel over snow and ice —***vi.*** to ride in or drive a sleigh —**sleigh′ing** ***n.***

sleight (slīt) ***n.*** [< ON. *slægth* < *slægr,* crafty] **1.** cunning used in deceiving **2.** skill or dexterity

sleight of hand **1.** skill in using the hands so as to confuse those watching, as in doing magic tricks **2.** tricks that deceive in or as in this way

slen·der (slen′dər) ***adj.*** [< ?] **1.** long and thin **2.** having a slim, trim figure **3.** small in amount, size, degree, etc.; slight *[slender earnings, slender hope]* —**slen′der·ly** ***adv.*** —**slen′der·ness** ***n.***

slen·der·ize (-īz′) ***vt.*** **-ized′, -iz′ing** to make or cause to seem slender —***vi.*** to become slender

slept (slept) *pt. & pp. of* SLEEP

sleuth (sl$\overline{oo}$th) ***n.*** [ON. *sloth*, a track, spoor] **1.** a bloodhound: in full, **sleuth′hound′** **2.** [Colloq.] a detective —***vi.*** to act as a detective

slew¹ (sl$\overline{oo}$) ***n.*** *same as* SLOUGH² (sense 4)

slew² (sl$\overline{oo}$) ***n., vt., vi.*** *same as* SLUE¹

slew³ (sl$\overline{oo}$) ***n.*** [Ir. *sluagh*, a host] [Colloq.] a large number or amount; a lot

slew⁴ (sl$\overline{oo}$) *pt. of* SLAY

slice (slīs) ***n.*** [OFr. *esclice*, ult. < Frank. *slizzan*, to slice] **1.** a thin, broad piece cut from something [a *slice* of cake] **2.** a part or share [a *slice* of the profits] **3.** a spatula or knife with a broad, flat blade **4.** *a)* the path of a hit ball that curves away to the right from a right-handed player or to the left from a left-handed player *b)* a ball that follows such a path —***vt.* sliced, slic′ing** **1.** to cut into slices **2.** *a)* to cut as a slice (with *off, from, away*, etc.) *b)* to cut through like a knife **3.** to separate into parts or shares **4.** to hit (a ball) in a slice —***vi.*** to cut (*through*) like a knife —**slic′er** ***n.***

slick (slik) ***vt.*** [OE. *slician*] **1.** to make sleek or smooth **2.** [Colloq.] to make smart, neat, or tidy (with *up*) —***adj.*** **1.** sleek; smooth **2.** slippery; oily, as a surface **3.** clever, skillful, or ingenious, esp. in a way considered tricky, smooth, etc. —***n.*** **1.** *a)* a smooth area on the surface of water, as resulting from a film of oil *b)* such a film of oil **2.** [Colloq.] a magazine printed on paper with a glossy finish —***adv.*** smoothly, cleverly, etc. —**slick′ly** ***adv.*** —**slick′ness** ***n.***

slick·er (-ər) ***n.*** **1.** a loose, waterproof coat **2.** [Colloq.] a person with smooth, tricky ways

slide (slīd) ***vi.* slid** (slid), **slid′ing** [OE. *slidan*] **1.** to move along in constant contact with a smooth surface, as on ice **2.** to move quietly and smoothly; glide **3.** to move stealthily or unobtrusively **4.** to slip [it *slid* from his hand] **5.** to pass gradually (*into* or *out of* some condition, habit, etc.) —***vt.*** **1.** to cause to slide **2.** to move or slip quietly or stealthily (*in* or *into*) —***n.*** **1.** an act of sliding **2.** a smooth, sloping track, surface, or chute down which to slide **3.** something that works by sliding **4.** a piece of film with a photograph on it, mounted for use with a viewer or projector **5.** a small glass plate on which objects are mounted for microscopic study **6.** *a)* the fall of a mass of rock, snow, etc. down a slope *b)* the mass that falls **7.** a U-shaped section of tubing which is moved to change the pitch of a trombone, etc. —**let slide** to fail to take care of (some matter) —**slid′er** ***n.***

slide fastener a zipper or a zipperlike device having two grooved edges joined or separated by a slide

slide rule an instrument consisting of a ruler with a central sliding piece, both marked with logarithmic scales: used for rapid mathematical calculations

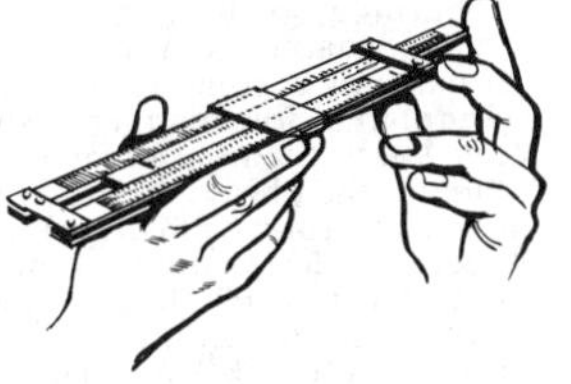
SLIDE RULE

sliding scale a scale or schedule, as of costs, wages, etc., that varies with given conditions or standards

slight (slīt) ***adj.*** [OE. *sliht*] **1.** *a)* light in build; slender *b)* frail; fragile **2.** having little weight, strength, substance, or significance **3.** small in amount or extent [a *slight* fever] —***vt.*** **1.** to do carelessly or poorly; neglect **2.** to treat with disrespect or indifference **3.** to treat as unimportant —***n.*** a slighting or being slighted by pointedly discourteous treatment —**slight′ing** ***adj.*** —**slight′ing·ly** ***adv.*** —**slight′ly** ***adv.*** —**slight′ness** ***n.***

sli·ly (slī′lē) ***adv.*** *var. of* SLYLY

slim (slim) ***adj.* slim′mer, slim′mest** [Du., crafty, bad] **1.** small in girth in proportion to height or length; slender **2.** small in amount, degree, or extent; slight; scant; meager —***vt., vi.* slimmed, slim′ming** to make or become slim —**slim′ly** ***adv.*** —**slim′ness** ***n.***

slime (slīm) ***n.*** [OE. *slim*] any soft, moist, slippery, often sticky matter, as thin mud, the mucous coating on fish, etc.; specif., any such matter considered disgusting —***vt.* slimed, slim′ing** **1.** to cover with slime **2.** to clean slime from

slim·y (slī′mē) ***adj.* slim′i·er, slim′i·est** **1.** of or like slime **2.** covered with slime **3.** disgusting; repulsive —**slim′i·ly** ***adv.*** —**slim′i·ness** ***n.***

sling¹ (sliŋ) ***n.*** [ME. *slinge(n)*, prob. < ON. *slyngva*, to throw] **1.** *a)* a primitive instrument for throwing stones, etc., consisting of a piece of leather tied to cords that are whirled for releasing the missile *b)* *same as* SLINGSHOT **2.** a throwing as with a sling; cast; fling **3.** *a)* a looped or hanging band, strap, etc., used in raising or lowering a heavy object, carrying a rifle, etc. *b)* a wide piece of cloth looped from the neck under an injured arm for support **4.** a woman's open-heeled slipper having a strap across the top of the heel: also **sling′-back′** —***vt.* slung, sling′ing** **1.** to throw (stones, etc.) with a sling **2.** to throw, cast, fling, etc. **3.** to raise, lower, etc. in a sling **4.** to hang loosely or in a sling; suspend —**sling′er** ***n.***

sling² (sliŋ) ***n.*** [< ?] a drink made with alcoholic liquor, water, sugar, and lemon juice

sling·shot (sliŋ′shät′) ***n.*** a Y-shaped piece of wood, metal, etc. with an elastic band fastened to the upper tips for shooting stones, etc.

slink (sliŋk) ***vi.* slunk, slink′ing** [OE. *slincan*, to creep] to move in a fearful or sneaky way, or as if ashamed —**slink′ing·ly** ***adv.***

slink·y (sliŋ′kē) ***adj.* slink′i·er, slink′i·est** **1.** sneaky in movement **2.** [Slang] sinuous and graceful in movement, line, etc. —**slink′i·ness** ***n.***

slip¹ (slip) ***vi.* slipped, slip′ping** [MLowG. *slippen*] **1.** to go quietly or secretly [to *slip* out of a room] **2.** *a)* to move or pass smoothly, quickly, or easily *b)* to get (*into* or *out of* clothes) quickly **3.** to pass gradually into or out of some condition, habit, etc. [to *slip* off to sleep] **4.** to escape from one's mind, power, etc. [to let a chance *slip* by] **5.** to shift or slide from position [the plate *slipped* from my hand] **6.** to slide accidentally, lose footing, etc. [to *slip* on ice] **7.** to make a mistake; err **8.** to become worse; weaken, lower, etc. [my memory is *slipping*, prices have *slipped*] —***vt.*** **1.** to put or move smoothly, easily, or quickly [to *slip* a bolt into place, to *slip* one's shoes off, to *slip* in a snide remark] **2.** to escape (one's mind) **3.** to get loose from [the dog *slipped* his leash] **4.** to let loose; release **5.** to transfer (a stitch) from one needle to another without knitting it, as in forming patterns **6.** to put out of joint; dislocate —***n.*** **1.** *a)* an inclined plane leading down to water, on which ships are built or repaired *b)* a water channel between piers or wharves for ship docking **2.** a leash for a dog **3.** *a)* a woman's sleeveless undergarment, suspended from shoulder straps to the hemline of the skirt *b)* a petticoat; half slip **4.** a pillowcase **5.** a slipping or falling down **6.** an error or mistake in judgment, conduct, speech, etc., esp. one made by accident in speaking, writing, etc. [a *slip* of the tongue] **7.** an accident or mishap **8.** *Cricket* a fielder placed behind the wickets on the off side **9.** *Geol.* *a)* a movement resulting in a small fault or landslide *b)* a smooth surface where such movement has taken place —**give someone the slip** to evade or escape from someone —**let slip** to say without intending to —**slip one over on** [Colloq.] to trick; hoodwink —**slip up** to make a mistake

slip² (slip) ***n.*** [< MDu. < *slippen*, to cut] **1.** a stem, root, twig, etc. cut off for planting or grafting **2.** a young, slim person [a *slip* of a girl] **3.** a long, narrow piece; strip **4.** a small piece of paper, esp. one for a specific use [an order *slip*] —***vt.* slipped, slip′ping** to take a slip from (a plant) for planting or grafting

slip³ (slip) ***n.*** [OE. *slypa*, a paste] *Ceramics* clay thinned to a watery paste for decorating, casting, or cementing

slip·case (-kās′) ***n.*** a boxlike container for a book or set of books, open at one end to expose the spine or spines

slip·cov·er (-kuv′ər) ***n.*** a removable, fitted cloth cover for an armchair, sofa, etc. —***vt.*** to cover (a chair, etc.) with a slipcover

slip·knot (-nät′) ***n.*** a knot made so that it will slip along the rope, etc. around which it is tied

slip-on (-än′) ***adj.*** easily put on or taken off, as shoes without laces, or a garment to be slipped on or off over the head —***n.*** a slip-on shoe or garment

slip·o·ver (-ō′vər) ***adj., n.*** *same as* PULLOVER

slip·page (slip′ij) ***n.*** **1.** a slipping, as of one gear past another **2.** the amount of this

slipped disk a herniated disk between two vertebrae, esp. in the lumbar region, often causing sciatica

slip·per (slip′ər) ***n.*** a light, low shoe easily slipped on the foot, esp. one for indoor wear —**slip′pered** ***adj.***

slip·per·y (slip′ər ē, slip′rē) ***adj.* -per·i·er, -per·i·est** [OE. *slipur*] **1.** causing or liable to cause slipping, as a wet surface **2.** tending to slip away, as from the grasp **3.** not reliable; tricky —**slip′per·i·ness** ***n.***

slippery elm **1.** a N. American elm with sticky inner bark and hard wood **2.** the wood or bark

slip·shod (slip′shäd′) ***adj.*** [SLIP¹ + SHOD] **1.** wearing shoes with worn-down heels **2.** careless; slovenly

slip·stream (-strēm′) ***n.*** the current of air thrust backward by the spinning propeller of an aircraft

slipt (slipt) *archaic or poetic pt. of* SLIP¹

slip-up (slip′up′) ***n.*** [Colloq.] an error, oversight, or mishap

slit (slit) ***vt.* slit, slit′ting** [akin to OE. *slitan*, to cut] **1.** to cut or split open, esp. by a straight, lengthwise incision

2. to cut lengthwise into strips —*n.* 1. a long, straight cut or tear 2. a narrow opening or crack —**slit′ter** *n.*
slith·er (slith′ər) *vi.* [< OE. *sliderian*, freq. < base of *slidan*, to slide] 1. to slip or slide on a loose, broken surface, as a gravelly slope 2. to move along by sliding or gliding, as a snake —*vt.* to cause to slither or slide —*n.* a slithering motion —**slith′er·y** *adj.*
sliv·er (sliv′ər) *n.* [OE. *slifan*, to cut] 1. a thin, sharp piece that has been cut, split, or broken off; splinter 2. a loose, thin, continuous fiber, as of flax, ready to be drawn and twisted —*vt., vi.* to cut or break into slivers
slob (släb) *n.* [Ir. *slab*, mud < Scand.] [Colloq.] a sloppy, coarse, or gross person
slob·ber (släb′ər) *vi.* [< or akin to LowG. *slubberen*, to swig] 1. to let saliva, food, etc. run from the mouth; slaver 2. to speak, write, etc. in a gushy or maudlin way —*vt.* to smear or dribble on with saliva —*n.* 1. saliva, etc. running from the mouth 2. gushy talk or writing —**slob′ber·er** *n.* —**slob′ber·y** *adj.*
sloe (slō) *n.* [OE. *sla*] 1. *same as* BLACKTHORN (sense 1) 2. the small, blue-black, plumlike fruit of the blackthorn 3. any of various wild plums
sloe-eyed (-īd′) *adj.* 1. having large, dark eyes 2. having almond-shaped eyes
sloe gin a red liqueur made of gin flavored with sloes
slog[1] (släg) *vt., vi.* **slogged, slog′ging** [var. of SLUG[4]] to hit hard; slug —**slog′ger** *n.*
slog[2] (släg) *vt., vi.* **slogged, slog′ging** [ME. *sluggen*: see SLUGGARD] 1. to make (one's way) with great effort; plod 2. to work hard (*at* something); toil —**slog′ger** *n.*
slo·gan (slō′gən) *n.* [< Gael. < *sluagh*, a host + *gairm*, a call] 1. orig., a battle cry of Scottish Highland and Irish clans 2. a catchword or motto associated with a political party or other group 3. a catch phrase used to advertise a product
slo·gan·eer (slō′gə nir′) *vi.* to coin or make use of slogans —*n.* a person who coins or uses slogans
slo·gan·ize (slō′gə nīz′) *vt.* **-ized′, -iz′ing** to express in the form of a slogan —**slo′gan·is′tic** *adj.*
sloid, slojd (sloid) *n. same as* SLOYD
sloop (slōōp) *n.* [< Du. < LowG. < *slupen*, to glide] a fore-and-aft rigged, single-masted sailing vessel
slop (släp) *n.* [OE. *sloppe* (only in comp.)] 1. watery snow or mud; slush 2. a splash or puddle of spilled liquid 3. liquid or semiliquid food that is unappetizing or of poor quality 4. [*often pl.*] *a*) liquid waste of any kind *b*) kitchen swill, used for feeding pigs 5. [Slang] a sloppy person —*vi.* **slopped, slop′ping** 1. to spill or splash 2. to walk or splash through slush or mud —*vt.* 1. to spill liquid on 2. to spill 3. to feed swill or slops to (pigs, etc.) —**slop over** 1. to overflow or spill 2. [Colloq.] to display sentimentality; gush

SLOOP

slope (slōp) *n.* [< OE. pp. of *aslupan*, to slip away < *slupan*, to glide] 1. ground that slants up or down, as a hillside 2. any inclined line, surface, position, etc.; slant 3. amount or degree of slant 4. the land area that drains into a given ocean —*vi., vt.* **sloped, slop′ing** to slant or cause to slant up or down —**slop′er** *n.*
slop·py (släp′ē) *adj.* **-pi·er, -pi·est** 1. wet and splashy; muddy or slushy 2. splashed or spotted with liquids 3. *a*) very untidy; slovenly or messy *b*) careless; slipshod 4. [Colloq.] gushingly sentimental —**slop′pi·ly** *adv.* —**slop′pi·ness** *n.*
sloppy Joe ground meat cooked with tomato sauce, etc. and served on a bun
slops (släps) *n.pl.* [< OE. *-slop*, as in *oferslop*, loose outer garment] 1. loose-fitting outer garments, esp. coveralls 2. clothing, bedding, etc. issued or sold to seamen 3. cheap, ready-made clothing
slosh (släsh) *vt.* [var. of SLUSH] 1. to shake or agitate (a liquid or something in it) 2. to apply (a liquid) carelessly or lavishly —*vi.* 1. to splash or move clumsily through water, mud, etc. 2. to splash about: said of a liquid —*n.* 1. *same as* SLUSH 2. the sound of liquid splashing about —**slosh′y** *adj.*
slot (slät) *n.* [< OFr. *esclot*, the hollow between the breasts] 1. a narrow notch, groove, or opening, as a slit for a coin in a vending machine 2. [Colloq.] a position in a group, series, schedule, etc. —*vt.* **slot′ted, slot′ting** 1. to make a slot in 2. [Colloq.] to place in a series, schedule, etc.
sloth (slôth, slōth, släth) *n.* [OE. *slæwth* < *slaw*, slow] 1. the condition of not liking to work or be active; indolence; laziness 2. any of several slow-moving mammals of Central and South America that live in trees, often hanging upside down from the branches
sloth·ful (-fəl) *adj.* characterized by sloth; indolent; lazy —**sloth′ful·ly** *adv.* —**sloth′ful·ness** *n.*
slot machine a machine, esp. a gambling device, worked by putting a coin in a slot
slouch (slouch) *n.* [ON. *slōkr*, lazy fellow < *slōka*, to droop] 1. *a*) a person who is awkward or lazy *b*) [Colloq.] a person who lacks skill [he's no *slouch* at golf] 2. *a*) a drooping or bending forward of the head and shoulders *b*) slovenly posture in general 3. a drooping, as of a hat brim —*vi.* 1. to sit, stand, walk, etc. in a slouch 2. to droop, as a hat brim —*vt.* to cause to slouch
slouch·y (-ē) *adj.* **slouch′i·er, slouch′i·est** slouching, esp. in posture —**slouch′i·ly** *adv.* —**slouch′i·ness** *n.*
slough[1] (sluf) *n.* [ME. *slouh*] 1. the skin of a snake, esp. the outer, castoff layer 2. any castoff layer, covering, etc.: often used figuratively 3. *Med.* the dead tissue that separates from living tissue or an ulceration —*vi.* 1. to be shed, cast off, etc. 2. to shed skin or other covering 3. *Med.* to separate from the surrounding tissue Often with *off* —*vt.* 1. to shed or throw (*off*); get rid of 2. *Bridge* to discard (a card considered valueless) —**slough over** to gloss over; minimize —**slough′y** *adv.*
slough[2] (slou; *for 4* slōō) *n.* [OE. *sloh*] 1. a place full of soft, deep mud 2. [< *Slough of Despond*, a swamp in Bunyan's *Pilgrim's Progress*] deep, hopeless discouragement 3. moral corruption 4. a swamp, bog, etc., esp. as part of an inlet —**slough′y** *adj.*
Slo·vak (slō′väk, -vak) *n.* 1. any of a Slavic people living chiefly in Slovakia 2. their West Slavic language, related to Czech —*adj.* of Slovakia, the Slovaks, or their language
Slo·va·ki·a (slō vä′kē ə, -vak′ē ə) region comprising E Czechoslovakia —**Slo·va′ki·an** *adj., n.*
slov·en (sluv′ən) *n.* [prob. < MDu. *slof*, lax] a person who is careless in his appearance, habits, work, etc.; dirty or untidy person
Slo·ve·ni·a (slō vē′nē ə, -vēn′yə) republic of Yugoslavia, in the NW part: 7,896 sq. mi.; cap. Ljubljana
Slo·ve·ni·an (slō vē′nē ən, -vēn′yən) *n.* 1. any of a Slavic people living chiefly in Slovenia 2. their South Slavic language —*adj.* of Slovenia, Slovenians, or their language Also **Slo·vene** (slō′vēn, slō vēn′)
slov·en·ly (sluv′ən lē) *adj.* **-li·er, -li·est** of or like a sloven; careless in appearance, habits, work, etc.; untidy —*adv.* in a slovenly manner —**slov′en·li·ness** *n.*
slow (slō) *adj.* [OE. *slaw*] 1. not quick or clever in understanding; dull; obtuse 2. taking a longer time than is expected or usual 3. marked by low speed, etc.; not fast 4. making speed difficult [a *slow* track] 5. showing a time that is behind the correct time: said of a timepiece 6. *a*) passing slowly or tediously *b*) not lively; dull 7. not active; slack [*slow* trading] 8. lacking in energy; sluggish 9. burning so as to give off low heat [a *slow* fire] 10. *Photog.* adapted to a relatively long exposure time —*vt., vi.* to make or become slow or slower (often with *up* or *down*) —*adv.* in a slow manner —**slow′ly** *adv.* —**slow′ness** *n.*
slow burn [Slang] a gradual working up or show of anger: often in the phrase **do a slow burn**
slow-mo·tion (-mō′shən) *adj.* 1. moving below usual speed 2. designating a motion-picture or taped television sequence in which the action is made to appear much slower than the actual action
slow·poke (-pōk′) *n.* [Slang] a person who acts or moves slowly
slow time *same as* STANDARD TIME
sloyd (sloid) *n.* [Sw. *slöjd*, skill] a system of manual training originating in Sweden, based upon the use of hand tools in woodcarving
slub (slub) *n.* [< ?] 1. a roll of fiber twisted slightly for use in spinning 2. a thick, irregular place in yarn
sludge (sluj) *n.* [var. of *slutch*, mud] 1. mud, mire, or ooze 2. spongy lumps of drift ice 3. any heavy, slimy deposit, sediment, or mass, as the waste resulting from oil refining, the sediment in a crankcase, etc. —**sludg′y** *adj.* **sludg′i·er, sludg′i·est**
sludge·worm (-wurm′) *n.* a small, freshwater worm able to live where there is little oxygen, as in polluted waters
slue[1] (slōō) *vt., vi.* **slued, slu′ing** [< ?] to turn or swing around a fixed point —*n.* 1. the act of sluing 2. the position to which a thing has been slued
slue[2] (slōō) *n. same as* SLOUGH[2] (sense 4)
slue[3] (slōō) *n. same as* SLEW[3]
slug[1] (slug) *n.* [ME. *slugge*, clumsy one < Scand.] 1. a small mollusk resembling a land snail, but usually having only a rudimentary internal shell 2. rarely, a larva resembling a slug 3. a person, vehicle, etc. that moves slowly
slug[2] (slug) *n.* [prob. < prec.] 1. a small piece of metal; specif., a bullet 2. a piece of metal used in place of a coin in automatic coin machines 3. *Printing* *a*) a strip of nonprinting metal used to space between lines *b*) a lino of type made in one piece, as by a linotype machine
slug[3] (slug) *n.* [prob. < or akin to Dan. *sluge*, to gulp] [Slang] a single drink, esp. of alcoholic liquor

slug[4] (slug) ***vt.*** **slugged, slug′ging** [ON. *slag*] [Colloq.] to hit hard, esp. with the fist or a bat —***n.*** [Colloq.] a hard blow or hit —**slug′ger** ***n.***

slug·gard (slug′ərd) ***n.*** [< ME. < *sluggen*, to be lazy] a habitually lazy or idle person —***adj.*** lazy or idle: also **slug′gard·ly**

slug·gish (-ish) ***adj.*** [SLUG[1] + -ISH] **1.** lacking energy or alertness; slothful **2.** slow or slow-moving **3.** below normal —**slug′gish·ly** ***adv.*** —**slug′gish·ness** ***n.***

sluice (slōōs) ***n.*** [< OFr. *escluse* < LL. < pp. of L. *excludere*, EXCLUDE] **1.** an artificial channel for water, with a gate at its head to regulate the flow, as in a canal **2.** the water held back by such a gate **3.** such a gate: also **sluice gate** **4.** any channel, esp. one for excess water **5.** a sloping trough through which water is run, as in carrying logs, etc. —***vt.*** **sluiced, sluic′ing** **1.** to draw off as by means of a sluice **2.** to wash with water from or as from a sluice **3.** to carry (logs, etc.) in a sluice —***vi.*** to run or flow as in a sluice

slum (slum) ***n.*** [< cant: orig. sense, a room < ?] a heavily populated area of a city having much poverty, poor housing, etc. —***vi.*** **slummed, slum′ming** to visit or tour slums —**slum′mer** ***n.*** —**slum′my** ***adj.*** **-mi·er, -mi·est**

slum·ber (slum′bər) ***vi.*** [< OE. < *sluma*, slumber] **1.** to sleep **2.** to be quiet or inactive —***vt.*** to spend in sleeping —***n.*** **1.** sleep **2.** an inactive state —**slum′ber·er** ***n.***

slum·ber·ous (-əs) ***adj.*** **1.** inclined to slumber; sleepy **2.** suggestive of slumber **3.** causing sleep **4.** calm; quiet [a *slumberous* town] Also **slum′brous** (-brəs)

slum·gul·lion (slum′gul′yən) ***n.*** [< ?] [Colloq.] any inexpensive stew or hash

slum·lord (slum′lôrd′) ***n.*** [SLUM + (LAND)LORD] an absentee landlord of slum dwellings, esp. one who charges rents that are too high and fails to make repairs, etc.

slump (slump) ***vi.*** [prob. < or akin to MLowG. *slumpen*, to come about by accident] **1.** to fall or sink suddenly **2.** to decline suddenly, as in value, etc. **3.** to have a drooping posture —***n.*** **1.** a sudden or sharp fall, decline, etc. **2.** a drooping posture **3.** a period during which a player, team, etc. performs below normal

slung (sluŋ) *pt. & pp. of* SLING[1]

slunk (sluŋk) *pt. & pp. of* SLINK

slur (slʉr) ***vt.*** **slurred, slur′ring** [prob. < MDu. *sleuren*, to drag] **1.** to pass (*over*) quickly and carelessly **2.** to pronounce rapidly in an unclear way **3.** to discredit or belittle **4.** *Music* *a)* to sing or play (successive notes) by gliding from one to another without a break *b)* to mark (notes) with a slur —***n.*** **1.** a slurring **2.** something slurred, as a pronunciation **3.** a remark that is harmful to a person's reputation; aspersion **4.** *Music* a curved symbol (‿) or (⁀) connecting slurred notes —**slur′ring·ly** ***adv.***

slurp (slʉrp) ***vt., vi.*** [Du. *slurpen*, to sip] [Slang] to drink or eat noisily —***n.*** [Slang] a loud sipping noise

slush (slush) ***n.*** [prob. < Scand.] **1.** partly melted snow or ice **2.** soft mud; mire **3.** grease **4.** overly sentimental talk or writing —***vi.*** to walk or move through slush —**slush′i·ness** ***n.*** —**slush′y** ***adj.*** **slush′i·er, slush′i·est**

slush fund money used for bribery, influencing politicians, voters, etc., or other corrupt purposes

slut (slut) ***n.*** [prob. akin to MLowG. *slote*, ditch] **1.** a dirty, slovenly woman; slattern **2.** a sexually promiscuous woman **3.** a female dog; bitch —**slut′tish** ***adj.*** —**slut′tish·ly** ***adv.*** —**slut′tish·ness** ***n.***

sly (slī) ***adj.*** **sli′er** or **sly′er, sli′est** or **sly′est** [ON. *slœgr*] **1.** [Dial.] skillful or clever **2.** skillful at tricking or fooling others, in a secretive or underhanded way **3.** tricking or teasing in a playful way —**on the sly** secretly —**sly′ly** ***adv.*** —**sly′ness** ***n.***

Sm *Chem.* samarium

smack[1] (smak) ***n.*** [OE. *smæc*] **1.** a slight but distinctive taste or flavor **2.** *a)* a small amount; bit *b)* a trace; touch —***vi.*** to have a smack (*of*) [actions that *smack* of treason]

smack[2] (smak) ***n.*** [< ? or akin to MDu. *smack*, of echoic orig.] **1.** a sharp noise made by parting the lips suddenly **2.** a loud kiss **3.** *a)* a sharp blow with a flat object; slap *b)* the sound of this —***vt.*** **1.** to part (the lips) suddenly so as to make a smack **2.** to kiss or slap loudly —***vi.*** to make a loud, sharp noise, as when hitting something —***adv.*** **1.** with a smack; violently **2.** directly; squarely: also [Colloq.] **smack′-dab′**

smack[3] (smak) ***n.*** [prob. < Du. *smak*] **1.** a small sailboat, usually rigged as a sloop **2.** a fishing boat with a well for keeping fish alive

smack·ing (-iŋ) ***adj.*** brisk; sharp; lively

small (smôl) ***adj.*** [OE. *smæl*] **1.** comparatively little in size; not large **2.** *a)* little in quantity, extent, value, duration, etc. [a *small* income] *b)* consisting of relatively few units; low in numbers [a *small* crowd] **3.** of little importance; trivial **4.** young [*small* children] **5.** having relatively little investment, capital, etc. [a *small* business] **6.** small-minded; petty **7.** of low or inferior rank **8.** gentle and low; soft, as a sound —***adv.*** **1.** in small pieces **2.** in a low tone; softly **3.** in a small manner —***n.*** **1.** the small or narrow part [the *small* of the back] **2.** [*pl.*] small articles —**feel small** to feel shame or humiliation —**small′ish** ***adj.*** —**small′ness** ***n.***

small arms firearms of small caliber, held in the hand or hands when fired, as pistols, rifles, etc.

small·clothes (smôl′klōz′, -klō*thz*′) ***n.pl.*** [Archaic] closefitting knee breeches of the 18th cent.

small hours the first few hours after midnight

small-mind·ed (-mīn′did) ***adj.*** selfish, petty, prejudiced, narrow-minded, etc. —**small′-mind′ed·ly** ***adv.*** —**small′-mind′ed·ness** ***n.***

small potatoes [Colloq.] a petty or insignificant person (or people) or thing (or things)

small·pox (-päks′) ***n.*** an acute, highly contagious virus disease causing fever, vomiting, and pustular eruptions that often leave pitted scars, or pockmarks

small-scale (-skāl′) ***adj.*** **1.** drawn to a small scale **2.** of limited scope; not extensive [*small-scale* trading]

small talk light conversation about common, everyday things; chitchat

small-time (-tīm′) ***adj.*** [Colloq.] of little importance or significance; minor or petty

smart (smärt) ***vi.*** [OE. *smeortan*] **1.** *a)* to cause sharp, stinging pain, as a slap, wound, etc. *b)* to feel such pain **2.** to feel mental distress, as in resentment, remorse, etc. —***vt.*** to cause to smart —***n.*** a smarting sensation or distress —***adj.*** **1.** causing sharp or stinging pain [a *smart* slap] **2.** sharp or stinging, as pain **3.** brisk; lively [a *smart* pace] **4.** *a)* intelligent, alert, clever, witty, etc. *b)* shrewd or sharp, as in one's dealings **5.** neat; trim; spruce **6.** in fashion; stylish **7.** [Colloq.] impertinent, flippant, or saucy **8.** [Dial.] quite strong, intense, etc.; considerable [a right *smart* rain] —***adv.*** in a smart way —**smart′ly** ***adv.*** —**smart′ness** ***n.***

smart al·eck, smart al·ec (al′ik) [SMART + *Aleck*, dim. of ALEXANDER] [Colloq.] a conceited, cocky person —**smart′-al′eck, smart′-al′eck·y** ***adj.***

smart·en (smärt′'n) ***vt.*** to make smart or smarter; specif., *a)* to improve in appearance *b)* to make more alert, aware, etc. Usually with *up*

smart set sophisticated, fashionable people

smart·weed (-wēd′) ***n.*** a knotgrass whose bitter juice is thought to cause skin irritation

smart·y (smär′tē) ***n.***, *pl.* **smart′ies** [Colloq.] *same as* SMART ALECK: also **smart′y-pants′**

smash (smash) ***vt.*** [prob. < *s-*, intens. + MASH] **1.** to break into pieces with noise or violence **2.** to hit (a tennis ball, etc.) with a hard overhand stroke **3.** to hit with a hard, heavy blow **4.** to ruin completely; destroy —***vi.*** **1.** to break into pieces **2.** to be destroyed **3.** to move or collide with force —***n.*** **1.** a hard, heavy hit; specif., a hard overhand stroke, as in tennis **2.** *a)* a violent, noisy breaking *b)* the sound of this **3.** *a)* a violent collision *b)* a wreck **4.** total failure, esp. in business **5.** an overwhelming popular success —***adj.*** that is a smash (*n.* 5) —**go to smash** [Colloq.] **1.** to become smashed **2.** to fail completely —**smash′er** ***n.***

smashed (smasht) ***adj.*** [Slang] drunk; intoxicated

smash·ing (smash′iŋ) ***adj.*** **1.** that smashes **2.** [Colloq.] extraordinary —**smash′ing·ly** ***adv.***

smash·up (-up′) ***n.*** **1.** a violent wreck or collision **2.** total failure; ruin **3.** any disaster

smat·ter (smat′ər) ***vt.*** [prob. akin to MHG. *smetern*, to chatter] [Now Rare] to speak, study, or learn superficially —***n.*** *same as* SMATTERING

smat·ter·ing (-iŋ) ***n.*** **1.** slight or superficial knowledge **2.** a small number

smear (smir) ***vt.*** [OE. *smerian*, to anoint] **1.** to cover or soil with something greasy, sticky, etc. **2.** to apply (something greasy, sticky, etc.) **3.** to make an unwanted mark on, or to obscure, by rubbing **4.** to make a smear with (the hand, a rag, etc.) **5.** to harm the reputation of; slander **6.** [Slang] to overwhelm or defeat decisively —***vi.*** to be or become smeared —***n.*** **1.** a mark made by smearing **2.** a small quantity of some substance smeared on a slide for microscopic study, etc. **3.** a slandering

smear·case (-kās′) ***n.*** [< G. *schmierkäse* < *schmieren*, to spread + *käse*, cheese] *same as* COTTAGE CHEESE

smear·y (smir′ē) ***adj.*** **smear′i·er, smear′i·est** **1.** covered with smears; smeared **2.** tending to smear, as wet ink —**smear′i·ness** ***n.***

smell (smel) ***vt.*** **smelled** or **smelt, smell′ing** [ME. *smellen*] **1.** to be aware of by means of the nose and the olfactory nerves; detect the odor of **2.** to sense the presence of [to *smell* trouble] **3.** to test by the odor; sniff [*smell* the milk to tell if it's sour] —*vi.* **1.** to use the sense of smell; sniff (often with *at* or *of*) **2.** *a*) to have a scent or odor *b*) to have an unpleasant odor **3.** to have the odor or a suggestion (*of*) [it *smells* of garlic] **4.** [Colloq.] *a*) to lack ability, worth, etc. *b*) to be foul, corrupt, etc. —*n.* **1.** that one of the five senses by which a substance is perceived through the stimulation of nerves (*olfactory nerves*) in the nasal cavity **2.** the stimulation of any specific substance upon the olfactory nerves; odor; scent **3.** an act of smelling **4.** that which suggests the presence of something; trace —**smell out** to look for or find as by smelling —**smell up** to cause to stink —**smell′er** *n.*

smelling salts carbonate of ammonium, inhaled to relieve faintness, headaches, etc.

smell·y (smel′ē) *adj.* **smell′i·er, smell′i·est** having an unpleasant smell —**smell′i·ness** *n.*

smelt[1] (smelt) *n., pl.* **smelts, smelt:** see PLURAL, II, D, 1 [OE.] a small, silvery, salmonlike food fish found in northern seas

smelt[2] (smelt) *vt.* [MDu. or MLowG. *smelten*] **1.** to melt or fuse (ore, etc.) so as to separate impurities from pure metal **2.** to refine or extract (metal) in this way —*vi.* to be smelted

smelt·er (smel′tər) *n.* **1.** a person engaged in the work of smelting **2.** a place where smelting is done: also **smelt′er·y,** *pl.* **-er·ies**

smidg·en (smij′ən) *n.* [prob. < dial. *smidge*, var. of *smitch*, a particle] [Colloq.] a small amount; a bit: also **smidg′in, smidg′eon**

smi·lax (smī′laks) *n.* [L. < Gr. *smilax*, bindweed] **1.** *same as* CAT BRIER **2.** a twining greenhouse vine of the lily family, with bright green leaves

smile (smīl) *vi.* **smiled, smil′ing** [ME. *smilen*] **1.** to show pleasure, amusement, affection, irony, etc. by an upward curving of the corners of the mouth and a sparkling of the eyes **2.** to regard with favor (with *on* or *upon*) —*vt.* **1.** to express with a smile **2.** to affect by smiling —*n.* **1.** the act or facial expression of smiling **2.** a favorable or agreeable appearance —**smile away** to get rid of by smiling —**smil′er** *n.* —**smil′ing·ly** *adv.*

smirch (smurch) *vt.* [prob. < OFr. *esmorcher*, to hurt] **1.** to soil or smear as with grime **2.** to dishonor (a reputation) —*n.* **1.** a smudge; smear **2.** a stain on a reputation

smirk (smurk) *vi.* [OE. *smearcian*, to smile] to smile in a conceited or self-satisfied way —*n.* such a smile —**smirk′er** *n.* —**smirk′ing·ly** *adv.*

smite (smīt) *vt.* **smote, smit′ten** or **smote, smit′ing** [OE. *smitan*] **1.** [Now Rare] *a*) to hit or strike hard *b*) to defeat, punish, or kill **2.** to attack with disastrous effect **3.** to affect strongly and suddenly (*with*) [*smitten* with dread] **4.** to distress [*smitten* by conscience] **5.** to impress favorably [*smitten* with her charms] —*vi.* [Now Rare] to hit or strike hard —**smit′er** *n.*

Smith (smith) **1. Adam,** 1723–90; Scot. economist **2.** Captain **John,** 1580–1631; Eng. colonist in America **3. Joseph,** 1805–44; U.S. founder of the Mormon Church

smith (smith) *n.* [OE.] **1.** a person who makes or repairs metal objects; metalworker: usually in combination [*silversmith*] **2.** *shortened form of* BLACKSMITH

smith·er·eens (smi*th*′ə rēnz′) *n.pl.* [Ir. *smidirīn*] [Colloq.] small fragments; bits

smith·y (smith′ē; *chiefly Brit.* smi*th*′ē) *n., pl.* **smith′ies** [OE. *smiththe*] **1.** the workshop of a smith, esp. a blacksmith **2.** *same as* BLACKSMITH

smit·ten (smit′'n) *alt. pp. of* SMITE

smock (smäk) *n.* [OE. *smoc* or ON. *smokkr*] a loose, shirtlike, outer garment worn to protect the clothes —*vt.* **1.** to dress in a smock **2.** to decorate with smocking

smock·ing (smäk′iŋ) *n.* shirred, decorative stitching used in gathering cloth, as to make it hang in even folds

smog (smôg, smäg) *n.* [SM(OKE) + (F)OG] a harmful mixture of fog and smoke —**smog′gy** *adj.* **-gi·er, -gi·est**

smoke (smōk) *n.* [OE. *smoca*] **1.** *a*) the vaporous matter, with suspended particles of carbon, arising from something burning *b*) a cloud of this **2.** any vapor, fume, etc. resembling smoke **3.** *a*) an act or period of smoking tobacco, etc. [time for a *smoke*] *b*) something to smoke, as a cigarette **4.** something fleeting, unreal, or obscuring —*vi.* **smoked, smok′ing** **1.** to give off smoke or a smokelike substance **2.** to discharge smoke excessively or improperly, as a fuel, a fireplace, etc. **3.** *a*) to draw the smoke of tobacco, etc. into the mouth and blow it out again *b*) to be a habitual smoker —*vt.* **1.** to stain or color with smoke **2.** to cure (meat, fish, etc.) with smoke **3.** to fumigate as with smoke **4.** to force out with smoke [to *smoke* an animal from its lair] **5.** to use (tobacco, a pipe, etc.) in smoking —**smoke out** to force out of hiding, secrecy, etc. —**smok′a·ble, smoke′a·ble** *adj.*

smoke·house (-hous′) *n.* a building where meats, fish, etc. are cured or flavored with smoke

smoke·less (-lis) *adj.* having or making little or no smoke

smok·er (smō′kər) *n.* **1.** a person or thing that smokes; specif., a person who habitually smokes tobacco **2.** a railroad car or compartment reserved esp. for smoking: also **smoking car** **3.** an informal party for men only

smoke screen **1.** a cloud of smoke spread to screen the movements of troops, ships, etc. **2.** anything said or done to conceal or mislead

smoke·stack (smōk′stak′) *n.* a pipe for the discharge of smoke from a steamship, factory, etc.

Smok·ies (smō′kēz) *same as* GREAT SMOKY MOUNTAINS

smoking jacket a man's lounging jacket for wear at home

smok·y (smō′kē) *adj.* **smok′i·er, smok′i·est** **1.** giving off smoke, esp. excessive smoke **2.** like, of, or as of smoke [a *smoky* haze] **3.** filled with smoke **4.** having the color of smoke **5.** flavored by smoking **6.** darkened or soiled by smoke —**smok′i·ly** *adv.* —**smok′i·ness** *n.*

Smoky Mountains *same as* GREAT SMOKY MOUNTAINS

smol·der (smōl′dər) *vi.* [ME. *smoldren* < Gmc.] **1.** to burn and smoke without flame **2.** to exist in a suppressed state **3.** to have or show suppressed anger or hate —*n.* the act or condition of smoldering

Smol·lett (smäl′it), **To·bi·as George** (tō bī′əs) 1721–71; Brit. novelist, born in Scotland

smolt (smōlt) *n.* [LME. (Scot.)] a young salmon when it first leaves fresh water and descends to the sea

smooch[1] (smo͞och) *vt., n. same as* SMUTCH

smooch[2] (smo͞och) *n.* [ult. akin to SMACK[2]] [Slang] a kiss —*vi., vt.* [Slang] to kiss or pet —**smooch′y** *adj.*

smooth (smo͞o*th*) *adj.* [OE. *smoth*] **1.** having an even surface with no roughness or projections **2.** without lumps [a *smooth* paste] **3.** even or gentle in flow or movement [a *smooth* voyage] **4.** free from interruptions, difficulties, etc. [*smooth* progress] **5.** calm; serene [a *smooth* temper] **6.** free from hair, beard, etc. **7.** not harsh to the taste **8.** having an easy, flowing rhythm or sound **9.** suave, polished, or ingratiating, esp. in an insincere way **10.** *Phonet.* not aspirated —*vt.* **1.** to make level or even **2.** to remove the lumps from **3.** to free from interruptions, difficulties, etc. **4.** to make calm; soothe **5.** to make less crude; refine —*vi.* to become smooth —*adv.* in a smooth manner —*n.* **1.** a smooth part **2.** an act of smoothing —**smooth away** to remove (difficulties, etc.) —**smooth down** to make or become smooth, or even, calm, etc. —**smooth over** to gloss over or make light of (an unpleasant situation) —**smooth′er** *n.* —**smooth′ly** *adv.* —**smooth′ness** *n.*

smooth·bore (-bôr′) *adj.* not rifled or grooved inside the barrel: said of guns —*n.* a smoothbore gun

smooth·en (-'n) *vt., vi.* to make or become smooth

smooth muscle unstriated involuntary muscle, occurring in the walls of the uterus, intestines, etc.

smooth-shav·en (-shā′v'n) *adj.* wearing no beard or mustache

smooth-spo·ken (-spō′k'n) *adj.* speaking in a pleasing, persuasive, or polished manner

smooth-tongued (-tuŋd′) *adj.* smooth-spoken, esp. in a plausible or flattering way

smor·gas·bord, smör·gås·bord (smôr′gəs bôrd′, smur′-) *n.* [Sw.] **1.** a wide variety of appetizers, cheeses, fishes, meats, salads, etc., served buffet style **2.** a meal composed of these **3.** a restaurant serving smorgasbord

smote (smōt) *pt. & alt. pp. of* SMITE

smoth·er (smu*th*′ər) *vt.* [ME. *smorthren* < *smorther*, dense smoke] **1.** to keep from getting enough air to breathe, or kill in this way; suffocate; stifle **2.** to cover (a fire), causing it to smolder or go out **3.** to cover over thickly [liver *smothered* in onions] **4.** to hide or suppress as by covering, as a yawn —*vi.* **1.** to be kept from getting enough air to breathe, or to die in this way **2.** to be hidden or suppressed —*n.* dense, suffocating smoke, dust, etc. —**smoth′er·er** *n.* —**smoth′er·y** *adj.*

smoul·der (smōl′dər) *vi., n. Brit. sp. of* SMOLDER

smudge (smuj) *n.* [prob. < ME. *smogen*] **1.** a stain, smear, etc.; dirty spot **2.** *a*) a fire made to produce dense smoke *b*) such smoke produced by burning a substance in containers (**smudge pots**), esp. for driving away insects or protecting plants from frost —*vt.* **smudged, smudg′ing** **1.** to protect (an orchard, etc.) with smudge **2.** to make dirty; soil —*vi.* **1.** to blur or smear **2.** to become smudged —**smudg′y** *adj.*

smug (smug) *adj.* **smug′ger, smug′gest** [prob. < LowG. *smuk*, trim] **1.** orig., neat, trim, etc. **2.** so pleased with oneself, one's opinions, etc. as to be annoying to others; too self-satisfied —**smug′ly** *adv.* —**smug′ness** *n.*

smug·gle (smug′'l) *vt.* **-gled, -gling** [< LowG. *smuggeln*] **1.** to bring into or take out of a country secretly or illegally **2.** to bring, take, etc. secretly —*vi.* to smuggle forbidden or taxable goods —**smug′gler** *n.*

smut (smut) *n.* [< or akin to LowG. *smutt*] **1.** *a*) sooty matter *b*) a particle of this **2.** a soiled spot **3.** pornographic or obscene talk, writing, etc. **4.** *Bot.* *a*) a plant disease in which certain fungi form masses of black spores that break up into a fine powder *b*) any fungus causing

smut —**vt., vi. smut′ted, smut′ting** to make or become smutty
smutch (smuch) **vt.** [akin to prec.] to smudge; soil —**n. 1.** a dirty mark; smudge **2.** soot, dirt, etc. —**smutch′y** ***adj.***
smut·ty (smut′ē) **adj. -ti·er, -ti·est 1.** soiled with smut **2.** affected with plant smut **3.** pornographic or obscene —**smut′ti·ly adv.** —**smut′ti·ness n.**
Smyr·na (smur′nə) *former name of* IZMIR
Sn [L. *stannum*] *Chem.* tin
SN *U.S. Navy* Seaman
snack (snak) **n.** [prob. < MDu. *snacken,* to snap] a light meal or refreshment taken between regular meals —**vi.** to eat a snack or snacks
snack bar a lunch counter, cafeteria, etc. serving snacks
snaf·fle (snaf′'l) **n.** [prob. < Du. < ODu. dim. of *snabbe,* bill of a bird] a bit, usually light and jointed, attached to a bridle and having no curb —**vt. -fled, -fling** to fit with or control by a snaffle

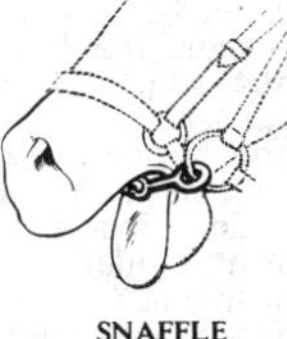
SNAFFLE

sna·fu (sna fo͞o′, snaf′o͞o) **adj.** [orig. military slang for phrase *s(ituation) n(ormal), a(ll) f(ouled)*–a euphemism–*u(p)*] [Slang] in disorder or confusion; completely mixed up —**vt. -fued′, -fu′ing** [Slang] to throw into confusion
snag (snag) **n.** [< Scand.] **1.** a sharp part, point, etc. that sticks out and may catch on things **2.** an underwater tree stump or branch dangerous to navigation **3.** a snaggletooth **4.** a small branch of an antler **5.** a tear or a pulled, looped-out thread in fabric, made by or as by a snag **6.** an unexpected or hidden difficulty —**vt. snagged, snag′ging 1.** to catch, tear, etc. on a snag **2.** to hinder; impede **3.** to catch quickly —**vi. 1.** to strike a snag in water **2.** to develop a snag —**snag′gy adj. -gi·er, -gi·est**
snag·gle·tooth (snag′'l to͞oth′) **n.,** *pl.* **-teeth′** [< prec.] **1.** a tooth that sticks out beyond the others **2.** a crooked or broken tooth —**snag′gle·toothed′ adj.**
snail (snāl) **n.** [OE. *snægl*] **1.** a slow-moving gastropod mollusk living on land or in water and having a spiral protective shell **2.** any lazy, slow-moving person or animal
snake (snāk) **n.** [OE. *snaca*] **1.** any of various limbless reptiles with a long, scaly body, lidless eyes, and a tapering tail: some species have a poisonous bite **2.** a treacherous or deceitful person **3.** a long, flexible rod of spiraled wire, used by a plumber to clear blocked pipes, etc. —**vi. snaked, snak′ing** to move, twist, etc. like a snake —**vt.** [Colloq.] to drag, pull, or jerk —**snake′like′ adj.**
snake dance an informal parade in which the celebrants join hands in a long, winding line
snake in the grass a treacherous person or harmful thing that is hidden or seemingly harmless
Snake River [transl. (prob. erroneous) of earlier *Shoshone River*] river in NW U.S., flowing from NW Wyo. into the Columbia River in Wash.: 1,038 mi.
snake·root (-ro͞ot′, -root′) **n. 1.** any of various plants reputed to be remedies for snake bites **2.** the roots of any of these plants
snake·skin (-skin′) **n.** a snake's skin or leather from it
snak·y (snā′kē) **adj. snak′i·er, snak′i·est 1.** of or like a snake or snakes **2.** sinuous; winding; twisting **3.** cunningly treacherous or evil **4.** infested with snakes
snap (snap) **vi., vt. snapped, snap′ping** [< MDu. or MLowG. *snappen*] **1.** to bite suddenly (often with *at*) **2.** to snatch or grasp quickly or eagerly (often with *at* or *up*) **3.** to speak or say in a sharp, abrupt way *[to snap out orders, to snap back at a person in anger]* **4.** to break or part suddenly, esp. with a sharp, cracking sound **5.** to break down suddenly under strain, as nerves, resistance, etc. **6.** to make or cause to make a sudden, sharp, cracking sound *[to snap one's fingers]* **7.** to close, fasten, etc. with a sound like this, as a lock **8.** to move or cause to move suddenly and smartly *[to snap to attention, snap the ball to me]* **9.** to take a snapshot (of) —**n. 1.** a sudden bite, grasp, snatch, etc. **2.** a sudden breaking or parting **3.** a sudden, sharp cracking or clicking sound **4.** a short, angry utterance or way of speaking **5.** a brief spell of cold weather **6.** any clasp or fastening that closes with a click **7.** a hard, thin cookie *[gingersnaps]* **8.** *same as* SNAPSHOT **9.** [Colloq.] alertness, vigor, or energy **10.** [Slang] an easy job, problem, etc. —**adj. 1.** made or done quickly without deliberation *[a snap decision]* **2.** that fastens with a snap **3.** [Slang] simple; easy —**adv.** with, or as with, a snap —**not a snap** not at all —**snap back** to recover quickly from an illness, disappointment, etc. —**snap one's fingers at** to show lack of concern for —**snap out of it** to recover quickly or regain one's senses
snap bean any of various green beans or wax beans
snap·drag·on (-drag′ən) **n.** [SNAP + DRAGON: from the mouth-shaped flowers] a plant with spikes of saclike two-lipped flowers in white, yellow, red, etc.
snap·per (-ər) **n. 1.** a person or thing that snaps **2.** *pl.* **-pers, -per:** see PLURAL, II, D, 1 *a) same as* SNAPPING TURTLE *b)* any of various bony fishes of warm seas; esp., the red snapper
snapping turtle any of several large, freshwater turtles of N. America, with powerful jaws that snap with great force
snap·pish (snap′ish) **adj. 1.** likely to snap or bite **2.** cross or irritable; sharp-tongued —**snap′pish·ly adv.** —**snap′pish·ness n.**
snap·py (snap′ē) **adj. -pi·er, -pi·est 1.** snappish; cross **2.** that snaps; snapping **3.** [Colloq.] *a)* brisk, vigorous, or lively *[a snappy pace]* *b)* sharply chilly *[snappy weather]* —**make it snappy** [Slang] be quick; hurry —**snap′pi·ly adv.** —**snap′pi·ness n.**
snap·shot (-shät′) **n.** a photograph taken with brief exposure by snapping the shutter of a hand camera
snare (sner) **n.** [OE. *sneare* < ON. *snara*] **1.** a trap for small animals, usually consisting of a noose which jerks tight upon the release of a spring trigger **2.** anything dangerous, risky, etc. that tempts or attracts; trap **3.** *a)* a length of spiraled wire or of gut strung across the bottom of a snare drum for added vibration *b)* [*pl.*] a set of snare drums —**vt. snared, snar′ing 1.** to catch in a trap or snare **2.** to lure into a situation that is dangerous, risky, etc. —**snar′er n.**
snare drum a small, double-headed drum with snares
snarl[1] (snärl) **vi.** [< earlier *snar,* to growl] **1.** to growl fiercely, baring the teeth, as a threatening dog **2.** to speak sharply, as in anger —**vt.** to utter with a snarl —**n. 1.** a fierce, harsh growl **2.** a harsh, angry utterance —**snarl′er n.** —**snarl′ing·ly adv.** —**snarl′y adj.**

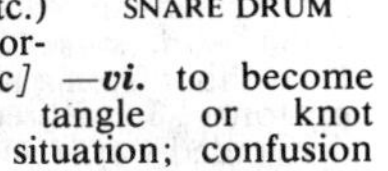
SNARE DRUM

snarl[2] (snärl) **vt.** [ME. *snarlen,* akin to SNARE] **1.** to make (thread, hair, etc.) knotted or tangled **2.** to make disordered or confused *[to snarl traffic]* —**vi.** to become knotted or tangled —**n. 1.** a tangle or knot **2.** a confused, disordered state or situation; confusion —**snarl′y adj.**
snatch (snach) **vt.** [prob. var. of ME. *snakken,* to seize] **1.** to grasp or seize suddenly, eagerly, or without right, warning, etc.; grab **2.** to remove abruptly or hastily **3.** to take, get, etc. hastily or while there is a chance **4.** [Slang] to kidnap —**vi.** to try to seize a thing suddenly; grasp (*at* something) —**n. 1.** the act of snatching **2.** a short time *[to sleep in snatches]* **3.** a fragment; bit *[snatches of gossip]* —**snatch′er n.**
snatch·y (-ē) **adj. snatch′i·er, snatch′i·est** done in snatches; not complete or continuous; disconnected
sneak (snēk) **vi. sneaked** or colloq. **snuck, sneak′ing** [prob. < OE. hyp. *snecan,* akin to *snican,* to crawl] **1.** to move quietly and stealthily so as to avoid notice **2.** to act in an underhanded or cowardly manner —**vt.** to give, put, take, etc. secretly or in a sneaking manner —**n. 1.** one who sneaks; sneaking, underhanded, contemptible person **2.** an act of sneaking —**adj.** without warning *[a sneak attack]* —**sneak out of** to avoid (a duty, etc.) craftily
sneak·er (snē′kər) **n. 1.** a person or animal that sneaks **2.** a cloth shoe with a heelless, soft rubber sole
sneak·ing (-kiŋ) **adj. 1.** cowardly, stealthy, underhanded, or furtive **2.** not admitted; secret *[a sneaking fondness for candy]* —**sneaking suspicion** a slight or growing suspicion —**sneak′ing·ly adv.**
sneak preview an advance single showing of a movie, as for getting audience reaction before regular showings
sneak thief a person who commits thefts in a sneaking way, without the use of force or violence
sneak·y (snē′kē) **adj. sneak′i·er, sneak′i·est** of or like a sneak; underhanded —**sneak′i·ly adv.** —**sneak′i·ness n.**
sneer (snir) **vi.** [ME. *sneren*] **1.** to look scornful or sarcastic, as by curling the lip **2.** to express scorn, derision, etc. in speech or writing —**vt.** to utter in a sneering way —**n. 1.** an act of sneering **2.** a sneering look, remark, etc. —**sneer′er n.** —**sneer′ing·ly adv.**
sneeze (snēz) **vi. sneezed, sneez′ing** [ME. *snesen,* altered < *fnesen* < OE. *fneosan*] to exhale breath from the nose and mouth in a sudden, uncontrolled way, as because the mucous membrane of the nose has been irritated —**n.** an act of sneezing —**not to be sneezed at** not to be disregarded —**sneez′er n.** —**sneez′y adj.**
snell (snel) **n.** [U.S. dial. < ?] a short length of gut, nylon, etc. used to attach a fishhook to a fish line —**vt.** to attach (a fishhook) to a snell

snick¹ (snik) *n.* [prob. < *snick or snee*, combat with knives] a small cut or notch; nick —*vt.* to nick

snick² (snik) *n., vt., vi.* [echoic] *same as* CLICK

snick·er (snik′ər) *vi.* [echoic] to laugh in a sly or partly stifled manner, as in disrespect or embarrassment —*vt.* to utter with a snicker —*n.* a snickering laugh —**snick′er·er** *n.* —**snick′er·ing·ly** *adv.*

snide (snīd) *adj.* [orig., counterfeit < thieves' slang, prob. of Du. dial. or G. origin] slyly malicious or derisive [a *snide* remark] —**snide′ly** *adv.* —**snide′ness** *n.*

sniff (snif) *vi.* [echoic] **1.** to draw air up the nose with enough force to be heard, as when trying to smell something **2.** to express disdain, skepticism, etc. by sniffing —*vt.* **1.** to draw (air, an inhalant, etc.) up the nose with some force **2.** to smell (a substance) by sniffing **3.** to detect, perceive, etc. as by sniffing (often with *out*) —*n.* **1.** an act or sound of sniffing **2.** something sniffed —**sniff′er** *n.*

snif·fle (snif′'l) *vi.* **-fled, -fling** to sniff repeatedly, as in checking mucus running from the nose —*n.* an act or sound of sniffling —**the sniffles** [Colloq.] a head cold, etc. in which there is much sniffling —**snif′fler** *n.*

sniff·y (-ē) *adj.* **sniff′i·er, sniff′i·est** [Colloq.] characterized by or having a tendency to sniff: also **sniff′ish** —**sniff′i·ly** *adv.* —**sniff′i·ness** *n.*

snif·ter (snif′tər) *n.* a globe-shaped goblet with a small opening to concentrate the aroma, as of brandy

snig·ger (snig′ər) *vi., vt., n.* [echoic] *same as* SNICKER

snip (snip) *vt.* **snipped, snip′ping** [Du. *snippen*] **1.** to cut with scissors, etc. in a short, quick stroke or strokes **2.** to remove by such cutting —*vi.* to make a short, quick cut or cuts —*n.* **1.** a small cut made with scissors, etc. **2.** the sound of this **3.** a small piece cut off **4.** [*pl.*] heavy hand shears for cutting sheet metal, etc. **5.** [Colloq.] a young, small, or insignificant person, esp. one regarded as impudent —**snip′per** *n.*

snipe (snīp) *n.* [ON. *snipa*] **1.** *pl.* **snipes, snipe:** see PLURAL, II, D, 1 any of certain wading birds with a long, flexible bill, living chiefly in marshy places **2.** a shot from a hidden position —*vi.* **sniped, snip′ing** **1.** to hunt or shoot snipe **2.** to shoot from a hidden position at individuals of an enemy force **3.** to direct an attack (*at* someone) in a sly or underhanded way —**snip′er** *n.*

snip·pet (snip′it) *n.* [dim. of SNIP] **1.** a small scrap or fragment, specif. of information, a writing, etc. **2.** [Colloq.] *same as* SNIP (*n.* 5) —**snip′pet·y** *adj.*

snip·py (snip′ē) *adj.* **-pi·er, -pi·est** **1.** made up of small scraps or snips; fragmentary **2.** [Colloq.] curt, sharp, etc., esp. in a rude or insolent way —**snip′pi·ly** *adv.* —**snip′pi·ness** *n.*

snit (snit) *n.* [< ? SN(IPPY) + (F)IT²] a fit of anger, pique, etc.: usually in the phrase **in** (or **into**) **a snit**

snitch (snich) *vt.* [< 18th-c. thieves' slang: orig. sense "a nose"] [Slang] to steal (usually something of little value); pilfer —*vi.* [Slang] to be an informer; tattle (*on*) —*n.* [Slang] an informer: also **snitch′er**

sniv·el (sniv′'l) *vi.* **-eled** or **-elled, -el·ing** or **-el·ling** [akin to OE. *snofl*, mucus] **1.** to have mucus running from the nose **2.** to cry and sniffle **3.** to complain in a whining, tearful manner **4.** to make a tearful, often false display of grief, sympathy, etc. —*n.* **1.** nasal mucus **2.** a sniffling **3.** a sniveling display of grief, etc. —**sniv′el·er** *n.*

snob (snäb) *n.* [< ? ON. *snāpr*, dolt] **1.** a person who attaches great importance to wealth, social position, etc., having contempt for those he considers inferior **2.** a person who feels and acts smugly superior about his particular tastes or interests [an intellectual *snob*] —**snob′ber·y** *n., pl.* **-ber·ies** —**snob′bish** *adj.* —**snob′bish·ly** *adv.* —**snob′bish·ness** *n.* —**snob′bism** *n.*

snood (sno͞od) *n.* [OE. *snod*] a baglike net worn at the back of a woman's head to hold the hair —*vt.* to bind (the hair) with a snood

snook (snook) *n., pl.* **snook, snooks:** see PLURAL, II, D, 2 [Du. *snoek*, pike] a pikelike fish of warm seas; esp., a game and food fish of the tropical Atlantic

snoop (sno͞op) *vi.* [Du. *snoepen*, to eat snacks on the sly] [Colloq.] to look about in a sneaking, prying way —*n.* [Colloq.] **1.** one who snoops: also **snoop′er** **2.** the act of snooping —**snoop′i·ness** *n.* —**snoop′y** *adj.* **snoop′i·er, snoop′i·est**

snoot (sno͞ot) *n.* [see SNOUT] [Colloq.] **1.** the nose **2.** the face **3.** a grimace —*vt.* to snub

snoot·y (-ē) *adj.* **snoot′i·er, snoot′i·est** [prec. + -Y²] [Colloq.] haughty; snobbish —**snoot′i·ly** *adv.* —**snoot′i·ness** *n.*

snooze (sno͞oz) *n.* [< ? LowG. *snusen*, to snore] [Colloq.] a brief sleep; nap —*vi.* **snoozed, snooz′ing** [Colloq.] to take a brief sleep; nap —**snooz′er** *n.*

snore (snôr) *vi.* **snored, snor′ing** [echoic] to breathe, while asleep, with harsh sounds caused by vibration of the soft palate, usually with the mouth open —*n.* the act or sound of snoring —**snor′er** *n.*

snor·kel (snôr′k'l) *n.* [G. *schnörkel*, spiral] **1.** a device for submarines, with air intake and exhaust tubes, permitting submergence for long periods **2.** a breathing tube extending above the surface of the water, used in swimming just below the surface —*vi.* **-keled, -kel·ing** to move or swim under water using a snorkel —**snor′kel·er** *n.*

SNORKEL

snort (snôrt) *vi.* [ME. *snorten*, akin to SNORE] **1.** to force breath from the nose in a sudden and noisy way **2.** to express anger, scorn, etc. by a snort **3.** to make a noise like a snort, as in laughing boisterously —*vt.* to express or utter with a snort —*n.* **1.** the act or sound of snorting **2.** [Slang] a drink of straight liquor, taken in one gulp —**snort′er** *n.* —**snort′ing·ly** *adv.*

snot (snät) *n.* [OE. (*ge*)*snot*, mucus] **1.** nasal mucus: a vulgar term **2.** [Slang] a young person who is insolent

snot·ty (-ē) *adj.* **-ti·er, -ti·est** **1.** of, like, or dirtied with snot **2.** [Slang] *a*) offensive; contemptible *b*) impudent, insolent, etc. —**snot′ti·ly** *adv.* —**snot′ti·ness** *n.*

snout (snout) *n.* [prob. < MDu. *snute*] **1.** the projecting nose and jaws, or muzzle, of an animal **2.** something like an animal's snout, as a nozzle or spout **3.** [Colloq.] a human nose, esp. a large one

snout beetle *same as* WEEVIL

snow (snō) *n.* [OE. *snaw*] **1.** particles of water vapor which when frozen in the upper air fall to earth as soft, white, crystalline flakes **2.** *a*) a falling of snow *b*) snowy weather **3.** a mass of fallen snow **4.** [Poet.] whiteness **5.** fluctuating spots appearing on a TV screen as a result of a weak signal **6.** [Slang] cocaine or heroin —*vi.* to fall as or like snow —*vt.* **1.** to shower or let fall as or like snow **2.** to cover, obstruct, etc. with or as with snow (usually with *in*, *under*, etc.) **3.** [Slang] to deceive, win over, etc. by glib talk, flattery, etc. —**snow under** to overwhelm as with work or defeat

snow·ball (-bôl′) *n.* **1.** a mass of snow packed together into a ball **2.** a cultivated European cranberry bush with round clusters of white or pinkish flowers —*vi.* **1.** to increase rapidly and out of control like a ball of snow rolling downhill **2.** to throw snowballs —*vt.* **1.** to throw snowballs at **2.** to cause to increase rapidly

snow·bank (-baŋk′) *n.* a large mound of snow

snow·ber·ry (-ber′ē) *n., pl.* **-ries** **1.** a hardy N. American plant with small, pink flowers and soft, white berries **2.** any of various other plants with white berries **3.** any of these berries

snow·bird (-burd′) *n.* **1.** a widely distributed N. American junco **2.** *same as* SNOW BUNTING

snow-blind (-blīnd′) *adj.* blinded temporarily by ultraviolet rays of the sun reflected from snow —**snow blindness**

snow blower a motorized, hand-guided machine on wheels, for removing snow as from walks: also **snow thrower**

snow·bound (-bound′) *adj.* shut in or blocked off by snow

snow bunting a small finch inhabiting cold regions in the Northern Hemisphere

snow·cap (-kap′) *n.* a cap of snow, as on a mountain, the top of a tree, etc. —**snow′capped′** *adj.*

snow·drift (-drift′) *n.* **1.** a smooth heap of snow blown together by the wind **2.** snow blown along by the wind

snow·drop (-dräp′) *n.* a low-growing, bulbous plant with small, bell-shaped white flowers

snow·fall (-fôl′) *n.* **1.** a fall of snow **2.** the amount of snow that falls in a given area or period of time

snow·field (-fēld′) *n.* a large expanse of snow

snow·flake (-flāk′) *n.* **1.** a single crystal of snow **2.** *same as* SNOW BUNTING **3.** a European bulbous plant with drooping white flowers

snow goose a white goose that breeds in the Arctic, having a red bill and black wing tips

snow leopard a large, whitish cat of the mountains of C Asia, having many dark blotches on its fur

snow line (or **limit**) the lower boundary of a high region in which snow never melts

snow·man (-man′) *n., pl.* **-men′** (-men′) a crude human figure made of snow packed together

snow·mo·bile (-mō bēl′) *n.* a motor vehicle for traveling over snow, usually with steerable runners at the front and tractor treads at the rear —*vi.* **-biled′, -bil′ing** to travel by snowmobile

snow-on-the-moun·tain (snō′än *thə* moun′t'n) *n.* a widely cultivated spurge of the western U.S., with small flowers and the margins of the upper leaves white

snow·plow (snō′plou′) *n.* **1.** any plowlike machine used to clear snow off a road, railroad, etc. **2.** *Skiing* a stemming of both skis, as for stopping, with the tips of the skis pointed at each other —*vi.* to stem with both skis

snow·shoe (-sho͞o′) ***n.*** a racket-shaped frame of wood crisscrossed with strips of leather, etc., worn on the feet to prevent sinking in deep snow —***vi.*** **-shoed′, -shoe′ing** to use snowshoes in walking —**snow′sho′er** ***n.***

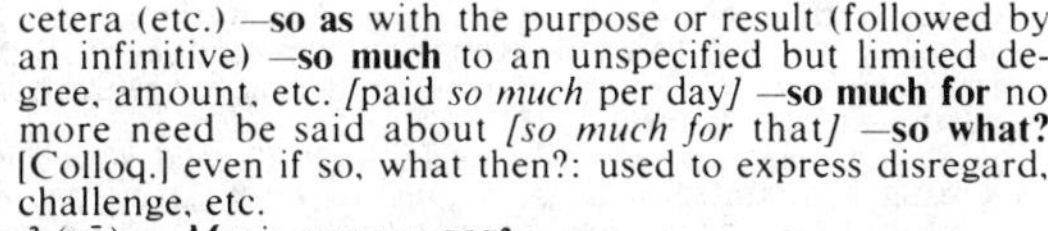

SNOWSHOES

snowshoe hare a hare of N America that is brown in summer and white in winter: also **snowshoe rabbit**

snow·slide (-slīd′) ***n.*** an avalanche of mainly snow

snow·storm (-stôrm′) ***n.*** a storm with a heavy snowfall

snow·suit (-so͞ot′) ***n.*** a heavily lined one-piece garment or set of pants and jacket, often with a hood, worn by children

snow tire a tire with a deep tread, and sometimes protruding studs, for added traction on snow or ice

snow-white (-hwīt′, -wīt′) ***adj.*** white as snow

snow·y (snō′ē) ***adj.*** **snow′i·er, snow′i·est** **1.** of or characterized by snow **2.** covered or filled with snow **3.** like snow; specif., *a)* pure; spotless *b)* white —**snow′i·ly** ***adv.*** —**snow′i·ness** ***n.***

snub (snub) ***vt.*** **snubbed, snub′bing** [ON. *snubba,* to chide] **1.** orig., to check with sharp words **2.** to treat with scorn, disregard, etc.; slight **3.** *a)* to check suddenly the movement of (a rope, etc.) by turning it around a post *b)* to make (a boat, etc.) fast in this way **4.** to put out (a cigarette) —***n.*** **1.** scornful, slighting action or treatment **2.** a snubbing, or checking —***adj.*** short and turned up; pug: said of the nose —**snub′ber** ***n.***

snub·by (-ē) ***adj.*** **-bi·er, -bi·est** turned up; snub

snub-nosed (-nōzd′) ***adj.*** having a snub nose

snuck (snuk) *colloq. pt. & pp. of* SNEAK

snuff[1] (snuf) ***n.*** [< ?] the charred end of a candlewick —***vt.*** **1.** to trim off the charred end of (a candlewick) **2.** to put out (a candle) —**snuff out** **1.** to put out (a candle, etc.); extinguish **2.** to destroy or cause to die suddenly

snuff[2] (snuf) ***vt.*** [MDu. *snuffen*] **1.** to inhale strongly through the nose; sniff **2.** to smell or sniff at —***vi.*** **1.** to sniff or snort **2.** [Rare] to use snuff —***n.*** **1.** the act or sound of snuffing; sniff **2.** *a)* a preparation of powdered tobacco taken up into the nose by sniffing or applied to the gums *b)* a pinch of this —**up to snuff** [Colloq.] up to the usual standard —**snuff′y** ***adj.*** **snuff′i·er, snuff′i·est**

snuff·box (-bäks′) ***n.*** a small box for holding snuff

snuff·er (-ər) ***n.*** **1.** a device with a cone on the end of a handle, for putting out a burning candle: in full, **candle snuffer** **2.** [*pl.*] an instrument like shears, for snuffing a candle: also **pair of snuffers**

snuf·fle (snuf′'l) ***vi.*** **-fled, -fling** [freq. of SNUFF[2]] **1.** to breathe audibly and with difficulty or by constant sniffing, as a dog in trailing; sniffle **2.** to speak or sing in a nasal tone —***vt.*** to utter by snuffling —***n.*** **1.** the act or sound of snuffling **2.** a nasal tone or twang —**the snuffles** *same as* the SNIFFLES —**snuf′fler** ***n.***

snug (snug) ***adj.*** **snug′ger, snug′gest** [prob. ult. < Scand.] **1.** protected from the weather; warm and cozy **2.** compact and convenient; neat *[a snug* cottage*]* **3.** large enough to provide ease: said of an income **4.** tight in fit *[a snug* coat*]* **5.** well-built; seaworthy **6.** hidden or concealed *[to lie snug]* —***adv.*** so as to be snug —***vt.*** **snugged, snug′ging** to make snug or secure —**snug′ly** ***adv.*** —**snug′ness** ***n.***

snug·gle (-'l) ***vi.*** **-gled, -gling** [freq. of SNUG] to lie closely and comfortably; cuddle, as for warmth, in affection, etc. —***vt.*** to cuddle

so[1] (sō) ***adv.*** [OE. *swa*] **1.** in the way shown, expressed, understood, etc. *[hold the bat just so]* **2.** *a)* to such an extent *[why are you so late?] b)* very *[they are so happy] c)* [Colloq.] very much *[she so wants to go]* **3.** for the reason specified; therefore *[they were tired, and so left]* **4.** more or less; approximately *[fifty dollars or so]* : in this sense often regarded as a pronoun **5.** also; likewise *[I'm going and so are you]* : also used colloquially in contradicting a negative statement *[I did so tell the truth!]* **6.** then *[and so to bed]* —***conj.*** **1.** in order that; with the purpose that: usually followed by *that [talk louder so* (that) all may hear*]* **2.** [Colloq.] with the result that *[he smiled, so I did too]* **3.** if only; as long as (*that*) —***pron.*** that which has been specified or named *[he is a friend and will remain so]* —***interj.*** an exclamation of surprise, approval, triumph, etc. —***adj.*** **1.** true; in reality *[that's so]* **2.** in proper order *[everything must be just so]* —**and so on** (or **forth**) and the rest; et cetera (etc.) —**so as** with the purpose or result (followed by an infinitive) —**so much** to an unspecified but limited degree, amount, etc. *[paid so much* per day*]* —**so much for** no more need be said about *[so much for* that*]* —**so what?** [Colloq.] even if so, what then?: used to express disregard, challenge, etc.

so[2] (sō) ***n.*** *Music same as* SOL[2]

So. **1.** south **2.** southern

soak (sōk) ***vt.*** [OE. *socian*] **1.** to make thoroughly wet; drench or saturate **2.** to submerge in a liquid, as for thorough wetting, softening, soothing, etc. **3.** *a)* to take in (liquid) by absorbing (usually with *up*) *b)* to absorb by exposure to it *[to soak* up sunshine*]* **4.** to take in mentally *[to soak* up knowledge*]* **5.** [Colloq.] to overcharge —***vi.*** **1.** to stay immersed in liquid for wetting, softening, etc. **2.** to pass (*into* or *through*) as a liquid does *[*rain *soaking* through his coat*]* **3.** to become absorbed mentally *[*the fact *soaked* into his head*]* —***n.*** **1.** a soaking or being soaked **2.** liquid used for soaking **3.** [Slang] a drunkard

so-and-so (sō′ən sō′) ***n.,*** *pl.* **so′-and-sos′** [Colloq.] some person or thing whose name is not specified: often used to avoid vulgar or offensive name-calling

soap (sōp) ***n.*** [OE. *sape*] **1.** a substance used with water to produce suds for washing, usually produced by the action of an alkali, as caustic soda, on fats or oils **2.** any metallic salt of a fatty acid **3.** [Slang] *same as* SOAP OPERA: also **soap′er** —***vt.*** to lather, scrub, etc. with soap —**no soap** [Slang] **1.** (it is) not acceptable **2.** to no avail

soap·ber·ry (-ber′ē) ***n.,*** *pl.* **-ries** **1.** any of various trees with fruits containing a soapy material **2.** the globe-shaped fruit, with yellowish flesh and a large, round seed

soap·box (-bäks′) ***n.*** **1.** a box for soap **2.** any improvised platform used by a person (**soapbox orator**) making an informal, often impassioned speech to a street audience

soap opera [Colloq.] a daytime radio or TV serial drama of a melodramatic, sentimental nature: originally, many of the sponsors were soap companies

soap·stone (-stōn′) ***n.*** *same as* STEATITE

soap·suds (-sudz′) ***n.pl.*** **1.** soapy water, esp. when stirred into a foam **2.** the foam on soapy water

soap·y (sō′pē) ***adj.*** **soap′i·er, soap′i·est** **1.** covered with or containing soap **2.** of or like soap **3.** [Slang] suave; oily —**soap′i·ly** ***adv.*** —**soap′i·ness** ***n.***

soar (sôr) ***vi.*** [OFr. *essorer,* ult. < L. *ex-,* out + *aura,* air] **1.** to rise or fly high into the air **2.** to sail or glide along high in the air, as a glider does on air currents **3.** to rise above the ordinary level *[soaring* prices*]* —***n.*** **1.** soaring range **2.** the act of soaring —**soar′er** ***n.***

sob (säb) ***vi.*** **sobbed, sob′bing** [ME. *sobben*] **1.** to weep aloud with short, gasping breaths **2.** to make a sound like this, as the wind —***vt.*** **1.** to put (oneself), as to sleep, by sobbing **2.** to utter with sobs —***n.*** the act or sound of sobbing —**sob′bing·ly** ***adv.***

so·ber (sō′bər) ***adj.*** [< OFr. < L. *sobrius*] **1.** temperate, esp. in the use of alcoholic liquor **2.** not drunk **3.** serious, solemn, sedate, etc. **4.** quiet; plain: said of color, clothes, etc. **5.** not distorted *[the sober* truth*]* **6.** showing mental and emotional balance —***vt., vi.*** to make or become sober (often with *up* or *down*) —**so′ber·ly** ***adv.*** —**so′ber·ness** ***n.***

so·ber-mind·ed (-mīn′did) ***adj.*** sensible and serious

so·bri·e·ty (sə brī′ə tē, sō-) ***n.*** a being sober; specif., *a)* temperance, esp. in the use of alcoholic liquor *b)* seriousness; sedateness

so·bri·quet (sō′brə kā′, sō′brə kā′) ***n.*** [Fr.] **1.** a nickname **2.** an assumed name

sob story [Colloq.] a very sad story; esp., an account of personal troubles meant to arouse sympathy

Soc., soc. **1.** social **2.** socialist **3.** society

so-called (sō′kôld′) ***adj.*** **1.** popularly known by this term *[the so-called* nuclear powers*]* **2.** inaccurately regarded as such *[a so-called* liberal*]*

soc·cer (säk′ər) ***n.*** [alt. < (AS)SOC(IATION FOOTBALL)] a kind of football played with a round ball moved chiefly by kicking

so·cia·ble (sō′shə b'l) ***adj.*** [Fr. < L. < *socius:* see ff.] **1.** enjoying or requiring the company of others; friendly; affable **2.** characterized by pleasant, informal conversation and companionship —***n.*** a social, esp. a church social —**so′cia·bil′i·ty** ***n.,*** *pl.* **-ties** —**so′cia·bly** ***adv.***

so·cial (sō′shəl) ***adj.*** [< Fr. < L. *socialis* < *socius,* companion] **1.** of or having to do with human beings living together in a situation or group relation affecting their common welfare *[social* problems*]* **2.** living in this way *[man as a social* being*]* **3.** of or having to do with the ranks of society, specif. the more fashionable ranks *[a social* event*]* **4.** getting along well with others; sociable **5.** of

or for companionship 6. of or engaged in welfare work *[a social agency]* 7. living in groups or communities *[the ant is a social insect]* —*n.* an informal gathering for recreation; party —**so′cial·ly** *adv.*
social climber a person who seeks higher social status by getting acquainted with distinguished or wealthy people
social disease any venereal disease
so·cial·ism (sō′shəl iz′m) *n.* **1.** any of various theories of the ownership and operation of the means of production and distribution by society rather than by private individuals, with all members of society sharing in the work and the products **2.** [*often* **S-**] *a)* a political movement for establishing such a system *b)* the doctrines, etc. of the Socialist parties **3.** the stage of society, in Marxist doctrine, coming between the capitalist stage and the communist stage (see COMMUNISM, sense 2), in which private ownership of the means of production and distribution has been eliminated
so·cial·ist (-ist) *n.* **1.** an advocate or supporter of socialism **2.** [**S-**] a member of a Socialist Party —*adj.* **1.** of or like socialism or socialists **2.** advocating or supporting socialism **3.** [**S-**] designating or of a political party advocating Socialism Also **so′cial·is′tic** —**so′cial·is′ti·cal·ly** *adv.*
so·cial·ite (sō′shə līt′) *n.* a socially prominent person
so·ci·al·i·ty (sō′shē al′ə tē) *n.* **1.** a being social or sociable **2.** *pl.* **-ties** the tendency to form social groups
so·cial·ize (sō′shə līz′) *vt.* **-ized′, -iz′ing 1.** to make social or fit for cooperative group living **2.** to adapt to the common needs of a social group **3.** to put under government ownership **4.** to cause to become socialist —*vi.* to take part in social activity —**so′cial·i·za′tion** *n.* —**so′cial·iz′er** *n.*
socialized medicine any system supplying complete medical and hospital care, through public funds, for all the people in a community, district, or nation
social science **1.** the study of people living together in groups, families, etc. **2.** any of several studies, as history, economics, civics, etc., dealing with society and the activity of its members —**social scientist**
social secretary a secretary employed by an individual to handle his social appointments and correspondence
social security a Federal system of old-age, unemployment, or disability insurance, financed by a fund maintained by employees, employers, and the government
social service *same as* SOCIAL WORK —**so′cial-serv′ice** *adj.*
social studies a course of study, esp. in elementary and secondary schools, including history, civics, geography, etc.
social welfare **1.** the welfare of society, esp. of those who are underprivileged or disadvantaged because of poverty, unemployment, etc. **2.** *same as* SOCIAL WORK
social work any activity designed to promote the welfare of the community and the individual, as through counseling services, recreation and rehabilitation centers, aid for the needy and aged, etc. —**social worker**
so·ci·e·ty (sə sī′ə tē) *n., pl.* **-ties** [< MFr. < L. *societas* < *socius,* companion] **1.** a group of persons regarded as forming a single community, esp. as forming a distinct social or economic class **2.** the system or condition of living together in such a group *[an agrarian society]* **3.** all people, collectively, regarded as a community of mutually dependent individuals **4.** companionship **5.** one's friends or associates **6.** any organized group of people with work, interests, etc. in common *[a medical society]* **7.** a group of persons regarded as a dominant class because of their wealth, birth, etc. —*adj.* of or involving society (*n.* 7) —**so·ci′e·tal** *adj.* —**so·ci′e·tal·ly** *adv.*
Society Islands group of French islands in the South Pacific: chief island, Tahiti
Society of Friends a Christian religious sect founded in England c. 1650 by George Fox: the Friends have no formal creed, rites, liturgy, or priesthood, and reject violence in human relations, including war
Society of Jesus *see* JESUIT
so·ci·o- (sō′sē ō′, -shē-; -ə) [Fr. < L. *socius,* companion] *a combining form meaning* social, society, sociological
so·ci·o·bi·ol·o·gy (sō′sē ō bī äl′ə jē, -shē-) *n.* the scientific study of the biological basis for animal and human social behavior —**so′ci·o·bi·ol′o·gist** *n.*
so·ci·o·e·co·nom·ic (-ē′kə näm′ik, -ek′ə-) *adj.* of or involving both social and economic factors
so·ci·ol·o·gy (sō′sē äl′ə jē, -shē-) *n.* [< Fr.: see SOCIO- & -LOGY] the science of human society and of social relations, organization, and change; specif., the study of the beliefs, values, etc. of groups in society —**so′ci·o·log′i·cal** (-ə läj′i k'l), **so′ci·o·log′ic** *adj.* —**so′ci·o·log′i·cal·ly** *adv.* —**so′ci·ol′o·gist** *n.*
so·ci·o·path (sō′sē ə path′, -shē-) *n.* [SOCIO- + (PSYCHO)PATH] a psychopathic personality whose behavior is aggressively antisocial —**so′ci·o·path′ic** *adj.*
so·ci·o·po·lit·i·cal (sō′sē ō pə lit′i k'l, -shē-) *adj.* of or involving both social and political factors
sock[1] (säk) *n.* [OE. *socc* < L. *soccus,* a light, low-heeled shoe] **1.** a light shoe worn by comic characters in ancient Greek and Roman drama **2.** comic drama **3.** *pl.* **socks, sox** a short stocking reaching only part way to the knee —**socked in** grounded (as aircraft) or closed (as an airfield) because of fog
sock[2] (säk) *vt.* [Slang] to hit with force, esp. with the fist —*n.* [Slang] a blow —*adv.* [Slang] directly; squarely —**sock away** to set aside (money)
sock·et (säk′it) *n.* [< Anglo-Fr., dim. < OFr. *soc,* plowshare < Gaul.] a hollow part into which something fits *[an eye socket, the socket for a light bulb]*
sock·eye (säk′ī′) *n.* [< AmInd. *suk-kegh*] a salmon of the N Pacific with red flesh, often canned
Soc·ra·tes (säk′rə tēz′) 470?–399 B.C.; Athenian philosopher & teacher —**So·crat·ic** (sə krat′ik, sō-) *adj., n.*
Socratic method a method of teaching, as used by Socrates, in which a series of questions leads the answerer to a logical conclusion foreseen by the questioner
sod (säd) *n.* [prob. < MDu. or MLowG. *sode*] **1.** a surface layer of earth containing grass plants with their matted roots; turf **2.** a piece of this layer —*vt.* **sod′ded, sod′ding** to cover with sod or sods
so·da (sō′də) *n.* [ML., ult. < Ar. *suwwād,* a plant burned to produce soda] **1.** *a)* sodium oxide, Na_2O *b) same as:* (1) SODIUM BICARBONATE (2) SODIUM CARBONATE (3) SODIUM HYDROXIDE **2.** *a) same as* SODA WATER (sense 1) *b)* [Chiefly Eastern] a drink of soda water flavored with syrup *c)* a confection of soda water flavored with syrup, fruit, etc. and served with ice cream in it
soda ash crude sodium carbonate (sense 1)
soda cracker a light, crisp cracker, usually salted, made from a dough of flour, water, and leavening, orig. baking soda and cream of tartar
soda fountain **1.** a counter for making and serving soft drinks, sodas, sundaes, etc. **2.** an apparatus for making soda water, with faucets for drawing it off
soda jerk [Slang] a person who works at a soda fountain: also **soda jerk·er** (jur′kər)
so·dal·i·ty (sō dal′ə tē) *n., pl.* **-ties** [< L. < *sodalis,* companion] **1.** an association or brotherhood **2.** *R.C.Ch.* a devotional or charitable lay society
soda pop a flavored, carbonated soft drink, esp. as sold in tightly capped bottles or in cans
soda water **1.** water charged under pressure with carbon dioxide gas, used in ice-cream sodas, as a chaser or mix, etc. **2.** *same as* SODA POP
sod·den (säd′'n) *obs. pp. of* SEETHE —*adj.* **1.** soaked through **2.** soggy from improper baking or cooking, as bread **3.** dull or stupefied, as from drunkenness —*vt., vi.* to make or become sodden —**sod′den·ness** *n.*
so·di·um (sō′dē əm) *n.* [ModL. < SODA] a silver-white, alkaline metallic chemical element, found in nature only in combined form: symbol, Na; at. wt., 22.9898; at. no., 11
sodium benzoate a sweet, white powder, the sodium salt of benzoic acid, used as a food preservative
sodium bicarbonate a white, crystalline compound, $NaHCO_3$, used in baking powder, as an antacid, etc.
sodium carbonate **1.** the anhydrous sodium salt of carbonic acid, Na_2CO_3 **2.** any of the hydrated carbonates of sodium; esp., *same as* SAL SODA
sodium chloride common salt, NaCl
sodium cyanide a white, highly poisonous salt, NaCN, used in electroplating, as an insecticide, etc.
sodium hydroxide a white, strongly caustic substance, NaOH, used in chemistry, etc.
sodium hyposulfite *see* SODIUM THIOSULFATE
sodium nitrate a clear, crystalline salt, $NaNO_3$, used in manufacturing explosives, fertilizers, etc.
sodium pentothal *same as* THIOPENTAL SODIUM
sodium thiosulfate a white, crystalline salt, $Na_2S_2O_3$, used as a fixing agent in photography, etc.: popularly but incorrectly called *(sodium) hyposulfite* or *hypo*
Sod·om (säd′əm) *Bible* a city destroyed by fire together with a neighboring city, Gomorrah, because of the sinfulness of the people: Gen. 18–19
Sod·om·ite (-īt′) *n.* **1.** an inhabitant of Sodom **2.** [**s-**] a person who practices sodomy
sod·om·ize (-īz′) *vt.* **-ized′, -iz′ing** [SODOM(Y) + -IZE] to engage in sodomy with; specif., to force sodomy upon
sod·om·y (-ē) *n.* [< SODOM] any sexual intercourse held to be abnormal, as between a person and an animal or between two persons of the same sex
so·ev·er (sō ev′ər) *adv.* **1.** in any way *[how dark soever it may be]* **2.** of any kind; at all *[no rest soever]*
-so·ev·er (sō ev′ər) *a combining form added for emphasis or generalization to* who, what, when, where, how, etc., *and meaning* any (person, thing, time, place, or manner) of all those possible
so·fa (sō′fə) *n.* [Fr. < Ar. *ṣuffah,* a cushion] an upholstered couch with fixed back and arms
So·fi·a (sō′fē ə, sō fē′ə; *Bulg.* sô′fē yä′) capital of Bulgaria, in the W part: pop. 868,000
S. of Sol. Song of Solomon

soft (sôft, säft) ***adj.*** [OE. *softe*] **1.** giving way easily under pressure, as a feather pillow or moist clay **2.** easily cut, shaped, or worn away [a *soft* wood or metal] **3.** not as hard as is normal, desirable, etc. [*soft* butter] **4.** smooth to the touch **5.** *a*) bland; not acid, sour, or sharp *b*) easy to digest because free from roughage: said of a diet **6.** nonalcoholic: said of drinks **7.** having few or none of the mineral salts that interfere with the lathering of soap: said of water **8.** mild or temperate, as a breeze, climate, etc. **9.** *a*) weak; not strong or vigorous *b*) having flabby muscles **10.** requiring little effort; easy [a *soft* job] **11.** *a*) kind or lenient; not severe *b*) easily influenced or imposed upon **12.** not bright; subdued: said of color or light **13.** showing little contrast or distinctness, as an etching **14.** gentle; low: said of sound **15.** *Finance* unstable and declining: said of a market, prices, etc. **16.** *Phonet.* *a*) sibilant: said of *c* and *g*, as in *cent* and *germ* *b*) voiced —***adv.*** softly; gently; quietly —***n.*** something soft; soft part —***interj.*** [Archaic] hush! stop! —**be soft on** **1.** to treat gently **2.** to feel amorous toward —**soft in the head** stupid or foolish —**soft′ish** ***adj.*** —**soft′ly** ***adv.*** —**soft′ness** ***n.***

soft·ball (sôft′bôl′, säft′-) ***n.*** **1.** a game like baseball played on a smaller diamond and with a larger and softer ball **2.** the ball used

soft-boiled (-boild′) ***adj.*** boiled only a short time so that the yolk is still soft: said of an egg

soft coal *same as* BITUMINOUS COAL

soft-cov·er (-kuv′ər) ***n.*** *same as* PAPERBACK —***adj.*** bound as a paperback

soft drink a nonalcoholic, esp. carbonated drink

sof·ten (sôf′'n, säf′-) ***vt., vi.*** **1.** to make or become soft or softer **2.** to make or become less resistant —**sof′ten·er** ***n.***

soft·goods (sôft′goodz′) ***n.pl.*** goods that last a relatively short time, esp. textile products: also **soft goods**

soft·head·ed (-hed′id) ***adj.*** stupid or foolish —**soft′-head′ed·ly** ***adv.*** —**soft′head′ed·ness** ***n.***

soft·heart·ed (-här′tid) ***adj.*** **1.** full of compassion or tenderness **2.** not strict or severe, as in discipline —**soft′-heart′ed·ly** ***adv.*** —**soft′heart′ed·ness** ***n.***

soft landing a safe landing, as of a spacecraft on the moon, in which the craft and its contents remain unharmed —**soft′-land′** ***vi., vt.***

soft palate the soft, fleshy part at the rear of the roof of the mouth; velum

soft-ped·al (-ped′'l) ***vt.*** **-aled** or **-alled, -al·ing** or **-al·ling** **1.** to soften the tone of (a musical instrument) by use of a special pedal (**soft pedal**) **2.** [Colloq.] to tone down; make less emphatic, less noticeable, etc.

soft sell selling that relies on subtle suggestion rather than high-pressure salesmanship —**soft′-sell′** ***adj.***

soft-shell (-shel′) ***adj.*** **1.** having a soft shell **2.** having an unhardened shell as the result of recent molting Also **soft′-shelled′**

soft-shoe (-shōō′) ***adj.*** designating a kind of tap dancing done without metal taps on the shoes

soft shoulder soft ground along the edge of a highway

soft-soap (-sōp′) ***vt.*** **1.** to apply soft soap to **2.** [Colloq.] to flatter —**soft′-soap′er** ***n.***

soft soap **1.** soap in liquid or semifluid form **2.** [Colloq.] flattery or smooth talk

soft-spo·ken (-spō′k'n) ***adj.*** **1.** speaking or spoken with a soft, low voice **2.** smooth; suave

soft touch [Slang] a person who is easily persuaded to give or lend money

soft·ware (-wer′) ***n.*** the programs, data, routines, etc. for a computer: cf. HARDWARE (3 *b*)

soft·wood (-wood′) ***n.*** **1.** *a*) any light, easily cut wood *b*) a tree yielding such wood **2.** *Forestry* wood from a needle-bearing conifer

soft·y, soft·ie (sôf′tē, säf′-) ***n.,*** *pl.* **soft′ies** [Colloq.] a person who is overly sentimental or trusting

sog·gy (säg′ē, sôg′ē) ***adj.*** **-gi·er, -gi·est** [prob. < or akin to ON. *sog,* lit., a sucking] **1.** saturated with moisture; soaked **2.** moist and heavy; sodden [a *soggy* cake] **3.** dull and boring —**sog′gi·ly** ***adv.*** —**sog′gi·ness** ***n.***

soil[1] (soil) ***n.*** [Anglo-Fr. < OFr. < L. *solum*] **1.** the surface layer of earth, supporting plant life **2.** any place for growth or development **3.** land; country [foreign *soil*] **4.** ground or earth —**the soil** life and work on a farm

soil[2] (soil) ***vt.*** [< OFr., ult. < L. *suculus,* dim. of *sus,* pig] **1.** to make dirty **2.** to smirch or stain **3.** to bring disgrace upon **4.** to corrupt or defile —***vi.*** to become soiled —***n.*** **1.** a soiled spot; stain **2.** excrement, sewage, etc. **3.** a soiling or being soiled

soi·ree, soi·rée (swä rā′) ***n.*** [< Fr. < *soir,* evening] a party or gathering in the evening

so·journ (sō′jurn; *also, for v.,* sō jurn′) ***vi.*** [< OFr. < L. *sub-,* under + *diurnus,* of a day < *dies,* day] to live somewhere temporarily; stay for a while —***n.*** a brief stay; visit —**so′journ·er** ***n.***

so·kol (sō′kôl) ***n.*** [Czech, lit., falcon] an organization promoting physical health, esp. through gymnastics

Sol (säl) [L.] **1.** *Rom. Myth.* the sun god: identified with the Greek god Helios **2.** the sun personified

sol[1] (sōl; *Sp.* sôl) ***n.,*** *pl.* **sols,** Sp. **so·les** (sô′les) [Sp., lit., sun] *see* MONETARY UNITS, table (Peru)

sol[2] (sōl) ***n.*** [< ML. *sol(ve)*: see GAMUT] *Music* a syllable representing the fifth tone of the diatonic scale

sol[3] (säl, sōl) ***n.*** a liquid colloidal solution

sol·ace (säl′is) ***n.*** [< OFr. < L. < *solari,* to comfort] **1.** an easing of grief, loneliness, etc. **2.** something that eases or relieves; comfort; relief Also **sol′ace·ment** —***vt.*** **-aced, -ac·ing** **1.** to give solace to; comfort **2.** to lessen (grief, sorrow, etc.) —**sol′ac·er** ***n.***

so·lar (sō′lər) ***adj.*** [L. *solaris* < *sol,* the sun] **1.** of or having to do with the sun **2.** produced by or coming from the sun [*solar* energy] **3.** depending upon the sun's light or energy [*solar* heating] **4.** measured by the earth's motion with relation to the sun [mean *solar* time]

solar battery an assembly of devices (**solar cells**) that convert the energy of sunlight into electricity

solar flare a short-lived increase of intensity in the light of the sun, usually near a sunspot

so·lar·i·um (sō ler′ē əm, sə-) ***n.,*** *pl.* **-i·a** (-ə) [L. < *sol,* the sun] a glassed-in porch, room, etc. where people sun themselves, as in treating illness

solar plexus **1.** a network of nerves in the abdominal cavity behind the stomach **2.** [Colloq.] the area of the belly just below the sternum

solar system the sun and all the heavenly bodies that revolve around it

solar wind streams of ionized gas particles constantly emitted by the sun

sold (sōld) *pt. & pp. of* SELL

sol·der (säd′ər) ***n.*** [< OFr. < L. *solidare,* to make firm] **1.** a metal alloy used when melted to join or patch metal parts or surfaces **2.** anything that joins or fuses; bond —***vt., vi.*** **1.** to join (things) with solder **2.** to unite or become united —**sol′der·er** ***n.***

sol·der·ing iron (säd′ər iŋ) a pointed metal tool heated for use in melting and applying solder

sol·dier (sōl′jər) ***n.*** [< OFr. < *solde,* pay < LL. *solidus,* a coin] **1.** a member of an army **2.** an enlisted man, as distinguished from an officer **3.** a man of much military experience **4.** a person who works for a specified cause —***vi.*** **1.** to serve as a soldier **2.** to shirk one's duty, as by pretending to work, to be ill, etc. —**sol′dier·li·ness** ***n.*** —**sol′dier·ly** ***adj.***

soldier of fortune **1.** a mercenary soldier, esp. one seeking adventure or excitement **2.** any adventurer

sol·dier·y (-ē) ***n.,*** *pl.* **-dier·ies** **1.** soldiers collectively **2.** military science: also **sol′dier·ship′**

sole[1] (sōl) ***n.*** [< OFr., ult. < L. *solum,* a base, bottom] **1.** the bottom surface of the foot **2.** the part of a shoe, sock, etc. corresponding to this **3.** the bottom surface of various objects, as a golf club —***vt.*** **soled, sol′ing** to furnish (a shoe, etc.) with a sole, esp. a new sole

sole[2] (sōl) ***adj.*** [< OE. < L. *solus*] **1.** *a*) without another; single; one and only *b*) acting, working, etc. alone without help **2.** of or having to do with only one (specified) person or group **3.** not shared; exclusive [*sole* rights to a patent] **4.** [Archaic] alone; solitary

sole[3] (sōl) ***n.,*** *pl.* **sole, soles:** see PLURAL, II, D, 2 [OFr. < L. *solea,* sole of a shoe, kind of fish: named from its shape] any of certain sea flatfishes, highly valued as food

sol·e·cism (säl′ə siz'm) ***n.*** [< L. < Gr. < *soloikos,* speaking incorrectly < dialect used in Soloi, city in Asia Minor] **1.** a violation of the conventional usage, grammar, etc. of a language (Ex.: "We done it" for "We did it") **2.** a mistake in etiquette —**sol′e·cist** ***n.*** —**sol′e·cis′tic** ***adj.*** —**sol′e·cis′ti·cal·ly** ***adv.***

sole·ly (sōl′lē) ***adv.*** **1.** without another or others; alone **2.** only, exclusively, merely, or altogether [to read *solely* for pleasure]

sol·emn (säl′əm) ***adj.*** [< OFr. < L. *sollemnis,* yearly < *sollus,* all + *annus,* year] **1.** *a*) observed or done according to ritual, as religious rites, etc. *b*) sacred **2.** according to strict form; formal **3.** serious; deeply earnest **4.** awe-inspiring; very impressive **5.** somber because dark in color —**sol′emn·ly** ***adv.*** —**sol′emn·ness** ***n.***

so·lem·ni·fy (sə lem′nə fī′) ***vt.*** **-fied′, -fy′ing** to make solemn

so·lem·ni·ty (-tē) ***n.,*** *pl.* **-ties** **1.** solemn ceremony, ritual, etc. **2.** seriousness; gravity

sol·em·nize (säl′əm nīz′) ***vt.*** **-nized′, -niz′ing** **1.** to celebrate formally or according to ritual **2.** to perform the

ceremony of (marriage, etc.) —**sol′em·ni·za′tion** ***n.***
so·le·noid (sō′lə noid′, säl′ə-) ***n.*** [< Fr. < Gr. *sōlēn*, a channel + *eidos*, a form] a coil of wire carrying an electric current and acting like a magnet —**so′le·noi′dal** ***adj.***
sole·plate (sōl′plāt′) ***n.*** [SOLE[1] + PLATE] the ironing surface of a flatiron
sol-fa (sōl′fä′) ***n.*** [It. *solfa* < *sol* + *fa:* see GAMUT] **1.** the syllables *do, re, mi, fa, sol, la, ti, do,* used for the tones of a scale, regardless of key **2.** the use of these syllables in vocal exercises —***vt., vi.*** **-faed′** (-fäd′), **-fa′ing** to sing (a scale, etc.) to these syllables —**sol′-fa′ist** ***n.***
sol·feg·gio (säl fej′ō, -fej′ē ō′) ***n.,*** *pl.* **-feg′gios, -feg′gi** (-fej′ē) [It. < *solfa:* see prec.] **1.** voice practice in which scales are sung to the sol-fa syllables **2.** the use of these syllables in singing
so·lic·it (sə lis′it) ***vt.*** [< MFr. < L.: see SOLICITOUS] **1.** to ask or seek earnestly; appeal to or for **2.** to entice (someone) to do wrong **3.** to approach for some immoral purpose, as a prostitute does —***vi.*** to solicit someone or something —**so·lic′i·ta′tion** ***n.***
so·lic·i·tor (-ər) ***n.*** **1.** a person who solicits; esp., one who seeks trade, contributions, etc. **2.** in England, a member of the legal profession who is not a barrister **3.** in the U.S., a lawyer serving as official law officer for a city, department, etc.
solicitor general *pl.* **solicitors general, solicitor generals** **1.** a law officer (in the Department of Justice in the U.S.) ranking next below the attorney general **2.** the chief law officer in some States
so·lic·i·tous (sə lis′ə təs) ***adj.*** [L. *sollicitus* < *sollus*, whole + pp. of *ciere*, to set in motion] **1.** showing care, attention, or concern *[solicitous* for her welfare*]* **2.** showing anxious desire; eager *[solicitous* to make friends*]* **3.** full of anxiety —**so·lic′i·tous·ly** ***adv.*** —**so·lic′i·tous·ness** ***n.***
so·lic·i·tude (-to͞od′, -tyo͞od′) ***n.*** the state of being solicitous; care, concern, etc.
sol·id (säl′id) ***adj.*** [< MFr. < L. *solidus*] **1.** tending to keep its form rather than to flow or spread out like a liquid or gas; relatively firm or compact **2.** not hollow **3.** having the three dimensions of length, breadth, and thickness **4.** firm and strong; substantial; sturdy **5.** serious; not trivial **6.** complete *[solid* satisfaction*]* **7.** having no breaks or divisions **8.** with no pauses *[*to talk for a *solid* hour*]* **9.** of one or the same color, material, etc. throughout **10.** showing unity; unanimous *[*a *solid* vote*]* **11.** thick or dense, as a fog **12.** firm or dependable *[*a *solid* friendship*]* **13.** [Colloq.] having a firmly favorable relationship **14.** [Colloq.] healthful and filling *[*a *solid* meal*]* **15.** [Slang] excellent **16.** *Printing* set without leads between the lines of type —***n.*** **1.** a substance that is solid, not a liquid or gas **2.** an object or figure having length, breadth, and thickness —**sol′id·ly** ***adv.*** —**sol′id·ness** ***n.***
sol·i·dar·i·ty (säl′ə dar′ə tē) ***n.,*** *pl.* **-ties** agreement of all elements or individuals, as of a group; complete unity
solid fuel a rocket fuel in solid form, consisting of both fuel and oxidizer combined or mixed
solid geometry geometry dealing with solid figures
so·lid·i·fy (sə lid′ə fī′) ***vt., vi.*** **-fied′, -fy′ing** **1.** to make or become solid, firm, hard, etc. **2.** to crystallize **3.** to make or become solid, strong, or united —**so·lid′i·fi·ca′tion** ***n.***
so·lid·i·ty (-tē) ***n.*** a being solid; firmness, hardness, etc.
sol·id-state (säl′id stāt′) ***adj.*** designating or of electronic devices, as semiconductors, that can control current without heated filaments, moving parts, etc.
sol·i·dus (säl′i dəs) ***n.,*** *pl.* **-i·di′** (-dī′) [LL. < L.] **1.** a gold coin of the Late Roman Empire **2.** *a)* a slant line (/) used to separate shillings from pence (Ex.: 7/6) *b) same as* VIRGULE
so·lil·o·quize (sə lil′ə kwīz′) ***vi.*** **-quized′, -quiz′ing** to deliver a soliloquy; talk to oneself —***vt.*** to utter in a soliloquy —**so·lil′o·quist** (-kwist) ***n.***
so·lil·o·quy (-kwē) ***n.,*** *pl.* **-quies** [< LL. < L. *solus*, alone + *loqui*, to speak] **1.** a talking to oneself **2.** lines in a drama in which a character reveals his thoughts to the audience by speaking as if to himself
sol·ip·sism (säl′ip siz′m) ***n.*** [< L. *solus*, alone + *ipse*, self + -ISM] **1.** the theory that the self can be aware only of its own experiences or states **2.** the theory that nothing exists but the self —**sol′ip·sist** ***n.*** —**sol′ip·sis′tic** ***adj.***
sol·i·taire (säl′ə ter′) ***n.*** [< Fr. < L.: see ff.] **1.** a single gem, esp. a diamond, set by itself **2.** any of many games, esp. card games, played by one person
sol·i·tar·y (-ter′ē) ***adj.*** [< OFr. < L. *solitarius* < *solus*, alone] **1.** living or being alone **2.** single; only *[*a *solitary* example*]* **3.** lacking companions; lonely **4.** with few or no people; remote *[*a *solitary* place*]* **5.** done in solitude —***n.,*** *pl.* **-tar′ies** **1.** a person who lives by himself; esp., a hermit **2.** [Colloq.] *same as* SOLITARY CONFINEMENT —**sol′i·tar′i·ly** ***adv.*** —**sol′i·tar′i·ness** ***n.***
solitary confinement confinement of a prisoner, usually as extra punishment, away from all others
sol·i·tude (säl′ə to͞od′, -tyo͞od′) ***n.*** [< MFr. < L. *solitudo* < *solus*, alone] **1.** a being solitary, or alone; seclusion **2.** a secluded place —**sol′i·tu′di·nous** ***adj.***
sol·mi·za·tion (säl′mi zā′shən) ***n.*** [< Fr. < *sol* + *mi:* see GAMUT] solfeggio, or any similar use of a system of syllables in singing
so·lo (sō′lō) ***n.,*** *pl.* **-los;** for *n.* 1 & 3, sometimes **-li** (-lē) [It. < L. *solus*, alone] **1.** a musical piece or passage to be played or sung by one person **2.** an airplane flight made by a pilot alone **3.** any performance by one person alone **4.** any card game in which there are no partners —***adj.*** **1.** for or by a single voice, person, or instrument **2.** performing a solo —***adv.*** alone —***vi.*** to make a solo flight —**so′lo·ist** ***n.***
Sol·o·mon (säl′ə mən) [LL. < Gr. < Heb. *shĕlōmōh*, lit., peaceful < *shālōm*, peace] **1.** a masculine name: dim. *Sol* **2.** *Bible* king of Israel; son & successor of DAVID: noted for his wisdom —***n.*** a very wise man
Solomon Islands **1.** country on a group of islands in the SW Pacific, east of New Guinea: c. 11,500 sq. mi.; pop. 206,000 **2.** group of islands including this country and other islands belonging to Papua New Guinea
Solomon's seal **1.** the Star of David used as a mystic symbol in the Middle Ages **2.** any of various plants with broad, waxy leaves and blue or black berries
So·lon (sō′lən, -län) 640?–559? B.C.; Athenian statesman & lawgiver —***n.*** [*sometimes* **s-**] a wise lawmaker
so long *colloq. term for* GOODBYE
sol·stice (säl′stis, sōl′-) ***n.*** [MFr. < L. *solstitium* < *sol*, the sun + *sistere*, to make stand still < *stare*, to stand] **1.** either of two points on the sun's ecliptic at which it is farthest north or farthest south of the celestial equator **2.** the time of reaching either of these points: see SUMMER SOLSTICE, WINTER SOLSTICE —**sol·sti′tial** (-stish′əl) ***adj.***
sol·u·ble (säl′yoo b′l) ***adj.*** [MFr. < L. *solubilis* < *solvere:* see SOLVE] **1.** that can be dissolved; able to pass into solution **2.** that can be solved —**sol′u·bil′i·ty** ***n.,*** *pl.* **-ties**
sol·ute (säl′yo͞ot, sō′lo͞ot) ***n.*** the substance dissolved in a solution —***adj.*** dissolved; in solution
so·lu·tion (sə lo͞o′shən) ***n.*** [< OFr. < L. < pp. of *solvere:* see ff.] **1.** *a)* the solving of a problem *b)* the answer to a problem *c)* an explanation, etc. *[*the *solution* of a mystery*]* **2.** *a)* the dispersion of one or more substances in another, usually a liquid, so as to form a homogeneous mixture; a dissolving *b)* a being dissolved *c)* the mixture, usually a liquid, so produced **3.** a breaking up; dissolution
solution set *Math.* the root or values that satisfy a given equation or inequality
solve (sälv) ***vt.*** **solved, solv′ing** [< L. *solvere*, to loosen < *se-*, apart + *luere*, to let go] to find a satisfactory answer for (a problem, mystery, etc.); make clear; explain —**solv′a·bil′i·ty** ***n.*** —**solv′a·ble** ***adj.*** —**solv′er** ***n.***
sol·vent (säl′vənt) ***adj.*** [< L. prp. of *solvere:* see SOLVE] **1.** able to pay all one's debts **2.** that can dissolve another substance —***n.*** **1.** a substance that can dissolve another one **2.** something that solves or explains —**sol′ven·cy** ***n.***
Sol·y·man (säl′i mən) *same as* SULEIMAN
So·ma·li (sō mä′lē, sə-) ***n.*** **1.** *pl.* **-lis, -li** a member of an Islamic, pastoral people of Somalia and nearby regions **2.** their Eastern Cushitic language
So·ma·li·a (sō mä′lē ə, sə-; -mäl′yə) country of E Africa, on the Indian Ocean & the Gulf of Aden: 246,201 sq. mi.; pop. 2,864,000
so·mat·ic (sō mat′ik) ***adj.*** [Gr. *sōmatikos* < *sōma*, the body] **1.** of the body; corporeal; physical **2.** of the cells (**somatic cells**) of an organism that become differentiated into the tissues, organs, etc. of the body **3.** of the outer walls of the body —**so·mat′i·cal·ly** ***adv.***
som·ber (säm′bər) ***adj.*** [Fr. *sombre*, ult. < L. *sub*, under + *umbra*, shade] **1.** dark and gloomy or dull **2.** mentally depressed or depressing; melancholy **3.** solemn; grave Also, chiefly Brit. sp., **som′bre** —**som′ber·ly** ***adv.*** —**som′ber·ness** ***n.***
som·bre·ro (säm brer′ō, səm-) ***n.,*** *pl.* **-ros** [Sp. < *sombra*, shade: see prec.] a broad-brimmed felt or straw hat, worn in Mexico, the Southwest, etc.

SOMBRERO

some (sum; *unstressed* səm) ***adj.*** [OE. *sum*] **1.** being a certain one or ones not specified or known *[some* people smoke*]* **2.** being of a certain unspecified quantity, degree, etc. *[*have *some* butter*]* **3.** about *[some* ten of us*]* **4.** [Colloq.] remarkable; striking *[*it was *some* fight*]* —***pron.*** **1.** a certain one or ones not specified or known *[some* agree*]* **2.** a certain unspecified number, quantity, etc. *[*take *some]* —***adv.*** **1.** about *[some* ten men*]* **2.** [Colloq.] to some extent *[*slept *some]* **3.** [Colloq.] to a great extent, at a great rate, etc. *[*must run *some* to catch up*]* —**and then some** [Colloq.] and more than that

-some[1] (səm) [OE. *-sum*] *a suffix meaning* like, tending to, tending to be *[tiresome, lonesome]*

-some[2] (səm) [< ME. *sum,* SOME] *a suffix meaning* (a specified) number together *[twosome]*

-some[3] (sōm) [< Gr. *sōma,* body] *a combining form meaning* body *[chromosome]*

some·bod·y (sum′bud′ē, -bäd′ē, -bəd ē) ***pron.*** a person unknown or not named; some person; someone —***n.,*** *pl.* **-bod′-ies** a person of importance

some·day (-dā′) ***adv.*** at some future time

some·how (-hou′) ***adv.*** in a way not known, stated, or understood *[*it was *somehow* damaged*]* : often in **somehow or other**

some·one (-wun′, -wən) ***pron.*** *same as* SOMEBODY

some·place (-plās′) ***adv.*** in, to, or at some place; somewhere

som·er·sault (sum′ər sôlt′) ***n.*** [altered < MFr. *sombresault* < L. *supra,* over + *saltus,* a leap] an acrobatic stunt done by turning the body one full revolution, heels over head: often used figuratively, as of a complete reversal of opinion —***vi.*** to do a somersault Also **som′er·set′** (-set′)

Som·er·ville (sum′ər vil′) [? after Capt. R. *Somers* (1778–1804)] city in E Mass.: suburb of Boston: pop. 77,000

some·thing (sum′thiŋ) ***n.*** **1.** a thing not definitely known, understood, etc. *[something* went wrong*]* **2.** some thing or things, definite but unspecified *[*have *something* to eat*]* **3.** a bit; a little *[something* over an hour*]* **4.** [Colloq.] a remarkable person or thing —***adv.*** **1.** somewhat **2.** [Colloq.] really *[*sounds *something* awful*]* Also used after a figure to indicate a fraction beyond *[*the bus leaves at six *something]* —**make something of 1.** to find a use for **2.** to treat as of great importance **3.** [Colloq.] to treat as a point of dispute —**something else** [Slang] a really remarkable person or thing

some·time (-tīm′) ***adv.*** **1.** at some time not known or specified **2.** at some future time **3.** [Archaic] *a)* sometimes *b)* formerly —***adj.*** **1.** former *[*his *sometime* friend*]* **2.** occasional *[*his wit is a *sometime* thing*]*

some·times (-tīmz′) ***adv.*** at times; occasionally

some·way (-wā′) ***adv.*** in some way or manner; somehow or other: also **some′ways′**

some·what (-hwut′, -hwät′, -wut′, -wət) ***n.*** some degree, amount, part, etc. *[somewhat* of a surprise*]* —***adv.*** to some extent, degree, etc.

some·where (-hwer′, -wer′) ***adv.*** **1.** in, to, or at some place not known or specified **2.** at some time, degree, age, figure, etc. (with *about, around, in,* etc.) —***n.*** an unspecified or undetermined place Also [Chiefly Dial.] **some′wheres′**

Somme (sum; *Fr.* sôm) river in N France flowing west into the English Channel

som·me·lier (sum′əl yā′) ***n.*** [Fr. < MFr., orig., person in charge of pack animals] a wine steward

som·nam·bu·late (säm nam′byoo lāt′, səm-) ***vt.*** **-lat′ed, -lat′ing** [< L. *somnus,* sleep + pp. of *ambulare,* to walk] to walk in a trancelike state while asleep —**som·nam′bu-lant** ***adj.*** —**som·nam′bu·la′tion** ***n.*** —**som·nam′bu·la′tor** ***n.***

som·nam·bu·lism (-liz′m) ***n.*** [see prec.] **1.** the act or practice of sleepwalking **2.** the trancelike state of a sleepwalker —**som·nam′bu·list** ***n.*** —**som·nam′bu·lis′tic** ***adj.***

som·nif·er·ous (säm nif′ər əs, səm-) ***adj.*** [< L. < *somnus,* sleep + *ferre,* to bring] causing sleep; soporific: also **som-nif′ic** —**som·nif′er·ous·ly** ***adv.***

som·no·lent (säm′nə lənt) ***adj.*** [< MFr. < L. *somnolentus* < *somnus,* sleep] **1.** sleepy; drowsy **2.** causing drowsiness —**som′no·lence** ***n.*** —**som′no·lent·ly** ***adv.***

son (sun) ***n.*** [OE. *sunu*] **1.** a boy or man as he is related to either or both parents: sometimes also used of animals **2.** a male descendant **3.** *a)* a son-in-law *b)* a stepson **4.** a male thought of as if in the relation of child to parent or to a formative influence *[*a *son* of revolution*]* **5.** a familiar form of address to a boy or younger man —**the Son** Jesus Christ, as the second person of the Trinity

so·nant (sō′nənt) ***adj.*** [< L. prp. of *sonare,* to SOUND[1]] **1.** of sound **2.** having sound; sounding —**so′nance** ***n.***

so·nar (sō′när) ***n.*** [*so(und) n(avigation) a(nd) r(anging)*] an apparatus that transmits high-frequency sound waves through water and registers the vibrations reflected back from an object: used to locate submarines, find depths, etc.

so·na·ta (sə nät′ə) ***n.*** [It. < L. *sonare,* to SOUND[1]] a musical composition for one or two instruments, usually in three or four movements in different tempos, etc.

sonde (sänd) ***n.*** [Fr., a sounding line] any of various devices for measuring and usually telemetering meteorological and other physical data during ascent and descent through the atmosphere

‡**son et lu·mière** (sōn nā lü myer′) [Fr., lit., sound and light] a historical spectacle at night before a monument, etc., using special lighting effects, narration, music, etc.

song (sôŋ) ***n.*** [OE. *sang*] **1.** the act or art of singing **2.** a piece of music sung or as if for singing **3.** *a)* poetry; verse *b)* a ballad or lyric that is or can be set to music **4.** a musical sound like singing *[*the *song* of the lark*]* —**for a song** cheaply —**song′ful** ***adj.*** —**song′less** ***adj.***

song·bird (-burd′) ***n.*** **1.** a bird that makes vocal sounds that are like music **2.** a woman singer

song·fest (-fest′) ***n.*** [SONG + -FEST] an informal gathering of people for singing songs, esp. folk songs

Song of Solomon a book of the Bible consisting of a love poem, dramatic and lyrical in character: also called **Song of Songs, Canticle of Canticles**

song sparrow a common N. American sparrow with a striped breast, noted for its sweet song

song·ster (sôŋ′stər) ***n.*** [OE. *sangestre*] **1.** a singer **2.** a writer of songs or poems **3.** a songbird —**song′stress** ***n.fem.***

song thrush a European songbird with brown wings and a white breast

song·writ·er (-rīt′ər) ***n.*** a person who writes words or music or both for songs, esp. popular songs

son·ic (sän′ik) ***adj.*** [< L. *sonus,* SOUND[1] + -IC] **1.** of or having to do with sound **2.** designating or of a speed equal to the speed of sound (about 1088 feet per second through air at sea level at 32° F)

sonic barrier the large increase in drag encountered by an aircraft approaching the speed of sound

sonic boom an explosive sound generated by the accumulation of pressure in a wave preceding an aircraft moving at or above the speed of sound

sonic depth finder *same as* FATHOMETER

son-in-law (sun′in lô′) ***n.,*** *pl.* **sons′-in-law′** the husband of one's daughter

son·net (sän′it) ***n.*** [Fr. < It. < Pr. dim. of *son,* a song < L. *sonus,* SOUND[1]] a poem normally of fourteen lines (typically in iambic pentameter) in any of several fixed verse and rhyme schemes, expressing a single theme: see SHAKESPEAREAN SONNET —***vt., vi.*** to write sonnets (about): also **son′net·ize′** (-ə tīz′) **-ized′, -iz′ing**

son·net·eer (sän′ə tir′) ***n.*** a person who writes sonnets

son·ny (sun′ē) ***n.,*** *pl.* **-nies** little son: used in addressing any young boy in a familiar way

son·o·buoy (sän′ō bo͞o′ē, sō′nō-; -boi′) ***n.*** [< L. *sonus,* SOUND[1] + BUOY] a buoy that transmits amplified sound signals picked up under water

so·no·rant (sə nôr′ənt, sō-) ***n.*** [SONOR(OUS) + (CONSON)ANT] *Phonet.* a voiced consonant that is less sonorous than a vowel but more sonorous than an unvoiced plosive, as *l, m, n, r, y, w:* sonorants may occur as syllabics

so·nor·i·ty (sə nôr′ə tē, sō-) ***n.,*** *pl.* **-ties** the quality or state of being sonorous; resonance

so·no·rous (sə nôr′əs, sän′ər əs) ***adj.*** [< L. < *sonor,* a sound] **1.** producing or capable of producing sound, esp. a full, deep, or rich sound; resonant **2.** full, deep, or rich: said of sound **3.** high-sounding; impressive *[sonorous* prose*]* —**so·no′rous·ly** ***adv.*** —**so·no′rous·ness** ***n.***

Soo (so͞o) [alteration of *Sault*] region in N Mich. & S Ontario, Canada, at the cities of Sault Ste. Marie & the ship canals (**Soo Locks**) that bypass a rapids of the St. Marys River: see SAULT STE. MARIE

soon (so͞on) ***adv.*** [OE. *sona,* at once] **1.** in a short time; shortly *[*we will *soon* be there*]* **2.** promptly; quickly *[*as *soon* as possible*]* **3.** ahead of time; early *[*he left too *soon]* **4.** readily; willingly *[*I would as *soon* go as stay*]* —**had sooner** would rather —**sooner or later** eventually

soot (soot, so͞ot) ***n.*** [OE. *sot*] a black substance consisting chiefly of carbon particles formed by the incomplete combustion of burning matter —***vt.*** to cover, soil, or treat with soot

sooth (so͞oth) ***adj.*** [OE. *soth*] **1.** [Archaic] true **2.** [Poet.] soothing; smooth —***n.*** [Archaic] truth —**in sooth** [Archaic] in truth —**sooth′ly** ***adv.***

soothe (so͞o*th*) ***vt.*** **soothed, sooth′ing** [OE. *sothian* < *soth,* truth] **1.** to make calm or composed, as by gentleness, flattery, etc. **2.** to relieve (pain, etc.) —***vi.*** to have a soothing effect —**sooth′er** ***n.*** —**sooth′ing** ***adj.*** —**sooth′ing·ly** ***adv.***

sooth·say·er (so͞oth′sā′ər) ***n.*** a person who claims to foretell the future —**sooth′say′ing** ***n.***

soot·y (soot′ē, so͞ot′ē) ***adj.*** **soot′i·er, soot′i·est** **1.** of, like, or covered with soot **2.** dark or black like soot —**soot′i-ness** ***n.***

sop (säp) ***n.*** [OE. *sopp*] **1.** a piece of food, as bread, soaked in milk, gravy, etc. **2.** *a)* something given by way of appeasement, etc. *b)* a bribe —***vt.*** **sopped, sop′ping** **1.** to soak, steep, etc. in or with liquid 2. to take (*up*), as liquid, by absorption —*vi.* 1. to soak (*in, into,* or *through* something) 2. to be or become thoroughly wet

SOP, S.O.P. standing (or standard) operating procedure

sop. soprano

So·phi·a (sō fē′ə) [< Gr. *sophia*, wisdom < *sophos*, wise] a feminine name: var. *Sophie, Sophy*

soph·ism (säf′iz'm) *n.* [< OFr. < L. < Gr. < *sophos*, clever] clever and reasonable argument that is, however, faulty or misleading; fallacy or sophistry

soph·ist (-ist) *n.* [< L. < Gr. *sophistēs*, wise man] 1. [*often* S-] in ancient Greece, any of a group of teachers of rhetoric, philosophy, etc., some of whom were notorious for their clever, specious arguments 2. a learned person 3. any person practicing clever, specious reasoning

so·phis·ti·cal (sə fis′ti k'l) *adj.* 1. of or characteristic of sophists or sophistry 2. clever and plausible but misleading Also **so·phis′tic** —**so·phis′ti·cal·ly** *adv.*

so·phis·ti·cate (sə fis′tə kāt′; *for n. usually* -kit) *vt.* **-cat′ed, -cat′ing** [< ML. < L. *sophisticus*, sophistical] 1. to change from being natural, simple, naive, etc. to being artificial, worldly-wise, etc. 2. to bring to a more developed, complex, or refined form, level, etc. —*n.* a sophisticated person

so·phis·ti·cat·ed (-kāt′id) *adj.* 1. not simple, natural, or naive; wise in the ways of the world; knowledgeable, subtle, etc. 2. appealing to sophisticated people 3. highly complex, refined, etc.; of an advanced form, technique, etc. —**so·phis′ti·cat′ed·ly** *adv.*

so·phis·ti·ca·tion (sə fis′tə kā′shən) *n.* 1. the act or process of sophisticating 2. the state or quality of being sophisticated

soph·is·try (säf′is trē) *n., pl.* **-tries** 1. unsound or misleading but subtle argument or reasoning 2. the methods of the Sophists

Soph·o·cles (säf′ə klēz′) 496?–406 B.C.; Gr. writer of tragedies

soph·o·more (säf′ə môr′) *n.* [altered (after Gr. *sophos*, wise + *mōros*, foolish) < obs. *sophumer*, lit., sophist] 1. a student in his second year of college or the tenth grade at high school 2. a person in his second year of some enterprise —*adj.* of or for sophomores

soph·o·mor·ic (säf′ə môr′ik) *adj.* of or like sophomores, often regarded as self-assured, opinionated, etc. though immature: also **soph′o·mor′i·cal** —**soph′o·mor′i·cal·ly** *adv.*

-so·phy (sə fē) [< Gr. *sophia*, skill, wisdom] *a combining form meaning* knowledge [*philosophy*]

sop·o·rif·ic (säp′ə rif′ik, sō′pə-) *adj.* [< Fr. < L. *sopor*, sleep + -FIC] 1. causing or tending to cause sleep 2. sleepy —*n.* a drug, etc. that causes sleep

sop·ping (säp′iŋ) *adj.* thoroughly wet; drenched

sop·py (säp′ē) *adj.* **-pi·er, -pi·est** 1. very wet; sopping 2. rainy 3. [Colloq.] sentimental —**sop′pi·ness** *n.*

so·pra·no (sə pran′ō, -prä′nō) *n., adj., pl.* **-nos, -ni** (-prä′nē) [It. < *sopra*, above] 1. the highest singing voice of women, girls, and young boys 2. *a*) a voice or singer with this range *b*) a musical instrument with this range *c*) a part for a soprano —*adj.* of, for, or having the range of a soprano

so·ra (sôr′ə) *n.* [< ? AmInd.] a small, short-billed wading bird of the rail family, living in marshes: also **sora rail**

sor·bic acid (sôr′bik) [ult. < L. *sorbus*, a kind of tree] a white, crystalline solid, $C_6H_8O_2$, used as a food preservative, fungicide, etc.

sor·bi·tol (sôr′bi tôl′, -tōl′) *n.* [see prec.] a white, sweet, crystalline alcohol, $C_6H_8(OH)_6$, used as a moistening agent in lotions, etc., and as a sugar substitute

Sor·bonne (sôr bän′; *Fr.* sôr bôn′) the liberal arts college of the University of Paris

sor·cer·er (sôr′sər ər) *n.* a person who practices sorcery; wizard —**sor′cer·ess** *n.fem.*

sor·cer·y (-ē) *n., pl.* **-cer·ies** [< OFr. < *sorcier*, sorcerer < L. *sors*, lot, share] 1. the supposed use of magical power by means of charms, spells, etc., usually for an evil purpose; witchcraft; black magic 2. seemingly magical power, charm, etc. —**sor′cer·ous** *adj.* —**sor′cer·ous·ly** *adv.*

sor·did (sôr′did) *adj.* [< Fr. < L. < *sordes*, filth] 1. *a*) dirty; filthy *b*) squalid; depressingly wretched 2. *a*) base; ignoble *b*) meanly selfish or grasping —**sor′did·ly** *adv.* —**sor′did·ness** *n.*

sore (sôr) *adj.* **sor′er, sor′est** [OE. *sar*] 1. *a*) giving pain; painful [*a sore* throat] *b*) feeling pain, as from bruises, etc. 2. *a*) filled with sadness, grief, etc. [*sore* at heart] *b*) causing sadness, grief, etc. [*sore* hardships] 3. provoking irritation [*a sore* point] 4. [Colloq.] angry; offended —*n.* 1. a sore, usually infected spot on the body, as an ulcer or blister 2. a source of pain, distress, etc. —*adv.* [Archaic] sorely —**sore′ness** *n.*

sore·head (-hed′) *n.* [Colloq.] a person who is angry, resentful, disgruntled, etc., or one easily made so

sore·ly (-lē) *adv.* 1. grievously; painfully [*sorely* vexed] 2. urgently; extremely [*sorely* needed]

sor·ghum (sôr′gəm) *n.* [< It. *sorgo*] 1. any of several tropical cereal grasses grown for grain, syrup, fodder, etc. 2. a syrup made from the sweet juices of a variety (**sorgo**) of sorghum

so·ror·al (sə rôr′'l) *adj.* [see ff.] of or like a sister or sisters; sisterly —**so·ror′al·ly** *adv.*

so·ror·i·ty (sə rôr′ə tē) *n., pl.* **-ties** [< ML. < L. *soror*, sister] a group of women or girls joined together for social or professional reasons; specif., a Greek-letter college organization

sor·rel[1] (sôr′əl, sär′-) *n.* [< OFr. < Frank. *sur*, sour] 1. any of several plants with sour, fleshy leaves; dock 2. *same as* WOOD SORREL

sor·rel[2] (sôr′əl, sär′-) *n.* [< OFr. < *sor*, light brown < ML. *saurus* < Gmc.] 1. light reddish brown 2. a horse, etc. of this color —*adj.* light reddish-brown

sor·row (sär′ō, sôr′ō) *n.* [OE. *sorg*] 1. mental suffering caused by loss, disappointment, etc.; sadness, grief, or regret 2. that which produces such suffering; trouble, misfortune, etc. 3. the outward expression of such suffering; mourning 4. earnest repentance —*vi.* to feel or show sorrow; grieve —**sor′row·er** *n.* —**sor′row·ing·ly** *adv.*

sor·row·ful (-ə fəl) *adj.* feeling, causing, or expressing sorrow; sad —**sor′row·ful·ly** *adv.* —**sor′row·ful·ness** *n.*

sor·ry (sär′ē, sôr′ē) *adj.* **-ri·er, -ri·est** [OE. *sarig* < *sar*, sore] 1. full of sorrow, pity, sympathy, etc.: also used in apologizing or in showing mild regret 2. *a*) inferior in worth or quality; poor *b*) wretched, pitiful, miserable, etc. —**sor′ri·ly** *adv.* —**sor′ri·ness** *n.*

sort (sôrt) *n.* [< MFr., ult. < L. *sors* (gen. *sortis*), a lot] 1. any group related by having something in common; kind; class 2. quality or type; nature [remarks of that *sort*] —*vt.* to arrange according to class or kind (often with *out*) —**of sorts** 1. of various kinds 2. of an inferior kind: also **of a sort** —**out of sorts** [Colloq.] cross, irritable, or ill —**sort of** [Colloq.] somewhat —**sort′a·ble** *adj.* —**sort′er** *n.*

sor·tie (sôr′tē) *n.* [Fr. < *sortir*, to issue] 1. a sudden attack or raid by troops from a besieged place; sally 2. one mission by a single military plane

SOS (es′ō′es′) 1. a signal of distress in code (···–––···) used internationally in wireless telegraphy, as by ships 2. [Colloq.] any urgent call for help

so-so (sō′sō′) *adv.* indifferently; just passably —*adj.* neither too good nor too bad; just fair Also **so so**

sos·te·nu·to (säs′tə no͞ot′ō) *n., adj., adv.* [It.] *Music* sustained or prolonged in tempo

sot (sät) *n.* [< Late OE. *sott* or OFr. *sot*, a fool < VL. *sottus*] a drunkard —**sot′tish** *adj.* —**sot′tish·ly** *adv.*

sot·ted (sät′id) *adj.* besotted; stupefied

sot·to vo·ce (sät′ō vō′chē) [It., under the voice] in an undertone, so as not to be overheard

sou (so͞o) *n., pl.* **sous** (so͞oz; *Fr.* so͞o) [Fr. < OFr. *sol* < LL. *solidus*, SOLIDUS] any of several former French coins, esp. one equal to five centimes

sou·brette (so͞o bret′) *n.* [Fr. < Pr. < *soubret*, sly, ult. < L. *superare*, to be above] *Theater* 1. the role of a lady's maid, esp. one involved in intrigue, or of any pretty, flirtatious young woman 2. an actress who plays such roles

sou·bri·quet (so͞o′brə kā′) *n. var. of* SOBRIQUET

souf·flé (so͞o flā′, so͞o′flā) *adj.* [Fr. < pp. of *souffler*, to blow] made light and puffy in cooking: also **souf·fléed′** (-flād′) —*n.* a baked food made light and puffy by adding beaten egg whites before baking [a cheese *soufflé*]

sough (sou, suf) *n.* [< OE. *swogan*, to sound] a soft, murmuring, sighing, or rustling sound —*vi.* to make a sough

sought (sôt) *pt. & pp. of* SEEK

souk (so͝ok) *n.* [Ar. *sūq*] an open-air marketplace in North Africa and the Middle East

soul (sōl) *n.* [OE. *sawol*] 1. the part of one's being that is thought of as the center of feeling, thinking, will, etc. apart from the body: in some religions the soul is believed to go on after death 2. the moral or emotional nature of man 3. spiritual or emotional warmth, force, etc. 4. vital or essential part, quality, etc. 5. the central or leading figure [Daniel Boone, *soul* of the frontier] 6. embodiment; personification [the very *soul* of kindness] 7. a person [a town of 1,000 *souls*] 8. [Colloq.] *a*) among U.S. Negroes, a sense of racial pride and social and cultural solidarity *b*) *short for* SOUL FOOD *or* SOUL MUSIC —*adj.* [Colloq.] of, for, like, or characteristic of U.S. Negroes —**upon my soul!** an exclamation of surprise

soul food [Colloq.] items of food popular orig. in the South esp. among Negroes, as chitterlings, ham hocks, yams, turnip greens, etc.

soul·ful (sōl′fəl) *adj.* full of or showing deep feeling —**soul′ful·ly** *adv.* —**soul′ful·ness** *n.*

soul·less (-lis) *adj.* lacking soul, sensitivity, or deep feeling —**soul′less·ly** *adv.* —**soul′less·ness** *n.*

soul music [Colloq.] *a form of* RHYTHM AND BLUES (with added elements of U.S. Negro gospel singing)

soul-search·ing (-sur′chiŋ) *n.* a close, honest examination of one's true feelings, motives, etc.

sound[1] (sound) *n.* [< OFr. *son* < L. *sonus*] **1.** *a)* vibrations in air, water, etc. that act on the nerves of the inner ear and produce the sensation of hearing *b)* the sensation that these vibrations stimulate in the ear **2.** *a)* any identifiable noise, tone, vocal utterance, etc. [the *sound* of a violin, speech *sounds*] *b)* such effects transmitted by or recorded for radio, television, movies, etc. **3.** the distance within which a sound may be heard; earshot **4.** the impression made by something said, etc.; drift [the *sound* of his report] **5.** meaningless noise —*vi.* **1.** to make a sound **2.** to seem or appear through sound or utterance [to *sound* troubled] —*vt.* **1.** *a)* to cause to sound *b)* to produce the sound of *c)* to utter distinctly [to *sound* one's r's] **2.** to express, signal, proclaim, etc. [*sound* the alarm, *sound* his praises] **3.** to examine (the chest) by percussion, etc. —**sound off 1.** to speak in turn, as in counting off **2.** [Slang] *a)* to give free voice to complaints, opinions, etc. *b)* to speak in a loud or offensive way —**sound′er** *n.*

sound[2] (sound) *adj.* [OE. (*ge*)*sund*] **1.** free from defect, damage, or decay [*sound* timber] **2.** normal and healthy [a *sound* body and mind] **3.** firm and safe; stable; secure [a *sound* bank] **4.** based on valid reasoning; sensible [*sound* advice] **5.** agreeing with established views or beliefs [*sound* doctrine] **6.** thorough, complete, forceful, etc. [a *sound* defeat] **7.** deep and undisturbed: said of sleep **8.** morally strong; honest, loyal, etc. **9.** *Law* valid —*adv.* completely; deeply [*sound* asleep] —**sound′ly** *adv.* —**sound′ness** *n.*

sound[3] (sound) *n.* [< OE. & ON. *sund*] **1.** a wide channel linking two large bodies of water or separating an island from the mainland **2.** a long arm of the sea **3.** the air bladder of certain fishes

sound[4] (sound) *vt.* [< MFr. *sonder* < VL. *subundare* < L. *sub,* under + *unda,* a wave] **1.** *a)* to measure the depth of (water), esp. with a weighted line (**sounding line**) *b)* to examine (the bottom of the sea, etc.) with a line that brings up particles that stick to it *c)* to probe (the atmosphere or space) so as to gain data **2.** to try to find out the opinions of (a person): often with *out* **3.** *Med.* to examine with a sound, or probe —*vi.* **1.** to sound water **2.** to dive suddenly downward through the water: said esp. of whales, etc. **3.** to try to find out something —*n. Med.* a long probe used in examining body cavities —**sound′a·ble** *adj.* —**sound′er** *n.*

sound barrier *same as* SONIC BARRIER

sound effects sounds, as of thunder, animals, etc., produced artificially or by recording as for radio, TV, etc.

sound·ing[1] (soun′diŋ) *adj.* **1.** giving forth sound **2.** resonant; sonorous **3.** high-sounding; bombastic

sound·ing[2] (soun′diŋ) *n.* **1.** *a)* the act of measuring the depth of water *b)* depth so measured *c)* [*pl.*] a place, usually less than 600 feet in depth, where a sounding line will touch bottom **2.** *a)* an examination of the atmosphere, as with a radiosonde *b)* a probe of space, as with a rocket **3.** [*pl.*] measurements or data learned by sounding **4.** [*often pl.*] a sampling, as of public opinion

sounding board 1. a thin plate of wood, etc. built into a musical instrument to increase its resonance: also **sound′board′** *n.* **2.** any structure designed to reflect sound **3.** a person on whom one tests one's ideas, opinions, etc.

sound·less (sound′lis) *adj.* without sound; noiseless —**sound′less·ly** *adv.* —**sound′less·ness** *n.*

sound·proof (-pro͞of′) *adj.* able to keep sound from coming through —*vt.* to make soundproof

sound track the area along one side of a motion-picture film, carrying the sound record of the film

sound wave *Physics* a pressure wave transported by an elastic medium, as air; esp., such a wave vibrating at a frequency that can be heard

soup (so͞op) *n.* [Fr. *soupe* < OFr., soup: of Gmc. origin] **1.** a liquid food made by cooking meat, vegetables, etc. in water, milk, etc. **2.** [Slang] a heavy fog **3.** [Slang] nitroglycerin —**in the soup** [Slang] in trouble —**soup up** [Slang] to increase the power, capacity for speed, etc. of (an engine, etc.) —**soup′y** *adj.* **soup′i·er, soup′i·est**

soup·çon (so͞op sôn′, so͞op′sôn′) *n.* [Fr.] **1.** a suggestion or trace, as of a flavor **2.** a tiny amount; bit

soupe du jour (so͞op′do͝o zho͝or′) [Fr., lit., soup of the day] the featured soup on a menu for that day: also **soup du jour**

soup kitchen a place where hot soup or the like is given to people in dire need

soup·spoon (so͞op′spo͞on′) *n.* a large-bowled spoon for eating soup

sour (sour) *adj.* [OE. *sur*] **1.** having the sharp, acid taste of lemon juice, vinegar, etc. **2.** made acid or spoiled by fermentation [*sour* milk] **3.** cross, bad-tempered, peevish, bitter, etc. **4.** below what is usual; poor [his game has gone *sour*] **5.** distasteful or unpleasant **6.** gratingly wrong or off pitch [a *sour* note] **7.** excessively acid: said of soil —*n.* **1.** something sour **2.** a cocktail made with lime or lemon juice [a whiskey *sour*] —*vt., vi.* to make or become sour —**sour′ish** *adj.* —**sour′ly** *adv.* —**sour′ness** *n.*

source (sôrs) *n.* [< OFr. < pp. of *sourdre* < L. *surgere,* to rise] **1.** a spring, etc. from which a stream arises **2.** that from which something originates, develops, etc. **3.** *a)* that by which something is supplied *b)* a person, book, etc. that provides information **4.** the point from which light rays, sound waves, etc. come forth

source·book (-bo͝ok′) *n.* a collection of selections from documents giving fundamental information about a subject to be studied or written about; also, a diary, journal, etc. giving such information

sour·dough (sour′dō′) *n.* **1.** [Dial.] fermented dough saved from one baking to the next, for use as leaven **2.** a prospector in the western U.S. or Canada: so called from his using sourdough

sour grapes [from Aesop's fable in which the fox, after futile efforts to reach some grapes, scorns them as being sour] a scorning or belittling of something only because it cannot be had or done

sour gum a hardy tree of E N. America, having purplish fruits and foliage that turns flaming red in autumn

sour·puss (sour′po͝os′) *n.* [Slang] a gloomy or disagreeable person

Sou·sa (so͞o′zə, -sə), **John Philip** 1854–1932; U.S. bandmaster & composer of marches

souse (sous) *n.* [< OFr. < OHG. *sulza,* brine] **1.** a pickled food, esp. the feet, ears, and head of a pig **2.** liquid for pickling; brine **3.** a plunging into a liquid **4.** [Slang] a drunkard —*vt., vi.* **soused, sous′ing 1.** to pickle **2.** to plunge or steep in a liquid **3.** to make or become soaking wet **4.** [Slang] to make or become intoxicated

sou·tane (so͞o tan′, -tän′) *n.* [Fr. < It. *sottana*] *same as* CASSOCK

south (south) *n.* [OE. *suth*] **1.** the direction to the left of a person facing the sunset (180° on the compass, opposite north) **2.** a region or district in or toward this direction **3.** [*often* **S-**] the southern part of the earth, esp. the antarctic regions —*adj.* **1.** in, of, to, or toward the south **2.** from the south **3.** [**S-**] designating the southern part of a country, etc. —*adv.* in or toward the south —**the South** that part of the U.S. bounded on the north by Pennsylvania, the Ohio River, and N Missouri

South Africa country in southernmost Africa: 472,358 sq. mi.; pop. 21,525,000; caps. Cape Town, Pretoria —**South African**

South African Dutch 1. the Boers **2.** *same as* AFRIKAANS

South America S continent in the Western Hemisphere: c. 6,864,000 sq. mi.; pop. 190,000,000 —**South American**

South·amp·ton (sou thamp′tən) seaport in S England: pop. 210,000

South Australia state of SC Australia

South Bend [from its being at the southernmost bend in the St. Joseph River] city in N Ind.: pop. 110,000

south·bound (south′bound′) *adj.* going southward

South Carolina [see CAROLINA[1]] Southern State of the U.S., on the Atlantic: 31,055 sq. mi.; pop. 3,119,000; cap. Columbia: abbrev. **S.C., SC** —**South Carolinian**

South China Sea arm of the W Pacific, touching Taiwan, the Philippines, Borneo, & SE Asia

South Dakota [see DAKOTA[2]] Middle Western State of the U.S.: 77,047 sq. mi.; pop. 690,000; cap. Pierre: abbrev. **S.Dak., SD** —**South Dakotan**

south·east (south′ēst′; *nautical* sou-) *n.* **1.** the direction halfway between south and east; 45° east of due south **2.** a region or district in or toward this direction —*adj.* **1.** in, of, to, or toward the southeast **2.** from the southeast, as a wind —*adv.* in, toward, or from the southeast —**the Southeast** the southeastern part of the U.S.

south·east·er (south′ēs′tər; *nautical* sou-) *n.* a storm or strong wind from the southeast

south·east·er·ly (-tər lē) *adj., adv.* **1.** in or toward the southeast **2.** from the southeast

south·east·ern (-tərn) *adj.* **1.** in, of, or toward the southeast **2.** from the southeast **3.** [**S-**] of or characteristic of the Southeast —**South′east′ern·er** *n.*

south·east·ward (-ēst′wərd) *adv., adj.* toward the southeast: also **south′east′wards** *adv.* —*n.* a southeastward direction, point, or region

south·east·ward·ly (-wərd lē) *adj., adv.* **1.** toward the southeast **2.** from the southeast, as a wind

south·er (sou′*th*ər) *n.* a storm or wind from the south

south·er·ly (su*th*′ər lē) *adj., adv.* **1.** toward the south **2.** from the south

south·ern (su*th*′ərn) *adj.* **1.** in, of, or toward the south **2.** from the south **3.** [**S-**] of or characteristic of the South —**south′ern·most′** *adj.*

Southern Cross a small S constellation with four bright stars in the form of a cross

south·ern·er (su*th*′ər nər, -ə nər) ***n.*** a native or inhabitant of the south, specif. **[S-]** of the southern part of the U.S.

Southern Hemisphere that half of the earth south of the equator

southern lights *same as* AURORA AUSTRALIS

Southern Rhodesia *former name of* RHODESIA

Southern Yemen *former name of* YEMEN (sense 2)

Sou·they (su*th*′ē, sou′*th*ē), **Robert** 1774–1843; Eng. poet & writer

South·field (south′fēld′) city in SE Mich.: suburb of Detroit: pop. 76,000

South Gate [< *South Gate Gardens,* south of Los Angeles] city in SW Calif.: suburb of Los Angeles: pop. 67,000

South Island S island of the two main islands of New Zealand

south·land (south′land′, -lənd) ***n.*** [*also* **S-**] the southern region of a country —**south′land′er** ***n.***

south·paw (-pô′) ***n.*** [SOUTH + PAW: in the Chicago ballpark (c. 1885) the pitcher's left arm was toward the south] [Slang] a person who is left-handed; esp., a left-handed baseball pitcher —***adj.*** [Slang] left-handed

South Pole the southern end of the earth's axis

South Sea Islands islands in temperate or tropical parts of the South Pacific —**South Sea Islander**

South Seas **1.** the South Pacific **2.** all the seas located south of the equator

south-south·east (south′south′ēst′; *nautical* sou′sou-) ***n.*** the direction halfway between due south and southeast; 22°30′ east of due south —***adj., adv.*** **1.** in or toward this direction **2.** from this direction

south-south·west (-west′) ***n.*** the direction halfway between due south and southwest; 22°30′ west of due south —***adj., adv.*** **1.** in or toward this direction **2.** from this direction

south·ward (south′wərd; *nautical* su*th*′ərd) ***adv., adj.*** toward the south: also **south′wards** ***adv.*** —***n.*** a southward direction, point, or region

south·ward·ly (-lē) ***adj., adv.*** **1.** toward the south **2.** from the south

south·west (south′west′; *nautical* sou-) ***n.*** **1.** the direction halfway between south and west; 45° west of due south **2.** a district or region in or toward this direction —***adj.*** **1.** in, of, to, or toward the southwest **2.** from the southwest —***adv.*** in, toward, or from the southwest —**the Southwest** the southwestern part of the U.S., esp. Okla., Tex., N.Mex., Ariz., and S Calif.

South West Africa territory in S Africa, on the Atlantic, formerly held as a mandate by South Africa (mandate revoked by the UN, 1966) See NAMIBIA

south·west·er (south′wes′tər; *nautical* sou-) ***n.*** **1.** a storm or strong wind from the southwest **2.** a sailor's waterproof hat, having a broad brim in the back

SOUTHWESTER

south·west·er·ly (-tər lē) ***adj., adv.*** **1.** in or toward the southwest **2.** from the southwest

south·west·ern (-tərn) ***adj.*** **1.** in, of, or toward the southwest **2.** from the southwest **3.** **[S-]** of or characteristic of the Southwest —**South′west′ern·er** ***n.***

south·west·ward (-west′wərd) ***adv., adj.*** toward the southwest: also **south′west′wards** ***adv.*** —***n.*** a southwestward direction, point, or region

south·west·ward·ly (-lē) ***adj., adv.*** **1.** toward the southwest **2.** from the southwest, as a wind

sou·ve·nir (sōō′və nir′, sōō′və nir′) ***n.*** [Fr., orig. inf., to remember < L. *subvenire,* to come to mind] something kept as a reminder of a place, person, or occasion; keepsake; memento

sou′·west·er (sou wes′tər) ***n.*** *same as* SOUTHWESTER

sov·er·eign (säv′rən, -ər in; *occas.* suv′-) ***adj.*** [< OFr. *soverain,* ult. < L. *super,* above] **1.** above or superior to all others; greatest **2.** supreme in power, rank, etc. **3.** of or being a ruler; reigning **4.** independent of all others *[a sovereign state]* **5.** excellent **6.** very effectual, as a remedy —***n.*** **1.** a person having sovereign authority; specif., a monarch or ruler **2.** esp. formerly, a British gold coin valued at 20 shillings —**sov′er·eign·ly** ***adv.***

sov·er·eign·ty (-tē) ***n., pl.*** **-ties** **1.** a being sovereign **2.** the status, rule, power, etc. of a sovereign **3.** supreme and independent political authority **4.** a sovereign state

so·vi·et (sō′vē it, -et′; sō′vē et′) ***n.*** [Russ., lit., council] **1.** in the Soviet Union, any of various elected governing councils, ranging from village and town soviets to the Supreme Soviet of the whole country **2.** **[S-]** [*pl.*] the Soviet people or their officials —***adj.*** **1.** of a soviet or soviets **2.** **[S-]** of or connected with the Soviet Union —**so′vi·et·ism** ***n.***

so·vi·et·ize (sō′vē ə tīz′) ***vt.*** **-ized′, -iz′ing** [*often* **S-**] **1.** to change to a soviet form of government **2.** to make conform to the system, principles, etc. of the Soviets —**so′vi·et·i·za′tion** ***n.***

Soviet Union *same as* UNION OF SOVIET SOCIALIST REPUBLICS: also **Soviet Russia**

sow[1] (sou) ***n.*** [OE. *sugu*] **1.** an adult female pig or hog **2.** an adult female of certain other mammals, as the bear

sow[2] (sō) ***vt.*** **sowed, sown** (sōn) or **sowed, sow′ing** [OE. *sawan*] **1.** to scatter or plant (seed) for growing **2.** to plant (a field, etc.) with seed **3.** to spread or scatter; disseminate **4.** to plant in the mind —***vi.*** to sow seed —**sow′er** ***n.***

sow·bel·ly (sou′bel′ē) ***n.*** [Colloq.] *same as* SALT PORK

sow bug (sou) any of several small crustaceans with a flat, oval body, living in damp places, as under rocks

sox (säks) ***n.*** *alt. pl. of* SOCK[1] (sense 3)

soy (soi) ***n.*** [Jap., colloq. for *shōyu* < Chin. < *chiang,* salted bean + *yu,* oil] **1.** a dark, salty sauce made from fermented soybeans steeped in brine, used esp. with Chinese and Japanese dishes: also **soy sauce** **2.** the soybean plant or its seeds Also, chiefly Brit., **soy·a** (soi′ə)

soy·bean (soi′bēn′) ***n.*** **1.** a plant of the legume family, native to China and Japan but widely grown for forage and cover and for its seeds, rich in protein and oil **2.** its seed

SP, S.P. Shore Patrol

Sp. **1.** Spain **2.** Spaniard **3.** Spanish

sp. **1.** special **2.** *pl.* **spp.** species **3.** spelling

spa (spä) ***n.*** [< *Spa,* a health resort in Belgium] **1.** a spring of mineral water, or a place with such a spring **2.** a commercial establishment with sauna, whirlpool baths, exercise rooms, etc. **3.** a large whirlpool bath with ledges for seating several people

space (spās) ***n.*** [< OFr. < L. *spatium*] **1.** *a)* the continuous, boundless expanse extending in all directions or in three dimensions, within which all things exist *b) same as* OUTER SPACE **2.** *a)* the distance, expanse, or area between, over, or within things *b)* area or room for something *[parking space]* **3.** an interval or period of time **4.** reserved accommodations, as on a ship **5.** *Music* the open area between any two lines of a staff **6.** *Printing a)* a blank piece of type metal used to separate characters, etc. *b)* the area left vacant by this on a printed or typed line —***adj.*** of space —***vt.*** **spaced, spac′ing** to arrange with spaces between —**space′less** ***adj.*** —**spac′er** ***n.***

Space Age [*also* **s- a-**] the period, since 1957, in which artificial satellites and manned space vehicles have been launched —**space′-age′** ***adj.***

space bar a bar, as on a typewriter keyboard, pressed to leave a blank space or spaces between words, etc.

space·craft (spās′kraft′) ***n., pl.*** **-craft′** a spaceship or satellite for use in outer space

space·flight (-flīt′) ***n.*** a flight through outer space

space heater a small heating unit for a room or small area

space·man (-man′, -mən) ***n., pl.*** **-men′** (-men′, -mən) an astronaut or any of the crew of a spaceship

space·port (-pôrt′) ***n.*** a center where spacecraft are assembled, tested, and launched

space·ship (-ship′) ***n.*** a rocket-propelled vehicle for travel in outer space

space station (or **platform**) a structure designed to orbit in space as a launching pad or as an observation center

space·suit (-sōōt′) ***n.*** *same as* G-SUIT, esp. one modified for use in spaceflights

space-time (continuum) (-tīm′) a continuum having the three dimensions of space and that of time, in which any event can be located

space·walk (-wôk′) ***n.*** the act of an astronaut in moving about in space outside his spacecraft —***vi.*** to engage in a spacewalk —**space′walk′er** ***n.***

spa·cial (spā′shəl) ***adj.*** *alt. sp. of* SPATIAL

spac·ing (spā′siŋ) ***n.*** **1.** the arrangement of spaces **2.** space or spaces, as between printed words **3.** the act of a person or thing that spaces

spa·cious (spā′shəs) ***adj.*** **1.** having more than enough space or room; vast; extensive **2.** not confined or limited; large —**spa′cious·ly** ***adv.*** —**spa′cious·ness** ***n.***

Spack·le (spak′′l) [ult. < L. *spatula,* SPATULA] *a trademark for* a powdery substance (**spackling compound**) that is mixed with water and dries hard, to cover wall seams, nail holes, etc. —***n.*** **[s-]** this substance —***vt.*** **-led, -ling** **[s-]** to put spackle on

spade[1] (spād) ***n.*** [OE. *spadu*] a heavy, long-handled digging tool with a flat blade that is pressed into the ground with the foot —***vt., vi.*** **spad′ed, spad′ing** to dig or cut as with a spade —**call a spade a spade** to use plain, blunt words —**spade′ful** ***n.***

spade[2] (spād) ***n.*** [Sp. *espada,* sword (sign used on Spanish cards) < L. *spatha,* SPATULA] **1.** the black figure (♠) marking one of the four suits of playing cards **2.** [*pl.*] this suit **3.** a card of this suit —**in spades** [Colloq.] in an extreme or emphatic way

spade·work (spād′wurk′) ***n.*** work done to get a project started, esp. when tiresome or difficult

spa·dix (spā′diks) *n., pl.* **-dix·es, -di·ces′** (spā′də sēz′, spā dī′sēz) [ModL. < L., a palm branch < Gr. *spadix*] a fleshy spike of tiny flowers, usually enclosed in a spathe

spa·ghet·ti (spə get′ē) *n.* [It., dim. pl. of *spago,* small cord] long, thin strings of pasta, cooked by boiling or steaming and served with a sauce

Spain (spān) country in SW Europe, on the Iberian Peninsula: 194,346 sq. mi.; pop. 34,134,000; cap. Madrid

spake (spāk) *archaic pt. of* SPEAK

span[1] (span) *n.* [OE. *sponn*] **1.** a measure of length, equal to nine inches, based on the distance between the tips of the extended thumb and little finger **2.** *a*) the full amount or extent between any two limits *b*) the distance between ends or supports [the *span* of an arch] *c*) the full duration, as of attention **3.** a part between two supports [a bridge of four *spans*] **4.** *shortened form of* WINGSPAN **5.** [borrowed in U.S. < Du. *span,* in same sense] a team of two animals used together —*vt.* **spanned, span′ning 1.** to measure, esp. by the hand with the thumb and the little finger extended **2.** to encircle with the hand or hands, as in measuring **3.** to extend, reach, or pass over or across [a bridge *spans* the river]

span[2] (span) *archaic pt. of* SPIN

Span. 1. Spaniard **2.** Spanish

span·dex (span′deks) *n.* [< EXPAND] an elastic fiber, chiefly a polymer of polyurethane, used in girdles, etc.

span·drel (span′drəl) *n.* [< dim. of Anglo-Fr. *spaundre* < OFr. *espandre,* to expand] **1.** the space between the exterior curve of an arch and a rectangular frame enclosing it **2.** any of the spaces between a series of arches and a cornice above

spang (spaŋ) *adv.* [< dial. *spang,* to leap] [Colloq.] abruptly, directly, or exactly

span·gle (spaŋ′g'l) *n.* [< dim. of ME. *spang,* a clasp < OE.] **1.** a small piece of bright metal, esp. any of those sewn on fabric for decoration **2.** any small, glittering object —*vt.* **-gled, -gling** to cover with spangles —*vi.* to glitter as with spangles —**span′gly** *adj.* **-gli·er, -gli·est**

Span·iard (span′yərd) *n.* a native or inhabitant of Spain

span·iel (span′yəl) *n.* [< MFr. *espagnol,* lit., Spanish, ult. < L. *Hispania,* Spain] **1.** any of several breeds of dog with a silky coat, drooping ears, and short legs and tail **2.** a servile, fawning person

SPRINGER SPANIEL (18 in. high at shoulder)

Span·ish (span′ish) *adj.* of Spain, its people, their language, etc. —*n.* the Romance language of Spain and of Spanish America —**the Spanish** the people of Spain

Spanish America Mexico and those countries in Central and South America in which Spanish is the chief language

Span·ish-A·mer·i·can (-ə mer′ə kən) *adj.* **1.** of both Spain and America **2.** of Spanish America or its people —*n.* a native or inhabitant of Spanish America, esp. one of Spanish descent

Spanish-American War the war between the U.S. and Spain (1898)

Spanish Armada *see* ARMADA (sense 1 *b*)

Spanish Civil War the civil war in Spain (1936–39)

Spanish Inquisition the Inquisition as reorganized in Spain in 1478: notorious for its cruel and extreme practices

Spanish Main 1. orig., the coastal region of the Americas along the Caribbean Sea; esp., the N coast of S. America **2.** later, the Caribbean Sea itself, or that part of it adjacent to the N coast of S. America

Spanish moss a rootless epiphytic plant often growing in long, graceful strands from the branches of trees in the SE U.S. and tropical America

Spanish omelet an omelet folded around a sauce of chopped onion, green pepper, and tomato

Spanish rice boiled rice cooked with tomatoes and chopped onions, green peppers, etc.

spank (spaŋk) *vt.* [echoic] to strike with something flat, as the open hand, esp. on the buttocks, as in punishment —*vi.* to move along swiftly —*n.* a smack given in spanking

spank·er (spaŋ′kər) *n.* **1.** a person or thing that spanks **2.** [Colloq.] an unusually fine, large, etc. person or thing **3.** *Naut. a*) a fore-and-aft sail on the after mast of a square-rigged vessel *b*) the after mast and its sail on a schooner-rigged vessel of more than three masts

spank·ing (-kiŋ) *adj.* **1.** rapid **2.** brisk: said of a breeze **3.** [Colloq.] unusually fine, large, etc. —*adv.* [Colloq.] altogether; completely [*spanking* new] —*n.* a series of smacks given by one who spanks

span·ner (span′ər) *n.* **1.** one that spans **2.** *chiefly Brit. term for* WRENCH (tool for turning nuts, bolts, etc.)

Span·sule (span′so͞ol, -syo͞ol) [SPAN[1] + (CAP)SULE] *a trademark for* a long-acting medicinal capsule whose tiny beads of medicine dissolve at spaced intervals —*n.* [s-] such a capsule

Spar, SPAR (spär) *n.* [< *s(emper) par(atus),* (always prepared), L. motto of the Coast Guard] a woman member of the U.S. Coast Guard

spar[1] (spär) *n.* [< MDu. or MLowG. *spar*] any shiny, crystalline mineral that cleaves easily into chips or flakes —**spar′ry** *adj.* **-ri·er, -ri·est**

spar[2] (spär) *n.* [< ON. *sparri* or MDu. *sparre*] **1.** any pole, as a mast, yard, or boom, for supporting the sails on a ship **2.** a lengthwise support for the ribs of an airplane wing —*vt.* **sparred, spar′ring** to equip with spars

spar[3] (spär) *vi.* **sparred, spar′ring** [prob. < MFr. < It. *sparare,* to kick < *parare,* to parry] **1.** to fight with the feet and spurs: said of a fighting cock **2.** to box with jabbing or feinting movements, landing few heavy blows, as in practice matches **3.** to dispute; argue —*n.* a sparring match

spare (sper) *vt.* **spared, spar′ing** [OE. *sparian*] **1.** to treat with mercy; refrain from killing, hurting, etc. **2.** to save or free (a person) from (something) [*spare* me the trouble] **3.** to omit, avoid using, or use frugally [*spare* no effort] **4.** to part with or give up (money, time, etc.) without trouble to oneself —*vi.* **1.** to be frugal **2.** to show mercy —*adj.* **1.** not in regular use; extra [a *spare* room] **2.** not taken up by regular work or duties; free [*spare* time] **3.** meager; scanty [*spare* rations] **4.** not fleshy; lean —*n.* **1.** an extra part, thing, etc. **2.** *Bowling a*) a knocking down of all the pins in two consecutive rolls of the ball *b*) a score so made —**(something) to spare** a surplus of (something) —**spare′ly** *adv.* —**spare′ness** *n.* —**spar′er** *n.*

spare·ribs (sper′ribz′) *n.pl.* [altered (after SPARE, *adj.*) < MLowG. *ribbesper*] a cut of meat, esp. pork, consisting of the thin end of the ribs with most of the meat cut away

spar·ing (sper′iŋ) *adj.* **1.** that spares **2.** frugal **3.** scanty; meager —**spar′ing·ly** *adv.* —**spar′ing·ness** *n.*

spark[1] (spärk) *n.* [OE. *spearca*] **1.** a glowing bit of matter, esp. one thrown off by a fire **2.** any flash or sparkle of light like this **3.** a tiny beginning or vestige, as of life, interest, etc.; particle or trace **4.** liveliness; vivacity **5.** *Elec. a*) a very brief flash of light accompanying an electric discharge through air or some other insulating material *b*) such a discharge, as in a spark plug —*vi.* **1.** to make or throw off sparks **2.** to come forth as or like sparks —*vt.* to stir into action; be the force that enlivens —**spark′er** *n.*

spark[2] (spärk) *n.* [ON. *sparkr,* lively] **1.** a dashing, gallant young man **2.** a beau or lover —*vt., vi.* [Colloq.] to court, woo, pet, etc. An old-fashioned term

spark gap a space between two electrodes through which a spark discharge may take place

spar·kle (spär′k'l) *vi.* **-kled, -kling** [< ME. freq. of *sparken,* to SPARK[1]] **1.** to throw off sparks **2.** to shine with flashes of light; glitter, as jewels **3.** to be brilliant and lively **4.** to bubble or effervesce, as some wines —*vt.* to make sparkle —*n.* **1.** a spark, or glowing particle **2.** a sparkling, or glittering **3.** brilliance; liveliness

spar·kler (-klər) *n.* one that sparkles; specif., *a*) a pencil-shaped firework that burns with bright sparks *b*) [*pl.*] [Colloq.] bright, clear eyes *c*) [Colloq.] a diamond or similar gem

spark plug 1. a piece fitted into a cylinder of an internal-combustion engine to make sparks that ignite the fuel mixture within **2.** [Colloq.] a person or thing that inspires, activates, etc. —**spark′plug′** *vt.* **-plugged′, -plug′ging**

TERMINAL
INSULATOR
ELECTRODES
GAP

SPARK PLUG (cutaway model)

sparring partner any person with whom a prizefighter boxes for practice

spar·row (spar′ō) *n.* [OE. *spearwa*] **1.** any of several old-world weaverbirds, esp. of a genus including the ENGLISH SPARROW, now common in the U.S. **2.** any of many finches native to both the Old and New Worlds; esp., any of various American species, as the SONG SPARROW

sparrow hawk 1. a small European hawk with short wings **2.** a small American falcon

sparse (spärs) *adj.* [< L. pp. of *spargere,* to scatter] thinly spread or scattered; not dense —**sparse′ly** *adv.* —**sparse′ness, spar·si·ty** (spär′sə tē) *n.*

Spar·ta (spär′tə) city in the S Peloponnesus, Greece, a powerful military city in ancient Laconia

Spar·ta·cus (spär′tə kəs) ?–71 B.C.; Thracian slave & gladiator in Rome: leader of a slave revolt

Spar·tan (spär′t'n) ***adj.*** **1.** of ancient Sparta, its people, or their culture **2.** like or characteristic of the Spartans; brave, stoical, frugal, highly disciplined, strict, etc. —***n.*** **1.** a citizen of Sparta **2.** a person with Spartan traits —**Spar′tan·ism *n.***

spar varnish a durable varnish for outdoor surfaces

spasm (spaz'm) ***n.*** [< MFr. < L. < Gr. *spasmos* < *span*, to pull] **1.** a convulsive, involuntary contraction of a muscle or muscles **2.** any short, sudden burst of activity, feeling, etc.

spas·mod·ic (spaz mäd′ik) ***adj.*** [ModL. *spasmodicus* < Gr. < *spasmos:* see prec.] of, like, or characterized by a spasm or spasms; sudden, violent, and temporary; fitful; intermittent Also **spas·mod′i·cal** —**spas·mod′i·cal·ly *adv.***

spas·tic (spas′tik) ***adj.*** [< L. < Gr. *spastikos*, pulling < *span:* see SPASM] of, marked by, or having spasm or spastic paralysis —***n.*** a person with spastic paralysis —**spas′ti·cal·ly *adv.***

spastic paralysis a condition, as in cerebral palsy, in which certain muscles stay contracted and movements are more or less uncontrollable

spat[1] (spat) ***n.*** [prob. echoic] **1.** a quick, slapping sound **2.** [Colloq.] a brief, petty quarrel or dispute —***vi.* spat′ted, spat′ting** **1.** to strike with a spat **2.** [Colloq.] to have a spat, or quarrel

spat[2] (spat) ***n.*** [contr. < SPATTERDASH] a short gaiter for the instep and ankle

spat[3] (spat) *alt. pt. & pp. of* SPIT[2]

spat[4] (spat) ***n.*** [Anglo-Fr. < ?] **1.** the spawn of the oyster or other bivalve shellfish **2.** a young oyster or young oysters —***vi.* spat′ted, spat′ting** to spawn: said of oysters

spate (spāt) ***n.*** [ME. < ?] **1.** [Chiefly Brit.] a sudden flood or heavy rain **2.** a large outpour, as of words

spathe (spā*th*) ***n.*** [< ModL. < L. < Gr. *spathē*, flat blade] a large, leaflike part or pair of such parts enclosing a flower cluster (esp. a spadix)

spa·tial (spā′shəl) ***adj.*** [< L. *spatium*, space] **1.** of space **2.** happening or existing in space —**spa′ti·al′i·ty** (-shē al′ə tē) ***n.*** —**spa′tial·ly *adv.***

spat·ter (spat′ər) ***vt.*** [akin to Fris. freq. of *spatten*, to splash] **1.** to scatter in drops or small blobs **2.** to splash with these **3.** to defame —***vi.*** **1.** to be scattered in drops, etc., as fat in frying **2.** to fall or strike as in a shower, as raindrops or pellets —***n.*** **1.** *a)* a spattering *b)* its sound **2.** a mark made by spattering

spat·ter·dash (-dash′) ***n.*** [prec. + DASH] a long legging formerly worn to protect the stocking or trouser leg, as in wet weather

spat·u·la (spach′ə lə) ***n.*** [L., dim. of *spatha*, flat blade] a knifelike implement with a flat, flexible blade used for spreading or blending foods, paints, etc., for scraping, etc.

spav·in (spav′in) ***n.*** [MFr. *esparvain*] a disease of horses in which a deposit of bone (**bone spavin**) or an infusion of lymph (**bog spavin**) develops in the hock joint, usually causing lameness —**spav′ined *adj.***

spawn (spôn) ***vt., vi.*** [< Anglo-Fr. < OFr. *espandre*, to shed < L.: see EXPAND] **1.** to produce or deposit (eggs, sperm, or young) **2.** to bring into being (esp. something regarded with contempt and produced in great quantity) —***n.*** **1.** the mass of eggs or young produced by fishes, mollusks, amphibians, etc. **2.** something produced; specif., offspring or progeny: usually contemptuous

spay (spā) ***vt.*** [< Anglo-Fr. < OFr. < *espee*, sword < L. *spatha:* see SPATHE] to sterilize (a female animal) by removing the ovaries

S.P.C.A. Society for the Prevention of Cruelty to Animals

speak (spēk) ***vi.* spoke** or archaic **spake, spo′ken** or archaic **spoke, speak′ing** [OE. *specan*, earlier *sprecan*] **1.** to utter words with the ordinary voice; talk **2.** to express opinions, feelings, ideas, etc. by or as by talking **3.** to make a request or reservation (*for*): usually in the passive *[*a seat not yet *spoken* for*]* **4.** to make a speech; discourse **5.** to be a spokesman (*for*) **6.** to converse **7.** to give out sound —***vt.*** **1.** to make known by or as by speaking **2.** to use or be able to use (a given language) in speaking **3.** to utter (words) orally —**so to speak** that is to say —**speak for itself** to be self-evident —**speak out** (or **up**) **1.** to speak audibly or clearly **2.** to speak freely or forcefully —**speak well for** to indicate something favorable about —**to speak of** worthy of mention *[*no gains *to speak of]* —**speak′a·ble *adj.***

speak-eas·y (-ē′zē) ***n.,*** *pl.* **-eas′ies** [SPEAK + EASY: so named from the secretive atmosphere] [Slang] a place selling alcoholic drinks illegally, esp. during Prohibition

speak·er (spē′kər) ***n.*** **1.** a person who speaks or makes speeches **2.** a person who serves as presiding officer of a lawmaking body; specif., [S-] the presiding officer of the U.S. House of Representatives: in full, **Speaker of the House** **3.** a loudspeaker —**speak′er·ship′ *n.***

speak·ing (-kiŋ) ***adj.*** **1.** that speaks, or seems to speak; expressive; vivid **2.** in or for speech —***n.*** **1.** the act or art of one who speaks **2.** utterance; discourse

speaking in tongues *same as* GLOSSOLALIA

spear (spir) ***n.*** [OE. *spere*] **1.** a weapon with a long shaft and sharp head, for thrusting or throwing **2.** any spearlike, often forked implement, as one used in fishing **3.** [var. of SPIRE] a long blade or shoot, as of grass —***vt.*** **1.** to pierce or stab as with a spear **2.** to catch (fish, etc.) as with a spear —***vi.*** **1.** to pierce like a spear **2.** to sprout into a long stem —**spear′er *n.***

spear·head (-hed′) ***n.*** **1.** the pointed head of a spear **2.** the person or persons leading an activity, esp. a military attack —***vt.*** to lead (an attack, etc.)

spear·man (-mən) ***n.,*** *pl.* **-men** a fighting man armed with a spear

spear·mint (-mint′) ***n.*** [from its flower spikes] a fragrant plant of the mint family, used for flavoring

spec. **1.** special **2.** specification **3.** speculation

spe·cial (spesh′əl) ***adj.*** [< OFr. < L. < *species*, kind] **1.** different, distinctive, or unique **2.** exceptional; extraordinary **3.** highly regarded *[*a *special* friend*]* **4.** of or for a particular occasion, purpose, etc. *[*a *special* edition*]* **5.** not general or regular; specific *[special* legislation*]* —***n.*** something special, as a featured item on a menu or in a sale, or a special TV program not part of a regular series —**spe′cial·ly *adv.***

special delivery delivery of mail by special postal messenger, for an extra fee

spe·cial·ist (-ist) ***n.*** **1.** a person who specializes in a particular branch of study, professional work, etc. **2.** *U.S. Army* any of six grades above private first class for enlisted personnel with technical duties —***adj.*** of a specialist: also **spe′cial·is′tic** —**spe′cial·ism *n.***

spe·ci·al·i·ty (spesh′ē al′ə tē) ***n.,*** *pl.* **-ties** *chiefly Brit. var. of* SPECIALTY

spe·cial·ize (spesh′ə līz′) ***vt.*** **-ized′, -iz′ing** **1.** to make special or specific **2.** to direct toward a specific end **3.** *Biol.* to adapt (parts or organs) to a special condition, use, etc. —***vi.*** **1.** to make a specialty of something; specif., to take up a special study or work in a special branch of a profession **2.** *Biol.* to become specialized —**spe′cial·i·za′tion *n.***

spe·cial·ty (-əl tē) ***n.,*** *pl.* **-ties** **1.** a special quality, feature, etc. **2.** a special field of study, branch of a profession, etc. **3.** the state of being special **4.** a product, line of products, etc. given special attention and care to make it attractive, superior, etc. *[*a bakery whose *specialty* is pie*]*

spe·ci·a·tion (spē′shē ā′shən, -sē-) ***n.*** *Biol.* the process of developing new species through evolution —**spe′ci·ate′** (-āt′) ***vi.*** **-at′ed, -at′ing**

spe·cie (spē′shē, -sē) ***n.*** [abl. of L. *species*, kind: cf. use in phr. below] coin, as distinguished from paper money —**in specie** **1.** in kind **2.** in coin

spe·cies (-shēz, -sēz) ***n.,*** *pl.* **-cies** [L., appearance, shape, kind, etc.] **1.** a distinctive kind; sort; variety; class **2.** *Biol.* a group of highly similar plants or animals that is part of a genus and that can reproduce fertile offspring only among themselves **3.** *Logic* a class of things with distinctive common attributes, grouped with similar classes in a genus **4.** *R.C.Ch.* *a)* the outward form of the consecrated Eucharistic bread and wine *b)* the bread or wine —**the species** the human race

specif. specifically

spe·cif·ic (spi sif′ik) ***adj.*** [LL. *specificus* < L. *species* (see SPECIES) + *-ficus*, -FIC] **1.** specifying or specified; precise; definite; explicit **2.** of or forming a species **3.** peculiar to or characteristic of something *[specific* traits*]* **4.** of a particular sort **5.** *Med.* *a)* specially indicated as a cure for a particular disease *[*a *specific* remedy*]* *b)* produced by a particular microorganism *[*a *specific* disease*]* **6.** *Physics* designating a constant characteristic in relation to a fixed standard —***n.*** **1.** something specially suited for a given use or purpose **2.** a specific cure or remedy **3.** a distinct item or detail; particular —**spe·cif′i·cal·ly *adv.*** —**spec·i·fic·i·ty** (spes′ə fis′ə tē) ***n.***

spec·i·fi·ca·tion (spes′ə fi kā′shən) ***n.*** **1.** a specifying; detailed mention **2.** [*usually pl.*] a statement of particulars as to size, materials, etc. *[specifications* for a new building*]* **3.** something specified; specified item, etc.

specific gravity the ratio of the weight or mass of a given volume of a substance to that of an equal volume of another substance (water for liquids and solids, air or hydrogen for gases) used as a standard

spec·i·fy (spes′ə fī′) ***vt.*** **-fied′, -fy′ing** [< OFr. < LL. < *specificus*, SPECIFIC] **1.** to mention or describe in detail; state definitely or explicitly **2.** to include as an item in a set of specifications —**spec′i·fi′a·ble *adj.*** —**spec′i·fi′er *n.***

spec·i·men (spes′ə mən) ***n.*** [L. < *specere*, to see] **1.** a part of a whole, or one individual of a group, used as a sample of the rest **2.** [Colloq.] a (specified kind of) individual or person *[*an odd *specimen]* **3.** *Med.* a sample, as of urine, for analysis

spe·cious (spē′shəs) ***adj.*** [< L. *speciosus* < *species*, appearance] seeming good, sound, etc., but not really so [*specious* logic] —**spe′cious·ly** ***adv.*** —**spe′cious·ness** ***n.***
speck (spek) ***n.*** [OE. *specca*] **1.** a small spot or mark **2.** a tiny bit; particle —***vt.*** to mark with specks
speck·le (spek′'l) ***n.*** [dim. of ME. *specke*, SPECK] a small mark of contrasting color; speck —***vt.*** **-led, -ling** to mark with speckles
specs (speks) ***n.pl.*** [Colloq.] **1.** eyeglasses **2.** specifications: see SPECIFICATION (sense 2)
spec·ta·cle (spek′tə k'l) ***n.*** [< OFr. < L. < *spectare*, freq. of *specere*, to see] **1.** something to look at, esp. a remarkable sight **2.** a public show on a grand scale **3.** [*pl.*] eyeglasses: old-fashioned term —**spec′ta·cled** ***adj.***
spec·tac·u·lar (spek tak′yə lər) ***adj.*** of or like a spectacle; strikingly grand or unusual —**spec·tac′u·lar·ly** ***adv.***
spec·ta·tor (spek′tāt ər, spek tāt′-) ***n.*** [L. < pp. of *spectare*, to behold] a person who watches something without taking part; onlooker [*spectators* at sports events]
spec·ter (spek′tər) ***n.*** [< Fr. < L. *spectrum*, appearance, apparition < *spectare*, to behold] **1.** a ghost; apparition **2.** any object of dread Also, Brit. sp., **spec′tre**
spec·tra (spek′trə) ***n.*** *alt. pl. of* SPECTRUM
spec·tral (-trəl) ***adj.*** **1.** of or like a specter; ghostly **2.** of a spectrum —**spec·tral′i·ty** (-tral′ə tē), **spec′tral·ness** ***n.*** —**spec′tral·ly** ***adv.***
spec·tro- [< SPECTRUM] *a combining form meaning:* **1.** of radiant energy as shown in a spectrum **2.** of or by a spectroscope
spec·tro·gram (spek′trə gram′) ***n.*** a photograph of a spectrum
spec·tro·graph (-graf′) ***n.*** an instrument for breaking up light into a spectrum and photographing the spectrum —**spec′tro·graph′ic** ***adj.*** —**spec′tro·graph′i·cal·ly** ***adv.***
spec·trom·e·ter (spek träm′ə tər) ***n.*** an instrument for measuring spectral wavelengths —**spec′tro·met′ric** (-trə met′rik) ***adj.*** —**spec·trom′e·try** (-ə trē) ***n.***
spec·tro·scope (spek′trə skōp′) ***n.*** an optical instrument for breaking up light from any source into a spectrum so that it can be studied —**spec′tro·scop′ic** (-skäp′ik) ***adj.*** —**spec′tro·scop′i·cal·ly** ***adv.***
spec·tros·co·py (spek träs′kə pē) ***n.*** the study of spectra by use of the spectroscope —**spec·tros′co·pist** ***n.***
spec·trum (spek′trəm) ***n.***, *pl.* **-tra** (-trə), **-trums** [ModL., special use of L. *spectrum*: see SPECTER] **1.** the series of colored bands into which white light is broken up by passing through a prism, etc.: it is arranged according to wavelength, from red, the longest wave visible, to violet, the shortest **2.** any like series of bands or lines formed from other kinds of radiant energy **3.** a range or extent, as of opinion **4.** *same as* RADIO SPECTRUM

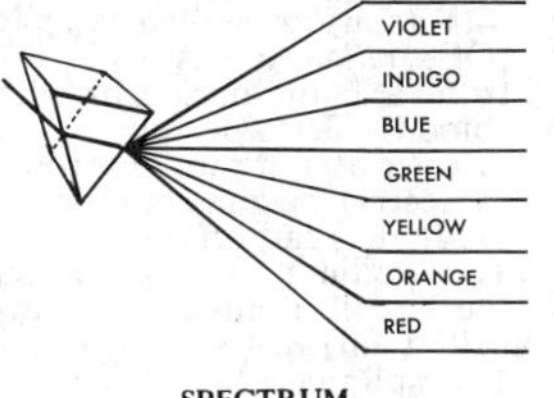

SPECTRUM

spec·u·late (spek′yə lāt′) ***vi.*** **-lat′ed, -lat′ing** [< L. pp. of *speculari*, to view < *specula*, watch tower < *specere*, to see] **1.** to think about the various aspects of a subject; ponder; esp., to conjecture **2.** to buy or sell stocks, land, etc., hoping to gain from price changes; also, to engage in any risky venture for possible huge profits —**spec′u·la′tion** ***n.*** —**spec′u·la′tive** (-lāt′iv, -lə tiv) ***adj.*** —**spec′u·la′tive·ly** ***adv.*** —**spec′u·la′tor** ***n.***
spec·u·lum (spek′yə ləm) ***n.***, *pl.* **-la** (-lə), **-lums** [L. < *specere*, to look] **1.** a mirror, esp. one of polished metal used as a reflector in a telescope, etc. **2.** *Med.* an instrument used to dilate a passage for easier examination —**spec′u·lar** (-lər) ***adj.*** —**spec′u·lar·ly** ***adv.***
sped (sped) *alt. pt. & pp. of* SPEED
speech (spēch) ***n.*** [OE. *spæc*, *spræc* < base of *sprecan*, to speak] **1.** the act of speaking **2.** the power or ability to speak **3.** the manner of speaking **4.** what is spoken; utterance, talk, etc. **5.** a talk given to an audience **6.** the language or dialect used by a certain group of people **7.** the study of the theory and practice of speaking
speech·i·fy (spē′chə fī′) ***vi.*** **-fied′, -fy′ing** to make a speech: used humorously or contemptuously —**speech′i·fi′er** ***n.***
speech·less (spēch′lis) ***adj.*** **1.** not able to speak **2.** silent, as from shock **3.** not expressed or expressible in words —**speech′less·ly** ***adv.*** —**speech′less·ness** ***n.***
speed (spēd) ***n.*** [OE. *spæd*, success] **1.** the act or state of moving rapidly; swiftness **2.** *a*) the rate of movement; velocity *b*) the rate or rapidity of any action [reading *speed*] **3.** an arrangement of gears for the drive of an engine **4.** [Colloq.] one's kind or level of taste, ability, etc. **5.** [Slang] any of various amphetamine compounds **6.** [Archaic] luck; success —***adj.*** of speed —***vi.*** **sped** or **speed′ed, speed′ing** **1.** to go fast, esp. at a speed greater than the legal limit **2.** [Archaic] *a*) to get along; fare *b*) to prosper —***vt.*** **1.** to help succeed; aid **2.** to wish Godspeed to **3.** to cause to go, move, etc. swiftly —**speed up** to go or make go faster —**speed′er** ***n.***
speed·boat (-bōt′) ***n.*** a motorboat built for speed
speed·om·e·ter (spi däm′ə tər) ***n.*** [< SPEED + -METER] a device attached to a motor vehicle, etc. to indicate speed, as in miles per hour
speed·ster (spēd′stər) ***n.*** a person or thing that speeds
speed·up (-up′) ***n.*** an increase in speed; esp., an increase in the rate of output, etc., as required by an employer
speed·way (-wā′) ***n.*** **1.** a track for racing cars or motorcycles **2.** a road for high-speed traffic
speed·well (-wel′) ***n.*** any of various plants of the figwort family, with spikes of white or bluish flowers
speed·y (spēd′ē) ***adj.*** **speed′i·er, speed′i·est** **1.** rapid; swift **2.** without delay; quick; prompt [a *speedy* reply] —**speed′i·ly** ***adv.*** —**speed′i·ness** ***n.***
spe·le·ol·o·gy (spē′lē äl′ə jē) ***n.*** [< L. < Gr. *spēlaion*, a cave + -LOGY] the scientific study and exploration of caves —**spe′le·ol′o·gist** ***n.***
spell¹ (spel) ***n.*** [OE., a saying] **1.** a word or formula supposed to have some magic power **2.** magical power or irresistible influence; charm; fascination —**cast a spell on** to enchant —**under a spell** enchanted
spell² (spel) ***vt.*** **spelled** or **spelt, spell′ing** [< OFr. *espeller*, to explain < Frank. *spellōn*] **1.** to name, write, or signal, esp. correctly, the letters of (a word, etc.) **2.** to make up, or form (a word, etc.): said of specified letters **3.** to mean [red *spells* danger] —***vi.*** to spell words, etc. —**spell out** **1.** to read letter by letter or with difficulty **2.** to discern as if by close reading **3.** to explain in detail
spell³ (spel) ***vt.*** **spelled, spell′ing** [OE. *spelian*] [Colloq.] to work in place of (another) while he rests; relieve —***n.*** **1.** a turn of working in place of another **2.** any period of work, duty, etc. **3.** a period (*of* being in some state) [a *spell* of gloom] **4.** a period of specified weather [a cold *spell*] **5.** [Colloq.] a period of time that is indefinite, short, etc. **6.** [Colloq.] a period of some illness **7.** [Dial.] a short distance
spell·bind (spel′bīnd′) ***vt.*** **-bound′, -bind′ing** to hold or affect as by a spell; fascinate; enchant —**spell′bind′er** ***n.***
spell·down (-doun′) ***n.*** a spelling contest in which each contestant who misspells a word must drop out: also **spelling bee**
spell·er (-ər) ***n.*** **1.** a person who spells words [a good *speller*] **2.** an exercise book used to teach spelling
spell·ing (-iŋ) ***n.*** **1.** the act of one who spells words **2.** the way a word is spelled
spelt¹ (spelt) *alt. pt. & pp. of* SPELL²
spelt² (spelt) ***n.*** [OE. < LL. *spelta*] a species of wheat with grains that do not thresh free of chaff
spe·lunk·er (spi luŋ′kər) ***n.*** [< obs. *spelunk*, a cave (ult. < Gr. *spēlynx*) + -ER] a person who explores caves as a hobby —**spe·lunk′ing** ***n.***
Spen·cer (spen′sər), **Herbert** 1820–1903; Eng. philosopher —**Spen·ce′ri·an** (-sir′ē ən) ***adj.***, ***n.***
spend (spend) ***vt.*** **spent, spend′ing** [< OE. *spendan* (in comp.) < ML. < L. *expendere*, to expend] **1.** to use up, exhaust, etc. [his fury was *spent*] **2.** to pay out (money) **3.** to give or devote (time, effort, etc.) to something **4.** to pass (time) [*spending* hours alone] **5.** to waste; squander —***vi.*** to pay out or use up money, etc. —**spend′a·ble** ***adj.*** —**spend′er** ***n.***
spend·thrift (-thrift′) ***n.*** a person who spends money carelessly; squanderer —***adj.*** wasteful; extravagant
Spen·ser (spen′sər), **Edmund** 1552?–99; Eng. poet —**Spen·se′ri·an** (-sir′ē ən) ***adj.***, ***n.***
spent (spent) *pt. & pp. of* SPEND —***adj.*** **1.** tired out; physically exhausted **2.** used up; worn out
sperm¹ (spurm) ***n.*** [< MFr. < LL. < Gr. *sperma*, seed < *speirein*, to sow] **1.** the fluid from the male reproductive organs; semen **2.** *same as* SPERMATOZOON
sperm² (spurm) ***n.*** *shortened form of:* **1.** SPERMACETI **2.** SPERM OIL **3.** SPERM WHALE
-sperm (spurm) [see SPERM¹] *a combining form meaning* seed [*gymnosperm*]
sper·ma·ce·ti (spur′mə set′ē, -sēt′ē) ***n.*** [ML. < LL. *sperma*, SPERM¹ + L. *ceti*, gen. of *cetus*, a whale] a white, waxlike substance from oil in the head of a sperm whale or dolphin, used in making cosmetics, ointments, candles, etc.
-sper·mal (spur′m'l) *same as* -SPERMOUS
sper·mat·ic (spər mat′ik) ***adj.*** of, like, or having to do with sperm or sperm cells

sper·mat·o- [< Gr. *sperma* (gen. *spermatos*), SPERM[1]] *a combining form meaning* seed or sperm

sper·mat·o·phyte (spər mat′ə fīt′, spʉr′mə tə-) ***n.*** [SPERMATO- + -PHYTE] any seed-bearing plant —**sper·mat′o·phyt′ic** (-fit′ik) ***adj.***

sper·mat·o·zo·on (spər mat′ə zō′än, -ən; spʉr′mə tə-) ***n., pl.*** **-zo′a** (-ə) [ModL. < SPERMATO- + Gr. *zōion*, animal] the male germ cell, found in semen: it penetrates and fertilizes the egg of the female —**sper·mat′o·zo′al, sper·mat′o·zo′an, sper·mat′o·zo′ic** ***adj.***

sperm oil a lubricating oil from the sperm whale

-sper·mous (spʉr′məs) *a combining form meaning* having (a specified number or kind of) seed

sperm whale a large, toothed whale of warm seas: a closed cavity in its roughly square head contains sperm oil

spew (spyōō) ***vt., vi.*** [OE. *spiwan*] **1.** to throw up from or as from the stomach; vomit **2.** to flow or gush forth —***n.*** something spewed —**spew′er** ***n.***

sp. gr. specific gravity

sphag·num (sfag′nəm) ***n.*** [ModL. < Gr. *sphagnos*, kind of moss] **1.** a spongelike moss found in bogs **2.** a mass of such mosses, used to improve soil, to pot plants, etc. —**sphag′nous** (-nəs) ***adj.***

sphal·er·ite (sfal′ə rīt′) ***n.*** [< G. < Gr. *sphaleros*, deceptive] native zinc sulfide, ZnS, the principal ore of zinc, usually brownish with a resinous luster

sphe·noid (sfē′noid) ***adj.*** [< ModL. < Gr. < *sphēn*, a wedge + -OID] *Anat.* designating or of the wedge-shaped compound bone at the base of the skull: also **sphe·noi′dal** —***n.*** the sphenoid bone

sphere (sfir) ***n.*** [< OFr. < L. < Gr. *sphaira*] **1.** any round body with a surface equally distant from the center at all points; globe; ball **2.** a star or planet **3.** the visible heavens; sky **4.** *short for* CELESTIAL SPHERE **5.** any of a series of transparent shells that ancient astronomers imagined as revolving one within another around the earth and containing the stars, planets, sun, and moon **6.** the place or range of action, knowledge, etc.; compass **7.** place in society —***vt.*** **sphered, spher′ing** [Chiefly Poet.] **1.** to put in or as in a sphere **2.** to put among the heavenly spheres **3.** to form into a sphere

-sphere (sfir) *a combining form meaning:* **1.** of or like a sphere *[hydrosphere]* **2.** of any of the layers of gas around the earth *[ionosphere]*

spher·i·cal (sfer′i k′l, sfir′-) ***adj.*** **1.** shaped like a sphere; globular **2.** of a sphere or spheres Also **spher′ic** —**spher′i·cal·ly** ***adv.*** —**sphe·ric·i·ty** (sfi ris′ə tē) ***n.***

sphe·roid (sfir′oid) ***n.*** a body that is almost but not quite a sphere —***adj.*** of this shape: also **sphe·roi′dal**

sphinc·ter (sfiŋk′tər) ***n.*** [LL. < Gr. *sphinktēr* < *sphingein*, to draw close] *Anat.* a ring-shaped muscle that surrounds a natural opening in the body and can open or close it by expanding or contracting —**sphinc′ter·al** ***adj.***

sphinx (sfiŋks) ***n., pl.*** **sphinx′es, sphin′ges** (sfin′jēz) [L. < Gr. *sphinx*, lit., the strangler] **1.** any ancient Egyptian statue having a lion's body and the head of a man, ram, or hawk; specif., [S-] a huge statue of this kind with a man's head, near Cairo, Egypt **2.** *a)* *Gr. Myth.* a winged monster with a lion's body and a woman's head and breasts; specif., [S-] such a monster at Thebes, who strangled passers-by unable to solve its riddle *b)* a person who is hard to know or understand

sphyg·mo·ma·nom·e·ter (sfig′mō mə näm′ə tər) ***n.*** [< Gr. *sphygmos*, the pulse + MANOMETER] a manometer with an attached inflatable band wrapped around an upper arm to compress the artery, used to measure blood pressure

spi·cate (spī′kāt) ***adj.*** [L. *spicatus*, spiked] *Bot., Zool.* formed or arranged like a spike or spikes

spice (spīs) ***n.*** [OFr. *espice* < L. *species*, sort] **1.** *a)* any of several vegetable substances, as clove, cinnamon, pepper, etc., used to season food *b)* such substances collectively **2.** a spicy aroma **3.** that which adds zest or interest —***vt.*** **spiced, spic′ing** **1.** to season or flavor with spice **2.** to add zest or interest to

spice·bush (-boosh′) ***n.*** an aromatic E N. American plant with small, yellowish flowers and red fruit

Spice Islands *former name of the* MOLUCCAS

spick-and-span (spik′'n span′) ***adj.*** [< *spick*, var. of SPIKE[1] + *span-new* < ON. < *spānn*, a chip + *nȳr*, new] **1.** new or fresh **2.** neat and clean

spic·ule (spik′yōōl) ***n.*** [< ModL. < ML. < L. dim. of *spica*, a point] **1.** *Bot.* a small spike **2.** *Zool.* a small, hard, needlelike piece or process, as in the skeleton of a sponge: also **spic′u·lum** (-yə ləm), *pl.* **-la** (-lə) —**spic′u·late′** (-yə lāt′), **spic′u·lar** (-lər) ***adj.***

spic·y (spī′sē) ***adj.*** **spic′i·er, spic′i·est** **1.** containing or full of spices **2.** having the flavor or aroma of spice **3.** lively, interesting, etc. **4.** risqué; racy —**spic′i·ly** ***adv.*** —**spic′i·ness** ***n.***

spi·der (spī′dər) ***n.*** [ME. *spithre*, ult. < OE. *spinnan*, to spin] **1.** any of various small arachnids with a body in two parts, the front part bearing the legs and the back part having organs that spin threads for making nests, cocoons, or webs **2.** a cast-iron frying pan, orig. one with legs **3.** any of various devices with leglike extensions —**spi′der·y** ***adj.***

spider monkey a monkey of South and Central America with long, spidery limbs and a long tail

spi·der·wort (-wʉrt′) ***n.*** any of various fleshy perennial plants with grasslike leaves and showy purplish, white, or pink flowers

spiel (spēl) ***n.*** [G., play] [Slang] a talk or harangue, as in selling —***vi.*** [Slang] to give a spiel —**spiel off** [Slang] to recite as by rote —**spiel′er** ***n.***

spi·er (spī′ər) ***n.*** a person who spies

spiff (spif) ***vt.*** [see ff.] [Slang] to make spiffy; spruce (*up*)

spiff·y (-ē) ***adj.*** **spiff′i·er, spiff′i·est** [< dial. *spiff*, well-dressed person] [Slang] spruce, smart, or dapper

spig·ot (spig′ət, spik′-) ***n.*** [ME. *spigote*] **1.** a plug or peg used to stop the vent in a barrel, etc. **2.** a faucet

spike[1] (spīk) ***n.*** [< ON. *spīkr* or < MDu. & MLowG. *spīker*] **1.** a long, heavy nail **2.** a sharp-pointed projection, as along the top of an iron fence **3.** *a)* any of the pointed metal projections on the bottoms of shoes used in baseball, golf, etc. *b)* [*pl.*] a pair of such shoes *c)* a high, very thin heel on a woman's shoe: also **spike heel** —***vt.*** **spiked, spik′ing** **1.** to fasten or equip as with a spike or spikes **2.** to pierce, cut, etc. with, or impale on, a spike or spikes **3.** to thwart or block (a scheme, etc.) **4.** [Slang] to add alcoholic liquor to (a drink) —**spik′y** ***adj.***

spike[2] (spīk) ***n.*** [L. *spica*] **1.** an ear of grain **2.** a long flower cluster with flowers attached directly to the stalk —**spiked** ***adj.***

spike·let (-lit) ***n.*** a small spike, as in a flower cluster

spike·nard (-nərd, -närd) ***n.*** [< LL. < L. *spica*, ear of grain + *nardus*, NARD] **1.** a fragrant ointment used in ancient times **2.** the Asiatic plant from which it is made

spile (spīl) ***n.*** [MDu., a splinter] **1.** a plug or spigot, as for a barrel **2.** a tap driven into a maple tree to draw off sap **3.** a heavy stake driven into the ground as a support —***vt.*** **spiled, spil′ing** **1.** to furnish with spiles, or stakes **2.** to set a spile into (a tree, barrel, etc.) **3.** to plug (a hole) with a spile

SPIKES (left, plantain; right, common mullein)

spill[1] (spil) ***vt.*** **spilled** or **spilt, spill′ing** [OE. *spillan*, to destroy] **1.** to let or make fall or flow over from a container, esp. without intending to **2.** to shed (blood) **3.** to lessen the pressure of (wind) on (a sail) **4.** to scatter at random from a container **5.** [Colloq.] to let (a secret) become known **6.** [Colloq.] to make (a rider, load, etc.) fall off —***vi.*** to be spilled from a container —***n.*** **1.** a spilling **2.** what is spilled **3.** a spillway **4.** [Colloq.] a fall; tumble —**spill over** to overflow

spill[2] (spil) ***n.*** [prob. via dial. *spil* < ON. *spila*, a splinter] **1.** a splinter **2.** a thin roll of paper, thin stick, etc. set on fire to light a pipe, candle, etc. **3.** a paper cone

spill·way (spil′wā′) ***n.*** [SPILL[1] + WAY] a channel to carry off excess water, as around a dam

spin (spin) ***vt.*** **spun** or archaic **span, spun, spin′ning** [OE. *spinnan*] **1.** *a)* to draw out and twist fibers of (wool, cotton, etc.) into thread *b)* to make (thread, yarn, etc.) thus **2.** to make (a web, cocoon, etc.) from a viscous fluid extruded from the body as a thread: said of spiders, etc. **3.** to produce in a way that suggests spinning **4.** to draw *out* (a story, etc.) to great length **5.** to make whirl *[to spin a top]* **6.** to make (wheels of a vehicle) rotate without traction, as on ice **7.** to extract water from (clothes) in a washer by swift rotation —***vi.*** **1.** to spin thread, etc. **2.** to fish with a spinning reel **3.** to whirl **4.** to feel dizzy and seem to be spinning **5.** to go into a spin: said of an aircraft **6.** to move along swiftly and smoothly **7.** to rotate freely without traction —***n.*** **1.** the spinning or rotating of something **2.** a moving along swiftly and smoothly **3.** a ride in a motor vehicle **4.** the descent of an airplane nose first along a spiral path **5.** any sudden, steep downward movement —**spin off** **1.** to produce as a secondary development **2.** to get rid of

spin·ach (spin′ich, -ij) ***n.*** [< MFr. < OSp. *espinaca* < Ar. < Per. *aspanākh*] **1.** a plant of the goosefoot family, with large, dark-green, edible leaves **2.** the leaves

spi·nal (spī′n'l) ***adj.*** of the spine or spinal cord —***n.*** a spinal anesthetic —**spi′nal·ly** ***adv.***

spinal anesthesia anesthesia of the lower part of the body by injection of an anesthetic into the spinal cord, usually in the lumbar region —**spinal anesthetic**

spinal column the series of joined vertebrae forming the axial support for the skeleton; spine

spinal cord the thick cord of nerve tissue of the central nervous system, in the spinal column

spin·dle (spin′d'l) ***n.*** [< OE. *spinel* < *spinnan*, to spin] **1.** a slender rod or pin for twisting, winding, or holding the thread in spinning by hand, on a spinning wheel, or in a spinning machine **2.** something spindle-shaped, as a slender, decorative rod in some chair backs **3.** any rod, pin, or shaft that revolves or serves as an axis for a revolving part **4.** in a lathe, a shaftlike part that rotates (**live spindle**) or does not rotate (**dead spindle**) while holding the thing to be turned **5.** a metal spike on a base, to stick papers on for temporary filing: also **spindle file** **6.** *Naut.* a metal rod or pipe topped with a lantern, etc. and fastened to a rock, shoal, etc. to warn vessels —***adj.*** of or like a spindle —***vi.*** **-dled, -dling** to grow in or into a long, slender shape or stem —***vt.*** **1.** to form into a spindle **2.** to stick on a spindle (*n.* 5) for filing

spin·dle·legs (-legz′) ***n.pl.*** **1.** thin legs **2.** [*with sing. v.*] [Colloq.] a person with thin legs —**spin′dle-leg′ged** (-leg′id, -legd′) ***adj.***

spin·dly (spin′dlē) ***adj.*** **-dli·er, -dli·est** long or tall and very thin or slender: also **spin′dling** (-dliŋ)

spin·drift (spin′drift′) ***n.*** [< Scot. var. of *spoondrift* < *spoon*, to scud (< ?) + DRIFT] spray blown from a rough sea or surf

spine (spīn) ***n.*** [< OFr. < L. *spina*, a thorn] **1.** any of the short, sharp, woody projections on a cactus, etc. **2.** *a*) a sharp process of bone *b*) any of the sharp, stiff projections on certain animals, as a porcupine quill *c*) anything like either of these **3.** the spinal column; backbone **4.** anything suggesting a backbone, as *a*) the crest of a hill *b*) the narrow back part of a bound book

spi·nel (spi nel′, spin′'l) ***n.*** [< MFr. < It. dim. of *spina*, spine < L. (see prec.)] a hard, crystalline mineral found in various colors: a red variety (**ruby spinel**) is used as a gem

spine·less (spīn′lis) ***adj.*** **1.** having no backbone; invertebrate **2.** having a weak backbone **3.** lacking courage, willpower, etc. **4.** having no spines or thorns —**spine′less·ly** ***adv.*** —**spine′less·ness** ***n.***

spin·et (spin′it) ***n.*** [< MFr. < It. *spinetta*, prob. < *spina*, a thorn] **1.** an obsolete, small harpsichord **2.** a small upright piano or electronic organ

spin·na·ker (spin′ə kər) ***n.*** [said to be altered < *Sphinx*, name of a yacht that carried the sail] a large, triangular forward sail used on some racing yachts

spin·ner (spin′ər) ***n.*** a person or thing that spins; specif., a fishing lure having blades that revolve or flutter when drawn through the water; also, any of its blades

spin·ner·et (spin′ə ret′) ***n.*** [dim. of SPINNER] **1.** the organ used by spiders, caterpillars, etc. to spin their silky threads **2.** a device with tiny holes through which a solution is forced in making synthetic fibers

spin·ning (spin′iŋ) ***n.*** **1.** the act of making thread, etc. from fibers or filaments **2.** fishing done with a rod that has a fixed spool, a light line, and light lures —***adj.*** that spins or is used in spinning

spinning jenny an early spinning machine with several spindles, for spinning more than one thread at a time

spinning wheel a simple spinning machine with a single spindle driven by a large wheel

spin·off (spin′ôf′) ***n.*** **1.** distribution to a corporation's shareholders of stock held in a subsidiary corporation **2.** a secondary benefit, development, etc.

spi·nose (spī′nōs) ***adj.*** [< L. < *spina*, spine] full of or covered with spines: also **spi′nous** (-nəs) —**spi′nose·ly** ***adv.*** —**spi·nos′i·ty** (-näs′ə tē) ***n.***, *pl.* **-ties**

Spi·no·za (spi nō′zə), **Ba·ruch** (bə ro͞ok′) or **Benedict** 1632–77; Du. philosopher —**Spi·no′zism** (-ziz'm) ***n.***

spin·ster (spin′stər) ***n.*** [ME. < *spinnen*, to spin + -STER] **1.** a woman who spins thread or yarn **2.** an unmarried woman, esp. an older one; old maid —**spin′ster·hood′** ***n.*** —**spin′ster·ish** ***adj.***

spin·y (spī′nē) ***adj.*** **spin′i·er, spin′i·est** **1.** covered with spines or thorns **2.** full of difficulties; troublesome **3.** spine-shaped —**spin′i·ness** ***n.***

spiny anteater *same as* ECHIDNA

spin·y-finned (spī′nē find′) ***adj.*** having fins supported by pointed, stiff spines

spiny lobster a sea crustacean similar to the common lobster, but lacking large pincers and having a spiny shell

spi·ra·cle (spī′rə k'l, spir′ə-) ***n.*** [L. *spiraculum* < *spirare*, to breathe] *Zool.* an opening for breathing, as one of the tracheal openings of arthropods, or the blowhole of a whale

spi·ral (spī′rəl) ***adj.*** [< ML. < L. *spira*, a coil < Gr. *speira*] **1.** circling or coiling around a central point in a flat curve that constantly increases (or decreases) in size **2.** circling an axis in a curve of conical or cylindrical form; helical —***n.*** **1.** a spiral curve occurring in a single plane **2.** a spiral curve occurring in a series of planes; helix **3.** something having a spiral form **4.** a spiral path or flight **5.** a section of a spiral **6.** a continuous, widening decrease or increase [an inflationary *spiral*] —***vi.***, ***vt.*** **-raled** or **-ralled**, **-ral·ing** or **-ral·ling** to move in or form (into) a spiral —**spi′ral·ly** ***adv.***

spi·rant (spī′rənt) ***n.***, ***adj.*** [< L. prp. of *spirare*, to breathe] *same as* FRICATIVE

spire (spīr) ***n.*** [OE. *spir*] **1.** a sprout, spike, or stalk of a plant, blade of grass, etc. **2.** the top part of a pointed, tapering object or structure, as a mountain peak **3.** anything that tapers to a point, as a steeple —***vi.*** **spired, spir′ing** to extend upward, tapering to a point

spi·re·a (spī rē′ə) ***n.*** [< ModL. genus name < L. < Gr. *speira*, a coil] any of several plants of the rose family, with dense clusters of small, pink or white flowers: also sp. **spi·rae′a**

spi·ril·lum (spī ril′əm) ***n.***, *pl.* **-la** (-ə) [ModL., dim. of L. *spira* (see SPIRAL)] a bacterium having the form of a spiral thread and moving by means of flagella

spir·it (spir′it) ***n.*** [< OFr. < L. *spiritus*, breath < *spirare*, to breathe] **1.** the life principle or the soul, esp. in man, sometimes regarded as immortal **2.** the thinking, feeling part of man; mind; intelligence **3.** [*also* **S-**] life, will, thought, etc., regarded as separate from matter **4.** a supernatural being, as a ghost, angel, demon, fairy, etc. **5.** an individual person or personality [a brave *spirit*] **6.** [*usually pl.*] disposition; mood [high *spirits*] **7.** vivacity, courage, enthusiasm, etc. **8.** enthusiasm and loyalty [school *spirit*] **9.** real meaning; true intention [to follow the *spirit* if not the letter of the law] **10.** an essential quality or prevailing tendency [the *spirit* of the Renaissance] **11.** [*usually pl.*] distilled alcoholic liquor **12.** [*often pl.*] any liquid produced by distillation **13.** an alcoholic solution of a volatile substance [*spirits* of camphor] —***vt.*** **1.** to inspirit, encourage, cheer, etc. **2.** to carry (*away*, *off*, etc.) secretly and swiftly —***adj.*** **1.** of spirits or spiritualism **2.** operating by the burning of alcohol [a *spirit* lamp] —**out of spirits** sad; depressed —**the Spirit** *same as* HOLY SPIRIT —**spir′it·less** ***adj.*** —**spir′it·less·ly** ***adv.*** —**spir′it·less·ness** ***n.***

spir·it·ed (-id) ***adj.*** **1.** full of spirit; lively; vigorous; animated **2.** having a (specified) character, mood, or disposition [low-*spirited*] —**spir′it·ed·ly** ***adv.*** —**spir′it·ed·ness** ***n.***

spir·it·ism (-iz'm) ***n.*** *same as* SPIRITUALISM —**spir′it·ist** ***n.***, ***adj.*** —**spir′it·is′tic** ***adj.***

spirit level *same as* LEVEL (*n.* 1)

spir·it·ous (spir′i təs) ***adj.*** *same as* SPIRITUOUS

spirits of ammonia a 10% solution of ammonia in alcohol: also **spirit of ammonia**

spir·it·u·al (spir′i cho͞o wəl, -cho͞ol) ***adj.*** **1.** of the spirit or soul as distinguished from the body or material matters **2.** of or consisting of spirit; not corporeal **3.** refined in thought or feeling **4.** of religion or the church; sacred, devotional, etc. **5.** spiritualistic or supernatural —***n.*** **1.** a religious folk song of U.S. Negro origin **2.** [*pl.*] religious or church matters —**spir′it·u·al′i·ty** (-wal′ə tē), *pl.* **-ties**, **spir′it·u·al·ness** ***n.*** —**spir′it·u·al·ly** ***adv.***

spir·it·u·al·ism (-iz'm) ***n.*** **1.** the belief that the dead survive as spirits which can communicate with the living, esp. with the help of a medium **2.** the philosophical doctrine that all reality is in essence spiritual **3.** spiritual quality —**spir′it·u·al·ist** ***n.*** —**spir′it·u·al·is′tic** ***adj.***

spir·it·u·al·ize (spir′i cho͞o wə līz′, -cho͞o līz′) ***vt.*** **-ized′, -iz′ing** **1.** to make spiritual; remove worldliness from **2.** to give a spiritual sense or meaning to —**spir′it·u·al·i·za′tion** ***n.***

‡spi·ri·tu·el (spē rē tü el′; *E.* spir′i cho͞o wel′) ***adj.*** [Fr.] having or showing a refined nature or, esp., a quick, graceful wit or mind —**spi·ri·tu·elle′** ***adj. fem.***

spir·it·u·ous (spir′i cho͞o wəs) ***adj.*** of, like, or containing alcohol: said of distilled beverages —**spir′it·u·os′i·ty** (-wäs′ə tē) ***n.***

spi·ro- [< Gr. *speira*, a coil] *a combining form meaning* spiral or coil [*spirochete*]

spi·ro·chete (spī′rə kēt′) ***n.*** [< ModL. < Gr. *speira*, a spiral + *chaitē*, hair] any of various spiral-shaped bacteria, some of which cause disease: also sp. **spi′ro·chaete′**

spirt (spurt) ***n.***, ***vt.***, ***vi.*** *same as* SPURT

spir·y (spīr′ē) ***adj.*** **spir′i·er, spir′i·est** **1.** of, or having the form of, a spire **2.** having many spires

spit[1] (spit) ***n.*** [OE. *spitu*] **1.** a thin, pointed rod on which meat is impaled for broiling or roasting over a fire or other direct heat **2.** a narrow point of land, or a narrow reef or shoal, extending into a body of water —***vt.*** **spit′ted, spit′ting** to impale as on a spit —**spit′ter** ***n.***

spit[2] (spit) ***vt.*** **spit** or, esp. Brit., **spat, spit′ting** [OE. *spittan*] **1.** to eject from the mouth **2.** to throw (*out*), emit, or utter explosively [to *spit* out an oath] —***vi.*** **1.** to eject saliva from the mouth; expectorate **2.** to make an explosive hissing noise, as an angry cat **3.** to express contempt by spitting saliva (*on* or *at*) **4.** to sputter, as frying fat —***n.*** **1.** the act of spitting **2.** saliva **3.** a salivalike, frothy secretion of certain insects **4.** [Colloq.] the perfect likeness, as of a person: in **spit and image** (spit′'n im′ij) —**spit up** to bring up from the stomach or throat —**spit′ter** ***n.***

spit·ball (-bôl′) ***n.*** **1.** a piece of paper chewed up into a wad for throwing **2.** *Baseball* a pitch, now illegal, made to curve by moistening one side of the ball as with saliva

spite (spīt) ***n.*** [short for DESPITE] **1.** a mean or evil feeling toward another, along with a desire to hurt, humiliate, etc.; malice **2.** an instance of this; a grudge —***vt.*** **spit′ed, spit′ing** to show one's spite for by hurting, frustrating, etc. —**in spite of** regardless of —**spite′ful** ***adj.*** —**spite′ful·ly** ***adv.*** —**spite′ful·ness** ***n.***

spit·fire (spit′fīr′) ***n.*** a person, esp. a woman or girl, who is easily aroused to violent outbursts of temper

Spits·ber·gen (spits′bur′gən) group of Norw. islands in the Arctic Ocean, east of Greenland

spit·ting im·age (spit′'n im′ij) *alteration of* SPIT AND IMAGE: see SPIT[2]

spit·tle (spit′'l) ***n.*** [< OE. *spætl*, var. of *spatl*] saliva; spit

spit·toon (spi to͞on′) ***n.*** a container to spit into

spitz (spits) ***n.*** [G. < *spitz*, pointed] a small Pomeranian dog with pointed muzzle and ears and a long, silky coat

splash (splash) ***vt.*** [intens. extension of PLASH[2]] **1.** to cause (a liquid) to scatter and fall in drops **2.** to dash or scatter a liquid, mud, etc. on, so as to wet or soil **3.** to cause to splash a liquid [to *splash* the oars] **4.** to make (one's way) by splashing **5.** to mark as by splashing [*splashed* with sunlight] **6.** to display conspicuously [scandal was *splashed* on the front page] —***vi.*** **1.** to dash or scatter a liquid about **2.** to move, fall, strike, or scatter with a splash —***n.*** **1.** the act or sound of splashing **2.** a mass of splashed water, mud, etc. **3.** a spot or mark made as by splashing **4.** a patch of color, light, etc. —**make a splash** [Colloq.] to attract great, often brief, attention —**splash′er** ***n.*** —**splash′i·ness** ***n.*** —**splash′y** ***adj.***

splash·down (-doun′) ***n.*** the landing of a spacecraft on water

splat[1] (splat) ***n.*** [via dial. < base of SPLIT] a thin, flat piece of wood, esp. as used in the back of a chair

splat[2] (splat) ***n., interj.*** a splattering or wet, slapping sound

splat·ter (-ər) ***n., vt., vi.*** [< SPATTER] spatter or splash

splay (splā) ***vt., vi.*** [< ME. *displaien*, to display] **1.** to spread out or apart; extend (often with *out*) **2.** to slope —***n.*** **1.** a sloping surface or angle **2.** a spreading; expansion —***adj.*** **1.** sloping, spreading, or turning outward **2.** broad and flat **3.** awkward

splay·foot (-foot′) ***n., pl.*** **-feet′** **1.** a foot that is flat and turned outward **2.** the condition of having such feet —***adj.*** of or having splayfoot: also **splay′foot′ed**

spleen (splēn) ***n.*** [< OFr. < L. < Gr. *splēn*, spleen] **1.** a large, vascular, lymphatic organ in the upper left part of the abdomen: it modifies the blood structure and was formerly regarded as the seat of certain emotions **2.** malice; spite; bad temper —**spleen′ful, spleen′ish, spleen′y** ***adj.***

splen·did (splen′did) ***adj.*** [L. *splendidus* < *splendere*, to shine] **1.** having or showing splendor; specif., *a*) shining; brilliant *b*) magnificent; gorgeous **2.** worthy of high praise; grand; glorious; illustrious **3.** [Colloq.] very good; excellent —**splen′did·ly** ***adv.*** —**splen′did·ness** ***n.***

splen·dif·er·ous (splen dif′ər əs) ***adj.*** [Colloq.] gorgeous; splendid: used jokingly —**splen·dif′er·ous·ly** ***adv.*** —**splen·dif′er·ous·ness** ***n.***

splen·dor (splen′dər) ***n.*** [< OFr. < L. < *splendere*, to shine] **1.** great luster; brilliance **2.** magnificent richness or glory; pomp; grandeur Also, Brit. sp., **splen′dour** —**splen′dor·ous, splen′drous** ***adj.***

sple·net·ic (spli net′ik) ***adj.*** [LL. *spleneticus*] **1.** of the spleen **2.** irritable; peevish; spiteful Also **sple·net′i·cal** —***n.*** a spleenful person —**sple·net′i·cal·ly** ***adv.***

splen·ic (splen′ik, splēn′-) ***adj.*** [< L. < Gr. *splēnikos*] **1.** of or having to do with the spleen **2.** in or near the spleen

splice (splīs) ***vt.*** **spliced, splic′ing** [MDu. *splissen*] **1.** to join (ropes or rope ends) by weaving together the end strands **2.** to join the ends of (timbers) by overlapping and binding or bolting together **3.** to fasten the ends of (wire, motion-picture film, etc.) together, as by cementing, twisting, etc. **4.** [Slang] to join in marriage —***n.*** a joint or joining made by splicing —**splic′er** ***n.***

SHORT SPLICE

splint (splint) ***n.*** [MDu. or MLowG. *splinte*] **1.** a thin strip of wood or cane woven together with others to make baskets, chair seats, etc. **2.** a thin, rigid strip of wood, metal, etc. used to keep a broken bone in place or to keep a part of the body in a fixed position —***vt.*** to fit, support, or hold in place as with a splint or splints

splin·ter (splin′tər) ***vt., vi.*** [< MDu., akin to *splinte*, splint] **1.** to break or split into thin, sharp pieces **2.** to break into groups with opposing views —***n.*** **1.** a thin, sharp piece of wood, bone, etc., made by splitting or breaking **2.** a splinter group —***adj.*** designating a group that separates from a main party, church, etc. because of opposing views —**splin′ter·y** ***adj.***

split (split) ***vt.*** **split, split′ting** [MDu. *splitten*] **1.** to separate, cut, etc. along the grain or length into two or more parts **2.** to break or tear apart by force **3.** to divide into parts or shares **4.** to cast (one's vote) for candidates of more than one party **5.** to cause (a group, political party, etc.) to separate into factions **6.** *a*) to break (a molecule) into atoms or into smaller molecules *b*) to produce nuclear fission in (an atom) **7.** *Finance* to divide (stock) by substituting some multiple of the original shares —***vi.*** **1.** to separate lengthwise into two or more parts **2.** to break apart; burst **3.** to separate because of failure to agree (often with *up*) **4.** [Slang] to leave a place; depart —***n.*** **1.** the act or result of splitting; specif., *a*) a break; crack *b*) a division in a group, between persons, etc. **2.** a splinter **3.** a confection made of a split banana or other fruit with ice cream, sauces, nuts, etc. **4.** [*often pl.*] the feat of spreading the legs apart until they lie flat on the floor, the body remaining upright **5.** [Colloq.] a small bottle of wine, etc., usually about six ounces **6.** [Colloq.] a share, as of loot **7.** *Bowling* an arrangement of pins after the first bowl, so separated as to make a spare extremely difficult —***adj.*** **1.** separated along the length or grain **2.** divided; separated —**split off** to break off or separate as by splitting —**split′ter** ***n.***

split infinitive *Gram.* an infinitive with the verbal and the *to* separated by an adverb (Ex.: he decided *to gradually change* his style): despite objections to this construction, many writers use it to avoid ambiguity or wrong emphasis

split-lev·el (-lev′'l) ***adj.*** designating or of a type of house with floor levels so staggered that each level is about a half story above or below the adjacent one

split pea a green or yellow pea that has been shelled, dried, and split: used esp. for making soup

split personality *a popular name for* SCHIZOPHRENIA

split second a fraction of a second —**split′-sec′ond** ***adj.***

split shift a shift, or work period, separated into two parts by a period longer than the usual one for a meal or rest

split ticket a ballot cast for candidates of more than one party

split·ting (split′iŋ) ***adj.*** **1.** that splits **2.** *a*) aching severely: said of the head *b*) severe, as a headache

split-up (-up′) ***n.*** a breaking up or separating into two or more parts, units, groups, etc.

splotch (splăch) ***n.*** [prob. a fusion of SPOT & BLOTCH] a spot, splash, or stain, esp. one that is irregular —***vt., vi.*** to mark or be marked with splotches —**splotch′y** ***adj.***

splurge (splurj) ***n.*** [echoic] [Colloq.] **1.** any very showy display or effort **2.** a spell of extravagant spending —***vi.*** **splurged, splurg′ing** [Colloq.] **1.** to make a splurge **2.** to spend money extravagantly —**splurg′er** ***n.***

splut·ter (splut′ər) ***vi.*** [var. of SPUTTER] **1.** to make hissing or spitting sounds; sputter **2.** to speak hurriedly and confusedly, as when excited —***vt.*** **1.** to utter hurriedly and confusedly **2.** to spatter —***n.*** a spluttering sound or utterance —**splut′ter·er** ***n.*** —**splut′ter·y** ***adj.***

spoil (spoil) ***vt.*** **spoiled** or **spoilt, spoil′ing** [< MFr. < L. *spoliare* < *spolium*, plunder] **1.** to damage or injure so as to make useless, valueless, etc.; destroy **2.** to impair the enjoyment, quality, etc. of [rain *spoiled* the picnic] **3.** to let (a person) have his own way so much that he demands or expects it —***vi.*** to be damaged or injured so as to become useless, valueless, etc.; decay, as food —***n.*** **1.** [*usually pl.*] *a*) goods, territory, etc. taken by plunder; booty *b*) public offices to which the political party that wins has the power to appoint people **2.** an object of plunder; prey —**be spoiling for a fight,** etc. to be aggressively eager for a fight, etc. —**spoil′a·ble** ***adj.*** —**spoil′er** ***n.***

spoil·age (-ij) ***n.*** **1.** a spoiling or being spoiled **2.** something spoiled or the amount spoiled

spoils·man (spoilz′mən) ***n., pl.*** **-men** a person who aids a political party in order to share in the spoils

spoil·sport (spoil′spôrt′) ***n.*** a person who behaves in such a way as to ruin the pleasure of others

spoils system the practice of treating public offices as the booty of the political party that wins an election, to be distributed among party workers

Spo·kane (spō kan′) [< ? AmInd. *spokanee*, sun] city in E Wash.: pop. 171,000

spoke[1] (spōk) ***n.*** [OE. *spaca*] **1.** any of the braces extending from the hub to the rim of a wheel **2.** a ladder rung **3.** any of the handholds along the rim of a ship's steering wheel —***vt.*** **spoked, spok′ing** to equip with spokes

spoke[2] (spōk) *pt. & archaic pp. of* SPEAK

spo·ken (spō′k'n) *pp. of* SPEAK —***adj.*** **1.** uttered; oral **2.** characterized by a (specified) kind of voice [*soft-spoken*]

spoke·shave (spōk′shāv′) ***n.*** a planing tool consisting of a blade with a handle at either end, used for shaping rounded surfaces, as, formerly, spokes

spokes·man (spōks′mən) ***n.,*** *pl.* **-men** a person who speaks or gives information for another or for a group

spo·li·a·tion (spō′lē ā′shən) ***n.*** [L. *spoliatio*] **1.** robbery; plundering **2.** the act of spoiling or damaging —**spo′li·a′tive** ***adj.***

spon·dee (spän′dē) ***n.*** [< L. < Gr. < *spondē*, solemn libation (one accompanied by a solemn melody)] a metrical foot consisting of two long or heavily accented syllables —**spon·da′ic** (-dā′ik) ***adj.***

sponge (spunj) ***n.*** [OE. < L. < Gr. *spongia*] **1.** a plantlike sea animal having a porous structure and a tough, fibrous skeleton and growing fixed to surfaces under water **2.** the skeleton of such animals, light in weight and highly absorbent, used for washing surfaces, in bathing, etc. **3.** any substance like this; specif., *a*) a piece of spongy plastic, cellulose, etc. *b*) a pad of gauze or cotton, as used in surgery *c*) a light, porous pudding *d*) a raised bread dough **4.** [Colloq.] a person who lives upon others as a parasite —***vt.*** **sponged, spong′ing 1.** to use a sponge on so as to dampen, wipe clean, etc. **2.** to remove as with a damp sponge (with *out*, *off*, etc.) **3.** to absorb with or like a sponge (often with *up*) **4.** [Colloq.] to get as by begging, imposition, etc. —***vi.*** **1.** to gather sponges from the sea **2.** to take up liquid like a sponge **3.** [Colloq.] to be a parasite (often with *off* or *on*) —**throw** (or **toss,** etc.) **in the sponge** [Colloq.] to admit defeat; give up —**sponge′like′** ***adj.*** —**spong′er** ***n.*** —**spon′gi·ness** ***n.*** —**spon′gy** ***adj.***

sponge bath a bath taken by using a wet sponge or cloth without getting into water or under a shower

sponge·cake (-kāk′) ***n.*** a light cake of spongy texture made of flour, beaten eggs, sugar, etc., but no shortening: also **sponge cake**

sponge rubber rubber processed to have a spongelike texture denser than foam rubber: used for gaskets, etc.

spon·son (spän′sən) ***n.*** [altered < ? EXPANSION] **1.** a structure that projects over the side of a ship or boat, as a gun platform **2.** a winglike piece attached to the hull of a seaplane to give stability in the water

spon·sor (spän′sər) ***n.*** [L. < *spondere*, to promise solemnly] **1.** a person or agency that acts as endorser, proponent, adviser, surety, etc. for a person, group, or activity **2.** a godparent; person who answers for a child, as at baptism, making the promises prescribed **3.** a business firm or other agency that alone or with others pays for a radio or TV program on which it advertises or promotes something —***vt.*** to act as sponsor for —**spon·so′ri·al** (-sôr′ē əl) ***adj.*** —**spon′sor·ship′** ***n.***

spon·ta·ne·i·ty (spän′tə nē′ə tē, -nā′-) ***n.*** **1.** the state or quality of being spontaneous **2.** *pl.* **-ties** spontaneous behavior, movement, action, etc.

spon·ta·ne·ous (spän tā′nē əs) ***adj.*** [< LL. < L. *sponte*, of free will] **1.** moved by a natural feeling or impulse, without constraint, effort, or forethought **2.** acting by internal energy, force, etc. **3.** growing naturally; wild —**spon·ta′ne·ous·ly** ***adv.*** —**spon·ta′ne·ous·ness** ***n.***

spontaneous combustion the process of catching fire as a result of heat generated by internal chemical action

spontaneous generation the theory, now discredited, that living organisms can originate from nonliving matter

spoof (spo͞of) ***n.*** [coined c. 1889] [Slang] **1.** a hoax, joke, or deception **2.** a light parody or satire —***vt., vi.*** [Slang] **1.** to fool; deceive **2.** to satirize in a playful manner

spook (spo͞ok) ***n.*** [Du.] [Colloq.] **1.** a specter; ghost **2.** any person suggestive of a specter, as an eccentric, a secret agent, etc. —***vt., vi.*** [Colloq.] to startle or be startled, frightened, etc. —**spook′i·ly** ***adv.*** —**spook′i·ness** ***n.*** —**spook′y** ***adj.*** **spook′i·er, spook′i·est**

spool (spo͞ol) ***n.*** [< MFr. < MDu. *spoele*] **1.** a cylinder, often hollowed and with a rim at either end, upon which thread, wire, etc. is wound **2.** something like a spool —***vt.*** to wind on a spool

spoon (spo͞on) ***n.*** [OE. *spon*, a chip] **1.** a utensil consisting of a small, shallow bowl with a handle, used for eating or stirring food or drinks **2.** something shaped like a spoon, as a shiny, curved fishing lure, usually of metal —***vt.*** to take up as with a spoon —***vi.*** [Colloq.] to make love, as by kissing or caressing: an old-fashioned term

spoon·bill (-bil′) ***n.*** **1.** a wading bird with a broad, flat bill that is spoon-shaped at the tip **2.** any of various other birds with a bill like this

spoon·drift (-drift′) ***n.*** *early form of* SPINDRIFT

spoon·er·ism (spo͞on′ər iz′m) ***n.*** [after Rev. W. A. *Spooner* (1844–1930), of Oxford Univ.] an unintentional interchange of sounds in two or more words (Ex.: "a well-boiled icicle" for "a well-oiled bicycle")

spoon·feed (spo͞on′fēd′) ***vt.*** **-fed′, -feed′ing 1.** to feed with a spoon **2.** to pamper; coddle **3.** to treat, instruct, etc. so as to discourage independent thought and action

spoon·ful (-fo͝ol′) ***n.,*** *pl.* **-fuls′** as much as a spoon will hold

spoor (spo͝or, spôr) ***n.*** [Afrik. < MDu.] the track or trail of a wild animal hunted as game —***vt., vi.*** to hunt by following a spoor

Spo·ra·des (spôr′ə dēz′; *Gr.* spô rä′*th*es) the Gr. islands along the W coast of Turkey, esp. the Dodecanese

spo·rad·ic (spô rad′ik, spə-) ***adj.*** [< ML. < Gr. *sporadikos* < *sporas*, scattered] **1.** happening from time to time; not regular **2.** appearing singly, apart, or in isolated instances —**spo·rad′i·cal·ly** ***adv.***

spo·ran·gi·um (spô ran′jē əm, spə-) ***n.,*** *pl.* **-gi·a** (-ə) [ModL. < *spora* (see ff.) + Gr. *angeion*, vessel] *Bot.* an organ or single cell producing spores —**spo·ran′gi·al** ***adj.***

spore (spôr) ***n.*** [ModL. *spora* < Gr. *spora*, a seed] a small reproductive body, usually a single cell, produced by bacteria, mosses, ferns, certain protozoans, etc. and capable of giving rise to a new individual —***vi.*** **spored, spor′ing** to develop spores

spore case *same as* SPORANGIUM

spo·ro- *a combining form meaning* spore [*sporophyte*]: also, before a vowel, **spor-**

spo·ro·go·ni·um (spôr′ə gō′nē əm) ***n.,*** *pl.* **-ni·a** (-ə) [ModL.: see SPORO- & -GONIUM] the sporophyte in mosses and liverworts, usually a spore-bearing capsule on a stalk

spo·ro·phyll (spôr′ə fil) ***n.*** [SPORO- + -PHYLL] a leaf or leaflike part producing one or more sporangia —**spo′ro·phyl′la·ry** (-fil′ə rē) ***adj.***

spo·ro·phyte (-fīt′) ***n.*** [SPORO- + -PHYTE] the asexual spore-bearing phase of some plants: cf. GAMETOPHYTE —**spo′ro·phyt′ic** (-fit′ik) ***adj.***

spor·ran (spär′ən, spôr′-) ***n.*** [ScotGael. *sporan*] a leather pouch or purse, usually fur-covered, worn hanging from the belt in the dress costume of Scottish Highlanders

sport (spôrt) ***n.*** [short for DISPORT] **1.** any recreational activity; diversion **2.** such an activity requiring bodily exertion and carried on according to a set of rules, whether outdoors, as golf, or indoors, as bowling **3.** fun or play **4.** *a*) an object of ridicule; laughingstock *b*) a thing or person buffeted about, as though a plaything **5.** [Colloq.] a gambler **6.** [Colloq.] *a*) a person who is sportsmanlike [be a *sport!*] *b*) a person judged according to his ability to take defeat, teasing, etc. [a good (or poor) *sport*] **7.** [Colloq.] a pleasure-loving, flashy person **8.** a plant or animal showing some marked variation from the normal type —***vt.*** [Colloq.] to wear or display [to *sport* a loud tie] —***vi.*** **1.** to play or frolic **2.** *a*) to joke or jest *b*) to trifle or play (*with*) *c*) to ridicule someone or something —***adj.*** **1.** of or for sports **2.** suitable for informal, casual wear [a *sport* coat] —**in** (or **for**) **sport** in joke or jest —**make sport of** to ridicule —**sport′er** ***n.*** —**sport′ful** ***adj.*** —**sport′ful·ly** ***adv.***

sport·ing (-iŋ) ***adj.*** **1.** of, interested in, or taking part in sports **2.** sportsmanlike; fair **3.** having to do with games, races, etc. involving gambling or betting **4.** *Biol.* inclined to mutate —**sport′ing·ly** ***adv.***

sporting chance [Colloq.] a fair or even chance

spor·tive (spôr′tiv) ***adj.*** **1.** fond of or full of sport or merriment **2.** done in fun or play, not in earnest —**spor′tive·ly** ***adv.*** —**spor′tive·ness** ***n.***

sports (spôrts) ***adj.*** *same as* SPORT [*sports* clothes]

sports (or **sport**) **car** a low, small automobile, typically with seats for two and a high-compression engine

sports·cast (spôrts′kast′) ***n.*** a radio or TV broadcast of sports news —**sports′cast′er** ***n.***

sports·man (-mən) ***n.,*** *pl.* **-men 1.** a man who is interested in or takes part in sports, esp. in hunting, fishing, etc. **2.** a person who plays fair and can take defeat without complaint or victory without gloating —**sports′man·like′, sports′man·ly** ***adj.*** —**sports′man·ship′** ***n.***

sports·wear (-wer′) ***n.*** clothes worn while engaging in sports or for informal, casual wear

sports·wom·an (-wo͝om′ən) ***n.,*** *pl.* **-wom′en** (-wim′ən) a woman who is interested in or takes part in sports

sports·writ·er (-rīt′ər) ***n.*** a reporter who writes about sports or sports events

sport·y (spôrt′ē) ***adj.*** **sport′i·er, sport′i·est** [Colloq.] **1.** sportsmanlike **2.** characteristic of a sport or sporting man **3.** loud, flashy, or showy, as clothes —**sport′i·ly** ***adv.*** —**sport′i·ness** ***n.***

spor·ule (spôr′yo͞ol) ***n.*** a small spore

spot (spät) ***n.*** [< or akin to MDu. *spotte*] **1.** a small area differing from the surrounding area, as in color **2.** a mark, stain, blot, speck, etc. **3.** a flaw, as in character; fault **4.** a locality; place [a good fishing *spot*] **5.** *shortened form of* SPOTLIGHT **6.** [Chiefly Brit. Colloq.] a small quantity; bit [a *spot* of tea] **7.** [Colloq.] a position or job **8.** [Colloq.] a position in a schedule —***vt.*** **spot′ted, spot′ting 1.** to mark with spots **2.** to stain; blemish **3.** to place in or on a given spot or spots; locate **4.** to remove (spots or marks), as in dry cleaning **5.** *a)* to pick out; recognize [to *spot* someone in a crowd] *b)* to determine the location of (a target, the enemy, etc.) **6.** [Colloq.] to allow as a handicap [I *spotted* him two points] —*vi.* **1.** to become marked with spots **2.** to make a stain, as ink, etc. —*adj.* **1.** *a)* ready; on hand [*spot* cash] *b)* involving immediate payment of cash **2.** made at random or by sampling [a *spot* survey] **3.** *a)* broadcast from the place of occurrence [*spot* news] *b)* inserted between regular radio or TV programs [a *spot* announcement] —**hit the spot** [Colloq.] to satisfy a craving —**in a (bad) spot** [Slang] in trouble —**on the spot** **1.** at the place mentioned **2.** at once **3.** [Slang] in trouble or in a demanding situation **4.** [Slang] in danger, esp. of being murdered —**spot′less** *adj.* —**spot′less·ly** *adv.* —**spot′less·ness** *n.*

spot-check (-chek′) *vt.* to check or examine at random or by sampling —*n.* an act or instance of such checking

spot·light (-līt′) *n.* **1.** a strong beam of light focused on a particular person, thing, etc., as on a stage **2.** a lamp used to project such a light, as on an automobile **3.** public notice —*vt.* to focus a spotlight on

spot·ted (-id) *adj.* **1.** marked with spots **2.** stained; blemished; sullied

spotted fever any of various diseases accompanied by fever and skin eruptions

spot·ter (spät′ər) *n.* a person who spots; specif., *a)* a person whose work is removing spots, etc. in dry cleaning *b)* a person hired to watch for dishonesty among employees, as in a store *c)* a person who watches for, and reports, enemy aircraft

spot·ty (-ē) *adj.* **-ti·er, -ti·est** **1.** having, occurring in, or marked with spots **2.** not uniform or consistent, as in quality; uneven —**spot′ti·ly** *adv.* —**spot′ti·ness** *n.*

spot welding a process in which metal pieces are held together between two electrodes and welded by a powerful surge of current —**spot′-weld′** *vt., vi.* —**spot′-weld′er** *n.*

spous·al (spou′z'l) *n.* [< ESPOUSAL] [*often pl.*] [Now Rare] a marriage ceremony —*adj.* [Now Rare] of marriage

spouse (spous; *also, esp. for vt.,* spouz) *n.* [< OFr. < L. pp. of *spondere:* see SPONSOR] a partner in marriage —*vt.* **spoused, spous′ing** [Archaic] to marry

spout (spout) *n.* [ME. *spute* < *spouten,* to spout] **1.** a lip or projecting tube, as of a teapot, drinking fountain, etc., by which a liquid is poured or discharged **2.** a stream, jet, etc. as of liquid from a spout **3.** *same as: a)* DOWNSPOUT *b)* WATERSPOUT —*vt.* **1.** to shoot out (liquid, etc.) from a spout **2.** to utter in a loud, pompous manner —*vi.* **1.** to shoot out with force in a jet: said of liquid, etc. **2.** to discharge liquid, etc. as from a spout **3.** to spout words, esp. (usually **spout off**) in a hasty or rash way —**spout′er** *n.*

sprain (sprān) *vt.* [< ? OFr. *espreindre,* to strain < L. < *ex-,* out + *premere,* to press] to wrench or twist a ligament or muscle of (a joint, as the ankle) without dislocating the bones —*n.* **1.** an act of spraining **2.** an injury resulting from this

sprang (spraŋ) *alt. pt. of* SPRING

sprat (sprat) *n.* [OE. *sprott*] **1.** a small, sardinelike, European fish of the herring family **2.** any of several other small herrings

sprawl (sprôl) *vi.* [OE. *spreawlian*] **1.** *a)* to spread the limbs in a relaxed or awkward position *b)* to sit or lie in such a position **2.** to crawl awkwardly **3.** to spread out awkwardly or unevenly, as handwriting, a line of men, etc. —*vt.* to cause to sprawl —*n.* a sprawling movement or position —**sprawl′er** *n.* —**sprawl′y** *adj.*

spray[1] (sprā) *n.* [< or akin to MDu. *spraeien,* to spray] **1.** a cloud or mist of fine liquid particles, as of water from breaking waves **2.** *a)* a jet of such particles, as from a spray gun *b)* a device for shooting out such a jet **3.** something likened to a spray [a *spray* of gunfire] —*vt., vi.* **1.** to direct a spray (upon) **2.** to shoot out in a spray —**spray′er** *n.*

spray[2] (sprā) *n.* [ME.] **1.** a small branch or sprig of a tree or plant, with leaves, berries, flowers, etc. **2.** a design or ornament like this

spray can a can in which gas under pressure is used to shoot out the contents as a spray

spray gun a device that shoots out a spray of liquid, as paint or insecticide, by air pressure

spread (spred) *vt.* **spread, spread′ing** [OE. *sprædan*] **1.** to open or stretch out so as to cover more space; unfold; unfurl **2.** to lay out in display **3.** to move apart (the fingers, arms, wings, etc.) **4.** *a)* to distribute over an area; scatter *b)* to distribute among a group **5.** *a)* to distribute in a thin layer; smear *b)* to cover by smearing (*with* something) **6.** to extend or prolong in time **7.** to cause to be widely or more widely known, felt, existent, etc. **8.** to cover or deck (*with* something) **9.** *a)* to set (a table) for a meal *b)* to set (food) on a table **10.** to push apart or farther apart —*vi.* **1.** to extend itself; be expanded **2.** to become distributed **3.** to be made widely or more widely known, felt, etc. **4.** to be pushed apart or farther apart **5.** to admit of being smeared, as butter —*n.* **1.** the act of spreading; extension **2.** *a)* the extent to which something can be spread *b)* the interval between the highest and lowest figures of a set **3.** an expanse; extent **4.** *a)* two facing pages of a magazine, etc., treated as a single sheet *b)* printed matter set across a page or several columns of a newspaper, etc. **5.** a cloth cover for a table, bed, etc. **6.** any soft substance, as jam, used for spreading on bread **7.** [Colloq.] a meal, esp. one with a wide variety of food **8.** [Colloq.] a pretentious display **9.** [Western] a ranch —**spread oneself** [Colloq.] **1.** to exert oneself in order to make a good impression, etc. **2.** to show off —**spread oneself thin** to try to do too many things at once —**spread′er** *n.*

spread-ea·gle (spred′ē′g'l) *adj.* **1.** having the figure of an eagle with the wings and legs spread **2.** [Colloq.] boastful about the U.S. —*vt.* **-gled, -gling** to stretch out in the form of a spread eagle, as for a flogging

spree (sprē) *n.* [18th-c. slang for earlier *spray* < ?] **1.** a lively, noisy frolic **2.** a drinking bout **3.** a period of unrestrained activity [a shopping *spree*]

sprig (sprig) *n.* [ME. *sprigge*] **1.** *a)* a little twig or spray *b)* a design or ornament like this **2.** a young fellow; stripling —*vt.* **sprigged, sprig′ging** to decorate with a design of sprigs —**sprig′gy** *adj.* **-gi·er, -gi·est**

spright·ly (sprīt′lē) *adj.* **-li·er, -li·est** [< *spright,* var. of SPRITE + -LY[1]] gay, lively, brisk, etc. —*adv.* in a sprightly manner —**spright′li·ness** *n.*

spring (spriŋ) *vi.* **sprang** or **sprung, sprung, spring′ing** [OE. *springan*] **1.** to move suddenly and rapidly; specif., *a)* to leap; bound *b)* to appear suddenly *c)* to be resilient; bounce **2.** to arise as from some source; specif., *a)* to grow or develop *b)* to come into existence [towns *sprang* up] **3.** to become bent, warped, split, etc. [the door has *sprung*] **4.** to rise up above surrounding objects; tower Often followed by *up* —*vt.* **1.** to cause to leap forth suddenly **2.** to cause to snap shut, as by a spring **3.** *a)* to cause to warp, bend, split, etc., as by force *b)* to stretch (a spring, etc.) too far **4.** to make known suddenly [to *spring* a surprise] **5.** [Slang] to get (someone) released from jail, as by paying bail —*n.* **1.** a springing; specif., *a)* a jump or leap, or the distance so covered *b)* a sudden darting or flying back **2.** *a)* elasticity; resilience *b)* energy or vigor, as in one's walk **3.** a device, as a coil of wire, that returns to its original form after being forced out of shape: used to absorb shock, etc. **4.** *a)* a flow of water from the ground, the source of a stream *b)* any source or origin **5.** *a)* that season of the year when plants begin to grow after lying dormant all winter *b)* any period of beginning **6.** *Naut.* a split or break, as in a mast —*adj.* **1.** of, for, appearing in, or planted in the spring **2.** of or like a spring; elastic; resilient **3.** having, or supported on, springs [a *spring* mattress] **4.** coming from a spring [*spring* water] —**spring a leak** to begin to leak suddenly

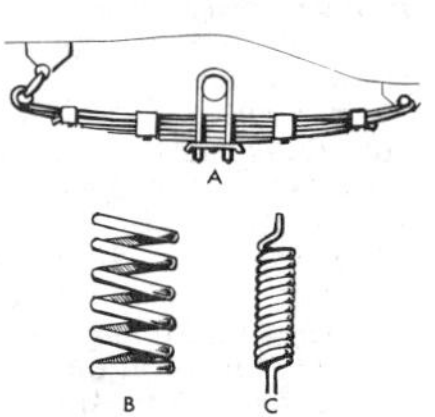

SPRINGS
(A, leaf; B, helical; C, expansion)

spring·board (spriŋ′bôrd′) *n.* **1.** a flexible, springy board used by acrobats as a takeoff in leaping **2.** *same as* DIVING BOARD **3.** a starting point

spring·bok (-bäk′) *n., pl.* **-bok′, -boks′:** see PLURAL, II, D, 2 [Afrik. < Du. *springen,* to spring + *bok,* a buck] a South African gazelle that leaps high in the air when startled: also **spring′buck′** (-buk′)

spring chicken **1.** a young chicken, esp. one only a few months old, used for broiling or frying **2.** [Slang] a young or inexperienced person

spring·er (-ər) *n.* **1.** a person or thing that springs **2.** *short for* SPRINGER SPANIEL **3.** *same as* SPRING CHICKEN

springer spaniel a breed of field spaniel used for flushing, or springing, game

spring fever the laziness and listlessness that many people feel during the first warm days of spring

Spring·field (spriŋ′fēld′) [sense 1 after *Springfield,* village in SE England; others prob. after sense 1] **1.** city in SW Mass.: pop. 152,000 **2.** city in SW Mo.: pop. 133,000 **3.** capital of Ill., in the C part: pop. 100,000 **4.** city in WC Ohio: pop. 73,000

spring lock a lock in which the bolt is snapped into place automatically by a spring

spring tide **1.** a tide occurring at the new and the full moon, normally the highest tide of the month **2.** any great flow, rush, or flood

spring·time (spriŋ′tīm′) *n.* the season of spring: also **spring′tide′** (-tīd′)

spring·y (-ē) *adj.* **spring′i·er, spring′i·est** **1.** flexible; elastic **2.** having many springs of water —**spring′i·ly** *adv.* —**spring′i·ness** *n.*

sprin·kle (spriŋ′k'l) ***vt.* -kled, -kling** [ME. *sprinklen*] **1.** to scatter (water, salt, etc.) in drops or particles **2.** *a*) to scatter drops or particles upon *b*) to dampen before ironing **3.** to distribute at random —***vi.*** **1.** to scatter something in drops or particles **2.** to fall in drops or particles **3.** to rain lightly —***n.*** **1.** the act of sprinkling, or a small amount sprinkled **2.** a light rain —**sprin′kler *n.***

sprin·kling (-kliŋ) ***n.*** **1.** a small number or amount, esp. when thinly distributed **2.** the act of one that sprinkles

sprint (sprint) ***vi.*** [< Scand.] to run or race at full speed, esp. for a short distance —***n.*** **1.** the act of sprinting **2.** a short race at full speed **3.** a brief period of intense activity —**sprint′er *n.***

sprit (sprit) ***n.*** [OE. *spreot*] a pole or spar extended diagonally upward from a mast to the topmost corner of a fore-and-aft sail

sprite (sprīt) ***n.*** [< OFr. *esprit* < L. *spiritus:* see SPIRIT] **1.** an elf, pixie, fairy, or goblin **2.** an elflike person

sprit·sail (sprit′sāl′, -s'l) ***n.*** a sail extended by a sprit

spritz (sprits; *G.* shprits) ***vt., vi., n.*** [ult. < MHG. *sprütze* < *sprützen,* to spray] squirt or spray

sprock·et (spräk′it) ***n.*** [< ?] **1.** any of the teeth or points, as on the rim of a wheel, arranged to fit into the links of a chain **2.** a wheel fitted with sprockets: in full, **sprocket wheel**

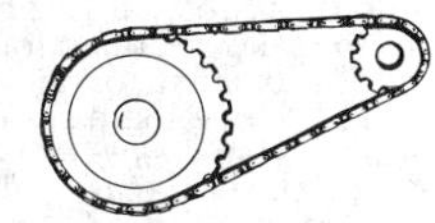
SPROCKET WHEELS

sprout (sprout) ***vi.*** [OE. *sprutan*] **1.** to begin to grow or germinate; give off shoots or buds **2.** to grow or develop rapidly —***vt.*** to cause to sprout or grow —***n.*** **1.** a young growth on a plant, as a stem or branch; shoot **2.** a new growth from a bud, rootstock, etc. **3.** any offshoot or scion **4.** [*pl.*] *shortened form of* BRUSSELS SPROUTS

spruce[1] (sprōōs) ***n.*** [< OFr. < ML. *Prussia:* prob. because first known as from Prussia] **1.** any of various evergreen trees of the pine family, having slender needles **2.** its wood

spruce[2] (sprōōs) ***adj.* spruc′er, spruc′est** [ME. *Spruce,* Prussia, esp. in phr. *Spruce leather,* fine leather imported from Prussia] neat and trim; smart; dapper —***vt., vi.* spruced, spruc′ing** to make or become spruce (usually with *up*) —**spruce′ly *adv.*** —**spruce′ness *n.***

sprung (spruŋ) *pp. & alt. pt. of* SPRING —***adj.*** having the springs broken, overstretched, or loose

spry (sprī) ***adj.* spri′er** or **spry′er, spri′est** or **spry′est** [< Scand.] full of life; active, brisk, and agile, esp. though elderly —**spry′ly *adv.*** —**spry′ness *n.***

spt. seaport

spud (spud) ***n.*** [prob. < Scand.] **1.** a sharp spade for rooting out weeds, etc. **2.** [Colloq.] a potato —***vt., vi.* spud′ded, spud′ding** to dig, etc. with a spud —**spud′der *n.***

spue (spyōō) ***vt., vi.* spued, spu′ing** *same as* SPEW

spume (spyōōm) ***n.*** [< MFr. < L. *spuma*] foam, froth, or scum —***vt., vi.* spumed, spum′ing** to foam or froth —**spu′mous, spum′y *adj.***

spu·mo·ni (spə mō′nē) ***n.*** [It.] an Italian frozen dessert of ice cream in layers of several flavors and colors, often containing bits of fruit and nuts: also sp. **spumone**

spun (spun) *pt. & pp. of* SPIN —***adj.*** formed by or as if by spinning

spunk (spuŋk) ***n.*** [IrGael. *sponc,* tinder < L. *spongia,* sponge] **1.** wood or fungus that smolders when ignited; punk **2.** [Colloq.] courage; spirit

spunk·y (spuŋ′kē) ***adj.* spunk′i·er, spunk′i·est** [Colloq.] having spunk; courageous; spirited —**spunk′i·ly *adv.*** —**spunk′i·ness *n.***

spur (spur) ***n.*** [OE. *spura*] **1.** a pointed device worn on the heel by horsemen and used to urge the horse forward **2.** anything that urges or incites; stimulus to action **3.** something like a spur; specif., *a*) a spinelike process, as on the wings or legs of certain birds *b*) a spinelike outgrowth of bone, as on the human heel, resulting from injury, disease, etc. *c*) a sharp metal device attached as a weapon to the leg of a gamecock *d*) a short branch or shoot of a tree, etc. **4.** a ridge projecting from the main mass of a mountain or mountain range **5.** a short side track (**spur track**) connected with the main track of a railroad **6.** *Bot.* a slender, tubelike structure formed by an extension of one or more petals or sepals, often holding nectar —***vt.* spurred, spur′ring** **1.** to prick with spurs **2.** to urge on; incite; stimulate **3.** to provide with a spur or spurs —***vi.*** **1.** to spur one's horse **2.** to hurry; hasten —**on the spur of the moment** abruptly and impulsively —**win one's spurs** to gain distinction or honor —**spur′like′ *adj.*** —**spur′rer *n.***

spurge (spurj) ***n.*** [< MFr. < *espurger,* to purge < L. *expurgare:* see EXPURGATE] any of a genus of plants having a milky juice and tiny flowers often protected by showy, scalelike leaves —***adj.*** designating a family of plants, usually with milky juice and diclinous flowers, including the poinsettia, cassava, rubber tree, etc.

spur gear **1.** a gearwheel with radial teeth parallel to the axle: also **spur wheel** **2.** gearing having this kind of gearwheel: also **spur gearing**

spu·ri·ous (spyoor′ē əs) ***adj.*** [L. *spurius*] **1.** [Now Rare] illegitimate **2.** not true or genuine; false; counterfeit —**spu′ri·ous·ly *adv.*** —**spu′ri·ous·ness *n.***

spurn (spurn) ***vt.*** [OE. *spurnan*] **1.** to push or drive away as with the foot **2.** to reject in a scornful way —***n.*** **1.** a kick **2.** scornful treatment or rejection —**spurn′er *n.***

spurred (spurd) ***adj.*** having, wearing, or fitted with spurs or spurlike parts

spurt (spurt) ***vt.*** [OE. *spryttan* < base of *sprutan,* to sprout] to expel suddenly in a stream or gushing flow; squirt; jet —***vi.*** **1.** to gush forth in a stream or jet **2.** to show a sudden, brief burst of energy or increased activity —***n.*** **1.** a sudden gushing or shooting forth; jet **2.** a sudden, brief burst of energy, etc.

sput·nik (spoot′nik, sput′-) ***n.*** [Russ., lit., co-traveler] an artificial satellite of the earth; specif., [S-] any of those put into orbit by the U.S.S.R. beginning in 1957

sput·ter (sput′ər) ***vi.*** [Du. *sputteren*] **1.** to spit out bits of saliva, food, etc., as when talking excitedly; splutter **2.** to talk in an excited, confused way, spitting out one's words **3.** to make sharp, sizzling or spitting sounds, as frying fat —***vt.*** **1.** to spit out (bits or drops) in an explosive manner **2.** to utter by sputtering —***n.*** **1.** the act or noise of sputtering **2.** matter thrown out in sputtering **3.** hasty, confused utterance —**sput′ter·ing·ly *adv.***

spu·tum (spyōōt′əm) ***n.,*** *pl.* **spu′ta** (-ə) [< L. < pp. of *spuere,* to SPIT[2]] saliva, usually mixed with mucus, spit out from the mouth

spy (spī) ***vt.* spied, spy′ing** [< OFr. < OHG. *spehōn,* to examine] to catch sight of; see —***vi.*** **1.** to watch closely and secretly; act as a spy **2.** to look carefully —***n.,*** *pl.* **spies** **1.** a person who keeps close and secret watch on another or others **2.** a person employed by a government to get secret information about the affairs, esp. military affairs, of another government, as of an enemy in wartime —**spy out** to discover or seek to discover by looking carefully

spy·glass (-glas′) ***n.*** a small telescope

sq. **1.** squadron **2.** square

sq. ft., sq. in., etc. square foot, square inch, etc.

squab (skwäb, skwôb) ***n.*** [prob. < Scand.] **1.** a very young pigeon **2.** a short, stout person **3.** [Brit.] a stuffed cushion or couch —***adj.*** short and stout: also **squab′by**

squab·ble (skwäb′'l, swôb′-) ***vi.* -bled, -bling** [< Scand.] to quarrel noisily over a small matter; wrangle —***n.*** a noisy, petty quarrel; wrangle —**squab′bler *n.***

squad (skwäd, skwôd) ***n.*** [< Fr. < Sp. *escuadra,* or It. *squadra,* a square, both ult. < L.: see SQUARE] **1.** *a*) a small group of soldiers assembled for drill, duty, etc. *b*) the smallest military tactical unit, often part of a platoon **2.** *a*) any small group of people working together [*a police squad*] *b*) an athletic team —***vt.* squad′ded, squad′ding** **1.** to form into a squad **2.** to assign to a squad

squad car a police patrol car, usually communicating with headquarters by radiotelephone

squad·ron (-rən) ***n.*** [< It. < *squadra:* see SQUAD] **1.** a group of warships assigned to special duty **2.** a unit of cavalry consisting of from two to four troops, etc. **3.** *a*) *U.S. Air Force* a unit consisting of two or more flights *b*) a formation of six or more aircraft **4.** any organized group

squal·id (skwäl′id, skwôl′-) ***adj.*** [< L. < *squalere,* to be foul] **1.** foul; filthy **2.** wretched; sordid —**squa·lid′i·ty, squal′id·ness *n.*** —**squal′id·ly *adv.***

squall[1] (skwôl) ***n.*** [< Scand.] **1.** a brief, violent windstorm, usually with rain or snow **2.** [Colloq.] trouble or disturbance —***vi.*** to storm briefly —**squall′y *adj.***

squall[2] (skwôl) ***vi., vt.*** [ON. *skvala,* to cry out] to cry or scream loudly or harshly —***n.*** a harsh, shrill cry or loud scream —**squall′er *n.***

squal·or (skwäl′ər, skwôl′-) ***n.*** [L., foulness] a being squalid; filth and wretchedness

squa·ma (skwā′mə) ***n.,*** *pl.* **-mae** (-mē) [L., a scale] a scale or scalelike part of an animal or plant —**squa′mate** (-māt), **squa′mous** (-məs), **squa′mose** (-mōs) ***adj.***

squan·der (skwän′dər, skwôn′-) ***vt., vi.*** [prob. < dial. *squander,* scatter] to spend or use (money, time, etc.) wastefully

square (skwer) ***n.*** [< OFr., ult. < L. *ex-,* out + *quadrare,* to square < *quadrus,* a square < *quattuor,* four] **1.** a plane figure having four equal sides and four right angles **2.** anything shaped like or nearly like this **3.** an area bounded by streets on four sides; also, the distance along one side of such an area; block **4.** an open area bounded by several streets, used as a park, plaza, etc. **5.** an instrument having two sides that form a 90° angle, used for drawing or testing right angles **6.** a solid piece with at least one face that is square *[a cake cut into squares]* **7.** the product of a number multiplied by itself *[9 is the square of 3]* **8.** [Slang] a person who is square (*adj.* 11) —*vt.* **squared, squar′ing 1.** *a)* to make into a square *b)* to make into any rectangle **2.** to test or adjust with regard to straightness or evenness **3.** to bring to or near to the form of a right angle *[square your shoulders]* **4.** *a)* to settle; adjust *[to square accounts]* *b)* to settle the accounts of **5.** to make equal *[to square the score of a game]* **6.** to bring into agreement *[to square a statement with the facts]* **7.** to mark off (a surface) in squares **8.** to bring into the correct position, as with reference to a line, course, etc. **9.** to multiply (a quantity) by itself **10.** to determine the square that is equal in area to (a figure) —*vi.* to fit; agree; accord (*with*) —*adj.* **1.** *a)* having four equal sides and four right angles *b)* more or less cubical, as a box **2.** forming a right angle, or having a rectangular part or cross section **3.** correctly adjusted; straight, level, even, etc. **4.** *a)* leaving no balance; balanced *b)* even in score; tied **5.** just; fair; honest **6.** clear; direct; straightforward *[a square refusal]* **7.** *a)* designating or of a unit of surface measure in the form of a square with sides of a specified length *b)* given or stated in terms of such measure **8.** having a shape broad for its length or height, with a solid, sturdy appearance *[a square build]* **9.** designating a number that is the product of another number multiplied by itself **10.** [Colloq.] satisfying; substantial *[a square meal]* **11.** [Slang] old-fashioned or unsophisticated —*adv.* **1.** honestly; fairly **2.** so as to be or form a square; at right angles **3.** directly; exactly **4.** so as to face **5.** firmly; solidly —**on the square 1.** at right angles **2.** [Colloq.] honest(ly), fair(ly), genuine(ly), etc. —**square away 1.** to bring a ship's yards around so as to sail before the wind **2.** *same as* SQUARE OFF —**square off** to get into position for attacking or for defending —**square oneself** [Colloq.] to make up for a wrong one has done —**square the circle 1.** to find a square equal in area to a circle: an insoluble problem **2.** to do or attempt something that seems impossible —**square up** to make a settlement, as by payment —**square′ly** *adv.* —**square′ness** *n.* —**squar′er** *n.* —**squar′ish** *adj.*

square dance a lively dance with various steps and figures, the couples forming squares, etc. —**square′-dance′** *vi.* **-danced′, -danc′ing**

square deal [Colloq.] any dealing that is honest and fair

square knot a double knot in which the free ends run parallel to the standing parts

square measure a system of measuring area, esp. the system in which 144 square inches = 1 square foot or that in which 10,000 square centimeters = 1 square meter: see TABLES OF WEIGHTS AND MEASURES in Supplements

square-rigged (-rigd′) *adj.* having square sails as principal sails —**square′-rig′ger** *n.*

square root the number that is multiplied by itself to produce a given number *[3 is the square root of 9]*

square sail a four-sided sail

square shooter [Colloq.] an honest, just person

square-shoul·dered (-shōl′dərd) *adj.* having shoulders jutting out squarely from the body's axis

squash¹ (skwäsh, skwôsh) *vt.* [< OFr. *esquasser*, ult. < L. *ex-*, intens. + pp. of *quatere*, to shake] **1.** *a)* to crush into a soft or flat mass *b)* to press tightly or too tightly **2.** to suppress; quash **3.** [Colloq.] to silence (another) crushingly —*vi.* **1.** to be squashed by pressure, etc. **2.** to make a sound of squashing **3.** to force one's way; squeeze —*n.* **1.** something squashed; crushed mass **2.** the act or sound of squashing **3.** either of two games (**squash rackets, squash tennis**) played in a four-walled court with rackets and a rubber ball **4.** [Brit.] fruit juice or fruit-flavored syrup with soda water —*adv.* with a squash

squash² (skwäsh, skwôsh) *n.* [< Algonquian] **1.** the fleshy fruit of various plants of the gourd family, cooked as a vegetable **2.** a plant, usually a vine, bearing this fruit

squash·y (-ē) *adj.* **-i·er, -i·est 1.** soft and wet; mushy **2.** easily squashed, as overripe fruit —**squash′i·ly** *adv.* —**squash′i·ness** *n.*

squat (skwät, skwôt) *vi.* **squat′ted, squat′ting** [< MFr. *esquatir*, ult. < L. *ex-*, intens. + *coactus*, pp. of *cogere*, to force] **1.** to crouch, with the knees bent and the weight on the balls of the feet **2.** to crouch close to the ground, as an animal **3.** to settle on land without any right or title to it **4.** to settle on public land under government regulation so as to get title to it —*adj.* **1.** crouched in a squatting position **2.** short and thick: also **squat′ty** —*n.* the act or position of squatting —**squat′ly** *adv.* —**squat′ness** *n.* —**squat′ter** *n.*

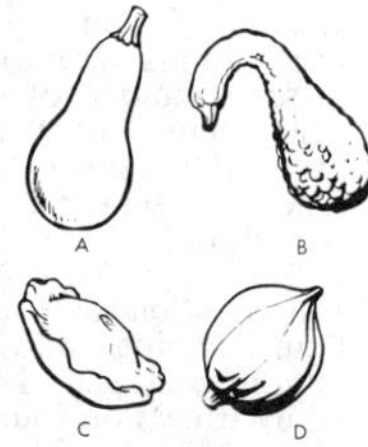

SQUASH (A, butternut; B, crookneck; C, white bush; D, acorn)

squaw (skwô) *n.* [< Algonquian] a N. American Indian woman, esp. a wife: now sometimes felt to be a contemptuous term

squawk (skwôk) *vi.* [echoic] **1.** to utter a loud, harsh cry, as a parrot **2.** [Colloq.] to complain or protest —*vt.* to utter in a squawk —*n.* **1.** a squawking cry **2.** [Colloq.] a complaint —**squawk′er** *n.*

squawk box [Slang] an intercom speaker

squaw man a white man married to a N. American Indian woman, esp. one living with her tribe

squeak (skwēk) *vi.* [prob. akin to ON. *skvakka*, to gurgle] to make or utter a short, sharp, high-pitched sound or cry —*vt.* to utter with a squeak —*n.* a short, shrill sound or cry —**narrow** (or **close**) **squeak** [Colloq.] a narrow escape —**squeak through** (or **by**, etc.) [Colloq.] to barely manage to succeed, survive, etc. —**squeak′i·ly** *adv.* —**squeak′y** *adj.* **-i·er, -i·est**

squeak·er (-ər) *n.* **1.** one that squeaks **2.** [Colloq.] a narrow escape, victory, etc.

squeal (skwēl) *vi.* [prob. akin to ON. *skvala:* see SQUALL²] **1.** to make or utter a long, shrill sound or cry **2.** [Slang] to inform against, or tell on, someone —*vt.* to utter with a squeal —*n.* a long, shrill sound or cry —**squeal′er** *n.*

squeam·ish (skwēm′ish) *adj.* [< Anglo-Fr. *escoimous*, orig., shy] **1.** easily nauseated **2.** easily shocked or offended; prudish **3.** too fastidious —**squeam′ish·ly** *adv.* —**squeam′ish·ness** *n.*

squee·gee (skwē′jē) *n.* [prob. akin to SQUEEZE] a T-shaped tool with a blade of rubber, etc., for wiping liquid off a surface —*vt.* **-geed, -gee·ing** to use a squeegee on

squeeze (skwēz) *vt.* **squeezed, squeez′ing** [OE. *cwysan*, to squeeze] **1.** to press hard or closely, esp. from two or more sides **2.** *a)* to press so as to extract liquid, etc. *[to squeeze oranges]* *b)* to extract (liquid, etc.) by pressure **3.** to force (*into, out,* etc.) as by pressing **4.** to get or extort by force or unfair means **5.** to oppress with taxes, etc. **6.** to put pressure on (someone) to do something, as to pay money **7.** to embrace closely; hug **8.** *Baseball* to score (a run or runner) by a squeeze play —*vi.* **1.** to yield to pressure *[a wet sponge squeezes easily]* **2.** to exert pressure **3.** to force one's way by pushing or pressing (*in, out, through,* etc.) —*n.* **1.** a squeezing or being squeezed **2.** *a)* a close embrace; hug *b)* a firm handclasp **3.** the state of being closely pressed or packed; crush **4.** a difficult situation; pinch **5.** a quantity extracted by squeezing **6.** [Colloq.] pressure exerted, as in extortion: esp. in **put the squeeze on 7.** *short for* SQUEEZE PLAY —**squeeze through** (or **by**, etc.) [Colloq.] to barely manage to succeed, survive, etc. —**squeez′er** *n.*

squeeze play 1. *Baseball* a play in which a bunter scores a runner from third base moving at the first pitching motion **2.** pressure or coercion exerted to achieve some goal

squelch (skwelch) *n.* [prob. echoic] **1.** the sound of liquid, mud, etc. moving under pressure or suction, as in wet shoes **2.** [Colloq.] a suppressing or silencing; esp., a crushing retort, rebuke, etc. —*vt.* **1.** to crush as by stamping upon; squash **2.** [Colloq.] to suppress or silence completely and crushingly —*vi.* **1.** to walk heavily through mud, etc., making a splashing sound **2.** to make such a sound —**squelch′er** *n.*

squib (skwib) *n.* [prob. echoic] **1.** a firecracker that hisses before exploding **2.** a short, witty writing that criticizes, etc. —*vt., vi.* **squibbed, squib′bing 1.** to shoot off (a squib) **2.** to put out a squib (against); criticize

squid (skwid) *n., pl.* **squids, squid:** see PLURAL, II, D, 1 [prob. akin to SQUIRT] any of various cephalopod mollusks having a slender body and ten arms, two arms being much longer than the others

SQUID (small species to 8 in. long)

squig·gle (skwig′'l) *n.* [SQU(IRM) + (W)IGGLE] **1.** a short curved or wavy line; curlicue **2.** an illegible or meaningless scribble —*vt.* **-gled, -gling** to form into or write as a squiggle or squiggles —*vi.* **1.** to make squiggles **2.** to squirm along; wriggle —**squig′gly** *adj.*

squil·gee (skwē′jē; skwil′jē *is a sp. pron.*) *n., vt.* **-geed, -gee·ing** *sailors' var. of* SQUEEGEE

squill (skwil) *n.* [< L. < Gr. *skilla*] **1.** *a)* the dried bulb of a plant of the lily family, formerly used in medicine *b)* this plant **2.** a strain of this plant having red bulbs that yield a powder used chiefly in rat poison

squinch (skwinch) *vt.* [SQU(INT) + (P)INCH] **1.** *a)* to squint (the eyes) *b)* to pucker or screw up (the face, nose, etc.) **2.** to squeeze or compress —*vi.* **1.** to squint or pucker

2. to crouch down or draw oneself together 3. to flinch
squint (skwint) *vi.* [see ASQUINT] **1.** to peer with the eyes partly closed, as in too strong light **2.** to look sidelong or askance **3.** to be cross-eyed **4.** to incline (*toward* a given direction, belief, etc.) —*vt.* to keep (the eyes) partly closed in peering —*n.* **1.** a squinting **2.** an inclination **3.** a being cross-eyed **4.** [Colloq.] a glance, often sidelong —*adj.* **1.** looking sidelong or askance **2.** cross-eyed — **squint′er** *n.* —**squint′y** *adj.*
squire (skwīr) *n.* [< OFr. *esquier:* see ESQUIRE] **1.** a young man of high birth who attended a knight **2.** in England, a country gentleman who owns much land **3.** a title of respect for a justice of the peace, etc., as in a rural district **4.** an attendant; esp., a man escorting a woman —*vt., vi.* to act as a squire (to)
squirm (skwurm) *vi.* [prob. echoic, infl. by WORM] **1.** to twist and turn the body in a snakelike movement; wriggle; writhe **2.** to show or feel distress, as from embarrassment —*n.* a squirming —**squirm′y** *adj.* **-i·er, -i·est**
squir·rel (skwur′əl; *chiefly Brit.* skwir′-) *n., pl.* **-rels, -rel:** see PLURAL, II, D, 1 [< OFr., ult. < L. *sciurus* < Gr. < *skia*, a shadow + *oura*, tail] **1.** *a)* any of a group of small, tree-dwelling rodents with heavy fur and a long, bushy tail *b)* any of various burrowing rodents, as chipmunks, related to these **2.** the fur of some of these animals —*vt.* **-reled** or **-relled, -rel·ing** or **-rel·ling** to store or hide (*away*)
squirt (skwurt) *vt.* [prob. < or akin to LowG. & Du. *swirtjen*, to squirt] **1.** to shoot out (a liquid) in a jet or narrow stream **2.** to wet with liquid thus shot out —*vi.* to be squirted out; spurt —*n.* **1.** a device for squirting, as a syringe **2.** a squirting **3.** a small amount of squirted liquid; jet **4.** [Colloq.] a small or young person, esp. one who is impudent —**squirt′er** *n.*
squirt gun a toy gun that shoots a stream of water
squish (skwish) *vi.* to make a soft, splashing sound when walked on, squeezed, etc. —*vt.* [Colloq.] to squeeze into a soft mass; squash —*n.* **1.** a squishing sound **2.** [Colloq.] a squashing; squash —**squish′y** *adj.*
squoosh (skwoosh) *vt.* [< SQUASH[1]] [Colloq.] **1.** to squeeze or crush into a soft, liquid mass **2.** *same as* SLOSH
Sr *Chem.* strontium
Sr. **1.** Senior **2.** [Sp.] *Señor* **3.** Sister
Sra. [Sp.] *Señora*
Sri Lan·ka (srē läŋ′kə) *official name of* CEYLON
S.R.O. standing room only
Srta. [Sp.] *Señorita*
SS. [L. *Sancti*] Saints
ss., ss *Baseball* shortstop
S.S., SS, S/S steamship
S.S.A. Social Security Administration
SSE, S.S.E., s.s.e. south-southeast
SSgt Staff Sergeant
S.S.R., SSR Soviet Socialist Republic
SSS Selective Service System
SSW, S.S.W., s.s.w. south-southwest
-st *same as* -EST
St. **1.** Saint: terms beginning with *St.* are entered in this dictionary as if spelled *St-* **2.** Strait **3.** Street
St., st. **1.** statute(s) **2.** stratus
Sta. Station
stab (stab) *n.* [ME. *stabbe*, prob. < var. of *stubbe*, stub] **1.** a wound made by piercing with a knife, dagger, etc. **2.** a thrust, as with a knife **3.** a sudden, sharp hurt or pain —*vt.* **stabbed, stab′bing** **1.** to pierce or wound as with a knife **2.** to thrust (a knife, etc.) into something **3.** to go into in a sharp, thrusting way —*vi.* **1.** to make a thrust or piercing wound as with a knife **2.** to feel like a stabbing knife: said of pain —**make** (or **take**) **a stab at** to make an attempt at —**stab in the back** to harm by treachery
sta·bile (stā′b'l, -bil; *also, and for n. usually,* -bēl) *adj.* [L. *stabilis:* see STABLE[1]] stable; stationary —*n.* a large stationary abstract sculpture, usually of metal, wire, wood, etc.
sta·bil·i·ty (stə bil′ə tē) *n., pl.* **-ties** **1.** a being stable, or fixed; steadiness **2.** firmness of character, purpose, etc. **3.** resistance to change **4.** the capacity of an object to return to equilibrium
sta·bi·lize (stā′bə līz′) *vt.* **-lized′, -liz′ing** **1.** to make stable, or firm **2.** to keep from changing, as in price **3.** to give stability to (an airplane, ship, etc.) with a stabilizer —*vi.* to become stabilized —**sta′bi·li·za′tion** *n.*
sta·bi·liz·er (-lī′zər) *n.* a person or thing that stabilizes; specif., *a)* an airfoil to keep an airplane steady in flight, specif. the horizontal part of the tail *b)* a gyrostabilizer or other device to steady a ship in rough waters *c)* any additive used in a substance to keep it stable, retard deterioration, etc.
sta·ble[1] (stā′b'l) *adj.* **-bler, -blest** [< OFr. < L. *stabilis* < *stare*, to stand] **1.** *a)* not easily moved or put off balance; firm; steady *b)* not likely to break down, fall apart, etc. **2.** firm in character, purpose, etc.; steadfast **3.** not likely to change or be affected adversely; enduring **4.** capable of returning to equilibrium **5.** *Chem., Physics* not readily decomposing —**sta′bly** *adv.*
sta·ble[2] (stā′b'l) *n.* [< OFr. < L. *stabulum* < *stare*, to stand] **1.** *a)* a building in which horses or cattle are sheltered and fed *b)* a group of animals kept in such a building **2.** *a)* all the racehorses of one owner *b)* the people who take care of and train these horses **3.** [Colloq.] all the athletes, performers, etc. under one management —*vt., vi.* **-bled, -bling** to keep or be kept in a stable
sta·ble·boy (-boi′) *n.* a boy who works in a stable
stac·ca·to (stə kät′ō) *adj.* [It., detached] **1.** *Music* with distinct breaks between successive tones **2.** made up of abrupt, distinct elements or sounds —*adv.* so as to be staccato —*n., pl.* **-tos** something staccato
stack (stak) *n.* [ON. *stakkr*] **1.** a large pile of straw, hay, etc., esp. one neatly arranged, as in the form of a cone **2.** any somewhat orderly pile **3.** a number of arms, esp. three rifles, leaned together on end to form a cone **4.** *a)* a grouping of chimney flues *b)* *same as* SMOKESTACK **5.** [*pl.*] the main area and shelves for shelving books in a library **6.** [Colloq.] a large amount —*vt.* **1.** to pile in a stack **2.** to load with stacks **3.** to assign (aircraft) to various altitudes for circling before landing **4.** to arrange in advance underhandedly for a desired result [*to stack a jury*] —**stack up** **1.** to come to as a total **2.** to stand in comparison (*with* or *against*) —**stack′a·ble** *adj.* —**stack′er** *n.*
stacked (stakt) *adj.* [Slang] having a full, shapely figure; curvaceous: said of a woman
stacked (or **stack**) **heel** a heel on a woman's shoe of several layers alternating in shade
stack·up (stak′up′) *n.* an arrangement of circling aircraft at various altitudes awaiting their turn to land
sta·di·um (stā′dē əm) *n., pl.* **-di·a** (-ə); also, and for sense 2 usually, **-di·ums** [L. < Gr. *stadion*, fixed standard of length] **1.** in ancient Greece and Rome, a track for footraces, about 607 feet long, with tiers of seats for spectators **2.** a large, open structure for football, baseball, etc. with tiers of seats for spectators
staff (staf) *n., pl.* **staffs;** also, for senses 1 & 5, **staves** [OE. *stæf*] **1.** a stick, rod, or pole used as for support, a weapon, a symbol of authority, a measure, etc. **2.** a group of people assisting a leader **3.** a group of officers serving a commanding officer as advisers and administrators **4.** a specific group of workers [*a teaching staff*] **5.** *Music* the five horizontal lines and four intermediate spaces on which music is written —*adj.* of, by, for, or on a staff —*vt.* to provide with a staff, as of workers
staff·er (-ər) *n.* a member of a staff
staff officer **1.** an officer on a staff **2.** *U.S. Navy* a commissioned officer with nonmilitary duties, as a surgeon
staff of life bread, regarded as the basic food
staff sergeant **1.** *U.S. Army & Marine Corps* an enlisted man ranking above sergeant **2.** *U.S. Air Force* an enlisted man ranking above airman first class
stag (stag) *n., pl.* **stags, stag:** see PLURAL, II, D, 1 [OE. *stagga*] **1.** *a)* a full-grown male deer *b)* the male of various other animals **2.** a male animal castrated in maturity **3.** *a)* a man who attends a social gathering unaccompanied by a woman *b)* a social gathering for men only —*adj.* for men only —**go stag** [Colloq.] **1.** to go as a stag (sense 3 *a*) **2.** to go unescorted by a man
stage (stāj) *n.* [< OFr. *estage*, ult. < L. pp. of *stare*, to stand] **1.** a platform or dock **2.** a workmen's scaffold **3.** a level, floor, or story **4.** *a)* a platform on which plays, speeches, etc. are presented *b)* any area, as in an arena theater, in which actors perform *c)* the whole working section of a theater, including the acting area, the backstage area, etc. *d)* the theater as a profession (with *the*) **5.** the scene of an event or events **6.** a stopping point on a route, esp. formerly for a stagecoach **7.** the distance between two such points **8.** *shortened form of* STAGECOACH **9.** a period or degree in a process of development, change, etc. **10.** any of two or more propulsion units used in sequence as the rocket of a spacecraft, etc. **11.** *Radio* an element or part in a complex arrangement —*vt.* **staged, stag′ing** **1.** to present as on a stage **2.** to plan and carry out [*stage an attack*] —*vi.* to be presented on the stage, as a play —**by easy stages** a little at a time, with many stops to rest
stage·coach (-kōch′) *n.* formerly, a horse-drawn coach on scheduled trips over a regular route
stage·craft (-kraft′) *n.* skill in writing or staging plays
stage door an outside door leading to the backstage part of a theater, used by actors, production staff, etc.
stage fright nervousness felt when appearing as a speaker or performer before an audience

stage·hand (-hand′) ***n.*** a person who helps to set and remove scenery and furniture, operate the curtain, etc. for a stage performance

stage-man·age (-man′ij) ***vt.*** **-aged, -ag·ing 1.** to be stage manager for **2.** to arrange or display with dramatic effect, esp. as if from behind scenes

stage manager an assistant to the director of a play, in overall charge backstage during an actual performance

stage-struck (-struk′) ***adj.*** having an intense desire to act or otherwise work in the theater

stage whisper 1. a loud whisper by an actor on the stage, thought of as being heard only by the audience and not by his fellow actors **2.** any similar loud whisper made at a social gathering

stag·ger (stag′ər) ***vi.*** [ON. *stakra,* to totter] **1.** to totter, sway, or reel, as from a blow, fatigue, drunkenness, etc. **2.** to waver in purpose, etc. —***vt.*** **1.** to make stagger **2.** to affect strongly, as with astonishment **3.** to set alternately, as on either side of a line; make zigzag *[to stagger the teeth of a saw]* **4.** to arrange (duties, vacations, etc.) so as to avoid crowding —***n.*** **1.** a staggering, tottering, etc. **2.** a staggered arrangement **3.** [*pl., with sing. v.*] a disease or toxic condition of horses, cattle, etc., marked by loss of coordination, staggering, etc. —**stag′ger·er** ***n.*** —**stag′ger·ing** ***adj.*** —**stag′ger·ing·ly** ***adv.***

stag·ing (stā′jiŋ) ***n.*** **1.** a temporary structure used for support; scaffolding **2.** the business of operating stagecoaches **3.** travel by stagecoach **4.** the act or process of presenting a play on the stage

stag·nant (stag′nənt) ***adj.*** [< L. prp. of *stagnare,* to stagnate] **1.** not flowing or moving **2.** foul from lack of movement: said of water, etc. **3.** lacking activity, etc.; sluggish —**stag′nan·cy** (-nən sē) ***n.*** —**stag′nant·ly** ***adv.***

stag·nate (-nāt) ***vi., vt.*** **-nat·ed, -nat·ing** [< L. pp. of *stagnare,* to stagnate < *stagnum,* a swamp] to become or make stagnant —**stag·na′tion** ***n.***

stag·y (stā′jē) ***adj.*** **stag′i·er, stag′i·est 1.** of the stage; theatrical **2.** affected; not real Also **stage′y** —**stag′i·ly** ***adv.*** —**stag′i·ness** ***n.***

staid (stād) *archaic pt. & pp. of* STAY[3] —***adj.*** sober; sedate —**staid′ly** ***adv.*** —**staid′ness** ***n.***

stain (stān) ***vt.*** [< OFr. < L. *dis-,* from + *tingere,* to color] **1.** to spoil the appearance of by discoloring or spotting **2.** to disgrace or dishonor (one's character, reputation, etc.) **3.** to change the appearance of (wood, glass, etc.) by applying a dye, pigment, etc. **4.** to treat (material for microscopic study) with a coloring matter, as to make transparent parts visible —***vi.*** to impart or take a stain —***n.*** **1.** a discoloration, spot, etc. resulting from staining **2.** a moral blemish; dishonor **3.** a dye, pigment, etc. for staining wood or for staining material for microscopic study —**stain′a·ble** ***adj.*** —**stain′er** ***n.***

stain·less (-lis) ***adj.*** **1.** without a stain **2.** that resists staining, rusting, etc. **3.** made of stainless steel —***n.*** flatware made of stainless steel —**stain′less·ly** ***adv.***

stainless steel steel alloyed with chromium, etc., virtually immune to rust and corrosion

stair (ster) ***n.*** [OE. *stæger*] **1.** [*usually pl.*] a flight of steps; staircase **2.** one of a series of steps leading from one level to another

stair·case (-kās′) ***n.*** a flight of stairs with a supporting structure and a handrail: also **stair′way′** (-wā′)

stair·well (-wel′) ***n.*** a vertical shaft (in a building) containing a staircase: also **stair well**

stake (stāk) ***n.*** [OE. *staca*] **1.** a length of wood or metal pointed at one end for driving into the ground, as for marking a boundary **2.** *a)* the post to which a person was tied for execution by burning *b)* such execution **3.** any of the posts fitted into sockets at the edge of a railway flatcar, truck bed, etc., to help hold a load **4.** [*often pl.*] something, esp. money, risked in a wager, game, or contest **5.** [*often pl.*] a prize given a winner, as in a race **6.** [*pl., with sing. v.*] a race in which a prize is offered **7.** a share or interest, as in property **8.** [Colloq.] a grubstake —***vt.*** **staked, stak′ing 1.** *a)* to mark the boundaries of as with stakes *b)* to establish (a claim) thus **2.** to support (a plant, etc.) by tying to a stake **3.** to tether to a stake **4.** to risk; gamble **5.** [Colloq.] *a)* to furnish with money or resources *b)* to grubstake —**at stake** being risked —**pull up stakes** [Colloq.] to change one's place of residence, business, etc. —**stake out** to station (police, etc.) in an attempt to capture a suspected criminal at (a specified place)

stake·hold·er (-hōl′dər) ***n.*** one who holds money, etc. bet by others and pays it to the winner

stake·out (-out′) ***n.*** **1.** the staking out of police, etc. in an attempt to capture a suspected criminal **2.** the place where police, etc. are staked out

Sta·kha·no·vism (stə khä′nə viz′m) ***n.*** [< A. G. *Stakhanov,* Soviet miner] in the Soviet Union, a system of working in teams to get higher production through greater efficiency, with bonuses, etc. given for success —**Sta·kha′no·vite′** (-vīt′) ***adj., n.***

sta·lac·tite (stə lak′tīt; *chiefly Brit.* stal′ək tīt′) ***n.*** [ModL. < Gr. *stalaktos,* dripping < *stalassein,* to drip] an icicle-shaped deposit hanging from the roof of a cave, formed by evaporation of dripping water full of lime —**stal·ac·tit·ic** (stal′ək tit′ik) ***adj.***

sta·lag·mite (stə lag′mīt; *chiefly Brit.* stal′əg mīt′) ***n.*** [ModL. < Gr. *stalagmos,* a dropping < *stalassein,* to drip] a cone-shaped deposit built up on the floor of a cave by dripping water full of lime, often from a stalactite above —**stal·ag·mit·ic** (stal′əg mit′ik) ***adj.***

stale (stāl) ***adj.*** **stal′er, stal′est** [prob. < LowG.] **1.** having lost freshness; specif., *a)* flat; tasteless *b)* hard and dry, as bread *c)* having little oxygen; stagnant *[stale air] d)* beginning to decay, as eggs **2.** no longer new or interesting; trite *[a stale joke]* **3.** ineffective, weakened, etc. from too much or too little activity —***vt., vi.*** **staled, stal′ing** to make or become stale —**stale′ly** ***adv.*** —**stale′ness** ***n.***

stale·mate (stāl′māt′) ***n.*** [OFr. *estal,* a fixed location + *mate* (to checkmate)] **1.** *Chess* any situation in which a player cannot move without placing his king in check: it results in a draw **2.** a deadlock; standstill —***vt.*** **-mat′ed, -mat′ing** to bring into a stalemate

Sta·lin (stä′lin), **Joseph** (born *Iosif Vissarionovich Dzhugashvili*) 1879–1953; premier of the U.S.S.R. (1941–53) —**Sta′lin·ism** ***n.*** —**Sta′lin·ist** ***adj., n.***

Sta·lin·grad (stä′lin grät′; *E.* stä′lin grad′) *former name of* VOLGOGRAD

stalk[1] (stôk) ***vi.*** [OE. *stealcian* < *stealc,* steep] **1.** *a)* to walk in a stiff, haughty, or grim manner *b)* to advance or spread grimly *[plague stalks across the land]* **2.** to pursue or approach game, etc. stealthily —***vt.*** **1.** to pursue or approach (game, etc.) stealthily **2.** to stalk through —***n.*** **1.** a slow, stiff, or haughty stride **2.** a stalking of game, etc. —**stalk′er** ***n.***

stalk[2] (stôk) ***n.*** [akin to OE. *stela,* stalk] **1.** any stem or stemlike part, as a slender rod or support **2.** *Bot. a)* the main stem or axis of a plant *b)* a lengthened part on which an organ grows or is supported, as the petiole of a leaf **3.** *Zool.* a lengthened support for an animal organ or for a whole body —**stalked** ***adj.*** —**stalk′i·ness** ***n.*** —**stalk′less** ***adj.*** —**stalk′y** ***adj.*** **-i·er, -i·est**

stalk·ing-horse (stôk′iŋ hôrs′) ***n.*** **1.** a horse, or a figure of one, used as cover by a hunter **2.** anything used to hide intentions, schemes, etc. **3.** a person put forth as a political candidate until the candidate actually preferred is announced

stall[1] (stôl) ***n.*** [OE. *steall*] **1.** *a)* formerly, a stable *b)* a compartment for one animal in a stable **2.** any of various compartments, sections, etc.; specif., *a)* a booth, etc. where goods are sold, as at a fair *b)* an enclosed seat in a church *c)* [Brit.] a theater seat near the stage *d)* a small, enclosed space, as for taking a shower *e)* any of the spaces marked off for parking cars in a garage, etc. **3.** a protective sheath for a finger; cot **4.** a stopping or standing still due to failure to work properly **5.** the tendency of an aircraft to drop or go out of control due to loss of lift and increase of drag —***vt., vi.*** **1.** to put, keep, or be kept in a stall **2.** to stick fast, as in mud **3.** to stop as from failure to work properly **4.** to put (an aircraft) into a stall, or go into a stall

stall[2] (stôl) ***vi.*** [< obs. *stale,* a decoy < Anglo-Fr. *estale*] to act or speak evasively so as to deceive or delay —***vt.*** to put off or delay by stalling (usually with *off*) —***n.*** [Colloq.] any trick used in stalling

stal·lion (stal′yən) ***n.*** [OFr. *estalon* < Gmc. *stal,* a stall] an uncastrated male horse, esp. one used as a stud

stal·wart (stôl′wərt) ***adj.*** [OE. *stælwyrthe* < *stathol,* foundation + *wyrthe,* worth] **1.** sturdy; robust **2.** brave; valiant **3.** resolute; firm —***n.*** **1.** a stalwart person **2.** a firm supporter of a cause, esp. that of a political party —**stal′wart·ly** ***adv.*** —**stal′wart·ness** ***n.***

sta·men (stā′mən) ***n., pl.*** **-mens, stam·i·na** (stam′ə nə) [ModL. < L., a thread, orig., warp] a pollen-bearing organ in a flower, made up of a slender stalk (*filament*) and a pollen sac (*anther*)

Stam·ford (stam′fərd) [after *Stamford,* town in NE England] city in SW Conn.: pop. 102,000

stam·i·na (stam′ə nə) ***n.*** [L., pl. of *stamen:* see STAMEN] resistance to fatigue, illness, hardship, etc.; endurance

stam·i·nate (stam′ə nit, -nāt′) ***adj.*** **1.** having stamens but no pistils, as male flowers **2.** having stamens

stam·mer (stam′ər) ***vt., vi.*** [OE. *stamerian*] to speak or say with pauses that one cannot control, often with rapid repetitions of syllables or initial sounds, as because of excitement, embarrassment, or mental conflicts —***n.*** the act or habit of stammering —**stam′mer·er** ***n.*** —**stam′mer·ing·ly** ***adv.***

stamp (stamp) ***vt.*** [ME. *stampen*] **1.** to bring (the foot) down forcibly on the ground, a floor, etc. **2.** *a*) to strike down on forcibly with the foot *b*) to beat, crush, etc. by treading on heavily *c*) to remove by stamping the feet *[stamped* the snow from his boots*]* *d*) to pulverize (ore, etc.) by grinding or crushing **3.** *a*) to imprint or cut out (a design, lettering, etc.) by bringing a form forcibly against a material *b*) to cut out or make as by applying a die to metal *[*to *stamp* auto bodies*]* **4.** to impress or imprint with a design, etc., as to decorate, show ownership, etc. **5.** to impress distinctly or indelibly *[*a face *stamped* with grief*]* **6.** to put an official seal or a stamp on (a document, letter, etc.) **7.** to characterize or reveal distinctly, as if by imprinting —***vi.*** **1.** to bring the foot down forcibly on the ground, etc. **2.** to walk with loud, heavy steps —***n.*** **1.** a stamping **2.** a machine, tool, etc. for stamping or crushing ore, etc. **3.** *a*) any implement, as a die, that is brought forcibly against something to mark or shape it *b*) the mark or form so made **4.** a mark, seal, etc. used to show officially that a tax has been paid, authority given, etc. **5.** *a*) a small piece of paper, distinctively imprinted and usually gummed, sold by a government and required to be put on a letter, parcel, document, etc. to show that the prescribed fee has been paid *b*) any similar piece of paper, issued by an organization, business, etc. *[*trading *stamps]* **6.** a characteristic sign or impression *[*the *stamp* of truth*]* **7.** character; kind; class; type —**stamp out** **1.** to crush or put out (a fire, etc.) by treading on forcibly **2.** to crush or put down (a revolt, etc.) —**stamp′er** ***n.***

stam·pede (stam pēd′) ***n.*** [AmSp. *estampida* < Sp. < *estampar*, to stamp < Gmc.] **1.** a sudden, headlong running away of a herd of frightened horses, cattle, etc. **2.** a confused, headlong rush of many people **3.** any sudden, spontaneous mass movement —***vi.*** **-ped′ed, -ped′ing** to move in a stampede —***vt.*** to cause to stampede —**stamped′er** ***n.***

stamp·ing ground (stam′piŋ) [Colloq.] a regular or favorite gathering place or resort

stance (stans) ***n.*** [< OFr., ult. < L. prp. of *stare*, to stand] **1.** a particular way of standing, esp. in regard to placing the feet **2.** an attitude adopted for dealing with a situation

stanch (stônch, stanch, stänch) ***vt., vi., adj. see*** STAUNCH

stan·chion (stan′chən, -shən) ***n.*** [< OFr. < *estance:* see STANCE] **1.** an upright bar, post, etc. used as a support **2.** a restraining device in a stall, fitted loosely about a cow's neck —***vt.*** **1.** to support with stanchions **2.** to confine with a stanchion

stand (stand) ***vi.*** **stood, stand′ing** [OE. *standan*] **1.** *a*) to be or stay upright on the feet *b*) to be or stay upright on its base, bottom, etc., as a vase *c*) to grow upright: said of plants **2.** to rise to an upright position, as from sitting **3.** *a*) to take, or be in, a (specified) upright position *[stand* straight*]* *b*) to take, keep, or be in a (specified) position or attitude *[*I *stand* opposed*]* **4.** to have a (specified) height when standing *[*he *stands* six feet*]* **5.** *a*) to be situated *b*) to stay where situated **6.** to gather and remain: said of a liquid **7.** to remain unchanged, valid, etc. *[*the law still *stands]* **8.** to be in a (specified) condition *[*they *stood* in awe, he *stands* to lose*]* **9.** to be of a (specified) rank, degree, etc. *[*to *stand* first in grades*]* **10.** to remain resolute or firm **11.** to make resistance **12.** *a*) to halt *b*) to remain stationary **13.** to show the (specified) relative position of those involved *[*the score *stands* at 10 to 8*]* **14.** [Chiefly Brit.] to be a candidate, as for office; run **15.** *Naut.* to take or hold a certain course —***vt.*** **1.** to make stand; put upright **2.** to put up with; endure **3.** to be unaffected by; withstand **4.** to undergo *[*to *stand* trial*]* **5.** to do the duty of *[stand* watch*]* **6.** [Colloq.] *a*) to bear the cost of (a meal, etc.), as when treating *b*) to treat (a person) to food, drink, etc. —***n.*** **1.** a standing; esp., a halt or stop; specif., *a*) a stopping to counterattack, resist, etc., as in retreat *b*) a halt by a touring theatrical company to give a performance; also, the place stopped at **2.** the place where one stands or is supposed to stand; position **3.** a view, opinion, etc., as on an issue **4.** a structure to stand or sit on; specif., *a*) a raised platform for a band, etc. *b*) [*often pl.*] a set of benches in tiers, as for spectators *c*) the place where a witness testifies in a courtroom **5.** *a*) a booth, stall, etc. where goods are sold *b*) a parking space reserved for taxicabs, etc. *c*) a business location **6.** a rack, small table, etc. for holding things **7.** a standing growth of trees or plants —**make a stand** **1.** to take a position for defense or opposition **2.** to support a definite position, opinion, etc. —**stand a chance** to have a chance —**stand by** **1.** to be near and ready to act as needed **2.** to aid or support **3.** to keep (a promise, etc.) **4.** to be present, esp. as an onlooker **5.** *Radio & TV* to stay tuned in, as for a program to continue —**stand for** **1.** to be a symbol for or sign of; represent **2.** [Colloq.] to put up with; endure —**stand in** [Colloq.] to be on good terms (usually with *with*) —**stand in for** to substitute for —**stand off** **1.** to keep at a distance **2.** to put off or evade —**stand on** **1.** to be founded on **2.** to insist upon (ceremony, one's rights, etc.) —**stand one's ground** to maintain one's position —**stand out** **1.** to project **2.** to show up clearly **3.** to be prominent or outstanding **4.** to refuse to give in —**stand up** **1.** to rise to or be in a standing position **2.** to prove valid, durable, etc. **3.** [Slang] to fail to keep an engagement with —**stand up for** to defend; support —**stand up to** to confront fearlessly —**stand′er** ***n.***

stand·ard (stan′dərd) ***n.*** [OFr. *estendard*, ult. < Gmc.] **1.** a flag, banner, etc. used as an emblem or symbol of a leader, people, military unit, etc. **2.** something established as a rule or basis of comparison in measuring or judging quantity, quality, value, etc. **3.** a usage or practice that is generally accepted or followed; criterion *[*moral *standards]* **4.** an upright support **5.** a piece of music that has remained popular for many years **6.** a tree or shrub with a single, tall stem —***adj.*** **1.** used as or conforming to an established rule, model, etc. **2.** generally accepted as reliable or authoritative *[standard* reference books*]* **3.** regular or typical; ordinary *[standard* procedure*]* **4.** suitable to speech or writing that is more or less formal; not slang, dialectal, obsolete, etc. *[standard* English*]*

stand·ard-bear·er (-ber′ər) ***n.*** **1.** a person carrying the standard, or flag, as of a military group **2.** a leader of a movement, political party, etc.

standard gauge **1.** a width of 56½ inches between the rails of a railroad track **2.** such a track, or a locomotive or car for it —**stand′ard-gauge′** ***adj.***

stand·ard·ize (stan′dər dīz′) ***vt.*** **-ized′, -iz′ing** **1.** to make standard or uniform; make the same in all cases **2.** to test by or adjust to a standard —**stand′ard·i·za′tion** ***n.*** —**stand′ard·iz′er** ***n.***

standard of living level of daily living, as of a nation, class, or person, with regard to the adequacy of necessities and comforts

standard time the time in any of the 24 time zones, each an hour apart, into which the earth is divided: it is based on distance east or west of Greenwich, England, and in North America, the eight zones (*Atlantic, Eastern, Central, Mountain, Pacific, Yukon, Alaska,* and *Bering*) use the mean solar times of the 60th, 75th, 90th, 105th, 120th, 135th, 150th, and 165th meridians, respectively: standard time is the official time for each zone except when daylight-saving time is in effect: see TIME, chart

stand·by (stand′bī′) ***n., pl.*** **-bys′** **1.** a person or thing that can always be depended on, or one ready to be used if needed **2.** a person waiting to board a plane, etc. if space becomes available —***adj.*** of, for, or being a standby —**on standby** ready or waiting as a standby

stand·ee (stan dē′) ***n.*** [Colloq.] a person who stands, usually because no seats are vacant

stand-in (stand′in′) ***n.*** **1.** a person who stands in a performer's place in movies, etc. while lights, cameras, etc. are being adjusted **2.** any substitute for another

stand·ing (stan′diŋ) ***n.*** **1.** the act, state, or position of one that stands **2.** status, rank, or reputation **3.** the time that something lasts; duration *[*of long *standing]* —***adj.*** **1.** that stands; upright **2.** in or from a standing position *[*a *standing* jump*]* **3.** not flowing; stagnant **4.** lasting; permanent **5.** stationary **6.** not in use

standing army a permanent army

standing room room in which to stand, esp. when there are no vacant seats, as in a theater

Stan·dish (stan′dish), **Miles** (or **Myles**) 1584?–1656; Eng. colonist; military leader of Plymouth Colony

stand·off (stand′ôf′) ***n.*** **1.** a standing off or being stood off **2.** an equalizing effect **3.** a tie or draw in a contest —***adj.*** **1.** that stands off **2.** *same as* STANDOFFISH

stand·off·ish (stand′ôf′ish) ***adj.*** reserved and cool; aloof —**stand′off′ish·ly** ***adv.*** —**stand′off′ish·ness** ***n.***

stand·out (stand′out′) ***n.*** [Colloq.] a person or thing of outstanding superiority —***adj.*** [Colloq.] outstandingly superior

stand·pat (-pat′) ***adj.*** [Colloq.] sticking firmly to an opinion, policy, etc. —**stand′pat′ter** ***n.*** —**stand′pat′tism** ***n.***

stand·pipe (-pīp′) ***n.*** a large vertical pipe or cylindrical tank for storing water

stand·point (-point′) ***n.*** the point or position from which something is seen or judged; point of view

stand·still (-stil′) ***n.*** a stop, halt, or cessation

stand-up (-up′) ***adj.*** **1.** upright; erect **2.** done, taken, etc. in a standing position **3.** designating or of a comedian who delivers monologues

Stan·ford-Bi·net test (stan′fərd bi nā′) a revision, wider in range, of the Binet-Simon test: developed at Stanford University (Calif.)

stan·hope (stan′hōp, -əp) ***n.*** [after F. *Stanhope*, 19th-c. Eng. clergyman] a light, open carriage with two or four wheels and usually one seat

Stan·hope (stan′əp), **Philip Dor·mer** (dôr′mər) *see* 4th Earl of CHESTERFIELD

Stan·i·slav·sky (stan′i släf′skē, stän′-), **Kon·stan·tin** (kän′stən tēn′) (born *Konstantin Sergeyevich Alekseyev*) 1863–1938; Russ. actor, director, & teacher of acting

stank (staŋk) *alt. pt. of* STINK

Stan·ley (stan′lē) **1.** [< OE. *stan leah,* stone lea] a masculine name **2.** Sir **Henry Morton,** (born *John Rowlands*) 1841–1904; Brit. journalist & explorer in Africa

stan·nic (stan′ik) ***adj.*** [< LL. *stannum,* tin + -IC] of or containing tin, specif. with a valence of four

stan·nous (-əs) ***adj.*** [< LL. *stannum,* tin + -OUS] of or containing tin, specif. with a valence of two

Stan·ton (stan′t'n), **Edwin Mc·Mas·ters** (mək mas′tərz) 1814–69; U.S. statesman; secretary of war (1862–68)

stan·za (stan′zə) ***n.*** [It., room, ult. < L. *stare,* to stand] a group of lines of verse, usually four or more and regular in pattern, forming one of the divisions of a poem or song —**stan·za′ic** (-zā′ik) ***adj.***

sta·pes (stā′pēz) ***n.,*** *pl.* **sta′pes, sta·pe·des** (stə pē′dēz, stā′pə dēz′) [ModL. < ML., a stirrup, prob. < Gmc.] *Anat.* a small, stirrup-shaped bone, the innermost of the three bones in the middle ear

staph (staf) ***n.*** *shortened form of* STAPHYLOCOCCUS

staph·y·lo·coc·cus (staf′ə lō käk′əs) ***n.,*** *pl.* **-coc′ci** (-käk′sī) [ModL. < Gr. *staphylē,* bunch of grapes + -COCCUS] any of a genus of spherical bacteria that generally occur in clusters or chains and cause pus to form in abscesses, etc. —**staph′y·lo·coc′cal** (-käk′'l), **staph′y·lo·coc′cic** (-käk′sik) ***adj.***

sta·ple[1] (stā′p'l) ***n.*** [< OFr. < MDu. *stapel,* mart] **1.** a chief commodity made, grown, etc. in a particular place **2.** a chief item or element **3.** raw material **4.** any common, regularly stocked item of trade, as salt, flour, etc. **5.** the fiber of cotton, wool, etc. with regard to length and fineness —***adj.*** **1.** regularly stocked **2.** produced or consumed regularly and in quantity **3.** chief; main [*a staple* industry] —***vt.*** **-pled, -pling** to sort (wool, cotton, etc.) according to staple —**sta′pler** ***n.***

sta·ple[2] (stā′p'l) ***n.*** [OE. *stapol,* a post] **1.** a U-shaped piece of metal with sharp-pointed ends, driven into a surface to hold a hook, wire, etc. in place **2.** a similar piece of thin wire driven through papers, etc. so that the ends bend over as a binding —***vt.*** **-pled, -pling** to fasten with a staple or staples —**sta′pler** ***n.***

star (stär) ***n.*** [OE. *steorra*] **1.** any heavenly body seen as a point of light in the night sky; specif., *Astron.* any self-luminous, gaseous, spheroidal heavenly body, as the sun, seen (except for the sun) as a fixed point of light **2.** a flat figure with usually five or six projecting points, representing a star **3.** a mark, emblem, etc. resembling such a figure, used as an award, insigne, etc. **4.** an asterisk **5.** *a)* *Astrol.* a planet, etc. regarded as influencing human fate *b)* [*often pl.*] fate; destiny **6.** a person who excels, esp. in a sport **7.** a leading actor or actress —***vt.*** **starred, star′ring** **1.** to decorate with stars **2.** to mark with a star or stars as a grade of quality **3.** to mark with an asterisk **4.** to present (a performer) in a leading role —***vi.*** **1.** to excel, esp. in a sport **2.** to have a leading role —***adj.*** **1.** excelling [*a star* athlete] **2.** of a star or stars —**star′less** ***adj.*** —**star′like′** ***adj.***

star·board (stär′bərd, -bôrd′) ***n.*** [< OE. < *steoran,* to steer (with a large oar used on the ship's right side) + *bord,* board] the right-hand side of a ship or airplane as one faces forward, toward the bow —***adj.*** of or on the starboard —***vt., vi.*** to move or turn (the helm) to the starboard side

starch (stärch) ***n.*** [ult. < OE. *stearc,* stiff] **1.** a white, tasteless, odorless food substance found in potatoes, grain, etc.: it is a complex carbohydrate $(C_6H_{10}O_5)_n$ **2.** a powdered form of this, used in laundering to stiffen cloth, etc. **3.** [*pl.*] starchy foods **4.** stiff formality **5.** [Colloq.] vigor —***vt.*** to stiffen as with starch —**starch′a·ble** ***adj.*** —**starch′less** ***adj.***

Star Chamber **1.** a royal English court or tribunal abolished in 1641, notorious for its harsh, arbitrary, and secret procedures **2.** [*also* s- c-] any similar tribunal, etc.

starch·y (stär′chē) ***adj.*** **starch′i·er, starch′i·est** **1.** of, containing, or like starch **2.** stiffened with starch **3.** formal; unbending —**starch′i·ly** ***adv.*** —**starch′i·ness** ***n.***

star-crossed (stär′krôst′) ***adj.*** [see STAR (*n.* 5)] ill-fated

star·dom (-dəm) ***n.*** **1.** the status of a star of stage, screen, etc. **2.** such stars collectively

stare (ster) ***vi.*** **stared, star′ing** [OE. *starian*] to look with a steady, fixed gaze, eyes wide open, as in wonder, curiosity, dullness, etc. —***vt.*** to inspect or affect in a given way by staring —***n.*** a staring look —**stare down** to stare back at (another) until he looks away —**stare one in the face** to be pressing or inescapable —**star′er** ***n.***

star·fish (stär′fish′) ***n.,*** *pl.* **-fish′, -fish′es:** see FISH a small sea animal with a hard, spiny skeleton and five or more arms or rays arranged like the points of a star

star·gaze (-gāz′) ***vi.*** **-gazed′, -gaz′ing** **1.** to gaze at the stars **2.** to daydream —**star′gaz′er** ***n.***

stark (stärk) ***adj.*** [OE. *stearc*] **1.** *a)* stiff or rigid, as a corpse *b)* harsh; severe **2.** sharply outlined or prominent [one *stark* tree] **3.** bleak; desolate **4.** *a)* emptied; stripped [*stark* shelves] *b)* totally naked **5.** grimly blunt; not softened, embellished, etc. [*stark* realism] **6.** sheer; utter [*stark* terror] —***adv.*** in a stark way; esp., utterly [*stark* mad] —**stark′ly** ***adv.*** —**stark′ness** ***n.***

star·let (stär′lit) ***n.*** **1.** a small star **2.** a young actress being promoted as a possible future star

star·light (-līt′) ***n.*** light from the stars

star·ling (stär′liŋ) ***n.*** [OE. *stærlinc,* dim. of *stær,* starling] any of a family of short-tailed, dark-colored birds, esp. the **common starling,** with iridescent plumage, brought into the U.S. from Europe

star·lit (stär′lit′) ***adj.*** lighted by the stars

Star of David a six-pointed star formed of two equilateral triangles: a symbol of Judaism

STAR OF DAVID

star·ry (stär′ē) ***adj.*** **-ri·er, -ri·est** **1.** set or marked with stars **2.** shining like stars; bright **3.** star-shaped **4.** lighted by or full of stars **5.** of, from, or like stars —**star′ri·ness** ***n.***

star·ry-eyed (-īd′) ***adj.*** with the eyes sparkling in a glow of wonder, romance, visionary dreams, etc.

Stars and Bars the original flag (1861) of the Confederacy, with three horizontal bars and a circle of stars

Stars and Stripes the red, white, and blue flag of the United States, with 13 stripes and 50 stars

Star-Span·gled Banner (stär′spaŋ′g'ld) **1.** the United States flag **2.** the United States national anthem: the words are by Francis Scott Key

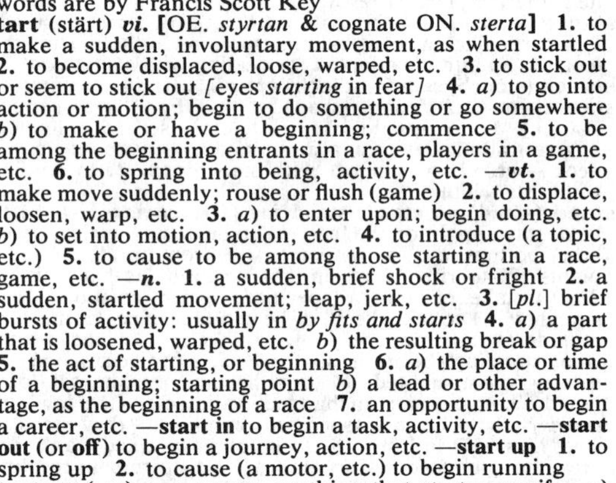

start (stärt) ***vi.*** [OE. *styrtan* & cognate ON. *sterta*] **1.** to make a sudden, involuntary movement, as when startled **2.** to become displaced, loose, warped, etc. **3.** to stick out or seem to stick out [eyes *starting* in fear] **4.** *a)* to go into action or motion; begin to do something or go somewhere *b)* to make or have a beginning; commence **5.** to be among the beginning entrants in a race, players in a game, etc. **6.** to spring into being, activity, etc. —***vt.*** **1.** to make move suddenly; rouse or flush (game) **2.** to displace, loosen, warp, etc. **3.** *a)* to enter upon; begin doing, etc. *b)* to set into motion, action, etc. **4.** to introduce (a topic, etc.) **5.** to cause to be among those starting in a race, game, etc. —***n.*** **1.** a sudden, brief shock or fright **2.** a sudden, startled movement; leap, jerk, etc. **3.** [*pl.*] brief bursts of activity: usually in *by fits and starts* **4.** *a)* a part that is loosened, warped, etc. *b)* the resulting break or gap **5.** the act of starting, or beginning **6.** *a)* the place or time of a beginning; starting point *b)* a lead or other advantage, as the beginning of a race **7.** an opportunity to begin a career, etc. —**start in** to begin a task, activity, etc. —**start out** (or **off**) to begin a journey, action, etc. —**start up** **1.** to spring up **2.** to cause (a motor, etc.) to begin running

start·er (-ər) ***n.*** a person or thing that starts; specif., *a)* the first in a series *b)* one starting in a race, etc. *c)* one giving the signal to start *d)* one supervising departing trucks, etc. *e)* any of various devices for starting an internal-combustion engine

star·tle (stärt′'l) ***vt.*** **-tled, -tling** [< ME. freq. of *sterten,* to start] to surprise, frighten, or alarm suddenly; esp., to make jump, jerk, etc. as from sudden fright —***vi.*** to be startled —***n.*** a startled reaction —**star′tler** ***n.*** —**star′tling** ***adj.*** —**star′tling·ly** ***adv.***

starve (stärv) ***vi.*** **starved, starv′ing** [OE. *steorfan,* to die] **1.** *a)* to die from lack of food *b)* to suffer or get weak from hunger *c)* [Colloq.] to be very hungry **2.** to suffer great need (with *for*) [*starving* for affection] —***vt.*** **1.** to cause to starve **2.** to force by starving [to *starve* an enemy into submission] —**star·va′tion** ***n.***

starve·ling (-liŋ) ***n.*** a starving person or animal —***adj.*** **1.** starving **2.** impoverished

stash (stash) ***vt.*** [prob. a blend of STORE & CACHE] [Colloq.] to put or hide in a secret or safe place —***n.*** [Slang] **1.** a place for hiding things **2.** something hidden away

sta·sis (stā′sis, stas′is) ***n.,*** *pl.* **-ses** (-sēz) [ModL. < Gr., a standing] **1.** *a)* a stoppage of the flow of a bodily fluid, as of blood *b)* reduced peristalsis of the intestines **2.** a state of equilibrium or stagnancy

-stat (stat) [< ModL. < Gr. *-statēs*] *a combining form meaning* stationary, making stationary [*thermostat*]

state (stāt) ***n.*** [< OFr. < L. *status* < pp. of *stare,* to stand] **1.** a set of circumstances or attributes characterizing a person or thing at a given time; condition [*a state* of poverty]

2. a particular mental or emotional condition [a *state* of bliss] **3.** condition as regards structure, form, etc. [liquid *state*] **4.** *a*) social status; esp., high rank *b*) ceremonious display; pomp **5.** [*sometimes* **S-**] *a*) a body of people politically organized under one government within a definite territory *b*) the authority represented by such a body of people **6.** [*usually* **S-**] any of the political units together constituting a federal government, as in the U.S. **7.** the territory of a state (senses 5 *a* & 6) **8.** civil government [church and *state*] **9.** the sphere of highest governmental authority [matters of *state*] **—*adj.*** **1.** ceremonial **2.** [*sometimes* **S-**] of the government or a state **—*vt.*** **stat′ed, stat′ing** **1.** to set or establish by specifying [the *stated* hour] **2.** to set forth or express in a specific, definite, or formal way [to *state* one's objections, *stating* a musical theme] **—in** (or **into**) **a state** [Colloq.] in (or into) an agitated emotional condition **—lie in state** to be displayed formally to the public before burial **—the States** the United States **—stat′a·ble *adj.*** **—state′less *adj.***

state·craft (-kraft′) ***n.*** the ability of a statesman

State·hood (-hood′) ***n.*** the condition of being a State of the U.S. rather than a Territory

State·house (-hous′) ***n.*** the official meeting place of the legislature of a State of the U.S.: also **State House** or **State Capitol**

state·ly (-lē) ***adj.*** **-li·er, -li·est** dignified, imposing, grand, or the like **—state′li·ness *n.***

state·ment (-mənt) ***n.*** **1.** *a*) the act of stating *b*) the thing stated or said **2.** *a*) a summary of a financial account *b*) a listing of charges for goods, etc.

Stat·en Island (stat′'n) [< Du. *Staaten Eylandt*, States Island, after States-General, name of the legislative assembly of the Netherlands] island between New Jersey and Long Island, forming the borough of Richmond, New York City

state·room (stāt′ro͞om′) ***n.*** **1.** a private cabin on a ship **2.** a private room in a railroad car

state's evidence *Law* evidence given by or for the prosecution in a criminal case, esp. by a criminal against his associates **—turn state's evidence** to give such evidence for the prosecution

state·side (stāt′sīd′) ***adj.*** [Colloq.] of or having to do with the U.S. (as viewed from abroad) **—*adv.*** [Colloq.] in, to, or toward the U.S.

states·man (stāts′mən) ***n.***, *pl.* **-men** a person who shows wisdom and skill in conducting state affairs or dealing with public issues, or one experienced in the business of government **—states′man·like′, states′man·ly *adj.*** **—states′man·ship′ *n.***

state socialism the theory, doctrine, or practice of an economy planned and controlled by the state, based on state ownership of public utilities, basic industries, etc.

States' rights all the rights and powers which the Constitution neither grants to the Federal government nor denies to the State governments: also **State rights**

state-wide (stāt′wīd′) ***adj.*** extending throughout a state

stat·ic (stat′ik) ***adj.*** [< ModL. < Gr. *statikos*, causing to stand < *histanai*, to cause to stand] **1.** acting through weight only: said of the pressure exerted by a motionless body **2.** of masses, forces, etc. at rest or in equilibrium: opposed to DYNAMIC **3.** at rest; inactive; stationary **4.** *Elec.* designating, of, or producing stationary electrical charges, as from friction **5.** *Radio* of or having to do with static Also **stat′i·cal —*n.*** **1.** *a*) electrical discharges in the atmosphere that interfere with radio or TV reception, etc. *b*) interference or noises produced by such discharges **2.** [Slang] remarks showing disapproval **—stat′i·cal·ly *adv.***

stat·ics (-iks) ***n.pl.*** [*with sing. v.*] [see prec.] the branch of mechanics dealing with bodies, masses, or forces at rest or in equilibrium

sta·tion (stā′shən) ***n.*** [< OFr. < L. < pp. of *stare*, to stand] **1.** the place where a person or thing stands or is located, esp. an assigned post, position, etc. [a guard's *station*, a police *station*] **2.** in Australia, a sheep or cattle ranch **3.** *a*) a regular stopping place, as on a bus line or railroad *b*) the building or buildings at such a place **4.** social standing or position **5.** *a*) a place equipped to transmit or receive radio waves; esp., the studios, technical installations, etc. of an establishment for radio or television transmission *b*) such an establishment, or the broadcasting frequency or channel assigned to it **—*vt.*** to assign to a station; post

station agent an official in charge of a small railroad station, or of a department in a larger station

sta·tion·ar·y (stā′shə ner′ē) ***adj.*** [< L. < *statio*: see STATION] **1.** not moving or movable; fixed **2.** unchanging in condition, value, etc. **3.** not migratory or itinerant **—*n.***, *pl.* **-ar′ies** a person or thing that is stationary

stationary engineer a person who operates and maintains stationary engines, such as steam boilers, turbines, etc.

sta·tion·er (stā′shə nər) ***n.*** [< ML. *stationarius* < L., STATIONARY] a person who sells office supplies, greeting cards, some books, etc.

sta·tion·er·y (-ner′ē) ***n.*** [see prec. & -ERY] writing materials; specif., paper and envelopes used for letters

sta·tion·mas·ter (stā′shən mas′tər) ***n.*** an official in charge of a large railroad station

station wagon an automobile with folding or removable rear seats and a tailgate that can be opened for loading luggage, packages, etc.

stat·ism (stāt′iz'm) ***n.*** the doctrine or practice of vesting economic control and planning in a centralized state government **—stat′ist *n., adj.***

sta·tis·tic (stə tis′tik) ***adj.*** *rare var. of* STATISTICAL **—*n.*** a statistical item or element

sta·tis·ti·cal (-ti k'l) ***adj.*** of, having to do with, consisting of, or based on statistics **—sta·tis′ti·cal·ly *adv.***

stat·is·ti·cian (stat′is tish′ən) ***n.*** an expert or specialist in statistics

sta·tis·tics (stə tis′tiks) ***n.pl.*** [< G. < ModL. *statisticus* < L. *status*: see STATE] **1.** facts or data of a numerical kind, assembled and classified so as to present significant information **2.** [*with sing. v.*] the science of compiling such facts

sta·tor (stāt′ər) ***n.*** [ModL. < L. < pp. of *stare*, to stand] the fixed part, as the housing, of a motor, dynamo, etc.

stat·u·ar·y (stach′o͞o wer′ē) ***n.*** **-ar′ies** **1.** statues collectively **2.** the art of making statues **—*adj.*** of or suitable for statues

stat·ue (stach′o͞o) ***n.*** [< OFr. < L. < *statuere*, to place < *stare*, to stand] the form of a person or animal carved in stone, wood, etc., modeled in clay, etc., or cast in plaster, bronze, etc., esp. when done in the round

stat·u·esque (stach′o͞o wesk′) ***adj.*** like a statue; specif., *a*) tall and well-proportioned *b*) having a stately grace and dignity **—stat′u·esque′ly *adv.*** **—stat′u·esque′ness *n.***

stat·u·ette (-wet′) ***n.*** a small statue

stat·ure (stach′ər) ***n.*** [OFr. < L. *statura* < *statuere*: see STATUE] **1.** the height of the body in a natural standing position **2.** growth or level of attainment, esp. as worthy of esteem [moral *stature*]

sta·tus (stāt′əs, stat′-) ***n.***, *pl.* **-tus·es** [L.: see STATE] **1.** condition or position with regard to law [the *status* of a minor] **2.** *a*) position; rank [high *status*] *b*) high position; prestige [seeking *status*] **3.** state or condition, as of affairs

status quo (kwō′) [L., lit., the state in which] the existing state of affairs: also **status in quo**

status symbol a possession, practice, etc. regarded as a mark of social status, esp. of high social status

stat·ute (stach′o͞ot, -oot) ***n.*** [< OFr. < LL. < L. pp. of *statuere*: see STATUE] **1.** an established rule **2.** *a*) a law passed by a legislative body and set forth in a formal document *b*) such a document

statute law law established by a legislative body

statute mile a unit of measure (5,280 feet): see MILE

statute of limitations a statute limiting the period within which a specific legal action may be taken

stat·u·to·ry (stach′oo tôr′ē) ***adj.*** **1.** of, or having the nature of, a statute **2.** fixed, authorized, or established by statute **3.** declared by statute to be punishable: said of an offense

St. Augustine [after St. AUGUSTINE, sense 2 *a*] seaport in NE Fla.: oldest city in the U.S.: pop. 12,000

staunch (stônch, stänch) ***vt.*** [OFr. *estanchier*, ult. < L. *stans*: see STANCE] **1.** to stop or check (the flow of blood or of tears, etc.) from (a wound, opening, etc.) **2.** *a*) to stop or lessen (a drain of resources, etc.) *b*) to stop up (a source of leakage, etc.) **—*vi.*** to cease flowing **—*adj.*** **1.** watertight; seaworthy [a *staunch* ship] **2.** firm; steadfast [a *staunch* supporter] **3.** strong; solidly made Also **stanch** For the *adj.*, **staunch** is now the prevailing form; for the *v.*, usage is about evenly divided between **staunch** and **stanch** **—staunch′ly *adv.*** **—staunch′ness *n.***

stave (stāv) ***n.*** [ME., taken as sing. of *staves*, pl. of *staf*, STAFF] **1.** *a*) any of the thin, shaped strips of wood, metal, etc. set edge to edge to form the wall of a barrel, bucket, etc. *b*) any similar slat, bar, rung, etc. **2.** a stick or staff **3.** a set of lines of a poem or song; stanza **4.** *Music same as* STAFF **—*vt.*** **staved** or **stove, stav′ing** **1.** to puncture or smash, esp. by breaking in staves **2.** to furnish with staves **—*vi.*** to be or become stove in, as a boat **—stave in** to break or crush inward **—stave off** to ward off or hold off, as by force, cleverness, etc.

STAVE

staves (stāvz) ***n.*** **1.** *alt. pl. of* STAFF **2.** *pl. of* STAVE

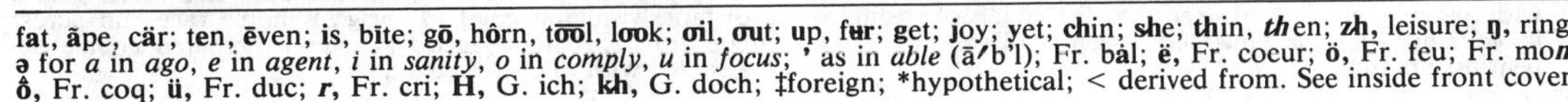

stay[1] (stā) *n.* [OE. *stæg*] a heavy rope or cable, usually of wire, used as a brace, as for a mast of a ship; guy *—vt.* to brace or support with stays

stay[2] (stā) *n.* [MFr. *estaie* < Frank.] **1.** a support; prop **2.** a strip of stiffening material used in a corset, shirt collar, etc. *—vt.* **1.** to support, or prop up **2.** to comfort in spirit **3.** to cause to rest (*on, upon,* or *in*)

stay[3] (stā) *vi.* **stayed** or archaic **staid, stay′ing** [< Anglo-Fr. < OFr. *ester* < L. *stare,* to stand] **1.** to continue in the place or condition specified; remain; keep *[*to *stay* at home, to *stay* healthy*]* **2.** to live, dwell, or reside, esp. temporarily **3.** to stop; halt **4.** to pause; wait; delay **5.** [Colloq.] to continue or endure; last **6.** [Colloq.] to keep up (*with* another contestant in a race, etc.) *—vt.* **1.** to stop, halt, or check **2.** to hinder, impede, or detain **3.** to postpone or delay (legal action) **4.** to satisfy for a time (thirst, appetite, etc.) **5.** *a)* to remain through (often with *out*) *[*to *stay* the week (out)*]* *b)* to be able to last through *[*to *stay* the distance*]* *—n.* **1.** *a)* a stopping or being stopped *b)* a halt, check, or pause **2.** a postponement in legal action *[*a *stay* of execution*]* **3.** the action of remaining, or the time spent, in a place *[*a long *stay* in Spain*]* **—stay put** [Colloq.] to remain in place or unchanged

staying power ability to last or endure; endurance

stay·sail (-sāl′, -s′l) *n.* a sail, esp. a triangular sail, fastened on a stay

St. Cath·a·rines (kath′rinz, -ər inz) city in SE Ontario, Canada, on the Welland Canal: pop. 123,000

St. Clair (kler), **Lake** [after Fr. *Sainte Claire* (St. Clare of Assisi, 1194–1253)] lake between SE Mich & Ontario, Canada

St. Clair Shores city in SE Mich., on Lake St. Clair: suburb of Detroit: pop. 76,000

St. Croix (kroi) [Fr., holy cross] largest island of the Virgin Islands of the U.S.

Ste. [Fr. *Sainte*] Saint (female)

stead (sted) *n.* [OE. *stede*] the place or position of a person or thing as filled by a substitute or successor *[*he came in my *stead]* **—stand (one) in good stead** to give (one) good use, service, etc.

stead·fast (sted′fast′, -fəst) *adj.* [OE. *stedefæste*] **1.** firm, fixed, or established **2.** not changing or wavering; constant **—stead′fast′ly** *adv.* **—stead′fast′ness** *n.*

stead·y (sted′ē) *adj.* **stead′i·er, stead′i·est** [see STEAD & -Y[2]] **1.** that does not shake, totter, etc.; firm; stable **2.** constant, regular, or continuous; not changing, faltering, etc. *[*a *steady* gaze*]* **3.** constant in behavior, loyalty, etc. **4.** habitual or regular *[*a *steady* customer*]* **5.** not easily excited; calm and controlled *[steady* nerves*]* **6.** sober; staid; reliable **7.** staying headed in the same direction: said of a ship *—interj.* keep calm! *—vt., vi.* **stead′ied, stead′y·ing** to make or become steady *—n.* [Colloq.] one's regular sweetheart **—go steady** [Colloq.] to be sweethearts **—stead′i·ly** *adv.* **—stead′i·ness** *n.*

stead·y-state theory (-stāt′) a theory of cosmology holding that as the universe expands, new matter is continuously created

steak (stāk) *n.* [ON. *steik* < base of *steikja,* to roast on a spit] a slice of meat, esp. beef, or of a large fish, cut thick for broiling or frying

steak tar·tare (tär tär′) [*tartare,* pseudo-Fr. for TARTAR: hence, steak in Tartar style] raw sirloin or tenderloin steak ground up and mixed with chopped onion, raw egg, salt, and pepper, and eaten uncooked

steal (stēl) *vt.* **stole, stol′en, steal′ing** [OE. *stælan*] **1.** to take (another's property, etc.) dishonestly, esp. in a secret manner **2.** to take slyly, surreptitiously, etc. *[*to *steal* a look*]* **3.** to gain slyly or artfully *[*he *stole* her heart*]* **4.** to be the outstanding performer in (a scene, act, etc.), esp. in a subordinate role **5.** to move, put, or convey stealthily (*in, into, from, away,* etc.) **6.** *Baseball* to gain (a base) safely without the help of a hit, walk, or error *—vi.* **1.** to be a thief **2.** to move, pass, etc. stealthily, quietly, etc. *—n.* [Colloq.] **1.** an act of stealing **2.** something stolen **3.** something obtained at an unusually low cost **—steal′er** *n.*

stealth (stelth) *n.* [ME. *stelthe* < base of *stelen,* to steal] secret, furtive, or artfully sly action or behavior **—stealth′i·ly** *adv.* **—stealth′i·ness** *n.* **—stealth′y** *adj.* **stealth′i·er, stealth′i·est**

steam (stēm) *n.* [OE.] **1.** orig., a vapor **2.** *a)* water as converted into a vapor or gas by being heated to the boiling point: used for heating, as a source of power, etc. *b)* the power supplied by steam under pressure *c)* [Colloq.] driving force; energy **3.** condensed water vapor; mist *—adj.* **1.** using steam; heated, operated, etc. by steam **2.** containing or conducting steam *—vi.* **1.** to give off steam or a vapor **2.** to be given off as steam **3.** to become covered with condensed steam, as a window (usually with *up*) **4.** to generate steam **5.** to move by steam power **6.** [Colloq.] to seethe with anger; fume *—vt.* to expose to the action of steam, as in cooking **—let** (or **blow**) **off steam** [Colloq.] to release pent-up emotion

steam·boat (-bōt′) *n.* a steamship, esp. a small one

steam engine **1.** an engine using steam under pressure to supply mechanical energy **2.** a locomotive powered by steam

steam·er (stē′mər) *n.* **1.** something operated by steam power, as a steamship or, formerly, a steam-powered automobile **2.** a container in which things are cooked, cleaned, etc. with steam

steam fitter a mechanic whose work (**steam fitting**) is installing and maintaining steam boilers, pipes, etc.

steam heat heat given off by steam in a closed system of pipes and radiators

steam iron an electric iron that releases steam through vents in the soleplate onto material being pressed

steam·roll·er (stēm′rōl′ər) *n.* **1.** a heavy, steam-driven roller used in building and repairing roads **2.** power which crushes opposition or forces its way relentlessly *—vt.* to crush, override, or force as if with a steamroller *—vi.* to move or act with overwhelming, crushing force Also **steam′roll′** *—adj.* relentlessly overpowering

steam·ship (-ship′) *n.* a ship driven by steam power

steam shovel a large, mechanically operated digger, powered by steam

steam table a serving table or counter, as in restaurants, having steam-heated compartments to keep foods warm

steam·y (stē′mē) *adj.* **steam′i·er, steam′i·est** **1.** of or like steam **2.** filled with steam **3.** giving off steam **—steam′i·ly** *adv.* **—steam′i·ness** *n.*

ste·ap·sin (stē ap′sin) *n.* [< Gr. *stea(r),* fat + (PE)PSIN] the lipase present in pancreatic juice

ste·ar·ic acid (stē ar′ik, stir′ik) [< Fr. < Gr. *stear,* tallow] a colorless, waxlike fatty acid, $C_{18}H_{36}O_2$, found in many animal and vegetable fats, and used in making candles, soaps, etc.

ste·a·rin (stē′ə rin, stir′in) *n.* [< Fr. < Gr.: see prec. & -INE[4]] a white, crystalline substance, $(C_{18}H_{35}O_2)_3C_3H_5$, found in the solid portion of most animal and vegetable fats: also **ste′a·rine** (-rin, -rēn′)

ste·a·tite (stē′ə tīt′) *n.* [L. *steatitis* < Gr. *stear,* tallow] a compact, massive variety of talc; soapstone **—ste′a·tit′ic** (-tit′ik) *adj.*

sted·fast (sted′fast′, -fəst) *adj. earlier var. of* STEADFAST **—sted′fast′ly** *adv.* **—sted′fast′ness** *n.*

steed (stēd) *n.* [OE. *steda*] a horse; esp., a high-spirited riding horse: literary term

steel (stēl) *n.* see PLURAL, II, D, 3 [OE. *stiele*] **1.** a hard, tough metal composed of iron alloyed with a small percentage of carbon and often variously with other metals, as nickel, chromium, etc., to produce hardness, etc. **2.** something made of steel; specif., [Poet.] a sword or dagger **3.** great strength or hardness *—adj.* of or like steel *—vt.* **1.** to cover or edge with steel **2.** to make hard, tough, unfeeling, etc. **—steel′i·ness** *n.* **—steel′y** *adj.* **-i·er, -i·est**

steel blue a metallic blue color like that of tempered steel **—steel′-blue′** *adj.*

Steele (stēl), Sir **Richard** 1672–1729; Brit. essayist & dramatist, born in Ireland

steel gray a bluish-gray color **—steel′-gray′** *adj.*

steel guitar a type of guitar, now esp. an electric guitar, with raised metal strings, held on the lap or mounted on legs and played by plucking while sliding a steel bar across the strings to change the pitch

steel mill a mill where steel is made, processed, and shaped: also **steel′works′** *n.*

steel wool long, hairlike shavings of steel in a pad or ball, used for scouring, smoothing, and polishing

steel·work·er (stēl′wur′kər) *n.* a worker in a steel mill

steel·yard (stēl′yärd′, stil′yərd) *n.* [STEEL & YARD[1] (in obs. sense of "rod")] a scale consisting of a metal arm suspended from above: the object to be weighed is hung from the shorter end and a weight is moved along the graduated longer end until the arm balances

steen·bok (stēn′bäk′, stān′-) *n., pl.* **-bok′, -boks′**: see PLURAL, II, D, 2 [Afrik. < Du. *steen,* a stone + *bok,* a buck] *same as* STEINBOK: also **steen′buck′** (-buk′)

steep[1] (stēp) *adj.* [OE. *steap,* lofty] **1.** having a sharp rise or slope; precipitous *[*a *steep* incline*]* **2.** [Colloq.] *a)* unreasonably high or great; excessive *[*a *steep* price*]* *b)* extreme *—n.* a steep slope **—steep′ly** *adv.* **—steep′ness** *n.*

steep[2] (stēp) *vt.* [akin to ON. *steypa*] **1.** to soak in liquid, as in order to extract the essence of **2.** to immerse, saturate, imbue, etc. *[steeped* in folklore*]* *—n.* **1.** a steeping or being steeped **2.** liquid in which something is steeped *—vi.* to be steeped, as tea leaves

steep·en (-′n) *vt., vi.* to make or become steep or steeper

stee·ple (stē′p′l) *n.* [OE. *stepel*] **1.** a tower rising above the main structure of a building, esp. of a church, usually capped with a spire **2.** *same as* SPIRE **—stee′pled** *adj.*

stee·ple·chase (-chās′) *n.* [the race orig. had as its goal a distant, visible steeple] **1.** orig., a horse race run across country **2.** a horse race run over a prepared course obstructed with ditches, hedges, etc.

stee·ple·jack (-jak′) ***n.*** a person whose work is building, painting, or repairing steeples, smokestacks, etc.

steer[1] (stir) ***vt.*** [OE. *stieran*] **1.** to guide (a ship or boat) by means of a rudder **2.** to direct the course of (an automobile, etc.) **3.** to oversee; direct *[he steered our efforts]* **4.** to set and follow (a course) —***vi.*** **1.** to steer a ship, automobile, etc. **2.** to be steered *[the car steers easily]* **3.** to set and follow a course —***n.*** [Colloq.] a suggestion; tip —**steer clear of** to avoid —**steer′a·ble** ***adj.*** —**steer′er** ***n.***

steer[2] (stir) ***n.*** [OE. *steor*] **1.** a castrated male of the cattle family **2.** loosely, any male of beef cattle

steer·age (stir′ij) ***n.*** **1.** *a)* the act of steering *b)* the response of a ship to the helmsman's guidance **2.** formerly, a section in some passenger ships occupied by passengers paying the lowest fare

steer·age·way (-wā′) ***n.*** the minimum forward speed needed to make a ship respond to the helmsman's guidance

steers·man (stirz′mən) ***n.***, *pl.* **-men** a person who steers a ship or boat; helmsman

Ste·fans·son (stef′an sən), **Vil·hjal·mur** (vil′hyoul′mər) 1879–1962; U.S. arctic explorer, born in Canada

stein (stīn) ***n.*** [G.] **1.** an earthenware beer mug, or a similar mug of pewter, glass, etc. **2.** the amount that a stein will hold

Stein (stīn), **Gertrude** 1874–1946; U.S. writer in France

Stein·beck (stīn′bek′), **John (Ernst)** 1902–68; U.S. novelist & short-story writer

stein·bok (stīn′bäk′) ***n.***, *pl.* **-bok′, -boks′**: see PLURAL, II, D, 2 [< G.] a small, reddish antelope found in grassy areas of S and E Africa

ste·le (stē′lē; *also, & for 2 usually,* stēl) ***n.*** [< L. < Gr. *stēlē*, a slab] **1.** an upright stone slab with an inscription or design, as a grave marker **2.** a prepared surface with an inscription or design, as on a façade

Stel·la (stel′ə) [L. *stella*, a star] a feminine name

stel·lar (stel′ər) ***adj.*** [< LL. < L. *stella*, a star] **1.** of the stars or a star **2.** like a star, as in shape **3.** by or as by a star performer; excellent **4.** leading; chief *[a stellar role]*

stel·late (stel′āt, -it) ***adj.*** [< L. pp. of *stellare*, to cover with stars < *stella*, a star] star-shaped; coming out in rays or points from a center: also **stel′lat·ed** —**stel′late·ly** ***adv.***

stem[1] (stem) ***n.*** [OE. *stemn*] **1.** the main stalk or trunk of a tree, shrub, or other plant, extending above the ground and bearing the leaves, flowers, etc. **2.** any stalk supporting leaves, flowers, or fruit **3.** a stemlike part; specif., *a)* the slender part of a tobacco pipe attached to the bowl *b)* a narrow supporting part above the foot of a wineglass, goblet, etc. *c)* the shaft projecting from a watch, with a knob for winding the spring *d)* the thick stroke of a letter, as in printing *e)* the vertical line of a musical note **4.** the prow of a ship; bow **5.** a branch of a family **6.** the part of a word to which inflectional endings are added —***vt.*** **stemmed, stem′ming** **1.** to remove the stem from (a fruit, etc.) **2.** to make headway against *[to row upstream, stemming the current]* —***vi.*** to originate or derive —**from stem to stern** **1.** from one end of a ship to another **2.** through the length of anything —**stem′less** ***adj.*** —**stem′like′** ***adj.***

stem[2] (stem) ***vt.*** **stemmed, stem′ming** [ON. *stemma*] **1.** to stop or check; esp., to dam up (a river, etc.), or to stop or check as if by damming up **2.** to turn (a ski) in stemming —***vi.*** to stop or slow down in skiing by turning the tip of the ski(s) inward

stemmed (stemd) ***adj.*** **1.** having a stem *[a thin-stemmed goblet]* **2.** with the stem or stems removed

stem-wind·ing (stem′wīn′diŋ) ***adj.*** wound, as a watch, by turning a knurled knob at the outer end of the stem —**stem′-wind′er** ***n.***

stench (stench) ***n.*** [OE. *stenc*] an offensive smell; stink

sten·cil (sten′s'l) ***vt.*** **-ciled** or **-cilled, -cil·ing** or **-cil·ling** [< OFr. < *estencele*, ult. < L. *scintilla*, a spark] to make, mark, or paint with a stencil —***n.*** **1.** a thin sheet, as of paper or metal, perforated or cut through in such a way that when ink, paint, etc. is applied to the sheet, the patterns, designs, letters, etc. are marked on the surface beneath **2.** a pattern, design, etc. made by stenciling —**sten′cil·er, sten′cil·ler** ***n.***

Sten·dhal (sten′däl; *Fr.* stan dål′) (pseud. of *Marie Henri Beyle*) 1783–1842; Fr. novelist & essayist

sten·o- [< Gr. *stenos*, narrow] *a combining form meaning* narrow, thin, small, etc. *[stenography]*

ste·nog·ra·pher (stə näg′rə fər) ***n.*** a person skilled in stenography

ste·nog·ra·phy (-fē) ***n.*** [STENO- + -GRAPHY] shorthand writing; specif., the skill or work of writing down dictation, testimony, etc. in shorthand and later transcribing it, as on a typewriter —**sten·o·graph·ic** (sten′ə graf′ik), **sten′o·graph′i·cal** ***adj.*** —**sten′o·graph′i·cal·ly** ***adv.***

sten·o·type (sten′ə tīp′) ***n.*** [STENO- + -TYPE] **1.** a symbol or symbols used in stenotypy **2.** a keyboard machine used in stenotypy —***vt.*** **-typed′, -typ′ing** to record by stenotype

sten·o·typ·y (-tī′pē) ***n.*** shorthand in which symbols representing sounds, words, or phrases are typed on a keyboard machine —**sten′o·typ′ist** ***n.***

Sten·tor (sten′tôr) a Greek herald in the *Iliad* having a very loud voice —***n.*** [*usually* **s-**] a person having a very loud voice

sten·to·ri·an (sten tôr′ē ən) ***adj.*** [< prec.] very loud

step (step) ***n.*** [OE. *stepe*] **1.** the act of moving and placing the foot, as in walking, dancing, climbing, etc. **2.** the distance covered by such a movement **3.** a short distance **4.** *a)* a manner of stepping; gait *b)* any pace or stride in marching *[the goose step]* *c)* a sequence of movements in dancing, usually repeated in a set pattern **5.** the sound of stepping; footfall **6.** a mark made by stepping; footprint **7.** a rest for the foot in climbing, as a stair or the rung of a ladder **8.** [*pl.*] a flight of stairs **9.** something resembling a stair step, as a raised frame supporting a mast **10.** a degree; rank; level; stage **11.** any of a series of acts, processes, etc. **12.** *Music* *a)* a degree of the staff or scale *b)* the interval between two consecutive degrees —***vi.*** **stepped, step′ping** **1.** to move by executing a step **2.** to walk, esp. a short distance **3.** to move with measured steps, as in dancing **4.** to move quickly: often with *along* **5.** to come or enter (*into* a situation, etc.) **6.** to put or press the foot down (*on* something) *[step on the brake]* —***vt.*** **1.** to take (one or more strides or paces) **2.** *a)* to set (the foot) down *b)* to move across or over by foot **3.** to execute the steps of (a dance) **4.** to measure by taking steps: usually with *off* *[step off ten paces]* **5.** to provide with steps; specif., *a)* to cut steps in *b)* to arrange in a series of degrees or grades —**break step** to stop marching in cadence —**in step** **1.** keeping to a set rhythm in marching, dancing, etc. **2.** in conformity or agreement —**keep step** to stay in step —**out of step** not in step —**step by step** by degrees; gradually —**step down** **1.** to resign (*from* an office, etc.) **2.** to decrease, as in rate —**step in** to start to participate; intervene —**step on it** [Colloq.] to go faster; hurry —**step out** [Colloq.] to go out for a good time —**step up** **1.** to approach **2.** to advance **3.** to increase, as in rate —**take steps** to adopt certain measures —**watch one's step** [Colloq.] to be careful

step·broth·er (step′bru*th*′ər) ***n.*** one's stepparent's son by a former marriage

step·child (-chīld′) ***n.***, *pl.* **-chil′dren** [OE. *steop-*, orphaned: orig. used of orphaned children] a child that one's husband or wife had by a former marriage

step·daugh·ter (-dôt′ər) ***n.*** a female stepchild

step-down (-doun′) ***adj.*** that steps down, or decreases, power, speed, etc., as a transformer, gear, etc. —***n.*** a decrease, as in intensity, etc.

step·fa·ther (-fä′*th*ər) ***n.*** a male stepparent

steph·a·no·tis (stef′ə nōt′is) ***n.*** [ModL. < Gr. < *stephanos*, a crown] a woody vine grown for its white, waxy, sweet-scented flowers

Ste·phen (stē′vən) [L. *Stephanus* < Gr. < *stephanos*, a crown] a masculine name: dim. *Steve*

step-in (step′in′) ***adj.*** put on by being stepped into —***n.*** a step-in garment or [*pl.*], esp. formerly, undergarment

step·lad·der (-lad′ər) ***n.*** a four-legged ladder having broad, flat steps

step·moth·er (-mu*th*′ər) ***n.*** a female stepparent

step·par·ent (-per′ənt, -par′-) ***n.*** [see STEPCHILD] the person who has married one's parent after the death or divorce of the other parent

steppe (step) ***n.*** [< Russ. *step′*] **1.** any of the great plains of SE Europe and Asia, having few trees **2.** any similar plain

stepped-up (stept′up′) ***adj.*** increased, as in tempo

step·per (step′ər) ***n.*** a person or animal that steps in a specified manner, as a dancer or a horse

step·ping·stone (step′iŋ stōn′) ***n.*** **1.** a stone, usually one of a series, used to step on, as in crossing a stream, etc. **2.** a means of advancement Also **stepping stone**

step·sis·ter (-sis′tər) ***n.*** one's stepparent's daughter by a former marriage

step·son (-sun′) ***n.*** a male stepchild

step-up (-up′) ***adj.*** that steps up, or increases, power, speed, etc., as a transformer, gear, etc. —***n.*** an increase, as in intensity, etc.

-ster (stər) [OE. *-estre*, orig. a fem. agent suffix] *a suffix meaning:* **1.** a person who is, does, or creates (something specified) *[oldster, punster]*: often derogatory *[rhymester]* **2.** a person associated with (something specified) *[gangster]*

stere (stir) *n.* [Fr. *stère* < Gr. *stereos,* solid, cubic] a cubic meter

ster·e·o (ster′ē ō′, stir′-) *n., pl.* **-os′** **1.** *a)* a stereophonic record player, radio, record, tape, etc. *b)* a stereophonic system **2.** a stereoscope or a stereoscopic picture, etc. **3.** *shortened form of: a)* STEREOTYPE *b)* STEREOTYPY —*adj. shortened form of* STEREOPHONIC

ster·e·o- [< Gr. *stereos,* hard, firm] *a combining form meaning* solid, firm, three-dimensional *[stereoscope]*

ster·e·o·phon·ic (ster′ē ə fän′ik, stir′-) *adj.* [prec. + PHONIC] designating or of sound reproduction, as in motion pictures, records, tapes, or broadcasting, using two or more channels to carry and reproduce through separate speakers a blend of sounds from separate sources —**ster′e·o·phon′i·cal·ly** *adv.*

ster·e·op·ti·con (-äp′ti kən, -kän′) *n.* [< Gr. *stereos,* solid + *optikon,* of sight] a kind of slide projector that allows one view to fade out while the next is fading in

ster·e·o·scope (ster′ē ə skōp′, stir′-) *n.* [STEREO- + -SCOPE] an instrument that gives a three-dimensional effect to photographs viewed through it: it has two eyepieces, through which two slightly different views of the same scene are viewed side by side —**ster′e·o·scop′ic** (-skäp′ik) *adj.* —**ster′e·o·scop′i·cal·ly** *adv.*

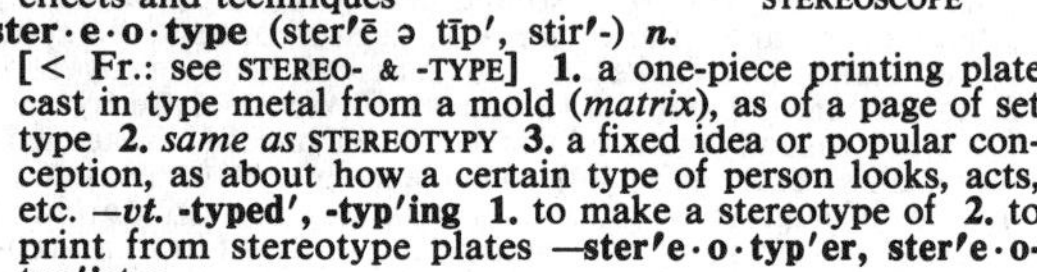

STEREOSCOPE

ster·e·os·co·py (ster′ē äs′kə pē, stir′-) *n.* the science of stereoscopic effects and techniques

ster·e·o·type (ster′ē ə tīp′, stir′-) *n.* [< Fr.: see STEREO- & -TYPE] **1.** a one-piece printing plate cast in type metal from a mold (*matrix*), as of a page of set type **2.** *same as* STEREOTYPY **3.** a fixed idea or popular conception, as about how a certain type of person looks, acts, etc. —*vt.* **-typed′, -typ′ing** **1.** to make a stereotype of **2.** to print from stereotype plates —**ster′e·o·typ′er, ster′e·o·typ′ist** *n.*

ster·e·o·typed (-tīpt′) *adj.* **1.** having the nature of a stereotype; esp., hackneyed; trite; not original **2.** printed from stereotype plates

ster·e·o·typ·y (-tī′pē) *n.* the process of making or printing from stereotype plates

ster·ile (ster′'l; *Brit. & Canad., usually* -īl) *adj.* [L. *sterilis*] **1.** incapable of producing others of its kind; barren **2.** producing little or nothing *[sterile* soil*]* **3.** lacking in interest or vitality *[*a *sterile* style*]* **4.** free from living microorganisms; esp., aseptic —**ster′ile·ly** *adv.* —**ste·ril·i·ty** (stə ril′ə tē) *n.*

ster·i·lize (ster′ə līz′) *vt.* **-lized′, -liz′ing** to make sterile; specif., *a)* to make incapable of producing others of its kind *b)* to make (land) unproductive *c)* to free from living microorganisms, as by subjecting to great heat or chemical action Also [Chiefly Brit.] **ster′i·lise′** —**ster′i·li·za′tion** *n.* —**ster′i·liz′er** *n.*

ster·ling (stur′liŋ) *n.* [ME. *sterlinge,* Norman silver penny < ?] **1.** sterling silver or articles made of it **2.** the standard of fineness of legal British coinage: for silver, 0.500; for gold, 0.91666 **3.** British money —*adj.* **1.** of standard quality: said of silver that is at least 92.5 percent pure **2.** of or payable in British money **3.** made of sterling silver **4.** worthy; excellent

Ster·ling Heights (stur′liŋ) [? ult. after Lord *Sterling,* general in the Am. Revolutionary Army] city in SE Mich.: suburb of Detroit: pop. 109,000

stern[1] (sturn) *adj.* [OE. *styrne*] **1.** hard; severe; strict *[stern* measures*]* **2.** grim; forbidding *[*a *stern* face*]* **3.** that cannot be changed *[stern* reality*]* **4.** unshakable; firm *[stern* determination*]* —**stern′ly** *adv.* —**stern′ness** *n.*

stern[2] (sturn) *n.* [ON. *stjorn,* steering < *styra,* to steer] **1.** the rear end of a ship, boat, etc. **2.** the rear end of anything

Sterne (sturn), **Laurence** 1713–68; Brit. novelist, born in Ireland

stern·most (sturn′mōst′) *adj.* **1.** nearest the stern **2.** farthest astern; rearmost

stern·post (sturn′pōst′) *n.* the main, upright piece at the stern of a vessel, usually supporting the rudder

ster·num (stur′nəm) *n., pl.* **ster′nums, ster′na** (-nə) [ModL. < Gr. *sternon*] a thin, flat structure of bone and cartilage to which most of the ribs are attached in the front of the chest in most vertebrates; breastbone —**ster′nal** *adj.*

ster·nu·ta·tion (stur′nyoo tā′shən) *n.* [< L. < freq. of *sternuere,* to sneeze] a sneeze or the act of sneezing —**ster·nu·ta·to·ry** (stər nyōōt′ə tôr′ē), **ster′nu·ta′tive** *adj.*

stern·ward (sturn′wərd) *adv., adj.* toward the stern; astern: also **stern′wards** *adv.*

stern·way (-wā′) *n.* backward movement of a ship

stern-wheel·er (-hwēl′ər, -wēl′ər) *n.* a steamer propelled by a paddle wheel at the stern

ster·oid (stir′oid, ster′-) *n.* [STER(OL) + -OID] any of a group of compounds including the sterols, sex hormones, etc., characteristically having the ring structure of the sterols —**ste·roi′dal** *adj.*

ster·ol (stir′ôl, ster′-; -ōl) *n.* [< (CHOLE)STEROL] any of a group of solid cyclic alcohols, as cholesterol, found in plant and animal tissues

ster·to·rous (stur′tə rəs) *adj.* [< L. *stertere,* to snore] characterized by loud, labored breathing, or snoring —**ster′to·rous·ly** *adv.* —**ster′to·rous·ness** *n.*

stet (stet) [L.] let it stand: a printer's term used to indicate that matter previously struck out is to remain —*vt.* **stet′ted, stet′ting** to cancel a change in or deletion of (a word, line, etc.), as by writing "stet" in the margin of a proof or manuscript

steth·o·scope (steth′ə skōp′) *n.* [< Fr. < Gr. *stēthos,* the chest + -SCOPE] *Med.* a hearing instrument placed against the body for examining the heart, lungs, etc. by listening to the sounds they make —**steth′o·scop′ic** (-skäp′ik), **steth′o·scop′i·cal** *adj.* —**steth′o·scop′i·cal·ly** *adv.* —**ste·thos·co·py** (stə thäs′kə pē) *n.*

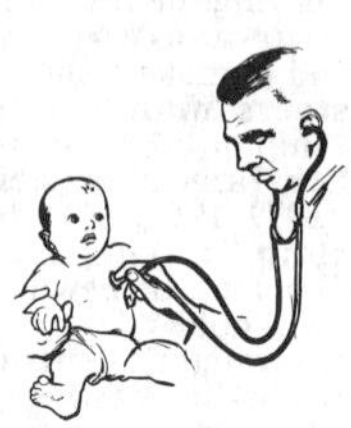

STETHOSCOPE

Stet·son (stet′s'n) *a trademark for* hats of various kinds —*n.* *[often* **s-**] a man's hat, worn esp. by Western cowboys, usually of felt, with a broad brim and a high crown

Steu·ben (stōō′b'n; *G.* shtoi′bən), Baron **Frederick William Augustus von** 1730–94; Prussian military officer: served as Am. general in the Revolutionary War

ste·ve·dore (stē′və dôr′) *n.* [< Sp. < *estivar,* to stow < L. *stipare,* to cram] a person employed at loading and unloading ships —*vt., vi.* **-dored′, -dor′ing** to load or unload the cargo of (a ship)

Ste·ven (stē′vən) [see STEPHEN] a masculine name

Ste·ven·son (stē′vən s'n), **Robert Louis (Balfour)** 1850–94; Scot. novelist, poet, & essayist

stew (stōō, styōō) *vt.* [< MFr. *estuver,* ult. < L. *ex,* out + Gr. *typhos,* steam] to cook by simmering slowly for a long time —*vi.* **1.** to undergo cooking in this way **2.** to live in hot, overcrowded conditions **3.** to fret or worry —*n.* **1.** a dish, esp. of meat and vegetables, cooked by stewing **2.** a state of anxiety or worry —**stew in one's own juice** to suffer from one's own actions

stew·ard (stōō′ərd, styōō′-) *n.* [OE. *stiweard* < *stig,* enclosure + *weard,* a keeper] **1.** a person in charge of the affairs of a large household, who supervises the kitchen and servants, manages the accounts, etc. **2.** one who acts as an administrator, as of finances and property, for another **3.** a person variously responsible for the food and drink, the service personnel, etc. in a club, restaurant, etc. **4.** a person in charge of arrangements for a ball, race, etc. **5.** an attendant on a ship, airplane, etc. who looks after the passengers' comfort **6.** *short for* SHOP STEWARD —*vi.* to act as a steward —**stew′ard·ship′** *n.*

stew·ard·ess (-ər dis) *n.* a woman steward (esp. sense 5)

Stew·art (stōō′ərt, styōō′-) [see STUART] a masculine name

stewed (stōōd) *adj.* **1.** cooked by stewing, as food **2.** [Slang] drunk; intoxicated

stew·pan (stōō′pan′, styōō′-) *n.* a pan for stewing

St. George's Channel strait between Ireland & Wales, connecting the Irish Sea with the Atlantic

St. He·le·na (hə lē′nə, hel′i nə) Brit. island in the S Atlantic, c. 1,200 mi. from Africa: site of Napoleon's exile (1815–21)

stick (stik) *n.* [OE. *sticca*] **1.** a twig or small branch broken or cut off, esp. a dead and dry one **2.** a long, slender piece of wood, often shaped for a specific purpose, as a wand, staff, club, cane, rod, etc. **3.** a stalk, as of celery **4.** something shaped like a stick *[*a *stick* of chewing gum*]* **5.** a separate article *[*every *stick* of furniture*]* **6.** an implement for striking a ball, puck, etc. *[*a hockey *stick]* **7.** a stab or thrust **8.** the power of adhering or making adhere **9.** [Colloq.] a dull or stupid person **10.** [Slang] a marijuana cigarette **11.** *Aeron.* a lever that controls the altitude and movement of an airplane: in full, **control stick** —*vt.* **stuck** or for *vt.* 8 **sticked, stick′ing** **1.** to pierce or puncture, as with a pointed instrument **2.** to kill by stabbing **3.** to pierce something with (a knife, pin, etc.) **4.** to thrust or push (*in, out,* etc.) **5.** *a)* to fasten or attach by gluing, pinning, etc. *b)* to decorate with things fastened in this way **6.** to transfix or impale **7.** to obstruct, bog down, etc.; also, to detain, delay, etc.: usually used in the passive *[*the wheels were *stuck,* he was *stuck* in town*]* **8.** to prop (a vine, etc.) with a stick **9.** [Colloq.] to place; put; set **10.** [Colloq.] to make sticky by smearing **11.** [Colloq.] to puzzle; baffle **12.** [Slang] *a)* to make pay excessively *b)* to impose a disagreeable task, burden, etc. upon —*vi.* **1.** to be or remain fixed or embedded by a pointed end, as a nail, etc. **2.** to be or remain attached by adhesion; adhere **3.** *a)* to remain in the same place *[*they *stick* at home*]* *b)* to remain fixed in the memory *c)* to remain in effect *[*to make charges *stick]* **4.** to keep or stay close *[*friends *stick* together, *stick* to the trail*]* **5.** to persevere *[*to *stick* at a job*]* **6.** to remain firm; endure **7.** to become fixed, blocked, embedded, jammed, etc. *[*my shoe *stuck* in the mud, the gears *stuck]* **8.** to be puzzled **9.** to hesitate; scruple *[*he'll *stick* at nothing*]* **10.** to protrude or extend (with *out, up,* etc.) —**be on the stick** [Slang] to be alert, efficient, etc. —**stick around** [Slang] to stay near at hand —**stick by** (or **to**) to remain loyal to —**stick it out** [Slang] to endure something to the end —**stick to one's ribs** to be nourishing: said of food —**stick up** [Slang] to commit armed robbery upon —**stick up for** [Colloq.] to uphold; defend —**the sticks** [Colloq.] the rural districts —**stick′like′** *adj.*

stick·ball (stik′bôl′) *n.* a game like baseball played by children, as on city streets, with improvised equipment such as a broom handle and a soft rubber ball

stick·er (-ər) *n.* a person or thing that sticks; specif., *a)* a bur, barb, or thorn *b)* a gummed label *c)* [Colloq.] *same as* STICKLER *d)* [Slang] a knife used as a weapon

stick·le (-′l) *vi.* **-led, -ling** [prob. < ME. *stightlen,* to dispose, ult. < OE. *stihtan,* to arrange] **1.** to raise objections, haggle, etc., esp. in a stubborn way, usually about trifles **2.** to scruple (*at*)

stick·le·back (stik′′l bak′) *n.* [< OE. *sticel,* a prick + ME. *bak,* back] a small, scaleless fish with sharp spines: the male builds a nest for the eggs

stick·ler (stik′lər) *n.* [cf. STICKLE] **1.** a person who insists on strict observance of something *[*a *stickler* for discipline*]* **2.** [Colloq.] something puzzling to solve

stick·pin (-pin′) *n.* a pin, esp. one set with a gem, worn as an ornament in a cravat or necktie

stick shift a gearshift for a motor vehicle operated manually, rather than automatically, by moving a lever, esp. one on the floor

stick-to-it·ive·ness (stik to͞o′it iv nis) *n.* [Colloq.] persistence; perseverance

stick-up (stik′up′) *n. slang term for* HOLDUP (sense 2)

stick·y (-ē) *adj.* **stick′i·er, stick′i·est** **1.** that sticks; adhesive; clinging **2.** covered with an adhesive substance **3.** [Colloq.] hot and humid **4.** [Colloq.] difficult; troublesome *[*a *sticky* problem*]* **5.** [Colloq.] overly sentimental —**stick′i·ly** *adv.* —**stick′i·ness** *n.*

sticky wicket **1.** *Cricket* a damp area between wickets, making play difficult and slow **2.** [Chiefly Brit.] a difficult or awkward situation

stiff (stif) *adj.* [OE. *stif*] **1.** hard to bend or stretch; rigid; firm **2.** hard to move or operate; not free or limber **3.** stretched tight; taut **4.** *a)* sore or limited in movement: said of joints or muscles *b)* having such joints or muscles **5.** not fluid or loose; thick; dense *[*a *stiff* sauce*]* **6.** moving swiftly, as a breeze **7.** containing much alcohol: said of a drink **8.** of high potency *[*a *stiff* dose of medicine*]* **9.** harsh *[*a *stiff* punishment*]* **10.** difficult *[*a *stiff* climb*]* **11.** constrained or awkward; not easy or graceful **12.** resolute or stubborn, as a person, a fight, etc. **13.** [Colloq.] high *[*a *stiff* price*]* **14.** [Slang] drunk —*adv.* **1.** to a stiff condition **2.** [Colloq.] completely *[*scared *stiff]* —*n.* [Slang] **1.** a corpse **2.** a drunken person **3.** an excessively formal person **4.** a rough person **5.** a hobo —*vt.* **stiffed, stiff′ing** [Slang] to cheat, as by leaving no tip or gratuity —**stiff′ish** *adj.* —**stiff′ly** *adv.* —**stiff′ness** *n.*

stiff-arm (-ärm′) *vt.* to push away (an opponent, etc.) with one's arm out straight —*n.* the act of stiff-arming

stiff·en (stif′′n) *vt., vi.* to make or become stiff or stiffer —**stiff′en·er** *n.*

stiff-necked (stif′nekt′) *adj.* stubborn; obstinate

sti·fle (stī′f′l) *vt.* **-fled, -fling** [ult. < MFr. *estouffer,* to smother] **1.** to suffocate; smother **2.** to suppress or check; stop *[*to *stifle* a sob*]* —*vi.* **1.** to die from lack of air **2.** to suffer from lack of fresh, cool air —**sti′fling** *adj.*

stig·ma (stig′mə) *n., pl.* **-mas**; also, and for 4, 5, & 6 usually, **stig·ma·ta** (stig mät′ə, stig′mə te) [L. < Gr., lit., a prick with a pointed instrument] **1.** formerly, a brand, as on a criminal **2.** a mark of disgrace or reproach **3.** a mark, sign, etc. indicating that something is not considered normal **4.** a small mark, scar, opening, etc., as a pore, on the surface of a plant or animal **5.** a spot on the skin, esp. one that bleeds because of nervous tension **6.** [*pl.*] marks resembling the Crucifixion wounds of Jesus **7.** *Bot.* the upper tip of the style of a flower, on which pollen falls —**stig·mat′ic** (-mat′ik), **stig·mat′i·cal** *adj.*

stig·ma·tize (stig′mə tīz′) *vt.* **-tized′, -tiz′ing** **1.** to mark with a stigma **2.** to mark as disgraceful —**stig′ma·ti·za′tion** *n.*

stile (stīl) *n.* [OE. *stigel* < *stigan,* to climb] **1.** a step or set of steps used in climbing over a fence or wall **2.** *shortened form of* TURNSTILE

sti·let·to (sti let′ō) *n., pl.* **-tos, -toes** [It., dim. of *stilo,* a dagger < L. *stilus:* see STYLE] a small dagger with a slender, tapering blade —*vt.* **-toed, -to·ing** to stab or kill with a stiletto

still[1] (stil) *adj.* [OE. *stille*] **1.** without sound; quiet; silent **2.** hushed, soft, or low in sound **3.** not moving; motionless: following *stand, sit, lie,* etc., sometimes regarded as an adverb **4.** calm; tranquil; unruffled *[still* water*]* **5.** not effervescent: said of wine **6.** *Motion Pictures* designating or of a single posed photograph or one made from a single frame of motion-picture film, for use as in publicity —*n.* **1.** silence; quiet *[*in the *still* of the night*]* **2.** a still photograph —*adv.* **1.** at or up to the time indicated, whether past, present, or future **2.** even; yet *[still* colder*]* **3.** nevertheless; yet *[*rich but *still* unhappy*]* **4.** [Archaic] ever; constantly —*conj.* nevertheless; yet —*vt.* to make still; specif., *a)* to make silent *b)* to make motionless *c)* to calm; relieve —*vi.* to become still —**still′ness** *n.*

still[2] (stil) *n.* [< obs. *still,* to DISTILL] **1.** an apparatus used for distilling liquids, esp. alcoholic liquors **2.** *same as* DISTILLERY —*vt., vi.* [Dial.] to distill (alcoholic liquor) illegally

STILL

still·born (stil′bôrn′) *adj.* **1.** dead at birth **2.** unsuccessful from the beginning; abortive —**still′birth′** *n.*

still life **1.** an arrangement of objects, as fruit in a bowl, flowers in a vase, etc. as the subject of a painting, drawing, etc. **2.** *pl.* **still lifes** such a painting, etc. —**still′-life′** *adj.*

Still·son wrench (stil′s′n) [after its U.S. inventor (in 1869), D. *Stillson*] *a trademark for* a wrench with a jaw that moves through a collar pivoted to the shaft, used for turning pipes, etc.: the jaw tightens as pressure is applied to the handle

still·y (stil′ē; *for adv.* stil′lē) *adj.* **still′i·er, still′i·est** [Literary] still; silent; calm —*adv.* in a still manner; quietly

stilt (stilt) *n.* [prob. < MLowG. or MDu. *stelte*] **1.** either of a pair of poles, each with a footrest somewhere along its length, used for walking with the feet above the ground, as in play **2.** any of a number of long posts used to hold a building, etc. above the ground or out of the water **3.** *pl.* **stilts, stilt:** see PLURAL, II, D, 1 any of several wading birds of the avocet family

stilt·ed (stil′tid) *adj.* **1.** raised on or as on stilts **2.** formal or dignified in a way that is not natural; pompous —**stilt′ed·ly** *adv.* —**stilt′ed·ness** *n.*

Stil·ton (cheese) (stil′t′n) [< *Stilton,* village in EC England] a rich, crumbly cheese with veins of blue-green mold

stim·u·lant (stim′yə lənt) *adj.* stimulating —*n.* anything that stimulates; specif., *a)* any drug, etc. that temporarily speeds up the heartbeat or some other body process *b)* popularly, an alcoholic drink: actually alcohol is a body depressant

stim·u·late (-lāt′) *vt.* **-lat′ed, -lat′ing** [< L. pp. of *stimulare,* to prick < *stimulus,* a goad] **1.** to make active or more active; stir up or spur on; arouse; excite **2.** to invigorate as by an alcoholic drink **3.** *Med., Physiol.* to excite (an organ, etc.) to activity or increased activity —*vi.* to act as a stimulant or stimulus —**stim′u·lat′er, stim′u·la′tor** *n.* —**stim′u·la′tion** *n.* —**stim′u·la′tive** *adj., n.*

stim·u·lus (-ləs) *n., pl.* **-u·li′** (-lī′) [L., a goad] **1.** something that stirs to action or increased action; incentive **2.** *Physiol., Psychol.* any action or agent that causes or changes an activity in an organism, organ, etc.

sti·my (stī′mē) *n., pl.* **-mies,** *vt.* **-mied, -my·ing** *same as* STYMIE

sting (stiŋ) *vt.* **stung, sting′ing** [OE. *stingan*] **1.** to prick or wound with a sting: said of plants and insects **2.** to cause sharp, sudden, smarting pain to *[*cold wind *stings* the face*]* **3.** to cause to suffer mentally *[*his conscience *stung* him*]* **4.** to stimulate suddenly and sharply *[stung* into action*]* **5.** [Slang] to cheat; esp., to overcharge —*vi.* **1.** to use a sting **2.** to cause or feel sharp, smarting pain, either physical or mental —*n.* **1.** the act or power of stinging **2.** a pain or wound resulting from or as from stinging **3.** a thing that stimulates; goad **4.** a sharp-pointed organ, as in insects, used to prick, wound, or inject poison **5.** any of the stinging, hollow hairs on some plants, as nettles —**sting′er** *n.* —**sting′ing·ly** *adv.* —**sting′less** *adj.*

sting·ray (stiŋ′rā′) *n.* a large ray (fish) having a whiplike tail with a sharp spine or spines that can inflict painful wounds: also **sting·a·ree** (stiŋ′ə rē′, stiŋ′ə rē′)

stin·gy[1] (stin′jē) *adj.* **stin′gi·er, stin′gi·est** [akin to STING] **1.** giving or spending grudgingly; miserly **2.** less than needed or expected —**stin′gi·ly** *adv.* —**stin′gi·ness** *n.*

sting·y[2] (stiŋ′ē) *adj.* stinging or capable of stinging

stink (stiŋk) *vi.* **stank** or **stunk, stunk, stink′ing** [OE. *stincan*] **1.** to give off a strong, bad smell **2.** to be offensive or hateful **3.** [Slang] to be no good, or of low quality —*n.* **1.** a strong, bad smell; stench **2.** [Slang] a strong public reaction, as of outrage, censure, or protest —**stink out** to drive out by a strong, bad smell —**stink up** to cause to stink —**stink′er** *n.* —**stink′ing** *adj.* —**stink′ing·ly** *adv.*

stink bomb a device made to burn or explode and give off an offensive smell

stink·bug (-bug′) *n.* any of various foul-smelling bugs

stink·weed (-wēd′) *n.* any of several foul-smelling plants, as the jimson weed

stint (stint) *vt.* [OE. *styntan,* to blunt] to limit to a certain, usually small, quantity or share —*vi.* to be sparing in giving or using —*n.* **1.** restriction; limit **2.** a task or share of work to be done —**stint′er** *n.* —**stint′ing·ly** *adv.*

stipe (stīp) *n.* [Fr. < L. *stipes,* tree trunk] a stalk, as that supporting a mushroom cap, fern frond, etc.

sti·pend (stī′pend, -pənd) *n.* [L. *stipendium* < *stips,* small coin + *pendere,* to weigh out, pay] **1.** a regular or fixed payment for services, as a salary **2.** any periodic payment, as an allowance

sti·pen·di·ar·y (stī pen′dē er′ē) *adj.* **1.** receiving, or performing services for, a stipend **2.** paid for by a stipend —*n., pl.* **-ar′ies** a person who receives a stipend

stip·ple (stip′'l) *vt.* **-pled, -pling** [< Du. < *stippel,* a speckle] **1.** to paint, draw, engrave, or apply in small dots rather than in lines or solid areas **2.** to mark with dots; fleck —*n.* **1.** *a)* the art of painting, drawing, etc. in dots *b)* the effect so produced, or an effect like it, as in nature **2.** stippled work Also **stip′pling** *n.* —**stip′pler** *n.*

stip·u·late (stip′yə lāt′) *vt.* **-lat′ed, -lat′ing** [< L. pp. of *stipulari,* to bargain] **1.** to arrange definitely, as in a contract **2.** to specify as an essential condition of an agreement —*vi.* to make a specific demand (*for* something) as a condition of an agreement —**stip′u·la′tion** *n.* —**stip′u·la′tor** *n.* —**stip′u·la·to′ry** (-lə tôr′ē) *adj.*

stip·ule (stip′yo͞ol) *n.* [ModL. *stipula* < L., a stalk] either of a pair of small, leaflike parts at the base of some leafstalks —**stip′u·lar** (-yoo lər) *adj.* —**stip′u·late** (-lit, -lāt′), **stip′u·lat′ed** *adj.*

stir[1] (stʉr) *vt.* **stirred, stir′ring** [OE. *styrian*] **1.** to move, shake, etc., esp. slightly **2.** to rouse from sleep, lethargy, etc. **3.** to make move or be active [*stirring* oneself to finish the work] **4.** to mix (a liquid, etc.) by moving a spoon, fork, spatula, etc. around **5.** to excite the feelings of; move deeply **6.** to incite or provoke (often with *up*) **7.** to evoke, or call up [to *stir* memories] —*vi.* **1.** to move, esp. only slightly **2.** to be busy and active **3.** to begin to show signs of activity **4.** to do or undergo mixing —*n.* **1.** a stirring, or the sound of this **2.** movement; activity **3.** excitement or commotion —**stir′rer** *n.*

stir[2] (stʉr) *n.* [prob. ult. < Romany] [Slang] a prison

stir-cra·zy (-krā′zē) *adj.* [see STIR[2]] [Slang] suffering nervous strain from being confined for a long time

stir-fry (-frī′) *vt.* **-fried′, -fry′ing** in Chinese cooking, to fry very quickly in a wok, with a little oil, while stirring constantly

stir·ring (stʉr′iŋ) *adj.* **1.** active; busy **2.** that stirs one's feelings; moving; rousing [*stirring* music]

stir·rup (stʉr′əp, stir′-) *n.* [OE. *stigrap*] **1.** a flat-bottomed ring hung by a strap from a saddle and used as a footrest **2.** any of various stirruplike supports, clamps, etc.

stirrup (bone) *same as* STAPES

stitch (stich) *n.* [OE. *stice,* a puncture] **1.** *a)* a single complete in-and-out movement of a threaded needle in sewing *b)* *same as* SUTURE (*n.* 3 *c*) **2.** a single loop of yarn worked off a needle in knitting, crocheting, etc. **3.** a loop, knot, etc. made by stitching **4.** a particular kind of stitch or stitching **5.** a sudden, sharp pain, as in the side **6.** a bit, as of work, or piece, as of clothing [not wearing a *stitch*] —*vi.* to make stitches; sew —*vt.* to fasten, repair, adorn, etc. with stitches; sew —**in stitches** laughing uproariously —**stitch′er** *n.*

stitch·er·y (-ər ē) *n.* ornamental needlework, as embroidery, crewelwork, etc.

sti·ver (stī′vər) *n.* [Du. *stuiver*] **1.** a former Dutch coin equal to 1/20 of a guilder **2.** a trifling sum

St. John **1.** seaport in S New Brunswick, Canada: pop. 86,000 **2.** island of the Virgin Islands of the U.S.

St. John's capital of Newfoundland; seaport on the SE coast: pop. 87,000

St. Joseph city in NW Mo., on the Missouri River: pop. 77,000

St-Lau·rent (san lô rän′) city in SW Quebec, Canada: suburb of Montreal: pop. 64,000

St. Lawrence [< Fr. *St. Laurent,* Rom. martyr (?–285)] **1.** river flowing from Lake Ontario into the Gulf of St. Lawrence **2. Gulf of,** inlet of the Atlantic in E Canada

St. Lawrence Seaway inland waterway for oceangoing ships, connecting the Great Lakes with the Atlantic: it consists of the St. Lawrence River & several locks & canals

St. Lou·is (lo͞o′is, lo͞o′ē) city & port in E Mo., on the Mississippi: pop. 453,000 (met. area 2,345,000)

St. Lu·ci·a (lo͞o′shē ə, -shə; lo͞o sē′ə) country on an island in the Windward group of the West Indies: 238 sq. mi.; pop. 112,000

St. Mo·ritz (sänt′ mō rits′; *Fr.* san mô rēts′) mountain resort town in SE Switzerland

stoat (stōt) *n., pl.* **stoats, stoat:** see PLURAL, II, D, 1 [ME. *stote*] a large European weasel, esp. in its brown summer coat: see ERMINE (sense 1)

sto·chas·tic (stō kas′tik) *adj.* [< Gr. *stochastikos,* proceeding by guesswork, ult. < *stochos,* a target] of, pertaining to, or arising from chance; random

stock (stäk) *n.* [OE. *stocc*] **1.** the trunk of a tree **2.** [Archaic] *a)* a tree stump *b)* a wooden block or log **3.** anything lacking life, motion, or feeling **4.** *a)* a plant stem into which a graft is inserted *b)* a plant from which cuttings are taken **5.** a rhizome or rootstock **6.** any of certain plants of the mustard family **7.** *a)* the first of a line of descent *b)* a line of descent; ancestry or family *c)* a strain, race, or other related group of animals or plants *d)* a group of related languages or families of languages **8.** a supporting or main part, as of an implement, etc., to which the working parts are attached, as the butt of a whip, the frame of a plow, the part of a rifle holding the barrel, etc. **9.** [*pl.*] a framework; specif., *a)* a former instrument of punishment consisting of a wooden frame with holes for confining an offender's ankles and, sometimes, his wrists *b)* a frame of timbers supporting a ship during construction **10.** raw material **11.** water in which meat, fish, etc. has been boiled, used as a base for soup or gravy **12.** paper of a specified weight, kind, etc. **13.** a store or supply; specif., *a)* all the animals, equipment, etc. kept on a farm *b)* *short for* LIVESTOCK *c)* the total amount of goods on hand in a store, etc.; inventory **14.** *a)* the capital invested in a company or corporation by individuals through the purchase of shares *b)* the proportionate share in the ownership of a corporation held by an individual stockholder, as represented by shares of this capital in the form of stock certificates *c)* [Colloq.] a part interest in something **15.** a stock company (sense 2), or its repertoire **16.** a former type of wide, stiff cravat —*vt.* **1.** to attach to a stock [to *stock* a plow] **2.** *a)* to furnish (a farm) with stock or (a shop, etc.) with stock *b)* to supply with [to *stock* a pond with fish] **3.** to keep a supply of, as for sale or for future use —*vi.* to put in a stock, or supply (often with *up*) —*adj.* **1.** continually kept in stock [*stock* sizes] **2.** common, hackneyed, or trite [a *stock* excuse] **3.** that deals with stock [a *stock* boy] **4.** of or relating to a stock company **5.** for breeding [a *stock* mare] **6.** of, or for the raising of, livestock [*stock* farming] —**in** (or **out of**) **stock** (not) available for sale or use —**take stock** **1.** to inventory the stock on hand **2.** to examine the situation before deciding or acting —**take** (or **put**) **stock in** to have faith in, regard as important, etc.

stock·ade (stä kād′) *n.* [< Fr. < Pr. *estacado* < *estaca,* a stake] **1.** a barrier of stakes driven into the ground side by side, for defense against attack **2.** an enclosure, as a fort, made with such stakes **3.** an enclosure for military prisoners —*vt.* **-ad′ed, -ad′ing** to surround, protect, or fortify with a stockade

stock·bro·ker (stäk′brō′kər) *n.* a person who acts as an agent for others in buying and selling stocks and bonds —**stock′bro′ker·age, stock′bro′king** *n.*

stock car a passenger automobile of standard make, modified in various ways for use in racing

stock company **1.** a company or corporation whose capital is divided into shares **2.** a commercial theatrical company that presents a repertoire of plays, usually at one theater

stock dividend **1.** a dividend in the form of additional shares of the same stock **2.** the payment of such a dividend

stock exchange **1.** a place where stocks and bonds are regularly bought and sold **2.** an association of stockbrokers who meet together for buying and selling stocks and bonds according to regulations

stock·fish (stäk′fish′) *n., pl.* **-fish′, -fish′es:** see FISH [< MDu. < *stok,* stick + *visch,* fish] a fish split and dried without salt in the open air

stock·hold·er (-hōl′dər) *n.* a person owning stock or shares in a given company

Stock·holm (stäk′hōm′, -hōlm′; *Sw.* stôk′hôlm′) capital of Sweden, on the Baltic: pop. 768,000 (met. area 1,280,000)

stock·i·nette, stock·i·net (stäk′ə net′) *n.* [prob. for earlier *stocking net*] an elastic, machine-knitted cloth used for making stockings, underwear, etc.

stock·ing (stäk′iŋ) ***n.*** [< STOCK, in obs. sense of leg covering + -ING] **1.** a closefitting covering, usually knitted, for the foot and, usually, most of the leg **2.** something like this, as a patch of color on an animal's leg —**in one's stocking feet** wearing stockings or socks but no shoes

stocking cap a long, tapered knitted cap

stock in trade **1.** merchandise stocked in a store **2.** tools, materials, etc. used in carrying on a trade or business **3.** any of the resources, practices, or devices always in use by a person or group

stock·man (-mən; *also, esp. for 2,* -man′) ***n., pl.*** **-men** (-mən, -men′) **1.** a man who owns or raises livestock **2.** a man who works in a stockroom or warehouse

stock market **1.** *same as* STOCK EXCHANGE **2.** the business carried on at a stock exchange **3.** the prices quoted on stocks and bonds

stock·pile (-pīl′) ***n.*** a supply of goods, raw material, etc., stored up esp. in anticipation of future shortage or emergency —***vt., vi.*** **-piled′**, **-pil′ing** to accumulate a stockpile (of) —**stock′pil′er** ***n.***

stock·room (-ro͞om′) ***n.*** a room in which a store of goods, materials, etc. is kept: also **stock room**

stock split the act or result of splitting stock: see SPLIT (*vt.* 7)

stock-still (-stil′) ***adj.*** perfectly motionless

Stock·ton (stäk′tən) [after R. F. *Stockton* (1795–1866), U.S. naval officer] city in C Calif.: pop. 150,000

stock·y (stäk′ē) ***adj.*** **stock′i·er, stock′i·est** **1.** heavily built; sturdy; short and thickset **2.** having a strong, thick stem: said of a plant —**stock′i·ness** ***n.***

stock·yard (stäk′yärd′) ***n.*** **1.** an enclosure for stock on a farm **2.** an enclosure with pens, sheds, etc. where cattle, hogs, etc. are kept just before slaughter or shipment: *usually used in pl.*

stodg·y (stäj′ē) ***adj.*** **stodg′i·er, stodg′i·est** [< dial. *stodge,* heavy food + -Y²] **1.** heavily built; bulky and slow in movement **2.** dull; uninteresting **3.** drab, unfashionable, or unattractive **4.** very old-fashioned or conventional —**stodg′i·ly** ***adv.*** —**stodg′i·ness** ***n.***

sto·gie, sto·gy (stō′gē) ***n., pl.*** **-gies** [contr. < *Conestoga,* town in Pa.] a long, thin, inexpensive cigar

Sto·ic (stō′ik) ***n.*** [< L. < Gr. < *stoa,* colonnade: Zeno taught under a colonnade at Athens] **1.** a member of a Greek school of philosophy founded by Zeno about 308 B.C., holding that all things, properties, relations, etc. are governed by unchanging natural laws, and that the wise man should be indifferent to the external world and to passion or emotion **2.** [**s-**] a stoical person —***adj.*** **1.** of the Stoics or their philosophy **2.** [**s-**] *same as* STOICAL

sto·i·cal (-i k′l) ***adj.*** **1.** showing austere indifference to joy, grief, pain, etc.; calm and unflinching under suffering, bad fortune, etc. **2.** [**S-**] *same as* STOIC —**sto′i·cal·ly** ***adv.***

Sto·i·cism (-siz′m) ***n.*** **1.** the philosophy of the Stoics **2.** [**s-**] indifference to pleasure or pain

stoke (stōk) ***vt., vi.*** **stoked, stok′ing** [< STOKER] **1.** to stir up and feed fuel to (a fire) **2.** to tend (a furnace, boiler, etc.) **3.** to feed or eat large quantities of food; fill (*up*)

stoke·hold (-hōld′) ***n.*** **1.** the room containing the boilers on a ship **2.** *same as* STOKEHOLE (sense 2)

stoke·hole (-hōl′) ***n.*** **1.** the opening in a furnace or boiler through which the fuel is put **2.** a space in front of a furnace or boiler from which the fire is tended, as on a ship

Stoke-on-Trent (stōk′än trent′) city in WC England, on the Trent River: pop. 271,000

stok·er (stō′kər) ***n.*** [Du. < *stoken,* to poke < *stok,* a stick] **1.** a man who tends a furnace, specif. of a steam boiler, as, esp. formerly, on a ship or locomotive **2.** a mechanical device that stokes a furnace

stole¹ (stōl) ***n.*** [OE. < L. < Gr. *stolē,* a garment] **1.** a long, decorated strip of cloth worn like a scarf by officiating clergymen of various churches **2.** a woman's long scarf of cloth or fur worn around the shoulders, with the ends hanging in front

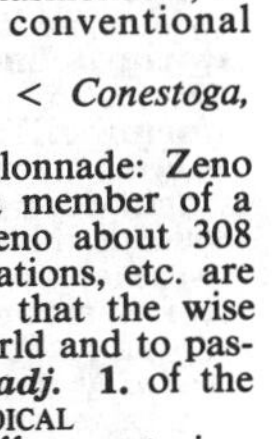

STOLE

stole² (stōl) *pt. of* STEAL

stol·en (stō′lən) *pp. of* STEAL

stol·id (stäl′id) ***adj.*** [L. *stolidus,* slow] having or showing little or no emotion or sensitivity; unexcitable —**sto·lid·i·ty** (stə lid′ə tē), **stol′id·ness** ***n.*** —**stol′id·ly** ***adv.***

sto·lon (stō′län) ***n.*** [ModL. *stolo* (gen. *stolonis*) < L., a shoot] *Bot.* a runner; esp., a stem running underground

sto·ma (stō′mə) ***n., pl.*** **-ma·ta** (-mə tə), **-mas** [ModL. < Gr. *stoma,* mouth] **1.** a microscopic opening in the epidermis of plants, serving for gaseous exchange **2.** *Zool.* a mouth or mouthlike opening —**sto·ma·tal** (stō′mə t′l, stäm′ə-) ***adj.***

stom·ach (stum′ək) ***n.*** [< OFr. < L. < Gr. *stomachos,* gullet < *stoma,* mouth] **1.** the large, saclike organ of vertebrates into which food passes from the esophagus or gullet for storage while undergoing the early processes of digestion: in cud-chewing animals it consists of four chambers **2.** any digestive cavity **3.** the abdomen, or belly **4.** appetite for food **5.** desire or inclination of any kind —***vt.*** **1.** to be able to eat or digest **2.** to tolerate; bear

stom·ach·ache (-āk′) ***n.*** pain in the stomach or abdomen

stom·ach·er (-ər) ***n.*** an ornamented, triangular piece of cloth formerly worn, esp. by women, as a covering for the chest and abdomen

sto·mach·ic (stə mak′ik) ***adj.*** **1.** of or having to do with the stomach **2.** acting as a digestive tonic Also **sto·mach′i·cal** —***n.*** a digestive tonic —**sto·mach′i·cal·ly** ***adv.***

-stome (stōm) [< Gr. *stoma,* mouth] *a combining form meaning* mouth

-sto·mous (stə məs) [< Gr. *stoma,* mouth] *a combining form meaning* having a (specified kind of) mouth

stomp (stämp) ***vt., vi.*** *var. of* STAMP; esp., to injure or kill by stamping (on) —***n.*** formerly, **1.** a jazz tune with a lively rhythm and a strong beat **2.** a dance to this music

-sto·my (-stə mē) [< Gr. < *stoma,* mouth] *a combining form meaning* a surgical opening into (a specified part)

stone (stōn) ***n.*** [OE. *stan*] **1.** the hard, solid, nonmetallic mineral matter of which rock is composed **2.** a small piece of rock **3.** a piece of rock shaped for some purpose; specif., *a)* a building block *b)* a gravestone *c)* a milestone *d)* a grindstone **4.** *a)* the stonelike seed of certain fruits, as of a date *b)* the hard endocarp and the enclosed seed of a drupe, as of a peach **5.** *short for* PRECIOUS STONE **6.** *pl.* **stone** in Great Britain, a unit of weight equal to 14 pounds **7.** *Med. same as* CALCULUS (sense 1) —***vt.*** **stoned, ston′ing** **1.** to throw stones at or kill with stones **2.** to furnish, pave, line, etc. with stones **3.** to remove the stone from (a peach, etc.) —***adj.*** of stone or stoneware —**cast the first stone** to be the first to censure or criticize —**leave no stone unturned** to do everything possible —**ston′er** ***n.***

stone- [< prec., with the sense of "like a stone"] *a combining form used in hyphenated compounds, meaning* very, completely [*stone*-blind]

Stone Age the early period in human culture during which stone implements were used

stone-blind (stōn′blīnd′) ***adj.*** completely blind

stone·crop (-kräp′) ***n.*** *popular name for* SEDUM

stone·cut·ter (-kut′ər) ***n.*** a person or machine that cuts stone and makes it smooth —**stone′cut′ting** ***n.***

stoned (stōnd) ***adj.*** **1.** having the stones removed [*stoned* peaches] **2.** [Slang] *a)* drunk; intoxicated *b)* under the influence of a drug

stone-deaf (stōn′def′) ***adj.*** completely deaf

stone·fly (-flī′) ***n., pl.*** **-flies′** any of various soft-bodied, winged insects in an undeveloped stage that live under stones in swift streams

Stone·henge (stōn′henj′) [< ME. *ston,* stone + OE. *henge,* (something) hanging] a circular arrangement of prehistoric monoliths in S England

stone·ma·son (-mā′s'n) ***n.*** a person who cuts stone to shape and uses it in making walls, buildings, etc. —**stone′ma′son·ry** (-rē) ***n.***

stone's throw a relatively short distance

stone·ware (stōn′wer′) ***n.*** a coarse, dense pottery containing much silica or sand and flint

stone·work (-wurk′) ***n.*** **1.** the art or process of working in stone **2.** something made or built in stone **3.** [*pl.*] a place where stonecutting is done

ston·y (stō′nē) ***adj.*** **ston′i·er, ston′i·est** **1.** covered with or having many stones **2.** of or like stone; specif., *a)* hard *b)* unfeeling; pitiless *c)* cold; fixed; rigid Also **ston′ey** —**ston′i·ly** ***adv.*** —**ston′i·ness** ***n.***

stood (stood) *pt. & pp. of* STAND

stooge (sto͞oj) ***n.*** [< ?] [Colloq.] **1.** an actor who aids a comedian by feeding him lines, being the victim of pranks, etc. **2.** anyone who acts as a foil, underling, etc. —***vi.*** **stooged, stoog′ing** [Colloq.] to be a stooge (*for* someone)

stool (sto͞ol) ***n.*** [OE. *stol*] **1.** *a)* a single seat having no back or arms *b)* *same as* FOOTSTOOL **2.** a toilet, or water closet **3.** the fecal matter eliminated in a single bowel movement **4.** *a)* a root or tree stump sending out shoots *b)* a cluster of such shoots —***vi.*** **1.** to put out shoots in the form of a stool **2.** [Colloq.] to act as a stool pigeon

stool pigeon **1.** a pigeon or other bird used as a decoy **2.** a person serving as a decoy **3.** [Colloq.] a spy or informer, esp. for the police: also **stool·ie** (sto͞ol′ē) ***n.***

stoop¹ (sto͞op) ***vi.*** [OE. *stupian*] **1.** to bend the body forward or in a crouch **2.** to carry the head and shoulders habitually bent forward **3.** to lower one's dignity or do something beneath one's dignity **4.** to swoop down, as a bird of prey —*vt.* to bend (the head, etc.) forward —*n.* **1.** the act or position of stooping the body, esp. habitually **2.** a lowering of one's dignity **3.** a swoop, as by a hawk at prey —**stoop′er** *n.* —**stoop′ing·ly** *adv.*

stoop[2] (st͞oop) *n.* [Du. *stoep*] a small porch or platform with steps, at the door of a house

stop (stäp) *vt.* **stopped, stop′ping** [< OE. *-stoppian* (in comp.) < WGmc. *stoppōn,* ult. < Gr. *styppē,* tow fibers] **1.** to close by filling, shutting off, covering, etc. **2.** to staunch (a wound, etc.) **3.** to block up (a passage, pipe, etc.); obstruct: often with *up* **4.** to close (a bottle, etc.) as with a cork **5.** to cause to cease motion, activity, etc. **6.** to prevent the passage of (water, light, etc.); block **7.** to halt the progress of (a person, vehicle, etc.) **8.** *a)* to check (a blow, stroke, etc.); parry; counter *b)* to defeat (an opponent) **9.** to baffle; perplex **10.** to cease; desist from (with a gerund) *[stop* talking*]* **11.** to cause to end *[stop* that racket*]* **12.** to cause (an engine, machine, etc.) to cease operation **13.** to close (a finger hole of a wind instrument) or press down (a violin string, etc.) to produce a desired tone **14.** to keep from beginning, acting, etc.; prevent **15.** to notify one's bank to withhold payment on (one's check) —*vi.* **1.** to cease moving, walking, etc.; halt **2.** to leave off doing something; desist **3.** to cease operating or functioning **4.** to come to an end **5.** to become clogged **6.** to tarry or stay for a while (often with *at* or *in*) —*n.* **1.** a stopping or being stopped; check; cessation **2.** a finish; end **3.** a stay or brief visit **4.** a place stopped at, as on a bus route **5.** something that stops; obstruction; specif., *a)* a plug or stopper *b)* an order to withhold payment on a check *c)* a mechanical part that stops or regulates motion *d)* [Chiefly Brit.] a punctuation mark, esp. a period **6.** *a)* a stopping of a violin string, finger hole of a wind instrument, etc. to produce a desired pitch *b)* such a hole **7.** *a)* a tuned set of organ pipes, reeds, or electronic devices of the same type and tone quality *b)* a pull, lever, or key for putting such a set into or out of operation **8.** *Phonet. a)* a complete stopping of the outgoing breath, as with the lips, tongue, or velum *b)* a consonant formed in this way, as *p, b, k, g, t,* and *d* —*adj.* that stops or is meant to stop *[*a *stop* signal*]* —**pull out all (the) stops 1.** to use all the stops in playing an organ **2.** to make an all-out effort —**put a stop to** to cause to cease —**stop off** to stop for a short visit on the way to a place —**stop over 1.** to visit for a while: also **stop in** (or **by**) **2.** to break a journey, as for rest

stop·cock (-käk′) *n.* a valve for stopping or regulating the flow of a fluid, as through a pipe

stope (stōp) *n.* [prob. < MLowG. *stōpe*] a steplike excavation formed by removing ore from around a mine shaft —*vt., vi.* **stoped, stop′ing** to mine in stopes

stop·gap (stäp′gap′) *n.* a person or thing serving as a temporary substitute —*adj.* used as a stopgap

stop·light (-līt′) *n.* **1.** a traffic light, esp. when red and signaling vehicles to stop **2.** a light at the rear of a vehicle, that lights up when the brakes are applied

stop·o·ver (-ō′vər) *n.* **1.** a brief stop or stay at a place in the course of a journey **2.** a place for such a stop Also **stop′-off′**

stop·page (-ij) *n.* **1.** a stopping or being stopped **2.** an obstructed condition; block

stop·per (-ər) *n.* **1.** a person or thing that stops **2.** something inserted to close an opening; plug —*vt.* to close with a plug or stopper

stop·ple (-'l) *n.* [< ME. dim. < *stoppen,* to stop] a stopper, or plug —*vt.* **-pled, -pling** to close with a stopple

stop street a street intersection at which vehicles must come to a complete stop before continuing

stop·watch (stäp′wäch′) *n.* a watch with a hand that can be started and stopped instantly so as to indicate fractions of seconds, as for timing races, etc.

stor·age (stôr′ij) *n.* **1.** a storing or being stored **2.** *a)* a place or space for storing goods *b)* the cost of keeping goods stored **3.** *same as* MEMORY (sense 7)

storage battery a battery of electrochemical cells for generating electric current: the cells can be recharged by passing a current through them in the direction opposite to the discharging flow of current

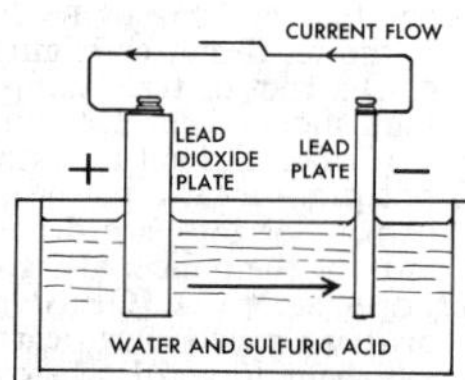

STORAGE BATTERY CELL (current flow when charging)

store (stôr) *vt.* **stored, stor′ing** [< OFr. *estorer* < L. *instaurare,* to restore] **1.** to put aside for use when needed **2.** to furnish with a supply or stock **3.** to put in a warehouse, etc. for safekeeping **4.** to be a place for the storage of **5.** to put or keep (information) in a computer memory unit —*vi.* to undergo storage in a specified manner —*n.* **1.** a supply (*of* something) for use when needed; reserve **2.** [*pl.*] supplies, esp. of food, clothing, etc. **3.** a retail establishment where goods are regularly offered for sale **4.** a storehouse; warehouse **5.** a great amount; abundance —*adj.* of a kind sold in stores —**in store** set aside for, or awaiting one in, the future —**set** (or **put** or **lay**) **store by** to value; esteem —**stor′a·ble** *adj.*

store·front (-frunt′) *n.* **1.** the front of a store **2.** a room at the ground front of a building, housing a retail store —*adj.* housed in a storefront *[*a *storefront* church*]*

store·house (-hous′) *n.* a place where things are stored; esp., a warehouse

store·keep·er (-kē′pər) *n.* **1.** a person in charge of stores, or supplies **2.** a retail merchant

store·room (-r͞oom′) *n.* a room where things are stored

sto·rey (stôr′ē) *n., pl.* **-reys** *Brit. sp. of* STORY[2]

sto·ried[1] (stôr′ēd) *adj.* **1.** ornamented with designs showing scenes from history, a story, etc. **2.** famous in story or history

sto·ried[2] (stôr′ēd) *adj.* having stories, or floors: usually in hyphenated compounds *[*many-*storied]*

stork (stôrk) *n., pl.* **storks, stork:** see PLURAL, II, D, 1 [OE. *storc*] a large, long-legged wading bird, having a long neck and bill

storm (stôrm) *n.* [OE.] **1.** a disturbance of the atmosphere in which there is a strong wind usually along with rain, snow, etc. and often with thunder and lightning **2.** any heavy fall of snow, rain, etc. **3.** anything resembling a storm *[*a *storm* of bullets*]* **4.** a strong emotional outburst **5.** a strong disturbance or upheaval of a political or social nature **6.** a sudden, strong attack on a fortified place **7.** *Meteorol.* a wind whose speed is 64 to 72 miles per hour —*vi.* **1.** to blow violently, rain, snow, etc. **2.** to rage; rant **3.** to rush or move violently *[*to *storm* into a room*]* —*vt.* **1.** to attack (someone) in a vigorous or angry outburst **2.** to capture or attempt to capture (a fortified place) with a sudden, strong attack

storm·bound (-bound′) *adj.* halted, delayed, or cut off by storms

storm cellar a deep cellar for shelter during heavy windstorms

storm door (or **window**) an extra door (or window) placed outside the regular one as added protection against winter weather

storm trooper a member of Hitler's Nazi party militia, notorious for their brutal and terroristic methods

storm·y (stôr′mē) *adj.* **storm′i·er, storm′i·est 1.** of, characteristic of, or affected by storms **2.** having or characterized by storms **3.** violent, raging, turbulent, etc. —**storm′i·ly** *adv.* —**storm′i·ness** *n.*

stormy petrel 1. any of several small petrels whose presence is thought to warn of coming storms: also **storm petrel 2.** a person thought to bring trouble wherever he goes

Stor·ting, Stor·thing (stôr′tiŋ′) *n.* [Norw. < *stor,* great + *ting,* assembly] the parliament of Norway

sto·ry[1] (stôr′ē) *n., pl.* **-ries** [< OFr. < L. < Gr. *historia:* see HISTORY] **1.** the telling of an event or series of events, whether true or fictitious; account; narration **2.** an anecdote or joke **3.** *a)* a fictitious literary composition shorter than a novel; narrative; tale *b)* such tales as a form of literature **4.** the plot of a novel, play, etc. **5.** *a)* a report or rumor *b)* [Colloq.] a falsehood or fib **6.** romantic legend or history **7.** a news event or a report of it, as in the newspapers —*vt.* **-ried, -ry·ing** to decorate with paintings, etc. of scenes from history or legend

sto·ry[2] (stôr′ē) *n., pl.* **-ries** [ML. *historia,* a picture (< L.: see HISTORY): prob. from use of "storied" windows or friezes marking the outside of different floors] **1.** a horizontal division of a building extending from a floor to the ceiling directly above it; floor *[*ten *stories* high*]* **2.** all the rooms on the same level of a building

sto·ry·book (stôr′ē bo͝ok′) *n.* a book of stories, esp. one for children —*adj.* typical of romantic tales in storybooks

sto·ry·tell·er (-tel′ər) *n.* **1.** a person who narrates stories **2.** [Colloq.] a fibber or liar —**sto′ry·tell′ing** *n.*

sto·tin·ka (stô tiŋ′kə) *n., pl.* **-tin′ki** (-kē) [Bulg.] *see* MONETARY UNITS, table (Bulgaria)

stoup (st͞oop) *n.* [ON. *staup*] **1.** [Brit. Dial.] a drinking cup; tankard **2.** a basin for holy water in a church

stout (stout) *adj.* [OFr. *estout,* bold, prob. < Frank. *stolt*] **1.** courageous; brave **2.** *a)* strong in body; sturdy *b)* firm; substantial *[*a *stout* wall*]* **3.** powerful; forceful **4.** fat; thickset; corpulent —*n.* **1.** a fat person **2.** a garment in a size for a fat man **3.** a heavy, dark-brown brew like porter, but with a higher percentage of hops —**stout′ish** *adj.* —**stout′ly** *adv.* —**stout′ness** *n.*

stout·heart·ed (-här′tid) *adj.* courageous; brave —**stout′heart′ed·ly** *adv.* —**stout′heart′ed·ness** *n.*

stove[1] (stōv) *n.* [MDu., a heated room] an apparatus using fuel or electricity for heating, cooking, etc.

stove[2] (stōv) *alt. pt. & pp. of* STAVE

stove·pipe (stōv′pīp′) *n.* **1.** a metal pipe used to carry off smoke or fumes from a stove **2.** [Colloq.] a man's tall silk hat: in full, **stovepipe hat**

stow (stō) *vt.* [OE. *stow,* a place] **1.** to pack or store away; esp., to pack in an orderly, compact way **2.** to fill by packing thus **3.** to hold: said of a container, etc. **4.** [Slang] to stop [*stow* the chatter!] —**stow away 1.** to put or hide away **2.** to be a stowaway **3.** to consume (food or drink), esp. in large amounts

stow·age (-ij) *n.* **1.** a stowing or being stowed **2.** place or room for stowing **3.** something stowed **4.** charges for stowing

stow·a·way (-ə wā′) *n.* a person who hides aboard a ship, airplane, etc. to get free passage, evade port officials, etc.

Stowe (stō), **Harriet (Elizabeth) Beecher** 1811–96; U.S. novelist: sister of Henry Ward BEECHER

St. Paul capital of Minn., on the Mississippi: pop. 270,000: see MINNEAPOLIS

St. Pe·ters·burg (pē′tərz burg′) **1.** *former name of* LENINGRAD **2.** city in WC Fla., on Tampa Bay: pop. 237,000

stra·bis·mus (strə biz′məs) *n.* [ModL. < Gr. < *strabizein,* to squint < *strabos,* twisted] a disorder of the muscles of the eyes, as cross-eye, in which both eyes cannot be focused on the same point at the same time —**stra·bis′mal, stra·bis′mic** *adj.* —**stra·bis′mal·ly** *adv.*

Strad (strad) *n. clipped form of* STRADIVARIUS

strad·dle (strad′'l) *vt.* **-dled, -dling** [freq. of STRIDE] **1.** to place oneself with a leg on either side of **2.** to spread (the legs) wide apart **3.** to take or appear to take both sides of (an issue); avoid committing oneself on —*vi.* **1.** to sit, stand, or walk with the legs wide apart **2.** to be spread apart: said of the legs **3.** to straddle an issue, etc. —*n.* **1.** the act or position of straddling **2.** a refusal to commit oneself definitely —**strad′dler** *n.*

Stra·di·va·ri (strä′dē vä′rē), **An·to·nio** (än tô′nyô) (L. name *Antonius Stradivarius*) 1644–1737; It. violin maker

Strad·i·var·i·us (strad′ə ver′ē əs) *n.* a string instrument, esp. a violin, made by A. Stradivari or his sons

strafe (strāf; *chiefly Brit.* sträf) *vt.* **strafed, straf′ing** [< G. phr. *Gott strafe England* (God punish England)] to attack with machine-gun fire from low-flying aircraft —**straf′er** *n.*

strag·gle (strag′'l) *vi.* **-gled, -gling** [prob. < ME. freq. of *straken,* to roam] **1.** to stray from the course or wander from the main group **2.** to be scattered over a wide area; ramble **3.** to leave, arrive, etc. at scattered irregular intervals **4.** to hang in an untidy way, as hair, clothes, etc. —*n.* a straggly arrangement or group —**strag′gler** *n.*

strag·gly (-lē) *adj.* **-gli·er, -gli·est** spread out in a straggling, irregular way

straight (strāt) *adj.* [< ME. pp. of *strecchen,* to STRETCH] **1.** having the same direction throughout its length [a *straight* line] **2.** not crooked, bent, wavy, etc. [*straight* hair] **3.** upright; erect [*straight* posture] **4.** level; even [a *straight* hemline] **5.** direct; undeviating, uninterrupted, etc. [to hold a *straight* course] **6.** supporting fully the principles, candidates, etc. of a political party [to vote a *straight* ticket] **7.** following a direct course of reasoning, etc.; methodical **8.** in order; properly arranged, etc. **9.** *a)* honest; sincere *b)* reliable [*straight* information] **10.** outspoken; frank **11.** *a)* without anything added; undiluted [a *straight* shot of whiskey] *b)* not blended with neutral grain spirits **12.** not qualified, slanted, etc. [a *straight* denial] **13.** at a fixed price per unit regardless of the quantity bought [apples at ten cents *straight*] **14.** [Slang] normal or conventional; specif., not a homosexual, not a drug addict, etc. —*adv.* **1.** in a straight line or direction; unswervingly **2.** upright; erectly **3.** *a)* without detour, delay, etc. *b)* directly [tell it *straight*] *c)* without alteration, etc. [play the role *straight*] —*n.* **1.** a being straight **2.** something straight; specif., *Poker* a hand consisting of any five cards in sequence —**straight away** (or **off**) at once; without delay —**the straight and narrow (path)** a strict code of morals —**straight′ly** *adv.* —**straight′ness** *n.*

straight angle an angle of 180 degrees

straight·a·way (-ə wā′) *adj.* extending in a straight line —*n.* **1.** a race track, or part of a track, that extends in a straight line **2.** a straight and level stretch of highway

straight chair a chair with a back that is straight, or almost vertical, and not upholstered

straight·edge (-ej′) *n.* a piece of wood, etc. with a straight edge used in drawing straight lines, testing plane surfaces, etc.

straight·en (-'n) *vt., vi.* to make or become straight —**straighten out 1.** to make or become less confused, easier to deal with, etc. **2.** to correct or reform the behavior of —**straight′en·er** *n.*

straight face a facial expression showing no amusement or other emotion —**straight′-faced′** *adj.*

straight·for·ward (strāt′fôr′wərd) *adj.* **1.** moving or leading straight ahead; direct **2.** honest; frank; open —*adv.* in a straightforward manner: also **straight′for′wards** —**straight′for′ward·ly** *adv.* —**straight′for′ward·ness** *n.*

straight·jack·et (strāt′jak′it) *n. same as* STRAITJACKET

straight-laced (-lāst′) *adj. same as* STRAIT-LACED (sense 2)

straight man an actor who serves as a foil for a comedian, feeding him lines

straight-out (-out′) *adj.* [Colloq.] **1.** straightforward **2.** unrestrained **3.** thoroughgoing; unqualified

straight razor a razor with a long, unguarded blade that can be folded into the handle

straight·way (-wā′) *adv.* at once; without delay

strain[1] (strān) *vt.* [< OFr. < L. *stringere,* to draw tight] **1.** to draw or stretch tight **2.** to exert, use, or tax to the utmost [to *strain* every nerve] **3.** to injure by overexertion; wrench [to *strain* a muscle] **4.** to injure or weaken by force, pressure, etc. [the wind *strained* the roof] **5.** to stretch beyond the normal limits [to *strain* a rule to one's advantage] **6.** *a)* to pass through a screen, sieve, etc.; filter *b)* to remove by filtration, etc. **7.** to hug: now only in **to strain to one's bosom** (or **heart,** etc.) —*vi.* **1.** to make violent efforts; strive hard **2.** to be or become strained **3.** to be subjected to great stress or pressure **4.** to pull or push with force **5.** to filter, ooze, etc. —*n.* **1.** a straining or being strained **2.** great effort, exertion, etc. **3.** an injury to a part of the body as a result of overexertion [heart *strain*] **4.** stress or force **5.** a great or excessive demand on one's emotions, resources, etc. —**strained** *adj.*

strain[2] (strān) *n.* [OE. *streon,* procreation < base of *strynan,* to produce] **1.** ancestry; lineage **2.** the descendants of a common ancestor; race; stock; line **3.** a group of individuals within a species, different in one or more characters from others in the species **4.** an inherited character or tendency **5.** a trace; streak **6.** the style or tone of a speech, book, action, etc. **7.** [*often pl.*] a passage of music; tune; air

strain·er (-ər) *n.* a person or thing that strains; specif., a device for straining, sifting, or filtering; sieve, filter, etc.

strait (strāt) *adj.* [< OFr. < L. pp. of *stringere:* see STRICT] **1.** [Archaic] *a)* narrow; tight *b)* strict; rigid **2.** [Now Rare] difficult; distressing —*n.* **1.** [*often pl.*] a narrow waterway connecting two large bodies of water **2.** [*often pl.*] difficulty; distress **3.** [Rare] an isthmus

strait·en (strāt′'n) *vt.* **1.** esp. formerly, *a)* to make strait or narrow *b)* to restrict or confine; hamper **2.** to bring into difficulties: usually in the phrase **in straitened circumstances,** lacking sufficient money

strait·jack·et (-jak′it) *n.* a coatlike device that binds the arms tight against the body: used to restrain persons in a violent state

strait-laced (-lāst′) *adj.* **1.** formerly, tightly laced, as a corset **2.** narrowly strict in behavior or moral views

Straits Settlements former Brit. crown colony in SE Asia, including Singapore, Malacca, etc.

strake (strāk) *n.* [akin to STRETCH] a single line of planking or plating extending along the length of a ship

strand[1] (strand) *n.* [OE.] shore, esp. ocean shore —*vt., vi.* **1.** to run or drive aground [a ship *stranded* by the storm] **2.** to leave or be put into a difficult, helpless position [*stranded* in a strange city with no money]

strand[2] (strand) *n.* [< ?] **1.** any of the threads, fibers, wires, etc. that are twisted together to form a string, rope, or cable **2.** a ropelike length of anything [a *strand* of pearls, *strands* of hair] **3.** any of the parts that are bound together to form a whole [the *strands* of one's life] —*vt.* to form (a rope, etc.) by twisting strands together —**strand′er** *n.*

strange (strānj) *adj.* **strang′er, strang′est** [< OFr. < L. *extraneus,* foreign < *extra,* outside] **1.** foreign; alien **2.** not previously known, seen, heard, etc.; unfamiliar **3.** unusual; extraordinary **4.** peculiar; odd **5.** reserved, distant, or cold in manner **6.** lacking experience; unaccustomed [*strange* to the job] —*adv.* in a strange manner —**strange′ly** *adv.* —**strange′ness** *n.*

stran·ger (strān′jər) *n.* **1.** an outsider or newcomer **2.** a person not known or familiar to one **3.** a person unaccustomed (*to* something) [a *stranger* to hate]

stran·gle (straŋ′g'l) *vt.* **-gled, -gling** [< OFr. < L. *strangulare* < Gr. < *strangalē,* halter] **1.** to kill by squeezing the throat as with the hands, a noose, etc., so as to shut off the breath **2.** to choke or suffocate in any way **3.** to suppress, stifle, or repress —*vi.* to be strangled; choke —**stran′gler** *n.*

stran·gle·hold (-hōld′) *n.* **1.** an illegal wrestling hold that chokes off an opponent's breath **2.** any force that restricts or suppresses freedom

stran·gu·late (straŋ′gyə lāt′) *vt.* **-lat′ed, -lat′ing** [< L. pp. of *strangulare*] **1.** *same as* STRANGLE **2.** *Med.* to cause (an intestine or other tube) to become squeezed so that a flow,

fat, āpe, cär, ten, ēven, is, bīte; gō, hôrn, tōōl, look; oil, out; up, fur; get; joy; yet; chin; she; thin, *th*en; zh, leisure; ŋ, ring; ə for *a* in *ago*, *e* in *agent*, *i* in *sanity*, *o* in *comply*, *u* in *focus*; ′ as in *able* (ā′b'l); Fr. bál; ë, Fr. coeur; ö, Fr. feu; Fr. mon; ô, Fr. coq; ü, Fr. duc; *r*, Fr. cri; H, G. ich; kh, G. doch; ‡foreign; *hypothetical; < derived from. See inside front cover.

as of blood, is cut off —*vi. Med.* to be strangulated —**stran′gu·la′tion** *n.*

strap (strap) *n.* [dial. form of STROP] **1.** a narrow strip of leather, plastic, cloth, etc. often with a buckle at one end, for tying or holding things together **2.** any of several straplike parts or things, as a shoulder strap, a razor strop, etc. —*vt.* **strapped, strap′ping 1.** to fasten with a strap **2.** to beat with a strap **3.** to strop (a razor) —**strap′less** *adj.* —**strap′per** *n.*

strapped (strapt) *adj.* [Colloq.] hard pressed for money

strap·ping (strap′iŋ) *adj.* [Colloq.] tall and sturdy; robust

Stras·bourg (stras′burg; *Fr.* stràz bo͞or′) city & port in NE France, on the Rhine: pop. 249,000

stra·ta (strāt′ə, strat′-) *n. alt. pl. of* STRATUM

strat·a·gem (strat′ə jəm) *n.* [< L. < Gr. *stratēgēma*, act of a general < *stratos*, army + *agein*, to lead] **1.** a trick, scheme, or plan for deceiving an enemy in war **2.** any trick or scheme for achieving some purpose

stra·te·gic (strə tē′jik) *adj.* **1.** of or having to do with strategy **2.** sound in strategy; advantageous **3.** *a*) needed for carrying out military strategy or carrying on war [*strategic* materials] *b*) directed against the military and industrial installations of the enemy [*strategic* bombing] Also **stra·te′gi·cal** —**stra·te′gi·cal·ly** *adv.*

strat·e·gist (strat′ə jist) *n.* one skilled in strategy

strat·e·gy (-jē) *n., pl.* **-gies** [< Fr. < Gr. < *stratēgos*, general: see STRATAGEM] **1.** *a*) the science of planning and directing large-scale military operations *b*) a plan or action based on this **2.** *a*) skill in managing or planning, esp. by using stratagems *b*) a stratagem or artful means to some end Also, esp. for sense 1, **stra·te·gics** (strə tē′jiks)

Strat·ford-on-A·von (strat′fərd än ā′vän) town in C England, on the Avon River: birthplace & burial place of Shakespeare: pop. 19,000: also **Strat′ford-up·on-A′von**

strat·i·fy (strat′ə fī′) *vt.* **-fied′, -fy′ing** [< Fr. < ModL. < L. *stratum*, layer + *facere*, to make] **1.** to form or arrange in layers or strata **2.** to classify (people) into groups graded according to status as determined by birth, income, education, etc. —*vi.* to become stratified —**strat′i·fi·ca′tion** (-fi kā′shən) *n.*

stra·to·cu·mu·lus (strāt′ō kyo͞om′yə ləs, strat′-) *n., pl.* **-li′** (-lī′) [ModL.: see STRATUS & CUMULUS] a cloud type arranged in horizontal patterns, with parts that are rounded, roll-shaped, etc.

strat·o·sphere (strat′ə sfir′) *n.* [< Fr. < ModL. *stratum*, STRATUM + Fr. *sphère*, SPHERE] the atmospheric zone extending from about six miles to about fifteen miles above the earth's surface, in which the temperature ranges from about −45°C to −75°C —**strat′o·spher′ic** (-sfer′ik, -sfir′-) *adj.*

stra·tum (strāt′əm, strat′-) *n., pl.* **stra′ta** (-ə), **-tums** [ModL. < L. < *stratus*, pp. of *sternere*, to spread] **1.** a horizontal layer of material, esp. any of several lying one upon another; specif., *Geol.* a single layer of sedimentary rock **2.** a section, level, or division, as of the atmosphere or ocean, regarded as like a stratum **3.** any of the socioeconomic groups of a society as determined by birth, income, education, etc. —**stra·tal** (strāt′'l) *adj.*

stra·tus (-əs) *n., pl.* **stra′ti** (-ī) [L., a strewing: see prec.] a cloud type extending in a long, low, gray layer with an almost uniform base

Strauss (shtrous; *E.* strous) **1. Jo·hann** (yō′hän), 1825–99; Austrian composer, esp. of waltzes **2. Rich·ard** (riH′ärt), 1864–1949; Ger. composer & conductor

Stra·vin·sky (strə vin′skē; *Russ.* strȧ vēn′ski), **I·gor (Fedorovich)** (ē′gôr) 1882–1971; U.S. composer & conductor, born in Russia

straw (strô) *n.* [OE. *streaw*] **1.** hollow stalks of grain after threshing, used for bedding, for weaving hats, baskets, etc. **2.** a single one of such stalks **3.** a tube used for sucking beverages **4.** something, as a hat, made of straw **5.** a worthless trifle —*adj.* **1.** straw-colored; yellowish **2.** made of straw **3.** worthless; meaningless —**a straw in the wind** a sign of what may happen —**grasp** (or **clutch, catch**) **at a straw** (or **straws**) to try anything that offers even the slightest hope —**straw′y** *adj.*

straw·ber·ry (-ber′ē, -bər ē) *n., pl.* **-ries** [< OE. < *streaw*, straw + *berige*, berry: prob. so called from the small achenes on the fruit] **1.** the small, red, fleshy fruit of a low plant of the rose family that puts out runners **2.** this plant

strawberry blonde reddish blonde

strawberry mark a small, red birthmark

straw·board (strô′bôrd′) *n.* a coarse cardboard made of straw pulp

straw boss [Colloq.] **1.** an assistant to a boss or foreman **2.** an overseer of work with little or no authority

straw color a pale-yellow color —**straw′-col′ored** *adj.*

straw·flow·er (-flou′ər) *n.* an annual plant whose brightly colored flower heads are dried for winter bouquets

straw-hat (-hat′) *adj.* [from the practice, esp. formerly, of wearing straw hats in summer] designating or of a summer theater or summer theaters

straw man 1. a scarecrow made of straw **2.** a weak argument, opponent, etc. set up by one so that he may in attacking gain an easy, showy victory **3.** a person used to disguise another's activities, etc.; blind

straw vote an unofficial vote or poll for sampling popular opinion on candidates or on an issue

stray (strā) *vi.* [< OFr. *estraier*, prob. ult. < L. *extra vagari*, to wander outside] **1.** to wander from a given place, course, etc.; roam **2.** to go wrong; deviate (*from* what is right) **3.** to wander from the subject; be inattentive or digress —*n.* a person or thing that strays; esp., a domestic animal wandering at large —*adj.* **1.** having strayed; lost **2.** isolated, occasional, or incidental [a few *stray* words] —**stray′er** *n.*

streak (strēk) *n.* [OE. *strica*] **1.** a line or long, thin mark; stripe or smear **2.** a ray of light or a flash, as of lightning **3.** a thin layer, as of fat in meat or ore in rock **4.** a tendency in one's nature [a jealous *streak*] **5.** a period, spell, or run [a *streak* of victories] —*vt.* to mark with streaks —*vi.* **1.** to become streaked **2.** to move swiftly **3.** to engage in the prank of dashing naked through a public place —**like a streak** [Colloq.] swiftly —**streak′er** *n.*

streak·y (-ē) *adj.* **streak′i·er, streak′i·est** marked with or occurring in streaks; uneven —**streak′i·ness** *n.*

stream (strēm) *n.* [OE.] **1.** a current or flow of water; specif., a small river **2.** a steady flow of any fluid [a *stream* of cold air] or of rays of energy [a *stream* of light] **3.** a moving line of things [a *stream* of cars] **4.** a trend or course [the *stream* of events] —*vi.* **1.** to flow as in a stream **2.** to flow (*with*) [eyes *streaming* with tears] **3.** to move steadily or swiftly **4.** to float or fly, as a flag in the breeze —*vt.* to cause to stream

stream·er (strē′mər) *n.* **1.** something that streams **2.** a long, narrow flag **3.** any long, narrow, flowing strip of material **4.** a stream of light extending up from the horizon **5.** a newspaper headline across the full page

stream·let (strēm′lit) *n.* a small stream; rivulet

stream·line (-līn′) *vt.* **-lined′, -lin′ing** to make streamlined —*adj. same as* STREAMLINED

stream·lined (-līnd′) *adj.* **1.** having a contour designed to offer the least resistance in moving through air, water, etc. **2.** arranged so as to be more efficient [a *streamlined* program] **3.** with no excess, as of weight, decoration, etc.; trim [a *streamlined* figure or design]

stream of consciousness individual conscious experience regarded as having continuity and flow: a principle made use of in novels, etc. in presenting the thoughts, inner feelings, etc. of a character in a natural, unrestrained flow

stream·y (strē′mē) *adj.* **stream′i·er, stream′i·est 1.** full of streams or currents **2.** flowing; streaming

street (strēt) *n.* [OE. *stræt* < LL. < L. *strata* (*via*), paved (road)] **1.** a public road in a city or town; esp., a paved thoroughfare with sidewalks and buildings along the sides **2.** such a road apart from its sidewalks **3.** the people living, working, etc. in the buildings along a given street —*adj.* **1.** of, in, on, or near the street [the *street* floor] **2.** suitable for everyday wear in public [*street* clothes]

street·car (-kär′) *n.* a large car on rails that provides public transportation on city streets

street·walk·er (-wôk′ər) *n.* a prostitute who solicits customers along the streets —**street′walk′ing** *n.*

street·wise (-wīz′) *adj.* [Colloq.] experienced or knowledgeable in dealing with the people in urban poverty areas, esp. those areas where crime is prevalent

strength (streŋkth, streŋth) *n.* [OE. *strengthu*] **1.** the state or quality of being strong; power; force; vigor **2.** the power to resist strain, stress, etc.; toughness; durability **3.** the power to resist attack **4.** legal, moral, or intellectual force **5.** *a*) capacity for producing an effect *b*) potency or concentration, as of drugs, liquors, etc. **6.** intensity, as of sound, color, etc. **7.** force as measured in numbers [an army at full *strength*] **8.** vigor of feeling or expression **9.** a source of strength or support —**on the strength of** based or relying on

strength·en (-'n) *vt., vi.* to make or become stronger —**strength′en·er** *n.*

stren·u·ous (stren′yoo wəs) *adj.* [L. *strenuus*] **1.** requiring or characterized by great effort or energy **2.** vigorous, arduous, etc. —**stren′u·ous·ly** *adv.* —**stren′u·ous·ness** *n.*

strep (strep) *n. shortened form of* STREPTOCOCCUS

strep·to·coc·cus (strep′tə käk′əs) *n., pl.* **-coc′ci** (-käk′sī) [ModL., genus name < Gr. *streptos*, twisted + COCCUS] any of a group of spherical bacteria that occur generally in chains: some species cause serious diseases —**strep′to·coc′cal** (-käk′əl), **strep′to·coc′cic** (-käk′sik) *adj.*

strep·to·my·cin (-mī′sin) *n.* [< Gr. *streptos*, twisted + *mykēs*, fungus] an antibiotic drug, $C_{21}H_{39}N_7O_{12}$, used in the treatment of various bacterial diseases, as tuberculosis

stress (stres) *n.* [< OFr., ult. < L. *strictus*, STRICT] **1.** strain or straining force; specif., force exerted upon a body, that tends to strain or deform its shape **2.** emphasis; importance **3.** *a*) mental or physical tension or strain *b*) urgency, pressure, etc. causing this **4.** *a*) the relative force of utterance given a syllable or word in pronunciation or, according to the meter, in verse *b*) an accented syllable **5.** *Music* emphasis on a note or chord **—*vt.*** **1.** to put stress, pressure, or strain on **2.** to give stress or accent to **3.** to emphasize **—stress′ful *adj.* —stress′ful·ly *adv.***

-stress (stris) [< -STER + -ESS] *a feminine suffix corresponding to* -STER *[songstress]*

stretch (strech) ***vt.*** [OE. *streccan*] **1.** to reach out; extend *[to stretch out a helping hand]* **2.** to cause (the body or limbs) to reach out to full length, as in relaxing, etc. **3.** to pull or spread out to full extent or to a greater size **4.** to cause to extend over a given space, distance, or time *[to stretch pipelines across a desert]* **5.** *a*) to extend farther or too far *b*) to strain in interpretation, scope, etc. to questionable or unreasonable limits *[to stretch a rule]* **6.** to make tense with effort; strain (a muscle, etc.) **—*vi.*** **1.** *a*) to spread out to full extent or beyond normal limits *b*) to extend over a given space, distance, or time **2.** *a*) to extend the body or limbs to full length, as in relaxing, etc. *b*) to lie down at full length (usually with *out*) **3.** to become stretched to greater size, as any elastic substance **—*n.*** **1.** a stretching or being stretched **2.** *a*) an unbroken period *[a stretch of ten days]* *b*) [Slang] a term served in prison **3.** the extent to which something can be stretched **4.** an unbroken length, tract, etc. *[a stretch of beach]* **5.** any of the sections of a race track; esp., *short for* HOMESTRETCH **—*adj.*** made of elasticized fabric **—stretch′a·bil′i·ty *n.* —stretch′a·ble *adj.***

stretch·er (-ər) ***n.*** **1.** one that stretches; specif., *a*) a brick or stone laid lengthwise in the face of a wall *b*) any of various devices for stretching or shaping garments, etc. **2.** *a*) a light frame covered with canvas, etc. and used for carrying the sick, injured, or dead *b*) any similar device, as a wheeled cot used in ambulances

stretch·y (-ē) ***adj.* stretch′i·er, stretch′i·est** **1.** that can be stretched; elastic **2.** tending to stretch too far **—stretch′i·ness *n.***

strew (stro͞o) ***vt.* strewed, strewed** or **strewn, strew′ing** [OE. *streawian*] **1.** to spread about here and there; scatter **2.** to cover as by scattering **3.** to be scattered over (a surface)

stri·a (strī′ə) ***n.,*** *pl.* **stri′ae** (-ē) [L.] **1.** a narrow groove or channel **2.** any of a number of parallel lines, stripes, furrows, etc.; specif., any of the cylindrical fibers in voluntary muscles

stri·ate (strī′āt; *for adj. usually* -it) ***vt.* -at·ed, -at·ing** [< L. pp. of *striare,* to groove] to mark with striae; stripe, furrow, etc. **—*adj.*** *same as* STRIATED **—stri·a′tion *n.***

stri·at·ed (strī′āt id) ***adj.*** marked with striae, as the voluntary muscles; striped, furrowed, etc.

strick·en (strik′'n) *alt. pp. of* STRIKE **—*adj.*** **1.** struck or wounded **2.** suffering, as from pain, trouble, etc.

strict (strikt) ***adj.*** [< L. pp. of *stringere,* to draw tight] **1.** exact or precise *[a strict translation]* **2.** perfect; absolute *[the strict truth]* **3.** *a*) enforcing rules with great care *b*) closely enforced or rigidly maintained *c*) disciplining severely **—strict′ly *adv.* —strict′ness *n.***

stric·ture (strik′chər) ***n.*** [< L. < pp. of *stringere,* to draw tight] **1.** strong criticism; censure **2.** a limiting or restricting condition; restriction **3.** *Med.* an abnormal narrowing of a passage in the body **—stric′tured *adj.***

stride (strīd) ***vi., vt.* strode, strid′den, strid′ing** [OE. *stridan*] **1.** to walk with long steps, esp. in a vigorous or swaggering manner **2.** to cross with a single, long step *[he strode over the log]* **3.** to straddle **—*n.*** **1.** the act of striding **2.** a long step **3.** *a*) a full step in a gait, as of a horse *b*) the distance covered by such a step **4.** [*usually pl.*] progress; advancement *[great strides in industry]* **—hit one's stride** to reach one's normal level of efficiency **—take in one's stride** to cope with easily and without undue effort **—strid′er *n.***

stri·dent (strīd′'nt) ***adj.*** [< L. prp. of *stridere,* to rasp] harsh-sounding; shrill; grating **—stri′dence, stri′den·cy *n.* —stri′dent·ly *adv.***

strid·u·late (strij′oo lāt′) ***vi.* -lat′ed, -lat′ing** [< ModL. pp. of *stridulare* < L. < *stridere,* to rasp] to make a shrill, grating or chirping sound by rubbing certain body parts together, as some insects do **—strid′u·la′tion *n.***

strid·u·lous (-ləs) ***adj.*** making a shrill, grating or chirping sound: also **strid′u·lant** (-lənt)

strife (strīf) ***n.*** [OFr. *estrif*] **1.** the act of striving; contention or competition **2.** the act or state of fighting or quarreling; struggle; conflict

strike (strīk) ***vt.* struck, struck** or occas. (but for *vt.* 12 commonly and for *vt.* 8 & 16 usually) **strick′en, strik′ing** [OE. *strican,* to go, proceed] **1.** *a*) to give a blow to; hit; smite *b*) to give (a blow, etc.) *c*) to remove as by a blow *[he struck the gun from her hand]* *d*) to make by stamping, printing, etc. *[to strike coins in a mint]* *e*) to pierce or penetrate *[struck in the head by a bullet]* **2.** to produce (a tone or chord) by hitting (a key or keys) or touching (a string or strings) on a musical instrument **3.** to announce (time), as with a bell: said of clocks, etc. **4.** *a*) to cause to come into forceful contact *[to strike one's head on a beam]* *b*) to thrust (a weapon, etc.) in or into something *c*) to bring forcefully into contact *[to strike cymbals together]* *d*) to ignite (a match) by friction **5.** to produce (a light, etc.) by friction **6.** to come into forceful contact with; crash into *[the stone struck his head]* **7.** to wound with the fangs: said of snakes **8.** to afflict, as with disease, pain, or death **9.** to attack **10.** to come into contact with; specif., *a*) to fall on; shine on, as light *b*) to reach (the eye or ear) *c*) to come upon *[we struck the main road]* *d*) to make (a path, etc.) as one goes along *e*) to notice or find suddenly *f*) to discover, as after drilling *[to strike oil]* **11.** to affect as if by contact, a blow, etc.; specif., *a*) to occur to *[struck by an idea]* *b*) to impress (one's fancy, sense of humor, etc.) *c*) to seem to *[it strikes me as silly]* *d*) to cause to become suddenly *[to be struck dumb]* *e*) to overcome suddenly with strong feeling *[to be struck with amazement]* *f*) to arouse *[to strike terror to the heart]* **12.** to remove (*from* a list, record, minutes, etc.) **13.** *a*) to make and ratify (a bargain, truce, etc.) *b*) to arrive at by figuring, etc. *[to strike a balance]* **14.** *a*) to lower (a sail, flag, etc.) *b*) to take down (a tent, etc.) *c*) to abandon (a camp) as by taking down tents **15.** to refuse to continue to work at (a factory, company, etc.) until certain demands have been met **16.** to level the top of (a measure of grain, etc.) as with a stick **17.** to assume (a pose, etc.) **18.** to put forth (roots): said of plants **19.** *Theater* *a*) to dismantle (a set) *b*) to turn (a light) down or off **—*vi.*** **1.** to deliver or aim a blow; hit (*at*) **2.** *a*) to attack *b*) to take part in a fight (*for* some objective) **3.** *a*) to make sounds as by being struck: said of a bell, clock, etc. *b*) to be announced by the striking of a bell, etc.: said of the time **4.** *a*) to hit; collide (*against, on,* or *upon*) *b*) to make an impression on the mind **5.** to ignite, as a match **6.** to seize a bait: said of a fish **7.** to dart in an attempt to wound, as a snake **8.** to penetrate or pierce (*to, through,* etc.) **9.** to come suddenly (*on* or *upon*) *[we struck on an idea]* **10.** to run upon a reef, rock, etc.: said of a ship **11.** *a*) to lower sail *b*) to lower a flag in token of surrender **12.** to refuse to continue to work until certain demands are met **13.** to take root: said of a plant **14.** to proceed, esp. in a new way or direction **15.** to move or pass quickly **16.** *U.S. Navy* to be in training (*for* a specified rating) **—*n.*** **1.** the act of striking; blow; specif., a military attack **2.** *a*) a concerted refusal by employees to go on working, in an attempt to get higher wages, better working conditions, etc. *b*) any similar refusal to do something, undertaken as a form of protest *[a hunger strike]* **3.** the discovery of a rich deposit of oil, coal, minerals, etc. **4.** any sudden success **5.** the pull on the line by a fish seizing bait **6.** *Baseball* a pitched ball which is struck at but missed, delivered through the strike zone but not struck at, hit foul but not caught, etc.: three strikes put the batter out **7.** *Bowling* *a*) the act of knocking down all the pins on the first bowl *b*) the score so made **—(out) on strike** striking (*vi.* 12) **—strike dumb** to amaze; astound **—strike home** **1.** to deliver an effective blow **2.** to have the desired effect **—strike it rich** **1.** to discover a rich deposit of ore, oil, etc. **2.** to become rich or successful suddenly **—strike off** **1.** to remove as by a cut or blow **2.** to print, stamp, etc. **—strike out** **1.** to remove from a record, etc.; erase **2.** to start out **3.** *Baseball* *a*) to be put out by three strikes *b*) to put (a batter) out by pitching three strikes **4.** to be a failure **—strike up** **1.** to begin playing, singing, etc. **2.** to begin (a friendship, etc.)

strike·break·er (-brā′kər) ***n.*** a person who tries to break up a strike, as by supplying scabs, threatening the strikers, etc. **—strike′break′ing *n.***

strik·er (strī′kər) ***n.*** **1.** a person who strikes; specif., a worker who is on strike **2.** a thing that strikes, as the clapper in a bell, etc.

strik·ing (strī′kiŋ) ***adj.*** **1.** that strikes or is on strike **2.** impressive; outstanding; remarkable **—strik′ing·ly *adv.***

Strind·berg (strind′burg, strin′-; *Sw.* strin′bar′y'), **(Johan) August** 1849–1912; Swed. dramatist & novelist

string (striŋ) ***n.*** [OE. *streng*] **1.** *a*) a thin length of twisted fiber or of wire, nylon, etc. used for tying, pulling, etc. *b*) a narrow strip of leather or cloth for fastening shoes, clothing, etc. **2.** a length of things on a string *[a string of pearls]* **3.** a line, row, or series of things *[a string of houses, a string of victories]* **4.** a number of business enterprises under one ownership **5.** a group of athletes arranged according to ability: the **first string** is more skilled than the **second string,** etc. **6.** *a)* a slender cord of wire, gut, nylon, etc., stretched on a violin, guitar, etc., and bowed, plucked, or struck to make a musical sound *b)* [*pl.*] all the stringed instruments of an orchestra, or their players **7.** a strong, slender, stringlike organ, structure, etc.; specif., a fiber of a plant **8.** [Colloq.] a condition or limitation attached to a plan, offer, etc.: *usually used in pl.* —*vt.* **strung, strung** or rare **stringed, string′ing 1.** to provide with strings **2.** to thread on a string **3.** to tie, pull, hang, etc. with a string **4.** to adjust or tune the strings of (a musical instrument) **5.** to make nervous or keyed (*up*) **6.** to remove the strings from (beans, etc.) **7.** to arrange in a row or series **8.** to extend like a string [*to string* a cable] —*vi.* **1.** to form into a string or strings **2.** to stretch out in a line —**on a** (or **the**) **string** completely under one's control —**pull strings 1.** to get someone to use influence in one's behalf, often secretly **2.** to direct action of others, often secretly —**string along** [Colloq.] **1.** to agree **2.** to fool or deceive —**string up** [Colloq.] to kill by hanging — **string′less** *adj.* —**string′like′** *adj.*

string bean *same as* SNAP BEAN

string·board (-bôrd′) *n.* a board placed along the side of a staircase to cover the ends of the steps

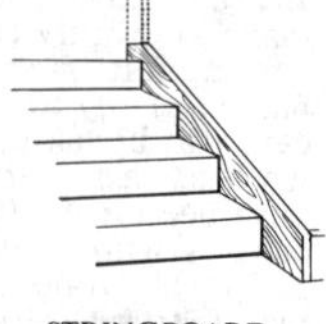

STRINGBOARD

string·course (-kôrs′) *n.* a decorative, horizontal band of brick or stone set in the wall of a building

stringed (striŋd) *rare pp. of* STRING — *adj.* having strings, as certain musical instruments

strin·gent (strin′jənt) *adj.* [< L. prp. of *stringere,* to draw tight] **1.** strict; severe **2.** tight in loan or investment money [*a stringent* money market] **3.** compelling; convincing —**strin′gen·cy** *n., pl.* **-cies** —**strin′gent·ly** *adv.* —**strin′gent·ness** *n.*

string·er (striŋ′ər) *n.* **1.** a person or thing that strings **2.** a long piece of timber used as a support, as to connect upright posts in a frame **3.** a long structural member of an airplane fuselage, wing, etc. **4.** a person ranked according to ability [second-*stringer*]

string·halt (striŋ′hôlt′) *n.* a condition in horses causing the hind legs to jerk spasmodically in walking

string·piece (-pēs′) *n.* a long, horizontal timber for supporting a framework

string quartet a quartet of or for players on stringed instruments, usually first and second violins, a viola, and a violoncello

string tie a narrow necktie, usually tied in a bow

string·y (striŋ′ē) *adj.* **string′i·er, string′i·est 1.** like a string or strings; long, thin, wiry, etc. **2.** consisting of strings or fibers **3.** having tough fibers [*stringy* meat, celery, etc.] **4.** forming strings; ropy [*stringy* molasses] — **string′i·ness** *n.*

strip[1] (strip) *vt.* **stripped, strip′ping** [OE. *strypan* (in comp.)] **1.** to remove (the clothing, covering, etc.) of or from (a person); make naked **2.** to dispossess (a person) of (honors, titles, attributes, etc.) **3.** to plunder; rob **4.** to peel or take off (the covering, skin, etc.) from (something) **5.** to make bare or clear by removing fruit, growth, removable parts, etc. [*to strip* a room of furniture] **6.** to take apart **7.** to break or damage the thread of (a nut, bolt, etc.) or the teeth of (a gear) —*vi.* **1.** to take off all clothing; undress **2.** to perform a striptease —**strip′per** *n.*

strip[2] (strip) *n.* [altered (after prec.) < STRIPE] **1.** a long, narrow piece, as of land, ribbon, wood, etc. **2.** *short for* COMIC STRIP **3.** a runway for the takeoff and landing of airplanes; landing strip —*vt.* to cut or tear into strips

stripe (strīp) *n.* [MLowG. & MDu. *stripe*] **1.** a long, narrow band, mark, or streak, differing as in color from the area around it **2.** [*often pl.*] a fabric or garment with a pattern of parallel stripes **3.** a strip of cloth or braid worn on the sleeve of a uniform to show rank, years served, etc. **4.** type; kind; sort [a man of his *stripe*] **5.** [Archaic] *a)* a stroke with a whip, etc. *b)* a long welt on the skin —*vt.* **striped, strip′ing** to mark with stripes

striped bass (bas) a silvery game and food fish with dark stripes along the sides, found along the coasts of N. America: it goes up rivers to spawn

strip·ling (strip′liŋ) *n.* a grown boy; youth

strip mining a method of mining, esp. for coal, by laying bare a mineral deposit near the earth's surface

stript (stript) *rare pt. & pp. of* STRIP[1]

strip·tease (strip′tēz′) *n.* an act, as in burlesque shows, in which a woman takes off her clothes slowly, usually while music is being played —**strip′tease′** *vi.* **-teased′, -teas′ing** —**strip′teas′er** *n.*

strip·y (strī′pē) *adj.* **strip′i·er, strip′i·est** characterized by, like, or marked with stripes

strive (strīv) *vi.* **strove** or **strived, striv·en** (striv′'n) or **strived, striv′ing** [< OFr. < *estrif,* effort < Gmc.] **1.** to make great efforts; try very hard [*to strive* to win] **2.** to struggle; contend [*to strive* against tyranny] —**striv′er** *n.*

strobe (strōb) *n.* **1.** *shortened form of* STROBOSCOPE **2.** an electronic tube that can emit extremely rapid, brief, and brilliant flashes of light: used in photography, the theater, etc.: also **strobe light**

stro·bi·lus (strō bī′ləs) *n., pl.* **-li** (-lē) [ModL. < LL. < Gr. *strobilos,* pine cone] *same as* CONE (*n.* 3): also **stro′bile** (-bil, -bīl)

stro·bo·scope (strō′bə skōp′, sträb′ə-) *n.* [< Gr. *strobos,* a twisting round + -SCOPE] **1.** an instrument for studying motion by illuminating a moving body, machine, etc. very briefly at frequent intervals **2.** *same as* STROBE (*n.* 2) —**stro′bo·scop′ic** (-skäp′ik), **stro′bo·scop′i·cal** *adj.* — **stro′bo·scop′i·cal·ly** *adv.*

strode (strōd) *pt. of* STRIDE

stro·ga·noff (strō′gə nôf′, strô′-) *adj.* [prob. after S. *Stroganoff,* 19th-c. Russ. gourmet] cooked with sour cream, bouillon, mushrooms, etc.: placed after the word it modifies [beef *stroganoff*]

stroke (strōk) *n.* [akin to OE. *strican,* to hit] **1.** a striking of one thing against another; blow of an ax, whip, etc. **2.** a sudden action resulting as if from a blow [a *stroke* of lightning, a *stroke* of luck] **3.** a sudden attack, esp. of apoplexy or paralysis **4.** *a)* a single effort to do or produce something, esp. a successful one *b)* something accomplished by such an effort *c)* a distinctive effect in an artistic, esp. literary, work **5.** the sound of striking, as of a clock **6.** *a)* a single movement, as with some tool, club, pen, etc. *b)* any of a series of repeated rhythmic motions made against water, air, etc. *c)* a type, manner, or rate of such a movement **7.** a mark made by a pen, etc. **8.** a beat of the heart **9.** a gentle, caressing motion with the hand **10.** *Mech.* any of the continuous, reciprocating movements of a piston, etc. **11.** *Rowing* the rower who sits nearest the stern and sets the rate of rowing —*vt.* **stroked, strok′ing 1.** to draw one's hand, a tool, etc. gently over the surface of **2.** to mark with strokes **3.** to hit (a ball), as in tennis, pool, etc. **4.** to set the rate of rowing for (a crew) —*vi.* **1.** to hit a ball in tennis, etc. **2.** to act as stroke (*for*) in rowing —**keep stroke** to make strokes in rhythm —**strok′er** *n.*

stroll (strōl) *vi.* [prob. < SwissG. dial. *strolen*] **1.** to walk in an idle, leisurely manner; saunter **2.** to go from place to place; wander —*vt.* to stroll along or through —*n.* a strolling; leisurely walk

stroll·er (-ər) *n.* **1.** a person who saunters **2.** *a)* an itinerant actor *b)* a vagrant **3.** a light, chairlike baby carriage

strong (strôŋ) *adj.* [OE. *strang*] **1.** *a)* physically powerful; having great muscular strength; robust *b)* healthy; sound; hale **2.** *a)* performing well [a *strong* heart] *b)* not easily upset [a *strong* stomach] **3.** morally or intellectually powerful [a *strong* will or mind] **4.** having special ability (*in* a specified area) [to be *strong* in French] **5.** governing firmly; authoritarian **6.** *a)* tough; firm; durable; able to resist *b)* holding firmly [a *strong* grip] *c)* binding tightly [*strong* glue] **7.** having many resources; powerful in wealth, numbers, supplies, etc. **8.** of a specified number [a force 6,000 *strong*] **9.** having a powerful effect; drastic [*strong* measures] **10.** having a large amount of its essential quality; not diluted [*strong* coffee] **11.** affecting the senses powerfully [*strong* light, odor, etc.] **12.** rancid; rank [*strong* butter] **13.** firm and loud [a *strong* voice] **14.** intense in degree or quality; specif., *a)* ardent; passionate *b)* forceful; persuasive *c)* felt deeply; decided [a *strong* opinion] *d)* zealous [a *strong* socialist] *e)* vigorous; forthright [*strong* language] *f)* distinct; marked [a *strong* resemblance] *g)* having emphasis or stress [a *strong* beat] **15.** moving rapidly and with force [a *strong* wind] **16.** magnifying highly [*strong* lenses] **17.** tending toward higher prices [a *strong* market] **18.** *Chem.* having a high ion concentration, as some acids and bases **19.** *Gram.* expressing variation in tense by internal change of vowel rather than by inflectional endings; irregular (Ex.: *swim, swam, swum*) —*adv.* in a strong manner; greatly; severely —**come on strong** [Slang] to make a striking impression —**strong′ish** *adj.* —**strong′ly** *adv.*

strong-arm (strôŋ′ärm′) *adj.* [Colloq.] using physical force —*vt.* [Colloq.] to use force upon, esp. in robbing

strong·box (-bäks′) *n.* a heavily made box or safe for storing valuables

strong·hold (-hōld′) *n.* **1.** a place having strong defenses; fortified place **2.** a place where a group having certain views, attitudes, etc. is concentrated

strong-mind·ed (-mīn′did) *adj.* having a strong, unyielding mind or will; determined —**strong′-mind′ed·ly** *adv.* —**strong′-mind′ed·ness** *n.*

strong-willed (-wild′) *adj.* having a strong or obstinate will

stron·ti·um (strän′shē əm, -shəm, -tē əm) *n.* [ModL. < *Strontian,* Scotland, where first found] a pale-yellow, metallic chemical element resembling calcium in properties and found only in combination: symbol, Sr; at. wt., 87.62; at. no., 38: a deadly radioactive isotope of strontium (**stron-**

tium 90) is present in the fallout of nuclear explosions —**stron′tic** ***adj.***

strop (sträp) ***n.*** [OE., ult. < L. *struppus* < Gr. *strophos*, a twisted band] **1.** *same as* STRAP **2.** a device, esp. a thick leather band, used for putting a fine edge on razors —***vt.*** **stropped, strop′ping** to sharpen on a strop —**strop′per** ***n.***

stro·phe (strō′fē) ***n.*** [< Gr. < *strephein*, to turn] **1.** in the ancient Greek theater, *a)* a turning of the chorus from right to left *b)* that part of the song sung by the chorus during this **2.** a stanza —**stroph·ic** (sträf′ik, strō′fik), **stroph′i·cal** ***adj.***

strove (strōv) *alt. pt. of* STRIVE

strow (strō) ***vt.*** **strowed, strown** (strōn) or **strowed, strow′·ing** *archaic form of* STREW

struck (struk) *pt. & pp. of* STRIKE —***adj.*** closed or affected by a labor strike

struc·tur·al (struk′chər əl) ***adj.*** **1.** of, having, or characterized by structure **2.** used in construction or building —**struc′tur·al·ly** ***adv.***

structural formula a chemical formula that illustrates the arrangement of atoms and bonds in a molecule

struc·tur·al·ist (-ist) ***n.*** an advocate of structural principles, as in the analysis or application of social, economic, or linguistic theory —***adj.*** of structuralists or their theories —**struc′tur·al·ism** ***n.***

structural linguistics the study of a language as a coherent, uniform system without comparing it to other languages or to its forms in early periods —**structural linguist**

struc·ture (struk′chər) ***n.*** [< L. < pp. of *struere*, to arrange] **1.** manner of building, constructing, or organizing **2.** something built or constructed, as a building or dam **3.** the arrangement of all the parts of a whole [the *structure* of the atom] **4.** something composed of interrelated parts —***vt.*** **-tured, -tur·ing** to put together according to a system; construct; organize —**struc′ture·less** ***adj.***

stru·del (stro͞o′d'l; *G.* shtro͞o′dəl) ***n.*** [G.] a kind of pastry made of a very thin sheet of dough filled with apple slices, cheese, etc., rolled up, and baked

strug·gle (strug′'l) ***vi.*** **-gled, -gling** [ME. *strogelen* < ?] **1.** to contend or fight violently with an opponent **2.** to make great efforts; strive **3.** to make one's way with difficulty —***n.*** **1.** great effort; exertion **2.** conflict; strife —**strug′gler** ***n.*** —**strug′gling·ly** ***adv.***

strum (strum) ***vt., vi.*** **strummed, strum′ming** [echoic] to play (a guitar, banjo, etc.), esp. in a casual way, or without much skill —***n.*** the act or sound of this —**strum′mer** ***n.***

strum·pet (strum′pit) ***n.*** [ME. < ?] a prostitute

strung (struŋ) *pt. & alt. pp. of* STRING

strut (strut) ***vi.*** **strut′ted, strut′ting** [OE. *strutian*, to stand rigid] to walk in a vain, stiff, swaggering manner —***vt.*** **1.** to provide with a strut or brace **2.** to make a display of —***n.*** **1.** a vain, swaggering walk **2.** a brace fitted into a framework to resist pressure in the direction of its length —**strut′ter** ***n.*** —**strut′ting·ly** ***adv.***

strych·nine (strik′nin, -nīn, -nēn) ***n.*** [Fr. < ModL. genus name < L. < Gr. *strychnos*, nightshade] a highly poisonous crystalline alkaloid, obtained from nux vomica and related plants: used in small doses as a stimulant

St. Thomas second largest island of the Virgin Islands of the U.S.

Stu·art (sto͞o′ərt) [< ? OE. *stigweard*, chamberlain] **1.** a masculine name **2.** ruling family of Scotland (1371–1603) & of England & Scotland (1603–1714), except during the Commonwealth (1649–60) **3. Gilbert (Charles)**, 1755–1828; U.S. portrait painter

stub (stub) ***n.*** [OE. *stybb*] **1.** a tree stump **2.** a short piece remaining after the main part has been removed or used up [a cigar *stub*] **3.** any short projection **4.** a pen with a short, blunt point **5.** a short piece of a ticket or of a leaf in a checkbook kept as a record —***vt.*** **stubbed, stub′bing** **1.** to root out (weeds, etc.) **2.** to clear (land) of stumps **3.** to strike (one's toe, etc.) against something by accident **4.** to put out (a cigarette, etc.) by pressing the end against a surface: often with *out*

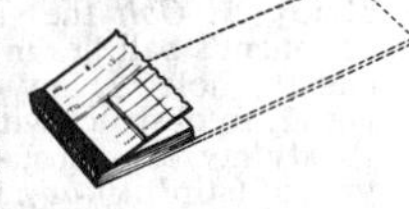

STUB (sense 5)

stub·ble (stub′'l) ***n.*** [OFr. *estouble* < VL. < L. *stipula*, a stalk] **1.** the short stumps of grain left standing after harvesting **2.** any growth like this [a *stubble* of beard] —**stub′bled** ***adj.*** —**stub′bly** ***adj.*** **-bli·er, -bli·est**

stub·born (stub′ərn) ***adj.*** [prob. < OE. *stubb*, var. of *stybb*, STUB] **1.** refusing to yield, obey, or comply; resisting; resolute or obstinate **2.** done or carried on in an obstinate or persistent manner [a *stubborn* campaign] **3.** hard to handle, treat, or deal with [a *stubborn* cold] —**stub′born·ly** ***adv.*** —**stub′born·ness** ***n.***

stub·by (stub′ē) ***adj.*** **-bi·er, -bi·est** **1.** covered with stubs or stubble **2.** short and heavy or dense **3.** short and thickset —**stub′bi·ly** ***adv.*** —**stub′bi·ness** ***n.***

stuc·co (stuk′ō) ***n.***, *pl.* **-coes, -cos** [It., prob. < Gmc.] **1.** plaster or cement, either fine or coarse, used for surfacing inside or outside walls, etc. **2.** work done in this: also **stuc′co·work′** —***vt.*** **-coed, -co·ing** to cover with stucco

stuck (stuk) *pt. & pp. of* STICK

stuck-up (stuk′up′) ***adj.*** [Colloq.] snobbish; conceited

stud[1] (stud) ***n.*** [OE. *studu*, post] **1.** any of a series of small knobs or rounded nailheads used to ornament a surface **2.** a small, buttonlike device used as an ornament or fastener on a shirt front **3.** an upright piece in the frame of a building, to which panels, laths, etc. are nailed **4.** a metal crossbar bracing a link, as in a chain cable **5.** a projecting pin or peg used as a support, pivot, etc., or, as in an automobile tire, to increase traction on ice —***vt.*** **stud′ded, stud′ding** **1.** to set or decorate with studs or studlike objects **2.** to be set thickly on [rocks *stud* the hillside] **3.** to scatter or cluster (something) thickly **4.** to provide (a building) with studs

stud[2] (stud) ***n.*** [OE. *stod*] **1.** *a)* a number of horses kept for breeding *b)* the place where these are kept **2.** *a) same as* STUDHORSE *b)* any male animal used esp. for breeding **3.** [Slang] a virile, sexually promiscuous man —***adj.*** of or having to do with a stud —**at stud** available for breeding: said of male animals

stud·book (-book′) ***n.*** a register of purebred animals, esp. racehorses: also **stud book**

stud·ding (stud′iŋ) ***n.*** **1.** studs collectively, esp. for walls **2.** material used for or as studs

stud·ding·sail (stud′iŋ sāl′, stun′s'l) ***n.*** [< ?] a light, auxiliary sail set at the edge of a working sail in light weather: also **studding sail**

stu·dent (sto͞od′'nt, styo͞od′-) ***n.*** [< OFr. < L. prp. of *studere*, to study] **1.** a person who studies something **2.** a person who is enrolled for study in a school, college, etc. —**stu′dent·ship′** ***n.***

student teacher a student in a college or university who teaches school under supervision as a requirement for a degree in education

stud·horse (stud′hôrs′) ***n.*** a stallion kept for breeding

stud·ied (stud′ēd) ***adj.*** **1.** prepared by careful study **2.** planned beforehand; deliberate [*studied* indifference] —**stud′ied·ly** ***adv.*** —**stud′ied·ness** ***n.***

stu·di·o (sto͞o′dē ō′, styo͞o′-) ***n.***, *pl.* **-di·os′** [It. < L. *studium*, a study] **1.** a place where an artist or photographer does his work **2.** a place where dancing or music lessons are given **3.** a place where motion pictures are made **4.** a place where radio or television programs are produced or where recordings are made

studio couch a kind of couch that can be opened into a full-sized bed

stu·di·ous (sto͞o′dē əs, styo͞o′-) ***adj.*** **1.** fond of study **2.** showing close attention **3.** zealous; wholehearted —**stu′di·ous·ly** ***adv.*** —**stu′di·ous·ness** ***n.***

stud poker a form of poker in which each player is dealt some cards face down and some face up

stud·y (stud′ē) ***n.***, *pl.* **stud′ies** [< OFr. < L. < *studere*, to study] **1.** the application of the mind to acquire knowledge, as by reading, investigating, etc. **2.** careful and critical examination of a subject, event, etc. **3.** a branch of learning **4.** [*pl.*] formal education; schooling **5.** an essay or thesis presenting results of an investigation **6.** a work of literature or art treating a subject in careful detail **7.** a first sketch for a story, picture, etc. **8.** *same as* ÉTUDE **9.** an earnest effort or intention **10.** a reverie; deep absorption **11.** a room designed for study, writing, etc. —***vt.*** **stud′ied, stud′y·ing** **1.** to try to learn by reading, thinking, etc. **2.** *a)* to investigate carefully [to *study* the problem of crime] *b)* to look at carefully; scrutinize [to *study* a map] **3.** *a)* to read (a book, lesson, etc.) so as to know and understand it *b)* to memorize **4.** to take a course in at a school **5.** to give attention or thought to —***vi.*** **1.** to study something **2.** to be a student **3.** to try hard **4.** to meditate —**study up on** [Colloq.] to make a careful study of

stuff (stuf) ***n.*** [< OFr. < *estoffer*, to cram, prob. < Frank.] **1.** the material out of which anything is or can be made **2.** basic elements; essence; character **3.** any kind of matter, unspecified **4.** cloth, esp. woolen cloth **5.** *a)* household goods *b)* personal belongings *c)* things; objects **6.** *a)* a medicine *b)* [Slang] a drug, as heroin **7.** worthless objects; junk **8.** *a)* talk or action of a specified kind *b)* foolish or worthless ideas, words, etc. [*stuff* and nonsense] **9.** [Colloq.] *a)* superior ability or special skill *b)* special control given to the ball in baseball, billiards, etc. —***vt.*** **1.** to fill the inside of (something); pack; specif., *a)* to fill (a cushion, etc.) with padding *b)* to fill the skin of (a dead animal, etc.) in order to mount and preserve it *c)* to fill (a fowl, etc.) with seasoning, bread crumbs, etc. before roasting **2.** *a)* to fill too full; cram *b)* to fill to excess with food **3.** to pack or cram with **4.** to fill with information, ideas, etc. **5.** to put fraudulent votes into (a ballot box) **6.** *a)* to plug; block *b)* to choke or stop up, as with phlegm **7.** to force or push *[to stuff money into a purse]* —*vi.* to eat too much —**stuff′er** *n.*

stuffed shirt [Slang] a pompous, pretentious person

stuff·ing (-iŋ) *n.* **1.** the action of one that stuffs **2.** something used to stuff; specif., *a)* soft, springy material used as padding in cushions, etc. *b)* a seasoned mixture for stuffing fowl, etc.

stuff·y (stuf′ē) *adj.* **stuff′i·er, stuff′i·est** **1.** poorly ventilated; having little fresh air; close **2.** having the nasal passages stopped up, as from a cold **3.** [Colloq.] *a)* dull; stodgy; old-fashioned *b)* prim; strait-laced *c)* pompous; pretentious —**stuff′i·ly** *adv.* —**stuff′i·ness** *n.*

stul·ti·fy (stul′tə fī′) *vt.* **-fied′, -fy′ing** [< LL. < L. *stultus,* foolish + *facere,* to make] **1.** *a)* to cause to appear foolish, stupid, absurd, etc. *b)* to make dull or sluggish **2.** to render worthless or useless —**stul′ti·fi·ca′tion** *n.*

stum·ble (stum′b'l) *vi.* **-bled, -bling** [< Scand.] **1.** to trip in walking, running, etc. **2.** to walk unsteadily, as when old and weak **3.** to speak, act, etc. in a confused, blundering manner **4.** to sin or err; do wrong **5.** to come by chance; happen *[to stumble across a clue]* —*vt.* **1.** to cause to stumble **2.** to perplex; confound —*n.* a stumbling —**stum′bler** *n.* —**stum′bling·ly** *adv.*

stumbling block an obstacle or difficulty

stump (stump) *n.* [prob. < or akin to MLowG. *stump*] **1.** the lower end of a tree or plant left in the ground after most of the stem or trunk has been cut off **2.** *a)* the part of an arm, leg, tooth, etc. left after the rest has been cut off or broken off *b)* a butt; stub *[the stump of a pencil]* **3.** the place where a political speech is made **4.** *a)* the sound of a heavy, tramping step *b)* such a step **5.** *Cricket* any of the three upright sticks of a wicket —*vt.* **1.** to reduce to a stump; lop **2.** to remove stumps from (land) **3.** to travel over (a district), making political speeches **4.** [Colloq.] to stub (one's toes, etc.) **5.** [Colloq.] to puzzle; baffle —*vi.* **1.** to walk heavily or clumsily, as with a wooden leg **2.** to travel about, making political speeches —**stump′er** *n.* —**stump′like′** *adj.*

stump·y (stum′pē) *adj.* **stump′i·er, stump′i·est** **1.** covered with stumps **2.** like a stump; short and thickset; stubby —**stump′i·ness** *n.*

stun (stun) *vt.* **stunned, stun′ning** [< OFr. *estoner,* to stun: see ASTONISH] **1.** to make senseless or unconscious, as by a blow **2.** to shock deeply; daze; astound **3.** to overpower as by a loud noise or explosion —*n.* the effect or condition of being stunned

stung (stuŋ) *pt. & pp. of* STING

stunk (stuŋk) *pp. & alt. pt. of* STINK

stun·ner (stun′ər) *n.* [Colloq.] a remarkably attractive, excellent, etc. person or thing

stun·ning (-iŋ) *adj.* **1.** that stuns **2.** [Colloq.] remarkably attractive, excellent, etc. —**stun′ning·ly** *adv.*

stun·sail, stun·s'le (stun′s'l) *n. same as* STUDDINGSAIL

stunt¹ (stunt) *vt.* [OE. *stunt,* stupid] **1.** to check the growth or development of; dwarf **2.** to hinder (growth or development) —*n.* **1.** a stunting **2.** something stunted

stunt² (stunt) *n.* [< ?] **1.** a display of skill or daring; trick **2.** something done to attract attention, etc. —*vi.* to perform a stunt or stunts

stunt man a professional acrobat who takes the place of an actor when dangerous scenes involving falls, leaps, etc. are filmed

stu·pe·fac·tion (sto͞o′pə fak′shən, styo͞o′-) *n.* **1.** a stupefying or being stupefied **2.** stunned amazement or utter bewilderment

stu·pe·fy (sto͞o′pə fī′, styo͞o′-) *vt.* **-fied′, -fy′ing** [< Fr. < L. < *stupere,* to be stunned + *facere,* to make] **1.** to make dull or lethargic; stun **2.** to amaze; astonish; bewilder —**stu′pe·fi′er** *n.*

stu·pen·dous (sto͝o pen′dəs, styo͝o-) *adj.* [< L. gerundive of *stupere,* to be stunned] **1.** astonishing; overwhelming **2.** astonishingly great or large —**stu·pen′dous·ly** *adv.* —**stu·pen′dous·ness** *n.*

stu·pid (sto͞o′pid, styo͞o′-) *adj.* [L. *stupidus* < *stupere,* to be stunned] **1.** dazed; stunned; stupefied **2.** lacking normal intelligence; slow-witted; dull **3.** showing or resulting from a lack of intelligence; foolish **4.** dull and boring *[a stupid party]* —*n.* a stupid person —**stu·pid′i·ty,** *pl.* **-ties, stu′pid·ness** *n.* —**stu′pid·ly** *adv.*

stu·por (sto͞o′pər, styo͞o′-) *n.* [L.] **1.** a state in which the mind and senses are so dulled, as by a drug, that one can barely think, act, feel, etc. **2.** mental or moral dullness or apathy —**stu′por·ous** *adj.*

stur·dy (stur′dē) *adj.* **-di·er, -di·est** [OFr. *estourdi,* stunned] **1.** firm; resolute; unyielding **2.** strong; hardy **3.** strongly built —**stur′di·ly** *adv.* —**stur′di·ness** *n.*

stur·geon (stur′jən) *n., pl.* **stur′geons, stur′geon:** see PLURAL, II, D, 1 [OFr. *esturjon* < Frank.] any of several large food fishes having rows of spiny plates along the body and a projecting snout: valuable as a source of caviar and isinglass

STURGEON
(to 7 ft. long)

stut·ter (stut′ər) *vt., vi.* [freq. of dial. *stut,* to stutter < ME. *stutten*] **1.** *same as* STAMMER **2.** to make (a series of repeated sounds) *[stuttering machine guns]* —*n.* the act or an instance of stuttering —**stut′ter·er** *n.*

Stutt·gart (stut′gärt; *G.* shto͝ot′gärt) city in S West Germany: pop. 628,000

Stuy·ve·sant (stī′və s'nt), **Peter** 1592–1672; Du. governor of New Netherland (1646–64)

St. Vincent country consisting of an island (*St. Vincent*) & a nearby island chain, in the Windward group of the West Indies: 150 sq. mi.; pop. 100,000

sty¹ (stī) *n., pl.* **sties** [OE. *sti, stig*] **1.** a pen for pigs **2.** any foul or depraved place —*vt., vi.* **stied, sty′ing** to lodge in or as in a sty

sty², stye (stī) *n., pl.* **sties** [< obs. dial. *styany* (taken as *sty on eye*) < dial. *styan,* rising < OE. *stigend,* prp. of *stigan,* to climb] a small, inflamed swelling of a sebaceous gland on the rim of the eyelid

Styg·i·an (stij′ē ən, stij′ən) *adj.* **1.** of or like the river Styx and the infernal regions **2.** [*also* **s-**] *a)* infernal or hellish *b)* dark or gloomy

style (stīl) *n.* [L. *stilus*] **1.** a pointed instrument used by the ancients in writing on wax tablets **2.** any device similar in shape or use; specif., *a)* [Obs.] a pen *b)* an etching needle *c)* a phonograph needle *d)* an engraving tool *e)* the pointer on a dial, chart, etc. *f) Bot.* the stalklike part of a carpel between the stigma and the ovary **3.** *a)* manner of expression in writing or speaking *b)* characteristic manner of expression, execution, or design, in any art, period, etc. *[Gothic style]* **4.** distinction, originality, etc. in artistic or literary expression *[this author lacks style]* **5.** the way in which anything is made or done; manner **6.** *a)* the current, fashionable way of dressing, acting, etc. *b)* something stylish *c)* a fashionable, luxurious manner *[to dine in style]* **7.** elegance of manner and bearing **8.** form of address; title *[entitled to the style of Mayor]* **9.** sort; kind; type **10.** a way of reckoning times, dates, etc.: see OLD STYLE (sense 2), NEW STYLE **11.** *Printing* a particular manner of dealing with spelling, punctuation, etc. —*vt.* **styled, styl′ing** **1.** to name; call *[Lincoln was styled the Great Emancipator]* **2.** to design the style of **3.** to make conform to a particular style —**style′less** *adj.* —**styl′er** *n.*

style·book (-bo͝ok′) *n.* a book consisting of examples or rules of style (esp. sense 11)

styl·ish (stī′lish) *adj.* conforming to current style, as in dress; fashionable —**styl′ish·ly** *adv.* —**styl′ish·ness** *n.*

styl·ist (-list) *n.* **1.** a writer, etc. whose work has style (sense 4) **2.** a person who designs, or advises on, current styles, as in dress —**sty·lis·tic** (stī lis′tik), **sty·lis′ti·cal** *adj.* —**sty·lis′ti·cal·ly** *adv.*

styl·ize (stī′līz) *vt.* **-ized, -iz·ing** to make conform to a given style rather than to nature; conventionalize —**styl′i·za′tion** *n.* —**styl′iz·er** *n.*

sty·lus (stī′ləs) *n., pl.* **-lus·es, -li** (-lī) [L., for *stilus,* pointed instrument] **1.** a style or other needlelike marking device **2.** any of various pointed tools, as for marking mimeograph stencils **3.** *a)* a sharp, pointed device for cutting the grooves of a phonograph record *b)* a phonograph needle

sty·mie (stī′mē) *n.* [prob. < Scot. *stymie,* a person partially blind] **1.** *Golf* the situation on a putting green when an opponent's ball lies in a direct line between the player's ball and the hole **2.** any frustrating situation —*vt.* **-mied, -mie·ing** **1.** to obstruct with a stymie **2.** to block; impede Also sp. **sty′my,** *pl.* **-mies; -mied, -my·ing**

styp·tic (stip′tik) *adj.* [< L. < Gr. *styptikos* < *styphein,* to contract] tending to halt bleeding by contracting the tissues or blood vessels; astringent —*n.* any styptic substance

sty·rene (stī′rēn, stir′ēn) *n.* [< L. *styrax,* a kind of tree + -ENE] a colorless or yellowish, aromatic liquid used in the manufacture of synthetic rubber and plastics

Sty·ro·foam (stī′rə fōm′) *a trademark for* rigid, lightweight, cellular polystyrene, used in insulation, commercial displays, etc. —*n.* [**s-**] this substance

Styx (stiks) [L., ult. < Gr. *stygein,* to hate] *Gr. Myth.* the river encircling Hades over which Charon ferried the souls of the dead

sua·sion (swā′zhən) *n.* [< L. < pp. of *suadere,* to persuade] *same as* PERSUASION: now chiefly in **moral suasion,** a persuading by appealing to one's sense of morality —**sua′sive** (-siv) *adj.* —**sua′sive·ly** *adv.* —**sua′sive·ness** *n.*

suave (swäv; *Brit. also* swāv) *adj.* [MFr. < L. *suavis,* sweet] smoothly gracious or polite; polished; urbane —**suave′ly** *adv.* —**suave′ness** *n.* —**suav·i·ty** (swä′və tē, swav′ə-) *n.*

sub (sub) ***n.*** *shortened form of:* **1.** SUBMARINE **2.** SUBSCRIPTION **3.** SUBSTITUTE **—*vi.*** **subbed, sub′bing** [Colloq.] to be a substitute (*for* someone)

sub- [< L. *sub,* under] *a prefix meaning:* **1.** under, beneath *[subsoil]* **2.** lower in rank or position than *[subaltern]* **3.** to a lesser degree than, somewhat *[subtropical]* **4.** by or forming a division into smaller parts *[subsection]* **5.** *Chem.* with less than the normal amount of (the specified substance) In words of Latin origin, *sub-* is assimilated to *suc-* before *c, suf-* before *f, sug-* before *g, sum-* before *m, sup-* before *p,* and *sur-* before *r: sub-* often changes to *sus-* before *c, p,* and *t*

sub. **1.** substitute(s) **2.** suburb(an)

sub·ac·id (sub as′id) ***adj.*** slightly acid **—sub′a·cid′i·ty** (-ə sid′ə tē) ***n.*** **—sub·ac′id·ly** ***adv.***

sub·al·tern (səb ôl′tərn, sub′əl tərn) ***adj.*** [< Fr. < LL. < L. *sub-,* under + *alternus,* alternate] **1.** subordinate **2.** [Brit.] holding an army commission below that of captain **—*n.*** **1.** a subordinate **2.** [Brit.] a subaltern officer

sub·ant·arc·tic (sub′ant ärk′tik, -är′-) ***adj.*** designating or of the area surrounding the Antarctic Circle

sub·arc·tic (sub ärk′tik, -är′-) ***adj.*** designating or of the area surrounding the Arctic Circle

sub·at·om (sub at′əm) ***n.*** one of the parts that make up an atom **—sub′a·tom′ic** (-ə täm′ik) ***adj.***

sub·base·ment (sub′bās′mənt) ***n.*** any floor or room below the principal basement

sub·branch (-branch′) ***n.*** a division of a branch

sub·class (-klas′) ***n.*** **1.** a division of a class; specif., *Biol.* any main natural subdivision of a class of plants or animals **2.** *Math. same as* SUBSET

sub·clin·i·cal (sub klin′i k′l) ***adj.*** without obvious clinical symptoms, as a disease in its early stages

sub·com·mit·tee (sub′kə mit′ē) ***n.*** any of the small committees with special duties into which a main committee may be divided

sub·com·pact (-käm′pakt) ***n.*** a model of automobile smaller than a compact

sub·con·scious (sub kän′shəs) ***adj.*** **1.** occurring with little or no conscious perception on the part of the individual: said of mental processes and reactions **2.** not fully conscious **—the subconscious** subconscious mental activity **—sub·con′scious·ly** ***adv.*** **—sub·con′scious·ness** ***n.***

sub·con·tract (-kän′trakt; *also, for v.,* sub′kən trakt′) ***n.*** a secondary contract undertaking some or all of the obligations of a primary or previous contract **—*vt., vi.*** to make a subcontract (for) **—sub·con′trac·tor** ***n.***

sub·crit·i·cal (-krit′i k′l) ***adj.*** unable to sustain a fission chain reaction: said of a nuclear reactor, etc.

sub·cul·ture (sub′kul′chər) ***n.*** **1.** a group of people of the same age, social or economic status, ethnic background, etc. and having its own interests, goals, etc. **2.** the distinct cultural patterns of such a group **—sub·cul′tur·al** ***adj.***

sub·cu·ta·ne·ous (sub′kyo͞o tā′nē əs) ***adj.*** being, used, or introduced beneath the skin **—sub′cu·ta′ne·ous·ly** ***adv.***

sub·dea·con (sub dē′k′n) ***n.*** a cleric ranking below a deacon

sub·deb (sub′deb′) ***n.*** [SUB- + DEB(UTANTE)] **1.** a girl in the years just preceding her debut into society **2.** any girl of such age **—*adj.*** of or suitable for a subdeb

sub·di·vide (sub′di vīd′, sub′di vīd′) ***vt., vi.*** **-vid′ed, -vid′ing** **1.** to divide further after previous division **2.** to divide (land) into small parcels for sale **—sub′di·vid′er** ***n.***

sub·di·vi·sion (sub′di vizh′ən, sub′di vizh′ən) ***n.*** **1.** a subdividing or being subdivided **2.** one of the parts resulting from subdividing **3.** a large tract of land subdivided into small parcels for sale

sub·dom·i·nant (sub däm′ə nənt) ***adj.*** less than or only partly dominant **—*n.*** **1.** something that is subdominant **2.** *Music* the fourth tone of a diatonic scale

sub·due (səb do͞o′, -dyo͞o′) ***vt.*** **-dued′, -du′ing** [< OFr. < L. *subducere,* to remove] **1.** to win control of; conquer; vanquish **2.** to overcome, as by persuasion or training; control **3.** to make less intense; diminish; soften **4.** to repress (emotions, passions, etc.) **—sub·du′a·ble** ***adj.***

sub·em·ploy·ed (sub′im ploid′) ***adj.*** designating or of those workers who are unemployed, underemployed, or employed at wages below a subsistence level

sub·fam·i·ly (sub′fam′ə lē) ***n.,*** *pl.* **-lies** **1.** any main natural subdivision of a family of plants or animals **2.** a subdivision of a language family

sub·freez·ing (sub′frē′ziŋ) ***adj.*** below freezing

sub·gum (sub′gum′) ***adj.*** [Cantonese, lit., mixed vegetables] designating any of various Chinese-American dishes, as chow mein, prepared with mushrooms, almonds, etc.

sub·head (sub′hed′) ***n.*** **1.** the title of a subdivision of a chapter, article, etc. **2.** a subordinate heading or title Also **sub′head′ing**

sub·hu·man (sub′hyo͞o′mən) ***adj.*** **1.** less than human **2.** nearly human

sub·in·dex (-in′deks) ***n.,*** *pl.* **-di·ces′** (-də sēz′) *same as* SUBSCRIPT

subj. **1.** subject **2.** subjunctive

sub·ja·cent (sub jā′s′nt) ***adj.*** [< L. prp. of *subjacere* < *sub-,* under + *jacere,* to lie] beneath; underlying **—sub·ja′cen·cy** ***n.*** **—sub·ja′cent·ly** ***adv.***

sub·ject (sub′jikt; *for v.* səb jekt′) ***adj.*** [< OFr. < L. pp. of *subjicere* < *sub-,* under + *jacere,* to throw] **1.** under the authority or control of, or owing allegiance to, another **2.** having a disposition or tendency (*to*) *[subject* to fits of anger*]* **3.** liable to receive *[subject* to censure*]* **4.** contingent upon *[subject* to his approval*]* **—*n.*** **1.** a person under the authority or control of another; esp., a person who owes allegiance to a ruler, government, etc. **2.** someone or something undergoing a treatment, experiment, etc. **3.** something dealt with in discussion, study, writing, painting, etc.; theme **4.** the main theme of a musical composition **5.** a cause; reason **6.** a branch of learning **7.** *Gram.* the noun, noun phrase, or noun substitute in a sentence about which something is said **8.** *Philos.* the mind, or ego, that thinks or feels, as distinguished from everything outside the mind **—*vt.*** **1.** to bring under the authority or control of **2.** to make liable or vulnerable *[*to *subject* one to contempt*]* **3.** to cause to undergo something **—sub·jec′tion** ***n.***

sub·jec·tive (səb jek′tiv) ***adj.*** **1.** of or resulting from the feelings of the subject, or person thinking; not objective; personal *[*a *subjective* opinion*]* **2.** determined by and emphasizing the ideas, feelings, etc. of the artist or writer **3.** *Gram. same as* NOMINATIVE **4.** *Med.* designating or of a symptom perceptible only to the patient **—sub·jec′tive·ly** ***adv.*** **—sub·jec·tiv·i·ty** (sub′jek tiv′ə tē), **sub·jec′tive·ness** ***n.***

sub·join (səb join′) ***vt.*** [< MFr. < L.: see SUB- & JOIN] to add (something) at the end of a statement

sub·ju·gate (sub′jə gāt′) ***vt.*** **-gat′ed, -gat′ing** [< L. pp. of *subjugare* < *sub-,* under + *jugum,* a yoke] **1.** to bring under control or subjection; conquer **2.** to cause to become submissive **—sub′ju·ga′tion** ***n.*** **—sub′ju·ga′tor** ***n.***

sub·junc·tive (səb juŋk′tiv) ***adj.*** [< LL. < L. pp. of *subjungere,* to SUBJOIN] designating or of that mood of a verb used to express supposition, desire, possibility, etc., rather than to state a fact *[were* in "if I *were* you" is in the *subjunctive* mood*]* **—*n.*** **1.** the subjunctive mood **2.** a verb in this mood **—sub·junc′tive·ly** ***adv.***

sub·lease (sub′lēs′; *for v.* sub lēs′) ***n.*** a lease granted by a lessee to another person of all or part of the property **—*vt.*** **-leased′, -leas′ing** to grant, obtain, or hold a sublease of **—sub′les·see′** (-les ē′) ***n.*** **—sub·les·sor** (sub-les′ôr, sub′les ôr′) ***n.***

sub·let (sub let′, sub′let′) ***vt.*** **-let′, -let′ting** **1.** to let to another (property which one is renting) **2.** to let out (work) to a subcontractor

sub·lieu·ten·ant (sub′lo͞o ten′ənt; *Brit. & Canad.* -leften′-) ***n.*** [Brit. & Canad.] a naval officer ranking below a lieutenant

sub·li·mate (sub′lə māt′; *for adj. & n., also* -mit) ***vt.*** **-mat′ed, -mat′ing** [< L. pp. of *sublimare:* see ff.] **1.** to sublime (a substance) **2.** to have an ennobling effect on **3.** to express (impulses, esp. sexual impulses, regarded as unacceptable) in ways that are acceptable **—*vi.*** to undergo subliming **—*adj.*** sublimated **—*n.*** a substance that is the product of subliming **—sub′li·ma′tion** ***n.***

sub·lime (sə blīm′) ***adj.*** [< L. < *sub-,* up to + *limen,* lintel] **1.** noble; exalted; majestic **2.** inspiring awe or admiration through grandeur, beauty, etc. **—*vt.*** **-limed′, -lim′ing** **1.** to make sublime **2.** to purify (a solid) by heating directly to a gaseous state and condensing the vapor back into solid form **—*vi.*** to go through this process **—the sublime** a sublime quality or thing **—sub·lime′ly** ***adv.*** **—sub·lim·i·ty** (sə blim′ə tē), **sub·lime′ness** ***n.***

sub·lim·i·nal (sub lim′ə n′l) ***adj.*** [< SUB- + L. *limen,* threshold + -AL] below the threshold of consciousness; specif., involving stimuli intended to take effect subconsciously through repetition **—sub·lim′i·nal·ly** ***adv.***

sub·ma·chine gun (sub′mə shēn′) a portable, automatic or semiautomatic firearm with a short barrel and a stock, using pistol ammunition and fired from the shoulder or hip

sub·mar·gin·al (sub mär′ji n′l) ***adj.*** **1.** below minimum requirements or standards **2.** not yielding a satisfactory return *[submarginal* land*]* **—sub·mar′gin·al·ly** ***adv.***

sub·ma·rine (sub′mə rēn′; *for n. & v., usually* sub′mə rēn′) ***adj.*** being, living, used, etc. beneath the surface of the sea **—*n.*** **1.** a submarine plant or animal **2.** a kind of warship, armed with torpedoes, etc., that can operate under water **—*vt.*** **-rined′, -rin′ing** to attack with a submarine

submarine sandwich *same as* HERO SANDWICH
sub·max·il·lar·y (sub mak′sə ler′ē) ***adj.*** [see SUB- & MAXILLARY] of or below the lower jaw; esp., designating or of either of two salivary glands, one on each side, beneath the lower jaw
sub·merge (səb murj′) ***vt.*** **-merged′, -merg′ing** [< L. < *sub-*, under + *mergere*, to plunge] **1.** to place under or as under water, etc. **2.** to cover over; suppress; hide **3.** to sink below a decent level of life —***vi.*** to sink or plunge beneath the surface of water, etc. —**sub·mer′gence** ***n.*** —**sub·mer′gi·ble** ***adj.***
sub·merse (-murs′) ***vt.*** **-mersed′, -mers′ing** [< L. pp. of *submergere*] *same as* SUBMERGE —**sub·mer′sion** ***n.***
sub·mers·i·ble (-mur′sə b'l) ***adj.*** that can be submersed —***n.*** any of various ships that can operate under water
sub·min·i·a·ture (sub min′ē ə chər) ***adj.*** designating or of a camera, electronic component, etc., smaller than one described as "miniature"
sub·mis·sion (səb mish′ən) ***n.*** [OFr. < L. < pp. of *submittere*] **1.** a submitting, yielding, or surrendering **2.** a submissive quality or state; resignation; obedience **3.** a submitting of something to another for decision, consideration, etc.
sub·mis·sive (-mis′iv) ***adj.*** having or showing a tendency to submit without resistance; docile —**sub·mis′sive·ly** ***adv.*** —**sub·mis′sive·ness** ***n.***
sub·mit (-mit′) ***vt.*** **-mit′ted, -mit′ting** [< L. < *sub-*, under + *mittere*, to send] **1.** to present to others for decision, consideration, etc. **2.** to yield to the control, power, etc. of another; also, to allow to be subjected to treatment, analysis, etc.: often used reflexively **3.** to offer as an opinion; suggest —***vi.*** **1.** *a)* to yield to the power, control, etc. of another *b)* to allow oneself to be subjected (*to* treatment, analysis, etc.) **2.** to defer to another's judgment or decision **3.** to be submissive, obedient, etc. —**sub·mit′ta·ble** ***adj.*** —**sub·mit′tal** ***n.*** —**sub·mit′ter** ***n.***
sub·nor·mal (sub nôr′m'l) ***adj.*** below the normal; less than normal, esp. in intelligence —***n.*** a subnormal person —**sub′nor·mal′i·ty** (-mal′ə tē) ***n.*** —**sub·nor′mal·ly** ***adv.***
sub·or·di·nate (sə bôr′də nit; *for v.* -nāt′) ***adj.*** [< ML. pp. of *subordinare* < L. *sub-*, under + *ordinare*, to order] **1.** below another in rank, power, importance, etc.; secondary **2.** under the power or authority of another **3.** subservient or submissive **4.** *Gram.* functioning as a noun, adjective, or adverb within a sentence *[a subordinate* phrase*]*: cf. SUBORDINATE CLAUSE —***n.*** a subordinate person or thing —***vt.*** **-nat′ed, -nat′ing** **1.** to place in a subordinate position **2.** to make obedient or subservient (*to*) —**sub·or′di·nate·ly** ***adv.*** —**sub·or′di·na′tion** ***n.*** —**sub·or′di·na′tive** (-nāt′iv) ***adj.***
subordinate clause in a complex sentence, a clause that cannot function syntactically as a complete sentence by itself; dependent clause (Ex.: She will visit us *if she can*)
subordinating conjunction a conjunction that connects subordinate words, phrases, or clauses to some other sentence element (Ex.: *if, as, so, unless, although, when*): also **subordinate conjunction**
sub·orn (sə bôrn′) ***vt.*** [< MFr. < L. *sub-*, under + *ornare*, to furnish] **1.** to get by bribery or other illegal methods **2.** to induce or urge (another) to do something illegal, esp. to commit perjury —**sub·or·na·tion** (sub′ôr nā′shən) ***n.*** —**sub·or′na·tive** ***adj.*** —**sub·orn′er** ***n.***
sub·plot (sub′plät′) ***n.*** a secondary or subordinate plot in a play, novel, etc.
sub·poe·na (sə pē′nə) ***n.*** [< ML. < L. *sub poena*, lit., under penalty: see SUB- & PAIN] a written legal order directing a person to appear in court to give testimony, etc. —***vt.*** **-naed, -na·ing** to summon with such an order Also sp. **sub·pe′na**
sub·ro·gate (sub′rə gāt′) ***vt.*** **-gat′ed, -gat′ing** [< L. pp. of *subrogare, surrogare:* see SURROGATE] to substitute (one person) for another; esp., to substitute (one creditor) for another —**sub′ro·ga′tion** ***n.***
sub ro·sa (sub rō′zə) [L., under the rose, an ancient symbol of secrecy] secretly; privately
sub·rou·tine (sub′ro͞o tēn′) ***n.*** a short set of instructions, often used repeatedly, that directs a digital computer in the solution of part of a problem
sub·scribe (səb skrīb′) ***vt.*** **-scribed′, -scrib′ing** [L. *subscribere:* see SUB- & SCRIBE] **1.** to sign (one's name) at the end of a document, etc. **2.** to write one's signature on (a document, etc.) as an indication of consent, etc. **3.** to support; consent to **4.** to promise to contribute (money) —***vi.*** **1.** to sign one's name to a document, etc. **2.** to give support or approval (*to*) **3.** to promise to contribute, or to give, a sum of money **4.** to agree to receive and pay for a periodical, theater tickets, etc. for a specified period (with *to*) —**sub·scrib′er** ***n.***
sub·script (sub′skript) ***adj.*** [< L. pp. of *subscribere*, SUBSCRIBE] written below —***n.*** a figure, letter, or symbol written below and to the side of another *[*in Y_3 and X_a, *3* and *a* are *subscripts]*
sub·scrip·tion (səb skrip′shən) ***n.*** **1.** a subscribing **2.** something subscribed; specif., *a)* a written signature *b)* a signed document, etc. *c)* consent or sanction, esp. in writing *d)* an amount of money subscribed *e)* a formal agreement to receive and pay for a periodical, theater tickets, etc. for a specified period
sub·se·quent (sub′si kwənt, -kwent′) ***adj.*** [< L. prp. of *subsequi* < *sub-*, after + *sequi*, to follow] coming after; following in time, place, or order —**subsequent to** after; following —**sub′se·quence′** ***n.*** —**sub′se·quent·ly** ***adv.***
sub·serve (səb surv′) ***vt.*** **-served′, -serv′ing** to be useful or helpful to (a cause, etc.); serve; aid
sub·ser·vi·ent (-sur′vē ənt) ***adj.*** **1.** that is useful or of service, esp. in a subordinate capacity **2.** submissive; obsequious —**sub·ser′vi·ence, sub·ser′vi·en·cy** ***n.*** —**sub·ser′vi·ent·ly** ***adv.***
sub·set (sub′set′) ***n.*** a mathematical set containing some or all of the elements of a given set
sub·side (səb sīd′) ***vi.*** **-sid′ed, -sid′ing** [< L. < *sub-*, under + *sidere*, to settle] **1.** to sink to the bottom; settle **2.** to sink to a lower level **3.** to become less active, intense, etc.; abate —**sub·sid′ence** (-sīd′'ns, sub′si dəns) ***n.***
sub·sid·i·ar·y (səb sid′ē er′ē) ***adj.*** [< L. < *subsidium:* see SUBSIDY] **1.** giving aid, service, etc.; acting as a supplement; auxiliary **2.** being in a subordinate capacity **3.** of, constituting, or maintained by a subsidy or subsidies —***n.***, *pl.* **-ar′ies** a person or thing that is subsidiary; specif., a company (**subsidiary company**) controlled by another company that owns all or most of its shares —**sub·sid′i·ar′i·ly** ***adv.***
sub·si·dize (sub′sə dīz′) ***vt.*** **-dized′, -diz′ing** **1.** to support with a subsidy **2.** to buy the aid of with a subsidy —**sub′si·di·za′tion** ***n.*** —**sub′si·diz′er** ***n.***
sub·si·dy (sub′sə dē) ***n.***, *pl.* **-dies** [< Anglo-Fr. < L. *subsidium*, reserve troops, support] a grant of money; specif., *a)* a grant of money from one government to another *b)* a government grant to a private enterprise considered of benefit to the public
sub·sist (səb sist′) ***vi.*** [< L. < *sub-*, under + *sistere*, to stand] **1.** *a)* to continue to be or exist *b)* to continue to be in use, force, etc. **2.** to continue to live (*on* sustenance, *by* specific means, etc.) **3.** to consist (*in*) —***vt.*** to maintain with sustenance
sub·sist·ence (-sis′təns) ***n.*** **1.** existence; being **2.** the act of providing sustenance **3.** means of support or livelihood; specif., the barest means needed, as just enough food, to sustain life —**sub·sist′ent** ***adj.***
sub·soil (sub′soil′) ***n.*** the layer of soil beneath the surface soil —***vt.*** to turn up the subsoil of —**sub′soil′er** ***n.***
sub·spe·cies (-spē′shēz) ***n.*** any natural subdivision of a species that exhibits small variations in form from other subdivisions of the same species living in different regions
sub·stance (sub′stəns) ***n.*** [< OFr. < L. < *substare* < *sub-*, under + *stare*, to stand] **1.** the real or essential part of anything; essence **2.** *a)* the physical matter of which a thing consists; material *b)* matter of a particular kind or chemical composition **3.** *a)* solid quality *b)* consistency; body **4.** the real content or meaning of something said or written **5.** material possessions; property; wealth —**in substance** **1.** essentially **2.** actually; really
sub·stand·ard (sub stan′dərd) ***adj.*** below standard; specif., *a)* below a legal standard *b) same as* NONSTANDARD; specif., designating or of a dialect regarded as below that used by educated speakers *[*"he don't" and "we ain't" are generally considered *substandard]*
sub·stan·tial (səb stan′shəl) ***adj.*** **1.** of or having substance **2.** real; actual; true **3.** strong; solid; firm **4.** ample; large **5.** of considerable value; important **6.** well-to-do **7.** with regard to essential elements —**sub·stan′ti·al′i·ty** (-shē al′ə tē), **sub·stan′tial·ness** ***n.*** —**sub·stan′tial·ly** ***adv.***
sub·stan·ti·ate (səb stan′shē āt′) ***vt.*** **-at′ed, -at′ing** **1.** to give substance to **2.** to give concrete form or body to **3.** to show to be true or real by giving evidence; prove —**sub·stan′ti·a′tion** ***n.*** —**sub·stan′ti·a′tive** ***adj.*** —**sub·stan′ti·a′tor** ***n.***
sub·stan·tive (sub′stən tiv) ***adj.*** [< LL. < L. *substantia*, SUBSTANCE] **1.** existing independently **2.** of considerable amount **3.** actual; real **4.** *a)* essential *b)* having direct bearing on a matter **5.** *Gram.* *a)* of or expressing existence *[*the *substantive* verb "to be"*]* *b)* of or used as a substantive —***n.*** **1.** something substantive **2.** a noun or any word or group of words functioning as a noun —**sub′stan·ti′val** (-tī′v'l) ***adj.*** —**sub′stan·ti′val·ly, sub′stan·tive·ly** ***adv.*** —**sub′stan·tive·ness** ***n.***
sub·sta·tion (sub′stā′shən) ***n.*** a branch station
sub·sti·tute (sub′stə to͞ot′, -tyo͞ot′) ***n.*** [< L. pp. of *substituere* < *sub-*, under + *statuere*, to put] a person or thing serving or used in place of another —***vt., vi.*** **-tut′ed, -tut′ing** to put, use, or serve in place of another —***adj.*** being a substitute —**sub′sti·tut′a·ble** ***adj.*** —**sub′sti·tu′tive** ***adj.***

sub·sti·tu·tion (sub′stə to͞o′shən, -tyo͞o′-) ***n.*** the substituting of one person or thing for another —**sub′sti·tu′tion·al, sub′sti·tu′tion·ar′y** ***adj.***

sub·stra·tum (sub′strāt′əm, -strat′-) ***n., pl.*** **-ta** (-ə), **-tums** [< L. pp. of *substernere* < *sub-*, under + *sternere*, to strew] **1.** a part, substance, etc. which lies beneath and supports another **2.** any basis or foundation **3.** loosely, *same as* SUBSOIL

sub·struc·ture (-struk′chər) ***n.*** a structure acting as a support, base, or foundation —**sub·struc′tur·al** ***adj.***

sub·sume (səb so͞om′, -syo͞om′) ***vt.*** **-sumed′, -sum′ing** [< ModL. < L. *sub-*, under + *sumere*, to take] **1.** to include within a larger class, group, etc. **2.** to show (an idea, instance, etc.) to be covered by a rule, principle, etc.

sub·sur·face (sub′sʉr′fis) ***adj.*** lying below the surface, esp. of the earth, the oceans, etc. —***n.*** a subsurface part

sub·sys·tem (-sis′təm) ***n.*** any system that is part of a larger system; component system

sub·teen (sub′tēn′) ***n.*** a child nearly a teen-ager

sub·tem·per·ate (sub tem′pər it) ***adj.*** of or occurring in the colder areas of the temperate zones

sub·ten·ant (-ten′ənt) ***n.*** one who rents from a tenant; tenant of a tenant —**sub·ten′an·cy** ***n.***

sub·tend (səb tend′) ***vt.*** [< L. < *sub-*, under + *tendere*, to stretch] **1.** to extend under or be opposite to in position *[*each side of a triangle *subtends* the opposite angle*]* **2.** *Bot.* to enclose in an angle, as between a leaf and its stem

sub·ter- [L. < *subter*, below, beneath] *a prefix meaning* below, under, less than, secretly

sub·ter·fuge (sub′tər fyo͞oj′) ***n.*** [< LL. < L. < *subter-*, below + *fugere*, to flee] any plan, action, etc. used to hide one's true objective, evade a difficult situation, etc.

sub·ter·ra·ne·an (sub′tə rā′nē ən) ***adj.*** [< L. < *sub-*, under + *terra*, earth] **1.** lying beneath the earth's surface; underground **2.** secret; hidden Also **sub′ter·ra′ne·ous** —***n.*** one who lives underground —**sub′ter·ra′ne·an·ly** ***adv.***

sub·tile (sut′'l, sub′til) ***adj.*** *now rare var. of* SUBTLE —**sub′tile·ly** ***adv.*** —**sub′tile·ness** ***n.*** —**sub′til·ty, sub·til·i·ty** (səb til′ə tē) ***n., pl.*** **-ties**

sub·til·ize (sut′'l īz′, sub′t'l-) ***vt., vi.*** **-ized′, -iz′ing** to make or become subtle; esp., to discuss or argue in a subtle way —**sub′til·i·za′tion** ***n.***

sub·ti·tle (sub′tīt′'l) ***n.*** **1.** a secondary title of a book, play, etc. **2.** a unit of lines of dialogue or description flashed on a movie or TV screen, esp. at the bottom in translation —***vt.*** **-ti′tled, -ti′tling** to add a subtitle or subtitles to

sub·tle (sut′'l) ***adj.*** **sub′tler** (-lər, -'l ər), **sub′tlest** (-list, -'l ist) [< OFr. < L. *subtilis*, orig., closely woven < *sub-*, under + *tela*, web] **1.** thin; tenuous; not dense **2.** making fine distinctions or marked by mental keenness **3.** delicately skillful; deft **4.** crafty; sly **5.** not grossly obvious *[*a *subtle* hint*]* **6.** not easily detected *[*a *subtle* poison*]* —**sub′tle·ness** ***n.*** —**sub′tly** ***adv.***

sub·tle·ty (-tē) ***n.*** **1.** the quality or condition of being subtle **2.** *pl.* **-ties** something subtle, as a fine distinction

sub·ton·ic (sub tän′ik) ***n.*** *Music* the seventh tone of a diatonic scale

sub·top·ic (sub′täp′ik) ***n.*** a topic that is a division of a main topic

sub·to·tal (-tōt′'l) ***n.*** a total forming part of a final, complete total —***vt., vi.*** **-taled** or **-talled, -tal·ing** or **-tal·ling** to add up so as to form a subtotal

sub·tract (səb trakt′) ***vt., vi.*** [< L. pp. of *subtrahere* < *sub-*, under + *trahere*, to draw] to take away or deduct (a part from a whole) or (one number or quantity from another) —**sub·tract′er** ***n.*** —**sub·trac′tive** ***adj.***

sub·trac·tion (-trak′shən) ***n.*** a subtracting or being subtracted; esp., the mathematical process of finding the difference between two numbers or quantities

sub·tra·hend (sub′trə hend′) ***n.*** [< L. gerundive of *subtrahere:* see SUBTRACT] a number or quantity to be subtracted from another

sub·treas·ur·y (sub′trezh′ər ē, sub trezh′-) ***n., pl.*** **-ur·ies** a branch treasury

sub·trop·i·cal (sub träp′i k'l) ***adj.*** designating, of, or characteristic of regions bordering on the tropical zone; nearly tropical: also **sub·trop′ic**

sub·trop·ics (-iks) ***n.pl.*** subtropical regions

sub·urb (sub′ərb) ***n.*** [< L. < *sub-*, under, near + *urbs*, town] **1.** a district on the outskirts of a city, often a separately incorporated city or town **2.** [*pl.*] a region of such districts (with *the*)

sub·ur·ban (sə bʉr′bən) ***adj.*** **1.** of or living in a suburb or the suburbs **2.** characteristic of the suburbs or suburbanites —**sub·ur′ban·ize′** (-īz′) ***vt., vi.*** **-ized′, -iz′ing**

sub·ur·ban·ite (-īt′) ***n.*** a person living in a suburb

sub·ur·bi·a (sə bʉr′bē ə) ***n.*** the suburbs or suburbanites collectively: used to connote suburban values, attitudes, etc.

sub·ven·tion (səb ven′shən) ***n.*** [< OFr. < LL. < L. < *sub-*, under + *venire*, to come] a grant of money; subsidy

sub·ver·sion (səb vʉr′zhən, -shən) ***n.*** a subverting or being subverted; ruin; overthrow

sub·ver·sive (-siv) ***adj.*** tending or seeking to subvert —***n.*** a person regarded as subversive —**sub·ver′sive·ly** ***adv.*** —**sub·ver′sive·ness** ***n.***

sub·vert (səb vʉrt′) ***vt.*** [< MFr. < L. < *sub-*, under + *vertere*, to turn] **1.** to overthrow or destroy (something established) **2.** to undermine or corrupt, as in morals —**sub·vert′er** ***n.***

sub·way (sub′wā′) ***n.*** **1.** an underground way **2.** an underground, metropolitan electric railway or the tunnel through which it runs

suc- *same as* SUB-: used before *c*

suc·ceed (sək sēd′) ***vi.*** [L. *succedere* < *sub-*, under + *cedere*, to go] **1.** *a)* to come next after another *b)* to follow another into office, possession, etc., as by election (often with *to*) **2.** to happen or turn out as planned **3.** to accomplish something planned or tried **4.** to have success; do well; attain wealth, fame, etc. —***vt.*** **1.** to follow into office, etc. **2.** to come after; follow

suc·cess (sək ses′) ***n.*** [< L. < pp. of *succedere:* see prec.] **1.** *a)* a favorable outcome *b)* something having a favorable outcome **2.** the gaining of wealth, fame, etc. **3.** a successful person

suc·cess·ful (-fəl) ***adj.*** **1.** turning out to be as was hoped for **2.** having gained wealth, fame, etc. —**suc·cess′ful·ly** ***adv.*** —**suc·cess′ful·ness** ***n.***

suc·ces·sion (sək sesh′ən) ***n.*** **1.** a succeeding or coming after another in sequence or to an office, etc. **2.** the right to succeed to an office, etc. **3.** a number of persons or things coming one after another; series; sequence **4.** *a)* a series of heirs or rightful successors *b)* the order or line of such a series —**in succession** one after another —**suc·ces′sion·al** ***adj.***

suc·ces·sive (sək ses′iv) ***adj.*** **1.** coming one after another; consecutive **2.** of succession —**suc·ces′sive·ly** ***adv.*** —**suc·ces′sive·ness** ***n.***

suc·ces·sor (-ər) ***n.*** a person or thing that succeeds, or follows, another; esp., one who succeeds to an office, etc.

suc·cinct (sək siŋkt′) ***adj.*** [< L. pp. of *succingere*, to tuck up < *sub-*, under + *cingere*, to gird] **1.** clearly and briefly stated; terse **2.** concise and to the point in speaking —**succinct′ly** ***adv.*** —**suc·cinct′ness** ***n.***

suc·cor (suk′ər) ***vt.*** [< OFr. < L. *succurrere* < *sub-*, under + *currere*, to run] to aid in time of need or distress —***n.*** **1.** aid; help **2.** a person or thing that succors Also, Brit. sp., **suc′cour**

suc·co·tash (suk′ə tash′) ***n.*** [< AmInd.] a dish consisting of lima beans and kernels of corn cooked together

Suc·coth (soo kōt′, sook′ōs) ***n.*** *same as* SUKKOT

suc·cu·bus (suk′yoo bəs) ***n., pl.*** **-bi′** (-bī′) [< ML., ult. < L. *sub-*, under + *cubare*, to lie] a female demon thought in medieval times to have sexual intercourse with sleeping men: also **suc′cu·ba** (-bə), *pl.* **-bae′** (-bē′)

suc·cu·lent (suk′yoo lənt) ***adj.*** [L. *succulentus* < *sucus*, juice] **1.** juicy **2.** full of interest, vigor, etc. **3.** *Bot.* having thick, fleshy tissues for storing water, as a cactus —***n.*** a succulent plant —**suc′cu·lence, suc′cu·len·cy** ***n.*** —**suc′cu·lent·ly** ***adv.***

suc·cumb (sə kum′) ***vi.*** [L. *succumbere* < *sub-*, under + *cumbere*, to lie] **1.** to give way (*to*); yield; submit **2.** to die *[*to *succumb* to a plague*]*

such (such) ***adj.*** [OE. *swilc, swelc*] **1.** *a)* of the kind mentioned or implied *[*one *such* as he*]* *b)* of the same or a similar kind *[*pens, pencils, and *such* supplies*]* **2.** certain but not specified; whatever *[*at *such* time as you go*]* **3.** so extreme, so much, etc. *[such* fun!*]* *Such* is used, with *as* or *that*, in making comparisons *[such* wit *as* his is rare*]* An article may occur between *such* and the noun it modifies *[such* a fool!*]* —***adv.*** to so great a degree *[such* good news*]* —***pron.*** such a one or ones —**as such** **1.** as being what is indicated **2.** in itself —**such as** **1.** for example **2.** like or similar to (what is specified)

such and such (being) something particular but not specified *[*he went to *such and such* a place*]*

such·like (-līk′) ***adj.*** of such a kind; of similar kind —***pron.*** persons or things of such kind

suck (suk) ***vt.*** [OE. *sucan*] **1.** *a)* to draw (liquid) into the mouth by making a vacuum with the lips, cheeks, and tongue *b)* to draw up (water, oil, etc.) by the action of a pump **2.** to take up or in as by sucking; absorb, inhale, etc. *[*to *suck* air into the lungs*]* **3.** to suck liquid from (a breast, fruit, etc.) **4.** to hold (candy, etc.) in the mouth and lick it **5.** to place (the thumb, etc.) in the mouth and draw on as if sucking —*vi.* **1.** to suck something in or up **2.** to suck milk from the breast or udder **3.** to make a sucking sound or movement —*n.* **1.** the act or sound of sucking **2.** *a)* something drawn in by sucking *b)* [Colloq.] the amount sucked at one time —**suck in 1.** to compress and pull inward *[*to *suck in* one's belly*]* **2.** [Slang] to fool, swindle, etc. —**suck up to** [Slang] to flatter or fawn upon

suck·er (-ər) *n.* **1.** one that sucks **2.** a carplike freshwater fish with a mouth adapted for sucking **3.** a part used for sucking; specif., *a)* a tube through which something is sucked *b)* the piston or piston valve of a suction pump *c)* an organ used by the leech, octopus, etc. for sucking or holding fast to a surface by suction **4.** a lollipop **5.** [Slang] *a)* a person easily fooled or cheated; dupe *b)* a person readily drawn to specified attractions **6.** *Bot.* a shoot from a root bud or stem bud —*vt.* **1.** to remove suckers, or shoots, from **2.** [Slang] to make a dupe of; trick —*vi.* to bear suckers, or shoots

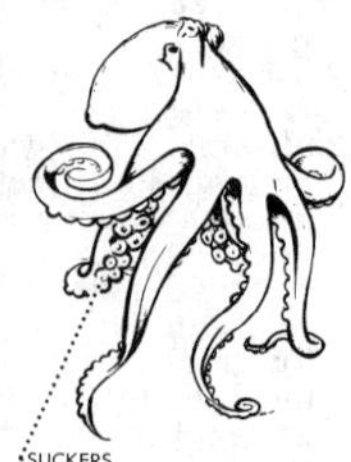
SUCKERS

suck·le (suk′'l) *vt.* **-led, -ling** [prob. < ff.] **1.** to give milk to from a breast or udder; nurse **2.** to nourish; foster —*vi.* to suck milk from its mother

suck·ling (-liŋ) *n.* [see SUCK & -LING[1]] an unweaned child or young animal

Su·cre (so͞o′kre) city in SC Bolivia; legal capital & seat of the judiciary (cf. LA PAZ): pop. 85,000

su·cre (so͞o′kre) *n.* [AmSp. after A.J. de *Sucre,* 19th-c. S. American liberator] *see* MONETARY UNITS, table (Ecuador)

su·crose (so͞o′krōs) *n.* [< Fr. *sucre,* sugar + -OSE[1]] *Chem.* pure crystalline sugar, $C_{12}H_{22}O_{11}$, extracted from sugar cane or sugar beets: it can be broken down into glucose and fructose

suc·tion (suk′shən) *n.* [OFr. < L. < *suctus,* pp. of *sugere,* to suck] **1.** the act or process of sucking **2.** the drawing of air out of a space to make a vacuum that will suck in surrounding air, liquid, etc. or cause something to stick to the surface **3.** the force so created —*adj.* causing or operating by suction

suction pump a pump that draws liquid up by suction created by pistons fitted with valves

suc·to·ri·al (suk tôr′ē əl) *adj.* [< ModL. < L.: see SUCTION] sucking or adapted for sucking

Su·dan (so͞o dan′) **1.** vast plains region in NC Africa, south of the Sahara **2.** country in the E part of this region, south of Egypt: 967,500 sq. mi.; pop. 15,595,000; cap. Khartoum —**Su′da·nese′** (-də nēz′) *adj., n., pl.* **-nese′**

Sud·bur·y (sud′ber′ē, -bər ē) city in SE Ontario, Canada: pop. 98,000

sud·den (sud′'n) *adj.* [OFr. *sodain* < L. *subitaneus,* ult. < *sub-,* under + *ire,* to go] **1.** *a)* happening or coming unexpectedly; not foreseen *b)* sharp or abrupt *[a sudden* turn*]* **2.** done, coming, or taking place quickly or abruptly —**all of a sudden** without warning; quickly —**sud′den·ly** *adv.* —**sud′den·ness** *n.*

sudden death *Sports* an extra period added to a tied game, the game ending as soon as one side scores

Su·de·ten·land (so͞o dāt′'n land′; *G.* zo͞o dā′tən länt′) mountainous region in N Czechoslovakia

su·dor·if·ic (so͞o′də rif′ik, syo͞o′-) *adj.* [< ModL. < L. *sudor,* sweat + *facere,* to make] causing or increasing sweating —*n.* a sudorific drug, etc.

suds (sudz) *n.pl.* [prob. < MDu. *sudse,* marsh water] **1.** foamy, soapy water **2.** foam, froth, or lather **3.** [Slang] beer or ale —*vi.* to make suds —*vt.* [Colloq.] to wash in suds —**suds′y** *adj.* **-i·er, -i·est**

sue (so͞o) *vt.* **sued, su′ing** [OFr. *sivre, suir,* ult. < L. *sequi,* to follow] **1.** to appeal to; petition **2.** to bring a lawsuit in court against **3.** [Archaic] to woo —*vi.* **1.** to petition; plead (*for* or *to*) **2.** [Archaic] to woo **3.** to bring legal suit —**su′er** *n.*

suede, suède (swād) *n.* [Fr. *Suède,* Sweden, in *gants de Suède,* Swedish gloves] **1.** tanned leather with the flesh side buffed into a nap **2.** a kind of cloth made to resemble this: also **suede cloth**

su·et (so͞o′it, syo͞o′-) *n.* [dim. < Anglo-Fr. *sue* < OFr. < L. *sebum,* fat] hard fat from around the kidneys and loins of cattle and sheep: used in cooking and as a source of tallow —**su′et·y** *adj.*

Su·ez (so͞o ez′, so͞o′ez) **1.** seaport in NE Egypt, on the Suez Canal: pop. 203,000 **2. Gulf of,** NW arm of the Red Sea **3. Isthmus of,** strip of land in NE Egypt, connecting Asia & Africa

Suez Canal ship canal across the Isthmus of Suez, joining the Mediterranean & the Gulf of Suez

suf- *same as* SUB-: used before *f*

suf·fer (suf′ər) *vt.* [< Anglo-Fr. < OFr. < L. *sufferre* < *sub-,* under + *ferre,* to bear] **1.** to undergo (something painful or unpleasant) **2.** to undergo (any process) **3.** to allow; tolerate **4.** to endure —*vi.* to undergo pain, harm, loss, etc. —**suf′fer·a·ble** *adj.* —**suf′fer·er** *n.* —**suf′fer·ing** *n.*

suf·fer·ance (suf′ər əns, suf′rəns) *n.* **1.** power or capacity to endure pain, etc. **2.** consent, toleration, etc. implied by failure to interfere or prohibit —**on sufferance** allowed or tolerated but not supported or encouraged

suf·fice (sə fīs′, -fīz′) *vi.* **-ficed′, -fic′ing** [< OFr. < L. *sufficere* < *sub-,* under + *facere,* to make] to be enough —*vt.* [Archaic] to be enough for

suf·fi·cien·cy (sə fish′ən sē) *n.* **1.** sufficient means, ability, or resources; an amount that is enough **2.** a being sufficient; adequacy

suf·fi·cient (-'nt) *adj.* [see SUFFICE] as much as is needed; enough —**suf·fi′cient·ly** *adv.*

suf·fix (suf′iks; *also for v.* sə fiks′) *n.* [< ModL. < L. pp. of *suffigere* < *sub-,* under + *figere,* to fix] a syllable or group of syllables added at the end of a word or word base to change its meaning or give it grammatical function (Ex.: *-ish* in *smallish, -ed* in *walked*) —*vt.* to add as a suffix —**suf′fix·al** *adj.* —**suf·fix′ion** *n.*

suf·fo·cate (suf′ə kāt′) *vt.* **-cat′ed, -cat′ing** [< L. pp. of *suffocare* < *sub-,* under + *fauces,* throat] **1.** to kill by cutting off the supply of oxygen to the lungs, gills, etc. **2.** to hinder the free breathing of **3.** to smother, suppress, etc. —*vi.* **1.** to die by being suffocated **2.** to be unable to breathe freely; choke, etc. —**suf′fo·cat′ing·ly** *adv.* —**suf′fo·ca′tion** *n.* —**suf′fo·ca′tive** *adj.*

suf·fra·gan (suf′rə gən) *n.* [MFr. < ML. < L. *suffragari,* to support] **1.** a bishop assisting another bishop **2.** a bishop as a subordinate of his archbishop —*adj.* **1.** designating or of such a bishop **2.** subordinate to a larger see

suf·frage (suf′rij) *n.* [MFr. < ML. < L. *suffragium,* a vote < *sub-,* under + *fragor,* loud applause] **1.** a short prayer of supplication **2.** a vote or voting **3.** the right to vote in political elections

suf·fra·gette (suf′rə jet′) *n.* a woman who works for women's right to vote —**suf′fra·get′tism** *n.*

suf·fra·gist (suf′rə jist) *n.* a person who believes in extending the right to vote, esp. to women

suf·fuse (sə fyo͞oz′) *vt.* **-fused′, -fus′ing** [< L. pp. of *suffundere* < *sub-,* under + *fundere,* to pour] to overspread so as to fill with a glow, color, fluid, etc.: said of light, a blush, air, etc. —**suf·fu′sion** *n.* —**suf·fu′sive** (-siv) *adj.*

sug- *same as* SUB-: used before *g*

sug·ar (shoog′ər) *n.* [OFr. *sucre,* ult. < Per. *šakar* < Sans. *śarkarā*] **1.** any of a class of sweet, soluble, crystalline carbohydrates, including sucrose, lactose, maltose, glucose, fructose, etc. **2.** sucrose in crystalline or powdered form: it is the common sugar used to sweeten food **3.** a bowl for sugar, specif. as forming a set with a creamer **4.** *short for* SUGAR DIABETES **5.** [Colloq.] sweetheart **6.** [Slang] money —*vt.* **1.** to put sugar on or in **2.** to make seem pleasant or less bad —*vi.* **1.** to form sugar **2.** to boil down maple syrup to form maple sugar (usually with *off*) —**sug′ar·less** *adj.* —**sug′ar·like′** *adj.*

sugar beet a variety of beet with a white root from which common sugar is got

sug·ar·bush (-boosh′) *n.* a grove of sugar maples

sugar cane a very tall, tropical grass cultivated as the main source of common sugar

sug·ar·coat (-kōt′) *vt.* **1.** to coat with sugar **2.** to make seem less unpleasant *[*to *sugarcoat* bad news*]*

sug·ar-cured (-kyoord′) *adj.* treated with a pickling preparation of sugar, salt, etc., as ham

sugar diabetes *popular term for* DIABETES MELLITUS

sugar loaf **1.** a conical mass of crystallized sugar **2.** a similarly shaped hill, etc.

sugar maple an E N. American maple valued for its hard wood and for its sap, which yields maple syrup

SUGAR CANE

sug·ar·plum (-plum′) *n.* a round or oval piece of sugary candy; bonbon

sug·ar·y (shoog′ər ē) *adj.* **1.** of, like, or containing sugar; sweet, granular, etc. **2.** too sweet or sentimental —**sug′ar·i·ness** *n.*

sug·gest (səg jest′; *also, & Brit. usually,* sə jest′) *vt.* [< L. pp. of *suggerere* < *sub-,* under + *gerere,* to carry] **1.** to mention as something to think over, act on, etc.; bring to the mind for consideration **2.** to call to mind through association of ideas *[*objects *suggested* by the shapes of clouds*]* **3.** to propose (someone or something) as a possibility **4.** to imply; intimate —**sug·gest′er** *n.*

sug·gest·i·ble (-jes′tə b'l) ***adj.*** easily influenced by suggestion —**sug·gest′i·bil′i·ty** ***n.***
sug·ges·tion (-jes′chən) ***n.*** **1.** a suggesting or being suggested **2.** something suggested **3.** the process by which one idea leads to another through association of ideas **4.** a faint hint; trace **5.** *Psychol.* the inducing of an idea that is accepted or acted on readily without questioning
sug·ges·tive (-jes′tiv) ***adj.*** **1.** that suggests or tends to suggest ideas **2.** tending to suggest something considered improper or indecent —**sug·ges′tive·ly** ***adv.*** —**sug·ges′tive·ness** ***n.***
su·i·ci·dal (sōō′ə sīd′əl) ***adj.*** **1.** of, involving, or leading to suicide **2.** having an urge to commit suicide **3.** rash to the point of being dangerous —**su′i·ci′dal·ly** ***adv.***
su·i·cide (sōō′ə sīd′) ***n.*** [L. *sui,* of oneself + -CIDE] **1.** the intentional killing of oneself **2.** ruin of one's interests through one's own actions **3.** a person committing suicide
su·i ge·ne·ris (sōō′ē jen′ər is, sōō′ī) [L., lit., of his (or her or its) own kind] altogether unique
suit (sōōt) ***n.*** [OFr. *suite,* ult. < L. *sequi,* to follow] **1.** *a)* a set of clothes to be worn together; esp., a coat and trousers (or skirt), usually of the same material *b)* any complete outfit [a *suit* of armor] **2.** a set or series of similar things; specif., any of the four sets of thirteen playing cards each (*spades, clubs, hearts, diamonds*) in a pack **3.** a lawsuit **4.** a suing, pleading, or wooing —***vt.*** **1.** to meet the needs of; be right for or becoming to **2.** to make fit; adapt [a dance *suited* to the music] **3.** to please; satisfy **4.** to furnish with clothes, esp. with a suit —***vi.*** to be suitable, convenient, or satisfactory —**bring suit** to start legal action; sue —**follow suit** **1.** to play a card of the same suit as the card led **2.** to follow the example set —**suit oneself** to do as one pleases
suit·a·ble (-ə b'l) ***adj.*** right for the purpose, occasion etc.; fitting; appropriate —**suit′a·bil′i·ty, suit′a·ble·ness** ***n.*** —**suit′a·bly** ***adv.***
suit·case (-kās′) ***n.*** a travel case for clothes, etc., esp. a rectangular one that opens into two hinged compartments
suite (swēt; *for 2 b, occas.* sōōt) ***n.*** [Fr.: see SUIT] **1.** a group of attendants or servants; retinue **2.** a set or series of related things; specif., *a)* a unit of connected rooms *b)* a set of matched furniture for a room [a bedroom *suite*] **3.** *Music* an instrumental composition made up of several movements or, in earlier times, dances
suit·ing (sōōt′iŋ) ***n.*** cloth for making suits
suit·or (-ər) ***n.*** **1.** a person who sues, petitions, pleads, etc. **2.** a man courting or wooing a woman
su·ki·ya·ki (sōō′kē yä′kē) ***n.*** [Jap.] a Japanese dish of thinly sliced meat, onions, and other vegetables cooked quickly, often at table, with soy sauce, sake, sugar, etc.
Suk·kot, Suk·koth (soo kōt′, sook′ōs) ***n.*** [Heb. *sukkōth,* lit., tabernacles] a Jewish festival in early fall, celebrating the harvest and commemorating the desert wandering of the Jews during the Exodus: also **Suk′kos** (sook′ōs)
Su·lei·man (I) (sōō′lā män′) 1494?–1566; sultan of the Ottoman Empire (1520–66)
sulf- *a combining form meaning* of or containing sulfur
sul·fa (sul′fə) ***adj.*** designating or of a family of drugs that are sulfonamides, used in combating certain bacterial infections
sul·fa·di·a·zine (sul′fə dī′ə zēn′, -zin) ***n.*** [prec. + DI-[1] + AZ(O) + -INE[4]] a sulfa drug, $C_{10}H_{10}N_4O_2S$, used in treating certain pneumococcal, streptococcal, and staphylococcal infections
sul·fate (sul′fāt) ***n.*** a salt or ester of sulfuric acid —***vt.*** **-fat·ed, -fat·ing** **1.** to treat with sulfuric acid or a sulfate **2.** to convert into a sulfate **3.** to form a lead sulfate deposit on (negative storage battery plates) —***vi.*** to become sulfated —**sul·fa′tion** ***n.***
sul·fide (sul′fīd) ***n.*** a compound of sulfur with another element or a radical
sul·fite (-fīt) ***n.*** a salt or ester of sulfurous acid
sul·fon·a·mide (sul fän′ə mīd′, -mid) ***n.*** [< *sulfon*(*yl*), the radical SO_2 + AMIDE] a compound, as sulfadiazine, containing the univalent radical $-SO_2NH_2$
sul·fur (sul′fər) ***n.*** [L. *sulphur, sulfur*] **1.** a pale-yellow, nonmetallic chemical element found in crystalline or amorphous form: it burns with a blue flame and a stifling odor: symbol, S; at. wt., 32.064; at. no., 16 **2.** any of numerous butterflies with dark-bordered, yellow or orange wings **3.** a greenish-yellow color —***vt.*** to sulfurize
sul·fu·rate (sul′fyoo rāt′, -fə-) ***vt.*** **-rat′ed, -rat′ing** *same as* SULFURIZE —**sul′fu·ra′tion** ***n.***
sul·fur-bot·tom (sul′fər bät′əm) ***n.*** *same as* BLUE WHALE
sulfur dioxide a heavy, colorless, suffocating gas, SO_2, easily liquefied and used as a bleach, preservative, etc.
sul·fu·re·ous (sul fyoor′ē əs) ***adj.*** **1.** of, like, or containing sulfur **2.** greenish-yellow
sul·fu·ret (sul′fyoo ret′) ***vt.*** **-ret′ed** or **-ret′ted, -ret′ing** or **-ret′ting** *same as* SULFURIZE
sul·fu·ric (sul fyoor′ik) ***adj.*** **1.** of or containing sulfur, esp. sulfur with a valence of six **2.** of or derived from sulfuric acid
sulfuric acid an oily, colorless, corrosive liquid, H_2SO_4, used in making explosives, fertilizers, chemicals, etc.
sul·fu·rize (sul′fyoo rīz′, -fə-) ***vt.*** **-rized′, -riz′ing** to combine or treat with sulfur or a sulfur compound —**sul′fu·ri·za′tion** ***n.***
sul·fu·rous (sul′fər əs; *for 1 usually* sul fyoor′əs) ***adj.*** **1.** of or containing sulfur, esp. sulfur with a valence of four **2.** like burning sulfur in odor, color, etc. **3.** of or suggesting the fires of hell **4.** violently emotional; fiery —**sul′fu·rous·ly** ***adv.*** —**sul′fu·rous·ness** ***n.***
sulfurous acid a colorless acid, H_2SO_3, known only in the form of its salts or in solution in water, and used as a chemical reagent, a bleach, etc.
sul·fur·y (sul′fər ē) ***adj.*** of or like sulfur
sulk (sulk) ***vi.*** [back-formation < ff.] to be sulky —***n.*** **1.** a sulky mood or state: also **the sulks** **2.** a sulky person
sulk·y (sul′kē) ***adj.*** **sulk′i·er, sulk′i·est** [prob. < OE. *solcen* (in comp.), idle] sullen in a pouting or peevish way [a *sulky* child] —***n., pl.*** **sulk′ies** a light, two-wheeled carriage for one person, esp., now, one used in harness races —**sulk′i·ly** ***adv.*** —**sulk′i·ness** ***n.***
Sul·la (sul′ə) (*Lucius Cornelius Sulla Felix*) 138?–78 B.C.; Rom. general; dictator of Rome (82–79)
sul·len (sul′ən) ***adj.*** [ult. < L. *solus,* alone] **1.** silent and keeping to oneself because one feels angry, bitter, hurt, etc. **2.** gloomy; dismal; depressing **3.** somber; dull **4.** sluggish —**sul′len·ly** ***adv.*** —**sul′len·ness** ***n.***
Sul·li·van (sul′ə vən), Sir **Arthur Sey·mour** (sē′môr) 1842–1900; Eng. composer: see Sir William GILBERT
sul·ly (sul′ē) ***vt.*** **-lied, -ly·ing** [prob. < OFr. *souiller:* see SOIL[2]] to soil, stain, etc., now esp. by disgracing
sulph- *var., now esp. Brit., sp. of* SULF-: for words beginning **sulph-**, see forms under **sulf-**
sul·phur (sul′fər) ***n.*** *var., now esp. Brit., sp. of* SULFUR
sul·tan (sul′t'n) ***n.*** [Fr. < Ar. *sulṭān*] a Moslem ruler; esp., [S-] formerly, the ruler of Turkey
sul·tan·a (sul tan′ə, -tä′nə) ***n.*** **1.** a sultan's wife, mother, sister, or daughter: also **sul′tan·ess** (-tən is) **2.** a small, white, seedless grape or raisin
sul·tan·ate (sul′t'n it, -āt′) ***n.*** the authority, office, reign, or dominion of a sultan
sul·try (sul′trē) ***adj.*** **-tri·er, -tri·est** [var. of *sweltry:* see SWELTER] **1.** oppressively hot and moist; sweltering **2.** fiery **3.** inflamed with passion, lust, etc. —**sul′tri·ly** ***adv.*** —**sul′tri·ness** ***n.***
Su·lu Archipelago (sōō′lōō) group of islands in the Philippines, southwest of Mindanao
sum (sum) ***n.*** [< MFr. < L. *summa,* fem. of *summus,* highest] **1.** an amount of money **2.** the whole amount; totality [the *sum* of one's experiences] **3.** gist; summary: usually in **sum and substance** **4.** *a)* the result gotten by adding numbers or quantities *b)* a series of numbers to be added up, or any problem in arithmetic —***vt.*** **summed, sum′ming** **1.** to add up **2.** to summarize —***vi.*** to get, or come to, a total —**in sum** to put it briefly; in short —**sum up** **1.** to add up or collect into a whole or total **2.** to summarize
sum- *same as* SUB-: used before *m*
su·mac, su·mach (shōō′mak, sōō′-) ***n.*** [MFr. < Ar. *summāq*] **1.** *a)* any of various nonpoisonous plants with compound leaves and cone-shaped clusters of hairy, red fruit *b)* the powdered leaves of some of these plants, used in tanning and dyeing **2.** any of several poisonous plants, as poison ivy

SUMAC

Su·ma·tra (soo mä′trə) large island of Indonesia, south of the Malay Peninsula: c. 165,000 sq. mi. —**Su·ma′tran** ***adj., n.***
Su·mer (sōō′mər) ancient region in the lower valley of the Euphrates River
Su·mer·i·an (soo mir′ē ən, -mer′-) ***adj.*** designating or of an ancient, non-Semitic people of Sumer —***n.*** **1.** any of the Sumerian people **2.** the language of the Sumerians
‡**sum·ma cum lau·de** (soom′ə koom lou′de, sum′ə kum lô′dē) [L.] with the greatest praise: phrase used to signify graduation with the highest honors from a college or university
sum·ma·rize (sum′ə rīz′) ***vt.*** **-rized′, -riz′ing** to make or be a summary of —**sum′ma·ri·za′tion** ***n.*** —**sum′ma·riz′er** ***n.***

sum·ma·ry (sum′ə rē) ***adj.*** [< ML. < L. *summa,* a sum] **1.** briefly giving the general idea; concise; condensed **2.** *a)* prompt and informal *b)* hasty and arbitrary —***n., pl.*** **-ries** a brief account covering the main points; digest —**sum·mar·i·ly** (sə mer′ə lē, sum′ə rə lē) ***adv.***

sum·ma·tion (sə mā′shən) ***n.*** **1.** a summing up, to find a total **2.** a total or aggregate **3.** a final summing up of arguments, as in a court trial

sum·mer (sum′ər) ***n.*** [OE. *sumor*] **1.** the warmest season of the year, following spring **2.** a year as reckoned by this season **3.** any period regarded, like summer, as a time of growth, development, etc. —***adj.*** of, typical of, or suitable for summer —***vi.*** to pass the summer —***vt.*** to keep or feed during the summer —**sum′mer·y** ***adj.***

sum·mer·house (-hous′) ***n.*** a small, open structure in a garden, park, etc., for providing a shady rest

summer house a house or cottage, as in the country, used during the summer

sum·mer·sault (sum′ər sôlt′) ***n., vi.*** *var. of* SOMERSAULT

summer sausage a type of hard, dried and smoked sausage that does not spoil easily

summer solstice the time in the Northern Hemisphere when the sun is farthest north of the celestial equator; June 21 or 22

summer squash any of various small garden squashes grown in summer and eaten before fully ripe

sum·mer·time (-tīm′) ***n.*** the season of summer

sum·mit (sum′it) ***n.*** [< OFr., ult. < L. *summus,* highest] **1.** the highest point or part; top; apex **2.** the highest degree or state; acme **3.** *a)* a top level of officials; specif., in diplomacy, the level restricted to heads of government *b)* a conference at this level —***adj.*** of the heads of government

sum·mon (sum′ən) ***vt.*** [< OFr., ult. < L. *summonere,* to remind secretly < *sub-,* secretly + *monere,* to warn] **1.** to call together; order to meet **2.** to call for or send for with authority **3.** to order, as by a summons, to appear in court **4.** to call upon to do something **5.** to call forth; rouse (often with *up*) *[summon* up strength*]* —**sum′mon·er** ***n.***

sum·mons (-ənz) ***n., pl.*** **-mons·es** [< Anglo-Fr. *somonse* < OFr.: see prec.] **1.** an order to come or do something; specif., *Law* an official order to appear in court, specif. as a defendant; also, the writ containing such an order **2.** a call, knock, etc. that summons

‡**sum·mum bo·num** (soom′əm bō′nəm) [L.] the highest, or supreme, good

su·mo (wrestling) (sōō′mō) [Jap. *sumō*] [*sometimes* **S-**] stylized Japanese wrestling engaged in by a hereditary class of large, extremely heavy men

sump (sump) ***n.*** [ME. *sompe,* a swamp] a pit, cistern, cesspool, etc. for draining or collecting liquid

sump pump a pump for removing liquid from a sump

sump·tu·ar·y (sump′choo wer′ē) ***adj.*** [< L. < *sumptus,* expense < pp. of *sumere,* to take] of or regulating expenses or expenditures

sump·tu·ous (sump′choo wəs) ***adj.*** [< OFr. < L. < *sumptus:* see prec.] **1.** involving great expense; costly; lavish **2.** magnificent, as in furnishings —**sump′tu·ous·ly** ***adv.***

sum total **1.** the total arrived at by adding up a sum or sums **2.** everything involved or included

sum·up (sum′up′) ***n.*** [Colloq.] a summarizing

sun (sun) ***n.*** [OE. *sunne*] **1.** *a)* the self-luminous, gaseous sphere about which the earth and other planets revolve and which furnishes light, heat, and energy for the solar system: it is about 93 million miles from earth and about 864,400 miles in diameter *b)* its heat or light **2.** any star that is the center of a planetary system **3.** something like the sun, as in warmth, brilliance, etc. **4.** [Poet.] *a)* a day *b)* a year *c)* a clime; climate —***vt., vi.*** **sunned, sun′ning** to expose or be exposed to the sun so as to warm, tan, bleach, etc. —**place in the sun** a prominent or favorable position —**under the sun** on earth; in the world

Sun. Sunday

sun·baked (-bākt′) ***adj.*** **1.** baked by the sun's heat, as bricks **2.** parched, cracked, etc. by the sun's heat

sun bath exposure of the body to sunlight or a sunlamp

sun·bathe (-bāth′) ***vi.*** **-bathed′, -bath′ing** to take a sun bath —**sun′bath′er** ***n.***

sun·beam (-bēm′) ***n.*** a ray or beam of sunlight

Sun·belt (sun′belt′) ***n.*** that part of the U.S. comprising most of the States of the South and the Southwest: also **Sun Belt**

sun·bon·net (-bän′it) ***n.*** a large-brimmed bonnet with a back flap, worn to shade the face and neck from the sun, esp. formerly, by women and girls

sun·burn (-burn′) ***n.*** an inflammation of the skin resulting from prolonged exposure to the sun's rays or a sunlamp —***vi., vt.*** **-burned′** or **-burnt′, -burn′ing** to get or cause to get a sunburn

sun·burst (-burst′) ***n.*** **1.** a burst of sunlight, as between clouds **2.** a decoration suggesting the sun and its rays

sun-cured (-kyoord′) ***adj.*** cured, as meat or fruit, by drying in the sun

sun·dae (sun′dē, -dā) ***n.*** [prob. < SUNDAY] a serving of ice cream covered with syrup, fruit, nuts, etc.

Sun·day (sun′dē, -dā) ***n.*** [OE. *sunnandæg,* lit., day of the sun] the first day of the week, observed by most Christians as a day of worship or as the Sabbath —***adj.*** **1.** of or typical of Sunday **2.** done, worn, performing, etc. usually or only on Sunday

Sunday best [Colloq.] one's best clothes

Sun·days (-dēz, -dāz) ***adv.*** on or during every Sunday

Sunday school **1.** a school giving religious instruction on Sunday at a church or synagogue **2.** the teachers and pupils of such a school

sun·der (sun′dər) ***vt., vi.*** [OE. *sundrian* < *sundor,* asunder] to break apart; split —**in sunder** into parts or pieces

Sun·der·land (sun′dər lənd) seaport in N England, on the North Sea: pop. 218,000

sun·di·al (sun′dī′əl, -dīl′) ***n.*** an instrument that shows time by the shadow of a pointer or gnomon cast by the sun on a dial marked in hours

SUNDIAL

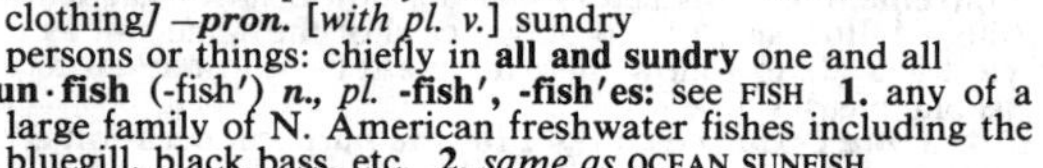

sun·dog (-dôg′) ***n.*** *same as* PARHELION

sun·down (-doun′) ***n.*** *same as* SUNSET

sun-dried (-drīd′) ***adj.*** dried by the sun

sun·dries (sun′drēz) ***n.pl.*** sundry items; miscellaneous things

sun·dry (-drē) ***adj.*** [OE. *syndrig,* separate < *sundor,* apart] various; miscellaneous *[sundry* articles of clothing*]* —***pron.*** [*with pl. v.*] sundry persons or things: chiefly in **all and sundry** one and all

sun·fish (-fish′) ***n., pl.*** **-fish′, -fish′es:** see FISH **1.** any of a large family of N. American freshwater fishes including the bluegill, black bass, etc. **2.** *same as* OCEAN SUNFISH

sun·flow·er (-flou′ər) ***n.*** any of various tall plants of the composite family, with large, yellow, daisylike flowers containing edible seeds from which an oil is extracted

sung (suŋ) *pp. & rare pt. of* SING

sun·glass·es (sun′glas′iz) ***n.pl.*** eyeglasses with tinted lenses to protect the eyes from the sun's glare

sunk (suŋk) *pp. & alt. pt. of* SINK —***adj.*** **1.** *same as* SUNKEN **2.** [Colloq.] utterly ruined, disgraced, etc.

sunk·en (-ən) *obs. pp. of* SINK —***adj.*** **1.** submerged *[a sunken* ship*]* **2.** below the level of the surrounding or adjoining area *[a sunken* patio*]* **3.** fallen in; hollow *[sunken* cheeks*]* **4.** dejected

sun·lamp (sun′lamp′) ***n.*** an electric lamp that radiates ultraviolet rays like those of sunlight

sun·less (-lis) ***adj.*** without sun or sunlight; dark

sun·light (-līt′) ***n.*** the light of the sun

sun·lit (-lit′) ***adj.*** lighted by the sun

sun·ny (sun′ē) ***adj.*** **-ni·er, -ni·est** **1.** bright with sunlight; full of sunshine **2.** bright and cheerful **3.** of or suggestive of the sun —**on the sunny side of** somewhat younger than (a specified age) —**sun′ni·ly** ***adv.*** —**sun′ni·ness** ***n.***

Sun·ny·vale (sun′ē vāl′) city in W Calif.: suburb of San Jose: pop. 107,000

sun parlor (or **porch** or **room**) a living room or enclosed porch with large windows to let sunlight in freely

sun·rise (-rīz′) ***n.*** **1.** the daily appearance of the sun above the eastern horizon **2.** the time of this **3.** the color of the sky at this time

sun·roof (-rōōf′, -roof′) ***n.*** an automobile roof with a panel that opens to let in light and air: also **sun roof**

sun·set (-set′) ***n.*** **1.** the daily disappearance of the sun below the western horizon **2.** the time of this **3.** the color of the sky at this time —***adj.*** designating or of a law requiring that a government agency or program end on a certain date unless it gets legislative reapproval

sun·shade (-shād′) ***n.*** a parasol, awning, broad hat, etc. used for protection against the sun's rays

sun·shine (-shīn′) ***n.*** **1.** the shining of the sun, or its light and heat **2.** cheerfulness, joy, etc. —***adj.*** designating or of a law requiring that certain meetings, records, etc. of public bodies be open to the public —**sun′shin′y** ***adj.***

sun·spot (-spät′) ***n.*** any temporarily cooler region appearing from time to time as a dark spot on the sun

sun·stroke (-strōk′) ***n.*** heatstroke caused by excessive exposure to the sun —**sun′struck′** (-struk′) ***adj.***

sun·suit (-sōōt′) ***n.*** a garment consisting of short pants with a bib and shoulder straps, for babies and children

sun·tan (-tan′) ***n.*** a darkened condition of the skin resulting from exposure to the sun or a sunlamp —**sun′-tanned′** ***adj.***

sun·up (-up′) ***n.*** *same as* SUNRISE

Sun Valley resort city in SC Ida.

sun·ward (-wərd) ***adv.*** toward the sun: also **sun′wards** —***adj.*** facing the sun

Sun Yat-sen (soon′ yät′sen′) 1866–1925; Chin. political & revolutionary leader

sup¹ (sup) ***n., vt., vi.*** **supped, sup′ping** [OE. *supan,* to drink] *same as* SIP

sup² (sup) ***vi.*** **supped, sup′ping** [< OFr. *souper* < *soupe*, soup] to have supper

sup- *same as* SUB-: used before *p*

sup. 1. superior **2.** supplement **3.** supply

su·per (so͞o′pər) ***n.*** [< ff.] **1.** *shortened form of: a)* SUPERNUMERARY *b)* SUPERINTENDENT **2.** [Colloq.] a product that is superior, extra large, etc.: a trade term —***adj.* 1.** outstanding; exceptionally fine **2.** great, extreme, or excessive

su·per- [L. < *super*, above] *a prefix meaning:* **1.** over, above, on top of *[superstructure]* **2.** higher in rank than, superior to *[superintendent]* **3.** *a)* surpassing *[superfine] b)* greater or better than others of its kind *[supermarket]* **4.** to a degree greater than normal *[supersaturate]* **5.** extra, additional *[supertax]*

su·per·a·ble (so͞o′pər ə b'l) ***adj.*** that can be overcome; surmountable —**su′per·a·bly *adv.***

su·per·a·bound (so͞o′pər ə bound′) ***vi.*** to be greatly or excessively abundant

su·per·a·bun·dant (-ə bun′dənt) ***adj.*** overly abundant —**su′per·a·bun′dance *n.*** —**su′per·a·bun′dant·ly *adv.***

su·per·an·nu·ate (-an′yoo wāt′) ***vt.*** **-at′ed, -at′ing** [backformation < ff.] **1.** to set aside as old-fashioned or obsolete **2.** to retire, esp. with a pension, because of old age or infirmity —**su′per·an′nu·a′tion *n.***

su·per·an·nu·at·ed (-id) ***adj.*** [< ML. pp. of *superannuari* < L. *super*, beyond + *annus*, year] **1.** *a)* too old for further work *b)* retired because of old age or infirmity **2.** obsolete; old-fashioned; outdated

su·perb (soo purb′, so͞o-) ***adj.*** [L. *superbus*, proud < *super*, above] **1.** noble, grand, or majestic **2.** rich; splendid **3.** excellent —**su·perb′ly *adv.*** —**su·perb′ness *n.***

su·per·car·go (so͞o′pər kär′gō) ***n.,*** *pl.* **-goes, -gos** [< Sp. *sobrecargo* < *sobre*, over + *cargo*, CARGO] an officer on a merchant ship who has charge of the cargo, representing the shipowner

su·per·charge (-chärj′) ***vt.*** **-charged′, -charg′ing 1.** to increase the power of (an engine), as with a supercharger **2.** *same as* PRESSURIZE (sense 1)

su·per·charg·er (-chär′jər) ***n.*** a blower or compressor used to increase the power of an internal-combustion engine by increasing the supply of air or fuel mixture to the cylinders

su·per·cil·i·ous (so͞o′pər sil′ē əs) ***adj.*** [< L. < *supercilium*, eyebrow, hence (with reference to raised brows), haughtiness < *super-*, above + *cilium*, eyelid] full of or showing pride or contempt; haughty —**su′per·cil′i·ous·ly *adv.*** —**su′per·cil′i·ous·ness *n.***

su·per·con·duc·tiv·i·ty (-kän′dək tiv′ə tē) ***n.*** *Physics* the ability of certain metals and alloys to conduct electricity continuously without resistance when chilled to near absolute zero: also **su′per·con·duc′tion** (-kən duk′shən) —**su′per·con·duct′ing, su′per·con·duc′tive *adj.*** —**su′per·con·duc′tor *n.***

su·per·cool (-ko͞ol′) ***vt.*** to lower the temperature of (a liquid) to below its freezing point without causing solidification —***vi.*** to become supercooled

su·per·e·go (so͞o′pər ē′gō) ***n.,*** *pl.* **-gos** *Psychoanalysis* that part of the psyche which is critical of the self or ego and enforces moral standards

su·per·em·i·nent (-em′ə nənt) ***adj.*** eminent beyond others —**su′per·em′i·nence *n.*** —**su′per·em′i·nent·ly *adv.***

su·per·er·o·ga·tion (-er′ə gā′shən) ***n.*** [< LL. < pp. of *supererogare* < *super*, above + *erogare*, to pay out] the act of doing more than what is required or expected

su·per·e·rog·a·to·ry (-i räg′ə tôr′ē) ***adj.* 1.** done beyond the degree required or expected **2.** superfluous

su·per·fi·cial (-fish′əl) ***adj.*** [< L. < *superficies*, a surface < *super-*, above + *facies*, face] **1.** *a)* of or being on the surface *b)* of surface area; plane **2.** concerned with and understanding only the easily apparent and obvious; not profound; shallow **3.** quick and cursory **4.** merely apparent —**su′per·fi′ci·al′i·ty** (-ē al′ə tē) ***n.,*** *pl.* **- ties** —**su′per·fi′cial·ly *adv.*** —**su′per·fi′cial·ness *n.***

su·per·fine (so͞o′pər fīn′, so͞o′pər fīn′) ***adj.* 1.** too subtle, delicate, or refined **2.** of very fine quality

su·per·flu·i·ty (so͞o′pər flo͞o′ə tē) ***n.,*** *pl.* **- ties 1.** a being superfluous **2.** a quantity beyond what is needed; excess **3.** something superfluous

su·per·flu·ous (soo pur′floo wəs) ***adj.*** [< L. < *superfluere* < *super-*, above + *fluere*, to flow] **1.** being more than is needed or wanted; excessive **2.** not needed; unnecessary —**su·per′flu·ous·ly *adv.*** —**su·per′flu·ous·ness *n.***

su·per·heat (so͞o′pər hēt′; *for n.* so͞o′pər hēt′) ***vt.* 1.** to make too hot **2.** to heat (a liquid) above its boiling point without its vaporizing **3.** to heat (steam not in contact with water) beyond its saturation point, so that a drop in temperature will not cause it to turn back to water

su·per·het·er·o·dyne (so͞o′pər het′ər ə dīn′) ***adj.*** [SUPER(SONIC) + HETERODYNE] designating or of radio reception in which some amplification is done at an intermediate supersonic frequency —***n.*** a radio set for this kind of reception

su·per·high frequency (so͞o′pər hī′) any radio frequency between 3,000 and 30,000 megahertz

su·per·high·way (-hī′wā′) ***n.*** *same as* EXPRESSWAY

su·per·hu·man (-hyo͞o′mən) ***adj.* 1.** having a nature above that of man; divine **2.** greater than normal for a human being —**su′per·hu′man·ly *adv.***

su·per·im·pose (-im pōz′) ***vt.*** **-posed′, -pos′ing 1.** to put or lay on top of something else **2.** to add as a feature that dominates or does not properly fit with the rest

su·per·in·duce (-in do͞os′, -dyo͞os′) ***vt.*** **-duced′, -duc′ing** to bring in as an addition —**su′per·in·duc′tion** (-duk′shən) ***n.***

su·per·in·tend (-in tend′) ***vt.*** to act as superintendent of; supervise —**su′per·in·tend′ence, su′per·in·tend′en·cy *n.***

su·per·in·tend·ent (-in ten′dənt) ***n.*** [< LL. prp. of *superintendere:* see SUPER- & INTEND] **1.** a person in charge of a department, institution, etc.; supervisor **2.** the custodian of a building, etc. —***adj.*** that superintends

Su·pe·ri·or (sə pir′ē ər, soo-), **Lake** [orig. so called from its position above Lake Huron] largest & westernmost of the Great Lakes, between Mich. & Ontario, Canada: 32,483 sq. mi.

su·pe·ri·or (sə pir′ē ər, soo-) ***adj.*** [OFr. < L., compar. of *superus*, that is above] **1.** higher in space; placed higher up **2.** higher in order, status, rank, etc. **3.** greater in quality or value than (with *to*) **4.** above average; excellent **5.** refusing to be affected by (something painful): with *to* **6.** haughty —***n.* 1.** a superior person or thing **2.** the head of a religious community —**su·pe′ri·or′i·ty** (-ôr′ə tē) ***n.***

superl. superlative

su·per·la·tive (sə pur′lə tiv, soo-) ***adj.*** [< MFr. < LL. < L. < *super-*, above + *latus*, pp. of *ferre*, to carry] **1.** excelling all others; supreme **2.** excessive **3.** *Gram.* designating or of the extreme degree of comparison of adjectives and adverbs: usually indicated by the suffix *-est* (*hardest*) or by the use of *most* (*most beautiful*) —***n.* 1.** the highest degree; acme **2.** something superlative **3.** *Gram. a)* the superlative degree *b)* a word or form in this degree —**su·per′la·tive·ly *adv.*** —**su·per′la·tive·ness *n.***

su·per·man (so͞o′pər man′) ***n.,*** *pl.* **-men′** (-men′) **1.** in Nietzsche's philosophy, a type of superior man regarded as the goal of the evolutionary struggle **2.** an apparently superhuman man

su·per·mar·ket (-mär′kit) ***n.*** a large, self-service, retail food store or market, often one of a chain

su·per·nal (soo pur′n'l) ***adj.*** [MFr. < L. *supernus*, upper] celestial, heavenly, or divine —**su·per′nal·ly *adv.***

su·per·nat·u·ral (so͞o′pər nach′ər əl) ***adj.* 1.** existing outside man's normal experience or the known laws of nature; specif., of or involving God or a god, or ghosts, the occult, etc. **2.** extraordinary —**the supernatural** supernatural beings, forces, happenings, etc. —**su′per·nat′u·ral·ly *adv.***

su·per·nat·u·ral·ism (-iz'm) ***n.* 1.** a supernatural quality or state **2.** a belief that some supernatural, or divine, force controls nature and the universe —**su′per·nat′u·ral·ist *n., adj.*** —**su′per·nat′u·ral·is′tic *adj.***

su·per·no·va (-nō′və) ***n.,*** *pl.* **-vae** (-vē), **-vas** [ModL.: see SUPER- & NOVA] an extremely bright nova that suddenly increases 10 million to 100 million times in brightness

su·per·nu·mer·ar·y (-no͞o′mə rer′ē, -nyo͞o′-) ***adj.*** [< LL. < L. *super*, above + *numerus*, number] beyond the regular or needed number; extra or superfluous —***n.,*** *pl.* **-ar′ies 1.** a supernumerary person or thing **2.** *Theater* a person with a small, nonspeaking part, as in a mob scene

su·per·pa·tri·ot (-pā′trē ət) ***n.*** a person who is or professes to be a devout patriot, often to the point of fanaticism —**su′per·pa′tri·ot′ic** (-pā′trē ät′ik) ***adj.*** —**su′per·pa′tri·ot·ism *n.***

su·per·pose (-pōz′) ***vt.*** **-posed′, -pos′ing** [< Fr. < L. pp. of *superponere:* see SUPER- & POSE¹] **1.** to lay or place on, over, or above something else **2.** *Geom.* to place (one figure) on top of another that is congruent so that corresponding sides coincide —**su′per·po·si′tion *n.***

su·per·pow·er (so͞o′pər pou′ər) ***n.*** any of the few most powerful nations of the world competing for spheres of influence

su·per·sat·u·rate (so͞o′pər sach′ə rāt′) ***vt.*** **-rat′ed, -rat′ing** to saturate beyond the normal point for the given temperature —**su′per·sat′u·ra′tion *n.***

su·per·scribe (-skrīb′) ***vt.*** **-scribed′, -scrib′ing** [< L.: see SUPER- & SCRIBE] to write or mark (an inscription, name, etc.) at the top or on an outer surface of something —**su′per·scrip′tion** (-skrip′shən) ***n.***

su·per·script (so͞o′pər skript′) ***adj.*** written above —***n.*** a figure, letter, or symbol written above and to the side of another *[in* y² *and* xⁿ, *2 and n are superscripts]*

su·per·sede (so͞o′pər sēd′) ***vt.*** **-sed′ed, -sed′ing** [< MFr. < L. *supersedere,* to preside over < *super-,* above + *sedere,* to sit] **1.** to cause to be set aside as inferior or obsolete and be replaced **2.** to take the place or office of; succeed **3.** to replace; supplant —**su′per·sed′er** ***n.*** —**su′per·se′dure** (-sē′jər), **su′per·sed′ence** ***n.***

su·per·sen·si·tive (-sen′sə tiv) ***adj.*** highly sensitive or too sensitive —**su′per·sen′si·tiv′i·ty** ***n.***

su·per·son·ic (-sän′ik) ***adj.*** [SUPER- + SONIC] **1.** designating, of, or moving at a speed in a surrounding fluid greater than that of sound in the same fluid: cf. SONIC **2.** *same as* ULTRASONIC —**su′per·son′i·cal·ly** ***adv.***

su·per·son·ics (-sän′iks) ***n.pl.*** [*with sing. v.*] the science dealing with supersonic phenomena

su·per·star (so͞o′pər stär′) ***n.*** a very prominent performer, as in sports, considered to have exceptional talent

su·per·sti·tion (so͞o′pər stish′ən) ***n.*** [< MFr. < L. *superstitio,* ult. < *super-,* over + *stare,* to stand] **1.** any belief, based on fear or ignorance, that is not in accord with the known laws of science or with what is considered true and rational; esp., such a belief in charms, omens, the supernatural, etc. **2.** any action or practice based on such a belief **3.** such beliefs collectively

su·per·sti·tious (-əs) ***adj.*** **1.** of, characterized by, or resulting from superstition **2.** having superstitions —**su′per·sti′tious·ly** ***adv.*** —**su′per·sti′tious·ness** ***n.***

su·per·struc·ture (so͞o′pər struk′chər) ***n.*** **1.** a structure built on top of another **2.** that part of a building above the foundation **3.** that part of a ship above the main deck

su·per·tax (-taks′) ***n.*** an additional tax; esp., a surtax

su·per·vene (so͞o′pər vēn′) ***vi.*** **-vened′, -ven′ing** [< L. < *super-,* over + *venire,* to come] to come or happen as something added or not expected —**su′per·ven′ient** (-vēn′yənt) ***adj.*** —**su′per·ven′tion** (-ven′shən), **su′per·ven′ience** (-vēn′yəns) ***n.***

su·per·vise (so͞o′pər vīz′) ***vt., vi.*** **-vised′, -vis′ing** [< ML. pp. of *supervidere* < L. *super-,* over + *videre,* to see] to oversee, direct, or manage (work, workers, a project, etc.); superintend —**su′per·vi′sion** (-vizh′ən) ***n.***

su·per·vi·sor (-vī′zər) ***n.*** **1.** a person who supervises; manager; director **2.** in certain school systems, an official in charge of the courses and teachers for a particular subject —**su′per·vi′so·ry** ***adj.***

su·pine (soo pīn′) ***adj.*** [L. *supinus*] **1.** lying on the back, face upward **2.** showing no concern or doing nothing about matters —**su·pine′ly** ***adv.*** —**su·pine′ness** ***n.***

supp., suppl. **1.** supplement **2.** supplementary

sup·per (sup′ər) ***n.*** [OFr. *souper,* orig. inf., to SUP²] **1.** an evening meal, as a dinner, or a late, light meal, as one eaten after the theater **2.** an evening social at which a meal is served *[a church supper]* —**sup′per·less** ***adj.***

sup·plant (sə plant′) ***vt.*** [< OFr. < L. *supplantare,* to trip up < *sub-,* under + *planta,* sole of the foot] **1.** to take the place of, esp. through force or plotting **2.** to remove and replace with something else —**sup·plan·ta·tion** (sup′lan tā′shən) ***n.*** —**sup·plant′er** ***n.***

sup·ple (sup′′l) ***adj.*** [< OFr. < L. *supplex,* humble] **1.** bending easily; flexible **2.** lithe; limber *[a supple body]* **3.** changing easily, as under new conditions or strong influences **4.** adaptable or yielding: said of the mind, etc. —**sup′ple·ly** ***adv.*** —**sup′ple·ness** ***n.***

sup·ple·ment (sup′lə mənt; *for v.* -ment′) ***n.*** [< L. < *supplere:* see SUPPLY¹] **1.** something added, esp. to make up for a lack **2.** a section added to a book, etc., as to give additional information **3.** a separate newspaper section containing feature stories, etc. **4.** *Math.* the number of degrees to be added to an angle or arc to make 180 degrees —***vt.*** to provide a supplement to; add to —**sup′ple·men·ta′tion** ***n.*** —**sup′ple·ment′er** ***n.***

sup·ple·men·ta·ry (sup′lə men′tər ē) ***adj.*** supplying what is lacking; additional: also **sup′ple·men′tal** —***n.,*** *pl.* **-ries** a supplementary person or thing

supplementary angle either of two angles that together form 180 degrees

sup·pli·ant (sup′lē ənt) ***n.*** [MFr., prp. of *supplier* < L.: see SUPPLICATE] a person who supplicates —***adj.*** supplicating; beseeching —**sup′pli·ance** ***n.*** —**sup′pli·ant·ly** ***adv.***

SUPPLEMENTARY ANGLES (angle BCA and angle DCB are supplementary)

sup·pli·cant (sup′lə kənt) ***adj., n.*** *same as* SUPPLIANT

sup·pli·cate (sup′lə kāt′) ***vt.*** **-cat′ed, -cat′ing** [< L. pp. of *supplicare,* to kneel down < *sub-,* under + *plicare,* to fold] **1.** to ask for humbly, as by prayer **2.** to make a humble request of —***vi.*** to make a humble request, esp. in prayer —**sup′pli·ca′tion** ***n.*** —**sup′pli·ca′tor** ***n.*** —**sup′pli·ca·to′ry** (-kə tôr′ē) ***adj.***

sup·ply¹ (sə plī′) ***vt.*** **-plied′, -ply′ing** [< MFr. < L. *supplere,* to fill up < *sub-,* under + *plere,* to fill] **1.** to give, furnish, or provide (what is needed) **2.** to meet the needs or requirements of **3.** to make up for (a deficiency, etc.) **4.** to act as a substitute in *[to supply another's pulpit]* —***vi.*** to serve as a substitute —***n.,*** *pl.* **-plies′** **1.** the act of supplying **2.** an amount available for use; stock; store **3.** [*pl.*] materials, provisions, etc. for supplying an army, a business, etc. **4.** a substitute, as for a minister **5.** *Econ.* the amount of a commodity available for purchase at a given price —***adj.*** **1.** having to do with a supply or supplies **2.** serving as a substitute —**sup·pli′er** ***n.***

sup·ply² (sup′lē) ***adv.*** in a supple manner; supplely

sup·port (sə pôrt′) ***vt.*** [< MFr. < LL. < L. < *sub-,* under + *portare,* to carry] **1.** *a)* to carry or bear the weight of; hold up *b)* to carry or bear (a specified weight, pressure, etc.) **2.** to give courage or faith to; help; comfort **3.** to give approval to or be in favor of; uphold **4.** to provide for (a person, institution, etc.) with money or subsistence **5.** to help prove or vindicate *[evidence to support a claim]* **6.** to bear; endure; tolerate **7.** to keep up; maintain; specif., to maintain (the price of a commodity) as by purchases **8.** *Theater* to act a subordinate role with (a specified star) —***n.*** **1.** a supporting or being supported **2.** a person or thing that supports; specif., *a)* a prop, base, brace, etc. *b)* a means of subsistence *c)* an elastic device to support or bind a part of the body —**sup·port′a·ble** ***adj.***

sup·port·er (-ər) ***n.*** **1.** a person who supports; advocate; adherent **2.** a thing that supports; esp., *a)* an elastic device to support the back, abdomen, etc. *b) same as* JOCKSTRAP: in full, **athletic supporter** *c) same as* GARTER

sup·port·ive (-iv) ***adj.*** that gives support, help, or approval

sup·pose (sə pōz′) ***vt.*** **-posed′, -pos′ing** [< MFr. < ML. *supponere,* ult. < L. *sub-,* under + *ponere,* to place] **1.** to take to be true, as for the sake of argument, etc. *[suppose A equals B]* **2.** to believe, think, guess, etc. **3.** to involve as a preceding condition; presuppose **4.** to consider as a suggested possibility *[suppose he doesn't come]* **5.** to expect: always in the passive *[she's supposed to telephone]* —***vi.*** to think or guess; conjecture —**sup·pos′a·ble** ***adj.*** —**sup·pos′a·bly** ***adv.*** —**sup·pos′er** ***n.***

sup·posed (sə pōzd′) ***adj.*** **1.** regarded as true, possible, etc., without actual knowledge **2.** merely imagined —**sup·pos′ed·ly** ***adv.***

sup·po·si·tion (sup′ə zish′ən) ***n.*** **1.** the act of supposing **2.** something supposed; assumption Also **sup·pos·al** (sə pōz′′l) —**sup′po·si′tion·al** ***adj.*** —**sup′po·si′tion·al·ly** ***adv.***

sup·pos·i·to·ry (sə päz′ə tôr′ē) ***n.,*** *pl.* **-ries** [< ModL. < L. < pp. of *supponere:* see SUPPOSE] a small, shaped piece of medicated substance, inserted into the rectum, vagina, etc., where it is melted and spread by the body heat

sup·press (sə pres′) ***vt.*** [< L. pp. of *supprimere* < *sub-,* under + *premere,* to press] **1.** to put down by force or authority; quell **2.** to keep from appearing or being known, published, etc. *[to suppress a news story, a book, etc.]* **3.** to keep back; restrain; check *[to suppress a laugh, cough, etc.]* **4.** to check the flow, secretion, etc. of **5.** *Electronics, Radio,* etc. to eliminate (an unwanted signal, etc.) **6.** *Psychiatry* to consciously dismiss (unacceptable ideas, impulses, etc.) from the mind —**sup·press′i·ble** ***adj.*** —**sup·pres′sive** ***adj.*** —**sup·pres′sive·ly** ***adv.*** —**sup·pres′sor** ***n.***

sup·pres·sion (sə presh′ən) ***n.*** **1.** a suppressing or being suppressed **2.** *Psychiatry a)* the mechanism by which unacceptable ideas, impulses, etc. are suppressed *b)* something suppressed in this way

sup·pu·rate (sup′yoo rāt′) ***vi.*** **-rat′ed, -rat′ing** [< L. pp. of *suppurare* < *sub-,* under + *pus* (gen. *puris*), pus] to form or discharge pus; fester —**sup′pu·ra′tion** ***n.*** —**sup′pu·ra′tive** ***adj.***

su·pra- [< L. *supra,* above, over] *a prefix meaning* above, over, beyond *[suprarenal]*

su·pra·na·tion·al (so͞o′prə nash′ə n′l) ***adj.*** of, for, involving, or over all or a number of nations *[supranational authority]* —**su′pra·na′tion·al·ism** ***n.***

su·pra·re·nal (-rē′n′l) ***adj.*** [< ModL.: see SUPRA- & RENAL] on or above the kidney; specif., designating or of an adrenal gland —***n.*** an adrenal gland

su·prem·a·cist (sə prem′ə sist, soo-) ***n.*** a person who believes in or promotes the supremacy of a particular group *[a white supremacist]*

su·prem·a·cy (sə prem′ə sē, soo-) ***n.,*** *pl.* **-cies** **1.** the quality or state of being supreme **2.** supreme power or authority

su·preme (sə prēm′, soo-) ***adj.*** [L. *supremus,* superl. of *superus,* that is above] **1.** highest in rank, power, etc. **2.** highest in quality, achievement, performance, etc.; most excellent **3.** highest in degree; utmost *[a supreme fool]*

4. final; ultimate —**su·preme′ly** *adv.* —**su·preme′ness** *n.*
Supreme Being God
Supreme Court 1. the highest Federal court, consisting of nine judges 2. the highest court in most States
supreme sacrifice the sacrifice of one's life
Supreme Soviet the parliament of the Soviet Union
Supt., supt. Superintendent
sur-[1] [OFr. < L. *super,* over, above] *a prefix meaning* over, upon, above, beyond *[surcharge]*
sur-[2] *same as* SUB-: used before *r*
Su·ra·ba·ja (sōō′rä bä′yä) seaport in NE Java, Indonesia: pop. 1,008,000
su·rah (soor′ə) *n.* [< *Surat,* a seaport in India] a soft, twilled fabric of silk or rayon
sur·cease (sur sēs′; *for n. usually* sur′sēs) *vt., vi.* **-ceased′, -ceas′ing** [< OFr. *sursis,* pp. of *surseoir,* to pause < L. *supersedere,* to refrain from] [Archaic] to stop; end —*n.* end; cessation
sur·charge (sur′chärj; *also for v.* sur chärj′) *vt.* **-charged′, -charg′ing** [< OFr.: see SUR-[1] & CHARGE] 1. to overcharge 2. to overload 3. to fill to excess 4. to mark (a postage stamp) with a surcharge —*n.* 1. *a)* an additional charge *b)* an overcharge 2. an extra or excessive load 3. a new face value overprinted on a postage stamp
sur·cin·gle (sur′siŋ′g'l) *n.* [< MFr. < *sur-,* over + L. *cingulum,* a belt] a strap passed around a horse's body to bind on a saddle, pack, etc.
sur·coat (-kōt′) *n.* [< MFr.: see SUR-[1] & COAT] an outer coat; esp., a short cloak worn over a knight's armor
surd (surd) *adj.* [L. *surdus,* deaf, mute] *same as:* 1. *Math.* IRRATIONAL 2. *Phonet.* VOICELESS —*n.* 1. *Math.* an irrational number or quantity, as a root that cannot be determined exactly *[√5 is a surd]* 2. *Phonet.* a voiceless sound
sure (shoor) *adj.* **sur′er, sur′est** [< OFr. < L. *securus:* see SECURE] 1. orig., secure or safe 2. that will not fail; always effective *[a sure method]* 3. that can be relied upon; trustworthy *[a sure friend]* 4. that cannot be doubted, questioned, etc.; absolutely true 5. having no doubt; positive; confident *[to be sure of the facts]* 6. that can be counted on to be or happen *[a sure defeat]* 7. bound to do, experience, etc. *[sure to lose]* 8. never missing *[a sure aim]* —*adv.* [Colloq.] 1. surely; inevitably 2. certainly; indeed: used as an intensive *[sure, I'll go]* —**for sure** certain(ly); without doubt —**make sure** to be or cause to be certain —**sure enough** [Colloq.] certainly; without doubt —**to be sure** surely; certainly —**sure′ness** *n.*
sure-fire (-fīr′) *adj.* [Colloq.] sure to be successful or as expected; that will not fail
sure-foot·ed (-foot′id) *adj.* not likely to stumble, fall, or err —**sure′-foot′ed·ly** *adv.* —**sure′-foot′ed·ness** *n.*
sure·ly (-lē) *adv.* 1. with confidence; in a sure, unhesitating manner 2. without a doubt; certainly *[surely you don't believe that!]* 3. without risk of failing: chiefly in **slowly but surely**
sure thing [Colloq.] 1. something certain to win, succeed, etc. 2. all right; O.K.: used as an interjection
sur·e·ty (shoor′ə tē, shoor′tē) *n., pl.* **-ties** 1. a being sure; assurance 2. something sure; certainty 3. something that makes sure or gives assurance, as against loss, default, etc.; security 4. a person who makes himself responsible for another; specif., *Law* one who makes himself liable for another's debts, etc. —**sur′e·ty·ship′** *n.*
surf (surf) *n.* [earlier *suffe,* prob. var. of SOUGH] 1. the waves of the sea breaking on the shore or a reef 2. the foam or spray caused by this —*vi.* to engage in the sport of surfing —**surf′er** *n.*
sur·face (sur′fis) *n.* [Fr. < *sur-* (see SUB-) + *face,* a face] 1. *a)* the outside or outer face of a thing *b)* any side of a thing having several sides *c)* the area of such a side 2. outward appearance 3. *Aeron.* an airfoil 4. *Geom.* an extent or magnitude having length and breadth, but no thickness —*adj.* 1. of, on, or at the surface 2. functioning or carried on land or sea, rather than in the air or under water *[surface forces, surface mail]* 3. seeming such on the surface; superficial —*vt.* **-faced, -fac·ing** 1. to treat the surface of, esp. so as to make smooth or level 2. to give a surface to, as in paving 3. to bring (a submarine, etc.) to the surface of the water —*vi.* 1. to rise to the surface of the water 2. to become known, esp. after being concealed —**sur′fac·er** *n.*
sur·face-ac·tive (-ak′tiv) *adj. Chem.* designating or of a substance, as a detergent, that lowers the surface tension of the solvent in which it is dissolved
surface noise noise produced by the friction of a phonograph needle moving in the grooves of a record
surface tension a property of liquids in which the surface tends to contract to the smallest possible area, so that the surface seems like a thin, elastic film under tension
surf·board (surf′bôrd′) *n.* a long, narrow board used in the sport of surfing —*vi.* to engage in this sport —**surf′board′er** *n.* —**surf′board′ing** *n.*

SURFBOARD

surf·boat (-bōt′) *n.* a sturdy, light boat used in heavy surf
surf-cast (-kast′) *vi.* **-cast′, -cast′·ing** to fish by casting into the ocean surf from or near the shore —**surf′-cast′er** *n.*
sur·feit (sur′fit) *n.* [< OFr. < *sorfaire,* to overdo < *sur-* (< L. *super*), over + *faire* (< L. *facere*), to make] 1. too great an amount or supply; excess *[a surfeit of compliments]* 2. an indulging in too much food, drink, etc. 3. disgust, nausea, etc. resulting from this —*vt.* to feed or supply to excess —*vi.* [Rare] to overindulge
surf·ing (surf′iŋ) *n.* the sport of riding in toward shore on the crest of a wave, esp. on a surfboard: also **surf′rid′ing**
surf·perch (surf′purch′) *n., pl.* **-perch′, -perch′es:** see PLURAL, II, D, 2 any of various fishes of N. American Pacific coastal waters, that bear living young
surge (surj) *n.* [prob. < OFr. < L. *surgere,* to rise] 1. a large wave of water, or the swelling or rushing motion of such a wave or series of waves 2. any sudden strong rush *[a surge of energy, electric power, etc.; the surge of the crowd]* —*vi.* **surged, surg′ing** to move in a surge
sur·geon (sur′jən) *n.* a doctor who specializes in surgery
sur·ger·y (sur′jər ē) *n., pl.* **-ger·ies** [< OFr. *cirurgie* < L. < Gr. *cheirourgia,* handicraft < *cheir,* the hand + *ergein,* to work] 1. *a)* the treatment of disease, injury, etc. by operations with the hands or instruments, as the removal of diseased parts by cutting, the setting of broken bones, etc. *b)* the branch of medicine dealing with this 2. the operating room of a surgeon or hospital
sur·gi·cal (-ji k'l) *adj.* 1. of surgeons or surgery 2. used in or connected with surgery 3. resulting from surgery —**sur′gi·cal·ly** *adv.*
Su·ri·nam·e (soor′i näm′, soor′i nam′; *Du.* soor′ə nä′mə) country on the NE coast of S. America: formerly part of the Netherlands: 55,144 sq. mi.; pop. 385,000: earlier **Su·ri·nam** (-näm′, soor′ə nam′)
sur·ly (sur′lē) *adj.* **-li·er, -li·est** [earlier *sirly,* imperious < *sir,* SIR] bad-tempered; sullenly rude; hostile and uncivil —**sur′li·ness** *n.*
sur·mise (sər mīz′; *for n. also* sur′mīz) *n.* [< OFr. pp. of *surmettre* < *sur-* (< L. *super*), upon + *mettre,* to put < L. *mittere,* to send] 1. an idea or opinion that is only a guess; conjecture 2. the act of surmising —*vt., vi.* **-mised′, -mis′ing** to imagine or infer (something) without conclusive evidence; guess —**sur·mis′er** *n.*
sur·mount (sər mount′) *vt.* [OFr. *surmonter:* see SUR-[1] & MOUNT[2]] 1. to overcome (a difficulty) 2. to be or lie at the top of; be or rise above 3. to climb up and across (a height, obstacle, etc.) —**sur·mount′a·ble** *adj.*
sur·name (sur′nām′; *for v. also* sur′nām′) *n.* [< OFr. < *sur-* (see SUR-[1]) + *nom* < L. *nomen,* name] 1. the family name, or last name, as distinguished from a given name 2. a name or epithet added to a person's given name (Ex.: Ivan *the Terrible*) —*vt.* **-named′, -nam′ing** to give a surname to
sur·pass (sər pas′) *vt.* [< MFr. < *sur-* (see SUR-[1]) + *passer,* to PASS[2]] 1. to be better or greater than; excel 2. to exceed in quantity, degree, etc. 3. to go beyond the limit, capacity, etc. of *[riches surpassing belief]* —**sur·pass′a·ble** *adj.*
sur·pass·ing (-iŋ) *adj.* that surpasses the average or usual; exceeding or excelling; unusually excellent —*adv.* [Archaic] exceedingly —**sur·pass′ing·ly** *adv.*
sur·plice (sur′plis) *n.* [< Anglo-Fr. < OFr. < ML. < L. *super-,* above + *pelliceum,* fur robe] a loose, white, wide-sleeved outer vestment worn by the clergy and choir in some churches —**sur′pliced** *adj.*

SURPLICE

sur·plus (sur′plus, -pləs) *n.* [OFr. < *sur-,* above + L. *plus,* more] 1. a quantity over and above what is needed or used; excess 2. the excess of the assets of a business over its liabilities —*adj.* that is a surplus; excess
sur·prise (sər prīz′) *vt.* **-prised′, -pris′ing** [< OFr. pp. of *sorprendre* < *sur-* (see SUR-[1]) + *prendre* < L. *prehendere,* to take] 1. to come upon suddenly or unexpectedly; take unawares 2. to attack or capture without warning 3. *a)* to cause to feel as-

tonishment by being unexpected *b*) to present (someone) unexpectedly with a gift, etc. **4.** *a*) to cause by some unexpected action to do or say something unintended: often with *into* *b*) to bring out (something) by such means —***n.*** **1.** [Rare] a surprising **2.** an unexpected seizure or attack **3.** a being surprised; astonishment **4.** something that surprises because unexpected, unusual, etc. —**take by surprise** **1.** to come upon suddenly or without warning **2.** to amaze; astound —**sur·pris′ed·ly** ***adv.*** —**sur·pris′er** ***n.***

sur·pris·ing (-iŋ) ***adj.*** causing surprise; amazing —**surpris′ing·ly** ***adv.***

sur·re·al·ism (sə rē′ə liz′m) ***n.*** [< Fr.: see SUR-[1] & REALISM] a modern movement in art and literature, in which an attempt is made to portray the workings of the subconscious mind, as by arranging material in unexpected, fantastic ways —**sur·re′al, sur·re′al·is′tic** ***adj.*** —**sur·re′al·ist** ***adj., n.*** —**sur·re′al·is′ti·cal·ly** ***adv.***

sur·ren·der (sə ren′dər) ***vt.*** [< MFr. < *sur-* (see SUR-[1]) + *rendre,* to RENDER] **1.** to give up possession of or power over; yield to another on compulsion **2.** to give up or abandon *[*to *surrender* all hope*]* **3.** to yield or resign (oneself) to an emotion, influence, etc. —***vi.*** **1.** to give oneself up, esp. as a prisoner; yield **2.** to give in (*to*) *[*to *surrender* to a whim*]* —***n.*** the act of surrendering —**sur·ren′der·er** ***n.***

sur·rep·ti·tious (sʉr′əp tish′əs) ***adj.*** [< L. < pp. of *surripere* < *sub-,* under + *rapere,* to seize] **1.** done, got, made, etc. in a secret, stealthy way; clandestine **2.** acting in a secret, stealthy way —**sur′rep·ti′tious·ly** ***adv.***

sur·rey (sʉr′ē) ***n.,*** *pl.* **-reys** [< *Surrey,* county in England] a light pleasure carriage having four wheels, two seats, and usually a flat top

sur·ro·gate (sʉr′ə gāt′, sur′-; *for n. also* -git) ***n.*** [< L. pp. of *surrogare* < *sub-,* in place of + *rogare,* to elect] **1.** a deputy or substitute for another person **2.** in some States, probate court, or a judge of this court —***vt.*** **-gat′ed, -gat′ing** to put in another's place as a substitute or deputy

sur·round (sə round′) ***vt.*** [< OFr. < LL. < L. *super,* over + *undare,* to rise < *unda,* a wave] **1.** to encircle on all or nearly all sides; enclose; encompass **2.** to cut off (a military unit, etc.) from communication or retreat by encircling —***n.*** [Chiefly Brit.] something that surrounds

sur·round·ing (-roun′diŋ) ***n.*** that which surrounds; esp., [*pl.*] the things, conditions, influences, etc. that surround a given place or person; environment —***adj.*** that surrounds

sur·tax (sʉr′taks; *for v. also* sʉr′taks′) ***n.*** an extra tax on something already taxed —***vt.*** to levy a surtax on

sur·tout (sər to͞o′, -to͞ot′) ***n.*** [Fr. < *sur,* over + *tout,* all] a man's long, closefitting overcoat

sur·veil·lance (sər vā′ləns, -vāl′yəns) ***n.*** [Fr. < *sur-* (see SUR-[1]) + *veiller,* to watch < L. *vigilare,* to watch] **1.** watch kept over a person, esp. a suspect **2.** supervision —**surveil′lant** ***n.***

sur·vey (sər vā′; *also, & for n. usually* sʉr′vā) ***vt.*** [< Anglo-Fr. < OFr. < *sur-* (see SUR-[1]) + *veoir* < L. *videre,* to see] **1.** to examine, inspect, or consider carefully **2.** to look at or consider, esp. in a comprehensive way **3.** to determine the location, form, or boundaries of (a tract of land) by measuring lines and angles with a chain, transit, etc. —***vi.*** to survey land —***n.,*** *pl.* **-veys** **1.** a detailed study made by gathering and analyzing information **2.** a comprehensive study or examination *[*a *survey* of Italian art*]* **3.** *a*) the process of surveying a tract of land *b*) a plan or written description of the area surveyed

sur·vey·ing (sər vā′iŋ) ***n.*** **1.** the act of one who surveys **2.** the science or work of surveying land

sur·vey·or (-ər) ***n.*** a person who surveys, esp. one whose work is surveying land

surveyor's measure a system of measurement used in surveying, based on the chain (**surveyor's chain**) as a unit: see CHAIN (*n.* 3)

sur·viv·al (sər vī′v'l) ***n.*** **1.** the act, state, or fact of surviving **2.** someone or something that survives, esp. an ancient belief, custom, usage, etc.

survival of the fittest *popular term for* NATURAL SELECTION

sur·vive (sər vīv′) ***vt.*** **-vived′, -viv′ing** [< OFr. < L. *super-,* above + *vivere,* to live] **1.** to live or exist longer than; outlive **2.** to continue to live after or in spite of *[*to *survive* a wreck*]* —***vi.*** to continue living or existing —**sur·viv′a·bil′i·ty** ***n.*** —**sur·viv′a·ble** ***adj.*** —**sur·vi′vor** ***n.***

Su·san (so͞o′z'n) [Fr. *Susanne* < LL. < Gr. < Heb. *shōshannāh,* lily] a feminine name: dim. *Sue;* var. *Susanna, Susannah*

sus·cep·ti·bil·i·ty (sə sep′tə bil′ə tē) ***n.,*** *pl.* **-ties** **1.** a being susceptible **2.** [*pl.*] sensitive feelings **3.** a susceptible temperament

sus·cep·ti·ble (sə sep′tə b'l) ***adj.*** [< ML. < L. pp. of *suscipere,* to receive < *sus-* (see SUB-), under + *capere,* to take] easily affected emotionally; having sensitive feelings —**susceptible of** admitting; allowing *[*testimony *susceptible of* error*]* —**susceptible to** easily influenced by or affected with *[susceptible to* disease*]* —**sus·cep′ti·ble·ness** ***n.*** —**sus·cep′ti·bly** ***adv.***

su·shi (so͞o′shē) ***n.*** [Jap.] a Japanese dish consisting of strips of raw fish wrapped about cakes of cold cooked rice

sus·pect (sə spekt′; *for adj. usually, & for n. always* sus′pekt) ***vt.*** [< L. pp. of *suspicere* < *sus-* (see SUB-), under + *spicere,* to look] **1.** to believe to be guilty of something specified, on little or no evidence **2.** to believe to be bad, wrong, harmful, etc.; distrust **3.** to think it likely; surmise; suppose —***vi.*** to be suspicious —***adj.*** viewed with suspicion; suspected —***n.*** a person who is suspected, esp. one suspected of a crime, etc.

sus·pend (sə spend′) ***vt.*** [< OFr. < L. < *sus-* (see SUB-), under + *pendere,* to hang] **1.** to remove (someone) from a position, school, team, etc., usually for a specified time, as a punishment **2.** to cause to become inoperative for a time **3.** to defer or hold back (judgment, a sentence, etc.) **4.** to hang by a support from above **5.** to hold (dust in the air, etc.) in suspension **6.** to keep in suspense, wonder, etc. —***vi.*** **1.** to stop temporarily **2.** to fail to pay debts or obligations **3.** to be suspended; hang —**sus·pend′i·ble** ***adj.***

sus·pend·ers (sə spen′dərz) ***n.pl.*** **1.** a pair of straps or bands passed over the shoulders to hold up trousers or a skirt **2.** [Brit.] garters for holding up stockings

sus·pense (sə spens′) ***n.*** [< MFr. < ML. < L. pp. of *suspendere,* to SUSPEND] **1.** the state of being undecided **2.** a state of usually anxious uncertainty, as in awaiting a decision **3.** the growing excitement felt as a story, play, etc. builds to a climax

sus·pen·sion (sə spen′shən) ***n.*** **1.** a suspending or being suspended; specif., *a*) a temporary removal from a position, school, etc. *b*) a temporary stoppage of payment, etc. *c*) a temporary canceling, as of rules *d*) a deferring of action on a sentence *e*) a holding back of a judgment, etc. **2.** a supporting device upon or from which something is suspended **3.** the system of springs, etc. supporting a vehicle upon its undercarriage **4.** *Chem.* *a*) the condition of a substance whose particles are dispersed through a fluid but not dissolved in it *b*) a substance in this condition *c*) a mixture of tiny, solid particles that are suspended in a liquid and settle out on standing **5.** *Music* *a*) the continuing of one or more tones of one chord into a following chord while the others are changed, creating a temporary dissonance *b*) the tone(s) so continued

suspension bridge a bridge suspended from cables anchored at either end and supported by towers at intervals

sus·pen·sive (-siv) ***adj.*** **1.** that suspends, defers, or temporarily stops something **2.** tending to suspend judgment; undecided **3.** of, characterized by, expressing, or in suspense —**sus·pen′sive·ly** ***adv.***

sus·pen·so·ry (-sə rē) ***adj.*** **1.** suspending, supporting, etc. *[*a *suspensory* muscle*]* **2.** suspending or delaying, esp. so as to leave something undecided —***n.,*** *pl.* **-ries** a suspensory muscle, bandage, support, etc.: also **sus·pen′sor**

sus·pi·cion (sə spish′ən) ***n.*** [< OFr. < LL. < L. < *suspicere,* to SUSPECT] **1.** a suspecting or being suspected **2.** the feeling or state of mind of a person who suspects **3.** a very small amount or degree; trace —***vt.*** [Dial.] to suspect —**above suspicion** not to be suspected; honorable —**on suspicion** on the basis of suspicion —**under suspicion** suspected

sus·pi·cious (-əs) ***adj.*** **1.** arousing or likely to arouse suspicion **2.** showing suspicion **3.** *a*) feeling suspicion *b*) tending habitually to suspect evil, etc. —**sus·pi′cious·ly** ***adv.*** —**sus·pi′cious·ness** ***n.***

Sus·que·han·na (sus′kwi han′ə) [< Iroquoian tribal or stream name] river flowing from C N.Y. through Pa. & Md. into Chesapeake Bay

sus·tain (sə stān′) ***vt.*** [< OFr. < L. *sustinere* < *sus-* (see SUB-), under + *tenere,* to hold] **1.** to keep in existence; maintain or prolong *[*to *sustain* a mood*]* **2.** to provide for the support of; specif., to provide nourishment for **3.** to support; carry the weight of **4.** to strengthen the spirits, courage, etc. of; comfort **5.** to endure; withstand **6.** to undergo; suffer (an injury, loss, etc.) **7.** to uphold the validity of *[*to *sustain* a verdict*]* **8.** to confirm; corroborate —**sus·tain′a·ble** ***adj.*** —**sus·tain′er** ***n.*** —**sus·tain′ment** ***n.***

sus·tain·ing program (-iŋ) any radio or TV program paid for by a station or network, not by a commercial sponsor

sus·te·nance (sus′ti nəns) ***n.*** **1.** a sustaining or being sustained **2.** means of livelihood; maintenance; support **3.** that which sustains life; nourishment; food

sut·ler (sut′lər) ***n.*** [< ModDu. < *soetelen,* to do dirty work] formerly, a person following an army to sell food, liquor, etc. to its soldiers

sut·tee (su tē′, sut′ē) ***n.*** [< Hindi < Sans. *satī,* virtuous wife] **1.** a Hindu widow who threw herself alive, and was cremated, on her husband's funeral pyre **2.** the former custom of such self-cremation: also **sut·tee′ism**

su·ture (so͞o′chər) ***n.*** [< L. < pp. of *suere,* to sew] **1.** *a*) the act of joining together by or as by sewing *b*) the line along which such a joining is made **2.** *Anat.* the line of junction of two bones, esp. of the skull **3.** *Surgery* *a*) the stitching together of the two edges of a wound or incision *b*) the gut, thread, wire, etc. used in such stitching *c*) any of the stitches so made —*vt.* **-tured, -tur·ing** to join together as with sutures —**su'tur·al** *adj.*

Su·wan·nee (sə wôn'ē, -wän'-; swô'nē, swä'-) [< AmInd. name] river flowing from S Ga. across N Fla. into the Gulf of Mexico

su·ze·rain (so͞o'zə rin, -rān') *n.* [Fr. < *sus,* above < L. *sursum,* upward + ending of Fr. *souverain,* SOVEREIGN] **1.** a feudal lord **2.** a state in its relation to another state over which it has political control —**su'ze·rain·ty** *n., pl.* **-ties**

s.v. [L. *sub verbo*] under the word (specified)

svelte (svelt, sfelt) *adj.* [Fr. < It., ult. < L. *evellere,* to pluck out] **1.** slender and graceful **2.** suave, polished, etc.

Sverd·lovsk (sferd lôfsk') city in W R.S.F.S.R., in the Ural Mountains: pop. 1,026,000

SW, S.W., s.w. 1. southwest **2.** southwestern

Sw. 1. Sweden **2.** Swedish

swab (swäb) *n.* [contr. < *swabber* < ModDu. *zwabber* < *zwabben,* to do dirty work] **1.** a mop for cleaning decks, floors, etc. **2.** *a*) a small piece of cotton, sponge, etc. used to apply medicine to, or clean discharged matter from, the throat, mouth, etc. *b*) matter collected in this way **3.** a brush for cleaning the barrel of a gun **4.** [Slang] *a*) a clumsy, loutish person *b*) a sailor, esp. an enlisted man in the U.S. Navy: also **swab'bie, swab'by** (-ē) —*vt.* **swabbed, swab'bing** to clean, medicate, etc. with a swab —**swab'ber** *n.*

Swa·bi·a (swā'bē ə) region in SW West Germany, formerly a duchy —**Swa'bi·an** *adj., n.*

swad·dle (swäd''l) *vt.* **-dled, -dling** [OE. *swethel*] **1.** to wrap (a newborn baby) in long, narrow bands of cloth (**swaddling clothes** or **bands**), as in former times **2.** to bind in or as in bandages; swathe —*n.* a cloth or bandage used for swaddling

swag (swag) *vi.* **swagged, swag'ging** [< or akin to Norw. *svagga,* to sway] **1.** to sway or lurch **2.** to sink down; sag —*vt.* **1.** to decorate with swags **2.** to hang in a swag —*n.* **1.** a swaying or lurching **2.** a valance, garland, chain, etc. hanging decoratively in a loop or curve **3.** [Slang] loot; plunder **4.** [Austral.] a bundle containing one's personal belongings

swage (swāj) *n.* [OFr. *souage*] **1.** a tool for bending or shaping metal **2.** a die or stamp for shaping metal by hammering —*vt.* **swaged, swag'ing** to shape, etc. with a swage

swag·ger (swag'ər) *vi.* [prob. < Norw. dial. *svagra,* freq. of *svagga,* to sway] **1.** to walk with a bold, arrogant stride; strut **2.** to boast, brag, or show off in a loud, superior manner —*n.* swaggering walk, manner, or behavior —*adj.* [Brit. Colloq.] stylish, esp. in an elegant way —**swag'ger·er** *n.* —**swag'ger·ing·ly** *adv.*

swagger stick a short stick or cane as carried by some army officers, etc.: also [Brit.] **swagger cane**

Swa·hi·li (swä hē'lē) *n.* [< Ar. *sawāḥil,* pl. of *sāḥil,* coast + *-i,* belonging to] **1.** *pl.* **-lis, -li** any of a Bantu people of Zanzibar and the nearby mainland **2.** their Bantu language, widely used as a lingua franca in E and C Africa

swain (swān) *n.* [< ON. *sveinn,* boy] [Poet. or Archaic] **1.** a country youth **2.** a young rustic lover or gallant **3.** a lover —**swain'ish** *adj.* —**swain'ish·ness** *n.*

swal·low[1] (swäl'ō) *n.* [OE. *swealwe*] **1.** any of various small, swift-flying birds with long, pointed wings and a forked tail, known for their regular migrations **2.** any of certain swifts resembling swallows —**swal'low·like'** *adj.*

BARN SWALLOW (to 7½ in. long)

swal·low[2] (swäl'ō) *vt.* [OE. *swelgan*] **1.** to pass (food, etc.) from the mouth through the esophagus into the stomach **2.** to take in; absorb; engulf (often with *up*) **3.** to take back (words said); retract **4.** to put up with; tolerate *[to swallow insults]* **5.** to refrain from expressing; suppress *[to swallow one's pride]* **6.** to utter (words) indistinctly **7.** [Colloq.] to accept as true without question —*vi.* to move the muscles of the throat as in swallowing, esp. when emotionally upset —*n.* **1.** the act of swallowing **2.** the amount swallowed at one time **3.** [Chiefly Brit.] the throat or gullet —**swal'low·er** *n.*

swal·low·tail (-tāl') *n.* **1.** something having a forked shape like that of a swallow's tail **2.** a butterfly having tail-like points on the hind wings

swal·low-tailed coat (-tāld') a man's full-dress coat, with long, tapering tails at the back

swam (swam) *pt. of* SWIM[1] & SWIM[2]

swa·mi (swä'mē) *n., pl.* **-mis** [< Hindi < Sans. *svāmin,* a lord] **1.** master: a title of respect for a Hindu religious teacher **2.** a learned man Also sp. **swa'my** *pl.* **-mies**

swamp (swämp, swômp) *n.* [< dial. var. of ME. *sompe,* SUMP] a piece of wet, spongy land; marsh; bog: also **swamp'land'** —*adj.* of or native to a swamp —*vt.* **1.** to plunge in a swamp, deep water, etc. **2.** to flood with or as with water **3.** to overwhelm; ruin *[swamped by debts]* **4.** to sink (a boat) by filling with water **5.** to clear of underbrush —*vi.* to sink as in a swamp —**swamp'i·ness** *n.* —**swamp'ish** *adj.* —**swamp'y** *adj.* **swamp'i·er, swamp'i·est**

swamp buggy an automotive vehicle for traveling over swampy or muddy terrain

swamp fever *same as* MALARIA

swan (swän, swôn) *n.* [OE.] **1.** *pl.* **swans, swan:** see PLURAL, II, D, 1 a large-bodied water bird with webfeet, a long, graceful neck, and, usually, pure white feathers **2.** a poet or singer of great ability: cf. SWAN SONG —**swan'like'** *adj.*

swan dive a forward dive in which the legs are held straight and together, the back is arched, and the arms are stretched out to the sides

Swa·nee (swô'nē, swä'-) *same as* SUWANNEE

swang (swaŋ) *archaic or dial. pt. of* SWING

swank (swaŋk) *n.* [akin to OE. *swancor,* pliant, supple] [Colloq.] **1.** stylish display or showiness in dress, etc. **2.** swaggering, showy behavior, speech, etc. —*adj.* [Colloq.] stylish in a showy way —*vi.* [Slang] to show off; boast

swank·y (swaŋ'kē) *adj.* **swank'i·er, swank'i·est** [Colloq.] stylish or expensive in a showy way —**swank'i·ly** *adv.* —**swank'i·ness** *n.*

swan's-down (swänz'doun', swônz'-) *n.* **1.** the soft, fine underfeathers, or down, of a swan, used for trimming clothes, etc. **2.** a soft, thick fabric of wool and silk, rayon, or cotton, used for making baby clothes, etc. **3.** a soft cotton flannel Also **swans'down'**

Swan·sea (swän'sē, -zē) seaport in S Wales, on Bristol Channel: pop. 171,000

swan song 1. the sweet song supposed in ancient legend to be sung by a dying swan **2.** the last act, final creative work, etc. of a person

swap (swäp, swôp) *vt., vi.* **swapped, swap'ping** [ME. *swappen,* to strike: hands were struck to conclude a bargain] [Colloq.] to exchange, trade, or barter —*n.* [Colloq.] an exchange, trade, or barter —**swap'per** *n.*

sward (swôrd) *n.* [OE. *sweard,* skin] grass-covered soil; turf —*vt.* to cover with sward

sware (swer) *archaic pt. of* SWEAR

swarm[1] (swôrm) *n.* [OE. *swearm*] **1.** a large number of bees, led by a queen, leaving a hive to start a new colony **2.** a colony of bees in a hive **3.** a moving mass or crowd —*vi.* **1.** to fly off in a swarm: said of bees **2.** to move, collect, etc. in large numbers; throng **3.** to be filled or crowded; teem —*vt.* to crowd; throng —**swarm'er** *n.*

swarm[2] (swôrm) *vi., vt.* [orig. nautical word < ?] to climb (a tree, mast, etc.); shin (*up*)

swart (swôrt) *adj.* [OE. *sweart*] *dial. var. of* SWARTHY

swarth (swôrth) *n. dial. var. of* SWARD —*adj. same as* SWARTHY

swarth·y (swôr'thē, -thē) *adj.* **swarth'i·er, swarth'i·est** [< dial. *swarth,* var. of SWART + -Y[2]] having a dark complexion; dusky —**swarth'i·ly** *adv.* —**swarth'i·ness** *n.*

swash (swäsh, swôsh) *vi.* [echoic] **1.** to dash, strike, wash, etc. with a splashing sound; splash **2.** to swagger —*vt.* to splash (a liquid), as in a container —*n.* **1.** a channel of water cutting through or behind a sandbank **2.** the splashing of water **3.** a swaggering action

swash·buck·ler (-buk'lər) *n.* [prec. + BUCKLER] a blustering, swaggering fighting man —**swash'buck'ling** *n., adj.*

swas·ti·ka (swäs'ti kə) *n.* [< Sans. < *svasti,* well-being] **1.** a design or ornament of ancient origin in the form of a cross with four equal arms, each bent in a right-angle extension **2.** this design with the extensions bent clockwise: used as the Nazi emblem

swat (swät) *vt.* **swat'ted, swat'ting** [echoic] [Colloq.] to hit with a quick, sharp blow —*n.* [Colloq.] a quick, sharp blow —**swat'ter** *n.*

swatch (swäch) *n.* [orig., a cloth tally < ?] **1.** a sample piece of cloth or other material **2.** a small amount or number in a cluster, bunch, or patch

swath (swäth, swôth) *n.* [OE. *swathu,* a track] **1.** the space covered with one cut of a scythe, etc. **2.** the strip or band of grass, wheat, etc. cut in a single trip across a lawn or field by a mower, etc. **3.** any long strip —**cut a wide swath** to make a big or showy impression

swathe[1] (swāth) *vt.* **swathed, swath'ing** [OE. *swathian*] **1.** to wrap or bind up in a bandage **2.** to wrap (a bandage, etc.) around something **3.** to surround or envelop —*n.* a bandage or wrapping —**swath'er** *n.*

swathe[2] (swāth) *n. same as* SWATH

sway (swā) ***vi.*** [ON. *sveigja,* to bend] **1.** *a)* to swing or move from side to side or to and fro *b)* to vacillate between one opinion, etc. and another **2.** *a)* to lean or incline to one side; veer *b)* to incline in judgment or opinion —***vt.*** **1.** to cause to sway, or swing to and fro, vacillate, incline to one side, etc. **2.** to change the thinking or actions of; influence in a certain direction [*swayed* by promises] **3.** [Archaic] to rule over; control —***n.*** **1.** a swaying or being swayed; a swinging, leaning, etc. **2.** influence or control **3.** rule; dominion —**hold sway** to reign or prevail —**sway′er** ***n.*** —**sway′ing·ly** ***adv.***

sway·backed (-bakt′) ***adj.*** having an abnormal sagging of the spine, usually as a result of strain or overwork, as some horses, etc. —**sway′back′** ***n.***

Swa·zi·land (swä′zē land′) country in SE Africa, surrounded on three sides by South Africa: 6,705 sq. mi.; pop. 421,000

swear (swer) ***vi.* swore, sworn, swear′ing** [OE. *swerian*] **1.** to make a solemn declaration, supporting it with an appeal to God or to something held sacred [to *swear* on one's honor] **2.** to make a solemn promise; vow **3.** to use profane or vulgar, offensive language; curse **4.** *Law* to give evidence under oath —***vt.*** **1.** to declare solemnly in the name of God or of something held sacred **2.** to pledge or vow on oath **3.** to assert with great emphasis **4.** to take (an oath) by swearing **5.** to administer a legal oath to —**swear by** **1.** to name (something held sacred) in taking an oath **2.** to have great faith in —**swear for** to give assurance for; guarantee —**swear in** to administer an oath to (a person taking office, a witness, etc.) —**swear off** to promise to give up [to *swear off* smoking] —**swear out** to obtain (a warrant for arrest) by making a charge under oath —**swear′er** ***n.***

swear·word (-wurd′) ***n.*** a word or phrase used in swearing or cursing; profane or vulgar, offensive word

sweat (swet) ***vi.* sweat** or **sweat′ed, sweat′ing** [OE. *swætan* < *swat,* sweat] **1.** to give out a salty moisture through the pores of the skin; perspire **2.** *a)* to give out moisture in droplets on its surface, as a ripening cheese *b)* to condense water in droplets on its surface [a glass of iced tea *sweats*] **3.** to ferment: said of tobacco leaves, etc. **4.** to come out in drops through pores; ooze **5.** to work hard enough to cause sweating **6.** [Colloq.] to suffer distress, anxiety, etc. —***vt.*** **1.** *a)* to give out (moisture) through a porous surface *b)* to condense (moisture) on the surface **2.** to cause to perspire, as by drugs, exercise, etc. **3.** to cause to give out moisture; esp., to ferment **4.** to make wet with perspiration **5.** to heat (an alloy) so as to extract an easily fusible constituent **6.** to unite (metal parts) by heating the solder applied to the ends until it melts **7.** *a)* to cause to work so hard as to sweat *b)* to cause (employees) to work long hours at low wages under poor working conditions **8.** [Colloq.] to get information from by torture or grueling questioning **9.** [Slang] to try hard or too hard to get or achieve —***n.*** **1.** the clear, salty liquid given out through the pores in the skin **2.** moisture given out or collected in droplets on a surface **3.** a sweating or being sweated **4.** a condition of eagerness, anxiety, impatience, etc. **5.** hard work; drudgery —**sweat blood** [Slang] **1.** to work very hard; overwork **2.** to be impatient, anxious, etc. —**sweat off** to get rid of (weight) by sweating —**sweat out** [Slang] **1.** to suffer through (something) **2.** to wait anxiously or impatiently for

sweat·band (-band′) ***n.*** a band of leather, etc. inside a hat to protect it against sweat from the brow

sweat·er (swet′ər) ***n.*** **1.** a person or thing that sweats **2.** a knitted outer garment for the upper part of the body, styled as a pullover or a jacket

sweat gland any of the many, tiny tubular glands just beneath the skin that secrete sweat

sweat shirt a heavy, long-sleeved cotton jersey, worn to absorb sweat during or after exercise, sometimes with loose trousers (**sweat pants**) of the same material

sweat·shop (-shäp′) ***n.*** a shop where employees work long hours at low wages under poor working conditions

sweat·y (-ē) ***adj.* sweat′i·er, sweat′i·est** **1.** wet with sweat; sweating **2.** of sweat [a *sweaty* odor] **3.** causing sweat [*sweaty* work] —**sweat′i·ly** ***adv.*** —**sweat′i·ness** ***n.***

Swed. **1.** Sweden **2.** Swedish

Swede (swēd) ***n.*** a native or inhabitant of Sweden

Swe·den (swē′d'n) country in N Europe, in the E part of the Scandinavian Peninsula: 173,620 sq. mi.; pop. 8,115,000; cap. Stockholm

Swe·den·borg (swēd′'n bôrg′; *Sw.* svād′'n bôr′y′), **E·man·u·el** (i man′yoo wəl) (born *Emanuel Swedberg*) 1688–1772; Swed. mystic & religious philosopher —**Swe′den·bor′gi·an** (-bôr′jē ən, -gē-) ***adj., n.***

Swed·ish (swē′dish) ***adj.*** of Sweden, its people, their language, etc. —***n.*** the North Germanic language of the Swedes —**the Swedish** the people of Sweden

Swedish turnip *same as* RUTABAGA

sweep (swēp) ***vt.* swept, sweep′ing** [akin to (or ? altered <) OE. *swapan:* see SWOOP] **1.** to clear or clean as by brushing with a broom [to *sweep* a floor] **2.** to remove or clear away (dirt, debris, etc.) as with a broom or brushing movement **3.** to strip, carry away, or destroy with forceful movement **4.** to carry along with a sweeping movement **5.** to touch or brush in moving across **6.** to pass swiftly over or across **7.** *a)* to drag (a river, pond, etc.) with a net, grapple, etc. *b)* to clear (waters) with a mine sweeper **8.** to rake with gunfire **9.** to win overwhelmingly [to *sweep* an election] —***vi.*** **1.** to clean a surface, room, etc. as with a broom **2.** to move or progress steadily with speed, force, or gracefulness [planes *swept* across the sky] **3.** to trail, as skirts or the train of a gown **4.** to extend in a long curve or line [a road *sweeping* up the hill] —***n.*** **1.** the act of sweeping, as with a broom **2.** a steady sweeping movement or stroke [the *sweep* of a scythe] **3.** a trailing, as of skirts **4.** range or scope **5.** extent or stretch [a *sweep* of meadow] **6.** a line, contour, curve, etc. that gives an impression of flow or movement **7.** a person whose work is sweeping; specif., *short for* CHIMNEY SWEEP **8.** [*usually pl.*] sweepings **9.** complete victory or success, as in a series of contests **10.** a long oar **11.** a long pole mounted on a pivot, with a bucket at one end, used for raising water **12.** *Electronics* a crossing by an electron beam of the screen of a cathode-ray tube —**sweep′er** ***n.***

sweep·ing (-iŋ) ***adj.*** **1.** that sweeps **2.** extending over a wide range **3.** *a)* extensive; comprehensive *b)* complete *c)* indiscriminate —***n.*** **1.** [*pl.*] things swept up, as dirt from a floor **2.** the act, work, etc. of one that sweeps —**sweep′ing·ly** ***adv.***

sweep·stakes (-stāks′) ***n., pl.* -stakes′** **1.** a lottery in which each participant puts up money in a common fund from which the money for the winners comes **2.** *a)* a contest, esp. a horse race, which determines the winners of such a lottery *b)* the prize or prizes won **3.** any of various other lotteries Also **sweep′stake′, sweeps**

sweet (swēt) ***adj.*** [OE. *swete*] **1.** *a)* having a taste of, or like that of, sugar *b)* containing sugar in some form [*sweet* wines] **2.** *a)* pleasant in taste, smell, sound, looks, etc. *b)* gratifying [*sweet* praise] *c)* having a friendly, pleasing disposition *d)* sentimental *e)* [Slang] good, delightful, nice, etc. **3.** *a)* not rancid, spoiled, or sour [*sweet* milk] *b)* not salty or salted: said of water or butter *c)* free from sourness or acidity: said of soil **4.** *Jazz* characterized by rather strict adherence to melody, blandness, moderate tempo, etc. —***n.*** **1.** a being sweet; sweetness **2.** something sweet; specif., *a)* [Chiefly Brit.] a candy; sweetmeat *b)* [Brit.] a sweet dessert **3.** a sweetheart; darling —***adv.*** in a sweet manner —**be sweet on** [Colloq.] to be in love with —**sweet′ish** ***adj.*** —**sweet′ly** ***adv.*** —**sweet′ness** ***n.***

sweet alyssum a short garden plant with small spikes of tiny flowers

sweet·bread (swēt′bred′) ***n.*** the thymus (**heart,** or **throat, sweetbread**) or the pancreas (**stomach sweetbread**) of a calf, lamb, etc., when used as food

sweet·bri·er, sweet·bri·ar (-brī′ər) ***n.*** *same as* EGLANTINE

sweet cherry **1.** an old-world cherry, widely grown for its sweet fruit **2.** its fruit

sweet clover any of various plants of the legume family, with small white or yellow flowers, and leaflets in groups of three: grown for hay, forage, etc.

sweet corn any of various strains of Indian corn with kernels rich in sugar, eaten unripe as a cooked vegetable

sweet·en (swēt′'n) ***vt.*** **1.** to make sweet with or as with sugar **2.** to make pleasant or agreeable **3.** to make less harsh, less acidic, etc. —***vi.*** to become sweet

sweet·en·er (-ər) ***n.*** a sweetening agent, esp. a synthetic substance, such as saccharin

sweet·en·ing (-iŋ) ***n.*** **1.** the process of making sweet **2.** something that sweetens

sweet flag a perennial marsh plant with sword-shaped leaves, small, green flowers, and a sweet-scented rhizome

sweet gum **1.** a large N. American tree with alternate maplelike leaves and spiny fruit balls **2.** the wood of this tree **3.** the aromatic balsam of this tree

sweet·heart (swēt′härt′) ***n.*** **1.** *a)* a person with whom one is in love *b)* darling: a term of endearment **2.** [Slang] a very agreeable person or an excellent thing

sweet marjoram *see* MARJORAM

sweet·meat (-mēt′) ***n.*** a bit of sweet food, esp. a candy, candied fruit, or the like

sweet pea a climbing annual plant of the legume family, with butterfly-shaped flowers

sweet pepper **1.** a variety of the red pepper producing a large, mild fruit **2.** the fruit

sweet potato **1.** a tropical, trailing plant with purplish flowers and a fleshy, orange or yellow, tuberlike root used as a vegetable **2.** its root **3.** [Colloq.] *same as* OCARINA

sweet-talk (-tôk′) ***vt., vi.*** [Colloq.] to talk in a flattering or blandishing way (to)

sweet tooth [Colloq.] a fondness or craving for sweets

sweet william, sweet William a perennial pink with dense, flat clusters of small flowers

swell (swel) ***vi.* swelled, swelled** or **swol′len, swell′ing** [OE. *swellan*] **1.** to become larger as a result of pressure from within; expand **2.** to curve out; bulge; protrude **3.** to extend above the normal level **4.** to form swells, or large waves: said of the sea **5.** to be filled (*with* pride, etc.) **6.** to increase within one [his anger *swelled*] **7.** to increase in size, force, intensity, etc. **8.** to increase in loudness **—*vt.*** to cause to swell; specif., *a*) to cause to increase in size, volume, etc. *b*) to cause to bulge *c*) to fill with pride, etc. *d*) to cause to increase in loudness **—*n.*** **1.** a part that swells; bulge; specif., *a*) a large wave that moves steadily without breaking *b*) a piece of rising ground **2.** a swelling or being swollen **3.** an increase in size, amount, degree, etc. **4.** [Colloq.] a person, esp. a man, of wealth and fashion: an old-fashioned term **5.** *Music a*) a crescendo usually followed by a decrescendo *b*) a sign (< >) indicating this *c*) a device for controlling the loudness of tones, as in an organ **—*adj.*** [Slang] first-rate; excellent: used in a general way to show approval

swelled head [Colloq.] great self-conceit

swell·ing (-iŋ) ***n.*** **1.** an increasing or being increased in size, volume, etc. **2.** a swollen part, as on the body

swel·ter (swel′tər) ***vi.*** [OE. *sweltan,* to die] to be or feel oppressively hot; sweat and wilt from great heat **—*vt.*** to cause to swelter **—*n.*** **1.** a sweltering **2.** oppressive heat

swel·ter·ing (-iŋ) ***adj.*** very hot, sweaty, sticky, etc.: also **swel′try** (-trē), **-tri·er, -tri·est —swel′ter·ing·ly *adv.***

swept (swept) *pt. & pp. of* SWEEP

swept·back (swept′bak′) ***adj.*** having a backward slant, as the wings of an aircraft

swept·wing (-wiŋ′) ***adj.*** *Aeron.* having sweptback wings

swerve (swurv) ***vi., vt.* swerved, swerv′ing** [OE. *sweorfan,* to scour] to turn aside suddenly from a straight line, course, etc. **—*n.*** the act or degree of swerving **—swerv′er *n.***

swift (swift) ***adj.*** [OE.] **1.** moving or capable of moving with great speed; fast **2.** coming, happening, or done quickly **3.** acting or responding quickly; prompt [*swift* to help] **—*adv.*** in a swift manner **—*n.*** an insect-eating, swift-flying bird resembling the swallow, as the chimney swift **—swift′ly *adv.* —swift′ness *n.***

Swift (swift), **Jonathan** 1667–1745; Eng. satirist, born in Ireland

swig (swig) ***vt., vi.* swigged, swig′ging** [< ?] [Colloq.] to drink in big gulps or amounts **—*n.*** [Colloq.] a big gulp, esp. of liquor **—swig′ger *n.***

swill (swil) ***vt.*** [OE. *swilian*] **1.** to flood with water so as to wash **2.** to drink greedily **3.** to feed swill to (pigs, etc.) **—*vi.*** to drink in large quantities **—*n.*** **1.** garbage, etc. mixed with liquid and fed to pigs, etc. **2.** garbage or slop **3.** the act of swilling **4.** a swig

swim[1] (swim) ***vi.* swam, swum, swim′ming** [OE. *swimman*] **1.** to move through water by movements of the arms and legs, or of flippers, fins, etc. **2.** to move along smoothly **3.** to float on the surface of a liquid **4.** to be immersed in a liquid **5.** to overflow [eyes *swimming* with tears] **—*vt.*** **1.** to move in or across (a body of water) by swimming **2.** to cause to swim **3.** to perform (a specified stroke) in swimming **—*n.*** an act, spell, or distance of swimming **—in the swim** conforming to the current fashions, or active in the main current of affairs **—swim′ma·ble *adj.* —swim′mer *n.***

swim[2] (swim) ***n.*** [OE. *swima*] the condition of being dizzy **—*vi.* swam, swum, swim′ming** **1.** to be dizzy **2.** to have a hazy, reeling, or whirling appearance

swim bladder a gas-filled sac in the body cavity of most bony fishes, giving buoyancy to the body

swim·mer·et (swim′ə ret′) ***n.*** any of the small abdominal appendages in certain crustaceans, used for swimming, etc.

swimming hole a pool or a deep place in a river, creek, etc. used for swimming

swim·ming·ly (swim′iŋ lē) ***adv.*** easily and with success

swimming pool a pool of water for swimming; esp., a tank specially built for the purpose

swim·suit (swim′so͞ot′) ***n.*** a garment worn for swimming

Swin·burne (swin′bərn), **Algernon Charles** 1837–1909; Eng. poet & critic

swin·dle (swin′d'l) ***vt.* -dled, -dling** [< G. *schwindeln,* to cheat] **1.** to get money or property from (another) under false pretenses; cheat; defraud **2.** to get by fraud **—*vi.*** to engage in swindling others **—*n.*** an act of swindling **—swin′dler *n.***

swine (swīn) ***n., pl.* swine** [OE. *swin*] **1.** a pig or hog: usually used collectively **2.** a vicious, contemptible, or disgusting person

swine·herd (-hurd′) ***n.*** one who tends swine

swing (swiŋ) ***vi.* swung, swing′ing** [OE. *swingan*] **1.** to sway or move backward and forward, as a freely hanging object **2.** to walk, trot, etc. with freely swaying movements **3.** to strike (*at*) **4.** to turn, as on a hinge or swivel **5.** *a*) to hang; be suspended *b*) [Colloq.] to be hanged in execution **6.** to move on a swing (*n.* 10) **7.** to have an exciting rhythmic quality [music that really *swings*] **8.** [Slang] to be very fashionable, active, etc., esp. in the pursuit of pleasure **—*vt.*** **1.** *a*) to move (a weapon, bat, etc.) with a sweeping motion; flourish *b*) to lift with a sweeping motion **2.** to cause (a freely hanging object) to move backward and forward **3.** to cause to turn or pivot, as on a hinge **4.** to cause to hang freely [to *swing* a scaffold from the roof] **5.** to cause to move in a curve [to *swing* a car around a corner] **6.** [Colloq.] to cause to come about successfully; manage with the desired results [to *swing* an election] **7.** to play (music) in the style of swing **—*n.*** **1.** the act of swinging **2.** the arc through which something swings **3.** the manner of swinging, as with a golf club, baseball bat, etc. **4.** freedom to do as one wishes **5.** a relaxed motion, as in walking **6.** a sweeping blow or stroke **7.** the course or movement of some activity, etc. **8.** the force behind something swung; impetus **9.** rhythm, as of poetry or music **10.** a seat hanging from ropes or chains, on which one can sit and swing **11.** a trip or tour [a *swing* around the country] **12.** a style of jazz music of about 1935 to 1945, characterized by large bands, improvised counterpoint, etc. **—*adj.*** of, in, or playing swing (music) **—in full swing** **1.** in complete and active operation **2.** going on without restraint **—swing′er *n.***

swin·gle (swiŋ′g'l) ***vt.* -gled, -gling** [< MDu. < *swinghel,* a swingle] to beat and clean (flax or hemp) with a swingle **—*n.*** a wooden, swordlike tool for beating and cleaning

swin·gle·tree (-trē′) ***n.*** *same as* SINGLETREE

swing shift [Colloq.] the evening work shift in some factories, from midafternoon to about midnight

swin·ish (swīn′ish) ***adj.*** of, like, or fit for swine; beastly, piggish, etc. **—swin′ish·ly *adv.* —swin′ish·ness *n.***

swipe (swīp) ***n.*** [prob. var. of SWEEP] [Colloq.] a hard, sweeping blow **—*vt.* swiped, swip′ing** **1.** [Colloq.] to hit with a hard, sweeping blow **2.** [Slang] to steal **—*vi.*** to make a sweeping blow or stroke

swirl (swurl) ***vi.*** [ME. *swyrl,* prob. < Norw. dial. *sverra,* to whirl] **1.** to move with a whirling motion **2.** to be dizzy **—*vt.*** to cause to swirl **—*n.*** **1.** a whirl; eddy **2.** a twist; curl; whirl **—swirl′ing·ly *adv.* —swirl′y *adj.***

swish (swish) ***vi.*** [echoic] **1.** to move with a sharp, hissing sound, as a cane swung through the air **2.** to rustle, as skirts **—*vt.*** to cause to swish **—*n.*** **1.** a hissing or rustling sound **2.** a movement that makes this sound **—*adj.*** [Slang] of, like, or for effeminate male homosexuals **—swish′y *adj.* swish′i·er, swish′i·est**

Swiss (swis) ***adj.*** of Switzerland, its people, or its culture **—*n.*** **1.** *pl.* **Swiss** a native or inhabitant of Switzerland **2.** [s-] a type of sheer fabric **—the Swiss** the people of Switzerland

Swiss chard *same as* CHARD

Swiss (cheese) a pale-yellow, hard cheese with many large holes, originally made in Switzerland

Swiss steak a thick cut of round steak, pounded with flour and braised, usually with tomatoes, onions, etc.

switch (swich) ***n.*** [prob. < MDu. or LowG.] **1.** a thin, flexible twig, stick, etc. used for whipping **2.** the bushy part of the tail of a cow, etc. **3.** a tress of detached hair used by women as part of a coiffure **4.** a sharp, lashing movement, as with a whip **5.** a device used to open, close, or divert an electric circuit **6.** a movable section of railroad track used in transferring a train from one track to another **7.** a shift or transference, esp. if sudden **—*vt.*** **1.** to whip as with a switch **2.** to jerk or swing sharply [a cow *switches* its tail] **3.** to shift; change; turn aside **4.** *a*) to operate the switch of (an electric current) *b*) to turn (an electric light, etc.) *on* or *off* in this way **5.** to transfer (a train, etc.) from one track to another by means of a switch **6.** [Colloq.] to change or exchange [to *switch* places] **—*vi.*** **1.** to move as from one track to another **2.** to shift; transfer **3.** to swing sharply; lash **—switch′er *n.***

switch·back (-bak′) ***n.*** a zigzag road up a steep grade

switch-blade knife (-blād′) a large jackknife that snaps open when a release button on the handle is pressed

switch·board (-bôrd′) ***n.*** a panel equipped with apparatus for controlling the operation of a system of electric circuits, as in a telephone exchange

switch-hit·ter (-hit′ər) ***n.*** a baseball player who bats sometimes right-handed and sometimes left-handed

switch·man (-mən) ***n., pl.* -men** a railroad employee who operates switches

switch·yard (-yärd′) ***n.*** a railroad yard where cars are shifted from one track to another by means of switches

Switz·er (swit′sər) ***n.*** **1.** a Swiss **2.** a Swiss mercenary soldier

Switz·er·land (swit′sər lənd) country in WC Europe, in the Alps: 15,941 sq. mi.; pop. 6,270,000; cap. Bern

swiv·el (swiv′'l) ***n.*** [< base of OE. *swifan,* to revolve] a coupling device that allows free turning of the parts attached to it; specif., a chain link in two parts, one piece fitting like a collar below the bolt head of the other and turning freely about it —***vt.*** **-eled** or **-elled, -el·ing** or **-el·ling** **1.** to cause to turn as on a swivel **2.** to fit or support with a swivel —***vi.*** to turn as on a swivel

swivel chair a chair whose seat turns horizontally on a pivot in the base

swiz·zle stick (swiz′'l) [< ?] a small rod for stirring mixed drinks

swob (swäb) ***n., vt.*** **swobbed, swob′bing** *var. sp. of* SWAB

swol·len (swō′lən) *alt. pp. of* SWELL —***adj.*** blown up; distended; bulging

swoon (swo͞on) ***vi.*** [< OE. *geswogen,* unconscious] **1.** to faint **2.** to feel strong, esp. rapturous emotion —***n.*** an act of swooning —**swoon′er** ***n.*** —**swoon′ing·ly** ***adv.***

swoop (swo͞op) ***vt.*** [OE. *swapan,* to sweep along] to snatch or seize suddenly: often with *up* —***vi.*** to pounce or sweep (*down* or *upon*) —***n.*** the act of swooping

swoosh (swo͝osh, swo͞osh) ***vi., vt.*** [echoic intens. of SWISH] to move, pour, etc. with a sharp, rustling or whistling sound —***n.*** such a sound

swop (swäp) ***n., vt., vi.*** **swopped, swop′ping** *var. sp. of* SWAP

sword (sôrd) ***n.*** [OE. *sweord*] **1.** a hand weapon having a long, sharp, pointed blade, set in a hilt **2.** *a)* power; esp., military power *b)* war —**at swords' points** ready to quarrel or fight —**cross swords** **1.** to fight **2.** to argue —**put to the sword** **1.** to kill with a sword **2.** to slaughter, esp. in war —**sword′like′** ***adj.***

sword·fish (-fish′) ***n., pl.*** **-fish′, -fish′es:** see FISH a large marine food and game fish with the upper jawbone extending in a long, flat, swordlike projection

SWORDFISH (to 15 ft. long)

sword grass any of a number of sedges or grasses with toothed or sword-shaped leaves

sword knot a loop of leather, ribbon, etc. attached to a sword hilt as an ornament or, orig., as a wrist support

sword·play (-plā′) ***n.*** the act or skill of using a sword in fencing or fighting

swords·man (sôrdz′mən) ***n., pl.*** **-men** **1.** a person who uses a sword in fencing or fighting **2.** a person skilled in using a sword Also [Archaic] **sword·man** (sôrd′mən), *pl.* **-men** —**swords′man·ship′** ***n.***

swore (swôr) *pt. of* SWEAR

sworn (swôrn) *pp. of* SWEAR —***adj.*** bound, pledged, promised, etc. by or as by an oath

swot (swät) ***n., vt.*** **swot′ted, swot′ting** *var. sp. of* SWAT

swum (swum) *pp. of* SWIM[1] & SWIM[2]

swung (swuŋ) *pp. & pt. of* SWING

syb·a·rite (sib′ə rīt′) ***n.*** [< *Sybarite,* a native of Sybaris, an ancient Greek city in S Italy, famed for its luxury] anyone very fond of luxury and self-indulgence —**syb′a·rit′ic** (-rit′ik) ***adj.*** —**syb′a·rit′i·cal·ly** ***adv.***

Syb·il (sib′'l) [< SIBYL] a feminine name

syc·a·more (sik′ə môr′) ***n.*** [< OFr. < L. < Gr. *sykomoros*] **1.** a shade tree native to Egypt and Asia Minor, with edible, figlike fruit **2.** a maple shade tree found in Europe and Asia **3.** *same as* PLANE[1]

syc·o·phant (sik′ə fənt) ***n.*** [< L. < Gr. *sykophantēs,* informer < *sykon,* a fig + *phainein,* to show] a person who seeks favor by flattering people of wealth or influence; toady —**syc′o·phan·cy** ***n., pl.*** **-cies** —**syc′o·phan′tic** (-fan′tik), **syc′o·phant′ish** ***adj.*** —**syc′o·phan′ti·cal·ly, syc′o·phant′ish·ly** ***adv.***

Syd·ney (sid′nē) **1.** [< SIDNEY] a masculine name **2.** seaport in SE Australia: pop. 2,713,000

syl- *same as* SYN-: used before *l*

syl·la·bar·y (sil′ə ber′ē) ***n., pl.*** **-bar′ies** [< ModL. < L. *syllaba:* see SYLLABLE] **1.** a table of syllables **2.** a set of the written characters of a language representing syllables

syl·lab·ic (si lab′ik) ***adj.*** **1.** of a syllable or syllables **2.** forming a syllable or the nucleus of a syllable; specif., standing by itself as the nucleus of a syllable without an accompanying vowel: said of a consonant, as the *l* in *tattle* **3.** pronounced with the syllables distinct —***n.*** a syllabic sound —**syl·lab′i·cal·ly** ***adv.***

syl·lab·i·cate (si lab′ə kāt′) ***vt.*** **-cat′ed, -cat′ing** *same as* SYLLABIFY —**syl·lab′i·ca′tion** ***n.***

syl·lab·i·fy (si lab′ə fī′) ***vt.*** **-fied′, -fy′ing** [< *syllabification* < L. *syllaba,* syllable + -FICATION] to form or divide into syllables —**syl·lab′i·fi·ca′tion** ***n.***

syl·la·ble (sil′ə b'l) ***n.*** [< OFr. < L. < Gr. *syllabē,* ult. < *syn-,* together + *lambanein,* to hold] **1.** a word or part of a word pronounced with a single, uninterrupted sounding of the voice **2.** any of the parts into which a written word is divided, in fairly close relation to its spoken syllables, to show where the word can be broken at the end of a line **3.** the least bit of detail, as of something said —***vt., vi.*** **-bled, -bling** to pronounce in or as in syllables

syl·la·bub (sil′ə bub′) ***n.*** [< ?] a dessert or beverage made of sweetened milk or cream mixed with wine or cider and beaten to a froth

syl·la·bus (sil′ə bəs) ***n., pl.*** **-bus·es, -bi′** (-bī′) [LL., a list < L. < Gr. *sillybos,* parchment label] a summary or outline, esp. of a course of study

syl·lo·gism (sil′ə jiz'm) ***n.*** [< MFr. < L. < Gr. *syn-,* together + *logizesthai,* to reason] **1.** a form of reasoning in which two statements or premises are made and a logical conclusion drawn from them Ex.: All mammals are warmblooded (*major premise*); whales are mammals (*minor premise*); therefore, whales are warmblooded (*conclusion*) **2.** reasoning from the general to the particular —**syl′lo·gis′tic, syl′lo·gis′ti·cal** ***adj.*** —**syl′lo·gis′ti·cal·ly** ***adv.***

sylph (silf) ***n.*** [ModL. *sylphus* < L., a spirit < ?] **1.** an imaginary being supposed to live in the air **2.** a slender, graceful woman or girl —**sylph′like′** ***adj.***

syl·van (sil′vən) ***adj.*** [< ML. < L. *silva,* a wood] **1.** of or characteristic of the woods or forest **2.** living, found, or carried on in the woods or forest **3.** wooded —***n.*** one who lives in the woods

Syl·vi·a (sil′vē ə) [< L. < *silva,* a wood] a feminine name

sym- *same as* SYN-: used before *m, p,* and *b*

sym·bi·o·sis (sim′bī ō′sis, -bē-) ***n.*** [ModL. < Gr. < *symbioun* < *syn-,* together + *bioun,* to live] **1.** *Biol.* the intimate living together of two kinds of organisms, esp. where such association is of mutual advantage **2.** a similar relationship in which persons or groups are dependent on each other —**sym′bi·ot′ic** (-ät′ik) ***adj.***

sym·bol (sim′b'l) ***n.*** [< Fr. < L. < Gr. *symbolon,* token, ult. < *syn-,* together + *ballein,* to throw] **1.** an object used to represent something abstract [the dove is a *symbol* of peace] **2.** a mark, letter, abbreviation, etc. standing for an object, quality, process, quantity, etc., as in music, chemistry, mathematics, etc. —***vt.*** **-boled** or **-bolled, -bol·ing** or **-bol·ling** *same as* SYMBOLIZE

sym·bol·ic (sim bäl′ik) ***adj.*** **1.** of or expressed in a symbol or symbols **2.** that serves as a symbol (*of* something) **3.** using symbolism Also **sym·bol′i·cal** —**sym·bol′i·cal·ly** ***adv.***

symbolic logic a modern type of formal logic using special mathematical symbols for propositions and relationships among propositions

sym·bol·ism (sim′b'l iz'm) ***n.*** **1.** the representation of things by use of symbols, esp. in art or literature **2.** a system of symbols **3.** symbolic meaning

sym·bol·ist (-ist) ***n.*** **1.** a person who uses symbols **2.** a person who practices symbolism in representing ideas, etc., esp. in art or literature —**sym′bol·is′tic** ***adj.*** —**sym′bol·is′ti·cal·ly** ***adv.***

sym·bol·ize (-īz′) ***vt.*** **-ized′, -iz′ing** **1.** to be a symbol of; typify; stand for **2.** to represent by a symbol or symbols —***vi.*** to use symbols —**sym′bol·i·za′tion** ***n.*** —**sym′bol·iz′er** ***n.***

sym·me·try (sim′ə trē) ***n., pl.*** **-tries** [< MFr. < L. < Gr., ult. < *syn-,* together + *metron,* a measure] **1.** similarity of form or arrangement on either side of a dividing line or plane; correspondence of opposite parts in size, shape, and position **2.** balance or beauty of form resulting from such correspondence —**sym·met·ri·cal** (si met′ri k'l), **sym·met′ric** ***adj.*** —**sym·met′ri·cal·ly** ***adv.***

sym·pa·thet·ic (sim′pə thet′ik) ***adj.*** **1.** of, resulting from, feeling, or showing sympathy; sympathizing **2.** in agreement with one's tastes, mood, etc.; congenial **3.** showing favor, approval, etc. [to be *sympathetic* to a plan] **4.** *Physiol.* designating or of that part of the autonomic nervous system involved in the involuntary response to alarm, as by speeding the heart rate, dilating the pupils of the eyes, etc. **5.** *Physics* designating or of vibrations caused by other vibrations having the same period that are transmitted from a neighboring vibrating body —**sym′pa·thet′i·cal·ly** ***adv.***

sym·pa·thize (sim′pə thīz′) ***vi.*** **-thized′, -thiz′ing** **1.** to share or understand the feelings or ideas of another; be in sympathy **2.** to feel or express sympathy, esp. in pity or compassion; commiserate **3.** to be in harmony or accord —**sym′pa·thiz′er** ***n.*** —**sym′pa·thiz′ing·ly** ***adv.***

sym·pa·thy (sim′pə thē) ***n., pl.*** **-thies** [< L. < Gr. < *syn-,* together + *pathos,* feeling] **1.** sameness of feeling; affinity between persons **2.** agreement in qualities; harmony; accord **3.** a mutual liking or understanding arising from sameness of feeling **4.** a sharing of, or the ability to share, another person's mental state, emotions, etc.; esp., [*often pl.*] pity or compassion felt for another's trouble, suffering, etc. **5.** a feeling of approval of an idea, cause, etc.

sympathy (or **sympathetic**) **strike** a strike by a group of workers in support of another group on strike

symphonic poem a composition of program music for full symphony orchestra, interpreting particular poetic or descriptive ideas, and free in form

sym·pho·ny (sim′fə nē) ***n., pl.* -nies** [< OFr. < L. < Gr. < *syn-*, together + *phōnē*, a sound] **1.** harmony of sounds, esp. of instruments **2.** any harmony, as of color **3.** *Music a*) an extended composition for full orchestra, having several (usually four) movements related in subject, but varying in form and execution *b*) *short for* SYMPHONY ORCHESTRA *c*) [Colloq.] a concert by a symphony orchestra —**sym·phon·ic** (sim fän′ik) ***adj.*** —**sym·phon′i·cal·ly *adv.***

symphony orchestra a large orchestra of string, wind, and percussion sections for playing symphonic works

sym·po·si·um (sim pō′zē əm) ***n., pl.* -si·ums, -si·a** (-ə) [L. < Gr. *syn-*, together + *posis*, a drinking] **1.** any meeting or social gathering at which ideas are freely exchanged **2.** a conference organized for the discussion of some particular subject **3.** a collection of opinions, esp. a group of essays, on a given subject —**sym·po′si·ac′** (-ak′) ***adj.***

symp·tom (simp′təm) ***n.*** [< ML. < LL. < Gr. *symptōma*, ult. < *syn-*, together + *piptein*, to fall] any circumstance, event, or condition that accompanies something and indicates its existence or occurrence; sign; specif., *Med.* any condition accompanying a disease or a physical disorder and serving as an aid in diagnosis —**symp′to·mat′ic** (-tə mat′ik) ***adj.*** —**symp′to·mat′i·cal·ly *adv.***

symp·tom·a·tize (-tə mə tīz′) ***vt.* -tized′, -tiz′ing** to be a symptom or sign of: also **symp′tom·ize′**

syn- [Gr. < *syn*, with] *a prefix meaning* with, together with, at the same time, by means of: *syn-* is assimilated to *syl-* before *l; sym-* before *m, p, b;* and *sys-* before *s* and aspirate *h*

syn. 1. synonym **2.** synonymous **3.** synonymy

syn·a·gogue (sin′ə gäg′, -gôg′) ***n.*** [< OFr. < LL. < Gr. *synagōgē*, an assembly, ult. < *syn-*, together + *agein*, to bring] **1.** an assembly of Jews meeting for worship and religious study **2.** a building or place used for such an assembly **3.** the Jewish religion as organized in such local congregations Also **syn′a·gog′** —**syn′a·gog′al** (-gäg′'l, -gôg′-), **syn′a·gog′i·cal** (-gäj′i k'l) ***adj.***

syn·apse (si naps′) ***n.*** [ModL. < Gr. *synapsis*, a union] the point of contact between adjacent neurons, where nerve impulses are transmitted from one to the other —**syn·ap′tic** (-nap′tik) ***adj.***

sync, synch (siŋk) ***vt., vi.*** *shortened form of* SYNCHRONIZE

syn·chro·mesh (siŋ′krə mesh′) ***adj.*** designating or employing a device by which gears to be meshed are automatically brought to the same speed of rotation before the shift is completed —***n.*** a synchromesh gear system

syn·chro·nism (siŋ′krə niz'm) ***n.*** **1.** the fact or state of being synchronous; occurrence at the same time **2.** a chronological listing of persons or events in history, showing existence or occurrence at the same time —**syn′chro·nis′tic *adj.*** —**syn′chro·nis′ti·cal·ly *adv.***

syn·chro·nize (siŋ′krə nīz′) ***vi.* -nized′, -niz′ing** [< Gr. < *synchronos*, contemporary < *syn-*, together + *chronos*, time] to move or occur at the same time or rate; be synchronous —***vt.*** **1.** to cause to agree in time or rate of speed; regulate (clocks, action and dialogue, etc.) so as to make synchronous **2.** to assign (events, etc.) to the same date or period —**syn′chro·ni·za′tion *n.*** —**syn′chro·niz′er *n.***

syn·chro·nous (-nəs) ***adj.*** [< LL. < Gr.: see prec.] **1.** happening at the same time; simultaneous **2.** having the same period between movements, occurrences, etc.; having the same rate and phase, as vibrations Also **syn′chro·nal** —**syn′chro·nous·ly *adv.*** —**syn′chro·nous·ness *n.***

syn·chro·tron (-trän′) ***n.*** [SYNCHRO(NOUS) + (ELEC)TRON] a circular machine for accelerating charged particles, esp. electrons, to very high energies through the use of a low-frequency magnetic field in combination with a high-frequency electrostatic field

syn·cline (siŋ′klīn) ***n.*** [< *synclinal* < Gr. *syn-*, together + *klinein*, to incline] *Geol.* a down fold in stratified rocks from whose central axis the beds rise upward and outward in opposite directions: opposed to ANTICLINE —**syn·cli·nal** (sin klī′n'l, siŋ′kli n'l) ***adj.***

syn·co·pate (siŋ′kə pāt′) ***vt.* -pat′ed, -pat′ing** [< ML. pp. of *syncopare*, to cut short < LL., to swoon < *syncope:* see SYNCOPE] **1.** to shorten (a word) by syncope **2.** *Music a*) to shift (the regular accent) as by beginning a tone on an unaccented beat and continuing it through the next accented beat, or on the last half of a beat and continuing it through the first half of the following beat *b*) to use such shifted accents in (a composition, etc.) —**syn′co·pa′tor *n.***

syn·co·pa·tion (siŋ′kə pā′shən) ***n.*** **1.** a syncopating or being syncopated **2.** syncopated music, a syncopated rhythm, etc. **3.** *Gram. same as* SYNCOPE

syn·co·pe (siŋ′kə pē) ***n.*** [LL. < Gr. < *syn-*, together + *koptein*, to cut] **1.** the dropping of sounds or letters from the middle of a word, as in *Wooster* for *Worcester* **2.** a fainting caused by an inadequate flow of blood to the brain

syn·cre·tize (siŋ′krə tīz′) ***vt., vi.* -tized′, -tiz′ing** [< ModL. < Gr. *synkrētizein*] to combine, unite, or reconcile

syn·dic (sin′dik) ***n.*** [Fr. < LL. < Gr. *syndikos*, advocate < *syn-*, together + *dikē*, justice] **1.** [Brit.] a business manager, esp. of a university **2.** a civil magistrate —**syn′di·cal *adj.***

syn·di·cal·ism (-di k'l iz'm) ***n.*** a theory of trade unionism in which all means of production and distribution would be brought under the control of federations of labor unions by the use of general strikes, etc. —**syn′di·cal·ist *adj., n.***

syn·di·cate (sin′də kit; *for v.* -kāt′) ***n.*** [Fr. *syndicat* < *syndic*, SYNDIC] **1.** a council of syndics **2.** *a*) an association of individuals or corporations formed to carry out some financial project requiring much capital *b*) any group organized to further some undertaking *c*) a group of similar organizations, as of newspapers, owned as a chain **3.** an organization that sells articles or features for publication by many newspapers —***vt.* -cat′ed, -cat′ing** **1.** to manage as or form into a syndicate **2.** to sell (an article, etc.) through a syndicate for publication in many newspapers, etc. —***vi.*** to form a syndicate —**syn′di·ca′tion *n.*** —**syn′di·ca′tor *n.***

syn·drome (sin′drōm) ***n.*** [ModL. < Gr. < *syn-*, with + *dramein*, to run] **1.** a set of symptoms characterizing a disease **2.** any set of characteristics identifying a type, condition, etc.

syne (sīn) ***adv., conj., prep.*** [Scot.] since; ago

syn·ec·do·che (si nek′də kē) ***n.*** [< ML. < L. < Gr., ult. < *syn-*, together + *ekdechesthai*, to receive] a figure of speech in which a part is used for a whole, an individual for a class, a material for a thing, or the reverse of any of these (Ex.: *bread* for *food, the army* for *a soldier*, or *copper* for *a penny*)

syn·er·gism (sin′ər jiz'm) ***n.*** [< ModL. < Gr. < *syn-*, together + *ergon*, work] the simultaneous action of separate agencies which, together, have greater total effect than the sum of their individual effects: said esp. of drugs: also **syn′er·gy** (-jē) —**syn′er·gis′tic *adj.***

Synge (siŋ), **(Edmund) John Mil·ling·ton** (mil′iŋ tən) 1871–1909; Ir. dramatist

syn·od (sin′əd) ***n.*** [OE. *sinoth*, ult. < Gr. *synodos*, lit., a meeting < *syn-*, together + *hodos*, way] **1.** a council of churches or church officials; specif., a high governing body in any of certain Christian churches **2.** any assembly or council —**syn′od·al *adj.***

syn·od·i·cal (si näd′i k'l) ***adj.*** **1.** of a synod **2.** *Astron.* of or having to do with conjunction, esp. with the interval between two successive conjunctions of the same heavenly bodies Also **syn·od′ic** —**syn·od′i·cal·ly *adv.***

syn·o·nym (sin′ə nim) ***n.*** [< L. < Gr. < *syn-*, together + *onyma*, a name] **1.** a word having the same or nearly the same meaning as another in the same language **2.** a word used in metonymy —**syn′o·nym′ic, syn′o·nym′i·cal *adj.***

syn·on·y·mous (si nän′ə məs) ***adj.*** [see prec.] of the same or nearly the same meaning —**syn·on′y·mous·ly *adv.***

syn·on·y·my (-mē) ***n., pl.* -mies** **1.** the study of synonyms **2.** a list or listing of synonyms, esp. one in which the terms are discriminated from one another **3.** the quality of being synonymous; sameness or near sameness of meaning

syn·op·sis (si näp′sis) ***n., pl.* -ses** (-sēz) [LL. < Gr. < *syn-*, together + *opsis*, a seeing] a short outline or review of the main points, as of a story; summary

syn·op·size (-sīz) ***vt.* -sized, -siz·ing** to make a synopsis of

syn·op·tic (-tik) ***adj.*** **1.** of or giving a synopsis, summary, or general view **2.** giving an account from the same point of view: said esp. [*often* S-] of the first three Gospels Also **syn·op′ti·cal** —**syn·op′ti·cal·ly *adv.***

syn·o·vi·a (si nō′vē ə) ***n.*** [ModL. < ?] the clear, albuminous lubricating fluid secreted by the membranes of joint cavities, tendon sheaths, etc. —**syn·o′vi·al *adj.***

syn·tac·tic (sin tak′tik) ***adj.*** of or in accordance with syntax: also **syn·tac′ti·cal** —**syn·tac′ti·cal·ly *adv.***

syn·tax (sin′taks) ***n.*** [< Fr. < LL. < Gr., ult. < *syn-*, together + *tassein*, to arrange] *Gram.* **1.** the arrangement of words as elements in a sentence to show their relationship to one another **2.** the organization and relationship of word groups, phrases, clauses, and sentences; sentence structure **3.** the branch of grammar dealing with this

syn·the·sis (sin′thə sis) ***n., pl.* -ses′** (-sēz′) [Gr. < *syn-*, together + *tithenai*, to place] **1.** the putting together of parts or elements so as to form a whole **2.** a whole formed in this way **3.** *Chem.* the formation of a complex compound by the combining of two or more simpler compounds, elements, or radicals —**syn′the·sist *n.***

syn·the·size (-sīz′) ***vt.* -sized′, -siz′ing** **1.** to bring togeth-

fat, āpe, cär; ten, ēven; is, bīte; gō, hôrn, tōōl, look; oil, out; up, fur; get; joy; yet; chin; she; thin, *th*en; zh, leisure; ŋ, ring; ə for *a* in *ago*, *e* in *agent*, *i* in *sanity*, *o* in *comply*, *u* in *focus*; ′ as in *able* (ā′b'l); Fr. bál; ë, Fr. coeur; ö, Fr. feu; Fr. mon; ô, Fr. coq; ü, Fr. duc; *r*, Fr. cri; H, G. ich; kh, G. doch; ‡foreign; *hypothetical; < derived from. See inside front cover.

er into a whole by synthesis **2.** to form by bringing together separate parts; specif., *Chem.* to produce by synthesis rather than by extraction, refinement, etc.

syn·the·siz·er (-sī′zər) ***n.*** a person or thing that synthesizes; specif., an electronic music device that produces sounds not made by ordinary musical instruments

syn·thet·ic (sin thet′ik) ***adj.*** **1.** of, involving, or using synthesis **2.** produced by synthesis; specif., produced by chemical synthesis, rather than of natural origin **3.** not real or genuine; artificial **4.** using inflection rather than word order and separate words to express syntactic relationships *[Latin is a synthetic language]* Also **syn·thet′i·cal** —***n.*** something synthetic —**syn·thet′i·cal·ly** ***adv.***

synthetic resin any of a large class of complex organic compounds formed from simpler molecules by polymerization, used esp. in making plastics

syph·i·lis (sif′ə lis) ***n.*** [ModL. < *Syphilus,* hero of a Latin poem (1530)] a disease, caused by a spirochete and usually passed on during sexual intercourse or gotten in the womb before birth —**syph′i·lit′ic** ***adj., n.***

sy·phon (sī′fən) ***n., vi., vt.*** *var. sp. of* SIPHON

Syr. **1.** Syria **2.** Syriac **3.** Syrian

Syr·a·cuse (sir′ə kyo͞os′, -kyo͞oz′) **1.** [after ff.] city in C N.Y.: pop. 170,000 (met. area 643,000) **2.** seaport on the SE coast of Sicily: pop. 105,000

Syr·i·a (sir′ē ə) **1.** region of ancient times at the E end of the Mediterranean **2.** country in the NW part of this region: 71,227 sq. mi.; pop. 6,451,000; cap. Damascus

Syr·i·ac (sir′ē ak′) ***n.*** the ancient Aramaic language of Syria, used from the 3d cent. to the 13th

Syr·i·an (sir′ē ən) ***adj.*** of Syria, its people, their language, etc. —***n.*** **1.** a member of the Semitic people of Syria **2.** their modern Arabic dialect

sy·rin·ga (sə riŋ′gə) ***n.*** [ModL., genus name < Gr. *syrinx* (see ff.): from former use in making pipes] **1.** *same as* LILAC (senses 1 & 2) **2.** *earlier name for* MOCK ORANGE

sy·ringe (sə rinj′, sir′inj) ***n.*** [< ML. < Gr. *syrinx* (gen. *syringos*), a reed, pipe] **1.** a device consisting of a narrow tube fitted at one end with a rubber bulb or piston by means of which a liquid can be drawn in and then pushed out in a stream: used to inject fluids into, or extract fluids from, body cavities, to cleanse wounds, etc. **2.** *short for* HYPODERMIC SYRINGE —***vt.*** **-ringed′, -ring′ing** to cleanse, inject, etc. with a syringe

SYRINGE

syr·inx (sir′iŋks) ***n., pl.*** **sy·rin·ges** (sə rin′jēz), **syr′inx·es** [ModL. < Gr., a pipe] **1.** the vocal organ of songbirds, at or near the base of the trachea **2.** *same as* PANPIPE

syr·up (sir′əp, sur′-) ***n.*** [< OFr. < ML. < Ar. *sharāb,* a drink] any sweet, thick liquid; specif., *a)* a solution made by boiling sugar with water and, often, flavored *b)* any such solution used in preparing medicines *c) short for* MAPLE SYRUP, CORN SYRUP, etc. —**syr′up·y** ***adj.***

sys·tem (sis′təm) ***n.*** [< LL. < Gr. *systēma,* ult. < *syn-,* together + *histanai,* to set] **1.** a group of things or parts working together or connected in some way so as to form a whole *[a solar system,* school *system, system* of highways*]* **2.** a set of principles, rules, etc. linked in an orderly way to show a logical plan *[an economic system]* **3.** a method or plan of classification or arrangement **4.** *a)* an established way of doing something; method; procedure *b)* orderliness or methodical planning in one's way of proceeding **5.** *a)* the body considered as a functioning organism *b)* a number of organs acting together to perform one of the main bodily functions *[the nervous system]* **6.** a related series of natural objects or elements, as rivers **7.** *Geol.* a major division of stratified rocks comprising the rocks laid down during a period

sys·tem·at·ic (sis′tə mat′ik) ***adj.*** **1.** based on or forming a system **2.** according to a system, method, or plan; regular; orderly **3.** orderly in planning or doing things; methodical **4.** of or having to do with classification Also **sys′tem·at′i·cal** —**sys′tem·at′i·cal·ly** ***adv.***

sys·tem·a·tize (sis′təm ə tīz′) ***vt.*** **-tized′, -tiz′ing** to form into a system; arrange according to a system; make systematic —**sys′tem·a·ti·za′tion** ***n.*** —**sys′tem·a·tiz′er** ***n.***

sys·tem·ic (sis tem′ik) ***adj.*** of a system; specif., *Physiol.* of or affecting the entire organism or bodily system —***n.*** any of a group of pesticides that are absorbed into the tissues of plants, making the plants poisonous to insects, etc. that feed on them —**sys·tem′i·cal·ly** ***adv.***

sys·tem·ize (sis′tə mīz′) ***vt.*** **-ized′, -iz′ing** *same as* SYSTEMATIZE —**sys′tem·i·za′tion** ***n.***

systems analysis an engineering technique that breaks down complex technical, social, etc. problems into basic elements whose interrelations are evaluated and programmed into a complete and integrated system —**systems analyst**

systems engineering a branch of engineering using computer science, facts from systems-analysis studies, etc. to design integrated operational systems for specific organizations —**systems engineer**

sys·to·le (sis′tə lē′) ***n.*** [ModL. < Gr. *systolē,* ult. < *syn-,* together + *stellein,* to send] the usual rhythmic contraction of the heart, esp. of the ventricles, during which the blood is driven onward from the chambers —**sys·tol·ic** (sis täl′ik) ***adj.***

Szcze·cin (shche tsēn′) river port in NW Poland, on the Oder: pop. 335,000

T

T, t (tē) ***n., pl.*** **T's, t's** **1.** the twentieth letter of the English alphabet **2.** the sound of *T* or *t*

T (tē) ***n.*** an object shaped like T —***adj.*** shaped like T —**to a T** to perfection; exactly

't it: a contraction, as in *'twas, do't*

-t *var. of* -ED (in some past participles and adjectives derived from them) *[slept, gilt]*

T. **1.** tablespoon(s) **2.** Territory **3.** Testament **4.** Tuesday

t. **1.** teaspoon(s) **2.** temperature **3.** tense **4.** time **5.** ton(s) **6.** town(ship) **7.** transitive **8.** troy

ta (tä) ***interj.*** [Brit.] thank you: orig. a child's term

Ta *Chem.* tantalum

tab¹ (tab) ***n.*** [< ?] **1.** a small, flat loop or strap fastened to something for pulling it, hanging it up, etc. **2.** an attached or projecting piece of a card or paper, useful in filing —***vt.*** **tabbed, tab′bing** **1.** to provide with tabs **2.** to choose or select

tab² (tab) ***n.*** [prob. < TABULATE] [Colloq.] **1.** a bill or check, as for expenses **2.** total cost or expenses —**keep tabs** (or **a tab**) **on** [Colloq.] to follow or watch every move of; check on —**pick up the tab** [Colloq.] to pay the bill or total cost

tab³ (tab) ***n.*** *shortened form of:* **1.** TABLET **2.** TABULATOR —***vt.*** **tabbed, tab′bing** *shortened form of* TABULATE

tab. table(s)

tab·ard (tab′ərd) ***n.*** [OFr. *tabart*] **1.** a loose, heavy jacket worn outdoors as by peasants in the Middle Ages **2.** a short-sleeved, blazoned cloak worn by a knight over his armor **3.** a herald's official coat, blazoned with his lord's arms

Ta·bas·co (tə bas′kō) [< *Tabasco,* a Mexican state] *a trademark for* a hot sauce made from a kind of red pepper

tab·by (tab′ē) ***n., pl.*** **-bies** [< Fr. < ML. < Ar. *'attābi,* quarter of Baghdad where it was made] **1.** a silk taffeta with wavy markings **2.** a gray or brown cat with dark stripes **3.** any pet cat, esp. a female —***adj.*** having dark stripes over gray or brown

tab·er·nac·le (tab′ər nak′′l) ***n.*** [< LL. < L. *tabernaculum,* a tent, dim. of *taberna,* a hut] **1.** formerly, a temporary shelter, as a tent **2.** [T-] *a)* the portable sanctuary carried by the Jews in their wanderings from Egypt to Palestine: Ex. 25–27 *b)* later, the Jewish Temple **3.** a shrine, niche, etc. with a canopy **4.** a place of worship, esp. one seating many people **5.** a cabinetlike enclosure on an altar, for consecrated Hosts —***vi.*** **-led, -ling** to dwell temporarily —***vt.*** to place in a tabernacle —**tab′er·nac′u·lar** (-yə lər) ***adj.***

ta·bes dor·sa·lis (tā′bēz dôr sā′lis, -sal′is) [ModL. < L. *tabes,* a wasting away + *dorsualis,* of the back] a chronic disease of the nervous system, usually caused by syphilis and characterized by loss of reflexes and of muscular coordination, etc.

ta·ble (tā′b′l) ***n.*** [OFr. < L. *tabula,* a board, tablet] **1.** orig., a thin slab of metal, stone, or wood, used for inscriptions; tablet **2.** *a)* a piece of furniture consisting of a flat, horizontal top set on legs *b)* such a table set with food for a meal *c)* food served at table *d)* the people seated at a table **3.** a large, flat-topped piece of furniture or equipment used for games, as a working surface, etc. *[pool table,* examining *table]* **4.** *a)* a compact, orderly list of details, contents, etc. *b)* a compact, orderly arrangement of facts, figures, etc., usually in rows and columns *[*the multiplication *table]* **5.** *same as* TABLELAND **6.** any of various flat surfaces, layers, or parts, as the upper, flat facet of a gem *—adj.* **1.** of, for, or on a table **2.** fit for serving at table *[table* salt*]* *—vt.* **-bled, -bling 1.** orig., to tabulate **2.** to put on a table **3.** to set aside the consideration of (a motion, bill, etc.) **4.** [Brit.] to put up for consideration **—at table** at a meal **—on the table** postponed or shelved: said of a bill, etc. **—the tables** laws, as the Ten Commandments, inscribed on flat stone slabs **—turn the tables** to reverse a situation completely **—under the table** [Colloq.] **1.** secretly, as a bribe **2.** drunk to the point of unconsciousness

tab·leau (tab′lō, ta blō′) *n., pl.* **-leaux** (-lōz, -blōz′), **-leaus** [Fr. < OFr. *tablel,* dim. of *table:* see prec.] **1.** a striking, dramatic scene or picture **2.** a representation of a scene, picture, etc. by a person or group posed in costume

ta·ble·cloth (tā′b'l klôth′, -kläth′) *n.* a cloth for covering a table, esp. at meals

ta·ble d'hôte (tä′b'l dōt′, tab′'l) *pl.* **ta′bles d'hôte′** (-b'lz, -'lz) [Fr., lit., table of the host] a complete meal with courses as specified, served at a restaurant or hotel for a set price: distinguished from ALA CARTE

ta·ble-hop (tā′b'l häp′) *vi.* **-hopped′, -hop′ping** to leave one's table in a restaurant, etc. and visit about at other tables **—ta′ble-hop′per** *n.*

ta·ble·land (-land′) *n.* a high, broad, level region; plateau

table linen tablecloths, napkins, etc.

ta·ble·spoon (-spo͞on′) *n.* **1.** *a)* a large spoon used for serving at table *b) same as* SOUPSPOON **2.** a spoon used as a measuring unit in cookery, equal to 3 teaspoonfuls or 1/2 fluid ounce **3.** *same as* TABLESPOONFUL

ta·ble·spoon·ful (-fo͝ol) *n., pl.* **-fuls** as much as a tablespoon will hold

tab·let (tab′lit) *n.* [< MFr. dim. of *table:* see TABLE] **1.** a flat, thin piece of stone, metal, etc., esp. one with an inscription **2.** a smooth, flat leaf of wood, metal, etc., used to write on **3.** a writing pad containing sheets of paper fastened at one edge **4.** a small, flat piece of some hard substance, as medicine, soap, etc.

table tennis a game somewhat like tennis in miniature, played on a table, with a small celluloid or plastic ball and short-handled, wooden paddles

ta·ble·ware (tā′b'l wer′) *n.* dishes, glassware, silverware, etc. for use at table

Tab·loid (tab′loid) [TABL(ET) + -OID] *a trademark for* a small tablet of medicine *—n.* **[t-]** a newspaper with pages about half the ordinary size, carrying many pictures and short, often sensational, news stories *—adj.* **[t-]** condensed; short

ta·boo (ta bo͞o′, tə-) *n.* [Tongan *tabu*] **1.** *a)* among some Polynesian peoples, a sacred prohibition which makes certain people or things untouchable, unmentionable, etc. *b)* the system of such prohibitions **2.** any social restriction resulting from convention or tradition *—adj.* **1.** sacred and forbidden by taboo **2.** forbidden by tradition, etc. *—vt.* **1.** to put under taboo **2.** to prohibit or forbid

ta·bor (tā′bər) *n.* [OFr. *tabur* < Per. *tabīrah*] a small drum, formerly used by a fife player to beat out his own rhythmic accompaniment Also sp. **ta′bour**

tab·o·ret (tab′ər it, tab′ə ret′) *n.* [OFr., a stool, dim. of *tabur:* see prec.] **1.** a small tabor **2.** a stool Also sp. **tab′ou·ret**

Ta·briz (tȧ brēz′) city in NW Iran: pop. 468,000

ta·bu (ta bo͞o′, tə-) *n., adj., vt. var. sp. of* TABOO

tab·u·lar (tab′yə lər) *adj.* [< L. < *tabula:* see TABLE] **1.** flat like a table **2.** *a)* of or arranged in tables or columns *b)* calculated by using tables **—tab′u·lar·ly** *adv.*

tab·u·late (tab′yə lāt′; *for adj.* -lit) *vt.* **-lat′ed, -lat′ing** [< L. *tabula* (see TABLE) + -ATE[1]] to put (facts, statistics, etc.) in a table or columns; arrange systematically *—adj.* having a flat surface **—tab′u·la′tion** *n.*

tab·u·la·tor (-lāt′ər) *n.* a person or thing that tabulates; specif., a device or key for setting stops on a typewriter carriage, as for typing columns

tac·a·ma·hac (tak′ə mə hak′) *n.* [< Sp. < Nahuatl *tecomahca*] **1.** a strong-smelling gum resin used in ointments and incenses **2.** any of several trees yielding this resin

ta·chom·e·ter (ta käm′ə tər, tə-) *n.* [< Gr. *tachos,* speed + -METER] a device that indicates or measures the revolutions per minute of a revolving shaft **—ta·chom′e·try** *n.*

tac·it (tas′it) *adj.* [< Fr. < L. pp. of *tacere,* to be silent] **1.** making no sound; saying nothing **2.** unspoken; silent **3.** not expressed openly, but implied or understood *[tacit* approval*]* **—tac′it·ly** *adv.* **—tac′it·ness** *n.*

tac·i·turn (tas′ə turn′) *adj.* [< Fr. < L. < *tacere:* see prec.] almost always silent; not liking to talk **—tac′i·tur′ni·ty** *n.* **—tac′i·turn′ly** *adv.*

Tac·i·tus (tas′ə təs), **(Publius Cornelius)** 55?–117? A.D.; Rom. historian

tack (tak) *n.* [MDu. *tacke,* a twig, point] **1.** a short nail or pin with a sharp point and a somewhat large, flat head **2.** *a)* a fastening, esp. in a slight or temporary way *b) Sewing* a stitch for marking darts, etc. from a pattern, clipped and later removed: in full, **tailor's tack** *c)* stickiness **3.** a zigzag course, or movement in such a course **4.** a course of action or policy **5.** *Naut. a)* a rope for holding securely the forward lower corner of some sails *b)* the corner thus held *c)* the direction in which a ship is moving in relation to the position of the sails *d)* a change of direction made by changing the position of the sails *e)* a course against the wind *f)* any of a series of zigzag movements in such a course **6.** a horse's equipment, as saddles, bridles, etc. *—vt.* **1.** to fasten with tacks **2.** to attach temporarily, as with long stitches **3.** to attach as a supplement *[*to *tack* an amendment onto a bill*]* **4.** *Naut. a)* to change the course of (a ship) by turning its head to the wind *b)* to maneuver (a ship) against the wind by a series of tacks *—vi.* **1.** *a)* to tack a ship *b)* to change its course by being tacked: said of a ship **2.** to go in a zigzag course **3.** to change suddenly one's course of action **—tack′er** *n.*

WIND

TACKING

tack·le (tak′'l; *in nautical usage, often* tā′k'l) *n.* [MDu. *takel,* pulley, rope] **1.** apparatus; equipment; gear *[*fishing *tackle]* **2.** a system of ropes and pulleys, used to lower, raise, or move weights **3.** the act or an instance of tackling, as in football **4.** *Football* the player next to either end on the offensive or defensive line **5.** *Naut.* the running rigging and pulleys used to operate a ship's sails *—vt.* **tack′led, tack′ling 1.** to fasten by means of tackle **2.** to harness (a horse) **3.** to take hold of; seize **4.** to undertake to do, solve, or deal with *[*to *tackle* a problem*]* **5.** *Football* to stop or throw (an opponent carrying the ball) *—vi. Football* to tackle an opponent **—tack′ler** *n.*

tack·y[1] (tak′ē) *adj.* **tack′i·er, tack′i·est** [TACK (*n.* 2) + -Y[2]] sticky, as varnish, glue, etc. before completely dry **—tack′i·ness** *n.*

tack·y[2] (tak′ē) *adj.* **tack′i·er, tack′i·est** [< *tacky,* a hillbilly < ?] [Colloq.] dowdy or shabby, as in appearance **—tack′i·ness** *n.*

ta·co (tä′kō) *n., pl.* **-cos** [AmSp.] a Mexican dish consisting of a fried, folded tortilla filled with chopped meat, shredded lettuce, etc.

Ta·co·ma (tə kō′mə) [AmInd., lit., snowy peak] seaport in W Wash., on Puget Sound: pop. 159,000

tac·o·nite (tak′ə nīt′) *n.* [< *Taconic* Range in Vt. and Mass., where such rock strata were first identified] a low-grade iron ore that is pelletized for blast-furnace reduction

tact (takt) *n.* [Fr. < L. pp. of *tangere,* to touch] a sense of the right thing to say or do without offending; skill in dealing with people

tact·ful (takt′fəl) *adj.* having or showing tact **—tact′ful·ly** *adv.* **—tact′ful·ness** *n.*

tac·tic (tak′tik) *n.* [< ModL. < Gr.: see TACTICS] **1.** *same as* TACTICS **2.** a detail or branch of tactics

tac·ti·cal (tak′ti k'l) *adj.* **1.** of or having to do with tactics, esp. in military or naval maneuvers **2.** characterized by or showing skill in tactics **—tac′ti·cal·ly** *adv.*

tac·ti·cian (tak tish′ən) *n.* an expert in tactics

tac·tics (tak′tiks) *n.pl.* [Gr. (*ta*) *taktika,* lit., (the) matters of arrangement < *tassein,* to arrange] **1.** *a)* [*with sing. v.*] the science of maneuvering military and naval forces in action, esp. with reference to short-range objectives *b)* actions in accord with this science **2.** any methods used to gain an end; esp., skillful methods

tac·tile (tak′t'l; *chiefly Brit.* -tīl) *adj.* [Fr. < L. *tactilis* < *tangere,* to touch] **1.** that can be perceived by the touch; tangible **2.** of, having, or related to the sense of touch **—tac·til′i·ty** (-til′ə tē) *n.*

tact·less (takt′lis) *adj.* not having or showing tact **—tact′less·ly** *adv.* **—tact′less·ness** *n.*

tad·pole (tad′pōl′) *n.* [ME. *tadde,* toad + *poll,* head] the larva of certain amphibians, as frogs and toads, having gills and a tail and living in water

Ta·dzhik Soviet Socialist Republic (tä′jik) republic of the U.S.S.R., in C Asia: 55,250 sq. mi.; pop. 2,900,000; cap. Dushanbe: also **Ta·dzhik·i·stan** (tä jēk′i stän′)

tael (tāl) *n.* [Port. < Malay *tahil,* a weight] **1.** any of various units of weight of E Asia **2.** formerly, a Chinese unit of money

ta'en (tān) [Poet.] taken

taf·fe·ta (taf′i tə) ***n.*** [< OFr., ult. < Per. < *tāftan,* to weave] a fine, rather stiff fabric of silk, nylon, acetate, etc., with a sheen —***adj.*** like or made of taffeta

taff·rail (taf′rāl′) ***n.*** [< Du. *tafereel,* a panel, ult. < L. *tabula:* see TABLE] the rail around a ship's stern

taf·fy (taf′ē) ***n.*** [< ?] a chewy candy made of sugar or molasses boiled down and pulled: cf. TOFFEE

Taft (taft), **William Howard** 1857–1930; 27th president of the U.S. (1909–13); chief justice of the U.S. (1921–30)

tag (tag) ***n.*** [prob. < Scand.] **1.** orig., a hanging end, as on a torn skirt **2.** any hanging part or loosely attached end **3.** a hard-tipped end, as of metal, on a cord or lace **4.** a card, paper, ticket, etc. attached to something as a label or for identification, etc. **5.** an epithet **6.** the sentence or sentences ending a speech, story, play, etc. **7.** a children's game in which one player, called "it," chases the others until he touches, or tags, one of them, making him "it" in turn —***vt.* tagged, tag′ging 1.** to provide with a tag; put a tag on **2.** to identify by an epithet **3.** to choose or select **4.** to overtake and touch as in the game of tag **5.** *Baseball* to touch (a base runner) with the ball, thus putting him out **6.** [Colloq.] to follow close behind —***vi.*** [Colloq.] to follow close behind a person or thing (usually with *along, after,* etc.) —**tag′ger *n.***

Ta·ga·log (tä gä′läg, -lôg) ***n.*** **1.** *pl.* **-logs, -log** a member of a Malayan people of the Philippine Islands **2.** their Indonesian language

Ta·gore (tä′gôr, tə gôr′), Sir **Ra·bin·dra·nath** (rə bēn′drə nät′) 1861–1941; Hindu poet

Ta·gus (tā′gəs) river flowing west across C Spain & Portugal into the Atlantic

Ta·hi·ti (tə hēt′ē, tä-) chief island of the Society Islands, in the South Pacific —**Ta·hi·ti·an** (tə hēsh′ən, tä-; -hēt′ē ən) ***adj., n.***

Ta·hoe (tä′hō), **Lake** [< AmInd. *tah-oo,* lake] lake on the border between Calif. & Nev.: a summer resort

Tai (tī) ***n., adj.*** *same as* THAI

tail[1] (tāl) ***n.*** [OE. *tægel*] **1.** the rear end of an animal's body, esp. when forming a distinct, flexible appendage to the trunk **2.** anything like an animal's tail in form or position [the *tail* of a shirt] **3.** a luminous train behind a comet **4.** the hind, last, bottom, or inferior part of anything **5.** [*often pl.*] the reverse side of a coin **6.** a long tress of hair **7.** *a)* the rear section of an aircraft, rocket, or missile *b)* a set of stabilizing planes at the rear of an airplane **8.** [*pl.*] [Colloq.] *a)* a swallow-tailed coat *b)* full-dress attire for men **9.** [Colloq.] a person or vehicle that follows another, esp. in surveillance —***adj.*** **1.** at the rear **2.** from the rear [a *tail* wind] —***vt.*** **1.** to provide with a tail **2.** to form the tail or end of, as a procession **3.** to fasten at or by the tail **4.** to fasten one end of (a brick, board, etc.) into a wall, etc. **5.** [Slang] to follow stealthily —***vi.*** **1.** to become gradually smaller or fainter (with *off* or *away*) **2.** to form, or become part of, a line or tail **3.** [Colloq.] to follow close behind, as in surveillance —**on one's tail** following one closely —**turn tail** to run from danger, difficulty, etc. —**tail′less *adj.*** —**tail′like′ *adj.***

tail[2] (tāl) ***n.*** [< OFr. < *taillier:* see TAILOR] *same as* ENTAIL (*n.* 2 & 3) —***adj.*** limited in a specific way as to inheritance

tailed (tāld) ***adj.*** having a (specified kind of) tail: usually in combination [*bobtailed*]

tail·gate (tāl′gāt′) ***n.*** a board or gate at the back of a wagon, truck, station wagon, etc.: it can be removed or swung down for loading, etc.: also **tail′board′** —***vi., vt.* -gat′ed, -gat′ing** to drive too closely behind (another vehicle) —**tail′gat′-er *n.***

TAILGATE

tail·ing (-iŋ) ***n.*** **1.** [*pl.*] refuse left in milling, mining, etc. **2.** the part of a projecting brick, stone, etc. fastened into a wall

tail·light (tāl′līt′) ***n.*** a light, usually red, at the rear of a vehicle to warn vehicles coming from behind

tai·lor (tā′lər) ***n.*** [< OFr. < *taillier,* to cut < LL. *taliare,* to split < L. *talea,* a twig] a person who makes, repairs, or alters clothes —***vi.*** to work as a tailor —***vt.*** **1.** to make (clothes) by tailor's work **2.** to make clothes for **3.** to form, alter, etc. so as to meet certain conditions [a novel *tailored* to popular taste] **4.** to fashion (women's garments) with trim, simple lines —**tai′lor·ing *n.***

tai·lor·bird (-burd′) ***n.*** any of several small Asiatic and African birds that stitch leaves together to camouflage and hold their nests

tai·lored (tā′lərd) ***adj.*** having trim, simple lines, as some women's garments, or specially fitted, as slipcovers

tai·lor-made (tā′lər mād′) ***adj.*** made by or as by a tailor; specif., *a)* having trim, simple lines; tailored *b)* made-to-order or handmade, rather than by machine in a factory

tail·piece (tāl′pēs′) ***n.*** **1.** a part forming the end of something **2.** the piece of wood at the lower end of a violin, etc., to which the strings are attached **3.** a short beam with one end tailed in a wall and the other supported by a header **4.** *Printing* an ornamental design at the end of a chapter, etc.

tail·pipe (-pīp′) ***n.*** **1.** an exhaust pipe at the rear of an automotive vehicle **2.** the exhaust duct of a jet engine

tail·race (-rās′) ***n.*** the lower part of a millrace, through which water flows after going over a water wheel

tail·spin (-spin′) ***n.*** **1.** *same as* SPIN (*n.* 4): also **tail spin** **2.** a state of rapidly increasing depression or confusion

tail wind a wind blowing in the same direction as the course of a ship or aircraft

taint (tānt) ***vt.*** [prob. a merging of ME. *taynten,* to touch + Anglo-Fr. *teinter,* to color, ult. < L. *tingere,* to wet] **1.** to affect with something injurious, unpleasant, etc.; spoil; infect **2.** to make morally corrupt —***vi.*** to become tainted —***n.*** **1.** a trace of corruption, disgrace, etc. **2.** an infectious or contaminating trace —**taint′less *adj.***

Tai·pei, Tai·peh (tī′pe′) capital of Taiwan, in the N part: pop. 1,700,000

Tai·wan (tī′wän′) island province of China, off the SE coast: seat of the Kuomintang government: 13,885 sq. mi.; pop. 14,964,000; cap. Taipei —**Tai′wan′i·an *adj., n.***

Tai·yü·an (tī′yü än′) city in N China: pop. 1,500,000

Taj Ma·hal (täzh′ mə häl′, täj′) mausoleum at Agra, India, built (1630?–48?) by a Mogul emperor for his favorite wife

ta·ka (tä′kä) ***n.,*** *pl.* **-ka** [< Sans. *ṭŏnkŏ,* silver coins] *see* MONETARY UNITS, table (Bangladesh)

take (tāk) ***vt.* took, tak′en, tak′ing** [OE. *tacan* < ON. *taka*] **1.** to get possession of by force or skill; capture, seize, etc. **2.** *a)* to win (a game, a trick at cards, etc.) *b)* to capture (an opponent's piece in chess or checkers) **3.** to get hold of; grasp or catch **4.** to affect; attack [*taken* with a fit] **5.** to capture the fancy of **6.** to obtain, acquire, assume, etc. **7.** to get into one's hand or hold **8.** to eat, drink, etc. for nourishment or as medicine **9.** to enter into a special relationship with [to *take* a wife] **10.** to rent, lease, etc. [to *take* a cottage] **11.** to get regularly by paying for [to *take* a newspaper] **12.** to assume as a responsibility, task, etc. [to *take* a job, *take* a vow] **13.** to assume (a symbol of duty or office, etc.) [the president *took* the chair] **14.** to join or support (one side in a contest, disagreement, etc.) **15.** to assume as if granted or due one [to *take* the blame, to *take* deductions] **16.** to get, adopt, etc. by selection or choice **17.** to use [*take* a mop to the floor] **18.** *a)* to travel by [to *take* a bus] *b)* to set out on [*take* that path] **19.** to go to for shelter, safety, etc. [to *take* cover] **20.** to consider [to *take* a matter seriously] **21.** *a)* to occupy [*take* a chair] *b)* to use up [it *took* all day] **22.** to require; need [it *takes* money] **23.** to derive (a name, quality, etc.) from something or someone **24.** to extract, as for quotation [he *took* a verse from the Bible] **25.** to obtain by observation, experiment, etc. [*take* a poll] **26.** to be enrolled as a student in (a course, etc.) **27.** to write down [to *take* notes] **28.** to make (a photograph, picture, etc.) **29.** to make an impression of [*take* his fingerprints] **30.** to win (a prize, etc.) **31.** to undergo [to *take* punishment] **32.** to occupy oneself or engage in [to *take* a nap] **33.** to accept (an offer, bet, etc.) **34.** to have a specified reaction to [to *take* a joke in earnest] **35.** to confront and get over, etc. [the horse *took* the jump] **36.** to be affected by [he *took* cold] **37.** to absorb (a dye, polish, etc.) **38.** to understand **39.** to suppose [he *took* her to be a clerk] **40.** to have or feel (an emotion, etc.) [*take* pity] **41.** to make (an objection, etc.) as the result of thought **42.** to conduct; lead [this path *takes* you home] **43.** to escort [*take* a friend to lunch] **44.** to carry [to *take* a book with one] **45.** to remove as by stealing **46.** to remove by death **47.** to subtract [*take* two from four] **48.** to direct (oneself) **49.** [Colloq.] to aim (a specified action) [he *took* a jab at me] **50.** [Slang] to cheat; trick **51.** *Gram.* to be used with in construction [a transitive verb *takes* an object] —***vi.*** **1.** to get possession **2.** to take root: said of a plant **3.** to catch [the fire *took* rapidly] **4.** to gain public favor; be popular **5.** to be effective in action, etc. [the vaccination *took*] **6.** to detract (*from*) [nothing *took* from the scene's beauty] **7.** to go [to *take* to the hills] **8.** [Colloq. or Dial.] to become (sick) —***n.*** **1.** the act or process of taking **2.** something taken **3.** *a)* the amount taken [the day's *take* of fish] *b)* [Slang] money received; receipts **4.** a movie scene photographed with an uninterrupted run of the camera **5.** a recording or tape of a performance —**on the take** [Slang] willing or seeking to take bribes or illicit income —**take after** **1.** to be, act, or look like **2.** to run after or pursue: also **take out** (or **off**) **after** —**take amiss** to become offended at (an act) as because of a misunderstanding —**take back** to retract (something said, promised, etc.) —**take down** **1.** to take apart **2.** to make less conceited; humble **3.** to put in writing; record —**take five** (or **ten,** etc.) take a five (or ten, etc.) minute break, as from working —**take for** 1. to consider to be 2. to mistake for —**take in** 1. to admit; receive 2. to make smaller 3. to include 4. to understand 5. to cheat; trick 6. to visit [to *take in* the sights] —**take it** [Slang] to withstand hardship, ridicule, etc. —**take it out on** [Colloq.] to make (another) suffer for one's own anger, irritation, etc. —**take off** 1. to go away 2. to deduct 3. to make a copy or likeness of 4. to leave the ground or water in flight: said of an aircraft 5. [Colloq.] to start 6. [Colloq.] to imitate; mimic —**take on** 1. to acquire; assume 2. to employ 3. to undertake (a task, etc.) 4. to play against; oppose 5. [Colloq.] to show violent emotion, esp. anger or sorrow —**take one's time** to be unhurried —**take out** 1. to remove 2. to apply for and get 3. [Colloq.] to escort —**take over** to begin controlling, managing, etc. —**take to** 1. to apply oneself to (work, etc.) 2. to become fond of —**take up** 1. to make tighter or shorter 2. to pay off (a mortgage, note, etc.) 3. to absorb (a liquid) 4. to accept (a challenge, etc.) 5. to become interested in (an occupation, belief, etc.) 6. to occupy (space or time) —**take upon** (or **on**) **oneself** 1. to take the responsibility for 2. to undertake Also **take upon** (or **on**) **one** —**take up with** [Colloq.] to become a friend or companion of —**tak′a·ble, take′a·ble** *adj.* —**tak′er** *n.*

take-home pay (tāk′hōm′) wages or salary after deductions for income tax, social security, etc. have been made

tak·en (tāk′′n) *pp. of* TAKE

take·off (-ôf′) *n.* 1. the act of leaving the ground, as in jumping or flight 2. the place from which one leaves the ground 3. the starting point or early stages of something; specif., *Econ.* the early stages of rapid, self-sustained growth and development 4. [Colloq.] an amusing or mocking imitation; burlesque Also **take′-off′**

take·out (-out′) *n.* a taking out —*adj.* designating or of prepared food sold by a restaurant to be eaten away from the premises Also **take′-out′**

take·o·ver (-ō′vər) *n.* the act of seizing power or assuming control in a nation, organization, etc.: also **take′-o′ver**

tak·ing (-iŋ) *adj.* attractive; winning —*n.* 1. the act of one that takes 2. something taken; catch 3. [*pl.*] earnings; profits —**tak′ing·ly** *adv.*

talc (talk) *n.* [Fr. < Ar. *ṭalq*] 1. a soft mineral, magnesium silicate, used to make talcum powder, lubricants, etc. 2. *shortened form of* TALCUM POWDER —*vt.* **talcked** or **talced, talck′ing** or **talc′ing** to use talc on

tal·cum (powder) (tal′kəm) a powder for the body and face made of powdered, purified talc, usually perfumed

tale (tāl) *n.* [OE. *talu*] 1. something told or related 2. a story of true or fictitious events; narrative 3. a piece of idle or malicious gossip 4. a falsehood; lie

tale·bear·er (-ber′ər) *n.* a person who spreads gossip, tells secrets, etc. —**tale′bear′ing** *adj., n.*

tal·ent (tal′ənt) *n.* [OE. *talente* < L. < Gr. *talanton,* a unit of money, weight] 1. any of various large units of weight or of money in ancient Greece, Rome, the Middle East, etc. 2. any natural ability or power 3. a special, superior ability in an art, science, craft, etc. 4. people who have talent —**tal′ent·ed** *adj.*

talent scout a person whose work is recruiting persons of superior ability in the theater, sports, etc.

ta·ler (tä′lər) *n., pl.* **ta′ler** [G.: see DOLLAR] a former German silver coin

ta·les·man (tālz′mən, tā′lēz-) *n., pl.* **-men** *Law* a person summoned to fill a vacancy in a jury when the regular jury panel lacks the proper number

ta·li (tā′lī) *n. alt. pl. of* TALUS[1]

tal·i·pes (tal′ə pēz′) *n.* [ModL. < L. *talus,* an ankle + *pes,* a foot] *same as* CLUBFOOT

tal·i·pot (tal′ə pät′) *n.* [Beng. *tālipāt,* palm leaf < Sans.] a palm tree of the East Indies, with gigantic leaves used for fans, umbrellas, etc., and seeds used for buttons: also **talipot palm**

tal·is·man (tal′is mən, -iz-) *n., pl.* **-mans** [Fr. < Ar. < MGr. *telesma,* a consecrated object] 1. a ring, stone, etc. bearing engraved figures supposed to bring good luck, keep away evil, etc. 2. anything supposed to have magic power; a charm —**tal′is·man′ic, tal′is·man′i·cal** *adj.*

talk (tôk) *vi.* [ME. *talken,* prob. freq. based on OE. *talian,* to reckon] 1. to put ideas into, or exchange ideas by, spoken words; speak 2. to express ideas by speech substitutes [*talk* by signs] 3. to speak trivially; chatter 4. to gossip 5. to confer; consult 6. to make noises suggestive of speech 7. to reveal secret information 8. to make a somewhat informal speech —*vt.* 1. to put into spoken words 2. to use in speaking [to *talk* Spanish, to *talk* nonsense] 3. to discuss 4. to put into a specified condition by talking [to *talk* oneself hoarse] —*n.* 1. *a)* the act of talking *b)* conversation 2. an informal speech 3. a conference 4. gossip 5. the subject of conversation, gossip, etc. 6. empty, frivolous discussion 7. a particular kind of speech; dialect, etc. 8. sounds, as by an animal, suggestive of speech —**big talk** [Slang] a bragging —**talk back** to answer impertinently —**talk big** [Slang] to boast —**talk down** to silence by talking louder, longer, or more effectively than —**talk down to** to talk to (a person) as if he were one's inferior in rank, intellect, etc. —**talk into** to persuade (someone) to do something —**talk out of** to dissuade (someone) from doing something —**talk over** 1. to discuss 2. to persuade (a person) by talking —**talk up** 1. to promote or praise in discussion 2. to speak loudly, boldly, etc. —**talk′er** *n.*

talk·a·thon (tôk′ə thän′) *n.* [TALK + (MAR)ATHON] any prolonged period of talking

talk·a·tive (-tiv) *adj.* talking, or fond of talking, a great deal; loquacious —**talk′a·tive·ness** *n.*

talking book a recording of a reading of a book, etc. for use esp. by the blind

talking picture *earlier name for* a motion picture with a synchronized sound track: also [Colloq.] **talk′ie** (-ē) *n.*

talking point a persuasive point to be emphasized, as in presenting an argument

talk·ing-to (tôk′iŋ to͞o′) *n.* [Colloq.] a rebuke; scolding

talk·y (tôk′ē) *adj.* 1. talkative 2. containing too much talk, or dialogue [a *talky* novel] —**talk′i·ness** *n.*

tall (tôl) *adj.* [< OE. (*ge*)*tæl,* swift] 1. of more than normal height or stature 2. having a specified height [five feet *tall*] 3. [Colloq.] hard to believe; exaggerated [a *tall* tale] 4. [Colloq.] large [a *tall* drink] —**tall′ish** *adj.* —**tall′ness** *n.*

Tal·la·has·see (tal′ə has′ē) [< Creek Indian name] capital of Fla., in the N part: pop. 82,000

Tal·ley·rand (tal′ē rand′; *Fr.* tȧ lā rän′) (born *Charles Maurice de Talleyrand-Périgord*) 1754–1838; Fr. statesman

Tal·linn (tȧl′lin) capital of the Estonian S.S.R., on the Gulf of Finland: pop. 363,000: also sp. **Tallin**

tal·lit, tal·lith (tä lēt′, täl′is) *n.* [< LHeb. < *ṭālal,* to cover] *Judaism* a fringed shawl worn by men during morning prayer: cf. Deut. 22:12

tal·low (tal′ō) *n.* [prob. < MLowG. *talg*] the pale yellow solid fat extracted from the natural fat of cattle, sheep, etc., used in making candles, soaps, lubricants, etc. —*vt.* to cover or smear with tallow —**tal′low·y** *adj.*

tal·ly (tal′ē) *n., pl.* **-lies** [Anglo-L. *talia* < L. *talea,* a stick] 1. *a)* orig., a stick with notches representing the amount of a debt *b)* anything used as a record for an account or score 2. an account, reckoning, or score 3. *a)* either of two corresponding parts; counterpart *b)* agreement; correspondence 4. an identifying tag or label —*vt.* **-lied, -ly·ing** 1. to put on or as on a tally 2. to count (usually with *up*) 3. to put a label or tag on —*vi.* 1. to tally something 2. to score a point or points in a game 3. to agree; correspond

tal·ly·ho (tal′ē hō′; *for n. & v.,* tal′ē hō′) *interj.* [altered < Fr. *taiaut*] the cry of a hunter on sighting the fox —*n., pl.* **-hos′** 1. a cry of "tallyho" 2. a coach drawn by four horses —*vi.* to cry "tallyho"

Tal·mud (täl′mood, tal′-; -məd) *n.* [LHeb. *talmūdh,* lit., learning < *lāmadh,* to learn] the writings constituting the Jewish civil and religious law —**Tal·mud′ic, Tal·mud′i·cal** *adj.* —**Tal′mud·ism** *n.* —**Tal′mud·ist** *n.*

tal·on (tal′ən) *n.* [< OFr., ult. < L. *talus,* an ankle] 1. the claw of a bird of prey, or, sometimes, of an animal 2. a human finger or hand when like a claw in appearance or grasp —**tal′oned** *adj.*

ta·lus[1] (tā′ləs) *n., pl.* **-lus·es, -li** (-lī) [ModL. < L., an ankle] 1. the anklebone 2. the entire ankle

ta·lus[2] (tā′ləs) *n.* [Fr. < OFr. *talu* < L. *talutium,* surface indication of gold under the earth] 1. a slope 2. the sloping face of a wall in a fortification 3. a pile of rock debris at the foot of a cliff or below a rock face

tam (tam) *n. short for* TAM-O'-SHANTER

ta·ma·le (tə mä′lē) *n.* [< MexSp. < Nahuatl *tamalli*] a native Mexican food of minced meat and red peppers rolled in cornmeal, wrapped in corn husks, and cooked by baking, steaming, etc.

tam·a·rack (tam′ə rak′) *n.* [< Algonquian] 1. an American larch tree, usually found in swamps 2. its wood

tam·a·rind (tam′ə rind) *n.* [< Sp. < Ar. *tamr hindī,* date of India] 1. a tropical leguminous tree with yellow flowers and brown pods with an acid pulp 2. its fruit, used in foods, medicine, etc.

tam·ba·la (täm bä′lä) *n., pl.* **ma′tam·ba′la** (mä′-) [native term, lit., rooster] *see* MONETARY UNITS, table (Malawi)

tam·bour (tam′boor) *n.* [< MFr. < OFr. < Ar. *ṭanbūr,* stringed instrument < Per.] 1. a drum 2. an embroidery frame of two hoops, one closely fitting inside the other, that hold the cloth stretched between them 3. a door, panel, etc. as in a cabinet, made of narrow, wooden slats that glide flexibly in grooves, as around curves —*vt., vi.* to embroider on a tambour

tam·bou·rine (tam′bə rēn′) ***n.*** [Fr., dim. of *tambour:* see TAMBOUR] a shallow, single-headed hand drum having jingling metal disks in the rim: played by shaking, hitting with the knuckles, etc. **—tam′bou·rin′ist *n.***

TAMBOURINE

tame (tām) ***adj.*** **tam′er, tam′est** [OE. *tam*] **1.** changed from a wild state, as an animal, for use by man **2.** gentle; docile **3.** crushed as by domestication; submissive **4.** without force or spirit; dull *—vt.* **tamed, tam′ing 1.** to make tame, or domestic **2.** to make gentle, docile, or spiritless **3.** to make less intense; soften *—vi.* to become tame **—tam′a·ble, tame′a·ble *adj.* —tame′ly *adv.* —tame′ness *n.* —tam′er *n.***

tame·less (-lis) ***adj.*** **1.** not tamed **2.** not tamable

Tam·er·lane (tam′ər lān′) [< *Timur lenk,* Timur the lame] 1336?–1405; Mongol warrior whose conquests extended from the Black Sea to the upper Ganges

Tam·il (tam′'l, täm′-, tum′-) ***n.*** **1.** *pl.* **-ils, -il** any of a Tamil-speaking people of S India and N Ceylon **2.** the Dravidian language of the Tamils, ancient or modern

Tam·ma·ny (tam′ə nē) ***n.*** [altered < *Tamanend,* a 17th-c. Am. Indian chief] a powerful Democratic political organization of New York City, incorporated in 1789: also **Tammany Society, Tammany Hall** *—adj.* of Tammany's practices, members, etc.

Tam·muz (tä′mooz) ***n.*** [Heb.] the tenth month of the Jewish year: see JEWISH CALENDAR

tam-o'-shan·ter (tam′ə shan′tər) ***n.*** [< main character of R. Burns's poem "Tam o'Shanter"] a Scottish cap with a round, flat top and, often, a center tassel

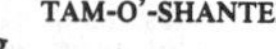
TAM-O'-SHANTER

tamp (tamp) ***vt.*** [< ? TAMPION] **1.** in blasting, to pack clay, sand, etc. around the charge in (the drill hole) **2.** to pack or pound (*down*) by a series of blows or taps

Tam·pa (tam′pə) [< AmInd. village name] seaport in WC Fla., on an arm **(Tampa Bay)** of the Gulf of Mexico: pop. 272,000 (met. area, incl. St. Petersburg, 1,550,000)

tamp·er[1] (tam′pər) ***n.*** a person or thing that tamps; specif., any of various tools for tamping

tam·per[2] (tam′pər) ***vi.*** [var. of TEMPER] [Archaic] to plot; scheme **—tamper with 1.** to make secret, illegal arrangements with, as by bribing **2.** to meddle with, esp. so as to damage, etc. **—tam′per·er *n.***

Tam·pi·co (tam pē′kō; *Sp.* täm pē′kô) seaport in E Mexico, on the Gulf of Mexico: pop. 196,000

tam·pi·on (tam′pē ən) ***n.*** [< Fr. *tampon* < *tapon,* a bung < Frank.] a plug or stopper put in the muzzle of a gun not in use

tam·pon (tam′pän) ***n.*** [Fr.: see prec.] a plug of cotton or other absorbent material put into a body cavity, wound, etc. to stop bleeding or absorb secretions *—vt.* to put a tampon into

tan (tan) ***n.*** [MFr. < ML. *tannum*] **1.** *same as* TANBARK **2.** tannin or a solution made from it **3.** *a)* a yellowish-brown color *b)* such a color given to fair skin as by exposure to the sun *—adj.* **tan′ner, tan′nest** yellowish-brown *—vt.* **tanned, tan′ning 1.** to change (hide) into leather by soaking in tannin **2.** to produce a tan color in, as by exposure to the sun **3.** [Colloq.] to whip severely; flog *—vi.* to become tanned

tan tangent

tan·a·ger (tan′ə jər) ***n.*** [ModL. *tanagra* < Port. < Tupi *tangara*] any of various small, new-world songbirds: the males usually are brilliantly colored

tan·bark (tan′bärk′) ***n.*** any bark containing tannin, used to tan hides and, after the tannin has been extracted, to cover circus rings, etc.

tan·dem (tan′dəm) ***adv.*** [orig. punning use of L. *tandem,* at length (of time)] one behind another; in single file *—n.* **1.** a two-wheeled carriage drawn by horses harnessed tandem **2.** a team, as of horses, harnessed tandem **3.** a bicycle with two seats and sets of pedals placed tandem **4.** a relationship between two persons or things involving cooperative action, mutual dependence, etc. *[to work in tandem] —adj.* having two parts or things placed tandem

Ta·ney (tô′nē), **Roger B(rooke)** 1777–1864; U.S. jurist; chief justice of the U.S. (1836–64)

tang (taŋ) ***n.*** [ON. *tangi,* a sting] **1.** a projecting point or prong on a knife, file, etc. that fits into the handle **2.** a strong, penetrating taste or odor **3.** a touch or trace (*of*) **4.** a special or characteristic flavor, quality, etc. *—vt.* to provide (a knife, etc.) with a tang

Tan·gan·yi·ka (taŋ′gan yē′kə) **1.** mainland region of Tanzania: formerly a Brit. trust territory **2. Lake,** lake in EC Africa, between Tanganyika and Zaire

tan·ge·lo (tan′jə lō′) ***n.,*** *pl.* **-los′** [TANG(ERINE) + (*pom*)*elo,* grapefruit] a fruit produced by crossing a tangerine with a grapefruit

tan·gent (tan′jənt) ***adj.*** [< L. prp. of *tangere,* to touch] **1.** touching **2.** *Geom.* touching and not intersecting a curved line or surface at one point only: said of a line or plane *—n.* **1.** *Geom.* a tangent line, curve, or surface **2.** *Trigonometry* the ratio of the side opposite a given acute angle in a right triangle to the adjacent side **—go** (or **fly**) **off at** (or **on**) **a tangent** to change suddenly from one line of action to another **—tan′gen·cy *n.***

tan·gen·tial (tan jen′shəl) ***adj.*** **1.** of or like a tangent **2.** drawn as a tangent **3.** going off at a tangent **4.** merely touching on a subject **—tan·gen′tial·ly *adv.***

tan·ge·rine (tan′jə rēn′, tan′jə rēn′) ***n.*** [< Fr. *Tanger,* Tangier] **1.** a variety of mandarin orange with a deep, reddish-yellow color and segments that are easily separated **2.** a deep, reddish-yellow color

tan·gi·ble (tan′jə b'l) ***adj.*** [< LL. *tangibilis* < L. *tangere,* to touch] **1.** that can be touched or felt by touch; having actual form and substance **2.** that can be appraised for value *[tangible* assets*]* **3.** definite; objective *—n.* [*pl.*] property that can be appraised for value; material things **—tan′gi·bil′i·ty, tan′gi·ble·ness *n.* —tan′gi·bly *adv.***

Tan·gier (tan jir′) seaport in N Morocco, on the Strait of Gibraltar: pop. 170,000

tan·gle (taŋ′g'l) ***vt.*** **-gled, -gling** [prob. var. of ME. *taglen,* to entangle] **1.** to hinder, obstruct, or confuse by circling, entwining, etc. **2.** to catch as in a net or snare; trap **3.** to make a snarl of; intertwist *—vi.* **1.** to become tangled **2.** [Colloq.] to quarrel or fight *—n.* **1.** an intertwisted, confused mass, as of string, branches, etc.; snarl **2.** a jumbled, confused condition **3.** a perplexed state **—tan′gler *n.***

tan·go (taŋ′gō) ***n.,*** *pl.* **-gos** [AmSp.] **1.** a S. American dance with long gliding steps and dips **2.** music for this *—vi.* **-goed, -go·ing** to dance the tango

tang·y (taŋ′ē) ***adj.*** **tang′i·er, tang′i·est** having a tang, or sharp flavor **—tang′i·ness *n.***

tank (taŋk) ***n.*** [< Sp. & Port. *tanque* < *estancar,* to stop the flow of] **1.** any large container for liquid or gas *[an oil tank,* a swimming *tank]* **2.** [name chosen to conceal secret manufacture] an armored, self-propelled combat vehicle armed with guns and moving on tractor treads **3.** [Slang] a jail cell, esp. one for new prisoners *—vt.* to put or store in a tank **—tank up** [Colloq.] **1.** to supply with or get a full tank of gasoline **2.** to drink much liquor **—tank′ful′ *n.,*** *pl.* **-fuls′**

tank·age (taŋ′kij) ***n.*** **1.** the capacity of a tank or tanks **2.** *a)* the storage of fluids, gases, etc. in tanks *b)* the charge for such storage **3.** slaughterhouse waste from which the fat has been rendered in tanks

tank·ard (taŋ′kərd) ***n.*** [ME.] a large drinking cup with a handle and, often, a hinged lid

tank car a large tank on wheels, for carrying liquids and gases by rail

tank·er (taŋ′kər) ***n.*** **1.** a ship for carrying a cargo of oil or other liquids in large tanks **2.** a plane with a cargo of gasoline for refueling another plane in flight

tank farming *same as* HYDROPONICS

tank top [orig. worn in swimming tanks] a casual shirt like an undershirt but with wider shoulder straps

tank town 1. a railroad stop for locomotives to get water **2.** any small or unimportant town

tan·ner (tan′ər) ***n.*** a person whose work is tanning hides

tan·ner·y (-ē) ***n.,*** *pl.* **-ner·ies** a place where hides are tanned

tan·nic (tan′ik) ***adj.*** of, like, or obtained from tanbark or tannin

tannic acid a yellowish, astringent substance, $C_{14}H_{10}O_9$, derived from oak bark, gallnuts, etc. and used in tanning, medicine, etc.

tan·nin (tan′in) ***n.*** *same as* TANNIC ACID

tan·sy (tan′zē) ***n.,*** *pl.* **-sies** [OFr. *tanesie,* ult. < LL. *tanacetum* < ?] any of various strong-smelling plants with clusters of small, yellow flowers

tan·ta·lize (tan′tə līz′) ***vt.*** **-lized′, -liz′ing** [< TANTALUS + -IZE] to tease or disappoint by promising or showing something and then withholding it **—tan′ta·li·za′tion *n.* —tan′ta·liz′er *n.* —tan′ta·liz′ing·ly *adv.***

tan·ta·lum (tan′tə ləm) ***n.*** [ModL. < TANTALUS: from the difficulty in extracting it from its ore] a rare, steel-blue, metallic chemical element that resists corrosion, used to make surgical instruments, parts for radio tubes, etc.: symbol, Ta; at. wt., 180.948; at. no., 73

Tan·ta·lus (tan′tə ləs) *Gr. Myth.* a king doomed in Hades to stand in water that always receded when he tried to drink it and under fruit branches he could never reach

tan·ta·mount (tan′tə mount′) ***adj.*** [< Anglo-Fr. < OFr. *tant* (< L. *tantus,* so much) + *amonter* (see AMOUNT)] having equal value, effect, etc.; equivalent (*to*)

tan·trum (tan′trəm) ***n.*** [< ?] a violent, willful outburst of annoyance, rage, etc.; childish fit of bad temper

Tan·za·ni·a (tan′zə nē′ə, tän′-) country in E Africa, consisting of a mainland section (*Tanganyika*) and Zanzibar: a member of the Commonwealth: 362,820 sq. mi.; pop. 13,634,000; cap. Dar es Salaam —**Tan′za·ni′an** *adj., n.*

Tao·ism (dou′iz'm, tou′-) *n.* [Chin. *tao*, the way + -ISM] a Chinese religion and philosophy based on the doctrines of Lao-tse and advocating simplicity, selflessness, etc. —**Tao′ist** *n., adj.* —**Tao·is′tic** *adj.*

tap[1] (tap) *vt.* **tapped, tap′ping** [OFr. *taper*, prob. echoic] **1.** to strike lightly **2.** to strike something lightly with **3.** to make or do by tapping *[to tap a message]* **4.** to choose, as for membership in a club **5.** to repair (a shoe) by adding a thickness of leather, etc. to the heel or sole —*vi.* **1.** to strike a light, rapid blow **2.** to perform a tap dance **3.** to move with a tapping sound —*n.* **1.** a light, rapid blow, or the sound made by it **2.** the leather, etc. added in tapping a shoe **3.** a small metal plate attached to the heel or toe of a shoe, as for tap dancing —**tap′per** *n.*

tap[2] (tap) *n.* [OE. *tæppa*] **1.** a device for controlling the flow of liquid in a pipe, barrel, etc.; faucet **2.** a plug, cork, etc. for stopping a hole in a container holding a liquid **3.** liquor of a certain kind, as drawn from a certain tap **4.** a draining of liquid from a body cavity **5.** a tool used to cut threads in a female screw **6.** the act of wiretapping **7.** a place in an electrical circuit where a connection can be made —*vt.* **tapped, tap′ping 1.** to put a tap or spigot on **2.** to make a hole in for drawing off liquid **3.** to pull out the plug from **4.** to draw (liquid) from a container, cavity, etc. **5.** to make use of *[to tap new resources]* **6.** to make a connection with (an electric circuit, telephone line, etc.); specif., to wiretap (a telephone line) **7.** to cut the inner threads of (a nut, etc.) **8.** [Slang] to borrow or get money from —**on tap 1.** in a tapped cask and ready to be drawn **2.** [Colloq.] ready for consideration or action —**tap′per** *n.*

ta·pa (tä′pä) *n.* [< native Polynesian name] an unwoven cloth made in the Pacific islands from the treated inner bark of a mulberry tree

tap dance a dance performed with sharp, loud taps of the foot, toe, or heel at each step —**tap′-dance′** *vi.* **-danced′, -danc′ing** —**tap′-danc′er** *n.*

tape (tāp) *n.* [OE. *tæppe*, a fillet] **1.** a strong, narrow, woven strip of cotton, linen, etc. used for binding, tying, etc. **2.** a narrow strip or band of steel, paper, etc. **3.** a strip of cloth stretched above the finishing line of a race **4.** *short for: a)* TAPE MEASURE *b)* ADHESIVE TAPE, MASKING TAPE, etc. —*vt.* **taped, tap′ing 1.** to put tape on or around, as for binding, tying, etc. **2.** to measure by using a tape measure **3.** to record (sound, video material, computer data, etc.) on magnetic tape —**tap′er** *n.*

tape deck a simplified magnetic-tape assembly, without an amplifier or speaker but having tape reels, drive, and recording and playback heads

tape measure a tape with marks in inches, feet, etc. for measuring: also **tape′line′** (-lin′) *n.*

ta·per (tā′pər) *n.* [OE. *tapur*] **1.** a slender candle **2.** a long wick coated with wax, used for lighting candles, lamps, etc. **3.** any feeble light **4.** *a)* a gradual decrease in width or thickness *[the taper of a pyramid]* *b)* a gradual decrease in action, power, etc. —*adj.* gradually decreased in size to a point —*vt., vi.* **1.** to decrease gradually in width or thickness **2.** to lessen; diminish Often with *off*

tape-re·cord (tāp′ri kôrd′) *vt.* to record on magnetic tape

tape recorder a device for recording on magnetic tape: see MAGNETIC RECORDING

tap·es·try (tap′is trē) *n., pl.* **-tries** [< MFr. < OFr. *tapis*, a carpet, ult. < Gr. dim. of *tapēs*, a carpet] a heavy woven cloth with decorative designs and pictures, used as a wall hanging, furniture covering, etc. —*vt.* **-tried, -try·ing** to decorate as with a tapestry: usually in the pp.

tape·worm (tāp′wurm′) *n.* any of various flatworms that live as parasites in the intestines of man and other vertebrates

tap·i·o·ca (tap′ē ō′kə) *n.* [Port. & Sp. < Tupi < *ty*, juice + *pŷa*, heart + *oc*, to squeeze out] a starchy, granular substance prepared from the root of the cassava plant, used for puddings, etc.

ta·pir (tā′pər) *n., pl.* **ta′pirs, ta′pir:** see PLURAL, II, D, 1 [Sp. < Tupi *tapyra*] any of various large, hoglike mammals found mostly in tropical America: tapirs have flexible snouts

TAPIR
(2½–3½ ft. high at shoulder)

tap·pet (tap′it) *n.* [TAP[1] + -ET] in an engine or machine, a projection or lever that moves or is moved by recurring contact, as with a cam

tap·room (tap′rōōm′) *n. same as* BARROOM

tap·root (-rōōt′, -root′) *n.* [TAP[2] + ROOT[1]] a main root, growing almost vertically downward, from which branch roots spread out

taps (taps) *n.* [< TAP[1], because orig. a drum signal] a bugle call to put out the lights for the night, as in an army camp: also sounded at a military funeral

tar[1] (tär) *n.* [OE. *teru*] **1.** a thick, sticky, brown to black liquid obtained by the destructive distillation of wood, coal, etc.: tars are used for protecting and preserving surfaces, in making many organic compounds, etc. **2.** loosely, any of the solids in smoke, as from tobacco —*vt.* **tarred, tar′ring** to cover or smear with or as with tar —*adj.* **1.** of or like tar **2.** tarred —**tar and feather** to cover (a person) with tar and feathers, as in punishment by mob action

tar[2] (tär) *n.* [< TAR(PAULIN)] [Colloq.] a sailor

tar·an·tel·la (tar′ən tel′ə) *n.* [It., dim. of ff.] **1.** a fast, whirling southern Italian dance for couples **2.** music for this

Ta·ran·to (tə ran′tō; *It.* tä′rän tô′) seaport in SE Italy, on an inlet (**Gulf of Taranto**) of the Ionian Sea: pop. 219,000

ta·ran·tu·la (tə ran′choo lə) *n., pl.* **-las, -lae** (-lē) [ML. < It. < prec.: because found nearby] **1.** a large, hairy, somewhat poisonous spider of the SW U.S. and tropical America **2.** a similar spider of S Europe

tar·boosh (tär bōōsh′) *n.* [Ar. *ṭarbūsh*] a brimless cap of cloth or felt shaped like a truncated cone, worn by Moslem men

tar·dy (tär′dē) *adj.* **-di·er, -di·est** [< OFr. < L. *tardus*, slow] **1.** slow in moving, acting, etc. **2.** late, delayed, or dilatory —**tar′di·ly** *adv.* —**tar′di·ness** *n.*

tare[1] (ter) *n.* [< or akin to MDu. *tarwe*, wheat] **1.** any of several vetches **2.** the seed of any of these plants **3.** *Bible* a weed, perhaps the darnel

tare[2] (ter) *n.* [< MFr. < It. < Ar. *taraḥa*, to reject] deduction of the weight of a container, wrapper, etc. from the total weight to determine the weight of the contents —*vt.* **tared, tar′ing** to find out, allow for, or mark the tare of

tar·get (tär′git) *n.* [< MFr. dim. of *targe*, a shield < Frank.] **1.** orig., a small, round shield **2.** *a)* a round, flat board, straw coil, etc., marked as with concentric circles, aimed at in archery, rifle practice, etc. *b)* any object that is shot at, bombarded, etc. **3.** an objective; goal **4.** an object of attack, criticism, or ridicule —*vt.* to establish a target, or goal, for

tar·iff (tar′if) *n.* [< It. < Ar. *ta'rīf*, information] **1.** a list or system of taxes upon exports or, esp., imports **2.** a tax of this kind, or its rate **3.** any list of prices, charges, etc. **4.** [Colloq.] any bill, charge, etc. —*vt.* **1.** to set a tariff on **2.** to fix the price of according to a tariff

Tar·king·ton (tär′kiŋ tən), (**Newton**) **Booth** 1869–1946; U.S. novelist

tar·la·tan, tar·le·tan (tär′lə tən) *n.* [Fr. *tarlatane*] a thin, stiff, open-weave muslin

Tar·mac (tär′mak) [< TAR[1] + MAC(ADAM)] *a trademark for* a coal-tar material used in paving —*n.* [**t-**] [Chiefly Brit.] a road, airport runway, etc. paved with crushed stone and tar

tarn (tärn) *n.* [< or akin to ON. *tjörn*] a small mountain lake

'tar·nal (tär′n'l) *adj. shortened dial. form of* ETERNAL: used chiefly as an intensive *[a 'tarnal fool]*

tar·na·tion (tär nā′shən) *interj., n.* [prob. < 'TAR(NAL) + (DAM)NATION] *dial. var. of* DAMNATION: used as an intensive *[what in tarnation is that?]*

tar·nish (tär′nish) *vt.* [< MFr. *ternir*, to make dim, prob. < OHG. *tarnjan*, to conceal] **1.** to dull the luster of (a metal) by exposure to the air **2.** to sully (a reputation, etc.) —*vi.* **1.** to lose luster; discolor, as from oxidation **2.** to become sullied —*n.* **1.** a being tarnished; dullness **2.** the film of discoloration on a tarnished surface **3.** a stain; blemish —**tar′nish·a·ble** *adj.*

ta·ro (tä′rō) *n., pl.* **-ros** [Tahitian] **1.** a large, tropical Asiatic plant, cultivated for its edible tubers, the source of poi **2.** the tuber of this plant

tar·ot (tar′ō, -ət; ta rō′) *n.* [Fr., ult. < Ar. *taraḥa*, to remove] [*often* **T-**] any of a set of playing cards with pictures of symbolic figures, used in fortunetelling

tarp (tärp) *n.* [Colloq.] *shortened form of* TARPAULIN

tar paper a heavy paper impregnated with tar, used as a base for roofing, etc.

tar·pau·lin (tär pô′lin, tär′pə lin) *n.* [TAR[1] + *-paulin*, prob. < *palling* < PALL[2]] **1.** canvas coated with a waterproofing compound **2.** a sheet of this spread over something to keep it dry

tar·pon (tär′pən, -pän) *n., pl.* **-pons, -pon:** see PLURAL, II, D, 1 [< ?] a large, silvery game fish of the herring group, found in the warmer parts of the W Atlantic

Tar·quin (tär′kwin) (*Lucius Tarquinius Superbus*) semilegendary Etruscan king of Rome (534?–510? B.C.)

tar·ra·gon (tar′ə gän′) ***n.*** [Sp. < Ar. < Gr. *drakōn*, dragon] **1.** an old-world wormwood whose fragrant leaves are used for seasoning **2.** these leaves

tar·ry[1] (tar′ē) ***vi.*** **-ried, -ry·ing** [prob. < OE. *tergan*, to vex, merged with OFr. *targer*, to delay < L. *tardus*, slow] **1.** to delay, linger, etc. **2.** to stay for a time, esp. longer than intended **3.** to wait —**tar′ri·er** ***n.***

tar·ry[2] (tär′ē) ***adj.*** **-ri·er, -ri·est** **1.** of or like tar **2.** covered or smeared with tar —**tar′ri·ness** ***n.***

tar·sal (tär′s'l) ***adj.*** of the tarsus —***n.*** a tarsal bone or plate

tar·si·er (tär′sē ər) ***n.*** [Fr. < *tarse*, TARSUS, from the foot structure] any of several small primates of the East Indies and the Philippines, with very large eyes and a long tail: they live in trees and are active at night

TARSIER (head & body 3–7 in. long; tail 5–10 in. long)

Tar·sus (tär′səs) city in S Turkey, near the Mediterranean: birthplace of the Apostle Paul: pop. 57,000

tar·sus (-səs) ***n., pl.*** **-si** (-sī) [ModL. < Gr. *tarsos*, flat of the foot] **1.** the human ankle, consisting of seven bones **2.** *Zool.* *a*) a group of bones in the ankle region of the hind limbs of vertebrates having four limbs *b*) the fifth segment from the base of an insect leg

tart[1] (tärt) ***adj.*** [OE. *teart*] **1.** sharp in taste; sour; acid **2.** sharp in meaning; cutting [*a tart answer*] —**tart′ly** ***adv.*** —**tart′ness** ***n.***

tart[2] (tärt) ***n.*** [MFr. *tarte*] **1.** a small shell of pastry filled with jam, jelly, etc. **2.** in England, a small pie filled with fruit or jam and often having a top crust

tart[3] (tärt) ***n.*** [< prec., orig. slang term of endearment] a prostitute or any woman of loose morals

tar·tan (tär′t'n) ***n.*** [prob. < MFr. *tiretaine*, a cloth of mixed fibers, ult. < L. *Tyrus*, TYRE] **1.** woolen cloth with a woven plaid pattern, esp. as worn in the Scottish Highlands, where each clan has its own pattern **2.** any plaid cloth or pattern **3.** a garment made of tartan —***adj.*** of or made of tartan

Tar·tar (tär′tər) ***n.*** [< ML. *Tartarus* < Per. *Tātār*] **1.** *same as* TATAR **2.** [*usually* **t-**] a bad-tempered person hard to deal with —***adj.*** of Tatary or the Tatars —**catch a tartar** to attack or oppose someone too strong for one

tar·tar (tär′tər) ***n.*** [< ML. < MGr. *tartaron* < ? Ar.] **1.** a potassium salt of tartaric acid forming a reddish, crustlike deposit in wine casks: in purified form called CREAM OF TARTAR **2.** a hard deposit on the teeth, consisting of saliva proteins, food deposits, calcium phosphate, etc.

tartar emetic a poisonous salt of tartaric acid used in medicine to cause vomiting, in dyeing as a mordant, etc.

tar·tar·ic (tär tar′ik, -tär′-) ***adj.*** of, containing, or derived from tartar or tartaric acid

tartaric acid a colorless, crystalline acid, $C_4H_6O_6$, found in fruit juices, etc. and obtained from tartar: it is used in dyeing, photography, medicine, etc.

tar·tar sauce (tär′tər) [< Fr.] a sauce, as for seafood, consisting of mayonnaise with chopped pickles, olives, capers, etc.: also sp. **tartare sauce**

tartar steak *same as* STEAK TARTARE

Tar·ta·rus (tär′tər əs) *Gr. Myth.* **1.** an infernal abyss below Hades **2.** Hades; hell —**Tar·tar′e·an** (-ter′ē ən) ***adj.***

Tar·ta·ry (tär′tər ē) *same as* TATARY

tar·trate (tär′trāt) ***n.*** a salt or ester of tartaric acid

Tar·zan (tär′zən, -zan) ***n.*** [after *Tarzan*, jungle-raised hero of stories by E. R. Burroughs (1875–1950), U.S. writer] [*also* **t-**] a very strong, virile, and agile man: often used humorously

Tash·kent (täsh kent′) capital of the Uzbek S.S.R., in the E part: pop. 1,385,000

task (task) ***n.*** [< ONormFr. < ML. *tasca*, for *taxa*, a tax < L. *taxare*, to rate, TAX] **1.** a piece of work that one must do **2.** any piece of work **3.** any difficult undertaking —***vt.*** **1.** to assign a task to **2.** to put a strain on; tax —**take to task** to reprimand or scold

task force a specially trained, self-contained military unit assigned a specific mission or task

task·mas·ter (-mas′tər) ***n.*** a person who assigns tasks to others, esp. when exacting or severe

Tas·man (täs′män; *E.* taz′mən), **A·bel Jans·zoon** (ä′bəl yän′sōn) 1603?–59; Du. navigator, esp. in the Pacific

Tas·ma·ni·a (taz mā′nē ə, -mān′yə) **1.** island south of Victoria, Australia **2.** state of Australia comprising this island & smaller nearby islands —**Tas·ma′ni·an** ***adj., n.***

Tass (täs) [< the initial letters of the full name] a Soviet agency for gathering and distributing news

tas·sel (tas′'l) ***n.*** [OFr., a knob] **1.** an ornamental tuft of threads, cords, etc. of equal length, hanging loosely from a knob or knot **2.** something resembling this; specif., a tassellike tuft, as of corn silk on an ear of corn —***vt.*** **-seled** or **-selled, -sel·ing** or **-sel·ling** to put tassels on —***vi.*** to grow tassels, as corn

Tas·so (täs′sô; *E.* tas′ō), **Tor·qua·to** (tôr kwä′tô) 1544–95; It. epic poet

taste (tāst) ***vt.*** **tast′ed, tast′ing** [OFr. *taster*, to touch, taste] **1.** to test the flavor of by putting a little in one's mouth **2.** to detect the flavor of by the sense of taste **3.** to eat or drink, esp. a small amount of **4.** to experience; have [*to taste defeat*] —***vi.*** **1.** to tell flavors by the sense of taste **2.** to eat or drink a small amount (*of*) **3.** to have the specific flavor (*of*) [*the salad tastes of garlic*] **4.** to have a sensation or limited experience (*of* something) —***n.*** **1.** the sense by which the taste buds on the tongue, when stimulated by a substance, distinguish it as sweet, sour, salty, or bitter **2.** the quality perceived through this sense; flavor; savor **3.** a small amount put into the mouth to test the flavor **4.** a slight experience of something; sample **5.** a bit; trace; touch **6.** *a*) the ability to appreciate and judge what is beautiful, appropriate, or excellent in art, dress, etc. *b*) a specific preference [*a taste for red ties*] *c*) a style or way that shows such ability or preferences **7.** a liking; inclination —**in bad, poor,** etc. (or **good, excellent,** etc.) **taste** in a form, style, or manner showing a bad (or good) sense of beauty, excellence, fitness, etc. —**in taste** in good taste —**to one's taste** **1.** pleasing to one **2.** so as to please one

taste bud any of the cells in the epithelium of the tongue that are the sense organs of taste

taste·ful (tāst′fəl) ***adj.*** having or showing good taste [*tasteful décor*] —**taste′ful·ly** ***adv.*** —**taste′ful·ness** ***n.***

taste·less (-lis) ***adj.*** **1.** *a*) without taste or flavor; flat; insipid *b*) dull; uninteresting **2.** lacking good taste; in poor taste —**taste′less·ly** ***adv.*** —**taste′less·ness** ***n.***

tast·er (tās′tər) ***n.*** a person who tastes; specif., one employed to test the quality of wines, teas, etc. by tasting

tast·y (-tē) ***adj.*** **tast′i·er, tast′i·est** **1.** that tastes good; flavorful **2.** [Now Rare] *same as* TASTEFUL —**tast′i·ly** ***adv.*** —**tast′i·ness** ***n.***

tat[1] (tat) ***vt.*** **tat′ted, tat′ting** [< TATTING] to make by tatting —***vi.*** to do tatting

tat[2] (tat) ***n.*** [< ? TAP[1]] *see* TIT FOR TAT

ta·ta·mi (tə tä′mē) ***n., pl.*** **-mi, -mis** [Jap.] a floor mat woven of rice straw, used traditionally in Japanese homes for sitting on, as when eating

Ta·tar (tät′ər) ***n.*** [Per.] **1.** a member of any of the Mongolian and Turkic tribes that invaded W Asia and E Europe in the Middle Ages **2.** any of a Turkic people living in a region of EC European Russia and in parts of Asia **3.** any of their Turkic languages —***adj.*** of the Tatars or their languages

Ta·ta·ry (tät′ə rē) vast region in Europe & Asia under the control of Tatar tribes in the late Middle Ages

'ta·ter, ta·ter (tāt′ər) ***n.*** *dial. form of* POTATO

tat·ter (tat′ər) ***n.*** [prob. < ON. *tötturr*, rags] **1.** a torn and hanging shred or piece, as of a garment **2.** a separate shred; rag **3.** [*pl.*] torn, ragged clothes —***vt., vi.*** to reduce to tatters; make or become ragged —**tat′tered** ***adj.***

tat·ter·de·mal·ion (tat′ər di māl′yən, -mal′-) ***n.*** [< prec. + ?] a person in torn, ragged clothes; ragamuffin

tat·ting (tat′iŋ) ***n.*** [prob. < Brit. dial. *tat*, to tangle] **1.** a fine lace made by looping and knotting thread that is wound on a hand shuttle **2.** the act of making this

TATTING

tat·tle (tat′'l) ***vi.*** **-tled, -tling** [prob. < MDu. *tatelen*, of echoic origin] **1.** to talk idly; chatter **2.** to tell others' secrets —***n.*** idle talk; chatter —**tat′tler** ***n.***

tat·tle·tale (-tāl′) ***n.*** an informer; talebearer: now chiefly a child's term

tat·too[1] (ta to͞o′) ***vt.*** **-tooed′, -too′ing** [< Tahitian *tatau*] **1.** to puncture (the skin) with a needle and insert indelible colors so as to leave permanent marks or designs **2.** to make (marks or designs) on the skin this way —***n., pl.*** **-toos′** a tattooed mark or design —**tat·too′er, tat·too′ist** ***n.***

tat·too[2] (ta to͞o′) ***n., pl.*** **-toos′** [< Du. < *tap toe*, shut the tap: a signal for closing barrooms] **1.** *a*) a signal on a drum, bugle, etc. summoning soldiers, etc. to their quarters at night *b*) in England, a military spectacle featuring marching, etc. **2.** any continuous drumming, rapping, etc. —***vt., vi.*** **-tooed′, -too′ing** to beat or tap

tat·ty (tat′ē) ***adj.*** **-ti·er, -ti·est** [prob. akin to OE. *taetteca*, a rag] [Chiefly Brit.] shabby, decrepit, tawdry, etc. —**tat′ti·ly** ***adv.*** —**tat′ti·ness** ***n.***

tau (tô, tou) ***n.*** [Gr.] the nineteenth letter of the Greek alphabet (Τ, τ)

taught (tôt) *pt. & pp. of* TEACH

taunt (tônt, tänt) ***vt.*** [< ? Fr. *tant pour tant*, tit for tat] **1.** to reproach in scornful or sarcastic language; jeer at **2.** to drive or provoke by taunting —***n.*** a scornful or jeering remark; gibe —**taunt′er** ***n.*** —**taunt′ing·ly** ***adv.***

taupe (tōp) ***n.*** [Fr. < L. *talpa*, a mole] a dark, brownish gray, the color of moleskin —***adj.*** of such a color

Tau·rus (tôr′əs) [L., a bull] **1.** a N constellation containing the Pleiades **2.** the second sign of the zodiac: see ZODIAC, illus.

taut (tôt) *adj.* [ME. *toght,* tight, prob. < pp. of *togen,* to pull] **1.** tightly stretched, as a rope **2.** strained; tense *[a taut smile]* **3.** trim, tidy, etc. *[a taut ship]* —**taut′ly** *adv.* —**taut′ness** *n.*

taut·en (tôt′ən) *vt., vi.* to make or become taut

tau·to- [< Gr. < *to auto,* the same] *a combining form meaning* the same *[tautology]*

tau·tog (tô täg′) *n.* [< Algonquian pl. of *tautau,* a blackfish] a black or greenish food fish found off the Atlantic coast of the U.S.

tau·tol·o·gy (tô täl′ə jē) *n., pl.* **-gies** [< LL. < Gr.: see TAUTO- & -LOGY] **1.** needless repetition of an idea in a different word, phrase, etc.; redundancy (Ex.: "necessary essentials") **2.** an instance of this —**tau′to·log′i·cal** *adj.* —**tau′to·log′i·cal·ly** *adv.*

tav·ern (tav′ərn) *n.* [< OFr. < L. *taberna*] **1.** a place where liquors, beer, etc. are sold and drunk; saloon; bar **2.** an inn

taw (tô) *n.* **1.** a fancy marble used to shoot with in playing marbles **2.** *a)* the game of marbles *b)* the line from which the players shoot

taw·dry (tô′drē) *adj.* **-dri·er, -dri·est** [< *St. Audrey,* esp. in *St. Audrey laces,* sold at St. Audrey's fair, Norwich, England] cheap and showy; gaudy; sleazy —**taw′dri·ly** *adv.* —**taw′dri·ness** *n.*

taw·ny (tô′nē) *adj.* **-ni·er, -ni·est** [< OFr. pp. of *tanner,* to tan] brownish-yellow; tan —*n.* tawny color —**taw′ni·ness** *n.*

tax (taks) *vt.* [< MFr. < L. *taxare,* to appraise < base of *tangere,* to touch] **1.** orig., to determine the value of; assess **2.** to require (a person) to pay a percentage of his income, property value, etc. for the support of a government **3.** to assess a tax on (income, property, purchases, etc.) **4.** to put a burden or strain on **5.** to accuse; charge *[to be taxed with negligence]* —*n.* **1.** a compulsory payment, usually a percentage of income, property value, sales price, etc., for the support of a government **2.** a heavy demand; burden; strain —**tax′a·bil′i·ty** *n.* —**tax′a·ble** *adj.* —**tax′er** *n.*

tax·a·tion (tak sā′shən) *n.* **1.** a taxing or being taxed **2.** the principle of levying taxes **3.** a tax or tax levy **4.** revenue from taxes

tax-de·duct·i·ble (taks′di duk′tə b′l) *adj.* allowed as a deduction in computing income tax

tax duplicate **1.** the certification of real-estate assessments to the taxing authorities **2.** the basis on which the tax collector prepares tax bills

tax-ex·empt (-ig zempt′) *adj.* **1.** exempt from taxation; that may not be taxed **2.** producing nontaxable income *[tax-exempt bonds]*

tax·i (tak′sē) *n., pl.* **tax′is** *shortened form of* TAXICAB —*vi.* **tax′ied, tax′i·ing** or **tax′y·ing** **1.** to go in a taxi **2.** to move slowly along the ground or on water as an airplane does before taking off or after landing —*vt.* **1.** to carry in a taxi **2.** to cause (an airplane) to taxi

tax·i·cab (-kab′) *n.* [< *taxi(meter) cab*] an automobile in which passengers are carried for a fare shown on a meter

tax·i·der·my (tak′si dur′mē) *n.* [< Gr. *taxis,* arrangement + *derma,* a skin] the art of preparing, stuffing, and mounting the skins of animals so as to give a lifelike effect —**tax′i·der′mal, tax′i·der′mic** *adj.* —**tax′i·der′mist** *n.*

tax·i·me·ter (tak′sē mēt′ər) *n.* [Fr. *taximètre* < G. < ML. *taxa,* a tax + *-meter,* -METER] an automatic device in taxicabs that registers fares due

taxi stand a place where taxicabs are stationed for hire

tax·on (tak′sän) *n., pl.* **tax′a** (-sə) [< TAXONOMY] a taxonomic category or unit, as a species, genus, etc.

tax·on·o·my (tak sän′ə mē) *n.* [< Fr. < Gr. *taxis,* arrangement + *nomos,* a law] the science of classification, esp. of plants and animals into natural, related groups such as species and genera —**tax′o·nom′ic** (-sə näm′ik), **tax′o·nom′i·cal** *adj.* —**tax′o·nom′i·cal·ly** *adv.* —**tax·on′o·mist** *n.*

tax·pay·er (taks′pā′ər) *n.* a person who pays taxes

tax shelter any financial investment made for the purpose of acquiring expenses, depreciation allowances, etc., which can be used to reduce one's income tax

tax stamp a stamp that shows a tax has been paid

Tay·lor (tā′lər) [after Zachary TAYLOR] city in SE Mich.: suburb of Detroit: pop. 78,000

Tay·lor (tā′lər) **1. Jer·e·my** (jer′ə mē), 1613–67; Eng. bishop & theological writer **2. Zach·a·ry** (zak′ər ē), 1784–1850; U.S. general in the Mexican War; 12th president of the U.S. (1849–50)

Tb *Chem.* terbium

TB, T.B., tb, t.b. tuberculosis

Tbi·li·si (t′bi lē sē′) capital of the Georgian S.S.R.: pop. 889,000

T-bone steak (tē′bōn′) a steak from the loin, with a T-shaped bone, containing some tenderloin

tbs., tbsp. tablespoon; tablespoons

Tc *Chem.* technetium

Tchai·kov·sky (chī kôf′skē), **Peter Il·ich** (il′yich) 1840–93; Russ. composer: also **Pëtr Il·yich Tschai·kow·sky** (pyô′tr′ il yēch′ chī kôf′skē)

Tchekov *var. sp. of* CHEKHOV: also **Tchekhov**

TD touchdown: also **td**

Te *Chem.* tellurium

tea (tē) *n.* see PLURAL, II, D, 3 [Chin. dial. *t'e,* for Mandarin *ch'a,* tea] **1.** a white-flowered, evergreen shrub grown in warm parts of Asia for its young leaves, which are prepared by drying, etc. for use in making a common drink **2.** the dried, prepared leaves **3.** the drink made by steeping these in hot water, etc. **4.** a tealike plant, or the tealike beverage made from it or from a meat extract *[camomile tea,* beef *tea]* **5.** [Chiefly Brit.] a light meal, usually with tea, in the late afternoon **6.** a social gathering in the afternoon at which tea, coffee, etc. are served

tea bag a small, porous bag with tea leaves in it, for making an individual cup of tea

tea ball a hollow, perforated metal ball used to hold tea leaves in making tea

tea·ber·ry (-ber′ē) *n., pl.* **-ries** **1.** *same as* WINTERGREEN (sense 1) **2.** a wintergreen berry

teach (tēch) *vt.* **taught, teach′ing** [OE. *tæcan*] **1.** to show or help to learn how to do something; instruct **2.** to give lessons to; guide the study of **3.** to give lessons in (a subject) **4.** to give knowledge, insight, etc. to; cause to know, understand, etc. *[the accident taught her to be careful]* —*vi.* to be a teacher —**teach′a·bil′i·ty, teach′a·ble·ness** *n.* —**teach′a·ble** *adj.*

teach·er (tē′chər) *n.* a person who teaches, esp. in a school or college —**teach′er·ship′** *n.*

teach·ing (-chiŋ) *n.* **1.** the action of one who teaches; profession of a teacher **2.** something taught; precept, doctrine, etc.: *usually in pl.*

tea·cup (tē′kup′) *n.* **1.** a cup for drinking tea, etc. **2.** a teacupful

tea·cup·ful (-fool′) *n., pl.* **-fuls′** as much as a teacup will hold, about four fluid ounces

tea·house (tē′hous′) *n.* in the Orient, a place where tea and other refreshments are served

teak (tēk) *n.* [< Port. < native word *tēkka*] **1.** a large East Indian tree with hard, yellowish-brown wood used for shipbuilding, furniture, etc. **2.** its wood: also **teak′wood′**

tea·ket·tle (tē′ket′′l) *n.* a covered kettle with a spout and handle, used to boil water for tea, etc.

teal (tēl) *n.* [ME. *tele*] **1.** *pl.* **teals, teal:** see PLURAL, II, D, 1 any of several small, short-necked freshwater wild ducks **2.** a dark greenish blue: also **teal blue**

team (tēm) *n.* [OE., offspring] **1.** two or more horses, oxen, etc. harnessed to the same vehicle or plow **2.** a draft animal or animals and the vehicle drawn **3.** a group of people working together on a project or playing together against opponents in games —*vt., vi.* to join together in a team (often with *up*)

team·mate (tēm′māt′) *n.* a fellow team member

team·ster (-stər) *n.* one whose occupation is driving teams or trucks for hauling loads

team teaching teaching by several teachers working together with a group of students to explore relationships among various subject areas

team·work (-wurk′) *n.* the action or effort of people working together as a group

tea party a social gathering at which tea is served

tea·pot (tē′pät′) *n.* a pot with a spout, handle, and lid, for brewing and pouring tea

tear[1] (ter) *vt.* **tore, torn, tear′ing** [OE. *teran,* to rend] **1.** to pull apart by force; rip; rend **2.** to make (a hole, etc.) by tearing **3.** to wound by tearing; lacerate **4.** to split into factions; disrupt *[ranks torn by dissension]* **5.** to divide by doubt, etc. *[torn between duty and desire]* **6.** to remove as by tearing, pulling, etc. (with *up, out, off,* etc.) —*vi.* **1.** to be torn **2.** to move with force or speed; rush —*n.* **1.** the act of tearing **2.** a torn place; rip **3.** a violent outburst **4.** [Slang] a spree —**tear at** to pull at violently in an effort to tear or remove —**tear down** to take apart; wreck, demolish, etc. —**tear into** [Colloq.] to attack or criticize violently —**tear′er** *n.*

tear[2] (tir) *n.* [OE.] **1.** a drop of the salty fluid that keeps the eyeball moist and flows from the eye in weeping **2.** any tearlike drop **3.** [*pl.*] sorrow; grief —*vi.* to shed, or fill with, tears —**in tears** weeping —**tear′less** *adj.*

tear·drop (tir′dräp′) *n.* a tear —*adj.* tear-shaped

tear·ful (-fəl) *adj.* **1.** in tears; weeping **2.** causing tears; sad —**tear′ful·ly** *adv.* —**tear′ful·ness** *n.*

tear gas (tir) a gas that makes the eyes sore and blinds them with tears —**tear′-gas′** *vt.* **-gassed′, -gas′sing**

tear-jerk·er (-jʉr′kər) *n.* [Slang] a play, movie, etc. that is sad in a too sentimental way —**tear′-jerk′ing** *adj.*

tea·room (tē′ro͞om′) *n.* a restaurant that serves tea, coffee, light lunches, etc. and caters chiefly to women

tear·y (tir′ē) *adj.* **-i·er, -i·est** 1. tearful; crying 2. of or like tears —**tear′i·ly** *adv.* —**tear′i·ness** *n.*

tease (tēz) *vt.* **teased, teas′ing** [OE. *tæsan*] 1. *a*) to card or comb (flax, wool, etc.) *b*) to raise a nap on (cloth) with teasels *c*) to fluff (the hair) by brushing or combing the hair ends toward the scalp 2. to bother or annoy by mocking, poking fun, etc. 3. to pester with repeated requests 4. to tantalize —*vi.* to tease someone —*n.* 1. a teasing or being teased 2. a person who teases —**teas′er** *n.*

tea·sel (tē′z′l) *n.* [< OE. < base of *tæsan*, to tease] 1. a bristly plant (esp. the **fuller's teasel**) with prickly, cylindrical flower heads 2. a dried flower head of the fuller's teasel, used to raise a nap on cloth 3. any device for raising a nap on cloth —*vt.* **-seled** or **-selled, -sel·ing** or **-sel·ling** to nap (cloth) with teasels —**tea′sel·er, tea′sel·ler** *n.*

tea·spoon (tē′spo͞on′) *n.* 1. a spoon for stirring tea, coffee, etc. and eating some soft foods 2. *same as* TEASPOONFUL

tea·spoon·ful (-fo͝ol′) *n.*, *pl.* **-fuls′** as much as a teaspoon holds; 1/3 tablespoonful ($1\frac{1}{3}$ fluid drams)

teat (tēt, tit) *n.* [< OFr. *tete* < Gmc.] the nipple of a breast or udder

tea·zel, tea·zle (tē′z′l) *n.*, *vt. same as* TEASEL

Te·bet, Te·beth (tā vāt′, tā′vəs) *n.* [Heb.] the fourth month of the Jewish year: see JEWISH CALENDAR

tech. 1. technical 2. technology

tech·ne·ti·um (tek nē′shē əm) *n.* [ModL. < Gr. < *technē*, an art + -IUM] a metallic chemical element obtained in the fission of uranium: symbol, Tc; at. wt., 97(?); at. no., 43

tech·nic (tek′nik; *for n. 1 also* tek nēk′) *adj.* [< Gr. < *technē*, an art] *same as* TECHNICAL —*n.* 1. *same as* TECHNIQUE 2. [*pl.*, *with sing. or pl. v.*] the study or principles of an art

tech·ni·cal (tek′ni k′l) *adj.* [prec. + -AL] 1. dealing with the practical, industrial, or mechanical arts or the applied sciences 2. of, used in, or peculiar to a specific science, art, craft, etc. [*technical* terms] 3. of or showing technique [*technical* skill] 4. according to principles or rules [a *technical* difference] 5. involving or using technicalities —**tech′ni·cal·ly** *adv.*

tech·ni·cal·i·ty (tek′nə kal′ə tē) *n.*, *pl.* **-ties** 1. the state or quality of being technical 2. a technical point, term, method, etc. 3. a minute, formal point or detail brought to bear upon a main issue

technical knockout *Boxing* a victory won when the opponent, though not knocked out, is so badly hurt that the referee stops the match

technical sergeant *U.S. Air Force* the second grade of enlisted man, just below master sergeant

tech·ni·cian (tek nish′ən) *n.* a person skilled in the technicalities of some subject or in the technique of some art or science

Tech·ni·col·or (tek′ni kul′ər) *a trademark for* a certain process of making color motion pictures —*n.* [t-] 1. this process 2. bright colors —**tech′ni·col′ored** *adj.*

tech·nique (tek nēk′) *n.* [Fr. < Gr.: see TECHNIC] 1. the method of procedure (as to practical or formal details) in creating an artistic work or carrying out a scientific or mechanical operation 2. the degree of expertness shown in this 3. any method of doing a thing

tech·no- [< Gr. *technē*, an art] *a combining form meaning:* 1. art, science, skill 2. technical, technological [*technocracy*]

tech·noc·ra·cy (tek näk′rə sē) *n.* [prec. + -CRACY] government by scientists and engineers —**tech′no·crat′** (-nə krat′) *n.* —**tech′no·crat′ic** *adj.*

tech·no·log·i·cal (tek′nə läj′i k′l) *adj.* 1. of technology 2. resulting from technical progress in the use of machinery and automation Also **tech′no·log′ic** —**tech′no·log′i·cal·ly** *adv.*

tech·nol·o·gy (tek näl′ə jē) *n.* [Gr. *technologia*, systematic treatment] 1. the science or study of the practical or industrial arts, applied sciences, etc. 2. the terms used in a science, art, etc. 3. applied science 4. a method, process, etc. for handling a specific technical problem —**tech·nol′o·gist** *n.*

tec·ton·ic (tek tän′ik) *adj.* [< LL. < Gr. < *tektōn*, a builder] designating, of, or pertaining to the processes that produce changes in the earth's crust

Te·cum·seh (ti kum′sə) 1768?–1813; chief of the Shawnee Indians

ted (ted) *vt.* **ted′ded, ted′ding** [prob. < ON. *tethja*, to manure] to spread or scatter (newly cut grass) for drying as hay —**ted′der** *n.*

ted·dy bear (ted′ē) [< *Teddy* (*Theodore*) Roosevelt] a child's stuffed toy made to look like a bear cub

Te De·um (tē dē′əm, tā dā′o͝om) [LL.] 1. a Christian hymn beginning *Te Deum laudamus* (We praise thee, O God) 2. music for this hymn

te·di·ous (tē′dē əs, tē′jəs) *adj.* full of tedium; tiresome; boring —**te′di·ous·ly** *adv.* —**te′di·ous·ness** *n.*

te·di·um (-dē əm) *n.* [L. *taedium* < *taedet*, it offends] the condition or quality of being tiresome, boring, or monotonous

tee^1 (tē) *n.*, *pl.* **tees** 1. the letter T, t 2. anything shaped like a T —*adj.* shaped like a T —**to a tee** exactly

tee^2 (tē) *n.* [< prec.: the mark was orig. T-shaped] a mark aimed at in quoits, curling, etc.

tee^3 (tē) *n.* [prob. < Scot. dial. *teaz*] 1. a small, pointed holder of wood, plastic, etc. on which a golf ball is put to be driven 2. the place at each hole from which a golfer makes his first stroke —*vt.*, *vi.* **teed, tee′ing** to put (a ball) on a tee —**tee off** 1. to play a golf ball from a tee 2. to begin 3. [Slang] to make angry or disgusted

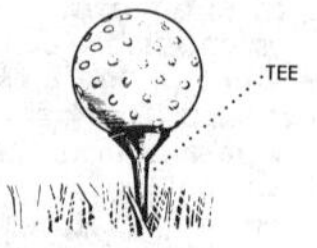

tee-hee (tē′hē′) *interj.*, *n.* [ME.: echoic] the sound of a titter or snicker —*vi.* **-heed′, -hee′ing** to titter or snicker

teem^1 (tēm) *vi.* [OE. *tieman*, to bear < base of *team*, progeny] to be full; abound; swarm [a river *teeming* with fish]

teem^2 (tēm) *vt.* [ON. *taema*] to empty; pour out —*vi.* to pour [a *teeming* rain]

teen (tēn) *n.* [< OE. *tien*, ten] 1. [*pl.*] the years from thirteen through nineteen (of a century or a person's age) 2. *same as* TEEN-AGER —*adj. same as* TEEN-AGE

teen-age (-āj′) *adj.* 1. in one's teens 2. of, like, or for persons in their teens Also **teen′age′**

teen-ag·er (-āj′ər) *n.* a person in his teens

tee·ny (tē′nē) *adj.* **-ni·er, -ni·est** *colloq. var. of* TINY: also **teen′sy**

teen·y-bop·per (tē′nē bäp′ər) *n.* [TEEN + -Y^1 + BOP^2 + -ER] [Slang] a young teen-ager, esp. a girl, of the 1960's, following the latest fads

tee·ny-wee·ny (-wē′nē) *adj.* [Colloq.] very small; tiny: also **teen·sy-ween·sy** (tēn′sē wēn′sē)

tee·pee (tē′pē) *n. alt. sp. of* TEPEE

tee shirt *same as* T-SHIRT

tee·ter (tēt′ər) *vi.* [dial. *titter* < ON. *titra*, to tremble] to totter, wobble, etc. —*vt.* to cause to teeter —*n. shortened form of* TEETER-TOTTER

tee·ter·board (-bôrd′) *n. same as* SEESAW

tee·ter-tot·ter (-tät′ər, -tôt′-) *n.*, *vi. same as* SEESAW

teeth (tēth) *n. pl. of* TOOTH

teethe (tē*th*) *vi.* **teethed, teeth′ing** to grow teeth; cut one's teeth

teeth·ing ring (tē′*th*iŋ) a ring of ivory, plastic, etc. for teething babies to bite on

teeth·ridge (tēth′rij′) *n.* the ridge of gum along the inside of the upper front teeth

tee·to·tal (tē tōt′'l, tē′tōt′'l) *adj.* [formed by redupl. of initial letter of TOTAL] 1. [Colloq.] entire; complete 2. of or in favor of teetotalism —**tee·to′tal·er, tee·to′tal·ler** *n.* —**tee·to′tal·ly** *adv.*

tee·to·tal·ism (-iz′m) *n.* the principle or practice of never drinking any alcoholic liquor —**tee·to′tal·ist** *n.*

Tef·lon (tef′län) *a trademark for* a tough, insoluble polymer used in making nonsticking coatings for cooking utensils, etc.

Te·gu·ci·gal·pa (te go͞o′sē gäl′pä) capital of Honduras, in the SC part: pop. 219,000

teg·u·ment (teg′yoo mənt) *n.* [< L. < *tegere*, to cover] *same as* INTEGUMENT

te-hee (tē′hē′) *interj.*, *n.*, *vi.* **-heed′, -hee′ing** *var. of* TEE-HEE

Teh·rán, Te·he·ran (te hrän′; *E.* te ə rän′, -ran′) capital of Iran, in the NC part: pop. 3,150,000

tek·tite (tek′tīt) *n.* [< Gr. *tēktos*, molten < *tēkein*, to melt + -ITE] any of certain small, dark green to black glassy bodies, assumed to have come to earth from outer space

tel- *same as:* 1. TELE- 2. TELO-

tel. 1. telegram 2. telegraph 3. telephone

Tel A·viv-Jaf·fa (tel′ä vēv′yäf′ə, tel′ə vēv′jaf′ə) seaport in W Israel, incorporating the former cities of Tel Aviv & Jaffa: pop. 383,000: usually called **Tel Aviv**

tel·e- *a combining form meaning:* 1. [< Gr. < *tēle*, far off] at, over, from, or to a distance [*telegraph*] 2. [< TELE(VISION)] of or by television [*telecast*]

tel·e·cast (tel′ə kast′) *vt.*, *vi.* **-cast′** or **-cast′ed, -cast′ing** [TELE- + (BROAD)CAST] to broadcast by television —*n.* a television broadcast —**tel′e·cast′er** *n.*

tel·e·com·mu·ni·ca·tion (tel′ə kə myo͞o′nə kā′shən) *n.* [*also pl.*, *with sing. or pl. v.*] communication by radio, telephone, telegraph, television, etc.

tel·e·gram (tel′ə gram′) *n.* [TELE- + -GRAM] a message transmitted by telegraph

tel·e·graph (-graf′) *n.* [< Fr.: see TELE- & -GRAPH] an apparatus or system for sending messages, orig. in Morse code, by electric impulses through a wire or by means of radio waves —*vt.* **1.** to send (a message) by telegraph to (someone) **2.** to let another know without meaning to (something one plans to do), as by a look —*vi.* to send a telegram —**te·leg·ra·pher** (tə leg′rə fər), **te·leg′ra·phist** *n.* —**tel′e·graph′ic** *adj.* —**tel′e·graph′i·cal·ly** *adv.*

te·leg·ra·phy (tə leg′rə fē) *n.* **1.** the operation of telegraph apparatus **2.** the sending of messages by telegraph

tel·e·ki·ne·sis (tel′ə ki nē′sis) *n.* [ModL. < TELE- + Gr. *kinēsis,* motion] the causing of an object to move supposedly by means of psychic forces —**tel′e·ki·net′ic** (-net′ik) *adj.*

Te·lem·a·chus (tə lem′ə kəs) *Gr. Legend* the son of Odysseus and Penelope, who helped his father slay his mother's suitors

Te·le·mann (te′lə män′), **Ge·org Phi·lipp** (gā ôrk′ fē′lip) 1681–1767; Ger. composer

tel·e·mark (tel′ə märk′) *n.* [after *Telemark,* region in S Norway] *Skiing* a turning movement during which the outer ski is advanced and turned in at a widening angle

tel·e·me·ter (tel′ə mēt′ər, tə lem′ə tər) *n.* [TELE- + -METER] a device for measuring temperature, radiation, etc. at a remote point, as in outer space, and transmitting the information obtained, esp. by radio, to a distant receiver on earth —*vt., vi.* to transmit by telemeter —**tel′e·met′ric** (-met′rik) *adj.* —**tel′e·met′ri·cal·ly** *adv.* —**te·lem·e·try** (tə lem′ə trē) *n.*

te·le·ol·o·gy (tē′lē äl′ə jē, tel′ē-) *n.* [ModL. < Gr. *telos,* an end + *-logia* (see -LOGY)] **1.** the fact or quality of having an ultimate purpose or goal **2.** a belief that what happens or occurs in nature is determined by an overall design or purpose, not just by mechanical causes —**te′le·o·log′i·cal** (-ə läj′i k′l) *adj.* —**te′le·ol′o·gist** *n.*

te·lep·a·thy (tə lep′ə thē) *n.* [TELE- + -PATHY] supposed communication between minds by some means other than the normal functioning of the senses —**tel·e·path·ic** (tel′ə path′ik) *adj.* —**tel′e·path′i·cal·ly** *adv.* —**te·lep′a·thist** *n.*

tel·e·phone (tel′ə fōn′) *n.* [TELE- + -PHONE] an instrument or system for conveying speech over distances by converting sound into electric impulses sent through a wire —*vi.* **-phoned′, -phon′ing** to talk over a telephone —*vt.* **1.** to convey (a message) by telephone **2.** to speak to or reach (a person) by telephone —**tel′e·phon′er** *n.* —**tel′e·phon′ic** (-fän′ik) *adj.* —**tel′e·phon′i·cal·ly** *adv.*

te·leph·o·ny (tə lef′ə nē) *n.* the science of communication by telephone

tel·e·pho·to (tel′ə fōt′ō) *adj.* **1.** telephotographic **2.** designating or of a camera lens producing a large image of a distant object

tel·e·pho·to·graph (tel′ə fōt′ə graf′) *n.* **1.** a photograph taken with a telephoto lens **2.** a photograph transmitted by telephotography —*vt., vi.* **1.** to take (photographs) with a telephoto lens **2.** to transmit (photographs) by telephotography

tel·e·pho·tog·ra·phy (-fə täg′rə fē) *n.* **1.** photography done with a telephoto lens **2.** the science or process of transmitting photographs over distances by converting light rays into electric signals which are sent over wire or radio channels —**tel′e·pho′to·graph′ic** (-fōt′ə graf′ik) *adj.*

tel·e·ran (tel′ə ran′) *n.* [*tele*(*vision*) *r*(*adar*) *a*(*ir*) *n*(*avigation*)] the televised transmission to aircraft of data received by radar concerning terrain, etc., as an aid to navigation

tel·e·scope (tel′ə skōp′) *n.* [< It. < ModL. < Gr.: see TELE- & -SCOPE] an instrument for making distant objects, as stars, appear nearer and larger: it consists of a tube or tubes containing lenses In a *refracting telescope,* the image is focused directly on a lens; in a *reflecting telescope,* the image is focused on a concave mirror —*adj.* having parts that slide one inside another —*vi.* **-scoped′, -scop′ing** to slide or be forced one inside another like tubes of a collapsible telescope —*vt.* **1.** to cause to telescope **2.** to condense; shorten

tel·e·scop·ic (tel′ə skäp′ik) *adj.* **1.** of a telescope **2.** seen or obtained by a telescope **3.** visible only through a telescope **4.** farseeing **5.** having sections that slide one inside another Also **tel′e·scop′i·cal** —**tel′e·scop′i·cal·ly** *adv.*

te·les·co·py (tə les′kə pē) *n.* the art or practice of using a telescope —**te·les′co·pist** *n.*

tel·e·thon (tel′ə thän′) *n.* [TELE(VISION) + (MARA)THON] a campaign, as on a lengthy telecast, asking for support for a cause, as by pledged donations made by telephone

Tel·e·type (tel′ə tīp′) *a trademark for* a form of teletypewriter —*n.* [*often* **t-**] communication by means of Teletype —*vt., vi.* **-typed′, -typ′ing** [*often* **t-**] to send (messages) by Teletype —**tel′e·typ′er, tel′e·typ′ist** *n.*

tel·e·type·writ·er (tel′ə tīp′rīt′ər) *n.* a form of telegraph in which the message is typed on a keyboard that sends electric signals to a machine that prints the words

tel·e·vise (tel′ə vīz′) *vt., vi.* **-vised′, -vis′ing** to transmit by television —**tel′e·vi′sor** *n.*

tel·e·vi·sion (-vizh′ən) *n.* [TELE- + VISION] **1.** the process of transmitting scenes or views by radio waves or, sometimes, by wire, in which light rays are converted by a camera tube into electric signals that are transmitted to a receiver that changes the signals into electron beams that are projected against the screen of a picture tube, reproducing the original image **2.** television broadcasting as an industry, art, etc.; also, its facilities and related activities **3.** a television receiving set —*adj.* of, in, or by television

tel·ex (tel′eks) *n.* [TEL(ETYPEWRITER) + EX(CHANGE)] **1.** a teletypewriter with a telephone dial for making connections **2.** a message sent by this —*vt.* to send (a message) by telex

tell (tel) *vt.* **told, tell′ing** [OE. *tellan,* lit., to calculate] **1.** orig., to enumerate; count **2.** to give an account of (a story, etc.) in speech or writing; narrate; relate **3.** to express in words; utter [to *tell* the truth] **4.** to report; announce **5.** to make known; disclose **6.** to recognize; distinguish [I can *tell* the difference] **7.** to decide; know [he can't *tell* when to go] **8.** to let know; inform **9.** to request; order [*tell* him to leave] **10.** to assure emphatically [it's there, I *tell* you] —*vi.* **1.** to give an account or description (*of* something) **2.** to be evidence or an indication (*of* something) **3.** to reveal something, esp. secrets **4.** to produce a result or have a marked effect —**tell off** **1.** to count and separate from the total **2.** [Colloq.] to rebuke severely —**tell on** **1.** to make weary, worn-out, etc. **2.** [Colloq.] to inform against —**tell′a·ble** *adj.*

Tell (tel), **William** in Swiss legend, a hero in the fight for independence from Austria, forced, on pain of death, to shoot an apple off his son's head with bow and arrow

tell·er (tel′ər) *n.* **1.** a person who tells (a story, etc.) **2.** a person who counts; specif., *a*) one who counts votes *b*) a bank clerk who pays out or receives money

tell·ing (tel′iŋ) *adj.* **1.** having an effect; forceful; striking **2.** that tells or reveals much —**tell′ing·ly** *adv.*

tell·tale (-tāl′) *n.* **1.** a talebearer or informer **2.** an outward indication of a secret **3.** a device that indicates or records information —*adj.* revealing a secret

tel·lu·ri·um (te loor′ē əm) *n.* [ModL. < L. *tellus,* the earth] a rare, tin-white, brittle, nonmetallic chemical element: symbol, Te; at. wt., 127.60; at. no., 52

tel·ly (tel′ē) *n.* [Brit. Colloq.] television

tel·o- [< Gr. *telos,* an end] *a combining form meaning* end

tel·pher, tel·fer (tel′fər) *n.* [< TEL(E)- + Gr. *pherein,* to BEAR[1]] an electrically driven car suspended from and run on overhead cables —**tel′pher·age** *n.*

Tel·star (tel′stär′) [TEL(E)- + STAR] a satellite for relaying microwaves in communication by telephone, television, etc., first put in earth orbit in 1962

Tel·u·gu (tel′ə gōō′) *n.* **1.** a Dravidian language of S India **2.** *pl.* **-gus′, -gu′** a member of a Dravidian people speaking this language —*adj.* of Telugu or the Telugus Also **Tel′e·gu′**

tem·blor (tem′blôr, -blər; *Sp.* tem blôr′) *n., pl.* **-blors;** Sp. **-blo′res** (-blô′res) [Sp. < *temblar,* to tremble] *same as* EARTHQUAKE

te·mer·i·ty (tə mer′ə tē) *n.* [< L. < *temere,* rashly] foolish or rash boldness; recklessness

temp. **1.** temperature **2.** temporary

Tem·pe (tem′pē) [after Vale of *Tempe,* river valley in E Greece] city in SC Ariz.: suburb of Phoenix: pop. 107,000

tem·per (tem′pər) *vt.* [< OE. & OFr., both < L. *temperare,* to regulate < *tempus,* a period] **1.** to make suitable or free from excess by mingling with another thing; moderate [*temper* criticism with reason] **2.** *a*) to bring to the proper texture, hardness, etc. by treating in some way [to *temper* steel by heating and sudden cooling] *b*) to toughen, as by hardship **3.** *Music* to adjust the pitch of (a note, instrument, etc.) to some temperament —*vi.* to become tempered —*n.* **1.** a being tempered; specif., the degree of hardness and resiliency of a metal **2.** frame of mind; disposition **3.** mental calm; composure: now only in **lose** (or **keep**) **one's temper** **4.** a tendency to get angry **5.** anger; rage **6.** something used to temper a mixture, etc.

tem·per·a (tem′pər ə) *n.* [It. < *temperare* < L.: see prec.] **1.** *a*) a way of painting that uses pigments mixed with size, casein, or egg to produce a dull finish *b*) the paint so used **2.** an opaque, water-base paint used as for posters

tem·per·a·ment (tem′prə mənt, -pər ə mənt, -pər mənt) *n.* [L. *temperamentum,* proper mixing < *temperare:* see TEMPER] **1.** one's customary frame of mind or natural disposition **2.** a nature that is excitable, moody, etc. **3.** *Music* a system of adjustment of the intervals between the tones of an instrument

tem·per·a·men·tal (tem′prə men′t'l, -pər ə men′t'l, -pər men′t'l) ***adj.*** **1.** of or caused by temperament **2.** excitable by temperament; easily upset **3.** erratic in behavior —**tem′per·a·men′tal·ly** ***adv.***

tem·per·ance (tem′pər əns, -prəns) ***n.*** **[**< MFr. < L. < prp. of *temperare:* see TEMPER**]** **1.** a being temperate or moderate; self-restraint **2.** moderation in drinking alcoholic liquor, or, esp., the avoiding of alcoholic liquor completely

tem·per·ate (tem′pər it, -prit) ***adj.*** **[**< L. pp. of *temperare,* to TEMPER**]** **1.** moderate in indulging the appetites; abstemious, esp. in using alcoholic liquor **2.** moderate in one's actions, speech, etc. **3.** characterized by restraint *[a temperate reply]* **4.** neither very hot nor very cold: said of a climate, etc. —**tem′per·ate·ly** ***adv.*** —**tem′per·ate·ness** ***n.***

Temperate Zone either of two zones of the earth (**North Temperate Zone** and **South Temperate Zone**) between the tropics and the polar circles

tem·per·a·ture (tem′prə chər, tem′pər ə-) ***n.*** **[**< L. < *temperatus,* temperate**]** the degree of hotness or coldness of anything, usually as measured on a thermometer; specif., *a*) the degree of heat of a living body; also, an excess of this over the normal (about 98.6°F or 37°C in man) *b*) the degree of heat of the atmosphere

tem·pered (tem′pərd) ***adj.*** **1.** having been given the desired texture, hardness, etc. **2.** modified by other qualities, etc. **3.** having a (specified) temper *[bad-tempered)* **4.** *Music* adjusted to a temperament

tem·pest (tem′pist) ***n.*** **[**< OFr., ult. < L. *tempestas,* portion of time, weather < *tempus,* time**]** **1.** a violent storm with high winds, esp. one accompanied by rain, hail, or snow **2.** a violent outburst; tumult

tem·pes·tu·ous (tem pes′choo wəs) ***adj.*** **1.** of or like a tempest; stormy **2.** violent; turbulent —**tem·pes′tu·ous·ly** ***adv.*** —**tem·pes′tu·ous·ness** ***n.***

Tem·plar (tem′plər) ***n.*** **[**from occupying quarters near the site of Solomon's Temple in Jerusalem**]** *same as* KNIGHT TEMPLAR

tem·plate, tem·plet (tem′plit) ***n.*** **[**< Fr., dim. of *temple* < L. *templum,* small timber**]** **1.** a pattern, usually a thin plate, for forming an accurate copy of an object or shape **2.** *Archit.* *a*) a short stone or timber placed under a beam to help distribute the pressure *b*) a beam for supporting joists over a doorway, etc.

tem·ple[1] (tem′p'l) ***n.*** **[**< OE. & OFr., both < L. *templum,* orig., space marked out**]** **1.** a building for the worship of a god or gods **2.** [T-] any of three buildings for worshiping Jehovah, successively built by the Jews in ancient Jerusalem **3.** the synagogue of a Reform, or sometimes Conservative, congregation **4.** a Christian church **5.** a building, usually of imposing size, serving some purpose *[a Masonic temple]* —**tem′pled** ***adj.***

tem·ple[2] (tem′p'l) ***n.*** **[**< OFr. < VL. < L. *tempora,* the temples, pl. of *tempus,* temple of the head**]** **1.** the flat area at either side of the forehead, above and behind the eye **2.** either of the sidepieces of a pair of glasses

tem·po (tem′pō) ***n.,*** *pl.* **-pos, -pi** (-pē) **[**It. < L. *tempus,* time**]** **1.** the speed at which a piece of music is performed **2.** rate of activity; pace *[the tempo of modern living]*

tem·po·ral[1] (tem′pər əl, -prəl) ***adj.*** **[**L. *temporalis* < *tempus,* time**]** **1.** lasting only for a time; transitory; not eternal **2.** of this world; not spiritual **3.** civil or secular; not ecclesiastical **4.** of or limited by time —***n.*** a temporal thing, power, etc. —**tem′po·ral·ly** ***adv.***

tem·po·ral[2] (tem′pər əl, -prəl) ***adj.*** **[**LL. *temporalis* < L. *tempora:* see TEMPLE[2]**]** of or near the temple or temples (of the head)

temporal bone either of a pair of compound bones forming the sides of the skull

tem·po·ral·i·ty (tem′pə ral′ə tē) ***n.,*** *pl.* **-ties** **1.** the quality or state of being temporal **2.** [*usually pl.*] secular properties of a church

tem·po·rar·y (tem′pə rer′ē) ***adj.*** **[**< L. < *tempus,* time**]** lasting only for a time; not permanent —**tem·po·rar·i·ly** (tem′pə rer′ə lē, tem′pə rer′ə lē) ***adv.*** —**tem′po·rar′i·ness** ***n.***

tem·po·rize (tem′pə rīz′) ***vi.*** **-rized′, -riz′ing** **[**MFr. *temporiser* < ML. < L. *tempus,* time**]** **1.** to act or speak in a way one thinks is expedient, ignoring principle **2.** *a*) to put off making a decision, or to agree for a while, so as to gain time *b*) to bargain or deal (*with* a person) so as to gain time —**tem′po·ri·za′tion** ***n.*** —**tem′po·riz′er** ***n.***

tempt (tempt) ***vt.*** **[**< OFr. < LL. *temptare* < L., to try the strength of**]** **1.** orig., to test; try **2.** to entice (a person) to do or want something that is wrong, forbidden, etc. **3.** to be inviting or enticing to; attract **4.** to provoke or risk provoking (fate, etc.) —**tempt′a·ble** ***adj.*** —**tempt′er** ***n.*** —**tempt′ress** ***n.fem.***

temp·ta·tion (temp tā′shən) ***n.*** **1.** a tempting or being tempted **2.** something that tempts

tempt·ing (temp′tiŋ) ***adj.*** that tempts; enticing; attractive —**tempt′ing·ly** ***adv.***

tem·pu·ra (tem′poo rä′, tem poor′ə) ***n.*** **[**Jap., lit., fried food**]** a Japanese dish of seafood or vegetables dipped in an egg batter and deep-fried *[shrimp tempura]*

‡**tem·pus fu·git** (tem′pəs fyoo′jit) **[**L.**]** time flies

ten (ten) ***adj.*** **[**OE.**]** totaling one more than nine —***n.*** **1.** the cardinal number between 9 and 11; 10; X **2.** anything having ten units or members, or numbered ten **3.** [Colloq.] a ten-dollar bill

ten. **1.** tenor **2.** *Music* tenuto

ten·a·ble (ten′ə b'l) ***adj.*** **[**Fr. < OFr. < *tenir:* see TENANT**]** that can be held, defended, or believed —**ten′a·bil′i·ty, ten′a·ble·ness** ***n.*** —**ten′a·bly** ***adv.***

te·na·cious (tə nā′shəs) ***adj.*** **[**< L. *tenax* (gen. *tenacis*) < *tenere,* to hold**]** **1.** holding firmly *[a tenacious grip]* **2.** that retains well *[a tenacious memory]* **3.** holding together strongly; cohesive **4.** clinging; adhesive **5.** persistent —**te·na′cious·ly** ***adv.*** —**te·na′cious·ness** ***n.***

te·nac·i·ty (tə nas′ə tē) ***n.*** the quality or state of being tenacious

ten·an·cy (ten′ən sē) ***n.,*** *pl.* **-cies** **1.** occupancy or duration of occupancy by a tenant **2.** any holding of property, an office, etc.

ten·ant (ten′ənt) ***n.*** **[**OFr., orig. prp. of *tenir,* to hold < L. *tenere***]** **1.** a person who pays rent to occupy or use land, a building, etc. **2.** an occupant of or dweller in a specified place —***vt.*** to occupy as a tenant —**ten′ant·a·ble** ***adj.*** —**ten′ant·less** ***adj.***

tenant farmer a person who farms land owned by another and pays rent in cash or in a share of the crops

ten·ant·ry (ten′ən trē) ***n.,*** *pl.* **-ries** **1.** a body of tenants **2.** occupancy by a tenant

ten-cent store (ten′sent′) *same as* FIVE-AND-TEN-CENT STORE

Ten Commandments *Bible* the ten laws forming the fundamental moral code of Israel, given to Moses by God on Mount Sinai: Ex. 20:2–17; Deut. 5:6–22

tend[1] (tend) ***vt.*** **[**see ATTEND**]** **1.** to take care of; watch over; attend to **2.** to be in charge of; manage —***vi.*** to pay attention; attend

tend[2] (tend) ***vi.*** **[**< OFr. < L. *tendere,* to stretch**]** **1.** to move or extend *[to tend east]* **2.** to be likely or apt; incline *[tending to boast]* **3.** to lead (*to* or *toward* a specified result)

tend·en·cy (ten′dən sē) ***n.,*** *pl.* **-cies** **[**< ML. < L. prp. of *tendere,* to stretch**]** **1.** an inclination to move or act in a particular direction or way; leaning; bias **2.** a course toward some purpose, object, or result; drift **3.** a definite purpose or point of view in something said or written

ten·den·tious (ten den′shəs) ***adj.*** **[**< G., ult. < ML. *tendentia,* TENDENCY**]** showing a deliberate tendency or aim; esp., advancing a definite point of view: also sp. **ten·den′cious** —**ten·den′tious·ly** ***adv.*** —**ten·den′tious·ness** ***n.***

ten·der[1] (ten′dər) ***adj.*** **[**< OFr. < L. *tener,* soft**]** **1.** soft or delicate and easily chewed, broken, cut, etc. **2.** physically weak; frail **3.** immature; young *[the tender age of five]* **4.** of soft quality or delicate tone **5.** needing careful handling; ticklish *[a tender subject]* **6.** gentle or light, as a touch **7.** *a*) affectionate, loving, etc. *[a tender smile]* *b*) careful; considerate **8.** *a*) that is hurt or feels pain easily; sensitive *[a tender skin]* *b*) sensitive to impressions, emotions, etc. *[a tender conscience]* *c*) sensitive to others' feelings; compassionate *[a tender heart]* —**ten′der·ly** ***adv.*** —**ten′der·ness** ***n.***

ten·der[2] (ten′dər) ***vt.*** **[**< Fr. < L. *tendere,* to stretch**]** **1.** to offer in payment of an obligation **2.** to present for acceptance; offer (an invitation, apology, etc.) —***n.*** **1.** an offer of money, services, etc. made to satisfy an obligation **2.** a formal offer, as of marriage, a contract, etc. **3.** money, etc. offered in payment —**ten′der·er** ***n.***

tend·er[3] (ten′dər) ***n.*** **1.** a person who tends, or has charge of, something **2.** *a*) a ship to supply or service another ship, a submarine, etc. *b*) a boat for carrying passengers, etc. to or from a ship close to shore **3.** the railroad car behind a steam locomotive for carrying its coal and water

ten·der·foot (-foot′) ***n.,*** *pl.* **-foots′, -feet′** **1.** a newcomer, specif. to the hardships of Western ranching **2.** a beginner in the Boy Scouts

ten·der·heart·ed (-här′tid) ***adj.*** having a tender heart; quick to feel pity —**ten′der·heart′ed·ly** ***adv.*** —**ten′der-heart′ed·ness** ***n.***

ten·der·ize (ten′də rīz′) ***vt.*** **-ized′, -iz′ing** to make (meat) tender, as by adding a substance that softens tissues —**ten′der·iz′er** ***n.***

ten·der·loin (ten′dər loin′) ***n.*** **1.** the tenderest muscle of a loin of beef or pork **2.** [*usually* **T-**] a vice-filled district of a city: so called because viewed as choice for graft

ten·di·ni·tis (ten′də nīt′əs) ***n.*** **[**< ModL.: see TENDON & -ITIS**]** inflammation of a tendon

ten·don (ten′dən) ***n.*** **[**ML. *tendo* (gen. *tendinis*) < Gr. < *teinein,* to stretch**]** any of the cords of tough, fibrous tissue connecting muscles to bones or other parts; sinew —**ten′dinous** (-də nəs) ***adj.***

ten·dril (ten′drəl) ***n.*** [prob. < OFr. *tendrum,* ult. < L. *tener,* soft] a threadlike part of a climbing plant, serving to support it by clinging to or coiling around an object

TENDRIL

ten·e·brous (ten′ə brəs) ***adj.*** [< L. < *tenebrae,* darkness] dark; gloomy: also **te·neb·ri·ous** (tə neb′rē əs)

ten·e·ment (ten′ə mənt) ***n.*** [< OFr. < ML. < L. *tenere,* to hold] **1.** *Law* land, buildings, etc. held by tenure **2.** a dwelling house **3.** a separately tenanted room or suite **4.** *same as* TENEMENT HOUSE —**ten′e·men′tal, ten′e·men′ta·ry** ***adj.***

tenement house an apartment building, now specif. one in the slums that is run-down and overcrowded

ten·et (ten′it) ***n.*** [L., he holds] a principle, doctrine, or belief held as a truth, as by some group

ten·fold (ten′fōld′) ***adj.*** **1.** having ten parts **2.** having ten times as much or as many —***adv.*** ten times as much or as many

ten-gal·lon hat (ten′gal′ən) a wide-brimmed felt hat with a high, round crown, orig. worn by cowboys

Ten·nes·see (ten′ə sē′) [< *Tanasi,* Cherokee village name] **1.** EC State of the U.S.: 42,244 sq. mi.; pop. 4,591,000; cap. Nashville: abbrev. **Tenn., TN** **2.** river flowing from NE Tenn. through N Ala. & W Tenn. into the Ohio River —**Ten′nes·se′an** ***adj., n.***

Tennessee walking horse any of a breed of saddle or light utility horse with an easy, ambling gait

ten·nis (ten′is) ***n.*** [prob. < Anglo-Fr. *tenetz,* hold (imperative) < OFr. *tenir:* see TENANT] **1.** a game (officially **lawn tennis**), usually played outdoors, in which two or four players using rackets hit a ball back and forth over a net dividing a marked rectangular area (**tennis court**) **2.** a similar but more complex old indoor game (**court tennis**), the ball being in addition bounced against walls

tennis shoe *same as* SNEAKER (sense 2)

Ten·ny·son (ten′ə s′n), **Alfred,** 1st Baron Tennyson, 1809–92; Eng. poet: called *Alfred, Lord Tennyson* —**Ten′ny·so′ni·an** (-sō′nē ən) ***adj.***

ten·on (ten′ən) ***n.*** [< MFr. < *tenir:* see TENANT] a part of a piece of wood, etc. cut to stick out so that it will fit into a hole (*mortise*) in another piece to make a joint: see MORTISE, illus. —***vt., vi.*** **1.** to make a tenon (on) **2.** to joint by mortise and tenon

ten·or (ten′ər) ***n.*** [< OFr. < L. < *tenere,* to hold] **1.** general course or tendency **2.** general meaning; drift **3.** general character or nature **4.** [because the tenor voice "held" the melody] *a)* the highest usual adult male voice, or its range: see also COUNTERTENOR *b)* a part for this voice *c)* a singer or instrument having this range —***adj.*** of, in, or for the tenor

tenor clef *see* C CLEF

ten·pen·ny (ten′pen′ē, -pə nē) ***adj.*** **1.** worth ten (esp. Brit.) pennies **2.** designating a size of nails, three inches long

ten·pins (-pinz′) ***n.pl.*** **1.** [*with sing. v.*] the game of bowling in which ten pins are used **2.** the pins

tense[1] (tens) ***adj.*** **tens′er, tens′est** [< L. pp. of *tendere,* to stretch] **1.** stretched tight; strained; taut **2.** feeling, showing, or causing mental strain; anxious —***vt., vi.*** **tensed, tens′ing** to make or become tense —**tense′ly** ***adv.*** —**tense′ness** ***n.***

tense[2] (tens) ***n.*** [< OFr. < L. *tempus,* time] any form or set of forms of a verb that show the time of the action or condition

ten·sile (ten′s′l) ***adj.*** **1.** of or under tension **2.** capable of being stretched: also **ten′si·ble** (-sə b′l) —**ten·sil′i·ty** (-sil′ə tē) ***n.***

ten·sion (ten′shən) ***n.*** **1.** a tensing or being tensed **2.** mental or nervous strain; tense feeling **3.** a state of strained relations **4.** a device to regulate tautness of thread, etc. **5.** *same as* VOLTAGE **6.** *a)* stress on a material by forces tending to cause extension *b)* a force exerting such stress —***vt.*** to subject to tension —**ten′sion·al** ***adj.***

ten·sor (ten′sər, -sôr) ***n.*** [ModL. < L. pp. of *tendere,* to stretch] any muscle that stretches a body part

tent (tent) ***n.*** [< OFr. < L. pp. of *tendere,* to stretch] **1.** a portable shelter consisting of canvas, skins, etc. stretched over poles and attached to stakes **2.** anything like a tent; specif., *short for* OXYGEN TENT —***adj.*** of or like a tent —***vi.*** to live in a tent —***vt.*** **1.** to lodge in tents **2.** to cover as with a tent

ten·ta·cle (ten′tə k′l) ***n.*** [ModL. *tentaculum* < L. *tentare,* to touch] **1.** any of various slender, flexible growths at or near the head or mouth, as of some invertebrates, used for grasping, feeling, moving, etc. **2.** *Bot.* any of the sensitive hairs on the leaves of insect-eating plants —**ten·tac′u·lar** (-tak′yə lər) ***adj.***

ten·ta·tive (ten′tə tiv) ***adj.*** [LL. *tentativus* < pp. of L. *tentare,* to try] made or done as a test or for the time being; not definite or final —**ten′ta·tive·ly** ***adv.*** —**ten′ta·tive·ness** ***n.***

tent caterpillar any of the caterpillars that live in colonies in large, tentlike webs spun among the tree branches that they defoliate

ten·ter (ten′tər) ***n.*** [see TENT] a frame to stretch cloth on for even drying —***vt.*** to stretch on a tenter

ten·ter·hook (-hook′) ***n.*** any of the hooked nails that hold cloth stretched on a tenter —**on tenterhooks** in suspense

tenth (tenth) ***adj.*** [OE. *teogotha*] **1.** preceded by nine others in a series; 10th **2.** designating any of the ten equal parts of something —***n.*** **1.** the one following the ninth **2.** any of the ten equal parts of something; 1/10 —**tenth′ly** ***adv.***

tent stitch [< ? TENT] an embroidery stitch forming a series of parallel slanting lines

ten·u·ous (ten′yoo wəs) ***adj.*** [< L. *tenuis,* thin + -OUS] **1.** slender or fine, as a fiber **2.** not dense; rare, as air high up **3.** not substantial; slight; flimsy *[tenuous* evidence*]* —**te·nu·i·ty** (tə nōō′ə tē, -nyōō′-), **ten′u·ous·ness** ***n.*** —**ten′u·ous·ly** ***adv.***

ten·ure (ten′yər, -yoor) ***n.*** [< MFr. < *tenir:* see TENANT] **1.** the act or right of holding property, an office, etc. **2.** the period or conditions of this **3.** the holding of a position in teaching, etc. on a permanent basis after meeting specified requirements

te·nu·to (tə nōōt′ō) ***adj.*** [It., pp. of *tenere,* to hold] *Music* held for the full value, as a note

te·pee (tē′pē) ***n.*** [< Siouan < *ti,* to dwell + *pi,* used for] a cone-shaped tent of animal skins, used by the Indians of the Great Plains

tep·id (tep′id) ***adj.*** [< L. < *tepere,* to be slightly warm] slightly warm; lukewarm —**te·pid·i·ty** (tə pid′ə tē), **tep′id·ness** ***n.*** —**tep′id·ly** ***adv.***

te·qui·la (tə kē′lə) ***n.*** [AmSp. < Nahuatl *Tequila,* a Mexican district] **1.** a strong alcoholic liquor of Mexico, distilled from pulque or mescal **2.** a Mexican agave that is a source of tequila and mescal

TEPEE

ter. **1.** terrace **2.** territory

ter·a- (ter′ə) [< Gr. *teras,* monster] *a combining form meaning* one trillion *[terahertz]*

ter·a·tism (ter′ə tiz′m) ***n.*** [< Gr. *teras* (gen. *teratos*), a monster] an abnormally formed fetus; monstrosity

ter·bi·um (tur′bē əm) ***n.*** [ModL. < *Ytterby,* town in Sweden] a metallic chemical element of the rare-earth group: symbol, Tb; at. wt., 158.924; at. no., 65

terce (turs) ***n.*** [< OFr. < L. *tertia,* fem. of *tertius,* third] [*often* **T-**] *Eccles.* the third of the seven canonical hours

ter·cen·te·nar·y (tur′sen ten′ər ē, tər sen′tə ner′ē) ***adj., n., pl.*** **-nar·ies** [L. *ter,* three times + CENTENARY] *same as* TRICENTENNIAL: also **ter′cen·ten′ni·al** (-ten′ē əl)

ter·cet (tur′sit, tər set′) ***n.*** [Fr. < It. dim. of *terzo,* a third < L. *tertius*] a group of three lines that rhyme or are connected by rhyme with an adjacent triplet

ter·e·binth (ter′ə binth′) ***n.*** [< MFr., ult. < Gr. *terebinthos*] a small European tree whose cut bark yields a turpentine

Ter·ence (ter′əns) [L. *Terentius,* name of a Roman gens] **1.** a masculine name: dim. *Terry* **2.** (L. name *Publius Terentius Afer*) 190?–159? B.C.; Rom. writer of comedies

Te·re·sa (tə rē′sə; *Sp.* te re′sä) **1.** [var. of THERESA] a feminine name **2.** Saint, 1515–82; Sp. Carmelite nun: called **Teresa of A·vi·la** (ä′vē lä′)

ter·gi·ver·sate (tur′ji vər sāt′) ***vi.*** **-sat′ed, -sat′ing** [< L. pp. of *tergiversari* < *tergum,* the back + *versari,* to turn] **1.** to desert a cause, party, etc. **2.** to use evasions or subterfuge —**ter′gi·ver·sa′tion** ***n.*** —**ter′gi·ver·sa′tor** ***n.***

ter·i·ya·ki (ter′ē yä′kē) ***n.*** [Jap.] meat or fish marinated or dipped in soy sauce and broiled, grilled, or barbecued: a Japanese dish

term (turm) ***n.*** [< OFr. < L. *terminus,* a limit] **1.** a set date, as for payment, termination of tenancy, etc. **2.** a set period of time; specif., *a)* a division of a school year, as a semester *b)* the period set for holding an office *c)* the normal period between conception and birth; also, the end of this period; childbirth **3.** [*pl.*] conditions of a contract, sale, etc. that limit or define it **4.** [*pl.*] personal relations *[*on speaking *terms]* **5.** a word or phrase having definite meaning in some science, art, etc. **6.** a word or phrase of a specified kind *[*a derogatory *term]* **7.** *Law a)* the time a court is in session *b)* the length of time for which an estate is granted *c)* the estate itself *d)* time allowed a debtor to pay **8.** *Logic a)* either of two concepts with a stated relation, as the subject and predicate of a proposition *b)* any one of the three parts of a syllogism **9.** *Math. a)* either of the two quantities of a fraction or ratio *b)* each quantity in a series or in an algebraic expression *—vt.* to call by a term; name **—bring to terms** to force to agree **—come to terms** to arrive at an agreement **—in terms of** regarding; concerning **—term′less** *adj.*

ter·ma·gant (tʉr′mə gənt) *n.* [< OFr. *Tervagant,* alleged Moslem deity] a quarrelsome, scolding woman; shrew

term·er (tʉr′mər) *n.* a person serving a specified term, esp. in prison *[a third-termer]*

ter·mi·na·ble (tʉr′mi nə b'l) *adj.* **1.** that can be terminated **2.** that terminates after a specified time, as a contract **—ter′mi·na·bil′i·ty, ter′mi·na·ble·ness** *n.*

ter·mi·nal (tʉr′mə n'l) *adj.* [L. *terminalis*] **1.** of, at, or forming the end or extremity of something **2.** occurring at the end of a series; concluding; final **3.** of or in the final stages of a fatal disease *[terminal* cancer*]* **4.** in or of a term or set period of time **5.** of, at, or forming the end of a transportation line *—n.* **1.** a terminating part; end; extremity **2.** a connective device or point on an electric circuit or conductor **3.** *a)* either end of a transportation line *b)* a station or city there or at any important point of the line **4.** a device, often with a keyboard and a cathode-ray screen, for feeding information into, or receiving information from, a computer **—ter′mi·nal·ly** *adv.*

ter·mi·nate (-nāt′) *vt.* **-nat′ed, -nat′ing** [< L. pp. of *terminare,* to end < *terminus,* a limit] **1.** to form the end or limit of; finish or bound **2.** to put an end to; stop *—vi.* to come to an end **—ter′mi·na′tive** *adj.* **—ter′mi·na′tor** *n.*

ter·mi·na·tion (tʉr′mə nā′shən) *n.* **1.** a terminating or being terminated **2.** the end or limit **3.** *Linguis.* the end of a word; specif., an inflectional ending

ter·mi·nol·o·gy (tʉr′mə näl′ə jē) *n., pl.* **-gies** the terms or special words used in some science, art, work, etc. **—ter′mi·no·log′i·cal** (-nə läj′i k'l) *adj.* **—ter′mi·no·log′i·cal·ly** *adv.* **—ter′mi·nol′o·gist** *n.*

ter·mi·nus (tʉr′mə nəs) *n., pl.* **-ni′** (-nī′), **-nus·es** [L., a limit] **1.** a boundary or limit **2.** a boundary stone or marker **3.** an end; final point or goal **4.** either end of a transportation line

ter·mite (tʉr′mīt) *n.* [L. *termes* (gen. *termitis*), wood-boring worm] a pale-colored, soft-bodied, antlike insect that lives in colonies and is very destructive to wooden structures

tern (tʉrn) *n.* [< ON. *therna*] any of several sea birds related to the gulls, but smaller, with a more slender body and beak and a deeply forked tail

ter·na·ry (tʉr′nər ē) *adj.* [< L. < *terni,* three each] **1.** threefold; triple **2.** third in rank, etc.

ter·nate (tʉr′nāt) *adj.* [ModL., ult. < L. *terni,* three each] **1.** consisting of three **2.** arranged in threes, as some leaves **—ter′nate·ly** *adv.*

ter·pene (tʉr′pēn) *n.* [G. *terpen*] any of a series of isomeric hydrocarbons of the general formula $C_{10}H_{16}$, found in resins, etc.

Terp·sich·o·re (tərp sik′ə rē′) *Gr. Myth.* the Muse of dancing

terp·si·cho·re·an (tʉrp′si kə rē′ən) *adj.* **1.** [T-] of Terpsichore **2.** having to do with dancing *—n.* a dancer: now only in humorous use

ter·race (ter′əs) *n.* [OFr., walled platform < It. *terrazzo* < L. *terra,* earth] **1.** *a)* a raised, flat mound of earth with sloping sides *b)* any of a series of flat platforms of earth with sloping sides, rising one above another, as on a hillside *c)* a geological formation of this nature **2.** an unroofed, paved area adjoining a house and overlooking a lawn or garden **3.** a gallery, portico, etc. **4.** a balcony or deck outside an apartment **5.** a flat roof, esp. of a house of Spanish architecture **6.** *a)* a row of houses on ground raised from the street *b)* a street in front of such houses *—vt.* **-raced, -rac·ing** to form into or surround with a terrace

ter·ra cot·ta (ter′ə kät′ə) [It., lit., baked earth < L.] **1.** a hard, brown-red, usually unglazed earthenware used for pottery, sculpture, etc. **2.** its brown-red color **—ter′ra-cot′ta** *adj.*

terra fir·ma (fʉr′mə) [L.] firm earth; solid ground

ter·rain (tə rān′, ter′ān) *n.* [Fr. < L. < *terra,* earth] ground or a tract of ground, esp. with regard to its features or fitness for some use

Ter·ra·my·cin (ter′ə mī′s'n) [< L. *terra,* earth + MYC(O)- + -IN¹] *a trademark for* an antibiotic derived from cultures of a soil fungus

ter·ra·pin (ter′ə pin) *n.* [< Algonquian] **1.** any of several American freshwater or tidewater turtles; specif., *same as* DIAMONDBACK **2.** its edible flesh

ter·rar·i·um (tə rer′ē əm) *n., pl.* **-i·ums, -i·a** (-ə) [ModL. < L. *terra,* earth + *-arium* as in *aquarium*] **1.** an enclosure for keeping small land animals **2.** a glass container for a garden of small plants

ter·raz·zo (tə raz′ō, tə rät′sō) *n.* [It., lit., TERRACE] flooring of small chips of marble set in cement and polished

Ter·re Haute (ter′ə hōt′, hut′) [Fr., lit., high land] city in W Ind., on the Wabash: pop. 61,000

ter·res·tri·al (tə res′trē əl) *adj.* [< L. *terrestris* < *terra,* earth] **1.** of this world; worldly; mundane **2.** of or constituting the earth **3.** consisting of land as distinguished from water **4.** living on land rather than in water, in the air, in trees, etc. **5.** growing in the ground *—n.* an inhabitant of the earth **—ter·res′tri·al·ly** *adv.*

ter·ret (ter′it) *n.* [< OFr. *toret,* dim. of *tour,* a turn] **1.** a ring for attaching a leash, as on a dog collar **2.** any of the rings on a harness, through which the reins pass

ter·ri·ble (ter′ə b'l) *adj.* [OFr. < L. *terribilis* < *terrere,* to frighten] **1.** causing terror; fearful; dreadful **2.** extreme; intense; severe **3.** [Colloq.] very bad, unpleasant, disagreeable, etc. **—ter′ri·ble·ness** *n.* **—ter′ri·bly** *adv.*

ter·ri·er (ter′ē ər) *n.* [MFr. (*chien*) *terrier,* hunting (dog) < *terrier,* hillock, ult. < L. *terra,* earth] any of various breeds of active, typically small dog, orig. bred to burrow after small game

ter·rif·ic (tə rif′ik) *adj.* [< L. < base of *terrere,* to frighten + -FIC] **1.** causing great fear; terrifying; dreadful **2.** [Colloq.] *a)* unusually great, intense, etc. *b)* unusually fine, enjoyable, etc. **—ter·rif′i·cal·ly** *adv.*

ter·ri·fy (ter′ə fī′) *vi.* **-fied′, -fy′ing** [L. *terrificare* < *terrificus,* TERRIFIC] to fill with terror; frighten greatly; alarm **—ter′ri·fy′ing·ly** *adv.*

ter·ri·to·ri·al (ter′ə tôr′ē əl) *adj.* **1.** of territory or land **2.** of or limited to a specific territory or district **3.** [T-] of a Territory or Territories **4.** [*often* **T-**] organized regionally for home defense *—n.* [T-] [Chiefly Brit.] a member of a Territorial force **—ter′ri·to′ri·al′i·ty** (-al′ə tē) *n.* **—ter′ri·to′ri·al·ly** *adv.*

ter·ri·to·ry (ter′ə tôr′ē) *n., pl.* **-ries** [L. *territorium* < *terra,* earth] **1.** the land and waters under the jurisdiction of a nation, state, ruler, etc. **2.** a part of a country or empire without the full status of a principal division; specif., *a)* [T-] formerly, a part of the U.S. without the status of a State and having an appointed governor *b)* [T-] a similar region in Canada or Australia **3.** any large tract of land; region **4.** an assigned area, as of a traveling salesman **5.** a sphere of action, existence, etc. **6.** the area occupied by an animal or pair of animals as for breeding, foraging, etc.

ter·ror (ter′ər) *n.* [< MFr. < L. < *terrere,* to frighten] **1.** intense fear **2.** *a)* a person or thing causing intense fear *b)* the quality of causing dread; terribleness **3.** a program of terrorism **4.** [Colloq.] a very annoying or unmanageable person, esp. a child

ter·ror·ism (-iz'm) *n.* **1.** the use of force and violence to intimidate, subjugate, etc., esp. as a political policy **2.** the intimidation produced in this way **—ter′ror·ist** *n., adj.* **—ter′ror·is′tic** *adj.*

ter·ror·ize (-īz′) *vt.* **-ized′, -iz′ing** **1.** to fill with terror **2.** to coerce, make submit, etc. by filling with terror **—ter′ror·i·za′tion** *n.* **—ter′ror·iz′er** *n.*

ter·ry (ter′ē) *n., pl.* **-ries** [prob. < Fr. pp. of *tirer,* to draw] cloth having a pile in which the loops are left uncut: also **terry cloth**

terse (tʉrs) *adj.* **ters′er, ters′est** [< L. pp. of *tergere,* to wipe] free of superfluous words; concise; succinct **—terse′ly** *adv.* **—terse′ness** *n.*

ter·tial (tʉr′shəl) *adj.* [< L. *tertius,* third] designating or of the third row of flight feathers on a bird's wing *—n.* a tertial feather

ter·tian (tʉr′shən) *adj.* [< L. < *tertius,* third] occurring every other day *—n.* a tertian fever or disease

ter·ti·ar·y (tʉr′shē er′ē, -shə rē) *adj.* [< L. < *tertius,* third] **1.** of the third rank, order, formation, etc.; third **2.** [T-] *Geol.* designating or of the first period in the Cenozoic Era **3.** *Zool. same as* TERTIAL *—n., pl.* **-ar′ies** *Zool. same as* TERTIAL **—the Tertiary** the Tertiary Period or its rocks: see GEOLOGY, chart

tes·sel·late (tes′ə lāt′; *for adj.* -lit) *vt.* **-lat′ed, -lat′ing** [< L. < *tessella,* little square stone] to lay out or pave in a mosaic pattern of small, square blocks *—adj.* tessellated

test¹ (test) *n.* [OFr., cup used in assaying < L. *testum,* earthen vessel < *testa,* shell] **1.** *a)* an examination or trial, as to prove the value or find out the nature of something *b)* a method or process, or a standard or criterion, used in this **2.** an event, situation, etc. that tries a person's qualities **3.** a set of questions, problems, etc. for determining a person's knowledge, abilities, etc.; examination **4.** *Chem. a)* a trial or reaction for identifying a substance *b)* the reagent used in the procedure *c)* a positive indication obtained by it *—vt.* to subject to a test; try *—vi.* **1.** to give or take a test for diagnosis, function, etc. *[to test* for blood sugar*]* **2.** to be rated as the result of a test *[to test* high*]* **—test′a·ble** *adj.*

test² (test) *n.* [L. *testa:* see prec.] the hard outer covering of certain invertebrate animals, as the shell of clams

Test. Testament

tes·ta (tes′tə) *n., pl.* **-tae** (-tē) [ModL. < L., a shell] *Bot.* the hard outer covering of a seed

tes·ta·ment (tes′tə mənt) *n.* [< OFr. < LL. < L., ult. < *testis,* a witness] **1.** orig., a covenant, esp. one between God and man **2.** [T-] *a)* either of the two parts of the Christian Bible, the *Old Testament* and the *New Testament* *b)* [Colloq.] a copy of the New Testament **3.** *a)* a testimonial *b)* an affirmation of beliefs, etc. **4.** *Law* a will: now rare except in **last will and testament** —**tes′ta·men′ta·ry** (-men′tə rē), **tes′ta·men′tal** *adj.*

tes·tate (tes′tāt) *adj.* [< L. pp. of *testari,* to testify, make a will] having made and left a legally valid will —*n.* a person who has died testate

tes·ta·tor (tes′tāt ər, tes tāt′-) *n.* a person who has made a will, esp. one who has died leaving a valid will —**tes·ta′trix** (-tā′triks) *n.fem., pl.* **-tri·ces′** (-tri sēz′)

test ban an agreement between or among nuclear powers to forgo tests of nuclear weapons, esp. in the atmosphere

test case *Law* **1.** a case that is likely to be used as a precedent **2.** a case entered into with the intention of testing the constitutionality of a particular law

test·er[1] (tes′tər) *n.* a person or thing that tests

tes·ter[2] (tes′tər) *n.* [< OFr. *testiere,* headpiece < L. *testa:* see TEST[1]] a canopy, as over a bed

tes·ti·cle (tes′ti k'l) *n.* [< L. dim. of *testis,* testicle] either of two oval sex glands in the male that are suspended in the scrotum and secrete spermatozoa —**tes·tic′u·lar** (-tik′yoo lər) *adj.*

tes·ti·fy (tes′tə fī′) *vi.* **-fied′, -fy′ing** [< L. *testificari* < *testis,* a witness + *facere,* to make] **1.** to bear witness or give evidence, esp. under oath in court **2.** to be evidence or an indication [*his look testifies to his rage*] —*vt.* **1.** to bear witness to; affirm; give as evidence, esp. under oath in court **2.** to be evidence of; indicate —**tes′ti·fi·ca′tion** *n.* —**tes′ti·fi′er** *n.*

tes·ti·mo·ni·al (tes′tə mō′nē əl) *n.* **1.** a statement testifying to a person's qualifications, character, etc. or to the merits of some product, etc. **2.** something given or done as an expression of gratitude or appreciation

tes·ti·mo·ny (tes′tə mō′nē) *n., pl.* **-nies** [< L. < *testis,* a witness] **1.** a statement made under oath in court to establish a fact **2.** any affirmation or declaration **3.** any form of evidence; indication [*his smile was testimony of his joy*] **4.** public avowal, as of faith

tes·tis (tes′tis) *n., pl.* **-tes** (-tēz) [L.] *same as* TESTICLE

tes·tos·ter·one (tes täs′tə rōn′) *n.* [TEST(IS) + *-o-* + STER(OL) + -ONE] a male sex hormone, $C_{19}H_{28}O_2$, a crystalline steroid obtained from animal testes or synthesized: used in medicine

test pilot a pilot who tests new or newly designed airplanes in flight, to determine their fitness for use

test-tube (test′to͞ob′, -tyo͞ob′) *adj.* **1.** made in or as in a test tube; experimental **2.** produced by artificial insemination [*a test-tube baby*]

test tube a tube of thin, clear glass closed at one end, used in chemical experiments, etc.

tes·tu·do (tes to͞o′dō, -tyo͞o′-) *n., pl.* **-di·nes′** (-də nēz′) [L., tortoise (shell)] in ancient Rome, **1.** a movable, roofed shelter used by soldiers **2.** a protection formed by a group of soldiers by overlapping shields above their heads

tes·ty (tes′tē) *adj.* **-ti·er, -ti·est** [< Anglo-Fr. < OFr. *teste,* the head < L. *testa:* see TEST[1]] irritable; touchy; peevish —**tes′ti·ly** *adv.* —**tes′ti·ness** *n.*

Tet (tet) *n.* [Vietnamese] a three-day Asian festival in winter, celebrating the arrival of the new year

tet·a·nus (tet′'n əs) *n.* [L. < Gr. *tetanos,* spasm, lit., stretched] an acute infectious disease, often fatal, caused by the toxin of a bacillus which usually enters the body through wounds: characterized by spasmodic contractions and rigidity of muscles; lockjaw —**te·tan·ic** (ti tan′ik) *adj.*

tetched (techt) *adj.* [Dial. or Humorous] touched; slightly demented

tetch·y (tech′ē) *adj.* **tetch′i·er, tetch′i·est** [prob. < OFr. *teche,* a spot + -Y[2]] touchy; irritable; peevish —**tetch′i·ly** *adv.* —**tetch′i·ness** *n.*

tête-à-tête (tāt′ə tāt′) *n.* [Fr., lit., head-to-head] **1.** a private conversation between two people **2.** an S-shaped seat on which two people can sit facing each other —*adj.* for or of two people in private —*adv.* together privately [*to speak tête-à-tête*]

teth·er (teth′ər) *n.* [prob. < ON. *tjōthr*] **1.** a rope or chain fastened to an animal so as to keep it within certain bounds **2.** the limit of one's abilities, resources, etc. —*vt.* to fasten with a tether —**at the end of one's tether** at the end of one's endurance, resources, etc.

teth·er·ball (-bôl′) *n.* **1.** a game for two who hit at a ball hanging by a cord from a pole in an attempt to make the cord coil around the pole **2.** the ball used

tet·ra (tet′rə) *n.* [< ModL. < old genus name] a colorful tropical American fish, often kept in aquariums

tet·ra- [Gr. < base of *tettares,* four] *a combining form meaning* four: also, before a vowel, **tetr-**

tet·ra·chord (tet′rə kôrd′) *n.* [< Gr.: see TETRA- & CHORD[2]] *Music* a series of four tones within the interval of a fourth —**tet′ra·chor′dal** *adj.*

tet·ra·cy·cline (tet′rə sī′klin, -klīn) *n.* [< TETRA- + CYCL(IC) + -INE[4]] a yellow, crystalline powder, prepared synthetically or obtained from certain microorganisms: used as an antibiotic

tet·rad (tet′rad) *n.* [< Gr. *tetras,* four] a group or set of four

tet·ra·eth·yl lead (tet′rə eth′'l) a heavy, colorless, poisonous compound of lead, added to gasoline to increase power and prevent engine knock

tet·ra·he·dron (-hē′drən) *n., pl.* **-drons, -dra** (-drə) [ModL. < LGr.: see TETRA- & -HEDRON] a solid figure with four triangular faces —**tet′ra·he′dral** *adj.*

TETRAHEDRON

te·tral·o·gy (te tral′ə jē) *n., pl.* **-gies** [< Gr.: see TETRA- & -LOGY] any series of four related plays, operas, novels, etc.

te·tram·e·ter (te tram′ə tər) *n.* [< LL. < Gr.: see TETRA- & -METER] **1.** a line of verse containing four metrical feet **2.** verse consisting of tetrameters —*adj.* having four metrical feet

te·trarch (te′trärk, tē′-) *n.* [< LL. < L. < Gr.: see TETRA- & -ARCH] **1.** in the ancient Roman Empire, the ruler of part (orig. a fourth part) of a province **2.** a subordinate prince, governor, etc. —**te·trarch′ic** *adj.*

te·trarch·y (-trär kē) *n., pl.* **-trarch·ies** **1.** the rule or territory of a tetrarch **2.** government by four persons

tet·ra·va·lent (tet′rə vā′lənt) *adj.* **1.** having a valence of four **2.** *same as* QUADRIVALENT (sense 1)

te·trox·ide (te träk′sīd) *n.* any oxide with four atoms of oxygen in each molecule

tet·ter (tet′ər) *n.* [OE. *teter*] any of various skin diseases, as eczema, characterized by itching

Teut. **1.** Teuton **2.** Teutonic

Teu·ton (to͞ot′'n, tyo͞ot′-) *n.* **1.** a member of the Teutones **2.** a member of any Teutonic people; esp., a German

Teu·to·nes (-ēz′) *n.pl.* [L.] an ancient tribe, either Teutonic or Celtic, that lived in Jutland

Teu·ton·ic (to͞o tän′ik, tyo͞o-) *adj.* **1.** of the ancient Teutons **2.** German **3.** designating or of a group of north European peoples including the German, Scandinavian, Dutch, English, etc. **4.** *Linguis. earlier var. of* GERMANIC —**Teu·ton′i·cal·ly** *adv.*

Tex·as (tek′səs) [Sp. < AmInd. *techas,* allies (against the Apaches)] SW State of the U.S., on the Gulf of Mexico & the Mexican border: 267,339 sq. mi.; pop. 14,228,000; cap. Austin: abbrev. **Tex., TX** —**Tex′an** *adj., n.*

Texas fever an infectious disease of cattle

Texas leaguer *Baseball* a safely hit fly ball that falls between the infield and outfield

Texas tower [from its resemblance to oil rigs off the *Texas* coast] an offshore platform on foundations planted in the sea bottom, for beacons, radar installations, etc.

text (tekst) *n.* [< OFr. < L. *textus,* fabric < pp. of *texere,* to weave] **1.** the exact or original words of an author or speaker, as distinguished from notes, paraphrase, etc. **2.** any of the forms, versions, or editions in which a written work exists **3.** the principal matter on a printed page, as distinguished from notes, pictures, etc. **4.** the words of a song, etc. **5.** *a)* a Biblical passage used as the topic of a sermon *b)* any topic or subject dealt with **6.** *shortened form of* TEXTBOOK

text·book (-book′) *n.* a book giving instructions in the principles of a subject of study

tex·tile (teks′tīl, -t'l, -til) *adj.* [< L. *textilis* < *textus:* see TEXT] **1.** having to do with weaving or woven fabrics **2.** that has been or can be woven —*n.* **1.** a fabric made by weaving, knitting, etc.; cloth **2.** raw material suitable for this, as cotton, wool, nylon, etc.

tex·tu·al (teks′choo wəl) *adj.* of, contained in, or based on a text —**tex′tu·al·ly** *adv.*

tex·ture (teks′chər) *n.* [< L. < *texere:* see TEXT] **1.** the character of a fabric as determined by the arrangement, size, etc. of its threads **2.** the structure or composition of anything, esp. in the way it looks or feels on the surface —*vt.* **-tured, -tur·ing** to cause to have a particular texture —**tex′tur·al** *adj.* —**tex′tur·al·ly** *adv.*

-th[1] [< OE.] *a suffix meaning:* **1.** the act of [*stealth*] **2.** the state or quality of being or having [*wealth*]

-th[2] [< OE.] a suffix used in forming ordinal numerals [*fourth*] : also, after a vowel, **-eth**

-th[3] [< OE.: see -ETH2] *contracted form of* -ETH2 *[hath, doth]*
Th *Chem.* thorium
Th. Thursday
Thack·er·ay (thak′ər ē), **William Make·peace** (māk′pēs′) 1811–63; Eng. novelist
Thai (tī) ***n.*** **1.** a group of Asian languages considered to belong to the Sino-Tibetan language family **2.** the official language of Thailand **3.** *pl.* **Thais, Thai** *a)* a member of a group of Thai-speaking peoples of SE Asia *b)* a native or inhabitant of Thailand —***adj.*** of Thailand, its people, etc.
Thai·land (tī′land, -lənd) **1.** country in SE Asia, on the Indochinese & Malay peninsulas: 198,456 sq. mi.; pop. 35,814,000; cap. Bangkok **2. Gulf of,** arm of the South China Sea between the Malay & Indochinese peninsulas
thal·a·mus (thal′ə məs) ***n., pl.*** **-mi′** (-mī′) [ModL. < L. < Gr. *thalamos,* inner room] **1.** *Anat.* a mass of gray matter at the base of the brain, involved in the transmission of certain sensations **2.** *Bot.* the receptacle of a flower —**tha·lam·ic** (thə lam′ik) ***adj.***
Tha·li·a (thə lī′ə, thāl′yə) *Gr. Myth.* **1.** the Muse of comedy and pastoral poetry **2.** one of the three Graces
thal·li·um (thal′ē əm) ***n.*** [ModL. < Gr. *thallos,* green shoot: from its green spectrum line] a rare, bluish-white, soft, metallic chemical element: symbol, Tl; at. wt., 204.37; at. no., 81
thal·lo·phyte (-ə fīt′) ***n.*** [see ff. & -PHYTE] any of a primary division of plants including the bacteria, algae, fungi, and lichens —**thal′lo·phyt′ic** (-fit′ik) ***adj.***
thal·lus (-əs) ***n., pl.*** **-li** (-ī), **-lus·es** [ModL. < Gr. *thallos,* young shoot] the plant body of a thallophyte, showing no distinction of roots, stem, or leaves —**thal′loid** (-oid) ***adj.***
Thames (temz) river in S England, flowing east through London into the North Sea
than (*th*an, *th*en; *unstressed th*ən, *th*′n) ***conj.*** [< OE. *thenne,* orig., then] a particle used: *a)* to introduce the second element in a comparison *[A is taller than B] b)* to express exception *[none other than Sam]* —***prep.*** compared to: in *than whom, than which [a writer than whom there is none finer]*
than·a·tol·o·gy (than′ə täl′ə jē) ***n.*** [< Gr. *thanatos,* death + -LOGY] the study of death, esp. of the medical, psychological, and social problems associated with dying —**than′a·tol′o·gist** ***n.***
thane (thān) ***n.*** [OE. *thegen*] **1.** in early England, one of a class of freemen who held land of the king or a lord in return for military services **2.** in early Scotland, a person of rank who held land of the king
thank (thaŋk) ***vt.*** [OE. *thancian*] **1.** to express appreciation to, as by saying "thank you" **2.** to hold responsible; blame: an ironic use *[he can be thanked for our failure]* —**thank you** *shortened form of* I thank you
thank·ful (-fəl) ***adj.*** feeling or expressing thanks —**thank′ful·ly** ***adv.*** —**thank′ful·ness** ***n.***
thank·less (-lis) ***adj.*** **1.** not feeling or expressing thanks; ungrateful **2.** unappreciated *[a thankless task]* —**thank′less·ly** ***adv.*** —**thank′less·ness** ***n.***
thanks (thaŋks) ***n.pl.*** an expression of gratitude —***interj.*** I thank you —**thanks to 1.** thanks be given to **2.** on account of
thanks·giv·ing (thaŋks′giv′iŋ) ***n.*** **1.** *a)* a giving of thanks *b)* an expression of this; esp., a formal, public expression of thanks to God **2.** [T-] *a)* a U.S. holiday on the fourth Thursday of November: it commemorates the Pilgrims' celebration of the good harvest of 1621 *b)* a similar Canadian holiday on the second Monday of October In full, **Thanksgiving Day**
Thant (thänt, thônt), **U** (o͞o) 1909–74; Burmese diplomat; secretary-general of the United Nations (1962–71)
that (*th*at; *unstressed th*ət) ***pron., pl.*** **those** [OE. *thæt*] *as a demonstrative pronoun:* **1.** the person or thing mentioned or understood *[that is John]* **2.** the thing farther away *[this is larger than that over there]* **3.** something being contrasted *[this possibility is more likely than that]* **4.** [*pl.*] certain people *[those who know] as a relative pronoun:* **1.** who, whom, or which: generally in restrictive clauses *[the road (that) we took]* **2.** where; at which *[the place that I saw him]* **3.** when; in which *[the year that he died]* —***adj., pl.*** **those 1.** designating the one mentioned or understood *[that man is John]* **2.** designating the thing farther away *[this house is larger than that one]* **3.** designating something being contrasted *[this possibility is more likely than that one]* **4.** designating a person or thing not described but well known *[that certain feeling]* —***conj.*** *used:* **1.** to introduce a noun clause *[that he's gone is obvious]* **2.** to introduce an adverbial clause expressing purpose *[they died that we might live]* **3.** to introduce an adverbial clause expressing result *[he ran so fast that I lost him]* **4.** to introduce an adverbial clause expressing cause *[I'm sorry that I won]* **5.** to introduce an incomplete sentence expressing surprise, desire, etc. *[oh, that he were here!]* —***adv.*** **1.** to that extent; so *[I can't see that far]* : also used colloquially before an adjective modified by a clause showing result *[I'm that tired I could drop]* **2.** [Colloq.] very; so very *[I don't like movies that much]* —**all that** [Colloq.] **1.** so very *[he isn't all that rich]* **2.** everything of the same sort *[sex and all that]* —**at that** [Colloq.] **1.** at that point: also **with that 2.** all things considered; even so —**that is 1.** to be specific **2.** in other words —**that's that!** that is settled!
thatch (thach) ***n.*** [OE. *thæc*] **1.** *a)* a roof or roofing of straw, rushes, palm leaves, etc. *b)* material for such a roof: also **thatch′ing 2.** any of various palms whose leaves are used for thatch: also **thatch palm 3.** a matted layer of leaves, etc. between growing vegetation and the soil **4.** the hair growing on the head —***vt.*** [OE. *theccan*] to cover with or as with thatch —**thatch′y** ***adj.*** **thatch′i·er, thatch′i·est**
thau·ma·tur·gy (thô′mə tʉr′jē) ***n.*** [< Gr. < *thauma,* a wonder + *ergon,* work] the supposed working of miracles; magic —**thau′ma·tur′gic, thau′ma·tur′gi·cal** ***adj.***
thaw (thô) ***vi.*** [OE. *thawian*] **1.** *a)* to melt: said of ice, snow, etc. *b)* to pass to an unfrozen state: said of frozen foods **2.** to rise in temperature above freezing, so that snow, etc. melts: with *it:* said of weather conditions *[it thawed today]* **3.** *a)* to get rid of the chill, stiffness, etc. resulting from extreme cold (often with *out*) *b)* to lose coldness or reserve of manner —***vt.*** to cause to thaw —***n.*** **1.** a thawing **2.** a spell of weather warm enough to allow thawing **3.** a becoming less reserved
Th.B. [L. *Theologiae Baccalaureus*] Bachelor of Theology
Th.D. [L. *Theologiae Doctor*] Doctor of Theology
the (*th*ə; *before vowels th*i, *th*ē) ***adj., definite article*** [OE. *se, the*] **1.** *the* (as opposed to *a, an*) refers to a particular person or thing, as *a)* that (one) being spoken of *[the story ended] b)* that (one) which is present, close, etc. *[the day is hot] c)* that (one) designated, as by a title *[the Ohio (River)] d)* that (one) considered outstanding, etc. *[that's the hotel in town]* : usually italicized in print *e)* that (one) belonging to a person previously mentioned *[take me by the hand] f)* that (one) considered as a unit of purchase, etc. *[ten cents the dozen] g)* one specified period of time *[the fifties] h)* [Colloq.] that (one) in a specified relationship to one *[the wife]* **2.** *the* is used to refer to that one of a number of persons or things which is identified by a modifier, as by an attributive adjective, a relative clause, a prepositional phrase, etc. **3.** *the* is used to refer to a person or thing considered generically, as *a)* one taken as the representative of the entire genus or type *[the cow is a domestic animal] b)* an adjective used as a noun *[the good, the true]* —***adv.*** **1.** that much; to that extent *[the better to see you with]* **2.** by how much . . . by that much; to what extent . . . to that extent: used in a correlative construction expressing comparison *[the sooner, the better]*
the·a·ter, the·a·tre (thē′ə tər) ***n.*** [< OFr. < L. < Gr. *theatron* < base of *theasthai,* to view] **1.** a place or structure where plays, motion pictures, etc. are presented **2.** any place like a theater, esp. in having ascending rows of seats **3.** any scene of events *[the Asian theater of war]* **4.** *a)* the art of writing or putting on plays *b)* people engaged in putting on plays, esp. live plays on a stage
the·a·ter-in-the-round (-in *th*ə round′) ***n.*** *same as* ARENA THEATER
the·at·ri·cal (thē at′ri k′l) ***adj.*** **1.** having to do with the theater, the drama, a play, etc. **2.** characteristic of the theater; dramatic; esp. (in disparagement), melodramatic or affected Also **the·at′ric** —**the·at′ri·cal·ism, the·at′ri·cal′i·ty** (-kal′ə tē) ***n.*** —**the·at′ri·cal·ly** ***adv.***
the·at·ri·cals (-k′lz) ***n.pl.*** performances of stage plays, esp. by amateurs
the·at·rics (thē at′riks) ***n.pl.*** **1.** [*with sing. v.*] the art of the theater **2.** things done or said for theatrical effect
Thebes (thēbz) **1.** ancient city in S Egypt, on the Nile **2.** city in ancient Greece —**The·ban** (thē′bən) ***adj., n.***
the·ca (thē′kə) ***n., pl.*** **-cae** (-sē) [ModL. < L. < Gr. *thēkē,* a case] **1.** *Bot.* a spore case, sac, or capsule **2.** *Zool., Anat.* any sac enclosing an organ or a whole organism, as the covering of an insect pupa —**the′cal** ***adj.*** —**the′cate** (-kit) ***adj.***
thee (*th*ē) ***pron.*** [OE. *the*] *objective case of* THOU: also used in place of *thou* by Friends (Quakers) *[thee is kind]*
theft (theft) ***n.*** [OE. *thiefth*] the act or an instance of stealing; larceny
thegn (thān) ***n.*** [OE.] *var. of* THANE
the·ine (thē′in, -ēn) ***n.*** [< ModL. < *thea,* tea] caffeine, esp. as found in tea
their (*th*er; *unstressed th*ər) ***possessive pronominal adj.*** [ON. *theirra*] of, belonging to, made by, or done by them: often used colloquially after a singular subject *[everyone has had their lunch]*
theirs (*th*erz) ***pron.*** that or those belonging to them: used with no following noun *[that cat is theirs, theirs are bet-*

ter]: also used after *of* to indicate possession [a friend of *theirs*]

the·ism (thē′iz'm) ***n.*** [THE(O)- + -ISM] **1.** belief in a god or gods **2.** belief in one God who is creator and ruler of the universe —**the′ist *n., adj.*** —**the·is′tic, the·is′ti·cal *adj.*** —**the·is′ti·cal·ly *adv.***

Thel·ma (thel′mə) [< ?] a feminine name

them (*th*em; *unstressed th*əm, *th*'m, əm) ***pron.*** [ON. *theim*] *objective case of* THEY: also used colloquially as a predicate complement with a linking verb (Ex.: that's *them*)

theme (thēm) ***n.*** [< OFr. < L. < Gr. *thema* < base of *tithenai*, to put] **1.** *a*) a topic, as of a lecture, essay, etc. *b*) a recurring, unifying subject or idea; motif **2.** a short essay, esp. one written as a school assignment **3.** *a*) a short melody used as the subject of a musical composition *b*) a musical phrase upon which variations are developed **4.** the principal song of a movie, musical, etc., or the music used to identify a radio or television program: also **theme song** —**the·mat·ic** (thē mat′ik) ***adj.*** —**the·mat′i·cal·ly *adv.***

The·mis·to·cles (thə mis′tə klēz′) 525?–460? B.C.; Athenian statesman & naval commander

them·selves (*th*em selvz′, *th*əm-) ***pron.*** a form of the 3d pers. pl. pronoun, used: *a*) as an intensive [they went *themselves*] *b*) as a reflexive [they hurt *themselves*] *c*) as a quasi-noun meaning "their real or true selves" [they are not *themselves* today]

then (*th*en) ***adv.*** [see THAN] **1.** at that time [he was young *then*] **2.** soon afterward; next in time [he took his hat and *then* left] **3.** next in order [first comes one and *then* two] **4.** in that case; accordingly [if it rains, *then* I will get wet] **5.** besides; moreover [I like to walk, and *then* it's cheaper] **6.** at another time [now it's warm, *then* cold] —***adj.*** being such at that time [the *then* director] —***n.*** that time [by *then*, they were gone] —**but then** but on the other hand —**then and there** at that time and in that place; at once —**what then?** what would happen in that case?

thence (*th*ens, thens) ***adv.*** [OE. *thanan*] **1.** from that place **2.** from that time; thenceforth **3.** on that account; therefore

thence·forth (-fôrth′) ***adv.*** from that time onward; thereafter: also **thence′for′ward, thence′for′wards**

the·o- [< Gr. *theos*, god] *a combining form meaning* a god or God: also, before a vowel, **the-**

the·oc·ra·cy (thē äk′rə sē) ***n.***, *pl.* **-cies** [< Gr.: see THEO- & -CRACY] **1.** lit., the rule of a state by God or a god **2.** government by priests or clergy claiming to rule with divine authority **3.** a country so governed —**the·o·crat** (thē′ə krat′) ***n.*** —**the′o·crat′ic, the′o·crat′i·cal *adj.*** —**the′o·crat′i·cal·ly *adv.***

the·od·o·lite (thē äd′'l īt′) ***n.*** [ModL. *theodelitus*] a surveying instrument used to measure vertical and horizontal angles —**the·od′o·lit′ic** (-ə lit′ik) ***adj.***

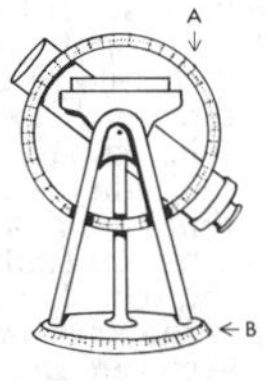

DIAGRAM OF THEODOLITE (A, vertical angles; B, horizontal angles)

The·o·dore (thē′ə dôr′) [< L. < Gr. < *theos*, god + *dōron*, gift] a masculine name: dim. *Ted, Teddy*

The·od·o·ric (thē äd′ər ik) 454?–526 A.D.; king of the Ostrogoths (474–526)

The·o·do·si·us I (thē′ə dō′shē əs, -shəs) (*Flavius Theodosius*) 346?–395 A.D.; Rom. general; emperor of Rome (379–395): called *the Great*

theol. **1.** theologian **2.** theology

the·o·lo·gi·an (thē′ə lō′jən, -jē ən) ***n.*** a student of or a specialist in theology or a theology

the·o·log·i·cal (-läj′i k'l) ***adj.*** of, based on, or offering instruction in, theology or a theology: also **the′o·log′ic** —**the′o·log′i·cal·ly *adv.***

theological virtues *Theol.* the three virtues (faith, hope, and charity) having God as their object

the·ol·o·gize (thē äl′ə jīz′) ***vt.*** **-gized′, -giz′ing** to put into theological terms —***vi.*** to speculate theologically —**the·ol′o·giz′er *n.***

the·ol·o·gy (thē äl′ə jē) ***n.***, *pl.* **-gies** [< LL. < Gr.: see THEO- & -LOGY] **1.** the study of God and of religious doctrines and matters of divinity **2.** a specific system of this study

the·o·rem (thē′ə rəm, thir′əm) ***n.*** [< Fr. < L. < Gr. *theōrēma* < *theōrein*, to view] **1.** a proposition that is not self-evident but that can be proved from accepted premises and so is established as a law or principle **2.** an expression of relations in an equation or formula **3.** *Math., Physics* a proposition embodying something to be proved —**the′o·re·mat′ic** (-rə mat′ik) ***adj.***

the·o·ret·i·cal (thē′ə ret′i k'l) ***adj.*** **1.** of or constituting theory **2.** limited to or based on theory; not practical; hypothetical **3.** tending to theorize; speculative Also **the′o·ret′ic** —**the′o·ret′i·cal·ly *adv.***

the·o·re·ti·cian (thē′ə rə tish′ən) ***n.*** a person who specializes in the theory of some art, science, etc.: also **the′o·rist** (-rist)

the·o·rize (thē′ə rīz′) ***vi.*** **-rized′, -riz′ing** to form a theory or theories; speculate —**the′o·ri·za′tion *n.*** —**the′o·riz′er *n.***

the·o·ry (thē′ə rē, thir′ē) ***n.***, *pl.* **-ries** [< Fr. < LL. < Gr. < *theōrein*, to view] **1.** a speculative idea or plan as to how something might be done **2.** a systematic statement of principles involved **3.** a formulation of apparent relationships or underlying principles of certain observed phenomena which has been verified to some degree **4.** that branch of an art or science consisting in a knowledge of its principles and methods rather than in its practice **5.** popularly, a mere conjecture, or guess

theory of games *same as* GAME THEORY

the·os·o·phy (thē äs′ə fē) ***n.***, *pl.* **-phies** [< ML. < LGr., ult. < Gr. *theos*, god + *sophos*, wise] **1.** any of various philosophies or religions that propose to establish direct, mystical contact with divine principle through contemplation, revelation, etc. **2.** [*often* **T-**] the doctrines of a modern sect (**Theosophical Society**) that incorporates elements of Buddhism and Brahmanism —**the′o·soph′ic** (-ə säf′ik), **the′o·soph′i·cal *adj.*** —**the′o·soph′i·cal·ly *adv.*** —**the·os′o·phist *n.***

ther·a·peu·tic (ther′ə pyōōt′ik) ***adj.*** [ModL. < Gr., ult. < *therapeuein*, to nurse] **1.** *a*) serving to cure or heal; curative *b*) serving to preserve health [*therapeutic* abortion] **2.** of therapeutics Also **ther′a·peu′ti·cal** —**ther′a·peu′ti·cal·ly *adv.***

ther·a·peu·tics (-iks) ***n.pl.*** [*with sing. v.*] the branch of medicine that deals with the treatment and cure of diseases; therapy

ther·a·py (ther′ə pē) ***n.***, *pl.* **-pies** [ModL. < Gr. < *therapeuein*, to nurse] the treatment of disease or of any physical or mental disorder by medical or physical means: often used in compounds [*hydrotherapy*] —**ther′a·pist *n.***

there (*th*er) ***adv.*** [OE. *ther*] **1.** at or in that place: often used as an intensive [John *there* is a good boy] **2.** toward, to, or into that place [go *there*] **3.** at that point in action, speech, etc. **4.** in that matter, respect, etc. [*there* you are wrong] **5.** right now [*there* goes the whistle] *There* is also used: *a*) in interjectional phrases of approval, etc. [*there's* a fine fellow!] *b*) in impersonal constructions in which the real subject follows the verb [*there* are three men here] —***n.*** that place or point [we left *there* at six] —***interj.*** an exclamation expressing defiance, dismay, satisfaction, sympathy, etc. [*there, there!* don't worry] —**(not) all there** [Colloq.] (not) mentally sound

there·a·bouts (*th*er′ə bouts′) ***adv.*** **1.** near that place **2.** near that time **3.** near that number, amount, degree, etc. Also **there′a·bout′**

there·af·ter (*th*er af′tər) ***adv.*** **1.** after that; subsequently **2.** [Archaic] accordingly

there·at (-at′) ***adv.*** **1.** at that place; there **2.** at that time **3.** for that reason

there·by (-bī′) ***adv.*** **1.** by that means **2.** connected with that [*thereby* hangs a tale]

there·for (-fôr′) ***adv.*** for this; for that; for it

there·fore (*th*er′fôr′) ***adv.*** for this or that reason; consequently; hence: often used like a conjunction

there·from (*th*er frum′, -främ′) ***adv.*** from this; from that; from it

there·in (-in′) ***adv.*** **1.** in there; in or into that place or thing **2.** in that matter, detail, etc.

there·in·to (*th*er in′tōō) ***adv.*** **1.** into that place or thing **2.** into that matter, condition, etc.

there·of (-uv′) ***adv.*** **1.** of that **2.** concerning that **3.** from that as a cause, reason, etc.

there·on (-än′) ***adv.*** **1.** on that **2.** *same as* THEREUPON

there's (*th*erz) **1.** there is **2.** there has

The·re·sa (tə rē′sə) **1.** [< Fr. or Port. < L. *Therasia* < ? Gr. *therizein*, to reap] a feminine name **2.** Saint, *same as* Saint TERESA

there·to (*th*er tōō′) ***adv.*** **1.** to that place, thing, etc.: also **there′un′to** **2.** [Archaic] besides

there·to·fore (*th*er′tə fôr′, *th*er′tə fôr′) ***adv.*** up to then; until that time; before that

there·un·der (*th*er un′dər) ***adv.*** **1.** under that; under it **2.** under the terms stated there

there·up·on (*th*er′ə pän′, *th*er′ə pän′) ***adv.*** **1.** immediately following that **2.** as a consequence of that **3.** concerning that subject, etc.

there·with (*th*er with′, -*with*′) ***adv.*** **1.** along with that **2.** in addition to that **3.** by that method or means **4.** immediately thereafter

fat, āpe, cär; ten, ēven; is, bīte; gō, hôrn, tōōl, look; oil, out; up, fur; get; joy; yet; chin; she; thin, *th*en; zh, leisure; ŋ, ring; ə for *a* in *ago*, *e* in *agent*, *i* in *sanity*, *o* in *comply*, *u* in *focus*; ' as in *able* (ā′b'l); Fr. bål; ë, Fr. coeur; ö, Fr. feu; Fr. mon; ô, Fr. coq; ü, Fr. duc; *r*, Fr. cri; H, G. ich; kh, G. doch; ‡foreign; *hypothetical; < derived from. See inside front cover.

there·with·al (*th*er′wi*th* ôl′) ***adv.*** **1.** in addition; besides **2.** [Obs.] along with that
ther·mal (thur′m'l) ***adj.*** [Fr. < Gr. *thermē*, heat] **1.** having to do with heat, hot springs, etc. **2.** warm or hot **3.** designating or of a loosely knitted material with air spaces to help retain body heat *[thermal* underwear*]* —***n.*** a rising column of warm air, caused by the uneven heating of the earth or sea by the sun —**ther′mal·ly** ***adv.***
thermal barrier the speed limit beyond which the high temperatures caused by atmospheric friction would damage or destroy a given spacecraft, rocket, etc.
thermal spring a spring whose water has a temperature higher than that of the air in the place where it is located
ther·mic (thur′mik) ***adj.*** of or caused by heat
therm·i·on·ic tube (thurm′ī än′ik, thur′mē-) [THERM(O)- + ION + -IC] an electron tube having a cathode electrically heated in order to cause electron or ion emission
therm·is·tor (thər mis′tər, thur′mis′-) ***n.*** [THERM(O)- + (RES)ISTOR] a resistor made of semiconductor material, whose resistance decreases as temperature rises: used to measure temperature, microwave power, etc.
ther·mo- [< Gr. *thermē*, heat] *a combining form meaning:* **1.** heat *[thermodynamics]* **2.** thermoelectric *[thermocouple]* Also, before a vowel, **therm-**
ther·mo·cou·ple (thur′mə kup′'l) ***n.*** a pair of dissimilar conductors joined together at their ends: when this junction is heated, the voltage across it is in proportion to the rise in temperature: also called **thermoelectric couple**
ther·mo·dy·nam·ic (thur′mō dī nam′ik) ***adj.*** **1.** of or having to do with thermodynamics **2.** caused or operated by heat converted into motive power —**ther′mo·dy·nam′i·cal·ly** ***adv.***
ther·mo·dy·nam·ics (-dī nam′iks) ***n.pl.*** [*with sing. v.*] the branch of physics dealing with the reversible transformation of heat into other forms of energy, esp. mechanical energy, and with the laws governing such conversions of energy
ther·mo·e·lec·tric (-i lek′trik) ***adj.*** of or having to do with the direct relations between heat and electricity: also **ther′mo·e·lec′tri·cal** —**ther′mo·e·lec′tri·cal·ly** ***adv.***
ther·mo·e·lec·tric·i·ty (-i lek′tris′ə tē) ***n.*** electricity produced by heating the junction between two dissimilar conductors so as to produce an electromotive force
ther·mo·gram (thur′mə gram′) ***n.*** [THERMO- + -GRAM] a record made by a thermograph
ther·mo·graph (-graf′) ***n.*** [THERMO- + -GRAPH] a thermometer for recording variations in temperature automatically
ther·mo·junc·tion (thur′mō juŋk′shən) ***n.*** the point of contact between the two conductors of a thermocouple
ther·mom·e·ter (thər mäm′ə tər) ***n.*** [< Fr.: see THERMO- & -METER] an instrument for measuring temperatures, as one consisting of a sealed glass tube, marked off in degrees, in which mercury, colored alcohol, etc. rises or falls as it expands or contracts from changes in temperature: see FAHRENHEIT, CELSIUS —**ther·mo·met·ric** (thur′mə met′rik) ***adj.*** —**ther′mo·met′ri·cal·ly** ***adv.***
ther·mo·nu·cle·ar (thur′mō nōō′klē ər, -nyōō′-) ***adj.*** *Physics* **1.** designating or of a reaction in which light atomic nuclei fuse at temperatures of millions of degrees into heavier nuclei **2.** designating, of, or employing the heat energy released in nuclear fusion
ther·mo·pile (thur′mə pīl′) ***n.*** [THERMO- + PILE[1]] a device consisting of a series of thermocouples, used for measuring minute changes in temperature or for generating thermoelectric current
ther·mo·plas·tic (thur′mə plas′tik) ***adj.*** soft and moldable when subjected to heat: said of certain plastics —***n.*** a thermoplastic substance
Ther·mop·y·lae (thər mäp′ə lē) in ancient Greece, a mountain pass on the E coast: scene of a battle (480 B.C.) in which the Persians destroyed a Spartan army
ther·mos (thur′məs) ***n.*** [Gr. *thermos*, hot] a bottle, flask, or jug with two walls enclosing a vacuum, used for keeping liquids at almost their original temperature for several hours: in full, **thermos bottle** (or **flask** or **jug**)
ther·mo·set·ting (thur′mō set′iŋ) ***adj.*** becoming permanently hard and unmoldable when once subjected to heat: said of certain plastics
ther·mo·stat (thur′mə stat′) ***n.*** [THERMO- + -STAT] **1.** an apparatus for regulating temperature, esp. one that automatically controls a heating unit **2.** a device that sets off a sprinkler, etc. at a certain heat —**ther′mo·stat′ic** ***adj.*** —**ther′mo·stat′i·cal·ly** ***adv.***
ther·mot·ro·pism (thər mät′rə piz'm) ***n.*** [THERMO- + -TROPISM] *Biol.* growth or movement toward or away from a source of heat —**ther·mo·trop·ic** (thur′mə träp′ik) ***adj.***
the·sau·rus (thi sôr′əs) ***n.***, *pl.* **-ri** (-ī), **-rus·es** [L. < Gr. *thēsauros*, a treasure] **1.** a treasury or storehouse **2.** a book containing a store of words; specif., a book of synonyms and antonyms **3.** a classified index of terms for use in information retrieval, as from a computer
these (*th*ēz) ***pron., adj.*** *pl. of* THIS
The·seus (thē′sōōs, -syōōs, -sē əs) *Gr. Legend* the principal hero of Attica, king of Athens, famed esp. for his killing of the Minotaur —**The·se·an** (thi sē′ən) ***adj.***
the·sis (thē′sis) ***n.***, *pl.* **the′ses** (-sēz) [L. < Gr. *thesis*, a placing < base of *tithenai*, to put] **1.** a proposition defended in argument **2.** a formal and lengthy research paper, esp. one presented as part of the requirements for a master's degree **3.** *Logic* an unproved statement assumed as a premise
Thes·pi·an (thes′pē ən) ***adj.*** [after *Thespis*, Greek poet of 6th c. B.C.] *[often* **t-**] having to do with the drama; dramatic —***n.*** [*often* **t-**] an actor or actress: a humorous or pretentious term
Thes·sa·lo·ni·ans (thes′ə lō′nē ənz) either of two books of the New Testament which were epistles from the Apostle Paul to the Christians of Thessalonica: abbrev. **Thess.**
Thes·sa·lon·i·ca (thes′ə län′i kə, -ə lə nī′kə) *ancient name of* SALONIKA
Thes·sa·ly (thes′ə lē) division of E Greece, on the Aegean Sea —**Thes·sa·li·an** (the sā′lē ən) ***adj., n.***
the·ta (thāt′ə, thēt′ə) ***n.*** the eighth letter of the Greek alphabet (Θ, θ, ϑ,)
thews (thyōōz) ***n.pl.***, *sing.* **thew** [OE. *theaw*, custom, habit] **1.** muscular power; bodily strength **2.** muscles or sinews —**thew′y** ***adj.*** **thew′i·er, thew′i·est**
they (*th*ā) ***pron.*** *for sing. see* HE, SHE, IT [< ON. *their*] **1.** the persons, animals, or things previously mentioned **2.** people in general *[they* say it's so*]* *They* is the nominative case form of the third personal plural pronoun
they'd (*th*ād) **1.** they had **2.** they would
they'll (*th*āl, *th*el) **1.** they will **2.** they shall
they're (*th*er, *th*ā′ər) they are
they've (*th*āv) they have
thi- *same as* THIO-
thi·a·mine (thī′ə mēn′, -min) ***n.*** [altered < THI(O)- + (VIT)AMIN] vitamin B_1, a white, crystalline compound, $C_{12}H_{17}ON_4SCl$, found in cereal grains, egg yolk, liver, etc., or prepared synthetically: a deficiency of this vitamin results in beriberi and certain nervous disorders: also **thi′a·min** (-min)
Thi·bet (ti bet′) *var. of* TIBET —**Thi·bet′an** ***adj., n.***
thick (thik) ***adj.*** [OE. *thicce*] **1.** of relatively great depth or extent from side to side *[*a *thick* board*]* **2.** having large diameter in relation to length *[*a *thick* pipe*]* **3.** measured between opposite surfaces *[*a wall six inches *thick]* **4.** dense; compact; specif., *a)* marked by profuse, close growth; luxuriant *[thick* woods*]* *b)* great in number and close together *[*a *thick* crowd*]* *c)* having much body; not thin *[thick* soup*]* *d)* dense and heavy *[thick* smoke*]* *e)* covered *[*a road *thick* with mud*]* *f)* studded profusely *[*a sky *thick* with stars*]* **5.** dark or obscure *[thick* shadows*]* **6.** *a)* slurred, muffled, or husky *[thick* speech, a *thick* voice*]* *b)* strongly marked *[*a *thick* accent*]* **7.** [Colloq.] stupid **8.** [Colloq.] close in friendship **9.** [Chiefly Brit. Colloq.] too much to be tolerated —***adv.*** in a thick way —***n.*** the thickest part or the period of greatest activity *[*in the *thick* of the fight*]* —**through thick and thin** in good times and bad times —**thick′ish** ***adj.*** —**thick′ly** ***adv.***
thick·en (thik′ən) ***vt., vi.*** **1.** to make or become thick or thicker **2.** to make or become more complex or involved —**thick′en·er** ***n.***
thick·en·ing (-iŋ) ***n.*** **1.** the action of one that thickens **2.** a substance used to thicken **3.** the thickened part
thick·et (thik′it) ***n.*** [OE. *thiccet* < *thicce*, thick] a thick growth of shrubs, underbrush, or small trees
thick·head·ed (thik′hed′id) ***adj.*** stupid —**thick′head′edness** ***n.***
thick·ness (-nis) ***n.*** **1.** the quality of being thick **2.** the measure of how thick a thing is **3.** a layer *[*three *thicknesses* of cloth*]*
thick·set (-set′) ***adj.*** **1.** planted thickly or closely **2.** thick in body; stocky —***n.*** [Archaic] a thicket
thick-skinned (-skind′) ***adj.*** **1.** having a thick skin **2.** not easily hurt by criticism, insults, etc.
thief (thēf) ***n.***, *pl.* **thieves** (thēvz) [OE. *theof*] a person who steals, esp. secretly
thieve (thēv) ***vt., vi.*** **thieved, thiev′ing** [OE. *theofian* < *theof*, a thief] to steal —**thiev′ish** ***adj.*** —**thiev′ish·ly** ***adv.*** —**thiev′ish·ness** ***n.***
thiev·er·y (thēv′ər ē) ***n.***, *pl.* **-er·ies** the act or practice of stealing or an instance of this; theft
thigh (thī) ***n.*** [OE. *theoh*] the part of the leg between the knee and the hip
thigh·bone (-bōn′) ***n.*** the largest and longest bone in the body, from the hip to the knee; femur: also **thigh bone**
thill (thil) ***n.*** [OE. *thille*, a stake, pole] either of the two shafts between which a horse is hitched to a wagon
thim·ble (thim′b'l) ***n.*** [OE. *thymel* < *thuma*, a thumb] **1.** a small cap of metal, plastic, etc. worn as a protection on the finger that pushes the needle in sewing **2.** anything like this; esp., a grooved metal ring inserted in a loop of rope, etc. to prevent wear

thim·ble·ful (-fool′) ***n.**, pl.* **-fuls′** **1.** as much as a thimble will hold **2.** a very small quantity
thim·ble·rig (-rig′) ***n.*** *same as* SHELL GAME ***—vt., vi.*** **-rigged′, -rig′ging** to cheat or swindle, as in this game — **thim′ble·rig′ger *n.***
thin (thin) ***adj.*** **thin′ner, thin′nest** [OE. *thynne*] **1.** of relatively little depth or extent from side to side [*a thin* board] **2.** having small diameter in relation to length [*thin* thread] **3.** having little fat or flesh; slender **4.** not dense or compact; specif., *a)* scanty in growth; sparse [*thin* hair] *b)* small in size or number [*thin* receipts] *c)* lacking body; watery [*thin* soup] *d)* not dense or heavy [*thin* smoke] *e)* rarefied, as air at high altitudes **5.** not deep and strong; weak [*thin* colors, a *thin* voice] **6.** light or sheer, as fabric **7.** easily seen through; flimsy [a *thin* excuse] **8.** slight, weak, vapid, etc. [a *thin* plot, a *thin* argument] ***—adv.*** in a thin way ***—vt., vi.*** **thinned, thin′ning** to make or become thin or thinner: often with *out, down,* etc. **—thin′ly *adv.*** **—thin′ness *n.*** **—thin′nish *adj.***
thine (*th*īn) ***pron.*** [OE. *thin*] [Archaic or Poet.] that or those belonging to thee (you): absolute form of THY [a friend of *thine,* this is *thine*] ***—possessive pronominal adj.*** [Archaic or Poet.] thy: used before a word beginning with a vowel or unvoiced *h*
thing[1] (thiŋ) ***n.*** [OE., a council, hence, "matter discussed, thing"] **1.** any matter, affair, or concern **2.** a happening, act, deed, incident, etc. [to do great *things*] **3.** an end to be achieved, a step in a process, etc. [the next *thing* is to mix thoroughly] **4.** an individual, distinguishable entity; specif., *a)* a tangible object, as distinguished from a quality, concept, etc. *b)* a lifeless object *c)* an item, detail, etc. [look at each *thing* on the list] *d)* the object or concept referred to by a word, symbol, or sign *e)* an object of thought; idea **5.** *a)* [*pl.*] personal belongings; also, clothes or clothing *b)* a dress, garment, etc. [not a *thing* to wear] **6.** a person or creature [poor *thing!*] **7.** something mentioned but unnamed [where did you buy that *thing?*] **8.** [Colloq.] a point of dispute; issue [he made a *thing* of it] **9.** [Colloq.] a strong, often neurotic liking, fear, aversion, etc. [to have a *thing* about flying] **—do one's (own) thing** [Colloq.] to express one's unique personality in one's own way of life, activities, etc. **—see things** [Colloq.] to have hallucinations **—the thing** **1.** that which is wise, essential, etc. **2.** that which is the height of fashion
‡**thing**[2] (tiŋ; *E.* thiŋ) ***n.*** [ON., assembly] a Scandinavian legislative body
thing·a·ma·bob, thing·um·a·bob (thiŋ′ə mə bäb′) ***n.*** [Colloq.] *same as* THINGAMAJIG: also **thing′um·bob′**
thing·a·ma·jig, thing·um·a·jig (-jig′) ***n.*** [extension of older *thingum,* THING[1]] [Colloq.] any device or gadget: jocular substitute for a name not known or temporarily forgotten
think[1] (thiŋk) ***vt.*** **thought, think′ing** [OE. *thencan*] **1.** to form or have in the mind [*think* good thoughts] **2.** to judge; consider [I *think* her charming] **3.** to believe; surmise; expect [I *think* I can go] **4.** to determine, work out, etc. by reasoning [to *think* a problem through] **5.** [Now Rare] to intend [*thinking* to do right] **6.** *a)* to have in mind; form an idea of [*think* what may be] *b)* to recall; recollect [*think* what joy was ours] **7.** to have constantly in mind [*think* success] ***—vi.*** **1.** to use the mind; reflect or reason [*think* before you act] **2.** to have an opinion, belief, judgment, etc. [I just *think* so, we *think* highly of him] **3.** to remember (with *of* or *about*) **4.** to consider or be considerate (with *of* or *about*) **5.** to invent; conceive (*of*) ***—n.*** [Colloq.] the act of thinking [give it a good *think*] ***—adj.*** [Colloq.] having to do with thinking **—think (all) the world of** to admire or love greatly **—think better of** **1.** to form a more favorable opinion of **2.** to make a more sensible decision about, after reconsidering **—think fit** to regard as proper **—think little (or nothing) of** **1.** to attach little (or no) importance to **2.** to have little (or no) hesitancy about **—think on (or upon)** [Archaic] to give thought to **—think out** **1.** to think about to a conclusion: also **think through** **2.** to work out by thinking **—think out loud** to speak one's thoughts as they occur: also **think aloud** — **think over** to give thought to; ponder well **—think twice** to reconsider **—think up** to invent, contrive, etc. by thinking **—think′a·ble *adj.*** **—think′er *n.***
think[2] (thiŋk) ***v.impersonal pt.*** **thought** [OE. *thyncan*] to seem: obs., except in archaic METHINKS, METHOUGHT
think·ing (-iŋ) ***adj.*** **1.** that thinks or can think; rational **2.** given to thought; reflective ***—n.*** thought
think tank (or **factory**) [Slang] a group of experts organized to do intensive research and problem solving, using computers, etc.
thin·ner (thin′ər) ***n.*** a person or thing that thins; esp., a substance added, as turpentine to paint, for thinning
thin-skinned (-skind′) ***adj.*** **1.** having a thin skin **2.** easily hurt by criticism, insults, etc.
thi·o- [< Gr. *theion,* brimstone] *a combining form meaning* sulfur, used to indicate the replacement of oxygen by sulfur
Thi·o·kol (thī′ə kôl′, -kōl′) [arbitrary coinage] *a trademark for* any of various synthetic rubbery compounds used as sealants and sealing adhesives
thi·o·pen·tal (sodium) (thī′ə pen′tal, -tôl, -t′l) [THIO- + PENT(A)- + -AL] a yellowish-white powder, $C_{11}H_{17}N_2O_2SNa$, injected intravenously in solution as a general anesthetic and hypnotic
thi·o·sul·fate (thī′ō sul′fāt) ***n.*** a salt of thiosulfuric acid; esp., sodium thiosulfate
thi·o·sul·fu·ric acid (-sul fyoor′ik) [THIO- + SULFURIC] an unstable acid, $H_2S_2O_3$, whose salts are used in photography, bleaching, etc.
third (thurd) ***adj.*** [OE. *thridda*] **1.** preceded by two others in a series; 3d or 3rd **2.** next below the second in rank, value, merit, etc. **3.** designating any of the three equal parts of something ***—adv.*** in the third place, rank, group, etc. ***—n.*** **1.** the one following the second **2.** any person, thing, class, etc. that is third **3.** any of the three equal parts of something; 1/3 **4.** the third forward gear ratio of a motor vehicle **5.** *Music* *a)* the third tone of an ascending diatonic scale, or a tone two degrees above or below any given tone in such a scale *b)* the interval between two such tones, or a combination of them **—third′ly *adv.***
third base *Baseball* the base between second base and home plate, located on the pitcher's right
third-class (thurd′klas′) ***adj.*** **1.** of the class, rank, excellence, etc. next below the second **2.** designating or of accommodations next below the second **3.** designating or of a lower-cost class of mail limited to merchandise weighing less than 16 oz. or bulk mailing of identical circulars, advertisements, etc. ***—adv.*** **1.** with third-class travel accommodations **2.** as or by third-class mail
third degree [Colloq.] harsh, grueling treatment and questioning of a prisoner in order to force a confession or information **—third′-de·gree′ *adj.***
third dimension **1.** *a)* the dimension of depth in something *b)* the quality of having, or of seeming to have, depth, or solidity **2.** the quality of being true to life or seeming real **—third′-di·men′sion·al *adj.***
third party **1.** a political party competing against the two major parties in a two-party system **2.** a person other than the principals in a case or matter
third person **1.** that form of a pronoun (as *he*) or verb (as *is*) which refers to the person or thing spoken of **2.** narration characterized by the general use of such forms
third rail an extra rail used in some electric railroads for supplying power
third-rate (-rāt′) ***adj.*** **1.** third in quality or other rating; third-class **2.** inferior; very poor **—third′-rat′er *n.***
third world [*often* **T- W-**] the underdeveloped or emergent countries of the world, esp. of Africa and Asia
thirst (thurst) ***n.*** [OE. *thurst*] **1.** the discomfort or distress caused by a desire or need for water, characterized generally by dryness in the mouth and throat **2.** [Colloq.] a craving for a specific liquid, esp. for alcoholic liquor **3.** any strong desire; craving ***—vi.*** **1.** to be thirsty **2.** to have a strong desire or craving
thirst·y (thur′stē) ***adj.*** **thirst′i·er, thirst′i·est** **1.** feeling thirst **2.** *a)* lacking water or moisture; dry [*thirsty* fields] *b)* very absorbent **3.** [Colloq.] causing thirst [*thirsty* work] **4.** having a strong desire; craving **—thirst′i·ly *adv.*** **—thirst′i·ness *n.***
thir·teen (thur′tēn′) ***adj.*** [OE. *threotyne*] three more than ten ***—n.*** the cardinal number between twelve and fourteen; 13; XIII
thir·teenth (-tēnth′) ***adj.*** **1.** preceded by twelve others in a series; 13th **2.** designating any of the thirteen equal parts of something ***—n.*** **1.** the one following the twelfth **2.** any of the thirteen equal parts of something; 1/13
thir·ti·eth (thur′tē ith) ***adj.*** **1.** preceded by twenty-nine others in a series; 30th **2.** designating any of the thirty equal parts of something ***—n.*** **1.** the one following the twenty-ninth **2.** any of the thirty equal parts of something; 1/30
thir·ty (thurt′ē) ***adj.*** [OE. *thritig* < *thri,* three + *-tig,* -TY[2]] three times ten ***—n.**, pl.* **-ties** **1.** the cardinal number between twenty-nine and thirty-one; 30; XXX **2.** this number used to signify the end of a dispatch, story, etc., as for a newspaper **—the thirties** the numbers or years, as of a century, from thirty through thirty-nine
thir·ty-sec·ond note (thurt′ē sek′ənd) *Music* a note having 1/32 the duration of a whole note: see NOTE, illus.
this (this) ***pron.**, pl.* **these** [OE. *thes,* masc., *this,* neut.] **1.** the person or thing mentioned or understood [*this* is

John*]* **2.** the thing that is nearer than another referred to as "that" *[this* is larger than that*]* **3.** the less remote in thought of two contrasted things *[this* is more likely than that*]* **4.** the fact, idea, etc. that is being, or is about to be, presented, etc. *[*now hear *this]* —***adj.***, *pl.* **these** **1.** designating the person or thing mentioned or understood *[this* man is John*]* **2.** designating the thing that is nearer than the one referred to as "that" *[this* desk is smaller than that one*]* **3.** designating the less remote in thought of two contrasted things *[this* possibility is more likely than that*]* **4.** designating something that is being, or is about to be, presented, etc. *[*hear *this* song*]* **5.** [Colloq.] designating a particular but unspecified person or thing *[*there's *this* lady in Iowa*]* —***adv.*** to this extent; so *[*it was *this* big*]*

this·tle (this′'l) ***n.*** [OE. *thistel*] any of various plants of the composite family, with prickly leaves and heads of white, purple, etc. flowers; esp., the **Scotch thistle** with white down and lavender flowers —**this·tly** (this′lē) ***adj.***

THISTLE

this·tle·down (-doun′) ***n.*** the down attached to the flower head of a thistle

thith·er (thi*th*′ər, thith′-) ***adv.*** [OE. *thider*] to or toward that place; there —***adj.*** on or toward that side; farther

thith·er·to (-to͞o′; thi*th*′ər to͞o′, thith′-) ***adv.*** until that time; till then

thith·er·ward (-wərd) ***adv.*** [Rare] toward that place; thither: also **thith′er·wards**

tho, tho' (*th*ō) ***conj., adv.*** *shortened sp. of* THOUGH

thole (thōl) ***n.*** [OE. *thol*] a pin or either of a pair of pins set vertically in the gunwale of a boat to serve as a fulcrum for an oar: also **thole′pin′** (-pin′)

Thom·as (täm′əs) [LL. < Gr. < Ar. *tĕ'ōma*, lit., a twin] **1.** a masculine name: dim *Tom, Tommy* **2.** *Bible* one of the twelve apostles, who doubted at first the resurrection of Jesus: John 20:24–29

Tho·mism (tō′miz'm) ***n.*** the theological and philosophical doctrines of Thomas Aquinas

Thomp·son (tämp′s'n, täm′-) **1. Benjamin,** Count Rumford, 1753–1814; Brit. scientist & statesman, born in America **2. Francis,** 1859–1907; Eng. poet

Thompson submachine gun [< the co-inventor, J. T. *Thompson* (1860–1940), U.S. army officer] *a trademark for* a type of submachine gun: see SUBMACHINE GUN

thong (thôŋ) ***n.*** [OE. *thwang*] **1.** a narrow strip of leather, etc. used as a lace, strap, etc. **2.** a whiplash, as of braided strips of hide

Thor (thôr) *Norse Myth.* the god of thunder, war, and strength, and the son of Odin

tho·rac·ic (thô ras′ik, thə-) ***adj.*** of, in, or near the thorax

tho·ra·co- (thôr′ə kō) *a combining form meaning* the thorax (and): also, before a vowel, **thorac-**

tho·rax (thôr′aks) ***n.***, *pl.* **-rax·es, -ra·ces′** (-ə sēz′) [L. < Gr. *thorax*] **1.** in man and other higher vertebrates, the part of the body between the neck and the abdomen; chest **2.** the middle one of the three main segments of an insect's body

Tho·ra·zine (thôr′ə zēn′) [*thor-* (< ?) + (CHLORPROM)-AZINE] *a trademark for* CHLORPROMAZINE

Thor·eau (thôr′ō, thə rō′), **Henry David** (born *David Henry Thoreau*) 1817–62; U.S. naturalist & writer

tho·ri·um (thôr′ē əm) ***n.*** [ModL. < THOR] a rare, grayish, radioactive chemical element, used in making electronic equipment and as a nuclear fuel: symbol, Th; at. wt., 232.038; at. no., 90 —**tho′ric** ***adj.***

thorn (thôrn) ***n.*** [OE.] **1.** *a)* a very short, hard, leafless branch or stem with a sharp point *b)* any small tree or shrub bearing thorns; esp., *same as* HAWTHORN **2.** anything that keeps troubling, vexing, or irritating one: usually in the phrase **thorn in one's side** (or **flesh**) **3.** in Old English, the runic character(Þ), corresponding to either the voiced or unvoiced sound of English *th*

thorn apple **1.** *a) same as* HAWTHORN *b)* its applelike fruit **2.** a jimson weed or similar plant

thorn·y (thôr′nē) ***adj.*** **thorn′i·er, thorn′i·est** **1.** full of thorns; prickly **2.** difficult or full of obstacles, vexations, pain, etc. —**thorn′i·ness** ***n.***

thor·o (thur′ō, -ə) ***adj.*** *shortened sp. of* THOROUGH

tho·ron (thôr′än) ***n.*** [ModL. < THORIUM] a radioactive isotope of radon, resulting from the disintegration of thorium

thor·ough (thur′ō, -ə) ***prep., adv.*** [ME. *thoruh*, a var. of *through*, THROUGH] *obs. var. of* THROUGH —***adj.*** **1.** done or proceeding through to the end; complete *[*a *thorough* checkup*]* **2.** that is completely (the thing specified); absolute *[*a *thorough* rascal*]* **3.** very exact, accurate, or painstaking, esp. about details —**thor′ough·ly** ***adv.*** —**thor′ough·ness** ***n.***

thor·ough·bred (thur′ə bred′) ***adj.*** **1.** purebred, as a horse or dog; pedigreed **2.** thoroughly trained, cultured, etc.; well-bred **3.** excellent; first-rate —***n.*** **1.** a thoroughbred animal; specif., [**T-**] any of a breed of racehorses **2.** a cultured, well-bred person

thor·ough·fare (-fer′) ***n.*** a public street open at both ends, esp. one through which there is much traffic; main road

thor·ough·go·ing (-gō′iŋ) ***adj.*** very thorough; specif., *a)* precise and painstaking *b)* absolute; out-and-out

those (*th*ōz) ***adj., pron.*** [OE. *thas*] *pl. of* THAT

thou (*th*ou) ***pron.*** [OE. *thu*] the nominative second person singular of the personal pronoun: formerly used in familiar address but now replaced by *you* except in poetic, religious, and some dialectal use

though (*th*ō) ***conj.*** [< OE. *theah* & cognate ON. *tho*] **1.** in spite of the fact that; notwithstanding that *[though* it rained, he went*]* **2.** and yet; nevertheless; however *[*they will probably win, *though* no one thinks so*]* **3.** even if; supposing that *[though* he may fail, he will have tried*]* —***adv.*** however; nevertheless *[*she sings well, *though]*

thought[1] (thôt) ***n.*** [OE. *thoht*] **1.** the act or process of thinking **2.** the power of reasoning; intellect; imagination **3.** what one thinks; idea, opinion, plan, etc. **4.** the ideas, opinions, etc. prevailing at a given time or place or among a given people *[*modern *thought* in education*]* **5.** attention; consideration *[*give it a moment's *thought]* **6.** intention or expectation *[*no *thought* of leaving*]* **7.** a little; trifle *[*be a *thought* more careful*]*

thought[2] (thôt) *pt. & pp. of* THINK

thought·ful (-fəl) ***adj.*** **1.** full of thought; meditative **2.** characterized by thought; serious **3.** heedful, careful, etc.; esp., considerate of others —**thought′ful·ly** ***adv.*** —**thought′ful·ness** ***n.***

thought·less (-lis) ***adj.*** **1.** not stopping to think; careless **2.** not given thought; rash **3.** not considerate of others **4.** [Rare] stupid —**thought′less·ly** ***adv.*** —**thought′less·ness** ***n.***

thou·sand (thou′z'nd) ***n.*** [OE. *thusend*] **1.** ten hundred; 1,000; M **2.** an indefinite but very large number —***adj.*** amounting to one thousand in number

thou·sand·fold (-fōld′) ***adj.*** [see -FOLD] having a thousand times as much or as many —***adv.*** a thousand times as much or as many: with *a*

Thousand Island dressing a salad dressing made of mayonnaise with ketchup, minced pickles, etc.

Thousand Islands group of c.1,000 islands in the St. Lawrence River at the outlet of Lake Ontario, some part of N.Y. State & some of Ontario, Canada

thou·sandth (thou′z'ndth) ***adj.*** **1.** coming last in a series of a thousand **2.** designating any of the thousand equal parts of something —***n.*** **1.** the thousandth one of a series **2.** any of the thousand equal parts of something; 1/1000

Thrace (thrās) **1.** ancient region in the E Balkan Peninsula **2.** modern region in the SE Balkan Peninsula divided between Greece & Turkey —**Thra·cian** (thrā′shən) ***adj., n.***

thrall (thrôl) ***n.*** [OE. *thræl* < ON.] **1.** orig., a slave or bondman **2.** a person under the moral or psychological domination of someone or something **3.** slavery

thrall·dom, thral·dom (-dəm) ***n.*** the condition of being a thrall; servitude; slavery

thrash (thrash) ***vt.*** [OE. *therscan*, to beat] **1.** *same as* THRESH **2.** to make move violently or wildly **3.** to give a severe beating to; flog —***vi.*** **1.** *same as* THRESH **2.** to move or toss about violently *[thrashing* in agony*]* **3.** to make one's way by thrashing —***n.*** the act of thrashing —**thrash out** to settle by much discussion —**thrash over** to go over (a problem, etc.) in great detail

thrash·er[1] (thrash′ər) ***n.*** a person or thing that thrashes

thrash·er[2] (thrash′ər) ***n.*** [E. dial. *thresher*] any of a group of gray to brownish American songbirds resembling the thrush by having a long, stiff tail and a long bill

thread (thred) ***n.*** [OE. *thræd*] **1.** *a)* a light, fine, stringlike length of two or more fibers or strands of spun cotton, silk, etc. twisted together and used in sewing *b)* a similar fine length of synthetic material, as of plastic, or of glass or metal *c)* the fine, stringy filament produced from itself by a spider, silkworm, etc. *d)* a fine, stringy length of syrup, etc. **2.** any thin line, stratum, vein, ray, etc. **3.** something like a thread in its length, sequence, etc. *[*the *thread* of a story*]* **4.** the spiral or helical ridge of a screw, bolt, nut, etc. **5.** [*pl.*] [Slang] a suit, or clothes generally —***vt.*** **1.** *a)* to put a thread through the eye of (a needle, etc.) *b)* to arrange thread for use on (a sewing machine) **2.** to string (beads, etc.) on or as if on a thread **3.** to fashion a thread (sense 4) on or in (a screw, pipe, etc.) **4.** to interweave with or as if with threads **5.** *a)* to pass through by twisting, turning, or weaving in and out *[*to *thread* the streets*]* *b)* to make (one's way) in this fashion —***vi.*** **1.** to go along in a winding way **2.** to form a thread when dropped from a spoon: said of boiling syrup beginning to thicken —**thread′er** ***n.*** —**thread′like′** ***adj.***

thread·bare (-ber′) ***adj.*** **1.** worn down so that the threads show; having the nap worn off **2.** wearing worn-out clothes; shabby **3.** that has lost freshness or novelty; stale

thread·y (-ē) ***adj.*** **thread′i·er, thread′i·est** **1.** of or like a thread; stringy; fibrous **2.** forming threads; viscid: said of liquids **3.** thin, weak, feeble, etc. *[a thready voice]* —**thread′i·ness** ***n.***

threat (thret) ***n.*** [OE. *threat,* a throng] **1.** an expression of intention to hurt, destroy, punish, etc., as in intimidation **2.** *a)* a sign of something dangerous or harmful about to happen *[the threat of war]* *b)* a source of possible danger, harm, etc.

threat·en (thret′'n) ***vt.*** [OE. *threatnian*] **1.** *a)* to make threats against *b)* to express one's intention to inflict (punishment, injury, etc.) **2.** *a)* to be a sign of (danger, harm, etc.) *[clouds threatening snow]* *b)* to be a source of possible danger, harm, etc. to *[an epidemic threatens the city]* —***vi.*** **1.** to make threats **2.** to be a sign or source of possible danger, etc. —**threat′en·er** ***n.*** —**threat′en·ing·ly** ***adv.***

three (thrē) ***adj.*** [OE. *threo, thrie*] totaling one more than two —***n.*** **1.** the cardinal number between two and four; 3; III **2.** anything having three units or members, or numbered three

three-base hit (thrē′bās′) a triple in baseball

3-D (thrē′dē′) ***adj.*** producing or designed to produce an effect of three dimensions *[a 3-D movie]* —***n.*** a system or effect that adds a three-dimensional appearance to visual images, as in movies

three-deck·er (-dek′ər) ***n.*** **1.** a ship with three decks **2.** any structure with three levels **3.** [Colloq.] a sandwich made with three slices of bread

three-di·men·sion·al (-də men′shən 'l) ***adj.*** **1.** *a)* of or having three dimensions *b)* appearing to have depth or thickness in addition to height and width **2.** having a life-like quality

three·fold (-fōld′) ***adj.*** [see -FOLD] **1.** having three parts **2.** having three times as much or as many —***adv.*** three times as much or as many

three-mile limit (-mīl′) the outer limit of a zone of water extending three miles offshore, sometimes regarded as the limit to a country's right to control, use, etc.

three·pence (thrip′'ns, thrup′-, threp′-) ***n.*** **1.** the sum of three British pennies **2.** a British coin of this value

three·pen·ny (thrē′pen′ē, thrip′ə nē) ***adj.*** **1.** worth or costing threepence **2.** of small worth; cheap

three-ply (-plī′) ***adj.*** having three thicknesses, interwoven layers, strands, etc.

three-quar·ter (-kwôr′tər) ***adj.*** of or involving three fourths

three·score (thrē′skôr′) ***adj.*** sixty

three·some (-səm) ***n.*** a group of three persons

thren·o·dy (thren′ə dē) ***n., pl.*** **-dies** [< Gr. < *thrēnos,* lamentation + *ōidē,* song] a song of lamentation; dirge —**thre·nod·ic** (thri näd′ik) ***adj.*** —**thren′o·dist** ***n.***

thresh (thresh) ***vt.*** [earlier form of THRASH] **1.** to beat out (grain) from its husk, as with a flail **2.** to beat grain out of (husks) **3.** to beat or strike as with a flail —***vi.*** **1.** to thresh grain **2.** to toss about; thrash —**thresh out** to settle by much discussion; thrash out

thresh·er (-ər) ***n.*** **1.** a person who threshes **2.** a machine for threshing grain: also **threshing machine** **3.** a large shark with a long tail

thresh·old (thresh′ōld, -hōld) ***n.*** [OE. *therscold* < base of *therscan* (see THRASH)] **1.** *same as* DOORSILL **2.** the entrance or beginning point of something **3.** *Physiol., Psychol.* the point at which a stimulus is just strong enough to be perceived or produce a response *[the threshold of pain]*

threw (thrōō) *pt. of* THROW

thrice (thrīs) ***adv.*** [ME. *thries*] **1.** three times **2.** threefold **3.** greatly; highly

thrift (thrift) ***n.*** [ON. < *thrifast,* to THRIVE] **1.** orig., a thriving **2.** careful management of one's money or resources; economy; frugality **3.** a small plant with narrow leaves and small white, pink, red, or purplish flowers —**thrift′less** ***adj.*** —**thrift′less·ly** ***adv.*** —**thrift′less·ness** ***n.***

thrift·y (-ē) ***adj.*** **thrift′i·er, thrift′i·est** **1.** practicing or showing thrift; economical **2.** thriving; prospering —**thrift′i·ly** ***adv.*** —**thrift′i·ness** ***n.***

thrill (thril) ***vi., vt.*** [OE. *thyr(e)lian,* to pierce < *thyrel,* hole < *thurh,* through] **1.** to feel or cause to feel keen emotional excitement; tingle with excitement **2.** to quiver or cause to quiver; tremble; vibrate —***n.*** **1.** a thrilling or being thrilled; tremor of excitement **2.** the quality of thrilling, or the ability to thrill **3.** something that causes emotional excitement **4.** a vibration; tremor; quiver

thrill·er (-ər) ***n.*** a suspenseful novel, movie, etc., esp. [Chiefly Brit.] one dealing with crime and detection

thrive (thrīv) ***vi.*** **thrived** or **throve, thrived** or **thriv·en** (thriv′'n), **thriv′ing** [< ON. *thrifast,* to prosper < *thrifa,* to grasp] **1.** to prosper or flourish; be successful, esp. by practicing thrift **2.** to grow vigorously or luxuriantly

thro′, thro (thrōō) ***prep., adv., adj.*** *archaic shortened sp. of* THROUGH

throat (thrōt) ***n.*** [OE. *throte*] **1.** the front part of the neck **2.** the upper part of the passage from the mouth and nose to the stomach and lungs, including the pharynx, upper larynx, trachea, and esophagus **3.** any narrow, throatlike passage or part —**jump down someone's throat** [Colloq.] to attack or criticize someone suddenly and violently —**stick in one's throat** to be hard for one to say, as from reluctance

-throat·ed (thrōt′id) *a combining form meaning* having a (specified kind of) throat *[ruby-throated]*

throat·y (-ē) ***adj.*** **throat′i·er, throat′i·est** **1.** produced in the throat, as some sounds or tones **2.** characterized by such sounds; husky *[a throaty voice]* —**throat′i·ly** ***adv.*** —**throat′i·ness** ***n.***

throb (thräb) ***vi.*** **throbbed, throb′bing** [ME. *throbben*] **1.** to beat, pulsate, vibrate, etc. **2.** to beat strongly or fast; palpitate, as the heart under exertion **3.** to tingle or quiver with excitement —***n.*** **1.** the act of throbbing **2.** a beat or pulsation, esp. a strong one of the heart —**throb′ber** ***n.*** —**throb′bing·ly** ***adv.***

throe (thrō) ***n.*** [prob. < OE. *thrawu,* pain] a spasm or pang of pain: *usually used in pl. [the throes of childbirth, death throes]* —**in the throes of** in the act of struggling with (a problem, task, etc.)

throm·bin (thräm′bin) ***n.*** [< Gr. *thrombos,* a clot] the enzyme of the blood, formed from prothrombin, that causes clotting by forming fibrin

throm·bo·sis (thräm bō′sis) ***n.*** [ModL. < Gr. < *thrombos,* a clot] coagulation of the blood in the heart or a blood vessel, forming a clot —**throm·bot′ic** (-bät′ik) ***adj.***

throne (thrōn) ***n.*** [< OFr. < L. < Gr. *thronos,* a seat] **1.** the chair on which a king, cardinal, etc. sits on formal or ceremonial occasions **2.** the power or rank of a king, etc.; sovereignty **3.** a sovereign ruler, etc. *[orders from the throne]* —***vt., vi.*** **throned, thron′ing** to enthrone or be enthroned

throng (thrôŋ) ***n.*** [OE. *(ge)thrang* < *thringan,* to crowd] **1.** a great number of people gathered together; crowd **2.** any great number of things massed or considered together; multitude —***vi.*** to gather together, move, or press in a throng; crowd —***vt.*** to crowd into; fill with a multitude

throt·tle (thrät′'l) ***n.*** [prob. dim. of THROAT] **1.** [Rare] the throat or windpipe **2.** the valve that regulates the amount of fuel vapor entering an internal-combustion engine or controls the flow of steam in a steam line: also **throttle valve** **3.** the lever or pedal that controls this valve —***vt.*** **-tled, -tling** **1.** to choke; strangle **2.** to stop the utterance or action of; suppress **3.** *a)* to reduce the flow of (fuel vapor, etc.) by means of a throttle *b)* to lessen the speed of (an engine, vehicle, etc.) by this or similar means —***vi.*** to choke or suffocate —**throt′tler** ***n.***

through (thrōō) ***prep.*** [OE. *thurh*] **1.** in one side and out the other side of; from end to end of **2.** in the midst of; among **3.** by way of **4.** over the entire extent of **5.** to various places in; around *[touring through France]* **6.** *a)* from the beginning to the end of *b)* up to and including *[through Friday]* **7.** without making a stop for *[to go through a red light]* **8.** past the difficulties of *[to come through hard times]* **9.** by means of **10.** as a result of; because of —***adv.*** **1.** in one side and out the other; from end to end **2.** from the beginning to the end **3.** completely to the end *[see it through]* **4.** thoroughly; completely: also **through and through** *[soaked through]* —***adj.*** **1.** extending from one place to another *[a through street]* **2.** traveling to the destination without stops *[a through train]* **3.** arrived at the end; finished **4.** at the end of one's usefulness, resources, etc. *[through in politics]* **5.** having no further dealings, etc. (*with* someone or something)

through·out (thrōō out′) ***prep.*** all the way through; in or during every part of —***adv.*** **1.** in or during every part; everywhere **2.** in every respect

through·way (-wā′) ***n.*** *same as* EXPRESSWAY

throve (thrōv) *alt. pt. of* THRIVE

throw (thrō) ***vt.*** **threw, thrown, throw′ing** [OE. *thrawan,* to twist] **1.** to twist strands of (silk, etc.) into thread or yarn **2.** to cause to fly through the air by releasing from the hand while the arm is in rapid motion; cast; hurl **3.** to discharge through the air from a catapult, gun, etc. **4.** to cause to fall; upset *[thrown by a horse]* **5.** to move or send rapidly *[they threw troops into the battle]* **6.** to put suddenly and forcibly into a specified place, condition, or situation *[thrown into confusion]* **7.** *a)* to cast (dice) *b)* to make (a specified cast) at dice *[to throw a five]* **8.** to cast off; shed *[snakes throw their skins]* **9.** to move (the lever of a switch, clutch, etc.) or connect, disconnect, etc. by so doing **10.** *a)* to direct, cast, turn, etc. (with *at, on, upon,* etc.) *[to* *throw* a glance, a light, a shadow, etc.*]* *b*) to deliver (a punch) **11.** to cause (one's voice) to seem to come from some other source **12.** to put (blame *on*, obstacles *before*, etc.) **13.** [Colloq.] to lose (a game, race, etc.) deliberately **14.** [Colloq.] to give (a party, dance, etc.) **15.** [Colloq.] to have (a fit, tantrum, etc.) **16.** [Colloq.] to confuse or disconcert *[*the question *threw* him*]* **17.** *Ceramics* to shape on a potter's wheel —***vi.*** to cast or hurl something —***n.*** **1.** the act of one who throws; a cast **2.** the distance something is or can be thrown *[*a stone's *throw]* **3.** *a*) a spread for draping over a sofa, etc. *b*) a woman's light scarf or wrap **4.** *a*) the motion of a moving part, as a cam, eccentric, etc. *b*) the extent of such a motion —**throw a monkey wrench into** to obstruct by direct interference; sabotage —**throw away** **1.** to rid oneself of; discard **2.** to waste **3.** to fail to make use of **4.** to deliver (a line or lines) in an offhand way: said of an actor or comedian —**throw back** **1.** to stop from advancing **2.** to revert to the type of an ancestor —**throw cold water on** to discourage by showing no interest or by criticizing —**throw in** **1.** to engage (a clutch) **2.** to add extra or free **3.** to add to others **4.** [Colloq.] to join (*with*) in cooperative action —**throw off** **1.** *a*) to rid oneself of *b*) to recover from **2.** to mislead **3.** to expel, emit, etc. —**throw on** to put on (a garment) hastily —**throw oneself at** to try very hard to win the affection or love of —**throw oneself into** to engage in with great vigor —**throw oneself on** (or **upon**) to rely on for support for aid —**throw open** **1.** to open completely and suddenly **2.** to remove all restrictions from —**throw out** **1.** to discard **2.** to reject or remove, often with force **3.** to emit **4.** to disengage (a clutch) **5.** *Baseball* to throw the ball to a teammate who in turn retires (a runner) —**throw over** **1.** to give up; abandon **2.** to jilt —**throw together** **1.** to make or assemble hurriedly **2.** to cause to become acquainted —**throw up** **1.** to give up or abandon **2.** to vomit **3.** to construct rapidly **4.** to mention repeatedly (*to* someone), as in reproach —**throw′er** ***n.***

throw·a·way (thrō′ə wā′) ***adj.*** designed to be discarded after use *[*a *throwaway* bottle*]*

throw·back (-bak′) ***n.*** **1.** a throwing back; check or stop **2.** reversion to an ancestral type **3.** an instance of this

throw rug *same as* SCATTER RUG

thru (thro͞o) ***prep., adv., adj.*** *shortened sp. of* THROUGH

thrum¹ (thrum) ***n.*** [OE., a ligament] **1.** *a*) the row of warp thread ends left on a loom when the web is cut off *b*) any of these ends **2.** any short end thread or fringe

thrum² (thrum) ***vt., vi.*** **thrummed, thrum′ming** [echoic] **1.** to strum (a guitar, banjo, etc.) **2.** to drum (on) with the fingers —***n.*** the act or sound of thrumming

thrush¹ (thrush) ***n.*** [OE. *thrysce*] any of a large group of songbirds, often plain-colored, including the robin, wood thrush, blackbird, etc.

thrush² (thrush) ***n.*** [prob. akin to Dan. *trøske*] a disease, esp. of infants, caused by a fungus that forms milky white lesions on the mouth, lips, and throat

thrust (thrust) ***vt.*** **thrust, thrust′ing** [ON. *thrysta*] **1.** to push with sudden force; shove **2.** to pierce; stab **3.** to force or impose (oneself or another) upon someone else or into some position or situation —***vi.*** **1.** to push or shove against something **2.** to make a stab or lunge, as with a sword **3.** to force one's way (*into, through*, etc.) **4.** to extend, as in growth —***n.*** **1.** a thrusting; specif., *a*) a sudden, forceful push *b*) a stab, as with a sword *c*) any sudden attack **2.** continuous pressure of one part against another, as of a rafter against a wall **3.** *a*) the driving force of a propeller in the line of its shaft *b*) the forward force produced by the gases escaping rearward from a jet or rocket engine **4.** *a*) forward movement; impetus *b*) energy; drive **5.** the basic meaning or purpose *[*the *thrust* of a speech*]* —**thrust′er** ***n.***

thru·way (thro͞o′wā′) ***n.*** *same as* EXPRESSWAY

Thu·cyd·i·des (tho͞o sid′ə dēz′) 460?–400? B.C.; Athenian historian

thud (thud) ***vi.*** **thud′ded, thud′ding** [prob. ult. < OE. *thyddan*, to strike] to hit or fall with a dull sound —***n.*** **1.** a heavy blow **2.** a dull sound, as of a heavy object dropping on a soft, solid surface

thug (thug) ***n.*** [Hindi *thag* < Sans. *sthaga*, a rogue] **1.** [*also* **T-**] a member of a former religious organization in India that murdered and robbed **2.** a rough, brutal hoodlum, gangster, robber, etc. —**thug′ger·y** ***n.*** —**thug′gish** ***adj.***

thu·li·um (tho͞o′lē əm) ***n.*** [ModL. < (ULTIMA) THULE] a metallic chemical element of the rare-earth group: symbol, Tm; at. wt., 168.934; at. no., 69

thumb (thum) ***n.*** [OE. *thuma*] **1.** the short, thick finger of the human hand that is nearest the wrist **2.** a corresponding part in some other animals **3.** that part of a glove, etc. which covers the thumb —***vt.*** **1.** to handle, turn, soil, etc. as with the thumb **2.** [Colloq.] to ask for or get (a ride) or make (one's way) in hitchhiking by gesturing with the thumb extended —**all thumbs** clumsy; fumbling —**thumb one's nose** to raise one's thumb to the nose in a coarse gesture of defiance or contempt —**thumbs down** a signal of disapproval —**thumbs up** a signal of approval —**under one's thumb** under one's influence

thumb index an index to the sections of a reference book, consisting of a series of rounded notches cut in the front edge of a book with a labeled tab at the base of each notch —**thumb′-in′dex** ***vt.***

thumb·nail (-nāl′) ***n.*** **1.** the nail of the thumb **2.** something as small as a thumbnail —***adj.*** very small or brief *[*a *thumbnail* sketch*]*

thumb·screw (-skro͞o′) ***n.*** **1.** a screw with a head shaped in such a way that it can be turned with the thumb and forefinger **2.** a former instrument of torture for squeezing the thumbs

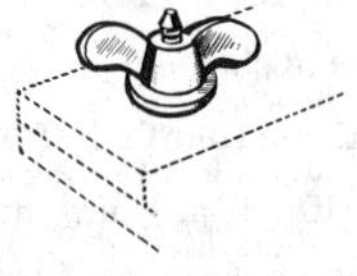

THUMBSCREW

thumb·tack (-tak′) ***n.*** a tack with a wide, flat head, that can be pressed into a board, etc. with the thumb

thump (thump) ***n.*** [echoic] **1.** a blow with something heavy and blunt **2.** the dull sound made by such a blow —***vt.*** **1.** to strike with a thump or thumps **2.** to thrash; beat severely —***vi.*** **1.** to hit or fall with a thump **2.** to make a dull, heavy sound; pound; throb —**thump′er** ***n.***

thump·ing (thum′piŋ) ***adj.*** **1.** that thumps **2.** [Colloq.] very large; whopping —**thump′ing·ly** ***adv.***

thun·der (thun′dər) ***n.*** [OE. *thunor*] **1.** the sound that is heard after a flash of lightning, caused by the sudden heating and expansion of air by electrical discharge **2.** any loud, rumbling sound like this **3.** an outburst of threatening or angry words Also used in mild oaths *[*yes, by *thunder!]*: also **thun′der·a′tion** —***vi.*** **1.** to produce thunder *[*it is *thundering]* **2.** to make, or move with, a sound like thunder **3.** to make strong denunciations, etc. —***vt.*** to utter, attack, etc. with a thundering sound —**steal someone's thunder** to lessen the effectiveness of someone's statement or action by anticipating him in its use —**thun′der·er** ***n.***

thun·der·bolt (-bōlt′) ***n.*** **1.** a flash of lightning with the thunder heard after it **2.** something that stuns or acts with sudden force or violence

thun·der·clap (-klap′) ***n.*** **1.** a clap, or loud crash, of thunder **2.** anything like this in being sudden, startling, violent, etc.

thun·der·cloud (-kloud′) ***n.*** a storm cloud charged with electricity and producing lightning and thunder

thun·der·head (-hed′) ***n.*** a round mass of cumulus clouds coming before a thunderstorm

thun·der·ous (-əs) ***adj.*** **1.** full of or making thunder **2.** making a noise like thunder —**thun′der·ous·ly** ***adv.***

thun·der·show·er (-shou′ər), **thun·der·squall** (-skwôl′), **thun·der·storm** (-stôrm′) ***n.*** a shower (or squall or storm) with thunder and lightning

thun·der·struck (-struk′) ***adj.*** amazed or shocked as if struck by a thunderbolt: also **thun′der·strick′en** (-strik′'n)

thu·ri·ble (thoor′ə b'l, thyoor′-) ***n.*** [< L. < *thus* (gen. *thuris*), incense < Gr. *thyos*, sacrifice] *same as* CENSER

Thu·rin·gi·a (thoo rin′jē ə) region of SW East Germany —**Thu·rin′gi·an** ***adj., n.***

Thurs., Thur. Thursday

Thurs·day (thurz′dē, -dā) ***n.*** [< OE. < ON. *Thorsdagr*, Thor's day] the fifth day of the week

Thurs·days (-dēz, -dāz) ***adv.*** on or during every Thursday

thus (*th*us) ***adv.*** [OE.] **1.** in this or that manner; in the way just stated or in the following manner **2.** to this or that degree or extent; so **3.** consequently; therefore; hence: often used with conjunctive force **4.** for example

thwack (thwak) ***vt.*** [prob. echoic] to strike with something flat; whack —***n.*** a blow with something flat

thwart (thwôrt) ***adj.*** [ON. *thvert*, transverse] lying across something else —***adv., prep.*** *archaic var. of* ATHWART —***n.*** **1.** a rower's seat extending across a boat **2.** a brace extending across a canoe —***vt.*** to keep from doing or being done; block or hinder (a person, plans, etc.)

thy (*th*ī) ***possessive pronominal adj.*** [ME. *thi*, contr. < *thin*, thy] of, belonging to, or done by thee: archaic or poet. var. of *your:* see also THINE, THOU

thyme (tīm) ***n.*** [< MFr. < L. < Gr. *thymon* < *thyein*, to offer sacrifice] any of various shrubby plants or aromatic herbs of the mint family, with white, pink, or red flowers and fragrant leaves used for seasoning —**thym′ic** ***adj.***

thy·mine (thī′mēn, -min) ***n.*** [G. *thymin* < Gr. *thymos*, spirit + G. *-in*, -INE⁴] a white, crystalline base, $C_5H_6N_2O_2$, one of the substances forming the genetic code in DNA molecules

thy·mol (thī′môl, -mōl) ***n.*** [THYM(E) + -OL¹] a colorless compound, $C_{10}H_{14}O$, extracted from thyme or made synthetically: used as an antiseptic, as in mouthwashes, etc.

thy·mus (thī′məs) ***n.*** [ModL. < Gr. *thymos*] a ductless, glandlike body near the throat, that has no known function and disappears in the adult: see also SWEETBREAD: also **thymus gland** —**thy′mic** ***adj.***

thy·roid (thī′roid) ***adj.*** [ModL. < Gr. < *thyreos*, door-shaped shield < *thyra*, door + *-eidēs*, -OID] **1.** designating or of a large ductless gland near the trachea, secreting the hormone thyroxine, which regulates body growth and metabolism **2.** designating or of the principal cartilage of the larynx, forming the Adam's apple —***n.*** **1.** the thyroid gland **2.** the thyroid cartilage **3.** a preparation of the thyroid gland of certain animals, used in treating goiter, etc.: also **thyroid extract**

thy·rox·ine (thī räk′sēn, -sin) ***n.*** [THYR(OID) + OX(Y)-[1] + -INE[4]] a colorless, crystalline compound, $C_{15}H_{11}I_4NO_4$, the active hormone of the thyroid gland, used in treating goiter, etc.: also **thy·rox′in** (-sin)

thyr·sus (thur′səs) ***n.***, *pl.* **-si** (-sī) [L. < Gr. *thyrsos*] *Gr. Myth.* a staff tipped with a pine cone and sometimes entwined with ivy, carried by Dionysus, the satyrs, etc.

thy·self (*thī* self′) ***pron.*** *reflexive or intensive form of* THOU: an archaic or poet. var. of *yourself*

ti (tē) ***n.*** [altered < *si:* see GAMUT, SOL-FA] *Music* a syllable representing the seventh tone of the diatonic scale

Ti *Chem.* titanium

ti·ar·a (tē er′ə, -ar′ə, -är′ə; tī-) ***n.*** [L. < Gr. *tiara*] **1.** an ancient Persian headdress **2.** the Pope's triple crown **3.** a woman's coronetlike headdress, often jeweled

Ti·ber (tī′bər) river in C Italy, flowing from the Apennines south through Rome into the Tyrrhenian Sea

Ti·ber·i·us (tī bir′ē əs) (*Tiberius Claudius Nero Caesar*) 42 B.C.–37 A.D.; Rom. emperor (14 A.D.–37 A.D.)

Ti·bet (ti bet′) autonomous region of SW China, north of the Himalayas: 471,660 sq. mi.; cap. Lhasa

Ti·bet·an (ti bet′'n) ***adj.*** of Tibet, its people, their language, etc. —***n.*** **1.** a member of the Mongolic people of Tibet **2.** the Sino-Tibetan language of Tibet

tib·i·a (tib′ē ə) ***n.***, *pl.* **-i·ae′** (-i ē′), **-i·as** [L.] **1.** the inner and thicker of the two bones of the leg below the knee; shinbone **2.** a corresponding bone in the leg of other vertebrates —**tib′i·al** ***adj.***

tic (tik) ***n.*** [Fr. < ?] a twitching of a muscle, esp. of the face, that is not consciously controlled

tick[1] (tik) ***n.*** [prob. < Gmc. echoic base] **1.** a light clicking or tapping sound, as that made by a clock **2.** a mark made to check off items; check mark (✓, /, etc.) **3.** [Brit. Colloq.] a moment; instant —***vi.*** **1.** to make a tick or ticks, as a clock **2.** [Colloq.] to function; work *[*what makes him *tick?]* —***vt.*** **1.** to indicate or count by a tick or ticks **2.** [Chiefly Brit.] to check off (an item in a list, etc.) with a tick (usually with *off*)

tick[2] (tik) ***n.*** [OE. *ticia*] any of a large group of bloodsucking arachnids that are parasitic on man, cattle, sheep, etc., including many species that transmit diseases

TICK
(¼ in. long)

tick[3] (tik) ***n.*** [ult. < L. < Gr. *thēkē*, a case] **1.** the cloth case that is filled with cotton, feathers, etc. to form a mattress or pillow **2.** [Colloq.] *same as* TICKING

tick[4] (tik) ***n.*** [contr. < TICKET] [Chiefly Brit. Colloq.] credit; trust *[*to buy something on *tick]*

tick·er (tik′ər) ***n.*** a person or thing that ticks; specif., *a)* a telegraphic device that records stock market quotations, etc. on paper tape (**ticker tape**) *b)* [Old Slang] a watch *c)* [Slang] the heart

tick·et (tik′it) ***n.*** [< obs. Fr. *etiquet* (now *étiquette*), a ticket] **1.** a printed card or piece of paper that gives one a specified right, as to attend a theater, ride a bus, etc. **2.** a label or tag, as on a piece of merchandise, giving the size, price, etc. **3.** the list of candidates nominated by a political party in an election; slate **4.** [Colloq.] a summons to court for a traffic violation —***vt.*** **1.** to label or tag with a ticket **2.** to issue a ticket to

tick·et-of-leave man (-əv lēv′) [Brit.] formerly, a person on parole from prison

tick·ing (tik′iŋ) ***n.*** [see TICK[3]] a strong, heavy cloth, often striped, used for casings of mattresses, pillows, etc.

tick·le (tik′'l) ***vt.*** **-led, -ling** [ME. *tikelen*] **1.** to please, gratify, etc.: often used in the passive voice with slang intensives, as **tickled pink** (or **silly, to death,** etc.) **2.** to amuse *[*the joke really *tickled* her*]* **3.** to touch or stroke lightly so as to cause twitching, laughter, etc. *[*to *tickle* someone's ear*]* —***vi.*** **1.** to have a scratching or tingling sensation *[*a throat that *tickles]* **2.** to be ticklish —***n.*** **1.** a tickling or being tickled **2.** a tickling sensation

tick·ler (tik′lər) ***n.*** **1.** a person or thing that tickles **2.** a memorandum pad, file, etc. for reminding one of things that need to be taken care of at certain future dates

tick·lish (-lish) ***adj.*** **1.** sensitive to tickling **2.** very sensitive or easily upset; touchy **3.** needing careful handling; delicate —**tick′lish·ly** ***adv.*** —**tick′lish·ness** ***n.***

tick-tack-toe, tic-tac-toe (tik′tak tō′) ***n.*** a game in which two players take turns marking either X's or O's in an open block of nine squares, the object being to complete a line of three of one's mark first

tick·tock (tik′täk′) ***n.*** the sound made by a clock —***vi.*** to make this sound

Ti·con·der·o·ga (tī′kän də rō′gə), **Fort** [< Iroquoian, lit., between two lakes] former fort in NE N.Y., taken from the British by Am. Revolutionary soldiers in 1775

tid·al (tīd′'l) ***adj.*** of, having, caused by, determined by, or dependent on a tide or tides —**tid′al·ly** ***adv.***

tidal wave **1.** in popular usage, an unusually great, destructive wave sent inshore by an earthquake or a very strong wind **2.** any great, widespread movement, expression of feeling, etc.

tid·bit (tid′bit′) ***n.*** [dial. *tid*, small object + BIT[2]] a choice bit of food, gossip, etc.

tid·dly·winks (tid′lē wiŋks′, tid′'l ē-) ***n.*** a game in which the players try to snap little colored disks into a cup by pressing their edges with a larger disk: also **tid′dle·dy·winks′** (-'l dē wiŋks′)

tide (tīd) ***n.*** [OE. *tid*, time] **1.** a period of time: now only in combination *[Eastertide]* **2.** *a)* the alternate rise and fall of the surface of oceans, seas, etc., caused by the attraction of the moon and sun: it occurs twice in each period of 24 hours and 50 minutes *b) same as* FLOOD TIDE **3.** something that rises and falls like the tide **4.** a stream, current, trend, etc. *[*the *tide* of public opinion*]* **5.** [Archaic] an opportune time —***adj.*** *same as* TIDAL —***vi.*** **tid′ed, tid′ing** to surge like a tide —***vt.*** to carry as with the tide —**tide over** to help along temporarily, as through a period of difficulty —**turn the tide** to reverse a condition

tide·land (-land′, -lənd) ***n.*** **1.** land covered by water at high tide and uncovered at low tide **2.** [*pl.*] loosely, land under water just beyond this and within territorial limits

tide·mark (-märk′) ***n.*** the high-water mark or, sometimes, the low-water mark of the tide

tide·wa·ter (-wôt′ər, -wät′-) ***n.*** **1.** water, as in some streams along a coastline, that is affected by the tide **2.** an area in which water is affected by the tide —***adj.*** of or along a tidewater

ti·dings (tī′diŋz) ***n.pl.*** [*sometimes with sing. v.*] [OE. *tidung*] news; information

ti·dy (tī′dē) ***adj.*** **-di·er, -di·est** [ult. < *tid*, time] **1.** neat in personal appearance, ways, etc.; orderly **2.** neat in arrangement; in order; trim **3.** [Colloq.] *a)* fairly good; satisfactory *b)* rather large; considerable *[*a *tidy* sum*]* —***vt., vi.*** **-died, -dy·ing** to make (things) tidy (often with *up*) —***n.***, *pl.* **-dies** *same as* ANTIMACASSAR —**ti′di·ly** ***adv.*** —**ti′di·ness** ***n.***

tie (tī) ***vt.*** **tied, ty′ing** [OE. *tigan* < base of *teag*, a rope] **1.** to fasten or bind together or to something else, as with string or rope made secure by knotting, etc. **2.** to tighten and knot the laces, strings, etc. of *[*to *tie* one's shoes*]* **3.** *a)* to make (a knot or bow) *b)* to make a knot or bow in *[*to *tie* a necktie*]* **4.** to join or bind in any way *[tied* by common interests*]* **5.** to confine; restrict **6.** to equal (the score, record, etc.) of (opponents, a rival, etc.) **7.** *Music* to connect with a tie —***vi.*** to make a tie —***n.*** **1.** a string, cord, etc. used to tie things **2.** something that joins, binds, etc.; bond **3.** something that confines or restricts *[*legal *ties]* **4.** *short for* NECKTIE **5.** a beam, rod, etc. that holds together and strengthens parts of a building **6.** any of the parallel crossbeams to which the rails of a railroad are fastened **7.** *a)* an equality of scores, votes, etc. in a contest *b)* a contest in which scores, etc. are equal **8.** [*pl.*] low, laced shoes **9.** *Music* a curved line joining two notes of the same pitch, indicating that the tone is to be held unbroken —***adj.*** that has been tied, or made equal *[*a *tie* score*]* —**tie down** to confine; restrain; restrict —**tie in** **1.** to bring into or have a connection **2.** to make or be consistent, harmonious, etc. —**tie off** to close off passage through by tying with something —**tie up** **1.** to tie securely **2.** to wrap up and tie with string, etc. **3.** to moor (a ship or boat) to a dock **4.** to block or hinder **5.** to cause to be already in use, committed, etc.

tie·back (-bak′) ***n.*** **1.** a sash, ribbon, tape, etc. used to tie curtains or draperies to one side **2.** a curtain with a tieback: *usually used in pl.*

tie beam a horizontal beam serving as a tie (*n.* 5)

tie clasp a decorative clasp for fastening a necktie to the shirt front: also **tie clip, tie bar**

tie-dye (tī′dī′) ***n.*** **1.** a method of dyeing designs on cloth by tightly tying bunches of it with thread, etc. so that the dye affects only exposed parts **2.** cloth so decorated or a design so made —***vt.*** **-dyed′, -dye′ing** to dye in this way

tie-in (-in′) ***adj.*** designating or of a sale in which an item in demand can be bought only along with some other item or items *—n.* **1.** a tie-in sale or advertisement **2.** a connection or relationship

tie line **1.** a direct telephone line between extensions in one or more PBX systems **2.** a line used to connect one electric power or transportation system with another

Tien Shan (tyen shän) mountain system in C Asia, extending across the Kirghiz S.S.R. & Sinkiang, China

Tien·tsin (tin′tsin′; *Chin.* tyen′jin′) seaport in NE China, on an arm of the Yellow Sea: pop. c. 4,000,000

tie·pin (tī′pin′) *n. same as* STICKPIN

Tie·po·lo (tye′pô lô), **Gio·van·ni Bat·tis·ta** (jô vän′nē bät tēs′tä) 1696–1770; Venetian painter

tier[1] (tir) *n.* [< MFr. *tire,* order] any of a series of layers or rows, as of seats, arranged one above or behind another *—vt., vi.* to arrange or be arranged in tiers

ti·er[2] (tī′ər) *n.* a person or thing that ties

tierce (turs) *n.* [*often* **T-**] *same as* TERCE

Tier·ra del Fue·go (tyer′rä del fwe′gô; *E.* tē er′ə del′ fo͞o ā′gō) **1.** group of islands at the tip of S. America, divided between Argentina & Chile **2.** chief island of this group

tie tack an ornamental pin with a short point that fits into a snap, used to fasten a necktie to the shirt front

tie-up (tī′up′) *n.* **1.** a temporary stoppage or interruption of work, traffic, etc. **2.** connection or relation

tiff (tif) *n.* [< ?] **1.** a slight fit of anger or bad humor **2.** a slight quarrel; spat *—vi.* to be in or have a tiff

tif·fin (tif′in) *n., vi. Anglo-Ind. term for* LUNCH

ti·ger (tī′gər) *n., pl.* **-gers, -ger:** see PLURAL, II, D, 1 [< OE. & OFr., both < L. < Gr. *tigris*] **1.** a large, flesh-eating animal of the cat family, native to Asia, having a tawny coat striped with black **2.** *a)* a very energetic or persevering person *b)* a fierce, belligerent person **—have a tiger by the tail** to find oneself in a situation more difficult to handle than one expected **—ti′ger·ish** *adj.*

tiger beetle any of various brightly colored, often striped beetles with burrowing larvae that feed on other insects

tiger lily a lily having purple-spotted, orange flowers

tiger moth any of a group of stout-bodied moths with brightly striped or spotted wings

tiger's eye a semiprecious, yellow-brown stone: also **ti′ger-eye′** *n.*

tight (tīt) *adj.* [< OE. *-thight,* strong] **1.** made so that water, air, etc. cannot pass through [a *tight* boat] **2.** drawn, packed, spaced, etc. closely together [a *tight* weave] **3.** [Dial.] snug; trim; neat **4.** fixed securely; firm [a *tight* joint] **5.** fully stretched; taut **6.** fitting so closely as to be uncomfortable **7.** strict [*tight* control] **8.** difficult to manage: esp. in the phrase **a tight corner** (or **squeeze,** etc.), a difficult situation **9.** showing strain [a *tight* smile] **10.** almost even or tied [a *tight* race] **11.** sharp: said of a spiral, turn, etc. **12.** *a)* difficult to get; scarce in relation to demand *b)* characterized by such scarcity [a *tight* market] **13.** concise: said of language, style, etc. **14.** [Colloq.] stingy **15.** [Slang] drunk **16.** [Slang] intimate; friendly (usually with *with*) *—adv.* in a tight manner; esp., *a)* securely or firmly [hold *tight*] *b)* [Colloq.] soundly [sleep *tight*] **—sit tight** to maintain one's opinion or position **—tight′ly** *adv.* **—tight′ness** *n.*

-tight (tīt) [< prec.] *a combining form meaning* not letting (something specified) in or out [*watertight, airtight*]

tight·en (tīt′'n) *vt., vi.* to make or become tight or tighter

tight end *Football* an end stationed next to the tackle on the offensive line

tight·fist·ed (tīt′fis′tid) *adj.* stingy

tight·fit·ting (-fit′iŋ) *adj.* fitting very tight

tight·knit (-nit′) *adj.* **1.** tightly knit **2.** well organized or put together in an efficient way

tight-lipped (-lipt′) *adj.* **1.** having the lips closed tightly **2.** not saying much; taciturn or secretive

tight·rope (-rōp′) *n.* a rope stretched tight on which acrobats do balancing acts

tights (tīts) *n.pl.* a garment that fits tightly over the legs and the lower part of the body, worn by acrobats, dancers, etc.

tight ship [Colloq.] any organization or business that is highly organized and efficiently run, like a naval vessel under strict discipline

tight·wad (tīt′wäd′, -wôd′) *n.* [TIGHT + WAD] [Slang] a stingy person; miser

ti·glon (tī′glän′, -glən) *n.* [TIG(ER) + L(I)ON] the offspring of a male tiger and a female lion: also **ti′gon′** (-gän′, -gən)

ti·gress (tī′gris) *n.* a female tiger

Ti·gris (tī′gris) river flowing from EC Turkey through Iraq, joining the Euphrates to form the Shatt-al-Arab

Ti·jua·na (tē wä′nə, tē′ə wä′-; *Sp.* tē hwä′nä) city in Baja California, on the U.S. border: pop. 335,000

tike (tīk) *n. same as* TYKE

til·bu·ry (til′bər ē) *n., pl.* **-ries** [< *Tilbury,* a London coach builder] a light, two-wheeled carriage for two persons

til·de (til′də) *n.* [Sp. < L. *titulus,* title, sign] a diacritical mark (~) used in various ways, as over an *n* in Spanish to indicate a palatal nasal sound (ny), as in *señor*

tile (tīl) *n.* [OE. *tigele,* ult. < L. *tegula*] **1.** *a)* a thin piece of glazed or unglazed, fired clay, stone, etc. used for roofing, flooring, decorative borders, bathroom walls, etc. *b)* a similar piece of plastic, asphalt, etc., used to cover floors, walls, etc. **2.** tiles collectively **3.** a drain of semicircular tiles or earthenware pipe **4.** burnt-clay, hollow blocks, used variously in construction **5.** any of the pieces in mah-jongg *—vt.* **tiled, til′ing** to cover with tiles **—on the tiles** [Brit. Colloq.] out carousing **—til′er** *n.*

til·ing (tīl′iŋ) *n.* **1.** the action of a person who tiles **2.** tiles collectively **3.** a covering of tiles

till[1] (til) *prep., conj.* [OE. *til*] *same as* UNTIL

till[2] (til) *vt., vi.* [OE. *tilian,* lit., to strive for] to work (land) in raising crops, as by plowing, fertilizing, etc.; cultivate **—till′a·ble** *adj.*

till[3] (til) *n.* [< ? ME. *tillen,* to draw] **1.** a drawer or tray, as in a store counter, for keeping money **2.** ready cash

till·age (til′ij) *n.* **1.** the tilling of land **2.** land that is tilled

till·er[1] (til′ər) *n.* [< OFr. < ML. *telarium,* weaver's beam < L. *tela,* a web] a bar or handle for turning a boat's rudder

till·er[2] (til′ər) *n.* a person who tills the soil

tilt (tilt) *vt.* [prob. < OE. *tealt,* shaky] **1.** to cause to slope or slant; tip **2.** *a)* to poise or thrust (a lance) in or as in a tilt *b)* to charge at (one's opponent) in a tilt *—vi.* **1.** to slope; incline **2.** to poise or thrust one's lance (*at* one's opponent) in a tilt **3.** to take part in a tilt or joust **4.** to dispute, argue, contend, etc. *—n.* **1.** a medieval contest in which two horsemen thrust with lances in an attempt to unseat each other **2.** any spirited contest, dispute, etc. between persons **3.** *a)* the act of tilting, or sloping *b)* a slope or slant **4.** [Colloq.] a leaning or inclination **—(at) full tilt** at full speed

tilth (tilth) *n.* [OE. < *tilian:* see TILL[2]] **1.** a tilling of land **2.** tilled land

Tim. Timothy

tim·bal (tim′b'l) *n.* [< Fr. < Sp. < Ar. < *al,* the + *ṭabl,* drum] *same as* KETTLEDRUM

tim·bale (tim′b'l) *n.* [Fr.: see prec.] **1.** a custardlike dish made with chicken, lobster, fish, etc. and baked in a small drum-shaped mold **2.** a type of fried or baked pastry shell, filled with a cooked food

tim·ber (tim′bər) *n.* [OE.] **1.** wood suitable for building houses, ships, etc. **2.** a large, heavy, dressed piece of wood used in building; beam **3.** [Brit.] *same as* LUMBER[1] (*n.* 2) **4.** trees or forests collectively **5.** personal quality or character [a man of his *timber*] **6.** a wooden rib of a ship *—vt.* to provide, build, or prop up with timbers *—adj.* of or for timber *—interj.* a warning shout by a lumberman that a cut tree is about to fall **—tim′bered** *adj.* **—tim′ber·ing** *n.*

timber hitch *Naut.* a knot used for tying a rope to a spar

tim·ber·land (tim′bər land′) *n.* land with trees suitable for timber; wooded land

tim·ber·line (-līn′) *n.* the line above or beyond which trees do not grow, as on mountains or in polar regions

timber wolf *same as* GRAY WOLF

tim·bre (tam′bər, tim′-) *n.* [Fr., earlier, sound of a bell < MFr. < OFr., ult. < Gr. *tympanon,* a drum] the quality of sound, apart from pitch or intensity, that makes one voice or musical instrument different from another

tim·brel (tim′brəl) *n.* [< OFr.: see prec.] an ancient type of tambourine

Tim·buk·tu (tim′buk to͞o′, tim buk′to͞o) town in C Mali, near the Niger River: pop. 9,000

time (tīm) *n.* [OE. *tima*] **1.** duration in which things happen in the past, present, and future; every minute there has been or ever will be **2.** a system of measuring the passing of hours [solar *time,* standard *time*] **3.** the period between two events or during which something exists, happens, or acts **4.** [*usually pl.*] a period of history [medieval *times,* Lincoln's *time*] **5.** *a)* a period characterized by a prevailing condition or specific experience [a *time* of peace, have a good *time*] *b)* [*usually pl.*] prevailing conditions [*times* are bad] **6.** a set period or term, as a lifetime or a term of imprisonment, apprenticeship, military service, etc. **7.** a period necessary, sufficient, measured, etc. for something [*time* for play, a baking *time* of ten minutes] **8.** *a)* the period worked or to be worked by an employee *b)* the hourly rate of pay for the regular working hours **9.** rate of speed in marching, driving, etc. **10.** a precise instant, minute, day, year, etc., determined by clock or calendar **11.** the point at which something happens; occasion [the game *time* is 2:00 P.M.] **12.** the usual or appointed

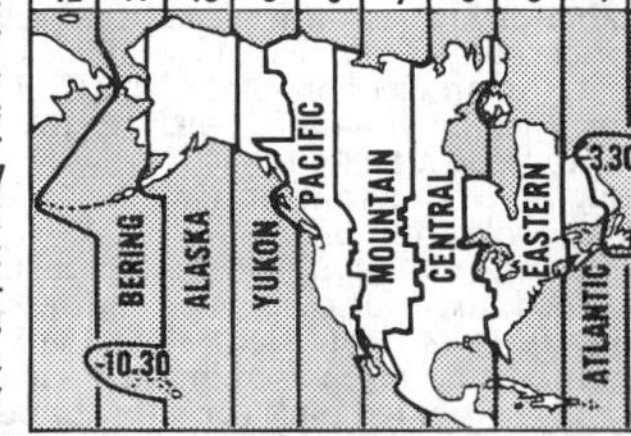

TIME ZONES

moment for something to happen, begin, or end [*time* to get up] **13.** the suitable or proper moment [now is the *time* to act] **14.** any one of a series of moments at which something recurs [for the fifth *time, time* and *time* again] **15.** *Music a*) the grouping of rhythmic beats into measures of equal length *b*) the characteristic rhythm of a piece of music in terms of this grouping *c*) the rate of speed at which a composition is played; tempo *d*) the duration of a note or rest —***interj.*** *Sports* a signal that a period of play or activity is ended or that play is temporarily suspended —***vt.*** **timed, tim′ing 1.** to arrange the time of so as to be acceptable or suitable, opportune, etc. **2.** to adjust, set, etc. so as to coincide in time [*time* your watch with mine] **3.** to set the duration of (a syllable or musical note) as a unit of rhythm **4.** to record the pace, speed, etc. of [to *time* a runner] —***adj.*** **1.** having to do with time **2.** set to explode, open, etc. at a given time [a *time* bomb] **3.** payable later [a *time* loan] **4.** designating or of any of a series of payments made over a period of time —**abreast of the times 1.** up to date **2.** informed about current matters —**against time** trying to finish in a given time —**ahead of time** sooner than due; early —**at one time 1.** together **2.** formerly —**at the same time 1.** together **2.** nonetheless; however —**at times** occasionally; sometimes —**behind the times** out of date; old-fashioned —**behind time** late —**do time** [Colloq.] to serve a prison term —**for the time being** for the present; temporarily —**from time to time** at intervals; now and then —**in good time 1.** at the proper time **2.** in a short time —**in no time** very quickly —**in time 1.** eventually **2.** before it is too late **3.** keeping the set tempo, pace, etc. —**make time** to travel, work, etc. at a fast rate of speed —**many a time** often; frequently —**on time 1.** at the appointed time; punctual(ly) **2.** to be paid for in installments over a period of time —**pass the time of day** to exchange a few words of greeting, etc. —**time after time** again and again; continually: also **time and again** —**time of one's life** [Colloq.] an experience of great pleasure for one —**time was** there was a time

time and a half a rate of payment one and a half times the usual rate, as for working overtime

time capsule a container holding articles of the present time, buried or preserved for a future age

time clock a clock with a mechanism for recording on a card (**timecard**) the time at which an employee begins and ends a work period

time exposure 1. a relatively long exposure of photographic film, generally for more than half a second **2.** a photograph taken in this way

time-hon·ored (tīm′än′ərd) ***adj.*** honored because in existence or usage for a long time

time·keep·er (-kē′pər) ***n.*** **1.** *same as* TIMEPIECE **2.** a person who keeps time; specif., *a*) one who keeps account of the hours worked by employees *b*) one who keeps account of the elapsed time in the periods of play in certain sports

time-lapse (-laps′) ***adj.*** of a technique of photographing a slow process on motion-picture film by exposing single frames at widely spaced intervals: the film is projected at regular speed to show the process speeded up

time·less (-lis) ***adj.*** **1.** unending **2.** eternal **3.** restricted to no specific time; always valid or true —**time′less·ly** ***adv.*** —**time′less·ness** ***n.***

time limit a fixed period of time during which something must be done or ended

time·ly (-lē) ***adj.*** **-li·er, -li·est** happening, done, said, etc. at a suitable time; well-timed; opportune —**time′li·ness** ***n.***

time·out (-out′) ***n.*** *Sports,* etc. any temporary suspension of play, as to discuss strategy, etc.

time·piece (-pēs′) ***n.*** any apparatus for measuring and recording time; esp., a clock or watch

tim·er (tī′mər) ***n.*** **1.** *same as: a*) TIMEKEEPER *b*) STOPWATCH **2.** in internal-combustion engines, a mechanism for causing the spark to be produced in the cylinder at the required instant **3.** a device for timing, or automatically starting and stopping, some mechanism

times (tīmz) ***prep.*** multiplied by: symbol, × [two *times* three is six]

time·sav·ing (tīm′sā′viŋ) ***adj.*** that saves time because of greater efficiency, etc. —**time′sav′er** ***n.***

time·serv·er (-sur′vər) ***n.*** a person who seeks to advance himself by altering his principles to suit the times or to gain support or favor —**time′serv′ing** ***n., adj.***

time signature *Music* a sign, usually like a numerical fraction, after the key signature, indicating the time, or tempo

time study study of operational or production procedures and the time consumed by them, with the intention of increasing efficiency: in full, **time and motion study**

time·ta·ble (-tā′b′l) ***n.*** a schedule of the times for things to happen, esp. of the times of arrival and departure of planes, trains, buses, etc.

time-test·ed (-tes′tid) ***adj.*** having value proved by long use or experience

time warp the condition or process of being displaced from one point in time to another, as in science fiction

time·worn (-wôrn′) ***adj.*** **1.** showing signs of wear or disrepair because of long use or existence **2.** hackneyed; trite

time zone *see* STANDARD TIME and chart at TIME

tim·id (tim′id) ***adj.*** [< L. < *timere,* to fear] **1.** easily frightened; shy **2.** showing lack of self-confidence —**ti·mid·i·ty** (tə mid′ə tē), **tim′id·ness** ***n.*** —**tim′id·ly** ***adv.***

tim·ing (tī′miŋ) ***n.*** **1.** *a*) the regulation of the speed with which something is performed so as to produce the most effective results *b*) the pacing of scenes, as of a play, for total effect **2.** measurement of time

Ti·mor (tē′môr, ti môr′) island of Indonesia, in the SE Malay Archipelago: c. 13,000 sq. mi.

tim·or·ous (tim′ər əs) ***adj.*** [< MFr. < ML. < L. *timor,* fear] **1.** full of or subject to fear; timid **2.** showing or caused by timidity —**tim′or·ous·ly** ***adv.*** —**tim′or·ous·ness** ***n.***

Tim·o·thy (tim′ə thē) [< Fr. < L. < Gr. < *timē,* honor + *theos,* god] **1.** a masculine name **2.** *Bible a*) a disciple of the Apostle Paul *b*) either of the epistles from the Apostle Paul to Timothy, books of the New Testament

tim·o·thy (tim′ə thē) ***n.*** [after *Timothy* Hanson, who took the seed to the Carolinas, c. 1720] a perennial grass with dense, cylindrical spikes, widely grown for hay

tim·pa·ni (tim′pə nē) ***n.pl.,*** *sing.* **-pa·no′** (-nō′) [It.: see TYMPANUM] kettledrums; esp., a set of kettledrums of different pitches played by one performer in an orchestra —**tim′pa·nist** ***n.***

tin (tin) ***n.*** [OE.] **1.** a soft, silver-white, metallic chemical element, easily shaped at ordinary temperatures: symbol, Sn; at. wt., 118.69; at. no., 50 **2.** *same as* TIN PLATE **3.** *a*) a pan, box, etc. made of tin plate *b*) [Chiefly Brit.] a can used for preserving food; also, its contents —***vt.*** **tinned, tin′ning 1.** to plate with tin **2.** [Chiefly Brit.] to put in cans for preservation

tin·a·mou (tin′ə mo͞o′) ***n.*** [Fr. < Carib name, *tinamu*] a bird of South and Central America resembling the partridge and quail, but related to the ostrich

tin can 1. a can used for preserving food **2.** [Slang] *same as* DESTROYER (sense 2)

tinc·ture (tiŋk′chər) ***n.*** [< L. *tinctura* < pp. of *tingere,* to dye] **1.** orig., a dye **2.** a light color; tint; tinge **3.** a slight trace, smattering, etc. **4.** a medicinal substance in a solution of alcohol or alcohol and water —***vt.*** **-tured, -tur·ing 1.** to color lightly; tint **2.** to give a slight trace to

tin·der (tin′dər) ***n.*** [OE. *tynder*] any dry, easily flammable material, esp. as formerly used for starting a fire from a spark made by flint and steel struck together

tin·der·box (-bäks′) ***n.*** **1.** formerly, a metal box for holding tinder, flint, and steel **2.** any highly flammable object, structure, etc. **3.** any place or situation in which trouble, war, etc. is likely to flare up

tine (tīn) ***n.*** [OE. *tind*] a sharp, projecting point; prong [the *tines* of a fork] —**tined** ***adj.***

tin ear [Colloq.] a sense of hearing that is so poorly developed that one seems deaf to certain sounds, music, etc.

tin·foil (tin′foil′) ***n.*** a very thin sheet or sheets of tin or an alloy of tin and lead, etc. used as a wrapping for food products, in insulation, etc.

ting[1] (tiŋ) ***n.*** [echoic] a single, light, ringing sound, as of a small bell —***vt., vi.*** to make or cause to make a ting

‡**ting**[2] (tiŋ) ***n.*** *same as* THING[2]

ting-a-ling (tiŋ′ə liŋ′) ***n.*** the sound of a small bell ringing repeatedly

tinge (tinj) ***vt.*** **tinged, tinge′ing** or **ting′ing** [L. *tingere,* to dye] **1.** to color slightly; give a tint to **2.** to give a trace, slight flavor or odor, shade, etc. to [joy *tinged* with sorrow] —***n.*** **1.** a slight coloring; tint **2.** a slight trace, flavor, odor, etc.

tin·gle (tiŋ′g'l) ***vi.*** **-gled, -gling** [< ME. var. of *tinklen,* to tinkle] **1.** to have a prickling or stinging feeling, as from cold, excitement, etc. **2.** to cause this feeling —***n.*** this feeling —**tin′gler** ***n.*** —**tin′gly** ***adj.*** **-gli·er, -gli·est**

tin god a person unworthy of the honor or respect he demands or receives

tin·horn (tin′hôrn′) ***adj.*** [Slang] cheap, showy, and phony —***n.*** [Slang] a tinhorn person, esp. a gambler

tin·ker (tiŋ′kər) ***n.*** [< ?] **1.** a person who mends pots, pans, etc., usually traveling at his trade **2.** a person who can make all kinds of minor repairs **3.** a clumsy or unskillful worker; bungler —*vi.* **1.** to work as a tinker **2.** to make clumsy attempts to mend something **3.** to putter aimlessly —*vt.* to mend as a tinker —**tin′ker·er** *n.*

tinker's damn (or **dam**) [< prec. + DAMN: with reference to the lowly status and profane speech of tinkers] something of no value: esp. in **not worth a tinker's damn**

Tin·ker·toy (tiŋ′kər toi′) *a trademark for* a toy set of wooden dowels, joints, wheels, etc., used by children to assemble structures —*n.* [t-] anything resembling or suggesting such a structure

tin·kle (tiŋ′k'l) *vi.* **-kled, -kling** [echoic] to make a series of light, clinking sounds like those of a very small bell —*vt.* **1.** to cause to tinkle **2.** to indicate, signal, etc. by tinkling —*n.* the act or sound of tinkling —**tin′kler** *n.* —**tin′kly** *adj.* **-kli·er, -kli·est**

tin liz·zie (liz′ē) [orig. nickname of an early model of Ford automobile] any cheap or old automobile

tin·ner (tin′ər) *n.* **1.** a tin miner **2.** *same as* TINSMITH

tin·ny (tin′ē) *adj.* **-ni·er, -ni·est 1.** of or yielding tin **2.** like tin; bright but cheap; not durable **3.** of or like the sound made in striking a tin object —**tin′ni·ly** *adv.* —**tin′ni·ness** *n.*

Tin Pan Alley 1. the center of popular music publishing in New York City **2.** the publishers, writers, and promoters of popular music

tin plate thin sheets of iron or steel plated with tin —**tin′-plate′** *vt.* **-plat′ed, -plat′ing**

tin·sel (tin′s'l, -z'l) *n.* [< MFr. *estincelle* < OFr.: see STENCIL] **1.** formerly, a cloth interwoven with glittering threads of gold, silver, etc. **2.** thin sheets, strips, or threads of tin, metal foil, etc., used for decoration, as on Christmas trees **3.** something that looks showy and fine but is really cheap and of little value —*adj.* **1.** of or decorated with tinsel **2.** showy; gaudy —*vt.* **-seled** or **-selled, -sel·ing** or **-sel·ling 1.** to make glitter as with tinsel **2.** to give a showy, gaudy look to —**tin′sel·ly** *adj.*

tin·smith (tin′smith′) *n.* a person who works in tin or tin plate; maker of tinware: also **tin′man,** *pl.* **-men**

tint (tint) *n.* [< L. pp. of *tingere,* to dye] **1.** a delicate color or hue; tinge **2.** a color or shading of a color, esp. with reference to its mixture with white **3.** a dye for the hair **4.** *Engraving* an even shading produced by fine parallel lines —*vt.* to give a tint to —**tint′er** *n.*

tin·tin·nab·u·la·tion (tin′ti nab′yoo lā′shən) *n.* [< L. *tintinnabulum,* little bell] the ringing sound of bells

Tin·to·ret·to (tēn′tô ret′tô; *E.* tin′tə ret′ō), **Il** (ēl) (born *Jacopo Robusti*) 1518–94; Venetian painter

tin·type (tin′tīp′) *n.* an old kind of photograph taken directly on a sensitized plate of enameled tin or iron

tin·ware (-wer′) *n.* pots, pans, etc. of tin plate

ti·ny (tī′nē) *adj.* **-ni·er, -ni·est** [< ME. *tine,* a little (something)] very small; diminutive —**ti′ni·ly** *adv.* —**ti′ni·ness** *n.*

-tion (shən) [< Fr. < OFr. < L. *-tio* (gen. *-tionis*)] *a suffix meaning:* **1.** the act of *[correction]* **2.** the state of being *[elation]* **3.** the thing that is *[creation]*

-tious (shəs) [< Fr. < L. *-tiosus*] a suffix used to form adjectives from nouns ending in -TION *[cautious]*

tip[1] (tip) *n.* [ME. *tippe*] **1.** the pointed or rounded end or top of something **2.** something attached to the end, as a cap, ferrule, etc. **3.** a top or apex, as of a mountain —*vt.* **tipped, tip′ping 1.** to make a tip on **2.** to cover the tip or tips of (*with* something) **3.** to serve as the tip of —**tip in** to insert (a map, picture, etc.) by pasting along the inner edge in bookbinding

tip[2] (tip) *vt.* **tipped, tip′ping** [akin ? to prec.] **1.** to strike lightly and sharply; tap **2.** to give a small present of money to (a waiter, porter, etc.) for some service **3.** [Colloq.] to give secret information to (often with *off*) **4.** *Baseball a)* to hit (the ball) a glancing blow *b)* to glance off (the bat, glove, etc.): said of the ball —*vi.* to give a tip or tips —*n.* **1.** a light, sharp blow; tap **2.** a piece of secret information *[a tip on the race]* **3.** a suggestion, hint, warning, etc. **4.** a small present of money given to a waiter, porter, etc. for services; gratuity —**tip one's hand** (or **mitt**) [Slang] to reveal one's plans, etc., often without intending to —**tip′per** *n.*

tip[3] (tip) *vt.* **tipped, tip′ping** [< ?] **1.** to overturn or upset (often with *over*) **2.** to cause to tilt or slant **3.** to raise (one's hat) slightly in greeting someone —*vi.* **1.** to tilt or slant **2.** to overturn or topple (often with *over*) —*n.* a tipping or being tipped; tilt; slant —**tip the scales at** to weigh (a specified amount)

tip-off (tip′ôf′) *n.* a giving of secret information, a hint, warning, etc.

tip·pet (tip′it) *n.* [prob. dim. of *tip,* TIP[1]] **1.** formerly, a long, hanging part of a hood, cape, or sleeve **2.** a scarflike garment of fur, wool, etc. for the neck and shoulders, hanging down in front

tip·ple[1] (tip′'l) *vi., vt.* **-pled, -pling** [prob. < ME. *tipelar,* tavern-keeper < ?] to drink (alcoholic liquor) habitually —*n.* alcoholic liquor —**tip′pler** *n.*

tip·ple[2] (tip′'l) *n.* [< obs. freq. of TIP[3]] an apparatus for emptying coal, etc. from a mine car

tip·py (tip′ē) *adj.* **-pi·er, -pi·est** [Colloq.] that tips easily; not steady; shaky

tip·py-toe, tip·py·toe (-tō′) *n., adj., adv., vi.* **-toed′, -toe′ing** *colloq. var. of* TIPTOE

tip·ster (tip′stər) *n.* [Colloq.] a person who sells tips, as to people betting on horse races, speculating in stocks, etc.

tip·sy (tip′sē) *adj.* **-si·er, -si·est 1.** that tips easily; not steady **2.** crooked; awry **3.** somewhat drunk —**tip′si·ly** *adv.* —**tip′si·ness** *n.*

tip·toe (tip′tō′) *n.* the tip of a toe or the tips of the toes —*vi.* **-toed′, -toe′ing** to walk stealthily or cautiously on one's tiptoes —*adj.* **1.** standing on one's tiptoes **2.** *a)* lifted up; exalted *b)* eager; alert *c)* stealthy; cautious —*adv.* on tiptoe —**on tiptoe 1.** on one's tiptoes **2.** eager or eagerly **3.** silently; stealthily

tip·top (-täp′) *n.* [TIP[1] + TOP[1]] **1.** the highest point; very top **2.** [Colloq.] the highest in quality or excellence; best —*adj., adv.* **1.** at the highest point, or top **2.** [Colloq.] at the highest point of excellence, health, etc.

ti·rade (tī′rād, tī rād′) *n.* [Fr. < It. *tirata,* a volley < pp. of *tirare,* to fire] a long, vehement speech or denunciation; harangue

Ti·ra·na (ti rä′nə) capital of Albania, in the C part: pop. 169,000: also, Albanian **Ti·ra·në** (tē *rä′*nə)

tire[1] (tīr) *vt., vi.* **tired, tir′ing** [OE. *tiorian*] **1.** to make or become weary or fatigued, as by exertion **2.** to make or become bored or impatient, as by dull talk

tire[2] (tīr) *n.* [prob. var. of ME. *atir,* equipment] a hoop of iron or rubber, or a rubber tube filled with air, fixed around the wheel of a vehicle to form a tread —*vt.* **tired, tir′ing** to furnish with tires

tired (tīrd) *adj.* **1.** fatigued; weary **2.** stale; hackneyed —**tired′ly** *adv.* —**tired′ness** *n.*

tire·less (tīr′lis) *adj.* that does not become tired —**tire′less·ly** *adv.* —**tire′less·ness** *n.*

tire·some (-səm) *adj.* **1.** tiring; boring **2.** annoying; irksome —**tire′some·ly** *adv.* —**tire′some·ness** *n.*

ti·ro (tī′rō) *n., pl.* **-ros** *var. sp. of* TYRO

Tir·ol (tir′äl, tī′rōl, ti rōl′) E Alpine region in W Austria & N Italy —**Ti·ro·le·an** (ti rō′lē ən) *adj., n.* —**Tir·o·lese** (tir′ə lēz′) *adj., n., pl.* **-lese′**

'tis (tiz) it is

Tish·ah b'Ab (tē shä′ bə äv′, tish′ə bôv′) a Jewish fast day commemorating the destruction of the Temple, observed on the 9th day of Ab

Tish·ri (tish rē′, tish′rē) *n.* the first month of the Jewish year: see JEWISH CALENDAR

tis·sue (tish′oo; *chiefly Brit.* tis′yoo) *n.* [< OFr. *tissu* < pp. of *tistre* < L. *texere,* to weave] **1.** cloth; esp., light, thin cloth, as gauze **2.** a tangled mass or series; mesh; network; web *[a tissue of lies]* **3.** a piece of soft, absorbent paper, used as a disposable handkerchief, as toilet paper, etc. **4.** *a) same as* TISSUE PAPER *b)* a sheet of tissue paper **5.** *Biol. a)* the substance of an organic body or organ, consisting of cells and the material between them *b)* any substance of this kind having a particular function *[epithelial tissue]* —*vt.* **-sued, -su·ing** to cover with tissue

tissue paper very thin, unglazed, nearly transparent paper, as for wrapping things, making tracings, etc.

tit[1] (tit) *n.* [TIT(MOUSE)] a titmouse or other small bird

tit[2] (tit) *n.* [OE.] *same as* TEAT

Tit. Titus

Ti·tan (tīt′'n) *poetic name for* HELIOS —*n.* **1.** *Gr. Myth.* any of a race of giant deities who were overthrown by the Olympian gods **2.** [t-] any person or thing of great size or power —*adj.* [*also* t-] *same as* TITANIC —**Ti′tan·ess** *n.fem.*

Ti·ta·ni·a (ti tā′nē ə, tī-) in early folklore, the queen of fairyland and wife of Oberon

Ti·tan·ic (tī tan′ik) *adj.* **1.** of or like the Titans **2.** [t-] of great size, strength, or power —**ti·tan′i·cal·ly** *adv.*

ti·ta·ni·um (tī tā′nē əm, ti-) *n.* [ModL. < Gr. pl. of *Titan,* a Titan] a silvery or dark-gray, lustrous, metallic chemical element found in various minerals and used as a deoxidizing agent in molten steel: symbol, Ti; at. wt., 47.90; at. no., 22

titanium dioxide a compound, TiO_2, used esp. as a white pigment

tit for tat [var. of earlier *tip for tap:* see TIP[2]] this in return for that, as blow for blow

tithe (tīth) *n.* [OE. *teothe,* a tenth] **1.** one tenth of the annual produce of one's land or of one's annual income, paid as a contribution to support a church or its clergy **2.** *a)* a tenth part *b)* any small part **3.** any tax or levy —*vt., vi.* **tithed, tith′ing** to pay a tithe of (one's income, etc.) —**tith′a·ble** *adj.* —**tith′er** *n.*

Ti·tian (tish′ən) (It. name *Tiziano Vecellio*) 1490?–1576; Venetian painter

ti·tian (tish′ən) *n.* [from the hair color in many of *Titian's* portraits] reddish yellow

Ti·ti·ca·ca (tit′ē kä′kə; *Sp.* tē′tē kä′kä), **Lake** largest lake in S. America, on the border of SE Peru & W Bolivia

tit·il·late (tit′'l āt′) *vt.* **-lat′ed, -lat′ing** [< L. pp. of *titillare,* to tickle] **1.** *same as* TICKLE **2.** to excite or stimulate pleasurably —**tit′il·lat′er** *n.* —**tit′il·la′tion** *n.* —**tit′il·la′tive** *adj.*

tit·i·vate (tit′ə vāt′) *vt., vi.* **-vat′ed, -vat′ing** [prob. < TIDY, with quasi-Latin suffix] to dress up; spruce up —**tit′i·va′tion** *n.*

tit·lark (tit′lärk′) *n.* [TIT[1] + LARK[1]] *same as* PIPIT

ti·tle (tīt′'l) *n.* [OFr. < L. *titulus*] **1.** the name of a book, chapter, poem, picture, piece of music, play, etc. **2.** *a)* *short for* TITLE PAGE *b)* a literary work having a particular title *[*50 new *titles* published in the fall*]* **3.** a descriptive name; epithet **4.** a word used to show the rank, office, occupation, etc. of a person *[*"Duke," "Mayor," and "Dr." are *titles]* **5.** a claim or right **6.** *Law a)* a right to ownership, esp. of real estate *b)* evidence of such right *c)* a document stating such a right; deed **7.** a championship, esp. in sports **8.** *Motion Pictures, TV* words shown on the screen that give credits, translations, etc. —*vt.* **-tled, -tling** to give a title to; name; entitle

ti·tle·hold·er (-hōl′dər) *n.* the holder of a title; specif., the winner of a championship, as in some sport

title page the page in the front of a book that gives the title, author, publisher, etc.

title role (or **part** or **character**) the character in a play, movie, etc. whose name is used as or in its title

ti·tlist (tīt′list) *n.* a titleholder in some sport

tit·mouse (tit′mous′) *n., pl.* **-mice′** (-mīs′) [ME. *titemose,* prob. < *tit-,* little + OE. *mase,* titmouse] a small bird found throughout the world except in S. America and Australia; esp., the **tufted titmouse,** with a crest on the head, common in the eastern U.S.

Ti·to (tē′tō), Marshal (born *Josip Broz*) 1892–1980; Communist party leader of Yugoslavia; president (1953–80)

ti·trate (tī′trāt) *vt., vi.* **-trat·ed, -trat·ing** [< Fr. *titrer* < *titre,* a standard < OFr. *title,* TITLE + -ATE[1]] to test by or be subjected to titration

ti·tra·tion (tī trā′shən) *n. Chem.* the process of finding out how much of a substance is in a known volume of a solution by measuring the volume of a solution of known concentration added to produce a given reaction

tit-tat-toe (tit′tat tō′) *n. same as* TICK-TACK-TOE

tit·ter (tit′ər) *vi.* [echoic] to laugh in a half-suppressed way, suggestive of silliness, nervousness, etc.; giggle —*n.* the act or an instance of tittering —**tit′ter·er** *n.*

tit·tle (tit′'l) *n.* [ME. *title,* orig. same word as TITLE] **1.** formerly, a dot or other small mark used as a diacritic **2.** a very small particle; iota; jot

tit·tle-tat·tle (tit′'l tat′'l) *n., vi.* **-tled, -tling** [redupl. of *tattle*] gossip; chatter

tit·u·lar (tich′ə lər; *chiefly Brit.* tit′yə-) *adj.* [< L. *titulus,* title] **1.** of, or having the nature of, a title **2.** having a title **3.** existing only in title; in name only *[*a *titular* leader*]* **4.** from whom or which the title or name is taken —**tit′u·lar·ly** *adv.*

Ti·tus (tīt′əs) *Bible* a book of the New Testament, which was an epistle of the Apostle Paul to his disciple Titus

tiz·zy (tiz′ē) *n., pl.* **-zies** [< ?] [Colloq.] a state of frenzied excitement, esp. over some trivial matter

TKO, T.K.O. *Boxing abbrev. of* TECHNICAL KNOCKOUT

Tl *Chem.* thallium

TLC, T.L.C., t.l.c. tender, loving care

Tm *Chem.* thulium

T-man (tē′man′) *n., pl.* **T′-men′** (-men′) [< *T(reasury)-man*] [Colloq.] a law-enforcement agent of the U.S. Department of the Treasury

TN Tennessee

tn. **1.** ton(s) **2.** training

TNT, T.N.T. trinitrotoluene

to (too͞; *unstressed* too, tə) *prep.* [OE.] **1.** *a)* in the direction of; toward *[*turn *to* the left*]* *b)* in the direction of and reaching *[*he went *to* Boston*]* **2.** as far as *[*wet *to* the skin*]* **3.** into a condition of *[*a rise *to* fame*]* **4.** on, onto, against, at, next, etc. *[*tie it *to* the post*]* **5.** *a)* until *[*from noon *to* night*]* *b)* before *[*the time is ten *to* six*]* **6.** for the purpose of *[*come *to* my aid*]* **7.** *a)* as concerns; in respect of *[*open *to* attack*]* *b)* in the opinion of *[*it seems *to* me*]* **8.** producing or resulting in *[*torn *to* pieces*]* **9.** with; along with *[*add this *to* the rest*]* **10.** belonging with *[*the key *to* this house*]* **11.** as compared with; as against *[*a score of 7 *to* 0*]* **12.** *a)* in agreement or correspondence with *[*not *to* my taste*]* *b)* in response to *[*come *to* my call*]* **13.** constituting; in *[*ten *to* the peck*]* **14.** to the limit of *[*moderate *to* high prices*]* **15.** with (a specified person or thing) as the recipient, or indirect object, of the action *[*give the book *to* her*]* **16.** in honor of *[*a toast *to* you*]* *To* is also used as a sign of the infinitive (Ex.: it is easy *to* read) —*adv.* **1.** forward *[*his hat is on wrong side *to]* **2.** in the normal or desired position or direction; esp., shut or closed *[*the door was blown *to]* **3.** to the matter at hand *[*let's all fall *to]* **4.** at hand *[*we were close *to* when it fell*]* —**to and fro** back and forth

toad (tōd) *n.* [OE. *tade*] **1.** any of a group of tailless, leaping amphibians with a rough, warty skin, that live on moist land rather than in water, except during breeding **2.** a person regarded as loathsome, contemptible, etc.

TOAD (1/2–9 in. long)

toad·fish (-fish′) *n., pl.* **-fish′, -fish′es:** see FISH any of various scaleless fishes with froglike heads, found in shallows off the Atlantic coast of N. America

toad·stool (-sto͞ol′) *n.* a mushroom; esp., in popular usage, any poisonous mushroom

toad·y (tōd′ē) *n., pl.* **toad′ies** [short for *toadeater,* quack doctor's assistant who pretended to eat toads and then drank the quack's cure-all] a person who flatters and serves others in any way to gain favor: also **toad′eat′er** —*vt., vi.* **toad′ied, toad′y·ing** to be a toady (to); flatter —**toad′y·ism** *n.*

to-and-fro (to͞o′ən frō′) *adj.* moving forward and backward; back-and-forth

toast[1] (tōst) *vt.* [< OFr., ult. < L. pp. of *torrere,* to parch] **1.** to brown the surface of (bread, etc.) by heating **2.** to warm thoroughly *[toast* yourself by the fire*]* —*vi.* to become toasted —*n.* sliced bread made brown and crisp by heat —**toast′er** *n.*

toast[2] (tōst) *n.* [< the toasted spiced bread formerly put in the wine] **1.** a person, thing, idea, etc. in honor of which glasses of wine, etc. are raised and drunk **2.** *a)* a proposal to drink to some person, etc. *b)* such a drink **3.** any person greatly acclaimed —*vt., vi.* to propose or drink a toast (to) —**toast′er** *n.*

toast·mas·ter (tōst′mas′tər) *n.* the person at a banquet who proposes toasts, introduces after-dinner speakers, etc. —**toast′mis′tress** (-mis′trəs) *n.fem.*

toast·y (tōs′tē) *adj.* **toast′i·er, toast′i·est** **1.** of or characteristic of toast **2.** warm and comfortable or cozy

Tob. Tobit

to·bac·co (tə bak′ō) *n., pl.* **-cos** [Sp. *tobaco* < WInd., pipe in which the Indians smoked the plant] **1.** any of various plants of the nightshade family, with large leaves and white, yellow, greenish, or purple flowers, esp. a species widely cultivated for its leaves **2.** these leaves, prepared for smoking, chewing, or snuffing **3.** cigars, cigarettes, snuff, etc. **4.** the use of tobacco for smoking, etc.

to·bac·co·nist (tə bak′ə nist) *n.* [Chiefly Brit.] a dealer in tobacco and other smoking supplies

To·ba·go (tō bā′gō, tə-) island in the West Indies, northeast of Trinidad: 116 sq. mi. See TRINIDAD AND TOBAGO

To·bit (tō′bit) a book of the Apocrypha

to·bog·gan (tə bäg′ən) *n.* [CanadFr. *tabagan* < Algonquian] a long, narrow, flat sled without runners, curved back at the front end: now used for coasting downhill —*vi.* **1.** to coast, travel, etc. on a toboggan **2.** to decline rapidly —**to·bog′gan·er, to·bog′gan·ist** *n.*

TOBOGGAN

To·by (tō′bē) *n., pl.* **-bies** [< *Toby,* dim. of *Tobias,* ult. < Heb. *tōbhīyāh,* lit., the lord is good] a jug or mug for ale or beer shaped like a stout man with a three-cornered hat: also **Toby jug**

toc·ca·ta (tə kät′ə) *n.* [It. < pp. of *toccare,* to touch < L.] a composition in free style for the organ, piano, etc., often used as a prelude of a fugue

to·coph·er·ol (tō käf′ə rôl′, -rōl′) *n.* [< Gr. *tokos,* childbirth + *pherein,* to BEAR[1] + -OL[1]] any of the four related oils that compose vitamin E and occur chiefly in wheat-germ oil, cottonseed oil, lettuce, etc.

Tocque·ville (tôk vēl′; *E.* tōk′vil), **A·lex·is (Charles Henri Maurice Clérel) de** (á lek sē′ də) 1805–59; Fr. writer & statesman

toc·sin (täk′sin) *n.* [Fr. < MFr. < Pr. < *toc,* a stroke + *senh,* a bell < L. *signum,* a sign] **1.** *a)* an alarm bell *b)* its sound **2.** any alarm

to·day (tə dā′) *adv.* [OE. *to dæg*] **1.** on or during the present day **2.** in the present time or age; nowadays —*n.* **1.** the present day **2.** the present time or period Also, esp. formerly, **to-day**

tod·dle (täd′'l) *vi.* **-dled, -dling** [? freq. of TOTTER] to walk with short, uncertain steps, as a child —*n.* a toddling —**tod′dler** *n.*

tod·dy (täd′ē) *n., pl.* **-dies** [Anglo-Ind. < Hindi *tārī,* fermented sap < *tār,* palm tree] **1.** the sweet or fermented sap of various East Indian palms, used as a beverage **2.** a drink of brandy, whiskey, etc. mixed with hot water, sugar, etc.: also **hot toddy**

to-do (tə do͞o′) *n.* [Colloq.] a commotion; fuss

toe (tō) *n.* [OE. *ta*] **1.** *a)* any of the digits of the foot *b)* the forepart of the foot *c)* that part of a shoe, sock, etc. which covers the toes **2.** anything like a toe in location, shape, or function —*vt.* **toed, toe′ing 1.** to touch, kick, etc. with the toes **2.** *a)* to drive (a nail) slantingly *b)* to fasten with nails so driven; toenail —*vi.* to stand, walk, or be formed so that the toes are in a specified position *[*to *toe* in*]* —**on one's toes** [Colloq.] mentally or physically alert —**step** (or **tread**) **on someone's toes** to offend someone, esp. by intruding on his rights —**toe the line** (or **mark**) to follow orders, rules, etc. strictly —**toe′like′** *adj.*

toed (tōd) *adj.* having (a specified kind or number of) toes: usually in hyphenated compounds *[*pigeon-*toed]*

toe dance a dance performed on the tips of the toes, as in ballet —**toe′-dance′** *vi.* **-danced′, -danc′ing —toe′-danc′er** *n.*

toe·hold (tō′hōld′) *n.* **1.** a small space or ledge for supporting the toe of the foot in climbing, etc. **2.** any means of surmounting obstacles, gaining entry, etc. **3.** a slight footing or advantage **4.** *Wrestling* a hold in which one wrestler twists the other's foot

toe·less (-lis) *adj.* **1.** having no toe or toes **2.** having the toe open *[toeless* shoes*]*

toe·nail (-nāl′) *n.* **1.** the nail of a toe **2.** *Carpentry* a nail driven slantingly —*vt. Carpentry* to fasten with a toenail

toff (täf, tôf) *n.* [< *toft,* var. of TUFT] [Brit. Slang] a fashionable, upper-class person; esp., a dandy

tof·fee, tof·fy (tôf′ē, täf′-) *n.* [later Brit. form of TAFFY] a hard, chewy candy made with brown sugar or molasses, often with nuts; kind of taffy

tog (täg, tôg) *n.* [prob. ult. < L. *toga,* TOGA] [*pl.*] [Colloq.] clothes —*vt., vi.* **togged, tog′ging** [Colloq.] to dress (usually with *up* or *out*)

to·ga (tō′gə) *n., pl.* **-gas, -gae** (-jē) [L. < *tegere,* to cover] **1.** in ancient Rome, a loose, one-piece outer garment worn in public by citizens **2.** a robe of office —**to′gaed** (-gəd) *adj.*

to·geth·er (tə geth′ər) *adv.* [< OE. < *to* (see TO) + *gædre,* together < base of *gaderian,* to gather] **1.** in or into one gathering, group, or place *[*the family ate *together]* **2.** in or into contact, collision, union, etc. *[*the cars skidded *together]* **3.** considered collectively *[*he won more than all of us *together]* **4.** *a)* with one another; in association *[*to live *together] b)* by joint effort *[together* they lifted the sofa*]* **5.** at the same time *[*shots fired *together]* **6.** in succession; continuously *[*he worked for two days *together]* **7.** in or into agreement, cooperation, etc. *[*let's get *together]* **8.** in or into a unified whole —*adj.* [Slang] having fully developed one's abilities, ambitions, etc.

to·geth·er·ness (-nis) *n.* the spending of much time together, as by a family in leisure-time activities, esp. in an effort to make the family more stable and unified

tog·ger·y (täg′ər ē, tôg′-) *n.* [Colloq.] clothes; togs

tog·gle (täg′'l) *n.* [prob. < dial. *tuggle,* freq. of TUG] **1.** a rod, pin, or bolt for insertion through a loop of a rope, a link of a chain, etc. to make an attachment, prevent slipping, etc. **2.** a toggle joint or a device having one —*vt.* **-gled, -gling** to provide or fasten with a toggle

toggle joint a knee-shaped joint consisting of two bars pivoted together at one end: pressure put on the joint to straighten it transmits opposite, outward pressure to the open ends

TOGGLE JOINT (arrows indicate direction of pressure)

toggle switch a switch consisting of a projecting lever moved back and forth through a small arc to open or close an electric circuit

To·go (tō′gō) country in W Africa, on the Atlantic, east of Ghana: 21,853 sq. mi.; pop. 1,914,000 —**To′go·lese′** (-lēz′) *adj., n., pl.* **-lese′**

toil[1] (toil) *vi.* [Anglo-Fr. *toiler,* to strive < OFr. < L. *tudiculare,* to stir about, ult. < *tudes,* mallet] **1.** to work hard and continuously **2.** to go or move slowly with pain or effort *[*to *toil* up a hill*]* —*vt.* [Now Rare] to accomplish with great effort *[*to *toil* one's way*]* —*n.* **1.** hard, exhausting work or effort **2.** a task performed by such effort —**toil′er** *n.*

toil[2] (toil) *n.* [OFr. *toile* < L. *tela,* a web] **1.** [Archaic] a net for trapping **2.** [*pl.*] any snare suggestive of a net

toi·let (toi′lit) *n.* [MFr. *toilette* < *toile,* cloth: see prec.] **1.** formerly, a dressing table **2.** the act of dressing or grooming oneself **3.** dress; attire **4.** *a)* a room, shelter, etc. for discharging wastes from the body; specif., a small room with a bowl-shaped fixture for this purpose that flushes with water *b)* such a fixture —*adj.* **1.** of or for grooming oneself **2.** for a toilet (*n.* 4*b*) —**make one's toilet** [Now Rare] to bathe, dress, arrange one's hair, etc.

toilet paper (or **tissue**) soft, absorbent paper, for cleaning oneself after discharging waste from the body

toi·let·ry (toi′lə trē) *n., pl.* **-ries** soap, lotion, cologne, etc. used in cleaning and grooming oneself

toi·lette (twä let′, toi-) *n.* [Fr.: see TOILET] **1.** the process of grooming oneself, including bathing, hairdressing, dressing, etc.: said of women **2.** dress or manner of dress; attire

toilet training the training of a young child to use a toilet when he needs to discharge bodily waste

toilet water a perfumed, slightly alcoholic liquid applied to the skin after bathing, shaving, etc.

toil·some (toil′səm) *adj.* requiring toil; laborious —**toil′some·ly** *adv.* —**toil′some·ness** *n.*

toil·worn (-wôrn′) *adj.* worn out by toil

To·kay (tō kā′) *n.* **1.** a sweet, rich wine made in Tokay, Hungary **2.** any wine like this **3.** a large, sweet grape used for the wine

toke (tōk) *n.* [? < ff.] [Slang] a puff on a cigarette, esp. one of marijuana or hashish

to·ken (tō′k'n) *n.* [OE. *tacn*] **1.** a sign, indication, or symbol *[*a *token* of one's affection*]* **2.** something serving as a sign of authority, identity, etc. **3.** a distinguishing mark or feature **4.** a keepsake **5.** a metal disk with a face value higher than its real value, issued as a substitute for currency, for use as fare on a bus, etc. —*vt.* to be a token of —*adj.* **1.** by way of a token, symbol, etc. **2.** merely simulated; slight or of no real account *[token* resistance*]* —**by the same** (or **this**) **token** following from this —**in token of** as evidence of

to·ken·ism (-iz'm) *n.* a pretending to act on a principle by doing so in a very small way; specif., token integration of Negroes, as in schools, jobs, etc.

To·ky·o (tō′kē ō′; *Jap.* tô′kyô′) capital of Japan, on the S coast of Honshu: pop. 8,907,000 (met. area 19,500,000) —**To′ky·o·ite′** (-īt′) *n.*

told (tōld) *pt. & pp. of* TELL —**all told** all (being) counted; in all *[*there were ten *all told]*

tole (tōl) *n.* [Fr. *tôle,* sheet iron < *table,* TABLE] a type of lacquered or enameled metalware used for trays, lamps, etc.

To·le·do (tə lē′dō; *also for 2, Sp.* tô lā′*th*ô) **1.** [after ff.] port in NW Ohio, on Lake Erie: pop. 355,000 (met. area 791,000) **2.** city in C Spain: pop. 40,000 —*n., pl.* **-dos** a fine-tempered sword or sword blade made in Toledo, Spain

tol·er·a·ble (täl′ər ə b'l) *adj.* **1.** that can be tolerated; endurable **2.** fairly good; passable **3.** [Colloq.] in fairly good health —**tol′er·a·bil′i·ty, tol′er·a·ble·ness** *n.* —**tol′er·a·bly** *adv.*

tol·er·ance (-əns) *n.* **1.** a tolerating or being tolerant of others' beliefs, practices, etc. **2.** the amount of variation allowed from a standard, accuracy, etc.; specif., the difference between the allowable maximum and minimum sizes of some mechanical part **3.** *Med.* the ability to resist the effects of a drug, etc. taken over a period of time or in larger and larger doses

tol·er·ant (-ənt) *adj.* **1.** having or showing tolerance of others' beliefs, practices, etc. **2.** *Med.* of or having tolerance —**tol′er·ant·ly** *adv.*

tol·er·ate (täl′ə rāt′) *vt.* **-at′ed, -at′ing** [< L. pp. of *tolerare,* to bear] **1.** to allow; permit **2.** to recognize and respect (others' beliefs, practices, etc.) without sharing them **3.** to put up with; bear **4.** *Med.* to have tolerance for (a specific drug, etc.) —**tol′er·a′tive** *adj.* —**tol′er·a′tor** *n.*

tol·er·a·tion (täl′ə rā′shən) *n.* tolerance; esp., freedom to hold religious views that differ from the established ones

toll[1] (tōl) *n.* [OE., prob. ult. < Gr. *telos,* tax] **1.** a tax or charge for a privilege, esp. for permission to use a bridge, highway, etc. **2.** the right to demand toll **3.** a charge for some service, as for a long-distance telephone call **4.** the number lost, taken, etc. *[*the storm took a heavy *toll* of lives*]* —*vt.* [Now Rare] **1.** to impose a toll on **2.** to gather (something) as toll

toll[2] (tōl) *vt.* [< ? OE. *-tillan,* to touch] **1.** to ring (a church bell, etc.) slowly with regular strokes, as for announcing a death **2.** to sound (the hour, a knell, etc.) by this **3.** to announce, summon, etc. by this —*vi.* to sound or ring slowly: said of a bell —*n.* **1.** the act or sound of tolling a bell **2.** a single stroke of the bell —**toll′er** *n.*

toll bar a bar, gate, etc. for stopping travel at a point where toll is taken

toll·booth (tōl′bo͞oth′) *n.* a booth at which toll is collected, as before entering a toll road

toll bridge a bridge at which toll is paid for passage

toll call a long-distance telephone call, for which there is a charge beyond the local rate

toll·gate (-gāt′) *n.* a gate for stopping travel at a point where toll is taken

toll·keep·er (-kēp′ər) *n.* a person who collects tolls at a tollgate

toll road a road on which toll must be paid

Tol·stoy (tôl stoi′; *E.* täl′stoi, tōl′-), Count **Lev** (E. **Leo**) **Ni·ko·la·ye·vich** (lyev nē′kô lä′ye vich) 1828–1910; Russ. novelist & social theorist: also sp. **Tolstoi**

Tol·tec (täl′tek, tōl′-) *n.* any of a group of Nahuatl Indians who were dominant in Mexico before the rise of the Aztecs —*adj.* of the Toltecs or their culture: also **Tol′tec·an**

to·lu (balsam) (tō lo͞o′) [< Sp. < *Tolú*, seaport in Colombia] a fragrant resin obtained from a S. American tree: it is used in cough syrups, etc.

tol·u·ene (täl′yoo wēn′) ***n.*** [TOLU + (BENZ)ENE] a liquid hydrocarbon, C_7H_8, first obtained from tolu balsam but now from coal tar, petroleum, etc.: it is used in making dyes, explosives, etc.: also **tol′u·ol′** (-wôl′, -wōl′)

tom (täm) ***n.*** [< *Tom*, dim. of THOMAS] the male of some animals, esp. of the cat —***adj.*** male [*a tom turkey*]

tom·a·hawk (täm′ə hôk′) ***n.*** [< Algonquian] a light ax with a head of stone, used by North American Indians as a tool and a weapon —***vt.*** to hit, cut, or kill with a tomahawk

Tom and Jerry (jer′ē) a hot drink made of rum, etc., beaten eggs, sugar, water or milk, and nutmeg

to·ma·to (tə māt′ō, -mät′ō) ***n.***, *pl.* **-toes** [< Sp. < Nahuatl *tomatl*] **1.** a red or yellowish fruit with a juicy pulp, used as a vegetable: botanically it is a berry **2.** the plant that it grows on

tomb (to͞om) ***n.*** [< Anglo-Fr. < LL. < Gr. *tymbos*] **1.** a vault, chamber, or grave for the dead **2.** a burial monument —**the tomb** death —**tomb′less** ***adj.*** —**tomb′like′** ***adj.***

tom·boy (täm′boi′) ***n.*** a girl who behaves or plays like an active boy —**tom′boy′ish** ***adj.*** —**tom′boy′ish·ly** ***adv.*** —**tom′boy′ish·ness** ***n.***

tomb·stone (to͞om′stōn′) ***n.*** a stone, usually with an inscription, marking a tomb or grave

tom·cat (täm′kat′) ***n.*** a male cat —***vi.*** **-cat′ted, -cat′ting** [Slang] to be sexually promiscuous: said of a man

Tom Collins *see* COLLINS

Tom, Dick, and Harry everyone; anyone: usually preceded by *every* and used disparagingly

tome (tōm) ***n.*** [Fr. < L. < Gr. *tomos*, piece cut off] **1.** orig., any volume of a work of several volumes **2.** a book, esp. a large or ponderous one

tom·fool (täm′fo͞ol′) ***n.*** a foolish, stupid, or silly person —***adj.*** foolish, stupid, or silly

tom·fool·er·y (-ər ē) ***n.***, *pl.* **-er·ies** foolish or silly behavior; nonsense

Tom·my (täm′ē) ***n.***, *pl.* **-mies** [< *Tommy Atkins* (for *Thomas Atkins*, fictitious name used in Brit. army sample forms)] [*also* **t-**] *epithet for* a private in the British army

Tommy gun *alternate trademark for* THOMPSON SUBMACHINE GUN —***n.*** a submachine gun

tom·my·rot (täm′ē rät′) ***n.*** [Slang] nonsense; foolishness

to·mor·row (tə mär′ō, -môr′ō) ***adv.*** [OE. *to morgen*] **1.** on the day after today **2.** at some time in the future —***n.*** **1.** the day after today **2.** some time in the future Also, esp. formerly, **to-morrow**

Tom Thumb **1.** a tiny hero of English folk tales **2.** any midget or small person

tom·tit (täm′tit′) ***n.*** [Chiefly Brit.] a titmouse or any of various other small birds

tom-tom (täm′täm′) ***n.*** [Hindi *ṭam-ṭam*] a simple kind of deep drum with a small head, usually beaten with the hands

-to·my (tə mē) [< Gr. < *temnein*, to cut] *a combining form meaning:* **1.** a dividing [*dichotomy*] **2.** a surgical operation [*lithotomy*]

ton (tun) ***n.*** [var. of TUN] **1.** a unit of weight equal to 2,000 pounds avoirdupois, commonly used in the U.S., Canada, South Africa, etc.: in full, **short ton** **2.** a unit of weight equal to 2,240 pounds avoirdupois, commonly used in Great Britain: in full, **long ton** **3.** *same as* METRIC TON **4.** a unit of internal capacity of ships, equal to 100 cubic feet: in full, **register ton** **5.** a unit of carrying capacity of ships, usually equal to 40 cubic feet: in full, **measurement ton, freight ton** **6.** a unit for measuring displacement of ships, equal to 35 cubic feet: it is nearly equal to the volume of a long ton of sea water: in full, **displacement ton** **7.** a unit of cooling capacity of an air conditioner, equal to 12,000 B.t.u. per hour **8.** [*often pl.*] [Colloq.] a very large amount or number Abbrev. **T., t., tn.** (*sing. & pl.*)

ton·al (tō′n′l) ***adj.*** of a tone or tonality —**ton′al·ly** ***adv.***

to·nal·i·ty (tō nal′ə tē) ***n.***, *pl.* **-ties** **1.** a quality of tone **2.** *Art* the color scheme in a painting **3.** *Music* *a*) *same as* KEY[1] *b*) tonal character as determined by the relationship of the tones to the keynote

ton·do (tän′dō) ***n.***, *pl.* **-di** (-dē), **-dos** [It., a plate] a round painting

tone (tōn) ***n.*** [< OFr. < L. < Gr. *tonos* < *teinein*, to stretch] **1.** *a*) a vocal or musical sound *b*) its quality **2.** an intonation, pitch, modulation, etc. of the voice that expresses a particular feeling [*a tone of contempt*] **3.** a way of wording or expressing things that shows a certain attitude [*the friendly tone of her letter*] **4.** normal resilience [*rubber that has lost its tone*] **5.** *a*) the style, character, spirit, etc. of a place or period *b*) distinctive style; elegance **6.** a quality of color; tint or shade **7.** *Linguis.* the relative height of pitch with which a syllable, word, etc. is pronounced **8.** *Music* *a*) a sound of distinct pitch (as distinguished from a noise) that may be put into harmonic relation with other such sounds *b*) the simple tone of a musical sound as distinguished from its overtones *c*) any one of the full intervals of a diatonic scale; whole step **9.** *Painting* the effect produced by the combination of light, shade, and color **10.** *Physiol.* the condition of an organism, organ, muscle, etc. with reference to its normal, healthy functioning: see also TONUS —***vt.*** **toned, ton′ing** **1.** [Rare] *same as* INTONE **2.** to give a tone to **3.** to change the tone of —***vi.*** to take on a tone —**tone down** **1.** to make or become less bright, sharp, etc.; soften **2.** to make (something written or said) less harsh —**tone in with** to harmonize with —**tone up** **1.** to give a more intense tone to **2.** to become strengthened or heightened —**tone′less** ***adj.*** —**tone′less·ly** ***adv.*** —**tone′less·ness** ***n.*** —**ton′er** ***n.***

tone arm the pivoted arm containing the pickup on a phonograph

tone color *same as* TIMBRE

tone-deaf (-def′) ***adj.*** not able to distinguish accurately differences in musical pitch —**tone′-deaf′ness** ***n.***

tone poem *same as* SYMPHONIC POEM

tone row (or **series**) *see* TWELVE-TONE

tong[1] (tôŋ, täŋ) ***vt.*** to seize, collect, handle, or hold with tongs —***vi.*** to use tongs

tong[2] (tôŋ, täŋ) ***n.*** [Chin. *t'ang*, a meeting place] a Chinese association, society, etc.

Ton·ga (täŋ′gə) country on a group of islands (**Tonga Islands**) in the South Pacific, east of Fiji: a member of the Commonwealth: 270 sq. mi.; pop. 86,000

Ton·gan (-gən) ***n.*** **1.** a native of Tonga **2.** the Polynesian language of the Tongans

tongs (tôŋz, täŋz) ***n.pl.*** [*sometimes with sing. v.*] [OE. *tange*] a device for seizing or lifting objects, with two arms pivoted or hinged together: also called **pair of tongs**

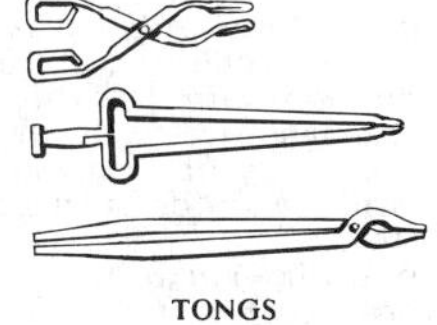

TONGS

tongue (tuŋ) ***n.*** [OE. *tunge*] **1.** the movable muscular structure attached to the floor of the mouth: it is used in eating, tasting, and (in man) speaking **2.** an animal's tongue used as food **3.** *a*) talk; speech *b*) a manner of speaking in regard to tone, diction, etc. [*a glib tongue*] **4.** a language or dialect **5.** [*pl.*] *see* GLOSSOLALIA **6.** something like a tongue in shape, position, motion, or use; specif., *a*) the flap under the laces of a shoe *b*) the clapper of a bell *c*) the pole of a wagon, etc. *d*) the projecting tenon of a tongue-and-groove joint *e*) the vibrating end of the reed in a wind instrument *f*) a narrow strip of land extending into a sea, river, etc. *g*) a long, narrow flame —***vt.*** **tongued, tongu′ing** **1.** [Archaic] to speak **2.** to touch, lick, etc. with the tongue **3.** *Music* to play by tonguing: see TONGUING —***vi.*** **1.** to project like a tongue **2.** *Music* to use tonguing: see TONGUING —**find one's tongue** to recover the ability to talk, as after shock —**hold one's tongue** to keep from speaking —**on everyone's tongue** spoken as common gossip —**on the tip of one's** (or **the**) **tongue** almost said or remembered —**speak in tongues** to be subject to glossolalia —**tongue′less** ***adj.*** —**tongue′like′** ***adj.***

tongue-and-groove joint (tuŋ′′n gro͞ov′) a kind of joint in which a tongue or tenon on one board fits exactly into a groove in another

tongued (tuŋd) ***adj.*** having a (specified kind of) tongue: usually in compounds [*sharp-tongued*]

tongue-lash (tuŋ′lash′) ***vt.*** [Colloq.] to scold or reprove harshly —**tongue′-lash′ing** ***n.***

tongue-tie (-tī′) ***n.*** limited motion of the tongue, caused by a short frenum —***vt.*** **-tied′, -ty′ing** to make tongue-tied

tongue-tied (-tīd′) ***adj.*** **1.** having a condition of tongue-tie **2.** speechless from embarrassment, etc.

tongue twister a phrase or sentence hard to speak fast (Ex.: six sick sheiks)

tongu·ing (tuŋ′iŋ) ***n.*** the use of the tongue in playing a musical wind instrument, esp. for more accurate intonation of rapid notes

ton·ic (tän′ik) ***adj.*** [< Gr. < *tonos*: see TONE] **1.** *a*) of or producing good muscle tone, or tension *b*) characterized by continuous muscular contraction [*a tonic spasm*] **2.** invigorating to the body or mind **3.** *Music* designating or based on a keynote —***n.*** **1.** anything that invigorates or stimulates; specif., *a*) a drug, medicine, etc. for increasing body tone *b*) a hair or scalp dressing **2.** a carbonated beverage flavored with a little quinine and served in a mixed drink with gin, vodka, etc.; quinine water **3.** *Music* the basic tone of a diatonic scale; keynote —**ton′i·cal·ly** *adv.*

to·nic·i·ty (tō nis′ə tē) *n.* the quality or condition of being tonic; esp., normal muscle tension; tonus

to·night (tə nīt′) *adv.* [OE. *to niht*] on or during the present or coming night —*n.* this night or the night about to come Also, esp. formerly, **to-night**

Ton·kin (tän′kin, täŋ′-) region & former Fr. state in NE Indochina: now part of North Vietnam

ton·nage (tun′ij) *n.* **1.** a duty or tax on ships, based on tons carried **2.** the total shipping, in tons, of a country or port **3.** the amount in tons a ship can carry **4.** weight in tons

ton·neau (tu nō′) *n., pl.* **-neaus′, -neaux′** (-nōz′) [Fr., lit., a cask] an enclosed rear compartment for passengers in an early type of automobile

ton·sil (tän′s'l) *n.* [L. *tonsillae, pl.*] either of a pair of oval masses of lymphoid tissue, one on each side of the throat at the back of the mouth —**ton′sil·lar** *adj.*

ton·sil·lec·to·my (tän′sə lek′tə mē) *n., pl.* **-mies** the surgical removal of the tonsils

ton·sil·li·tis (-līt′əs) *n.* inflammation of the tonsils —**ton′sil·lit′ic** (-lit′ik) *adj.*

ton·so·ri·al (tän sôr′ē əl) *adj.* [< L. < *tonsor,* clipper < pp. of *tondere,* to clip] of a barber or barbering: often used humorously

ton·sure (tän′shər) *n.* [< MFr. < L. *tonsura* < pp. of *tondere,* to clip] **1.** the act of shaving a man's head, esp. on top, when he becomes a priest or monk **2.** the part of the head left bare by doing this —*vt.* **-sured, -sur·ing** to shave the head of, esp. in this way

ton·tine (tän′tēn, tän tēn′) *n.* [Fr. < It., after L. *Tonti,* 17th-c. banker of Naples] a fund to which a group of persons contribute, benefits finally going to the last survivor or to those surviving after a specified time

to·nus (tō′nəs) *n.* [ModL. < L. < Gr. *tonos:* see TONE] the slight continuous contraction characteristic of a normal muscle at rest

ton·y (tō′nē) *adj.* **ton′i·er, ton′i·est** [Slang] high-toned; luxurious; stylish: often ironic

too (to͞o) *adv.* [< TO] **1.** in addition; also **2.** more than enough; excessively, overly, etc. *[*the hat is *too* big*]* **3.** very; extremely *[*it's *too* good!*]* Often used only to emphasize *[*I will *too* go*]* or as an adjective with *much, many [too* much to see*]*

took (to͝ok) *pt. of* TAKE

tool (to͞ol) *n.* [OE. *tol*] **1.** any implement, instrument, etc. held in the hand and used for some work, as a knife, saw, or shovel **2.** *a)* the working part of a power-driven machine, as a drill, jigsaw blade, etc. *b)* the whole machine; machine tool **3.** anything that serves as a means to get something done *[*books are *tools* of education*]* **4.** a person used by another to accomplish his purposes, esp. when these are illegal or unethical —*vt.* **1.** to shape or work with a tool **2.** to provide tools or machinery for (a factory, etc.): often with *up* **3.** to impress designs, etc. on (leather, etc.) with tools —*vi.* **1.** to use a tool or tools **2.** to get or install the tools, equipment, etc. needed (often with *up*) **3.** to go in a vehicle —**tool′er** *n.* —**tool′ing** *n.*

tool·box (-bäks′) *n.* a box or chest in which tools are kept: also **tool chest**

tool·mak·er (-mā′kər) *n.* a machinist who makes, maintains, and repairs machine tools —**tool′mak′ing** *n.*

tool·room (-ro͞om′) *n.* a room, as in a machine shop, where tools are stored, kept in repair, issued to workmen, etc.

toot (to͞ot) *vi.* [prob. via LowG. *tuten* < echoic base] **1.** to blow a horn, whistle, etc. in short blasts **2.** to sound in short blasts: said of a horn, etc. —*vt.* **1.** to cause to sound in short blasts **2.** to sound (tones, etc.) as on a horn —*n.* **1.** a short blast of a horn, etc. **2.** [Slang] a drinking spree

tooth (to͞oth; *for v. also* to͞o*th*) *n., pl.* **teeth** (tēth) [OE. *toth*] **1.** *a)* any of a set of hard, bonelike structures in the jaws of most vertebrates, used for biting, tearing, and chewing *b)* any similar structure in invertebrates *c)* [*pl.*] *same as* DENTURE **2.** a toothlike part, as on a saw, comb, gearwheel, etc. **3.** an appetite or taste for something *[*a sweet *tooth]* **4.** something biting, piercing, etc. like a tooth *[*the *teeth* of the storm*]* **5.** an effective means of enforcing something *[*to put *teeth* into a law*]* —*vt.* **1.** to provide with teeth **2.** to make jagged; indent —*vi.* to mesh or interlock, as gears —**armed** (or **dressed**) **to the teeth** as armed (or dressed up) as one can be —**get** (or **sink**) **one's teeth into** to become fully occupied with —**in the teeth of 1.** directly against **2.** defying —**tooth and nail** with all one's strength or resources —**tooth′less** *adj.*

CROWN
DENTIN
PULP
ROOT

TOOTH

tooth·ache (-āk′) *n.* pain in or near a tooth

tooth·brush (-brush′) *n.* a brush for cleaning the teeth

toothed (to͞otht, to͞o*th*d) *adj.* **1.** having teeth: often used in hyphenated compounds (big-*toothed*) **2.** notched

toothed whale any of a main division of whales, as the sperm whale, that have cone-shaped teeth

tooth·paste (to͞oth′pāst′) *n.* a paste used in cleaning the teeth with a toothbrush

tooth·pick (-pik′) *n.* a very small, pointed stick for getting bits of food free from between the teeth

tooth powder a powder used like toothpaste

tooth·some (-səm) *adj.* pleasing to the taste; tasty —**tooth′some·ly** *adv.* —**tooth′some·ness** *n.*

tooth·y (-ē) *adj.* **tooth′i·er, tooth′i·est** showing prominent teeth —**tooth′i·ly** *adv.* —**tooth′i·ness** *n.*

too·tle (to͞ot′'l) *vi.* **-tled, -tling** [freq. of TOOT] to keep tooting softly —*n.* the act or sound of tootling

top[1] (täp) *n.* [OE.] **1.** the head or the crown of the head *[*from *top* to toe*]* **2.** the highest part, point, or surface of anything **3.** the part of a plant growing above the ground *[*beet *tops]* **4.** an uppermost part or covering; specif., *a)* a lid, cap, cover, etc. *b)* a folding roof of an automobile *c)* the upper part of a two-piece garment *d)* a platform around the head of each lower mast on a sailing ship **5.** one first in order, excellence, importance, etc.; specif., *a)* the highest degree, pitch, rank, position, etc. *b)* a person of highest rank, etc. *c)* the choicest part; pick *[*the *top* of the crop*]* *d)* the beginning, as of something being rehearsed *e) Baseball* the first half (*of* an inning) **6.** *Sports a)* a stroke hitting the ball near its top *b)* the forward spin given the ball by such a stroke —*adj.* of or at the top; highest, greatest, foremost, etc. —*vt.* **topped, top′ping 1.** to take off the top of (a plant, etc.) **2.** to put a top on *[*to *top* a cake with icing*]* **3.** to be a top for **4.** to reach or go over the top of **5.** to exceed in amount, height, etc. *[topped* 75 pounds*]* **6.** to be better, more effective, etc. than; outdo **7.** to be at the top of; head; lead **8.** *Sports* to hit (a ball) near its top, giving it a forward spin —*vi.* to top someone or something —**off the top** [Slang] from gross income —**off the top of one's head** speaking offhand, without careful thought —**on top** at the top; successful —**on top of 1.** on or at the top of **2.** resting upon **3.** in addition to; besides **4.** right after **5.** controlling successfully —**over the top 1.** over the front of a trench, as in attacking **2.** exceeding the quota or goal —**(the) tops** [Slang] the very best —**top off** to complete by adding a finishing touch —**top out** to level off

top[2] (täp) *n.* [OE.] a child's cone-shaped toy, spun on its pointed end —**sleep like a top** to sleep soundly

to·paz (tō′paz) *n.* [< OFr. < L. < Gr. *topazos*] **1.** a crystalline mineral that is a silicate of aluminum and fluorine; esp., a clear, yellow variety used as a gem **2.** a yellow variety of quartz

top banana [prob. from the banana-shaped soft club carried by burlesque comedians] [Slang] **1.** a top performer in show business; specif., the star comedian in a burlesque show **2.** the most important person in any group

top boot a boot reaching to just below the knee, esp. such a boot topped with a band of contrasting color

top brass important officials: see BRASS (sense 5)

top·coat (täp′kōt′) *n.* a lightweight overcoat

top dog [Slang] the person, company, etc. in a dominant or leading position, esp. in a competitive situation

top-drawer (-drôr′) *adj.* of first importance, rank, etc.

top-dress·ing (-dres′iŋ) *n.* material applied to a surface, as fertilizer —**top′-dress′** *vt.*

tope (tōp) *vt., vi.* **toped, top′ing** [Fr. *toper,* to accept a bet] [Archaic] to drink much (alcoholic liquor)

to·pee (tō pē′, tō′pē) *n.* [Hindi *ṭopī*] in India, a pith helmet worn as a sunshade

To·pe·ka (tə pē′kə) [? Siouan, lit., good place to dig potatoes] capital of Kans., on the Kansas River: pop. 115,000

top·er (tō′pər) *n.* a person who topes; drunkard

top-flight (täp′flīt′) *adj.* [Colloq.] best; first-rate

top·gal·lant (täp′gal′ənt; *naut.* tə gal′-) *adj.* next above the topmast —*n.* a topgallant mast, sail, etc.

top hat a tall, black, cylindrical hat, usually of silk, worn by men in formal dress

top-heav·y (täp′hev′ē) *adj.* too heavy at the top and so likely to fall over —**top′-heav′i·ness** *n.*

to·pi (tō pē′, tō′pē) *n. same as* TOPEE

to·pi·ar·y (tō′pē er′ē) *adj.* designating or of the art of trimming and training shrubs or trees into unnatural, ornamental shapes —*n., pl.* **-ar′ies** topiary art or work

top·ic (täp′ik) *n.* [< L. < Gr. *ta topika,* title of work by Aristotle, ult. < *topos,* a place] **1.** the subject of a writing, speech, discussion, etc. **2.** a heading or item in an outline

top·i·cal (-i k'l) *adj.* **1.** of a particular place; local **2.** of, using, or arranged by topics **3.** having to do with topics of the day; of current or local interest **4.** *Med.* of or for a particular part of the body *[*a *topical* lotion*]* —**top′i·cal′i·ty** (-kal′ə tē) *n.* —**top′i·cal·ly** *adv.*

top kick [Mil. Slang] *same as* FIRST SERGEANT

top·knot (täp′nät′) *n.* **1.** a knot of feathers, ribbons, etc. worn as a headdress **2.** a tuft of hair or feathers on the crown of the head

top·less (-lis) ***adj.*** without a top; specif., designating or wearing a costume that exposes the breasts

top-lev·el (-lev′'l) ***adj.*** **1.** of or by persons of the highest office or rank **2.** in highest office or rank

top·loft·y (-lôf′tē) ***adj.*** [Colloq.] lofty in manner; haughty —**top′loft′i·ly** ***adv.*** —**top′loft′i·ness** ***n.***

top·mast (täp′məst, -mast′) ***n.*** the second mast above the deck of a sailing ship, supported by the lower mast

top·most (täp′mōst′) ***adj.*** at the very top

top-notch (-näch′) ***adj.*** [Colloq.] first-rate; excellent

to·pog·ra·phy (tə päg′rə fē) ***n.,*** *pl.* **-phies** [< LL. < Gr.: see TOPIC & -GRAPHY] **1.** *a)* the science of showing on maps, charts, etc. the surface features of a region, such as hills, rivers, and roads *b)* such features **2.** surveying done to discover and measure such features **3.** a study of some part or system of the body showing the relationship, size, shape, etc. of its parts **4.** a similar study of some whole, as the mind or the atom, in relation to its parts —**to·pog′ra·pher** ***n.*** —**top·o·graph·ic** (täp′ə graf′ik), **top′o·graph′i·cal** ***adj.*** —**top′o·graph′i·cal·ly** ***adv.***

to·pol·o·gy (tə päl′ə jē) ***n.,*** *pl.* **-gies** [< Gr. *topos,* a place + -LOGY] **1.** *same as* TOPOGRAPHY (senses 3 & 4) **2.** *Math.* the study of those properties of geometric figures that remain unchanged even when under distortion —**top·o·log·i·cal** (täp′ə läj′i k'l) ***adj.*** —**to·pol′o·gist** ***n.***

top·per (täp′ər) ***n.*** **1.** a person or thing that tops **2.** [Colloq.] *a) same as* TOP HAT *b)* a woman's short topcoat **3.** [Slang] a remark, joke, etc. that tops, or surpasses, all preceding ones

top·ping (-iŋ) ***n.*** something that forms the top of, or is put on top of, something else, as a sauce on food —***adj.*** [Brit. Colloq.] excellent; first-rate

top·ple (täp′'l) ***vi.*** **-pled, -pling** [< TOP[1], *v.* + freq. *-le*] **1.** to fall (*over*) from top-heaviness, etc. **2.** to totter —***vt.*** **1.** to cause to topple **2.** to overthrow

top·sail (täp′s'l, -sāl′) ***n.*** **1.** in a square-rigged vessel, the square sail, or either of a pair of square sails, next above the lowest sail on a mast **2.** in a fore-and-aft-rigged vessel, the small sail set above the gaff

top-se·cret (-sē′krit) ***adj.*** designating or of the most highly restricted military or government information

top sergeant *colloq. var. of* FIRST SERGEANT

top·side (-sīd′) ***n.*** [*usually pl.*] the part of a ship's side above the waterline —***adv.*** on or to an upper deck or the main deck of a ship

top·soil (-soil′) ***n.*** the upper layer of soil, usually darker and richer than the subsoil

top·sy-tur·vy (täp′sē tur′vē) ***adv. adj.*** [prob. < *top,* highest part + ME. *terven,* to roll] **1.** upside down; reversed **2.** in confusion or disorder —***n.*** a topsy-turvy condition —**top′sy-tur′vi·ly** ***adv.*** —**top′sy-tur′vi·ness** ***n.***

toque (tōk) ***n.*** [Fr.] a woman's small, round hat

to·rah, to·ra (tō′rə, tō rä′) ***n.*** [Heb.] *Judaism* **1.** *a)* learning, law, instruction, etc. *b)* [*also* **T-**] the whole of Jewish religious literature, including the Scripture, the Talmud, etc. **2.** [*usually* **T-**] *a)* the Pentateuch *b) pl.* **-roth, -rot** (-rəs, -rōt′) a parchment scroll containing the Pentateuch

torch (tôrch) ***n.*** [OFr. *torche,* ult. < L. *torquere,* to twist] **1.** a portable light consisting of a long piece of resinous wood, etc. flaming at one end **2.** anything viewed as enlightening, inspiring, etc. **3.** a portable device for producing a very hot flame, used in welding, etc. **4.** [Brit.] a flashlight —***vt.*** [Slang] to set fire to, as in arson —**carry a** (or **the**) **torch for** [Slang] to love (someone), esp. without having one's love returned

torch·bear·er (-ber′ər) ***n.*** **1.** a person who carries a torch **2.** a person or leader who enlightens or inspires others

torch·light (tôrch′līt′) ***n.*** the light of a torch or torches —***adj.*** done or carried on by torchlight

tore (tôr) *pt. of* TEAR[1]

tor·e·a·dor (tôr′ē ə dôr′) ***n.*** [Sp. < *torear,* to fight bulls, ult. < L. *taurus,* a bull] a bullfighter: term no longer used in bullfighting

to·re·ro (tə rer′ō; *Sp.* tô re′rô) ***n.,*** *pl.* **-ros** (-rōz; *Sp.* -rôs) [Sp. < LL. < L. *taurus,* a bull] a bullfighter, esp. a matador

to·ri·i (tôr′i ē′) ***n.,*** *pl.* **-ri·i′** [Jap.] a gateway at the entrance to a Shinto temple, consisting of two uprights supporting a curved horizontal beam, with a straight crosspiece just below

To·ri·no (tô rē′nô) *It. name of* TURIN

tor·ment (tôr′ment; *for v., usually* tôr ment′) ***n.*** [< OFr. < L. *tormentum,* a rack, torture < *torquere,* to twist] **1.** great pain, physical or mental; agony **2.** a source of pain, anxiety, or annoyance —***vt.*** **1.** to make suffer greatly, in body or mind **2.** to annoy, harass, or tease —**tor·ment′ing·ly** ***adv.*** —**tor·men′tor, tor·ment′er** ***n.***

torn (tôrn) *pp. of* TEAR[1]

tor·na·do (tôr nā′dō) ***n.,*** *pl.* **-does, -dos** [< Sp. *tronada,* thunder < L. *tonare,* to thunder] **1.** a rapidly whirling column of air, usually seen as a slender, funnel-shaped cloud that usually destroys everything in its narrow path **2.** any whirlwind or hurricane —**tor·nad′ic** (-nad′ik) ***adj.***

To·ron·to (tə rän′tō) capital of Ontario, Canada, on Lake Ontario: pop. 633,000 (met. area 2,803,000)

tor·pe·do (tôr pē′dō) ***n.,*** *pl.* **-does** [L., numbness < *torpere,* to be stiff] **1.** *same as* ELECTRIC RAY **2.** a large, cigar-shaped, self-propelled projectile launched under water against enemy ships as from a submarine: it explodes on contact **3.** any of various other explosive devices, as an underwater mine **4.** a small firework that explodes when thrown against a hard surface —***vt.*** **-doed, -do·ing** to attack, destroy, etc. as with a torpedo

torpedo boat a small, fast warship for attacking with torpedoes

tor·pid (tôr′pid) ***adj.*** [< L. < *torpere,* to be numb] **1.** having lost temporarily all or some ability to feel or move, as a hibernating animal; dormant **2.** sluggish or slow and dull —**tor·pid′i·ty, tor′pid·ness** ***n.*** —**tor′pid·ly** ***adv.***

tor·por (tôr′pər) ***n.*** **1.** a state of being dormant or inactive **2.** sluggishness; dullness; apathy

torque (tôrk) ***n.*** [< L. *torques,* a twisted metal necklace] **1.** *Physics* a twisting effect exerted on a body by a force acting at a distance, equal to the force times its distance from the center of rotation **2.** popularly, any force that causes rotation

Tor·que·ma·da (tôr′ke mä′*th*ä; *E.* tôr′ki mä′də), **To·más de** (tô mäs′ *th*e) 1420–98; Sp. Dominican monk; first Grand Inquisitor of the Spanish Inquisition

Tor·rance (tôr′əns) [after J. *Torrance,* local landowner] city in SW Calif.: suburb of Los Angeles: pop. 131,000

tor·rent (tôr′ənt, tär′-) ***n.*** [Fr. < L. *torrens,* burning, rushing, prp. of *torrere,* to parch] **1.** a swift, violent stream, esp. of water **2.** a flood or rush of words, mail, etc. **3.** a very heavy fall of rain —**tor·ren·tial** (tô ren′shəl, tə-) ***adj.***

Tor·ri·cel·li (tôr′rē chel′lē; *E.* tôr′i chel′ē), **E·van·ge·lis·ta** (e′vän je lēs′tä) 1608–47; It. physicist: discovered principle of the barometer

tor·rid (tôr′id, tär′-) ***adj.*** [< L. < *torrere,* to parch] **1.** dried by or subjected to intense heat, esp. of the sun; scorched; parched; arid **2.** so hot as to parch or scorch **3.** highly passionate, ardent, etc. —**tor·rid·i·ty** (tô rid′ə tē), **tor′rid·ness** ***n.*** —**tor′rid·ly** ***adv.***

Torrid Zone the area of the earth's surface between the Tropic of Cancer & the Tropic of Capricorn and divided by the equator

tor·sion (tôr′shən) ***n.*** [< MFr. < LL. < pp. of L. *torquere,* to twist] **1.** a twisting or being twisted **2.** *Mech. a)* the stress produced in a rod, wire, etc. from having one end twisted while the other is held firm or twisted in the opposite direction *b)* the tendency of a rod, etc. so twisted to untwist again —**tor′sion·al** ***adj.*** —**tor′sion·al·ly** ***adv.***

tor·so (tôr′sō) ***n.,*** *pl.* **-sos, -si** (-sē) [It. < L. < Gr. *thyrsos,* a stem] **1.** the trunk of the human body **2.** a statue representing this, esp. one lacking head and limbs

tort (tôrt) ***n.*** [< OFr. < ML. < L. pp. of *torquere,* to twist] *Law* a wrongful act, injury, or damage (not involving a breach of contract), for which a civil action can be brought

torte (tôrt) ***n.*** [G. < It. < LL. *torta,* a twisted bread] a rich cake, variously made, as of eggs, chopped nuts, and crumbs or a little flour

tor·til·la (tôr tē′ə) ***n.*** [Sp., dim. of *torta,* a cake: see TORTE] a griddlecake of unleavened cornmeal, now sometimes of flour: a staple food throughout Mexico

tor·toise (tôr′təs) ***n.,*** *pl.* **-tois·es, -toise:** see PLURAL, II, D, 1 [< ML. *tortuca,* ult. < ? LGr. *tartarouchos,* demon] a turtle, esp. one that lives on land: see TURTLE

tortoise shell **1.** the hard, mottled, yellow-and-brown shell of some turtles used, esp. formerly, in making combs, etc. **2.** a synthetic substance like this

tor·to·ni (tôr tō′nē) ***n.*** [prob. altered < It. *tortone,* lit., big tart] an ice cream made with heavy cream, maraschino cherries, almonds, etc.

tor·tu·ous (tôr′choo wəs) ***adj.*** [Anglo-Fr. < L. *tortuosus* < pp. of *torquere,* to twist] **1.** full of twists and turns; winding; crooked **2.** not straightforward; devious or deceitful —**tor′tu·os′i·ty** (-wäs′ə tē) ***n.,*** *pl.* **-ties** —**tor′tu·ous·ly** ***adv.*** —**tor′tu·ous·ness** ***n.***

tor·ture (tôr′chər) ***n.*** [Fr. < LL. *tortura* < pp. of L. *torquere,* to twist] **1.** the inflicting of severe pain, as to force information or confession **2.** a method of doing this **3.** any severe physical or mental pain, or a cause of it —***vt.*** **-tured, -tur·ing** **1.** to subject to torture **2.** to cause extreme physical or mental pain to **3.** to twist or distort (meaning, language, etc.) —**tor′tur·er** ***n.*** —**tor′tur·ous** ***adj.*** —**tor′tur·ous·ly** ***adv.***

to·rus (tôr′əs) ***n.***, *pl.* **-ri** (-ī) [L., a bulge] **1.** a large, convex molding used at the base of columns, etc. **2.** *Bot.* the receptacle of a flower stalk

To·ry (tôr′ē) ***n.***, *pl.* **-ries** [< Ir. *tōruidhe*, robber < *tōir*, to pursue] **1.** formerly, a member of one of the two major political parties of England: orig. opposed to Whig: changed officially c. 1830 to *Conservative* **2.** in the American Revolution, a person who showed or favored continued loyalty to Great Britain **3.** [*often* **t-**] any very conservative person —***adj.*** [*also* **t-**] of or being a Tory —**To′ry·ism** ***n.***

toss (tôs, täs) ***vt.*** [prob. < Scand.] **1.** to throw or pitch about; buffet [*a boat tossed by a storm*] **2.** to mix (esp. a salad) lightly **3.** to disturb; agitate **4.** to throw; specif., to throw upward lightly from the hand **5.** to throw in or bandy (ideas, remarks, etc.) **6.** to lift quickly; jerk upward [*tossed her head in disdain*] **7.** to toss up with (someone *for* something): see phrase below —***vi.*** **1.** to be tossed or thrown about **2.** to fling oneself about in sleep, etc. **3.** to go impatiently, angrily, etc., as from a room **4.** to toss up: see phrase below —***n.*** **1.** a tossing or being tossed **2.** a tossing up: see phrase below **3.** the distance that something is or can be tossed —**toss off** **1.** to make, do, write, etc. quickly and casually **2.** to drink up in one draft —**toss up** to toss a coin to decide something according to which side lands uppermost —**toss′er** ***n.***

toss·up (-up′) ***n.*** **1.** the act of tossing a coin to decide something according to which side lands uppermost **2.** an even chance

tost (tôst, täst) *archaic pt. & pp. of* TOSS

tot[1] (tät) ***n.*** [prob. < Scand.] **1.** a young child **2.** [Chiefly Brit.] a small drink of alcoholic liquor

tot[2] (tät) ***vt., vi.*** **tot′ted, tot′ting** [contr. < TOTAL] [Chiefly Brit. Colloq.] to add; total (usually with *up*)

tot. total

to·tal (tōt′'l) ***adj.*** [< MFr. < ML. < L. *totus*, all] **1.** constituting the (or a) whole; entire **2.** complete; utter —***n.*** the whole amount or number —***vt.*** **-taled** or **-talled, -tal·ing** or **-tal·ling** **1.** to find the total of; add **2.** to equal a total of; add up to **3.** [Slang] to wreck completely —***vi.*** to amount (*to*) as a whole —**to′tal·ly** ***adv.***

to·tal·i·tar·i·an (tō tal′ə ter′ē ən, tō′tal ə-) ***adj.*** [TOTAL + (AUTHOR)ITARIAN] designating, of, or like a government or state in which one political group maintains complete control under a dictatorship and bans all others Also **to·tal·is·tic** (tōt′'l is′tik), **to′tal·ist** —***n.*** a person favoring such a government or state —**to·tal′i·tar′i·an·ism** ***n.***

to·tal·i·ty (tō tal′ə tē) ***n.***, *pl.* **-ties** **1.** the fact or condition of being total **2.** the total amount or sum

to·tal·i·za·tor (tōt′'l i zāt′ər) ***n.*** a machine used in pari-mutuel betting to register bets and, usually, compute odds and payoffs while bets are being placed: also **to′tal·i·sa′tor, to′tal·iz′er**

tote[1] (tōt) ***vt.*** **tot′ed, tot′ing** [prob. of Afr. orig.] [Colloq.] **1.** to carry or haul **2.** to be armed with (a gun, etc.) —***n.*** **1.** [Colloq.] *a*) a toting *b*) something toted; load **2.** *short for* TOTE BAG —**tot′er** ***n.***

tote[2] (tōt) ***vt.*** **tot′ed, tot′ing** *shortened form of* TOTAL (usually with *up*)

tote[3] (tōt) ***n.*** *shortened form of* TOTALIZATOR

tote bag a large, open handbag of cloth, etc. in which women can carry shoes, small packages, etc.

tote board [Colloq.] a large board facing the grandstand at a race track, on which the bets, odds, and payoffs recorded by a totalizator are flashed

to·tem (tōt′əm) ***n.*** [< Algonquian] **1.** among primitive peoples, an animal or natural object considered to be related by blood to a given family or clan and taken as its symbol **2.** an image of this —**to·tem·ic** (tō tem′ik) ***adj.*** —**to′tem·ism** ***n.*** —**to′tem·ist** ***n.***

totem pole a pole or post carved and painted with totems, often erected in front of their dwellings, by Indian tribes of northwestern N. America

TOTEM POLE

toth·er, t'oth·er, 'toth·er (tu*th*′ər) ***adj., pron.*** [Chiefly Dial.] that (or the) other

tot·ter (tät′ər) ***vi.*** [prob. < Scand.] **1.** to rock or shake as if about to fall **2.** to be on the point of collapse **3.** to be unsteady on one's feet; stagger —***n.*** a tottering —**tot′ter·ing** ***adj.*** —**tot′ter·ing·ly** ***adv.*** —**tot′ter·y** ***adj.***

tou·can (to͞o′kan) ***n.*** [Fr. < Port. < Tupi *tucana*] a brightly colored, fruit-eating bird of tropical America, with a very large beak

touch (tuch) ***vt.*** [OFr. *tochier*] **1.** to put the hand, finger, etc. on, so as to feel **2.** to bring into contact with something else [*touch a match to kindling*] **3.** to be or come into contact with **4.** to border on; adjoin **5.** to strike lightly **6.** to affect by contact [*water won't touch these grease spots*] **7.** to injure slightly [*frost touched these plants*] **8.** to give a light tint, aspect, etc. to [*clouds touched with pink*] **9.** to stop at (a port, etc.) in passing: said of a ship **10.** to lay hands on; handle; use **11.** to manhandle or molest **12.** to partake of [*didn't touch his supper*] **13.** to come up to; reach **14.** to compare with; equal [*cooking that can't touch hers*] **15.** to take or use wrongfully **16.** to deal with or refer to, esp. in passing **17.** to affect; concern [*a subject that touches our welfare*] **18.** to arouse an emotion in, esp. one of sympathy or gratitude **19.** to hurt the feelings of; pain [*touched him to the quick*] **20.** [Slang] to ask for, or get by asking, a loan or gift of money from **21.** *Geom.* to be tangent to —***vi.*** **1.** to touch a person or thing **2.** to be or come in contact **3.** to approach; verge (*on, upon*) **4.** to pertain; bear (*on, upon*) **5.** to treat a topic slightly or in passing (with *on, upon*) **6.** to stop briefly (*at* a port, etc.) during a voyage **7.** *Geom.* to be tangent —***n.*** **1.** a touching or being touched; specif., a light tap, stroke, etc. **2.** the sense by which physical objects are felt **3.** a sensation so caused; feel **4.** a special quality, skill, or manner [*he lost his touch*] **5.** an effect of being touched; specif., *a*) a mark, impression, etc. left by touching *b*) a subtle change or addition in a painting, story, etc. **6.** a very small amount, degree, etc.; specif., *a*) a trace, tinge, etc. [*a touch of humor*] *b*) a slight attack [*a touch of the flu*] **7.** formerly, a touchstone **8.** any test or criterion **9.** contact or communication [*keep in touch*] **10.** [Slang] *a*) the act of asking for a loan or gift of money, or a getting of it thus *b*) money so gotten *c*) a person with regard to how easily money can be so gotten from him **11.** *Music* *a*) the way that a performer strikes the keys of a piano, etc. *b*) the way that the keys of a piano, etc. respond to the fingers —**touch down** to land: said of an aircraft or spacecraft —**touch off** **1.** to represent accurately or aptly **2.** to make explode; fire **3.** to produce (esp. a violent reaction, etc.) —**touch up** to improve or finish (a painting, story, etc.) by minor changes or additions —**touch′a·bil′i·ty** ***n.*** —**touch′a·ble** ***adj.*** —**touch′er** ***n.***

touch and go an uncertain, risky, or dangerous situation —**touch-and-go** (tuch′ən gō′) ***adj.***

touch·back (-bak′) ***n.*** *Football* a play in which a player grounds the ball behind his own goal line when the ball was caused to pass the goal line by an opponent

touch·down (-doun′) ***n.*** **1.** a touching down, or landing **2.** *Football* *a*) a scoring play in which a player grounds the ball on or past the opponent's goal line *b*) a score of six points so made

tou·ché (to͞o shā′) ***interj.*** [Fr.] *Fencing* touched: said when one's opponent scores a point by a touch: also used in congratulating someone for his witty reply, etc.

touched (tucht) ***adj.*** **1.** emotionally moved **2.** slightly unbalanced mentally: also **touched in the head**

touch football a kind of football in which the ball carrier is stopped by touching rather than tackling him

touch·hole (tuch′hōl′) ***n.*** in early firearms, the hole in the breech through which the charge was touched off

touch·ing (tuch′iŋ) ***adj.*** arousing tender emotion; affecting —***prep.*** with regard to —**touch′ing·ly** ***adv.***

touch-me-not (-mē nät′) ***n.*** *same as* JEWELWEED

touch·stone (-stōn′) ***n.*** **1.** a black stone formerly used to test the purity of gold or silver by the streak left on it when it was rubbed with the metal **2.** any test of genuineness

touch-type (-tīp′) ***vi.*** **-typed′, -typ′ing** to type without looking at the keys, by a system (**touch system**) in which a given key is touched with a specific finger —**touch′-typ′ist** ***n.***

touch·wood (-wood′) ***n.*** dried, decayed wood or dried fungus used as tinder; punk

touch·y (tuch′ē) ***adj.*** **touch′i·er, touch′i·est** [TOUCH + -Y[2]] **1.** easily offended or irritated; oversensitive **2.** very risky —**touch′i·ly** ***adv.*** —**touch′i·ness** ***n.***

tough (tuf) ***adj.*** [OE. *toh*] **1.** strong but pliant; that will bend, twist, etc. without tearing or breaking **2.** not easily cut or chewed [*tough steak*] **3.** sticky; viscous [*tough putty*] **4.** *a*) physically strong; hardy *b*) mentally or morally firm **5.** hard to influence; stubborn **6.** practical and realistic **7.** overly aggressive; rough **8.** *a*) very difficult *b*) vigorous or violent [*a tough fight*] **9.** [Colloq.] unfavorable; bad [*a tough break*] **10.** [Slang] fine; excellent —***n.*** a tough person; thug —**tough′ly** ***adv.*** —**tough′ness** ***n.***

tough·en (-'n) ***vt., vi.*** to make or become tough or tougher

tough·ie, tough·y (-ē) ***n.***, *pl.* **-ies** [Colloq.] **1.** a tough person; ruffian **2.** a difficult problem or situation

tough-mind·ed (-mīn′did) ***adj.*** shrewd and unsentimental; practical; realistic —**tough′-mind′ed·ness** ***n.***

Tou·lon (to͞o län′; *Fr.* to͞o lōn′) seaport in SE France, on the Mediterranean: pop. 175,000

Tou·louse (to͞o lo͞oz′) city in S France: pop. 371,000

Tou·louse-Lau·trec (to͞o lo͞oz′lō trek′), **Hen·ri (Marie Raymond) de** (än rē′ də) 1864–1901; Fr. painter

tou·pee (to͞o pā′) ***n.*** [Fr. *toupet*, dim. of OFr. *toup*, tuft of hair] a man's wig, esp. one for a small bald spot

tour (toor) ***n.*** [< MFr. < OFr. < *tourner*, to TURN] **1.** a turn or shift of work; esp., a period of duty or military service at a single place: in full, **tour of duty** **2.** a long trip, as for sightseeing **3.** any trip, as for inspection; round; circuit; specif., a trip, as by a theatrical company, to give performances, etc. in various cities —***vi.*** to go on a tour —***vt.*** **1.** to take a tour through **2.** to take (a play, etc.) on tour —**on tour** touring, as to give performances, lectures, etc.

tour de force (toor′ də fôrs′) *pl.* **tours′ de force′** (toor) [Fr.] an unusually skillful or ingenious production, performance, etc., sometimes a merely clever one

touring car an early type of open automobile, often with a folding top, seating five or more passengers

tour·ism (toor′iz'm) ***n.*** tourist travel, esp. when regarded as a business —**tour·is′tic** ***adj.***

tour·ist (-ist) ***n.*** **1.** a person who makes a tour, esp. for pleasure **2.** tourist class —***adj.*** **1.** of or for tourists **2.** designating or of the lowest-priced accommodations, as on a ship —***adv.*** in or by means of tourist class

tourist court *same as* MOTEL

tourist home a private home in which bedrooms are rented to tourists or travelers

tour·ma·line (toor′mə lin, -lēn′) ***n.*** [Fr., ult. < Sinh. *tōramalli*, a carnelian] a crystalline mineral that is a complex silicate, commonly black but also colored or transparent, used as a gemstone and in optical equipment

tour·na·ment (toor′nə mənt, tur′-) ***n.*** [< OFr. < *torneier:* see TOURNEY] **1.** in the Middle Ages, a contest in which knights on horseback tried to unseat one another with lances **2.** a series of contests in a sport, chess, or bridge, usually a competition for championship

tour·ney (toor′nē, tur′-) ***n.,*** *pl.* **-neys** [< OFr. *torneier* < base of *tourner:* see TURN] *same as* TOURNAMENT —***vi.*** to take part in a tournament; joust

tour·ni·quet (toor′nə kit, tur′-; -kā′) ***n.*** [Fr. < MFr. *turniquet*, coat of mail < OFr. *tunicle* < L. dim. of *tunica*, tunic] any device for compressing a blood vessel to stop bleeding, as a bandage twisted about a limb or a pad pressed down by a screw

Tours (toor; *Fr.* toor) city in WC France, on the Loire: pop. 128,000

tou·sle (tou′z'l) ***vt.*** **-sled, -sling** [freq. of ME. *tusen* (in comp.), to pull] to disorder, dishevel, rumple, etc. —***n.*** a tousled condition, mass of hair, etc.

Tous·saint L'Ou·ver·ture (too san′ loo ver tür′) (born *Pierre François Dominique Toussaint*) 1743?–1803; Haitian Negro liberator & general

tout (tout) ***vi., vt.*** [OE. *totian*, to peep] [Colloq.] **1.** to solicit (customers, votes, etc.) **2.** to praise or recommend (a person or thing) highly **3.** *a)* esp. in England, to spy on (racehorses) to get betting tips *b)* to provide such tips on (racehorses) —***n.*** [Colloq.] a person who touts —**tout′er** ***n.***

‡**tout de suite** (toot swēt′) [Fr.] immediately

tou·zle (tou′z'l) ***n., vt.*** **-zled, -zling** *var. of* TOUSLE

tow[1] (tō) ***vt.*** [OE. *togian*] to pull as by a rope or chain —***n.*** **1.** a towing or being towed **2.** something towed **3.** a towline —**in tow** **1.** being towed **2.** as one's companion or follower **3.** under one's control

tow[2] (tō) ***n.*** [OE. *tow-*, for spinning] the coarse and broken fibers of hemp, flax, etc. before spinning

to·ward (tôrd; *also for prep.* tə wôrd′; *also, and for adj. usually,* tō′ərd) ***prep.*** [OE. *toweard:* see TO & -WARD] **1.** in the direction of **2.** facing **3.** in a way aimed at or tending to *[*steps *toward* peace*]* **4.** concerning; regarding *[*my attitude *toward* it*]* **5.** close to *[toward* noon*]* **6.** in order to get; for *[*saving *toward* a car*]* **7.** so as to help pay for *[*to contribute *toward* a new library*]* —***adj.*** [Archaic or Rare] **1.** favorable **2.** docile **3.** at hand **4.** in progress

to·wards (tôrdz, tə wôrdz′) ***prep.*** *same as* TOWARD

tow·boat (tō′bōt′) ***n.*** *same as* TUGBOAT

tow·el (tou′'l, toul) ***n.*** [< OFr. *toaille* < Frank.] a piece of absorbent cloth or paper for wiping or drying things —***vt.*** **-eled** or **-elled, -el·ing** or **-el·ling** to wipe or dry with a towel —**throw** (or **toss,** etc.) **in the towel** [Colloq.] to admit defeat —**towel off** to dry oneself, as after bathing

tow·el·ing, tow·el·ling (-iŋ) ***n.*** material for making towels

tow·er[1] (tou′ər) ***n.*** [OE. *torr* & OFr. *tur*, both < L. *turris*] **1.** a structure that is relatively high for its length and width, either standing alone or as part of another building **2.** such a structure used as a fortress or prison **3.** a person or thing like a tower in height, strength, etc. —***vi.*** to rise high or stand high like a tower —**tow′ered** ***adj.***

tow·er[2] (tō′ər) ***n.*** a person or thing that tows

tow·er·ing (tou′ər iŋ) ***adj.*** **1.** that towers; very high or tall **2.** very great, intense, etc. *[*a *towering* rage*]*

tow·head (tō′hed′) ***n.*** **1.** a head of pale-yellow hair **2.** a person having such hair —**tow′head′ed** ***adj.***

tow·hee (tou′hē, tō′-) ***n.*** [echoic] any of various small, N. American sparrows that feed on the ground

tow·line (tō′līn′) ***n.*** a rope, chain, etc. for towing

town (toun) ***n.*** [OE. *tun*] **1.** a group of houses and buildings, larger than a village but smaller than a city **2.** a city or other thickly populated urban place **3.** *a)* in parts of the U.S., *same as* TOWNSHIP *b)* in New England and some others States, a unit of local government whose affairs are conducted by a town meeting **4.** the business center of a city **5.** the people of a town —***adj.*** of or for a town —**go to town** [Slang] **1.** to go on a spree **2.** to act fast and efficiently **3.** to be very successful —**on the town** [Colloq.] out for a good time

town clerk an official in charge of the records, legal business, etc. of a town

town crier a person who formerly cried public announcements through the streets of a village or town

town hall a building in a town, housing the offices of public officials, the council chamber, etc.

town house **1.** a city residence, esp. of a person who also owns a country residence **2.** a dwelling, usually two-story, that is one of a number of adjoining dwellings built as a unit

town meeting **1.** a meeting of the people of a town **2.** esp. in New England, a meeting of the qualified voters of a town to act upon town business

town·ship (-ship′) ***n.*** **1.** orig., in England, a parish or division of a parish **2.** in parts of the U.S., a division of a county constituting a unit of local government **3.** in New England, *same as* TOWN (sense 3 *b*) **4.** a unit of territory in the U.S. land survey, generally six miles square **5.** in Canada, a subdivision of a province

towns·man (tounz′mən) ***n.,*** *pl.* **-men** **1.** a person who lives in, or has been reared in, a town **2.** a person who lives in the same town as one

towns·peo·ple (-pē′p'l) ***n.pl.*** **1.** the people of a town **2.** people reared in a town or city Also **towns′folk′** (-fōk′)

tow·path (tō′path′) ***n.*** a path alongside a canal, for men or animals towing canalboats

tow·rope (-rōp′) ***n.*** a rope used in towing

tow truck a truck equipped for towing away vehicles that are disabled, illegally parked, etc.

tox·e·mi·a (täk sē′mē ə) ***n.*** [ModL.: see TOXIC & -EMIA] a condition in which poisonous substances, esp. toxins from bacteria, etc., are in the bloodstream: also sp. **tox·ae′mi·a** —**tox·e′mic** (-mik) ***adj.***

tox·ic (täk′sik) ***adj.*** [< ML. < L. *toxicum*, a poison < Gr. *toxikon*, orig., poison for arrows < *toxon*, a bow] **1.** of, affected by, or caused by a toxin **2.** acting as a poison —**tox·ic′i·ty** (-sis′ə tē) ***n.***

tox·i·co- [< Gr. *toxikon:* see prec.] *a combining form meaning* poison: also, before a vowel, **tox′ic-**

tox·i·col·o·gy (täk′si käl′ə jē) ***n.*** [< Fr.: see TOXIC & -LOGY] the science of poisons, their effects, antidotes, etc. —**tox′i·co·log′ic** (-kə läj′ik), **tox′i·co·log′i·cal** ***adj.*** —**tox′i·co·log′i·cal·ly** ***adv.*** —**tox′i·col′o·gist** ***n.***

tox·in (täk′sin) ***n.*** [TOX(IC) + -IN[1]] **1.** any of various poisonous compounds produced by some microorganisms and causing certain diseases **2.** any of various similar poisons produced by certain plants or animals Toxins injected into animals or man usually cause antitoxins to form

tox·oid (täk′soid) ***n.*** [TOX(IN) + -OID] a toxin that has been treated, as with chemicals, so that its toxic qualities are removed but it can still act as an antigen

toy (toi) ***n.*** [< ? MDu. *toi*, finery] **1.** a thing of little value or importance; trifle **2.** a bauble; trinket **3.** a plaything, esp. one for children **4.** anything small; specif., a dog of a small breed —***adj.*** **1.** being or like a toy **2.** of or for toys **3.** made as a toy or as a small model *[*a *toy* stove*]* —***vi.*** to play or trifle (*with* a thing, idea, etc.)

to·yon (tō′yən) ***n.*** [AmSp.] a large evergreen shrub or tree of the rose family, with clusters of white flowers and bright-red berries, native to California

toy·shop (toi′shäp′) ***n.*** a shop where toys are sold

tp. township

T-R transmit-receive

tr. **1.** trace **2.** transitive **3.** translated **4.** translation **5.** translator **6.** transpose **7.** treasurer **8.** trustee

trace[1] (trās) ***n.*** [< OFr. *tracier*, ult. < L. pp. of *trahere*, to draw] **1.** a mark, footprint, etc. left by the passage of a person, animal, or thing **2.** a beaten path or trail **3.** a perceptible mark left by a past person, thing, or event; sign *[traces* of war*]* **4.** a barely perceptible amount *[*a *trace* of anger*]* **5.** something traced, drawn, recorded, etc. **6.** the visible line or spot moving across the face of a cathode-ray tube —***vt.*** **traced, trac′ing** **1.** [Now Rare] to move along (a path, route, etc.) **2.** to follow the trail of; track **3.** *a)* to follow the development or history of *b)* to determine (a source, date, etc.) thus **4.** to discover by investigating traces of (a prehistoric thing, etc.) **5.** to draw, outline, etc. **6.** to ornament with tracery **7.** to copy (a drawing, etc.) by following its lines on a transparent sheet placed over it **8.** to record by a curved, broken, or wavy line, as in a seismograph —*vi.* **1.** to follow a path, route, etc. **2.** to go back or date back (*to* something past) —**trace′a·bil′i·ty, trace′a·ble·ness** *n.* —**trace′a·ble** *adj.* —**trace′a·bly** *adv.*

trace² (trās) *n.* [< OFr. pl. of *trait:* see TRAIT] either of two straps, chains, etc. connecting a draft animal's harness to the vehicle drawn —**kick over the traces** to shake off control

trace element **1.** a chemical element, as iron, copper, zinc, etc., essential in nutrition, but only in minute quantities **2.** any element present in minute quantities in an organism, soil, water, etc.

trac·er (trā′sər) *n.* **1.** one that traces; specif., *a)* a person who traces designs, etc. on transparent paper *b)* a person who traces lost or missing articles, persons, etc. *c)* an instrument for tracing designs on cloth, etc. **2.** an inquiry sent out for a letter, package, etc. missing in transport **3.** *same as* TRACER BULLET (or SHELL) **4.** an element or other substance used to follow biochemical reactions, as in an animal body, to locate diseased cells, etc.

tracer bullet (or **shell**) a bullet or shell that leaves a trail of smoke or fire to mark its course and help in adjusting aim

trac·er·y (-ē) *n., pl.* **-er·ies** [TRACE¹ + -ERY] any graceful design of lines that come together or cross in various ways, as in a stained glass window

TRACERY

tra·che·a (trā′kē ə; *chiefly Brit.* trə kē′ə) *n., pl.* **-che·ae′** (-ē′), **-che·as** [ML. < LL. < Gr. *tracheia* (*arteria*), rough (windpipe)] **1.** the tube through which most land vertebrates breathe, coming from the larynx and dividing into the bronchi **2.** any of the minute tubes branching through the bodies of insects, etc. and bringing in air —**tra′che·al** *adj.*

tra·che·o- [< prec.] *a combining form meaning:* **1.** of the trachea **2.** the trachea and Also, before a vowel, **trache-**

tra·che·ot·o·my (trā′kē ät′ə mē) *n., pl.* **-mies** [see -TOMY] surgical incision of the trachea

tra·cho·ma (trə kō′mə) *n.* [< Gr. < *trachys*, rough] a contagious infection of the conjunctiva and cornea, caused by a virus and producing granulation —**tra·cho′ma·tous** (-käm′ə təs, -kō′mə-) *adj.*

trac·ing (trā′siŋ) *n.* **1.** the action of one that traces **2.** something made by tracing, as a copy of a drawing, or a line traced by a recording instrument

track (trak) *n.* [MFr. *trac*, a track] **1.** a mark or marks left by a person, animal, or thing, as a footprint or rut **2.** a trace or vestige **3.** a beaten path or trail **4.** a course or line of motion or action; route **5.** a sequence of ideas, events, etc. **6.** a path or circuit laid out for running, horse racing, etc. **7.** a pair of parallel metal rails on which trains, etc. run **8.** the distance in inches between parallel wheels, as of an automobile **9.** either of the two endless belts on tanks, some tractors, etc. on which they move **10.** *a)* athletic sports performed on a track, as running, hurdling, etc. *b)* track and field sports together **11.** *a)* *same as* SOUND TRACK *b)* the part of a magnetic tape or drum passing under a given recording or reading head —*vt.* **1.** *a)* to follow the track or footprints of *b)* to follow (a path, etc.) **2.** to trace by means of vestiges, evidence, etc. **3.** to plot the path of and record data from (an aircraft, spacecraft, etc.) using a telescope, radar, etc. **4.** to tread or travel **5.** *a)* to leave footprints, etc. on (often with *up*) *b)* to leave in the form of tracks [to *track* dirt over the floor] —*vi.* to be in alignment, as wheels, or a phonograph pickup in a record groove —**in one's tracks** where one is at the moment —**keep track of** to keep an account of; stay informed about —**lose track of** to fail to stay informed about —**make tracks** [Colloq.] to go or leave hurriedly —**on** (or **off**) **the track** keeping to (or straying from) the subject or goal —**track down** **1.** to pursue until caught **2.** to investigate fully —**track′er** *n.* —**track′less** *adj.*

track·age (-ij) *n.* **1.** all the tracks of a railroad **2.** *a)* permission for a railroad to use the tracks of another *b)* a charge for this

track·man (-mən) *n., pl.* **-men** one whose work is laying and repairing railroad tracks: also **track′lay′er**

track man an athlete who competes in track or field events, as a runner, hurdler, discus thrower, etc.

tract¹ (trakt) *n.* [< L. < pp. of *trahere*, to draw] **1.** formerly, *a)* duration of time *b)* a period of time **2.** a continuous expanse of land, etc. **3.** *Anat.*, *Zool.* a system of parts or organs having some special function [the digestive *tract*]

tract² (trakt) *n.* [< LL. < L. pp. of *tractare:* see ff.] a pamphlet, esp. one on a religious or political subject

trac·ta·ble (trak′tə b′l) *adj.* [< L. < *tractare*, to drag, freq. of *trahere*, to draw] **1.** easily managed, taught, etc.; docile **2.** easily worked or shaped; malleable —**trac′ta·bil′i·ty, trac′ta·ble·ness** *n.* —**trac′ta·bly** *adv.*

trac·tion (trak′shən) *n.* [< ML. < L. *tractus*, pp. of *trahere*, to draw] **1.** a pulling or drawing, as of a load, or a being pulled or drawn **2.** the power used by a locomotive, etc. **3.** the power, as of tires on pavement, to grip or hold to a surface while moving, without slipping —**trac′tive** *adj.*

trac·tor (trak′tər) *n.* [ModL. < L.: see prec.] **1.** a powerful, motor-driven vehicle with large rear wheels or endless belt treads, for pulling farm machinery, hauling loads, etc. **2.** a truck with a driver's cab and no body, for hauling one or more trailers

trac·tor-trail·er (-trā′lər) *n.* a combination of a tractor and a trailer or semitrailer, used in trucking

trade (trād) *n.* [MLowG., a track < OS. *trada*, a trail] **1.** *a)* a means of earning one's living; occupation *b)* skilled work; craft *c)* all the persons or companies in a particular line of business **2.** buying and selling, or bartering; commerce **3.** business of a specified kind [the tourist *trade*] **4.** customers; clientele **5.** a purchase or sale; deal **6.** an exchange; swap **7.** [*pl.*] the trade winds —*adj.* **1.** of trade or commerce **2.** of, by, or for the trade (*n.* 1 *c*) [a *trade* journal] **3.** of the members in the trades, or crafts, etc. [*trade* unions]: also **trades** —*vi.* **trad′ed, trad′ing** **1.** to carry on a business **2.** to have business dealings (*with* someone) **3.** to make an exchange (*with* someone) **4.** [Colloq.] to be a customer (*at* a specified store, etc.) —*vt.* **1.** to exchange; barter **2.** to buy and sell (stocks, etc.) —**trade in** to give (one's used car, etc.) as part of the purchase price of a new one —**trade on** (or **upon**) to take advantage of; exploit —**trad′a·ble, trade′a·ble** *adj.*

trade-in (trād′in′) *n.* **1.** a used car, etc. given or taken as part payment toward a new one **2.** a deal involving such a car, etc. **3.** the amount allowed as part payment

trade·mark (-märk′) *n.* a symbol, design, word, etc. used by a manufacturer or dealer to distinguish his products from those of competitors: usually registered and protected by law —*vt.* **1.** to put a trademark on (a product) **2.** to register (a symbol, word, etc.) as a trademark

trade name **1.** the name by which a commodity is commonly known in trade **2.** a name, often a trademark or service mark, used by a company to describe a product, service, etc. **3.** the name under which a company carries on business

trad·er (trā′dər) *n.* **1.** a person who trades; merchant **2.** a ship used in trade

trade route a regular route used by trading ships, caravans, etc.

trade school a school where a trade or trades are taught

trades·man (trādz′mən) *n., pl.* **-men** [Chiefly Brit.] a person engaged in trade; esp., a storekeeper —**trades′wom′an** *n.fem., pl.* **-wom′en**

trades·peo·ple (-pē′p′l) *n.pl.* people engaged in trade; esp., storekeepers: also **trades′folk′**

trade union *same as* LABOR UNION: also [Chiefly Brit.] **trades union** —**trade′-un′ion** *adj.* —**trade unionism** —**trade unionist**

trade wind [earlier *trade*, adv., steadily, in phr. *to blow trade*] a wind that blows steadily toward the equator from the northeast in the tropics north of the equator and from the southeast in the tropics south of the equator

trading post a store or station in an outpost, settlement, etc., where trading is done, as with natives

trading stamp a stamp given by some merchants as a premium to customers, redeemable in merchandise

tra·di·tion (trə dish′ən) *n.* [< MFr. < L. < pp. of *tradere*, to deliver] **1.** *a)* the handing down orally of beliefs, customs, stories, etc. from generation to generation *b)* a belief, custom, etc. so handed down **2.** any long-established custom or practice **3.** any unwritten religious teachings regarded as coming from the founder or earliest prophet of a religion —**tra·di′tion·less** *adj.*

tra·di·tion·al (-′l) *adj.* of, handed down by, or conforming to tradition; conventional: also **tra·di′tion·ar′y** (-er′ē) —**tra·di′tion·al·ly** *adv.*

tra·di·tion·al·ism (-′l iz′m) *n.* the following of tradition or a clinging to traditions —**tra·di′tion·al·ist, tra·di′tion·ist** *n.* —**tra·di′tion·al·is′tic** *adj.*

tra·duce (trə do͞os′, -dyo͞os′) *vt.* **-duced′, -duc′ing** [L. *traducere*, to disgrace < *tra*(*ns*), across + *ducere*, to lead] **1.** to say untrue or mean things about; defame **2.** to turn against; betray —**tra·duce′ment** *n.* —**tra·duc′er** *n.*

Tra·fal·gar (trə fal′gər; *Sp.* trä′fäl gär′), **Cape** cape on the SW coast of Spain, at the entrance of the Strait of Gibraltar: site of a naval battle (1805) in which Nelson's Brit. fleet defeated Napoleon's fleet

traf·fic (traf′ik) *n.* [< Fr. < It. < *trafficare*, to trade < L. *trans*, across + It. *ficcare*, to bring] **1.** buying and selling; trade, sometimes of a wrong or illegal kind [*traffic* in drugs] **2.** dealings or business (*with* someone) **3.** *a)* the movement or number of cars along a street, pedestrians along a sidewalk, etc. *b)* the cars, pedestrians, etc. **4.** the amount of business done in a given period, as measured by the number of passengers or customers, the amount of freight handled, etc. —*adj.* of traffic or its regulation —*vi.* **-ficked, -fick·ing** **1.** to carry on traffic (*in* something) **2.** to have dealings (*with* someone) —**traf′fick·er** *n.*

traffic circle a circular street where several streets meet, with vehicles traveling in one direction only

traffic light (or **signal**) a set of signal lights at intersections of streets to regulate traffic

trag·a·canth (trag′ə kanth′) *n.* [< Fr. < L. < Gr. < *tragos*, goat + *akantha*, thorn] **1.** a tasteless gum used as a thickener and emulsifier in foodstuffs, drugs, etc. **2.** any of certain Asiatic plants that yield this gum

tra·ge·di·an (trə jē′dē ən) *n.* an actor of tragedy

tra·ge·di·enne (trə jē′dē en′) *n.* an actress of tragedy

trag·e·dy (traj′ə dē) *n., pl.* **-dies** [< MFr. < L. < Gr. *tragōidia* < *tragos*, goat + *ōidē*, song: prob. from the goatskin dress of the performers representing satyrs] **1.** a serious play having a sad or disastrous ending brought about by fate, moral weakness in a character, social pressures, etc. **2.** the branch of drama consisting of such plays **3.** the writing or acting of such plays **4.** a novel or any narrative having a tragic theme, tone, etc. **5.** the tragic element in literature or life **6.** a very sad or tragic event

trag·ic (traj′ik) *adj.* **1.** of, like, or having to do with tragedy **2.** bringing great harm, suffering, etc.; very sad, disastrous, etc. **3.** suitable to tragedy [a *tragic* voice] Also **trag′i·cal** —*n.* the tragic element in art or life —**trag′i·cal·ly** *adv.* —**trag′i·cal·ness** *n.*

trag·i·com·e·dy (traj′ə käm′ə dē) *n., pl.* **-dies** **1.** a play, novel, etc. combining tragic and comic elements **2.** a situation or incident in life like this —**trag′i·com′ic, trag′i·com′i·cal** *adj.* —**trag′i·com′i·cal·ly** *adv.*

trail (trāl) *vt.* [< MFr., ult. < L. *tragula*, sledge < *trahere*, to drag] **1.** *a)* to drag or let drag behind one *b)* to bring along behind [*trailing* exhaust fumes] *c)* to pull or tow **2.** *a)* to make (a path, etc.), as by treading down *b)* to make a path in (grass, etc.) **3.** to follow the tracks of **4.** to hunt by tracking **5.** to follow or lag behind (another or others) in movement, a contest, etc. **6.** *Mil.* to carry (a rifle, etc.) in one hand, with the muzzle tilted forward and the butt near the ground —*vi.* **1.** to be drawn along behind one, as the train of a gown **2.** to grow along the ground, etc., as some plants **3.** to extend in an irregular line; straggle **4.** to flow behind in a long, thin stream, wisp, etc., as smoke **5.** *a)* to follow or lag behind *b)* to be losing, as in a sports contest **6.** to track game: said of hounds **7.** to grow gradually weaker, dimmer, etc. (with *off* or *away*) —*n.* **1.** something that trails behind **2.** a mark, scent, etc. left by a person, animal, or thing that has passed **3.** a rough path made across country, as by repeated passage **4.** a train of events, etc. following something [a *trail* of debts followed his illness] **5.** a part of a gun carriage, which may be lowered to the ground to form a rear brace

trail·blaz·er (-blāz′ər) *n.* **1.** a person who blazes a trail **2.** a pioneer in any field —**trail′blaz′ing** *n.*

trail·er (trā′lər) *n.* **1.** one that trails another **2.** a cart or van designed to be pulled by an automobile or truck (esp. a tractor, *n.* 2) **3.** a closed vehicle designed to be pulled by a motor vehicle and equipped as a place to live or work in: see also MOBILE HOME **4.** a selection of scenes from a coming motion picture, used to advertise it

trailer park an area, usually with piped water, electricity, etc., designed to accommodate trailers, esp. mobile homes: also **trailer camp, trailer court**

trailing arbutus (trā′liŋ) *same as* ARBUTUS (sense 2)

trailing edge *Aeron.* the rear edge of an airfoil, propeller blade, etc.

train (trān) *n.* [< OFr. < *trahiner*, to draw on, ult. < L. *trahere*, to pull] **1.** something that drags along behind, as a part of a gown that trails **2.** a group of followers or attendants in a procession; retinue **3.** a group of persons, animals, vehicles, etc. moving in a line; procession; caravan **4.** the persons, vehicles, etc. carrying supplies, ammunition, food, etc. for combat troops **5.** a series of events that follow some happening [war brought famine in its *train*] **6.** any connected sequence; series [a *train* of thought] **7.** a line of gunpowder used to set off an explosive charge **8.** a series of connected parts for transmitting motion [a gear *train*] **9.** a line of connected railroad cars pulled or pushed by a locomotive —*vt.* **1.** to guide the growth of (a plant) by tying, pruning, etc. **2.** to subject to certain action, exercises, etc. so as to bring to a desired condition **3.** to guide the mental, moral, etc. development of; bring up; rear **4.** to teach so as to make fully skilled [to *train* airplane pilots] **5.** to discipline (animals) to do tricks or obey commands **6.** to make fit for some sport, as by exercise, practice, etc. **7.** to aim (a gun, binoculars, etc.) at something (usually with *on*) **8.** [Colloq.] to condition (a child, puppy, etc.) to defecate and urinate in the required place —*vi.* to give or get training —**train′a·ble** *adj.* —**train′er** *n.*

train·ee (trā nē′) *n.* a person undergoing vocational training, military training, etc. —**train·ee′ship′** *n.*

train·ing (trān′iŋ) *n.* **1.** the lessons, practice, drills, etc. given by one who trains or received by one who is being trained **2.** the process of being trained for some sport, as by exercise, practice, etc.

train·man (-mən) *n., pl.* **-men** a person who works on a railroad train or in a railroad yard; esp., a brakeman

traipse (trāps) *vi., vt.* **traipsed, traips′ing** [< ?] [Dial. or Colloq.] to walk, wander, tramp, or gad —*n.* [Dial. or Colloq.] the act of traipsing

trait (trāt) *n.* [Fr., a line < L. pp. of *trahere*, to draw] a distinct quality or feature, as of personality

trai·tor (trāt′ər) *n.* [OFr. < L. < pp. of *tradere*, to betray] a person who betrays his country, cause, friends, etc.; one guilty of treason or treachery —**trai′tress** *n.fem.*

trai·tor·ous (-əs) *adj.* **1.** of or like a traitor; treacherous **2.** of or involving treason; treasonable —**trai′tor·ous·ly** *adv.* —**trai′tor·ous·ness** *n.*

Tra·jan (trā′jən) (L. name *Marcus Ulpius Trajanus*) 53?–117 A.D.; Rom. emperor (98–117), born in Spain

tra·jec·to·ry (trə jek′tə rē) *n., pl.* **-ries** [< ML. < L. pp. of *trajicere* < *tra(ns)*, across + *jacere*, to throw] the curved path of something hurtling through space, esp. that of a projectile

tram (tram) *n.* [prob. < LowG. *traam*, a beam] **1.** an open railway car used in mines: also **tram′car′** **2.** [Brit.] *a)* a streetcar; trolley car: also **tram′car′** *b)* a streetcar line: also **tram′line′, tram′way′** —*vt., vi.* **trammed, tram′ming** to carry or ride in a tram

tram·mel (tram′'l) *n.* [< MFr. < ML. *tremaculum*, kind of fishing net < L. *tres*, three + *macula*, a mesh] **1.** *a)* a three-ply fishing net *b)* a fowling net Also **trammel net** **2.** a shackle for a horse, esp. one to teach ambling **3.** [*usually pl.*] something that hinders freedom of action **4.** a device with links, etc. for hanging a pothook in a fireplace **5.** an instrument for drawing ellipses —*vt.* **-meled** or **-melled, -mel·ing** or **-mel·ling** **1.** to entangle as in a trammel **2.** to hinder, restrain, or shackle —**tram′mel·er, tram′mel·ler** *n.*

tramp (tramp) *vi.* [< or akin to LowG. *trampen*, to trample] **1.** *a)* to walk with heavy steps *b)* to step heavily (*on* something); stamp **2.** *a)* to travel about on foot; hike *b)* to travel as or like a vagabond, hobo, etc. —*vt.* **1.** to step on heavily; trample **2.** to walk or ramble through —*n.* **1.** a person who travels about on foot doing odd jobs or begging; hobo; vagrant **2.** the sound of heavy steps **3.** a journey on foot; hike **4.** a freight ship that has no regular schedule, arranging for cargo, etc. as it goes along **5.** [Slang] a sexually promiscuous woman —**tramp′er** *n.*

tram·ple (tram′p'l) *vi.* **-pled, -pling** [< ME. freq. of *trampen*: see prec.] to tread heavily —*vt.* to crush, destroy, etc. as by treading heavily on —*n.* the sound of trampling —**trample under foot** to crush or hurt by or as by trampling: also **trample on** (or **upon**) —**tram′pler** *n.*

tram·po·line (tram′pə lēn′, -lin; tram′pə lēn′) *n.* [< It. *trampolino*, a springboard] a sheet of strong canvas stretched tightly on a frame, used as a kind of springboard in acrobatic tumbling —**tram′po·lin′er, tram′po·lin′ist** *n.*

trance (trans) *n.* [< OFr. < L. *transire*, to die: see TRANSIT] **1.** a state brought on by hysteria, hypnosis, etc., in which a person seems to be conscious but is unable to move or act of his own will **2.** any daze, stupor, etc. **3.** the condition of being completely lost in thought or meditation **4.** the state a spiritualist medium is in while allegedly communicating with the dead —*vt.* **tranced, tranc′ing** *chiefly poet. var. of* ENTRANCE[2]

tran·quil (traŋ′kwəl, tran′-) *adj.* **-quil·er** or **-quil·ler, -quil·est** or **-quil·lest** [L. *tranquillus*] free from disturbance or agitation; calm, quiet, peaceful, etc. [*tranquil* waters, a *tranquil* mood] —**tran′quil·ly** *adv.*

tran·quil·ize, tran·quil·lize (traŋ′kwə līz′, tran′-) *vt., vi.* **-ized′** or **-lized′, -iz′ing** or **-liz′ing** to make or become tranquil; specif., to calm by the use of a tranquilizer —**tran′quil·i·za′tion, tran′quil·li·za′tion** *n.*

tran·quil·iz·er, tran·quil·liz·er (-lī′zər) *n.* any of certain drugs used in calming persons suffering from nervous tension, anxiety, etc.

tran·quil·li·ty, tran·quil·i·ty (traŋ kwil′ə tē, tran-) *n.* the quality or state of being tranquil; calmness, etc.

trans- [L. < *trans*, across] *a prefix meaning:* **1.** on or to the other side of, over, across, through [*transatlantic*] **2.** so as to change thoroughly [*transliterate*] **3.** above and beyond, transcending

trans. 1. transaction(s) 2. transitive 3. translated 4. translation 5. transportation

trans·act (tran sakt′, -zakt′) ***vt.*** [< L. pp. of *transigere* < *trans-*, across + *agere*, to drive] to carry on, conduct, or complete (business, etc.) —**trans·ac′tor** ***n.***

trans·ac·tion (-sak′shən, -zak′-) ***n.*** 1. a transacting or being transacted 2. something transacted; specif., *a)* a business deal *b)* [*pl.*] a record of the proceedings of a society, convention, etc. —**trans·ac′tion·al** ***adj.***

trans·al·pine (trans al′pīn, tranz-; -pin) ***adj.*** on the other (the northern) side of the Alps, from Rome

trans·at·lan·tic (trans′ət lan′tik, tranz′-) ***adj.*** 1. crossing or spanning the Atlantic 2. on the other side of the Atlantic

Trans·cau·ca·sia (trans′kô kā′zhə, -shə) that part of the Caucasus south of the Caucasus Mountains, containing the republics of Armenia, Azerbaijan, & Georgia —**Trans′cau·ca′sian** ***adj., n.***

trans·ceiv·er (tran sē′vər) ***n.*** [TRANS(MITTER) + (RE)CEIVER] an apparatus in a single housing, functioning alternately as a radio transmitter and receiver

tran·scend (tran send′) ***vt.*** [L. *transcendere* < *trans-*, over + *scandere*, to climb] 1. to go beyond the limits of; exceed [his story *transcends* belief] 2. to be superior to; surpass; excel —***vi.*** to be transcendent

tran·scend·ent (-sen′dənt) ***adj.*** 1. transcending; surpassing; excelling 2. *Theol.* existing apart from the material universe —**tran·scend′ence, tran·scend′en·cy** ***n.*** —**tran·scend′ent·ly** ***adv.***

tran·scen·den·tal (tran′sen den′t'l) ***adj.*** 1. *same as: a)* TRANSCENDENT (sense 1) *b)* SUPERNATURAL 2. abstract; metaphysical 3. of transcendentalism —**tran′scen·den′tal·ly** ***adv.***

tran·scen·den·tal·ism (-iz'm) ***n.*** 1. any of various philosophies seeking to discover the nature of reality by investigating the process of thought rather than the things that are thought about 2. the philosophical ideas of Emerson and some other 19th-cent. New Englanders, based on a search for reality through spiritual intuition 3. popularly, any obscure, visionary, or idealistic thought —**tran′scen·den′tal·ist** ***n., adj.***

trans·con·ti·nen·tal (trans′kän tə nen′t'l) ***adj.*** 1. that crosses a (or the) continent 2. on the other side of a (or the) continent —**trans′con·ti·nen′tal·ly** ***adv.***

tran·scribe (tran skrīb′) ***vt.*** **-scribed′, -scrib′ing** [< L. < *trans-*, over + *scribere*, to write] 1. to write or type out in full (shorthand notes, a speech, etc.) 2. to translate or transliterate 3. to arrange (a piece of music) for an instrument, etc. other than that for which it was originally written 4. *Radio & TV* to record (a program, commercial, etc.) for broadcast later —**tran·scrib′er** ***n.***

tran·script (tran′skript′) ***n.*** 1. something made by transcribing; written, typewritten, or printed copy 2. any copy or reproduction, esp. one that is official, as a copy of a student's record in school or college

tran·scrip·tion (tran skrip′shən) ***n.*** 1. the act or process of transcribing 2. a transcript; copy 3. an arrangement of a piece of music for an instrument, voice, etc. other than that for which it was originally written 4. a recording made for radio or television broadcasting; also, the act of using such recordings —**tran·scrip′tion·al** ***adj.***

tran·sect (tran sekt′) ***vt.*** [< TRANS- + pp. of L. *secare*, to cut] to cut across —**tran·sec′tion** ***n.***

tran·sept (tran′sept) ***n.*** [< ModL. < L. *trans-*, across + *septum*, enclosure] 1. the part of a cross-shaped church at right angles to the long, main section, or nave 2. either arm of this part, outside the nave

trans·fer (trans fur′; *also, & for n. always,* trans′fər) ***vt.*** **-ferred′, -fer′ring** [< L. < *trans-*, across + *ferre*, to bear] 1. to convey, carry, send, etc. from one person or place to another 2. to make over (title to property, etc.) to another 3. to move (a picture, design, etc.) from one surface to another, as by making wet and pressing —***vi.*** 1. to transfer oneself or be transferred; move 2. to change from one school, college, etc. to another 3. to change from one bus, train, etc. to another —***n.*** 1. a transferring or being transferred 2. one that is transferred; specif., a picture or design transferred or to be transferred from one surface to another 3. a ticket entitling the bearer to change from one bus, train, etc. to another 4. a document effecting a transfer 5. a person who transfers or is transferred —**trans·fer′a·ble, trans·fer′ra·ble** ***adj.*** —**trans·fer′al, trans·fer′ral** ***n.*** —**trans·fer′ence** ***n.*** —**trans·fer′rer,** *Law* **trans·fer′or** ***n.***

trans·fer·ee (trans′fər ē′) ***n.*** a person who is transferred or to whom something is transferred

trans·fig·u·ra·tion (trans fig′yoo rā′shən, trans′fig-) ***n.*** a transfiguring or being transfigured —[T-] 1. *Bible* the change in the appearance of Jesus on the mountain: Matt. 17 2. a church festival (Aug. 6) commemorating this

trans·fig·ure (trans fig′yər) ***vt.*** **-ured, -ur·ing** [L. *transfigurare:* see TRANS- & FIGURE] 1. to change the figure, form, or appearance of; transform 2. to transform so as to exalt or glorify —**trans·fig′ur·er** ***n.***

trans·fix (trans fiks′) ***vt.*** [< L. pp. of *transfigere* < *trans-*, through + *figere*, to fix] 1. to pierce through as with something pointed 2. to fasten in this way; impale 3. to make unable to move, as if impaled [*transfixed* with horror] —**trans·fix′ion** ***n.***

trans·form (trans fôrm′) ***vt.*** [L. *transformare*, ult. < *trans-*, over + *forma*, a shape] 1. to change the form or appearance of 2. to change the condition, character, or function of 3. *Elec.* to change (voltage, current, etc.) by use of a transformer 4. *Math.* to change (an algebraic expression or equation) to a different form having the same value 5. *Physics* to change (one form of energy) into another —***vi.*** [Rare] to be or become transformed —**trans·form′a·ble** ***adj.*** —**trans′for·ma′tion** ***n.*** —**trans′for·ma′tion·al** ***adj.*** —**trans·form′a·tive** ***adj.***

trans·form·er (-fôr′mər) ***n.*** 1. a person or thing that transforms 2. *Elec.* a device for transferring electric energy from one alternating-current circuit to another, usually with a change in voltage, current, etc.

trans·fuse (trans fyo͞oz′) ***vt.*** **-fused′, -fus′ing** [< L. pp. of *transfundere* < *trans-*, across + *fundere*, to pour] 1. to pour in or spread through; instill, imbue, infuse, permeate, etc. 2. *Med. a)* to transfer or introduce (blood, saline solution, etc.) into a blood vessel, usually a vein *b)* to give a transfusion to —**trans·fus′er** ***n.*** —**trans·fus′i·ble** ***adj.*** —**trans·fu′sive** ***adj.***

trans·fu·sion (-fyo͞o′zhən) ***n.*** a transfusing, esp. of blood

trans·gress (trans gres′, tranz-) ***vt.*** [< Fr. < L. pp. of *transgredi* < *trans-*, over + *gradi*, to step] 1. to overstep or break (a law, commandment, etc.) 2. to go beyond (a limit, boundary, etc.) —***vi.*** to break a law, commandment, etc.; sin —**trans·gres′sive** ***adj.*** —**trans·gres′sor** ***n.***

trans·gres·sion (-gresh′ən) ***n.*** a transgressing; breach of a law, duty, etc.; sin

tran·ship (tran ship′) ***vt.*** *var. sp. of* TRANSSHIP

tran·sient (tran′shənt) ***adj.*** [< L. prp. of *transire:* see TRANSIT] 1. *a)* passing away with time; temporary; transitory *b)* passing quickly; fleeting; ephemeral 2. staying for only a short time [a *transient* lodger] —***n.*** a transient person or thing [*transients* at a hotel] —**tran′sience, tran′sien·cy** ***n.*** —**tran′sient·ly** ***adv.***

tran·sis·tor (tran zis′tər, -sis′-) ***n.*** [TRAN(SFER) + (RE)SISTOR] a small, solid-state electronic device used instead of an electron tube

tran·sis·tor·ize (-tə rīz′) ***vt.*** **-ized′, -iz′ing** to equip with transistors

trans·it (tran′sit, -zit) ***n.*** [< L. pp. of *transire* < *trans-*, over + *ire*, to go] 1. *a)* passage through or across *b)* a transition; change 2. *a)* a carrying or being carried from one place to another [goods in *transit*] *b)* a system of public transportation in a city: cf. RAPID TRANSIT 3. a surveying instrument for measuring horizontal angles: in full, **transit theodolite** 4. *Astron. a)* the apparent passage of a heavenly body across a given meridian or through the field of a telescope *b)* the apparent passage of a smaller heavenly body across the disk of a larger one —***vt., vi.*** to make a transit (through or across)

tran·si·tion (tran zish′ən, -sish′-; *Brit.* -sizh′-) ***n.*** 1. *a)* a passing from one condition, activity, place, etc. to another *b)* the period of this 2. a word, phrase, sentence, etc. that relates one element or topic to another that follows 3. *Music a)* a shifting from one key to another; modulation *b) same as* BRIDGE —**tran·si′tion·al** ***adj.*** —**tran·si′tion·al·ly** ***adv.***

tran·si·tive (tran′sə tiv, -zə-) ***adj.*** taking a direct object to complete the meaning: said of certain verbs —***n.*** a transitive verb —**tran′si·tive·ly** ***adv.***

tran·si·to·ry (tran′sə tôr′ē, -zə-) ***adj.*** of a passing nature; not enduring; temporary; fleeting —**tran′si·to′ri·ly** ***adv.*** —**tran′si·to′ri·ness** ***n.***

transl. 1. translated 2. translation

trans·late (trans lāt′, tranz-; trans′lāt, tranz′-) ***vt.*** **-lat′ed, -lat′ing** [< L. *translatus*, used as pp. of *transferre*, to TRANSFER] 1. to change from one place or condition to another; specif., *Theol.* to carry up to heaven without death 2. to put into the words of a different language 3. to change into another medium or form [*translate* ideas into action] 4. to put into different words; rephrase —***vi.*** 1. to make a translation into another language 2. to be capable of being translated —**trans·lat′a·ble** ***adj.*** —**trans·la′tor** ***n.***

trans·la·tion (-lā′shən) ***n.*** 1. a translating or being translated 2. writing or speech translated into another language —**trans·la′tion·al** ***adj.***

trans·lit·er·ate (trans lit′ə rāt′, tranz-) ***vt.*** **-at′ed, -at′ing** [< TRANS- + L. *litera*, letter + -ATE[1]] to write or spell (words, etc.) in corresponding characters of another alphabet —**trans·lit′er·a′tion** ***n.***

trans·lu·cent (trans lo͞o′s'nt, tranz-) ***adj.*** [< L. prp. of *translucere* < *trans-*, through + *lucere*, to shine] 1. orig., shining through 2. letting light pass but diffusing it so that objects on the other side cannot be clearly distinguished, as frosted glass: also **trans·lu′cid** (-sid) —**trans·lu′cence, trans·lu′cen·cy** *n.* —**trans·lu′cent·ly** *adv.*

trans·mi·grate (-mī′grāt) *vi.* **-grat·ed, -grat·ing** [< L. pp. of *transmigrare:* see TRANS- & MIGRATE] **1.** to move from one habitation, country, etc. to another **2.** in some religions, to pass into another body at death: said of the soul —**trans′mi·gra′tion** *n.* —**trans·mi′gra·tor** *n.* —**trans·mi′gra·to′ry** (-grə tôr′ē) *adj.*

trans·mis·si·ble (trans mis′ə b'l, tranz-) *adj.* capable of being transmitted —**trans·mis′si·bil′i·ty** *n.*

trans·mis·sion (-mish′ən) *n.* **1.** *a)* a transmitting or being transmitted *b)* something transmitted **2.** the part of an automobile, etc. that transmits motive force from the engine to the wheels, as by gears **3.** the passage of radio waves through space between the transmitting station and the receiving station —**trans·mis′sive** *adj.*

trans·mit (-mit′) *vt.* **-mit′ted, -mit′ting** [< L. < *trans-*, over + *mittere*, to send] **1.** to send or cause to go from one person or place to another; transfer; convey **2.** to pass along (a disease, etc.) **3.** to hand down to others by heredity, inheritance, etc. **4.** to communicate (news, etc.) **5.** *a)* to cause (light, heat, etc.) to pass through some medium *b)* to conduct [water *transmits* sound] **6.** to convey (force, movement, etc.) from one mechanical part to another **7.** to send out (radio or television broadcasts, etc.) by electromagnetic waves —*vi.* to send out radio or television signals —**trans·mit′tal, trans·mit′tance, trans·mit′tan·cy** *n.* —**trans·mit′ti·ble, trans·mit′ta·ble** *adj.*

trans·mit·ter (trans mit′ər; *for 2, often* trans′mit ər, tranz′-) *n.* **1.** a person who transmits **2.** a thing that transmits; specif., *a)* the part of a telegraphic instrument by which messages are sent *b)* the part of a telephone, behind the mouthpiece, that converts sound into electric impulses for transmission *c)* the apparatus that generates, modulates, and sends out radio waves

trans·mu·ta·tion (trans′myo͞o tā′shən, tranz′-) *n.* **1.** a transmuting or being transmuted **2.** the conversion of base metals into gold and silver as sought in alchemy **3.** *Chem.* the conversion of atoms of one element into atoms of a different isotope, or element, as by nuclear bombardment —**trans′mu·ta′tion·al** *adj.* —**trans·mut′a·tive** (-myo͞ot′ə-tiv) *adj.*

trans·mute (trans myo͞ot′, tranz-) *vt., vi.* **-mut′ed, -mut′ing** [< L. < *trans-*, over + *mutare*, to change] to change from one form, nature, substance, etc. into another; transform —**trans·mut′a·bil′i·ty** *n.* —**trans·mut′a·ble** *adj.* —**trans·mut′a·bly** *adv.*

trans·o·ce·an·ic (trans′ō shē an′ik, tranz′-) *adj.* **1.** crossing or spanning the ocean **2.** from or on the other side of the ocean

tran·som (tran′səm) *n.* [prob. < L. *transtrum*, crossbeam] **1.** a horizontal crossbar across the top or middle of a window or the top of a door **2.** a small window directly over a door or window, usually hinged to the transom **3.** any crosspiece, as the horizontal beam of a gallows

tran·son·ic (tran sän′ik) *adj.* designating, of, or moving at a speed within the range of change from subsonic to supersonic speed

trans·pa·cif·ic (trans′pə sif′ik) *adj.* **1.** crossing or spanning the Pacific **2.** on the other side of the Pacific

trans·par·en·cy (trans per′ən sē, -par′-) *n.* **1.** a transparent state or quality: also **trans·par′ence** **2.** *pl.* **-cies** something transparent; specif., a piece of material having a picture, etc. that is visible when light shines through it

trans·par·ent (-ənt) *adj.* [< ML. prp. of *transparere* < L. *trans-*, through + *parere*, to appear] **1.** transmitting light rays so that objects on the other side may be distinctly seen **2.** so fine in texture or open in mesh as to be seen through; sheer; gauzy **3.** easily understood, recognized, or detected; obvious **4.** open; frank —**trans·par′ent·ly** *adv.* —**trans·par′ent·ness** *n.*

tran·spire (tran spīr′) *vt.* **-spired′, -spir′ing** [< Fr. < ML. < L. *trans*, through + *spirare*, to breathe] to cause (vapor, moisture, etc.) to pass through tissue or other permeable substances, esp. through the pores of the skin or the surface of leaves, etc. —*vi.* **1.** to give off vapor, moisture, etc. as through pores **2.** to be given off, exhaled, etc. **3.** to leak out; become known **4.** to come to pass; happen: regarded by some as a loose usage —**tran′spi·ra′tion** (-spə-rā′shən) *n.*

trans·plant (trans plant′; *for n.* trans′plant′) *vt.* [< LL.: see TRANS- & PLANT] **1.** to remove from one place and plant or put in another **2.** to remove (people) from one place and resettle in another **3.** *Surgery* to transfer (tissue or an organ) from one individual or part of the body to another; graft —*vi.* to be capable of being transplanted —*n.* **1.** a transplanting **2.** something transplanted, as a body organ or seedling —**trans·plant′a·ble** *adj.* —**trans′plan·ta′tion** *n.* —**trans·plant′er** *n.*

tran·spon·der (tran spän′dər) *n.* [TRAN(SMITTER) + (RE)SPONDER] a radio or radar transceiver that automatically transmits electrical signals when actuated by a specific signal

trans·port (trans pôrt′; *for n.* trans′pôrt) *vt.* [< MFr. < L. < *trans-*, over + *portare*, to carry] **1.** to carry from one place to another, esp. over long distances **2.** to carry away with emotion; enrapture **3.** to banish or deport to a penal colony, etc. —*n.* **1.** a transporting; transportation **2.** strong emotion, esp. of delight or joy **3.** a ship, airplane, train, etc. used for transporting soldiers, freight, etc. **4.** a transported convict —**trans·port′a·bil′i·ty** *n.* —**trans·port′a·ble** *adj.* —**trans·port′er** *n.*

trans·por·ta·tion (trans′pər tā′shən) *n.* **1.** a transporting or being transported **2.** *a)* a means or system of conveyance *b)* the work or business of conveying passengers or goods **3.** fare or a ticket for being transported **4.** banishment for crime, as to a penal colony

trans·pose (trans pōz′) *vt.* **-posed′, -pos′ing** [MFr. *transposer:* see TRANS- & POSE[1]] **1.** to change the usual, relative, or respective order or position of; interchange **2.** to transfer (an algebraic term) from one side of an equation to the other, reversing the plus or minus value **3.** to rewrite or play (a musical composition) in a different key —*vi.* to play music in a different key —**trans·pos′a·bil′i·ty, trans·pos′a·ble·ness** *n.* —**trans·pos′a·ble** *adj.* —**trans·pos′er** *n.* —**trans′po·si′tion** (-pə zish′ən) *n.*

trans·sex·u·al (tran sek′sho͞o wəl, trans-) *n.* a person who tends to identify with the opposite sex, or one whose sex has been changed by means of surgery and hormone injections —**trans·sex′u·al·ism** *n.*

trans·ship (tran ship′, trans-) *vt.* **-shipped′, -ship′ping** to transfer from one ship, train, truck, etc. to another for reshipment —**trans·ship′ment** *n.*

trans·son·ic (-sän′ik) *adj. same as* TRANSONIC

tran·sub·stan·ti·a·tion (tran′səb stan′shē ā′shən) *n.* [< ML. < pp. of *transubstantiare* < L. *trans-*, over + *substantia*, substance] **1.** a changing of one substance into another **2.** *R.C. & Orthodox Eastern Ch.* the doctrine that, in the Eucharist, the whole substance of the bread and wine are changed into the body and blood of Christ, while only the appearance, taste, etc. of bread and wine remain

trans·u·ran·ic (trans′yoo ran′ik, tranz′-) *adj.* designating or of the elements, as plutonium, having atomic numbers higher than that of uranium: also **trans′u·ra′ni·um** (-rā′nē əm)

Trans·vaal (trans väl′, tranz-) province of South Africa, in the NE part

trans·ver·sal (trans vur′səl) *adj. same as* TRANSVERSE —*n.* a line that intersects two or more other lines —**trans·ver′sal·ly** *adv.*

trans·verse (trans vurs′, tranz-; *also, and for n. usually,* trans′vurs, tranz′-) *adj.* [< L. pp. of *transvertere:* see TRAVERSE] lying, situated, placed, etc. across; crosswise —*n.* a transverse part, beam, etc. —**trans·verse′ly** *adv.*

transverse colon the central portion of the large intestine, crossing the abdomen: see INTESTINE, illus.

trans·ves·tite (trans ves′tīt, tranz-) *n.* [< TRANS- + L. *vestire*, to clothe + -ITE] a person who derives sexual pleasure from dressing in the clothes of the opposite sex —**trans·ves′tism, trans·ves′ti·tism** *n.*

Tran·syl·va·ni·a (tran′sil vā′nē ə, -vān′yə) plateau region in C Romania —**Tran′syl·va′ni·an** *adj., n.*

trap[1] (trap) *n.* [OE. *træppe*] **1.** any device for catching animals; gin, snare, etc. **2.** any stratagem or ambush designed to catch or trick unsuspecting persons **3.** any of various devices for preventing the escape of gas, offensive odors, etc., as a U-shaped part in a drainpipe **4.** an apparatus for throwing disks into the air to be shot at in trapshooting **5.** a light, two-wheeled carriage with springs **6.** *same as* TRAPDOOR **7.** [*pl.*] the cymbals, blocks, etc. attached to a set of drums, as in a jazz band **8.** [Slang] the mouth **9.** *Golf same as* SAND TRAP —*vt.* **trapped, trap′ping** **1.** to catch as in a trap; entrap **2.** to hold back or seal off by a trap **3.** to furnish with a trap or traps **4.** *Sports* to seize (a ball) just as it bounces from the ground —*vi.* to set traps to catch animals, esp. for their furs

trap[2] (trap) *n.* [< Sw. < *trappa*, stair] **1.** any of several dark-colored, igneous rocks; esp., such a rock, as basalt, used in road making **2.** a geologic structure enclosing oil or gas Also **trap′rock′**

trap[3] (trap) *vt.* **trapped, trap′ping** [< OFr. *drap*, cloth] to cover with trappings; caparison —*n.* [*pl.*] [Colloq.] personal belongings, clothes, etc.

trap·door (trap′dôr′) *n.* a hinged or sliding door in a roof, ceiling, or floor

tra·peze (tra pēz′, trə-) ***n.*** **[**Fr. < ModL.: see ff.**]** a short horizontal bar, hung at a height by two ropes, on which gymnasts, acrobats, etc. swing and do stunts
tra·pe·zi·um (trə pē′zē əm) ***n.,*** *pl.* **-zi·ums, -zi·a** (-ə) **[**ModL. < Gr. dim. of *trapeza,* table < *tra-,* for *tetra,* four + *peza,* a foot**]** **1.** a plane figure with four sides no two of which are parallel **2.** [Brit.] *same as* TRAPEZOID (sense 1) **3.** a small bone of the wrist near the base of the thumb

TRAPEZIUM

trap·e·zoid (trap′ə zoid′) ***n.*** **[**ModL. < Gr.: see prec. & -OID**]** **1.** a plane figure with four sides only two of which are parallel **2.** [Brit.] *same as* TRAPEZIUM (sense 1) **3.** a small bone of the wrist near the base of the index finger —***adj.*** shaped like a trapezoid: also **trap′e·zoi′dal**

TRAPEZOID

trap·per (trap′ər) ***n.*** a person who traps; esp., one who traps fur-bearing animals for their skins
trap·pings (-iŋz) ***n.pl.*** [see TRAP[3]] **1.** a highly decorated covering for a horse; caparison **2.** highly decorated clothing **3.** things accompanying something that are an outward sign of it *[trappings* of success*]*
Trap·pist (trap′ist) ***n.*** **[**< Fr. < (*La*) *Trappe,* abbey in Normandy**]** a monk of a branch of the Cistercian order, living under a vow of silence —***adj.*** of the Trappists
trap·shoot·ing (trap′sho͞ot′iŋ) ***n.*** the sport of shooting at clay pigeons, or disks, sprung into the air from traps —**trap′shoot′er** ***n.***
trash (trash) ***n.*** **[**prob. < Scand.**]** **1.** parts that have been broken off, stripped off, etc., esp. leaves, twigs, etc. **2.** discarded or worthless things; rubbish **3.** worthless, unnecessary, offensive, or foolish matter *[*literary *trash]* **4.** a person or people regarded as disreputable —***vt.*** [Slang] to destroy (property) as by vandalism, arson, etc.
trash·y (-ē) ***adj.*** **trash′i·er, trash′i·est** containing, consisting of, or like trash; worthless —**trash′i·ness** ***n.***
‡**trat·tor·i·a** (trät′tô rē′ä) ***n.,*** *pl.* **-i·e** (-e) **[**It. < *trattore,* innkeeper**]** a small, inexpensive restaurant in Italy
trau·ma (trou′mə, trô′-) ***n.,*** *pl.* **-mas, -ma·ta** (-mə tə) **[**ModL. < Gr.**]** **1.** *Med.* a bodily injury, wound, or shock **2.** *Psychiatry* an emotional shock which has a lasting effect on the mind —**trau·mat′ic** (-mat′ik) ***adj.*** —**trau·mat′i·cal·ly** ***adv.***
trau·ma·tize (-tīz′) ***vt.*** **-tized′, -tiz′ing** **1.** *Med.* to injure or wound (tissues) **2.** *Psychiatry* to subject to a trauma
trav·ail (trav′āl, trə vāl′) ***n.*** **[**OFr. < VL. *tripalium,* a torture device < *tria,* three + *palus,* a stake**]** **1.** very hard work **2.** the pains of childbirth **3.** intense pain; agony —***vi.*** **1.** to toil **2.** to suffer the pains of childbirth
trav·el (trav′'l) ***vi.*** **-eled** or **-elled, -el·ing** or **-el·ling** **[**var. of prec.**]** **1.** to go from one place to another; make a journey **2.** to go from place to place as a traveling salesman **3.** to walk or run **4.** to move, pass, or be transmitted **5.** to move in a given course: said of mechanical parts, etc. **6.** to advance or progress **7.** *Basketball* to move (usually more than two steps) while holding the ball **8.** [Colloq.] to associate (*with*) **9.** [Colloq.] to move with speed —***vt.*** **1.** to make a journey over or through **2.** [Colloq.] to cause to pass along —***n.*** **1.** the act or process of traveling **2.** [*pl.*] trips, journeys, tours, etc. **3.** movement of any kind **4.** *a*) mechanical motion, esp. reciprocating motion *b*) the distance of a mechanical stroke, etc. —**trav′el·er, trav′el·ler** ***n.***
trav·eled, trav·elled (-'ld) ***adj.*** **1.** that has traveled much **2.** much used by travelers *[*a *traveled* road*]*
traveler's check a check, usually one of a set, issued by a bank, etc. and sold to a traveler who signs it when it is issued and again in the presence of the one cashing it
traveling salesman a salesman who travels for a business firm, soliciting orders
trav·e·logue, trav·e·log (trav′ə lôg′, -läg′) ***n.*** **1.** a lecture on travels, accompanied by the showing of pictures **2.** a motion picture of travels
trav·erse (tra vurs′, trə-; *also, & for n. & adj. always,* trav′ərs) ***vt.*** **-ersed′, -ers′ing** **[**< OFr. < L. pp. of *transvertere* < *trans-,* over + *vertere,* to turn**]** **1.** *a*) to pass or extend over, across, or through *b*) to go back and forth over or along **2.** to go counter to; oppose **3.** to examine carefully **4.** to turn (a gun, etc.) laterally **5.** *Law* to deny formally (an allegation) —***vi.*** **1.** to cross over **2.** to move back and forth over a place, etc. **3.** to swivel or pivot **4.** to move across a mountain slope, as in skiing, in an oblique direction —***n.*** **1.** something that traverses or crosses; specif., *a*) a crossbar, crossbeam, etc. *b*) a gallery, loft, etc. crossing a building **2.** a traversing or passing across **3.** a device that causes a traversing movement **4.** a way across **5.** a zigzag course taken by a vessel —***adj.*** **1.** extending across **2.** designating or of drapes hung in pairs so that they can be drawn by pulling cords at the side —**trav·ers′a·ble** ***adj.*** —**trav·ers′al** ***n.*** —**trav·ers′er** ***n.***
trav·er·tine (trav′ər tēn′, -tin) ***n.*** **[**< It., ult. < L. (*lapis*) *Tiburtinus,* (stone) by Tibur, ancient It. city**]** a light-colored limestone deposited around limy springs, lakes, etc.
trav·es·ty (trav′is tē) ***n.,*** *pl.* **-ties** **[**< Fr. pp. of *travestir,* to disguise < It. < L. *trans-,* over + *vestire,* to dress**]** **1.** a grotesque or exaggerated imitation for purposes of ridicule; burlesque **2.** a crude or ridiculous representation —***vt.*** **-tied, -ty·ing** to make a travesty of
trawl (trôl) ***n.*** **[**< ? MDu. *traghel,* a dragnet**]** **1.** a large, baglike net dragged by a boat along the bottom of a fishing bank: also **trawl′net′** **2.** a long line supported by buoys, from which many short fishing lines are hung: also **trawl line** —***vt., vi.*** to fish or catch with a trawl
trawl·er (trô′lər) ***n.*** a boat used in trawling
tray (trā) ***n.*** **[**OE. *treg,* wooden board**]** **1.** a flat receptacle with low sides, for holding or carrying articles **2.** a tray with its contents *[*a *tray* of food*]* **3.** a shallow, removable compartment of a trunk, cabinet, etc.
treach·er·ous (trech′ər əs) ***adj.*** **1.** full of or showing treachery; traitorous **2.** untrustworthy; unreliable *[treacherous* rocks*]* —**treach′er·ous·ly** ***adv.*** —**treach′er·ous·ness** ***n.***
treach·er·y (-ē) ***n.,*** *pl.* **-er·ies** **[**< OFr. < *trichier,* to trick, cheat**]** **1.** betrayal of trust, faith, or allegiance; disloyalty or treason **2.** an act of disloyalty or treason
trea·cle (trē′k'l) ***n.*** **[**< OFr. < L. < Gr. *thēriakē,* remedy for venomous bites < *thērion,* dim. of *thēr,* wild beast**]** [Brit.] molasses —**trea′cly** (-klē) ***adj.***
tread (tred) ***vt.*** **trod, trod′den** or **trod, tread′ing** **[**OE. *tredan***]** **1.** to walk on, in, along, over, etc. **2.** to do or follow by walking, dancing, etc. *[*to *tread* the measures gaily*]* **3.** to press or beat with the feet; trample **4.** to oppress or subdue **5.** to copulate with: said of male birds —***vi.*** **1.** to move on foot; walk **2.** to set one's foot (*on, across,* etc.) **3.** to trample (*on* or *upon*) **4.** to copulate: said of birds —***n.*** **1.** the act, manner, or sound of treading **2.** something on which a person or thing treads or moves, as the part of a shoe sole, wheel, etc. that touches the ground, the endless belt over cogged wheels of a tractor, etc., the horizontal surface of a stair step, etc. **3.** *a*) the thick outer layer of an automotive tire *b*) the depth or pattern of grooves in this layer —**tread the boards** to act in plays —**tread water** *pt. & pp. now usually* **tread′ed** to keep the body upright and the head above water in swimming by moving the legs up and down —**tread′er** ***n.***
trea·dle (tred′'l) ***n.*** **[**< OE. < *tredan:* see prec.**]** a lever or pedal moved by the foot as to turn a wheel —***vi.*** **-dled, -dling** to work a treadle
tread·mill (tred′mil′) ***n.*** **1.** a mill wheel turned by persons treading steps built around its outer edge, or by an animal treading an endless belt **2.** any monotonous routine of duties, work, etc.
treas. **1.** treasurer **2.** treasury
trea·son (trē′z'n) ***n.*** **[**< OFr. < L. < pp. of *tradere,* to deliver up < *trans-,* over + *dare,* to give**]** **1.** [Now Rare] betrayal of trust or faith **2.** betrayal of one's country, esp. by helping the enemy in time of war
trea·son·a·ble (-ə b'l) ***adj.*** of or involving treason; traitorous: also **trea′son·ous** —**trea′son·a·ble·ness** ***n.*** —**trea′son·a·bly** ***adv.***
treas·ure (trezh′ər) ***n.*** **[**< OFr. < L. < Gr. *thēsauros***]** **1.** accumulated wealth, as money, gold, jewels, etc. **2.** any person or thing considered valuable —***vt.*** **-ured, -uring** **1.** to save up (money, etc.) for future use **2.** to value greatly; cherish
treas·ur·er (trezh′ər ər) ***n.*** a person in charge of a treasure or treasury; specif., an officer in charge of the funds of a government, corporation, society, etc. —**treas′ur·er·ship′** ***n.***
treas·ure-trove (-trōv′) ***n.*** **[**< Anglo-Fr. < OFr. *tresor,* treasure + *trové,* pp. of *trover,* to find**]** **1.** treasure found hidden, the original owner of which is not known **2.** any valuable discovery
treas·ur·y (-ē) ***n.,*** *pl.* **-ur·ies** **1.** a place where treasure is kept **2.** a place where public or private funds are kept, recorded, etc. **3.** the funds or revenues of a state, corporation, etc. **4.** [T-] the governmental department in charge of revenue, taxation, etc. **5.** a collection of treasures in art, literature, etc.
treasury note any of the interest-bearing notes or obligations of the U.S. Treasury
treat (trēt) ***vi.*** **[**< OFr. *traiter* < L. *tractare,* freq. of *trahere,* to draw**]** **1.** to discuss terms (*with* a person or *for* a settlement) **2.** to deal with a subject; speak or write (*of*) **3.** to stand the cost of another's entertainment —***vt.*** **1.** to deal with (a subject) in writing, music, etc. in a specified style **2.** to act toward (a person, animal, etc.) in a specified manner **3.** to regard in a specified way *[*he *treated* it as a joke*]* **4.** *a*) to pay for the food, drink, etc. of (another) *b*) to provide with something that pleases **5.** to subject to some process or substance, as in a chemical procedure **6.** to give medical or surgical care to (someone) or for (some dis-

order) *—n.* **1.** a meal, drink, etc. paid for by someone else **2.** anything that gives great pleasure **3.** *a)* the act of treating or entertaining *b)* one's turn to treat **—treat′a·bil′i·ty** *n.* **—treat′a·ble** *adj.* **—treat′er** *n.*

trea·tise (trēt′is) *n.* [< Anglo-Fr., ult. < OFr. *traiter:* see TREAT] a formal, systematic article or book dealing with some subject in a detailed way

treat·ment (-mənt) *n.* **1.** act, manner, method, etc. of treating **2.** medical or surgical care

trea·ty (trēt′ē) *n., pl.* **-ties** [< OFr. *traité,* ult. < pp. of L. *tractare,* to manage] a formal agreement between two or more nations, relating to peace, alliance, trade, etc.

tre·ble (treb′'l) *adj.* [< OFr. < L. *triplus,* triple] **1.** threefold; triple **2.** of, for, or performing the treble **3.** high-pitched or shrill *—n.* **1.** the highest part in musical harmony; soprano **2.** a singer or instrument that takes this part **3.** a high-pitched voice or sound *—vt., vi.* **-bled, -bling** to make or become threefold **—tre′bly** *adv.*

treble clef *Music* a sign on a staff, indicating the position of G above middle C on the second line

tree (trē) *n.* [OE. *treow*] **1.** a large, woody perennial plant with one main trunk which develops many branches **2.** a treelike bush or shrub **3.** a wooden beam, bar, post, etc. **4.** anything resembling a tree; specif., *short for* FAMILY TREE *—vt.* **treed, tree′ing 1.** to chase up a tree **2.** to stretch on a shoe tree **—up a tree** [Colloq.] in a situation without escape; cornered **—tree′less** *adj.* **—tree′like′** *adj.*

tree fern a tropical fern with a woody trunk

tree frog any of various frogs that live in trees: many are called *tree toads*

tree lawn in some cities, the strip of ground between a street and its parallel sidewalk, often planted with lawns and trees: also **tree′lawn′** *n.*

tree·nail (trē′nāl′; tren′'l, trun′-) *n.* [< ME. < *tre,* wood + *nayle,* nail] a dry wooden peg used to join timbers, esp. in shipbuilding: it swells when wet so as to fit tight

tree of heaven a fast-growing ailanthus

tree squirrel any of various squirrels that live in trees, as the gray squirrel, the red squirrel, etc.

tree surgery treatment of damaged trees as by filling cavities, pruning, etc. **—tree surgeon**

tree toad *see* TREE FROG

tree·top (trē′täp′) *n.* the topmost part of a tree

tre·foil (trē′foil) *n.* [< Anglo-Fr. < L. < *tri-,* three + *folium,* a leaf] **1.** a plant with leaves divided into three leaflets, as the clover **2.** any ornamental figure shaped like such a leaf

trek (trek) *vi.* **trekked, trek′king** [Afrik. < Du. *trekken,* to draw] **1.** in South Africa, to travel by ox wagon **2.** to travel slowly or laboriously **3.** [Colloq.] to go, esp. on foot *—n.* **1.** in South Africa, a journey made by ox wagon **2.** a journey or leg of a journey **3.** a migration **4.** [Colloq.] a short trip, esp. on foot **—trek′ker** *n.*

trel·lis (trel′is) *n.* [< OFr., ult. < L. *trilix,* triple-twilled] an openwork structure of thin, crossed strips, esp. of wood, on which vines are trained; lattice *—vt.* **1.** to furnish with, or train on, a trellis **2.** to cross or interweave like a trellis

trem·a·tode (trem′ə tōd′, trē′mə-) *n.* [< ModL. < Gr. < *trēma* (gen. *trēmatos*), a hole + *eidos,* form] any of various parasitic flatworms; fluke *—adj.* of a trematode

trem·ble (trem′b'l) *vi.* **-bled, -bling** [< OFr. < VL., ult. < L. < *tremere*] **1.** to shake involuntarily from cold, fear, excitement, etc.; shiver **2.** to feel great fear or anxiety **3.** to quake, totter, vibrate, etc. **4.** to quaver [*a trembling voice*] *—n.* **1.** a trembling **2.** [*sometimes pl.*] a fit or state of trembling **—trem′bler** *n.* **—trem′bling·ly** *adv.* **—trem′bly** *adj.*

tre·men·dous (tri men′dəs) *adj.* [< L. *tremendus* < *tremere,* to TREMBLE] **1.** such as to make one tremble; terrifying **2.** *a)* very large; great *b)* [Colloq.] wonderful, amazing, etc. **—tre·men′dous·ly** *adv.* **—tre·men′dous·ness** *n.*

trem·o·lo (trem′ə lō′) *n., pl.* **-los′** [It. < L.: see TREMULOUS] **1.** a trembling effect produced by rapidly repeating the same musical tone **2.** a device, as in an organ, for producing such a tone

trem·or (trem′ər; *occas.* trē′mər) *n.* [< OFr. < L. < *tremere,* to TREMBLE] **1.** a trembling, shaking, etc. **2.** a vibratory motion **3.** a nervous thrill; trembling sensation **4.** a trembling sound **—trem′or·ous** *adj.*

trem·u·lous (trem′yoo ləs) *adj.* [L. *tremulus* < *tremere,* to TREMBLE] **1.** trembling; quivering **2.** fearful; timid **3.** marked by or showing trembling or quivering Also **trem′u·lant —trem′u·lous·ly** *adv.* **—trem′u·lous·ness** *n.*

tre·nail (trē′nāl′; tren′'l, trun′-) *n. same as* TREENAIL

trench (trench) *vt.* [< OFr. < ? L. *truncare,* to cut off] **1.** to cut, slice, gash, etc. **2.** to dig a ditch or ditches in **3.** to surround or fortify with trenches *—vi.* **1.** to dig a ditch or ditches **2.** to infringe (*on* or *upon* another's land, rights, etc.) **3.** to verge or border (*on*); come close *—n.* **1.** a deep furrow **2.** a long, narrow ditch with earth banked in front as a parapet, used in battle for cover, etc.

trench·ant (tren′chənt) *adj.* [< OFr.: see prec.] **1.** orig., cutting; sharp **2.** keen; penetrating; incisive [*trenchant words*] **3.** forceful; vigorous [*a trenchant argument*] **4.** clear-cut; distinct [*a trenchant pattern*] **—trench′an·cy** *n.* **—trench′ant·ly** *adv.*

trench coat a belted raincoat in a military style

trench·er (tren′chər) *n.* [Archaic] **1.** a wooden platter for carving and serving meat **2.** *a)* food served on a trencher *b)* a supply of food

trench·er·man (-mən) *n., pl.* **-men** an eater; esp., one who eats much and heartily

trench fever an infectious disease transmitted by body lice, in which there is remittent fever, muscular pains, etc.

trench foot a diseased condition of the feet from prolonged exposure to wet and cold, as of soldiers in trenches

trench mortar (or **gun**) any of various portable mortars for shooting projectiles at a high trajectory and short range

trench mouth an infectious disease of the mouth and throat in which the mucous membranes become ulcerated

trend (trend) *vi.* [OE. *trendan*] **1.** to extend, turn, bend, etc. in a specific direction **2.** to have a general tendency: said of events, opinions, etc. *—n.* **1.** the general direction of a river, road, etc. **2.** the general tendency or course, as of events, a discussion, etc. **3.** a vogue, or current style, as in fashions

trend·y (-ē) *adj.* **trend′i·er, trend′i·est** [Colloq.] of or in the latest style, or trend; faddish **—trend′i·ly** *adv.* **—trend′i·ness** *n.*

Trent (trent) **1.** city in N Italy: pop. 87,000: It. name **Tren·to** (tren′tô) **2.** river in C England, flowing northeast into the North Sea **3. Council of,** the council of the Roman Catholic Church held intermittently at Trent, 1545–63, to counteract the Reformation

Tren·ton (tren′tən) [after Wm. *Trent* (1655–1724), colonist] capital of N.J., on the Delaware River: pop. 92,000

tre·pan (tri pan′) *n.* [< ML. < Gr. < *trypan,* to bore] **1.** an early form of the trephine **2.** a heavy boring tool *—vt.* **-panned′, -pan′ning** *same as* TREPHINE **—trep·a·na·tion** (trep′ə nā′shən) *n.*

tre·pang (tri paŋ′) *n.* [Malay *tĕripang*] a boiled, smoked, and dried sea cucumber, used in the Orient for making soup

tre·phine (tri fīn′, -fēn′) *n.* [formed (after TREPAN) < L. *tres,* three + *fines,* ends] a type of small circular saw used in surgery to remove disks of bone from the skull *—vt.* **-phined′, -phin′ing** to operate on with a trephine **—treph·i·na·tion** (tref′ə nā′shən) *n.*

trep·i·da·tion (trep′ə dā′shən) *n.* [< L. < pp. of *trepidare,* to tremble < *trepidus,* disturbed] **1.** tremulous or trembling movement **2.** fearful uncertainty or anxiety

tres·pass (tres′pəs; *also, esp. for v.,* -pas′) *vi.* [< OFr., ult. < L. *trans-,* across + VL. hyp. *passare,* to pass] **1.** to go beyond the limits of what is considered right or moral; transgress **2.** to go on another's property without permission or right **3.** to intrude; encroach **4.** *Law* to commit a trespass *—n.* a trespassing; specif., *a)* a moral offense *b)* an encroachment; intrusion *c) Law* an illegal act done with force against another's person, rights, or property **—tres′pass·er** *n.*

tress (tres) *n.* [< OFr. < ? Frank.] **1.** orig., a braid of hair **2.** a lock of human hair **3.** [*pl.*] a woman's or girl's hair, esp. when long and falling loosely

-tress (tris) *a suffix meaning* female [*actress*] : see also -ESS

tres·tle (tres′'l) *n.* [< OFr., ult. < L. *transtrum,* a beam] **1.** a frame consisting of a horizontal beam fastened to two pairs of spreading legs, used to support planks to form a table, etc. **2.** a framework of uprights and crosspieces, supporting a bridge, etc.; also, such a bridge

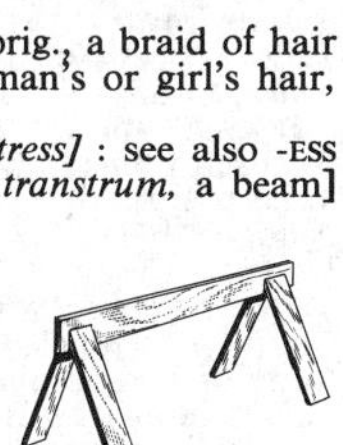

TRESTLE

tres·tle·work (-wurk′) *n.* a system of trestles for supporting a bridge, etc.

trey (trā) *n.* [< OFr. < L. *tres,* three] **1.** a playing card with three spots **2.** the side of a die bearing three spots, or a throw of the dice totaling three

tri- [< Fr., L., or Gr.] *a combining form meaning:* **1.** having or involving three [*triangular*] **2.** triply, in three ways [*trilingual*] **3.** three times, into three [*trisect*] **4.** every third [*triannual*] **5.** *Chem.* having three atoms, groups, or equivalents of (the thing specified) [*tribasic*]

tri·a·ble (trī′ə b'l) *adj.* **1.** that can be tried or tested **2.** subject to trial in a law court **—tri′a·ble·ness** *n.*

tri·ac·e·tate (trī as′ə tāt′) *n.* a compound containing three acetate radicals in the molecule

tri·ad (trī′ad) ***n.*** [< LL. < Gr. < *treis*, three] **1.** a group of three persons, things, etc. **2.** a musical chord of three tones, esp. one consisting of a root tone and its third and fifth: a triad with a major third and perfect fifth is called a *major triad;* a triad with a minor third and perfect fifth is called a *minor triad* —**tri·ad′ic** ***adj.***

tri·age (trē äzh′) ***n.*** [Fr. < *trier*, to sift] a system of deciding in what order battlefield casualties will receive medical treatment, according to urgency, chance of survival, etc.

tri·al (trī′əl, trīl) ***n.*** [Anglo-Fr. < *trier*, to try] **1.** *a)* a trying, testing, etc.; test *b)* a testing of qualifications, progress, etc.; probation *c)* an experiment **2.** *a)* a being tried by suffering, temptation, etc. *b)* suffering, hardship, trouble, etc., or the cause of this **3.** a formal examination of the facts of a case by a court of law to decide the validity of a charge or claim **4.** an attempt; effort —***adj.*** **1.** of a trial **2.** of or for trying, testing, etc. —**on trial** in the process of being tried

trial and error a trying or testing over and over again until the right result is found —**tri′al-and-er′ror** ***adj.***

trial balance a statement of the debit and credit balances of all open accounts in a double-entry bookkeeping ledger to test their equality

trial balloon **1.** *same as* PILOT BALLOON **2.** an action, statement, etc. made to test public opinion on an issue

trial jury *same as* PETIT JURY

tri·an·gle (trī′aŋ′g'l) ***n.*** [< MFr. < L.: see TRI- & ANGLE[1]] **1.** a plane figure having three angles and three sides **2.** any three-sided or three-cornered figure, area, etc. **3.** a situation involving three persons **4.** a musical instrument consisting of a steel rod bent in a triangle: it makes a high-pitched, tinkling sound when struck —**tri·an′gu·lar** (-aŋ′gyə-lər) ***adj.*** —**tri·an′gu·lar′i·ty** (-ler′ə tē) ***n.***

TRIANGLES

tri·an·gu·late (trī aŋ′gyə lāt′; *for adj. usually* -lit) ***vt.*** **-lat′ed, -lat′ing** **1.** to divide into triangles **2.** to survey (a region) by triangulation **3.** to make triangular **4.** to measure by trigonometry —***adj.*** of, like, or marked with triangles

tri·an·gu·la·tion (trī aŋ′gyə lā′shən) ***n.*** a triangulating or being triangulated; specif., *Surveying* the determining of distance between points on the earth's surface by calculations based on the division of an area into connected triangles and the measurement of their angles

Tri·as·sic (trī as′ik) ***adj.*** [< ModL. < LL. *trias*, TRIAD (because divisible into three groups) + -IC] designating or of the first period of the Mesozoic Era —**the Triassic** the Triassic Period or its rocks: see GEOLOGY, chart

trib·al·ism (trī′b'l iz'm) ***n.*** tribal organization, culture, loyalty, etc. —**trib′al·ist** ***n., adj.***

tribe (trīb) ***n.*** [L. *tribus*, any of the divisions (orig. three) of the ancient Romans] **1.** a group of persons, families, or clans believed to have a common ancestor: many tribes form a close community under a leader or chief **2.** any group of people with the same occupation, ideas, etc. **3.** a subdivision of a subfamily of plants or animals **4.** loosely, any group of plants or animals classified together **5.** [Colloq.] a family —**trib′al** ***adj.*** —**trib′al·ly** ***adv.***

tribes·man (trībz′mən) ***n., pl.*** **-men** a member of a tribe

trib·u·la·tion (trib′yə lā′shən) ***n.*** [< OFr. < LL. < *tribulare*, to afflict < L., to press < *tribulum*, threshing sledge] **1.** great misery or distress, as from oppression **2.** the cause of this; affliction; trial

tri·bu·nal (trī byo͞o′n'l, tri-) ***n.*** [L.: see TRIBUNE[1]] **1.** the judge's bench **2.** a court of justice **3.** any seat of judgment

trib·une[1] (trib′yo͞on; *in a newspaper name often* tri byo͞on′) ***n.*** [< L. *tribunus* < *tribus*, tribe] **1.** in ancient Rome, *a)* any of several magistrates whose duty it was to protect the rights and interests of the plebeians *b)* any of six officers rotating command over a legion **2.** a champion of the people —**trib′une·ship′** ***n.***

trib·une[2] (trib′yo͞on) ***n.*** [Fr. < It. < L.: see TRIBUNAL, sense 1] a raised platform or dais for speakers

trib·u·tar·y (trib′yoo ter′ē) ***adj.*** **1.** paying tribute **2.** under another's control; subject [*a tributary* nation] **3.** owed or paid as tribute **4.** *a)* making additions; contributory *b)* flowing into a larger one [*a tributary* stream] —***n., pl.*** **-tar′ies** **1.** a tributary nation or ruler **2.** a tributary stream or river

trib·ute (trib′yo͞ot) ***n.*** [< MFr. < L. pp. of *tribuere*, to allot, pay < *tribus*, tribe] **1.** money that one nation is forced to pay to another, more powerful nation **2.** any forced payment **3.** the obligation to pay tribute **4.** something given, done, or said to show gratitude, honor, or praise

trice (trīs) ***vt.*** **triced, tric′ing** [MDu. *trisen*, to pull < *trise*, windlass] to haul up and secure (a sail, etc.): usually with *up* —***n.*** [< *at a trice*, with one pull] a very short time; instant: now only in **in a trice**

tri·cen·ten·ni·al (trī′sen ten′ē əl) ***adj.*** happening once in, or lasting for, 300 years —***n.*** a 300th anniversary

tri·ceps (trī′seps) ***n., pl.*** **-ceps·es, -ceps** [ModL. < L. < *tri-*, three + *caput*, a head] a muscle having three points of origin, esp. the muscle at the back of the upper arm that extends the forearm

tri·chi·na (tri kī′nə) ***n., pl.*** **-nae** (-nē) [ModL. < Gr. *trichinos*, hairy < *thrix*, hair] a very small worm whose larvae infest the intestines and muscles of man, pigs, etc., causing trichinosis —**tri·chi′nal** ***adj.***

trich·i·no·sis (trik′ə nō′sis) ***n.*** a trichinal disease marked by fever, diarrhea, muscular pains, etc. and usually acquired by eating undercooked infested pork

trick (trik) ***n.*** [ONormFr. *trique* < OFr. *trichier*, to cheat] **1.** something that is done to fool, cheat, outwit, etc.; ruse; stratagem **2.** *a)* a piece of playful mischief; prank *b)* a deception or illusion [the light played a *trick* on his eyes] **3.** a freakish, foolish, or mean act **4.** a clever or skillful act intended to amuse; specif., *a)* an act of jugglery, sleight of hand, etc. *b)* a feat done by a trained animal **5.** the art or knack of doing a thing easily, skillfully, quickly, etc. **6.** a personal mannerism **7.** a turn at work; shift **8.** *Card Games* the cards played and won in a single round —***vt.*** to deceive, cheat, outwit, fool, etc. —***adj.*** **1.** of, for, or using tricks [*trick* photography] **2.** that tricks **3.** not always working right [a *trick* knee] —**do** (or **turn**) **the trick** to bring about the desired result —**trick out** (or **up**) to dress up; adorn

trick·er·y (-ər ē) ***n., pl.*** **-er·ies** the use of tricks to cheat, outwit, etc.; deception; stratagem

trick·le (trik′'l) ***vi.*** **-led, -ling** [prob. < freq. of ME. *striken*, to strike] **1.** to flow slowly in a thin stream or fall in drops **2.** to move little by little [the crowd *trickled* away] —***vt.*** to cause to trickle —***n.*** **1.** a trickling **2.** a thin flow or drip

trick·ster (trik′stər) ***n.*** a person who tricks; cheat

trick·sy (-sē) ***adj.*** **-si·er, -si·est** **1.** mischievous; prankish **2.** *same as* TRICKY —**trick′si·ness** ***n.***

trick·y (trik′ē) ***adj.*** **trick′i·er, trick′i·est** **1.** given to or full of trickery **2.** intricate; difficult **3.** needing special skill or care —**trick′i·ly** ***adv.*** —**trick′i·ness** ***n.***

tri·clin·ic (trī klin′ik) ***adj.*** [< TRI- + Gr. *klinein*, to incline + -IC] designating a crystalline form that has three unequal axes intersecting at oblique angles

tri·col·or (trī′kul′ər) ***n.*** a flag consisting of three stripes, each of a different color, esp. the flag of France —***adj.*** having three colors

tri·corn, tri·corne (-kôrn′) ***adj.*** [< Fr. < L. < *tri-*, three + *cornu*, horn] having three horns or corners —***n.*** a tricorn hat

tri·cot (trē′kō) ***n.*** [Fr. < *tricoter*, to knit, ult. < MDu.] **1.** a thin fabric that is knitted or woven to look knitted **2.** a type of ribbed cloth for dresses

tri·cus·pid (trī kus′pid) ***adj.*** [< L.: see TRI- & CUSP] **1.** having three cusps, or points [a *tricuspid* tooth]: also **tri·cus′pi·date** (-pə dāt′) **2.** designating or of a valve with three flaps, between the right auricle and right ventricle of the heart —***n.*** a tricuspid tooth or valve

tri·cy·cle (trī′si k'l) ***n.*** [Fr.] a light, three-wheeled vehicle worked by pedals, esp. one for children

tri·dent (trīd′'nt) ***n.*** [< L. < *tri-*, three + *dens* (gen. *dentis*), a tooth] a three-pronged spear

tri·den·tate (trī den′tāt) ***adj.*** having three teeth, prongs, or points

tried (trīd) *pt. & pp. of* TRY —***adj.*** **1.** tested; proved **2.** trustworthy; faithful **3.** having endured trials and troubles

tri·en·ni·al (trī en′ē əl) ***adj.*** [< L. < *tri-*, three + *annus*, a year] **1.** happening every three years **2.** lasting three years —***n.*** a triennial event —**tri·en′ni·al·ly** ***adv.***

tri·er (trī′ər) ***n.*** a person or thing that tries

Tri·este (trē est′; *It.* trē es′te) seaport in NE Italy, on an inlet (**Gulf of Trieste**) of the Adriatic: pop. 278,000

tri·fa·cial (trī fā′shəl) ***adj., n.*** *same as* TRIGEMINAL

tri·fid (trī′fid) ***adj.*** [< L. < *tri-*, three + base of *findere*, to divide] divided into three lobes by deep clefts, as some leaves

tri·fle (trī′f'l) ***n.*** [< OFr. dim. of *truffe*, deception] **1.** something of little value or importance **2.** a small amount; bit **3.** a small sum of money —***vi.*** **-fled, -fling** **1.** to talk or act in a joking way; deal lightly [not a person to *trifle* with] **2.** to play or toy (*with* something) —***vt.*** to spend idly; waste [*trifling* time away] —**tri′fler** ***n.***

tri·fling (-fliŋ) ***adj.*** **1.** frivolous; fickle **2.** trivial

tri·fo·cal (trī fō′k'l, trī′fō′-) ***adj.*** having three focal lengths —***n.*** **1.** a lens with one part ground for close focus, one for intermediate focus, and one for distant focus **2.** [*pl.*] a pair of glasses with such lenses

trig[1] (trig) ***adj.*** [< ON. *tryggr*, true] [Chiefly Brit.] **1.** trim; neat **2.** in good condition —***vt.*** **trigged, trig′ging** [Chiefly Brit. Dial.] to make trig (often with *out, up*)

trig[2] (trig) ***n.*** *shortened form of* TRIGONOMETRY

trig., trigon. **1.** trigonometric(al) **2.** trigonometry

tri·gem·i·nal (trī jem′ə n'l) ***adj.*** [< ModL. < L. < *tri-*, three + *geminus,* twin] designating or of either of a pair of cranial nerves, each dividing into three branches supplying the head and face —*n.* a trigeminal nerve

trig·ger (trig′ər) *n.* [< Du. < *trekken,* to pull] a lever, etc. which when pulled or pressed releases a catch, spring, etc.; esp., the small lever pressed back by the finger in firing a gun —*vt.* **1.** to fire or set into action with a trigger **2.** to set off (an action) [the fight *triggered* a riot] —**quick on the trigger** [Colloq.] **1.** quick to fire a gun **2.** quick to act, retort, etc.; alert

trig·ger-hap·py (-hap′ē) *adj.* [Colloq.] quick to resort to force, make war, etc.

tri·glyc·er·ide (trī glis′ər īd′) *n.* [TRI- + GLYCERIDE] any of a group of esters of fatty acids and glycerol, found in the blood and thought to be a factor in atherosclerosis

trig·o·nom·e·try (trig′ə näm′ə trē) *n.* [< ModL. < Gr. *trigōnon,* triangle + *-metria,* measurement] the branch of mathematics dealing with the ratios between the sides of a right triangle with reference to either acute angle (*trigonometric functions*), the relations between these ratios, and use of these facts in finding the unknown sides or angles of any triangle —**trig′o·no·met′ric** (-nə met′rik), **trig′o·no·met′ri·cal** *adj.* —**trig′o·no·met′ri·cal·ly** *adv.*

tri·he·dral (trī hē′drəl) *adj.* [TRI- + -HEDRAL] having three sides or faces [a *trihedral* angle] —*n.* a figure formed by three lines, each in a different plane, that intersect at a point

trike (trīk) *n.* [Colloq.] *same as* TRICYCLE

tri·lat·er·al (trī lat′ər əl) *adj.* three-sided

tri·lin·gual (-liŋ′gwəl) *adj.* in or using three languages

trill (tril) *n.* [< It. < *trillare,* of echoic origin] **1.** a rapid alternation of a tone with one just above it **2.** a bird's warble **3.** *a)* a rapid vibration of the tongue or uvula, as in pronouncing *r* in some languages *b)* an *r,* etc. so pronounced —*vt., vi.* to sound with a trill —**trill′er** *n.*

tril·lion (tril′yən) *n.* [Fr. < *tri-,* TRI- + (*mi*)*llion*] **1.** in the U.S. and France, the number represented by 1 followed by 12 zeros **2.** in Great Britain and Germany, the number represented by 1 followed by 18 zeros —*adj.* amounting to one trillion —**tril′lionth** *adj., n.*

tril·li·um (tril′ē əm) *n.* [ModL., genus name < L. *tri-,* three] a plant of the lily family with an erect stem bearing a whorl of three leaves and a single, three-petaled flower

tri·lo·bate (trī lō′bāt) *adj.* having three lobes, as some leaves: also **tri·lo′bat·ed, tri′lobed′** (-lōbd′)

tri·lo·bite (trī′lə bīt′) *n.* [< ModL.: see TRI-, LOBE, & -ITE] an extinct sea arthropod with the body divided by two furrows into three parts: a common fossil in Paleozoic rocks —**tri′lo·bit′ic** (-bit′ik) *adj.*

TRILLIUM

tril·o·gy (tril′ə jē) *n., pl.* **-gies** [Gr. *trilogia:* see TRI- & -LOGY] a set of three plays, novels, etc. which form a related group, although each is a complete work

trim (trim) *vt.* **trimmed, trim′ming** [OE. *trymman,* to make firm < *trum,* strong] **1.** to put in proper order; make neat or tidy, esp. by clipping, etc. [to *trim* hair] **2.** to clip, lop, cut, etc. [to *trim* dead branches off a tree] **3.** to cut (something) down to the required size or shape **4.** *a)* to decorate with ornaments, colorful materials, etc. [to *trim* a Christmas tree] *b)* to arrange an attractive display of merchandise in or on [to *trim* a store window] **5.** *a)* to balance (a ship) by shifting cargo, etc. *b)* to put (sails, etc.) in order for sailing **6.** to balance (an aircraft in flight) by adjusting stabilizers, tabs, etc. **7.** [Colloq.] *a)* to scold *b)* to beat, thrash, etc. *c)* to defeat *d)* to cheat —*vi.* **1.** *a)* to take a middle position between opposing sides *b)* to change one's opinions, policy, etc. in a way that is expedient **2.** to keep a ship, etc. in balance —*n.* **1.** condition or order [in proper *trim*] **2.** good condition or order [keep in *trim*] **3.** a trimming by clipping, cutting, etc. **4.** *a)* *same as* WINDOW DRESSING *b)* decorative molding or borders, esp. around windows and doors *c)* the interior furnishings or ornamental metalwork of an automobile *d)* any ornamental trimming **5.** *a)* the condition of being ready to sail: said of a vessel *b)* the position of a vessel in relation to the horizontal *c)* correct position in the water: a ship is **in trim** if stable and floating on an even keel, **out of trim** if not *d)* the adjustment of sails, etc. in a vessel **6.** something trimmed off —*adj.* **trim′mer, trim′mest 1.** orderly; neat **2.** well-proportioned; smartly designed **3.** in good condition —*adv.* in a trim way —**trim one's sails** to adjust

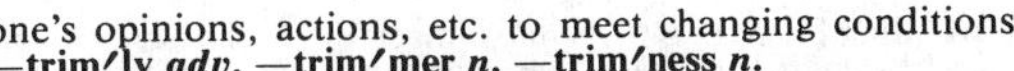

one's opinions, actions, etc. to meet changing conditions —**trim′ly** *adv.* —**trim′mer** *n.* —**trim′ness** *n.*

tri·mes·ter (trī mes′tər, trī′mes-) *n.* [< Fr. < L. < *tri-,* three + *mensis,* month] **1.** a three-month period **2.** in some colleges and universities, any of three periods into which the academic year is divided

trim·e·ter (trim′ə tər) *n.* [< L. < Gr.: see TRI- & METER[1]] **1.** a line of verse containing three metrical feet **2.** verse consisting of trimeters —*adj.* having three metrical feet

trim·ming (trim′iŋ) *n.* **1.** the action of one that trims **2.** that which trims; specif., *a)* decoration *b)* [*pl.*] side dishes or garnishes **3.** [*pl.*] parts trimmed off

tri·month·ly (trī munth′lē) *adj.* happening or appearing every three months

tri·nal (trī′n'l) *adj.* [< LL. < L. *trinus,* triple < *tres,* three] threefold; triple: also **tri′na·ry** (-nər ē), **trine** (trīn)

Trin·i·dad (trin′ə dad′; *Sp.* trē nē *thäth′*) island in the West Indies, off the NE coast of Venezuela: see ff.: 1,864 sq. mi. —**Trin′i·dad′i·an** *adj., n.*

Trinidad and Tobago country in the West Indies, comprising the islands of Trinidad & Tobago: a member of the Commonwealth: 1,980 sq. mi.; pop. 1,030,000; cap. Port-of-Spain

Trin·i·tar·i·an (trin′ə ter′ē ən) *adj.* **1.** of, about, or believing in the Trinity **2.** [t-] of a trinity —*n.* one who believes in the Trinity —**Trin′i·tar′i·an·ism** *n.*

tri·ni·tro·tol·u·ene (trī nī′trō täl′yoo wēn′) *n.* [TRI- + NITRO- + TOLUENE] a high explosive, $CH_3C_6H_2(NO_2)_3$, derived from toluene and used for blasting, in artillery shells, etc.: also **tri·ni′tro·tol′u·ol′** (-wōl′, -wôl′): abbrev. **TNT**

trin·i·ty (trin′ə tē) *n., pl.* **-ties** [< OFr. < L. < *trinus,* triple] **1.** a unit formed of three persons or things **2.** [T-] *Christian Theol.* the union of the three divine persons (Father, Son, and Holy Spirit, or Holy Ghost) in one Godhead

Trinity Sunday the Sunday after Pentecost, dedicated to the Trinity

trin·ket (triŋ′kit) *n.* [ONormFr. *trenquet*] **1.** a small piece of cheap jewelry, etc. **2.** a trifle or toy

tri·no·mi·al (trī nō′mē əl) *adj.* [TRI- + (BI)NOMIAL] composed of three terms —*n.* **1.** a mathematical expression consisting of three terms connected by plus or minus signs **2.** a three-word scientific name of a plant or animal, noting the genus, species, and subspecies

tri·o (trē′ō) *n., pl.* **tri′os** [Fr. < It. < *tri-,* TRI- (after *duo,* DUO)] **1.** a group of three **2.** *Music* *a)* a composition for three voices or instruments *b)* the three performers of such a composition *c)* the middle section of a minuet, scherzo, etc., orig. for three parts

tri·ode (trī′ōd) *n.* [TRI- + (ELECTR)ODE] an electron tube containing three electrodes (an anode, cathode, and control grid)

tri·ox·ide (trī äk′sīd) *n.* an oxide having three oxygen atoms to the molecule

trip (trip) *vi.* **tripped, trip′ping** [OFr. *treper* < Gmc.] **1.** to walk, run, or dance with light, rapid steps; skip; caper **2.** to stumble, esp. by catching the foot **3.** to make a mistake **4.** to go past an escapement catch: said of an escape wheel tooth **5.** [Slang] to experience a trip (*n.* 6) —*vt.* **1.** to make stumble **2.** to cause to make a mistake **3.** to catch in a lie, error, etc. (often with *up*) **4.** *a)* to release (a spring, wheel, etc.), as by moving a catch *b)* to start or operate by such action —*n.* **1.** a light, quick tread **2.** a going to or from a place, or to a place and returning; journey, esp. a short one **3.** *a)* a stumble *b)* a maneuver to cause this **4.** a mistake **5.** *a)* a contrivance, as a pawl, to trip a part *b)* its action **6.** [Slang] the hallucinations, sensations, etc. produced by a psychedelic drug, esp. LSD —**trip the light fantastic** to dance

tri·par·tite (trī pär′tīt) *adj.* [< L. < *tri-,* three + *partitus,* PARTITE] **1.** divided into three parts **2.** having three corresponding parts or copies **3.** made or existing between three parties, as an agreement —**tri·par′tite·ly** *adv.*

tripe (trīp) *n.* [< MFr., prob. ult. < Ar. *tharb,* entrails, lit., fold of fat] **1.** part of the stomach of an ox, etc., used as food **2.** [Slang] nonsense; rubbish

trip·ham·mer (trip′ham′ər) *n.* a heavy, power-driven hammer with a tripping device making it alternately rise and fall: also **trip hammer**

tri·ple (trip′'l) *adj.* [Fr. < L. *triplus:* see the *v.*] **1.** consisting of three; threefold **2.** done, said, etc. three times **3.** three times as much, as many, etc. **4.** *Music* having three beats to the measure [*triple* time] —*n.* **1.** a triple amount, number, etc. **2.** *Baseball* a hit getting the batter to third base —*vt.* **tri′pled,**

TRIPHAMMER

fat, āpe, cär; ten, ēven; is, bīte; gō, hôrn, tōōl, look; oil, out; up, fur; get; joy; yet; chin; she; thin, *th*en; zh, leisure; ŋ, ring; ə for *a* in *ago, e* in *agent, i* in *sanity, o* in *comply, u* in *focus;* ′ as in *able* (ā′b'l); Fr. bål; ë, Fr. coeur; ö, Fr. feu; Fr. mon; ô, Fr. coq; ü, Fr. duc; r, Fr. cri; H, G. ich; kh, G. doch; ‡foreign; *hypothetical; < derived from. See inside front cover.

tri′pling [< ML. < L. *triplus*, threefold < *tri-*, TRI- + *-plus*, as in *duplus*, double] to make three times as much or as many —*vi.* 1. to be tripled 2. *Baseball* to hit a triple —**tri′ply** *adv.*
triple play *Baseball* a play in which three players are put out
tri·ple-space (-spās′) *vt., vi.* **-spaced′, -spac′ing** to type (copy) so as to leave two full spaces between lines
tri·plet (trip′lit) *n.* [TRIPL(E) + -ET] 1. a group of three, usually of one kind; specif., *a*) a group of three lines of poetry, usually rhyming *b*) a group of three musical notes to be performed in the time of two of the same value 2. any of three offspring born at a single birth
trip·li·cate (trip′lə kit; *for v.* -kāt′) *adj.* [< L. pp. of *triplicare*, to treble < *triplex*, threefold] 1. threefold 2. designating the third of identical copies —*n.* any of three identical copies —*vt.* **-cat′ed, -cat′ing** to make three identical copies of —**in triplicate** in three identical copies —**trip′li·ca′tion** *n.*
tri·pod (trī′päd) *n.* [< L. < Gr. < *tri-*, three + *pous*, a foot] 1. a three-legged caldron, stool, etc. 2. a three-legged support for a camera, etc.
Trip·o·li (trip′ə lē) 1. one of the two capitals of Libya, on the NW coast: pop. 245,000 2. seaport on the NW coast of Lebanon: pop. 150,000
trip·per (trip′ər) *n.* 1. one that trips; specif., a device for tripping or releasing a catch, pawl, etc. 2. [Brit. Colloq.] a tourist
trip·ping (-iŋ) *adj.* moving lightly and quickly —**trip′ping·ly** *adv.*
trip·tych (trip′tik) *n.* [< Gr. *triptychos*, threefold < *tri-*, three + *ptychē*, a fold] 1. an ancient writing tablet of three leaves hinged together 2. a set of three panels with pictures, carvings, etc., often hinged and used as an altarpiece
tri·reme (trī′rēm) *n.* [< L. < *tri-*, three + *remus*, an oar] an ancient Greek or Roman galley, usually a warship, with three banks of oars on each side
tri·sect (trī sekt′, trī′sekt) *vt.* [< TRI- + L. pp. of *secare*, to cut] 1. to cut into three parts 2. *Geom.* to divide into three equal parts —**tri·sec′tion** *n.* —**tri·sec′tor** *n.*
tri·shaw (trī′shô′) *n.* [< TRI- + (JINRIKI)SHA] *same as* PEDICAB
Tris·tram (tris′trəm) *Medieval Legend* a knight who is involved in a tragic romance with a princess, Isolde: also **Tris′tam** (-təm), **Tris′tan** (-tən)
tri·syl·la·ble (trī sil′ə b′l, trī′sil′-) *n.* a word of three syllables —**tri·syl·lab·ic** (trī′si lab′ik) *adj.*
trite (trīt) *adj.* **trit′er, trit′est** [L. *tritus*, pp. of *terere*, to wear out] worn out by constant use; no longer fresh, original, etc. —**trite′ly** *adv.* —**trite′ness** *n.*
trit·i·um (trit′ē əm, trish′-) *n.* [ModL. < Gr. *tritos*, third] a radioactive isotope of hydrogen with an atomic weight of 3: it decays by beta-particle emission and is used in thermonuclear bombs, as a radioactive tracer, etc.
Tri·ton (trīt′′n) 1. *Gr. Myth.* a sea god with the head and upper body of a man and the tail of a fish 2. the larger of Neptune's two moons —*n.* [t-] 1. *a*) a sea snail with a long, spiral shell *b*) the shell 2. an old-world salamander
trit·u·rate (trich′ə rāt′) *vt.* **-rat′ed, -rat′ing** [< LL. pp. of *triturare*, to grind < L. *tritus:* see TRITE] to rub, crush, or grind into very fine particles; pulverize —*n.* something triturated —**trit′u·ra·ble** (-ər ə b′l) *adj.* —**trit′u·ra′tion** *n.* —**trit′u·ra′tor** *n.*
tri·umph (trī′əmf) *n.* [< OFr. < L. *triumphus*, akin to Gr. *thriambos*, hymn to Bacchus] 1. in ancient Rome, a procession celebrating a victorious general's return 2. a victory; success 3. exultation or joy over a victory, etc. —*vi.* 1. to be victorious, successful, etc. 2. to rejoice or exult over victory, etc. —**tri·um′phal** (-um′f′l) *adj.*
tri·um·phant (trī um′fənt) *adj.* 1. victorious; successful 2. exulting in victory, etc. —**tri·um′phant·ly** *adv.*
tri·um·vir (trī um′vər) *n., pl.* **-virs, -vi·ri′** (-vi rī′) [L. < *trium virum*, of three men] in ancient Rome, any of three administrators sharing authority equally —**tri·um′vi·ral** *adj.*
tri·um·vi·rate (-it) *n.* 1. the office or term of a triumvir 2. government by three men 3. any association of three in authority 4. any group of three
tri·une (trī′yo͞on) *adj.* [< TRI- + L. *unus*, one] being three in one [*a triune God*] —**tri·u′ni·ty** *n.*
tri·va·lent (trī vā′lənt) *adj.* [TRI- + -VALENT] 1. having a valence of three 2. having three valences —**tri·va′lence, tri·va′len·cy** *n.*
triv·et (triv′it) *n.* [OE. *trefet* < L. *tripes*, tripod] 1. a three-legged stand for holding pots, kettles, etc. over or near a fire 2. a short-legged plate for hot dishes to rest on
triv·i·a (triv′ē ə) *n.pl.* [*often with sing. v.*] [ModL. < ff.] unimportant matters; trivialities
triv·i·al (triv′ē əl, triv′yəl) *adj.* [L. *trivialis*, of the crossroads, commonplace < *tri-*, three + *via*, a road] of little value or importance; trifling —**triv′i·al·ly** *adv.*
triv·i·al·i·ty (triv′ē al′ə tē) *n.* 1. a being trivial 2. *pl.* **-ties** a trivial thing, idea, etc.; trifle
triv·i·al·ize (triv′ē ə līz′) *vt., vi.* **-ized′, -iz′ing** to treat as or make seem trivial —**triv′i·al·i·za′tion** *n.*
-trix (triks) *pl.* **-trix·es, -tri·ces′** (tri sēz′, trī′sēz) [L.] an ending of some feminine nouns of agent
TRM trademark
tro·che (trō′kē) *n.* [< Fr. < LL. *trochiscus*, a pill < Gr. < *trochos*, a wheel] a small, usually round, medicinal lozenge
tro·chee (trō′kē) *n.* [< L. < Gr. *trochaios*, running < *trechein*, to run] a metrical foot of two syllables, the first accented and the other unaccented, as in English verse (Ex.: "Pétĕr, | Pétĕr, | púmpkĭn | éatĕr") —**tro·cha′ic** (-kā′ik) *adj.*
trod (träd) *pt. & alt. pp. of* TREAD
trod·den (-'n) *alt. pp. of* TREAD
trode (trōd) *archaic pt. of* TREAD
trog·lo·dyte (träg′lə dīt′) *n.* [< L. < Gr. < *trōglē*, a cave + *dyein*, to enter] 1. any of the prehistoric people who lived in caves 2. a person who lives alone in seclusion 3. anyone who lives in a crude, primitive way —**trog′lo·dyt′ic** (-dit′ik), **trog′lo·dyt′i·cal** *adj.*
tro·gon (trō′gän) *n.* [ModL. < Gr. prp. of *trōgein*, to gnaw] any of various bright-colored tropical birds
troi·ka (troi′kə) *n.* [Russ. < *troe*, three] 1. *a*) a Russian vehicle drawn by three horses abreast *b*) the horses 2. any group of three; esp., an association of three in authority
Troi·lus (troi′ləs, trō′i ləs) *Gr. Legend* a son of King Priam: in Chaucer and Shakespeare, Troilus was the lover of the faithless Cressida
Trois-Ri·vières (trwȧ rē vyer′) city in S Quebec, Canada, on the St. Lawrence: pop. 58,000: Eng. name *Three Rivers*
Tro·jan (trō′jən) *adj.* of ancient Troy, its people, etc. —*n.* 1. a native or inhabitant of ancient Troy 2. a strong, hard-working, determined person
Trojan horse *Gr. Legend* a huge, hollow wooden horse filled with Greek soldiers and left at the gates of Troy: when the Trojans brought it into the city, the soldiers crept out and opened the gates to the Greek army
Trojan War *Gr. Legend* the ten-year war waged against Troy by the Greeks to get back Helen: see HELEN OF TROY
troll[1] (trōl) *vt., vi.* [ME. *trollen*, to roll, wander] 1. to roll; revolve 2. *a*) to sing the parts of (a round, etc.) in succession *b*) to sing in a strong or full voice 3. *a*) to fish (*for* or *in*) with a moving line, esp. with a revolving lure trailed from a moving boat *b*) to move (a lure, etc.) thus —*n.* 1. a trolling 2. a lure, or a lure and line, used in trolling —**troll′er** *n.*
troll[2] (trōl) *n.* [ON.] in Scandinavian folklore, any of certain supernatural beings, giants or dwarfs, living underground or in caves
trol·ley (träl′ē) *n., pl.* **-leys** [< TROLL[1]] 1. a wheeled carriage, basket, etc. that runs suspended from an overhead track 2. a device, as a grooved wheel at the end of a pole, to carry electric current from an overhead wire to the motor of a streetcar, etc. 3. a trolley car; streetcar 4. [Brit.] a low cart —*vt., vi.* **-leyed, -ley·ing** to carry or go on a trolley
trolley bus an electric bus that gets its power from overhead wires by means of trolleys but does not run on tracks
trolley car an electric streetcar that gets its power from an overhead wire by means of a trolley
trol·lop (träl′əp) *n.* [prob. < G. *trolle*, a wench] a sexually promiscuous woman; specif., a prostitute
Trol·lope (träl′əp), **Anthony** 1815–82; Eng. novelist
trol·ly (träl′ē) *n., pl.* **-lies**, *vt., vi.* **-lied, -ly·ing** *var. of* TROLLEY
trom·bone (träm bōn′, träm′bōn) *n.* [It. < *tromba*, a trumpet < OHG. *trumba*] a large brass-wind instrument with a bell mouth and a long tube bent parallel to itself twice and having either a section that slides in or out (**slide trombone**) or valves (**valve trombone**) —**trom·bon′ist** *n.*

TROMBONE

tromp (trämp) *vi., vt. var. of* TRAMP
‡**trompe l'oeil** (trōnp lë′y′) [Fr., lit., trick of the eye] 1. a painting, etc. so realistic that it gives the illusion of being the actual thing depicted 2. any such illusion or effect
-tron (trän) [Gr. *-tron*, suffix of instrument] *a combining form meaning* instrument
troop (tro͞op) *n.* [< Fr. < OFr. < ML. *troppus*, a flock] 1. a group of persons or animals; band, herd, etc. 2. loosely, a great number; lot 3. [*pl.*] *a*) a body of soldiers *b*) soldiers [*45 troops*] 4. a subdivision of a cavalry regiment, corresponding to an infantry company 5. a unit of Boy Scouts or Girl Scouts under an adult leader —*vi.* 1. to gather or go as in a group 2. to walk, go, etc. —*vt.* to form into troops
troop·er (tro͞o′pər) *n.* [prec. + -ER] 1. an enlisted cavalryman 2. a cavalry horse 3. a mounted policeman 4. [Colloq.] a member of the police force of a State

troop·ship (tro͞op′ship′) ***n.*** a ship for carrying troops

trope (trōp) ***n.*** [< L. < Gr. *tropos,* a turning < *trepein,* to turn] **1.** a figure of speech **2.** the use of figures of speech

tro·phy (trō′fē) ***n., pl.* -phies** [< MFr. < L. < Gr. *tropaion,* token of an enemy's defeat, ult. < *trepein,* to turn] **1.** something taken from a defeated enemy and kept as a memorial of victory **2.** an animal skin, head, etc. displayed to show one's hunting prowess **3.** a prize, usually a silver cup, awarded as in a sports contest **4.** any memento

-tro·phy (trə fē) [Gr. *-trophia* < *trephein,* to nourish] *a combining form meaning* nutrition, growth *[hypertrophy]*

trop·ic (träp′ik) ***n.*** [< LL. < Gr. *tropikos,* of a turn (of the sun at the solstices) < *tropē,* a turn] **1.** *Astron.* either of two circles of the celestial sphere (the **Tropic of Cancer,** c. 23½° north and the **Tropic of Capricorn,** c. 23½° south) parallel to the celestial equator: they are the limits of the apparent north-and-south journey of the sun **2.** *Geog. a)* either of two parallels of latitude corresponding to these, on either side of the earth's equator *b)* [*also* **T-**] [*pl.*] the region of the earth between these latitudes, noted for its hot climate —***adj.*** of the tropics; tropical

-trop·ic (träp′ik, trō′pik) [< Gr. < *trepein,* to turn + -IC] *a combining form meaning* turning, changing, or otherwise responding to a (specified kind of) stimulus *[phototropic]* : also **-troph·ic** (träf′ik)

trop·i·cal (träp′i k'l) ***adj.*** of, in, characteristic of, or suitable for the tropics —**trop′i·cal·ly** ***adv.***

tropical fish any of various usually brightly colored fish, orig. from the tropics, kept in an aquarium (**tropical aquarium**) maintained at a constant, warm temperature

Tropical Zone *same as* TORRID ZONE

tropic bird any of various tropical sea birds having white feathers with black markings and a pair of long tail feathers

tro·pism (trō′piz'm) ***n.*** [< ff.] the tendency of a plant or animal to grow or turn toward or away from an external stimulus such as light —**tro·pis′tic** ***adj.***

-tro·pism (trə piz'm) [< Gr. *-tropos* (see TROPE) + -ISM] *a combining form meaning* tropism *[heliotropism]* : also **-tro·py** (trə pē)

trop·o·sphere (träp′ə sfir′, trō′pə-) ***n.*** [< Fr. < Gr. *tropos* (see TROPE) + Fr. *sphère* (see SPHERE)] the atmosphere from the earth's surface to the stratosphere, reaching from 6 to 12 miles, in which clouds form and in which temperature usually decreases as altitude increases —**trop′o·spher′ic** (-sfer′ik, -sfir′-) ***adj.***

‡**trop·po** (trôp′pô) ***adv.*** [It.] too; too much so: a direction in music, as in *allegro non troppo,* not too fast

trot (trät) ***vi.*** **trot′ted, trot′ting** [< OFr. < OHG. *trottōn,* to tread] **1.** to move, ride, go, etc. at a trot **2.** to hurry; run —***vt.*** to make trot —***n.*** **1.** a gait of a horse, etc. in which the legs are lifted in alternating diagonal pairs **2.** a person's gait between a walk and a run **3.** a horse race for trotters **4.** [Slang] *same as* PONY (*n.* 3) —**trot out** [Colloq.] to bring out for others to see or admire

troth (trôth, trōth, träth) ***n.*** [ult. < OE. *treowth,* truth] [Archaic] **1.** faithfulness; loyalty **2.** truth: chiefly in **in troth,** truly; indeed **3.** one's pledged word; promise: see also PLIGHT ONE'S TROTH (at PLIGHT[2]) —***vt.*** [Archaic] to pledge to marry

trot·line (trät′līn′) ***n.*** a strong fishing line suspended over the water and hung with short lines bearing baited hooks

Trot·sky (trät′skē; *Russ.* trôt′-), **Le·on** (lē′än) (born *Lev Davidovich Bronstein*) 1879–1940; Russ. revolutionist & writer: exiled (1929) —**Trot′sky·ism** ***n.*** —**Trot′sky·ist, Trot′sky·ite′** (-īt′) ***adj., n.***

trot·ter (trät′ər) ***n.*** **1.** an animal that trots; esp., a horse bred and trained for trotting races **2.** the foot of a sheep or pig used as food

trou·ba·dour (tro͞o′bə dôr′) ***n.*** [Fr. < Pr. < *trobar,* to compose in verse] any of a class of lyric poets who lived in southern France and northern Italy in the 11th, 12th, and 13th cent. and wrote poems of love and chivalry

trou·ble (trub′'l) ***vt.*** **-bled, -bling** [OFr. *trubler,* ult. < LL. *turbidare,* to trouble < L. *turbidus,* turbid] **1.** to disturb or agitate *[troubled* waters*]* **2.** to worry; harass; perturb **3.** to cause pain or discomfort to *[troubled* by headaches*]* **4.** to cause difficulty or inconvenience to **5.** to annoy, tease, bother, etc. —***vi.*** **1.** to take pains; bother *[*don't *trouble* to return it*]* **2.** to be distressed; worry —***n.*** **1.** a state of mental distress; worry **2.** *a)* a misfortune or mishap *b)* a difficult situation *c)* a condition of needing to be repaired, fixed, etc. *[*tire *trouble]* **3.** a cause of annoyance, distress, etc. **4.** public disturbance **5.** bother; pains *[*he took the *trouble* to listen*]* **6.** an illness —**in trouble** [Colloq.] pregnant when unmarried —**trou′bler** ***n.***

trou·ble·mak·er (-mā′kər) ***n.*** a person who habitually makes trouble for others —**trou′ble·mak′ing** ***n.***

trou·ble-shoot·er (-sho͞ot′ər) ***n.*** a person whose work is to find and repair or eliminate mechanical breakdowns or other sources of trouble —**trou′ble-shoot′ing** ***n.***

trou·ble·some (-səm) ***adj.*** full of or causing trouble —**trou′ble·some·ly** ***adv.*** —**trou′ble·some·ness** ***n.***

trou·blous (trub′ləs) ***adj.*** [Chiefly Literary] **1.** troubled; disturbed **2.** *same as* TROUBLESOME

trough (trôf) ***n.*** [OE. *trog*] **1.** a long, narrow, open container for holding water or food for animals **2.** a vessel of similar shape, as for kneading something **3.** a gutter, esp. under the eaves of a building, for carrying off rainwater **4.** a long, narrow hollow, as between waves **5.** a low point in business activity, etc. **6.** a long, narrow area of low barometric pressure

trounce (trouns) ***vt.*** **trounced, trounc′ing** [< ?] **1.** to beat; thrash **2.** [Colloq.] to defeat —**trounc′er** ***n.***

troupe (tro͞op) ***n.*** [Fr.] a group, esp. of actors, singers, etc.; company —***vi.*** **trouped, troup′ing** to travel as a member of a troupe —**troup′er** ***n.***

trou·sers (trou′zərz) ***n.pl.*** [< obs. *trouse* < ScotGael. *triubhas*] an outer garment, esp. for men and boys, reaching from the waist usually to the ankles and divided into separate coverings for the legs; pants —**trou′ser** ***adj.***

trous·seau (tro͞o′sō, tro͞o sō′) ***n., pl.*** **-seaux** (-sōz), **-seaus** [Fr. < OFr., dim. of *trousse,* a bundle] a bride's outfit of clothes, linen, etc.

trout (trout) ***n., pl.*** **trout, trouts:** see PLURAL, II, D, 2 [OE. *truht* < LL. < Gr. *trōktēs,* kind of fish < *trōgein,* to gnaw] any of various food and game fishes related to but smaller than the salmon and found chiefly in fresh water

trove (trōv) ***n.*** *short for* TREASURE-TROVE

trow (trō, trou) ***vi., vt.*** [OE. *treowian* < *treow,* faith] [Archaic] to believe, think, suppose, etc.

trow·el (trou′əl) ***n.*** [< MFr. < LL. < L. *trulla* < *trua,* ladle] **1.** a tool with a thin, flat, rectangular blade for smoothing plaster **2.** a tool with a thin, flat, pointed blade for applying and shaping mortar **3.** a tool with a pointed scoop for digging holes in a garden —***vt.*** **-eled** or **-elled, -el·ing** or **-el·ling** to spread, smooth, shape, dig, etc. with a trowel

TROWELS (A, brick; B, garden)

Troy (troi) **1.** ancient city in NW Asia Minor **2.** [after prec.] city in E N.Y., on the Hudson: pop. 57,000

troy (troi) ***adj.*** by or in troy weight

troy weight [< *Troyes,* a city in France] a system of weights for gold, silver, precious stones, etc.: see TABLES OF WEIGHTS AND MEASURES in Supplements

tru·ant (tro͞o′ənt) ***n.*** [OFr., a beggar < Celt.] **1.** a pupil who stays away from school without permission **2.** a person who shirks his duties —***adj.*** **1.** that is a truant **2.** idle; shiftless **3.** errant; straying —***vi.*** to be truant —**tru′an·cy** (-ən sē) ***n., pl.*** **-cies** —**tru′ant·ly** ***adv.***

truant officer a school official dealing with pupils who are truants: now usually called *attendance officer*

truce (tro͞os) ***n.*** [OE. *treow,* compact, faith] **1.** a period during a war in which the nations or peoples engaged in it agree to stop fighting for a time **2.** any pause in quarreling, conflict, etc.

truck[1] (truk) ***n.*** [prob. < L. < Gr. *trochos,* a wheel < *trechein,* to run] **1.** a small solid wheel, esp. for a gun carriage **2.** a small wooden disk with holes for halyards, esp. at the top of a flagpole or mast **3.** a frame with wheels at one end and handles at the other, used to carry trunks, crates, etc.: also **hand truck** **4.** a low frame or platform on wheels, for carrying heavy loads **5.** an automotive vehicle for hauling loads along highways, streets, etc. **6.** a swiveling frame, with two or more pairs of wheels, under each end of a railroad car, etc. —***vt.*** to carry on a truck —***vi.*** **1.** to do trucking **2.** to drive a truck as one's work

truck[2] (truk) ***vt., vi.*** [MFr. *troquer* < ?] to exchange; barter —***n.*** **1.** *same as* BARTER **2.** payment of wages in goods instead of money **3.** small commercial articles **4.** small articles of little value **5.** vegetables raised for sale in markets **6.** [Colloq.] dealings **7.** [Colloq.] rubbish

truck·age (truk′ij) ***n.*** **1.** transportation of goods by truck **2.** the charge for this

truck·er[1] (-ər) ***n.*** **1.** a truck driver **2.** a person or company doing trucking Also **truck′man** (-mən), *pl.* **-men**

truck·er[2] (-ər) ***n.*** **1.** a truck farmer **2.** a person who sells commodities or engages in barter

truck farm a farm where vegetables are grown to be marketed —**truck farmer** —**truck farming**

truck·ing (-iŋ) ***n.*** the business of carrying goods by truck

truck·le (truk′'l) ***n.*** [< L. *trochlea,* a pulley < Gr. < *trochos,* a wheel] **1.** orig., a small wheel **2.** *short for* TRUCKLE BED —***vi.*** **-led, -ling** to give in or yield too easily (*to*)
truckle bed *same as* TRUNDLE BED
truc·u·lent (truk′yoo lənt) ***adj.*** [< L. < *trux* (gen. *trucis*)] **1.** fierce; savage **2.** rude; harsh; scathing **3.** ready to fight —**truc′u·lence, truc′u·len·cy** ***n.*** —**truc′u·lent·ly** ***adv.***
Tru·deau (trōō′dō; *Fr.* trü dō′), **Pierre El·li·ott** (el′ē ət) 1921– ; prime minister of Canada (1968–79; 1980–)
trudge (truj) ***vi.*** **trudged, trudg′ing** [< ?] to walk, esp. wearily or laboriously —***n.*** a trudging —**trudg′er** ***n.***
true (trōō) ***adj.*** **tru′er, tru′est** [OE. *treowe*] **1.** faithful; loyal **2.** reliable; certain **3.** in accordance with fact; not false **4.** *a*) conforming to an original, standard, etc. *b*) exact; accurate; correct **5.** rightful; lawful *[*the *true* heirs*]* **6.** accurately fitted, placed, or shaped *[*the board is *true]* **7.** *a*) genuine; authentic *b*) rightly so called *[*a *true* scholar*]* **8.** [Archaic] honest, virtuous, or truthful —***adv.*** truly, truthfully, accurately, etc. —***vt.*** **trued, tru′ing** or **true′ing** to fit, place, or shape accurately (often with *up*) —***n.*** that which is true; truth or reality (with *the*) —**come true** to happen as predicted or expected —**in** (or **out of**) **true** that is (or is not) properly set, adjusted, etc. —**true to form** behaving as might be expected —**true′ness** ***n.***
true bill a bill of indictment endorsed by a grand jury
true-blue (trōō′blōō′) ***adj.*** very loyal; staunch
true·bred (-bred′) ***adj.*** *same as:* **1.** WELL-BRED **2.** PUREBRED
true-false test (trōō′fôls′) a test, as of knowledge, consisting of a series of statements to be identified as either "true" or "false"
true·heart·ed (-här′tid) ***adj.*** **1.** loyal; faithful **2.** honest or sincere —**true′heart′ed·ness** ***n.***
true-life (-līf′) ***adj.*** like what happens in real life; true to reality *[*a *true-life* story*]*
true·love (-luv′) ***n.*** (one's) sweetheart; a loved one
truelove knot a kind of bowknot that is hard to untie, a symbol of lasting love: also **true′-lov′er's knot**
true ribs ribs that are attached by cartilage directly to the breastbone; in man, the upper seven pairs of ribs
truf·fle (truf′'l, trōō′f'l) ***n.*** [< Fr. < OIt. *truffa,* ult. < L. *tuber,* a knob] any of certain related fleshy, edible fungi that grow underground, esp. a European kind regarded as a delicacy
tru·ism (trōō′iz'm) ***n.*** a statement the truth of which is obvious and well known —**tru·is′tic** ***adj.***
trull (trul) ***n.*** [G. *trolle*] a prostitute or trollop
tru·ly (trōō′lē) ***adv.*** **1.** in a true manner; genuinely, faithfully, rightfully, etc. **2.** really; indeed
Tru·man (trōō′mən), **Harry S.** 1884–1972; 33d president of the U.S. (1945–53)
trump[1] (trump) ***n.*** [altered < TRIUMPH] **1.** any playing card of a suit that ranks higher than any other suit during the playing of a hand **2.** [*occas. pl. with sing. v.*] a suit of trumps **3.** any advantage held in reserve until needed **4.** [Colloq.] a fine person —***vt.*** **1.** to take (a trick, card, etc.) with a trump **2.** to outdo; surpass —***vi.*** to play a trump —**trump up** to make up (a charge against someone, an excuse, etc.) in order to deceive
trump[2] (trump) ***n., vi., vt.*** [OFr. *trompe*] *archaic or poet. var. of* TRUMPET
trump·er·y (trum′pər ē) ***n., pl.*** **-er·ies** [< MFr. < *tromper,* to deceive] **1.** something showy but worthless **2.** nonsense —***adj.*** showy but worthless
trum·pet (trum′pit) ***n.*** [< MFr. dim. of *trompe,* trumpet] **1.** a brass-wind instrument with a blaring tone, consisting of a tube in an oblong loop or loops, flared at the end opposite the mouthpiece **2.** something shaped like a trumpet; esp., *same as* EAR TRUMPET **3.** a sound like that of a trumpet —***vi.*** **1.** to blow a trumpet **2.** to make a sound like a trumpet —***vt.*** **1.** to sound on or as on a trumpet **2.** to proclaim loudly

TRUMPET

trumpet creeper **1.** a vine of the southern U.S., with red, trumpet-shaped flowers **2.** a related vine of China Also **trumpet vine**
trum·pet·er (-ər) ***n.*** **1.** a trumpet player **2.** a person who proclaims or heralds something **3.** a long-legged, long-necked S. American bird having a loud cry **4.** *same as* TRUMPETER SWAN **5.** a domestic pigeon with feathered feet and a rounded crest
trumpeter swan a N. American wild swan with a loud cry
trumpet honeysuckle an American honeysuckle with red-dish, trumpet-shaped flowers
trun·cate (truŋ′kāt) ***vt.*** **-cat·ed, -cat·ing** [< L. pp. of *truncare,* to cut off < *truncus,* a stem] to shorten by cutting; lop —***adj.*** *same as* TRUNCATED —**trun·ca′tion** ***n.***
trun·cat·ed (-id) ***adj.*** **1.** cut short or appearing as if cut short **2.** having the vertex cut off by a plane
trun·cheon (trun′chən) ***n.*** [< OFr., ult. < L. *truncus,* a stem] **1.** a staff carried as a symbol of authority **2.** [Chiefly Brit.] a policeman's stick
trun·dle (trun′d'l) ***n.*** [OE. *trendel,* a circle < *trendan,* to roll] **1.** a small wheel **2.** *short for* TRUNDLE BED —***vt., vi.*** **-dled, -dling** to roll along
trundle bed a low bed on casters, that can be rolled under a higher bed when not in use
trunk (truŋk) ***n.*** [< OFr. < L. *truncus,* trunk, orig., mutilated] **1.** the main stem of a tree **2.** a human body or animal body, not including the head and limbs **3.** the thorax of an insect **4.** the main body of a nerve, blood vessel, etc. **5.** a long, flexible snout, as of an elephant **6.** a large, reinforced box for carrying a traveler's clothes, etc. **7.** a large, long, boxlike pipe, etc. that conveys air, water, etc. **8.** [*pl.*] *same as* TRUNK HOSE **9.** [*pl.*] men's shorts worn for athletics, as boxing, swimming, etc. **10.** *short for* TRUNK LINE **11.** a compartment in an automobile, usually in the rear, for a spare tire, luggage, etc. **12.** *Archit.* the shaft of a column
trunk·fish (-fish′) ***n., pl.*** **-fish′, -fish′es:** see FISH a tropical fish whose body is encased in fused bony plates
trunk hose full, baggy breeches reaching about halfway down the thigh, worn in the 16th and 17th cent.
trunk line a main line of a railroad, telephone system, etc.
trun·nion (trun′yən) ***n.*** [Fr. *trognon,* a stump] either of two projecting pins on each side of a cannon, on which it pivots
truss (trus) ***vt.*** [OFr. *trousser*] **1.** orig., to tie into a bundle **2.** to tie or bind (often with *up*) **3.** to skewer or bind the wings, etc. of (a fowl) before cooking **4.** to support or strengthen with a truss —***n.*** **1.** a bundle or pack **2.** an iron band around a mast, to which a yard is fastened **3.** a rigid framework of beams, struts, etc. for supporting a roof, bridge, etc. **4.** an appliance worn for supporting a hernia, usually a pad on a belt
trust (trust) ***n.*** [ON. *traust*] **1.** *a*) firm belief in the honesty, reliability, etc. of another *b*) the one trusted **2.** confident expectation, hope, etc. *[*have *trust* in the future*]* **3.** *a*) the fact of having confidence placed in one *b*) the responsibility resulting from this **4.** care; custody **5.** something entrusted to one; charge **6.** confidence in a purchaser's intention or future ability to pay for goods, etc.; credit **7.** *a*) an industrial or business combination of corporations, with control vested in a single board of trustees who are able to eliminate competition, fix prices, etc. *b*) *same as* CARTEL (sense 3) **8.** *Law a*) confidence placed in a person by giving him nominal ownership of property that he is to keep, use, or administer for another's benefit *b*) the property involved —***vi.*** **1.** to have trust or faith; be confident **2.** to hope (*for*) **3.** to give business credit —***vt.*** **1.** to have trust in; rely on, etc. **2.** to commit (*to* a person's care) **3.** to put something confidently in the charge of *[*to *trust* a lawyer with one's case*]* **4.** to allow to do something without fear of the outcome **5.** to believe or suppose **6.** to hope **7.** to grant business credit to —***adj.*** **1.** relating to a trust or trusts **2.** held in trust **3.** acting as a trustee —**in trust** in the condition of being entrusted to another's care —**trust to** to rely on —**trust′a·ble** ***adj.***
trus·tee (trus tē′) ***n.*** **1.** a person to whom another's property or the management of another's property is entrusted **2.** a nation under whose control a trust territory is placed **3.** any of a group of persons appointed to manage the affairs of a college, hospital, etc. —***vt.*** **-teed′, -tee′ing** to commit (property or management) to a trustee or trustees
trus·tee·ship (-ship′) ***n.*** **1.** the position or function of a trustee **2.** *a*) a commission from the United Nations to a country to administer a trust territory *b*) the state or fact of being a trust territory
trust·ful (trust′fəl) ***adj.*** full of trust or confidence in another or others; trusting —**trust′ful·ly** ***adv.*** —**trust′ful·ness** ***n.***
trust fund money, stock, etc. held in trust
trust·ing (trus′tiŋ) ***adj.*** that trusts; trustful —**trust′ing·ly** ***adv.*** —**trust′ing·ness** ***n.***
trust territory a territory placed by the United Nations under the control of a country that manages the affairs of the territory
trust·wor·thy (trust′wur′*th*ē) ***adj.*** **-thi·er -thi·est** worthy of trust; dependable; reliable —**trust′wor′thi·ly** ***adv.*** —**trust′wor′thi·ness** ***n.***
trust·y (trus′tē) ***adj.*** **trust′i·er, trust′i·est** that can be relied upon; dependable —***n., pl.*** **trust′ies** a trusted person; specif., a convict granted special privileges as a trustworthy person —**trust′i·ly** ***adv.*** —**trust′i·ness** ***n.***
truth (trōōth) ***n., pl.*** **truths** (trōō*th*z, trōōths) [OE. *treowth*] **1.** the quality or state of being true; specif., *a*) orig., loyalty *b*) sincerity; honesty *c*) the quality of being in agreement with reality or facts *d*) reality; actual existence *e*) agreement with a standard, rule, etc.; correctness **2.** that which is true **3.** an established or verified fact, etc. **4.** a particular belief or teaching regarded by the speaker as the true one (often with *the*) —**in truth** truly; in fact —**of a truth** certainly

truth drug an anesthetic or hypnotic, as thiopental sodium, regarded as tending to make a person taking it willing to answer questions: also **truth serum**

truth·ful (tro͞oth′fəl) ***adj.*** **1.** telling the truth; honest **2.** agreeing with fact or reality —**truth′ful·ly** ***adv.*** —**truth′ful·ness** ***n.***

try (trī) ***vt.*** **tried, try′ing** [OFr. *trier,* ult. < ? L. pp. of *terere,* to thresh grain] **1.** to melt or render (fat, etc.) to get (the oil): usually with *out* **2.** *a)* to examine and decide (a case) in a law court *b)* to determine legally the guilt or innocence of (a person) **3.** to put to the proof; test **4.** to test the faith, patience, etc. of; afflict *[he was sorely tried]* **5.** to subject to a severe test or strain **6.** to test the effect of; experiment with *[try this recipe]* **7.** to attempt; endeavor *[try to forget]* —***vi.*** **1.** to make an effort, attempt, etc. **2.** to experiment —***n.,*** *pl.* **tries** an attempt; effort; trial —**try on** to test the fit, etc. of (a garment) by putting it on —**try one's hand at** to attempt (to do something), esp. for the first time —**try out** **1.** to test the quality, value, etc. of, as by using **2.** to test one's fitness, as to be on a team, act a role, etc.

try·ing (-iŋ) ***adj.*** that tries one's patience; annoying; exasperating; irksome —**try′ing·ly** ***adv.***

try·out (trī′out′) ***n.*** [Colloq.] **1.** a chance to prove, or a test to determine, one's fitness to be on a team, act a role, etc. **2.** a performance of a play before its official opening, as to test audience reaction

tryp·sin (trip′sin) ***n.*** [G., prob. < Gr. *tryein,* to wear away + G. *(pe)psin:* see PEPSIN] a digestive enzyme in the pancreatic juice: it changes proteins into polypeptides —**tryp′tic** ***adj.***

try·sail (trī′s'l, -sāl′) ***n.*** [< naut. phr. *a try,* position of lying to in a storm] a small, stout, fore-and-aft sail used for keeping a vessel's head to the wind in a storm

try square an instrument for testing the accuracy of square work and for marking off right angles

tryst (trist, trīst) ***n.*** [OFr. *triste,* hunting station] **1.** an appointment to meet at a specified time and place, esp. one made secretly by lovers **2.** *a)* a meeting held by appointment *b)* the place of such a meeting: also **trysting place** —**tryst′er** ***n.***

tsar (tsär, zär) ***n.*** *var. sp. of* CZAR —**tsar′dom** ***n.*** —**tsar′ism** ***n.*** —**tsar′ist** ***adj., n.***

Tschaikowsky *see* TCHAIKOVSKY

tset·se fly (tset′sē, tsēt′-, set′-, sēt′-) [Afrik. < the Bantu name] any of several small flies of central and southern Africa, including the one that carries sleeping sickness

T-shirt (tē′shurt′) ***n.*** [so named because T-shaped] a collarless pullover shirt with short sleeves

Tsing·tao (chiŋ′dou′) seaport in NE China, on the Yellow Sea: pop. 1,144,000

tsk ***interj., n.*** a clicking or sucking sound made with the tongue, to express disapproval, sympathy, etc.

tsp. **1.** teaspoon(s) **2.** teaspoonful(s)

T square a T-shaped ruler for drawing parallel lines

T-strap (tē′strap′) ***n.*** **1.** a T-shaped strap over the instep of a shoe **2.** a woman's or girl's shoe with such a strap

tsu·na·mi (tso͞o nä′mē) ***n.*** [Jap. < *tsu,* a harbor + *nami,* wave] a huge sea wave caused by a disturbance under water, as an earthquake: popularly, but inaccurately, called *tidal wave* —**tsu·na′mic** (-mik) ***adj.***

Tu. Tuesday

tu·a·ta·ra (to͞o′ə tä′rə) ***n.*** [< Maori < *tua,* back + *tara,* spine] a primitive, lizardlike reptile of islands near New Zealand, with a row of spines in the middle of the back

tub (tub) ***n.*** [MDu. *tubbe*] **1.** *a)* a round, open, wooden container, usually formed of staves and hoops fastened around a flat bottom *b)* any large, open container of metal, etc., as for washing *c)* as much as a tub will hold **2.** *a) short for* BATHTUB *b)* [Brit. Colloq.] a bath in a tub **3.** [Colloq.] a slow-moving, clumsy ship or boat —***vt., vi.*** **tubbed, tub′bing** **1.** [Colloq.] to wash in a tub **2.** [Brit. Colloq.] to bathe (oneself) —**tub′ba·ble** ***adj.*** —**tub′ber** ***n.***

tu·ba (to͞o′bə, tyo͞o′-) ***n.,*** *pl.* **tu′bas, tu′bae** (-bē) [L., a trumpet] a large, brass-wind musical instrument having three to five valves

tub·al (to͞o′b'l, tyo͞o′-) ***adj.*** of or in a tube, esp. a Fallopian tube *[a tubal pregnancy]*

tub·by (tub′ē) ***adj.*** **-bi·er, -bi·est** **1.** shaped like a tub **2.** short and fat —**tub′bi·ness** ***n.***

tube (to͞ob, tyo͞ob) ***n.*** [Fr. < L. *tubus,* a pipe] **1.** *a)* a slender, hollow cylinder or pipe of metal, glass, rubber, etc., in which gases and liquids can flow or be kept *b)* an instrument, part, organ, etc. resembling a tube *[a bronchial tube]* **2.** a rubber casing inflated with air and used, esp. formerly, with an outer casing to form an automotive tire **3.** an enclosed, hollow cylinder of thin, pliable metal, etc. with a screw cap at one end, used for holding pastes or semiliquids **4.** *short for: a)* ELECTRON TUBE *b)* VACUUM TUBE **5.** *a)* an underground tunnel for a railroad, subway, etc. *b)* [Brit. Colloq.] a subway —***vt.*** **tubed, tub′ing** **1.** to provide with, place in, or pass through a tube or tubes **2.** to make tubular —**down the tube** (or **tubes**) [Colloq.] in or into a condition of failure, defeat, loss, etc. —**the tube** [Colloq.] television —**tu′bate** ***adj.*** —**tube′like′** ***adj.***

tube foot any of numerous projecting, water-filled tubes in most echinoderms, used in moving about, handling food, etc.

tube·less tire (-lis) a tire for an automotive vehicle, consisting of a single air-filled unit without an inner tube

tu·ber (to͞o′bər, tyo͞o′-) ***n.*** [L., lit., a swelling] **1.** a short, thickened, fleshy part of an underground stem, as a potato **2.** a tubercle or swelling

tu·ber·cle (-k'l) ***n.*** [L. *tuberculum,* dim. of *tuber:* see prec.] **1.** a small, rounded part growing out from a bone or from the root of a plant **2.** any abnormal hard nodule or swelling; specif., the typical nodular lesion of tuberculosis

tubercle bacillus the bacterium causing tuberculosis

tu·ber·cu·lar (too bur′kyə lər, tyoo-) ***adj.*** **1.** of, like, or having tubercles **2.** of or having tuberculosis **3.** caused by the tubercle bacillus Also **tu·ber′cu·lous** (-ləs) —***n.*** a person having tuberculosis

tu·ber·cu·lin (-lin) ***n.*** a sterile solution prepared from a culture of the tubercle bacillus and injected into the skin as a test for tuberculosis

tu·ber·cu·lo·sis (too bur′kyə lō′sis, tyoo-) ***n.*** [ModL.: see TUBERCLE & -OSIS] an infectious disease caused by the tubercle bacillus and causing tubercles to form in body tissues; specif., tuberculosis of the lungs; consumption

tube·rose (to͞ob′rōz′, tyo͞ob′-) ***n.*** [ModL. < L. *tuberosus,* TUBEROUS] a perennial Mexican plant with a tuberous rootstock and white, sweet-scented flowers

tu·ber·ous (to͞o′bər əs, tyo͞o′-) ***adj.*** [< Fr. < L. *tuberosus:* see TUBER & -OUS] **1.** covered with rounded, wartlike swellings; knobby **2.** of, like, or having a tuber or tubers Also **tu′ber·ose′** (-ōs′) —**tu′ber·os′i·ty** (-bə räs′ə tē) ***n.,*** *pl.* **-ties**

tu·bi·fex (to͞o′bə feks′, tyo͞o′-) ***n.,*** *pl.* **-fex′es, -fex′** [ModL. < L. *tubus,* a pipe + *-fex* < *facere,* to make] a small freshwater worm, found esp. in polluted waters and often used as food for aquarium fish

tub·ing (to͞ob′iŋ, tyo͞ob′-) ***n.*** **1.** a series or system of tubes **2.** material in the form of a tube **3.** a length of tube

tu·bu·lar (to͞o′byə lər, tyo͞o′-) ***adj.*** [< L. dim. of *tubus,* a pipe] **1.** of or shaped like a tube **2.** made with tubes Also **tu′bu·late** (-lit) —**tu′bu·lar′i·ty** (-lar′ə tē) ***n.***

tu·bule (to͞ob′yool, tyo͞ob′-) ***n.*** a small tube

tuck (tuk) ***vt.*** [< MDu. *tucken,* to tuck & cognate OE. *tucian,* to tug] **1.** to pull up or gather up in a fold or folds, as to make shorter **2.** to sew a fold or folds in (a garment) **3.** *a)* to thrust the edges of (a sheet, napkin, etc.) under or in, in order to make secure (usually with *up, in,* etc.) *b)* to cover or wrap snugly *[tuck the baby in bed]* **4.** to put or press snugly into a small space; cram *[to tuck shoes in a suitcase]* **5.** to put into a secluded, empty, or isolated spot —***vi.*** **1.** to draw together; pucker **2.** to make tucks —***n.*** a sewed fold in a garment —**tuck away** **1.** to eat or drink heartily **2.** to put aside, as for future use —**tuck in** **1.** to pull in or contract (one's chin, stomach, etc.) **2.** to eat or drink heartily

tuck·er[1] (tuk′ər) ***n.*** **1.** a person or device that makes tucks **2.** a neck and shoulder covering formerly worn with a low-cut bodice by women **3.** [Austral. Slang] food

tuck·er[2] (tuk′ər) ***vt.*** [prob. < *tuck,* in obs. sense "to punish, rebuke"] [Colloq.] to tire (*out*); weary

Tuc·son (to͞o′sän, to͞o sän′) [Sp. < Pima *tu-uk-so-on,* black base, after a dark stratum in a nearby mountain] city in S Ariz.: pop. 331,000 (met. area 532,000)

Tu·dor (to͞o′dər, tyo͞o′-) ruling family of England (1485–1603) —***adj.*** designating or of a style of architecture popular under the Tudors, characterized by shallow moldings, extensive paneling, etc.

Tues., Tue. Tuesday

Tues·day (to͞oz′dē, tyo͞oz′-; -dā) ***n.*** [OE. *Tiwes dæg,* lit., day of the god of war *Tiw*] the third day of the week

Tues·days (-dēz, -dāz) ***adv.*** on or during every Tuesday

tu·fa (to͞o′fə, tyo͞o′-) ***n.*** [It. *tufo* < L. *tofus*] a porous rock formed of calcium carbonate, etc. deposited by springs —**tu·fa′ceous** (-fā′shəs) ***adj.***

tuff (tuf) ***n.*** [< Fr. < It. *tufo,* TUFA] a porous rock formed from volcanic ash, dust, etc. —**tuff·a′ceous** (-ā′shəs) ***adj.***

tuf·fet (tuf′ət) ***n.*** [< TUFT] **1.** a tuft of grass **2.** [by misunderstanding of a nursery rhyme] a low stool

tuft (tuft) ***n.*** [OFr. *tufe,* prob. < L. *tufa,* helmet crest] **1.** a bunch of hairs, feathers, grass, etc. growing or tied closely together **2.** *a)* the fluffy ball forming the end of any of the clusters of threads drawn tightly through a quilt, etc. to hold the padding in place *b)* a decorative button to which

fat, āpe, cär, ten, ēven, is, bīte; gō, hôrn, to͞ol, look; oil, out; up, fur; get; joy; yet; chin; she; thin, *th*en; zh, leisure; ŋ, ring; ə for *a* in *ago, e* in *agent, i* in *sanity, o* in *comply, u* in *focus;* ′ as in *able* (ā′b'l); Fr. bål; ë, Fr. coeur; ö, Fr. feu; Fr. mon; ô, Fr. coq; ü, Fr. duc; r, Fr. cri; H, G. ich; kh, G. doch; ‡foreign; *hypothetical; < derived from. See inside front cover.

a tuft is fastened —*vt.* **1.** to provide or decorate with a tuft or tufts **2.** to keep the padding of (a quilt, mattress, etc.) in place by regularly spaced tufts —*vi.* to grow in or form into tufts —**tuft'ed** *adj.* —**tuft'er** *n.* —**tuft'y** *adj.*

tug (tug) *vi.* **tugged, tug'ging** [prob. < ON. *toga,* to draw] **1.** to pull hard (often with *at*) **2.** to labor; toil; struggle —*vt.* **1.** to pull at with force; strain at **2.** to drag; haul **3.** to tow with a tugboat —*n.* **1.** a hard pull **2.** a great effort or a struggle, strain, etc. **3.** a rope, chain, strap, etc. used for pulling **4.** *shortened form of* TUGBOAT —**tug'ger** *n.* —**tug'ging·ly** *adv.*

tug·boat (-bōt') *n.* a small, powerful boat used for towing or pushing ships, barges, etc.

tug of war **1.** a contest in which two teams pull at opposite ends of a rope, each trying to drag the other across a central line **2.** any hard struggle

tu·grik (to͞o'grik) *n.* [Mongol. *dughurik,* lit., wheel] *see* MONETARY UNITS, table (Mongolia)

tu·i·tion (too wish'ən, tyoo-) *n.* [< OFr. < L. *tuitio,* protection < pp. of *tueri,* to protect] **1.** the fee for instruction, esp. at a college or private school **2.** [Now Rare] teaching; instruction —**tu·i'tion·al** *adj.*

tu·la·re·mi·a (to͞o'lə rē'mē ə) *n.* [ModL. < *Tulare* County, California + -EMIA] an infectious disease of rodents, esp. rabbits, sometimes transmitted to man: also sp. **tu'la·rae'mi·a** —**tu'la·re'mic** *adj.*

tu·lip (to͞o'lip, tyo͞o'-) *n.* [< Fr. < Turk. *tülbend,* TURBAN: the flower resembles a turban] **1.** any of various spring-blooming bulb plants, with long, pointed leaves and a large, cup-shaped flower **2.** the flower or bulb

tulip tree a tree of the magnolia family with tulip-shaped, greenish-yellow flowers, and long, conelike fruit: also called **tulip poplar**

tu·lip·wood (-wood') *n.* **1.** the light, soft wood of the tulip tree, used for furniture, etc. **2.** any of several woods having streaks of color

tulle (to͞ol; *Fr.* tül) *n.* [< *Tulle,* city in France] a thin, fine netting of silk, rayon, nylon, etc., used for veils, scarfs, etc.

Tul·ly (tul'ē) *Englished name of* (Marcus) Tullius (CICERO)

Tul·sa (tul'sə) [< Creek Indian name] city in NE Okla., on the Arkansas River: pop. 361,000 (met. area 679,000)

tum·ble (tum'b'l) *vi.* **-bled, -bling** [OE. *tumbian,* to jump, dance] **1.** to do somersaults, handsprings, or similar acrobatic feats **2.** *a)* to fall suddenly or helplessly *b)* to undergo a sudden drop or downfall *[prices tumbled,* the government *tumbled]* **3.** to stumble or trip **4.** to toss or roll about **5.** to move in a hasty, disorderly manner **6.** [Colloq.] to understand suddenly (with *to*) —*vt.* **1.** to cause to tumble **2.** to put into disorder as by tossing here and there —*n.* **1.** a tumbling; specif., *a)* a somersault, handspring, etc. *b)* a fall **2.** disorder; confusion **3.** a confused heap —**give** (or **get**) **a tumble** [Colloq.] to give (or get) some favorable or affectionate notice, attention, etc.

tum·ble·bug (-bug') *n.* any of various beetles that roll balls of dung, in which they deposit their eggs and in which the larvae develop

tum·ble·down (-doun') *adj.* ready to tumble down; dilapidated

tum·bler (tum'blər) *n.* **1.** an acrobat or gymnast who does somersaults, handsprings, etc. **2.** a kind of pigeon that does somersaults in flight **3.** *a)* an ordinary drinking glass with no foot or stem *b)* its contents **4.** a part of a lock whose position must be changed by a key in order to release the bolt **5.** a device for tumbling things about

tum·ble·weed (tum'b'l wēd') *n.* any of various plants which break off near the ground in autumn and are blown about by the wind

tum·brel, tum·bril (tum'brəl) *n.* [< MFr. < *tomber,* to fall] **1.** a farmer's cart that can be tilted for emptying **2.** any of the carts used to carry the condemned to the guillotine during the French Revolution

tu·me·fy (to͞o'mə fī', tyo͞o'-) *vt., vi.* **-fied', -fy'ing** [< Fr., ult. < L. < *tumere,* to swell + *facere,* to make] to swell or cause to swell —**tu'me·fac'tion** (-fak'shən) *n.*

tu·mes·cence (to͞o mes''ns, tyo͞o-) *n.* [< L. prp. of *tumescere,* to swell up] **1.** a swelling; distention **2.** a swollen or distended part —**tu·mes'cent** *adj.*

tu·mid (to͞o'mid, tyo͞o'-) *adj.* [< L. < *tumere,* to swell] **1.** swollen; bulging **2.** inflated; pompous —**tu·mid'i·ty, tu'mid·ness** *n.* —**tu'mid·ly** *adv.*

tum·my (tum'ē) *n., pl.* **-mies** stomach: a child's word

tu·mor (to͞o'mər, tyo͞o'-) *n.* [L. < *tumere,* to swell] an abnormal growth of tissue in some part of the body, that is either benign or malignant: Brit. sp. **tu'mour** —**tu'mor·ous** *adj.*

tump·line (tump'līn) *n.* [*tump,* a tumpline < AmInd.] a broad band passed across the forehead and behind across the shoulders to support a pack on the back

tu·mult (to͞o'mult, tyo͞o'-) *n.* [< MFr. < L. *tumultus* < *tumere,* to swell] **1.** noisy commotion, as of a crowd; uproar **2.** confusion; agitation; disturbance **3.** great emotional disturbance

tu·mul·tu·ous (too mul'choo wəs) *adj.* **1.** full of or characterized by tumult; wild and noisy; uproarious **2.** making a tumult **3.** greatly disturbed —**tu·mul'tu·ous·ly** *adv.* —**tu·mul'tu·ous·ness** *n.*

tu·mu·lus (to͞o'myə ləs, tyo͞o'-) *n., pl.* **-li'** (-lī'), **-lus·es** [L., a mound] an artificial mound, esp. an ancient burial mound

tun (tun) *n.* [OE. *tunne,* large cask & OFr. *tonne,* both < ML. *tunna* < Celt.] **1.** a large cask for liquids **2.** a measure of capacity for liquids, usually 252 wine gallons —*vt.* **tunned, tun'ning** to store in a tun or tuns

tu·na[1] (to͞o'nə, tyo͞o'-) *n., pl.* **tu'na, tu'nas:** see PLURAL, II, D, 2 [AmSp. < Sp. < Ar. < L. *thunnus:* see TUNNY] **1.** a large, ocean, food and game fish of the mackerel group: also called **bluefin tuna** **2.** any of various related fishes, as the albacore **3.** the flesh of the tuna, often canned for food: also called **tuna fish**

tu·na[2] (to͞o'nə, tyo͞o'-) *n.* [Sp., of WInd. origin] any of various prickly pears

tun·a·ble (to͞on'ə b'l, tyo͞on'-) *adj.* capable of being tuned: also sp. **tune'a·ble** —**tun'a·ble·ness** *n.*

tun·dra (tun'drə, toon'-) *n.* [Russ.] any of the vast, nearly level, treeless plains of the arctic regions

tune (to͞on, tyo͞on) *n.* [ME., var. of *tone,* TONE] **1.** a succession of musical tones forming a rhythmic, catchy whole; melody; air **2.** the condition of having correct musical pitch, or of being in key; also, harmony; concord: now chiefly in phrases **in tune, out of tune** —*vt.* **tuned, tun'ing** **1.** to adjust (a musical instrument) to some standard of pitch **2.** to adapt (music, the voice, etc.) to some pitch, tone, etc. **3.** to adapt to some condition, mood, etc. **4.** to adjust (an electronics circuit, a motor, etc.) to the proper or desired performance —*vi.* to be in tune; harmonize —**call the tune** to be in control —**change one's tune** to change one's attitude or manner: also **sing a different tune** —**to the tune of** [Colloq.] to the amount of —**tune in** **1.** to adjust a radio or television receiver to a given frequency or channel so as to receive (a specified station, program, etc.) **2.** [Slang] to become or make aware, knowing, etc. —**tune out** **1.** to adjust a radio or television receiver so as to get rid of (interference, etc.) **2.** [Slang] to turn one's attention, sympathies, etc. away from —**tune up** **1.** to adjust (musical instruments) to the same pitch **2.** to put (an engine) into good working condition —**tun'er** *n.*

tune·ful (-fəl) *adj.* full of tunes or melody; musical; melodious —**tune'ful·ly** *adv.* —**tune'ful·ness** *n.*

tune·less (-lis) *adj.* not musical or melodious —**tune'less·ly** *adv.* —**tune'less·ness** *n.*

tune·up, tune-up (-up') *n.* an adjusting, as of an engine, to the proper condition

tung oil (tuŋ) [< Chin. *yu-t'ung* < *yu,* oil + *t'ung,* name of the tree] a fast-drying oil from the seeds of a subtropical tree (**tung tree**), used in paints, varnishes, etc.

tung·sten (tuŋ'stən) *n.* [Sw. < *tung,* heavy + *sten,* stone] a hard, heavy, gray-white, metallic chemical element, used in steel, electric lamp filaments, etc.: symbol, W; at. wt., 183.85; at. no., 74 —**tung'stic** (-stik) *adj.*

tu·nic (to͞o'nik, tyo͞o'-) *n.* [L. *tunica*] **1.** a loose, gownlike garment worn by men and women in ancient Greece and Rome **2.** a blouselike garment extending to the hips or lower, often belted **3.** [Chiefly Brit.] a short coat forming part of the uniform of soldiers, policemen, etc. **4.** a short vestment worn by a subdeacon **5.** *Biol.* a covering membrane or tissue

tu·ni·cate (to͞o'ni kit, tyo͞o'-; -kāt') *adj.* [< L. pp. of *tunicare,* to put on a tunic] *Bot., Zool.* covered with or having a tunic or tunics: also **tu'ni·cat'ed** (-kāt'id) —*n.* any of several sea animals having a saclike body enclosed by a thick cellulose tunic

tuning fork a small steel instrument with two prongs, which when struck sounds a certain fixed tone: it is used as a guide in tuning instruments, etc.

Tu·nis (to͞o'nis, tyo͞o'-) capital of Tunisia, on an inlet (**Gulf of Tunis**) of the Mediterranean: pop. 642,000

Tu·ni·sia (to͞o nē'zhə, tyo͞o-; -nish'ə, -nish'ē ə) country in N Africa, on the Mediterranean: 48,332 sq. mi.; pop. 5,137,000; cap. Tunis —**Tu·ni'sian** *adj., n.*

tun·nage (tun'ij) *n. same as* TONNAGE

tun·nel (tun''l) *n.* [MFr. *tonnelle,* vault < OFr. dim. of *tonne,* a tun] **1.** an underground or underwater passageway for automobiles, trains, etc. **2.** an animal's burrow **3.** any tunnellike passage, as one in a mine —*vt.* **-neled** or **-nelled, -nel·ing** or **-nel·ling** **1.** to make a tunnel through or under **2.** to make (one's way) by digging a tunnel —*vi.* to make a tunnel —**tun'nel·er, tun'nel·ler** *n.*

tun·ny (tun'ē) *n., pl.* **-nies, -ny:** see PLURAL, II, D, 1 [< MFr. < Pr. < L. < Gr. *thynnos*] *same as* TUNA[1] (senses 1 & 2)

tu·pe·lo (to͞o'pə lō') *n., pl.* **-los'** [< Creek Indian *ito,* tree + *opilwa,* a swamp] **1.** any of several gum trees of the southern U.S. **2.** the fine-textured wood of any of these trees, used for mallets, furniture, etc.

Tu·pi (to͞o pē', to͞o'pē) *n.* [Tupi, comrade] **1.** *pl.* **Tu-**

pis′, Tu·pi′ any member of a group of S. American Indian tribes living chiefly along the lower Amazon **2.** their language

tup·pence (tup′'ns) ***n.*** *same as* TWOPENCE

tuque (to͞ok, tyo͞ok) ***n.*** [CanadFr. < Fr. *toque,* a cap] a kind of knitted winter cap

tur·ban (tʉr′bən) ***n.*** [< MFr. < It. or Port. < Turk. *tülbend,* dial. form of *dülbend* < Per.] **1.** a headdress of Moslem origin, consisting of a cloth wound in folds about the head, often over a cap **2.** any head covering or hat made like or resembling this —**tur′baned** ***adj.***

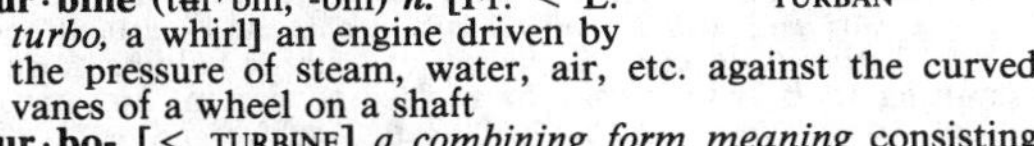

TURBAN

tur·bid (tʉr′bid) ***adj.*** [< L. < *turba,* a crowd] **1.** muddy or cloudy from having the sediment stirred up **2.** thick or dark, as clouds or smoke **3.** confused or perplexed; muddled —**tur·bid′i·ty, tur′bid·ness** ***n.*** —**tur′bid·ly** ***adv.***

tur·bine (tʉr′bin, -bīn) ***n.*** [Fr. < L. *turbo,* a whirl] an engine driven by the pressure of steam, water, air, etc. against the curved vanes of a wheel on a shaft

tur·bo- [< TURBINE] *a combining form meaning* consisting of or driven by a turbine

tur·bo·fan (tʉr′bō fan′) ***n.*** **1.** a turbojet engine in which additional thrust is obtained from the part of the air that bypasses the engine and is accelerated by a fan: in full, **turbofan engine** **2.** a fan driven by a turbine

tur·bo·jet (-jet′) ***n.*** **1.** a jet engine with a turbine-driven air compressor that compresses air for fuel combustion, the resulting hot gases being used to rotate the turbine before forming the propulsive jet: in full, **turbojet engine** **2.** an aircraft propelled by such an engine

tur·bo·prop (-präp′) ***n.*** [TURBO- + PROP(ELLER)] **1.** a turbojet engine whose turbine shaft drives a propeller that develops most of the thrust, some being added by a jet of the turbine exhaust gases: in full, **turboprop engine** **2.** an aircraft propelled by such an engine

tur·bot (tʉr′bət) ***n.,*** *pl.* **-bot, -bots:** see PLURAL, II, D, 2 [< OFr. *tourbout*] **1.** a large European flatfish, highly regarded as food **2.** any of several American flounders

tur·bu·lent (tʉr′byə lənt) ***adj.*** [Fr. < L. < *turba,* a crowd] full of commotion or wild disorder; specif., *a)* marked by or causing turmoil; disorderly *b)* violently agitated or excited *c)* marked by wildly irregular motion —**tur′bu·lence, tur′bu·len·cy** ***n.*** —**tur′bu·lent·ly** ***adv.***

tu·reen (to͝o rēn′) ***n.*** [MFr. *terrine,* earthen vessel, ult. < L. *terra,* earth] a deep dish with a lid, for serving soup, etc.

turf (tʉrf) ***n.,*** *pl.* **turfs,** esp. Brit. **turves** (tʉrvz) [OE.] **1.** *a)* a surface layer of earth containing grass plants with their matted roots; sod *b)* a piece of this layer **2.** peat **3.** [Slang] one's territory —***vt.*** to cover with turf —**the turf** **1.** a track for horse racing **2.** the sport of horse racing —**turf out** [Brit. Colloq.] to throw out

turf·man (-mən) ***n.,*** *pl.* **-men** an owner, trainer, etc. of racehorses

Tur·ge·nev (to͝or gā′nyif), **I·van (Sergeevich)** (ē vän′) 1818–83; Russ. novelist: also sp. **Turgenieff, Turgeniev**

tur·ges·cent (tʉr jes′'nt) ***adj.*** [< L. prp. of *turgescere,* to swell up] becoming turgid or swollen —**tur·ges′cence** ***n.***

tur·gid (tʉr′jid) ***adj.*** [< L. *turgidus* < *turgere,* to swell] **1.** swollen; distended **2.** bombastic; grandiloquent —**tur·gid′i·ty, tur′gid·ness** ***n.*** —**tur′gid·ly** ***adv.***

Tu·rin (to͝or′in, tyo͝or′-; to͝o rin′, tyo͝o-) city in NW Italy, on the Po River: pop. 1,177,000

Turk (tʉrk) ***n.*** **1.** a native or inhabitant of Turkey; esp., a member of the Moslem people of Turkey or, formerly, of the Ottoman Empire **2.** a member of any of the peoples speaking Turkic languages See also YOUNG TURK

Turk. **1.** Turkey **2.** Turkish

Tur·ke·stan (tʉr′ki stan′, -stän′) region in C Asia, extending from the Caspian Sea to the Gobi Desert, inhabited by Turkic-speaking peoples

Tur·key (tʉr′kē) country occupying Asia Minor & a SE part of the Balkan Peninsula: 301,381 sq. mi.; pop. 36,162,000; cap. Ankara

tur·key (tʉr′kē) ***n.,*** *pl.* **-keys, -key:** see PLURAL, II, D, 1 [orig. applied to the guinea fowl, sometimes imported through Turkey and for a time identified with the Am. fowl] **1.** *a)* a large, wild or domesticated, N. American bird with a small head and spreading tail, bred as poultry *b)* its flesh **2.** [Slang] a failure: said esp. of a theatrical production **3.** [Slang] a stupid or unpleasant person **4.** *Bowling* three strikes in a row —**talk turkey** [Colloq.] to talk bluntly and directly

turkey buzzard a dark-colored vulture of temperate and tropical America, having a naked, reddish head: also called **turkey vulture**

Tur·ki (to͝or′kē, tʉr′-) ***n.*** **1.** the Turkic languages collectively or any Turkic language **2.** a member of any Turkic people —***adj.*** designating or of the Turkic languages or the peoples who speak them

Tur·kic (tʉr′kik) ***adj.*** **1.** designating or of a subfamily of Altaic languages, including Turkish **2.** designating or of the peoples who speak any of these languages —***n.*** the Turkic subfamily of languages

Turk·ish (tʉr′kish) ***adj.*** of Turkey, the Turks, their language, etc. —***n.*** **1.** the Turkic language of Turkey: in full, **Ottoman-Turkish** **2.** loosely, *same as* TURKIC

Turkish bath a public bath in which the bather, after a period of heavy perspiration in a room of hot air or steam, is washed and massaged

Turkish Empire *same as* OTTOMAN EMPIRE

Turkish towel [*also* **t-**] a thick cotton towel of terry cloth

Tur·ki·stan (tʉr′ki stan′, -stän′) *same as* TURKESTAN

Turk·men Soviet Socialist Republic (tʉrk′men) republic of the U.S.S.R., in C Asia, on the Caspian Sea: 188,400 sq. mi.; pop. 2,200,000: also **Turk′men·i·stan′** (-i stan′, -i stän′) —**Turk·me·ni·an** (tʉrk mē′nē ən) ***adj.***

Tur·ko- *a combining form meaning:* **1.** of Turkey or the Turks **2.** Turkey and **3.** the Turks and Also **Tur′co-**

tur·mer·ic (tʉr′mər ik) ***n.*** [< MFr. < ML. *terra merita,* lit., deserving earth < ?] **1.** an East Indian plant whose rhizome in powdered form is used as a yellow dye or a seasoning, and in medicine **2.** its aromatic rhizome or the powder made from it

tur·moil (tʉr′moil) ***n.*** [*tur-* (< ? TURBULENT) + MOIL] a very excited or confused condition; tumult; uproar

turn (tʉrn) ***vt.*** [< OE. *turnian* & OFr. *tourner,* both < L. *tornare,* to turn in a lathe, ult. < Gr. *tornos,* a lathe] **1.** to make (a wheel, etc.) move about a center or axis; rotate; revolve **2.** to move around or partly around [to *turn* a key, handle, etc.] **3.** to do (a somersault, cartwheel, etc.) **4.** to give a rounded shape to, as on a lathe **5.** to give a graceful form to [to *turn* a pretty phrase] **6.** to change the position or direction of [*turn* your chair around] **7.** to revolve in the mind; ponder (often with *over*) **8.** *a)* to bend, fold, etc. [*turn* the sheet back] *b)* to twist (one's ankle) **9.** to move so that the underside is on top, and vice versa; reverse; invert [to *turn* pages, a collar, the soil, etc.] **10.** to make topsy-turvy **11.** to upset (the stomach) **12.** to deflect; divert **13.** *a)* to convert or persuade *b)* to prejudice **14.** to go around (a corner, etc.) **15.** to reach or pass (a certain age, amount, etc.) **16.** to reverse the course of; repel or make recoil [to *turn* an attack] **17.** to drive, set, let go, etc. in some way [the dog was *turned* loose] **18.** to direct, point, aim, etc. [eyes *turned* ahead, thoughts *turned* to the past] **19.** to put to a specified use; apply [he *turned* his hand to writing] **20.** to change from one form, condition, etc. to another [to *turn* cream into butter] **21.** to exchange for [to *turn* produce into hard cash] **22.** to translate or paraphrase **23.** to derange, distract, or infatuate **24.** to make sour **25.** to affect in some way [*turned* sick by the sight] **26.** to change the color of —***vi.*** **1.** to rotate, revolve, pivot, etc. **2.** to move around or partly around **3.** to reel; whirl [my head is *turning*] **4.** to become curved or bent **5.** to become reversed or inverted **6.** to become upset, as the stomach **7.** to change or reverse one's or its course or direction [the tide *turned*] **8.** to refer (*to*) **9.** to go or apply (*to*) for help **10.** to direct or shift one's attention, abilities, etc. [he *turned* to music] **11.** to make a sudden attack (*on* or *upon*) [the dog *turned* on him] **12.** to reverse one's feelings, allegiance, etc. [he *turned* against his sister] **13.** to depend or hinge (*on* or *upon*) **14.** to become [to *turn* bitter with age] **15.** to change into another form [the rain *turned* into sleet] **16.** to become rancid, sour, etc. **17.** to change color, as leaves in the fall —***n.*** **1.** a turning around; rotation, as of a wheel, handle, etc. **2.** a single twist, coil, winding, etc. **3.** a musical ornament of four tones, with the tones above and below the principal tone alternating with it **4.** a change or reversal of position, course, or direction **5.** a short walk or ride around an area, as for exercise or inspection **6.** the place where a change in direction occurs; bend; curve **7.** *a)* a change in trend, events, health, etc. *b)* *same as* TURNING POINT **8.** the time of change [the *turn* of the century] **9.** a sudden, brief shock **10.** an action or deed [a good *turn*] **11.** a spell of activity **12.** an attack of illness, dizziness, etc. **13.** the right, duty, or chance to do something, esp. in regular order [his *turn* at bat] **14.** an act in a variety show **15.** a distinctive form, manner, detail, etc. [a quaint *turn* to her speech] **16.** natural inclination [a curious *turn* of mind] —**at every turn** in every instance; constantly —**by turns** one after another in regular order —**call the turn** to predict successfully —**in turn** in proper sequence or succession —**out of turn** **1.** not in proper sequence or order **2.** imprudently *[to talk out of turn]* —**take turns** to speak, do, etc. one after another in regular order —**to a turn** perfectly —**turn and turn about** alternately —**turn down** **1.** to reject (the request, etc. of someone) **2.** to lessen the intensity or volume of —**turn in** **1.** to make a turn into; enter **2.** to deliver; hand in **3.** to inform on or hand over, as to the police **4.** to give back **5.** [Colloq.] to go to bed —**turn off** **1.** *a)* to leave (a road, etc.); *b)* to branch off: said of a road, etc. **2.** to shut off; stop from functioning **3.** to stop displaying suddenly *[to turn off a smile]* **4.** [Slang] to cause (someone) to become uninterested, annoyed, etc. —**turn on** **1.** to start; make go on or start functioning **2.** to display suddenly *[to turn on the charm]* **3.** [Slang] to stimulate with or as with a psychedelic drug; make elated, euphoric, etc. —**turn out** **1.** to put out (a light) **2.** to put outside **3.** to dismiss **4.** to come or gather *[to turn out for a picnic]* **5.** to produce **6.** to result **7.** to prove to be **8.** to become **9.** to equip, dress, etc. **10.** [Colloq.] to get out of bed —**turn over** **1.** to change or reverse the position of **2.** to shift one's position **3.** to begin, or make begin, to operate, as an engine **4.** to consider; ponder **5.** to hand over; give **6.** to convert **7.** to sell and replenish (a stock of goods) **8.** to do business to the amount of —**turn to** to get to work —**turn up** **1.** to fold back or over upon itself **2.** to lift up or turn face up **3.** to increase the speed, intensity, etc. of, as by turning a control **4.** to make a turn onto or into (a street, etc.) **5.** to have an upward direction **6.** to happen **7.** to make an appearance; arrive **8.** to find or be found —**turn′er** *n.*

turn·a·bout (turn′ə bout′) *n.* **1.** a turning about, as to face the other way **2.** a sharp change, as of opinion

turn·buck·le (-buk′′l) *n.* a metal loop with opposite internal threads in each end for the threaded ends of two rods or ringbolts, forming a coupling that can be turned to tighten or loosen the rods or two wires attached to the ringbolts

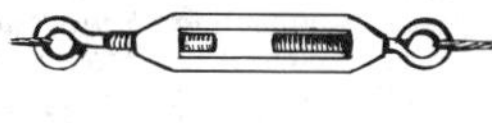
TURNBUCKLE

turn·coat (-kōt′) *n.* a renegade; traitor

turn·down (-doun′) *adj.* **1.** that can be turned down **2.** having the upper part folded down *[a turndown collar]* —*n.* **1.** a rejection **2.** a decline; downturn

Tur·ner (tur′nər), **J(oseph) M(allord) W(illiam)** 1775–1851; Eng. painter

turn·ing (tur′niŋ) *n.* **1.** the action of a person or thing that turns **2.** a place where a road, etc. turns **3.** the art or process of shaping things on a lathe

turning point **1.** a point at which something turns or changes direction **2.** a point in time at which a decisive change occurs; crisis

tur·nip (tur′nip) *n.* [prob. < TURN or < Fr. *tour,* in sense of "round" + ME. *nepe* < OE. < L. *napus,* a turnip] **1.** *a)* a plant of the mustard family, with edible, hairy leaves and a roundish, light-colored root used as a vegetable *b)* *same as* RUTABAGA **2.** the root of either of these plants

turn·key (turn′kē′) *n., pl.* **-keys′** a person in charge of the keys of a prison; warder; jailer

turn·off (-ôf′) *n.* **1.** a turning off **2.** a place where one turns off; esp., a road or ramp leading off a highway

turn·out (-out′) *n.* **1.** a turning out **2.** *a)* a gathering of people, as for a meeting *b)* the number of people **3.** an amount produced **4.** *a)* a wider part of a narrow road, as for passing *b)* a railroad siding **5.** a carriage with its horse or horses **6.** *a)* equipment *b)* a set of clothes

turn·o·ver (-ō′vər) *n.* **1.** a turning over; specif., *a)* an upset *b)* a change from one side, opinion, etc. to another **2.** a small pie made by folding one half of the crust back over the other **3.** *a)* the selling out and replacing of a stock of goods *b)* the amount of business done during a given period in terms of the money used in buying and selling **4.** *a)* the number of workers hired as replacements during a given period *b)* the ratio of this to the average number of workers employed **5.** *Basketball, Football* loss of possession of the ball due to an error by the offensive team —*adj.* that turns over

turn·pike (-pīk′) *n.* [ME. *turnpyke,* a spiked barrier across a road: see TURN & PIKE[4]] **1.** *same as* TOLLGATE **2.** a toll road, esp. one that is an expressway

turn·stile (-stīl′) *n.* a post with revolving horizontal bars, often coin-operated, used at an entrance to admit persons one at a time

turn·stone (-stōn′) *n.* a small, ploverlike shore bird that turns over pebbles to seek food

turn·ta·ble (-tā′b′l) *n.* a circular rotating platform; specif., *a)* such a platform for supporting a phonograph record being played *b)* such a platform carrying tracks to turn a locomotive around

turn·up (turn′up′) *n.* something turned up —*adj.* that turns up or is turned up

‡**Turn·ver·ein** (to͝orn′fer īn′; *E.* turn′fə rīn′) *n.* [G. < *turnen,* to exercise + *verein,* a club] a club of gymnasts

tur·pen·tine (tur′pən tīn′) *n.* [< OFr. < L., ult. < Gr. *terebinthos,* the terebinth] **1.** an oleoresin from the terebinth **2.** any of various oleoresins obtained from pines and other conifers: in full, **gum turpentine** **3.** a colorless, volatile oil distilled from such oleoresins and used in paints, in medicine, etc.: in full, **spirits** (or **oil**) **of turpentine** —*vt.* **-tined′, -tin′ing** to apply turpentine to —**tur′pen·tin′ic** (-tin′ik), **tur′pen·tin′ous** (-tī′nəs) *adj.*

tur·pi·tude (tur′pə to͞od′, -tyo͞od′) *n.* [MFr. < L. < *turpis,* vile] the condition of being wicked, evil, or depraved

turps (turps) *n.pl.* [*with sing. v.*] *same as* TURPENTINE (*n.* 2)

tur·quoise (tur′koiz, -kwoiz) *n.* [< MFr. fem. of OFr. *turqueis,* Turkish: orig. brought to W Europe through Turkey] **1.** a greenish-blue, semiprecious stone, a hydrous phosphate of aluminum containing a small amount of copper **2.** a greenish blue —*adj.* greenish-blue Also sp. **tur′quois**

tur·ret (tur′it) *n.* [< OFr. dim. of *tour:* see TOWER[1]] **1.** a small tower projecting from a building, usually at a corner **2.** *a)* a low, armored, usually revolving, towerlike structure for guns, as on a warship, tank, etc. *b)* a transparent dome for a gun and gunner, as on a bomber **3.** an attachment for a lathe, drill, etc., consisting of a block holding several cutting tools, which may be rotated to present any of the tools to the work: also **tur′ret·head′** —**tur′ret·ed** *adj.*

tur·tle (tur′t′l) *n., pl.* **-tles, -tle:** see PLURAL, II, D, 1 [altered (after TURTLEDOVE) < Fr. *tortue,* tortoise] **1.** any of various land and water reptiles having a toothless beak and a soft body encased in a hard shell into which, in most species, it can pull its head, tail, and four legs: land species are usually called *tortoise* **2.** the flesh of some turtles, used as food **3.** *archaic var. of* TURTLEDOVE —*vi.* **-tled, -tling** to hunt for turtles —**turn turtle** to turn upside down

tur·tle·back (-bak′) *n.* an arched structure over the deck of a ship as a protection against heavy seas

tur·tle·dove (-duv′) *n.* [OE. *turtle* < L. *turtur,* of echoic origin] **1.** any of several wild doves noted for their sad cooing and the devotion that the mates seem to show toward each other **2.** *same as* MOURNING DOVE

tur·tle·neck (-nek′) *n.* **1.** a high, snugly fitting, turndown collar on a pullover sweater, shirt, etc. **2.** a sweater, shirt, etc. with such a neck

Tus·ca·loo·sa (tus′kə lo͞o′sə) [< Choctaw < *taska,* warrior + *lusa,* black] city in WC Ala., near Birmingham: pop. 75,000

Tus·ca·ny (tus′kə nē) region of C Italy, on the Ligurian & Tyrrhenian seas: chief city, Florence —**Tus′can** *adj., n.*

Tus·ca·ro·ra (tus′kə rôr′ə) *n.* [< the native name, lit., hemp gatherers] **1.** *pl.* **-ras, -ra** a member of a tribe of Iroquoian Indians at one time living in Virginia and North Carolina, but later in New York and Ontario **2.** their Iroquoian language

tush (tush) *interj., n.* [ME. *tussch*] an exclamation expressing impatience, reproof, contempt, etc.

tusk (tusk) *n.* [OE. *tucs*] **1.** in elephants, wild boars, etc., a long, pointed tooth, usually one of a pair, that sticks out of the mouth **2.** any tusklike tooth or part —*vt.* to dig, gore, etc. with a tusk or tusks —**tusked** *adj.* —**tusk′like′** *adj.*

tus·sah (tus′ə) *n.* [< Hindi < Sans. *tasara,* lit., a shuttle] **1.** an Asiatic silkworm that produces a coarse, tough silk **2.** this silk: also **tussah silk** Also sp. **tus′sore, tus′sor** (tus′ôr)

tus·sle (tus′′l) *n., vi.* **-sled, -sling** [LME. freq. of *tusen,* to pull] struggle; wrestle; scuffle

tus·sock (tus′ək) *n.* [prob. < ME. (*to*)*tusen,* to rumple + -OCK] a thick tuft or clump of grass, twigs, etc. —**tus′sock·y** (-ē) *adj.*

tut (tut) *interj., n.* an exclamation of impatience, annoyance, rebuke, etc. —*vi.* **tut′ted, tut′ting** to utter "tuts"

Tut·ankh·a·men (to͞ot′äŋk ä′mən) fl. c. 1355 B.C.; Egyptian king of the 18th dynasty: also sp. **Tutankhamon**

tu·tee (to͞o tē′, tyo͞o-) *n.* [TUT(OR) + -EE] a person who is being tutored

tu·te·lage (to͞ot′′l ij, tyo͞ot′-) *n.* [< L. *tutela,* protection] **1.** guardianship; care, protection, etc. **2.** teaching; instruction **3.** the condition of being under a guardian or tutor

tu·te·lar·y (-er′ē) *adj.* [< L. < *tutela:* see prec.] **1.** that watches over or protects **2.** of or serving as a guardian Also **tu′te·lar** (-ər) —*n., pl.* **-lar′ies** a tutelary god, spirit, etc.

tu·tor (to͞ot′ər, tyo͞ot′-) *n.* [< MFr. < L. < pp. of *tueri,* to guard] **1.** a teacher who teaches one student at a time **2.** a legal guardian of a minor **3.** in English universities, an official in charge of the studies of an undergraduate **4.** in some U.S. colleges, a teacher ranking below an instructor —*vt.* **1.** to act as a tutor to; esp., to teach (students) one at a time **2.** to discipline; admonish —*vi.* **1.** to act as a tutor **2.** [Colloq.] to be tutored —**tu′tor·age, tu′tor·ship′** *n.* —**tu·to·ri·al** (to͞o tôr′ē əl, tyo͞o-) *adj.*

tut·ti (to͞ot′ē) *adj.* [It., ult. < L. *totus,* all] *Music* for all instruments or voices —*n., pl.* **-tis** **1.** a passage played or sung by all performers 2. the tonal effect of such a passage

tut·ti-frut·ti (to͞ot′ē fro͞ot′ē) *n.* [It., all fruits] 1. ice cream or other sweet food containing bits of candied fruits 2. a flavoring combining a number of fruit flavors

tu·tu (to͞o′to͞o) *n.* [Fr.] a very short, full, projecting skirt worn by women ballet dancers

Tu·tu·i·la (to͞o′to͞o ē′lä) chief island of American Samoa, in the South Pacific: chief town, Pago Pago

Tu·va·lu (to͞o′və lo͞o′) country consisting of a group of islands in the WC Pacific: 10 sq. mi.; pop. 6,000

tu-whit tu-whoo (to͞o hwit′ to͞o hwo͞o′; -wit′, -wo͞o′) the characteristic vocal sound made by an owl

tux (tuks) *n. same as* TUXEDO

tux·e·do (tək sē′dō) *n., pl.* **-dos** [< the name of a country club near *Tuxedo* Lake, N.Y.] 1. a man's tailless jacket for semiformal evening wear, orig. black 2. a suit with such a jacket, worn with a dark bow tie —*adj.* designating or of a sofa, chair, etc. with a straight back and sides at the same height

TV (tē′vē′) *n., pl.* **TVs, TV's** television or a television receiving set

TVA, T.V.A. Tennessee Valley Authority

TV dinner [because it can conveniently be eaten while viewing television] a frozen, precooked dinner packaged in a tray for heating and serving

twa (twä) *adj., n.* [OE.] *Scot. var. of* TWO

twad·dle (twäd′'l) *n.* [prob. akin to TATTLE] foolish, empty talk or writing; nonsense —*vt., vi.* **-dled, -dling** to talk or write in a foolish or senseless manner; prattle —**twad′dler** *n.*

twain (twān) *n., adj.* [OE. *twegen,* two] *archaic var. of* TWO

Twain (twān), **Mark** *see* Samuel Langhorne CLEMENS

twang (twaŋ) *n.* [echoic] 1. a quick, sharp, vibrating sound, as of a plucked string 2. *a)* a sharp, nasal speech sound *b)* a dialect using such sounds —*vi., vt.* 1. to make or cause to make a twang, as a bowstring, banjo, etc. 2. to speak or say with a twang 3. to shoot or be released with a twang, as an arrow —**twang′y** *adj.*

'twas (twuz, twäz; *unstressed* twəz) it was

twat·tle (twät′'l) *n., vi., vt.* **-tled, -tling** *var. of* TWADDLE

tweak (twēk) *vt.* [OE. *twiccan,* to twitch] to give a sudden, twisting pinch to (someone's nose, ear, cheek, etc.) —*n.* such a pinch

tweed (twēd) *n.* [< misreading of *tweel,* Scot. form of TWILL: later assoc. with the *Tweed,* river in Scotland] 1. a wool fabric with a rough surface, in a twill weave of two or more colors 2. a suit, etc. of this 3. [*pl.*] clothes of tweed

twee·dle·dum and twee·dle·dee (twēd′'l dum′'n twēd′'l dē′) [echoic of musical notes] two persons or things so much alike that it is hard to tell them apart

tweed·y (twēd′ē) *adj.* **tweed′i·er, tweed′i·est** 1. of or like tweed 2. having the casually tailored look, fondness of the outdoors, etc. of a person given to wearing tweeds —**tweed′i·ness** *n.*

'tween (twēn) *prep.* [Poet.] between

tweet (twēt) *n., interj.* [echoic] the thin, chirping sound of a small bird —*vi.* to make this sound

tweet·er (-ər) *n.* a small, high-fidelity loudspeaker for reproducing high-frequency sounds: cf. WOOFER

tweeze (twēz) *vt.* **tweezed, tweez′ing** [back-formation < ff.] [Colloq.] to pluck with or as with tweezers

tweez·ers (twē′zərz) *n.pl.* [*with sing. or pl. v.*] [< obs. *tweeze,* surgical set < Fr. pl. of *étui,* a case] small pincers for plucking out hairs, handling little objects, etc.: also **tweezer** or **pair of tweezers**

twelfth (twelfth) *adj.* [OE. *twelfta*] 1. preceded by eleven others in a series; 12th 2. designating any of the twelve equal parts of something —*n.* 1. the one following the eleventh 2. any of the twelve equal parts of something; 1/12

Twelfth Day the twelfth day (Jan. 6) after Christmas; Epiphany: the evening before, or sometimes the evening of, this day is called **Twelfth Night**

twelve (twelv) *adj.* [OE. *twelf*] two more than ten —*n.* 1. the cardinal number between eleven and thirteen; 12; XII 2. any group of twelve persons or things; dozen —**the Twelve** the Twelve Apostles

Twelve Apostles the twelve disciples chosen by Jesus to go forth to teach the gospel

twelve·fold (twelv′fōld′) *adj.* 1. having twelve parts 2. having twelve times as much or as many —*adv.* twelve times as much or as many

twelve·mo (-mō) *adj., n., pl.* **-mos** *same as* DUODECIMO

twelve·month (-munth′) *n.* a year

twelve-tone (-tōn′) *adj. Music* designating or of a system of composition in which the twelve tones of the chromatic scale are arranged into some arbitrary, fixed succession (*tone row*) as a basis for further thematic development

twen·ti·eth (twen′tē ith) *adj.* 1. preceded by nineteen others in a series; 20th 2. designating any of the twenty equal parts of something —*n.* 1. the one following the nineteenth 2. any of twenty equal parts of something; 1/20

twen·ty (twen′tē) *adj.* [OE. *twegentig*] two times ten —*n., pl.* **-ties** 1. the cardinal number between nineteen and twenty-one; 20; XX 2. [Colloq.] a twenty-dollar bill —**the twenties** the numbers or years, as of a century, from twenty through twenty-nine

twen·ty·fold (-fōld′) *adj.* 1. having twenty parts 2. having twenty times as much or as many —*adv.* twenty times as much or as many

twen·ty-one (-wun′) *n.* a gambling game at cards in which each player's aim is to obtain from the dealer cards totaling twenty-one points or close to that total without exceeding it; blackjack

twen·ty-twen·ty (or **20/20**) **vision** (twen′tē twen′tē) normal keenness of vision, which is the ability to see clearly at twenty feet what the normal eye can see

'twere (twʉr) [Poet.] it were

twerp (twʉrp) *n.* [< ? or akin to Dan. *tver,* perverse] [Slang] a person regarded as insignificant, contemptible, etc.

twice (twīs) *adv.* [OE. *twiges* < *twiga*] 1. on two occasions or in two instances 2. two times 3. two times as much or as many; twofold; doubly

twid·dle (twid′'l) *vt.* **-dled, -dling** [prob. < TW(IST) + (D)IDDLE[1]] to twirl or play with lightly —*vi.* 1. to toy with some object 2. to be busy about trifles —*n.* a light, twirling motion, as with the thumbs —**twiddle one's thumbs** 1. to twirl one's thumbs idly around one another 2. to be idle —**twid′dler** *n.* —**twid′dly** *adj.*

twig (twig) *n.* [OE. *twigge*] a small branch or shoot of a tree or shrub —**twigged** *adj.* —**twig′gy** *adj.* **-gi·er, -gi·est**

twi·light (twī′līt′) *n.* [ME. < *twi-,* two + LIGHT[1]] 1. *a)* the soft, dim light just after sunset or, sometimes, just before sunrise *b)* the period from sunset to dark 2. any growing darkness 3. a condition of gradual decline —*adj.* of or like twilight

twi·lit (twī′lit) *adj.* full of or bathed in the soft, dim light of twilight

twill (twil) *n.* [OE. *twilic,* woven of double thread, ult. < L. *bilix,* double-threaded] 1. a cloth woven so as to have parallel diagonal lines or ribs 2. the pattern of this weave —*vt.* to weave with a twill —**twilled** *adj.*

'twill (twil) [Poet.] it will

twin (twin) *adj.* [OE. *twinn* & ON. *tvinnr,* double] 1. consisting of, or being one of a pair of, two separate but similar or closely related things; paired 2. being two, or either of two, that have been born at the same birth [*twin* girls, a *twin* sister] —*n.* 1. either of two born at the same birth: twins are either *identical* (produced from the same ovum) or *fraternal* (produced from separate ova) 2. either of two persons or things very much alike in appearance, shape, etc. —*vi.* **twinned, twin′ning** 1. to give birth to twins 2. to be paired (with another) —*vt.* 1. to give birth to as twins 2. to pair or couple

twin bill [Colloq.] *same as:* 1. DOUBLE FEATURE 2. DOUBLE-HEADER

twine (twīn) *n.* [OE. *twin,* double thread] 1. a strong thread, string, or cord of two or more strands twisted together 2. a twining or being twined 3. a twined thing or part; twist —*vt.* **twined, twin′ing** 1. *a)* to twist together; intertwine *b)* to form in this way 2. to wreathe or wind (one thing) around or with another 3. to enfold, embrace, etc. [a wreath *twining* his brow] —*vi.* 1. to twist, interlace, etc. 2. to twist and turn —**twin′ing·ly** *adv.*

twin-en·gined (twin′en′jənd) *adj.* powered by two engines: said of an airplane: also **twin′-en′gine**

twinge (twinj) *vt., vi.* **twinged, twing′ing** [OE. *twengan,* to squeeze] to have or cause to have a sudden, brief, darting pain or pang —*n.* 1. a sudden, brief, darting pain or pang 2. a sudden, brief feeling of remorse, shame, etc.; qualm

twin·kle (twiŋ′k'l) *vi.* **-kled, -kling** [OE. *twinclian*] 1. to shine with quick flashes of light at intervals, as some stars; sparkle 2. to light up, as with amusement: said of the eyes 3. to move quickly and lightly, as a dancer's feet; flicker —*vt.* 1. to make twinkle 2. to emit (light) in quick flashes at intervals —*n.* 1. a wink of the eye 2. a quick flash of amusement, etc. in the eye 3. a quick flash of light; sparkle 4. the instant it takes to wink —**twin′kler** *n.*

twin·kling (-kliŋ) *n.* 1. the action of a thing that twinkles 2. *a)* the winking of an eye *b)* the very brief time it takes to wink; instant

twirl (twʉrl) *vt., vi.* [prob. < Scand.] 1. to rotate rapidly; spin 2. to whirl in a circle 3. to twist or coil 4. *Baseball* to pitch —*n.* 1. a twirling or being twirled 2. something twirled; specif., a twist, coil, flourish, etc. —**twirl′er** *n.*

twist (twist) *vt.* [< OE. *-twist,* a rope (in *mæst-twist,* rope to stay a mast)] 1. to wind (strands of cotton, silk, etc.)

around one another, as in spinning or in making thread, cord, etc. **2.** to wreathe; twine **3.** to wind (thread, rope, etc.) around something **4.** to make (one's or its way) by turning one way and then another **5.** to give spiral shape to **6.** *a)* to subject to torsion *b)* to wrench; sprain **7.** *a)* to contort or distort (the face, etc.) *b)* to cause to be malformed *[fingers twisted with arthritis]* **8.** to confuse or disturb mentally or emotionally **9.** to distort or pervert the meaning of **10.** to cause to turn around or rotate **11.** to break off by turning the end (often with *off*) **12.** to make (a ball) go in a curve by giving it a spinning motion *—vi.* **1.** to undergo twisting and thus take on a spiral or coiled form **2.** to spiral, coil, twine, etc. (*around* or *about* something) **3.** to revolve or rotate **4.** to turn to one side **5.** to wind or meander, as a path **6.** to squirm; writhe **7.** to move in a curved path, as a ball *—n.* **1.** a strong, closely twisted silk thread **2.** a twisted roll of tobacco leaves **3.** a loaf of bread or roll made of twisted pieces of dough **4.** a knot, etc. made by twisting **5.** a sliver of peel from a lemon, lime, etc. twisted and added to a drink **6.** a twisting or being twisted **7.** a spin given to a ball in throwing or striking it **8.** stress due to torsion, or the degree of this **9.** a contortion, as of the face **10.** a wrench or sprain **11.** a turning aside; turn; bend **12.** a place at which something twists *[a twist in the road]* **13.** a personal tendency; eccentricity; quirk **14.** distortion, as of meaning **15.** a different or unexpected meaning, method, slant, etc. *[a new twist to an old story]*

twist·er (twis′tər) *n.* **1.** a person or thing that twists; specif., a thrown or batted ball that has been given a twist **2.** a tornado or cyclone

twit[1] (twit) *vt.* **twit′ted, twit′ting** [< OE. *ætwitan* < *æt,* at + *witan,* to accuse] to reproach, tease, taunt, etc., esp. by reminding of a fault or mistake *—n.* a reproach or taunt

twit[2] (twit) *n.* [< TWITTER[1]] a state of nervous excitement

twitch (twich) *vt., vi.* [< OE. *twiccian,* to pluck] **1.** to pull (at) with a quick, slight jerk; pluck **2.** to move with a quick, slight jerk, often due to muscle spasm **3.** to ache with a sudden, sharp pain *—n.* **1.** a quick, slight jerk **2.** a sudden, quick motion, esp. one caused by muscle spasm; tic **3.** a sudden, sharp pain; twinge

twit·ter[1] (twit′ər) *vi.* [ME. *twiteren:* orig. echoic] **1.** to make a series of light, sharp vocal sounds; chirp, as birds do **2.** *a)* to talk in a rapid or agitated manner; chatter *b)* to giggle **3.** to tremble with excitement, etc. *—vt.* to say in a twittering manner *—n.* **1.** the act or sound of twittering **2.** a condition of trembling excitement; flutter **—twit′ter·er** *n.* **—twit′ter·y** *adj.*

twit·ter[2] (twit′ər) *n.* a person who twits

'twixt (twikst) *prep.* [Poet.] betwixt

two (to͞o) *adj.* [OE. *twa*] totaling one more than one *—n.* **1.** the cardinal number between one and three; 2; II **2.** anything having two units or members, or numbered two **—in two** in two parts **—put two and two together** to reach an obvious conclusion by considering several facts together

two-base hit (to͞o′bās′) a double in baseball

two-bit (-bit′) *adj.* **1.** [Colloq.] worth twenty-five cents **2.** [Slang] *a)* cheap; tawdry *b)* mediocre, inferior, etc.

two bits [Colloq.] twenty-five cents

two-by-four (to͞o′bə fôr′, -bī-) *adj.* **1.** that measures two inches (or feet, etc.) by four inches (or feet, etc.) **2.** [Colloq.] small, narrow, cramped, etc. *—n.* any length of untrimmed lumber two inches thick and four inches wide: in the building trades, a trimmed piece 1 5/8 by 3 5/8 inches

two-edged (-ejd′) *adj.* **1.** that has two cutting edges **2.** that can have two different meanings, as a remark

two-faced (-fāst′) *adj.* **1.** having two faces **2.** deceitful; hypocritical **—two′-fac′ed·ly** (-fās′id lē) *adv.*

two-fist·ed (-fis′tid) *adj.* [Colloq.] **1.** able to use both fists **2.** vigorous; virile

two·fold (-fōld′) *adj.* **1.** having two parts; double **2.** having twice as much or as many *—adv.* twice as much or as many

two-hand·ed (-han′did) *adj.* **1.** that needs to be used or wielded with both hands **2.** worked by two people *[a two-handed saw]* **3.** for two people, as a card game **4.** having two hands **5.** using both hands equally well

two-leg·ged (-leg′id, -legd′) *adj.* having two legs

two·pence (tup′′ns) *n.* **1.** two pence, or two British pennies **2.** a former British coin of this value

two·pen·ny (tup′ə nē; *also, esp. of nails,* to͞o′pen′ē) *adj.* **1.** worth or costing twopence **2.** cheap; worthless **3.** designating a size of nails one inch long

two-piece (to͞o′pēs′) *adj.* consisting of two separate parts *[a two-piece bathing suit]*

two-ply (-plī′) *adj.* **1.** having two thicknesses, layers, strands, etc. **2.** woven double

two-sid·ed (-sīd′id) *adj.* **1.** having two sides **2.** having two aspects *[a two-sided question]*

two·some (-səm) *n.* **1.** two people; a couple **2.** *Golf* a game involving two players

two-step (-step′) *n.* **1.** a ballroom dance in 2/4 time **2.** a piece of music for this dance

two-time (to͞o′tīm′) *vt.* **-timed′, -tim′ing** [Slang] to deceive; esp., to be unfaithful to **—two′-tim′er** *n.*

'twould (two͝od) [Poet.] it would

two-way (to͞o′wā′) *adj.* **1.** having separate lanes for vehicles going in opposite directions **2.** involving the same obligations, privileges, etc. toward each other by two parties, nations, etc. *[a two-way cultural exchange]* **3.** involving two persons, groups, etc. *[a two-way political race]* **4.** *a)* used for both transmitting and receiving *[a two-way radio]* *b)* moving, operating, etc. in either of two directions

twp. township

TX Texas

-ty[1] (tē, ti) [< OFr. *-té* < L. *-tas*] *a suffix meaning* quality of, condition of *[novelty]*

-ty[2] (tē, ti) [OE. *-tig*] *a suffix meaning* tens, times ten *[sixty]*

ty·coon (tī ko͞on′) *n.* [< Jap. < Chin. *ta,* great + *kiun,* prince] **1.** a title applied by foreigners to the former shogun of Japan **2.** a wealthy and powerful industrialist, financier, etc.

ty·ing (tī′iŋ) *prp. of* TIE

tyke (tīk) *n.* [ON. *tik,* a bitch] **1.** [Colloq.] a small child **2.** [Chiefly Brit. Dial.] a dog, esp. a mongrel or cur

Ty·ler (tī′lər) [after ff.] city in E Tex.: pop. 71,000

Ty·ler (tī′lər), **John** 1790–1862; 10th president of the U.S. (1841–45)

tym·pa·ni (tim′pə nē) *n.pl., sing.* **-no′** (-nō′) *var. of* TIMPANI **—tym′pa·nist** *n.*

tym·pan·ic membrane (tim pan′ik) a thin membrane that separates the middle ear from the external ear and vibrates when struck by sound waves; eardrum

tym·pa·num (tim′pə nəm) *n., pl.* **-nums, -na** (-nə) [L., a drum < Gr. *tympanon*] **1.** *Anat. same as: a)* MIDDLE EAR *b)* TYMPANIC MEMBRANE **2.** a drum or drumhead **3.** *Archit. a)* the recessed space, usually triangular, enclosed by the slanting cornices of a pediment *b)* the space enclosed by an arch and the top of the door or window below it **—tym·pan′ic** (-pan′ik) *adj.*

Tyn·dale (tin′d′l), **William** 1494?–1536; Eng. religious reformer & translator of the Bible: executed for heresy

typ·al (tīp′′l) *adj.* of, pertaining to, or serving as a type

type (tīp) *n.* [< LL. < L. < Gr. *typos,* a figure, model < *typtein,* to strike] **1.** a person, thing, or event that represents another, esp. another that it is thought will appear later; symbol; token; sign **2.** the characteristic form, plan, style, etc. of a particular class or group **3.** a class, group, etc. having characteristics in common *[a new type of truck]* : colloquially, *of* is often omitted **4.** a person, animal, or thing that is representative or characteristic of a class or group **5.** a perfect example; model; pattern **6.** *Biol.* a specimen designated as the one serving as the basis for the original description and name of a taxon **7.** *Printing a)* a rectangular piece of metal or, sometimes, wood, with a raised letter, figure, etc. in reverse on its upper end *b)* such pieces collectively *c)* a printed or photographically reproduced character or characters *—vt.* **typed, typ′ing** **1.** to classify according to type *[to type a blood sample]* **2.** to write with a typewriter; typewrite *—vi.* to use a typewriter **—typ′a·ble, type′a·ble** *adj.*

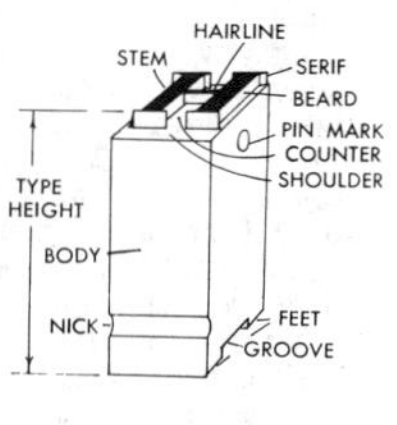

TYPE

-type (tīp) [< Gr. *typos:* see TYPE] *a combining form meaning:* **1.** type, example *[prototype]* **2.** stamp, print, printing type *[monotype]*

type·cast (tīp′kast′) *vt.* **-cast′, -cast′ing** to cast (an actor) repeatedly in the same type of part

type-cast (tīp′kast′) *vt., vi.* **-cast′, -cast′ing** to cast (type)

type·face (-fās′) *n. same as* FACE (*n.* 10)

type metal an alloy of tin, lead, and antimony, and sometimes copper, used for making type, etc.

type·script (-skript′) *n.* typewritten matter or copy

type·set (-set′) *vt.* **-set′, -set′ting** to set in type

type·set·ter (-set′ər) *n.* **1.** a person who sets type; compositor **2.** a machine for setting type **—type′set′ting** *n., adj.*

type·write (-rīt′) *vt., vi.* **-wrote′, -writ′ten, -writ′ing** to write with a typewriter: now usually clipped to *type*

type·writ·er (-rīt′ər) *n.* **1.** a writing machine with a keyboard for reproducing letters, figures, etc. that resemble printed ones **2.** *earlier term for* TYPIST

ty·phoid (tī′foid) *n.* [TYPH(US) + -OID] **1.** orig., any typhus-like disorder **2.** an infectious disease caused by a bacillus and acquired by eating food or drinking water contaminated by excreta: it causes fever, intestinal disorders, etc.: in full, **typhoid fever** **—ty·phoi′dal** *adj.*

ty·phoon (tī fo͞on′) *n.* [< Chin. dial. *tai-fung,* lit., great wind] any violent tropical cyclone originating in the W Pacific, esp. in the South China Sea **—ty·phon′ic** (-fän′ik) *adj.*

ty·phus (tī′fəs) ***n.*** [ModL. < Gr. *typhos*, a fever] an acute infectious disease caused by a rickettsia transmitted to man by fleas, lice, etc., and causing fever, red spots on the skin, etc.: in full, **typhus fever** —**ty′phous** (-fəs) ***adj.***
typ·i·cal (tip′i k'l) ***adj.*** **1.** serving as a type; symbolic **2.** having the distinguishing characteristics, qualities, etc. of a class, group, etc.; representative **3.** belonging to a type; characteristic Also **typ′ic** —**typ′i·cal·ly** ***adv.*** —**typ′i·cal·ness, typ′i·cal′i·ty** (-kal′ə tē) ***n.***
typ·i·fy (tip′ə fī′) ***vt.*** **-fied′, -fy′ing** [see TYPE & -FY] **1.** to be a type or emblem of; symbolize **2.** to have or show the distinctive characteristics of; be typical of —**typ′i·fi·ca′tion** ***n.*** —**typ′i·fi′er** ***n.***
typ·ist (tīp′ist) ***n.*** a person who operates a typewriter, esp. one whose work is typing
ty·po (tī′pō) ***n.,*** *pl.* **-pos** [Colloq.] a typographical error; mechanical mistake made in setting type or in typing
ty·po- [< Gr. *typos*: see TYPE] *a combining form meaning* type
ty·pog·ra·pher (tī päg′rə fər) ***n.*** a person skilled in typography; printer, compositor, etc.
ty·po·graph·i·cal (tī′pə graf′i k'l) ***adj.*** of typography; having to do with the setting of type, printing, etc.: also **ty′po·graph′ic** —**ty′po·graph′i·cal·ly** ***adv.***
ty·pog·ra·phy (tī päg′rə fē) ***n.*** [< Fr. < ML.: see TYPO- & -GRAPHY] **1.** the art or process of printing from type **2.** the art or process of setting and arranging type for printing **3.** the arrangement, style, or appearance of matter printed from type
Tyr (tir) *Norse Myth.* the god of war and son of Odin
ty·ran·ni·cal (ti ran′i k'l, tī-) ***adj.*** **1.** of or suited to a tyrant; arbitrary; despotic **2.** harsh, cruel, unjust, etc. Also **ty·ran′nic** —**ty·ran′ni·cal·ly** ***adv.***
ty·ran·ni·cide (-ə sīd′) ***n.*** **1.** the act of killing a tyrant **2.** a person who kills a tyrant
tyr·an·nize (tir′ə nīz′) ***vi.*** **-nized′, -niz′ing** **1.** to govern as a tyrant **2.** to use authority harshly or cruelly —***vt.*** to treat tyrannically; oppress —**tyr′an·niz′er** ***n.***
ty·ran·no·saur (ti ran′ə sôr′, tī-) ***n.*** [< ModL. < Gr. *tyrannos*, tyrant + -SAURUS] any of various huge, two-footed, flesh-eating dinosaurs of the Cretaceous Period in N. America: also **ty·ran′no·saur′us** (-əs)
tyr·an·nous (tir′ə nəs) ***adj.*** tyrannical; despotic, oppressive, unjust, etc. —**tyr′an·nous·ly** ***adv.***
tyr·an·ny (tir′ə nē) ***n.,*** *pl.* **-nies** **1.** the office, authority, government, etc. of a tyrant, or absolute ruler **2.** oppressive and unjust government; despotism **3.** very cruel and unjust use of power or authority **4.** harshness; severity **5.** a tyrannical act
ty·rant (tī′rənt) ***n.*** [< OFr. < L. < Gr. *tyrannos*] **1.** an absolute ruler **2.** a cruel, oppressive ruler; despot **3.** any person who uses his authority in an oppressive manner
Tyre (tīr) seaport in SW Lebanon, on the Mediterranean: center of ancient Phoenician culture: pop. 12,000 —**Tyr·i·an** (tir′ē ən) ***adj., n.***
Tyrian purple (or **dye**) **1.** a purple or crimson dye used by the ancient Romans and Greeks: it was made from certain mollusks, orig. at Tyre **2.** bluish red
ty·ro (tī′rō) ***n.,*** *pl.* **-ros** [ML. < L. *tiro*, recruit] a beginner in learning something; novice
Tyr·ol (tir′äl, tī′rōl, ti rōl′) *same as* TIROL —**Ty·ro·le·an** (ti rō′lē ən) ***adj., n.*** —**Tyr·o·lese** (tir′ə lēz′) ***adj., n.,*** *pl.* **-lese′**
Tyr·rhe·ni·an Sea (ti rē′nē ən) part of the Mediterranean, between the W coast of Italy & Corsica & Sardinia
tzar (tsär, zär) ***n.*** *var. of* CZAR —**tzar′dom** ***n.*** —**tzar′ism** ***n.*** —**tzar′ist** ***adj., n.***
tzar·e·vitch (tsär′ə vich, zär′-) ***n.*** *var. of* CZAREVITCH
tza·ri·na (tsä rē′nə, zä-) ***n.*** *var. of* CZARINA: also **tza·rit′za** (-rēt′sə)
tzet·ze fly (tset′sē, tsē′tsē) *var. of* TSETSE FLY
‡**tzi·gane** (tsē gȧn′) ***n.*** [Fr. < Hung.] a gypsy

U

U, u (yo͞o) ***n.,*** *pl.* **U's, u's** **1.** the twenty-first letter of the English alphabet **2.** a sound of *U* or *u*
U (yo͞o) ***n.*** **1.** something shaped like U **2.** *Chem.* uranium —***adj.*** shaped like U
U., U **1.** Union **2.** United **3.** University
U., U, u., u unit; units
U.A.R. United Arab Republic
U.A.W., UAW United Automobile, Aerospace, and Agricultural Implement Workers of America
U·ban·gi (o͞o bäŋ′gē, yo͞o baŋ′-) river in C Africa, flowing from N Zaire west & south into the Congo River
u·biq·ui·tous (yo͞o bik′wə təs) ***adj.*** [see ff. & -OUS] present, or seeming to be present, everywhere at the same time; omnipresent —**u·biq′ui·tous·ly** ***adv.*** —**u·biq′ui·tous·ness** ***n.***
u·biq·ui·ty (-tē) ***n.*** [< Fr. < L. *ubique*, everywhere] the state, fact, or capacity of being, or seeming to be, everywhere at the same time; omnipresence
U-boat (yo͞o′bōt′) ***n.*** [< G. *U-boot*, abbrev. of *Unterseeboot*, undersea boat] a German submarine
u.c. *Printing* upper case
ud·der (ud′ər) ***n.*** [OE. *udr*] a mammary gland with two or more teats, as in cows
U·fa (o͞o fä′) city in E European R.S.F.S.R., in the W foothills of the Urals: pop. 773,000
UFO (yo͞o′fō, yo͞o′ef ō′) ***n.,*** *pl.* **UFOs, UFO's** [*u(nidentified) f(lying) o(bject)*] any of a number of unidentified objects reported, esp. since 1947, to have been seen flying at varying heights and speeds and variously regarded as hallucinations, spacecraft from another planet, etc.
U·gan·da (yo͞o gan′də, o͞o gän′dä) country in EC Africa: a member of the Commonwealth: 93,981 sq. mi.; pop. 10,127,000 —**U·gan′dan** (-dən) ***adj., n.***
ugh (ookh, uH, oo, ug, *etc.*) ***interj.*** [echoic] an exclamation of disgust, horror, etc.
ug·li (ug′lē) ***n.*** [altered < UGLY: from its misshapen appearance] a Jamaican citrus fruit that is a three-way cross between a grapefruit, orange, and tangerine: also called **ugli fruit**
ug·li·fy (ug′lə fī′) ***vt.*** **-fied′, -fy′ing** to make ugly; disfigure
ug·ly (ug′lē) ***adj.*** **-li·er, -li·est** [< ON. *uggligr*, fearful < *uggr*, fear] **1.** unpleasing to look at; unsightly **2.** bad, vile, repulsive, offensive, etc. [an *ugly* lie] **3.** ominous; dangerous [*ugly* storm clouds] **4.** [Colloq.] ill-tempered; cross [an *ugly* disposition] —**ug′li·ly** ***adv.*** —**ug′li·ness** ***n.***
ugly duckling [from a story by H. C. Andersen] a very plain child or unpromising thing that in time becomes or could become beautiful, important, etc.
U·gri·an (o͞o′grē ən, yo͞o′-) ***adj.*** **1.** designating or of a group of Finno-Ugric peoples of W Siberia and Hungary **2.** *same as* UGRIC (*adj.* 1) —***n.*** **1.** a member of any of the Ugrian peoples **2.** *same as* UGRIC
U·gric (-grik) ***adj.*** **1.** designating or of a branch of the Finno-Ugric subfamily of languages including Hungarian (Magyar) **2.** *same as* UGRIAN (*adj.* 1) —***n.*** the Ugric languages
uh (u, un) ***interj.*** **1.** *same as* HUH **2.** a prolonged sound made in speaking, as while searching for a word
UHF, U.H.F., uhf, u.h.f. ultrahigh frequency
uh-huh (ə hu′; *for 2* un′un′) ***interj.*** **1.** an exclamation indicating: *a)* an affirmative response *b)* that one is listening attentively **2.** *var. of* UH-UH
uh-uh (un′un′, -un′) ***interj.*** an exclamation indicating a negative response
uit·land·er (üt′län′dər; *E.* īt′lan′dər, āt′-) ***n.*** [Afrik. < Du. *uit*, out + *land*, land] [*sometimes* U-] in South Africa, a foreigner; specif., one not a Boer in the Transvaal
U.K. United Kingdom
u·kase (yo͞o′kās, -kāz; yo͞o kās′, -kāz′) ***n.*** [Russ. *ukaz*, edict] **1.** in Czarist Russia, an imperial order or decree **2.** any official, esp. arbitrary, decree or proclamation
U·krain·i·an (yo͞o krā′nē ən, -krī′-) ***adj.*** of the Ukraine, its people, their language, etc. —***n.*** **1.** a native or inhabitant of the Ukraine **2.** the East Slavic language of the Ukrainians, very closely related to Russian
Ukrainian Soviet Socialist Republic republic of the U.S.S.R., in the SW European part: 231,990 sq. mi.; pop. 47,100,000; cap. Kiev: also called **the U·kraine** (yo͞o krān′)

u·ku·le·le (yo͞o′kə lā′lē; *Haw.* o͞o′ko͞o lā′lā) ***n.*** [Haw., lit., flea] a musical instrument with four strings, like a small guitar: also [Colloq.] **uke** (yo͞ok)

UKULELE

UL, U.L. Underwriters' Laboratories

ul·cer (ul′sər) ***n.*** [L. *ulcus* (gen. *ulceris*)] **1.** an open sore on the skin or some mucous membrane, that festers, damages the tissue, etc. **2.** any corrupting condition or influence

ul·cer·ate (ul′sə rāt′) ***vt., vi.*** **-at′ed, -at′ing** [< L. pp. of *ulcerare*] to make or become ulcerous —**ul′cer·a′tion** ***n.*** —**ul′cer·a′tive** ***adj.***

ul·cer·ous (-sər əs) ***adj.*** **1.** having an ulcer or ulcers **2.** of or like an ulcer or ulcers

-ule (yo͞ol, yool) [< Fr. < L. *-ulus, -ula, -ulum*] *a suffix meaning* little *[sporule]*

-u·lent (yoo lənt) [< Fr. < L. *-ulentus*] *a suffix meaning* full of, abounding in *[fraudulent]*

ul·na (ul′nə) ***n.***, *pl.* **-nae** (-nē), **-nas** [ModL. < L., the elbow] **1.** the larger of the two bones of the forearm, on the side opposite the thumb **2.** a corresponding bone in the forelimb of other vertebrates —**ul′nar** (-nər) ***adj.***

-u·lose (yoo lōs′) [< L. *-ulosus*] *a suffix meaning* characterized by, marked by *[granulose]*

-u·lous (yoo ləs) [< L. *-ulosus*] *a suffix meaning* tending to, characterized by *[populous]*

Ul·ster (ul′stər) **1.** former province of Ireland, divided to form Northern Ireland and a province (*Ulster*) of Ireland **2.** [Colloq.] Northern Ireland —**Ul′ster·man** (-mən) ***n.***, *pl.* **-men**

ul·ster (ul′stər) ***n.*** [< prec., where the fabric was orig. made] a long, loose, heavy overcoat

ult. **1.** ultimate **2.** ultimately **3.** ultimo

ul·te·ri·or (ul tir′ē ər) ***adj.*** [L., compar. of hyp. *ulter*, beyond] **1.** lying beyond or on the farther side **2.** later, subsequent, or future **3.** beyond what is openly said or made known *[an ulterior motive]* —**ul·te′ri·or·ly** ***adv.***

ul·ti·ma (ul′ti mə) ***n.*** [L., fem. of *ultimus*, last] the last syllable of a word

ul·ti·mate (ul′tə mit) ***adj.*** [< LL. pp. of *ultimare*, to come to an end < L. *ultimus*, last] **1.** beyond which it is impossible to go; farthest **2.** final; last **3.** most basic; fundamental; primary **4.** greatest or highest possible; maximum —***n.*** something ultimate *[the ultimate in pleasure]* —**ul′ti·ma·cy** (-mə sē), **ul′ti·mate·ness** ***n.*** —**ul′ti·mate·ly** ***adv.***

ul·ti·ma Thu·le (ul′ti mə tho͞o′lē) [L.] **1.** among the ancients, the northernmost region of the world **2.** any far-off, unknown region

ul·ti·ma·tum (ul′tə māt′əm) ***n.***, *pl.* **-tums, -ta** (-ə) [ModL. < LL., neut. pp.: see ULTIMATE] a final offer or demand presented to another in a dispute, esp. with a threat to break off relations, use force, etc.

ul·ti·mo (ul′tə mō′) ***adv.*** [L. *ultimo* (*mense*), (in the) last (month)] in the preceding month: an old-fashioned usage *[yours of the 13th (day) ultimo received]*

ul·tra (ul′trə) ***adj.*** [L., beyond] going beyond the usual limit; extreme —***n.*** an extremist, as in opinions held

ul·tra- [L.] *a prefix meaning:* **1.** beyond *[ultraviolet]* **2.** to an extreme degree *[ultramodern]* **3.** beyond the range of *[ultramicroscopic]*

ul·tra·con·serv·a·tive (ul′trə kən sur′və tiv) ***adj.*** conservative to an extreme degree —***n.*** an ultraconservative person

ul·tra·high frequency (ul′trə hī′) any radio frequency between 300 and 3,000 megahertz

ul·tra·ma·rine (ul′trə mə rēn′) ***adj.*** [< ML.: see ULTRA- & MARINE] **1.** beyond the sea **2.** deep-blue —***n.*** **1.** a blue pigment orig. made from powdered lapis lazuli **2.** any similar pigment made from other substances **3.** a deep blue

ul·tra·mi·cro·scope (-mī′krə skōp′) ***n.*** an instrument for observing by dispersed light objects, as colloidal particles, too small to be seen with an ordinary microscope —**ul′tra·mi·cros′co·py** (-mī kräs′kə pē) ***n.***

ul·tra·mi·cro·scop·ic (-mī′krə skäp′ik) ***adj.*** **1.** too small to be seen with an ordinary microscope **2.** of an ultramicroscope —**ul′tra·mi′cro·scop′i·cal·ly** ***adv.***

ul·tra·mod·ern (-mäd′ərn) ***adj.*** modern to an extreme degree —**ul′tra·mod′ern·ism** ***n.*** —**ul′tra·mod′ern·ist** ***n.***

ul·tra·na·tion·al·ism (-nash′ən ′l iz′m) ***n.*** nationalism that is excessive or extreme —**ul′tra·na′tion·al·ist** ***adj., n.*** —**ul′tra·na′tion·al·is′tic** ***adj.***

ul·tra·son·ic (-sän′ik) ***adj.*** [ULTRA- + SONIC] designating or of a frequency of mechanical vibrations above the range audible to the human ear, i.e., above 20,000 vibrations per second —**ul′tra·son′i·cal·ly** ***adv.***

ul·tra·son·ics (-sän′iks) ***n.pl.*** [*with sing. v.*] the science dealing with ultrasonic phenomena

ul·tra·sound (ul′trə sound′) ***n.*** ultrasonic waves, used in medical diagnosis and therapy, in surgery, etc.

ul·tra·vi·o·let (ul′trə vī′ə lit) ***adj.*** **1.** lying just beyond the violet end of the visible spectrum and having wavelengths shorter than 4,000 angstroms **2.** of or producing light rays of such wavelengths —***n.*** ultraviolet radiation

ul·u·late (yo͞ol′yoo lāt′, ul′-) ***vi.*** **-lat′ed, -lat′ing** [< L. pp. of *ululare*, to howl: echoic] **1.** to howl or hoot **2.** to wail or lament loudly —**ul′u·lant** (-lənt) ***adj.*** —**ul′u·la′tion** ***n.***

U·lys·ses (yoo lis′ēz) [L.] *same as* ODYSSEUS

um·bel (um′b′l) ***n.*** [L. *umbella:* see UMBRELLA] a cluster of flowers with stalks of nearly equal length which spring from the same point —**um′bel·late** (-it, -āt′), **um′bel·lat′ed** ***adj.*** —**um′bel·late′ly** ***adv.***

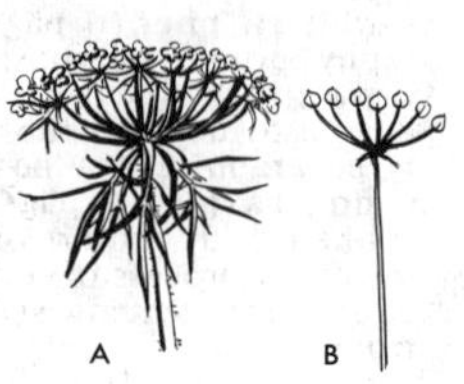

UMBEL (A, compound; B, simple)

um·ber (um′bər) ***n.*** [< Fr. < It. (*terra d'*)*ombra*, lit., (earth of) shade, prob. < L. *umbra*, a shade] **1.** a kind of earth containing oxides of manganese and iron, used as a pigment: raw umber is yellowish-brown; burnt, or calcined, umber is reddish-brown **2.** a yellowish-brown or reddish-brown color —***adj.*** of the color of raw umber or burnt umber —***vt.*** to color with or as with umber

um·bil·i·cal (um bil′i k′l) ***adj.*** **1.** of or like an umbilicus or an umbilical cord **2.** situated at or near the navel **3.** linked together by or as if by an umbilical cord

umbilical cord a cordlike structure that connects a fetus with the placenta: it is severed at birth, the navel being formed at the point where it was attached to the fetus

um·bil·i·cus (um bil′i kəs, um′bi lī′kəs) ***n.***, *pl.* **-ci′** (-sī′, -sī) [L.] **1.** *same as* NAVEL **2.** a navellike depression, as the hilum of a seed

um·bra (um′brə) ***n.***, *pl.* **-brae** (-brē), **-bras** [L., a shade] **1.** a shade or shadow **2.** the dark cone of shadow projecting from a planet or satellite on the side opposite the sun

um·brage (um′brij) ***n.*** [OFr. < L. < *umbra*, a shade] **1.** [Obs.] shade; shadow **2.** foliage, considered as shade-giving **3.** offense or resentment *[to take umbrage at a remark]* —**um·bra′geous** (-brā′jəs) ***adj.*** —**um·bra′geous·ly** ***adv.***

um·brel·la (um brel′ə) ***n.*** [< It. < L. < *umbella*, parasol, dim. of *umbra*, shade] **1.** cloth, plastic, etc. stretched over a folding radial frame at the top of a stick, carried for protection against the rain or sun **2.** something that looks like this or is suggestive of this, as in its overall coverage; specif., a force of aircraft sent up to screen ground or naval forces

umbrella tree **1.** an American magnolia with clusters of long leaves at the ends of the branches, foul-smelling white flowers, and reddish fruit **2.** any of various trees that have an umbrellalike shape

u·mi·ak, u·mi·ack (o͞o′mē ak′) ***n.*** [Esk.] an open Eskimo boat made of skins stretched on a wooden frame

um·laut (oom′lout) ***n.*** [G. < *um*, about + *laut*, a sound] *Linguis.* **1.** *a*) a change in sound of a vowel, caused by its assimilation to another vowel or semivowel originally in the next syllable but later generally lost *b*) a vowel resulting from such assimilation **2.** the diacritical mark (¨) placed over such a vowel, esp. in German, to indicate umlaut —***vt.*** to sound or write with an umlaut

ump (ump) ***n., vt., vi.*** *shortened form of* UMPIRE

um·pire (um′pīr) ***n.*** [ME. *oumpere* (by faulty separation of *a noumpere*) < MFr. *nomper*, uneven, hence third person < *non*, not + *per*, even] **1.** a person chosen to give a decision in a dispute; arbiter **2.** an official who rules on the plays of a game, as in baseball —***vt., vi.*** **-pired, -pir·ing** to act as umpire (in or of)

ump·teen (ump′tēn′) ***adj.*** [Slang] a great number of; very many —**ump′teenth′** ***adj.***

UMW, U.M.W. United Mine Workers of America

un- (un; *unstressed, also* ən) *either of two prefixes meaning:* **1.** [OE. *un-*] not, lack of, the opposite of *[unhappy, untruth]* **2.** [OE. *un-, on-, and-*] the reverse or removal of: added to verbs to indicate a reversal of the action of the verb *[unfasten]* and to nouns to indicate a removal or release from the thing, state, etc. indicated by the noun *[unbosom]*; sometimes *un-* is merely intensive *[unloosen]* The list at the bottom of the following pages includes many of the more common compounds formed with *un-* (either prefix) that do not have special meanings

UN, U.N. United Nations

un·a·ble (un ā′b'l) ***adj.*** not able; lacking the ability, means, or power to do something

un·a·bridged (un′ə brijd′) ***adj.*** not abridged, or shortened: often applied to a large, extensive dictionary that is not abridged from a larger work

un·ac·count·a·ble (un′ə koun′tə b'l) ***adj.*** **1.** that cannot be explained or accounted for; strange **2.** not responsible —**un′ac·count′a·bil′i·ty** ***n.*** —**un′ac·count′a·bly** ***adv.***

un·ac·cus·tomed (-ə kus′təmd) ***adj.*** **1.** not accustomed (*to*) **2.** not usual; strange [an *unaccustomed* action]

un·ad·vised (-əd vīzd′) ***adj.*** **1.** without counsel or advice **2.** thoughtlessly hasty; indiscreet —**un′ad·vis′ed·ly** (-vīz′id lē) ***adv.*** —**un′ad·vis′ed·ness** ***n.***

un·af·fect·ed (-ə fek′tid) ***adj.*** **1.** not affected, or influenced **2.** without affectation; sincere and natural —**un′af·fect′ed·ly** ***adv.*** —**un′af·fect′ed·ness** ***n.***

un-A·mer·i·can (-ə mer′ə kən) ***adj.*** not American; esp., thought of as not conforming to the principles, policies, etc. of the U.S. —**un′-A·mer′i·can·ism** ***n.***

U·na·mu·no (o͞o′nä mo͞o′nô), **Mi·guel de** (mē gel′ *th*e) 1864–1936; Sp. philosopher & writer

u·nan·i·mous (yoo nan′ə məs) ***adj.*** [< L. < *unus*, one + *animus*, the mind] **1.** agreeing completely; united in opinion **2.** showing, or based on, complete agreement —**u·na·nim·i·ty** (yo͞o′nə nim′ə tē) ***n.*** —**u·nan′i·mous·ly** ***adv.***

un·ap·proach·a·ble (un′ə prōch′ə b'l) ***adj.*** **1.** not approachable or accessible, friendly, etc. **2.** having no rival or equal; unmatched —**un′ap·proach′a·bil′i·ty** ***n.*** —**un′approach′a·bly** ***adv.***

un·arm (un ärm′) ***vt.*** *same as* DISARM

un·armed (-ärmd′) ***adj.*** having no weapons, esp. firearms, or armor; defenseless

un·as·sail·a·ble (un′ə sāl′ə b'l) ***adj.*** not assailable; specif., *a*) that cannot be successfully attacked *b*) that cannot be successfully denied —**un′as·sail′a·ble·ness, un′assail′a·bil′i·ty** ***n.*** —**un′as·sail′a·bly** ***adv.***

un·as·sum·ing (-ə so͞o′miŋ, -syo͞o′-) ***adj.*** not assuming, pretentious, or forward; modest —**un′as·sum′ing·ly** ***adv.*** —**un′as·sum′ing·ness** ***n.***

un·at·tached (-ə tacht′) ***adj.*** **1.** not attached or fastened **2.** not connected with any organization **3.** not engaged or married **4.** *Law* not taken as security for a judgment

un·a·vail·ing (-ə vā′liŋ) ***adj.*** not availing; useless; futile; —**un′a·vail′ing·ly** ***adv.***

un·a·void·a·ble (-ə voi′də b'l) ***adj.*** that cannot be avoided; inevitable —**un′a·void′a·ble·ness** ***n.*** —**un′a·void′a·bly** ***adv.***

un·a·ware (-ə wer′) ***adj.*** not aware or conscious [*unaware* of danger] —***adv.*** *same as* UNAWARES —**un′a·ware′ness** ***n.***

un·a·wares (-ə werz′) ***adv.*** **1.** without knowing or being aware **2.** unexpectedly; by surprise [to sneak up on someone *unawares*]

un·backed (un bakt′) ***adj.*** **1.** without a back or backing **2.** having no backers, supporters, etc.

un·bal·ance (-bal′əns) ***vt.*** **-anced, -anc·ing** **1.** to throw out of balance **2.** to derange (the mind) —***n.*** the condition of being unbalanced

un·bal·anced (-bal′ənst) ***adj.*** **1.** not balanced or equal **2.** not sane or normal in mind

un·bar (-bär′) ***vt.*** **-barred′, -bar′ring** to unbolt or unlock

un·bear·a·ble (-ber′ə b'l) ***adj.*** that cannot be endured or tolerated —**un·bear′a·ble·ness** ***n.*** —**un·bear′a·bly** ***adv.***

un·beat·a·ble (-bēt′ə b'l) ***adj.*** that cannot be defeated or surpassed

un·beat·en (-bēt′'n) ***adj.*** **1.** not struck, pounded, etc. **2.** untrodden or untraveled **3.** undefeated or unsurpassed

un·be·com·ing (un′bi kum′iŋ) ***adj.*** not suited to one's appearance, status, character, etc. [an *unbecoming* dress, *unbecoming* behavior] —**un′be·com′ing·ly** ***adv.*** —**un′be·com′ing·ness** ***n.***

un·be·known (-bi nōn′) ***adj.*** unknown or unnoticed; without one's knowledge (usually with *to*): also **un′be·knownst′** (-nōnst′)

un·be·lief (-bə lēf′) ***n.*** a withholding or lack of belief, esp. in religion

un·be·liev·a·ble (-bə lēv′ə b'l) ***adj.*** beyond belief; astounding; incredible —**un′be·liev′a·bly** ***adv.***

un·be·liev·er (-bə lē′vər) ***n.*** **1.** a person who does not believe; doubter **2.** a person who does not accept any, or any particular, religious belief

un·be·liev·ing (-bə lē′viŋ) ***adj.*** doubting; skeptical; incredulous —**un′be·liev′ing·ly** ***adv.***

un·bend (un bend′) ***vt., vi.*** **-bent′** or **-bend′ed, -bend′ing** **1.** to make or become less tense, less formal, etc. **2.** to make or become straight again

un·bend·ing (-ben′diŋ) ***adj.*** not bending; specif., *a*) rigid; stiff *b*) firm; resolute *c*) aloof; austere —***n.*** a relaxation of restraint, severity, etc. —**un·bend′ing·ly** ***adv.*** —**un·bend′ing·ness** ***n.***

un·bid·den (-bid′'n) ***adj.*** **1.** not commanded **2.** not invited Also **un·bid′**

un·bind (-bīnd′) ***vt.*** **-bound′, -bind′ing** **1.** to untie; unfasten **2.** to release from restraints

un·blessed, un·blest (-blest′) ***adj.*** **1.** not blessed **2.** wretched; unhappy

un·blush·ing (-blush′iŋ) ***adj.*** **1.** not blushing **2.** shameless —**un·blush′ing·ly** ***adv.***

un·bolt (-bōlt′) ***vt., vi.*** to draw back the bolt or bolts of (a door, etc.); unbar; open

un·bolt·ed[1] (-bōlt′id) ***adj.*** not fastened with a bolt

un·bolt·ed[2] (-bōlt′id) ***adj.*** not bolted or sifted, as flour

un·born (-bôrn′) ***adj.*** **1.** not born **2.** still within the mother's womb **3.** yet to come or be; future

un·bos·om (-booz′əm, -bo͞o′zəm) ***vt., vi.*** to tell or reveal (one's feelings, secrets, etc.) —**unbosom oneself** to express (oneself) openly about one's feelings, etc.

un·bound·ed (-boun′did) ***adj.*** **1.** without bounds or limits **2.** not restrained; uncontrolled

un·bowed (-boud′) ***adj.*** **1.** not bowed or bent **2.** not yielding or giving in; unsubdued

un·bri·dled (-brī′d'ld) ***adj.*** **1.** having no bridle on, as a horse **2.** not controlled; unrestrained

un·bro·ken (-brō′k'n) ***adj.*** not broken; specif., *a*) whole; intact *b*) not tamed or subdued *c*) continuous; uninterrupted *d*) not surpassed [an *unbroken* record]

un·buck·le (-buk′'l) ***vt.*** **-led, -ling** to unfasten the buckle or buckles of

un·bur·den (-burd′'n) ***vt.*** **1.** to free from a burden **2.** to relieve (oneself or one's mind) by disclosing (something hard to bear)

un·but·ton (-but′'n) ***vt., vi.*** to unfasten the buttons of

---

unabashed
unabated
unabbreviated
unabetted
unabsolved
unabsorbed
unacademic
unaccented
unacceptable
unacclimated
unaccommodating
unaccompanied
unaccomplished
unaccounted-for
unaccredited
unacknowledged
unacquainted
unadaptable
unadjustable
unadorned
unadulterated
unadventurous
unadvertised
unadvisable
unaffiliated
unafraid
unaggressive
unaided
unaimed
unalike
unallied
unallowable
unalloyed
unalterable
unaltered
unambiguous
unambitious
unamplified
unamusing
unannounced
unanswerable
unanticipated
unapologetic
unapparent
unappealable
unappealing
unappeasable
unappetizing
unappreciated
unappreciative
unapproached
unapt
unarmored
unartistic
unascertained
unashamed
unasked
unaspiring
unassigned
unassimilated
unassisted
unassociated
unassorted
unassured
unattainable
unattempted
unattended
unattested
unattired
unattractive
unauthentic
unauthenticated
unauthorized
unavailable
unavenged
unawed
unbaked
unbaptized
unbathed
unbefitting
unbelted
unbiased
unblamable
unbleached
unblemished
unblinking
unbought
unbound
unbraced
unbraid
unbranched
unbranded
unbreakable
unbreathable
unbridgeable
unbrotherly
unbruised
unbrushed
unbudgeted
unbuilt
unburied
unburned
unburnt
unbusinesslike

---

fat, āpe, cär; ten, ēven; is, bīte; gō, hôrn, to͞ol, look; oil, out; up, fur; get; joy; yet; chin; she; thin, *th*en; zh, leisure; ŋ, ring; ə for *a* in *ago*, *e* in *agent*, *i* in *sanity*, *o* in *comply*, *u* in *focus*; ′ as in *able* (ā′b'l); Fr. bál; ë, Fr. coeur; ö, Fr. feu; Fr. mo*n*; ô, Fr. coq; ü, Fr. duc; *r*, Fr. cri; H, G. ich; kh, G. doch; ‡foreign; *hypothetical; < derived from. See inside front cover.

un·called-for (un kôld′fôr′) ***adj.*** **1.** not required **2.** unnecessary and out of place; impertinent
un·can·ny (-kan′ē) ***adj.*** **1.** mysterious in an eerie way; weird **2.** so remarkable, acute, etc. as to seem unnatural *[uncanny* vision*]* —**un·can′ni·ly** ***adv.*** —**un·can′ni·ness** ***n.***
un·cap (-kap′) ***vt.*** **-capped′, -cap′ping** **1.** to remove the cap from the head of (a person) **2.** to remove the cap from (a bottle, etc.)
un·cared-for (-kerd′fôr′) ***adj.*** not cared for or looked after; neglected
un·cer·e·mo·ni·ous (un′ser ə mō′nē əs) ***adj.*** **1.** less ceremonious than is expected; informal **2.** so curt or abrupt as to be discourteous —**un′cer·e·mo′ni·ous·ly** ***adv.*** —**un′cer·e·mo′ni·ous·ness** ***n.***
un·cer·tain (un sʉrt′'n) ***adj.*** **1.** *a)* not surely or certainly known; questionable *b)* not sure or certain in knowledge; doubtful **2.** not definite; vague **3.** liable to change; not dependable or reliable **4.** not steady or constant; varying —**un·cer′tain·ly** ***adv.*** —**un·cer′tain·ness** ***n.***
un·cer·tain·ty (-tē) ***n.*** **1.** lack of certainty; doubt **2.** *pl.* **-ties** something uncertain
un·char·i·ta·ble (-char′i tə b'l) ***adj.*** harsh or severe, as in opinion; unforgiving, ungenerous, or faultfinding —**un·char′i·ta·ble·ness** ***n.*** —**un·char′i·ta·bly** ***adv.***
un·chris·tian (-kris′chən) ***adj.*** **1.** not having or practicing a Christian religion **2.** not in accord with the principles of Christianity **3.** [Colloq.] outrageous; dreadful
un·church (-chʉrch′) ***vt.*** **1.** to deprive (a person) of membership in a given church **2.** to deprive (a congregation) of its rights as a church
un·ci·al (un′shē əl, -shəl) ***adj.*** [< L. < *uncia,* an inch] designating or of a form of large, rounded letter used in the script of Greek and Latin manuscripts between 300 and 900 A.D. —***n.*** **1.** an uncial letter **2.** an uncial manuscript **3.** uncial script
un·cir·cum·cised (un sʉr′kəm sīzd′) ***adj.*** **1.** not circumcised; specif., not Jewish; gentile **2.** [Archaic] heathen
un·civ·il (un siv′'l) ***adj.*** **1.** not civilized; barbarous **2.** not civil or courteous; ill-mannered —**un·civ′il·ly** ***adv.***
un·civ·i·lized (-siv′ə līzd′) ***adj.*** **1.** not civilized; barbarous **2.** far from civilization
un·clad (-klad′) ***adj.*** wearing no clothes; naked
un·clasp (-klasp′) ***vt.*** **1.** to unfasten the clasp of **2.** to release from a clasp or grasp —***vi.*** **1.** to become unfastened **2.** to relax the clasp or grasp
un·cle (uŋ′k'l) ***n.*** [OFr. < L. *avunculus,* one's mother's brother] **1.** the brother of one's father or mother **2.** the husband of one's aunt **3.** [Colloq.] any elderly man: a term of address —**say** (or **cry**) **uncle** to surrender or admit defeat
un·clean (un klēn′) ***adj.*** **1.** dirty; filthy; foul **2.** not pure according to religious laws **3.** morally impure; unchaste; obscene —**un·clean′ness** ***n.***
un·clean·ly[1] (-klen′lē) ***adj.*** not cleanly; unclean; dirty —**un·clean′li·ness** ***n.***
un·clean·ly[2] (-klēn′lē) ***adv.*** in an unclean manner
un·clench (-klench′) ***vt., vi.*** to open: said of something clenched, or clinched: also **un·clinch′** (-klinch′)
Uncle Sam [< abbrev. U.S.] [Colloq.] the U.S. (government or people), personified as a tall man with chin whiskers, dressed in a red, white, and blue suit
Uncle Tom [after an elderly Negro slave in H. B. STOWE's antislavery novel, *Uncle Tom's Cabin* (1852)] a Negro whose behavior toward whites is regarded as fawning or servile: a term of contempt —**Uncle Tom′ism**
un·cloak (un klōk′) ***vt., vi.*** **1.** to remove a cloak or other covering (from) **2.** to reveal; expose
un·close (-klōz′) ***vt., vi.*** **-closed′, -clos′ing** **1.** to open **2.** to disclose or reveal
un·clothe (-klōth′) ***vt.*** **-clothed′** or **-clad′, -cloth′ing** to strip of or as of clothes; uncover; divest
un·coil (-koil′) ***vt., vi.*** to unwind or release from being coiled
un·com·fort·a·ble (-kumf′tər b'l, -kum′fər tə b'l) ***adj.*** **1.** not comfortable; feeling discomfort **2.** not pleasant; causing discomfort **3.** ill at ease —**un·com′fort·a·ble·ness** ***n.*** —**un·com′fort·a·bly** ***adv.***
un·com·mit·ted (un′kə mit′id) ***adj.*** **1.** not committed, as a crime **2.** not bound or pledged **3.** not having taken a position **4.** not imprisoned **5.** not committed to a mental hospital
un·com·mon (-käm′ən) ***adj.*** **1.** not common; rare; not usual **2.** strange; remarkable; extraordinary —**un·com′mon·ly** ***adv.*** —**un·com′mon·ness** ***n.***
un·com·mu·ni·ca·tive (un′kə myōō′nə kāt′iv, -ni kə tiv) ***adj.*** not communicative; reserved; taciturn —**un′com·mu′ni·ca′tive·ly** ***adv.*** —**un′com·mu′ni·ca′tive·ness** ***n.***
un·com·pro·mis·ing (un käm′prə mī′ziŋ) ***adj.*** not yielding or giving in at all; firm; inflexible
un·con·cern (un′kən sʉrn′) ***n.*** **1.** lack of interest; indifference **2.** lack of concern, or worry
un·con·cerned (-kən sʉrnd′) ***adj.*** not concerned; specif., *a)* not interested *b)* not solicitous or anxious —**un′con·cern′ed·ly** (-sʉr′nid lē) ***adv.*** —**un′con·cern′ed·ness** ***n.***
un·con·di·tion·al (-kən dish′ən 'l) ***adj.*** without conditions or stipulations; absolute —**un′con·di′tion·al·ly** ***adv.***
un·con·di·tioned (-kən dish′ənd) ***adj.*** **1.** *same as* UNCONDITIONAL **2.** *Psychol.* natural; inborn *[an unconditioned* reflex*]*
un·con·scion·a·ble (un kän′shən ə b'l) ***adj.*** **1.** not guided or restrained by conscience; unscrupulous **2.** unreasonable, excessive, etc. —**un·con′scion·a·bly** ***adv.***
un·con·scious (-kän′shəs) ***adj.*** **1.** deprived of consciousness *[unconscious* from a blow on the head*]* **2.** not aware (*of*) **3.** not realized or intended by the person himself *[unconscious* humor*]* —**the unconscious** *Psychoanalysis* the sum of all memories, thoughts, feelings, etc. of which the individual is not conscious but which influence his emotions and behavior —**un·con′scious·ly** ***adv.*** —**un·con′scious·ness** ***n.***
un·con·sti·tu·tion·al (un′kän stə tōō′shən 'l, -tyōō′-) ***adj.*** not in accordance with or permitted by a constitution, specif. the U.S. Constitution —**un′con·sti·tu′tion·al′i·ty** (-shə nal′ə tē) ***n.*** —**un′con·sti·tu′tion·al·ly** ***adv.***
un·con·ven·tion·al (un′kən ven′shən 'l) ***adj.*** not conforming to customary, formal, or accepted practices, standards, etc. —**un′con·ven′tion·al′i·ty** (-shə nal′ə tē) ***n.*** —**un′con·ven′tion·al·ly** ***adv.***
un·cork (un kôrk′) ***vt.*** to pull the cork out of
un·count·ed (-kount′id) ***adj.*** **1.** not counted **2.** too many to be counted; innumerable
un·cou·ple (-kup′'l) ***vt.*** **-pled, -pling** to unfasten (things coupled); disconnect —***vi.*** to become unfastened
un·couth (-kōōth′) ***adj.*** [OE. *uncuth,* unknown < *un-,* not + *cuth,* pp. of *cunnan,* to know] **1.** awkward; clumsy; ungainly **2.** uncultured; crude; boorish —**un·couth′ly** ***adv.*** —**un·couth′ness** ***n.***
un·cov·er (-kuv′ər) ***vt.*** **1.** to make known; disclose **2.** to lay bare by removing a covering **3.** to remove the cover or protection from **4.** to remove the hat, cap, etc. from

uncaged
uncanceled
uncaring
uncarpeted
uncataloged
uncaught
unceasing
uncelebrated
uncensored
uncensured
uncertified
unchain
unchallenged
unchangeable
unchanged
unchaperoned
uncharacteristic
uncharged
uncharted
unchartered
unchaste
unchastened
unchecked
uncherished
unchewed
unchilled
unchivalrous
unchosen
unchristened
unclaimed
unclarified
unclassifiable
unclassified
uncleaned
unclear
uncleared
unclipped
unclog
unclouded
uncluttered
uncoated
uncocked
uncollectable
uncollected
uncollectible
uncolonized
uncolored
uncombed
uncombinable
uncombined
uncomely
uncomforted
uncommissioned
uncompensated
uncomplaining
uncompleted
uncomplicated
uncomplimentary
uncomplying
uncompounded
uncomprehending
uncompressed
unconcealed
unconciliated
unconcluded
uncondemned
uncondensed
unconfessed
unconfined
unconfirmed
unconformity
unconfused
uncongenial
unconnected
unconquerable
unconquered
unconscientious
unconsecrated
unconsidered
unconsoled
unconsolidated
unconstrained
unconstricted
unconsumed
uncontaminated
uncontemplated
uncontested
uncontradictable
uncontrived
uncontrollable
uncontrolled
unconverted
unconvinced
unconvincing
uncooked
uncooperative
uncoordinated
uncorrected
uncorroborated
uncorrupted
uncountable
uncrate
uncredited
uncritical

(the head), as in showing respect —*vi.* to bare the head, as in showing respect

unc·tion (uŋk′shən) ***n.*** [L. *unctio* < *ungere*, to anoint] **1.** *a*) the act of anointing, as in medical treatment or a religious ceremony *b*) the oil, ointment, etc. used for this **2.** anything that soothes or comforts **3.** *a*) a very earnest manner of speaking or behaving, esp. about religious matters *b*) such a manner when it is pretended or seems put on

unc·tu·ous (uŋk′choo wəs) ***adj.*** [< ML. < L. *unctum*, ointment < *ungere*, to anoint] **1.** of, like, or characteristic of an ointment; oily or greasy **2.** like oil, soap, or grease to the touch: said of certain minerals **3.** characterized by a smug, smooth pretense of spiritual feeling or earnestness, as in seeking to persuade; too suave or oily in speech or manner —**unc′tu·os′i·ty** (-wäs′ə tē), **unc′tu·ous·ness** ***n.*** —**unc′tu·ous·ly** ***adv.***

un·cut (un kut′) ***adj.*** not cut; specif., *a*) having untrimmed margins: said of the pages of a book *b*) not ground to shape: said of a gem *c*) not abridged

un·daunt·ed (-dôn′tid, -dän′-) ***adj.*** not daunted; not afraid or discouraged —**un·daunt′ed·ly** ***adv.***

un·de·ceive (un′di sēv′) ***vt.*** **-ceived′, -ceiv′ing** to cause to be no longer deceived, mistaken, or misled

un·de·cid·ed (-di sīd′id) ***adj.*** **1.** that is not decided or settled **2.** not having come to a decision —**un′de·cid′ed·ly** ***adv.*** —**un′de·cid′ed·ness** ***n.***

un·de·ni·a·ble (-di nī′ə b′l) ***adj.*** **1.** that cannot be denied **2.** unquestionably good or excellent —**un′de·ni′a·bly** ***adv.***

un·der (un′dər) ***prep.*** [OE.] **1.** in, at, or to a position down from; below **2.** beneath the surface of [*under* water] **3.** below and to the other side of [to drive *under* a bridge] **4.** covered or concealed by [a vest *under* a coat] **5.** *a*) lower in authority, position, etc. than *b*) lower in value, amount, etc. than *c*) lower than the required degree of [*under* age] **6.** *a*) subject to the control, government, direction, influence, etc. of *b*) bound by [*under* oath] *c*) subjected to; undergoing [*under* repair] **7.** with the character, disguise, etc. of [*under* an alias] **8.** in (the designated category) [spiders are classified *under* arachnids] **9.** during the rule of [France *under* Louis XV] **10.** being the subject of [the question *under* discussion] **11.** because of [*under* the circumstances] **12.** authorized or attested by [*under* her signature] —***adv.*** **1.** in or to a lower position; beneath **2.** beneath the surface, as of water **3.** in or to a subordinate condition **4.** so as to be covered or concealed **5.** less in amount, value, etc. —***adj.*** lower in position, authority, rank, amount, degree, etc.

un·der- [OE.] *a prefix meaning:* **1.** in, on, to, or from a lower place or side; beneath or below [*undershirt*] **2.** in an inferior or subordinate position or rank [*undergraduate*] **3.** too little, not enough, below normal [*underdeveloped*]: the list below includes some common compounds formed with *under* that can be understood if *too little* or *insufficiently* is added to the meaning of the base word

underactive	**undermanned**
underbake	**underprice**
undercook	**undersubscribe**
underemphasize	**undersupply**
underexercise	**undertrained**

un·der·a·chieve (un′dər ə chēv′) ***vi.*** **-chieved′, -chiev′ing** to fail to do as well in school studies as might be expected from scores made on intelligence tests —**un′der·a·chieve′ment** ***n.*** —**un′der·a·chiev′er** ***n.***

un·der·act (-akt′) ***vt., vi.*** to act (a theatrical role) with too little emphasis or too great restraint

un·der·age (-āj′) ***adj.*** **1.** not of full or mature age **2.** below the age required by law

un·der·arm (un′dər ärm′) ***adj.*** **1.** under the arm; in the armpit **2.** *same as* UNDERHAND (sense 1) —***adv.*** *same as* UNDERHAND (sense 1)

un·der·bel·ly (-bel′ē) ***n.*** **1.** the lower, posterior part of an animal's belly **2.** any vulnerable or unprotected area or part

un·der·bid (un′dər bid′; *for n.* un′dər bid′) ***vt., vi.*** **-bid′, -bid′ding** **1.** to bid lower than (another person) **2.** to bid less than the worth of —***n.*** a lower or inadequate bid

un·der·bod·y (un′dər bäd′ē) ***n.*** **1.** the underpart of an animal's body **2.** the undersurface of a vehicle

un·der·brush (-brush′) ***n.*** small trees, shrubs, etc. that grow beneath large trees in woods or forests

un·der·buy (un′dər bī′) ***vt., vi.*** **-bought′, -buy′ing** **1.** to buy at less than the real value **2.** to buy more cheaply than (another or others)

un·der·cap·i·tal·ize (-kap′ə tə līz′) ***vt., vi.*** **-ized′, -iz′ing** to provide (a business) with too little capital for successful operation —**un′der·cap′i·tal·i·za′tion** ***n.***

un·der·car·riage (un′dər kar′ij) ***n.*** a supporting frame or structure, as of an automobile

un·der·charge (un′dər chärj′; *for n.* un′dər chärj′) ***vt., vi.*** **-charged′, -charg′ing** **1.** to charge too low a price (to) **2.** to provide with too little or low a charge —***n.*** a charge that is too little or low

un·der·class·man (un′dər klas′mən) ***n.***, *pl.* **-men** a freshman or sophomore

un·der·clothes (un′dər klōz′, -klōthz′) ***n.pl.*** *same as* UNDERWEAR: also **un′der·cloth′ing** (-klōth′iŋ)

un·der·coat (-kōt′) ***n.*** **1.** a coating of tarlike material applied to the undersurface of a car, etc. to retard rust, etc. **2.** a coat of paint, varnish, etc. applied before the final coat Also **un′der·coat′ing** —***vt.*** to apply an undercoat to

un·der·cov·er (-kuv′ər) ***adj.*** acting or done in secret

un·der·cur·rent (-kur′ənt) ***n.*** **1.** a current flowing below another or beneath the surface **2.** a hidden or underlying tendency, opinion, etc., usually conflicting with a more obvious one

un·der·cut (un′dər kut′; *for v.* un′dər kut′) ***n.*** **1.** a cut made below another so as to leave an overhang **2.** *Sports* an undercutting —***adj.*** that is undercut —***vt.*** **-cut′, -cut′ting** **1.** to make an undercut (sense 1) in **2.** to cut out the underpart of **3.** to undersell or work for lower wages than **4.** to weaken the position of; undermine **5.** *Sports* to strike (a ball) with an oblique downward motion, as in golf, or to chop with an underhand stroke, as in tennis, esp. so as to impart backspin —***vi.*** to undercut someone or something

un·der·de·vel·op (un′dər di vel′əp) ***vt.*** **1.** to develop to a point below what is needed **2.** *Photog.* to develop (a film, etc.) too short a time or with a weak developer

un·der·de·vel·oped (-əpt) ***adj.*** not developed to a desirable degree; specif., inadequately developed economically and industrially [*underdeveloped* nations]

un·der·do (-do͞o′) ***vt.*** **-did′, -done′, -do′ing** to do less than is usual, needed, or desired

un·der·dog (un′dər dôg′) ***n.*** **1.** the one that is losing, as in a contest **2.** a person who is handicapped or a victim of injustice, discrimination, etc.

un·der·done (un′dər dun′) ***adj.*** not cooked enough, as meat

un·der·em·ployed (-im ploid′) ***adj.*** **1.** employed at less than full time **2.** working at low-skilled, poorly paid jobs when one can do more skilled work —**the underemployed** underemployed people —**un′der·em·ploy′ment** ***n.***

un·der·es·ti·mate (-es′tə māt′; *for n.* -mit) ***vt., vi.*** **-mat′ed, -mat′ing** to set too low an estimate on or for —***n.*** an estimate that is too low —**un′der·es′ti·ma′tion** ***n.***

un·der·ex·pose (-ik spōz′) ***vt.*** **-posed′, -pos′ing** to expose (a photographic film, etc.) to inadequate light or for too short a time —**un′der·ex·po′sure** (-spō′zhər) ***n.***

un·der·feed (-fēd′) ***vt.*** **-fed′, -feed′ing** to feed less than is needed

un·der·foot (un′dər foot′) ***adv., adj.*** **1.** under the foot or feet **2.** in the way, as of one walking

un·der·fur (un′dər fur′) ***n.*** the softer, finer fur under the outer coat of some animals, as beavers or seals

un·der·gar·ment (-gär′mənt) ***n.*** a piece of underwear

un·der·gird (un′dər gurd′) ***vt.*** **-gird′ed** or **-girt′, -gird′ing** **1.** to gird or strengthen from the bottom side **2.** to supply support for

un·der·go (-gō′) ***vt.*** **-went′, -gone′, -go′ing** to experience; endure; go through

un·der·grad·u·ate (-graj′oo wit) ***n.*** a student at a university or college who has not yet received a bachelor's degree

un·der·ground (un′dər ground′; *for n.* -ground′) ***adj.*** **1.** occurring, working, etc. beneath the surface of the earth **2.** secret; undercover **3.** designating or of noncommercial newspapers, movies, etc. that are unconventional, experi-

uncross	**uncurl**	**undecorated**	**undemanding**
uncrowded	**undamaged**	**undefeatable**	**undemocratic**
uncrowned	**undated**	**undefeated**	**undemonstrable**
uncrystallized	**undebatable**	**undefended**	**undemonstrative**
uncultivated	**undecayed**	**undefiled**	**undenied**
uncultured	**undecipherable**	**undefinable**	**undenominational**
uncurbed	**undeclared**	**undefined**	**undependable**
uncured	**undeclinable**	**undeliverable**	**undepreciated**

mental, radical, etc. —*adv.* **1.** beneath the surface of the earth **2.** in or into secrecy or hiding —*n.* **1.** the entire region beneath the surface of the earth **2.** a secret movement organized to oppose the government in power or enemy forces of occupation **3.** [Brit.] a subway

underground railroad **1.** a subway: also **underground railway** **2.** [*often* U- R-] in the U.S. before the Civil War, a system set up by abolitionists to help fugitive slaves to escape to free States and Canada

un·der·growth (-grōth′) *n. same as* UNDERBRUSH

un·der·hand (un′dər hand′) *adj.* **1.** performed with the hand below the level of the elbow or shoulder **2.** *same as* UNDERHANDED (sense 1) —*adv.* **1.** with an underhand motion **2.** underhandedly

un·der·hand·ed (un′dər han′did) *adj.* **1.** secret, sly, deceitful, etc. **2.** lacking workers, players, etc.; shorthanded —**un′der·hand′ed·ly** *adv.* —**un′der·hand′ed·ness** *n.*

un·der·lay (un′dər lā′; *for n.* un′dər lā′) *vt.* **-laid′, -lay′-ing** **1.** to cover the bottom of **2.** to raise or support with something laid underneath —*n.* something laid underneath; specif., patches of paper laid under type to raise it

un·der·lie (-lī′) *vt.* **-lay′, -lain′, -ly′ing** **1.** to lie under or beneath **2.** to form the basis or foundation of

un·der·line (un′dər līn′; *also, for v.,* un′dər līn′) *vt.* **-lined′, -lin′ing** **1.** to draw a line beneath; underscore **2.** to stress or emphasize —*n. same as* UNDERSCORE

un·der·ling (un′dər liŋ) *n.* [OE.: see UNDER- & -LING[1]] a person who must carry out the orders of others above him; inferior: a disparaging term

un·der·lin·ing (-līn′iŋ) *n.* a garment lining formed of pieces cut to the shape of and attached to the sections of a garment, which are then sewed together

un·der·ly·ing (un′dər lī′iŋ) *adj.* **1.** lying under; placed beneath **2.** fundamental; basic

un·der·mine (un′dər mīn′, un′dər mīn′) *vt.* **-mined′, -min′ing** **1.** to dig beneath, so as to form a tunnel or mine **2.** to wear away and weaken the supports of **3.** to injure, weaken, or impair, esp. in a slow or stealthy way

un·der·most (un′dər mōst′) *adj., adv.* lowest in place, position, rank, etc.

un·der·neath (un′dər nēth′) *adv.* **1.** under; below; beneath **2.** at a lower level —*prep.* **1.** under; below; beneath **2.** under the form, guise, or authority of —*adj.* under or lower —*n.* the underpart

un·der·nour·ish (-nur′ish) *vt.* to provide with less food than is needed for health and growth —**un′der·nour′ish-ment** *n.*

un·der·pants (un′dər pants′) *n.pl.* an undergarment, long or short, for the lower part of the body, with a separate opening for each leg

un·der·part (-pärt′) *n.* the lower part or side, as of an animal's body or an airplane's fuselage

un·der·pass (-pas′) *n.* a passageway under something; esp., a road that runs under a railway or highway

un·der·pay (un′dər pā′) *vt., vi.* **-paid′, -pay′ing** to pay too little, or less than is right —**un′der·pay′ment** *n.*

un·der·pin (-pin′) *vt.* **-pinned′, -pin′ning** to support or strengthen from beneath, as with props

un·der·pin·ning (un′dər pin′iŋ) *n.* **1.** a supporting structure, esp. one placed beneath a wall **2.** a support or prop **3.** [*pl.*] [Colloq.] the legs

un·der·play (un′dər plā′) *vt., vi.* **1.** to act (a role or scene) with subtlety or little emphasis, in an intentionally restrained manner **2.** *same as* UNDERACT

un·der·priv·i·leged (-priv′'l ijd, -priv′lijd) *adj.* deprived of basic social rights and security through poverty, discrimination, etc. —**the underprivileged** underprivileged people

un·der·pro·duce (-prə do͞os′, -dyo͞os′) *vt., vi.* **-duced′, -duc′ing** to produce in a quantity that fails to meet the need or demand —**un′der·pro·duc′tion** *n.*

un·der·rate (-rāt′) *vt.* **-rat′ed, -rat′ing** to rate, assess, or estimate too low

un·der·score (un′dər skôr′; *for n.* un′dər skôr′) *vt.* **-scored′, -scor′ing** *same as* UNDERLINE —*n.* a line drawn under a word, passage, etc., as for emphasis

un·der·sea (-sē′) *adj., adv.* beneath the surface of the sea: also **un′der·seas′** (-sēz′) *adv.*

un·der·sec·re·tar·y (-sek′rə ter′ē) *n., pl.* **-tar′ies** an assistant secretary: in U.S. government, **under secretary**

un·der·sell (-sel′) *vt.* **-sold′, -sell′ing** **1.** to sell at a lower price than (another seller) **2.** to promote in a restrained or inadequate manner

un·der·sexed (-sekst′) *adj.* having a weaker than normal sexual drive or interest

un·der·shirt (un′dər shurt′) *n.* a usually sleeveless undergarment worn under an outer shirt, esp. by men and boys

un·der·shoot (un′dər sho͞ot′) *vt.* **-shot′, -shoot′ing** **1.** to shoot or fall short of (a target, mark, etc.) **2.** to bring an aircraft down short of (the runway, etc.) —*vi.* to shoot or go short of the mark

un·der·shorts (un′dər shôrts′) *n.pl.* short underpants worn by men and boys

un·der·shot (-shät′) *adj.* **1.** with the lower part jutting out past the upper [an *undershot* jaw] **2.** driven by water flowing along the lower part [an *undershot* water wheel]

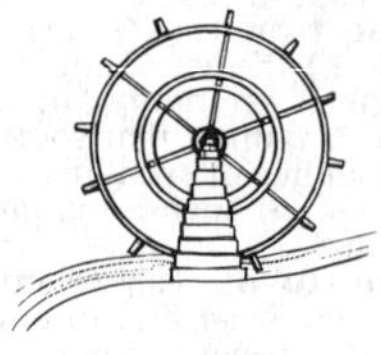

UNDERSHOT WHEEL

un·der·side (-sīd′) *n.* the side or surface underneath

un·der·sign (un′dər sīn′) *vt.* to sign one's name at the end of (a letter, document, etc.) —**the undersigned** the person or persons undersigning

un·der·sized (-sīzd′) *adj.* smaller in size than is usual, average, or proper: also **un′der·size′**

un·der·slung (-sluŋ′) *adj.* attached to the underside of the axles: said of an automobile frame

un·der·staffed (un′dər staft′) *adj.* having too small a staff; having fewer personnel than needed

un·der·stand (un′dər stand′) *vt.* **-stood′, -stand′ing** [OE. *understandan,* lit., to stand under] **1.** to get or know the meaning of **2.** to gather or assume from what is heard, known, etc.; infer **3.** to take as meant or meaning; interpret **4.** to take for granted or as a fact **5.** to supply mentally (an idea, word, etc.), as for grammatical completeness **6.** to be informed of; learn **7.** to know clearly or fully the nature, character, etc. of **8.** to have a sympathetic rapport with [no one *understands* me] —*vi.* **1.** to have understanding, comprehension, etc., either in general or with reference to something specific **2.** to be informed; believe —**un′der·stand′a·ble** *adj.* —**un′der·stand′a·bly** *adv.*

un·der·stand·ing (-iŋ) *n.* **1.** the act, state, or feeling of a person who understands; comprehension, knowledge, sympathetic awareness, etc. **2.** the power to think, learn, judge, etc.; intelligence; sense **3.** an explanation or interpretation [one's *understanding* of the matter] **4.** *a)* mutual comprehension, as of ideas, intentions, etc. *b)* an agreement, esp. one that settles differences or is informal —*adj.* that understands; having or showing comprehension, sympathy, etc. —**un′der·stand′ing·ly** *adv.*

un·der·state (un′dər stāt′) *vt.* **-stat′ed, -stat′ing** **1.** to make a weaker statement of than is warranted by truth, accuracy, or importance **2.** to express in a restrained style —**un′der·state′ment** *n.*

un·der·stud·y (un′dər stud′ē) *n., pl.* **-stud′ies** an actor who learns the part of another actor so that he can serve as a substitute when necessary —*vt., vi.* **-stud′ied, -stud′y-ing** **1.** to act as an understudy (to) **2.** to learn (a part) as an understudy

un·der·sur·face (-sur′fis) *n. same as* UNDERSIDE

un·der·take (un′dər tāk′) *vt.* **-took′, -tak′en, -tak′ing** **1.** to enter into or upon (a task, journey, etc.); take upon oneself; agree to do **2.** to give a promise or pledge that; contract **3.** to promise; guarantee

un·der·tak·er (un′dər tā′kər; *for 2* un′dər tā′kər) *n.* **1.** a person who undertakes something **2.** *earlier term for* FUNERAL DIRECTOR

un·der·tak·ing (un′dər tā′kiŋ; *also, & for 3 always,* un′dər tā′kiŋ) *n.* **1.** something undertaken; task; enterprise **2.** a promise; guarantee **3.** the business of an undertaker (sense 2) **4.** the act of one who undertakes a task, etc.

un·der-the-count·er (un′dər *thə* koun′tər) *adj.* [Colloq.] done, sold, given, etc. secretly in an unlawful or unethical way: also **un′der-the-ta′ble**

un·der·things (-thiŋz′) *n.pl.* women's or girls' underwear

un·der·tone (-tōn′) *n.* **1.** a low tone of sound or voice **2.** a subdued or background color **3.** any underlying quality, factor, element, etc. [an *undertone* of horror]

un·der·tow (-tō′) *n.* [UNDER- + TOW[1]] a current of water moving beneath the surface water and in a different direction, as seaward under the surf

un·der·val·ue (un′dər val′yo͞o) *vt.* **-ued, -u·ing** **1.** to value too low, or below the real worth **2.** to regard or esteem too lightly —**un′der·val′u·a′tion** *n.*

un·der·waist (un′dər wāst′) *n.* an undergarment worn under a waist

un·der·wa·ter (un′dər wôt′ər, -wät′ər) *adj.* **1.** being, done, etc. beneath the surface of the water **2.** used or for use under water —*adv.* beneath the surface of the water

un·der·way (un′dər wā′) *adj.* *Naut.* not at anchor or moored or aground

un·der·wear (un′dər wer′) *n.* clothing worn under one's outer clothes, usually next to the skin, as undershirts, undershorts, slips, bras, etc.

un·der·weight (un′dər wāt′; *also for adj.,* un′dər wāt′) *adj.* below the normal, desirable, or allowed weight —*n.* less weight than is needed, desired, or allowed

un·der·went (un′dər went′) *pt. of* UNDERGO

un·der·world (un′dər wurld′) *n.* **1.** the mythical world of the dead; Hades **2.** the criminal members of society, or people living by vice or crime, regarded as a group

un·der·write (un′dər rīt′) ***vt.*** **-wrote′, -writ′ten, -writ′ing** **1.** to write under something written; subscribe to, as by signature **2.** to agree to buy (an issue of stocks, bonds, etc.) on a given date and at a fixed price, or to guarantee the purchase of (stocks or bonds to be made available to the public) **3.** to pledge to support (an undertaking, etc.) financially **4.** *a)* to sign one's name to (an insurance policy), thus assuming liability *b)* to insure *c)* to assume liability to the amount of (a specified sum) —**un′der·writ′er** ***n.***

un·de·sir·a·ble (un′di zīr′ə b'l) ***adj.*** not desirable; objectionable —***n.*** an undesirable person —**un′de·sir′a·bil′i·ty** ***n.*** —**un′de·sir′a·bly** ***adv.***

un·dies (un′dēz) ***n.pl.*** [Colloq.] women's or girls' underwear

un·do (un dōō′) ***vt.*** **-did′, -done′, -do′ing** **1.** *a)* to release or untie (a fastening) *b)* to open (a parcel, door, etc.) by this means **2.** to reverse or do away with (something done or its effect) **3.** to ruin or destroy **4.** to upset or perturb —**un·do′er** ***n.***

un·do·ing (-iŋ) ***n.*** **1.** a reversal of something done or its effect **2.** ruin or the cause of ruin

un·done[1] (un dun′) *pp. of* UNDO —***adj.*** **1.** ruined, disgraced, etc. **2.** emotionally upset; greatly perturbed

un·done[2] (un dun′) ***adj.*** not done; not performed, accomplished, completed, etc.

un·doubt·ed (-dout′id) ***adj.*** not doubted or called in question; certain —**un·doubt′ed·ly** ***adv.***

un·draw (-drô′) ***vt., vi.*** **-drew′, -drawn′, -draw′ing** to draw (a curtain, drapes, etc.) open, back, or aside

un·dreamed (-drēmd′) ***adj.*** not even dreamed (*of*) or imagined; inconceivable: also **un·dreamt′** (-dremt′)

un·dress (un dres′; *for n. usually* un′dres′) ***vt.*** **1.** to take off the clothing of; strip **2.** to remove the dressing from (a wound) —***vi.*** to take off one's clothes; strip —***n.*** **1.** the state of being naked, partly clothed, in a robe, etc. **2.** ordinary or informal dress, as opposed to uniform, etc.

Und·set (oon′set), **Si·grid** (si′gri; *E.* si′grid) 1882–1949; Norw. novelist

un·due (un dōō′, -dyōō′) ***adj.*** **1.** not yet due or payable **2.** not suitable; improper [*undue* flippancy] **3.** too much; excessive [*undue* haste]

un·du·lant (un′joo lənt, -dyoo-; -doo-) ***adj.*** moving in or as in waves; undulating

undulant fever a form of brucellosis, transmitted to man from domestic animals or their products, and marked by recurrent fever, sweating, and pains in the joints

un·du·late (-lāt′; *for adj. usually* -lit) ***vt.*** **-lat′ed, -lat′ing** [< L. *undulatus*, undulated, ult. < *unda*, a wave] **1.** to cause to move in waves **2.** to give a wavy form, surface, etc. to —***vi.*** **1.** to move in waves **2.** to have a wavy form, surface, etc. —***adj.*** having a wavy form, margin, or surface: also **un′du·lat′ed** —**un′du·la·to′ry** ***adj.***

un·du·la·tion (un′joo lā′shən, -dyoo-, -doo-) ***n.*** **1.** an undulating or undulating motion **2.** a wavy, curving form or outline, esp. one of a series **3.** *Physics* wave motion, as of light or sound, or a wave or vibration

un·du·ly (un dōō′lē, -dyōō′-) ***adv.*** beyond what is proper or right; too much [*unduly* alarmed]

un·dy·ing (-dī′iŋ) ***adj.*** not dying; immortal or eternal

un·earned (-urnd′) ***adj.*** **1.** not earned by work or service; specif., obtained as a return on an investment [*unearned* income] **2.** not deserved; unmerited

un·earth (-urth′) ***vt.*** **1.** to dig up from out of the earth **2.** to bring to light; discover or disclose

un·earth·ly (-urth′lē) ***adj.*** **1.** not, or as if not, of this earth **2.** supernatural **3.** weird; mysterious **4.** [Colloq.] fantastic, outlandish, etc. —**un·earth′li·ness** ***n.***

un·eas·y (-ē′zē) ***adj.*** **-eas′i·er, -eas′i·est** **1.** having, showing, or allowing no ease of body or mind; uncomfortable **2.** awkward; constrained **3.** worried; anxious —**un·ease′, un·eas′i·ness** ***n.*** —**un·eas′i·ly** ***adv.***

un·ed·it·ed (-ed′it id) ***adj.*** **1.** not edited for publication **2.** not assembled for presentation [an *unedited* film]

un·em·ploy·a·ble (un′im ploi′ə b'l) ***adj.*** not employable; specif., that cannot be employed because of age, physical or mental deficiency, etc. —***n.*** an unemployable person

un·em·ployed (-im ploid′) ***adj.*** **1.** not employed; without work **2.** not being used; idle —**the unemployed** people who are out of work

un·em·ploy·ment (-im ploi′mənt) ***n.*** **1.** the state of being unemployed; lack of employment **2.** the number or percentage of persons in the normal labor force out of work

un·e·qual (un ē′kwəl) ***adj.*** **1.** not equal, as in size, strength, ability, value, rank, amount, etc. **2.** *a)* not balanced or symmetrical *b)* that matches unequal contestants [an *unequal* battle] **3.** not even, regular, etc.; variable **4.** not equal or adequate [*unequal* to the task] —***n.*** one that is not equal to another —**un·e′qual·ly** ***adv.***

un·e·qualed, un·e·qualled (-ē′kwəld) ***adj.*** not equaled; unmatched; unrivaled; supreme

un·e·quiv·o·cal (un′i kwiv′ə k'l) ***adj.*** not equivocal; not ambiguous; plain; clear —**un′e·quiv′o·cal·ly** ***adv.***

un·err·ing (un ur′iŋ, -er′-) ***adj.*** **1.** free from error **2.** not missing or failing; sure; exact —**un·err′ing·ly** ***adv.***

UNESCO (yoo nes′kō) United Nations Educational, Scientific, and Cultural Organization

un·e·ven (un ē′vən) ***adj.*** not even; specif., *a)* not level, smooth, or flat; rough; irregular *b)* not equal in size, amount, etc. *c)* not uniform; varying *d)* not equally balanced or matched *e)* *Math.* not evenly divisible by two —**un·e′ven·ly** ***adv.*** —**un·e′ven·ness** ***n.***

un·ex·am·pled (un′ig zam′p'ld) ***adj.*** with nothing like it before; with no other example; unprecedented

un·ex·cep·tion·a·ble (-ik sep′shə nə b'l) ***adj.*** not exceptionable; without flaw or fault; not warranting even the slightest criticism —**un′ex·cep′tion·a·bly** ***adv.***

un·ex·cep·tion·al (-ik sep′shən 'l) ***adj.*** **1.** not uncommon or unusual; ordinary **2.** not admitting of any exception **3.** *same as* UNEXCEPTIONABLE: regarded by some as a loose usage —**un′ex·cep′tion·al·ly** ***adv.***

un·ex·pect·ed (-ik spek′tid) ***adj.*** not expected; unforeseen —**un′ex·pect′ed·ly** ***adv.*** —**un′ex·pect′ed·ness** ***n.***

---

undeserving
undesignated
undesigning
undesired
undesirous
undestroyed
undetachable
undetected
undeterminable
undeterred
undeveloped
undeviating
undevoured
undevout
undifferentiated
undiffused
undigested
undigestible
undignified
undiluted
undiminished
undimmed
undiplomatic
undirected
undiscernible
undiscerning
undischarged
undisciplined
undisclosed
undiscouraged
undiscoverable
undiscovered
undiscriminating
undiscussed
undisguised
undismayed
undispelled
undisposed
undisputed
undissected
undissolved
undistilled
undistinguishable
undistinguished
undistorted
undistracted
undistressed
undistributed
undisturbed
undiversified
undiverted
undivested
undivided
undivulged
undocumented
undogmatic
undomestic
undomesticated
undrained
undramatic
undraped
undried
undrinkable
undutiful
undyed
uneatable
uneaten
uneclipsed
uneconomical
unedifying
uneducated
uneffaced
unemancipated
unembarrassed
unembellished
unemotional
unemphatic
unemptied
unenclosed
unencumbered
unending
unendorsed
unendowed
unendurable
unenforceable
unengaged
unenjoyable
unenlightened
unenriched
unenrolled
unenslaved
unentangled
unenterprising
unentertaining
unenthusiastic
unentitled
unenviable
unenvious
unequipped
unescorted
unessential
unestablished
unestimated
unethical
uneventful
unexacting
unexaggerated
unexamined
unexcelled
unexchangeable
unexcitable
unexciting
unexcused
unexecuted
unexercised
unexpendable
unexpired
unexplainable
unexplained
unexploded
unexploited
unexplored
unexposed
unexpressed

un·fail·ing (un fāl′iŋ) *adj.* **1.** not failing **2.** never ceasing or falling short; inexhaustible **3.** always reliable; certain —**un·fail′ing·ly** *adv.*

un·fair (-fer′) *adj.* **1.** not just or impartial; biased; inequitable **2.** dishonest or unethical in business dealings —**unfair′ly** *adv.* —**un·fair′ness** *n.*

un·faith·ful (-fāth′fəl) *adj.* **1.** failing to stay loyal or to keep a vow, promise, etc.; faithless **2.** not true, accurate, etc.; untrustworthy **3.** guilty of adultery —**un·faith′ful·ly** *adv.* —**un·faith′ful·ness** *n.*

un·fa·mil·iar (un′fə mil′yər) *adj.* **1.** not familiar or well-known; strange *[unfamiliar* lands*]* **2.** not acquainted (*with* something) —**un′fa·mil′i·ar′i·ty** (-yar′ə tē, -ē ar′-) *n.* —**un′fa·mil′iar·ly** *adv.*

un·fas·ten (un fas′'n) *vt.* to open or make loose; untie, unlock, undo, etc. —*vi.* to become unfastened

un·fa·vor·a·ble (-fā′vər ə b'l, -fāv′rə b'l) *adj.* not favorable; opposed, harmful, disadvantageous, inauspicious, etc. —**un·fa′vor·a·bly** *adv.*

un·feel·ing (-fēl′iŋ) *adj.* **1.** without feeling **2.** hard-hearted; cruel —**un·feel′ing·ly** *adv.*

un·feigned (-fānd′) *adj.* genuine; real; sincere

un·fin·ished (-fin′isht) *adj.* **1.** not finished or completed **2.** having no finish, or final coat, as of paint

un·fit (-fit′) *adj.* **1.** not meeting requirements; not fit or suitable **2.** not physically or mentally fit **3.** not fitted for a given purpose —*vt.* **-fit′ted, -fit′ting** to make unfit —**unfit′ly** *adv.* —**un·fit′ness** *n.*

un·fix (-fiks′) *vt.* to unfasten; loosen

un·flap·pa·ble (-flap′ə b'l) *adj.* [see FLAP, *n.* 4] [Colloq.] not easily excited or upset; calm

un·fledged (-flejd′) *adj.* **1.** not fully fledged; unfeathered, as a young bird **2.** immature; undeveloped

un·flinch·ing (-flin′chiŋ) *adj.* steadfast; resolute; unyielding —**un·flinch′ing·ly** *adv.*

un·fold (-fōld′) *vt.* **1.** to open and spread out (something folded) **2.** to lay open to view; reveal, disclose, display, or explain **3.** to open up; unwrap —*vi.* **1.** to become unfolded **2.** to develop fully

un·for·tu·nate (-fôr′chə nit) *adj.* **1.** *a)* having bad luck; unlucky *b)* bringing, or coming by, bad luck; unfavorable **2.** not suitable or successful —*n.* an unfortunate person —**un·for′tu·nate·ly** *adv.*

un·found·ed (-foun′did) *adj.* **1.** not founded on fact or truth; baseless **2.** not established

un·freeze (-frēz′) *vt.* **-froze′, -froz′en, -freez′ing** **1.** to cause to thaw **2.** to remove financial controls from (prices, wages, etc.)

un·friend·ed (-fren′did) *adj.* having no friends; friendless

un·friend·ly (-frend′lē) *adj.* **1.** not friendly or kind; hostile **2.** not favorable or propitious —**un·friend′li·ness** *n.*

un·frock (-fräk′) *vt.* **1.** to remove a frock from **2.** to deprive of the rank or function of priest or minister

un·furl (-furl′) *vt., vi.* to open or unfold from a furled state

un·gain·ly (-gān′lē) *adj.* **1.** awkward; clumsy **2.** coarse and unattractive —**un·gain′li·ness** *n.*

un·glued (-glōōd′) *adj.* broken open; separated: said of things glued together

un·god·ly (-gäd′lē) *adj.* **1.** not godly or religious; impious **2.** sinful; wicked **3.** [Colloq.] outrageous; dreadful —*adv.* [Colloq.] outrageously; dreadfully —**un·god′li·ness** *n.*

un·gov·ern·a·ble (-guv′ər nə b'l) *adj.* that cannot be governed or controlled; unruly —**un·gov′ern·a·bly** *adv.*

un·gra·cious (-grā′shəs) *adj.* **1.** rude; discourteous; impolite **2.** unpleasant; unattractive —**un·gra′cious·ly** *adv.* —**un·gra′cious·ness** *n.*

un·guard·ed (-gärd′id) *adj.* **1.** unprotected **2.** without guile or cunning; open **3.** careless; thoughtless; imprudent —**un·guard′ed·ly** *adv.*

un·guent (uŋ′gwənt) *n.* [L. *unguentum* < *unguere,* to anoint] a salve or ointment —**un′guen·tar′y** (-gwən ter′ē) *adj.*

un·guis (uŋ′gwis) *n., pl.* **un′gues** (-gwēz) [L., a nail] a nail, claw, or hoof: also **un′gu·la** (-gyoo lə), *pl.* **-lae′** (-lē′)

un·gu·late (-gyoo lit, -lāt′) *adj.* [< L. *ungula,* a hoof] having hoofs; of or belonging to a former group of all mammals having hoofs —*n.* a mammal having hoofs

un·hal·lowed (un hal′ōd) *adj.* **1.** not hallowed or consecrated; unholy **2.** wicked; profane

un·hand (-hand′) *vt.* to loose or release from the hand or hands or one's grasp; let go of

un·hand·y (-han′dē) *adj.* **-hand′i·er, -hand′i·est** **1.** not handy, convenient, or easy to reach **2.** not clever with the hands; awkward —**un·hand′i·ly** *adv.* —**un·hand′i·ness** *n.*

un·hap·py (-hap′ē) *adj.* **-pi·er, -pi·est** **1.** unlucky; unfortunate **2.** sad; wretched; sorrowful **3.** not suitable —**unhap′pi·ly** *adv.* —**un·hap′pi·ness** *n.*

un·health·y (-hel′thē) *adj.* **-health′i·er, -health′i·est** **1.** having or showing poor health; sickly; not well **2.** harmful to health; unwholesome **3.** harmful to morals **4.** dangerous or risky *[*an *unhealthy* situation*]* —**un·health′i·ly** *adv.* —**un·health′i·ness** *n.*

un·heard (-hurd′) *adj.* **1.** not perceived by the ear **2.** not given a hearing

un·heard-of (-hurd′uv′) *adj.* **1.** not heard of before; unprecedented **2.** unacceptable or outrageous *[unheard-of* behavior*]*

un·hinge (-hinj′) *vt.* **-hinged′, -hing′ing** **1.** to remove from the hinges **2.** to dislodge or detach **3.** to throw (the mind, etc.) into confusion; unbalance or upset

un·his·tor·ic (un′his tôr′ik, -tär′-) *adj.* not historic or historical; specif., *Linguis.* not having a historical basis; accidental, as the *b* in *thumb:* also **un′his·tor′i·cal**

un·hitch (un hich′) *vt.* **1.** to free from a hitch **2.** to unfasten; release; detach

un·ho·ly (-hō′lē) *adj.* **-li·er, -li·est** **1.** not sacred, hallowed, or consecrated **2.** wicked; profane; impious **3.** [Colloq.] outrageous; dreadful —**un·ho′li·ness** *n.*

un·hook (-hook′) *vt.* **1.** to remove or loosen from a hook **2.** to undo or unfasten the hook or hooks of —*vi.* to become unhooked

un·horse (-hôrs′) *vt.* **-horsed′, -hors′ing** **1.** to throw (a rider) from a horse **2.** to overthrow

un·hu·man (-hyōō′mən, -yōō′-) *adj.* **1.** *rare var. of: a)* INHUMAN *b)* SUPERHUMAN **2.** not human in kind, quality, etc. —**un·hu′man·ly** *adv.*

u·ni- [< L. *unus,* one] *a combining form meaning* having or consisting of one only *[unicellular]*

U·ni·ate, U·ni·at (yōō′nē ət, -at′) *n.* [< Russ. *uniyat,* ult. < L. *unus,* one: from union with the Roman Church] a member of the Eastern Church (sense 1 *b*)

u·ni·cam·er·al (yōō′nə kam′ər əl) *adj.* [< UNI- + LL. *camera,* a chamber] of or having a single legislative chamber

UNICEF (yōō′nə sef′) United Nations International Children's Emergency Fund

u·ni·cel·lu·lar (yōō′nə sel′yoo lər) *adj.* having or consisting of a single cell

---

unexpurgated
unextended
unextinguished
unfading
unfaltering
unfashionable
unfathomable
unfathomed
unfeared
unfeasible
unfeathered
unfed
unfederated
unfelt
unfeminine
unfenced
unfermented
unfertilized
unfettered
unfilial
unfilled
unfiltered
unfired
unfitting
unflagging
unflattering
unflavored
unforbidden
unforced
unforeseeable
unforeseen
unforested
unforfeited
unforged
unforgettable
unforgivable
unforgiven
unforgiving
unforgotten
unformed
unformulated
unforsaken
unfortified
unfought
unframed
unfree
unfrequented
unfruitful
unfulfilled
unfunded
unfunny
unfurnished
ungarnished
ungathered
ungenerous
ungentlemanly
ungenuine
ungifted
ungird
unglazed
unglorified
ungloved
ungraceful
ungraded
ungraduated
ungrammatica
ungrateful
ungratified
ungreased
ungrounded
ungrudging
unguessable
unguided
unhampered
unhandled
unhandsome
unhanged
unhardened
unharmed
unharmful
unharmonious
unharness
unharrowed
unharvested
unhatched
unhealed
unhealthful
unheated
unheeded
unheeding
unhelpful
unheralded
unheroic
unhesitating
unhindered
unhired
unhonored
unhoped-for
unhoused
unhung
unhurried
unhurt
unhygienic
unhyphenated

u·ni·corn (yo͞o′nə kôrn′) *n.* [< OFr. < L. < *unus,* one + *cornu,* a horn] a mythical horselike animal with a single horn growing from the center of its forehead

UNICORN

u·ni·cy·cle (yo͞o′nə sī′k'l) *n.* a riding device with only one wheel, which is straddled by the rider

u·ni·fi·ca·tion (yo͞o′nə fi kā′shən) *n.* the act of unifying or the state of being unified

u·ni·form (yo͞o′nə fôrm′) *adj.* [< MFr. < L. < *unus,* one + *-formis,* -form] **1.** always the same; not varying in form, rate, degree, manner, etc. **2.** having the same form, appearance, etc. as others of the same class **3.** consistent in action, intention, effect, etc. *[a uniform* policy*]* —*n.* the official or distinctive clothes worn by the members of a particular group, as policemen or soldiers —*vt.* to clothe or supply with a uniform —**uniform with** having the same form, appearance, etc. as —**u′ni·form′ly** *adv.*

u·ni·form·i·ty (yo͞o′nə fôr′mə tē) *n., pl.* **-ties** state, quality, or instance of being uniform

u·ni·fy (yo͞o′nə fī′) *vt., vi.* **-fied′, -fy′ing** [< MFr. < LL. *unificare:* see UNI- & -FY] to combine into one; become or make united —**u′ni·fi′a·ble** *adj.* —**u′ni·fi′er** *n.*

u·ni·lat·er·al (yo͞o′nə lat′ər əl) *adj.* **1.** of, occurring on, or affecting one side only **2.** involving one only of several parties; done by one only *[a unilateral* contract*]* **3.** taking into account one side only of a matter; one-sided **4.** turned to, or having its parts on, one side —**u′ni·lat′er·al·ism** *n.* —**u′ni·lat′er·al·ly** *adv.*

u·ni·lin·e·ar (-lin′ē ər) *adj.* of or following a single, consistent path of development or progression

un·im·peach·a·ble (un′im pēch′ə b'l) *adj.* that cannot be doubted, questioned, or discredited; irreproachable —**un′im·peach′a·bly** *adv.*

un·im·proved (un′im pro͞ovd′) *adj.* **1.** not bettered, improved, or developed, as land by planting, building, etc. **2.** not used to good advantage **3.** not improved in health

un·in·hib·it·ed (-in hib′it id) *adj.* without inhibition; esp., free from the usual social or psychological restraints

un·ion (yo͞on′yən) *n.* [< MFr. < LL. < L. < *unus,* one] **1.** a uniting or being united; combination; junction; specif., *a)* a grouping together of nations, political groups, etc. for some specific purpose *b)* marriage **2.** something united; a whole made up of united parts; specif., *a)* an organization or confederation uniting various individuals, political units, etc. *b) short for* LABOR UNION **3.** a device symbolizing political union, used in a flag or ensign, as the white stars on a blue field in the U.S. flag **4.** a facility for social recreation on a college campus: in full, **student union** **5.** a device for joining together parts; esp., a coupling for linking the ends of pipes **6.** *Math.* a set containing all the elements of two or more given sets, with no element listed more than once —**the Union** the United States of America

Union City [formed by the union of two older towns] city in NE N.J.: suburb of Jersey City: pop. 56,000

un·ion·ism (yo͞on′yən iz'm) *n.* **1.** *a)* the principle of union *b)* support of this principle or of a specified union **2.** the system or principles of labor unions **3.** [U-] loyalty to the Federal union of the U.S., esp. during the Civil War —**un′ion·ist** *n.* —**un′ion·is′tic** *adj.*

un·ion·ize (-īz′) *vt.* **-ized′, -iz′ing** **1.** to organize (a group of workers) into a labor union **2.** to bring into conformity with the rules, standards, etc. of a labor union —*vi.* to join or organize a labor union —**un′ion·i·za′tion** *n.*

union jack **1.** a jack or flag consisting only of a union, esp. of the union of a national flag **2.** [U- J-] the national flag of the United Kingdom

Union of South Africa *former name of* SOUTH AFRICA

Union of Soviet Socialist Republics country in E Europe & N Asia, extending from the Baltic Sea to the Pacific: it is a union of fifteen republics: 8,603,000 sq. mi.; pop. 258,000,000; cap. Moscow

union shop a factory, business, etc. operating under a contract with a labor union, which requires that new workers join the union after being hired

union suit a suit of men's or boys' underwear uniting shirt and drawers in a single garment

u·nique (yo͞o nēk′) *adj.* [Fr. < L. *unicus,* single < *unus,* one] **1.** one and only; sole **2.** having no like or equal; unparalleled **3.** highly unusual, extraordinary, etc.: a common usage still objected to by some —**u·nique′ly** *adv.* —**u·nique′ness** *n.*

u·ni·sex (yo͞o′nə seks′) *adj.* [Colloq.] designating or of a fashion, as in garments, hair styles, etc., adopted by persons of either sex

u·ni·sex·u·al (yo͞o′nə sek′sho͞o wəl) *adj.* having one sex (male or female) only; not hermaphroditic —**u′ni·sex′u·al′i·ty** (-sho͞o wal′ə tē) *n.* —**u′ni·sex′u·al·ly** *adv.*

u·ni·son (yo͞o′nə sən, -zən) *n.* [MFr. < ML. < L. *unus,* one + *sonus,* a sound] **1.** identity of musical pitch, as of two or more voices or tones **2.** agreement; concord; harmony —**in unison** **1.** sounding the same note at the same time **2.** with all the voices or instruments performing the same part **3.** uttering the same words, or producing the same sound, at the same time

u·nit (yo͞o′nit) *n.* [< UNITY] **1.** *a)* the smallest whole number; one *b)* the number in the position just to the left of the decimal point **2.** any fixed quantity, amount, measure, etc. used as a standard; specif., the amount of a drug, vaccine, etc. needed to produce a given result **3.** *a)* a single person or group, esp. as distinguished from others or as part of a whole *b)* a single, distinct part, esp. one used for a specific purpose *[*the lens *unit* of a camera*]*

U·ni·tar·i·an (yo͞o′nə ter′ē ən) *n.* **1.** a person who denies the doctrine of the Trinity, rejecting the divinity of Jesus and holding that God exists as one person or being **2.** a member of a Christian denomination based on these beliefs and showing tolerance of differing religious views —*adj.* **1.** of Unitarians or their beliefs **2.** [u-] *same as* UNITARY —**U′ni·tar′i·an·ism** *n.*

u·ni·tar·y (yo͞o′nə ter′ē) *adj.* **1.** of a unit or units **2.** of, based on, or characterized by unity **3.** having the nature of or used as a unit

unit character *Genetics* a character or trait determined by a single gene or gene pair

u·nite (yoo nīt′) *vt., vi.* **-nit′ed, -nit′ing** [< L. pp. of *unire,* to unite < *unus,* one] **1.** to put or join together so as to make one; combine into a whole **2.** *a)* to bring or come together in common cause, interest, action, etc.; join through fellowship, legal bonds, etc. *b)* to join in marriage

u·nit·ed (yoo nīt′id) *adj.* **1.** combined; joined **2.** of or resulting from joint action or association **3.** in agreement —**u·nit′ed·ly** *adv.* —**u·nit′ed·ness** *n.*

United Arab Emirates country consisting of seven Arab sheikdoms in E Arabia: 32,300 sq. mi.; pop. 179,000

United Arab Republic *former name* (1961–71) *of* EGYPT

United Church of Christ a Protestant denomination formed by a merger of denominations in 1957

United Kingdom country in W Europe, consisting of England, Scotland, Wales, Northern Ireland, the Channel Islands, & the Isle of Man: 94,217 sq. mi.; pop. 55,730,000; cap. London: in full, **United Kingdom of Great Britain and Northern Ireland**

United Nations an international organization of nations pledged to promote world peace and security under a charter signed in 1945 by 50 nations: 104 additional members had been admitted by 1980

United States of America country made up of the N. American area extending from the Atlantic Ocean to the Pacific Ocean between Canada and Mexico, together with Alaska & Hawaii: 3,615,211 sq. mi.; pop. 226,505,000 (1980); cap. Washington: also called **United States**

unidentified
unidiomatic
unilluminated
unillustrated
unimaginable
unimaginably
unimaginative
unimitated
unimpaired
unimpassioned
unimpeded
unimplemented
unimportance
unimportant
unimposing
unimpregnated
unimpressed
unimpressionable
unimpressive
unincorporated
unindulged
unindustrialized
unindustrious
uninfected
uninfested
uninflected
uninfluenced
uninformed
uninhabitable
uninhabited
uninitiated
uninjured
uninspired
uninspiring
uninstructed
uninsurable
uninsured
unintegrated
unintelligent
unintelligible
unintended
unintentional
uninterested
uninteresting
uninterrupted
unintimidated
uninventive
uninvested
uninvited
uninviting
uninvolved
unissued

u·ni·tive (yo͞o′nə tiv) ***adj.*** tending to produce unity

u·nit·ize (yo͞o′nə tīz′) ***vt.*** **-ized′, -iz′ing** to make into a single unit —**u′nit·i·za′tion** ***n.***

unit pricing a supplementary system of pricing commodities, esp. food items, by showing the prices in terms of standard units, as of an ounce or pint

u·ni·ty (yo͞o′nə tē) ***n.,*** *pl.* **-ties** [< OFr. < L. *unitas* < *unus,* one] **1.** the state of being one, or united; oneness **2.** a single, separate thing **3.** harmony; agreement; concord **4.** *a*) unification *b*) a unified group or body **5.** a complex that is a union of related parts **6.** *a*) an arrangement of parts that will produce a single, harmonious effect in an artistic or literary production *b*) an effect so produced **7.** constancy or continuity of purpose, action, etc. **8.** *Math.* any quantity, magnitude, etc. identified as a unit, or 1

Univ. 1. Universalist **2.** University

u·ni·va·lent (yo͞o′nə vā′lənt, yo͝o niv′ə lənt) ***adj.*** *Chem.* **1.** having one valence **2.** having a valence of one —**u′ni·va′lence, u′ni·va′len·cy** ***n.***

u·ni·valve (yo͞o′nə valv′) ***n.*** **1.** a mollusk having a one-piece shell, as a snail **2.** such a one-piece shell —***adj.*** **1.** having a one-piece shell **2.** having one valve only

u·ni·ver·sal (yo͞o′nə vur′s'l) ***adj.*** [< OFr. < L.: see UNIVERSE] **1.** of the universe; present or occurring everywhere **2.** of, for, or including all or the whole; not limited **3.** entire; whole **4.** broad in knowledge, interests, etc. **5.** that can be used for all kinds, forms, sizes, etc. **6.** used, intended to be used, or understood by all **7.** *Logic* predicating something of every member of a specified class —***n.*** **1.** *short for* UNIVERSAL JOINT **2.** *Logic* a universal proposition —**u′ni·ver′sal·ness** ***n.***

u·ni·ver·sal·ism (-iz'm) ***n.*** **1.** *same as* UNIVERSALITY **2.** [U-] the theological doctrine that all souls will eventually find salvation —**U′ni·ver′sal·ist** ***adj., n.***

u·ni·ver·sal·i·ty (yo͞o′nə vər sal′ə tē) ***n.,*** *pl.* **-ties 1.** quality, state, or instance of being universal **2.** unlimited range, application, occurrence, etc.; comprehensiveness

u·ni·ver·sal·ize (-vur′sə līz′) ***vt.*** **-ized′, -iz′ing** to make universal —**u′ni·ver′sal·i·za′tion** ***n.***

universal joint (or **coupling**) a joint or coupling that permits a swing of limited angle in any direction, esp. one used to transmit rotary motion from one shaft to another not in line with it, as in the drive shaft of an automobile

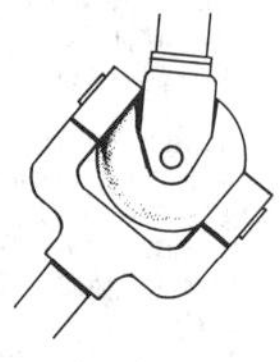

UNIVERSAL JOINT

u·ni·ver·sal·ly (-vur′s'l ē) ***adv.*** **1.** in every instance **2.** in every part or place

universal suffrage suffrage for all adult citizens

u·ni·verse (yo͞o′nə vurs′) ***n.*** [L. *universum* < *unus,* one + pp. of *vertere,* to turn] **1.** the totality of all the things that exist; the cosmos **2.** the world

u·ni·ver·si·ty (yo͞o′nə vur′sə tē) ***n.,*** *pl.* **-ties** [< MFr. < ML. < L. *universitas,* the whole, a society: see prec.] **1.** an educational institution of the highest level, typically having one or more undergraduate colleges and also graduate and professional schools **2.** the buildings, students, faculty, or administrators of a university

un·joint (un joint′) ***vt.*** **1.** to separate (a joint) **2.** to separate the joints of

un·just (-just′) ***adj.*** not just or right; unfair —**un·just′ly** ***adv.*** —**un·just′ness** ***n.***

un·kempt (-kempt′) ***adj.*** [UN- + *kempt,* pp. of dial. *kemben,* to comb] **1.** not combed **2.** not tidy, neat, or groomed —**un·kempt′ness** ***n.***

un·kind (-kīnd′) ***adj.*** **1.** not sympathetic to or considerate of others **2.** harsh, severe, cruel, etc. —**un·kind′ness** ***n.***

un·kind·ly (-kīnd′lē) ***adj.*** *same as* UNKIND —***adv.*** in an unkind manner —**un·kind′li·ness** ***n.***

un·known (-nōn′) ***adj.*** **1.** not in one's knowledge, acquaintance, etc.; unfamiliar (*to*) **2.** not discovered, identified, etc. —***n.*** an unknown person, thing, or quantity

un·lace (-lās′) ***vt.*** **-laced′, -lac′ing** to undo or unfasten the laces of

un·lade (-lād′) ***vt., vi.*** **-lad′ed, -lad′ed** or **-lad′en, -lad′ing 1.** to unload (a ship, etc.) **2.** to discharge (a cargo, etc.)

un·latch (-lach′) ***vt., vi.*** to open by release of a latch

un·law·ful (-lô′fəl) ***adj.*** **1.** against the law; illegal **2.** against ethical standards; immoral —**un·law′ful·ly** ***adv.***

un·lead·ed (-led′id) ***adj.*** not mixed with tetraethyl lead: said of gasoline

un·learn (-lurn′) ***vt., vi.*** to forget (something learned) by a conscious effort, as in retraining

un·learn·ed (-lur′nid; *for 2* -lurnd′) ***adj.*** **1.** *a*) not learned or educated; ignorant *b*) showing a lack of learning or education **2.** known or acquired without conscious study [*unlearned* tact] —**un·learn′ed·ly** ***adv.***

un·leash (-lēsh′) ***vt.*** to release from or as from a leash

un·less (ən les′) ***conj.*** [earlier *on lesse that,* at less than] in any case other than; except if [he won't go *unless* she does] —***prep.*** except [no one, *unless* the doctor, knows]

un·let·tered (un let′ərd) ***adj.*** **1.** *a*) uneducated *b*) illiterate **2.** not marked with letters

un·like (-līk′) ***adj.*** not alike; different; dissimilar —***prep.*** **1.** not like; different from **2.** not characteristic of [it's *unlike* her to cry] —**un·like′ness** ***n.***

un·like·ly (-līk′lē) ***adj.*** **1.** not likely to happen or be true; improbable **2.** not likely to succeed —***adv.*** improbably —**un·like′li·hood′, un·like′li·ness** ***n.***

un·lim·ber[1] (-lim′bər) ***adj.*** not limber; stiff —***vi., vt.*** to make or become limber

un·lim·ber[2] (-lim′bər) ***vt., vi.*** **1.** to prepare (a field gun) for use by detaching the limber **2.** to get ready for action

un·lim·it·ed (-lim′it id) ***adj.*** **1.** without limits or restrictions **2.** without boundaries

un·load (-lōd′) ***vt.*** **1.** *a*) to remove (a load, cargo, etc.) *b*) to take a load, etc. from **2.** *a*) to express or tell (one's troubles, etc.) freely *b*) to relieve of something that troubles, burdens, etc. **3.** to remove the charge from (a gun) **4.** to get rid of —***vi.*** to unload something

un·lock (-läk′) ***vt.*** **1.** *a*) to open (a lock) *b*) to open the lock of (a door, etc.) **2.** to let loose as if by opening a lock [to *unlock* a flood of tears] **3.** to cause to separate [to *unlock* clenched jaws] **4.** to lay open [to *unlock* a secret] —***vi.*** to get unlocked

un·looked-for (-lo͝okt′fôr′) ***adj.*** not expected or foreseen

un·loose (-lo͞os′) ***vt.*** **-loosed′, -loos′ing** to make or set loose: also **un·loos′en**

un·luck·y (-luk′ē) ***adj.*** **-luck′i·er, -luck′i·est** not lucky; having or marked by bad luck; unfortunate —**un·luck′i·ly** ***adv.***

un·make (-māk′) ***vt.*** **-made′, -mak′ing 1.** to cause to be as before; make revert to original condition **2.** to ruin; destroy **3.** to depose from a position or authority

un·man (-man′) ***vt.*** **-manned′, -man′ning 1.** to deprive of manly courage, confidence, etc. **2.** to castrate

un·man·ly (-man′lē) ***adj.*** **-li·er, -li·est** not manly; specif., cowardly, weak, effeminate, etc. —**un·man′li·ness** ***n.***

un·manned (-mand′) ***adj.*** not manned; specif., without men aboard and operating by automatic or remote control

un·man·ner·ly (-man′ər lē) ***adj.*** having or showing poor manners; rude; discourteous —***adv.*** rudely

un·mask (-mask′) ***vt., vi.*** **1.** to remove a mask or disguise (from) **2.** to show or appear in true character

un·mean·ing (-mēn′iŋ) ***adj.*** **1.** lacking in meaning or sense **2.** showing no sense or intelligence; expressionless

un·meet (-mēt′) ***adj.*** not meet, or fit; unsuitable

un·men·tion·a·ble (un men′shən ə b'l) ***adj.*** not fit to be mentioned; not nice to talk about —***n.*** [*pl.*] unmentionable things; specif., underwear: a humorous usage

un·mer·ci·ful (-mur′si fəl) ***adj.*** **1.** having or showing no mercy; cruel; pitiless **2.** excessive —**un·mer′ci·ful·ly** ***adv.***

un·mind·ful (-mīnd′fəl) ***adj.*** not mindful; heedless

un·mis·tak·a·ble (un′mis tāk′ə b'l) ***adj.*** that cannot be mistaken or misunderstood; clear; plain —**un′mis·tak′a·bly** ***adv.***

---

unjoined
unjudicial
unjustifiable
unkept
unkissed
unknit
unknot
unknowable
unknowing
unlabeled
unlabored
unladylike
unlamented
unlaundered
unleased
unleavened
unlevied
unlicensed
unlifelike
unlighted
unlikable
unlikeable
unlined
unlisted
unlit
unlively
unlocated
unlovable
unloved
unlovely
unloving
unlubricated
unmagnified
unmalleable
unmanageable
unmanifested
unmanufacturable
unmanufactured
unmarked
unmarketable
unmarred
unmarried
unmastered
unmatchable
unmatched
unmated
unmatted
unmeant
unmeasurable
unmeasured
unmechanical
unmedicated
unmeditated
unmelodious
unmelted
unmended
unmentioned
unmercenary
unmerited
unmethodical
unmilitary
unmilled
unmingled
unmistaken

un·mit·i·gat·ed (un mit′ə gāt′id) ***adj.*** **1.** not lessened or eased *[unmitigated* suffering*]* **2.** out-and-out; absolute *[*an *unmitigated* fool*]* —**un·mit′i·gat′ed·ly** ***adv.***
un·mor·al (-môr′′l) ***adj.*** *var. of* AMORAL
un·muz·zle (-muz′′l) ***vt.*** **-zled, -zling** **1.** to free (a dog, etc.) from a muzzle **2.** to stop restraining or censoring
un·nat·u·ral (-nach′ər əl) ***adj.*** not natural; specif., *a)* abnormal; strange *b)* artificial; strained *c)* abnormally evil or cruel —**un·nat′u·ral·ly** ***adv.*** —**un·nat′u·ral·ness** ***n.***
un·nec·es·sar·y (-nes′ə ser′ē) ***adj.*** not necessary or required; needless —**un·nec′es·sar′i·ly** ***adv.***
un·nerve (-nurv′) ***vt.*** **-nerved′, -nerv′ing** **1.** to cause to lose one's courage, confidence, etc. **2.** to make nervous
un·num·bered (-num′bərd) ***adj.*** **1.** not counted **2.** *same as* INNUMERABLE **3.** having no identifying number
un·oc·cu·pied (-äk′yə pīd′) ***adj.*** **1.** having no occupant; vacant; empty **2.** at leisure; idle
un·or·gan·ized (-ôr′gə nīzd′) ***adj.*** **1.** having no organic structure **2.** not having or following any regular order or system **3.** not having or belonging to a labor union
un·pack (-pak′) ***vt.*** **1.** to open and remove the packed contents of **2.** to take from a crate, trunk, etc. **3.** to remove a pack or load from —***vi.*** to empty a packed trunk, etc.
un·paged (-pājd′) ***adj.*** having the pages unnumbered: said of a book, etc.
un·par·al·leled (-par′ə leld′) ***adj.*** that has no parallel, equal, or counterpart; unmatched
un·par·lia·men·ta·ry (-pär′lə men′tər ē, -trē) ***adj.*** contrary to parliamentary law or usage
un·peg (-peg′) ***vt.*** **-pegged′, -peg′ging** **1.** to remove a peg or pegs from **2.** to unfasten or detach in this way
un·peo·ple (-pē′p′l) ***vt.*** **-pled, -pling** to reduce the population of; depopulate
un·pin (-pin′) ***vt.*** **-pinned′, -pin′ning** **1.** to remove a pin or pins from **2.** to unfasten or detach in this way
un·pleas·ant (-plez′′nt) ***adj.*** not pleasant; offensive; disagreeable —**un·pleas′ant·ly** ***adv.*** —**un·pleas′ant·ness** ***n.***
un·plumbed (-plumd′) ***adj.*** **1.** not sounded or measured with a plumb **2.** not fully plumbed or understood
un·polled (-pōld′) ***adj.*** **1.** *a)* not canvassed in a poll *b)* not cast or registered: said of votes **2.** unshorn
un·pop·u·lar (-päp′yə lər) ***adj.*** not popular; not liked by the public or the majority —**un′pop·u·lar′i·ty** (-yə lar′ə tē) ***n.***
un·prac·ticed (-prak′tist) ***adj.*** **1.** not practiced; not regularly done, etc. **2.** not skilled or experienced
un·prec·e·dent·ed (-pres′ə den′tid) ***adj.*** having no precedent or parallel; unheard-of; novel
un·prej·u·diced (-prej′ə dist) ***adj.*** **1.** without prejudice or bias; impartial **2.** not impaired
un·prin·ci·pled (-prin′sə p′ld) ***adj.*** characterized by lack of moral principles; unscrupulous
un·print·a·ble (-print′ə b′l) ***adj.*** not printable; not fit to be printed, as because of obscenity
un·pro·fes·sion·al (un′prə fesh′ən ′l) ***adj.*** **1.** violating the ethical code of a given profession **2.** not of, typical of, or belonging to a profession —**un′pro·fes′sion·al·ly** ***adv.***
un·qual·i·fied (un kwäl′ə fīd′) ***adj.*** **1.** lacking the necessary qualifications; not fit **2.** not limited; absolute *[*an *unqualified* success*]* —**un·qual′i·fied′ly** ***adv.***
un·ques·tion·a·ble (-kwes′chən ə b′l) ***adj.*** **1.** not to be questioned, doubted, or disputed; certain **2.** with no exception or qualification —**un·ques′tion·a·bly** ***adv.***
un·ques·tioned (-kwes′chənd) ***adj.*** not questioned; specif., *a)* not interrogated *b)* not disputed; accepted
un·qui·et (-kwī′ət) ***adj.*** not quiet; restless, disturbed, uneasy, anxious, etc. —***n.*** an unquiet state —**un·qui′et·ly** ***adv.*** —**un·qui′et·ness** ***n.***
un·quote (un′kwōt′) ***interj.*** I end the quotation: used in speech after a quotation
un·rav·el (un rav′′l) ***vt.*** **-eled** or **-elled, -el·ing** or **-el·ling** **1.** to undo (something woven, tangled, etc.); separate the threads of **2.** to make clear; solve —***vi.*** to become unraveled —**un·rav′el·ment** ***n.***
un·read (-red′) ***adj.*** **1.** not read, as a book **2.** having read little or nothing **3.** unlearned (*in* a subject)
un·read·y (-red′ē) ***adj.*** **1.** not ready; unprepared, as for action **2.** not prompt or alert; slow —**un·read′i·ly** ***adv.*** —**un·read′i·ness** ***n.***
un·real (-rē′əl, -rēl′) ***adj.*** not real; imaginary, false, etc. —**un′re·al′i·ty** (-rē al′ə tē) ***n.***, *pl.* **-ties**
un·re·al·is·tic (un′rē ə lis′tik) ***adj.*** not realistic; impractical; visionary —**un′re·al·is′ti·cal·ly** ***adv.***
un·rea·son (un rē′z′n) ***n.*** lack of reason; irrationality
un·rea·son·a·ble (-ə b′l) ***adj.*** not reasonable; specif., *a)* having or showing little sense *b)* excessive; immoderate —**un·rea′son·a·ble·ness** ***n.*** —**un·rea′son·a·bly** ***adv.***
un·rea·son·ing (-iŋ) ***adj.*** lacking reason or judgment; irrational —**un·rea′son·ing·ly** ***adv.***

---

unmixed
unmodified
unmoistened
unmolested
unmollified
unmoor
unmortgaged
unmotivated
unmounted
unmourned
unmovable
unmoved
unmoving
unmown
unmuffle
unmurmuring
unmusical
unmystified
unnail
unnamable
unnameable
unnamed
unnaturalized
unnavigable
unnavigated
unneeded
unneedful
unneighborly
unnoted
unnoticeable
unnoticed
unnurtured
unobjectionable
unobliged
unobliging
unobscured
unobservant
unobserved
unobserving
unobstructed
unobtainable
unobtrusive
unoffending
unoffensive
unoffered
unofficial
unofficious
unoiled
unopen
unopened
unopposed
unoppressed
unordained
unoriginal
unornamental
unorthodox
unostentatious
unowned
unoxidized
unpacified
unpaid
unpaid-for
unpainful
unpainted
unpaired
unpalatable
unpardonable
unpardoned
unparted
unpasteurized
unpatched
unpatented
unpatriotic
unpaved
unpeaceful
unpenetrated
unpensioned
unperceived
unperceiving
unperceptive
unperfected
unperformed
unperplexed
unpersuadable
unpersuaded
unpersuasive
unperturbed
unphilosophic
unphilosophical
unpicked
unpierced
unpile
unpitied
unpitying
unplaced
unplanned
unplanted
unplayable
unplayed
unpleasing
unpledged
unpliable
unploughed
unplowed
unplucked
unplug
unpoetic
unpoetical
unpointed
unpoised
unpolished
unpolitical
unpolluted
unpopulated
unposted
unpredictable
unpremeditated
unprepared
unprepossessing
unprescribed
unpresentable
unpreserved
unpressed
unpretending
unpretentious
unpreventable
unpriced
unprinted
unprivileged
unprobed
unprocessed
unprocurable
unproductive
unprofaned
unprofessed
unprofitable
unprogressive
unpromising
unprompted
unpronounceable
unpronounced
unpropitious
unproportionate
unproposed
unprosperous
unprotected
unproved
unproven
unprovided
unprovoked
unpruned
unpublished
unpunctual
unpunished
unpurged
unpurified
unquenchable
unquenched
unquestioning
unquotable
unquoted
unransomed
unrated
unratified
unreachable
unreadable
unrealized
unreasoned

---

un·re·con·struct·ed (un′rē kən struk′tid) ***adj.*** **1.** not reconstructed **2.** holding to an outmoded practice or attitude; specif., not reconciled to the Reconstruction
un·reel (un rēl′) ***vt., vi.*** to unwind as from a reel
un·re·gen·er·ate (un′ri jen′ər it) ***adj.*** **1.** not spiritually reborn **2.** not converted to a particular belief, etc. **3.** recalcitrant or obstinate Also **un′re·gen′er·at′ed**
un·re·lent·ing (-ri len′tiŋ) ***adj.*** **1.** refusing to yield or relent **2.** without mercy or compassion **3.** not relaxing, as in effort —**un′re·lent′ing·ly** ***adv.***
un·re·li·gious (-ri lij′əs) ***adj.*** **1.** *same as* IRRELIGIOUS **2.** not involving religion; nonreligious
un·re·mit·ting (-ri mit′iŋ) ***adj.*** not stopping, relaxing, or slackening; persistent —**un′re·mit′ting·ly** ***adv.***
un·re·served (-ri zʉrvd′) ***adj.*** not reserved; specif., *a)* frank; open *b)* unlimited *c)* not set aside for advance sale, as seats —**un′re·serv′ed·ly** (-zʉr′vid lē) ***adv.***
un·rest (un rest′) ***n.*** a troubled or disturbed state; restlessness; specif., a state of discontent close to revolt
un·rid·dle (-rid′'l) ***vt.*** **-dled, -dling** to solve or explain (a riddle, mystery, etc.)
un·rig (-rig′) ***vt.*** **-rigged′, -rig′ging** to strip of rigging
un·right·eous (-rī′chəs) ***adj.*** **1.** not righteous; wicked; sinful **2.** not right; unjust; unfair —**un·right′eous·ly** ***adv.*** —**un·right′eous·ness** ***n.***
un·rip (-rip′) ***vt.*** **-ripped′, -rip′ping** to rip open; take apart or detach by ripping
un·ripe (-rīp′) ***adj.*** **1.** not ripe or mature; green **2.** not yet fully developed *[unripe* plans*]* —**un·ripe′ness** ***n.***
un·ri·valed, un·ri·valled (-rī′v'ld) ***adj.*** having no rival, equal, or competitor; matchless; peerless
un·roll (-rōl′) ***vt.*** **1.** to open or extend (something rolled up) **2.** to present to view; display —***vi.*** to become unrolled
un·ruf·fled (-ruf′'ld) ***adj.*** not ruffled, disturbed, or agitated; calm; smooth; serene
un·rul·y (-ro͞o′lē) ***adj.*** **-rul′i·er, -rul′i·est** [< ME. < *un-*, not + *reuly,* orderly] hard to control, restrain, or keep in order; disobedient, disorderly, etc. —**un·rul′i·ness** ***n.***
un·sad·dle (-sad′'l) ***vt.*** **-dled, -dling** **1.** to take the saddle off (a horse, etc.) **2.** to throw from the saddle; unhorse —***vi.*** to take the saddle off a horse, etc.
un·said (-sed′) *pt. & pp. of* UNSAY —***adj.*** not expressed
un·sat·u·rat·ed (-sach′ə rāt′id) ***adj.*** **1.** not saturated **2.** *Chem. a)* capable of dissolving more of the solute than has been dissolved *b)* designating on organic compound with a double or triple bond between carbon atoms, capable of combining with other elements or compounds by adding on at the bond
un·sa·vor·y (-sā′vər ē) ***adj.*** **1.** orig., tasteless **2.** unpleasant to taste or smell **3.** morally offensive —**un·sa′vor·i·ly** ***adv.*** —**un·sa′vor·i·ness** ***n.***
un·say (-sā′) ***vt.*** **-said′, -say′ing** to take back or retract (what has been said)
un·scathed (-skāthd′) ***adj.*** not hurt; unharmed
un·scram·ble (-skram′b'l) ***vt.*** **-bled, -bling** to cause to be no longer scrambled, disordered, etc.; specif., *Electronics* to make (incoming scrambled signals) intelligible at the receiver —**un·scram′bler** ***n.***
un·screw (-skro͞o′) ***vt.*** **1.** to remove a screw or screws from **2.** *a)* to remove or loosen by removing a screw or screws, or by turning *b)* to remove a threaded top, cover, etc. from (a jar, etc.) —***vi.*** to be or become unscrewed
un·scru·pu·lous (-skro͞o′pyə ləs) ***adj.*** not scrupulous; heedless of what is right, just, etc.; unprincipled —**un·scru′pu·lous·ly** ***adv.*** —**un·scru′pu·lous·ness** ***n.***
un·seal (-sēl′) ***vt.*** **1.** to break or remove the seal of **2.** to open by or as by breaking a seal
un·seam (-sēm′) ***vt.*** to open the seam or seams of; rip
un·search·a·ble (-sʉrch′ə b'l) ***adj.*** that cannot be searched into; inscrutable —**un·search′a·bly** ***adv.***
un·sea·son·a·ble (-sē′z'n ə b'l) ***adj.*** **1.** not usual for the season **2.** coming at the wrong time; untimely; inopportune —**un·sea′son·a·ble·ness** ***n.*** —**un·sea′son·a·bly** ***adv.***
un·seat (-sēt′) ***vt.*** **1.** to throw or dislodge from a seat, saddle, etc. **2.** to remove from office, deprive of rank, etc.
un·seem·ly (-sēm′lē) ***adj.*** not seemly; not proper; unbecoming —***adv.*** unbecomingly —**un·seem′li·ness** ***n.***
un·self·ish (-sel′fish) ***adj.*** not selfish; altruistic; generous —**un·self′ish·ly** ***adv.*** —**un·self′ish·ness** ***n.***
un·set·tle (-set′'l) ***vt.*** **-tled, -tling** to make unsettled, insecure, etc.; disturb, displace, disorder, etc. —***vi.*** to become unsettled —**un·set′tle·ment** ***n.***
un·set·tled (-set′'ld) ***adj.*** **1.** not settled; not in order, not stable, not decided or determined, etc. **2.** not paid or disposed of, as a debt or estate **3.** having no settlers **4.** not established in a place or abode —**un·set′tled·ness** ***n.***
un·sex (-seks′) ***vt.*** to deprive of the qualities considered characteristic of one's sex
un·shack·le (-shak′'l) ***vt.*** **-led, -ling** **1.** to loosen or remove the shackles from **2.** to free
un·sheathe (-shēth′) ***vt.*** **-sheathed′, -sheath′ing** to remove (a sword, knife, etc.) from a sheath
un·ship (-ship′) ***vt.*** **-shipped′, -ship′ping** **1.** to unload from a ship **2.** to remove (an oar, etc.) from position
un·sight·ly (-sīt′lē) ***adj.*** not pleasant to look at; ugly —**un·sight′li·ness** ***n.***

---

unrebuked
unreceived
unreceptive
unreciprocated
unreclaimable
unreclaimed
unrecognizable
unrecognized
unrecommended
unrecompensed
unreconcilable
unreconciled
unrecorded
unrecoverable
unrectified
unredeemed
unrefined
unreflected
unreflecting
unreformed
unrefreshed
unregarded
unregistered
unregretted
unregulated
unrehearsed
unrelated
unrelaxed
unreliability
unreliable
unrelieved
unremedied
unremembered
unremorseful
unremovable
unremoved
unremunerated
unremunerative
unrenewed
unrenowned
unrentable
unrented
unrepaid
unrepairable
unrepaired
unrepealed
unrepentant
unrepenting
unreplaceable
unreplaced
unreplenished
unreported
unrepresentative
unrepresented
unrepressed
unreprieved
unreprimanded
unrequested
unrequited
unresentful
unresigned
unresistant
unresisting
unresolved
unresponsive
unrested
unrestful
unrestrainable
unrestrained
unrestraint
unrestricted
unretarded
unretentive
unretracted
unretrieved
unreturned
unrevealed
unrevenged
unreversed
unreviewed
unrevised
unrevoked
unrewarded
unrewarding
unrhetorical
unrhymed
unrhythmic
unrhythmical
unrightful
unromantic
unroof
unrounded
unruled
unsafe
unsaintly
unsalable
unsalaried
unsaleable
unsalted
unsampled
unsanctified
unsanctioned
unsanitary
unsated
unsatiable
unsatiated
unsatisfactory
unsatisfied
unsatisfying
unsaved
unscalable
unscaled
unscanned
unscarred
unscented
unscheduled
unscholarly
unschooled
unscientific
unscorched
unscraped
unscratched
unscreened
unscriptural
unsculptured
unseasoned
unseaworthy
unseconded
unsecured
unseeded
unseeing
unseen
unsegmented
unsegregated
unselected
unselective
unsent
unsentimental
unseparated
unserved
unserviceable
unset
unsevered
unsewn
unshaded
unshadowed
unshakable
unshakeable
unshaken
unshamed
unshaped
unshapely
unshared
unsharpened
unshaved
unshaven
unshed
unshelled
unsheltered
unshielded
unshod
unshorn
unshortened
unshrinkable
unshrinking
unshriven
unshrunk
unshuffled
unshut
unshuttered
unsifted
unsighted

un·skilled (-skild′) ***adj.*** not skilled; specif., having, showing, or requiring no special skill or training

un·skill·ful (-skil′fəl) ***adj.*** not skillful; awkward; clumsy —**un·skill′ful·ly** ***adv.*** —**un·skill′ful·ness** ***n.***

un·sling (-sliŋ′) ***vt.*** **-slung′, -sling′ing** **1.** to take (a rifle, etc.) from a slung position **2.** to release from slings

un·snap (-snap′) ***vt.*** **-snapped′, -snap′ping** to undo the snap or snaps of, so as to loosen or detach

un·snarl (-snärl′) ***vt.*** to free of snarls; untangle

un·so·cia·ble (-sō′shə b'l) ***adj.*** **1.** avoiding others; not sociable **2.** not conducive to sociability —**un·so′cia·bil′i·ty, un·so′cia·ble·ness** ***n.*** —**un·so′cia·bly** ***adv.***

un·so·cial (-sō′shəl) ***adj.*** having or showing a dislike for the society of others —**un·so′cial·ly** ***adv.***

un·sol·der (-säd′ər) ***vt.*** **1.** to take apart (things soldered together) **2.** to disunite; separate

un·so·phis·ti·cat·ed (un′sə fis′tə kāt′id) ***adj.*** not sophisticated; artless, simple, unworldly, unrefined, etc. —**un′so·phis′ti·cat′ed·ly** ***adv.*** —**un′so·phis′ti·ca′tion** ***n.***

un·sound (un sound′) ***adj.*** not sound or free from defect; specif., *a*) not normal or healthy *b*) not safe or secure *c*) not safe and secure financially *d*) not accurate, sensible, etc. *e*) light: said of sleep —**un·sound′ly** ***adv.*** —**un·sound′ness** ***n.***

un·spar·ing (-sper′iŋ) ***adj.*** **1.** not sparing or stinting; lavish **2.** not merciful; severe —**un·spar′ing·ly** ***adv.***

un·speak·a·ble (-spēk′ə b'l) ***adj.*** **1.** that cannot be spoken **2.** marvelous, awesome, etc. beyond expression **3.** indescribably bad, evil, etc. —**un·speak′a·bly** ***adv.***

un·sta·ble (-stā′b'l) ***adj.*** not stable; specif., *a*) easily upset, unbalanced, disturbed, etc. *b*) changeable *c*) unreliable; fickle *d*) *Chem., Physics* readily decomposing —**un·sta′ble·ness** ***n.*** —**un·sta′bly** ***adv.***

un·stead·y (-sted′ē) ***adj.*** not steady; specif., *a*) not firm or stable *b*) changeable or erratic —***vt.*** **-stead′ied, -stead′y·ing** to make unsteady —**un·stead′i·ly** ***adv.*** —**un·stead′i·ness** ***n.***

un·stick (-stik′) ***vt.*** **-stuck′, -stick′ing** to loosen or free (something stuck)

un·stop (-stäp′) ***vt.*** **-stopped′, -stop′ping** **1.** to remove the stopper from **2.** to clear (an obstructed pipe, etc.)

un·strap (-strap′) ***vt.*** **-strapped′, -strap′ping** to loosen or remove the strap or straps of

un·string (-striŋ′) ***vt.*** **-strung′, -string′ing** **1.** to loosen or remove the string or strings of **2.** to remove from a string **3.** to make nervous, weak, upset, etc.

un·struc·tured (-struk′chərd) ***adj.*** not formally or systematically organized; loose, free, open, etc.

un·strung (-struŋ′) ***adj.*** **1.** nervous, upset, etc. **2.** having the string(s) loosened or detached, as a bow

un·stud·ied (-stud′ēd) ***adj.*** **1.** not got by study or conscious effort **2.** spontaneous; natural; unaffected **3.** not having studied; unlearned or unversed (*in*)

un·sub·stan·tial (un′səb stan′shəl) ***adj.*** not substantial; specif., *a*) having no material substance *b*) flimsy; light *c*) unreal; visionary —**un′sub·stan′ti·al′i·ty** (-stan′shē al′ə tē) ***n.*** —**un′sub·stan′tial·ly** ***adv.***

un·suit·a·ble (un so͞ot′ə b'l, -syo͞ot′-) ***adj.*** not suitable; unbecoming; inappropriate —**un·suit′a·bly** ***adv.***

un·sung (-suŋ′) ***adj.*** **1.** not sung **2.** not honored or celebrated, as in song or poetry

un·sus·pect·ed (un′sə spek′tid) ***adj.*** **1.** not believed guilty, bad, harmful, etc. **2.** not imagined existent, probable, etc. —**un′sus·pect′ed·ly** ***adv.***

un·tan·gle (un taŋ′g'l) ***vt.*** **-gled, -gling** **1.** to free from a snarl or tangle; disentangle **2.** to free from confusion; clear up; put in order

un·taught (-tôt′) ***adj.*** **1.** not taught or educated **2.** got without being taught; natural

un·ten·a·ble (-ten′ə b'l) ***adj.*** **1.** not tenable; that cannot be defended **2.** incapable of being tenanted or occupied —**un′ten·a·bil′i·ty, un·ten′a·ble·ness** ***n.***

un·thank·ful (-thaŋk′fəl) ***adj.*** **1.** not thankful; ungrateful **2.** thankless; unappreciated —**un·thank′ful·ly** ***adv.*** —**un·thank′ful·ness** ***n.***

un·think·a·ble (-thiŋk′ə b'l) ***adj.*** **1.** beyond thought or imagination; inconceivable **2.** not to be considered; impossible —**un·think′a·bly** ***adv.***

un·think·ing (-thiŋk′iŋ) ***adj.*** **1.** showing little or no thought or consideration; thoughtless **2.** lacking the ability to think; not rational —**un·think′ing·ly** ***adv.***

un·thread (-thred′) ***vt.*** **1.** to draw the thread from **2.** to disentangle; unravel **3.** to find one's way through (a maze, etc.)

un·throne (-thrōn′) ***vt.*** **-throned′, -thron′ing** *same as* DETHRONE —**un·throne′ment** ***n.***

un·ti·dy (-tī′dē) ***adj.*** **-di·er, -di·est** not tidy or neat; slovenly; messy —**un·ti′di·ly** ***adv.*** —**un·ti′di·ness** ***n.***

un·tie (-tī′) ***vt.*** **-tied′, -ty′ing** **1.** to loosen or undo (something tied or knotted) **2.** to free, as from difficulty, restraint, etc. **3.** to untangle —***vi.*** to become untied

un·til (un til′, ən-) ***prep.*** [ME. *untill* < *un-* (see UNTO) + *till*, till] **1.** up to the time of; till [*until* payday] **2.** before (a specified time) [not *until* tomorrow] —***conj.*** **1.** up to the time when or that [*until* I go] **2.** to the point, degree, etc. that [heat water *until* it boils] **3.** before [don't leave *until* he does]

un·time·ly (un tīm′lē) ***adj.*** **1.** before the usual or expected time; premature [his *untimely* death] **2.** at the wrong time; inopportune —***adv.*** **1.** prematurely **2.** inopportunely —**un·time′li·ness** ***n.***

un·to (un′to͞o, -too) ***prep.*** [ME. *un-*, until + *to*, to] *archaic or poet. var. of:* **1.** TO **2.** UNTIL

un·told (un tōld′) ***adj.*** **1.** not told or revealed **2.** too great, numerous, etc. to be counted, measured, or described

un·touch·a·ble (-tuch′ə b'l) ***adj.*** that cannot or should not be touched —***n.*** **1.** an untouchable person or thing **2.** in India, formerly, one whose touch was regarded as defiling to higher-caste Hindus —**un′touch·a·bil′i·ty** ***n.***

un·to·ward (un tō′ərd, -tôrd′) ***adj.*** **1.** inappropriate, im-

unsigned
unsilenced
unsimplified
unsingable
unsinkable
unsisterly
unsized
unskeptical
unslackened
unslaked
unsleeping
unsliced
unsmiling
unsmoked
unsoftened
unsoiled
unsold
unsoldierly
unsolicited
unsolidified
unsolvable
unsolved
unsorted
unsought
unsounded
unsowed
unsown
unspecialized
unspecific
unspecified
unspectacular
unspent
unspilled
unspiritual
unspoiled
unspoken
unsporting
unsportsmanlike
unspotted
unsprung
unsquandered
unstained
unstamped
unstandardized
unstarched
unstarred
unstated
unstatesmanlike
unstemmed
unsterilized
unstinted
unstitched
unstoppable
unstrained
unstratified
unstressed
unstriated
unstuffed
unsubdued
unsubmissive
unsubsidized
unsubstantiated
unsuccessful
unsuited
unsullied
unsunk
unsupervised
unsupportable
unsupported
unsuppressed
unsure
unsurmountable
unsurpassable
unsurpassed
unsurprised
unsusceptible
unsuspecting
unsuspicious
unsustained
unswayed
unsweetened
unswept
unswerving
unswollen
unsworn
unsymmetrical
unsympathetic
unsympathizing
unsystematic
unsystematized
untabulated
untack
untactful
untagged
untainted
untalented
untalked-of
untamable
untamed
untanned
untapped
untarnished
untasted
untaxed
unteachable
untechnical
untempered
untenanted
untended
unterrified
untested
untethered
unthanked
unthatched
unthawed
untheatrical
unthoughtful
unthought-of
unthrifty
unticketed
untillable
untilled
untinged
untired
untiring
untitled
untorn
untouched

proper, unseemly, etc. [an *untoward* remark] **2.** not favorable or fortunate [*untoward* circumstances]
un·true (un trōō′) ***adj.*** **1.** not correct; false **2.** not agreeing with a standard or rule **3.** not faithful or loyal
un·truth (-trōōth′) ***n.*** **1.** the quality or state of being untrue **2.** an untrue statement; falsehood; lie
un·truth·ful (-trōōth′fəl) ***adj.*** **1.** not in accordance with the truth **2.** telling a lie or lies, esp. habitually —**un·truth′ful·ly** ***adv.*** —**un·truth′ful·ness** ***n.***
un·tu·tored (-tōōt′ərd, -tyōōt′-) ***adj.*** **1.** not tutored or taught; uneducated **2.** simple; naive; unsophisticated
un·twine (-twīn′) ***vt.*** **-twined′, -twin′ing** to undo (something twined or twisted); disentangle or unwind —***vi.*** to become untwined
un·twist (-twist′) ***vt., vi.*** to turn in the opposite direction so as to loosen or separate; untwine
un·used (-yōōzd′) ***adj.*** **1.** not in use **2.** that has never been used **3.** unaccustomed (*to*)
un·u·su·al (-yōō′zhoo wəl) ***adj.*** not usual or common; rare —**un·u′su·al·ly** ***adv.*** —**un·u′su·al·ness** ***n.***
un·ut·ter·a·ble (-ut′ər ə b'l) ***adj.*** that cannot be expressed or described —**un·ut′ter·a·bly** ***adv.***
un·var·nished (-vär′nisht) ***adj.*** **1.** not varnished **2.** plain; simple; unadorned [the *unvarnished* truth]
un·veil (un vāl′) ***vt.*** to reveal as by removing a veil or covering from —***vi.*** to take off a veil; reveal oneself
un·veil·ing (-iŋ) ***n.*** a formal or ceremonial removal of a covering from a new statue, tombstone, etc.
un·voiced (un voist′) ***adj.*** **1.** not uttered or expressed **2.** *Phonet. same as* VOICELESS
un·war·y (-wer′ē) ***adj.*** not wary or cautious; not alert to possible danger, trickery, etc. —**un·war′i·ly** ***adv.***
un·wea·ried (-wir′ēd) ***adj.*** **1.** not weary or tired **2.** never wearying; tireless; indefatigable
un·well (-wel′) ***adj.*** not well; ailing; ill; sick
un·wept (-wept′) ***adj.*** **1.** not shed [*unwept* tears] **2.** not wept for; unmourned
un·whole·some (-hōl′səm) ***adj.*** not wholesome; specif., *a*) harmful to body or mind *b*) unhealthy or unhealthy-looking *c*) morally bad —**un·whole′some·ness** ***n.***
un·wield·y (-wēl′dē) ***adj.*** hard to wield, manage, handle, etc. because of weight, shape, etc. —**un·wield′i·ness** ***n.***
un·will·ing (-wil′iŋ) ***adj.*** **1.** not willing; reluctant **2.** done, given, etc. against one's will —**un·will′ing·ly** ***adv.***
un·wind (-wīnd′) ***vt.*** **-wound′, -wind′ing** **1.** to wind off or undo (something wound) **2.** to uncoil **3.** to untangle **4.** to relax —***vi.*** to become unwound, relaxed, etc.
un·wise (-wīz′) ***adj.*** not wise; foolish or imprudent
un·wit·ting (-wit′iŋ) ***adj.*** **1.** not knowing; unaware **2.** not intended; unintentional —**un·wit′ting·ly** ***adv.***
un·wont·ed (-wun′tid, -wôn′-) ***adj.*** not common, usual, or habitual —**un·wont′ed·ly** ***adv.***
un·world·ly (-wurld′lē) ***adj.*** **1.** unearthly or otherworldly **2.** not worldly-wise; unsophisticated
un·wor·thy (-wur′*th*ē) ***adj.*** **-thi·er, -thi·est** **1.** lacking merit or value; worthless **2.** not deserving (often with *of*) **3.** not fit or becoming (usually with *of*) **4.** not deserved —**un·wor′thi·ly** ***adv.*** —**un·wor′thi·ness** ***n.***
un·wrap (-rap′) ***vt.*** **-wrapped′, -wrap′ping** to take off the wrapping of; open or undo (something wrapped) —***vi.*** to become unwrapped
un·writ·ten (-rit′'n) ***adj.*** **1.** not in writing; not written or printed **2.** operating only through custom or tradition [an *unwritten* rule] **3.** not written on; blank
unwritten law law based on custom, usage, court decisions, etc. rather than on the action of a lawmaking body
un·yoke (-yōk′) ***vt.*** **-yoked′, -yok′ing** **1.** to release from a yoke **2.** to separate or disconnect —***vi.*** **1.** to become unyoked **2.** to remove a yoke
un·zip (-zip′) ***vt., vi.*** **-zipped′, -zip′ping** **1.** to open (a zipper) **2.** to open the zipper of (a garment, etc.)
up[1] (up) ***adv.*** [OE.] **1.** to a higher place **2.** in or on a higher position or level **3.** in a direction or place thought of as higher or above **4.** above the horizon **5.** to a later period [from childhood *up*] **6.** to a higher condition or rank **7.** to a higher amount, degree, etc. **8.** *a*) in or into a standing or upright position *b*) out of bed **9.** in or into action, view, consideration, etc. [to bring a matter *up*] **10.** aside; away; by [lay *up* grain] **11.** so as to be even with in space, time, degree, etc. [keep *up* with the times] **12.** so as to be tightly closed, bound, packed, etc. [tie it *up*] **13.** completely [eat it *up*] **14.** so as to stop [to rein *up* a horse] **15.** *Baseball* to one's turn at batting; at bat **16.** *Naut.* windward **17.** *Sports & Games* ahead (by a specified number of points, goals, etc.) **18.** [Colloq.] served in a cocktail glass without ice cubes The adverb *up* is also used with verbs *a*) to form combinations having special meanings (Ex.: show *up*) *b*) as an intensive (Ex.: dress *up*) *c*) as a virtually meaningless addition (Ex.: light *up* a cigarette) —***prep.*** **1.** to, toward, or at a higher place, condition, rank, etc. on or in **2.** at, along, or toward a more distant part of [*up* the road] **3.** toward the source or against the flow, etc. of [*up* the river] **4.** in or toward the interior or more northerly part of (a country, territory, etc.) —***adj.*** **1.** being in or directed toward a higher position, condition, etc. **2.** *a*) above the ground *b*) above the horizon **3.** higher in amount, degree, etc. [rents are *up*] **4.** *a*) standing or upright *b*) out of bed **5.** active, excited, etc. **6.** even with in space, time, etc. **7.** in the inner or higher part of a country, etc. **8.** at an end; over [time is *up*] **9.** [Colloq.] happening [what's *up?*] **10.** *Baseball* at bat —***n.*** **1.** an upward slope, movement, course, etc. **2.** a train, bus, etc. headed up **3.** a period or state of prosperity, good luck, etc. —***vi.*** **upped, up′ping** [Colloq.] to get up; rise: sometimes used without inflection to emphasize a second verb [he *up* and left] —***vt.*** [Colloq.] to put up, lift up, or take up —**on the up and up** [Slang] honest —**up against** [Colloq.] faced with —**up against it** in difficulty, esp. financially —**up and around** (or **about**) out of bed and again active, as after an illness —**up and doing** busy; active —**up for** **1.** presented or considered for (an elective office, election, sale, auction, etc.) **2.** before a court for (trial) or on (a charge) —**up front** [Colloq.] **1.** very honest or forthright; candid **2.** in advance [to pay for something *up front*] —**up on** (or **in**) [Colloq.] well-informed about —**ups and downs** good periods and bad periods —**up to** [Colloq.] **1.** occupied with; doing; scheming [*up to* mischief] **2.** equal to (a task, etc.); capable of (doing, undertaking, etc.) **3.** as many as [*up to* four] **4.** as far as [*up to* here] **5.** dependent upon; incumbent upon —**up with!** give or restore power, favor, etc. to!
up[2] (up) ***adv.*** [phonetic respelling of AP(IECE)] apiece; each [the score is seven *up*]
up- *a combining form meaning* up [*uphill*]
up-and-com·ing (up′'n kum′iŋ) ***adj.*** **1.** enterprising, alert, and promising **2.** gaining in importance or status
up-and-down (-doun′) ***adj.*** **1.** going alternately up and down, to and fro, etc. **2.** variable; changing; fluctuating
u·pas (yōō′pəs) ***n.*** [short for Malay *pohon upas*, tree of

untraceable
untraced
untracked
untrained
untrammeled
untransferable
untransferred
untranslatable
untranslated
untransmitted
untrapped
untraveled
untraversed
untreated
untried
untrimmed
untrod
untroubled
untrustworthy
untufted
untunable
untuned
untuneful
unturned
untwilled
untypical
unusable
unutilizable
unutilized
unuttered
unvaccinated
unvacillating
unvalued
unvanquished
unvaried
unvarying
unventilated
unverifiable
unverified
unversed
unvexed
unvindicated
unviolated
unvisited
unvocalized
unvulcanized
unwakened
unwalled
unwaning
unwanted
unwarlike
unwarmed
unwarned
unwarped
unwarrantable
unwarranted
unwashed
unwasted
unwatched
unwatchful
unwatered
unwavering
unwaxed
unweakened
unweaned
unwearable
unweary
unwearying
unweathered
unweave
unwed
unwedded
unweeded
unweighed
unwelcome
unwelded
unwetted
unwifely
unwilled
unwincing
unwinking
unwished
unwished-for
unwithered
unwithering
unwitnessed
unwomanly
unwon
unwooded
unwooed
unworkable
unworked
unworkmanlike
unworn
unworried
unworshiped
unwounded
unwoven
unwrinkled
unwrought
unyielding
unyouthful
unzealous
unzoned

poison] 1. a tall Javanese tree of the mulberry family, whose whitish bark yields a poisonous juice 2. the juice
up·beat (up′bēt′) ***n.*** 1. an upward trend; upswing 2. *Music* an upward stroke made by a conductor to show an unaccented beat —***adj.*** lively; cheerful
up·braid (up brād′) ***vt.*** [< OE. < *up-*, up + *bregdan*, to pull, shake] to rebuke severely; censure sharply
up·bring·ing (up′briŋ′iŋ) ***n.*** the training and education received while growing up; rearing; nurture
up·chuck (-chuk′) ***vi., vt., n.*** [Slang] *same as* VOMIT
up·com·ing (-kum′iŋ) ***adj.*** coming soon; forthcoming
up·coun·try (-kun′trē) ***adj.*** of or located in the interior of a country —***n.*** the interior of a country —***adv.*** in or toward the interior of a country
up·date (up dāt′) ***vt.*** **-dat′ed, -dat′ing** to bring up to date; make conform to the most recent facts, methods, ideas, etc.
up·draft (up′draft′) ***n.*** an upward air current
up·end (up end′) ***vt., vi.*** 1. to turn or stand on end 2. to upset or topple
up·grade (up′grād′; *for v. usually* up grād′) ***n.*** an upward slope, esp. in a road —***adj., adv.*** uphill; upward —***vt.*** **-grad′ed, -grad′ing** 1. to promote to a more skilled job at higher pay 2. to raise in importance, value, etc. —**on the upgrade** advancing or improving in status, health, etc.
up·heav·al (up hē′v′l) ***n.*** 1. an upheaving, as of the earth's crust by an earthquake 2. a sudden, violent change
up·heave (-hēv′) ***vt.*** **-heaved′** or **-hove′, -heav′ing** to heave or lift up —***vi.*** to rise as if forced up
up·hill (up′hil′) ***adv.*** 1. toward the top of a hill 2. with difficulty —***adj.*** 1. going or sloping up 2. requiring great effort
up·hold (up hōld′) ***vt.*** **-held′, -hold′ing** 1. to hold up; raise 2. to keep from falling; support 3. to give moral support to 4. to decide in favor of; support against opposition —**up·hold′er** ***n.***
up·hol·ster (up hōl′stər, ə pōl′-) ***vt.*** [altered < ME. *upholder*, dealer in small wares < *upholden*, to repair] to fit out (furniture, etc.) with covering, padding, springs, etc. —**up·hol′ster·er** ***n.***
up·hol·ster·y (-stər ē, -strē) ***n., pl.*** **-ster·ies** 1. the materials used in upholstering 2. the business or work of upholstering
up·keep (up′kēp′) ***n.*** 1. the keeping up of buildings, equipment, etc.; maintenance 2. the cost of this 3. state of repair
up·land (-lənd, -land′) ***n.*** land elevated above other land —***adj.*** of or situated in upland
up·lift (up lift′; *for n.* up′lift′) ***vt.*** 1. to lift up; elevate 2. to raise to a higher moral, social, or cultural level —***n.*** 1. *a*) an uplifting *b*) any influence, movement, etc. aimed at uplifting society 2. a brassiere designed to lift and support the breasts —**up·lift′er** ***n.*** —**up·lift′ment** ***n.***
up·most (up′mōst′) ***adj.*** *same as* UPPERMOST
up·on (ə pän′) ***prep.*** on, or up and on: generally interchangeable with *on*, the choice depending on idiom, sentence rhythm, etc. —***adv.*** on: used only for completing a verb *[*a canvas not painted *upon]*
up·per (up′ər) ***adj.*** 1. higher in place or physical position 2. farther north or farther inland 3. higher in rank, authority, etc. 4. [U-] *Geol.* later: used of a division of a period —***n.*** the part of a shoe or boot above the sole —**on one's uppers** [Colloq.] 1. wearing shoes with soles worn through 2. in need; poor
upper case [from their being kept in the upper of two cases of type] capital-letter type used in printing, as distinguished from small letters (*lower case*) —**up′per-case′** ***adj.*** —**up′per-case′** ***vt.*** **-cased′, -cas′ing**
upper class the social class above the middle class; rich, socially prominent, or aristocratic class
up·per·class·man (up′ər klas′mən) ***n., pl.*** **-men** a junior or senior in a high school or college
up·per·cut (up′ər kut′) ***n.*** *Boxing* a short, swinging blow directed upward —***vt., vi.*** **-cut′, -cut′ting** to hit with an uppercut
upper hand the position of advantage or control
Upper House [*often* **u- h-**] the smaller and less representative branch of a bicameral legislature, as the U.S. Senate
up·per·most (up′ər mōst′) ***adj.*** highest in place, power, authority, etc.; predominant; foremost —***adv.*** in the highest place, rank, etc.
Upper Vol·ta (väl′tə) country in W Africa, north of Ghana: 108,880 sq. mi.; pop. 5,384,000
up·pish (up′ish) ***adj.*** [Colloq.] inclined to be arrogant, snobbish, etc.: also **up′pi·ty** (-ə tē) —**up′pish·ness** ***n.***
Upp·sa·la (oop′sä′lä; *E.* up′sə le) city in EC Sweden: pop. 102,000: also sp. **Up′sa·la**
up·raise (up rāz′) ***vt.*** **-raised′, -rais′ing** to raise up
up·rear (-rir′) ***vt.*** 1. to lift up 2. to erect; build 3. to exalt 4. to bring up; rear —***vi.*** to rise up
up·right (up′rīt′; *also for adv.* up rīt′) ***adj.*** 1. standing or directed straight up; erect 2. honest and just; honorable —***adv.*** in an upright position —***n.*** 1. a being upright or vertical 2. something having an upright position 3. *short for* UPRIGHT PIANO —**up′right′ly** ***adv.*** —**up′right′ness** ***n.***
upright piano a piano with a vertical rectangular body
up·rise (up rīz′; *for n.* up′rīz′) ***vi.*** **-rose′, -ris′en, -ris′ing** 1. to rise; get up, move up, rise into view, swell, etc. 2. to rise in revolt —***n.*** 1. a rising up 2. an upward slope
up·ris·ing (up′rīz′iŋ) ***n.*** a rising up; specif., a revolt
up·roar (-rôr′) ***n.*** [Du. *oproer*, a stirring up] 1. a violent disturbance; tumult 2. loud, confused noise; din
up·roar·i·ous (up rôr′ē əs) ***adj.*** 1. making, or marked by, an uproar; tumultuous 2. *a*) loud and boisterous, as laughter *b*) causing such laughter *[*an *uproarious* joke*]* —**up·roar′i·ous·ly** ***adv.*** —**up·roar′i·ous·ness** ***n.***
up·root (up ro͞ot′, -ro͝ot′) ***vt.*** 1. to tear up by the roots 2. to destroy or remove utterly; eradicate
up·sa·dai·sy (up′sə dā′zē) ***interj.*** *var. of* UPSY-DAISY
up·set (up set′; *for n. and occas. adj.* up′set′) ***vt.*** **-set′, -set′ting** 1. *a*) to tip over; overturn *b*) to defeat, esp. unexpectedly 2. *a*) to disturb the functioning, fulfillment, or completion of *b*) to disturb mentally, emotionally, or physically —***vi.*** to become overturned —***n.*** an upsetting or being upset; specif., *a*) an overturning *b*) a defeat, esp. when unexpected *c*) a disturbance; disorder —***adj.*** 1. overturned 2. defeated 3. disturbed —**up·set′ter** ***n.***
up·shot (up′shät′) ***n.*** [orig., the final shot in an archery match] the conclusion; result; outcome
up·side (-sīd′) ***n.*** the upper side or part
upside down 1. with the top side or part underneath 2. in disorder; topsy-turvy —**up′side′-down′** ***adj.***
upside-down cake a cake baked with a bottom layer of fruit and turned upside down before serving
up·si·lon (yo͞op′sə län′, up′-; -lən) ***n.*** [Gr.] the twentieth letter of the Greek alphabet (Υ, υ)
up·stage (up′stāj′; *for v.* up stāj′) ***adv.*** toward or at the rear of a stage —***adj.*** 1. of or having to do with the rear of a stage 2. haughty and aloof —***vt.*** **-staged′, -stag′ing** to draw attention, as of an audience, to oneself at the expense of (another)
up·stairs (up′sterz′) ***adv.*** 1. up the stairs 2. on or to an upper floor or higher level —***adj.*** situated on an upper floor —***n.*** an upper floor or floors —**kick upstairs** [Colloq.] to promote from a position of power to a higher but less powerful position
up·stand·ing (up stan′diŋ) ***adj.*** 1. standing straight; erect 2. upright in character and behavior; honorable
up·start[1] (up′stärt′) ***n.*** a person who has recently come into wealth, power, etc., esp. one who is aggressive; parvenu —***adj.*** of or characteristic of an upstart
up·start[2] (up stärt′) ***vi., vt.*** to start, or spring, up or cause to spring up
up·state (up′stāt′) ***n.*** that part of a State farther to the north or away from a large city; esp., the northern part of New York —***adj., adv.*** in, to, or from upstate
up·stream (-strēm′) ***adv., adj.*** in the direction against the current of a stream
up·surge (up surj′; *for n.* up′surj′) ***vi.*** **-surged′, -surg′ing** to surge up —***n.*** a surge upward
up·sweep (up′swēp′; *for v.* up swēp′) ***n.*** 1. a sweep or curve upward 2. an upswept hairdo —***vt., vi.*** **-swept′, -sweep′ing** to sweep or curve upward
up·swept (up′swept′) ***adj.*** 1. curved upward 2. designating or of a style of hairdo in which the hair is combed up in the back and piled on the top of the head
up·swing (up′swiŋ′; *for v.* up swiŋ′) ***n.*** a swing or trend upward; specif., an upward trend in business —***vi.*** **-swung′, -swing′ing** 1. to swing upward 2. to advance
up·sy-dai·sy (up′sə dā′zē, up′sē-) ***interj.*** [baby-talk extension of UP!] up you go: used playfully in lifting a baby
up·take (up′tāk′) ***n.*** the act of taking up; a drawing up, absorbing, etc. —**quick** (or **slow**) **on the uptake** [Colloq.] quick (or slow) to understand or comprehend
up·thrust (-thrust′) ***n.*** 1. an upward push or thrust 2. an upheaval of a part of the earth's crust
up-tight, up·tight (up′tīt′) ***adj.*** [Slang] 1. very tense, nervous, anxious, etc. 2. overly conventional or strict in attitudes 3. in a bad way or state Also **up tight**
up-to-date (up′tə dāt′) ***adj.*** 1. extending to the present time 2. keeping up with what is most recent, modern, etc. —**up′-to-date′ness** ***n.***

up·town (up′toun′) ***adj., adv.*** of, in, like, to, or toward the upper part of a city or town —***n.*** the uptown part

up·turn (up tʉrn′; *for n.* up′tʉrn′) ***vt., vi.*** to turn up, upward, or over —***n.*** an upward turn, curve, or trend —**up′turned′** ***adj.***

up·ward (up′wərd) ***adv., adj.*** **1.** toward a higher place, position, degree, etc. **2.** from an earlier to a later time **3.** beyond (an indicated price, amount, etc.) *[*tickets cost one dollar and *upward]* Also **up′wards** ***adv.*** —**upwards** (or **upward**) **of** more than —**up′ward·ly** ***adv.***

up·wind (up′wind′) ***adv., adj.*** in the direction from which the wind is blowing or usually blows

Ur (ʉr) ancient Sumerian city on the Euphrates River, in what is now S Iraq

u·ra·cil (yoor′ə sil) ***n.*** [UR(O)- + AC(ETIC) + -IL(E)] a crystalline base, $C_4H_4O_2N_2$, found in ribonucleic acid

U·ral (yoor′əl) **1.** [*pl.*] mountain system in the W R.S.F.S.R., traditionally regarded as the boundary between Europe & Asia: also **Ural Mountains** **2.** river flowing from the S section of these mountains into the Caspian Sea

U·ral-Al·ta·ic (-al tā′ik) ***n.*** the group of languages which includes, among others, the Uralic and Altaic families —***adj.*** **1.** designating or of this group of languages **2.** of the peoples speaking these languages

U·ral·ic (yoo ral′ik, -rā′lik) ***adj.*** designating or of the family of languages including Finno-Ugric and Samoyed —***n.*** this family of languages Also **U·ra′li·an** (-rā′lē ən)

U·ra·ni·a (yoo rā′nē ə) *Gr. Myth.* the Muse of astronomy

u·ra·ni·um (yoo rā′nē əm) ***n.*** [ModL. < URANUS, the planet] a very hard, heavy, radioactive metallic chemical element: it is found only in combination, and its isotopes are important in work on atomic energy: symbol, U; at. wt., 238.03; at. no., 92

U·ra·nus (yoor′ə nəs, yoo rā′nəs) **1.** *Gr. Myth.* a god who personified the heavens and was the father of the Titans, Furies, and Cyclopes: he was overthrown by his son Cronus (Saturn) **2.** a planet of the solar system, seventh in distance from the sun: diameter, c. 29,500 mi.

u·rate (yoor′āt) ***n.*** a salt of uric acid

ur·ban (ʉr′bən) ***adj.*** [< L. < *urbs*, a city] **1.** of, in, or constituting a city or town **2.** characteristic of the city as distinguished from the country

Ur·ban II (ʉr′bən) 1042?–99; Pope (1088–99)

ur·bane (ʉr bān′) ***adj.*** [< L.: see URBAN] polite and courteous in a smooth, polished way; refined —**ur·bane′ly** ***adv.*** —**ur·bane′ness** ***n.***

ur·ban·ism (ʉr′bən iz′m) ***n.*** **1.** *a)* the character of life in the cities *b)* the study of this **2.** concentration of the population in the cities —**ur′ban·ist** ***n., adj.***

ur·ban·ite (-īt′) ***n.*** a person living in a city

ur·ban·i·ty (ʉr ban′ə tē) ***n.,*** *pl.* **-ties** **1.** the quality of being urbane **2.** [*pl.*] civilities, courtesies, or amenities

ur·ban·ize (ʉr′bə nīz′) ***vt.*** **-ized′, -iz′ing** to change from rural to urban —**ur′ban·i·za′tion** ***n.***

ur·ban·ol·o·gist (ʉr′bə näl′ə jist) ***n.*** [URBAN + *-o-* + -LOG(Y) + -IST] a specialist in urban problems

urban renewal the renewal of urban areas suffering from neglect and decay, as by clearing slums and constructing new housing projects, etc.

ur·chin (ʉr′chin) ***n.*** [< OFr. < L. *ericius*, a hedgehog < *er*, hedgehog] **1.** *same as* SEA URCHIN **2.** a small boy, or any youngster, esp. one who is mischievous

Ur·du (oor′doo) ***n.*** an Indic language, a variant of Hindi written with Arabic characters: an official language of Pakistan

-ure (ər) [Fr. < L. *-ura*] *a suffix meaning:* **1.** act or result of being *[exposure]* **2.** agent, instrument, or scope of *[legislature]* **3.** state of being *[composure]*

u·re·a (yoo rē′ə, yoor′ē ə) ***n.*** [ModL. < Fr. < Gr. *ouron*, urine] a soluble, crystalline solid, $CO(NH_2)_2$, found in the urine of mammals or produced synthetically: used in making plastics, adhesives, etc. —**u·re′al, u·re′ic** ***adj.***

u·re·mi·a (yoo rē′mē ə, -rēm′yə) ***n.*** [ModL. < Gr. *ouron*, urine + *haima*, blood] a toxic condition caused by the presence in the blood of waste products normally eliminated in the urine —**u·re′mic** ***adj.***

u·re·ter (yoo rēt′ər) ***n.*** [ModL. < Gr. < *ourein*, to urinate] a duct or tube that carries urine from a kidney to the bladder or cloaca —**u·re′ter·al, u·re·ter·ic** (yoor′ə ter′ik) ***adj.***

u·re·thra (yoo rē′thrə) ***n.,*** *pl.* **-thrae** (-thrē), **-thras** [LL. < Gr. < *ouron*, urine] the canal through which urine is discharged from the bladder in most mammals: in the male, semen is also discharged through the urethra —**u·re′thral** ***adj.***

U·rey (yoor′ē), **Harold Clay·ton** (klā′t'n) 1893– ; U.S. chemist

urge (ʉrj) ***vt.*** **urged, urg′ing** [L. *urgere*, to press hard] **1.** *a)* to press upon the attention; speak in favor of *[*to *urge* caution*]* *b)* to entreat or plead with; exhort **2.** to stimulate or incite; provoke **3.** to drive or force onward; impel —***vi.*** **1.** to make an earnest presentation of arguments, claims, charges, etc. **2.** to exert a force that impels, as to action —***n.*** **1.** the act of urging **2.** an impulse to do a certain thing —**urg′er** ***n.***

ur·gen·cy (ʉr′jən sē) ***n.,*** *pl.* **-cies** **1.** an urgent quality or state; need for action, haste, etc. **2.** insistence; importunity **3.** something urgent

ur·gent (-jənt) ***adj.*** [MFr. < L. prp. of *urgere*, to urge] **1.** calling for haste, immediate action, etc.; pressing **2.** insistent —**ur′gent·ly** ***adv.***

-ur·gy (ʉr′jē) [< Gr. < *-ourgos*, worker < *ergon*, work] *a combining form meaning* a working with or by means of (something specified) *[zymurgy]*

-u·ri·a (yoor′ē ə) [ModL. < Gr. < *ouron*, urine] *a combining form meaning* a (diseased) condition of the urine *[hematuria]*

u·ric (yoor′ik) ***adj.*** of, contained in, or derived from urine

uric acid a white, odorless, crystalline substance, $C_5H_4N_4O_3$, found in urine

u·ri·nal (yoor′ə n'l) ***n.*** **1.** a portable container used for urinating **2.** a place for urinating; specif., a fixture for use by men in urinating

u·ri·nal·y·sis (yoor′ə nal′ə sis) ***n.,*** *pl.* **-ses′** (-sēz′) chemical or microscopic analysis of the urine

u·ri·nar·y (yoor′ə ner′ē) ***adj.*** **1.** of urine **2.** of the organs involved in secreting and discharging urine

u·ri·nate (yoor′ə nāt′) ***vi.*** **-nat′ed, -nat′ing** to discharge urine from the body —***vt.*** to discharge as or with the urine —**u′ri·na′tion** ***n.*** —**u′ri·na′tive** ***adj.***

u·rine (yoor′in) ***n.*** [OFr. < L. *urina*] in mammals, the yellowish fluid containing urea and other waste products, secreted from the blood by the kidneys, passed to the bladder, and periodically discharged through the urethra

u·ri·no- [< L. *urina*, urine] *a combining form meaning* urine, urinary tract: also, before a vowel, **urin-**

u·ri·no·gen·i·tal (yoor′ə nō jen′ə t'l) ***adj.*** *same as* UROGENITAL

urn (ʉrn) ***n.*** [L. *urna*] **1.** *a)* a vase, esp. one with a foot or pedestal *b)* a container for the ashes of a cremated body **2.** a metal container with a faucet, used for making or serving coffee, tea, etc.

u·ro- [< Gr. *ouron*, urine] *a combining form meaning* urine, urination, urinary tract: also, before a vowel, **ur-**

u·ro·gen·i·tal (yoor′ō jen′ə t'l) ***adj.*** designating or of the urinary and genital organs; genitourinary

u·rol·o·gy (yoo räl′ə jē) ***n.*** the branch of medicine dealing with the urogenital or urinary system and its diseases —**u·ro·log·ic** (yoor′ə läj′ik), **u′ro·log′i·cal** ***adj.*** —**u·rol′o·gist** ***n.***

u·ros·co·py (yoo räs′kə pē) ***n.,*** *pl.* **-pies** examination of the urine, as for the diagnosis of disease —**u·ro·scop·ic** (yoor′ə skäp′ik) ***adj.***

Ur·sa Major (ʉr′sə) [L., lit., Great Bear] the most conspicuous constellation in the northern sky: it contains the seven stars which form the Big Dipper

Ursa Minor [L., lit., Little Bear] the northernmost constellation: it contains the Little Dipper, with the North Star at the end of its handle

ur·sine (ʉr′sīn, -sin) ***adj.*** [< L. < *ursus*, a bear] of or like a bear or the bear family; bearlike

Ur·su·la (ʉr′sə lə) [ML., dim. of L. *ursa*, she-bear] **1.** a feminine name **2.** Saint, a legendary Christian Brit. princess said to have lived in the 4th cent.

Ur·su·line (-lin, -līn′) ***n.*** [< ModL.: after Saint URSULA] *R.C.Ch.* any member of a teaching order of nuns founded c.1537 —***adj.*** of this order

ur·ti·car·i·a (ʉr′tə ker′ē ə) ***n.*** [ModL. < L. *urtica*, a nettle] *same as* HIVES —**ur′ti·car′i·al** ***adj.***

U·ru·guay (yoor′ə gwā′, -gwī′; *Sp.* oo′roo gwī′) **1.** country in SE S. America, on the Atlantic: 72,171 sq. mi.; pop. 2,886,000; cap. Montevideo **2.** river in SE S. America, flowing into the Río de la Plata —**U′ru·guay′an** ***adj., n.***

us (us) ***pron.*** [OE.] *objective case of* WE: also used colloquially as a predicate complement with a linking verb (Ex.: that's *us*)

U.S., US United States

USA, U.S.A. **1.** United States of America **2.** United States Army

us·a·ble, use·a·ble (yoo′zə b'l) ***adj.*** that can be used; fit, convenient, or available for use —**us′a·bil′i·ty, us′a·ble·ness** ***n.*** —**us′a·bly** ***adv.***

USAF, U.S.A.F. United States Air Force

us·age (yoo′sij, -zij) ***n.*** **1.** the act, way, or extent of using; treatment **2.** a long-continued or established practice; custom; habit **3.** the way in which a word, phrase, etc. is used in speaking or writing, or an instance of this

USCG, U.S.C.G. United States Coast Guard

USDA United States Department of Agriculture

use (yooz; *for n.* yoos) ***vt.*** **used** (yoozd; *for vt. 6 & vi., with the following "to,"* yoos′tə *or* yoos′too), **us′ing** [< OFr., ult. < L. *usus*, pp. of *uti*, to use] **1.** to put or bring into action or service **2.** to practice; exercise *[use* your judgment*]* **3.** to behave toward; treat *[*to *use* a friend badly*]* **4.** to do away with by using; consume, expend, etc. *[*to *use* up one's energy*]* **5.** *a)* to smoke or chew (tobacco) *b)* to take or consume habitually *[*to *use* drugs*]* **6.** to accustom (used in the passive with *to) [*to become *used* to certain ways*]* **7.** to exploit (a person) *—vi.* to be accustomed (now only in the past tense, with an infinitive, meaning "did at one time") *[*he *used* to live in Iowa*]* *—n.* **1.** a using or being used **2.** the ability to use *[*he lost the *use* of his leg*]* **3.** the right or permission to use **4.** the need or opportunity to use *[*no further *use* for his services*]* **5.** an instance or way of using **6.** usefulness; utility **7.** the object or purpose for which something is used **8.** function, service, or benefit **9.** custom; habit; practice **10.** *Law a)* the enjoyment of property, as from occupying or employing it *b)* profit or benefit, esp. that of property held in trust by another **—have no use for 1.** to have no need of **2.** to dislike strongly **—in use** being used **—make use of** to use: also **put to use** **—us′er** *n.*

used (yo͞ozd) *pt. & pp. of* USE *—adj.* **1.** that has been used **2.** *same as* SECONDHAND

use·ful (yo͞os′fəl) *adj.* that can be used; serviceable; helpful **—use′ful·ly** *adv.* **—use′ful·ness** *n.*

use·less (-lis) *adj.* **1.** having no use; unserviceable; worthless **2.** to no purpose; ineffectual; of no avail **—use′less·ly** *adv.* **—use′less·ness** *n.*

U-shaped (yo͞o′shāpt′) *adj.* having the shape of a U

ush·er (ush′ər) *n.* [OFr. *uissier* < L. *ostiarius* < *ostium,* door] **1.** an official doorkeeper **2.** a person whose duty it is to show people to their seats in a theater, church, etc. **3.** any of the groom's attendants at a wedding **4.** [Obs.] in Great Britain, an assistant teacher *—vt.* **1.** to escort or conduct (others) to seats, etc. **2.** to herald or bring (*in*) *—vi.* to act as an usher

ush·er·ette (ush′ə ret′) *n.* a woman or girl usher, as in a theater

USIA, U.S.I.A. United States Information Agency

USIS, U.S.I.S. United States Information Service

U.S.M., USM **1.** United States Mail **2.** United States Mint

USMC, U.S.M.C. United States Marine Corps

USN, U.S.N. United States Navy

USNG, U.S.N.G. United States National Guard

USO, U.S.O. United Service Organizations

U.S.P., U.S.Pharm. United States Pharmacopoeia

U.S.S. United States Ship, Steamer, or Steamship

U.S.S.R., USSR Union of Soviet Socialist Republics

u·su·al (yo͞o′zho͞o wəl, -zhwəl, -zhəl) *adj.* [< MFr. < LL. *usualis* < L. *usus:* see USE] such as is most often seen, heard, used, etc.; common; ordinary; customary **—as usual** in the usual way **—u′su·al·ly** *adv.* **—u′su·al·ness** *n.*

u·su·fruct (yo͞o′zyo͞o frukt′, -zo͞o-, -so͞o-) *n.* [< LL. < L. *usus,* a use + *fructus,* a fruit] *Law* the right to use and enjoy the advantages and profits of the property of another without altering or damaging the substance **—u′su·fruc′tu·ar′y** (-fruk′cho͞o wer′ē) *adj., n., pl.* **-ar′ies**

u·su·rer (yo͞o′zho͞o rər) *n.* a person who engages in usury

u·su·ri·ous (yo͞o zhoor′ē əs) *adj.* **1.** practicing usury **2.** of or involving usury **—u·su′ri·ous·ly** *adv.* **—u·su′ri·ous·ness** *n.*

u·surp (yo͞o sʉrp′, -zʉrp′) *vt., vi.* [< MFr. < L. *usurpare* < *usus,* a use + *rapere,* to seize] to take or assume and hold (power, position, rights, etc.) by force or without right **—u·surp′er** *n.* **—u·surp′ing·ly** *adv.*

u·sur·pa·tion (yo͞o′sər pā′shən, -zər-) *n.* unlawful or violent seizure of a throne, power, etc.

u·su·ry (yo͞o′zho͞o rē) *n., pl.* **-ries** [< ML. < L. *usura* < *usus:* see USE] **1.** the lending of money at interest, now specif. at a rate of interest that is excessively or unlawfully high **2.** interest at such a high rate

usw, u.s.w. [G. *und so weiter*] and so forth

U·tah (yo͞o′tô, -tä) [< Sp. < tribal name, lit. ? hill dwellers] Western State of the U.S.: 84,916 sq. mi.; pop. 1,461,000; cap. Salt Lake City: abbrev. **Ut., UT** **—U′tah·an** *adj., n.*

Ute (yo͞ot, yo͞ot′ē) *n.* **1.** *pl.* **Utes, Ute** any member of a tribe of Shoshonean Indians living mainly in Colorado and Utah **2.** their Shoshonean language

u·ten·sil (yo͞o ten′s'l) *n.* [< MFr. < L. < *utensilis,* fit for use < *uti,* to use] an implement or container used for a particular purpose, now esp. one used in a kitchen *[*cooking *utensils]*

u·ter·ine (yo͞ot′ər in, yo͞o′tə rīn′) *adj.* **1.** of the uterus **2.** having the same mother but a different father *[uterine* sisters*]*

u·ter·us (yo͞ot′ər əs) *n., pl.* **u′ter·i′** (-ī′) [L.] a hollow, muscular organ of female mammals in which the ovum is deposited and the embryo and fetus are developed; womb

U Thant *see* THANT

U·ti·ca (yo͞o′ti kə) [after an ancient city in N Africa] city in C N.Y., on the Mohawk River: pop. 76,000

u·til·i·tar·i·an (yo͞o til′ə ter′ē ən) *adj.* **1.** of or having utility; useful **2.** stressing usefulness over beauty, etc. **3.** of or believing in utilitarianism *—n.* a person who believes in utilitarianism

u·til·i·tar·i·an·ism (-iz'm) *n.* **1.** the doctrine that the value of anything is determined solely by its utility **2.** the doctrine that the purpose of all action should be to bring about the greatest happiness of the greatest number **3.** utilitarian character or quality

u·til·i·ty (yo͞o til′ə tē) *n., pl.* **-ties** [< OFr. < L. < *utilis,* useful < *uti,* to use] **1.** usefulness **2.** something useful **3.** *a)* something useful to the public, esp. the service of electricity, gas, water, etc. *b)* a company providing such a service: see also PUBLIC UTILITY **4.** *Econ.* the power to satisfy the wants of humanity *—adj.* **1.** for practical use with little attention to beauty **2.** useful or used in a number of ways **3.** *Baseball* able to substitute in several positions *[utility* infielder*]*

utility room a room containing various household appliances and equipment, as for heating, laundry, cleaning, etc.

u·ti·lize (yo͞ot′'l īz′) *vt.* **-lized′, -liz′ing** to put to use; make practical or profitable use of: Brit. sp. **u′ti·lise** **—u′ti·liz′a·ble** *adj.* **—u′ti·li·za′tion** *n.* **—u′ti·liz′er** *n.*

ut·most (ut′mōst′) *adj.* [OE. *utemest,* double superl. of *ut,* out] **1.** most extreme or distant; farthest **2.** of or to the greatest or highest degree, amount, number, etc.; greatest *—n.* the most or the greatest that is possible; extreme limit or degree

U·to-Az·tec·an (yo͞ot′ō az′tek ən) *adj.* designating or of a large American Indian linguistic family of the W U.S., Mexico, and Central America *—n.* the Uto-Aztecan family of languages, including Shoshone, Nahuatl, Pima, etc.

U·to·pi·a (yo͞o tō′pē ə) [ModL. < Gr. *ou,* not + *topos,* a place] an imaginary island described in a book of the same name by Sir Thomas More (1516) as having a perfect political and social system *—n.* [*often* **u-**] **1.** any idealized place, state, or situation of perfection **2.** any visionary scheme for an ideally perfect society

U·to·pi·an (-ən) *adj.* **1.** of or like Utopia **2.** [*often* **u-**] having or based on ideas envisioning perfection in social and political organization; idealistic; visionary *—n.* **1.** an inhabitant of Utopia **2.** [*often* **u-**] a person who believes in a utopia, esp. of a social or political nature; visionary **—u·to′pi·an·ism** *n.*

U·trecht (yo͞o′trekt; *Du.* ü′treHt) city in the C Netherlands: pop. 279,000

u·tri·cle (yo͞o′tri k'l) *n.* [< Fr. < L. dim. of *uter,* leather bag] a small sac, vesicle, or baglike part: also **u·tric·u·lus** (yo͞o trik′yə ləs), *pl.* **-li′** (-lī′) **—u·tric′u·lar** *adj.*

U·tril·lo (o͞o tril′ō; *Fr.* o͞o trē lō′), **Maurice** 1883–1955; Fr. painter

ut·ter[1] (ut′ər) *adj.* [OE. *uttera,* compar. of *ut,* out] **1.** complete; total **2.** unqualified; absolute; unconditional **—ut′ter·ly** *adv.* **—ut′ter·ness** *n.*

ut·ter[2] (ut′ər) *vt.* [< ME. < *utter,* outward < *ut,* out] **1.** orig., to give out; put forth; now esp., to pass (counterfeit money, forged checks, etc.) **2.** to make or express with the voice *[*to *utter* a cry, to *utter* a thought*]* **3.** to express in any way **4.** to make known; divulge **—ut′ter·a·ble** *adj.* **—ut′ter·er** *n.*

ut·ter·ance (ut′ər əns, ut′rəns) *n.* **1.** the act, power, or way of uttering **2.** something uttered or said

ut·ter·most (ut′ər mōst′) *adj., n. same as* UTMOST

U-turn (yo͞o′tʉrn′) *n.* a turning completely around, esp. of a vehicle within the width of a street or road, so as to head in the opposite direction

UV, uv ultraviolet

u·vu·la (yo͞o′vyə lə) *n., pl.* **-las, -lae′** (-lē′) [ML., dim. of L. *uva,* a grape] the small, fleshy part of the soft palate hanging down above the back of the tongue

u·vu·lar (-lər) *adj.* **1.** of or having to do with the uvula **2.** *Phonet.* pronounced with a vibration of the uvula, or with the back of the tongue near or touching the uvula *—n.* a uvular sound **—u′vu·lar·ly** *adv.*

UVULA

ux·o·ri·al (ək sôr′ē əl, əg zôr′-) *adj.* [see ff.] of, befitting, or characteristic of a wife **—ux·or′i·al·ly** *adv.*

ux·o·ri·ous (-əs) *adj.* [< L. < *uxor,* wife] dotingly fond of or submissive to one's wife **—ux·o′ri·ous·ly** *adv.* **—ux·o′ri·ous·ness** *n.*

Uz·bek (ooz′bek, uz′-) *n.* **1.** a member of a Turkic people living in the region of the Uzbek S.S.R. **2.** the Turkic language of the Uzbeks Also **Uz′beg** (-beg)

Uzbek Soviet Socialist Republic republic of the U.S.S.R., in C Asia: 173,546 sq. mi.; pop. 12,000,000; cap. Tashkent: also **Uz′bek·i·stan′** (-i stan′, -stän′)

V

V, v (vē) ***n., pl.*** **V's, v's** **1.** the twenty-second letter of the English alphabet **2.** the sound of *V* or *v*

V (vē) ***n.*** **1.** something shaped like V **2.** a Roman numeral for 5 **3.** [Colloq.] a five-dollar bill **4.** *Chem.* vanadium —***adj.*** shaped like V

V, v **1.** *Math.* vector **2.** velocity **3.** victory **4.** volt(s)

v. **1.** [L. *vice*] in the place of **2.** [G. *von*] of **3.** [L. *vide*] see **4.** verb **5.** *pl.* **vv.** verse **6.** version **7.** versus **8.** vice- **9.** *pl.* **vv.** violin **10.** voice **11.** volt **12.** voltage **13.** volume

VA, V.A. Veterans Administration

Va., VA Virginia

va·can·cy (vā′kən sē) ***n., pl.*** **-cies** **1.** the state of being vacant; emptiness **2.** *a)* empty space *b)* a vacant space; gap, blank, opening, etc. **3.** lack of intelligence, interest, or thought **4.** an unoccupied position or office **5.** a room, apartment, etc. available for rent

va·cant (vā′kənt) ***adj.*** [< OFr. < L. prp. of *vacare*, to be empty] **1.** having nothing in it, as a space; empty **2.** not held, filled, or occupied, as a position, a seat, a house, etc. **3.** free from work or activity *[vacant* time*]* **4.** without thought, interest, etc. *[a vacant* mind, stare, etc.*]* —**va′cant·ly** ***adv.*** —**va′cant·ness** ***n.***

va·cate (vā′kāt) ***vt.*** **-cat·ed, -cat·ing** [< L. pp. of *vacare*, to be empty] **1.** to make vacant; specif., to leave (an office, position, etc.) or move out of (a house, room, etc.) **2.** *Law* to make void; annul —***vi.*** to make an office, position, house, etc. vacant

va·ca·tion (və kā′shən, vā-) ***n.*** [< MFr. < L. *vacatio*] **1.** a rest or respite from something **2.** a period of time when one stops working, going to school, etc. in order to rest and have recreation **3.** [Rare] a vacating **4.** *Law* a formal recess between terms of court —***vi.*** to take one's vacation —**va·ca′tion·er, va·ca′tion·ist** ***n.***

vac·ci·nate (vak′sə nāt′) ***vt.*** **-nat′ed, -nat′ing** to inoculate with a specific vaccine in order to prevent disease, as in immunizing against smallpox —***vi.*** to practice vaccination —**vac′ci·na′tor** ***n.***

vac·ci·na·tion (vak′sə nā′shən) ***n.*** **1.** the act or practice of vaccinating **2.** the scar on the skin where the vaccine has been applied

vac·cine (vak sēn′; vak′sēn, -sin) ***n.*** [L. *vaccinus*, from cows < *vacca*, a cow: from use of cowpox virus in smallpox vaccine] any preparation of killed microorganisms, living weakened organisms, etc. introduced into the body to produce immunity to a specific disease by causing antibodies to be formed —**vac′ci·nal** ***adj.***

vac·il·late (vas′ə lāt′) ***vi.*** **-lat′ed, -lat′ing** [< L. pp. of *vacillare*] **1.** to sway to and fro; waver **2.** to fluctuate or oscillate **3.** to waver in mind; show indecision —**vac′il·lat′ing** ***adj.*** —**vac′il·lat′ing·ly** ***adv.*** —**vac′il·la′tion** ***n.***

va·cu·i·ty (va kyo͞o′ə tē) ***n., pl.*** **-ties** [< L. < *vacuus*, empty] **1.** a being empty; emptiness **2.** an empty space; void or vacuum **3.** lack of intelligence, interest, or thought **4.** something inane; inanity

vac·u·ole (vak′yoo wōl′) ***n.*** [Fr. < L. *vacuus*, empty] *Biol.* a fluid-filled cavity within the plasma membrane of a cell, believed to have the function of discharging excess water or wastes —**vac′u·o·lar** (-wə lər, vak′yoo wō′lər) ***adj.***

vac·u·ous (vak′yoo wəs) ***adj.*** [L. *vacuus*] **1.** empty **2.** stupid; senseless; inane **3.** lacking purpose; idle —**vac′u·ous·ly** ***adv.*** —**vac′u·ous·ness** ***n.***

vac·u·um (vak′yoo wəm; *also, & for adj. & v. usually,* vak′yoom) ***n., pl.*** **-u·ums, -u·a** (-yoo wə) [L., neut. sing. of *vacuus*, empty] **1.** a space with nothing at all in it **2.** an enclosed space, as that inside a vacuum tube, out of which most of the air or gas has been taken, as by pumping **3.** a space left empty as by the removal of something; void: often used figuratively **4.** *short for* VACUUM CLEANER —***adj.*** **1.** of a vacuum **2.** used to make a vacuum **3.** having a vacuum **4.** working by suction or the creation of a partial vacuum —***vt., vi.*** to clean with a vacuum cleaner: in full, **vac′u·um-clean′**

vacuum bottle (or **flask** or **jug**) *same as* THERMOS

vacuum cleaner a machine for cleaning carpets, floors, upholstery, etc. by suction: also **vacuum sweeper**

vacuum-packed (-pakt′) ***adj.*** packed in an airtight container from which most of the air was exhausted before sealing, so as to keep the contents fresh

vacuum pump a pump used to draw air or gas out of a sealed space

vacuum tube an electron tube from which the air has been evacuated to the highest possible degree

va·de me·cum (vā′dē mē′kəm, vä′-) [L., lit., go with me] something carried about by a person for constant use, reference, etc., as a handbook

vag·a·bond (vag′ə bänd′) ***adj.*** [< MFr. < L. *vagabundus*, strolling about < *vagari*, to wander] **1.** moving from place to place; wandering **2.** of, having to do with, or living an unsettled, drifting, irresponsible life; vagrant; shiftless **3.** aimlessly following an irregular course —***n.*** **1.** a person who wanders from place to place, having no fixed abode **2.** a tramp **3.** an idle, disreputable, or shiftless person —***vi.*** to wander —**vag′a·bond′age, vag′a·bond′ism** ***n.***

va·gar·y (və ger′ē, -gar′-; vā′gər ē) ***n., pl.*** **-gar′ies** [< L. *vagari*, to wander] **1.** an odd, eccentric, or unexpected action **2.** an odd, whimsical, or freakish idea or notion —**va·gar′i·ous** ***adj.*** —**va·gar′i·ous·ly** ***adv.***

va·gi·na (və jī′nə) ***n., pl.*** **-nas, -nae** (-nē) [L., a sheath] a sheath or sheathlike structure; specif., in female mammals, the canal leading from the vulva to the uterus —**vag·i·nal** (vaj′ə n'l, və jī′n'l) ***adj.***

vag·i·nate (vaj′ə nit, -nāt′) ***adj.*** **1.** having a vagina or sheath; sheathed **2.** like a sheath

va·got·o·my (vā gät′ə mē) ***n., pl.*** **-mies** [VAG(US) + -TOMY] the surgical cutting of the vagus nerve

va·gran·cy (vā′grən sē) ***n., pl.*** **-cies** [< ff.] **1.** a wandering in thought or talk; digression **2.** a wandering from place to place **3.** shiftless or idle wandering without money or work, as of tramps, beggars, etc.: often a statutory offense chargeable as a misdemeanor

va·grant (vā′grənt) ***n.*** [prob. < Anglo-Fr. < OFr. *walcrer*, to wander: infl. prob. by L. *vagari*, to wander] a person who wanders from place to place; esp., one without a regular job, supporting himself by begging, etc.; vagabond, tramp, etc. —***adj.*** **1.** wandering from place to place; roaming; nomadic **2.** of, characteristic of, or living the life of a vagrant **3.** following no fixed direction or course; random, wayward, etc. —**va′grant·ly** ***adv.***

vague (vāg) ***adj.*** **va′guer, va′guest** [Fr. < L. *vagus*, wandering] **1.** not clearly or precisely expressed or stated **2.** indefinite in shape or form **3.** not sharp, certain, or precise in thought or expression **4.** not known or determined; uncertain —**vague′ly** ***adv.*** —**vague′ness** ***n.***

va·gus (vā′gəs) ***n., pl.*** **va′gi** (-jī) [ModL. < L., wandering] either of a pair of cranial nerves acting upon the larynx, lungs, heart, esophagus, and most of the abdominal organs: also **vagus nerve** —**va′gal** (-g'l) ***adj.***

vain (vān) ***adj.*** [< OFr. < L. *vanus*, empty] **1.** having no real value or significance; worthless, empty, etc. *[vain* pomp*]* **2.** without force or effect; futile, fruitless, etc. *[a vain* attempt*]* **3.** having or showing an excessively high regard for one's self, looks, ability, etc.; conceited —**in vain** **1.** unsuccessfully; fruitlessly **2.** lightly; profanely —**vain′ly** ***adv.*** —**vain′ness** ***n.***

vain·glo·ri·ous (vān′glôr′ē əs) ***adj.*** [< ML.: see ff.] **1.** boastfully vain and proud of oneself **2.** characterized by boastful vanity —**vain′glo′ri·ous·ly** ***adv.*** —**vain′glo′ri·ous·ness** ***n.***

vain·glo·ry (vān′glôr′ē, vān glôr′ē) ***n.*** [< OFr. < L. *vana gloria*, empty boasting: see VAIN & GLORY] **1.** extreme self-pride and boastfulness **2.** vain show or empty pomp

val·ance (val′əns, vāl′-) ***n.*** [< ? *Valence*, city in France] **1.** a short drapery or curtain hanging from the edge of a bed, shelf, etc., often to the floor **2.** a short drapery or facing of wood or metal across the top of a window —**val′anced** ***adj.***

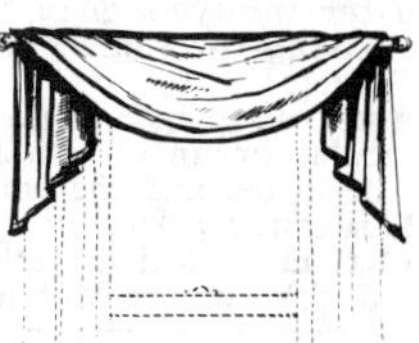

VALANCE

vale¹ (vāl) ***n.*** [< OFr. < L. *vallis*] [Poet.] *same as* VALLEY

‡**va·le²** (vā′lē, wä′lā) ***interj., n.*** [L.] farewell

val·e·dic·tion (val′ə dik′shən) ***n.*** [< L. pp. of *valedicere* < *vale*, farewell (imper. of *valere*, to be well) + *dicere*, to say] **1.** a bidding farewell **2.** something said in parting

val·e·dic·to·ri·an (val'ə dik tôr'ē ən) *n.* in schools and colleges, the student, usually the one ranking highest in the class in scholarship, who delivers the valedictory

val·e·dic·to·ry (val'ə dik'tər ē) *adj.* said or done at parting, by way of farewell; uttered as a valediction —*n., pl.* **-ries** a farewell speech, esp. one delivered at graduation

va·lence (vā'ləns) *n.* [< ML., ult. < L. prp. of *valere,* to be strong] *Chem.* **1.** the combining capacity of an element or radical, as measured by the number of hydrogen or chlorine atoms which one radical or one atom of the element will combine with or replace **2.** any of the units of valence which an element may have Also **va'len·cy,** *pl.* **-cies**

valence electrons the mobile electrons in the outermost shell of an atom which largely determine its properties

Va·len·ci·a (və len'shē ə, -shə, -sē ə; *Sp.* vä len'thyä) seaport in E Spain, on the Mediterranean: pop. 624,000

-va·lent (vā'lənt) [< L. *valens*] *Chem. a suffix meaning:* **1.** having a specified valence **2.** having a specified number of valences

Val·en·tine (val'ən tīn'), Saint 3d cent. A.D.; Christian martyr of Rome

val·en·tine (val'ən tīn') *n.* **1.** a sweetheart chosen or complimented on Saint Valentine's Day **2.** a greeting card or gift sent on this day

Va·ler·i·an (və lir'ē ən) (L. name *Publius Licinius Valerianus*) 190?–260 A.D.; Roman emperor (253–260)

va·le·ri·an (və lir'ē ən) *n.* [< MFr. < ML. *valeriana*] **1.** any of various plants with clusters or spikes of white, pink, red, or purplish flowers **2.** a drug made from the roots of some of these plants, formerly used as a sedative

val·et (val'it, val'ā; *Fr.* vȧ lā') *n.* [Fr., a groom < OFr. *vaslet,* young man, page] **1.** a man's personal manservant who takes care of the man's clothes, helps him in dressing, etc. **2.** an employee, as of a hotel, who cleans or presses clothes, etc. **3.** a rack for coats, pants, etc. —*vt., vi.* to serve (a person) as a valet

val·e·tu·di·nar·i·an (val'ə to͞o'də ner'ē ən) *n.* [< L. < *valetudo,* state of health, sickness < *valere,* to be strong] **1.** a person in poor health; invalid **2.** a person who worries constantly about his health —*adj.* **1.** in poor health; sickly **2.** anxiously concerned about one's health

Val·hal·la (val hal'ə) *Norse Myth.* the great hall where Odin receives and feasts the souls of heroes fallen bravely in battle: also **Val·hall'**

val·iant (val'yənt) *adj.* [< OFr. prp. of *valoir* < L. *valere,* to be strong] courageous; brave —**val'iance, val'ian·cy** *n.* —**val'iant·ly** *adv.*

val·id (val'id) *adj.* [< Fr. < L. *validus,* strong < *valere,* to be strong] **1.** having legal force; binding under law **2.** well-grounded on principles or evidence, as an argument; sound **3.** effective, cogent, etc. **4.** *Logic* correctly derived or inferred according to the rules of logic —**val'id·ly** *adv.* —**val'id·ness** *n.*

val·i·date (val'ə dāt') *vt.* **-dat'ed, -dat'ing** [< ML. pp. of *validare*] **1.** to give legal force to; declare legally valid **2.** to prove to be valid —**val'i·da'tion** *n.*

va·lid·i·ty (və lid'ə tē) *n., pl.* **-ties** the state, quality, or fact of being valid in law or in argument, proof, etc.

va·lise (və lēs') *n.* [Fr. < It. *valigia* < ?] a piece of hand luggage: an old-fashioned term

Val·kyr·ie (val kir'ē, val'ki rē) *n. Norse Myth.* any of the maidens of Odin who conduct the souls of heroes slain in battle to Valhalla —**Val·kyr'i·an** *adj.*

Val·le·jo (və lā'hō, -ō) [after M. *Vallejo* (1807–90), owner of the site] seaport in W Calif., north of Oakland: pop. 80,000

val·ley (val'ē) *n., pl.* **-leys** [< OFr. < L. *vallis*] **1.** a stretch of low land lying between hills or mountains **2.** the land drained or watered by a great river system [the Nile *valley*] **3.** any long dip or hollow

Valley Forge [after an iron *forge* on *Valley* Creek] village in SE Pa.: the place where Washington and his troops camped in the winter of 1777–78

val·or (val'ər) *n.* [< OFr. < LL. < L. *valere,* to be strong] great courage or bravery: also, Brit. sp., **val'our** —**val'or·ous** *adj.* —**val'or·ous·ly** *adv.* —**val'or·ous·ness** *n.*

val·or·i·za·tion (val'ər i zā'shən) *n.* [Port. *valorização,* ult. < LL. *valor,* VALOR] a fixing of prices, usually by government action, as by buying up a commodity at the fixed price, etc. —**val'or·ize'** (-ə rīz') *vt., vi.* **-ized', -iz'ing**

Val·pa·rai·so (val'pə rā'zō, -rī'sō) seaport in C Chile: pop. 296,000: also **Val·pa·ra·í·so** (*Sp.* väl'pä rä ē'sô)

‡**valse** (vȧls) *n.* [Fr.] a waltz

val·u·a·ble (val'yoo b'l, -yoo wə b'l) *adj.* **1.** *a*) being worth money *b*) having great value in terms of money **2.** highly regarded as precious, useful, worthy, etc. —*n.* an article of value, as a piece of jewelry —**val'u·a·ble·ness** *n.* —**val'u·a·bly** *adv.*

val·u·ate (val'yoo wāt') *vt.* **-at'ed, -at'ing** to set a value on; appraise —**val'u·a'tor** *n.*

val·u·a·tion (val'yoo wā'shən) *n.* **1.** the act of determining the value of anything; evaluation **2.** determined or estimated value **3.** estimation of the worth, merit, etc. of anything —**val'u·a'tion·al** *adj.* —**val'u·a'tion·al·ly** *adv.*

val·ue (val'yo͞o) *n.* [< OFr. pp. of *valoir,* to be strong, to be worth < L. *valere*] **1.** a fair equivalent in money, etc. for something sold or exchanged **2.** the worth of a thing in money or goods at a certain time **3.** estimated or appraised worth **4.** purchasing power **5.** that quality of a thing that makes it more or less desirable, useful, etc. **6.** [*pl.*] the social principles, goals, or standards held by an individual, class, society, etc. **7.** precise meaning, as of a word **8.** numerical order assigned to a playing card, etc. **9.** *Art a*) relative lightness or darkness of a color *b*) the effect produced by the use of light and shade **10.** *Math.* the quantity for which a symbol stands **11.** *Music* the relative duration of a note, tone, or rest **12.** *Phonet.* the quality of a speech sound —*vt.* **-ued, -u·ing** **1.** to estimate the value of; appraise **2.** to place a certain estimate of worth on in a scale of values [to *value* health above wealth] **3.** to think highly of; prize [I *value* your friendship] —**val'ue·less** *adj.* —**val'ue·less·ness** *n.* —**val'u·er** *n.*

val·ued (-yo͞od) *adj.* **1.** estimated; appraised **2.** highly thought of; esteemed

value judgment an estimate made of the worth, goodness, etc. of a person, action, event, etc., esp. when such a judgment is not called for or desired

val·vate (val'vāt) *adj.* [L. *valvatus,* having folding doors < *valva:* see ff.] **1.** having a valve or valves **2.** *Bot. a*) meeting without overlapping, as petals, etc. *b*) opening by valves, as a pea pod

valve (valv) *n.* [L. *valva,* leaf of a folding door] **1.** a sluice gate **2.** *Anat.* a membranous structure which permits body fluids to flow in one direction only, or opens and closes a tube, etc. **3.** *Bot.* any of the segments into which a seed capsule separates **4.** *Mech. a*) any device in a pipe, etc. that permits a flow in one direction only, or regulates or stops the flow by means of a flap, lid, plug, etc. *b*) this flap, lid, plug, etc. **5.** *Music* a device, as in the trumpet, that opens an auxiliary to the main tube, lengthening the air column and lowering the pitch **6.** *Zool.* one of the parts making up the shell of a mollusk, clam, etc. —*vt., vi.* **valved, valv'ing** **1.** to fit with a valve or valves **2.** to regulate the flow of (a fluid) by means of a valve —**valve'less** *adj.* —**valve'like'** *adj.*

VALVE
(in a faucet)

val·vu·lar (val'vyə lər) *adj.* **1.** having the form or function of a valve **2.** having a valve or valves **3.** of a valve or valves; esp., of the valves of the heart

va·moose (va mo͞os') *vi., vt.* **-moosed', -moos'ing** [Sp. *vamos,* let us go] [Old Slang] to leave quickly; go away (from) hurriedly: also **va·mose'** (-mōs') **-mosed', -mos'ing**

vamp¹ (vamp) *n.* [< OFr. *avampié* < *avant,* before + *pié,* a foot] **1.** the part of a boot or shoe covering the instep and, in some styles, also the toes **2.** something patched up to seem new **3.** *Music* a simple, improvised introduction or interlude —*vt.* **1.** to put a vamp on (a shoe, etc.) **2.** to patch (*up*); repair **3.** to invent; fabricate **4.** *Music* to improvise —*vi. Music* to play a vamp

vamp² (vamp) *n. shortened form of* VAMPIRE (sense 3) —*vt.* to seduce or beguile (a man) by the use of feminine charms —*vi.* to act the part of a vamp

vam·pire (vam'pīr) *n.* [Fr. < G. *vampir;* of Slav. orig.] **1.** *Folklore* a corpse that comes alive at night and sucks the blood of sleeping persons **2.** a person who preys on others in a dishonest, evil, or wicked way **3.** a beautiful but wicked woman who seduces men and leads them to their ruin **4.** *shortened form of* VAMPIRE BAT —**vam'pir·ism** *n.*

vampire bat **1.** a tropical American bat that lives on the blood of animals **2.** any of various other bats mistakenly believed to be bloodsuckers

van¹ (van) *n.* [abbrev. < VANGUARD] **1.** the front of an army or fleet when advancing **2.** the foremost position in a line, movement, endeavor, etc., or those in this position

van² (van) *n.* [< CARAVAN] **1.** a closed truck or wagon for carrying furniture, etc. **2.** [Brit.] *a*) a closed railway car for baggage, etc. *b*) a delivery wagon or truck

va·na·di·um (və nā′dē əm) ***n.*** [ModL. < ON. *Vanadis,* a name of Freya, goddess of love] a rare, ductile metallic chemical element: cf. VANADIUM STEEL: symbol, V; at. wt., 50.942; at. no., 23

vanadium steel a steel alloy containing 0.15 to 0.25 percent vanadium to harden and toughen it

Van Al·len (radiation) belt (van al′ən) [after J. A. *Van Allen* (1914–), U.S. physicist] a doughnut-shaped belt of high-intensity radiation encircling the earth at varying levels, starting at c. 600 mi.

Van Bu·ren (van byoor′ən), **Martin** 1782–1862; 8th president of the U.S. (1837–41)

Van·cou·ver (van ko͞o′vər) **1.** island of British Columbia, Canada, off the SW coast **2.** seaport in SW British Columbia, opposite this island: pop. 410,000 (met. area 1,166,000)

Van·dal (van′d'l) ***n.*** **1.** a member of an East Germanic tribe that ravaged Gaul, Spain, etc. and sacked Rome (455 A.D.) **2.** [**v-**] a person who destroys or spoils things on purpose, esp. works of art, public property, etc. —***adj.*** **1.** of the Vandals: also **Van·dal·ic** (van dal′ik) **2.** [**v-**] like a vandal; ruthlessly destructive

van·dal·ism (-iz′m) ***n.*** willful destruction of public or private property, esp. of that which is beautiful —**van′dal·is′tic** ***adj.***

van·dal·ize (-īz′) ***vt.*** **-ized′, -iz′ing** to destroy or damage (public or private property) on purpose

Van·der·bilt (van′dər bilt), **Cor·nel·ius** (kôr nēl′yəs) 1794–1877; U.S. capitalist & industrialist

Van Dyck (van dīk′), Sir **Anthony** 1599–1641; Fl. painter, in England after 1632: also sp. **Van·dyke′**

Van·dyke (beard) (van dīk′) a closely trimmed, pointed beard, as seen in portraits by Van Dyck

vane (vān) ***n.*** [OE. *fana,* a flag] **1.** *same as* WEATHER VANE **2.** any of several flat or curved pieces set around an axle and rotated about it by moving air, water, etc. [the *vanes* of a windmill] or mechanically rotated to move the air, water, etc. [the *vanes* of a turbine] **3.** a projecting plate or strip of metal fixed to a rocket, missile, etc. to give stability or guidance **4.** the web or flat part of a feather —**vaned** ***adj.***

VANDYKE BEARD

van Eyck (vän īk′), **Jan** (yän) 1385?–1441; Fl. painter

van Gogh (van gō′, gôkh′; *Du.* vän khôkh′), **Vincent** 1853–90; Du. painter

van·guard (van′gärd′) ***n.*** [< OFr. < *avant,* before + *garde,* guard] **1.** the front part of an army in an advance; the van **2.** the leading position or persons in a movement

va·nil·la (və nil′ə) ***n.*** [ModL., genus name < Sp. dim. of *vaina,* a pod < L. *vagina,* a sheath] **1.** any of various climbing tropical American orchids with fragrant flowers **2.** the podlike capsule (**vanilla bean**) of some of these plants **3.** a flavoring made from these capsules —**va·nil′lic** ***adj.***

va·nil·lin (və nil′in, van′ə lin) ***n.*** a fragrant, white, crystalline substance, $C_8H_8O_3$, produced from the vanilla bean or made synthetically and used for flavoring

van·ish (van′ish) ***vi.*** [< OFr., ult. < L. *evanescere:* see EVANESCE] **1.** to go or pass suddenly from sight **2.** to cease to exist; come to an end —**van′ish·er** ***n.***

vanishing point **1.** the point where parallel lines receding from the observer seem to come together **2.** a time, place, or stage at which something disappears

van·i·ty (van′ə tē) ***n.,*** *pl.* **-ties** [< OFr. < L. < *vanus,* vain] **1.** any thing or act that is vain, futile, or worthless **2.** a being vain, or worthless; futility **3.** a being vain, or excessively proud of oneself, one's possessions, etc. **4.** *short for* VANITY CASE **5.** *same as* DRESSING TABLE **6.** a cabinet in a bathroom with a washbowl set in the top

vanity case a woman's small traveling case fitted for carrying cosmetics, toilet articles, etc.

van·quish (vaŋ′kwish, van′-) ***vt.*** [< OFr. < L. *vincere,* to conquer] **1.** to conquer or defeat in battle **2.** *a)* to defeat in any conflict *b)* to overcome (a feeling, condition, etc.); suppress —**van′quish·er** ***n.***

van·tage (van′tij) ***n.*** [see ADVANTAGE] **1.** a position more advantageous than that of an opponent **2.** a position that allows a clear and broad view, understanding, etc.: also **vantage point**

Van·ua·tu (vän wä to͞o′) country on a group of islands in the SW Pacific: 5,700 sq. mi.; pop. 112,000

van·ward (van′wərd) ***adj.*** in the van, or front, as of an army —***adv.*** toward the van

vap·id (vap′id) ***adj.*** [L. *vapidus*] **1.** having no taste or flavor **2.** lifeless; dull; boring —**vap·id·i·ty** (va pid′ə tē), *pl.* **-ties, vap′id·ness** ***n.*** —**vap′id·ly** ***adv.***

va·por (vā′pər) ***n.*** [< Anglo-Fr. < MFr. < L. *vapor*] **1.** *a)* visible particles of moisture floating in the air, as fog, mist, or steam *b)* anything, as smoke, fumes, etc., given off in a cloud **2.** the gaseous form of any substance that is usually a liquid or solid **3.** [*pl.*] [Archaic] depressed spirits (often with *the*) —***vi.*** **1.** to rise or pass off as vapor; evaporate **2.** to give off vapor **3.** to brag or bluster —***vt.*** *same as* VAPORIZE —**va′por·er** ***n.*** —**va′por·ish** ***adj.*** —**va′por·like′** ***adj.***

va·por·ing (vā′pər iŋ) ***adj.*** boastful, bombastic, etc. —***n.*** boastful or extravagant talk or behavior

va·por·ize (vā′pə rīz′) ***vt., vi.*** **-ized′, -iz′ing** to change into vapor, as by heating or spraying —**va′por·iz′a·ble** ***adj.*** —**va′por·i·za′tion** ***n.*** —**va′por·iz′er** ***n.***

vapor lock a blocking of the flow of fuel in an internal-combustion engine as the result of vaporized fuel in the fuel line, caused by excessive heat

va·por·ous (vā′pər əs) ***adj.*** **1.** giving off or forming vapor **2.** full of vapor; foggy **3.** like vapor **4.** *a)* fleeting, fanciful, etc.: said of things, ideas, etc. *b)* given to such ideas or talk Also **va′por·y** —**va′por·ous·ly** ***adv.*** —**va′por·ous·ness, va′por·os′i·ty** (-pə räs′ə tē) ***n.***

va·pour (-pər) ***n., vi., vt.*** *Brit. sp. of* VAPOR

va·que·ro (vä ker′ō) ***n.,*** *pl.* **-ros** [Sp. < *vaca,* a cow < L. *vacca*] in the Southwest, a man who herds cattle; cowboy

var. **1.** variant(s) **2.** variation **3.** variety **4.** various

Va·ra·na·si (və rän′ə sē′) city in NE India, on the Ganges: pop. 490,000

var·i·a·ble (ver′ē ə b'l, var′-) ***adj.*** **1.** apt to change or vary; changeable, inconstant, etc. **2.** that can be changed or varied **3.** *Biol.* tending to deviate in some way from the type **4.** *Math.* having no fixed value —***n.*** **1.** anything changeable; thing that varies **2.** *Math. a)* a quantity that may have a number of different values *b)* a symbol for such a quantity **3.** *Naut.* a shifting wind —**var′i·a·bil′i·ty, var′i·a·ble·ness** ***n.*** —**var′i·a·bly** ***adv.***

variable star a star whose brightness varies from time to time, usually in regular periods

var·i·ance (ver′ē əns, var′-) ***n.*** **1.** a varying or being variant **2.** degree of change or difference; discrepancy **3.** official permission to bypass regulations, esp. zoning laws of a city **4.** a quarrel; dispute **5.** *Accounting* the difference between actual costs of production and the expected costs —**at variance** not in agreement; conflicting

var·i·ant (-ənt) ***adj.*** varying; different; esp., different in some way from others of the same kind —***n.*** anything that is variant, as a different spelling of the same word

var·i·a·tion (ver′ē ā′shən, var′-) ***n.*** **1.** *a)* the act, fact, or process of varying; change in form, condition, extent, etc. *b)* the degree or extent of such change **2.** *same as* DECLINATION (sense 3) **3.** a thing that is somewhat different from another of the same kind **4.** *Biol.* a deviation from the usual or parental type in structure or form **5.** *Music* the repetition of a melody or theme with changes in harmony, rhythm, key, etc. —**var′i·a′tion·al** ***adj.***

var·i·cel·la (var′ə sel′ə) ***n.*** [ModL., dim. of *variola:* see VARIOLA] *same as* CHICKEN POX —**var′i·cel′loid** (-oid) ***adj.***

var·i·col·ored (ver′i kul′ərd, var′-) ***adj.*** of several or many colors

var·i·cose (var′ə kōs′) ***adj.*** [L. *varicosus* < *varix* (gen. *varicis*), enlarged vein] **1.** abnormally and irregularly swollen [*varicose* veins] **2.** resulting from varicose veins [*varicose* ulcer] —**var′i·cos′i·ty** (-käs′ə tē) ***n.***

var·ied (ver′ēd, var′-) ***adj.*** **1.** of different kinds; various **2.** variegated **3.** changed; altered —**var′ied·ly** ***adv.***

var·i·e·gate (ver′ē ə gāt′, ver′ə gāt′; var′-) ***vt.*** **-gat′ed, -gat′ing** [< L. pp. of *variegare* < *varius,* various] **1.** to make varied in appearance by differences, as in colors **2.** to give variety to —**var′i·e·gat′ed** ***adj.*** —**var′i·e·ga′tion** ***n.***

va·ri·e·tal (və rī′ə t'l) ***adj.*** of or being a variety

va·ri·e·ty (və rī′ə tē) ***n.,*** *pl.* **-ties** [< Fr. < L. *varietas*] **1.** a being various or varied; absence of monotony or sameness **2.** any of the various forms of something; sort; kind [*varieties* of cloth] **3.** a number of different kinds [a *variety* of fruits, a *variety* of merchandise] **4.** a subdivision of a species; subspecies or variant; specif., *Bot.* a recognized variant of a wild plant, even though brought under cultivation —***adj.*** of or in a variety show

variety meat meat other than flesh; specif., any of the edible organs, as the liver, kidneys, heart, etc.

variety show a show made up of different kinds of acts, as comic skits, songs, dances, etc.

variety store a retail store that sells a wide variety of relatively small and inexpensive items

var·i·form (ver′ə fôrm′, var′-) ***adj.*** having various forms

va·ri·o·la (və rī′ə lə) ***n.*** [ModL. < ML. < L. *varius,* various, mottled] any of a group of virus diseases characterized by pustular eruptions and including smallpox, cowpox, etc.

var·i·om·e·ter (ver′ē äm′ə tər, var′-) ***n.*** [VARIO(US) + -METER] **1.** a device for determining variations of magnetic force esp. at different places on the earth **2.** *Radio* a unit consisting of a coil that can be rotated within a fixed coil to vary inductance

var·i·o·rum (ver′ē ôr′əm, var′-) ***n.*** [L., of various (scholars)] **1.** an edition or text, as of a literary work, with notes by various editors, scholars, etc. **2.** an edition containing variant texts —***adj.*** of or being a variorum

var·i·ous (ver′ē əs, var′-) ***adj.*** [L. *varius,* diverse] **1.** differing one from another; of several kinds **2.** *a)* several or

many [found in *various* parts of the country] *b*) individual; distinct [bequests to the *various* heirs] **3.** many-sided; versatile **4.** characterized by variety; varied in nature or appearance —**var′i·ous·ly** ***adv.***
va·ris·tor (və ris′tər) ***n.*** [VAR(IOUS) + (RES)ISTOR] a semiconductor device whose resistance drops as the voltage is increased
var·let (vär′lit) ***n.*** [OFr., var. of *vaslet:* see VALET] [Archaic] **1.** an attendant **2.** a scoundrel; knave
var·mint, var·ment (vär′mənt) ***n.*** [dial. var. of VERMIN] [Dial. or Colloq.] a person or animal regarded as troublesome or objectionable
var·nish (vär′nish) ***n.*** [< OFr. < ML. *veronix,* a resin < Gr. *Berenikē,* an ancient city] **1.** *a*) a preparation made of resinous substances dissolved in oil (**oil varnish**) or in alcohol, turpentine, etc. (**spirit varnish**), used to give a hard, glossy surface to wood, etc. *b*) any of various natural or prepared products similarly used **2.** the hard, glossy surface produced **3.** a surface gloss or smoothness, as of manner —***vt.*** **1.** to cover with varnish **2.** to smooth over in a false way —**var′nish·er** ***n.***
va·room (və ro͞om′) ***n., vi.*** *var. of* VROOM
var·si·ty (vär′sə tē) ***n., pl.*** **-ties** [contr. & altered < UNIVERSITY] the main team representing a university, college, or school in some competition, esp. an athletic one —***adj.*** designating or of such a team
var·y (ver′ē, var′-) ***vt.*** **var′ied, var′y·ing** [< OFr. < L. *variare* < *varius,* various] **1.** to change in form, nature, etc.; alter **2.** to make different from one another **3.** to give variety to —***vi.*** **1.** to be or become different; differ or change **2.** to deviate or depart (*from*) —**var′i·er** ***n.***
vas (vas) ***n., pl.*** **va·sa** (vā′sə) [L., a vessel] *Anat., Biol.* a vessel or duct —**va·sal** (vā′s'l) ***adj.***
vas·cu·lar (vas′kyə lər) ***adj.*** [< ModL. < L. *vasculum,* dim. of *vas,* a vessel] **1.** *Anat., Zool.* of or consisting of vessels carrying blood or lymph **2.** *Bot.* of, consisting of, or having special cells, xylem, and phloem that carry water and food, as ferns and seed plants
vascular bundle a unit of the conducting system of higher plants, consisting chiefly of xylem and phloem
vas de·fe·rens (vas def′ə renz′) *pl.* **va·sa de·fe·ren·ti·a** (vā′sə def′ə ren′shē ə) [ModL. < L. *vas,* a vessel + *deferens,* carrying down] the duct that carries sperm from the testicle to the ejaculatory duct of the penis
vase (vās, vāz; *chiefly Brit.* väz) ***n.*** [< Fr. < L. *vas,* a vessel, dish] an open container of metal, glass, pottery, etc. used for decoration, holding flowers, etc.
vas·ec·to·my (vas ek′tə mē) ***n., pl.*** **-mies** [VAS(O)- + -ECTOMY] the cutting, tying, and removing of part of the vas deferens for the purpose of sterilizing sexually
Vas·e·line (vas′ə lēn′) [coinage < G. *was(ser),* water + Gr. *el(aion),* oil + -INE[4]] *a trademark for* PETROLATUM —***n.*** [v-] petrolatum, or petroleum jelly
vas·o- [< L. *vas,* a vessel] *a combining form meaning:* **1.** blood vessels [*vasomotor*] **2.** vas deferens [*vasectomy*] **3.** vasomotor [*vasoinhibitor*] Also, before a vowel, **vas-**
vas·o·con·stric·tor (vas′ō kən strik′tər) ***adj.*** [prec. + CONSTRICTOR] *Physiol.* constricting the blood vessels —***n.*** a nerve or drug doing this —**vas′o·con·stric′tion** ***n.***
vas·o·di·la·tor (-dī′lāt′ər) ***adj.*** [VASO- + DILATOR] *Physiol.* dilating the blood vessels —***n.*** a nerve or drug doing this —**vas′o·dil′a·ta′tion** (-dil′ə tā′shən), **vas′o·di·la′tion** ***n.***
vas·o·in·hib·i·tor (-in hib′ə tər) ***n.*** [VASO- + INHIBITOR] a drug or agent inhibiting the action of the vasomotor nerves —**vas′o·in·hib′i·to′ry** (-tôr′ē) ***adj.***
vas·o·mo·tor (-mōt′ər) ***adj.*** [VASO- + MOTOR] *Physiol.* regulating the diameter of blood vessels by causing contraction or dilatation, as certain nerves or nerve centers
vas·o·pres·sin (-pres′'n) ***n.*** [< VASO- + PRESS(URE) + -IN[1]] a hormone of the pituitary gland that increases blood pressure
vas·o·pres·sor (-pres′ər) ***n.*** [VASO- + PRESS(URE) + -OR] a substance causing a rise in blood pressure
vas·sal (vas′'l) ***n.*** [OFr. < ML. *vassalus* < *vassus,* servant < Celt.] **1.** a person in the feudal system who held land in return for fealty, military help, etc. to an overlord **2.** a subordinate, servant, slave, etc. —***adj.*** of, like, or being a vassal —**vas′sal·age** (ij) ***n.***
vast (vast) ***adj.*** [L. *vastus*] very great in size, extent, amount, degree, etc. —**vast′ly** ***adv.*** —**vast′ness** ***n.***
Väs·te·rås (ves′tə rôs′) city in SC Sweden: pop. 113,000
vast·y (vas′tē) ***adj.*** **-i·er, -i·est** [Archaic] vast; immense
vat (vat) ***n.*** [< OE. *fæt,* a cask] a large tank, tub, or cask for holding liquids as for use in a manufacturing process —***vt.*** **vat′ted, vat′ting** to put in or store in a vat
Vat·i·can (vat′i k'n) **1.** the papal palace, a group of buildings in Vatican City **2.** the papal government or authority —***adj.*** **1.** of the Vatican **2.** designating either of the Roman Catholic Ecumenical Councils held in Vatican City in 1869–70 (**Vatican I**) or 1962–65 (**Vatican II**)
Vatican City independent papal state constituted as an enclave in Rome: it includes the Vatican & St. Peter's Basilica: 108 acres: pop. c. 1,000
vaude·ville (vōd′vil, vôd′-; vō′də-, vô′də-) ***n.*** [Fr. < *Vau-de-Vire,* a valley in Normandy, famous for light, convivial songs] **1.** a stage show consisting of mixed specialty acts, including songs, dances, comic skits, acrobatics, etc. **2.** such entertainment generally —**vaude·vil′lian** (-vil′yən) ***n., adj.***
vault[1] (vôlt) ***n.*** [< OFr., ult. < L. *volvere,* to roll] **1.** an arched roof, ceiling, etc. of masonry **2.** an arched chamber or space, esp. when underground **3.** a cellar room used for storage **4.** *a*) a burial chamber *b*) a concrete or metal enclosure in the ground, into which the casket is lowered at burial **5.** a secure room for the safekeeping of valuables or money, as in a bank **6.** the sky as a vaultlike canopy —***vt.*** **1.** to cover with a vault **2.** to build as a vault —***vi.*** to curve like a vault —**vault′ed** ***adj.***

GROINED VAULT

vault[2] (vôlt) ***vi.*** [< MFr. < OIt. *voltare,* ult. < L. *volvere,* to roll] to leap as over a barrier, esp. putting the hands on the barrier or using a long pole —***vt.*** to vault over —***n.*** a vaulting —**vault′er** ***n.***
vault·ing[1] (vôl′tiŋ) ***n.*** **1.** the arched work forming a vault **2.** a vault or vaults
vault·ing[2] (vôl′tiŋ) ***adj.*** **1.** that vaults or leaps **2.** reaching too far or beyond one's abilities [*vaulting* ambition]
vaunt (vônt, vänt) ***vi., vt.*** [< OFr. < LL. *vanitare* < L. *vanus,* vain] to boast or brag (of) —***n.*** a boast or brag —**vaunt′ed** ***adj.*** —**vaunt′er** ***n.***
v.aux. auxiliary verb
vb. **1.** verb **2.** verbal
VC, V.C. Viet Cong
V.C. **1.** Vice-Consul **2.** Victoria Cross
VD, V.D. venereal disease
V-Day (vē′dā′) ***n.*** Victory Day
've *contraction of* HAVE [*we've* seen it]
Ve·a·dar (vā′ä där′, vē′ä där′) ***n.*** [Heb.] a recurring extra month of the Jewish year: see JEWISH CALENDAR
veal (vēl) ***n.*** [OFr. *veel* < L. dim. of *vitulus,* a calf] **1.** the flesh of a young calf, used as food **2.** a vealer
veal·er (-ər) ***n.*** a calf, esp. as intended for food
Veb·len (veb′lən), **Thor·stein (Bunde)** (thôr′stīn) 1857–1929; U.S. political economist & social scientist
vec·tor (vek′tər) ***n.*** [ModL. < L., a carrier < pp. of *vehere,* to carry] **1.** *Biol.* an animal, as an insect, that transmits a disease-producing organism from one host to another **2.** *Math.* *a*) a physical quantity with both magnitude and direction, such as a force or velocity: distinguished from SCALAR *b*) a directed line segment representing such a quantity —**vec·to′ri·al** (-tôr′ē əl) ***adj.***
Ve·da (vā′də, vē′-) ***n.*** [Sans. *veda,* knowledge] **1.** any of four ancient sacred books of Hinduism, consisting of psalms, chants, sacred formulas, etc. **2.** these books collectively —**Ve·da·ic** (vi dā′ik), **Ve′dic** ***adj.***
Ve·dan·ta (vi dän′tə, -dan′-) ***n.*** [< Sans. < *veda,* knowledge + *anta,* an end] a system of Hindu monistic or pantheistic philosophy based on the Vedas —**Ve·dan′tic** ***adj.*** —**Ve·dan′tism** ***n.***
V-E Day (vē′ē′) May 8, 1945, the official date of Germany's surrender ending the European phase of World War II
Veep (vēp) ***n.*** [< *veepee* (for V.P.)] [*sometimes* **v-**] [Colloq.] a vice-president; specif., the U.S. Vice President
veer (vir) ***vi.*** [altered < Fr. *virer,* to turn around] **1.** to change direction; shift; turn **2.** to change sides, as from one opinion to another **3.** to shift clockwise: said of the wind —***vt.*** to turn or swing; change the course of —***n.*** a change of direction —**veer′ing·ly** ***adv.***
veer·y (vir′ē) ***n., pl.*** **veer′ies** [prob. echoic] a brown and cream-colored thrush of the eastern U.S.
Ve·ga (vē′gə, vā′-) [ML. < Ar.] a very bright star in the constellation Lyra
Ve·ga (ve′gä), **Lo·pe de** (lô′pe *th*e) 1562–1635; Sp. dramatist & poet
veg·e·ta·ble (vej′tə b'l, vej′ə tə-) ***adj.*** [< ML. *vegetabilis,* vegetative < LL., animating < L. *vegetare:* see VEGETATE] **1.** of plants in general [the *vegetable* kingdom] **2.** of, like, or from vegetables [*vegetable* oil] —***n.*** **1.** any plant, as distinguished from something animal or inorganic **2.** *a*) any plant that is eaten whole or in part, raw or cooked, generally with an entree or in a salad *b*) the edible part of such a plant, as the root (e.g., a carrot), tuber (a potato),

seed (a pea), fruit (a tomato), stem (celery), leaf (lettuce), etc. **3.** a person thought of as vegetablelike because living in or as in a coma

vegetable ivory the fully ripe, ivorylike seed of a S. American palm, used to make buttons, ornaments, etc.

vegetable oil any of various liquid fats derived from the fruits or seeds of plants, used in food products, etc.

veg·e·tal (vej′ə t'l) *adj. same as:* **1.** VEGETABLE **2.** VEGETATIVE (sense 3)

veg·e·tar·i·an (vej′ə ter′ē ən) *n.* [VEGET(ABLE) + -ARIAN] a person who eats no meat; strictly, one who believes in a diet of only vegetables, fruits, grains, and nuts as the proper one for people *—adj.* **1.** of vegetarians, their principles, etc. **2.** consisting only of vegetables, fruits, etc. **—veg′e·tar′i·an·ism** *n.*

veg·e·tate (vej′ə tāt′) *vi.* **-tat′ed, -tat′ing** [< L. pp. of *vegetare,* to enliven < *vegetus,* lively < *vegere,* to quicken] **1.** to grow as plants **2.** to exist with little mental and physical activity; lead a dull, inactive life

veg·e·ta·tion (vej′ə tā′shən) *n.* **1.** the act or process of vegetating **2.** plant life in general **3.** dull, passive, unthinking existence **—veg′e·ta′tion·al** *adj.*

veg·e·ta·tive (vej′ə tāt′iv) *adj.* **1.** of plants or plant growth **2.** growing as plants **3.** designating or of the functions or parts of plants not related to reproduction **4.** helping plant growth *[vegetative* loams*]* **5.** dull and inactive *[a vegetative* life*]* **6.** *Zool.* of or pertaining to asexual reproduction Also **veg′e·tive** (-tiv) **—veg′e·ta′tive·ly** *adv.* **—veg′e·ta′tive·ness** *n.*

ve·he·ment (vē′ə mənt) *adj.* [< MFr. < L. *vehemens,* eager < *vehere,* to carry] **1.** acting or moving with great force; violent; impetuous **2.** full of or showing very strong feeling; intense, fervent, impassioned, etc. **—ve′he·mence, ve′he·men·cy** *n.* **—ve′he·ment·ly** *adv.*

ve·hi·cle (vē′ə k'l, vē′hi-) *n.* [< Fr. < L. *vehiculum,* carriage < *vehere,* to carry] **1.** a means of carrying persons or things, esp. over land or in space, as an automobile, bicycle, sled, spacecraft, etc. **2.** a means of expressing ideas **3.** a play as a means of presenting a specified actor or company **4.** *Painting* a liquid, as water or oil, with which pigments are mixed for use **5.** *Pharmacy* a substance, as a syrup, in which medicines are given **—ve·hic·u·lar** (vē hik′yoo lər) *adj.*

veil (vāl) *n.* [< ONormFr. < L. *vela,* pl. of *velum,* cloth] **1.** a piece of light fabric, as net or gauze, worn, esp. by women, over the face or head to hide the features or as an ornament **2.** any cloth, curtain, etc. used to conceal or separate **3.** anything that covers or conceals *[a veil* of mist, a *veil* of silence*]* **4.** *a)* a part of a nun's headdress, draped along the face and over the shoulders *b)* the state or life of a nun: chiefly in **take the veil,** to become a nun *—vt.* to cover, conceal, etc. with or as with a veil **—veiled** *adj.* **—veil′like′** *adj.*

veil·ing (-iŋ) *n.* **1.** a veil **2.** fabric for veils

vein (vān) *n.* [< OFr. < L. *vena*] **1.** any blood vessel bringing blood back to the heart from some part of the body **2.** any riblike support in an insect wing **3.** any of the fine lines, or ribs, in a leaf **4.** a layer of mineral, rock, etc. in a fissure or zone of different rock; lode **5.** a streak or marking of a color or substance different from the surrounding material, as in marble **6.** *a)* a distinctive quality or strain running through something *[a vein* of humor*]* *b)* course or tenor of thought, feeling, action, etc. **7.** a temporary state of mind; mood *[in a serious vein]* *—vt.* **1.** to mark as with veins **2.** to branch out through like veins

vein·ing (-iŋ) *n.* formation or arrangement of veins

vein·let (-lit) *n. same as* VENULE: also **vein′ule** (-yo͞ol)

vein·y (-ē) *adj.* **vein′i·er, vein′i·est** full of veins or veinlike markings

ve·lar (vē′lər) *adj.* **1.** of a velum; esp., of the soft palate **2.** *Phonet.* pronounced with the back of the tongue touching or near the soft palate, as the sound of *k* followed by a back vowel like (o͞o) *—n.* a velar sound

Ve·láz·quez (ve läth′keth; *E.* və las′kes, -kwez), **Die·go (Rodríguez de Silva y)** (dye′gô) 1599–1660; Sp. painter: also **Ve·lás·quez** (ve läs′keth)

Vel·cro (vel′krō) [arbitrary formation < VEL(VET)] *a trademark for* a nylon material made with both a surface of tiny hooks and one of pile: matching strips are used in garments, etc. as fasteners, easily pressed together or pulled apart *—n.* this material

veld, veldt (velt) *n.* [Afrik. < MDu. *veld,* a field] in South Africa, open grassy country

vel·lum (vel′əm) *n.* [MFr. *velin,* vellum < OFr. *veel:* see VEAL] **1.** a fine parchment used for writing on or for binding books **2.** a manuscript on vellum **3.** a strong paper resembling vellum *—adj.* of or like vellum

ve·loc·i·pede (və läs′ə pēd′) *n.* [< Fr. < L. *velox* (gen. *velocis*), swift + *pes* (gen. *pedis*), a foot] **1.** any of various early bicycles or tricycles **2.** [Now Rare] a child's tricycle

ve·loc·i·ty (-tē) *n., pl.* **-ties** [< Fr. < L. < *velox:* see prec.] **1.** quickness of motion or action; speed **2.** rate of change of position, or rate of motion in a particular direction, in relation to time

ve·lour, ve·lours (və loor′) *n., pl.* **ve·lours′** [Fr.: see VELURE] a fabric with a soft nap like velvet, used for upholstery, draperies, hats, clothing, etc.

ve·lum (vē′ləm) *n., pl.* **-la** (-lə) [L., a veil] *Biol.* any of various veillike membranous partitions or coverings; specif., *same as* SOFT PALATE

ve·lure (və loor′) *n.* [Fr. *velours* < OFr. < LL. *villosus,* shaggy < *villus,* shaggy hair] velvet or velvetlike fabric

vel·vet (vel′vit) *n.* [< OFr. < VL. *villutus* < L. *villus,* shaggy hair] **1.** a rich fabric of silk, rayon, nylon, etc. with a soft, thick pile **2.** anything with a surface like that of velvet **3.** [Old Slang] extra or clear profit or gain *—adj.* **1.** made of or covered with velvet **2.** smooth or soft like velvet **—vel′vet·y** *adj.*

velvet ant any of various wasps that resemble ants, often covered with brightly colored hairs: females are wingless

vel·vet·een (vel′və tēn′) *n.* a velvetlike cotton cloth

ve·na ca·va (vē′nə kā′və) *pl.* **ve′nae ca′vae** (vē′nē kā′vē) [ModL. < L. *vena,* vein + *cava,* fem. of *cavus,* hollow] *Anat.* either of two large veins carrying blood to the right atrium of the heart

ve·nal (vē′n'l) *adj.* [L. *venalis,* salable < *venum,* sale] **1.** that can readily be bribed or corrupted **2.** characterized by bribery or corruption **—ve·nal′i·ty** (-nal′ə tē) *n., pl.* **-ties** **—ve′nal·ly** *adv.*

ve·na·tion (vē nā′shən) *n.* [< L. *vena,* a vein] **1.** an arrangement or system of veins, as in an insect's wing or a leaf **2.** such veins collectively

vend (vend) *vt., vi.* [< Fr. < L. *vendere,* contr. < *venum dare,* to offer for sale] to sell, esp. by peddling

vend·ee (ven′dē′) *n.* the person to whom a thing is sold

ven·det·ta (ven det′ə) *n.* [It. < L. *vindicta,* vengeance] **1.** a feud in which relatives of a murdered or wronged person seek vengeance on the guilty person or his family **2.** any bitter quarrel or feud **—ven·det′tist** *n.*

vend·i·ble, vend·a·ble (ven′də b'l) *adj.* [see VEND] capable of being sold *—n.* something vendible **—vend′i·bil′i·ty** *n.* **—vend′i·bly** *adv.*

vending machine a coin-operated machine for selling certain kinds of articles, refreshments, etc.

ven·dor, vend·er (ven′dər) *n.* **1.** one who vends, or sells; seller **2.** *same as* VENDING MACHINE

ve·neer (və nir′) *vt.* [G. *furnieren* < Fr. *fournir,* to furnish] **1.** to cover with a thin layer of finer material; esp., to cover (wood) with wood of a finer quality **2.** to make outwardly attractive **3.** to glue (thin wood layers) together to form plywood *—n.* **1.** a thin layer used to veneer something; also, any of the layers used in making plywood **2.** a surface appearance that hides what is below

ve·neer·ing (-iŋ) *n.* material used for veneer

ven·er·a·ble (ven′ər ə b'l, ven′rə b'l) *adj.* [see VENERATE] **1.** worthy of respect or reverence by reason of age, dignity, character, etc. **2.** impressively ancient, historic, or hallowed **—ven′er·a·bil′i·ty** *n.* **—ven′er·a·bly** *adv.*

ven·er·ate (ven′ə rāt′) *vt.* **-at′ed, -at′ing** [< L. pp. of *venerari,* to worship] to feel or show deep respect for; revere **—ven′er·a′tor** *n.*

ven·er·a·tion (ven′ə rā′shən) *n.* **1.** a venerating or being venerated **2.** a feeling of deep respect and reverence **3.** an act showing this

ve·ne·re·al (və nir′ē əl) *adj.* [< L. *venereus* < *venus* (gen. *veneris*), love] **1.** *a)* relating to sexual love or intercourse *b)* arousing sexual desire **2.** *a)* transmitted only or chiefly by sexual intercourse with an infected individual, as syphilis and gonorrhea *b)* infected with a venereal disease *c)* of or dealing with venereal disease

ven·er·y[1] (ven′ər ē) *n.* [< L. *Venus* (gen. *Veneris*), Venus, love] [Archaic] sexual intercourse

ven·er·y[2] (ven′ər ē) *n.* [< MFr. < *vener,* to hunt < L. *venari*] [Archaic] the hunting of game; the chase

Ve·ne·tian (və nē′shən) *adj.* of Venice, its people, culture, etc. *—n.* a native or inhabitant of Venice

Venetian blind [*also* **v- b-**] a window blind made of a number of thin, horizontal slats that can be set at any angle to regulate the light and air passing through or drawn up by cords to the window top

VENETIAN BLIND

Ve·ne·zi·a (ve ne′tsyä) *It. name of* VENICE

Ven·e·zue·la (ven′i zwā′lə, -zwē′-; *Sp.* ve′ne swe′lä) country in N S. America, on the Caribbean: 352,143 sq. mi.; pop. 10,399,000; cap. Caracas **—Ven′e·zue′lan** *adj., n.*

venge·ance (ven′jəns) *n.* [OFr. < *venger,* to avenge < L. *vindicare:* see VINDICATE] **1.** the return of an injury for an injury, in punishment; an avenging; revenge **2.** the desire to make such a return **—with a vengeance 1.** with great force or fury **2.** to an excessive or unusual extent

venge·ful (venj′fəl) *adj.* 1. desiring or seeking vengeance; vindictive 2. arising from a desire for vengeance: said of actions or feelings 3. inflicting vengeance —**venge′ful·ly** *adv.* —**venge′ful·ness** *n.*

ve·ni·al (vē′nē əl, vēn′yəl) *adj.* [OFr. < LL. *venialis* < L. *venia,* grace] 1. that can be forgiven, pardoned, or excused, as an error or fault 2. *R.C.Ch.* not causing spiritual death: said of sins not regarded as serious —**ve′ni·al·ly** *adv.*

Ven·ice (ven′is) seaport in N Italy built on more than 100 small islands in an inlet (**Gulf of Venice**) at the N end of the Adriatic: pop. 368,000

ven·in (ven′in) *n.* [< VEN(OM) + -IN¹] any of the specific toxic constituents of animal venoms

ve·ni·re (və nī′rē) *n.* [L., to come] 1. *short for* VENIRE FACIAS 2. a list or group of people from among whom a jury or juries will be selected

venire fa·ci·as (fā′shē as′) [ML., cause to come] *Law* a writ issued by a judge to a sheriff or coroner, instructing him to summon persons to serve as jurors

ve·ni·re·man (və nī′rē mən) *n., pl.* **-men** a member of a venire (sense 2)

ven·i·son (ven′i s'n, -z'n; *Brit.* ven′zən) *n.* [< OFr. < L. < pp. of *venari,* to hunt] the flesh of deer, used as food

‡**ve·ni, vi·di, vi·ci** (vā′nē vē′dē vē′chē, wā′nē wē′dē wē′kē, vē′nī vī′dī vī′sī) [L.] I came, I saw, I conquered: Julius Caesar's report to the Roman Senate of a victory

ven·om (ven′əm) *n.* [< OFr. < L. *venenum,* a poison] 1. the poison secreted by some snakes, spiders, insects, etc., injected into the victim by bite or sting 2. spite; malice

ven·om·ous (-əs) *adj.* 1. full of venom; poisonous 2. full of spite or ill will; malicious 3. *Zool.* able to inject venom by bite or sting —**ven′om·ous·ly** *adv.* —**ven′om·ous·ness** *n.*

ve·nous (vē′nəs) *adj.* [L. *venosus*] 1. *Biol. a)* of a vein or veins *b)* having veins or full of veins; veiny 2. *Physiol.* designating blood being carried in the veins back to the heart and lungs —**ve′nous·ly** *adv.*

vent¹ (vent) *n.* [OFr. *venter,* to blow, ult. < L. *ventus,* a wind] 1. an issuing, as of air, or the means of this; outlet; passage; escape 2. expression; release *[giving vent to emotion]* 3. *a)* a small opening to let gas, etc. out *b)* a small triangular window, as in a car door, for letting air in without a direct draft 4. the opening in a volcano through which it erupts 5. *Zool.* the excretory opening in animals —*vt.* 1. to make a vent in 2. to let (steam, gas, etc.) out through an opening 3. to give release or expression to 4. to unburden by giving vent to feelings

vent² (vent) *n.* [< OFr., ult. < L. pp. of *findere,* to split] a vertical slit in a garment, esp. one put in the back or sides of a coat —*vt.* to make a vent or vents in

ven·ti·late (ven′t'l āt′) *vt.* **-lat′ed, -lat′ing** [< L. pp. of *ventilare,* to fan < *ventus,* a wind] 1. *a)* to circulate fresh air in (a room, etc.) *b)* to circulate in (a room, etc.): said of fresh air 2. to put a vent in, to let air, gas, etc. escape 3. to examine and discuss (a grievance, etc.) openly 4. to aerate (blood); oxygenate —**ven′ti·la′tion** *n.*

ven·ti·la·tor (-ər) *n.* a thing that ventilates; esp., any device used to bring in fresh air and drive out foul air

ven·tral (ven′trəl) *adj.* [Fr. < L. *ventralis* < *venter,* belly] of, on, or near the belly —**ven′tral·ly** *adv.*

ven·tri·cle (ven′tri k'l) *n.* [< L. dim. of *venter,* belly] *Anat., Zool.* a cavity; specif., *a)* either of the two lower chambers of the heart which receive blood from the atria and pump it into the arteries *b)* any of the four small continuous cavities within the brain —**ven·tric′u·lar** (-trik′yə lər) *adj.*

ven·tril·o·quism (ven tril′ə kwiz′m) *n.* [< L. < *venter,* belly + *loqui,* to speak + -ISM] the art or practice of speaking so that the voice seems to come from some source other than the speaker: also **ven·tril′o·quy** (-kwē) —**ven·tril′o·quist** *n.* —**ven·tril′o·quis′tic** *adj.* —**ven·tril′o·quize′** (-kwīz′) *vi., vt.* **-quized′, -quiz′ing**

Ven·tu·ra (ven toor′ə) [< *(San Buena)ventura* (the official name) < Sp., lit., saint of good fortune] city in SW Calif., northwest of Los Angeles: pop. 74,000

ven·ture (ven′chər) *n.* [< ME. *aventure:* see ADVENTURE] 1. a risky undertaking; esp., a business enterprise in which there is danger of loss as well as chance for profit 2. something on which a risk is taken 3. chance; fortune: now only in **at a venture,** by mere chance —*vt.* **-tured, -tur·ing** 1. to risk; hazard 2. to take the risk of; brave 3. to express (an opinion, etc.) at the risk of being criticized, etc. —*vi.* to do or go at some risk —**ven′tur·er** *n.*

venture capital funds invested or for investment at considerable risk in potentially very profitable enterprises

ven·ture·some (-səm) *adj.* 1. inclined to venture; daring 2. risky; hazardous —**ven′ture·some·ly** *adv.* —**ven′ture·some·ness** *n.*

ven·tu·ri (tube) (ven toor′ē) [after G. B. *Venturi* (1746–1822), It. physicist] a short tube with a narrow throat that increases the velocity and lowers the pressure of a fluid flowing through it: used to measure fluid flow, to regulate the mixture in a carburetor, etc.

ven·tur·ous (ven′chər əs) *adj. same as* VENTURESOME —**ven′tur·ous·ly** *adv.* —**ven′tur·ous·ness** *n.*

ven·ue (ven′yoo, -oo) *n.* [OFr., arrival < *venir,* to come < L. *venire*] 1. *Law a)* the county or locality in which a cause of action or a crime occurs *b)* the county or locality in which a jury is drawn and a case tried 2. the site of an event or activity, as of a sports contest —**change of venue** *Law* the substitution of another place of trial, as when the jury or court is likely to be prejudiced

ven·ule (ven′yool) *n.* [< L. dim. of *vena,* vein] 1. *Anat.* a small vein 2. *Biol.* any small branch of a vein in a leaf or in an insect wing —**ven′u·lar** (-yoo lər) *adj.*

Ve·nus (vē′nəs) [L., lit., love] 1. *Rom. Myth.* the goddess of love and beauty: identified with the Greek goddess Aphrodite 2. a planet in the solar system, second in distance from the sun: diameter, c.7,600 mi —*n.* 1. a statue or image of Venus 2. a very beautiful woman

Ve·nus′ fly·trap (vē′nəs flī′trap′) a white-flowered swamp plant native to the Carolinas, having leaves with two hinged blades that snap shut and so trap insects

VENUS' FLYTRAP

Ver·a (vir′ə) [Russ. *Vjera,* faith; also L. fem. of *verus,* true] a feminine name

ve·ra·cious (və rā′shəs) *adj.* [< L. < *verus,* true] 1. habitually truthful; honest 2. true; accurate —**ve·ra′cious·ly** *adv.* —**ve·ra′cious·ness** *n.*

ve·rac·i·ty (və ras′ə tē) *n., pl.* **-ties** [< ML. < L. *verus,* true] 1. habitual truthfulness; honesty 2. accordance with truth; accuracy of statement 3. accuracy or precision, as of perception 4. that which is true; truth

Ver·a·cruz (ver′ə krooz′; *Sp.* ve′rä kroos′) seaport in E Mexico, on the Gulf of Mexico: pop. 242,000

ve·ran·da, ve·ran·dah (və ran′də) *n.* [Anglo-Ind. < Port. *varanda,* a balcony < *vara,* a pole < L., forked stick] an open porch, usually roofed, along the outside of a building

verb (vurb) *n.* [< OFr. < L. *verbum,* a word] 1. any of a class of words expressing action, existence, or occurrence, and acting as the main part of a predicate: see also AUXILIARY VERB, LINKING VERB 2. any phrase or construction used as a verb —*adj.* of, or functioning as, a verb

ver·bal (vur′b'l) *adj.* 1. of, in, or by means of words 2. concerned merely with words rather than with facts, ideas, or actions 3. oral rather than written 4. *Gram.* of, like, or derived from a verb —*n. Gram.* a verbal noun or other word derived from a verb: in English, gerunds, infinitives, and participles are verbals —**ver′bal·ly** *adv.*

ver·bal·ism (-iz′m) *n.* 1. an expression in one or more words; word or word phrase 2. words only, without any real meaning 3. any virtually meaningless phrase

ver·bal·ist (-ist) *n.* 1. a person skilled in verbal expression 2. a person who gives more importance to words than to the facts or ideas they convey

ver·bal·ize (vur′bə līz′) *vi.* **-ized′, -iz′ing** 1. to be wordy, or verbose 2. to communicate in words —*vt.* 1. to express in words 2. to change (a noun, etc.) into a verb —**ver′bal·i·za′tion** *n.* —**ver′bal·iz′er** *n.*

verbal noun *Gram.* a noun derived from a verb and acting in some respects like a verb: in English it is either a noun ending in *-ing* (a gerund) or an infinitive (Ex.: *walking* is healthful, *to err* is human)

ver·ba·tim (vər bāt′əm) *adv.* [ML. < L. *verbum,* a word] word for word; in exactly the same words —*adj.* following the original, word for word *[a verbatim account]*

ver·be·na (vər bē′nə) *n.* [ModL., genus name < L., foliage] any of a group of ornamental plants with spikes or clusters of red, white, or purplish flowers

ver·bi·age (vur′bē ij) *n.* [Fr. < OFr. < L. *verbum,* a word] an excess of words beyond those needed to express concisely what is meant; wordiness

ver·bose (vər bōs′) *adj.* [L. *verbosus,* full of words < *verbum,* a word] using or containing too many words; wordy; long-winded —**ver·bose′ly** *adv.* —**ver·bos′i·ty** (-bäs′ə tē), **ver·bose′ness** *n.*

‡**ver·bo·ten** (fer bō′tən) *adj.* [G.] forbidden; prohibited

ver·dant (vur′d'nt) *adj.* [prob. < VERD(URE) + -ANT] 1. green 2. covered with green vegetation 3. inexperienced; immature —**ver′dan·cy** (-d'n sē) *n.*

Verde (vurd), **Cape** peninsula on the Atlantic coast of Senegal: westernmost point of Africa

Ver·di (ver′dē), **Giu·sep·pe (Fortunino Francisco)** (jōō zep′pe) 1813–1901; It. operatic composer
ver·dict (vur′dikt) *n.* [< Anglo-Fr. < ML. < L. *vere,* truly + *dictum,* a thing said < *dicere,* to say] **1.** *Law* the decision reached by a jury at the end of a trial **2.** any decision or judgment
ver·di·gris (vur′di grēs′, -gris) *n.* [< MFr. < OFr. < *verd,* green + *de,* of + *Grece,* Greece] a green or greenish-blue coating that forms on brass, bronze, or copper
Ver·dun (ver dun′, vur-; *Fr.* ver dën′) **1.** city in NE France, on the Meuse River: scene of a battle of World War I **2.** city in SW Quebec, Canada: suburb of Montreal: pop. 77,000
ver·dure (vur′jər) *n.* [OFr. < *verd,* green] **1.** the fresh green color of growing things **2.** green vegetation **3.** vigorous or flourishing condition —**ver′dured** *adj.* —**ver′dur·ous** *adj.*
verge[1] (vurj) *n.* [< OFr. < L. *virga,* rod] **1.** *a*) the edge, brink, or margin [the *verge* of a forest, on the *verge* of hysteria] *b*) [Brit.] a grassy border, as along a road **2.** *a*) an enclosing line or border, esp. of something circular *b*) the area enclosed **3.** a rod or staff symbolic of an office —*vi.* **verged, verg′ing** to be on the verge, brink, or border (usually with *on* or *upon*)
verge[2] (vurj) *vi.* **verged, verg′ing** [L. *vergere*] **1.** to tend or incline (*to* or *toward*) **2.** to be in the process of change into something else; pass gradually (*into*) [dawn *verging* into daylight]
verg·er (vur′jər) *n.* [see VERGE[1] & -ER] **1.** a person who carries a staff of office before a bishop, etc. **2.** a church caretaker or usher
Ver·gil (vur′jəl) *var. of* VIRGIL —**Ver·gil′i·an** (-jil′ē ən) *adj.*
ver·i·est (ver′ē ist) *adj.* [superl. of VERY, *adj.*] being such to the highest degree; utter [the *veriest* nonsense]
ver·i·fi·ca·tion (ver′ə fi kā′shən) *n.* a verifying or being verified; establishment or confirmation of the truth or accuracy of a fact, theory, etc.
ver·i·fy (ver′ə fī′) *vt.* **-fied′, -fy′ing** [< MFr. < ML. < L. *verus,* true + *-ficare,* -FY] **1.** to prove to be true by demonstration, evidence, etc.; confirm or substantiate **2.** to test the accuracy of, as by comparison with a standard **3.** *Law* to affirm on oath —**ver′i·fi′a·ble** *adj.* —**ver′i·fi′a·bly** *adv.* —**ver′i·fi′er** *n.*
ver·i·ly (ver′ə lē) *adv.* [Archaic] in very truth; truly
ver·i·sim·i·lar (ver′ə sim′ə lər) *adj.* [< L. < *verus,* true + *similis,* like] seeming to be true or real; likely
ver·i·si·mil·i·tude (ver′ə si mil′ə tōōd′, -tyōōd′) *n.* [< L.: see prec.] **1.** the appearance of being true or real **2.** something having the mere appearance of being true or real
ver·i·ta·ble (ver′i tə b′l) *adj.* [< OFr. < L. *veritas,* truth] being such in truth or fact; actual [a *veritable* feast] —**ver′i·ta·bly** *adv.*
ver·i·ty (ver′ə tē) *n., pl.* **-ties** [< OFr. < L. *veritas,* truth < *verus,* true] **1.** conformity to truth or fact **2.** a principle, belief, etc. taken to be fundamentally and permanently true; a truth; a reality
ver·juice (vur′jōōs′) *n.* [< MFr. < *vert,* green + *jus,* juice] **1.** the sour, acid juice of green, or unripe, fruit **2.** sourness of temper, looks, etc.
Ver·laine (ver len′), **Paul** (pôl) 1844–96; Fr. poet
Ver·meer (vər mer′; *E.* vər mir′), **Jan** (yän) 1632–75; Du. painter: also called *Jan van der Meer van Delft*
ver·mi- [< L. *vermis*] *a combining form meaning* worm
ver·mi·cel·li (vur′mə sel′ē, -chel′ē) *n.* [It., little worms < L. dim. of *vermis,* a worm] pasta like spaghetti, but in thinner strings
ver·mi·cide (vur′mə sīd′) *n.* [VERMI- + -CIDE] a drug or other agent used to kill worms, esp. intestinal worms
ver·mic·u·lar (vər mik′yə lər) *adj.* [< ModL. < L. dim. of *vermis,* a worm] **1.** *a*) wormlike in shape or movement *b*) having twisting lines, ridges, etc. that look like worm tracks **2.** of, made by, or caused by worms Also **ver·mic′u·late** (-lit), **ver·mic′u·lat′ed** (-lāt′id)
ver·mic·u·lite (vər mik′yə līt′) *n.* [< L.: see prec. & -ITE] any of various hydrous silicate minerals, usually as mica in tiny scales that expand when heated: used for insulation, water adsorption, etc.
ver·mi·form (vur′mə fôrm′) *adj.* [VERMI- + FORM] shaped like a worm
vermiform appendix *see* APPENDIX (sense 2)
ver·mi·fuge (vur′mə fyōōj′) *adj.* [VERMI- + -FUGE] serving to expel worms and other parasites from the intestinal tract —*n.* a vermifuge drug
ver·mil·ion (vər mil′yən) *n.* [< OFr. < *vermeil,* bright-red < L. dim. of *vermis,* a worm] **1.** *a*) bright-red mercuric sulfide, used as a pigment *b*) any of several other red pigments resembling this **2.** a bright red or scarlet —*adj.* of the color vermilion
ver·min (vur′min) *n., pl.* **-min** [< OFr. < L. *vermis,* a worm] **1.** *a*) any of various insects, bugs, or small animals regarded as pests because destructive, disease-carrying, etc., as flies, lice, or rats *b*) such pests collectively **2.** [Chiefly Brit.] collectively, birds or animals that kill game on preserves **3.** *a*) a vile, loathsome person *b*) such persons collectively —**ver′min·ous** *adj.*
Ver·mont (vər mänt′) [< Fr. *Verd Mont,* green mountain] New England State of the U.S.: 9,609 sq. mi.; pop. 511,000; cap. Montpelier: abbrev. **Vt., VT** —**Ver·mont′er** *n.*
ver·mouth (vər mōōth′) *n.* [Fr. < G. *wermut,* wormwood] a sweet or dry, fortified white wine flavored with aromatic herbs, used in cocktails and as an aperitif
ver·nac·u·lar (vər nak′yə lər) *adj.* [L. *vernaculus,* native < *verna,* a homeborn slave] **1.** using the native language of a place [a *vernacular* writer] **2.** commonly spoken by the people of a particular country or place [a *vernacular* dialect] **3.** of or in the native language **4.** native to a place [*vernacular* arts] **5.** designating or of the common name, rather than the scientific Latin name, of an animal or plant —*n.* **1.** the native language or dialect of a country or place **2.** the common, everyday language of ordinary people in a particular locality **3.** the shoptalk of a profession or trade **4.** a vernacular word or term —**ver·nac′u·lar·ism** *n.* —**ver·nac′u·lar·ly** *adv.*
ver·nal (vur′n′l) *adj.* [L. *vernalis* < *vernus* < *ver,* spring] **1.** of, relating to, or appearing or occurring in, the spring **2.** springlike; fresh, warm, and mild **3.** fresh and young; youthful —**ver′nal·ly** *adv.*
ver·nal·ize (-īz′) *vt.* **-ized′, -iz′ing** to stimulate the growth and flowering of (a plant) by artificially shortening the dormant period —**ver′nal·i·za′tion** *n.*
ver·na·tion (vər nā′shən) *n.* [ModL. < pp. of L. *vernare,* to flourish] *Bot.* the arrangement of leaves in a leaf bud
Verne (vurn; *Fr.* vern), **Jules** (jōōlz; *Fr.* zhül) 1828–1905; Fr. novelist
ver·ni·er (vur′nē ər, -nir) *n.* [after P. *Vernier,* 17th-c. Fr. mathematician] a short, graduated scale that slides along a longer graduated instrument and is used to indicate fractional parts of divisions: also **vernier scale**
Ve·ro·na (və rō′nə; *It.* ve rô′nä) city in N Italy: pop. 259,000 —**Ver·o·nese** (ver′ə nēz′) *adj., n.*
Ve·ro·ne·se (ve′rô ne′se; *E.* ver′ə nēz′), **Pa·o·lo** (pä′ô lô′) (born *Paolo Cagliari*) 1528–88; Venetian painter, born in Verona
Ve·ron·i·ca (və rän′i kə) [ML.] a feminine name —*n.* [**v-**] **1.** [ModL.] *same as* SPEEDWELL **2.** *Bullfighting* a move in which the matador holds his cape out and pivots slowly as the bull charges past him
Ver·sailles (vər sī′, -sālz′; *Fr.* ver sä′y′) city in NC France, near Paris: the Allies & Germany signed a peace treaty here (1919) ending World War I: pop. 95,000
ver·sa·tile (vur′sə t′l; *chiefly Brit.* -tīl′) *adj.* [Fr. < L. < pp. of *versare,* freq. of *vertere,* to turn] **1.** *a*) competent in many things; able to turn easily from one subject or occupation to another *b*) adaptable to many uses or functions **2.** *Biol.* moving freely, as the anther of a flower or the antenna of an insect —**ver′sa·tile·ly** *adv.* —**ver′sa·til′i·ty** (-til′ə tē) *n.*
verse (vurs) *n.* [< OE. & OFr. < L. *versus,* a turning, row, pp. of *vertere,* to turn] **1.** a single line of poetry **2.** *a*) poetry in general; sometimes, specif., poems of a light or amusing nature *b*) poetry of a specified kind [blank *verse*] **3.** *a*) a single poem *b*) the poetry of a particular writer, period, etc. **4.** a stanza or other short subdivision of a poem **5.** any of the single, usually numbered, short divisions of a chapter of the Bible —*vt., vi.* **versed, vers′ing** [Now Rare] *same as* VERSIFY
versed (vurst) *adj.* [< L. pp. of *versari,* to be busy] acquainted by experience and study; skilled or learned (*in* a specified subject)
ver·si·cle (vur′si k′l) *n.* [< L. *versiculus,* dim. of *versus,* a verse] a short verse or sentence, esp. one said or sung in a religious service and followed by a response
ver·si·fi·ca·tion (vur′sə fi kā′shən) *n.* **1.** the act of versifying **2.** the art, practice, or theory of poetic composition **3.** the form or metrical structure of a poem
ver·si·fy (vur′sə fī′) *vi.* **-fied′, -fy′ing** [< MFr. < L. < *versus:* see VERSE & -FY] to compose verses —*vt.* **1.** to tell about or describe in verse **2.** to put into verse form —**ver′si·fi′er** *n.*
ver·sion (vur′zhən, -shən) *n.* [Fr. < ML. < L. *versus:* see VERSE] **1.** *a*) a translation *b*) [*often* **V-**] a translation of the Bible **2.** an account giving one point of view [two *versions* of the accident] **3.** a particular form or variation, esp. as adapted to another art form [the movie *version* of the novel] —**ver′sion·al** *adj.*
‡**vers li·bre** (ver lē′br′) *French term for* FREE VERSE
ver·so (vur′sō) *n., pl.* **-sos** [ModL. (*folio*) *verso* < L., abl. of *versus:* see VERSE] *Printing* any left-hand page of a book; back of a leaf: opposed to RECTO
verst (vurst, verst; *Russ.* vyôrst) *n.* [< Russ. *versta*] a former Russian unit of linear measure, equal to c.3,500 feet
ver·sus (vur′səs) *prep.* [ML. < L., toward < *vertere,* to turn] **1.** in contest against [our team *versus* theirs] **2.** in contrast with; as an alternative to [peace *versus* war]

ver·te·bra (vur′tə brə) ***n., pl.*** **-brae′** (-brē′), **-bras** [L., a joint < *vertere,* to turn] any of the single bones or segments of the spinal column —**ver′te·bral** ***adj.***

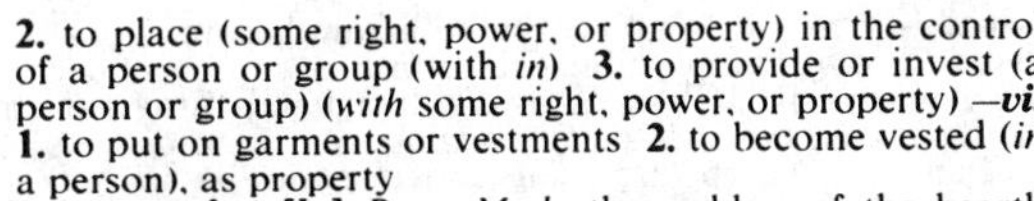

VERTEBRAE (A, section of spinal column; B, single vertebra)

ver·te·brate (-brit, -brāt′) ***adj.*** [< L.: see prec.] **1.** having a backbone, or spinal column **2.** of or belonging to the vertebrates —***n.*** any of a large group of animals, including all mammals, fishes, birds, reptiles, and amphibians, that have a backbone and a brain and cranium

ver·tex (vur′teks) ***n., pl.*** **-tex·es, -ti·ces′** (-tə sēz′) [L., the top, the turning point < *vertere,* to turn] **1.** *a)* the highest point; top; apex *b) same as* ZENITH **2.** *Geom. a)* the point where the two sides of an angle intersect *b)* a corner point of a triangle, square, cube, etc.

ver·ti·cal (vur′ti k'l) ***adj.*** **1.** of or at the vertex, or highest point; directly overhead **2.** perpendicular to the plane of the horizon or to a level surface; upright; straight up or down **3.** of or including the different levels, as in the manufacture or distribution of some product **4.** *Biol.* lengthwise —***n.*** **1.** a vertical line, plane, etc. **2.** upright position —**ver′ti·cal′i·ty** (-kal′ə tē) ***n.*** —**ver′ti·cal·ly** ***adv.***

vertical union *same as* INDUSTRIAL UNION

ver·ti·cil (vur′tə sil) ***n.*** [L. *verticillus,* dim. of *vertex,* a whirl] *Bot.* a circle of leaves, flowers, etc. on a stem; whorl —**ver·tic·il·late** (vər tis′'l it, -āt′) ***adj.***

ver·tig·i·nous (vər tij′ə nəs) ***adj.*** **1.** of, affected by, or causing vertigo; dizzy or dizzying **2.** whirling; spinning **3.** unstable; inconstant —**ver·tig′i·nous·ly** ***adv.***

ver·ti·go (vur′ti gō′) ***n., pl.*** **-goes′, ver·tig·i·nes** (vər tij′ə nēz′) [L. < *vertere,* to turn] *Med.* dizziness in an individual who feels as if he is whirling or as if his surroundings are

ver·tu (vər to͞o′, vur′to͞o) ***n.*** *same as* VIRTU

ver·vain (vur′vān) ***n.*** [< OFr. < L. *verbena,* foliage] any of a number of verbenas

verve (vurv) ***n.*** [Fr. < OFr., caprice < L. *verba,* words] **1.** vigor and energy **2.** vivacity; spirit; dash

ver·y (ver′ē) ***adj.*** **ver′i·er, ver′i·est** [< OFr., ult. < L. *verus,* true] **1.** in the fullest sense; complete; utter *[*the *very* opposite of the truth*]* **2.** same; identical *[*the *very* hat he lost*]* **3.** exactly right, suitable, etc.; precise *[*the *very* one I want*]* **4.** even (the): used as an intensive *[*the *very* rafters shook*]* **5.** actual *[*caught in the *very* act*]* —***adv.*** **1.** in a high degree; exceedingly **2.** truly; really: used as an intensive *[*the *very* same man*]*

very high frequency any radio frequency between 30 and 300 megahertz

very low frequency any radio frequency between 10 and 30 kilohertz

Ver·y signal (or **light**) (ver′ē, vir′ē) [after E. W. *Very,* 19th-c. U.S. ordnance expert] a colored flare fired from a special pistol (**Very pistol**) for signaling at night

ves·i·cant (ves′i kənt) ***adj.*** [< L. *vesica,* a blister] causing blisters —***n.*** a vesicant agent Also **ves′i·ca·to′ry** (-kə tôr′ē) ***adj., n., pl.*** **-to′ries**

ves·i·cate (-kāt′) ***vt., vi.*** **-cat′ed, -cat′ing** [< L. *vesica,* a bladder, blister] to blister —**ves′i·ca′tion** ***n.***

ves·i·cle (ves′i k'l) ***n.*** [< Fr. < L. dim. of *vesica,* bladder] **1.** a small, membranous cavity, sac, or cyst; specif., a blister **2.** *Geol.* a small, spherical cavity in volcanic rock —**ve·sic·u·lar** (və sik′yə lər), **ve·sic′u·late** (-lit) ***adj.***

Ves·pa·si·an (ves pā′zhē ən, -zhən) (L. name *Titus Flavius Sabinus Vespasianus*) 9–79 A.D.; Roman emperor (69–79)

ves·per (ves′pər) ***n.*** [L.] **1.** *a)* orig., evening *b)* [Poet.] [V-] *same as* EVENING STAR **2.** an evening prayer or service; specif., [*pl.*] [*often* **V-**] *a) R.C.Ch.* the sixth of the seven canonical hours, recited or sung in the late afternoon *b) Anglican Ch. same as* EVENSONG —***adj.*** **1.** of evening **2.** of vespers

Ves·puc·ci (ves po͞ot′chē), **A·me·ri·go** (ä′me rē′gô) (L. name *Americus Vespucius*) 1451?–1512; It. navigator

ves·sel (ves′'l) ***n.*** [< OFr. < LL. dim. of L. *vas,* a vessel] **1.** a utensil for holding something, as a bowl, pot, tub, etc. **2.** a ship or large boat **3.** *a) Anat., Zool.* a tube or duct containing or circulating a body fluid *b) Bot.* a waterconducting tube in the xylem

vest (vest) ***n.*** [< Fr. < It. < L. *vestis,* a garment] **1.** *a)* a short, tightfitting, sleeveless garment worn, esp. under a suit coat, by men; waistcoat *b)* a similar, jacketlike garment worn by women *c)* a piece set into a bodice, resembling the front of a man's vest **2.** a girl's undershirt **3.** [Brit.] any undershirt —***vt.*** **1.** to dress, as in church vestments; clothe **2.** to place (some right, power, or property) in the control of a person or group (with *in*) **3.** to provide or invest (a person or group) (*with* some right, power, or property) —***vi.*** **1.** to put on garments or vestments **2.** to become vested (*in* a person), as property

Ves·ta (ves′tə) [L.] *Rom. Myth.* the goddess of the hearth

ves·tal (ves′t'l) ***adj.*** **1.** of or sacred to Vesta **2.** of the vestal virgins **3.** chaste; pure —***n.*** **1.** *short for* VESTAL VIRGIN **2.** a chaste woman; specif., a virgin

vestal virgin in ancient Rome, any of the virgin priestesses of Vesta, who tended the sacred fire in her temple

vest·ed interest (ves′tid) **1.** an established right that cannot be done away with, as to some future benefit **2.** [*pl.*] the powerful persons and groups that own and control industry, business, etc.

vest·ee (ves tē′) ***n.*** *dim. of* VEST (*n.* 1 *c*)

ves·ti·ar·y (ves′tē er′ē) ***n., pl.*** **-ar′ies** [< OFr. < L. *vestiarium:* see VESTRY] a supply room for clothing, as in a monastery

ves·ti·bule (ves′tə byo͞ol′) ***n.*** [L. *vestibulum,* entrance hall] **1.** a small entrance hall, either to a building or a room **2.** the enclosed passage between passenger cars of a train **3.** *Anat., Zool.* any cavity or space serving as an entrance to another cavity or space

ves·tige (ves′tij) ***n.*** [Fr. < L. *vestigium,* a footprint] **1.** a trace or remaining bit of something once present or whole *[vestiges* of an ancient wall, not a *vestige* of hope*]* **2.** *Biol.* an organ or part not so fully developed or functional as it once was in the embryo or species: also **ves·tig·i·um** (ves tij′ē əm), *pl.* **-i·a** (-ə) —**ves·tig′i·al** (-tij′ē əl, -tij′əl) ***adj.***

vest·ment (vest′mənt) ***n.*** [< OFr. < L. *vestimentum* < *vestire,* to clothe] **1.** a garment; esp., an official robe or gown **2.** *Eccles.* any of the garments worn by clergymen, etc. during religious services

vest-pock·et (vest′päk′it) ***adj.*** **1.** small enough to fit into a vest pocket *[*a *vest-pocket* dictionary*]* **2.** very small

ves·try (ves′trē) ***n., pl.*** **-tries** [< OFr. < L. *vestiarium,* a wardrobe < *vestis,* a garment] **1.** a room in a church, where vestments and sacred vessels are kept **2.** a room in a church, used for meetings, Sunday school, etc. **3.** *Anglican & Episcopal Ch.* a group of church members who manage the business affairs of the church

ves·try·man (-mən) ***n., pl.*** **-men** a member of a vestry

ves·ture (ves′chər) ***n.*** [< OFr. < VL. < L. *vestire,* to clothe] [Now Rare] **1.** clothing **2.** a covering —***vt.*** **-tured, -tur·ing** [Rare or Archaic] to clothe or cover

Ve·su·vi·us (və so͞o′vē əs) active volcano in S Italy, on the Bay of Naples (see POMPEII) —**Ve·su′vi·an** ***adj.***

vet[1] (vet) ***n.*** *shortened form of* VETERINARIAN —***vt.*** **vet′ted, vet′ting** [Colloq.] **1.** to examine or treat as a veterinarian does **2.** to examine or evaluate thoroughly

vet[2] (vet) ***n.*** *shortened form of* VETERAN

vet. **1.** veteran **2.** veterinarian **3.** veterinary

vetch (vech) ***n.*** [< ONormFr. < L. *vicia,* vetch] any of a number of leafy, climbing or trailing plants of the legume family, used chiefly as fodder or fertilizer

vet·er·an (vet′ər ən, vet′rən) ***adj.*** [L. *veteranus* < *vetus* (gen. *veteris*), old] **1.** having had long experience in some kind of work or in military service **2.** of a veteran or veterans —***n.*** **1.** a person with much experience in some kind of work **2.** a person who has served in the armed forces of a country, esp. in war

Veterans Administration a consolidated Federal agency administering all laws on benefits for military veterans

Veterans Day a legal holiday in the U.S. honoring all veterans of the armed forces: observed (except 1971–77) on ARMISTICE DAY

vet·er·i·nar·i·an (vet′ər ə ner′ē ən, vet′rə ner′-) ***n.*** a person who practices veterinary medicine or surgery

vet·er·i·nar·y (vet′ər ə ner′ē, vet′rə-) ***adj.*** [< L. < *veterina,* beasts of burden] designating or of the branch of medicine dealing with the treatment of diseases and injuries in animals, esp. domestic animals —***n., pl.*** **-nar′ies** *same as* VETERINARIAN

ve·to (vē′tō) ***n., pl.*** **-toes** [L., I forbid < *vetare,* to forbid] **1.** *a)* an order forbidding some proposed act; prohibition *b)* the power to prevent action thus **2.** the constitutional right or power of a ruler or legislature to reject bills passed by another branch of the government; specif., in the U.S., *a)* the power of the President to refuse to sign a bill passed by Congress *b)* a similar power held by the governors of States *c)* the exercise of this power **3.** a document or message giving the reasons of the executive for rejecting a bill: also **veto message** **4.** the power of any of the five permanent members of the Security Council of the United Nations to prevent an action by casting a negative vote —***vt.***

-toed, -to·ing 1. to prevent (a bill) from becoming law by veto 2. to forbid; prohibit —**ve′to·er** *n.*
vex (veks) *vt.* [< MFr. < L. *vexare,* to agitate] 1. to disturb, irritate, etc., esp. in a petty, nagging way 2. to distress or afflict 3. to keep discussing and disputing (a matter) —**vex·ed·ly** (vek′sid lē) *adv.* —**vex′er** *n.*
vex·a·tion (vek sā′shən) *n.* 1. a vexing or being vexed 2. something that vexes; cause of annoyance or distress
vex·a·tious (-shəs) *adj.* characterized by or causing vexation; annoying, troublesome, etc. —**vex·a′tious·ly** *adv.*
vex·ing (vek′siŋ) *adj.* that vexes —**vex′ing·ly** *adv.*
V.F.W., VFW Veterans of Foreign Wars
VHF, V.H.F., vhf, v.h.f. very high frequency
VI, V.I. Virgin Islands (of the United States)
vi., v.i. intransitive verb
v.i. [L. *vide infra*] see below
vi·a (vī′ə, vē′ə) *prep.* [L., abl. sing. of *via,* a way] 1. by way of; passing through [from Rome to London *via* Paris] 2. by means of [*via* airmail]
vi·a·ble (vī′ə b'l) *adj.* [< Fr. < *vie,* life < L. *vita*] 1. *a*) able to live; specif., developed enough to be able to live outside the uterus [a premature but *viable* infant] *b*) capable of growing [*viable* seeds] 2. workable; likely to survive [*viable* ideas] —**vi′a·bil′i·ty** *n.* —**vi′a·bly** *adv.*
vi·a·duct (vī′ə dukt′) *n.* [L. *via* (see VIA) + (AQUE)DUCT] a bridge consisting of a series of short spans supported on piers or towers, usually to carry a road or railroad over a valley, gorge, etc.
vi·al (vī′əl) *n.* [< OFr. < OPr., ult. < Gr. *phialē,* shallow cup] a small bottle, usually of glass, for holding medicine or other liquids; phial —*vt.* **-aled** or **-alled, -al·ing** or **-al·ling** to put or keep in or as in a vial
‡**vi·a me·di·a** (vī′ə mē′dē ə, vē′ə mā′-) [L.] a middle way; course between two extremes
vi·and (vī′ənd) *n.* [< OFr., ult. < L. *vivenda,* neut. pl. gerundive of *vivere,* to live] 1. an article of food 2. [*pl.*] food; esp., choice dishes
vi·at·i·cum (vī at′i kəm) *n., pl.* **-ca** (-kə), **-cums** [L. < *viaticus,* of a way or road < *via,* way] 1. money or supplies for a journey 2. [*often* V-] the Eucharist as given to a person dying or in danger of death
vibes (vībz) *n.pl.* 1. [Colloq.] a vibraphone 2. [< VIBRATION(S)] [Slang] qualities in a person or thing that produce an emotional response in one
vi·bra·harp (vī′brə härp′) *n. same as* VIBRAPHONE
vi·brant (vī′brənt) *adj.* [< L. prp. of *vibrare,* vibrate] 1. quivering; vibrating 2. produced by vibration; resonant: said of sound 3. active; lively [*vibrant* streets] 4. energetic, sparkling, vivacious, etc. [a *vibrant* woman] —**vi′bran·cy** *n.* —**vi′brant·ly** *adv.*
vi·bra·phone (vī′brə fōn′) *n.* [VIBRA(TE) + -PHONE] a musical instrument resembling the marimba, but with electrically operated valves in the resonators, that produce a gentle vibrato —**vi′bra·phon′ist** *n.*
vi·brate (vī′brāt) *vt.* **-brat·ed, -brat·ing** [< L. pp. of *vibrare,* to vibrate] 1. to give off (light or sound) by vibration 2. to set in to-and-fro motion; oscillate 3. to cause to quiver —*vi.* 1. to swing back and forth, as a pendulum 2. to move rapidly back and forth; quiver, as a plucked string 3. to resound 4. to feel very excited; thrill
vi·bra·tile (vī′brə til, -tīl′) *adj.* 1. of or characterized by vibration 2. capable of vibrating or being vibrated 3. having a vibrating motion —**vi′bra·til′i·ty** *n.*
vi·bra·tion (vī brā′shən) *n.* 1. a vibrating; esp., rapid movement back and forth; quivering 2. *Physics a*) rapid, periodic, to-and-fro motion or oscillation of an elastic body or the particles of a fluid, as in transmitting sound *b*) a single, complete oscillation —**vi·bra′tion·al** *adj.*
vi·bra·to (vi brät′ō, vē-) *n., pl.* **-tos** [It.] *Music* the pulsating effect of a rapid, hardly noticeable variation in pitch, produced by a slight oscillation of the finger on a violin string, by a slight wavering of the tone in singing, etc.
vi·bra·tor (vī′brāt′ər) *n.* something that vibrates, as an electrical device used in massage, etc.
vi·bra·to·ry (vī′brə tôr′ē) *adj.* 1. of, like, or causing vibration 2. vibrating or capable of vibration
vi·bur·num (vī bur′nəm) *n.* [ModL., genus name < L., the wayfaring tree] 1. any of various shrubs or small trees related to the honeysuckle and bearing white flowers 2. the bark of several species, sometimes used in medicine
vic·ar (vik′ər) *n.* [< OFr. < L. *vicarius* < *vicis,* a change] 1. a person who acts in place of another; deputy 2. *Anglican Ch.* a parish priest who is not a rector and receives a stipend instead of the tithes 3. *Protestant Episcopal Ch.* a minister in charge of one chapel in a parish 4. *R.C.Ch. a*) a church officer acting as deputy of a bishop *b*) [V-] the Pope: in full, **Vicar of Christ** —**vi·car·i·al** (vī ker′ē əl, vi-) *adj.* —**vi·car′i·ate** (-it, -āt′), **vic′ar·ate** (-ər it, -ə rāt′) *n.*
vic·ar·age (-ij) *n.* 1. the residence of a vicar 2. the salary of a vicar 3. the position or duties of a vicar
vicar apostolic *pl.* **vicars apostolic** *R.C.Ch.* a titular bishop in a region where no regular see has yet been organized
vic·ar-gen·er·al (vik′ər jen′ər əl) *n., pl.* **vic′ars-gen′er·al** 1. *Anglican Ch.* a layman serving as administrative deputy to an archbishop or bishop 2. *R.C.Ch.* a priest, etc. acting as administrative deputy to a bishop or to the general superior of a religious order
vi·car·i·ous (vī ker′ē əs, vi-) *adj.* [L. *vicarius,* substituted < *vicis,* a change] 1. *a*) taking the place of another *b*) delegated [*vicarious* powers] 2. *a*) done or undergone by one person in place of another *b*) felt as if one were actually taking part in another's experience [a *vicarious* thrill] —**vi·car′i·ous·ly** *adv.* —**vi·car′i·ous·ness** *n.*
vice[1] (vīs) *n.* [< OFr. < L. *vitium*] 1. *a*) an evil or wicked action, habit, etc. *b*) depravity or corruption *c*) prostitution 2. any fault, failing, defect, etc. —**vice′less** *adj.*
vi·ce[2] (vī′sē, -sə) *prep.* [L.: see VICE-] in the place of; as the deputy or successor of
vice[3] (vīs) *n., vt. chiefly Brit. sp. of* VISE
vice- [< L. *vice,* in the place of another, abl. of *vicis:* see VICAR] *a prefix meaning* one who acts in the place of; subordinate; deputy [*vice*-president]
vice admiral a naval officer next in rank above a rear admiral and below an admiral —**vice admiralty**
vice-con·sul (vīs′kän′s'l) *n.* an officer who is subordinate to or a substitute for a consul —**vice′-con′su·lar** *adj.* —**vice′-con′su·late** (-it) *n.* —**vice′-con′sul·ship′** *n.*
vice·ge·rent (vīs′jir′ənt) *n.* [< ML. < L. < *vice* (see VICE-) + *gerere,* to direct] a person appointed by another to exercise the latter's power and authority; deputy —*adj.* of a vicegerent: also **vice′ge′ral** —**vice′ge′ren·cy** *n.*
vice-pres·i·dent (vīs′prez′i dənt) *n.* 1. *a*) an officer next in rank below a president, acting in his place during his absence or incapacity *b*) [V- P-] the elected officer of this rank in the U.S. government: he succeeds to the Presidency if the President dies or otherwise leaves office: usually written **Vice President** 2. any of several officers of a company, etc., each in charge of a department —**vice′-pres′i·den·cy** *n.* —**vice′-pres′i·den′tial** *adj.*
vice·re·gal (vīs′rē′g'l) *adj.* of a viceroy
vice·re·gent (-rē′jənt) *n.* a deputy of a regent
vice·roy (vīs′roi) *n.* [MFr. < *vice-* (see VICE-) + *roy,* a king < L. *rex*] a person ruling a country, province, etc. as the deputy of a sovereign —**vice′roy′al·ty,** *pl.* **-ties, vice′roy·ship′** *n.*
vice squad a police squad assigned to the suppression or control of prostitution, gambling, etc.
vi·ce ver·sa (vī′sē vur′sə, vī′sə; vīs′) [L.] the order or relation being reversed; conversely
Vi·chy (vish′ē, vē′shē; *Fr.* vē shē′) city in C France: capital of unoccupied France (1940–44): pop. 31,000
vi·chy·ssoise (vē′shē swäz′, vish′ē-) *n.* [Fr.] a thick cream soup of potatoes, etc., usually served cold
Vichy (water) 1. a mineral water found at Vichy 2. a natural or processed water like this
vic·i·nage (vis′ə nij) *n.* [< MFr., ult. < L. *vicinus:* see ff.] 1. *same as* VICINITY 2. the people in a neighborhood
vi·cin·i·ty (və sin′ə tē) *n., pl.* **-ties** [< L. < *vicinus,* near < *vicus,* village] 1. a being close by; nearness [two theaters in close *vicinity*] 2. nearby region; neighborhood
vi·cious (vish′əs) *adj.* [< OFr. < L. < *vitium,* a vice] 1. *a*) characterized by vice or evil; depraved *b*) debasing; corrupting 2. ruined by defects, flaws, etc. [a *vicious* argument] 3. having bad habits; unruly [a *vicious* horse] 4. malicious; spiteful; mean [a *vicious* rumor] 5. very intense, sharp, etc. —**vi′cious·ly** *adv.* —**vi′cious·ness** *n.*
vicious circle 1. a situation in which the solution of one problem gives rise to another, but the solution of this brings back the first, etc. 2. *Logic* an argument which is not valid, because its conclusion rests on a premise which itself depends on the conclusion
vi·cis·si·tude (vi sis′ə to͞od′, -tyo͞od′) *n.* [Fr. < L. *vicissitudo* < *vicis,* a turn] 1. a condition of constant change or alternation, as a natural process 2. [*pl.*] unpredictable changes or variations that keep occurring in life, fortune, etc.; shifting circumstances; ups and downs —**vi·cis′si·tu′di·nar′y, vi·cis′si·tu′di·nous** *adj.*
Vicks·burg (viks′burg) [after Rev. N. *Vick* (?–1819), early settler] city in W Miss., on the Mississippi: besieged by Grant in the Civil War (1863): pop. 25,000
vic·tim (vik′təm) *n.* [L. *victima*] 1. a person or animal killed as a sacrifice to a god 2. someone or something killed, destroyed, etc. [*victims* of war] 3. a person who suffers some loss, esp. by being swindled; dupe
vic·tim·ize (vik′tə mīz′) *vt.* **-ized′, -iz′ing** to make a victim of —**vic′tim·i·za′tion** *n.* —**vic′tim·iz′er** *n.*
vic·tim·less crime (vik′təm lis) a statutory crime, such as prostitution or gambling, regarded as having no clearly identifiable victim
Vic·tor (vik′tər) [L.: see ff.] a masculine name

vic·tor (vik′tər) *n.* [L. < pp. of *vincere,* to conquer] the winner in a battle, struggle, etc. *—adj. same as* VICTORIOUS

Victor Emmanuel III 1869–1947; king of Italy (1900–46): abdicated & the monarchy dissolved (1946)

Vic·to·ri·a[1] (vik tôr′ē ə, -tôr′yə) **1.** [L., VICTORY] a feminine name: dim. *Vicky* **2.** (**Alexandrina**), 1819–1901; queen of Great Britain & Ireland (1837–1901) *—n.* [**v-**] **1.** a four-wheeled carriage for two passengers, with a folding top and a high seat for the coachman **2.** a S. American waterlily with large leaves and large, night-blooming flowers

VICTORIA

Vic·to·ri·a[2] (vik tôr′ē ə, -tôr′yə) **1.** state of Australia, in the SE part **2.** capital of Hong Kong: pop., of met. area, 2,800,000 **3.** capital of British Columbia, Canada, on Vancouver Island: pop. 63,000 **4. Lake,** lake in E Africa, bounded by Kenya, Uganda, & Tanzania

Victoria Cross the highest British military decoration, given for deeds of exceptional valor

Victoria Day a legal holiday in Canada, celebrated on the Monday immediately preceding May 25

Vic·to·ri·an (-ən) *adj.* **1.** of or characteristic of the time when Victoria was queen of England **2.** showing the middle-class respectability, prudery, etc. regarded as typical of Victorians *—n.* a person, esp. a British writer, of the time of Queen Victoria **—Vic·to′ri·an·ism** *n.*

vic·to·ri·ous (vik tôr′ē əs, -tôr′yəs) *adj.* **1.** having won a victory; winning; triumphant **2.** of, typical of, or bringing about victory

vic·to·ry (vik′tər ē, -trē) *n., pl.* **-ries** [< OFr. < L. *victoria* < *victor,* VICTOR] **1.** the decisive winning of a battle or war **2.** success in any contest or struggle involving the defeat of an opponent or the overcoming of obstacles

vict·ual (vit′'l) *n.* [< MFr. < LL. < L. *victualis,* of food < *victus,* food < pp. of *vivere,* to live] **1.** [Archaic or Dial.] food or other provisions **2.** [*pl.*] [Dial. or Colloq.] articles of food *—vt.* **-ualed** or **-ualled, -ual·ing** or **-ual·ling** to supply with food *—vi.* to lay in a supply of food

vict·ual·er, vict·ual·ler (-ər) *n.* **1.** formerly, one who supplied victuals, as to an army **2.** [Brit.] an innkeeper

vi·cu·ña (vī ko͞on′yə, -ko͞o′nə; vi-) *n., pl.* **-ñas, -ña:** see PLURAL, II, D, 1 [Sp., of Quechuan origin] **1.** an animal found wild in the S. American Andes, related to the llama and alpaca, with soft, shaggy wool **2.** this wool **3.** a fabric made from it or in imitation of it

VICUÑA
(to 40 in. high at shoulder)

‡vi·de (vī′dē, vē′dā) [L.] see: used to direct attention to a particular page, book, etc.

‡vide an·te (an′tē) [L.] see before (in the book, etc.)

‡vide in·fra (in′frə) [L.] see below; see further on (in the book, etc.)

‡vi·de·li·cet (vi del′ə sit) *adv.* [L. < *videre licet,* it is permitted to see] that is; namely

vid·e·o (vid′ē ō′) *adj.* [L., I see] **1.** of or used in television **2.** designating or of the picture portion of a telecast: cf. AUDIO *—n. same as* TELEVISION

vid·e·o·cas·sette (-ka set′, -kə-) *n.* a cassette with videotape, for playing back recorded material on a TV set

video game an electronic device attached to a television set, that produces images on the screen, which are controlled by players competing in any of various games

vid·e·o·phone (vid′ē ō fōn′) *n.* a telephone combined with a television receiver and transmitter so that users can see, as well as speak with, each other

vid·e·o·tape (vid′ē ō tāp′) *n.* a magnetic tape on which a telecast can be recorded as for later broadcasting

‡vide su·pra (so͞o′prə) [L.] see above; see earlier (in the book, etc.)

vid·i·con (vid′ə kän) *n.* [VID(EO) + ICON(OSCOPE)] a TV camera pickup tube in which optical images are scanned by an electron beam for transmission

vie (vī) *vi.* **vied, vy′ing** [< OFr. < L. *invitare,* to invite] to be a rival or rivals; compete (*with* someone) **—vi′er** *n.*

Vi·en·na (vē en′ə) capital of Austria, on the Danube: pop. 1,642,000 **—Vi·en·nese** (vē′ə nēz′) *adj., n., pl.* **-nese′**

Vien·tiane (vyen tyän′) capital of Laos, on the Mekong River: pop. c.150,000

Vi·et Cong (vē′et käŋ′, vyet) [< Vietnamese *Viet Nam Cong San,* Vietnamese Communist] **1.** collectively, the native military force in South Vietnam, which sought national independence (1954–76) **2.** any member of this force

Vi·et·nam (vē′ət näm′, vyet′-; -nam′) country on the E coast of the Indochinese Peninsula: divided, 1954–76, into two republics (**North Vietnam** and **South Vietnam**): 129,607 sq. mi.; pop. 47,872,000; cap. Hanoi Also sp. **Viet-Nam, Viet Nam —Vi′et·nam·ese′, Vi′et-Nam·ese′** (-nə mēz′, -mēs′) *adj., n., pl.* **-ese′**

view (vyo͞o) *n.* [< OFr. < *veoir,* to see < L. *videre*] **1.** a seeing or looking, as in inspection **2.** sight or vision; esp., range of vision **3.** mental examination or survey [*a correct view* of the situation] **4.** *a*) a scene or prospect, as of a landscape *b*) a picture of such a scene **5.** visual appearance of something **6.** manner of regarding something; opinion **7.** an object; aim; goal [*with a view* to helping] **8.** a general survey *—vt.* **1.** to inspect; scrutinize **2.** to see; behold **3.** to survey mentally; consider **4.** to regard in a particular way **—in view 1.** in sight **2.** under consideration **3.** as an object aimed at **4.** in expectation; as a hope **—in view of** in consideration of; because of **—on view** displayed publicly **—with a view to 1.** with the purpose of **2.** with a hope of; looking forward to

view·er (-ər) *n.* **1.** a person who views something; spectator **2.** an optical device for individual viewing as of slides

view·find·er (-fīn′dər) *n. same as* FINDER (sense 2)

view·less (-lis) *adj.* **1.** affording no view, or prospect **2.** [Rare] invisible **3.** having or expressing no opinions

view·point (-point′) *n.* the mental position from which things are viewed and judged; point of view

vi·ges·i·mal (vī jes′ə m'l) *adj.* [< L., ult. < *viginti,* twenty] **1.** of or based on the number twenty **2.** twentieth

vig·il (vij′əl) *n.* [< OFr. < L. *vigil,* awake < *vigere,* to be lively] **1.** *a*) a watchful staying awake during the usual hours of sleep *b*) a watch kept, or the period of this **2.** *Eccles.* the evening or day before a festival, or the devotional services held then

vig·i·lance (vij′ə ləns) *n.* the quality or state of being vigilant; watchfulness

vigilance committee a group that sets itself up, without legal authority, to punish crime, etc. independently of the usual law-enforcement agencies

vig·i·lant (vij′ə lənt) *adj.* [Fr. < L. prp. of *vigilare,* to watch < *vigil,* awake] staying watchful and alert to danger or trouble **—vig′i·lant·ly** *adv.*

vig·i·lan·te (vij′ə lan′tē) *n.* [Sp., vigilant] a member of a vigilance committee

vig·i·lan·tism (vij′ə lan tiz'm) *n.* the lawless, violent methods, spirit, etc. of vigilantes **—vig′i·lan′tist** *adj.*

vi·gnette (vin yet′) *n.* [Fr., dim. < *vigne,* a vine] **1.** an ornamental design or illustration used in a book, magazine, etc., as at the beginning or end of a chapter or section **2.** a picture or photograph shading off gradually at the edges **3.** a short, delicate literary sketch *—vt.* **-gnet′ted, -gnet′ting** to make a vignette of **—vi·gnet′tist** *n.*

vig·or (vig′ər) *n.* [< OFr. < L. < *vigere,* to be strong] **1.** active physical or mental force; vitality **2.** active or healthy growth **3.** intensity, force, or energy **4.** effective legal force; validity Also, Brit. sp., **vig′our**

vig·or·ous (vig′ər əs) *adj.* **1.** strong; robust **2.** of, characterized by, or requiring vigor **3.** forceful; energetic; powerful **—vig′or·ous·ly** *adv.* **—vig′or·ous·ness** *n.*

vik·ing (vī′kiŋ) *n.* [ON. *vikingr*] [*also* **V-**] any of the Scandinavian pirates who ravaged the coasts of Europe from the 8th to the 10th centuries

vile (vīl) *adj.* [< OFr. < L. *vilis,* cheap, base] **1.** morally evil; wicked **2.** repulsive; disgusting **3.** degrading; low **4.** very bad [*vile* weather] **—vile′ly** *adv.* **—vile′ness** *n.*

vil·i·fy (vil′ə fī′) *vt.* **-fied′, -fy′ing** [LL. *vilificare:* see VILE & -FY] to use abusive or slanderous language about; revile; defame **—vil′i·fi·ca′tion** *n.* **—vil′i·fi′er** *n.*

vil·la (vil′ə) *n.* [It. < L.] **1.** a country house or estate, esp. when large or luxurious and used as a retreat or summer house **2.** [Brit.] a small suburban house

Vi·lla (vē′yä), **Fran·cis·co** (frän sēs′kô) 1877?–1923; Mex. revolutionary leader: called *Pancho Villa*

vil·lage (vil′ij) *n.* [< OFr. < L. < *villa,* a country house] **1.** a group of houses in the country, larger than a hamlet and smaller than a town **2.** such a community incorporated as a municipality **3.** the people of a village, collectively *—adj.* of a village **—vil′lag·er** *n.*

vil·lain (vil′ən) *n.* [< OFr. < VL. *villanus,* a servant < L. *villa,* a farm] **1.** a person guilty of great crimes; evil person **2.** a wicked character in a novel, play, etc. who opposes the hero **3.** *same as* VILLEIN **—vil′lain·ess** *n.fem.*

vil·lain·ous (-əs) *adj.* **1.** of or like a villain; evil; wicked **2.** very bad or disagreeable **—vil′lain·ous·ly** *adv.*

vil·lain·y (-ē) *n., pl.* **-lain·ies** **1.** the fact or state of being villainous **2.** villainous conduct **3.** a villainous act; wicked, detestable, or criminal deed

-ville (vil) [< Fr. *ville*, town, city] *a combining form meaning:* **1.** town, city *[Evansville]* **2.** place or condition characterized by: freely used in coining slang terms *["dullsville"]*

vil·lein (vil′ən) *n.* [see VILLAIN] in feudal England, any of a class of serfs who by the 13th cent. had become freemen in their legal relations to all except their lord —**vil′lein·age, vil′len·age** *n.*

Vil·lon (vē yōn′), **Fran·çois** (frän swȧ′) (born *François de Montcorbier* or *des Loges*) 1431–?; Fr. poet

vil·lus (vil′əs) *n., pl.* **vil′li** (-ī) [L., shaggy hair] **1.** *Anat.* any of numerous hairlike growths on certain mucous membranes of the body, as of the small intestines, serving to secrete mucus and absorb fats, etc. **2.** *Bot.* any of the long, soft hairs on certain plants —**vil·los·i·ty** (vi läs′ə tē) *n., pl.* **-ties** —**vil′lous** (-əs) *adj.*

Vil·ni·us (vil′nē oos′) capital of the Lithuanian S.S.R.: pop. 372,000: Russ. name **Vil·na** (vēl′nä; *E.* vil′nə)

vim (vim) *n.* [L., acc. of *vis*, strength] energy; vigor

‡**vin** (van; *Anglicized* vin) *n.* [Fr.] wine

vi·na·ceous (vī nā′shəs) *adj.* [< L. < *vinum*, wine] **1.** of or like wine or grapes **2.** wine-colored; red

vin·ai·grette (vin′i gret′) *n.* [Fr. < *vinaigre*, vinegar] a small ornamental box or bottle with a perforated lid, used for holding aromatic vinegar, smelling salts, etc.

vinaigrette sauce a savory sauce made of vinegar, oil, herbs, etc. and used esp. on cold meats

Vin·cent (vin′s′nt) [< LL. < prp. of *vincere*, to conquer] a masculine name

Vin·cent's angina (vin′s′nts) [after J. H. *Vincent* (1862–1950), Fr. physician] *same as* TRENCH MOUTH: also called **Vincent's infection**

Vinci, Leonardo da *see* DA VINCI

vin·ci·ble (vin′sə b'l) *adj.* [< L. < *vincere*, to overcome] that can be overcome or defeated —**vin′ci·bil′i·ty** *n.*

vin·di·ca·ble (vin′di kə b'l) *adj.* that can be vindicated; justifiable

vin·di·cate (vin′də kāt′) *vt.* **-cat′ed, -cat′ing** [< L. pp. of *vindicare*, to claim < *vim*, acc. of *vis*, force + *dicere*, to say] **1.** to clear from criticism, blame, suspicion, etc. **2.** to defend (a cause, etc.) against opposition **3.** to justify *[he vindicated their belief in him]* —**vin′di·ca′tive** (-kāt′iv, vin dik′ə tiv), **vin′di·ca·to′ry** *adj.* —**vin′di·ca′tor** *n.*

vin·di·ca·tion (vin′də kā′shən) *n.* **1.** a vindicating or being vindicated **2.** a fact or circumstance that vindicates

vin·dic·tive (vin dik′tiv) *adj.* [< L. *vindicta*, revenge (see VINDICATE) + -IVE] **1.** revengeful in spirit **2.** said or done in revenge *[vindictive punishment]* —**vin·dic′tive·ly** *adv.* —**vin·dic′tive·ness** *n.*

vine (vīn) *n.* [< OFr. < L. < *vinum*, wine] **1.** *a)* any plant with a long, thin stem that grows along the ground or climbs a wall or other support by means of tendrils, etc. *b)* the stem of such a plant **2.** *same as* GRAPEVINE (sense 1) —**vine′like′** *adj.*

vin·e·gar (vin′i gər) *n.* [< MFr. < *vin*, wine + *aigre*, sour < L. *acris*, acrid] **1.** a sour liquid containing acetic acid, made by fermenting cider, wine, malt, etc.: it is used as a condiment and preservative **2.** ill-tempered speech, character, etc. **3.** forceful vigor —**vin′e·gar·y, vin′e·gar·ish** *adj.*

vin·er·y (vīn′ər ē) *n., pl.* **-er·ies** **1.** an enclosed area or building in which grapevines are grown **2.** vines collectively

vine·yard (vin′yərd) *n.* land devoted to cultivating grapevines

‡**vingt-et-un** (van tā ēn′) *n.* [Fr., lit., twenty-one] *same as* TWENTY-ONE

vin·i- [< L. *vinum*, wine] *a combining form meaning* wine grapes or wine *[viniculture]*

vin·i·cul·ture (vin′i kul′chər) *n.* [prec. + CULTURE] the cultivation of wine grapes —**vin′i·cul′tur·al** *adj.* —**vin′i·cul′tur·ist** *n.*

Vin·land (vin′lənd) region, now believed to be part of N. America, discovered by Norsemen c.1000 A.D.

‡**vi·no** (vē′nô) *n.* [It. & Sp.] wine

vi·nous (vī′nəs) *adj.* [< L. < *vinum*, wine] **1.** of, having the nature of, or characteristic of wine **2.** *a)* fond of drinking wine *b)* resulting from drinking wine —**vi·nos′i·ty** (-näs′ə tē) *n.*

Vin·son (vin′sən), **Fred(erick) M(oore)** 1890–1953; U.S. jurist; chief justice of the U.S. (1946–53)

vin·tage (vin′tij) *n.* [< OFr. < L. *vindemia* < *vinum*, wine + *demere*, to remove] **1.** *a)* the crop of grapes or the resultant wine of a vineyard or grape-growing region in a single season *b)* the wine, esp. a prized wine, of a particular region in a specified year **2.** the act or season of gathering grapes or of making wine **3.** the type or model of a particular year or period *[a car of prewar vintage]* —*adj.* **1.** *a)* of choice vintage *[vintage wine]* *b)* representative of the best **2.** dating from a period long past *[vintage clothes]*

vint·ner (vint′nər) *n.* [< OFr. < ML. < L. *vinetum*, a vineyard] a wine merchant

vin·y (vī′nē) *adj.* **vin′i·er, vin′i·est** **1.** of or like vines **2.** filled or covered with vines

vi·nyl (vī′n'l) *n.* [< L. *vinum*, wine + -YL] the univalent radical, CH_2:CH–, derived from ethylene: various vinyl compounds are polymerized to form resins and plastics

vi·ol (vī′əl) *n.* [MFr. *viole* < OPr. *viula* < ?] any of an early family of stringed instruments, usually with six strings, frets, and a flat back: used in sizes from the treble viol to the bass viol

vi·o·la[1] (vē ō′lə, vī-) *n.* [It. < OPr. *viula*, viol] a stringed instrument of the violin family, slightly larger than a violin and tuned a fifth lower

vi·o·la[2] (vī′ə lə, vī ō′lə) *n.* [< L., a violet] any of various violets developed from a pansy

vi·o·la·ble (vī′ə lə b'l) *adj.* that can be, or is likely to be, violated —**vi′o·la·bil′i·ty, vi′o·la·ble·ness** *n.* —**vi′o·la·bly** *adv.*

viola da gam·ba (də gam′bə, gäm′-) [It., lit., viol for the leg] an early instrument of the viol family, held between the knees and comparable in range to the cello

vi·o·late (vī′ə lāt′) *vt.* **-lat′ed, -lat′ing** [< L. pp. of *violare*, to use force] **1.** to break (a law, rule, promise, etc.); fail to observe; infringe on **2.** to assault sexually; esp., to rape (a woman) **3.** to desecrate or profane (something sacred) **4.** to break in on; disturb *[to violate one's privacy]* **5.** to offend, insult, etc. *[to violate one's sense of decency]* —**vi′o·la′tive** *adj.* —**vi′o·la′tor** *n.*

vi·o·la·tion (vī′ə lā′shən) *n.* a violating or being violated; specif., *a)* infringement or breach, as of a law *b)* rape *c)* desecration of something sacred *d)* disturbance

vi·o·lence (vī′ə ləns) *n.* [< MFr. < L. < *violentus*, violent] **1.** physical force used so as to injure or damage **2.** intense, powerful force, as of a hurricane, etc. **3.** *a)* unjust or callous use of force or power, as in violating another's rights, privacy, etc. *b)* the harm done by this **4.** vehemence; fury **5.** a twisting of a sense, phrase, etc. so as to distort meaning **6.** a violent deed or act

vi·o·lent (-lənt) *adj.* **1.** *a)* acting with or characterized by great physical force, so as to injure, etc. *b)* acting with or characterized by unlawful force **2.** caused by violence **3.** *a)* furious; passionate; immoderate *[violent language]* *b)* emotionally disturbed and uncontrollable **4.** extreme; intense *[a violent storm]* —**vi′o·lent·ly** *adv.*

vi·o·let (vī′ə lit) *n.* [< OFr. < L. *viola*, a violet] **1.** *a)* any of a number of related short plants with white, blue, purple, or yellow flowers *b)* the flower of any of these plants **2.** any of various similar but unrelated plants, as the African violet **3.** a bluish-purple color —*adj.* bluish-purple

violet ray **1.** the shortest ray of the visible spectrum **2.** loosely, an ultraviolet ray

vi·o·lin (vī′ə lin′) *n.* [< It. dim. of *viola*, a viol] any instrument of the modern family of stringed instruments played with a bow and having four strings and no frets; specif., the smallest and highest-pitched instrument of this family, held horizontally under the chin

VIOLIN
(A, scroll; B, pegs; C, neck; D, fingerboard; E, waist; F, tailpiece; G, chinboard)

vi·o·lin·ist (-ist) *n.* a violin player

vi·ol·ist (vī′əl ist; *for 2* vē ō′list) *n.* **1.** a viol player **2.** a viola player

vi·o·lon·cel·lo (vē′ə län chel′ō, vī′ə lən-) *n., pl.* **-los** [It., dim. of *violone*, bass viol < *viola*, viol] *same as* CELLO —**vi′o·lon·cel′list** *n.*

VIP, V.I.P. [Colloq.] very important person

vi·per (vī′pər) *n.* [OFr. < L. *vipera* < ? *vivus*, living + *parere*, to bear] **1.** *a)* any of a family of venomous snakes found in Europe, Africa, and Asia, including the puff adder (sense 1), etc. *b) same as* PIT VIPER *c) same as* ADDER (sense 1) **2.** a malicious or treacherous person —**vi′per·ine** (-in, -īn′) *adj.*

vi·per·ous (-əs) *adj.* of, having the nature of, or like a viper; esp., spiteful or malicious: also **vi′per·ish** —**vi′per·ous·ly** *adv.* —**vi′per·ous·ness** *n.*

vi·ra·go (vi rā′gō, vī-; -rä′-) *n., pl.* **-goes, -gos** [OE. < L., a manlike maiden < *vir*, a man] a quarrelsome, shrewish woman; scold

vi·ral (vī′rəl) *adj.* of, involving, or caused by a virus

vir·e·o (vir′ē ō′) *n., pl.* **-e·os′** [L., a type of finch] any of a number of small, insect-eating, American songbirds, with olive-green or gray plumage

vi·res·cent (vī res′'nt, vi-) *adj.* [< L. prp. of *virescere* < *virere*, to be green] **1.** turning or becoming green **2.** greenish —**vi·res′cence** *n.*

Vir·gil (vʉr′jəl) [< L. *Vergilius,* name of the Roman gens to which the poet belonged] **1.** a masculine name **2.** (L. name *Publius Vergilius Maro*) 70–19 B.C.; Roman poet: author of the *Aeneid* —**Vir·gil′i·an** (-jil′ē ən) *adj.*

vir·gin (vʉr′jin) *n.* [< OFr. < L. *virgo* (gen. *virginis*), a maiden] **1.** a person, esp. a woman, who has not had sexual intercourse **2.** an unmarried girl or woman —[**V-**] *Astron. same as* VIRGO —*adj.* **1.** being a virgin **2.** like a virgin; chaste; modest **3.** untouched, pure, clean, etc. *[virgin* snow*]* **4.** as yet unused, untrod, unexplored, etc. by man *[a virgin* forest*]* **5.** being the first *[a virgin* effort*]* —**the Virgin** Mary, the mother of Jesus

vir·gin·al[1] (vʉr′ji n′l) *adj.* **1.** of or like a virgin; maidenly **2.** pure; fresh; unsullied —**vir′gin·al·ly** *adv.*

vir·gin·al[2] (vʉr′ji n′l) *n.* [prob. akin to prec.] [*sometimes pl.*] a harpsichord; esp., a small, rectangular harpsichord of the 16th cent., placed on a table or in the lap to be played: also **pair of virginals**

Virgin Birth *Christian Theol.* the doctrine that Jesus was born to Mary, a virgin, and that she was his only human parent

Vir·gin·ia (vʉr jin′yə, -ē ə) **1.** [L., fem. of *Virginius,* name of a Roman gens] a feminine name **2.** [after ELIZABETH I, the *Virgin* Queen] Southern State of the U.S., on the Atlantic: 40,815 sq. mi.; pop. 5,346,000; cap. Richmond: abbrev. **Va., VA** —**Vir·gin′ian** *adj., n.*

Virginia Beach city in SE Va., on the Atlantic, near Norfolk: pop. 262,000

Virginia cowslip (or **bluebell**) a perennial woodland plant with clusters of blue or purple bell-shaped flowers

Virginia creeper *same as* WOODBINE (sense 2)

Virginia deer *same as* WHITE-TAILED DEER

Virginia reel **1.** a country dance, the American variety of the reel, performed by a number of couples facing each other in two parallel lines **2.** music for this dance

Virgin Islands group of islands in the West Indies, east of Puerto Rico: *a)* **British Virgin Islands** easternmost islands of this group, constituting a Brit. territory: 59 sq. mi.; pop. 10,000 *b)* **Virgin Islands of the United States** the islands of this group closest to Puerto Rico, constituting a territory of the U.S.: 132 sq. mi.; pop. 63,000; cap. Charlotte Amalie: abbrev. **VI, V.I.**

vir·gin·i·ty (vər jin′ə tē) *n.* **1.** the state or fact of being a virgin; maidenhood, chastity, etc. **2.** the state of being virgin, pure, clean, etc.

Virgin Mary Mary, the mother of Jesus

Virgin Queen *epithet of* ELIZABETH I

vir·gin's-bow·er (vʉr′jinz bou′ər) *n.* a white-flowered, rambling variety of clematis

virgin wool wool that has never before been processed

Vir·go (vʉr′gō) [L., lit., virgin] **1.** a large constellation between Leo and Libra **2.** the sixth sign of the zodiac: see ZODIAC, illus.

vir·gule (vʉr′gyo͞ol) *n.* [Fr. < L. dim. of *virga,* a twig] a short, diagonal line (/) placed between two words to show that either can be used (and/or), in dates or fractions (3/8), to express "per" (feet/second), etc.

vir·i·des·cent (vir′ə des′nt) *adj.* [< LL., ult. < *viridis,* green] greenish —**vir′i·des′cence** *n.*

vir·ile (vir′əl; *chiefly Brit.* -īl) *adj.* [< L. < *vir,* a man] **1.** of or characteristic of an adult man; masculine; male **2.** having manly strength or vigor **3.** of or capable of copulation; sexually potent —**vir′ile·ly** *adv.* —**vi·ril·i·ty** (vi ril′ə tē) *n.*

vi·rol·o·gy (vī räl′ə jē) *n.* [< VIR(US) + *-o-* + -LOGY] the study of viruses and virus diseases —**vi·ro·log·ic** (vī′rə läj′ik), **vi′ro·log′i·cal** *adj.* —**vi·rol′o·gist** *n.*

vir·tu (vər to͞o′, vʉr′to͞o) *n.* [It. < L. *virtus,* virtue] **1.** a love of, or taste for, artistic objects **2.** such objects, collectively **3.** the quality of being so artistic, beautiful, rare, etc. as to interest a collector

vir·tu·al (vʉr′cho͞o wəl) *adj.* being such practically or in effect, although not in actual fact or name *[a virtual* dictator*]* —**vir′tu·al′i·ty** (-wal′ə tē) *n.*

vir·tu·al·ly (-cho͞o wəl ē, -cho͞o lē) *adv.* in effect although not in fact; for all practical purposes *[virtually* identical*]*

vir·tue (vʉr′cho͞o) *n.* [< OFr. < L. *virtus,* manliness, worth] **1.** general moral excellence; goodness of character **2.** a specific moral quality regarded as good **3.** chastity **4.** *a)* excellence in general; merit *b)* a specific excellence; good quality **5.** efficacy; potency; esp., healing power, as of a medicine —**by** (or **in**) **virtue of** because of; on the grounds of —**make a virtue of necessity** to do what has to be done as if one really wanted to

vir·tu·os·i·ty (vʉr′cho͞o wäs′ə tē) *n., pl.* **-ties** [< ff. + -ITY] great technical skill in some fine art, esp. in the performance of music

vir·tu·o·so (vʉr′cho͞o wō′sō) *n., pl.* **-sos, -si** (-sē) [It., skilled] **1.** orig., *a)* a person with a broad interest in the arts or sciences *b)* a person with highly cultivated tastes concerning art **2.** a person having great technical skill in some fine art, esp. in the performance of music —*adj.* of or like that of a virtuoso: also **vir′tu·os′ic** (-wäs′ik, -wō′sik)

vir·tu·ous (vʉr′cho͞o wəs) *adj.* **1.** having, or characterized by, moral virtue **2.** chaste: said of a woman —**vir′tu·ous·ly** *adv.* —**vir′tu·ous·ness** *n.*

vir·u·lent (vir′yo͞o lənt, -o͞o-) *adj.* [< L. *virulentus* < *virus,* a poison] **1.** *a)* extremely poisonous or injurious; deadly *b)* bitterly spiteful; full of hate and enmity **2.** *Med. a)* violent and rapid in its course: said of a disease *b)* highly infectious: said of a microorganism —**vir′u·lence, vir′u·len·cy** *n.* —**vir′u·lent·ly** *adv.*

vi·rus (vī′rəs) *n.* [L., a poison] **1.** orig., venom, as of a snake **2.** *a)* any of a group of ultramicroscopic infective agents that cause various diseases in animals or plants: see also FILTERABLE VIRUS *b)* a disease caused by a virus **3.** an evil or harmful influence

‡**vis** (vis) *n., pl.* **vi·res** (vī′rēz) [L.] force; strength

vi·sa (vē′zə) *n.* [Fr. < L. pp. of *videre,* to see] an endorsement on a passport, showing that it has been examined by the proper officials of a country and granting entry into that country —*vt.* **-saed, -sa·ing** **1.** to put a visa on (a passport) **2.** to give a visa to (someone)

vis·age (viz′ij) *n.* [< OFr. < L. *visus,* a look < pp. of *videre,* to see] **1.** the face; countenance **2.** appearance; aspect —**vis′aged** *adj.*

vis-à-vis (vē′zə vē′) *adj., adv.* [Fr.] face to face; opposite —*prep.* **1.** face to face with **2.** in relation to

Visc. **1.** Viscount **2.** Viscountess Also **Vis., Visct.**

vis·cer·a (vis′ər ə) *n.pl., sing.* **vis′cus** (-kəs) [L.] the internal organs of the body, as the heart, lungs, liver, intestines, etc.; specif., in popular usage, the intestines

vis·cer·al (-əl) *adj.* **1.** of, like, or affecting the viscera **2.** intuitive, emotional, etc. rather than intellectual —**vis′cer·al·ly** *adv.*

vis·cid (vis′id) *adj.* [< LL. < L. *viscum,* birdlime] being a cohesive and sticky fluid; viscous —**vis·cid·i·ty** (vi sid′ə tē) *n.* —**vis′cid·ly** *adv.*

vis·cose (vis′kōs) *adj.* **1.** *same as* VISCOUS **2.** of viscose —*n.* a syruplike solution made by treating cellulose with sodium hydroxide and carbon disulfide: used in making cellophane and rayon thread and fabrics (**viscose rayon**)

vis·cos·i·ty (vis käs′ə tē) *n., pl.* **-ties** **1.** a viscous quality or state **2.** *Physics* the internal friction of a fluid, caused by molecular attraction

vis·count (vī′kount) *n.* [< OFr. < ML. *vice comes:* see VICE- & COUNT[2]] a nobleman next below an earl or count and above a baron —**vis′count·cy, vis′count·y, vis′count·ship′** *n.*

vis·count·ess (vī′koun tis) *n.* **1.** the wife of a viscount **2.** a peeress having the same rank as a viscount

vis·cous (vis′kəs) *adj.* [< LL. < L. *viscum,* birdlime] **1.** being a cohesive and sticky fluid; viscid **2.** *Physics* having viscosity —**vis′cous·ly** *adv.* —**vis′cous·ness** *n.*

vise (vīs) *n.* [< OFr. < L. *vitis,* a vine, lit., that which winds] a device consisting of two jaws opened and closed by a screw, lever, etc., used for holding firmly an object being worked on —*vt.* **vised, vis′ing** to hold or squeeze with or as with a vise —**vise′like′** *adj.*

VISE

vi·sé (vē′zā, vē zā′) *n., vt.* **-séed, -sé·ing** [Fr.] *same as* VISA

Vish·nu (vish′no͞o) *Hindu Theol.* the second member of the trinity (Brahma, Vishnu, and Siva), called "the Preserver": see also KRISHNA —**Vish′nu·ism** *n.*

vis·i·bil·i·ty (viz′ə bil′ə tē) *n., pl.* **-ties** **1.** a being visible **2.** *a)* the relative possibility of being seen under the conditions of distance, light, and atmosphere that exist at a certain time *b)* range of vision

vis·i·ble (viz′ə b′l) *adj.* [< OFr. < L. *visibilis* < pp. of *videre,* to see] **1.** that can be seen **2.** that can be perceived; evident; manifest **3.** on hand *[visible* supply*]* —**vis′i·ble·ness** *n.* —**vis′i·bly** *adv.*

Vis·i·goth (viz′ə gäth′, -gôth′) *n.* any of the West Goths who invaded the Roman Empire late in the 4th cent. A.D. and set up a kingdom in France and Spain —**Vis′i·goth′ic** *adj.*

vi·sion (vizh′ən) *n.* [< OFr. < L. *visio* < pp. of *videre,* to see] **1.** the act or power of seeing **2.** *a)* something supposedly seen by other than normal sight, as in a dream, trance, etc. *b)* the experience of having seen something in

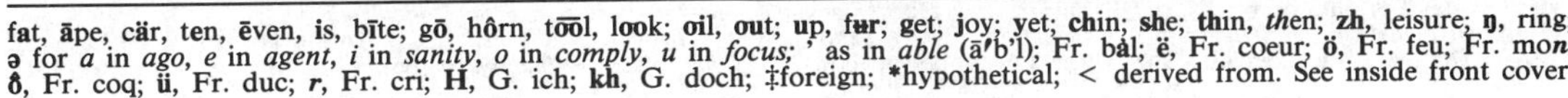

this way 3. a mental image *[visions* of power*]* 4. *a)* the ability to perceive something not actually visible, as through mental acuteness *b)* force or power of imagination *[*a statesman of great *vision]* 5. something or someone of great beauty —*vt.* to see as in a vision —**vi′sion·al** *adj.*

vi·sion·ar·y (-er′ē) *adj.* 1. of, having the nature of, or seen in a vision 2. *a)* imaginary *b)* not realistic; impractical, as an idea 3. seeing or disposed to see visions 4. characterized by impractical ideas or schemes —*n., pl.* **-ar′ies** 1. a person who sees visions 2. a person who has impractical ideas; dreamer

vis·it (viz′it) *vt.* [< OFr. < L. *visitare,* freq. < *visere,* to go to see < pp. of *videre,* to see] 1. to go or come to see (someone) out of friendship or for business or professional reasons 2. to stay with as a guest 3. to go or come to (a place) as in order to inspect or look at 4. to occur or come to *[visited* by an odd idea*]* 5. to come upon or afflict *[*a drought *visited* the land*]* 6. to inflict (punishment, suffering, etc.) upon (someone) —*vi.* to visit someone or something; specif., *a)* to make a social call (often with *with) b)* to stay with someone as a guest *c)* [Colloq.] to converse, as during a visit —*n.* a visiting; specif., *a)* a social call *b)* a stay as a guest *c)* an official call, as of a doctor, inspector, etc. *d)* [Colloq.] a friendly conversation or chat —**vis′it·a·ble** *adj.*

vis·it·ant (-ənt) *n.* 1. a visitor 2. a migratory bird in any of its temporary resting places

vis·it·a·tion (viz′ə tā′shən) *n.* 1. a visiting; esp., an official visit as to inspect 2. any trouble looked on as punishment sent by God —**the Visitation** *R.C.Ch.* 1. the visit of the Virgin Mary to Elizabeth: Luke 1:39–56 2. a church feast (July 2) commemorating this —**vis′it·a′tion·al** *adj.* —**vis·it·a·to·ri·al** (viz′i tə tôr′ē əl), **vis′i·to′ri·al** *adj.*

vis·it·ing card (viz′i tiŋ) *same as* CALLING CARD

visiting fireman [Colloq.] 1. an important visitor, esp. any of a group, given special treatment 2. a free-spending tourist, etc.

vis·i·tor (viz′it ər) *n.* a person making a visit

vi·sor (vī′zər) *n.* [< Anglo-Fr. < OFr. < *vis,* a face] 1. *a)* in armor, the movable part of a helmet that could be lowered to cover the upper part of the face *b)* a movable section of safety glass, that is part of a protective head covering 2. a mask 3. the projecting brim of a cap, for shading the eyes 4. an adjustable shade in a car, over the windshield, for shading the eyes —**vis′ored** *adj.*

VISORS

VISTA (vis′tə) [*V(olunteers) i(n) S(ervice) t(o) A(merica)*] a U.S. government program using volunteers who work at improving living conditions in poverty-stricken areas of the U.S.

vis·ta (vis′tə) *n.* [< It., ult. < L. *videre,* to see] 1. a view, esp. one seen through a long passage, as between rows of houses or trees 2. a comprehensive mental view of a series of events —**vis′taed** *adj.*

Vis·tu·la (vis′choo lə) river in Poland, flowing from the Carpathian Mountains into the Baltic Sea

vis·u·al (vizh′oo wəl) *adj.* [< LL. < L. *visus,* a sight < pp. of *videre,* to see] 1. of, connected with, based on, or used in seeing 2. that is or can be seen; visible —**vis′u·al·ly** *adv.*

visual aids motion pictures, slides, charts, etc. (but not books) used in teaching, illustrating lectures, etc.

vis·u·al·ize (vizh′oo wə līz′, -oo līz′) *vt.* **-ized′, -iz′ing** to form a mental image of (something not visible) —*vi.* to form a mental image —**vis′u·al·i·za′tion** *n.*

vi·tal (vīt′'l) *adj.* [< MFr. < L. < *vita,* life] 1. of or concerned with life 2. *a)* essential to life *[vital* organs*] b)* destroying life; fatal *[vital* wounds*]* 3. *a)* essential; indispensable *b)* of crucial importance 4. affecting the validity, truth, etc. of something *[*a *vital* error*]* 5. full of life and vigor; energetic —*n.* [*pl.*] 1. the vital organs, as the heart, brain, etc. 2. the essential parts of anything —**vi′tal·ly** *adv.* —**vi′tal·ness** *n.*

vi·tal·ism (-iz′m) *n.* the doctrine that the life in living organisms is caused and sustained by a basic force (**vital force** or **principle**) that is distinct from all physical and chemical forces —**vi′tal·ist** *n., adj.* —**vi′tal·is′tic** *adj.*

vi·tal·i·ty (vī tal′ə tē) *n., pl.* **-ties** 1. power to live or go on living 2. power to endure or survive 3. mental or physical energy; vigor

vi·tal·ize (vīt′'l īz′) *vt.* **-ized′, -iz′ing** 1. to make vital; give life to 2. to give vigor or animation to; make lively —**vi′tal·i·za′tion** *n.*

Vi·tal·li·um (vī tal′ē əm) *a trademark for* an alloy of cobalt, chromium, and molybdenum, used in bone surgery, etc.

vital statistics data on births, deaths, marriages, etc.

vi·ta·min (vīt′ə min; *Brit.* vit′-) *n.* [< L. *vita,* life + AMINE: from the orig. mistaken idea that these substances all contain amino acids] any of a number of complex organic substances found variously in foods and essential for the normal functioning of the body —**vi′ta·min′ic** *adj.*

vitamin A a fat-soluble alcohol found in fish-liver oil, egg yolk, butter, etc. or derived from carotene in carrots and other vegetables: a deficiency of this vitamin results in night blindness: it occurs in two forms, **vitamin A_1,** and **vitamin A_2**

vitamin B (complex) a group of unrelated water-soluble substances, including: *a)* **vitamin B_1** (*see* THIAMINE) *b)* **vitamin B_2** (*see* RIBOFLAVIN) *c)* **vitamin B_6** (*see* PYRIDOXINE) *d)* NIACIN *e)* PANTOTHENIC ACID *f)* BIOTIN: also called **vitamin H** *g)* INOSITOL *h)* PARA-AMINOBENZOIC ACID *i)* CHOLINE *j)* FOLIC ACID *k)* **vitamin B_{12}** a complex vitamin, essential for normal growth and used esp. in treating pernicious anemia

vitamin C *same as* ASCORBIC ACID

vitamin D any of several fat-soluble vitamins occurring in fish-liver oils, milk, egg yolk, etc.: a deficiency of this vitamin tends to produce rickets: this group includes **vitamin D_2, vitamin D_3, vitamin D_4,** and **vitamin D_5**

vitamin E the tocopherols collectively, necessary for fertility in some animals

vitamin H *same as* BIOTIN

vitamin K a fat-soluble vitamin that promotes blood clotting: **vitamin K_1** is found chiefly in alfalfa leaves and **vitamin K_2** chiefly in fish meal: **vitamin K_3** and **vitamin K_4** are prepared synthetically

vi·ti·ate (vish′ē āt′) *vt.* **-at′ed, -at′ing** [< L. pp. of *vitiare* < *vitium,* a VICE[1]] 1. to make imperfect or faulty; spoil 2. to weaken morally; debase 3. to make legally ineffective —**vi′ti·a′tion** *n.* —**vi′ti·a′tor** *n.*

vit·i·cul·ture (vit′ə kul′chər, vīt′-) *n.* [< L. *vitis,* a vine + CULTURE] the cultivation of grapes —**vit′i·cul′tur·al** *adj.* —**vit′i·cul′tur·ist** *n.*

vit·re·ous (vit′rē əs) *adj.* [< L. < *vitrum,* glass] 1. *a)* of or like glass; glassy *b)* derived from or made of glass 2. of the vitreous body —**vit′re·ous·ness** *n.*

vitreous body (or **humor**) the transparent, colorless, jellylike substance that fills the eyeball between the retina and lens

vit·ri·fy (vit′rə fī′) *vt., vi.* **-fied′, -fy′ing** [< Fr. < L. *vitrum,* glass + Fr. *-fier,* -FY] to change into glass or a glasslike substance by fusion due to heat —**vit′ri·fi′a·ble** *adj.* —**vit′ri·fi·ca′tion, vit′ri·fac′tion** *n.*

vit·rine (vi trēn′) *n.* [Fr., ult. < L. *vitrum,* glass] a glass-paneled cabinet or glass display case for art objects, curios, etc.

vit·ri·ol (vit′rē əl, -ōl′) *n.* [< MFr. < ML. *vitriolum* < LL. < L. *vitreus,* glassy] 1. *a)* any of several sulfates of metals, as of copper (*blue vitriol*), of iron (*green vitriol*), of zinc (*white vitriol*), etc. *b) same as* SULFURIC ACID: in full, **oil of vitriol** 2. sharpness or bitterness, as in speech or writing —*vt.* **-oled** or **-olled, -ol·ing** or **-ol·ling** to treat as with vitriol

vit·ri·ol·ic (vit′rē äl′ik) *adj.* 1. of, like, or derived from a vitriol 2. extremely biting or caustic *[vitriolic* talk*]*

vit·ri·ol·ize (vit′rē ə līz′) *vt.* **-ized′, -iz′ing** 1. to convert into vitriol 2. to subject to the action of vitriol

vit·tle (vit′'l) *n., v. obs. or dial. var. of* VICTUAL

vi·tu·per·ate (vī tōō′pə rāt′, vi-; -tyōō′-) *vt.* **-at′ed, -at′ing** [< L. pp. of *vituperare* < *vitium,* a fault + *parare,* to make ready] to speak abusively to or about; berate —**vi·tu′per·a′tion** *n.* —**vi·tu′per·a′tive** *adj.* —**vi·tu′per·a′tive·ly** *adv.* —**vi·tu′per·a′tive·ness** *n.* —**vi·tu′per·a′tor** *n.*

‡**vi·va** (vē′vä) *interj.* [It., Sp.] (long) live (someone or something specified)!: an exclamation of praise

vi·va·ce (vi vä′chā) *adj., adv.* [It.] *Music* in a lively, spirited manner: a direction to the performer

vi·va·cious (vi vā′shəs, vī-) *adj.* [< L. *vivax* (gen. *vivacis*) < *vivere,* to live] full of animation; spirited; lively —**vi·va′cious·ly** *adv.* —**vi·va′cious·ness** *n.*

vi·vac·i·ty (vi vas′ə tē, vī-) *n.* the quality or state of being vivacious; liveliness; animation

Vi·val·di (vē väl′dē; *E.* vi-), **An·to·nio** (än tô′nyô) 1675?–1741; It. composer

vi·var·i·um (vī ver′ē əm) *n., pl.* **-i·ums, -i·a** (-ə) [L., ult. < *vivere,* to live] an enclosed place for animals to live as if in their natural environment

vi·va vo·ce (vī′və vō′sē) [ML., with living voice] by word of mouth; orally —**vi′va-vo′ce** *adj.*

‡**vive** (vēv) *interj.* [Fr.] (long) live (someone or something specified)!: an exclamation of praise

Viv·i·an (viv′ē ən, viv′yən) [L. *Vivianus* < *vivus,* alive] a masculine or feminine name

viv·id (viv′id) *adj.* [< L. < *vivere,* to live] 1. full of life; lively; striking *[*a *vivid* personality*]* 2. bright; intense: said of colors, light, etc. 3. forming or suggesting clear or striking mental images *[*a *vivid* imagination, a *vivid* description*]* 4. clearly perceived, as a recollection —**viv′id·ly** *adv.* —**viv′id·ness** *n.*

viv·i·fy (viv′ə fī′) *vt.* **-fied′, -fy′ing** [< Fr. < LL. < L. *vivus,* alive + *facere,* to make] 1. to give life to; animate

2. to make more lively, active, striking, etc. —**viv′i·fi·ca′tion** *n.* —**viv′i·fi′er** *n.*

vi·vip·a·rous (vī vip′ər əs) *adj.* [< L. < *vivus,* alive + *parere,* to produce] bearing living young (as most mammals and some other animals do) instead of laying eggs —**vi·vip′a·rous·ly** *adv.*

viv·i·sect (viv′ə sekt′) *vt., vi.* [< ff.] to practice vivisection (on) —**viv′i·sec′tor** *n.*

viv·i·sec·tion (viv′ə sek′shən) *n.* [< L. *vivus,* alive + SECTION] medical research consisting of surgical operations or other experiments done on living animals to study the living organs and to investigate the effects of diseases and therapy —**viv′i·sec′tion·al** *adj.*

viv·i·sec·tion·ist (-ist) *n.* a person who practices or favors the practice of vivisection for the good of science

vix·en (vik′s′n) *n.* [ME. (southern dial.) *fixen* < OE. *fyxe,* she-fox] **1.** a female fox **2.** an ill-tempered, shrewish woman —**vix′en·ish** *adj.* —**vix′en·ish·ly** *adv.*

viz., viz (viz; *often read* "namely") [ML., altered < contr. for L. *videlicet*] videlicet; that is; namely

viz·ard (viz′ərd) *n.* [altered < *visar,* var. of VISOR] a mask, as for disguise

vi·zier (vi zir′, viz′yər) *n.* [< Turk. < Ar. *wazīr,* lit., bearer of burdens < *wazara,* to bear a burden] in Moslem countries, a high officer in the government; esp., a minister of state: also sp. **vi·zir′** —**vi·zier′ate** (-it, -āt), **vi·zier′ship** *n.*

vi·zor (vī′zər) *n. alt. sp. of* VISOR

V-J Day (vē′jā′) the day on which the fighting with Japan officially ended in World War II (Aug. 15, 1945) or the day of formal surrender (Sept. 2, 1945)

VL. Vulgar Latin

Vla·di·vos·tok (vlad′i väs′täk; *Russ.* vlä′di vôs tôk′) seaport in SE R.S.F.S.R., on the Pacific: pop. 442,000

Vla·minck (vlȧ maṅk′), **Mau·rice de** (mô rēs′ də) 1876–1958; Fr. painter

VLF, V.L.F., vlf, v.l.f. very low frequency

Vl·ta·va (v′l′tä vä) river in W Czechoslovakia, flowing northward into the Elbe

V-neck (vē′nek′) *n.* a neckline V-shaped in front

voc. vocative

vo·ca·ble (vō′kə b′l) *n.* [Fr. < L. *vocabulum* < *vocare,* to call] a word; esp., a word regarded as a unit of sounds or letters rather than as a unit of meaning

vo·cab·u·lar·y (vō kab′yə ler′ē, və-) *n., pl.* **-lar′ies** [< ML. < L. *vocabulum,* a word: see prec.] **1.** a list of words, usually arranged in alphabetical order and defined or otherwise identified, as in a dictionary or glossary **2.** all the words of a language, or all those used by a particular person, class, profession, etc.

vo·cal (vō′k′l) *adj.* [< L. *vocalis* < *vox* (gen. *vocis*), a voice] **1.** *a)* uttered by the voice; esp., spoken; oral *[vocal* sounds*]* *b)* sung or to be sung *[vocal* music*]* **2.** having a voice; able to speak or make oral sounds **3.** of, used in, connected with, or belonging to the voice *[vocal* organs*]* **4.** full of voices **5.** speaking freely or strongly —*n.* **1.** a vocal sound **2.** the part of a popular song that is sung, as distinguished from the parts played by the instruments —**vo′cal·ly** *adv.*

vocal cords either of two pairs of membranous cords or folds in the larynx, consisting of a thicker upper pair (**false vocal cords**) and a lower pair (**true vocal cords**): voice is produced when air from the lungs causes the lower (true) cords to vibrate

vo·cal·ic (vō kal′ik) *adj.* **1.** *a)* of, or having the nature of, a vowel *b)* composed mainly or entirely of vowels **2.** producing or involving vowel change —**vo·cal′i·cal·ly** *adv.*

vo·cal·ist (vō′k′l ist) *n.* a singer

vo·cal·ize (vō′k′l īz′) *vt.* **-ized′, -iz′ing** **1.** *a)* to give utterance to; express with the voice *b)* to make capable of vocal expression **2.** *Phonet. a)* to change into or use as a vowel *b)* to voice —*vi.* to make vocal sounds; speak or sing; specif., to do a singing exercise, using various vowel sounds —**vo′cal·i·za′tion** *n.* —**vo′cal·iz′er** *n.*

vo·ca·tion (vō kā′shən) *n.* [< LL. < L. < *vocare,* to call] **1.** *a)* a call or will to carry on some work or enter a certain career, esp. a religious one *b)* the work or career toward which one believes himself to be called **2.** any trade, profession, or occupation

vo·ca·tion·al (-′l) *adj.* **1.** of a vocation, trade, occupation, etc. **2.** designating or of education, training, etc. intended to prepare one for an occupation, sometimes specif. in a trade —**vo·ca′tion·al·ism** *n.* —**vo·ca′tion·al·ly** *adv.*

vocational guidance the work of testing and interviewing persons in order to guide them toward the choice of a suitable vocation

voc·a·tive (väk′ə tiv) *adj.* [< OFr. < L. < pp. of *vocare,* to call < *vox,* the voice] *Gram.* in certain inflected languages, designating or of the case indicating the person or thing addressed —*n.* **1.** the vocative case **2.** a word in this case

vo·cif·er·ate (vō sif′ə rāt′) *vt., vi.* **-at′ed, -at′ing** [< L. pp. of *vociferari* < *vox,* voice + *ferre,* to bear] to utter or shout loudly or vehemently; bawl; clamor —**vo·cif′er·ant** (-ər ənt) *adj.* —**vo·cif′er·a′tion** *n.* —**vo·cif′er·a′tor** *n.*

vo·cif·er·ous (vō sif′ər əs) *adj.* loud, noisy, or vehement in making one's feelings known; clamorous —**vo·cif′er·ous·ly** *adv.* —**vo·cif′er·ous·ness** *n.*

vod·ka (väd′kə) *n.* [Russ., dim. of *voda,* water] a colorless alcoholic liquor distilled from wheat, rye, etc.

vogue (vōg) *n.* [Fr., a fashion, lit., a rowing < *voguer,* to row < MLowG.] **1.** the accepted fashion at any particular time; mode: often with *the* **2.** general acceptance; popularity —*adj.* in vogue: also **vogu·ish** (vō′gish)

voice (vois) *n.* [< OFr. < L. *vox* (gen. *vocis*)] **1.** sound made through the mouth, esp. by human beings in talking, singing, etc. **2.** the ability to make such sounds *[*to lose one's *voice]* **3.** any sound, influence, etc. regarded as like vocal utterance *[*the *voice* of the sea, the *voice* of one's conscience*]* **4.** a specified or distinctive quality of vocal sound *[*an angry *voice]* **5.** *a)* an expressed wish, choice, opinion, etc. *[*the *voice* of the people*]* *b)* the right to express one's choice, opinion, etc.; vote **6.** utterance or expression *[*giving *voice* to his joy*]* **7.** the means by which something is expressed *[*a newspaper known to be the *voice* of the administration*]* **8.** *Gram.* a form of a verb showing the connection between the subject and the verb, either as performing (**active voice**) or receiving (**passive voice**) the action **9.** *Music a)* the quality of a person's singing *[*a good *voice]* *b)* a singer *c)* any of the individual parts sung or played together in a musical composition **10.** *Phonet.* sound made by vibrating the vocal cords with air forced from the lungs, as in pronouncing all vowels and such consonants as (b), (d), (g), (m), etc. —*vt.* **voiced, voic′ing** **1.** to utter or express in words **2.** *Music* to regulate the tone of (organ pipes, etc.) **3.** *Phonet.* to utter with voice —**in voice** with the voice in good condition, as for singing —**with one voice** unanimously —**voic′er** *n.*

voiced (voist) *adj.* **1.** having a voice **2.** having (a specified kind of) voice *[*deep-*voiced]* **3.** expressed by the voice **4.** *Phonet.* made by vibrating the vocal cords with air forced from the lungs: said of certain consonants

voice·less (vois′lis) *adj.* **1.** having no voice; mute **2.** not speaking or spoken **3.** *Phonet.* uttered without voice *[p, t, k,* etc. are *voiceless* consonants*]* —**voice′less·ly** *adv.* —**voice′less·ness** *n.*

voice-o·ver (-ō′vər) *n.* the voice commenting or narrating off camera, as for a television commercial

voice·print (-print′) *n.* the distinctive pattern of wavy lines, etc. formed by a person's voice as recorded by an electronic device

void (void) *adj.* [< OFr., ult. < L. *vacivus* < *vacare,* to be empty] **1.** not occupied; vacant: said of a position or office **2.** *a)* having nothing in it; empty *b)* lacking; devoid (*of*) *[void* of sense*]* **3.** useless; ineffective **4.** *Law* of no legal force; not binding; invalid —*n.* **1.** an empty space or vacuum **2.** *a)* total absence of something normally present *b)* a feeling of emptiness or loss —*vt.* **1.** *a)* to empty (the contents of something) *b)* to discharge (urine or feces) **2.** to make void; annul —*vi.* to defecate or, esp., to urinate —**void′a·ble** *adj.* —**void′er** *n.*

‡**voi·là** (vwȧ lȧ′) [Fr., see there] behold; there it is: often used as an interjection

voile (voil) *n.* [Fr., a veil] a thin, sheer fabric, as of cotton

vol. **1.** volcano **2.** *pl.* **vols.** volume **3.** volunteer

vo·lant (vō′lənt) *adj.* [Fr. < L. prp. of *volare,* to fly] **1.** flying or capable of flying **2.** nimble; quick **3.** *Heraldry* represented as flying

vol·a·tile (väl′ə t′l; *chiefly Brit.* -tīl′) *adj.* [MFr. < L. < *volare,* to fly] **1.** vaporizing or evaporating quickly, as alcohol **2.** *a)* unstable or explosive *[*a *volatile* social condition*]* *b)* moving capriciously from one idea, interest, etc. to another; fickle *c)* not lasting long; fleeting —**vol′a·til′i·ty** (-til′ə tē), **vol′a·tile·ness** *n.*

vol·a·til·ize (väl′ə t′l īz′) *vt., vi.* **-ized′, -iz′ing** to make or become volatile; evaporate —**vol′a·til·i·za′tion** *n.*

vol·can·ic (väl kan′ik) *adj.* **1.** of, from, or produced by a volcano **2.** having volcanoes **3.** like a volcano; likely to explode; violent —**vol·can′i·cal·ly** *adv.*

vol·can·ism (väl′kə niz′m) *n.* volcanic activity or phenomena

vol·ca·no (väl kā′nō) *n., pl.* **-noes, -nos** [It. < L. *Volcanus,* VULCAN] **1.** a vent in the earth's crust through which molten rock (*lava*), rock fragments, gases, ashes, etc. erupt or burst from the earth's interior **2.** a cone-shaped hill or mountain, chiefly of volcanic materials, built up around the vent, usually so as to form a crater

vole (vōl) ***n.*** **[**earlier *vole mouse* < Scand., as in Norw. *voll,* field + MOUSE**]** any of a number of small rodents with a stout body and short tail

Vol·ga (väl′gə, vōl′-; *Russ.* vôl′gä) river in western R.S.F.S.R., flowing southeastward into the Caspian Sea

Vol·go·grad (väl′gə grad′; *Russ.* vôl′gô grät′) city in SC European R.S.F.S.R., on the Volga: pop. 818,000

vo·li·tion (vō lish′ən, və-) ***n.*** **[**Fr. < ML. *volitio,* ult. < L. *velle,* to will**]** **1.** the act or power of using the will **2.** a conscious or deliberate decision —**vo·li′tion·al** ***adj.***

vol·i·tive (väl′ə tiv) ***adj.*** **1.** of the will **2.** *Gram.* expressing a wish, as a verb, mood, etc.

vol·ley (väl′ē) ***n., pl.*** **-leys [**MFr. *volee,* ult. < L. pp. of *volare,* to fly**]** **1.** *a)* the simultaneous discharge of a number of guns or other weapons *b)* the missiles discharged in this way **2.** a burst of words or acts suggestive of this [a *volley* of curses] **3.** *Sports a)* the flight of a ball, etc. before it touches the ground *b)* a return of a ball, etc. before it touches the ground *c)* loosely, any extended exchange of shots, as in tennis, esp. in warming up —***vt., vi.*** **-leyed, -ley·ing** **1.** to discharge or be discharged as in a volley **2.** *Sports* to return (the ball, etc.) as a volley; engage in a volley —**vol′ley·er** ***n.***

vol·ley·ball (-bôl′) ***n.*** **1.** a game played on a court by two teams who hit a large, light, inflated ball back and forth over a high net with the hands, each team trying to return the ball before it touches the ground **2.** this ball

vol·plane (väl′plān′) ***vi.*** **-planed′, -plan′ing [**Fr. *vol plané* < *voler,* to fly + *plané,* pp. of *planer,* to glide**]** to glide down as or in an airplane with the engine cut off —***n.*** such a glide

vols. volumes

volt[1] (vōlt) ***n.*** **[**< Fr. < It. < L. pp. of *volvere,* to turn about**]** **1.** a turning movement of a horse, sideways around a center **2.** *Fencing* a leap to avoid a thrust

volt[2] (vōlt) ***n.*** **[**after A. *Volta* (1745–1827), It. physicist**]** the mks unit of electromotive force or difference in potential between two points in an electric circuit that will send a current of one ampere through a resistance of one ohm

volt·age (vōl′tij) ***n.*** electromotive force, or difference in electrical potential, expressed in volts

vol·ta·ic (väl tā′ik, vōl-) ***adj.*** **1.** designating or of electricity produced by chemical action; galvanic **2.** used in so producing electricity

voltaic battery **1.** a battery composed of voltaic cells **2.** *same as* VOLTAIC CELL

voltaic cell a device for producing an electric current by the action of two plates of different metals in an electrolyte

Vol·taire (vōl ter′, väl-; *Fr.* vôl ter′) (born *François Marie Arouet*) 1694–1778; Fr. writer & philosopher

vol·tam·e·ter (väl tam′ə tər, vōl-) ***n.*** an electrolytic cell for measuring an electric current by the amount of gas liberated or metal deposited from an electrolyte

volt·am·me·ter (vōlt′am′mēt′ər) ***n.*** an instrument for measuring either voltage or amperage

volt-am·pere (-am′pir) ***n.*** a unit of electric power equal to the product of one volt and one ampere

volt·me·ter (vōlt′mēt′ər) ***n.*** an instrument for measuring voltage

vol·u·ble (väl′yoo b'l) ***adj.*** **[**Fr. < L. *volubilis* < pp. of *volvere,* to roll**]** talking very much and easily; talkative, glib, etc. —**vol′u·bil′i·ty** ***n.*** —**vol′u·bly** ***adv.***

vol·ume (väl′yoom, -yəm) ***n.*** **[**MFr. < L. *volumen,* a scroll < pp. of *volvere,* to roll**]** **1.** *a)* a collection of written or printed sheets bound together; book *b)* any of the books of a set **2.** a set of the issues of a periodical over a fixed period of time, usually a year **3.** the amount of space occupied in three dimensions; cubic contents **4.** *a)* a quantity, bulk, mass, or amount *b)* a large quantity **5.** the strength or loudness of sound **6.** *Music* fullness of tone —**speak volumes** to be very meaningful

vol·u·met·ric (väl′yoo met′rik) ***adj.*** of or based on the measurement of volume: also **vol′u·met′ri·cal** —**vol′u·met′ri·cal·ly** ***adv.***

vo·lu·mi·nous (və lo͞o′mə nəs) ***adj.*** **1.** writing, producing, or consisting of enough to fill volumes **2.** of great volume; large; bulky; full —**vo·lu′mi·nos′i·ty** (-näs′ə tē) ***n.*** —**vo·lu′mi·nous·ly** ***adv.***

vol·un·tar·y (väl′ən ter′ē) ***adj.*** **[**< L. < *voluntas,* free will, ult. < *velle,* to will**]** **1.** brought about by one's own free choice; given or done of one's own free will **2.** acting willingly or of one's own accord [a *voluntary* guide] **3.** intentional [*voluntary* manslaughter] **4.** controlled by the will [*voluntary* muscles] **5.** having free will or the power of free choice [man is a *voluntary* agent] **6.** made up of volunteers [a *voluntary* army] —***n., pl.*** **-tar′ies** an organ solo played for a church service —**vol′un·tar′i·ly** (-ə lē, väl′ən ter′-) ***adv.***

vol·un·teer (väl′ən tir′) ***n.*** **[**< obs. Fr. *volontaire,* a voluntary**]** **1.** a person who offers to do something of his own free will **2.** a person who enlists in the armed forces of his own free will —***adj.*** **1.** of or made up of volunteers **2.** serving as a volunteer **3.** *same as* VOLUNTARY —***vt.*** to offer or give of one's own free will —***vi.*** to enter or offer to enter into any service of one's own free will; enlist

vo·lup·tu·ar·y (və lup′cho͞o wer′ē) ***n., pl.*** **-ar′ies [**see ff.**]** a person devoted to luxurious living and sensual pleasures —***adj.*** of or characterized by luxury and sensual pleasures

vo·lup·tu·ous (-cho͞o wəs) ***adj.*** **[**< L. < *voluptas,* pleasure**]** **1.** full of, producing, or characterized by sensual pleasures **2.** fond of luxury, the pleasures of the senses, etc. **3.** suggesting, or arising from, sensual pleasure **4.** sexually attractive because of a full, shapely figure —**vo·lup′tu·ous·ly** ***adv.*** —**vo·lup′tu·ous·ness** ***n.***

vo·lute (və lo͞ot′) ***n.*** **[**< L. < pp. of *volvere,* to roll**]** **1.** a spiral or twisting form; whorl **2.** *Archit.* a spiral scroll, as of an Ionic capital **3.** *Zool.* any of the whorls of a spiral shell —***adj.*** spiraled: also **vo·lut′ed** —**vo·lu′tion** ***n.***

vom·it (väm′it) ***n.*** **[**< L. < pp. of *vomere***]** matter thrown up from the stomach —***vi., vt.*** **1.** to throw up (the contents of the stomach) through the mouth **2.** to throw out or be thrown out with force; belch forth —**vom′it·er** ***n.***

vom·i·tive (-ə tiv) ***adj.*** of or causing vomiting; emetic

‡**von** (fôn; *E.* vän) ***prep.*** **[**G.**]** of; from: a prefix occurring in many names of German and Austrian families, esp. of the nobility

voo·doo (vo͞o′do͞o) ***n., pl.*** **-doos [**Creole Fr. < a WAfr. word**]** **1.** a primitive religion based on a belief in sorcery, fetishism, etc.: it originated in Africa and is still practiced, chiefly by natives of the West Indies **2.** a person who practices voodoo **3.** a voodoo charm, fetish, etc. —***adj.*** of voodoos or their practices, beliefs, etc. —***vt.*** to affect by voodoo magic —**voo′doo·ism** ***n.*** —**voo′doo·ist** ***n.*** —**voo′doo·is′tic** ***adj.***

vo·ra·cious (vô rā′shəs, və-) ***adj.*** **[**L. *vorax* (gen. *voracis*) < *vorare,* to devour**]** **1.** greedy in eating; ravenous; gluttonous **2.** very greedy or eager in some desire or pursuit [a *voracious* reader] —**vo·ra′cious·ly** ***adv.*** —**vo·rac′i·ty** (-ras′ə tē), **vo·ra′cious·ness** ***n.***

Vo·ro·nezh (vô rô′nesh) city in SC European R.S.F.S.R., near the Don: pop. 660,000

-vo·rous (və rəs) **[**< L. < *vorare,* to devour**]** *a combining form meaning* feeding on, eating [*omnivorous*]

vor·tex (vôr′teks) ***n., pl.*** **vor′tex·es, vor′ti·ces′** (-tə sēz′) **[**L. < *vertere,* to turn**]** **1.** a whirling mass of water forming a vacuum at its center, into which anything caught in the motion is drawn; whirlpool **2.** a whirl of air; whirlwind **3.** any activity, situation, etc. that is like a whirl in its rush, catastrophic power, etc. —**vor′ti·cal** ***adj.*** —**vor′ti·cal·ly** ***adv.***

Vosges (Mountains) (vōzh) mountain range in NE France, west of the Rhine

vo·ta·ry (vōt′ə rē) ***n., pl.*** **-ries [**< L. pp. of *vovere,* to vow + -ARY**]** **1.** *a)* a person bound by religious vows, as a monk *b)* a devout worshiper **2.** a devoted supporter; one who is devoted to some cause or interest Also **vo′ta·rist** —**vo′ta·ress** (-ris) ***n.fem.***

vote (vōt) ***n.*** **[**L. *votum,* a vow < pp. of *vovere,* to vow**]** **1.** a decision on a proposal, etc., or a choice between candidates for office **2.** *a)* the expression of such a decision or choice *b)* the ballot, voice, etc. by which it is expressed **3.** the right to exercise such a decision, etc.; suffrage **4.** *a)* votes collectively *b)* a specified group of voters, or their votes [the farm *vote*] **5.** [Archaic] a voter —***vi.*** **vot′ed, vot′ing** to express preference in a matter by ballot, etc. —***vt.*** **1.** *a)* to decide, choose, enact, or authorize by vote *b)* to confer by vote *c)* to support (a specified party) in voting **2.** to declare by general opinion **3.** [Colloq.] to suggest —**vote down** to defeat by voting —**vote in** to elect —**vote out** to defeat (an incumbent) in an election —**vote′less** ***adj.***

vot·er (vōt′ər) ***n.*** a person who has a right to vote; elector, esp. one who actually votes

voting machine a machine on which the votes in an election are cast, registered, and counted

vo·tive (vōt′iv) ***adj.*** **[**L. *votivus* < *votum:* see VOTE**]** given, done, etc. in fulfillment of a vow [*votive* offerings]

vouch (vouch) ***vt.*** **[**< OFr. < L. *vocare,* to call < *vox,* a voice**]** to uphold by demonstration or evidence —***vi.*** **1.** to give assurance, a guarantee, etc. (with *for*) [to *vouch* for his honesty] **2.** to serve as evidence or assurance (*for*)

vouch·er (vou′chər) ***n.*** **1.** a person who vouches, as for the truth of a statement **2.** a paper giving evidence of or attesting to the expenditure or receipt of money, the accuracy of an account, etc.

vouch·safe (vouch sāf′) ***vt.*** **-safed′, -saf′ing [**< ME. *vouchen safe,* to vouch as safe**]** to be kind or gracious enough to give or grant —**vouch·safe′ment** ***n.***

vous·soir (vo͞o swär′) ***n.*** **[**Fr. < OFr., ult. < L. pp. of *volvere,* to roll**]** *Archit.* any of the wedge-shaped stones of which an arch or vault is built

vow (vou) ***n.*** **[**< OFr. < L. *votum:* see VOTE**]** **1.** a solemn promise or pledge, as one made to God or with God as one's witness, binding oneself to an act, way of life, etc. [marriage *vows*] **2.** a solemn affirmation —***vt.*** **1.** to promise solemnly **2.** to swear solemnly to do, get, etc. **3.** to declare in a forceful or earnest way *—vi.* to make a vow —**take vows** to enter a religious order —**vow′er** *n.*

vow·el (vou′əl, voul) *n.* [< MFr. < L. *vocalis* (*littera*), vocal (letter) < *vox,* a voice] **1.** any speech sound made by letting the voiced breath pass in a continuous stream through the pharynx and opened mouth **2.** a letter, as *a, e, i, o, u,* and sometimes *y,* representing such a sound *—adj.* of a vowel or vowels

‡**vox** (väks) *n., pl.* **vo·ces** (vō′sēz) [L.] voice

‡**vox po·pu·li** (päp′yoo lī′) [L.] the voice of the people; public opinion or sentiment: abbrev. **vox pop.**

voy·age (voi′ij) *n.* [< OFr. < L. *viaticum,* provision for a journey < *via,* way] **1.** a relatively long journey by water or, formerly, by land **2.** a journey by aircraft or spacecraft *—vi.* **-aged, -ag·ing** to make a voyage; travel *—vt.* to sail or travel over or on —**voy′ag·er** *n.*

‡**vo·ya·geur** (vwà yà zhėr′) *n., pl.* **-geurs′** (-zhėr′) [Fr.] in Canada, **1.** formerly, a person who transported goods and men for the fur companies **2.** any woodsman or boatman of the wilds

vo·yeur (vwä yur′, voi ur′) *n.* [Fr. < *voir,* to see] a person who has an exaggerated interest in viewing sexual objects or activities to obtain sexual gratification; peeping Tom —**vo·yeur′ism** *n.* —**vo′yeur·is′tic** *adj.*

V.P., VP Vice-President

V.Rev. Very Reverend

vroom (vro͞om) *n.* [echoic] the sound made by a motor vehicle in accelerating *—vi.* [Colloq.] to make, or move off with, such a sound

vs. versus

v.s. [L. *vide supra*] see above

V-shaped (vē′shāpt′) *adj.* shaped like the letter V

Vt., VT Vermont

vt., v.t. transitive verb

VTOL [*v*(*ertical*) *t*(*ake*)*o*(*ff and*) *l*(*anding*)] an aircraft, usually other than a helicopter, that can take off and land vertically

V-type engine (vē′tīp′) a gasoline engine in which the cylinders are set at an angle in two banks forming a V

Vul·can (vul′k'n) *Rom. Myth.* the god of fire and of metalworking —**Vul·ca′ni·an** (-kā′nē ən) *adj.*

vul·can·ite (vul′kə nīt′) *n.* [< prec. + -ITE] a hard rubber made by treating crude rubber with a large amount of sulfur and subjecting it to intense heat; ebonite: used in combs, electrical insulation, etc.

vul·can·ize (-nīz′) *vt., vi.* **-ized′, -iz′ing** [< VULCAN + -IZE] to treat (crude rubber) with sulfur and subject it to heat in order to increase its strength and elasticity —**vul′can·i·za′tion** *n.* —**vul′can·iz′er** *n.*

Vulg. Vulgate

vul·gar (vul′gər) *adj.* [< L. *vulgaris* < *vulgus,* the common people] **1.** of the great mass of people in general; common; popular *[a vulgar* superstition*]* **2.** of or in the vernacular **3.** *a)* characterized by a lack of culture, refinement, taste, etc.; crude; boorish *b)* indecent or obscene —**vul′gar·ly** *adv.* —**vul′gar·ness** *n.*

vul·gar·i·an (vul ger′ē ən, -gar′-) *n.* a vulgar person; esp., a rich person with coarse, showy manners or tastes

vul·gar·ism (vul′gər iz'm) *n.* **1.** a word, phrase, etc. that is used widely but is regarded as nonstandard, coarse, or obscene **2.** vulgar behavior, quality, etc.; vulgarity

vul·gar·i·ty (vul gar′ə tē) *n.* **1.** the state or quality of being vulgar, crude, etc. **2.** *pl.* **-ties** a vulgar act, habit, usage in speech, etc.

vul·gar·ize (vul′gə rīz′) *vt.* **-ized′, -iz′ing** to make vulgar; specif., *a)* to make coarse, crude, etc. *b)* to popularize —**vul′gar·i·za′tion** *n.* —**vul′gar·iz′er** *n.*

Vulgar Latin the everyday speech of the Roman people, from which the Romance languages developed

Vul·gate (vul′gāt, -git) *n.* [ML. *vulgata* (*editio*), popular (edition)] **1.** a Latin version of the Bible prepared in the 4th cent., serving as an authorized version of the Roman Catholic Church **2.** [**v-**] the vernacular, or common speech *—adj.* **1.** of or in the Vulgate **2.** [**v-**] of or in the vernacular

vul·ner·a·ble (vul′nər ə b'l) *adj.* [< LL. < L. *vulnerare,* to wound < *vulnus* (gen. *vulneris*), a wound] **1.** that can be wounded or physically injured **2.** *a)* open to, or easily hurt by, criticism or attack *b)* affected by a specified influence, etc. *[vulnerable* to political pressure*]* **3.** open to attack by armed forces **4.** *Bridge* open to increased penalties or increased bonuses: said of a team which has won one game —**vul′ner·a·bil′i·ty** *n.* —**vul′ner·a·bly** *adv.*

vul·pine (vul′pīn, -pin) *adj.* [< L. < *vulpes,* a fox] **1.** of or like a fox or foxes **2.** clever, cunning, etc.

vul·ture (vul′chər) *n.* [L. *vultur*] **1.** a large bird related to the eagles and hawks, with a naked head: vultures feed on carrion **2.** *same as* TURKEY BUZZARD **3.** a greedy, ruthless person who preys on others —**vul′tur·ous** *adj.*

VULTURE
(to 32 in. long; wingspread to 6 ft.)

vul·va (vul′və) *n., pl.* **-vae** (-vē), **-vas** [ModL. < L., womb] the external genital organs of the female —**vul′val, vul′var** *adj.* —**vul′vate** (-vāt, -vit) *adj.*

vv. **1.** verses **2.** violins

v.v. vice versa

vy·ing (vī′iŋ) *adj.* that vies; that competes

W

W, w (dub′'l yo͞o, -yə) *n., pl.* **W's, w's** **1.** the twenty-third letter of the English alphabet **2.** the sound of *W* or *w*

W *Chem.* tungsten

W, w watt; watts

W, W., w, w. **1.** west **2.** western

W. **1.** Wales **2.** Washington **3.** Wednesday **4.** Welsh

W., w. **1.** watt(s) **2.** weight **3.** width **4.** won

w. **1.** week(s) **2.** wide **3.** wife **4.** with

WA Washington (State)

Wa·bash (wô′bash) [< Algonquian stream and tribal name] river flowing from W Ohio across Ind. into the Ohio River

wab·ble (wäb′'l) *n., vt., vi.* **-bled, -bling** *var. of* WOBBLE

Wac (wak) *n.* a member of the Women's Army Corps

WAC Women's Army Corps

wack·y (wak′ē) *adj.* **wack′i·er, wack′i·est** [< ? WHACK + -Y²] [Slang] odd, silly, or crazy —**wack′i·ly** *adv.* —**wack′i·ness** *n.*

Wa·co (wā′kō) [< AmInd. tribal name] city in EC Tex.: pop. 101,000

wad (wäd, wôd) *n.* [ML. *wadda,* wadding < ?] **1.** a small, soft mass or ball, as a handful of cotton, crumpled paper, etc. **2.** a lump or small, compact mass *[a wad* of chewing tobacco*]* **3.** a mass of soft material used for padding, packing, etc. **4.** a plug stuffed against a charge to keep it firmly in place, as in a muzzleloading gun **5.** [Colloq.] a roll of paper money **6.** [Slang] a large amount, esp. of money *—vt.* **wad′ded, wad′ding** **1.** to compress, or roll up, into a wad **2.** *a)* to plug with a wad *b)* to force or stuff *[to wad* oakum into a crack*]* **3.** to pad with wadding **4.** to hold (a charge) in place by a wad —**wad′der** *n.*

Wad·den·zee, Wad·den Zee (väd′ən zā′) section of the North Sea extending into the Netherlands: formerly, the N part of the Zuider Zee

wad·ding (wäd′iŋ, wôd′-) *n.* any soft material for use in padding, packing, stuffing, etc.; esp., cotton made up into loose, fluffy sheets

wad·dle (wäd′'l, wôd′-) *vi.* **-dled, -dling** [freq. of WADE] to walk with short steps, swaying from side to side, as a duck *—n.* **1.** the act of waddling **2.** a waddling gait —**wad′dler** *n.*

wade (wād) *vi.* **wad′ed, wad′ing** [OE. *waden,* to go] **1.** to walk through a substance, as water, mud, tall grass, etc., that slows one down **2.** to walk and splash about in shallow water in play **3.** to get through with difficulty *[to wade* through a book*]* **4.** [Colloq.] to start or attack with vigor (with *in* or *into*) *—vt.* to go across or through by wading *—n.* an act of wading

wad·er (wād′ər) ***n.*** **1.** a person or thing that wades **2.** *same as* WADING BIRD **3.** *a)* [*pl.*] high waterproof boots *b)* [*usually pl.*] waterproof trousers with bootlike parts for the feet, worn by fishermen

wa·di (wä′dē) ***n.,*** *pl.* **-dis, -dies** [Ar. *wādī*] in Arabia, N Africa, etc., **1.** a valley, ravine, etc. that is dry except during the rainy season **2.** the rush of water that flows through it Also sp. **wa′dy,** *pl.* **-dies**

wading bird any of various unrelated, long-legged shore birds that wade the shallows and marshes for food, as the crane, heron, rail, coot, sandpiper, and snipe

Waf (waf) *n.* a member of the WAF

WAF Women in the Air Force

wa·fer (wā′fər) ***n.*** [< ONormFr. *waufre* < MDu. *wafel*] **1.** *a)* a thin, flat, crisp cracker or cookie *b)* anything resembling this, as a thin, flat disk of candy **2.** a thin cake of unleavened bread used in the Eucharist **3.** a small disk of sticky paper, used as a seal on letters, documents, etc.

waf·fle[1] (wäf′'l, wôf′-) ***n.*** [Du. *wafel*] a crisp batter cake with small, square hollows, baked in a waffle iron —***adj.*** having a surface like a waffle: also **waf′fled**

waf·fle[2] (wäf′'l, wôf′-) ***vi.*** **-fled, -fling** [orig., to yelp < echoic *waff,* to yelp] [Chiefly Brit. Colloq.] to speak or write in a wordy, vague, or indecisive manner —***n.*** [Chiefly Brit. Colloq.] talk or writing of this kind

waffle iron a utensil or appliance for cooking waffles, having two flat, studded plates pressed together so that the waffle bakes between them

waft (waft, wäft) ***vt.*** [< obs. *wafter,* a convoy < Du. *wachter,* lit., a watcher] **1.** to carry or move (objects, sounds, etc.) lightly through the air or over water **2.** to transport as if in this manner —***vi.*** **1.** to float, as in the air **2.** to blow gently: said of breezes —***n.*** **1.** an odor, sound, etc. carried through the air **2.** a puff or gust of wind **3.** a wafting movement —**waft′er** ***n.***

wag[1] (wag) ***vt.*** **wagged, wag′ging** [prob. < ON. *vaga,* to rock] **1.** *a)* to cause to move rapidly back and forth, up and down, etc. *[*the dog *wagged* his tail*]* *b)* to shake (a finger) or nod (the head), as in reproving, etc. **2.** to move (the tongue) in talking, esp. in idle gossip —***vi.*** **1.** to move rapidly back and forth, up and down, etc. **2.** to keep moving in talk: said of the tongue **3.** to walk or move with a swaying motion; waddle —***n.*** the act or an instance of wagging —**wag′ger** ***n.***

wag[2] (wag) ***n.*** [prob. < obs. *waghalter,* a gallows bird, rogue] a comical or humorous person; joker; wit

wage (wāj) ***vt.*** **waged, wag′ing** [< ONormFr. *wagier* < *wage* (OFr. *gage*), a pledge < Frank.] to engage in or carry on (a war, campaign, etc.) —***n.*** **1.** [*often pl.*] money paid to an employee for work done, usually on an hourly, daily, or piecework basis **2.** [*usually pl., formerly with sing. v.*] what is given in return; recompense; requital *[*"The *wages* of sin is death"*]*

wage earner a person who works for wages

wa·ger (wā′jər) ***n.*** [< ONormFr.: see WAGE] *same as* BET (*n.* 1, 2) —***vt., vi.*** *same as* BET —**wager of battle** a challenge by a defendant to prove his innocence by personal combat —**wa′ger·er** ***n.***

wag·ger·y (wag′ər ē) ***n.,*** *pl.* **-ger·ies** **1.** roguish humor or merriment **2.** a joke; esp., a practical joke

wag·gish (-ish) ***adj.*** **1.** of or like a wag; roguishly merry **2.** playful; jesting *[*a *waggish* remark*]* —**wag′gish·ly** ***adv.***

wag·gle (wag′'l) ***vt.*** **-gled, -gling** [freq. of WAG[1]] to wag, esp. with short, quick movements —***vi.*** to wobble —***n.*** the act of waggling —**wag′gly** ***adj.***

wag·gon (wag′ən) ***n., vt., vi.*** *Brit. var. of* WAGON

Wag·ner (väg′nər), **(Wilhelm) Rich·ard** (riH′ärt) 1813–83; Ger. composer

Wag·ne·ri·an (väg nir′ē ən) ***adj.*** **1.** of or like Richard Wagner or his music, theories, etc. **2.** designating or of a soprano, tenor, etc. specializing in Wagner's operas —***n.*** an admirer of Wagner's music, theories, etc.

wag·on (wag′ən) ***n.*** [Du. *wagen*] **1.** *a)* a four-wheeled vehicle for hauling heavy loads *b)* a small cart used by children at play **2.** *short for:* *a)* PATROL WAGON *b)* STATION WAGON **3.** [Brit.] a railroad freight car —***vt., vi.*** to carry or move (goods) in a wagon —**fix someone's wagon** [Slang] to hurt someone so as to get even with him —**hitch one's wagon to a star** to set oneself an ambitious goal —**on** (or **off**) **the wagon** [Slang] no longer (or once again) drinking alcoholic liquors

wag·on·er (-ər) ***n.*** a person who drives a wagon

wag·on·ette (wag′ə net′) ***n.*** [dim. of WAGON] a four-wheeled carriage with two seats set lengthwise facing each other behind the driver's seat

‡**wag·on-lit** (vå gōn lē′) ***n.,*** *pl.* **wag·ons-lits′** (-gōn lē′) [Fr. < *wagon,* a car + *lit,* a bed] in Europe, a railroad sleeping car

wag·on·load (wag′ən lōd′) ***n.*** the amount a wagon holds

wagon train a line of wagons traveling together, as one carrying military supplies, or one in which pioneers crossed the Western plains

wag·tail (wag′tāl′) ***n.*** **1.** a small bird related to the pipits, having a long tail that wags up and down **2.** any of various similar birds

Wah·ha·bi, Wa·ha·bi (wä hä′bē) ***n.*** [Ar. *Wahhabi*] a member of a strict Moslem sect in Saudi Arabia —**Wah·ha′bism, Wa·ha′bism** ***n.*** —**Wah·ha′bite** (-bīt) ***n., adj.***

wa·hi·ne (wä hē′nā) ***n.*** [Maori & Haw.] a Polynesian woman, esp. of Hawaii

wa·hoo[1] (wä′hōō, wä hōō′) ***n.*** [< Dakota *wanhu*] a N. American shrub or small tree having red fruits and purple flowers

wa·hoo[2] (wä′hōō, wä hōō′) ***n.,*** *pl.* **-hoo, -hoos:** see PLURAL, II, D, 2 [< ?] a large game and food fish, related to the mackerels and found in warm seas

wa·hoo[3] (wä hōō′, wä′hōō) ***interj.*** [Western] a shout expressing unrestrained enthusiasm, exhilaration, etc.

waif (wāf) ***n.*** [ONormFr., prob. < ON.] **1.** anything found that is without an owner **2.** a person without home or friends; esp., a homeless child **3.** a stray animal

Wai·ki·ki (wī′kē kē′, wī′kē kē′) [Haw., spurting water] famous bathing beach in Honolulu, Hawaii

wail (wāl) ***vi.*** [< ON. *væla* < *væ,* woe] **1.** to express grief or pain by long, loud cries **2.** to make a sad, crying sound *[*the wind *wails]* **3.** *Jazz* [Slang] to play in an intense or inspired manner —***vt.*** [Archaic] **1.** to lament; mourn **2.** to cry out in mourning —***n.*** **1.** a long cry of grief or pain **2.** a sound like this **3.** the act of wailing —**wail′er** ***n.*** —**wail′ful** ***adj.*** —**wail′ful·ly** ***adv.***

wain (wān) ***n.*** [OE. *wægn*] [Archaic or Dial.] a wagon or cart

wain·scot (wān′skət, -skät′) ***n.*** [< MDu. *wagenschot*] **1.** a lining or paneling of wood, etc. on the walls of a room, often on the lower part only **2.** the lower part of the walls of a room when finished differently from the upper part —***vt.*** **-scot·ed** or **-scot·ted, -scot·ing** or **-scot·ting** to line (a wall, etc.) with wainscoting

wain·scot·ing, wain·scot·ting (-iŋ) ***n.*** **1.** *same as* WAINSCOT **2.** material used to wainscot

wain·wright (wān′rīt′) ***n.*** [WAIN + WRIGHT] a person who builds or repairs wagons

waist (wāst) ***n.*** [< base of OE. *weaxan,* to grow] **1.** the part of the body between the ribs and the hips **2.** *a)* the part of a garment that covers the waist *b)* *same as* WAISTLINE (sense 2) *c)* the part of a garment covering the body from the shoulders to the waistline *d)* a blouse **3.** the middle, narrow part of something

waist·band (wāst′band′) ***n.*** a band encircling the waist, esp. one at the top of a skirt, trousers, etc.

waist·coat (wes′kət, wāst′kōt) ***n.*** **1.** [Brit.] a man's vest **2.** a similar garment worn by women —**waist′coat·ed** ***adj.***

waist·line (wāst′līn′) ***n.*** **1.** the line of the waist, between the ribs and the hips **2.** *a)* the narrow part of a woman's dress, etc., worn at the waist or above or below it as styles change *b)* the line where the waist and skirt of a dress join **3.** the distance around the waist

WAISTLINES

wait (wāt) ***vi.*** [ONormFr. *waitier* < Frank.] **1.** to stay in place or remain in readiness or in anticipation (often with *until* or *for*) **2.** to be ready *[*dinner is *waiting* for us*]* **3.** to remain undone for a time *[*that job will have to *wait]* **4.** to serve food (with *at* or *on*) —***vt.*** **1.** to be, remain, or delay in expectation of *[*to *wait* orders*]* **2.** [Colloq.] to delay serving (a meal) as in waiting for someone *[*to *wait* dinner*]* —***n.*** the act or a period of waiting —**lie in wait (for)** to wait so as to catch after planning an ambush or trap (for) —**wait on** (or **upon**) **1.** to act as a servant to **2.** to call on or visit (esp. a superior) in order to pay one's respects, ask a favor, etc. **3.** to be a consequence of **4.** to serve (a customer, etc.) as a clerk, waiter, etc. **5.** [Dial. or Colloq.] to wait for; await —**wait out** to remain inactive during the course of —**wait table** to serve food as a waiter or servant to people at a table —**wait up** **1.** to put off going to bed until someone expected arrives or something expected happens **2.** [Colloq.] to stop and wait for someone to catch up

wait·er (wāt′ər) ***n.*** **1.** a person who waits or awaits **2.** a man who waits on table, as in a restaurant **3.** a tray for carrying dishes; salver

wait·ing (-iŋ) ***adj.*** **1.** that waits **2.** of or for a wait —***n.*** **1.** the act of one that waits **2.** a period of waiting —**in waiting** in attendance, as on a king or other royal person

waiting game a delaying or postponing action until one has the advantage

waiting list a list of applicants, as for a vacancy or an item in short supply, in the order of their application

waiting room a room in which people wait, as in a railroad station, a dentist's office, etc.

wait·ress (wā′tris) ***n.*** a woman or girl who waits on table, as in a restaurant

waive (wāv) ***vt.*** **waived, waiv′ing** [< Anglo-Fr. *waiver,* to renounce < ON. *veifa,* to fluctuate] **1.** to give up or forgo (a right, claim, etc.) **2.** to refrain from insisting on or taking advantage of **3.** to postpone; defer

waiv·er (wā′vər) ***n.*** *Law* **1.** a waiving, or giving up voluntarily, of a right, claim, etc. **2.** a written statement of this

wake[1] (wāk) ***vi.*** **woke** or **waked, waked** (or, occas. Brit., **wok′en** or **woke**), **wak′ing** [< OE. *wacian,* to be awake & *wacan,* to arise] **1.** to come out of sleep or a state like sleep; awake (often with *up*) **2.** to be or stay awake **3.** to become active again (often with *up*) **4.** to become alert *[to wake* to a peril*]* **5.** [Chiefly Dial.] *pt. & pp.* **waked** to hold a wake —***vt.*** **1.** to cause to wake from or as from sleep (often with *up*) **2.** to arouse or excite (passions, etc.) **3.** [Chiefly Dial.] *pt. & pp.* **waked** to hold a wake over (a corpse) —***n.*** an all-night vigil over a corpse before burial

wake[2] (wāk) ***n.*** [ON. *vök,* a hole in the ice] **1.** the track left in the water by a moving boat or ship **2.** any track left behind —**in the wake of** following close behind

wake·ful (wāk′fəl) ***adj.*** **1.** keeping awake **2.** alert; watchful **3.** *a)* unable to sleep *b)* sleepless —**wake′ful·ly** ***adv.*** —**wake′ful·ness** ***n.***

Wake Island (wāk) coral atoll in the N Pacific between Midway & Guam: a U.S. territory

wake·less (-lis) ***adj.*** unbroken; deep: said of sleep

wak·en (wāk′'n) ***vi., vt.*** [OE. *wacnian*] to become awake or cause to wake; wake up; rouse —**wak′en·er** ***n.***

wake-rob·in (wāk′räb′in) ***n.*** **1.** *same as* TRILLIUM **2.** [Brit.] any of several plants of the arum family

Wa·la·chi·a (wä lā′kē ə) region in S Romania

Wald·heim (väld′hīm′), **Kurt** (koort) 1918– ; Austrian diplomat; secretary general of the United Nations (1972–)

Wal·dorf salad (wôl′dôrf) [after the old *Waldorf*-Astoria hotel in New York City] a salad made of diced raw apples, celery, and walnuts, with mayonnaise

wale (wāl) ***n.*** [OE. *walu,* a weal] **1.** a raised line made on the skin by a slash of a whip, etc.; welt **2.** *a)* a ridge on the surface of cloth, as corduroy *b)* texture of cloth **3.** [*pl.*] heavy planks fastened to the outside of the hull of a wooden ship —***vt.*** **waled, wal′ing** **1.** to mark (the skin) with wales **2.** to make (cloth, etc.) with wales

Wales (wālz) division of the United Kingdom, occupying a peninsula of WC Great Britain, on St. George's Channel: 8,016 sq. mi.; pop. 2,662,000; chief city, Cardiff

walk (wôk) ***vi.*** [OE. *wealcan,* to roll] **1.** to move along on foot at a moderate pace by placing one foot (or, with quadrupeds, two feet) on the ground before lifting the other (or others) **2.** to appear after death as a ghost **3.** to follow a certain course, way of life, etc. *[let us walk* in peace*]* **4.** *Baseball* to be advanced to first base as a result of being pitched four balls **5.** *Basketball same as* TRAVEL —***vt.*** **1.** to go along, over, etc. by walking *[to walk* the deck*]* **2.** to cause (a horse, dog, etc.) to walk, as for exercise **3.** to push (a bicycle, etc.) while walking alongside **4.** to go along with (a person) on a walk *[I'll walk* you home*]* **5.** to bring to a specified state by walking *[to walk* oneself to exhaustion*]* **6.** *Baseball a)* to advance (a batter) to first base by pitching four balls *b)* to force (a run) *in* by doing this when the bases are loaded —***n.*** **1.** the act of walking **2.** a stroll or hike **3.** a route taken in walking **4.** a distance to walk *[an* hour's *walk* from here*]* **5.** the pace of one who walks **6.** a way of walking *[I* knew her by her *walk]* **7.** a particular station in life, sphere of activity, etc. *[people* from all *walks* of life*]* **8.** a path set apart for walking **9.** an enclosure for grazing animals **10.** *Baseball* an advancing to first base on four balls —**walk (all) over** [Colloq.] **1.** to defeat decisively **2.** to domineer over —**walk away with** **1.** to steal **2.** to win easily —**walk off** **1.** to go away, esp. without warning **2.** to get rid of (fat, etc.) by walking —**walk off with** **1.** to steal **2.** to win (something), esp. easily —**walk out** to go on strike —**walk out on** [Colloq.] to leave; desert; abandon —**walk′ing** ***adj., n.***

walk·a·way (-ə wā′) ***n.*** an easily won victory

walk·er (-ər) ***n.*** **1.** a person or animal that walks **2.** a frame on wheels for babies learning to walk, or one without wheels used as a support in walking by convalescents, etc.

walk·ie-talk·ie (wôk′ē tôk′ē) ***n.*** a compact radio transmitter and receiver that can be carried by one person: also **walk′y-talk′y,** *pl.* **-talk′ies**

walk-in (-in′) ***adj.*** large enough for one to walk inside *[a walk-in* closet*]* —***n.*** a walk-in closet, etc.

walking papers [Colloq.] dismissal from a job

walking stick **1.** a stick carried when walking; cane **2.** an insect resembling a twig: also **walk′ing·stick′** ***n.***

walk-on (wôk′än′) ***n.*** a minor role in which an actor has no speaking lines or just a very few

walk·out (-out′) ***n.*** **1.** a strike of workers **2.** an abrupt departure of people as a show of protest

walk·o·ver (-ō′vər) ***n.*** an easily won victory

walk-through (-thro͞o′) ***n.*** an early rehearsal of a play in which the actors begin to carry out actions on stage

walk-up (-up′) ***n.*** **1.** an upstairs apartment in a building without an elevator **2.** the building itself

walk·way (-wā′) ***n.*** a path, passage, etc. for pedestrians, esp. one that is sheltered

wall (wôl) ***n.*** [OE. *weall* < L. *vallum,* a rampart < *vallus,* a stake] **1.** an upright structure of wood, stone, etc., serving to enclose, divide, support, or protect *[the walls* of a room, building, garden, etc.*]* **2.** [*usually pl.*] a surrounding fortification **3.** anything like a wall in appearance or function —***adj.*** of, on, in, or along a wall —***vt.*** **1.** to furnish, enclose, divide, etc. with or as with a wall (often with *off, in,* etc.) **2.** to close up (an opening) with a wall (usually with *up*) —**drive** (or **push**) **to the wall** to place in a desperate position —**drive** (or **send,** etc.) **up the wall** [Colloq.] to make frantic, tense, etc. —**go to the wall** **1.** to suffer defeat **2.** to fail in business —**off the wall** [Slang] 1. unsound of mind; crazy **2.** very eccentric or unconventional —**walled** ***adj.***

wal·la·by (wäl′ə bē) ***n.,*** *pl.* **-bies, -by:** see PLURAL, II, D, 1 [< Australian native name] a small or medium-sized marsupial related to the kangaroo

Wal·lace (wôl′is, wäl′-) **1.** [ult. < Anglo-Fr. *Waleis* or ME. *Walisc,* foreign, WELSH] a masculine name: dim. *Wally* **2. Alfred Rus·sel** (rus′'l), 1823–1913; Eng. naturalist **3. Henry A(gard),** 1888–1965; U.S. politician

Wal·la·chi·a (wä lā′kē ə) *same as* WALACHIA

wal·la·roo (wäl′ə ro͞o′) ***n.*** [< Australian native name] a large kangaroo that has a stocky body and broad, thickly padded feet

wall·board (wôl′bôrd′) ***n.*** fibrous material made in thin slabs for making or covering walls and ceilings in place of plaster, etc.

wal·let (wôl′it, wäl′-) ***n.*** [ME. *walet* < ?] **1.** formerly, a knapsack **2.** a flat pocketbook, as of leather, with compartments for paper money, cards, etc.; billfold

wall·eye (wôl′ī′) ***n.*** [< ff.] **1.** an eye, as of a horse, with a whitish iris or white, opaque cornea **2.** an eye that turns outward, showing more white than is normal **3.** any of several fishes with large, staring eyes; esp., a N. American food fish of the perch family (in full, **walleyed pike**)

wall·eyed (-īd′) ***adj.*** [< ON., ult. < *vagl,* a beam + *eygr,* having eyes] **1.** having a walleye or walleyes **2.** having large, staring eyes, as some fishes

wall·flow·er (-flou′ər) ***n.*** **1.** any of a number of garden plants having racemes of yellow, orange, etc. flowers **2.** [Colloq.] a person, esp. a girl, who merely looks on at a dance from lack of a partner

Wal·loon (wä lo͞on′) ***n.*** [Fr. *Wallon*] **1.** a member of a people living mostly in S and SE Belgium and nearby parts of France **2.** the French dialect of the Walloons

wal·lop (wäl′əp, wôl′-) ***vi.*** [< ONormFr. *waloper* (OFr. *galoper*), to gallop < Frank.] [Dial. or Colloq.] **1.** to move along in a rapid, reckless, awkward way **2.** to boil vigorously and noisily —***vt.*** [Colloq.] **1.** to beat soundly **2.** to strike hard **3.** to defeat crushingly —***n.*** [Colloq.] **1.** a hard blow **2.** the power to strike a hard blow **3.** a thrill

wal·lop·ing (-iŋ) ***adj.*** [Colloq.] impressively large; enormous —***n.*** [Colloq.] **1.** a thrashing **2.** a crushing defeat

wal·low (wäl′ō, wôl′-) ***vi.*** [OE. *wealwian,* to roll around] **1.** to roll about, as in mud, dust, etc. **2.** to roll and pitch, as a ship **3.** to give oneself over to, or revel in, some feeling, way of life, etc. *[to wallow* in self-pity, to *wallow* in riches*]* —***n.*** **1.** a wallowing **2.** a place where animals wallow

wall·pa·per (wôl′pā′pər) ***n.*** paper for covering the walls or ceiling of a room —***vt.*** to put wallpaper on or in

Wall Street **1.** a street in lower Manhattan, New York City: main U.S. financial center **2.** U.S. financiers and their power, policies, etc., or the U.S. money market

wall-to-wall (wôl′tə wôl′) ***adj.*** **1.** that completely covers a floor *[wall-to-wall* carpeting*]* **2.** [Colloq.] *a)* pervasive *b)* comprehensive; all-inclusive *[wall-to-wall* health care*]*

wal·nut (wôl′nut′, -nət) ***n.*** [< OE. < *wealh,* foreign + *hnutu,* a nut] **1.** any of a number of related trees, valued for their nuts and wood **2.** their edible nut, having a hard, crinkled shell and a two-lobed seed **3.** their wood, used for furniture, etc. **4.** the brown color of the heartwood of black walnut **5.** *local name for* SHAGBARK

Wal·pur·gis Night (väl poor′gis) the eve of May Day (April 30), when witches supposedly gathered for a demonic orgy

wal·rus (wôl′rəs, wäl′-) *n., pl.* **-rus·es, -rus:** see PLURAL, II, D, 1 [Du. < Dan. *hvalros,* prob. < ON. *hrosshvalr,* lit., horse whale] a massive sea mammal of the seal family, having two tusks jutting from the upper jaw, a thick mustache, a thick hide, and a heavy layer of blubber *—adj.* like that of a walrus *[a walrus* mustache*]*

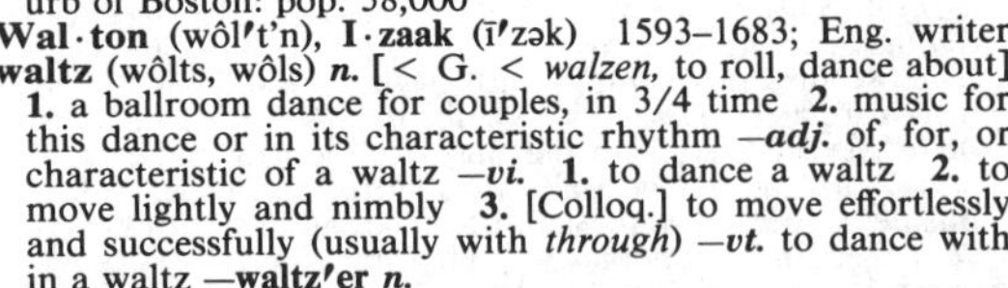

WALRUS (to 12 ft. long & 5 ft. high)

Wal·ter (wôl′tər) [< ONormFr. < Frank. < *waldan,* to rule + *heri,* army; also < G. *Walther* < OHG.] a masculine name: dim. *Walt*

Wal·tham (wôl′tham, -thəm) [? after *Waltham* Abbey, England, home of the 1st settlers] city in E Mass.: suburb of Boston: pop. 58,000

Wal·ton (wôl′t'n), **I·zaak** (ī′zək) 1593–1683; Eng. writer

waltz (wôlts, wôls) *n.* [< G. < *walzen,* to roll, dance about] **1.** a ballroom dance for couples, in 3/4 time **2.** music for this dance or in its characteristic rhythm *—adj.* of, for, or characteristic of a waltz *—vi.* **1.** to dance a waltz **2.** to move lightly and nimbly **3.** [Colloq.] to move effortlessly and successfully (usually with *through*) *—vt.* to dance with in a waltz —**waltz′er** *n.*

Wal·vis Bay (wôl′vis) **1.** seaport on the coast of South West Africa **2.** small exclave of South Africa surrounding this seaport

wam·pum (wäm′pəm) *n.* [< Algonquian] **1.** small beads made of shells and used by N. American Indians as money, for ornament, etc. **2.** [Slang] money

wan (wän, wôn) *adj.* **wan′ner, wan′nest** [OE. *wann,* dark] **1.** sickly pale; pallid *[a wan* complexion*]* **2.** suggestive of a sickly condition or great weariness; feeble *[a wan* smile*]* —**wan′ly** *adv.* —**wan′ness** *n.*

wand (wänd, wônd) *n.* [ON. *vondr*] **1.** a slender, supple switch, as of a young tree **2.** a rod carried as a symbol of authority; scepter **3.** any rod of supposed magic power

wan·der (wän′dər, wôn′-) *vi.* [OE. *wandrian*] **1.** to move or go about aimlessly; ramble; roam **2.** to go to a place in a casual or indirect way; idle **3.** *a)* to stray (*from* a path, course, etc.) *b)* to stray from home, friends, etc. (often with *off*) **4.** to go astray in mind or purpose; specif., *a)* to drift away from a subject, as in discussion *b)* to be disordered, incoherent, etc. **5.** to meander, as a river **6.** to move idly from one object to another: said of the eyes, etc. *—vt.* to roam through, in, or over —**wan′der·er** *n.* —**wan′der·ing** *adj., n.* —**wan′der·ing·ly** *adv.*

wan·der·lust (-lust′) *n.* [G.] an impulse, longing, or urge to wander or travel

wane (wān) *vi.* **waned, wan′ing** [OE. *wanian*] **1.** to grow gradually less in extent: said of the moon after it has become full **2.** to grow dim or faint: said of light, etc. **3.** to decline in power, importance, etc. **4.** to approach the end *[*the day *wanes]* *—n.* **1.** a waning **2.** a period of waning —**on the wane** declining, decreasing, etc.

wan·gle (waŋ′g'l) *vt.* **-gled, -gling** [altered < ? WAGGLE] [Colloq.] **1.** to get, make, or bring about by persuasion, influence, manipulation, etc. **2.** to falsify or juggle (accounts, etc.) *—vi.* [Colloq.] to make use of tricky and indirect methods to achieve one's aims —**wan′gler** *n.*

Wan·kel engine (väŋ′k'l, waŋ′-) [after F. *Wankel* (1902–), G. engineer] a rotary combustion engine having a spinning piston and requiring fewer parts and less fuel than a comparable turbine engine

want (wänt, wônt) *vt.* [ON. *vanta*] **1.** to have too little of; lack **2.** to be short by (a specified amount) *[*it *wants* two minutes of noon*]* **3.** to feel the need of; crave *[*to *want* love*]* **4.** to desire or wish (followed by the infinitive) *[*to *want* to travel*]* **5.** *a)* to wish to see or speak with (someone) *[wanted* on the phone*]* *b)* to wish to apprehend, as for arrest *[wanted* by the police*]* **6.** [Chiefly Brit.] to require; need *Want* is also used colloquially as an auxiliary meaning *ought* or *should [*you *want* to be careful*]* *—vi.* **1.** to have a need or lack (usually with *for*) **2.** to be destitute or very poor *—n.* **1.** a scarcity; shortage; lack **2.** poverty; destitution **3.** a wish for something; craving **4.** something needed; need —**want′er** *n.*

want ad [Colloq.] a classified advertisement, as in a newspaper, stating that one wants a job, an apartment, an employee, etc.

want·ing (wän′tiŋ, wôn′-) *adj.* **1.** absent; lacking *[*a coat with buttons *wanting]* **2.** not up to some standard *[*weighed and found *wanting]* *—prep.* **1.** lacking (something); without **2.** minus —**wanting in** having not enough of (some quality, etc.)

wan·ton (wän′t'n, wôn′-) *adj.* [< OE. < *wan,* lacking + *togen,* pp. of *teon,* to bring up] **1.** orig., undisciplined *[wanton* boys*]* **2.** *a)* sexually loose *b)* [Poet.] frisky; playful *c)* [Poet.] capricious *[wanton* winds*]* **3.** senseless, unprovoked, or deliberately malicious *[wanton* cruelty*]* **4.** recklessly ignoring justice, decency, morality, etc. **5.** lavish, luxurious, or extravagant *—n.* a wanton person or thing; esp., a sexually loose woman *—vi.* to be wanton —**wan′ton·ly** *adv.* —**wan′ton·ness** *n.*

wap·i·ti (wäp′ə tē) *n., pl.* **-tis, -ti:** see PLURAL, II, D, 1 [< Algonquian] the American elk, the largest N. American deer, with large, branching antlers and a short tail

war (wôr) *n.* [ONormFr. *werre,* strife < Frank.] **1.** open armed conflict between countries or between factions within the same country **2.** any active hostility, contention, or struggle *[*the *war* against poverty*]* **3.** military operations as a science *—adj.* of, used in, or resulting from war *—vi.* **warred, war′ring 1.** to carry on war **2.** to contend; strive —**at war** in a state of active armed conflict —**declare war (on) 1.** to make a formal declaration of being at war (with) **2.** to announce one's hostility (to) —**go to war 1.** to enter into a war **2.** to join the armed forces during a war

War between the States the U.S. Civil War (1861–65): term used by those sympathetic to the Confederacy

war·ble (wôr′b'l) *vt.* **-bled, -bling** [ONormFr. *werbler* < Frank.] **1.** to sing (notes, etc.) with trills, quavers, runs, etc., as a bird **2.** to express in song *—vi.* **1.** to sing melodiously, with trills, etc. **2.** to make a musical sound; babble, as a stream **3.** *same as* YODEL *—n.* **1.** an act of warbling **2.** a warbling sound; trill

war·bler (wôr′blər) *n.* **1.** a bird or person that warbles **2.** any of a family of small, insect-eating, new-world birds, many of which are brightly colored **3.** any of a family of small songbirds related to the thrushes

war bonnet a headdress with long feathers, worn by some N. American Indian warriors

war cry 1. a name, phrase, etc. shouted in a charge or battle **2.** a phrase or slogan adopted by a party in any conflict, contest, election, etc.

ward (wôrd) *vt.* [OE. *weardian,* to protect, guard] **1.** to turn aside; fend off (usually with *off*) **2.** [Rare] to guard *—n.* **1.** a guarding: now only in *watch and ward* **2.** a being under guard **3.** *a)* a child or person not able to manage his own affairs who is placed under the care of a guardian or court *b)* any person under another's care **4.** each of the divisions of a jail or prison **5.** a division of a hospital *[*a maternity *ward]* **6.** a division of a city or town, for purposes of administration, voting, etc. **7.** a means of defense **8.** a defensive posture, as in fencing **9.** *a)* a ridge in a lock that allows only the right key to enter *b)* the notch in a key that fits this ridge

-ward (wərd) [< OE. *-weard* < base of *weorthan,* to become] *a suffix meaning* in a (specified) direction or course *[backward]*

Ward (wôrd), **Ar·te·mus** (är′ti məs) (pseud. of *Charles Farrar Browne*) 1834–67; U.S. humorist

war dance a ceremonial dance performed as by some American Indian tribes before battle or after victory

war·den (wôr′d'n) *n.* [< ONormFr. < OFr. *gardein*] **1.** a person who guards, or has charge of, something; keeper *[*a game *warden]* **2.** the chief administrative official of a prison **3.** in England, a governing officer in certain hospitals, colleges, etc. **4.** in Connecticut, the chief executive of a borough **5.** *same as* CHURCHWARDEN —**war′den·ship′** *n.*

ward·er (wôr′dər) *n.* **1.** a watchman **2.** a person who guards an entrance **3.** [Chiefly Brit.] a warden in a jail

ward heeler a person who works in a ward for a political party or boss, as in getting votes: a contemptuous term

ward·robe (wôrd′rōb′) *n.* **1.** a closet or tall cabinet with hangers for holding clothes **2.** a room where clothes are kept, as a room in a theater for costumes **3.** one's supply of clothes

ward·room (wôrd′ro͞om′) *n.* in a warship, a compartment used for eating and lounging by commissioned officers, except, usually, the captain

-wards (wərdz) *same as* -WARD

ward·ship (wôrd′ship′) *n.* **1.** guardianship; custody, as of a minor **2.** the condition of being a ward

ware (wer) *n.* [OE. *waru*] **1.** any thing or service that one has to sell: *usually used in pl.* **2.** things that are for sale, esp. a (specified) kind of merchandise *[hardware, glassware]* **3.** pottery or a specified kind of pottery

ware·house (wer′hous′; *for v., usually* -houz′) *n.* **1.** a building where wares, or goods, are stored **2.** [Chiefly Brit.] a wholesale store, or, sometimes, a large retail store *—vt.* **-housed′, -hous′ing** to place or store in a warehouse —**ware′house′man** (-mən) *n., pl.* **-men**

war·fare (wôr′fer′) *n.* **1.** the action of waging war; armed conflict **2.** conflict of any kind

war·far·in (wôr′fə rin) *n.* [*W(isconsin) A(lumni) R(esearch) F(oundation)* + *(coum)arin,* a chemical] **1.** a crystalline powder used as a rat poison **2.** this drug neutralized and used in medicine as an anticoagulant

war game 1. training in military tactics in which maps and small figures are used to represent terrain, troops, etc. **2.** [*pl.*] practice maneuvers for military troops

war hawk *same as* HAWK[1] (*n.* 2)

war·head (wôr′hed′) *n.* the forward section of a self-propelled projectile, etc. containing the explosive charge
war horse **1.** a horse used in battle **2.** [Colloq.] a person who has engaged in many battles or struggles; veteran **3.** [Colloq.] a symphony, play, opera, etc. that has been performed so often as to seem stale and trite For 2 & 3 now usually **war′horse′** *n.*
war·i·ly (wer′ə lē) *adv.* in a wary manner; cautiously
war·i·ness (-ē nis) *n.* the quality or state of being wary
war·like (wôr′līk′) *adj.* **1.** fit for, fond of, or ready for war **2.** of or appropriate to war **3.** threatening war
war·lock (wôr′läk′) *n.* [OE. *wærloga,* a traitor, liar] a sorcerer or wizard: male equivalent of a *witch*
war·lord (wôr′lôrd′) *n.* **1.** a high military officer in a warlike nation **2.** a local ruler or leader with a military following, as formerly in China
warm (wôrm) *adj.* [OE. *wearm*] **1.** *a)* having or giving off a moderate degree of heat [a *warm* iron] *b)* giving off pleasurable heat [a *warm* fire] *c)* hot [a *warm* night] **2.** *a)* overheated, as with exercise *b)* such as to make one heated [*warm* work] **3.** effective in keeping body heat in [*warm* clothing] **4.** marked by lively disagreement, as an argument **5.** ardent; enthusiastic [*warm* encouragement] **6.** lively, vigorous, etc. **7.** quick to anger **8.** *a)* cordial or sincere [a *warm* welcome] *b)* sympathetic or loving **9.** suggesting warmth: said of yellow, orange, or red colors **10.** newly made; fresh, as a scent or trail **11.** [Colloq.] close to discovering something **12.** [Colloq.] disagreeable [we'll make it *warm* for him] *—adv.* so as to be warm *—vt., vi.* **1.** to make or become warm **2.** to make or become excited, ardent, lively, etc. **3.** to make or become friendly, affectionate, etc. *—n.* [Colloq.] a warming or being warmed —**warm up** **1.** *a)* to make or become warm *b)* to make or become warm enough to operate efficiently **2.** to reheat (cooked food, etc.): also **warm over** **3.** to make or become more animated, excited, ardent, etc. **4.** *Sports* to practice or exercise before going into a game —**warm′er** *n.* —**warm′ish** *adj.* —**warm′ly** *adv.* —**warm′ness** *n.*
warm·blood·ed (-blud′id) *adj.* **1.** having a relatively constant body temperature, independent of and usually warmer than that of the surroundings, as mammals and birds **2.** ardent; fervent —**warm′blood′ed·ness** *n.*
warmed-o·ver (wôrmd′ō′vər) *adj.* **1.** reheated [*warmed-over* hash] **2.** presented again, without significant change [*warmed-over* ideas]
warm front *Meteorol.* the forward edge of an advancing mass of warm air replacing colder air
warm·heart·ed (wôrm′här′tid) *adj.* kind, sympathetic, friendly, etc. —**warm′heart′ed·ly** *adv.* —**warm′heart′edness** *n.*
warming pan a long-handled, covered pan for holding live coals: formerly used to warm beds
war·mon·ger (wôr′muŋ′gər, -mäŋ′-) *n.* a person or agency that advocates war or tries to bring about a war —**war′mon′ger·ing** *adj., n.*
warmth (wôrmth) *n.* **1.** *a)* the state or quality of being warm *b)* mild heat **2.** *a)* excitement or vigor of feeling; enthusiasm *b)* cordial or affectionate feelings or nature *c)* slight anger **3.** a glowing effect obtained by using red, yellow, or orange
warm-up (wôrm′up′) *n.* the act or an instance of warming up
warn (wôrn) *vt.* [OE. *wearnian*] **1.** to tell (a person) of a danger, coming evil, etc. **2.** to caution about certain acts [*warned* against smoking] **3.** to notify in advance **4.** to give notice to (a person) to stay or keep (*off, away,* etc.) *—vi.* to give warning —**warn′er** *n.*
warn·ing (wôr′niŋ) *n.* **1.** the act of one that warns, or the state of being warned **2.** something that serves to warn *—adj.* that warns —**warn′ing·ly** *adv.*
War of American Independence *Brit. name for* AMERICAN REVOLUTION
War of 1812 a war (1812–15) between the U.S. and Great Britain
war of nerves a conflict or campaign using psychological means to unsettle an opponent or destroy his morale
warp (wôrp) *n.* [OE. *wearp,* the base of *weorpan,* to throw] **1.** *a)* a distortion, as a twist or bend in wood *b)* any similar distortion **2.** a mental twist, quirk, bias, etc. **3.** a rope run from a ship to a dock, etc., used to haul the vessel into position **4.** *a)* *Weaving* the threads running lengthwise in the loom and crossed by the weft or woof *b)* foundation; base *—vt.* **1.** to bend or twist out of shape **2.** to distort, pervert, bias, etc. [a *warped* mind] **3.** to move (a ship) by hauling on a line fastened to a dock, etc. *—vi.* **1.** to become bent or twisted out of shape **2.** to turn aside from the natural or right course —**warp′er** *n.*
war paint **1.** a pigment applied to the face and body, as by some American Indian tribes, in preparation for war **2.** [Slang] *a)* ceremonial dress *b)* women's cosmetics
war·path (wôr′path′) *n.* the path taken by American Indians on a warlike expedition —**on the warpath** **1.** at war, ready for war, etc. **2.** angry; ready to fight
war·plane (wôr′plān′) *n.* any airplane for use in war
war·rant (wôr′ənt, wär′-) *n.* [< ONormFr. (OFr. *garant*), a warrant < Frank.] **1.** *a)* authorization, as by the law *b)* justification for some act, belief, etc. **2.** something that serves as a guarantee of some event or result **3.** a written authorization or certification for something; specif., *a)* authorization for the payment or receipt of money *b)* *Law* a writ authorizing an arrest, seizure, search, etc. *c)* *Mil.* the certificate of appointment to the grade of warrant officer *—vt.* **1.** *a)* to give (someone) authorization to do something *b)* to authorize (the doing of something) **2.** to serve as justification for (an act, belief, etc.) **3.** *a)* to guarantee the quality, quantity, etc. of (goods) to a purchaser *b)* to guarantee to (the purchaser) that goods sold are as represented **4.** [Colloq.] to state with confidence [I *warrant* he'll be late]
war·ran·tee (wôr′ən tē′, wär′-) *n.* *Law* a person to whom a warranty is given
warrant officer a U.S. military officer ranking above an enlisted man but below a commissioned officer and holding his office on a warrant instead of a commission
war·ran·tor (wôr′ən tôr′, wär′-; -tər) *n.* *Law* a person who warrants, or gives warranty: also **war′rant·er** (-tər)
war·ran·ty (-tē) *n., pl.* **-ties** [see WARRANT] **1.** official authorization **2.** justification, as for an opinion or action **3.** *Law* a guarantee; specif., *a)* a guarantee of something in a contract, as to a purchaser that goods sold him are as represented *b)* a covenant by which the seller of real estate gives assurance of the security of the title
War·ren[1] (wôr′ən, wär′-) **1.** [< ONormFr. < ? OHG. *Warin,* name of a people mentioned by Tacitus] a masculine name **2. Earl,** 1891–1974; U.S. jurist; chief justice of the U.S. (1953–69)
War·ren[2] (wôr′ən, wär′-) **1.** [after Dr. J. *Warren* (1741–75)] city in SE Mich.: suburb of Detroit: pop. 161,000 **2.** [after M. *Warren,* 19th-cent. U.S. surveyor] city in NE Ohio: pop. 57,000: see YOUNGSTOWN
war·ren (wôr′ən, wär′-) *n.* [< ONormFr. < OFr. *warir,* to preserve < Frank.] **1.** a space or limited area in which rabbits breed or are numerous **2.** any building or buildings crowded like a rabbit warren
war·ri·or (wôr′ē ər, wär′-; -yər) *n.* [< ONormFr. < *werrier,* to make war < *werre,* WAR] a man experienced in conflict or war; soldier
War·saw (wôr′sô) capital of Poland, on the Vistula River: pop. 1,284,000
war·ship (wôr′ship′) *n.* any ship constructed or armed for combat use, as a battleship, destroyer, etc.
wart (wôrt) *n.* [OE. *wearte*] **1.** a small, usually hard, tumorous growth on the skin **2.** a small growth on a plant **3.** an imperfection, failing, flaw, etc. [a lovable person, *warts* and all] —**wart′y** *adj.* **wart′i·er, wart′i·est**
wart hog a wild African hog with large, incurved tusks, and a number of warts below the eyes
war·time (wôr′tīm′) *n.* a time of war *—adj.* of or characteristic of such a time
War·wick (wôr′wik) [after an Earl of *Warwick* (England), friend of the founder] city on the SE coast of R.I.: suburb of Providence: pop. 87,000
War·wick (wôr′ik, wär′-), Earl of, (*Richard Neville*) 1428–71; Eng. statesman & military leader
war·y (wer′ē) *adj.* **war′i·er, war′i·est** [< archaic adj. *ware,* watchful + -Y[2]] **1.** cautious; on one's guard **2.** characterized by caution —**wary of** careful of
was (wuz, wäz; *unstressed* wəz) [OE. *wæs*] *1st and 3d pers. sing., pt., of* BE
wash (wôsh, wäsh) *vt.* [OE. *wæscan*] **1.** to clean by means of water or other liquid, often with soap, etc. **2.** to make clean in a religious or moral sense; purify **3.** to wet; moisten **4.** to cleanse by licking, as a cat does **5.** to flow over, past, or against: said of a sea, waves, etc. **6.** to soak (*out*), flush (*off*), or carry (*away*) by the action of water **7.** *a)* to make by flowing over and wearing away substance [rain *washed* gullies in the bank] *b)* to erode [the flood *washed* out the road] **8.** to be a cleansing agent for [soap that will *wash* silks] **9.** to cover with a thin coating of paint or metal **10.** *Chem.* to pass (a gas) over or through a liquid in order to remove soluble matter **11.** *Mining* to pass water through or over (earth, etc.) in order to separate (ore, precious stones, etc.) *—vi.* **1.** to wash oneself or one's hands, face, etc. (often with *up*) **2.** to wash clothes **3.** to undergo washing, esp. without fading, etc. **4.** to be removed by washing [the stain *washed* out] **5.** to be worn or carried

away by the action of water [the bridge *washed* out] **6.** [Brit. Colloq.] to withstand a test [his story won't *wash*] —*n.* **1.** *a*) the act or an instance of washing *b*) a place where something is washed [an auto *wash*] **2.** a quantity of clothes, etc. washed, or to be washed **3.** refuse liquid food; hogwash **4.** *a*) the rush or surge of water or waves *b*) the sound of this *c*) the eddy of water caused by a propeller, oars, etc. *d*) a slipstream **5.** erosion caused by the action of water **6.** silt, mud, etc. carried and dropped by running water **7.** earth from which metals, ores, etc. may be washed **8.** *a*) low ground which is flooded part of the time and partly dry the rest *b*) a bog; marsh **9.** in the western U.S., the bed of a stream when it runs dry **10.** a thin coating of paint or metal **11.** any of various liquids for cosmetic or medicinal use [*mouthwash*] **12.** weak liquor or liquid food **13.** [Colloq.] water, beer, etc. drunk after strong liquor; chaser —*adj.* that can be washed without damage [a *wash* dress] —**come out in the wash** [Slang] to be revealed or explained sooner or later —**wash down** **1.** to clean by washing **2.** to follow (food, a drink of whiskey, etc.) with a drink, as of water —**wash out** [Slang] to drop or be dropped from a course, esp. in military aviation, because of failure

Wash. Washington (State)

wash·a·ble (wôsh′ə b'l, wäsh′-) *adj.* that can be washed without damage —*n.* a washable fabric or garment

wash-and-wear (-'n wer′) *adj.* designating or of fabrics or garments that need little or no ironing after washing

wash·board (-bôrd′) *n.* **1.** a board or frame with a ridged surface of metal, glass, etc. used for scrubbing dirt out of clothes **2.** the worn surface of a paved road

wash·bowl (-bōl′) *n.* a bowl or basin for use in washing one's hands and face, etc., esp. a bathroom fixture fitted with water faucets and a drain: also **wash′ba′sin** (-bā′s'n)

wash·cloth (-klôth′) *n.* a small cloth, usually of terry, used in washing the face or body

wash·day (-dā′) *n.* a day when the clothes and linens of a household are washed

washed-out (wôsht′out′, wäsht′-) *adj.* **1.** faded in color, specif. from washing **2.** [Colloq.] tired; spiritless **3.** [Colloq.] tired-looking; pale and wan

washed-up (-up′) *adj.* **1.** cleaned up **2.** [Colloq.] tired; exhausted **3.** [Slang] finished; done for; having failed

wash·er (wôsh′ər, wäsh′-) *n.* **1.** a person who washes **2.** a flat disk or ring of metal, rubber, etc., used to make a seat for the head of a bolt or for a nut or faucet valve, to lock a nut in place, to provide packing, etc. **3.** a machine for washing something

wash·er·wom·an (-woom′ən) *n., pl.* **-wom′en** a woman whose work is washing clothes, etc. —**wash′er·man** (-mən) *n.masc., pl.* **-men**

wash goods washable fabrics or garments

wash·ing (wôsh′iŋ, wäsh′-) *n.* **1.** the act of a person or thing that washes; a cleaning, flushing, etc. in water or other liquid **2.** clothes, etc. washed or to be washed, esp. at one time **3.** matter obtained or removed by washing **4.** a thin coating, as of metal, put on in liquid form

washing machine a machine for washing clothes, linens, etc., now usually operated automatically; washer

washing soda a crystalline form of sodium carbonate

Wash·ing·ton (wôsh′iŋ tən, wäsh′-) [after G. WASHINGTON] **1.** NW coastal State of the U.S.: 68,192 sq. mi.; pop. 4,130,000; cap. Olympia: abbrev. **Wash., WA** **2.** capital of the U.S., coextensive with the District of Columbia: pop. 638,000 (met. area 3,045,000) —**Wash′ing·to′ni·an** (-tō′nē ən) *adj., n.*

Wash·ing·ton (wôsh′iŋ tən, wäsh′-) **1. Book·er T(aliaferro)** (book′ər), 1856–1915; U.S. Negro educator & author **2. George,** 1732–99; 1st president of the U.S. (1789–97); commander in chief of the Continental army

Washington's Birthday February 22, George Washington's birthday: it is celebrated as a legal holiday in most States on the third Monday in February

wash·out (wôsh′out′, wäsh′-) *n.* **1.** the washing away of soil, rocks, etc. by a sudden, strong flow of water **2.** a hole made by such washing away, as in a road **3.** [Slang] a complete failure

wash·rag (-rag′) *n. same as* WASHCLOTH

wash·room (-room′) *n.* **1.** a room for washing **2.** *same as* RESTROOM

wash·stand (-stand′) *n.* **1.** a table holding a bowl and pitcher, etc. for washing the face and hands **2.** a washbowl that is a bathroom fixture

wash·tub (-tub′) *n.* a tub for washing clothes, etc.; often, a stationary metal tub fitted with water faucets and a drain

wash·wom·an (-woom′ən) *n., pl.* **-wom′en** *same as* WASHERWOMAN

wash·y (-ē) *adj.* **wash′i·er, wash′i·est** **1.** watery; weak **2.** weak in color; pale **3.** without force or substance; insipid

was·n't (wuz′'nt, wäz′-) was not

WASP, Wasp (wäsp, wôsp) *n.* a white Anglo-Saxon Protestant

wasp (wäsp, wôsp) *n.* [OE. *wæsp*] any of a large, worldwide group of winged insects with a slender body, biting mouthparts, and, in the females and workers, a sharp sting —**wasp′like′** *adj.* —**wasp′y** *adj.* **wasp′i·er, wasp′i·est**

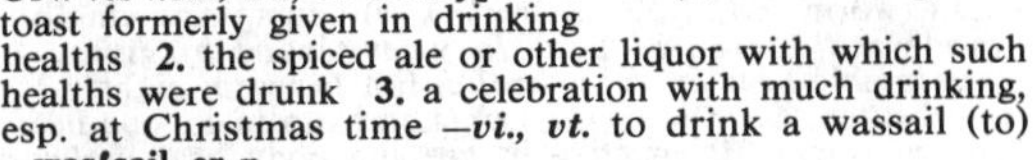

WASP (1/2–3 in. long)

wasp·ish (wäs′pish, wôs′-) *adj.* **1.** of or like a wasp **2.** having a slender waist **3.** bad-tempered; snappish —**wasp′ish·ly** *adv.* —**wasp′ish·ness** *n.*

wasp waist a very slender or tightly corseted waist

was·sail (wäs′'l, was′-; -āl) *n.* [< ON. *ves heill,* lit., be hearty] **1.** a toast formerly given in drinking healths **2.** the spiced ale or other liquor with which such healths were drunk **3.** a celebration with much drinking, esp. at Christmas time —*vi., vt.* to drink a wassail (to) —**was′sail·er** *n.*

Was·ser·mann test (or **reaction**) (wäs′ər mən) [after A. von *Wassermann* (1866–1925), G. bacteriologist] a test for syphilis by determining the presence of syphilitic antibodies in the blood serum

wast (wäst; *unstressed* wəst) *archaic 2d pers. sing., past indic., of* BE: *used with* thou

wast·age (wās′tij) *n.* **1.** loss by use, decay, etc. **2.** the process of wasting **3.** anything wasted, or the amount of this; waste

waste (wāst) *vt.* **wast′ed, wast′ing** [ONormFr. *waster* < L. *vastare,* to lay waste] **1.** to destroy; devastate; ruin **2.** to wear away; use up **3.** to make weak or feeble [a man *wasted* by age and disease] **4.** to use up or spend without need, gain, or purpose; squander **5.** to fail to take advantage of [to *waste* an opportunity] —*vi.* **1.** to lose strength, health, flesh, etc., as by disease (often with *away*) **2.** to be used up or worn down gradually **3.** to be wasted, or not put to full or proper use —*adj.* **1.** uncultivated or uninhabited, as a desert; wild; barren; desolate **2.** left over; no longer of use [a *waste* product] **3.** excreted from the body, as feces or urine **4.** used to carry off or hold waste [a *waste* pipe, *wastebasket*] —*n.* **1.** uncultivated or uninhabited land, as a desert **2.** *a*) a desolate or devastated area *b*) a vast expanse, as of the sea **3.** a wasting or being wasted; specif., *a*) a squandering, as of money, time, etc. *b*) a failure to take advantage (*of* something) *c*) a gradual loss or decrease by use, wear, decay, etc. **4.** useless or discarded material, as ashes, garbage, etc. **5.** matter excreted from the body, as feces **6.** refuse cotton fiber or yarn, used for wiping machinery, etc. —**go to waste** to be or become wasted —**lay waste (to)** to destroy; devastate —**wast′er** *n.*

waste·bas·ket (wāst′bas′kit) *n.* a basket or other open container for wastepaper, bits of trash, etc.: also **wastepaper basket**

waste·ful (-fəl) *adj.* in the habit of wasting or characterized by waste; squandering; extravagant —**waste′ful·ly** *adv.* —**waste′ful·ness** *n.*

waste·land (-land′) *n.* land that is uncultivated, barren, unproductive, devastated, etc.

waste·pa·per (-pā′pər) *n.* paper thrown away after use or as useless: also **waste paper**

wast·ing (wās′tiŋ) *adj.* **1.** desolating; destructive [a *wasting* war] **2.** destructive to health, as a disease —**wast′ing·ly** *adv.*

wast·rel (wās′trəl) *n.* **1.** a person who wastes; esp., a spendthrift **2.** a good-for-nothing

watch (wäch, wôch) *n.* [OE. *wæcce* < base of *wacian,* to be awake] **1.** the act or fact of keeping awake, esp. in order to protect or guard **2.** *a*) close observation for a time, as to find out something *b*) vigilant, careful guarding **3.** a person or group on duty to protect or guard **4.** [*pl.*] hours (of the night): only in **watches of the night** **5.** the period of duty of a guard **6.** a small timepiece carried in the pocket, worn on the wrist, etc. **7.** *Naut. a*) any of the periods of duty (usually four hours) into which the day is divided on shipboard *b*) the part of the crew on duty during any such period —*vi.* **1.** to stay awake at night; keep vigil **2.** to be on the alert; keep guard **3.** to look; observe **4.** to be looking or waiting attentively (with *for*) [*watch* for your chance] —*vt.* **1.** to guard **2.** to observe carefully and constantly **3.** to keep informed about **4.** to wait for and look for [to *watch* one's chance] **5.** to keep watch over; tend —**on the watch** watching; on the lookout —**watch oneself** to be careful or cautious —**watch out** to be alert and on one's guard; be careful —**watch over** to protect from harm or danger —**watch′er** *n.*

watch·band (-band′) *n.* a band of leather, metal, cloth, etc. for holding a watch on the wrist

watch·case (-kās′) *n.* the metal case, or outer covering, of a watch

watch·dog (-dôg′, -däg′) *n.* **1.** a dog kept to guard property **2.** a person or group that keeps watch to prevent waste, dishonest practices, etc.

watch fire a fire kept burning at night as a signal or for the use of those staying awake to guard

watch·ful (-fəl) ***adj.*** **1.** watching closely; alert **2.** characterized by vigilance **—watch′ful·ly** ***adv.*** **—watch′ful·ness** ***n.***

watch·mak·er (-mā′kər) ***n.*** a person who makes or repairs watches **—watch′mak′ing** ***n.***

watch·man (-mən) ***n., pl.*** **-men** a person hired to watch or guard, esp. at night

watch night a religious service held on New Year's Eve: also **watch meeting** or **watch-night service**

watch pocket a small pocket, usually in a vest or trousers, for carrying a watch

watch·tow·er (-tou′ər) ***n.*** a high tower from which a sentinel watches for enemies, forest fires, etc.; lookout

watch·word (-wurd′) ***n.*** **1.** a password **2.** a slogan; esp., the slogan or cry of a group or party

wa·ter (wôt′ər, wät′-) ***n.*** [OE. *wæter*] **1.** the colorless, transparent liquid occurring on earth as rivers, lakes, oceans, etc., and falling as rain: chemically a compound of hydrogen and oxygen, H_2O, it freezes at 32° F (0° C) and boils at 212° F (100° C) **2.** [*often pl.*] a large body of water, as a river, lake, sea, etc. **3.** water with reference to its depth, its surface, its level, etc. [ten feet of *water,* under *water,* high *water*] **4.** [*pl.*] the water of mineral springs **5.** any body fluid or secretion, as urine, saliva, tears, etc. **6.** a solution of any substance, often a gas, in water [ammonia *water*] **7.** *a)* the degree of transparency and luster of a precious stone [a diamond of the first *water*] *b)* degree of quality or conformity to type [an artist of the first *water*] **8.** a wavy, lustrous finish given to linen, silk, etc., or to a metal surface **9.** *Finance* an illegal issue of watered stock **—*vt.*** **1.** to supply with water; specif., *a)* to give (animals) water to drink *b)* to give water to (soil, crops, etc.), as by sprinkling, irrigating, etc. *c)* to soak or moisten with water (often with *down*) *d)* to dilute with water **2.** to give a wavy luster to the finish of (silk, etc.) **3.** *Finance* to add illegally to the total face value of (stock) without increasing assets to justify this valuation **—*vi.*** **1.** to fill with tears: said of the eyes **2.** to secrete or fill with saliva [his mouth *watered*] **3.** to take on a supply of water **4.** to drink water: said of animals **—*adj.*** **1.** of or having to do with water **2.** in or on water [*water* sports] **3.** growing in or living on or near water [*water* plants, *water* birds] **4.** *a)* operated by water [a *water* wheel] *b)* derived from running water [*water* power] **—by water** by ship or boat **—hold water** to remain sound, logical, etc. [the argument won't *hold water*] **—like water** lavishly; freely: said of money spent, etc. **—make one's mouth water** to create a desire or appetite in one **—make** (or **pass**) **water** to urinate **—water down** to weaken the power or effectiveness of **—wa′ter·er** ***n.*** **—wa′ter·less′** ***adj.***

Water Bearer *same as* AQUARIUS

water bed a heavy vinyl bag filled with water and used as a bed or as a mattress in a special frame

water beetle any of various beetles that live in freshwater ponds and streams

water bird a swimming or wading bird

water boatman any of various water bugs that swim about by movement of their fringed, oarlike hind legs

wa·ter·borne (-bôrn′) ***adj.*** floating on or carried by water

wa·ter·buck (-buk′) ***n., pl.*** **-buck′, -bucks′:** see PLURAL, II, D, 2 an African antelope having lyre-shaped horns, found near rivers and streams

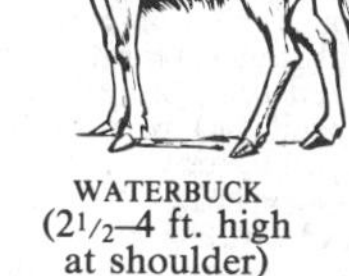

WATERBUCK
(2½–4 ft. high at shoulder)

water buffalo a slow, powerful, oxlike draft animal native to S Asia, Malaya, and the Philippine Islands

Wa·ter·bur·y (wôt′ər ber′ē, wät′-) [from the many streams there] city in WC Conn.: pop. 103,000

water chestnut **1.** a Chinese sedge, growing in clumps in water **2.** its button-shaped tuber, used in cooking

water clock a mechanism for measuring time by the fall or flow of water; clepsydra

water closet *same as* TOILET (*n.* 4)

wa·ter·col·or (-kul′ər) ***n.*** **1.** a pigment or coloring matter mixed with water for use as a paint **2.** (a) painting done with such paints **—*adj.*** painted with watercolors **—wa′ter·col′or·ist** ***n.***

wa·ter-cooled (-ko͞old′) ***adj.*** kept from overheating by having water circulated around or through it, as in pipes or a water jacket [a *water-cooled* engine] **—wa′ter·cool′** ***vt.***

water cooler a device for cooling water, esp. by refrigeration, for drinking

wa·ter·course (-kôrs′) ***n.*** **1.** a stream of water; river, brook, etc. **2.** a channel for water, as a canal

wa·ter·craft (-kraft′) ***n.*** **1.** skill in water sports, boating, etc. **2.** *pl.* **-craft′** a boat, ship, or other water vehicle

wa·ter·cress (-kres′) ***n.*** a plant of the mustard family, growing generally in running water: its leaves are used in salads, etc.

water cure *same as:* **1.** HYDROPATHY **2.** HYDROTHERAPY

wa·ter·fall (-fôl′) ***n.*** a steep fall of water, as of a stream, from a height; cascade

wa·ter·fowl (-foul′) ***n., pl.*** **-fowls′, -fowl′:** see PLURAL, II, D, 1 a bird that lives on or near the water, esp. one that swims

wa·ter·front (-frunt′) ***n.*** **1.** land at the edge of a stream, harbor, etc. **2.** the part of a city or town on such land

water gap a break in a mountain ridge, with a stream flowing through it

water gas a fuel gas that is a poisonous mixture of hydrogen, carbon dioxide, carbon monoxide, and nitrogen, made by forcing steam through hot coke

Wa·ter·gate (-gāt′) ***n.*** [after *Watergate,* D.C. building housing Dem. party hdqrs., burglarized (1972) under govt. direction] a scandal that involves officials violating public trust through various crimes and abuses of power in order to maintain their positions of authority

water gate a gate controlling the flow of water; floodgate

water gauge **1.** a gauge for measuring the level or flow of water in a stream or channel **2.** a device, as a glass tube, that shows the water level in a tank, boiler, etc.

water glass **1.** a drinking glass; tumbler; goblet **2.** *same as* WATER GAUGE (sense 2) **3.** sodium silicate or, sometimes, potassium silicate, usually dissolved in water to form a syrupy liquid used as an adhesive, as a preservative for eggs, etc. Also **wa′ter·glass′** ***n.***

water hole **1.** a dip or hole in the ground, in which water collects; pool; pond **2.** a hole in the ice on a body of water

water hyacinth a floating plant with showy lavender flowers, native to S. America: now often a hindrance to water traffic in the southern U.S., esp. Florida

water ice [Brit.] water and sugar flavored and frozen

wa·ter·i·ness (-ē nis) ***n.*** the state or quality of being watery

wa·ter·ing place (-iŋ) **1.** a place at a stream, lake, etc. where animals go to drink **2.** [Chiefly Brit.] a resort or spa with mineral springs for drinking or bathing or with a beach for swimming, water sports, etc.

watering pot (or **can**) a can with a spout, often having a perforated nozzle, for watering plants, etc.

water jacket a casing for holding water that circulates, as around the cylinders of an internal-combustion engine

water jump a strip, ditch, or channel of water that a horse must jump, as in a steeplechase

water level **1.** *a)* the surface of still water *b)* the height of this **2.** *same as* WATERLINE (senses 1 & 2)

wa·ter·lil·y (-lil′ē) ***n., pl.*** **-lil′ies** **1.** any of various water plants having large, flat, floating leaves and showy flowers in many colors **2.** the flower of such a plant

WATERLILY

wa·ter·line (-līn′) ***n.*** **1.** the line to which the surface of the water comes on the side of a ship or boat **2.** any of several lines parallel to this, marked on the hull of a ship, indicating how far the ship has sunk in the water when it is fully or partly loaded, or unloaded **3.** a pipe, tube, etc. connected to a source of water

wa·ter·logged (-lôgd′, -lägd′) ***adj.*** **1.** soaked or filled with water so as to be heavy and sluggish in movement: said of boats or floating objects **2.** soaked with water; swampy

Wa·ter·loo (wôt′ər lo͞o′, wät′-; wôt′ər lo͞o′, wät′-) **1.** [after ff.] city in NE Iowa: pop. 76,000 **2.** town in C Belgium: scene of Napoleon's final defeat (1815) **—*n.*** any disastrous or decisive defeat

water main a main pipe in a system of water pipes

wa·ter·man (wôt′ər mən, wät′-) ***n., pl.*** **-men** a person who works on or with boats; esp., an oarsman

wa·ter·mark (-märk′) ***n.*** **1.** a mark showing the limit to which water has risen **2.** *Papermaking a)* a faint mark in paper, produced by pressure of a projecting design, as in the mold *b)* the design **—*vt.*** **1.** to mark (paper) with a watermark **2.** to impress (a design) as a watermark

wa·ter·mel·on (-mel′ən) ***n.*** **1.** a large, edible fruit with a hard, green rind and juicy, pink or red pulp having many seeds **2.** the vine on which it grows

water mill a mill whose machinery is driven by water

fat, āpe, cär, ten, ēven, is, bīte; gō, hôrn, to͞ol, look; oil, out; up, fur; get; joy; yet; chin; she; thin, *th*en; zh, leisure; ŋ, ring; ə for *a* in *ago*, *e* in *agent*, *i* in *sanity*, *o* in *comply*, *u* in *focus;* ′ as in *able* (ā′b'l); Fr. bål; ë, Fr. coeur; ö, Fr. feu; Fr. mon; ô, Fr. coq; ü, Fr. duc; *r*, Fr. cri; H, G. ich; kh, G. doch; ‡foreign; *hypothetical; < derived from. See inside front cover.

water moccasin a large, poisonous, olive-brown pit viper found along or in rivers and swamps in the SE U.S.: often confused with various harmless water snakes
water nymph *Gr. & Rom. Myth.* a goddess having the form of a lovely young girl, supposed to dwell in a stream, pool, lake, etc.
water of crystallization water that occurs in crystalline substances and can be removed by heat: the loss of water usually results in the loss of crystalline structure
water ouzel any of several birds of Europe, Asia, and America; esp., the **American dipper** of western N. America that dives and swims in mountain streams
water pipe 1. a pipe for carrying water 2. a smoking pipe in which the smoke is drawn through water; hookah
water pistol a toy gun that shoots water in a stream
water plant any plant living under water or with only the roots in or under water
water polo a water game played with a round, partly inflated ball by two teams of seven swimmers
water power 1. the power of running or falling water, used to drive machinery, etc. 2. a fall of water that can be so used Also **wa′ter·pow′er** *n.*
wa·ter·proof (wôt′ər pro͞of′, wät′-) *adj.* that keeps out water completely; esp., treated with rubber, plastic, etc. so that water will not penetrate —*n.* 1. waterproof material 2. [Chiefly Brit.] a raincoat, etc. of waterproof material —*vt.* to make waterproof —**wa′ter·proof′er** *n.*
water rat 1. any of various rodents that live on the banks of streams and ponds 2. *same as* MUSKRAT
wa·ter-re·pel·lent (-ri pel′ənt) *adj.* that repels water but is not thoroughly waterproof
wa·ter·shed (-shed′) *n.* 1. a ridge dividing the areas drained by different river systems 2. the area drained by a river system 3. a crucial turning point
wa·ter·side (-sīd′) *n.* land at the edge of a body of water —*adj.* of, at, or on the waterside
wa·ter-ski (-skē′) *vi.* **-skied′, -ski′ing** to be towed, as a sport, on skilike boards (**water skis**) by a line attached to a speedboat —**wa′ter·ski′er** *n.*
water snake any of numerous saltwater or freshwater snakes; esp., a thick-bodied, nonpoisonous freshwater snake that feeds on fish and amphibians
wa·ter-soak (-sōk′) *vt.* to soak with or in water
water softener 1. a chemical compound added to hard water to make it soft, or free from mineral salts 2. a tank, etc. in which water is filtered through chemicals to make it soft
water spaniel either of two breeds of spaniel having a curly coat and used in hunting to retrieve waterfowl
wa·ter·spout (-spout′) *n.* 1. a hole, pipe, or spout from which water runs 2. a tornado occurring over water, appearing as a rapidly rotating column of spray
water sprite in folklore, a spirit, nymph, etc. dwelling in or haunting the water
water table the level below which the ground is saturated with water
wa·ter·tight (-tīt′) *adj.* 1. so snugly put together that no water can get in or through 2. well thought out, with no weak points: said of an argument, plan, etc. —**wa′ter-tight′ness** *n.*
water tower 1. an elevated tank used for water storage and for keeping equal pressure on a water system 2. a firefighting apparatus that can be used to lift high-pressure hoses, etc. to great height
water vapor water in the form of mist or tiny diffused particles, esp. when below the boiling point, as in the air: distinguished from STEAM
wa·ter·way (-wā′) *n.* 1. a channel through or along which water runs 2. any body of water wide enough and deep enough for boats, ships, etc.
water wheel 1. a wheel with paddles turned by running water, used to give power 2. a wheel with buckets on its rim, used for lifting water
water wings a device, inflated with air, used to keep one afloat while learning to swim
wa·ter·works (-wurks′) *n.pl.* [*often with sing. v.*] 1. a system of reservoirs, pumps, etc. used to bring a water supply to a city, etc. 2. a pumping station in such a system
wa·ter·worn (-wôrn′) *adj.* worn, smoothed, or polished by the action of running water
wa·ter·y (-ē) *adj.* 1. of or like water 2. containing or full of water 3. thin, diluted, weak, etc. [*watery* tea] 4. tearful 5. in or consisting of water [a *watery* grave] 6. soft or soggy
Wat·ling Island (wät′liŋ) *same as* SAN SALVADOR (island): also **Wat′lings Island**
watt (wät, wôt) *n.* [after ff.] the mks unit of electrical power equal to the power used by a direct current of one ampere flowing through a resistance of one ohm
Watt (wät, wôt), **James** 1736–1819; Scot. engineer & inventor: noted for his development of the steam engine
watt·age (wät′ij, wôt′-) *n.* 1. amount of electrical power, expressed in watts 2. the amount of watts required to operate a given appliance or device
Wat·teau (vȧ tō′; *E.* wä tō′), **(Jean) An·toine** (än twȧn′) 1684–1721; Fr. painter
watt-hour (wät′our′, wôt′-) *n.* a unit of electrical energy or work, equal to one watt acting for one hour
wat·tle (wät′'l, wôt′-) *n.* [OE. *watul*] 1. a woven work of sticks intertwined with twigs or branches, used for walls, roofs, etc. 2. [Brit. Dial.] a stick, twig, etc. 3. in Australia, any of various acacias 4. a fleshy, often brightly colored piece of skin that hangs from the throat of a cock, turkey, etc., or of some lizards —*adj.* made of or roofed with wattle —*vt.* **-tled, -tling** 1. to intertwine (sticks, twigs, etc.) so as to form an interwoven structure 2. to construct (a fence) by intertwining twigs, etc. 3. to build of wattle

watt·me·ter (wät′mēt′ər, wôt′-) *n.* an instrument for measuring in watts the power in an electric circuit
Wa·tu·si (wä to͞o′sē) *n., pl.* **-sis, -si** any member of a tall, slender, cattle-owning people of Burundi and Rwanda: also **Wa·tut′si** (-to͞ot′sē)
Wau·ke·gan (wô kē′gən) [< Algonquian, lit., trading place] city in NE Ill., on Lake Michigan: pop. 68,000
waul (wôl) *vi., n.* wail, squall, or howl
Wau·wa·to·sa (wô′wə tō′sə) [< AmInd. *wawatosi,* ? firefly] city in SE Wis.: suburb of Milwaukee: pop. 51,000
Wave (wāv) *n.* a member of the WAVES
wave (wāv) *vi.* **waved, wav′ing** [OE. *wafian*] 1. to move up and down or back and forth in a curving motion; sway to and fro [the flag *waves*] 2. to signal by moving a hand, arm, etc. to and fro 3. to have the form of a series of curves [hair that *waves* naturally] —*vt.* 1. to cause to wave or sway to and fro 2. to brandish (a weapon) 3. *a)* to move or swing (something) as a signal *b)* to signal (something) by doing this [to *wave* farewell] *c)* to signal to (someone) by doing this [he *waved* us on] 4. to arrange (hair, etc.) in a series of curves —*n.* 1. *a)* a ridge or swell moving along the surface of a body of water, etc. *b)* something that suggests this as when wind blows over a field of grain 2. a curve or series of curves, as in the hair, etc. 3. a motion to and fro or up and down, as that made by the hand in signaling 4. something like a wave in action or effect; specif., an upsurge or rise [a crime *wave*] 5. [Poet.] water; esp., the sea 6. *Physics* a state of motion that periodically advances and retreats as it is transmitted progressively from one particle in a medium to the next in a given direction, as in the propagation of light, sound, etc. —**wave′less** *adj.* —**wave′like′** *adj.* —**wav′er** *n.*
wave band *Radio & TV* a specific range of wave frequencies
wave·length (wāv′leŋkth, -leŋth) *n. Physics* the distance, measured in the direction of the progression of a wave, from any given point to the next point characterized by the same phase: also **wave length**
wave·let (-lit) *n.* a little wave; ripple
wa·ver (wā′vər) *vi.* [< ME. < *waven,* to WAVE] 1. to sway to and fro; flutter 2. to show indecision; vacillate 3. to become unsteady; falter 4. to tremble: said of the voice, etc. 5. to flicker: said of light —*n.* a wavering —**wa′ver·er** *n.* —**wa′ver·ing·ly** *adv.*
WAVES (wāvz) [orig. *W*(*omen*) *A*(*ppointed for*) *V*(*oluntary*) *E*(*mergency*) *S*(*ervice*)] the women's branch of the U.S. Navy
wav·y (wā′vē) *adj.* **wav′i·er, wav′i·est** 1. having waves 2. moving in a wavelike motion 3. having curves; forming waves and hollows 4. like or characteristic of waves 5. wavering; fluctuating; unsteady —**wav′i·ly** *adv.* —**wav′i·ness** *n.*
wax[1] (waks) *n.* [OE. *weax*] 1. an easily molded, dull-yellow substance secreted by bees for building cells; beeswax: it is used for candles, modeling, etc. 2. any substance like this; specif., *a)* paraffin *b)* earwax *c)* sealing wax —*vt.* to rub, polish, cover, or treat with wax —*adj.* made of wax —**wax′er** *n.* —**wax′like′** *adj.*
wax[2] (waks) *vi.* **waxed, waxed** or archaic **wax′en, wax′ing** [OE. *weaxan,* to grow] 1. to increase in strength, intensity, volume, etc. 2. to become gradually full: said of the moon 3. to become [to *wax* angry]
wax bean 1. a variety of kidney bean with long, narrow, yellow pods 2. the immature pod cooked as a vegetable
wax·ber·ry (waks′ber′ē) *n., pl.* **-ries** *same as:* 1. SNOWBERRY (senses 1 & 3) 2. BAYBERRY (sense 1)
wax·en (wak′s'n) *adj.* 1. made of, or covered with, wax 2. like wax, as in being pale, soft, easily molded, etc.
wax myrtle *same as* BAYBERRY; esp., an evergreen shrub native to eastern N. America and having grayish-white berries coated with a wax used for candles
wax palm 1. *same as* CARNAUBA 2. a palm of the Andes that yields a wax used to make candles, polishes, etc.

wax paper a kind of paper made moistureproof by a wax, or paraffin, coating: also **waxed paper**

wax·wing (waks′wiŋ′) ***n.*** any of a group of birds with silky-brown plumage, a showy crest, and scarlet spines, suggesting sealing wax, at the ends of the secondary quill feathers

wax·work (-wʉrk′) ***n.*** **1.** work, as objects, figures, etc., made of wax **2.** a human figure made of wax

wax·works (-wʉrks′) ***n.pl.*** [*with sing. v.*] an exhibition of wax figures made to look like famous or notorious persons: also **wax museum**

wax·y (wak′sē) ***adj.*** **wax′i·er, wax′i·est** **1.** full of, covered with, or made of wax **2.** like wax in nature or appearance —**wax′i·ness *n.***

way (wā) ***n.*** [OE. *weg*] **1.** a road, highway, street, path, etc. **2.** room for passing; an opening, as in a crowd **3.** a course from one place to another [*highway*, one-*way* street] **4.** a specified route or direction [on the *way* to town] **5.** course or habits of life [to fall into evil *ways*] **6.** a method of doing something **7.** a customary or characteristic manner of living, acting, etc. [to change one's *ways*] **8.** manner; style **9.** distance [a long *way* off]: also [Colloq.] **ways** **10.** direction of movement, etc. [look this *way*] **11.** respect; point; particular [to be right in some *ways*] **12.** wish; will [to get one's *way*] **13.** range, as of experience [that never came my *way*] **14.** relationship as to those taking part [a four-*way* agreement] **15.** [Colloq.] a (specified) state or condition [he is in a bad *way*] **16.** [Colloq.] a district; locality [out our *way*] **17.** [*pl.*] a timber framework on which a ship is built and along which it slides in launching **18.** *Naut.* a ship's movement or momentum through water —***adv.*** [Colloq.] away; far [*way* behind] —**by the way** **1.** incidentally **2.** on or beside the way —**by way of** **1.** passing through; via **2.** as a way, method, or means of —**come one's way** **1.** to come to one **2.** to turn out successfully for one: also **go one's way** —**give way** **1.** to withdraw; yield **2.** to break down —**give way to** to yield to —**go out of the** (or **one's**) **way** to make a special effort —**in the way** in such a position as to obstruct, hinder, etc. —**lead the way** to be a guide or example —**make one's way** **1.** to proceed **2.** to succeed by one's own efforts —**make way** **1.** to clear a passage **2.** to make progress —**on the way out** **1.** becoming unfashionable or unpopular **2.** dying —**out of the way** **1.** in a position so as not to hinder, etc. **2.** disposed of **3.** not on the right or usual route **4.** *a*) improper; amiss *b*) unusual —**the way** according to the way that [with things *the way* they are] —**under way** **1.** moving; advancing **2.** *Naut. see* UNDERWAY

way·bill (wā′bil′) ***n.*** a paper giving a list of goods and shipping instructions, sent with the goods being shipped

way·far·er (-fer′ər) ***n.*** a person who travels, esp. from place to place on foot —**way′far′ing *adj., n.***

way·lay (wā′lā′, wā′lā′) ***vt.*** **-laid′, -lay′ing** **1.** to lie in wait for and attack; ambush **2.** to wait for and accost (a person) on the way —**way′lay′er *n.***

Wayne (wān) **1.** [< surname *Wayne*] a masculine name **2. Anthony,** 1745–96; Am. general in the Revolutionary War: called *Mad Anthony Wayne*

way-out (wā′out′) ***adj.*** [Colloq.] very unusual, unconventional, experimental, nonconformist, esoteric, etc.

-ways (wāz) [< *way* (see WAY) + adv. genit. *-s*] *a suffix meaning* in a (specified) direction, position, or manner [*endways*]: equivalent to -WISE (sense 1)

ways and means **1.** methods and resources at the disposal of a person, company, etc. **2.** methods of raising money, as for government

way·side (wā′sīd′) ***n.*** the area close to the side of a road —***adj.*** on, near, or along the side of a road —**go by the wayside** to be put aside or discarded

way station a small railroad station between more important ones, where through trains stop only on signal

way·ward (-wərd) ***adj.*** [see AWAY & -WARD] **1.** insistent upon having one's own way; headstrong, willful, disobedient, etc. **2.** unpredictable; erratic —**way′ward·ly *adv.*** —**way′ward·ness *n.***

way·worn (-wôrn′) ***adj.*** tired from traveling

W.B., W/B waybill

w.c. **1.** water closet **2.** without charge

W.C.T.U. Women's Christian Temperance Union

we (wē) ***pron. for sing. see*** I [OE.] **1.** the persons speaking or writing: sometimes used by a person in referring to two or more persons including himself and often the person or persons addressed, or by a monarch, author, editor, etc. in referring to himself **2.** you: used in direct address as to a child, invalid, etc. [shall *we* take a nap now?] *We* is the nominative case form of the first personal plural pronoun

weak (wēk) ***adj.*** [ON. *veikr*] **1.** *a*) lacking in strength of body or muscle; not physically strong *b*) lacking vitality; feeble; infirm **2.** lacking in skill or strength for combat or competition [a *weak* team] **3.** lacking in moral strength or will power **4.** lacking in mental power **5.** *a*) lacking ruling power, or authority *b*) having few resources, little wealth, etc. [a *weak* nation] **6.** lacking in force or effectiveness **7.** *a*) not strong in material or construction; easily broken, bent, etc. *b*) not sound or secure [a *weak* fort] **8.** *a*) not functioning normally or well: said of a body organ or part [*weak* eyes] *b*) easily upset; queasy [a *weak* stomach] **9.** suggesting moral or physical lack of strength [*weak* features] **10.** lacking in volume, intensity, etc.; faint [a *weak* voice] **11.** lacking the usual or proper strength [*weak* tea] **12.** poor or deficient in something specified [*weak* in grammar] **13.** ineffective; faulty [a *weak* argument] **14.** *Chem.* having a low ion concentration, as certain acids and bases **15.** *Gram.* inflected by adding a suffix such as *-ed, -d* rather than by an internal vowel change: said of regular verbs **16.** *Phonet.* unstressed or lightly stressed **17.** *Prosody* designating or of a verse ending in which the stress falls on a word or syllable normally unstressed —**weak′ish *adj.***

weak·en (-'n) ***vt., vi.*** to make or become weak or weaker

weak·fish (-fish′) ***n., pl.*** **-fish′, -fish′es:** see FISH [< obs. Du. < *week*, soft + *visch*, a fish] any of several ocean food fishes, esp. a species off the eastern coast of the U.S.

weak-kneed (wēk′nēd′) ***adj.*** **1.** having weak knees **2.** lacking courage, determination, resistance, etc.

weak·ling (-liŋ) ***n.*** **1.** a person or animal low in physical strength or vitality **2.** a person of weak character or intellect —***adj.*** weak; feeble

weak·ly (-lē) ***adj.*** **-li·er, -li·est** sickly; feeble; weak —***adv.*** in a weak way —**weak′li·ness *n.***

weak-mind·ed (-mīn′did) ***adj.*** **1.** not firm of mind; indecisive **2.** mentally retarded **3.** showing weakness of thought —**weak′-mind′ed·ness *n.***

weak·ness (-nis) ***n.*** **1.** a being weak **2.** a weak point; fault **3.** a liking or an unreasonable fondness (*for* something) **4.** something of which one is unreasonably fond

weak sister [Slang] one who is cowardly, unreliable, etc.

weal[1] (wēl) ***n.*** [var. of WALE] a mark, line, or ridge raised on the skin, as by a blow; welt

weal[2] (wēl) ***n.*** [OE. *wela*] a prosperous state; well-being

weald (wēld) ***n.*** [OE.] [Poet.] **1.** a wooded area; forest **2.** wild, open country

wealth (welth) ***n.*** [see WEAL[2] & -TH[1]] **1.** *a*) much money or property; riches *b*) the state of being rich; affluence **2.** a large amount; abundance [a *wealth* of ideas] **3.** valuable products, contents, or derivatives [the *wealth* of the oceans] **4.** *Econ.* *a*) everything having value in money or a price *b*) any useful material thing capable of being bought and sold

wealth·y (wel′thē) ***adj.*** **wealth′i·er, wealth′i·est** **1.** having wealth; rich **2.** of or suggestive of wealth **3.** abounding (*in* something) —**wealth′i·ly *adv.*** —**wealth′i·ness *n.***

wean (wēn) ***vt.*** [OE. *wenian*] **1.** to accustom (a child or young animal) to food other than its mother's milk; now, often, to cause to give up drinking milk from a bottle with a nipple **2.** to withdraw (a person) by degrees (*from* a habit, object of affection, etc.) as by substituting something else —**wean′er *n.***

wean·ling (-liŋ) ***n.*** a child or young animal that has just been weaned —***adj.*** recently weaned

weap·on (wep′ən) ***n.*** [OE. *wæpen*] **1.** any instrument or device used for fighting, as specif. in warfare **2.** any organ or part (of an animal or plant) used for attacking or defending **3.** any means of attack or defense

weap·on·ry (-rē) ***n.*** **1.** the design and production of weapons **2.** weapons collectively, esp. of a nation for use in war

wear[1] (wer) ***vt.*** **wore, worn, wear′ing** [OE. *werian*] **1.** *a*) to have or carry (clothing, jewelry, a weapon, etc.) on the body *b*) to hold the position symbolized by [to *wear* the heavyweight crown] **2.** to have or show in one's expression or appearance [to *wear* a smile] **3.** to damage, impair, diminish, etc. by constant use, friction, etc. (often with *away*) **4.** to bring by use to a specified state [to *wear* a coat to rags] **5.** to make by the friction of rubbing, flowing, etc. [to *wear* a hole in the rug] **6.** to tire or exhaust —***vi.*** **1.** to become damaged, impaired, diminished, etc. by constant use, friction, etc. **2.** to hold up in spite of use; last [a fabric that *wears* well] **3.** to become in time; grow gradually [courage *wearing* thin] **4.** to pass away gradually: said of time [the day *wore* on] **5.** to have an irritating or exhausting effect (*on*) [noise *wearing* on his nerves] —***n.*** **1.** a wearing or being worn **2.** things, esp. clothes, worn, or for wearing, on the body [men's *wear*]: often in combination [*sportswear*] **3.** damage, impairment, loss, etc. from use, friction, etc. **4.** the ability to last in spite of use [a lot of *wear* left in the tire] —**wear down** **1.** to lose or cause to lose thickness or height by use, friction, etc. **2.** to tire out; exhaust **3.** to overcome by constant effort —**wear off** to pass away or diminish by degrees —**wear out 1.** to make or become useless from continued wear or use **2.** to waste or consume by degrees **3.** to tire out; exhaust —**wear′er** *n.*

wear[2] (wer) *vt.* **wore, worn, wear′ing** [altered < *veer* (to let out)] to turn (a ship) about by swinging its bow away from the wind —*vi.* to turn about by having the bow swung away from the wind

wear·a·ble (wer′ə b'l) *adj.* that can be worn; suitable for wear —*n.* [*pl.*] garments; clothing —**wear′a·bil′i·ty** *n.*

wear and tear loss and damage resulting from use

wear·ing (-iŋ) *adj.* **1.** of or for wear *[wearing* apparel*]* **2.** causing wear or loss **3.** tiring —**wear′ing·ly** *adv.*

wea·ri·some (wir′ē səm) *adj.* causing weariness; tiring; tiresome —**wea′ri·some·ly** *adv.* —**wea′ri·some·ness** *n.*

wear·proof (wer′pro͞of′) *adj.* that resists wearing out

wea·ry (wir′ē) *adj.* **-ri·er, -ri·est** [OE. *werig*] **1.** tired; worn out **2.** no longer liking, patient, tolerant, etc.; bored (with *of*) *[weary* of jokes*]* **3.** tiring *[weary* work*]* **4.** irksome; tedious *[weary* excuses*]* —*vt., vi.* **-ried, -ry·ing** to make or become weary —**wea′ri·ly** *adv.* —**wea′ri·ness** *n.*

wea·sand (wē′z'nd) *n.* [OE. *wæsend*] the gullet; esophagus

wea·sel (wē′z'l) *n., pl.* **-sels, -sel:** see PLURAL, II, D, 1 [OE. *wesle*] **1.** an agile, flesh-eating mammal related to the marten, with a long, slender body, short legs, and a long, bushy tail: they feed on rats, birds, eggs, etc. **2.** a sly or sneaky person —*vi.* **1.** to use weasel words **2.** [Colloq.] to evade a commitment or responsibility (with *out*) —**wea′sel·ly** *adj.*

WEASEL (6–14 in. long, including tail)

weasel words words or remarks that are deliberately misleading because they can be understood in more than one way

weath·er (we*th*′ər) *n.* [OE. *weder*] **1.** the general condition (as to temperature, moisture, cloudiness, etc.) of the atmosphere at a particular time and place **2.** disagreeable atmospheric conditions; storm, rain, etc. —*vt.* **1.** to expose to the weather or atmosphere, as for airing, drying, seasoning, etc. **2.** to wear away, discolor, etc. by exposure to the atmosphere **3.** to get through safely *[*to *weather* a storm*]* **4.** to slope (sills, etc.) so as to throw off rain, etc. **5.** *Naut.* to pass to the windward of (a cape, reef, etc.) —*vi.* **1.** to become worn, discolored, etc. by exposure to the weather **2.** to endure such exposure in a specified way *[*it *weathers* well*]* —*adj.* **1.** designating or of the side of a ship, etc. toward the wind; windward **2.** exposed to the elements *[weather* deck*]* —**under the weather** [Colloq.] **1.** not feeling well; ailing **2.** somewhat drunk —**weather through** to go safely through a storm, difficulty, etc.

weath·er-beat·en (-bēt′'n) *adj.* showing the effect of weather, as *a)* stained, damaged, or worn *b)* sunburned, roughened, etc.: said of a person, his face, etc.

weath·er·board (-bôrd′) *n.* a clapboard; piece of siding —*vt.* to put weatherboards on (a wall, etc.)

weath·er-bound (-bound′) *adj.* delayed or halted by bad weather, as a ship, airplane, etc.

Weather Bureau *former name of the* NATIONAL WEATHER SERVICE

weath·er·cock (-käk′) *n.* **1.** a weather vane in the form of a rooster **2.** a fickle or changeable person or thing

weather eye 1. an eye alert to signs of changing weather **2.** a close watch for any change

weath·er·ing (-iŋ) *n. Geol.* the effects of the forces of weather on rock surfaces, as in forming soil, sand, etc.

weath·er·man (-man′) *n., pl.* **-men′** (-men′) a person who forecasts the weather, or, esp., one who reports weather conditions and forecasts, as on television

weather map a map or chart showing weather conditions in a certain area at a given time by indicating barometric pressures, temperatures, wind direction, etc.

weath·er·proof (-pro͞of′) *adj.* that can be exposed to wind, rain, snow, etc. without being damaged —*vt.* to make weatherproof

weather station a post or office where weather conditions are recorded and studied and forecasts are made

weath·er·strip (-strip′) *n.* a thin strip of metal, felt, wood, etc. used to cover the joint between a door or window and its casing, so as to keep out drafts, rain, etc.: also **weather strip** —*vt.* **-stripped′, -strip′ping** to provide with this: also **weath′er-strip′**

weath·er·strip·ping (-strip′iŋ) *n.* **1.** *same as* WEATHERSTRIP **2.** weatherstrips collectively

weather vane a shaped piece of metal, etc., set up high to swing in the wind and show which way it is blowing

weath·er-wise (-wīz′) *adj.* **1.** skilled in predicting the weather **2.** skilled in predicting shifts of opinion, feeling, etc.

weath·er·worn (-wôrn′) *adj. same as* WEATHER-BEATEN

weave (wēv) *vt.* **wove** or, chiefly for *vt.* 6 & *vi.* 3, **weaved, wo′ven** or **wove** or, chiefly for *vt.* 6 & *vi.* 3, **weaved, weav′ing** [OE. *wefan*] **1.** *a)* to make (a fabric), esp. on a loom, by interlacing threads or yarns *b)* to form (threads) into a fabric **2.** *a)* to construct in the mind *b)* to form (incidents, etc.) into a story, poem, etc. **3.** *a)* to make by interlacing twigs, straw, etc. *[*to *weave* baskets*]* *b)* to interlace (twigs, straw, etc.) so as to make something **4.** to twist (something) into, through, or among *[*to *weave* flowers into one's hair*]* **5.** to spin (a web): said of spiders, etc. **6.** *a)* to cause (a vehicle, etc.) to move from side to side or in and out *b)* to make (one's way) by moving thus —*vi.* **1.** to do weaving **2.** to become interlaced **3.** to move from side to side or in and out *[weaving* through traffic*]* —*n.* a method or pattern of weaving

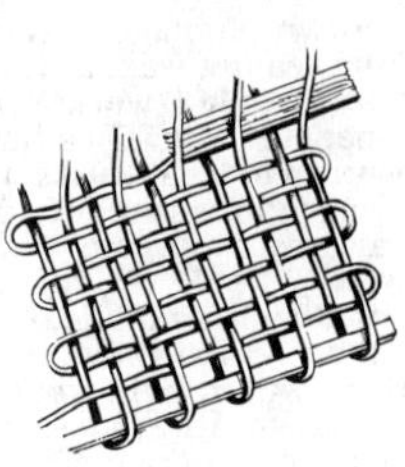
WEAVING

weav·er (wē′vər) *n.* **1.** a person who weaves; esp., one whose work is weaving **2.** *same as* WEAVERBIRD

weav·er·bird (-burd′) *n.* any of a number of related old-world, finchlike birds that weave elaborate domed nests of sticks, grass, and other vegetation

web (web) *n.* [OE. *webb*] **1.** any woven fabric; esp., a length of cloth being woven on a loom or just taken off **2.** the network spun by a spider or by the larvae of certain insects **3.** a carefully woven trap **4.** anything contrived in an intricate way *[*a *web* of lies*]* **5.** *Anat.* a tissue or membrane **6.** *Mech.* the plate joining the flanges of a girder, rail, etc. **7.** *Printing* a large roll of paper for continuously feeding a type of rotary press **(web press) 8.** *Zool. a)* the vane of a feather *b)* a membrane joining the digits of various water birds, water animals, etc. —*vt.* **webbed, web′bing 1.** to join by a web **2.** to cover as with a web **3.** to snare in a web —**web′like′** *adj.*

web·bing (-iŋ) *n.* **1.** a strong, tough fabric, as of jute, woven in strips and used for belts, in upholstery, etc. **2.** a membrane joining the digits, as of a duck or frog **3.** a part like this **4.** a netlike structure of interwoven cord, etc.

web·by (-ē) *adj.* **web′bi·er, web′bi·est 1.** of or like a web **2.** webbed or web-footed

We·ber (vā′bər), **Carl Ma·ri·a (Friedrich Ernst) von** (mä-rē′ä fôn) 1786–1826; Ger. composer

We·bern (vā′bərn), **An·ton (von)** (än′tôn) 1883–1945; Austrian composer

web·foot (web′foot′) *n., pl.* **-feet′ 1.** a foot with the toes webbed **2.** an animal with webfeet —**web′-foot′ed** *adj.*

Web·ster (web′stər) **1. Daniel,** 1782–1852; U.S. statesman & orator **2. John,** 1580?–1625?; Eng. dramatist **3. Noah,** 1758–1843; U.S. lexicographer —**Web·ster′i·an** (-stir′ē ən) *adj.*

web-toed (web′tōd′) *adj.* having webfeet

wed (wed) *vt.* **wed′ded, wed′ded** or **wed, wed′ding** [OE. *weddian*] **1.** to marry; specif., *a)* to take as husband or wife *b)* to join in marriage **2.** to join closely —*vi.* to get married

we'd (wēd) **1.** we had **2.** we should **3.** we would

Wed. Wednesday

wed·ded (wed′id) *adj.* **1.** married **2.** devoted *[wedded* to one's work*]* **3.** joined *[wedded* by common interests*]*

wed·ding (-iŋ) *n.* [OE. *weddung*] **1.** the act or ceremony of getting married, or the festivities that go with it **2.** a marriage anniversary **3.** a joining together

wedding ring a ring put on the bride's finger by the groom during the marriage ceremony; also, a ring sometimes given to the groom by the bride during the ceremony

wedge (wej) *n.* [OE. *wecg*] **1.** a piece of wood, metal, etc. tapering to a thin edge that can be driven into a narrow opening, as to split wood **2.** anything with a wedgelike shape or part; specif., *a)* *Golf* an iron with much loft, as for shots out of bunkers *b)* same as WEDGIE **3.** any action or procedure used to open the way for a change —*vt.* **wedged, wedg′ing 1.** to split as with a wedge **2.** to fix in place by driving a wedge under, beside, etc. **3.** to pack (*in*) or crowd together —*vi.* to push or be forced as or like a wedge —**wedge′like′** *adj.* —**wedg′y** *adj.*

WEDGE

wedg·ie (wej′ē) *n.* a woman's shoe having a wedgelike piece under the heel so as to form a solid sole, flat from heel to toe

Wedg·wood (ware) (wej′wood′) [after J. *Wedgwood,* 18th-c. E. potter] *a trademark for* a fine English pottery, typically with neoclassical figures applied in relief

wed·lock (wed′läk′) *n.* [< OE. < *wed,* a pledge + *-lac,* an offering] the state of being married

Wednes·day (wenz′dē, -dā) ***n.*** [OE. *Wodnes dæg*, Woden's day] the fourth day of the week

Wednes·days (-dēz, -dāz) ***adv.*** on or during every Wednesday

wee (wē) ***adj.*** **we′er, we′est** [OE. *wege*] **1.** very small; tiny **2.** very early [the *wee* hours] —***n.*** [Scot. & Eng. Dial.] a little bit; esp., a short time

weed (wēd) ***n.*** [OE. *weod*] **1.** any undesired, uncultivated plant, esp. one growing in profusion and crowding out a desired crop, spoiling a lawn, etc. **2.** [Colloq.] *a*) tobacco: with *the* *b*) a cigar or cigarette *c*) a marijuana cigarette **3.** something useless —***vt.*** **1.** to remove weeds from (a garden, etc.) **2.** to remove as useless, harmful, etc.: often with *out* **3.** to rid of useless or harmful elements —***vi.*** to remove weeds, etc. —**weed′er** ***n.*** —**weed′like′** ***adj.***

weed·kill·er (-kil′ər) ***n.*** *same as* HERBICIDE

weeds (wēdz) ***n.pl.*** [< OE. *wæde*, a garment] black mourning clothes, esp. those worn by a widow

weed·y (wēd′ē) ***adj.*** **weed′i·er, weed′i·est** **1.** full of weeds **2.** of or like a weed, as in rapid growth **3.** lean, lanky, ungainly, etc. —**weed′i·ness** ***n.***

week (wēk) ***n.*** [OE. *wicu*] **1.** a period of seven days, esp. one beginning with Sunday and ending with Saturday **2.** the hours or days of work in a seven-day period [a 40-hour *week*] —**week after week** every week —**week by week** each week —**week in, week out** every week

week·day (-dā′) ***n.*** **1.** any day of the week except Sunday (or, as in Judaism, Saturday) **2.** any day not in the weekend —***adj.*** of, for, or on a weekday

week·days (-dāz′) ***adv.*** on or during every weekday or most weekdays

week·end, week-end (-end′) ***n.*** the period from Friday night or Saturday to Monday morning: also **week end** —***adj.*** of, for, or on a weekend —***vi.*** to spend the weekend (*at* or *in* a specified place)

week·end·er (-en′dər) ***n.*** **1.** a person who takes a vacation or goes for a visit on a weekend **2.** a small piece of luggage for use on a weekend trip: also **weekend case** (or **bag**)

week·ends (-endz′) ***adv.*** on or during every weekend or most weekends

week·ly (-lē) ***adj.*** **1.** continuing or lasting for a week **2.** done, happening, appearing, etc. once a week or every week [a *weekly* visit] **3.** of a week, or of each week [a *weekly* wage] —***adv.*** once a week; every week —***n., pl.*** **-lies** a periodical published once a week

ween (wēn) ***vi., vt.*** [OE. *wenan*] [Archaic] to think; suppose; imagine

wee·nie, wee·ny[1] (wē′nē) ***n., pl.*** **-nies** [Colloq.] *same as* WIENER

wee·ny[2] (wē′nē) ***adj.*** **-ni·er, -ni·est** [WEE + (TI)NY] [Colloq.] small; tiny

weep (wēp) ***vi.*** **wept, weep′ing** [OE. *wepan*] **1.** to show or express strong emotion, usually grief or sorrow, by crying, wailing, or, esp., shedding tears **2.** to lament or mourn (with *for*) **3.** to drip or form liquid drops, esp. of moisture condensed from the air **4.** to exude liquid —***vt.*** **1.** to weep for; lament **2.** to shed (tears, etc.) —***n.*** [*often pl.*] a fit of weeping —**weep′er** ***n.***

weep·ing (wē′piŋ) ***n.*** the act of one who or that which weeps —***adj.*** **1.** that weeps tears or other liquid **2.** having graceful, drooping branches —**weep′ing·ly** ***adv.***

weeping willow a Chinese willow widely grown as an ornamental tree for its delicate, drooping branches

weep·y (wē′pē) ***adj.*** **weep′i·er, weep′i·est** **1.** *a*) inclined to weep; tearful *b*) exuding liquid **2.** characterized by or apt to cause weeping —**weep′i·ness** ***n.***

wee·vil (wē′v'l) ***n.*** [OE. *wifel*] any of numerous beetles, esp. those with projecting beaks, including many pest species that feed, esp. as larvae, on cotton, fruits, grain, etc. —**wee′vil·y, wee′vil·ly** ***adj.***

weft (weft) ***n.*** [OE. *weft* < base of *wefan*, to weave] **1.** in weaving, the woof **2.** something woven

weigh[1] (wā) ***vt.*** [OE. *wegan*, to carry] **1.** to determine the weight of by means of a scale or balance **2.** to have a (specified) weight [it *weighs* ten pounds]: orig., and still when used with an adverb, construed as a *vi.* **3.** *same as* WEIGHT (*vt.* 1) **4.** to lift or balance (an object) in the hand(s) in order to estimate its heaviness **5.** to measure out as by weight (often with *out*) **6.** *a*) to consider and choose carefully [to *weigh* one's words] *b*) to consider in order to make a choice [to *weigh* one plan against another] **7.** *Naut.* to hoist, or lift (an anchor) —***vi.*** **1.** to have significance, importance, or influence **2.** to be a burden (with *on* or *upon*) [his crime *weighed* on his mind] **3.** *Naut.* to hoist anchor —**weigh down** **1.** to make bend down as with added weight **2.** to bear down on so as to oppress —**weigh in** **1.** to weigh (a boxer, jockey, etc.) before or after a contest so as to verify his declared weight **2.** to be so weighed —**weigh′a·ble** ***adj.*** —**weigh′er** ***n.***

weigh[2] (wā) ***n.*** *var. of* WAY, in **under weigh,** progressing, advancing: cf. UNDERWAY

weight (wāt) ***n.*** [OE. *wiht* < *wegan:* see WEIGH[1]] **1.** a quantity weighing a specified amount **2.** heaviness as a quality; specif., the force of gravity acting on a body **3.** how much a thing weighs or should weigh **4.** *a*) any unit of heaviness *b*) any system of such units [troy *weight*]: see TABLES OF WEIGHTS AND MEASURES in Supplements *c*) a piece of metal, etc. of a specific standard heaviness, used on a balance or scale in weighing **5.** any block or mass used for its heaviness; specif., *a*) one used to hold light things down *b*) one used to drive a mechanism [clock *weights*] *c*) one lifted for exercise **6.** *a*) any heavy thing or load *b*) a burden of responsibility, sorrow, etc. **7.** importance or consequence **8.** influence, power, or authority **9.** the relative thickness or heaviness of a fabric or article of clothing **10.** *Printing* the relative thickness of the lines in fonts **11.** *Sports* *a*) any of the classifications for boxers and wrestlers based on what they weigh *b*) how many pounds a horse must carry for a race, including the weight of the jockey, saddle, and, often, added lead weights —***vt.*** **1.** to add weight to **2.** to load down; burden **3.** to control or manipulate so as to favor a particular side [*weighted* evidence] —**by weight** as determined by weighing —**carry weight** to be important, influential, etc. —**pull one's weight** to do one's share —**throw one's weight around** to use one's authority to gain an advantage

weight·less (-lis) ***adj.*** having little or no apparent weight; specif., free of or offsetting the pull of gravity —**weight′less·ly** ***adv.*** —**weight′less·ness** ***n.***

weight lifting the athletic exercise or competitive sport of lifting barbells —**weight lifter**

weight·y (-ē) ***adj.*** **weight′i·er, weight′i·est** **1.** very heavy **2.** burdensome; oppressive **3.** of great significance; serious **4.** of great importance —**weight′i·ness** ***n.***

Wei·ma·ra·ner (vī′mə rän′ər, wī′-) ***n.*** [< *Weimar*, where the breed was developed: see ff.] any of a breed of lean, medium-sized hunting dog with a smooth, gray coat

Wei·mar Republic (vī′mär; *E.* wī′mär) German Republic (1919–33), created at the city of Weimar (in what is now SW East Germany) & dissolved after Hitler became chancellor

weir (wir) ***n.*** [OE. *wer*] **1.** a low dam built in a river to back up or divert water, as for a mill **2.** a fence built in a stream or channel to catch fish

weird (wird) ***adj.*** [ult. < OE. *wyrd*, fate] **1.** of or suggestive of ghosts or other supernatural things; unearthly, mysterious, eerie, etc. **2.** strikingly odd, strange, etc.; fantastic; bizarre —**weird′ly** ***adv.*** —**weird′ness** ***n.***

Welch (welch, welsh) ***adj., n.*** *var. of* WELSH

welch (welch, welsh) ***vt., vi.*** [Slang] *var. of* WELSH

wel·come (wel′kəm) ***adj.*** [< OE. *wilcuma*, orig. *n.*, a welcome guest < *willa*, pleasure + *cuma*, a guest] **1.** gladly received [a *welcome* guest] **2.** agreeable or gratifying [*welcome* news] **3.** willingly permitted or invited [*welcome* to use the library] **4.** under no obligation [you're *welcome*]: used in a conventional response to thanks —***n.*** an act or expression of welcoming [a hearty *welcome*] —***interj.*** you are welcome: an expression of cordial greeting —***vt.*** **-comed, -com·ing** **1.** to greet with pleasure and hospitality **2.** to receive with pleasure or satisfaction [to *welcome* criticism] **3.** to meet, receive, or acknowledge in a specified way —**bid welcome** to receive with cordial greetings —**wear out one's welcome** to come too often or stay too long —**wel′com·er** ***n.***

welcome mat a doormat: chiefly in **put out the welcome mat,** to welcome enthusiastically

weld (weld) ***vt.*** [altered < obs. *well*, to weld] **1.** to unite (pieces of metal, etc.) by heating until molten and fused or until soft enough to hammer or press together **2.** to unite closely —***vi.*** to be welded or capable of being welded —***n.*** **1.** a welding or being welded **2.** the joint formed by welding —**weld′a·bil′i·ty** ***n.*** —**weld′a·ble** ***adj.*** —**weld′er** ***n.***

wel·fare (wel′fer′) ***n.*** [see WELL[2] & FARE] **1.** condition of health, happiness, and comfort; well-being **2.** aid by government agencies for the poor, unemployed, etc. **3.** *same as* WELFARE WORK —**on welfare** receiving government aid because of poverty, unemployment, etc.

welfare state a nation in which the government assumes responsibility for the welfare of the citizens, with regard to employment, medical care, social security, etc.

welfare work the organized effort of a community or organization to improve the living conditions and standards of its needy members —**welfare worker**

wel·far·ism (wel′fer′iz'm) ***n.*** **1.** the policies and practices of a welfare state or of public welfare agencies **2.** aid given by such a state or such agencies —**wel′far′ist** ***n., adj.***

wel·kin (wel′kin) ***n.*** [OE. *wolcen*] [Archaic or Poet.] the vault of heaven, the sky, or the upper air

well[1] (wel) ***n.*** [OE. *wella,* akin to *weallan,* to boil up] **1.** a natural spring and pool **2.** a hole sunk into the earth to get water, gas, oil, etc. **3.** an abundant source **4.** any shaft like a well; esp., *a)* an open shaft in a building for a staircase *b)* a shaft to let light and air into a building or between buildings *c)* an elevator shaft *d) Naut.* an enclosure for the pumps in the hold of a ship *e)* in a fishing boat, a compartment for freshly caught fish **5.** any of various containers for liquid, as an inkwell **6.** a depression in a platter, broiler, etc. for catching meat juices —***vi., vt.*** to pour forth as from a well; gush (*up, forth, down, out,* etc.)

well[2] (wel) ***adv.*** **bet′ter, best** [OE. *wel*] **1.** in a pleasing or desirable way; satisfactorily **2.** in a proper or friendly way **3.** skillfully **4.** fittingly **5.** *a)* in comfort and plenty *b)* to one's advantage **6.** with good reason; in justice **7.** to a considerable degree, extent, etc. **8.** thoroughly **9.** with certainty; definitely [you know very *well* why] **10.** intimately; closely [to know a person *well*] **11.** in good spirit; with good grace *Well* is also used in hyphenated compounds, to mean *properly, satisfactorily, thoroughly,* etc. [*well*-defined] —***adj.*** **1.** proper, right, etc. [it is *well* that he came] **2.** in good health **3.** in good condition —***interj.*** an exclamation used to express surprise, agreement, resignation, etc., or to introduce a remark —**as well 1.** besides; in addition **2.** with equal reason or effect —**as well as 1.** just as much or as good as **2.** in addition to —**wish someone well** to wish someone success or good luck

we'll (wēl, wil) **1.** we shall **2.** we will

well-ad·vised (wel′əd vīzd′) ***adj.*** showing or resulting from careful consideration or sound advice; wise

Wel·land (Ship) Canal (wel′ənd) canal of the St. Lawrence Seaway, in Ontario, Canada, between Lake Ontario & Lake Erie

well-ap·point·ed (wel′ə poin′tid) ***adj.*** excellently furnished or equipped [a *well-appointed* office]

well·a·way (wel′ə wā′) ***interj.*** [ME. *wei la wei,* lit., woe! lo! woe!] [Archaic] alas!: also **well′a·day′** (-dā′)

well-bal·anced (wel′bal′ənst) ***adj.*** **1.** carefully balanced, adjusted, etc. [a *well-balanced* meal] **2.** sane; sensible

well-be·haved (-bi hāvd′) ***adj.*** behaving well; polite

well-be·ing (-bē′iŋ) ***n.*** the state of being well, happy, or prosperous; welfare

well-be·loved (-bi luvd′, -luv′id) ***adj.*** **1.** deeply loved **2.** highly respected: used on formal occasions

well·born (-bôrn′) ***adj.*** born into a family of high social position

well-bred (-bred′) ***adj.*** **1.** showing good breeding; courteous and considerate **2.** of good stock: said of animals

well-cho·sen (-chō′z'n) ***adj.*** chosen with care; proper

well-con·tent (-kən tent′) ***adj.*** thoroughly pleased or satisfied: also **well′-con·tent′ed**

well-dis·posed (-dis pōzd′) ***adj.*** **1.** suitably or properly placed or arranged **2.** inclined to be friendly, kindly, or favorable (*toward* a person) or receptive (*to* an idea, etc.)

well-done (-dun′) ***adj.*** **1.** performed with skill and efficiency **2.** thoroughly cooked: said esp. of meat —***interj.*** an exclamation of approval of another's action

well-fa·vored (-fā′vərd) ***adj.*** handsome; pretty

well-fed (-fed′) ***adj.*** showing the effect of eating much good food; specif., plump or fat

well-fixed (-fikst′) ***adj.*** [Colloq.] wealthy; well-to-do

well-found·ed (-foun′did) ***adj.*** based on facts, good evidence, or sound judgment [a *well-founded* suspicion]

well-groomed (-groomd′) ***adj.*** **1.** carefully cared for [a *well-groomed* horse, a *well-groomed* lawn] **2.** clean and neat; carefully washed, combed, dressed, etc.

well-ground·ed (-groun′did) ***adj.*** **1.** having a thorough basic knowledge of a subject **2.** based on good reasons

well·head (wel′hed′) ***n.*** **1.** the source of a spring of water; spring **2.** any source; fountainhead

well-heeled (wel′hēld′) ***adj.*** [Slang] rich; prosperous

well-in·formed (-in fôrmd′) ***adj.*** **1.** having thorough knowledge of a subject **2.** having considerable knowledge of many subjects, esp. those of current interest

Wel·ling·ton (wel′iŋ tən) capital of New Zealand; seaport on S North Island: pop. (of urban area) 179,000

Wel·ling·ton (wel′iŋ tən), 1st Duke of, (*Arthur Wellesley*) 1769–1852; Brit. general & statesman, born in Ireland

Wellington (boot) [after prec.] [*also* **w- b-**] a high boot, traditionally extending just above the knee in front and just below in back, now usually just below the knee

well-in·ten·tioned (-in ten′shənd) ***adj.*** having or showing good or kindly intentions, but often with bad results

well-knit (-nit′) ***adj.*** having a strong, compact, or sturdy structure

well-known (-nōn′) ***adj.*** **1.** widely or generally known; famous **2.** thoroughly known

well-made (-mād′) ***adj.*** **1.** skillfully and strongly built **2.** skillfully contrived or plotted [a *well-made* play]

well-man·nered (-man′ərd) ***adj.*** polite; courteous

well-mean·ing (-mē′niŋ) ***adj.*** **1.** having good or kindly intentions **2.** said or done with good intentions, but often unwisely or with bad results: also **well′-meant′** (-ment′)

well-nigh (-nī′) ***adv.*** very nearly; almost

well-off (-ôf′) ***adj.*** **1.** in a favorable or fortunate condition or circumstance **2.** prosperous; well-to-do

well-or·dered (-ôr′dərd) ***adj.*** properly or carefully organized

well-pre·served (-pri zurvd′) ***adj.*** in good condition or of good appearance, in spite of age

well-read (-red′) ***adj.*** **1.** having read much (*in* a subject) **2.** having a wide knowledge of books through having read much

well-round·ed (-roun′did) ***adj.*** **1.** well planned for proper balance [a *well-rounded* program] **2.** showing interest, ability, etc. in many fields **3.** shapely

Wells (welz), **H**(**erbert**) **G**(**eorge**) 1866–1946; Eng. novelist & historian

well-spo·ken (wel′spō′k'n) ***adj.*** **1.** speaking fluently, graciously, etc. **2.** properly or aptly spoken

well·spring (wel′spriŋ′) ***n.*** **1.** a spring or fountainhead **2.** a source of abundant supply

well-thought-of (wel′thôt′uv′) ***adj.*** having a good reputation; of good repute

well-timed (-tīmd′) ***adj.*** timely; opportune

well-to-do (-tə do͞o′) ***adj.*** prosperous; well-off; wealthy

well-turned (-turnd′) ***adj.*** **1.** gracefully shaped **2.** expressed or worded well [a *well-turned* phrase]

well-wish·er (-wish′ər) ***n.*** a person who wishes well to another or to a cause, etc. —**well′-wish′ing *adj., n.***

well-worn (-wôrn′) ***adj.*** **1.** much worn; much used **2.** overused; trite [a *well-worn* joke]

Welsh (welsh, welch) ***adj.*** of Wales, its people, their language, etc. —***n.*** the Brythonic language spoken in Wales —**the Welsh** the people of Wales

welsh (welsh, welch) ***vt., vi.*** [< ?] [Slang] **1.** to cheat by failing to pay a bet or other debt **2.** to evade (an obligation) Often with *on* —**welsh′er *n.***

Welsh cor·gi (kôr′gē) [WELSH + W. *corgi* < *corr,* dwarf + *ci,* dog] either of two breeds of short-legged dog with a fox-like head, orig. from Wales

Welsh·man (welsh′mən, welch′-) ***n., pl.*** **-men** a native or inhabitant of Wales

Welsh rabbit [orig., a humorous usage] a dish of melted cheese, often mixed with ale or beer, served on crackers or toast: also **Welsh rarebit**

Welsh terrier a wire-haired terrier closely resembling the Airedale but smaller, orig. from Wales

welt (welt) ***n.*** [ME. *welte*] **1.** a strip of leather in the seam between the sole and upper of a shoe to strengthen the joining **2.** a strip of material at an edge or seam of a garment, etc. to reinforce or trim it **3.** *a)* a ridge raised on the skin by the blow of a whip, etc. *b)* such a blow —***vt.*** **1.** to furnish with a welt **2.** to raise welts on (the body) **3.** [Colloq.] to beat severely; thrash

wel·ter (wel′tər) ***vi.*** [MDu. *welteren*] **1.** to roll about or wallow, as a pig in mud **2.** to be deeply involved [to *welter* in sin] **3.** to be soaked, stained, etc. [to *welter* in blood] —***n.*** **1.** a tossing and tumbling **2.** a turmoil

wel·ter·weight (wel′tər wāt′) ***n.*** [prob. < WELT + -ER + WEIGHT] a boxer or wrestler between a lightweight and a middleweight (in boxing, 136–147 pounds)

wen (wen) ***n.*** [OE. *wenn*] a harmless skin tumor, esp. of the scalp, consisting of a sebaceous cyst

wench (wench) ***n.*** [OE. *wencel,* a child] **1.** a girl or young woman: now a somewhat derogatory or jocular term **2.** [Archaic] *a)* a country girl *b)* a female servant *c)* a prostitute or loose woman —***vi.*** to be sexually promiscuous with prostitutes or loose women —**wench′er *n.***

wend (wend) ***vt.*** **wend′ed** or archaic **went, wend′ing** [OE. *wendan,* to turn] to proceed on (one's way)

went (went) [old pt. of WEND, used to replace missing form of GO] *pt. of* GO

wept (wept) *pt. & pp. of* WEEP

were (wur; *unstressed* wər) [OE. *wæron*] *pl. & 2d pers. sing., past indic., and the past subj., of* BE

we're (wir) we are

weren't (wurnt) were not

were·wolf (wir′woolf′, wur′-, wer′-) ***n., pl.*** **-wolves′** (-woolvz′) [< OE. < *wer,* a man + *wulf,* a wolf] *Folklore* a person changed into a wolf or able to take the form of a wolf at will: also sp. **wer′wolf′**, *pl.* **wer′wolves′**

wert (wurt; *unstressed* wərt) *archaic 2d pers. sing., past indic. & subj., of* BE: *used with* thou

wes·kit (wes′kit) ***n.*** [< WAISTCOAT] a vest or waistcoat

Wes·ley (wes′lē, wez′-) **1.** [< the surname *Wesley*] a masculine name **2. Charles,** 1707–88; Eng. clergyman: brother of *ff.* **3. John,** 1703–91; Eng. clergyman & founder of the Methodist Church

Wes·ley·an (wes′lē ən, wez′-) ***adj.*** of John Wesley or the Methodist Church —***n.*** a follower of John Wesley; Methodist —**Wes′ley·an·ism *n.***

Wes·sex (wes′iks) former Anglo-Saxon kingdom in S England

west (west) ***n.*** [OE.] **1.** the direction to the left of a person facing north; direction in which sunset occurs (270° on the compass, opposite east) **2.** a region or district in or toward this direction **3.** **[W-]** the Western Hemisphere, or the Western Hemisphere and Europe; the Occident **4.** **[W-]** the Western Roman Empire —***adj.*** **1.** in, of, to, or toward the west **2.** from the west **3.** **[W-]** designating the western part of a country, etc. —***adv.*** in or toward the west —**the West** **1.** the western part of the U.S., esp. the region west of the Mississippi **2.** the U.S. and its non-Communist allies in Europe and the Western Hemisphere

West (west), **Benjamin** 1738–1820; Am. painter in England

West Al·lis (al′is) [after the *Allis*-Chalmers Co. there] city in SE Wis.: suburb of Milwaukee: pop. 64,000

West Berlin W section of Berlin, constituting a city associated with West Germany: pop. 2,141,000: cf. BERLIN

west·bound (-bound′) ***adj.*** going westward

West Co·vi·na (kō vē′nə) [*Covina* said locally to mean "place of vines"] city in SW Calif.: pop. 80,000

West End W section of London, England

west·er·ly (wes′tər lē) ***adj., adv.*** **1.** toward the west **2.** from the west —***n., pl.*** **-lies** a wind from the west

west·ern (-tərn) ***adj.*** **1.** in, of, or toward the west **2.** from the west **3.** **[W-]** of or characteristic of the West —***n.*** a story, motion picture, etc. about cowboys or frontiersmen in the western U.S. —**west′ern·most′** (-mōst′) ***adj.***

Western Australia state of Australia, occupying the W third of the continent

Western Church that part of the Catholic Church which recognizes the Pope and follows the Latin Rite; the Roman Catholic Church

west·ern·er (wes′tər nər) ***n.*** a native or inhabitant of the west, specif. **[W-]** of the western part of the U.S.

Western Hemisphere that half of the earth that includes North & South America

west·ern·ize (wes′tərn īz′) ***vt.*** **-ized′, -iz′ing** to make western in character, etc. —**west′ern·i·za′tion** ***n.***

Western (omelet) an omelet prepared with diced green pepper, onion, and ham

Western Roman Empire the W part of the Roman Empire, from its separation (395 A.D.) to its overthrow (476)

Western saddle [also **w- s-**] a heavy saddle of the kind used by cowboys, with a high cantle and pommel and a horn projecting above the pommel

Western Samoa country in the South Pacific, consisting of two large islands & several small ones: a member of the Commonwealth: 1,130 sq. mi.; pop. 146,000

West Germany W section of Germany, constituting a country in NC Europe: 95,735 sq. mi.; pop. 59,974,000; cap. Bonn: cf. GERMANY

West Haven city in SW Conn., on Long Island Sound: suburb of New Haven: pop. 53,000

West Indies large group of islands between N. America & S. America: it includes the Greater Antilles, Lesser Antilles, & Bahamas —**West Indian**

West·ing·house (wes′tiŋ hous′), **George** 1846–1914; U.S. inventor & manufacturer

West Ir·i·an (ir′ē ən) province of Indonesia, occupying the W half of the island of New Guinea: c.160,000 sq. mi.

West·land (west′lənd, -land′) [from its location in the county] city in SE Mich.: suburb of Detroit: pop. 85,000

West·min·ster Abbey (west′min′stər) Gothic church in London where English monarchs are crowned: burial place for English monarchs and other famous persons

west-north·west (west′nôrth′west′; *nautical* -nôr′-) ***n.*** the direction halfway between due west and northwest; 22°30′ north of due west —***adj., adv.*** **1.** in or toward this direction **2.** from this direction

West Palm Beach city in SE Fla., on a lagoon opposite Palm Beach: pop. 63,000 (met. area 552,000)

West Point military reservation in SE N.Y., on the west bank of the Hudson: site of the U.S. Military Academy

west-south·west (west′south′west′; *nautical* -sou′-) ***n.*** the direction halfway between due west and southwest; 22°30′ south of due west —***adj., adv.*** **1.** in or toward this direction **2.** from this direction

West Virginia E State of the U.S., northwest of Va.: 24,181 sq. mi.; pop. 1,950,000; cap. Charleston: abbrev. **W.Va., WV** —**West Virginian**

west·ward (-wərd) ***adv., adj.*** toward the west: also **west′wards** ***adv.*** —***n.*** a westward direction, point, or region

west·ward·ly (-lē) ***adv., adj.*** **1.** toward the west **2.** from the west

wet (wet) ***adj.*** **wet′ter, wet′test** [OE. *wæt*] **1.** covered or soaked with water or other liquid **2.** rainy; misty **3.** not yet dry [*wet* paint] **4.** preserved in liquid **5.** using, or done with or in, water or other liquid **6.** permitting or favoring the sale of alcoholic liquors —***n.*** water, rain, moisture, etc. —***vt., vi.*** **wet** or **wet′ted, wet′ting** **1.** to make or become wet (often with *through* or *down*) **2.** to make (a bed, oneself, etc.) wet by urination —**all wet** [Slang] wrong; in error —**wet behind the ears** [Colloq.] young and inexperienced —**wet′ly** ***adv.*** —**wet′ness** ***n.*** —**wet′ta·ble** ***adj.***

wet·back (wet′bak′) ***n.*** [from the fact that many enter by swimming or wading the Rio Grande] [Colloq.] a Mexican agricultural laborer who illegally enters the U.S. to work

wet bar a bar or serving counter, as in a recreation room, equipped with running water

wet blanket a person or thing that dampens or lessens the enthusiasm or gaiety of others

wet cell a voltaic cell in which the electrolyte is a liquid

weth·er (we*th*′ər) ***n.*** [OE.] a castrated male sheep

wet·land (wet′land′) ***n.*** [*usually pl.*] swamps or marshes

wet nurse a woman hired to suckle another woman's child —**wet-nurse** (wet′nurs′) ***vt.*** **-nursed′, -nurs′ing**

wet suit a closefitting, usually one-piece suit of rubber, worn by skin divers for warmth

we've (wēv) we have

wf, w.f. *Printing* wrong font

WGmc. West Germanic

whack (hwak, wak) ***vt., vi.*** [echoic] [Colloq.] to strike or slap with a sharp, resounding blow —***n.*** [Colloq.] a sharp, resounding blow, or its sound —**at a** (or **one**) **whack** [Colloq.] at one time and quickly or without pausing —**have** (or **take**) **a whack at** [Colloq.] **1.** to aim a blow at **2.** to make an attempt at —**out of whack** [Colloq.] not in proper condition —**whack off** [Colloq.] to separate or remove as by a chopping blow —**whack′er** ***n.***

whacked (hwakt, wakt) ***adj.*** **1.** [Chiefly Brit. Colloq.] very tired; exhausted **2.** [Slang] intoxicated

whack·ing (hwak′iŋ, wak′-) ***adj.*** [Chiefly Brit. Colloq.] big; great

whack·y (-ē) ***adj.*** **-i·er, -i·est** [Slang] *same as* WACKY

whale[1] (hwāl, wāl) ***n., pl.*** **whales, whale:** see PLURAL, II, D, 1 [OE. *hwæl*] any of various large mammals that live in the sea and have a fishlike form, with a flat, horizontal tail and with front limbs modified into flippers; esp., any of the larger mammals of this kind (up to 100 ft. in length), as distinguished from the porpoises and dolphins: see TOOTHED WHALE, WHALEBONE WHALE —***vi.*** **whaled, whal′ing** to hunt whales —**a whale of a** [Colloq.] an exceptionally large, fine, etc. example of (a class of persons or things)

whale[2] (hwāl, wāl) ***vt.*** **whaled, whal′ing** [prob. var. of WALE] [Colloq.] to beat; whip; thrash

whale·back (hwāl′bak′, wāl′-) ***n.*** **1.** something rounded on top like a whale's back **2.** a freight steamer with the bow and upper deck rounded so water runs off

whale·boat (-bōt′) ***n.*** **1.** a long rowboat, pointed at both ends: used formerly by whalers **2.** a similar lifeboat

whale·bone (-bōn′) ***n.*** **1.** horny, elastic material hanging in fringed sheets from the upper jaw or palate of whalebone whales and straining the tiny sea animals they feed on **2.** something made of this, as a corset stay

whalebone whale any of a main division of whales, as the blue whale, having whalebone in the mouth and no teeth

whal·er (hwā′lər, wā′-) ***n.*** **1.** a ship used in whaling **2.** a man whose work is whaling: also **whale′man,** ***pl.*** **-men**

whal·ing (-liŋ) ***n.*** the work or trade of hunting and killing whales for their blubber, whalebone, etc.

wham (hwam, wam) ***interj.*** a sound imitating a heavy blow or explosion —***n.*** a heavy blow or impact —***vt., vi.*** **whammed, wham′ming** to strike, explode, etc. loudly

wham·my (-ē) ***n., pl.*** **-mies** [Slang] a jinx or the evil eye: usually in **put a** (or **the**) **whammy on**

whang (hwaŋ, waŋ) ***vt.*** [echoic] **1.** to strike with a resounding blow **2.** [Dial.] to thrash —***vi.*** to make a loud noise by hitting —***n.*** the noise or blow so made

wharf (hwôrf, wôrf) ***n., pl.*** **wharves** (hwôrvz, wôrvz), **wharfs** [OE. *hwerf,* a dam < base of *hweorfan,* to turn] a platform built along or out from the shore, where ships can dock and load or unload; pier; dock —***vt.*** **1.** to bring to a wharf **2.** to unload or store on a wharf

wharf·age (-ij) ***n.*** **1.** the use of a wharf **2.** a fee charged for this **3.** wharves collectively

Whar·ton (hwôr′t'n, wôr′-), **Edith** (born *Edith Newbold Jones*) 1862–1937; U.S. novelist

what (hwut, hwät, wut, wät; *unstressed* hwət, wət) ***pron.*** [OE. *hwæt,* neut. of *hwa,* who] **1.** which thing, event, etc.: used in asking questions or in asking someone to repeat, explain, specify, etc. [*what* is that object? you told him *what?*] **2.** that which or those which: used as a relative pronoun [to know *what* one wants, not *what* it was] : also used elliptically for "what it is," "what to do," etc. [I'll tell you *what*] —***n.*** the nature (*of* an event) [the *what* and

fat, āpe, cär, ten, ēven, is, bīte; gō, hôrn, tōōl, look; oil, out; up, fur; get; joy; yet; chin; she; thin, *th*en; zh, leisure; ŋ, ring; ə for *a* in *ago*, *e* in *agent*, *i* in *sanity*, *o* in *comply*, *u* in *focus*; ′ as in *able* (ā′b'l); Fr. bål; ë, Fr. coeur; ö, Fr. feu; Fr. mon; ô, Fr. coq; ü, Fr. duc; *r*, Fr. cri; H, G. ich; kh, G. doch; ‡foreign; *hypothetical; < derived from. See inside front cover.

why of his exile*]* **—*adj.*** **1.** which or which kind of: used interrogatively or relatively *[what* man told you that? I know *what* books you like*]* **2.** as much, or as many, as *[*take *what* time (or men) you need*]* **3.** how great, surprising, etc.: in exclamations *[what* joy!*]* **—*adv.*** **1.** in what respect? to what degree? how? *[what* does it matter?*]* **2.** in some manner or degree; in part; partly (usually with *with) [what* with singing and joking, the time passed quickly*]* **3.** how greatly, surprisingly, etc. *[what* sad news!*]* **—*conj.*** that: in **but what,** but that *[*never doubt *but what* he loves you*]* **—*interj.*** an exclamation of surprise, anger, etc. *[what!* no dinner?*]* **—and what not** and other things of all sorts **—what about** what do you think, know, etc. concerning? **—what for 1.** why? **2.** [Slang] punishment *[*you'll get *what for]* **—what have you** [Colloq.] anything similar *[*games, toys, or *what have you]* **—what if 1.** what would happen if **2.** what difference would it make if **—what's what** [Colloq.] the true state of affairs **—what the (heck, devil,** etc.) **1.** an exclamation of surprise **2.** what: used emphatically **—what though** no matter if

what·ev·er (hwət ev′ər, wət-) ***pron.*** **1.** what: used for emphasis; specif., *a)* which thing, event, etc.: used in questions *[whatever* can it be?*]* *b)* anything that *[*tell her *whatever* you like*]* *c)* no matter what *[whatever* you do, don't rush*]* **2.** [Colloq.] anything of the sort *[*use pen, pencil, or *whatever]* **—*adj.*** **1.** of no matter what type, degree, etc. *[*make *whatever* repairs are needed*]* **2.** being who it may be *[whatever* man told you that, it isn't true*]* **3.** of any kind *[*no plans *whatever]* Also [Poet.] **what·e'er′** (-er′)

what·not (hwut′nät′, hwät′-, wut′-, wät′-) ***n.*** **1.** a nondescript thing **2.** a set of open shelves, as for bric-a-brac

what's (hwuts, hwäts, wuts, wäts) what is

what·so·ev·er (hwut′sō ev′ər, hwät′-, wut′-, wät′-) ***pron., adj.*** whatever: used for emphasis: also [Poet.] **what′so·e'er′** (-er′)

wheal[1] (hwēl, wēl) ***n.*** **[**akin to OE. *hwelian,* to suppurate**]** **1.** formerly, a pustule; pimple **2.** a small, raised patch of skin, as from an insect bite or hives

wheal[2] (hwēl, wēl) ***n.*** *same as* WEAL[1]

wheat (hwēt, wēt) ***n.*** see PLURAL, II, D, 3 **[**OE. *hwæte***]** **1.** any of a group of cereal grasses with dense spikes that grow upright and bear grains that are threshed to remove the chaff **2.** such grain, used for flour, cereals, pasta, etc.

wheat cake a pancake of whole-wheat flour

wheat·en (-'n) ***adj.*** **1.** made of wheat or wheat flour **2.** of the pale-yellow color of wheat

wheat germ **1.** the wheat-kernel embryo, rich in vitamins, milled out as an oily flake **2.** the milled flakes

WHEAT

whee (hwē, wē: *with prolonged vowel*) ***interj.*** an exclamation expressing joy, exultation, etc.

whee·dle (hwē′d'l, wē′-) ***vt., vi.*** **-dled, -dling** **[**< ? G. *wedeln,* to wag the tail, hence to flatter**]** **1.** to influence or persuade (a person) by flattery, soothing words, coaxing, etc. **2.** to get (something) by coaxing or flattery **—whee′dler *n.***

wheel (hwēl, wēl) ***n.*** **[**OE. *hweol***]** **1.** a solid disk, or a circular frame connected by spokes to a central hub, capable of turning on a central axis **2.** anything like a wheel in shape, movement, etc. **3.** a device having as its main part a wheel or wheels; specif., *a)* a medieval torture instrument that was a circular frame on which a victim was painfully stretched *b)* a wheel with projecting handles, to control a ship's rudder *c) short for* POTTER'S WHEEL, SPINNING WHEEL, etc. *d)* [Colloq.] a bicycle *e)* [*pl.*] [Slang] an automobile **4.** [*usually pl.*] the moving, propelling, or controlling forces or agencies *[*the *wheels* of progress*]* **5.** a turning movement **6.** [Slang] an important or influential person: also **big wheel —*vt., vi.*** **1.** to move or roll on wheels or in a wheeled vehicle **2.** to turn round; rotate, revolve, pivot, etc. **3.** to turn so as to reverse direction, attitude, etc. (often with *about*) **—at the wheel 1.** steering a ship, motor vehicle, etc. **2.** in charge; directing activities **—wheel and deal** [Slang] to behave in an aggressive, flamboyant way, as in a business deal **—wheel of fortune** the changes, good and bad, that occur in life **—wheeled *adj.***

wheel and axle a grooved wheel fixed to a shaft or drum, used for lifting weights: the turning of the wheel by a rope in the groove winds a rope on the shaft or drum

wheel·bar·row (-bar′ō, -ber′ō) ***n.*** a shallow, open box for moving small loads, having a single wheel in front, two legs in back, and two shafts with handles for raising the vehicle off its legs and pushing or pulling it

wheel·base (-bās′) ***n.*** in a motor vehicle, the distance in inches from the center of the hub of a front wheel to the center of the hub of the corresponding back wheel

wheel·chair (-cher′) ***n.*** a chair mounted on large wheels, used in moving about by persons unable to walk

wheel·er (-ər) ***n.*** **1.** a person or thing that wheels **2.** *same as* WHEEL HORSE (sense 1) **3.** something having a specified kind or number of wheels *[*two-*wheeler]*

wheel·er-deal·er (hwēl′ər dēl′ər, wēl′-) ***n.*** [Slang] a person who wheels and deals: see phrase at entry WHEEL

wheel horse **1.** the horse, or one of the horses, harnessed nearest the front wheels of a vehicle **2.** a person who works especially hard and effectively in any enterprise

wheel·house (-hous′) ***n.*** *same as* PILOTHOUSE

wheel·ie (-ē) ***n.*** a stunt performed on a motorcycle or bicycle, in which the front wheel is raised so that the vehicle is balanced for a moment on its rear wheel.

wheel·wright (-rīt′) ***n.*** a person who makes and repairs wagon and carriage wheels

wheeze (hwēz, wēz) ***vi.*** **wheezed, wheez′ing** **[**ON. *hvaesa,* to hiss**]** **1.** to breathe hard with a whistling, breathy sound, as in asthma **2.** to make a sound like this *[*the old organ *wheezed]* **—*vt.*** to utter with a sound of wheezing **—*n.*** **1.** an act or sound of wheezing **2.** [Slang] a trite remark, joke, or gag **—wheez′er *n.* —wheez′ing·ly *adv.***

wheez·y (hwē′zē, wē′-) ***adj.*** **wheez′i·er, wheez′i·est** wheezing or characterized by wheezing **—wheez′i·ly *adv.***

whelk[1] (hwelk, welk) ***n.*** **[**OE. *wioluc***]** any of various large sea snails with spiral shells, esp. those species used in Europe for food

WHELK
(3 in. long)

whelk[2] (hwelk, welk) ***n.*** **[**OE. *hwylca***]** **1.** a pimple or pustule **2.** *same as* WEAL[1]

whelm (hwelm, welm) ***vt.*** **[**? merging of OE. *-hwelfan,* to overwhelm, with *helmian,* to cover**]** **1.** to submerge or engulf **2.** to overwhelm

whelp (hwelp, welp) ***n.*** **[**OE. *hwelp***]** **1.** a young dog; puppy **2.** a young lion, tiger, wolf, etc.; cub **3.** a youth or child: contemptuous usage **—*vt., vi.*** to give birth to whelps

when (hwen, wen; *unstressed* hwən, wən) ***adv.*** **[**OE. *hwænne***]** **1.** *a)* at what time? *b)* on what occasion or under what circumstances? *c)* at what point? *[when* shall I stop pouring?*]* **2.** earlier and in other circumstances *[*I knew him *when]* **—*conj.*** **1.** at the time or point that *[*he told us *when* we sat down*]* **2.** at which *[*a time *when* men must speak out*]* **3.** as soon as *[*come *when* I call*]* **4.** at whatever time that *[*he rested *when* he could*]* **5.** although *[*to object *when* there's no reason to do so*]* **6.** if *[*how can he help *when* they won't let him?*]* **—*pron.*** what time or which time *[*until *when* will you stay?*]* **—*n.*** the time or moment (*of* an event) *[*the *when* and where of his arrest*]*

when·as (hwen az′, wen-) ***conj.*** [Archaic] **1.** when **2.** inasmuch as **3.** whereas

whence (hwens, wens) ***adv.*** **[**OE. *hwanan***]** from what place, source, cause, etc.; from where *[whence* do you come? *whence* did he get his facts?*]* **—*conj.*** **1.** to the place from which *[*return *whence* you came*]* **2.** because of which fact

whence·so·ev·er (hwens′sō ev′ər, wens′-) ***adv., conj.*** from whatever place, source, or cause

when·ev·er (hwen ev′ər, wen-, hwən-, wən-) ***adv.*** [Colloq.] when: used for emphasis *[whenever* will he learn?*]* **—*conj.*** at whatever time; on whatever occasion *[*visit us *whenever* you can*]* Also [Poet.] **when′e'er′** (-er′)

when·so·ev·er (hwen′sō ev′ər, wen′-) ***adv., conj.*** whenever: used for emphasis: also [Poet.] **when′so·e'er′** (-er′)

where (hwer, wer; *unstressed* hwər, wər) ***adv.*** **[**OE. *hwær***]** **1.** in or at what place? *[where* is the car?*]* **2.** to or toward what place? *[where* did he go?*]* **3.** in what situation? *[where* will we be if we lose?*]* **4.** in what respect? *[where* is she to blame?*]* **5.** from what place or source? *[where* did you find out?*]* **—*conj.*** **1.** in or at what place *[*he knows *where* it is*]* **2.** in or at which place *[*we came home, *where* we ate dinner*]* **3.** in or at the place or situation in which *[*he is *where* he should be*]* **4.** in whatever place, situation, or respect in which *[*there is never peace *where* men are greedy*]* **5.** *a)* to or toward the place to which *[*he'll go *where* we go*]* *b)* to a place in which *[*send help *where* it's needed*]* **6.** to or toward whatever place *[*go *where* you please*]* **7.** [Colloq.] *same as* WHEREAS The use of *where* in place of *that* to introduce a noun clause is objected to by some *[*I see *where* taxes are going up*]* **—*pron.*** **1.** the place or situation in, at, or to which *[*it is a mile from *where* he lives*]* **2.** what or which place *[where* are you from?*]* **—*n.*** the place (*of* an event) *[*tell us the *where* of the party*]*

where·a·bouts (hwer′ə bouts′, wer′-) ***adv.*** near or at what place? where? **—*n.*** the place where a person or thing is *[*do you know his *whereabouts?]*

where·as (hwer az′, wer-, hwər-, wər-) ***conj.*** **1.** in view of the fact that: used in a formal document **2.** but on the other hand; while *[*she is slender, *whereas* he is stout*]* **—*n., pl.*** **-as·es** a statement beginning with "whereas"

where·at (-at′) ***adv.*** [Archaic] at what? *[whereat* was he angry?*]* **—*conj.*** [Archaic] at which point *[*he left, *whereat* she began to weep*]*

where·by (-bī′) ***adv.*** [Archaic] by what? how? *[whereby* did

you expect to profit?] —*conj.* by which; by means of which [a plan *whereby* to make money]
where·fore (hwer′fôr′, wer′-) *adv.* [Archaic] for what reason or purpose? why? [*wherefore* are you angry?] —*conj.* **1.** for which [the reason *wherefore* we have met] **2.** because of which; therefore [we won, *wherefore* rejoice] —*n.* the reason; cause
where·from (hwer frum′, wer-) *adv., conj.* from which
where·in (-in′) *adv.* [Archaic] in what way? how? [*wherein* is it wrong?] —*conj.* in which [the room *wherein* he lay]
where·of (-uv′) *adv., conj.* of what, which, or whom
where·on (-än′) *adv.* [Archaic] on what? [*whereon* do you rely?] —*conj.* on which [the hill *whereon* we stand]
where·so·ev·er (hwer′sō ev′ər, wer′-) *adv., conj.* wherever: used for emphasis: also [Poet.] **where′so·e'er′** (-er′)
where·to (-to͞o′) *adv.* to what? toward what place, direction, or end? —*conj.* to which
where·up·on (hwer′ə pän′, wer′-; hwer′ə pän, wer′-) *adv.* [Archaic] upon what? whereon? —*conj.* **1.** upon which [the ground *whereupon* he had fallen] **2.** at which [she told a joke, *whereupon* he laughed]
wher·ev·er (hwer ev′ər, wer-, hwər-, wər-) *adv.* [Colloq.] where: used for emphasis [*wherever* did you hear that?] —*conj.* in, at, or to whatever place or situation [he thinks of us, *wherever* he is] Also [Poet.] **wher·e'er′** (-er′)
where·with (hwer with′, wer-) *adv.* [Archaic] with what? [*wherewith* shall he be saved?] —*conj.* with which [lacking the money *wherewith* to pay him] —*pron.* that with which [to have *wherewith* to build]
where·with·al (hwer′with ôl′, wer′-; -with-) *n.* that with which something can be done; necessary means, esp. money (usually with *the*) [the *wherewithal* to continue one's education] —*adv., conj. archaic var. of* WHEREWITH
wher·ry (hwer′ē, wer′-) *n., pl.* **-ries** [< ? ME. *whirren*, to whir, with idea of fast movement] **1.** a light rowboat used on rivers **2.** a racing scull for one person **3.** [Brit.] a large, broad, but light barge —*vt.* **-ried, -ry·ing** to transport in a wherry
whet (hwet, wet) *vt.* **whet′ted, whet′ting** [OE. *hwettan* < *hwæt*, keen] **1.** to sharpen by rubbing or grinding (the edge of a knife or tool); hone **2.** to stimulate [to *whet* the appetite] —*n.* **1.** an act of whetting **2.** something that whets —**whet′ter** *n.*
wheth·er (hweth′ər, weth′ər) *conj.* [OE. *hwæther*] **1.** if it be the case or fact that [ask *whether* she will help] **2.** in case; in either case that: used to introduce alternatives [*whether* it rains or snows] **3.** either [*whether* by accident or design] —**whether or no** in any case
whet·stone (hwet′stōn′, wet′-) *n.* an abrasive stone for sharpening knives or other edged tools
whew (hyo͞o, hwyo͞o) *interj.* [echoic] an exclamation of relief, surprise, dismay, etc.
whey (hwā, wā) *n.* [OE. *hwæg*] the thin, watery part of milk, which separates from the thicker part (curds) after coagulation —**whey′ey** (-ē) *adj.*
whey·face (-fās′) *n.* **1.** a pale or pallid face **2.** a person having such a face —**whey′faced′** *adj.*
which (hwich, wich) *pron.* [OE. *hwylc*] **1.** what one (or ones) of the persons, things, or events mentioned or implied? [*which* do you want?] **2.** the one (or ones) that [he knows *which* he wants] **3.** that: used as a relative referring to the thing or event specified in the antecedent [her hat, *which* is blue; the boat *which* sank] **4.** any that; whichever [take *which* you like] **5.** a thing or fact that [you are late —*which* reminds me, where is Joe?] —*adj.* **1.** what one or ones (of the number mentioned or implied) [*which* man (or men) came?] **2.** whatever [try *which* plan you like] **3.** being the one just mentioned [he is old, *which* fact is important]
which·ev·er (hwich ev′ər, wich-) *pron., adj.* **1.** any one (of two or more) [he may choose *whichever* (desk) he likes] **2.** no matter which [*whichever* (desk) he chooses, they won't be pleased]
which·so·ev·er (hwich′sō ev′ər, wich′-) *pron., adj.* whichever: used for emphasis
whick·er (hwik′ər, wik′-) *vi.* [echoic] **1.** to utter a partly stifled laugh; snicker; titter **2.** to neigh or whinny
whiff (hwif, wif) *n.* [echoic] **1.** a light puff or gust of air or wind; breath **2.** a slight gust of odor [a *whiff* of garlic] **3.** an inhaling or exhaling of tobacco smoke —*vt.* **1.** to blow with a puff or gust; waft **2.** to smoke (a pipe, etc.) —*vi.* **1.** to blow or move in puffs **2.** to inhale or exhale whiffs, as in smoking —**whiff′er** *n.*
whif·fet (-it) *n.* [dim. of prec.] **1.** a little whiff **2.** a small dog **3.** [Colloq.] an insignificant person
whif·fle (-'l) *vi.* **-fled, -fling** [freq. of WHIFF] **1.** to blow in gusts: said of the wind **2.** to shift; veer; vacillate —*vt.* to blow or scatter with or as with a puff of wind —**whif′fler** *n.*
whif·fle·tree (-'l trē′) *n. var. of* WHIPPLETREE
Whig (hwig, wig) *n.* [< *whiggamore* (applied to Scot. Presbyterians who marched on Edinburgh in 1648) < WScot. < *whig*, a cry to urge on horses + *mare*, a horse] **1.** a member of a political party in England (fl. 18th to mid-19th cent.) which championed popular rights: it later became the Liberal Party **2.** in the American Revolution, a person who opposed Great Britain and supported the Revolution **3.** a member of an American political party (c.1836–1856) opposing the Democratic Party —*adj.* of or being a Whig —**Whig′gish** *adj.* —**Whig′gism, Whig′ger·y** *n.*
while (hwīl, wīl) *n.* [OE. *hwil*] a period of time [a short *while*] —*conj.* **1.** during or throughout the time that [we talked *while* we ate] **2.** at the same time that [*while* you're up, close the door] **3.** *a*) although [*while* she isn't pretty, she is charming] *b*) whereas [the walls are green, *while* the ceiling is white] —*vt.* **whiled, whil′ing** to spend (time) in a pleasant way [to *while* away the hours] —**between whiles** at intervals —**the while** during this very time —**worth (one's) while** worth one's time; profitable
whiles (hwīlz, wīlz) *adv.* [Chiefly Scot.] *same as* SOMETIMES —*conj.* [Archaic or Dial.] *same as* WHILE
whi·lom (hwī′ləm, wī′-) *adv.* [OE. *hwilum*, dat. pl. of *hwil*, while] [Archaic] at one time; formerly —*adj.* formerly such; former [their *whilom* friends]
whilst (hwīlst, wīlst) *conj.* [Dial.] *same as* WHILE
whim (hwim, wim) *n.* [short for WHIM-WHAM] a sudden fancy; idle and passing notion; caprice
whim·per (hwim′pər, wim′-) *vi.* [? akin to WHINE] to cry with low, whining, broken sounds —*vt.* to utter with a whimper —*n.* a whimpering sound or cry —**whim′per·er** *n.* —**whim′per·ing·ly** *adv.*
whim·si·cal (hwim′zi k'l, wim′-) *adj.* **1.** full of whims or whimsy; having odd notions **2.** different in an odd way; freakish **3.** unpredictable —**whim′si·cal′i·ty** (-kal′ə tē), *pl.* **-ties, whim′si·cal·ness** *n.* —**whim′si·cal·ly** *adv.*
whim·sy (hwim′zē, wim′-) *n., pl.* **-sies** [prob. < ff.] **1.** an odd fancy; idle notion; whim **2.** quaint or fanciful humor Also sp. **whim′sey,** *pl.* **-seys**
whim-wham (hwim′hwam′, wim′wam′) *n.* [< ?] **1.** a bauble; trinket **2.** an odd notion; whim —**the whim-whams** [Colloq.] a nervous feeling; the jitters
whin (hwin, win) *n.* [prob. < Scand.] *same as* FURZE
whin·chat (hwin′chat′, win′-) *n.* [prec. + *chat*, a warbler] a brown and buff migrating European songbird
whine (hwīn, wīn) *vi.* **whined, whin′ing** [OE. *hwinan*] **1.** *a*) to utter a peevish, high-pitched sound, as in complaint, distress, etc. *b*) to make a drawn-out, high-pitched sound **2.** to complain or beg in a childish, undignified way —*vt.* to utter with a whine —*n.* **1.** the act or sound of whining **2.** a complaint uttered in a whining tone —**whin′er** *n.* —**whin′i·ness** *n.* —**whin′ing·ly** *adv.* —**whin′y, whin′ey** *adj.* **whin′i·er, whin′i·est**
whing·ding (hwiŋ′diŋ′, wiŋ′-) *n.* [Slang] *same as* WINGDING
whin·ny (hwin′ē, win′ē) *vi.* **-nied, -ny·ing** [prob. < or akin to WHINE] to neigh in a low, gentle way: said of a horse —*vt.* to express with a whinny —*n., pl.* **-nies** the whinnying of a horse, or a similar sound
whip (hwip, wip) *vt.* **whipped, whip′ping** [MDu. *wippen*, to swing] **1.** to move, pull, throw, etc. suddenly (usually with *out, off, up*, etc.) [to *whip* out a knife] **2.** to strike, as with a strap, rod, etc.; lash; beat **3.** to drive, urge, etc. by or as by whipping **4.** to strike as a whip does [the rain *whipped* her face] **5.** to wind (cord or thread) around (a rope, etc.), so as to prevent fraying **6.** to fish (a stream, etc.) by making repeated casts **7.** to beat (eggs, cream, etc.) into a froth with a fork, mixer, etc. **8.** to sew (a seam, etc.) with a loose, overcasting or overhand stitch **9.** [Colloq.] to defeat or outdo —*vi.* **1.** to move, go, etc. quickly and suddenly [he *whipped* out the door] **2.** to flap about in a whiplike manner [flags *whip* in high wind] —*n.* **1.** an instrument for striking or flogging, consisting of a rod with a lash attached to one end **2.** a blow, cut, etc. made with or as with a whip **3.** a person who uses a whip, as a coachman **4.** an officer of a political party in Congress, Parliament, etc. who enforces party discipline, attendance, etc.: also **party whip** **5.** a whipping motion **6.** a dessert made of sugar and whipped cream, beaten egg whites, etc., and often fruit **7.** something resembling a whip in its action —**whip into shape** [Colloq.] to bring by vigorous action into a desired condition —**whip up** **1.** to rouse; excite **2.** [Colloq.] to prepare quickly and efficiently —**whip′like′** *adj.* —**whip′per** *n.*
whip·cord (-kôrd′) *n.* **1.** a hard, twisted or braided cord used for whiplashes, etc. **2.** a strong worsted cloth with a hard, diagonally ribbed surface
whip hand **1.** the hand in which a driver holds his whip **2.** the position of advantage or control

whip·lash (-lash′) ***n.*** **1.** the lash of a whip **2.** a sudden, severe jolting of the neck backward and then forward, as caused by the impact of a rear-end automobile collision

whipped cream rich sweet cream stiffened as by whipping and used as a topping on desserts, etc.: also **whip cream**

whip·per·snap·per (hwip′ər snap′ər, wip′-) ***n.*** [< *whip-snapper*, one who snaps whips] a young or unimportant person who does not seem to show proper respect for those older or more important than himself

whip·pet (hwip′it, wip′-) ***n.*** [dim. < WHIP] a swift dog resembling a small greyhound, used in racing

whip·ping (-iŋ) ***n.*** **1.** a flogging or beating, as in punishment **2.** cord, twine, etc. used to whip, or bind

whipping boy *same as* SCAPEGOAT (sense 2)

whipping cream sweet cream with a high percentage of butterfat, that can be whipped until stiff

whipping post a post to which offenders are tied to be whipped as a legal punishment

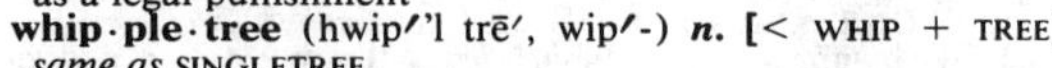

WHIPPET (18–22 in. high at shoulder)

whip·ple·tree (hwip′′l trē′, wip′-) ***n.*** [< WHIP + TREE] *same as* SINGLETREE

whip·poor·will (hwip′ər wil′, wip′-) ***n.**, pl.* **-wills′, -will′**: see PLURAL, II, D, 1 [echoic] a grayish bird of eastern N. America, one of the goatsuckers

whip·saw (hwip′sô′, wip′-) ***n.*** a long-bladed saw; esp., one with a handle at each end for use by two persons —***vt.*** to cut with a whipsaw

whip·stitch (-stich′) ***vt., vi.*** *Sewing* to overcast or whip —***n.*** a stitch made in this way

whip·stock (-stäk′) ***n.*** the handle of a whip

whir, whirr (hwʉr, wʉr) ***vi., vt.*** **whirred, whir′ring** [prob. < Scand.] to fly, revolve, vibrate, etc. with a whizzing or buzzing sound —***n.*** a sound like this, as of a propeller

whirl (hwʉrl, wʉrl) ***vi.*** [ON. *hvirfla*] **1.** to move rapidly in a circular manner or as in an orbit **2.** to rotate or spin fast; gyrate **3.** to move, go, etc. swiftly **4.** to seem to spin; reel [my head is *whirling*] —***vt.*** **1.** to cause to rotate, revolve, etc. rapidly **2.** to move, carry, etc. with a rotating motion [the wind *whirled* the leaves] —***n.*** **1.** the act of whirling **2.** a whirling motion **3.** something whirling or being whirled **4.** a round of parties, etc. **5.** a tumult; uproar; stir **6.** a confused or giddy condition [my head is in a *whirl*] —**give it a whirl** [Colloq.] to make an attempt —**whirl′er** ***n.***

whirl·i·gig (hwʉr′li gig′, wʉr′-) ***n.*** [see WHIRL & GIG[1]] **1.** a child's toy that whirls or spins **2.** a merry-go-round **3.** a whirling motion

whirl·pool (hwʉrl′po͞ol′, wʉrl′-) ***n.*** **1.** water in rapid, violent, whirling motion tending to form a circle into which floating objects are drawn; eddy of water **2.** anything like a whirlpool, as in violent motion

whirlpool bath a bath, as used in hydrotherapy, in which an agitating device causes a current of warm water to swirl around

whirl·wind (-wind′) ***n.*** **1.** a current of air whirling violently upward in a spiral that has a forward motion **2.** anything resembling a whirlwind, as in violent or destructive force, etc. —***adj.*** carried on as fast as possible [a *whirlwind* courtship]

whirl·y·bird (hwʉr′lē bʉrd′, wʉr′-) ***n.*** *colloq. term for* HELICOPTER

whish (hwish, wish) ***vi.*** [echoic] to move with a soft, rushing sound; whiz; swish —***n.*** a sound so made

whisk (hwisk, wisk) ***n.*** [ON. *visk*, a brush] **1.** *a)* the act of brushing with a quick, light, sweeping motion *b)* such a motion **2.** a small bunch of straw, hair, etc. used for brushing **3.** a kitchen utensil consisting of wire loops fixed in a handle, for whipping eggs, etc. —***vt.*** **1.** to move, remove, brush (*away, off, out*, etc.) with a quick, sweeping motion **2.** [Chiefly Brit.] to whip (eggs, cream, etc.) —***vi.*** to move quickly, nimbly, or briskly

whisk broom a small, short-handled broom for brushing clothes, etc.

whisk·er (hwis′kər, wis′-) ***n.*** [see WHISK & -ER] **1.** [*pl.*] the hair growing on a man's face; esp., the beard on the cheeks **2.** *a)* a hair of a man's beard *b)* any of the long, bristly hairs growing on the upper lip of a cat, rat, etc. —**whisk′ered, whisk′er·y** ***adj.***

whis·key (hwis′kē, wis′kē) ***n.**, pl.* **-keys, -kies** [short for *usquebaugh* < IrGael. *uisce*, water + *beathadh*, life] **1.** a strong alcoholic liquor distilled from the fermented mash of grain, esp. of rye, wheat, corn, or barley **2.** a drink of whiskey —***adj.*** of, for, or made with whiskey Also sp. **whis′ky**, *pl.* **-kies** *Note:* in the U.S. and Ireland, the usual spelling is **whiskey**; in Great Britain and Canada, it is **whisky**

whis·per (hwis′pər, wis′-) ***vi.*** [OE. *hwisprian*] **1.** to speak very softly, esp. without vibration of the vocal cords **2.** to talk in a quiet or sneaky way, as in gossiping or plotting **3.** to make a soft, rustling sound —***vt.*** **1.** to say very softly, esp. by whispering **2.** to tell as a secret —***n.*** **1.** a whispering; soft, low speech produced with breath but, usually, without voice **2.** something whispered; a secret, hint, rumor, etc. **3.** a soft, rustling sound —**whis′per·er** ***n.*** —**whis′per·ing** ***adj., n.*** —**whis′per·ing·ly** ***adv.*** —**whis′per·y** ***adj.***

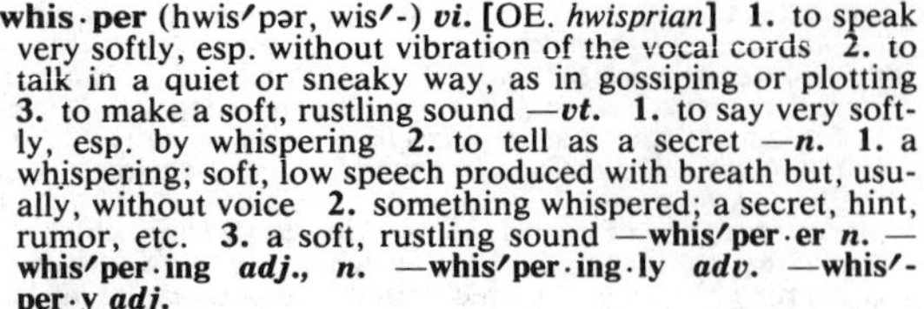

whispering campaign the spreading, by word of mouth, of nasty rumors intended to discredit a political candidate, cause, etc.

whist[1] (hwist, wist) ***interj.*** [echoic] [Archaic or Dial.] hush! silence! —***vt., vi.*** to be or become quiet

whist[2] (hwist, wist) ***n.*** [< earlier *whisk*] a card game usually played by two pairs of players, similar to, and the forerunner of, bridge

whis·tle (hwis′'l, wis′-) ***vi.*** **-tled, -tling** [OE. *hwistlian*] **1.** *a)* to make a clear, shrill sound by forcing breath between the teeth or through puckered lips *b)* to make a similar sound by sending steam through a small opening **2.** to make a clear, shrill cry: said of some birds and animals **3.** to move, pass, go, etc. with a high, shrill sound, as the wind **4.** *a)* to blow a whistle *b)* to have its whistle blown, as a train —***vt.*** **1.** to produce (a tune, etc.) by whistling **2.** to summon, signal, etc. by whistling —***n.*** **1.** an instrument for making whistling sounds **2.** the act or sound of whistling —**wet one's whistle** to take a drink —**whistle for** to seek or expect in vain —**whistle in the dark** to pretend to be confident —**whis′tler** ***n.*** —**whis′tling** ***adj., n.***

Whis·tler (hwis′lər, wis′-), **James Ab·bott Mc·Neill** (ab′ət mək nēl′) 1834–1903; U.S. painter & etcher in England —**Whis·tle′ri·an** (-lir′ē ən) ***adj.***

whistle stop **1.** a small town, orig. one at which a train stopped only upon signal **2.** a brief stop in a small town as part of a tour, esp. in a political campaign —**whis′tle-stop′** ***vi.*** **-stopped′, -stop′ping**

whit (hwit, wit) ***n.*** [Early ModE. resp. of OE. *wiht*, a wight] the least bit; jot; iota: chiefly in negative constructions [not a *whit* the wiser]

white (hwīt, wīt) ***adj.*** **whit′er, whit′est** [OE. *hwit*] **1.** having the color of pure snow or milk; of the color of reflected light containing all of the visible rays of the spectrum: opposite to black: see COLOR **2.** of a light or pale color; specif., *a)* gray; silvery *b)* very blond *c)* pale; wan [a face *white* with terror] *d)* light-yellow or amber [*white* wines] *e)* blank, as a space unmarked by printing *f)* snowy **3.** colorless [*white* creme de menthe] **4.** clothed in white [the *White* Friars] **5.** pure; innocent **6.** free from evil intent; harmless [*white* magic] **7.** *a)* having a light-colored skin; Caucasoid *b)* of or controlled by Caucasoids **8.** [Slang] honest; fair —***n.*** **1.** white color **2.** the state of being white; specif., *a)* fairness of complexion *b)* purity; innocence **3.** a white or light-colored part or thing, as the albumen of an egg, the white part of the eyeball, the light-colored part of meat, wood, etc., a white garment, white wine, white pigment, etc. **4.** a person with a light-colored skin; Caucasoid —***vt.*** **whit′ed, whit′ing** to make white; whiten —**bleed white** to drain (a person) completely of money, resources, etc. —**white′ly** ***adv.*** —**white′ness** ***n.***

white ant *popular name for* TERMITE

white·bait (-bāt′) ***n.**, pl.* **-bait′** **1.** any of various small, silvery European fishes, as young herring, used as food **2.** a smelt of the Pacific coast of N. America

white bass (bas) a silvery, freshwater, food and game fish of eastern N. America

white birch **1.** *same as* PAPER BIRCH **2.** a European birch with silvery-white bark, widely grown in the U.S.

white blood cell *same as* LEUKOCYTE: also called **white blood corpuscle**

white bread bread of a light color, made from finely sifted wheat flour

white bush (scallop) a variety of summer squash having a saucer-shaped, white fruit, scalloped around the edges

white·cap (-kap′) ***n.*** a wave with its crest broken into white foam

white cedar **1.** *a)* an evergreen tree growing in swampy land in the eastern U.S. *b)* its soft, light-colored wood, used for shingles, etc. **2.** *a)* the American arborvitae, growing in the northeastern U.S. *b)* its soft, brittle wood

white clover a creeping species of clover with white flower clusters, grown as a forage plant

white-col·lar (-käl′ər) ***adj.*** [from the formerly typical white shirt worn by such workers] designating or of clerical or professional workers or the like

whited sepulcher a hypocrite: Matt. 23:27

white elephant **1.** an albino elephant, regarded as sacred by the Thais, Burmese, etc. **2.** something that is of little profit or use but costs a lot to maintain **3.** any object that its owner no longer wants to keep but that others may want to own or buy

white feather [from belief that a white feather in a gamecock's tail shows bad breeding, hence cowardice] an indication of cowardice: chiefly in **show the white feather**
white·fish (-fish′) ***n.***, *pl.* **-fish′, -fish′es:** see FISH **1.** any of various white or silvery food fishes of the salmon family, found in the lakes of the northern U.S. and Canada **2.** any of various other whitish fishes, as the **ocean whitefish** of southern California waters **3.** *same as* BELUGA (sense 2)
white flag a white banner or cloth hoisted as a signal of truce or surrender
white·fly (-flī′) ***n.***, *pl.* **-flies′** any of various tiny whitish insects, often harmful to plants
White Friar a Carmelite friar: so called from the white mantle worn by these friars
white gold gold alloyed with nickel, zinc, etc., to give it a white, platinumlike appearance for use in jewelry
white-haired (-herd′) ***adj.*** **1.** having white or very light hair **2.** [Colloq.] *same as* FAIR-HAIRED (sense 2)
White·hall (hwīt′hôl′, wīt′-) a street in London, site of several government offices —***n.*** the British government
white heat **1.** the degree of intense heat (beyond red heat) at which metal, etc. glows white **2.** a state of intense emotion, excitement, etc.
White·horse (hwīt′hôrs′, wīt′-) capital of the Yukon Territory, Canada, in the S part: pop. 13,000
white-hot (hwīt′hät′, wīt′-) ***adj.*** **1.** glowing white with heat **2.** extremely angry, excited, enthusiastic, etc.
White House, the **1.** official residence of the President of the U.S.: a white mansion in Washington, D.C. **2.** the executive branch of the U.S. government
white lead **1.** a poisonous, heavy, white powder, basic lead carbonate, $2PbCO_3 \cdot Pb(OH)_2$, used as a paint pigment, for pottery glazes, etc. **2.** any of several white pigments containing lead, as lead sulfate
white lie a lie about something unimportant, often one told to spare someone's feelings
white light *Physics* light, as sunlight, composed of rays of all the wavelengths ranging from red to violet
white lightning [Slang] homemade whiskey, esp. corn whiskey, usually unaged and strong and typically colorless
white-liv·ered (-liv′ərd) ***adj.*** cowardly; craven
white matter whitish nerve tissue of the brain and spinal cord, consisting chiefly of nerve fibers
white meat any light-colored meat, as veal, pork, the breast of poultry, etc.
White Mountains [from the appearance of the higher peaks] range of the Appalachian system, in N N.H.
whit·en (hwīt′′n, wīt′-) ***vt., vi.*** to make or become white or whiter —**whit′en·er** ***n.*** —**whit′en·ing** ***n.***
white oak **1.** any of a number of oaks having whitish or grayish bark and hard wood **2.** the wood of any such tree, used in barrels, furniture, etc.
white·out (-out′) ***n.*** a weather condition occurring in polar regions in which the snowy ground and white sky merge so that one's sense of direction and distance disappears
white pepper pepper ground from the husked, dried seeds of the nearly ripe pepper berry
white pine **1.** *a)* a pine of eastern N. America, with needles in bundles of five and soft, light wood *b)* this wood **2.** any of various pines with needles in bundles of five
White Plains [? after the AmInd. *quaropas,* white marshes] city in SE N.Y., near New York City: pop. 47,000
white poplar **1.** a large old-world poplar having lobed leaves with white or gray down on the undersides, now widespread in the U.S. **2.** *same as: a)* TULIP TREE *b)* TULIPWOOD (sense 1)
white potato *same as* POTATO (sense 2 *a*)
white race loosely, the Caucasoid group of mankind
White Russia *same as* BYELORUSSIAN SOVIET SOCIALIST REPUBLIC
White Russian **1.** a native or inhabitant of White Russia; Byelorussian **2.** any of the Russians who fought against the Bolsheviks (Reds) in the Russian civil war
white sale a sale of sheets, towels, linens, etc. held in a store
white sauce a sauce for vegetables, meat, fish, etc., made of fat or butter, flour, milk or stock, and seasoning
White Sea arm of the Arctic Ocean, extending into NW U.S.S.R.
white slave a woman enticed or forced into or held in prostitution for the profit of others —**white′-slave′** ***adj.*** —**white slaver** —**white slavery**
white-tailed deer (-tāld′) a common American deer having a tail that is white on the undersurface, a white-spotted red coat in summer, and a brownish-gray coat in winter: also **white′tail′** ***n.***
white tie **1.** a white bow tie, properly worn with a swallow-tailed coat **2.** a swallow-tailed coat and its accessories
white·wall (-wôl′) ***adj.*** designating or of a pneumatic tire with a circular white band on the outer sidewall: also **white′-wall′** —***n.*** a whitewall tire
white·wash (-wôsh′, -wäsh′) ***n.*** **1.** a mixture of lime, whiting, size, water, etc., for whitening walls, etc. **2.** *a)* a concealing of faults or defects as in an effort to avoid blame *b)* something said or done for this purpose **3.** [Colloq.] *Sports* a defeat in which the loser scores no points —***vt.*** **1.** to cover with whitewash **2.** to conceal the faults or defects of **3.** [Colloq.] *Sports* to defeat (an opponent) without permitting him to score —**white′wash′er** ***n.*** —**white′wash′ing** ***n.***
white whale *same as* BELUGA (sense 2)
whith·er (hwith′ər, with′-) ***adv.*** [OE. *hwider*] to what place, condition, etc.? where? —***conj.*** **1.** to which place, condition, etc. **2.** wherever *Where* is now almost always used in place of *whither*
whit·ing¹ (hwīt′iŋ, wīt′-) ***n.***, *pl.* **-ings, -ing:** see PLURAL, II, D, 1 [MDu. *wijting* < *wit,* white] any of numerous unrelated ocean food fishes of N. America, Europe, and Australia, including several hakes and kingfishes
whit·ing² (hwīt′iŋ, wīt′-) ***n.*** [see WHITE, *v.* + -ING] powdered chalk used in making paints, inks, etc.
whit·ish (-ish) ***adj.*** somewhat white —**whit′ish·ness** ***n.***
whit·low (hwit′lō, wit′-) ***n.*** [ME. *whitflawe:* of disputed origin] *same as* FELON²
Whit·man (hwit′mən, wit′-), **Walt(er)** 1819–92; U.S. poet
Whit·ney (hwit′nē, wit′-), **Eli** 1765–1825; U.S. inventor, esp. of the cotton gin
Whit·ney (hwit′nē), **Mount** [after J. *Whitney* (1819–96), U.S. geologist] mountain of the Sierra Nevada Range, EC Calif.: highest in the U.S. outside of Alas., 14,495 ft.
Whit·sun (hwit′s'n, wit′-) ***adj.*** of or observed on Whitsunday or at Whitsuntide
Whit·sun·day (hwit′sun′dē, wit′-; -dā; -s'n dā′) ***n.*** [OE. *Hwita Sunnandæg,* white Sunday] *same as* PENTECOST (sense 2)
Whit·sun·tide (-s'n tīd′) ***n.*** the week beginning with Whitsunday, esp. the first three days of that week
Whit·ti·er (hwit′ē ər, wit′-) [after ff.] city in SW Calif.: suburb of Los Angeles: pop. 69,000
Whit·ti·er (hwit′ē ər, wit′-), **John Green·leaf** (grēn′lēf′) 1807–92; U.S. poet
whit·tle (hwit′′l, wit′-) ***vt.*** **-tled, -tling** [OE. *thwitan,* to cut] **1.** *a)* to cut thin shavings from (wood) with a knife *b)* to carve (an object) in this manner **2.** to reduce, destroy, etc. gradually, as if by whittling: usually with *down, away,* etc. *[to whittle down costs]* —***vi.*** to whittle wood —**whit′tler** ***n.***
whit·y (hwīt′ē, wīt′-) ***adj.*** **whit′i·er, whit′i·est** *same as* WHITISH
whiz, whizz (hwiz, wiz) ***vi.*** **whizzed, whiz′zing** [echoic] **1.** to make the buzzing or hissing sound of something moving swiftly through the air **2.** to speed by with or as with this sound *[the bus whizzed by him]* —***vt.*** to cause to whiz —***n.*** **1.** a whizzing sound or movement **2.** [Slang] a person who is very adroit or skilled at something *[a whiz at math]*
who (hōō) ***pron.***, obj. **whom,** poss. **whose** [OE. *hwa*] **1.** what or which person or persons: used to introduce a question *[who is he? I don't know who he is]* **2.** *a)* (the, or a, person or persons) that: used to introduce a relative clause *[the man who came to dinner]* *b)* any person or persons that: used as an indefinite relative *["who steals my purse steals trash"]* The use of *who* rather than *whom* as the object of a verb or preposition *[who did you see? who was it written by?],* although widespread, is objected to by some —**who's who** the important people are
WHO World Health Organization
whoa (hwō, wō, hō) ***interj.*** [for HO] stop!: used esp. in directing a horse to stand still
who·dun·it (hōō dun′it) ***n.*** [Colloq.] a mystery novel, play, etc.: cf. MYSTERY¹ (sense 2 *b*)
who·ev·er (-ev′ər) ***pron.*** **1.** any person that; whatever person **2.** no matter what person *[whoever said it, it's not so]* **3.** what person? who?: used for emphasis *[whoever told you that?]*
whole (hōl) ***adj.*** [OE. *hal*] **1.** healthy; not diseased or injured **2.** not broken, damaged, defective, etc.; intact **3.** containing all the elements or parts; complete **4.** not divided up; in a single unit **5.** constituting the entire amount, extent, etc. *[the whole week]* **6.** having both parents in common *[a whole brother]* **7.** in all aspects of one's being *[the whole man]* **8.** *Arith.* not mixed or fractional *[25 is a whole number]* —***n.*** **1.** the entire amount, etc.; totality **2.** a complete organization of parts; unity, entirety, etc. —**as a whole** as a complete unit; altogether —**made out of whole cloth** completely fictitious or false —**on the whole** all things considered; in general —**whole′ness** ***n.***
whole·heart·ed (-här′tid) ***adj.*** doing or done with all one's energy, enthusiasm, etc.; sincere —**whole′heart′ed·ly** ***adv.*** —**whole′heart′ed·ness** ***n.***

whole-hog (hōl′hôg′, -häg′) ***adj., adv.*** [Slang] without reservation; complete(ly)

whole milk milk from which none of the butterfat or other elements have been removed

whole note *Music* a note having four times the duration of a quarter note: see NOTE, illus.

whole number zero or any positive or negative multiple of 1; integer *[28 is a whole number]*

whole·sale (hōl′sāl′) ***n.*** the selling of goods in relatively large quantities, esp. to retailers who then sell them at higher prices to consumers *—adj.* **1.** of, connected with, or engaged in such selling **2.** extensive or sweeping *[wholesale criticism]* *—adv.* **1.** in wholesale amounts or at wholesale prices **2.** extensively or sweepingly *—vt., vi.* **-saled′, -sal′ing** to sell wholesale **—at wholesale** in wholesale quantities or at wholesale prices **—whole′sal′er** ***n.***

whole·some (-səm) ***adj.*** [see WHOLE & -SOME[1]] **1.** good for one's health or well-being; healthful *[wholesome food]* **2.** tending to improve the mind or character **3.** full of health and vigor **4.** suggesting health *[a wholesome smile]* **—whole′some·ly** ***adv.*** **—whole′some·ness** ***n.***

whole tone *Music* an interval consisting of two adjacent semitones: also **whole step**

whole-wheat (-hwēt′) ***adj.*** **1.** made of the entire cleaned kernels of wheat *[whole-wheat flour]* **2.** made of whole-wheat flour *[whole-wheat bread]*

who'll (ho͞ol) **1.** who shall **2.** who will

whol·ly (hō′lē, hōl′lē) ***adv.*** to the whole amount or extent; totally; entirely

whom (ho͞om) ***pron.*** *objective case of* WHO: see note at WHO on the use of *who* and *whom*

whom·ev·er (ho͞om ev′ər) ***pron.*** *objective case of* WHOEVER

whomp (hwämp) ***vt.*** [echoic] **1.** to beat, strike, thump, etc. **2.** to defeat decisively *—n.* the act or sound of whomping

whom·so·ev·er (ho͞om′sō ev′ər) ***pron.*** *objective case of* WHOSOEVER

whoof (hwo͝of, wo͝of) ***n.*** [echoic] a deep, abrupt, breathy sound *[the bear's startled whoof]* *—vi.* to make this sound *—interj.* an exclamation of relief, surprise, etc.

whoop (ho͞op, hwo͞op, wo͞op, wo͝op) ***n.*** [OFr. *houper,* to cry out] **1.** a loud shout, cry, etc., as of excitement, joy, etc. **2.** a hoot, as of an owl **3.** the gasping sound made when a breath of air is taken in following a fit of coughing in whooping cough *—vi., vt.* to utter, or utter with, a whoop or whoops *—interj.* an exclamation of excitement, joy, etc. **—not worth a whoop** [Colloq.] worth nothing at all **—whoop it** (or **things**) **up** [Slang] **1.** to create a noisy disturbance, as in celebrating **2.** to create enthusiasm (*for*) **—whoop′er** ***n.***

whoop-de-do, whoop-de-doo (ho͞op′dē do͞o′, hwo͞op′-) ***n.*** [extended < prec.] [Colloq.] noisy or excited activity, commotion, or fuss; hoopla, ballyhoo, to-do, etc.

whoop·ee (wo͞o′pē, hwo͞o′-, wo͝o′-, hwo͝o′-) ***interj.*** [< prec.] an exclamation of great joy, gay abandonment, etc. *—n.* **1.** a shout of "whoopee!" **2.** noisy fun **—make whoopee** [Slang] to revel or have fun in a noisy way

whoop·ing cough (ho͞o′piŋ, ho͝o′-) an acute infectious disease, usually affecting children, in which there are repeated attacks of coughing that end in a whoop

whooping crane a large, white N. American crane noted for its whooping call: now nearly extinct

whoops (hwo͝ops, wo͝ops, hwo͞ops, wo͞ops) ***interj.*** an exclamation uttered as in regaining one's balance after stumbling or one's composure after a slip of the tongue

whoosh (hwo͝osh, wo͝osh) ***vi., vt.*** [echoic] to make or cause to make a hissing or rushing sound while moving swiftly through the air *—n.* this sound *—interj.* an exclamation imitating this or expressing surprise, fatigue, etc.

whop (hwäp, wäp) ***vt., vi.*** **whopped, whop′ping** [prob. echoic] [Colloq.] **1.** to beat, strike, etc. **2.** to defeat decisively *—n.* [Colloq.] a sharp, loud blow, thump, etc.

whop·per (-ər) ***n.*** [< prec.] [Colloq.] **1.** anything extraordinarily large **2.** a great lie

whop·ping (-iŋ) ***adj.*** [< WHOP + -ING] [Colloq.] extraordinarily large or great; colossal

whore (hôr) ***n.*** [OE. *hore* < or akin to ON. *hora*] a sexually promiscuous woman; esp., a prostitute *—vi.* **whored, whor′·ing** **1.** to be a whore **2.** to fornicate with whores **—whor′·ish** ***adj.***

who're (ho͞o′ər, ho͝or) who are

whore·mon·ger (hôr′muŋ′gər, -mäŋ′gər) ***n.*** a pimp; pander: also **whore′mas′ter**

whorl (hwôrl, wôrl, hwurl, wurl) ***n.*** [< dial. var. of WHIRL] anything with a coiled or spiral appearance; specif., *a)* any of the circular ridges that form the design of a fingerprint *b) Bot.* a circular growth of leaves, petals, etc. about the same point on a stem *c) Zool.* any of the turns in a spiral shell **—whorled** ***adj.***

whor·tle·ber·ry (hwur′t'l ber′ē, wur′-) ***n., pl.*** **-ries** [< Brit. dial. form of earlier *hurtleberry* < OE. *horte*] **1.** *a)* a European plant having pink flowers and blue or blackish berries *b)* any of these berries **2.** *same as* HUCKLEBERRY

who's (ho͞oz) **1.** who is **2.** who has

whose (ho͞oz) ***pron.*** [OE. *hwæs*] that or those belonging to whom *[whose is this?]* ***—possessive pronominal adj.*** of, belonging to, made, or done by whom or which *[the man whose car was stolen]*

who·so (ho͞o′sō) ***pron.*** [OE. *hwa swa*] [Archaic] whoever; whosoever

who·so·ev·er (ho͞o′sō ev′ər) ***pron.*** whoever: used for emphasis

whr. watt-hour

why (hwī, wī) ***adv.*** [OE. *hwi,* instrumental case of *hwæt,* what] for what reason, cause, or purpose? *[why did he go? he told her why he went]* *—conj.* **1.** because of which *[there is no reason why you should go]* **2.** the reason for which *[that is why he went]* *—n., pl.* **whys** the reason, cause, etc. *[never mind the why]* *—interj.* an exclamation used to show surprise, impatience, etc. or to introduce a remark

WI Wisconsin

Wich·i·ta (wich′ə tô′) [< AmInd.] city in S Kans., on the Arkansas River: pop. 279,000

Wichita Falls [see prec.] city in NC Tex.: pop. 94,000

wick (wik) ***n.*** [OE. *weoca*] a piece of cord or tape, or a thin bundle of threads, in a candle, oil lamp, etc., that absorbs the fuel and, when lighted, burns with a steady flame

wick·ed (wik′id) ***adj.*** [ME. < *wikke,* evil, akin to OE. *wicce,* witch] **1.** morally bad or wrong; acting or done with evil intent **2.** generally painful, unpleasant, etc. *[a wicked blow on the head]* **3.** naughty; mischievous **4.** [Slang] skillful *[he plays a wicked game of golf]* **—wick′ed·ly** ***adv.*** **—wick′ed·ness** ***n.***

wick·er (wik′ər) ***n.*** [< Scand.] **1.** a thin, flexible twig; withe **2.** *a)* such twigs or long, woody strips woven together, as in making baskets or furniture *b) same as* WICKERWORK (sense 1) *—adj.* made of wicker

wick·er·work (-wurk′) ***n.*** **1.** things made of wicker **2.** *same as* WICKER (sense 2 *a*)

wick·et (wik′it) ***n.*** [ONormFr. *wiket* < Gmc.] **1.** a small door or gate, esp. one set in or near a larger one **2.** a small window or opening, as in a box office **3.** a small gate for regulating the flow of water, as to a water wheel **4.** *Cricket a)* either of two sets of three stumps each, with two bails resting on top of them *b)* the playing space between the two wickets *c)* a player's turn at bat **5.** *Croquet* any of the wire arches through which the balls must be hit; hoop

wick·et·keep·er (-kē′pər) ***n.*** *Cricket* the fielder stationed immediately behind the wicket

Wick·liffe, Wic·lif (wik′lif) *variants of* WYCLIFFE

wide (wīd) ***adj.*** **wid′er, wid′est** [OE. *wid*] **1.** extending over a large area; esp., extending over a larger area from side to side than is usual **2.** of a specified extent from side to side *[two miles wide]* **3.** of great extent, range, etc. *[a wide variety]* **4.** roomy; ample; full *[wide pants]* **5.** opened as far as possible *[eyes wide with fear]* **6.** far from the point, issue, etc. aimed at *[wide of the mark]* *—adv.* **1.** over a relatively large area; widely **2.** to a large or full extent; fully *[wide open]* **3.** so as to miss the point, issue, etc. aimed at; astray **—wide′ly** ***adv.*** **—wide′ness** ***n.***

-wide (wīd) *a combining form meaning* existing or extending throughout *[nationwide]*

wide-an·gle (wīd′aŋ′g'l) ***adj.*** **1.** designating or of a kind of camera lens covering a wide angle of view **2.** designating or of any of several systems using one or more movie cameras (and projectors) and a very wide, curved screen

wide-a·wake (-ə wāk′) ***adj.*** **1.** completely awake **2.** alert **—wide′-a·wake′ness** ***n.***

wide-eyed (-īd′) ***adj.*** with the eyes wide open

wid·en (wīd′'n) ***vt., vi.*** to make or become wide or wider

wide-o·pen (wīd′ō′p'n) ***adj.*** **1.** opened wide **2.** not having or enforcing laws against prostitution, gambling, liquor sales, etc. *[a wide-open city]*

wide receiver *Football* a player eligible to receive a pass who takes a position at some distance from the rest of the offensive team

wide·spread (-spred′) ***adj.*** spread widely; esp., *a)* widely extended *[with widespread arms]* *b)* occurring over a wide area or extent *[widespread benefits]*

widg·eon (wij′ən) ***n., pl.*** **-eons, -eon:** see PLURAL, II, D, 1 [prob. < MFr. *vigeon*] any of various wild, freshwater ducks having a head with a cream-colored or white crown

wid·get (wij′it) ***n.*** [altered < GADGET] a small gadget or device, esp. one without a specific description

wid·ow (wid′ō) ***n.*** [OE. *widewe*] **1.** a woman whose husband has died and who has not remarried **2.** *Cards* a group of cards dealt to the table, typically for the use of the highest bidder **3.** *Printing* an incomplete line, as that ending a paragraph, carried over to the top of a new page or column **4.** [Colloq.] a woman whose husband is often away *[a golf widow]* *—vt.* to cause to become a widow *[widowed by the war]* **—wid′ow·hood′** ***n.***

wid·ow·er (wid′ə wər) ***n.*** a man whose wife has died and who has not remarried

widow's mite a small gift or contribution freely given by one who can scarcely afford it: Mark 12:41–44

widow's peak a point formed by hair growing down in the middle of a forehead
width (width, witth) *n.* [< WIDE, by analogy with LENGTH] **1.** a being wide; wideness **2.** the distance from side to side **3.** a piece having a certain width *[two widths of cloth]*
wield (wēld) *vt.* [OE. *wealdan* & *wieldan*] **1.** to handle and use (a tool or weapon), esp. with skill and control **2.** to exercise (power, influence, etc.) —**wield′er** *n.*
wield·y (wēl′dē) *adj.* **wield′i·er, wield′i·est** that can be wielded easily; manageable
Wien (vēn) *Ger. name of* VIENNA
wie·ner (wē′nər) *n.* [short for G. *Wiener wurst,* Vienna sausage] a smoked link sausage of beef or beef and pork; frankfurter: also **wie′ner·wurst′** (-wurst′)
Wies·ba·den (vēs′bäd′'n) city in W West Germany, on the Rhine: pop. 261,000
wife (wīf) *n., pl.* **wives** (wīvz) [OE. *wif*] **1.** orig., a woman: still so used in *midwife, housewife,* etc. **2.** a married woman —**take to wife** to marry (a specified woman) —**wife′hood′** *n.* —**wife′less** *adj.* —**wife′ly** *adj.* **-li·er, -li·est**
wig (wig) *n.* [shortened < PERIWIG] **1.** *a)* a false covering of real or synthetic hair for the head, worn as part of a costume, to hide baldness, etc. *b) same as* TOUPEE **2.** [Slang] the hair, head, or mind —*vt.* **wigged, wig′ging 1.** to furnish with a wig or wigs **2.** [Slang] *a)* to annoy, upset, anger, etc. *b)* to make excited, frenzied, crazy, etc. (often with *out*) **3.** [Brit. Colloq.] to scold, rebuke, etc. —*vi.* [Slang] to be or become wigged, or upset, frenzied, etc. (often with *out*) —**wig′less** *adj.*
wi·geon (wij′ən) *n. var. of* WIDGEON
wig·gle (wig′'l) *vt., vi.* **-gled, -gling** [prob. < MDu. & MLowG. *wiggelen,* freq. of *wiggen,* to move from side to side] to move with short, jerky or twisting motions from side to side —*n.* the act or an instance of wiggling
wig·gler (wig′lər) *n.* **1.** a person or thing that wiggles **2.** the larva of a mosquito; wriggler
wig·gly (-lē) *adj.* **-gli·er, -gli·est 1.** that wiggles; wiggling **2.** wavy *[a wiggly line]*
wig·gy (wig′ē) *adj.* **-gi·er, -gi·est** [Slang] wild, exciting, crazy, etc.
wight (wīt) *n.* [OE. *wiht*] [Archaic] a human being; person: now sometimes used in a patronizing way
Wight (wīt), **Isle of** island in the English Channel, off the S coast of England, that is an English county
wig·let (wig′lit) *n.* a small wig; specif., a woman's hairpiece for use along with her own hair
wig·wag (wig′wag′) *vt., vi.* **-wagged′, -wag′ging** [< obs. *wig,* to move + WAG[1]] **1.** to move back and forth; wag **2.** to send (a message) by waving flags, lights, etc. back and forth in accordance with a code —*n.* **1.** the sending of messages in this way **2.** a message so sent
wig·wam (wig′wäm, -wôm) *n.* [< Algonquian] a dwelling made by the Indians of E and C N. America, consisting typically of a framework of arched poles covered with bark

WIGWAM

Wil·ber·force (wil′bər fôrs′), **William** 1759–1833; Eng. statesman & vigorous opponent of slavery
Wil·bur (wil′bər) [OE. *Wilburh:* prob. < a place name meaning "willow town"] a masculine name
wil·co (wil′kō) *interj.* [*wil(l) co(mply)*] I will comply with your request: used in radiotelephony
wild (wīld) *adj.* [OE. *wilde*] **1.** living or growing in its original, natural state; not domesticated or cultivated *[wild flowers, wild animals]* **2.** not lived in or cultivated; overgrown, waste, etc. *[wild land]* **3.** not civilized; savage *[a wild tribe]* **4.** not controlled; unruly, rough, lawless, etc. *[wild children]* **5.** lacking social or moral restraint; dissolute, orgiastic, etc. *[a wild rake, a wild party]* **6.** turbulent; stormy *[wild seas]* **7.** *a)* very excited or enthusiastic *[wild with delight]* *b)* angered, frantic, crazed, etc. *[wild with desperation]* **8.** in a state of disorder, confusion, etc. *[wild hair]* **9.** reckless, fantastic, crazy, etc. *[a wild scheme]* **10.** missing the target *[a wild shot]* **11.** *Cards* having any value specified by the holder: said of a card —*adv.* in a wild manner *[to shoot wild]* —*n.* [*usually pl.*] a wilderness or wasteland —**run wild** to grow, exist, or behave in an uncontrolled way —**wild′ly** *adv.* —**wild′ness** *n.*
wild boar a variety of hog living wild in Europe, Asia, and Africa, from which domestic hogs have been derived
wild-card (kärd) *adj. Sports* designating or of any of the teams, other than those that finish in first and sometimes second place, that qualify for a championship play-off
wild carrot a common weed, with finely divided leaves and white flower umbels: the ancestor of the garden carrot
wild·cat (wīld′kat′) *n., pl.* **-cats′, -cat′:** see PLURAL, II, D, 1 **1.** *a)* any of various fierce, medium-sized, undomesticated animals of the cat family, as the lynx or bobcat *b)* a house cat that has escaped from domestication: in this sense, usually **wild cat 2.** a fierce, aggressive person **3.** an unsound or risky business scheme **4.** an oil well drilled in an area not known before to have oil **5.** *Naut.* a drum on a windlass, that engages chain cable links **6.** *Railroading* a locomotive and tender without cars —*adj.* **1.** unsound or financially risky **2.** *a)* operating in an illegal or unethical way *b)* not officially authorized *[a wildcat strike]* —*vi.* **-cat′ted, -cat′ting 1.** to drill for oil in an area considered unproductive before **2.** to engage in wildcat enterprises —**wild′cat′ter** *n.*
Wilde (wīld), **Oscar (Fingal O'Flahertie Wills)** 1854–1900; Brit. playwright, poet, & novelist, born in Ireland
wil·de·beest (wil′də bēst′, vil′-) *n., pl.* **-beests′, -beest′:** see PLURAL, II, D, 1 [Afrik. < Du. *wild,* wild + *beeste,* beast] *same as* GNU
wil·der·ness (wil′dər nis) *n.* [< ME. *wilderne,* wild place (< OE. < *wilde,* wild + *deor,* animal) + *-nesse,* -NESS] **1.** wasteland or overgrown land with no settlers **2.** a large, confused mass or tangle of persons or things
wild-eyed (wīld′īd′) *adj.* **1.** staring in a wild, distracted, or demented way **2.** fantastically impractical
wild·fire (-fīr′) *n.* a fire that spreads fast and is hard to put out *[the rumors spread like wildfire]*
wild·flow·er (-flou′ər) *n.* any flowering plant growing without cultivation in fields, woods, etc. Also **wild flower**
wild·fowl (-foul′) *n., pl.* **-fowls′, -fowl′:** see PLURAL, II, D, 1 a wild bird, esp. a game bird: also **wild fowl**
wild-goose chase (-gōōs′) any search or undertaking as futile as trying to catch a wild goose by chasing it
wild·life (wīld′līf′) *n.* wild animals and birds, collectively
wild oats any of several wild grasses, having twisted awns and occurring as a weed in the western U.S.: also **wild oat** —**sow one's wild oats** to be sexually promiscuous in youth before settling down: usually said of a man
wild pansy an uncultivated pansy, esp. a European species with petals in combinations of white, yellow, and purple
wild pitch *Baseball* a pitch too erratic for the catcher to control, allowing a runner to advance to another base
wild rice 1. a tall grass of the U.S. and Canada, found in swampy borders of lakes and streams **2.** its edible grain
wild rose any of various roses growing wild, as eglantine
Wild West [*also* **w- W-**] the western U.S. in its early frontier period of lawlessness
wild·wood (wīld′wood′) *n.* a natural woodland or forest, esp. when unfrequented by man
wile (wīl) *n.* [Late OE. *wil* < OE. *wigle,* magic] **1.** a sly trick; stratagem **2.** a beguiling or coquettish trick *Usually used in pl.* —*vt.* **wiled, wil′ing** to beguile; lure —**wile away** to while away (time): by confusion with *while*
Wil·fred, Wil·frid (wil′frid) [< OE. < *willa,* a wish, WILL[1] + *frith,* peace] a masculine name
wil·ful (wil′fəl) *adj. var. of* WILLFUL
Wil·hel·mi·na (wil′hel mē′nə; *Du.* vil′hel mē′nä) [< G. fem. of *Wilhelm:* see WILLIAM] **1.** a feminine name **2.** (*Wilhelmina Helena Pauline Maria*) 1880–1962; queen of the Netherlands (1890–1948)
Wilkes-Bar·re (wilks′bar′ē, -ber′ē; -ə) [after J. *Wilkes,* 18th-c. Eng. political reformer & Col. I. *Barré,* Brit. officer] city in NE Pa.: pop. 52,000
will[1] (wil) *n.* [OE. *willa*] **1.** the power of making a reasoned choice or decision or of controlling one's own actions **2.** *a)* strong and fixed purpose; determination *[where there's a will there's a way]* *b)* energy and enthusiasm *[to work with a will]* **3.** attitude toward others *[good will]* **4.** *a)* the desire, purpose, choice, etc. of a certain person or group *[what is your will?]* *b)* a compelling command or decree *[the will of the people]* **5.** *a)* the legal statement of a person's wishes concerning the disposal of his property after death *b)* the document containing this —*vt.* **1.** to have as the object of one's will **2.** to control or influence by the power of the will **3.** to bequeath by a will —*vi.* **1.** to exert one's will **2.** to choose or prefer —**at will** when one wishes —**will′a·ble** *adj.* —**will′-less** *adj.*
will[2] (wil; *unstressed* wəl) *v., pt.* **would** [OE. *willan*] **1.** an auxiliary regularly used to express the future: in the rules of some grammarians, esp. formerly, *will* is to be used in the second and third persons for simple future and in the first person to show determination or obligation, and *shall* is to be used in the first person for simple future and in the second and third persons to show determination or obligation: in actual practice *will* and *shall* are used interchangeably, with *will* more common in all persons **2.** an auxiliary

used to express: *a)* willingness [*will* you do me a favor?] *b)* ability or capacity [it *will* hold another quart] *c)* habit, custom, inclination, or inevitability [boys *will* be boys] *d)* expectation, surmise, etc. [that *will* be his wife with him, I suppose] See also SHALL *—pt., vi.* to wish; desire [do what (or as) you *will*]

will call the department, as of a large store, at which articles are held to be picked up, as when paid for

willed (wild) ***adj.*** having a will, esp. a specified kind of will: used in hyphenated compounds [strong-*willed*]

will·ful (wil′fəl) ***adj.*** **1.** done deliberately or intentionally **2.** always wanting one's own way; doing as one pleases; self-willed **—will′ful·ly *adv.* —will′ful·ness *n.***

Wil·liam (wil′yəm) [< ONormFr. < OHG. < *willeo,* WILL[1] + *helm,* protection] **1.** a masculine name **2. William I** *a)* 1027?–87; duke of Normandy who conquered England (see Battle of HASTINGS); king of England (1066–87): called *William the Conqueror b)* 1533–84; prince of Orange (1544–84); founder of the Netherlands republic: called *William the Silent* **3. William II** 1859–1941; emperor of Germany & king of Prussia (1888–1918): called *Kaiser Wilhelm* **4. William III** 1650–1702; king of England, Scotland, & Ireland (1689–1702): see MARY II

Wil·liams (wil′yəmz) **1. Roger,** 1603?–83; Eng. colonist in America: founder of Rhode Island **2. Tennessee,** (born *Thomas Lanier Williams*) 1914– ; U.S. playwright

Wil·liams·burg (wil′yəmz burg′) [after WILLIAM III] city in SE Va.; colonial capital of Va., now restored to its 18th-cent. appearance

wil·lies (wil′ēz) ***n.pl.*** [< ?] [Slang] a state of nervousness; jitters: with *the*

will·ing (wil′iŋ) ***adj.*** **1.** ready or agreeing (*to* do something) [*willing* to try] **2.** doing, giving, etc. or done, given, etc. readily or gladly **—will′ing·ly *adv.* —will′ing·ness *n.***

wil·li·waw, wil·ly·waw (wil′i wô′) ***n.*** [< ?] a sudden, violent, cold wind blowing down from mountain passes toward the coast in far northern or southern latitudes

will-o'-the-wisp (wil′ə *thə* wisp′) ***n.*** [earlier *Will* (personal name) *with the wisp*] **1.** a light seen moving over marshes at night: see also IGNIS FATUUS **2.** any hope or goal that leads one on but is impossible to reach

wil·low (wil′ō) ***n.*** [OE. *welig*] **1.** *a)* any of a genus of trees and shrubs bearing catkins and usually narrow leaves: the flexible twigs of certain species are used in weaving baskets, chair seats, etc. *b)* the wood of any of these **2.** [orig. made of willow] [Colloq.] a baseball bat or cricket bat

wil·low·y (wil′ə wē) ***adj.*** **1.** covered or shaded with willows **2.** like a willow; specif., slender, supple, lithe, etc.

will·pow·er (wil′pou′ər) ***n.*** strength of will, mind, or determination; self-control

wil·ly-nil·ly (wil′ē nil′ē) ***adv.*** [contr. < *will I, nill I: nill* < OE. *nyllan* < *ne,* not + *willan,* to WILL[1]] whether one wishes it or not; willingly or unwillingly *—adj.* that is or happens whether one wishes it or not

Wil·ming·ton (wil′miŋ tən) [after S. Compton (1673?–1743), Earl of *Wilmington*] seaport in N Del., on the Delaware River: pop. 70,000 (met. area 523,000)

Wil·son (wil′s'n) **1. Edmund,** 1895–1972; U.S. writer & critic **2. (Thomas) Wood·row** (wood′rō), 1856–1924; 28th president of the U.S. (1913–21)

wilt[1] (wilt) ***vi.*** [var. of obs. *welk,* to wither] **1.** to become limp, as from heat or lack of water; wither; droop: said of plants **2.** to become weak or faint; languish **3.** to lose courage; quail *—vt.* to cause to wilt *—n.* a being wilted

wilt[2] (wilt) *archaic 2d pers. sing., pres. indic., of* WILL[2]

Wil·ton (wilt′'n) ***n.*** [< *Wilton,* England, where first made] a kind of carpet with a velvety pile of cut loops: also **Wilton carpet, Wilton rug**

wil·y (wī′lē) ***adj.* wil′i·er, wil′i·est** full of wiles; crafty; sly **—wil′i·ness *n.***

wim·ble (wim′b'l) ***n.*** [< Anglo-Fr. < MDu. *wimmel,* an auger] a tool for boring, as a gimlet, auger, etc.

Wim·ble·don (wim′b'l dən) city in SE England: suburb of London: scene of international lawn tennis matches

wimp (wimp) ***n.*** [< ?] [Slang] a weak, ineffectual, or insipid person **—wimp′y *adj.***

wim·ple (wim′p'l) ***n.*** [OE. *wimpel*] a woman's head covering of medieval times consisting of a cloth arranged about the head, cheeks, chin, and neck: now worn only by certain nuns *—vt.* **-pled, -pling 1.** to clothe as with a wimple **2.** to lay in folds **3.** to cause to ripple *—vi.* **1.** to lie in folds **2.** to ripple

WIMPLE

win (win) ***vi.* won, win′ning** [OE. *winnan,* to fight] **1.** *a)* to gain a victory; be victorious; triumph (sometimes with *out*) *b)* to finish in first place in a race, contest, etc. **2.** to succeed in reaching or achieving a specified state or place (with various prepositions, adverbs, etc.) [to *win* back to health] *—vt.* **1.** to get by effort, struggle, etc.; specif., *a)* to gain through accomplishment [to *win* distinctions] *b)* to achieve (one's point, demands, etc.) *c)* to gain (a prize or award) in competition *d)* to earn (a livelihood, etc.) **2.** to be victorious in (a contest, dispute, etc.) **3.** to get to with effort [they *won* the hilltop by noon] **4.** to influence or persuade: often with *over* [to *win* someone over to one's side] **5.** *a)* to gain the sympathy, favor, etc. of [to *win* a supporter] *b)* to gain (someone's sympathy, etc.) **6.** to persuade to marry one *—n.* **1.** [Colloq.] an act of winning; victory, as in a contest **2.** *Racing* first position at the finish

wince (wins) ***vi.* winced, winc′ing** [< Anglo-Fr. var. of OFr. *guenchir* < Frank.] to draw back slightly, usually grimacing, as in pain *—n.* a wincing **—winc′er *n.***

winch (winch) ***n.*** [OE. *wince*] **1.** a crank with a handle for transmitting motion **2.** a hoisting or hauling apparatus consisting of a drum or cylinder on which is to be wound a rope or cable attached to the object to be lifted or moved *—vt.* to hoist or haul with a winch

Win·ches·ter (rifle) (win′ches′tər, -chis-) [after O. F. *Winchester* (1810–80), U.S. manufacturer] *a trademark for* a type of repeating rifle with a tubular magazine set horizontally under the barrel

wind[1] (wīnd) ***vt.* wound** or rarely **wind′ed, wind′ing** [OE. *windan*] **1.** *a)* to turn, or make revolve [to *wind* a crank] *b)* to move as by cranking **2.** *a)* to coil (string, ribbon, etc.) around itself or around something else [*winding* a bandage around his toe] *b)* to cover by encircling with something [to *wind* a spool with thread] **3.** *a)* to make (one's way) in a winding or twisting course *b)* to make move in such a course **4.** to introduce deviously [*winding* his prejudices throughout] **5.** to hoist or haul as with a winch (often with *up*) **6.** to tighten the spring of (a clock, etc.) as by turning a stem *—vi.* **1.** to move or go in a twisting or curving course **2.** to appear in a way that is circuitous, devious, etc. **3.** to coil or spiral (*about* or *around* something) **4.** to undergo winding [this clock *winds* easily] *—n.* **1.** the act of winding **2.** a single turn of something wound **3.** a turn; twist; bend; curve **—wind up 1.** to wind into a ball, etc. **2.** to entangle or involve **3.** to bring or come to an end; finish **4.** to make very tense, nervous, excited, etc. **5.** *Baseball* to swing the arm in getting ready to pitch the ball **—wind′er *n.***

wind[2] (wind; *for n., also poet.* wīnd) ***n.*** [OE.] **1.** air that is moving **2.** a strong, fast-moving air current; gale **3.** an air current regarded as bearing a scent, as in hunting [to lose (the) *wind* of the fox] **4.** figuratively, air regarded as bearing information, indicating trends, etc. [rumors in the *wind*] **5.** breath or the power of breathing [to get the *wind* knocked out of one] **6.** *a)* idle or empty talk *b)* bragging; pomposity **7.** gas in the stomach or intestines **8.** [*pl.*] the wind instruments of an orchestra, or the players of these *—vt.* **1.** to expose to the wind, as for drying; air **2.** to get or follow the scent of **3.** to put out of breath [to be *winded* by a long run] **4.** to rest (a horse, etc.) so as to allow recovery of breath **—break wind** to expel gas from the bowels **—get** (or **have**) **wind of** to get (or have) information or a hint about **—how the wind blows** (or **lies**) what the trend of affairs, public opinion, etc. is **—in the teeth of the wind** straight against the wind: also **in the wind's eye —in the wind** happening or about to happen **—into the wind** in the direction from which the wind is blowing **—take the wind out of one's sails** to remove one's advantage, nullify one's argument, etc. suddenly **—wind′less *adj.***

wind[3] (wīnd, wind) ***vt., vi.* wound** or rarely **wind′ed, wind′ing** [< prec.] [Poet.] **1.** to blow (a horn, etc.) **2.** to sound (a signal, etc.), as on a horn

wind·age (win′dij) ***n.*** **1.** the disturbance of air around a moving projectile **2.** deflection of a projectile by the wind, or the degree of this

wind·bag (wind′bag′) ***n.*** [Colloq.] a person who talks much and pretentiously but says little of importance

wind·blown (-blōn′) ***adj.*** **1.** blown by the wind **2.** twisted in growth by the prevailing wind: said of a tree

wind-borne (-bôrn′) ***adj.*** carried by the wind, as pollen

wind·break (-brāk′) ***n.*** a hedge, fence, or row of trees that serves as a protection from wind

Wind·break·er (-brā′kər) *a trademark for* a warm sports jacket of leather, wool, etc., having a closefitting elastic waistband and cuffs *—n.* **[w-]** such a jacket

wind·burn (-burn′) ***n.*** a roughened, reddened, sore condition of the skin, caused by overexposure to the wind

wind chimes (or **bells**) a cluster of small chimes or pendants of glass, ceramic, etc., hung so that they strike one another and tinkle when blown by the wind

wind cone *same as* WINDSOCK

wind·fall (-fôl′) ***n.*** **1.** something blown down by the wind, as fruit from a tree **2.** any unexpected money or gain

wind·flaw (-flô′) ***n.*** a gust of wind: see FLAW[2]

wind·flow·er (-flou′ər) ***n.*** *same as* ANEMONE (sense 1)

wind·hov·er (-huv′ər, -häv′-) ***n.*** [Brit.] a kestrel

wind·i·ly (win′də lē) ***adv.*** in a windy manner

wind·i·ness (-dē nis) ***n.*** a windy quality or condition

wind·ing (wīn′diŋ) ***n.*** **1.** the action or effect of a person or thing that winds; a coiling, twining, turn, bend, etc. **2.** something that winds or is wound around an object —***adj.*** that winds, turns, coils, spirals, etc.

winding sheet a cloth in which the body of a dead person is wrapped for burial; shroud

wind instrument (wind) a musical instrument sounded by blowing air, esp. breath, through it, as an oboe

wind·jam·mer (wind′jam′ər) ***n.*** *Naut.* a sailing ship, esp. a large one, or one of its crew

wind·lass (wind′ləs) ***n.*** [ON. *vindass* < *vinda,* to WIND[1] + *ass,* a beam] a winch, esp. a simple one worked by a crank —***vt., vi.*** to hoist, etc. with a windlass

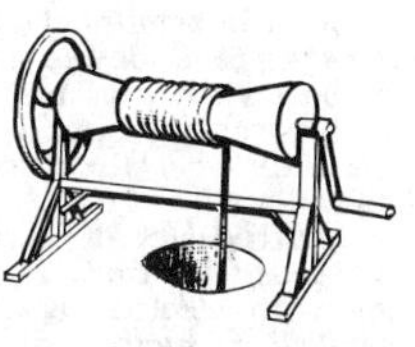
WINDLASS

wind·mill (wind′mil′) ***n.*** a machine made to go by the wind blowing on vanes fixed like spokes of a wheel on a shaft at the top of a tower: it gives power for grinding grain, pumping water, etc. —**fight** (or **tilt at**) **windmills** to fight imaginary opponents: from Don Quixote's mistaking windmills for giants

win·dow (win′dō) ***n.*** [< ON. < *vindr,* WIND[2] + *auga,* an eye] **1.** *a)* an opening in a building, vehicle, etc., to let in light or air or to look through, usually having a pane or panes of glass, etc. set in a frame that is usually movable *b)* any such pane or frame **2.** any similar opening **3.** the transparent panel of a window envelope **4.** any portion of the frequency spectrum of the earth's atmosphere through which light, heat, or radio waves can penetrate to the earth's surface —***vt.*** to provide with a window or windows —**win′dow·less** ***adj.***

window box a long, narrow box on or outside a window ledge, for growing plants

window dressing **1.** the display of goods and trimmings in a store window to attract customers **2.** any display or attempt to make something seem better than it really is

window envelope an envelope with a transparent panel, through which the address on the enclosure can be seen

win·dow·pane (-pān′) ***n.*** a pane of glass in a window

window seat a seat built in beneath a window or windows

window shade a shade for a window, esp. one of stiffened cloth or heavy paper on a roller

win·dow-shop (-shäp′) ***vi.*** **-shopped′, -shop′ping** to look at displays of goods in store windows without entering the stores to buy —**win′dow-shop′per** ***n.***

win·dow·sill (-sil′) ***n.*** the sill of a window

wind·pipe (wind′pīp′) ***n.*** *same as* TRACHEA (sense 1)

wind·proof (-pro͞of′) ***adj.*** that the wind cannot blow through, blow out, etc. *[a windproof lighter]*

wind·row (-rō′) ***n.*** **1.** a row of hay or of grain, etc. raked together to dry **2.** a row of dry leaves, dust, etc. swept together by the wind —***vt.*** to rake or sweep into windrows

wind·shield (-shēld′) ***n.*** in automobiles, etc., a transparent screen in front, as of glass, to protect the riders from wind, etc.: also, chiefly Brit., **wind′screen′**

wind·sock (-säk′) ***n.*** a long, cone-shaped cloth bag, open at both ends and attached to the top of a mast, as at an airfield, to show wind direction: also called **wind sleeve**

Wind·sor[1] (win′zər) ruling family of Great Britain since 1917

Wind·sor[2] (win′zər) **1.** city in SE England, on the Thames: site of Windsor Castle **2.** port in SE Ontario, Canada, opposite Detroit: pop. 193,000

Windsor Castle residence of English sovereigns since the time of William the Conqueror, located in Windsor

Windsor chair a style of wooden chair, esp. popular in 18th-cent. England and America, with spreading legs, a spindle back, and usually a saddlelike seat

WINDSOR chair

Windsor knot a form of double slipknot in a four-in-hand necktie, resulting in a wider, bulkier knot

Windsor tie a wide necktie of silk cut on the bias, tied in a loose double bow

wind·storm (wind′stôrm′) ***n.*** a storm with a strong wind but little or no rain, hail, etc.

wind-swept (-swept′) ***adj.*** swept by or exposed to winds

wind tee a large T-shaped weather vane placed on a landing field to show wind direction to aircraft

wind tunnel a tunnellike chamber through which air is forced and in which scale models of airplanes, etc. are tested to determine the effects of wind pressure

wind·up (wīnd′up′) ***n.*** **1.** a winding up, or conclusion; close; end **2.** *Baseball* the swinging of the arm when getting ready to pitch the ball

wind·ward (wind′wərd; *nautical* win′dərd) ***n.*** the direction from which the wind blows —***adv.*** toward the wind —***adj.*** **1.** moving windward **2.** on the side from which the wind blows Opposed to LEEWARD

Wind·ward Islands (wind′wərd) S group of islands in the Lesser Antilles of the West Indies

wind·y (win′dē) ***adj.*** **wind′i·er, wind′i·est** **1.** characterized by wind *[a windy day]* **2.** swept by strong winds *[a windy city]* **3.** violent like wind *[windy anger]* **4.** *a)* without substance; empty, flimsy, etc. *b)* long-winded, pompous, boastful, etc. **5.** *same as* FLATULENT

wine (wīn) ***n.*** [OE. *win,* ult. < L. *vinum*] **1.** the fermented juice of grapes, used as an alcoholic beverage and in cooking, etc. **2.** the fermented juice of other fruits or plants, used as a beverage *[dandelion wine]* **3.** anything that exhilarates one **4.** a dark, purplish red like that of red wine —***vt., vi.*** **wined, win′ing** to provide with or drink wine: usually in **wine and dine,** to entertain with food, drink, etc.

wine·bib·ber (-bib′ər) ***n.*** a person who drinks much wine

wine cellar **1.** a cellar where wine is stored **2.** a stock of wine

wine-col·ored (-kul′ərd) ***adj.*** having the color of red wine; dark purplish-red

wine gallon the old English gallon of 231 cu. in., now the standard gallon in the U.S.

wine·glass (-glas′) ***n.*** a small glass, usually stemmed, for serving wine —**wine′glass·ful′** ***n.,*** *pl.* **-fuls′**

wine·grow·ing (-grō′iŋ) ***n.*** the art or process of cultivating grapes and making wine from them —**wine′grow′er** ***n.***

wine press a vat in which grapes are trodden, or a machine for pressing them, to extract the juice for making wine

win·er·y (wīn′ər ē) ***n.,*** *pl.* **-er·ies** an establishment where wine is made

Wine·sap (wīn′sap′) ***n.*** a dark-red winter apple

wine·skin (wīn′skin′) ***n.*** in Eastern countries, a large bag for holding wine, made of the skin of an animal

wing (wiŋ) ***n.*** [< ON. pl. of *vaengr*] **1.** *a)* either of the two feathered forelimbs of a bird, developed in most birds for use in flying *b)* either of a pair of structures on a bat or an insect used for flying *c)* any of various winglike structures used by certain animals for gliding, as the pectoral fin of a flying fish **2.** either of a pair of winglike structures that angels, dragons, etc. are thought of as having **3.** something used as or like a wing; esp., a (or the) main supporting surface of an airplane **4.** something like a wing in its position or relation to the main part; esp., *a)* a distinct part of a building, often at one side or added later or having a special use *b)* either side of a theater stage out of sight of the audience *c)* any winglike part, as on some seeds **5.** a group having a winglike relation to another group; specif., *a)* the right or left section of an army, fleet, etc. *b)* a section or faction, as of a political party, viewed as radical or conservative **6.** in hockey, a position or player forward and right (or left) of center **7.** *a)* any of various air force units; specif., *U.S. Air Force,* a unit larger than a group *b)* [*pl.*] the insignia worn by pilots and crew of military aircraft **8.** a flying, or a means or way of flying: now chiefly in **give wing to, take wing** (see phrases below) **9.** [Slang] a person's arm; specif., *Baseball* a pitcher's throwing arm —***vt.*** **1.** to provide with wings **2.** *a)* to cause to fly or speed as on wings *b)* to make (one's way) by flying *c)* to go through or over by flying **3.** to transport as by flight **4.** to wound, as with a bullet, in the wing, arm, etc. —***vi.*** to go swiftly as on wings; fly —**give wing** (or **wings**) **to** to enable to fly or soar on or as if on wings —**on the wing** **1.** flying, or while in flight **2.** in motion or while moving or traveling —**on wings of** filled with joy or rapture by *[on wings of song]* —**take wing** **1.** to take flight; fly away **2.** to become joyous or enraptured —**under one's wing** under one's protection, patronage, etc. —**wing it** [Colloq.] to act, speak, etc. with little or no planning or preparation; improvise —**wing′less** ***adj.***

wing chair an upholstered armchair with a high back from each side of which high sides, or wings, extend forward

wing·ding (wiŋ′diŋ′) ***n.*** [< ?] [Slang] an event, party, etc. that is very festive, lively, etc.

winged (wiŋd; *often poet.* wiŋ′id) ***adj.*** **1.** having wings or winglike parts **2.** moving, esp. swiftly, on or as if on wings **3.** lofty; sublime *[winged words]*

wing nut a nut with flared sides for turning with the thumb and forefinger

wing·span (wiŋ′span′) *n.* the distance between the tips of an airplane's wings
wing·spread (-spred′) *n.* **1.** the distance between the tips of a pair of fully spread wings **2.** *same as* WINGSPAN
wing tip **1.** a man's shoe with a decorative piece of leather over the vamp, peaked toward the tongue, with perforations on it and along the sides extending back from it **2.** this piece of leather Also **wing′-tip′, wing′tip′** *n.*
wink (wiŋk) *vi.* [OE. *wincian*] **1.** to close the eyelids and open them again quickly **2.** *a*) to close and open an eyelid quickly so as to signal, etc. *b*) to be closed and opened thus: said of the eye **3.** to shine or twinkle in flashes of light —*vt.* **1.** to make (the eyes or an eye) wink **2.** to move, remove, etc. by winking [to *wink* back tears] **3.** to signal, etc. by winking —*n.* **1.** a winking, or the instant of time it takes **2.** a tiny interval (of sleep) [didn't sleep a *wink*] **3.** a signal, etc. given by winking **4.** a twinkle —**wink at** to pretend not to notice (some wrongdoing)
wink·er (-ər) *n.* **1.** a person or thing that winks **2.** a blinder (for a horse) **3.** [Colloq.] an eyelash or an eye
win·kle[1] (wiŋ′k'l) *n.* **1.** *short for* PERIWINKLE[2] **2.** a large whelk very destructive to oysters and clams
win·kle[2] (wiŋ′k'l) *vt.* **-kled, -kling** [< ?] [Colloq.] to pry or rout from cover, secrecy, etc. (with *out, out of,* etc.)
win·ner (win′ər) *n.* one that wins; esp., [Colloq.] one that seems destined to win or be successful
win·ning (-iŋ) *adj.* **1.** that wins; victorious **2.** attractive; charming —*n.* **1.** victory **2.** [*pl.*] something won, esp. money —**win′ning·ly** *adv.*
Win·ni·peg (win′ə peg′) **1.** capital of Manitoba, Canada, on the Red River: pop. 561,000 (met. area 578,000) **2. Lake,** large lake in SC Manitoba
win·now (win′ō) *vt.* [OE. *windwian* < *wind,* WIND[2]] **1.** *a*) to blow the chaff from (grain) *b*) to blow off (chaff) **2.** to blow away; scatter **3.** to analyze or examine carefully so as to separate the various elements; sift **4.** *a*) to separate out (poor or useless parts) *b*) to sort out or extract (good or useful parts) —*vi.* to winnow grain —*n.* **1.** a winnowing **2.** an apparatus for winnowing —**win′now·er** *n.*
win·o (wī′nō) *n., pl.* **-os** [Slang] a person who habitually gets drunk on wine; esp., an alcoholic derelict who drinks only cheap wine
win·some (win′səm) *adj.* [OE. *wynsum,* pleasant] attractive in a sweet, engaging way; charming —**win′some·ly** *adv.* —**win′some·ness** *n.*
Win·ston-Sa·lem (win′stən sā′ləm) [ult. after Maj. J. *Winston* (1746–1815) & SALEM] city in north central N.C., near Greensboro: pop. 132,000
win·ter (win′tər) *n.* [OE.] **1.** the coldest season of the year, following autumn **2.** a year as reckoned by this season **3.** any period regarded, like winter, as a time of decline, dreariness, etc. —*adj.* **1.** of, typical of, or suitable for winter **2.** that will keep during the winter [*winter* apples] **3.** planted in the fall to be harvested in the spring [*winter* wheat] —*vi.* **1.** to pass the winter **2.** to be supplied with food and shelter in the winter —*vt.* to keep or maintain during the winter —**win′ter·er** *n.*
win·ter·feed (-fēd′) *vt.* **-fed′, -feed′ing** to feed (animals, esp. livestock) during the winter
win·ter·green (-grēn′) *n.* **1.** an evergreen plant with small, rounded leaves, white flowers, and red, edible berries **2.** an aromatic compound (**oil of wintergreen**) made from these leaves or from birch bark or synthetically, used in medicine and as a flavoring **3.** its flavor
win·ter·ize (-īz′) *vt.* **-ized′, -iz′ing** to put into condition for winter [to *winterize* a car with antifreeze]
win·ter·kill (-kil′) *vt., vi.* to kill or die by exposure to winter cold: said of plants
winter solstice the time in the Northern Hemisphere when the sun is farthest south of the celestial equator; December 21 or 22
winter squash any of several squashes, as the acorn squash, with a hard rind and good keeping qualities
win·ter·time (-tīm′) *n.* the season of winter
Win·throp (win′thrəp), **John** **1.** 1588–1649; Eng. colonist in America; 1st governor of the colony (*Massachusetts Bay Colony*) founded at Salem, Mass. **2.** 1606–76; governor of Connecticut colony (1657, 1659–76): son of *prec.*
win·try (win′trē) *adj.* **-tri·er, -tri·est** of or like winter; cold, bleak, etc. [a *wintry* day, a *wintry* stare] : also **win′ter·y** (-tər ē, -trē) —**win′tri·ness** (-trē nis) *n.*
win·y (wī′nē) *adj.* **win′i·er, win′i·est** like wine in taste, smell, color, etc.
wipe (wīp) *vt.* **wiped, wip′ing** [OE. *wipian*] **1.** *a*) to rub with a cloth, etc., as for cleaning or drying *b*) to clean or dry in this manner **2.** to rub or pass (a cloth, etc.) over something **3.** to apply by wiping **4.** to remove as by wiping (with *away, off,* etc.) —*n.* a wiping —**wipe out** **1.** to remove; erase **2.** to kill off **3.** to destroy —**wip′er** *n.*
wipe·out (-out′) *n.* [Slang] any fall, failure, etc.
wire (wīr) *n.* [OE. *wir*] **1.** metal that has been drawn into a long thread **2.** a length of this, used for conducting electric current, etc. **3.** wire netting or other wirework **4.** anything made of wire or wirework, as a telephone cable, a snare, etc. **5.** *a*) telegraph [reply by *wire*] *b*) a telegram **6.** *Horse Racing* a wire above the finish line of a race —*adj.* made of wire or wirework —*vt.* **wired, wir′ing** **1.** to furnish, connect, bind, etc. with wire **2.** to supply with a system of wires for electric current **3.** to telegraph —*vi.* to telegraph —**down to the wire** to the very last moments —**get (in) under the wire** to enter or achieve barely on time —**pull wires** to get what one wants through one's friends' influence —**wire′like′** *adj.*
wire·draw (-drô′) *vt.* **-drew′, -drawn′, -draw′ing** **1.** to draw (metal) into wire **2.** to reduce to the finest subtleties; strain (a point in argument)
wire gauge a device for measuring the diameter of wire, thickness of sheet metal, etc.: it usually consists of a disk with notches of graduated sizes along its edge
wire·hair (-her′) *n.* a fox terrier with a wiry coat: also **wire-haired terrier**
wire-haired (-herd′) *adj.* having coarse, or wiry, hair
wire·less (-lis) *adj.* **1.** without wire or wires; specif., operating with electromagnetic waves and not with conducting wire **2.** [Chiefly Brit.] *same as* RADIO —*n.* **1.** *same as: a*) WIRELESS TELEGRAPHY *b*) [Chiefly Brit.] RADIO **2.** a message sent by wireless —*vt., vi.* to communicate (with) by wireless
wireless telegraphy (or **telegraph**) telegraphy by radio-transmitted signals
wireless telephone a telephone operating by radio-transmitted signals —**wireless telephony**
Wire·pho·to (-fōt′ō) *a trademark for:* **1.** a system of reproducing photographs at a distance by means of electric impulses transmitted by wire **2.** a photograph so produced
wire·pull·er (-pool′ər) *n.* a person who gets what he wants through his friends' influence —**wire′pull′ing** *n.*
wire service a business organization that sends news stories, features, etc. by direct telegraph to subscribing or member newspapers and radio and television stations
wire·tap (-tap′) *vi., vt.* **-tapped′, -tap′ping** to tap (a telephone wire, etc.) to get information secretly or underhandedly —*n.* **1.** the act or an instance of wiretapping **2.** a device used in wiretapping —*adj.* of or relating to wiretapping —**wire′tap′per** *n.*
wire·work (-wʉrk′) *n.* netting, mesh, etc. made of wire
wir·ing (wīr′iŋ) *n.* **1.** the action of a person or thing that wires **2.** a system of wires, as to provide a house with electricity —*adj.* **1.** that wires **2.** used in wiring
wir·y (wīr′ē) *adj.* **wir′i·er, wir′i·est** **1.** of wire **2.** like wire in shape and substance; stiff **3.** lean, sinewy, and strong: said of persons and animals **4.** produced by or as if by a vibrating wire [a *wiry* sound] —**wir′i·ness** *n.*
wis (wis) *vt.* [< ME. *iwis,* certainly: erroneously understood as "I know"] [Archaic] to suppose; imagine; deem
Wis·con·sin (wis kän′s'n) [< Fr. < Algonquian] Middle Western State of the U.S.: 56,154 sq. mi.; pop. 4,705,000; cap. Madison: abbrev. **Wis., WI** —**Wis·con′sin·ite′** (-īt′) *n.*
wis·dom (wiz′dəm) *n.* [OE. < *wis,* WISE[1] + *-dom,* -DOM] **1.** the quality of being wise; good judgment, based on knowledge, etc.; sagacity **2.** learning; knowledge; erudition **3.** wise teaching **4.** a wise plan or course of action
Wisdom of Solomon one of the books of the Apocrypha: called **Wisdom** in the Douay Bible
wisdom tooth the back tooth on each side of each jaw in human beings, appearing usually between the ages of 17 and 25
wise[1] (wīz) *adj.* **wis′er, wis′est** [OE. *wis*] **1.** having or showing good judgment; sagacious **2.** judicious; sound [a *wise* saying] **3.** informed [none the *wiser*] **4.** learned; erudite **5.** shrewd; cunning **6.** [Slang] conceited, impudent, fresh —**be** (or **get**) **wise to** [Slang] to be (or become) aware of —**get wise** [Slang] **1.** to become aware of the true facts **2.** to become impudent —**put wise (to)** [Slang] to give (someone) information, etc. (about) —**wise up** [Slang] to make or become informed —**wise′ly** *adv.* —**wise′ness** *n.*
wise[2] (wīz) *n.* [OE.] way; manner: used chiefly in phrases, as **in no wise, in this wise,** etc.
-wise (wīz) [< prec.] *a suffix meaning:* **1.** in a (specified) direction, position, or manner [*sidewise*] **2.** in the same way or direction as [*clockwise*] **3.** with regard to; in connection with [*weatherwise, budgetwise*]
wise·a·cre (wīz′ā′kər) *n.* [< MDu. < OHG. *wizzago,* a prophet] a person who acts as though he were much wiser than he really is
wise·crack (-krak′) *n.* [Slang] a flippant or joking remark, often a gibe or retort —*vi.* [Slang] to make wisecracks —*vt.* [Slang] to say as a wisecrack —**wise′crack′er** *n.*
wise guy [Slang] a person who is brashly and annoyingly conceited, knowing, etc.; smart aleck
wish (wish) *vt.* [OE. *wyscan*] **1.** to have a longing for; want; desire **2.** to have or express a desire concerning [to *wish* the day were over, to *wish* her good luck] **3.** to bid [to *wish* a person good morning] **4.** to request [he *wishes* her to leave] **5.** to impose (with *on*) [he *wished* hard jobs on

me*]* —***vi.*** **1.** to long; yearn **2.** to make a wish —***n.*** **1.** a wishing; desire for something **2.** something wished for *[*he got his *wish]* **3.** a polite request with some of the force of an order **4.** [*pl.*] expressed desire for a person's health, etc. *[*to offer one's best *wishes]* —**wish′er** ***n.***

wish·bone (-bōn′) ***n.*** the forked bone in front of the breastbone of most birds

wish·ful (-fəl) ***adj.*** having or showing a wish; desirous; longing —**wish′ful·ly** ***adv.*** —**wish′ful·ness** ***n.***

wishful thinking thinking in which one interprets facts in terms of what he would like to believe

wish·y-wash·y (wish′ē wôsh′ē, -wäsh′ē) ***adj.*** **[**redupl. of WASHY**]** [Colloq.] **1.** watery; insipid; thin **2.** not strong or decisive in character; weak —**wish′y-wash′i·ly** ***adv.***

wisp (wisp) ***n.*** **[**prob. < Scand.**]** **1.** a small bunch or tuft *[*a *wisp* of straw, hair, etc.*]* **2.** a thin, filmy bit or puff *[*a *wisp* of smoke*]* **3.** something delicate, frail, etc. *[*a *wisp* of a girl*]* **4.** *same as* WILL-O'-THE-WISP —***vt.*** to roll into a wisp —**wisp′y** ***adj.*** **wisp′i·er, wisp′i·est**

wist (wist) *pt. & pp. of* WIT[2]

wis·ter·i·a (wis tir′ē ə) ***n.*** **[**ModL., after C. *Wistar* (1761–1818), U.S. anatomist**]** a twining shrub of the legume family, with showy clusters of bluish, white, pink, or purple flowers: also **wis·tar′i·a** (-ter′-)

wist·ful (wist′fəl) ***adj.*** **[**altered (after WISHFUL) < earlier *wistly,* attentive**]** showing or expressing vague yearnings or pensive longing —**wist′ful·ly** ***adv.*** —**wist′ful·ness** ***n.***

wit[1] (wit) ***n.*** **[**OE.**]** **1.** [*pl.*] powers of thinking and reasoning, esp. in a normal, effective way **2.** alert, practical intelligence; good sense **3.** *a)* the ability to make lively, clever remarks expressed in a surprising, epigrammatic, or ironic way *b)* a person having this ability, or speech or writing in which it is expressed —**at one's wits' end** at a loss as to what to do —**keep** (or **have**) **one's wits about one** to remain mentally alert, as in an emergency —**live by one's wits** to live by trickery or craftiness

wit[2] (wit) ***vt., vi.*** **wist, wit′ting** **[**OE. *witan***]** [Archaic] to know or learn *Wit* is conjugated in the present indicative: (I) *wot,* (thou) *wost* or *wot(t)est,* (he, she, it) *wot* or *wot(t)eth,* (we, ye, they) *wite* or *witen* —**to wit** that is to say; namely

witch (wich) ***n.*** **[**OE. *wicce,* fem. of *wicca,* sorcerer**]** **1.** a person, now specif. a woman, who is supposed to have magic power, esp. with the help of evil spirits: cf. WARLOCK **2.** an ugly and ill-tempered old woman **3.** [Colloq.] a bewitching or fascinating woman or girl —***vt.*** **1.** to put a magic spell on **2.** to charm; fascinate

witch·craft (-kraft′) ***n.*** **1.** *a)* the power or practices of witches; black magic; sorcery *b)* an instance of this **2.** bewitching attraction or charm

witch doctor among certain tribes, esp. in Africa, a person who practices a type of primitive medicine involving the use of magic, witchcraft, etc.

witch·er·y (wich′ər ē) ***n.,*** *pl.* **-er·ies** **1.** witchcraft; sorcery **2.** bewitching charm; fascination

witch hazel **[**OE. *wice***]** **1.** a shrub with yellow flowers and woody fruit **2.** an alcoholic lotion containing an extract from the leaves and bark of this shrub

witch hunt **[**after the cruel treatment of persons once imagined to be witches**]** an investigation usually carried on with much publicity, supposedly to uncover activities aimed at overthrowing the government but really to harass and weaken political opposition —**witch hunter**

witch·ing (wich′iŋ) ***n.*** witchcraft —***adj.*** that witches; bewitching —**witch′ing·ly** ***adv.***

with (wi*th,* with) ***prep.*** **[**OE., orig., against**]** **1.** against *[*to argue *with* a friend*]* **2.** *a)* alongside of; near to *b)* in the company of *c)* into; among *[*mix blue *with* red*]* **3.** as an associate, or companion, of *[*he played golf *with* me*]* **4.** *a)* as a member of *[*to sing *with* a quartet*]* *b)* working for *[with* the firm 20 years*]* **5.** in regard to; concerning *[*pleased *with* her gift*]* **6.** in the same terms as; compared to *[*having equal standing *with* the others*]* **7.** as well as *[*he can run *with* the best*]* **8.** of the same opinions as *[*I'm *with* you*]* **9.** on the side of *[*he voted *with* the Tories*]* **10.** in the opinion of *[*it's all right *with* me*]* **11.** as a result of *[*faint *with* hunger*]* **12.** *a)* by means of; using *[*stir *with* a spoon*]* *b)* by *[*filled *with* air*]* **13.** having received *[with* your permission, he'll go*]* **14.** having or showing *[*a boy *with* red hair, to enter *with* confidence, to play *with* skill*]* **15.** in the keeping, care, etc. of *[*leave the baby *with* me*]* **16.** *a)* added to *[*the boy, *with* his friend, arrived*]* *b)* including *[with* the newcomers, the class is large*]* **17.** in spite of *[with* all her faults, I love her still*]* **18.** *a)* at the same time as *[*to rise *with* the chickens*]* *b)* in the same direction as *[*to travel *with* the sun*]* *c)* in proportion to *[*wages varying *with* skills*]* *d)* in the course of *[*grief lessens *with* time*]* **19.** to; onto *[*join one end *with* the other*]* **20.** from *[*to part *with* money*]* **21.** after *[with* that remark, he left*]* —**with that** after that

with- **[**OE. < prec.**]** *a combining form meaning:* **1.** away, back *[withdraw]* **2.** against, from *[withhold]*

with·al (wi*th* ôl′, with-) ***adv.*** **1.** besides **2.** despite that; notwithstanding **3.** [Archaic] with that; therewith —***prep.*** [Archaic] with: used following its object

with·draw (-drô′) ***vt.*** **-drew′, -drawn′, -draw′ing** **1.** to take back or draw back; remove **2.** to take back (something said, offered, etc.) —***vi.*** **1.** to move back; go away; retreat **2.** to remove oneself *[from* an organization, activity, association with other people, etc.*)* —**with·draw′er** ***n.***

with·draw·al (-drô′əl) ***n.*** **1.** the act of withdrawing **2.** a giving up the use of a narcotic drug to which one has become addicted, typically accompanied by distress of body and mind (**withdrawal symptoms**)

with·drawn (-drôn′) *pp. of* WITHDRAW —***adj.*** withdrawing within oneself; shy, reserved, unsociable, etc.

withe (with, wi*th,* wī*th*) ***n.*** **[**OE. *withthe***]** a tough, flexible twig of willow, etc., used for binding things —***vt.*** **withed, with′ing** to bind with withes

with·er (wi*th*′ər) ***vi.*** **[**< ME. var. of *wederen,* lit., to weather**]** **1.** to dry up; shrivel *[*plants *withering* in the heat, a face *withering* with age*]* **2.** to lose strength; weaken *[*our hopes soon *withered]* —***vt.*** **1.** to cause to wither **2.** to make feel abashed, as by a scornful glance

with·ers (wi*th*′ərz) ***n.pl.*** **[**OE. *withre,* resistance < *wither,* against**]** the highest part of the back of a horse, etc., between the shoulder blades

with·hold (with hōld′, wi*th*-) ***vt.*** **-held′, -hold′ing** **1.** *a)* to hold back; restrain *b)* to take out or deduct (taxes, etc.) from wages or salary **2.** to keep from giving; refuse *[*to *withhold* approval*]* —***vi.*** to refrain; forbear

withholding tax the amount of income tax withheld from employees' wages or salaries

with·in (wi*th* in′, with-) ***adv.*** **[**OE. *withinnan***]** **1.** on or to the inside **2.** indoors **3.** inside the body, mind, spirit, etc. —***prep.*** **1.** in the inner part of; inside **2.** not more than; not beyond *[within* a mile of home*]* **3.** inside the limits of *[within* the law*]* —***n.*** the inside or the interior

with·out (-out′) ***adv.*** **[**OE. *withutan***]** **1.** on or to the outside **2.** outdoors —***prep.*** **1.** at, on, or to the outside of **2.** beyond the limits of **3.** not with; lacking *[*shoes *without* laces*]* **4.** free from *[*a man *without* fear*]* **5.** with avoidance of *[*to pass by *without* speaking*]* —***n.*** the outside or the exterior —***conj.*** [Dial.] unless —**go** (or **do**) **without** to manage although lacking something

with·stand (with stand′, wi*th*-) ***vt., vi.*** **-stood′, -stand′ing** to oppose, resist, or endure, esp. in a successful way

with·y (wi*th*′ē, with′ē) ***n.,*** *pl.* **with′ies** **[**OE. *withig***]** a tough, flexible twig of willow, etc.; withe

wit·less (wit′lis) ***adj.*** lacking wit or intelligence; foolish —**wit′less·ly** ***adv.*** —**wit′less·ness** ***n.***

wit·ling (wit′liŋ) ***n.*** one who fancies himself a wit

wit·ness (wit′nis) ***n.*** **[**OE. *gewitnes,* knowledge, testimony**]** **1.** evidence; testimony **2.** a person who saw, or can give a firsthand account of, something **3.** a person who testifies in court **4.** a person who watches a contract, will, etc. being signed and then, as proof that he did, signs it himself **5.** something serving as evidence —***vt.*** **1.** to testify to **2.** to serve as evidence of **3.** to act as witness of (a contract, will, etc.) **4.** to be present at; see personally **5.** to be the scene of *[*this field *witnessed* a battle*]* —***vi.*** **1.** to give, or serve as, evidence **2.** to testify to religious beliefs or faith —**bear witness** to be or give evidence

witness stand the place from which a witness gives his testimony in a law court: also, Brit., **wit′ness-box′** ***n.***

wit·ted (wit′id) ***adj.*** having (a specified kind of) wit: used in hyphenated compounds *[*slow-*witted]*

wit·ti·cism (wit′ə siz′m) ***n.*** **[**< WITTY + *-cism,* as in CRITICISM**]** a witty remark

wit·ting (wit′iŋ) ***adj.*** **[**ME. *wytting***]** done knowingly; intentional —**wit′ting·ly** ***adv.***

wit·ty (wit′ē) ***adj.*** **-ti·er, -ti·est** **[**OE. *wittig***]** having or showing wit; cleverly amusing —**wit′ti·ly** ***adv.*** —**wit′ti·ness** ***n.***

Wit·wa·ters·rand (wit wôt′ərz rand′, -wät′-; -ränt′) region in NE South Africa, containing rich gold fields

wive (wīv) ***vi., vt.*** **wived, wiv′ing** **[**OE. *wifian***]** [Archaic] to marry (a woman)

wives (wīvz) ***n.*** *pl. of* WIFE

wiz (wiz) ***n.*** *shortened form of* WIZARD (*n.* 2)

wiz·ard (wiz′ərd) ***n.*** **[**ME. *wisard,* prob. < *wis,* WISE[1] + *-ard,* -ARD**]** **1.** a magician; sorcerer **2.** [Colloq.] a person exceptionally gifted or clever at a specified activity —***adj.*** **1.** of wizards or wizardry **2.** magic **3.** [Chiefly Brit.] outstanding; excellent —**wiz′ard·ly** ***adv.***

wiz·ard·ry (-rē) ***n.*** witchcraft; magic; sorcery

wiz·en (wiz′'n, wēz′-) *vt., vi.* [OE. *wisnian*] to dry up; wither; shrivel —***adj.*** *same as* WIZENED
wiz·ened (-'nd) ***adj.*** dried up; withered; shriveled
wk. *pl.* **wks.** **1.** week **2.** work
WL, w.l. **1.** waterline **2.** wavelength
Wm. William
WNW, W.N.W., w.n.w. west-northwest
WO, W.O. Warrant Officer
woad (wōd) ***n.*** [OE. *wad*] any of a group of plants of the mustard family, esp. a plant (**dyer's woad**) with yellow flowers and leaves that yield a blue dye
wob·ble (wäb′'l) ***vi.*** **-bled, -bling** [prob. < LowG. *wabbeln*] **1.** to move from side to side in an unsteady way **2.** to shake as jelly does **3.** to waver in mind —***vt.*** to cause to wobble —***n.*** a wobbling motion —**wob′bler** ***n.*** —**wob′bli·ness** ***n.*** —**wob′bly** ***adj.*** **-bli·er, -bli·est**
Wo·den, Wo·dan (wōd′'n) the chief Germanic god, identified with the Norse god Odin
woe (wō) ***n.*** [OE. *wa*] **1.** great sorrow; grief **2.** a cause of sorrow; trouble —***interj.*** alas! Also [Archaic] **wo**
woe·be·gone (wō′bi gôn′, -gän′) ***adj.*** **1.** [Archaic] woeful **2.** showing woe; looking sad or mournful
woe·ful (-fəl) ***adj.*** **1.** full of woe; sad; mournful **2.** of, causing, or involving woe **3.** pitiful; wretched; miserable —**woe′ful·ly** ***adv.*** —**woe′ful·ness** ***n.***
wok (wäk) ***n.*** [Chin.] a metal cooking pan with a convex bottom, often used with a ringlike stand
woke (wōk) *alt. pt. & occas. Brit. pp. of* WAKE[1]
wok·en (wō′k'n) *occas. Brit. pp. of* WAKE[1]
wold (wōld) ***n.*** [OE. *wald*] a treeless, rolling plain, esp. a high one
wolf (wo͝olf) ***n.,*** *pl.* **wolves** [OE. *wulf*] **1.** *a)* any of a group of wild, flesh-eating, doglike mammals, esp. the gray wolf, found throughout the Northern Hemisphere *b)* the fur of a wolf **2.** *a)* a fierce, cruel, or greedy person *b)* [Slang] a man who boldly approaches women for sexual purposes —***vt.*** to eat greedily (often with *down*) —**cry wolf** to give a false alarm —**keep the wolf from the door** to provide the necessities of life —**wolf′ish** ***adj.*** —**wolf′ish·ly** ***adv.*** —**wolf′ish·ness** ***n.***
wolf·ber·ry (-ber′ē) ***n.,*** *pl.* **-ries** a hardy plant with pink flowers and white, spongy berries
Wolfe (wo͝olf) **1. James,** 1727–59; Eng. general: defeated the Fr. forces under Montcalm at Quebec (1759) **2. Thomas (Clayton),** 1900–38; U.S. novelist
wolf·hound (wo͝olf′hound′) ***n.*** a large dog of any of several breeds formerly used for hunting wolves: see IRISH WOLFHOUND, BORZOI (*Russian wolfhound*)
wolf·ram (wo͝ol′frəm) ***n.*** [G. < *wolf,* wolf + MHG. *ram,* dirt] *same as* TUNGSTEN
wolf·ram·ite (-frə mīt′) ***n.*** [< G.: see prec.] a brownish or blackish mineral, a compound of tungsten (wolfram), iron, and manganese: the principal ore of tungsten
wolfs·bane (wo͝olfs′bān′) ***n.*** *same as* ACONITE (sense 1)
Wol·sey (wo͝ol′zē), **Thomas** 1475?–1530; Eng. statesman & cardinal; chief Chancellor (1515–29) under Henry VIII
Wol·ver·hamp·ton (wo͝ol′vər hamp′tən) city in WC England, near Birmingham: pop. 264,000
wol·ver·ine (wo͝ol′və rēn′, wo͝ol′və rēn′) ***n.,*** *pl.* **-ines′, -ine′:** see PLURAL, II, D, 1 [irreg. dim. < WOLF] **1.** a stocky, ferocious, flesh-eating mammal with thick fur, found in the northern U.S., northern Eurasia, and Canada: the European variety is the GLUTTON (sense 3) **2.** its fur Also, Brit. sp., **wol′ver·ene′**

WOLVERINE (2½–3½ ft. long, including tail; 12–16 in. high at shoulder)

wolves (wo͝olvz) ***n.*** *pl. of* WOLF
wom·an (wo͝om′ən) ***n.,*** *pl.* **wom′en** (wim′in) [OE. *wifmann* < *wif,* a female + *mann,* a human being] **1.** an adult, female human being **2.** women as a group [*"Woman's* work is never done"] **3.** a female servant **4.** *a)* [Dial.] a wife *b)* a sweetheart or a mistress **5.** womanly qualities [it's the *woman* in her] —***adj.*** female
wom·an·hood (-ho͝od′) ***n.*** **1.** the condition of being a woman **2.** womanly qualities **3.** women; womankind
wom·an·ish (-ish) ***adj.*** like, characteristic of, or suitable to a woman; feminine or effeminate —**wom′an·ish·ly** ***adv.*** —**wom′an·ish·ness** ***n.***
wom·an·ize (-īz′) ***vt.*** **-ized′, -iz′ing** to make effeminate —***vi.*** [Colloq.] to be sexually promiscuous with women —**wom′an·iz′er** ***n.***
wom·an·kind (-kīnd′) ***n.*** women in general
wom·an·like (-līk′) ***adj.*** womanly
wom·an·ly (-lē) ***adj.*** **1.** like a woman; womanish **2.** characteristic of or fit for a woman —**wom′an·li·ness** ***n.***
woman suffrage the right of women to vote in governmental elections —**wom′an-suf′fra·gist** ***n.***
womb (wo͞om) ***n.*** [OE. *wamb*] **1.** *same as* UTERUS **2.** any place in which something is contained, developed, etc.
wom·bat (wäm′bat) ***n.*** [altered < Australian native name] a burrowing marsupial that looks like a small bear, found in Australia, Tasmania, and several Pacific islands
wom·en (wim′in) ***n.*** *pl. of* WOMAN
wom·en·folk (-fōk′) ***n.pl.*** [Dial. or Colloq.] women; womankind: also **wom′en·folks′**
women's rights the rights claimed by and for women of equal privileges and opportunities with men: cf. FEMINISM: also **woman's rights**
won[1] (wun) *pt. & pp. of* WIN
won[2] (wän) ***n.,*** *pl.* **won** [Korean < Chin. *yüan,* round] the monetary unit of North Korea and South Korea: see MONETARY UNITS, table
won·der (wun′dər) ***n.*** [OE. *wundor*] **1.** a person, thing, or event so unusual as to cause surprise, amazement, etc.; marvel **2.** the feeling of surprise, amazement, etc. caused by something strange, remarkable, etc. **3.** a miracle —***vi.*** **1.** to feel wonder; marvel **2.** to have curiosity, sometimes mixed with doubt —***vt.*** to have curiosity or doubt about; want to know [I *wonder* what he meant] —**do wonders for** to make a remarkable improvement in —**no wonder!** now I know why! —**won′der·er** ***n.***
won·der·ful (-fəl) ***adj.*** **1.** that causes wonder; marvelous; amazing **2.** [Colloq.] very good; excellent —**won′der·ful·ly** ***adv.*** —**won′der·ful·ness** ***n.***
won·der·land (-land′) ***n.*** an imaginary land or place full of wonders, or a real place like this
won·der·ment (-mənt) ***n.*** wonder or amazement
won·der-struck (-struk′) ***adj.*** struck with wonder, surprise, admiration, etc.: also **won′der-strick′en** (-strik′'n)
won·der·work (-wurk′) ***n.*** **1.** a wonderful work; wonder **2.** a miraculous act; miracle —**won′der·work′er** ***n.***
won·drous (wun′drəs) ***adj.*** [Now Rare] wonderful —***adv.*** [Now Rare] wonderfully; remarkably —**won′drous·ly** ***adv.***
wont (wōnt, wônt, wunt, wänt) ***adj.*** [ult. < OE. *wunian,* to be used to] accustomed [he was *wont* to rise early] —***n.*** usual practice; habit
won't (wōnt) [contr. < ME. *wol not*] will not
wont·ed (wōn′tid, wôn′-, *etc.*) ***adj.*** customary; accustomed
won ton (wän′ tän′) a Chinese dish consisting of casings of noodle dough filled with ground meat and boiled: served in a broth (**won-ton soup**) or fried
woo (wo͞o) ***vt.*** [OE. *wogian*] **1.** to try to get the love of; seek as a mate; court **2.** to try to get; seek [to *woo* fame] **3.** to entreat; coax; urge —***vi.*** **1.** to court a person **2.** to make entreaty —**woo′er** ***n.***
wood (wo͝od) ***n.*** [OE. *wudu*] **1.** [*usually pl.*] a thick growth of trees; forest or grove **2.** the hard, fibrous substance beneath the bark of trees and shrubs **3.** lumber or timber **4.** wood used as fuel; firewood **5.** something made of wood; specif., *a)* a wooden cask [whiskey aged in *wood*] *b)* [*pl.*] woodwind instruments *c)* *Golf* any of a set of numbered clubs with wooden heads having various lofts —***adj.*** **1.** made of wood; wooden **2.** for cutting, shaping, or holding wood **3.** growing or living in woods —***vt.*** **1.** to plant trees thickly over **2.** to furnish with wood, esp. for fuel —***vi.*** to get a supply of wood —**out of the woods** [Colloq.] out of difficulty, danger, etc.
wood alcohol *same as* METHANOL
wood·bine (wo͝od′bīn′) ***n.*** [OE. *wudubinde:* see WOOD & BIND] **1.** a European climbing honeysuckle **2.** a tendril-climbing vine growing in eastern N. America, with green flower clusters and dark-blue, inedible berries
wood block a block of wood, esp. one used in making a woodcut —**wood′block′** ***adj.***
wood·carv·ing (-kär′viŋ) ***n.*** **1.** the art or craft of carving wood by hand to make art objects, decorative moldings, etc. **2.** an object so made —**wood′carv′er** ***n.***
wood·chuck (-chuk′) ***n.*** [altered < Algonquian name] a common N. American marmot, an animal that burrows in the ground and sleeps all winter; groundhog

WOODCHUCK (head & body to 15 in. long; tail to 6 in. long)

wood·cock (-käk′) ***n.,*** *pl.* **-cocks′, -cock′:** see PLURAL, II, D, 1 **1.** a widespread, European, migratory game bird with short legs and a long bill **2.** a smaller, related game bird of eastern N. America
wood·craft (-kraft′) ***n.*** **1.** matters relating to the woods, as camping, hunting, etc. **2.** *same as: a)* WOODWORKING *b)* WOODCARVING **3.** skill in any of these
wood·cut (-kut′) ***n.*** **1.** a wooden block engraved with a design, etc. **2.** a print made from this
wood·cut·ter (-kut′ər) ***n.*** a person who fells trees, cuts wood, etc. —**wood′cut′ting** ***n.***
wood·ed (-id) ***adj.*** covered with trees or woods
wood·en (wo͝od′'n) ***adj.*** **1.** made of wood **2.** stiff, clum-

sy, or lifeless **3.** dull; insensitive —**wood′en·ly** *adv.* —**wood′en·ness** *n.*
wood engraving **1.** the art or process of engraving on wood **2.** *same as* WOODCUT —**wood engraver**
wood·en·head·ed (wood′'n hed′id) *adj.* [Colloq.] dull; stupid —**wood′en·head′ed·ness** *n.*
wooden horse *same as* TROJAN HORSE
wood·en·ware (-wer′) *n.* bowls, dishes, etc. made of wood
wood·land (wood′land′; *also, and for adj. always,* -lənd) *n.* land covered with woods or trees —*adj.* of, living in, or relating to the woods —**wood′land·er** *n.*
wood louse *same as* SOW BUG
wood·man (-mən) *n., pl.* **-men** *same as* WOODSMAN
wood·note (-nōt′) *n.* a sound of a forest bird or animal
wood nymph a nymph that lives in the woods; dryad
wood·peck·er (-pek′ər) *n.* any of various tree-climbing birds that have a strong, pointed bill used to drill holes in bark to get insects
wood·pile (-pīl′) *n.* a pile of wood, esp. of firewood
wood pulp pulp from wood fiber, used in making paper
wood·ruff (-ruf′) *n.* [OE. *wudurofe*] a plant with small white, pink, or blue, lily-shaped flowers
wood screw a metal screw with a sharp point and a coarse thread, for use in wood
wood·shed (-shed′) *n.* a shed for storing firewood
woods·man (woodz′mən) *n., pl.* **-men** **1.** a person who lives or works in the woods, as a hunter, woodcutter, etc. **2.** a person at home in the woods or skilled in woodcraft
wood sorrel any of a group of creeping plants with white, pink, red, or yellow, five-petaled flowers
wood·sy (wood′zē) *adj.* **-si·er, -si·est** of, characteristic of, or like the woods —**wood′si·ness** *n.*
wood tar a dark, sticky, syruplike substance obtained by the destructive distillation of wood
wood thrush a large, brown thrush of eastern N. America, having a sweet, clear song: also called **wood robin**
wood turning the art or process of turning, or shaping, wood on a lathe —**wood′-turn′er** *n.* —**wood′-turn′ing** *n.*
wood·wind (-wind′) *n.* **1.** [*pl.*] the wind instruments of an orchestra made, esp. originally, of wood: clarinets, oboes, bassoons, flutes, and English horns **2.** any of these instruments —*adj.* of or for such instruments
wood·work (-wurk′) *n.* **1.** work done in wood **2.** things made of wood, esp. interior moldings, doors, stairs, etc.
wood·work·ing (-wur′kiŋ) *n.* the art or work of making things out of wood —*adj.* of woodworking —**wood′work′er** *n.*
wood·worm (-wurm′) *n.* any of a number of insect larvae that live on and burrow in wood
wood·y (wood′ē) *adj.* **wood′i·er, wood′i·est** **1.** covered with trees; wooded **2.** consisting of or forming wood [a *woody* plant] **3.** like wood —**wood′i·ness** *n.*
woof[1] (woof, wōōf) *n.* [OE. *owef* < *o-* (< *on*) + *-wef* < base of *wefan,* to weave] **1.** the horizontal threads crossing the warp in a woven fabric; weft **2.** a woven fabric
woof[2] (woof) *n.* a gruff barking sound of or like that of a dog —*vi.* to make such a sound
woof·er (woof′ər) *n.* [prec. + -ER] in an assembly of two or more loudspeakers, a large speaker for reproducing low-frequency sounds: cf. TWEETER
wool (wool) *n.* see PLURAL, II, D, 3 [OE. *wull*] **1.** *a*) the soft, curly hair of sheep *b*) the hair of some other animals, as the goat, llama, or alpaca **2.** *a*) yarn spun from the fibers of such hair *b*) cloth, clothing, etc. made of this yarn **3.** anything that looks or feels like wool —*adj.* of wool or woolen goods —**all wool and a yard wide** genuine —**pull the wool over someone's eyes** to deceive or trick someone —**wool′like′** *adj.*
wool·en (-ən) *adj.* **1.** made of wool **2.** of or relating to wool or woolen cloth —*n.* [*pl.*] woolen goods or clothing Also, chiefly Brit. sp., **wool′len**
wool·gath·er·ing (-ga*th*′ər iŋ) *n.* absent-mindedness or daydreaming —**wool′gath′er·er** *n.*
wool·grow·er (-grō′ər) *n.* a person who raises sheep for wool —**wool′grow′ing** *n.*
wool·ly (wool′ē) *adj.* **-li·er, -li·est** **1.** of or like wool **2.** bearing wool **3.** covered with wool or something like wool in texture **4.** rough and uncivilized: chiefly in **wild and woolly** **5.** confused; fuzzy [*woolly* ideas] —*n., pl.* **-lies** **1.** [Western] a sheep **2.** a woolen garment; specif., [*pl.*] long underwear —**wool′li·ness** *n.*
wool·sack (wool′sak′) *n.* **1.** a sack of wool **2.** a cushion stuffed with wool, on which the British Lord Chancellor sits in the House of Lords
wool·y (wool′ē) *adj.* **wool′i·er, wool′i·est,** *n., pl.* **wool′ies** *same as* WOOLLY —**wool′i·ness** *n.*
wooz·y (wōō′zē, wooz′ē) *adj.* **wooz′i·er, wooz′i·est** [prob. < *wooze,* var. of OOZE[1]] [Colloq.] **1.** dizzy, faint, and sickish **2.** befuddled, as from drink —**wooz′i·ly** *adv.* —**wooz′i·ness** *n.*
Worces·ter (woos′tər) [after *Worcester,* city in E England] city in C Mass.: pop. 162,000
Worces·ter·shire sauce (woos′tər shir′) [orig. made in *Worcester,* England] a spicy sauce for meats, poultry, etc., containing soy, vinegar, etc.
word (wurd) *n.* [OE.] **1.** *a*) a speech sound, or series of speech sounds, serving to communicate meaning; unit of language consisting of a single morpheme or a group of morphemes *b*) a letter or group of letters, written or printed, representing such a unit of language **2.** a brief expression; remark [a *word* of advice] **3.** a promise [he gave his *word*] **4.** news; information [no *word* from home] **5.** *a*) a password or signal *b*) a command; order **6.** [*usually pl.*] *a*) talk; speech *b*) lyrics; text; libretto **7.** [*pl.*] a quarrel; dispute **8.** an ordered combination of characters with meaning, regarded as a unit and stored in a computer —*vt.* to express in words; phrase —**a good word** a favorable comment, or commendation —**by word of mouth** by speech; orally —**have a word with** to have a brief conversation with —**have no words for** to be incapable of describing —**have words with** to argue angrily with —**in a word** in short; briefly —**in so many words** precisely; succinctly —**man (or woman) of his (or her) word** one who keeps his promises —**of many (or few) words** talkative (or untalkative) —**take the words out of one's mouth** to say what one was about to say oneself —**the Word** **1.** the Bible: also **Word of God** **2.** the spirit of God as revealed in Jesus: John 1:1 **3.** *same as* GOSPEL (sense 1) —**(upon) my word!** indeed! really! —**word for word** in precisely the same words —**word′less** *adj.* —**word′less·ly** *adv.* —**word′less·ness** *n.*
word·age (-ij) *n.* **1.** words collectively, or the number of words (*of* a story, novel, etc.) **2.** wordiness **3.** wording
word·book (-book′) *n.* a dictionary, lexicon, or vocabulary
word-for-word (-fər wurd′) *adj.* in exactly the same words
word·ing (-iŋ) *n.* choice and arrangement of words; diction
word of honor pledged word; solemn promise
word order the arrangement of words in a phrase, clause, or sentence
word processing an automated, computerized system in which letters, records, etc. are prepared, stored, or reproduced, as by using an electronic typewriter
word square a square made of letters so arranged that they spell the same words horizontally and vertically
Words·worth (wurdz′wərth), **William** 1770–1850; Eng. poet
word·y (wur′dē) *adj.* **word′i·er, word′i·est** containing or using many or too many words; verbose —**word′i·ly** *adv.* —**word′i·ness** *n.*
wore (wôr) *pt. of* WEAR[1]
work (wurk) *n.* [OE. *weorc*] **1.** physical or mental effort exerted to do or make something; labor; toil **2.** employment at a job [out of *work*] **3.** occupation, profession, business, trade, craft, etc. **4.** *a*) something one is making, doing, or acting upon; task [to take *work* home] *b*) the amount of this [a day's *work*] **5.** something that has been made or done; specif., *a*) an act; deed: *usually used in pl.* [good *works*] *b*) [*pl.*] collected writings *c*) [*pl.*] engineering structures, as bridges, dams, etc. *d*) a fortification *e*) needlework; embroidery *f*) *same as* WORK OF ART **6.** [*pl., with sing. v.*] a place where work is done, as a factory **7.** workmanship **8.** the action of, or effect produced by, natural forces **9.** *Mech.* transference of force from one body or system to another, measured by the product of the force and the amount of displacement in the line of force —*adj.* of, for, or used in work —*vi.* **worked** or **wrought, work′ing** **1.** to do work; labor; toil **2.** to be employed **3.** *a*) to perform its function; operate; act *b*) to operate effectively **4.** to undergo fermentation **5.** to produce results or exert an influence [let it *work* in his mind] **6.** to be manipulated, kneaded, etc. [putty that *works* easily] **7.** to move, proceed, etc. slowly and with or as with difficulty **8.** to move, twitch, etc. as from agitation [his face *worked* with emotion] **9.** to change into a specified condition, as by repeated movement [the handle *worked* loose] —*vt.* **1.** to cause; bring about [his idea *worked* wonders] **2.** to mold; shape [to *work* silver] **3.** to sew, embroider, etc. [to *work* a sampler] **4.** to solve (a mathematical problem or a puzzle) **5.** to manipulate; knead [to *work* dough] **6.** to bring into a specified condition, as by moving back and forth [to *work* a nail loose] **7.** to cultivate (soil) **8.** to cause to function; operate; use **9.** to cause fermentation in **10.** to cause to work [to *work* a crew hard] **11.** to influence; persuade [*work* him to your ideas] **12.** to make (one's way, etc.) by work or effort **13.** to provoke; rouse [to *work* oneself into a rage] **14.** to carry on activity in, along, etc.; cover [a salesman who has been successfully *working* this territory] **15.**

[Colloq.] to make use of, esp. by clever dealing *[work* your connections*]* —**at work** working —**get** (or **give one**) **the works** [Slang] to be (or cause one to be) the victim of an ordeal —**in the works** [Colloq.] in the process of being planned or done —**make short** (or **quick**) **work of** to deal with or dispose of quickly —**out of work** unemployed —**shoot the works** [Slang] **1.** to risk everything on one chance **2.** to make a supreme effort —**the works** **1.** the working parts (*of* a watch, clock, etc.) **2.** [Colloq.] everything —**work in** to insert or be inserted —**work off** **1.** to get rid of, as by exertion **2.** to pay (a debt or obligation) by work instead of money —**work on** (or **upon**) **1.** to influence **2.** to try to persuade —**work out** **1.** to make its way out, as from being embedded **2.** to exhaust (a mine, etc.) **3.** *same as* WORK OFF (sense 2) **4.** to accomplish **5.** to solve **6.** to result in some way **7.** to develop; elaborate **8.** to engage in a workout —**work over** [Colloq.] to subject to harsh or cruel treatment —**work up** **1.** to advance; rise **2.** to develop; elaborate **3.** to arouse; excite

work·a·ble (wʉr′kə b'l) ***adj.*** **1.** that can be worked **2.** practicable; feasible —**work′a·bil′i·ty** ***n.***

work·a·day (wʉr′kə dā′) ***adj.*** **1.** of or suitable for working days; everyday **2.** commonplace; ordinary

work·a·hol·ic (wʉr′kə hôl′ik, -häl′-) ***n.*** [WORK + *-a-* + (ALCO)HOLIC] a person having a compulsive need to work

work·bench (wʉrk′bench′) ***n.*** a table at which work is done, as by a mechanic, carpenter, etc.

work·book (-book′) ***n.*** **1.** a book containing questions and exercises to be worked by students **2.** a book of operating instructions **3.** a book containing a record of work planned or done

work·day (-dā′) ***n.*** **1.** a day on which work is done; working day **2.** the part of a day during which work is done *[a 7-hour workday]* —***adj.*** *same as* WORKADAY

work·er (wʉr′kər) ***n.*** **1.** a person, animal, or thing that works; specif., a person who works for a living **2.** a person who works for a cause, etc. **3.** any of various sterile female ants, bees, etc. that do work for the colony

work force the total number of workers actively employed in, or available for work in, a nation, region, plant, etc.

work·horse (wʉrk′hôrs′) ***n.*** **1.** a horse used for working, as for pulling a plow **2.** a steady, responsible worker with a heavy workload **3.** a durable machine, vehicle, etc.

work·house (-hous′) ***n.*** **1.** in England, formerly, a poorhouse **2.** a kind of prison where petty offenders are confined and made to work

work·ing (wʉr′kiŋ) ***adj.*** **1.** that works **2.** of, for, or used in work **3.** sufficient to get work done *[a working majority]* **4.** on which further work may be based *[a working hypothesis]* —***n.*** **1.** the act or process of a person or thing that works **2.** [*usually pl.*] a part of a mine, quarry, etc. where work is or has been done

working capital the part of a company's capital that can be converted readily into cash

working class workers as a class; esp., industrial or manual workers as a class; proletariat —**work′ing-class′** ***adj.***

working day **1.** a day on which work is done, esp. as distinguished from a Sunday, holiday, etc. **2.** the part of a day during which work is done; specif., the number of hours each day that an employee is required to work

work·ing·man (-man′) ***n.,*** *pl.* **-men′** (-men′) a worker; esp., an industrial or manual worker; wage earner; laborer

work·ing·wom·an (-woom′ən) ***n.,*** *pl.* **-wom′en** a woman worker; esp., a woman industrial or manual worker

work·load (wʉrk′lōd′) ***n.*** the amount of work assigned to be completed within a given period of time

work·man (wʉrk′mən) ***n.,*** *pl.* **-men** **1.** *same as* WORKINGMAN **2.** a craftsman

work·man·like (-līk′) ***adj.*** characteristic of a good workman; skillful: also **work′man·ly**

work·man·ship (-ship′) ***n.*** **1.** skill of a workman; craftsmanship **2.** something produced by this skill

work of art **1.** something produced in one of the fine arts, as a painting, sculpture, etc. **2.** anything made, performed, etc. with great skill and beauty

work·out (wʉrk′out′) ***n.*** **1.** a period of doing exercises intended to develop physical fitness or athletic skill **2.** any exercise, work, etc. requiring great effort

work·room (-ro͞om′) ***n.*** a room in which work is done

work·shop (-shäp′) ***n.*** **1.** a room or building where work is done **2.** a seminar or series of meetings for intensive study, work, etc. in some field *[a writers' workshop]*

work song a folk song sung by laborers, as in the fields, with a marked rhythm matching the rhythm of their work

work·week (-wēk′) ***n.*** the total number of hours or days worked in a week for the regular wage or salary

work·wom·an (-woom′ən) ***n.,*** *pl.* **-wom′en** *same as* WORKINGWOMAN

world (wʉrld) ***n.*** [OE. *werold*] **1.** *a)* the planet earth *b)* the whole universe *c)* any heavenly body imagined as being inhabited **2.** the earth and its inhabitants **3.** *a)* mankind *b)* people generally *[the news startled the world]* **4.** *a)* [*also* **W-**] some part of the earth *[the Old World]* *b)* some period of history, its society, etc. *[the ancient world]* *c)* any sphere or domain *[the animal world]* *d)* any sphere of human activity *[the world of music]* **5.** individual experience, outlook, etc. *[his world is narrow]* **6.** *a)* the usual social life of people, as apart from a life devoted to religious or spiritual matters *b)* people leading the usual social life **7.** [*often pl.*] a large amount; great deal *[to do a world* (or *worlds*) of good*]* —**bring into the world** to give birth to —**come into the world** to be born —**for all the world** **1.** for any reason or consideration at all **2.** in every respect; exactly —**in the world** **1.** on earth or in the universe; anywhere **2.** at all; ever

world·beat·er (-bēt′ər) ***n.*** [Colloq.] one that is, or has the qualities needed to become, a great success

world·ling (-liŋ) ***n.*** a worldly person

world·ly (wʉrld′lē) ***adj.*** **-li·er, -li·est** **1.** of or limited to this world; temporal or secular **2.** devoted to or concerned with the affairs, pleasures, interests, etc. of this world: also **world′ly-mind′ed** **3.** worldly-wise —**world′li·ness** ***n.***

world·ly-wise (-wīz′) ***adj.*** wise in the ways or affairs of the world; sophisticated

world power a nation or organization large or powerful enough to have a worldwide influence

World Series [*also* **w- s-**] an annual series of games between the winning teams of the two major U.S. baseball leagues to decide the championship

world-shak·ing (wʉrld′shā′kiŋ) ***adj.*** of great importance, effect, or influence; momentous

World War I the war (1914–18) between the Allies (Great Britain, France, Russia, the U.S., Italy, Japan, etc.) and the Central Powers (Germany, Austria-Hungary, etc.)

World War II the war (1939–45) between the United Nations (Great Britain, France, the Soviet Union, the U.S., etc.) and the Axis (Germany, Italy, Japan, etc.)

world-wea·ry (wʉrld′wir′ē) ***adj.*** weary of the world; bored

world·wide (-wīd′) ***adj.*** extending throughout the world

worm (wʉrm) ***n.*** [OE. *wyrm,* serpent] **1.** any of many long, slender, soft-bodied, creeping animals, as the annelids, roundworms, etc. **2.** popularly, *a)* an insect larva, as a grub *b)* any of several mollusks, as the shipworms *c)* any of various wormlike animals, as the rotifer **3.** a person looked down on as being too meek, wretched, etc. **4.** something thought of as being wormlike because of its spiral shape; specif., a short, rotating screw that meshes with the teeth of a worm wheel or a rack **5.** [*pl.*] *Med.* any disease or disorder caused by parasitic worms in the intestines, etc. —***vi.*** to move, proceed, etc. like a worm, in a winding, creeping, or roundabout manner —***vt.*** **1.** to bring about, get, make, etc. in a winding, creeping, or roundabout manner **2.** to rid of worms; esp., to purge of intestinal worms —**worm′er** ***n.*** —**worm′like′** ***adj.***

worm-eat·en (-ēt′'n) ***adj.*** **1.** eaten into by worms, termites, etc. **2.** worn-out, out-of-date, etc.

worm gear **1.** *same as* WORM WHEEL **2.** a gear consisting of a worm and worm wheel

worm·hole (-hōl′) ***n.*** a hole made, as in wood, by a worm, termite, etc.

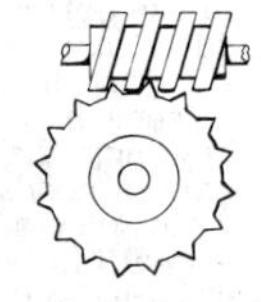

WORM GEAR

Worms (vôrmz; *E.* wʉrmz) city in West Germany, on the Rhine: scene of an assembly (*Diet of Worms*), 1521, at which Martin Luther was condemned for heresy

worm wheel a toothed wheel designed to gear with the thread of a worm

worm·wood (wʉrm′wood′) ***n.*** [altered by folk etym. < OE. *wermod*] **1.** any of various strong-smelling plants; esp., a Eurasian perennial that yields a bitter-tasting, dark-green oil (**wormwood oil**) used in making absinthe **2.** a bitter experience

worm·y (wʉr′mē) ***adj.*** **worm′i·er, worm′i·est** **1.** containing a worm or worms; worm-infested **2.** *same as* WORM-EATEN **3.** like a worm **4.** debased; groveling —**worm′i·ness** ***n.***

worn (wôrn) *pp. of* WEAR[1] —***adj.*** **1.** showing the effects of use, wear, etc. **2.** damaged by use or wear **3.** showing the effects of worry or anxiety **4.** exhausted; spent

worn-out (-out′) ***adj.*** **1.** used or worn until no longer effective, usable, or serviceable **2.** exhausted; tired out

wor·ri·ment (wʉr′ē mənt) ***n.*** **1.** a worrying or being worried; mental disturbance; anxiety **2.** a cause of worry

wor·ri·some (-səm) ***adj.*** **1.** causing worry or anxiety **2.** having a tendency to worry —**wor′ri·some·ly** ***adv.***

wor·ry (wʉr′ē) ***vt.*** **-ried, -ry·ing** [OE. *wyrgan,* to strangle] **1.** *a)* to treat roughly, as with continual biting *[a dog worrying a bone]* *b)* to pluck at, touch, etc. repeatedly in a nervous way *[to worry a loose tooth with the tongue]* **2.** to annoy; bother **3.** to cause to feel troubled or uneasy —***vi.*** **1.** to bite, pull, or tear (*at* an object) with the teeth **2.** to be anxious, troubled, etc. 3. to manage to get (*along* or *through*) in the face of difficulties —*n., pl.* **-ries** 1. the act of worrying 2. a troubled state of mind; anxiety 3. something that causes anxiety —**wor′ri·er** *n.*

wor·ry·wart (-wôrt′) *n.* [WORRY + WART] [Colloq.] a person who tends to worry, esp. over trivial details

worse (wʉrs) *adj. compar. of* BAD[1] & ILL [OE. *wiersa*] 1. *a*) bad, evil, harmful, etc. in a greater degree *b*) of inferior quality or condition 2. in poorer health; more ill 3. in a less satisfactory situation —*adv. compar. of* BADLY & ILL in a worse manner; to a worse extent —*n.* that which is worse —**for the worse** to a worse condition

wors·en (wʉr′s'n) *vt., vi.* [orig., a dial. word < prec. + -EN] to make or become worse

wor·ship (wʉr′ship) *n.* [< OE.: see WORTH & -SHIP] 1. *a*) reverence or devotion for a deity; veneration *b*) a church service or other rite showing this 2. intense love or admiration of any kind 3. something worshiped 4. [Chiefly Brit.] a title of honor (preceded by *your* or *his*) used in addressing magistrates, etc. —*vt.* **-shiped** or **-shipped, -ship·ing** or **-ship·ping** 1. to show religious reverence for 2. to have intense love or admiration for —*vi.* to engage in worship —**wor′ship·er, wor′ship·per** *n.*

wor·ship·ful (-fəl) *adj.* 1. [Chiefly Brit.] honorable; respected: used as a title of respect 2. feeling or offering great devotion or respect —**wor′ship·ful·ly** *adv.* —**wor′ship·ful·ness** *n.*

worst (wʉrst) *adj. superl. of* BAD[1] & ILL [OE. *wyrsta*] 1. *a*) bad, evil, harmful, etc. in the greatest degree *b*) of the lowest quality or condition 2. in the least satisfactory situation —*adv. superl. of* BADLY & ILL in the worst manner; to the worst extent —*n.* that which is worst —*vt.* to get the better of; defeat —**at worst** under the worst circumstances —**if (the) worst comes to (the) worst** if the worst possible thing happens —**(in) the worst way** [Slang] very much; greatly —**make the worst of** to be pessimistic about

wor·sted (woos′tid, wʉr′stid) *n.* [after *Worsted,* now *Worstead,* England, where first made] 1. a smooth, hard-twisted thread or yarn made from long-staple wool 2. fabric made from this —*adj.* made of worsted

wort[1] (wʉrt) *n.* [< OE. *wyrt-* (in compounds)] a liquid prepared with malt which, after fermenting, becomes beer, ale, etc.

wort[2] (wʉrt) *n.* [OE. *wyrt,* a root] a plant or herb: now usually in compounds [*liverwort*]

worth (wʉrth) *n.* [OE. *weorth*] 1. material value, esp. as expressed in terms of money 2. the esteem in which a person or thing is held; importance, value, etc. 3. the quantity of something that may be had for a given sum [*a dime's worth* of nuts] 4. wealth; possessions —*adj.* [*with prepositional force*] 1. deserving or worthy of; meriting 2. equal in value to (something specified) 3. having wealth amounting to —**for all one is worth** to the utmost —**put in one's two cents' worth** to give one's opinion

worth·less (-lis) *adj.* without worth or merit; useless, valueless, etc. —**worth′less·ly** *adv.* —**worth′less·ness** *n.*

worth·while (-hwīl′, -wīl′) *adj.* important or valuable enough to repay time or effort spent; of true value

wor·thy (wʉr′*th*ē) *adj.* **-thi·er, -thi·est** 1. having worth, value, or merit 2. deserving; meriting (often with *of* or an infinitive) —*n., pl.* **-thies** a person of outstanding worth or importance: often used humorously —**wor′thi·ly** *adv.* —**wor′thi·ness** *n.*

wot (wät) *1st & 3d pers. sing., pres. indic., of* WIT[2]

would (wood; *unstressed* wəd) *v.* [OE. *wolde,* pt. of *willan,* to will] 1. *pt. of* WILL[2] 2. an auxiliary used: *a*) to express condition [*he would go if you would*] *b*) in indirect discourse to express futurity [*he said he would come*] *c*) to express habitual action [*Sundays he would sleep late*] *d*) to soften a request [*would you please leave?*] 3. I wish [*would that she were here*] See also SHOULD

would-be (wood′bē′) *adj.* 1. wishing or pretending to be [*a would-be expert*] 2. intended to be [*a would-be help*]

would·n't (wood′n't) would not

wouldst (woodst) *archaic 2d pers. sing. of* WILL[2]: *used with* thou: also **would·est** (wood′ist)

wound[1] (wōōnd) *n.* [OE. *wund*] 1. an injury in which the skin or other tissue is broken, cut, torn, etc. 2. any hurt to the feelings, honor, etc. —*vt., vi.* to inflict a wound (*on* or *upon*); injure —**the wounded** persons wounded, esp. in warfare

wound[2] (wound) 1. *pt. & pp. of* WIND[1] 2. *pt. & pp. of* WIND[3]

wove (wōv) *pt. & alt. pp. of* WEAVE

wo·ven (-'n) *alt. pp. of* WEAVE

wow[1] (wou) *interj.* an exclamation of surprise, pleasure, pain, etc. —*n.* [Slang] a remarkable, successful, exciting, etc. person or thing —*vt.* [Slang] to be a great success with

wow[2] (wou) *n.* [echoic] a distortion in reproduced sound, caused by variations in speed of the turntable, tape, etc. either in recording or playing

WPA, W.P.A. Works Progress (later, Work Projects) Administration

wpm words per minute

wrack[1] (rak) *n.* [< OE. *wræc,* misery & MDu. *wrak,* a wreck] 1. ruin; destruction: now chiefly in **wrack and ruin** 2. seaweed, etc. cast up on shore

wrack[2] (rak) *vt.* [< RACK[1]] *same as* RACK[1]; esp., to subject to extreme mental or physical suffering; torture

wraith (rāth) *n.* [Scot., ult. < ON. *vǫrthr,* guardian < *vartha,* to guard] 1. a ghost 2. a ghostlike figure of a person supposedly seen just before his death

wran·gle[1] (raŋ′g'l) *vi.* **-gled, -gling** [< ME. freq. of *wringen,* to WRING] 1. to quarrel angrily and noisily 2. to argue; dispute —*vt.* to argue (a person) *into* or *out of* something —*n.* an angry, noisy dispute or quarrel

wran·gle[2] (raŋ′g'l) *vt.* **-gled, -gling** [< WRANGLER[2]] to herd (livestock, esp. saddle horses)

wran·gler[1] (raŋ′glər) *n.* [WRANGLE[1] + -ER] a person who wrangles, or argues, esp. in a noisy or angry way

wran·gler[2] (raŋ′glər) *n.* [< (*horse*) *wrangler,* partial transl. of AmSp. *caballerango,* a groom] a cowboy who herds livestock, esp. saddle horses

wrap (rap) *vt.* **wrapped** or **wrapt, wrap′ping** [ME. *wrappen*] 1. *a*) to wind or fold (a covering) around something *b*) to cover by this means 2. to envelop; hide; conceal [*a town wrapped in fog*] 3. to enclose and fasten in a wrapper of paper, etc. 4. to wind or fold [*to wrap one's arms around someone*] —*vi.* to twine, extend, coil, etc. (usually with *over, around,* etc.) —*n.* 1. an outer covering; esp., an outer garment worn by being wrapped around the body 2. [*pl.*] secrecy; censorship [*plans kept under wraps*] —**wrapped up in** 1. devoted to; absorbed in (work, etc.) 2. involved in —**wrap up** 1. to enfold in a covering 2. to put on warm clothing 3. [Colloq.] *a*) to bring to an end *b*) to give a concluding report, etc.

wrap·a·round (rap′ə round′) *adj.* 1. that has a full-length opening and is wrapped around the body [*a wraparound skirt*] 2. molded, etc. so as to curve [*a wraparound windshield*] —*n.* a wraparound garment, esp. a skirt

wrap·per (-ər) *n.* 1. a person or thing that wraps 2. that in which something is wrapped; covering; cover 3. a woman's dressing gown 4. a baby's robe

wrap·ping (-iŋ) *n.* [*often pl.*] the material, as paper, in which something is wrapped

wrap-up (-up′) *adj.* [Colloq.] 1. making final; concluding 2. that comes at the end and summarizes —*n.* 1. [Colloq.] *a*) the concluding event, action, etc. in a sequence *b*) a concluding, summarizing report, etc. 2. [Slang] a quick, easy sale or the customer to whom the sale is made

wrasse (ras) *n., pl.* **wrass′es, wrasse:** see PLURAL, II, D, 1 [Corn. *wrach*] any of various fishes with spiny fins and bright coloring, found esp. in tropical seas

wras·tle (ras′'l) *n., vi., vt.* **-tled, -tling** *dial. or colloq. var. of* WRESTLE: also **wras′sle -sled, -sling**

wrath (rath; *chiefly Brit.* rôth) *n.* [OE. *wræththo* < *wrath,* wroth] 1. intense anger; rage 2. any action carried out in great anger, esp. for punishment or vengeance

wrath·ful (-fəl) *adj.* 1. full of wrath 2. resulting from or expressing wrath —**wrath′ful·ly** *adv.* —**wrath′ful·ness** *n.*

wreak (rēk) *vt.* [OE. *wrecan,* to revenge] 1. to give vent or free play to (anger, malice, etc.) 2. to inflict (vengeance), cause (havoc), etc. —**wreak′er** *n.*

wreath (rēth) *n., pl.* **wreaths** (rē*th*z) [OE. *writha,* a ring < *writhan,* to twist] 1. a twisted band or ring of leaves, flowers, etc. 2. something suggesting this in shape [*wreaths of smoke*] —**wreath′like′** *adj.*

wreathe (rē*th*) *vt.* **wreathed, wreath′ing** 1. to coil, twist, or entwine, esp. so as to form a wreath 2. to coil, twist, or entwine around; encircle [*clouds wreathe the hills*] 3. to decorate with wreaths 4. to cover or envelop [*a face wreathed in smiles*] —*vi.* 1. to have a twisting or coiling movement 2. to form a wreath

wreck (rek) *n.* [Anglo-Fr. *wrec* < ON. *vrek,* driftwood, wreckage] 1. goods or wreckage cast ashore after a shipwreck 2. *a*) the disabling or destruction of a ship by a storm or other disaster; shipwreck *b*) a ship thus disabled or destroyed 3. the remains of anything that has been destroyed or badly damaged 4. a person in very poor health 5. a wrecking or being wrecked; ruin —*vt.* 1. to destroy or damage badly 2. to tear down (a building, etc.) 3. to overthrow; thwart 4. to destroy the health of —*vi.* 1. to be wrecked 2. to work as a wrecker

wreck·age (-ij) *n.* 1. a wrecking or being wrecked 2. the remains of something that has been wrecked

wreck·er (-ər) *n.* 1. a person or thing that wrecks 2. a person who causes ruin, obstruction, etc. **3.** a person, car, train, etc. that salvages or clears away wrecks; specif., a truck equipped to tow away wrecked or disabled automobiles **4.** a person whose work is tearing down and salvaging buildings, etc.

wreck·ing (-iŋ) ***n.*** the act or work of a wrecker —***adj.*** engaged or used in dismantling or salvaging wrecks

wrecking bar a crowbar with a chisellike point at one end and a curved claw at the other

wren (ren) ***n.*** [OE. *wrenna*] any of various small, insect-eating songbirds having a long bill, rounded wings, and a stubby, erect tail

Wren (ren), Sir **Christopher** 1632–1723; Eng. architect

wrench (rench) ***n.*** [OE. *wrenc,* a trick] **1.** a sudden, sharp twist or pull **2.** an injury caused by a twist or jerk, as to the back **3.** a sudden feeling of anguish, grief, etc., as at parting with someone **4.** any of a number of tools used for holding and turning nuts, bolts, pipes, etc. —***vt.*** **1.** to twist, pull, or jerk violently **2.** to injure (a part of the body) with a twist or wrench **3.** to distort (a meaning, statement, etc.) —***vi.*** to pull or tug (*at* something) with a wrenching movement

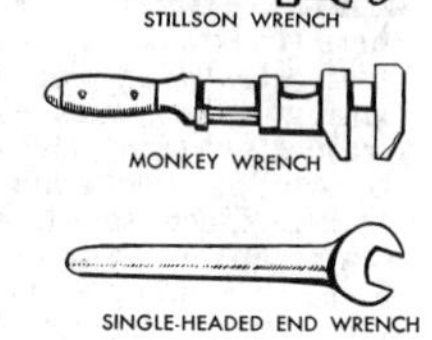

TYPES OF WRENCH

wrest (rest) ***vt.*** [OE. *wræstan*] **1.** to pull or force away violently with a twisting motion **2.** to take by force; usurp **3.** to distort or change the true meaning, purpose, etc. of —***n.*** a wresting; a twist; wrench

wres·tle (res′'l) ***vi., vt.*** **-tled, -tling** [< OE. freq. of *wræstan,* to twist] **1.** to struggle hand to hand with (an opponent) in an attempt to throw or force him to the ground without striking blows **2.** to struggle hard (*with* a problem, etc.) or struggle to move or lift (something) —***n.*** **1.** a wrestling; wrestling bout **2.** a struggle or contest —**wres′tler** ***n.***

wres·tling (-liŋ) ***n.*** a form of sport in which the opponents wrestle, or struggle hand to hand

wretch (rech) ***n.*** [OE. *wrecca,* an outcast] **1.** a miserable or unhappy person **2.** a person who is despised or scorned

wretch·ed (-id) ***adj.*** [OE. *wræcc*] **1.** very unhappy; miserable; unfortunate **2.** causing misery [*wretched* slums] **3.** very inferior [a *wretched* meal] **4.** deserving to be despised —**wretch′ed·ly** ***adv.*** —**wretch′ed·ness** ***n.***

wrig·gle (rig′'l) ***vi.*** **-gled, -gling** [MLowG. *wriggeln*] **1.** to twist and turn to and fro; squirm **2.** to move along with a twisting, writhing motion **3.** to make one's way by subtle or shifty means; dodge —***vt.*** **1.** to cause to wriggle **2.** to bring into a specified condition by wriggling —***n.*** a wriggling —**wrig′gly** ***adj.*** **-gli·er, -gli·est**

wrig·gler (-lər) ***n.*** **1.** a person or thing that wriggles **2.** the larva of a mosquito; wiggler

wright (rīt) ***n.*** [OE. *wyrhta* < *wyrcan,* to work] a person who makes, constructs, or repairs: used chiefly in compounds [*shipwright*]

Wright (rīt) **1. Frank Lloyd,** 1869–1959; U.S. architect **2. Or·ville** (ôr′vil), 1871–1948 & his brother **Wilbur,** 1867–1912; U.S. airplane inventors

wring (riŋ) ***vt.*** **wrung** or rare **wringed, wring′ing** [OE. *wringan*] **1.** *a)* to squeeze, press, or twist, esp. so as to force out water or other liquid *b)* to force out (water, etc.) by this means (usually with *out*) **2.** to clasp and twist (the hands) together as an expression of distress **3.** to clasp (another's hand) forcefully in greeting **4.** to wrench or twist forcibly **5.** to get or extract by force, threats, persistence, etc. **6.** to afflict with anguish, pity, etc. [the story *wrung* her heart] —***vi.*** to squirm or twist with force or great effort —***n.*** a wringing

wring·er (-ər) ***n.*** **1.** a person or thing that wrings **2.** a device with two rollers close together between which wet clothes are run to squeeze out the water

wrin·kle[1] (riŋ′k'l) ***n.*** [prob. < OE. (*ge*)*wrinclod,* pp. of (*ge*)*wrinclian,* to wind about] **1.** a small ridge or furrow in a normally smooth surface, caused by contraction, folding, etc. **2.** a crease or pucker in the skin —***vt., vi.*** **-kled, -kling** to contract or pucker into small ridges or creases —**wrin′kly** ***adj.*** **-kli·er, -kli·est**

wrin·kle[2] (riŋ′k'l) ***n.*** [prob. ult. < OE. *wrenc,* a trick] [Colloq.] a clever or novel trick, idea, or device

wrist (rist) ***n.*** [OE.] **1.** the joint or part of the arm between the hand and the forearm; carpus **2.** the corresponding part in an animal —**a slap** (or **tap**) **on the wrist** a token punishment, less severe than seems called for

wrist·band (rist′band′) ***n.*** a band that goes around the wrist, as on the cuff of a sleeve

wrist·let (-lit) ***n.*** **1.** a closefitting band or strip of material worn around the wrist, as for warmth **2.** a bracelet

wrist pin the stud or pin by which the connecting rod is attached to a wheel, crank, etc.

wrist·watch (-wäch′, -wôch′) ***n.*** a watch worn on a strap or band that fits around the wrist

writ (rit) ***n.*** [OE. < *writan,* to write] **1.** [Rare or Archaic] something written **2.** a formal legal document ordering or prohibiting some action

write (rīt) ***vt.*** **wrote, writ′ten, writ′ing;** archaic pt. & pp. **writ** [OE. *writan,* to scratch, write] **1.** *a)* to form (words, letters, etc.) on a surface, esp. with a pen or pencil *b)* to form the words, letters, etc. of [*write* your name] **2.** to spell (a word, etc.) [words *written* the same are often pronounced differently] **3.** to know (a specific language, etc.) well enough to communicate in writing **4.** to be the author or composer of (literary or musical material) **5.** to fill in (a check, form, etc.) with the writing required **6.** to cover with writing [he *wrote* 10 pages] **7.** to communicate in writing [he *wrote* that he was ill] **8.** to communicate with in writing [*write* me every day] **9.** to record (information) in a computer's memory or on a tape, etc. for use by a computer **10.** to leave signs or evidence of [greed was *written* on his face] —***vi.*** **1.** to form words, letters, etc. on a surface, esp. with a pen or pencil **2.** to write books or other literary matter **3.** to write a letter **4.** to produce writing of a specified kind [to *write* legibly] —**write down** **1.** to put into written form **2.** to discredit in writing **3.** to write in a very simple style so as to be easily understood —**write in** to vote for (someone not officially on a ballot) by inserting his name on the ballot —**write off** **1.** to cancel or remove from accounts (bad debts, etc.) **2.** to drop from consideration —**write out** **1.** to put into writing **2.** to write in full —**write up** **1.** to write an account of **2.** to praise in writing

writ·er (rīt′ər) ***n.*** a person who writes, esp. as a business or occupation; author, journalist, etc.

write-up (rīt′up′) ***n.*** [Colloq.] a written report or description, often a favorable account, as for publicity

writhe (rīth) ***vt.*** **writhed, writh′ing** [OE. *writhan,* to twist] to cause to twist or turn; contort —***vi.*** **1.** to make twisting or turning movements; squirm **2.** to suffer great emotional distress —***n.*** a writhing movement

writ·ing (rīt′iŋ) ***n.*** **1.** the act of a person who writes **2.** something written, as a letter, document, etc. **3.** written form **4.** *short for* HANDWRITING **5.** a literary work **6.** the profession or occupation of a writer **7.** the art, style, etc. of literary composition —***adj.*** **1.** that writes **2.** used in writing

writ·ten (rit′'n) *pp. of* WRITE —***adj.*** put down in a form to be read; not spoken or oral

Wroc·ław (vrôts′läf) city in SW Poland, on the Oder River: pop. 514,000

wrong (rôŋ) ***adj.*** [OE. *wrang* < ON. *rangr,* twisted] **1.** not just, moral, etc.; unlawful, immoral, or improper **2.** not in accordance with an established standard, etc. [the *wrong* method] **3.** not suitable or appropriate [the *wrong* thing to say] **4.** *a)* contrary to fact, reason, etc.; incorrect *b)* acting, believing, etc. incorrectly; mistaken **5.** in an unsatisfactory or bad condition **6.** not functioning properly [what's *wrong* with the light?] **7.** designating the unfinished, inner, or under side [the *wrong* side of a fabric] —***adv.*** in a wrong manner, direction, etc.; incorrectly —***n.*** **1.** something wrong, esp. an unjust or immoral act **2.** *Law* a violation of a legal right —***vt.*** **1.** to treat badly or unjustly; injure **2.** to think badly of without real justification —**get (someone** or **something) wrong** [Colloq.] to fail to understand (someone or something) properly —**go wrong** **1.** to turn out badly **2.** to change from good behavior to bad —**in the wrong** not on the side supported by truth, justice, etc. —**wrong′er** ***n.*** —**wrong′ly** ***adv.*** —**wrong′ness** ***n.***

wrong·do·ing (-dōō′iŋ) ***n.*** any act or behavior that is wrong; transgression —**wrong′do′er** ***n.***

wrong·ful (-fəl) ***adj.*** **1.** full of wrong; unjust, unfair, or injurious **2.** without legal right; unlawful —**wrong′ful·ly** ***adv.*** —**wrong′ful·ness** ***n.***

wrong·head·ed (-hed′id) ***adj.*** stubborn in sticking to wrong opinions, ideas, etc.; perverse —**wrong′head′ed·ly** ***adv.*** —**wrong′head′ed·ness** ***n.***

wrong number a telephone number reached through error, as by dialing incorrectly, or the person reached

wrote (rōt) *pt. of* WRITE

wroth (rôth; *chiefly Brit.* rōth) ***adj.*** [OE. *wrath*] angry; wrathful; incensed

wrought (rôt) *alt. pt. & pp. of* WORK —***adj.*** **1.** formed; fashioned **2.** shaped by hammering or beating: said of metals **3.** elaborated with care **4.** decorated; ornamented

wrought iron a kind of iron that contains some slag and very little carbon: it is tough but easy to work or shape —**wrought′-i′ron** ***adj.***

wrought-up (rôt′up′) ***adj.*** very disturbed or excited

wrung (ruŋ) *pt. & pp. of* WRING

wry (rī) ***vt., vi.*** **wried, wry′ing** [OE. *wrigian,* to turn] to writhe or twist —***adj.*** **wri′er, wri′est** **1.** turned or bent to one side; twisted; distorted **2.** made by twisting or distort-

ing the features [a *wry* face] **3.** perverse; ironic [*wry* humor] —**wry'ly** *adv.* —**wry'ness** *n.*
wry·neck (-nek') *n.* **1.** a condition in which the neck is twisted by a muscle spasm **2.** a bird related to the woodpecker, noted for its habit of twisting its neck
WSW, W.S.W., w.s.w. west-southwest
wt. weight
Wu·han (wōō'hän') city in EC China, on the Yangtze: pop. 2,500,000
‡**Wun·der·kind** (voon'dər kint') *n., pl.* **-kin'der** (-kin'dər) [G. < *wunder,* wonder + *kind,* child] a child prodigy
Wup·per·tal (voop'ər täl') city in the Ruhr Basin of West Germany: pop. 414,000
wurst (wurst, woorst; *G.* voorsht) *n.* [G.] sausage: often used in combination [*bratwurst, knackwurst*]
W.Va., WV West Virginia
Wy·an·dotte (wī'ən dät') *n.* [< Iroquoian < ?] any of a breed of American chickens
Wy·att (wī'ət), Sir **Thomas** 1503?–42; Eng. poet
wych-elm (wich'elm') *n.* [< OE. *wice,* applied to trees with pliant branches + ELM] **1.** a small variety of elm native to Europe and N Asia **2.** its wood
Wych·er·ley (wich'ər lē), **William** 1640?–1716; Eng. dramatist
Wyc·liffe (or **Wyc·lif**) (wik'lif), **John** 1324?–84; Eng. religious reformer: made the first complete translation of the Bible into English
Wy·o·ming (wī ō'miŋ) [< Algonquian, lit., large plains] **1.** Western State of the U.S.: 97,914 sq. mi.; pop. 471,000; cap. Cheyenne: abbrev. **Wyo., WY** **2.** city in SW Mich.: suburb of Grand Rapids: pop. 60,000 —**Wy·o'ming·ite'** (-īt') *n.*

X

X, x (eks) *n., pl.* **X's, x's** **1.** the twenty-fourth letter of the English alphabet **2.** a sound of *X* or *x*
X (eks) *n.* **1.** a mark shaped like X, used to represent the signature of a person who cannot write, to mark a particular point on a map or diagram, etc. **2.** the Roman numeral for 10 **3.** a person or thing unknown or unrevealed —*adj.* shaped like X
X a motion-picture rating meaning that no one under the age of seventeen is to be admitted
x *a symbol for:* **1.** *Math. a*) an unknown quantity *b*) times (in multiplication) [3 × 3 = 9] *c*) an abscissa **2.** *a*) by [3 ft. × 4 ft.] *b*) power of magnification (in optical instruments) *c*) one's choice or answer (on a ballot, test, etc.)
x (eks) *vt.* **x-ed** or **x'd, x-ing** or **x'ing** **1.** to indicate (one's choice, etc.) by marking with an X **2.** to cross (*out*) words or letters with an X or X's
xan·the·in (zan'thē in) *n.* [Fr. *xanthéine*] the water-soluble part of the yellow pigment in some plants
xan·thic (zan'thik) *adj.* [< Fr.: see XANTHO- & -IC] **1.** yellow **2.** of or having to do with xanthine
xan·thine (-thēn, -thin) *n.* [Fr.: cf. XANTHO- & -IN[1]] a white, crystalline nitrogenous compound present in blood, urine, and certain plants
Xan·thip·pe (zan tip'ē) 5th cent. B.C.; wife of Socrates: her name has become proverbial for the nagging wife
xan·tho- (zan'thō, -thə) [< Gr. *xanthos,* yellow] *a combining form meaning* yellow: also, before a vowel, **xanth-**
xan·thous (zan'thəs) *adj.* [Gr. *xanthos*] yellow
Xa·vi·er (zā'vē ər, zav'ē-; zāv'yər), Saint **Francis** 1506–52; Sp. Jesuit missionary
x-ax·is (eks'ak'sis) *n., pl.* **x'-ax'es** (-sēz) *Math.* the horizontal axis along which the abscissa is measured
X chromosome *Genetics* one of the sex chromosomes: see SEX CHROMOSOME
Xe *Chem.* xenon
xe·bec (zē'bek) *n.* [< Fr. *chébec,* ult. < Ar. *shabbāk*] a small, three-masted ship with overhanging bow and stern: once common in the Mediterranean
xen·o- [< Gr. *xenos*] *a combining form meaning:* **1.** stranger, foreigner [*xenophobia*] **2.** strange, foreign Also, before a vowel, **xen-**
xe·non (zē'nän, zen'än) *n.* [Gr., neut. of *xenos,* strange] a heavy, colorless, gaseous chemical element present in the air in minute quantities: used in electron tubes, lasers, etc.: symbol, Xe; at. wt., 131.30; at. no., 54
xen·o·pho·bi·a (zen'ə fō'bē ə) *n.* [ModL.: see XENO- & -PHOBIA] fear or hatred of strangers or foreigners —**xen'o·phobe'** (-fōb') *n.* —**xen'o·pho'bic** (-fō'bik) *adj.*
Xen·o·phon (zen'ə fən) 430?–355? B.C.; Gr. historian, essayist, & military leader
xe·rog·ra·phy (zi räg'rə fē) *n.* [< Gr. *xēros,* dry + -GRAPHY] a process for copying printed or written material, etc., in which an image of the material is electrically charged on a surface and attracts oppositely charged dry ink particles, which are then fused in place —**xe·ro·graph·ic** (zir'ə graf'ik) *adj.*
xe·roph·i·lous (zi räf'ə ləs) *adj.* [< Gr. *xēros,* dry + -PHILOUS] thriving in a hot, dry climate —**xe·roph'i·ly** *n.*
xe·ro·phyte (zir'ə fīt') *n.* [< Gr. *xēros,* dry + -PHYTE] a plant adapted to grow under very dry or desert conditions —**xe'ro·phyt'ic** (-fit'ik) *adj.*
Xe·rox (zir'äks) *a trademark for* a device for copying printed or written material, etc. by xerography —*n.* a copy made by such a device —*vt., vi.* to reproduce by such a device
Xer·xes I (zurk'sēz) 519?–465? B.C.; king of Persia (486?–465?): son of DARIUS I: called *the Great*
Xho·sa (kō'sä, -zä; *the* k *is actually a click*) *n.* **1.** *pl.* **Xho'sas, Xho'sa** any member of a people living in Cape Province, South Africa **2.** their Bantu language, characterized by clicks Also sp. **Xo'sa**
xi (zī, sī; *Gr.* ksē) *n.* [Gr.] the fourteenth letter of the Greek alphabet (Ξ, ξ)
Xmas (kris'məs; *popularly* eks'məs) *n.* [X (chi), 1st letter in Gr. *Christos,* Christ + -MAS] *same as* CHRISTMAS
X-ray (eks'rā') *n.* **1.** an electromagnetic ray or radiation of very short wavelength produced by the bombardment of a metal by a stream of electrons, as in a vacuum tube: X-rays can penetrate solid substances and are widely used in medicine to study the bones, organs, etc. inside the body and to diagnose and treat certain disorders **2.** a photograph made by means of X-rays —*adj.* of, by, or having to do with X-rays —*vt.* to examine, treat, or photograph with X-rays Also **X ray, x-ray, x ray**
xy·lem (zī'ləm, -lem) *n.* [G. < Gr. *xylon,* wood] the woody tissue of a plant, which gives support to softer tissues and contains vessels or cells that conduct water, minerals, etc.
xy·lo- [< Gr. *xylon*] *a combining form meaning* wood [*xylophone*] : also, before a vowel, **xyl-**
xy·lo·phone (zī'lə fōn') *n.* [XYLO- + -PHONE] a musical instrument consisting of a series of wooden bars graduated in length so as to sound the notes of the scale when struck with small wooden hammers —**xy'lo·phon'ist** (-fō'nist, zī läf'ə nist) *n.*

XYLOPHONE

xy·lose (zī'lōs) *n.* [XYL(O)- + -OSE[1]] a colorless sugar derived from wood, straw, corncobs, etc. and used in dyeing, diabetic foods, etc.

Y

Y, y (wī) ***n.***, *pl.* **Y's, y's** **1.** the twenty-fifth letter of the English alphabet **2.** a sound of *Y* or *y*
Y (wī) ***n.*** **1.** something shaped like Y **2.** *Chem.* yttrium —***adj.*** shaped like Y
y *Math. a symbol for:* **1.** the second of a set of unknown quantities, *x* usually being the first **2.** an ordinate
-y[1] (ē, i) **[**ME. *-y, -i, -ie*, prob. < OFr.**]** *a suffix meaning* little, dear: used in forming diminutives, nicknames, and terms of endearment *[kitty, Billy]*
-y[2] (ē, i) **[**OE. *-ig***]** *a suffix meaning:* **1.** having, full of, or characterized by *[dirty]* **2.** somewhat; rather *[chilly]* **3.** tending to *[sticky]* **4.** suggestive of, somewhat like *[wavy]* In some words, *-y* simply adds force without changing the meaning *[vasty]*
-y[3] (ē, i) **[**< OFr. *-ie* < L. *-ia* < or akin to Gr. *-ia***]** *a suffix meaning:* **1.** quality or condition of (being) *[jealousy]* **2.** a shop or goods of a specified kind *[bakery]* **3.** a collective body of a specified kind *[soldiery]*
-y[4] (ē, i) **[**< Anglo-Fr. *-ie* < L. *-ium***]** *a suffix meaning* action of *[inquiry, entreaty]*
Y, Y. *short for* YMCA *or* YWCA
y. **1.** yard(s) **2.** year(s)
yacht (yät) ***n.*** **[**Du. *jacht*, short for *jaghtschip*, pursuit ship**]** a large boat or small ship for pleasure cruises, races, etc. —***vi.*** to sail in a yacht —**yacht′ing** ***n.***
yachts·man (yäts′mən) ***n.***, *pl.* **-men** a person who owns or sails a yacht —**yachts′man·ship′** ***n.***
yack (yak) ***vi.***, ***n.*** *var. of* YAK[2]
yah (yä, ya) ***interj.*** a shout of scorn, defiance, etc.
Ya·hoo (yä′ho͞o) ***n.*** **1.** in Swift's *Gulliver's Travels*, any of a race of coarse, brutish creatures having the form and vices of man **2.** [y-] a vicious, coarse person
Yah·weh, Yah·we (yä′we) **[**Heb.: see JEHOVAH**]** God: a form of the Hebrew name in the Scriptures: also **Yah·ve, Yah·veh** (yä′ve)
yak[1] (yak) ***n.***, *pl.* **yaks, yak:** see PLURAL, II, D, 1 **[**Tibet. *gyak***]** a stocky, long-haired wild ox of Tibet and C Asia, often used as a beast of burden
yak[2] (yak; *also, for n.* 2, yäk) ***vi.*** **yakked, yak′king** **[**echoic**]** [Slang] to talk much or idly; chatter —***n.*** [Slang] **1.** idle talk or chatter **2.** *a)* a loud laugh, esp. as audience response to comedy *b)* a joke or comic bit that gets such a laugh Also, for *vi.* & *n.* (sense 1), **yak′-yak′, yak·e·ty-yak** (yak′ə tē yak′) —**yak′ker** ***n.***
Ya·lu (yä′lo͞o′; *Chin.* yä′lü′) river flowing along the Manchuria–North Korea border into the Yellow Sea
yam (yam) ***n.*** **[**Port. *inhame*, prob. < WAfr. name**]** **1.** *a)* the edible, starchy root of a climbing plant grown in tropical regions *b)* this plant **2.** [South] the sweet potato
ya·mal·ka, ya·mul·ka (yäm′əl kə) ***n.*** *var. of* YARMULKE
yang (yäŋ, yaŋ) ***n.*** **[**< Chin. dial.**]** in Chinese philosophy, the active, positive, masculine force or principle in the universe, complementary to the *yin:* see YIN
Yang·tze (yaŋ′sē; *Chin.* yäŋ′tse′) river in C China, flowing from Tibet into the East China Sea: c. 3,400 mi.
Yank (yaŋk) ***n.*** [Slang] a Yankee; esp., a U.S. soldier in World Wars I and II —***adj.*** of or like a Yank or Yanks
yank (yaŋk) ***n.*** **[**< ?**]** [Colloq.] a sudden, strong pull; jerk —***vt.***, ***vi.*** [Colloq.] to jerk
Yan·kee (yaŋ′kē) ***n.*** **[**< ? Du. *Jan Kees* (taken as pl.) < *Jan*, John + *Kees* < *kaas*, cheese: a disparaging nickname applied by Dutch colonists in America to English settlers**]** **1.** a native or inhabitant of New England **2.** *a)* a native or inhabitant of a Northern State; Northerner *b)* a Union soldier in the Civil War **3.** a native or inhabitant of the U.S. —***adj.*** of or like Yankees —**Yan′kee·dom** ***n.***
Yankee Doo·dle (do͞o′d'l) an old American song, popular during the Revolutionary War
‡**Yan·qui** (yäŋ′kē) ***n.***, *pl.* **-quis** (-kēs) *American Spanish respelling of* YANKEE (sense 3)
yap (yap) ***vi.*** **yapped, yap′ping** **[**echoic**]** **1.** to make a sharp, shrill bark or yelp **2.** [Slang] to talk noisily and stupidly —***n.*** **1.** a sharp, shrill bark or yelp **2.** [Slang] *a)* noisy, stupid talk *b)* a crude, noisy person *c)* the mouth —**yap′per** ***n.*** —**yap′ping·ly** ***adv.***
yard[1] (yärd) ***n.*** **[**OE. *gierd*, a rod**]** **1.** *a)* a measure of length, equal to 3 feet, or 36 inches *b)* a cubic yard *[a yard of topsoil]* **2.** *Naut.* a slender rod or spar fastened across a mast to support a sail or to hold signal flags, lights, etc. **3.** [Slang] one hundred dollars or, sometimes, one thousand dollars
yard[2] (yärd) ***n.*** **[**OE. *geard*, enclosure**]** **1.** the ground around or next to a house or other building **2.** a pen, etc. for livestock or poultry **3.** a place in the open used for a particular purpose, work, etc. *[a navy yard, a lumberyard]* **4.** a railroad center where trains are made up, serviced, switched, etc. —***vt.*** to put, keep, or enclose in a yard (often with *up*)
yard·age (yär′dij) ***n.*** **1.** measurement in yards **2.** the extent of something so measured **3.** distance covered in advancing a football
yard·arm (yärd′ärm′) ***n.*** *Naut.* either end of a yard supporting a square sail, signal lights, etc.
yard·bird (-burd′) ***n.*** [Slang] **1.** a military recruit, esp. a rookie assigned to menial duties **2.** a convict
yard goods textiles made in standard width, usually sold by the yard
yard·man (-mən) ***n.***, *pl.* **-men** a man who works in a yard
yard·mas·ter (-mas′tər) ***n.*** a man in charge of a railroad yard
yard·stick (-stik′) ***n.*** **1.** a measuring stick one yard long **2.** any standard used in judging, comparing, etc.
yar·mul·ke (yär′məl kə) ***n.*** **[**Yid. < Pol. *yarmulka***]** a skullcap often worn by Jewish men and boys at prayer or study, at meals, etc.: also **yar′mal·ke, yar′mel·ke**
yarn (yärn) ***n.*** **[**OE. *gearn***]** **1.** a continuous strand or thread of spun wool, silk, cotton, nylon, glass, etc., for weaving, knitting, rope-making, etc. **2.** [Colloq.] a tale or story, esp. one that seems exaggerated —***vi.*** [Old Colloq.] to tell yarns —**spin a yarn** [Colloq.] to tell a yarn
Ya·ro·slavl, Ya·ro·slavl' (yä′rô släv′l') city in W European R.S.F.S.R., on the Volga: pop. 517,000
yar·row (yar′ō) ***n.*** **[**OE. *gæruwe***]** a plant of the composite family, having a strong smell, finely divided leaves, and clusters of small, pink or white flower heads
yat·a·ghan, yat·a·gan (yat′ə gan′, -gən) ***n.*** **[**Turk. *yatağan***]** a type of Turkish short saber with a double-curved blade and a handle without a guard
yat·ter (yat′ər) ***vi.*** **[**prob. < YA(K)[2] + (CHA)TTER**]** [Slang] to talk idly about trivial things —***n.*** [Slang] a yattering
yaw (yô) ***vi.*** **[**ON. *jaga*, to sway**]** **1.** to swing back and forth across its course, as a ship pushed by high waves **2.** to rotate or swing about the vertical axis, as an aircraft, spacecraft, etc. —***vt.*** to cause to yaw —***n.*** a yawing
yawl (yôl) ***n.*** **[**< MLowG. *jolle* or Du. *jol***]** **1.** a ship's boat **2.** a sailboat like a ketch, but with the short mizzenmast behind the rudderpost
yawn (yôn) ***vi.*** **[**prob. merging of OE. *ginian* & *ganian*, to gape**]** **1.** to open the mouth wide and breathe in deeply, as one often does automatically when sleepy or tired **2.** to open wide; gape *[a yawning chasm]* —***vt.*** to express with a yawn —***n.*** a yawning —**yawn′er** ***n.***
yawp (yôp) ***vi.*** **[**ME. *yolpen***]** **1.** to utter a loud, harsh call or cry **2.** [Slang] to talk noisily and stupidly —***n.*** the act or sound of yawping —**yawp′er** ***n.***
yaws (yôz) ***n.pl.*** *[with sing. v.]* **[**of Carib origin**]** a tropical infectious disease caused by a spirochete and characterized by raspberrylike skin eruptions followed by destructive lesions
y-ax·is (wī′ak′sis) ***n.***, *pl.* **y′-ax′es** (-sēz) *Math.* the vertical axis along which the ordinate is measured
Yb *Chem.* ytterbium
Y chromosome *Genetics* one of the sex chromosomes: see SEX CHROMOSOME
y·clept, y·cleped (i klept′) ***pp.*** **[**OE. *geclypod*, pp. of *clipian*, to call**]** [Archaic] called; named
yd. *pl.* **yd., yds.** yard
ye[1] (*thə, thi, thē*; *now often* yē) ***adj.*** *archaic form of* THE: *y* was substituted for the thorn (þ), the Old and Middle English character representing the sound (*th*)
ye[2] (yē; *unstressed* yi) ***pron.*** **[**OE. *ge***]** [Archaic] you
yea (yā) ***adv.*** **[**OE. *gea***]** **1.** yes: used to express affirmation **2.** indeed; truly —***n.*** an answer or vote of "yes" —***interj.*** a cry used in cheering on an athletic team
yeah (ya, ye, ye′ə, *etc.*) ***adv.*** [Colloq.] yes
yean (yēn) ***vt.***, ***vi.*** **[**< OE. hyp. *ge-eanian***]** to bring forth (young): said of a sheep or goat
yean·ling (-liŋ) ***n.*** a lamb or kid —***adj.*** newborn

year (yir) ***n.*** [OE. *gear*] **1.** a period of 365 days (in leap year, 366 days) divided into 12 months (from Jan. 1 through Dec. 31) **2.** the period (365 days, 5 hours, 48 minutes, and 46 seconds) spent by the sun in its apparent passage from vernal equinox to vernal equinox: the year of the seasons: also **tropical** or **solar year** **3.** the period (365 days, 6 hours, 9 minutes, and 9.54 seconds) spent by the sun in its apparent passage from a fixed star and back to the same position again: also **sidereal year** **4.** a period of 12 lunar months, as in the Jewish calendar: also **lunar year** **5.** the period of time in which any planet makes its revolution around the sun **6.** a period of 12 calendar months starting from any date *[six years ago]* **7.** a calendar year of a specified number in an era *[the year 500 B.C.]* **8.** a particular annual period of less than 365 days *[a school year]* **9.** [*pl.*] *a)* age *[old for his years]* *b)* time; esp., a long time *[years ago]* —**year after year** every year —**year by year** each year —**year in, year out** every year

year·book (-book′) ***n.*** a book published each year, as one with statistics and data of the past year, one with pictures and reports of a school's graduating class, etc.

year·ling (yir′liŋ, yur′-) ***n.*** an animal one year old or in its second year —***adj.*** being a year old

year·long (yir′lôŋ′) ***adj.*** continuing for a full year

year·ly (-lē) ***adj.*** **1.** lasting a year **2.** done, happening, etc. once a year, or every year **3.** of a year, or each year —***adv.*** annually; every year

yearn (yurn) ***vi.*** [OE. *gyrnan* < *georn,* eager] **1.** to be filled with longing or desire **2.** to feel tenderness or sympathy —**yearn′er** ***n.*** —**yearn′ing** ***n., adj.*** —**yearn′ing·ly** ***adv.***

year-round (yir′round′) ***adj.*** open, in use, operating, etc. throughout the year

yea·say·er (yā′sā′ər) ***n.*** [YEA + SAY + -ER] a person who is affirmative, positive, etc. in his attitude toward life

yeast (yēst) ***n.*** [OE. *gist*] **1.** any of various single-celled fungi that live on sugary solutions, ferment sugars to form alcohol and carbon dioxide, and are used in making beer, whiskey, etc. and as a leavening in baking: also **yeast plant** **2.** *a)* the yellowish, moist mass of yeast plants occurring as a froth on fermenting solutions *b)* this substance dried in flakes or granules or compressed into cakes **3.** foam; froth **4.** *a)* something that agitates or causes ferment; leaven *b)* ferment; agitation —**yeast′like′** ***adj.***

yeast·y (yēs′tē) ***adj.*** **yeast′i·er, yeast′i·est** **1.** of, like, or containing yeast **2.** frothy; foamy **3.** light; frivolous **4.** in a ferment; restless —**yeast′i·ness** ***n.***

Yeats (yāts), **William Butler** 1865–1939; Ir. poet, playwright, & essayist

yegg (yeg) ***n.*** [Old Slang] a safecracker or burglar

yell (yel) ***vi.*** [OE. *giellan*] to cry out loudly; shout; scream —***vt.*** to utter by yelling —***n.*** **1.** a loud outcry or shout; scream **2.** a rhythmic cheer given in unison, as by students at a football game —**yell′er** ***n.***

yel·low (yel′ō) ***adj.*** [OE. *geolu*] **1.** of the color of gold, butter, or ripe lemons **2.** having a yellowish skin; Mongoloid **3.** [Colloq.] cowardly **4.** cheaply sensational *[yellow journalism]* —***n.*** **1.** a yellow color; color between orange and green in the spectrum **2.** a yellow pigment or dye **3.** the yolk of an egg —***vt., vi.*** to make or become yellow —**yel′low·ish** ***adj.*** —**yel′low·ness** ***n.***

yel·low-bel·ly (-bel′ē) ***n.,*** *pl.* **-lies** [Slang] a contemptible coward —**yel′low-bel′lied** ***adj.***

yel·low·bird (-burd′) ***n.*** a bird yellow in color, as the yellow warbler, the American goldfinch, etc.

yel·low-dog contract (-dôg′) a contract, now illegal, by which a new employee agrees not to join a labor union

yellow fever a tropical disease caused by a virus carried to man by the bite of the **yellow-fever mosquito,** and marked by fever, jaundice, vomiting, etc.

yel·low·ham·mer (-ham′ər) ***n.*** [ult. < OE. *geolu,* yellow + *amore,* kind of finch] **1.** a small European finch having a yellow head, neck, and breast: also called **yellow bunting** **2.** the golden-winged flicker

yellow jack **1.** *same as* YELLOW FEVER **2.** a yellow flag used as a signal of quarantine

yellow jacket any of several social wasps or hornets having bright-yellow markings

Yel·low·knife (yel′ō nīf′) town on Great Slave Lake, NW Canada; capital of Northwest Territories: pop. 8,000

yellow metal **1.** gold **2.** brass that is 60 parts copper and 40 parts zinc

Yellow Pages [*also* **y- p-**] the section or volume of a telephone directory, on yellow paper, containing classified listings of subscribers according to business, profession, etc.

yellow pine **1.** any of several N. American pines having yellowish wood **2.** this wood

Yellow River *same as* HWANG HO

Yellow Sea arm of the East China Sea, between China & Korea

Yel·low·stone (yel′ō stōn′) [ult. ? Fr. transl. of native name] river flowing from NW Wyo. through Mont. into the Missouri River

Yellowstone National Park national park mostly in NW Wyo., containing geysers, boiling springs, etc.

yellow streak a tendency to be cowardly

yellow warbler a small, bright-yellow N. American warbler

yel·low·wood (-wood′) ***n.*** **1.** any of several trees with yellow wood, esp. one of the southeastern U.S. **2.** its wood

yel·low·y (yel′ə wē) ***adj.*** somewhat yellow

yelp (yelp) ***vi.*** [OE. *gielpan,* to boast] **1.** to utter a short, sharp cry or bark, as a dog **2.** to cry out sharply, as in pain —***vt.*** to express by yelping —***n.*** a short, sharp cry or bark

Yem·en (yem′ən) **1.** country in S Arabia, on the Red Sea: c. 75,000 sq. mi.; pop. 5,000,000: in full, **Yemen Arab Republic** **2.** country in S Arabia, on the Arabian Sea, east of Yemen (sense 1): c. 110,000 sq. mi.; pop. 1,475,000: in full, **People's Democratic Republic of Yemen** —**Yem′en·ite′** (-ə nīt′), **Yem′e·ni** (-ə nē) ***adj., n.***

yen[1] (yen) ***n.,*** *pl.* **yen** [Jap. < Chin. *yüan,* round] the monetary unit of Japan: see MONETARY UNITS, table

yen[2] (yen) ***n.*** [Chin. *yán,* opium] [Colloq.] a strong longing or desire —***vi.*** **yenned, yen′ning** [Colloq.] to have a yen (*for*); long; yearn

Ye·ni·sei, Ye·ni·sey (ye′ni sā′) river in C Siberian R.S.F.S.R., flowing north into the Arctic Ocean: c. 2,600 mi.

yen·ta, yen·te (yen′tə) ***n.*** [Yid.] a woman gossip or busybody

yeo·man (yō′mən) ***n.,*** *pl.* **-men** [ME. *yeman,* prob. contr. < *yung man,* young man] **1.** orig., *a)* a manservant in a royal or noble household *b)* a freeholder of a class below the gentry **2.** [Brit.] *a)* a small landowner *b)* *same as* YEOMAN OF THE GUARD *c)* a member of the yeomanry (sense 2) **3.** *U.S. Navy* a petty officer assigned to clerical duty —***adj.*** of or like yeomen: see also YEOMAN'S SERVICE

yeo·man·ly (-lē) ***adj.*** **1.** of, like, or befitting a yeoman **2.** brave; sturdy —***adv.*** in a yeomanly manner

yeoman of the (royal) guard any of the 100 men forming a ceremonial guard for the English royal family

yeo·man·ry (-rē) ***n.*** **1.** yeomen collectively **2.** a British volunteer cavalry force, orig. a home guard, but now part of the Territorial Army

yeoman's service very good, useful, or loyal service or assistance: also **yeoman service**

yep (yep) ***adv.*** [Slang] yes: an affirmative reply

-yer (yər) *same as* -IER: usually after *w,* as in *lawyer*

Ye·re·van (ye re vän′) capital of the Armenian S.S.R., at the foot of Mt. Ararat: pop. 767,000

yes (yes) ***adv.*** [OE. *gese,* prob. < *gea,* yea + *si,* be it so] **1.** aye; yea; it is so: the opposite of NO, used to express agreement, consent, affirmation, etc. **2.** not only that, but more; moreover *[ready, yes, eager to help]* *Yes* is sometimes used alone in inquiry to signify "What is it?" or as a polite expression of interest —***n.,*** *pl.* **yes′es** **1.** the act of saying *yes* **2.** an affirmative vote, voter, etc. —***vt., vi.*** **yessed, yes′sing** to say *yes* (to)

yes man [Slang] a person who indicates approval of every suggestion or opinion offered by his superior

yes·ter (yes′tər) ***adj.*** [< ff.] **1.** of yesterday **2.** previous to this Usually in combination *[yestereve, yesteryear]*

yes·ter·day (yes′tər dē, -dā′) ***n.*** [< OE. < *geostran,* yesterday + *dæg,* day] **1.** the day before today **2.** a recent day or time **3.** [*usually pl.*] time gone by —***adv.*** **1.** on the day before today **2.** recently —***adj.*** of yesterday

yes·ter·year (-yir′) ***n., adv.*** [Poet.] **1.** last year **2.** (in) recent years

yet (yet) ***adv.*** [OE. *giet*] **1.** up to now or to the time specified; thus far *[he hasn't gone yet]* **2.** at the present time; now *[we can't leave yet]* **3.** still; even now *[there is yet a chance for peace]* **4.** at some future time; sooner or later *[she will thank you yet]* **5.** now or at a particular time, as continuing from a preceding time *[we could hear her yet]* **6.** in addition; still *[he was yet more kind]* **7.** as much as; even *[he did not come, nor yet write]* **8.** now, after all the time that has elapsed *[hasn't he finished yet?]* **9.** nevertheless *[he was rich, yet lonely]* —***conj.*** nevertheless; however *[she seems happy, yet she is troubled]* —**as yet** up to now

ye·ti (yĕt′ē) ***n.*** [Tibet.] [*often* **Y-**] *same as* ABOMINABLE SNOWMAN

yew (yōō) ***n.*** [OE. *iw*] **1.** an evergreen shrub or tree with red, waxy cones and a fine-grained, elastic wood **2.** the wood, used esp. for making archers' bows

fat, āpe, cär, ten, ēven, is, bīte; gō, hôrn, tōōl, look; oil, out; up, fur; get; joy; yet; chin; she; thin, *th*en; zh, leisure; ŋ, ring; ə for *a* in *ago, e* in *agent, i* in *sanity, o* in *comply, u* in *focus;* ′ as in *able* (ā′b'l); Fr. bål; ë, Fr. coeur; ö, Fr. feu; Fr. mon; ô, Fr. coq; ü, Fr. duc; r, Fr. cri; H, G. ich; kh, G. doch; ‡foreign; *hypothetical; < derived from. See inside front cover.

Yid·dish (yid′ish) *n.* [Yid. *yidish* < G. *jüdisch,* Jewish, ult. < L. *Judaeus,* a Jew] a language derived from medieval High German, spoken by East European Jews and their descendants in other countries: it is written in the Hebrew alphabet and contains vocabulary borrowings from Hebrew, Russian, Polish, English, etc.: abbrev. **Yid.** *—adj.* of or in this language

yield (yēld) *vt.* [OE. *gieldan,* to pay] **1.** to produce; specif., *a)* to give or furnish as a natural process *[*the orchard *yields* a good crop*] b)* to give in return; produce as a result, profit, etc. **2.** to give up under pressure; surrender **3.** to concede; grant *—vi.* **1.** to produce or bear **2.** to give up; surrender **3.** to give way to physical force **4.** to give place; lose precedence, etc. (often with *to*); specif., *a)* to let another (motorist) have the right of way *b)* to give up willingly a right, etc. *—n.* **1.** the amount yielded or produced **2.** the earnings received from investment in stocks, bonds, etc. **3.** the force in kilotons or megatons of a nuclear or thermonuclear explosion **—yield′er** *n.*

yield·ing (yēl′diŋ) *adj.* **1.** producing a good yield; productive **2.** bending easily; flexible **3.** submissive

yin (yin) *n.* [< Chin. dial.] in Chinese philosophy, the passive, negative, feminine force or principle in the universe, complementary to the *yang:* see YANG

yip (yip) *n.* [echoic] [Colloq.] a yelp, or bark *—vi.* **yipped, yip′ping** [Colloq.] to yelp, or bark

yipe (yīp) *interj.* an exclamation of pain, dismay, alarm, etc.

yip·pee (yip′ē) *interj.* an exclamation of joy, delight, etc.

-yl (il; *now rarely* ēl) [< Gr. *hylē,* wood] *Chem. a combining form meaning:* **1.** a univalent hydrocarbon radical *[ethyl]* **2.** a radical containing oxygen *[hydroxyl]*

YMCA, Y.M.C.A. Young Men's Christian Association

YMHA, Y.M.H.A. Young Men's Hebrew Association

yob (yäb) *n.* [inversion of BOY] [Brit. Slang] a hoodlum or lout: also **yob·bo** (yä′bō)

yock (yäk) *n.* [var. of YAK[2]] [Slang] a loud laugh or something evoking loud laughter; yak: also sp. **yok**

yo·del (yō′d'l) *vt., vi.* **-deled** or **-delled, -del·ing** or **-del·ling** [G. *jodeln*] to sing with sudden changes back and forth between the normal chest voice and the falsetto *—n.* **1.** the act or sound of yodeling **2.** a song sung in this way **—yo′del·er, yo′del·ler** *n.*

yo·ga (yō′gə) *n.* [Sans., union] **1.** *Hinduism* a discipline by which one seeks to achieve union with the universal soul through deep meditation, prescribed postures, controlled breathing, etc. **2.** a system of exercising involving such postures, breathing, etc. **—yo′gic** (-gik) *adj.*

yo·gi (yō′gē) *n., pl.* **-gis** a person who practices yoga: also **yo′gin** (-gin)

yo·gurt (yō′gərt) *n.* [Turk. *yōghurt*] a thick, semisolid food made from milk fermented by a bacterium, believed to have a beneficial effect on the intestines: often prepared with various flavors: also sp. **yo′ghurt, yo′ghourt**

yo-heave-ho (yō′hēv′hō′) *interj.* a chant formerly used by sailors while pulling or lifting together in rhythm

yoicks (yoiks) *interj.* [earlier *hoik, hike,* also *yoaks*] [Brit.] a cry used for urging on the hounds in fox hunting

yoke (yōk) *n., pl.* **yokes;** for 2, usually **yoke** [OE. *geoc*] **1.** a wooden frame with bows at either end, fitted around the necks of a pair of oxen, etc. to harness them **2.** a pair of animals harnessed together **3.** the condition of being under another's power or control; bondage **4.** something that binds, unites, etc. **5.** something like a yoke, as a frame fitting over the shoulders for carrying pails, etc. **6.** a part of a garment fitted closely around the shoulders or hips to support the gathered parts below *—vt.* **yoked, yok′ing 1.** to put a yoke on **2.** to harness (an animal) to (a plow, etc.) **3.** to join together *—vi.* to be joined together

YOKE (on pair of oxen)

yo·kel (yō′k'l) *n.* [prob. < dial. *yokel,* green woodpecker] a country person; rustic: a contemptuous term

Yo·ko·ha·ma (yō′kə hä′mə; *Jap.* yô′kô hä′mä) seaport on the S coast of Honshu, Japan: pop. 1,789,000

yolk (yōk) *n.* [OE. *geolca*] the yellow, principal substance of an egg **—yolked, yolk′y** *adj.*

yolk sac a sac containing yolk that is attached to and supplies nourishment for the embryos of birds, fishes, and reptiles

Yom Kip·pur (yäm kip′ər, yôm-; *Heb.* yōm′ kē po͞or′) a Jewish holiday, the Day of Atonement, a fast day observed on the 10th day of Tishri

yon (yän) *adj., adv.* [OE. *geon*] [Archaic or Dial.] yonder

yon·der (yän′dər) *adj.* [ME.] **1.** farther; more distant (with *the*) **2.** being at a distance, but within, or as within, sight *—adv.* at or in that place; over there

Yon·kers (yäŋ′kərz) [< Du. *De Jonkers* (*Land*), the young nobleman's (land)] city in SE N.Y., on the Hudson: suburb of New York City: pop. 195,000

yoo-hoo (yo͞o′ho͞o′) *interj., n.* a shout or call used to attract someone's attention

yore (yôr) *adv.* [OE. *geara*] [Obs.] long ago *—n.* time long past: now only in **of yore,** formerly

York[1] (yôrk) ruling family of England (1461–85)

York[2] (yôrk) [after ff.] city in SE Pa.: pop. 45,000

York·shire (yôrk′shir) former county of N England, on the North Sea: now divided into three counties (*North Yorkshire, South Yorkshire,* and *West Yorkshire*)

Yorkshire pudding a batter of flour, eggs, and milk baked in the drippings of roasting meat

Yorkshire terrier a long-haired toy terrier of a breed originating in Yorkshire, England

York·town (yôrk′toun′) [after the Duke of *York,* later CHARLES I] town in SE Va.: scene of the surrender of Cornwallis to Washington (1781)

Yo·sem·i·te National Park (yō sem′ə tē) [< AmInd., lit., grizzly bears, killers] national park in EC Calif., in the Sierra Nevadas: notable for its steep-walled valley **(Yosemite Valley)** & its high waterfalls **(Yosemite Falls)**

you (yo͞o; *unstressed* yoo, yə) *pron.* [OE. *eow,* dat. & acc. pl. of *ge,* YE[2]] **1.** the person or persons to whom one is speaking or writing: *you* is the nominative and objective form (sing. & pl.) of the second personal pronoun **2.** a person or people generally *[you* never can tell!*]*

you-all (yo͞o ôl′, yôl) *pron. Southern colloq. for* YOU: chiefly used as a pl. form

you'd (yo͞od; *unstressed* yood, yəd) **1.** you had **2.** you would

you'll (yo͞ol; *unstressed* yool, yəl) **1.** you will **2.** you shall

young (yuŋ) *adj.* [OE. *geong*] **1.** being in an early period of life or growth **2.** characteristic of youth in quality, appearance, etc.; fresh; vigorous **3.** representing or embodying a new tendency, social movement, etc. **4.** of youth or early life **5.** lately begun; in an early stage **6.** lacking experience or practice; immature; green **7.** younger than another of the same name or family *—n.* **1.** young people **2.** offspring, esp. young offspring, collectively *[*a bear and her *young]* **—with young** pregnant

Young (yuŋ), **Brig·ham** (brig′əm) 1801–77; U.S. Mormon leader

young·ber·ry (yuŋ′ber′ē) *n., pl.* **-ries** [after B. *Young,* 19th-c. U.S. horticulturist] **1.** a large, sweet, dark-purple berry, a cross between a blackberry and a dewberry **2.** the trailing bramble bearing this fruit

young blood 1. young people **2.** youthful vigor, ideas, etc.

young·ish (yuŋ′ish) *adj.* rather young

young·ling (-liŋ) *n.* **1.** a young person; youth **2.** a young animal or plant *—adj.* young

young·ster (-stər) *n.* **1.** a child **2.** a youth **3.** a young animal

Youngs·town (yuŋz′toun′) [after J. *Young,* an early (c. 1800) settler] city in NE Ohio: pop. 115,000 (met. area, with Warren, 530,000)

Young Turk [orig., member of early 20th-c. revolutionary party in Turkey] [*also* **y- T-**] any of a group of younger people seeking to take control of an organization, political party, etc. from the older, usually conservative, people in power

your (yoor, yôr; *unstressed* yər) ***possessive pronominal adj.*** [OE. *eower*] of, belonging to, or done by you: also used before some titles *[your* Honor*]*

you're (yoor, yo͞or; *unstressed* yər) you are

yours (yoorz, yôrz) *pron.* that or those belonging to you: the absolute form of *your,* used without a following noun *[*that book is *yours, yours* are better*]* : also used after *of* to indicate possession *[*a friend of *yours]*

your·self (yər self′, yoor-) *pron., pl.* **-selves′** (-selvz′) **1.** a form of the 2d pers. sing. pronoun, used: *a)* as an intensive *[*you *yourself* went*] b)* as a reflexive *[*you hurt *yourself] c)* as a quasi-noun meaning "your real or true self" *[*you are not *yourself* today*]* **2.** *same as* ONESELF *[*it is best to do it *yourself]*

yours truly 1. a phrase used before the signature in ending a letter **2.** [Colloq.] I or me

youth (yo͞oth) *n., pl.* **youths** (yo͞oths, yo͞o*thz*) [OE. *geoguthe*] **1.** the state or quality of being young **2.** the period of life coming between childhood and maturity; adolescence **3.** an early stage of growth or existence **4.** young people collectively **5.** a young person; esp., a young man

youth·ful (-fəl) *adj.* **1.** young; possessing youth **2.** of, characteristic of, or suitable for youth **3.** fresh; vigorous **4.** new; early; in an early stage **—youth′ful·ly** *adv.* **—youth′ful·ness** *n.*

youth hostel any of a system of supervised shelters providing cheap lodging on a cooperative basis for young people on bicycle tours, hikes, etc.

you've (yo͞ov; *unstressed* yoov, yəv) you have

yow (you) *interj.* an exclamation of pain, surprise, etc.

yowl (youl) *vi.* [< ON. *gaula*] to utter a long, mournful cry; howl *—n.* such a cry

yo-yo (yō′yō′) *n.* [< Tagalog name: the toy came to the U.S. from the Philippines] **1.** a spoollike toy attached to

one end of a string upon which it may be made to spin up and down **2.** [Slang] a person who is dull or stupid
Y·pres (ē′pr′) town in NW Belgium, near the Fr. border: center of heavy fighting in World War I
yr. **1.** year(s) **2.** younger **3.** your
yrs. **1.** years **2.** yours
yt·ter·bi·um (i tur′bē əm) ***n.*** [ModL. < *Ytterby,* Sweden] a scarce, silvery, metallic chemical element of the rare-earth group: symbol, Yb; at. wt., 173.04; at. no., 70
yt·tri·um (it′rē əm) ***n.*** [ModL. < *Ytterby,* Sweden] a rare, silvery, metallic chemical element: symbol, Y; at. wt., 88.905; at. no., 39
yu·an (yōō än′) ***n.*** [Chin. *yüan,* round] *see* MONETARY UNITS, table (China)
Yu·ca·tán, Yu·ca·tan (yōō′kä tän′; *E.* yōō′kə tan′) peninsula comprising SE Mexico, British Honduras, & part of W Guatemala: it extends north into the Gulf of Mexico
yuc·ca (yuk′ə) ***n.*** [ModL., genus name < Sp. *yuca*] **1.** a plant of the U.S. and Latin America, having stiff, sword-shaped leaves and white flowers in an erect raceme **2.** its flower
yuck·y (yuk′ē) ***adj.*** **-i·er, -i·est** [Slang] unpleasant, disgusting, etc.
Yu·go·slav (yōō′gō släv′, -gə-) ***adj.*** of Yugoslavia or its people: also **Yu′go·slav′ic** —***n.*** a member of a Slavic people, including Serbs, Croats, and Slovenes, who live in Yugoslavia Also **Yu′go·sla′vi·an**
Yu·go·sla·vi·a (yōō′gō slä′vē ə, -gə släv′yə) country in the NW Balkan Peninsula, on the Adriatic: 98,766 sq. mi.; pop. 20,672,000; cap. Belgrade
yuk (yuk) ***n.*** [echoic] [Slang] a loud laugh of amusement, or something evoking such a laugh —***vi.*** **yukked, yuk′king** [Slang] to laugh loudly Also sp. **yuck**
Yu·kon (yōō′kän) **1.** territory of NW Canada, east of Alas.: 207,076 sq. mi.; pop. 22,000; cap. Whitehorse: in full, **Yukon Territory:** abbrev. **Y.T.** **2.** river flowing through this territory & Alas. into the Bering Sea
Yukon Standard Time *see* STANDARD TIME
yule (yōōl) ***n.*** [OE. *geol*] Christmas or the Christmas season
yule log a large log formerly used as a foundation for the ceremonial Christmas Eve fire
yule·tide (-tīd′) ***n.*** Christmas time
yum (yum) ***interj.*** [echoic] delicious; excellent
yum·my (yum′ē) ***adj.*** **-mi·er, -mi·est** [echoic] [Colloq.] very tasty; delectable; delicious
yup (yup) ***adv.*** [Slang] yes: an affirmative reply
yurt (yoort) ***n.*** [< Russ. *yurta,* lit., dwelling] a circular tent on a framework of poles, used by the nomads of Mongolia
YWCA, Y.W.C.A. Young Women's Christian Association
YWHA, Y.W.H.A. Young Women's Hebrew Association

Z

Z, z (zē; *Brit. & Canad.* zed) ***n.,*** *pl.* **Z's, z's** **1.** the twenty-sixth and last letter of the English alphabet **2.** the sound of *Z* or *z* **3.** *a symbol for* the last in a sequence or group
Z (zē; *Brit. & Canad.* zed) ***n.*** an object shaped like Z —***adj.*** shaped like Z
z *Math. a symbol for:* **1.** the third in a set of unknown quantities, *x* and *y* usually being the first two **2.** a variable
Z., z. **1.** zero **2.** zone
Za·greb (zä′greb) city in NW Yugoslavia; capital of Croatia: pop. 457,000
Za·ire, Za·ïre (zä ir′) **1.** country in C Africa, on the equator: a former Belgian colony: 905,563 sq. mi.; pop. 22,477,000; cap. Kinshasa **2.** *same as* CONGO (River)
za·ire (zä ir′) ***n.,*** *pl.* **-ire′** [< Port., prob. < Bantu *nzadi,* big river] *see* MONETARY UNITS, table (Zaire)
Zam·be·zi (zam bē′zē) river in S Africa, flowing through Zambia & Mozambique into the Indian Ocean: c. 1,600 mi.
Zam·bi·a (zam′bē ə) country in S Africa: a member of the Commonwealth: 290,323 sq. mi.; pop. 4,336,000
za·ny (zā′nē) ***n.,*** *pl.* **-nies** [< Fr. < It. *zanni,* orig., an abbrev. pronun. of *Giovanni,* John] **1.** a clown or buffoon **2.** a silly or foolish person; simpleton —***adj.*** **-ni·er, -ni·est** of or like a zany; specif., *a*) comical in a crazy way *b*) foolish or crazy —**za′ni·ly** ***adv.*** —**za′ni·ness** ***n.***
Zan·zi·bar (zan′zə bär′) **1.** group of islands off the E coast of Africa, constituting a part of Tanzania **2.** largest island of this group: 640 sq. mi.
zap (zap) ***vt., vi.*** **zapped, zap′ping** [echoic] [Slang] to move, strike, stun, kill, etc. with sudden speed and force —***n.*** [Slang] energy, verve, pep, etc. —***interj.*** an exclamation used to express sudden, swift action
Za·po·rozh·e, Za·po·rozh·ye (zä′pô rôzh′ye) city in the SE Ukrainian S.S.R., on the Dnepr: pop. 658,000
Za·ra·go·za (thä′rä gô′thä) city in NE Spain: pop. 657,000
Zar·a·thus·tra (zar′ə thōōs′trə) *Persian name of* ZOROASTER
zarf (zärf) ***n.*** [Ar. *zarf,* a saucer] a small, cuplike holder, used in the Levant for a hot coffee cup
zeal (zēl) ***n.*** [< LL. *zelus* < Gr. *zēlos*] intense enthusiasm; ardent endeavor or devotion; fervor
Zea·land (zē′lənd) largest island of Denmark, between Jutland & Sweden: 2,912 sq. mi.; chief city, Copenhagen
zeal·ot (zel′ət) ***n.*** [< LL. < Gr. *zēlōtēs* < *zēlos,* zeal] a person who is zealous, esp. to an extreme or excessive degree; fanatic —**zeal′ot·ry** ***n.***
zeal·ous (zel′əs) ***adj.*** full of or showing zeal; fervent; enthusiastic —**zeal′ous·ly** ***adv.*** —**zeal′ous·ness** ***n.***
ze·bec, ze·beck (zē′bek) ***n.*** *same as* XEBEC
ze·bra (zē′brə; *Brit. & Canad., also* zeb′rə) ***n.,*** *pl.* **-bras, -bra:** see PLURAL, II, D, 1 [Port., prob. ult. < L. *equiferus,* a wild horse] any of several swift African mammals related to and resembling the horse but with dark stripes on a white or tawny body
zebra fish any of a number of unrelated fishes with barred, zebralike markings, often kept in aquariums
ze·bu (zē′byōō) ***n.,*** *pl.* **-bus, -bu:** see PLURAL, II, D, 1 [Fr. *zébu* < ?] an oxlike domestic animal of Asia and Africa: it has a large hump and short, curving horns: see BRAHMAN (sense 2)
Zech·a·ri·ah (zek′ə rī′ə) *Bible* **1.** a Hebrew prophet of the 6th cent. B.C. **2.** the book containing his prophecies: abbrev. **Zech.**
zed (zed) ***n.*** [< MFr. < LL. < Gr. *zēta*] *Brit. & usual Canad. name for* the letter Z, z
zee (zē) ***n.,*** *pl.* **zees** the letter Z, z
‡Zeit·geist (tsīt′gīst′) ***n.*** [G., time spirit] the trend of thought and feeling in a period of history
Zen (zen) ***n.*** [Jap. < Chin., ult. < Sans. *dhyāna,* meditation] **1.** a Japanese Buddhist sect that seeks enlightenment through meditation and intuition rather than in traditional scripture **2.** the beliefs and practices of this sect
Zend (zend) ***n.*** [Per., interpretation] the Middle Persian translation of and commentary on the Zoroastrian Avesta
Zend-A·ves·ta (-ə ves′tə) ***n.*** the sacred writings of the Zoroastrians
ze·nith (zē′nith; *Brit.* zen′ith) ***n.*** [< MFr. < ML. *cenit* < Ar. *semt,* road < L. *semita,* path] **1.** the point in the sky directly overhead: that point of the celestial sphere directly opposite to the nadir **2.** the highest point; peak
Ze·no (zē′nō) 334?–261? B.C.; Gr. philosopher: founder of Stoicism
Zeph·a·ni·ah (zef′ə nī′ə) *Bible* **1.** a Hebrew prophet of the 7th cent. B.C. **2.** the book containing his prophecies: abbrev. **Zeph.**
zeph·yr (zef′ər) ***n.*** [< L. < Gr. *zephyros*] **1.** the west wind **2.** a soft, gentle breeze **3.** a fine, soft, lightweight yarn, cloth, or garment
zep·pe·lin (zep′ə lin, zep′lin) ***n.*** [after F. von *Zeppelin* (1838–1917), G. inventor] [*often* **Z-**] a type of dirigible airship designed around 1900
ze·ro (zir′ō, zē′rō) ***n.,*** *pl.* **-ros, -roes** [Fr. *zéro* < It. < Ar. *ṣifr,* CIPHER] **1.** the symbol or numeral 0; cipher; naught **2.** the point, marked 0, from which positive or negative quantities are reckoned on a graduated scale, as on thermometers **3.** a temperature that causes a thermometer to register zero **4.** nothing **5.** the lowest point [*his chances sank to zero*] —***adj.*** **1.** of or at zero **2.** without measurable value **3.** designating or of visibility, as in flying, thought to extend no farther than a few feet —***vt.*** **-roed, -ro·ing** to adjust

(an instrument, etc.) to a zero point from which all positive or negative readings are to be made —**zero in** **1.** to adjust the sight settings of (a rifle) by calibrated firing on a standard range **2.** to aim (a gun or guns) directly at (a target) —**zero in on** **1.** to adjust gunfire so as to be aiming directly at (a target) **2.** to concentrate attention on
ze·ro-base (-bās′) *adj.* [from the idea of starting at zero] designating or of budgeting in which each item is evaluated on its merits without considering previous budgets: also **ze′ro-based′**
zero gravity a condition of weightlessness
zero hour **1.** the time set for the beginning of an attack or other military operation **2.** any critical point
zero (population) growth a condition in a given population in which the birthrate equals the death rate so that the population remains constant
ze·ro-sum (-sum′) *adj.* in game theory, designating or of a situation, competition, etc. in which a gain for one must result in a loss for another or others
zest (zest) *n.* [Fr. *zeste,* orange peel used to give flavor] **1.** stimulating or exciting quality; flavor; relish **2.** keen enjoyment; gusto (often with *for*) *[a zest* for life*]* —**zest′ful** *adj.* —**zest′ful·ly** *adv.* —**zest′ful·ness** *n.* —**zest′y** *adj.*
ze·ta (zāt′ə, zēt′ə) *n.* [Gr.] the sixth letter of the Greek alphabet (Z, ζ)
Zeus (zo͞os) the supreme deity of the ancient Greeks, son of Cronus and Rhea: identified with the Roman god Jupiter
zig·gu·rat (zig′o͝o rat) *n.* [Assyr. *ziqquratu,* height] an ancient Assyrian or Babylonian temple built as a pyramid with steplike stories
zig·zag (zig′zag′) *n.* [Fr.] **1.** a series of short, sharp angles or turns in alternate directions, as in a line or course **2.** a design, path, etc. having a series of such angles or turns —*adj.* having the form of a zigzag —*adv.* in a zigzag course —*vt., vi.* **-zagged′, -zag′ging** to move or form in a zigzag
zilch (zilch) *n.* [nonsense syllable, orig. used in the 1930's as name of a magazine character] [Slang] nothing; zero
zil·lion (zil′yən) *n.* [arbitrary coinage, after MILLION] [Colloq.] a very large, indefinite number
Zim·ba·bwe (zim bä′bwe) country in S Africa, north of South Africa: 150,333 sq. mi.; pop. 6,930,000; cap. Salisbury
zinc (ziŋk) *n.* [G. *zink*] a bluish-white, metallic chemical element, used as a protective coating for iron, in electric batteries and in alloys, and, in the form of salts, in medicines: symbol, Zn; at. wt., 65.37; at. no., 30 —*vt.* **zincked** or **zinced, zinck′ing** or **zinc′ing** to coat or treat with zinc; galvanize —**zinc′ic** (-ik), **zinck′y, zink′y, zinc′y** *adj.*
zinc ointment an ointment containing zinc oxide
zinc oxide a white powder, ZnO, used as a pigment and in making glass, cosmetics, ointments, etc.
zinc white zinc oxide used as a white pigment
zing (ziŋ) *n.* [echoic] [Slang] **1.** a shrill, high-pitched sound, as of something moving at high speed **2.** vitality, vigor, zest, etc. —*vi.* [Slang] to make a shrill, high-pitched sound —**zing′y** *adj.* **zing′i·er, zing′i·est**
zing·er (ziŋ′ər) *n.* [Slang] something said or done that has zing, as a retort, punch line, etc.
zin·ni·a (zin′ē ə, zin′yə) *n.* [ModL., after J. G. *Zinn,* 18th-c. G. botanist] a plant of the composite family, having colorful flowers, native to N. and S. America
Zi·on (zī′ən) **1.** the hill in Jerusalem on which the Temple was built: a symbol of the center of Jewish national life **2.** *a)* Jerusalem *b)* the land of Israel **3.** the Jewish people **4.** heaven **5.** the theocracy of God
Zi·on·ism (-iz'm) *n.* a movement formerly for reestablishing, now for supporting, the Jewish national state of Israel —**Zi′on·ist** *n., adj.* —**Zi′on·is′tic** *adj.*
zip (zip) *n.* [echoic] **1.** a short, sharp hissing sound, as of a passing bullet **2.** [Colloq.] energy; vim **3.** [Slang] a score of zero —*vi.* **zipped, zip′ping** **1.** to make, or move with, a zip **2.** [Colloq.] to act or move with speed or energy **3.** to become fastened or unfastened by means of a zipper —*vt.* to fasten or unfasten with a zipper
ZIP code (zip) [*z(oning) i(mprovement) p(lan)*] a system devised to speed mail deliveries, under which the post office assigns a code number to individual areas and places
zip·per (zip′ər) *n.* **1.** a person or thing that zips **2.** a device used to fasten and unfasten two edges of material: it consists of two rows of interlocking tabs worked by a part that slides up or down —*vt., vi.* to fasten with a zipper
zip·py (-ē) *adj.* **-pi·er, -pi·est** [< ZIP + -Y²] [Colloq.] full of vim and energy; brisk
zir·con (zʉr′kän) *n.* [G. *zirkon,* ult. < Per. *zargūn,* gold-colored < *zar,* gold] a crystalline silicate of zirconium, $ZrSiO_4$, colored yellow, brown, red, etc.: transparent varieties are used as gems
zir·co·ni·um (zər kō′nē əm) *n.* [ModL.: see prec.] a soft, gray or black metallic chemical element used in alloys, ceramics, etc.: symbol, Zr; at. wt., 91.22; at. no., 40
zit (zit) *n.* [< ?] a pimple, esp. one on the face
zith·er (zith′ər, zith′-) *n.* [G. < L. < Gr. *kithara,* a lute] a musical instrument having from thirty to forty strings stretched across a flat soundboard and played with a plectrum and the fingers
zlo·ty (zlô′tē) *n., pl.* **-tys** [Pol., lit., golden] *see* MONETARY UNITS, table (Poland)
Zn *Chem.* zinc
zo- *same as* ZOO-: used before a vowel
-zo·a (zō′ə) [ModL. < Gr. *zōia,* pl. of *zōion,* an animal] *a combining form used in zoology to form names of groups [Protozoa]*
zo·di·ac (zō′dē ak′) *n.* [< MFr. < L. < Gr. *zōdiakos (kyklos),* lit., (circle) of animals < *zōidion,* dim. of *zōion,* animal] **1.** an imaginary belt in the heavens extending on either side of the apparent path of the sun and including the paths of the moon and the planets: it is divided into twelve equal parts, or signs, each named for a different constellation **2.** a diagram representing the zodiac and its signs: used in astrology —**zo·di′a·cal** (-dī′ə k'l) *adj.*

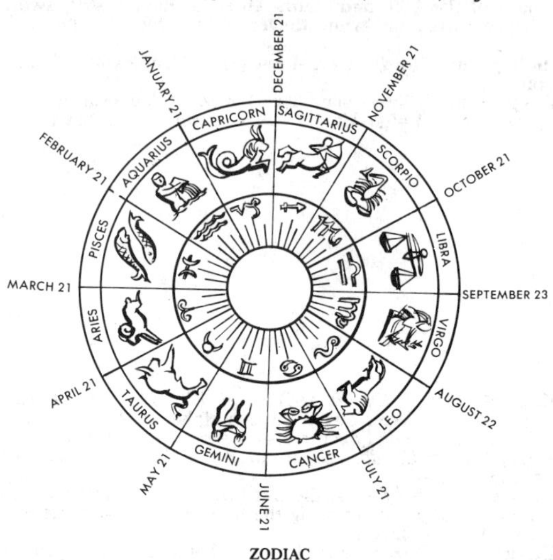

ZODIAC

Zo·la (zô lä′; *E.* zō′lə), **É·mile (Édouard Charles Antoine)** (ā mēl′) 1840–1902; Fr. novelist
zom·bie (zäm′bē) *n.* [of Afr. origin] **1.** in West Indian superstition, a dead person supposedly brought back by magic power to a form of life in which he can be made to move or act as he is ordered: also sp. **zom′bi** **2.** [Slang] *a)* a person like a zombie as in seeming to be half dead, to move automatically, etc. *b)* an eccentric person
zone (zōn) *n.* [Fr. < L. < Gr. *zōnē* < *zōnnynai,* to gird] **1.** *a)* an encircling band, stripe, etc. distinct in color, structure, etc. from what surrounds it *b)* formerly, a belt or girdle **2.** any of the five great divisions into which the earth's surface is marked off by imaginary lines: see TORRID ZONE, TEMPERATE ZONE, and FRIGID ZONE **3.** any region considered with reference to its particular use, crops, geological features, etc. *[a* canal *zone,* cotton *zone]* **4.** *a)* any area of a city restricted by law for a particular use, as for homes, businesses, etc. *b)* any space along a street or road restricted by traffic regulations *[*no parking *zone]* **5.** *a)* any of the numbered sections into which a metropolitan area is divided to make mail delivery easier *b)* any of a series of concentric areas about a given point, each having a different postage rate **6.** *short for* TIME ZONE **7.** *Sports* any of the areas into which a football field, basketball court, etc. is divided —*vt.* **zoned, zon′ing** **1.** to mark off into zones; specif., *a)* to divide (a city, etc.) into zones for particular uses *b)* to limit (an area of a city, etc.) as a zone for a particular use **2.** to encircle —**zon′al** *adj.*

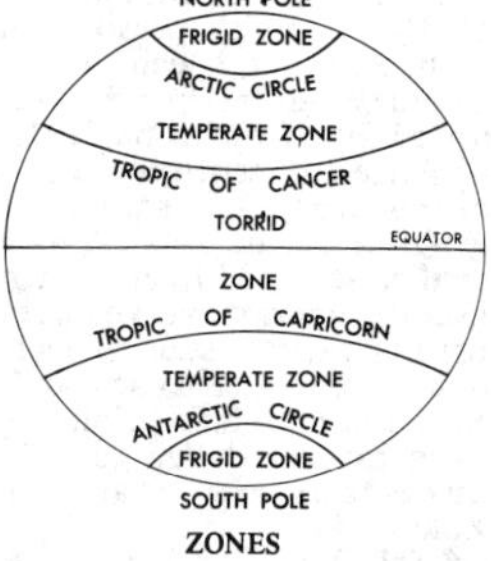

ZONES

zonked (zäŋkt) *adj.* [pp. of *zonk,* to strike, beat] [Slang] highly intoxicated or under the influence of a drug
zoo (zo͞o) *n.* [< ZOO(LOGICAL GARDEN)] a place where a collection of wild animals is kept for public showing
zo·o- [< Gr. *zōion,* animal] *a combining form meaning:* **1.**

animal, animals **2.** zoology and *[zoogeography]* Words beginning with *zoo-* are sometimes written **zoö-**

zo·o·ge·og·ra·phy (zō'ə jē äg'rə fē) ***n.*** the science dealing with the geographical distribution of animals **—zo'o·ge'o·graph'ic** (-jē'ə graf'ik), **zo'o·ge'o·graph'i·cal** ***adj.***

zo·og·ra·phy (zō äg'rə fē) ***n.*** [ZOO- + -GRAPHY] the branch of zoology concerned with the description of animals, their habits, etc. **—zo·og'ra·pher** ***n.*** **—zo·o·graph·ic** (zō'ə graf'ik), **zo'o·graph'i·cal** ***adj.***

zo·oid (zō'oid) ***n.*** [ZO(O)- + -OID] **1.** a comparatively independent animal organism produced by fission, gemmation, etc. rather than by sexual means **2.** any of the individual members of a colonial or compound organism, as a coral or hydroid ***—adj.*** of, or having the nature of, an animal: also **zo·oi'dal**

zool. 1. zoological **2.** zoology

zoological garden *same as* ZOO (sense 1)

zo·ol·o·gy (zō äl'ə jē) ***n.*** [< ModL.: see ZOO- & -LOGY] **1.** the branch of biology that deals with animals, their life, growth, classification, etc. **2.** the animal life of an area; fauna **3.** the characteristics of an animal or an animal group **—zo'o·log'i·cal** (-ə läj'i k'l), **zo'o·log'ic** ***adj.*** **—zo'o·log'i·cal·ly** ***adv.*** **—zo·ol'o·gist** ***n.***

zoom (zōōm) ***vi.*** [echoic] **1.** to make a loud, low-pitched, buzzing or humming sound **2.** to move with a zooming sound **3.** to climb suddenly and sharply: said of an airplane **4.** to rise rapidly *[prices zoomed]* **5.** to focus a camera by using a zoom lens ***—vt.*** to cause to zoom ***—n.*** **1.** a zooming or a zooming sound **2.** *same as* ZOOM LENS ***—adj.*** equipped with a zoom lens

zoom lens a system of lenses, as in a movie or TV camera, that can be rapidly adjusted for close-up shots or distance views while keeping the image in focus

zo·oph·i·lism (zō äf'ə liz'm) ***n.*** [ZOO- + PHIL(O)- + -ISM] extreme love for animals; specif., abnormal sexual attraction to animals: also **zo·oph'i·ly**

zo·o·phyte (zō'ə fīt') ***n.*** [< ModL. < Gr.: see ZOO- & -PHYTE] any animal, as a coral, sponge, etc., that looks and grows somewhat like a plant **—zo'o·phyt'ic** (-fit'ik), **zo'o·phyt'i·cal** ***adj.***

zo·o·plank·ton (zō'ə plaŋk'tən) ***n.*** plankton consisting of animals, as protozoans

zo·o·spore (zō'ə spôr') ***n.*** *Bot.* an asexual spore, esp. of certain fungi or algae, capable of independent motion usually by means of cilia or flagella **—zo'o·spor'ic, zo·os'po·rous** (-äs'pə rəs) ***adj.***

zo·ri (zôr'ē) ***n.,*** *pl.* **zo'ris, zo'ri** [Jap.] a sandal of a Japanese style, consisting of a flat sole held on the foot with a thong between the big toe and the toe next to it

Zo·ro·as·ter (zō'rō as'tər, zôr'ō as'-) ? 6th or 7th cent. B.C.; Per. religious leader: founder of Zoroastrianism **—Zo'ro·as'tri·an** (-trē ən) ***adj., n.***

Zo·ro·as·tri·an·ism (-trē ən iz'm) ***n.*** the religious system of the ancient Persians, teaching the eventual triumph of the spirit of good over the spirit of evil

Zou·ave (zōō äv', zwäv) ***n.*** [Fr. < Ar. *Zwāwa,* an Algerian tribe] **1.** a member of a former infantry unit in the French army that wore a colorful Oriental uniform **2.** a member of any military group wearing a similar colorful uniform

zounds (zoundz) ***interj.*** [altered < the oath *(by) God's wounds*] [Archaic] a mild oath expressing surprise or anger

zow·ie (zou'ē) ***interj.*** an exclamation expressing excitement, enthusiasm, admiration, etc.

zoy·si·a (zoi'sē ə) ***n.*** [ModL., after Karl von *Zois,* 18th-c. G. botanist] a creeping, wiry grass used for lawns in warm, dry regions

Zr *Chem.* zirconium

zuc·chet·to (zōō ket'ō, -ə; *It.* tsōō ket'tô) ***n.,*** *pl.* **-tos;** It. **-ti** (-tē) [< It. < *zucca,* a gourd] *R.C.Ch.* a skullcap worn by clergymen: a priest's is black, a bishop's purple, a cardinal's red, and the Pope's white

zuc·chi·ni (zōō kē'nē) ***n.,*** *pl.* **-ni, -nis** [It., pl. of *zucchino,* dim. of *zucca,* a gourd] a variety of summer squash that is green-skinned and shaped somewhat like a cucumber

Zui·der Zee, Zuy·der Zee (zī'dər zē'; *Du.* zöi'dər zā') former arm of the North Sea, which extended into the Netherlands: the S section (now called IJSSELMEER) was shut off from the North Sea by dikes: cf. WADDENZEE

Zu·lu (zōō'lōō) ***n.*** **1.** *pl.* **-lus, -lu** any member of a cattle-owning people living in Natal, South Africa **2.** their Bantu language ***—adj.*** of the Zulus, their language, etc.

Zu·lu·land (zōō'lōō land') region, formerly a Zulu kingdom, in Natal province, South Africa, on the Indian Ocean

Zu·ñi (zōōn'yē) ***n.*** [AmSp. < AmInd.] **1.** *pl.* **-ñis, -ñi** any member of a tribe of American Indians living in a pueblo in W New Mexico **2.** their language **—Zu'ñi·an** ***adj., n.***

Zur·ba·rán (thōōr'bä rän'), **Fran·cis·co de** (frän thēs'kô the) 1598–1664; Sp. painter

Zur·ich (zoor'ik) city in N Switzerland: pop. 428,000: also written **Zür·ich** (*G.* tsü'rIH)

zwie·back (swē'bak, swī'-, tswē'-, zwī'-; -bäk; *G.* tsvē'bäk') ***n.*** [G. < *zwie-,* twice + *backen,* to bake] a kind of rusk or biscuit that is sliced and toasted after baking

Zwing·li (tsviŋ'lē; *E.* zwiŋ'glē, swiŋ'-), **Ul·rich** (ool'rIH) or **Hul·dreich** (hool'drIH) 1484–1531; Swiss Protestant reformer **—Zwing'li·an** ***adj., n.***

zy·gote (zī'gōt, zig'ōt) ***n.*** [< Gr. *zygōtos,* yoked < *zygon,* a yoke] a cell formed by the union of male and female gametes; fertilized egg cell before cleavage **—zy·got'ic** (-gät'ik) ***adj.*** **—zy·got'i·cal·ly** ***adv.***

zy·mase (zī'mās) ***n.*** [Fr.: see ff. & -ASE] an enzyme, present in yeast, that promotes fermentation by breaking down glucose and some other carbohydrates into alcohol and carbon dioxide

zyme (zīm) ***n.*** [Gr. *zymē,* a leaven] [Obs.] a ferment or enzyme

zy·mo- [< Gr. *zymē,* a leaven] *a combining form meaning* fermentation *[zymology]* : also, before a vowel, **zym-**

zy·mo·gen (zī'mə jən) ***n.*** *Biochem.* an inactive form of an enzyme that can be made active

zy·mol·o·gy (zī mäl'ə jē) ***n.*** [ZYMO- + -LOGY] the science dealing with fermentation **—zy'mo·log'ic** (-mə läj'ik), **zy'mo·log'i·cal** ***adj.*** **—zy·mol'o·gist** ***n.***

zy·mur·gy (zī'mər jē) ***n.*** [ZYM(O)- + -URGY] the branch of chemistry dealing with fermentation, as applied in wine making, brewing, etc.

---

fat, āpe, cär, ten, ēven, is, bīte; gō, hôrn, tōōl, look; oil, out; up, fur; get; joy; yet; chin; she; thin, *th*en; zh, leisure; ŋ, ring; ə for *a* in *ago, e* in *agent, i* in *sanity, o* in *comply, u* in *focus;* ' as in *able* (ā'b'l); Fr. bàl; ë, Fr. coeur; ö, Fr. feu; Fr. mon; ô, Fr. coq; ü, Fr. duc; r, Fr. cri; H, G. ich; kh, G. doch; ‡foreign; *hypothetical; < derived from. See inside front cover.

TABLES OF WEIGHTS AND MEASURES

Linear Measure

1 mil	= 0.001 inch	=	0.0254 millimeter
1 inch	= 1,000 mils	=	2.54 centimeters
12 inches	= 1 foot	=	0.3048 meter
3 feet	= 1 yard	=	0.9144 meter
5½ yards or 16½ feet	= 1 rod (or pole or perch)	=	5.029 meters
40 rods	= 1 furlong	=	201.168 meters
8 furlongs or 1,760 yards or 5,280 feet	= 1 (statute) mile	=	1.6093 kilometers
3 miles	= 1 (land) league	=	4.83 kilometers

Square Measure

	1 square inch	=	6.452 square centimeters
144 square inches	= 1 square foot	=	929.03 square centimeters
9 square feet	= 1 square yard	=	0.8361 square meter
30¼ square yards	= 1 square rod (or square pole or square perch)	=	25.292 square meters
160 square rods or 4,840 square yards or 43,560 square feet	= 1 acre	=	0.4047 hectare
640 acres	= 1 square mile	=	259.00 hectares or 2.590 square kilometers

Cubic Measure

	1 cubic inch	=	16.387 cubic centimeters
1,728 cubic inches	= 1 cubic foot	=	0.0283 cubic meter
27 cubic feet	= 1 cubic yard	=	0.7646 cubic meter
(in units for cordwood, etc.)			
16 cubic feet	= 1 cord foot	=	0.453 cubic meter
128 cubic feet or 8 cord feet	= 1 cord	=	3.625 cubic meters

Nautical Measure

6 feet	= 1 fathom	= 1.829 meters
100 fathoms	= 1 cable's length (ordinary) (In the U.S. Navy 120 fathoms or 720 feet, or 219.456 meters, = 1 cable's length; in the British Navy, 608 feet, or 185.319 meters, = 1 cable's length.)	
10 cables' length	= 1 international nautical mile (6,076.11549 feet, by international agreement)	= 1.852 kilometers (exactly)
1 international nautical mile	= 1.150779 statute miles (the length of a minute of longitude at the equator)	
3 nautical miles	= 1 marine league (3.45 statute miles)	= 5.56 kilometers
60 nautical miles	= 1 degree of a great circle of the earth = 69.047 statute miles	

Dry Measure

	1 pint	= 33.60 cubic inches	= 0.5506 liter
2 pints	= 1 quart	= 67.20 cubic inches	= 1.1012 liters
8 quarts	= 1 peck	= 537.61 cubic inches	= 8.8098 liters
4 pecks	= 1 bushel	= 2,150.42 cubic inches	= 35.2390 liters

According to United States government standards, the following are the weights avoirdupois for single bushels of the specified grains: for wheat, 60 pounds; for barley, 48 pounds; for oats, 32 pounds; for rye, 56 pounds; for shelled corn, 56 pounds. Some States have specifications varying from these.

The British dry quart = 1.032 U.S. dry quarts

Liquid Measure

1 gill	= 4 fluid ounces (see next table)	= 7.219 cubic inches	= 0.1183 liter
4 gills	= 1 pint	= 28.875 cubic inches	= 0.4732 liter
2 pints	= 1 quart	= 57.75 cubic inches	= 0.9464 liter
4 quarts	= 1 gallon	= 231 cubic inches	= 3.7854 liters

The British imperial gallon (4 imperial quarts) = 277.42 cubic inches = 4.546 liters. The barrel in Great Britain equals 36 imperial gallons, in the United States, usually 31½ gallons.

Apothecaries' Fluid Measure

	1 minim	= 0.0038 cubic inch	= 0.0616 milliliter
60 minims	= 1 fluid dram	= 0.2256 cubic inch	= 3.6966 milliliters
8 fluid drams	= 1 fluid ounce	= 1.8047 cubic inches	= 0.0296 liter
16 fluid ounces	= 1 pint	= 28.875 cubic inches	= 0.4732 liter

See table immediately preceding for quart and gallon equivalents.
The British pint = 20 fluid ounces.

Circular (or Angular) Measure

60 seconds (″)	= 1 minute (′)
60 minutes	= 1 degree (°)
90 degrees	= 1 quadrant or 1 right angle
180 degrees	= 2 quadrants or 1 straight angle
4 quadrants or 360 degrees	= 1 circle

Avoirdupois Weight

(The grain, equal to 0.0648 gram, is the same in all three tables of weight.)

1 dram or 27.34 grains		=	1.772 grams
16 drams or 437.5 grains	= 1 ounce	=	28.3495 grams
16 ounces or 7,000 grains	= 1 pound	=	453.59 grams
100 pounds	= 1 hundredweight	=	45.36 kilograms
2,000 pounds	= 1 ton	=	907.18 kilograms

In Great Britain, 14 pounds (6.35 kilograms) = 1 stone, 112 pounds (50.80 kilograms) = 1 hundredweight, and 2,240 pounds (1,016.05 kilograms) = 1 long ton.

Troy Weight

(The grain, equal to 0.0648 gram, is the same in all three tables of weight.)

	3.086 grains	= 1 carat	=	200.00 milligrams
	24 grains	= 1 pennyweight	=	1.5552 grams
20 pennyweights or	480 grains	= 1 ounce	=	31.1035 grams
12 ounces or	5,760 grains	= 1 pound	=	373.24 grams

Apothecaries' Weight

(The grain, equal to 0.0648 gram, is the same in all three tables of weight.)

20 grains	= 1 scruple	=	1.296 grams
3 scruples	= 1 dram	=	3.888 grams
8 drams or 480 grains	= 1 ounce	=	31.1035 grams
12 ounces or 5,760 grains	= 1 pound	=	373.24 grams

THE METRIC SYSTEM

Linear Measure

	1 millimeter	=	0.03937 inch
10 millimeters	= 1 centimeter	=	0.3937 inch
10 centimeters	= 1 decimeter	=	3.937 inches
10 decimeters	= 1 meter	=	39.37 inches or 3.2808 feet
10 meters	= 1 decameter	=	393.7 inches
10 decameters	= 1 hectometer	=	328.08 feet
10 hectometers	= 1 kilometer	=	0.621 mile or 3,280.8 feet
10 kilometers	= 1 myriameter	=	6.21 miles

Square Measure

	1 square millimeter	=	0.00155 square inch
100 square millimeters	= 1 square centimeter	=	0.15499 square inch
100 square centimeters	= 1 square decimeter	=	15.499 square inches
100 square decimeters	= 1 square meter	=	1,549.9 square inches or 1.196 square yards
100 square meters	= 1 square decameter	=	119.6 square yards
100 square decameters	= 1 square hectometer	=	2.471 acres
100 square hectometers	= 1 square kilometer	=	0.386 square mile or 247.1 acres

Land Measure

1 square meter	= 1 centiare	=	1,549.9 square inches
100 centiares	= 1 are	=	119.6 square yards
100 ares	= 1 hectare	=	2.471 acres
100 hectares	= 1 square kilometer	=	0.386 square mile or 247.1 acres

Volume Measure

1,000 cubic millimeters	= 1 cubic centimeter	=	0.06102 cubic inch
1,000 cubic centimeters	= 1 cubic decimeter	=	61.023 cubic inches or 0.0353 cubic foot
1,000 cubic decimeters	= 1 cubic meter (the unit is called a *stere* in measuring firewood)	=	35.314 cubic feet or 1.308 cubic yards

Capacity Measure

10 milliliters	= 1 centiliter	=	0.338 fluid ounce
10 centiliters	= 1 deciliter	=	3.38 fluid ounces or 0.1057 liquid quart
10 deciliters	= 1 liter	=	1.0567 liquid quarts or 0.9081 dry quart
10 liters	= 1 decaliter	=	2.64 gallons or 0.284 bushel
10 decaliters	= 1 hectoliter	=	26.418 gallons or 2.838 bushels
10 hectoliters	= 1 kiloliter	=	264.18 gallons or 35.315 cubic feet

Weights

10 milligrams	= 1 centigram	=	0.1543 grain or 0.000353 ounce (avdp.)
10 centigrams	= 1 decigram	=	1.5432 grains
10 decigrams	= 1 gram	=	15.432 grains or 0.035274 ounce (avdp.)
10 grams	= 1 decagram	=	0.3527 ounce
10 decagrams	= 1 hectogram	=	3.5274 ounces
10 hectograms	= 1 kilogram	=	2.2046 pounds
10 kilograms	= 1 myriagram	=	22.046 pounds
10 myriagrams	= 1 quintal	=	220.46 pounds
10 quintals	= 1 metric ton	=	2,204.6 pounds

GUIDE TO THE MECHANICS OF WRITING

MARKS OF PUNCTUATION

The Period [.]

1. Use a period at the end of declarative sentences, indirect questions, and most imperative sentences.
 This book is very helpful. (*declarative sentence*)
 He asked what the score was. (*indirect question*)
 Write your name at the top of each sheet. (*imperative sentence*)
2. Use a period after most abbreviations. (See the section on abbreviations, p. 881)
3. Use three periods (called *suspension points* or *ellipsis marks*) to show that material has been omitted from a quotation. Use four periods when the omission comes at the end of a sentence.
 "There are four ways . . . to remedy the situation."
 Original: "There are four ways, none of which has been mentioned by my opponent, to remedy the situation."
4. A period may be used after a polite request phrased as a question.
 Would you please send me a copy of your catalog.
5. Do *not* use a period at the end of the title of a book, magazine, article, poem, or essay.
6. In a typed manuscript there should be two spaces between a period and the beginning of the next sentence.
7. In a typed manuscript, abbreviations do not have internal spacing.
 U.S.A.
 Ph.D.
 e.g.

The Question Mark [?]

1. Use a question mark at the end of a direct question.
 Do you have the money?
 "Do you have the money?" he asked. (Note that a comma is not used after the question mark.)
2. Use a question mark after each query in a series if you wish to emphasize each element.
 Have you heard the candidate give her views on civil rights? the war? urban problems? or the farm problem?
3. Use a question mark enclosed in parentheses to show uncertainty about a word, fact, or number.
 He was born in 1572(?) and died in 1622.
4. In a typed manuscript there should be two spaces between a question mark and the beginning of the next sentence.

The Exclamation Mark [!]

1. Use the exclamation mark after a forceful interjection or imperative sentence.
 Help!
 Please! Don't leave now!
2. In a typed manuscript there should be two spaces between an exclamation mark and the beginning of the next sentence.

The Comma [,]

1. Use a comma before the conjunctions *and, but, for, or, yet,* and *nor* when they join the clauses of a compound sentence.
 We inquired for him at the address she gave us, but no one there had ever heard of a person by that name.
 Note: Between most short clauses and between many long ones when the meaning is clear, the comma is omitted.
 First he stopped at the bank and then he went home.
2. Use a comma to separate an introductory clause or phrase from a main clause.
 When he had tired of the mad pace of New York, he moved to Dubuque.
 In the beginning, he liked the work.
 Note: If the introductory clause or phrase is short, or if there is no danger of ambiguity, the comma may be omitted. The following examples require commas because their omission slows up comprehension.
 In spite of all that, she got a passing grade.
 If the police shoot, the woman may be wounded.
3. Use a comma to set off introductory *yes* and *no*, mild exclamations, words of direct address, and introductory words that serve as a transition (*however, anyway,* etc.)
 Yes, I am going too.
 Jane, bring the book with you.
 Nevertheless, he was there when the trouble started.
4. Use a comma to set off a question at the end of a statement.
 You are coming too, aren't you?
5. Use a comma to set off dates, addresses, and titles.
 The letter was dated June 20, 1973, and was sent airmail.
 He lived at 21 Baker Street, Elyria, Ohio, for twenty years.
 Dr. Mary Harris, Director of Admissions.
6. Use a comma to set off contrasted sentence elements.
 Fred, not Jim, was first in his class.
7. Use a comma to indicate an omitted word or words in parallel constructions within a sentence.
 Irene is studying hard; Susan, scarcely at all.
8. Use a comma to set off sentence elements out of natural order.
 That he would accept the money, none of us seriously doubted.
9. Use a comma to separate words, phrases, and clauses in a series.
 The menu offered the usual choice of steak, chops, or chicken.
 If he studies hard, if he takes good notes, and if he participates in class discussion, he will probably pass.
 Note: In the style of some individuals and publications, the final comma before the conjunction is omitted.
 The daffodils, hyacinths, tulips and lilacs were in bloom.
10. Use a comma to set off absolute and parenthetical elements in the sentence.
 We finished within the allotted time, however.
 He did not say that, as you will realize when we play the recording, but he did imply it.
11. Use a comma to separate coordinate adjectives modifying the same noun. (If you can substitute *and* for the comma, the adjectives are coordinate.)
 It was a quaint, old-fashioned, vine-covered cottage.
 She had bright, mischievous, laughing brown eyes.
 But do not use a comma to separate noncoordinate adjectives modifying the same noun.
 Professor Jones is a kind old gentleman.
12. Use a comma or commas to set off nonrestrictive phrases or clauses from the rest of the sentence. (A nonrestrictive phrase or clause is one not essential to the meaning of the sentence.)
 My gun, which is now over the mantlepiece, hasn't been used for years.
 He found the paper on the roof, where the newsboy had thrown it.
13. Use a comma to set off direct quotations from such expressions as *he said, she replied,* etc.
 He said, "I'll never believe you again."
 "I know you can pass this course," he said, "if you will only try."
 But note: If the *he said* (or similar expression) comes between two independent clauses, then it must be followed by a period or semicolon, not by a comma.
 "Try this book," he said. "I think you will like it."
14. Use a comma following the salutation of a personal letter and following the closing phrase of every letter.
 Dear Jean,
 Very truly yours,
15. Use a comma before and after a dependent clause that comes in the middle of a sentence.
 The apples, although they had been freshly picked, became spoiled in shipment.
16. Use a comma after terms (*e.g., i.e., namely*) that introduce a series or an example.
 Some of our presidents, e.g., Jefferson, J. Q. Adams, and Buchanan, had previously been secretaries of state.
 But note: "Such as" should not have a comma preceding or following it.
 I enjoy sports such as football, basketball, and track.
17. Use a comma to set off the one spoken to in direct address.
 "John, you're the troublemaker in this class."
 "Yes, sir, I guess I am."
18. Use a comma to separate thousands in numbers of one thousand or over.
 The area of the earth is approximately 196,950,000 sq. mi.
19. Use a comma to separate inverted names, phrases, etc., as in a bibliography, index, or catalog.
 Jones, Harold T.
 Persia, architecture of
 radios, portable
20. In a typed manuscript a comma is followed by one space.

Misused and Unnecessary Commas

1. Do not use a comma to separate independent clauses not joined by a conjunction. This error is called the *comma splice* or *comma fault*.
 Evanston is by no means a resort city; however, its recreation facilities are of the finest. (*not* . . . a resort city, however, . . .)
 John told me he was an officer in the army; that isn't what I heard from others, however. (*not* . . . in the army, that isn't what . . .)

2. Do not use a comma or commas to set off restrictive phrases or clauses—that is, phrases or clauses necessary to the proper identification of the words they modify.
The book which I am reading is a history text.
3. Do not use a comma to separate a verb from a noun clause used as its subject or as its object.
That the professor enjoyed his subject was evident.
(*not* That the professor enjoyed his subject, was evident.)
I cannot imagine what made me do it. (*not* I cannot imagine, what made me do it.)
4. Do not use a comma between a noun and an adjective that comes directly before it.
It was a cold, wet, miserable day. (*not* . . . a cold, wet, miserable, day.)
5. Do not use a comma before *that* introducing an indirect statement.
He said that he would be there. (*not* He said, that he would be there.)

The Semicolon [;]

1. Use a semicolon between two independent clauses when they are not joined by a coordinating conjunction and the ideas expressed are very closely connected.
Good English requires more than correctness; it demands clarity, precision, and smoothness.
2. Use a semicolon to separate independent clauses joined only by conjunctive adverbs (*however, furthermore, nevertheless, consequently, also, besides, thus, otherwise, accordingly, hence, moreover, than,* etc.)
The bill was sent to the Senate; however, it was buried there in committee.
3. Use a semicolon with a coordinating conjunction if the independent clauses themselves contain commas.
The war, which was an abomination, had ended; and the battle for peace was to begin, at long last.
4. Use a semicolon to separate elements of a series when the elements themselves contain internal punctuation.
The participants came from Albany, New York; Cleveland, Ohio; and London, England.
5. Do *not* use a semicolon as the equivalent of a colon. Although a semicolon is often interchangeable with a period, it is never interchangeable with a colon.
6. Do *not* use a semicolon as the equivalent of a comma. Except for the special uses described in 3 and 4 above, the semicolon should never be used as a substitute for the comma.
7. In a typed manuscript a semicolon is followed by one space.

The Colon [:]

1. Use a colon before a long, formal quotation, formal statement, or list of items.
Lincoln arose and spoke as follows: "Fourscore and seven years ago . . . ."
The court's rules were simply stated: no television, no photographs, no demonstrations.
The following materials will be needed: pen, pencil, notebook, paper, and typewriter.
2. Use a colon after a main clause when the succeeding clause or clauses explain the first clause.
English usage is like table etiquette: it is conventional and its sanction is a social one.
3. Use a colon following the salutation of a formal letter. In informal letters a comma may be used.
Dear Ms. Brown:
Dear Sir:
Dear Bob,
4. Use a colon to separate chapter and verse of a Biblical citation, volume and page numbers in references, numerals designating hours and minutes, and the parts of a ratio.
Exodus 4:6
U.S. Encyclopedia 12:587
10:45 A.M.
11:10 odds
5. In a typed manuscript a colon is followed by one space.

The Dash [—]

1. Use a dash to indicate an abrupt break in the structure of the sentence or an unfinished statement.
He is—how shall I say it?—an officious zealot.
He said, "I am at a loss to understand—"
Note: When the dash comes at the end of the sentence, it is not followed by a period.
2. Use a dash to set off a summary or a long appositive.
Behind his apparent solicitude for her health, comfort, and happiness, one motive was evident to us—his eagerness for a bequest in her will.
3. Use a dash to set off strongly parenthetical expressions.
I was offended—no, enraged would be more accurate—by his actions.
4. Use a dash between numbers, dates, times, places, etc. that mark limits.
Look at pages 17—34.
Franklin lived 1706—90.
The office hours are 8:00—5:00 daily.
He will arrive on the New York—Chicago express.
5. Do not use dashes indiscriminately as a substitute for other marks of punctuation.
6. A dash is made in typing by using two hyphens with no space between them and the preceding and following words.

Parentheses [( )]

1. Use parentheses to enclose material that serves as an explanation, supplement, or example.
He ran 1500 meters (a little less than a mile).
2. Use parentheses to enclose figures and letters in the text of a piece of writing to indicate order of enumeration.
The subjects for this course are (1) English, (2) shorthand, (3) bookkeeping, (4) typewriting.
3. Use parentheses to enclose cross-references.
The amount of this yearly increase is astonishing (see Appendix A).
"Unexceptionable" is not to be confused with "unexceptional" (consult the dictionary).
4. Use parentheses in formal business writing to confirm a sum previously given in words.
I enclose my check for five hundred dollars ($500.00) to cover payment in full.
5. The conventions governing the use of parentheses with other marks of punctuation are as follows:
a. When a complete sentence within parentheses stands alone (that is, not as part of another sentence), the terminal punctuation is enclosed within parentheses.
He said that knowledge is sometimes useful. (That must be the unexceptionable statement of the century.)
b. When a complete sentence within parentheses is part of another sentence:
- It does not begin with a capital letter unless the first word is a proper noun.
- No period is used within the parentheses.
- If it is a question, a question mark is used within the parentheses.

Later in his analysis he stated that quality control was uneconomical (does he think this true for all lines?) and that its enforcement was ineffective.
c. When a word, phrase, or clause within parentheses is part of a sentence:
- A comma, semicolon, or period is never used after the last word in the parentheses.
- A comma, semicolon, or period is used following the second parenthesis only if the sentence without the parenthetical material requires punctuation at that point.
- A question mark or exclamation mark is used within the parentheses if it applies to the material within the parentheses.

He considered reporting Jim's threat (could it have been just so much bluster?) but then decided to have a heart-to-heart talk with him first.
6. In a typed manuscript matter in parentheses within a sentence is separated from the words on either side of the parentheses by a single space. A sentence standing by itself within parentheses is separated from the preceding and following sentences by two spaces.

Quotation Marks [" "]

1. Use quotation marks to enclose all direct quotations.
"Are you," she asked, "the man who helped my son?"
"Yes," he said, "I helped him. I didn't do much, though."
2. Use single quotation marks to enclose a quotation within another quotation.
The teacher said, "William Hazlitt's dying words were 'It was a happy life.' "
3. Use quotation marks to enclose titles of articles, chapters of a book, essays, short stories, short poems, and musical compositions.
The third chapter, "Some Solutions to the Problem," is perhaps the most valuable in the book.
One of Emerson's characteristic essays is "Self Reliance."
I enjoyed Steinbeck's short story "The Leader of the People."
She made us memorize the poem "Dover Beach," which none of us liked.
She sang "Over the Bounding Waves" loudly and with appropriate gestures.
4. Use quotation marks to enclose words spoken of as words, words used in special senses, or words emphasized. (Italics may also be used in such cases.)
Such words as "good," "bad," "beautiful," and "ugly" are merely judgment words.
What was the "real" meaning of her question?

5. A long quotation of a number of lines is usually placed in a paragraph that is indented on both sides, single-spaced, and without quotation marks.
6. Generally speaking, do not use quotation marks to redeem slang. If the slang expression is the best and most exact expression for the context, then use it without the apology of quotation marks; if it is not, putting it in quotation marks probably will not improve it or make it acceptable.
7. The conventions governing the use of quotation marks with other forms of punctuation are as follows:
a. The comma and the period are *always* enclosed within quotation marks.
"I'm sorry," he said, "but I don't believe you."
b. The colon and semicolon are *never* enclosed within quotation marks.
I had not read Francis Bacon's essay, "Of Truth"; in fact, I had never heard of it.
c. The dash, question mark, and exclamation mark are enclosed within quotation marks if they apply to the quoted material. They are placed after the quotation marks if they apply to the whole sentence.
"Am I going too?" she asked.
Did she say, "I am going too"?

Brackets [ ]

1. Use brackets to enclose matter which you insert in the text of a quoted passage to explain, comment, or correct.
"He was born in 1805 [actually in 1802] in . . . ."
According to *Time* magazine, "It [*Rabbit, Run*] was a flawlessly turned portrait of a social cripple who understood somehow that, running, he was more alive than he would be standing still."
2. Use brackets to enclose the Latin word *sic*, meaning "thus," when you insert it into a quotation following a mistake in fact, spelling, grammar, etc. to indicate to the reader that you are quoting verbatim from your source and that the mistake was in your source and was not yours.
"Andrew Johnson never attended school and was scarcely able to read when he met Eliza McCardle, whom he married on May 5, 1927 [sic]."
3. In a typed manuscript insert brackets in ink if your typewriter lacks these characters.

Apostrophe [']

1. Use the apostrophe to indicate the possessive case of the noun or pronoun.
the student's book
John's golf clubs
one's obligation
2. **a.** For nouns not ending in *s* add the apostrophe followed by *s*.
children's shoes
dog's collar
men's suits
b. For singular nouns ending in an *s*, *sh*, or *z* sound, the possessive is formed either by adding the apostrophe to the final *s* or by adding the apostrophe and another *s*.
James' book *or* James's book
conscience' sake *or* conscience's sake
c. For plural nouns ending in an *s*, *sh*, or *z* sound, use the apostrophe alone.
the Joneses' house
dogs' collars
the ladies' purses
d. In compound constructions place the apostrophe and *s* on the word standing immediately before the word being modified.
the King of England's daughter
anyone else's opinion
sister-in-law's cousin
e. Joint possession is shown by adding the apostrophe and *s* to the last name only or to all the names.
Wendy, Tony, and Christopher's home
Wendy's, Tony's, and Christopher's home
f. Separate ownership is denoted by the apostrophe and *s* after each name and the plural form of the modified word.
Wendy's, Tony's, and Christopher's homes
Selma's and Debbie's typewriters
3. Use the apostrophe to indicate the omission of letters or figures.
we've, won't, it's, can't, '73
4. Use an apostrophe to indicate the plurals of figures, letters, and words referred to as such.
Watch your p's and q's.
There are several 5's in the number.
There are too many "and's" in your sentence.
It was a party of V.I.P.'s.
5. Do not use the apostrophe with the personal pronouns to indicate possession.
Is it yours? (*not* Is it your's?)
Its color is faded. (*not* It's color is faded.)
6. The apostrophe is often omitted in the names of organizations.
Teachers College
Citizens Bank
Lions International
Veterans Administration

Italics

Italics (slanted type in printing) are indicated in a typed or handwritten manuscript by underlining.
1. Use italics for titles of books, magazines, plays, movies, long musical compositions, and names of trains, planes, and ships.
I read Austin Warren's *Rage for Order*.
Esquire is one of my favorite magazines.
We saw Alec Guinness in *The Horse's Mouth*.
We sailed on the *Cristoforo Colombo*.
Jim Frantz gave us Menotti's *The Medium* for Christmas.
Mort Walker directed García Lorca's *Blood Wedding*.
2. Use italics to emphasize a word or larger element in a sentence or to refer to a word as a word.
Moderation and *pragmatism* are the key terms to describe his fiscal policies.
The dictionary under the word *run* lists dozens of meanings.
Note: Do not overuse italics for emphasis.
3. Use italics to indicate a foreign word or phrase which has not been fully adopted as an English word. Check the dictionary to see whether the foreign word or phrase you want to use is so regarded.
His motto was *ars gratia artis*, which means "art for art's sake."
I thought the bullfighter would never deliver the *coup de grâce*.
He received a per diem allowance while on the trip.
(Note that the phrase "per diem," a Latin phrase, is now a fully naturalized English term and, hence, is not italicized.)

The Hyphen [-]

1. Use a hyphen to divide a word at the end of a line.
But note:
- Words of one syllable cannot be divided (this includes verbs such as "worked").
- Words of more than one syllable can be divided only between syllables. (Consult the dictionary.)
- Suffixes of fewer than three letters should not be separated from the rest of the word.
- Never divide a word so that only one letter stands at the end of the line.
- Hyphenated words should be divided only at the hyphen.

2. Use a hyphen between parts of a compound modifier preceding a noun except when the compound includes an adverb ending in *ly*. Compound modifiers following a noun are usually not hyphenated.
It was their twenty-fifth anniversary.
(All compound numerical modifiers between twenty-one and ninety-nine are hyphenated.)
She was a well-dressed woman.
The woman was well dressed.
(Here the compound follows the noun.)
She was a smartly dressed woman.
(Here the compound includes an adverb ending in *ly*.)
3. Use the dictionary to check on the hyphenation of other compound words. The practice of hyphenating words varies, and dictionaries seek to show the prevailing current practices. The main thing is to be consistent in one's treatment of any particular compound word.

NUMBERS

1. Use figures to express dates, hours, street numbers, decimals, measures, percentages, and volume, chapter, and page numbers.

April 22, 1969	Vol. II
12:05 P.M. or p.m.	Chapter V
21 Baker Street	p. 83
.3715	73% or 73 percent
16 pounds	80° or 80 degrees

2. Use figures to record uneven sums of money, and numbers over one hundred except when the numbers can be written as two words.
$4.19
122 *but* five thousand
3. Be consistent in your use of numbers within any piece of writing; do not, for example, spell out a number which can be expressed in two words (fifteen thousand) and later use figures for the same kind of number (20,000).
4. Usually spell out ordinal numbers.

Third Reich	Tenth Street
eighteenth century	Twenty-third Psalm

5. Do not begin a sentence with a figure. If spelling out the

number, however, would be awkward, recast the sentence so that it does not begin with a number.

Nine hundred and sixty students attended the rally.

He received 2,694,386 votes. (*not* Two million six hundred and ninety-four thousand three hundred and eighty-six votes were cast for him.)

CAPITALIZATION

1. Capitalize the first word of a sentence.
2. Capitalize the pronoun *I* and the interjection *O*.
3. Capitalize the first word in a quotation.
   He asked, "Are you going too?"
4. Capitalize the first word of a direct question falling within a sentence.
   This story answers the question, Where does true happiness really lie?
5. Capitalize all nouns referring to the deity and to the Bible and other sacred books and persons. Pronouns referring to the deity are capitalized by many, but not all, writers.

God	The Ten Commandments	the Holy Bible
Christ	The Blessed Virgin	the Koran
The Holy Spirit	the Incarnate Word	

6. Capitalize the names of gods and goddesses of polytheistic religions.
   Zeus, Thor, Venus
7. Use a capital letter for *President* and *Presidency* when these refer to the office of President of the United States.
   The President will speak 9:00 P.M.
   But note: The president [of a company] will address the luncheon.
8. Use a capital letter for official titles before the names of officials.
   Mayor Davis, President Kennedy, Governor Blair
   But note: Mr. Williams was governor of Michigan.
9. Capitalize proper nouns, and adjectives formed from proper nouns. (Consult the dictionary when in doubt.)

Michael Mardikes	Germany	Catholicism	Fifth Avenue
London	Maine	Protestant	Shakespearean

10. Capitalize every word except conjunctions, articles, and short prepositions in the titles of books and magazines, music and art, etc. The first word of the title is always capitalized.
   The Decline and Fall of the Roman Empire
   The Taming of the Shrew
   The Atlantic Monthly
   The Magic Flute
11. Capitalize every word except conjunctions, articles, and short prepositions in the names (or derived adjectives, verbs, etc.) of organizations, institutions, businesses, agencies, movements, religions, holidays, holy days, etc. Sometimes the initial article is capitalized as part of the official name.

The World Publishing Company	Memorial Day
the Boy Scouts of America	Corpus Christi
Internal Revenue Service	Buddhism
Yom Kippur	Library of Congress

12. Capitalize the names of nationalities, languages, and the anthropological terms for major groups of mankind.

Italian	Mongoloid
English	Negroid
Latin	Caucasoid

   But note: Do not capitalize *white, black, yellow,* or *red* when referring to groups of mankind.
13. Capitalize the names of all heavenly bodies.

Mars	Virgo
Sirius	Big Dipper

   But note: Earth, sun, and *moon* are not capitalized except when cited along with other heavenly bodies. The moon shines by means of light reflected from the sun. (*But:* Mercury is the planet closest to the Sun.)
14. Capitalize a title, rank, etc. followed by a proper name or of an epithet used with or in place of a proper name.

Lord Byron	General MacArthur
The Great Emancipator	Catherine the Great

15. Capitalize the names of trademarks.
   Dacron, Vaseline
16. Capitalize compass directions and adjectives derived from them when they refer to a specific geographical area.
   He lives in the East.
   She lives in the Middle West.
   He is a Southern congressman.
   But note: Chicago is east of Kansas City.
17. Capitalize words denoting family relationships only when they precede the name of a person or when they stand unmodified as a substitute for a person's name.
   I wrote to Grandfather Smith.
   I wrote Mother a letter.
   I wrote my mother a letter.
18. Capitalize the names of abstract or inanimate things that are personified.
   It has been said that Justice is lame as well as blind.
   It was the work of Fate.
   And now Spring came scattering her vexatious dandelions.
19. Capitalize geographical terms when they are part of a proper name.

Long Island Sound	the Gobi Desert
the Great Lakes	Mount Hood
the Dead Sea	the Straits of Mackinac

   But note: Do not capitalize geographical terms when they are used with two or more proper names (e.g., the Missouri River, *but* the Missouri and Mississippi rivers).
20. Capitalize government departments and offices.

Senate	Supreme Court
House of Representatives	Court of Appeals

ABBREVIATIONS

In general, do not use abbreviations in formal or informal writing (including business letters), except for the universally recognized cases given below.

1. Use abbreviations for the titles *Mr., Ms., Mrs., Dr.* These are never spelled out.
2. You may use abbreviations for the titles of college faculty, clergy, government officials, military personnel, etc. if the title is followed by a full name (first name and surname); if only the surname is used, the title must be written out.

Prof. Ralph King, Jr.	*but* Professor King (*never* Professor King, Jr. Use *Jr.* and *Sr.* only with full names)
Rev. William Clancy	*but* The Reverend Dr. *or* Mr. *or* Father Clancy (*never* Reverend Clancy)
Gov. Warren Hearnes	*but* Governor Hearnes
Hon. Warren Hearnes	*but* The Honorable Warren Hearnes or The Honorable Mr. Hearnes
Col. John Daniel	*but* Colonel Daniel

3. Use abbreviations for titles of religious orders, following the full name and a comma. Women's names are preceded by their title and followed by a surname if that is the custom of the order. Men's names may or may not be preceded by a title, according to one's choice.
   Sister Bede Sullivan, O.S.B.
   Mother Angela Therese, I.H.M.
   Father James Agattas, S.J. *or* Fr. James Agattas, S.J. *or* James Agattas, S.J. *or* Rev. James Agattas, S.J. (the last form is now the most usual)
4. Abbreviate the names of organizations when the full names the abbreviations stand for are universally known.

AFL-CIO	NAACP
DAR	UNESCO

5. Abbreviate the names of government agencies and military services and terms when the abbreviations are universally used. These abbreviations do not usually have periods (consult the dictionary entry for an abbreviation when in doubt about the use of periods with it).

CIA	USN
FBI	USAF
NATO	MP
HEW	PX

6. Abbreviate certain foreign terms in frequent use.
   etc., e.g., i.e.
7. Do *not* abbreviate in formal writing, except in footnotes or bibliographies, the days of the week, months of the year, States, countries (except U.S. and U.S.S.R.), weights and measures, or the words *street* and *avenue.*

SPELLING

The general principles or rules given here apply primarily to American usage. They are not complete but should provide practical helps for the spelling of many common words.

Words Ending in -e

Words that end in a silent *-e* usually drop the *-e* when a suffix beginning with a vowel is added.

assume — assuming	sense — sensible
grope — groping	style — stylish
purple — purplish	rogue — roguish

However, the *-e* is kept in a few words, as in these common exceptions.

shoeing	hoeing	toeing
dyeing	singeing	mileage

Words that end in a silent *-e* usually keep the *-e* when a suffix beginning with a consonant is added.

awe — awesome	improve — improvement
fate — fateful	time — timely

However, many words that end in a silent *-e* immediately preceded by a vowel other than *-e* drop the *-e* when a suffix is added.

true — truly	argue — argument
value — valuation	pursue — pursuant

Other exceptions:

awful	wisdom	ninth	wholly

Words Ending in -ce or -ge

Words that end in *-ce* or *-ge* retain the *-e* when suffixes that begin with *a*, *o*, or *u* are added, so that the *c* or *g* will not be pronounced with the hard sound.

peace — peaceable	advantage — advantageous
service — serviceable	change — changeable
notice — noticeable	courage — courageous

Words Ending in a Consonant

Words that end in a single consonant preceded by a single vowel usually double that consonant when a suffix beginning with a vowel is added. This rule applies to words of one syllable as well as to words of more than one syllable that are accented on the last syllable.

spin — spinning	propel — propellant
big — biggest	recur — recurrence
trot — trotter	permit — permitted
abet — abetted	regret — regrettable

When the addition of the suffix shifts the accent from the last syllable to a prior syllable, the consonant is not doubled.

prefer — preference	refer — reference

Words that end in two or more consonants, words that end in a single consonant preceded by more than one vowel, and words that are not accented on the last syllable usually do not double the final consonant when a suffix beginning with a vowel is added.

hurl — hurling	sprout — sprouted
count — counter	profit — profiteer
return — returned	benefit — benefited
conceal — concealed	prosper — prosperous
prevail — prevailing	combat — combative

Words Ending in -y

Words that end in *-y* preceded by a consonant usually change the *y* to an *i* when a suffix that does not begin with an *i* is added.

charity — charities	duty — dutiful
dizzy — dizziness	ply — plies
marry — married	study — studious
marrying	studying

Words that end in *-y* preceded by a vowel usually remain unchanged when a suffix is added.

convey — conveyance	boy — boyish
enjoy — enjoying	play — playing

Exceptions:

paid	said	laid
daily	gaiety	slain

Words Ending in -ie

Words that end in *-ie* change the *-ie* to *y* when the suffix *-ing* is added.

lie — lying	die — dying	vie — vying

Words Ending in -c

Words that end in *-c* usually take on a *k* when a suffix beginning with *i*, *e*, or *y* is added.

picnic — picnicker	shellac — shellacked
mimic — mimicking	panic — panicky
colic — colicky	rollic — rollicking

Words Containing ie or ei

Words that contain *ie* or *ei* usually are spelled with the *i* before the *e* when the combination represents the sound (ē), except after the letter *c* where the *e* usually precedes the *i*.

grief	believe	perceive	ceiling
piece	siege	receipt	conceit
brief	hygiene	deceive	receive
field	achieve		

Exceptions:

either	neither	leisure
seize	weird	financier

In those words in which *ie* and *ei* have the sounds (ā), (e), (i), or (ī), the spelling *ei* is usually found.

weigh	heifer	forfeit
neighbor	foreign	counterfeit
vein	sovereign	height
sleigh	heir	sleight

Exceptions:

handkerchief	friend	sieve
mischief	kerchief	

In those words in which the *ie* and *ei* combinations have two vowel sounds, the spelling corresponds with the pronunciation.

scientist	diet	society
theist	deity	de-ice

The Ending -ful

The word *full* when used as a suffix drops one *l*.

roomful	cupful	spoonful	eyeful

The Endings -ceed, -sede, -cede

Three words end in *-ceed*. One ends in *-sede*. The other verbs with the final sound (sēd) end in *-cede*.

exceed	supersede	recede
proceed		intercede
succeed		precede, etc.

FORMATION OF PLURALS

Most nouns in English form the plural by adding *-s* or *-es*. When the singular noun ends in a sound that allows *-s* to be added and pronounced without the formation of a new syllable, *-s* is used. When the singular noun ends in such a sound that *-s* cannot be joined to it and pronounced without the formation of an additional syllable, *-es* is used.

book — books	torch — torches
cake — cakes	kiss — kisses
doctor — doctors	tax — taxes
room — rooms	bush — bushes

Nouns Ending in -o

Nouns that end in *-o* preceded by a vowel form the plural by adding *-s* to the singular.

radio — radios	tattoo — tattoos
folio — folios	vireo — vireos

Most nouns that end in *-o* preceded by a consonant form the plural by adding *-es* to the singular. Some, however, add *-s* only. There is no fixed rule that deals with this distinction.

hero — heroes	solo — solos
potato — potatoes	piano — pianos
tomato — tomatoes	octavo — octavos

Nouns Ending in -f

Most nouns that end in *-f* or the sound of *-f* form their plurals regularly, but some common words drop the *-f* and add *-ves*. A few nouns have both forms.

calf — calves	life — lives
knife — knives	loaf — loaves
leaf — leaves	thief — thieves
shelf — shelves	wife — wives
hoof — hoofs, hooves	wharf — wharfs, wharves

Nouns Ending in -y

Nouns that end in *-y* preceded by a consonant usually form the plural by dropping the *-y* and adding *-ies*.

lady — ladies	story — stories
army — armies	study — studies
fly — flies	library — libraries

However, the plural of proper nouns ending in *-y* is formed by adding *-s*: both Harrys, the three McNallys.

Nouns that end in *-y* preceded by a vowel form the plural regularly, by adding *-s*.

boy — boys	quay — quays
tray — trays	toy — toys
key — keys	buy — buys

Change of Vowel

Some nouns form the plural by a vowel change.

man — men	goose — geese
mouse — mice	foot — feet
tooth — teeth	woman — women

Compounds that end with these words form the plural by the same vowel change.

postman — postmen	dormouse — dormice
bucktooth — buckteeth	splayfoot—splayfeet

Nouns that end in *-man* but are not compounds form the plural regularly, by adding *-s*.

human — humans	German — Germans
cayman — caymans	Norman — Normans
talisman — talismans	Ottoman — Ottomans

Similarly the noun *mongoose* is not a compound of *goose* and has the plural *mongooses*, while *goose* in the sense of a tailor's pressing iron has the plural *gooses*.

Nouns from Foreign Languages

Nouns derived from foreign languages often keep their original plurals.

alumna — alumnae	datum — data
alumnus — alumni	kibbutz — kibbutzim
analysis — analyses	monsieur — messieurs
basis — bases	phylum — phyla

Many such nouns, however, have an Anglicized plural as well as the original plural. Either is correct.

appendix — appendices, appendixes
cherub — cherubim, cherubs
criterion — criteria, criterions
focus — foci, focuses
index — indices, indexes
radius — radii, radiuses

KEY TO PRONUNCIATION

An abbreviated form of this key appears at the bottom of every alternate page of the vocabulary. A fuller explanation of the symbols will be found on pp. ix–xi of the Guide to the Use of the Dictionary.

SYMBOL	KEY WORDS	SYMBOL	KEY WORDS	SYMBOL	KEY WORDS
a	fat, lap	**u**	up, cut	**p**	put, tap
ā	ape, date	**ū**	use, cute	**r**	red, dear
â	bare, care	**ūr**	fur, turn	**s**	sell, pass
ä	car, father			**t**	top, hat
		ə	a *in* ago	**v**	vat, have
e	ten, let		e *in* agent	**w**	will, always
ē	even, meet		i *in* sanity	**y**	yet, yard
ê	here, dear		o *in* comply	**z**	zebra, haze
ēr	over, under		u *in* focus		
				ch	chin, arch
i	is, hit	**b**	bed, dub	**ŋ**	ring, drink
ī	bite, mile	**d**	did, had	**sh**	she, dash
		f	fall, off	**th**	thin, truth
o	lot, top	**g**	get, dog	***th***	then, father
ō	go, tone	**h**	he, ahead	**zh**	azure, leisure
ô	horn, fork	**j**	joy, jump		
o͞o	tool, troop	**k**	kill, bake	**'**	[see explanatory note on p. ix]
oo	book, moor	**l**	let, ball		
oi	oil, boy	**m**	met, trim		
ou	out, doubt	**n**	not, ton		

FOREIGN SOUNDS

ȧ	This symbol, representing the *a* in French *bal* (bȧl), can perhaps best be described as intermediate between (a) and (ä).
ë	This symbol represents the sound of *eu* in French *leur* (lër) and can be approximated by rounding the lips for (ô) and trying to pronounce (e).
ö	This symbol represents the sound of *eu* in French *feu* (fö) or *ö* (*oe*) in German *Göthe* (*Goethe*) (gö'tə) and can be approximated by rounding the lips for (ō) and trying to pronounce (ā).
ô	This symbol represents a range of sounds varying from (ō) to (ô) and heard with such varying quality in French *coq* (kôq), German *doch* (dôkh), Russian *gospodin* (gôs'-pô-dēn'), Italian *poco* (pô'kô), etc.
ü	This symbol represents the sound of *u* in French *duc* (dük) and German *grün* (grün) and can be approximated by rounding the lips for (o͞o) and trying to pronounce (ē).
kh	This symbol represents the unvoiced velar or uvular fricative, as in German *doch* (dôkh) or Scottish *loch* (lôkh) and can be approximated by arranging the speech organs as for (k) but allowing the breath to escape in a continuous stream, as in pronouncing (h).
H	This symbol represents a sound similar to the preceding but formed forward in the mouth, as in German *ich* (iH), and frequently misheard by English speakers as (sh).
n	This symbol indicates that the vowel sound immediately preceding it is nasalized; that is, the nasal passage is left open so that the breath passes through both the mouth and the nose in voicing the vowel [examples: Fr. *mon* (mō*n*), *en passant* (ä*n*' pȧ'sä*n*')].